New Bible Dictionary

NEW BIBLE DICTIONARY

THIRD EDITION

Organizing editor (first edition)
J. D. Douglas
formerly Lecturer, Singapore Bible College

Revision editor (second edition)
N. Hillyer
formerly Librarian, Tyndale House, Cambridge

Revision editor (third edition)
D. R. W. Wood
formerly Senior Editor, Inter-Varsity Press

Consulting editors for the third edition:
I. H. Marshall
Honorary Professor, Department of Divinity and Religious Studies, University of Aberdeen

A. R. Millard
Professor, School of Archaeology, Classics and Oriental Studies, University of Liverpool

J. I. Packer
Board of Governers, Professor of Theology, Regent College, Vancouver

D. J. Wiseman
Emeritus Professor of Assyriology, University of London

INTER-VARSITY PRESS, LEICESTER, ENGLAND

INTERVARSITY PRESS, DOWNERS GROVE, ILLINOIS

INTER-VARSITY PRESS
38 De Montfort Street, Leicester LE1 7GP, England
Email: ivp@uccf.org.uk
Website: www.ivpbooks.com

Published and sold in the USA and Canada by
INTERVARSITY PRESS, USA
5206 Main Street, PO Box 1400, Downers Grove, Illinois 60515, USA.

First edition May 1962
Reprinted 1962, 1963
Reprinted (with bibliographical revision) 1965
Reprinted 1967, 1968, 1970, 1972, 1974, 1975, 1976, 1977, 1978, 1980
Second edition 1982
Reprinted 1984, 1985, 1986, 1987, 1988, 1990, 1992, 1993, 1994
Third edition 1996
Reprinted 1997, 1999, 2000, 2001, 2003

British Library Cataloguing in Publication Data
A catalogue record for this book is available from the British Library.

Library of Congress Cataloguing-in-Publication Data
New Bible dictionary / revision editor, D. R. W. Wood: consulting
editors, I. H. Marshall . . . [et al.]—3rd ed.
p. cm.
Includes bibliographical references and index.
ISBN 0-8308-1439-6 (cloth: alk. paper)
1. Bible—Dictionaries. I. Wood, D. R. W. II. Marshall, I. Howard.
BS440N42 1996 96-24002
220.3—dc20 **CIP**

UK ISBN 0-85110-659-5
USA ISBN 0-8308-1439-6

Set in Times New Roman
Typeset by RefineCatch Limited, Bungay, Suffolk
Printed in Great Britain by The Bath Press, Bath

Inter-Varsity Press, England, is the publishing division of the Universities and Colleges Christian Fellowship (formerly the Inter-Varsity Fellowship), a student movement linking Christian Unions in universities and colleges throughout Great Britain, and a member movement of the International Fellowship of Evangelical Students. For information about local and national activities write to UCCF, 38 DeMontfort Street, Leicester LE1 7GP, email us at email@uccf.org.uk or visit the uccf website at www.uccf.org.uk.

InterVarsity Press®, USA, is the book-publishing division of InterVarsity Christian Fellowship®, a student movement active on campus at hundreds of universities, colleges and schools of nursing in the United States of America, and a member movement of the International Fellowship of Evangelical Students. For information about local and regional activities, write Public Relations Dept., InterVarsity Christian Fellowship, 6400 Schroeder Rd., PO Box 7895, Madison, WI 53707-7895.

Contents

Preface

We have been very greatly encouraged by the continuing and consistent demand for the *New Bible Dictionary* since it was first published in 1962 and revised in 1982. The major part of this reference work still stands and has required little or no modification to maintain its claim to be 'New' and up-to-date. Recent research, however, especially in the cultural and archaeological areas, needed to be incorporated. This has been done in this third edition wherever possible, subject to the limits imposed by the existing format. The opportunity has been taken to update the bibliographical entries and to make them more relevant for the reader of today. Also the work now makes reference to the *New International Version* of the Bible and other more recent translations in addition to the *Revised Standard Version*.

The revised volume reflects the same evangelical viewpoint as the previous editions and continues to embody loyalty to Holy Scripture as God's Word to humankind. The contributors are drawn largely, but not exclusively, from the membership of the Tyndale Fellowship for Biblical Research, part of the Universities and Colleges Christian Fellowship (formerly Inter-Varsity Fellowship). Individual authors and revisers are responsible only for their own contributions and do not necessarily endorse all the opinions expressed by their colleagues; no attempt has been made to impose any rigid uniformity upon the work as a whole or to exclude the expression of different opinions within the bounds of our basic understanding of Holy Scripture.

We are grateful to many academic colleagues for their helpful co-operation. In most cases the original authors of articles have been responsible for updating their entries. Where this has not been possible, other contributors have made the necessary revisions. In addition, a number of fresh entries have been written for this volume.

We are indebted above all to Derek Wood for undertaking the hard task of organizing this revision; also to Philip Hillyer and Andrew Warren for their painstaking work on the bibliographies, to Steve Carter for patient labour on both the bibliographies and the index and to Lyn Saville for checking both manuscripts and proofs.

This new edition of the *New Bible Dictionary* builds on the foundations laid by the editors of former editions and we gratefully acknowledge our indebtedness to J. D. Douglas, the Organizing Editor of the original work and Norman Hillyer, Revision Editor for the second edition. We remember too with gratitude the masterful work of our late colleagues R. V. G. Tasker (first edition), F. F. Bruce and Donald Guthrie (first and second editions). The patient care, consistent labour and wide understanding of these and other fellow-labourers have ensured a continuing life for a volume that is still, we believe, much needed for on-going Christian witness in the church today.

Our desire and prayer is that this new edition will, like its predecessors, enable all its users, teachers and students of the Bible alike, to reach a fuller understanding of the Word of God and its message for us today.

I.H.M.
A.R.M.
J.I.P.
D.J.W.

How to use this Dictionary

Articles are arranged in alphabetical order and are easily found under the headline at the top of each page. Where the reference required does not appear as an article, reference should be made to the index.

Index
A comprehensive index containing the significant references to each topic is to be found on p. 1273. This includes locations on maps and an index to the illustrations.

Cross-references
An asterisk before a word indicates that further relevant information will be found in the article under that title and is equivalent to the abbreviation *q.v.*

Abbreviations
A full list of abbreviations used in the Dictionary will be found on pp. (x)–(xiv).

Authorship of articles
The authors and co-authors of articles are indicated by their initials at the foot of each article. A full index of contributors is to be found on pp. (xv)–(xviii). The entries are listed in alphabetical order of initials, not of surnames.

Bibliographies
To assist those wishing to study subjects in greater detail, bibliographies appear at the end of most of the longer articles. These usually provide references to the recent general works on the subject and may include detailed studies or books which take up a position different from that of the contributor.

Acknowledgments
The source and/or holders of copyright for the illustrations are listed on p. 1297.

Bible versions
The Bible translation adopted for this Dictionary is the Revised Standard Version. In a few cases contributors have selected quotations from the King James (Authorized) Version, or, when available at the time of writing, the New International Version.

Maps
There is no map supplement to the Dictionary, but maps are to be found alongside the articles themselves for easy reference.

Names of regions, provinces, kingdoms, *etc.*, are printed in large roman capitals, *e.g.* BABYLONIA.

Tribes and ethnic groups: large italic capitals, *e.g. AMORITES*.

Towns and villages: lower case roman, *e.g.* Jerusalem.

Geographical features such as mountains, rivers, lakes, seas, *etc.*: lower case italic, *e.g. Great Sea*.

Modern place-names: as above but in brackets, *e.g.* (*Mediterranean Sea*). Absolute consistency has not been possible but, in general, where the modern name is clearly derived from the ancient (*e.g.* Creta = Crete, Italia = Italy) or where it would be pedantic to place modern names in brackets (*e.g.* Egypt, Jerusalem) brackets have been omitted. In a few other cases, where nearly all the place-names are modern, the principle has been abandoned for the sake of simplicity.

Features to be noted particularly, such as the subject of the article concerned, are underlined, *e.g.* Ashdod.

Where a site was known by two or more alternative names they are divided by an oblique stroke, *e.g.* Ezion-geber/Elath.

The word 'or' indicates uncertainty about the name or the location, as does a question mark.

Transliteration

The following systems have been adopted throughout the volume. In fairness to our contributors it should be said that some have disagreed on philological grounds with our transliteration of Hebrew words generally and of the divine name *Yahweh* in particular, but have graciously subordinated their convictions to editorial policy.

Hebrew

א	=	ʾ	ד	=	ḏ	י	=	y	ס	=	s	ר	= r
בּ	=	b	ה	=	h	כּ	=	k	ע	=	ʿ	שׂ	= ś
ב	=	ḇ	ו	=	w	כ	=	ḵ	פּ	=	p	שׁ	= š
גּ	=	g	ז	=	z	ל	=	l	פ	=	p̄	תּ	= t
ג	=	ḡ	ח	=	ḥ	מ	=	m	צ	=	ṣ	ת	= ṯ
דּ	=	d	ט	=	ṭ	נ	=	n	ק	=	q		

Long Vowels				Short Vowels	Very Short Vowels
(ה)ָ	= â	ָ	= ā	ַ = a	ֲ = ᵃ
ֵי	= ê	ֵ	= ē	ֶ = e	ֱ = ᵉ
ִי	= î			ִ = i	ְ = ᵉ (if vocal)
וֹ	= ô	ֹ	= ō	ָ = o	ֳ = ᵒ
וּ	= û			ֻ = u	

Greek

α	= a		ι	= i		ρ	= r		ῥ	= rh
β	= b		κ	= k		σ, ς	= s		ʽ	= h
γ	= g		λ	= l		τ	= t		γξ	= nx
δ	= d		μ	= m		υ	= y		γγ	= ng
ε	= e		ν	= n		φ	= ph		αυ	= au
ζ	= z		ξ	= x		χ	= ch		ευ	= eu
η	= ē		ο	= o		ψ	= ps		ου	= ou
θ	= th		π	= p		ω	= ō		υι	= yi

Arabic

ا	= ʾ	خ	= ḫ	ش	= š	غ	= ġ	ن	= n
ب	= b	د	= d	ص	= ṣ	ف	= f	ه	= h
ت	= t	ذ	= ḏ	ض	= ḍ	ق	= ḳ	و	= w
ث	= ṯ	ر	= r	ط	= ṭ	ك	= k	ى	= y
ج	= ǧ	ز	= z	ظ	= ẓ	ل	= l	ة	= t
ح	= ḥ	س	= s	ع	= ʿ	م	= m		

Abbreviations

I. Books and Journals

AASOR — *Annual of the American Schools of Oriental Research*
AB — *Anchor Bible*
ABD — D. M. Freedman *et al.* (eds.), *Anchor Bible Dictionary*, 6 vols., 1992
ACA — Sir Moses Finley, *Atlas of Classical Archaeology*, 1977
AfO — *Archiv für Orientforschung*
AJA — *American Journal of Archaeology*
AJBA — *Australian Journal of Biblical Archaeology*
AJSL — *American Journal of Semitic Languages and Literatures*
AJT — *American Journal of Theology*
ALASP — *Abhandlungen zur Literatur Alt – Syrien Palastinas*
ALUOS — *Annual of the Leeds University Oriental Society*
ANEP — J. B. Pritchard, *The Ancient Near East in Pictures*, 1954; [2]1965
ANET — J. B. Pritchard, *Ancient Near Eastern Texts*, 1950; [2]1965; [3]1969
ANRW — *Aufstieg und Niedergang der römischen Welt*
ANT — M. R. James, *The Apocryphal New Testament*, 1924
AOTS — D. W. Thomas (ed.), *Archaeology and Old Testament Study*, 1967
ARAB — D. D. Luckenbill, *Ancient Records of Assyria and Babylonia*, 1926
ARE — J. H. Breasted, *Ancient Records of Egypt*, 5 vols., 1906–7
ARV — *American Revised Version* (see ASV)
AS — *Anatolian Studies*
ASAE — *Annales du Service des Antiquités de l'Égypte*
ASV — *American Standard Version*, 1901 (American version of RV)
ATR — *Anglican Theological Review*
AUSS — *Andrews University Seminar Studies*
AV — *Authorized Version* (*King James'*), 1611
BA — *Biblical Archaeologist*
BA1CS — *The Book of Acts in its First Century Setting*, 6 vols.
BAGD — W. Bauer, *A Greek-English Lexicon of the New Testament and Other Early Christian Literature,* revised and augmented by F. W. Gingrich and F. W. Danker from 5th ed., 1979
BANE — G. E. Wright (ed.), *The Bible and the Ancient Near East*, 1961
BAR — *Biblical Archaeology Review*
BASOR — *Bulletin of the American Schools of Oriental Research*
BC — F. J. Foakes-Jackson and K. Lake, *The Beginnings of Christianity*, 5 vols., 1920–33
BDB — F. Brown, S. R. Driver and C. A. Briggs, *Hebrew and English Lexicon of the Old Testament*, 1906
BECNT — *Baker Exegetical Commentary on the New Testament*
Bib — *Biblica*
BibRes — *Biblical Research*
BIES — *Bulletin of the Israel Exploration Society*
BJRL — *Bulletin of the John Rylands Library*
BNTC — *Black's New Testament Commentaries*
BO — *Bibliotheca Orientalis*
BRD — W. M. Ramsay, *The Bearing of Recent Discovery on the Trustworthiness of the New Testament*, 1914
BRev — *Bible Review*
BS — *Bibliotheca Sacra*
BSOAS — *Bulletin of the School of Oriental and African Studies*
BST — *Bible Speaks Today*
BTh — *Biblical Theology*
BZ — *Biblische Zeitschrift*
BZAW — *Beiheft, Zeitschrift für die alttestamentliche Wissenschaft*
CAH — *Cambridge Ancient History*, 12 vols., 1923–39; revised ed. 1970–
CB — *Century Bible*
CBP — W. M. Ramsay, *Cities and Bishoprics of Phrygia*, 1895–7
CBQ — *Catholic Biblical Quarterly*
CBSC — *Cambridge Bible for Schools and Colleges*
CD — Qumran Damascus Document
CDC — Cairo Geniza Documents of the Damascus Covenanters
CE — *Chronique d'Égypte*
CGT — *Cambridge Greek Testament*
CIG — *Corpus Inscriptionum Graecarum*
CIL — *Corpus Inscriptionum Latinarum*
CML — G. R. Driver (ed.), *Canaanite Myths and Legends*[2], 1978
CQ — *Classical Quarterly; Crozer Quarterly*
CRE — W. M. Ramsay, *The Church in the Roman Empire before AD 170*, 1903
CTJ — *Calvin Theological Journal*
DAC — J. Hastings (ed.), *Dictionary of the Apostolic Church*, 2 vols., 1915–18
DBA — E. M. Blaiklock *et al.* (eds.), *Dictionary of Biblical Archaeology*, 1983.
DBS — *Dictionnaire de la Bible*, Supplément, 1928–
DBT — X. Leon-Dufour (ed.), *Dictionary of Biblical Theology*[2], 1973, reprinted with corrections 1988
DCG — J. Hastings (ed.), *Dictionary of Christ and the Gospels*, 2 vols., 1906–08

ABBREVIATIONS

DJG	J. B. Green, S. McKnight and I. H. Marshall (eds.), *Dictionary of Jesus and the Gospels*, 1993
DOTT	D. W. Thomas (ed.), *Documents of Old Testament Times*, 1958
EB	*Expositor's Bible*
EBC	*Expositor's Bible Commentary*
EBi	*Encyclopaedia Biblica*
EBr	*Encyclopaedia Britannica*
EBT	J. B. Bauer (ed.), *Encyclopaedia of Biblical Theology*, 3 vols., 1970
EDNT	H. Balz and G. Schneider (eds.), *Exegetical Dictionary of the New Testament*, 3 vols., E.T. 1990–93
EEP	K. Lake, *The Earlier Epistles of St Paul*, 1911
EGT	W. R. Nicoll, *The Expositor's Greek Testament*[6], 1910
EIs	*Encyclopaedia of Islam*, 1954–
EJ	C. Roth (ed.), *Encyclopaedia Judaica*, 15 vols., 1971
EQ	*Evangelical Quarterly*
ERE	J. Hastings (ed.), *Encyclopaedia of Religion and Ethics*, 13 vols., 1908–26
ETL	*Ephemerides theological lovanienses*
ExpT	*Expository Times*
FOTL	*Forms of Old Testament Literature*
FRLANT	*Forschungen zur Religion und Literatur des Alten und Neuen Testaments*
FT	*Faith and Thought* (formerly *JTVI*)
GB	*Ginsburg's Bible* (New Masoretico-Critical Text of the Hebrew Bible), 1896
GNB	*Good News Bible* (=TEV)
GTT	J. Simons, *Geographical and Topographical Texts of the Old Testament*, 1959
HAT	*Handbuch zum Alten Testament*
HDB	J. Hastings (ed.), *Dictionary of the Bible*, 5 vols., 1898–1904
HES	*Harvard Expedition to Samaria*, 1924
HHT	J. Lightfoot, *Horae Hebraicae et Talmudicae*, 1658–64
HJ	*Hibbert Journal*
HJP	E. Schürer, *A History of the Jewish People in the Time of Christ*, 2 vols., E.T. 1885–1901; revised ed., M. Black, G. Vermes and F. Millar (eds.), 3 vols., 1973–
HNT	H. Lietzmann, *Handbuch zum Neuen Testament*
HSS	*Harvard Semitic Series*
HTKNT	*Herders Theologischer Kommentar zum Neuen Testament*
HTR	*Harvard Theological Review*
HUCA	*Hebrew Union College Annual*
IB	G. A. Buttrick *et al.* (eds.), *Interpreter's Bible*, 12 vols., 1952–7
IBA	D. J. Wiseman, *Illustrations from Biblical Archaeology*, 1958
ICC	*International Critical Commentary*
IDB	G. A. Buttrick *et al.* (eds.), *The Interpreter's Dictionary of the Bible*, 4 vols., 1962
IDBS	*IDB*, Supplement vol., 1976
IEBP	F. N. Hepper, *Illustrated Encyclopedia of Bible Plants*, 1992
IEJ	*Israel Exploration Journal*
IG	*Inscriptiones Graecae*
IGRR	*Inscriptiones Graecae ad res Romanas pertinentes*
Int	*Interpretation*
INT	*Introduction to the New Testament*
IOSCS	*International Organization for Septuagint and Cognate Studies*
IOT	*Introduction to the Old Testament*
ISBE	*International Standard Bible Encyclopaedia*[3], 4 vols., 1979–88
IVPNTC	*IVP New Testament Commentary*
JAOS	*Journal of the American Oriental Society*
JB	*Jerusalem Bible*, 1966
JBL	*Journal of Biblical Literature*
JBQ	*Jewish Bible Quarterly*
JCS	*Journal of Cuneiform Studies*
JCSBR	*Journal of the Chicago Society of Biblical Research*
JEA	*Journal of Egyptian Archaeology*
JEH	*Journal of Ecclesiastical History*
JewE	I. Singer *et al.* (eds.), *Jewish Encyclopaedia*, 12 vols., 1901–06
JHS	*Journal of Hellenic Studies*
JJS	*Journal of Jewish Studies*
JNES	*Journal of Near Eastern Studies*
JNSL	*Journal of Northwest Semitic Languages*
JPOS	*Journal of the Palestine Oriental Society*
JQR	*Jewish Quarterly Review*
JRAS	*Journal of the Royal Asiatic Society*
JRS	*Journal of Roman Studies*
JSOT(SS)	*Journal for the Study of the Old Testament (supplements)*
JSS	*Journal of Semitic Studies*
JTS	*Journal of Theological Studies*
JTVI	*Journal of the Transactions of the Victoria Institute* (now *FT*)
JWH	*Journal of World History*
KAT	*Kommentar zum Alten Testament*
KB	L. Köhler and W. Baumgartner, *Hebräisches und aramäisches Lexicon zum Alten Testament*[3], 1967
KEK	H. A. W. Meyer (ed.), *Kritischexegetischer Kommentar über das Neue Testament*
KJV	*King James' Version* (= AV)
KTU	*Die keilalphabetischen Texte aus Ugarit*
LA	*Liber Annus* (Jerusalem)
LAE	A. Deissmann, *Light from the Ancient East*[4], 1927
LAPO	*Litteratures anciennes du proche orient*
LBC	*Layman's Bible Commentary*
LOB	Y. Aharoni, *The Land of the Bible*[2], 1979
LOT	S. R. Driver, *Introduction to the Literature of the Old Testament*[9], 1913
LSJ	H. G. Liddell, R. Scott and H. S. Jones, *Greek–English Lexicon*[9], 1940
MM	J. H. Moulton and G. Milligan, *The Vocabulary of the Greek Testament illustrated from the Papyri and other non-literary sources,* 1930
MNTC	*Moffatt New Testament Commentary*
Moffatt	J. Moffatt, *A New Translation of the Bible*[2], 1936
NAC	*New American Commentaries*
NASB	*New American Standard Bible*, 1963
NBC	F. Davidson (ed.), *The New Bible Commentary*, 1953
NBCR	D. Guthrie *et al.* (eds.), *The New Bible Commentary Revised*, 1970

NCB *New Century Bible*
NClB *New Clarendon Bible*
NEAEHL E. Stern (ed.), *New Encyclopedia of Archaeological Excavations in the Holy Land*, 4 vols., 1993
NEB *New English Bible*: NT, 1961; OT, Apocrypha, 1970
Nestle *Nestle's Novum Testamentum Graece*[22], 1956
NIBC *New International Biblical Commentary*
NIC *New International Commentary*
NIDNTT C. Brown (ed.), *The New International Dictionary of New Testament Theology*, 3 vols., 1975–8
NIGTC *New International Greek Testament Commentary*
NIV *New International Version*: NT, 1974; complete Bible, 1978
NLC *New London Commentary*
NovT *Novum Testamentum*
NTC *New Testament Commentary*
NTD *Das Neue Testament Deutsch*
NTS *New Testament Studies*
OCD M. Cary *et al.* (eds.), *The Oxford Classical Dictionary*, 1949
ODCC F. L. Cross and E. A. Livingstone (eds.), *The Oxford Dictionary of the Christian Church*[2], 1974
Or *Orientalia*
OTL *Old Testament Library*
OTMS H. H. Rowley (ed.), *The Old Testament and Modern Study*, 1951
OTS *Oudtestamentische Studiën*
Pauly-Wissowa See *RE*
Pelican *Pelican Commentaries*
PEQ *Palestine Exploration Quarterly*
PG J. P. Migne, *Patrologia Graeca*
Phillips J. B. Phillips, *The New Testament in Modern English*, 1958; revised ed. 1972
PJB *Palästina-Jahrbuch*
PL J. P. Migne, *Patrologia Latina*
POTT D. J. Wiseman (ed.), *Peoples of Old Testament Times*, 1973
P.Oxy. Papyrus Oxyrhynchus
PRU *Le Palais Royal d'Ugarit*
PTR *Princeton Theological Review*
RA *Revue d'Assyriologie*
RAC T. Klausner *et al.* (eds.), *Reallexicon für die Antike und Christentum*, 1941–
RAr *Revue d'Archéologie*
RB *Revue Biblique*
RE A. F. Pauly, G. Wissowa *et al.* (eds.), *Real-Encyclopädie der klassischen Altertumwissenschaft*, 1893–
R&E *Review and Expositor*
RGG K. Galling (ed.), *Die Religion in Geschichte und Gegenwart*[3], 7 vols., 1957–65
RHR *Revue de l'Histoire des Religions*
RQ *Revue de Qumran*
RSP *Ras Shamra Parallels*
RSR *Recherches de Science Religieuse*
RSV *Revised Standard Version*: NT, 1946; OT, 1952; *Common Bible*, 1973
RTR *Reformed Theological Review* (Australia)
RV *Revised Version*: NT, 1881; OT, 1885
SB H. L. Strack and P. Billerbeck, *Kommentar zum Neuen Testament aus Talmud und Midrasch*, 6 vols., 1926–61
SBET *Scottish Bulletin of Evangelical Theology*
SBLR *Society of Biblical Literature*
SBLDS *Society of Biblical Literature Dissertation Series*
SBT *Studies in Biblical Theology*
Schürer See *HJP*
SHERK *The New Schaff-Herzog Encyclopaedia of Religious Knowledge*[2], 1949–52
SIG W. Dittenberger (ed.), *Sylloge Inscriptionum Graecarum*, 1915–24
SJOT *Scandinavian Journal of the Old Testament*
SJT *Scottish Journal of Theology*
SNTSMS *Society for New Testament Studies Monograph Series*
SP Samaritan Pentateuch
SPEM G. S. Duncan, *St Paul's Ephesian Ministry*, 1929
SPT W. M. Ramsay, *St Paul the Traveller and Roman Citizen*[4], 1920
ST *Studia Theologica*
Strack-Billerbeck See *SB*
TB Babylonian Talmud
TBC *Torch Bible Commentary*
TCERK *The Twentieth Century Encyclopaedia of Religious Knowledge*, 1955
TDNT G. Kittell and G. Friedrich (eds.), *Theologisches Wörterbuch zum Neuen Testament*, 1932–74; E. T. *Theological Dictionary of the New Testament*, ed. G. W. Bromiley, 10 vols., 1964–76
TDOT G. J. Botterweck and H. Ringgren (eds.), *Theologisches Wörterbuch zum Alten Testament*, 1970– ; E.T. *Theological Dictionary of the Old Testament*, trans. by J. T. Willis, 1974–
TEV *Today's English Version*[4], 1976 (= GNB)
Th *Theology*
THAT E. Jenni and C. Westermann (eds.), *Theologisches Handwörterbuch zum Alten Testament*, 2 vols., 1971–6
THB *Tyndale House Bulletin* (now *TynB*)
Them *Themelios*
ThL *Theologische Literaturzeitung*
THNT *Theologische Handbuch zum Neuen Testament*
TJ Jerusalem Talmud
TNT *Translators' New Testament* (Bible Society)
TNTC *Tyndale New Testament Commentary*
TOTC *Tyndale Old Testament Commentary*
TPINTC *Trinity Press International New Testament Commentary*
TR *Theologische Rundschau*
TS *Texts and Studies*
TSFB *Theological Students' Fellowship Bulletin*
TU *Texte und Untersuchungen zur Geschichte der altchristlichen Literatur*
TWBR A. Richardson (ed.), *A Theological Word Book of the Bible*, 1950
TynB *Tyndale Bulletin* (formerly *THB*)
TZ *Theologisches Zeitung*
UBL *Ugaritisch-Biblische Literatur*
UF *Ugarit-Forschungen: Internationales Jahrbuch für die Altertumskunde*
UG *Ugaritica*, 7 vols., in C. F. A. Schaeffer, *Mission de Ras Shamra*, 1–18, 1929–78
UT *Ugaritic Textbook*
VC *Vigiliae Christianae*
VT *Vetus Testamentum*
VT Supp. *Vetus Testamentum*, Supplementary vol.

ABBREVIATIONS

WBC	*Word Biblical Commentary*
WC	*Westminster Commentary*
WDB	*Westminster Dictionary of the Bible*, 1944
Wett.	J. J. Wettstein, *Novum Testamentum Graecum*, 1751–2
Weymouth	R. F. Weymouth, *The New Testament in Modern Speech*, 1903
WH	B. F. Westcott and F. J. A. Hort, *The New Testament in Greek*, 1881
WTJ	*Westminster Theological Journal*
ZA	*Zeitschrift für Assyriologie*
ZAW	*Zeitschrift für die alttestamentliche Wissenschaft*
ZDMG	*Zeitschrift der deutschen morgenländischen Gesellschaft*
ZDPV	*Zeitschrift des deutschen Palästina-Vereins*
ZNW	*Zeitschrift für die neutestamentliche Wissenschaft*
ZPEB	M. C. Tenney (ed.), *The Zondervan Pictorial Encyclopaedia of the Bible*, 5 vols., 1975
ZTK	*Zeitschrift für Theologie und Kirche*

Editions are indicated by small superior figures: *LOT*[9]

II. Classical Works

ad Fam.	Cicero, *Epistulae ad Familiares*
Adv. Haer.	Irenaeus, *Adversus Haereses*
Ann.	Tacitus, *Annales*
Ant.	Josephus, *Antiquities of the Jews*
Apol.	Justin Martyr, *Apologia*; Tertullian, *Apologia*
BJ	Josephus, *Jewish Wars*
Clem. Recog.	Rufinus, *Clementine Recognitions*
Contra Pelag.	Jerome, *Contra Pelagium*
Eccles. Hist.	Sozomen, *History of the Church*
EH	Eusebius, *Ecclesiastical History*
Epig.	Martial, *Epigrammaticus Latinus*
Ep. Mor.	Seneca, *Epistulae Morales ad Lucilium*
Eus.	Eusebius
Ev. Petr.	*Gospel of Peter* (apocryphal)
Exc. Theod.	Clement of Alexandria, *Excerpta ex Theodoto*
Geog.	Ptolemy, *Geography*; Strabo, *Geography*
Hist.	Dio Cassius, *History*; Tacitus, *History*
Hypot.	Clement of Alexandria, *Hypotyposes*
Il.	Homer, *Iliad*
Iul.	Suetonius, *C. Julius Caesar* (*Lives of the Caesars*)
In Verr.	Cicero, *In Verrem Actio*
Jos.	Josephus
Juv.	Juvenal
Lk. Hom.	Origen, *Homily on Luke*
Magn.	Ignatius, *Magnesians*
NH	Pliny, *Natural History*
Od.	Horace, *Odes*
Onom.	Eusebius, *Onomasticon de Locis Hebraicis*
Philad.	Ignatius, *Philadelphians*
Praep. Ev.	Eusebius, *Praeparatio Evangelica*
Quaest	Seneca, *Quaestiones Naturales*
Sat.	Juvenal, *Satires*; Persius, *Satires*
Strom.	Clement of Alexandria, *Stromateis*
Trall.	Ignatius, *Trallians*
Vesp.	Suetonius, *Vespasian* (*Lives of the Caesars*)
Vit. Mos.	Philo, *De Vita Mosis* (*Life of Moses*)

III. Biblical Books

Books of the Old Testament
Gn., Ex., Lv., Nu., Dt., Jos., Jdg., Ru., 1, 2 Sa., 1, 2 Ki., 1, 2 Ch., Ezr., Ne., Est., Jb., Ps. (Pss.), Pr., Ec., Ct., Is., Je., La., Ezk., Dn., Ho., Joel, Am., Ob., Jon., Mi., Na., Hab., Zp., Hg., Zc., Mal.

Books of the New Testament
Mt., Mk., Lk., Jn., Acts, Rom., 1, 2 Cor., Gal., Eph., Phil., Col., 1, 2 Thes., 1, 2 Tim., Tit., Phm., Heb., Jas., 1, 2 Pet., 1, 2, 3 Jn., Jude, Rev.

IV. General Abbreviations

ad loc.	*ad locum* (Lat.), at the place
Akkad.	Akkadian
Apoc.	Apocrypha(l)
Aq.	Aquila's Gk. tr. of OT, *c.* AD 140
Arab	Arabic
Aram	Aramaic
Assyr.	Assyrian
b.	*bar/ben* (Aram./Heb.), son of
Bab.	Babylonian
BM	British Museum
c.	*circa* (Lat.), about, approximately
ch.(chs.)	chapter(s)
cf.	*confer* (Lat.), compare
Copt.	Coptic
D	Deuteronomist
diss.	dissertation
DSS	Dead Sea Scrolls
E	East, eastern; Elohist
eccl. Lat.	ecclesiastical Latin
Ecclus.	Ecclesiasticus (Apoc.)
ed. (eds.)	edited by, edition, editor(s)
Egyp.	Egyptian
Eng.	English
E.T.	English translation
et al.	*et alii* (Lat.), and others
Eth.	Ethiopic
EVV	English versions
f. (ff.)	and the following (verse(s), *etc.*)
f.c.	forthcoming
fig.	figuratively
Ger.	German
Gk.	Greek
H	Law of Holiness
Heb.	Hebrew

ibid.	*ibidem* (Lat.), the same work
idem	*idem* (Lat.), the same author
J	Yahwist
Lat.	Latin
lit.	literally
L.L.	Late Latin
loc. cit.	*loco citato* (Lat.), in the place already quoted
LXX	Septuagint (Gk. version of OT)
Macc.	Maccabees (Apoc.)
mg.	margin
mod.	modern
MS (MSS)	manuscript(s)
MT	Massoretic text
N	North, northern
n.f.	*neue Folge* (Ger.), new series
n.s.	new series
NT	New Testament
OE	Old English
OL	Old Latin
op.cit.	*opere citato* (Lat.), in the work cited above
OT	Old Testament
P	Priestly Narrative
par.	and parallel(s)
passim	to be found at various places throughout the text
Pent.	Pentateuch
per se	by or in itself
Pesh	Peshitta
Phoen.	Phoenician
pl.	plate (illustration)
Q	*Quelle* (Ger.), source thought to be behind sayings of Jesus common to Mt. and Lk.
q.v.	*quod vide* (Lat.), which see
R.	Rabbi
Rom.	Roman
S	South, southern
Sem.	Semitic
Suppl.	supplementary volume
s.v.	*sub verbo* (Lat.), under the word
Symm.	Symmachus' Gk. tr. of OT, 2nd century AD
Syr.	Syriac
Targ.	Targum
Theod.	Theodotion's Gk. tr. of OT, 2nd century AD
TR	Textus Receptus
tr.	translated, translation
Turk.	Turkish
v. (vv.)	verse(s)
v.l.	*vario lectio* (Lat.), variant reading
vol.	volume
vss	versions
Vulg.	Vulgate
W	West, western

List of Contributors

The information given below was correct at the time of publication of the third edition of this Dictionary.

A.A.J. A. A. Jones, M.A., B.D., Ph.D., formerly Head of Department of Religious Studies, Avery Hill College, London.

A.C. R. A. Cole, M.Th., Ph.D., formerly Lecturer in Old Testament Language and Literature, University of Sydney, Moore College, Sydney, and Trinity College, Singapore.

A.E.C. A. E. Cundall, B.A., B.D., formerly Principal, Bible College of Victoria, Australia.

A.E.W. A. E. Willingale, B.A., B.D., M.Th., Romford, Essex.

A.F. The late A. Flavelle, B.A., B.D., formerly Minister of Finaghy Presbyterian Church, Belfast.

A.F.W. A. F. Walls, O.B.E., M.A., B.Litt., D.D., F.S.A. Scot., Director of the Centre for the Study of Christianity in the Non-Western World, and Honorary Professor in the University of Edinburgh.

A.G. A. Gelston, M.A., Reader in Theology, University of Durham.

A.K.C. A. K. Cragg, M.A., D.Phil., D.D., Assistant Bishop of Wakefield and formerly Vicar of Helme, Huddersfield.

A.R. The late A. Ross, M.A., B.D., D.D., formerly Professor of New Testament, Free Church College, Edinburgh.

A.R.M. A. R. Millard, M.A., M.Phil., F.S.A., Rankin Professor of Hebrew and Ancient Semitic Languages, University of Liverpool.

A.S. The late A. Stuart, M.Sc., Dip.R.M.S., formerly Emeritus Professor of Geology, University of Exeter.

A.S.W. The late A. S. Wood, B.A., Ph.D., F.R.Hist.S., formerly Principal, Cliff College, Calver, Derbyshire.

A. van S. The late A. van Selms, Th.D., formerly Emeritus Professor of Semitic Languages, University of Pretoria.

B.A.M. B. A. Milne, M.A., B.D., Ph.D., Senior Minister, First Baptist Church, Vancouver, B.C.

B.F.C.A. The late B. F. C. Atkinson, M.A., Ph.D., formerly Under-Librarian, University of Cambridge.

B.F.H. B. F. Harris, B.A., M.A., B.D., Ph.D., formerly Associate Professor of History, Macquarie University, New South Wales.

B.L.S. B. L. Smith, B.D., Th.Schol., Lecturer in Biblical and Historical Theology, Sydney Missionary and Bible College.

B.O.B. B. O. Banwell, B.A., M.A., formerly Lecturer in Old Testament, Rhodes University; Methodist Minister, Fort Beaufort, S. Africa.

C.D.W. C. de Wit, Docteur en philologie et histoire orientales; Conservateur honoraire Musées Royaux d'Art et Histoire, Brussels; Emeritus Professor of the University of Louvain.

C.F.P. The late C. F. Pfeiffer, B.A., B.D., Ph.D., formerly Associate Professor of Old Testament, Gordon Divinity School, Beverly Farms, Massachusetts.

C.H.D. C. H. Duncan, M.A., B.D., Ph.D., Th.D., Lecturer in Philosophy, State College of Victoria, Australia; Canon of St Paul's Cathedral, Melbourne.

C.J.D. C. J. Davey, B.Sc., M.A., Inspector of Mines, Victoria, Australia.

C.J.H. The late C. J. Hemer, M.A., Ph.D., formerly Librarian and Research Fellow, Tyndale House, Cambridge.

C.L.F. C. L. Feinberg, A.B., A.M., Th.B., Th.M., Ph.D., Emeritus Professor of Semitics and Old Testament and Dean of Talbot Theological Seminary, La Mirada, California.

D.A.H. The late D. A. Hubbard, B.A., B.D., Th.M., Ph.D., D.D., L.H.D., formerly President, Fuller Theological Seminary, Pasadena, California.

D.A.Ha D. A. Hagner, B.D., Th.M., Ph.D., George Eldon Ladd Professor of New Testament, Fuller Theological Seminary, Pasadena, California.

D.B.K. The late D. B. Knox, B.A., B.D., M.Th., D.Phil, A.L.C.D., formerly Founding Principal, George Whitefield College, Cape Town.

D.F. The late D. Freeman, B.A., Th.B., Th.M., Ph.D., formerly Professor, Rhode Island Junior College.

D.F.P. D. F. Payne, B.A., M.A., Academic Dean, London Bible College.

D.F.W D. F. Wright, M.A., Senior Lecturer in Ecclesiastical History, New College, University of Edinburgh.

D.G. The late D. Guthrie, B.D., M.Th., Ph.D., formerly President, London Bible College.

LIST OF CONTRIBUTORS

D.G.P. D. G. Peterson, M.A., B.D., Ph.D., Th.Schol., Principal of Oak Hill College, London.

D.G.S. D. G. Stradling, Magdalen College, Oxford.

D.H.F. D. H. Field, B.A., Vice-Principal, Oak Hill College, London.

D.H.T. The late D. H. Tongue, M.A., formerly Lecturer in New Testament, Trinity College, Bristol.

D.H.W. D. H. Wheaton, M.A., B.D., Vicar of Christ Church, Ware; formerly Principal, Oak Hill College, London; Canon of St Alban's Cathedral.

D.J.A.C. D. J. A. Clines, M.A., Professor of Biblical Studies, University of Sheffield.

D.J.V.L. D. J. V. Lane, Ll.B., B.D., International Minister, Overseas Missionary Fellowship.

D.J.W. D. J. Wiseman, O.B.E., M.A., D.Lit., F.B.A., F.K.A., F.S.A., Emeritus Professor of Assyriology, University of London.

D.K.F. D. K. Falk, B.A., M.C.S., Ph.D., Kennicott Fellow in Hebrew, Oriental Institute, University of Oxford, and Junior Research Fellow in Qumran, Oxford Centre for Hebrew and Jewish Studies.

D.K.I. D. K. Innes, M.A., B.D., Vicar of Doddington, Newnham and Wychling, Kent.

D.O.S. D. O. Swann, B.A., B.D., formerly Minister of Ashford Evangelical Congregational Church, Middlesex.

D.R. de L. D. R. de Lacey, M.A., Ph.D., Computer Officer, School of Arts and Humanities, University of Cambridge; formerly Lecturer in New Testament, Ridley Hall, Cambridge.

D.R.H. D. R. Hall, M.A., M.Th., Superintendent Minister of the Rhyl and Prestatyn Circuit of the Methodist Church.

D.T. D. H. Trapnell, M.A., M.D., F.R.C.P., F.R.C.R., Consultant Radiologist, Westminster Hospital, London.

D.W. D. Wenham, M.A., Ph.D., Lecturer in New Testament, Wycliffe Hall, Oxford.

D.W.B. D. W. Baker, A.B., M.C.S., M.Phil., Ph.D., Professor of Old Testament and Semitic Languages, Ashland Theological Seminary, Ohio.

D.W.B.R. D. W. B. Robinson, A.O., M.A., Th.D., formerly Archbishop of Sydney, New South Wales.

D.W.G. D. W. Gooding, M.A., Ph.D., M.I.R.A., Emeritus Professor of Old Testament Greek, The Queen's University, Belfast.

E.A.J. E. A. Judge, M.A., Professor of History, Macquarie University, New South Wales.

E.E.E. E. E. Ellis, Ph.D., Research Professor of Theology, Southwestern Baptist Theological Seminary, Forth Worth, Texas.

E.J.Y. The late E. J. Young, B.A., Th.M., Ph.D., formerly Professor of Old Testament, Westminster Theological Seminary, Philadelphia.

E.M.B. The late E. M. Blaiklock, O.B.E., M.A., Litt.D., formerly Professor of Classics, University of Auckland.

E.M.B.G. E. M. B. Green, M.A., B.D., Archbishops' Advisor in Evangelism.

E.M.Y. E. M. Yamauchi, B.A., M.A., Ph.D., Professor of History, Miami University, Oxford, Ohio.

F.C.F. The late F. C. Fensham, M.A., Ph.D., D.D., formerly Professor in Semitic Languages, University of Stellenbosch.

F.D.K. F. D. Kidner, M.A., A.R.C.M., formerly Warden, Tyndale House, Cambridge.

F.F. F. Foulkes, B.A., B.D., M.A., M.Sc., formerly Warden of the College of St John the Evangelist, Auckland, New Zealand, and Lecturer in Biblical History and Literature, University of Auckland.

F.F.B. The late F. F. Bruce, M.A., D.D., F.B.A., formerly Emeritus Rylands Professor of Biblical Criticism and Exegesis, University of Manchester.

F.H.P. F. H. Palmer, M.A., formerly Diocesan Missioner and Minister of St Matthew's Church, Walsall, West Midlands.

F.N.H. F. N. Hepper, F.I.Biol., B.Sc., F.L.S., formerly Assistant Keeper, The Herbarium, Royal Botanic Gardens, Kew.

F.S.F. F. S. Fitzsimmonds, B.A., B.D., M.Th., formerly Vice-Principal, Spurgeon's College, London.

G.C.D.H. The late G. C. D. Howley, formerly Consulting Editor of *The Witness*.

G.G.G. G. G. Garner, B.A., B.D., formerly Director, Australian Institute of Archaeology, Melbourne.

G.I.D. G. I. Davies, M.A., Ph.D., Lecturer in Old Testament and Intertestamental Studies, University of Cambridge.

G.I.E. G. I. Emmerson, M.A., Ph.D., Dip.Or. Lang., Lecturer, Department of Theology, University of Birmingham.

G.J.W. G. J. Wenham, M.A., Ph.D., Professor of Old Testament, Cheltenham and Gloucester College of Higher Education.

G.M. G. McFarlane, Ph.D., Lecturer in Systematic Theology, London Bible College.

G.R.B.-M. G. R. Beasley-Murray, M.A., Ph.D., D.D., D. Litt., formerly Principal of Spurgeon's College, London.

G.S.C. The late G. S. Cansdale, B.A., B.Sc., F.L.S., former Consultant Biologist.

G.S.M.W. The late G. S. M. Walker, M.A., B.D., Ph.D., formerly Lecturer in Church History, University of Leeds.

G.T.M. The late G. T. Manley, M.A., sometime Fellow, Christ's College, Cambridge.

G.W. G. Walters, B.A., B.D., Ph.D., Emeritus Professor of Ministry, Gordon-Conwell Theological Seminary, South Hamilton, Massachusetts.

G.W.G. G. W. Grogan, B.D., M.Th., Principal Emeritus, Glasgow Bible College.

H.A.G.B. H. A. G. Belben, M.A., B.D., formerly Principal, Cliff College, Calver, Derbyshire.

H.D.McD. H. D. McDonald, B.A., B.D., Ph.D., D.D., formerly Vice-Principal, London Bible College.

H.G.M.W. H. G. M. Williamson, M.A., Ph.D., D.D., Regius Professor of Hebrew, University of Oxford.

H.L.E. The late H. L. Ellison, B.A., B.D., formerly Senior Tutor, Moorlands Bible College.

H.M.C. H. M. Carson, B.A., B.D., formerly Minister of Knighton Evangelical Free Church, Leicester.

H.R. H. N. Ridderbos, D.Theol., Emeritus Professor of New Testament, Kampen Theological University, The Netherlands.

H.W.H. H. W. Hoehner, Ph.D., Professor of New Testament Studies, Dallas Theological Seminary.

I.H.M. I. H. Marshall, B.A., M.A., B.D., Ph.D., D.D., Professor of New Testament Exegesis, University of Aberdeen.

J.A.M. J. A. Motyer, M.A., B.D., formerly Principal, Trinity College, Bristol.

J.A.T. J. A. Thompson, M.A., M.Sc., B.D., B.Ed., Ph.D., formerly Reader and Chairman in Department of Middle Eastern Studies, University of Melbourne.

J.B.J. J. B. Job, M.A., B.D., Minister in the South Bedford and Ampthill Methodist Circuit; formerly Vice-Principal of Emmanuel College, Ibadan, and Tutor in Old Testament, Cliff College, Calver, Derbyshire.

J.B.P. The late J. B. Payne, Ph.D., formerly Professor of Old Testament, Covenant Theological Seminary, St Louis, Missouri.

J.B.T. J. B. Torrance, M.A., B.D., Emeritus Professor of Systematic Theology, University of Aberdeen.

J.B.Tr. J. B. Taylor, M.A., Bishop of St Albans.

J.C.C. J. C. Connell, B.A., M.A., formerly Director of Studies and Lecturer in New Testament Exegesis, London Bible College.

J.C.J.W. J. C. J. Waite, B.D., Minister of Wycliffe Independent Chapel, Sheffield; formerly Principal, South Wales Bible College.

J.C.W. J. C. Whitcomb, Jr, Th.D., formerly Professor of Theology and Old Testament, Grace Theological Seminary, Winona Lake, Indiana.

J.D.D. J. D. Douglas, M.A., B.D., S.T.M., Ph.D., Lecturer, Singapore Bible College.

J.D.G.D. J. D. G. Dunn, M.A., B.D., Ph.D., D.D., Lightfoot Professor of Divinity, University of Durham.

J.E.G. J. E. Goldingay, B.A., Ph.D., Principal, St John's College, Nottingham.

J.G.B. The late J. G. Baldwin, B.A., B.D., formerly Principal, Trinity College, Bristol.

J.G.G.N. The late J. G. G. Norman, B.D., M.Th.

J.G.McC. J. G. McConville, M.A., B.D., Ph.D., Senior Lecturer in Religious Studies, Cheltenham and Gloucester College of Higher Education.

J.G.S.S.T. J. G. S. S. Thomson, B.A., M.A., B.D., Ph.D., Minister of the Church of Scotland.

J.H. J. W. L. Hoad, M.A., Clinical Supervisor, Princeton, New Jersey.

J.H.H. J. H. Harrop, M.A., formerly Lecturer in Classics, Fourah Bay College, University of Sierra Leone.

J.H.P. J. H. Paterson, M.A., Emeritus Professor of Geography, University of Leicester.

J.H.S. J. H. Skilton, B.A., M.A., M.Div., Ph.D., D.D., Emeritus and Adjunct Professor of New Testament, Westminster Theological Seminary, Philadelphia.

J.H.Sr. The late J. H. Stringer, M.A., B.D., formerly Tutor, London Bible College.

J.I.P. J. I. Packer, M.A., D.Phil., D.D., Professor of Theology, Regent College, Vancouver, BC.

J.J.H. J. J. Hughes, B.A., M.Div., Assistant Professor of Religious Studies, Westmont College, Santa Barbara, California.

J.L.K. The late J. L. Kelso, B.A., Th.M., M.A., Th.D., D.D., Ll.D., formerly Professor of Old Testament History and Biblical Archaeology, Pittsburgh Theological Seminary, Pennsylvania.

J.M. The late J. Murray, M.A., Th.M., formerly Professor of Systematic Theology, Westminster Theological Seminary, Philadelphia.

J.McK J. McKeown, B.D., Ph.D., Vice-Principal, Belfast Bible College.

LIST OF CONTRIBUTORS

J.M.H. J. M. Houston, M.A., B.Sc., D.Phil., Chancellor, formerly Principal, Regent College, Vancouver, BC.

J.N.B. J. N. Birdsall, M.A., Ph.D., F.R.A.S., Professor Emeritus of New Testament Studies and Textual Criticism, University of Birmingham.

J.N.G. The late J. N. Geldenhuys, B.A., B.D., Th.M.

J.P. J. Philip, M.A., Minister of Holyrood Abbey, Edinburgh.

J.P.B. The late J. P. Baker, M.A., B.D., formerly Rector of Newick, East Sussex.

J.P.K. J. P. Kane, Ph.D., Dip.Ed., Lecturer in Hellenistic Greek, University of Manchester.

J.P.U.L. J. P. U. Lilley, M.A., A.T.I.I., Magdalen College, Oxford.

J.R. J. Rea, M.A., Th.D., Professor of Old Testament, Melodyland School of Theology, Anaheim, California.

J.Ru J. Ruffle, M.A., Keeper, Oriental Museum, University of Durham.

J.S.W. The late J. S. Wright, M.A., formerly Principal, Tyndale Hall, Bristol; Canon of Bristol Cathedral.

J.T. J. A. Thompson, B.A., M.Div., Th.M., Ph.D., Research Consultant, American Bible Society.

J.T.W. The late J. T. Whitney, M.A., L.C.P., Ph.D., formerly Head of Religious Studies, South East Essex Sixth Form College.

J.W. J. Woodhead, Assistant Director, British School of Archaeology in Jerusalem, University of Edinburgh.

J.W.C. J. W. Charley, M.A., Priest in Charge of Great Malvern Priory, Herefordshire and Worcestershire.

J.W.D. J. W. Drane, M.A., Ph.D., Lecturer in Religious Studies, University of Stirling.

J.W.M. The late J. W. Meiklejohn, M.B.E., M.A., formerly Secretary of the Inter-School Christian Fellowship in Scotland.

K.A.K. K. A. Kitchen, B.A., Ph.D., formerly Personal and Brunner Professor of Egyptology, University of Liverpool.

K.E.B. K. E. Brower, M.A., Ph.D., Dean, Nazarene Theological College, Manchester.

K.L.McK. K. L. McKay, B.A., M.A., formerly Reader in Classics, The Australian National University, Canberra.

L.C.A. L. C. Allen, M.A., Ph.D., D.D., Professor of Old Testament, Fuller Theological Seminary, Pasadena, California.

L.M. L. L. Morris, M.Sc., M.Th., Ph.D., formerly Principal, Ridley College, Melbourne; Canon Emeritus of St Paul's Cathedral, Melbourne.

M.A.M. The late M. A. MacLeod, M.A., formerly Director, Christian Witness to Israel.

M.B. M. Beeching, B.A., B.D., M.Ed., formerly Principal Lecturer and Head of Department of Divinity, Cheshire College of Education, Alsager.

M.G.K. M. G. Kline, Th.M., Ph.D., Professor of Old Testament, Gordon-Conwell Theological Seminary, South Hamilton, Mass.; visiting Professor at Westminster West, Escondido, Califormia.

M.H.C. M. H. Cressey, M.A., Principal of Westminster College, Cambridge.

M.J.S. M. J. Selman, B.A., M.A., Ph.D., Director of Postgraduate Studies, Spurgeon's College, London.

M.J.S.R. M. J. S. Rudwick, M.A., Ph.D., Sc.D., formerly Professor of History of Science, The Free University, Amsterdam.

M.R.G. The late M. R. Gordon, B.D., formerly Principal, Bible Institute of South Africa, Kalk Bay, South Africa.

M.R.W.F. M. R. W. Farrer, M.A., formerly Vicar of St Paul's Church, Cambridge.

M.T. M. Turner, M.A., Ph.D., Vice-Principal (Academic) and Senior Lecturer in New Testament, London Bible College.

M.T.F. M. T. Fermer, B.A., B.Sc., A.R.C.S., formerly Vicar of Loscoe, Derbyshire.

N.H. N. Hillyer, B.D., S.Th., A.L.C.D., formerly Librarian, Tyndale House, Cambridge.

N.H.R. The late N. H. Ridderbos, D.D., formerly Emeritus Professor of Old Testament, The Free University, Amsterdam.

P.A.B. P. A. Blair, M.A., Rector of Barking, Essex.

P.E. P. Ellingworth, Ph.D., Translation Consultant, United Bible Societies, Aberdeen.

P.E.H. The late P. E. Hughes, M.A., B.D., Th.D., D.Litt., formerly Visiting Professor at Westminster Theological Seminary, Philadelphia; formerly Associate Rector of St John's Episcopal Church, Huntingdon Valley, Pennsylvania.

P.F.J. P. F. Jensen, M.A., B.D., D.Phil., Principal, Moore Theological College, Sydney, Australia.

P.H.D. P. H. Davids, B.A., M.Div., Ph.D., Researcher and Theological Teacher, Langley Vineyard Christian Fellowship, Langley, B.C., Canada.

P.T. P. Trebilco, Ph.D., Professor of New Testament Studies, Knox Theological Hall, Dunedin, New Zealand.

P.W. The late P. Woolley, B.A., Th.M., D.D., formerly Emeritus Professor of Church History, Westminster Theological Seminary, Philadelphia.

P.W.L.W. P. W. L. Walker, M.A., Ph.D., Lecturer in New Testament, Wycliffe Hall, Oxford.

R.A.F. The late R. A. Finlayson, M.A., formerly Emeritus Professor of Systematic Theology, Free Church College, Edinburgh.

R.A.H.G. R. A. H. Gunner, B.A., M.Th., formerly Lecturer in French, Brooklands Technical College, Weybridge, Surrey.

R.A.S. The late R. A. Stewart, M.A., B.D., M.Litt., formerly Church of Scotland Minister.

R.E.N. The late R. E. Nixon, M.A., formerly Principal, St John's College, Nottingham.

R.H.M. R. H. Mounce, B.A., B.D., Th.M., Ph.D., President, Whitworth College, Spokane, Washington State.

R.J.A.S. R. J. A. Sheriffs, B.A., B.D., Ph.D., formerly Lecturer in Old Testament, Rhodes University, Grahamstown, Cape Province.

R.J.B. R. J. Bauckham, M.A., Ph.D., Professor of New Testament Studies, University of St Andrews.

R.J.C. The late R. J. Coates, M.A., sometime Warden, Latimer House, Oxford.

R.J.McK. R. J. McKelvey, B.A., M.Th., D.Phil., formerly Principal, Northern College, Manchester.

R.J.T. R. J. Thompson, M.A., B.D., Th.M., D. Theol., formerly Tutor, Spurgeon's College, London, Whitley College, Melbourne and Tyndale College, Auckland, and Principal, New Zealand Baptist Theological College, Auckland.

R.J.W. R. J. Way, M.A., formerly Minister of St Columba's United Reformed Church, Leeds.

R.K.H. The late R. K. Harrison, M.Th., Ph.D., D.D., formerly Professor of Old Testament, Wycliffe College, University of Toronto.

R.N.C. R. N. Caswell, M.A., Ph.D., formerly Head of Religious Education, The Academical Institution, Coleraine, Northern Ireland.

R.P.G. R. P. Gordon, M.A., Ph.D., Lecturer in Divinity, University of Cambridge.

R.P.M. R. P. Martin, M.A., Ph.D., Professor of Biblical Studies, University of Sheffield.

R.S.H. R. S. Hess, B.A., M.Div., Th.M., Ph.D., Reader in Old Testament, Roehampton Institute London.

R.S.W. R. S. Wallace, M.A., B.Sc., Ph.D., formerly Professor, Columbia Theological Seminary, Decatur, Georgia.

R.T.B. R. T. Beckwith, M.A., D.D., Librarian, Latimer House, Oxford.

R.T.F. R. T. France, M.A., B.D., Ph.D., Rector of Wentnor, Shropshire; formerly Principal of Wycliffe Hall, Oxford.

R.V.G.T. The late R. V. G. Tasker, M.A., D.D., formerly Professor of New Testament Exegesis, University of London.

S.M. S. Motyer, M.A., M. Litt., Ph.D., Lecturer in New Testament, London Bible College.

S.S.S. S. S. Smalley, M.A., B.D., Ph.D., Dean of Chester Cathedral.

T.C.M. T. C. Mitchell, M.A., formerly Keeper, Department of Western Asiatic Antiquities, British Museum.

T.H.J. T. H. Jones, M.A., B.D., A.M.B.I.M., formerly Archdeacon of Loughborough.

T.L. T. Longman III, B.A., M.Div., M.Phil., Ph.D., Associate Professor of Old Testament, Westminster Theological Seminary, Philadelphia.

T.R.S. T. R. Schreiner, Ph.D., Professor of New Testament, Bethel Theological Seminary, St. Paul, Minnesota.

V.M.S. V. M. Sinton, M.A., Cert.Ed., Dip.H.E.Theol., Director of Pastoral Studies, Wycliffe Hall, Oxford.

W.G.P. The late W. G. Putman, B.A., B.D., formerly Methodist Minister, Walton-on-Thames, Surrey.

W.H.G. W. H. Gispen, D.Theol., Doctorandus Semitic Languages, Emeritus Professor of Hebrew and Old Testament, The Free University, Amsterdam.

W.J.C. The late W. J. Cameron, M.A., B.D., formerly Professor of New Testament Language, Literature, Exegesis and Theology, Free Church of Scotland College, Edinburgh.

W.J.M. The late W. J. Martin, M.A., Th.B., Ph.D., formerly Head of the Department of Hebrew and Ancient Semitic Languages, University of Liverpool.

W.O. W. Osborne, M.A., M.Phil., Head of Department, Hebrew and Old Testament, The Bible College of New Zealand.

W.W.W. W. W. Wessel, M.A., Ph.D., Professor of New Testament, Bethel College, St Paul, Minnesota.

AARON (Heb. *'ah^{a}rôn*). According to the genealogy of Ex. 6:14ff., Aaron was one of the two sons of Amram and Jochebed (the other being Moses) and third in line of descent from Levi (Levi-Kohath-Amram-Aaron); according to Ex. 7:7 he was 3 years older than Moses. Miriam, their sister, was older still, if she is Moses' unnamed 'sister' of Ex. 2:4, 7ff.

Aaron first appears in the Exodus narrative as 'Aaron the Levite' who went to meet his brother Moses on the latter's return to Egypt after the theophany at the burning bush; because of his superior eloquence he was to be Moses' spokesman to the Israelites and to Pharaoh (Ex. 4:14ff.). Throughout his career he was very much a lay figure alongside his dynamic brother; on the one occasion when he acted independently of Moses' instructions he acted wrongly (Ex. 32:1–6). In addition to being Moses' spokesman he also filled a thaumaturgic role: it was he who wielded the rod which became a serpent and swallowed up the rod-serpents of the Egyptian magicians (Ex. 7:8ff.) and which, when he stretched it out, turned the Nile into blood and then brought forth the successive plagues of frogs and gnats (Ex. 7:19; 8:5f., 16f.).

After the crossing of the Sea of Reeds Aaron was one of Moses' two supporters during the battle with the Amalekites (Ex. 17:8ff.), and ascended Mt Sinai in his company (Ex. 19:24), together with his sons, Nadab and Abihu, and seventy elders of Israel; there they had a vision of the God of Israel and shared a meal in his presence (Ex. 24:9ff.). On the next occasion, however, when Moses went up Mt Sinai attended by Joshua only (Ex. 24:12ff.), Aaron was persuaded by the people to make a visible image of the divine presence and fashioned the golden bull-calf, thus incurring Moses' severe displeasure (Ex. 32:1ff.). His formula of presentation of the bull-calf to the people, 'These are your gods, O Israel, who brought you up out of the land of Egypt!' (Ex. 32:4), provided a precedent for Jeroboam I when he installed the golden bull-calves at Bethel and Dan (1 Ki. 12:28).

In the priestly legislation of the Pentateuch Aaron is installed as high priest and his sons as priests, to minister in the wilderness tabernacle (Ex. 28:1ff.; Lv. 8:1ff.). Aaron is anointed with holy oil and is henceforth 'the anointed priest' (Lv. 4:3, *etc.*; *cf.* the oil on Aaron's beard in Ps. 133:2). He and his sons receive special vestments, but Aaron's are distinctive. The headband of his turban is inscribed 'Holy to Yahweh' (Ex. 28:36); his scapular (ephod) incorporates a breastpiece with twelve jewels (one for each tribe) and accommodation for the Urim and Thummim, the objects with which the sacred lot was cast to ascertain Yahweh's will for his people (Ex. 28:15ff.).

The outstanding day of the year for Aaron (and for each 'anointed priest' who succeeded him) was the Day of Atonement (Tishri 10), when he passed through the curtain separating the outer compartment of the sanctuary (the holy place) from the inner (the holy of holies) and presented the blood of an expiatory sacrifice in the latter for the sins of the people (Lv. 16:1ff.). On this occasion he did not wear his colourful vestments of 'glory and beauty' but a white linen robe.

Aaron's wife was Elisheba, of the tribe of Judah. Their elder sons Nadab and Abihu died in the wilderness after using 'unholy fire' for the incense-offering (Lv. 10:1ff.); from their two surviving sons, Eleazar and Ithamar, rival priestly families later traced their descent (1 Ch. 24:3).

Despite Aaron's status, Moses remained Yahweh's prophet to Israel and Israel's prevailing intercessor with Yahweh, and this excited the envy of Aaron and Miriam (Nu. 12:1ff.). Aaron himself (with Moses) attracted the envy of other Levitical families, whose leader was Korah (Nu. 16:1ff.). Their doubts about Aaron's privileges were answered by the phenomenon of *Aaron's rod.

Aaron, like Moses, was debarred from entering Canaan at the end of the wilderness wanderings; he died and was buried on Mt Hor, on the Edomite border, and his functions and vestments passed to Eleazar (Nu. 20:22ff.).

The priesthood in Israel came to be known comprehensively as 'the sons of Aaron'. The 'sons of Zadok', who served as priests in the Jerusalem Temple from its dedication under Solomon to 171 BC (apart from the hiatus of the Babylonian exile), are incorporated into the family of Aaron, among the descendants of Eleazar, in the genealogy of 1 Ch. 6:1ff. Ten years after the abolition of the Zadokite priesthood Alcimus, appointed high priest by the Seleucid authorities, was recognized by the Hasidaeans as 'a priest of the line of Aaron' (1 Macc. 7:12ff.), his genealogy being reckoned perhaps through Ithamar. Ben Sira pronounces Aaron's encomium in Ecclus. 45:6ff. The men of Qumran formed a community of 'Israel and Aaron', *i.e.* of Jewish laymen and priests (CD 1:7), the priests constituting an 'Aaronic holy of holies' (1QS 8:5f., 8f.), and looked forward to the coming of an Aaronic (priestly) Messiah alongside the (lay) 'Messiah of Israel' (1QS 9:11; CD 12:23f.; 20:1).

In NT Aaron is named as the ancestor of Elizabeth, mother of John the Baptist (Lk. 1:5), and receives incidental mention in Stephen's retrospect of the history of Israel (Acts 7:40). The writer to the Hebrews contrasts Aaron's circumscribed and hereditary priesthood with the perfect and perpetual ministry of Jesus in the heavenly sanctuary (Heb. 5:4; 7:11, *etc.*).

BIBLIOGRAPHY. R. de Vaux, *Ancient Israel*², 1965, pp. 345–401. F.F.B.

AARON'S ROD. The rebellion of Korah and his associates (Nu. 16:1ff.) made it clear that the sacral status of the tribe of Levi, and the priestly status of Aaron and his descendants within that tribe, should be publicly established. Accordingly, the leader of each of the tribes had his name written on the rod or sceptre (*maṭṭeh*) belonging to his tribe—Aaron's name being written on that of the tribe of Levi—and the twelve rods were placed 'in the tent of meeting before the testimony' (*i.e.* the tables of the law contained in the ark). Next morning the rod bearing Aaron's name was found to have put forth buds, blossoms and ripe almonds—a token that he was God's chosen priest. His rod was then put back 'before the testimony' as a warning against further rebellion (Nu. 17:1–11). According to Heb. 9:4 it was kept with the 'tables of the covenant' inside the ark. It was apparently the same rod that was used to strike the rock in Kadesh (Nu. 20:7–11); *cf.* the 'rod of God' (Ex. 4:20; 17:9). F.F.B.

ABADDON. The satanic angel of the bottomless pit (Rev. 9:11) whose Greek name is given as Apollyon, 'destroyer'. In Hebrew *'ᵃḇaddôn* means '(place of) destruction', and in the OT it is used as a synonym of *death and Sheol. (*HELL.) J.D.D.

ABANA. One of two Syrian rivers mentioned by the leprous Naaman in 2 Ki. 5:12. Named Chrysorrhoas ('golden river') by the Greeks, it is probably identical with the modern Barada, which rises in the Anti-Lebanon mountains 29 km NW of Damascus, and then, after flowing through the city, enters a marshy lake, Bahret-el-Kibliyeh, some 29 km to the E. The fertile gardens and orchards which it waters may explain Naaman's boast. J.D.D.

ABARIM. A name for the mountains which rise from the E shore of the Dead Sea, where the edge of the *Moabite plateau is broken up by a succession of E–W wadis: literally it means 'the regions beyond', *i.e.* beyond the Dead Sea from the point of view of Judah. At the N end of the range stands Mt *Nebo, from which Moses could look across over the land of Canaan (Nu. 27:12; Dt. 32:49). According to the itinerary in Nu. 33 the Israelites' last encampment before they reached the Jordan valley was in these mountains (vv. 47–48). *Iye-abarim (vv. 44–45; *cf.* Nu. 21:11) must have lain near the S end of the Dead Sea. In accordance with modern translations, against AV which translates 'passages' (*cf.* Targ.), this name should also be read in Je. 22:20, where two other mountains which overlook Canaan are mentioned.

BIBLIOGRAPHY. G. Adam Smith, *The Historical Geography of the Holy Land*[25], 1931, pp. 380–381; *GTT*, pp. 261, 444. G.I.D.

ABBA. An Aramaic word, in the emphatic state, meaning 'father'. The word passed into Hebrew, and occurs frequently in TB, where it is used by a child to its father and also as a style of address to rabbis. The term conveyed both a sense of warm intimacy and also filial respect; but in Jewish circles it has never been a form of address to the Almighty.

In the NT the word occurs 3 times, transliterated into Greek; in each instance it is a vocative, addressed to God, and the Greek equivalent is appended (Mk. 14:36; Rom. 8:15; Gal. 4:6). It appears that the double phrase was common in the Greek-speaking church, where its use may well have been liturgical. (The Lord's Prayer in its Aramaic form probably began with *'abba*.)

It appears that it was Jesus who first applied the term to God, and who gave authority to his disciples to do so. Paul sees in its use a symbol of the Christian's adoption as a son of God and his possession of the Spirit.

BIBLIOGRAPHY. J. Jeremias, *Abba*, 1966, pp. 1–67, *idem*, *New Testament Theology*, E.T. 1971, pp. 61–68; *TDNT* 1, pp. 5ff.; 5, p. 1006; *NIDNTT* 1, pp. 614ff. D.F.P.

ABDON (Heb. *'aḇdôn*). **1.** A levitical town in Asher (Jos. 21:30, spelt *Ebron* in 19:28); Kh. 'Abdeh (Avdon), 6 km inland from *Achzib, commanding a way into the hills. **2.** Last of the minor judges; from *Pirathon (Jdg. 12:13ff.). **3.** Head of a father's house in Benjamin (1 Ch. 8:23). **4.** A Benjaminite ancestor of Saul (1 Ch. 8:30; 9:36). **5.** A member of Josiah's court (2 Ch. 34:20). J.P.U.L.

ABEDNEGO. The name given to Azariah, companion of Daniel in exile (Dn. 1:7). Made an official of a Babylonian province until deposed on refusing to bow to an image (Dn. 3:13), but restored after escaping the furnace (3:30). He is mentioned in 1 Macc. 2:59 and, by implication, in Heb. 11:33–34. The name may be an Aramaic (Chaldean?) equivalent of a Babylonian one meaning 'servant of the shining one', perhaps making word-play on the name of the Babylonian god Nabû (*NEBO). D.J.W.

ABEL. The second son of Adam and Eve, and the brother (perhaps the twin, Gn. 4:1–2) of *Cain. The name is sometimes connected with Akkadian *aplu*, Sumerian *ibila*, 'son', or Akkadian *ibilu*, 'camel', but these remain conjectures. Abel was a righteous (*dikaios*, Mt. 23:35) man and when he, as a shepherd (Gn. 4:2), brought an offering of the firstlings of his flock, God accepted it (Gn. 4:4; Heb. 11:4). He was subsequently murdered by Cain, leaving, so far as we know, no offspring. It is clear that to Christ he was a historical person (Mt. 23:35; Lk. 11:51).

BIBLIOGRAPHY. *KB*, p. 227; and *cf.* S. Landersdorfer, *Sumerisches Sprachgut im Alten Testament*, 1916, pp. 67–68. T.C.M.

ABEL. An element of certain place-names, chiefly in Transjordan. The traditional interpretation 'meadow' is not at all certain, and Baumgartner (*KB*, p. 7) prefers 'brook, watercourse', comparing Heb. *'ûḇāl*, *yûḇāl*, *yāḇāl*. 'Abel' of *MT* of 1 Sa. 6:18 (*cf.* AV) is probably a textual error, and *'eḇen* = 'stone' should be read (*cf.* LXX and modern versions). In 2 Sa. 20:18 'Abel' stands for 'Abel (of) Beth-maacah' (vv. 14–15), and in 2 Ch. 16:4 (corrupt text?) Abel-maim seems to be the same place (*cf.* 1 Ki. 15:20). The exact locations of Abel-mizraim 'beyond (or 'beside', with NEB) the Jordan' (Gn. 50:11) and Abel-keramim (Jdg. 11:33: somewhere in Ammon) are unknown, but see Skinner and Kidner on Gn. 50:11, and *LOB*, pp. 243, 371 for possible sites. G.I.D.

ABEL-BETH-MAACAH (Heb. *'āḇēl bêṯ ma'ᵃḵâ*, 'meadow of the house of oppression'). The town in N Naphtali in which Joab besieged Sheba, son of Bichri (2 Sa. 20:14); captured by the Syrians under Ben-hadad (*c.* 879 BC, 1 Ki. 15:20; 2 Ch. 16:4) where it is called Abel-maim. Captured by the Assyrians under Tiglath-pileser III (*c.* 733 BC, 2 Ki. 15:29). Possibly part of the Syrian state of *Maacah. It has been identified with Tell Abil 20 km N of Lake Huleh. The use of the name Abel alone in the Egyp. Execration Texts and in 2 Sa. 20:18, as well as the use of the explicative conjunction in 2 Sa. 20:14 ('Abel, *i.e.* Beth-maacah'), shows that these are two alternative names rather than one consisting of three parts. D.W.B.

ABEL-MEHOLAH. A town named in conjunction with the flight of the Midianites from Gideon (Jdg. 7:22). It became part of Solomon's fifth district (1 Ki. 4:12) and was Elisha's birthplace (1 Ki. 19:16). The site is unknown, but is usually placed in the Jordan valley S of Beth-shean. D.W.B.

ABIATHAR (Heb. *'eḇyāṯār*, 'father of excellence'). Son of Ahimelech and with him priest at Nob, he escaped alone from the massacre of his family by Saul to join David at Keilah, bringing with him an ephod (1 Sa. 22:20–22; 23:6, 9). He helped to take the ark to Jerusalem, where he was one of David's counsellors (1 Ch. 15:11; 27:34). He was sent back to Jerusalem with his son Jonathan, when David fled, to act in the king's interests against Absalom (2 Sa. 15:25ff.; 17:15). At the close of David's reign he conspired to make Adonijah king, and was expelled from office by Solomon (1 Ki. 1–2), ending Eli's line. High priest during David's reign, he seems to have been senior to Zadok (1 Ki. 2:35; *cf.* Mk. 2:26). It is uncertain whether he had a son Ahimelech or whether the two names have been transposed in 2 Sa. 8:17; 1 Ch. 24:6. In Mk. 2:26, 'when Abiathar was high priest' is better rendered 'in the passage about Abiathar', by analogy with Mk. 12:26. A.R.M.

ABIEL (Heb. *'ᵃḇî'ēl*, 'God is my father'). **1.** Saul's grandfather (1 Sa. 9:1 and 14:51). **2.** One of David's heroes (1 Ch. 11:32), called Abi-albon (2 Sa. 23:31), *albon* being a copyist's transference from the following verse. Some codices of LXX have Abiel here. R.A.H.G.

ABIEZER (Heb. *'ᵃḇî'ezer*, 'my father is help'). **1.** A clan of Manasseh (Jos. 17:2) of which Gideon was a member (Jdg. 6:11). In Gideon's time the clan was centred on Ophrah (Jdg. 6:11, 24), probably to be identified with al-Ṭayibeh N of Beth-shean. A district of Abiezer is mentioned in the Samaria Ostraca (nos. 13, 28) from *c.* 800 BC and is located SW of Shechem (see *LOB*, pp. 315–327). Iezer (Nu. 26:30) is a contraction.

2. One of the thirty mighty men of David (2 Sa. 23:27; 1 Ch. 11:28) and a native of Anathoth, 4 km N of Jerusalem. He commanded the ninth division of David's militia in the ninth month (1 Ch. 27:12). R.P.G.

ABIGAIL (Heb. *'ᵃḇîḡayil*, 'my father is joy'(?)).

1. The wife of Nabal the Carmelite or Calebite, a wealthy boor who lived in Maon, was a contrast to her husband. She realized that his veiled insult in his refusal to give gifts to David's men, at the time of sheep-shearing, endangered the whole household, and so, on her own responsibility, she took gifts of loaves, wine, sheep, corn, raisins and figs, and waylaid David as he was planning his attack, thus preventing bloodshed. Her wisdom, beauty and dignity impressed him and he blessed God. When she told Nabal of her action he appreciated the narrowness of their escape, and from fright fell into an apoplectic fit and died—at the hand of God. David then married her and thus secured a new social position and a rich estate. With Ahinoam, the Jezreelite, she shared David's life at Gath. They were captured by the Amalekites near Ziklag and rescued (1 Sa. 30:18). She was the mother of Chileab (2 Sa. 3:3), or Daniel (1 Ch. 3:1), David's second son.

2. The wife of Ithra (2 Sa. 17:25) or Jether (1 Ch. 2:17; 1 Ki. 2:5) the Ishmaelite—terms easily confused in Hebrew—and mother of Amasa. She was a daughter of Nahash (2 Sa. 17:25) or Jesse (1 Ch. 2:13–16). Modern critics dismiss *Nahash as a scribal error. M.B.

ABIHAIL (Heb. *'ᵃḇîḥayil*, 'my father is might'). Man's and woman's name. **1.** A Levite, father of Zuriel (Nu. 3:35). **2.** The wife of Abishur (1 Ch. 2:29). **3.** A Gadite living in Bashan (1 Ch. 5:14). **4.** The mother of Rehoboam's wife Mahalath, and daughter of Eliab, David's eldest brother (2 Ch. 11:18). **5.** Father of Esther and uncle of Mordecai (Est. 2:15; 9:29). R.A.H.G.

ABIHU (Heb. *'ᵃḇîhû'*, 'my father is he' [*sc.* Yahweh]). Son of Aaron, a priest. He saw God in his glory (Ex. 24:1, 9) yet acted independently of the requirements of the ritual law and was killed by holy fire (Lv. 10:1–8). A.R.M.

ABIJAH (Heb. *'ᵃḇîyâ*, 'my father is Yahweh', or 'Yahweh is father'). A name borne by several men and women in the OT. Chief among them are the second son of Samuel (1 Sa. 8:2; 1 Ch. 6:28), a descendant of Eleazar who gave his name to the eighth of the twenty-four courses of priests (1 Ch. 24:10; *cf.* Lk. 1:5), the son of Jeroboam I (1 Ki. 14:1–18), and the son and successor of Rehoboam king of Judah (1 Ch. 3:10; 2 Ch. 11:20; 13:1). The name of the latter appears as Abijam (*'ᵃḇîyām*, 'father of sea', or 'father of west') in 1 Ki. 14:31; 15:1, 7–8. Several Heb. MSS, however, read Abijah here and this reading is supported by the LXX *Abiou*.

Abijah reigned 3 years over Judah (1 Ki. 15:2; 2 Ch. 13:2). The accounts of his reign in Kings and Chronicles stand in marked yet reconcilable contrast to each other. In the former he is censured for his adherence to the corrupt religious policy of his father (1 Ki. 15:3). The account in Chronicles (2 Ch. 13) is almost wholly concerned with a decisive victory with Yahweh's help over the numerically stronger army of Jeroboam I. Abijah's oration before the battle condemns the apostasy of the N kingdom and affirms the divine sanction attaching to the Davidic dynasty and the worship offered at the Temple at Jerusalem. J.C.J.W.

ABILENE. A region of Anti-Lebanon, attached to the city of Abila (*cf.* Heb. *'āḇēl*, 'meadow'), on the bank of the Abana (mod. Barada), some 29 km NW of Damascus (its ruins still stand round the village of Es-Suk). Abilene belonged to the Ituraean kingdom of Ptolemy Mennaeus (*c.* 85–40 BC) and his son Lysanias I (40–36 BC); it was later detached to form the tetrarchy of a younger *Lysanias, mentioned in Luke 3:1. In AD 37 it was given by the emperor Gaius to Herod Agrippa I as part of his kingdom, and in 53 by Claudius to Herod Agrippa II. *Cf.* Jos., *BJ* 2. 215, 247; *Ant.* 18. 237; 19. 275; 20. 138.

BIBLIOGRAPHY. *HJP*, 1, 1973, pp. 561–573. F.F.B.

ABIMELECH (Heb. *'ᵃḇîmelek*, 'the (divine) king is my father'). **1.** Philistine kings of Gerar bearing this name figure in episodes involving Abraham (Gn. 20:1–18) and Isaac (Gn. 26:1–33). The similarities between the accounts have led many to suppose that they are doublets, but Abimelech may have been a cognomen of Philistine kings (*cf.* Egyptian 'Pharaoh'); there are also significant differences in the stories (and note the relevance of Gn. 20:13 for both Abraham and Isaac). Nor need the reference to the presence of Philistines in Canaan in patriarchal days be anachronistic, for 'Philistine' may mean that the Gerarites were an advance party of the Sea Peoples who later settled in Palestine; of these the Philistines were to become the dominant element. In the superscription to Ps. 34 the name Abimelech is given to Achish king of Gath.

2. A son of Gideon by a Shechemite concubine (Jdg. 8:31). With the aid of his mother's family he murdered all seventy of his brothers, with the exception of Jotham. Although he proclaimed himself 'king'—a title which his father had repudiated (Jdg. 8:23)—his territory cannot have extended beyond W Manasseh. After 3 years the Shechemites turned against their king and sided with Gaal. Abimelech responded vigorously and cruelly; he later died somewhat ingloriously while besieging Thebez. For the archaeological background to Jdg. 9, see G. E. Wright, *Shechem*, 1965, pp. 123–128.

3. A priest, the son of Abiathar (1 Ch. 18:16) according to *MT*, but perhaps a scribal error for A*h*imelech (so RSV; *cf.* 2 Sa. 8:17). R.P.G.

ABIRAM (Heb. *'ᵃḇîrām*, 'my father is exalted'). **1.** A son of Eliab, a Reubenite, who with his brother, *Dathan, and *Korah, a Levite, and others instigated a rebellion against Moses (Nu. 16). **2.** The eldest son of *Hiel of Bethel whose life was lost during the rebuilding of the fortress of Jericho *c.* 870 BC (1 Ki. 16:34; *cf.* Jos. 6:26). D.W.B.

ABISHAG (Heb. *'ᵃḇîšaḡ*; possibly, 'father has wandered'). A beautiful *Shunammite girl brought to David to nurse him in his old age. After he died, Adonijah, his eldest son, wished to marry her, but Solomon, seeing this as an attempt to gain the throne, since apparently a king's harem were inherited by his successor (*cf.* R. de Vaux, *Ancient Israel*, 1961, p. 116), had his brother killed (1 Ki. 2:13–25). D.W.B.

ABISHAI (Heb. *'ᵃḇîšay*, 'father of gift' or 'my father is Jesse'). Son of Zeruiah and brother of Joab and Asahel (2 Sa. 2:18). 2 Sa. 23:18; 1 Ch. 11:20–21 show him to be chief of 'the three', which must mean (as the Vulgate translates) 'the second group of three', next in order to 'the three' of 2 Sa. 23:8–12. However, two Hebrew MSS and the Syriac of 2 Sa. 23:18-19 and 1 Ch. 11:20 make him the chief of 'the thirty'. He had an eventful career as a high officer in David's army. G.W.G.

ABNER (Heb. *'aḇnēr*, but *'ᵃḇînēr* in 1 Sa. 14:50). Saul's cousin and the commander-in-chief of his army (1 Sa. 14:50); one of the very few state officials mentioned in connection with Saul's reign. On Saul's death Abner secured for his remaining son Eshbaal (Ishbosheth) the allegiance of all but the Judahites (2 Sa. 2:8–10), installing him in a new capital (Mahanaim) on the E side of the Jordan. In the ensuing struggle between the house of Saul and the house of David (*cf.* 2 Sa. 3:1) Abner loyally supported his protégé until the latter insinuated that, by taking Saul's concubine, Abner was himself staking a claim to the throne. He now began to make overtures to David, promising to unite all Israel behind their rightful king. But Joab did not trust Abner and, partly to avenge the death of his brother Asahel (2 Sa. 2:18–23), murdered him in the gate of Hebron (2 Sa. 3:27). R.P.G.

ABOMINATION. Four Hebrew words are translated thus. **1.** *piggûl* is used of sacrificial flesh which has been left too long (Lv. 7:18, *etc.*). **2.** *šiqqûṣ* refers to idols ('Milcom the abomination of the Ammonites', 1 Ki. 11:5), and to customs derived from idolatry (Je. 16:18). **3.** The related word *šeqeṣ* is used in much the same way, a notable extension of meaning being its application to food prohibited for Israelites as being 'unclean' (Lv. 11:10f.). **4.** *tô'ēḇâ* is the most important word of the group. This may denote that which offends anyone's religious susceptibilities: 'every shepherd is an abomination to the Egyptians' (Gn. 46:34; so with eating with foreigners, Gn. 43:32). Or it may be used of idols (in 2 Ki. 23:13 *šiqqûṣ* is used of Ashtoreth and Chemosh and *tô'ēḇâ* of Milcom). It denotes practices derived from idolatry, as when Ahaz 'burned his son as an offering, according to the abominable practices of the nations whom the Lord drove out' (2 Ki. 16:3), and all magic and divination (Dt. 18:9–14). But the word is not confined to heathen customs. Sacrifice offered to Yahweh in the wrong spirit is 'abomination' (Pr. 15:8; Is. 1:13). So is sexual sin (Lv. 18:22). And the word attains a strongly ethical connotation when such things as 'lying lips' and 'diverse weights' are said to be an abomination to the Lord (Pr. 12:22; 20:23, *cf.* also 6:16ff., *etc.*). L.M.

ABRAHAM. A descendant of Shem and son of Terah; husband of Sarah and, as father of Isaac, ancestor of the Hebrew nation and, through Ishmael, of other Semites (Gn. 17:5; 25:10–18). His life (Gn. 11:26–25:10; summarized in Acts 7:2–8) is taken as an example of outstanding faith in God (Heb. 11:8–12) by Jew, Christian and Muslim.

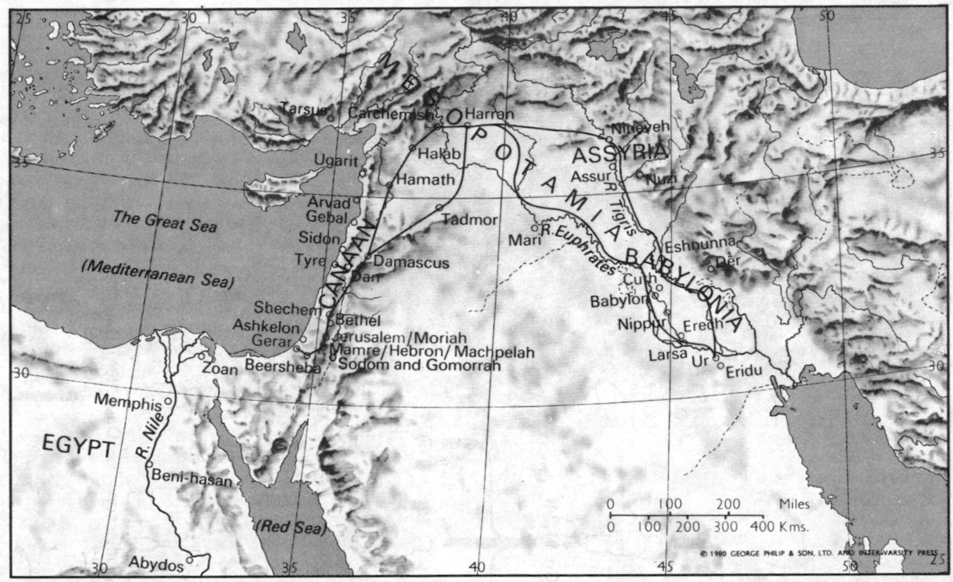

Possible routes for Abraham's journey from Ur into Canaan.

I. The name

The etymology of the name Abram (Heb. *'aḇrām*; used Gn. 11:26-17:4 and rarely elsewhere, *e.g.* 1 Ch. 1:27; Ne. 9:7) is uncertain. It probably means 'the father is exalted' and is a typical specific early W Semitic personal name form of Ab(i)ram. After the covenant of Gn. 17:5 his name is changed to Abraham (*'aḇrāhām*) and explained as 'father of a multitude' of nations. Both these name forms occur in cuneiform and Egyptian texts from the 19th century BC onwards, but not as identical persons. The latter form, possibly as popular etymology, is generally considered a dialectical variant of Abram, though a distinct new name is implied (which may incorporate an early form of Arabic *rhm* = 'multitude').

II. His career

Abraham was born in *Ur and moved with his wife Sarai, his father, brother Nahor, and nephew Lot to Harran (Gn. 11:26–32). At the age of 75, on his father's death, Abraham moved on to Palestine (Canaan) near Bethel, to Mamre near Hebron, and to Beersheba. At each place he set up an altar and tent-shrine.

His relations with foreigners while staying near Shechem, in Egypt, Gerar and Machpelah, portray him as a respected leader of a group with whom they dealt as with an equal. He acted as acknowledged leader of a coalition which rescued his nephew Lot who had been taken from Sodom by a group of 'kings' (Gn. 14). Stress is laid on his life, not so much as a 'pilgrim', but as a 'resident-alien' (*gēr*) without a capital city. He was a wealthy man with servants (14:14) and possessions (13:2), living amicably among Canaanites (12:6), Perizzites (13:7), Philistines (21:34) and Egyptians, and negotiating with Hittites (23).

III. *Covenants

In accordance with the form of early treaty-covenants, Abraham is granted a covenant-treaty by the 'Great King' Yahweh (15:17–21) and entered into parity-treaties with contemporary powers.

(*i*) *The land*

By covenant Yahweh promised Abraham and his successors the land from the river Euphrates and SW for ever. Abraham's faith was shown both by taking steps to appropriate this divine land-grant from Beersheba (21:33) to Dan (14:14) by symbolic acts, or by taking it over as 'leader' of its multiracial inhabitants by virtue of defeating others who had once controlled it. Yet he did not set up any capital and had to purchase a place to bury his wife (Gn. 23).

(*ii*) *The family*

The same divine covenant promised and reaffirmed to him a family and nations as successors (13:16). Being childless, he first made his major-domo Eliezer of Damascus his heir (15:2). He treated his nephew like an heir, giving him a preferential share in his 'promised' land until Lot chose to move outside to Sodom (13:8–13). Then, aged 86, he had a son, Ishmael, by an Egyptian concubine, Hagar, given him by his wife. They were later expelled. Then, when Abraham was 99, the promise of family, nation and law was repeated, and Yahweh gave him his change of name and the covenant sign of male circumcision (17). Again the covenant-promise was confirmed by another theophany at Mamre, despite Sarah's disbelief (18:1–19). A year later Isaac was born.

The great test of Abraham's faith came when Yahweh ordered him to sacrifice Isaac at Moriah. He obeyed, his hand being stayed at the moment of slaughter when a ram was provided as a substitute (22:1–14). Thereupon the covenant between Yahweh and Abraham was reaffirmed (vv. 15–20). Sarah died, aged 127, and was buried in a cave at

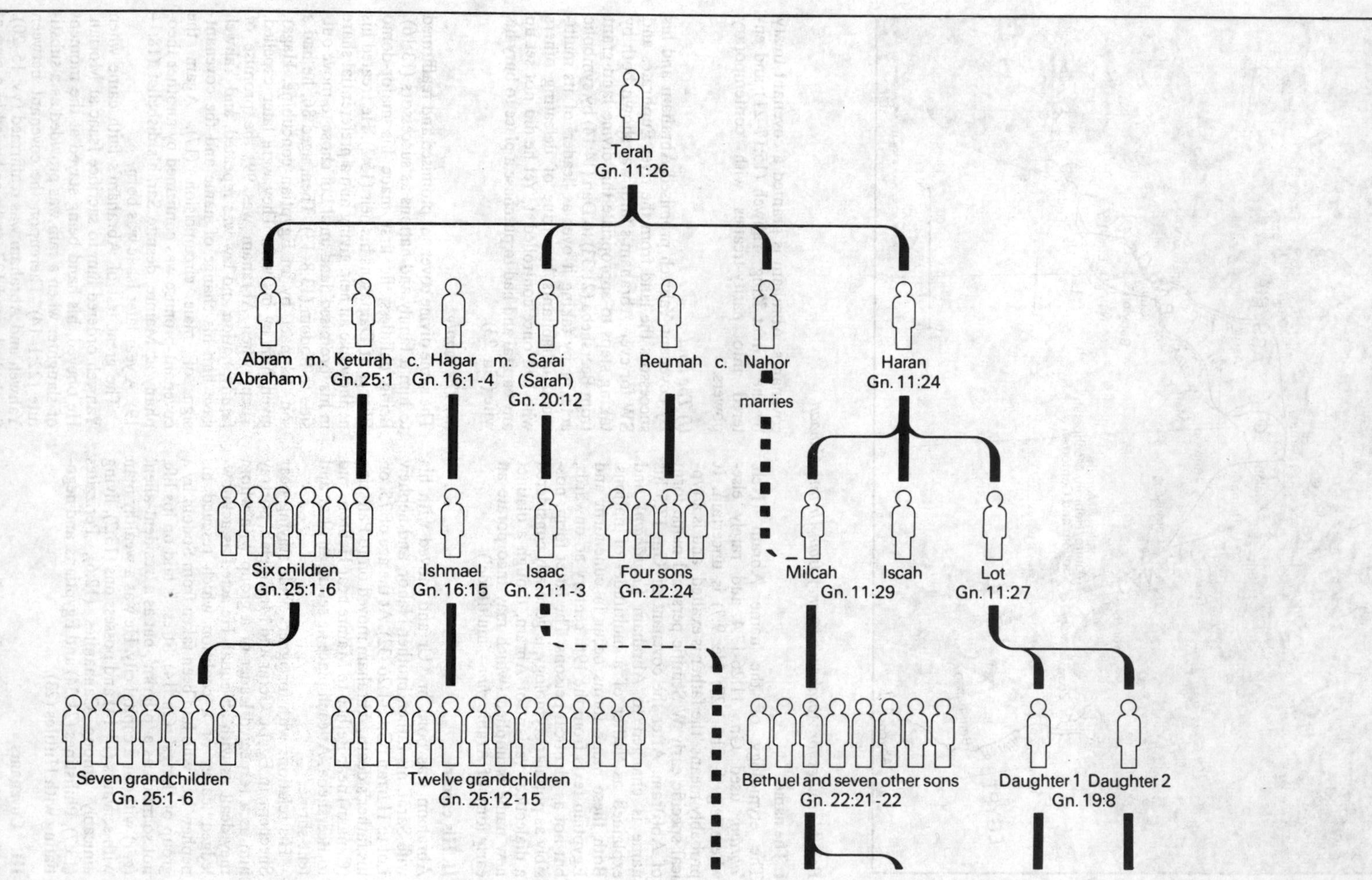
Terah
Gn. 11:26
Abram m. Keturah c. Hagar m. Sarai
(Abraham) Gn. 25:1 Gn. 16:1-4 (Sarah)
Gn. 20:12
Reumah c. Nahor
marries
Haran
Gn. 11:24
Six children
Gn. 25:1-6
Ishmael
Gn. 16:15
Isaac
Gn. 21:1-3
Four sons
Gn. 22:24
Milcah Iscah
Gn. 11:29
Lot
Gn. 11:27
Seven grandchildren
Gn. 25:1-6
Twelve grandchildren
Gn. 25:12-15
Bethuel and seven other sons
Gn. 22:21-22
Daughter 1 Daughter 2
Gn. 19:8

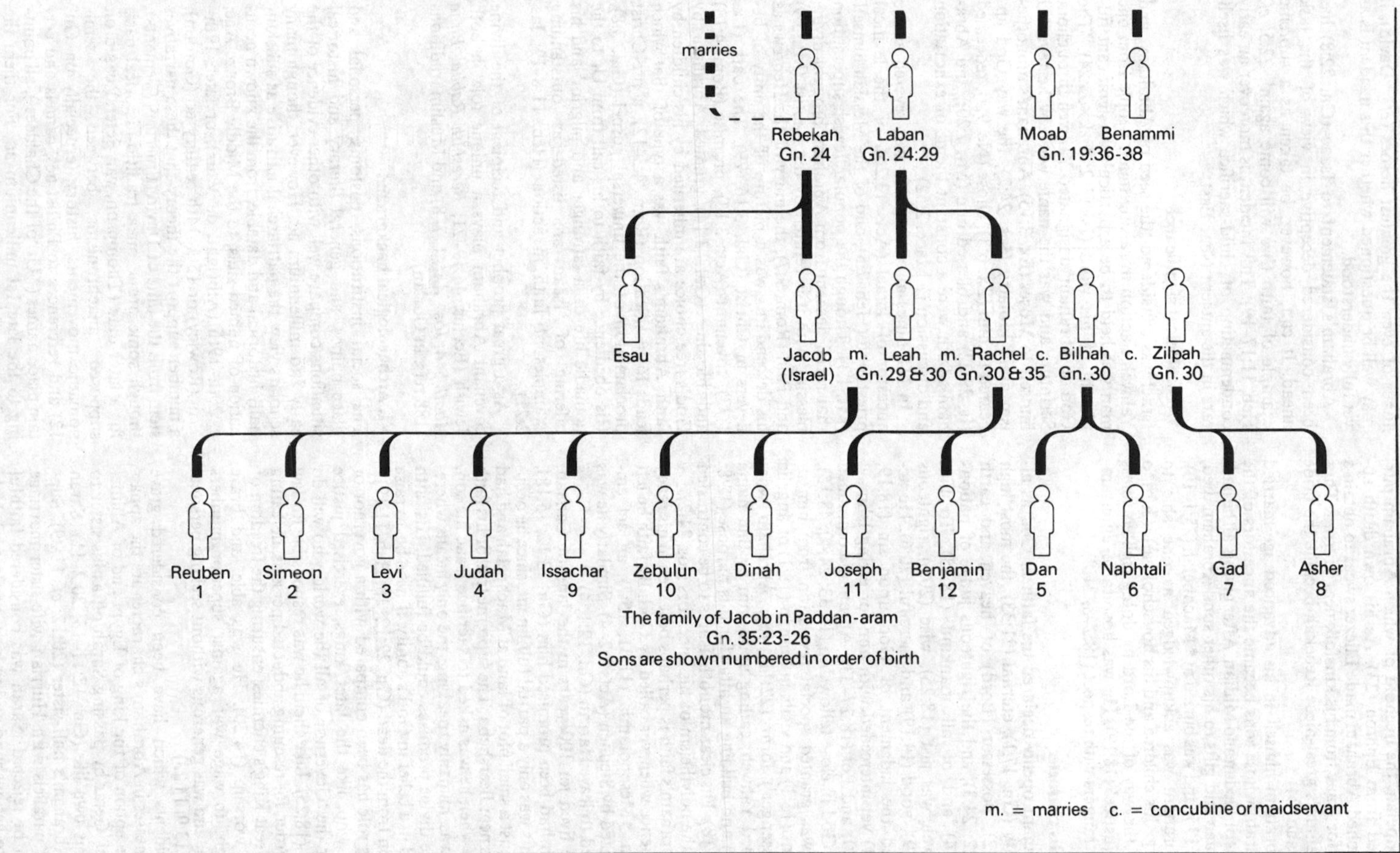

Genealogical table of Abraham and his family.

Machpelah, the freehold of which Abraham purchased from Ephron (23). As his own death approached Abraham made Eliezer swear to obtain a wife for Isaac from his kinsfolk near Harran. Thus Abraham's great-niece Rebekah became the bride of Isaac (24).

Abraham himself in his advanced age married Keturah, whose sons became the ancestors of the tribes of Dedan and Midian. After giving 'all he had' to Isaac and gifts to his other sons Abraham died, aged 175, and was buried at *Machpelah (25:1–10).

Abraham was acknowledged as one able to 'charge his children and his household after him to keep the way of the Lord by doing righteousness and justice' (18:19). He was hospitable, entertaining strangers with respect (18:2–8; 21:8).

IV. His character

Abraham openly declared his faith in God as almighty (Gn. 17:1), eternal (21:33), the most high (14:22), possessor (Lord) of heaven and earth (14:22; 24:3), and the righteous judge of nations (15:14) and of all mankind (18:25). To him Yahweh was just (18:25), wise (20:6), righteous (18:19), good (19:19) and merciful (20:6). He accepted the judgment of God upon sin (18:19; 20:11) yet interceded with him for erring Ishmael (17:20) and Lot (18:27–33). Abraham communed with God in close fellowship (18:33; 24:40; 48:15), and was granted special revelation from him in visions (15:1) and visits in human (18:1) or angelic ('messenger') form (22:11, 15). Abraham worshipped Yahweh, calling upon him by that name (13:4) and building an altar for this purpose (12:8; 13:4, 18). His clear monotheism is to be contrasted with the polytheism of his ancestors (Jos. 24:2).

Abraham's faith is perhaps best seen in his ready obedience whenever called by God. By faith he left Ur in *Mesopotamia (11:31; 15:7), an act emphasized by Stephen (Acts 7:2–4). Similarly he was guided to leave Harran (Gn. 12:1, 4).

He lived for 100 years in the land of Canaan, which had been promised him (Gn. 13:12; 15:18), but this was only a partial fulfilment, since he occupied just a small plot of land at Machpelah and had rights near Beersheba. The supreme trial of his faith came when he was asked to sacrifice Isaac his son, who was, humanly speaking, the only means whereby the divine promises could be fulfilled. His faith rested in a belief in God's ability, if need be, to raise his son from the dead (Gn. 22:12, 18; Heb. 11:19).

His role has been compared with a governor or ruler who, like the later kings, exercised justice under the 'Governor of all the world who will do right' (18:25). Like them he was responsible for law and order, for rescuing abducted persons, defeating the Great King's enemies, ensuring the freedom of local worship (14:20). He was able, and brave enough, to wage war against superior numbers (14:5), and was generous without seeking personal gain (13:9; 14:23).

Incidents which have been considered grave weaknesses in Abraham's character are the apparent deception of the king of Egypt and of Abimelech of Gerar by passing Sarah off as his sister to save his own life (Gn. 12:11–13; 20:2–11). Sarah was Abraham's half-sister (20:12; *cf.* 11:29). Supposed parallels with Hurrian wife-sister marriage are to be rejected. Sarah was considered faithful both to her husband and to his God (Is. 51:2; Heb. 11:11; 1 Pet. 3:6), so that, while this might be an example of the way the Scriptures portray the fortunes of even the greatest heroes (*cf.* *David), it may well be questioned whether this incident is as yet fully understood.

Abraham's statement to Isaac (Gn. 22:8) has been considered deceptive in view of the task ahead. It can, however, be taken as a supreme example of faith ('*we* will come again', 22:5; *cf.* Heb. 11:17–19). This incident is moreover an early condemnation of child-sacrifice which was itself rare in the ancient Near East.

V. Theological significance

Israel was considered 'the seed of Abraham', and Yahweh's action in raising much people from one man was held to be a particularly significant fulfilment of his word (Is. 51:2; Ezk. 33:24). 'The God of Abraham' designated Yahweh throughout Scripture and was the name whereby he revealed himself to Moses (Ex. 3:15). Abraham's monotheism amid idolatry (Jos. 24:2), the way God appeared to him (Ex. 6:3), chose (Ne. 9:7), redeemed (Is. 29:22) and blessed him (Mi. 7:20), and Abraham's faith were a constant theme of exhortation and discussion (1 Macc. 2:52).

In NT times also Abraham was revered as the ancestor of Israel (Acts 13:26), of the levitical priesthood (Heb. 7:5), and of the Messiah himself (Mt. 1:1). Though the popular Jewish superstition that racial descent from Abraham brought divine blessing with it is refuted by the Baptist (Mt. 3:9) and Paul (Rom. 9:7), the unity of the Hebrews as his descendants was a picture of the unity of believers in Christ (Gal. 3:16, 29). The oath (Lk. 1:73), covenant (Acts 3:13), promise (Rom. 4:13) and blessing (Gal. 3:14) granted Abraham by God's free choice are inherited by his children by faith. Abraham's faith was a type of that which leads to justification (Rom. 4:3–12), a pre-Christ proclamation of the universal gospel (Gal. 3:8). His obedience by faith to his call from Ur to the nomadic life of a 'stranger and pilgrim' and his offering of Isaac are listed as outstanding examples of faith in action (Heb. 11:8–19; Jas. 2:21).

As a great prophet and recipient of the divine covenant Abraham plays a unique role in both Jewish (Ecclus. 44:19–21; *Bereshith Rabba*; *Pirqe Aboth* 5. 4; Jos., *Ant.* 1. 7–8) and Muslim traditions (188 refs. in Qur'an).

VI. Archaeological background

The social institutions, customs, personal and place names, and general literary and historical situations compare well with other evidence of the early 2nd millennium BC. However, though many scholars view the patriarchal narrative as substantially historical and datable, from the known occupation of named sites, to the Middle Bronze Age, *c.* 20th–19th (Albright, de Vaux), or later, 19th–17th (Rowley) or 15th–14th century BC (Gordon), a number support the theory that these narratives stem from the time of David (Emerton, Clements), though some argue on a traditio-historical basis for a later date (Thompson, van Seters) based on supposed anachronisms between the semi-nomadic movements, history (especially on Gn. 12) and references to Philistines, camels and certain place names (*Ur 'of the Chaldees'), all pointing to the late 1st millennium BC. For them the tradition is of later composition (Thompson, van Seters). Most of these points can be answered individually on the basis of all available evidence (details of the *Ebla texts, *c.* 2300 BC, may provide additional data). It is to be noted that the precise details, the absence of 'saga' personification of Abraham as a tribe, and the fact that the majority of Abraham's deeds are recorded as those of an individual, are indications of early sources.

BIBLIOGRAPHY. A. R. Millard and D. J. Wiseman, eds., *Essays on the Patriarchal Narratives*, 1980; T. L. Thompson, *Historicity of the Patriarchal Narratives*, 1974; A. R. Millard, *ABD* 1, pp. 35–41. D.J.W.

ABRAHAM'S BOSOM. A figure of speech used by Jesus in the parable of *Lazarus and Dives (Lk. 16:22–23), illustrating the 'great gulf fixed' between the bliss of paradise and the misery of Hades (*cf.* Mt. 8:11–12). The dead Lazarus is portrayed as reclining next to Abraham at the feast of the blessed, after the Jewish manner, which brought the head of one person almost into the bosom of the one who sat above him, and placed the most favoured guest in such a relation to his host (*e.g.* Jn. 13:23). To sit in Abraham's bosom, in Talmudic language, was to enter *Paradise (*cf.* 4 Macc. 13:17). Such Oriental imagery should not be regarded as evidence of Jewish belief in an interim state. J.D.D.

ABRECH. An obscure term proclaimed before Joseph as Pharaoh's chief minister (Gn. 41:43). W. Spiegelberg interpreted it as Egyp. *lb-r.k*, 'attention!', 'look out!' J. Vergote suggests *l.brk*, 'pay homage!', 'kneel!', an Egyptian imperative of a Semitic loan-word (*Joseph en Égypte*, 1959, pp. 135–141, 151). Recent discussions add nothing to these suggestions. K.A.K.

ABSALOM (Heb. *'aḇšālôm*, 'father is/of peace'). **1.** Third son of David, with a foreign mother, Maacah, daughter of Talmai, king of Geshur (2 Sa. 3:3). His personal comeliness was shared by Tamar, his sister, and was the cause of her being violated by Amnon, David's first-born son by another mother (2 Sa. 13:1-18). When Absalom learnt of this incident, he brought about the death of Amnon, thus incurring the displeasure of his father, before which he fled to Geshur (2 Sa. 13:19–39). The first part of Nathan's prophecy had come true (2 Sa. 12:10). After 3 years of exile, and a further 2 years of banishment from the court, David received his son back into favour, and was repaid by a plot against his throne (2 Sa. 15:1–15). The 'forty years' of v. 7 does not seem to square with 18:5, and the reading 'four' has been suggested. The second part of Nathan's prophecy now came true (2 Sa. 12:11a). The third part (v. 11b) was also soon fulfilled (2 Sa. 16:20–23) and there was now no turning back. There is pathos and spiritual profit in the words of David when the Levites sought to take the Ark into flight with the deposed king (2 Sa. 15:25–26). The end of Absalom is well known. With the help of Hushai (2 Sa. 15:32–37 and 17:1–16) and Joab (2 Sa. 18:1–21; see also 19:1–7) David was able to defeat him in battle. 2 Sa. 18:9–17 describes his ignominious death. The third Psalm purports to come from the period of Absalom's rebellion.

2. Rehoboam's father-in-law (2 Ch. 11:20–21; called 'Abishalom' in 1 Ki. 15:2, 10).

3. In the Apocrypha, an ambassador of Judas Maccabaeus, the father of Mattathias and Jonathan (1 Macc. 11:70; 13:11; 2 Macc. 11:17). T.H.J.

ABYSS. The Greek word *abyssos* ('bottomless [pit]', 'deep') appears 9 times in the NT. It is translated in RSV as 'abyss' (the abode of demons, Lk. 8:31; the place of the dead, Rom. 10:7) and 'bottomless pit' (the place of torment, Rev. 9:1–2, 11; 11:7; 17:8; 20:1, 3). LXX renders Heb. *tᵉhôm*, 'deep place', as 'abyss' (Gn. 1:2, *etc.*), with reference to the primitive idea of a vast mass of water on which the world floated, or to the underworld (Ps. 71:20). (*HELL.) J.D.D.

ACCAD, AKKAD. One of the major cities, with Babylon and Erech, founded by Nimrod (Gn. 10:10). It bore the Semitic name of *Akkadu*, Sumerian *Agade*. Its precise location near Sippar or Babylon is uncertain, though some identify it with the ruins of Tell *Šešubār* or even Babylon itself.

Inscriptions show that an early Semitic dynasty founded by Sargon I (*c.* 2350 BC) flourished here. At this time Akkad controlled all Sumer (S Babylonia), and its armies reached Syria, Elam and S Anatolia. With the great trade and prosperity which followed the rule of Sargon and his successor Naram-Sīn the dynasty became symbolic of a 'golden age'. When Babylon later became the capital, the term 'Akkad' continued to be used to describe the whole of N Babylonia until the late Persian period in the records of the kings of *Assyria and *Babylonia.

Akkadian (Accadian) is now used as a convenient term for the Semitic Assyrian and Babylonian languages, the dialect of the famous dynasty of Agade being designated 'Old Akkadian'. D.J.W.

ACCEPTANCE. The English words 'accept', 'accepted', 'acceptable' and 'acceptance' translate a variety of Hebrew and Greek words of cognate meaning. God is normally the subject; and the object may be the worshipper's sacrifices (Ps. 119:108), his prayers (Gn. 19:21), the whole tenor of his life, and particularly his person. In contrary distinction to the pagan viewpoint, the biblical doctrine is that the prayers and sacrifices are acceptable to God because a man's person is acceptable. Thus 'the Lord had regard for Abel and his offering: but for Cain and his offering he had no regard' (Gn. 4:4–5). The acceptance of Abel's offering was a witness that Abel's person had already been accepted. Through his offerings 'he received approval as righteous, God bearing witness by accepting his gifts' (Heb. 11:4), and Cain was admonished that his offering would be accepted if his life were acceptable (Gn. 4:7).

The OT prophets inveighed against the notion, so congenial to the natural man, that God can be persuaded to accept a man's person through accepting a correctly-offered ritual worship. They constantly affirmed that the divine order was the reverse. The offerings were acceptable only when the persons were acceptable (Ho. 8:13; Mal. 1:10, 13). Throughout the Bible the teaching is underlined that God does not accept a man's person because of his social status or importance. He does not respect persons (Gal. 2:6). This is a virtue which all are to imitate. However, it was not till the Cornelius incident that the early church apprehended the truth that God does not require Jewish nationality, nor circumcision, as a prerequisite for acceptance with him (Acts 10:35).

The well-doing that God requires for acceptance must not in any point fall short of his perfections. Only those who by patience persist in well-doing may claim the reward of eternal life for their works (Rom. 2:6–7). None achieves this. All fall short of the glory of God through sin (Rom. 3:9–23). Our Lord alone is accepted. He alone has merited God's verdict: 'With thee I am well pleased.'

Ezekiel foretold that it would be the work of God to make sinners acceptable to him (Ezk. 20:40–41; 36:23–29). It is through incorporation into Christ, and the gift of his righteousness (Rom. 5:17), that believers are accepted with God. This is the work of God, who through his grace makes us 'accepted in the beloved' (Eph. 1:6, AV). D.B.K.

ACCESS. An intermediary in the Oriental court introduced suppliants and guaranteed their genuineness (*cf.* Barnabas, Acts 9:27–28). The OT portrait of God as King (Ps. 47:7) posed to NT writers the problem of the sinner's *prosagōgē* or access into his presence. He has no independent right of personal approach, and obtains introduction only through Christ (Rom. 5:2; Eph. 2:18; 3:12; 1 Pet. 3:18), whose death removes the barriers of hostility (Eph. 2:16), and enables believers to draw near with confidence to the throne of grace (Heb. 4:16). D.H.T.

ACHAIA. A small region of Greece, on the S coast of the gulf of Corinth, which twice gave its name to the whole country. In Homer the Greeks are frequently called Achaeans. Again, in the age of the Hellenistic kings, the Achaean confederacy championed the freedom of the republics, and after its defeat by the Romans (146 BC) the name was used by them for Greece in general. The area was administered with Macedonia at first, and even after organization as a separate province (27 BC) is linked in common usage with Macedonia (Acts 19:21; Rom. 15:26; 1 Thes. 1:8). The province was in the regular senatorial allotment, and was hence governed by a proconsul (*anthypatos*, Acts 18:12), with two exceptions: from AD 15 to 44 it was under the Caesarian legate of Moesia; and from AD 67 Roman supervision was entirely suspended for several years by Nero's benevolence, and the 40 or so republics in the area enjoyed their liberty without even the appearance of permission.

The old confederacy was maintained under the Romans, with its capital at Argos, the seat of the imperial cult, but the much larger province was governed from Corinth. It is always in connection with Corinth that the name occurs in the NT, and it is uncertain whether anything more is meant (see 2 Cor. 1:1; 9:2; 11:10). We know, however, that there was a church at Cenchreae (Rom. 16:1), and there were believers at Athens (Acts 17:34). We may assume, therefore, that in referring to the household of Stephanas as the 'first converts in Achaia' (1 Cor. 16:15), Paul is applying the term to Corinth as having a primacy due to its position as the Roman capital. He is not thinking of the rest of the province.

BIBLIOGRAPHY. Pausanias 8. 16.10—17.4; Strabo 8; J. Keil, *CAH* 11, pp. 556–565; D. W. J. Gill, *BA1CS* 2, pp. 453–454. E.A.J.

ACHAICUS. A Corinthian Christian (1 Cor. 16:17): on his position see *FORTUNATUS. The name suggests a slave or ex-slave of Achaia, or possibly in the service of the Mummii: it was the title of L. Mummius, creator of Roman Achaia (and destroyer of *Corinth), and was retained in his family in Paul's lifetime (*cf.* Suetonius, *Galba* 3). A.F.W.

ACHAN (Heb. *'āḵān*). A Judahite of clan Zerah, who was in the assault on Jericho and violated the sacrificial ban, stealing gold, silver and fine clothing. This was discovered when inquiry was made by lot after the failure to take Ai. Achan with his family and possessions was stoned and cremated in the Vale of *Achor (Jos. 7). Joshua, in pronouncing sentence, used the similarity of his name to the verb *'āḵar*, 'to distress'; the chronicler spells his name thus (Achar, 1 Ch. 2:7). The event is recalled in Jos. 22:20. J.P.U.L.

ACHISH. The king of Gath (called Abimelech in the title of Ps. 34) with whom David lived *incognito* when fleeing from Saul and from whom he escaped by pretending to be mad (1 Sa. 21:10–15). The second time David went for refuge in Gath, Achish gave him the town of *Ziklag on his border with Israel (1 Sa. 27). He appointed David as his bodyguard in a battle against Israel (1 Sa. 28:1–2), but the other Philistines would not have David fight with them (1 Sa. 29). Achish continued as king into the reign of Solomon (1 Ki. 2:39–40). D.W.B.

ACHOR (Heb. *'āḵôr*). The valley near Jericho where *Achan was executed. Jewish and Christian tradition placed it N of Jericho (Eusebius, *Onom.* 18, 84; J. T. Milik, *Discoveries in the Judaean Desert*, 1962, vol. 3, p. 262), probably in the W Nu'eima. If so, Jos. 15:7 refers to another valley, S of the Judah–Benjamin border; el-Buqei'a is likely (*GTT*, pp. 137, 139, 271; L. E. Stager, *RB* 81, 1974, pp. 94–96; *NEAEHL*, pp. 267–269; see *SECACAH). The W Qilt has been suggested on the assumption that Jos. 7 and 15 mean the same place, but it suits neither. Is. 65:10; Ho. 2:15 are perhaps most pointed if referred to the W Nu'eima. J.P.U.L.

ACHSAH (Heb. *'aḵsâ*, 'anklet'). The daughter of Caleb who, on being married to Othniel, Caleb's nephew, as a reward for Othniel's capture of Kiriath-sepher, encouraged him to ask Caleb for extra territory and herself asked for springs of water (Jos. 15:16–17; Jdg. 1:12–15; 1 Ch. 2:49). A.E.C.

ACHSHAPH (Heb. *'aḵšāp̄*). An important Canaanite city (Jos. 11:1; 12:20), mentioned in Egyptian lists and *Papyrus Anastasi*, I (*ANET*, p. 477);

near Acco, apparently E or SE. The alternatives most favoured are Tell Keisan (W. Albright, *BASOR* 83, 1941, p. 33) and Khirbet Harbaj (Tell Regev) (*LOB*, pp. 22, *etc*.). Occupied by Asher (Jos. 19:25). J.P.U.L.

ACHZIB. 1. A Canaanite harbour town assigned to Asher (Jos. 19:29) which they never occupied (Jdg. 1:31). Taken by Sennacherib in 701 BC (*ANET*, p. 287). Identified with the modern ez-Zib, 14 km N of Acco (Acre). **2.** A town of Judah (Jos. 15:44) in the Shephelah. Probably the Chezib of Gn. 38:5; conquered by Sennacherib (*cf*. Mi. 1:14); tentatively identified as the modern Tell el-Beida (see *NEAEHL*, pp. 32–36). D.W.B.

ACTS, BOOK OF THE. 'The Acts of the Apostles' (Gk. *praxeis apostolōn*) is the title given, since the latter years of the 2nd century AD, to the second volume of a history of Christian beginnings whose first volume we know as 'The Gospel according to Luke'.

I. Outline of contents

The book takes up the story where the Gospel (the 'first book' of Acts 1:1) ends, with the resurrection appearances of Jesus, and goes on to record his ascension, the coming of the Holy Spirit and the rise and early progress of the church of Jerusalem (1–5). Then it describes the dispersal of the Hellenistic members of that church which followed the execution of their leader Stephen, their evangelization of more distant regions as far N as Antioch, and the beginning of the Gentile mission in that city. In the course of this narrative we have also the account of Paul's conversion and Peter's evangelization of the plain of Sharon, culminating in the conversion of the first Gentile household in Caesarea. This section of Acts ends with Paul's arrival in Antioch to take part in the Gentile mission there, and Peter's departure from Jerusalem after his escape from death at the hands of Herod Agrippa I (6–12). From then on Paul's apostolic ministry is the main subject of Acts: with Barnabas he evangelizes Cyprus and S Galatia (13–14), takes part in the Council of Jerusalem (15), with Silas crosses to Europe and evangelizes Philippi, Thessalonica and Corinth (16–18), with other colleagues evangelizes provincial Asia from his headquarters in Ephesus (19), pays a visit to Palestine, where he is rescued from mob-violence and kept in custody for 2 years (20–26), is sent to Rome to have his case heard by the emperor at his own request, and spends 2 years there under house arrest, with complete liberty to make the gospel known to all who visit him (27–28). While the gospel was no doubt carried along all the roads which branched out from its Palestinian homeland, Acts concentrates on the road from Jerusalem to Antioch and thence to Rome.

II. Origin and purpose

The preface to the 'first book' (Lk. 1:1–4) applies equally to both parts of the work: the whole work was undertaken in order that one *Theophilus might have a consecutive and reliable account of the rise and progress of Christianity—a subject on which he already possessed a certain amount of information.

The date is not indicated precisely; Acts cannot have been written earlier than the latest event it records, Paul's spending 2 years in custody in Rome (Acts 28:30), covering probably the years 60 and 61, but how much later it was written is uncertain. If its dependence on the *Antiquities* of Josephus were established, then its date could not be earlier than AD 93, but such a dependence is improbable. We might think of a time when something had happened to stimulate special interest in Christianity among responsible members of Roman society, of whom Theophilus may be regarded as a representative. One such time was the latter part of Domitian's principate (AD 81–96), when Christianity had penetrated the imperial family. It has even been suggested that Theophilus might be a pseudonym for Domitian's cousin, Flavius Clemens. An earlier occasion may be found in the later sixties, when the moment seemed opportune to dissociate Christianity from the Jewish revolt in Palestine, or even earlier in the sixties, when the leading propagator of Christianity came to Rome as a Roman citizen to have his appeal heard by the imperial tribunal. The optimistic note on which Acts ends, with Paul proclaiming the kingdom of God in Rome without let or hindrance, might suggest a date before the outbreak of persecution in AD 64. The internal evidence for the dating of Luke is relevant here, but if it be felt that Luke, as we have it now, must be dated after AD 70, it might be considered whether the 'first book' of Acts 1:1 could not be 'Proto-Luke' (so C. S. C. Williams and others). The remitting of Paul's case to Rome would certainly make it needful for imperial officials to look more seriously into the nature of Christianity than had previously been necessary; the author of Acts may well have thought it wise to provide such people with an account of the matter.

The author, from the 2nd century onwards, has been identified (rightly, in all probability) with Luke, Paul's physician and fellow-traveller (Col. 4:14; Phm. 24; 2 Tim. 4:11). Luke was a Greek of Antioch, according to the late 2nd century anti-Marcionite prologue to his Gospel (his Antiochene origin is also implied by the 'western' reading of Acts 11:28). His presence at some of the events which he records is indicated unobtrusively by the transition from the third person to the first person plural in his narrative; the three 'we-sections' of Acts are 16:10–17; 20:5–21:18; 27:1–28:16. Apart from the periods covered by these sections, he had ample opportunity of tracing the course of events from the first, as he had access to first-hand information from people he met from time to time, not only in Antioch but also in Asia Minor and Macedonia, in Jerusalem and Caesarea, and finally in Rome. Among these informants an important place should doubtless be given to his hosts in various cities, such as Philip and his daughters in Caesarea (21:8f.) and Mnason, a foundation-member of the church in Jerusalem (21:16). He does not appear to have used Paul's Epistles as a source.

III. Historical character

The historical trustworthiness of Luke's account has been amply confirmed by archaeological discovery. While he has apologetic and theological interests, these do not detract from his detailed accuracy, although they control his selection and presentation of the facts. He sets his narrative in the framework of contemporary history; his pages are full of references to city magistrates, provincial governors, client kings and the like, and these references time after time prove to be just right for the place and time in question. With a minimum of words he conveys the true local colour of the widely differing cities mentioned in his story. And his description of Paul's voyage to Rome (27) remains to this day one of our most important documents on ancient seamanship.

IV. Apologetic emphasis

Luke is obviously concerned, in both parts of his work, to demonstrate that Christianity is not a menace to imperial law and order. He does this particularly by citing the judgments of governors, magistrates and other authorities in various parts of the empire. In the Gospel Pilate thrice pronounces Jesus not guilty of sedition (Lk. 23:4, 14, 22), and when similar charges are brought against his followers in Acts they cannot be sustained. The praetors of Philippi imprison Paul and Silas for interference with the rights of private property, but have to release them with an apology for their illegal action (16:19ff., 35ff.). The politarchs of Thessalonica, before whom Paul and his companions are accused of sedition against the emperor, are content to find citizens of that place who will guarantee the missionaries' good behaviour (17:6–9). A more significant decision is taken by Gallio, proconsul of Achaia, who dismisses the charge of propagating an illicit religion brought against Paul by the Jewish leaders of Corinth; the practical implication of his decision is that Christianity shares the protection assured by Roman law to Judaism (18:12ff.). At Ephesus, Paul enjoys the friendship of the *Asiarchs and is exonerated by the town clerk from the charge of insulting the cult of Ephesian *Artemis (19:31, 35ff.). In Judaea the governor Festus and the client king Agrippa II agree that Paul has committed no offence deserving either death or imprisonment, and that in fact he might have been liberated forthwith had he not taken the jurisdiction out of their hands by appealing to Caesar (26:32).

It might well be asked, however, why the progress of Christianity had so frequently been marked by public riots if Christians were as law-abiding as Luke maintained. His reply is that, apart from the incident at Philippi and the demonstration stirred up by the silversmiths' guild at Ephesus, the tumults which attended the proclamation of the gospel were invariably instigated by its Jewish opponents. Just as the Gospel represents the Sadducean chief priests of Jerusalem as prevailing upon Pilate to sentence Jesus to death against his better judgment, so in Acts it is Jews who are Paul's bitterest enemies in one place after another. While Acts records the steady advance of the gospel in the great Gentile centres of imperial civilization, it records at the same time its progressive rejection by the majority of the Jewish communities throughout the Empire.

V. Theological interest

On the theological side, the dominating theme of Acts is the activity of the Holy Spirit. The promise of the outpouring of the Spirit, made by the risen Christ in 1:4ff., is fulfilled for Jewish disciples in ch. 2 and for Gentile believers in ch. 10. The apostles discharge their commission in the power of the Spirit, which is manifested by supernatural signs; their converts' acceptance of the gospel is likewise attended by visible manifestations of the Spirit's power. The book might indeed be called 'The Acts of the Holy Spirit', for it is the Spirit who controls the advance of the gospel throughout; he guides the movements of the preachers, *e.g.* of Philip (8:29, 39), Peter (10:19f.), Paul and his companions (16:6ff.); he directs the church of Antioch to set Barnabas and Saul apart for the more extended service to which he himself has called them (13:2); he receives pride of place in the letter conveying the decision of the Jerusalem *Council to the Gentile churches (15:28); he speaks through prophets (11:28; 20:23; 21:4, 11) as he did in OT days (1:16; 28:25); he it is in the first instance who appoints the elders of a church to take spiritual charge of it (20:28); he is the principal witness to the truth of the gospel (5:32).

The supernatural manifestations which accompany the spread of the gospel signify not only the Spirit's activity but also the inauguration of the new age in which Jesus reigns as Lord and Messiah. The miraculous element, as we should expect, is more prominent in the earlier than in the later part of the book: 'we have a steady reduction of the emphasis on the miraculous aspect of the working of the Spirit which corresponds to the development in the Pauline Epistles' (W. L. Knox, *The Acts of the Apostles*, 1948, p. 91).

VI. Acts in the early church

Unlike most of the NT books, the two parts of Luke's history do not appear to have been primarily associated with Christian churches, whether as addressed to them or as circulating within them. Martin Dibelius may be right in thinking that the work circulated through the contemporary book trade for the benefit of the Gentile reading public for which it was intended. There may thus have been some lapse of time between the first publication of the twofold work and its more general circulation in the churches as an authoritative Christian document.

Early in the 2nd century, when the four Gospel writings were collected and circulated as a fourfold group, the two parts of Luke's history were separated from each other, to pursue their several paths. While the future of Luke was assured by reason of its incorporation with the other three Gospels, Acts proved increasingly to be such an important document that it can justly be called, in Harnack's words, the pivot-book of the NT.

The wider circulation of Acts in the churches may have had much to do, towards the end of the 1st century, with the move to collect the Pauline Epistles to form a *corpus*. If Paul tended to be forgotten in the generation following his death, Acts would certainly bring him back to Christian memory and also emphasize what an interesting and extraordinarily important man he was. But, while emphasizing the importance of Paul's role, Acts bore witness to the work of other apostles too, especially Peter.

For this last reason Marcion (*c.* AD 140) could not include Acts in his Canon, although he did include his edition of Luke as a preface to the Pauline *corpus*. Acts, while it bore eloquent witness to the apostleship of Paul, at the same time cut right across Marcion's insistence that the original apostles of Jesus had proved unfaithful to their Master's teaching. Marcion and his followers are probably the main target of Tertullian's charge of inconsistency against those heretics who confidently appeal to the exclusive apostolic authority of Paul while rejecting the one book above all others which provides independent testimony of his apostleship (*Prescription* 22f.).

To the champions of the catholic faith, on the other hand, the value of Acts now appeared greater than ever. For not only did it present irrefragable evidence of Paul's status and achievement as an apostle, but it also safeguarded the position of the other apostles and justified the inclusion of non-Pauline apostolic writings alongside the Pauline collection in the volume of Holy Writ. It was from this time that it came to be known as 'The Acts of the Apostles', or even, as the Muratorian list calls it with anti-Marcionite exaggeration, 'The Acts of *all* the Apostles'.

VII. Its abiding value

The title of Acts to occupy its traditional place between the Gospels and the Epistles is clear. On the one hand, it is the general sequel to the fourfold Gospel (as it is the proper sequel to one of the four); on the other hand, it supplies the historical background to the earlier Epistles, and attests the apostolic character of most of the writers whose names they bear.

Moreover, it remains a document of incalculable value for the beginnings of Christianity. When we consider how scanty is our knowledge of the progress of the gospel in other directions in the decades following AD 30, we may appreciate our indebtedness to Acts for the relatively detailed account which it gives of the progress of the gospel along the road from Jerusalem to Rome. The rise and progress of Christianity is a study beset with problems, but some of these problems would be even more intractable than they are if we had not the information of Acts to help us. For example, how did it come about that a movement which began in the heart of Judaism was recognized after a few decades as a distinctively Gentile religion? And how has it come about that a faith which originated in Asia has been for centuries predominantly associated, for better or worse, with European civilization? The answer is largely, though not entirely, bound up with the missionary career of Paul, apostle to the Gentiles and citizen of Rome; and of that career Luke, in Acts, is the historian. His narrative is, in fact, a source-book of the highest value for a significant phase of the history of world civilization.

BIBLIOGRAPHY. *BC*, 5 vols., 1920–33; H. J. Cadbury, *The Book of Acts in History*, 1955; M. Dibelius, *Studies in the Acts of the Apostles*, 1956; R. P. C. Hanson, *The Acts in the Revised Standard Version*, 1967; E. Haenchen, *The Acts of the Apostles*, 1971; W. W. Gasque, *A History of the Interpretation of the Acts of the Apostles*, 1989; F. F. Bruce, *The Acts of the Apostles*[3], 1991; *idem*, *The Book of the Acts*[2], *NIC*, 1988; *BA1CS*.

F.F.B.

ADAH (Heb. *ada*, meaning uncertain). **1.** One of the wives of Lamech and mother of Jabal and Jubal (Gn. 4:19ff.). **2.** One of the wives of Esau, daughter of Elon a Hittite and mother of Eliphaz (Gn. 36:2ff.).

T.C.M.

ADAM (Heb. *'āḏām*). A town 28 km N of Jericho, near *Zarethan, controlling the Jordan fords just below the confluence of the Jabbok; modern Tell ed-Damiyeh. The blocking of the Jordan here made it possible for the Israelites to cross at Jericho (Jos. 3:10ff.).

J.P.U.L.

ADAM.

I. In the Old Testament

The first man, created (*bārā'*, Gn. 1:27) by God in his own image (*ṣelem*), on the sixth day by means of forming him (as a potter forms, *yāṣar*, Gn. 2:7) of dust from the ground (*'ᵃḏāmâ*), and uniquely breathing into his nostrils the breath of life (*nišmaṯ hayyîm*; see *b*, below). The result of this was that 'the man' became a living being (*nep̄eš ḥayyâ*). Sumerian and Babylonian myths of the creation of man are known, but compared with the creation story in the Bible all are crude and polytheistic.

a. Etymology

The name Adam (*'āḏām*), in addition to being a proper name, also has the connotation 'man-kind', a sense in which it occurs in the OT some 500 times, so that when the noun occurs with the definite article (*hā'āḏām*) it is to be translated as the proper noun rather than as the name. The word *'adm* occurs also in Ugaritic in the sense 'mankind'. In the accounts of the *creation in Gn. 1 and 2 the article is used with *'āḏām* in all but three cases: 1:26, where 'man' in general is evidently intended; 2:5, where 'a man' (or 'no man') is clearly the most natural sense; and 2:20, the first permissible use of the proper name according to the text. The AV has projected this use back into the preceding verse (2:19) in spite of the article there, whereas RV, RSV, observing that in this occurrence, and indeed in all those (3:17, 21) without the article up to Gn. 4:25 the name is prefixed by the preposition *lᵉ-*, which might be read (*lā-<lᵉhā-*) to include the article without alteration to the consonantal text, prefer to assume that the Massoretes have wrongly pointed the text and that the proper name does not occur until Gn. 4:25. Though attempts have been made to determine the etymology of the name, there is no agreement, and the fact that the original language of mankind was not Hebrew renders such theories academic. It is clear, however, that the use of the word *'ᵃḏāmâ*, 'ground', in juxtaposition to the name *'āḏām* in Gn. 2:7 is intentional, a conclusion reinforced by Gn. 3:19.

b. Adam's early condition

Adam was distinguished from the animals, but this not because the epithets *nep̄eš* and *rûaḥ* were applied to him, for these terms are also used on occasion of the animals, but because he was made in God's image, given dominion over all the animals, and perhaps also because God individually breathed the breath (*nᵉšāmâ*) of life into his nostrils (*VT* 11, 1961, pp. 177–187). God made a garden for Adam in *Eden (Gn. 2:8–14) and put him in it to work it and watch over it. The word 'to work it' (*'āḇaḏ*) is that commonly used for labour (*e.g.* Ex. 20:9), so Adam was not to be idle. His food was apparently to be fruit from the trees (Gn. 2:9, 16), berries and nuts from the shrubs (*śîaḥ*, EVV plant') and cereals from the herbs (*'ēśeḇ*, Gn. 2:5). God then brought all the animals and birds to Adam for him to give them names, and presumably in the process to familiarize himself with their characteristics and potentialities

(Gn. 2:19–20). It is possible that some dim reflection of this is to be found in a Sumerian literary text which describes how the god Enki set the world in order, and among other things put the animals under the control of two minor deities.

c. The Fall

God said 'It is not good that the man should be alone' (Gn. 2:18), so he made a woman (2:22), to be a help to him (*EVE). At the inducement of the serpent the woman persuaded Adam to eat from the fruit of the tree which he had been commanded by God not to touch (Gn. 3:1–7) (*FALL), and as a result he and the woman were banished from the garden (Gn. 3:23–24). It is evident that until this time Adam had had direct communion with God. When Adam and the woman recognized their nakedness they took fig leaves and sewed them together to make loin cloths (*ḥᵃg̱ôrâ*, Gn. 3:7), evidence perhaps for the practice of such simple skills as sewing. Adam was punished by expulsion from the garden and subjection to the future lot of obtaining his livelihood in painful toil and in the sweat of his face, since the ground (*ᵃḏāmâ*), to which he would now return at his death, was cursed and would bring forth thorn bushes and thistles. He was still to be a farmer, therefore, though his labours would be now more arduous than they had been (Gn. 3:17–19, 23). Parallels have been drawn between these episodes and the Akkadian myth of Adapa, who mistakenly refused the bread and water of life, thus losing immortality for mankind; but the connections are remote. God provided the two with leather tunics (Gn. 3:21), implying that they would now need protection from uncontrolled vegetation or cold weather.

Adam had two sons, *Cain and *Abel, but as Cain killed Abel he had another son, *Seth, to take Abel's place (Gn. 4:25) and to carry on the faithful line of descent. Adam was 130 (LXX 230) years old when Seth was born and he lived 800 (LXX 700) years after this event, making 930 years in all (Gn. 5:2–5 agreeing with LXX and Samaritan Pentateuch, the latter agreeing with *MT* in all three figures) (*GENEALOGY). In comparison, it is to be noted that the first pre-flood king, Alulim, in the Sumerian king list is given a reign of 28,800 years (a variant text gives 67,200), and his counterpart, Alōros, in Berossos' *Babylōniaka*, is credited with 36,000 years. It is to be presumed that Adam had other children than the three specifically mentioned in Genesis. The date of Adam's existence and the exact area in which he lived are at present disputed.

BIBLIOGRAPHY. *KB*³, p. 14; C. Westermann, *Biblischer Kommentar AT*, I/1, 1976; for the creation of man, see A. Heidel, *The Babylonian Genesis*², 1951, pp. 46–47, 66–72, 118–126; W. G. Lambert and A. R. Millard, *Atraḫasīs. The Babylonian Story of the Flood*, 1969, pp. 8–9, 15, 54–65; S. N. Kramer, 'Sumerian Literature and the Bible', *Analecta Biblica* 12, 1959, pp. 191–192; for Enki and the world order, see *History Begins at Sumer*, 1958, pp. 145–147; for Adapa, see Heidel, *Genesis*, pp. 147–153; E. A. Speiser in *ANET*, pp. 101–103; for king list, see T. Jacobsen, *The Sumerian King List*, 1939, pp. 70–71; A. L. Oppenheim in *ANET*, p. 265. T.C.M.

II. In the New Testament

Adam's name appears in only seven verses in the NT (Lk. 3:38; Rom. 5:14; 1 Cor. 15:22, 45; 1 Tim. 2:13–14; Jude 14), but his significance is far greater than this implies, particularly for Paul. He is seen as:

(i) *The prototype of the human race*. Luke's geneaology of Jesus goes right back to Adam, 'the son of God' (Lk. 3:38). This geneaology underlines the *single relatedness* of the whole human family, not just to one human ancestor, but to God (and now also to Jesus, who is also God's son, Lk. 3:22). 'We have borne the image of the man of dust!' (1 Cor. 15:49) expresses in a nutshell Paul's perception of the human problem. His comparison of Adam and Christ in Rom. 5:12–21 also rests on our relatedness to Adam – a fatal bond arising from our common humanity.

In the teaching about marriage in Mt. 19:4–6 Adam and Eve set the pattern for all humankind. It is widely maintained that the teaching in 1 Tim. 2:12–14 depends on a 'headship' of Adam over Eve, because Paul apparently uses it to argue that women should not teach men in church. But he may well be countering a 'feminist' rewriting of the Genesis genealogy (*cf.* Tim. 1:4) which emphasized Eve's supremacy and thus sought to justify bossy and disruptive behaviour by women in the church.

(ii) *The archetype of disobedience*. Paul shared the Jewish belief that 'sin came into the world through one man and death through sin' (Rom. 5:12 – referring to Adam). But views on the *level of Adam's culpability* differed. The author of 4 Ezra blamed Adam wholly for the corruption of humanity (4 Ezra 3:20–22). The author of 2 Baruch tried to make Adam the *origin* of death ('Adam sinned first and brought death upon all') but not the *cause*: 'Adam is not the cause, except only for himself, but each of us has become the Adam of his own soul' (2 Baruch 54:15, 19).

Paul straddles the two traditions. On the one hand, he cites Adam to underline our responsibility. Probable allusions are: in Rom. 1:21–23 to the fall as he describes the corruption of the Gentile world for which 'they are without excuse' (1:20); in Rom. 3:23 to the Jewish tradition that Adam in the Garden shone with the glory of God, which he lost when he sinned: 'fall short of' could be translated 'are deprived of'; in Rom. 7:8–11 to the story of the deception of Eve by the serpent, who used the commandment to 'kill' her and Adam. Paul universalizes it with an 'I' which speaks for all; supremely, in Rom. 5:12 Paul makes Adam the door of sin into the world, but immediately disqualifies a rigid determinism: 'death spread to all, *because all sinned*'.

On the other hand, Paul underlines the compulsive effect of Adam's sin in his comparisons between Adam and Christ: 'By one man's sin, many died' (5:15); 'God's judgment spread from one man and produced condemnation' (5:16); 'By one man's sin, death reigned' (5:17); 'through one man's disobedience a vast crowd were made sinners' (5:19); or, tersely, in 1 Cor. 15:22, 'in Adam all die'.

Paul thus maintains a careful balance between our responsibility and the culpability of Adam. How should we interpret his teaching? There are two respects in which he stands out from his Jewish background:

1. in the emphasis he lays on *death* as the focus of our inheritance from Adam;
2. in the *cosmic scope* of his thought.

In Rom. 8:20–22 he explains that *the whole cre-*

ation fell with Adam: so 'sin entered the world' in 5:12 does not merely mean 'sin entered the human race'. And in Rom. 5:13–14 he explains that it is the universal presence of *death* which supremely testifies to the effect of Adam's disobedience.

Paul thought of *the human race* as a 'solidarity', bound with Adam in the disobedience which cut him off from God, but also of *the world* as indwelt by 'sin', the alien power which Adam introduced. We partake of the world's now *mortal* substance, and share and reinforce its alienation from God, unless delivered by Christ. Notably in 1 Cor. 15 it is not just our *sin* which stops us from inheriting the Kingdom of God, but our *flesh and blood* (1 Cor. 15:50).

(iii) *The antitype of Christ.* Paul's understanding of *the solidarity of humanity in Adam*, which he inherited (and developed) from Judaism, was one of the sources of his understanding of God's action through Christ. In three ways:

1. *The person of Christ.* When Paul calls Jesus 'the image of God' (2 Cor. 4:4, Col. 1:15), he is referring to Adam and Eve as bearing God's 'image' (Gn. 1:26f., 9:6). 'Form' is a closely related word: 'who being in the *form* of God, did not count equality with God a prize to be hoarded, but emptied himself, taking the form of a servant . . .' (Phil. 2:6f.). Many scholars have pointed to 'Adam' ideas in this hymn in Philippians (2:6–11). God's image is seen in Christ as he takes on himself the image of 'a servant' and binds himself to mortal humanity.

Paul applies Ps. 8 to Jesus: he is the true (and *only*) 'man' to whom everything is *really* submitted (Ps. 8:4–6; 1 Cor. 15:27, Eph. 1:22, Heb. 2:6–9). This promise was made to Adam (Gn. 1:28–30), but lost by him (Gn. 3:17–19) and fulfilled in Christ.

2. *The obedience of Christ.* The contrast between Christ's obedience and Adam's disobedience is drawn out in Rom. 5:19. This obedience is not submission to the law, but a life of unbroken union with, and submission to, God, 'obedience unto death, even death on a cross' (Phil. 2:8). By this obedience Jesus expresses both the 'forms' that he bears – the form of God, whose will he obeys, and the form of humankind, whose death he shares.

3. *The people of Christ.* Because he bears both these 'forms', Jesus is qualifed to be the head of a new humanity. We touch here on the heart of Paul's understanding of the atonement. United to Christ, the Adam promise of rule over the earth is fulfilled in us too: 'If by the sin of one man death reigned through that one man, how much more will those who receive this massive gift of grace and righteousness *reign in life* through the one man Jesus Christ!' (Rom. 5:17).

BIBLIOGRAPHY: M. D. Hooker, *From Adam to Christ*, 1990, chs. 5–7; N. T. Wright, 'Adam, Israel and the Messiah' in *The Climax of the Covenant*, 1991, pp. 18–40. S.M.

ADAMAH (Heb. *ʼᵃḏāmāh*). A town in Naphtali (Jos. 19:36). Possibly at Qarn Hattin (Y. Aharoni, *JNES* 19, 1960, pp. 179–181, identifying it with Shemesh-adam of Egyptian sources). J.P.U.L.

ADAMI-NEKEB. A place mentioned in Jos. 19:33, on the border of Naphtali. It was apparently a pass and has been identified with the modern Kh. ed-Dâmiyeh. See *LOB*. R.A.H.G.

ADMAH. One of the Cities of the *Plain (Gn. 14:2, 8; Dt. 29:23), linked specially with *Zeboiim (Ho. 11:8). The association with Gaza (Gn. 10:19) suggests the correctness of the modern locating of the pentapolis as submerged beneath the S waters of the Dead Sea. J.A.M.

ADONI-BEZEK (Heb. *ʼᵃḏōnî-ḇezeq*, 'lord of Bezek'). Judah and Simeon, preparatory to conquering their own territory, combined to defeat 10,000 Canaanites at Bezek, probably modern Khirbet Ibziq, 21 km NE of Shechem (Jdg. 1:4–7). Their king, Adoni-bezek, not to be equated with *Adoni-zedek (Jos. 10:1–27), fled, but was recaptured and incapacitated in the contemporary customary manner. He acknowledged a certain rough justice in this, as he had inflicted similar mutilations upon seventy kings. He was brought to Jerusalem, where he died. As the Israelites were not able to hold and develop all captured cities, Jerusalem was later occupied by the Jebusites (Jdg. 1:21).

BIBLIOGRAPHY. *LOB*, p. 197. A.E.C.

ADONIJAH (Heb. *ʼᵃḏōniyyâ*, 'my lord is Yahweh'). **1.** The fourth son of David, by his wife Haggith. After the death of the three eldest he regarded himself as the heir-presumptive. (Amnon had been murdered by his brother Absalom, who himself died in the rebellion against his father. As no mention is made of Chileab, the son of Abigail, it is assumed that he died before any question of the succession arose.) It would appear, however, that David had promised Bathsheba (1 Ki. 1:17) that her son Solomon should succeed him. It may have been knowledge of this that provoked Adonijah to make his futile attempt at gaining the crown while his father was alive. His supporters included two of his father's right-hand men, Joab the commander-in-chief of the army, and Abiathar the priest, and no doubt Adonijah hoped that they would draw the power of the army and the sanction of the priesthood. But before that hope materialized those faithful to the king, Nathan his prophet-counsellor, Zadok the priest and Benaiah the commander of the royal bodyguard, took action. While Adonijah was making a feast for his supporters, Bathsheba was instructed to approach David and remind him of his oath, and while she was yet speaking Nathan came in and reproached the king for his not having told him of his (supposed) plans for Adonijah. David confirmed his oath to Bathsheba and secured the accession of Solomon. The noise and the news of the acclamation reached Adonijah and his guests in En-rogel, and threw them into a panic. The would-be aspirant for the throne fled for sanctuary to the altar, and Solomon promised to spare his life on condition of future loyalty (1 Ki. 1). No sooner was his father dead than his former ambitions again made themselves apparent. Thus at least did Solomon interpret his request for Abishag, his father's young concubine who had nursed him in his old age. This charge of a renewed attempt on the throne was probably not without foundation in the light of oriental custom (*cf.* 2 Sa. 3:7; 16:21). The sentence of death on the ambitious and tactless Adonijah was speedily carried out (1 Ki. 2:13–25).

2. One of the Levites whom Jehoshaphat sent to teach in the cities of Judah (2 Ch. 17:8).

3. One of those who sealed the covenant (Ne. 10:16). This is the same as Adonikam (Ezr. 2:13, *etc.*). M.A.M.

ADONIRAM (Heb. *ᵃᵈōnîrām*, 'my lord is exalted'). The official in charge of forced labour during Solomon's reign (1 Ki. 4:6; 5:14). Probably the Adoram who had the same responsibility during the reigns of David (2 Sa. 20:24) and Rehoboam (1 Ki. 12:18; 'Hadoram' in 2 Ch. 10:18). People of Israel stoned him to death as the first act of their revolt and the division of the monarchy under Jeroboam *c.* 922 BC. D.W.B.

ADONI-ZEDEK (Heb. *ᵃᵈōnî-ṣeḏeq*, 'my lord is righteous'). An Amorite king of Jerusalem who led four other Canaanite kings against the Israelites and their allies of Gibeon. The five kings were defeated by divine intervention and hid themselves in a cave at *Makkedah. They were humbled in common oriental style, then executed by Joshua and buried in the cave (Jos. 10). The meaning of the name may be compared with Melchizedek ('my king is righteous'), king of *Salem (Gn. 14:18). There is not sufficient evidence for the existence of a god Zedek to give a meaning 'my king is Zedek'. A.R.M.

ADOPTION.

I. In the Old Testament

Adoption occurs comparatively rarely in the OT. Hebrew possesses no technical term for the practice, and it makes no appearance in the laws of the OT. This situation is probably explained by the existence among the Israelites of several alternatives to the problem of infertile marriage. Polygamy and levirate *marriage lessened the need for adoption, while the principle of maintaining property within the tribe (Lv. 25:23ff.; Nu. 27:8–11; Je. 32:6ff.) allayed some of the fears of childless parents.

Adoption in the OT is considerably illuminated by comparative material from Mesopotamia and Syria. Ancient Near Eastern adoption was a legal act by which a person was brought into a new family relationship, with the full privileges and responsibilities of one who participated in that relationship by birth. Applying this description to the OT, a small number of adoptions can be identified, the majority in Gn. 12–50. A preference for adoption within the family is discernible, and it seems that the OT, in common with ancient Near Eastern texts, included adrogation and legitimation alongside adoption within a single umbrella concept, whereas Roman law made clear distinctions between these practices.

According to cuneiform legal custom, adoption would have been required for Eliezer to become Abraham's heir (Gn. 15:3) and for the sons of Hagar, Bilhah and Zilpah to participate in the inheritance of Abraham and Jacob (Gn. 16:1–4; 30:1–13; *cf.* 21:1–10). Although Eliezer's apparent removal from the inheritance is untypical (Gn. 24:36; 25:5–6), his case is paralleled by an Old Babylonian letter from Larsa (*Textes cunéiformes du Louvre* 18, 153) which indicates that a man without sons could adopt his own slave. The adoptive status of the concubines' sons is supported by Sarah's and Rachel's declarations, 'I shall be built up' (Gn. 16:2; 30:3; *cf.* RVmg.), and by Rachel's statement, 'God has . . . given *me* a son' (Gn. 30:6). Although no evidence exists for Jacob's adoption by Laban (*cf.* Gn. 31:3, 18, 30; 32:3ff.), Jacob himself probably adopted Ephraim and Manasseh. The adoption of a grandson also occurred in Ugarit (*PRU* 3, 70–71). Elsewhere in the OT, Moses (Ex. 2:10) and Esther (Est. 2:7, 15) were almost certainly adopted, probably according to non-Israelite law, though the case of Genubath (1 Ki. 11:20) is more doubtful.

An adoption formula seems to occur in Ps. 2:7 ('you are my son'; *cf.* Gn. 48:5, 'your two sons . . . are mine'). A similar phrase appears in an Elephantine adoption contract (E. G. Kraeling, *The Brooklyn Museum Aramaic Papyri*, 1953, No. 8), and a negative equivalent also occurs, chiefly in Old Babylonian texts. The OT contains no reference to adoption rites, however, since the custom of 'bearing upon the knees' (Gn. 30:3; 50:23; Jb. 3:12) is associated with birth and recognition by the head of the family.

Adoption also had a theological aspect. The nation Israel was regarded as God's son (Is. 1:2f.; Je. 3:19; Ho. 11:1), especially as his first-born (Ex. 4:22; Je. 31:9), and the Davidic king was similarly privileged, though his humanity and accountability were equally emphasized (2 Sa. 7:14; 1 Ch. 28:6f.; Ps. 89:19ff.). It was this divine choice that lay behind Paul's statement that sonship belonged to the Israelites (Rom. 9:4).

BIBLIOGRAPHY. H. J. Boecker, *ZAW* 86, 1974, pp. 86–89; S. Paul, *Maarav* 2, 1979–80, pp. 173–185; F. Lyall, *Slaves, Citizens, Sons*, 1984, pp. 67–99. M.J.S.

II. In the New Testament

Adoption in the NT has as its background not Roman law, in which its chief aim was to continue the adoptive parent's line, but Jewish custom, which conferred the benefits of the family on the adoptee. It occurs only in Paul, and is a relationship conferred by God's act of free grace which redeems those under the law (Gal. 4:5). Its intention and result is a change of status, planned from eternity and mediated by Jesus Christ (Eph. 1:5), from slavery to sonship (Gal. 4:1ff.). The cry 'Abba! Father!' (Rom. 8:15 and Gal. 4:6; in the context of adoption) may perhaps be the traditional cry of the adopted slave. The adopted son of God possesses all family rights, including access to the Father (Rom. 8:15) and sharing with Christ in the divine inheritance (Rom. 8:17). The presence of the Spirit of God is both the instrument (Rom. 8:14) and the consequence (Gal. 4:6) of this sonship. However complete in status this adoption may be, it has yet to be finally made real in the deliverance of the creation itself from bondage (Rom. 8:21ff.).

Adoption is implicit as a relationship of grace in John's teaching about 'becoming a son' (Jn. 1:12; 1 Jn. 3:1–2), in the prodigal's acceptance into full family rights (Lk. 15:19ff.) and in Jesus' oft-repeated title of God as Father (Mt. 5:16; 6:9; Lk. 12:32).

BIBLIOGRAPHY. W. H. Rossell, 'New Testament Adoption—Graeco-Roman or Semitic?', *JBL* 71, 1952, pp. 233ff.; D. J. Theron, '"Adoption" in the Pauline Corpus', *EQ* 28, 1956, pp. 1ff.; F. Lyall, 'Roman Law in the Writings of Paul—Adoption', *JBL* 88, 1969, pp. 458ff. F.H.P.

ADORAIM. City of SW Judah fortified by Rehoboam (2 Ch. 11:9), identified today with the village of Dura, some 8 km SW of Hebron. It became a major Idumaean city, and as such figured in various historical events in the intertestamental period. D.F.P.

ADRAMMELECH. 1. A god brought from *Sepharvaim to Samaria, where the colonists sacrificed children to him (2 Ki. 17:31). Attempts to identify the name include *'ddr mlk*, 'The king (or Molek) is powerful'. There is no need to change to read Adad-Malik.

2. One of the sons of Sennacherib, brother of Sharezer, who murdered their father in 681 BC (2 Ki. 19:37; Is. 37:38). This event is also recorded in the Babylonian Chronicle without naming the son (*DOTT*, pp. 70–73). A W Semitic name for one of the sons is likely, as Sennacherib's wife Naqi'a-Zakutu was of W Semitic origin; *cf.* the name *'drmlk*, king of Byblos, on a Phoen. coin of the 4th century BC. D.J.W.

ADRAMYTTIUM. Seaport in Mysia, in Roman Asia, facing Lesbos: the site is Karatash, but the modern inland town, Edremit, preserves the name. Rendel Harris (unconvincingly) suggested a S Arabian origin for the original settlement (*Contemporary Review* 128, 1925, pp. 194ff.). Its commercial importance, once high, was declining by NT times.

An Adramyttian ship conveyed Julius and Paul from Caesarea (Acts 27:2). It was doubtless homeward bound, engaging in coastwise traffic with 'the ports along the coast of Asia', where a connection for Rome might be obtained—an expectation soon justified (vv. 5f.).

BIBLIOGRAPHY. Strabo, 13. 1. 51, 65–66; Pliny, *NH* 13. 1. 2 (for a local export); W. Leaf, *Strabo on the Troad*, 1923, pp. 318ff. A.F.W.

ADRIA. The 'sea of Adria' (Acts 27:27), across which the ship of the Alexandrian grain fleet, which was taking Paul to Italy, drifted in a W direction for 14 days, was the Central Mediterranean, including the Ionian Sea (*cf.* Strabo, *Geog.* 2. 5. 20; Jos. *Vita* 15; Pausanias, *Description of Greece* 5. 25. 3; Ptolemy, *Geog.* 3. 4. 1; 15. 1). It is to be distinguished from the *gulf* of Adria (*cf.* the town of Adria or Hadria N of the Po), which is known to us as the Adriatic Sea. F.F.B.

ADULLAM. A Canaanite city in Judah (Jos. 12:15); fortified by Rehoboam (2 Ch. 11:7); mentioned by Micah (Mi. 1:15) and inhabited after the Exile (Ne. 11:30). Identified with Tell esh-Sheikh Madhkur (Ḥorvat 'Adullam), midway between Jerusalem and Lachish, the place is usually associated with the cave in which David hid when pursued by Saul (1 Sa. 22:1). J.W.M.

ADUMMIM. A steep pass on the boundary between Judah and Benjamin (Jos. 15:7; 18:17) on the road from Jericho to Jerusalem. Traditionally the scene of the Good Samaritan story (Lk. 10:34), it is known today as Tal'at ed-Damm ('ascent of blood'), probably from the red marl of the soil, though Jerome attributed the name to the murders and robberies said to have taken place there. J.D.D.

AENON (from Gk. *'ainōn*, 'fountain'). A place W of Jordan where John baptized (Jn. 3:23), perhaps to be identified with 'Ainun, NE of Nablus, near the headwaters of the Wadi Far'ah (hence 'there was much water there'). (*SALIM.) F.F.B.

AFRICA

I. Early knowledge and nomenclature

The Greeks designated the continent 'Libya', but of its extent and its relation to Asia there was doubt. Herodotus (5th century BC) is already convinced of its being almost surrounded by sea, and cites (*Hist.* 4. 42) an alleged circumnavigation by a Phoenician crew in the service of Pharaoh *Neco. A translation of a Punic document, the Periplus of the Erythraean Sea, recounts a Carthaginian voyage, evidently as far as Sierra Leone, before 480 BC. The Romans applied 'Africa' to the whole continent (Pomponius Mela, 1. 4), but far more regularly to Proconsular Africa, comprising the area (roughly modern Tunisia) annexed from Carthage in 146 BC, plus the Numidian and Mauretanian domains later added. But, though the Carthaginians may have known more about the Trans-Sahara than we realize, the knowledge of Africa possessed by the ancient peoples who have left most literary remains was largely confined to the areas participating in, or accessible to, the Mediterranean civilizations, rarely penetrating the colossal barriers of the Atlas Mountains, the Sahara and the perils of the Upper Nile.

II. Africa in the Old Testament

Similarly, Israel's main concerns in Africa were naturally with her powerful neighbour, Egypt. Whether as the granary of the Patriarchs, the oppressor of the bondage or the broken reed of the period of Assyrian advance, the changing roles of Egypt could not be ignored. Despite the cruel past, a tender feeling towards Egypt remained (Dt. 23:7), which prepares us for the prophecies of Egypt's eventually sharing with Israel, in the knowledge and worship of the Lord (Is. 19—note the changing tone as the chapter proceeds). Other African peoples are mentioned from time to time (*LIBYA, *PUT), but the most frequent allusions are to Cush (*ETHIOPIA), the general designation for the lands beyond Egypt. The characteristic skin and physique of the inhabitants was remarked (Je. 13:23; Is. 45:14, and probably Is. 18:2, 7).

At some periods historical circumstances linked Egypt and Ethiopia in Hebrew eyes, and they stand together, sometimes with other African peoples, as representative nations on which God's righteous judgments will be executed (Is. 43:3; Ezk. 30:4ff.; Na. 3:9), as those who will one day recognize the true status of God's people (Is. 45:14), and as those who will ultimately receive Israel's God (Ps. 87:4, and especially Ps. 68:31). The picture of Ethiopia, symbol of the great African unknown beyond the Egyptian river, stretching out hands to God, was like a trumpet-call in the missionary revival of the 18th and 19th centuries. Even within the biblical period it had a measure of fulfilment; not only were there Jewish settlements in Africa (*cf.* Zp. 3:10) but an Ethiopian in Jewish service did more for God's prophet than true-born Israelites (Je. 38), and the high-ranking Ethiopian of Acts 8 was evidently a devout proselyte.

Despite a long tradition of perverted exegesis in some quarters, there is nothing to connect the curse of Ham (Gn. 9:25) with a permanent divinely instituted malediction on the negroid peoples; it is explicitly applied to the Canaanites.

III. Africa in the New Testament

Jesus himself received hospitality on African soil (Mt. 2:13ff.). The Jewish settlements in Egypt and Cyrene, prefigured, perhaps, in Is. 19:18f. *et alia*, were evidently a fruitful field for the early church. Simon who bore the cross was a Cyrenian, and that his relationship with Christ did not stop there may be inferred from the fact that his children were apparently well known in the primitive Christian community (Mk. 15:21). Egyptian and Cyrenian Jews were present at Pentecost (Acts 2:10); the mighty *Apollos was an Alexandrian Jew (Acts 18:24); Cyrenian converts, probably including the prophet *Lucius, shared in the epoch-making step of preaching to pure pagans at Antioch (Acts 11:20f.). But we know nothing certain about the foundation of the Egyptian and N African churches, some of the most prominent in the world by the late 2nd century. The tradition, which cannot be traced very early, that Mark was the pioneer Evangelist of Alexandria (Eusebius, *EH* 2. 16) is itself, when applied to 1 Pet. 5:13, the only support for the theory of Peter's residence there (but *cf.* G. T. Manley, *EQ* 16, 1944, pp. 138ff.). Luke's vivid picture in Acts of the march of the gospel through the N lands of the Mediterranean may obscure for us the fact that the march through the S lands must have been quite as effective and probably almost as early. There were Christians in Africa about as soon as there were in Europe.

But Luke does not forget Africa. He shows how, by means the apostolic church never anticipated, and before the real Gentile mission began, the gospel went to the kingdom of Meroë (Acts 8:26ff.), as if in earnest of the fulfilment of the purpose of God for Africa declared in the OT.

BIBLIOGRAPHY. M. Cary and E. H. Warmington, *The Ancient Explorers*, 1929; B. H. Warmington, *The North African Provinces*, 1954; C. K. Meek, *Journal of African History* 1, 1960, pp. 1ff.; C. P. Groves, *The Planting of Christianity in Africa*, 1, 1948, pp. 31ff; *idem, Carthage*[2], 1968–9. A.F.W.

AGABUS. Derivation uncertain; possibly equals OT Hagab, Hagabah.

A Jerusalem prophet whose prediction of 'a great famine' was fulfilled in the reign of Claudius (Acts 11:27–28). Suetonius, Dio Cassius, Tacitus and Eusebius mention famines at that time. At Caesarea he acted a prediction of Paul's fate at Jerusalem (Acts 21:10–11). In late traditions, one of the 'Seventy' (Lk. 10:1) and a martyr. G.W.G.

AGAG. From Balaam's use of the name (Nu. 24:7, *etc.*) it would appear to be the common title of the kings of Amalek as 'Pharaoh' was in Egypt. In particular, the name is used of the king of the Amalekites taken by Saul and, contrary to God's command, spared along with the spoil. He was slain by Samuel. Saul's disobedience was the occasion of his rejection by God (1 Sa. 15). M.A.M.

AGAGITE. An adjective applied to Haman in Est. 3:1, 10; 8:3, 5; 9:24. Josephus (*Ant.* 11. 209) makes him an Amalekite, presumably descended from *Agag, whom Saul spared (1 Sa. 15). Mordecai, who brought about Haman's fall, was, like Saul, descended from Kish (Est. 2:5; 1 Sa. 9:1). The LXX has *Bougaios* (meaning obscure) in Est. 3:1, and *Makedōn* (Macedonian) in 9:24; elsewhere it omits the adjective. J.S.W.

AGE, OLD AGE. Throughout the ancient Near East the aged were held in honour for their experience and wisdom (Jb. 12:12; 32:7). Among the Hebrews this was not simply because of the outward sign of the grey beard (hence 'aged', *zāqēn*) or of grey hair (*sbh*), but because the attainment of 'fullness of days' or 'entering into (many) days' was considered to be a sign of divine favour for fearing the Lord and keeping his commands (Lv. 19:32; Dt. 30:19–20) and thus showing dependence on the God-appointed authority (Ex. 20:12). Yet without righteousness the hoary head is no crown of glory (Pr. 16:31; *cf.* Ec. 4:13). Christ in glory is depicted as with 'white hair' (Rev. 1:14) and identified with the 'Ancient of Days' (*cf.* Dn. 7:9).

Older men were expected to lead in positions of authority and responsibility as *elders. 'The beauty of old age' is grey hair (Pr. 20:29). Age should equally be marked by wisdom (1 Ki. 12:6–8; Jb. 12:20; 15:10; 32:7). Thus failure to respect the aged is a mark of a decadent society (Is. 3:5), as of the Babylonians who 'had no compassion on old man or aged', lit. 'the one who stooped through age' (2 Ch. 36:17; but *cf.* Herodotus 2. 80). Conversely respect for age brings blessing to the community (Is. 65:20; Zc. 8:4).

The disabilities of old age are not overlooked (Ps. 71:9) and are pictured in Ec. 12:2-7 as a loss of vision, vigour and teeth, as well as increasing insomnia, anxiety and waning ambition. Abraham and Sarah were believed to be beyond the age of child-bearing (Gn. 18:11–14; *cf.* Lk. 1:18), and blindness afflicted Isaac (Gn. 27:1), Jacob (Gn. 48:10), Eli (1 Sa. 3:2; 4:15) and Ahijah (1 Ki. 14:4). Barzillai lost his sense of taste and hearing (2 Sa. 19:35), while David suffered from poor circulation, or hyperthermia (1 Ki. 1:1–4). Apart from the unusual years attributed by the pre-flood *genealogies of Gn. 5 and 11, as to early Babylonian rulers, the Patriarchs attained great age (Abraham 175, Gn. 25:7; Isaac 180, Gn. 35:28; Jacob 147, Gn. 47:28; and Joseph 110, Gn. 50:22). Yet men like Moses at age 120 (Dt. 34:7), or Jehoiada at 130 (2 Ch. 24:15), were still full of vigour.

The change from maturity to 'old age' was considered as age 60 (*cf.* Lv. 27:1–8; Ps. 90:10). Thus 'at 60 one attains old age; at 70 the hoary head, at 80 special strength, at 90 bending, and at 100 (is) as though already dead' (*Pirqē Aboth* 21). This may be compared with a contemporary Babylonian view in which '60 is maturity; 70 length of days (long life); 80 old age; 90 extreme old age' (Sultan Tepe Tablet 400:45–49). D.J.W.

AGRICULTURE. The excavations of OT Jericho have demonstrated that Palestine was one of the earliest agricultural centres yet discovered. Good farming can be dated here around 7500 BC. Jericho represents irrigation culture which was common in the prehistoric period in the Jordan valley, not along the river itself but beside the streams that flowed into it. About the same time the hill country also was showing signs of agriculture, for the Natufian culture shows flint sickle-blades and hoes. Irrigation as an ancient science reached its peak and held it in Egypt and Babylonia. By Abraham's time, however, in Palestine irrigation farming was declining in importance, and even dry farming, as in the Negeb, was coming in.

Most of Palestine's farmers depended on rain. The drought of a 6 months' summer ended with the 'early rains', and as soon as the sun-baked earth could be farmed (late November or December) the seed was broadcast and ploughed under. Sometimes the land was also ploughed before seeding. The heavy winter rains gave the crops their major moisture, but the 'latter rains' of March and April were needed to bring the grain to head.

The principal grain crops were wheat and barley, the former the more valuable, but the latter had the advantage of a shorter growing season and the ability to grow on poorer soil. Various legumes, such as lentils, peas and beans, formed a secondary crop. *Vegetables added variety to the meal, with onions and garlic playing a prominent part. *Herbs, seeds and other condiments gave variety to a menu that was basically bread. Newly-sprouting wild *plants served as salads.

After the invention of the sickle, where flint teeth were set into a bone or wooden haft, the next improvement was the plough. The best tree from which to fashion a wooden plough was the oak. The poorest farmer never had a metal ploughshare (Heb. *'ēt*, as 'coulter' AV in 1 Sa. 13:20f.). By the time of David, however, iron was sufficiently plentiful, and a good-sized iron one could be used. The result was much better crops and a heavier population on the same land area.

The single-handled wooden plough had a virtue in its lightness, as the fields were often stony and the plough could be easily lifted over boulders. On level land, as in Bashan, excess rocks were gathered into piles in the fields. But on the hillsides they were built into terraces to keep the good soil from washing away and to conserve moisture. Large stones served as boundary marks of a grain field, and no fencing was used. The single-handled plough left the farmer's other hand free to use the ox-goad.

Grain crops matured first in the deep hot Jordan valley, and then the harvest season followed up the rising elevation of the land, first the coastal and Esdraelon areas, then the low hills and finally the higher mountains. The barley harvest of April and May preceded the wheat by several weeks or even a month. By that time a summer crop of millet had often been sown on other land which had been left fallow through the winter.

To harvest the crop, the grain was grasped in one hand and then cut with the sickle held in the other hand. These bundles were tied into sheaves, which in turn were loaded on to donkeys or camels to be carried to the threshing-floor. Amos mentions the use of wagons. Gleaners followed the reapers, and then animals were let into the stubble in the following order: sheep, goats and camels.

Threshing-floors were located near the village at a point where the winds would be helpful for winnowing. The floor itself was either a rock outcropping or a soil area coated with marly clay. The sheaves were scattered about a foot deep over the floor and protected at the edges by a ring of stones. The animals, which were sometimes shod for this purpose, were driven round and round until the grain was loosened. A faster method was to use a wooden sled with stones or iron fragments fastened into the under side. The grain was winnowed by tossing it into the wind with wooden shovels or fans. The grain might be sifted with sieves (Heb. *k^{e}ḇārâ* in Am. 9:9 and *nāpâ* in Is. 30:28) to remove grit before being bagged for human use. The straw was saved as fodder for the animals. Fire in a ripening field or a threshing-floor was a major crime, as that year's food supply was lost. Samson's fox-fire episode (Jdg. 15:4–5) was a catastrophe to the Philistines. Threshing might last to the end of August or even later with bumper harvests.

The best grain lands were the benches of the Jordan valley that could be irrigated by the tributaries of the Jordan, the Philistine plain, Esdraelon (although part of it was then marshy), Bashan and Moab. But since bread was the principal food of the country, even poor bench land was often cultivated to produce grain. Narrow stair-like terraces were erected on the mountainside, and in Lebanon today they still creep up the mountains to the very snow-line. The lower hills, such as the Shephelah, gave a wider distribution to crops, adding the *vine and the *olive to the grains, making a famous trio of crops often referred to in OT. The better sections of the higher land were farmed, but much was left for grazing or forestry.

The heavy summer dews in many parts of the country supplemented the sub-soil moisture from the winter rains and made possible the cultivation of grapes, cucumbers and melons. These were far more valuable crops than many Bible readers realize, for Palestine has no summer rain, and most of the streams dry up. These fruits and vegetables then become an extra water ration to both man and beast. Many varieties of grapes were grown, and they were not only a valuable food item in summer but, when dried as raisins, they were also winter food. The wine made from the grape was an item of export. Grapes were usually a hillside crop, with beans and lentils often grown between the vines. Is. 5:1–6 provides a good picture of the vineyard.

Fruits and nuts were other means of adding variety to the menu. The olive tree and the sesame plant were principal sources of cooking oil; animal fat was very expensive. Nuts, although rich in oil, were primarily used as condiments. The pods of the carob tree were an excellent food for animals. *Flax was the only plant grown for cloth.

The farmer's major enemy was drought. The failure of any one of the three rain seasons was serious, and prolonged droughts were not uncommon, especially in certain sections of the land. The farmer was also plagued by locust invasions, plant diseases, such as the mildew, and the hot sirocco winds. War, too, was a common enemy of the farmer, for war was usually conducted at the harvest season so that the invading army could live off the land. Palestine's chief exports were wheat, olive oil and wine. These were not only shipped to other countries, but large quantities of these items were consumed by the caravans traversing the land of Palestine itself.

The levitical laws of Moses laid down certain agricultural principles, some of which have been mentioned above. These were often sound agricultural practice for soil conservation, *e.g.* fallow in the seventh year (Lv. 25), or social reasons, *e.g.* leaving the residual grain for the poor to glean (Lv. 23:22). If God's principles were not observed, the crops would not grow and famine would follow (Lv. 26:14ff.): moral and practical lessons that are still relevant and yet to be learnt throughout the world.

BIBLIOGRAPHY. D. Baly, *The Geography of the Bible*², 1974; A. Reifenberg, *The Desert and the Sown*, 1956; F. N. Hepper, *IEBP*; P. J. Ucko and G. W. Dimbleby (eds.), *The Domestication and Exploitation of Plants and Animals*, 1969.

J.L.K.
F.N.H.

AHAB (Heb. *'aḥ'āḇ*; Assyr. *Aḫābu*, 'the (divine) brother is father').

1. The son and successor of Omri, founder of the dynasty, who reigned as seventh king of Israel for 22 years, *c.* 874–852 BC (1 Ki. 16:28ff.). He married Jezebel, daughter of Ethbaal, king of Sidon and priest of Astarte.

I. Political history

Ahab fortified Israelite cities (1 Ki. 16:34; 22:39) and undertook extensive work at his own capital, *Samaria, as is shown also by excavation (1 Ki. 16:32). His own palace was adorned with ivory (1 Ki. 21:1; 22:39; *cf.* Am. 3:15). Throughout his reign there were frequent wars with Syria (*cf.* 1 Ki. 22:1) especially against Ben-hadad who, with his allies, besieged Samaria but was driven off (1 Ki. 20:21). Later, in battle near Aphek, Ahab heavily defeated Ben-hadad but spared his life (1 Ki. 20:26–30), perhaps in return for commercial concessions in Damascus similar to those allowed to Syrian merchants in Samaria. Economic ties were maintained with Phoenician ports through his marriage.

The Assyrian annals show that in 853 BC, at the battle of Qarqar on the Orontes, Ahab supported Ben-hadad with 2,000 chariots and 10,000 men in the successful, though temporary, effort to stay the advance SW by *Shalmaneser III (*cf. ANET*, pp. 278–281). This intervention was one of the first causes of the later Assyrian advances against Israel. The preoccupation with Syrian affairs enabled Moab, once Ahab's vassal, to revolt (*MOABITE STONE). Later in his reign, however, Ahab, with Jehoshaphat of Judah, once more warred against Syria (1 Ki. 22:3). Though warned by Micaiah's prophecy of the fatal outcome, Ahab entered the final battle at Ramoth-gilead, but in disguise. He was mortally wounded by a random arrow, and his body taken to Samaria for burial. His son Ahaziah succeeded to the throne (1 Ki. 22:28–40).

II. Religious affairs

Elijah was the principal prophet of the reign. Ahab was influenced by his wife Jezebel whom he allowed to build a temple dedicated to Baal (of Tyre) in Samaria with its pagan altar, *asherah* and attendants (1 Ki. 16:32). She encouraged a large group of false prophets together with the devotees of Baal (1 Ki. 18:19–20), and later instigated open opposition to Yahweh. The true prophets were slain, altars of the Lord were torn down and Elijah forced to flee for his life. One hundred prophets were, however, hidden by Obadiah, Ahab's godly minister (1 Ki. 18:3–4).

Ahab's failure to stand for the law and true justice was exemplified in the fake trial and subsequent death of Naboth, whose vineyard was annexed to the adjacent palace grounds at Jezreel (1 Ki. 21:1–16). This brought Elijah once again into open opposition; his stand was vindicated by Yahweh at the test at Carmel which routed the claims of the false prophets. Elijah prophesied the fate of Ahab, his wife and the dynasty (1 Ki. 21:20–24). The reign, marked by idolatry and the evil influence of Jezebel (1 Ki. 21:25–26), affected succeeding generations for evil, and was also condemned by Hosea (1:4) and Micah (6:16).

2. Ahab, son of Kolaiah, was one of the two false prophets denounced by Jeremiah for using the name of Yahweh. His death, by fire, at the hand of the king of Babylon was foretold by the prophet (Je. 29:21). D.J.W.

AHASUERUS (*ᵃḥašwērôš*, the Heb. equivalent of the Persian *khshayarsha*). In the Elephantine Aramaic papyri the consonants appear as *ḥsy'rš*. The resemblance of the latter to the Greek Xerxes is reasonably close, and the Babylonian version of Xerxes' name on the Behistun inscription is close to the Hebrew as above. Xerxes I was king of Persia (485–465 BC). The name occurs in three different contexts:

1. Ezra 4:6. It is probable that in Ezr. 4:6–23 the author has deliberately introduced two later examples of opposition in the reigns of Xerxes I and his successor, Artaxerxes I. The context speaks of opposition to the building of the city walls, and not of the Temple, as in 4:1-5, 24 (see J. Stafford Wright, *The Date of Ezra's Coming to Jerusalem*, 1958). An alternative but improbable theory is that the king here is Cambyses, the successor of Cyrus (529–522 BC).

2. The book of *Esther. Almost certainly Xerxes I, although the LXX reads throughout 'Artaxerxes', and some identify Ahasuerus here with Artaxerxes II (404–359 BC).

3. Dn. 9:1. The father of *Darius the Mede. J.S.W.

AHAVA. A Babylonian town and also, probably, a canal named after the town, where Ezra assembled returning exiles (Ezr. 8:15–31). The site may well be the classical Scenae (Strabo, *Geog.* 16. 1. 27), an important caravan junction not far from Babylon.

D.J.A.C.

AHAZ (Heb. *'āḥaz*, 'he has grasped'). **1.** King of Judah (732–715 BC), son of Jotham. The name Ahaz is an abbreviated form of Jehoahaz. This is confirmed by an inscription of Tiglath-pileser III (*Yauhazi*, see *ANET*, p. 282). His age at the time of his accession and the length of his reign (2 Ki. 16:2; 2 Ch. 28:1) both give rise to chronological problems (*CHRONOLOGY OF THE OLD TESTAMENT).

Early in his reign, Pekah, king of Israel, and Rezin, king of Syria, tried to force him to join their anti-Assyrian alliance. Failing in this, the allies invaded Judah (2 Ki. 16:5). The Judaeans suffered heavy casualties and many were taken prisoner. The intervention of the prophet Oded secured the repatriation of the prisoners (2 Ch. 28:5–15). Isaiah sought vainly to encourage Ahaz at the height of the crisis to put his trust in Yahweh (Is. 7:1–12), but the faithless king preferred to appeal to Assyria for help. The price of Assyrian aid, besides being a heavy drain on the exchequer, was a century of vassalage for Judah. The Philistines and the Edomites took advantage of Judah's weakened condition to make hostile incursions (2 Ch. 28:17–18).

These calamities are represented as divine judgment on Ahaz for his flagrant apostasy. He 'even burned his son as an offering', encouraged corrupt worship of the high places, placed an Assyrian-type altar in the temple court, used the displaced Solomonic bronze altar for divination and closed the temple sanctuary (2 Ki. 16:3–4, 10–16; 2 Ch. 28:2–4, 23–25).

2. Ahaz was also the name of a son of Micah, great-grandson of King Saul (1 Ch. 8:35–36; 9:41–42). J.C.J.W.

AHAZIAH (Heb. *'ªḥazyâ* or *'ªḥazyāhû*, 'Yahweh has grasped'). **1.** Son and successor of *Ahab, king of Israel, whose religious policy he continued unchanged (1 Ki. 22:51–2 Ki. 1:18). Consequently, the main interest in his 2-year reign for the biblical narrator is his clash with *Elijah after he had sent to consult with *Baalzebub, god of Ekron. At his accession, the revolt of Moab, which the *Moabite Stone suggests may have started during the closing years of Ahab's reign, was successfully concluded (2 Ki. 1:1; 3:5). Ahaziah also faced failure in his ill-fated attempt at a maritime alliance with Jehoshaphat, king of Judah (2 Ch. 20:35–36; 1 Ki. 22:48–49). He died prematurely after a fall, and, having no son, was succeeded by his brother Jehoram.

2. Also called Jehoahaz (2 Ch. 21:17), a variant form of the same name: the youngest son of Jehoram, king of Judah. Complementary accounts of his accession and assassination, based on independent sources which reflect differing interests, are found in 2 Ki. 8:25–29; 9:16–29; and 2 Ch. 22:1–9. He was placed on the throne by the inhabitants of Jerusalem as the sole surviving heir. His reign of less than a year was characterized by a close association with his uncle, Jehoram, king of Israel, no doubt under the influence of his mother, *Athaliah. He was murdered during the purge of Jehu whilst visiting Jehoram, who was convalescing in Jezreel. H.G.M.W.

AHIJAH, AHIAH. 1. A prophet from Shiloh who protested against the idolatry of Solomon. Ahijah symbolically divided his robe into 12 parts, 10 of which he gave to Jeroboam, a minor official in Solomon's government (1 Ki. 11:28ff.). Ahijah stated that the kingdom of Solomon would be divided and that 10 of the tribes would become subject to Jeroboam (1 Ki. 11:30–40). To escape the wrath of Solomon, Jeroboam fled to Egypt, where he was granted asylum by Pharaoh Shishak. After Solomon's death, Ahijah's prophecy was fulfilled when the 10 N tribes revolted from Rehoboam, Solomon's son, and Jeroboam became king of Israel (922–901 BC). Jeroboam, however, led Israel into idolatry and was also denounced by Ahijah. The prophet foretold the death of Jeroboam's son, the extinction of his house and the future captivity of Israel (1 Ki. 14:6–16).

2. In 1 Sa. 14:3, 18 Ahiah appears as the name of the great-grandson of Eli. He is elsewhere called Ahimelech, priest of Nob and father of Abiathar (1 Sa. 21:1ff.; 22:9ff.).

3. Other men bearing the name are mentioned briefly: one of Solomon's secretaries (1 Ki. 4:3); the father of Baasha (1 Ki. 15:27, 33); the son of Jerahmeel (1 Ch. 2:25, where the rendering is uncertain); the son of Ehud (1 Ch. 8:4, 7, AV respectively 'Ahoah' and 'Ahiah'); one of David's heroes (1 Ch. 11:36); a guardian of the Temple treasure (1 Ch. 26:20, where again the text is dubious); and one of Nehemiah's fellow-signatories to the covenant (Ne. 10:26, RSV 'Ahiah'). C.F.P.

AHIKAM (Heb. *'ªḥîqām*, 'my brother has arisen'). Son of Shaphan (probably not Shaphan the scribe, 2 Ki. 22:12), and father of *Gedaliah, whom Nebuchadrezzar appointed governor in 587 BC (2 Ki. 25:22; Je. 39:14). One of those sent by Josiah to enquire of *Huldah the prophetess (2 Ki. 22:14; 2 Ch. 34:20–22), he later saved Jeremiah from death (Je. 26:24). D.W.B.

AHIMAAZ (Heb. *'ªḥîma'aṣ*, 'my brother is wrath'). **1.** Father of Saul's wife, Ahinoam (1 Sa. 14:50).

2. Son of Zadok. Famed for his swift running (2 Sa. 18:27). With Jonathan, Abiathar's son, he acted as messenger from David's secret allies in Jerusalem during Absalom's rebellion (2 Sa. 15:27, 36), and escaped capture at En-rogel only by hiding in a well (2 Sa. 17:17–21). He was one of the two messengers who brought news of Absalom's defeat, though he did not report his death, either through ignorance of the fact or a natural reluctance to tell David (2 Sa. 18:19–32).

3. Solomon's commissariat officer for Naphtali, who married his daughter, Basemath (1 Ki. 4:15). Some identify with Zadok's son. J.G.G.N.

AHIMELECH (Heb. *'ªḥîmeleḵ*, 'brother of a king', 'my brother is king'). The name is also found on the ostraca from Samaria and an ancient Hebrew seal. **1.** Son of Ahitub and father of Abiathar. He was priest at Nob and gave David the showbread and Goliath's sword, for which he was killed by Saul (1 Sa. 21–22) (*AHIJAH). **2.** Son of *Abiathar, a priest under David, perhaps grandson of **1** (2 Sa. 8:17). **3.** A Hittite in David's service before he became king (1 Sa. 26:6). A.R.M.

AHIRAM. A son of Benjamin (Nu. 26:38), possibly corrupted to Ehi in Gn. 46:21 and to Aharah in 1 Ch. 8:1. J.D.D.

AHITHOPHEL (Heb. *'ªḥîṯōpel*, possibly 'brother of foolish talk'). A native of Giloh and David's respected counsellor (2 Sa. 16:23). When he conspired with Absalom, David prayed that his advice might be rendered useless, perhaps playing on the name (2 Sa. 15:12, 31ff.). Ahithophel suggested that Absalom should assert his authority by taking possession of his father's harem. His plan for attacking David before he could muster his forces was thwarted by the king's friend Hushai. Ahithophel, perceiving that Absalom had taken a disastrous course, went home and hanged himself lest he fall into the hands of his former lord (2 Sa. 16–17). Jehoiada and Abiathar took his place as David's counsellors (1 Ch. 27:33–34). His son, Eliam, evidently remained faithful to David, as he was one of the thirty heroes (2 Sa. 23:34). A.R.M.

AHITUB (Heb. *'ᵃḥîṭûḇ*, 'brother of good', 'my brother is good'. LXX *Achitōb* and Assyr. *Aḫuṭāb* suggest a reading Ahitob). **1.** Son of Phinehas, grandson of Eli, father of *Ahijah (1 Sa. 14:3). **2.** Father of Ahimelech, perhaps the same person as **1** (1 Sa. 22:9). **3.** A Levite, son of Amariah (1 Ch. 6:7–8), father of Meraioth and 'chief officer of the house of God' (1 Ch. 9:11). Zadok was evidently his grandson (2 Sa. 8:17; 1 Ch. 18:16; Ezr. 7:2; *cf.* 1 Ch. 9:11; Ne. 11:11). A.R.M.

AHLAB. Situated in the territory of Asher (Jdg. 1:31), it is possibly the Mehebel of Jos. 19:29. Probably to be identified with Khirbet el-Maḥālib, 8 km NE of Tyre, the Mahalib captured by *Tiglathpileser III in 734 BC and later by *Sennacherib. See D. J. Wiseman, *Iraq* 18, 1956, p. 129. D.J.W.

AI. The name is always written with the definite article in Hebrew, *hā'ay*, the heap, ruin. The city lay E of Bethel and the altar which Abram built (Gn. 12:8) adjacent to Beth-aven (Jos. 7:2) and N of Michmash (Is. 10:28). The Israelite attack upon it, immediately following the sack of Jericho, was at first repulsed, but after Achan's sin had been punished a successful stratagem was employed. The people of Ai were killed, their king executed, and their city burned and made into 'a heap' (Heb. *tēl*; Jos. 7:1–8:29). It became an Ephraimite town (1 Ch. 7:28, 'Ayyah'), but was inhabited by the Benjaminites after the Exile (Ne. 11:31). Isaiah pictured the Assyrian armies advancing on Jerusalem by way of Ai (Is. 10:28, 'Aiath').

Modern Et-Tell (Arab. *tall*, heap, mound) about 3 km SE of Bethel (Tell Beitīn) is usually identified with Ai on topographical grounds and on the correspondence in the meanings of the ancient and modern names. Excavations in 1933–5 by Mme J. Marquet-Krause and in 1964–72 by J. A. Callaway revealed a city which prospered in the 3rd millennium BC. There was a strong city-wall and a temple containing stone bowls and ivories imported from Egypt. It was destroyed *c.* 2400 BC, perhaps by Amorite invaders. No traces of later occupation were found except for a small settlement which made use of the earlier ruins about 1200–1050 BC. Those who believe in this identification have made various attempts to explain the discrepancy between the biblical account of Joshua's conquest and the archaeological evidence. It has been suggested that the story originally referred to Bethel but was later adapted to suit Ai or even invented to explain the impressive ruin as the result of an attack by the hero Joshua. There is no evidence to support these hypotheses; indeed, it would be strange to credit a hero with failure at first. More plausible is the explanation that Ai, with its massive old walls, was used as a temporary stronghold by the surrounding population; but the account points rather to an inhabited town with its own king. While it is possible that Ai is to be located elsewhere, no completely satisfactory solution has yet been proposed (for the question of identification see D. Livingston, *WTJ* 33, 1970, pp. 20–44; A. F. Rainey, *WTJ* 33, pp. 175–188; D. Livingston, *WTJ* 34, 1971, pp. 39–50). The later town (Ezr. 2:28; Ne. 7:32) may be identified with some other site in the vicinity. For references to the excavation results and proposed solutions of the problem they raise, see J. A. Callaway, *NEAEHL*, 1, pp. 39–45; J. M. Grintz, *Bib* 42, 1961, pp. 201–216.

Ai is also the name of a city in Moab (Je. 49:3) of unknown location. A.R.M.

AIJALON, AJALON (Heb. *'ayyālôn*). **1.** A town on a hill commanding from the S the entrance to the valley of Aijalon. The earliest traces (2000 BC) are at Tell el-Qoq'a, near Yalo. In successive phases of Israel's history it was inhabited by Danites (who could not expel the Amorites), Ephraimites and Benjaminites (Jos. 19:42; Jdg. 1:35; 1 Ch. 6:69; 8:13). A levitical town, fortified by Rehoboam to guard the NW approach to Jerusalem, it was occupied by the Philistines in the reign of Ahaz (2 Ch. 11:10; 28:18).

BIBLIOGRAPHY. D. Baly, *Geog. Companion*, 1963, pp. 92f.; *LOB*, pp. 174, 311f., *etc.*

2. A town in Zebulun (Jdg. 12:12), where the judge Elon (same Heb. letters) was buried; LXX *Ailom*. Possibly Kh. el-Lōn; *cf.* F. M. Abel, *Géographie de la Palestine*, 2, 1937, p. 241. J.P.U.L.

AKELDAMA. Acts 1:19 gives the meaning of the word (in AV Aceldama) as 'field of blood'—the Aramaic phrase being *ḥᵃqēl dᵉmâ*. The ground was previously known as the Potter's Field, and this has been equated with the Potter's House (Je. 18:2) in the Hinnom Valley. Jerome placed it on the S side of this valley; and the site accepted today is there. Eusebius, however, said this ground was N of Jerusalem. The traditional site certainly can provide potter's clay; and it has long been used for burials. See J. A. Motyer in *NIDNTT* 1, pp. 93–94, for bibliography and a brief discussion of the problems. D.F.P.

AKRABBIM (Heb. *'aqrabbîm*, 'scorpions'). A mountain pass at the S end of the Dead Sea (Nu. 34:4; Jos. 15:3 ['Maaleh-acrabbim', AV]; Jdg. 1:36) between the Arabah and the hill-country of Judah, identified with the modern Naqb eṣ-ṣāfā. J.D.D.

ALALAH (Akkad., Hurrian *a-la-la-aḫ*; Egypt. *'irrḫ*). Capital of a city-state on the river Orontes in the Amq plain of N Syria from which 468 texts from Level VII (*c.* 1900–1750 BC) and IV (*c.* 1500–1470 BC) provide details which may be compared with the patriarchal period of Gn. (also *EBLA, *MARI, *UGARIT). The site of Tell Aṭšānâ (Turk. Açana) was excavated by Sir Leonard

Woolley, who in 1937–9 and 1946–9 uncovered sixteen levels of occupation since *c.* 3100 BC (XVI) to *c.* 1200 (I) with early affinities with both Palestine and Mesopotamia.

The 172 texts from Yarimlim's palace (VII) were primarily contracts and ration lists. The city was controlled by a W Semitic family ruling Aleppo (Halab) whose governor Abba'el (or Abban) suppressed a revolt at Irrid near Carchemish and, *c.* 1720, gave Alalah to his brother Yarimlim (AT 1). This early covenant-treaty text, and associated agreements, describes the historical situation, stipulations, divine witnesses and curses, as is common in the later *covenant formulae. A separate document by the same scribe lists the religious obligations (AT 126). Yarimlim left the city to his son in his will (AT 6), attested by state officials, perhaps to avoid rivalry on his death (*cf.* 1 Ki. 1:17–36). However, another son, Irkabtum, succeeded and made peace with the semi-nomadic Hapiru (*HEBREW, *ABRAHAM). The city fell to the Hittite Mursilis I when he captured Aleppo (*c.* 1600 BC).

After a gap (V), Idrimi, the youngest son of a king of Aleppo, was driven into exile, as he tells in his autobiography, inscribed as a speech on his statue. After living among the Hapiru in Canaan for 7 years he received divine assurance to mount an amphibious operation to recapture Mukish. He re-entered his capital Alalah to popular acclaim, was made king and built a palace and temple with spoil taken in war (*c.* 1470 BC). This narrative has been compared with the experiences of David (1 Sa. 22:3ff.). Idrimi made treaties with neighbouring states regulating the extradition of runaway slaves (AT 3, *ANET*[3], p. 532). Similarly Shimei entered Philistine territory to search for his two slaves and Achish of Gath returned them on demand (1 Ki. 2:39–40). This would imply a similar type of treaty, perhaps between Solomon and Gath, following David's experience there (1 Sa. 27:5ff.). It would also throw light on the provision prohibiting the extradition of Hebrew fugitives in Dt. 23:15–16 (*IEJ* 5, 1955, pp. 65–72). Another treaty makes city elders responsible for returning fugitives (AT 2, *ANET*[3], pp. 531f.; Dt. 23:15–16). Alalah later came under Hittite control (Level III), as it had earlier been governed by northerners in the 20th–19th centuries BC. There is no reason to doubt that *Hittites might be resident in S Palestine in the days of Abraham (Gn. 23:5–7; *JTVI*, 1956, p. 124). Alalah was finally destroyed by 'Sea-peoples', perhaps those allied to the *Philistines.

The main interest in these texts for the OT lies in the comparison of customs and language with the Gn. narratives. In marriage contracts (AT 91–94), the future father-in-law was 'asked' for the bride (*cf.* Gn. 29:18), to whom betrothal gifts were made (AT 17). Some contracts state that failing a son within 7 years the husband could marry a concubine (*cf.* Gn. 29:18–21); however, if the first wife later bore a son he would be the first-born (AT 92; *cf.* Gn. 21:10).

The king held a firm control legally and economically over citizens of all classes including the élite *maryanu*-warriors (who also had religious obligations, AT 15), the freedmen and the semi-free rural retainers, among whom were listed the *hupšu* (*ḥopšî*, Dt. 15:12–18).

Some individuals were made to work off their debt by going to the palace to 'dwell in the house of the king' (AT 18–27, 32; *cf.* Ps. 23:6). Slaves were not numerous and could be received as prisoners of war or as gifts (AT 224). They were shekels and some contracts included clauses against release at a royal amnesty (AT 65). The *corvée* (*mas*) was enforced at Alalah as in later Israel (AT 246; Jos. 17:13). All this would be in the mind of Samuel at least when the Israelites asked for a similar type of kingship (1 Sa. 8).

Other customs which may illustrate biblical practices are the exchange of villages to preserve inter-state boundaries along natural and defensible features. This may be reflected in Solomon's 'gift' of 20 villages to Hiram of Tyre in return for wood and gold (1 Ki. 9:10–14; *JBL* 79, 1960, pp. 59–60). Treaty ceremonies involved the slaughter of sheep over which the participants declared: 'If ever I take back what I have given . . .', implying 'may the gods cut off my life', a similar idea to that in OT oaths (*e.g.* 1 Sa. 3:17). In some contracts clothes were given as additional payment, as also in Syria later according to 2 Ki. 5:5–27. Ahab may have attempted to justify his action in confiscating Naboth's property (1 Ki. 21:15) on the basis of the practice whereby a rebel against the king had his property taken by the palace after the execution of an evil-doer (AT 17, *ANET*[3], p. 546, no. 15). The use of *mištannu*, 'equivalent' (AT 3, *ANET*[3], p. 532), in the manumission of slaves (*cf. mišneh*, Dt. 15:18) argues against Je. 16:18 as 'stigmatizing God as unreasonable and unjust' (*HUCA* 29, 1958, pp. 125f.).

The mixed Semitic and Hurrian population of the area from early times (VII) gives significant Hurrian (*HORITE) parallels to such names as Anah, Aholibamah, Alian, Ajah, Dishon, Ezer (Gn. 36), Anah and Shamgar (Jdg. 3:31), To'i (2 Sa. 8:9), Agee (2 Sa. 23:11), Eli-hepa (2 Sa. 23:32) (*JTVI* 82, 1950, p. 6).

BIBLIOGRAPHY. C. L. Woolley, *A Forgotten Kingdom*, 1953; *Alalakh*, 1955; D. J. Wiseman, *The Alalakh Tablets*, 1953 (=AT); *AOTS*, 1967, pp. 119–135; *IDBS*, 1976, pp. 16–17; Sidney Smith, *The Statue of Idrimi*, 1949; *cf. ANET*, 1969, pp. 557–558.

D.J.W.

ALEXANDER. A common Hellenistic name. Its widespread adoption among Jews displeased some strict rabbis and gave rise to an amusing aetiological story that a demand by Alexander the Great for a golden statue in the Temple was countered with the proposal that all boys born that year should be called Alexander (see E. Nestle, *ExpT* 10, 1898–9, p. 527). The frequency is reflected in the NT.

1. The son of Simon of Cyrene (*RUFUS). **2.** A member of the high priestly family, unknown apart from Acts 4:6. **3.** The would-be spokesman of the Jewish interest in the Ephesian riot (Acts 19:33f.). His function was presumably to dissociate the regular Jewish community from the Christian trouble-makers: the anti-Semitism of the mob, however, allowed him no voice. **4.** A pernicious teacher of subverted morals (1 Tim. 1:20), whom Paul 'delivers to Satan' (*HYMENAEUS).

5. A bitter enemy of Paul and the gospel (2 Tim. 4:14f.), evidently (since Timothy is put on guard against him) operating in the Ephesus–Troas area. Had he been responsible for an arrest in Ephesus? He was a coppersmith (the word was then used to designate all kinds of metal-worker), though some have read the title as a proper name, 'Alexander

Chalceus'. When Paul adds 'the Lord will requite him for his deeds', the tense marks this as a prediction (RSV, TEV), not a curse (AV).

Those identifying **3** and **5** (*e.g.* P. N. Harrison, *Problem of the Pastoral Epistles*, 1921, pp. 118f.) can point to the Ephesian location, the origin of the riot with the craft-guilds, and the introduction of Alexander in Acts 19:33 as if well known; but nothing there indicates the sort of opposition betokened in 2 Tim. 4:14. Little can be said for or against identifying **4** and **5**; but **3** and **4** cannot be identical, for the latter would claim to be a Christian. A.F.W.

ALEXANDER THE GREAT. The youthful king of Macedon whose pan-hellenic expedition of 336 BC to liberate the Greeks of Asia Minor unexpectedly demolished the Persian Empire. Only the mutiny of his troops turned him back in India, and he died in 323 while planning the conquest of the W. His generals established the concert of Hellenistic kingdoms to which the Herods performed the epilogue. Probably from necessity rather than idealism, Alexander abandoned the isolationism of the Greeks in favour of racial co-operation. Hellenism became an international norm of civilization. Hence the agonies of the Jews in the Maccabean age, and the tensions that surrounded the crucifixion. Hence also the inspiration of the cosmopolitan philosophies that chimed in with Christian ideals.

Presumably it is Alexander to whom reference is made in Dn. 8:21; 11:3.

BIBLIOGRAPHY. Arrian, *Anabasis*; Plutarch, *Life of Alexander*; C. B. Welles, *Alexander and the Hellenistic World*, 1970; R. L. Fox, *Alexander the Great*, 1973; J. R. Hamilton, *Alexander the Great*, 1973; P. Green, *Alexander of Macedon*, 1974.

E.A.J.

ALEXANDRIA.

I. The city

a. Location

A great seaport on the NW coast of the Egyptian Delta, on the narrow isthmus between the sea and Lake Mareotis. It was founded in 332 BC by Alexander (the Great) of Macedon and named after himself. A small Egyptian settlement, Rakotis, was its only predecessor on the site and was absorbed into the W side of the new city; in native Egyptian parlance (exemplified by Coptic, centuries later), the name Rakotis was extended to Alexandria. The city was apparently laid out on a 'grid' plan of cross-streets and *insulae*; but as the remains of the ancient city are inextricably buried underneath its modern successor, any reconstruction of its lay-out and location of its great buildings must draw heavily on the none-too-precise literary references virtually by themselves, and hence cannot be exact. Not until the time of Ptolemy II (*c.* 285–246 BC) did Alexandria first attain to the architectural splendours so famed in later writers' accounts. Between the shore and the Pharos island stretched a connecting causeway, the 'Heptastadion' ('seven stadia', 1,300 m long); this divided the anchorage into a W harbour and an E or Great harbour, whose entrance was dominated by the Pharos lighthouse-tower. It contained also the royal harbour, and was flanked on the E by the royal palace. S of the shore-line, extending all along behind it and as far as Lake Mareotis, stretched the city.

b. Population

Right from the start, Alexandria was a thoroughly cosmopolitan city. Besides its Greek citizens and numerous poor Greek immigrants, there was a considerable Jewish community (*cf.* later, Acts 6:9; 18:24) under their own ethnarch and having their own quarter (though not restricted to it until AD 38), and quite a large native Egyptian populace, especially in the Rakotis district in the W. In Rakotis was localized the Serapeum, temple of the Egypto-Hellenistic deity Sarapis, whose cult was specially promoted by Ptolemy I, just possibly to serve as a common bond for both Greeks and Egyptians (Sir H. I. Bell).

c. The city's role

Politically, Alexandria became capital of Egypt under the *Ptolemies, Graeco-Macedonian kings of Egypt, *c.* 323–30 BC. Under the first and energetic kings of this line it became the greatest Hellenistic city of the day. Alexandria continued as Egypt's administrative capital into the Roman imperial and Byzantine epochs. Alexandria was the banking-centre of all Egypt, an active manufacturing city (cloths, glass, papyrus, *etc.*) and a thriving port. Thence were transhipped the exotic products of Arabia, India and the East, and thence in Roman times sailed the great grain-ships of Alexandria (*cf.* Acts 27:6; 28:11) to bring cheap corn for the Roman plebeians. Finally, Alexandria quickly became and long remained a brilliant seat of learning. To the reign of either Ptolemy I (323–285 BC) or Ptolemy II (285–246 BC) belongs the founding of the 'Museum', where scholars researched and taught in arts and sciences, and of the Library which eventually contained thousands of works upon many tens of thousands of papyrus rolls.

II. Judaism and Christianity

Alexandria's very large Jewish community was concentrated in the E sector, but with places of worship all over the city (Philo, *Legatio ad Gaium* 132). One famous synagogue, magnificently fitted, was so vast that flags had to be used to signal the Amen (TB *Sukkah* 51b, cited in *BC*, 1, pp. 152f.). But beyond this, Alexandria was the intellectual and literary centre of the Dispersion. It was there that the Greek OT, the Septuagint (*TEXTS AND VERSIONS), was produced, and from there came such works as the Book of Wisdom (*APOCRYPHA) with its Platonic modifications of OT categories and its Greek interest in cosmology and immortality. It was the home of the voluminous *Philo, perhaps the first considerable scholar to use the biblical material as philosophic data—though 'his object is not to investigate but to harmonize' (Bigg, p. 32)—and the first major exponent of the allegorical exegesis of Scripture. Whatever the demerits of the attempted synthesis of Athens and Jerusalem by Alexandrian Jews (and some of them amount to enormities), the literary remains testify to intellectual energy, missionary concern and, despite audacious departures from traditional formation, a profound seriousness about the Scriptures.

These features had considerable indirect influence on early Greek Christianity. It is significant that the eloquent travelling preacher *Apollos, who became an important figure in the apostolic church, was an Alexandrian Jew, and 'well versed in the Scriptures' (Acts 18:24). The Epistle to the Hebrews, because of its use of terminology beloved at Alexandria, and its characteristic use of OT, has been associated, if not necessarily with him, at least with an Alexandrian background; and so, with less reason, have other NT books (*cf.* J. N. Sanders, *The Fourth Gospel in the Early Church*, 1943; S. G. F. Brandon, *The Fall of Jerusalem and the Christian Church*, 1951). Apart, however, from unreliable traditions about the agency of the Evangelist Mark (which may relate originally to the reception of his Gospel in Alexandria), the origin and early history of the Alexandrian church are completely hidden (*AFRICA).

It has been suggested that Alexandrian Judaism had so philosophized away the Messianic hope that the earliest Christian preaching made slow headway there. There is not sufficient evidence to test this hypothesis. It is unmistakable, however, that when Alexandrian Christianity comes into full view it is patently the heir of Alexandrian Judaism. The missionary zeal, the philosophic apologetic, the allegorical exegesis, the application to biblical commentary and the passion for intellectual synthesis which sometimes leads doctrine to disaster, are common to both. Some thoroughfare, at present unlit, links Philo and Clement of Alexandria; but it is hardly too bold a conjecture that the road lies through the conversion to Christ of a substantial number of Jews or their adherents in Alexandria during the apostolic or sub-apostolic period.

BIBLIOGRAPHY. For a standard historical and cultural background for Alexandria, Ptolemaic and Byzantine, see respectively *CAH*, 7, 1928, ch. IV, sect. vii, pp. 142–148, and chs. VIII–IX, pp. 249–311, and *ibid.*, 12, 1939, ch. XIV, sect. i, pp. 476–492. Useful and compact, with reference to actual remains is E. Breccia, *Alexandrea ad Aegyptum, A Guide* . . ., 1922. A popular account of the history and manner of life in ancient Alexandria is H. T. Davis, *Alexandria, the Golden City*, 2 vols., 1957. An excellent study of paganism, Judaism and the advent and triumph of Christianity in Egypt generally, and Alexandria also, is Sir Harold Idris Bell, *Cults and Creeds in Graeco-Roman Egypt*, 1953. On Alexandria and Christianity, see also J. M. Creed in S. R. K. Glanville (ed.), *The Legacy of Egypt*, 1942, pp. 300-316; A. F. Shore in J. R. Harris (ed.), *The Legacy of Egypt*[2], 1971, pp. 390–398; C. Bigg, *The Christian Platonists of Alexandria*[2], 1913; J. E. L. Oulton and H. Chadwick, *Alexandrian Christianity*, 1954; L. W. Barnard, 'St Mark and Alexandria', *HTR* 57, 1964, pp. 145-150; P. M. Fraser, *Ptolemaic Alexandria*, 3 vols., 1972.

A.F.W.

ALMIGHTY. Used of God 48 times in the OT (31 of them in Job) to translate Heb. *šaddai*, and following LXX in some verses, Gk. *pantokratōr*. Interpreted by early Jewish commentators as 'the all-sufficient' (*hikanos* in Jewish–Greek OT versions of 2nd century AD and later). Modern scholars offer a wide range of derivations, none certain. Outside the OT the name apparently occurs in the Tell Deir Alla Aramaic text *c.* 700 BC (*WRITING) in the plural form *šdyn*, denoting supernatural beings. Within the OT *šaddai* carries ideas of power to injure and protect (Pss. 68:14; 91:1; Is. 13:6; Joel 1:15). The name is used six times in relation to the Patriarchs, as stated in Ex. 6:3, sometimes in the compound *'ēl šaddai*, 'God Almighty'. Each case concerns the promise of blessing upon Abraham and his descendants, again with the note of power. In Job 'the Almighty' stands as a poetic parallel to 'God', as also in Ruth 1:20–21 to Yahweh, showing their identity for the writers of these books.

Gk. *pantokratōr* ('all-powerful') occurs in 2 Cor. 6:18, and nine times in Rev., where the power of God is stressed (1:8; 4:8; 11:17; 15:3; 16:7, 14; 19:6, 15; 21:22).

BIBLIOGRAPHY. N. Walker, *ZAW* 72, 1960, pp. 64–66; L. Morris in A. E. Cundall and L. Morris, *Judges and Ruth*, *TOTC*, 1968, pp. 264–268; K. Koch, *VT* 26, 1976, pp. 299–332; W. Michaelis, *TDNT* 3, pp. 914–915.

A.R.M.

ALMS, ALMSGIVING. From Gk. *eleēmosynē via* eccl. Lat. *eleemosyna* and Old English *ælmysse*. The Gk. word signifies pity, prompting relief given in money or kind to the poor.

Though not explicitly mentioned in the English OT, almsgiving is implied as an expression of compassion in the presence of God. It had a twofold development: (*a*) The Mosaic legislation looked on compassion as a feeling to be cherished in ideal conduct (*cf.* Dt. 15:11); (*b*) The prophets considered almsgiving as a right which the needy might justly claim.

From the fusion of these two concepts there arose in the intertestamental age the idea of righteousness secured through almsgiving as efficacious in annulling the guilt of sin, and as ensuring divine favour in time of trouble (*cf.* Ps. 112:9; Dn. 4:27). Righteousness and almsgiving were at times regarded as synonymous terms, as in the LXX (and in our modern use of 'charity' to denote almsgiving), but this is scarcely justifiable from either the Hebrew OT or the true text of the NT.

After the cessation of sacrifice, almsgiving seems to have ranked among the Jews as the first of religious duties. In every city there were collectors who distributed alms of two kinds, *i.e.* money collected in the synagogue chest every sabbath for the poor of the city, and food and money received in a dish. 'Therefore no disciple should live in a city where there is no alms-box' (*Sanhedrin* 17b). It is significant that in the OT scarcely a trace of beggars and begging in the street can be found (but see 1 Sa. 2:36; Ps. 109:10). Ps. 41:1 can be taken as not merely an exhortation to almsgiving, but also as an adjuration to take a personal interest in the poor.

Jesus does not reject almsgiving as futile in the search for right standing with God, but stresses the necessity for right motive, 'in my name'. He rebuked the ostentatious charity of his day (Mt. 6:1–4; note RSV 'piety', translating *dikaiosynēn* for AV 'alms', translating TR *eleēmosynēn*), and emphasized the blessedness of giving (*cf.* Acts 20:35), and its opportunities.

In the early Christian community the first election of officers was made to ensure a fair distribution of alms; the needs of the poor were met (Acts 4:32, 34); and every Christian was exhorted to lay by on the first day of each week some portion of his profits to be applied to the wants of the needy (Acts 11:30; Rom. 15:25–27; 1 Cor. 16:1–4).

'Alms' are equated with 'righteousness', not because they justify a man (Rom. 3–4), but because they constitute an action which is right and for which our neighbour has a rightful claim on us in the eyes of God who gives us means for this very end (Eph. 4:28).

(*POVERTY; *COMMUNION; *COMPASSION.)

J.D.D.

ALPHA AND OMEGA. This juxtaposition of the first and last letters of the Gk. alphabet, corresponding to the Heb. *'alep̄* and *tāw*, is used in Rev. alone as a self-designation of both God (Rev. 1:8; 21:6, where 'the Alpha and the Omega' is explained by the parallel 'the beginning and the end') and Christ (22:13, with the same parallel, and the additional phrase 'the first and the last'). In Rev. 22:13 the Son's divinity is confirmed by applying to him what is said of the Father. In each of these cases the term refers to the eternal, dynamic and comprehensive activity of God or Christ in creation and salvation; that is, the origin, preservation and goal of all things are to be found in the Godhead (*cf.* Rom. 11:36). The Hebrews, Greeks and Romans all used their alphabetic letters as numerals, so that 'alpha and omega' could easily stand for 'first and last' (*cf.* Is. 44:6, 'Thus says the Lord, ... "I am the first and I am the last"'; also Rev. 2:8). S.S.S.

ALPHAEUS. 1. The father of Levi, the tax collector (Mk. 2:14) who is generally identified with the apostle Matthew. Nothing else is known about him.

2. The father of the apostle James, who is called 'the son of Alphaeus', to distinguish him from James the son of Zebedee (Mt. 10:3; Mk. 3:18; Lk. 6:15; Acts 1:13). There is no valid reason for identifying him with the father of *Levi **1**. Attempts have also been made to identify him with Cleopas (Lk. 24:18) and Clopas (Jn. 19:25). However, it is improbable that *Cleopas and *Clopas are the same person and that Alphaeus is the same as either of them. The Aramaic of Alphaeus is *Halphai*, which could be transliterated as *Klōpas*, but even if the same individual is signified, we cannot assume from Jn. 19:25 that this James was in any way related to our Lord and certainly not that he was James the Lord's brother. R.E.N.

ALTAR.

I. In the Old Testament

In all but four of the OT occurrences of the word 'altar', the Heb. is *mizbēaḥ*, which means 'place of sacrifice' (from *zāḇaḥ*, 'to slaughter for sacrifice'), and one of the remaining occurrences (Ezr. 7:17) is simply its Aram. cognate *maḏbaḥ*. While etymologically the term involves slaughter, in usage it was not always so restricted, being applied also to the altar for burning incense (Ex. 30:1). For other occurrences of 'altar' in the EVV, see *g*, below.

a. The Patriarchs

The Patriarchs built their own altars and offered their own sacrifices on them without having any recourse to a priesthood. Noah built one after the flood and made burnt-offerings on it (Gn. 8:20). Abraham built altars to Yahweh at Shechem, between Bethel and Ai, at Hebron and at Moriah, where he offered a ram instead of Isaac (Gn. 12:6–8; 13:18; 22:9). Isaac did likewise at Beersheba (Gn. 26:25), Jacob erected altars at Shechem and Bethel (Gn. 33:20; 35:1–7), and Moses erected one at Rephidim after the victory of the Israelites over Amalek (Ex. 17:15). The altars were evidently erected mainly to commemorate some event in which the principal had had dealings with God.

b. Pre-Israelite altars in Palestine

Discounting domestic, agricultural or industrial installations formerly believed to be altars, true altars have been uncovered from different periods. At Ai, Mme J. Marquet-Krause discovered a small temple of the Early Bronze Age in which was an altar of plastered stones, against the wall, on which animal and food-offerings had been made. In Middle Bronze Age *Megiddo (level XV) two temples were found containing rectangular altars, one of mud bricks and the other of lime-plastered stones. Temples of the Late Bronze Age containing altars of similar type have been found at Lachish, Beth-shean and Hazor. In the levels of this period at Hazor a great hewn block of stone was discovered, with two hollowed basins on one face, perhaps for catching the blood of sacrificed animals. At Megiddo and Nahariyeh great platforms of stones which were probably used as places of sacrifice were uncovered, but these were more *'high places' than they were true altars.

A number of hewn limestone altars with four horns at the upper corners, dating from about the period of the conquest, were found at Megiddo. These, however, to judge from their relatively small size (largest *c.* 70 cm high), were probably incense altars. Numerous clay stands which may have been for burning incense have been uncovered at such sites as Megiddo, Beth-shean and Lachish, from Bronze and Iron Age Levels.

Thus altars were in use among the Canaanites in the Promised Land, a fact that gives point to the careful regulations on this matter in the Sinai revelation. That altars were not limited to Palestine is shown by the discoveries at such sites as Eridu, Ur, Khafajah and Assur in Mesopotamia, and the episode in which Balaam erected, and offered bullocks on, 7 altars at Kiriath-huzoth (Nu. 23) may perhaps be understood in this light.

c. The altars of the tabernacle

At Sinai God revealed to Moses the specifications for two altars which were to be used in the *tabernacle: the altar of burnt-offering and the altar of incense.

d. Built altars

In Ex. 20:24–26, God instructed Moses to tell the people to make an altar of earth (*mizbaḥ *ᵃḏāmâ) or (unhewn) stones (*mizbaḥ *ᵃḇānîm*), upon which to sacrifice their offerings. In neither case were there to be steps, so that the 'nakedness' of the offerer might not be uncovered. The form of this passage, in which God tells Moses to pass on this instruction to the people, suggests that it, like the Ten Commandments at the beginning of the chapter, was addressed to each Israelite individually, rather than to Moses as their representative as in Ex. 27. It may be that under this provision the layman was permitted to perform this himself, and it is perhaps in the light of this that the altars built by Joshua on Mt Ebal (Jos. 8:30–31; *cf.* Dt. 27:5), by Gideon in Ophrah (Jdg. 6:24–26), by David on the threshing-floor of Araunah (2 Sa. 24:18–25) and by Elijah on Mt Carmel (1 Ki. 18), as well as the episodes described in Jos. 22:10–34 and 1 Sa. 20:6, 29, are to be viewed (*cf.* Ex. 24:4).

e. The Temple of Solomon

In building his *Temple, Solomon, though influenced by his Phoenician associates, sought to follow the basic layout of the tabernacle and its court. Though David had already built an altar of burnt-offerings (2 Sa. 24:25), Solomon probably built a new one, as is indicated by 1 Ki. 8:22, 54, 64 and 9:25 (not mentioned in the main description, 1 Ki. 6–7). Altars of this period are well illustrated by the finds (IA II period) at Arad where in the temple courtyard stood an altar made of brick and rubble for burnt-offerings (*cf.* Ex. 20:25) which measured 5 cubits sq. (2.5 m) like that of the tabernacle (Ex. 17:1; *cf.* 2 Ch. 6:13). Two stone incense-altars with concave bowl-shaped tops were found on a step leading up to the 'holy of holies'. Other Israelite incense-altars of the Israelite period have been recovered from Beersheba, and also a large altar which was probably used for burnt offerings. This large altar had been destroyed in the 8th century and its stones used to repair the wall of a storehouse. Protrusions at its top corners illustrate what is meant by 'the horns' of an altar.

f. False altars

Unlawful altars were in use in both Israel and Judah, as is shown by the condemnations of the prophets (Am. 3:14; Ho. 8:11) and the account of Jeroboam's sins in 1 Ki. 12:28–33, as well as by archaeological finds.

g. Ezekiel's vision

During the Exile, Ezekiel had a vision of Israel restored and the Temple rebuilt (Ezk. 40-44), and while no incense altar is mentioned, the altar of burnt offering in this visionary temple is described in detail (43:13–17). It consisted of 3 stages reaching to a height of 11 cubits on a base 18 cubits square. It was thus in form reminiscent of a Babylonian ziggurat, and this impression is furthered by the names of some of its parts. The base, *ḥêq hā'āreṣ* (Ezk. 43:14, AV 'bottom upon the ground', literally 'bosom of the earth') recalls the Akkadian *irat irṣiti* with the same meaning, and the terms *har'ēl* and *ᵃri'êl* translated 'altar' in vv. 15–16 may be Hebraized forms of Akkadian *arallu*, one of the names for the underworld, which had the secondary meaning 'mountain of the gods'. Such borrowings from the Babylonian vocabulary, which would be independent of their etymological meaning, would have been normal after an exile of many years in Babylonia. The altar was ascended by a flight of steps, and the 4 upper corners bore horns.

h. The second Temple

When the Temple was rebuilt after the Return it was presumably provided with altars. These are referred to in Josephus (*Contra Apionem* 1. 198) and in the *Letter of Aristeas*, but on this period neither of these authors can be followed uncritically. In 169 BC Antiochus Epiphanes carried off the 'golden altar' (1 Macc. 1:21), and 2 years later he surmounted the altar of burnt offering with a 'desolating sacrilege' (1 Macc. 1:54), probably an image of Zeus. The Maccabees built a new altar and restored the incense altar (1 Macc. 4:44–49), and these must have continued in use when Herod enlarged the *Temple in the latter part of the 1st century BC. In his time the altar of burnt offering was a great pile of unhewn stones, approached by a ramp.

II. In the New Testament

In the NT two words for altar are used, that most frequently found being *thysiastērion*, which is used often in the LXX for *mizbēaḥ*. This word is used of the altar on which Abraham prepared to offer Isaac (Jas. 2:21), of the altar of burnt offering in the Temple (Mt. 5:23–24; 23:18–20, 35; Lk. 11:51; 1 Cor. 9:13; 10:18; Heb. 7:13; Rev. 11:1), and of the altar of incense, not only in the earthly Temple (Lk. 1:11) but also in the heavenly (Rev. 6:9; 8:5; 9:13; 14:18; 16:7; *cf.* also Rom. 11:3; Heb. 13:10). The other word, *bōmos*, is used once (Acts 17:23). It was used in the LXX for both *mizbēaḥ* and *bāmâ* (*HIGH PLACE), and had primarily the meaning of a raised place.

BIBLIOGRAPHY. R. de Vaux, *Ancient Israel. Its Life and Institutions*, 1961, pp. 406–414, 546; Y. Aharoni, 'Arad: Its Inscriptions and Temple', *BA* 31, 1968, pp. 2–32; *idem*, 'The Horned Altar of Beersheba', *BA* 37, 1974, pp. 2-6; A. Biran, 'An Israelite Horned Altar at Dan', *BA* 37, 1974, pp. 106–107.

J.McK.
T.C.M.

AMALEK, AMALEKITES. Amalek (Heb. *ᵃmālēq*) was the son of Eliphaz and the grandson of Esau (Gn. 36:12, 16). The name is used as a collective noun for his descendants, Amalekites (Ex. 17:8; Nu. 24:20; Dt. 25:17; Jdg. 3:13, *etc.*).

Some writers distinguish the nomadic Amalekites normally found in the Negeb and Sinai area, from the descendants of Esau, because Gn. 14:7, which pre-dates Esau, refers to 'the country of the Amalekites' (Heb. *ᵃmālēqî*). The distinction is unnecessary if we regard the phrase as a later editorial description.

Israel first met the Amalekites at Rephidim in the wilderness of Sinai (Ex. 17:8–13; Dt. 25:17–18). Because of this attack, the Amalekites came under a permanent ban and were to be destroyed (Dt. 25:19; 1 Sa. 15:2–3). On that occasion Aaron and Hur held up Moses' hands and Israel prevailed. A year later, after the report of the spies, Israel ignored Moses' command and sought to enter S Palestine. The Amalekites defeated them at Hormah (Nu. 14:43, 45).

From the days of the Judges two encounters are recorded. The Amalekites assisted Eglon, king of Moab, to attack Israelite territory (Jdg. 3:13), and later combined forces with the Midianites and the children of the E to raid Israelite crops and flocks. Gideon drove them out (Jdg. 6:3–5, 33; 7:12; 10:12).

From the Exodus onwards, Amalekites were to be found in the Negeb, but for a time they gained a foothold in Ephraim (Jdg. 12:15). Balaam, the foreign prophet, looked away to their lands from his vantage-point in Moab, and described them as 'the first of the nations' (Nu. 24:20), which may mean in regard either to origin or to status.

Samuel commanded Saul to destroy the Amalekites in the area S of *Telaim. Booty was forbidden. Saul pursued them from Havilah to Shur but captured their king alive. Later, Samuel slew Agag and rebuked Saul (1 Sa. 15).

David fought the Amalekites in the area of

Ziklag which Achish, king of Gath, had given him (1 Sa. 27:6; 30:1–20). The Amalekites declined later, and in Hezekiah's day the sons of Simeon attacked 'the remnant of the Amalekites that had escaped', taking their stronghold in Mt Seir (1 Ch. 4:43).

BIBLIOGRAPHY. F. M. Abel, *Géographie de la Palestine*, 2, 1933, pp. 270–273; D. Baly, *The Geography of the Bible*², 1974. J.A.T.

AMARNA. (Tell) el-Amarna is the modern name of Akhetaten, capital of Egypt under Amenophis IV (Akhenaten) and his immediate successors, *c.* 1375–1360 BC. The ruins lie some 320 km S of Cairo on the E bank of the river Nile. The site extends about 8 × 1 km and has been partially excavated. The impressive remains include temples, administrative buildings, tombs with wall paintings as well as the buildings of many prosperous estates with houses often of uniform plan.

The importance of Amarna for biblical studies lies in the series of letters written in cuneiform on clay tablets found by chance in 1887. With subsequent discoveries, the number of documents recovered now totals about 380. The majority are letters from various Asiatic rulers to the pharaohs Amenophis III and IV in the period *c.* 1385–1360 BC; nearly half come from Palestine and Syria. They supply important information concerning the history of the area, providing a vivid picture of the intrigues and inter-city strife which followed the weakening of Egyptian control shortly before the Israelites entered the land.

In S Syria, Abdi-ashirta and his son Aziru, though protesting their loyalty to their Egyptian overlords, were in reality increasing their own domains with the connivance of the Hittites of N Syria, and thus preparing the way for the eventual conquest of all Syria by the Hittite Suppiluliumas. Rib-ḫaddi of Byblos, a loyalist who wrote 53 letters to the Egyptian court, describes the uncertainty and chaos which followed his unanswered pleas for military assistance. He reports the capture by Aziru of an adjacent town, where the Egyptian resident had been slain, and the attack on Byblos from which he was forced to flee. Similarly Lab'ayu of Shechem, despite his protests of innocence (EA 254), was increasing his hold in the central hills in league with the semi-nomadic 'Apiru, who are frequently named in the texts, mainly as small armed bands (*HEBREWS). The activities of these 'Apiru are reported by many cities. When Lab'ayu threatened Megiddo, its ruler, Biridiya, begged Egypt for help.

Abdi-ḫeba of Jerusalem makes frequent reports, complaining that Milkilu of Gezer and others are engaged in raids. He cannot, therefore, understand why the pharaoh should allow Gezer, Lachish and Ashkelon to escape from the duty of providing the Egyptian garrison with food when they have plenty. He himself has been robbed by Egyptian troops and warns the pharaoh that his tribute and slaves being sent to Egypt will probably not arrive, as Lab'ayu and Milkilu have planned an ambush (EA 287). The latter might be a ruse to avoid sending any gifts, for in another letter Shuwardata of Hebron warns the pharaoh that Abdi-ḫeba of Jerusalem is a rogue.

Our knowledge of the political geography of Palestine at this time is helped by references to various local rulers, such as Ammunira of Beirut, Abimilki of Tyre, Akizzi of Qatna and Abdi-tirši of Hazor. Some of these names can be correlated with contemporary texts from *Ugarit (Ras Shamra). In addition to the local historical evidence, these letters are important for the wider implications of alliances between Egypt and the rulers of Mitanni and Babylon, often concluded, or supported, by marriages between the ruling families.

References to an Egyptian official named Yanḫamu, who attained high office, remind one of the position of Joseph, though the two cannot be identified. Yanḫamu's name is a Semitic form, and one of his functions was the supervision of the grain supply during a time of scarcity for the pharaoh's Syrian subjects.

The tablets are also of great linguistic importance. All but two are written in Akkadian, the *lingua franca* of the whole ancient Near East in this period. The presence at Amarna of Mesopotamian literature (myths of Nergal and Adapa, a story of Sargon of Akkad) and lexical texts including a list of Egyptian and Akkadian words indicates the influence of Akkadian, and this is supported by the discovery in 1946 of a fragment of the Gilgamesh Epic (*c.* 1400 BC) at Megiddo. The letters from Palestine and Syria are written mainly in local W Semitic dialects of Akkadian, and they provide valuable information about the Canaanite language in its various local forms before the arrival of the Israelites. Letters from King Tushratta of Mitanni have also added considerably to our knowledge of the non-Semitic Hurrian language (*HORITES).

Since some have argued that the 'Apiru of these texts are to be identified with the Hebrews under Joshua, instead of being evidence of the state of the land prior to the Conquest, the following aspects of the Amarna evidence should perhaps be stressed. The *ḫablpiru* (SA.GAZ) (= 'Apiru) here, as indicated also by the Ras Shamra and *Alalaḫ texts, were occupying the areas not strictly controlled by the larger towns; they operated usually in small numbers throughout Palestine and Syria, and do not appear as besiegers of cities. Moreover, these texts show a situation different from that under Joshua: Lachish and Gezer, far from being destroyed (Jos. 10), are in active support of the 'Apiru. The names of the rulers also differ, the king of Jerusalem at this time being Abdi-ḫeba, and whereas the 'Apiru were very active in the Jerusalem area, the city did not become Israelite until the time of David. Finally, the 'Apiru made use of chariots, but the Israelites knew nothing of this method of warfare until David's reign.

BIBLIOGRAPHY. W. F. Albright, *ANET*, pp. 483–490; *idem*, 'The Amarna Letters from Palestine', *CAH* 2/2, 1975, pp. 98–116; F. F. Bruce, *AOTS*, pp. 1–20; B. J. Kemp, *Lexikon der Agyptologie*, 6, pp. 309–319; W. L. Moran, *The Amarna Letters*, 1992. M.J.S.

AMASA. 1. Son of Jether (or Ithra) an Ishmaelite, and of David's sister Abigail, Amasa commanded Absalom's rebel army (2 Sa. 17:25), was defeated by Joab (2 Sa. 18:6–8), pardoned by David, and replaced Joab as commander of the army (2 Sa. 19:13). Taken off his guard, he was slain by the double-dealing Joab at 'the great stone of Gibeon' (2 Sa. 20:9–12). Amasa may possibly be the

Amasai of 1 Ch. 12:18, but the evidence is inconclusive.

2. An Ephraimite who, among others, obeyed the prophet Oded and opposed the entry into Samaria of the Jewish prisoners taken by Pekah, king of Israel, in his campaign against Ahaz (2 Ch. 28:9–15). J.D.D.

AMAZIAH (Heb. *'ᵃmaṣyâ* or *'ᵃmaṣyāhû*, 'Yahweh is mighty'). **1.** Son and successor of Joash, king of Judah (2 Ki. 14:1–20; 2 Ch. 25). He inflicted a severe defeat on Edom, which had previously regained its independence from Judah (2 Ki. 8:20–22), though apparently without subduing it completely (*cf.* 2 Ki. 14:22). Elated with his success, and perhaps also angered by the raiding of some dismissed Israelite mercenaries, he challenged Jehoash of Israel to a battle which proved his undoing. His overwhelming defeat led to the dismantling of part of Jerusalem's defences and the plundering of the Temple and palace. He himself was captured (2 Ki. 14:13). It has been suggested that at this time his son Azariah began to rule as co-regent, a suggestion which certainly eases some of the difficulties of the *chronology of his reign. He was eventually assassinated for reasons which are not disclosed.

2. The priest of Jeroboam II who sought to silence the prophet Amos at Bethel (Am. 7:10–17).

3. A Simeonite (1 Ch. 4:34).

4. A Levite of the family of Merari (1 Ch. 6:45). H.G.M.W.

AMBASSADOR (Heb. *mal'āk*, 'messenger'; *lûṣ*, 'interpreter'; *ṣîr*, 'to go'). A term used to describe envoys sent to other nations on special occasions, *e.g.* to congratulate (1 Ki. 5:1; 2 Sa. 8:10), solicit favours (Nu. 20:14), make alliances (Jos. 9:4), or protest against wrongs (Jdg. 11:12). Usually men of high rank, ambassadors became more common after Israel had developed relations with Syria, Babylon, *etc.* They did not represent the person of their sovereign, nor, as a general rule, were they empowered to negotiate (but see 2 Ki. 18:17–19:8). They were nevertheless treated with respect, and the only biblical infringement of this brought severe retribution (2 Sa. 10:2–5). The word (Gk. *presbeuō*, 'to be a senior') occurs metaphorically in the NT (2 Cor. 5:20; Eph. 6:20), applied to the representative of Christ in carrying his message of reconciliation. The collective term 'ambassage' is found in Lk. 14:32 (AV; RSV 'embassy'). J.D.D.

AMBER. Heb. *ḥašmal*, occurring only in Ezk. 1:4, 27; 8:2 (AV). The context requires *ḥašmal* to be something shining, but the exact denotation of the word has puzzled scholars from the rabbinic to present times. LXX renders *ēlektron*, meaning 'amber' or 'an alloy of gold and silver' (*LSJ*). Delitzsch suggests the Assyrian *ešmaru* as a cognate, which is phonologically possible, and which denotes a shining metallic alloy. G. R. Driver suggests 'brass', comparing Akkadian *elmešu*. See *VT* 1, 1951, pp. 60–62; *VT Supp.* 16, pp. 190–198. R.J.W.

AMEN. Heb. *'āmēn*, 'surely', from a root meaning 'to be firm, steady, trustworthy'; *cf.* *'ᵉmûnâ*, 'faithfulness', *'ᵉmeṯ*, 'truth'. It is used in the OT as a liturgical formula in which a congregation or individual accepts both the validity of an oath or curse and its consequences (Nu. 5:22; Dt. 27:15ff.; Ne. 5:13; Je. 11:5). It was also the response to a benediction (1 Ch. 16:36; Ne. 8:6), and is found incorporated in the doxologies which conclude the first four books of Psalms (Ps. 41:13; 72:19; 89:52; 106:48). Other uses are Jeremiah's ironic response to Hananiah's prophecy of a brief exile (Je. 28:6) and Benaiah's willing acceptance of David's command to make Solomon king (1 Ki. 1:36); in both cases it introduces a prayer for God's blessing on the proposal. Its connection with both blessings and cursings is sufficient explanation for the description of God as 'the God of truth (lit. amen)' in Is. 65:16. Outside the OT, the word is used in a 7th-century BC document to introduce a sworn declaration of innocence: 'Amen, I am free of guilt . . .'

By NT times the word is regularly used at the close of prayers and doxologies and is a natural response to be expected in public worship (1 Cor. 14:16). Christ's use of it in the introductory 'Amen, I say to you' was probably peculiar to himself, there being no evidence that the apostles followed his example, and gave his words their distinctive Messianic authority. Hence the association of the term with the promises of God, uniquely fulfilled in him (2 Cor. 1:20), and the attribution to him of the title 'the Amen' (Rev. 3:14).

BIBLIOGRAPHY. H. Bietenhard, *NIDNTT* 1, pp. 97–99; S. Talmon, *Textus* 7, 1969, pp. 124–129. J.B.Tr.

AMMON, AMMONITES. Ammon (Heb. *'ammôn*) was the name of the descendants of Ben-ammi, Lot's younger son by his daughter, born in a cave near Zoar (Gn. 19:38). They were regarded as relatives of the Israelites, who were commanded to treat them kindly (Dt. 2:19).

At an early date the Ammonites occupied the territory of the Zamzummim between the Arnon and Jabbok rivers (Dt. 2:20–21, 37; 3:11). Later, part of this territory was taken from them by the Amorites, and they were confined to an area to the E of the Jabbok (Nu. 21:24; Dt. 2:37; Jos. 12:2; 13:10, 25; Jdg. 11:13, 22). Archaeology shows that the Ammonites, like others, surrounded their territories by small fortresses (Nu. 21:24).

At the time of the Exodus, Israel did not conquer Ammon (Dt. 2:19, 37; Jdg. 11:15). However, the Ammonites were condemned for joining the Moabites in hiring Balaam, and were forbidden to enter the congregation of Israel to the 10th generation (Dt. 23:3–6).

Their chief town was Rabbath Ammon, mod. Amman (*RABBAH), where the ironstone sarcophagus ('bedstead of iron') of Og, the king of Bashan, rested (Dt. 3:11).

In the days of the Judges, the Ammonites assisted Eglon of Moab to subdue Israelite territory (Jdg. 3:13). Again, at the time of Jephthah they encroached on Israelite lands E of Jordan (Jdg. 11) and were driven out. Their religion influenced some of the Israelites (Jdg. 10:6), and this caused the Ammonite oppression in Gilead which led to Jephthah's campaign (Jdg. 10). Later Nahash, king of the Ammonites, besieged Jabesh-gilead just before Saul became king. Saul rallied Israel and drove off Nahash (1 Sa. 11:1–11; 12:12; 14:47). A few years later Nahash was a friend of David (2 Sa. 10:1–2), but his son Hanun rejected a kindly visit of David's ambassadors and insulted them. He hired Syrian mercenaries and went to war, but David's generals Joab and Abishai defeated them (2 Sa. 10; 1 Ch. 19). A year later the Israelites captured Rabbah, the Ammonite capital (2 Sa. 12:26–31; 1 Ch. 20:1–3) and put the people to work. Some Ammonites befriended David, however, *e.g.* Shobi son of Nahash, who cared for him when he fled from Absalom (2 Sa. 17:27, 29) and Zelek, who was one of his 30 mighty men (2 Sa. 23:37; 1 Ch. 11:39).

Solomon included Ammonite women in his harem, and worshipped *Milcom (*MOLECH) their god (1 Ki. 11:1, 5, 7, 33). An Ammonitess, Naamah, was the mother of Rehoboam (1 Ki. 14:21, 31; 2 Ch. 12:13).

In the days of Jehoshaphat, the Ammonites joined Moabites and Edomites in a raid on Judah (2 Ch. 20:1–30). About 800 BC, Zabad and Jehozabad, both sons of an Ammonitess, conspired to slay Joash king of Judah (2 Ch. 24:26). Later in the century, both Uzziah and Jotham of Judah received tribute from the Ammonites (2 Ch. 26:8; 27:5). Josiah defiled the high place that Solomon erected (2 Ki. 23:13). Ammonites joined others in troubling Jehoiakim (2 Ki. 24:2), and after the fall of Jerusalem in 586 BC, Baalis their king provoked further trouble (2 Ki. 25:25; Je. 40:11–14). They were bitterly attacked by the prophets as inveterate enemies of Israel (Je. 49:1-6; Ezk. 21:20; 25:1–7; Am. 1:13–15; Zp. 2:8–11).

After the return from exile Tobiah, the governor of Ammon, hindered the building of the walls by Nehemiah (Ne. 2:10, 19; 4:3, 7). Intermarriage between the Jews and the Ammonites was censured by both Ezra and Nehemiah (Ezr. 9:1–2; Ne. 13:1, 23–31). The Ammonites survived into the 2nd century BC at least, since Judas Maccabaeus fought against them (1 Macc. 5:6).

Sedentary occupation of the area was resumed about the beginning of the 13th century BC after an almost complete break of some centuries. A few Middle Bronze tombs from the 17th to 16th century BC, a shrine near Amman and occupation levels in the city of the Late Bronze Age suggest some limited occupation, prior to the 13th century. There was a vigorous resurgence of urban life at the start of the Iron Age which is evidenced by a string of small circular tower fortresses built of large stones. Other structures from the period were square or rectangular. Several settlements have been investigated, each consisting of several flint-block houses together with one or more towers, *e.g.* Khirbet Morbat Bedran. Clearly Ammonite occupation was vigorous during the Iron II period (840–580 BC). During the 7th century BC Ammon flourished under Assyrian control, as numerous references in Assyrian documents show. Ammon paid considerable tribute to Assyria. Tombs found in the region of Amman give evidence of a high material culture, to judge from the pottery, anthropoid coffins, seals, statues, figures, *etc.* A growing volume of written material including seals (7th century BC), an inscribed copper bottle from Siran (*c.* 600 BC) and an eight-line fragmentary inscription from the Amman citadel (9th century BC) display a language similar to Heb., but a script influenced by Aram. The copper bottle contained seeds of emmer wheat, bread wheat and hulled six-row barley, three domesticated grasses in use by the Ammonites of the 6th century BC. At least eleven Ammonite kings can now be listed from various sources.

Archaeological work suggests that sedentary occupation was interrupted by the Babylonian campaigns of the 6th century BC and did not resume until the 3rd century. Bedouin groups occupied the area until the Tobiads (4th–2nd century BC), the Nabataeans (1st century BC) and the Romans (1st century BC–3rd century AD).

BIBLIOGRAPHY. P. Bordreuil, *Syria* 50, 1973, pp. 181–195 (seals); G. Garbini, *Ann. de l'Inst. Or. Napoli* 20, 1970, pp. 249–257; *idem, JSS* 19, 1974, pp. 159–168; N. Glueck, *The Other Side of Jordan*, 1940; *idem*, *AASOR* 18, 19, 25–28; P. C. Hammond, *BASOR* 160, 1960, pp. 38–41; S. H. Horn, *BASOR* 193, 1967, pp. 2–13; G. M. Landes, *BA* 24.3, 1961, pp. 66–86; H. O. Thompson, *AJBA* 2.2, 1973, pp. 23–38; *idem* and F. Zayadine, *BASOR* 212, 1973, pp. 5–11; *POTT*, pp. 229–258 and index.

J.A.T.

AMON. The son of Manasseh, Amon reigned for 2 years over Judah (2 Ki. 21:19–26; 2 Ch. 33:21–25). Before his reign was cut short by assassination, he gave the clearest evidence of his complete acceptance of the gross idolatry of his father's earlier years. It is not certainly known what motive inspired his assassins, but the fact that they were in turn put to death by 'the people of the land' suggests that Amon was the victim of court intrigue rather than of a popular revolution. J.C.J.W.

AMON (Egyp. *Amūn*, 'the hidden'). An Egyptian god whose essential nature is as unclear as his name indicates. Often associated with the wind, and in certain forms embodying the power of generation, he was first prominent as a local god of *Thebes, whence came the powerful 12th Dynasty pharaohs (1991–1786 BC). Through union with the cosmic and royal sun-god Rēʿ as Amen-Rēʿ, Amūn became chief god. Later, when the 18th Dynasty Theban pharaohs established the Egyptian Empire (1552 BC ff.), Amūn became state god, 'king of the gods', gathering up many of their powers and attributes, while his priesthood accumulated vast wealth and lands. Hence, the fall of Thebes (No) and the wealth of its priesthoods to the Assyrians in 663 BC was fittingly selected by Nahum (3:8) in prophesying the crash of equally mighty Nineveh. After this, Amūn and Thebes, still his holy city, regained some measure of prosperity, but even this was doomed by prophecy of Jeremiah (46:25). (*EGYPT.) K.A.K.

AMORITES. A people of Canaan (Gn. 10:16) often listed with the Hittites, Perizzites, *etc.*, as opponents of Israel (Ex. 33:2). They were scattered throughout the hill country on either side of the Jordan (Nu. 13:29). Abraham had an alliance with the Amorites of Hebron and, with their aid, routed the four kings who had attacked the Dead Sea plain, including the Amorite town of Hazazon-tamar (Gn. 14:5–7). The name was also used as a general term for the inhabitants of Canaan (Gn. 48:22; Jos. 24:15). Ezekiel well indicates the mixed population of Palestine (caused largely by continuous infiltrations from the eastern steppes), describing Jerusalem as the offspring of Amorite and Hittite (Ezk. 16:3, 45).

During the latter half of the 3rd millennium BC, Sumerian and Akkadian inscriptions refer to the Amorites (Sum. *mar-tu*, Akkad. *amurru*) as a desert people unacquainted with civilized life, grain, houses, cities, government. Their headquarters were in the mountain of Basar, probably Jebel Bishri N of Palmyra. About 2000 BC these people, who had been infiltrating for centuries, moved into Babylonia in force. They were partly responsible for the collapse of the powerful 3rd Dynasty of Ur and took over the rule of several towns (*e.g.* Larsa). An 'Amorite' dynasty was established at *Babylon, and its most powerful king, Hammurapi, conquered the two other important 'Amorite' states of Assur and Mari (*c.* 1750 BC). Amorites are traceable by linguistic, mainly onomastic, evidence. Such is not always reliable or conclusive, but these dynasties were clearly of western origin, Hammurapi's being termed Amorite in a contemporary text. The 20,000 texts found at *Mari are mostly written in Akkadian with many W Semitic features. Personal name forms common in these texts show that the names of the Patriarchs followed well-known styles. The Mari texts give information about nomadic tribes in Syria, notably the *Mare-Yamina* (or possibly *Bene-Yamina*) connected with the area of Mt Basar. Another group had settled in the Lebanon and engaged in the trading of horses. This kingdom survived into the period of the Amarna letters and the 19th Dynasty of Egypt when tribute is recorded from the state of Amor. The capital of this seems to have been the port of Ṣumur (modern Tell Kazel) S of Arvad. This is the country mentioned in Jos. 13:4.

The general unrest of the years *c.* 2100–1800 BC both in Mesopotamia and in Palestine was closely connected with increased Amorite movement. The break in occupation of several Palestinian cities between the Early and Middle Bronze Age was caused by an influx of nomadic folk who left many graves behind them, but little trace of buildings. The pottery of these people has clear affinities with pottery from Syria, which may indicate that they were related 'Amorites' (see K. M. Kenyon, *Amorites and Canaanites*, 1966; W. G. Dever, *HTR* 64, 1971, pp. 197–226). The journeys of Abraham may be associated with the latter part of this period.

At the time of the Israelite invasion of Palestine, Amorite kings (Sihon of Heshbon and Og of Bashan) ruled most of Transjordan (Jos. 12:1–6; Jdg. 1:36). The conquest of these two kings was the first stage of the possession of the Promised Land and was looked upon as a most important event in Israelite history (Am. 2:9; Pss. 135:11; 136:19). Gad, Reuben and half of Manasseh occupied this territory (Nu. 32:33), and it later formed one of the twelve regions supporting Solomon's court (1 Ki. 4:19). The men of Ai are called Amorites (Jos. 7:7) and Jerusalem, Hebron, Jarmuth, Lachish and Eglon were Amorite principalities which Israel overcame (Jos. 10:1–27). Northern Amorites aided the king of *Hazor (Jos. 11:1–14). After the land was settled, the Amorites became menials and were gradually absorbed (1 Ki. 9:20). Their evil memory remained, providing comparison for the idolatry of Ahab and Manasseh (1 Ki. 21:26; 2 Ki. 21:11; *cf.* Gn. 15:16).

Invasions of other peoples, the Kassites, Hurrians and Indo-Europeans in Mesopotamia, the Israelites in Palestine and the Aramaeans in Syria weakened the Amorites as a power by 1000 BC. The name survived in Akkadian as a designation for Syria–Palestine until superseded by *Ḫatti* (Hittite), and was also a word for 'West'.

BIBLIOGRAPHY. S. Moscati, *The Semites in Ancient History*, 1959; J. R. Kupper, *Les Nomades en Mésopotamie au temps des Rois de Mari*, 1957; review by A. Goetze, *JSS* 4, 1959, pp. 142–147; I. J. Gelb, *JCS* 15, 1961, pp. 24–47; M. Liverani in *POTT*, pp. 100–133. A.R.M.

AMOS, BOOK OF.

I. Outline of contents

On the whole the Hebrew text of Amos' prophecies has been well preserved. In addition, the progressive orderliness of his writings makes it possible to divide the book up into sections which are not artificial. It falls into four parts.

a. 1:1–2:16. After a simple introduction (1:1f.) in which Amos tells who he is, when he prophesied and wherein resided his authority to preach, he announces judgment upon the surrounding peoples (1:3–2:3), upon his native Judah and upon Samaria (2:4–16). Judgment falls on Gentile nations for offences against humanity, violations of those conscience-taught standards which make people human; Judah and Israel are judged for turning away from divine revelation (2:4, 11-12) with consequent moral and social collapse.

b. 3:1–6:14. The series of addresses in this section are each introduced by a clearly defined formula (3:1; 4:1; 5:1; 6:1). Here the emphasis is upon Samaria's privileges, but the nation's sinfulness has turned privilege into a ground upon which Amos bases his doctrine of judgment. Privilege involves God's people in penalty, hence Amos' insistence that status does not save (3:1–2) and that the 'day of Yahweh' will bring darkness and not the light complacently expected (5:16–20).

c. 7:1–9:10. A series of five visions of judgment, in each of which the judgment is set forth under a symbol: locusts (7:1–3), fire (7:4–6), a plumbline (7:7–9), summer fruit (8:1–14) and a smitten sanctuary (9:1–10). In 7:10–17 Amos displays his credentials for thus addressing the people of God.

d. 9:11–15. An epilogue which describes the restoration of the Davidic kingdom.

II. Authorship and date

Nothing is known of the prophet Amos outside of his writings. He was a native of Tekoa (1:1; *cf.* 2 Sa. 14:2; 2 Ch. 11:6), situated about 16 km S of Jerusalem. The surrounding countryside yielded pasture for the flocks, to tend which was part of Amos' calling (1:1). In addition, he was a fig farmer (*TREES, Sycomore; 7:14). The significance of this information is that Amos had no background in prophetic activity: he had not previously considered himself a prophet, nor was he trained in the prophetic schools (7:14f.). We know from 1:1 that he lived during the reigns of Uzziah, king of Judah (779–740 BC) and Jeroboam II, king of Samaria (783–743 BC). Uzziah and Jeroboam II reigned concurrently for 36 years (779–743). We do not know the date of the earthquake (1:1) and can place the ministry of Amos only by general indications. The level of prosperity and security which seems to have been enjoyed by Israel would indicate a date possibly about the middle of the reign of Jeroboam, *c.* 760 BC.

III. Circumstances

A Hebrew prophet's ministry and message were intimately bound up with the conditions in which the people to whom he preached lived, and in this Amos' book is no exception.

a. Political and social conditions. Over 40 years before Amos' ministry Assyria had crushed Syria, Samaria's N neighbour. This permitted Jeroboam II to extend his frontiers (2 Ki. 14:25), and to build up a lucrative trade which created a powerful merchant class in Samaria. Unfortunately the wealth that came to Samaria was not evenly distributed among the people. It remained in the hands of the merchant princes, who spent the new-found riches on improving their own living standards (3:10, 12, 15; 6:4), and neglected completely the peasant class which had hitherto been the backbone of Samaria's economy. The unmistakable symptoms of a morally sick society began to declare themselves in Samaria. In Amos' day oppression of the poor by the rich was common (2:6f.), and heartless indifference among the wealthy towards the affliction of the hungry (6:3–6). Justice went to the highest bidder (2:6; 8:6). In drought (4:7–9) the poor had recourse only to the moneylender (5:11f.; 8:4–6), to whom he was often compelled to mortgage his land and his person.

b. The state of religion. Naturally the social conditions in Samaria affected religious habits. Religion was being not neglected but perverted. At the national religious shrines (5:5) ritual was being maintained (4:4f.), but it went hand in hand with godlessness and immorality. Far from pleasing Yahweh it invited his judgment (3:14; 7:9; 9:1–4); it did not remove but increased transgression (4:4). God was not to be found at the national shrines (5:4f.) because he could not accept the worship there (5:21–23); the true preoccupations of the people were with other gods (8:14). In addition, this rich ceremonial and the costly sacrifices were being offered at the expense of the poor (2:8; 5:11).

IV. Amos and the sacrificial system

Amos was well aware of the traditions of his own nation, historical (2:9ff.; 3:1, 13; 4:11; 5:6, 25; 7:16), religious (4:4ff.; 5:22; 8:5) and legal (2:8, *cf.* Ex. 22:26; Am. 8:5, *cf.* Lv. 19:35; Am. 2:4, *cf.* Dt. 17:19). This helps to give background to an understanding of his apparently hostile attitude to the religion he saw around him, and particularly to what is often thought of as his rejection of the whole system of sacrifices as lacking divine authorization (5:25). In company with other occasional verses in the pre-exilic prophets (*cf.* Is. 1:10–15; Je. 7:21f.; Ho. 6:6; Mi. 6:7f.) we have here, however, not a condemnation of the sacrificial code as such but of the way in which it was currently abused (*PROPHECY). On any reading of the Pentateuch, the people of Amos' day would have been instructed in the patriarchal and Mosaic traditions that sacrifice had ever been part of the religion of God's people and that he had accepted this with approval. Bearing in mind, then, that in 5:25 Amos does not make an assertion but asks a rhetorical question, only one answer is possible: an immediate affirmative. The balance of the Hebrew, however, suggests that Amos did not aim his question at the institution of sacrifice but at the prominence currently given to it: 'Was it sacrifices and offerings you brought me . . .?' The implication ('Was that the sum total of your religion then as it is now?') suits the context in Amos. Verses 22–23 and verse 24 are an either/or in appearance only (a frequent biblical mode of emphasizing a due priority in things, *e.g.* Pr. 8:10a, 10b; Lk. 14:26); they are an appeal for the restoration of a true balance wherein, as in the Mosaic norm, the sacrifices act as a divine provision for the lapses of a people committed to a life of ethical obedience to the law of God.

V. The prophet's message

a. Amos' concept of God is fundamental to an understanding of his message to Samaria. The Lord is the Creator of the world (4:13), but he is still actively present as its Sustainer. He it is who brings day and night to pass, and controls the waves of the sea (5:8; 9:6). He determines whether famine (4:6–11) or plenty (9:13) shall prevail. In the light of this knowledge of the God of creation there is no need to reject as later insertions 4:13; 5:8–9; 9:5–6. They are neither theologically premature, as used to be asserted, nor contextually misplaced: each in turn relates the foregoing declaration of judgment to a clear understanding of the divine nature and capability. The Lord also controls the destinies of the nations. He restrains this nation (1:5), raises up that (6:14) and puts down another (2:9). He also controls their distribution (9:7). He is therefore their Judge (1:3–2:3) when they offend against his moral laws.

b. Naturally Amos' message betrays a particular interest in Israel. In a quite special sense it was Yahweh's will to elect her to covenant relation with himself (3:2). Through his servants he has made known his will to her (2:11; 3:7). But these high privileges involve Israel in heavy responsibility; and failure to accept this brings upon his people a far more severe judgment than that which was to fall upon pagan nations. When Israel broke Yahweh's laws (2:4) there could be only a fearful looking forward to judgment (4:12).

c. Amos was also concerned to proclaim that a law broken through unrighteousness could not be mended by means of ritual, festival or offering alone. Indeed, Yahweh was already standing at the altar waiting to smite it (9:1–4). The most elaborate ritual was an abomination to him so long as it was offered by a people who had no intention of measuring up to the ethical standards laid down in his holy laws. Such a religion of ceremonial and ritual was divorced from morality, and this Yahweh could only hate (5:21f.).

d. The foregoing means that Amos' main concern was to demand righteousness in the name of the Lord from the people of the Lord (5:24). Righteousness was for Amos the most important moral attribute of the divine nature. Every outrage of the moral law, whether perpetrated by pagan nations (1:3–2:3) or by Israel (2:4–16), was an outrage upon the nature of God and was, therefore, a provocation of divine justice. If Yahweh is righteous, then injustice, dishonesty, immorality, cannot be tolerated by him, and must receive stern retribution from him.

e. But judgment was not Amos' final word to Samaria (5:4). Indeed, he closes with a promise of a brighter day for her (9:11–15). The prevailing fashion for refusing these verses to Amos ought to be resisted. It is not out of place for a Judahite to assert the Davidic hope nor inappropriate for Amos (notwithstanding his stress on judgment) to crown the negative ruling out of final loss (7:1–6) with a matching positive statement of final glory.

BIBLIOGRAPHY. W. R. Harper, *A Critical and Exegetical Commentary on Amos and Hosea*, 1910; S. R. Driver, *Joel and Amos*, 1915; R. M. Gwynn, *The Book of Amos*, 1927; R. S. Cripps, *A Critical and Exegetical Commentary on the Book of Amos*, 1929; E. A. Edghill, *The Book of Amos*, 1914; J. Marsh, *Amos and Micah*, 1959; J. L. Mays, *Amos*, 1969; J. A. Motyer, *NBCR*, 'Amos', 1970; *idem*, *BST, The Message of Amos*, 1974; H. W. Wolff, *Amos the Prophet*, 1973; R. Gordis, 'The Composition and Structure of Amos', *HTR* 33, 1940, pp. 239–251; H. H. Rowley, 'Was Amos a Nabi?' Eissfeldt *Festschrift*, 1947; J. D. Watts, *Vision and Prophecy in Amos*, 1958; E. Hammershaimb, *The Book of Amos*, 1970. J.G.S.S.T.

J.A.M.

AMPHIPOLIS. An important strategic and commercial centre at the N of the Aegean, situated on the river Strymon (Struma) about 5 km inland from the seaport Eion. Prized by the Athenians and Macedonians as the key both to the gold, silver and timber of Mt Pangaeus and also to the control of the Dardanelles, it became under the Romans a free town and the capital of the first district of Macedonia. Amphipolis is about 50 km WSW of Philippi on the Via Egnatia, a great Roman highway, and Paul passed through it on his way to Thessalonica (Acts 17:1). K.L.McK.

AMPLIATUS. Paul's friend, affectionately greeted (Rom. 16:8). The best MSS show 'Ampliatus', a Latin slave name: 'Amplias' (AV) is a Gk. pet-form. Lightfoot (*Philippians*, p. 174) finds the name in inscriptions of 'Caesar's household' (*cf.* Phil. 4:22); but it was common. Those addressing Rom. 16 to Ephesus can find one there (*CIL*, 3, 436). A tomb-inscription 'Ampliati', perhaps late 1st century, in the catacomb of Domitilla, is ornate for a slave, perhaps reflecting his honour in the church (*cf.* Sanday and Headlam, *Romans*, p. 424). A connection with Paul's Ampliatus or his family is not impossible (*cf.* R. Lanciani, *Pagan and Christian Rome*, 1895, pp. 342ff.). Ampliatus, Stachys and Urbanus (*cf.* v. 9) were commemorated together as martyrs (*Acta Sanctorum*, Oct. 13, p. 687). A.F.W.

AMRAM (Heb. *'amrām*, 'people exalted'). **1.** The husband of Jochebed, and father of Moses, Aaron and Miriam (Ex. 6:20; Nu. 26:59; 1 Ch. 6:3; 23:13). He was a 'son' (*i.e.* probably descendant, *cf.* 1 Ch. 7:20–27) of Kohath (Ex. 6:18; Nu. 3:19), and so of Levi. **2.** An Amram is mentioned in Ezr. 10:34 as having taken a foreign wife. E.J.Y.

AMRAPHEL. A king of *Shinar who attacked Sodom and its neighbours with the aid of *Chedorlaomer and other kings, but was repulsed by Abram (Gn. 14:1ff.). His identity is uncertain. The equation with *Hammurapi is unlikely. D.W.B.

AMULETS. The practice of wearing on the person a small symbolic object as a charm or protection against evil was common throughout the ancient Near East. Such amulets were usually in the form of small ornaments, gems, stones, seals, beads, plaques or emblems, sometimes inscribed with an incantation or prayer. The Hebrews were unique in condemning their use and Is. 3:18–23 gives a list of such trinkets worn by women. These include 'soul boxes' and 'amulets' (*lᵉḥāšîm*—a word meaning 'whisper', either an incantation or perhaps snake-charming) (Is. 3:20, AV 'earrings'; *cf.* Ps. 58:5; Ec. 10:11; Je. 8:17). The presence of amulets may also be inferred in 'stones conferring favour' (Pr. 17:8; AVmg. 'stones of grace') for most stones were thought to have magical properties. Thus all stones and rings used as *seals were considered as amulets (*cf.* Je. 22:24; Hg. 2:23), as were most personal ornaments like those used to make the golden calf (Ex. 32:2) or buried by Jacob (Gn. 35:4). In common with the condemnation of those who employed charms (as Is. 3:3, RSV), the bronze serpent made by Moses was destroyed as soon as it became an object of superstitious reverence in itself (2 Ki. 18:4).

Archaeological evidence reveals the common use of ornaments in the shape of the sun disk or inverted moon crescent, a symbol of the goddess Ishtar-Astarte, worn by women or animals to increase their fertility (Jdg. 8:21). Egyptian-style figurines, and animal and fruit symbols (*ankh* for life, sacred eye) also generally relate to fertility and protection. The frontlets between the eyes (*ṭôṭāpôṯ*, Ex. 13:16; Dt. 6:8; 11:18) and fringes (*ṣîṣiṯ*, Nu. 15:38–39; Mt. 23:5) on garments were designed to act as a reminder of the law and as a deterrent to superstition and idolatry, which it condemned (Ex. 13:9; Dt. 6:8ff.; Pr. 3:3). These crimson cords have been compared with the Hittite use of blue and red cords as amuletic fringes, and some have thought that the bells on the fringe of the high priest's garment had a similar function (Ex. 28:33) as they had on horses in Assyria (*cf.* Zc. 14:20). Judas Maccabeus found amulets on the bodies of his dead soldiers (2 Macc. 12:40), presumably used as *phylacteries (Gk. *phylaktērion*, 'safeguard'), much as the small box containing a tiny scroll with a biblical passage and fixed to the doorpost (*mᵉzûzâ*; Dt. 6:9) came to be regarded by later Jews. D.J.W.

ANAH. 1. RSV, following Samaritan LXX, and Syr. Pesh., reads 'son' (AV, with Heb., 'daughter') of Zibeon, the Hivite, and father of Oholibamah, one of Esau's Canaanite wives (Gn. 36:2, also vv. 14, 18, 24–25; 1 Ch. 1:40). If in Gn. 36 Hivite and Horite (Hurrian) may be equated, Anah found the hot springs in the wilderness as he pastured his father's asses (v. 24). Further, if Oholibamah of Gn. 36:2 may be identified with Judith (Gn. 26:34), Beeri the Hittite of this verse will be another name for Anah, and commemorates the discovery of the hot springs, Heb. *bᵉ'ēr* meaning 'well'.

2. A Horite chief, brother of Zibeon and son of Seir (Gn. 36:20, 29; 1 Ch. 1:38). R.A.H.G.

ANAK, ANAKIM. The Anakim (Heb. *ᵃnāqîm*), descendants of an eponymous ancestor Anak, were among the pre-Israelite inhabitants of Palestine. The name Anak occurs without the article only in Nu. 13:33 and Dt. 9:2, but elsewhere it appears in the form 'the Anak' (*hā ᵃnāq*), where it is presumably to be taken as the collective, equivalent to Anakim. The phrase 'the city of Arba (*qiryaṯ 'arba'*, *KIRIATH-ARBA), father of Anak' in Jos. 15:13 apparently indicates that an individual named Arba was the ultimate ancestor of the Anakim, unless the noun 'father' is taken to qualify the city, in which case this city, later known as *Hebron, was considered the ancestral home of the Anakim.

The stature and formidable nature of the Anakim were almost proverbial, for they were taken as a standard for comparison to stress the size of such other peoples as the Emim (Dt. 2:10) and the Rephaim (Dt. 2:21), and there was a saying, 'Who can stand before the sons of Anak?' (Dt. 9:2). In the account of the Promised Land brought back by the ten faint-hearted spies, emphasis was laid on the fact that the Anakim were there (Dt. 1:28; the LXX here renders *ʿănāqîm* by *gigantes*, *GIANT). It was even stated that they were descended from the Nephilim, who were also claimed as sons of Anak, and the spies said that they felt like grasshoppers beside them (Nu. 13:33). They were settled in the hill-country, particularly at Hebron (Nu. 13:22), where Ahiman, Sheshai and Talmai, 'descendants of Anak', were found. Joshua cut off the Anakim from the hill-country (from Hebron, Debir and Anab), but some were left in Gaza, Gath and Ashdod (Jos. 11:21f.), and it fell to Caleb finally to drive them out from Hebron, which had been allotted to him. Nothing is known of these people outside the Bible, unless they are, as some scholars hold, among the peoples mentioned in the Egyp. 18th-century Execration Texts, or they represent an early 'Philistinian-type' title.

BIBLIOGRAPHY. *ANET*, p. 328; *VT* 15, 1965, pp. 468–474. T.C.M.

ANAMMELECH. A deity worshipped, with *Adrammelech, by Sepharvaim colonists placed in Samaria by the Assyrians (2 Ki. 17:31). If *Sepharvaim is interpreted as Babylonian Sippar the name is 'Anu is king'. However, as the name has initial ' the link with Anu is unlikely, because Akkadian divine names with initial vowels are written with ' in Aramaic transcriptions (as is Anu in 3rd century BC Uruk). More probable is identification with 'An, male counterpart of 'Anat, known in Ugaritic and Phoenician (F. Gröndahl, *Die Personennamen der Texte aus Ugarit*, 1967, pp. 83, 110). D.J.W.

ANANIAS, Gk. form of Hananiah ('Yahweh has dealt graciously'). **1.** In Acts 5:1ff. a member of the primitive church of Jerusalem whose contribution to the common fund was less than he pretended; he fell dead when his dishonesty was exposed. **2.** In Acts 9:10ff. a follower of Jesus in Damascus, 'a devout man according to the law', who befriended Saul of Tarsus immediately after his conversion and conveyed Christ's commission to him. **3.** In Acts 23:2; 24:1, Ananias the son of Nedebaeus, high priest AD 47–58, president of the Sanhedrin when Paul was brought before it, notorious for his greed; killed by Zealots in 66 for his pro-Roman sympathies. F.F.B.

ANATHEMA. 1. Gk. *anathēma* originally meant 'something set up (in a temple)', hence a votive offering, a form and sense preserved in Lk. 21:5 (AV 'gifts').

2. Gk. *anathema* (short *e*) is later; the forms are distinguished by lexicographers such as Hesychius, but are related in meaning and often confused in practice.

The LXX often uses *anathema* to represent Heb. *ḥērem*, *curse, 'the devoted thing', the thing to be put to the *ban, involving total destruction (*e.g.* Lv. 27:28f.; Nu. 21:3, of Hormah; Dt. 7:26, and *cf.* the striking Judith 16:19). Pagan imprecatory texts show that the word was used as a cursing formula outside Judaism (see Deissmann, *LAE*, pp. 95ff.; and *MM*).

So it was that Christians might hear, Hellenistic syncretism being what it was, the horrid blasphemy 'Anathema Jesus' from the lips of apparently 'inspired' preachers (1 Cor. 12:3): whether as an abjuration of allegiance (Pliny, *Ep.* 10. 96 and other sources show persecuted Christians were called on to 'curse Christ'), or by way of disparaging the earthly Jesus in contrast to the exalted Christ. Whatever the condition of the speaker, no message degrading Jesus came from the Holy Spirit. Again, Paul could wish himself for the sake of his unconverted brethren 'under the ban', involving separation from Christ (Rom. 9:3), and could call the ban, involving the abolition of Christian recognition, on preachers of 'any other gospel' (Gal. 1:8–9). In all these cases RV transliterates *anathema*, while AV and RSV render it 'accursed' or 'cursed'.

In one place, 1 Cor. 16:22, AV has transliterated *anathema* putting haters of Christ under the ban, attaching the following **maranatha* to it. This would perhaps give the general sense 'and may our Lord swiftly execute his judgments' (*cf.* C. F. D. Moule, *NTS* 6, 1960, pp. 307ff.). But *maranatha* may be a separate sentence (*cf.* RSV). In view of the contents of 1 Cor., these words amid the affectionate closing greetings are quite appropriate, without any special connection of the anathema with the dismissal before the Eucharist, which some find (*cf.* G. Bornkamm, *ThL* 75, 1950, pp. 227ff.; J. A. T. Robinson, *JTS* n.s. 4, 1953, pp. 38ff.).

The conspirators in Acts 23:14 put themselves under an *anathema* (RSV 'oath'; AV, RV 'curse'): *i.e.* they called the curse upon themselves if they failed (*cf.* the OT phrase 'May the Lord do so to me and more also if I do not . . .').

The ecclesiastical sense of excommunication is an extension, not an example, of biblical usage, though it is not impossible that synagogue practice (*cf. SB*, 4, pp. 293ff.) gave some early colouring to it.

The cognate verb appears in Mk. 14:71; Acts 23:12, 14, 21.

BIBLIOGRAPHY. H. Aust, D. Müller, *NIDNTT* 1, pp. 413–415; J. Behm, *TDNT* 1, pp. 354f. A.F.W.

ANATHOTH. A town in Benjamite territory assigned to Levites (Jos. 21:18). It was the home of Abiezer (2 Sa. 23:27), Abiathar (1 Ki. 2:26) and Jehu, David's warriors (1 Ch. 12:3). Sennacherib conquered it (Is. 10:30). Jeremiah had property there (Je. 1:1; 32:7–9). Excavations at Anāta, Deīr es-Sid, about 5 km NE of Jerusalem, uncovered buildings and pottery of the 7th and 6th centuries BC, whereas Ras el-Kharrūbeh, another site proposed for Anathoth, yielded very little from that date. The area was repopulated after the exile.

BIBLIOGRAPHY. A. Biran, *EI* 18, 1985, pp. 209–214. D.J.W. A.R.M.

ANCESTOR WORSHIP. Most primitive pagan peoples believe in the existence of spirits, good and evil, and many consider that among these are the spirits of the dead. The desire to provide for the comfort of the benevolent, and to placate the ill-will of the malevolent, among these, often leads to a 'cult of the dead', where such services as fitting burial and provision of food and drink are performed to achieve these ends. The overt worship of the dead in the sense of adoration or even deification is, however, comparatively rare; the best-known example is that of Confucian China. It is more appropriate therefore to speak of a 'cult of the dead' than of 'ancestor worship', since there is no question of the latter's being found in the Bible.

In the latter part of the 19th and early years of the 20th century the reports of travellers and missionaries of the beliefs of modern primitive peoples gave material for anthropologists to speculate on the 'development' of religion. In the light of the resultant theories the Bible was re-examined, and the supposed traces of early stages in the development of Israelite religion detected. Among these traces were indications of ancestor worship. Thus it was claimed that evidence of this was to be found in the translation of *Enoch to be with God (Gn. 5:24), an indication that he was deified, but this is entirely gratuitous. It was suggested likewise that the *teraphim were originally worshipped as ancestor images, but there is again no foundation for such a view.

With the rediscovery of the civilizations of the ancient Near East, which formed the *milieu* of the OT, the customs of modern primitive peoples were seen to be largely irrelevant, but many of the theories of the development of religion remained, though now the religion of the OT was viewed as something of an amalgam of the beliefs and practices of the surrounding peoples.

In the ancient Near East belief in the after-life led to widespread cult practices connected with the dead. The provisions by the Egyptians for the comfort of the deceased, in what was believed to be a basically enjoyable future existence, were elaborate. In Mesopotamia less is known of the funeral rites of individuals, but a gloomy view was taken of the life to come, and it was in consequence important to ensure, by the provision of necessities as well as by ritual and liturgy, that the dead did not return as dissatisfied spirits to molest the living. The case of kings was different, and there was a tendency, in form at least, to their deification. The names, for example, of such early rulers as Lugalbanda and Gilgamesh were written with the divine determinative, an honour also accorded particularly to the kings of the 3rd Dynasty of Ur, and prayers were on occasion offered to them. In Syria also a cult of the dead is well attested, as, for instance, in the discoveries at Ras Shamra, where tombs were found provided with pipes and gutters to make it possible for libations to be poured from the surface into the tomb vaults.

Few cemeteries or tombs of the Israelite period have been excavated in Palestine, but those which have show, perhaps, a decline in furniture from the Canaanite Bronze Age or, in other words, a decline in the cult of the dead. That the Israelites, however, were continually falling away from the right path and adopting the religious practices of their neighbours is clearly stated by the Bible. It is to be expected that among these practices should have been some associated with the cult of the dead. Thus, the declarations in Dt. 26:14 suggest that it was necessary to prohibit offerings to the dead; it appears that it was expected that incense would be burned for (*lᵉ*) Asa at his burial (2 Ch. 16:14), and at Zedekiah's funeral (Je. 34:5); and Ezk. 43:7-9 implies that there was worship of the dead bodies of kings. The practice of necromancy (*DIVINATION) is also attested (1 Sa. 28:7), though clearly condemned (Is. 8:19; 65:4).

Other biblical passages are sometimes cited as evidence that such practices were acquiesced in, or accepted as legitimate. Thus, in Gn. 35:8 it is described how the oak under which Rebekah's nurse was buried was called Allon-bacuth, 'Oak of weeping', and again in Gn. 35:20 Jacob set up a *maṣṣēḇâ* (*PILLAR) over Rachel's grave. These actions have been taken to indicate a belief in the sanctity of graves, and, as a consequence, cult practices associated with the dead. But weeping over the dead may just as well be genuine as ritual, and there is no evidence to suggest that the raising of a memorial pillar necessarily implies a cult practice. The custom of levirate marriage (Dt. 25:5–10; *MARRIAGE, IV) has been interpreted as partly aimed at providing someone to carry out the cult of the dead for the deceased. This interpretation, however, is again one which exceeds the simple testimony of the text. Despite various theories, the participation in family sacrifices (*e.g.* 1 Sa. 20:29) provides no evidence of a cult of the dead. It has been further suggested that some of the mourning customs (*BURIAL AND MOURNING) show signs of a cult of, or even worship of, the dead. But such of these practices as were legitimate (*cf.* Lv. 19:27–28; Dt. 14:1) may just as well be explained as manifestations of sorrow over the loss of a dear one.

It is thus clear that neither ancestor worship nor a cult of the dead played any part in the true religion of Israel.

BIBLIOGRAPHY. R. H. Lowie, *An Introduction to Cultural Anthropology*, 1940, pp. 308–309 (modern primitives); J. N. D. Anderson (ed.), *The World's Religions*[4], 1975, pp. 40 (modern primitives), 202–203 (Shinto), 223–224 (Confucian); A. H. Gardiner, *The Attitude of the Ancient Egyptians to Death and the Dead*, 1935; H. R. Hall in *ERE*, 1, pp. 440–443 (Egypt); A. Heidel, *The Gilgamesh Epic and Old Testament Parallels*[2], 1949, pp. 137–223; H. W. F. Saggs, 'Some Ancient Semitic Conceptions of the After-life', *Faith and Thought* 90, 1958, pp. 157–182; C. F. A. Schaeffer, *The Cuneiform Texts of Ras Shamra*, 1939, pp. 49–54; G. Margoliouth in *ERE*, 1, pp. 444–450; M. Burrows, *What Mean These Stones?*, 1941, pp. 238–242; R. de Vaux, *Ancient Israel*, E.T. 1961, p. 38.

T.C.M.

ANDREW. One of the twelve apostles. The name is Greek (meaning 'manly'), but it may have been a 'Christian name' like 'Peter'. He was the son of Jonas or John and came from Bethsaida in Galilee (Jn. 1:44), but afterwards went to live with his brother Simon Peter at Capernaum (Mk. 1:29), where they were in partnership as fishermen (Mt. 4:18). As a disciple of John the Baptist (Jn. 1:35–40) he was pointed by him to Jesus as the Lamb of God. He then found Simon and brought him to Jesus (Jn. 1:42). Later he was called to full-time discipleship (Mt. 4:18–20; Mk. 1:16–18) and became one of the twelve apostles (Mt. 10:2; Mk. 3:18; Lk. 6:14). His practical faith is shown in Jn. 6:8–9; 12:21–22. He was one of those who asked about the judgment coming on Jerusalem (Mk. 13:3–4). He is last mentioned as being with the other apostles after the ascension (Acts 1:13).

It is probable that he was crucified in Achaia. The Synoptic Gospels say little about him, but in John he is shown as the first home missionary (1:42) and the first foreign missionary (12:21–22). Of the former, William Temple wrote, 'Perhaps it is as great a service to the Church as ever any man did' (*Readings in St John's Gospel*, p. 29).

R.E.N.

ANDRONICUS AND JUNIAS, JUNIA. (AV 'Junia' is feminine—perhaps Andronicus' wife? RSV 'Junias' would be masculine, contracted from Junianus.) Affectionately greeted by Paul (Rom. 16:7) as (1) 'kinsmen', *i.e.* probably fellow-Jews, as in Rom. 9:3 (but see *MM*, *syngenēs*, for this word as a title of honour); Ramsay (*Cities of St Paul*, pp. 176ff.) infers membership of the same Tarsian civic tribe; (2) 'fellow-prisoners of war', probably to be understood of literal imprisonment (see Abbott, *ICC*, on Col. 4:10), but at what time this occurred is unknown; (3) 'distinguished among the apostles' ('well known *to* the apostles' is improbable): on this see *Apostle, and (4) Christians before him, as one might expect of apostles. For hypotheses connecting them with the foundation of the Ephesian or Roman churches, see B. W. Bacon, *ExpT* 42, 1930–1, pp. 300ff., and G. A. Barton, *ibid.*, 43, 1931–2, pp. 359ff.

A.F.W.

ANGEL. A biblical angel (Heb. *mal'āḵ*, Gk. *angelos*) is, by derivation and function, a messenger of God, familiar with him face to face, therefore of an order of being higher than that of man. He is a creature certainly, holy and uncorrupted spirit in original essence, yet endowed with free will, therefore not necessarily impervious to temptation and sin. There are many indications of an angelic fall, under the leadership of Satan (Jb. 4:18; Is. 14:12-15; Ezk. 28:12–19; Mt. 25:41; 2 Pet. 2:4; Rev. 12:9), though this belongs properly to the realm of demonology. The Qumran Scrolls have a double hierarchy of angels, with associated mortals, those from the respective realms of light and darkness. Both Testaments use the selfsame word for mortal and for quite mundane messengers. The biblical material will be considered roughly in its time order, but without discussing chronological problems.

I. In the Old Testament

Apart perhaps from the *angel of the Lord, the executive or even manifestation of Yahweh, angels are spiritual beings separate from God, yet, unless they be fallen, of unquestioned integrity, goodwill and obedience to him (*cf.* 1 Sa. 29:9; 2 Sa. 14:17, 20; 19:27). Angels may appear to men as bearers of God's specific commands and tidings (Jdg. 6:11–23; 13:3–5, *etc.*; see **II**, below). They may bring specific succour to needy mortal servants of God (1 Ki. 19:5–7; see **II**, below). They may undertake commissions of military assistance (2 Ki. 19:35, *etc.*) or, more rarely, active hostility (2 Sa. 24:16f.) towards Israel. The men of Sodom (Gn. 19 *passim*) or any other evildoers may be smitten by them. Their warlike potential, implied in Gn. 32:1f.; 1 Ki. 22:19, is more specific in Jos. 5:13–15; 2 Ki. 6:17—hence the familiar title of deity, Lord God of hosts.

Man's early thinking associated angels with stars. This prompted one of the poetic thoughts of Job, where the angels are also witnesses of creation (Jb. 38:7, see below; *cf.* Jdg. 5:20; Rev. 9:1). Balaam's ass is more aware of the presence of the angel of the Lord than her greedy, blinded master, who merits divine rebuke (Nu. 22:21–35). Very familiar are the angels in converse with Abraham (Gn. 18:1–16) or on Jacob's ladder (Gn. 28:12). Individual guardian angels are probably reflected in Ps. 91:11; some discern the angel of death in Jb. 33:23 (*cf. ICC*, *ad loc.*). These ideas, rudimentary in OT, become strong speculative tenets in the uninspired rabbinic literature. The term 'sons of God' means simply angels—the descent implied is mental or spiritual, not physical. The beings thus denoted may be clearly good angels (Jb. 38:7; see above), possibly good angels (Jb. 1:6; 2:1) or clearly fallen angels (Gn. 6:4). Another special term is *qᵉḏôšîm*, 'holy ones', AV 'saints' (Jb. 5:1; Ps. 89:5, 7; Dn. 8:13, *etc.*). This latter term is perhaps a little technical, for it may be used even in a context of potential criticism (*cf.* Jb. 15:15). The word *'ᵉlōhîm* (Ps. 8:5; *cf.* Heb. 2:7) is rendered 'God' (RSV) or 'divine' (Moffatt), yet the familiar AV rendering 'angels' remains arguable. Noteworthy also is Nebuchadrezzar's Aram. term 'wakeful one' or 'watcher', *'îr*; *cf.* Dn. 4:13, 17. *Cf.* also *Cherubim, *Seraphim.

Excepting minor references to Dn., the material so far examined is broadly pre-exilic, in origin at least. Here the angels still remain echoes of a higher will, lacking in that independent personality which will broaden in the later writings.

In the post-exilic books, the angel unquestionably gains in firmness and contour. The 'man' who acts as Ezekiel's divinely appointed guide to the ideal temple is a midway concept (chs. 40ff.), his counterpart becomes explicitly an interpreting angel in Zc. 1–6. The intercessory ministry on behalf of Israel in Zc. 1:12 calls for special mention. If it be remembered that 'saints' means 'angels' in that context, the last words of Zc. 14:5 make interesting reading in the light of the Synoptic predictions of the second coming.

OT angelology reaches its fullest development in Daniel, the earliest Jewish apocalypse. Here angels are first endowed with proper names, and attain to something like personality. Gabriel explains many things to Daniel, much in the spirit of Zechariah's divine visitant (Dn. 8:16ff.; 9:21ff.). In both books the angel is the fluent mouthpiece of God, and may be questioned, but Daniel's Gabriel is more rounded and convincing. Michael has a special function as guardian angel of Israel (Dn. 10:13, 21; 12:1), and other nations are similarly equipped (Dn. 10:20). This became rabbinic commonplace. There is a visionary glimpse into the heavenly places, where there are countless myriads of throne angels (Dn. 7:10; *cf.* Dt. 33:2; Ne. 9:6; Ps. 68:17 for slighter echoes).

II. In the New Testament

The NT largely endorses and underlines the OT, though developments in the intervening uninspired literature are historically important. Heb. 1:14 defines the angel both as messenger of God and as minister to man; the NT as a whole suggests a deepening bond of sympathy and service (*cf.* Rev. 19:10; Lk. 15:10). The concept of the personal guardian angel has sharpened, as in the rabbinic literature (Mt. 18:10; *cf. SB, ad loc.*; and on Acts 12:15). Special missions of communication to individuals are not lacking: the visitation of Gabriel to Daniel may be compared with that to Zechariah (Lk. 1:11–20) and Mary (Lk. 1:26–38; *cf.* also Mt. 1–2 *passim*; Acts 8:26; 10:3ff.; 27:23, *etc.*). The role of active succour to humanity is perceived in Acts 5:19f.; 12:7–10, which recalls Elijah under the juniper tree. God's throne is surrounded by countless myriads of angels, as Daniel had already declared (Heb. 12:22; Rev. 5:11, *etc.*).

The OT implies that angels were the joyful witnesses of, though not necessarily active participants in, God's act of creation (Jb. 38:7). In the NT they are closely associated with the giving of the law (Acts 7:53; Gal. 3:19; Heb. 2:2), and it is not inconsistent that they should be coupled with final judgment (Mt. 16:27; Mk. 8:38; 13:27; Lk. 12:8f.; 2 Thes. 1:7f., *etc.*). It may be their special task also to carry the righteous dead into Abraham's bosom (Lk. 16:22f.). Little is attempted by way of direct description of the angelic form. There are hints of lustrous countenance and apparel, of awesome, other-worldly beauty, which Christian art has attempted to express in its own way (Mt. 28:2f. and parallels; Lk. 2:9; Acts 1:10). The OT shows a comparable restraint in dealing with the *cherubim (Ezk. 10) and *seraphim (Is. 6). The splendour on the face of the condemned Stephen reflects the angelic loveliness (Acts 6:15). The incarnate Christ received the angelic ministry on several occasions (Mt. 4:11; Lk. 22:43), and he could have commanded thousands of angels, had he been prepared, at Gethsemane or anywhere else, to deviate from the appointed sacrificial path (Mt. 26:53).

There is a strange undertone of hostility or suspicion towards angels in certain passages. This has interesting though unconnected parallels in the rabbinic literature. Rom. 8:38 refers to fallen angels, and this explains also the puzzling passage 1 Cor. 11:10, which should be read in the light of Gn. 6:1ff. Some special exegesis is still necessary for Gal. 1:8 and 1 Cor. 13:1, also for the stern warning of Col. 2:18. It was doubtless through doctrinal errors on the part of his readers that the writer to the Hebrews urged so forcefully the superiority of the Son to any angel (Heb. 1).

The essential meaning of Jude 9 (partial parallel 2 Pet. 2:10f.) would seem to be that fallen angels retain from their first condition a status and dignity such that even their unfallen former companions may not revile them, but must leave the final condemnation to God. The incident referred to by Jude is said to have been recorded in the *Assumption of Moses*, a fragment of apocalyptic midrash. There Satan claims the body of Moses for his kingdom of darkness, because Moses killed the Egyptian (Ex. 2:12), and was therefore a murderer, whatever his subsequent virtues may have been. The final honours do not go to Satan, but even Michael the archangel must bridle his tongue before the foe of mankind.

Bibliography. L. Berkhof, *Systematic Theology*, 1949, pp. 141–149, and similar manuals; H. Heppe, *Reformed Dogmatics*, 1950, pp. 201–219; *TDNT* 1, pp. 74–87; *NIDNTT* 1, pp. 101–105, 449–454 (with biblios.). For rabbinic background, see *SB*, under particular NT passages; R. A. Stewart, *Rabbinic Theology*, 1961. For Qumran aspect, Y. Yadin, *The Scroll of the War of the Sons of Light against the Sons of Darkness*, 1962, pp. 229-242.

R.A.S.

ANGEL OF THE LORD. The angel of the Lord, sometimes 'the angel of God' or 'my (or 'his') angel', is represented in Scripture as a heavenly being sent by God to deal with men as his personal agent and spokesman. In many passages he is virtually identified with God and speaks not merely in the name of God but as God in the first person singular (*e.g.* with Hagar, Gn. 16:7ff.; 21:17f.: at the sacrifice of Isaac, Gn. 22:11ff.; to Jacob, Gn. 31:13, 'I am the god of Beth-el'; to Moses at the burning bush, Ex. 3:2; with Gideon, Jdg. 6:11ff.). Sometimes he is distinguished from God, as in 2 Sa. 24:16; Zc. 1:12f.; but Zechariah does not consistently maintain the distinction (*cf.* Zc. 3:1f.; 12:8).

In the NT there is no possibility of the angel of the Lord being confused with God. He appears as *Gabriel in Lk. 1:19, though from Acts 8:26, 29 some would infer an identification with the Holy Spirit. In function, the angel of the Lord is the agent of destruction and judgment (2 Sa. 24:16; 2 Ki. 19:35; Ps. 35:5f.; Acts 12:23); of protection and deliverance (Ex. 14:19; Ps. 34:7; Is. 63:9, 'the angel of his presence'; Dn. 3:28; 6:22; Acts 5:19; 12:7, 11); he offers guidance and gives instructions (Gn. 24:7, 40; Ex. 23:23; 1 Ki. 19:7; 2 Ki. 1:3, 15; Mt. 2:13, 19; Acts 8:26); he gives advance warning about the birth of Samson (Jdg. 13:3ff.), John the Baptist (Lk. 1:11ff.) and Jesus (Mt. 1:20, 24; Lk. 2:9). He is not recognized at once in Jdg. 13:3ff. and is not even visible to Balaam (Nu. 22:22ff.); but mostly when appearing to men he is recognized as a divine being, even though in human form, and is addressed as God (Gn. 16:13, *etc.*). J.B.Tr.

ANGELS OF THE CHURCHES. The 'seven stars' of the Patmos vision are explained as referring to 'the angels (*angeloi*) of the seven churches' (Rev. 1:20), to whom the letters of Rev. 2 and 3 are then addressed. The 'angel' concept is problematic. It is often taken either of guardian angels or of human leaders or bishops of the churches. Both suggestions involve difficulty. Elsewhere in Rev. *angelos* certainly means 'angel', but the 'angel' can scarcely be made to share responsibility for the sins of the church. The interpretation 'bishop' seems contrary to usage, and unsupported by effective parallels. There is no such emphasis on episcopacy as later in Ignatius. Nor can this view be based on the inferior reading 'your wife' in 2:20 (*sou* inserted by dittography). And again it would be strange to hold one man individually and absolutely responsible for the church. *angelos* is literally 'messenger', but the initially attractive idea that the *angeloi* might be messengers appointed by the churches breaks down for a combination of similar reasons.

The real difficulty is probably that the image belongs to a context and genre which eludes the logic of modern categories. *angelos* must be rendered verbally as 'angel', but the verbal equivalence does not sufficiently explain the underlying thought. The 'angel' is perhaps something like a heavenly counterpart of the church. In practice we may visualize this as amounting to a personification of the church, even if this does less than justice to the connotations of the original concept. C.J.H.

ANIMALS OF THE BIBLE.

(For an alphabetical list see page 1295.) In the earliest EVV, especially AV, lack of precise knowledge of the Palestine fauna was a major reason for inaccuracy and it is not surprising that translators used the names of European species with which they were familiar. The precise study of animal life began only in the 19th century, and it was formerly usual to give names only to animals which were obvious or of practical importance. Animals resembling each other in general appearance or usage would thus be called by the same or by similar names. These general principles apply to animal life as a whole. There is usually little difficulty in identifying animals mentioned several times in varying contexts likely to provide clues, but the correct translation of many names found only in the various lists of Lv. and Dt. will always be difficult. EVV published since about 1900 have corrected some early mistakes, but there is lack of uniformity within and among the EVV and most include some strange translations. Not all of these names, some now obsolete or indefinite, are mentioned below but most are discussed. Two major sections may be recognized – the wild animals that usually form part of the incidental background, and the domestic animals that were a basic part of daily life. The latter is the more important and is treated first.

Two Heb. words are translated **ASS**: *'āṯôn*, referring to its endurance, and *ḥ^amôr* from the reddish coat of the most usual colour form. The latter is used much more frequently than the former, which is found mainly in the two incidents of Balaam's ass (Nu. 22) and the asses of Kish (1 Sa. 9–10). These words refer only to the domesticated ass. **DONKEY**, of unknown origin, is not found before the end of the 18th century: applied only to the domesticated form, it is used in some modern EVV, including JB and NEB.

In addition, two words are generally translated **WILD ASS** – *'ārôḏ* and *pere'*. The former is found both in the Aram. form *'arād* (Dn. 5:21), and as Heb. *'ārôḏ* (Jb. 39:5), but the translation is questioned by some authorities. *pere'* occurs 9 times and its translation 'wild ass' in Jb. 39:5–8 is well endorsed by the context. This species is known today as the **ONAGER** (*Equus onager*) and it is still found in parts of W and Central Asia. A form closely related to the sub-species that became extinct about mid-19th century has now been successfully introduced into the Hay Bar Nature Reserve in the S Negeb.

The **ASS** is descended from the Nubian wild ass (*Equus asinus*) and is thought to have been domesticated in Neolithic times in NE Africa. The first biblical mention is during Abram's stay in Egypt (Gn. 12:16), but he had probably used asses as transport from Mesopotamia, where several distinct breeds were recognizable by *c.* 1800 BC. 'Asses' which drew wheeled carts in ancient Mesopotamia more than 1,000 years earlier are now known from stone carvings and drawings to have been onagers, but this species was never fully domesticated. Asses were vitally important to poor nomadic peoples and provided their basic transport, allowing an average journey of about 30 km a day. A text from Mari shows that as early as the 17th century BC it was considered improper for royalty to ride a horse rather than an ass. The biblical picture is consistent, that royal persons rode asses on peaceful occasions, while horses are associated with war. In the light of this, *cf.* Zc. 9:9 and Mt. 21:2f.

Both **COLT** and **FOAL** are correctly used for the young of members of the horse tribe; in EVV they refer only to the ass, except for Gn. 32:15 where colt applies to a young camel.

The OT contains numerous references to the **HORSE** (*sûs*), many of them figurative, and its use is especially frequent in the prophetic literature and poetic books. Throughout OT and NT the horse is regularly associated with war and power, and very seldom mentioned singly. A further word, *pārāš*, translated 'horseman' in most EVV, could mean a mounted horse of the cavalry or perhaps a horse with rider; *sûs* is a more general word, used in particular for horses drawing chariots.

Of all the animals that have become beasts of burden, the horse is the most important, though it was domesticated long after cattle and the ass. In contrast to the wild ass, which lived in the semi-desert of N Africa, the ancestors of the horse were native to the grasslands of Europe and Asia. It is likely that domestication took place independently in several different areas – W Europe, SW Asia and Mongolia. Horses in the biblical record presumably come from the second of these.

A Bab. tablet of the period of Hammurapi, *c.* 1750 BC, gives the first record of the horse, referred to as 'the ass from the east'. Horses were already in Egypt when Joseph was in power, and they were used in pursuit at the Exodus. It is unlikely that the children of Israel owned horses, but in any case they would have been unsuited to a desert journey.

The nations living in Canaan had horses and rode them in battle (Jos. 11:4, *etc.*). David frequently fought against them: 'David hamstrung all the chariot horses (of 1,700 horsemen), but left enough for 100 chariots' (2 Sa. 8:4), which seems to be the first record that he owned any. (In AV the obsolete word 'hough' is used for hamstring; now spelt, as pronounced, 'hock', it is the joint between knee and fetlock in the hind leg. Cutting this tendon permanently crippled a horse.) David's sons ignored the prohibition in Dt. 17:16 (referring to the time when the people would demand a king), 'He must not multiply horses for himself'; *e.g.* 'Absalom got himself a chariot and horses' (2 Sa. 15:1), while Solomon later had great numbers of horses, kept in special establishments at Hazor, Megiddo and Gezer. These were imported from Egypt and Kue (S Anatolia) and exported to neighbouring states, the price of a horse being 150 shekels of silver (1 Ki. 10:28f.).

Although the Eng. word **MULE** has a number of other meanings it was first, and still is primarily, applied to the offspring of a horse by a donkey. These hybrids were probably first bred soon after the horse was introduced into areas where the donkey was kept, although such breeding seems to be specifically forbidden by Lv. 19:19, 'You shall not let your cattle breed with a different kind' (cattle, *b^ehēmâ*, here means any domesticated stock). This may explain why it was not until towards the end of David's reign (2 Sa. 13:29) that mules appear in the record. It is generally agreed that Heb. *yēmîm* (Gn. 36:24) should be translated 'hot springs' (RSV) and not 'mule' (AV). *pereḏ* and *pirdâ* are used for the male and female, but this hybrid is always sterile. Mules are valuable in that they combine the strength of the horse with the endurance and sure-footedness of the donkey, as well as its ability to thrive on poorer food; they also have the extra vigour characteristic of hybrids, both plant and animal.

In Est. 8:14 Heb. *reḵeš* is better translated 'swift horses' (RSV).

Although the early history of the **CAMEL** (Heb. *gāmāl*; Gr. *kamēlos*) has major gaps and its wild ancestor is unknown, there is ample evidence of early domestication. The one-humped camel, usually known as Arabian, is often called dromedary, though this name strictly refers to the fast riding breed; it is typical of the deserts of the Middle East and features in the biblical narrative. The two-humped, or Bactrian, camel (named after Bactria, probably near the Oxus river in SW Asia) is now associated with Central and NE Asian deserts, where winters are very cold. This form was sometimes brought farther S and an obelisk at Nimrod (841 BC) shows it as part of the booty taken by Shalmaneser III. Anatomically there is little difference between the two and they are known to interbreed.

The camel is wonderfully fitted to life in dry zones. The hump is a storage organ which is drawn on when food is short, as it often is on desert crossings. Its water economy allows it to go for a week without drinking, a feat made possible by a camel's ability to lose up to one-third of its body weight without danger; when given access to water this is replaced in about 10 minutes. There is also an unusual physiological mechanism whereby body temperature rises from a morning reading of 34°C to 40°C in the afternoon, thus avoiding water loss through sweating. Mouth, nose, eyes and feet are all anatomically adapted to desert life. The camel's products are widely used; the winter hair is woven into rough cloth and the droppings are collected for fuel. The camel chews the cud but is not cloven-hoofed, so under Mosaic law it was unclean; it is not certain that this ban applied to the milk, which is a valuable source of food, for the cow may stay in milk for nearly 2 years. Camel hides are made into leather. Camels can live on poor vegetation, of which the high fibre content makes the droppings useful.

A camel can carry about 200 kg and its rider, but only half that for desert reaches. Freight camels can average 45 km a day but a fast riding camel has covered 150 km in 13 hours.

There has been much argument about the use of camels by the Patriarchs, but archaeology has now shown that there were domesticated camels in Egypt at least 1,200 years earlier. The problem arises largely because there were long periods when the camel seems to have been unknown in Egypt, possibly for reasons of taboo; it was in one such period that Abram went there (Gn. 12:16), and the inclusion of camels in the list of presents from the pharaoh is considered a scribal addition, but there is no reason to reject later mentions. The evidence for the camel's early use is detailed in Zeuner (ch. 13) and Cansdale (ch. 4). More recent excavations in Oman confirm its occurrence there *c.* 2500 BC.

In the narrative from Gn. 24:35 onwards camels formed an important part of wealth and were also used for long-distance transport (Gn. 24:10ff. and 31:34), but camel nomadism and the regular use of camels did not become general until *c.* 16th century BC. David appointed an Ishmaelite as his camel master (1 Ch. 27:30) and the Queen of Sheba's baggage was carried on camels from SW Arabia (1 Ki. 10:2).

Camels were valuable for transport in and around deserts but were never popular with the Hebrews. There is no clear biblical reference to camels as draught animals, but they have been widely used in cultivation, sometimes paired oddly with a donkey. In contrast to the 57 wholly literal OT mentions only two of the six NT references are literal – the material for John the Baptist's clothes in Mt. 3:4 and Mk. 1:6. The others are in colourful comments by Christ which are perhaps proverbial in origin – 'straining out a gnat' (Mt. 23:24) and 'the eye of a needle' (Mt. 19:24). See also separate article on *Camel.

The importance of the domestic **SHEEP** to the Israelites is shown by its being mentioned some 400 times, with 12 Heb. words. Of these some are simple alternatives; others refer to age and sex, while at least one word (*kar*, Aram. *dᵉkar*) may denote a separate breed. *ṣō'n*, the most common word, is a collective term, discussed under 'Goat', to which it refers equally. *keḇeś* occurs over 100 times and with only 5 exceptions applies to sacrificial animals; the frequent qualification 'a year old' suggests that it may refer to a lamb of 1 year and upwards. Four Gk. words cover the more than 70 NT occurrences, in which *probaton* is most used. For a complete list of Heb. and Gk. words and their usage, see Cansdale, pp. 53–55.

The origins and early history of the sheep are complex and disputed. It was kept by Neolithic man *c.* 5000 BC and by 2000 BC at least five different breeds had reached Mesopotamia. Its ancestors were probably mountain sheep, perhaps from more than one source; a wide range of breeds has now been developed which serve many purposes and utilize habitats ranging from marshland to near desert. Sheep were first domesticated for their meat and fat, especially the latter, of which the earlier goat provided little. The wool was developed by careful breeding and became very valuable, being the most useful and easily available fibre for clothing. Mesha, king of Moab (2 Ki. 3:4), paid as annual tribute the wool of 100,000 rams, with fleeces perhaps averaging 1 kg. The tanned skins were used for clothes and also for the inner covering of the tabernacle (Ex. 25:5, *etc.*). The milk was mostly used in the form of curds and as a basic food it was probably more important than the meat, which was usually eaten only as part of sacrificial meals.

The sheep is mainly a grazer, *i.e.* it feeds on grasses and is thus more selective than the grazing goat. The fat-tailed breed is now the most common in Palestine. This strange feature, which may weigh 5 kg, is known from Egyp. mummies of *c.* 2000 BC; it is a storage organ, analogous to the camel's hump, and is useful in the hot dry summer and cold winter. The main limiting factor was probably winter feed, and in NT times flocks were often kept under cover from the November rains until Passover and fed on chaff and barley.

It is clear from Gn. 30:32 that both sheep and goats were already in various colours and patterns, and possibly few were pure white. This suggests that the correct translation of Heb. *tāmîm* (Nu. 28:3) is 'without blemish' (most modern EVV) and not 'without spot' (AV), referring to general imperfections rather than to colour markings.

Although archaeological material is rich in tools and other objects made from sheep bones, there is no biblical reference other than to the use of rams' horns as containers of oil (1 Sa. 16:1) and as musical instruments (Jos. 6:4, *etc.*).

Throughout the Bible the sheep has deep metaphorical significance and in the NT the only entirely non-figurative references are to their being sold in the Temple (Jn. 2:14, *etc.*). Sheep were always a familiar part of the scene, with the shepherd leading and protecting his sheep and building folds for them. It is therefore not surprising that the sheep is consistently a picture of man – helpless, easily led astray and lost, essentially sociable, unable to fend for itself or find its way home, *e.g.* Is. 53:6, 'All we like sheep have gone astray; we have turned every one to his own way.' The alternative, of man restored, is stated in Ps. 23, written by David from his early experience as a shepherd. The NT unfolds the great paradox of Jn. 1:29, 'Behold, the Lamb of God, who takes away the sin of the world!' and Jn. 10:14, 'I am the good shepherd', with Rev. 5:6, 'a lamb standing, as though it had been slain'.

The meaning of separating the sheep from the goats (Mt. 25:32) becomes clear when a mixed flock is inspected; the two may look alike, and close scrutiny is needed to distinguish them. Of the highly figurative passage in Ct. 4:2 it is enough to say that although the phrase 'all of which bear twins' is a disputed translation, the shepherd's ambition is for all ewes to have twin lambs and lose none by abortion.

CATTLE (from OE *catel*) first meant property, of which livestock was then a major part. This usage is close to Heb. *miqneh*. Today cattle are wild and domesticated bovines, *i.e.* members of the ox tribe, but biblical reference is confined to domestic animals. Ten Heb. words apply to cattle, which between them are mentioned over 450 times. The following are the most important: *b^{e}hēmâ* (sing. and collective) denotes larger domestic animals and not only bovines. *šôr*, usually a bull, though occasionally female, is the basic word for a single animal. *bāqār* is another collective term for adult horned cattle, often translated herd, while *b^{e}'îr* is a collective term used mostly for beasts of burden, which could include oxen. *par* is a bull; its feminine, *pārâ*, is used of the red heifer of Nu. 19. *'ēḡel* and *'eglâ* (fem.) (from a root 'to roll') are used of young animals. *m^{e}rî'*, translated fat beast, almost always refers to animals for sacrifice.

Six Gk. words are used. *damalis*, the (red) heifer; *thremma*, *moschos* and *sitistos* mostly refer to fattened cattle; *tauros*, ox; and *bous*, bull.

All domestic cattle are thought to be derived from the aurochs or wild ox (see below). It was first tamed in Neolithic times, probably in several different parts of the world independently, and later than sheep and goats. The primary reason for domestication was for meat; later the cows were used for milking and the bulls for draught purposes, which greatly increased the area of land that could be cultivated. Their size and the need for good grazing limited the range of cattle-keeping and they did best in the hilly country of Upper Galilee. However, they seem to have been widely kept in small numbers and were everywhere used as multipurpose animals.

Several humanitarian rules about oxen are recorded in both OT and NT. They were included in the sabbath rest (Ex. 23:12). A straying ox should be led to safety (Ex. 23:4). Watering cattle was permitted on the sabbath (Lk. 13:15). Paul twice quoted the Mosaic injunction (Dt. 25:4) not to muzzle the ox treading out corn (1 Cor. 9:9; 1 Tim. 5:18). These and other precepts show a concern for animal welfare still unknown in many countries and not recognized in the West until well into the 19th century.

Domesticated in antiquity – from the **WILD GOAT** (*Capra aegagrus*) – the **GOAT** was useful to the Patriarchs (Gn. 15:9), for though kept with sheep it had the advantage of being able to thrive on poorer ground. The story of Jacob and Esau (Gn. 27:9) stresses its value as meat, but normally only kids were used for food. The she-goats provided milk, skins were used for leather and as bottles, and the hair of some varieties was woven into cloth; but goats have also done untold damage to the habitat of lands where they have been introduced and not properly controlled. This is especially true of hilly terrain of the E Mediterranean, with hot, dry summers and winter rains.

As would be expected, such an important animal has a range of Heb. names for male (*ṣāp̄îr*, *śā'îr*, *tayiš*), female (*'ez*, *ś^{e}'îrâ*), young (*g^{e}ḏî*, *g^{e}ḏî 'izzîm*, pl. *b^{e}nê 'izzîm*), *etc.* In addition, two collective nouns, *ṣō'n* or *ṣ^{e}'ôn* 'flock' and *śeh* or *śê* 'member of the flock', are found more often than any other names. Unless specified by attaching *'ez*, 'goat', or *keḇeś*, 'sheep', these words may refer equally to either sheep or goats, or to a mixture of both. It is therefore often difficult to speak of relative numbers.

The domestic **SWINE** of Palestine was derived from *Sus scrofa*, the wild boar of Europe and W Asia. The children of Israel were divinely prohibited from eating swine (*ḥ^{a}zîr*, Lv. 11:7; Dt. 14:8). This was for two hygienic reasons. First, the pig, as a frequent scavenger, may pick up diseased material and either carry infection mechanically or itself become infected. Secondly, the pig is host of the tapeworm causing trichinosis; this passes one stage in the muscles of a pig and can be transmitted only by being eaten. The tape worms then invade various tissues in man and can even cause death. Thorough cooking kills the worms but this is not always possible when firewood is scarce, so that only a complete ban is safe. This relationship was proved only in the 20th century.

This prohibition became a national loathing with the Jews, with the pig standing for what is despicable and hated. Thus in Pr. 11:22 a woman of doubtful character is associated with a swine, and the prodigal son had reached the utter depths when feeding the swine (*choiros*) of a Gentile (Lk. 15:15). Herds were kept by local Gentile communities in NT times (Mt. 8:30ff., *etc.*). The demons' plea to be sent into a nearby herd of swine would not appear strange to a Jew, who considered swine and demons of the same order. Similarly, in Mt. 7:6 Jesus warns his followers not to throw pearls before swine. The author of 2 Pet. 2:22 regards false teachers as those who will return to their (swinish) pagan nature.

Pig, which once meant young swine, is now the name in general use; swine is obsolete other than in some technical terms, but is still retained in most EVV.

The contempt and disgust with which the **DOG** is regarded in the OT cannot easily be understood by Western people, to whom the dog is a companion and auxiliary. It is generally agreed that it was the first animal to be domesticated and that by the late Stone Age it was being kept in many parts of the world. Most authorities regard the wolf as the ancestor of all the many and varied breeds of domestic dog.

In many parts of the East the dog is still basically a scavenger. It was useful in disposing of refuse but was by its very nature unclean and a potential carrier of disease, and therefore could not be touched without defilement. Heb. *kebeḇ* and Gr. *kyōn* are without doubt the semi-wild dogs which roamed outside the city walls waiting for rubbish or dead bodies to be thrown over. Dogs were differently regarded in other lands, especially in Egypt, where they were used in hunting and also held in reverence. A second Gk. word, the diminutive *kynarion*, is used in the incident of the Syro-Phoenician woman (Mt. 15:26ff.). The context suggests that this was a pet dog allowed about the house.

The 'dogs' of Phil. 3:2 are Judaizing intruders who disturb the peace of the church; the 'dogs' who are excluded from the new Jerusalem in Rev. 22:15 are people of unclean lives, probably an echo of Dt. 23:18, where 'dog' seems to be a technical term for a male temple prostitute.

In OT times Palestine was fairly rich in wild **RUMINANTS** (animals that chew the cud) that were allowed as food. There is frequent mention of *hunting and hunting methods, with a wide range of nets, traps, pitfalls, *etc.* Many of these are in figurative contexts and cannot always be identified exactly, but they were certainly the tools of the hunter, and it must be assumed that hunting yielded useful meat. It seems likely that all the major species find mention in the Heb. text, but there has been no consistency in the EVV, only in part because the Palestine fauna was not known when the early translations were made, for even in modern EVV the treatment is often erratic. The wild ruminants known to have occurred in Palestine will be listed, with brief notes, but there is no point in tabulating all the EVV translations. For a fuller discussion see Cansdale, ch. 5, 'Beasts of the Chase'.

Heb. *r^{e}'ēm* is without doubt the **AUROCHS** or **WILD OX**, ancestor of domestic cattle. It had disappeared from Palestine before the Christian era, and the last-known specimen was killed in Poland early in the 17th century. EVV now generally translate 'wild ox', and the AV 'unicorn' is rightly dropped. Heb. *te'ô* is translated 'wild ox' and 'wild bull' (AV) and more widely 'antelope'. JB has **ORYX**, which is correct. Properly called the Arabian or desert oryx, it is a specialized desert animal able to survive long periods without water; almost white in coat, it stands 1 m high and both sexes have long, straight horns. Modern weapons and transport brought disaster and this oryx may already be extinct in the wild. Is. 51:20 speaks of its being taken in a net, a method of hunting practised by Arabs up to the end of the 19th century.

The **ADDAX** is another rare desert antelope; it still survives in the Sahara, but was lost to Bible lands before 1900. Heb. *dîšôn* is translated 'pygarg' (AV) via the Gk. in LXX. Long tradition, and its placing between two desert species in the food lists suggest that this is probably the addax. 'Ibex' (RSV) cannot be right.

Heb. *yaḥmûr* is the most difficult in the list of clean animals in Dt. 14:5. Tradition, backed by LXX, suggests the **BUBAL HARTEBEEST**, now extinct in the N part of its range, but this is made less likely by its inclusion in Solomon's daily provision for the table (1 Ki. 4:23), for this seems to imply a herd animal or one that could be penned. 'Fallow deer' (AV) and 'roedeer' (RSV) are unlikely.

The last name in this food list is also difficult. *zemer* ('leaper') is translated 'chamois' (AV, RV), which cannot be right, for this is an animal of the high mountains. **MOUNTAIN SHEEP** (RSV) is acceptable but this name is not precise. It cannot be the Barbary sheep, confined to N Africa and the Sahara, but it would be one of the now extinct forms of **MOUFLON**, of which other sub-species are still found in S Europe and SW Asia.

The **NUBIAN IBEX** can be seen today in its true habitat on the rocky slopes above the oasis of En-gedi – the 'spring of the wild kid'. There is no doubt that this is the correct translation of *y^{e}'ēlîm*, 'wild goats' (AV). The root means 'climber'; it is always associated with mountains and the name is always plural, as befits a herd animal: 'The high mountains are for the wild goats' (Ps. 104:18). It seems probable that Heb. *'aqqô* (Dt. 14:5) is a synonym for *yā'ēl*, the singular form; it is not unusual for well-known animals to have two names.

To many Eng.-speaking people any hoofed animal with horns or antlers is just a **DEER**. In fact, deer form a large well-defined group of ruminants; they are distinguished by having antlers that are shed and regrown annually, and most typical of the N temperate regions. There are many species and to be meaningful the word must be qualified.

Three kinds once lived in Palestine. The **RED DEER**, the species found commonly through much of Europe and SW Asia, is the largest, standing about 1.5 m. It could not have been common, for Palestine offered little shelter, and it disappeared early, perhaps before the arrival of the Israelites. The **FALLOW DEER**, which is a common park deer in many countries today, stands only 1 m at the shoulder and is distinguished by having a coat more or less spotted at all ages and not just when young. This kind was lost to Palestine by about 1922. The **ROE DEER** is no taller than 80 cm; unlike the other two it is found only in ones and twos, and it is hard to see, so its presence may not be noticed. The last Palestine specimen was reported on Mt Carmel early in the 20th century. It is likely that Heb. *'ayyāl* and its feminine forms, translated stag, hart, hind, *etc.*, in most EVV, refer to both fallow and roe deer generally and are therefore best translated deer.

The key to Heb. *ṣ^{e}ḇî* is found in Acts 9:36, 'Tabitha, which means Dorcas' (*dorkas*, **GAZELLE**). This latter word had not reached England when the AV translated 'roe' and 'roedeer', but later EVV are fairly consistent with gazelle. Two species are found in Palestine: the dorcas and Palestine gazelles, both standing under 70 cm. Once seriously in danger of extermination, they have recovered under protection, and today can be seen in the Judaean hills and the central plains, as well as around the desert. Gazelles are typically dry-zone antelopes, pale coloured and often with forward-pointing horns.

The **WILD BOAR** is mentioned above as the ancestor of the domestic pig. Heb. *ḥ^{a}zîr* refers to both forms. The wild boar is still common in parts of the Middle East, where the food habits of both Jew and Muslim give no extra incentive for control. Its main habitat is forest and reed beds; *e.g.* Ps. 80:13, 'the boar from the forest ravages it'. In Ps. 68:30 'the beasts that dwell among the reeds' are thought to be wild boars.

The **ELEPHANT** is not directly mentioned in Scripture but there are 12 references to *ivory, which came from both African and Asiatic species. Methods of taming and training elephants were worked out in India in the 3rd millennium BC. But this was not true domestication, for the animals were caught young and reared to become beasts of burden or, frequently, for use in war. The books of Maccabees (*e.g.* 1 Macc. 6:30, 35) have several references to the fighting elephants used against the Jews by the Seleucid, Antiochus Epiphanes. The Asiatic elephant was once found as far W as the upper reaches of the Euphrates where, according to Assyrian records, it was taken in pits; in such country it is not likely to have been common and it was killed out late in the 1st millennium BC.

At one time **LIONS** were found from Asia Minor through the Middle East and Persia to India, with a similar form in Greece up to nearly AD 100. This European/Asiatic lion resembles the African lion closely. Of all the carnivorous animals only the lion has certainly disappeared from Bible lands, though the cheetah and bear have almost gone. The last Palestine lion was probably killed near Megiddo in the 13th century; lions were still known in Persia in 1900; they had gone by 1930 at the latest. Lions were reported in Syria up to 1851 by Burton (*Travels in Syria*) and in parts of Iraq up to the early 1920s. The few Asiatic lions surviving today are in a small patch of forest in the Kathiawar peninsula of India.

The word 'lion' occurs some 130 times in AV/RSV, with one general Heb. word *'aryeh* and 8 other words, perhaps applied to various ages of the two sexes, though at least some are probably poetical names. This rich vocabulary suggests that the lion was common and well known in OT times, and many contexts confirm this, even though the usage is largely metaphorical for strength. The lion was also a symbol of royalty in the ancient Near East (*LION OF JUDAH). Lions were frequently kept in captivity (*cf.* Dn. 6:7ff.). They were being bred by Ashurnasirpal II (883–859 BC) at Nimrud (*CALAH) and kept in large numbers (E. W. Budge and L. W. King, *Annals of the Kings of Assyria*, 1901).

In popular Eng. usage the word **LEOPARD**, usually with a qualifying word, stands for a number of different spotted cats. It is possible that Heb. *nāmēr* refers to both the true leopard and the **CHEETAH**, or hunting leopard, and also to one or two other spotted wild cats of Palestine. All the few references are proverbial and figurative, and the precise species is therefore immaterial. Perhaps the most familiar use of the word is in the proverb of Je. 13:23, 'Can the Ethiopian change his skin or the leopard his spots?'

The **JUNGLE CAT** (*Felis chaus*) still lives in the more wooded parts, especially in Galilee. The leopard (*Panthera pardus*) is now very rare in Israel and Jordan, but several were seen or killed in the late 1960s, including two near the shore of the Dead Sea and one in Galilee.

Heb. *z^e'ēḇ* (Is. 11:6, *etc.*) and Gk. *lykos* (Mt. 7:15, *etc.*) refer to the SE Asiatic form of the **WOLF**. Its range and numbers have been drastically reduced by the growth of population and modern methods of control, but up to NT times it was common enough to be a menace to livestock, though it is now agreed that wolves have never been the danger to man that popular legend suggested. Their carnivorous nature is implied in most passages but the wolf is mentioned only metaphorically throughout. It is notable that in more than half the references the wolf stands for someone in authority who is misusing his position, *e.g.* Zp. 3:3, 'Her judges are evening wolves'. The wolf of Palestine is similar to, though rather smaller than, the wolf that is found in Central and N Europe.

Both **FOXES** and **JACKALS** are found throughout the Middle East. They are members of the *Canidae*, the dog family, and closely related, but the fox is usually solitary, whereas jackals often go in packs. It is likely that Heb. *šû'āl* and Gk. *alōpēx* include both fox and jackal, and modern EVV translate fox in some passages and jackal in others. Both species eat fruit and other vegetable matter, including grapes (Ct. 2:15). In Jdg. 15:4 the 300 animals caught by Samson were probably jackals.

Another Heb. word *tannîm*, always plural, which AV translates 'dragon' is now translated 'jackal' in RV/RSV. It is possible that this is a poetical name used to suggest desolation.

The Syrian form of the widely distributed **BROWN BEAR** may still be found in parts of the Middle East though no longer within the actual area of Palestine, but its status is doubtful and it may already be extinct. The last bear in Palestine was killed in Upper Galilee in the 1930s but a few lived around Mt Hermon for a further 10 years or so. It is clearly Heb. *dōḇ* (Arab. *dub*). It is paler than the typical race and usually referred to as a sub-species *Ursus arctos syriacus*. Like most bears other than the polar bear, the brown bear is omnivorous or vegetarian for most of the year, so its attacks on livestock, especially sheep, would be most likely during winter when wild fruits are scarce.

The term 'bear robbed of her cubs' (2 Sa. 17:8; Pr. 17:12) seems to be proverbial; also the expression in Am. 5:19, 'as if a man fled from a lion and a bear met him'. The bear is more feared than the lion because its strength is greater and its actions less predictable.

The **WEASEL** is mentioned only in Lv. 11:29, translating *ḥōleḏ*. Several members of the weasel tribe are found in Palestine, and also a mongoose; there is nothing to confirm that *ḥōleḏ* refers to all or any of them but it is widely thought to refer to the actual weasel.

It is obvious that smaller animals are hard to identify unless the context includes some clues. Heb. *šāp̄ān* is clearly recognizable from its 4 OT occurrences (Lv. 11:5; Dt. 14:7; Ps. 104:18; Pr. 30:26) as the **SYRIAN ROCK HYRAX**. This belongs to a small order classified nearest to the elephants and is about the size of a rabbit, 30–40 cm long. It feeds on a variety of plants and lives in rocky hills where it can shelter in crevices. This identification was clearly made last century and confirmed by Tristram in his *The Natural History of the Bible* (1867). It is thus hard to understand why modern EVV, though rightly dropping 'coney' because of its confusion with 'rabbit', use such non-names as 'rock-rabbit' and 'rock-badger'. JB gives 'hyrax' in the Mosaic lists, though 'rock-badger' elsewhere, and is one of the few EVV to translate *šāp̄ān* correctly.

Heb. *taḥaš* is the material used for covering the tabernacle when erected (Ex. 25) and the Ark of the Covenant when being carried (Nu. 4). This is translated badgers' skin (AV), sealskin (RV), goatskin (RSV). Tristram (1867) seems to have been the first to suggest that the most likely source of this skin was the **DUGONG**, a large marine mammal belonging to the *Sirenia* which, until the early 19th century, was fairly common in the Gulf of Aqaba. NEB translates 'porpoise hide', with mg. note '*strictly* sea-cow'. The latter is a popular name for dugong, which is not at all related to the porpoise, one of the toothed whales.

Heb. *'akbār* is found 6 times in OT and uniformly translated **MOUSE**. In popular usage this name is applied to a wide range of small rodents, and one would expect *'akbār* to have this force when used as a prohibited item of food in Lv. 11:29, *i.e.* it probably covered voles, jerboas, gerbils, *etc.*, as well as true rats and mice. Four occurrences are in 1 Sa. 6, the incident of the pestilence that struck the Philistines. The symptoms seem to fit bubonic plague precisely, which suggests that *'akbār* here refers to the **BLACK RAT** (*Rattus rattus*) whose flea is the main carrier for this lethal disease, which was the black death of the Middle Ages in Europe.

Heb. *'arnebet* is mentioned only as a forbidden food but the similarity to Arab. *'arneb* and the reason for the ban suggests that this is the Palestine **HARE**. Lv. 11:6, 'because it chews the cud but does not part the hoof' (*i.e.* is not cloven-hoofed), was long misunderstood, for clearly the hare, related to rodents, does not really chew the cud. However, it is now known that hares, like the closely related rabbit, pass two different kinds of droppings, one of which is chewed and swallowed again, giving the appearance of cud-chewing. This strange habit serves somewhat the same purpose as rumination, for it allows digestion of material otherwise hard to utilize.

BAT is a reasonable translation for *'ᵃṭellēp̄* (Lv. 11:19 and Dt. 14:18) among the flying animals in the Mosaic lists. Many species are found abundantly throughout the Middle East, some of which roost communally in large numbers in caves, either hanging from the roof or clustering in crevices. They would have been some of the most obvious animals at certain seasons and logically included in the forbidden foods, for most species are insectivorous. The only other mention of bats is in Is. 2:20, 'men will cast forth their idols . . . to the bats', where this unclean animal is used almost to signify desolation.

Heb. *qôp̄*, generally translated **APE**, is usually taken to be a loan-word from Egyp. *g(i)f*, *gwf*, **MONKEY**. These animals were included in cargoes brought to Egypt by her Red Sea fleets from 'Punt', a land possibly located in SE Sudan and Eritrea. These would have been baboons or vervet monkeys. Another suggestion is that this word is derived from Tamil and therefore indicates an E origin, in which case the monkeys would have been **MACAQUES** or **LANGURS**. None of these is, technically, an ape.

Heb. *tannîn* is discussed under ***DRAGON**, which is the commonest translation in most EVV, though serpent, whale and sea monster are also found. (See Cansdale, Appendix B, for detailed analysis.) There has been some confusion with Heb. *tannîm*, which is probably a poetic name for jackal, but it is unlikely that the two words are related. *tannîn* is mostly found in wholly figurative contexts and it is not at all certain that a living animal is intended; these therefore merit no comment here. However, *tannîn* is also found in the creation narrative, 5th day (Gn. 1:21), 'great whales' (AV), 'sea monsters' (RSV). In this context it is a general word and not specific, and 'giant marine animals' is perhaps the best translation. It is also translated 'serpent' in the incident where the rods became serpents (Ex. 7:9–10, 12). In two other vv. AV has 'whale' where the context is clearly figurative.

In Mt. 12:40 Gk. *kētos* is translated **WHALE** (most EVV) referring to the great fish (Heb. *dāḡ*) of Jon. 1:17. For anatomical reasons it seems most unlikely that 'fish' is correct, but several toothed whales are recorded from the E Mediterranean, including some that are capable of swallowing a man. In the early part of this century there were one or two reasonably authenticated cases of men surviving after being swallowed (*PTR* 25, 1927, pp. 636ff.). This is the only NT occurrence of *kētos*, which is used by Homer and Herodotus for a wide range of sea animals, real and mythical, and the precise meaning must remain in doubt.

The word **BEHEMOTH** came into the Eng. language when the early translators failed to find an animal that seemed to fit the context of Jb. 40:15. It is the plural of Heb. *bᵉhēmâ*, a common general word for beast. This is found 9 times and in all but one it has the normal plural meaning of animals or cattle. The passage in Jb. 40, however, is a special case, for the plural seems to be used for intensive effect and a specific animal is probably meant. Although various suggestions have been made, the opinion of most scholars over the years is that Job was writing about the **HIPPOPOTAMUS**, an animal that received its Eng. name after the AV appeared. This comes from the Gk., meaning 'river horse', though the two species are not at all related. This huge water animal lived in the lower Nile until the 12th century AD and, much earlier, in the Orontes river in Syria (and perhaps elsewhere in SW Asia) until after the time of Joseph, so it was well known in Bible lands. This passage is a difficult one, but several points in the RSV translation seem helpful. It is aquatic and powerful (vv. 21–23) and vegetarian (v. 15). 'The mountains yield food for him' (v. 20). It is true that hippos can climb steep slopes as they leave the water in search of food. This problem is discussed fully in Cansdale, pp. 100f.

Heb. *qippōd* is one of a number of difficult words applied to creatures of desolation, and it is found 3 times in connection with God's judgment on Babylon (Is. 14:23), Idumaea (Is. 34:11) and Nineveh (Zp. 2:14). Numerous alternatives have been suggested, such as bittern, heron, bustard, porcupine, hedgehog and lizard. Neither philology nor the context gives much help. Bittern and heron are marsh and water birds, and most unlikely, while the bustards are rarely seen in the region. Perhaps **HEDGEHOG** is the most probable. In Zp. 2:14 Nineveh was to become a waste and the city has actually been buried in sand, so it is literally possible for hedgehogs to 'lodge in her capitals'. Three kinds of hedgehog live in the region, two being desert or semi-desert forms, with one in the N of Palestine similar to the British species.

The **PORCUPINE** is still found in Israel, where it is by far the largest rodent, with a weight of some 20 kg. Nothing connects it with *qippōd* or any other Heb. word in the Bible.

Palestine is a land very rich in **BIRDS**. It has a great range of habitats, varying from semi-tropical to true desert; moreover, one of the main migration routes from Africa into Europe and W Asia runs from the N point of the Red Sea through the whole length of Israel. The resident birds therefore are augmented by numerous migrants, and there is some movement in progress in almost every month.

This wealth of bird life makes it difficult to identify with certainty some of the birds named in the Bible, and in some cases it is not possible to state whether the Heb. words refer to birds or other classes of animals. With the exception of 'hawk', which is also mentioned in Jb. 39:26, the following birds are found only in the food lists of Lv. and Dt.: **SEA GULL** (*šaḥap̄*), **HAWK** (*nēṣ*), **NIGHT-HAWK** (*taḥmās*), **CORMORANT** (*šālāḵ*), **HOOPOE** (*dûḵîp̄eṯ*), **OSPREY** (*'ozniyyâ*) and **WATER HEN** (*tinšemeṯ*). These may not indicate even the major group to which each bird belongs, and Driver (1955) gives an interesting new list of translations.

Palestine is still rich in large birds of prey, and outside the main towns the traveller is likely to see some of them in the air almost every day.

Heb. *rāḥām* (Lv. 11:18; Dt. 14:17), 'gier eagle' (AV), 'vulture' (RSV), rendered by R. Young as 'parti-coloured vulture', is likely to be the Egyp. **VULTURE**, a conspicuous black-and-white bird frequently seen scavenging on garbage tips.

Among several birds of prey forbidden as food (Lv. 11:13) is the **OSSIFRAGE** or bone-breaker (Heb. *peres*). This accurately describes the **LAMMERGEIER** or **BEARDED VULTURE**, which drops bones from a height on to rocks in order to break them and get the marrow within.

Some true **EAGLES** are still found in, or travel through, Palestine: Heb. *nešer* is probably as much a generic term as the Eng. word 'eagle'. It could include all large birds of prey, and the many references, most of them figurative, give few clues to the species. Mi. 1:16, 'make yourselves as bald as the eagle', clearly suggests the **GRIFFON VULTURE**, whose pale down-covered head contrasts with the well-feathered heads of all eagles. Some authorities consider that in all cases *nešer* should be the griffon vulture, just as Gk. *aetos*, translated 'eagle' in Mt. 24:28 ('there the eagles will be gathered together'), should be so rendered. This clearly describes the flocking of vultures to a carcass.

Heb. *'ayyâ* (Jb. 28:7), *dā'â* (Lv. 11:14) and *dayyâ* (Dt. 14:13; Is. 34:15) is probably the **KITE**, of which both the black and the red species are common.

OWLS are referred to 8 times in the OT by 4 Heb. words. The translation is probably correct, and several different species may be intended.

Heb. *lîlîṯ* is found only in Is. 34:14 among several other much disputed names which together seem to signify a setting of desolation. It is thought to be a loan-word from the Assyr. female demon of the night, *lilitu*. The following translations have been suggested – screech owl (AV), night monster (AVmg., RV), night hag (RSV), nightjar (NEB), *Lilith (JB). According to rabbinical tradition it was a ghost in the form of a well-dressed woman which lay in wait at night. Israeli zoologists suggest 'tawny owl'. *lîlîṯ* may be a real animal, but in the absence of further evidence it must be left as 'unidentified'.

The **WHITE STORK** is one of the most striking migratory birds of Palestine, slowly travelling N, especially along the Jordan valley in March and April. Je. 8:7, 'the stork in the heavens knows her times', suggests *ḥᵃsîḏâ* may well be the stork, though it could refer to several other large birds, including the kite and heron.

The **CRANE** is a bird of similar build to the white stork and is also a migrant. It is thought that in Is. 38:14 and Je. 8:7 *'āḡûr* should be translated 'crane' and *sûs* 'swallow', from its note. Both are migrants as Je. 8:7 suggests. Another word, *dᵉrôr*, is translated **SWALLOW** in Ps. 84:3 and Pr. 26:2, and in the former it is implied that it nests within the temple buildings. This would be true of several species of swallow and also of the **SWIFT**, a bird of similar build and habits, but unrelated to the swallow. At least 4 species of swallow, 4 species of **MARTIN** and 3 species of swift occur in Palestine.

SPARROWS are associated with human habitations in many parts of the world, and the house sparrow so common in Palestine today is almost identical with the W European form. This could well have been the bird to which our Lord referred (Mt. 10:29, *etc.*), though Gk. *strouthion* implies assorted small birds such as were, and still are, killed and offered for sale in Palestine. In Ps. 84:3 Heb. *ṣippôr* is translated 'sparrow'; Ps. 102:7, 'a sparrow alone upon the house top' (AV) hardly suggests the sociable house sparrow, and it could refer to the **BLUE ROCK THRUSH**, a solitary bird which sometimes perches on houses.

The absence of any mention of the **DOMESTIC FOWL** from the OT is at first surprising, since there is some evidence that Assyria paid tribute to Egypt in the form of **HENS**, *c.* 1500 BC, and **COCKS** are shown on seals of the 7th century BC. However, Homer (*c.* 9th century BC) does not refer to hens, though he mentions **GEESE**. Some authorities consider that the fatted fowl of 1 Ki. 4:23 could be domestic fowls. The importation of **PEACOCKS** (1 Ki. 10:22), if this translation is correct, suggests that Solomon had traffic with Ceylon or India, the original home of the domestic fowl, and he could therefore have introduced them.

The only mention of the hen in the NT is in Mt. 23:37 and Lk. 13:34, where in one of our Lord's most poignant similes it is obvious that Gk. *ornis* is the domestic hen. The cock (*alektōr*) is mentioned in two incidents. In Mk. 13:35 Jesus mentioned the four night-watches, including 'at cockcrow' (midnight to 3 a.m. by Roman reckoning). The crowing of the cock was thought to take place at set times, and in many countries the domestic cock was regarded as an alarm clock, but it would be unwise to read any specific hours into the incident of Peter and the cock-crowing, Mt. 26:74–75, *etc*. See W. L. Lane, *The Gospel according to Mark*, *NIC*, 1974, p. 512, n. 69, and p. 543, for some remarkable observations on the conscientious time-keeping of cocks in Jerusalem.

The **PEACOCK** is native to the jungles of the Indo-Malayan region. There is no independent evidence to confirm the identification *tukkiyyim*; it is suggested that this word is derived from the Tamil *tokai*, but this means 'tail' and is not now known to refer to the peacock itself. This splendid bird had reached Athens by 450 BC, and had been kept on the island of Samos earlier still.

The **QUAIL**, almost the smallest of the game birds, features in only one incident, Ex. 16:13, *etc.*, 'In the evening quails (*śᵉlāw*) came up and covered the camp'. There has been speculation as to the correct translation, but the quail fits better than any other. Ps. 78:27, 'winged birds', confirms that *śᵉlāw* were birds; they also belonged to one of the few groups regarded as clean. Quails are migrants, and at certain seasons travel in large flocks a metre or two above the ground. Their migrations take them across the route followed after the Exodus.

The only other gallinaceous bird identifiable is the **PARTRIDGE**: 1 Sa. 26:20, 'like one who hunts a partridge in the mountains'. Heb. *qôrē'* is the rock partridge (*Alectoris graeca*), which is hunted regularly in many parts of the Middle East and SE Europe. It is similar to the red-legged partridge (*A. rufa*) of SW Europe. The significance of the proverb in Je. 17:11 is not clear.

Two members of the **CROW** family can be seen very frequently in Palestine – the **RAVEN** and the hooded crow. Heb. *'ôrēḇ* and Gk. *korax* are analagous to the Eng. 'crow' in that they probably refer primarily to the raven but are also used of crows as a whole. Both raven and hooded crow are similar in appearance and habits to the British birds.

The **OSTRICH** finds mention in several passages, but the general view is that *baṯ ya'ᵃnâ* should be 'ostrich' and not 'owl' (AV) in 8 passages. Jb. 39:13–18 is clearly a description of the ostrich, a bird which once lived in the Middle East. Heb. *yᵉ'ēnîm* is also translated 'ostriches' in La. 4:3, but a bird such as an ostrich may well have several native names.

'A **PELICAN** of the wilderness' (Ps. 102:6) (most EVV except RSV, 'vulture') has been thought a contradiction, but *wilderness does not always connote desert. A swamp could also be described in this way, and the drained swamps of the N Jordan valley are still visited by flocks of white pelicans passing on migration.

Several species of **DOVES** and **PIGEONS** are found in Palestine, and there is some confusion of names (so the Eng. wood-pigeon is also known as ring-dove). Heb. *yônâ* is usually translated 'dove', but in the sacrificial passages of Lv. and Nu. it is always translated '(young) pigeon'. In the same verses is the *tôr*, turtle or turtle dove; this has the scientific generic name *Turtur*, from its call, and this can be identified with both the common turtle dove and the collared turtle dove, mostly the latter, which has long been domesticated with the name Barbary dove. Heb. *yônâ* is therefore the rock dove (*Columba livia*), which was domesticated in antiquity and has been used widely as a source of food and for message-carrying.

Speckled bird (*ṣāḇûa'*), Je. 12:9, is considered by many authorities to be better rendered **'HYENA'**.

BIBLIOGRAPHY. G. R. Driver, 'Birds in the Old Testament', *PEQ* 86, 1954, pp. 5ff.; 87, 1955, pp. 129ff.; 'Once Again, Birds in the Bible', *PEQ* 90, 1958, pp. 56ff.; G. S. Cansdale, *Animals of Bible Lands*, 1970, chs. 10–15.

LIZARDS are by far the most conspicuous reptiles in Palestine, with some 40 species, and they are the only reptiles that the traveller can be sure of seeing. The two most obvious are the **AGAMA** or **RAINBOW LIZARD**, which frequents roadsides and the vicinity of humans; it is easily recognized by its habit of doing 'press-ups'; and the **ROCK GECKO** that often basks on boulders in the early morning. Mention of lizards may therefore be expected and there are, in fact, 6 Heb. words that EVV generally translate lizard. Each occurs only in the food list of Lv. 11:29f., with no help from the context other than that they are unclean; this suggests that they are carnivorous but any identification is largely conjecture, from slender philological evidence and tradition, that this is a series of reptiles.

1. *ṣāḇ*. Tortoise (AV) is incorrect. RV, RSV translate 'great lizard', a non-specific name. Tradition identifies this with the spiny-tailed lizards, reaching some 50 cm. Arab. *dhubb* or *dhabb* may be sufficiently alike to give some confirmation.

2. *'ᵃnāqâ*. Ferret (AV) is not correct. **GECKO** (RV, RSV) is more probable.

3. *kōaḥ*. Chameleon (AV) and land crocodile (RV, RSV). The latter expression is meaningless but was once applied to the desert monitor, the largest lizard of the region.

4. *lᵉṭā'â*. Lizard (most EVV). Perhaps lizards of the *Lacertid* family.

5. *ḥōmeṭ*. Snail (AV) is not correct. RV, RSV translate 'sand lizard'. Perhaps the fast, streamlined **SKINKS** so typical of sandy areas.

6. *tinšemeṯ* is very difficult. Mole (AV) is not correct. RV, RSV translate chameleon.

In addition *śᵉmāmîṯ* (Pr. 30:28) is translated spider (AV) or lizard (RV, RSV). This could well be a **GECKO**, or house lizard; several species, some of which live on and inside buildings, are found in Palestine. The specially modified feet allow them to cling to smooth walls and even ceilings.

One of the geckos, *Ptyodactylus hasselquisti*, was called *abubrais* (Arab.), 'father of leprosy', perhaps because of its fleshy colour, perhaps because of (incorrectly) supposed poisonous qualities. The **CHAMELEON** is small (up to 15 cm) and rather uncommon, living in the more wooded areas of Palestine. Its colour, shape and habits make it inconspicuous and one would not expect it to feature in the food lists.

Several species of **TORTOISE** are found in the Middle East. The tortoise could be the *ṣāḇ* (AV) in Lv. 11:29, for it is a reptile that would be seen from time to time, but other authorities translate 'lizard' and the identity must be considered doubtful. Tortoises were known in ancient Assyria, whence a curse runs, 'May you be turned upside down like a tortoise (and die)' (*Iraq* 20, 1958, p. 76).

The words ***SERPENT** and **SNAKE** are of roughly equal age: snake has always had a specific meaning, a member of the sub-order of reptiles known as *Ophidia*, but serpent, while having been popularly used for snake, also had a wide application, including many mythical creatures. Although serpent is obsolescent it is retained generally by modern EVV, even in literal passages. NEB and JB use both snake and serpent.

Three Heb. words are translated serpent (RSV) of which *nāḥāš* occurs most often and is a general word, probably including other creeping reptiles also. The Heb. word translated 'divination' *etc.* is from the same root – to foretell by observing serpents. The first mention of *nāḥāš* is in Gn. 3:1, introducing the fall of man. *śārāp̄* is a common root usually translated fiery or burning; in Nu. 21:6 it qualifies *nāḥāš* and is translated fiery serpent, but stands alone in vv. 8 and 9 for the bronze serpent cast by Moses. It is translated flying serpent in Is. 14:29; 30:6. *tannîn*, usually translated dragon, is translated serpent only in the incident of Aaron's rod (Ex. 7:9ff.).

Gk. *ophis*, specific for snake, is found 14 times in a variety of NT contexts, including the reference to the serpent in the wilderness (Jn. 3:14) and the serpent of Gn. 3 (Rev. 12:9).

Snakes are found in all habitats from desert to

closed woodland and marsh, with a wide range of species, some under 30 cm while others may reach 2 m. Most are harmless; about 6 species are potentially lethal, but only a low percentage of bites prove fatal if given any treatment. All feed only on animals, from insects to mammals, which they swallow whole with no chewing. They can pass long periods, sometimes over one year, without food but need water more often.

Snakes are today widely regarded with terror and are a common object of phobias. This has probably always been true. One cannot expect snakes to be clearly identified in the Bible or their habits described, but contexts and roots sometimes allow deductions to be made.

Heb. *peṯen* must represent a poisonous species. It occurs 6 times and while most EVV, including RSV, translate adder and asp, NEB has cobra twice and asp 4 times. There is general agreement that **COBRA** is correct, since the bite of the **ASP** (now obsolete) was used in Egypt to commit suicide; a cobra's neurotoxic venom would usually cause a quick death. Is. 11:8 speaks of the 'hole of the asp'; cobras typically live in holes. Snake-charming is clearly mentioned in Ps. 58:4–5, 'the voice of charmers', referring to *peṯen*; cobras are traditionally used for this purpose.

The figurative importance of the fiery serpent is emphasized by our Lord's reference to it in Jn. 3:14. The context of Nu. 21, where both *nāḥāš* and *śārāp̄* are used, allows some deductions, and 4 facts suggest the **CARPET VIPER** *Echis*. It is notorious for striking without provocation, which is rare in snakes; its venom is largely haemolytic, causing death after several days; it is more active by day than other desert vipers; in parts of Asia and Africa it is known to become very numerous over limited areas. When the Israelites cried for help God told Moses to cast a serpent in bronze and put it on a pole so that those who looked in faith would live. It seems that the brazen serpent, or a copy of it, later became a focus for heathen worship, so that Hezekiah destroyed it in his reformation (2 Ki. 18:4). There is evidence of a snake-cult in early Palestine and a direct statement in Wisdom 11:15 that they worshipped 'irrational serpents'. A flat relief stela of the serpent goddess was found at Beit Mirsin. A bronze snake, *c.* 15th century BC, from Gezer has the expanded neck of a cobra and there are many examples of jars and incense vessels with relief patterns of snakes. It is likely that snakes were among 'all kinds of creeping things' worshipped by the Jerusalem elders (Ezk. 8:10).

Five futher Heb. words are translated **ADDER** and **VIPER**. *ṣip̄'ônî* (Pr. 23:32) translated adder (RSV), adder, asp, basilisk (RV), is found only in figurative passages from which little can be inferred; but in Je. 8:17 'adders which cannot be charmed' suggest **DESERT VIPERS**. *ṣep̄a'* (Is. 14:29) was earlier translated cockatrice (AV) and basilisk (RV), both words indefinite and now obsolete; RSV now translates adder. *š^e^p̄îp̄ôn* is found only in Gn. 49:17, 'a viper by the path that bites the horses' heels'. (Arrowsnake *(*AVmg.*)* has no known meaning.)

The desert vipers *Cerastes cerastes* and *C. vipera* became the Egyp. hieroglyph for 'f' from the onomatopoeic *fy*, *fyt*; the above 3 names may be related to this. Tristram notes that *shiphon* is Arab. for the horned viper. Although the words adder and viper are nearly synonymous and refer to the Old World viperine snakes, adder first referred to snakes generally (a **NADDER** [OE] became an adder). Viper, derived from viviparous (live-bearing), was first used by Tyndale in the early 16th century.

Both *'ep̄'eh* and *'aḵšûḇ* are translated viper (RSV) in figurative passages. The former is identical with Arab. *afa'â*, used sometimes of snakes generally, sometimes of vipers. *'aḵšûḇ* is related to an Arab. root 'to coil itself', which describes a habit of the desert vipers.

Palestine's largest viper (*Vipera palestina*) is found over much of the country except the desert; it cannot be identified with any of the above but it is common in Galilee and Judaea and could be the species to which Gk. *echidna* largely refers. Four of its 5 mentions are to a 'brood of vipers' used by Christ and John the Baptist of the Pharisees. This is apt, for these vipers bear live young in batches. The fifth mention is the only literal one, in Acts 28:3; the snake which bit Paul is traditionally held to be the common viper, which is still found on Sicily and other islands, though not on Malta.

For further details on biology and distribution see Cansdale, pp. 202–210.

The word **CROCODILE** is not found in any EV other than RSVmg. where it translates leviathan (Jb. 41:1) and though this passage is wholly figurative there are several points suggesting crocodile is correct: *e.g.* vv. 13 and 15, 'Who can penetrate his double coat of mail? . . . his back is made of rows of shields.' The precise setting of Job is uncertain but it is likely to have been somewhere around the E Mediterranean. In biblical times the Nile crocodile was found from source to mouth of the Nile. While its distribution N of Egypt in that period is unknown, returning Crusaders reported crocodiles in the Zerka river, which runs into the Mediterranean near Caesarea and is still known locally as the Crocodile river. Crocodilians are eaten in various parts of the world and though they cannot be identified in the Mosaic food lists it is certain that their carnivorous habits would make them unclean.

Apart from one figurative use in Rev. 16:13 (Gk. *batrachos*), the word **FROG** (Heb. *ṣ^e^p̄ardēa'*) occurs only in connection with the second of God's plagues upon Egypt (Ex. 8:2ff.). Frogs belong to the class *Amphibia*, all members of which must pass their early stages in water. Several frogs, especially of the genus *Rana*, are common in the Nile valley, and more than one species could have been the *ṣ^e^p̄ardēa'* which caused this plague.

LOCUSTS are the most important biblical insects, with some 56 appearances under 9 Heb. names and one Gk. To the ancient Heb. the locust was primarily a destroyer but it was also a useful source of animal protein. Three suggestions for interpreting the Heb. names are:

1. They refer to different species. This cannot be wholly true, for only 3 species of true locust are involved – migratory, desert and Moroccan locusts.

2. They represent various colour phases and/or the stages through which locusts pass as they mature. The list in Joel 1:4 is sometimes taken to describe such a series.

3. These names are descriptive nicknames, for all with identifiable roots refer to one or other attribute of locusts. This is most likely, though (1) and (2) may be true in part.

Locusts, of the section *Saltatoria* (leapers) of the

order *Orthoptera*, were the only insects regarded as 'clean', described vividly as having 'legs above their feet, with which to leap on the earth' (Lv. 11:21). Locusts are, in fact, **GRASSHOPPERS** and 2 of the Heb. words may refer to species other than true locusts – *ḥāgāḇ*, from a root 'to hide', could have been a recognizable smaller species, for 3 of its 5 occurrences refer to smallness. *sol'ām*, from a root 'to swallow up or destroy', is sometimes translated 'bald locust' from old Talmudic statements that its head is smooth in front, which would well fit the *Tryxalinae*, a distinct family of grasshoppers.

The EVV handle these names so variously, especially in the food lists and Joel 1:4, that it is not useful to tabulate them. *'arḇeh* (24 times) is the general term, from a root 'to multiply', always used of the 8th plague and often considered to be specific for migratory locust. The other Heb. words are *ḥargōl*, incorrectly beetle (AV) and cricket (RSV), probably from root 'to run swiftly'; *gāzām*, from root 'to cut off'; *yeleq*, perhaps from root 'to lick or eat up'; *ḥāsîl*, from root 'to consume'; *ṣᵉlāṣal* from root 'to whir'; and *gôḇ*, literally 'a swarm'.

Locusts are typically highly gregarious but there is now evidence that they also have solitary phases and that swarming is probably a physiological response to conditions. Migrations follow no precise pattern and swarms are largely wind-driven, certainly over long distances ('the east wind had brought the locusts', Ex. 10:13). The biology of all species is roughly the same. The female lays packets of eggs just beneath the surface of the soil where they may stay for many months before moisture allows them to hatch. The locust does not pass through the 3 distinct stages of a typical insect; when the egg hatches, the larva has the general shape of the adult, but without wings, which it acquires gradually over the 5 or 6 moults. The young are often known as hoppers. Locusts are wholly vegetarian and exist in such numbers that disastrous damage is done to crops; in 1889 a desert locust swarm that crossed the Red Sea was reckoned to cover 5,000 sq. km.

There is no direct statement that the Israelites ate locusts, but the reference in the food lists implies it. Their potential food value in ancient times is often forgotten but there is much evidence in the literature for their wide use. Until recent years large numbers have been eaten by desert and other tribes and at some seasons it was probably a main source of protein, as well as of fat and minerals.

The locust was almost synonymous with 'destroyer' and a plague of locusts was often regarded as God's judgment; in 3 cases, apart from the 8th plague, locusts were sent or threatened by God as punishment.

ANTS, BEES and **WASPS** form the insect order *Hymenoptera* (membranous-winged), many of whose species have complex social organization. Numerous kinds are found in Palestine and of these the most important is the honey bee, for until the 18th century honey was the basic material for sweetening. The general name **BEE** is properly given today to several families of this order, including solitary and bumble bees as well as honey bees. Heb. *dᵉḇôrâ* could have covered an even larger range of insects, including bee-like flies, but it is clear from their contexts that 3 out of 4 OT occurrences refer to the honey bee (Jdg. 14:8; Ps. 118:12; Dt. 1:44). The fourth passage using this word is a figurative one – Is. 7:18, 'The Lord shall whistle ... for the bee that is in the land of Assyria.' This translation for *šāraq* is preferred to 'hiss' (AV). A tradition that the natives of Palestine called their bees by making a whistling or hissing sound suggests that *dᵉḇōrâ* here also refers to the honey bee.

The numerous references to *honey in OT and NT imply that its use was common and widespread. It is likely that much of the honey was produced by wild bees nesting in hollow trees or rocky holes, but from very early times bees have been encouraged to occupy simple hives of basket or earthenware.

All EVV translate Heb. *ṣir'â* as **HORNET**, which is a large colonial wasp with a very painful or even dangerous sting, still common in parts of Palestine, including the desert around the Dead Sea. All the mentions are in rather similar contexts, as Ex. 23:28, 'I will send hornets before you'. The reference could be literal, for there are records of hornets, and even bees, causing horses and cattle to panic and stampede. J. Garstang's suggestion (*Joshua–Judges*, 1931, pp. 112ff., 285ff.) that the hornet of Jos. 24:12, *etc*., represents the Egyptian empire in Canaan has not found much acceptance.

The **ANT** (Heb. *nᵉmālâ*) is mentioned only in Pr. 6:6 and 30:25. Ants vary widely in size and habits, but all are social, living in colonies of a dozen or so to hundreds of thousands. Many types of ants occur in Palestine, but the context clearly identifies this as the harvester ant, sometimes called the agricultural ant, which is about 6 mm long. Its colonies are common and conspicuous in many parts of Israel outside the actual desert. It collects seeds of many kinds, especially grasses, during spring and early summer and stores them in underground galleries, often after removing the husks and letting them blow away in the wind, which clearly indicates the nest entrance.

MOTH is the name given correctly to the larger section of the order *Lepidoptera* (scale-winged insects) which includes the most colourful and conspicuous insects. Palestine has many species of both butterfly and moth, but the only biblical reference is to the atypical clothes moth, Heb. *'āš* and Gk. *sēs* (Jb. 4:19; Lk. 12:33, *etc*.). The contexts all confirm identification of this pest, which is always associated with man and his goods. In countries with fairly high average temperatures for much of the year, where clothes were regarded as a form of wealth and therefore stored in quantity, damage by the larvae of these clothes moths could be serious. When the moths emerge the damage has already been done, for the adults do not feed.

FLEAS, belonging to a wingless insect order, have always been parasitic on man and his domestic stock and they are particularly numerous among nomadic peoples. Heb. *par'ōš* occurs only in 1 Sa. 24:14; 26:20. The metaphor is clear and the jumping habit of the flea confirms the translation. Although mostly known just as nuisances, fleas are also potential carriers of serious diseases, notably bubonic plague (see 'Mouse', above).

Although the word **FLY** is widely and loosely used it is strictly applied only to *Diptera*, a large insect order having only one pair of wings. The word occurs only twice in AV/RSV, each time translating Heb. *zᵉḇûḇ*, but nothing in the context of either allows more precise identification. In Is. 7:18 it is used figuratively, while Ec. 10:1 is the familiar proverb, 'Dead flies cause the ointment of the apothecary to send forth a stinking savour' (AV). A wide variety of insects, and not only true flies, might be attracted to embalmers' spices and unguents. Heb. *'ārōḇ* is translated 'swarms of flies' (Ex. 8:21ff.; Pss. 78:45; 105:31). These passages refer to the plague of flies in Egypt; many species have mass hatchings into profuse swarms that are dangerous or gravely inconvenient from sheer weight of numbers. These swarms could well have consisted of 'divers sorts of flies' (AV).

GNAT is an imprecise word given to several groups of small two-winged insects, similar to and sometimes including midges and mosquitoes. The only NT occurrence of Gk. *kōnōps* is in Mt. 23:24, which should be read as in RSV 'straining out a gnat'. (AV 'strain *at* a gnat' seems to be a printer's error.) This comment was based on the Pharisaic practice of drinking water through a straining cloth to avoid swallowing an insect regarded as unclean. Many small insects breed in and near water and their larval forms are common in stagnant water. *kōnōps* probably had as wide a meaning as the Eng. 'gnat'.

RSV prefers 'gnat' to 'louse' (Heb. *kinnām*) in Ex. 8:16–18, but the most probably translation is **TICK**. The louse is a wingless insect but the tick is an eight-legged arthropod more nearly related to spiders. Both are specialized blood-sucking parasites and vectors of dangerous human diseases. This problem is discussed in Cansdale, p. 229.

The **SCORPION** (Heb. *'aqrāḇ*; Gk. *skorpios*) is one of the arthropods that can be identified with certainty. Members of this order vary widely in size and toxicity; though the largest of the Palestine species is up to 15 cm, most of the 12 species are much smaller and none has a sting likely to be fatal under normal conditions. All have the typical scorpion shape – heavy pincers, 4 pairs of legs and a long up-turned tail ending in a sting. Scorpions are largely nocturnal, especially in desert country, spending the day hidden under stones or in holes and emerging at night to hunt the small animals on which they feed. Several mentions in the OT and NT are in proverbial form, *e.g.* 1 Ki. 12:11, 'I will chastise you with scorpions', possibly a reference to a many-tailed whip, loaded with hooked knobs of metal and known as a scorpion (*cf.* 1 Macc. 6:51; 'machines [Gk. *skorpidia*] to shoot arrows'). Our Lord vividly likens a scorpion to an egg in Lk. 11:12; the main segment of some scorpions is fat and almost egg-shaped.

Palestine has a large range of **SPIDERS**, another order of eight-legged arthropods, of which the web-spinners are clearly referred to in Jb. 8:14 and Is. 59:5–6 (Heb. *'akkāḇîš*). *śᵉmāmîṯ* also is translated 'spider' in Pr. 30:28, 'The spider taketh hold with her hands' (AV). A more likely translation is **GECKO**.

Finally, there is a series of names that refer to less easily identified invertebrates (animals without backbones). The context clearly confirms **SNAIL** as the translation for Heb. *šaḇlûl* 'as a snail which melteth' (AV), 'like the snail which dissolves into slime' (RSV), Ps. 58:8. Both translations reflect an ancient belief that in leaving a visible trail behind it the snail was gradually melting away. There is nothing to confirm 'snail' as the translation of Heb. *ḥōmeṭ* in the list of forbidden meats in Lv. 11:30. RSV renders it 'sand lizard' and there is general agreement in modern EVV that it is a **LIZARD** of some kind.

The word **WORM** is technically correct only for several phyla of invertebrate animals, but popular language uses it much more widely. Wire-worms and wood-worms are beetles; cut-worms are moth caterpillars; slow-worms are lizards, and so on. In ancient times and among less-developed peoples the usage is even more vague. Five Heb. words are translated 'worm' and in the popular sense this translation can be accepted. In most passages the use is solely figurative and more precise identification is difficult, but see Cansdale, pp. 235f., for discussion. There is no word for 'worms' in the Heb. text of the well-known passage in Jb. 19:16 and the AVmg. and RSV should be followed: 'after my skin has been destroyed'.

Found only in Pr. 30:15 the word 'horseleach' (AV), 'leech' (RSV), is a translation of Heb. *'ᵃlûqâ*, 'sucking'; but in most EVV there is mg. comment that the text is obscure. Two interpretations are found. 1. Most scholars, following AV, RSV, assume a reference to the **LEECH**, probably of some aquatic type such as the horse leech (*Limnatis nilotica*), still found in stagnant waters of Egypt and the Near East, which is a serious menace to men and animals when swallowed with drinking-water. Leeches belong to the world-wide *Phylum Annelida*, or segmented worms. 2. Others, noting the similarity to the Arab. word *'alaqeh*, identify it with a female demon, perhaps a blood-sucking vampire (*cf.* RVmg.) which the Arabs call *'Alūq*; this latter cannot be accepted, for blood-sucking bats, the true vampires, are found only in Central and S America.

The phrase **CREEPING THINGS** is a non-specific term in EVV translating two Heb. words which are used particularly in the *creation narrative. The comments below refer mainly to AV. In RSV the translation of these two words is not uniform and in one case (1 Ki. 4:33) *šereṣ* is translated reptiles.

1. *remeś*, from the verb *rāmaś*, to creep, move', and having, with *rōmēś*, the participle of that verb, the meaning 'creeping or moving thing'. It is apparently applied to all animals in Gn. 9:3, but is sometimes used of sea (Gn. 1:21; Ps. 104:25) or land (Gn. 1:24–25; 6:20; 7:8, 14, 21, 23) creatures exclusively, and in 1 Ki. 4:33 and Ezk. 38:20 it is distinguished from beasts (*bᵉhēmâ*), fowls (*'ôp̄*) and fishes (*dāḡ*). Though some commentators have argued that in the creation account it refers to reptiles, it cannot correspond exactly to any modern scientific category, referring rather to all creatures moving close to the ground.

2. *šereṣ*, from the verb *šāraṣ*, 'to swarm, teem', and meaning 'swarming thing', translated in the AV as 'creeping thing' (Gn. 7:21; Lv. 5:2; 11:21, 23, 29, 41–44; 22:5; Dt. 14:19) and 'moving creature' (Gn. 1:20; *CREATION). It could be applied to water (Gn. 1:20; Lv. 11:10) and land (Gn. 8:21) creatures, and in Lv. 11:29 is specifically defined as including weasels, mice and lizards. In short, *šereṣ*, like *remeś*, seems to refer to creatures which appear to move close to the ground with a range of possibilities according to the context.

In NT Gk. *herpeton*, derived from *herpō*, 'to creep, crawl' (not in the Bible), and therefore meaning 'creeping thing', is used 4 times (Acts 10:12; 11:6; Rom. 1:23; Jas. 3:7), probably meaning 'reptile' in each case. In the LXX it is used chiefly as a translation for *remeś* and *šereṣ*.

BIBLIOGRAPHY. G. S. Cansdale, *Animals of Bible Lands*, 1970; F. E. Zeuner, *A History of Domesticated Animals*, 1963; *ABD*, *s.v.* G.S.C.

ANNA (Gk. form of Heb. *ḥannâ*, 'grace'). An aged widow, daughter of Phanuel, of the tribe of Asher (Lk. 2:36–38). Like Simeon, who also belonged to the remnant which 'waited for the consolation of Israel', she had prophetic insight, and was a regular attender at the morning and evening services in the Temple. On hearing Simeon's words at the presentation of Jesus, she commended the child as the long-awaited Messiah, and praised God for the fulfilment of his promises. J.D.D.

ANNAS. Annas or Ananos, son of Seth, was appointed high priest in AD 6 and deposed in AD 15. In the NT he is still referred to as high priest after AD 15. This may be for one of three reasons. First, though the Romans deposed high priests and appointed new ones, the Jews thought of the high priesthood as a life office. The Mishnah (*Horayoth* 3. 4) says: 'A high priest in office differs from the priest that is passed from his high priesthood only in the bullock that is offered on the Day of Atonement and the tenth of the ephah.' Secondly, the title 'high priest' is given in Acts and Josephus to members of the few priestly families from which most high priests were drawn, as well as to those exercising the high-priestly office. Thirdly, Annas had great personal influence with succeeding high priests. Five of his sons and Caiaphas his son-in-law became high priest. At the trial of Jesus we find Annas conducting a preliminary investigation before the official trial by Caiaphas (Jn. 18:13–24). When Lk. 3:2 says that the high priest was Annas and Caiaphas, the singular is probably deliberate, indicating that, though Caiaphas was the high priest officially appointed by Rome, his father-in-law shared his high-priestly power, both *de facto* by his personal influence and, according to strict Jewish thought, also *de jure* (*cf.* Acts 4:6). D.R.H.

ANNUNCIATION. The vision of Mary (Lk. 1:26–38) 'announces' the conception of a Messiah-Son and describes with poetic imagery Messiah's human (Lk. 1:32) and divine (Lk. 1:34f.) character and the eternal nature of his kingdom (Lk. 1:33). Machen and Daube give the most helpful treatment of the literary questions. See also *VIRGIN BIRTH, *INCARNATION.

BIBLIOGRAPHY. R. E. Brown, *The Birth of the Messiah*, 1977; D. Daube, *The New Testament and Rabbinic Judaism*, 1956; E. E. Ellis, *The Gospel of Luke*[2], 1974; J. G. Machen, *The Virgin Birth*, 1931; J. McHugh, *The Mother of Jesus in the New Testament*, 1975; *DCG*; *ODCC*. E.E.E.

ANOINTING, ANOINTED. Persons and things were anointed, in the OT, to signify holiness, or separation unto God: pillars (*cf.* Gn. 28:18); the tabernacle and its furniture (Ex. 30:22ff.); shields (2 Sa. 1:21; Is. 21:5: probably to consecrate them for the 'holy war', see Dt. 23:9ff.); kings (Jdg. 9:8; 2 Sa. 2:4; 1 Ki. 1:34); priests (Ex. 28:41); prophets (1 Ki. 19:16). The importance and solemnity of the anointing is shown, first, by the fact that it was an offence meriting excommunication to compound the holy oil for a common purpose (Ex. 30:32–33); secondly, by the authority which the anointing carried, such that, for example, while Jehu's fellow-commanders scorned the prophet as a 'madman', they did not dare resist the implications of his action, but accepted without question that he who was anointed as king must indeed be king (2 Ki. 9:11–13); thirdly, by the effect produced in the anointed, the person or thing becoming holy (Ex. 30:22–33) and sacrosanct (1 Sa. 24:7, *etc.*). Fundamentally the anointing was an act of God (1 Sa. 10:1), and the word 'anointed' was used metaphorically to mean the bestowal of divine favour (Pss. 23:5; 92:10) or appointment to a special place or function in the purpose of God (Ps. 105:15; Is. 45:1) (*MESSIAH). Further, the anointing symbolized equipment for service, and is associated with the outpouring of the Spirit of God (1 Sa. 10:1, 9; 16:13; Is. 61:1; Zc. 4:1–14). This usage is carried over into the NT (Acts 10:38; 1 Jn. 2:20, 27). The use of oil in anointing the sick (Jas. 5:14) is best understood thus, as pointing to the Holy Spirit, the Lifegiver. Or, on the OT model of setting aside kings by anointing, the oil may signify a separating off of the sickness from the patient to Christ (*cf.* Mt. 8:17).

BIBLIOGRAPHY. E. Kutsch, *Salbung als Rechtsakt im A.T.* (*ZAW* Beiheft 87), 1963; W. Brunotte, D. Müller, *NIDNTT* 1, pp. 119–124. J.A.M.

ANTICHRIST. The expression *antichristos* is found in the Bible only in the Johannine Epistles (1 Jn. 2:18, 22; 4:3; 2 Jn. 7), but the idea behind it is widespread. We should probably understand the force of *anti* as indicating opposition, rather than a false claim, *i.e.* the antichrist is one who opposes Christ rather than one who claims to be the Christ. If this is so, then we should include under the heading 'antichrist' such OT passages as Dn. 7:7f., 21f., and those in 2 Thes. 2 and Revelation which deal with the strong opposition that the forces of evil are to offer Christ in the last days.

The concept is introduced in John as already well known ('you have heard that antichrist is coming', 1 Jn. 2:18). But though he does not dispute the fact that at the end of this age there will appear an evil being, called 'antichrist', John insists that there is a temper, an attitude, characteristic of antichrist, and that already exists. Indeed, he can speak of 'many antichrists' as already in the world (1 Jn. 2:18). He gives something in the nature of a definition of antichrist when he says, 'This is the antichrist, he who denies the Father and the Son' (1 Jn. 2:22). This becomes a little more explicit when the criterion is made the refusal to acknowledge 'the coming of Jesus Christ in the flesh' (2 Jn. 7). For John it is basic that in Jesus Christ we see God acting for man's salvation (1 Jn. 4:9f.). When a man denies this he is not simply guilty of doctrinal error. He is undercutting the very foundation of the Christian faith. He is doing the work of Satan in opposing the things of God. At the end of the age this will characterize the work of the supreme embodiment of evil. And those who in a small way do the same thing now demonstrate by that very fact that they are his henchmen.

Paul does not use the term 'antichrist', but the 'man of lawlessness' of whom he writes in 2 Thes. 2:3ff. clearly refers to the same being. The characteristic of this individual is that he 'opposes and exalts himself against every so-called god or object of worship' (v. 4). He claims to be God (*ibid.*). He is not Satan, but his coming is 'by the activity of Satan' (v. 9). It cannot be said that all the difficulties of this passage have been cleared up, and, in particular, the identification of the man of lawlessness is still hotly debated. But for our present purpose the main points are clear enough. Paul thinks of the supreme effort of Satan as not in the past, but in the future. He does not think of the world as gradually evolving into a perfect state, but of evil as continuing right up till the last time. Then evil will make its greatest challenge to good, and this challenge will be led by the mysterious figure who owes his power to Satan, and who is the instrument of Satan's culminating challenge to the things of God. Paul is sure of the outcome. Christ will consume the man of lawlessness 'with the breath of his mouth' (v. 8). The last, supreme challenge of Satan will be defeated.

That is surely the meaning of some, at least, of the imagery of the book of Revelation. Biblical students are far from unanimous about the right way to interpret this book, but nearly all are agreed that some of the visions refer to the final struggle of the forces of evil with Christ. Sometimes the symbolism refers plainly to Satan. Thus the 'great red dragon' of Rev. 12:3 is expressly identified with Satan (v. 9). But the 'beast' of Rev. 11:7 is not. He is closely related to Satan, as his works show. Other similar figures appear (Rev. 13:11, *etc*.). It is not our purpose here to identify any particular one with the antichrist, but simply to point to the fact that this book too knows of one empowered by Satan who will oppose Christ in the last days. This may fairly be said to be characteristic of the Christian view of the last days.

BIBLIOGRAPHY. W. Bousset and A. H. Keane, *The Antichrist Legend*, 1896; art. 'Antichrist' in *EBi*; M. R. James, art. 'Man of Sin and Antichrist' in *HDB*; G. Vos, *The Pauline Eschatology*², 1961, pp. 94–135; *NIDNTT* 1, pp. 124–126; G. C. Berkouwer, *The Return of Christ*, 1972, pp. 260–290.

L.M.

ANTIOCH (PISIDIAN). This Asia Minor city located in Phrygia towards Pisidia, according to Strabo, was one of a number of Antiochs founded by a Macedonian cavalry leader, Seleucus I Nicator (312–280 BC), probably on the site of a Phrygian temple-village. Situated astride a main trading route between Ephesus and Cilicia, it became a prominent centre of Hellenism in the pre-Christian period. The Seleucids brought Jewish colonists into Phrygia for political and commercial reasons, and the more tolerant descendants of these settlers received Paul kindly on his first missionary journey (Acts 13:14). The Romans included Pisidian Antioch in the province of Galatia, and Augustus made it one of a series of Roman colonies in Pisidia.

In Phrygia, women enjoyed considerable prestige and sometimes occupied civic offices. Paul's enemies employed some of these to obtain his expulsion from Antioch (Acts 13:50). The ruined site is near Yalvaç in modern Turkey, and from that locality have come inscriptions, damaged stelae and other artifacts relating to the cult of the god Mên, which was prominent in Pisidian Antioch in the 1st century AD.

BIBLIOGRAPHY. B. Levick, *JHS* 91, 1971, pp. 80–84.

R.K.H.

ANTIOCH (SYRIAN). Antioch on the Orontes, now Antakya in SE Turkey, some 500 km N of Jerusalem, was founded *c.* 300 BC by Seleucus I Nicator after his victory over Antigonus at Issus (310 BC). It was the most famous of sixteen Antiochs established by Seleucus in honour of his father. Built at the foot of Mt Silpius, it overlooked the navigable river Orontes and boasted a fine seaport, Seleucia Pieria. While the populace of Antioch was always mixed, Josephus records that the Seleucids encouraged Jews to emigrate there in large numbers, and gave them full citizenship rights (*Ant*. 12. 119).

Antioch fell to Pompey in 64 BC, and he made it a free city. It became the capital of the Roman province of Syria, and was the third largest city of the empire. The Seleucids and Romans erected magnificent temples and other buildings.

Even under the Seleucids the inhabitants had gained a reputation for energy, insolence and instability, which manifested itself in a series of revolts against Roman rule. Nevertheless, Antioch was renowned for its culture, being commended in this respect by no less a person than Cicero (*Pro Archia* 4). Close by the city were the renowned groves of Daphne, and a sanctuary dedicated to Apollo, where orgiastic rites were celebrated in the name of religion. Despite the bad moral tone, life in Antioch at the beginning of the Christian era was rich and varied.

Apart from Jerusalem itself, no other city was so intimately connected with the beginnings of Christianity. Nicolas, one of the seven 'deacons' of Acts 6:5, was of Antioch, and had been a Gentile convert to Judaism. During the persecution which followed the death of Stephen, some of the disciples went as far north as Antioch (Acts 11:19), and preached to the Jews. Later arrivals also took Christianity to the Greek populace, and when numerous conversions occurred the Jerusalem church sent Barnabas to Antioch. When he had assessed the situation he went to Tarsus and brought Saul back with him, and both of them taught in Antioch for a whole year. The disciples were first called 'Christians' there (Acts 11:26).

The energetic nature of the Christians in Antioch was displayed in the way in which alms were sent to the mother church in Jerusalem when famine struck (Acts 11:27–30). It was fitting that the city in which the first Gentile church was founded, and where the Christians were given, perhaps sarcastically, their characteristic name, should be the birthplace of Christian foreign missions (Acts 13:1–3). Paul and Barnabas set out from the seaport of Antioch and sailed for Cyprus. This first journey into Asia Minor concluded when Paul and Barnabas returned to Antioch and reported to the assembled church.

Some of the refugees from the persecution over Stephen had taken the lead in preaching at Antioch to Gentiles equally with Jews (Acts 11:20). The Gentile problem came to a head when some Jews visited Antioch and proclaimed the necessity of circumcision for Gentiles as a prerequisite to becoming Christians. Resisting this principle, the church at Antioch sent a deputation headed by Paul and Barnabas to Jerusalem to debate the matter (Acts 15:1–2).

With James presiding, the question of whether or not circumcision was to be obligatory for Gentile Christians was thoroughly discussed. Peter had already encountered the difficulties involved in the relationships between Jews and Gentiles at other than commercial levels (Acts 10:28). Although ap-

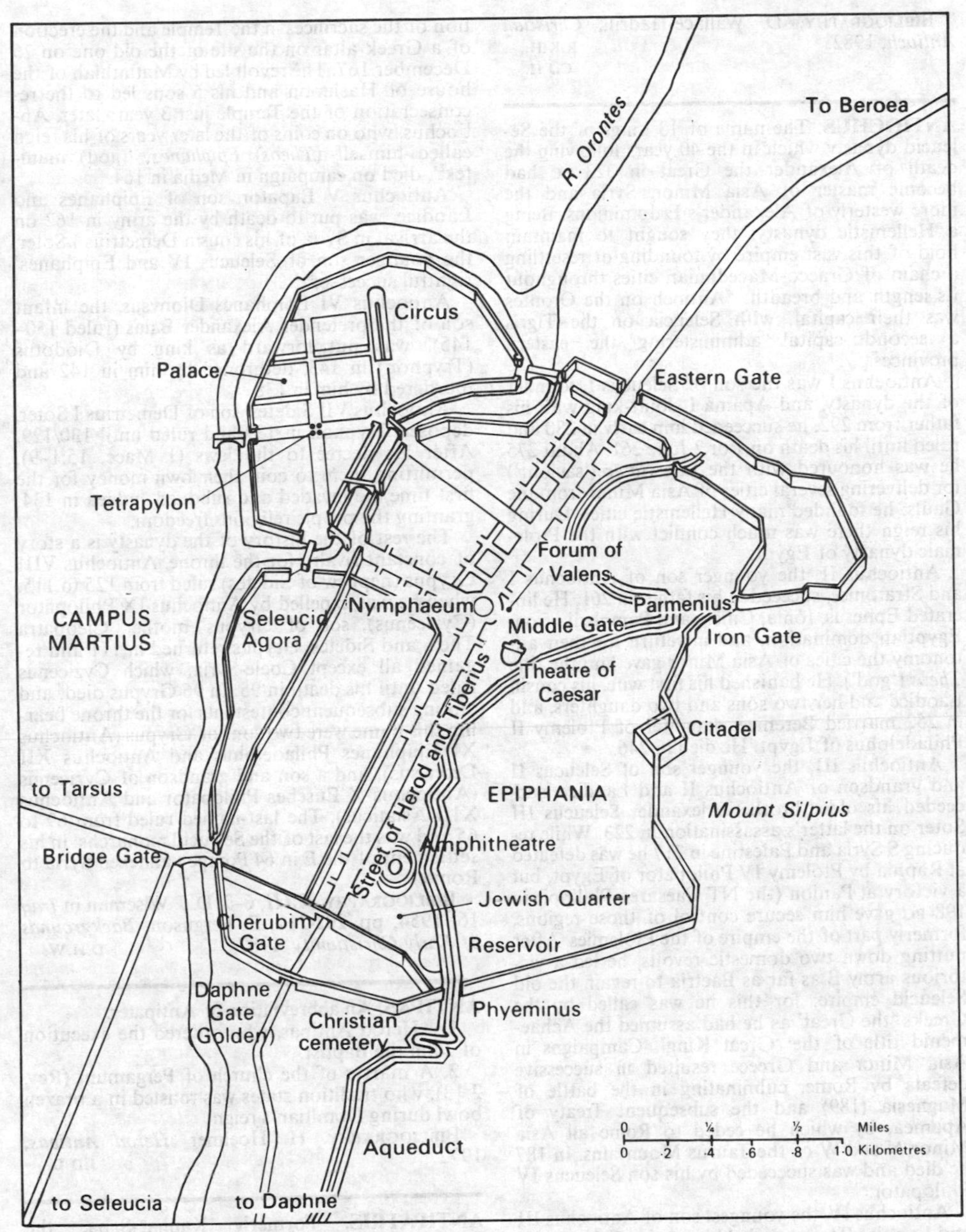

Plan of the city of Antioch in the 1st cent. AD.

pouring favourable to such contacts, he had been censured by the Jerusalem church for eating in uncircumcised company (Acts 11:3; *cf.* Gal. 2:12). He now acknowledged that God had not differentiated between Jew and Gentile after Pentecost.

After Paul had related the blessings which the Gentiles had received, James gave his opinion that abstinence from blood, things strangled, idolatry and immorality should alone be required of Gentile converts. These provisions were written into the apostolic letter to the churches of Antioch and its province. Paul returned to Antioch as the recognized apostle to the uncircumcision (Acts 15:22–26).

There is good reason for the view that *Galatians was written on the eve of this Jerusalem Council, possibly from Antioch. It appears that the Council settled in principle the contentions for which Paul had to battle in Galatians.

Paul began and ended his second missionary journey at Antioch. This notable city saw also the start of his third missionary visitation. Its evangelistic zeal afforded Antioch great status in the subsequent history of the church. Archaeological excavations at the site have unearthed over twenty ruined churches dating from the 4th century AD.

BIBLIOGRAPHY. D. Wallace-Hadrill, *Christian Antioch*, 1982. R.K.H. C.J.H.

ANTIOCHUS. The name of 13 kings of the Seleucid dynasty which in the 40 years following the death of Alexander the Great in 323 BC had become master of Asia Minor, Syria and the more westerly of Alexander's E dominions. Being a Hellenistic dynasty, they sought to maintain hold of this vast empire by founding or resettling a chain of Graeco-Macedonian cities throughout its length and breadth. *Antioch on the Orontes was their capital, with Seleucia on the Tigris a second capital administering the eastern provinces.

Antiochus I was the son of Seleucus I, founder of the dynasty, and Apama I. Joint-king with his father from 292, he succeeded him early in 280 and ruled until his death on 1 or 2 June 261. About 275 he was honoured with the title *Sōtēr* ('saviour') for delivering several cities of Asia Minor from the Gauls: he founded many Hellenistic cities. During his reign there was much conflict with the Ptolemaic dynasty of Egypt.

Antiochus II, the younger son of Antiochus I and Stratonice, succeeded his father in 261. He liberated Ephesus, Ionia, Cilicia and Pamphylia from Egyptian domination, and in return for their autonomy the cities of Asia Minor gave him the title *Theos* ('god'). He banished his first wife, his cousin Laodice and her two sons and two daughters, and in 252 married Berenice, daughter of Ptolemy II Philadelphus of Egypt. He died in 246.

Antiochus III, the younger son of Seleucus II and grandson of Antiochus II and Laodice, succeeded his older brother Alexander Seleucus III Soter on the latter's assassination in 223. While reducing S Syria and Palestine in 217 he was defeated at Raphia by Ptolemy IV Philopator of Egypt, but a victory at Panion (the NT Caesarea Philippi) in 198 BC gave him secure control of those regions, formerly part of the empire of the Ptolemies. After putting down two domestic revolts, he led a victorious army E as far as Bactria to regain the old Seleucid empire: for this he was called by the Greeks 'the Great' as he had assumed the Achaemenid title of the 'Great King'. Campaigns in Asia Minor and Greece resulted in successive defeats by Rome, culminating in the battle of Magnesia (189) and the subsequent Treaty of Apamea, by which he ceded to Rome all Asia Minor N and W of the Taurus Mountains. In 187 he died and was succeeded by his son Seleucus IV Philopator.

Antiochus IV, the youngest son of Antiochus III and Laodice III, succeeded his brother Seleucus IV in 175. Until 170/169 he reigned with his nephew Antiochus, Seleucus' baby son, who was murdered in Antiochus' absence by Andronicus, who arranged also the assassination of Onias III, the illegally deposed high priest, and was himself rewarded with execution (2 Macc. 4:32-38). During his reign there was much intrigue for the high priesthood on the part of Jason and Menelaus, and because of their misbehaviour Antiochus visited Jerusalem in 169 and insisted on entering the holy of holies, and carried off some of the gold and silver vessels. Pressure from Egypt convinced him of the necessity to hellenize Palestine, and measures against the old religion resulted in the cessation of the sacrifices in the Temple and the erection of a Greek altar on the site of the old one on 25 December 167. The revolt led by Mattathiah of the house of Hashmon and his 5 sons led to the reconsecration of the Temple just 3 years later. Antiochus, who on coins of the later years of his reign called himself (*Theos*) *Epiphanēs*, '(god) manifest', died on campaign in Media in 164.

Antiochus V Eupator, son of Epiphanes and Laodice, was put to death by the army in 162 on the arrival in Syria of his cousin Demetrius I Soter, the younger son of Seleucus IV and Epiphanes' rightful successor.

Antiochus VI Epiphanes Dionysus, the infant son of the pretender Alexander Balas (ruled 150–145), was put forward as king by Diodotus (Tryphon) in 143, dethroned by him in 142 and murdered by him in 138.

Antiochus VII Sidetes, son of Demetrius I Soter, deposed Tryphon in 139 and ruled until 130/129. After his decree to the Jews (1 Macc. 15:1–9), permitting them to coin their own money for the first time, he invaded and subdued Judaea in 134, granting the people religious freedom.

The rest of the history of the dynasty is a story of constant rivalry for the throne. Antiochus VIII Grypus (nephew of Sidetes) ruled from 125 to 115, when he was expelled by Antiochus IX Philopator (Cyzicenus), son of Grypus' mother, Cleopatra Thea, and Sidetes. Grypus returned in 111 and regained all except Coele-Syria, which Cyzicenus ruled until his death in 95. In 96 Grypus died, and among subsequent contestants for the throne bearing this name were two sons of Grypus (Antiochus XI Epiphanes Philadelphus and Antiochus XII Dionysus), and a son and grandson of Cyzicenus (Antiochus X Eusebes Philopator and Antiochus XIII Asiaticus). The last-named ruled from 69 to 65 and was the last of the Seleucid monarchs: in his settlement of the E in 64 Pompey annexed Syria to Rome.

BIBLIOGRAPHY. *CAH*, 6–9; D. J. Wiseman in *Iraq* 16, 1954, pp. 202-211; E. Ferguson, *Backgrounds of Early Christianity*, 1987. D.H.W.

ANTIPAS. An abbreviation of Antipater.

1. *Herod Antipas, who ordered the execution of John the Baptist.

2. A martyr of the church of Pergamum (Rev. 2:13), who tradition states was roasted in a brazen bowl during Domitian's reign.

BIBLIOGRAPHY. H. Hoehner, *Herod Antipas*, 1972. J.D.D.

ANTIPATRIS. Formerly Kaphar-Saba, the modern Ras el-Ain, this city, about 42 km S of Caesarea on the road to Lydda, was rebuilt by Herod the Great in memory of his father Antipater (Josephus, *Ant.* 16. 143; *BJ* 1. 417). Paul was taken there on his way from Jerusalem to Caesarea (Acts 23:31). Vespasian occupied it in AD 68 (*BJ* 4. 443). Codex Sinaiticus reads *Antipatris* instead of *patris* (home-country) in Mt. 13:54, with *anti-* subsequently crossed out. (*APHEK.) D.H.W.

APELLES. Greeted by Paul as a tried Christian (Rom. 16:10). Lightfoot (*Philippians*, p. 174) found the name – which was often adopted by Jews (*cf.* Horace, *Sat.* 1. 5. 100) – in Imperial household circles: Lagrange *in loc.* notes the sculptured contemporary Apelles in *CIL*, VI, 9183, just possibly Christian. Some MSS have 'Apelles' for 'Apollos' at Acts 18:24; 19:1, perhaps through Origen's guess that they may have been identical. A.F.W.

APHEK, APHEKAH (Heb. *ʼăpēq(â)*, 'fortress'). Name of several places in Palestine. **1.** Jos. 13:4. Defining the land remaining to be occupied to the N. Probably Afqa, NE of Beirut at the source of Nahr Ibrahim (*BDB*; Abel, *Géographie de la Palestine*, p. 247; *LOB*, p. 217). A different view places it at *Ras el-ʻAin (*cf. GTT*, p. 110).

2. Jos. 12:18; 1 Sa. 4:1; 29:1. Later *Antipatris, now Ras el-Ain, Heb. Tel Afeq, at the source of Nahr el-Auga (Jarkon, Jos. 19:46) on the trunk road to Egypt. Listed by Tuthmosis III, Amenophis II, Ramesses II and III, probably the Execration Texts. Esarhaddon mentions '*Apku* in the territory of Samaria', and it occurs in the Aramaic letter of Adon, *c.* 600 BC (see *ANET*, 242, 246, 292, 329). Excavations by Tel Aviv University since 1972 have found important Late Bronze Age and Philistine remains (*NEAEHL*, pp. 87–89).

3. Jos. 19:30; Jdg. 1:31 (Aphik). In Asher, modern Tell Kurdaneh, Heb. Tel Afeq, at the source of Nahr Na'amein which flows into the Bay of Haifa.

4. 1 Ki. 20:26, 30; 2 Ki. 13:17. Fīq or Afīq at the head of Wadi Fīq, E of the sea of Galilee may preserve the name, the place being 'En-Gev, a tell on the shore (*LOB*, p. 304, n. 60).

5. Jos. 15:53 (Aphekah). SW of Hebron, either Khirbet ed-ḍarrame (A. Alt, *Palästinajahrbuch*, 28, pp. 16f.) or Khirbet Kana'an (Abel, *op. cit.*, p. 247). A.R.M.

APOCALYPTIC. The word designates both a genre of literature (the Jewish and Christian apocalypses) and also the characteristic ideas of this literature. Within the Canon apocalyptic is represented especially by the books of *Daniel and *Revelation, but there are many other apocalypses from the intertestamental and early Christian periods.

Already within the OT prophetic books there are passages which must be classified as apocalyptic in some respects at least. Apocalyptic *eschatology can be found especially in Is. 24–27; 56–66; Joel; Zc. 9–14. In these passages the eschatological future is envisaged in terms of direct divine intervention, a universal judgment of the nations and a new age of salvation, in which the cosmos will be radically transformed. This transcendent eschatology is the central core of apocalyptic belief. The apocalyptic doctrine of the resurrection of the dead is also probably found already in Is. 26:19, as well as in Dn. 12:2. The literary forms of the apocalypse, however, are anticipated especially in the visions of Ezekiel and Zc. 1–6.

It was after the cessation of prophecy that apocalyptic flourished as a literature distinct from prophecy. Its first great flowering was in the mid-2nd-century crisis of Jewish faith under Antiochus Epiphanes, when apocalyptic was the literary vehicle of the Hasidic movement, which stood for national repentance, uncompromising opposition to hellenization and eschatological faith in God's imminent intervention on behalf of his people. Thereafter apocalyptic probably characterized various groups within Judaism, including Essenes, Pharisees, Zealots, Jewish Christians. (The *variety* of the apocalyptic literature should be remembered whenever generalizations about apocalyptic are attempted.) Apocalyptic flourished especially in times of national crisis, and the last great Jewish eschatological apocalypses come from the period between the fall of Jerusalem in AD 70 and the failure of Bar Kokhba's revolt.

The most important post-canonical Jewish apocalypses are: *1 Enoch, a collection of writings of which the earliest may date from the 5th century BC and the latest from the 1st century AD; *The Testament of Moses* (also called *Assumption of Moses*), which should be dated either *c.* 165 BC or early 1st century AD; *4 Ezra* (or *2 Esdras*, in the English Apocrypha), *2 Baruch* and the *Apocalypse of Abraham*, all from the period AD 70–140. The Jewish *Sibylline Oracles* contain apocalyptic material cast in the style of the pagan oracles of the Sibyls. Other works, such as *Jubilees and *The Testaments of the Twelve Patriarchs*, contain apocalyptic passages, and some new apocalyptic texts have been found at Qumran.

The apocalypses just listed are largely eschatological in content, continuing, in some sense, the tradition of OT prophecy. They reveal (Gk. *apokalyptō*) the secrets of God's plans for history and for his coming triumph at the end of history. But the apocalyptic literature also includes a tradition of *cosmological apocalyptic*, which reveals the mysteries of the cosmos. This tradition has its origin in parts of *1 Enoch*, where Enoch is taken by angels on journeys through the heavens and the realms of the dead. Cosmology really comes into its own in hellenistic apocalypses of the Christian era, such as *2 Enoch* and *3 Baruch*, where the eschatological hope has largely faded. In the rest of this article we confine our attention to *eschatological* apocalyptic.

In *literary* terms, apocalyptic is a highly stylized form of literature, with its own conventions of symbolism and terminology, continually feeding on OT sources. It is a literature of dreams and visions, often centred on a vision of the heavenly throne-room. Eschatological prophecy may take the form of long discourses or of symbolic imagery, which is sometimes very artificial, sometimes vivid and effective. Probably the apocalyptists never intended to depict the End in literal terms. In their attempt to portray a future salvation which transcends ordinary historical experience, they seem to have borrowed symbols from Canaanite myth and from the mythology they encountered in the Eastern Diaspora and in hellenistic Palestine. Apocalyptic literature often exhibits a close but critical interaction with the international culture of its time.

If Jewish apocalyptic was often indebted for its imagery and forms to its non-Jewish environment, its eschatological content derived from OT prophecy. In this respect apocalyptic was the *heir of prophecy*. Its role was to reassert the prophetic promises for the future in their relevance to the apocalyptist's own generation. The apocalyptists were not themselves prophets. They lived in an age when prophecy had ceased, and probably for that reason they adopted the device of *pseudonymity*, writing under the name of an OT saint from the period of prophetic revelation. This need not be regarded as a fraudulent device, as though they wished to pass off their work as belonging to the age of prophecy; rather it should be seen as a literary form expressing the apocalyptists' role as interpreters of the revelation given in the prophetic age.

From this fictional standpoint in the past, the apocalyptists often give reviews of history up to their own time in the form of predictive prophecy. Again, this device need not be intended to deceive. It is the apocalyptist's means of penetrating the divine plan of history and presenting an interpretation of the prophecies of the past, which he rewrites in the light of their fulfilment in order to show how they have been fulfilled and what still remains to be fulfilled.

The apocalyptists, then, are interpreters of OT prophecy. This does not mean they do not claim inspiration. There is good reason to think that the visionary experiences attributed to the pseudonym often reflect the real experience of the apocalyptist himself. The apocalyptist's inspiration, however, was the source not so much of fresh prophetic revelation as of interpretation of the revelation already given through the prophets. The authority of his message is thus derivative from that of the prophets.

If this view of the apocalyptists' self-understanding is adopted, it will be seen that they occupy an essentially *intertestamental* position. They interpret the prophets to an age when prophecy has ceased but fulfilment is still awaited. Their exclusion from the Canon is not therefore a negative judgment on their value for the intertestamental development of Jewish religion. On the contrary, by sustaining and intensifying the eschatological hope they played a decisively important role as a bridge between the Testaments.

The apocalyptic understanding of *history and eschatology* developed in the context of the post-exilic experience of history, in which Israel remained under the domination of the Gentile powers and the prophetic promises of glorious restoration remained largely unfulfilled. In the extended period of contradiction between God's promises and the reality of Israel's historical experience, the apocalyptists sought to assure the faithful that God had not abandoned his people, that the promised salvation was coming. To this end they stressed the divine *sovereignty over history*: God has predetermined the whole course of world history and the End will come at the time he has appointed. The power of the pagan empires survives only so long as he permits. This strongly deterministic view of history does not, however, become a fatalism which contradicts human freedom and responsibility, for the apocalyptists also call their readers to repentance and intercession and ethical action. Only rarely do they venture to set a date for the End.

The coming eschatological salvation is envisaged in transcendent and universal terms. It is an event which far transcends the great events of the salvation-history of the past. It amounts to a new creation, in which all forms of evil and suffering will be eliminated. It is characteristic of the apocalyptists to believe that even death will be conquered: this belief appears in the form both of bodily resurrection and of spiritual immortality. The eschatological age will be the kingdom of God, replacing all earthly empires for ever. Expectations of the fate of the Gentiles vary. The oppressors of Israel will be condemned, but frequently the nations may come to share in the salvation of the righteous in Israel, while the apostates in Israel will be judged. The universalism of apocalyptic results both from post-exilic Israel's involvement in the history of the world-empires, and from the apocalyptists' intense awareness of the universal problem of evil.

The negative experience of present history, in which apocalyptic arose, contrasted with the transcendent future salvation, gives rise to the *temporal dualism* of apocalyptic: its distinction between this age and the age to come which follows the new creation. This dualism became fully developed only at a late stage. The terminology of the two ages appears only in the 1st century AD (when it is also found in the NT). It is never an absolute dualism, for although the powers of evil have become dominant in this age, God remains in sovereign control over them. The new creation is seen as a renewal of *this* world (though the degree of continuity envisaged seems to vary). Apocalyptic dualism is at its starkest in *2 Baruch* and *4 Ezra*, where there is a deepening pessimism and a strong tendency to view the history of this age in wholly negative terms. From this extreme eschatological dualism it is not too great a step to the cosmological dualism of Gnosticism.

The relation between *apocalyptic and the NT* has been much debated. There are passages which strongly resemble the Jewish apocalypses in both form and content: especially Mt. 24; Mk. 13; Lk. 21; 1 Thes. 4:16f.; 2 Thes. 2; Rev. But even apart from these apocalyptic passages it is clear that both Jesus and the early church were broadly indebted to the apocalyptic world of thought, as is evident from their use of such apocalyptic concepts as resurrection, the two ages, the Son of man, the time of tribulation, the kingdom of God.

On the other hand, the purely future orientation of Jewish apocalyptic is modified in the NT by the conviction that eschatological *fulfilment has already begun* in the historical event of Jesus Christ. Christians live between the 'already' and the 'not yet'. In this way the apocalyptic tendency to a negative evaluation of present history is superseded by the conviction that God's redemptive purpose is already at work within the history of this age.

Moreover, NT apocalyptic is *Christ-centred*. God's decisive act of eschatological salvation has taken place in the history of Jesus, and Jesus is therefore also the focus of the future hope of Christians. For NT writers apocalyptic becomes primarily a means of declaring the significance of Jesus Christ for the destiny of the world.

One aspect of eschatological fulfilment is the renewal of prophecy, and so NT apocalyptic is a form of fresh prophetic revelation. It is no longer pseudonymous and no longer takes a fictional standpoint in the past: the prophet John, for example, writes in his own name (Rev. 1:1) and abandons the convention of writing for the distant future (22:10).

Bibliography. K. Koch, *The Rediscovery of Apocalyptic*, 1972; P. D. Hanson, *The Dawn of Apocalyptic*, 1975; C. Rowland, *The Open Heaven*, 1982; P. D. Hanson (ed.), *Visionaries and their Apocalypses*, 1983; D. Hellholm (ed.), *Apocalypticism*, 1983; J. J. Collins, *The Apocalyptic Imagination*, 1984; H.Kvanvig, *Roots of Apocalyptic*, 1987; D. S. Russell, *Divine Disclosure*, 1992.

R.J.B.

APOCRYPHA.

I. Definition

The term 'apocrypha' (neuter plural of the Gk. adjective *apokryphos*, 'hidden') is a technical term concerning the relation of certain books to the OT Canon, signifying that, while they are not approved for public lection, they are nevertheless valued for private study and edification. The term covers a number of additions to canonical books in their LXX form (*viz*. Esther, Daniel, Jeremiah, Chronicles), and other books, legendary, historical or theological, many originally written in Hebrew or Aramaic but preserved or known until recently only in Greek; these figure in the loosely defined LXX Canon, but were rejected from the Hebrew *Canon at Jamnia. Christian usage and opinion about their status were somewhat ambiguous until the 16th century, when twelve works were included in the Canon of the Roman Church by the Council of Trent; but Protestant thought (*e.g.* Luther, and the Anglican Church in the Thirty-Nine Articles) admitted them only for private edification. Works other than the twelve here under discussion are nowadays usually termed *'pseudepigrapha'. These, too, were freely drawn upon before the 16th century in the outlying Eastern churches in whose languages alone they have been preserved (*e.g.* Ethiopic, Armenian, Slavonic).

II. Contents

We may proceed to summarize the contents and chief critical problems of the twelve books which go to make up what we know today as the Apocrypha.

1 Esdras in EVV is called *2 Esdras* in the Lucianic recension of the LXX, and *3 Esdras* in Jerome's Vulg. This gives a parallel account of events recorded in Chronicles–Ezra–Nehemiah, with one large addition (*viz.* the 'Debate of the Three Youths' in 3:1–5:6). 1:1–20, 23–25 = 2 Ch. 35:1–36:21; 2:1–11 = Ezr. 1:1–11; 2:12–26 = Ezr. 4:7–24; 5:7–71 = Ezr. 2:1–4:5; 6:1–9:36 = Ezr. 5:1–10:44; 9:37–55 = Ne. 7:72–8:13. The 'Debate of the Three Youths' is an adaptation of a Persian tale, and in its details evidence of this may still be discerned: it is adapted as the means whereby Zerubbabel, guardsman of Darius, by winning a debate on the strongest power (wine, women or Truth?), gains opportunity to remind the Persian monarch of his obligation to allow the Temple to be rebuilt. Detailed comparison of it with the LXX Ezra shows that the two are independent translations from the *MT*. 1 Esdras is probably the earlier of the two. They present contrasts not only of text but also in chronological order of events and of the Persian kings. In a number of these cases scholarship is still undecided as to which work to follow. Certainly in some cases 1 Esdras provides good textual evidence. It is a free and idiomatic translation, and was known to Josephus.

2 Esdras in EVV is *4 Esdras* in the Vulg.; it is also called the *Apocalypse of Ezra* or *4 Ezra.* This version, as it now stands in the Old Latin, is an expansion by Christian writers of an original Jewish apocalyptic work found in chs. 4–14. The other chapters, *i.e.* the Christian additions, are lacking in some oriental versions. The original body of the book consists of seven visions. In the first (3:1–5:19) the seer demands an explanation of the suffering of Zion, whose sin is not greater than that of her oppressor. The angel Uriel answers that this cannot be understood, but that the era shortly to dawn will bring salvation. The second (5:20–6:34) deals with a similar problem – why Israel, God's chosen, has been delivered up to other nations; this, too, is declared to be incomprehensible to men. The age to come will follow this age without interval, preceded by signs of the end and a time of conversion and salvation. This should give comfort to the seer. The third vision (6:35–9:25) asks why the Jews do not possess the earth; the answer is given that they will inherit it in the age to come. Various other matters about the after-life and the age to come are dealt with, including the fewness of the elect. The fourth vision (9:26–10:59) is of a mourning woman who recounts her woes, and is thereupon transformed into a glorious city. This is a symbol of Jerusalem. The fifth vision (10:60–12:51) is of a twelve-winged and three-headed eagle – the symbol of Rome, which is explicitly declared by the interpreting angel to be the fourth kingdom of Dn. 7. The Messiah is to supplant it. By the most probable interpretation, this vision is to be dated in the reign of Domitian. The sixth vision (13:1-58) is of a man arising from the sea, and annihilating an antagonistic multitude. This is an adaptation of the Son of man vision of Dn. 7. The final vision (14) deals with the distinct topic of Ezra's restoration of the sacred books of the Hebrews, by means of a vision and with the help of supernaturally aided scribes. There are 94 such books, *viz.* the 24 of the Hebrew Canon and 70 esoteric or apocalyptic works.

Tobit is a pious short story of a righteous Hebrew of the northern captivity, Tobit, and his son Tobias. Tobit suffers persecution and privations because of his succour of fellow Israelites under the tyranny of Esarhaddon. At length he is blinded accidentally; and to his shame, his wife is obliged to support him. He prays that he may die. At the same time, prayer is offered by Sarah, a young Hebrew woman in Ecbatana, who is haunted by the demon Asmodaeus, who has slain seven suitors on their wedding night with her. The angel Raphael is sent 'to heal them both'. Tobias is sent by his father to collect 10 silver talents left in Media. Raphael takes on the form of Azariah, who is hired as a travelling companion. In the Tigris a fish is caught, and its heart, liver and gall are preserved by Tobias on Azariah's advice. Tobias arrives in Ecbatana and becomes betrothed to Sarah, who is found to be his cousin. On the bridal night he burns the heart and liver of the fish, the stench of which drives the demon away to Egypt. On his return home (preceded by his dog), where he had been given up as lost, Tobias anoints his father's eyes with the fish-gall and restores his sight. The story apparently originated in the Babylonian or Persian Exile, and its original language is likely to have been Aramaic. Three Greek recensions are known, and fragments in Hebrew and Aramaic have been found by the Dead Sea.

Judith tells the story of a courageous young Jewess, a widow, and the overthrow of Nebuchadrezzar's host by her guile. A native of Bethulia, besieged by Holofernes, she visits him in his camp, under the ruse of giving military secrets away: she then begins to entice him by her charms, until at length, banqueting with him alone at night, she is able to behead him. She then returns with his head to the city, greeted by rejoicing. The Assyrian(!) host retreats on the discovery of its general's assassination. Judith and the women of Bethulia rejoice in a psalm before God. The story is frank fiction – otherwise its inexactitudes would be incredible – and dates from the 2nd century BC. Its original was Hebrew, and a Greek translation in 4 recensions has preserved the tale for us.

Additions to Daniel are found in the LXX and Theodotion's translation. To chapter 3 is added the **Prayer of Azariah** uttered in the furnace and the **Song of the Three Holy Children** (*i.e. paidōn*, 'servants') sung to God's praise as the three walk about in the fire. This is the Benedicite of Christian worship. These two additions evidently existed in a Hebrew original. Prefaced to Daniel in Theodotion but following in LXX, is the story of **Susanna**. She is the beautiful and virtuous wife of a wealthy Jew in Babylon. Two elders of the people who lust after her come upon her bathing and offer her the alternatives of yielding to their desire or facing false accusation as an adulteress. She chooses the latter: her detractors are believed, and she is condemned protesting her innocence. Daniel, though but a mere youth, cries out against the injustice of this, and in a second trial before him the lie is uncovered and the woman justified.

The stories of **Bel and the Dragon** are plainly written to ridicule idolatry. Daniel shows that the priests of Bel, and not the image of the god, devour the nightly offering of food; the king thereupon destroys the image. A mighty dragon worshipped in Babylon is destroyed by Daniel. He is thrown into the lions' den and is preserved alive for 6 days; on the 6th the prophet Habakkuk is miraculously transported from Judaea to give him food; on the 7th he is released by the king. These two stories are probably translated from a Semitic original, but the matter is not finally decided. These additions are examples of pious legendary embroidery of the Daniel story and date from about 100 BC.

Additions to Esther considerably increase the size of the Greek version of the book. There are 6 additional passages. The first deals with Mordecai's dream and his prevention of a conspiracy against the king; it precedes chapter 1. The second is the king's edict for the destruction of all Jews in his realm. This follows 3:13 of the Hebrew. The third comprises prayers of Esther and Mordecai to follow chapter 4. The fourth describes Esther's audience with the king, to supplement 5:12. The fifth is the king's edict permitting Jewish self-defence, to follow 8:12. The sixth includes the interpretation of Mordecai's dream; and a historical note giving the date of the bringing of the Greek version into Egypt. The majority of scholars consider that all this is in fact addition to the shorter work of the Hebrew Canon, and that some, if not all, was composed in Greek. Scholars of the Roman obedience and a minority of others (including C. C. Torrey) argue, however, that the Hebrew is an abbreviation of a larger work, in Hebrew or Aramaic, of which the Greek is a translation. The colophon claims that the work was translated in Palestine some time before 114 BC, by one Lysimachus, son of Ptolemy, a Jerusalemite.

The Prayer of Manasses claims to give the prayer of which record is made in 2 Ch. 33:11–19. In the opinion of most scholars it is a Jewish composition and probably was written originally in Hebrew. However this may be, it is first attested in the Syriac Didascalia (3rd century AD), and found also among the Odes (*i.e.* hymns from OT and NT used in Christian worship) appended to the Psalms in some LXX MSS, such as the Codex Alexandrinus.

The Epistle of Jeremiah is a typical Hellenistic–Jewish attack on idolatry in the guise of a letter from Jeremiah to the exiles in Babylon, similar to that mentioned in Je. 29. Idols are ridiculed; the evils and follies connected with them are exposed, and the captive Jews are told neither to worship nor to fear them. It is written in good Greek, but it may have had an Aramaic original.

The Book of Baruch is allegedly the work of the friend and scribe of Jeremiah. The work is brief, but, in the opinion of most scholars, it is a composite work, variously attributed to two, three or four authors. It falls into the following sections. (*a*) 1:1–3:8. In the setting of the Babylonian Exile of 597, Baruch is depicted as addressing the exiles, setting out a confession of sins, a prayer for forgiveness and a prayer for salvation. (*b*) 3:9–4:4. This section sets out the praises of Wisdom which may be found in the law of Moses, and without which the heathen have come to naught, but with which Israel will be saved. (*c*) 4:5–5:9. A lament of Jerusalem over the exiles, followed by an exhortation to Jerusalem to be comforted, since her children will be brought back to their home. The first part was patently written in Hebrew, and, although the Greek of the two later sections is more idiomatic, a plausible case for a Hebrew original can be made.

Ecclesiasticus is the name given in its Greek dress to the Wisdom of Joshua ben-Sira. He was a Palestinian living in Jerusalem, and parts of his work survive in the original Hebrew in MSS of the Cairo Geniza. The work figures in Greek among the apocrypha in the translation made by his grandson, who furnishes chronological details in a preface. The most likely date for Ben-Sira himself is *c.* 180 BC, since his grandson apparently migrated to Egypt in the reign of Ptolemy VII Euergetes (170–117 BC). The author composed his work in two parts, chapters 1–23 and 24–50, with a short appendix, chapter 51. Like the Wisdom books, it is advice for a successful life conceived in the widest sense; fear of the Lord and the observance of his law are allied in the author's experience and teaching with practical 'wisdom' drawn from observation and his own life. Personal piety will express itself in the observance of the law, in which Wisdom is revealed; and in daily living moderation will be the keynote of all aspects of life. The second book concludes with the praise of famous men, a list of the worthies of Israel, ending with Simon II the high priest (*c.* 200 BC), who is known also from the Mishnah (*Aboth* 1:2) and Josephus (*Ant.* 12. 224). The book represents the beginnings of the ideal of the scribe, such as Ben-Sira himself, which became the type of orthodox Jewry – devoted to God, obedient to the law, sober in living and setting the highest value on learning in the law. It became a favourite Christian book, as its title ('The Church-book') shows; and though never canonical among the Jews, it was held in high honour by them, being occasionally cited by the Rabbis as if it were Scripture. The Syriac version is of Jewish origin and is based upon the Hebrew text.

The Wisdom of Solomon is perhaps the highlight of Jewish Wisdom writing. Its roots are in the stream of Wisdom literature which is to be found in the OT and Apocrypha, but here under the influence of Greek thought the book achieves a greater formality and precision than other examples of this literary type. The book is an exhortation to seek Wisdom. Chapters 1–5 declare the blessings which accrue upon the Jews who are the seekers after Wisdom; chapters 6–9 speak the praises of the divine Wisdom, hypostatized as a feminine celestial being, foremost of the creatures and servants of God; chapters 10–19 review OT history in illustration of the theme that throughout it Wisdom has helped her friends the Jews, and has brought punishment and damnation upon her adversaries. The work may thus be interpreted as an encouragement to Jews not to forsake their ancestral faith, but the missionary motive so evident in Hellenistic Judaism is not lacking. The author drew on sources in Hebrew, but it appears clear that the work as it stands was composed in Greek, since its prosody is Greek, and it makes use of Greek terms of philosophy and depends on the Greek version of the OT. The description of Wisdom, in which Stoic and Platonic terminology is utilized, and the author's convictions about the immortality of the soul, are the points at which his dependence on Greek thought is most clearly in evidence. In the opinion of most scholars there are no conclusive arguments for subdividing the authorship of the book, but various sources may be discerned. The author of the book is unknown, but an Alexandrian origin is most likely.

Several works are entitled **Maccabees**: of these, two figure in the Apocrypha as printed in the English versions. These are the historical works **1 and 2 Maccabees**. 1 Maccabees covers events between 175 and 134 BC, *i.e.* the struggle with Antiochus Epiphanes, the wars of the Hasmonaeans, and the rule of John Hyrcanus. The book ends with a panegyric on John and was evidently written just after his death in 103 BC. Originally written in Hebrew, it is translated in the literal style of parts of the LXX. The aim of the work is to glorify the family of the Maccabees seen as the champions of Judaism. **2 Maccabees** is a work of different origin: its subject-matter covers much of the same history as its namesake, but does not continue the history beyond the campaigns and defeat of Nicanor. Its unknown author is sometimes called the 'epitomist', since much of his book is excerpted from the otherwise unknown work of Jason of Cyrene. There are a number of discrepancies in chronological and numerical matters between the two works, and it is customary to place more reliance on 1 Maccabees. There is debate also over the historical value of the letters and edicts which figure in the two works. Nevertheless, neither work is to be discredited as an historical source. **3 and 4 Maccabees** are found in a number of MSS of the LXX. The former is an account of pogroms and counter-pogroms under Ptolemy IV (221-204 BC) not unlike the book of Esther in tone and ethos. 4 Maccabees is not a narrative but a diatribe or tract on the rule of reason over the passions, illustrated from biblical stories and the martyr stories of 2 Macc. 6–7. The writer seeks to enhance the law, though he is greatly influenced by Stoicism. (See also * NEW TESTAMENT APOCRYPHA.)

BIBLIOGRAPHY. R. H. Charles (ed.), *The Apocrypha and Pseudepigrapha of the Old Testament*, 1913; C. C. Torrey, *The Apocryphal Literature*, 1945; *HJP*, 3 *passim*; M. E. Stone (ed.), *Jewish Writings of the Second Temple Period*, 1984.

J.N.B.

APOLLONIA. A town on the Via Egnatia some 43 km WSW of Amphipolis. It lay between the rivers Strymon and Axius (Vardar), but its site is not known for certain. Paul and Silas passed through it on their way from Philippi to Thessalonica (Acts 17:1). There were several other towns named Apollonia in the Mediterranean area.

K.L.McC.

APOLLOS. An Alexandrian Jew (Acts 18:24). The name is abbreviated from Apollonius. He came to Ephesus in AD 52 during Paul's hasty visit to Palestine (Acts 18:22). He had accurate knowledge of the story of Jesus, which may have come to him (possibly at Alexandria) either from Galilean disciples of our Lord or from some early written Gospel. He combined natural gifts of eloquence (or learning) with a profound understanding of the OT, and he was enthusiastic in proclaiming such truth as he knew (Acts 18:24–25). The conspicuous gap in his knowledge concerned the outpouring of the Holy Spirit and the consequent rite of Christian baptism. This was made good by the patient instruction of Priscilla and Aquila (Acts 18:26). From Ephesus Apollos went on to Corinth, where he showed himself to be an expert at Christian apologetics in dealing with the Jews (Acts 18:27-28). At Corinth there sprang up factions in the names of Paul, Apollos, Cephas and Christ himself (1 Cor. 1:12). Paul seeks to show that this was not due to himself or Apollos, who were both working together under the hand of God (1 Cor. 3:4–6). All belonged to the Corinthians, including himself and Apollos (1 Cor. 3:21–23), and there could be no cause for party spirit (1 Cor. 4:6). The factions were probably due to the preference of some for the polished eloquence of Apollos. His desire to lessen the controversy may be the reason for his not returning to Corinth despite Paul's request (1 Cor. 16:12). He is last mentioned in Tit. 3:13 as making some sort of journey.

Since the time of Luther, Apollos has often been suggested as the author of the Epistle to the Hebrews. This is possible, if he used the allegorical exegesis of his native Alexandria, but it is by no means proved.

BIBLIOGRAPHY. H. W. Montefiore, *A Commentary on the Epistle to the Hebrews*, 1964, pp. 9ff.; F. F. Bruce, *New Testament History*, 1969, pp. 304ff.; idem, 'Apollos in the NT', *Ekklesiastikos Pharos* 57, 1975, pp. 354ff.; L. D. Hurst, 'Apollos, Hebrews and Corinth', *SJT* 38, 1985, pp. 505–513.

A.S.W.

APOSTASY. In classical Gk. *apostasia* is a technical term for political revolt or defection. In LXX it always relates to rebellion against God (Jos. 22:22; 2 Ch. 29:19), originally instigated by Satan, the apostate dragon of Jb. 26:13.

There are two NT instances of the Gk. word. Acts 21:21 records that Paul was maliciously accused of teaching the Jews to forsake Moses by abandoning circumcision and other traditional observances. 2 Thes. 2:3 describes the great apostasy of prophecy, alongside or prior to the revelation of the man of lawlessness (*cf.* Mt. 24:10–12). The allusion is neither to the political nor to the religious infidelity of the Jews, but is entirely eschatological in character and refers to 'the final catastrophic revolt against the authority of God which in apocalyptic writings is a sign of the end of the world' (E. J. Bicknell, *The First and Second Epistles to the Thessalonians*, 1932, p. 74). It may be regarded as the earthly counterpart of the heavenly rebellion in Rev. 12:7–9.

Apostasy is a continual danger to the church, and the NT contains repeated warnings against it (*cf.* 1 Tim. 4:1–3; 2 Thes. 2:3; 2 Pet. 3:17). Its nature is made clear: falling 'from the faith' (1 Tim. 4:1) and 'from the living God' (Heb. 3:12). It increases in times of special trial (Mt. 24:9–10; Lk. 8:13) and is encouraged by false teachers (Mt. 24:11; Gal. 2:4), who seduce believers from the purity of the Word with 'another gospel' (Gal. 1:6–8; *cf.* 2 Tim. 4:3–4; 2 Pet. 2:1–2; Jude 3–4). The impossibility of restoration after deliberate apostasy is solemnly urged (Heb. 6:4–6; 10:26).

BIBLIOGRAPHY. *NIDNTT* 1, pp. 606–611; I. H. Marshall, *Kept by the Power of God: A Study of Perseverance and Falling Away*, 1969. A.S.W.

APOSTLE. There are over 80 occurrences of the Gk. word *apostolos* in the NT, mostly in Luke and Paul. It derives from the very common verb *apostellō*, to send, but in non-Christian Gk., after Herodotus in the 5th century BC, there are few recorded cases where it means 'a person sent', and it generally means 'fleet', or perhaps occasionally 'admiral'. The sense of 'sent one, messenger' may have survived in popular speech: at least, isolated occurrences in the LXX and Josephus suggest that this meaning was recognized in Jewish circles. Only with Christian literature, however, does it come into its own. In NT it is applied to Jesus as the Sent One of God (Heb. 3:1), to those sent by God to preach to Israel (Lk. 11:49) and to those sent by churches (2 Cor. 8:23; Phil. 2:25); but above all it is applied absolutely to the group of men who held the supreme dignity in the primitive church. Since *apostellō* seems frequently to mean 'to send with a particular purpose', as distinct from the neutral *pempō* (save in the Johannine writings, where the two are synonyms), the force of *apostolos* is probably 'one commissioned' – it is implied, by Christ.

It is disputed whether *apostolos* represents in NT a Jewish term of similar technical force. Rengstorf, in particular, has elaborated the theory that it reflects the Jewish *šālîaḥ*, an accredited representative of religious authority, entrusted with messages and money and empowered to act on behalf of the authority (for the idea, *cf.* Acts 9:2); and Gregory Dix and others have applied ideas and expressions belonging to the *šālîaḥ* concept (*e.g.* 'a man's *šālîaḥ* is as himself') to the apostolate and eventually to the modern episcopate. Such a process is full of perils, and not least because there is no clear evidence that *šālîaḥ* was used in this sense until post-apostolic times. *apostolos*, in fact, may well be the earlier as a technical term, and it is safest to seek its significance in the meaning of *apostellō* and from the contexts of the NT occurrences.

a. The origin of the Apostolate

Essential to the understanding of all the Gospels as they stand is the choice by Jesus, out of the wider company of his followers, of a group of 12 men whose purpose was to be with him, to preach, and to have authority to heal and to exorcize (Mk. 3:14f.). The only occasion on which Mark uses the word 'apostle' is on the successful return of the Twelve from a mission of preaching and healing (Mk. 6:30; *cf.* Mt. 10:2ff.). This is usually taken as a non-technical use (*i.e.* 'those sent on this particular assignment'), but it is unlikely that Mark would use it without evoking other associations. This preparatory mission is a miniature of their future task in the wider world. From this preliminary training they return 'apostles' indeed. There is then nothing incongruous in Luke (who speaks of the 'apostles' in 9:10; 17:5; 22:14; 24:10) declaring that Jesus conferred the title (already in Gk.?) himself (6:13).

b. The functions of the Apostolate

Mark's first specification on the choice of the Twelve is for them 'to be with him' (Mk. 3:14). It is no accident that the watershed of Mark's Gospel is the apostolic confession of the Messiahship of Jesus (Mk. 8:29), or that Matthew follows this with the 'Rock' saying about the apostolic confession (Mt. 16:18f.; *PETER). The primary function of the apostles was witness to Christ, and the witness was rooted in years of intimate knowledge, dearly bought experience and intensive training.

This is complementary to their widely recognized function of witness to the resurrection (*cf.*, *e.g.*, Acts 1:22; 2:32; 3:15; 13:31); for the special significance of the resurrection lies, not in the event itself, but in its demonstration, in fulfilment of prophecy, of the identity of the slain Jesus (*cf.* Acts 2:24ff., 36; 3:26; Rom. 1:4). Their witness *of* the resurrection of Christ made them effective witnesses *to* his Person, and he himself commissions them to world-wide witness (Acts 1:8).

The same commission introduces a factor of profound importance for the apostolate: the coming of the Spirit. Curiously enough, this is most fully treated in Jn. 14–17, which does not use the word 'apostle' at all. This is the great commissioning discourse of the Twelve (*apostellō* and *pempō* are used without discrimination): their commission from Jesus is as real as his from God (*cf.* Jn. 20:21); they are to bear witness from their long acquaintance with Jesus, yet the Spirit bears witness of him (Jn. 15:26–27). He will remind them of the words of Jesus (Jn. 14:26), and guide them into all the truth (a promise often perverted by extending its primary reference beyond the apostles) and show them the age to come (of the church) and Christ's glory (Jn. 16:13–15). Instances are given in the Fourth Gospel of this process, where the significance of words or actions was recalled only after Christ's 'glorification' (Jn. 2:22; 12:16; *cf.* 7:39). That is, the witness of the apostles to Christ is not left to their impressions and recollections, but to the guidance of the Holy Spirit, whose witness it is also – a fact of consequence in assessing the recorded apostolic witness in the Gospels.

For this reason the apostles are the norm of doctrine and fellowship in the NT church (Acts 2:42; *cf.* 1 Jn. 2:19). In their own day they were regarded as 'pillars' (Gal. 2:9 – *cf.* C. K. Barrett in *Studia Paulina*, 1953, pp. 1ff.) – perhaps translate 'marking posts'. The church is built on the foundation of the apostles and prophets (Eph. 2:20; probably the witness of the OT is intended, but the point remains if Christian prophets are in mind). The apostles are the assessors at the Messianic judgment (Mt. 19:28), and their names are engraved on the foundation stones of the holy city (Rev. 21:14).

Apostolic doctrine, however, originating as it does with the Holy Spirit, is the *common* witness of the apostles, not the perquisite of any individual. (For the common preaching, *cf.* C. H. Dodd, *The Apostolic Preaching and its Developments*, 1936; for the common use of the OT, C. H. Dodd, *According to the Scriptures*, 1952.) The chief apostle could by implication betray a fundamental principle he had accepted, and be withstood by a colleague (Gal. 2:11ff.).

The Synoptists, as already noted, view the incident of Mk. 6:7ff. and parallels as a miniature of the apostolic mission, and healing and exorcism, as well as preaching, were included. Healing, and other spectacular gifts, such as prophecy and tongues, are abundantly attested in the apostolic church, related, like the apostolic witness, to the special dispensation of the Holy Spirit; but they are strangely missing in the 2nd-century church, the writers of those days speaking of them as a thing in the past – in the apostolic age, in fact (*cf.* J. S. McEwan, *SJT* 7, 1954, pp. 133ff.; B. B. Warfield, *Miracles Yesterday and Today*, 1953). Even in the NT, we see no signs of these gifts except where apostles have been at work. Even where there has previously been genuine faith, it is only in the presence of apostles that these gifts of the Spirit are showered down (Acts 8:14ff.; 19:6 – the contexts show that visual and audible phenomena are in question).

By contrast, the NT has less to say than might be expected of the apostles as ruling the church. They are the touchstones of doctrine, the purveyors of the authentic *tradition about Christ: apostolic delegates visit congregations which reflect new departures for the church (Acts 8:14ff.; 11:22ff.). But the Twelve did not appoint the Seven; the crucial Jerusalem Council consisted of a large number of elders as well as the apostles (Acts 15:6; *cf.* 12, 22): and two apostles served among the 'prophets and teachers' of the church at Antioch (Acts 13:1). Government was a distinct gift (1 Cor. 12:28), normally exercised by local elders: apostles were, by virtue of their commission, mobile. Nor are they even prominent in the administration of the sacraments (*cf.* 1 Cor. 1:14). The identity of function which some see between apostle and 2nd-century bishop (*cf.* K. E. Kirk in *The Apostolic Ministry*, p. 10) is by no means obvious.

c. Qualifications

It is obvious that the essential qualification of an apostle is the divine call, the commissioning by Christ. In the case of the Twelve, this was given during his earthly ministry. But with Matthias, the sense of the divine commissioning is not less evident: God has already chosen the apostle (Acts 1:24), even though his choice is not yet known. No laying on of hands is mentioned. The apostle, it is assumed, will be someone who has been a disciple of Jesus from the time of John's baptism ('the beginning of the gospel') to the ascension. He will be someone acquainted with the whole course of the ministry and work of Jesus (Acts 1:21–22). And, of course, he must be specifically a witness of the resurrection.

Paul equally insists on his direct commission from Christ (Rom. 1:1; 1 Cor. 1:1; Gal. 1:1, 15ff.). He in no sense derived his authority from the other apostles; like Matthias, he was accepted, not appointed by them. He did not fulfil the qualifications of Acts 1:21f., but the Damascus road experience was a resurrection appearance (*cf.* 1 Cor. 15:8), and he could claim to have 'seen the Lord' (1 Cor. 9:1); he was thus a witness of the resurrection. He remained conscious that his background – an enemy and persecutor, rather than a disciple – was different from that of the other apostles, but he counts himself with their number and associates them with his own gospel (1 Cor. 15:8–11).

d. The number of the apostles

'The Twelve' is a regular designation of the apostles in the Gospels, and Paul uses it in 1 Cor. 15:5. Its symbolic appropriateness is obvious, and recurs in such places as Rev. 21:14. The whole Matthias incident is concerned with making up the number of the Twelve. Yet Paul's consciousness of apostleship is equally clear. Further, there are instances in the NT where, *prima facie*, others outside the Twelve seem to be given the title. James the Lord's brother appears as such in Gal. 1:19; 2:9, and, though he was not a disciple (*cf.* Jn. 7:5), received a resurrection appearance personal to himself (1 Cor. 15:7). Barnabas is called an apostle in Acts 14:4, 14, and is introduced by Paul into an argument which denies any qualitative difference between his own apostleship and that of the Twelve (1 Cor. 9:1–6). The unknown *Andronicus and Junias are probably called apostles in Rom. 16:7, and Paul, always careful with his personal pronouns, may so style Silas in 1 Thes. 2:6. Paul's enemies in Corinth evidently claim to be 'apostles of Christ' (2 Cor. 11:13).

On the other hand, some have argued strongly for the limitation of the title to Paul and the Twelve (*cf., e.g.*, Geldenhuys, pp. 71ff.). This involves giving a subordinate sense ('accredited messengers of the church') to 'apostles' in Acts 14:14 and Rom. 16:7, and explaining otherwise Paul's language about James and Barnabas. Some have introduced more desperate expedients, suggesting that James replaced James bar-Zebedee as Matthias replaced Judas, or that Matthias was mistakenly hurried into the place which God intended for Paul. Of such ideas there is not the remotest hint in the NT. However it may be explained, it seems safest to allow that there *were*, at an early date, apostles outside the Twelve. Paul's own apostleship makes such a breach in any more restrictive theory that there is room for others of God's appointment to pass with him. A hint of this may be given in the distinction between 'the Twelve' and 'all the apostles' in 1 Cor. 15:5, 7. But everything suggests that an apostle was a witness of the resurrection, and the resurrection appearance to Paul was clearly exceptional. Whether, as old writers suggested, some who are later called 'apostles' belonged to the Seventy sent out by the Lord (Lk. 10:1ff.), is another matter. The special significance of the Twelve for the first establishment of the church is beyond question.

e. Canonicity and continuity

Implied in apostleship is the commission to witness by word and sign to the risen Christ and his completed work. This witness, being grounded in a unique experience of the incarnate Christ, and directed by a special dispensation of the Holy Spirit, provides the authentic interpretation of Christ, and has ever since been determinative for the universal church. In the nature of things, the office could not be repeated or transmitted: any more than the underlying historic experiences could be transmitted to those who had never known the incarnate Lord, or received a resurrection appearance. The origins of the Christian ministry and the succession in the Jerusalem church are beyond the scope of this article; but, while the NT shows the apostles taking care that a local ministry is provided, there is no hint of the transmission of the peculiar apostolic functions to any part of that ministry.

Nor was such transmission necessary. The apostolic witness was maintained in the abiding work of the apostles and in what became normative for later ages, its written form in the NT (see Geldenhuys, pp. 100ff.; O. Cullmann, 'The Tradition', in *The Early Church*, 1956). No renewal of the office or of its special gifts has been called for. It was a foundational office: and church history ever since has been its superstructure. (*BISHOP; *TRADITION.)

BIBLIOGRAPHY. K. H. Rengstorf, *TDNT* 1, pp. 398–447; J. B. Lightfoot, *Galatians*, pp. 92ff.; K. Lake in *BC*, 5, pp. 37ff.; K. E. Kirk (ed.), *The Apostolic Ministry*², 1957, especially essays 1 and 3; A. Ehrhardt, *The Apostolic Succession*, 1953; J. N. Geldenhuys, *Supreme Authority*, 1953; W. Schneemelcher, *etc.*, in *New Testament Apocrypha*, ed. E. Hennecke, W. Schneemelcher, R. McL. Wilson, 1, 1965, pp. 25–87; C. K. Barrett, *The Signs of an Apostle*, 1970; R. Schnackenburg, in *Apostolic History and the Gospel*, ed. W. W. Gasque and R. P. Martin, 1970, pp. 287–303; W. Schmithals, *The Office of Apostle in the Early Church*, 1971; J. A. Kirk, *NTS* 21, 1974–5, pp. 249–264; D. Müller, C. Brown, *NIDNTT* 1, pp. 126–137; F. H. Agnew, 'The Origin of the NT Apostle-Concept: A Review of Research', *JBL* 105, pp. 75–96; *BAICS* 6 f.c.

A.F.W.

APPEAL TO CAESAR. When *Festus succeeded *Felix as Roman procurator of Judaea in AD 59 (Acts 24:27) and re-opened Paul's case, which Felix had left unsettled, Paul soon had reason to fear that the new governor's inexperience might be exploited by the high priest to his own disadvantage. Accordingly, he availed himself of his privilege as a Roman citizen and 'appealed to Caesar' – *i.e.* appealed for the transfer of his case from the provincial court to the supreme tribunal in Rome (Acts 25:10f.).

The citizen's right of appeal (*prouocatio*) to the emperor appears to have developed from the earlier right of appeal in republican times to the sovereign Roman people. According to Dio Cassius (*Hist*. 51. 19), Octavian in 30 BC was granted the right to judge on appeal. It was in this period, too, that the *lex Iulia de ui publica* (Julian law on the public use of force) was enacted, which forbade any magistrate vested with *imperium* or *potestas* to kill, scourge, chain or torture a Roman citizen, or to sentence him *aduersus prouocationem* ('in the face of an appeal') or prevent him from going to Rome to lodge his appeal there within a fixed time. A. H. M. Jones (*Studies in Roman Government and Law*, 1960, p. 96) concluded that, from the date of this enactment, a Roman citizen anywhere in the empire was protected against summary magisterial punishment (*coercitio*), although the provincial magistrate might deal with cases which involved a plain breach of established statute law (which Paul's case manifestly did not). By the beginning of the 2nd century AD it evidently became the regular practice for Roman citizens in the provinces, charged with offences *extra ordinem* (not covered by the standard code of procedure), to be sent to Rome almost automatically, without going through the formality of appealing to Caesar. In this, as in many other respects, the picture of Roman practice given in Acts is true to the dramatic date of the book; the case of Paul's appeal fits in with what we know of conditions in the late fifties of the 1st Christian century, and Luke's account of it is a substantial contribution to the available evidence.

It was with some relief that Festus heard Paul's appeal to Caesar: he himself would now be quit of the responsibility of adjudicating in a case where he knew himself to be out of his depth. One responsibility remained, however: he had to send to Rome along with the accused man an explanatory statement (*litterae dimissoriae*) outlining the nature of the case and its history to date. In drafting this statement he was glad to have the timely aid of one who was reputed to be an expert in Jewish religious affairs, the younger Agrippa, who came to Caesarea about this time with his sister Bernice to greet the emperor's new representative.

After the normal exchange of courtesies, Festus acquainted Agrippa with his problem. The charges against Paul, he said, seemed to revolve around 'one Jesus, who was dead, but whom Paul asserted to be alive' (Acts 25:19). Agrippa's interest was immediately aroused and he expressed a desire to meet Paul. Festus was only too glad to arrange an interview. After listening to Paul, Agrippa agreed with Festus that he could not reasonably be convicted on any of the serious charges brought against him. Indeed, said the king, Paul might have been discharged on the spot had he not appealed to Caesar, but for Festus to prejudge the issue now by releasing him would have been *ultra vires* (Acts 26:30–32). But Agrippa presumably gave Festus the help he required in drafting the *litterae dimissoriae*.

Paul did not appeal to Caesar while Felix was in office, presumably because Felix had virtually decided on his innocence and was simply postponing his formal acquittal and release. One day (Paul might have hoped) Felix's procrastination would come to an end and Paul would be discharged and be able to carry out his long-cherished plan of travelling to Rome and the West. But with the recall of Felix and his supersession by Festus a new and dangerous situation was developing for Paul; hence his decision to appeal.

The uppermost consideration in Paul's appeal to Caesar was not his own safety, but the interests of the gospel. 7 or 8 years previously he had experienced the benevolent neutrality of Roman law in the tacit decision of *Gallio, proconsul of Achaia, that there was nothing illegal in his preaching (Acts 18:12–16). He might reasonably expect a similarly favourable verdict from the supreme court in Rome. Not only so: even a man of smaller intelligence than Paul must have realized that the consideration which moved Gallio would not be valid much longer. Gallio had ruled in effect that what Paul preached was a variety of Judaism, and therefore not forbidden by Roman law. But, thanks in large measure to Paul's own activity, it would soon be impossible to regard Christianity as a variety of Judaism, since it was now manifestly more Gentile than Jewish. A favourable hearing from the emperor in Rome might win recognition for Christianity, if not as the true fulfilment of Israel's ancestral religion (which Paul believed it to be), at least as a permitted association (*collegium licitum*, or group of *collegia licita*) in its own right. Besides, if Caesar in person heard Paul's defence, what might the outcome not be? The younger Agrippa had politely declined to admit the logic of Paul's argument, but Gentiles had regularly shown themselves more amenable to the gospel than Jews, and a Roman emperor might be more easily won than a Jewish client-king. It would be precarious to set limits to Paul's high hopes, however impracticable they may appear to us in retrospect.

But the fact that it was to Caesar that Paul appealed does not necessarily mean that Caesar would hear the case personally. According to Tacitus (*Annals* 13. 4. 2), Nero announced at the beginning of his principate that he would not judge cases *in propria persona*, as his predecessor Claudius had done; and indeed, during his first 8 years he generally delegated them to others. Thus, 'if Paul came to trial some time after the period of 2 years mentioned in Acts 28:30, it is probable that his case was heard by someone other than the Princeps' (A. N. Sherwin-White, *Roman Society and Roman Law in the New Testament*, 1963, p. 366). This 'someone other' might be the prefect of the praetorian guard, 'representing the Emperor in his capacity as the fountain of justice, together with the assessors and high officers of the court' (W. M. Ramsay, *SPT*, p. 357). But this is a matter on which we have no information.

Neither have we any information on the outcome of the appeal – whether Paul was heard and condemned, or heard and acquitted. We do not even know whether his appeal was ever heard. The prolongation of his stay in Rome over 2 full years could have been due to congestion of court business as much as anything else; and if indeed he was discharged without coming to trial, this would probably have been the result of an act of *imperium* on Caesar's part. 'Perhaps Paul benefited from the clemency of Nero, and secured a merely casual release. But there is no necessity to construe Acts to mean that he was released at all' (A. N. Sherwin-White, *op. cit.*, p. 109). By the account of Paul's night vision at sea, in which he was assured that he would stand before Caesar (Acts 27:23f.), Luke probably implies that Paul's appeal did at length come up for hearing, whatever the outcome was.

BIBLIOGRAPHY. H. J. Cadbury, 'Roman Law and the Trial of Paul', *BC* 5, pp. 297ff.; A. H. M. Jones, *Studies in Roman Government and Law*, 1960; T. Mommsen, *Römisches Strafrecht*, 1899; A. N. Sherwin-White, *Roman Society and Roman Law in the New Testament*, 1963; *idem*, *The Roman Citizenship*², 1973; *BA1CS* 3. F.F.B.

APPHIA. Addressed in Phm. 2 in a manner suggesting that she was Philemon's wife, and hostess to the Colossian church (but see *PHILEMON, EPISTLE to). RSV's text 'our sister' is probably to be preferred to AV's 'our beloved'. The name was common in W Asia and is probably native Phrygian. (See examples in Lightfoot, *Colossians*, p. 304, *MM*, and the Colossian inscription, *CIG*, 3, 4380K, 3.) A.F.W.

AQUILA AND PRISCA, PRISCILLA. A Jewish leatherworker (RSV 'tent-maker', Acts 18:3) and his wife, staunch friends of Paul. Aquila came from Pontus, but the couple were in Rome when Claudius' edict of *c.* AD 49 expelled all Jews from the city. Obscure words of Suetonius (*Claudius* 25. 4) suggest that the purge followed disturbances in the Roman Jewish community over Christianity, and there is every likelihood that Aquila and Prisca were already Christians on meeting Paul in Corinth. He stayed with them and shared in their craft (Acts 18:1–3; an inferior reading in v. 7 adds that Paul left them after the split in the synagogue). It was doubtless in this period that they endangered their lives for his sake (Rom. 16:3); perhaps, too, they turned the apostle's mind to the needs and opportunities of Rome.

When Paul left, they accompanied him as far as Ephesus, where they received and assisted to a fuller faith the very influential *Apollos (Acts 18:18–28). They were still at Ephesus, and a church was meeting in their house, when 1 Cor. was written, and they had not forgotten their Corinthian friends (1 Cor. 16:19 – a gloss claims that Paul was again their guest). Not long afterwards, perhaps taking advantage of relaxations towards Jews after Claudius' death, they seem to be back in Rome (Rom. 16:3). Since 2 Tim. 4:19 evidently indicates a renewal of the Ephesian residence, the references to the couple have been a primary argument for regarding Rom. 16 as a separate letter to Ephesus (*cf.* especially K. Lake, *EEP*, pp. 327ff.); but the force of it is much reduced by the obvious propensity of Aquila and Prisca for travel.

Aquila's name is attested in Pontus (*cf. MM*) – his namesake, the translator, also came from there. The best MSS indicate that Paul uses the proper form, Prisca, for the lady, Luke, characteristically, the diminutive, Priscilla.

Rom. 16:3 shows how widely this peripatetic and ever-hospitable Jewish couple were known and loved in the Gentile churches, and the temptation to fill in the blanks in our knowledge about them has proved irresistible. The curious fact that Prisca is usually named first has been interpreted as indicating that she was a Roman lady of higher rank than her husband (*cf.* Ramsay, *CBP*, 1, p. 637, for a contemporary analogy), or that she was more prominent in the church. The true reason is undiscoverable. Attempts have been made to trace their final return to Rome (*cf.* Sanday and Headlam, *Romans*, pp. 418ff., for archaeological data), or even Pontus, or to show that Aquila was a member or freedman of the *gens Pontia* or the *gens Acilia*. While some are attractive, none is conclusive; and still less is Harnack's attribution to the couple, with the lady in the lead, of the Epistle to the Hebrews.

BIBLIOGRAPHY. F. F. Bruce, *The Pauline Circle*, 1985, pp. 44–51. A.F.W.

AR. The chief city of Moab, E of the Dead Sea near the Arnon river (site unknown). Something of the early history of the city was known to the Hebrews from records in the Book of the Wars of the Lord (Nu. 21:15), and popular proverbs (Nu. 21:28). Isaiah appears to have had access to similar sources (Is. 15:1). In the later stages of the wilderness wanderings the Hebrews were forbidden to dispossess the Moabite inhabitants of the city and settle there themselves, for this was not the land which the Lord their God had given them. (Dt. 2:9, 18, 29; LXX 'Seir'.) R.J.W.

ARABAH (Heb. *ʿărāḇâ*). In the AV the word is used only once in its original form (Jos. 18:18), although it is of frequent occurrence in the Hebrew text.

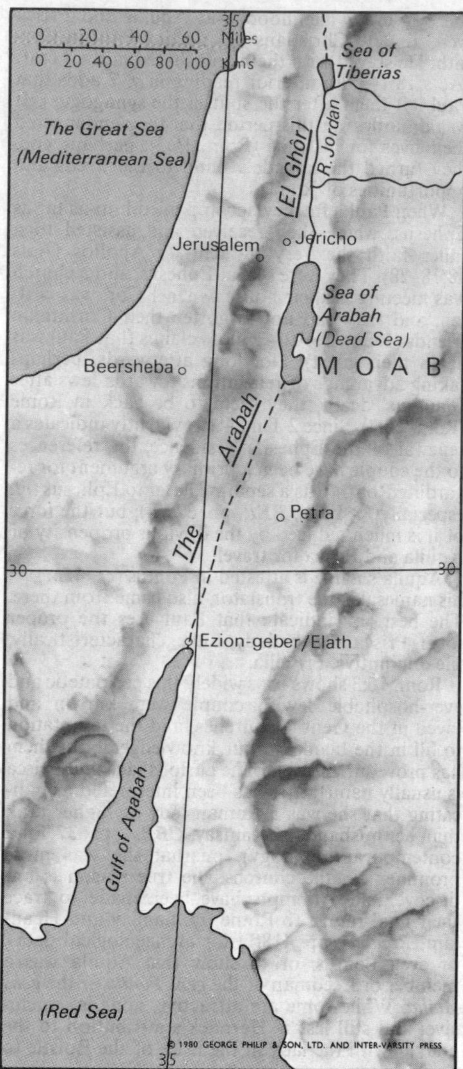

The Arabah: the rift valley running from the Sea of Tiberias to the Gulf of Aqabah.

1. The root *rb*, meaning 'dry', 'burnt up' and therefore 'waste land', is used to describe the desert steppe (Jb. 24:5; 39:6; Is. 33:9; 35:1, 6; Je. 51:43; RSV usually translates as 'wilderness' or 'desert').

2. Used with the article (*hā-ʿărāḇâ*), the name is applied generally to the rift valley which runs from the Sea of Tiberias to the Gulf of Aqabah. Although the topographical significance of this word was ignored by the earlier commentators, it has a precise connotation in many OT references. Its location is connected with the lake of Tiberias (Dt. 3:17; Jos. 11:2; 12:3) and as far S as the Red Sea and Elath (Dt. 1:1; 2:8). The Dead Sea is called the Sea of Arabah (Jos. 3:16; 12:3; Dt. 4:49; 2 Ki. 14:25). Today, the valley of the Jordan downstream to the Dead Sea is called the Ghôr, the 'depression', and the Arabah more properly begins S of the Scorpion cliffs and terminates in the Gulf of Aqabah. For its physical features see *JORDAN.

3. The plural of the same word, 'Araboth, without the article, is used in its primary meaning to describe certain waste areas within the Arabah, especially around Jericho (Jos. 5:10, RSV 'plains'; 2 Ki. 25:5; Je. 39:5, RSV 'plains'), and the wilderness of Moab. The Araboth Moab ('plains of Moab', RSV) is plainly distinguished from the pastoral and cultivated lands of the plateaux above the Rift Valley, the Sede-Moab (see Nu. 22:1; 26:3, 63; 31:12; 33:48–50; Dt. 34:1, 8; Jos. 4:13; 5:10, *etc.*).

4. Beth-arabah (the house of Arabah) refers to a settlement situated near Ain el-Gharba (Jos. 15:6, 61; 18:22).

BIBLIOGRAPHY. D. Baly, *Geography of the Bible*², 1974, pp. 191–209. J.M.H.

ARABIA.

I. In the Old Testament

a. Geography

In structure the Arabian peninsula consists of a mass of old crystalline rock which forms a range of mountains on the W, rising above 3,000 m in places, with a series of strata of younger formation uptilted against its E side. In the W mountains, and particularly in the SW corner of the peninsula, where the annual rainfall exceeds 500 mm in parts, settled life based on irrigation is possible, and it was in this area, the modern Yemen, that the ancient kingdoms of S Arabia chiefly flourished. The capitals of three of these, Qarnāwu (of Maʿīn), Mārib (of Saba') and Timnaʿ (of Qatabān), were situated on the E slopes of the mountain range, on water-courses running off to the E, and Shabwa the capital of Ḥaḍramaut lay farther to the SE on a water-course running NW off the Ḥaḍramaut table-land. An area of rainfall of 100–250 mm extends N along the W mountains and E along the coast, and here settled life is also possible. In the whole of the rest of the peninsula the annual rainfall is negligible and life depends upon oases and wells.

Between the escarpments formed by the uptilted strata and the E coast the scarp slope of the uppermost provides level areas ranging from steppe to sandy desert. The zones of desert which exist in this area and between the central escarpments widen out in the S into the barren sand desert of al-Rubʿ al-Ḫāli ('the empty quarter'), with the smaller sand sea, the Ramlat Sabatayu, to the SW, round which lay Marib, Timnaʿ and Shabura, and in the N to the smaller desert of al-Nafud. At various points along the foot of the escarpments springs provide oases, and consequent trade routes. Apart from the areas of sandy and rocky desert, the terrain of the peninsula is largely steppe, yielding grass under the sporadic annual rains, and supporting a poor nomadic population (*NOMADS), particularly in the N area between Syria and Mesopotamia. It was where this zone graded into the settled areas of Syria that such metropolises as Petra, Palmyra and Damascus flourished.

b. Exploration

The first notable European explorer in the Arabian peninsula was the Danish orientalist, Carsten Niebuhr, who visited the Yemen in 1763. In the N, J. L.

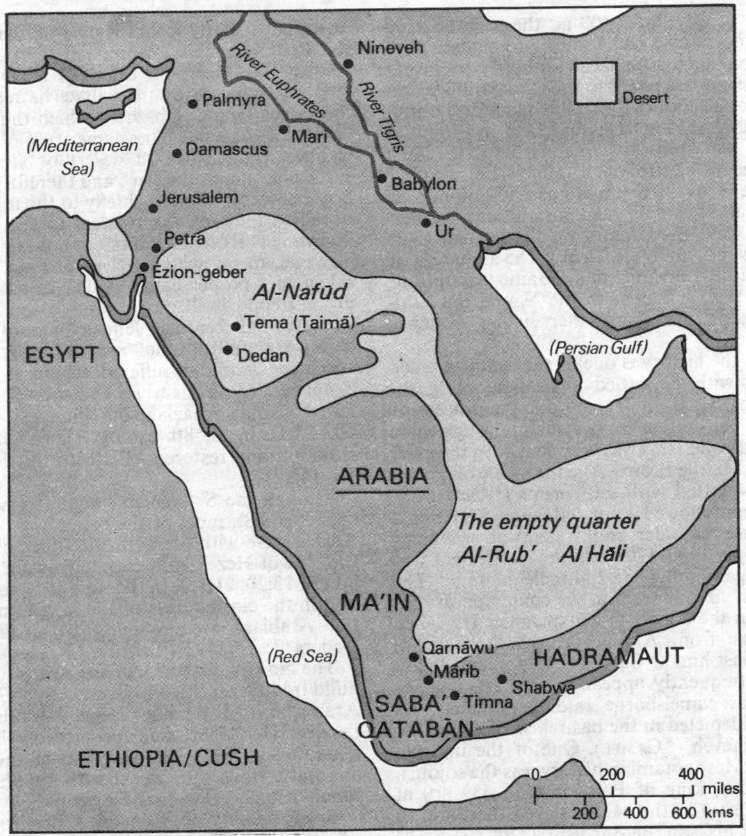

Ancient Arabia

Burckhardt rediscovered Petra in 1812, but interest was focused on the S when J. R. Wellsted published in 1837 the first S Arabian inscriptions to be seen in Europe, an event which led to their decipherment in 1841 by W. Gesenius and E. Rödiger. These inscriptions were known as 'Ḥimyaritic', from the name of the kingdom which dominated the whole of the SW of the peninsula in the last centuries BC, and was therefore considered by later historians to be the source of the inscriptions, though in fact they stemmed from the earlier kingdoms. Some thousands of these inscriptions are now known, many as a result of the explorations of J. Halévy and E. Glaser in the second half of the last century, but also from more recent expeditions and from numerous individual explorers. Since then a considerable amount of survey work has been undertaken in S Arabia, with some archaeological soundings and a number of full-scale excavations. Other international excavations have been undertaken in E Arabia.

Many explorations have been made in other parts of Arabia, notable among which are those of A. Musil, in central and N Arabia (1909–14), of N. Glueck, in Transjordan and Sinai (1932–71), and those of G. Ryckmans and H. St J. Philby, who collected some thousands of Arabic inscriptions from Sa'udi Arabia in 1951–2, not to mention the travels on a lesser scale of such men as Burton, Hurgronje, Doughty, Rutter and Thomas. Important among inscriptions from the N are the Taima' Stone, which bears an Aramaic inscription of about the 5th century BC, obtained by Huber in 1883 (*TEMA), and a second Aramaic inscription of the 4th century BC, found at Taima' in 1982.

c. History and civilization

Apart from the *nomads of the steppe lands of Arabia, whose life has continued with little change for millennia, the main areas of historical civilization were in the SW corner of the peninsula, and in the zone to the N where the steppe merges into the settled regions of Syria.

In the 2nd millennium BC various Semitic-speaking tribes arrived from the N in the area of modern Yemen, and formed the settlements which were later to emerge as the kingdoms of Saba' (*SHEBA, 7), Ma'īn (*MINAEANS), Qatabān and Ḥaḍramaut (Hazarmaveth, Gn. 10:26). The main cause of their prosperity was their intermediate position on the trade routes from the frankincense lands of the S coast and Ethiopia (*HERBS, Frankincense), to the civilizations in the N. The first of these kingdoms to emerge was Saba', as revealed by the appearance in about the 9th-8th century of native inscriptions which indicate a well-organized polity under a ruler who evidently combined certain priestly functions in his office. Religion was involved in most aspects of life, and there were annual festivals at the shrines of national deities. Its prosperity is indicated by the fact that it paid tribute to Sargon and Sennacherib, possibly from a

N trading colony. In *c.* 400 BC the neighbouring kingdom of Ma'īn came into prominence and infringed on much of Sabaean authority. In the 4th century the monarchy was founded in Qatabān, and in the last quarter of the 1st millennium the dominion of Saba', Ma'īn, Qatabān and Ḥaḍramaut fluctuated with turns of fortune, until the area came under the control of the Ḥimyarites. At their height, the S Arabian kingdoms had colonies as far afield as N Arabia, and inscriptions in their characters have been found on the Persian Gulf and in Mesopotamia (Ur, Uruk). The alphabets of the Thamūdic, Liḥyānite and Ṣafāitic inscriptions also show their influence in the N, and the Ethiopic language and script offer similar evidence from Africa.

In the N the history is one of the contacts made by nomads with the settled civilizations of Mesopotamia and Syria. In Transjordan the process of infiltration and settlement is evident, though there were periods when this was very sparse. In the early part of the Middle Bronze Age the whole of Transjordan was dotted with settlements (*ABRAHAM), but this was followed by a reduction (but not a total absence, as older books state) of sedentary occupation, *c.* 1900–1200 BC, until settlement was increased again in the late 2nd millennium BC. The name 'Arab' first appears in the contemporary inscriptions in the annals of Shalmaneser III, when one Gindibu from 'Arabia' (Kurkh Stele 2. 94) fought against him at Qarqar (853 BC), and thereafter they frequently appear in the Assyrian inscriptions as camel-borne raiding nomads, and they are so depicted in the bas-reliefs of Ashurbanipal at Nineveh (*CAMEL). One of the unusual episodes in Mesopotamian history was the sojourn of Nabonidus, king of Babylon (556–539 BC) at Taima' (*TEMA) in the N. He stayed there for 10 years while his son Bel-šar-uṣur (*BELSHAZZAR) ruled for him in Babylon.

In the latter part of the 4th century BC the Aramaic-speaking Arab kingdom of the *Nabataeans, with its capital at Petra, began to emerge, and it flourished as a trading state from the 2nd century until well into the Roman period. Farther S in the same period the Liḥyānite kingdom of *Dedan was formed by Arabs settling at an ancient Minaean colony. In the 1st century BC another Arab state, which adopted Aramaic as its official language, began to come to prominence at Palmyra (*TADMOR), and in the Christian era it largely eclipsed Petra as a trading state, and became a serious rival to Rome.

d. Biblical references

Arabia is not often referred to by this name in the Bible, since its inhabitants were generally known by the political or tribal names of the smaller groups to which they belonged. The Table of the *Nations in Gn. 10 lists a number of S Arabian peoples as the descendants of *Joktan and of *Cush. A number of mainly N Arabian tribes are listed as being descendants of Abraham through *Keturah and *Hagar (Gn. 25). Again among the descendants of Esau (Gn. 36) a number of Arabian peoples are mentioned. In the time of Jacob two groups of Abraham's descendants, the Ishmaelites (*ISHMAEL) and the *Midianites, are found as caravan merchants (Gn. 37:25–36; *NOMADS). It is, however, in the time of Solomon that contacts with Arabia become prominent in the OT narrative, mainly as a result of his extensive trade relations, particularly from his port of Eziongeber on the Red Sea. This is emphasized by the famous visit of the Queen of *Sheba (1 Ki. 9:26 28; 10), and nearer home by the tribute he received from the *malkê ʻ^{a}rab̲* (2 Ch. 9:14) which the EVV render 'kings of Arabia'. The name *ʻ^{a}rāb̲, ʻ^{a}rāb̲î* seems to have originally meant 'desert' or 'steppe' and by extension 'steppe dweller', and therefore in the biblical context it referred chiefly to those people who occupied the semi-desert areas to the E and S of Palestine (*EAST, CHILDREN OF). It is not possible, however, to say whether the word is always to be taken as a proper name 'Arab', or as a collective noun 'steppe dweller'.

In the 9th century, Jehoshaphat of Judah received tribute from the *ʻ^{a}rāb̲î* (2 Ch. 7:11), but his successor Jehoram suffered a raid in which the *ʻ^{a}rāb̲î* carried off his wives and sons (2 Ch. 21:16–17), and only Ahaziah, the youngest, was left (2 Ch. 22:1). In the 8th century Uzziah reversed the situation and restored *Elath to his dominion (2 Ki. 14:22).

Though the S Arabian kingdoms were known (*e.g.* Joel 3:8), most of the contacts of Israel with Arabia were with the nomadic tribes of the N. In the time of Hezekiah these people were very familiar (Is. 13:20; 21:13). In the time of Josiah (Je. 3:2), and in the closing days of the kingdom of Judah, the Arabians were coming to prominence as traders (Je. 25:23–24; Ezk. 27; *KEDAR).

The growing tendency of the Arabs to settle and build trading centres is illustrated by *Geshem, the Arab who tried to hinder Nehemiah rebuilding Jerusalem (Ne. 2:19; 6:1), presumably because he feared trade rivals. The kingdom of the Nabataeans was to follow, and in the Apocrypha the term 'Arab' usually refers to these people.

BIBLIOGRAPHY. (*a*) General: J. Bright, *A History of Israel*[2], 1972; I. Eph'al, *The Ancient Arabs*, 1982; W. C. Brice, *South-West Asia*, 1966, pp. 246–276; P. K. Hitti, *History of the Arabs*[6], 1956, pp. 1-86; M. Hoffner in H. W. Hausseg (ed.), *Wörtebuch der Mythologie*, I. 1, n. d., c. 1962, pp. 407–552; A. Grohmann, *Arabien*, 1963; G. W. van Beek in G. E. Wright (ed.), *The Bible and the Ancient Near East*, 1961, pp. 229–248; A. K. Irvine in *POTT*, pp. 287–311; S. Moscati, *The Semites in Ancient History*, 1959, pp. 104–132; G. Ryckmans, *Les religions arabes préislamiques*, 1951; *Proceedings of the Seminar for Arabian Studies*, 1- (1970–); *Atlal*, 1– (1977–); *Raydan*, 1– (1978–); *Arabian Archaeology and Epigraphy*, 1– (1990–); *Archäeologische Berichte aus dem Yemen*, 1– (1982–).

(*b*) S Arabia: A. F. L. Beeston, *Sabaic Grammar*, 1984; Beeston *et al*, *Sabaic Dictionary*, 1982; S. D. Ricks, *Lexicon of Inscriptional Qatabanian*, 1989; 'Theocracy in the Sayhad Culture', *Proceedings of the Seminar for Arabian Studies*, 7 (1977), pp. 5–10; B. Doe, *Southern Arabia*, 1971; *Monuments of South Arabia*, 1983; K. A. Kitchen, *Documents from Ancient Arabia*, I (1994), II–IV (in preparation).

(*c*) N Arabia: W. Wright, *A Grammar of the Arabic Language*[3], rev. by W. R. Smith and M. J. de Goeje, 1896; A. Musil, *Oriental Explorations and Studies*, 1–6, 1926–8; N. Glueck, *Explorations in Eastern Palestine*, I–IV (*AASOR* 14, 15, 18, 19, 25, 28), 1934–51; and more popular accounts – *The Other Side of the Jordan*[2], 1970; *The River Jordan*, 1946; and *Rivers in the Desert*, 1959; see also *BA* 22, 1959, pp. 98–108; F. V. Winnett and W. L. Reed, *Ancient Records from North Arabia*, 1970; on

Tema, see W. G. Lambert, *Proceedings of the Seminar for Arabian Studies*, 2 (1972), pp. 53–64 and C. J. Gadd, in *Anatolian Studies* 8, 1958, pp. 79–89. T.C.M.

II. In the New Testament

Arabia did not, as it does today, denote the whole of the great peninsula between the Red Sea and the Persian Gulf, but only the area to the immediate E and S of Palestine. This territory was occupied by an Arab tribe or tribes called the * Nabataeans, who had settled in the area during the 3rd century BC. By the 1st century they had established their control over an area which stretched from Damascus on the N to Gaza to the S and far into the desert to the E. Their capital was the red-rock city of Petra.

Arabia is mentioned only twice in the NT. Paul relates how, after his conversion, he went away into Arabia (Gal. 1:17). No other account of this incident occurs in the NT. The exact location of this event is very uncertain. Since Arabia to the Graeco-Roman mind meant the Nabataean kingdom, it is likely that he went there, possibly to Petra, the capital city. Why he went is not revealed. Perhaps his purpose was to be alone to commune with God. K. Lake suggests that Paul conducted a preaching mission there, because in the Epistle to the Galatians, where he mentions this incident, the antithesis is not between conferring with the Christians at Jerusalem and conferring with God in the desert, but between obeying immediately his commission to preach to the Gentiles and going to Jerusalem to obtain the authority to do this (*The Earlier Epistles of St Paul*, 1914, pp. 320f.).

In the only other occurrence of the word Arabia in the NT (Gal. 4:25) it is used in the narrower sense to denote the Sinai Peninsula, or the territory immediately to the E, across the Gulf of Aqabah.

BIBLIOGRAPHY. G. A. Smith, *The Historical Geography of the Holy Land*, 1931, pp. 547f., 649; *HDAC*; *IDB*; J. A. Montgomery, *Arabia and the Bible*, 1934. W.W.W.

ARAD. 1. A Canaanite town in the wilderness of Judah whose king vainly attacked Israel during the Wandering. Arad was destroyed, and renamed * Hormah (Nu. 21:1–3; 33:40). Jos. 12:14 lists a king of Arad and a king of Hormah amongst the conquered, while Jdg. 1:16–17 tells of Kenites settling in the area, and of Judah and Simeon destroying Zephath, renamed Hormah. Now Tell Arad 30 km NE of Beersheba, excavated from 1962 to 1974 by Y. Aharoni and R. B. K. Amiran. A large fortified city existed in the Early Bronze Age (Lower City), then the site was deserted until Iron Age I, when a mound at one side was occupied. Here a fortress was built in the 10th century BC that was used until the 6th century. During several phases of remodelling a shrine with stone altars and pillars existed in one corner. Potsherds inscribed in Hebrew found there include the names of the priestly families Pashhur and Meremoth. More texts were recovered from other parts of the fort, dealing with military affairs and supplies in the troubled years about 600 BC. One mentions 'the house of YHWH'. Arad of the Late Bronze Age (Canaanite Arad) may have been the present Tell Malḥatah, 12 km to the SW. Two Arads, Arad Rabbat and Arad of Yeruham, were listed by * Shishak after his invasion. See *NEAEHL*, pp. 62–72 and Y. Aharoni, *Arad Inscriptions*, 1981.

2. A Benjaminite, son of Beriah (1 Ch. 8:15–16). A.R.M.

ARAM, ARAMAEANS.

I. Ancestral and personal

a. The son of Shem, so named with Elam, Assyria and others in Gn. 10:22–23 and 1 Ch 1:17, having four others grouped under him. On this association of Aram with the E and NE parts of the ancient East, see section **II.***a*, below.

b. A personal name borne by individuals and heads of later clans in the patriarchal age and after, thus: Aram, grandson of Nahor, Abraham's brother (Gn. 22:21); an 'Aramitess' was mother of Machir by Manasseh (1 Ch. 7:14); another Aram is mentioned as a descendant of Asher (1 Ch. 7:34).

In the genealogies of Mt. 1:3–4 and Lk. 3:33 (AV) Aram is simply the misleading Gk. form of Ram (RSV), an entirely different name.

II. People, lands and language

a. Origins

Aram and Aramaeans are usually called 'Syria(ns)' in the English OT – a misleading appellation when applied to the period before *c.* 1000 BC. From the 3rd millennium BC, W Semitic-speaking seminomadic peoples are known from cuneiform sources to have been constantly infiltrating into Syria and Mesopotamia from almost the whole of the Arabian desert-fringe. In Mesopotamia under the kings of Akkad and of the 3rd Dynasty of Ur (*c.* 2400-2000 BC) these 'Westerners' (*MAR.TU* in Sumerian, *Amurru* in Babylonian) eventually penetrated right across the Tigris to the steppelands farther E, reaching the Iranian mountains. Evidence shows that they became well established there. (For a good discussion of this see J.-R. Kupper, *Les Nomades en Mésopotamie au Temps des Rois de Mari*, 1957, pp. 147f., 166, 177f., 196.) But these NE regions were no empty land. In the steppes and hills beyond, the Hurrians were at home, and the two populations doubtless mingled. These facts provide an illuminating background for the origins of the Aramaeans of biblical and external sources.

At this period mention is made of a settlement called Aram(e.i) in the E Tigris region N of Elam and ENE of Assyria. If this fact is linked with the presence of W Semitic-speaking settlers there, these may justifiably be considered as proto-Aramaeans. Kupper rejects this interpretation, but has apparently overlooked the importance of some OT passages here. This association of the earliest 'Aramaeans' with the E and NE is evident in Gn. 10:22–23, where Aram, Elam and Assyria occur together – a mark of very early date. Am. 9:7 carries on this tradition in later times: God brought Israel from Egypt (S), the Philistines from Caphtor (W) and the Aramaeans from Qir (NE). Qir occurs only once more (Is. 22:6) – standing for Assyria – - along with Elam, so Amos is in line with Gn. 10 and with the ascertainable NE occurrences of proto-Aramaeans. On the cuneiform evidence (but not using the biblical passages adduced here), these earliest Aramaeans were accepted by A. Dupont-Sommer, *VT Supp*. Vol. I, 1953, pp. 40–49; by S. Moscati, *The Semites in Ancient History*, 1959, pp. 66–67, and in earlier works; and by M. McNamara, *Verbum Domini* 35, 1957, pp. 129–142; but rejected (*e.g.*) by I. J. Gelb, *JCS* 15, 1961,

p. 28, n. 5; D. O. Edzard, *Die zweite Zwischenzeit Babyloniens*, 1957, p. 43, n. 188.

Aramu is attested as a personal name in the 3rd Dynasty of Ur (*c.* 2000 BC) and at Mari (18th century 196 BC); at Alalaḫ in N Syria about this time occurs the form Arammú for the doubled 'm' *cf.* the Heb. *'ᵉrammî*, 'Aramaean'. This corresponds with Aram as an OT personal name about that time. The name Aram may even be Hurrian; at Alalaḫ and at Nuzi appear a series of Hurrian-type names compounded with initial Aram- or Arim- (Kupper, *Nomades*, p. 113). 'Aram' may have been the name of a tribal group that first crossed the Tigris into the Hurrian regions, and its name has been applied by the Hurrians to all such W Semitic-speaking infiltrators and settlers (*cf.* Sumerian and Babylonian use of terms *MAR.TU* and *Amurru*, above) – hence its occurrence in place-names, or it might even have been a Hurrian epithet, which would better explain its occurrence in personal names. As the Hurrians spread right across upper Mesopotamia and into Syria by the beginning of the 2nd millennium, they would then perhaps use this term of the many W Semitic settlers in these regions – known from non-Hurrian cuneiform sources (*e.g.* Mari), Haneans, Suteans and others; but this remains wholly uncertain.

b. Early history, 19th–12th centuries BC

The Hebrew Patriarchs, after leaving Ur, first settled in this upper Mesopotamian area, at Harran (Gn. 11:28–32), in 'Aram-naharaim' (see below). One part of the family stayed on here (Nahor, Bethuel, Laban) as 'Aramaeans' (*i.e.*, named after the place where they lived), while the other (Abraham) went on to Canaan. But the wives of both Isaac and Jacob came from the Aramaean branch of the family (Gn. 24:28ff.), thoroughly justifying the later Israelite confession of descent from 'a wandering Aramaean' (= Jacob) in Dt. 26:5. The speech of Jacob's and Laban's families already showed dialectal differences ('Canaanite' and 'Aramaic'), see Gn. 31:47; note the early form of this Aramaic phrase, using direct (construct) genitive and not circumlocution with *dī*.

Aram-naharaim ('Aram of the two rivers') or Paddan-aram was basically the area within the great bend of the river Euphrates past Carchemish bounding it on the W, with the river Habur as limit in the E. In this area arose the Hurrian kingdom of Mitanni (16th–14th centuries BC). In the *Amarna Letters (*c.* 1360 BC) it is called *Naḫrima* with Canaanitic dual in 'm' (like Heb.), while in Egyptian texts of *c.* 1520–1170 BC appears the form *Nhrn*, clearly exhibiting an Aramaic-type dual in 'n', not assimilated to Canaanite as in the Amarna letters. The form in Egyptian is clear evidence – deriving directly from Egyptian military contact with Aram-naharaim – for Aramaic dialect-forms there from the 16th century BC. The forms *Naḫrima*/*Nhrn* are mentioned briefly in Gelb, *Hurrians and Subarians*, 1944, p. 74 and n. 208. Further hints of (proto-)Aramaic forms in the early 2nd millennium in this area are found in Albright, *AfO* 6, 1930–1, p. 218, n. 4.

From Ugarit (14th–13th centuries BC) come personal names Armeya and B(e)n-Arm(e)y(a), and a plot of land called 'fields of Aramaeans' (Kupper, *Nomades*, p. 114), which continue the story. An Egyptian mention of Aram occurs under Amenophis III (*c.* 1370 BC), *cf.* E. Edel, *Die Ortsnamenlisten aus dem Totentempel Amenophis III*, 1966, pp. 28f. Thus the place-name 'the Aram' or 'Pa-Aram' in the Egyptian Papyrus Anastasi III (13th century BC) probably stands for Aram, not Amurru. It was in the 13th century BC that Balaam was hired from *Pethor (in 'Amaw?) by the Euphrates in Aram (-naharaim) and the 'mountains of the east', in order to curse Israel (Nu. 22:5, RSV; 23:7; Dt. 23:4).

In the chaos that befell the W part of the ancient E just after *c.* 1200 BC when the sea peoples destroyed the Hittite empire and disrupted Syria-Palestine (*CANAAN; *EGYPT, History), one of Israel's oppressors was the opportunist *Cushan-rishathaim, king of Aram-naharaim, whose far-flung but fragile dominion lasted only 8 years (Jdg. 3:7–11). Still later in the Judges' period, the gods of Syria proper could already be called 'the gods of Aram' (*c.* 1100 BC?) in Jdg. 10:6 (Heb.); this ties up with the accelerating inflow of Aramaeans and settling in the later 12th and 11th centuries BC in Syria and Mesopotamia, culminating in the founding of Aramaean states. Just at this time, Tiglath-pileser I of Assyria (1100 BC) was trying unavailingly to stem the advance of 'Akhlamu, Aramaeans' across the length of the middle Euphrates (*ANET*, p. 275). The Akhlamu occur in the 13th, 14th and (as personal name) 18th centuries BC as Aramaean-type people, thus further witnessing to an Aramaean continuity from earlier to later times. On this section see also Kupper, *Nomades*; R. T. O'Callaghan, *Aram Naharaim*, 1948; M. F. Unger, *Israel and the Aramaeans of Damascus*, 1957; *ANET*, p. 259 and n. 11; W. T. Pitard, *Ancient Damascus*, 1987.

c. Israel and the Aramaean States (*c. 1000–700 BC*)

(i) *Saul* (*c. 1050–1010 BC*). During his reign, Saul had to fight many foes for Israel: Moab, Ammon and Edom in the E, the Philistines in the SW and the 'kings of Zobah' in the N (1 Sa. 14:47; or 'king', if LXX be followed). This was probably at the height of his power (*c.* 1025 BC?), before the final disasters of his reign.

(ii) *David* (*c. 1010–970 BC*). David's first known Aramaean contact is with Talmai son of Ammihur, king of Geshur, whose daughter he married (Absalom being her son by him) within his first 7 years' reign at Hebron (1010–1003 BC), 2 Sa. 3:3, 5. Talmai still ruled Geshur late in David's reign when Absalom fled there for 3 years (2 Sa. 13:37–39). In the second half of his reign, David clashed with Hadadezer son of Rehob, king of Aram-zobah (N of Damascus). This king had already extended his rule as far as the Euphrates (subduing the hostile Toi, king of Hamath, 2 Sa. 8:10), but his N subjects must have revolted, for when David attacked him Hadadezer was then going to 'restore' his conquests there (2 Sa. 8:3). Perhaps David and Toi found Hadadezer too dangerous; at any rate, David annexed Damascus and Toi of Hamath became his (subject-) ally, 2 Sa. 8:5–12. The revolt against Hadadezer probably followed the two heavy defeats that David inflicted on him as ally of Ammon (2 Sa. 10; 1 Ch. 19) with other Aramaean states (see Unger, pp. 42–46). No direct time-relation between 2 Sa. 8:3-12 and 2 Sa. 9–12 is stated – but the Ammonite war probably preceded that of 2 Sa. 8. Henceforth, David was doubtless overlord of Hadadezer and all Syria. The earlier wide but ephemeral power of Hadadezer may be reflected in later Assyrian texts which report how, under Ashur-rabi II (*c.* 1012–972 BC), 'the king of Aram' gained control of Pethor (Pitru) and

Mutkinu on either side of the Euphrates; this may mark the foundation there of the Aramaean kingdom of Bit-Adini – perhaps the source of Hadadezer's troops from beyond the Euphrates. For further discussion, see Landsberger, *Sam'al I*, 1948, p. 35, n. 74; and Malamat, *BA* 21, 1958, pp. 101–102.

(iii) *Solomon* (*c. 970–930 BC*). Probably it was in the first half of his reign that Solomon overcame 'Hamath-zobah', *i.e.* presumably crushed a revolt in the S part of the country of Hamath that adjoined Zobah – perhaps a rising against Hamath's subject-ally status? At any rate Solomon's overlordship was effective enough for him to have store-cities built there (2 Ch. 8:3–4). But in the last part of David's reign, after the discomfiture of Hadadezer of Zobah, a mere youth, Rezon, went off and gathered a marauding band around himself. For some time, into Solomon's earlier years, he was probably little more than a petty, roving insurgent. But for the latter half of Solomon's reign he gained control of Damascus and became king there, briefly surviving Solomon, whom he had always opposed (1 Ki. 11:23–25); Rezon, it seems, played bandit till *c.* 955 BC, reigning in Damascus perhaps *c.* 955–925 BC, till at last – full of years – - he passed away, and a new 'strong man', Hezion, seized the Damascus throne.

(iv) *The Dynasty of Hezion*. The new opportunist founded a dynasty that lasted a century. Hezion (*c.* 925–915?), his son Tabrimmon (*c.* 915–900?) and grandson Ben-hadad I (*c.* 900–860?) are attested in this order and relationship, from 1 Ki. 15:18. (The Melqart Stele, commonly held to show the same line (*DOTT*, pp. 239–41; *ANET*, p. 501), is in fact impossible to read with confidence.) These kings speedily made of Damascus the paramount kingdom in Syria proper, rivalled only by Hamath. When attacked by Baasha of Israel, Asa of Judah sought aid from Ben-hadad I (1 Ki. 15:18ff.).

The *Ben-hadad who clashed with Ahab (1 Ki. 20) and was murdered by Hazael in Joram's time, *c.* 843 BC (2 Ki. 6:24ff.; 8:7–15) is probably a different king, a Ben-hadad II (*c.* ?860–843), but it is possible to argue, with Albright, that this is still Ben-hadad I (then, *c.* 900–843 BC – a long reign but not unparalleled). This Ben-hadad II/I is almost certainly the Adad-idri ('Hadad-ezer') of Damascus whom Shalmaneser III attacked in 853, 849, 848 and 845 BC, and whose murder and replacement by *Hazael are also alluded to by the Assyrian. Double names are common among ancient Near Eastern rulers; Ben-hadad/Adad-idri is but one more example. It was Ben-hadad of Damascus and Urhileni of Hamath who led the opposition to Assyria and contributed the largest armed contingents, though their efforts were handsomely matched in this respect by Ahab of Israel in 853 BC at Qarqar (*ANET*, pp. 278–281; Wiseman in *DOTT*, p. 47).

(v) *Hazael to Rezin*. The usurper *Hazael (*c.* 843–796 BC) almost immediately clashed with Joram of Israel (842/1 BC), *cf.* 2 Ki. 8:28–29; 9:15. Jehu gained the Israelite throne at this time, but he and others paid tribute to Assyria (*ANET*, p. 280; *DOTT*, p. 48; *IBA*, p. 57, fig. 51), leaving Hazael of Damascus to oppose Assyria alone in 841 and 837 BC (Unger, *op. cit.*, pp. 76–78). Thereafter, Hazael savagely attacked Israel under Jehu, seizing Transjordan (2 Ki. 10:32–33), and throughout the reign of Jehoahaz, *c.* 814/3–798 BC (2 Ki. 13:22). But temporary relief did occur; the 'deliverer' sent by God then (2 Ki. 13:5) may have been Adad-nirari III of Assyria who intervened against Hazael (called 'Mari') about 805–802 BC.

In the Israelite Joash's early years the pressure was at first maintained by Hazael's son Ben-hadad III (2 Ki. 13:3). But as promised by God through Elisha, Joash (*c.* 798–782/1 BC) was able to recover from Ben-hadad the lands previously lost to Hazael (2 Ki. 13:14–19, 22–25). Ben-hadad acceded *c.* 796 BC, and reigned till roughly 770 BC on evidence of Zakur's stele (see Unger, *op. cit.*, pp. 85–89; *DOTT*, pp. 242–250). Ben-hadad headed a powerful coalition against Zakur of Hamath, a usurper from Lu'ash who had seized control of the whole kingdom Hamath-Lu'ash. But Zakur and his allies defeated Ben-hadad's coalition and so spelt the end of the dominance in Syria of the Aramaean kingdom of Damascus.

Shortly after this, discredited Damascus came under the overlordship of Jeroboam II of Israel (2 Ki. 14:28). Still later, perhaps after Jeroboam II's death in 753 BC, a king *Rezin (Assyrian *Raḫianu*) appeared in Damascus and menaced Judah as Israel's ally, even (like Hazael) conquering Transjordan again; but Ahaz of Judah appealed to Tiglath-pileser III of Assyria, who then in 732 BC defeated and slew Rezin (2 Ki. 16:5-9; *ANET*, p. 283), deporting the unhappy Aramaeans to Qir, ironically their ancient homeland, as prophesied by Amos (1:4–5).

(vi) *Other Aramaean kingdoms* are rarely mentioned in Scripture. Sennacherib in 701 BC mocked Hezekiah over the impotence of the kings and gods of *Arpad, *Hamath, *Gozan, *Harran, *Rezeph (Assyr. *Raṣappa*) and the 'children of Eden in Telassar' (2 Ki. 18:34; 19:12–13). The last-named are the people of the Aramaean province (former kingdom) of Bit-Adini, the 'House of Eden' or Beth-eden of Am. 1:5.

BIBLIOGRAPHY. M. F. Unger, R. T. O'Callaghan, A. Malamat (works cited at end of **II.** *b*); A. Dupont-Sommer, *Les Araméens*, 1949. Specific studies include: R. de Vaux, *RB* 43, 1934, pp. 512–518, and A. Jepsen, *AfO* 14, 1941–4, pp. 153–172, and *ibid.* 16, 1952–3, pp. 315–317; B. Mazar, *BA* 25, 1962, pp. 98–120, for Aram-Damascus and Israel; E. O. Forrer, in Ebeling and Meissner, *Reallexikon der Assyriologie*, 1, 1932, pp. 131–139 (*Aramu*), and B. Landsberger, *Sam'al I*, 1948; W. F. Albright in *AS* 6, 1956, pp. 75–85, on Assyrian penetration of Aramaean politics and art; A. Malamat, in *POTT*, pp. 134–155. Inscriptions, *cf.* J. C. L. Gibson, *Textbook of Syrian Semitic Inscriptions*, 2, 1975.

d. Language

See *LANGUAGE OF THE OLD TESTAMENT.

It should be recognized that the occurence of Aramaisms in OT Hebrew often indicates an *early*, not a late, date. Note the 2nd-millennium traces of Aramaic forms (**II.***b*, above). Aramaean states in Syria which existed from at least Saul's reign, and marriages in the time of David (Talmai), imply Aramaic linguistic influence in Palestine then. Finally, some 'Aramaisms' are actually Hebraisms (or Canaanisms) in Aramaic (*cf.* K. A. Kitchen, *Ancient Orient and Old Testament*, 1966, pp. 143–146; A. Hurwitz, *IEJ* 18, 1968, pp. 234–240).

e. Aramaean culture

The Aramaeans' one major contribution to ancient Oriental culture was their language: at first, in commerce and diplomacy, then for communication over wide areas (see above), but also as a literary medium (see R. A. Bowman, 'Aramaic, Arameans and the Bible', *JNES* 7, 1948, pp. 65–99). The story and proverbs of Ahiqar are set in the Assyria of Sennacherib and certainly go back in origin to almost that time; from the 5th century BC come the religious texts in demotic (Egyptian) script (Bowman, *JNES* 3, 1944, pp. 219–231) and the Papyri Blacassiani (G. A. Cooke, *A Textbook of North-Semitic Inscriptions*, 1903, pp. 206–210, No. 76). Still later come magical texts, including one in cuneiform script of the Seleucid era (C. H. Gordon, *AfO* 12, 1937–9, pp. 105–117). Syriac in the Christian epoch was a great province of Christian literature. The chief gods of the Aramaeans were Baal-shamain and other forms of Baal, Hadad the storm-god, Canaanite deities such as Ashtar, and Mesopotamian ones, including Marduk, Nebo, Shamash, *etc.* (J. A. Fitzmyer, *The Aramaic Inscriptions of Sefîre*, 1967, pp. 33ff.). See Dupont-Sommer, *Les Araméens*, pp. 106–119; Dhorme and Dussaud, *Religions, Babylonie, etc.*, 1949, pp. 389ff. K.A.K.

ARARAT.

I. Biblical evidence

The name Ararat occurs four times in the Bible. It was the mountainous or hilly area (*hārê ʾărāṭ*, 'mountains of Ararat') where Noah's ark came to rest (Gn. 8:4. Reports linking supposed remains of wood from Lake Kop on Mt Ararat with the ark of Noah's *flood have not been confirmed archaeologically nor dated prior to *c.* 2500 BC); the land (*'ereṣ*) to which Adrammelech and Sharezer, the parricides of Sennacherib, fled for asylum (2 Ki. 19:37 = Is. 37:38); and a kingdom (*mamlāḵâ*) grouped by Jeremiah with Minni and Ashkenaz in a prophetic summons to destroy Babylon (Je. 51:27). The AV reads 'Armenia' in both Kings and Isaiah, following *Armenian* in the LXX of Isaiah.

II. Extra-biblical evidence

There is little doubt that biblical *ʾărāṭ* was the *Urarṭu* of the Assyrian inscriptions, a kingdom which flourished in the time of the Assyrian empire in the neighbourhood of Lake Van in Armenia. While it is frequently mentioned by the Assyrian kings as a troublesome N neighbour, it was much influenced by Mesopotamian civilization, and in the 9th century the cuneiform script was adopted and modified for writing Urarṭian (also called 'Vannic' or 'Chaldian', not to be confused with 'Chaldean'), a language unrelated to Akkadian. Nearly 200 Urarṭian inscriptions are known, and in these the land is referred to as *Biainae* and the people as 'children of Ḫaldi', the national god. Excavations, notably at Toprak Kale, part of the ancient capital, Ṭušpa, near the shore of Lake Van, at Karmir Blur, a town site near Erivan in the USSR, and at Alting Tepe, near Erzincan, have revealed examples of art and architecture.

III. Uraru

In the 13th century, when Urarṭu is first mentioned in the inscriptions of Shalmaneser I, it appears as a small principality between the lakes of Van and Urmia, but it seems to have grown in power in the following centuries when Assyria was suffering a period of decline. In the 9th century reports of Assyrian campaigns against Urarṭu, whose territory now extended well to the N and W, become more frequent, and about 830 BC a new dynasty was founded by Sardur I, who established his capital at Ṭušpa. His immediate successors held the frontiers, but the kingdom was badly shaken at the end of the 8th century by the Cimmerian (*GOMER) invasions, and was only briefly revived in the mid-7th century by Rusa II, who may have been the king who gave asylum to Sennacherib's assassins. The end of Urarṭu is obscure, but the Indo-European-speaking Armenians must have been established there by the late 6th century BC, as is shown by the Behistun inscription which gives *arminiya* in the Old Persian version where the Babylonian version reads *urašṭu*, and the Aramaic version from Elephantine gives *'rrṭ*. Urarṭu probably disappeared as a state in the early 6th century, at about the time of Jeremiah's prophetic summons.

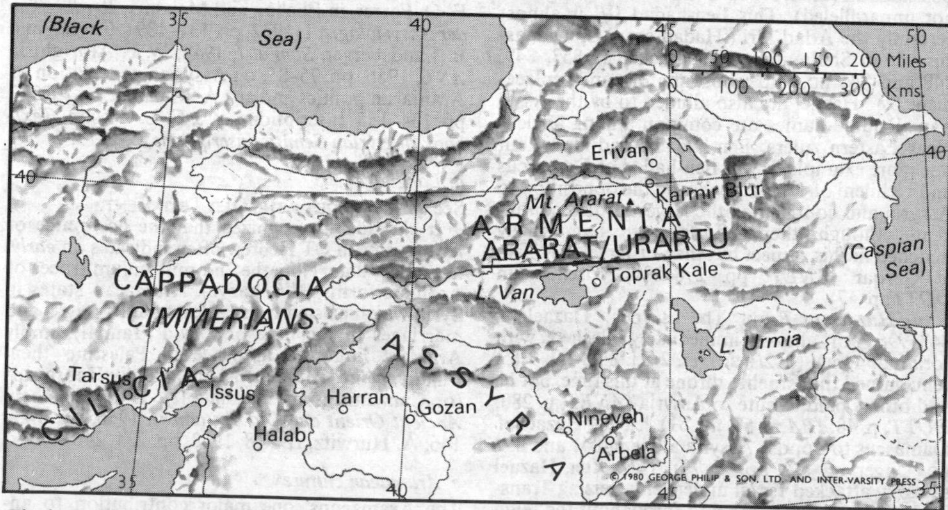

The location of Ararat in Armenia.

BIBLIOGRAPHY. A. Goetze, *Kleinasien*², 1957, pp. 187-200, 215–216; F. W. König, *Handbuch der chaldischen Inschriften* (*AfO*, Beiheft 8), I, 1955, II, 1957; M. N. van Loon, *Urartian Art*, 1966. T.C.M.

ARAUNAH (Heb. *'ᵃrawnâ*, also *hā'ᵃwarnâ*, *'ᵃranyâ*). In 2 Sa. 24:16ff. a Jebusite whose threshing-floor was bought by David when he saw the destroying angel hold his hand there, so that he might build an altar on the spot and offer a sacrifice to check the pestilence which broke out after his numbering of the people. In 1 Ch. 21:18ff. (where Araunah is called Ornan) David buys the area surrounding the threshing-floor too, to be the site of the future Temple which, in due course, Solomon built there (1 Ch. 22:1; 2 Ch. 3:1). Araunah's name has been derived from Hittite *arawanis*, 'freeman', 'noble'. H. A. Hoffner (*POTT*, p. 225) suggests rather reading *'wrnh* (*cf.* Ch. and LXX) = Hurrian *ewri-ne*, 'the lord'. Ugarit supplies both *iwrn* (Hurrian) and *arwn* (Hittite) as personal names (F. Gröndahl, *Die Personennamen der Texte aus Ugarit*, 1967, pp. 224, 272). In 2 Sa. 24:16 the name is preceded by the definite article, and in v. 23 it is glossed by *hammeleḵ* ('the king'), whence it has been conjectured that he was the last king of Jebusite Jerusalem. (*HITTITES.) F.F.B.

ARCHAEOLOGY.

I. General

Within the rapidly developing science of archaeology the special study of 'Biblical Archaeology' selects those material remains of Palestine and its neighbouring countries which relate to the biblical period and narrative. These include the remains of buildings, art, inscriptions and every artefact which helps the understanding of the history, life and customs of the Hebrews and those peoples who, like the Egyptians, Phoenicians, Syrians, Assyrians and Babylonians, came into contact with and influenced them. Interest in places and times mentioned in the Bible provided the initial incentive to many of the earlier excavations, and the broad picture of the historical, religious and ethical background to the Bible now available from archaeological discoveries has done much to explain, illustrate and sometimes to corroborate biblical statements and counteract theories insufficiently based on facts.

The limitations of archaeology are due to the vast span of time and area to be covered and to the hazards of preservation. Objects of wood, leather or cloth rarely survive and their existence has to be assumed. No biblical site has ever been, or probably can be, completely excavated. Only in recent years have accurate methods of stratification and recording enabled detailed comparisons to be made between sites. This has led to the revision of some earlier conclusions, *e.g.* Garstang's dating of Jericho walls to centuries earlier by Kenyon. Moreover, the dearth of inscriptions from Palestine itself means that direct extra-biblical insight into the thoughts and life of the early peoples is rare. As archaeology deals primarily with materials, it can never test such great biblical truths as the existence and redeeming activity of God and Christ, the incarnate Word.

In Palestine (taking this term to include the modern states of Israel and Jordan) the archaeological technique of sequence dating was first worked out. At Tell el-Hesi in 1890 Flinders Petrie realized that different levels of occupation could be distinguished by the characteristic pottery and other features found in them. This scheme of stratigraphy and typology is now applied throughout the world; in Palestine it has been improved by later excavators, especially at Tell Beit Mirsim, Samaria, Lachish and Jericho. By comparison between sites within Palestine and farther afield a network of related finds has been established, linking with historical records, to give a remarkably close-knit chronology from the 4th millennium BC. Dates before that time are still imprecise, even when the Carbon 14 method supplies some evidence. The accompanying table (p. 74) gives the currently-accepted designations for these archaeological periods:

II. Prehistory

The Near East was the scene of man's first emergence as a food-gatherer in the Palaeolithic period of which remains are found in the Carmel caves (Wadi al-Mughârah), 'Eynan and 'Oren. After a gap he is traced as a food-gatherer in the so-called 'Neolithic revolution'. Many find early associations with pre-historic Europe rather than Africa and physical relationships with European Neanderthal types. Open settlements with huts dated *c.* 9000 BC are found at Shanidar (Iraq), 'Eynan (Lake Huleh), Jericho and Beidha (near Petra). These lead on to the pre-pottery Neolithic B with the development of the economy of production. At Jericho at this time (*c.* 7500 BC) there are found massive defences and unusually plastered skulls and figurines of unidentified purpose. Neolithic sites have been traced in Yarmuk and Galilee (Sh'ar Haggolan) and at Ain Ghazzal in Jordan. These are contemporary with settlements in the Nile Valley, on Cyprus, in Anatolia (Çayönü, Çatal Hüyük) and in N Mesopotamia (Jarmo, Nemrik).

In the Chalcolithic period wall paintings, painted pottery and simple copper come from the Jordan Valley, Telulat Ghassul, Esdraelon, near Gaza, and in the N Negeb. Elaborate objects were cast in copper for cultic purposes (Nahal Mishmar) and gold was worked. Clay models show that curved vaulted roofs were a feature of underground stores (Abu Matar), rock cisterns and some dwellings.

The transition to the Early Bronze Age is ill-defined in Palestine. Some trace this at a number of settlements which later grew into city states (Megiddo, Jericho, Beth-shan, Beth-yeraḥ and Tell el-Far'a near Shechem) or were later abandoned for a time (Samaria and Tell en-Nasbeh). Invaders, probably former nomads from the N or E, brought a new type of pottery and buried their dead in mass graves cut in the rocks. These tombs sometimes included pottery types known from the previous Late Chalcolithic period, Esdraelon burnished wares and painted pottery later found in abundance (EB I). The term Proto-Urban, corresponding to the Protoliterate (Jemdet Nasr) period in Iraq *c.* 3200 BC has been used to describe this phase.

III. The Canaanite (Bronze) Age

Towns with mud-brick walls begin to appear in the Early Bronze Age I. At the same time the pottery in the N (Beth-yeraḥ, level II; Beth-shan, level XI) differs from that in the S, found at Ophel (Jerusalem), Gezer, Ai, Jericho (VI–VII) and Tell en-Nasbeh. The towns in the N continued to flourish in EB II *c.* 2900 BC (Megiddo, XVI–XVII; Beth-yeraḥ, III; Beth-shan, XII) although in the S some Egyptian influence can be seen (Jericho, IV). The well-developed lower city at Arad (IV–I) with its twin temples shows affinities with the N Canaanite towns (*cf.* *AI). There were striking developments, notably in a fine new 'Khirbet Kerak' ware which shows the gradual improvement in pottery technique in Palestine and Syria.

About 2200 BC saw the appearance of a people with distinctive burial customs, pottery and weapons. These were local nomadic groups thought to have been new arrivals to the land and were identified with the Amorites (e.g. Tel Ajjul, Jericho, Megiddo). The incoming Israelites later noted the Amorites (Nu. 13:29; Jos. 5:1; 10:6) as people of the hill-country, and earlier the Execration Texts (*Egypt IV *b*1) attest an Amorite presence there.

Other types of pottery, weapons and burial customs show there were people connected with the city-states of Syria and Phoenicia, and soon the numerous city-states begin to appear which are characteristically Canaanite. Their kings probably included the Asiatic 'Foreign Rulers' (Hyksos) who overran Egypt *c.* 1730 BC. It was a time of wealth, though of frequent inter-city warfare. Major cities had a citadel and a lower town enclosed by high ramparts (*e.g.* Carchemish, Qatna, Hazor).

This Middle Bronze Age was a time when semi-nomadic groups, including Habiru, among whom may well have been the Patriarchs, infiltrated the scrub-land between the defended towns (*PATRIARCHAL AGE). The tombs of such people have been found at Jericho. The towns and their houses (*e.g.* Beit Mirsim, Megiddo and Jericho) remained small but with little change until they were violently destroyed (LB) probably by the Egyptians (Tuthmosis III) repulsing the Hyksos, *c.* 1450 BC. Despite trade contacts with the E Mediterranean (Mycenaean pottery), the hill towns of Palestine were now poorer and fewer than the neighbouring coastal cities.

Once again the major cities were reoccupied, but only to be sacked again later in the 13th century. Traces of the Israelite attack under Joshua have been seen in the burnt ruins of Hazor, Bethel, Beit Mirsim and Lachish, but it is impossible to substantiate this claim. According to the OT, Joshua did not set fire to many places. At Jericho the town has been found to have been abandoned *c.* 1325 BC, but the fallen walls once thought to belong to this LB period (Garstang) are now known to have been destroyed in EB (Kenyon).

Examples of at least six different types of *writing have been found in the LB sites of Canaan: Babylonian cuneiform, Egyp. hieroglyphic and hieratic, the Canaanite linear alphabet (ancestor of the Heb. and Gk. alphabets), and an alphabet of 25 to 30 cuneiform signs related to that of *Ugarit, the syllabic script of Byblos and scripts of Cypriot or Cretan type.

Canaanite religious practices can be glimpsed in the remains of temples and shrines at Hazor, Lachish, Megiddo, and other places, with *altars, offering tables and cultic furniture. Metal figurines represent *Baal, and clay ones Astarte. These are commonly found. Cylinder *seals also show gods and goddesses, one from Bethel bearing the name Astarte in Egyptian.

(For a new statement of the archaeological and

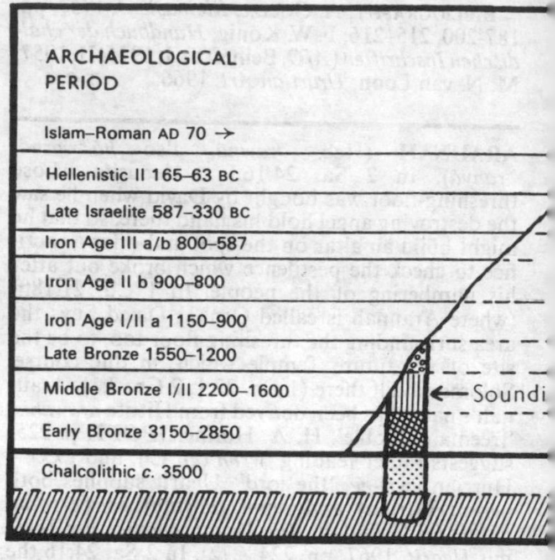

Schematic drawing of an ancient Palestinian site showin

other evidence for a 15th-century-BC date for the Exodus, see J. J. Bimson, *Redating the Exodus and Conquest*[2], 1981.)

IV. The Israelite (Iron) Age

By the 12th century the Philistine settlement in SW Canaan is attested by a new range of decorated pottery inspired by Late Mycenean forms yet with local Palestinian, Cypriote and Egyp. elements. Philistine pottery occurs throughout Philistia, the Shephela from Beit Mirsim to Gezer and as far N as Joppa. Other than small amounts attributable to trade, it is not found at first in the central hills (Tell en-Nazbeh, Gibeah, Jerusalem, Beth-zur), but by 1050 BC traces of their inroads to Shiloh and Beth-shan have been discovered. Such pottery found along the coast N of Philistia, in Dor, Akko, and Megiddo, probably belong to other groups of the Sea People. The Bible relates that the Philistines were the first people to use iron in Palestine. The Israelites were slow to break this monopoly and their consequent economic superiority (1 Sa. 13:18–22). Wealthy and well-constructed Canaanite strongholds held out for at least another century (Beth-shan). The Israelites at this time lived in small villages throughout the central hill-country ('zbet Sartah) and Galilee (Dan). They are recognized by their four-roomed houses (three parallel to each other and the fourth at right angles to them at one end), by the large number of storage pits for grain around the houses, and large storage jars with thick collar rims.

Archaeologically it is very difficult to attribute the construction of cities to any specific king of the United Monarchy. Saul had a citadel at Gibeah (Tell el-Fûl), and the first fortification there has been attributed to him. It shows the adoption of a new fortification system of casemate walls which were a characteristic feature of this period of *architecture. Similar casemate walls have been found at a number of sites including Shechem, Beth-shemesh and Beit Mirsim. A small town at Megiddo, whose houses form a defensive ring around the perimeter of the mound, has been attributed to David.

1 Ki. 9:15 relates how Solomon had built up

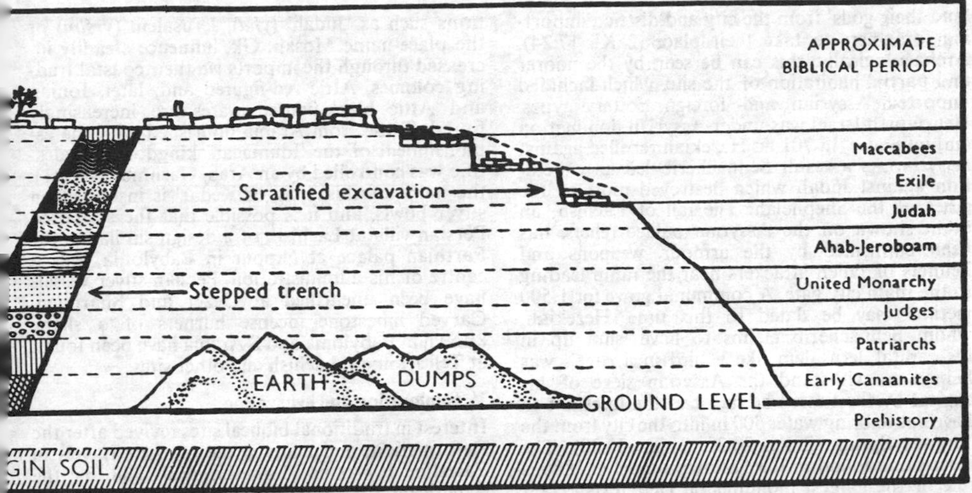

hods of excavation and levels (strata) of occupation (see also p. 73).

Hazor, Megiddo and Gezer. Hazor of the period of the monarchy has a casemate wall, a six-chambered gate and a 'governor's residence'. On the basis of this it was attributed to Solomon. At Megiddo the first fortified city also has a six-chambered gate, and another has been found at Gezer. Lachish had a fortified tower which controlled the collection of taxes and the storage of grain in the region. The material prosperity of Solomon's reign must have been largely due to the construction and development of many copper- and iron-smelting *mines. Ezion-geber at Aqabah was used for importing many commodities by *ship. A potsherd found at Tell Qasileh inscribed 'gold from Ophir' attests this trade at a slightly later date.

The defeat of the Philistines opened the way for an undisputed expansion of Phoenician trade, and this is reflected in the building of Solomon's Temple. The plan followed a Syro-Phoenician style already adopted at Hazor and Tell Tainat. The entrance, flanked by twin free-standing pillars (*cf.* *JACHIN AND BOAZ), led by a direct axis through a vestibule into the large sanctuary (*hêkl̲āl*) into the small, inner sanctuary (*dᵉḇîr*). A peculiar Solomonic development was the provision of considerable storage space for the treasuries along the sides of this building. The decoration of the *Temple, with its cherubim, palms, open-work patterns or furnishings, can be paralleled from contemporary ivories found at Samaria, Arslan Tash (Syria) or Nimrud (Iraq), and attested in earlier *art also at *Ugarit. Other items, altars, stands, tongs and utensils, have been found during excavations.

The invasion of Shishak I of Egypt, *c.* 926 BC, resulted in destruction as far N as Tell Abu Hawan and at Beit Mirsim (B) and Beth-shemesh (IIa). The period of the divided Monarchy has been illuminated by a number of excavations. At Tirzah (Tell el-Far'a) de Vaux has shown that after the 10th century the town was abandoned, as would be expected when Omri transferred his capital to Samaria (1 Ki. 16:23–24) which gave him better communications with the Phoenician sea-ports.

At Samaria the summit was laid out as a royal quarter surrounded by a wall of fine masonry.

Many ivories found in the Omri-Ahab palace may have come from the decorations or furnishings of Ahab's 'ivory house' (1 Ki. 22:39; Am. 6:4), and some are inscribed with Phoenician marks common in the working of *ivory. The script is identical with that of the inscription of Mesha, found at Dibhan, describing relations between him and Israel *c.* 825 BC (*MOABITE STONE). In the palace courtyard at Samaria was an open cistern or 'pool', perhaps that in which Ahab's chariot was washed down (1 Ki. 22:38). Sixty-three inscribed ostraca, accounts of wine and oil brought to the royal stores, testify to the administrative organization, probably under Jeroboam II.

Official buildings similar to those at Samaria (I) have been found at Beth-shan (V) and Megiddo (V). At Megiddo, Hazor and Beer-sheba large storehouses have been uncovered where the taxes paid in kind were kept. At Hazor (VIII) Ahab appears to have extended the town by building new fortifications round the whole of the high ground around the citadel. There, as at Samaria (II = Jehu), the solid defence walls now built were to stand until the Hellenistic reconstructions, *c.* 150 BC. About 800 BC Tell el-Far'a was reoccupied as a local residence for a governor with excellent private houses near by. The pottery found there is similar to that at Samaria (IV), where Jeroboam II was in residence.

Tell en-Nasbeh (Mizpah) and Gibeah were strongly refortified as frontier towns during the divided Monarchy. Both sites were reconstructed on an identical plan and with similar material which may show that this was the work of Asa after he had destroyed the nearby fort of Baasha at Ramah (1 Ki. 15). The invasion of Tiglath-pileser III of Assyria, *c.* 734 BC, resulted in the heavy destruction of Hazor (V) and Megiddo (IV). In the debris of the former a sherd inscribed *lpqḥ* ('belonging to Pekah') recalls that, according to 2 Ki. 15:29; 16:5–8 and the Assyrian Annals, Pekah ruled there at this time. The same Assyrian king mentioned (Jeho)ahaz whose tribute is recorded in 2 Ki. 16:8.

In 722 BC Sargon II concluded the siege of Samaria and, as he claims, removed 27,290 prisoners 'and their gods' from the city and district, importing foreigners to take their place (2 Ki. 17:24). Archaeologically, this can be seen by the poorer and partial habitation of the site, which included imported Assyrian and foreign pottery types. Henceforth Israel was under Assyrian domination and influence. In 701 BC Hezekiah rebelled against Assyria. As a result Sennacherib led an expedition against Judah which destroyed most of the cities of the Shephelah. The fall of Lachish, an event shown on the Assyrian palace reliefs, has been confirmed by the armour, weapons and helmets of fallen attackers near the ramp leading to the main city gate. A communal grave for 1,500 victims may be dated to this time. Hezekiah, whom Sennacherib claims to have 'shut up in his capital Jerusalem like a bird in a cage', was helped to withstand the Assyrian siege of his capital by the tunnel he had had the foresight to have cut to bring water 500 m into the city from the Virgin's Spring (2 Ki. 20:20; 2 Ch. 32:30). The inscription found in the *Siloam tunnel in 1880 is one of the longest monumental Heb. texts extant (*DOTT*, pp. 209–211). Other contemporary Heb. *writing includes a possible inscription of *Shebna.

The ardour of Josiah's opposition to Egypt is seen in the destruction of Megiddo (II) by Neco in 609 BC while on his way to Carchemish, a city which excavation shows to have been destroyed by fire soon afterwards. This was during the battle in 605 BC when Nebuchadrezzar II captured the city and overran Syria and Palestine, which became subject to the Babylonians. When Judah rebelled, stern punishment was inevitable. The Babylonian Chronicle describes the capture of Jerusalem on 16 March 597 BC. Many towns and fortresses in Judah, but not in the N, show the ravages of the Babylonian attacks at this time and, following Zedekiah's revolt, during the war of 589–587, some were destroyed and never again reoccupied (Beth-shemesh, Tell Beit Mirsim). In the debris at *Lachish (III) 21 inscribed potsherds bear witness to the anxiety of the defenders (*DOTT*, pp. 211–217).

Archaeological surveys show that the country was greatly impoverished during the Exile, although the royal estates in Judah continued to be administered on behalf of Jehoiachin, who is named in texts from his prison in Babylon. Stamp sealings of 'Eliakim, steward of Yaukin'; *seals of Jaazaniah from Tell en-Nasbeh and of Gedaliah from Lachish (2 Ki. 25:22–25) are witnesses to the activities of these leaders.

The resettlement of Judah was slow, and excavations show that it was not until the 3rd century that Judah was repopulated to the same density as in former times. Samaria, Bethel, Tell en-Nasbeh, Beth-zur and Gezer were, however, occupied almost continuously, and cemeteries at 'Athlit (Carmel) and Tell el-Far'a (Negeb) produced Iron Age III pottery and Persian objects. The Persians allowed a measure of local autonomy, and locally minted coins begin to appear in the 5th and are abundant by the 3rd century. Most are imitations of Attic drachmas, but some bear Hebrew–Aramaic inscriptions (*yehud*, 'Judah') similar to those found on the Jewish coin which shows also a male deity seated on a chariot holding a hawk (early 4th century BC; see *IBA*, fig. 96). This may be an early instance of the use of *money. Many jar handles of this period are stamped with inscriptions such as 'Judah' (*yhd*), Jerusalem (*yršlm*) or the place-name Mosah. Gk. influence steadily increased through the imports *via* their coastal trading colonies. Attic red-figured and, later, Ionian and Attic black-figured wares are increasingly found. Trade from Arabia flourished with the establishment of the 'Idumaean' kingdom. S Palestine was controlled by an Arab, Gashmu (Ne. 6:1); the name of this 'king of Kedar' is inscribed on silver bowls, and it is possible that the supposed Persian villa at Lachish, of a design similar to the Parthian palace at Nippur in Babylonia, was a centre of his administration. Persian silver vessels have been unearthed at Gezer and Sharuhen. Carved limestone incense burners of a shape known in Babylonia and S Arabia have been found at Tell Jemmeh, Lachish and other sites.

V. Exploration and excavation

Interest in traditional biblical sites revived after the Reformation, and many wrote of their travels in Palestine. It was not, however, until 1838 that the Americans Edward Robinson and Eli Smith carried out the first planned surface exploration, identifying several ancient sites with places named in the Bible. The first excavation was undertaken by the Frenchman De Saulcy, near Jerusalem in 1863, and this was followed by a series of surveys on behalf of the Palestine Exploration Fund in 1865–1914. The areas visited and mapped included W Palestine, Kadesh (Conder), Galilee and the Arabah (Kitchener), the desert of the Exodus (Palmer) and sites including Capernaum, Samaria and Caesarea (Wilson). Interest centred on Jerusalem itself, where underground tunnelling revealed the foundations of walls, and rock levels and parts of the S wall and gates and Ophel were explored between 1867 and 1928. Following the excavation in 1890 by Sir Flinders Petrie of Tell el-Hesi, which established the first ceramic index and stratigraphical chronology based on comparisons with Egypt, many scientific expeditions led by American, British, French, German and Israeli scholars have worked at a variety of sites, principally *Gezer, *Taanach, *Megiddo, *Samaria, *Shechem and *Beth-shemesh. Subsequent surface surveys by N. Glueck in Jordan (1930s) and the Israelis in the Negeb have made detailed archaeological maps possible.

In 1920 the Department of Antiquities of Palestine encouraged the development of careful techniques of excavation and interpretation. A pottery chronology was established by Albright and further developed by Amiran, and is constantly being revised as new data emerges. The data has been compared with similar data from the rest of the ancient Near East. Excavation has continued at a great number of sites and those listed here are just a small number of the more important biblical sites. Pre-1967 excavations included, Abu Hawam, Achziv, *Ai, *Arad, *Ashdod, Azeqah, Beit Mirsim, *Bethel, *Beth-zur, *Dothan, *En-gedi, *Gibeah, *Gibeon, *Hazor, *Jericho, Masada, en-Nasbeh, Samaria, Shechem, and *Tirzah. Sites excavated or re-excavated since 1967 include Akko, *Aphek, *Ashqelon, *Beer-sheba, *Beth-shan, *Beth-shemesh, *Caesarea, *Dan, Dor, Ekron, *Gezer, Haror, *Hebron, Jemmeh, *Jerusalem, *Jezreel, Kinneret, *Lachish, *Megiddo, Qasileh, Qeisan, ash-Shariah, *Shiloh, and Yoqne'am. Large-scale surface surveys have also been undertaken covering much of the land including lower

	Archaeological Periods	Sometimes known as	Approx. Period
Islamic AD 636 →	Islamic		AD 636 –
Byzantine AD 324 – 636	Byzantine		AD 324 – 636
Roman 63 BC – AD 324	Roman III		AD 180 – 324
	Roman II		AD 70 – 180
	Roman I	Herodian	63 BC – AD 70
Hellenistic 330 – 63 BC	Hellenistic II	Hasmonaean/Maccabean	152 – 63 BC
	Hellenistic I		330 – 152 BC
Iron Age 1200 – 330 BC Sometimes known as Israelite Period	Babylonian/Persian	Late Iron (= LI)/Persian	587 330 BC
	Iron Age III b		720 – 587 BC
	Iron Age III a		800 – 720 BC
	Iron Age II b	Middle Iron (= MI)	900 – 800 BC
	Iron Age II a		1000 – 900 BC
	Iron Age I b		1150 – 1000 BC
	Iron Age (= IA) I a	Early Iron/Israelite (= EI)	1200 – 1150 BC
Bronze Age 3150 – 1200 BC Sometimes known as Canaanite Period	Late Bronze II b		1300 – 1200 BC
	Late Bronze II a		1400 – 1300 BC
	Late Bronze (= LBA) I	(Late Canaanite (= LC))	1550 – 1400 BC
	Middle Bronze II c		1600 – 1550 BC
	Middle Bronze II b		1750 – 1600 BC
	Middle Bronze II a	(Middle Canaanite (= MC))	1950 – 1750 BC
	Middle Bronze (= MBA) I	Early – Middle Bronze Age	2200 – 1950 BC
	Early Bronze IV	Early Bronze Age III b	2350 – 2200 BC
	Early Bronze III	(Early Canaanite III)	2650 – 2350 BC
	Early Bronze II	(Early Canaanite II)	2850 – 2650 BC
	Early Bronze (= EBA) I	(Early Canaanite (= EC) I)	3150 – 2850 BC
Chalcolithic 4000 – 3150 BC	Chalcolithic	Ghassulian	4000 – 3150 BC
Stone Age → 4000 BC	Neolithic (Pottery)		5000 – 4000 BC
	Neolithic (Pre-Pottery)	New Stone Age	7500 – 5000 BC
	Mesolithic	Middle Stone Age/Natufian	10,000 – 7500 BC
	Palaeolithic	Old Stone Age	– 10,000 BC

Classification of archaeological periods.

Galilee, the central hill-country, the Negev, and Sinai.

In Jordan important work has been undertaken at Buseirah (*BOZRAH), *Heshbon (Hesban), Madeba, Petra, Deir 'Alla, Tell es-Sa'idiyeh, Amman and Ezion-geber. The results of all this work have been reported regularly in journals (some listed in the bibliography), encyclopaedias of archaeology and in special volumes devoted to specific sites. A continued enlargement of the knowledge of biblical lands and times is to be expected.

VI. Inscriptions (Old Testament)

Many excavations have resulted in the discovery of documents, both in archives and in isolation. These employ various forms of writing on diverse materials. It is to be expected that such inscriptions, especially those from *Egypt, *Assyria and *Babylonia which can be closely dated, will be of much value in comparison with the documents preserved in the OT. Some bring direct reference, others illustrate the widespread nature of literacy and literary styles spread through the whole of the ancient Near East. Products of these schools of writing are also found in Palestine in addition to indigenous and local writing on papyri and ostraca, *seals, and *money in the form of coins, stone, wood and other surfaces.

Some collections of documents or archives are of particular importance for comparison with the OT. These include for *Egypt the Execration Texts (*c*. 1800 BC) and for Syria the texts from *Ebla (*c*. 2300 BC), *Mari and *Ugarit (Ras Shamra). While these, and the texts from *Nuzi (15th century) and *Amarna (14th century), illustrate the early history down to the patriarchal period, later ostraca from *Samaria and *Lachish give background to the later kingdoms of Israel and Judah. Other inscriptions illustrate the development of *writing throughout the OT period.

The study of biblical (Palestinian) archaeology requires comparisons to be made with both the general evidence of neighbouring *Egypt, *Syria, *Assyria and *Babylonia, and with the particular aspects, *e.g.* *art and *architecture, and its specific aspects, building, *palace, *house and artefacts (*e.g.* *altar, *amulets, *glass, *pottery, *money) and sites (*e.g.* *Jerusalem, *etc.*).

BIBLIOGRAPHY. *Sites: NEAEHL*; Current details are given in such periodicals as *The Biblical Archaeologist* (American Schools for Oriental Research); *Israel Exploration Journal*, *Iraq*, *Levant*, *Palestine Exploration Quarterly*.

Texts: *ANET*, *ANEP*, *DOTT*.

Selected bibliography: W. F. Albright, *The Archaeology of Palestine*, 1960; E. Anati, *Palestine before the Hebrews*, 1962; M. Avi-Yonah, *Encyclopedia of Archaeological Excavations in the Holy Land*, 1976–7; P. Bienkowski (ed.), *Treasures from an Ancient Land. The Art of Jordan*, 1991; W. B. Dever, *ABD* 1, pp. 354–367; M. Burrows, *What Mean these Stones?*, 1957; K. M. Kenyon, *Archaeology in the Holy Land*[4], 1979; K. A. Kitchen, *Ancient Orient and Old Testament*, 1966; A. Mazar, *Archaeology of the Land of the Bible*, 1990; P. R. S. Moorey, *The Bible Lands*, 1975; S. M. Paul and W. G. Devers, *Biblical Archaeology*, 1973; D. Winton Thomas (ed.), *Archaeology and Old Testament Study*, 1967; D. J. Wiseman, *Illustrations from Biblical Archaeology*, 1962; *Peoples of Old Testament Times*, 1973; G. F. Wright, *Biblical Archaeology*, 1962; E. Yamauchi, *The Stones and the Scriptures*, 1973.

D.J.W.

VII. The Hellenistic–Roman period

When the Macedonian Alexander the Great won Palestine as part of the former Persian empire in 332 BC, the country was yet further opened to Hellenistic influence. However, after his death internecine warfare between his generals retarded this development. Only isolated pottery and coins can be assigned with confidence to the ruling Lagides in 332–200 BC. At Mareshah (Marisa) in Idumaea a carefully laid-out Greek town has been uncovered. The streets set at right angles and parallel to each other led near the city gate to a market square (*agora*), round three sides of which were shops. Near the city were tombs of Greek, Phoenician and Idumaean traders (*c*. 250–200 BC).

The stern days in which the Maccabees fought for Jewish independence (165–37 BC) are attested by refugee camps and caves (Wadi Ḥabsa) and forts like that built at Gezer by Simon Maccabaeus. Traces of the N line of forts said to have been created by Alexander Jannaeus (Jos., *BJ* 7. 170) have been found near Tel Aviv-Jaffa. At Beth-zur, commanding the road from Hebron to Jerusalem, Judas (165–163 BC) had built a fort on top of an earlier Persian structure, and this in turn was later rebuilt by the general Bacchides. Shops, houses, fortifications, reservoirs, Rhodian stamped jar handles and coins help to illustrate the life of the Hasmonaean princes, one of whom, John Hyrcanus (134–104 BC), destroyed the pagan Greek cities of Samaria and Marisa.

Herod the Great (37–4 BC), an able and ambitious ruler, carried through many grandiose building projects. At Jerusalem the massive walls which he built around the Temple Mount, enlarged and embellished, have been found *in situ* on bedrock and rising above the present ground-level to a considerable height. The upper parts of the wall were surrounded by pilasters, and would have looked exactly like the wall—still standing—at Hebron (Machpelah). This wall too surrounded a sacred place, where the Patriarch Abraham and his wife Sarah had been buried. Recent work around the Temple Mount at Jerusalem has also located a complex of streets and terraces, as well as ornamental fragments from gates and cloisters (reconstructions and plans on pp. 26–31, 34–35 in *Jerusalem Revealed*). In the Upper City remains of wall-paintings and polychrome mosaics from luxurious upper-class houses have been excavated by Avigad (*ibid.*, pp. 41–51; colour-plate before p. 41) together with various items of furniture, tableware and so on. The so-called *Tower of David* in the Upper City, excavated long ago by Johns, is also Herodian work *in situ*, built over Hasmonaean walls. This was one of three Herodian towers which defended the NW angle of the city; just inside the city-wall at this point was the palace of Herod (in the Upper City), and the substructures of this too have recently been excavated. Outside the palace was the site of *Gabbatha*, and the Pavement where Jesus was tried by Pilate. On the other side of the city, at the N end of the Temple Mount, was the Antonia tower. The various remains at the Convent of the Sisters of Zion are now thought to be too far N to come from the Antonia; they are probably from the re-founded Hadrianic city, Aelia Capitolina. The Pools of Bethesda were outside the city-wall just N of the Temple Mount in the time of Jesus; they were brought into the city by Agrippa's Wall (the 3rd N Wall of Jerusalem) *c.* AD 41–44. The respective lines of the 2nd and 3rd N Walls of Jerusalem are not agreed by scholars; but certainly, whether one assumes the Sukenik/Mayer line or the British School line, the sites of Golgotha and the tomb at the traditional *Holy Sepulchre* were outside the 2nd N Wall. These have a strong claim to be the sites of the crucifixion and burial of Jesus, supported by a tradition which seems to go back at least to Hadrian (AD 135). But the form of the burial-chamber with its trough-arcosolium, as described by the pilgrim Arculf, is atypical for the period, and constitutes a problem. The other site, the *Garden Tomb*, is congenial, but can't be authentic as it dates to the 8th century BC. Very many tombs of the 1st century BC/AD have been located at Jerusalem, some of them monumental. The groups at 'Dominus Flevit' (Mt of Olives) and at Sanhedria are interesting; the tomb of a convert to Judaism, Queen Helena of Adiabene, is the most impressive. The ossuaries (small chests for bones) from these tombs are often inscribed. Recently an ossuary was found which contained the bones of a crucified man; a nail still transfixed two of the bones. Various attempts to restore the position of the body at crucifixion have followed (*e.g. IEJ* 1970, pl. 24).

Outside Jerusalem the most important Herodian remains have been found in cities established by King Herod (Sebaste, Caesarea Maritima), at his winter-resort (Jericho) and in his fortresses (Masada, Herodium). In the Samaritan hills the old city of Samaria was re-founded by Herod as Sebaste in honour of the Roman emperor Augustus (the Gk. equivalent of Lat. *augustus* is *sebastos*). Ancient Israelite walls were rebuilt and reinforced with round towers, a temple of Augustus was dedicated and a sports-stadium founded; all have been located by excavation, including painted wall-panels in the stadium just like other wall-paintings at Jericho, Masada and Herodium. At Caesarea the great Herodian harbour or mole has been explored by an underwater team; its lines are clearly visible in air-photographs. Italian excavators have found part of the city-wall of Strato's Tower and the Herodian theatre with its seats and stage and a series of painted-plaster floors (almost unique). At Jericho the Herodian palace is on both sides of the Wadi Qelt with a sunken garden and a pool between the two wings, a magnificent conception. Even more unusual is the use of the native technique of building in dried brick together with special Roman concrete techniques characteristic of Augustan Italy. Only at Jericho has this Roman technique been found; so far as is known Herod used it nowhere else. At Jericho even the flower-pots from the garden were still there! Interior embellishments of the Herodian palaces include painted wall-panels, marquetry floors and mosaics. Open or vaulted pools, stepped and plastered, are present on many Herodian sites, but together with these one finds the Roman technique of underfloor heating and a steam-room. Such baths are found in Herod's fortresses, which were also provided with luxurious dwelling-space. The polychrome mosaics are perhaps the most interesting feature of the administrative palace at Masada. The small palace (villa) at the N end of Masada perches on terraces at the edge of sheer cliffs; again the painted Herodian wall-panels are there. In the fortresses at Masada and at Herodium Israeli archaeologists claim to have found at last the remains of 1st century AD synagogues (otherwise the earliest known are usually dated to the late 2nd century AD or 3rd century AD). In all this Herodian art human and animal motifs have never been found until very recently in Broshi's excavations near the Zion Gate at Jerusalem.

VIII. Other inscriptions (New Testament)

Certain inscriptions found at Jerusalem are to be connected with Herod's Temple. Some of these occur on the small stone chests (ossuaries) in which the dry bones of the dead were re-buried (1st century BC/AD). One such ossuary contained the bones of 'Simon, builder of the Temple', presumably a mason rather than Herod's architect. On another ossuary one reads 'Bones of the sons of Nikanor the Alexandrian, who provided the gates'; this must refer to the Jew, famed for his piety, who paid for the most splendid of the gates within the new Temple. An important inscription which was actually set up within the Temple enclosure has been found. Two examples are known, both in Gk., one fragmentary. The text (1st century BC/AD) reads: 'No non-Jew to proceed beyond the barrier and enclosure which surrounds the Sacred Place; any man who [does so and] is caught is himself responsible for his death, which is the consequence.' Josephus refers to these plaques, which were set up in Gk. and Lat. round the Sacred Place (Inner Temple); he uses almost the same words as one finds in the inscriptions (*BJ* 5. 194; *Ant.* 15. 417). The incidents of Acts 21:26–29 must be connected with the same prohibition. The riot which broke out was caused by pious Jews who believed that Paul had brought a Greek within the forbidden area.

Other ossuary-inscriptions are also relevant. One must now discount the words said to be 'Jesus! Woe!', which many have connected with the crucifixion. These words, written on the ossuary of a Jew within his family tomb, are in fact merely his name, 'Jesus, son of Judas' (identifying the bones of the dead as usual). It may be of interest to note the combination 'Jesus, son of Joseph', which occurs on another ossuary; both names were common ones of the period. Indeed the list of names derived from these ossuaries is much as one would expect from reading the NT: John, Judas, Lazarus (Eliezer), Jesus, Mary, Martha, *etc.* Finally, one may mention the tomb and ossuaries of 'Alexander, son of Simon, of Cyrene' and his sister Sarah from Cyrenaican Ptolemais. It seems quite possible that this man's father was the 'man called Simon, from Cyrene, the father of Alexander and Rufus' (Mk. 15:21).

The ruins of many ancient synagogues are to be found in Palestine. For a long time the earliest were thought to be those at Capernaum, Chorazin and Kefar Biram in Galilee (usually dated late 2nd/early 3rd century AD). Now it is claimed that assembly-halls of the 1st century AD in Masada and Herodium were synagogues; and Franciscan excavators have argued that the ruins at Capernaum are later than was thought (late 4th/early 5th century AD). Be all this as it may, the earliest certain evidence for a synagogue in Palestine comes from Jerusalem, and is a Gk. inscription (1st century BC/AD). It declares that a certain Theodotus, a priest, paid part of the expenses involved in building a meeting-house (synagogue), over which he presided as 'archisynagogos'. It was a family affair:

his father and grandfather before him had also been heads of the same synagogue. The inscription further declares that this place was built 'for the reading of the Law and study of (its) precepts'; and that a hospice was attached to it for visitors from abroad, who had their own baths and chambers.

In Italian excavations at Caesarea, Herod's re-foundation of the old Phoenician strongpoint, Strato's Tower, the ancient theatre was found to have gone through various phases of construction and rebuilding. When in the later Roman period the original Herodian remains were dumped under steps as 'rubble', an inscribed stone was included. The excavators found that this refers to Pontius *Pilate. He is named 'prefect of Judaea', and the wording states that he set up a shrine in honour of Tiberius, the Roman emperor. It must have been about this time that the term 'prefect' was dropping out of use as the title of minor (equestrian) governors like Pilate; the word 'procurator' (formerly reserved for the emperor's fiscal agents) supplanted it.

The inscriptions so far described relate mainly to the Gospels. Others—from Greece, Turkey, *etc.*—are connected with events described in Acts or Paul's Epistles. A decree of Claudius found at Delphi (Greece) describes Gallio as proconsul of Achaia in AD 51, thus giving a correlation with the ministry of Paul in Corinth (Acts 18:12). In Corinth also a door inscription—'Synagogue of the Hebrews'—may indicate the place where Paul preached (Acts 18:4). Excavations there revealed a text naming a benefactor, Erastus, perhaps the city-treasurer of Rom. 16:23; shops similar to those in which Paul worked (Acts 18:2–3), and an inscription of 'Lucius the butcher', which probably marks the site of the 'meat-market' (*makellon*) to which Paul referred in 1 Cor. 10:25.

At Ephesus parts of the temple of Artemis, the 'Diana of the Ephesians', have been recovered together with the agora and open-air theatre capable of seating more than 25,000 persons. A votive text of Salutaris, dedicating a silver image of Artemis 'to be erected in the theatre during a full session of the *ecclēsia*', shows that the full assembly met here as implied by Acts 19:28–41. The historical trustworthiness of Luke has been attested by a number of inscriptions. The 'politarchs' of Thessalonica (Acts 17:6, 8) were magistrates and are named in five inscriptions from the city in the 1st century AD. Similarly Publius is correctly designated *prōtos* ('first man') or Governor of Malta (Acts 28:7). Near Lystra inscriptions record the dedication to Zeus of a statue of Hermes by some Lycaonians, and near by was a stone altar for 'the Hearer of Prayer' (Zeus) and Hermes. This explains the local identification of Barnabas and Paul with Zeus (Jupiter) and Hermes (Mercury) respectively (Acts 14:11). Derbe, Paul's next stopping-place, was identified by Ballance in 1956 with Kaerti Hüyük near Karaman (*AS* 7, 1957, pp. 147ff.). Luke's earlier references to *Quirinius as governor of Syria before the death of Herod I (Lk. 2:2) and to *Lysanias as tetrarch of Abilene (Lk. 3:1) have likewise received inscriptional support.

BIBLIOGRAPHY. Only recent, non-technical works in English are listed. Y. Yadin, *Masada*, 1966; K. M. Kenyon, *Jerusalem: Excavating 3,000 Years of History*, 1967 (chs. 6-11); P. Benoit, *HTR* 1971, pp. 135–167 (Antonia); *Inscriptions Reveal*, 1973, incl. nos. 169–170, 182, 216 (published by the Israel Museum, Jerusalem); K. M. Kenyon, *Digging Up Jerusalem*, 1974 (chs. 1–3, 10–15); B. Mazar, *The Mountain of the Lord*, 1975; L. I. Levine, *Roman Caesarea: an Archaeological-Topographical Study*, 1975; Y. Yadin, *Jerusalem Revealed: Archaeology in the Holy City*, 1968–74, pp. 1–91; J. McRay, *Archaeology and the New Testament*, 1991; *NEAEHL*, *s.v.* Caesarea, Herodium, Jericho, Jerusalem.

J.P.K.
J.W.

ARCHIPPUS. 'Fellow soldier' of Paul and Timothy (Phm. 2); the phrase implies previous service together (*cf.* Phil. 2:25). He is addressed with Philemon and Apphia in a manner suggesting that he may have been their son. This does not necessarily exclude the early suggestion (*cf. Theodore of Mopsuestia*, ed. Swete, I, p. 311) based on the context of Col. 4:17, and adopted with divergent conclusions by Lightfoot and Goodspeed, that the 'ministry' that the Colossians must exhort him to fulfil was exercised in nearby Laodicea; but the context does not demand, and may not support, this. Even if he ministered at Colossae, and the charge is to root out the heresy there (*cf.* W. G. Rollins, *JBL* 78, 1959, pp. 277f.), it is curious that the *church* is bidden to convey it. Even more dubious is J. Knox's suggestion that Archippus was host to the Colossian house-church, the owner of Onesimus and the principal addressee of Philemon. The expressions in Col. 4:17 imply the reception of a tradition, and can hardly be interpreted in terms of the release of Onesimus. The precise nature of the ministry is unknown, but perhaps Paul's old comrade-in-arms, while still linked with his home church, was again on missionary service. The solemn charge need not imply actual dereliction (*cf.* 2 Tim. 4:5). (*PHILEMON, EPISTLE TO.)

BIBLIOGRAPHY. J. Knox, *Philemon among the Letters of Paul*[2], 1960.

A.F.W.

ARCHITECTURE. Compared with many ancient cultures, the architectural remains of Palestine are for most of its history unimpressive. The perishable nature of the normal building materials used is partly to blame for this deficiency as is the frequent lack of indigenous prosperity, without which monumental structures cannot be attempted. While most building in Palestine was performed on a non-professional basis, a few periods are outstanding for their architectural splendour: the Middle Bronze II, Solomonic, Herodian and Omayyad periods. The biblical account includes Egypt, Mesopotamia, Persia and the classical world, which together possess the most imposing ancient architectural remains.

a. Materials and construction

Because of the quantities involved, it was not normal for building materials to be transported long distances. This is true of most stone, although not marble which during the Roman period was transported up to 1500 km. The base rock of the hill country of *Palestine is limestone and the normal building stone for that area. It may even have been quarried on the building site itself, as at *Samaria and Ramat Raḥel (*BASOR* 217, 1975, p. 37). Sandstone was used in the coastal areas of Palestine, while in S Syria, basalt is a common building stone. The comparatively wet climate of

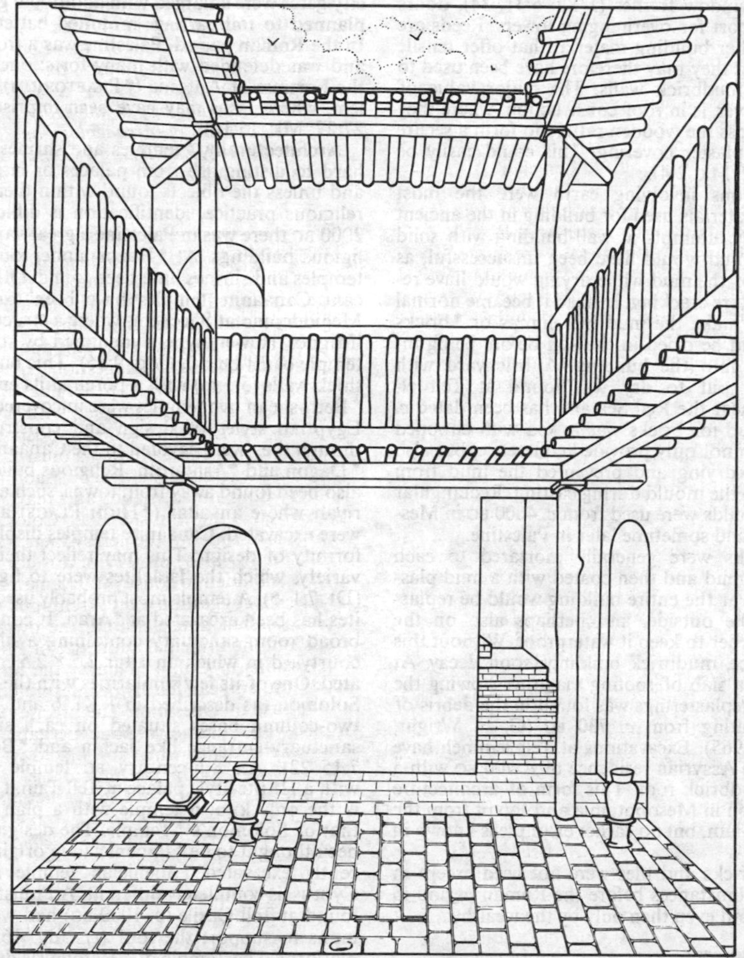

Reconstruction of a private house excavated at Ur. The living quarters were on the first floor, the ground floor being used for servants and storage. c. 1900 BC.

Palestine necessitated the laying of *foundations consisting of rubble walls, which were erected above ground level to protect the mudbrick structure from rising damp. Some *fortifications were constructed almost entirely of rubble; the earliest known example is a Neolithic tower at *Jericho (*c.* 7000 BC). It was, however, not until *c.* 1400 BC that squared masonry was employed for building in Palestine. Solomon used coursed rectangular masonry in many of his buildings, examples of which are the gates at *Megiddo and Gezer. The production of this building stone was expensive and required a large workforce (2 Ch. 2:18). Later examples of fine masonry have been found at Samaria and Ramat Raḥel, and can be seen in the 'wailing wall' in Jerusalem built by *Herod the Great. During the Israelite monarchy, stone was carved into a variety of architectural elements such as the proto-aeolic *pillars (*PEQ* 109, 1977, pp. 39–52) and the balustrade from Ramat Raḥel which probably formed the lower part of a window. (*ARTS AND CRAFTS.)

Most types of stone were used for building somewhere in the ancient world. From the classical period marble was one of the most valued building stones and the remains of *Corinth, *Ephesus, *Pergamum and *Athens give a good impression of the magnificence of architecture which employed it during the NT age.

Timber was also a plentiful commodity in Palestine (Jos. 17:15, 18). Royal buildings were constructed and decorated with expensive woods such as cedar and fir (1 Ki. 5:6, 8) imported from Lebanon, almug (1 Ki. 10.11–12) from Ophir and the local olive (1 Ki. 6:23, 31, 33). (*TREES.) General work was normally done with the most suitable local wood, which may have been sycamore (Is. 9:10), pine or oak. The excavation of a small fortress at *Gibeah from *c.* 1000 BC showed that cypress and pine were used in the first construction, but, possibly because of deforestation, almond was used in later rebuilding. The large amount of charred wood found may indicate that the superstructure was predominantly wood. Because of its tensile strength, wood performed such vital architectural functions as roof support, wall stresses, door and window frames (1 Ki. 6:31, 34), doors and as support for overhanging towers. Reeds are the only other building material that offer tensile strength and they may therefore have been used to strengthen mudbrick walls. The major value of reeds, however, is in roof construction, where they are laid across the wooden rafters to form a secure base for a plaster covering. This could easily be removed (*cf.* Mk. 2:4).

Preparations involving earth were the most common materials used for building in the ancient world. Early attempts at wall-building with solid masses of mud would have been unsuccessful, as shrinkage of the mud while drying would have resulted in severe cracking. Instead it became normal practice to make the mud into lumps or *bricks which would be dried in the sun before being incorporated into the building. A brickyard with bricks laid out to dry was found at Tell el-Kheleifeh near the Red Sea and has been dated *c.* 850 BC. Mud for bricks was mixed with chopped straw which not only provided coherence, but also accelerated drying and prevented the mud from adhering to the mould during casting. Rectangular wooden moulds were used from *c.* 4000 BC in Mesopotamia, and sometime later in Palestine.

Mudbricks were generally mortared to each other with mud and then coated with a mud plaster. Each year the entire building would be replastered on the outside, and perhaps also on the inside, in order to keep it waterproof. Without this maintenance, mudbrick buildings soon decay. At *Shechem a slab of roofing material showing the successive replasterings was found in the debris of a house dating from *c.* 730 BC (G. E. Wright, *Shechem*, 1965). Excavations at Tell Jemmeh have revealed an Assyrian residence of *c.* 700 BC with a vaulted mudbrick roof. This form of architecture was common in Mesopotamia and Egypt from the 3rd millennium, but no earlier example is known in Palestine.

Baked bricks and tiles were not used except in special circumstances before the Roman period in Palestine, and even then only by the wealthy.

b. General survey

The efficiency of community life produces wealth which must be protected, and so as soon as man began living in settlements, *fortifications were required. The walls of houses on the perimeter of the village were strengthened as the earliest form of defence. The gate was always the most vulnerable feature of fortification and the special attention given to it can be seen at Jawa in the Syrian desert where all the basic plans of gates later employed in Palestine were in use by *c.* 3200 BC. After 3000 BC it was common for cities to have secondary walls to cover the base of the main wall, as well as towers situated at all strategic points along the main wall. Earth embankments were also used, but were not utilized to their full potential until after 2000 BC, when steep slopes outside the city walls were built up and stabilized with consolidated limestone chips.

Cities in this period were large. The walls of *Hazor enclosed *c.* 700,000 sq. m; this included an upper town area (or tell), enclosed within a second main wall. It continued to be normal for cities to have a number of lines of defence, either enclosing the entire city as at *Lachish (*c.* 700 BC), or protecting different sections, as in NT *Jerusalem. During the Assyrian expansion (after *c.* 850 BC) city gates were enlarged with additional gatehouses planned to foil carriage-mounted battering rams. In the Roman period, Palestine was a frontier area and was defended with many forts; one such was the Fortress of Antonia (*PRAETORIUM) in Jerusalem, where Jesus may have been imprisoned (Mt. 27:27; Mk. 15:16).

Architecturally, *temples and shrines are often hard to distinguish from palaces or large houses, and unless the objects found within them indicate religious practice, identification is difficult. After 2000 BC there was in Palestine a great variety of religious buildings. At *Hazor alone, four separate temples and shrines have been found. Other significant Canaanite temples have been excavated at Megiddo and at Shechem, where a structure of the 'Migdol' (tower) type is identified by some as the temple of El-be'rith (Jdg. 9:46). This building had thick walls (5.1 m) with a porch at its entrance. At *Beth-shean two temples were uncovered revealing Egyptian styles of design and construction, although they were devoted to the Canaanite deities, *Dagon and *Ashtaroth. Religious buildings have also been found away from towns, such as at Nahariyah where an altar (*HIGH PLACE) and temple were excavated. Canaanite temples display no uniformity of design. This may reflect their religious variety, which the Israelites were to fight against (Dt. 7:1–5). A temple most probably used by Israelites has been excavated at *Arad. It consisted of a broad room sanctuary containing a niche and a courtyard in which an altar 2.5 × 2.5 m was situated. One of its few similarities with the Temple of Solomon (as described in 1 Ki. 6 and 7) was the two-column bases situated on each side of the sanctuary-entrance like Jachin and *Boaz (1 Ki. 7:15–22). An 8th-century BC temple associated with a Hittite-style palace at Tell Tainat in N Syria is the only known temple with a plan similar to that of Solomon's *Temple. The design has often been thought to be *Phoenician in origin, but a recently excavated Phoenician temple at Kition, Cyprus, is completely different. A Philistine temple found at Tell Qasile (*c.* 1000 BC) had wooden columns to support the roof (*cf.* Jdg. 16:29) and a platform. The Temple of *Herod was described by Josephus and with reference to the present remains, a reasonable reconstruction can be made. The massive stonework of Herod's substructure is still visible in the Haram esh-Sherif (*cf.* Mk. 13:1–2).

Substantial *palaces are not common in Palestine. One building which may have been a local monarch's residence was uncovered at Megiddo, near the gate. It had a number of storeys arranged around a courtyard and was in use between *c.* 1500 and 1200 BC, during which time it was reconstructed at least once. Solomon's palaces in Jerusalem are undiscovered and little has been found of the palaces of *Omri and *Ahab at *Samaria. The palace of *Jehoiakim at Ramat Raḥel, probably referred to by Jeremiah (22:13–19), has been excavated, but no precise plan could be determined. The vast palaces of the Assyrian and Babylonian kings have been excavated extensively at *Nineveh, Nimrud, Khorsabad and *Babylon. These were considerable administrative complexes, having large state rooms richly decorated with relief sculpture, and also numerous offices and official residences. The spectacularly sited N palace of Herod the Great at Masada has been uncovered revealing its imitation marble decoration.

The normal *house plan in Palestine has always been of the courtyard variety. Houses at Arad (*c.* 2800 BC) consisted of a main room and one or two smaller rooms built round an irregular walled courtyard. The Israelites used a very regular form of courtyard house in which a number of rooms were built around three sides of a rectangular courtyard. On the fourth side was a doorway leading to the street. This design used space economically and provided the protection and warmth required in the hill country of Palestine. Upper storeys were added when required (2 Ki. 4:10). Some of the largest and most comfortable ancient houses were excavated at *Ur. They were in use *c.* 1900 BC and consisted of two storeys arranged around a courtyard.

A common building in Israelite cities is the store-house. When these were first excavated at Megiddo they were thought to be stables.

BIBLIOGRAPHY. S. M. Paul and W. G. Dever, *Biblical Archaeology*, 1973; H. and R. Leacroft, *The Buildings of Ancient Mesopotamia*, 1974; A. Kempinski & R. Reich (eds.), *The Architecture of Ancient Israel*, 1982. C.J.D.

AREOPAGUS (Gk. *Areios pagos*, 'the hill of Ares', the Greek god of war, corresponding to the Roman Mars).

1. A little hill NW of the Acropolis in Athens, called 'Mars' hill' in Acts 17:22 (AV).

2. The Council of the Areopagus, so called because the hill of Ares was its original meeting-place. In NT times, except for investigating cases of homicide, it met in the 'Royal Porch' (*stoa basileios*) in the Athenian market-place (*agora*), and it was probably here that Paul was brought before the Areopagus (Acts 17:19) and not, as AV puts it, 'in the midst of Mars' hill' (v. 22). It was the most venerable institution in Athens, going back to legendary times, and, in spite of the curtailment of much of its ancient powers, it retained great prestige, and had special jurisdiction in matters of morals and religion. It was therefore natural that 'a preacher of foreign divinities' (Acts 17:18) should be subjected to it adjudication.

The Areopagus address delivered by Paul on the occasion referred to (Acts 17:22–31) is a discourse on the true knowledge of God. Taking as his point of departure an altar inscription 'To an *unknown god', he tells his audience that he has come to make known to them the God of whose nature they confess themselves ignorant. The true God is Creator and Lord of the universe; he does not inhabit material shrines; he is not dependent on the offerings of his creatures but bestows on them life and everything else that they need. He who is Creator of all things in general is Creator of mankind in particular; and so the speech goes on to make certain affirmations about man in relation to God. Man is one; the habitable zones of earth and the seasons of the year have been appointed for his advantage; God's purpose in these appointments is that men might seek and find him, the more so because they are his offspring. While the wording and citations of the speech are Hellenistic, the emphases are thoroughly biblical. In the peroration Paul calls his hearers to repent and submit to the knowledge of God, since he is not only Creator of all but Judge of all; the pledge of his coming judgment has been given in his raising from the dead the Man empowered to execute that judgment. Hearing this reference to resurrection, the Council dismissed Paul as unworthy of serious consideration.

BIBLIOGRAPHY. N. B. Stonehouse, *Paul before the Areopagus*, 1957; M. Dibelius, *Studies in the Acts of the Apostles*, 1956, pp. 26–83; B. Gärtner, *The Areopagus Speech and Natural Revelation*, 1955; H. Conzelmann, 'The Address of Paul on the Areopagus', in L. E. Keck and J. L. Martyn (eds.), *Studies in Luke–Acts*, 1966, pp. 217-230; T. D. Barnes, 'An Apostle on Trial', *JTS* n.s. 20, 1969, pp. 407–419; C. J. Hemer, 'Paul at Athens: A Topographical Note', *NTS* 20, 1973–4, pp. 341–349. F.F.B.

ARETAS. The reference in 2 Cor. 11:32 is to Aretas IV Philopatris, the last and most famous *Nabataean king of that name (*c.* 9 BC–AD 40). He was confirmed in the tenure of his client kingdom by Augustus, albeit somewhat reluctantly, for he had seized it without permission. His daughter married *Herod Antipas, who divorced her when he wanted to marry *Herodias (Mk. 6:17). Aretas declared war on Herod and defeated him in AD 36. Rome sided with Herod, but the punitive expedition which was eventually despatched under Vitellius, governor of Syria, had reached only Jerusalem when news of the death of the emperor Tiberius in AD 37 caused it to be abandoned.

From 2 Cor. 11:32 it seems probable, though very surprising, that Aretas had at some stage held Damascus, the old Syrian capital. It is commonly assumed that he was given the city by Gaius (AD 37–41), whose policy it was to encourage client kingdoms. In fact no Roman coinage is known to have been minted at Damascus between AD 34 and AD 62. This gap may or may not be significant. An occupation by Aretas may well have intervened at some stage between 34 (or 37) and 40, or the activity of his 'ethnarch' may possibly admit of some other explanation. The reference is potentially important for Pauline chronology, but on the evidence now available the indications are too uncertain and the possibilities too various to permit any conclusion. If we may equate the occasion of 2 Cor. 11:32 with the events both of Gal. 1:17–18 and Acts 9:23–29, this may be set '3 years' after Paul's conversion. This option might, on some readings of the case, accord more easily with the early dating of the apostle's conversion which seems probable on other grounds. E.M.B.G. J.H.

ARGOB. A district of Transjordan which was ruled over by Og, king of Bashan, before the Israelite conquest under Moses (Dt. 3:3–5). It contained sixty strongly fortified, walled cities and many unwalled towns. The exact location of the areas has been a matter of dispute. One view which had the support of Jewish tradition and derived additional weight from an unlikely etymology of Argob identified the region with the volcanic tract of land known as el-Leja (*TRACHNITIS). This view is no longer favoured. The name probably indicates a fertile area of arable land (*'argōḇ* probably from *regeḇ*, 'a clod'. *Cf.* Jb. 21:33; 38:38). Its W extent is given as the border of the petty kingdoms of Geshur and Maacah (Dt. 3:14), *i.e.* the Golan Heights. Some difficulty arises over the reference to the renaming of the cities of Argob, *Havvoth-jair, by Jair the Manassite. In 1 Ki. 4:13

the towns of Jair are located in Gilead (*cf.* Jdg. 10:3–4). C.J.W.

ARIEL (Heb. *'ᵃrî'ēl*, 'hearth of El [God]'). **1.** A name for the altar of burnt-offering described by Ezekiel (43:15–16). Several interpretations of this name have been given; 'altar-hearth' (RV); 'mount of God' (*cf.* Ezk. 43:15–16) or, less likely, 'Lion of God'. In this sense *'r'l* is named on the *Moabite Stone (1:12, *c.* 830 BC). **2.** A cryptic name applied to Jerusalem (Is. 29:1–2, 7) as the principal stronghold and centre of the worship of God (see **1** above). **3.** A Moabite whose sons were slain by Benaiah, one of David's warriors (2 Sa. 23:20; 1 Ch. 11:22). AV translates 'lionlike man' (see **1** above). **4.** A delegate sent by Ezra to Casiphia to bring men to accompany him to Jerusalem for the Temple ministry (Ezr. 8:16). J.W.

ARIMATHEA. 'A city of the Jews', and home of *Joseph, in whose sepulchre the body of Jesus was laid (Mt. 27:57; Mk. 15:43; Lk. 23:51; Jn. 19:38). Identified by Eusebius and Jerome with *Ramah or Ramathaim-zophim, the birth-place of Samuel (1 Sa. 1:19). It is probably identical with the Samaritan toparchy called Rathamein (1 Macc. 11:34) or Ramathain (Jos., *Ant.* 13. 127), which Demetrius II added to Jonathan's territory. Possibly the modern Rentis, *c.* 15 km NE of Lydda. See K. W. Clark, 'Arimathaea', in *IDB*. J.W.M.
F.F.B.

ARIOCH. 1. Name of the king of *Ellasar, an ally of *Chedorlaomer of Elam and *Amraphel of Shinar, who warred against Sodom and Gomorrah (Gn. 14:1, 9) and was defeated by Abraham. Although this person is unidentified, the name can be compared with *Arriwuk*, a son of Zimri-Lim, mentioned in the Mari letters (*c.* 1770 BC) or with the later Hurrian *Ariukki* of the Nuzi texts (15th century BC).

2. The Babylonian king's bodyguard in 588 BC (Dn. 2:14–15). He was commanded to slay the 'wise men' who had failed to interpret the royal dream but avoided this command by introducing Daniel to King Nebuchadrezzar II. D.J.W.

ARISTARCHUS. All the references undoubtedly relate to the same person. The first, Acts 19:29, describes him as already Paul's fellow-traveller when seized by the Ephesian mob (though it has been argued that this is proleptic). In Acts 20:4 he accompanies Paul to Jerusalem, probably as an official Thessalonian delegate with the collection; and in Acts 27:2 he is on Paul's ship from Caesarea. W. M. Ramsay argued that he could have travelled only as Paul's slave (*SPT*, pp. 315f.), though Lightfoot's suggestion still deserves mention, that the manner of reference indicates that he was on his way home to Thessalonica. However (assuming a Roman origin for Colossians), he rejoined Paul, and became his 'fellow prisoner-of-war' (Col. 4:10), possibly alternating with Epaphras in voluntary imprisonment (*cf.* Col. 4:10–12 with Phm. 23–24). On the 'Ephesian imprisonment' theory he will have gone home after the riot and the writing of Colossians (*cf.* G. S. Duncan, *St Paul's Ephesian Ministry*, 1929, pp. 196, 237ff.). His association with the collection has suggested an identification with the 'brother' of 2 Cor. 8:18 (Zahn, *INT*, 1, p. 320). The most natural reading of Col. 4:10–11 implies a Jewish origin. A.F.W.

ARK. 1. The ark of Noah (Heb. *tēḇâ*, probably from Egyp. *ḏb'.t*, 'chest, coffin', Gn. 6–9; *kibōtos*, 'box, chest' in the NT) was evidently intended to be no more than a floating repository, measuring, if the cubit is taken at *c.* 46 cm (*WEIGHTS AND MEASURES), about 150 × 25 × 15 m (Gn. 6:15). It is possible to read *qānîm*, 'reeds', for *qinnîm*, 'nests', in Gn. 6:14, without interfering with the consonantal text, giving the sense that the gopher wood components were bound together and caulked with reeds, and the whole then finished off with *bitumen. While the statement in 6:16 (literally, 'thou shalt make it lower, second, and third') can be taken in the traditional sense as describing three storeys, it is also possible to understand it to indicate three layers of logs laid cross-wise, a view which would accord well with a construction of wood, reeds and bitumen. The ark also had an opening (*peṯaḥ*) in the side, and a *ṣōhar*, a word not properly understood, but most commonly taken to mean an opening for light, running right round the vessel just below the roof.

The ark came to rest on 'the mountains of *Ararat' (Gn. 8:4) or, according to the Babylonians, Mt Nisir ('Salvation') in NW Persia. Attempts to find the remains of the Noahic ark on modern Mount Ararat are probably misconceived (*Flood, *g*). Radio-carbon analysis of wood samples collected there yield dates in the 7th and 8th centuries AD.

2. The ark of Moses (Heb. *tēḇâ*, Ex. 2:3-6) may perhaps be pictured as a miniature version of that of Noah, but only of sufficient size to take a small infant. It was made of reeds (*gōme'*, /PAPYRI), and sealed with bitumen (*ḥēmār*) and pitch (*zep̄eṯ*, *BITUMEN) and from the fact that it was necessary to open it (Ex. 2:6) it was apparently, as was probably Noah's ark, completely closed in.

BIBLIOGRAPHY. A. Heidel, *The Gilgamesh Epic and Old Testament Parallels*², 1949, pp. 232–237; E. Ullendorff, *VT* 4, 1954, pp. 95–96; L. R. Bailey, *BA* 40, 1977, pp. 137–146. T.C.M.

ARK OF THE COVENANT. Called also 'ark of the Lord', 'ark of God', 'ark of the covenant of the Lord' (Dt. 10:8) and 'ark of the testimony' (*ēḏûṯ* = covenant-terms: *WITNESS). The ark was a rectangular box (*'ārôn*) made of acacia wood, and measured 2½ × 1½ × 1½ cubits (*i.e. c.* 4 × 2½ × 2½ feet or *c.* 1.22 m × 76 cm × 76 cm). The whole was covered with gold and was carried on poles inserted in rings at the four lower corners. The lid, or 'mercy-seat', was a gold plate surrounded by two antithetically-placed cherubs with outspread wings.

The ark served (i) as receptacle for the two tablets of the Decalogue (Ex. 25:16, 21; 40:20; Dt. 10:1–5) and also for the pot of manna and Aaron's rod (Heb. 9:4–5); (ii) as the meeting-place in the inner sanctuary where the Lord revealed his will to his servants (Moses: Ex. 25:22; 30:36; Aaron: Lv. 16:2; Joshua: Jos. 7:6). Thus it served as the symbol of the divine presence guiding his people. The ark was made at Sinai by Bezalel to the pattern given to Moses (Ex. 25:8ff.). It was used as a depository for the written law (Dt. 31:9; Jos. 24:26) and played a significant part at the crossing of Jordan (Jos. 3–4), the fall of Jericho (Jos. 6) and the ceremony of remembering the covenant at Mt Ebal (Jos. 8:30ff.).

From Gilgal the ark was moved to Bethel (Jdg. 2:1; 20:27), but was taken to Shiloh in the time of the Judges (1 Sa. 1:3; 3:3), remaining there till captured by the Philistines on the battlefield at Ebenezer (1 Sa. 4). Because its presence caused 7 months of plagues, the Philistines returned it to Kiriath-jearim, where it remained for 20 years (2 Sa. 5:1–7:2), except possibly for a temporary move to Saul's camp near Beth-aven (1 Sa. 14:18—where, however, LXX indicates that the original reading was probably 'ephod').

David installed the ark in a tent at Jerusalem (2 Sa. 6), and would not remove it during Absalom's rebellion (2 Sa. 15:24–29). It was placed in the Temple with great ceremony in the reign of Solomon (1 Ki. 8:1ff.), and re-sited in the sanctuary during Josiah's reforms (2 Ch. 35:3) when Jeremiah anticipated an age without its presence (3:16). It was presumably lost during the destruction of Jerusalem by the Babylonians in 587 BC. There was no ark in the second Temple (Josephus, *BJ* 5. 219).

Gold-overlaid wooden receptacles or portable shrines are known from the ancient Near East in pre-Mosaic times. The ark is unique, however, as the repository of the covenant-tablets, *i.e.* documents bearing the 'covenant-stipulations' (*'ēḏûṯ*). K.A.K.

ARKITE. Gn. 10:17; 1 Ch. 1:15. A descendant of Ham through Canaan, and the eponymous ancestor of the inhabitants of a Phoenician city, modern Tell 'Arqa, 20 km NE of Tripolis. The place is mentioned in Egyptian records, including the *Amarna letters, and by Shalmaneser III (853 BC) and Tiglath-pileser III. Called Caesari Libani in Roman times. G.G.G.

ARM (Heb. *zᵉrōa'*, common throughout the OT, with parallels in other Near Eastern languages, of the human arm or shoulder as a symbol of strength: paralleled, less frequently, in the NT by Gk. *brachiōn*).

The symbol of the arm outstretched, or made bare (much the same idea in view of E dress), is used especially of the Lord to portray his mighty acts, referring often to the deliverance of Israel from Egypt (Ex. 6:6, *etc.*), also to other acts of judgment or salvation evidenced or sought (Is. 51:9; Ezk. 20:33). Thus, logically, the arm or arms of the Lord become the symbol of safe refuge (Dt. 33:27). The powerful arm of the Lord is contrasted with the puny arm of man, 'an arm of flesh' (2 Ch. 32:8). The arms of the wicked are broken, or withered (Ps. 37:17; Zc. 11.17), but the Lord can strengthen the arms of those whom he chooses to enable them to do wonders (Ps. 18:34).

In Dn. 11:22 (AV) the symbol is used of impersonal force, 'the arms of a flood'. The parallelism with *'hand' or 'right hand' is natural (Ps. 44:3). B.O.B.

ARMAGEDDON (*WH*, RV, *Har Magedon*; TR *Armageddon*; Lat. *Hermagedon*; Syr.[Gwy.] *Magedon*). The assembly-point in the apocalyptic scene of the great Day of God Almighty (Rev. 16:16; unknown elsewhere). If it is symbolic, geographical exactness is unimportant. The earliest known interpretation, extant only in Arabic, is 'the trodden, *level* place (Arab. *'lmwḍ' 'lwṭv* = the Plain?)' (Hippolytus, ed. Bonwetsch). Of four modern interpretations, namely, 'mountain of Megiddo', 'city of Megiddo', 'mount of assembly' (C. C. Torrey) and 'his fruitful hill', most scholars prefer the first. The fact that the tell of Megiddo was about 21 m high in John's day, and was in the vicinity of Carmel Range, justifies the use of Heb. *har*, used loosely in the OT for 'hill' and 'hill country' (*BDB*, p. 249; *cf.* Jos. 10:40; 11:16). The 'waters of Megiddo' (Jdg. 5:19) and the 'valley-plain of Megiddo' (2 Ch. 35:22) have witnessed important battles, from one fought by Tuthmosis III in 1468 BC to that of Lord Allenby of Megiddo in 1917. The 'mountains of Israel' witness Gog's defeat in Ezk. 39:1–4. This may be in the writer's mind. R.J.A.S.

ARMOUR AND WEAPONS. The comprehensive terms in Hebrew and Greek are *kēlîm* (Gn. 27:3; 1 Sa. 17:54; more specifically *kᵉlê milḥāmâ*, 'weapons of war', as Dt. 1:41, *etc.*) and *hopla* (LXX *passim*; 2 Cor. 10:4). References to armour-bearers in Jdg. 9:54; 1 Sa. 14:1; 17:7, and to armouries in 1 Ki. 10:17; Ne. 3:19. The Qumran *War Scroll* furnishes a detailed description of the armour to be used by the 'sons of light' in their eschatological war with the 'sons of darkness'. Yadin (see bibliography) maintains that the descriptions reflect Roman military practice in the second half of the 1st century BC. Various items of armour are given a figurative, spiritual significance in Is. 59:17; Eph. 6:10–17, *etc.*

I. Armour (defensive)

a. Shield

The use of shields in battle is attested in the earliest battle scenes from Egypt and Mesopotamia; for Egypt *cf.* the pre-dynastic mural from Hierakonpolis, now in Cairo Museum, and, for Mesopotamia, Eannatum's Stele of the Vultures (*c.* 2500 BC). Various shapes and sizes were in vogue depending on the country and period in question. The advent of the smaller, circular shield is associated with the appearance of the Sea Peoples in the Levant in the late 2nd millennium BC. In Hebrew the commonest term is *māḡēn*, often denoting this type of shield; *ṣinnâ* is used for the larger version. It was the latter which was used by Goliath, who had his own shield-bearer (1 Sa. 17:7). The smaller shield was carried by archers such as the Benjaminites in Asa's army (2 Ch. 14:8, 'bucklers'). Shields commonly consisted of a wooden frame covered with hide which was oiled before use in battle (*cf.* 2 Sa. 1:21; Is. 21:5). Metal provided greater protection, but impeded movement; for its use *cf.* 1 Ki. 14:27. As a compromise, leather shields might be studded with metal discs to increase their effectiveness.

b. Helmet

Metal helmets were worn by Sumerian and Akkadian soldiery in the 3rd millennium BC. The Hebrew term is *qôḇa'/kôḇa'*, and may be of foreign origin. Metal helmets were expensive to make, and in some periods their use was restricted to kings and other military leaders; Saul offered David his own bronze helmet for the contest with

Goliath (1 Sa. 17:38). 2 Ch. 26:14 could be interpreted to mean that (leather?) helmets were general issue in the army of Judah in the time of Uzziah. According to 1 Macc. 6:35 the rank and file were supplied with bronze helmets in the Seleucid period. The Assyrian army attacking Palestine often wore the conical, reinforced helmet with an elongation to protect the neck.

c. Coat of mail

The coat of mail was worn in the first instance by charioteers (*cf.* Je. 46:4) and archers (*cf.* Je. 51.3), who were not in a position to protect themselves with shields. Scale armour, more protective than leather and lighter than plate-armour, was in widespread use in the Near East by the middle of the 2nd millennium BC. It was expensive, and Tuthmosis III (1490–1436 BC) was pleased to include more than 200 coats of mail in the spoil taken by his army after the battle of Megiddo. Nuzi (15th century BC) provides both material and textual evidence for the composition of the coat of mail. One text mentions a coat consisting of 680 scales and another of 1,035 scales. The size of the scales depended on their place in the coat; they were affixed to the leather or cloth by means of thread which was inserted in holes pierced in them for this purpose. The joins of the sleeves were weak points, as is illustrated by the story of Ahab (1 Ki. 22:34f.) and by a relief on a chariot belonging to Tuthmosis IV. In Hebrew the usual term is *širyôn*, which probably comprised both breastplate and backplate. One such was worn by Goliath (1 Sa. 17:5), while coats of mail also provided protection for Nehemiah's workmen (Ne. 4:16).

The Greek equivalent was the *thōrax*, also used in 1 Macc. 6:43 of armour protecting the Seleucid war-elephants.

Targum Onkelos' translation of *taḥrā'* in Ex. 28:32; 39:23 by 'coat of mail' has been shown to be correct in the light of the Samaritan use of *taḥrā'* with precisely this meaning; see J. M. Cohen, *VT* 24, 1974, pp. 361–366.

d. Greaves

It is said in 1 Sa. 17:6 that Goliath wore *miṣḥôṯ* (*MT miṣḥaṯ*) of bronze upon his legs, and LXX translates by *knēmides*, 'greaves' (armour for shins). The Hebrew word is a *hapax legomenon*, but the sense does not seem to be in doubt. Greaves were commonly used by Greek and Roman soldiers at a later date.

II. Weapons (offensive)

a. Sword

The sword (Heb. *ḥereḇ*) is the most frequently mentioned weapon in the Bible. The earliest swords in the ancient world were usually straight, double-edged and more akin to daggers, being used for stabbing (*cf.* the examples from the Royal Cemetery at Ur and from Dorak (Anatolia), all dated *c.* 2500 BC). About the middle of the 3rd millennium the sickle-shaped sword begins to appear; examples from somewhat later have been found at Byblos, Shechem and Abydos. In the first half of the 2nd millennium blades were still quite short, and it was only in the time of the Egyptian New Kingdom that the longer-bladed sword began to be used widely. With the arrival of the Sea Peoples the long, straight sword began to enjoy popularity; *cf.* the sword bearing the name of Pharaoh Merenptah discovered at Ugarit (late 13th century BC). The sword played no small part in the Israelite conquest of Canaan just about this time (*cf.* Jos. 10:11; 11:11, *etc.*). It was usually housed in a sheath which was suspended from a belt (*cf.* 2 Sa. 20:8); hilts were often ornamented, to judge from the various finds in Egypt and Mesopotamia.

The word most often used in the NT is *machaira* (*cf.* Mt. 26:47). The *rhomphaia*, occurring, with one exception, only in Revelation, was a large, broad sword, used originally by the Thracians. The revolutionary Jewish assassins, the *sicarii*, carried short, slightly curved daggers under their clothing (Jos., *BJ* 2. 255). In both Testaments the sword is frequently used, by metonymy, for war, or as a symbol for the word of God (*cf.* Ezk. 21:9; Eph. 6:17).

b. Spear and javelin

The spear (Heb. *ḥ^{a}nîṯ*), consisting of a wooden shaft and a metallic head, in later times of iron (*cf.* 1 Sa. 13:19; 17:7), was greatly favoured by the Sumerians in the 3rd millennium. It remained the basic weapon of the infantry, the lighter javelin or lance being used by the charioteers (*cf.* the Egyptian practice in the 19th Dynasty and subsequently). Hebrew also has the word *rōmaḥ* (*e.g.* Jdg. 5:8), by which a light spear or lance (*cf.* Nu. 25:7) may be intended. The Hebrew *kîḏôn* has traditionally been rendered 'javelin' (*e.g.* 1 Sa. 17:6), but the translation has been disputed (*cf.* NEB 'dagger'), and the evidence of the Qumran *War Scroll* supports the meaning 'sword'. In certain circumstances the spear was a symbol of royal authority (*cf.* 1 Sa. 22:6; 26:7). Pikes and throw-spears were also used by the Assyrian *army.

The Greek *longchē* of Jn. 19:34 is the equivalent of the Hebrew *ḥ^{a}nîṯ*. It has been conjectured that 'hyssop' in Jn. 19:29 has replaced an original reading 'javelin' (*hyssōpos* for *hyssos*), but there is good reason to retain the traditional text.

c. Bow and arrow

The basic Hebrew words are *qešeṯ* and *ḥēṣ*. The ancient bow could have a single curve or be double-convex (examples of the latter from as early as pre-dynastic Egypt). Development of the composite bow meant a considerable increase in power and range, and may partly account for the military superiority of the Semitic Akkadians over the Sumerians in the late 3rd millennium BC. However, it was fully another millennium before the composite bow came into more general use. Animal horn and sinews were bonded with strips of wood to make up the frame (*cf.* the description of Anat's bow in the Ugaritic Aqhat legend); bronze might also be used as a strengthener (*cf.* Ps. 18:34). Arrows were usually made of reed and fitted with metal heads; they might be carried in leather quivers, and sometimes chariots were also fitted with quivers. A quiver is usually depicted as holding thirty arrows (Amarna, Nuzi), or fifty when attached to a chariot (Assyrian reliefs). To string the bow the lower end was pressed down by the foot, while the upper end was bent so as to permit the string to be fastened in a notch, hence the Hebrew expression 'to tread the bow'; archers were called 'bow-treaders' (Je. 50:14). Among the Israelites the tribes of Benjamin, Reuben, Gad and Manasseh were especially famed for their bowmen (*cf.* 1 Ch. 5:18; 12:2; 2 Ch. 14:8).

d. The sling

The sling (*qela*) was carried chiefly by shepherds (*e.g.* David, 1 Sa. 17:40), to ward off wild beasts from their flocks or to prevent animals from straying. It was used as a weapon of war by the Egyptian, Assyrian and Babylonian armies, though monumental evidence in the case of the Assyrians begins only in the 8th century BC. The Israelites also employed companies of slingers in their armies, the ambidextrous Benjaminites being the leading exponents of this method of warfare (1 Ch. 12:2). The sling consisted of a patch of cloth or leather with cords attached at opposite ends. The ends of the cords were held firmly in the hand as the loaded sling was whirled above the head, until one end was suddenly released. Graphic metaphorical use of this is made in Je. 10:18. Sling-stones (pointed or round pebbles) fired by Assyrian besiegers were found in the Lachish excavations.

e. The battle-axe

The battle-axe, like the mace, was designed for hand-to-hand combat and varied greatly in shape and size. Biblical references are few. In Je. 51:20 *mappēṣ* (lit. 'shatterer', *BDB*) is translated 'hammer' in RSV and 'battle-axe' in NEB. A similar word occurs in the expression 'weapon for slaughter' in Ezk. 9:2. (*ARMY, *WAR.)

BIBLIOGRAPHY. Y. Yadin, *The Scroll of the War of the Sons of Light against the Sons of Darkness*, 1962; *idem*, *The Art of Warfare in Biblical Lands in the Light of Archaeological Discovery*, 1963; K. Galling, *SVT* 15, 1966, pp. 150–169.

R.P.G.

ARMY. Unlike their Egyptian and Mesopotamian counterparts, the monarchs of Israel appear not to have been interested in having their military exploits commemorated in propagandist reliefs and paintings. Our description of the Israelite military machine must therefore largely be dependent on the verbal accounts of battles and the incidental references which the OT offers.

a. Composition

As the story of Deborah and Barak well illustrates, the Israelite army began as a tribal militia assembled in times of crisis and led by someone of charismatic stamp. The basis of organization was the tribal clan which, in theory, provided a contingent of a thousand men (1 Sa. 10:19). Certain tribes gained reputations for proficiency in the use of particular weapons (*e.g.* Jdg. 20:16; *cf.* 1 Ch. 12). It was Saul who provided Israel with the nucleus of a standing army, numbering in the first instance no more than 3,000 (1 Sa. 13:2). Like the institution of kingship itself, the creation of this regular force owed much to the continuing menace of the Philistines. Duels between champions as a means of avoiding excessive bloodshed seem to have been more familiar to the Philistines than to the Israelites (1 Sa. 17), but we do read of a representative encounter between two groups of *nᵉʿārîm* (lit. 'young men', but occasionally used as a technical term meaning 'picked troops') from the armies of David and Ishbosheth (2 Sa. 2:12–17). David's army comprised both regular contingents (2 Sa. 15:18) and a militia force. 2 Sa. 23:8ff. lists the commanding officers in David's army—'The Three' and 'The Thirty'. In the main these were men who had distinguished records from the days when David was in hiding from Saul and at the head of a band of freebooters. Included in the regular contingents were Aegean mercenaries (Cherethites and Pelethites) who acted as the royal bodyguard (2 Sa. 15:18–22, mentioning also Philistines of Gath). The militia was divided into twelve battalions each of which served for a month at a time (1 Ch. 27:1–15). If David had a chariot force it must have been quite small (*cf.* 2 Sa. 8:3–4); it is in Solomon's reign that chariots come into their own (1 Ki. 4:26; 10:26). There is little evidence to suggest that Israel ever had a cavalry force worthy of the name. Most of the chariots were appropriated by the N kingdom after the Disruption but, thanks to the Syrian depredations, the advantage had largely been lost by the end of the 9th century (2 Ki. 13:7). (*CAPTAIN.)

b. Camp

The camp (Heb. *maḥᵃneh*) was probably in the shape of a circle or square (*cf.* Nu. 2); the king and his commanding officers would in any case be in the centre (1 Sa. 26:5). That the soldiers slept in booths (Heb. *sukkôṯ*; *cf.* 2 Sa. 11:11; 1 Ki. 20:12, 16) is disputed by Yadin (pp. 274–275, 304–310) who prefers to read Succoth, *i.e.* the place-name. During an engagement the baggage at base would be guarded by a detachment (1 Sa. 25:13). It was possible for civilians to visit the camp and bring supplies of food—as well as exchange news (1 Sa. 17:17–30).

c. Roman army

The main division was the *legion, in theory numbering 6,000 men but actually somewhere between 4,000 and 6,000. There were ten cohorts to a legion and each cohort was made up of six centuries; each centurion commanded between seventy and a hundred men. There were also auxiliary cohorts and small cavalry units called *alae*, these mainly composed of provincials, though not Jews (Josephus, *Ant.* 14. 204). There is inscriptional evidence for the presence of an 'Italian Cohort' (Acts 10:1) in Syria *c.* AD 69; this was an auxiliary cohort and was composed of Roman freedmen.

d. Spiritual armies

The original sense of the OT expression 'Lord of hosts' (*Yahweh ṣᵉḇā'ôṯ*) is uncertain; the title may refer to God's sovereignty over the armies of Israel (1 Sa. 17:45) or to spiritual armies under his command (Jos. 5:13–15; 1 Ki. 22:19; 2 Ki. 6:17). It is the latter sense which predominates in the OT. In the final battle between good and evil Christ appears as leader of the armies of heaven (Rev. 19:14), defeating the armies of the beast and of the kings of the earth (Rev. 19:19).

BIBLIOGRAPHY. Y. Yadin, *The Art of Warfare in Biblical Lands*, 1963; R. de Vaux, *Ancient Israel*², 1965, pp. 213–228; A. F. Rainey in L. R. Fisher (ed.), *Ras Shamra Parallels*, 2, 1975, pp. 98–107.

R.P.G.

ARNON. A wadi running into the E side of the Dead Sea opposite En-gedi. This formed the S border of Reubenite territory at the time of the settlement (Dt. 3:12, 16), and previously marked the boundary between Moab to the S and Ammon to the N (Jdg. 11:18–19). The invading Hebrews crossed the Arnon from S to N, and this proved a turning-point in their career, for they took their first territorial possessions on the N side (Dt. 2:24). However, the *Moabite Stone (line 10) mentions Moabites living in Ataroth, which is to the N of the wadi, suggesting either incomplete conquest on the part of the settlers or later Moabite infiltration. The importance of the river is confirmed by the number of forts and fords which are found there, the latter being mentioned by Isaiah (Is. 16:2).

R.J.W.

AROER. 1. In Transjordan, on the N bank of the river Arnon (Wadi Môjib) overlooking its deep gorge (D. Baly, *The Geography of the Bible*, 1957, fig. 72 on p. 237), at modern 'Ara'ir (D. Homès-Fredericq and J. B. Hennessy, *Archaeology of Jordan, I. Bibliography*, 1986, p. 199); *c.* 22 km E of the Dead Sea (Dt. 2:36; 3:12; 4:48; Jos. 12:2). It symbolized the S limit, first, of the Amorite kingdom of Sihon, second, of the tribal territory of Reuben (Jos. 13:9, 16; Jdg. 11:26 and probably 33) being the seat of a Reubenite family (1 Ch. 5:8), and third, of the Transjordanian conquests of Hazael of Damascus in Jehu's time (2 Ki. 10:33). About this time, Mesha, king of Moab, 'built Aroer and made the road by the Arnon' (Moabite Stone, line 26); Aroer remained Moabite down to Jeremiah's time (Je. 48:18–20). In Nu. 32:34 Gad apparently helped to repair newly conquered cities, including Aroer, before formal allotment of Reubenite and Gadite territories by Moses. In 2 Sa. 24:5 probably read with RSV that Joab's census for David started from Aroer and the city in the valley *towards* Gad and on to Jazer. Isaiah (17:1–3) prophesied against (Moabite-held) Aroer, alongside Damascus and Ephraim. The 'city that is in the valley' (Dt. 2:36; Jos. 13:9, 16, all RV [but not 12:2, see AV, RSV*)*; 2 Sa. 24:5, RV] may be present Khirbet el-Medeiyineh *c.* 11 km SE of Aroer (Simons, *Geographical and Topographical Texts of the Old Testament*, 1959, § 298, pp. 116–117; see *NEAEHL*, pp. 92–93).

2. In Transjordan, 'before Rabbah' (Jos. 13:25, AV, RV, against RSV); could be modern es-Ṣweiwinā, *c.* 3½ km SW of Rabbah (Glueck, *Explorations in Eastern Palestine* III (= *AASOR* 18, 19), 1939, pp. 247, 249; for a description, see *ibid.*, pp. 168–170 and fig. 55). But the existence of this Aroer separate from **1** above is doubtful, as Jos. 13:25 might perhaps be rendered '... half the land of the Ammonites unto Aroer, which (land is/extends) towards/as far as Rabbah' (Glueck, *op. cit.*, p. 249).

3. In Negeb (southland) of Judah, 19 km SE of Beersheba, present Khirbet Ar'areh (N. Glueck, *Rivers in the Desert*, 1959, pp. 131–132, 184–185). Among the Judaeans receiving presents from David at Ziklag (1 Sa. 30:26–28) were 'them which were in Aroer'; among his mighty men were two sons of 'Hotham the Aroerite' (1 Ch. 11:44) (see *NEAEHL*, pp. 89–92).

K.A.K.

ARPACHSHAD, ARPHAXAD (Heb. *'arpaḵšaḏ*; LXX and NT *Arphaxad*). A son of Shem (Gn. 10:22; 1 Ch. 1:17, 24), who was born 2 years after the Flood (Gn. 11:10). The *MT* states that he was the father of Shelah, who was born when he was 35 years old (Gn. 10:24; 11:12; 1 Ch. 1:18, 24; LXX and Samaritan Pentateuch read 135), but some MSS of the LXX interpose a *Kainan* between Arpachshad and Shelah, and this has evidently been followed by Lk. 3:36. Arpachshad lived for a total of 438 years (Gn. 11:13; LXX gives 430, but the Samaritan Pentateuch agrees in the total in spite of disagreement on the component figures). Several theories about the identification of the name have been put forward, perhaps the commonest connecting it with *Arrapḫu* of the cuneiform inscriptions, Gk. *Arrapachitis*, probably modern Kirkuk. Other theories see the end of the name, *-kšad*, as a corruption from *keśeḏ*, *kaśdîm*, *'Chaldeans', therefore referring to S Mesopotamia. An Iranian etymology has also been suggested, in which connection it is to be noted that it is stated in the Apocrypha (Judith 1:1) that one Arphaxad (*cf.* LXX *Arphaxad*) ruled over the Medes in Ecbatana. This book is, however, largely fiction, and in the absence of a Hebrew original there is no guarantee that the name is the same. The name continues therefore to be unknown outside the Bible.

BIBLIOGRAPHY. J. Skinner, *ICC*, *Genesis*², 1930, pp. 205, 231, 233; W. F. Albright, *JBL* 43, 1924, pp. 388–389; W. Brandenstein, in *Sprachgeschichte und Wortbedeutung: Festschrift Albert Debrunner*, 1954, pp. 59–62; and for another theory G. Dossin, *Muséon* 47, 1934, pp. 119–121; *KB*, p. 87.

T.C.M.

ARPAD. Name of city and Aramaean province in N Syria, now Tell Rif'at, *c.* 30 km NW of Aleppo, excavated in 1956–64. From *c.* 1000 BC Arpad (Akkad. *Arpaddu*, Old Aram. *'rpd*), capital of an *Aramaean tribal territory known as Bit Agusi, opposed Assyria as an ally of Hamath, Damascus, and in 743 BC Urartu. (*ARARAT.) Annexed by *Tiglath-pileser III after a 2-year siege in 740 BC, it rebelled with Hamath, Damascus and Samaria in 720, and was reconquered by Sargon II. This lies behind the boast of *Rabshakeh to Jerusalem (2 Ki. 18:34; Is. 36:19; 37:13, AV 'Arphad'). Its destruction symbolized the overwhelming might of Assyria (Is. 10:9; Je. 49:23). The last ruler of Arpad, Mati'el, signed a vassal treaty under Ashur-nirari V of Assyria in 754 BC, which survives in Assyrian, and another with an unidentified king, 'Bar-Ga'yah of KTK', which was inscribed on stone stelae found at Sefire (*cf.* Jos. 8:32).

BIBLIOGRAPHY. *Excavations:* V. M. S. Williams, *Iraq* 23, 1961, pp. 68–87; *idem*, *AASOR* 17, 1967, pp. 69–84; *Iraq* 29, 1967, pp. 16–33; *Treaty: ANET*, pp. 532f., 659–661; J. Mathers, *The River Qoveiq: the Tell Rif'at Survey*, 1981. D.J.W.

ART. Throughout their long history Palestine and Syria were occupied by mixed peoples and cultures, and it is not easily possible to distinguish Heb. or Jewish art from the contemporary Egyp., Syrian, Mesopotamian or Phoenician art, or the later Jewish art from the Hellenistic and Graeco-Roman importations, imitations or influences. In each period, however, certain local styles found in a defined context supplied by *archaeology can be traced.

a. Prehistoric art

Natufian bone carvings from the Carmel region (*c.* 8000 BC), carved sickle handle or red ochre painting of a gazelle on limestone or the decoration of skulls with cowrie shells, a practice followed in pre-pottery Neolithic Jericho (*c.* 6500 BC), are, with figurines and votive figures, a portent of a long history of art. The earliest extant wall-painting comes from Teleilat Ghassul in the Jordan valley (*c.* 3500 BC). One polychrome fresco uses geometrical patterns centring on an eight-pointed star encircled by figures and dragons(?). Others depict a bird or a group of figures, possibly worshippers. The style is reminiscent of contemporary Assyria (Tell Halaf). The Neolithic people of Jericho also decorated red burnished pottery with geometric designs. Elsewhere *ivory and bone was worked to make precious objects like figurines and furniture (*e.g.* Abu Matar, *c.* 3900–3300 BC).

b. Canaanite art (3000–c. 1200 BC)

This now has to be studied according to its regional developments which range from the fine engraved statue from Tell Mardiḥ (*EBLA) and the engraved silver cup from Ain Samiyeh (both reflecting Mesopotamian influence) to the more common local versions of figurines and images. Metal figurines from Byblos, inlaid and silhouette ivories from an El Jisr tomb (MB II) show strong Egyptian inspiration, while the basalt relief orthostats from the 18th-century palace of Yarimlim of *Alalah are not dissimilar to those also found in Anatolia and Palestine (Hazor). The figure of Yarimlim, like that of the later sculpture of the seated figure of Idrimi of Alalaḫ (*c.* 1460 BC), seems to show a Sumerian-type ancestry.

By the Late Bronze Age there are many local composite art forms in sculpture, as on the Baal stela, which is a cross between Egyptian (stance and part dress), Anatolian (helmet and hairstyle) and Syrian (dress). Ivory carvings from this period have been compared with both Mycenean and Mesopotamian art. A finely-worked gold plate from *Ugarit uses mythological motifs. Towards the end of this period come a number of reliefs following the tradition of the Beth-shean sculptured stela (MN II under Egyp. influence) and votive plaques dedicated to the local god Mekal of Khirbet Balu'a (Transjordan). Such images of *idols include a gold-covered bronze statue from Megiddo and ivory carvings, ably executed, from Lachish, Tell el-Farah or Megiddo (12th century). From this period also comes a steady flow of painted pottery using local motifs though some were already known from Syria and Mesopotamia. A characteristic spiral and 'bird' decoration marks out the jugs and craters of the Philistines in the coastal area.

c. Hebrew art (c. 1200–586 BC)

There seems to be little change in the local products, which were in a period of decline throughout the ancient Near East, when the Israelites entered the land. They do not appear to have imported indigenous forms, though they were not devoid of appreciation of art or its employment in *arts and crafts. They had accepted fine Egyp. jewellery as gifts (Ex. 12:35) and had used gold and silver for fashioning an Egyptianizing bull-calf in the round after the Exodus (Ex. 32:2-4). The Israelites gave their finer possessions to adorn the *tabernacle which was constructed under the direction of a native of Judah, Bezalel, himself capable of designing and working in wood, metal and *embroidery (Ex. 35:30–33).

With increasing prosperity under David and Solomon the Hebrews turned to Phoenician artists to train their native workers. Since the plans for the *architecture and building of David's *palace and Solomon's *Temple in Jerusalem received royal approval, it may be indicative that local Heb. tastes did not differ significantly from their neighbours in Syro-Phoenicia.

The second commandment forbidding the making of 'a graven image, or any likeness of anything that is in heaven . . . earth . . . or the water' (Ex. 20:4) did not condemn art but the practice of idolatry to which it might lead (v. 5). In practice it seems to have been interpreted as precluding only the representation of the human form and significantly none such which can be said to be indubitably Heb. or Jewish has yet been discovered. The Temple, as the tabernacle, was decorated with winged human-headed lions (*CHERUBIM), winged griffins, palmettes, and floral and arboreal patterns. Elsewhere Egyptianized figures and symbols, as well as birds and reptiles and a variety of animals (lions, bulls) and patterns (*e.g.* guilloche), are found on temple decoration (1 Ki. 6:18) and on contemporary ivories from Samaria and Hazor, drawn on pottery and engraved on seals.

Both kings and the wealthy employed craftsmen to beautify their homes (1 Ki. 22:39), and where this is condemned it is on the grounds of the inappropriateness of such luxury, an expression of self-interest, while God's house and work lie neglected (Am. 3:15; Ps. 45:8; Hg. 1:4). It must always be remembered that the Hebrews, by their encouragement of *music, literature (both prose and poetry) and speech, set a high standard of 'artistic expression' which has profoundly influenced later art.

d. Media

(i) *Painting.* Since the Egyptians and Amorites (*e.g.* the Investiture fresco from Mari) commonly painted scenes on plastered walls, it is possible that the Hebrews may have done so, though few examples are yet known. Pigments have been found in excavations (see also Dyer under *ARTS AND CRAFTS) and red ochre (Heb. *šāšēr*) was used for painting on walls and wood (Je. 22:14; Ezk. 23:14). Oholibah in the 6th century saw Chaldeans painted (*māšaḥ*, 'to smear, anoint') on a wall in vermilion (Ezk. 23:14).

(ii) *Wood-carving.* Bezalel and his assistant Oholiab directed the wood-cutting (*ḥ^a^rōšeṯ 'ēṣ*) for the tabernacle, which included pillars with curved capitals (Ex. 36:38; 35:33), and a horned altar recessed to take a grating (38:2–4). The Temple built by Solomon was roofed with pine with appliqué palmettes and guilloche borders (2 Ch. 3:5) and panelled in cedar (1 Ki. 6:15–16). The walls and doors were sculptured in bas-relief with carvings (*miqlā'ôṯ*) of lotus buds and 'fleur-de-lis' or 'Prince-of-Wales' feathers forming a triple flower (AV 'knops and open flowers'), palm designs and representations of *cherubim (1 Ki. 6:18, 29). The doors of olive-wood had similar designs etched (*ḥāqâ*) and in intaglio work (vv. 32–35); the whole, as so often with fine wood or ivory work, was overlaid with gold. Since hard woods, such as almug (sandalwood) and ebony, had to be imported (1 Ki. 10:11), and skilled carvers were rare, the use of panelling (*sāp̄an*), elaborate woodwork, and carved windows was considered an extravagant display of wealth (Je. 22:14; Hg. 1:4). Ezekiel's Temple was conceived as having carved panels of two-faced cherubim alternating with palm-trees and young lions, the outer doors being veneered (*š*ᵉ*ḥîp̄*) with wood (Ezk. 41:16–26).

Elaborately carved furniture and other objects of wood, boxes, spoons and vessels have been found in the 'Amorite' tombs at *Jericho. Since ancient Egyp. wood-carving (*c.* 2000–500 BC) 'both on a large and miniature scale reached a standard not equalled in Europe until the Renaissance', something of this work must have been known to wealthy Hebrews. See also Carpenter under *ARTS AND CRAFTS.

(iii) *Ivory-carving.* As early as 34th–33rd centuries BC (Abu Matar) ivory and bone was worked in Palestine to make precious objects, figurines and furniture. It was incised (mostly in panels), sculptured in the round, or cut as open work, or relief. 'Canaanite' ivories include an ointment vase in female form with a hand-shaped (Lachish, 14th century BC) or Hathor-headed stopper (Hazor, 13th century BC), an unguent spoon shaped as a swimming lady catching a duck (Tell Beit Mirsim) and several pyxides show human figures. After a period of decline in the art, incised panels from Megiddo, probably of local workmanship in the 12th to 10th centuries, show lively scenes in one of which the king seated on a throne, which must have been similar to that later made for Solomon (2 Ch. 9:17–18), receives tribute.

Ivories found at Samaria, of the time of Ahab, show the influence of Phoenician art with its Egyp., Syro-Hittite and Assyr. elements. They compare closely with contemporary ivories found at Arslan Tash (Syria) and Nimrud (Iraq), and may have been from the same 'school' or guild of craftsmen. Some are overlaid with gold or inlaid with gold, lapis-lazuli, coloured stones and glass. Commonly recurring designs include the 'lotus' patterns and cherubim already noted in a wood-carving and allied art; also panels with a woman's head (Astarte?) at a window, couchant and suckling animals, and 'Egyptian' figures and symbols, especially the kneeling infant Horus. A matching cosmetic palette and jar from Hazor (8th century) bears a simple hatched pattern and is of Israelite manufacture.

(iv) *Sculpture*. A few sculptures from the 'Canaanite' period in Palestine have been recovered. The seated basalt figure of a Baal, the roughly engraved stele with its pair of upraised hands and the altars from Hazor, and the serpent-coiled goddess on a stele from Beit Mirsim must be considered alongside the well-sculptured feet of a statue from Hazor (13th century BC) to show that good as well as moderate artists were at work there. A stone incense ladle in the form of a hand clasping a bowl from the same city (8th century) shows affinities with contemporary Assyr. art. The boulder in the Lachish water-shaft (9th century BC) worked into the likeness of a bearded man shows that the people of Palestine were never without an inventive spirit. But little has so far survived, and the work of their neighbours (*e.g.* the sculptured sarcophagus of Ahiram from Byblos) is better known. Volute capitals, forerunners of the Ionic type, found at Megiddo and Samaria, were probably similar to those used in the Temple. In the Maccabean period Hellenistic–Jewish ornamentalists of stone carved the fruits of the land (grapes, ethrog and acanthus leaves), symbols which are also found on coins used for *money.

A special guild of ossuary workers at Jerusalem has bequeathed us several chests engraved with six-pointed stars, rosettes, flowers and even architectural designs.

(v) *Seal-engraving*. Cylinder, scarab, stamp and cylinder seals from Palestine bear typical 'Phoenician' motifs as found on ivories, though here the winged disc and winged scarab occur more frequently. The human figure is often engraved up to the Monarchy, and the inclusion of personal names seems to be more customary in Israel than among her neighbours. Pictorial representations are rare on Judaean seals, which may show a growing awareness of the religious prohibition (see section *c*, above).

(vi) *Metal-work*. There is every indication that the Hebrews were expert metal-workers, but little has survived. This impression is borne out by the miniature bronze stand from Megiddo in openwork style showing the invocation of a seated god (*c.* 1000 BC). The bronze 'sea' of Solomon's Temple is computed to have weighed about 23,000 kg and have been of cast bronze 8 cm thick with a bowl 4.6 m in diameter and 2.3 m high with a 'pet-alled' rim. The whole rested on the backs of twelve oxen separately cast and arranged in four supporting triads (1 Ki. 7:23ff.). It held about 50,000 litres of water and must have been a remarkable technological achievement (*JACHIN AND BOAZ).

Many of the motifs in the materials used in i–vi are similar to those employed in other *arts and crafts such as metal-working and are known from representations of art from outside Palestine. It is not possible to judge how far *dance was considered an art form so much as part of sacred ritual.

BIBLIOGRAPHY. A. Reifenberg, *Ancient Hebrew Arts*, 1950; H. H. Frankfort, *The Art and Architecture of the Ancient Orient*, 1963; A. Moortgart, *The Art of Ancient Mesopotamia*, 1969. D.J.W.

ARTAXERXES (Heb. *'artaḥšastâ'*, with variant vocalizations, from Old Persian *arta-xša ra*, 'kingdom of righteousness'). **1.** Artaxerxes I (Longimanus), 464–424 BC. In his reign Ezra and Nehemiah came to Jerusalem, according to Ezr. 7:1; Ne. 2:1; *etc*. It has been argued that in the former case the Chronicler has confused him with Artaxerxes II (Mnemon), 404–359 BC, but there is no need to doubt the biblical record. (See J. Stafford Wright, *The Date of Ezra's Coming to Jerusalem*, 1958.)

2. Ezr. 4:7. This also is likely to be Artaxerxes I, and the date is shortly before Ne. 1:1f., when the king reverses the edict of Ezr. 4:21. Others (improbably) identify him with the pseudo-Smerdis, who reigned for a few months in 522–521 BC.

3. The LXX has Artaxerxes in place of *Ahasuerus in *Esther and some believe that the king here is Artaxerxes II, 404–359 BC.

BIBLIOGRAPHY. A. T. Olmstead, *History of the Persian Empire*, 1948. J.S.W.

ARTEMIS. This was the Greek name of the goddess identified with the Latin Diana of classical mythology. The name Artemis is pre-Greek. She first appears in Greek literature as mistress and protectress of wild life. (*Cf.* W. K. C. Guthrie, *The Greeks and their Gods*, 1950, pp. 99ff.) In Greece proper she was worshipped as the daughter of Zeus and Leto, and twin sister of Apollo. Horror at the pains her mother endured at her birth is supposed to have made her averse to marriage. She was goddess of the moon and of hunting, and is generally portrayed as a huntress, with dogs in attendance. Her temple at *Ephesus was one of the seven wonders of the world, and here worship of the 'virgin goddess' appears to have been fused with some kind of fertility-cult of the mother-goddess of Asia Minor. The temple was supported on 100 massive columns, some of which were sculptured. Tradition claims that her image fell there from the sky (Acts 19:35), and is thought to refer to a meteorite; Pliny tells of a huge stone above the entrance, said to have been placed there by Diana herself. Her worship was conducted by eunuch priests, called *megabyzoi* (Strabo, 14. 1. 23), and archaeologists have discovered statues depicting her with many breasts. The silversmiths who made small votary shrines, portraying the goddess in a recess with her lions in attendance, or possibly souvenir models of the temple, caused the riot when Paul was ministering there (Acts 19:23–20:1). Their cry of 'Great is Artemis of the Ephesians!' (Acts 19:28, 34) is attested by inscriptions from Ephesus which call her 'Artemis the Great' (*CIG*, 2963c; *Greek Inscriptions in the British Museum*, iii, 1890, 481. 324).

See also *DEMETRIUS; J. T. Wood, *Discoveries at Ephesus*, 1877; E. Ferguson, *Backgrounds of Early Christianity*, 1987. D.H.W.

ARTS AND CRAFTS. Throughout their history the inhabitants of Palestine maintained the same basic trades as their neighbours and were able to make most of their artefacts by the use of clay, metal, fibres, wood and stone. Working with these materials was the task of any able-bodied peasant, supported by the women in the home spinning and weaving cloth and cooking. Contacts with countries which were more advanced technologically meant that the Hebrews were quick to learn and adapt for their own use more specialized crafts, and were thus probably never without some outstanding craftsmen, though archaeology has revealed few examples of their work.

There is evidence that the Israelites, while not of outstanding inventiveness or artistry, themselves appreciated good workmanship. The possession of such skill by the Judaean Bezalel was considered a divine gift (Ex. 31:3; 35:31; 28:3). Iron-working was learnt from the Philistines (1 Sa. 13:20) and the secrets of dyeing from the Phoenicians, who supplied designers, foremen and craftsmen to supplement the local labour force available for work on such major projects as the building of David's royal palace and the Temple at Jerusalem (see section **III.** *c*, below). In the 1st century BC the art of glass-making was similarly imported from Tyre.

I. Trades and trade guilds

For reasons of economy and supply the more skilled artisans lived in the larger towns and cities, usually working in special quarters, as in the modern bazaar (*sūq*). This led to the organization of craft unions or guilds called 'families' which were sometimes located at a town where their work was centred, as the scribes at Jabez (1 Ch. 2:55) or dyers and weavers at Tell Beit Mirsim (Debir?; 1 Ch. 4:21). At Jerusalem certain areas were allotted to the wood and stone-workers (1 Ch. 4:14; Ne. 11:35); potters (Mt. 27:7) and fullers (2 Ki. 18:17) had fields of their own outside the city walls. A guild member was called 'a son' of his craft (*e.g.* the goldsmiths in Ne. 3:8, 31). By NT times the guilds were powerful political groups working under imperial licence. Demetrius led the guild of silversmiths at Ephesus (Acts 19:24), and the designation of Alexander as coppersmith (Gk. *chalkeus*) implies his membership of such a union (2 Tim. 4:14).

A general term (Heb. *ḥārāš*, 'one who cuts in, devises') is used both of craftsmen (AV 'artificers') in general (Ex. 38:23; 2 Sa. 5:11) or of a skilled worker in metal, whether copper (2 Ch. 24:12; Is. 40:19) or iron (Is. 44:12; 2 Ch. 24:12). It includes those who prepared and refined the basic metal (Je. 10:9) and was also applied to wood-workers (Is. 44:13; 2 Ki. 12:12), stonemasons (2 Sa. 5:11), engravers of gems (Ex. 28:11) or those specially devoted to manufacturing idols (Is. 44:9–20).

II. Basic tools

From prehistoric times in Palestine worked flint knives, scrapers and hoes have been found, and these long continued in use for rough tools, for reaping-hooks, in which the flints are set in a semicircle of plaster, or for striking lights. Wooden implements and stone hammers and pestles were of early origin. Meteoric iron was utilized when available (Gn. 4:22), as was native copper from *c.* 6000 BC. In Palestine copper was regularly employed from 3200 BC, and iron tools were plentiful after the arrival of the Philistines, *c.* 1190 BC (*cf.* 1 Ki. 6:7). Axe-heads, fitted on wooden handles, were used for felling trees (Dt. 19:5), and knives (Gn. 22:6) for a variety of purposes, including eating (Pr. 30:14). Tools are sometimes mentioned under the collective Heb. *k^e^lî*, 'vessels, instruments', or *ḥereḇ*, which includes the sword, knife or any sharp cutter. Iron axe-heads (2 Ki. 6:5), saws (1 Ki. 7:9), adzes, hoes, scrapers, chisels, awls, bow-drills and nails (Je. 10:3–4) were in constant use and have left their traces on objects recovered by excavation.

III. Archaeological evidence

a. The potter

The earliest known pottery comes from N Syria and is dated *c.* 8000 BC. It was, however, not until *c.* 4000 BC that a slow wheel was used by the potter and *c.* 3000 BC before the fast wheel was developed. The *potter, whose work is described in Je. 18:3–4, sat on a stone seat with his feet working a large stone or wooden wheel, set in a pit, which turned an upper stone on which the vessel was thrown. A potter's workshop, with its 'two stones' (v. 3), has been found at Lachish (*c.* 1200 BC). Smaller wheels of stone or clay which revolve in a socketed disc date from the time of the monarchy at Megiddo, Gezer and Hazor. The clay used for finer vessels or slips was prepared by treading out coarser clay in water with the feet (Is. 41:25). For the development and types of pottery in use, see *POTTER. Pottery kilns have been found at many sites in Palestine, although only rarely does more than the 'fire-box' remain. Outside a potter's shop at Megiddo lay three U-shaped *furnaces (8th–7th century BC).

b. The builder

The manufacture of sun-dried *brick for use in building the ordinary dwelling was part of the seasonal work of the peasant, who covered his house with clay or thatch spread over roof timbers. Such buildings require constant attention. In a few cases bricks made in a mould were fired, and this was probably the potters' work.

The Heb. *bānâ*, meaning 'to build' and 'to rebuild, to repair' and 'builder' (so AV), is used both of skilled and unskilled workmen (2 Ch. 34:11) who were needed for work on any large project which involved the labours of stonemasons, carpenters, and many porters and untrained men. Large buildings were both planned and constructed under the close supervision of a master-builder (Gk. *architektōn*; 1 Cor. 3:10).

A site was first surveyed with a measuring-line consisting of a rope or cord (2 Sa. 8:2; Zc. 2:1), string (1 Ki. 7:15), or twisted linen thread (Ezk. 40:3) marked in cubits (1 Ki. 7:15, 23). In Hellenistic times a reed rod marked in furlongs was similarly used (Rev. 11:1; 21:15). More than one line might be used to mark out a site (2 Sa. 8:2), the survey of which was recorded in plan and writing. The work of the surveyor was taken as a symbol of divine judgment (Is. 28:17; Je. 31:39).

The progress of the building was checked by the chief builder using a 'plumb-line', or cord weighted with lead or tin (*'anāḵ*; Am. 7:7–8), a stone (Zc. 4:10), or any heavy object (Heb. *mišqeleṯ*, AV 'plummet'; 2 Ki. 21:13), to test any vertical structure. This was a symbol of testing the truth (Is. 28:17). The metaphor of building is frequently used, for God as Builder establishes the nation (Ps. 69:35), the house of David (Ps. 89:4) and his city of Jerusalem (Ps. 147:2). So the church is compared to a building (1 Cor. 3:9; 1 Pet. 2:4–6). Paul uses the word 'to build (up), edify' (Gk. *oikodomeō*) about 20 times. The believers are both built up (*epoikodomeō*) into Christ (Col. 2:7) and exhorted to build themselves up in their faith (Jude 20).

c. The carpenter

Both Joseph (Mt. 13:55) and Jesus (Mk. 6:3) followed the ancient trade of carpenter (Gk. *tektōn*). A skilled worker in wood (Heb. *ḥārāš 'ēṣîm*) undertook all the carpentry tasks required in building operations, making roof, door, window and stair fittings. Of the furniture he constructed couches, beds, chairs, tables and footstools. Examples of some of these and of finely carved bowls, spoons and boxes have survived in the tombs at Jericho (*c.* 1800 BC). The same carpenter would manufacture agricultural implements, ploughs, yokes, threshing instruments (2 Sa. 24:22) or boards (Is. 28:27–28) and irrigation machines. In the large cities groups of carpenters who made carts would, in time of war, build chariots (Ct. 3:9). In the Levant ship-building seems to have remained a Phoenician monopoly centred at Tyre, where boats were constructed of local cypress with masts of cedar and oars of oak (Ezk. 27:5–6). (*SHIPS.) Some carpenters made idols (Is. 44:13–17). Though the Israelites undertook their own wood-working for the tabernacle fitments (Ex. 25), wood and experienced carpenters were supplied by agreement with Tyre for the construction of David's palace (2 Sa. 5:11) and the Temple built by Solomon. The same practice was followed for the later Temple (Ezr. 3:7) and possibly for the repair of the Temple recorded in 2 Ch. 24:12.

Wood-carving was undertaken by a few specialists (Ex. 31:5; 35:33), who may have also worked on bone and ivory. These worked the cherubim for the first Temple (1 Ki. 6:23) and other *objets d'art*. For this hard woods, ebony, sandal and boxwood, were imported, while the local woods, cedar, cypress, oak, ash (Is. 44:14) and acacia (AV 'shittim') were used for most joinery, the mulberry being commonly worked for agricultural implements. (*TREES.)

The carpenter's special tools included a marking tool (*śereḏ*, AV 'rule'), compass or dividers (*meḥûgâ*), an adze (*maqṣu'â*—'a scraping instrument', AV 'plane', Is. 44:13), small chopper (*ma'aṣāḏ*), iron saw (some two-edged), and files (Je. 10:4), bow-drill and wooden mallet (*halmûṯ*, Jdg. 5:26, AV 'hammer') and hammer (*maqqāḇâ*, Is. 44:12) as well as the various chisels and awls, examples of which have been recovered. Both nail and dowel joints can be seen on wooden objects from Middle Bronze Age and Monarchy period sites. By Roman times various types of wood plane and spoke-shave were also in use.

d. The mason

Stone, being costly to transport and work, was considered an extravagance in a private house (Am. 5:11), and for the more important public buildings would be used only sparingly for essential constructional features. (*CORNERSTONE, *ARCHITECTURE.) While in Egypt, granite, sandstone, quartzite and limestone were quarried for building stone, only limestone was available in Palestine for this purpose. Blocks of harder stones for the Temple and other splendid buildings were worked in the Lebanon prior to importation (1 Ki. 6:7). The stonemason used many of the same tools as the carpenter, sawing the limestone (1 Ki. 7:9) and trimming it with a mallet and chisel or walling

n'y — rope-maker
ps insj — dyer (of red cloth)
gnwty — sculptor
ḥmw — carpenter

Various occupations of Ancient Egypt with their names in hieroglyphs and transliteration.

hammer. In quarrying large blocks of stone wooden wedges were knocked in with wooden hammers and soaked until the stone cracked under the force of their expansion; a method commonly used in the ancient Near East. Hard stone was shaped by repeated pounding with a large metal forge-hammer (Heb. *paṭṭîš*). Such a hammer is used to describe the action of the divine Word (Je. 23:29) and of mighty Babylon (Je. 50:23).

The mason also quarried out tombs in the natural caves in the hills or drove shafts into the hillside off which chambers were excavated (Is. 22:16). Particularly fine examples of such family mausolea have been found at Bethshemesh (8th century) and round Jerusalem (both 8th century BC and 1st century BC–2nd century AD). Deep silos or cisterns as cut at Lachish, Megiddo and Gibeon involved the removal of as much as 400,000 cubic m of limestone by hand. There, and in the water tunnels cut by masons and miners, the marks of their chisels remain visible. (*MINING, *ARCHITECTURE, *SILOAM.)

In the Monarchy large stone pillar bases were cut, and from the 10th century BC pecked and marginally drafted masonry was used. By the Hellenistic period Herodian buildings at Jerusalem, Machpelah and other sites show the use of immense blocks of stone so carefully dressed as to be aligned without mortar, and it is still impossible to insert a knife blade between the joins. Such careful work can also be seen at Megiddo in the 9th century BC. Masons' marks can be seen on a number of constructions such as the steps of the Capernaum synagogue. Masons were also employed to cut inscriptions on rock surfaces, and for this seem to have copied cursive inscriptions, for surviving examples at Shebna's tomb, the Siloam tunnel and the Samaria fragment show no adaptation to the *writing material. Finer engraving can be seen on *seals.

e. The metalworker

Copper was regularly smelted and cast in Palestine from *c.* 3200 BC. After *c.* 2000 BC it was normal to use bronze rather than copper and this material remained popular even after the introduction of iron. Solomon had large objects, such as the pillars for the Temple, made from bronze by a Tyrian smith who cast them in the clay of the Jordan valley between Succoth and Zarethan (1 Ki. 7:46; 2 Ch. 4:17). Because of its strength iron was preferred for agricultural tools and weapons, but it required more sophisticated techniques of manufacture and maintenance. Initially Israel was without the knowledge of iron-working and relied on the Philistines for their iron tools (1 Sa. 13:19–22).

The smith worked within the city with the aid of a furnace supplied with a forced draught provided by skin or pottery bellows (Heb. *mappuaḥ*, 'a blowing instrument'). Thus the smith was commonly designated as 'he who blows (the coals)', a title akin to the common Akkadian *nappāḫu* (Is. 54:16). Copper and bronze were refined in crucibles (Heb. *maṣrēp̄*, Pr. 17:3; 27:21), and then poured into stone or clay moulds. Iron, on the other hand, was forged by being beaten on an anvil (Heb. *pa'am*, Is. 41:7). The ironsmith is naturally called 'he who strikes the anvil', while the bronzeworker, who had to trim rough castings by hammering, is called 'he who smooths with the hammer' (Is. 41:7). Techniques of soldering, riveting and casting-on were practised by these craftsmen, enabling them to manufacture intricate objects. Such an object is the small bronze stand from Megiddo which, if Israelite, indicates that their technical skill was as good as any of their neighbours.

The smiths manufactured a variety of metal vessels and implements, plough-blades, tips for oxgoads, forks, axle-trees and axes, as well as the smaller pins, fibulae (from 10th century BC), images, figurines and small instruments. The manufacture of knives, which were a close relation to daggers and swords, lance and spear-heads, and other weapons of war (*ARMOUR AND WEAPONS), reminds us how easily these same craftsmen could turn their hand to making implements for war or peace (Is. 2:4; Joel 3:10; Mi. 4:3).

Jewellery was possessed from an early period by women for whom it was the only method by which they could possess and preserve their personal wealth. Gold and silver-smiths used blow-pipes to ventilate their small furnaces and cast their products with the aid of steatite or clay moulds. *Cire perdue*, granulation, filigree and *cloisonné* inlay were all techniques practised by early gold and silver-smiths.

f. The tanner

Leather, the treated skins of sheep and goats, was used for certain items of clothing (Lv. 13:48; Nu. 31:20), including sandals and girdles (2 Ki. 1:8; Mt. 3:4). The sewn skins were specially suitable at low cost for vessels or containers for water (Gn. 21:14), wine (Mt. 9:17) or other liquids (Jdg. 4:19). Sometimes the skins were sewn into true 'bottle' shapes. Leather was rarely used for tents (Ex. 25:5; Nu. 4:6) but commonly for military articles, such as helmets, quivers, chariot fittings, slings and shields, the latter well oiled to prevent cracking or the penetration of missiles (2 Sa. 1:21; Is. 21:5). Sandals of seal or porpoise skin (AV 'badgers' skin') were a sign of luxury (Ezk. 16:10), though it is likely that, as in Egypt and Assyria, fine leather was used for beds, chair covers and other furnishings.

Since tanning was a malodorous task, it was usually undertaken outside a town and near abundant water. Peter's visit to Simon the tanner outside Joppa (Acts 9:43; 10:6, 32) illustrates how far he had overcome his scruples against contact with what was ceremonially unclean. The process began by removing the animal fat from the skin by stone scrapers or metal knives. The hair was removed by scraping, soaking in urine or rubbing with lime. The skin was then either dressed by smoking or by being rubbed with an oil, or tanned with suitable wood, bark or leaves. If the hair or fur was not removed, the skin was dressed with alum which was obtained from the Dead Sea or Egypt, sun-dried and then oil-dressed to alleviate the stiffness.

g. The dyer

The ancient craft of dyeing was known to the Israelites at the Exodus, when skins used for the tabernacle were dyed scarlet by the juices of crushed cochineal insects found in oak-trees (Ex. 26:1, 31; 36:8; Lv. 14:4). The black-purple or red-violet 'Tyrian' or 'Imperial' dye, prepared from the molluscs *purpura* and *murex* found on the E Mediterranean coast, was mainly a Phoenician monopoly and used for dyeing the highly-priced garments which were a mark of rank and nobility (Jdg. 8:26;

Pr. 31:22; Lk. 16:19; Rev. 18:12, 16). The trade is attested in Ras Shamra texts (*c.* 1500 BC). This was also the 'purple' used in the tabernacle fabric (Ex. 26:31, 28:5), for the Temple veil, the 'blue and purple and crimson' being variants of the same dye (2 Ch. 3:14), and for the garment put upon Jesus at his trial (Jn. 19:2, 5). Native Israelites were taught the trade by Tyrian workmen at Solomon's request (2 Ch. 2:7). Lydia traded in cloth similarly treated in Thyatira (Acts 16:14). See *JNES* 22, 1963, pp. 104ff.

In Palestine yellow dyes were made from ground pomegranate rind, the Phoenicians also using safflower and turmeric. Blue was obtained from indigo plants (*Indigofera tinctoria*) imported from Syria or Egypt, where it had been originally transplanted from India. Woad was known after 300 BC.

At Tell Beit Mirsim (= Debir?) six or seven dye-plants were excavated indicating that textile-fabrication was a major industry at that site. At Tell Amal near Beth-shean many pottery vessels, in which skeins of thread were dyed, have been found, together with weaving artefacts such as loom weights.

h. The fuller

The art of fulling, cleansing and bleaching cloth was of importance because of the high cost of clothing and the need to cleanse the fibres of their natural oil or gums before dyeing. In some places the fuller was also the dyer.

It was customary for a fuller to work outside a town within reach of water in which clothes could be cleaned by treading them on a submerged stone. Hence the fuller was characteristically called a 'trampler' (Heb. *kāḇas*). At Jerusalem the locality outside the E wall where garments were spread to dry in the sun was called the 'fuller's field' (2 Ki. 18:17; Is. 7:3; 36:2). Christ's garments at the transfiguration were described as brighter than it was possible for any fuller (Gk. *gnapheus*, 'cloth dresser') to whiten them (Mk. 9:3).

For cleansing, natron (nitre) was sometimes imported from Egypt, where, mixed with white clay, it was used as soap (Pr. 25:20; Je. 2:22). Alkali was plentifully available in plant ash, and 'soap' (Heb. *bōrîṯ*, *kâlî*) was obtained by burning the soda plant (*Salsola kali*). The 'fullers' soap' of Mal. 3:2 was probably 'cinders of *bōrîṯ*', since potassium and sodium nitrate do not seem to have been known in Syria or Palestine, though found in Babylonia.

Other crafts, *ART, *COSMETICS AND PERFUMERY, *IVORY, *SPINNING AND WEAVING, *EMBROIDERY; glass-making, *GLASS; other references to crafts, *MUSIC, *EGYPT, *ASSYRIA and *BABYLONIA.

BIBLIOGRAPHY. C. Singer (ed.), *A History of Technology*, 1, 1958; G. E. Wright, *Biblical Archaeology*, 1957, pp. 191–198; R. J. Forbes, *Studies in Ancient Technology*, 1–8, 1955–64; A. Reifenberg, *Ancient Hebrew Arts*, 1950; A. Lucas, *Ancient Egyptian Materials and Industries*, 1962; J. Jeremias, *Jerusalem in the Time of Jesus*, 1969; D. Strong and D. Brown, *Roman Crafts*, 1976.

D.J.W.

ARVAD. Ezk. 27:8, 11; 1 Macc. 15:23 (Aradus) and its inhabitants, the Arvadites, Gn. 10:18; 1 Ch. 1:16. Modern Ruād, a small island 3 km off the coast of Syria (anciently Phoenicia) and about 80 km N of Byblos. The most N of the four great Phoenician cities, it paid tribute to some Assyrian kings, who noted its seafaring skills. A period of independence from *c.* 627 BC was ended by Nebuchadrezzar (*ANET*, p. 308). During these eras it was secondary to Tyre and Sidon. Its commercial fortunes revived under the Persians and Seleucids, but it was displaced by Antaradus (mod. Tartûs) in Roman times.

G.G.G.

ASA (Heb. *'āsā'*). **1.** Third king over the independent state of Judah, reigned 41 years (*c.* 911–870 BC). The problem of synchronizing his reign with that of *Baasha (1 Ki. 16:8, Baasha dies in 26th year of Asa; 2 Ch. 16:1, Baasha attacks Judah in Asa's 36th year) is at present most plausibly solved by assuming Chronicles is computing from the disruption of the united monarchy. The early part of his reign was characterized by religious zeal which led to the abolition of heathen gods and cultic prostitution. The extent of his zeal and of the pervasiveness of pagan cults is indicated by Asa's removal of his (grand-)mother *Maacah from her official postion (1 Ki. 15:13). He did not destroy all the high places in Israel, but his devotion was said to be the reason for a period of peace in the country (2 Ch. 15:15, 19). The Chronicler contrasts his notable victory over *Zerah the Ethiopian (2 Ch. 14:9), attributed to his faith in Yahweh, with his dependence on Syrian aid to overcome Baasha. This latter action, which may have been sparked off by defection of large numbers of Israelites to Asa (2 Ch. 15:9), enabled him to fortify Mizpah and Geba (not Gibea with LXX), which thereafter became the N border of Judah. The latter part of his reign was marred by illness (2 Ch. 16:12) and continued warfare, which were viewed by Chronicles as the outcome of his failure to continue in dependence on Yahweh (2 Ch. 16:7ff.).

2. A Levite, son of Elkanah, among the first to return from the Exile and settle again in Palestine.

W.O.

ASAHEL (Heb. *'ᵃśāh'ēl*, 'God has made'). **1.** A son of David's sister Zeruiah, and brother of Joab and Abishai (1 Ch. 2:16). He was famous for his amazing speed, but when he used it to pursue *Abner following the clash at Gibeon, the latter was forced to use his greater experience in warfare to kill him (2 Sa. 2:18ff.). This gave rise to a blood feud in which Abner was treacherously murdered by Joab (2 Sa. 3:27ff.). He is among David's thirty select warriors (2 Sa. 23:24), and is listed as being in charge of 24,000 men appointed to serve David during the fourth month (1 Ch. 27:7). This list may originally have been drawn up in outline early in David's reign, so that Asahel is now represented by his son Zebadiah.

2. One of nine Levites whom Jehoshaphat sent together with priests and officials on a teaching mission throughout the cities of Judah (2 Ch. 17:8). **3.** An overseer assisting in the control of tithes for the Temple in Hezekiah's time (2 Ch. 31:13). **4.** Father of Jonathan who opposed the appointment of a select body to represent the returned Exiles in determining the removal of foreign wives (Ezr. 10:15).

W.O.

ASAPH (Heb. *'āsāp̄*). **1.** A descendant of Gershom, son of Levi (1 Ch. 6:39); nominated by the chief Levites as a leading singer, using cymbals, when the ark was brought to Jerusalem (1 Ch. 15:17, 19). David made him leader of the choral worship (16:4–5). The 'sons of Asaph' remained the senior family of musicians until the Restoration (1 Ch. 25; 2 Ch. 20:14; 35:15; Ezr. 3:10; Ne. 11:17, 22; 12:35), primarily as singers and cymbalists. Asaph himself had a reputation as a seer, and was recognized as the author of psalms used when Hezekiah revived the Temple-worship (2 Ch. 29:30; *cf.* the traditional ascriptions of Pss. 50, 73–83; *cf.* also the prophecy of Jahaziel, 2 Ch. 20:14ff.). It is not clear whether Asaph lived to see the Temple consecrated, or if 2 Ch. 5:12 simply means 'the families of Asaph', *etc.* **2.** Warden of forests in Palestine under the Persian king Artaxerxes (Ne. 2:8). J.P.U.L.

ASCENSION. The story of the ascension of the Lord Jesus Christ is told in Acts 1:4–11. In Lk. 24:51 the words 'and was carried up into heaven' are less well attested, as is also the description in Mk. 16:19. There is no alternative suggestion in the NT of any other termination to the post-resurrection appearances, and the fact of the ascension is always assumed in the frequent references to Christ at the right hand of God, and to his return from heaven. It would be unreasonable to suppose that Luke would be grossly mistaken or inventive about such an important fact so long as any of the apostles were alive to note what he had written. For other allusions to the ascension see Jn. 6:62; Acts 2:33–34; 3:21; Eph. 4:8–10; 1 Thes. 1:10; Heb. 4:14; 9:24; 1 Pet. 3:22; Rev. 5:6.

Objections are made to the story on the ground that it rests upon out-dated ideas of heaven as a place above our heads. Such objections are beside the point for the following reasons:

1. The act of ascension could have been an acted parable for the sake of the disciples who held this idea of heaven. Jesus thus indicated decisively that the period of post-resurrection appearances was now over, and that his return to heaven would inaugurate the era of the presence of the Holy Spirit in the church. Such acted symbolism is perfectly natural.

2. The terms 'heaven' and 'the right hand of the Father' have some necessary meaning in relation to this earth, and this meaning can best be expressed with reference to 'above'. Thus Jesus lifted up his eyes to heaven when he prayed (Jn. 17:1; *cf.* 1 Tim. 2:8), and taught us to pray, 'Our Father who art in heaven … Thy will be done on earth, as it is in heaven.' In one sense heaven is away from this earth, whatever may be its nature in terms of a different dimension. In passing from the earthly space-time to the heavenly state, Jesus was observed to move away from the earth, just as at his second coming he will be observed to move towards the earth. This doctrine of bodily absence is balanced in the NT by the doctrine of spiritual presence. (*SPIRIT, HOLY.) Thus the Lord's Supper is in memory of One who is bodily absent 'until he comes' (1 Cor. 11:26), yet, as at all Christian gatherings, the risen Lord is spiritually present (Mt. 18:20).

The concept of God above on the throne has special reference to the difference between God and man, and to the approach to him by the sinner, whose sin bars access to the King. Thus we may see the purpose of the ascension as follows:

1. 'I go to prepare a place for you' (Jn. 14:2).

2. Jesus Christ is seated, a sign that his atoning work is complete and final. Those who believe that as Priest he continues to offer himself to the Father, say that one must not mix together the two metaphors of king and priest. Yet this is precisely what is done in Heb. 10:11–14 to show the finality of Christ's offering.

3. He intercedes for his people (Rom. 8:34; Heb. 7:25), though nowhere in the NT is he said to be offering himself in heaven. The Greek word for intercede, *entynchanō*, has the thought of looking after someone's interests.

4. He is waiting until his enemies are subdued, and will return as the final act in the establishment of the kingdom of God (1 Cor. 15:24–26).

BIBLIOGRAPHY. W. Milligan, *The Ascension and Heavenly Priesthood of our Lord*, 1891; H. B. Swete, *The Ascended Christ*, 1910; C. S. Lewis, *Miracles*, ch. 16, 1947. J.S.W.

ASENATH. Daughter of 'Potiphera priest of On' in Egypt, given in marriage to Joseph by Pharaoh (Gn. 41:45) and so mother of Manasseh and Ephraim (Gn. 41:50–52; 46:20). The name Asenath (Heb. *'āsᵉnaṯ*) is good Egyptian, of the pattern *'I(w).s-n-X*, 'she belongs to X', X being a deity or parent, or a pronoun referring to one of these. Three equally good possibilities would be: *'Iw.s-(n)-Nt*, 'she belongs to (the goddess) Neit', *'Iw.s-n-'t*, 'she belongs to (her) father', or *'Iw.s-n.t* (*t* for *ṯ*), 'she belongs to thee' (fem., either a goddess or the mother). Such names are well attested in the Middle Kingdom and Hyksos periods (*c.* 2100–1600 BC) of Egyptian history, corresponding to the age of the Patriarchs and Joseph. K.A.K.

ASHDOD. Tel Ashdod, 6 km SE of the modern village, was a major Philistinian city, first mentioned in Late Bronze Age texts (Jos. 11:22) dealing with Ugarit. It may have withstood attempts by Judah to conquer it and settle there (Jos. 13:3; 15:46–47). It had a principal port (Ashdod-Yam; in Akkadian sources *Asdudimmu*; *cf. ANET*, p. 286) and a temple of Dagon to which the ark was taken (1 Sa. 5:1ff.). It was attacked by Uzziah of Judah (2 Ch. 26:6). When it rebelled against Assyria, who replaced King Azuri by his brother, *Asdudu* was sacked, according to Assyr. inscriptions, by Sargon II in 711 BC. These calamities were noted by Amos (1:8) and Isaiah (20:1). Later besieged by Psamtik I of Egypt for 29 years (Herodotus 2. 157), it became a Bab. province and was weak (Je. 25:20) and derelict (Zp. 2:4; Zc. 9:6). It was partially repopulated after the Exile (Ne. 13:23–24). As Azotus, its idolatry provoked attacks by the Maccabeans (John the Hasmonean and John Hyrcanus, 1 Macc. 5:68; 10:84). Separated from Judaea by Pompey (Jos., *BJ* 1. 156), reconstructed by Gabinius, and given to Salome, Herod's sister, by Augustus, it flourished (Acts 8:40) until it surrendered to Titus.

Excavations (1962–72) confirm this history and show Canaanite, Philistinian (temple) and possibly Solomonic occupation (gateway).

BIBLIOGRAPHY. *NEAEHL*, 1, pp. 93–102; *BASOR* 175, 1964, pp. 48–50; M. Dothan, *Ashdod* 1–4, 1967–82. D.J.W.

ASHER (Heb. *'āšēr*, 'happy, blessed'). **1.** Jacob's eighth son, his second by Leah's maid Zilpah (Gn. 30:13; 35:26). Asher himself fathered four sons and a daughter (Gn. 46:17; Nu. 26:46; with descendants, 1 Ch. 7:30–40). His descendants' prosperity was foreshadowed in Jacob's last blessing (Gn. 49:20). As an authentic NW Semitic personal name Asher is attested at precisely Jacob's period, as that of a female servant (*c.* 1750 BC in an Egyptian papyrus list; see W. C. Hayes, *A Papyrus of the Late Middle Kingdom in the Brooklyn Museum*, 1955, pp. 88, 97, and especially W. F. Albright, *JAOS* 74, 1954, pp. 229, 231: *išr*, *'šra*). This particular philological discovery rules out the commonly adduced equation of biblical Asher with the *isr* in Egyptian texts of the 13th century BC as a Palestinian place-name: *isr* would represent *'ṯr* not *'šr* (*cf.* Albright, *loc. cit.*). This eliminates the consequent suggestion that the Egyptian *isr* of 1300 BC (Sethos I) indicated an 'Asher'-settlement in Palestine prior to the Israelite invasion later in the 13th century BC.

2. An Israelite tribe descended from **1**, and its territory. Consisting of five main families or clans (Nu. 26:44–47), Asher shared the organization and fortunes of the tribes in the wilderness journeyings (Nu. 1:13; 2:27; 7:72; 13:13, *etc.*), and shared in Moses' blessing (Dt. 33:24). Asher's territory as assigned by Joshua was principally the Plain of Acre, the W slopes of the Galilean hills behind it and the coast from the tip of Carmel N to Tyre and Sidon (Jos. 19:24–31, 34). On the S, Asher bordered on Manasseh, *ex*cluding certain border cities (Jos. 17:10–11; translate v. 11, 'Manasseh had *beside* Issachar and *beside* Asher . . . (various towns) . . .'). See Y. Kaufmann, *The Biblical Account of the Conquest of Palestine*, 1953, p. 38. (*Cf.* also *HELKATH and *IBLEAM.) In Asher the Gershonite Levites had four cities (1 Ch. 6:62, 74–75). However, the Asherites failed to expel the Canaanites, and merely occupied parts of their portion among them (Jdg. 1:31–32). On topography and resources of Asher's portion, *cf.* D. Baly, *The Geography of the Bible*, 1974, pp. 121–127. In the Judges' period Asher failed to help Deborah but rallied to Gideon's side (Jdg. 5:17; 6:35; 7:23). Asher provided warriors for David (1 Ch. 12:36) and formed part of an administrative district of Solomon (1 Ki. 4:16). After the fall of the N kingdom some Asherites responded to Hezekiah's call to revive the Passover at Jerusalem (2 Ch. 30:11). In much later times the aged prophetess Anna, who rejoiced to see the infant Jesus, was of the tribe of Asher (Lk. 2:36).

3. Possibly a town on the border of Manasseh and Ephraim, location uncertain (Jos. 17:7).

K.A.K.

ASHERAH. A Canaanite mother-goddess mentioned in the Ras Shamra texts (*'aṯrt*) as a goddess of the sea and the consort of El, but associated in the OT with Baal (*e.g.* Jdg. 3:7). While the OT sometimes refers to Asherah as a goddess (*e.g.* 1 Ki. 18:19; 2 Ki. 23:4; 2 Ch. 15:16), the name is used also of an image made for that goddess (*e.g.* 1 Ki. 15:13) which consequently came to represent her. The Israelites were commanded to cut down (*e.g.* Ex. 34:13) or burn (Dt. 12:3) the *asherim* of the Canaanites, and were likewise forbidden themselves to plan 'an Asherah of any kind of tree' beside God's altar (Dt. 16:21). From these references it appears that the object was of wood, and was presumably an image of some kind. A piece of carbonized wood about 1.2 m long, discovered in the Early Bronze Age shrine at Ai, has been interpreted as a possible asherah, but many scholars would now reject the view that the object was a post, and would give the translation 'Asherah-image' in all occurrences. In the AV the word is consistently translated 'grove'.

BIBLIOGRAPHY. W. L. Reed, *The Asherah in the Old Testament*, 1949; A. Caquot, M. Sznycer and A. Herdner, *Textes Ougaritiques*, 1, 1974, pp. 68–73; J. C. de Moor in *TDOT* I, pp. 438–444; R. Patai, *JNES* 24, 1965, pp. 37–52; W. F. Albright, *Archaeology and the Religion of Israel*[3], 1953, pp. 77–79; J. Marquet-Krause, *Les Fouilles de 'Ay (et-Tell) 1933–1934* . . ., 1949, p. 18.

T.C.M.

ASHES. 1. Heb. *'ēper.* This is the most commonly used term to indicate powdery ashes. As such it occurs alone or in connection with *sackcloth as a symbol of mourning (2 Sa. 13:19; Est. 4:3; Is. 58:5; Je. 6:26; Dn. 9:3). It also signifies worthless or debased objects or ideas (Ps. 102:9; Is. 44:20), and in this connection it is linked with *'dust', *'āpār* (Gn. 18:27; Jb. 13:12; 30:19). *'āpār*, 'dust', is translated 'ashes' in Nu. 19:17, and 2 Ki. 23:4, where it refers to the ashes of a burnt sin offering and those of pagan vessels respectively. **2.** Heb. *dešen*, 'fatness', is translated 'ashes' referring to the admixture of the fat of sacrifices and the fuel used to consume them (Lv. 1:16; 6:10; 1 Ki. 13:3, 5). It is used also of burnt corpses. **3.** Heb. *pîaḥ*, 'soot', is rendered 'ashes' in reference to the residual deposits of a kiln, used by Moses to create the plague of boils (Ex. 9:8, 10). **4.** Gk. *spodos* is used in the NT for ashes employed in mourning (Mt. 11:21; Lk. 10:13) or purification (Heb. 9:13).

W.O.

ASHIMA. The god or idol of the people of Hamath (2 Ki. 17:30), which they made in the territory of Samaria, whence they had been deported by the Assyrians. Not known outside the OT, though some have suggested identity with the Syrian Semios or the *'šm* of the Elephantine papyri. See A. Vincent, *La Religion des Judéo-Araméens d'Elephantine*, 1937, pp. 654ff.; P. Grelot, *Documents Araméens d'Égypte*, 1972, pp. 353, 464.

T.C.M.

ASHKELON. Lies on the southern coast of Israel between Jaffa and Gaza. This is one of the largest sites of ancient Israel, excavated by Stager since 1985. The earliest settlements are Neolithic huts, and from then on occupation has been continuous.

Ashkelon is mentioned in Egyptian texts (19th–15th centuries BC). In this period the city was surrounded on its three sides by a 2 km long and 40 m high fortified rampart, including gates, and at least one temple in which a silver calf was found. A seal from the Old Assyrian colony in Kanesh in Anatolia shows the extent of trading links. In the *Amarna letters (14th century BC) Widiya sent at least seven letters to Pharaoh; in others he was accused of helping the Habiru. In the 13th century BC Ashkelon joined others in a rebellion against Merenptah.

From the 12th century BC until its destruction by the Babylonians in 604 BC, Ashkelon was Philistine, and one of the five major cities including *Ashdod, *Ekron, *Gath, and *Gaza. During the period of the Judges, Samson killed thirty men of the city. In 734 BC it became a vassal of the Assyrians (*asqaluna*), and in 701 BC Sennacherib had to put down a revolt by Sidqa, replacing him with Sharruludar. In 630 BC the city once again came under Egyptian domination, until it was captured by Nebuchadrezzar. Its king, Aga', was killed and prisoners were taken to Babylon in 598 BC. This event, predicted by Jeremiah (47:5–7) and Zephaniah (2:4–7), affected Jerusalem (Je. 52:4–11) which was soon to suffer a similar fate.

BIBLIOGRAPHY. *NEAEHL*, pp. 103–112; L. E. Stager, *IEJ* 37, 1987, pp. 68–72; *BAR* 17, 1991, pp. 25–43. J.W.

ASHKENAZ. A descendant of Noah through Japheth and Gomer (Gn. 10:3; 1 Ch. 1:6). Eponymous ancestor of the successive inhabitants of an area between the Black and Caspian Seas. *Ascanius* occurs as the name of a Mysian and Phrygian prince, while elsewhere these people are said to live in the district of *Ascania*. Assyrian texts tell of *Aškuzai* in the NE from *c.* 720 BC onwards. Later they joined other tribes in the conquest of Babylon reflected in Je. 51:27. The Ashkenaz are to be identified with the *Skythai* (*SCYTHIANS) mentioned by Herodotus (1. 103–107; 4. 1). R.J.W.

ASHTAROTH, ASHTORETH. 1. Heb. *'aštōreṯ*, *'aštārōṯ*, a mother goddess with aspects as goddess of fertility, love and war, known to the Israelites through the Canaanites (1 Ki. 11:5). The name was common in one form or another, among many of the Semitic-speaking peoples of antiquity. In Mesopotamia Ištar was identified with the Sumerian mother goddess Inanna. The name occurs in the form *'ṯtrt* in the Ugaritic texts, and as *'štrt* in the (later) Phoenician inscriptions, transcribed in the Gk. script as *Astartē*. It has been suggested that the Heb. *'aštōreṯ* is an artificial form created from *'štrt*, by analogy with the vowel pattern of *bōšeṯ* 'shame', to show a fitting attitude among the Israelites to the goddess, whose cult as practised by the Canaanites was depraved in the extreme. *'aštārôṯ* is the plural form of the name. The Israelites turned to the worship of Ashtoreth soon after arriving in the land (Jdg. 2:13; 10:6); it was rife in the time of Samuel (1 Sa. 7:3–4; 12:10) and was given royal sanction by Solomon (1 Ki. 11:5; 2 Ki. 23:13). After Saul had been killed by the Philistines, his armour was placed in the temple of Ashtaroth at Beth-shan (1 Sa. 31:10), and the excavators of this site have suggested that the N temple in level V there may have been the one in question, though this remains an inference. Numerous clay plaques depicting naked female images have been discovered in Palestinian sites of the Bronze and Iron Ages, and it is probable that some of these are representations of the goddess Ashtoreth-Astarte.

BIBLIOGRAPHY. J. B. Pritchard, *Palestinian Figurines in Relation to Certain Goddesses Known through Literature*, 1943, esp. pp. 65–72; W. F. Albright, *Mélanges Syriens . . . Dussaud*, 1, 1939, pp. 107–120; *Archaeology and the Religion of Israel*, 1953, pp. 74ff.; A. Caquot, M. Sznycer and A. Herdner, *Textes Ougaritiques*, I, 1974, pp. 92–95; H. Ringgren, *Religions of the Ancient Near East*, 1973, pp. 141–142; A. Rowe, *The Four Canaanite Temples of Beth-Shan*, Part I, 1940, pp. 31–34.

2. *'ašt'rôṯ ṣō'neḵā*, a phrase occurring in Dt. 7:13; 28:4, 18, 51 and rendered variously 'flocks of thy sheep' (AV) and 'young of thy flock' (RV, RSV). It may be that from her fertility aspect the name of Astarte was associated by the Canaanites with sheep-breeding, and came to mean 'ewe' or something similar, the word being later borrowed by the Israelites without the cultic overtones.

BIBLIOGRAPHY. W. F. Albright, *Archaeology and the Religion of Israel*, 1953, pp. 75, 220.

3. *'aštarôṯ*. A city, presumably a centre of the worship of the goddess Ashtaroth, which is probably to be identified with Tell Ashtarah some 30 km E of the Sea of Galilee. The city, probably *Ashteroth-karnaim of Abraham's day, was the capital of Og, king of Bashan (Dt. 1:4). It was in the territory allotted to Manasseh by Moses (Jos. 13:31), but, though Joshua conquered Og (Jos. 9:10) and took Ashtaroth (Jos. 12:4), it was evidently not held, for it remained among the territories yet to be possessed when Joshua was an old man (Jos. 13:12). It later became a levitical city (1 Ch. 6:71; Jos. 21:27, *b''ešt'râ*, possibly a contraction of *bêṯ 'aštārâ*, which appears in EVV as Beeshterah), and is only subsequently mentioned in the Bible as the home of Uzzia, one of David's mighty men (1 Ch. 11:44). It is perhaps to be identified with the *'s[t']rtm* ('As[ta]rtum?) in the Egyp. Execration Texts of about the 18th century, and with more certainty with the *strt* of the records of Tuthmosis III, the *aš-tar-te* of the Amarna letters and the *as-tar-tu* of the Assyr. inscriptions. A stylized representation of a city with crenellated towers and battlements standing on a mound below the name *as-tar-tu* is given on a bas-relief of Tiglath-pileser III which was discovered at Nimrud (BM 118908; *ANEP*, no. 306). G. Pettinato (*BA* 39, 1976, p. 46 and n. 7) reports that the 3rd-millennium *Ebla texts repeatedly refer to the place Ashtaroth.

BIBLIOGRAPHY. N. Glueck, *AASOR* 18–19, 1937–9, p. 265; F. M. Abel, *Géographie de la Palestine*, 2, 1938, p. 255; W. F. Albright, *BASOR* 83, 1941, p. 33; J. A. Knudtzon, *Die el-Amarna Tafeln*, 1, 1907, pp. 726, 816; 2, 1915, p. 1292; Honigman, *Reallexikon der Assyriologie*, 1, 1932, p. 304; W. Helck, *Die Beziehungen ägyptens zu Vorderasien*, 1962, p. 57; R. D. Barnett and N. Falkner, *The Sculptures of Tiglath-Pileser III (745–727 BC)*, 1962, pl. LXIX, p. 30. T.C.M.

ASHTEROTH-KARNAIM. A city inhabited by the Rephaim, sacked by Chedorlaomer in the time of Abraham (Gn. 14:5). Some scholars interpret the name as 'Astarte of the Two Horns' and identify this goddess with representations in art of a female with two horns of which Palestinian examples have been found at Gezer and Beth-shan. It is more probable, however, that the name is to be taken as 'Ashteroth near Karnaim' and identified with the city of *Ashtaroth (3), which lies in the vicinity of Karnaim (mentioned in 1 Macc. 5:43–44).

BIBLIOGRAPHY. F. M. Abel, *Géographie de la Palestine*, 2, 1938, p. 255; D. Baly, *The Geography of the Bible*, 1974, pp. 97, 216; H. Tadmor, *IEJ* 12, 1962, p. 121 and n. 30; W. C. Graham and H. G.

May, *Material Remains of the Megiddo Cult*, 1935, p. 12. T.C.M.

ASHURBANIPAL (Assyr. *Aššur-bān-apli*, 'Ashur has made a son'). He was created crown prince in May 672 BC by his father Esarhaddon whom he succeeded in 669 BC as king of *Assyria. Early in his reign he warred against Egypt, where he captured *Thebes in 663 BC (*cf.* Na. 3:8), and to hold this distant land had to make a number of punitive raids against the Syrians, Phoenicians and Arabs. He is probably the king who freed Manasseh from exile in Nineveh (2 Ch. 33:13) and thus had a vassal king serving him in Judah. About 645 BC Ashurbanipal sacked *Susa, capital of Elam, and for this reason is thought to be the 'great and noble Osnappar (AV Asnappar)', whom the Samaritans claimed had brought men from Susa and Elam to their city (Ezr. 4:9–10). Since this is a reference in an Aramaic letter more than 200 years after the event, the rendering of the Assyrian royal name as *'as(rb)npr* (LXX *Asennaphar*; Gk. [Lucian] interprets as *Shalmaneser) is not unlikely.

From 652 to 648 BC the last of the great Assyrian kings was at war with his twin brother Šamaš-šum-ukin of Babylon and the Assyrian hold on Palestine weakened. The end of his reign is obscure for *c.* 627 BC he died or had his son Aššur-eṭil-ilāni as co-regent. Ashurbanipal is well known for his library of Akkadian literature collected at Nineveh.

BIBLIOGRAPHY. *CAH*, 3/2, 1991. D.J.W.

ASHURITES. The translation of *Ashuri* (2 Sa. 2:9) by Ashurites, taking it as a gentilic collective, has raised problems. It seems clear that there is no connection with the Ashurites of Gn. 25:3. Some would read Asherites and connect it with Jdg. 1:32, since the Targum of Jonathan reads Beth-Asher. Some scholars would emend to Geshurites, finding support (*cf. POTT*, p. 26, n. 45) in the Syr. and Vulg. The objection to this reading is that Geshur had its own king Talmai (*cf.* 2 Sa. 13:37), whose daughter David had married (1 Ch. 3:2). The LXX has *thaseiri*, possibly due to the misreading of the definite article *h* as a *t*.

The use, however, of the preposition *'el* in 2 Sa. 2:9 with the names Gilead, Ashuri and Jezreel rather indicates place-names, as this preposition can have the sense of 'at'. The meaning would then be that these are the names of three administrative centres. In the choice of such centres consideration would be given to geographical accessibility. In the case of Ashuri, otherwise unknown, this could have been the decisive factor. With the following three names the preposition *'al* is used, as commonly with 'people' in the phrase 'to reign over', thus, and over Ephraim, and over Benjamin, even over all Israel'. The use of the definite article with Ashuri is not unusual with proper names (*cf.* Gilead), and there are other examples of place-names with the ending *i* (*e.g.* Edrei, Ophni). If the three towns formed a triangle, then Ashuri would be the S point, with Jezreel N and Gilead E. Thus geographically an identification with Asher (Jos. 17:7) might be possible. W.J.M.

ASIA. To Greeks the name either of the continent or more commonly of the region in Asia Minor based on Ephesus. The latter embraced a number of Greek states which in the 3rd century BC fell under the control of the kings of Pergamum. In 133 BC the royal possessions were bequeathed to the Romans, and the area was subsequently organized as a province including the whole W coast of Asia Minor together with adjacent islands, and stretching inland as far as the Anatolian plateau. There was a galaxy of wealthy Greek states which suffered at first from Roman exploitation, but recovered in the NT period to become the most brilliant centres of Hellenism in the world. The Roman jurisdiction was exercised through nine or more assizes (*agoraioi*, Acts 19:38) presided over by the senatorial proconsul or his legates

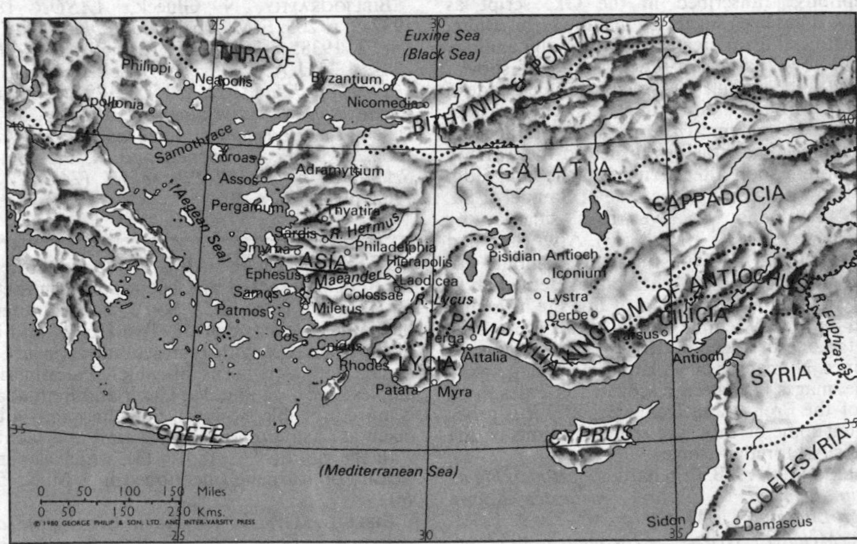

The Roman province of proconsular Asia (after 133 BC).

(*anthypatoi*, *ibid*.). The Greek republics formed a confederation whose chief expression was the cult of Rome and Augustus established initially at Pergamum. It is not certain whether the 'Asiarchs' (Acts 19:31) were the ex-high priests of the cult or the members of the federal assembly. In either case they represent a pro-Roman political élite. (J. A. O. Larsen, *Representative Government in Greek and Roman Antiquity*, 1955, pp. 117–120.)

Churches were established only in the administrative heart of the province at first. All three metropolitan centres, Pergamum, Smyrna and Ephesus, had churches. Beyond that we know for certain of churches in only two of the nearer assize centres, Sardis in the Hermus valley (Thyatira and Philadelphia being important cities in the same region) and Laodicea (on the Lycus) at the head of the Maeander valley (with the smaller towns of Colossae and Hierapolis near by).

BIBLIOGRAPHY. Pliny, *NH* 5. 28–41; Strabo 12–14; J. Keil, *CAH*, 11, pp. 580–589; D. Magie, *Roman Rule in Asia Minor*, 2 vols., 1950; P. Trebilco, 'Asia', in *BA1CS* 2, pp. 291–362.

E.A.J.

ASIARCH. In Acts 19:31 some of the Asiarchs (Gk. *asiarchēs*), described as friends of Paul, warn him not to risk his life by going into the Ephesian theatre during the riotous demonstration in honour of Artemis. The league (*koinon*) of cities of the province of Asia was administered by the Asiarchs, who were chosen annually from the wealthiest and most aristocratic citizens. From their ranks were drawn the honorary high priests of the provincial cult of 'Rome and the Emperor', established by the league with its headquarters at Pergamum in 29 BC. They are further mentioned by Strabo (*Geography* 14. 1. 42) and in inscriptions.

BIBLIOGRAPHY. R. A. Kearsley, 'The Asiarchs', in *BA1CS* 2, pp. 363–376.

F.F.B.

ASSASSINS. A term in Acts 21:38 to render the Gk. *sikarioi*, here used of the followers of an *Egyptian impostor. The term was applied specially to groups of militant Jewish nationalists in the middle years of the 1st century AD who armed themselves with concealed daggers (Lat. *sicae*, whence *sicarii*, 'dagger-men') to despatch unawares men whom they regarded as enemies of the nation (Josephus, *BJ* 2. 254–257; *Ant*. 20. 163–165, 186–188).

F.F.B.

ASSOS. A seaport of NW Asia Minor, at the modern Behram Köy on the S coast of the Troad, directly opposite the island of Lesbos. The city was built on a commanding cone of rock over 230 m high and impressive remains survive of its superb 4th-century-BC fortifications. The shore below is sheltered from the prevalent northerlies, but the harbour was artificial, protected by a mole (Strabo 13. 1. 57 = p. 610). Acts 20:13–14 records that Paul's companions sailed ahead of him from *Troas to Assos, where he rejoined them after making the swifter 30 km land journey, perhaps wishing to spend as long as possible at Troas without deferring his voyage to Jerusalem. A harbour village with dwindling trade persisted at Assos into modern times.

C.J.H.

ASSURANCE. 1. Grounds for certainty (a pledge, token or proof). **2.** The state of certainty. Both Testaments depict faith as a state of assurance founded upon divinely given assurances.

Sense **1** is found in Acts 17:31, where Paul says that by raising Jesus God has 'given assurance to all men' (*pistis*, objectively adequate grounds for belief) that Jesus will judge the world. *Cf.* 2 Tim. 3:14 AV, where Timothy is told to continue in what he has 'been assured of' (passive of *pistoō*, render certain)—the assurance deriving in this case from Timothy's knowledge of his teachers and of the Scriptures.

Sense **2** is regularly expressed by the noun *plērophoria* (fullness of conviction and confidence), which EVV translate 'full assurance'. We read of the 'riches of the *plērophoria* of understanding' ('a wealth of assurance, such as understanding brings', Arndt) (Col. 2:2); of approaching God with *plērophoria* of faith (Heb. 10:22); of maintaining *plērophoria* of hope (Heb. 6:11); and of the gospel being preached 'in the Holy Spirit and with full *plērophoria*'—*i.e.* with strong, Spirit-wrought conviction in both preacher and converts (1 Thes. 1:5). Paul uses the passive of the corresponding verb *plērophoreō* (lit., 'be filled full; be fully resolved', Ec. 8:11, LXX; 'be fully satisfied', papyri [see *LAE*, p. 82]) to denote the state of being fully assured as to God's will (Rom. 14:5) and his ability to perform his promises (Rom. 4:21). Another passive (*pepeismai*, 'I am persuaded') introduces Paul's conviction that God can guard him (2 Tim. 1:12), and that nothing can separate him from God's love (Rom. 8:38f.). This passive points to the fact that Christian assurance is not an expression of human optimism or presumption, but a persuasion from God. It is, indeed, just one facet of the gift of *faith (*cf.* Heb. 11:1). God's witness is its ground and God's Spirit its author.

Assured faith in the NT has a double object: first, God's revealed truth, viewed comprehensively as a promise of salvation in Christ; second, the believer's own interest in that promise. In both cases, the assurance is correlative to and derived from divine testimony.

1. God testifies to sinners that the gospel is his truth. This he does, both by the miracles and charismata which authenticated the apostles as his messengers (Heb. 2:4), and by the Spirit-given illumination which enabled their hearers to recognize and receive their message 'not as the word of men but as what it really is, the word of God' (1 Thes. 2:13, *cf.* 1:5).

2. God testifies to believers that they are his sons. The gift to them of the Spirit of Christ (see Acts 2:38; 5:32; Gal. 3:2) is itself God's testimony to them that he has received them into the Messianic kingdom (Acts 15:8), and that now they know him savingly (1 Jn. 3:24). This gift, the 'guarantee of our inheritance' (Eph. 1:14), seals them as God's permanent possession (Eph. 1:13; 4:30), and assures them that through Christ they are now his children and heirs. The Spirit witnesses to this by prompting them to call God 'Father' (Rom. 8:15f.; Gal. 4:6) and giving them a sense of his fatherly love (Rom. 5:5). Hence the boldness and joy before God and men that everywhere characterize NT religion.

Self-deception is, however, a danger here, for strong persuasions of a saving relationship with God may be strong delusions of demonic origin. Inward assurance must therefore be checked by external moral and spiritual tests (*cf.* Tit. 1:16). John's Epistles deal directly with this. John specifies right belief about Christ, love to Christians and righteous conduct as objective signs of being a child of God and knowing him savingly (1 Jn. 2:3–5, 29; 3:9f., 14, 18f.; 4:7; 5:1, 4, 18). Those who find these signs in themselves may assure (lit., persuade) their hearts in the presence of God when a sense of guilt makes them doubt his favour (1 Jn. 3:19). But absence of these signs shows that any assurance felt is delusive (1 Jn. 1:6; 2:4, 9–11, 23; 3:6–10; 4:8, 20; 2 Jn. 9; 3 Jn. 11).

BIBLIOGRAPHY. L. Berkhof, *The Assurance of Faith*; G. Delling, *TDNT* 6, pp. 310f.; R. Schippers, *NIDNTT* 1, pp. 733ff.; and, among older works, W. Guthrie, *The Christian's Great Interest*, 1658.

J.I.P.

ASSYRIA. The name of the ancient country whose inhabitants were called Assyrians. It lay in the upper Mesopotamian plain, bounded on the W by the Syrian desert, on the S by the Jebel Hamrin and Babylonia, and on the N and E by the Urarṭian (Armenian) and Persian hills. The most fertile and densely populated part of Assyria lay E of the central river Tigris ('Hiddekel', Gn. 2:14, AV). The Heb. *'aššûr* (Assyr. *aššur*) is used both of this land and of its people. The term Assyria was sometimes applied to those territories which were subject to the control of its kings dwelling at Nineveh, Assur and Calah, the principal cities. At the height of its power in the 8th–7th centuries BC, these territories included Media and S Anatolia, Cilicia, Syria, Palestine, Arabia, Egypt, Elam and Babylonia.

In the OT Asshur was considered the second son of Shem (Gn. 10:22) and was distinct from Ashuram ('Asshurim'), an Arab tribe descended from Abraham and Keturah (Gn. 25:3), and from the *Ashurites of 2 Sa. 2:9 (where 'Asherites' or 'Geshur' is perhaps to be read; *cf.* Jdg. 1:31–32). Assyria, which is always carefully distinguished from Babylonia, stands for the world power whose invasions of Israel and Judah were divinely permitted, though later it too suffered destruction for its godlessness. There are frequent references to the land (Is. 7:18; Ho. 11:5) and to the kings of Assyria (Is. 8:4; 2 Ki. 15–19).

I. History

a. Early history down to 900 BC

Assyria was inhabited from prehistoric times (*e.g.* Jarmo, *c.* 5000 BC) and pottery from the periods known as Hassuna, Samarra, Halaf and 'Ubaid (*c.* 5000–3000 BC) has been found at a number of sites, including Assur, Nineveh and Calah, which, according to Gn. 10:11–12, were founded by immigrants from Babylonia. Although the origins of the Assyrians are still disputed, the Sumerians were present at Assur by 2900 BC and Assyrian language and culture owes much to the southerners. According to the Assyrian king list, the first seventeen kings of Ashur 'lived in tents'. One of these, Tudiya, made a treaty with *Ebla *c.* 2300 BC, so cannot be a mere 'eponymous ancestor'.

The kings of Babylonia, including Sargon of Agade (*ACCAD), *c.* 2350 BC built in Assyria at Nineveh, and a building inscription of Amar-Su'en of Ur (*c.* 2040 BC) has been found at Assur. After the fall of Ur to Amorite invaders Assur, according to the Assyrian king list, was ruled by independent princes. These established trade connections with Cappadocia (*c.* 1920–1870 BC). Šamši-Adad I (1813–1781 BC) gradually increased his lands, his sons Yasmaḫ-Adad and Zimrilim ruling at *Mari until that city was captured by *Hammurapi of Babylon. With the advent of the Mitanni and Hurrian groups in the Upper Euphrates the influence of Assyria declined, though it remained a prosperous agricultural community whose typical life and customs can be seen in the tablets recovered from *Nuzi. Under Ashur-uballiṭ I (1365–1330 BC) Assyria began to recover something of its former greatness. He entered into correspondence with Amenophis IV of Egypt whereupon Burnaburias II of Babylon objected, declaring him to be his vassal (Amarna letters). However, the decline of the Mitanni allowed the trade routes to the N to be reopened and in the reigns of Arik-den-ili (1319–1308 BC) and Adad-nirari I (1307–1275 BC) territories as far W as Carchemish, lost since the days of Šamši-Adad, were recovered.

Shalmaneser I (1274–1245 BC) made constant expeditions against the tribes in the E hills and against new enemies in Urarṭu. He also sought to contain the Hurrian forces by campaigns in Hanigalbat to the NW. He rebuilt *Calah as a new capital. His son Tukulti-Ninurta I (1244–1208 BC) had to devote much of his attention to Babylonia, of which he was also king for 7 years until murdered by his son Aššurnadinapli. Soon afterwards Babylonia became independent again and there was a revival of fortune for a while under Tiglath-pileser I (1115–1077 BC). He vigorously campaigned against the Muški (*MESHECH) and Subarian tribes, thrusting also as far as Lake Van in the N and to the Mediterranean, where he received tribute from Byblos, Sidon and Arvad, and making expeditions as far as Tadmor (Palmyra) in his efforts to control the Aramaean (Aḫlame) tribes of the desert. It was the activities of these latter tribes which contained Assyria from *c.* 1100 to 940 BC and left David and Solomon free to strike into Syria (Aram).

b. The Neo-Assyrian period (900–612 BC)

The Assyrians under Tukulti-Ninurta II (890–884 BC) began to take more vigorous military action against the tribes oppressing Assyria. His son, Ashurnasirpal II (883–859 BC), in a series of brilliant campaigns subdued the tribes on the Middle Euphrates, and reached the Lebanon and Philistia, where the coastal cities paid him tribute. He also sent expeditions into N Babylonia and the E hills. His reign marked the commencement of a sustained pressure by Assyria against the W which was to bring her into conflict with Israel. More than 50,000 prisoners were employed on the enlargement of Calah, where Ashurnasirpal built a new citadel, palace and temples, and commenced work on the ziggurat. He employed artists to engrave sculptures in his audience chambers and skilled men to maintain botanical and zoological gardens and a park.

Ashurnasirpal's son Shalmaneser III (858–824 BC) continued his father's policy and greatly extended Assyria's frontiers, making himself the master from Urarṭu to the Persian Gulf and from Media to the Syrian coast and Cilicia (Tarsus). In 857 BC he captured Carchemish and his attack on Bit-Adini (*EDEN, HOUSE OF) alerted the major city-states to the SW. Irhuleni of Hamath and Hadadezer of Damascus formed an anti-Assyrian coalition of 10 kings who faced the Assyrian army in the indecisive battle of Qarqar in 853 BC. According to the Assyrian annals, 'Ahab the Israelite (*sir'alaia*)' supplied 2,000 chariots and 10,000 men on this occasion. 3 years later Shalmaneser undertook a further series of operations directed mainly against Hadadezer (probably *BEN-HADAD I). By 841 BC, Shalmaneser's 18th year, the coalition had split up, so that the full force of the Assyrian army could be directed against *Hazael of Damascus who fought a rearguard action in the Anti-Lebanon mountains and withdrew into Damascus. When the siege of this city failed, Shalmaneser moved through the Hauran to the Nahr el-Kelb in the Lebanon and there received tribute from the rulers of Tyre, Sidon and 'Jehu (*Ya-ú-a*), son of Omri', an act, in the reign of Jehu, rather than Jehoram, not mentioned in the OT but depicted on Shalmaneser's 'Black Obelisk' at Nimrud (Calah). He had scenes from the other campaigns engraved on the bronze plating of the gates of the temple at Imgur-Bel (Balawat). (These are now in the British Museum.)

Šamši-Adad V (823–811 BC) was obliged to initiate reprisal raids in Nairi to counteract the plots of the rebel Ispuini of Urarṭu, and also launched three campaigns against Babylonia and the fortress Der on the Elamite frontier. Šamši-Adad died young, and his influential widow Sammuramat (Semiramis) acted as regent until 805 BC, when their son Adad-nirari III was old enough to assume authority. Meanwhile the army undertook expeditions in the N and W, and Guzana (*GOZAN) was incorporated as an Assyrian province. Adad-nirari set out to support Hamath in 804 by attacking Damascus, where *Hazael, son of Ben-hadad II—whom he called by his Aramaic title *Mari'*—was ruling. This gave Israel a respite from the attacks from Aram (2 Ki. 12:17; 2 Ch. 24:23f.), and many rulers brought the Assyrian gifts in recognition of his aid. He claims that among those bringing tribute were 'Hatti (N Syria), Amurru (E Syria), Tyre, Sidon, Omri-land (Israel), Edom and Philistia as far as the Mediterranean'. A stela from Rimah (Assyria) names 'Joash of Samaria' (*Ya'usu samerinaia*) among these, *c.* 796 BC. The Assyrian action seems to have enabled Joash to recover towns on his N border which had previously been lost to Hazael (2 Ki. 13:25). Affairs at home appear to have been peaceful, for the Assyrian king built a new palace outside the citadel walls at Calah.

Shalmaneser IV (782–773 BC), though harassed by the Urarṭian Argistis I on his N border, kept up the pressure against Damascus, and this doubtless helped Jeroboam II to extend the boundaries of Israel to the Beqa' ('entrance of Hamath', 2 Ki. 14:25–28). But Assyria was now being weakened by internal dissension, for the succession was uncertain, since Shalmaneser had died when young and childless. A notable defeat in the N was marked by that 'sign of ill omen', an eclipse of the sun, in 763 BC, a date of importance in Assyrian chronology. Once again the W was free to re-group to withstand further attacks, as indicated by the Aramaic treaty of Mati'el of Bit-Agusi (Arpad) with Barga'ayah.

The records of Tiglath-pileser III (744–727 BC) are fragmentary, and the order of events in his reign uncertain. He was, however, a strong ruler who set out to regain, and even extend, the territories which owed allegiance to the national god Ashur. Early in his reign he was proclaimed king of Babylon under his native name Pul(u) (2 Ki. 15:19; 1 Ch. 5:26). In the N he fought Sardur II of Urarṭu, who was intriguing with the Syrian states. By relentless campaigning Tiglath-pileser defeated the rebels in towns along the Anti-Taurus (Kashiari) mountains as far as Kummuḫ, organizing the subdued country in a series of provinces owing allegiance to the king. *Arpad was besieged for 2 years (742–740 BC), and during this time Rezin of Damascus and other neighbouring rulers brought in their tribute. While Tiglath-pileser was absent in the N hills in 738 a revolt was stimulated by 'Azriau of Yaudi' in league with Hamath. Yaudi was a small city-state in N Syria, though there is a possibility that the reference is to Azariah of Judah. At this time Tiglath-pileser claims to have received tribute from Menahem (*Meni ḫimmu*) of Samaria and Hiram of Tyre. This event is not mentioned in the OT, which records a later payment. Then the amount of 50 shekels of silver extorted from the leading Israelites to meet this demand is shown by contemporary Assyrian contracts to be the price of a slave. It was evidently a ransom to avoid deportation (2 Ki. 15:20).

A series of campaigns 2 years later ended with the capture of Damascus in 732 BC. Tiglath-pileser, according to his annals, replaced Pekah, the murderer of Pekahiah, son of Menahem, by 'Ausi (Hoshea). *Cf.* 2 Ki. 15:30. This was probably in 734 BC, when the Assyrians marched down the Phoenician coast and through 'the border of Israel' as far as Gaza, whose king, Hanunu, fled across the 'River of *Egypt'. This action in Palestine was at least in part a response to the appeal of *Iauḫazi* ([Jeho]Ahaz) of Judah, whose tribute is listed with that of Ammon, Moab, Ashkelon and Edom, for help against Rezin of Damascus and Pekah of Israel (2 Ki. 16:5–9). Israel (*Bit-Humria*) was attacked, Hazor in Galilee destroyed (2 Ki. 15:29), and many prisoners taken into exile. Ahaz, too, paid dearly for this bid and had to accept religious obligations (2 Ki. 16:10ff.), the imported altar being but one symbol of vassalage, another being an image of the king such as Tiglath-pileser set up in conquered Gaza.

Shalmaneser V (726–722 BC), son of Tiglath-pileser III, also warred in the W. When the Assyrian vassal Hoshea failed to pay his annual tribute after listening to overtures of help promised by Egypt (2 Ki. 17:4), Shalmaneser laid siege to Samaria (v. 5). After 3 years, according to the Babylonian Chronicle, 'he broke the resistance of the city of *Samara'in*' (Samaria?) so 'the king of Assyria (who) took Samaria' (v. 6) and carried off the Israelites to exile in the Upper Euphrates and Media may be this same Assyrian king. However, since his successor Sargon II later claims the capture of Samaria as his own act, it may be that the unnamed king of v. 6 was Sargon, who could have been associated with Shalmaneser in the siege and have completed the operation on the latter's death.

Sargon II (721–705 BC) was a vigorous leader like Tiglath-pileser III. He records that, when the citizens of Samaria were led by Iau-bi'di of Hamath to withhold their taxes, he removed 27,270 (or 27,290) people from the area of Samaria, 'with the gods in which they trusted'. The exact date of this exile, which broke Israel as an independent nation, cannot be determined as yet from Assyrian records. Hanunu of Gaza had returned from Egypt with military support so Sargon marched to Raphia, where, in the first clash between the armies of the two great nations, he defeated the Egyptians. Despite this, the Palestinian rulers and peoples still leaned on Egypt for support, and the history of this period is an essential background for the prophecies of Isaiah. In 715 Sargon intervened once more, sacking Ashdod and Gath and claiming to have 'subjugated Judah'; but there is no evidence in the OT that he entered the land at this time. Sargon defeated Pisiris of Carchemish in 717 and campaigned in Cilicia. He continued Assyrian raids on the Mannai and tribes in the Lake Van area (714 BC) who were restless under Cimmerian pressure. In the S he invaded Elam, sacked Susa and drove Marduk-apla-iddina II (*MERODACH-BALADAN) back into the marshland at the head of the Persian Gulf. Sargon died before his new palace at Dur-Šarrukin (Khorsabad) could be completed.

The first years of Sennacherib (704–681 BC) were occupied in suppressing revolts which broke out on his father's death. While crown-prince he had been responsible for safeguarding the N frontier, and this knowledge proved invaluable in his dealings with Urarṭu and Media, and in his military expeditions, which reached as far W as Cilicia, where Tarsus was captured in 698 BC. Marduk-apla-iddina seized the throne of Babylon (703–701 BC), and it required a concentrated military expedition to dislodge him. It was probably during these years that the Chaldean asked Hezekiah for help (2 Ki. 20:12–19). Isaiah's disapproval of this alliance was justified, for by 689 BC the Assyrians had driven Merodach-baladan out of the country and sacked Babylon. A naval operation which was planned to cross the Gulf in pursuit of the rebel was called off on receipt of the news of his death in Elam. Moreover, in 701 BC Sennacherib had marched to Syria, besieged Sidon and moved S to attack rebellious Ashkelon. It was probably at this time that the Assyrians successfully besieged Lachish (2 Ki. 18:13–14), a victory depicted on the bas-reliefs in Sennacherib's palace at Nineveh. The army next moved to meet the Egyptians at Eltekeh. During these moves in Judah, Hezekiah paid tribute (2 Ki. 18:14–16), an act which is recorded in the Assyrian annals. The majority opinion is that it was later in this same campaign and year that Sennacherib 'shut up Hezekiah the Judaean in Jerusalem as a bird in a cage', and demanded his surrender (2 Ki. 18:17–19:9). On any interpretation, the Assyrians raised the siege suddenly and withdrew (2 Ki. 19:35–36, *cf.* Herodotus, 2. 141). Another view connects the siege of Jerusalem with a later campaign, perhaps that against the Arabs in 686 BC. This minority view assumes no time lapse, as is probable between the return to Nineveh and the assassination of *Sennacherib by his sons in the month Tebet 681 BC (Is. 37:38; 2 Ki. 19:37). The Babylonian Chronicle states that Sennacherib was murdered by 'his son', and Esarhaddon, his younger son and successor, claimed to have pursued his rebel brothers, presumably the murderers, into S Armenia (for a fuller discussion of the seeming discrepancy between the OT and Assyrian texts on the place and number of the assassins, see *DOTT*, pp. 70–73).

Sennacherib, with his W Semitic wife Naqi'a-Zakutu, extensively rebuilt Nineveh, its palaces, gateways and temples, and to ensure water-supplies aqueducts (Jerwan) and dams were built. This was also used to irrigate large parks around the city. Prisoners from his campaigns, including Jews, were used on these projects and are depicted on the palace reliefs.

Esarhaddon (680–669 BC) had been designated crown-prince by his father 2 years before he came to the throne, and had served as viceroy in Babylon. When the S Babylonians rebelled, a single campaign sufficed to subdue them, and Na'id-Marduk was appointed as their new chief in 678. But a series of campaigns was needed to counteract the machinations of their neighbours, the Elamites. In the hills farther N also periodic raids kept the tribesmen of Zamua and the Median plain subject to Assyrian overlordship. The N tribes were more restless, due to the plotting of Teušpa and the Cimmerians. Esarhaddon also came into conflict with Scythian tribes (*Išguzai*).

In the W Esarhaddon continued his father's policy of exacting tribute from the city-states, including those in Cilicia and Syria. Baal of Tyre refused payment and was attacked, and Abdi-Milki was besieged in Sidon for 3 years from 676. This opposition to Assyrian domination was incited by Tirhakah of Egypt and provoked a quick reaction. Esarhaddon increased the amount payable, collecting in addition wood, stone and other supplies for his new palace at *Calah and for his reconstruction of Babylon. It may have been in connection with the latter that Manasseh was taken there (2 Ch. 33:11). 'Manasseh (*Menasi*) of Judah' is named among those from whom Esarhaddon claimed tribute at this time. These included 'Baal of Tyre, Qauš-(Chemosh)-gabri of Edom, Muṣuri of Moab, Ṣili-Bel of Gaza, Metinti of Ashkelon, Ikausu of Ekron, Milki-ašapa of Gebel, . . . Aḫi-Milki of Ashdod as well as 10 kings of Cyprus (*Iadnana*)'.

With these states owing at least a nominal allegiance, the way was open to the fulfilment of Assyria's ambition to control the Egyptian Delta from which so much opposition was mounted. This was accomplished by a major expedition in 672 BC, which resulted in Assyrian governors being installed in Thebes and Memphis. In this same year Esarhaddon summoned his vassals to hear his declaration of Ashurbanipal as crown-prince of Assyria and Šamaš-šum-ukin as crown-prince of Babylonia. In this way he hoped to avoid disturbances similar to those which marked his own succession to the throne. Copies of the terms and oaths imposed at this ceremony are of interest as indicative of the *'covenant' form of relationship between a suzerain and his vassals. Many parallels can be drawn between this and OT terminology (D. J. Wiseman, *Vassal-Treaties of Esarhaddon*, 1958). It shows that Manasseh, as all the other rulers, would have had to swear eternal allegiance to Ashur, the national god of his overlord (2 Ki. 21:2-7, 9). The end of Esarhaddon's reign saw the beginning of the very revolts these 'covenants' were designed to forestall. Pharaoh Tirhakah incited the native chiefs of Lower Egypt to break away. It was at Harran, while on his way to crush this insurrection, that Esarhaddon died and was succeeded by his sons as planned.

Ashurbanipal (668–*c.* 627 BC) immediately took up his father's unfinished task and marched against Tirhakah (*Tarqu*); but it required three hard campaigns and the sack of Thebes in 663 (Na. 3:8, 'No' AV) to regain control of Egypt. In his reign Assyria reached its greatest territorial extent. Punitive raids on the rebels in Tyre, Arvad and Cilicia brought Assyria into contact with another rising power—Lydia, whose king Gyges sent emissaries to Nineveh seeking an alliance against the Cimmerians. The raids on the Arab tribes and the restoration of Manasseh of Judah, called *Minse* by Ashurbanipal, probably had the one aim of keeping the route open to Egypt. Nevertheless, Assyria was doomed to fall swiftly. The Medes were increasing their hold over neighbouring tribes and threatening the Assyrian homeland. By 652 BC Šamaš-šum-ukin had revolted and the resultant struggle with Babylonia, which restrained the army from needed operations farther afield, ended in the sack of the S capital in 648 BC. This rebellion had been supported by Elam, so Ashurbanipal marched in to sack *Susa in 645 and henceforth made it an Assyrian province. Free from the frequent incursions of the Assyrian army in support of its local officials and tax-collectors, the W city-states gradually loosed from Assyria, and in Judah this new-found freedom was to be reflected in the reforms initiated by Josiah. Once again Egypt was independent and intriguing in Palestine.

The date of Ashurbanipal's death is uncertain (*c*. 631–627 BC), and very few historical texts for this period have yet been found. The hordes of the Scythians (Umman-manda) began to dominate the Middle Euphrates area and Kyaxares the Mede besieged Nineveh. Ashurbanipal may have delegated power to his sons Aššur-eṭel-ilāni (632–628 BC) and Šin-šar-iškun (628–612 BC). Ashurbanipal himself was interested in the arts. He built extensively in *Nineveh, where in his palace and in the Nabu temple he collected libraries of tablets (see section **III**, Literature, below).

With the rise of Nabopolassar, the *Chaldeans drove the Assyrians out of Babylonia in 625 BC. The Babylonians joined the Medes to capture Assur (614 BC) and in July/August 612 BC, as foretold by Nahum and Zephaniah, Nineveh fell to their attack. These campaigns are fully told in the Babylonian Chronicle. The walls were breached by floods (Na. 1:8; Xenophon, *Anabasis* 3. 4) and Šin-šar-iškun (Sardanapalus) perished in the flames. For 2 years the government under Ashur-uballiṭ held out at Harran, but no help came from Egypt, Neco marching too late to prevent the city falling to the Babylonians and Scythians in 609 BC. Assyria ceased to exist and her territory was taken over by the Babylonians.

In later years 'Assyria' formed part of the Persian, Hellenistic (Seleucid) and Parthian empires, and during this time 'Assyria' (Persian *Athura*) continued to be used as a general geographical designation for her former homelands (Ezk. 16:28; 23:5–23).

II. Religion

The Assyrian king acted as regent on earth for the national god Ashur, to whom he reported his activities regularly. Thus Assyrian campaigns were conceived, at least in part, as a holy war against those who failed to avow his sovereignty or breached the borders of his land, and were ruthlessly pursued in the event of rebellion. Ashur's primary temple was at the capital Assur, and various deities were thought to guard the interests of the other cities. Anu and Adad resided at Assur, having temples and associated ziggurats there, while Ishtar, goddess of war and love, was worshipped at Nineveh, though as 'Ishtar of Arbela' she also held sway at Erbil. Nabu, god of wisdom and patron of the sciences, had temples at both Nineveh and Calah (Nimrud), where there were libraries collected by royal officials and housed in part in the Nabu (*NEBO) temple. Sin, the moon-god, and his priests and priestesses had a temple and cloisters at Ehulhul in Harran and were in close association with their counterpart in Ur. In general, divine consorts and less prominent deities had shrines within the major temples; thus at Calah, where the temples of Ninurta, god of war and hunting, Ishtar and Nabu have been discovered, there were places for such deities as Shala, Gula, Ea and Damkina. In most respects Assyrian religion differed little from that of *Babylonia, whence it had been derived. For the part played by religion in daily life, see the next section.

III. Literature

The daily life and thought of the Assyrians is to be seen in the many hundreds of letters, economic and administrative documents, and literary texts found during excavations. Thus the early 2nd millennium BC is illuminated by the letters from Mari and Shemshara and *c*. 1500, during the period of Hurrian influence, from *Nuzi. The best-known period is, however, that of the Neo-Assyrian empire, when many texts, including some copied from the Middle Assyrian period, enable a detailed reconstruction to be made of the administration and civil service. Thus the historical annals, recorded on clay prisms, cylinders and tablets, though originally intended as introductions to inscriptions describing the king's building operations, can be supplemented by texts which record the royal requests to a deity (often Shamash) for oracles to guide in decisions concerning political and military affairs. A number of the letters and legal texts, as well as the annals, make reference to Israel, Judah and the W city-states (*DOTT*, pp. 46–75; *Iraq* 17, 1955, pp. 126–154).

Ashurbanipal, an educated man, created a library by importing or copying texts both from the existing archives at Nineveh, Assur and Calah and from Babylonian religious centres. Thus, in 1852/3 in his palace at Nineveh and in the Nabu temple there, Layard and Rassam discovered 26,000 fragmentary tablets, representing about 10,000 different texts. This find and its subsequent publication laid the foundation for the study of the Semitic Assyrian language and of Babylonian, from which it differs mainly dialectally. The cuneiform script, employing 600 or more signs as ideographs, syllables or determinatives, was taken over from the earlier Sumerians. Assyro-Babylonian (Akkadian) now provides the major bulk of ancient Semitic inscriptions. Since some texts had interlinear Sumerian translations, this find has been of importance in the study of that non-Semitic tongue which survived, as did Latin in England, for religious purposes.

The discovery among the Nineveh (Kuyunjik) collection, now housed in the British Museum, of a Babylonian account of the flood (Gilgamesh XI), later published by George Smith in December 1872, proved a stimulus to further excavations, and much has been written with special reference to the bearing of these finds on the OT. The library texts represent scholarly handbooks, vocabularies, sign and word lists, and dictionaries. The mythological texts written in poetic form include the series of twelve tablets now called the 'Epic of Gilgamesh' which describes his quest for eternal life and the story he was told by Uta-napishtim of his own survival of the *Flood in a specially constructed ship. The Epic of *Creation, called *Enuma eliš* after the opening phrase, is principally concerned with the exaltation of Marduk as the head of the Babylonian pantheon. An old Babylonian epic (*Atrahasīs*) describes the creation of man following a strike against the gods and also the Flood. This provides closer parallels with OT than either *Enuma eliš* or Gilgamesh epics. Other epics include the Descent of Ishtar into the underworld in search of her husband Tammuz. Contrary to many recent theories, no text describing the resurrection of Tammuz has yet been found. Legends, including that of Sargon of Agade, who was saved at birth by being placed in a reed basket on the river Euphrates until rescued by a gardener, who brought him up to be king, have been compared with OT incidents. These Akkadian literary texts also contain the legend of Etana, who flew to heaven on an eagle, and that of the plague god Era, who fought against Babylon. Wisdom literature includes the poem of the righteous sufferer (*Ludlul bēl nēmeqi*) or the so-called 'Babylonian Job', the Babylonian theodicy, precepts and admonition, among which are counsels of wisdom, sayings and dialogues of a pessimist, and advice to a prince of the same *genre*, but not spirit, as OT Wisdom literature. There are also collections of hymns, fables, popular sayings, parables, proverbs and tales ('The poor man of Nippur') which are precursors of later literary forms.

Religious literature is also well represented by tablets grouped in series of up to ninety with their number and title stated in a colophon. The majority are omens derived from the inspection of the liver or entrails of sacrificial animals, or the movements and features of men, animals, birds, objects and planets. Many tablets give instructions for rituals to ensure the king's welfare and that of his country. Closely allied to these texts are the carefully recorded observations which formed the basis of Akkadian science, especially medicine (prognosis and diagnosis), botany, geology, chemistry, mathematics and law. For chronological purposes lists covering many of the years from *c.* 1100 to 612 BC gave the name of the eponym or *limmu*-official by whom each year was designated. These, together with the recorded king lists and astronomical data, provide a system of dating which is accurate to within a few years.

IV. Administration

The government derived from the person of the king who was also the religious leader and commander-in-chief. He exercised direct authority, although he also delegated local jurisdiction to provincial governors (*e.g.* *RABSHAKEH, *RABSARIS) and district-governors who collected and forwarded tribute and taxes, usually paid in kind. They were supported by the expeditions of the Assyrian army, the nucleus of which was a highly-trained and well-equipped regular force of chariots, siege-engineers, bowmen, spearmen and slingers. Conquered territories were made vassal-subjects of the god Ashur on oath and forced to render both political and religious allegiance to Assyria. Offenders were punished by reprisals and invasion, which resulted in the loot and destruction of their cities, death to the rebel leaders, and slavery and exile for the skilled citizens. The remainder were subjected to the surveillance of pro-Assyrian deputies. This helps to explain both the attitude of the Hebrew prophets to Assyria and the fear of 'this cauldron boiling over from the north' (*cf.* Je. 1:13) by the small states of Israel and Judah.

V. Art

Many examples of Assyrian art, wall-paintings, painted glazed panels, sculptured bas-reliefs, statues, ornaments, cylinder seals, ivory carvings, as well as bronze and metal work, have been preserved following excavation. Some of the reliefs are of particular interest in that the stele and obelisk of Shalmaneser III from Nimrud mention Israel and may portray Jehu. Sennacherib, on his palace sculptures at Nineveh, depicts the siege of Lachish and the use of Judaean captives to work on his building projects; while the bronze gates at Balawat show the Assyrian army engaged in Syria and Phoenicia. Other reliefs of Ashurnasirpal II at Nimrud and Ashurbanipal in the 'Lion Hunt' from Nineveh are a pictorial source for the costume, customs, and military and civilian operations of the Assyrians from the 9th to the 7th centuries BC.

VI. Excavations

Early explorers searched for biblical *Nineveh (Kuyunjik and Nebi Yunus) opposite Mosul, which was surveyed by C. J. Rich in 1820 and excavated in 1842–3 by Botta, in 1846–7, 1849–51 and 1853–4 by Layard and Rassam, by the British Museum in 1903–5, 1927–32 and subsequently by Iraqi archaeologists. Other major cities excavated include Assur (Qala'at Shergat) by German expeditions (1903–14); *Calah (Nimrud) by the British—Layard (1842–52), Loftus (1854–5), Mallowan and Oates (1949–63)—and by Iraqis and Poles (1969-76); and Dūr-Sharrukīn (Khorsabad) by the French (1843–5) and Americans (1929-35). Outlying prehistoric sites include Jarmo, Hassuna, Thalathat, Umm Dabaghiyah, Arpachiyah and Tepe Gawra. The principal Middle Assyrian occupations uncovered in addition to Assur are Tell Rimah and Billa (Shibaniba). Later Assyrian sites of note include Balawat (Imgur-Bēl).

For sites explored 1842–1939, see S. A. Pallis, *The Antiquity of Iraq*, 1956; for 1932–56 see M. E. L. Mallowan, *Twenty-Five Years of Mesopotamian Discovery*, 1956; and subsequently, reports in the journals *Iraq*, *Sumer* (*passim*).

BIBLIOGRAPHY. *History: CAH* 3:1, 1982; 3:2, 1991. *Inscriptions:* A. K. Grayson, *Assyrian Royal Inscriptions*, 1975–6; W. W. Hallo and W. K. Simpson, *The Ancient Near East: A History*, 1971, ch. 5; A. L. Oppenheim, *Letters from Mesopotamia*, 1967; *Ancient Mesopotamia*, 1964. *Relation to OT: ANET*, *DOTT*. *General: Reallexikon der Assyriologie*, 1932–78. *Art:* R. D. Barnett, *The Assyrian Palace Reliefs*, 1976; *The Sculptures of Ashurbanipal*, 1976; M. E. L. Mallowan, *Nimrud and its Remains*, 1966. *Various:* G. van Driel, *The Cult of Aššur*, 1976; J. N. Postgate, *Taxation and Conscription in the Assyrian Empire*, 1974.

D.J.W.

ATAROTH (Heb. *ᵃṭārôṯ*, lit. 'crowns'). **1.** A city on the E of Jordan in Reubenite territory (Nu. 32:3, 34), modern Khirbet 'Attarus; *cf.* *ARNON. A city called Atroth occurs in Nu. 32:35, but this may be an accidental repetition from the previous verse, or else should be taken with the following word, giving the otherwise unknown place-name Atroth-Shophan. **2.** A city in Ephraim, perhaps the same as Ataroth-Addar (Jos. 16:2, 5, 7; 18:13). **3.** 'Ataroth, the house of Joab' is mentioned in a Judaean genealogy (1 Ch. 2:54). This may be understood as 'the crowns (scions, chiefs) of the house of Joab', a description of Bethlehem and Netophathi, whose names immediately precede. See *LOB*. R.J.W.

ATHALIAH (Heb. *ʿaṯalyāhû*, 'Yahweh is exalted'). **1.** The daughter of Ahab, and the granddaughter of Omri (2 Ki. 8:26). Her marriage with Jehoram, king of Judah, marked an alliance between N and S, and implied the superiority of Israel. The death of her son, Ahaziah, after a reign of 1 year, at the hand of Jehu, in the 'Prophetic Revolution' (2 Ki. 8:25–10:36), revealed her as 'that wicked woman' (2 Ch. 24:7). To retain the power she had enjoyed as queen-mother, she 'destroyed all the royal family' (2 Ki. 11:1); and began to reign (*c.* 842 BC). For 6 years her authority was unchallenged, then the priest Jehoiada put the child Joash on the throne. She came out to meet her enemies, and was put to death outside the Temple.

2. A person named in the genealogy of Benjamin (1 Ch. 8:26).

3. One of the exiles who returned from Babylon with Ezra (Ezr. 8:7). M.B.

ATHENS. Acts 17:15–34; 1 Thes. 3:1. In the 5th and 4th centuries BC Athens was famous for its culture, the home of great dramatists, and of great philosophers like Plato and Aristotle. After the Roman conquest of Greece, Athens became a *civitas foederata* (a city linked to Rome by treaty), entirely independent of the governor of Achaia, paying no taxes to Rome and with internal judicial autonomy. Of the three great university cities Athens, Tarsus and Alexandria, Athens was the most famous. Philo the Alexandrian said that the Athenians were the keenest-sighted mentally of the Greeks. It was also famous for its temples, statues and monuments. The first 168 pages of the

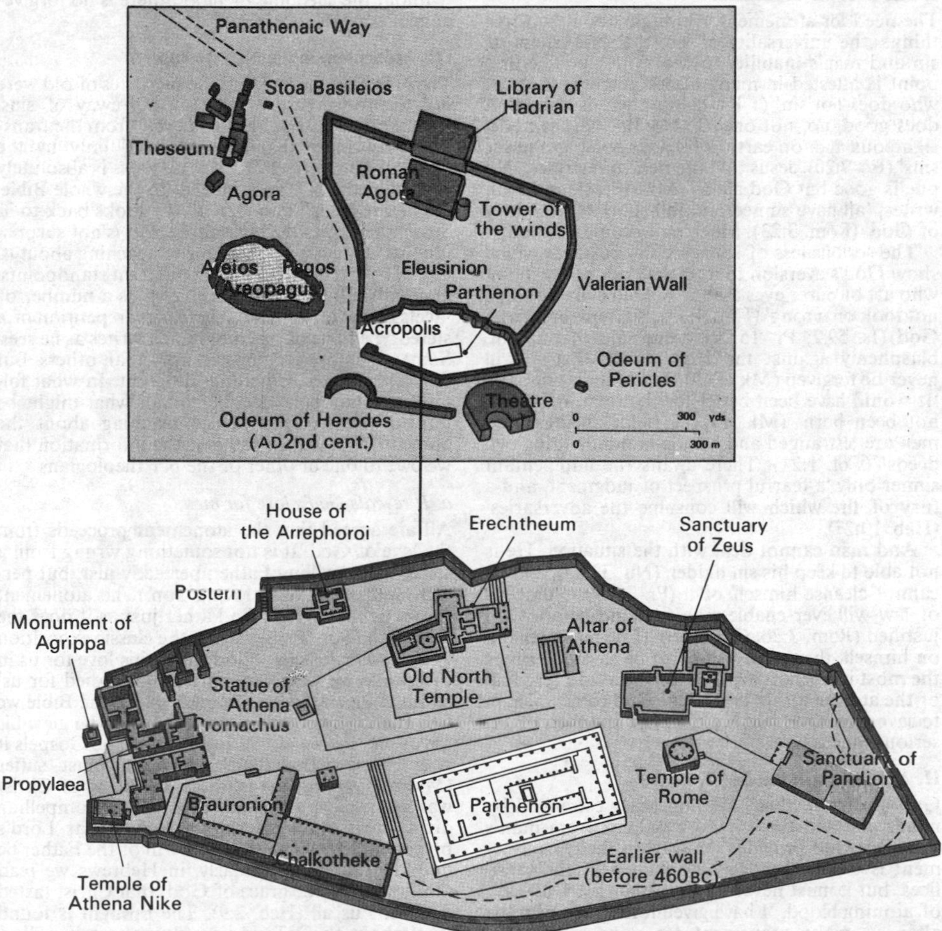

Ancient Athens incorporating the Acropolis.

Loeb edition of the *Description of Greece*, by Pausanias, written a century after Paul's visit, are a good tourists' guide to the antiquities of Athens. Though the Athenians were religious and eager to discuss religion, their spiritual level was not exceptionally high. Apollonius the philosopher, a contemporary of Paul, rebuked them for their lascivious jigs at the festival of Dionysus and for their love of human slaughter in the gladiatorial games. D.R.H.

ATONEMENT. The word 'atonement' is one of the few theological terms which derive basically from Anglo-Saxon. It means 'a making at one', and points to a process of bringing those who are estranged into a unity. The word occurs in the OT to translate words from the *kpr* word group, and it is found once in the NT (AV), rendering *katallagē* (which is better translated 'reconciliation' as RSV). Its use in theology is to denote the work of Christ in dealing with the problem posed by the sin of man, and in bringing sinners into right relation with God.

I. The need for atonement

The need for atonement is brought about by three things, the universality of sin, the seriousness of sin and man's inability to deal with sin. The first point is attested in many places: 'there is no man who does not sin' (1 Ki. 8:46); 'there is none that does good, no, not one' (Ps. 14:3); 'there is not a righteous man on earth, who does good and never sins' (Ec. 7:20). Jesus told the rich young ruler, 'No one is good but God alone' (Mk. 10:18), and Paul writes, 'all have sinned and fall short of the glory of God' (Rom. 3:23). Much more could be cited.

The seriousness of sin is seen in passages which show God's aversion to it. Habakkuk prays 'Thou who art of purer eyes than to behold evil and canst not look on wrong' (Hab. 1:13). Sin separates from God (Is. 59:2; Pr. 15:29). Jesus said of one sin, blasphemy against the Holy Spirit, that it will never be forgiven (Mk. 3:29), and of Judas he said, 'It would have been better for that man if he had not been born' (Mk. 14:21). Before being saved men are 'estranged and hostile in mind, doing evil deeds' (Col. 1:21). There awaits the unrepentant sinner only 'a fearful prospect of judgment, and a fury of fire which will consume the adversaries' (Heb. 10:27).

And man cannot deal with the situation. He is not able to keep his sin hidden (Nu. 32:23), and he cannot cleanse himself of it (Pr. 20: 9). No deeds of law will ever enable man to stand before God justified (Rom. 3:20; Gal. 2:16). If he must depend on himself, then man will never be saved. Perhaps the most important evidence of this is the very fact of the atonement. If the Son of God came to earth to save men, then men were sinners and their plight serious indeed.

II. Atonement in the Old Testament

God and man, then, are hopelessly estranged by man's sin, and there is no way back from man's side. But God provides the way. In the OT atonement is usually said to be obtained by the sacrifices, but it must never be forgotten that God says of atoning blood, 'I have given it for you upon the altar to make atonement for your souls' (Lv. 17:11). Atonement is secured, not by any value inherent in the sacrificial victim, but because sacrifice is the divinely appointed way of securing atonement. The sacrifices point us to certain truths concerning atonement. Thus the victim must always be unblemished, which indicates the necessity for perfection. The victims cost something, for atonement is not cheap, and sin is never to be taken lightly. The death of the victim was the important thing. This is brought out partly in the allusions to *blood, partly in the general character of the rite itself and partly in other references to atonement. There are several allusions to atonement, either effected or contemplated by means other than the cultus, and where these bear on the problem they point to death as the way. Thus in Ex. 32:30–32 Moses seeks to make an atonement for the sin of the people, and he does so by asking God to blot him out of the book which he has written. Phinehas made an atonement by slaying certain transgressors (Nu. 25:6–8, 13). Other passages might be cited. It is clear that in the OT it was recognized that death was the penalty for sin (Ezk. 18:20), but that God graciously permitted the death of a sacrificial victim to substitute for the death of the sinner. So clear is the connection that the writer of the Epistle to the Hebrews can sum it up by saying 'without the shedding of blood there is no forgiveness of sins' (Heb. 9:22).

III. Atonement in the New Testament

The NT takes the line that the sacrifices of old were not the root cause of the putting away of sins. Redemption is to be obtained even 'from the transgressions under the first covenant' only by the death of Christ (Heb. 9:15). The cross is absolutely central to the NT, and, indeed, to the whole Bible. All before leads up to it. All after looks back to it. Since it occupies the critical place, it is not surprising that there is a vast volume of teaching about it. The NT writers, writing from different standpoints, and with different emphases, give us a number of facets of the atonement. There is no repetition of a stereotyped line of teaching. Each writes as he sees. Some saw more and more deeply than others. But they did not see something different. In what follows we shall consider first of all what might be termed the common, basic teaching about the atonement, and then some of the information that we owe to one or other of the NT theologians.

a. It reveals God's love for men

All are agreed that the atonement proceeds from the love of God. It is not something wrung from a stern and unwilling Father, perfectly just, but perfectly inflexible, by a loving Son. The atonement shows us the love of the Father just as it does the love of the Son. Paul gives us the classic exposition of this when he says, 'God shows his love for us in that while we were yet sinners Christ died for us' (Rom. 5:8). In the best-known text in the Bible we find that 'God so loved the world that he gave his only Son . . .' (Jn. 3:16). In the Synoptic Gospels it is emphasized that the Son of man 'must' suffer (Mk. 8:31, *etc*.). That is to say, the death of Christ was no accident: it was rooted in a compelling divine necessity. This we see also in our Lord's prayer in Gethsemane that the will of the Father be done (Mt. 26:42). Similarly, in Hebrews we read that it was 'by the grace of God' that Christ tasted death for us all (Heb. 2:9). The thought is found throughout the NT, and we must bear it well in mind when we reflect on the manner of the atonement.

b. The sacrificial aspect of Christ's death

Another thought that is widespread is that the death of Christ is a death for sin. It is not simply that certain wicked men rose up against him. It is not that his enemies conspired against him and that he was not able to resist them. He 'was put to death for our trespasses' (Rom. 4:25). He came specifically to die for our sins. His blood was shed 'for many for the forgiveness of sins' (Mt. 26:28). He 'made purification for sins' (Heb. 1:3). He 'bore our sins in his body on the tree' (1 Pet. 2:24). He is 'the propitiation for our sins' (1 Jn. 2:2; so, rightly, AV). The cross of Christ will never be understood unless it is seen that thereon the Saviour was dealing with the sins of all mankind.

In doing this he fulfilled all that the old sacrifices had foreshadowed, and the NT writers love to think of his death as a sacrifice. Jesus himself referred to his blood as 'blood of the covenant' (Mk. 14:24), which points us to the sacrificial rites for its understanding. Indeed, much of the language used in the institution of the Holy Communion is sacrificial, pointing to the sacrifice to be accomplished on the cross. Paul tells us that Christ 'loved us and gave himself up for us, a fragrant offering and sacrifice to God' (Eph. 5:2). On occasion he can refer, not to sacrifice in general, but to a specific sacrifice, as in 1 Cor. 5:7, 'For Christ our paschal lamb (better, passover) has been sacrificed.' Peter speaks of 'the precious blood of Christ, like that of a lamb without blemish or spot' (1 Pet. 1:19), which indicates that in one aspect Christ's death was a sacrifice. And in John's Gospel we read the words of John the Baptist, 'Behold, the Lamb of God, who takes away the sin of the world' (Jn. 1:29). Sacrifice was practically the universal religious rite of the 1st century. Wherever men were and whatever their background, they would discern a sacrificial allusion. The NT writers made use of this, and employed sacrificial terminology to bring out what Christ had done for men. All that to which the sacrifices pointed, and more, he had fully accomplished by his death.

c. The representative nature of Christ's death

It is agreed by most students that Christ's death was vicarious. If in one sense he died 'for sin', in another he died 'for us'. But 'vicarious' is a term which may mean much or little. It is better to be more precise. Most scholars today accept the view that the death of Christ is representative. That is to say, it is not that Christ died and somehow the benefits of that death become available to men (did not even Anselm ask to whom more fittingly than to us could they be assigned?). It is rather that he died specifically for us. He was our representative as he hung on the cross. This is expressed succinctly in 2 Cor. 5:14, 'one died for all; therefore all have died'. The death of the Representative counts as the death of those he represents. When Christ is spoken of as our 'advocate with the Father' (1 Jn. 2:1) there is the plain thought of representation, and as the passage immediately goes on to deal with his death for sin it is relevant to our purpose. The Epistle to the Hebrews has as one of its major themes that of Christ as our great High Priest. The thought is repeated over and over. Now whatever else may be said about a High Priest, he represents men. The thought of representation may thus be said to be very strong in this Epistle.

d. Substitution taught in the New Testament

But can we say more? There is a marked disinclination among many modern scholars (though not by any means all) to use the older language of substitution. Nevertheless, this seems to be the teaching of the NT, and that not in one or two places only, but throughout. In the Synoptic Gospels there is the great ransom saying, 'the Son of man also came not to be served but to serve, and to give his life as a ransom for many' (Mk. 10:45). Both the details ('ransom' has a substitutionary connotation, and *anti*, 'for', is the preposition of substitution) and the general thought of the passage (men should die, Christ dies instead, men no longer die) point to substitution. The same truth is indicated by passages which speak of Christ as the suffering Servant of Is. 53, for of him it is said, 'he was wounded for our transgressions, he was bruised for our iniquities; upon him was the chastisement that made us whole, and with his stripes we are healed . . . the Lord has laid on him the iniquity of us all' (Is. 53:5f.). The shrinking of Christ in Gethsemane points in the same direction. He was courageous, and many far less worthy than he have faced death calmly. The agony seems to be inexplicable other than on the grounds disclosed by Paul, that for our sake God 'made him to be sin, who knew no sin' (2 Cor. 5:21). In his death he took our place, and his holy soul shrank from this identification with sinners. And it seems that no less than this gives meaning to the cry of dereliction, 'My God, my God, why hast thou forsaken me?' (Mk. 15:34).

Paul tells us that Christ 'redeemed us from the curse of the law, having become a curse for us' (Gal. 3:13). He bore our curse, which is but another way of saying substitution. The same thought lies behind Rom. 3:21–26, where the apostle develops the thought that God's justice is manifested in the process whereby sin is forgiven, *i.e.* the cross. He is not saying, as some have thought, that God's righteousness is shown in the *fact* that sin is forgiven, but that it is shown in the *way* in which sin is forgiven. Atonement is not a matter of passing over sin as had been done previously (Rom. 3:25). The cross shows that God is just, at the same time as it shows him justifying believers. This must mean that God's justice is vindicated in the way sin is dealt with. And this seems another way of saying that Christ bore the penalty of men's sin. This is also the thought in passages dealing with sin-bearing as Heb. 9:28; 1 Pet. 2:24. The meaning of bearing sin is made clear by a number of OT passages where the context shows that the bearing of penalty is meant. For example, in Ezk. 18:20 we read, 'The soul that sins shall die. The son shall not suffer for (Heb. 'bear') the iniquity of the father . . .', and in Nu. 14:34 the wilderness wanderings are described as a bearing of iniquities. Christ's bearing of our sin, then, means that he bore our penalty.

Substitution lies behind the statement in 1 Tim. 2:6 that Christ gave himself 'a ransom for all'. *antilytron*, translated 'ransom', is a strong compound meaning 'substitute-ransom'. Grimm–Thayer define it as 'what is given in exchange for another as the price of his redemption'. It is impossible to empty the word of substitutionary associations. A similar thought lies behind John's recording of the cynical prophecy of Caiaphas, 'it is expedient for you that one man should die for the people, and that the whole nation should not perish' (Jn. 11:50). For Caiaphas the words were sheer political expediency, but John sees in them a prophecy that Christ would die instead of the people.

This is a formidable body of evidence (and is not exhaustive). In the face of it it seems impossible to deny that substitution is one strand in the NT understanding of the work of Christ.

c. Other NT aspects of the atonement

Such are the main points attested throughout the NT. Other important truths are set forth in individual writers (which does not, of course, mean that they are any the less to be accepted; it is simply a method of classification). Thus Paul sees in the cross the way of deliverance. Men naturally are enslaved to sin (Rom. 6:17; 7:14). But in Christ men are free (Rom. 6:14, 22). Similarly, through Christ men are delivered from the flesh, they 'have crucified the flesh' (Gal. 5:24), they 'do not war after the flesh' (2 Cor. 10:3, AV), that flesh which 'lusteth against the Spirit' (Gal. 5:17, AV), and which apart from Christ spells death (Rom. 8:13). Men are under the wrath of God on account of their unrighteousness (Rom. 1:18), but Christ delivers from this, too. Believers are 'justified by his blood', and thus will 'be saved by him from the wrath of God' (Rom. 5:9). The law (*i.e.* the Pentateuch, and hence the whole Jewish Scripture) may be regarded in many ways. But considered as a way of salvation it is disastrous. It shows a man his sin (Rom. 7:7), and, entering into an unholy alliance with sin, slays him (Rom. 7:9–11). The end result is that 'all who rely on works of the law are under a curse' (Gal. 3:10). But 'Christ redeemed us from the curse of the law' (Gal. 3:13). Death to men of antiquity was a grim antagonist against whom none might prevail. But Paul sings a song of triumph in Christ who gives victory even over death (1 Cor. 15:55–57). It is abundantly plain that Paul sees in Christ a mighty Deliverer.

The atonement has many positive aspects. It must suffice simply to mention such things as redemption, reconciliation, justification, adoption and propitiation. These are great concepts and mean much to Paul. In some cases he is the first Christian of whom we have knowledge to make use of them. Clearly he thought of Christ as having wrought much for his people in his atoning death.

For the writer to the Hebrews the great thought is that of Christ as our great High Priest. He develops thoroughly the thought of the uniqueness and the finality of the offering made by Christ. Unlike the way established on Jewish altars and ministered by priests of the Aaronic line, the way established by Christ in his death is of permanent validity. It will never be altered. Christ has dealt fully with man's sin.

In the writings of John there is the thought of Christ as the special revelation of the Father. He is One sent by the Father, and all that he does must be interpreted in the light of this fact. So John sees Christ as winning a conflict against the darkness, as defeating the evil one. He has much to say about the working out of the purpose of God in Christ. He sees the true glory in the lowly cross whereon such a mighty work was done.

From all this it is abundantly apparent that the atonement is vast and deep. The NT writers strive with the inadequacy of language as they seek to present us with what this great divine act means. There is more to it by far than we have been able to indicate. But all the points we have made are important, and none is to be neglected. Nor are we to overlook the fact that the atonement represents more than something negative. We have been concerned to insist on the place of Christ's sacrifice of himself in the putting away of sin. But that opens up the way to a new life in Christ. And that new life, the fruit of the atonement, is not to be thought of as an insignificant detail. It is that to which all the rest leads. (*EXPIATION, *FORGIVENESS, *PROPITIATION, *RECONCILIATION, *REDEEMER, *SACRIFICE.)

BIBLIOGRAPHY. J. Denney, *The Death of Christ*, 1951; G. Aulen, *Christus Victor*, 1931; E. Brunner, *The Mediator*; K. Barth, *Church Dogmatics*, 4, i; *The Doctrine of Reconciliation*; J. S. Stewart, *A Man in Christ*; Anselm, *Cur Deus Homo*; L. Morris, *The Cross in the New Testament*, 1967; *The Atonement*, 1983; M. Hengel, *The Atonement*, 1981; J. Stott, *The Cross of Christ*, 1986; R. Letham, *The Work of Christ*, 1993; J. Knox, *The Death of Christ*; J. I. Packer, 'What did the Cross achieve? The Logic of Penal Substitution', *TynB* 25, 1974, pp. 3–45.

L.M.

ATONEMENT, DAY OF (Heb. *yôm hakkippurîm*). On the 10th day of the 7th month (Tishri, September/October), Israel observed its most solemn holy day. All work was forbidden and a strict fast was enjoined on all of the people.

I. Purpose

The Day of Atonement served as a reminder that the daily, weekly and monthly sacrifices made at the altar of burnt offering were not sufficient to atone for sin. Even at the altar of burnt offering the worshipper stood 'afar off', unable to approach the holy Presence of God, who was manifest between the cherubim in the holy of holies. On this one day in the year, atoning blood was brought into the holy of holies, the divine throneroom, by the high priest as the representative of the people.

The high priest made atonement for 'all the iniquities of the children of Israel and all their transgressions in all their sins'. Atonement was first made for the priests because the mediator between God and his people had to be ceremonially clean. The sanctuary was also cleansed, for it, too, was ceremonially defiled by the presence and ministration of sinful men.

II. Ancient observance

To prepare for the sacrifices of the day, the high priest put aside his official robes and dressed in a simple white garment. He then offered a bullock as a sin-offering for himself and the priesthood. After filling his censer with live coals from the altar, the high priest entered the holy of holies, where he placed incense on the coals. The incense sent forth a cloud of smoke over the mercy seat, which served as a covering for the ark of the covenant. The high priest took some of the blood of the bullock and sprinkled it on the mercy seat and on the ground in front of the ark. In this way atonement was made for the priesthood.

The high priest next sacrificed a he-goat as a sin offering for the people. Some of the blood was taken into the holy of holies, and it was sprinkled there in the manner in which the sin offering for the priests had been sprinkled (Lv. 16:11–15).

After purifying the holy place and the altar of burnt offering with the mingled blood of the bullock and the goat (Lv. 16:18–19) the high priest took a second goat, laid his hands upon its head and confessed over it the sins of Israel. This goat, commonly called the *scapegoat (*i.e.* escape goat), was then driven into the desert, where it symbolically carried away the sins of the people.

The carcasses of the two burnt offerings—the bullock and the he-goat—were taken outside the city and burnt. The day was concluded with additional sacrifices.

III. Significance

The Epistle to the Hebrews interprets the ritual of the Day of Atonement as a type of the atoning work of Christ, emphasizing the perfection of the latter by contrast with the inadequacy of the former (Heb. 9–10). Jesus himself is termed our 'great high priest', and the blood shed on Calvary is seen as typified in the blood of bulls and goats. Unlike the OT priesthood, the sinless Christ did not have to make sacrifice for any sins of his own.

As the high priest of the OT entered the holy of holies with the blood of his sacrificial victim, so Jesus entered heaven itself to appear before the Father on behalf of his people (Heb. 9:11–12).

The high priest had to offer sin offerings each year for his own sins and the sins of the people. This annual repetition of the sacrifices served as a reminder that perfect atonement had not yet been provided. Jesus, however, through his own blood effected eternal redemption for his people (Heb. 9:12).

The Epistle to the Hebrews notes that the levitical offerings could effect only 'the purification of the flesh'. They ceremonially cleansed the sinner, but they could not bring about inward cleansing, the prerequisite for fellowship with God. The offerings served as a type and a prophecy of Jesus, who, through his better sacrifice, cleanses the conscience from dead works (Heb. 9:13–14).

The OT tabernacle was designed, in part, to teach Israel that sin hindered access to the presence of God. Only the high priest, and he only once a year, could enter the holy of holies, and then 'not without taking blood' offered to atone for sins (Heb. 9:7). Jesus, however, through a 'new and living way' has entered heaven itself, the true holy of holies, where he ever lives to make intercession for his people. The believer need not stand afar off, as did the Israelite of old, but may now through Christ approach the very throne of grace.

In Heb. 13:11–12 we are reminded that the flesh of the sin offering of the Day of Atonement was burnt outside the camp of Israel. Jesus, also, suffered outside the gate of Jerusalem that he might redeem his people from sin.

IV. Modern observance

In modern Jewish usage the Day of Atonement, *Yom Kippur*, is the last of the '10 Days of Penitence' which begin with *Rosh Hashanah*—the Jewish New Year's Day. This 10-day period is devoted to the spiritual exercises of penitence, prayer and fasting in preparation for the most solemn day of the year, *Yom Kippur*. Although the sacrificial aspects of the Day of Atonement have not been in effect since the destruction of the Temple, Jews still observe the day by fasting and refraining from all types of work.

The shophar, or ram's horn, is blown to assemble the people for worship in the synagogue on the eve of *Yom Kippur*. At this time the impressive *Kol Nidre* ('all vows') service is chanted. The congregation penitently asks God to forgive them for breaking the vows which they were unable to fulfil.

Services are held on the next day from early morning until nightfall. At sunset the Day of Atonement is ended by a single blast of the shophar, after which the worshippers return to their homes.

BIBLIOGRAPHY. M. Noth, *Leviticus*, 1965, pp. 115–126; N. H. Snaith, *The Jewish New Year Festival*, 1947, p. 121 *et passim*; *idem*, *Leviticus and Numbers*, 1967, pp. 109–118; R. de Vaux, *Ancient Israel*, 1961, pp. 507–510; *idem*, *Studies in Old Testament Sacrifice*, 1964, pp. 91–97. C.F.P.

ATTALIA, modern Antalya, near the mouth of the river Cataractes (mod. Aksu), was the chief port of Pamphylia. Founded by Attalus II of Pergamum (159–138 BC), it was bequeathed by Attalus III to Rome. Paul and Barnabas returned from their missionary journey through Attalia (Acts 14:25). There was another Attalia in N Lydia. K.L.McK.

AUGUSTUS. An additional name adopted by *Caesar Octavianus upon the regularization of his position in 27 BC, and apparently intended to signalize that moral authority in terms of which he defined his primacy in the Roman republic (*Res Gestae* 34). It passed to his successors as a title of office rather than a name, and was hence translated into Greek (*sebastos*, 'His Reverence', Acts 25:21, 25: RSV 'the emperor') when referring to them, though transliterated when referring to him (Lk. 2:1).

Augustus embodied the Roman ideal: personal merit should win dignity and power. But his success put an end to competition, and left him with the burden of universal responsibility. His 57 years of rule (43 BC to AD 14) saw the foundation of a new era of peace under the *Roman empire.

BIBLIOGRAPHY. A. H. M. Jones, *Augustus*, 1970. E.A.J.

AUTHORITIES, CITY. The senior board of magistrates, five in number and later six, at Thessalonica. Their title (Gk. *politarchai*) is epigraphically attested for a number of Macedonian states (E. D. Burton, *American Journal of Theology* 2, 1898, pp. 598–632). As is nicely illustrated by the Acts (17:6–9), they controlled the republic under Roman supervision. E.A.J.

AUTHORITY. The NT word is *exousia*, meaning rightful, actual and unimpeded power to act, or to possess, control, use or dispose of, something or somebody. Whereas *dynamis* means physical power simply, *exousia* properly signifies power that is in some sense lawful. *exousia* may be used with the stress on either the rightfulness of power really held, or the reality of power rightfully possessed. In the latter case, EVV often translate it as 'power'. *exousia* sometimes bears a general secular sense (*e.g.* in 1 Cor. 7:37, of self-control; Acts 5:4, of disposing of one's income), but its significance is more commonly theological.

AUTHORITY

The uniform biblical conviction is that the only rightful power within creation is, ultimately, the Creator's. Such authority as men have is delegated to them by God, to whom they must answer for the way they use it. Because all authority is ultimately God's, submission to authority in all realms of life is a religious duty, part of God's service.

I. The authority of God

God's authority is an aspect of his unalterable, universal and eternal dominion over his world (for which see Ex. 15:18; Pss. 29:10; 93:1f.; 146:10; Dn. 4:34f., *etc.*). This universal Kingship is distinct from (though basic to) the covenanted relationship between himself and Israel by which Israel became his people and kingdom (*cf.* Ex. 19:6), and so heirs of his blessing. His regal authority over mankind consists in his unchallengeable right and power to dispose of men as he pleases (compared by Paul to the potter's *exousia* over the clay, Rom. 9:21; *cf.* Je. 18:6), plus his indisputable claim that men should be subject to him and live for his glory. Throughout the Bible, the reality of God's authority is proved by the fact that all who ignore or flout this claim incur divine judgment. The royal Judge has the last word, and so his authority is vindicated.

In OT times, God exercised authority over his people through the agency of prophets, priests and kings, whose respective work it was to proclaim his messages (Je. 1:7ff.), teach his laws (Dt. 31:11; Mal. 2:7) and rule in accordance with those laws (Dt. 17:18ff.). So doing, they were to be respected as God's representatives, having authority from him. Also, written Scripture was acknowledged as God-given and authoritative, both as instruction (*tôrâ*) to teach Israelites their King's mind (*cf.* Ps. 119) and as the statute-book by which he ruled and judged them (*cf.* 2 Ki. 22–23).

II. The authority of Jesus Christ

The authority of *Jesus Christ is also an aspect of kingship. It is both personal and official, for Jesus is both Son of God and Son of man (*i.e.* the Messianic man). As man and Messiah, his authority is real because delegated to him by the God at whose command he does his work (Christ applauded the centurion for seeing this, Mt. 8:9f.). As the Son, his authority is real because he is himself God. Authority to judge has been given him, both that he may be honoured as the Son of God (for *judgment is God's work), and also because he is the Son of man (for judgment is the Messiah's work) (Jn. 5:22f., 27). In short, his authority is that of a divine Messiah: of a God-man, doing his Father's will in the double capacity of (*a*) human servant, in whom meet the saving offices of prophet, priest and king, and (*b*) divine Son, co-creator and sharer in all the Father's works (Jn. 5:19ff.).

This more-than-human authority of Jesus was manifested during his ministry in various ways, such as the finality and independence of his teaching (Mt. 7:28f.); his exorcizing power (Mk. 1:27); his mastery over storms (Lk. 8:24f.); his claiming to forgive sins (a thing which, as the bystanders rightly pointed out, only God can do) and, when challenged, proving his claim (Mk. 2:5–12; *cf.* Mt. 9:8). After his resurrection, he declared that he had been given 'all *exousia* in heaven and on earth'—a cosmic Messianic dominion, to be exercised in such a way as effectively to bring the elect into his kingdom of salvation (Mt. 28:18ff.; Jn. 17:2; *cf.* Jn. 12:31ff.; Acts 5:31; 18:9f.). The NT proclaims the exalted Jesus as 'both Lord and Christ' (Acts 2:36)—divine Ruler of all things, and Saviour-king of his people. The gospel is in the first instance a demand for assent to this estimate of his authority.

III. Apostolic authority

Apostolic authority is delegated Messianic authority; for the *apostles were Christ's commissioned witnesses, emissaries and representatives (*cf.* Mt. 10:40; Jn. 17:18; 20:21; Acts 1:8; 2 Cor. 5:20), given *exousia* by him to found, build up and regulate his universal church (2 Cor. 10:8; 13:10; *cf.* Gal. 2:7ff.). Accordingly, we find them giving orders and prescribing discipline in Christ's name. *i.e.* as his spokesmen and with his authority (1 Cor. 5:4; 2 Thes. 3:6). They appointed deacons (Acts 6:3, 6) and presbyters (Acts 14:23). They presented their teaching as Christ's truth, Spirit-given in both content and form of expression (1 Cor. 2:9–13; *cf.* 1 Thes. 2:13), a norm for faith (2 Thes. 2:15; *cf.* Gal. 1:8) and behaviour (2 Thes. 3:4, 6, 14). They expected their *ad hoc* rulings to be received as 'the commandment of the Lord' (1 Cor. 14:37). Because their authority depended on Christ's direct personal commission, they had, properly speaking, no successors; but each generation of Christians must show its continuity with the first generation, and its allegiance to Christ, by subjecting its own faith and life to the norm of teaching which Christ's appointed delegates provided and put on record for all time in the documents of the NT. Through the NT, apostolic *exousia* over the church has been made a permanent reality.

IV. Authority delegated to man

Besides the church, where 'leaders' (presbyters) may claim obedience because they are Christ's servants, tending his flock under his authority (Heb. 13:17; 1 Pet. 5:1f.), the Bible mentions two other spheres of delegated divine authority.

a. Marriage and the family

Men have authority over women (1 Cor. 11:3; *cf.* 1 Tim. 2:12) and parents over children (*cf.* 1 Tim. 3:4, 12). Hence, wives must obey their husbands (Eph. 5:22; 1 Pet. 3:1–6) and children their parents (Eph. 6:1ff.). This is God's order.

b. Civil government

Secular (Roman) governors are called *exousiai*, and described as God's servants to punish evildoers and encourage law-abiding citizens (Rom. 13:1–6). Christians are to regard the 'powers that be' as God-ordained (see Jn. 19:11), and dutifully subject themselves to civil authority (Rom. 13:1; 1 Pet. 2:13f.; *cf.* Mt. 22:17–21) so far as is compatible with obedience to God's direct commands (Acts 4:19; 5:29).

V. Satanic power

The exercise of *power by Satan and his hosts is sometimes termed *exousia* (*e.g.* Lk. 22:53; Col. 1:13). This indicates that, though Satan's power is usurped from God and hostile to him, Satan holds it only by God's permission and as God's tool.

BIBLIOGRAPHY. Arndt; *MM*; T. Rees in *ISBE* and J. Denney in *DCG*, *s.v.* 'Authority'; N. Geldenhuys, *Supreme Authority*, 1953; O. Betz, *NIDNTT* 2, pp. 606–611; W. Foerster, *TDNT* 2, pp. 562–575.

J.I.P.

AVEN. 1. Abbreviated (Ho. 10:8) for *Beth-aven, epithet of Bethel (Ho. 4:15, *etc.*). **2.** In Am. 1:5, probably the Beqa' valley between Lebanon and Anti-lebanon in the Aramaean kingdom of Damascus. **3.** For Ezk. 30:17, see *On. K.A.K.

AVENGER OF BLOOD (Heb. *gō'ēl haddām*, lit. 'redeemer of blood'). Even before the time of Moses, a basic feature of primitive life was the system of blood revenge for personal injury. It is mentioned with approval as early as Gn. 9:5. All members of the clan were regarded as being of one blood, but the chief responsibility for avenging shed blood devolved upon the victim's next-of-kin, who might under other circumstances be called on to redeem the property or person of a poor or captive relative (Lv. 25:25, 47–49; Ru. 4:1ff., though in the latter case other factors were involved also). The Mosaic penal code authorized the avenger to execute the murderer but no-one else (Dt. 24:16; 2 Ki. 14:6; 2 Ch. 25:4), and made provision for accidental homicide. Blood revenge seems to have persisted into the reigns of David (2 Sa. 14:7–8) and Jehoshaphat (2 Ch. 19:10). (*KIN, *CITIES OF REFUGE.) J.D.D.

AZARIAH (Heb. *ᵃzaryāhû*, *ᵃzaryâ*, 'Yahweh has helped'). **1.** One of Solomon's ministers, son of Zadok (1 Ki. 4:2; *cf.* 1 Ch. 6:9). **2.** Another of Solomon's ministers, son of Nathan; he was over the officers (1 Ki. 4:5). **3.** Alternative name for King *Uzziah (2 Ki. 14:21, *etc.*). Montgomery (*Kings*, *ICC*, p. 446) calls it the 'throne-name', Uzziah representing the popular or adopted name. For his reign, see H. Tadmor, 'Azriyau of Yaudi', *Scripta Hierosolymitana* 8, 1961, pp. 232–271. **4, 5.** Son of Ethan (1 Ch. 2:8) and son of Jehu (1 Ch. 2:38) in the genealogical table of Judah.

6–8. Son of Johanan (1 Ch. 6:10; *cf.* Ezr. 7:3), son of Hilkiah (1 Ch. 6:13; *cf.* 9:11; Ezr. 7:1) and son of Zephaniah (1 Ch. 6:36) in the genealogical table of Levi. **9.** The prophet, son of Oded, who encouraged Asa in his reformation (2 Ch. 15:1–8). **10, 11.** Two of Jehoshaphat's sons, slain by Jehoram on his accession (2 Ch. 21:2, 4). **12.** Scribal error for Ahaziah (2 Ch. 22:6).

13, 14. Two of the 'centurions' who helped to restore Joash (2 Ch. 23:1). **15.** High priest who withstood Uzziah's attempt to offer incense in the Temple (2 Ch. 26:16–20). **16.** An Ephraimite chief who supported the prophet Oded's plea for clemency (2 Ch. 28:12). **17, 18.** Two Levites connected with Hezekiah's cleansing of the Temple (2 Ch. 29:12). **19.** A chief priest in Hezekiah's reign (2 Ch. 31:10).

20. A workman repairing the city wall (Ne. 3:23). **21.** One of Zerubbabel's companions (Ne. 7:7; *cf.* Ezr. 2:2—'Seraiah'). **22.** One who expounded the law after Ezra had read it (Ne. 8:7). **23.** A priest who sealed the covenant with Nehemiah (Ne. 10:2; *cf.* Ne. 12:33). **24.** Son of Hoshaiah and supporter of Gedaliah, who later rejected Jeremiah's advice to remain in Palestine (Je. 43:2). Called Jezaniah in Je. 42:1 (*cf.* Je. 40:8; 2 Ki. 25:23). **25.** Heb. name of Abed-nego (Dn. 1:6f., 11, 19; 2:17). J.G.G.N.

AZEKAH. A Judaean conurbation (Jos. 15:35), lying in the low agricultural plains along the W coast, perhaps modern Tell ez-Zahariyeh. Joshua pursued the Amorites as far as Azekah on the day they attacked the newly settled Gibeonite group (Jos. 10:10–11). In the days of Rehoboam it was a fortified border city (2 Ch. 11:5ff.), and in later times was one of the few strong points to resist the Babylonian incursion under Nebuchadrezzar (Je. 34:7). Azekah is mentioned, and its capture by Nebuchadrezzar probably implied, in one of the Lachish Letters (*DOTT*, pp. 216f.). See *NEAEHL*, pp. 123–124. R.J.W.

B

BAAL. The Hebrew noun *ba'al* means 'master', 'possessor' or 'husband'. Used with suffixes, *e.g.* Baal-peor or Baal-berith, the word may have retained something of its original sense; but in general Baal is a proper name in the OT, and refers to a specific deity, Hadad, the W Semitic storm-god, the most important deity in the Canaanite pantheon. It is not clear to what extent local Baals were equated with or distinguished from Hadad. The Baal confronted at Mt Carmel (1 Ki. 18) was probably Melqart, the god of Tyre. The OT use of the plural (*e.g.* 1 Ki. 18:18) may suggest that more Baals than one were clearly distinguished; but in any case there was fluidity in the pagan conception of deities.

The Baal cults affected and challenged the worship of Yahweh throughout Israelite history. The limited OT data about Baal can now be supplemented by the information from the Ras Shamra documents. One of his consorts was *Ashtaroth, another *Asherah; and Baal is called the son of *Dagon. The texts reveal him as a nature deity; myths describe him in conflict with death, infertility and flood waters, emerging victorious as 'king' of the gods.

Yahweh was 'master' and 'husband' to Israel, and therefore they called him 'Baal', in all innocence; but naturally this practice led to confusion of the worship of Yahweh with the Baal rituals, and presently it became essential to call him by some different title; Hosea (2:16) proposed *'îš*, another word meaning 'husband'. Once the title 'Baal' was no longer applied to Yahweh, personal names incorporating the word were likely to be misunderstood. So *bōšeṯ* ('shame') tended to replace *ba'al* in such names. Thus Esh-baal and Merib-baal (1 Ch. 8:33f.) are better known as Ishbosheth (2 Sa. 2:8) and Mephibosheth (2 Sa. 9:6).

The word Baal also occurs once or twice as a man's name and as a place-name (*cf.* 1 Ch. 5:5; 4:33).

BIBLIOGRAPHY. N. C. Habel, *Yahweh versus Baal*, 1964; W. F. Albright, *Yahweh and the Gods of Canaan*, 1968; H. Ringgren, *Religions of the Ancient Near East*, E.T. 1973, ch. 3; J. C. De Moor and M. J. Mulder, *TDOT* 2, pp. 181–200; and see *CANAAN. D.F.P.

BAAL-BERITH (Heb. *ba'al b^{e}rîṯ*, 'Lord of the covenant'). The Canaanite Baal-deity worshipped originally at Shechem (Jdg. 8:33; 9:4), probably to be equated with El-berith (Jdg. 9:46). The capture of Shechem by Joshua is nowhere recorded; it came under Habiru control in the 14th century BC and was probably incorporated into Israel by treaty. The Abimelech episode (Jdg. 9) illustrates the tension between the true Israelites and this basically Canaanite enclave. The Shechemites are called 'the sons of Hamor' ('ass', Jdg. 9:28) which is equivalent to 'the sons of the covenant' since the sacrifice of an ass was essential to the ratification of a treaty amongst the Amorites. A.E.C.

BAAL-GAD. The N limit of Israelite conquest lying at the foot of and to the W of Mt Hermon (Jos. 11:17; 13:5; 21:7). It may be Hasbeiyah (so F. M. Abel, *Géographie de la Palestine*, 2, 1938, p. 258) or Tell Hauš (so *GTT*, 509), 19 km farther N, both in the Wadi et-Teim. Archaeological evidence favours the latter. A.R.M.

BAAL-HAZOR. A mountain 1,016 m high, 9 km NNE of Bethel, mod. Jebel el-'Aṣûr. Absalom gathered his half-brothers to this mountain, perhaps to a settlement of the same name at its foot, at sheep-shearing time and killed Amnon (2 Sa. 13:23). (*OPHRAH.) A.R.M.

BAAL-MEON, known also as Beth-baal-meon (Jos. 13:17), Beth-meon (Je. 48:23) and Beon (Nu. 32:3), was one of several towns built by the Reubenites in the territory of Sihon the Amorite (Nu. 32:38). It was later captured by the Moabites and was still in their hands in the 6th century BC (Je. 48:23; Ezk. 25:9). Today the site is known as Ma'în. (*MOABITE STONE.) J.A.T.

BAAL-ZEBUB, BEELZEBUL. 1. In OT Heb. *ba'al z^{e}ḇûḇ* ('lord of flies'), probably a mocking alteration of *ba'al z^{e}ḇûl* ('Prince *Baal'), appears as the name of the god of Ekron, whom Ahaziah, king of Israel, tried to consult in his last illness (2 Ki. 1:1–6, 16).

2. In NT Gk. *beelzeboul, beezeboul* (Beelzebub in TR and AV) is the prince of the demons (Mt. 12:24, 27; Mk. 3:22; Lk. 11:15, 18f.), identified with Satan (Mt. 12:26; Mk. 3:23, 26; Lk. 11:18). In contemporary Semitic speech it may have been understood as 'the master of the house'; if so, this phrase could be used in a double sense in Mt. 10:25b. F.F.B.

BAAL-ZEPHON ('Baal *(*lord*)* of the north'). The name of a place in the Egyptian E Delta near which the Israelites camped during their Exodus (Ex. 14:2, 9; Nu. 33:7), deriving from the name of the Canaanite god Baal-Zephon. The 'waters of Baal' were in the general area of the Delta residence Pi-R'messē (Qantir) in the 13th century BC; a Phoen. letter of the 6th century BC alludes to 'Baal-Zephon and all the gods of Tahpanhes'. This has led to the suggestion that Tahpanhes, modern Tell Defneh some 43 km SSW of Port Said, was earlier the Baal-Zephon of the 'waters of Baal' near Ra'amses and of the Israelite Exodus. Eissfeldt and Cazelles identify Baal-Zephon and Baal-Hasi (in Ugaritic; later Zeus Casios) and place the Egyptian Zephon/Casios at Ras Qasrun on the Mediterranean shore some 70 km due E of Port Said, backed by Lake Serbonis. However, the deity Baal-Zephon/Casios was worshipped at various places in Lower Egypt, as far S as Memphis, which leaves several possibilities open.

BIBLIOGRAPHY. R. A. Caminos, *Late-Egyptian Miscellanies*, 1954; N. Aimé-Giron, *Annales du Service des Antiquités de l'Égypte* 40, 1940/41, pp. 433–460; W. F. Albright in *BASOR* 109, 1948, pp. 15–16, and in *Festschrift Alfred Bertholet*, 1950, pp. 1–14; *RB* 62, 1955, pp. 332ff. C.D.W.

BAASHA. The founder of the second brief dynasty of N Israel (*c*. 900–880 BC). Though of humble origin (1 Ki. 16:2), Baasha usurped the throne following his assassination of Nadab, son of Jeroboam I, during the siege of the Philistine town of Gibbethon (1 Ki. 15:27ff.). His extermination of the entire house of Jeroboam fulfilled the prophecy of Ahijah (1 Ki. 16:5ff.). Active hostility between Israel and Judah continued steadily throughout the 24 years of his reign (1 Ki. 15:32). His provocative action in fortifying Ramah, 6 km N of Jerusalem, prompted Asa's appeal for Syrian intervention. He continued the religious policy of Jeroboam and earned a stern prophetic rebuke (1 Ki. 16:1ff.). J.C.J.W.

BABEL (Heb. *Bāḇel*, 'gate of god'; also *BABYLON). The name of one of the chief cities founded by Nimrod in the land of Shinar (Sumer), ancient Babylonia. It is named with Erech and Accad (Gn. 10:10) and according to Babylonian tradition was founded by the god Marduk and destroyed by Sargon *c*. 2350 BC when he carried earth from it to found his new capital Agade (*ACCAD). The history of the building of the city and its lofty tower is given in Gn. 11:1–11, where the name Babel is explained by popular etymology based on a similar Heb. root *bālal*, as 'confusion' or 'mixing'. Babel thus became a synonym for the confusion caused by language differences which was part of the divine punishment for the human pride displayed in the building.

There is as yet no archaeological evidence to confirm the existence of a city at Babylon prior to the 1st Dynasty (*c*. 1800 BC) but Babylonian tradition and a text of Sharkalisharri, king of Agade *c*. 2250 BC, mentioning his restoration of the temple-tower (*ziggurat*) at Babylon, implies the existence of an earlier sacred city on the site. Sargon's action would confirm this. The use of burnt clay for bricks and of bitumen (AV 'slime') for mortar (Gn. 11:3) is attested from early times. The latter was probably floated down the Euphrates from Hit.

The 'Tower of Babel', an expression not found in the OT, is commonly used to describe the tower (*migdōl*) intended to be a very high landmark associated with the city and its worshippers. It is generally assumed that, like the city, the tower was incomplete (v. 8), and that it was a staged temple tower or multi-storeyed *ziggurat* first developed in Babylonia in the early 3rd millennium BC from the low temenos or platform supporting a shrine set up near the main city temples (as at Erech and 'Uqair). After Sharkalisharri the earliest reference to the *ziggurat* at Babylon is to its restoration by Esarhaddon in 681–665 BC. This was named in Sumerian 'Etemenanki'—'the Building of the Foundation–platform of Heaven and Earth' whose 'top reaches to heaven' and associated with the temple of Marduk Esagila, 'the Building whose top is (in) heaven'. It is very probable that such a sacred edifice followed an earlier plan. The tower was severely damaged in the war of 652–648 BC but restored again by Nebuchadrezzar II (605–562 BC). It was this building, part of which was recovered by Koldewey in 1899, which was described by Herodotus on his visit *c*. 460 BC and is discussed in a cuneiform tablet dated 229 BC (Louvre, AO 6555). These enable an approximate picture of the later tower to be given. The base stage measured 90 × 90 m and was 33 m high. Above this were built five platforms, each 6–18 m high but of diminishing area. The whole was crowned by a temple where the god was thought to descend for intercourse with mankind. Access was by ramps or stairways. A late Babylonian plan of a seven-staged *ziggurat* shows that the architectural form was a height equal to the width at base with a cubic temple on the summit. Among others, ziggurats were found in *UR, *ERECH, *NINEVEH and elsewhere in *ASSYRIA and *BABYLONIA.

The *ziggurat* at Babylon was demolished by Xerxes in 472 BC, and though Alexander cleared

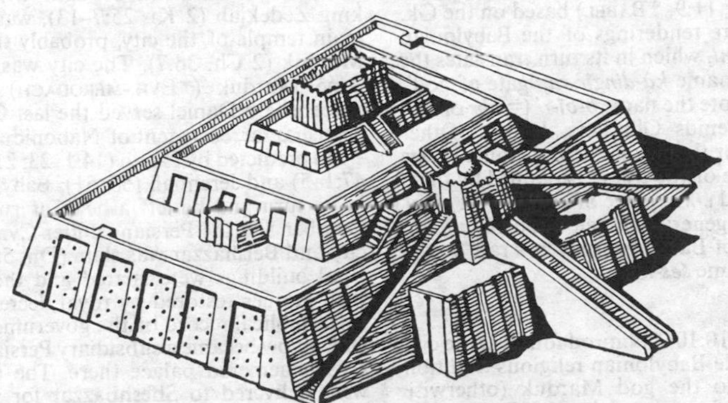

A reconstruction of the temple-tower, or ziggurat, as built by Ur-Nammu, king of Ur, c. 2100 BC*. The platforms were of different colours (black, red, blue), the temple at the top being covered with silver.*

the rubble prior to its restoration this was thwarted by his death. The bricks were subsequently removed by the local inhabitants, and today the site of Etemenanki is a pit (*Es-Saḥn*) as deep as the original construction was high.

Travellers of all ages have sought to locate the ruined tower of Babel. Some identify it with the site described above and others with the vitrified remains of a *ziggurat* still visible at Borsippa (mod. Birs Nimrūd) 11 km SSW of Babylon, which is probably of Neo-Babylonian date. Yet others place the biblical tower at Dūr-Kurigalzu (Aqar Quf), W of Baghdad, a city which was, however, built *c.* 1400 BC. All that can certainly be said is that the Gn. 11 account bears all the marks of a reliable historical account of buildings which can no longer be traced.

Some scholars associate Jacob's vision of a ladder and a 'gate of heaven' (Gn. 28:11–18) with a *ziggurat* of the kind once built at Babel.

According to Gn. 11:9, the intervention of Yahweh at the building of Babel led to the confusion of tongues and the subsequent dispersion of mankind, possibly in the days of Peleg (Gn. 10:25). (*NATIONS, TABLE OF; Gn. 10.)

Babel, as *Babylon throughout its history, became a symbol of the pride of man and his inevitable fall. Babel was also theologically linked with the confusion and broken fellowship between men and nations when separated from God. Its effects are to be reversed in God's final kingdom, but there is no certainty that the *tongues or glossolalia of Acts 2:4 (*cf.* the interpretation of Joel in vv. 16–21), which were confined to Jews and proselytes and largely Aramaic- and Greek-speaking peoples, were other than known 'foreign languages' (*JTS* n.s. 17, 1966, pp. 299–307).

BIBLIOGRAPHY. D. J. Wiseman, *Nebuchadrezzar and Babylon*, 1985, pp. 68–73.

D.J.W.

BABYLON.

I. In the Old Testament

The city on the river Euphrates (80 km S of modern Baghdad, Iraq) which became the political and religious capital of Babylonia and of the empire and civilization based upon it.

a. Name

The Heb. *Bāḇel* is translated by EVV as Babylon (except Gn. 10:10; 11:9, *BABEL) based on the Gk. *Babylōn*. These are renderings of the Babylonian *bâb-ili*; pl. *bâb-ilāni*, which in its turn translates the earlier Sumerian name *kà-dingir-ra*, 'gate of god'. The Egyptians wrote the name *b-bī-r'* (= *bbr* or *bbl*) and the Achaemenids Old Pers. *babiruš*. Other common names for the city in the Babylonian texts are *tin-tir* (*ki*), 'life of the trees', explained by them as 'seat of life' and *e-ki*, 'place of canals'. *Šešaḵ* of Je. 25:26; 51:41 is generally taken to be an '*atbash*' cypher rendering of Babel, but may be a rare occurrence of an old name *šeš-ki*.

b. Foundation

According to Gn. 10:10, *Nimrod founded the city as his capital, while Babylonian religious tradition gives the credit to the god Marduk (otherwise apart from the reference to the building of the Tower of *Babel (the *ziggurat*) there are no records of its foundation).

c. History

Sargon I of Agade (*c.* 2400 BC) and his successor Sharkalisharri built temples for the gods Anunitum and Amal and restored the temple-tower according to tradition. It is possible that their city of Agade was built on part of the ruins of the earlier city of Babylon. In the time of Shulgi of Ur (*c.* 2000 BC) Babylon was attacked and then ruled by governors (*patensi*) appointed from Ur. With the advent of the Amorite 1st Dynasty of Babylon under Sumu-abum the city walls were restored and Hammurapi and his successors enlarged the town, which flourished as capital of their realm until its overthrow by the Hittites *c.* 1595 BC. After a period under Kassite domination the city revolted and was attacked on several occasions, notably by Tiglath-pileser I of Assyria *c.* 1100 BC. Babylon repeatedly strove for its independence, and once a Chaldean ruler, Marduk-apla-iddina II (722–710, 703–702 BC), sent embassies to enlist the help of Judah (2 Ki. 20:12–18). Isaiah's account of the fate of the city (Is. 13) is very similarly worded to the account by Sargon II of Assyria of his sack of the place. In an attempt to remove the chief rebels, some of the leading citizens were deported to Samaria, where they introduced the worship of local Babylonian deities (2 Ki. 17:24–30). Sennacherib made his son king of Babylon but he was killed by pro-Babylonian Elamites in 694 BC. In an attempt to end this upsurge of Babylonian nationalism Sennacherib sacked the city in 689 BC and removed the sacred statues. His son, Esarhaddon, sought to restore the holy city to which he transported Manasseh as prisoner (2 Ch. 33:11). He made Babylon a vassal-city under a son, Šamaš-šum-ukīn, who, however, quarrelled with his brother *Ashurbanipal of Assyria. In the subsequent war of 652–648 BC Babylon was severely damaged by fire, and once again the Assyrians tried appointing a local chief, Kandalanu, as governor.

The decline of the Assyrian empire enabled Nabopolassar, a Chaldean, to recover the city and found a new dynasty in 626 BC. His work of restoring the city was ably continued by his successors, especially his son, Nebuchadrezzar II, king of Babylonia (2 Ki. 24:1), whose boast was of the great city he had rebuilt (Dn. 4:30). It was to Babylon that the victorious Babylonian army brought the Jewish captives after the wars against Judah. Among these was Jehoiachin, whose captivity there is confirmed by inscriptions found in the ruins of Babylon itself. The plunder from the Temple at Jerusalem, brought with the blinded king Zedekiah (2 Ki. 25:7–13), was stored in the main temple of the city, probably that of the god Marduk (2 Ch. 36:7). The city was later ruled by Amēl-Marduk (*EVIL-MERODACH) and was the place where Daniel served the last Chaldean ruler *Belshazzar, co-regent of Nabonidus.

As predicted by Isaiah (14:1–23; 21:1–10; 46:1–2; 47:1–5) and Jeremiah (50–51), Babylon was to fall in its turn and be left a heap of ruins (see *d*). In October 539 the Persians under Cyrus entered the city and Belshazzar was slain (Dn. 5:30). The principal buildings were spared and the temples and their statues restored by royal decree. There is no extra-biblical record of the government of the city, which now became a subsidiary Persian capital with an Achaemenid palace there. The temple vessels were delivered to Sheshbazzar for restoration to Jerusalem, and the discovery of the record of this, probably in the record office at Babylon, in the reign of Darius I (Ezr. 5:16ff.) was the cause of a further return of exiles rallied at Babylon by Ezra (8:1). Babylon, as of old, was the centre of a number of rebellions, by Nidintu-Bēl in 522 BC, and Araka (521 BC), and by Bel-shimanni and Shamash-eriba in 482 BC. In suppressing the latter, Xerxes destroyed the city (478 BC); although Alexander planned to restore it, he met his death there before work had progressed far, and with the founding of Seleucia on the river Tigris as the capital of the Seleucid rulers after the capture of Babylon in 312 BC, the city once again fell into disrepair and ruins, although, according to cuneiform texts, the temple of Bel continued in existence at least until AD 75.

d. Exploration

Many travellers since Herodotus of Halicarnassus *c.* 460 BC (*History* 1. 178–188) have left accounts of their visits to Babylon. Benjamin of Tudela (12th century), Rauwolf (1574), Niebuhr (1764), C. J. Rich (1811–21) and Ker Porter (1818) were among those who were followed by the more scientific explorers who made soundings and plans of the ruins. The preliminary work by Layard (1850) and Fresnel (1852) was succeeded by systematic excavation of the inner city by the Deutsche Orient-Gesellschaft under Koldewey (1899–1917) and more recently by Lenzen in 1956–8 and since 1962 by the Iraqis (including the preservation and restoration of the Ninmah temple).

This work, combined with evidence of more than 10,000 inscribed tablets, recovered from the site by natives digging for bricks, enables a fair picture of the city of Nebuchadrezzar's day to be reconstructed. The deep overlay of debris, the frequent destruction and rebuilding, together with the change in the course of the river Euphrates and a rise in the water-table, means that, excepting only a few parts of it, the city of the earlier period has not been uncovered.

The site is now covered by a number of widely scattered mounds. The largest, Qasr, covers the citadel, Merkes a city quarter; to the N, Bāwil the N or summer palace of Nebuchadrezzar; Amran ibn 'Ali the temple of Marduk; and Saḥn the site of the *ziggurat* or temple-tower.

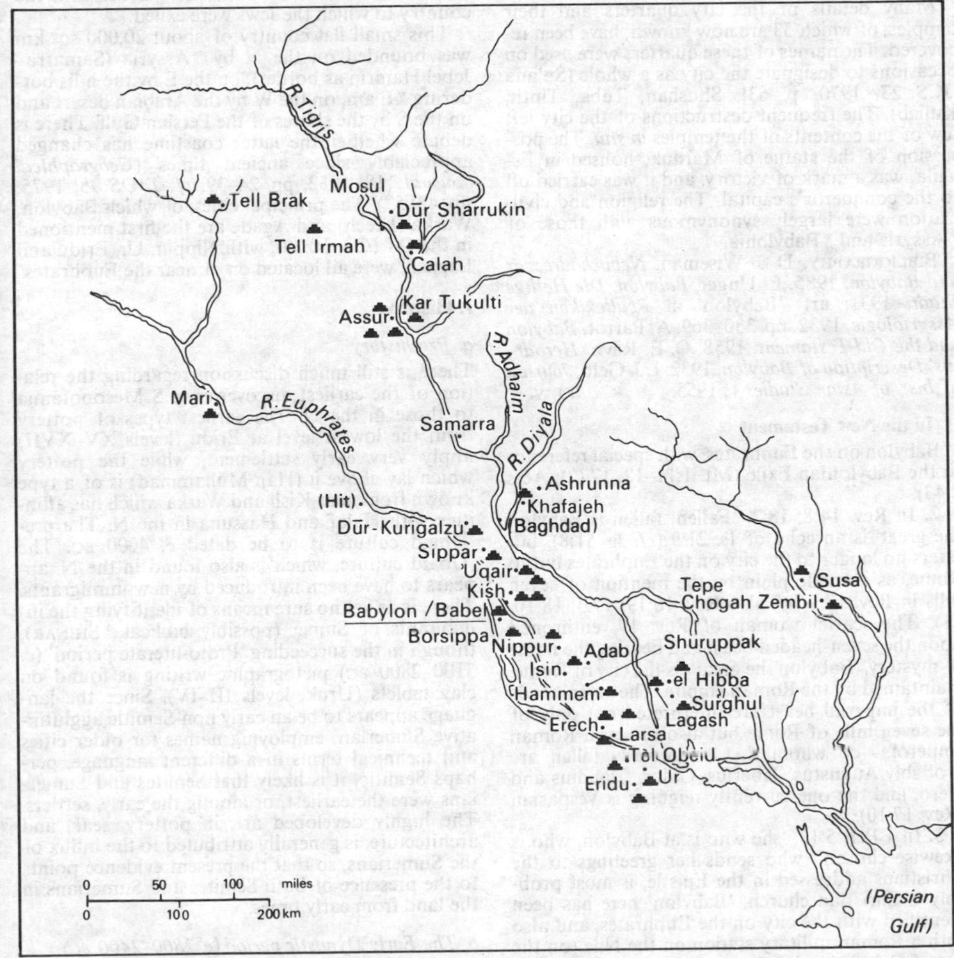

Sites of Mesopotamian stepped/staged temple-towers (ziggurats).

The city was surrounded by an intricate system of double walls, the outer range covering 27 km, strong and large enough for chariots to pass upon the top, buttressed by defence towers and pierced by 8 gates. On the N side the massive Ishtar gates marked the procession way leading S to the citadel to Esagila, the temple of Marduk and the adjacent *ziggurat* Etemenanki. This paved roadway was *c.* 920 m long, its walls decorated with enamelled bricks showing 120 lions (symbol of Ishtar) and 575 *mušruššu*—dragons (Marduk) and bulls (Bel) ranged in alternate rows. From this road another ran W to cross the river Euphrates by a bridge which linked the New Town on the W bank with the ancient capital. The main palaces on which successive kings lavished attention are now represented by the complex of buildings in the citadel, among which the throne-room (52 × 17 m) may have been in use in the time of Daniel. At the NE angle of the palace are the remains of vaults thought by Koldewey to be supports for the terraced 'hanging gardens' built by Nebuchadrezzar for Amytis, his Median wife, as a reminder of her homeland.

The temple-tower of Babylon became famous as the Tower of *Babel.

Many details of the city quarters and their temples, of which 53 are now known, have been recovered. The names of these quarters were used on occasions to designate the city as a whole (Šu'ana [JCS 23, 1970, p. 63], Shushan, Tuba, Tintir, Kullab). The frequent destructions of the city left few of the contents of the temples *in situ*. The possession of the statue of Marduk, housed in Esagila, was a mark of victory, and it was carried off to the conqueror's capital. The religion and civilization were largely synonymous with those of *Assyria and *Babylonia.

BIBLIOGRAPHY. D. J. Wiseman, *Nebuchadrezzar and Babylon*, 1985. E. Unger, *Babylon, Die Heilige Stadt*, 1931; art. 'Babylon' in *Reallexikon der Assyriologie*, 1932, pp. 330–369; A. Parrot, *Babylon and the Old Testament*, 1958; O. E. Ravn, *Herodotus' Description of Babylon*, 1932; I. J. Gelb, *Journal of Inst. of Asian Studies* 1, 1955. D.J.W.

II. In the New Testament

1. Babylon on the Euphrates, with special reference to the Babylonian Exile (Mt. 1:11–12, 17 (2); Acts 7:43).

2. In Rev. 14:8; 18:2, 'Fallen, fallen is Babylon the great' is an echo of Is. 21:9 (*cf.* Je. 51:8), but refers no longer to the city on the Euphrates but to Rome, as is made plain by the mention of seven hills in Rev. 17:9 (*cf.* also Rev. 16:19; 17:5; 18:10, 21). The scarlet woman of Rev. 17, enthroned upon the seven-headed beast and bearing the name of mystery, 'Babylon the great', is the city of Rome, maintained by the Roman empire. The seven heads of the imperial beast are interpreted not only of the seven hills of Rome but also of seven Roman emperors—of whom the five already fallen are probably Augustus, Tiberius, Gaius, Claudius and Nero, and the one currently reigning is Vespasian (Rev. 17:10).

3. In 1 Pet. 5:13, 'she who is at Babylon, who is likewise chosen', who sends her greetings to the Christians addressed in the Epistle, is most probably a Christian church. 'Babylon' here has been identified with the city on the Euphrates, and also with a Roman military station on the Nile (on the site of Cairo); but it is best to accept the identification with Rome.

BIBLIOGRAPHY. E. G. Selwyn, *The First Epistle of St Peter*, 1946, pp. 243, 303ff.; O. Cullmann, *Peter: Disciple, Apostle, Martyr*, 1953, pp. 70ff. *et passim*; I. T. Beckwith, *The Apocalypse of John*, 1919, pp. 284ff., 690ff.; G. B. Caird, *The Revelation of St John the Divine*, 1966, pp. 211ff.; C. P. Thiede, *Bib* 67, pp. 532–538. F.F.B.

BABYLONIA. The territory in SW Asia, now S Iraq, which derived its name from the capital city of *Babylon. It was also called *Shinar (Gn. 10:10; 11:2; Is. 11:11; Jos. 7:21, AV 'Babylonish') and, later, 'the land of the Chaldeans' (Je. 24:5; Ezk. 12:13). In earlier antiquity it bore the name of Akkad (Gn. 10:10, AV *ACCAD) for the N reaches and Sumer for the S alluvium and the marshes bordering the Persian Gulf; a territory which was later strictly called 'Chaldaea', a term for the whole country after the rise of the 'Chaldean' dynasty (see **I.***h*, below). Thus the Babylonians (*bᵉnê bāḇel*, 'sons of Babylon') are also qualified as Chaldeans (Ezk. 23:15, 17, 23). Babylonia, watered by the Tigris and Euphrates rivers, was the probable site of Eden (Gn. 2:14) and of the tower of *Babel, and the country to which the Jews were exiled.

This small flat country of about 20,000 sq. km was bounded on the N by *Assyria (Samarra–Jebel Hamrîn as border), on the E by the hills bordering *Elam, on the W by the Arabian desert and on the S by the shores of the Persian Gulf. There is debate whether the latter coastline has changed appreciably since ancient times (*Geographical Journal* 118, 1952, pp. 24–39; *cf. JAOS* 95, 1975, pp. 43–57). The principal cities, of which Babylon, Warka (Erech) and Agade are the first mentioned in the OT (Gn. 10:10), with Nippur, Ur, Eridu and Lagash, were all located on or near the Euphrates.

I. History

a. Pre-history

There is still much discussion regarding the relation of the earliest discoveries in S Mesopotamia to those in the N. The earliest types of pottery from the lowest level at Eridu (levels XV–XVII) imply very early settlement, while the pottery which lay above it (Haji Muhammad) is of a type known from near Kish and Warka which has affinities with Halaf and Hassuna in the N. The pre-'Ubaid culture is to be dated *c.* 4000 BC. The 'Ubaid culture, which is also found in the N, appears to have been introduced by new immigrants. There is as yet no sure means of identifying the inhabitants of Sumer (possibly biblical *SHINAR), though in the succeeding 'Proto-literate period' (*c.* 3100–2800 BC) pictographic writing is found on clay tablets (Uruk, levels III–IV). Since the language appears to be an early non-Semitic agglutinative Sumerian, employing names for older cities and technical terms in a different language, perhaps Semitic, it is likely that Semites and Sumerians were the earliest, or among the early, settlers. The highly developed art, in pottery, seals and architecture, is generally attributed to the influx of the Sumerians, so that the present evidence points to the presence of both Semites and Sumerians in the land from early times.

b. The Early Dynastic period (*c. 2800–2400* BC)

This period saw the advent of kingship and the foundation of great cities. According to the Sumerian king list, 8 or 10 kings ruled before the Flood at the cities of Eridu, Badtibirra, Larak, Sippar and Shuruppak. The governor of the latter was the hero of the Sumerian flood story (*cf.* *NOAH). The 'flood' deposit found by Woolley at Ur is dated in the 'Ubaid period, and therefore does not correspond with similar levels found at Kish and Shuruppak (Proto-literate—Early Dynastic I; *cf. Iraq* 26, 1964, pp. 62–82). There was, however, a strong literary tradition of a *flood in Babylonia from *c.* 2000 BC.

After the Flood 'kingship came down again from heaven' and the rulers at Kish and Uruk (Erech) include Gilgamesh and Agga, the heroes of a series of legends, who may well be historical characters. City-states flourished with centres at Uruk, Kish, Ur (Royal Graves), Lagash, Shuruppak, Abu Ṣalabīkh and as far N as Mari. Often more than one powerful ruler sought to dominate Babylonia at the same time, and clashes were frequent. Thus the 1st Dynasty at Lagash founded by Ur-Nanše ended when Urukagina, a social reformer (*c.* 2351 BC), defeated Enannatum and soon afterwards Lugalzagesi of Umma, who had taken over the cities of Lagash, Ur and Uruk, established the first or 'proto-' imperial domination of Sumer as far as the Mediterranean.

c. The Akkadians (c. 2400–2200 BC)

A strong Semitic family founded a new city at Agade and about this time may have restored Babylon. This 'Akkadian' or Sargonid dynasty (2371–2191 BC), so called after the name of its founder *Sargon, developed a new technique of war with the bow and arrow and soon defeated the despot Lugalzagesi of Umma, Kish and Uruk to gain the whole of Sumer. This king carried his arms to the Mediterranean and Anatolia. His widespread authority was maintained by his grandson Naram-Sin before the Gutians from the E hills overran N Babylonia (2230–2120 BC) and kept their hold over the economy until defeated by a coalition led by Utuḫegal of Uruk. Their rule was, however, somewhat local and strongest E of the river Tigris. Lagash under its *ensi*, or ruler, Gudea (*c.* 2150 BC) remained independent and dominated Ur and the S cities. Gudea gradually extended his territory and expeditions as far as Syria (*EBLA) to win wood, precious stones and metals, and so increased the prosperity of his city. The Sumerian renaissance or 'Golden Age' which followed was one of economic and artistic wealth.

d. 3rd Dynasty of Ur (2113–2006 BC)

Following the reign of Utuḫegal of Uruk and Namaḫani, the son-in-law of Gudea, in Lagash, Ur once more became the centre of power. Ur-Nammu (2113–2096 BC) rebuilt the citadel with its ziggurat and temples at *Ur and in Uruk, Isin and Nippur set up statues of himself in the temples which were controlled by his nominees. Gradually Ur extended its influence as far as Assur and Byblos, and for a while his successors were accorded divine honours, depicted on their monuments and seals by the horned headgear of divinity (C. J. Gadd, *Ideas of Divine Rule in the Ancient Near East*, 1944). Similar honours appear to have been granted to Naram-Sin earlier. Many thousands of documents reveal the administration and religion of this period when Ur traded with places

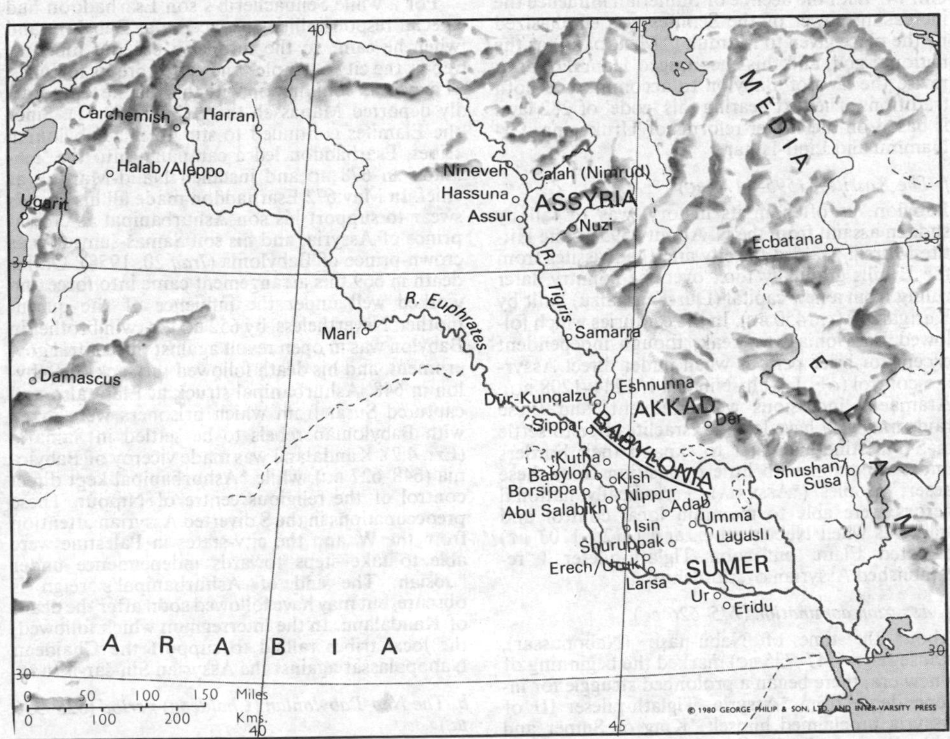

Babylonia and the major area under its influence.

as far distant as India. The end came after severe famines, and the Sumerian rulers were displaced by invaders from Elam and Semitic semi-nomads from the W deserts. It is possible that the migration of Terah and Abraham (Gn. 11:31) took place at this time of change in Ur's fortune.

e. The Amorites (*2000–1595 BC*)

The territories formerly controlled by Ur were divided among the local chiefs at Assur, Mari on the Upper Euphrates and Eshnunna. Independent rule was established by Ishbi-Irra in Isin and Naplanum in Larsa, thus dividing the loyalties of the previously united Sumerians. Then Kudurmabug of Yamutbal, E of the river Tigris, made his son Warad-Sin ruler of Larsa. He was followed by Rim-Sin, who took over Isin but failed to make headway against the growing power of Babylon, where a series of vigorous rulers in the 1st (Amorite) Dynasty of Babylon (1894–1595 BC) held sway. The sixth of the line, *Hammurapi (1792–1750 BC; according to the most accepted *Chronology), eventually defeated Rim-Sin and for the last decade of his reign ruled from the Persian Gulf to *Mari, where he defeated Zimrilim, a Semite who had previously driven out Yasmaḫ-Adad, son of Shamshi-Adad I of Assyria. Despite this victory, Hammurapi was not as powerful as his namesake in Aleppo, and the Mari letters, which afford a remarkable insight into the diplomacy, trade, history and religion of those days, show that he did not subdue Assyria, Eshnunna or other cities in Babylonia (*ARCHAEOLOGY). The relations between Babylon, Elam and the W at this time made possible a coalition such as that described in Gn. 14. With the decline of Sumerian influence the increasing power of the Semites was emphasized by the place given to Marduk (*MERODACH) as the national god, and this encouraged Hammurapi to revise the laws of Babylon to accommodate both traditions. The text bearing this 'code' of 282 laws is based on the earlier reforms of Urukagina, Ur-Nammu and Lipit-Ishtar.

f. The Kassites (*1595–1174 BC*)

Babylon, as often in its history, was to fall by sudden assault from the N. About 1595 BC the Hittite Mursili I raided the city and the Kassites from the E hills gradually took over the country, later ruling from a new capital (Dur-Kurigalzu) built by Kurigalzu I (*c.* 1450 BC). In the centuries which followed Babylonia was weak, though independent except for brief periods when under direct Assyrian control (*e.g.* Tukulti-Ninurta I, 1244–1208 BC). Aramaean incursions were frequent, and these raids may well have left the Israelites free to settle in S Palestine and later to expand their borders under Solomon with little opposition from these desert peoples (*ASSYRIA). Periodically national heroes were able to maintain local control and trade, as when Nebuchadrezzar I (1124–1103 BC) defeated Elam, but soon Tiglath-pileser I re-established Assyrian overlordship.

g. Assyrian domination (*745–626 BC*)

About the time of Nabû-naṣir (Nabonassar), whose reign (747–735 BC) marked the beginning of a new era, there began a prolonged struggle for independence from *Assyria. Tiglath-pileser III of Assyria proclaimed himself 'King of Sumer and Akkad', took the hands of Bel(= Marduk) and thus claimed the throne in Babylon in 745 BC, using his other name Pul(u) (1 Ch. 5:26). 15 years later he had to bring the Assyrian army to fight the rebel Ukin-zēr of Bît-Amuk-kani. He defeated him in Sapia and deported many prisoners. A rival sheikh, Marduk-apla-iddina II, of the S district of Bît-Yakin, paid Tiglath-pileser tribute at this time (*Iraq* 17, 1953, pp. 44–50). However, the preoccupation with the siege of *Samaria by *Shalmaneser V and *Sargon II in 726–722 gave Marduk-apla-iddina (*MERODACH-BALADAN) his opportunity for intrigue. For 10 years (721–710 BC) he held the throne in Babylon until the Assyrian army attacked Der, defeated Ḫumbanigaš of Elam and occupied Babylon. The Assyrian army moved S, but Merodach-baladan was retained as local ruler. It says much for Sargon's diplomacy that he kept him a loyal subject for the rest of his reign.

On Sargon's death in 705 BC, however, Merodach-baladan again plotted against his masters, and it is likely that it was he, rather than Hezekiah, who initiated the overtures for an alliance against Assyria (2 Ki. 20:12–19; Is. 39). Isaiah's opposition was well founded, for the Babylonians themselves set their own citizen Marduk-zakir-šum on the throne in 703 BC. This freed Merodach-baladan's hand and he had himself proclaimed king of Babylon, though he lived in the more friendly city of Borsippa. Sennacherib marched against him, defeated the rebels and their Elamite supporters in battles at Kutha and Kish, and entered Babylon, where he set a pro-Assyrian, Bel-ibni, on the throne. Bît-Yakin was ravaged, but Merodach-baladan had already fled to Elam, where he died before Sennacherib was able to assemble a punitive naval force in 694 BC.

For a while Sennacherib's son Esarhaddon had special responsibilities as viceroy at Babylon, and when he came to the throne in 681 did much to repair the city's temples and to restore its fortunes. It may be in conjunction with this that he temporarily deported Manasseh there (2 Ch. 33:11). Since the Elamites continued to stir up the Babylonian tribes, Esarhaddon led a campaign into the 'sea-lands' in 678 BC and installed Na'id-Marduk as chief. In May 672 Esarhaddon made all his vassals swear to support his son Ashurbanipal as crown-prince of Assyria, and his son Šamaš-šum-ukin as crown-prince of Babylonia (*Iraq* 20, 1958). On his death in 669 this arrangement came into force and worked well under the influence of the queen-mother. Nevertheless, by 652 BC the twin brother in Babylon was in open revolt against the central government, and his death followed the sack of Babylon in 648. Ashurbanipal struck at Elam also and captured Susa, from which prisoners were taken with Babylonian rebels to be settled in Samaria (Ezr. 4:2). Kandalanu was made viceroy of Babylonia (648–627 BC), while *Ashurbanipal kept direct control of the religious centre of Nippur. These preoccupations in the S diverted Assyrian attention from the W, and the city-states in Palestine were able to take steps towards independence under *Josiah. The end of Ashurbanipal's reign is obscure, but may have followed soon after the death of Kandalanu. In the interregnum which followed, the local tribes rallied to support the Chaldean Nabopolassar against the Assyrian Sin-šar-iškun.

h. The Neo-Babylonian (*Chaldean*) *period* (*626–539 BC*)

Nabopolassar, a governor of the 'sea-lands' near the Persian Gulf, was a Chaldean (*kaldu* hence

* CHALDEA), occupied the throne in Babylon on 22 November 626, and at once made peace with Elam. In the following year he defeated the Assyrians at Sallat, and by 623 Der had broken from their yoke. The Babylonian Chronicle, the principal and reliable source for this period, is silent on the years 623–616 BC, by which time Nabopolassar had driven the Assyrians back along the rivers Euphrates and Tigris. In 614 the Medes joined the Babylonians to attack Assur, and the same allies, perhaps with Scythian support, captured Nineveh in the summer of 612 BC, the Babylonians pursuing the refugees westwards. Babylonian campaigns in Syria were followed by the assault on Harran in 609 and raids on the N hill-tribes in 609–606 BC. Nabopolassar, now aged, entrusted the Babylonian army to his crown-prince Nebuchadrezzar, who fought the Egyptians at Kumuḫi and Quramati (Upper Euphrates).

In May–June 605 BC Nebuchadrezzar made a surprise attack on Carchemish, sacked the city and annihilated the Egyptian army at Hamath. Thus the Babylonians now overran all Syria as far as the Egyptian border but do not appear to have entered the hill-country of Judah itself (2 Ki. 24:7; Jos., *Ant.* 10. 6; *cf.* Dn. 1:1). Jehoiakim, a vassal of Neco II, submitted to Nebuchadrezzar, who carried off hostages, including Daniel, to Babylon. While in Palestine, Nebuchadrezzar heard of the death of his father (15 August 605 BC) and at once rode across the desert to 'take the hands of Bel', thus claiming the throne, on 6 September 605 BC.

In 604 BC Nebuchadrezzar received the tribute of 'all the kings of Hatti-land (Syro-Palestine)', among whom must have been Jehoiakim. Ashkelon, however, refused and was sacked, an event which had a profound effect on Judah (Je. 47:5–7). An Aramaic letter appealing for help from the pharaoh against the advancing Babylonian army may be assigned to this time (*cf. DOTT*, pp. 251–255). In 601 the Babylonians fought the Egyptians, both sides sustaining heavy losses; the Babylonians remained at home to re-equip the army during the next year. It was probably as a result of this that Jehoiakim, contrary to the word of Jeremiah (Je. 27:9–11), transferred his allegiance to Neco II after submitting to Babylon for 3 years (2 Ki. 24:1).

In preparation for further campaigns the Babylonian army raided the Arab tribes in 599/8 (Je. 49:28–33). In the month Kislev in his 7th year (December 598) Nebuchadrezzar called out his army once more and, according to the Babylonian Chronicle, 'besieged the city of Judah, capturing it on the second day of Adar. He captured its king, appointed a ruler of his own choice and, having taken much spoil from the city, sent it back to Babylon' (BM 21946). The fall of Jerusalem on 16 March 597, the capture of Jehoiachin, the appointment of Mattaniah-Zedekiah and the commencement of the Jewish Exile are thus recorded as in the OT (2 Ki. 24:10–17; 2 Ch. 36:8–10).

In the following year Nebuchadrezzar appears to have marched against Elam (*cf.* Je. 49:34–38). The Babylonian Chronicle is missing from 595 BC, but further Babylonian operations against Judah when Zedekiah rebelled are recorded by Jeremiah (52:3ff.; 2 Ki. 25:7). Jerusalem was destroyed in 587 BC and a further deportation effected in 581 (2 Ki. 25:8–21), leaving Judah a dependent province under Gedaliah (vv. 22–26). A Babylonian text gives a glimpse of an invasion of Egypt in 568/7 BC (Je. 46). The exiled Jehoiachin, who is named in ration-tablets from Babylon (dated 595–570 BC), was favourably treated by Nebuchadrezzar's successor Amēl-Marduk (* EVIL-MERODACH, 562–560 BC; 2 Ki. 25:27). This king was assassinated by Nebuchadrezzar's son-in-law Neriglissar (* NERGAL-SHAREZER, 560–556 BC), who campaigned in Cilicia in an effort to stem the rising power of Lydia. His son, Labaši-Marduk, reigned only 9 months before Nabonidus took the throne and immediately marched to Cilicia, where, according to Herodotus, he mediated between the Lydians and Medes. The latter now threatened Babylonia, from which Nabonidus was driven by the people's unwillingness to accept his reforms. He campaigned in Syria and N Arabia, where he lived at Tema for 10 years while his son * Belshazzar acted as co-regent in Babylon. About 544 his people and the kings of Arabia, Egypt and the Medes being favourably disposed, Nabonidus returned to his capital (*AS* 8, 1958), but by this time the country was weak and divided.

i. The Achaemenids (539–332 BC)

Cyrus, who had taken over Media, Persia and Lydia, entered Babylon on 16 October 539 BC, following its capture by his general Gobryas. The course of the river Euphrates had been diverted at Opis to enable the invaders to penetrate the defences along the dried-up river-bed. Belshazzar was killed (Dn. 5:30) and Nabonidus was exiled to Carmania. The identity of * Darius the Mede with Cyrus (as Dn. 6:28) or with Gubaru has been proposed.

The rule of Cyrus in Babylon (539–530 BC) was just and favourable to the Jews, whose return from exile he encouraged (Ezr. 1:1–11; *cf.* Is. 44:24–28; 45:13; Mi. 5). For a brief time his son Cambyses acted as co-regent until his father died fighting in the NE hills. He invaded Egypt but his death (522 BC) brought insurgence, and pretenders seized the throne (*AJSL* 58, 1941, pp. 341ff.), until in December 522 Darius I restored law and order. During his reign (522–486 BC) he allowed the Jews to rebuild the Temple at Jerusalem under Zerubbabel (Ezr. 4:5; Hg. 1:1; Zc. 1:1).

Henceforth Babylonia was ruled by kings of * Persia; Xerxes (* AHASUERUS, 486–470 BC), Artaxerxes I (464–423 BC) and Darius II (423–408 BC), who may be the 'Darius the Persian' so named in Ne. 12:22 to distinguish him from 'Darius the Mede'.

Following the capture of Babylon, which he planned to rebuild, Alexander III (the Great) ruled the city (331–323 BC) and was followed by a Hellenistic line; Philip Arrhidaeus (323–316 BC) and Alexander IV (316–312 BC). The country then passed in turn into the hands of the Seleucids (312–64 BC) and then of the Parthians (Arsacids) and Sassanians until its conquest by the Arabs in AD 641.

From the Neo-Babylonian period onwards there were a number of Jewish settlements in Babylonia maintaining links with Judaea (Acts 2:9), and after the fall of Jerusalem in AD 70 these became influential in the *diaspora*.

II. Religion

From the 3rd millennium BC onwards lists of the names of deities with their titles, epithets and temples were compiled. Although in the final library version at Nineveh in the 7th century BC these numbered more than 2,500, many can be identified as earlier Sumerian deities assimilated by the Semites after the time of the 1st Dynasty of Babylon (*c.* 1800 BC), so that the actual number of deities worshipped in any one period was considerably less.

a. The Pantheon

The chief gods were Anu (Sumerian, *An*) the heaven-god, with his principal temple É.anna at Uruk (*ERECH). He was the Semitic 'El, and his wife Innana, or Innin, was later confused with Ishtar. Similar syncretistic tendencies can be traced over Enlil, the air-god, whose attributes were later taken over by Bel (Baal) or Marduk (*MERODACH). His wife, called Ninlil or Ninhursag, was later identified also with Ishtar. The third deity of the supreme triad was Ea (Sum. *Enki*), 'lord of the deep waters', god of wisdom and thus especially favourable to mankind, to whom he revealed the means of learning the mind of the gods through divination, and for whom he interceded. His temple É.abzu was at Eridu, and his wife bore the names of Dam-gal, Nin-mah or Damkina, the great wife of earth and heaven.

Among the other principal deities was the Semitic Ishtar, at first perhaps a male deity (*cf.* Arab. *'Athtar*). But later, by the assumption of the powers of Innana through the same process of syncretism, Ishtar became supremely the goddess of love and the heroine of war and was considered to be the daughter of Sin. Sin, the Babylonian moon-god (Sum. *su'en*), was worshipped with his wife Ningal in temples at Ur and Harran. He was said to be the son of Anu or of Enlil. Shamash, whose wife Aya was also later considered to be a form of Ishtar, was the sun in his strength (Sum. *utu*), the son of Sin, the god of power, justice and of war. His main temples (É.babbar, 'the House of the Sun') were at Sippar and Larsa, though like that of all the principal deities his worship was perpetuated in shrines in other cities.

Adad, of W Semitic origin, was the god of storms, the Canaanite-Aramaean Addu or *Hadad. Nergal and his wife Ereshkigal ruled the underworld, and thus he was the lord of plagues (Irra), fevers and maladies. With the rise of the Amorites the worship of Marduk (Sum. *amar.utu*, 'the young bull of the sun'?), the eldest son of Enki, became paramount in Babylon. The Epic of Creation (*enuma eliš*) is a poem concerning the creation of the universe and of order restored by Marduk, whose 50 titles are given. Nabu (*NEBO), god of science and writing, had his temple (É.zida) in many cities, including *Nineveh, *Calah and Borsippa. Many deities were of importance in certain localities. Thus Ashur (*an.šar*) became the national god of Assyria. Amurru (*mar.tu*, 'the west'), who is identified with Anu, Sin and Adad, was a W Semitic deity as was *Dagon (*TAMMUZ). Dummuzi was a god of vegetation whose death, but not resurrection, forms the subject of an Ishtar myth. Ninurta was the Babylonian and Assyrian god of war and hunting (perhaps reflected in the biblical *NIMROD).

The upper world was peopled with Igigu-gods and the lower by Annunaku. The whole spiritual and material realm was regulated by divine laws (*me*), over a hundred of which are known, ranging from 'godship' to 'victory' and 'a musical instrument', *i.e.* cultural traits and complexes. The gods were immortal yet of limited power. The myths, in which but few of the principal deities figure, illustrate their anthropomorphic character and the conception of any object (*e.g.* a stone) being imbued with 'life'. Spirits and demons abound. The Sumerians sought by various theological devices to resolve the problems inherent in their polytheistic system. Thus the myths are primarily concerned with such questions as the origin of the universe, the foundation and government of the world and the *creation of man and the search for immortality, as in the Epic of the Flood, and man's relationship to the spiritual world.

b. Priesthood

There were many classes of temple servants, with the king or ruler as the supreme pontiff at certain solemn festivals. In early Sumerian times the whole economy was centred on the temple, where the chief official (*ênû*) was 'the lord of the manor'. In the worship of Sin, the high-priestess (*entu*) was usually a royal princess. The chief priests (*maḫḫu*) had many priests (*šangu*), males of sound body and often married, to assist them. The chief liturgist (*urigallu*) was supported by a host of minor officials who had access to the temple (*ēreb bīti*). In the ceremonial, chanters, psalmists, dirge-singers and musicians played a great part.

In man's approach to the god many specialists might play a role. The exorcist (*ašipu*) could remove the evil spirit or spell with the incantations or ritual prescribed in the texts (*šurpu*; *maqlu*) involving symbolic substitutions (*kuppuru*), purification by *mašmašu*-priests or by those who cleansed by water (*ramku*). There are many documents describing the action to be taken against evil spirits (*utukki limnūti*), demons of fate (*namtaru*), demons plaguing women (*lamaštu*) or taboos. The extensive medical literature of the early period was closely allied to religion, as was the astronomy or astrology of the later 'Chaldean' dynasty. The latter was based on the equation of deities with planets or stars (*e.g.* Nabu = Mercury), or with parts of the heavens ('The Way of Anu' = fixed stars).

Others were engaged in ascertaining the will of the gods by omens from livers (the *barû*-priest or 'seer'), or by inquiry by oracle (*ša'ilu*), or by offering prayers. Many women, including sanctuary prostitutes, were attached to the temples (H. A. Hoffner, *Orient and Occident*, 1973, pp. 213–222) and local shrines where travellers prayed have been found at Ur (*Iraq* 22, 1960).

The regular service (*dullu*) included giving the gods something to eat and drink. Statues were dressed and ornamented and votive figures of worshippers set near by. Sacrifices placed on altars were subsequently allocated, wholly or in part, to the priests. The gods had their own chairs, chariots and boats for use in processions.

c. Festivals

Most cities and temples had their own distinctive festivals and sacred days. At Babylon, Erech and Ur, as at Assur, Nineveh and Calah, the New Year Festival (*akitu*) was the most outstanding, held in the spring, but not exclusively, and with varying practices at different centres and periods. At Babylon the ceremonies lasted 2 weeks with numerous rites including a procession of gods to Marduk's temple, the humiliation and restoration of the king who later 'took the hand of Bēl' to lead him in procession to the *akitu*-house outside the city where a re-enactment of the assembly of the gods, the creation debate and struggle (in ritual combat?) and the fixing of the fates for the ensuing year took place. This was sometimes followed by a 'sacred marriage' (king and priestess representing the god) and days of general rejoicing. The Epic of Creation was recited during this time and also at other times later in the year.

Royal festivals included the coronation of the king (texts of Ur-Nammu, Nabopolassar, *etc.*, survive), celebration of victories and the inauguration of a city or temple. Personal festivals include celebration of birth, marriage and the installation of girls as priestesses.

d. Literature

Babylonian literature is already well developed in the Abū Ṣalabīkh tablets (*c.* 2800–2500 BC) with evidence of Semitic scribes copying earlier Sumerian texts and using literary techniques (colophons, *etc.*) commonly taught in schools. Throughout its long history (to AD 100) this literature was influential throughout the ancient Near East, copies being found in Anatolia (*HITTITE), Syria (*EBLA, *UGARIT), Palestine (Megiddo, Hazor, *etc.*), Egypt (*AMARNA) and later even Greece. Originals or copies were taken to, or made for, the royal libraries of *Assyria at Assur, Nineveh and Calah.

The range covered some 50 epics about ancient heroes and myths in Akkadian (some translated from Sumerian, and relating to creation, the flood and establishment of civilization). 'Wisdom literature' includes compositions about 'man and his god', the Babylonian 'Job' (*ludlul bēl nēmeqi*), theodices, disputations, dialogues, practical instructions, proverbs, parables, fables and folk-tales, miniature essays and love-songs. These are also found as part of the school curriculum besides the series of handbooks necessary to a skilled scribe (sign-lists, syllabaries, grammatical paradigms, phrase books, dictionaries and numerous lists, *e.g.* personal and place-names).

'Religious' literature includes psalms, hymns and prayers (to gods and some kings), rituals, incantations, as well as catalogues of such literature, much of which is still lost. 'Scientific' literature covers medicine (prognosis, diagnosis, prescriptions, *vade mecum*, surgery and veterinary texts), chemistry (mainly perfume and glass-making), geology (lists of stones with colour and hardness), alchemy, botany (drug and plant lists) and zoology (lists of fauna). Mathematics (including geometry and algebra) is represented by both problem and practical texts and is closely related also to astronomy with its tables, procedure, ephemerides and goal-year texts, almanacs and diaries. Texts include predictions for intercalated months to maintain the *calendar.

In Babylonia the historical Chronicle was highly developed; extracts from it were included in a whole range of literature (epics, 'dynastic prophecies' and astronomical diaries). Collections of laws (but not law codes) from the 2nd millennium BC (*e.g.* Eshnunna, Hammurapi) are well known and can be compared with practice in more than a quarter of a million texts—letters, legal, economic and administrative from *c.* 3000 to 300 BC. From the 4th century BC developments include horoscopes, the zodiac, and texts written in Greek letters on clay tablets, among other *writing materials.

III. Exploration and excavation

Many travellers, from the time of Herodotus in the 5th century BC, have described their journeys in Babylonia. From the 19th century AD interest in the location of Babylon and the 'Tower of Babel' was increased by the objects and drawings brought to Europe by travellers such as C. J. Rich (1811–25), Ker Porter (1818) and Costin and Flandin (1841). Excavation soon followed at Babylon, Erech and Borsippa (Layard, Loftus), and the good results led to more scientific expeditions, notably at Erech (Warka), *Kish, *Babylon, *Ur, Lagash and Nippur from 1850 onwards. More recent and still continuing excavation has added largely to our knowledge of all periods, *e.g.* the Early Dynastic period—Erech (Warka), Abū Ṣalabīkh, Girsu (Telloh), Lagash (Tell Hiba); Ur III (Adab, Drehem and Ur); Old Babylonian (Tell Harmal, Dēr, Sippar (Abu Habbah), Larsa, Eshnunna, Umma); Kassite (Dūr-Kurigalzu); Neo-Babylonian (Erech, Nippur, Kutha, Sippar) and later periods (Dilbat, Seleucia). Reports and texts are published regularly in the journals *Archiv für Orientforschung*, *Orientalia*, *Iraq*, *Sumer*, *Journal of Cuneiform Studies*.

BIBLIOGRAPHY. *General and History:* S. N. Kramer, *History Begins at Sumer*, 1958; H. W. F. Saggs, *The Greatness that was Babylon*, 1961; D. J. Wiseman, *Chronicles of Chaldaean Kings*, 1956; A. L. Oppenheim, *Ancient Mesopotamia*, 1964; *CAH* 1/2, 1971, pp. 238–290; 417–463, 595–643; 2/1, 1973, pp. 176–227; 2/2, 1975, pp. 21–48, 443–481; 3/1, 1982, pp. 282–313; 3/2, 1991, pp. 1–30, 229–321. *Texts:* A. K. Grayson, *Assyrian and Babylonian Chronicles*, 1975; *Babylonian Historical-Literary Texts*, 1975; *ANET* for translations of historical, religious, law and other texts. *Religion:* J. Bottéro, *La religion babylonienne*, 1952; T. Jacobsen, *Treasures of Darkness*, 1976; *Art: ANEP*; H. Frankfort, *The Art and Architecture of the Ancient Orient*, 1954; Seton Lloyd, *The Archaeology of Mesopotamia*, 1978. *Other:* R. S. Ellis, *A Bibliography of Mesopotamian Sites*, 1972. D.J.W.

BACA, VALLEY OF (Heb. *'ēmeq habbāḵā'*), a place near Jerusalem mentioned in Ps. 84:6, so translated in AV, RSV. The traditional rendering 'valley of Weeping' (RV; *cf.* 'Valley of the Weeper', JB), as though from *beḵeh* (*cf.* Ezr. 10:1), goes back through Jerome's Gallican Psalter to LXX; it is accepted by G. R. Driver, who suggests the valley may have been so called because it was lined with tombs. Other renderings are 'valley of mulberry (balsam) trees' (AVmg., RVmg.), as though from *b^eḵā'îm* (2 Sa. 5:23f.); these are supposed to grow in arid districts, whence perhaps the paraphrase 'thirsty valley' (NEB).

BIBLIOGRAPHY. G. R. Driver, 'Water in the Mountains!', *PEQ* 102, 1970, pp. 87ff. F.F.B.

BADGERS' SKINS (Heb. *taḥaš*, probably from Egyp. *ṯḥś*, 'leather', and Arab. *tuḫasun*, 'dolphin'). Mentioned in AV as the upper covering of the tabernacle, *etc.* (Ex. 25:5; 26:14, *etc.*, in all of which cases RSV has 'goatskins'), and as the material used in making sandals (Ezk. 16:10, where RV has 'sealskin', RVmg. 'porpoise-skin', NIV 'hides of sea cows', ASV 'sealskin', RSV 'leather'). LXX has *hyakinthos*, probably meaning 'skins with the colour of the hyacinth', the colour of which is difficult to ascertain because classical authors differ about it. The common opinion of modern scholars is that *taḥaš* means 'dolphin' or 'porpoise'. (*ANIMALS.)

The *taḥaš*-skin was precious in OT times as is indicated by Ezk. 16:10, where it is mentioned along with embroidered cloth, fine linen and silk. The skins are included among the gifts for the erecting of the sanctuary (Ex. 25:5); they were used with tanned rams' skins for the covering of the tent of the tabernacle and the ark (*e.g.* Nu. 4:6).

F.C.F.

BAG. 1. Heb. *kîs* (similarly Arab.) is a bag for money, or shopkeeper's stone weights, the latter sometimes used deceitfully (Dt. 25:13; Mi. 6:11). In Is. 46:6; Pr. 1:14, AV uses bag, RSV purse.

2. Heb. *ḥārîṭ* (rare word; used in Arabic), 2 Ki. 5:23; Is. 3:22. In the latter passage, AV has crisping pins, RSV handbags, which may be a good approximation. Arabic Bible uses *kîs* in both contexts.

3. Heb. *yalqûṭ* (1 Sa. 17:40) is a shepherd's bag or wallet, synonymous with *kᵉlî hārō'îm*, lit. bag of shepherds (1 Sa. 17:40, 49). *kᵉlî* can mean article, utensil, vessel, sack, bag, according to context. *Cf.* Mt. 10:10 and parallels, where Gk. has *pēra*.

4. Heb. *ṣᵉrôr* sometimes means bag (Jb. 14:17; Pr. 7:20; Hg. 1:6), quite often bundle (*e.g.* Gn. 42:35; Ct. 1:13; metaphorically, 1 Sa. 25:29).

5. Gk. *ballantion* (Lk. 10:4; 12:33, *etc.*) is a money-bag or purse.

6. Gk. *glōssokomon*, Jn. 12:6, is a moneybox (RSV), rather than bag (AV). LXX uses it for the Temple tax chest of Joash (2 Ch. 24:8, 10–11), Aquila's Gk. version for the ark of the covenant (Ex. 37:1; 1 Sa. 6:19). The Mishnah uses the Gk. loanword for bookcase or coffin.

R.A.S.

BAHURIM. Modern Ras eṭ-Ṭmim, to the E of Mt Scopus, Jerusalem. Phaltiel, the husband of Michal, accompanied his wife as far as Bahurim when she went to David to become his wife (2 Sa. 3:14–16). Shimei, a man of Bahurim, met and cursed David as he reached this locality in his flight from Jerusalem before Absalom (2 Sa. 16:5), and David's soldiers hid in a well in Bahurim when pursued by Absalom's men (2 Sa. 17:17–21).

R.J.W.

BALAAM. The name *Bilām* occurs 50 times in Nu. 22–24; it is mentioned also in Nu. 31:8, 16; Dt. 23:4–5; Jos. 13:22; 24:9–10; Ne. 13:2; Mi. 6:5. In the Greek of the NT the name is written *Balaam* (2 Pet. 2:15; Jude 11; Rev. 2:14). Whereas Albright, in his attempt to date the oracles of Balaam in the 12th century, tried to explain the name as derived from Amorite *Yabilammu*, 'the (divine) uncle brings', most scholars derive the name from Hebrew *bāla*, 'to swallow down', comparing Arabic *balam*, 'glutton'. Taking the last two consonants as representing *am*, 'nation', Rev. 2:6, 15 translated the name as *Nicolaus, 'he that inflicts defeat on the nation'.

Balaam's father is called Beor, but against his identification with Bele the son of Beor, a king in Edom (Gn. 36:32), there are serious objections: the one is a seer, the other is a king; the one lives in Dinhaba, the other in Pethor (Akkad. *Pitru*, on the river Euphrates, 20 km S of Carchemish); the one is connected with Edom, the other with Moab and Midian.

The narrative in Nu. 22 is rather intricate. Balak, king of Moab, summons Balaam from the land of Amaw or Amae (*BASOR* 118, 1950, p. 15). The elders of Midian in vv. 4, 7 are perhaps mentioned to prelude on Nu. 31:16; they play no role in the further story. God first forbids and later on allows Balaam to follow the summons; still later God's angel opposes his going, and after the show-down between man, beast and angel, Balaam is again allowed to proceed on his voyage. It is a total misconception of ancient oriental story-telling to unravel the story into different strands. The author wants to heighten the suspense of his hearers, for whom the arrival of a soothsayer (Jos. 13:22), whose *curses might have a fatal effect on the future of Israel, represented a lethal danger. Such belief in the magical working of curses (*cf.* the Egyptian execration texts, *ANET*, pp. 328ff.) was widespread, but the faithful worshippers of the Lord believed that God could turn a human curse into a blessing; Ps. 109:28, *cf.* 2 Sa. 16:12; 1 Ch. 4:9–10; Pr. 26:2. According to Dt. 23:5 and Ne. 13:2 this was what happened with Balaam's curses, and the story in Nu. 22–24 illustrates Israel's belief that under the protection of the Lord no human curse or other form of magic is to be feared. It is therefore, also, that both Balak and Balaam are ridiculed, the latter especially in the episode with the ass.

The oracles of Balaam, embedded in a poetical form reminiscent of 2 Sa. 23:1–7, predict Israel's future greatness under David, who is meant by the star that should come forth out of Jacob (24:17). As there is a very strong relation between the story in prose and the oracles in poetry, it looks improbable that the oracles were older than the prose-narrative. The whole is best placed under David, who made Moab subject (2 Sa. 8:2). In that case Asshur in Nu. 24:22, 24 is to be understood not as the Assyrian empire, but as the Arabian tribe of Gn. 25:3; *cf.* Ps. 83:8.

Though Nu. 24:25 seems to indicate that Balaam returned to his town, we find him later (Nu. 31:8, 16) among the Midianites, whom he advised to lure the Israelites into the cult of Baal of Peor (*cf.* Nu. 25). For this reason he was killed, together with the kings of the Midianites, by Israel. In the NT his name is a symbol of avarice (2 Pet. 2:15; Jude 11) and of participation in pagan cult and immorality (Rev. 2:14).

A fragmentary Aramaic text written on wall-plaster at Tell Deir 'Alla in the Jordan valley about 700 BC relates another story about Balaam. Here he is involved with several gods and goddesses whose will he conveys to a disobedient audience. This text rewards the seer's continued fame in Transjordan.

BIBLIOGRAPHY. W. F. Albright, 'The Oracles of Balaam', *JBL* 63, 1944, pp. 207–233; A. H. van Zyl, *The Moabites*, 1960, pp. 10–12, 121–125; J. Hoftijzer and G. van der Koolj, *Aramaic Texts from Deir 'Alla*, 1976; J. A. Hackett, 'The Balaam Text from Deir Alla', *BA* 49, 1986, pp. 216–223.

A.van S.
D.W.B.

BALAK. The king of Moab who employed *Balaam to put a curse on the Israelites (Nu. 22–

24). He was remembered as an example of the folly of seeking to thwart God's will (Jos. 24:9; Jdg. 11:25). N.H.

BAMOTH, BAMOTH-BAAL. Bamoth (lit. 'heights') is mentioned as a stage in Israel's journey (Nu. 21:19–20). The important shrine on the height was known as Bamoth-baal (Nu. 22:41) and the settlement is later given among the cities of Reuben (Jos. 13:17). The exact location is unknown but the site was near the river Arnon and on a commanding position for, from it, *Balaam could 'see the full extent of the Israelite host'. *Baal is probably used here in the general sense of 'lord' relating to the Moabite god Chemosh. Balaam built his own altars on which to invoke God. The *Moabite Stone refers to another Moabite *'high place' ('bamah'). J.T.W.

BAN. The OT ban (Heb. *ḥerem*) denotes in practice to 'ban, exterminate, consecrate to God'. Thus people devoted to idolatry as the *Canaanites (Ex. 23:31; 34:13; Dt. 7:2; 20:10–17) or places (Jericho, Jos. 6:17–21; *cf.* Dt. 2:34f.; Jos. 11:14) were to be destroyed. The ban was extended to an Israelite household (Achan, Jos. 7:24–26; *cf.* Dt. 20:10ff.) and threatened against Israel for her idolatry (Dt. 8:19; Jos. 23:15). The ban involves an aspect of taboo forbidding contact with an abomination (Dt. 7:26) or holy thing (Lv. 27:28). In Israel it was primarily religious, objects being devoted to the Lord and his service (Nu. 18:14).

Similar impositions of taboo on spoils of war to be devoted to the deity are known from extra-biblical sources from *Mari and the *Moabite Stone. The practice seems to have been neglected after the monarchy, though the prophets called for it (1 Sa. 15:9; 1 Ki. 20:31, 42; Mi. 4:13; Is. 34:5). The English 'ban' is used only in Ezr. 10:8 (AV 'separate') where the idea of excommunication or banishment is introduced. Thus Christians were banned from synagogues (Jn. 9:22; 12:42; 16:2; *cf.* Acts 28:16–22). The NT instances reinforce the view that such a ban or exclusion was for the ultimate welfare of the banned person also (1 Cor. 5:1–5).

BIBLIOGRAPHY. A. Malamat, 'The Ban', in *Mari and the Early Israelite Experience*, 1989, pp. 70–76. D.J.W.

BANK, BANKER. There was no bank in Israel in the sense of an establishment for the custody of private money or the granting of commercial credit. For safe keeping a private person would either bury his valuables (Jos. 7:21) or deposit them with a neighbour (Ex. 22:7). Commerce remained largely a royal monopoly (2 Sa. 5:11; 1 Ki. 10:14–29; *cf.* 2 Ch. 20:35ff.). The palace and the Temple were the repositories of the national wealth (1 Ki. 14:26); later private property also was deposited for safe keeping in temples (2 Macc. 3:6, 10ff.). A banking system existed in Babylonia in 2000 BC, but the Jews did not use it until the Exile. The money-changers in Mt. 21:12; Mk. 11:15; Jn. 2:14–15 converted Roman money into orthodox coinage for the Temple half-shekel (Mt. 17:24). Mt. 25:27 (Lk. 19:23) refers to a money-lender. A.E.W.

BANNER. 1. Heb. *deḡel*, meaning 'standard' or 'flag', is rendered 'banner' 4 times and 'standard'

Three Egyptian army banners, with (second from right) a 9th–8th-century Assyrian standard. The individual symbols were probably the distinctive signs of the unit carrying them.

14 times in RSV. In the wilderness each tribe was marked by its own banner (Nu. 1:52; 2:2–3, *etc.*). In Ps. 20:5 the word is used for a flag of battle. In the Song of Solomon it is used figuratively by the Shulammite to denote the distinguished appearance of her beloved (Ct. 5:10, AVmg.), and by him in referring to her overpowering beauty (Ct. 6:4, 10; *cf.* 2:4).

2. Heb. *nēs*, meaning 'ensign', is often rendered 'banner' in RSV. It is usually employed to designate a rallying-standard. In Is. 11:12 the Messiah is said to raise up such a standard, while in v. 10 he is himself said to be one. Perhaps this latter reference is intended to be a link with 'The Lord is my banner' (Jehovah-nissi, AV) in Ex. 17:15. The RSV is probably correct in removing references to a banner in Is. 10:18 and 59:19. G.W.G.

Assyrian military standard bearing the figure of Ashur or Ninurta as the god of war.

BANQUET. The words translated 'banquet' in AV (variously in RSV, as 'dinner', 'banquet(ing)', '(to) feast', 'carousing') are *mišteh* (*e.g.* Est. 5:4ff.; Dn. 5:10), *šāṯâ* (Est. 7:1), *yayin* (Ct. 2:4) and *potos* (1 Pet. 4:3). These terms refer primarily to wine-drinking; in the 1 Pet. reference *potos* means precisely this. In the OT the 'banquet' motif is used to represent the happiness of the coming Messianic kingdom (so Is. 25:6; *cf.* Mt. 8:11; Lk. 14:15ff.). Similarly, the 'common meal' of the Qumran sectarians seems to have been a ritual anticipation of the Messianic banquet (*cf.* 1QS 2). Such a banquet is also alluded to in the NT at the Last Supper, where Jesus tells the disciples that the meal which they were sharing was a foretaste of the true Messianic glory to come, made possible by his death (Mt. 26:27–29; *cf.* Lk. 22:29f.; Rev. 3:20; 19:9).

S.S.S.

BAPTISM.

I. The gospel and baptism

Since baptism focuses and symbolizes the gospel in a formalized rite, it is well to begin by highlighting the relationship between the two. There can be little dispute regarding two aspects of the gospel as presented in the NT.

a. The gospel as an offer of forgiveness and acceptance. This is how Jesus characterized his own ministry (*e.g.* Mk. 2:17 and Lk. 7:36–50). It was precisely the sinners, including those discounted by the righteous within Israel, whom Jesus welcomed. Similarly, Paul's message of justification by faith was the offer of God's acceptance to the Gentiles, equally discounted by the righteous as standing outside the covenant people (*e.g.* Rom. 4, 9–11).

b. The gospel as a summons to repentance and/or faith. Again we find common ground between Jesus and Paul, as such passages as Mk. 1:15 and Rom. 1:16–17 make clear.

Both aspects are deeply rooted in the biblical traditions and have given rise to the main either/or in the Christian understanding of baptism—either paedo/infant-baptism or believers' baptism. Characteristically, the paedo-baptist tradition emphasizes the faith of the parent(s), sponsors (godparents) and believing community. Equally characteristic is the baptist emphasis on the God-givenness of faith, faith as a necessary response to the prior grace of God.

However, there is a third aspect of the gospel, prominent in the NT, which is often neglected.

c. The openness of the gospel offer as itself a criticism of those who would restrict the grace of God. Jesus proclaimed his gospel in opposition to those who restricted God's grace to the righteous and denied it to the sinner (*e.g.* Lk. 18:9–14; 19:1–10), and who restricted it by reference to the law and by their ritual practice (Mk. 2:23–25; 7:1–23; Lk. 13:10–17). Paul similarly maintained his gospel in opposition to those who wanted to restrict God's grace to the chosen race and to deny it to the Gentiles, and who did so by making the ritual act of circumcision the make or break issue (Gal. 2–5). The covenant community of God's people is made such by God's call and grace (Rom. 9:6–12; 11:6), and its composition is not determined by the community's ritual observances (Gal. 2:14–21; Eph. 2:8–16), however much they may express its boundaries (*cf.* Rom. 4:11; Acts 10:47–48).

There is clearly a warning here that the openness of the gospel's offer can become too restricted by ritual requirements or practices.

II. The baptismal texts

a. Disputed passages. There are a number of texts where a reference to baptism is disputed, especially in Paul. In particular, the washing imagery of 1 Cor. 6:11, Eph. 5:26 and Tit. 3:5: is it a spiritual or physical cleansing which is envisaged, or both (*cf.* also Acts 15:9; Tit. 2:14; Heb. 9:14; 10:22; 1 Jn. 1:7, 9)? These exegetical disputes will never be completely settled. In 2 Cor. 1:22, Eph. 1:13 and 4:30 it is more likely that Paul is referring to the vividness of his converts' experience of the Spirit, making a visible impact on their lives, like the stamp of a seal (*cf.* Acts 8:17–18; 10:44–46; 19:6; Gal. 3:2–5; 4:6–7; Phil. 3:3). But a long tradition from Patristic times has referred the imagery of the seal to baptism itself.

However, there are sufficient passages where baptismal language is used so that an informed view can be achieved.

b. Passages where the divine initiative comes to the fore. Particularly relevant are those passages where the 'divine passive' (denoting an action accomplished by God) appears: 'baptized into Christ' (Rom. 6:3–4; Gal. 3:27; similarly Col. 2:12; and *cf.* Jn. 3:5). It is also possible to argue that God was declared to mediate his forgiveness through baptism in Acts 2:38 and 22:16.

It is here that the more involved argument for the solidarity of the household of faith is usually brought in. The inference drawn is that those given by birth to the members of the covenant people are to be regarded also as members of that people. Reference is usually made to Acts 2:39 and 1 Cor. 7:14. That baptism is the inevitable corollary to this covenant status can be argued from the parallel with circumcision in the old covenant (but see **II***e* below). From the household baptisms in Acts 16:15, 33; 18:8 and 1 Cor. 1:16, it is perfectly possible that 'household' in these passages denotes retainers and slaves without necessarily implying the presence of under-age children.

There is, however, insufficient evidence that in the 1st century spiritual birth was identified with baptism, particularly where it is the creative power of the word which is being given prominence (*cf.* Jas. 1:18; 1 Pet. 1:3, 23; 1 Jn. 3:9); though this observation should not be allowed to pose an antithesis between word and sacrament.

c. Passages where the repentance/faith of the baptisand is to the fore. John's baptism was characterized as a baptism of repentance (Mt. 3:11; Mk. 1:4; Lk. 3:3; Acts 13:24; 19:4). A similar emphasis with regard to Christian baptism is clear in Acts 2:38, 41; 8:12–13; 16:14–15, 33–34; 18:8 and 19:2–3 (*cf.* Heb. 6:1–2). The term 'to be baptized into the name of Christ' (Acts 8:16; 19:5) is probably drawn from the commercial world, where 'into the name of' was used in transactions (as today we write cheques 'to the name of'). So, 'to be baptized in/into the name of' someone was to be made over to him, to become his disciple (1 Cor. 1:12–13). The nearest thing to a definition of baptism in the NT defines it as an 'appeal to God for a clear conscience' or 'a pledge to God of a clear conscience' (1 Pet. 3:21).

At the same time, the fact that these references all appear in contexts in which the gospel was being preached to non-Christians in a pre-

Christian culture, raises the question of whether they would be equally applicable where Christianity has been the 'established' religion.

In short, in neither case is the evidence so clear-cut as to require or enable the expositor to make an either/or choice between paedo-baptism and believers' baptism.

d. The consistent emphasis on the once-for-allness of Christian baptism. It was precisely the 'once-for-allness' of John's baptism which distinguished it from the regular ablutions of ritual purification in contemporary Judaism, not least as practised by the (nearby?) Qumran community (but *cf.* Heb. 6:2; 10:22). John also gave the rite a profound eschatological significance—baptism as a way of preparing for, or escaping from, the wrath to come (Mt. 3:7, Lk. 3:7), as symbolizing and preparing for the decisive acts of final judgment by the Coming One (Mt. 3:10–12; Lk. 3:9, 16–17).

The finally decisive nature of entering upon discipleship of Jesus, of transfer to Christ's Lordship, is stressed in the 'already' emphasis of such passages as Jn. 5:24 and Col. 1:13. It is also linked with baptism, particularly in the death and burial imagery of Rom. 6:3–4 and Col. 2:12, and probably also in the birth imagery of Jn. 3:5. It is important that the same imagery can be used for the decisive beginnings of the Christian life and for its ongoing discipline of renewal (*cf.* Gal. 3:27 with Rom. 13:14; *cf.* Rom. 6:5 with Phil. 3:10). But there is no suggestion that repeated baptism was ever thought of as an option for Christians.

In contrast we may note the emphasis on 'one baptism' in Eph. 4:5. There is a 'once-for-allness' about entry into the new age, into the new covenant, which Heb. 6:4–6 is concerned to safeguard, and which baptism was seen to express.

The lack of a NT precedent for a repetition of baptism in the name of Christ is a striking feature of the NT witness. The twelve 'disciples' of Acts 19:1–7 had previously known only John's baptism, and were baptized in the name of the Lord Jesus, presumably because they had not received the Spirit. But Apollos, in Acts 18:24–28, who also knew only John's baptism, was apparently not 're-baptized', presumably because he was already 'aglow with the Spirit' (18:25). We may also note that the disciples at Pentecost had previously received only John's baptism.

Most striking of all is the case of the Samaritans in Acts 8. Like the twelve at Ephesus (Acts 19), they had not received the Spirit. But they were *not* re-baptized by Peter and John, because presumably they had been baptized 'in the name of Jesus' (8:16). Although they had not received the gift of the Spirit at their baptism, they were not re-baptized.

e. At the same time, bound up with the whole complex is a warning, sometimes explicit, sometimes implicit, *not to put too much weight on the ritual moment* in the whole process.

John the Baptist used the imagery of baptism to describe the Coming One's work—'he will baptize you with the Holy Spirit and with fire' (Mt. 3:11; Lk. 3:16). It is clear that something other than John's baptism in water is in view (*cf.* Is. 30:27–28; Mk. 10:38; Lk. 12:49–50). The accounts of Jesus' encounter with John at the River Jordan are consistent in focusing on Jesus' anointing with the Spirit rather than the act of baptism (particularly Lk. 3:21–22; Jn. 1:32–34; *cf.* Acts 10:37–38). No NT writer even hints that Jesus received the Spirit through his baptism by John, thereby transforming John's baptism into Christian baptism (a popular line of interpretation in later centuries). Moreover, in rather striking contrast to John the Baptist, although Jesus may have practised baptism initially, he soon abandoned it (Jn. 3:22; 4:1).

Acts 1:5 and 11:16 repeat John the Baptist's contrast between his baptizing in water and Christians' experience of being baptized in the Spirit. A related disjunction between baptism and the gift of the Spirit is attested in Acts 8:12–17 and 10:44–48, where it is the gift of the Spirit on which the issue of discipleship and salvation really hangs (8:16; 11:14–18; 19:2). Similarly, the single reference in John's Gospel (Jn. 3:5) has to be set alongside the stronger emphasis on birth as from the Spirit (3:5–8), and on the Spirit as life-giver (6:63), as symbolized by a river of living water (4:10, 14; 7:38–39).

More to the point is Paul's argument against the necessity of circumcision, despite the explicit warnings of Gn. 17:9–14. What mattered was the circumcision 'made without hands' (Col. 2:11—hardly a description of baptism), the circumcision of the heart (Rom. 2:28–29), which the gift of the Spirit effected (Phil. 3:3). In fact it was the presence of the Spirit which defined the Christian (Rom. 8:9 em;the nearest definition of a Christian in the NT). Reception of the Spirit rendered circumcision unnecessary (Gal. 3:3; 5:3–5; Rom. 2:28–29). For Paul, the Spirit had replaced circumcision as the hallmark of the covenant people (2 Cor. 3:3, 6), the evidence of the Spirit in a person's life serving as a sign and seal of the new covenant just as circumcision served for the old covenant (Jer. 31:31–34; 2 Cor. 1:22; *cf.* Rom. 4:11).

With such an emphasis, Paul's relative depreciation of baptism in 1 Cor. 1:17, following his congratulations on the Corinthians' spiritual endowment in 1:4–7, should not occasion any surprise. In 1 Cor. 12:13 (both 13a and 13c) it is likely that Paul was thinking of the outpouring of the Spirit on the Corinthians without implying that this was tied to the ritual act of baptism. Most commentators, however, assume that Paul is speaking of baptism as such, though usually without taking into account the texts noted in the preceding paragraphs.

In all this it is not clear where we should fit in one of the texts most often cited in 'baptismal' liturgies—Jesus' acceptance and blessing of children (Mk. 10:13–16). The episode certainly indicates Jesus' readiness to receive and bless little children; but that is not disputed by any Christian. What remains unclear is whether baptism is the equivalent today, or whether the equivalent blessing for children brought to him should not be tied to baptism (bearing in mind that Jesus himself did not baptize).

III. Conclusions

a. The NT evidence is not sufficiently clear to resolve the question whether paedo-baptism or believers' baptism is the more appropriate expression of and response to the gospel. On the other hand, a baptismal practice such as 'indiscriminate baptism', which does not hold grace and faith in sufficient balance, is much less easy to justify from the NT precisely for that reason.

b. There is no suggestion in the NT that baptism in the name of Christ is repeatable. On the contrary, the 'once-for-allness' of its symbolism of death and birth is a prominent feature of the NT teaching. Any precedent for a second Christian baptism is lacking, even where the reality of the Spirit came significantly later than the ritual act of baptism. Indeed, Christian baptism was only given to those who had already received John's baptism with water when the Spirit had *not* been received. The gift of the Spirit so fulfilled the expectation even of a less-than-Christian baptism, that a further baptism 'in the name of Christ' was evidently considered unnecessary. For those who regard the NT as providing their rule of faith and life, this must be a weighty consideration.

c. The danger of making too much of the ritual moment does not provide a decisive argument in determining the either/or of paedo-baptism or believers' baptism. It could be developed as an argument against paedo-baptism. But it could equally be developed as an argument against any insistence that baptism must provide expression for newly-awakened faith. Its force is rather to warn against pushing the choice between paedo-baptism and believers' baptism to an either/or. It is the insistence that only one of these teachings is right which offends against the openness of Jesus and the NT's qualification of the ritual moment, rather than the teachings themselves. It is not so much that believers' baptism is commended, as the vitality of faith and the Spirit's activity in a life, without these being tied necessarily to the ritual moment.

BIBLIOGRAPHY. *Baptism, Eucharist and Ministry*, 1982; K. Aland, *Did the Early Church Baptize Infants?*, 1963; J. Baillie, *Baptism and Conversion*, 1964; K. Barth, *Church Dogmatics*, IV/4, 1970; G. R. Beasley-Murray, *Baptism in the New Testament*, 1962; C. Buchanan, *A Case for Infant Baptism*, 1973; J. D. G. Dunn, *Baptism in the Holy Spirit*, 1970; A. George, *et al.*, *Baptism in the New Testament*, 1964; L. Hartman, *ABD* 1, pp. 583–594; J. Jeremias, *Infant Baptism in the First Four Centuries*, 1960; *The Origins of Infant Baptism*, 1963; G. W. H. Lampe, *The Seal of the Spirit*, 1967; J. Murray, *Christian Baptism*, 1962; J. K. Parratt, 'Holy Spirit and Baptism', *ExpT* 82, 1970–71, pp. 231–235, 266–271; A. Schmemann, *Of Water and the Spirit*, 1976; R. Schnackenburg, *Baptism in the Thought of St Paul*, 1964; G. Wainwright, *Christian Initiation*, 1969; A. J. M. Wedderburn, *Baptism and Resurrection*, 1987; World Council of Churches, *Baptism, Eucharist and Ministry*, 1982.

J.D.G.D.

BARABBAS. A bandit (Jn. 18:40), arrested for homicidal political terrorism (Mk. 15:7; Lk. 23:18f.). Mark's language could indicate a well-known incident, and the epithet 'notable' (Mt. 27:16, AV) some reputation as a species of hero. The priests, possibly taking up an initial demand from his supporters (*cf.* Mk. 15:8), engineered a movement for his release to counter Pilate's intended offer of that of Jesus (Mt. 27:20; Mk. 15:11) and Barabbas became an exemplification of the effects of substitutionary atonement.

The name is a patronymic ('son of Abba'). It occurs as 'Jesus Barabbas' (*cf.* 'Simon Barjonah') in some authorities at Mt. 27:16f., and Origen *in loc.* notes this reading as ancient. It adds pungency to Pilate's offer, 'Jesus Barabbas or Jesus Christ?', but, however attractive, this must remain uncertain.

The privilege of the release of a prisoner at Passover time is independently attested by Mark and John, but remains obscure. Blinzler associates it with Mishnah *Pesaḥim* 8. 6, which ordains that the Passover lamb may be offered 'for one whom they have promised to bring out of prison'.

BIBLIOGRAPHY. Deissmann in G. K. A. Bell and A. Deissmann, *Mysterium Christi*, pp. 12ff. (for the text: *contra*, *cf.* M. J. Lagrange, *S. Matthieu*, pp. 520ff.) R. L. Merritt, *JBL* 104, pp. 57–68 (a romance); C. E. B. Cranfield, *St Mark*, pp. 449ff. (a sensitive reading of the incident); J. Blinzler, *The Trial of Jesus*, 1959, pp. 218ff.; F. F. Bruce, *New Testament History*, 1971, pp. 203ff. A.F.W.

BARAK (Heb. *bārāq*, 'lightning'; *cf.* Carthaginian *Barca*). In Jdg. 4:6ff. the son of Abinoam, from Kedesh in Naphtali, summoned by the prophetess *Deborah to muster the tribes of Israel and lead them to battle against *Sisera, commander-in-chief of the confederate Canaanite forces. He consented to act on condition that Deborah accompanied him, for which reason he was told that not he, but a woman, would have the honour of despatching Sisera. The details of his victory, when a sudden downpour flooded the river *Kishon and immobilized Sisera's chariotry, are graphically depicted in the Song of Deborah (Jdg. 5:19–22). In Heb. 11:32 Barak is listed among the 'elders' whose faith is attested in the sacred record. In 1 Sa. 12:11 'Bedan' should perhaps be emended to 'Barak', following LXX and Syr. (so RSV, NEB). F.F.B.

BARBARIAN. A term applied by the Greeks to all non-Greek-speaking peoples. It was not originally, or necessarily, pejorative. Luke actually praises the 'barbarians' of *Malta for their exceptional kindness (Acts 28:2–4). Inscriptions show that a Phoenician dialect was spoken on Malta. Perhaps Luke recalls the first frustration of failure to communicate in the cosmopolitan Latin and Greek. In 1 Cor. 14:11 the use of uninterpreted tongues is seen ironically as creating linguistic barriers. 'Greeks and barbarians' together (Rom. 1:14) comprise all kinds of men without discrimination (*cf.* Col. 3:11). C.J.H.

BAR-JESUS ('son of Joshua' or 'son of Ishvah'). In Acts 13:6ff. a magician and false prophet, attached to the court of Sergius Paulus, proconsul of Cyprus. He is given the alternative name Elymas in v. 8, possibly from a Semitic root meaning 'sage', 'wise man'. In the Western Text his names appear as Bariesouan and Hetoimas. He tried to dissuade Sergius Paulus from paying attention to Paul and Barnabas, but came off worse in an encounter with Paul. His temporary blinding may have been intended to have the same salutary effect as Paul's similar experience on the Damascus road.

F.F.B.

BARN. The AV rendering of 4 Heb. words, each of them used only once. They are: **1.** *gōren*, 'an open threshing-floor' (Jb. 39:12). RV renders 'threshing-floor' (*AGRICULTURE). **2.** *mᵉgûrâ*, 'a granary' (Hg. 2:19). **3.** *'āsām*, 'a storehouse' (Pr. 3:10). **4.** *mammᵉgōrâ*, 'a repository' (Joel 1:17). Often a dry cistern in the ground was used, covered with a thick layer of earth. Grain could keep for years under such conditions. (*STORE-CITIES.)

In the NT, Gk. *apothēkē*, 'a place for putting away', is used literally (Mt. 6:26; Lk. 12:18, 24), and metaphorically to signify heaven (Mt. 13:30).

J.D.D.

BARNABAS. The cognomen of Joseph, a foremost early missionary. Luke (Acts 4:36) interprets 'son of *paraklēsis*', 'one who encourages, or exhorts' (*cf.* 'son of peace' in Lk. 10:6). *Nabas* may reflect Aramaic *nᵉwaḥâ*, 'pacification', 'consolation' (the abnormal Greek transcription being eased by the contemporary soft pronunciation of *b*), or some derivative of the root *nb'*, 'to prophesy'. Strictly, this would be 'son of a prophet' or 'of prophecy', but exhortation was supremely a prophetic function (Acts 15:32; 1 Cor. 14:3), and Luke is concerned, not to provide a scientific etymology, but to indicate the man's character. We find him engaged in *paraklēsis* in Acts 11:23. Deissmann equates the name with *Barnebous* (Aramaic *Barnᵉbō*, 'son of Nebo') found in Syrian inscriptions; but Luke states that the apostles gave it, and they would hardly confer a name redolent of a pagan deity.

He came from a Jewish–Cypriot priestly family, but the Jerusalemite John Mark was his cousin (Col. 4:10), and he himself an early member of the Jerusalem church, selling his property (in Cyprus?) for the common good (Acts 4:36ff.). Clement of Alexandria calls him one of the Seventy (*Hypot.* 7; *Stromateis* 2. 20. 116). The Western Text of Acts 1:23 confounds him with Joseph-Barsabas in the apostolic election; but later Luke (Acts 14:4, 14) and Paul (1 Cor. 9:6, in context) regard him as an *apostle.

'A good man,' says Luke, 'full of the Holy Spirit and of faith' (Acts 11:24), and on at least four occasions his warm-heartedness and spiritual insight, and the apparently universal respect for him, had momentous results.

a. When the converted Saul arrived in Jerusalem only to discover that the Christians thought him a spy, it was Barnabas who introduced him to the 'pillar' apostles and convinced them of his conversion and sincerity (Acts 9:27; *cf.* Gal. 1:18).

b. It was Barnabas who represented the apostles at Antioch when, for the first time, Gentiles had been evangelized in significant numbers, and where fellow-Cypriots had been prominent (Acts 11:19ff.). He saw the movement as a work of God—and as a fitting sphere for the forgotten Saul, whom he brought to share his labours. On their visiting Jerusalem with famine-relief, their call to Gentile missionary work was recognized (Gal. 2:9; *CHRONOLOGY OF THE NEW TESTAMENT). But Barnabas was not the man to withstand Peter to his face when he succumbed to Judaizing pressure: 'even Barnabas' temporarily broke table-fellowship with the Antiochene Gentiles (Gal. 2:13).

c. Barnabas' third great contribution, however, showed him committed to full acceptance of Gentiles on faith in Christ (*cf.* Acts 13:46). The journey with Paul (Acts 13–14), beginning in his own Cyprus, resulted in a chain of predominantly Gentile churches far into Asia Minor and a surging Jewish opposition.

For the church and for Barnabas it was a milestone. Hitherto he had been leader, Paul his protégé. Luke's consistent order up to the departure from Cyprus is 'Barnabas and Saul'. Thereafter he usually says, 'Paul and Barnabas'. (Acts 13:43, 46, 50; 15:2, twice, 22, 35. The order in 14:14 is probably due to the order of the deities.) This doubtless reflects the progress of events.

d. But Barnabas had another crucial task. Back at Antioch, the circumcision question became so acute that he and Paul were appointed to bring the matter before the Jerusalem Council. Their policy was triumphantly vindicated (Acts 15:1–29). Significantly, Barnabas stands before Paul both in the account of the proceedings (v. 12) and in the Council's letter (v. 25, contrast 22); probably the words of the original apostolic representative in Antioch carried greater weight with many in the Council. Barnabas insisted on including Mark, who had previously deserted them, on a proposed second journey. Paul refused, and the itinerary was divided, Barnabas taking Cyprus (Acts 15:36–40). Paul's later testimonies to Mark (*e.g.* 2 Tim. 4:11) may mean that the latter greatly profited from working under his cousin. The close partnership was broken, but not the friendship. 'Whenever Paul mentions Barnabas, his words imply sympathy and respect' (Lightfoot on Gal. 2:13). In principles and practice they were identical, and we shall never know how much Paul owed to Barnabas. When 1 Corinthians was written, Barnabas was still alive, and, like Paul and unlike most of their colleagues, supporting himself without drawing on the churches (1 Cor. 9:6). After this, we hear only insubstantial traditions associating him with Rome and Alexandria.

His name was early attached to an anonymous letter of Alexandrian provenance, but there is nothing else to connect it with him (*PATRISTIC LITERATURE). The Epistle to the Hebrews has often been ascribed to him, at least from Tertullian's time (Tert., *De pudicitia* 20; *cf.* Zahn, *INT*, 2, pp. 301ff.), and 1 Peter by A. C. McGiffert (*Christianity in the Apostolic Age*, 1897, pp. 593ff.). There is a late Cypriot martyrology (see James, *ANT*, p. 470). The *Gospel of Barnabas* (ed. L. Ragg, 1907) is a medieval work in Muslim interest.

BIBLIOGRAPHY. A. Klostermann, *Probleme im Aposteltexte neu erörtert*, 1883; A. Deissmann, *Bible Studies*, pp. 307ff.; H. J. Cadbury in *Amicitiae Corolla* (Rendel Harris Festschrift), 1933, pp. 45ff.; *BC*, 4; F. F. Bruce, *The Acts of the Apostles*³, 1990; *idem*., *The Book of the Acts*², *NIC*, 1990.

A.F.W.

BARRENNESS. To be a wife without bearing children has always been regarded in the East, not only as a matter of regret, but as a reproach which could lead to divorce. This is the cause of Sarah's despairing laughter (Gn. 18:12), Hannah's silent prayer (1 Sa. 1:10ff.), Rachel's passionate alternative of children or death (Gn. 30:1) and Elizabeth's cry that God had taken away her reproach (Lk. 1:25). The awfulness of the coming judgment on Jerusalem is emphasized by the incredible statement, 'Blessed are the barren . . .' (Lk. 23:29). It was believed that the gift of children or the withholding of them indicated God's blessing or curse (Ex. 23:26; Dt. 7:14), as also did the barrenness or fruitfulness of the land (Ps. 107:33–34). J.W.M.

BARTHOLOMEW (Gk. *bartholomaios*, 'son of Talmai' or, in Graeco-Roman times, 'son of Ptolemy'). The bearer of this patronymic appears in each list of the Twelve (Mt. 10:3; Mk. 3:18; Lk. 6:14; Acts 1:13), but is otherwise unmentioned in NT. His association in all lists but the last with Philip has suggested to many readers from the 9th century onwards that he may be identical with Philip's friend *Nathanael of Cana (Jn. 1:45ff.; *cf.* 21:2); on this certainty is unattainable. F.F.B.

BARTIMAEUS. A blind beggar who was healed by Jesus (Mk. 10:46–52). The name means 'Son of Timaeus' and may have been recorded by Mark because he was a well-known figure in the early church. The incident took place on Jesus' last journey to Jerusalem as he left Jericho, and is found in the other Synoptic Gospels, though with a number of differences. In Mt. 20:29–34 there are two blind men, while in Lk. 18:35–43 the healing takes place as Jesus is approaching Jericho. The story has been variously reconstructed, and it may be that Matthew and Mark refer to Old Jericho and Luke to New Jericho, which was to the S of it. The incident is remarkable for the persistence of Bartimaeus' faith in Jesus as the Messiah.

R.E.N.

BARUCH (Heb. *bārûḵ*, 'blessed'). **1.** The son of Neriah (Je. 36:4), and brother of Seraiah, quartermaster to King Zedekiah (Je. 51:59). He was a faithful attendant on the prophet Jeremiah (36:10), wrote his master's prophecies (36:4, 32) and read them to the people (vv. 14–15). He acted as witness to the purchase by the imprisoned prophet of his family estate at Anathoth (Je. 32). Following the sack of Jerusalem, he is said to have resided with Jeremiah at Masphatha (Mizpah, Josephus, *Ant.* 10. 158) but after the murder of Gedaliah was arrested for influencing Jeremiah's departure (43:3). He was taken with Jeremiah to Egypt (43:6), where according to one tradition he and Jeremiah died (Jerome on Is. 30:6). Josephus, however, implies that they were both carried captive to Babylon after Nebuchadrezzar had invaded Egypt in 583 BC (*Ant.* 10. 182). Josephus also says that Baruch was of noble family (as Baruch 1:1). His association with Jeremiah resulted in his name being given to a number of apocryphal books, notably *The Apocalypse of Baruch*, a work probably of Heb. or Aram. origin of which Gk. (2nd century AD) and Syr. versions survive; *The Book of Baruch*, a deuterocanonical book found in LXX between Jeremiah and Lamentations, of which various vss (Lat. and Gnostic) are known; and *The Rest of the Works of Baruch*. Jewish tradition (*Mid. Rabba* on Ct. 5:5) speaks of Baruch as Ezra's teacher.

Clay bulla (enlarged 3×), bearing the impression of the inscribed seal of 'Berechiah (Baruch), son of Neriah the scribe' (lbrkyhw bn nryhw hspr). *Late 7th cent. BC.*

2. A priest, son of Zabbai, who assisted Nehemiah in rebuilding work (Ne. 3:20) and as witness to a covenant (10:6).

3. Son of Col-hozeh, a Judaean, father of Maaseiah (Ne. 11:5). D.J.W.

BARZILLAI ('Man of iron'). **1.** 'The Gileadite of Rogelim' (2 Sa. 17:27, *etc.*), a faithful follower of David. **2.** A relation of the above by marriage who took the family name (Ezr. 2:61), and is called 'Jaddus' in 1 Esdras 5:38. **3.** 'The Meholathite', whose son Adriel married Saul's daughter Merab (1 Sa. 18:19; 2 Sa. 21:8; LXX and two Heb. MSS), or Michal (2 Sa. 21:8, RSVmg., *MT*). G.W.G.

BASEMATH (Bashemath, AV). Probably from Semitic stem *bsm*, 'fragrant'. **1.** According to Gn. 26:34, Esau married Basemath, the daughter of Elon, the Hittite. According to Gn. 36:3, he was married to a certain Basemath who was the daughter of Ishmael and the sister of Nebaioth. *Cf.* Gn. 28:9, where she is called Mahalath, and Gn. 36:2, where Elon's daughter is called Adah. It is possible that both Mahalath and Adah were given the nickname Basemath, 'fragrant', or else it is a scribal error (*cf.* some MSS of the LXX). **2.** Basemath, daughter of Solomon, married Ahimaaz of Naphtali (1 Ki. 4:15).

BIBLIOGRAPHY. J. Hoftijzer & C.-F. Jean, *Dictionnaire des Inscriptions Sémitiques de l'Ouest*, 1960–62. F.C.F.

BASHAN. A region E of Jordan lying to the N of Gilead, from which it was divided by the river Yarmuk. Its fertility was famous; see Ps. 22:12; Ezk. 39:18; Am. 4:1; and Is. 2:13; Je. 50:19; Ezk. 27:5–6. The name, nearly always written with the article (*habbāšān*), had varying connotations. In the wide sense it was counted as extending N to Mt Hermon and E to *Salecah; and in the narrower sense it comprised roughly the area called today en-Nuqra. It included the cities of *Ashtaroth, *Golan and *Edrei, and the regions of *Argob and *Havvoth-jair. At the time of the conquest Bashan was under the rule of Og, who had his capital at Ashtaroth. He was defeated by the Israelites at Edrei (Dt. 1:4; 3:1–3) and the territory fell to the lot of Manasseh. It formed part of the dominions of David and Solomon, falling within the sixth administrative district of the latter (1 Ki. 4:13). It was lost during the Syrian wars, but was regained by Jeroboam II (2 Ki. 14:25), only to be taken by Tiglath-pileser III (2 Ki. 15:29), after which it formed part of the successive Assyrian, Babylonian and Persian empires. Under the Persians it roughly coincided with the district of Qarnaim, and in the Greek period with that of Batanaea.

BIBLIOGRAPHY. G. A. Smith, *The Historical Geography of the Holy Land* [11], 1904, pp. 542, 548–553, 575ff.; F. M. Abel, *Géographie de la Palestine*, 1, 1933, pp. 274f. T.C.M.

BASKET. The following Heb. words are translated 'basket'. **1.** *dûḏ*, a round basket large enough to hold a human head (2 Ki. 10:7), but normally used for carrying figs, *etc*. (Ps. 81:6; Je. 24:1–2). **2.** *ṭene'* (loan-word from Egyp. *dnyt*, 'basket'), used for storing produce (Dt. 26:2, 4) parallel to kneading-trough (Dt. 28:5, 17) as an item in the household. **3.** *kᵉlûḇ*, which held fruit in Amos' vision (8:1) but was originally used for trapping birds, as in Je. 5:27 and the Canaanite letters from Amarna. **4.** *sal*, a flat, open basket for carrying bread (unleavened, Ex. 29:3, 23, 32; Lv. 8:2, 26, 31; Nu. 6:15, 17, 19; Jdg. 6:19). Pharaoh's baker dreamt he was carrying three full of white *bread (Heb. *ḥōrî*) on his head (Gn. 40:16; *cf*. *IBA*, fig. 28). **5.** *salsillôṯ* (Je. 6:9, AV) are more probably branches (RSV) which are being thoroughly plucked, rather than 'baskets'.

The distinction between the feeding of the four thousand and of the five thousand is emphasized by the Gospel writers' use of Gk. *kophinos* for basket in the former miracle (Mt. 14:20; 16:9; Mk. 6:43; 8:19; Lk. 9:17; Jn. 6:13), but Gk. *spyris* in the latter (Mt. 15:37; 16:10; Mk. 8:8, 20). Both words denote a hamper, *kophinos* appearing elsewhere in a Jewish context, and *spyris*, in which Paul was lowered from the wall of Damascus, being the larger (Acts 9:25; parallel to Gk. *sarganē*, a plaited container, 2 Cor. 11:33). A.R.M.

BATH, BATHING. Heb. *rāḥaṣ*, occasionally *qādaš* (*e.g.* Ex. 19:10, 14, 22) and *hizzāh* 'sprinkle'. Gk. *louō*/*niptō*.

The dusty heat of the Middle East made washing desirable. Bathing in rivers or pools was practised by those who lived near them (*e.g.* Ex. 2:5; 1 Ki. 22:38; 2 Ki. 5:10; Jn. 9:7). Otherwise people used drawn water, stored in jars (*cf*. Jn. 2:6), to wash themselves and especially the feet of visitors (*e.g.* Gn. 18:4; *cf*. Jn. 13:1–10).

Washing was an essential prerequisite to worship, as it was a means of eliminating uncleanness. Thus the priests always had to wash their hands and feet prior to worship (Ex. 30:21; 40:30–32). Sometimes immersion to cleanse the whole body was required, *e.g.* on the day of atonement (Lv. 16:4). The 'sea', a huge laver, was used by priests for this purpose (2 Ch. 4:2–6).

Laity coming to worship were expected to wash themselves (Ex. 19:10), especially if they had been suffering from a complaint, *e.g.* skin disease (Lv. 14:8) or discharge (Lv. 15:13). Polluted vessels could also be purified by washing with water (*e.g.* Lv. 11:32; Nu. 31:23). Purification could also be effected sometimes by sprinkling with water (Lv. 14:7, 51) or a water mixture (Nu. 19:18–20).

By NT times special baths called miqvehs, fed by running water, were used to cleanse people from bodily uncleanness. They are still used by Jews today. The Jewish practice of washing hands before meals (*cf*. Mt. 15:2) may reflect OT practice.

Washing often has symbolic significance in Scripture. It represents a turning away from evil (Is. 1:16) and a purification from sin (Ps. 26:6; 73:13) which is central to the use of water in baptism (1 Pet. 3:21). G.J.W.

BATHSHEBA (called, in 1 Ch. 3:5, 'Bathshua, daughter of Ammiel'). She was the daughter of Eliam (2 Sa. 11:3), and, if he is the 'mighty man' of 2 Sa. 23:34, granddaughter of Ahithophel. David took her while her husband, Uriah the Hittite, was in command of the army which was besieging Rabbah, the Ammonite capital. This led to Uriah's murder, Bathsheba's entry into the royal harem and the rebuke by Nathan the prophet (2 Sa. 12). In David's old age Bathsheba allied with Nathan to secure Solomon's accession and become queen-mother. She petitioned Solomon, on Adonijah's behalf, for Abishag, David's concubine (1 Ki. 2:19–21). This was interpreted as a bid for the throne, and resulted in Adonijah's death. M.B.

BDELLIUM. A fragrant, transparent, yellowish gum-resin, the sap from trees of the genus *Commiphora*, valued for its use as a perfume. It was found in the land of *Havilah, near Eden (Gn. 2:12), and its colour was the same as that of *manna (Nu. 11:7). The Heb. *bᵉḏōlaḥ* was taken over into Gk. as *bdellion*. Although this loan-word is found in the later Gk. translations of the OT, the LXX translates by *anthrax* and *krystallos*, possibly because the hardened gum resembled a precious stone, or because of the associated substances in Gn. 2:11f. (*JEWELS.)

BIBLIOGRAPHY. *KB*; *RAC*, 2, pp. 34f.; *EJ*, 4, p. 354. I.H.M.

BEARD. 1. Heb. *zāqān*. Israelites and their neighbours generally wore full round beards which they tended scrupulously. The beard was a mark of vitality and of manly beauty (Ps. 133:2; *cf*. 2 Sa. 19:24); to shave or cover it was a sign of grief or mourning (Is. 15:2; Je. 48:37, *etc*.; *cf*. Lv. 19:27; 21:5, enacted probably against idolatrous practices), or of leprosy (Lv. 14:9). To mutilate another's beard was to dishonour him (2 Sa. 10:4; Is. 50:6). Jeremiah criticizes those who shave their temples (Je. 9:26, *etc*.). (*HAIR; *BURIAL AND MOURNING.)

2. Heb. *śāpām* (2 Sa. 19:24), denoting the moustache. J.D.D.

BEAST. Although found widely in most modern EVV, including RSV, the word 'beast' is now largely obsolete as a precise term. Coming from Old French, it was in general use when the Bible was first translated into English: 'animal', which has now replaced it, is from Latin and first appeared early 16th century but was not widely used until later. It is still used on farms in a semi-technical way, especially as 'fat beasts' and also, more widely, as 'beasts of burden'; otherwise it is found only in literary works or used figuratively, *i.e.* a cruel or rough man is a beast and his behaviour is beastly or bestial.

There is little uniformity in its use in EVV. In general both RV and RSV follow AV in the OT, and this is a notable exception to the RV policy of translating Heb. words consistently. Two Heb. words are usually translated 'beast'; *bᵉhēmâ* (coll.) is also translated *'cattle': *ḥayyâ* is translated 'beast' 96 times (AV), but in 35 other passages it is translated by 10 different Eng. words. *bᵉ'îr* is often translated 'beast' but sometimes 'cattle'.

In some passages *bᵉhēmâ* and *ḥayyâ* are hard to differentiate as, for instance, where in the same chapter (Lv. 11) and very similar contexts they are both used of clean animals: v. 2 (AV) 'the beasts (*ḥayyâ*) which ye shall eat', but v. 39 'any beast (*bᵉhēmâ*) of which ye shall eat'. In v. 47 *ḥayyâ* has a wider meaning, so that RV and RSV often translate as 'living thing', but this is reversed in v. 2: 'These are the living things (*ḥay*) which you may eat among all the beasts (*bᵉhēmâ*) that are on the earth.'

In the NT both RV and RSV follow the Greek more closely than AV. *zōon*, always 'beast' in AV, is translated 'living creature' in RV and RSV in Rev. 4:6. Except for RSV in Acts 23:24 (mounts) and 28:4–5 (creature), Acts 10:12 and 1 Cor. 15:39 (animals), and Rev. 18:13 (cattle), all common EVV retain 'beast' for *ktēnos* (domestic animal, especially beast of burden) and *thērion* (wild beast). RV and RSV thus correctly distinguish between the four living creatures on the one hand and the beast of Rev. 11:7 and all literal passages on the other.

The word 'animal' was current before AV was published but is not used in this or in RV. Animal now has two usages. Strictly it is any living being with sensation and voluntary movement, *i.e.* the animal kingdom in contrast with the plant kingdom; more popularly it refers to four-footed animals, often only to four-footed mammals, in contrast with man, birds, *etc.* As used in RSV the meaning is nearer the latter, but in the 34 OT occurrences there is no uniformity. For instance, the first 12 instances translate 6 different Heb. words, which AV translates 'beast', 'cattle', 'of the herd' and 'of the flock'. The NT pattern is similar; the 7 occurrences are from 4 Greek words: *thērion*, *tetrapous*, *ktēnos* and *zōon*. (*ANIMALS.)

G.S.C.

BEAST (APOCALYPSE). 1. The 'beast that ascends from the bottomless pit' (Rev. 11:7) is the apocalyptic symbol of the last anti-Christian power (Rev. 13:1ff.; 17:3ff.; 19:19f.), portrayed as a composite picture of the 4 beasts of Dn. 7:3ff. His 10 horns are borrowed from Daniel's fourth beast; his 7 heads mark his derivation of authority from the dragon of Rev. 12:3, and go back ultimately to Leviathan (*cf.* Ps. 74:14; Is. 27:1); John reinterprets them once of the 7 hills of Rome (Rev. 17:9), otherwise of 7 Roman emperors. The beast is usually the persecuting empire, occasionally the final emperor, a reincarnation of one of the first 7, probably Nero. He claims divine honours, wages war on the saints and is destroyed by Christ at his parousia (*cf.* 2 Thes. 2:8).

2. The 'beast from the earth' (Rev. 13:11ff.), also called the 'false prophet' (Rev. 16:13; 19:20; 20:10), is public relations officer of the former beast, persuades men to worship him and ultimately shares his fate. The imperial cult in the province of Asia (*ASIARCH) evidently suggested some of his features to John.

F.F.B.

BEER (*bᵉ'ēr*, lit. 'a well', 'cistern', usually manmade). **1.** Nu. 21:16. A point on the itinerary of the wandering Hebrews, reached soon after leaving Arnon. This verse records an otherwise unknown story of the provision of water; an important event, for v. 18b suggests that Beer was in a desert place. The site is unknown. **2.** Jdg. 9:21. The place to which Jotham fled after having denounced the *coup d'état* of his brother Abimelech. The site is unknown.

R.J.W.

BEER-LAHAI-ROI. The name itself and certain elements of Gn. 16:13–14, where it first appears, defy certain translation. As it stands, the name may mean 'The well of the living one who sees me' or 'The well of "He who sees me lives"'. However, the original place-name may have suffered a degree of distortion in transmission, putting the original beyond our discovery. This is not the only proper name in the OT to have suffered in this way. The exact site is not known, but Gn. 16:7, 14 places it towards the Egyptian border, whither Hagar, the Egyptian maid, was fleeing from the wrath of Sarai her mistress. God appeared to Hagar here and announced the birth of Ishmael. Isaac passed through Beer-lahai-roi when waiting for Eliezer to bring him a wife from Mesopotamia (Gn. 24:62), and settled there after the death of Abraham.

R.J.W.

BEERSHEBA. The name given to an important well, and also to the local town and district (Gn. 21:14; Jos. 19:2). The present town lies 77 km SW of Jerusalem and approximately midway between the Mediterranean and the S part of the Dead Sea. There are several wells in the vicinity, the largest 3.75 m in diameter. The digging of this well involved cutting through 5 m of solid rock. On one stone of the masonry lining the shaft Conder found a date indicating that repairs had been carried out in the 12th century AD. At the time of his visit in 1874, it was 11 m to the surface of the water.

Excavations at Tel es-Seba', 5 km W of the town, have revealed a planned and fortified town of the Judaean monarchy. A well outside the gateway is dated to the 12th century BC by the excavator, and associated with Abraham, setting the stories of the Patriarchs after the Israelite conquest. There is no evidence to support this speculation. No pottery of Bronze Age date has been found at the site, nor anything to prove the place's ancient name. Iron Age pottery has been found in the modern town (Bir es-Seba'), which was called Berosaba in Roman times, and may yet prove to be the patriarchal site.

The meaning of the name is given in Gn. 21:31, 'The well of seven' (*i.e.* lambs). The alternative interpretation, 'The well of the oath', arises through a misunderstanding of the use of the Heb. word for 'therefore', which can refer only to an antecedent statement (Gn. 11:9 is not really an exception), and a mistranslation of the Heb. particle *kî* by 'because', whereas it here introduces an independent temporal clause and should be rendered 'when', or even 'then'. The antecedent statement tells *why* it was done; this clause, *when* it was done. (For a similar use of *kî*, *cf.* Gn. 24:41; *cf.* König, *Heb. Syntax*, 387 h.) The explanation of the alleged second account of the naming of the well by Isaac (Gn. 26:33) is given in v. 18: 'And Isaac dug again the wells of water which had been dug in the days of Abraham his father; for the Philistines had stopped them after the death of Abraham; and he gave them the names which his father had given them.' Since the digging of a well was often a major achievement, filial respect alone would insist that the work of a great father would be thus remembered. In v. 33 the actual wording is: 'He called it Shibah.' The use here of the feminine of the numeral may merely express the numerical group, roughly equivalent to 'It, of the seven'.

Beersheba has many patriarchal associations. Abraham spent much time there (Gn. 22:19). It was probably a part of Palestine without an urban population, since the seasonal nature of the pasturage would not have been conducive to settled conditions. From here he set out to offer up Isaac. Isaac was dwelling here when Jacob set out for Harran (Gn. 28:10). On his way through to Joseph in Egypt, Jacob stopped here to offer sacrifices (Gn. 46:1). In the division of the land it went to the tribe of Simeon (Jos. 19:2).

In the familiar phrase 'from Dan to Beersheba' (Jdg. 20:1, *etc.*) it denoted the southernmost place of the land. The town owed its importance to its position on the trade-route to Egypt.

The reference to it in Amos (5:5 and 8:14) indicates that it had become a centre for undesirable religious activities.

Beersheba and its villages (Heb. 'daughters') were resettled after the captivity (Ne. 11:27).

The place referred to by Josephus (*BJ* 2. 573 and 3. 39), which Winckler wanted to identify with the Beersheba of the OT, was a village in lower Galilee (Jos., *Life* 5. 188).

BIBLIOGRAPHY. W. Zimmerli, *Geschichte u. Tradition von Beer-sheba im A.T.*, 1932. Y. Aharoni, *Beer-sheba*, 1, 1973; Herzog, *Beer-sheba*, 2, 1984; *NEAEHL*, pp. 167–173.

W.J.M.
A.R.M.

BEHEMOTH. Morphologically the Heb. plural of *b^e^hēmâ*, occurring 9 times in the OT (Dt. 32:24; Jb. 12:7; 40:15; Pss. 49:12, 20; 50:10; 73:22; Je. 12:4; Hab. 2:17), and in all but one of these occurrences 'beasts', 'animals' or 'cattle' is apparently the intended meaning. In Jb. 40:15, however, the reference is so qualified in the following verses as to suggest some specific animal, and it is usual to take the plural here as having intensive force, 'great beast', and referring to the hippopotamus which seems to fit the description best. A derivation has been suggested from a hypothetical Egyptian *p'.iḥ.mw*, 'the ox of the water', but the fact that Egyptian has other words for hippopotamus renders this unlikely. While other theories have been put forward, the hippopotamus identification may be tentatively accepted in the present state of knowledge. The LXX renders the word here by *ktēnos*. (*BEAST.)

BIBLIOGRAPHY. S. R. Driver and G. B. Gray, *The Book of Job*, *ICC*, 1921, 1, pp. 351–358; *KB*, p. 111; for another theory, see G. R. Driver in Z. V. Togan (ed.), *Proceedings of the Twenty-Second Congress of Orientalists ... Istanbul ... 1951*, 2, 1957, p. 113; G. S. Cansdale, *Animals of Bible Lands*, 1970, p. 100; J. V. Kinnier Wilson, *VT* 25, 1975, pp. 1–14.

T.C.M.

BEL. The name or title of the principal Babylonian deity, Marduk (*MERODACH), whose overthrow was synonymous with the end of Babylon and its domination (Je. 50:2; 51:44). In this connection Bel is named with the god Nabû (*NEBO), who was considered his son (Is. 46:1). Bēl (Sumerian *en*, 'lord'; Heb. *Ba'al*) was one of the original Sumerian triad of deities, with Anu and Enki, his name being a title or epithet of the wind and storm god Enlil. When Marduk became the chief god of Babylon in the 2nd millennium he was given the additional name of Bēl. It was the idol of this god whom Daniel and his companions were commanded to worship (Bel and the Dragon 3ff.).

D.J.W.

BELIAL. The sense of this word is generally clear from its context: 'son of' or 'man of' Belial plainly means a very wicked person. The word occurs in Heb. of Ps. 18:4, parallel to the word 'death'; hence the RSV translation 'perdition'. In intertestamental literature and NT it is a synonym for Satan (often spelled 'Beliar'). The derivation is, however, obscure. The Heb. text, with the Massoretic vowels, read *b^e^lîya'al*, apparently from *b^e^lî* ('without') and *ya'al* ('profit'), and so means 'worthlessness'; this is still a strong possibility, although one cannot easily account for its having become a proper name. A number of scholars have sought a mythological background, *e.g.* Baal-yam ('Lord Sea'), but none of the suggestions has been very convincing. A third type of approach is to ignore the Massoretic vowels and derive the word from a Heb. verb *bāla'* ('swallow up, engulf'); the name would then primarily describe Sheol, as 'the Engulfer' (the etymology of English 'infernal' is comparable).

Modern EVV chiefly use such words as 'scoundrel', 'base', 'godless' and 'abominable' to render phrases which contain 'Belial' in Heb.

BIBLIOGRAPHY. D. W. Thomas in *Biblical and Patristic Studies in Memory of R. P. Casey*, 1963, pp.11–19; V. Maag, *TZ* 21, 1965, pp. 287–299; *TDOT*.

D.F.P.

BELL. Two Hebrew words are thus translated. **1.** *pa'^a^môn* ('striking', 'beating'). Small gold bells, alternating with pomegranates of blue, purple and scarlet stuff, were attached to the hem of the high priest's ephod (Ex. 28:33–34; 39:25–26), their ringing announced his going into the sanctuary. Bells for religious purposes are known from Assyria (see B. Meissner, *Babylonien und Assyrien*, 1, 1920, p. 268, and photograph, Abb. 142). Bells are also attested for personal adornment in Egypt, from at least the Bubastite period (*c.* 800 BC) to Roman and Coptic times, and were often attached to children to announce their whereabouts. See, with illustrations, Petrie, *Objects of Daily Use*, 1927, pp. 24, 57–58, plates 18:33–37 and 50:292–305. Bells with clappers appear in the 1st millennium BC; earlier small 'bell rattles' were current, openwork metal containers with a small metal ball inside.

2. Heb. *m^e^ṣillâ* ('tinkling'). These are little bells. In Zc. 14:20 they are part of the trappings of horses, prophesied to become 'Holy to the Lord' (and so inscribed). Little bells often appeared among horse-trappings in antiquity; they can be seen at the necks of Assyrian war-horses in Grollenberg, *Shorter Atlas of the Bible*, 1959, p. 113, bottom photograph. See also J. Rimmer, *Ancient Musical Instruments of Western Asia in the British Museum*, 1969, pp. 37ff., pls. xvii–xx.

K.A.K.

BELSHAZZAR. The ruler of Babylon who was killed at the time of its capture in 539 BC (Dn. 5). Bēl-šar-uṣur ('Bel has protected the king [ship]') is named in Babylonian documents by his father Nabonidus, king of Babylon in 556–539 BC. Other texts give details of Belshazzar's administration and religious interests in Babylon and Sippar up to the 14th year of his father's reign. He was possibly a grandson of Nebuchadrezzar II and, according to the Nabonidus Chronicle, his father 'entrusted the army and the kingship' to him *c.* 556 BC, while Nabonidus campaigned in central Arabia, where he eventually remained for 10 years. Belshazzar ruled in Babylonia itself. It is possible that Daniel dated events by the years of this co-regency (Dn. 7:1; 8:1), though the official dating of documents continued to use the regnal years of Nabonidus himself. Legal texts dated to the 12th and 13th years of Nabonidus include the name of the Bēl- šar-uṣur, the crown prince, in unique oaths. Since a Harran inscription (*AS* 8, 1958, pp. 35–92; *ANET*³, pp. 562f.) gives 10 years for the exile of Nabonidus, this would confirm other sources since the 'king' who died in October 539 BC was Belshazzar (Dn. 5:30), whose father was captured on his subsequent return to the capital (Xenophon, *Cyropaedia*, 7. 5. 29–30, does not give names). Belshazzar (Aram. *Bēlša'ṣṣar*) is also called Balthasar (Gk. Baruch 1:11–12; Herodotus, 1. 188) or Baltasar (Jos., *Ant.* 10. 254).

BIBLIOGRAPHY. R. P. Dougherty, *Nabonidus and Belshazzar*, Yale Oriental Series 15, 1929; P. A. Beaulieu, *The Reign of Nabonidus King of Babylon 556–539* bc, 1989. D.J.W.

BELTESHAZZAR (Heb. *bēlṭᵉša'aṣṣar*; Gk. *Baltasar*). The name given to Daniel in Babylon (Dn. 1:7; 2:26; 4:8–9, 19; 5:12; 10:1). The Heb. may be a transliteration of the common Babylonian name *Belet/Belti-šar-uṣur* (May the Lady [wife of the god *Bel] protect the king'). For the form of the name, *Belshazzar, *Sharezer, and see A. R. Millard, *EQ* 49, 1977, p. 72. D.J.W.

BENAIAH (Heb. *bᵉnāyāhû*, *bᵉnāyâ*, 'Yahweh has built up'). **1.** Son of Jehoiada from Kabzeel in S Judah (2 Sa. 23:20). Captain of David's foreign bodyguard (2 Sa. 8:18; 20:23), he commanded the host for the third month (1 Ch. 27:5–6). He was renowned among 'the thirty' of David's mighty men (2 Sa. 23:20–23; 1 Ch. 11:22–25), and probably accompanied David during Absalom's rebellion (2 Sa. 15:18). He helped to thwart Adonijah and establish Solomon as king (1 Ki. 1) and later executed Adonijah, Joab and Shimei (1 Ki. 2:25, 29ff., 46), replacing Joab as commander-in-chief (1 Ki. 2:35).

2. One of 'the thirty' who formed the second group of David's mighty men, from Pirathon in Ephraim (2 Sa. 23:30; 1 Ch. 11:31), and commanded the host for the eleventh month (1 Ch. 27:14).

Ten other persons bearing this name are known only from the following references: 1 Ch. 4:36; 15:18, 20, 24; 16:5–6; 2 Ch. 20:14; 31:13; Ezr. 10:25, 30, 35, 43 (*cf.* 1 Esdras 9:26, 34–35); Ezk. 11:1, 13. J.G.G.N.

BEN-AMMI ('son of my kinship'). The name given to the child born of Lot's incestuous union with his younger daughter (Gn. 19:38), from whom sprang the children of *Ammon. Moses recognized their kinship, through Lot, with the children of Israel; and so directed that they should not be disturbed in the land which had been 'given them for a possession' (Dt. 2:19). Nevertheless, 'the children of Lot' in later times became their enemies (2 Ch. 20:1; Ps. 83:6–8). G.T.M.

BENE-BERAK. A town in the territory of Dan (Jos. 19:45), identified with modern el-Kheirîyeh (till recently Ibn Ibrâq), about 6 km E of Jaffa. According to Sennacherib it was one of the cities belonging to Ashkelon besieged and taken by him (*DOTT*, p. 66; *ANET*, p. 237). See *NEAEHL*, pp. 186–187. J.D.D.

BENEDICTUS. The prophecy of Zechariah (Lk. 1:68–79), named from the first word in the Latin version, is one of six visions (Lk. 1:5–25, 26–38; 2:1–20), and prophecies (Lk. 1:46–56; 2:29–35) in the Lucan infancy narrative. It is a recurrent pattern in Hebrew prophecy to reflect upon or elaborate former revelations (*cf.* Ps. 105; Mi. 4:4; Zc. 3:10). In the NT the Revelation of John is a mosaic of OT language and concepts. Likewise the Benedictus alludes to a number of passages in the Psalms and Isaiah.

The first division of the passage (Lk. 1:68–75), in parallelisms characteristic of Jewish poetry, extols God for his Messianic deliverance and rejoices in its results. The second section (Lk. 1:76–79) describes the place which John will have in this mighty act of God. In the Benedictus Messiah's work is particularly a spiritual deliverance. Does this mean that Zechariah's thought has itself been radically changed in the light of the interpretation of the OT by Christ and his apostles? Not necessarily. While the mass of Jews viewed the Messiah as a political Redeemer, his role as a religious or priestly Redeemer was not absent in Judaism (*cf. Test. Judah* 21. 1–3; *Test. Levi* 18. 2f.; *Test. Simeon* 7. 1f.; 1QS 9. 10f.; CD 19. 10; 20. 1). This would be central in the thoughts of a pious priest; therefore, it is quite in keeping with his personality and background that, 'filled with the Holy Spirit', Zechariah should utter this particular revelation. (*ANNUNCIATION.) E.E.E.

BENEFACTOR. The Gk. *euergetēs* was used as a title by kings of Egypt (*e.g.* Ptolemy IX, 147–117 BC) and of Syria (*e.g.* Antiochus VII, 141–129 BC) and appears on their coins; also on 1st century inscriptions, *e.g.* to the people of Cos (*LAE*, p. 253). Disciples of Jesus should not seek the title (Lk. 22:25) but should help the needy without thought of return.

BIBLIOGRAPHY. B. W. Winter, *Seek the Welfare of the City, Christians as Benefactors and Citizens*, 1994. A.R.M.

BENE-JAAKAN. A camping-ground of the Israelites (Nu. 33:31–32; Dt. 10:6). Formally it is a tribal name and refers to one of the clans of Seir (1 Ch. 1:42), which is a name for the mountainous region W of Wadi Arabah. No more exact location is possible, as the section of the itinerary in Nu. 33 in which it occurs could refer to one of a number of routes.

BIBLIOGRAPHY. J. R. Bartlett, *JTS* n.s. 20, 1969, pp. 1–12. G.I.D.

BEN-HADAD. Heb. form of Aramaic Bar- or Bir-Hadad, 'son of Hadad', name of either two or three rulers of the Aramaean kingdom of Damascus.

1. Ben-hadad I is called 'son of Tabrimmon, son of Hezion, king of Aram' in 1 Ki. 15:18. In his 15th year (35th of the divided Monarchy), Asa of Judah vanquished *Zerah the Ethiopian and held a great thanksgiving-feast in Jerusalem, inviting Israelites also (2 Ch. 14:9–15:19); therefore in the 16th (36th) year, Baasha of Israel attacked Judah (2 Ch. 16:1–10), and so Asa sought aid from Ben-hadad I of Aram (1 Ki. 15:18ff., as above). Hence Ben-hadad I was already ruling by *c.* 895 BC, say *c.* 900. For this period, see E. R. Thiele, *Mysterious Numbers of the Hebrew Kings*, 1951, pp. 58–60; 1965 ed., pp. 59–60.

2. Ben-hadad, the opponent of Ahab (*c.* 874/3–853 BC), 1 Ki. 20, died by the hand of *Hazael in the days of Joram (*c.* 852–841 BC) and Elisha (2 Ki. 6:24ff.; 8:7–15). Hazael succeeded Ben-hadad about 843 BC (Shalmaneser III of Assyria already mentions Hazael in 841 BC) (see M. F. Unger, *Israel and the Aramaeans of Damascus*, p. 75). Two problems here arise. First, is the Ben-hadad of Ahab and Joram Asa's Ben-hadad I (implying a long but not unparalleled 57 years' reign, *c.* 900–843 BC), or is he a separate Ben-hadad II? Albright (*BASOR* 87, 1942, pp. 23–29) would identify them as a single Ben-hadad (I), but his only positive reason is a possible date about 850 BC (limits, *c.* 875–825 BC) for the Melqart Stele on the style of its script. But the most natural interpretation of 1 Ki. 20:34 is that Omri had earlier been defeated by Ben-hadad I, father of a Ben-hadad II the contemporary of Ahab; Albright's interpretation of this passage is distinctly forced, and the non-mention by the OT of an event like Omri's discomfiture is well paralleled by its similar omission of Jehu's paying tribute to Shalmaneser III. Secondly, Shalmaneser III's annals for 853 BC (Wiseman, in *DOTT*, p. 47) and for 845 BC (*ANET*, p. 280a; *ARAB*, 1, §§ 658, 659) call the king of Damascus [d]IM-idri, probably to be read as Adad-idri ('Hadad-ezer'); this must be almost certainly another name for Ben-hadad (I/II), Ahab's contemporary; *cf.* Michel, *Welt des Orients*, 1, 1947, p. 59, n. 14. If two Ben-hadads are admitted, 'I' may be dated roughly 900–860 BC, and 'II' about 860–843 BC. The so-called Melqart Stele dates to this general period; attribution to a specific Ben-hadad is precluded by the illegibility of his ancestry on the monument, despite attempted solutions (*e.g.* Gross, *BASOR* 205, 1972, pp. 36–42).

3. Ben-hadad III, *c.* 796–770 BC, son of Hazael, continued his father's oppression of Israel (*temp.* Jehoahaz, *c.* 814/3–798 BC, 2 Ki. 13:22) into the reign of Jehoash (*c.* 798–782/1 BC), who, in fulfilment of Elisha's dying prophecy, was able successfully to repel Ben-hadad (2 Ki. 13:14–19, 25); this Aramaean king is also mentioned on the contemporary stele of Zakur, king of Hamath and Lu'ash (*cf.* Black, in *DOTT*, pp. 242–250). The unnamed 'deliverer' against Syria at this time (to Israel's benefit) may be a veiled reference to intervention by Adad-nirari III of Assyria against *Aram; *cf.* W. Hallo, *BA* 23, 1960, p. 42, n. 44, following H. Schmökel, *Geschichte des Alten Vorderasien*, 1957, p. 259, no. 4. Amos (1:4) prophesied the destruction of the 'palaces of (Hazael and) Ben-hadad', and their memory is evoked by Jeremiah (49:27) in his prophecy against the *Damascus province.

BIBLIOGRAPHY. For these kings, see A. Malamat, in *POTT*, pp. 143ff.; W. T. Pitard, *Ancient Damascus*, 1987.

K.A.K.

BENJAMIN. 1. The youngest son of Jacob, called *binyāmîn* ('son of the right hand', *i.e.* 'lucky') by his father, though his mother Rachel, dying in child-birth, called him *ben-'ônî* ('son of my sorrow') (Gn. 35:18, 24). After Joseph's disappearance, he took first place in his father's affections as the surviving son of Rachel; this was a major factor in bringing about the eventual surrender of Joseph's brothers (Gn. 42:4, 38; 44:1–34).

2. The tribe descended from Benjamin; Heb. *binyāmîn*, as collective, or pl. *b[e]nê binyāmîn*; also *b[e]nê y[e]mînî*, Jdg. 19:16; 1 Sa. 22:7; and sing. *ben y[e]mînî* or *ben hayy[e]mînî* (*cf.* *'îš y[e]mînî*, 1 Sa. 9:1; *'ereṣ y[e]mînî*, v. 4). A similar name *bīnū* (or *mārū*) *yamina*, possibly meaning 'sons of (dwellers in) the south', is found in the Mari texts (18th century BC), and some scholars, *e.g.* Alt, Parrot, have sought here the antecedents of the biblical tribe; but the difference in time and origin makes this very uncertain.

Much detail is given of Benjaminite genealogies, though they are nowhere complete; ten families are enumerated in Gn. 46:21, but the Chronicler names only three clans (1 Ch. 7:6ff.), of which Jediael does not appear as such in the Pentateuch. The pre-invasion reckoning of 'fathers' houses' is given in Nu. 26:38ff.; for details recorded under the Monarchy, see 1 Ch. 8.

The tribe occupied a strip of land in the passes between Mt Ephraim and the hills of Judah. The boundary with Judah is clearly defined (Jos. 18:15ff.; *cf.* 15:5ff.) and passed S of Jerusalem, which however became a Jebusite town until David captured it. Thence it ran to Kiriath-jearim, at one time in Benjamin (Jos. 18:28; RSV 'and' follows LXX, but the text is unclear). Jos. 15:9 supports this, while identifying with Baalah of Judah; Noth (*Josua*[2], *ad loc.*) considers this a gloss, but it is repeated in Jos. 15:60; 18:14; Jdg. 18:12; 1 Ch. 13:6; *cf.* 1 Ch. 2:50ff. The N border ran from Jericho to the N of *Ophrah, then roughly SW to the ridges S of *Beth-horon, leaving Luz in Ephraim (but perhaps originally not the sanctuary of *Bethel; Jos. 18:13). Under the Divided Monarchy, 'Ephraim' (*i.e.* the N kingdom) occupied Bethel and part of E Benjamin, but the border fluctuated; *cf.* 2 Ch. 13:9. The W border is given as a straight line from Beth-horon to Kiriath-jearim, but there was settlement farther W (1 Ch. 8:12f.).

'Benjamin is a ravenous wolf'—so ran the ancient blessing of Jacob (Gn. 49:27). The tribe earned a high reputation for bravery and skill in war, and was noted for its slingers with their traditional left-handed action (Jdg. 3:15; 20:16; 1 Ch. 8:40). Ehud, who delivered Israel from the Moabites, was of Benjamin; so also were Saul, the first king (1 Sa. 9:1), Queen Esther (Est. 2:5) and the apostle Paul (Rom. 11:1). Lying right in the path of Philistine expansion, the tribe played its chief part in Israelite history under Saul's leadership, and on the whole remained loyal to him, though a number came over to David in his exile (1 Ch. 12:2–7, 29). Indeed, the feud was remembered long after (2 Sa. 16:5; 20:1). Such clan loyalty was evident in their disastrous resistance to the national demand for justice in the matter of the Levite's concubine (Jdg. 20–21) many years before the Monarchy (20:26f.).

With the capital established at Jerusalem, Benjamin was drawn closer to Judah (1 Ch. 8:28), and after the division Rehoboam retained its allegiance (1 Ki. 12:21; 2 Ch. 11; note 1 Ki. 11:32, 'for the sake of Jerusalem'). There were two 'Benjamin' gates in the city, one in the Temple (Je. 20:2), the other perhaps the same as the 'sheep gate' in the N city wall (Je. 37:13; Zc. 14:10). Despite the varying fortunes of war, Benjamin remained part of Judah (1 Ki. 15:16ff.; 2 Ki. 14: 11ff.; *cf.* 2 Ki. 23:8, 'Geba'). From the Restoration, the distinction is confined to personal genealogy (*cf.* Ne. 7 with 11:7ff.).

In the vision of Ezekiel, the portion of Benjamin lies just S of the city (Ezk. 48:22ff.).

3. A descendant of Jediael (1 Ch. 7:10).

4. A Benjaminite of the Restoration who took a foreign wife (Ezr. 10:32). Ne. 3:23; 12:34 may refer to the same person.

BIBLIOGRAPHY. *Mari texts:* J. Gibson, *JSS* 7, 1962, pp. 57f.; I. Gelb, *JCS* 15, 1961, pp. 37f. *Topography:* Z. Kallai, *IEJ* 6, 1956, pp. 180–187; *VT* 8, 1958, pp. 139f.; *GTT*, pp. 164ff., 170ff.; *LOB* pp. 255f., 315, 349ff. *General:* K-D. Schunck, *ZAW Suppl.* 86, 1963; S. Yeivin, *IEJ* 21, 1971, pp. 141–154; *Israelite Conquest of Canaan*, 1971.

J.P.U.L.

BERACAH (lit. 'blessing'). **1.** One of the warriors who joined David at Ziklag when he was in straits because of the enmity of Saul (1 Ch. 12:1–3). **2.** A valley where Jehoshaphat and his people gave God thanks for the victory which they had gained over the Ammonites, Moabites and Edomites (2 Ch. 20:26). It is identified with Wadi Bereikūt between Jerusalem and Hebron, and W of Tekoa. The modern name suggests an earlier form which was pronounced slightly differently from that in the Heb. text with the meaning 'water pool' (*bereḵâ*).

R.J.W.

BERNICE. The eldest daughter of Herod Agrippa I, and sister of Drusilla, born in AD 28. Having been engaged, if not married, previously, she married at the age of 13 her uncle Herod of Chalcis. Upon his death in AD 48, she went to live with her brother Herod Agrippa II (an incestuous relationship with him is alleged in Juvenal, *Sat.* 6. 156–160). She then married Polemon king of Cilicia, deserted him and returned to her brother, in whose company she heard Paul (Acts 25:13). She subsequently became the mistress of the future emperor Titus. Josephus shows her in a more favourable light: in Jerusalem in AD 66 she intervened courageously in the attempt to prevent a massacre of the Jews by the procurator Florus (*BJ* 2. 309–314).

E.M.B.G.
C.J.H.

BEROEA, BEREA. 1. The modern Verria, a city of S Macedonia probably founded in the 5th century BC. In NT times it was evidently a prosperous centre with a Jewish colony. When Paul and Silas were smuggled out of Thessalonica to avoid Jewish opposition (Acts 17:5–11), they withdrew to Beroea, 80 km away. Here they received a good hearing until the pursuit caught up with them. Beroea was the home of Sopater (Acts 20:4). **2.** The Hellenistic name of Aleppo (2 Macc. 13:4).

BIBLIOGRAPHY. Strabo 7; *BC*, 4, pp. 188f., 206f.

J.H.P.

BETEN. One of the towns of Asher listed in Jos. 19:25. Its location is uncertain. Eusebius's *Onomasticon*, calling it Bethseten, puts it 8 Roman miles E of Ptolemais (Acco). It may be the modern Abtûn, E of Mt Carmel.

J.D.D.

BETHABARA (probably from Heb. *bêṯ ʿᵃḇārâ*, 'house of (the) ford'). This place is read in many Gk. MSS at Jn. 1:28 for *'Bethany beyond Jordan': hence it is found in AV and RVmg. Origen preferred this reading while admitting that the majority of contemporary MSS were against him. He gives its etymology as 'house of preparation', which he associated with the Baptist's 'preparation'. In his day, he says, this place was shown as the place of John's baptism. It is probably the present Qasr el-Yehud, on the right bank of the Jordan, E of Jericho, where a monastery of St John stands.

BIBLIOGRAPHY. R. E. Brown, *The Gospel According to John*, *AB*, 1971, pp. 44f., 71f.

J.N.B.

BETH-ANATH (Heb. *bêṯ ʿᵃnāṯ*, 'temple of Anat'). Perhaps Safed el-Battikh, NW of Galilee, and the *bt ʿnt* listed by Seti I and Ramesses II. The city was allotted to Naphtali (Jos. 19:38); the original inhabitants were not expelled, but made tributary (Jdg. 1:33).

BIBLIOGRAPHY. *LOB*, pp. 200, 214.

A.R.M.

BETH-ANOTH (Heb. *bêṯ ʿᵃnôṯ*, probably 'temple of Anat'). A conurbation (a city with its villages, Jos. 15:59) which was allotted to Judah. Modern Beit ʿAnûn 6 km NNE of Hebron.

J.D.D.

BETHANY. 1. A village (present population 726) on the farther side of the Mount of Olives, about 3 km from Jerusalem on the road to Jericho. It is first mentioned in the Gospels, especially as the home of Jesus' beloved friends, Mary, Martha and Lazarus; hence the modern Arabic name 'el-ʿAzariyeh. Its most central role in the Gospel history is as the place of Jesus' anointing (Mk. 14:3–9). Outside the Gospels it figures largely in Christian itineraries, traditions and legends.

2. The place where John baptized 'beyond the Jordan' (Jn. 1:28). Its identification remains uncertain. Already by the time of Origen (*c.* AD 250) it was unknown (see his *Commentary on John* 6:40, p. 157, ed. Brooke). Origen preferred the reading *Bethabara, since this place was known in his day and, moreover, this choice might in his opinion be corroborated by allegory. 'Bethany', however, should be accepted as the more difficult reading. The mention of a place so soon unknown is frequently adduced as a token of knowledge of 1st-century Palestine by the Evangelist or his source.

J.N.B.

BETH-ARBEL. A city described (Ho. 10:14) as having been destroyed by *Shalman in the 'day of battle'. The name is known only from this reference, so that the common identification with modern Irbid, probably the Arbela of Eusebius, some 30 km SE of the Sea of Galilee, remains uncertain. Note: *NEAEHL*, pp. 87–89, identifies it with a place W of the Sea of Galilee.

BIBLIOGRAPHY. W. F. Albright, *BASOR* 35, 1929, p. 10; G. L. Harding, *The Antiquities of Jordan*, 1959, pp. 54–56. T.C.M.

BETH-AVEN (Heb. *bêṯ 'āwen*, 'house of iniquity'). Lying to the W of Michmash (1 Sa. 13:5) and possibly to be distinguished from the Beth-aven said to lie to the E of Bethel (Jos. 7:2). If these two are to be distinguished, it is impossible to be certain which is referred to as a N boundary mark for Benjamin's allotment (Jos. 18:12). In Hosea (4:15; 5:8; 10:5) the name may be a derogatory synonym for *Bethel, 'House of the false (god)'. R.J.W.

BETH-DAGON (Heb. *bêṯ dāḡôn*). **1.** In the lowland of Judah S of *Azekah (Jos. 15:41). **2.** In Asher, probably N of *Helkath (Jos. 19:27). There were others; that taken by Sennacherib is now Bet Dagan near Tel Aviv (Z. Kallai, *VT* 8, 1958, pp. 153ff.; B. Mazar, *IEJ* 10, 1960, p. 72). J.P.U.L.

BETHEL. Identified by most scholars with Tell Beitīn on the watershed route 19 km N of Jerusalem. Although traces of earlier occupation have been found, the city seems to have been established early in the Middle Bronze Age. During this period, Abram camped to the E of Bethel, where he built an altar to Yahweh (Gn. 12:8). After his visit to Egypt, he returned for this site (Gn. 13:3). For Jacob, Bethel was the starting-point of his realization of God, who is for him 'God of Bethel' (Gn. 31:13; 35:7). As a result of his vision of Yahweh he named the place 'House of God' (Heb. *bêṯ 'ēl*) and set up a *pillar (Heb. *maṣṣēḇâ*, Gn. 28:11–22). He was summoned to Bethel on his return from Harran, and both built an altar and set up a pillar, reiterating the name he had given before (Gn. 35:1–15). The site is perhaps Burġ Beitīn, SE of Tell Beitīn, the 'shoulder of Luz' (Jos. 18:13).

Excavations yielded some Early Bronze Age traces, with, the excavator claimed, a blood-stained rock high place. This seems to be an improbable interpretation, and the claim that a Middle Bronze Age shrine replaced it is also dubious. The Middle Bronze Age city was prosperous, destroyed about 1550 BC, and followed by well-built Late Bronze Age houses. These in turn were sacked, and the subsequent Iron Age buildings marked a complete cultural change, which the excavator related to the Israelite conquest (Jos. 12:16; Jdg. 1:22–26). Bethel was allotted to the Joseph tribes who captured it, particularly to Ephraim (1 Ch. 7:28), and bordered the territory of Benjamin (Jos. 18:13). The Israel-

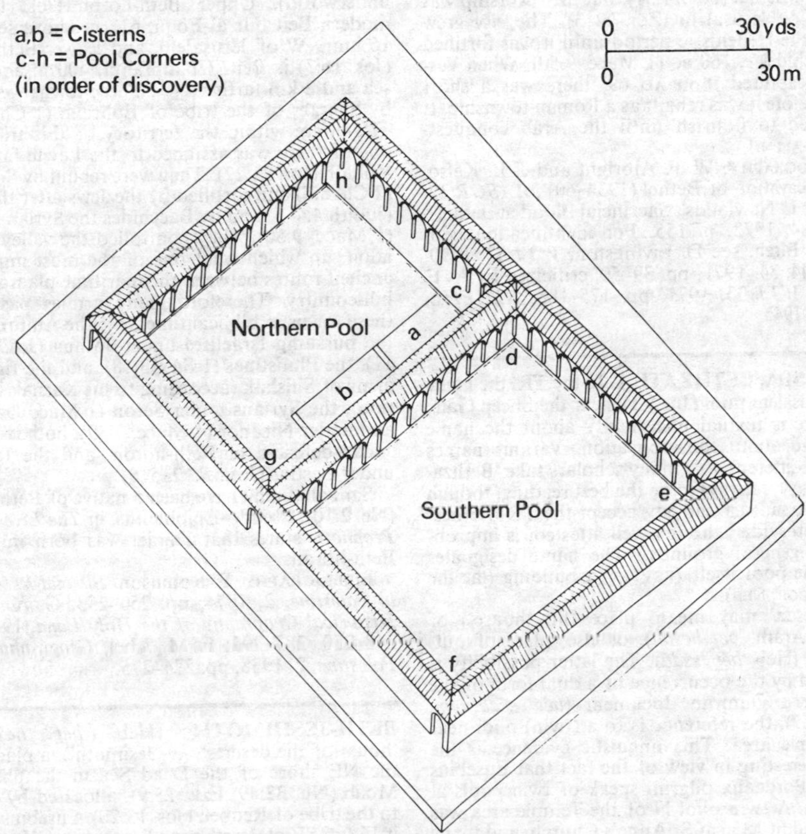

A proposed reconstruction of Bethesda pool (see p. 132).

ites soon resettled the town, calling it by the name Jacob had given to the scene of his vision instead of Luz (Jdg. 1:23). When it was necessary for Israel to punish Benjamin, the people sought advice on the conduct of the battle and worshipped at Bethel 'for the ark . . . was there' (Jdg. 20:18–28; 21:1–4). It was a sanctuary too in the time of Samuel, who visited it annually (1 Sa. 7:16; 10:3). The material remains of this period indicate an unsophisticated and insecure community. The settlement was twice burnt, possibly by the Philistines.

Under the early monarchy the city prospered, presently becoming the centre of Jeroboam's rival cult, condemned by a man of God from Judah (1 Ki. 12:28–13:32). The Judaean Abijah captured it (2 Ch. 13:19), and his son, Asa, may have destroyed it (2 Ch. 14:8). Elisha met a group of the 'sons of the prophets' from Bethel but also the mocking boys (2 Ki. 2:3, 23). Amos condemned the rites of the Israelite royal sanctuary (Am. 4:4; 5:5–6; 7:13; *cf.* Ho. 10:15), and Jeremiah showed their futility (Je. 48:13). The priest sent to instruct the Assyrian settlers in Samaria settled at Bethel (2 Ki. 17:28), and worship evidently continued there until Josiah took advantage of Assyrian weakness to invade Israel and destroy its sanctuaries. No traces of Jeroboam's shrine have been unearthed; it may well have been outside the city proper on the site of the patriarchal altars. In the 6th century BC the city was destroyed by fire. Returning exiles settled in Bethel (Ne. 11:31), but their worship was centred on Jerusalem (Zc. 7:2–3). The city grew during the Hellenistic period until it was fortified by Bacchides *c.* 160 BC (1 Macc. 9:50). When Vespasian captured it in AD 69, there was a short break before it was rebuilt as a Roman township. It continued to flourish until the Arab conquest. (*BETH-AVEN.)

BIBLIOGRAPHY. W. F. Albright and J. L. Kelso, 'The Excavation of Bethel (1934–60)', *AASOR* 39, 1968; D. L. Newlands, 'Sacrificial Blood at Bethel?' *PEQ* 104, 1972, p. 155. For identification with modern Bireh, see D. Livingston, *WTJ* 33, 1970, pp. 20–44; 34, 1971, pp. 39–50; criticized by A. F. Rainey, *WTJ* 33, 1971, pp. 175–188; *NEAEHL*, pp. 192–194.

A.R.M.

BETHESDA, BETHZATHA. In the TR, the name of a Jerusalem pool (Jn. 5:2), near the Sheep Gate; but there is textual uncertainty about the name itself and about its application. Various names occur in different MSS; many scholars take 'Bethzatha' (so RSV, JB, TEV) to be the best reading, though AV, RV, NASB, NEB and NIV accept the TR 'Bethesda'. ('Bethsaida', though well attested, is improbable on general grounds.) The name designates either the pool itself (RSV) or a building ('at the Sheep-Pool', NEB).

'Bethesda' may mean 'place (lit. 'house') of mercy' (Aram. *bêṯ ḥesdâ*), or else 'place of outpouring' (Heb. *bêṯ 'ešdâ*). The latter possibility is enhanced by the occurrence of a dual form of the name in a Qumran document (*bêṯ 'ešdāṯayin*, 3Q15, §57); the reference is to a (twin) pool near the Temple area. This linguistic evidence is the more interesting in view of the fact that Eusebius and the Bordeaux pilgrim speak of twin pools at Bethesda. A twin pool N of the Temple area was discovered in 1856 at St Anne's Church, and many have since identified it with the locale of Jn. 5:2; remains of magnificent porticoes seem to have survived. However, the identification remains uncertain; other pools in the same general area have been proposed; and some scholars have thought the Pool of *Siloam a possibility. If so, the word *probatikē* cannot refer to the 'Sheep *(Gate)*', which lay N of the Temple area; but other renderings are possible (*cf.*, *e.g.*, NEB).

BIBLIOGRAPHY. J. Jeremias, *The Rediscovery of Bethesda*, E.T. 1966; B. M. Metzger, *A Textual Commentary on the Greek New Testament*, 1971, *ad loc.*; D. Bahat, *Illustrated Atlas of Jerusalem*, 1990; and standard commentaries.

D.F.P.

BETH-HARAN (Nu. 32:36, to be identified with Beth-aram, Jos. 13:27). This site formed part of the allotment of Gad, and so lay on the E of the Jordan. It was probably a border strong-point which the Gadites built (Nu. 32:36) or else an existing settlement which they fortified (Jos. 13:27) to protect themselves and their cattle. The settlement was in good pasture (Nu. 32:1) but in the valley (Jos. 13:27), and so lacked the security of hill fastnesses which those who crossed the river enjoyed. Identified with modern Tell Iktanû 12 km NE of the mouth of the Jordan.

R.J.W.

BETH-HORON. A Canaanite place-name meaning 'house of Hauron' (a Canaanite god of the underworld). Upper Beth-horon (Jos. 16:5) is modern Beit 'Ûr al-Fôqâ, 617 m above sea-level, 16 km NW of Jeruṣalem, and Lower Beth-horon (Jos. 16:3) is Beit 'Ûr al-Taḥtâ, 400 m above the sea and 2 km farther NW. These towns were built by Sherah, of the tribe of Ephraim (1 Ch. 7:24). They were within the territory of this tribe, and one of them was assigned to the Levite family of Kohath (Jos. 21:22). They were rebuilt by Solomon (2 Ch. 8:5) and fortified by the Jews after the Exile (Judith 4:4–5) and by Bacchides the Syrian general (1 Macc. 9:50). They controlled the valley of Aijalon, up which went one of the most important ancient routes between the maritime plain and the hill-country. Therefore many armies passed by these towns in biblical times, *e.g.* the Amorites and the pursuing Israelites under Joshua (Jos. 10:10–11), the Philistines (1 Sa. 13:18), and the Egyptian army of Shishak (according to his Karnak inscription), the Syrians under Seron (1 Macc. 3:16, 24) and under Nicanor (1 Macc. 7:39), both of whom Judas defeated at Beth-horon, and the Romans under Cestius (Jos., *BJ* 2. 516).

Sanballat may have been a native of Beth-horon (Ne. 2:10). Pseudo-Epiphanius, in *The Lives of the Prophets*, states that Daniel was born in Upper Beth-horon.

BIBLIOGRAPHY. E. Robinson, *Biblical Researches in Palestine*, 2, 1874, pp. 250–253; G. A. Smith, *Historical Geography of the Holy Land*, 1931, pp. 248–250, 287–292; F. M. Abel, *Géographie de la Palestine*, 2, 1938, pp. 274–275.

J.T.

BETH-JESHIMOTH (Heb. *bêṯ hayšîmôṯ*, 'house of the deserts', AV 'Jesimoth'), a place near the NE shore of the Dead Sea in the plains of Moab (Nu. 33:49; Ezk. 25:9), allocated by Moses to the tribe of Reuben (Jos. 13:20). Eusebius places it 16 km SE of Jericho, and Josephus (*War* 4. 438) mentions it by its Greek name *Bēsimōth* (the nearby Khirbet Sueimeh), captured by the Roman tribune Placidus during the Jewish revolt. A well and some ruins (Tell el-'Azeimeh) remain. N.H.

BETHLEHEM (Heb. *bêṯ leḥem*, 'house of bread', the latter word probably in the wider sense, 'food'). It has been suggested that the final word *leḥem* is Lakhmu, an Assyrian deity; but there is no evidence that this god was ever revered in Palestine. There are two towns of the name in the OT, both today given the Arabic name Bayt Lahm, the exact equivalent of the Hebrew.

1. The famed city of David, as it came to be styled. It lies 9 km S of Jerusalem. Its earlier name was Ephrath (Gn. 35:19), and it was known as Bethlehem Judah, or Bethlehem Ephrathah, to distinguish it from the other city of the same name. Rachel's tomb was near it; David's ancestors lived there; the Philistines placed a garrison there; and the Messiah was destined to be born there. Jesus was accordingly born there, and the stories of the shepherds and the Magi centre upon it. Bethlehem suffered at the hands of Hadrian in the 2nd century AD, and all Jews were expelled from it; and it seems that the site of the nativity grotto was lost for two centuries; so the Church of the Nativity erected by Helena in the reign of Constantine may or may not mark the true site.

2. The second Bethlehem lay in Zebulunite territory (Jos. 19:15); it is 11 km NW of Nazareth. Most scholars think the judge Ibzan (Jdg. 12:8) was a resident of it, but ancient tradition favours Bethlehem Judah.

BIBLIOGRAPHY. *NEAEHL*, pp. 203–210; C. Kopp, *Holy Places of the Gospels*, 1963. D.F.P.

BETH-MARCABOTH (Heb. *bêṯ hammarkāḇôṯ*, 'house of chariots'). A part of the allotment to Simeon (Jos. 19:5; 1 Ch. 4:31). The site is uncertain but, being connected with Ziklag and Hormah, was probably a strong-point on the Judaean–Philistine border. The name suggests that the settlement may have been a Canaanite arsenal in the days of the conquest. The possession of chariots by the Canaanites prevented the unmounted Hebrew soldiers from entirely occupying the land (Jdg. 19). R.J.W.

BETH-NIMRAH. 'House of pure water' or 'House of leopard', a city in Gad (Nu. 32:36), probably equalling Nimrah (Nu. 32:3) and Nimrim (Is. 15:6; Je. 48:34). By Eusebius, called Betham-Naram and located 8 km N of Livias. Possibly either modern Tell Nimrin beside the Wadi Shaîb or nearby Tell Bileibil, some 24 km E of Jericho. G.W.G.

BETH-PEOR (lit. 'Temple of Peor'). A place in the hill country in the land of Moab (Jos. 13:20) or of the Amorites (Dt. 4:46), to the E of Jordan, which was part of Reubenite territory. The historical framework of Deuteronomy describes the Hebrews gathering at Mt Pisgah near to Beth-peor to receive their final exhortation before going over into the Promised Land (Dt. 3:29; 4:44–46). Having repeated the law to the immigrants, Moses died, and was buried nearby (Dt. 34:5–6). Beth-peor may be near, or even the same as, Peor, where Balaam built seven altars (Nu. 23:28). Nu. 25:1–5 mentions the worship of a god Baal Peor (Lord of Peor) by the Moabites. The site is uncertain. R.J.W.

BETHPHAGE (in Aram. 'place of young figs'). A village on the Mount of Olives, on or near the road from Jericho to Jerusalem and near Bethany (Mt. 21:1; Mk. 11:1; Lk. 19:29). Its site is unknown. See *ZPEB*, p. 112. J.W.M.

BETH-SAIDA. A town on the N shores of Galilee, near the Jordan. The name is Aramaic, meaning 'house of fishing' (if *bêṯ ṣaydâ*) or else 'fisherman's house' (if *bêṯ ṣayyāḏâ*). Philip the tetrarch rebuilt it and gave it the name Julias, in honour of Julia the daughter of Augustus. Pliny and Jerome tell us that it was on the E of the Jordan, and there are two likely sites, al-Tell or Mas'adiya. (The two are close together, the latter being nearer the actual shore.) But in Mk. 6:45 the disciples were sent from E of the Jordan to Beth-saida, towards Capernaum (*cf.* Jn. 6:17); hence a second Beth-saida has been postulated W of the Jordan—perhaps to be located at 'Ayn al-Tabigha. This is also claimed to be Beth-saida 'of Galilee' (Jn. 12:21), since the political division Galilee may not have extended E of the Jordan. But this is unlikely; 'Galilee' is not necessarily used in the technical sense. A suburb of Julias on the W bank may suit Mk. 6:45 best; Capernaum was not far away. D.F.P.

BETHSHEAN, BETHSHAN. A city situated at the important junction of the Valley of *Jezreel with the Jordan valley. The name occurs in the Bible as *bêṯ šᵉʼān* (Jos. 17:11, 16; Jdg. 1:27; 1 Ki. 4:12; 1 Ch. 7:29) and *bêṯ šan* (1 Sa. 31:10, 12; 2 Sa. 21:12). The name is preserved in the modern village of Beisân, adjacent to which stands Tell el-Husn, the 80 m high ruin mound which covers nineteen successive layers of occupation, excavated by C. S. Fisher (1921–3), A. Rowe (1925-8), G. M. Fitzgerald (1930–3), Y. Yadin and J. Geva (1983) and A. Mazar (1989–). The city was almost continuously occupied from Chalcolithic to modern times and for a long time was the most important Egyptian stronghold in the north.

Though a deep sounding was made, revealing settlements of the 4th millennium and an important Canaanite city of the Early Bronze Age, the main excavations were devoted to the 9 upper levels which extended from the 14th century BC to Islamic times. During much of the earlier part of this period, Bethshean was an Egyp. fortified outpost. Already in the 15th century Tuthmosis III mentions it as under his control (scarabs bearing his name were found there), and in the following century one of the Amarna letters speaks of reinforcements sent to garrison *bît-sa-a-ni* on behalf of Egypt. The earliest main level (IX) probably belongs to this century (the levels have been redated on the basis of pottery sequence, since the original dates of the excavators relied on less certain criteria), and in this an extensive temple dedicated to 'Mekal, the Lord (Ba'al) of Bethshan' was uncovered, in which were found the remains of a sacrificed 3-year-old bull (*SACRIFICE AND OFFERING).

Level VIII was comparatively unimportant, dating from about the end of the 14th century, but at this time Sethos (Seti) I was seeking to restore Egyp. control in Asia, and in his first year he retook Bethshean. Two of his royal stelae have been found there, one of them recording that he had a clash nearby with the *'pr.w* (*HEBREWS). Level VII (*c.* 13th century) contained a temple in which was found a stela depicting a goddess with a two-horned headdress (*ASHTEROTH-KARNAIM), and in level VI a similar temple was uncovered. This level probably dates to the 12th century, the time of Rameses III, of whom a statue was found there, and the discovery in the city cemetery of anthropoid clay coffins characteristic of the *Philistines suggests that these people were stationed as a mercenary garrison at Bethshean by Rameses. Arriving in Palestine, Manasseh was allotted Bethshean (Jos. 17:11), found it too formidable to take (Jos. 17:16; Jdg. 1:27), so that it remained in Canaanite hands until the time of David. The Bible refers to it as Bethshan 'and her daughters' (*i.e.* dependent villages) so it was clearly important. It was still in Philistine hands at the time of Saul, for it was upon its walls that his body and those of his sons were hung, and from which the men of Jabesh-gilead recovered them (1 Sa. 31:10, 12).

In level V (*c.* 11th century) two temples were uncovered, one (the S) dedicated to the god Resheph and the other to the goddess Antit, and Rowe has suggested that these are the temples of Dagon and Ashteroth in which Saul's head and armour were displayed by the Philistines (1 Ch. 10:10; 1 Sa. 31:10). The city must have fallen finally to the Israelites in the time of David, and the excavations have revealed little material settlement (level IV) from then until the Hellenistic Period (level III). During this time it is mentioned with its environs ('all of Bethshean', *kolbêṯ šᵉ'ān*) as belonging to Solomon's fifth administrative district (1 Ki. 4:12), and in the reign of Rehoboam (1 Ki. 14:25) Sheshonq (*SHISHAK) claimed it among his conquests. The city was refounded as the Hellenistic centre of Scythopolis, and this later became a part of the *Decapolis.

BIBLIOGRAPHY. A. Rowe, *Beth-shan*, 1, *The Topography and History of Beth-shan*, 1930; 2, i, *The Four Canaanite Temples of Beth-shan*, 1940; with which see G. E. Wright, *AJA* 45, 1941, pp. 483–485; G. M. Fitzgerald, *Beth-shan*, 2, ii, 1930; 3, 1931; *ANET*, pp. 242, 249, 253; J. Knudtzon, *Die El-Amarna Tafeln* 1, 1907, pp. 874f., no. 289. 20; 2, 1915, p. 1343 (= *ANET*, p. 489); W. F. Albright, 'The Smaller Beth-Shan Stele of Sethos I (1309–1290 BC)', *BASOR* 125, 1952, pp. 24–32; G. Posener in J. Bottéro, *Le Problème des Habiru*, 1954, p. 168 (= *ANET*, p. 255); G. E. Wright, *BA* 22, 1959, pp. 53–56, 65; (on anthropoid coffins) G. M. Fitzgerald, in *AOTS*, pp. 185–196; *NEAEHL*, pp. 214–235; Y. Yadin, *IEJ* 34, 1984, pp. 187–189; F. W. James and P. E. McGovern, *The Late Bronze II Egyptian Garrison at Beth Shan*, 1986.

T.C.M.

BETH-SHEMESH (Heb. *bêṯ šemeš*, 'house [temple] of the sun'), a name applied to 4 places in the Bible.

1. An important city of Judah (2 Ki. 14:11; 2 Ch. 25:21) on its N border with Dan (Jos. 15:10), situated in a W-facing valley of the hill-country some 24 km W of Jerusalem and consequently commanding a route from the uplands to the coast plain. The site is probably to be identified with modern Tell er-Rumeileh, situated on the saddle of a hill spur to the W of the later settlement of 'Ain Shems. Excavations were conducted in 1911–12, and more extensively in 1928–32. The site was first settled near the end of the Early Bronze Age, some time before 2000 BC, and flourished as a strongly fortified Canaanite city throughout the Middle and Late Bronze Ages, reaching its zenith in the time of the Egyptian domination under the pharaohs of Dynasty 19. Connections with the N are illuminated by the discovery in the Late Bronze Age levels of a clay tablet inscribed in the cuneiform alphabet of *Ugarit (Ras Shamra). The close of the Bronze Age is marked by quantities of *Philistine pottery, showing that these people, who settled initially along the coast, also established themselves well inland, where they became the chief rivals of the newly arrived Israelites. The city must have been taken by the Israelites in the period of the Judges, as it was set aside as a levitical city (Jos. 21:16; 1 Ch. 6:59), and was certainly in their hands by the time of Samuel, for thither the captured ark came when the Philistines released it (1 Sa. 6). It is probable that David strengthened this city in the later phases of his struggle with the Philistines, and it is likely that the casemate *walls discovered there date from this period. There is evidence that the city was destroyed in the 10th century, probably at the hands of the Egyptian king *Shishak, who invaded Judah in Rehoboam's fifth year (1 Ki. 14:25–28). About a century after this, Beth-shemesh was the scene of the great victory of Joash of Israel over Amaziah of Judah (2 Ki. 14:11–13; 2 Ch. 25:21–23). In the reign of Ahaz, Beth-shemesh was with other cities again taken by the Philistines (2 Ch. 28:18), but they were driven out by Tiglath-pileser III, to whom Ahaz had appealed and of whom Judah now became a vassal. Life in the city during the period of the monarchy was illuminated by the discovery of a refinery for olive-oil and installations for copper-working, which last had already existed in the Bronze Age. The city was now in decline, however, and it was finally destroyed by Nebuchadrezzar in the 6th century BC.

It is probable that Ir-shemesh, 'city of the sun' (Jos. 19:41), is to be equated with Beth-shemesh.

BIBLIOGRAPHY. D. Mackenzie, 'Excavations at Ain Shems', *Annual Report of the Palestine Exploration Fund*, 1, 1911, pp. 41–94; 2, 1912–13, pp. 1–100; E. Grant (and G. E. Wright), *Ain Shems Excavations*, 1–5, 1931–9; *NEAEHL*, pp. 249–253; J. A. Emerton, *AOTS*, pp. 197–206.

2. A city on the border of Issachar (Jos. 19:22), from which the Canaanites were not driven out, but became tributary to the Israelites (Jdg. 1:33), perhaps to be identified with modern el-'Abēdîyeh, which commands a ford over the Jordan some 3 km S of the Sea of Galilee.

BIBLIOGRAPHY. A. Saarisalo, *The Boundary between Issachar and Naphtali*, 1927, pp. 71–73, 119f.

3. A fortified city allotted to Naphtali (Jos. 19:38), whose site is unknown, unless it is to be identified with **2.**

4. A city in Egypt (Je. 43:13) probably to be identified with Heliopolis (which is here given in RSV) (*ON).

T.C.M.

BETH-SHITTAH (Heb. *bêṯ šiṭṭâ*, 'house of [the] acacia'). A town near Abel-meholah, to which the Midianites fled from Gideon (Jdg. 7:22). No definitive identification has yet been made.

J.D.D.

BETH-ZUR (Heb. *bêṯ ṣûr*). A city in Judah (Jos. 15:58), not mentioned in the account of the conquest, but settled by the descendants of *Caleb the son of Hezron (1 Ch. 2:45). It was fortified by Rehoboam in the 10th century (2 Ch. 11:7), was of some importance in the time of Nehemiah (3:16), and was a strategic fortified city during the Maccabean wars (1 Macc.).

The name is preserved at the site called Burj eṣ- Ṣur, but the ancient city is represented today by the neighbouring mound of Khirbet eṭ-Ṭubeiqah, about 6 km N of Hebron. The site was identified in 1924, and in 1931 an American expedition under the direction of O. R. Sellers and W. F. Albright carried out preliminary excavations, which, due to the troubled times, were not resumed until 1957, when a further season was undertaken under Sellers.

There was little settlement on the site until Middle Bronze Age II (*c.* 19th–16th century BC), in the latter part of which the Hyksos dominated Palestine, and it is probably to them that a system of massive defensive walls on the slope of the mound is to be attributed. When the Egyptians finally expelled the Hyksos from Egypt and pursued them well into Palestine, Beth-zur was destroyed and largely abandoned, and it evidently remained so throughout the Late Bronze Age (*c.* 1550–1200) and therefore offered no resistance to the armies of Joshua, as indicated by its absence from the conquest narratives. The Israelites evidently settled there, for in the 12th and 11th centuries the city was flourishing, though the population seems to have declined towards the end of the 10th century. No certain evidence of Rehoboam's fortifications has come to light, so it may be that he re-used the Middle Bronze Age walls and stationed only a small garrison there. The site was occupied throughout the Monarchy, abandoned during the Exile and resettled in the Persian period, but its zenith of importance came during the Hellenistic period. It was then a garrison city commanding the Jerusalem–Hebron road at the boundary between Judaea and Idumaea, and figured prominently in the Maccabean wars. A large fortress was uncovered on the summit, in which were found a great number of coins, including many of Antiochus IV Epiphanes, and several stamped Rhodian jar handles, indicating that it had been garrisoned by Greek troops. The fort had seen three main phases, the second probably due to Judas Maccabaeus, who fortified it after having defeated Antiochus' deputy Lysias there (1 Macc. 4:26–34, 61), and the third probably to be ascribed to the Macedonian general Bacchides, who fortified it around 161 BC (1 Macc. 9:52).

BIBLIOGRAPHY. O. R. Sellers, *The Citadel of Beth-zur*, 1933; W. F. Albright, *The Archaeology of Palestine*, revised edition, 1960, *passim*, esp. pp. 150–152; F. M. Abel, *Géographie de la Palestine*, 2, 1938, p. 283; R. W. Funk, *NEAEHL*, pp. 259–261.

T.C.M.

BEULAH. When the Lord saves Zion, her land shall receive this symbolic name, meaning 'married' (Is. 62:4, AV, RSVmg.). Expressing the closeness of the relation between Zion and her sons (v. 5a), and the restoration of Zion to her God (v. 5b, *cf.* Is. 49:18; 54:1–6; Ho. 2:14–20; contrast Ho. 1:2), the name foretells the fertility of the Messianic age. The Lord will be the *ba'al*, Husband, Guarantor of fruitfulness, on the basis of righteousness (Is. 62:1–2; Dt. 28:1–14).

J.A.M.

BEZALEL, BEZALEEL (Heb. *bᵉṣal'ēl*, 'in the shadow [protection] of God'). **1.** A Judahite, of Hezron's family in Caleb's house, Uri's son, Hur's grandson; gifted by God as a skilled craftsman in wood, metal and precious stones, and placed in charge of the making of the tabernacle; he also taught other workers. See Ex. 31:1–11; 35:30–35. **2.** A son of Pahath-moab, who was persuaded by Ezra to put away his foreign wife (Ezr. 10:30).

D.W.G.

BIBLE. Derived through Latin from Gk. *biblia* ('books'), the books which are acknowledged as canonical by the Christian church. The earliest Christian use of *ta biblia* ('the books') in this sense is said to be *2 Clement* 14:2 (*c.* AD 150): 'the books and the apostles declare that the church . . . has existed from the beginning'. *Cf.* Dn. 9:2, 'I Daniel perceived in the books' (Heb. *bassᵉpārîm*), where the reference is to the corpus of OT prophetic writings. Gk. *biblion* (of which *biblia* is the plural) is a diminutive of *biblos*, which in practice denotes any kind of written document, but originally one written on papyrus (Gk. *byblos*; *cf.* the Phoen. port of Byblus, through which in antiquity papyrus was imported from Egypt).

A term synonymous with 'the Bible' is 'the writings' or 'the Scriptures' (Gk. *hai graphai, ta grammata*), frequently used in the NT to denote the OT documents in whole or in part; *cf.* Mt. 21:42, 'Have you never read in the scriptures?' (*en tais graphais*); the parallel passage Mk. 12:10 has the singular, referring to the particular text quoted, 'have you not read this scripture?' (*tēn graphēn tautēn*); 2 Tim. 3:15, 'the sacred writings' (*ta hiera grammata*), v. 16, 'all scripture is inspired by God' (*pasa graphē theopneustos*). In 2 Pet. 3:16 'all' the letters of Paul are included along with 'the other scriptures' (*tas loipas graphas*), by which the OT writings and probably also the Gospels are meant.

The OT and NT—the *tawrat* (from Heb. *tôrâ*) and the *injīl* (from Gk. *euangelion*)—are acknowledged in the Qur'an (Sura 3) as earlier divine revelations. The OT in Hebrew is the Jewish Bible. The Pentateuch in Hebrew is the Samaritan Bible.

I. Content and authority

Among Christians, for whom the OT and NT together constitute the Bible, there is not complete agreement on their content. Some branches of the Syriac church do not include 2 Peter, 2 and 3 John, Jude and Revelation in the NT. The Roman and Greek communions include a number of books in the OT in addition to those which make up the Hebrew Bible; these additional books formed part of the Christian Septuagint.

While they are included, along with one or two others, in the complete Protestant English Bible, the Church of England (like the Lutheran Church) follows Jerome in holding that they may be read 'for example of life and instruction of manners; but yet doth it not apply them to establish any doctrine' (Article VI). Other Reformed Churches accord them no canonical status at all (*APOCRYPHA). The Ethiopic Bible includes *1 Enoch* and the book of *Jubilees*.

In the Roman, Greek and other ancient communions the Bible, together with the living tradition of the church in some sense, constitutes the ultimate authority. In the churches of the Reformation, on the other hand, the Bible alone is the final court of appeal in matters of doctrine and practice. Thus Article VI of the Church of England affirms: 'Holy Scripture containeth all things necessary to salvation: so that whatsoever is not read therein, nor may be proved thereby, is not to be required of any man, that it should be believed as an article of the Faith, or be thought requisite or necessary to salvation.' To the same effect the *Westminster Confession of Faith* (1. 2) lists the 39 books of the OT and the 27 of the NT as 'all ... given by inspiration of God, to be the rule of faith and life'.

II. The two Testaments

The word 'testament' in the designations 'Old Testament' and 'New Testament', given to the two divisions of the Bible, goes back through Latin *testamentum* to Gk. *diathēkē*, which in most of its occurrences in the Greek Bible means 'covenant' rather than 'testament'. In Je. 31:31ff. a new covenant (Heb. *b^e^rîṯ*, LXX *diathēkē*) is foretold which will supersede that which Yahweh made with Israel in the wilderness (*cf.* Ex. 24:7f.). 'In speaking of a new covenant, he treats the first as obsolete' (Heb. 8:13). The NT writers see the fulfilment of the prophecy of the new covenant in the new order inaugurated by the work of Christ; his own words of institution (1 Cor. 11:25) give the authority for this interpretation. The OT books, then, are so called because of their close association with the history of the 'old covenant'; the NT books are so called because they are the foundation documents of the 'new covenant'. An approach to our common use of the term 'Old Testament' appears in 2 Cor. 3:14, 'in the reading of the old covenant', although Paul probably means the law, the basis of the old covenant, rather than the whole volume of Hebrew Scripture. The terms 'Old Testament' (*palaia diathēkē*) and 'New Testament' (*kainē diathēkē*) for the two collections of books came into general Christian use in the later part of the 2nd century; in the W, Tertullian rendered *diathēkē* into Latin now by *instrumentum* (a legal document) and now by *testamentum*; it was the latter word that survived—unfortunately, since the two parts of the Bible are not 'testaments' in the ordinary sense of the term.

III. The Old Testament

In the Hebrew Bible the books are arranged in three divisions—the Law (*tôrâ*), the Prophets (*n^e^ḇî'îm*) and the Writings (*k^e^ṯûḇîm*). The Law comprises the Pentateuch, the five 'books of Moses'. The Prophets fall into two subdivisions—the 'Former Prophets' (*n^e^ḇî'îm rî'šônîm*), comprising Joshua, Judges, Samuel and Kings, and the 'Latter Prophets' (*n^e^ḇî'îm 'aḥ^a^rônîm*), comprising Isaiah, Jeremiah, Ezekiel and 'The Book of the Twelve Prophets'. The Writings contain the rest of the books—first, Psalms, Proverbs and Job; then the five 'Scrolls' (*m^e^ḡillôṯ*), namely Canticles, Ruth, Lamentations, Ecclesiastes and Esther; and finally Daniel, Ezra-Nehemiah and Chronicles. The total is traditionally reckoned as 24, but these 24 correspond exactly to our common reckoning of 39, since in the latter reckoning the Minor Prophets are counted as 12 books, and Samuel, Kings, Chronicles and Ezra-Nehemiah as two each. There were other ways of counting the same 24 books in antiquity; in one (attested by Josephus) the total was brought down to 22; in another (known to Jerome) it was raised to 27.

The origin of the arrangement of books in the Hebrew Bible cannot be traced; the threefold division is frequently believed to correspond to the three stages in which the books received canonical recognition, but there is no direct evidence for this (*CANON OF THE OLD TESTAMENT).

In the LXX the books are arranged according to similarity of subject-matter. The Pentateuch is followed by the historical books, these are followed by the books of poetry and wisdom, and these by the prophets. It is this order which, in its essential features, is perpetuated (*via* the Vulgate) in most Christian editions of the Bible. In some respects this order is truer to chronological sequence of the narrative contents than that of the Hebrew Bible; for example, Ruth appears immediately after Judges (since it records things which happened 'in the days when the judges ruled'), and the work of the Chronicler appears in the order Chronicles, Ezra, Nehemiah.

The threefold division of the Hebrew Bible is reflected in the wording of Lk. 24:44 ('the law of Moses ... the prophets ... the psalms'); more commonly the NT refers to 'the law and the prophets' (see Mt. 5:17, *etc.*) or 'Moses and the prophets' (Lk. 16:29, *etc.*).

The divine revelation which the OT records was conveyed in two principal ways—by mighty works and prophetic words. These two modes of revelation are bound up indissolubly together. The acts of mercy and judgment by which the God of Israel made himself known to his covenant people would not have carried their proper message had they not been interpreted to them by the prophets—the 'spokesmen' of God who received and communicated his word. For example, the events of the Exodus would not have acquired their abiding significance for the Israelites if Moses had not told them that in these events the God of their fathers was acting for their deliverance, in accordance with his ancient promises, so that they might henceforth be his people and he their God. On the other hand, Moses' words would have been fruitless apart from their vindication in the events of the Exodus. We may compare the similarly significant role of Samuel at the time of the Philistine menace, of the great 8th-century prophets when Assyria was sweeping all before her, of Jeremiah and Ezekiel when the kingdom of Judah came to an end, and so forth.

This interplay of mighty work and prophetic word in the OT explains why history and prophecy are so intermingled throughout its pages; it was no doubt some realization of this that led the Jews to include the chief historical books among the Prophets.

But not only do the OT writings record this progressive twofold revelation of God; they record at the same time men's response to God's revelation—a response sometimes obedient, too often disobedient; expressed both in deeds and in words. In this OT record of the response of those to whom the word of God came the NT finds practical instruction for Christians; of the Israelites' rebellion in the wilderness and the disasters which ensued Paul writes: 'these things happened to them as a warning, but they were written down for our instruction, upon whom the end of the ages has come' (1 Cor. 10:11).

As regards its place in the Christian Bible, the OT is preparatory in character: what 'God . . . spoke of old to our fathers by the prophets' waited for its completion in the word which 'in these last days' he has 'spoken unto us by a Son' (Heb. 1:1f.). Yet the OT was the Bible which the apostles and other preachers of the gospel in the earliest days of Christianity took with them when they proclaimed Jesus as the divinely sent Messiah, Lord and Saviour: they found in it clear witness to Christ (Jn. 5:39) and a plain setting forth of the way of salvation through faith in him (Rom. 3:21; 2 Tim. 3:15). For their use of the OT they had the authority and example of Christ himself; and the church ever since has done well when it has followed the precedent set by him and his apostles and recognized the OT as Christian scripture. 'What was indispensable to the Redeemer must always be indispensable to the redeemed' (G. A. Smith).

IV. The New Testament

The NT stands to the OT in the relation of fulfilment to promise. If the OT records what 'God . . . spoke of old to our fathers by the prophets', the NT records that final word which he spoke in his Son, in which all the earlier revelation was summed up, confirmed and transcended. The mighty works of the OT revelation culminate in the redemptive work of Christ; the words of the OT prophets receive their fulfilment in him. But he is not only God's crowning revelation to man; he is also man's perfect response to God—the high priest as well as the apostle of our confession (Heb. 3:1). If the OT records the witness of those who saw the day of Christ before it dawned, the NT records the witness of those who saw and heard him in the days of his flesh, and who came to know and proclaim the significance of his coming more fully, by the power of his Spirit, after his rising from the dead.

The NT has been accepted by the great majority of Christians, for the past 1,600 years, as comprising 27 books. These 27 fall naturally into 4 divisions: (*a*) the four Gospels, (*b*) the Acts of the Apostles, (*c*) 21 letters written by apostles and 'apostolic men', (*d*) the Revelation. This order is not only logical, but roughly chronological so far as the subject-matter of the documents is concerned; it does not correspond, however, to the order in which they were written.

The first NT documents to be written were the earlier Epistles of Paul. These (together, possibly, with the Epistle of James) were written between AD 48 and 60, before even the earliest of the Gospels was written. The four Gospels belong to the decades between 60 and 100, and it is to these decades too that all (or nearly all) the other NT writings are to be ascribed. Whereas the writing of the OT books was spread over a period of 1,000 years or more, the NT books were written within a century.

The NT writings were not gathered together in the form which we know immediately after they were penned. At first the individual *Gospels had a local and independent existence in the constituencies for which they were originally composed. By the beginning of the 2nd century, however, they were brought together and began to circulate as a fourfold record. When this happened, *Acts was detached from Luke, with which it had formed one work in two volumes, and embarked on a separate but not unimportant career of its own.

Paul's letters were preserved at first by the communities or individuals to whom they were sent. But by the end of the 1st century there is evidence to suggest that his surviving correspondence began to be collected into a Pauline corpus, which quickly circulated among the churches—first a shorter corpus of 10 letters and soon afterwards a longer one of 13, enlarged by the inclusion of the 3 *Pastoral Epistles. Within the Pauline corpus the letters appear to have been arranged not in chronological order but in descending order of length. This principle may still be recognized in the order found in most editions of the NT today: the letters to churches come before the letters to individuals, and within these two subdivisions they are arranged so that the longest comes first and the shortest last. (The only departure from this scheme is that Galatians comes before Ephesians, although Ephesians is slightly the longer of the two.)

With the Gospel collection and the Pauline corpus, and Acts to serve as a link between the two, we have the beginnings of the NT *Canon as we know it. The early church, which inherited the Hebrew Bible (or the Greek version of the LXX) as its sacred Scriptures, was not long in setting the new evangelic and apostolic writings alongside the Law and the Prophets, and in using them for the propagation and defence of the gospel and in Christian worship. Thus Justin Martyr, about the middle of the 2nd century, describes how Christians in their Sunday meetings read 'the memoirs of the apostles or the writings of the prophets' (*Apology* 1. 67). It was natural, then, that when Christianity spread among people who spoke other languages than Greek, the NT should be translated from Greek into those languages for the benefit of new converts. There were Latin and Syriac versions of the NT by AD 200, and a Coptic one within the following century.

V. The message of the Bible

The Bible has played, and continues to play, a notable part in the history of civilization. Many languages have been reduced to writing for the first time in order that the Bible, in whole or in part, might be translated into them in written form. And this is but a minor sample of the civilizing mission of the Bible in the world.

This civilizing mission is the direct effect of the central message of the Bible. It may be thought surprising that one should speak of a central message in a collection of writings which reflects the history of civilization in the Near East over several millennia. But a central message there is, and it is the recognition of this that has led to the common treatment of the Bible as a book, and not simply a collection of books—just as the Greek plural *biblia* ('books') became the Latin singular *biblia* ('the book').

The Bible's central message is the story of salvation, and throughout both Testaments three strands in this unfolding story can be distinguished: the bringer of salvation, the way of salvation and the heirs of salvation. This could be reworded in terms of the covenant idea by saying that the central message of the Bible is God's covenant with men, and that the strands are the mediator of the covenant, the basis of the covenant and the covenant people. God himself is the Saviour of his people; it is he who confirms his covenant mercy with them. The bringer of salvation, the Mediator of the covenant, is Jesus Christ, the Son of God. The way of salvation, the basis of the covenant, is God's grace, calling forth from his people a response of faith and obedience. The heirs of salvation, the covenant people, are the Israel of God, the church of God.

The continuity of the covenant people from the OT to the NT is obscured for the reader of the common English Bible because 'church' is an exclusively NT word, and he naturally thinks of it as something which began in the NT period. But the reader of the Greek Bible was confronted by no new word when he found *ekklēsia* in the NT; he had already met it in the LXX as one of the words used to denote Israel as the 'assembly' of Yahweh. To be sure, it has a new and fuller meaning in the NT. Jesus said 'I will build my church' (Mt. 16:18), for the old covenant people had to die with him in order to rise with him to new life—a new life in which national restrictions had disappeared. But he provides in himself the vital continuity between the old Israel and the new, and his faithful followers were both the righteous remnant of the old and the nucleus of the new. The Servant Lord and his servant people bind the two Testaments together (*CHURCH; *ISRAEL OF GOD).

The message of the Bible is God's message to man, communicated 'in many and various ways' (Heb. 1:1) and finally incarnated in Christ. Thus 'the authority of the holy scripture, for which it ought to be believed and obeyed, dependeth not upon the testimony of any man or church, but wholly upon God (who is truth itself), the author thereof; and therefore it is to be received, because it is the word of God' (*Westminster Confession of Faith*, 1. 4). (*BIBLICAL CRITICISM; *CANON OF NEW TESTAMENT; *CANON OF OLD TESTAMENT; *ENGLISH VERSIONS; *INSPIRATION; *INTERPRETATION (BIBLICAL); *LANGUAGE OF APOCRYPHA, OF OLD TESTAMENT, OF NEW TESTAMENT; *REVELATION; *SCRIPTURE; *TEXTS AND VERSIONS.)

BIBLIOGRAPHY. B. F. Westcott, *The Bible in the Church*, 1896; H. H. Rowley (ed.), *A Companion to the Bible*[2], 1963; B. B. Warfield, *The Inspiration and Authority of the Bible*, 1948; A. Richardson and W. Schweitzer (eds.), *Biblical Authority for Today*, 1951; C. H. Dodd, *According to the Scriptures*, 1952; H. H. Rowley, *The Unity of the Bible*, 1953; F. F. Bruce, *The Books and the Parchments*, 1953; A. M. Chirgwin, *The Bible in World Evangelism*, 1954; J. Bright, *The Kingdom of God in Bible and Church*, 1955; J. K. S. Reid, *The Authority of the Bible*, 1957; S. H. Hooke, *Alpha and Omega*, 1961; *The Cambridge History of the Bible*, 1–3, 1963–70; J. Barr, *The Bible in the Modern World*, 1973.

F.F.B.

BIBLICAL CRITICISM today involves various disciplines whose goal is the exact interpretation of the Bible. Most types of criticism aim to clarify the meaning of the text: they are not critical in the sense of challenging the text and its meaning. Traditionally, biblical criticism has been largely concerned with historical issues: who wrote the text? when was it written? what errors may have crept in through copying? what sources were used? *etc*. These are still the concerns of the majority of academic biblical scholars, but increasingly other forms of criticism are coming to the fore. These more modern criticisms tend to focus on the text in itself or on the reader. Text-oriented criticisms include rhetorical, canon, and the new criticism, while reader-oriented criticisms include audience, liberationist and feminist approaches.

Conventionally the relationship between a text, its author, its reader and the world is portrayed as follows:

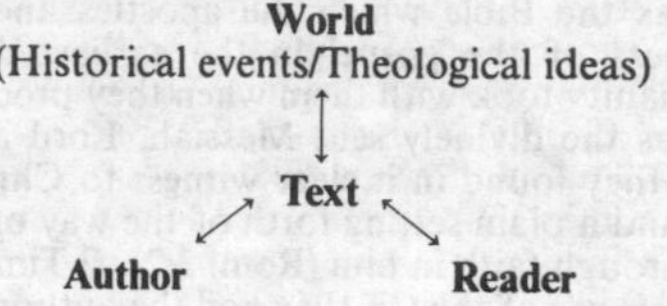

To understand the different types of biblical criticism it is preferable to work with a simplified diagram:

Author ⟶ **Text** ⟶ **Reader**
in his world   in our world

In the simplest form of communication a speaker sends a message, words, which are then heard by the listener. In this oral situation the worlds of speaker and hearer are usually the same, and communication is relatively simple. But when communication takes the form of writing, the possibility of misunderstanding the author's meaning is increased, especially in the case of biblical literature where language, culture, and a gap of thousands of years separate author and reader. The task of the biblical critic is to appreciate these gaps and to attempt to bridge them.

Traditional biblical criticisms concentrate their attention on the left-hand side of this diagram, on the author, his world, and his production of the text. Under the heading 'Author-centred approaches' we shall look at source criticism, redaction criticism, form criticism and textual and historical criticism.

I. Author-centred approaches

a. Historical criticism

The primary task of historical criticism is to determine who wrote a book and when. From the book of Nahum we can determine that it was probably written before the fall of Nineveh (612 BC) and after the fall of Thebes (663 BC *cf.* 3:8–9). It affects the interpretation of Revelation and the gospels whether they were written before or after the fall of Jerusalem (AD 70), so historical critics will try to determine their dates too. Historical criticism may involve evaluating claims for authorship within a book, *e.g.* the apostolic authorship of John or the trustworthiness of some books.

b. Source criticism

If a book was written long after the events it records, it could enhance its credibility to know what sources it was using and whether they were written close to the events they recount. The book of Kings often refers to the royal annals of Judah and Israel. Regrettably, these annals are lost, but their use by the author of Kings does make his narrative of distant events more trustworthy. It is often argued that the Pentateuch was composed from a variety of earlier sources (J, E, P, *etc.*) which take us closer to the events recorded; but this view is not unanimously held. Similarly, gospel source critics postulate sources such as Q, L and M, which they hope preserve the words of Jesus more exactly than the present gospels.

c. Form criticism

Behind the written sources, or the present texts, in the Bible may lie oral traditions. Many of the psalms may have been used in temple worship before being incorporated into the Psalter. Form critics examined the psalms to discover groups of them exhibiting similar patterns in phraseology or content. Groups of psalms with a particular form may have been used on similar occasions. National laments may have been used when Israel was facing a famine or defeat in war (*e.g.* Ps. 79), while individual thanksgivings (*e.g.* Ps. 116) may have been used when someone's prayer for healing was answered. Form criticism has also been used to establish the original setting of OT laws, or early Christian hymns lying behind parts of the epistles (*e.g.* Phil. 2:5–11) or sermons used in the writing of the gospels.

d. Redaction criticism

Parallel versions of history, gospels, or poems raise interesting issues. If the writer of Chronicles used the book of Kings, and the gospels of Matthew and Luke used Mark, what changes did Chronicles make to Kings or Luke to Mark and why? These are the questions redaction critics ask, and in formulating their answers they often shed light on the circumstances of writing, and the interests and theologies of the later writer. When redaction criticism is used where the earlier sources are not extant, as in the Pentateuch, the enterprise becomes much more speculative.

e. Textual criticism

If we possessed the original autographs of Genesis or Paul's epistles, textual criticism would be unnecessary. Unfortunately we do not. The earliest complete manuscript of the NT dates from about 300 years after its composition, while in the case of the OT the gap is more than 1,000 years. Whenever a text wore out, it had to be copied, and in the course of copying a number of mistakes were introduced. It is the aim of textual criticism to identify and, if possible, eliminate these mistakes. Jewish scribes were particularly scrupulous in copying the OT, so fewer mistakes have crept in than might be imagined, as the Dead Sea Scrolls from the turn of the era prove. Even in the less carefully copied NT, textual criticism can be fairly confident of restoring the text to its near-original purity.

All these branches of criticism essentially deal with the development of the text over time. If one imagines the growth of a biblical book, form criticism would deal with the earliest phase of its existence, source criticism the next, then historical criticism, and finally textual criticism. These types of criticism are diachronic, *i.e.* concerned with changes to the text over time. Recent critical study has a literary focus and tends to be synchronic, *i.e.* concerned with the text and its meaning at one point in time.

II. Text-centred approaches

a. Rhetorical criticism

Text-centred approaches focus on the text as it exists now, rather than on the processes whereby it has come into being. These synchronic approaches have a variety of emphases. Some, like rhetorical criticism, focus on surface features of texts, such as repetition and keywords, others deal with methods of storytelling, of writing poetry, and yet others claim to elucidate underlying structures of literature.

By rhetorical criticism I understand not just the study of persuasive techniques, but all approaches which are concerned with surface features of the text. We now realize that Hebrew writers had a range of tricks or devices that they used, maybe unconsciously, in composing poems or stories. Parallelism is the best known poetic device. In prose, repetition of phrases or keywords is very important. The beginning and end of sections may be marked by inclusion (repetition of the opening). Writing in parallel panels (ABCDABCD), or chiastically (ABBA), or in longer palistrophes (mirror-image patterns ABCDEDCBA, *etc.*) are some of the devices that have been noted in both OT and NT.

b. New criticism

New criticism holds that a literary work should be interpreted as a text on its own, without reference to its historical background or the author's intention. To this end, new critics pay very close attention to the way a book is composed: its plot, themes, its use of ambiguity and irony, the portrayal of character, the viewpoints of the actors and the narrator, *etc.* This involves close reading of the text, attention to subtle detail, such as slight variation in wording when material is repeated. Often new critics take account of the clues rhetorical criticism relies on (*e.g.* keywords), but try to integrate them within a total understanding of the work. This approach has led to some rich and powerful interpretations of biblical texts.

c. Structuralism

Whereas rhetorical and new criticism pay attention to textual features that may be presumed to have been consciously employed by writers, structuralists argue that literature also expressed deep structures that characterize all communication (*e.g.* binary contrasts). The jargon of structuralism makes many of its ideas difficult to grasp, but it is concerned to elucidate recurrent patterns of thought, *e.g.* in grammar, law, folk-tales and parables.

III. Reader-centred approaches

A message is encoded and sent by a speaker, then received and decoded by a listener. Similarly, a writer encodes a message in a text which is then read and decoded by a reader. The recognition that hearers or readers are involved in the reception of messages, though not a new insight, has become much more prominent in recent critical discussion. Previously, most attention had been given to trying to discover what the text said or what the author intended. Now it is recognized that the reader's input may significantly affect his understanding of the message. It is, of course, obvious that if a reader is a poor Hebraist, he or she could easily misunderstand an OT text. Or if a reader were insensitive to genre, he or she might misunderstand the parable of the Good Samaritan as history. Readerly incompetence will lead to misinterpretation. But the reader contributes much more than this. The reader brings to the text the pre-understanding, the questions, the cultural assumptions, the religious and ethical convictions, that are bound to affect his conclusions.

a. Audience criticism

When prophets preached, or apostles wrote epistles, they were addressing real people with particular outlooks and problems which the writer tried to address. Sometimes these beliefs were explicitly referred to, as Paul does in writing to the Corinthians: he seems to have received a letter to which 1 Cor. is a reply. In the case of Amos, there are few allusions to what his hearers were thinking, but if we are to make sense of the book's message, we must read it as a kind of dialogue between him and his listeners. Though the term 'audience criticism' is new, scholars have long been aware of the importance of establishing the original situation a text envisages if it is to be correctly understood.

b. Indeterminacy and deconstructionism

It is one thing to envisage the situation of the original readers: they knew the writer, his language, and the situation he was addressing. But the situation of the 20th-century reader is very different. There are many 'gaps' in the text, that is things left unsaid, which a modern reader must supply. And different readers will fill these gaps in different ways. Can we be sure who is right on how these gaps should be filled? The world of ideas we inhabit is quite different from the biblical, and our knowledge of the original setting of the texts is so patchy that we may completely misconstrue them. Furthermore, according to deconstructionists, there are contradictions within texts, which make establishing a determinate meaning impossible.

c. Ideological criticism

Not only is it very difficult for moderns to understand the biblical world, but it must be recognized that our preconceptions affect our reading of the text. Rather than pretend that we have no preunderstanding that we bring to the text, ideological critics believe that they should be openly acknowledged and that their effect on our readings be explored. One may approach the text as a materialist or a vegetarian. What would materialists make of the frequent references to the supernatural in the Bible? How would a vegetarian react to the concept of animal sacrifice? Criticism of biblical texts from these perspectives is rare, but liberationist/Marxist and feminist criticism is much more popular. Liberationists insist that texts be read from the standpoint of the poor and oppressed in the Third World, not, as is often done, from the standpoint of the comfort of the Western middle classes. What do the texts have to say about poverty and oppression? Feminist critics urge that texts be read from a woman's standpoint. Some insist that texts should be evaluated against the principles of modern feminism and the patriarchy of many biblical passages exposed. Others merely highlight those passages that acknowledge the equality of the sexes or laud women's achievements.

d. Concluding observations

The issues raised by modern criticism are highly complex and cannot be adequately dealt with here. Though author-centred approaches have dominated biblical studies for more than two centuries, and still do, there is much more validity in the other critical methods than has been recognized. In particular, the text-oriented approaches offer much of great value. Studies emanating from this school are gold-mines of exegetical insight (*e.g.* Alter, Berlin). Though many proponents of this school have wanted to divorce text from author and historical context, this is not really possible when we are reading an ancient text, as Sternberg has shown.

Reader-oriented approaches have drawn proper attention to the subjective input of the reader to all criticism. All readers come with their own agenda and preconceptions, which will inevitably colour their reading of a text. But this does not mean all readings are equally valid, or that texts are of indeterminate meaning. If that happened in everyday life, we should cease to communicate. Obviously it is easier to understand friends than those we meet for the first time, or those who speak a foreign language. But that does not mean we cannot understand someone or a text better if we work at it.

Reader-oriented critics are right to draw attention to the ideology of the reader. What we bring to a text in the way of assumptions and questions will influence what we find in them. In the post-modern world, where all truth is held to be relative, this does mean that any ideology may be brought to a text. But from a Christian perspective, there is only one God and therefore truth must be one, too. So it is essential for Christian critics to approach the text with a Christian ideology, not a secular one, or we will read against the grain of the text, imposing our own ideas on the Bible instead of letting it address us with God's message for us. Its agenda is to show us how to love God with all our heart, soul and mind, and our neighbour as ourselves. Unless we readers make that our priority, we are likely to distort its meaning at many points.

BIBLIOGRAPHY. All older introductions to the OT and NT are devoted to author-oriented criticisms. Evangelical evaluations of these approaches include: F. F. Bruce, *The NT Documents: Are They Reliable?*, 1960; C. Brown (ed.), *History, Criticism and Faith*, 1976; I. H. Marshall (ed.), *New Testament Interpretation*, 1977. Text and reader-oriented approaches are discussed by the following: R. Alter, *The Art of Biblical Narrative*, 1981; A. Berlin, *Poetics and Interpretation of Biblical Narrative*, 1983; J. Barton, *Reading the OT*, 1984; M. Sternberg, *The Poetics of Biblical Narrative*, 1985; R. Alter & F. Kermode, *A Literary Guide to the Bible*, 1987; T. Longman, *Literary Approaches to Biblical Interpretation*, 1987; L. Ryken, *Words of Delight: A Literary Introduction to the Bible*, 1987; *idem. Words of Life: A Literary Introduction to the New Testament*, 1987; A. C. Thiselton, *New Horizons in Hermeneutics*, 1992; F. Watson, *Text, Church and World*, 1994. G.J.W.

BILHAH (Heb. *bilhâh*). **1.** A servant-girl in Laban's household, given to Rachel on her marriage; in her mistress' place she bore Dan and Naphtali to Jacob (Gn. 29:29ff.). Theories which start from the assumption that the 'sons of Israel' never actually existed as one family must suppose 'sons of Bilhah' to have a special meaning; *e.g.* Steuernagel (followed by Burney, *Judges*, pp. cvif., cx n.) equates them with 'Canaanite tribes which amalgamated with Rachel tribes'; but there is no common factor in the records concerning Dan and Naphtali which would support such a hypothesis. **2.** A Simeonite settlement, 1 Ch. 4:29, spelt *bālāh* in Jos. 19:3, *ba'ᵃlâh* in Jos. 15:29; site unknown.

J.P.U.L.

BINDING AND LOOSING (Aram. *'ᵃsar* and *šᵉrā'*; Gk. *deō, lyō*). Rabbinic terms used in Mt. 16:19 of Peter's doctrinal authority to declare things forbidden or permitted; and in Mt. 18:18 of the disciples' disciplinary authority to condemn or absolve. The disciplinary authority differs from personal rabbinic power in being inseparable from the gospel proclaimed; so in Mt. 10:12–15 the preaching disciples pronounce no human judgment; and in Mt. 13:30; 22:13, the 'binding' symbolism signifies divine judgment. The doctrinal authority is exercised through the apostolic teaching (Acts 2:42) and a teaching ministry (2 Tim. 2:24–26), not indiscriminately.

deō (alone) is used symbolically of marriage (1 Cor. 7:29), legal ties (Rom. 7:2), and Paul's service (Acts 20:22). *lyō* (alone) is used of laws relaxed (Mt. 5:19), sins forgiven (Rev. 1:5), and (*cf. deō*) of deliverance (Lk. 13:16).

BIBLIOGRAPHY. *IDB*, 1, p. 438; R. Bultmann, *The History of the Synoptic Tradition*², 1968; *JewE*, 3, p. 215; O. Cullmann, *Peter: Disciple–Apostle–Martyr*, 1953, pp. 204–206.

D.H.T.

BIRTHDAY. The day of birth and its anniversaries were usually a day of rejoicing and often of feasting. Only two such anniversaries are recorded in Scripture, that of Joseph's pharaoh (Gn. 40:20) and that of Herod Antipas (Mt. 14:6; Mk. 6:21). In Egypt, celebration of birthdays is mentioned at least as early as the 13th century BC, and probably goes back much earlier (Helck and Otto, *Kleines Wörterbuch der Ägyptologie*, 1956, p. 115, with textual references). Pharaoh's accession was likewise kept as a feast-day, as is indicated by a text of Amenophis II, *c.* 1440 BC (Helck, *JNES* 14, 1955, pp. 22–31); observation of the royal birthday is attested under Ptolemy V (*c.* 205–182 BC; Budge, *The Rosetta Stone*, 1951, p. 8). An amnesty on a royal birthday is mentioned in a wisdom-papyrus of the 4th/5th century BC (S. R. K. Glanville, *The Instructions of 'Onchsheshonqy*, 1, 1955, p. 13). The birthday celebrations of the Herods were well known in Rome; see H. Hoehner, *Herod Antipas*, 1972, pp. 160–161, n. 5.

K.A.K.

BISHOP.

I. Application of the term

In classical Greek, both gods and men can be described as *episkopoi* or 'overseers' in a general and non-technical sense; inscriptions and papyri of wide distribution use the word to denote magistrates, who sometimes appear to have administered the revenues of heathen temples; Plutarch (*Numa* 9) calls the Roman pontifex *episkopos* of the Vestal Virgins; and the word can apply also to philosophers, especially Cynics, when acting as spiritual directors. The LXX employs the same term to describe taskmasters or officers (Ne. 11:9; Is. 60:17), and *episkopē* in reference to a visitation of God (Gn. 50:24; *cf.* Lk. 19:44). In the NT the name is applied pre-eminently to Christ (1 Pet. 2:25), next to the apostolic office (Acts 1:20, quoting Ps. 109:8), and finally to the leaders of a local congregation (Phil. 1:1).

II. Qualifications and function

It is improbable that the Christian use of the term was directly copied from either pagan or Jewish sources; taken over as a generic description of responsible office, its meaning was defined in accordance with the qualifications demanded by the church. These are listed in 1 Tim. 3:1ff. and Tit. 1:7ff.: blameless moral character, teaching ability, a hospitable nature, patience, experience, sobriety, leadership and complete integrity, or in other words, the qualities required in a good teacher, pastor and administrator. It appears to be virtually certain that the terms 'bishop' and *'presbyter' are synonymous in the NT. In Acts 20:17, 28 Paul describes the presbyters of Ephesus as *episkopoi*; he says that the Holy Spirit has made them overseers of the flock, and this might be thought to imply that only now in his absence are they to succeed to the episcopal duties which he himself has previously performed; but the usage elsewhere current is against this interpretation. Thus, in Tit. 1:5 Titus is enjoined to ordain elders, and immediately afterwards (v. 7), in obvious reference to the same persons, the qualifications of a bishop are described; again, the verb *episkopein* is used to describe the elders' function in 1 Pet. 5:2; and while 1 Tim. 3 confines itself to bishops and deacons, the mention of elders in 5:17 suggests that the eldership is another name for the episcopate. There was a plurality of bishops in the single congregation at Philippi (Phil. 1:1), from which we may conclude that they acted corporately as its governing body.

III. The rise of monarchical episcopacy

There is no trace in the NT of government by a single bishop; the position of James at Jerusalem (Acts 15:13; 21:18; Gal. 2:9, 12) was quite exceptional, and the result of his personal relationship to Christ; but influence is a different thing from office. Among the Apostolic Fathers, Ignatius is the only one who insists on monarchical episcopacy, and even he never states that this is of divine institution—an argument which would have been decisive, if it had been available for him to use. Jerome, commenting on Tit. 1:5, remarks that the supremacy of a single bishop arose 'by custom rather than by the Lord's actual appointment', as a means of preventing schisms in the church (*cf. Ep.* 146). It seems most probable that monarchical episcopacy appeared in the local congregations when some gifted individual acquired a permanent chairmanship of the board of presbyter-bishops, or when the church expanded, and the presbyters were scattered to outlying congregations, leaving only one of their number in the mother church. Harnack thought that the elders were the ruling body, while the bishops and deacons were the liturgical leaders and administrators employed by them. Others have seen the origins of the later episcopate in the position held by Paul's lieutenants Timothy and Titus; but these men are never called bishops, and we meet them in letters of recall, which make no clear provision for the appointment of personal successors. Whatever may have been the reason for the rise of the monarchical episcopate, its effect was to divide up the tasks and attributes of the presbyter-bishop, some of them adhering to the bishop and some to the presbyter.

We do not know how bishops were at first instituted to their office; but the emphasis on popular election in Acts 6, Clement of Rome and the *Didache* suggests that this was an early practice; and it was doubtless followed by prayer and imposition of hands (*CHURCH GOVERNMENT).

BIBLIOGRAPHY. See under *MINISTRY and *PRESBYTER. G.S.M.W.
R.T.B.

BITHYNIA. A territory on the Asiatic side of the Bosporus, bequeathed by its last king to the Romans in 74 BC and subsequently administered with Pontus as a single province. The area was partitioned between a number of flourishing Greek republics. It early attracted the attention of Paul (Acts 16:7), though he apparently never fulfilled his ambition of preaching there. Others did so, however (1 Pet. 1:1), and by AD 111 there was a thoroughly well-established church, even extending to rural areas, which had excited a good deal of local opposition (Pliny, *Ep*. 10. 96). E.A.J.

BITUMEN. In the EVV of the OT the Hebrew words *kōp̄er* (Gn. 6:14) and *zep̄eṯ* (Ex. 2:3; Is. 34:9) are rendered 'pitch', and *ḥēmār* (Gn. 11:3; 14:10; Ex. 2:3) 'bitumen' (AV 'slime'). It would seem better, however, to render all three terms by 'bitumen', since, while pitch is strictly the product of a distillation process, bitumen, a natural derivative of crude petroleum, is found ready to hand in Mesopotamia and Palestine, and is therefore more probably the material referred to. The word *kōp̄er* is derived from Akkadian *kupru* (from *kapāru*, 'to smear'), an outside origin for *zep̄eṯ* is suggested by its W and S Semitic cognates, while *ḥēmār* may be a native Hebrew word from the verb *ḥāmar*, 'to ferment, boil up'. In view of the diverse origins of the three terms, it seems probable that they all meant the same thing and that no scientific distinctions are to be observed. (*ARK.)

BIBLIOGRAPHY. R. J. Forbes, *Studies in Ancient Technology*, 1, 1955, pp. 1–120; *KB*[3], p. 471.
T.C.M.

BLASPHEMY.

I. In the Old Testament

Here the root meaning of the word is an act of effrontery in which the honour of God is insulted by man. The proper object of the verb is the name of God, which is cursed or reviled instead of being honoured. (Compare the common biblical and rabbinical phrase, 'Blessed art thou, O Lord.') The penalty of the outrage of blasphemy is death by stoning (Lv. 24:10–23; 1 Ki. 21:9ff.; Acts 6:11; 7:58).

In the first reference it is a half-caste Israelite who sins in this way; and, generally speaking, blasphemy is committed by pagans (2 Ki. 19:6, 22 = Is. 37:6, 23; Pss. 44:16; 74:10, 18; Is. 52:5), sometimes incited to it by the bad example and moral lapses of the Lord's people (2 Sa. 12:14). It follows also that when God's people fall into idolatry they are regarded as committing the blasphemy of the heathen (Is. 65:7; Ezk. 20:27). The name of Yahweh which it is Israel's peculiar destiny to hallow (see G. F. Moore, *Judaism*, 2, 1927–30, p. 103) is profaned by the faithless and disobedient people.

II. In the New Testament

Here there is an extension of the meaning. God is blasphemed also in his representatives. So the word is used of Moses (Acts 6:11); Paul (Rom. 3:8; 1 Cor. 4:12; 10:30); and especially the Lord Jesus, in his ministry of forgiveness (Mk. 2:7 and parallels), at his *trial (Mk. 14:61–64), and at Calvary (Mt. 27:39; Lk. 23:39). Because these representatives embody the truth of God himself (and our Lord in a unique way), an insulting word spoken against them and their teaching is really directed against the God in whose name they speak (so Mt. 10:40; Lk. 10:16). Saul of Tarsus fulminated against the early followers of Jesus and tried to compel them to blaspheme, *i.e.* to curse the saving name (Acts 24:11), and thereby to renounce their baptismal vow in which they confessed that 'Jesus is Lord' (*cf.* 1 Cor. 12:3; Jas. 2:7). His misdirected zeal, however, was not simply against the church, but against the Lord himself (1 Tim. 1:13; *cf.* Acts 9:4).

The term is also used, in a weaker sense, of slanderous language addressed to men (*e.g.* Mk. 3:28; 7:22; Eph. 4:31; Col. 3:8; Tit. 3:2). Here the best translation is 'slander, abuse'. These verses condemn a prevalent vice; but their warning may be grounded in a theological as well as an ethical context if we remember Jas. 3:9. Men are not to be cursed because on them, as men, the 'formal' image of God is stamped and the human person is, in some sense, God's representative on earth (*cf.* Gn. 9:6).

There are two problem texts. 2 Pet. 2:10–11 speaks of blasphemy against 'the glorious ones' whom angels dare not revile. These are probably evil angelic powers against whom false teachers presumed to direct their insults (*cf.* Jude 8). The blasphemy against the Holy Spirit (Mt. 12:32; Mk. 3:29) carries with it the awful pronouncement that the sinner is 'guilty of an eternal sin' which cannot be forgiven. The verse is a solemn warning against persistent, deliberate rejection of the Spirit's call to salvation in Christ. Human unresponsiveness inevitably leads to a state of moral insensibility and to a confusion of moral issues wherein evil is embraced as though it were good ('Evil, be thou my Good'; *cf.* Is. 5:18–20; Jn. 3:19). The example of this attitude is that of the Pharisees, who attributed Jesus' works of mercy to Satan. In such a frame of mind repentance is not possible to the hardened heart because the recognition of sin is no longer possible, and God's offer of mercy is in effect peremptorily refused. To be in this perilous condition is to cut oneself off from the source of forgiveness. Hebert adds a helpful pastoral note: 'People who are distressed in their souls for fear that they have committed the sin against the Holy Ghost should in most cases be told that their distress is proof that they have not committed that sin' (*TWBR*, p. 32).

BIBLIOGRAPHY. H. W. Beyer, *TDNT* 1, pp. 621–625; H. Währisch, *et al.*, *NIDNTT* 3, pp. 340–347; G. H. Twelftree, *DJG*, pp. 75–77; O. Hofius, *EDNT* 1, pp. 220–221. R.P.M.

BLESSED. The most frequent OT word is *bārûḵ*. When applied to God it has the sense of praise (Gn. 9:26; 1 Ki. 1:48; Ps. 28:6, *etc.*), and when used of man denotes a state of happiness (1 Sa. 26:25; 1 Ki. 2:45). *'ašrê* ('how happy!', Ps. 1:1) is always used of man and has for its NT equivalent *maka-*

rios. The latter is used in pagan Greek literature to describe the state of happiness and well-being such as the gods enjoy. In the NT it is given a strong spiritual content, as revealed in the Beatitudes (Mt. 5:3–11) and elsewhere (Lk. 1:45; Jn. 20:29; Acts 20:35; Jas. 1:12). The word seems also to contain a congratulatory element, as a note in *Weymouth's New Testament* suggests: 'People who are blessed may outwardly be much to be pitied, but from the higher and therefore truer standpoint they are to be envied, congratulated, and imitated.' *eulogētos* is used only of Christ and God (Rom. 9:5; Eph. 1:3).

BIBLIOGRAPHY. J. Pedersen, *Israel: Its Life and Culture*, 1926; *TDOT* 1, pp. 445–448; *TDNT* 4, pp. 362–370; *NIDNTT* 1, pp. 215–217. W.W.W.

BLESSING. The OT word is *b^e rāḵâ*, and generally denotes a bestowal of good, usually conceived of as material (Dt. 11:26; Pr. 10:22; 28:20; Is. 19:24, *etc*.). Often it is contrasted with the curse (Gn. 27:12; Dt. 11:26–29; 23:5; 28:2; 33:23), and sometimes is used of the formula of words which constitute a 'blessing' (Gn. 27:36, 38, 41; Dt. 33:1). The NT word *eulogia* is used also in the latter sense (Jas. 3:10), but in addition denotes both the spiritual good brought by the gospel (Rom. 15:29 mg.; Eph. 1:3) and material blessings generally (Heb. 6:7; 12:17; 2 Cor. 9:5, 'gift').

BIBLIOGRAPHY. H. W. Beyer, *TDNT* 2, pp. 754–764; H.-G. Link, U. Becker, *NIDNTT* 1, pp. 206–218. W.W.W.

BLOOD. The point chiefly to be determined is whether 'blood' in biblical usage points basically to life or to death. There are those who hold that in the sacrificial system of the OT 'blood' represents life liberated from the limitations of the body and set free for other purposes. The ceremonial manipulation of blood on this view represents the solemn presentation to God of life, life surrendered, dedicated, transformed. The death occupies a subordinate place or even no place at all. On this view 'the blood of Christ' would mean little more than 'the life of Christ'. The evidence, however, does not seem to support it.

In the first place there is the statistical evidence. Of the 362 passages in which the Hebrew word *dam* occurs in the OT, 203 refer to death with violence. Only six passages connect life and blood (17 refer to the eating of meat with blood). From this it is clear enough that death is the association most likely to be conjured up by the use of the term.

Then there is the lack of evidence adduced in support of the life theory. Exponents of this view regard it as self-evident from passages such as Lv. 17:11, 'the life of the flesh is in the blood'. But the scriptural passages can just as well be interpreted of life yielded up in death, as of life set free.

It is undeniable that in some places atonement is said to have been secured by death, *e.g.* Nu. 35:33, 'for blood pollutes the land, and no expiation can be made for the land (lit. for the land it will not be atoned) for the blood that is shed in it, except by the blood of him who shed it'. See also Ex. 29:33; Lv. 10:17.

The OT, then, affords no grounds for the far-reaching statements that are sometimes made. *Atonement is secured by the death of a victim rather than by its life. This carries over into the NT. There, as in the OT, blood is more often used in the sense of death by violence than in any other sense. When we come to the blood of Christ there are some passages which indicate in the plainest possible fashion that death is meant. Such are the references to being 'justified by his blood' (Rom. 5:9; parallel to 'reconciled . . . by the death of his Son' in v. 10), 'the blood of his cross' (Col. 1:20), the reference to coming 'by water and blood' (1 Jn. 5:6), and others.

Sometimes the death of Christ is thought of as a sacrifice (*e.g.* the blood of the covenant). But a close examination of all these passages indicates that the term is used in the same way as in the OT. That is to say, the sacrifices are still understood to be efficacious by virtue of the death of the victim. 'The blood of Christ' accordingly is to be understood of the atoning death of the Saviour.

BIBLIOGRAPHY. *TDNT* 1, pp. 172–177; S. C. Gayford, *Sacrifice and Priesthood*[2], 1953; L. Morris, *The Apostolic Preaching of the Cross*[3], 1965; F. J. Taylor, in *TWBR*; H. C. Trumbull, *The Blood Covenant*, 1887; A. M. Stibbs, *The Meaning of the Word 'Blood' in Scripture*, 1947. L.M.

BOANERGES. The name given by Jesus to the sons of Zebedee and recorded only in Mk. 3:17. Its derivation is uncertain, but it is most likely to be the equivalent of the Heb. *b^e nê reḡeš* ('sons of confusion or thunder') but might be from *b^e nê r^e gaz* ('sons of wrath'; *cf.* Jb. 37:2). It is strange that *b^e nê* should be transliterated by *boanē-* in Gk.; a dialect pronunciation is probably indicated.

The title seems not to have been greatly used. It is variously seen to be appropriate in their fiery temper (Lk. 9:54–56), which may have caused James' death (Acts 12:2), and in the heavenly resonance of the Johannine writings. R.E.N.

BOAZ. The hero of the book of *Ruth, a wealthy landowner of Bethlehem, a benevolent farmer who had a concern for his workers' welfare and a sense of family responsibility. This led him to redeem Ruth, the widow of a distant relative, in place of her next-of-kin, under the levirate marriage law. He thus became the great-grandfather of David (Ru. 4:17–22; *cf.* Mt. 1:5). M.B.

BODY. The principal Hebrew words translated 'body' are *g^e wiyyâ*, used primarily of a 'corpse', though also of the living human body (Gn. 47:18), and *bāśār*, which means *'flesh'. Contrary to Greek philosophy and much modern thought, the emphasis in Hebrew is not on the body as distinct from the soul or spirit. J. A. T. Robinson (*The Body*, 1952) maintains that the Hebrews did not rigidly differentiate (*i*) form and matter, (*ii*) the whole and its parts, (*iii*) body and soul, or (*iv*) the body from the next self or object. 'The flesh-body was not what partitioned a man off from his neighbour, it was rather what bound him in the bundle of life with all men and nature.' In Aramaic sections of Daniel, often regarded as late and influenced by Greek thought, there may be more of a distinction between body and spirit (7:15), where the word (*niḏneh*) translated 'within *me*' is probably a loan-word, from Persian, meaning 'sheath'.

The common Hebrew word for flesh (*bāśār*) comes near to presenting a distinction from spirit

(Is. 31:3), and may have influenced Paul in his theological use of the term. The usage of the term for *'heart' in Heb. could perhaps be said to approach what we would mean by spirit (Ps. 84:2), but it is significant that it is at the same time a physical organ. It is noteworthy that much modern psychology is realizing the essential unity of the whole man.

On the other hand, in Hebrew thought there were no clearly defined physiologically unifying concepts, such as the nervous or circulatory systems, and the various organs are sometimes spoken of as having a seeming independence of action (Mt. 5:29, 30) (*EYE, *HAND, *LIP, *etc.*), though this is obviously synecdoche in certain passages, *e.g.* Dt. 28:4, *beṭen* = 'belly', translated 'body' in RSV. Likewise La. 4:7, *'eṣem* = 'bone'.

The NT usage of *sōma*, 'body', keeps close to the Hebrew and avoids the thought of Greek philosophy, which tends to castigate the body as evil, the prison of the soul or reason, which was seen as good. Paul however does use 'body of sin' as a theological term parallel to 'flesh' indicating the locality of operation of sin. There is, however, a clearer distinction in the NT between body and soul or spirit (Mt. 10:28; 1 Thes. 5:23; Jas. 2:26).

But it may be doubted whether the Bible gives us a view of man as existing apart from the body, even in the future life after death. The clearly-enunciated belief in a physical resurrection found in the NT (1 Cor. 15:42–52; 1 Thes. 4:13–18), foreshadowed in the OT (Dn. 12:2), militates against any idea of man enduring apart from some bodily manifestation or form of expression, though this does not imply the regrouping of the self-same material atoms (1 Cor. 15:44). A passage which at first sight seems to suggest separation from the body (2 Cor. 5:1–8) is perhaps best explained by J. A. T. Robinson (*In the End God*, 1950) as referring not to death, but the parousia, thus not to the distinction between soul or spirit and body, but between the future resurrection body and the present mortal body. Yet it is at least arguable that Lk. 23:43; Phil. 1:23; Heb. 12:23; Rev. 6:9–11, *cf.* 20:4–6 teach that departed Christians are in conscious joy with Christ, prior to resurrection.

The form of the resurrection body—the 'spiritual body' of 1 Cor. 15—can only be glimpsed from what we know of Christ's risen body, which left no corpse in the tomb, and, it seems, passed through the graveclothes (Lk. 24:12, 31). His bodily ascension does not necessarily suppose movement to a certain locality known as heaven, but suggests the emergence of his body into a larger life transcending the space-time limitations which bind us.

The metaphor of the church as the *body of Christ (1 Cor. 12:12ff., *etc.*) develops the idea of the body as the essential form and means of expression of the person.

BIBLIOGRAPHY. E. C. Rust, *Nature and Man in Biblical Thought*, 1953; A. R. Johnson, *The Vitality of the Individual in the Thought of Ancient Israel*, 1949; J. A. T. Robinson, *The Body*, 1952; H. G. Schütz, S. Wibbing, J. A. Motyer, *NIDNTT* 1, pp. 229–242. B.O.B.

BODY OF CHRIST. This phrase has a threefold use in the NT.

1. The human body of Jesus Christ, insisted on by the NT writers in the face of docetism as real (denial that Jesus Christ came in the flesh is 'of antichrist', 1 Jn. 4:2-3). The reality of Christ's body is the proof of his true manhood. That the Son should take a human body is thus a fact essential for salvation (*cf.* Heb. 2:14ff.) and specifically for atonement (Heb. 10:20). The transformation (not relinquishment) of it at the resurrection is a guarantee and prototype of the resurrection body for believers (1 Cor. 15; Phil. 3:21).

2. The bread at the Last Supper over which Christ spoke the words 'This is my body' (recorded in Mt. 26; Mk. 14; Lk. 22; 1 Cor. 11, *cf.* 1 Cor. 10:16). The words have been interpreted historically as meaning both 'This represents my sacrifice' and also 'This is myself'. Interpretation must be controlled by reference to the person of Christ, to his sacrifice, and to the church, in that order.

3. The exact phrase is used by Paul in 1 Cor. 10:16; 12:27 as a description of a group of believers—*cf.* 'one body in Christ' (Rom. 12:5) and 'body' in verses referring to a local church, or to the universal church, *i.e.* 1 Cor. 10:17; 12:12; Eph. 1:23 (but see C. F. D. Moule, *Colossians*, p. 168); 2:16; 4:4, 12, 16; 5:23; Col. 1:18, 24; 2:19; 3:15. It should be noted that the phrase is 'body of Christ', not 'of Christians', and that it has visible, congregational and also eschatological significance. In Rom. and 1 Cor. it defines the unity existing between members of each local congregation; in Col. and Eph. the whole church is in view, with Christ as the head.

The origin of Paul's image has been sought in the OT idea that as each part receives its function from the whole so the whole is weakened when any part fails; also in Gk. Stoic ideas; or, more likely, through Acts 9, it expresses the conviction that Christ is totally identified with all Christians.

The exegetical problem is to establish the amount of metaphor in the phrase. If it is literal, the church is viewed as the extension of the incarnation. Paul's diverse usage on the one hand, and the probable OT background on the other, point rather to its being a metaphor instructing church members that their existence and unity depend on Christ, and that each member has power to promote or to imperil unity.

BIBLIOGRAPHY. Arndt; E. Schweizer, *TDNT* 7, pp. 1067–1094; H. G. Schütz, *et al.*, *NIDNTT* 1, pp. 229–242; D. G. Stewart, *ZPEB* 1, pp. 800–801; C. B. Bass, *ISBE* 1, pp. 530–531. M.R.W.F.

BONES (Heb. *'eṣem*, common in the OT; Gk. *osteon*, in the NT only 5 times). As the basic and most durable part of the human body, the bones are used to describe the deepest feelings, affections and affiliations (Gn. 29:14; Jdg. 9:2; Jb. 2:5; 30:30; Ps. 22:17) often with 'flesh' as a parallel. The decent burial of the bones, or corpse, was regarded as an important matter (Gn. 50:25; Ezk. 39:15; Heb. 11:22 RSVmg.). Contact with them caused defilement (Nu. 19:16); to burn men's bones on altars was a most effective way of deconsecrating the altars (2 Ki. 23:20).

The bones preserved some of the vitality of the individual (2 Ki. 13:21), but dry bones less so (Ezk. 37:1–2, and figuratively v. 11). To break or scatter the bones was utterly to defeat an enemy (Ps. 53:5; Is. 38:13) but to burn his bones was wrong (Am. 2:1). B.O.B.

BOOK OF LIFE (Heb. *sēper ḥayyîm*; Gk. *biblos* or *biblion zōēs*, 'the roll of the living').

1. It is used of natural life, Ps. 69:28, where 'let them be blotted out of the book of the living' means 'let them die'. *Cf.* Ex. 32:32f., where Moses prays to be blotted out of God's book if Israel is to be destroyed; Ps. 139:16 ('in thy book were written . . . the days that were formed for me'); Dn. 12:1, where all the righteous who 'shall be found written in the book' will survive the eschatological tribulation.

2. In later Judaism and the NT it is used of the life of the age to come. Thus Is. 4:3, where 'every one who has been enrolled for life in Jerusalem' refers to natural life, is re-interpreted in the Targum as speaking of 'eternal life'. So in the NT the book of life is the roster of believers, *e.g.* Phil. 4:3; Rev. 3:5; 22:19, *etc.* At the last judgment everyone not enrolled in the book of life is consigned to the fiery lake (Rev. 20:12, 15); this is the book of life of the slaughtered Lamb (Rev. 13:8; 21:27), in which the names of the elect have been inscribed 'from the foundation of the world' (17:8). The same idea is expressed in Lk. 10:20, 'your names are written in heaven'; Acts 13:48, 'as many as were ordained (*i.e.* inscribed) to eternal life believed'. F.F.B.

BOOTH. A word sometimes used in the EVV to translate the Hebrew term *sukkâ*, a booth or rude temporary shelter made of woven boughs (Ne. 8:14–17). This type of structure figured particularly in the annual Feast of *Tabernacles (Lv. 23:34; Dt. 16:13, AV, RV 'tabernacles'), but was also used by armies in the field (*PAVILION, *TENT), and in agriculture as a shelter from the sun (see Jb. 27:18; Jon. 4:5); or for cattle (Gn. 33:17; *SUCCOTH). T.C.M.

BOWELS (Heb. *mē'îm*; Gk. *splanchna*). The Hebrews had no clear idea of the physiology of the internal organs. RSV translates *mē'îm* and *splanchna* variously by 'belly', Jon. 1:17; *'body', 2 Sa. 7:12; *'breast', Ps. 22:14; *'heart', Jb. 30:27; 1 Jn. 3:17; *'soul', Is. 16:11; *'stomach', Ezk. 3:3; *'womb', Ps. 71:6; and only by 'bowels' where the reference is clearly to 'intestines', usually as visible by reason of death or an abdominal wound, 2 Sa. 20:10; Acts 1:18.

The translation is also sometimes figurative, 'anguish' (Je. 4:19); especially in NT, 'affections' (2 Cor. 6:12). Gk. has a cognate verb *splanchnizomai* (Lk. 10:33), 'to feel compassion'. B.O.B.

BOX. 1. Heb. *paḵ*, 'flask', used as an oil container by Samuel when anointing Saul (1 Sa. 10:1, AV 'vial') and by one of the sons of the prophets when anointing Jehu (2 Ki. 9:1, 3). Narrow-necked juglets found on Iron Age sites may have been called *paḵ*, but the LXX *phakos*, lentil shaped, suggests a lentoid flask with two handles, of similar date. (*ARK OF THE COVENANT.)

2. Gk. *alabastron*, a perfume bottle, not necessarily of alabaster. The woman at Simon the leper's house may have broken off the narrow neck (Mt. 26:7; Mk. 14:3; *cf.* Lk. 7:37). A.R.M.

BOZRAH. 1. A city of Edom whose early king was Jobab (Gn. 36:33; 1 Ch. 1:44). Its later overthrow was predicted by Amos (1:12) and taken as symbolic of the defeat of powerful Edom and of God's avenging all his enemies (Is. 34:6; 63:1). Bozrah is usually identified with modern Buseirah, a fortified city of 19 acres atop a crag at the head of Wadi Hamayideh, *c.* 60 km N of Petra and *c.* 40 km SSE of the Dead Sea, controlling the *King's Highway from Elath and thus able to deny passage to the Israelites (Nu. 20:17). Excavations at Buseirah 1971–6 have uncovered three principal levels of occupation in the 8th century BC and later, though not as yet earlier (C. Bennett, *Levant* 7, 1975, pp. 1–19; 9, 1977, pp. 1–10; *NEAEHL*, pp. 264–266.

2. A city of Moab (Je. 48:24; LXX Bosor), perhaps to be identified with Bezer, a town rebuilt by *Mesha *c.* 830 BC, possibly Umm al-'Amad, NE of Medeba, used as a levitical city of refuge.

3. A town of SE Hauran, *c.* 120 km S of Damascus at the head of the King's Highway, captured by Judas Maccabeus (165–160 BC; 1 Macc. 5:26–28; Jos., *Ant.* 12. 336). Bozrah (mod. Busra eski-Sham, and probably the Busruna [Bozrah] of the 14th century BC *Amarna texts) became the most N provincial capital of Roman Arabia in NT times. D.J.W.

BRANCH. 1. The word represents various Heb. and Gk. words meaning shoot, twig, bough, palm-branch, *etc.* It occurs frequently in passages where Israel is spoken of under the figure of a tree, *e.g.* a vine (Ps. 80:11; Ezk. 17:6; Na. 2:2; *cf.* Jn. 15:1ff.) or a cedar (Ezk. 17:23) or an olive (Ho. 14:6; *cf.* Rom. 11:16ff.). Branches of trees, palm, myrtle and willow were used ceremonially at the Feast of Tabernacles for making *booths (*sukkôṯ*) (Lv. 23:40; Ne. 8:15), and for carrying in procession with cries of *Hosanna (Ps. 118:27; Mishnah, *Sukkah* 4). *Cf.* Jesus' triumphal entry into Jerusalem (Mt. 21:8–9; Mk. 11:8–10; Jn. 12:13).

2. Of special interest is the Messianic use of the word (Heb. *ṣemaḥ*) for the scion of the family of David who would come to rule Israel in righteousness. Explicitly prophesied in Je. 23:5; 33:15, the expression looks back to Is. 4:2 (*cf.* Is. 11:1, Heb. *nēṣer*). Zc. 3:8; 6:12 show that the title 'branch' was a recognized Messianic term after the Exile, used to incorporate the idea of priest-king.

3. In Ex. 25:31ff.; 37:17ff. the word is used of the golden lampstand in the tabernacle, which is traditionally depicted with a central stem and three branches on either side. The Heb. *qāneh* 'reed' may have been misunderstood here, for the seven-branched candlestick is not known earlier than the 1st century BC.

BIBLIOGRAPHY. J. G. Baldwin, '*Ṣemaḥ* as a Technical Term in the Prophets', *VT* 14, 1964, pp. 93–97; R. North, 'Zechariah's Seven-Spout Lampstand', *Biblica* 51, 1970, pp. 183ff. J.G.B.

BREAD. Bread was the all-important commodity of the ancient Near East, and the price of grain is an infallible index to economic conditions at any given time. In early Babylonia the grain of corn provided the basic unit for the system of weights, and cereal took the place of money in commerce. Hosea paid part of the price of his wife in grain.

While we possess much information about the price of grain, references to the price of bread are extremely rare because it was usually made by each housewife. One reference from the Hammurapi period (18th century BC) gives 10 *še* (about a twentieth of a shekel) as the price of about 2½ litres (4 *sila*) of bread, and half this amount was a man's daily ration. (B. Meissner, *Warenpreise in Babylonien*, p. 7.) In 2 Ki. 7:1 the price quoted for cereal seems abnormally high, but it was doubtless considerably lower than in the preceding famine. In Rev. 6:6 the prices describe graphically the grim conditions of famine.

Barley bread was probably the most widely used. The fact that barley was also fed to horses (1 Ki. 4:28) does not necessarily imply that it was considered inferior, any more than is oats in our day. Wheat bread was more highly prized and was probably fairly common. Spelt was also used, but rye does not seem to have been cultivated. On occasions various cereals may have been mixed together and, as Ezk. 4:9 shows, even lentil and bean meal were added.

The general term for grain was *dāḡān*. After threshing and winnowing, the grain was either crushed in a *mortar with a pestle or was ground in a *mill by rubbing the upper stone to and fro on the nether millstone. The term for flour or meal in general was *qemaḥ*, and when necessary this was qualified by the addition of the name of the cereal (Nu. 5:15). What was probably a finer quality was called *sōleṯ* (*cf.* 1 Ki. 4:22), but some scholars take this word to mean 'groats'. This was the meal used in the offerings (Ex. 29:40; Lv. 2:5, *etc.*).

The word *qālî*, often translated 'parched corn', was probably roasted grains, which were eaten without further preparation.

The flour, mixed with water and seasoned with salt, was kneaded in a special trough. To this, leaven in the form of a small quantity of old fermented dough was added until the whole was leavened. Unleavened bread also was baked. Leaven was not used in the offerings made by fire (Lv. 2:11, *etc.*), and its use was forbidden during Passover week. The baking was done either over a fire on heated stones or on a griddle, or in an oven. Leavened bread was usually in the form of round, flat loaves, and unleavened in the form of thin cakes. The form called *'uḡâ* was probably the griddle cake, since it required turning (Ho. 7:8).

When bread was kept too long it became dry and crumbly (Jos. 9:5 and 12). In Gilgamesh 11. 225–229, there is an interesting account of the deterioration of bread (*ANET*, p. 95). (*FOOD.)

That so vital a commodity should leave its mark on language and symbolism is not surprising. From earliest times the word 'bread' was used for food in general (Gn. 3:19 and Pr. 6:8, where Heb. has 'bread'). Since it was the staple article of diet, it was called 'staff' of bread (Lv. 26:26), which is probably the origin of our phrase 'staff of life'. Those who were responsible for bread were important officials, as in Egypt (Gn. 40:1), and in Assyria a chief baker is honoured with an eponymy. Bread was early used in sacred meals (Gn. 14:18), and loaves were included in certain offerings (Lv. 21:6, *etc.*). Above all, it had a special place in the sanctuary as the 'bread of the Presence'. The manna was later referred to as 'heavenly bread' (see Ps. 105:40). Our Lord referred to himself as the 'bread of God' and as the 'bread of life' (Jn. 6:33, 35), and he chose the bread of the Passover to be the symbolic memorial of his broken body.

W.J.M.

BREAST. Four uses of the word may be distinguished. **1.** Heb. *daḏ* or *šaḏ* (Jb. 3:12; Ezk. 23:21, *etc.*); Gk. *mastos*, with reference to sucking, *etc.*, as of a woman, or an animal (La. 4:3; Lk. 11:27). **2.** The same used figuratively (Is. 60:16; 66:11), symbolic of riches. **3.** Heb. *ḥāzeh* (Ex. 29:26; Lv. 8:29, *etc.*), the breast portion of an animal, often offered as a wave-offering. **4.** Aram. *ḥᵃḏî* (Dn. 2:32), the chest, equivalent to the Gk. *stēthos* in the NT, where smiting upon the breast is a sign of anguish (Lk. 18:13), and leaning upon the breast a sign of affection (Jn. 13:23, 25). The word 'bosom', Heb. *ḥêq* (Mi. 7:5), presents a close parallel in this sense. Ho. 13:8 RSV, 'tear open their breast', Heb. *lēḇ* 'their *heart*'.

B.O.B.

BREASTPIECE OF THE HIGH PRIEST. Heb. *ḥōšen*, interpretatively translated 'breastplate', 'breastpiece' (Ex. 28:4, 15–30; 39:8–21; *cf.* LXX, *peristēthion*, Ex. 28:4), is, however, etymologically obscure. The former relation to Arab. cognates with the sense 'beauty' is not now usually given credence and no other cognate attracts confidence. Most commentators tend towards the contextual translation 'pouch'. Made of the same materials as the ephod (Ex. 28:15), the breastpiece was a square pouch (v. 16), with gold rings at the 4 corners (vv. 23, 26). The lower rings were fastened by blue laces to rings above the girdle of the ephod (v. 28). On the breastpiece were set 12 gems engraved with the names of the tribes (vv. 17–21), and gold cords fastened the upper rings to the two similarly engraved gems on the shoulders of the ephod (vv. 9–12, 22–25). Thus, symbolically, on the one hand the nation, in God's sight, rested on a high-priestly person and work; on the other hand, the priest carried continually into God's presence the people, as a loved responsibility (v. 29); and equally, as containing the oracular *Urim and Thummim (v. 30)—hence the title 'breastpiece of judgment' (v. 15; *cf.* the customary LXX, *logion tēs kriseōs*, 'oracle of judgment')—the breastpiece symbolizes the priest as the announcer of God's will to man (*cf.* Mal. 2:6–7).

BIBLIOGRAPHY. Josephus, *Ant.* 3. 162; B. S. Childs, *Exodus*, 1974, p. 526; U. Cassuto, *A Commentary on the Book of Exodus*, 1967, p. 375.

J.A.M.

BRETHREN OF THE LORD. Four men are described in the Gospels as 'brothers' of Jesus, *viz.* James, Joses, Simon and Judas (Mt. 13:55; Mk. 6:3). The native townsmen of Jesus expressed amazement that a brother of these men should possess such wisdom and such power (Mk. 6:2–3). On the other hand, Jesus contrasted his brothers and his mother, who were bound to him by physical ties, with his disciples, who in virtue of their obedience to the will of his Father were regarded by him as his spiritual 'brothers' and 'mother' (Mt. 12:46–50). Three views have been held as to the nature of the relationship between these men and Jesus.

a. The 'brothers' were the younger children of Joseph and Mary. This view is supported by the *prima facie* meaning of 'firstborn' in Lk. 2:7, and by the natural inference from Mt. 1:25 that after the birth of Jesus normal marital relations between Joseph and Mary followed. It was strongly advocated by Helvidius in the 4th century, but came to be regarded as heretical in the light of the doctrine, increasingly attractive as the ascetic movement developed, that Mary was always virgin. Since the Reformation it has been the view most commonly held by Protestants.

b. The 'brothers' were the children of Joseph by a former wife. This view, first promulgated in the 3rd century and defended by Epiphanius in the 4th, became the accepted doctrine of the Eastern Orthodox Church. It has no direct support from the NT. Its advocates have usually supposed, however, that the opposition of the brothers to Jesus during his earthly life was largely due to jealousy of the achievements of their younger half-brother.

c. The 'brothers' were the cousins of Jesus. This view, put forward by Jerome in defence of the doctrine of the perpetual virginity of the mother of Jesus, has remained the official teaching of the Roman Catholic Church. It is based on the following series of arbitrary assumptions: (i) that the correct interpretation of Jn. 19:25 is that there were three, not four, women standing near the cross, *viz.* Mary the mother of Jesus, her sister identified with 'Mary of Clopas', and Mary of Magdala; (ii) that the second Mary in the Johannine passage is identical with the Mary described in Mk. 15:40 as 'the mother of James the less and of Joses'; (iii) that this 'James the less' is the apostle called in Mk. 3:18 'the son of Alphaeus'; (iv) that the second Mary in Jn. 19:25 was married to Alphaeus. Why she should be described as 'of Clopas', which presumably means 'the wife of Clopas', Jerome admitted that he was ignorant. The theory would seem to demand either that Clopas is another name for Alphaeus, or that this Mary was married twice. By this ingenious but unconvincing exegesis Jerome reduced the number of men called James in the NT to two—the son of Zebedee, and James the Lord's brother, who was also an apostle and known as 'the less' to distinguish him from the son of Zebedee! It is probable that 'my brethren' in Mt. 28:10 refers to a wider group than 'the brothers' already mentioned.

BIBLIOGRAPHY. See the excursus by J. B. Lightfoot 'The Brethren of the Lord' in *Saint Paul's Epistle to the Galatians*[2], 1866, pp. 247–282; J. J. Gunther, 'The Family of Jesus', *EQ* 46, 1974, pp. 25ff.; J. W. Wenham, 'The Relatives of Jesus', *EQ* 47, 1975, pp. 6ff.; and the introductions to the commentaries mentioned under *JAMES, EPISTLE OF.

R.V.G.T.

BRICK. A lump of mud or clay, usually rectangular, sun-dried or kiln-baked ('burnt'); the commonest building material of the ancient biblical world. At first moulded by hand, bricks early began to be made ('struck') with open, rectangular, wooden moulds. The mud was mixed with sand, chopped straw, *etc.*, the bricks struck off in long rows, and left to dry out; see Petrie, *Egyptian Architecture*, 1938, pp. 3–13; Lucas, *Ancient Egyptian Materials and Industries*[4], 1962, pp. 48–50. Bricks often bore stamped impressions: in Egypt, the name of the pharaoh or of the building they were used in; in Babylonia, also the king's name and dedication; *e.g.* Nebuchadrezzar, of whom five different stamps are known. For these and Nebuchadrezzar's brick-making techniques, see R. Koldewey, *Excavations at Babylon*, 1914, pp. 75–82 and figures.

Sun-dried brick was the universal building material of Mesopotamia, where kiln-baked bricks were often used for facings and pavements (*cf.* also Gn. 11:3). In Egypt sun-dried brick was usual for all but the most important and permanent buildings (*i.e.* stone temples and tombs); kiln-baked bricks are almost unknown before Roman times. Various forms of bonding were practised.

Ex. 5:6–19 accurately reflects brick-making usage in ancient Egypt; straw or stubble was regularly used in the 19th and 20th Dynasties (13th–12th centuries BC), as bricks so made proved much stronger. In contemporary papyri one official reports of his workmen, 'they are making their quota of bricks daily', while another complains, '. . . at Qenqenento, . . . there are neither men to make bricks nor straw in the neighbourhood'; *cf.* R. A. Caminos, *Late-Egyptian Miscellanies*, 1954, pp. 106, 185. The straw itself is not so much a binding-agent, but its chemical decay in the clay released an acid which (like glutamic or gallotannic acid) gave the clay greater plasticity for brick-making. This effect (but not, of course, the chemistry) was evidently a well-known one. See A. A. McRae in *Modern Science and Christian Faith*, 1948, pp. 215–219, after E. G. Acheson, *Transactions of the American Ceramic Society* 6, 1904, p. 31; further comment and references in Lucas, *op. cit.*, p. 49; and *cf.* also C. F. Nims, *BA* 13, 1950, pp. 21–28.

In Palestine sun-dried brick was also the norm; city and house walls were often of brick upon a stone foundation.

For 'burning incense upon bricks' (Is. 65:3), *cf.* mud-brick altars from a very early period at Megiddo, *ANEP*, p. 229, fig. 729. (*ARCHITECTURE, *WALLS.)

BIBLIOGRAPHY: K. A. Kitchen, 'From the Brick-fields of Egypt', *TynB* 27, 1976, pp. 137–147.

K.A.K.

BRICK-KILN. Oven for baking mud bricks. In the biblical East sun-dried mud bricks were always the cheapest and commonest building material, but were not specially durable (*e.g.* in rainy weather). Burnt *bricks were almost indestructible. They were used in Mesopotamia for facings, pavements, *etc.*, in important buildings from very early times, but are hardly known in Palestine or Egypt before Roman times. Hence brick-kilns are regularly found in Mesopotamia but not by the Nile or Jordan. In the AV of 2 Sa. 12:31; Je. 43:9; Na. 3:14 the term *malbēn* is rendered 'brickkiln', but this seems to be incorrect. The *malbēn* is the rectangular, hollow wooden brick-mould for making ordinary sun-dried bricks in 2 Sa. and Na., and is used figuratively to describe the rectangular brick pavement in Tahpanhes in Jeremiah. In 2 Sa. 12:31 the meaning is that David put the Ammonites to hard labour (in the verb, reading *d* for *r*, very similar letters in Heb.), with saws, harrows, axes and brick-moulds (*malkēn* is probably for *malbēn*, *MT* margin/*Q*^e^*rê*).

The 'fiery furnace' into which Daniel's three friends were cast as punishment (Dn. 3:6, 11, 15, 19–23) was very likely a brick-kiln, one of those that must have supplied burnt bricks to Nebuchadrezzar's Babylon. The word used, *'attûn*, 'furnace', is probably identical with the Assyro-Babylonian word *utūnum*, 'furnace, kiln'. Outside of Daniel, Nebuchadrezzar's cruel punishment is attested not only in Je. 29:22 but also by actual inscriptions: in a

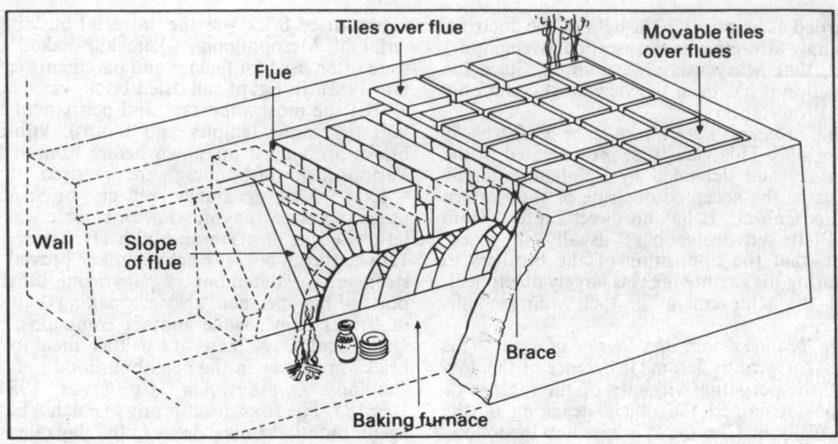

A pottery kiln, excavated at Nippur.

Babylonian letter of *c.* 1800 BC and in an Assyrian court regulation of *c.* 1130 BC people were (or might be) thrown into a furnace as a punishment; see G. R. Driver, *AfO* 18, 1957, p. 129, and E. F. Weidner, *AfO* 17, 1956, pp. 285–286. The practice is used as a comparison in Ps. 21:9. On the 'fiery furnace' being a brick-kiln, compare the reference to the flames of similar modern brick-kilns lighting up the sky near Babylon by R. Koldewey, *The Excavations at Babylon*, 1914, pp. 81–82. The brick-kilns of ancient Babylonia may have looked like the large pottery-kiln excavated in Nippur and pictured in B. Meissner, *Babylonien und Assyrien*, 1, 1920, p. 234 and figs. 55–56. K.A.K.

BRIDE, BRIDEGROOM. These two words are quite naturally complementary to each other (Jn. 3:29a) and are found side by side in Is. 62:5; Je. 7:34; 16:9; 25:10; 33:11; Rev. 18:23. 'The voice of the bridegroom and the voice of the bride' in these references is parallel with 'the voice of mirth and gladness', and illustrates the rich concept of marital joy of which the Bible often speaks (*e.g.* Ps. 128; Pr. and Ct.). Is. 62:5 extends this significance to include a comparison between human relationships and God's joy in his people Israel, who are regarded as his bride (*cf.* Is. 54:6; Je. 2:2; 3:20; Ezk. 16:8; 23:4; Ho. 2:16). This metaphor prepares the way for the NT allusions to the church as the bride of Christ, especially in the Epistles (2 Cor. 11:2; Eph. 5:25–27, 31f.; *cf.* Rev. 19:7; 21:2; 22:17). According to this picture the Lord is the divine Bridegroom who seeks his bride in love and enters into covenant relations with her.

Whether this allegory of Christ and the church is derived from the teaching of Jesus or not is a debatable point. Some deny the allegorical interpretation of Mt. 25:1–12 on the ground that the Messiah is not represented in the OT and in the rabbinical literature as a Bridegroom (so J. Jeremias, *TDNT* 4, pp. 1099–1106, and *The Parables of Jesus*, E.T. 1954, p. 46). But, on the other hand, there is the witness of Mk. 2:19–20 (*cf.* Mt. 9:15; Lk. 5:34–35), which shows that the term Bridegroom was used by the Lord as a Messianic designation and corresponds to his use of the third person in speaking of himself as 'the Son of man' (so V. Taylor, *The Gospel according to St Mark*, 1952, *ad loc.*). This is further confirmed if the variant reading of Mt. 25:1, 'to meet the bridegroom and the bride', is accepted; and there is early and important attestation of it (see A. H. McNeile, *The Gospel according to St Matthew*, 1915, *ad loc.*; F. C. Burkitt, *JTS* 30, 1929, pp. 267–270; T. W. Manson, *The Sayings of Jesus*, 1949, pp. 243f., who makes an interesting and plausible suggestion to explain the identity of the bride). See also Jn. 3:29b for John the Baptist as 'the friend of the bridegroom', *i.e.* the groomsman (Heb. *šôšᵉḇîn*), who acted as 'best man' (*cf.* 1 Macc. 9:39). He was the agent for the bridegroom in arranging the marriage and played an important part in the wedding festivities, as did also the bridegroom's attendants, who are referred to in Mk. 2:19 (AV) as 'the sons of the bridechamber'.

BIBLIOGRAPHY. A. Isaksson, *Marriage and Ministry in the New Temple*, 1965; R. Batey, *NT Nuptial Imagery*, 1971; J. P. Sampley, *And the Two Shall Become One Flesh*, 1971; D. J. Williams, *DJG*, pp. 86–88. R.P.M.

BRIMSTONE (Heb. *goprîṯ*, Gk. *theion*, 'sulphur'), a yellow crystalline solid, with medicinal and fumigating properties, which occurs in the natural state in regions of volcanic activity such as the valley of the Dead Sea (*cf.* Gn. 19:24). The element burns readily in air, and is consequently associated in the Bible with fire (*e.g.* Gn. 19:24; Ps. 11:6; Ezk. 38:22; Lk. 17:29; Rev. 9:17–18; 14:10; 19:20; 20:10; 21:8), and appears in figures of the burning wrath of God (Is. 30:33; 34:9; Rev. 14:10). The usual environment of its natural occurrence also led to the use of the word to indicate barrenness of land (Dt. 29:23; Jb. 18:15). That the substance was well known in the ancient world is suggested by the occurrence of cognates to *goprîṯ* in Akkadian, Aramaic and Arabic. *theion* occurs already in Homer, and is regularly used in the LXX to translate *goprîṯ*. 'Brimstone' was the form current in 1611 of a Middle English word, meaning 'burn(ing)-stone', which had appeared, for instance, in Wyclif's Bible as (among other spellings) 'brunston'. The word, though archaic in modern extra-biblical usage, has been retained by the RV and RSV.

BIBLIOGRAPHY. R. Campbell Thompson, *A Dic-*

tionary of Assyrian Chemistry and Geology, 1936, pp. 38–39; *KB*³, p. 193. T.C.M.

BROOK. The word *naḥal* is used variously of a perennial stream, the flow of water and the dried course of a river-bed. Apart from the Jordan itself, nearly all the perennial streams are left-bank tributaries of the Jordan fed by springs. Such is the Kishon (1 Ki. 18:40), the second largest river by volume, and the Jabbok, modern Zerka (Gn. 32:22–23). The brook in full spate is used metaphorically (*e.g.* Am. 5:24), while the ephemeral nature of the dried-up brook is also used (Jb. 6:15). A severe drought will terminate the flow even of spring-fed brooks (*e.g.* 1 Ki. 17:2–7). Sometimes the stream-bed has a mantle of vegetation owing to the shallow water-table. Thus 'the brook of the willows' (Is. 15:7) may describe the cover of oleander bushes and other vegetation. In poetry *mayim*, 'water', is frequently used of the channel bed (Jb. 12:15; Ps. 42:1; Is. 8:7; Joel 1:20). (*EGYPT, RIVER OF.) J.M.H.

BROTHERLY LOVE. Gk. *philadelphia* (Rom. 12:10; 1 Thes. 4:9; Heb. 13:1; 1 Pet. 1:22; 2 Pet. 1:7) means, not figurative brother-*like* love, but the love of those united in the Christian brotherhood (*adelphotēs*, 1 Pet. 2:17; 5:9; *cf.* the adjective *philadelphos*, 1 Pet. 3:8). Outside Christian writings (*e.g.* 1 Macc. 12:10, 17) *philadelphia* is used only of men of common descent. In the OT, 'brother', like 'neighbour', meant 'fellow Israelite' (Lv. 19:17f.; *cf.* Acts 13:26). Jesus widened the scope of love for fellow men (Mt. 5:43–48; Lk. 10:27–37), but also, by calling his followers his own (Mk. 3:33ff.; Mt. 28:10; Jn. 20:17) and one another's (Mt. 23:8; Lk. 22:32) brethren, and by the Johannine command to love one another (Jn. 13:34; 15:12, 17), established the special love of fellow Christians which *philadelphia* describes (*cf.* Rom. 8:29).

This is shown in the common life of the church (*cf. homothymadon*, 'with one accord, together', Acts 1:14; 2:46; 4:24; 5:12; 15:25). It is an outworking of Christ's love (Eph. 5:1f.) which it is natural to find among Christians (1 Thes. 4:9f.), but which must be increased (1 Thes. 4:10) and deepened (Rom. 12:10) so as to be lasting (Heb. 13:1), genuine (*anypokritos*, 1 Pet. 1:22; *cf.* Rom. 12:9), and earnest (*ektenēs*, 1 Pet. 1:22; *cf.* 4:8). It is shown in a common way of thinking (*to auto phronein*, Rom. 12:16; 15:5; 2 Cor. 13:11; Phil. 4:2; *cf.* Gal. 5:10; Phil. 2:2, 5; 3:15) and living (*tō autō stoichein*, Phil. 3:16), especially in hospitality (Heb. 13:1f.; 1 Pet. 4:8f.) and help to needy Christians (Rom. 12:9–13). It proves, to Christians themselves (1 Jn. 3:14) and to the world (Jn. 13:35), the genuineness of their faith (1 Jn. 2:9–11; 3:10; 4:7, 11, 20; 5:1.)

philadelphia cannot by definition be realized outside the 'household of faith', but it is associated with honouring (1 Pet. 2:17) and doing good to (Gal. 6:10) all. Its converse is not exclusiveness or indifference to those outside (*hoi exō*, Mk. 4:11; 1 Cor. 5:12f.; Col. 4:5; 1 Thes. 4:12), but the constraining, dividing and still unconsummated love of Christ (2 Cor. 5:14; *cf.* Lk. 12:50–53). (*LOVE, *FAMILY, *NEIGHBOUR.)

BIBLIOGRAPHY. *TDNT* 1, pp. 144–146; *NIDNTT* 1, pp. 254–260; 2, pp. 547–550; M. J. Wilkins, *ABD* 1, pp. 782b–783b. P.E.

BURDEN. A noun used about 80 times to translate several Heb. and Gk. words. **1.** Heb. *maśśā'*, 'thing lifted up', and other cognate words from the root *nāśā'*, 'he lifted up'. This word occurs most frequently, notably of prophetic utterances. (*ORACLE.) **2.** Heb. *sāḇal*, 'to bear a load' (in various derivative forms). **3.** Heb. *yāhaḇ*, 'to give' (Ps. 55:22 only). **4.** Heb. *'ᵃḡuddâ*, 'bundle' (Is. 58:6, AV, only). **5.** Gk. *baros*, 'something heavy'. **6.** Gk. *phortion*, 'something to be borne'. **7.** Gk. *gomos*, 'the freight' of a ship (Acts 21:3, AV).

Those terms which occur more than once vary little in meaning, and seem at times to be interchangeable. A burden is whatever renders body or mind uneasy (*e.g.* Zp. 3:18); as much as one can bear (2 Ki. 5:17); government in church or state (Nu. 11:17); prediction of heavy judgment (Is. 13); labour, bondage, affliction, fear (Ps. 81:6; Ec. 12:5; Mt. 20:12); Christ's laws (Mt. 11:30; Rev. 2:24); God's ceremonial law and men's superstitious ceremonies (Mt. 23:4; Acts 15:28); men's infirmities (Gal. 6:2). J.D.D.

BURIAL AND MOURNING.

I. In the Old Testament

a. The times of the Patriarchs

Successive generations were buried in the family tomb (cave or rock-cut); thus Sarah (Gn. 23:19), Abraham (Gn. 25:9), Isaac and Rebekah, Leah (Gn. 49:31) and Jacob (Gn. 50:13). Death far from the family tomb required individual burial; so Deborah near Bethel (Gn. 35:8) and Rachel on the road to Ephrath (Gn. 35:19–20). Besides weeping, mourning already included rending one's garments and donning sackcloth (Gn. 37:34–35), for up to 7 days (Gn. 50:10). The embalming of Jacob and Joseph and the use of a coffin for Joseph in Egyptian fashion was exceptional (Gn. 50:2–3, 26). Mummification required removal of the viscera for separate preservation, and desiccation of the body by packing in salt (not brine); thereafter the body was packed with impregnated linen and entirely wrapped in linen. Embalming and mourning usually took 70 days, but the period for embalming could be shorter, as for Jacob.

b. The Pentateuchal legislation

Prompt burial, including that of hung criminals, was the norm (Dt. 21:22–23). Contact with the dead and formal mourning brought ceremonial defilement. Mourning by weeping, rending the garments and unbinding the hair was permitted to the Aaronic priests (Lv. 21:1–4), but not to the high priest (Lv. 21:10–11) or the Nazirite under vow (Nu. 6:7). Expressly forbidden to priests (Lv. 21:5) and people (Lv. 19:27–28; Dt. 14:1) were laceration ('cuttings in the flesh'), cutting the corners of the beard, baldness between the eyes and 'rounding' (mutilation?) of the corner(s) of the head. Eating of tithes in mourning or offering them to the dead (Dt. 26:14) was also forbidden. Women captured in war might mourn their parents for one month before marrying their captors (Dt. 21:11–13). The national leaders Aaron (Nu. 20:28–29; Dt. 10:6) and Moses (Dt. 34:5–8) were each accorded 30 days' national mourning after burial.

c. Israel in Palestine

(i) *Burial.* When possible, people were buried in the ancestral family tomb: so Gideon and Samson (Jdg. 8:32; 16:31), Asahel and Ahithophel (2 Sa. 2:32; 17:23), and eventually Saul (2 Sa. 21:12–14). Burial in one's 'house', as of Samuel (1 Sa. 25:1, *cf.* 28:3) and Joab (1 Ki. 2:34), may merely mean the same, unless it was more literally under the house or yard floor. The body was borne to rest on a bier (2 Sa. 3:31). Lack of proper burial was a great misfortune (1 Ki. 13:22; Je. 16:6). Tombs were usually outside the town. The Late Bronze Age used pit-tombs in the plains and valleys, but family tombs (with benches) in the hill-country (R. Gonen, *Burial Patterns & Cultural Diversity in Late Bronze Age Canaan*, 1992). Cremation was Phoenician and northern; P. Bienkowski, *Levant* 14, 1982, pp. 80–89. Persian-age burials, see E. Stern, *Material Culture of the Land of the Bible in the Persian Period, 538–332* BC, 1973, pp. 68–92. Tomb-inscriptions occur from the 7th century BC; *cf.* W. G. Dever, *HUCA* 40/41, 1969–70, pp. 139–204, and R. Deutsch & M. Heltzer, *Forty New Ancient West Semitic Inscriptions*, 1994, pp. 27–30. The upstart treasurer *Shebna drew Isaiah's condemnation in hewing himself an ostentatious rock-tomb (Is. 22:15–16). Pottery and other objects left with the dead became a pure formality during the Israelite period, by contrast with elaborate Canaanite funerary provision. Memorial pillars were sometimes erected in Israel as elsewhere in antiquity; 2 Sa. 18:18 is an anticipatory example. Outside Jerusalem was a tract of land set aside for 'the graves of the common people' (2 Ki. 23:6; Je. 26:23).

The grave of an executed criminal or foe was sometimes marked by a heap of stones. Examples are Achan (Jos. 7:26), Absalom (2 Sa. 18:17), the king of Ai, and the five Canaanite kings (Jos. 8:29; 10:27). Cremation was not a Hebrew practice, but a corpse might be burnt pending proper burial in the ancestral tomb, as with Saul (1 Sa. 31:12–13) and in Am. 6:10. For royal burials, *SEPULCHRE OF THE KINGS.

(ii) *Mourning.* In Palestine in the 2nd and 1st millennia this included: (1) baldness of head and cutting the beard; (2) lacerating the body; (3) rending garments and wearing sackcloth; (4) scattering dust on the head and wallowing in ashes; and (5) weeping and lamentation. Not all of these were favoured by the law. (See section *b*, above.) For Hebrew mourning, see the action of David (2 Sa. 1:11–12; 13:31), the woman of Tekoah (2 Sa. 14:2), and note the allusions in the prophets (Is. 3:24; 22:12; Je. 7:29; Ezk. 7:18; Joel 1:8; Am. 8:10; Mi. 1:16). For Tyrian seafarers, Philistia and Moab, see Ezk. 27:30, 32; Je. 47:5; Is. 15:2–3 and Je. 48:37.

David lamented over Saul and Jonathan (2 Sa. 1:17–27) and Jeremiah and others over Josiah (2 Ch. 35:25). For professional mourners, *cf.* Je. 9:17–18; Am. 5:16. After a funeral a breaking-fast meal was possibly given to mourners (Je. 16:7; *cf.* Ho. 9:4). A 'great burning' sometimes marked the funeral of Judaean kings (2 Ch. 16:14; 21:19–20; Je. 34:5).

d. Non-funereal mourning

Mourning was associated with repentance or contrition (*e.g.* Ex. 33:4; Joel 1:13; 2:12–13; Ezr. 9: 3, 5) or took place because of misfortune (*e.g.* 2 Sa. 13:19; 15:32; Jb. 2:12–13). There are also references to laceration, weeping, *etc.*, in pagan(izing) cult-practices. *Cf.* the actions of Baal's prophets on Mt Carmel (1 Ki. 18:28), and those of the men of Israel who came with oblations for God (Je. 41:5). Ezekiel saw in a vision the women of Jerusalem weeping for the god Tammuz (Ezk. 8:14); and Isaiah depicts pagan observances at graves being performed by the rebellious Israelites (Is. 65:4).

BIBLIOGRAPHY. For the late Judaean royal caves, see A. Kloner, *Levant* 18, 1986, pp. 126–129. For Canaanite tombs of the patriarchal age, see K. M. Kenyon, *Digging up Jericho*, 1957, pp. 233–255. For laceration in Ugaritic (N Canaanite) epics, see *DOTT*, 1958, p. 130; see also J. A. Callaway, 'Burial in Ancient Palestine from the Stone Age to Abraham', *BA* 26, 1963, pp. 74–91; E. M. Myers, 'Secondary Burials in Palestine', *BA* 33, 1970, pp. 2–29.

K.A.K.

II. In the New Testament

The corpse. Tabitha was washed and displayed in an upstairs room (Acts 9:39). The arms and legs of Lazarus and Jesus were bound in linen bands (*keiriai*, *othonia*) impregnated with aromatic perfumes, and a piece of linen was wrapped around their heads (Jn. 11:44; 20:6–7). That Palestinian Jews borrowed Lat. *sudarium* (handkerchief, napkin) to describe a 'turban' is evident from this Johannine usage and from Mishnaic *ṣûdārîn*, which Jastrow (*Lexicon*, p. 962) defines as 'a scarf wound around the head and hanging down over the neck'. One must presume also that the body itself was clothed; perhaps the sing. *sindōn* (Mk. 15:46 and par.) indicates a linen shift (contrast *Apoc. Moses* 40:1–7 in 1st century AD: plur. *sindones* = winding-bands). If *M.Shabbath* 23. 5 reflects normal 1st century practice the corpse was anointed immediately, and its chin bound 'not to raise it, but so that it does not sink lower'; similarly *Semahoth* 1. 2 describes an immediate binding of the jaws, indicating the function of the *sudarium*. Jesus recognized an anticipation of normal burial-customs among the Jews when his feet or head were anointed at Bethany (Mk. 14:3–9; Jn. 11:2; 12:7); but the preparations of the women to anoint him were thwarted (Mk. 16:1; Lk. 23:56). The Mishnaic plural *taḵrîḵîn* confirms the sense 'bindings', 'wrappings' for Johannine *keiriai*, *othonia* (S. Safrai, *The Jewish People in the First Century*, 1974, 1. 2, p. 777, *e.g. M.Kilaim* 9. 4, *Maaser Sheni* 5. 12); and the corresponding verb is even more explicit at *Semahoth* 12. 10: 'A man may wrap (*meḵārēḵ*) and bind (the corpse of) a man, but not (the corpse of) a woman . . .' However, at *M.Sanhedrin* 6. 5 H. Danby (*Mishnah*, 1933) translated 'garments'; and D. Zlotnik (*Tractate Mourning*, 1966, p. 22) assumes a 'linen garment' at the death of Gamaliel II *c.* AD 130. Perhaps too one should note R. Nathan (late 2nd century AD): 'In the same clothes (*keṣût*) which go with him to Sheol will a man appear in the age to come.' All of this seems to suggest both wrappings and garments.

Burial and mourning. Those who mourned at the house of Jairus 'wept and lamented' (Mk. 5:38), forming a large throng (Mt. 9:23) and making a great disturbance; presumably they beat their breasts in grief (as Lk. 18:13; 23:48). Similarly when Stephen was buried there was 'great lamentation' (Acts 8:2). One is reminded of the 2nd century BC Wisdom of Jesus ben Sirach (Ecclus.) 38:16–18:

'My son, shed tears over a dead man,
and intone the lament to show your own deep grief;
bury his body with due ceremonial,
and do not neglect to honour his grave.
Weep bitterly, wail most fervently;
observe the mourning the dead man deserves' (JB).

Jairus hired pipers for the mourning (Mt. 9:23), presumably to accompany a formal dirge both at the house and during the procession; for Josephus indicates that in AD 67 in Jerusalem (when the Jewish revolt in Galilee had failed), '. . . many hired pipers who accompanied their dirges' (*BJ* 3. 435–437). Later rabbinic law exacted special obligations from a husband to his dead wife; R. Judah (late 2nd century AD) said: 'Even the poorest in Israel should hire not less than two flutes and one wailing woman' (*M.Ketuboth* 4. 4). That no corpse was permitted to stay overnight within the walls of Jerusalem was a rabbinic *dictum* rather than normal practice (A. Guttmann, *HUCA* 60, 1969–70, pp. 251–275); nevertheless many texts indicate burial the same day. Jn. 11:39 expects the stench of decomposition within 4 days (probably earlier). At Nain Jesus met a procession on its way to the tomb including the mother and many townspeople. The body was on a bier (*soros*) carried by bearers. *Semahoth* 4. 6 refers to the use of the bier at Jerusalem, and to a eulogist who preceded it and spoke the praises of the dead. Similarly *M.Berakoth* 3. 1 mentions those who carried the *miṭṭah* (bier), those who relieved them, those who went before and those who went behind. One may contrast with this the funeral of King Herod (4 BC), whose body was displayed on a golden couch (*klinē*) studded with precious stones and wore the royal purple and a golden crown (*Ant.* 17. 196–199; *BJ* 1. 670–673). His son Archelaus gave a sumptuous funerary banquet to the people, as was the custom of the more well-to-do, whose pious generosity 'impoverished' them (*BJ* 2. 1). King Herod himself had spent lavishly on the funeral of Antigonus (whom he murdered)—on the furnishing of the burial-vault, costly spices burnt as incense, the personal adornment (*kosmos*) of the corpse (*Ant.* 15. 57–61). But Josephus was aware that expense was not the point:

> The pious rites which the Law provides for the dead do not consist of costly obsequies or the erection of notable monuments. The funeral ceremony is undertaken by the nearest kin, and all who pass while burial is in progress must join the procession and mourn with the family. After the funeral the house and its inhabitants must be purified (*Contra Apionem* 2. 205).

Mourning continued after the funeral. In the 2nd century BC its rules and sanctions held for 7 days (Ecclus. 22:12); at the end of the 1st century BC Archelaus mourned 7 days for Herod (*BJ* 2. 1), and in the 1st century AD this remained the norm (*Ant.* 17. 200). In the 2nd century AD the rabbis still refer to *šiḇ'āh* or 'the seven days of mourning' (*Semahoth* 7). A longer period of 30 days was exceptional (*BJ* 3. 435–437).

Tombs. Ancient rock-cut tombs of the period *c.* 40 BC–AD 135 surround the walls of Jerusalem on three sides (but not on the W, from where the prevailing winds blew), including those of more well-to-do families at Sanhedriyya (*PEQ* 84, 1952, pp. 23–38; *ibid.* 86, 1954, pp. 16–22; *Atiqot* 3, 1961, pp. 93–120), and the poorer tombs, rich in finds, at '*Dominus flevit*' on the Mt of Olives. Most magnificent of all is the tomb of queen Helena of Adiabene. A few stone sarcophagi are found, but mostly the dead were laid in *koḵin*, sometimes on bench-*arcosolia*; a rock-cut sarcophagus beneath an *arcosolium* (recessed archway in tomb-wall) is extremely rare, the only well-known example being in tomb 7 at Sanhedriyya in Jerusalem. The *koḵ* is the only type of burial-place referred to in the Mishnah (*M.Baba Bathra* 6. 8); the ideal rabbinic arrangement—two *kôḵîm* opposite the tomb-entry and three in either side-wall—is rarely found. A *kôḵ* was a burial-tunnel cut vertically into the wall of the chamber like a deep oven, set back over projecting rock-ledges around the chamber-walls (interrupted only by the entry-step), which left an oblong pit at the centre of the chamber to give a standing man head-room. The sarcophagus (rare), projecting continuous ledge and *kôḵ* are the only possible resting-places for a body in the smaller and less pretentious rock-cut tombs. These consisted of one or more chambers with a low square entry, such that one had to crawl through it. The closing-stone was either like an enormous cork, slotting into a rebate round the small entry as into the neck of a bottle; or it was a rough boulder. For this type of tomb see *AJA* 51, 1947, pp. 351–365, *Atiqot* (English) 3, 1961, pp. 108–116 (many in Heb. journals). It is clear that such a tomb—which one stooped to enter, which was closed by a stone that had to be rolled aside, and in which the body might have been placed initially on the projecting ledge—would match the Gospel descriptions of the place where Joseph put the body of Jesus. More elaborate tombs are much rarer, but combined the 'pit-ledge-*kôḵ*' arrangement with one or more bench-*arcosolia* (*Bankbogengräber*), where the body was visible on a flat ledge cut lengthwise into the wall of the burial chamber—*i.e. along* the wall, not deep into it—making a space *c.* 2 m long beneath an archway along the whole length of the wall. Such tombs usually consist of several chambers, not one, and often had an entry-vestibule with a wide, tall entry, giving access to the usual small square entry into the burial-chamber(s). Often too there was an ornamented façade, even a pediment, frieze, cornice, distyle inantis colonnade or separate monument. Beyond this the tomb of Helena had an elaborate system of chambers with both *kôḵîm* and bench-*arcosolia*. This tomb and the royal Herodian tomb are the only ones of this period (up to AD 135) to have a closing-stone like a large round cheese or a millstone.

All undisturbed tombs of this period also contain ossuaries, small limestone chests in which the bones were gathered up and reburied. *M.Sanhedrin* 6. 5b refers to this custom in the case of criminals, first buried in two special cemeteries by the Sanhedrin of Jerusalem (after the death penalty), then formally reburied in the family tomb. The bones of a crucified man have been found in his family tomb (*IEJ* 21, 1970, pp. 18–59). More general discussion of the 'gathering of bones' (*ossilegium*) in early rabbinic documents is particularly detailed in *Semahoth* 12–13, and involves the rabbis of *c.* AD 120 and later. Possibly it was the elder Eleazar bar Zadok whose father—before AD 70—urged that his bones must be gathered and reburied in a *dᵉlôsqōmā'* (ossuary), as his own father's bones had been buried. The archaeological evidence from

Jerusalem dates the use of ossuaries from *c.* 30 BC to AD 135, succeeding the large Hasmonaean bone-chambers (*IEJ* 8, 1958, pp. 101–105; 17, 1967, pp. 61–113). In the Tomb of Helena bones were also put into small box-like compartments near the *kokim*. E. M. Meyers has tried to prove continuous secondary burial from a very ancient period (*Jewish Ossuaries: Reburial and Rebirth*, 1971); see the important review by L. Y. Rahmani, *IEJ* 23, 1973, pp. 121–126, rejecting the identity of the Jerusalemite ossuary-burial with earlier practices.

Holy Sepulchre, *Garden tomb*, *Turin shroud*. Of these three the *Holy Sepulchre* has by far the greatest claim to authenticity—see especially articles by C. W. Wilson in *PEQ*, 1902–04. It is extremely unlikely that the site of 'Skull Place' (Golgotha) was lost before AD 135. Moreover in the early 4th century AD Eusebius was confident that the tomb of Jesus had been buried beneath a Roman temple dedicated to Aphrodite (*Life of Constantine* 3. 26), perhaps a Temple of Venus built by Hadrian (*PEQ* 1903, pp. 51–56, 63-65). The Christian pilgrim Arculf (AD 670) visited the Holy Sepulchre, and describes the burial-place in detail; unfortunately it has since been covered by marble panels. The description of Arculf indicates either a regular trough-arcosolium (impossible to date before the 2nd century AD) or perhaps the type shown here. This latter is extremely rare before AD 135 and therefore unlikely *c.* AD 30 (but not impossible; perhaps the last Jewish monumental tombs at Jerusalem date before the revolts of AD 66–70 and 132–5, and even before the unrest of the 50s and early 60s). Other tombs very close to the traditional one (and still within the Holy Sepulchre) are of the regular 1st-century type (see R. H. Smith, *BA* 30, 1967, pp. 74–90, especially pp. 83–85, and the articles by C. Clermont-Ganneau, C. W. Wilson and C. R. Conder, *PEQ* 1877, pp. 76–84, 128–132, 132–134).

The Garden tomb was first said to be the tomb of Jesus in the 19th century, and has been an attractive site for evangelical devotions ever since. It has the merit of displaying a simple rock-cut tomb in a garden, a setting obviously similar to that described in the Gospels. But it has no claim to authenticity, and was 'identified' on the basis of generalities. The burial-forms—single troughs cut round 3 sides of a chamber into which they project (*i.e.* they are not beneath *arcosolia*)—are unknown in Jerusalem in the NT period. Current Israeli research suggests an Iron Age date.

The Turin shroud, a piece of linen *c.* 3 m × 1 m, has on it a painting or impression of a human corpse, said to be the body of Jesus. The fact that natural facial highlights are reversed on film has been interpreted in two quite different ways — either that paint was used and has deteriorated (details: H. Thurston, *Catholic Encyclopaedia*, 13, 1912, p. 763), or that chemical emanations were produced by human agony (argued by Vignon in 1902; see A. J. Otterbein, *New Catholic Encyclopaedia*, 13, 1967, p. 187). The shroud is certainly the one which was displayed at Lirey in France in the 14th century, perhaps also at Constantinople from the 12th century. But NT and other early texts do not indicate the use of a shroud in the 1st century; rather winding-bands for the head and limbs and a linen shift or other garments for the body. The suggestion of Thurston that the shroud of Turin had the corpse of Jesus painted on it to be displayed at a liturgical Easter drama seems most reasonable (other 'shrouds' were certainly used in this way). J.P.K.

BURNING BUSH. The call of Moses to be Israel's deliverer took place when he turned to see the marvel of the bush which burned and yet was not consumed (Ex. 3:3). Like all such manifestations which the Bible records—*e.g.* the smoking-flashing oven (Gn. 15:17) and the cloudy-fiery pillar (Ex. 13:21)—the burning bush is a self-revelation of God, and not, as some hold, of Israel in the furnace of affliction. The story commences by saying that 'the *angel of the Lord appeared to him' (Ex. 3:2); the Hebrew translated 'in a flame' more aptly signifies 'as' or 'in the mode of' a flame (v. 2); Moses (v. 6) 'was afraid to look at God'; Dt. 33:16 speaks of 'him that dwelt in the bush'. The revelation thus conveyed may be summarized in the three words 'living', 'holy' and 'indwelling'. The bush is not consumed because the flame is self-sufficient, self-perpetuating. Equally, and by a consistent symbolism (*e.g.* Gn. 3:24; Ex. 19:18), the flame is the unapproachable holiness of God (v. 5), being, indeed, the first overt expression of the divine holiness in Scripture. Thirdly, so as to reveal the sovereign grace of God who, though self-sufficient, freely chooses and empowers instruments of service, the flame in the bush declares that the living, holy God is the Indweller. Thus the revelation at the bush is the background of the promise of the divine presence to Moses (v. 12), of the implementation of the covenant with the fathers (Ex. 2:24; 3:6; 6:5), of the divine name (v. 14), and of the holy law of Sinai.

BIBLIOGRAPHY. U. Cassuto, *A Commentary on the Book of Exodus*, 1967; B. S. Childs, *Exodus*, 1974. J.A.M.

BUZI. The father of Ezekiel (Ezk. 1:3). The Jewish tradition that he was Jeremiah must be firmly rejected, being based on an unwarranted supposition and fanciful etymology. He was a priest, probably a Zadokite and most likely of a more important priestly family, since his son was carried into captivity with Jehoiachin (2 Ki. 24:14–16). H.L.E.

C

CABUL. Identified with Ḥorvat Rosh Zayit, 1·5 km from mod. village of Kābūl, 13 km SE of Acco. Excavations since 1988 have found Iron Age II buildings and a later fortress marking the border between Phoenicia and Israel. It was a frontier village exchanged by Solomon's treaty with Hiram of Tyre (1 Ki. 9:13) to rectify the border. The name may be a play on words 'as nothing, defective' or simply 'borderland' (*cf.* Heb. *yᵉḇūl*).

BIBLIOGRAPHY. *NEAEHL*, pp. 1289–1291; *BA* 53, 1990, pp. 88–97; *BAR* 19, 1993, pp. 39–44, 84. D.J.W.

CAESAR. The name of a branch of the aristocratic family of the Julii which established an ascendancy over the Roman republic in the triumph of Augustus (31 BC) and kept it till Nero's death (AD 68). This hegemony (as it is nicely called in Lk. 3:1, Gk.; RSV 'reign' is too precise a term) was an unsystematic compound of legal and social powers, novel to Roman tradition in its monopoly of leadership rather than its form or theory. It was not technically a monarchy. Its success produced so thorough a reorientation of government, however, that, on the elimination of the Caesarian family, their position was institutionalized and their name assumed by its incumbents.

One of the bases of a Caesar's power was his extended tenure of a provincial command embracing most of Rome's frontier forces. Judaea always fell within this area, hence Paul's appeal (Acts 25:10–11) against the procurator, which would not have been possible where the governor was a fully competent proconsul and thus Caesar's equal. Hence also the Jewish custom of referring to Caesar as a king (Jn. 19:12, 15). The dynastic family was from their point of view monarchical. Even where the technical powers were not in Caesarian hands, however, the same terminology occurs (Acts 17:7; 1 Pet. 2:13, 17). The force of Hellenistic traditions of royal suzerainty over the republics, redirected through the universal oath of personal allegiance to the Caesarian house and their association in the imperial cult, nullified the strict Roman view of the Caesar's position. His quasi-monarchical role in any case simplified Rome's imperial task. But the cult of the Caesar came to pose an agonizing problem for Christians (Pliny, *Ep.* 10. 96–97 and perhaps Rev. 13).

The Caesars referred to in the NT are, in the Gospels, Augustus (Lk. 2:1), and elsewhere Tiberius, and in the Acts, Claudius (Acts 11:28; 17:7; 18:2), and elsewhere Nero.

BIBLIOGRAPHY. Suetonius, *Lives of the Caesars*; Tacitus, *Annals*; *CAH*, 10–11; F. Millar, *The Emperor in the Roman World*, 1977. E.A.J.

CAESAREA. This magnificent city, built by Herod the Great on the site of Strato's Tower, stood on the Mediterranean shore 37 km S of Mt Carmel and about 100 km NW of Jerusalem. Named in honour of the Roman emperor Caesar Augustus, it was the Roman metropolis of Judaea and the official residence both of the Herodian kings and the Roman procurators. It stood on the great caravan route between Tyre and Egypt, and was thus a busy commercial centre for inland trade. But Caesarea was also a celebrated maritime trading-centre, due largely to the construction of elaborate stone breakwaters N and S of the harbour.

The city was lavishly adorned with palaces, public buildings and an enormous amphitheatre, dominated by Herod's huge temple dedicated to Caesar and Rome. Archaeologists have found ruins of Herod's structures beneath later houses and fortresses. Herod's aqueduct, bringing fresh water 9 km from springs in the hills, still stands. In the theatre was found the only known inscription of Pontius Pilate.

Like other NT Mediterranean communities, Caesarea had a mixed population, making for inevitable clashes between Jews and Gentiles. When Pilate was procurator of Judaea he occupied the governor's residence in Caesarea. Philip, the evangelist and deacon, brought Christianity to his home city, and subsequently entertained Paul and his companions (Acts 21:8). Paul departed from Caesarea on his way to Tarsus, having escaped his Jewish enemies in Damascus (Acts 9:30). Caesarea was the abode of the centurion Cornelius and the locale of his conversion (Acts 10:1, 24; 11:11). At Caesarea Peter gained greater insight into the nature of the divine kingdom by realizing that God had disrupted the barriers between Gentile and Jewish believers (Acts 10:35), and had dispensed with such classifications as 'clean' and 'unclean'.

Paul landed at Caesarea when returning from his second and third missionary journeys (Acts 18:22; 21:8). Paul's fateful decision to visit Jerusalem was made here also (Acts 21:13), and it was to Caesarea that he was sent for trial by Felix (Acts 23:23–33) before being imprisoned for 2 years. Paul made his defence before Festus and Agrippa in Caesarea, and sailed from there in chains when sent by Festus to Rome on his own appeal (Acts 25:11).

BIBLIOGRAPHY. L. I. Levine, *Roman Caesarea: An Archeological-Topographical Study*, 1975; *NEAEHL*, pp. 270–291; R. L. Hohlfelder, *ABD* 1, pp. 798–803. A.R.M. R.K.H.

CAESAREA PHILIPPI. A beautiful locality at the foot of Mt Hermon, on the main source of the

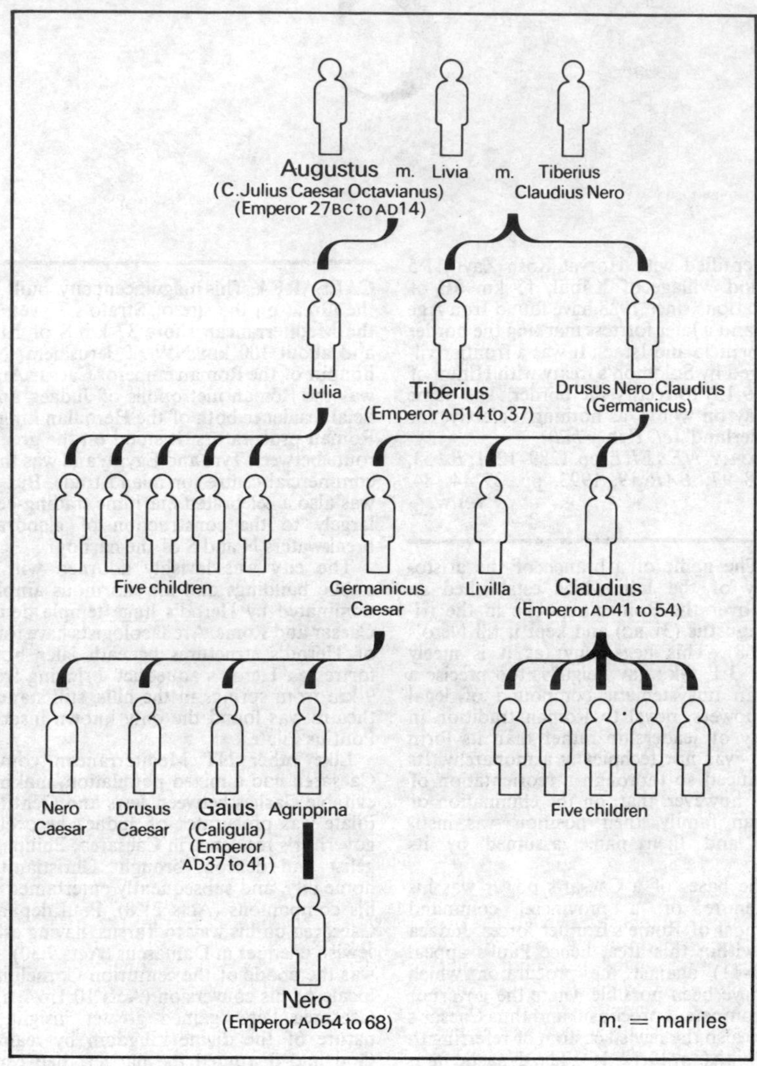

Simplified family tree of the Julio-Claudians.

river Jordan, famed as the place of Peter's confession (Mt. 16:13ff.). It may be the OT Baal-gad. Baal was the deity worshipped there in OT times; the Greeks later substituted their god Pan, and the town took the name Paneas, the shrine itself being called Panion. When the Seleucid ruler Antiochus III wrested Palestine (together with the whole of Coelesyria) from the Ptolemies, Paneas was the scene of one of the decisive battles (200 BC). Herod the Great built a marble temple to Augustus Caesar, who had given him the town; and Philip the tetrarch later in the same emperor's reign further adorned the town, renaming it Caesarea in the emperor's honour. The addition 'Philippi'—*i.e.* of Philip—was to distinguish it from the coastal *Caesarea (*cf.* Acts 8:40). Agrippa II then rebuilt the town in Nero's reign, and gave it another name, Neronias; but this name was soon forgotten. The town had a considerable history in Crusader times. Its ancient name persists as Banias today. There is a shrine there to the Muslim al-Khidr, equated with St George. D.F.P.

CAESAR'S HOUSEHOLD. A Roman aristocrat's household (Gk. *oikia*, Lat. *familia*) was his staff of servants, primarily those held in slavery, but probably also including those manumitted and retaining obligations of clientship as his freedmen. Their duties were extremely specialized, and covered the full range of domestic service, professional duties (medicine, education, *etc.*), and business, literary and secretarial assistance. In the case of the Caesars, their permanent political leadership made their household the equivalent of a modern civil service, providing the experts in most fields of state. Its servile origins, and the eastern responsibilities of the Caesars, made it largely

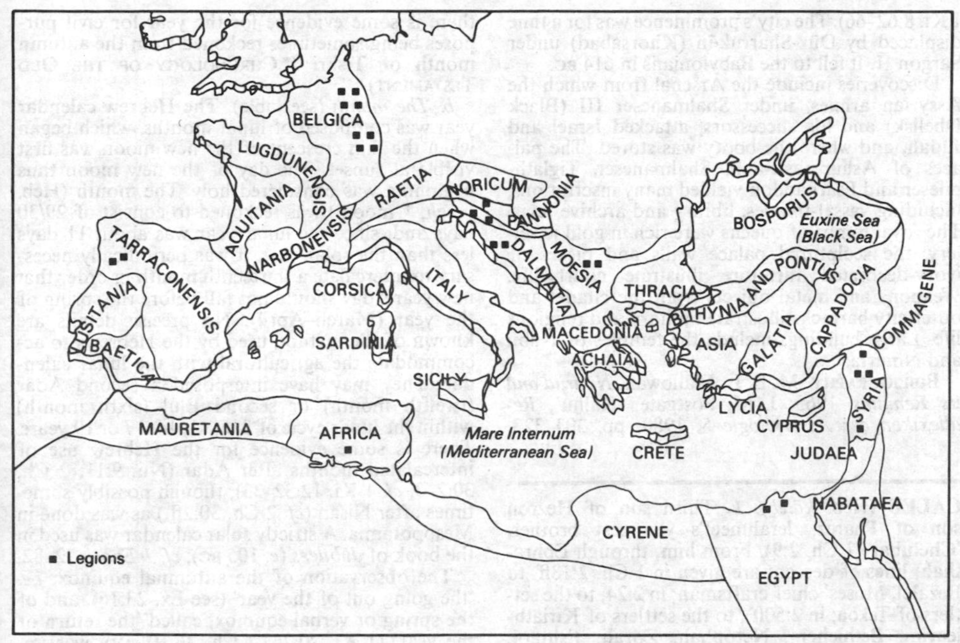

The Roman Empire at the beginning of the reign of Tiberius Caesar in AD *14. The gradual extension of direct Roman rule in the East led to a somewhat changed provincial organization, especially in Asia Minor, by the time of Paul (see p. 155).*

Greek and oriental in its composition. It is not therefore surprising to find it well represented amongst the believers in Rome (Phil. 4:22).

Bibliography. J. B. Lightfoot, *Philippians*[7], 1883, pp. 171–178; P. R. C. Weaver, *Familia Caesaris*, 1972. E.A.J.

CAIAPHAS Joseph Caiaphas was high priest from AD 18 to 36. He was son-in-law to Annas (Jn. 18:13). Caiaphas interrogated Jesus and handed him over to Pilate (Mt. 26:57–68; Jn. 11:49). An ossuary of the Second Temple Period, inscribed 'Yosef bar Qayafa'', perhaps Caiaphas, has been found in a family tomb in the Peace Forest near Jerusalem (*BAR* 18, 1992, pp. 28–45).

Bibliography. Z. Greenhut *et al.*, 'The Caiaphas Tomb in North Talpiyot, Jerusalem', *Atiqot*, 21, 1992, pp. 63–87. D.J.W.

CAIN (Heb. *qayin*). **1.** The eldest son of Adam and Eve (Gn. 4:1), at whose birth Eve said, 'I have gotten (*qānîṯî*) a man' (AV). Since this account is unlikely to have been originally couched in Heb., no judgment can be made on the validity of the pun, and nothing can be concluded from apparent etymologies of the name. He was an agriculturalist (Gn. 4:2), unlike *Abel, who was a shepherd, and being 'of the evil one' (*ek tou ponērou*, 1 Jn. 3:12) and out of harmony with God (Heb. 11:4), his offering (*minḥâ*) was rejected (Gn. 4:3–7) and he subsequently killed his brother (Gn. 4:8). God punished him by sending him to become a wanderer, perhaps a nomad, in the land of *Nod (Gn. 4:9–16), and to protect him from being slain himself God set a 'mark' (*'ôṯ*, 'sign, token', *cf.* Gn. 9:12–13) 'for' (*l[e]*) him. The nature of the 'mark' is unknown. Cain was the father of *Enoch. Parallels to the conflict between Cain and Abel have been drawn from Sumerian literature, where disputations concerning the relative merits of agriculture and herding are found, but in none of those known does the farmer kill the herdsman, and such a conflict probably only reflects the historical situation in Mesopotamia from late prehistoric times onwards. (*Nomads.)

Bibliography. S. N. Kramer, 'Sumerian Literature and the Bible', in *Analecta Biblica* 12, 1959, p. 192; *History Begins at Sumer*, 1958, pp. 164–166, 185–192; C. J. Gadd, *Teachers and Students in the Oldest Schools*, 1956, pp. 39ff.; S. H. Hooke, 'Cain and Abel', in *The Siege Perilous*, 1956, pp. 66ff.

2. The name of a town, written with the article (*haqqayin*), in the S of the territory allotted to Judah (Jos. 15:57), and probably to be identified with modern Khirbet Yaqin to the SE of Hebron. See A. Alt, *Palästina-jahrhbuch* 22, 1926, pp. 76–77. T.C.M.

CALAH. The Assyrian state and provincial capital on the E bank of the River Tigris *c.* 35 km S of Nineveh (Assyr. *Kalhu*, mod. Tell Nimrūd). Deep soundings show that it was founded by migrants from Sumer (Gn. 10:11–12). Excavations by the British in 1845–8 (Layard), 1948–63 (Mallowan and Oates), Iraqis and others (1969–80) have traced its use from prehistoric to Hellenistic times.

Rebuilt by Shalmaneser I (*c.* 1250 BC), it was redeveloped as the military capital of the Assyrian Empire by Ashurnasirapli II. His inauguration ceremony in 879 BC was attended by 69,574 persons (the Banquet Stela, *ANET*[3], pp. 558–560, *cf.*

1 Ki. 8:62–66). The city's prominence was for a time displaced by Dūr-Sharrukēn (Khorsabad) under Sargon II. It fell to the Babylonians in 614 BC.

Discoveries include the Arsenal from which the Assyrian armies, under Shalmaneser III (Black Obelisk) and his successors, attacked Israel and Judah, and where the booty was stored. The palaces of Ashur-nasir-apli, Shalmaneser, Tiglath-pileser and Esarhaddon yielded many inscriptions, including vassal-treaties, library and archive texts. The royal tombs of queens were rich in gold jewellery, the sculptured palace walls and pieces of ivory-decorated furniture illustrate court life. Weapons and metal objects from the citadel and outer city barracks illustrate military and religious life. Large buildings include the temples of Nabû and Ninurta.

BIBLIOGRAPHY. M. E. L. Mallowan, *Nimrud and its Remains*, 1965; J. M. Postgate, 'Kalḫu', *Reallexikon der Assyriologie* 5, 1980, pp. 303–323.

D.J.W.

CALEB (Heb. *kālēḇ*). **1.** Third son of Hezron son of Pharez: Jerahmeel's youngest brother; 'Chelubai' (1 Ch. 2:9). From him, through Ephrathah, lines of descent are given in 1 Ch. 2:18ff. to Bezalel, Moses' chief craftsman; in 2:24, to the settlers of Tekoa; in 2:50ff., to the settlers of Kiriath-jearim, Bethlehem, Netophah, Zorah, Eshtaol, Beth-gader and others (the Kenite families named in 2:55 may be loosely connected).

2. 'Brother of Jerahmeel' (1 Ch. 2:42), possibly the same as **1**, from whom descent was traced in the towns of Ziph, Maon and Beth-zur (the names Hebron and Tappuach also occur). This list may refer in part to Caleb **3**, father of Achsah (v. 49).

3. Caleb ben Jephunneh, an outstanding leader of Judah, whose faithfulness in the mutiny at Kadesh won him exemption from the curse pronounced there (Nu. 14:24). He directed the invasion of Judaea and settled at Hebron (Jos. 1; 15). From Jos. 14:6, *etc.*; 1 Ch. 4:14–15, we learn that he was a *Kenizzite. *Nabal was his descendant.

4. 'Brother of Shuhah', spelt 'Chelub' in 1 Ch. 4:11.

J.P.U.L.

CALENDAR.

I. In the Old Testament

There is no precise Heb. equivalent of the Lat. *calendarium*, the passage of the year being generally marked by reference to the months, agricultural seasons or the principal festivals.

a. The year (Heb. *šānâ*—so named from the change or succession of the seasons) was at first reckoned to begin with the autumn (seventh) month of Tishri (Ex. 23:16; 34:22), the time also of the commencement of the sabbatical year (Lv. 25:8–10). While in Egypt the Hebrews may have conformed to the solar year of 12 months, each of 30 days + 5 additional days, *i.e.* 365 days (Herodotus, 2. 4), but if so a change was made thereafter and the 'beginning of months' or first month of the year was fixed in the spring (Ex. 12:2; 13:3–4; 23:15; Dt. 16:1, 6). Thereafter the Hebrew year followed the W Semitic Calendar with a year of 12 lunar months (1 Ki. 4:7; 1 Ch. 27:1–15). It is not certain whether the commencement of the year in spring (Nisan) was for use only in the ritual, since there is some evidence for the year for civil purposes being sometimes reckoned from the autumn month of Tishri (*CHRONOLOGY OF THE OLD TESTAMENT).

b. The month (see table). The Hebrew calendar year was composed of lunar months, which began when the thin crescent of the new moon was first visible at sunset. The day of the new moon thus beginning was considered holy. The month (Heb. *yeraḥ*, *'moon') was reckoned to consist of 29/30 days and, since the lunar year was about 11 days less than the solar year, it was periodically necessary to intercalate a thirteenth month in order that new year's day should not fall before the spring of the year (March–April). No precise details are known of the method used by the Hebrews to accommodate the agricultural with the lunar calendar. They may have interposed a second Adar (twelfth month) or second Elul (sixth month) within the lunar cycle of 3, 6, 11, 14, 17 or 19 years. There is some evidence for the Hebrew use of intercalated months after Adar (Nu. 9:11; 2 Ch. 30:2–3; *cf.* 1 Ki. 12:32–33), though possibly sometimes after Nisan (*cf.* 2 Ch. 30:2ff.) as was done in Mesopotamia. A strictly solar calendar was used in the book of *Jubilees* (*c.* 105 BC); *cf. 1 Enoch* 72–82.

The observation of the autumnal equinox, *i.e.* 'the going out of the year' (see Ex. 23:16), and of the spring or vernal equinox, called 'the return of the year' (1 Ki. 20:26; 2 Ch. 36:10, AV), was important for controlling the calendar and consequently the festivals. Thus the year began with the new moon nearest to the vernal equinox when the sun was in Aries (Jos., *Ant.* 3. 201), and the Passover on the fourteenth day of Nisan coincided with the first full moon (Ex. 12:2–6).

The early month names were probably local Palestinian references to the seasons, and differ from the designation of the months named in texts from Syria (Ras Shamra, Alalaḫ, Mari). Some are known from Phoenician also. *Abib*, 'ripening of corn' (Ex. 13:4); *Ziv* (AV Zif; 1 Ki. 6:1, 37); *Ethanim* (1 Ki. 8:2) and *Bul* (1 Ki. 6:38) of uncertain meaning, are the only names extant from this period. At all periods the months were usually designated numerically; first, Ex. 12:2; second, Gn. 7:11; third, Ex. 19:1; fourth, 2 Ki. 25:3; fifth, Nu. 33:38; sixth, 1 Ch. 27:9; seventh, Gn. 8:4; eighth, Zc. 1:1; ninth, Ezr. 10:9; tenth, Gn. 8:5; eleventh, Dt. 1:3; twelfth, Est. 3:7. In post-exilic times the month-names of the Babylonian calendar were followed (see table).

c. The seasons—the agricultural calendar. Although the Hebrews adopted a calendar based on lunar months, they also, as agriculturalists, commonly indicated time of year by the season rather than by the names or numeration of the months. Thus, the year which in Palestine divided approximately into the dry season (April–September) and the rainy season (October–March) could be again subdivided generally into 'seed-time' (November–December) and 'harvest' (April–June; Gn. 8:22). More specific designations would indicate to the local inhabitants actual months, *e.g.* wheat (Gn. 30:14; Jdg. 15:1) or barley harvest (2 Sa. 21:9; Ru. 1:22) denotes March–April; the 'earing time' (Ex. 34:21) would be March; and 'the first ripe grapes' (Nu. 13: 20) the month *Tammuz* (June–July). 'The first rains' (based on the old civil calendar beginning in *Tishri*) fell in September–October, and the 'latter rains' in March–April. The 'summer-fruit' (*qāyiṣ*) of August–September gave its name to the 'summer', also called the 'heat'. The months *Ṭebet*

	Month	Pre-exilic name	Post-exilic name	Modern equivalent	Season	Festivals
Rain	1	ABIB Ex. 13:4; 23:15; 34:18; Dt. 16:1	NISAN Est. 3:7 Ne. 2:1	Mar.–Apr.	Spring Latter rains Barley harvest Flax harvest	14 Passover (Ex. 12:18; Lv. 23:5) 15–21 Unleavened Bread (Lv. 23:6) 16 Firstfruits (Lv. 23:10f.)
Dry	2	ZIV 1 Ki. 6:1, 37	IYYAR	Apr.–May	Dry season begins	14 Later Passover (Nu. 9:10–11)
	3		SIVAN Est. 8:9	May–June	Early figs ripen	6 Pentecost (Lv. 23:15ff.) Feast of Weeks Harvest
	4		TAMMUZ	June–July	Grape harvest	
	5		AB	July–Aug.	Olive harvest	
	6		ELUL Ne. 6:15	Aug.–Sept.	Dates and summer figs	
Rain	7	ETHANIM 1 Ki. 8:2	TISHRI	Sept.–Oct.	Early rains	1 Trumpets (Nu. 29:1; Lv. 23:24) 10 Day of Atonement (Lv. 16:29ff.; 23:27ff.) 15–21 Tabernacles (Lv. 23:34 ff.) 22 Solemn assembly (Lv. 23:36)
	8	BUL 1 Ki. 6:38	MARCHESVAN	Oct.–Nov.	Ploughing Winter figs	
	9		CHISLEV Ne. 1:1	Nov.–Dec.	Sowing	25 Dedication (1 Macc. 4:52f.; Jn. 10:22)
Cold	10		TEBETH Est. 2:16	Dec.–Jan.	Rains (snow on high ground)	
	11		SHEBAT Zc. 1:7	Jan.–Feb.	Almond blossom	
Rain	12		ADAR Est. 3:7	Feb.–Mar.	Citrus fruit harvest	

The Hebrew calendar, showing seasons and festivals with modern equivalents.

and *Šebaṭ* were the 'cold' months (see table under heading 'Seasons').

With the above OT references may be compared the agricultural calendar roughly written on stone, perhaps a palimpsest inscribed by a schoolboy in the 10th century BC, found at Gezer in 1908. The translation is uncertain, but it lists the agricultural operations for the 12 months of the year beginning with the autumn: 'Two months of storage. Two months of sowing. Two months of spring growth. Month of pulling flax. Month of barley harvest. Month when everything (else) is harvested. Two months of pruning (vines). Month of summer fruit' (*cf.* *DOTT*, pp. 201–203).

d. Other ways of accounting times and seasons are covered by general words for a specified 'time' or festival (*'iddān*, Dn. 7:25; *mō'ēḏ*, Dn. 12:7; *zᵉmān*, Ec. 3:1; Ne. 2:6), *cf.* Ps. 104:27. Historical events are normally dated by the regnal years of rulers or by synchronism with some memorable national event, *e.g.* the Exodus; the sojourn in Egypt (Ex. 12:40); the construction of the first Temple (1 Ki. 6:1); or the 70–year Exile in Babylon (Ezk. 33:21); or the earthquake in the reign of Uzziah (Am. 1:1; Zc. 14:5).

BIBLIOGRAPHY. J. Finegan, *Handbook of Biblical Chronology*, 1964; J. B. Segal, *VT* 7, 1957, pp. 250–307; *JSS* 7, 1962, pp. 212–221.

D.J.W.

II. Between the Testaments

The 'year of the kingdom of the Greeks' (1 Macc. 1:10) is the Seleucid era, dating officially from the first day of the Macedonian month Dios (September/October) in 312 BC. This era is followed in 1 Macc., though in some of the sources used in that book (under the influence of the Babylonian reckoning of the beginning of the year from Nisan) the era is dated from March/April, 311 BC.

III. In the New Testament

Dates in the NT are occasionally reckoned by reference to Gentile rulers. The most elaborate example is in Lk. 3:1f., where the beginning of the ministry of John the Baptist is dated not only 'in the fifteenth year of the reign of Tiberius Caesar' (*i.e.* AD 27–28, according to the reckoning retained in the former Seleucid realm, where a new regnal year was held to start in September/October), but also by reference to rulers then in office, whether secular or sacerdotal, in Judaea and the neighbouring territories. *Cf.* datings by reference to the emperors Augustus (Lk. 2:1) and Claudius (Acts 11:28), the provincial governors Quirinius (Lk. 2:2) and Gallio (Acts 18:12), and Herod, king of the Jews (Mt. 2:1; Lk. 1:5).

For the most part, however, the NT writers measure time in terms of the current Jewish calendar (or calendars). The record is punctuated by reference to Jewish festivals and other sacred occasions. This is especially so in the Fourth Gospel; *cf.* Jn. 2:13, 23 (Passover); 5:1 (perhaps the New Year); 6:4 (Passover); 7:2 (Tabernacles; in v. 37 'the last day, that great day of the feast' is the eighth day; *cf.* Lv. 23:36; Nu. 29:35; Ne. 8:18); 10:22 (Dedication, on 25th Kislew; *cf.* 1 Macc. 4:59); 11:55ff. (Passover). *Cf.* also Mt. 26:2; Mk. 14:1; Lk. 22:1 (Passover and Unleavened Bread); Acts 2:1 (Pentecost); 12:3f. (Passover and Unleavened Bread); 18:21, AV (perhaps Passover); 20:6 (Unleavened Bread); 20:16 (Pentecost); 27:9 (where 'the fast' is the Day of Atonement, about which time sailing in the Mediterranean came to an end for the winter); 1 Cor. 16:8 (Pentecost).

Among days of the week, the sabbath is frequently mentioned. The 'second first sabbath' (Lk. 6:1 mg.) is probably a technical term whose meaning can no longer be determined with certainty. Friday is 'the day of Preparation (Gk. *paraskeuē*), that is, the day before the sabbath (Gk. *prosabbaton*)' (Mk. 15:42; *cf.* Jn. 19:31); 'the day of Preparation of the Passover' (Jn. 19:14) means 'Friday of Passover week' (Gk. *paraskeuē tou pascha*). The 'first day of the week' (Gk. *mia sabbatou* or *mia tōn sabbatōn*, *i.e.* one day after the sabbath) receives a new significance from its being the resurrection day; *cf.* (in addition to the resurrection narratives in the Gospels) Acts 20:7; 1 Cor. 16:2; also 'the *Lord's day' (Gk. *kyriakē hēmera*) in Rev. 1:10.

In general, the Jewish calendar in NT times (at least before AD 70) followed the Sadducean reckoning, since it was by that reckoning that the Temple services were regulated. Thus the day of Pentecost was reckoned as the fiftieth day after the presentation of the first harvested sheaf of barley, *i.e.* the fiftieth day (inclusive) from the first Sunday after Passover (*cf.* Lv. 23:15f.); hence it always fell on a Sunday, as it does in the Christian calendar. The Pharisaic reckoning, which became standard after AD 70, interpreted 'sabbath' in Lv. 23:15 as the festival day of Unleavened Bread and not the weekly sabbath; in that case Pentecost always fell on the same day of the month (an important consideration for those in whose eyes it marked the anniversary of the law-giving) but not on the same day of the week.

Even more important than the minor calendrical differences between Sadducees and Pharisees was the cleavage between the Sadducees and Pharisees, on the one hand, and those, on the other hand, who followed the 'sectarian' calendar known from the book of *Jubilees* and now also from the Qumran literature. If Jesus and his disciples followed this 'sectarian' calendar, that might explain how they kept the Passover before his arrest, while the chief priests and their associates did not keep it until after his crucifixion (Jn. 18:28).

BIBLIOGRAPHY. A. Jaubert, *La Date de la Cène*, 1957, and 'Jésus et le calendrier de Qumrân', *NTS* 7, 1960–1, pp. 1ff.; J. van Goudoever, *Biblical Calendars*, 1959; J. B. Segal, *The Hebrew Passover from the Earliest Times to AD 70*, 1963; J. Finegan, *Handbook of Bible Chronology*, 1963; E. J. Bickerman, *Chronology of the Ancient World*, 1968; E. J. Wiesenberg and others, 'Calendar' in *EJ*; W. M. O'Neil, *Time and the Calendars*, 1975; T. Talley, 'Liturgical Time in the Ancient Church: The State of Research', *Studia Liturgica* 14, 1982, pp. 34–51; R. T. Beckwith, 'The Essene Calendar and the Moon: A Reconsideration', *RQ* 15, 1992, pp. 457–466; S. Talmon, 'The Calender of the Covenanters', *The World of Qumram from Within*, 1989, pp. 147–185.

F.F.B.

CALF, GOLDEN. 1. The golden image made after the Exodus by Aaron and the Israelites at Sinai while Moses was in the mountain. On finding that they were idolatrously worshipping it as God with sacrifices, feasting and revelry, Moses destroyed it (Ex. 32:4–8, 18–25, 35; Dt. 9:16, 21; Ne. 9:18; Ps. 106:19–20; Acts 7:41). This idol is sometimes thought to be the Egyptian Apis-bull of Memphis (see *IBA*, p. 39, fig. 33) or the Mnevis bull of Heliopolis, but these are too far away from Goshen to have been really familiar to the Hebrews. In fact, there were several not dissimilar bull-cults in the E Delta, much closer to the Hebrews in Goshen, which they could have aped later at Sinai. To the SW of *Goshen (Tumilat-area), in the 10th Lower Egyptian nome or province, called 'the Black Bull', there was an amalgam of Horus-worship and bull-or calf-cult; farther N and extending along the NW of Goshen itself, the 11th Lower Egyptian nome also possessed a bull-cult linked with Horus-worship; other traces are known. (See E. Otto, *Beiträge zur Geschichte der Stierkulte in Aegypten*, 1938, pp. 6–8, 32–33.) In Egypt, the bull or calf was a symbol of fertility in nature, and of physical strength (*cf.* Otto, *op. cit.*, pp. 1–2, 24f., and *passim*), and, as elsewhere in the Near East, could even perhaps have had links with the worship of the host of heaven. (*Cf.* Wainwright, *JEA* 19, 1933, pp. 42–52, especially pp. 44–46. For certain reserves, see Otto, *op. cit.*, p. 7, n. 4. Perhaps *cf.* also Acts 7:41–42 in conjunction?)

In nearby Canaan, however, the bull or calf was the animal of Baal or Hadad, god(s) of storm, fertility and vegetation, and, as in Egypt, symbolized fertility and strength. Bearing in mind the close links between Canaan and the Egyptian E Delta (*EGYPT, *MOSES) and the presence of many Semites in the Delta besides the Israelites, it is possible to view the idolatry at Sinai as a blending of contemporary, popular bull- and calf-cults, Egyptian and Canaanite alike, with their emphasis on natural strength and fertility. In any case, it represented a reduction of the God of Israel (*cf.* 'feast to the Lord', Ex. 32:5) to the status of an amoral (tending to immoral) nature-god like those of the surrounding nations, and meant that he could then all too easily be identified with the Baals. This God rejected, refusing to be identified with the god of the calf, hence condemning it as the worship of an 'other' god, and therefore idolatry (Ex. 32:8).

2. At the division of the Hebrew kingdom, Israel's first king, Jeroboam I, wishing to counteract the great attraction of the Temple at Jerusalem in Judah, set up two golden calves, in Bethel and Dan, to be centres of Israel's worship of Yahweh (1 Ki. 12:28–33; 2 Ki. 17:16; 2 Ch. 11:14–15; 13:8). In Syria-Palestine the gods Baal or Hadad were commonly thought of (and shown) as standing upon a bull or calf, emblem of their powers of fertility and strength (see *ANEP*, pp. 170, 179, figs. 500, 501, 531), and Jeroboam's action had the same disastrous implications as Aaron's golden calf: the reduction of Yahweh to a nature-god, and his subsequent identification with the Baals of Canaan. With this would go a shift in emphasis from righteousness, justice and an exemplary moral standard to purely physical and material considerations, sliding easily into immorality with a religious backing, with social disintegration, and total loss of any sense of the divinely appointed mission of the chosen people in a darkened world. All this was bound up in the idolatry that was 'the sin of Jeroboam, son of Nebat'.

Jehu (2 Ki. 10:29) removed the more obvious and explicit Baal-worship in Israel, but not the calves of a Baalized Yahweh. Hosea (8:5–6; 13:2) prophesied the coming end of such 'worship'.

K.A.K.

CALL, CALLING. In OT and NT there are some 700 occurrences of the word as verb, noun or adjective. The principal Heb. root is *qr'*; in Gk. *kalein* (with its compounds, and derivatives *klētos*, 'called', and *klēsis*, 'calling'), *legein* and *phōnein* are used. In both languages other verbs are occasionally rendered by parts of 'to call', *e.g.* *'mr* in Is. 5:20, and *chrēmatizein* in Rom. 7:3.

I. In the Old Testament

a. 'Call to', hence 'invite or summon (by name)' (Gn. 3:9, *etc.*); 'summon an assembly' (La. 1:15). 'Call upon the name' is found from Gn. 4:26 onwards ('men began to call upon the name of the Lord'), and denotes the claiming of God's protection either by summoning assistance from one whose name (*i.e.* character) was known, or by calling oneself by the name of the Lord (*cf.* Gn. 4:26 AVmg.; Dt. 28:10; Is. 43:7).

b. 'Give a name to' is found in such verses as Gn. 1:5 ('God called the light Day'). Those verses where God is the subject indicate the underlying unity of the two senses of *qr'*, thereby revealing its theological meaning. The first sense implies a call to serve God in some capacity and for some particular purpose (1 Sa. 3:4; Is. 49:1). The meaning of the sense is not simply to identify; it is both to describe (Gn. 16:11; *cf.* Mt. 1:21) and to indicate a relationship between God the nominator and his nominee, especially Israel. Is. 43:1 epitomizes God's call and naming of Israel to be his, separated from other nations, granted the work of bearing witness, and the privilege of the protection afforded by his name. God alone initiates this call, and only a minority (remnant) respond (*e.g.* Joel 2:32).

II. In the New Testament

Here the same usages are found, and the call of God is now 'in Christ Jesus' (Phil. 3:14). It is a summons to bear the name of Christian (1 Pet. 4:16; Jas. 2:7; Acts 5:41; Mt. 28:19) and to belong to God in Christ (1 Pet. 2:9). 'Call to' is found in, *e.g.*, Mk. 2:17 and 'give a name to' in Lk. 1:59. The present passive participle is in frequent use, as in Lk. 7:11. Jesus called disciples and they followed him (Mk. 1:20). The Epistles, especially Paul's, make clear the theological meaning of Christ's call. It comes from God, through the gospel for salvation through sanctification and belief (2 Thes. 2:14) to God's kingdom (1 Thes. 2:12), for fellowship (1 Cor. 1:9) and service (Gal 1:15). Other writers impart this full meaning to God's call through Jesus (*cf.* Heb. 3:1; 9:15; 1 Pet. 2:21; 1 Jn. 3:1 especially—'. . . that we should be called children of God; and so we are'). Those who respond are 'called' (1 Cor. 1:24; Lightfoot translates as 'believers'). Paul equates call and response (Rom. 8:28ff.) to emphasize God's unchanging purpose (Rom. 9:11), *i.e.*, Paul sees the call as effective. The saying of Jesus in Mt. 22:14 distinguishes 'the called', those who hear, from 'the chosen', those who respond and become 'choice'.

Many commentators interpret 'calling' in 1 Cor. 7:20ff. as a particular occupation. Rather *klēsis* here means the divine calling of each man as a concrete historical event, *i.e.* as including in itself the outward circumstances in which it was received. Slavery as such is not incompatible with faith in Christ.

BIBLIOGRAPHY. K. L. Schmidt, *TDNT* 3, pp. 487–536; L. Coenen, *NIDNTT* 1, pp. 271–276; C. H. Horne, *ZPEB* 1, p. 694; G. W. Bromiley, *ISBE* 1, pp. 580–582. M.R.W.F.

CALNEH, CALNO. 1. Calneh. The name of a city founded by Nimrod in the land of *Shinar (Gn. 10:10, AV). Since no city of this name is known in Babylonia, some scholars propose to point the Heb. *kullānâ*, 'all of them', as in Gn. 42:36; 1 Ki. 7:37. This would then be a comprehensive clause to cover such ancient cities as Ur and Nippur (identified with Calneh in TB). Those who locate Shinar in N Mesopotamia equate this city with **2** and also with *CANNEH.

2. Calno (Kalno), Is. 10:9; Kalneh, Am. 6:2 (LXX *pantes*, 'all', see **1**). A town Kullania mentioned in Assyr. tribute lists. Associated with Arpad. Modern Kullan Köy 16 km SE of Arpad (*AJSL* 51, 1935, pp. 189–191).

BIBLIOGRAPHY. *JNES* 3, 1944, p. 254. D.J.W.

CALVARY. The name occurs once only in the AV, in Lk. 23:33, and not at all in most EVV. The word comes from the Vulgate, where the Lat. *calvaria* translates the Gk. *kranion*; both words translate Aramaic *gulgoltâ*, the 'Golgotha' of Mt. 27:33, meaning 'skull'. Three possible reasons for such a name have been propounded: because skulls were found there; because it was a place of execution; or because the site in some way resembled a skull. All we know of the site from Scripture is that it was outside Jerusalem, fairly conspicuous, probably not far from a city gate and a highway, and that a garden containing a tomb lay near by.

Two Jerusalem localities are today pointed out as the site of the Lord's cross and tomb; the one is the Church of the Holy Sepulchre, the other Gordon's Calvary, commonly known as the Garden Tomb. Unfortunately it has always proved difficult to debate the question objectively; in some quarters the identification one accepts is almost the touchstone of one's orthodoxy. The Church of the Holy Sepulchre marks the site of a temple to Venus which the emperor Constantine removed, understanding that it stood over the sacred site. The tradition thus goes back at least to the 4th century. But in view of the operations and activities of Titus in the 1st century and Hadrian in the 2nd, the identification must still be viewed as precarious. It has at least been clarified by recent excavations that the traditional site lay outside the city walls in the time of Christ. On the other hand, the evidence of the church itself may indicate a tomb of slightly too late a date to be authentic: see *BURIAL AND MOURNING (NT).

The Garden Tomb was first pointed out in 1849; a rock formation there resembles a skull; and admittedly the site accords with the biblical data. But there is no tradition nor anything else to support its claim. The more ancient site is much more likely; but any identification must remain conjectural.

BIBLIOGRAPHY. L. E. Cox Evans, *PEQ* 1968, pp. 112–136; D. Bahat, *Illustrated Atlas of Jerusalem*, 1990, pp. 54–57; and other bibliography under *JERUSALEM. D.F.P.

CAMEL (Heb. *gāmāl*; Gk. *kamēlos*). A desert quadruped, famous for its ability to cross desert regions through being able to carry within itself several days' water-supply. The Heb. term (like the popular use of the word 'camel' in English) does *not* distinguish between the two characteristic kinds of camel: the one-humped animal (*Camelus dromedarius*) or 'dromedary' of Arabia, and the two-humped beast (*Camelus bactrianus*) or Bactrian camel from NE of Iran (Bactria, now in Turkmen and NW Afghanistan). In antiquity, both kinds are represented on the monuments.

In Scripture, camels are first mentioned in the days of the Patriarchs (*c.* 1900–1700 BC). They formed part of the livestock wealth of Abraham and Jacob (Gn. 12:16; 24:35; 30:43; 32:7, 15) and also of Job (1:3, 17; 42:12). On only two notable occasions are the Patriarchs actually shown using camels for transport: when Abraham's servant went to Mesopotamia to obtain a wife for Isaac (Gn. 24:10ff.), and when Jacob fled from Laban (Gn. 31:17, 34)—neither an everyday event. Otherwise, camels are attributed only to the Ishmaelites/Midianites, desert traders, at this time (Gn. 37:25). This very modest utilization of camels in the patriarchal age corresponds well with the known rather limited use of camels in the early 2nd millennium BC (see below).

In the 13th century BC the Egyptian beasts of burden smitten with disease included horses (the most valuable), asses (the most usual) and camels (a rarity), besides others (Ex. 9:3); and in the law camels were forbidden as food (Lv. 11:4; Dt. 14:7).

The mention of camels in the Pentateuch, especially in Genesis, has been often and persistently dismissed as anachronistic by some but stoutly defended by others. The truth appears to be as follows. From the 12th century BC the camel (and camel-nomadism) becomes a regular feature in the biblical world (other than Egypt, where it remains rare). Before this date, definite but very limited use was made of the camel. Though limited and imperfect, the extant evidence clearly indicates that the domesticated camel was known by 3000 BC, and continued in limited use as a slow-moving burden-carrier down through the 2nd millennium BC, the ass being the main beast of burden. (*ANIMALS OF THE BIBLE.)

Archaeological evidence. From the evidence available, only a few items bearing on Genesis and Exodus can be cited here. First and foremost, a mention of the (domesticated) camel occurs in a cuneiform tablet from Alalaḫ in N Syria (18th century BC) as GAM.MAL; see Wiseman, *JCS* 13, 1959, p. 29 and Goetze, *ibid.*, p. 37, on text 269, line 59. Lambert (*BASOR* 160, 1960, pp. 42–43), however, disputes the Alalaḫ camel-reference, and instead produces evidence for knowledge of the camel in the Old Babylonian period (*c.* 19th century BC) in a text from Ugarit. Then there is the kneeling camel-figure from Byblos of similar date (Montet, *Byblos et l'Égypte*, 1928, p. 91 and plate 52, No. 179). Albright's objection (*JBL* 64, 1945, p. 288) that it has no hump (hence not a camel) is ruled out because the figure is incomplete and has a socket by which a separately-fashioned hump and load were once fixed (this is also noted by R. de Vaux, *RB* 56, 1949, p. 9, nn. 4–5). A camel's jaw was found in a Middle Bronze Age tomb at Tell el-Fara' by Nablus (*c.* 1900–1550 BC) (de Vaux, *op. cit.*, p. 9, n. 8). Nor does this exhaust the evidence for the patriarchal period.

In the Egyptian Fayum province was found a camel-skull dated to the 'Pottery A' stage, *i.e.* within the period *c.* 2000–1400 BC, the period from the Patriarchs practically to Moses; see O. H. Little, *Bulletin de l'Institut d'Égypte* 18, 1935–6, p. 215. From the Memphis region comes a figure of a camel with two water-jars (clear evidence of its domestication in Egypt) datable by associated archaeological material to about the 13th century BC (Petrie, *Gizeh and Rifeh*, 1907, p. 23 and plate 27). Albright (*JBL* 64, 1945, pp. 287–288) wished to lower the date of this example; but as he fails to offer specific evidence of any kind in support of his contention, it must be dismissed. Palestine also affords some evidence of camels at this general period. Hence the references in Exodus, Leviticus and Deuteronomy are no more objectionable than those in Genesis.

In the Judges' period Israel was troubled by camel-riding Midianites (repelled by Gideon, Jdg. 6–8) and others, *e.g.* the Hagarites (1 Ch. 5:21); likewise Saul and David fought camel-using Amalekites (1 Sa. 15:3; 27:9; 30:17). The Arabians made particular use of camels in peace and war—so did the Queen of Sheba (1 Ki. 10:2; 2 Ch. 9:1) and the people of Kedar and 'Hazor' (Je. 49:29, 32). Hazael the Aramaean brought 40 camel-loads of gifts from king Ben-hadad to Elisha (2 Ki. 8:9). *Cf.* the pictures of Assyrian, Arabian and Aramaean camels cited at the end of this article. The Jews who returned to Judaea with Zerubbabel after the Exile had 435 camels (Ezr. 2:67; Ne. 7:69). In NT times camel's hair furnished clothing for John the Baptist (Mt. 3:4; Mk. 1:6), while the camel featured in two of Christ's most striking word-pictures (Mt. 19:24 = Lk. 18:25; Mt. 23:24).

Bibliography. For one-humped camels, see *ANEP*, p. 20, fig. 63, p. 52, fig. 170, p. 58, fig. 187, p. 132, fig. 375 (Assyrian and Arabian ones), p. 59, fig. 188 (Aramaean). For two-humped camels, see *ANEP*, p. 122, fig. 355 = *IBA*, p. 57, fig. 51, for Assyrian times, and H. Frankfort, *Art and Architecture of the Ancient Orient*, 1954, plate 184B of Persian period.

Specially valuable for the camel in antiquity are the richly-documented studies by R. Walz, in *Zeitschrift der Deutschen Morgenländischen Gesellschaft* 101, n.s. 26, 1951, pp. 29–51; *ibid*, 104, n.s. 29, 1954, pp. 45–87; and in *Actes du IVᵉ Congrès Internationale des Sciences Anthropologiques et Ethnologiques*, 3, Vienna, 1956, pp. 190–204. More recent are: G. S. Cansdale, *Animals of Bible Lands*, 1970; M. Ripinsky, *JEA* 71, 1985, pp. 134–141; G. Stone, *Buried History* 27, 1991, pp. 100–106, 28, 1992, pp. 3–14. K.A.K.

CANA (Gk. *kana*, probably from Heb. *qānâ*, 'place of reeds'). A Galilean village in the uplands W of the lake, mentioned in John's Gospel only. It was the scene of Jesus' first miracle (Jn. 2:1, 11), the place where with a word he healed the nobleman's son who lay sick at Capernaum (4.46, 50), and the home of Nathanael (21:2). Not definitely located, it has been identified by some with Kefr Kenna, about 6 km NNE of Nazareth on the road to Tiberias. This site, where excavations have been made, is a likely place for the events of Jn. 2:1–11, having ample water springs, and providing such shady fig trees as that suggested in Jn. 1:48. Many modern scholars, however, prefer an identification with Khirbet Kănā, a ruined site 14 km N of Nazareth, which local Arabs still call Cana of Galilee. J.D.D.

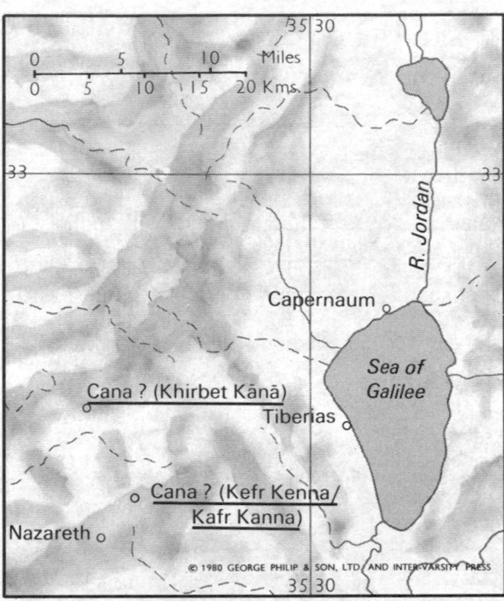

Sites suggested as ancient Cana.

CANAAN. Son of Ham, grandson of Noah, who laid a curse upon him (Gn. 9:18, 22–27). In Gn. 10:15–19 eleven groups who historically inhabited Phoenicia in particular and Syria–Palestine in general are listed as his descendants. See also the following article. K.A.K.

CANAAN, CANAANITES. A Semitic-speaking people and their territory, principally in Phoenicia. Their racial affinities are at present uncertain.

I. The name

The name Canaan (Heb. *kᵉna'an*) of people and land derives from that of their forebear Canaan or Kna' (see previous article) according to both Gn. 10:15–18 and native Canaanite–Phoenician tradition as transmitted by Sanchuniathon and preserved by Philo of Byblos. *Kna'(an)* is the native name of the Canaanites–Phoenicians applied to them both in Greek sources and by the Phoenicians themselves (*e.g.* on coins; see W. F. Albright, p. 1, n. 1, in his paper, 'The Rôle of the Canaanites in the History of Civilization', in *The Bible and the Ancient Near East, Essays for W. F. Albright*, 1961, pp. 328–362; cited hereafter as *BANE* Vol.). The meaning of *Kn'(n)* is unknown. Outside the Bible, the name occurs both with and without the final *n*. This *n* could be either a final *n* of a common Semitic type, or else a Hurrian suffix (Albright, *op. cit.*, p. 25, n. 50). Formerly, some linked *kn'(n)* with words for 'purple dye', esp. in Hurrian (with Speiser, *Language* 12, 1936, p. 124), but this was disproved by Landsberger (*JCS* 21, 1967, p. 106f.).

II. Extent of Canaan

'Canaan' in both Scripture and external sources has threefold reference. **1.** Fundamentally it indicates the land and inhabitants of the Syro-Palestinian coastland, especially Phoenicia proper. This is indicated within Gn. 10:15–19 by its detailed enumeration of Sidon 'the first-born', the *Arkite, the Sinite, the Zemarite and Hamath in

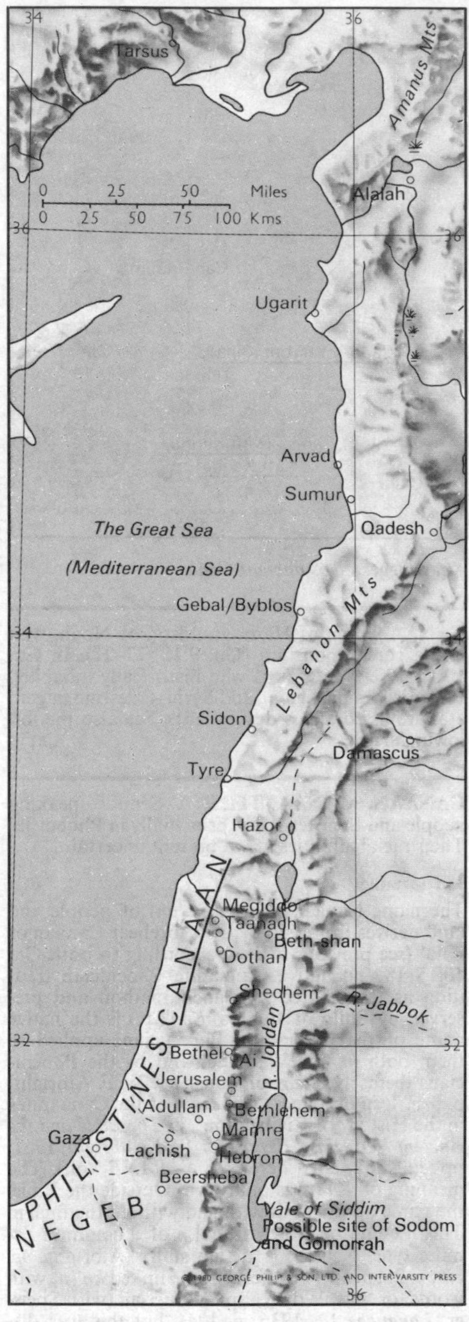

Canaan and its neighbours.

the Orontes valley. More specifically Nu. 13:29; Jos. 5:1; 11:3; Jdg. 1:27ff. put the Canaanites on the coastlands, in the valleys and plains, and the Jordan valley, with Amorites and others in the hills. Notably the inscription of Idrimi, king of Alalaḫ in the 15th century BC, mentions his flight to Ammia in coastal Canaan (S. Smith, *The Statue of Idrimi*, 1949, pp. 72–73; *ANET*[3], pp. 557–558).

2. 'Canaan(ite)' can also cover, by extension, the hinterland and so Syria–Palestine in general. Thus, Gn. 10:15–19 includes also the Hittite, Jebusite, Amorite, Hivite and Girgashite, explaining that 'the families of the Canaanite spread abroad' (v. 18); this wider area is defined as extending coastally from Sidon to Gaza, inland to the Dead Sea cities Sodom and Gomorrah and apparently back up N to *Lasha (location uncertain). See also Gn. 12:5; 13:12; or Nu. 13:17–21; 34:1–2, with the following delimitation of W Palestinian boundaries; Jdg. 4:2, 23–24 calls Jabin (II) of Hazor titular 'king of Canaan'. This wider use is also encountered in early external sources. In their Amarna letters (14th century BC) kings of Babylon and elsewhere sometimes use 'Canaan' for Egypt's Syro-Palestinian territories generally. And the Egyptian Papyrus Anastasi IIIA (lines 5–6) and IV (16: line 4) of 13th century BC mention 'Canaanite slaves from Huru' (= Syria–Palestine generally) (R. A. Caminos, *Late-Egyptian Miscellanies*, 1954, pp. 117, 200).

3. The term 'Canaanite' can bear the more restricted meaning of 'merchant, trafficker', trading being a most characteristic Canaanite occupation. In Scripture this meaning may be found in Jb. 41:6; Is. 23:8; Ezk. 17:4; Zp. 1:11; the word *kn't* in Je. 10:17 is even used for 'wares, merchandise'. A stele of the pharaoh Amenophis II (*c.* 1440 BC) lists among his Syrian captives '550 *maryannu* (= noble chariot-warriors), 240 of their wives, 640 *Kn'nw*, 232 sons of princes, 323 daughters of princes', among others (*ANET*, p. 246). From this, Maisler (*BASOR* 102, 1946, p. 9) infers that the 640 *Kn'nw* (Canaaneans) found in such exalted company are of the merchant 'plutocracy of the coastal and the trading centres of Syria and Palestine'; but this is uncertain.

III. Canaanites and Amorites

Alongside the specific, wider and restricted uses of 'Canaan(ite)' noted above, *'Amorite(s)' also has both a specific and a wider reference. Specifically, the Amorites in Scripture are part of the hill-country population of Palestine (Nu. 13:29; Jos. 5:1; 11:3). But in its wider use 'Amorite' tends to overlap directly the term 'Canaanite'. 'Amorite' comes in under 'Canaan' in Gn. 10:15–16 for a start. Then, Israel is to conquer Canaan (= Palestine) in Nu. 13:17–21, *etc.*, and duly comes to dwell in the land of the Amorites, overcoming 'all the people' there, namely Amorites (Jos. 24:15, 18). Abraham reaches, and is promised, Canaan (Gn. 12:5, 7; 15:7, 18), but occupation is delayed as 'the iniquity of the Amorites is not yet complete' (Gn. 15:16). Shechem is a Canaanite principality under a Hivite ruler (Gn. 12:5–6; 34:2, 30), but can be called 'Amorite' (Gn. 48:22).

The documentary theory of literary criticism has frequently assayed to use these overlapping or double designations, Canaanites and Amorites (and other 'pairs'), as marks of different authorship (see, *e.g.*, S. R. Driver, *Introduction to the Literature of the Old Testament*[9], 1913, p. 119, or O. Eissfeldt, *The Old Testament, an Introduction*, 1965, p. 183). But any such use of these terms does not accord with the external records which have no underlying 'hands', and it must therefore be questioned.

In the 18th century BC Amurru is part of Syria in the Alalaḫ tablets, while Amorite princes are mentioned in a Mari document in relation to Hazor in

Palestine itself (*cf.* J.-R. Kupper, *Les Nomades en Mésopotamie au temps des Rois de Mari*, 1957, pp. 179–180). As Hazor is the Canaanite city *par excellence* of N Palestine, the mingling of people and terms is already attested in Abraham's day. In the 14th/13th centuries BC the specific kingdom of Amurru of Abdi-aširta, Aziru, and their successors in the Lebanon mountain region secured a firm hold on a section of the Phoenician coast and its Canaanite seaports by conquest and alliance 'from Byblos to Ugarit' (Amarna Letter No. 98). This *Amorite control in coastal Canaan is further attested by the Battle of Qadesh inscriptions of Rameses II (13th century BC) mentioning the timely arrival inland of a battle force from a 'port in the land of Amurru' (see Gardiner, *Ancient Egyptian Onomastica* I, 1947, pp. 188*–189*, and Gardiner, *The Kadesh Inscriptions of Ramesses II*, 1960, on this incident). This is independent evidence for a contiguous use of Amor(ites) and Canaan(ites) in Moses' time. The use of these terms as the distinguishing marks of different literary hands is thus erroneous. In any case the situation reflected in the Pentateuch and Joshua by this usage was radically changed by the impact of the sea peoples at the end of the 13th century BC, after which date the emergence of that usage would be inexplicable.

IV. The language

The definition of what is or is not 'Canaanite' is much controverted. Within the general group of the NW Semitic languages and dialects, biblical Hebrew (*cf.* Is. 19:18) and the W Semitic glosses and terms in the Amarna tablets can correctly be termed 'S Canaanite' along with Moabite and Phoenician. Separate but related are Aramaic and Ya'udic. Between these two groups comes Ugaritic. Some hold this latter to be a separate NW Semitic language, others that it is Canaanite to be classed with Hebrew, *etc.* Ugaritic itself betrays historical development linguistically, and thus the Ugaritic of the 14th/13th centuries BC is closer to Hebrew than is the archaic language of the great epics (Albright, *BASOR* 150, 1958, pp. 36–38). Hence it is provisionally possible to view NW Semitic as including S Canaanite (Hebrew, *etc.*), N Canaanite (Ugaritic) and Aramaic. *Cf.* S. Moscati (*The Semites in Ancient History*, 1959, pp. 97–100), who (rather radically) would abolish 'Canaanite'; and J. Friedrich (*Scientia* 84, 1949, pp. 220–223), on this question. The distinction between 'Canaanite' and 'Amorite' is almost illusory, and little more than dialectal. On NW Semitic *ā* versus Canaanite *ō*, *cf.* Gelb, *JCS* 15, 1961, pp. 42f. They differ in little more than the sibilants. Texts from the N Syrian city of *Ebla are written in a dialect that appears to be W Semitic and to show affinities with S Canaanite, according to the decipherer, G. Pettinato, who calls it 'Palaeo-Canaanite' (*Orientalia* n.s. 44, 1975, pp. 361–374, esp. 376ff.). (*LANGUAGE OF THE OLD TESTAMENT.)

V. Canaanite history

The presence of Semitic-speaking people in Palestine in the 3rd millennium BC is so far explicitly attested only by two Semitic place-names in a text of that age: *Ndi'* which contains the element *'il(u)*, god', and *n..k..* which begins with *ain*, 'spring, well', both these names occurring in an Egyptian tomb-scene of 5th/6th Dynasty, *c.* 2400 BC.

However, the question as to whether these indicate the presence of Canaanites, and just when Canaanites appeared in Palestine, is a matter of dispute. It is certain that Canaaanites and Amorites were well established in Syria-Palestine by 2000 BC, and a NW-Semitic-speaking element at Ebla in N Syria by *c.* 2300 BC.

Throughout the 2nd millennium BC, Syria–Palestine was divided among a varying number of Canaanite/Amorite city-states. For the 19th/18th century BC, many names of places and rulers are recorded in the Egyptian Execration Texts. On the organization of some of the separate states in Palestine in this, the patriarchal period, see also A. van Selms, *Oudtestamentische Studiën* 12, 1958 (*Studies on the Book of Genesis*), pp. 192–197.

During the period roughly 1500–1380 BC, these petty states were part of Egypt's Asiatic empire; in the 14th century BC the N ones passed under Hittite suzerainty, while the S ones remained nominally Egyptian. Early in the 13th century BC Egypt regained effectual control in Palestine and coastal Syria (the Hittites retaining N and inner Syria), but this control evaporated as time passed (*cf.* H. Klengel, *Geschichte Syriens*, 1–3, 1965–70). Thus Israel in the late 13th century met Canaanite/Amorite, but not specifically Egyptian, opposition (except for Merenptah's abortive raid). The 'conquest' by Rameses III, *c.* 1180 BC, was a sweeping raid, mainly *via* the coast and principal routes, and was superficial.

At the end of the 13th century BC the sway of the Canaanite/Amorite city-states, now decadent, was shattered by political upheavals. The Israelites, under Joshua, entered W Palestine from across the Jordan, gaining control of the hill-country first and defeating a series of Canaanite kings. For the Hebrews, the conquest of Canaan was the fulfilment of an ancient promise to their forefathers (Gn. 17:8; 28:4, 13–14; Ex. 6:2–8). They were to dispossess the peoples of the land as expelled by God, and to destroy those who remained (*cf.* Dt. 7:1, 2ff.); this was in consequence of divine judgment on long centuries of persistent wickedness by these peoples (Dt. 9:5, *cf.* Gn. 15:16), and not from any merit on Israel's part.

Meantime, the sea-peoples of the Egyptian records (including Philistines) had destroyed the Hittite empire and swept through Syria and Palestine to be halted on the Egyptian border by Rameses III; some, especially *Philistines, establishing themselves on the Palestinian coast. Finally, Aramaean penetration of inland Syria swiftly increased in the century or so following. The result was that the Canaanites now ruled only in Phoenicia proper with its ports and in isolated principalities elsewhere. From the 12th century BC onwards, the former Bronze Age Canaanites in their new, restricted circumstances emerged as the more-than-ever maritime *Phoenicians of the 1st millennium BC, centred on the famous kingdom of *Tyre and *Sidon. On the history of the Canaanites, especially as continuing as Phoenicians, see Albright, *BANE* Vol., pp. 328–362.

VI. Canaanite culture

Our knowledge of this is derived from two main sources: first, literary, from the N Canaanite and Babylonian texts discovered at *Ugarit (Ras Shamra, on the Syrian coast) with odd fragments elsewhere; and second, archaeological, in the sense of being derived from the excavated objects and remains from and of towns and cemeteries in Syria and Palestine.

a. Canaanite society

Most of the Canaanite city-states were monarchies. The king had extensive powers of military appointment and conscription, of requisitioning lands and leasing them in return for services, of taxation, including tithes, customs-dues, real-estate tax, *etc*., and of corvée to requisition the labour of his subjects for state purposes. This is directly reflected in Samuel's denunciation of a kingship like that of the nations round about (1 Sa. 8, *c.* 1050 BC), and clearly evident in the tablets from Alalaḫ (18th–15th centuries BC) and Ugarit (14th–13th centuries BC) (see I. Mendelsohn, *BASOR* 143, 1956, pp. 17–22). Military, religious and economic matters were under the king's direct oversight; the queen was an important personage sometimes appealed to by high officials; the court was elaborately organized in larger states like Ugarit (for the latter, *cf.* A. F. Rainey, *The Social Stratification of Ugarit*, 1962).

The basic unit of society was the family. For the period of the 19th–15th centuries BC, the great N Canaanite epics from Ugarit (see *Literature*, below) betray the main features of family life (see A. van Selms, *Marriage and Family Life in Ugaritic Literature*, 1954). Further information is afforded by legal documents for the 14th/13th centuries BC. Among larger social units, besides the obvious ones of towns with their associated villages (in Ugarit state, see Virolleaud, *Syria* 21, 1940, pp. 123–151, and *cf.* briefly, C. H. Gordon, *Ugaritic Literature*, p. 124), for which compare the assignment of towns with their villages ('suburbs') in Jos. 13ff., one may note the widespread organization of guilds. These include primary producers (herdsmen, fowlers, butchers and bakers), artisans (smiths, working in copper (or bronze) and silver, potters, sculptors, and house-, boat-and chariot-builders), and traders, both local and long-distance. Priests and other cult-personnel (see below), also musicians, had guilds or groups; and there were several special classes of warriors. Several inscribed javelin-or spearheads found in Palestine perhaps belonged to late-Canaanite mercenary troops of the 12/11th centuries BC, the sort of people commanded by a Sisera or Jabin (Jdg. 4, *etc.*); these also illustrate the free use of early W Semitic alphabetic script in the Palestine of the Judges. It has been suggested that in Canaanite society in 13th-century BC Palestine there was a sharp class distinction between upper-class patricians and lower-class, half-free serfs, the contrast with the relatively humble and homogeneous Israelites possibly being reflected in the excavated archaeological sites.

b. Literature

This is principally represented by N Canaanite texts from *Ugarit. These include long, but disordered and fragmentary, sections of the Baal Epic (deeds and fortunes of Baal or Hadad), which goes back linguistically to perhaps *c.* 2000 BC; the legend of Aqhat (vicissitudes of the only son of good king Dan'el) perhaps from *c.* 1800 BC; the story of King Keret (bereft of family, he gains a new wife virtually by conquest, and also incurs the wrath of the gods) perhaps about 16th century BC; and other fragments. All extant copies date from the 14th/13th centuries BC. The high-flown poetry of the early epics has clearly demonstrated the archaic flavour of much Hebrew OT poetry in its vocabulary and turns of speech. For full translations of the epics, so important for early Canaanite religions, see C. H. Gordon, *Ugaritic Literature*, 1949; G. R. Driver, *Canaanite Myths and Legends*, 1956; A. Caquot, M. Sznycer, A. Herdner, *Textes Ougaritiques* I, 1974. Selections are given in *ANET*, pp. 129–155, by H. L. Ginsberg, and in *DOTT* by J. Gray.

c. Religion

The Canaanites had an extensive pantheon, headed by El. More prominent in practice were *Baal (lord'), *i.e.* Hadad the storm-god, and *Dagon, with temples in Ugarit and elsewhere. The goddesses *Asherah, Astarte (*Ashtaroth) and Anath—like Baal—had multi-coloured personalities and violent characters; they were goddesses of sex and war. Kothar-and-Hasis was artificer-god (*cf.* Vulcan), and other and lesser deities abounded.

Actual temples in Palestine include remains at Beth-shan, Megiddo, Lachish, Shechem and especially Hazor (which had at least three), besides those in Syria at Qatna, Alalaḫ or Ugarit. The Ugaritic texts mention a variety of animals sacrificed to the gods: cattle, sheep (rams and lambs) and birds (including doves)—plus, of course, libations. Animal bones excavated in several Palestinian sites support this picture.

The title of high priest (*rb khnm*) is attested for Canaanite religion at Ugarit. That the *qdšm* of the Ugaritic texts were cult prostitutes is very possible; at any rate, the *qdšm* were as much an integral part of Canaanite religion there as they were forbidden to Israel (Dt. 23:17–18, *etc.*). Human sacrifice in 2nd-millennium Canaanite religion has not yet been isolated archaeologically with any certainty, but there are indications that it was customary. That Canaanite religion appealed to the bestial and material in human nature is clearly evidenced by the Ugaritic texts and in Egyptian texts of Semitic origin or inspiration; *cf.* Albright, *Archaeology and Religion of Israel*[3], 1953, pp. 75–77, 158–159, 197, n. 39; see also *CALF, GOLDEN. When the full import of this is realized it will be the more evident that physically and spiritually the sophisticated crudities of decaying Canaanite culture and emergent Israel with a unique mission could not coexist.

BIBLIOGRAPHY. A. R. Millard, 'The Canaanites', in *POTT*, pp. 29–52. For discoveries at Ugarit, see Schaeffer's reports in *Syria* since 1929, and the fully documented series of volumes, *Mission de Ras Shamra* by Schaeffer, Virolleaud and Nougayrol. K.A.K.

CANANAEAN (Gk. *Kananaios*, from Heb. and Aram. *qannā'* or Aram. *qan'ān*, 'zealot', 'zealous'). In Mt. 10:4; Mk. 3:18 (RV and RSV rightly for AV 'Canaanite'), the surname of Simon, one of the Twelve. In Lk. 6:15; Acts 1:13 he is called by the equivalent Greek term *Zēlōtēs*, 'zealot'. The presence of a *Zealot (or past Zealot) among the apostles gives rise to interesting speculation; he may not, of course, have been a Zealot proper, but received the designation from Jesus or his fellow apostles because of his temperament. The fact that Mark, followed by Matthew, used the Semitic form suggests, however, the more technical sense. F.F.B.

CANDACE. The name or, more properly, title of the Ethiopian queen whose minister was converted under the ministry of Philip (Acts 8:27). For the extent of her kingdom, which probably centred in the region of Upper Nubia (Meroë) rather than in modern-day Ethiopia, see *ETHIOPIA. Women rulers, probably queen mothers, bearing this title during the Hellenistic period, are well attested in ancient literature, *e.g.* Pseudo-Callisthenes (3. 18), Strabo (17. 820), Pliny (*NH* 6. 186).

BIBLIOGRAPHY. *BAGD*; E. Ullendorff in *NTS* 2, 1955–6, pp. 53–56. D.A.H.

CANNEH. The name of a settlement or town mentioned, with *Haran and *Eden, as trading with Tyre (Ezk. 27:23). The site is unknown, but the above association suggests the area of the middle Euphrates, and this has support from Assyr. documents of the 7th century BC.

T.C.M.

CANON OF THE OLD TESTAMENT.

I. The Canon and Canonicity

'Canon' is borrowed from Gk., in which *kanōn* means a rule. Since the 4th century *kanōn* has been used by Christians to denote an authoritative list of the books belonging to the OT or NT. What qualifies a book for a place in the Canon of the OT or NT is not just that it is ancient, informative and helpful, and has long been read and valued by God's people, but that it has God's authority. God spoke through its human author to teach his people what to believe and how to behave. It is not just a record of revelation, but the permanent written form of revelation. The Bible is 'inspired' (*INSPIRATION), and it makes the books of the Bible in this respect different from all other books.

There has long been some difference of opinion about the books which should be included in the OT Canon. The Samaritans rejected all its books except the Pentateuch; while, from about the 3rd century BC onwards, pseudonymous works, usually apocalyptic, claimed to be inspired writings and found credence in certain circles. In the rabbinical literature it is related that in the first few centuries of the Christian era certain sages disputed, on internal evidence, the canonicity of five OT books (Ezekiel, Proverbs, Song of Songs, Ecclesiastes, Esther). In the patristic period there was uncertainty among Christians whether the Apocrypha of the Gk. and Latin Bible were to be regarded as inspired or not. Difference on the last point came to a head at the Reformation, when the church of Rome insisted that the Apocrypha were part of the OT, on an equal footing with the rest, while the Protestant churches denied this. Though some of the Protestant churches regarded the Apocrypha as edifying reading (the Church of England, for example, continuing to include them in its lectionary 'for example of life but not to establish any doctrine'), they were all agreed that, properly speaking, the OT Canon consists only of the books of the Heb. Bible—the books acknowledged by the Jews and endorsed in the teaching of the NT. The Eastern Orthodox Church was for a time divided on this, but is now tending to come down on the Protestant side.

II. The first emergence of the Canon

The doctrine of biblical inspiration is fully developed only in the NT. But far back in Israel's history certain writings were being recognized as having divine authority, and serving as a written rule of faith and practice for God's people. This is seen in the people's response when Moses reads to them the book of the covenant (Ex. 24:7), or when the book of the Law found by Hilkiah is read, first to the king and then to the congregation (2 Ki. 22–23; 2 Ch. 34), or when the book of the Law is read to the people by Ezra (Ne. 8:9, 14–17; 10:28–39; 13:1–3). These form a part or the whole of the Pentateuch—in the first case quite a small part of Exodus, probably chapters 20–23. The Pentateuch is treated with the same reverence in Jos. 1:7f.; 8:31; 23:6–8; 1 Ki. 2:3; 2 Ki. 14:6; 17:37; Ho. 8:12; Dn. 9:11, 13; Ezr. 3:2, 4; 1 Ch. 16:40; 2 Ch. 17:9; 23:18; 30:5, 18; 31:3; 35:26.

The Pentateuch presents itself as basically the work of Moses, one of the earliest, and certainly the greatest of the OT prophets (Nu. 12:6–8; Dt. 34:10–12). God often spoke through Moses orally, as he did through later prophets, but Moses' activity as a writer is also frequently mentioned (Ex. 17:14; 24:4, 7; 34:27; Nu. 33:2; Dt. 28:58, 61; 29:20f., 27; 30:10; 31:9–13, 19, 22, 24–26). There were other prophets in Moses' lifetime and more were expected to follow (Ex. 15:20; Nu. 12:6; Dt. 18:15–22; 34:10), as they did (Jdg. 4:4; 6:8), though major prophetic activity began with Samuel. The literary work of these prophets started, as far as we know, with Samuel (1 Sa. 10:25; 1 Ch. 29:29), and their earliest writing was mostly history, which afterwards became the basis of the books of Chronicles (1 Ch. 29:29; 2 Ch. 9:29; 12:15; 13:22; 20:34; 26:22; 32:32; 33:18f.), and probably of Samuel and Kings too, which have so much material in common with Chronicles. It is possible that Joshua and Judges were also based on prophetic histories of this kind. That the prophets on occasion wrote down oracles also is clear from Is. 30:8; Je. 25:13; 29:1; 30:2; 36:1–32; 51:60–64; Ezk. 43:11; Hab. 2:2; Dn. 7:1; 2 Ch. 21:12. Of course, to say all this is to accept the *prima facie* evidence of the OT books as historical: for discussion of other views, see *PENTATEUCH, *DEUTERONOMY, *CHRONICLES, *etc.*

The reason why Moses and the prophets wrote down God's message, and did not content themselves with delivering it orally, was sometimes to send it to another place (Je. 29:1; 36:1–8; 51:60f.; 2 Ch. 21:12); but quite as often to preserve it for the future, as a memorial (Ex. 17:14), or a witness (Dt. 31:24–26), that it might be for the time to come for ever and ever (Is. 30:8). The unreliability of oral tradition was well known to the OT writers. An object-lesson here was the loss of the book of the Law during the reigns of Manasseh and Amon: when it was rediscovered by Hilkiah its teaching came as a great shock, for it had been forgotten (2 Ki. 22–23; 2 Ch. 34). The permanent form of God's message was therefore not its spoken but its written form, hence the rise of the OT Canon.

How long the *Pentateuch took to reach its final shape we cannot be sure. However, we saw in the case of the book of the covenant, referred to in Ex. 24, that it was possible for a short document like Ex. 20–23 to become canonical before the whole book was complete. The book of Genesis also embodies earlier documents (Gn. 5:1), Numbers includes an item from an ancient collection of poems (Nu. 21:14f.), and the main part of Deuteronomy was laid up as canonical beside the ark in Moses'

	Hebrew Bible	Christian Bible
I The Law (Pentateuch)	Genesis	Genesis
	Exodus	Exodus
	Leviticus	Leviticus
	Numbers	Numbers
	Deuteronomy	Deuteronomy
II The Prophets	Joshua	Joshua
	Judges	Judges
	Samuel	Ruth
	Kings	Samuel (1 and 2)
	Isaiah	Kings (1 and 2)
	Jeremiah	Chronicles (1 and 2)
	Ezekiel	Ezra
	Hosea	Nehemiah
	Joel	Esther
	Amos	Job
	Obadiah	Psalms
	Jonah	Proverbs
	Micah	Ecclesiastes
	Nahum	Song of Solomon
	Habakkuk	Isaiah
	Zephaniah	Jeremiah
	Haggai	Lamentations
	Zechariah	Ezekiel
	Malachi	Daniel
III The Writings (Hagiographa)	Psalms	Hosea
	Proverbs	Joel
	Job	Amos
	Song of Solomon	Obadiah
	Ruth	Jonah
	Lamentations	Micah
	Ecclesiastes	Nahum
	Esther	Habakkuk
	Daniel	Zephaniah
	Ezra	Haggai
	Nehemiah	Zechariah
	Chronicles	Malachi

Wisdom Writings

Historical

See also article on Apocrypha

The canonical arrangement of the books of the OT according to Christian tradition, compared with the original order in Hebrew.

lifetime (Dt. 31:24–26), before the account of his death can have been added. The analogy between the *covenants of Ex. 24; Dt. 29–30 and the ancient Near Eastern treaties is suggestive, since the treaty documents were often laid up in a sacred place, like the tables of the Ten Commandments and the book of Deuteronomy; and this was done when the treaty was made. The covenants between God and Israel were undoubtedly made when the Pentateuch says they were made, at the Exodus, when God formed Israel into a nation; so it is in that period that the laying up of the Decalogue and Deuteronomy in the sanctuary should be dated, in accordance with the Pentateuchal account. This means that their public recognition as binding and indeed divine should also be dated as from then. The preservation of sacred books in the sanctuary was a custom which continued right down to the destruction of the second temple in AD 70.

While there was a succession of prophets it was possible for earlier sacred writings to be added to and edited in the manner indicated above, without committing the sacrilege spoken of in Dt. 4:2; 12:32; Pr. 30:6. The same applies to other parts of the OT. Joshua embodies the covenant of its last chapter, vv. 1–25, originally written by Joshua himself (v. 26). Samuel embodies the document on the manner of the kingdom (1 Sa. 8:11–18), originally written by Samuel (1 Sa. 10:25). Both these documents were canonical from the outset, the former written in the very book of the Law at the sanctuary of Shechem, and the latter laid up before the Lord at Mizpeh. There is a sign of the growth of the book of Proverbs in Pr. 25:1. Items from an ancient collection of poems are included in Joshua (10:12f.), Samuel (2 Sa. 1:17–27) and Kings (1 Ki. 8:53, LXX). Kings names as its sources the *Book of the Acts of Solomon*, the *Book of the Chronicles of the Kings of Israel* and the *Book of the Chronicles of the Kings of Judah* (1 Ki. 11:41; 14:19, 29, *etc.*; 2 Ki. 1:18; 8:23, *etc.*). The latter two works, combined together, are probably the same as the *Book of the Kings of Israel and Judah*, often named as a source by the canonical books of Chronicles (2 Ch. 16:11; 25:26; 27:7; 28:26; 35:27; 36:8; and, in abbreviated form, 1 Ch. 9:1; 2 Ch. 24:27). This source book seems to have incorporated many of the prophetic histories which are also named as sources in Chronicles (2 Ch. 20:34; 32:32).

Not all the writers of the OT books were prophets, in the narrow sense of the word; some of them were kings and wise men. But their experience of inspiration led to their writings also finding a place in the Canon. The inspiration of psalmists is spoken of in 2 Sa. 23:1–3; 1 Ch. 25:1, and of wise men in Ec. 12:11f. Note also the revelations made by God in Job (38:1; 40:6), and the implication of Pr. 8:1–9:6 that the book of Proverbs is the work of the divine Wisdom.

III. The closing of the first section (the Law)

The references to the Pentateuch (in whole or part) as canonical, which we saw in the other books of the OT, and which continue in the intertestamental literature, are remarkably numerous. This is doubtless due in part to its fundamental importance. References to other books as inspired or canonical are, within the OT, largely confined to their authors: the chief exceptions are probably Is. 34:16; Ps. 149:9; Dn. 9:2. The Pentateuch may have been the first section of the OT to be written and recognized as canonical. It was basically the work of a single prophet of very early date, which was edited after his death but was not open to continual addition, whereas the other sections of the OT were produced by authors of later date, whose number was not complete until after the return from the Exile. No one doubts that the Pentateuch was both complete and canonical by the time of Ezra and Nehemiah, in the 5th century BC, and it may have been so considerably earlier. In the 3rd century BC it was translated into Gk., thus becoming the first part of the LXX. In the mid-2nd century BC we have evidence of all 5 books, including Genesis, being attributed to Moses (see Aristobulus, as cited by Eusebius, *Preparation for the Gospel* 13.12). Later in the same century the breach between Jews and Samaritans seems to have become complete, and the preservation of the Heb. Pentateuch by both parties since proves that it was already their common property. All this is evidence that the first section of the Canon was now closed, consisting of the 5 familiar books, neither more nor less, with only minor textual variations persisting.

IV. The evolution of the second and third sections (the Prophets and Hagiographa)

The rest of the Heb. Bible has a different structure from the English. It is divided into two sections: the Prophets, and the Hagiographa or (other) Scriptures. The Prophets comprise 8 books: the historical books Joshua, Judges, Samuel and Kings, and the oracular books Jeremiah, Ezekiel, Isaiah and the Twelve (the Minor Prophets). The Hagiographa comprise 11 books: the lyrical and wisdom books, Psalms, Job, Proverbs, Ecclesiastes, Song of Songs and Lamentations; and the historical books, Daniel (see below), Esther, Ezra–Nehemiah and Chronicles. This is the traditional order, according to which the remaining book of the Hagiographa, Ruth, is prefaced to Psalms, as ending with the genealogy of the psalmist David, though in the Middle Ages it was moved to a later position, alongside the other 4 books of similar brevity (Song of Songs, Ecclesiastes, Lamentations and Esther). In Jewish tradition Samuel, Kings, the Minor Prophets, Ezra–Nehemiah and Chronicles are each reckoned as a single book. This may indicate the capacity of an average Hebrew leather scroll at the period when the canonical books were first listed and counted.

Doubt has sometimes been thrown on the antiquity of this way of grouping the OT books. More commonly, but with equally little real reason, it has been assumed that it reflects the gradual development of the OT Canon, the grouping having been a historical accident, and the Canon of the Prophets having been closed about the 3rd century BC, before a history like Chronicles and a prophecy like Daniel (which, it is alleged, naturally belong there) had been recognized as inspired or even written. The Canon of the Hagiographa, according to this popular hypothesis, was not closed until the Jewish synod of Jamnia or Jabneh about AD 90, after an open OT Canon had already been taken over by the Christian church. Moreover, a broader Canon, containing many of the Apocrypha, had been accepted by the Greek-speaking Jews of Alexandria, and was embodied in the LXX; and the LXX was the OT of the early Christian church. These two facts, and the Essene fondness for the pseudonymous apocalypses, are responsible for the fluidity of the OT Canon in patristic Christianity. Such is the theory.

The reality is rather different. The grouping of the books is not arbitrary, but according to literary character. Daniel is half narrative, and in the Hagiographa, as the traditional order arranged them, it seems to be placed with the histories. There are histories in the Law (from the creation to Moses) and in the Prophets (Joshua to the end of the Monarchy), so why should there not be histories in the Hagiographa also, dealing with the period of the Exile and return? Chronicles is put last among the histories, as a summary of the whole biblical narrative, from Adam to the return. The Canon of the Prophets was *not* completely closed when Chronicles was written, for the sources it quotes are not Samuel and Kings but the fuller prophetic histories which seem to have served as sources for Samuel and Kings as well. The earliest elements in the Prophets, incorporated in books such as Joshua and Samuel, are certainly very old, but so are the earliest elements in the Hagiographa, incorporated in books such as Psalms, Proverbs and Chronicles. These elements may have been recognized as canonical before the completion of even the first section of the Canon. The latest elements in the Hagiographa, such as Daniel, Esther and Ezra–Nehemiah, belong to the end of OT history. But the same is true of the latest elements in the Prophets, such as Ezekiel, Haggai, Zechariah and Malachi. The books of the Hagiographa *tend* to be later than the Prophets, but the overlap is considerable. Indeed, the very assumption that the Hagiographa are a late collection may have led to their individual books being dated later than they otherwise would have been.

Since the books in both these sections are by a variety of authors and are usually independent of one another, they may have been recognized as canonical individually, at different dates, and at first formed a single miscellaneous collection. Then, when the prophetic gift had been for some while withdrawn, and their number was seen to be complete, they were more carefully classified, and were divided into two sections. 'The books', spoken of in Dn. 9:2, may have been one growing body of literature, loosely organized, and containing not only prophecy like Jeremiah's, but also psalms like David's. The tradition in 2 Macc. 2:13 about Nehemiah's library reflects such a mixed collection: 'he, founding a library, gathered together the books about the kings and prophets, and the books of David, and letters of kings about sacred gifts'. The antiquity of this tradition is shown by the likelihood that some such action would be necessary after the calamity of the Exile, and also by the fact that the 'letters of kings about sacred gifts' are simply being preserved because of their importance, and have not yet been embodied in the book of Ezra (6:3–12; 7:12–26). Time had to be given after this for books like Ezra to be completed, for the recognition of the latest books as canonical, and for the realization that the prophetic gift had ceased, and only when these things had happened could the firm division between Prophets and Hagiographa and the careful arrangement of their contents be made. The division had already been made towards the end of the 2nd century BC, when the prologue to the Gk. translation of Ecclesiasticus was composed, for this prologue repeatedly refers to the three sections of the Canon. But the division seems recent, for the third section of the Canon had not yet been given a name: the writer calls the first section 'the Law', the second 'the Prophets' or 'the Prophecies', but the third he simply describes. It is 'the others that have followed in their steps', 'the other ancestral books', 'the rest of the books'. This language implies a complete group of books, but one less old and well-established than the books it contains. The three sections are also referred to, in the 1st century AD, by Philo (*De Vita Contemplativa* 25) and by Christ (Lk. 24:44), both of whom give the third section its earliest name of 'the Psalms' (or, as at Qumran, 'David').

V. The closing of the second and third sections

The date when the Prophets and Hagiographa were organized in their separate sections was probably about 165 BC. 2 Maccabees speaks of the second great crisis in the history of the Canon: 'And in the same way Judas (Maccabaeus) collected all the books that had been lost on account of the war which had come upon us, and they are still in our possession' (2 Macc. 2:14). The 'war' in question is the Maccabaean war of liberation from the Syrian persecutor Antiochus Epiphanes. Antiochus hated the Scriptures (1 Macc. 1:56f.), and it is probable that Judas would have needed to gather copies of them together when the persecution was over. Judas knew that the prophetic gift had ceased a long time before (1 Macc. 9:27), so he probably arranged and listed the now complete collection in the way which became traditional. Since the books were as yet in separate scrolls, which had to be 'collected', what he would have produced would not have been a volume but a collection, and a list of the books in the collection, divided into three.

In drawing up his list, Judas probably established not only the firm division into Prophets and Hagiographa, but also the traditional order and number of the books within them. A list of books has to have an order and number, and the traditional order, recorded as a *baraita* from an older source in the Babylonian Talmud (*Baba Bathra* 14b–15a), is the one given earlier in this article, making Chronicles the last of the Hagiographa. This position for Chronicles can be traced back to the 1st century AD, since it is reflected in a saying of Christ's in Mt. 23:35 and Lk. 11:51, where the phrase 'from the blood of Abel to the blood of Zechariah' probably means all the martyred prophets from one end of the Canon to the other, from Gn. 4:3–15 to 2 Ch. 24:19–22. The traditional number of the canonical books is 24 (the 5 books of the Law, together with 8 books of the Prophets and the 11 books of the Hagiographa listed above), or 22 (Ruth being in that case appended to Judges, and Lamentations to Jeremiah. The number 24 is first recorded in 2 Esdras 14:44–48, about AD 100, but may also be alluded to in Rev. 4:4, 10, *etc.*, for the *baraita* in *Baba Bathra* seems to imply that the authors of the OT books, as well as the books themselves, were 24, like the elders of Revelation. The number 22 is first recorded in Josephus (*Contra Apion* 1.8), just before AD 100, but also, probably, in the fragments of the Gk. translation of the book of *Jubilees* (1st century BC?). If the number 22 goes back to the 1st century BC, so does the number 24, for the former is an adaptation of the latter to the number of letters in the Heb. alphabet. And since the number 24, which combines some of the smaller books into single units but not others, seems to have been influenced in this by the traditional order, the order too must be equally old. There is no doubt about the identity of the 24 or 22 books—they are the books of the Heb. Bible. Josephus says that they have all been accepted as canonical from time immemorial. Individual attestation can be provided for the canonicity of nearly all of them from writings of the 1st century AD or earlier. This is true even of 4 out of the 5 disputed by certain of the rabbis: only the Song of Songs, perhaps because of its shortness, remains without individual attestation.

So, by the beginning of the Christian era the identity of all the canonical books was well known and generally accepted. How, then, has it come to be thought that the third section of the Canon was not closed until the synod of Jamnia, some decades after the birth of the Christian church? The main reasons are that the rabbinical literature records disputes about 5 of the books, some of which were settled at the Jamnia discussion; that many of the LXX MSS mix apocryphal books among the canonical, thus prompting the theory of a wider Alexandrian Canon; and that the Qumran discoveries show the apocalyptic pseudepigrapha to have been cherished, and perhaps reckoned canonical, by the Essenes. But the rabbinical literature records similar academic objections to many other canonical books, so it must have been a question of removing books from the list (had this been possible), not adding them. Moreover, one of the 5 disputed books (Ezekiel) belongs to the second section of the Canon, which admittedly closed long before the Christian era. As to the Alexandrian Canon, Philo of Alexandria's writings show it to have been the same as the Palestinian. He refers to the 3 familiar sections, and he ascribes inspiration to many books in all 3, but never to any of the Apocrypha. In the LXX MSS, the Prophets and Hagiographa have been rearranged by Christian hands in a non-Jewish manner, and the intermingling of Apocrypha there is a Christian phenomenon, not a Jewish. At Qumran the pseudonymous apocalypses were probably viewed as an Essene appendix to the standard Jewish Canon. Philo mentions such an appendix in his account of the Therapeutae (*De Vita Contemplativa* 25), in MMT and so do 2 Esdras 14:44–48. It was also discovered at Qumran that the Essenes, though at rivalry with mainstream Judaism since the 2nd century BC, reckoned as canonical some at least of the Hagiographa, and had presumably done so since before the rivalry began.

VI. From Jewish Canon to Christian

The LXX MSS are paralleled by the writings of the early Christian Fathers, who (at any rate outside Palestine and Syria) normally used the LXX or the derived Old Latin version. In their writings, there is both a wide and a narrow Canon. The former comprises those books from before the time of Christ which were generally read and esteemed in the church (including the Apocrypha), but the latter is confined to the books of the Jewish Bible, which scholars like Melito, Origen, Epiphanius and Jerome distinguish from the rest as alone inspired. The Apocrypha were known in the church from the start, but the further back one goes, the more rarely are they treated as inspired. In the NT itself, one finds Christ acknowledging the Jewish Scriptures, by various of their current titles, and accepting the three sections of the Jewish Canon and the traditional order of its books; one finds Revelation perhaps alluding to their number; and throughout the NT one finds most of the books being referred to individually as having divine authority; but none of the Apocrypha. The only apparent exception is the reference to *Enoch* in Jude 14f., which may be just an *argumentum ad hominem* to converts from the apocalyptic school of thought.

What evidently happened was this. Christ passed on to his followers, as Holy Scripture, the Bible which he had received, containing the same books as the Heb. Bible today. The first Christians shared with their Jewish contemporaries a full knowledge of the canonical books. However, the Bible was not yet between two covers: it was a memorized list of scrolls. The breach with Jewish oral tradition (in some matters very necessary), the alienation between Jew and Christian, and the general ignorance of Semitic languages in the church outside Palestine and Syria, led to increasing doubt on the OT Canon among Christians, which was accentuated by the drawing up of new lists of the biblical books, arranged on other principles, and the introduction of new lectionaries. Such doubt about the Canon could only be resolved, and can only be resolved today, in the way it was resolved by Jerome and at the Reformation—by returning to the teaching of the NT, and the Jewish background against which it is to be understood.

BIBLIOGRAPHY. S. Z. Leiman, *The Canonization of Hebrew Scripture*, 1976; A. C. Sundberg, *The OT of the Early Church*, 1964; J. P. Lewis, *Journal of Bible and Religion* 32, 1964, pp. 125–132; M. G. Kline, *The Structure of Biblical Authority*, 1972; J. D. Purvis, *The Samaritan Pentateuch and the Origin of the Samaritan Sect*, 1968; B. F. Westcott, *The Bible in the Church*, 1864; W. H. Green, *General Introduction to the OT: the Canon*, 1899; R. T. Beckwith, *The OT Canon of the NT Church*, 1985; *idem*, *VT* 41, 1991, pp. 385–395; M. L. Margolis, *The Hebrew Scriptures in the Making*, 1922; S. Zeitlin, *A Historical Study of the Canonization of the Hebrew Scriptures*, 1933; R. L. Harris, *Inspiration and Canonicity of the Bible*, 1957. R.T.B.

CANON OF THE NEW TESTAMENT.

I. The earliest period

Biblical theology demands as its presupposition a fixed extent of biblical literature: this extent is traditionally fixed, since the era of the great theological controversies, in the Canon of the NT. 'Canon' is here the latinization of the Gk. *kanōn*, 'a reed', which, from the various uses of that plant for measuring and ruling, comes to mean a ruler, the line ruled, the column bounded by the line, and hence, the list written in the column. Canon is the list of books which the church uses in public worship. *kanōn* also means rule or standard: hence a secondary meaning of Canon is the list of books which the church acknowledges as inspired Scripture, normative for faith and practice. Our understanding of inspiration requires, then, not only that we fix the text of Scripture and analyse the internal history of scriptural books, but also that we trace as accurately as possible the growth of the concept of a canon and of the Canon itself.

In this investigation, especially of the earliest period, three matters must be distinguished clearly: the knowledge of a book evinced by a particular Father or source; the attitude towards such a book as an inspired Scripture on the part of the Father or source (which may be shown by introductory formulae such as 'It is written' or 'As the scripture says'); and the existence of the concept of a list or canon in which the quoted work figures (which will be shown, not only by actual lists but also by reference to 'the books' or 'the apostles', where a literary corpus is intended). This distinction has not always been made, with resultant confusion. Quotations, even in the earliest period, may be discovered; but whether quotation implies status as inspired Scripture is a further question for which precise criteria are frequently lacking. This being so, it is not surprising that a decision about the existence of any canonical list or concept of a canon often fails to find any direct evidence at all, and depends entirely upon inference.

The earliest point at which we can take up the investigation is in the data provided by the NT itself. The apostolic church was not without Scripture—it looked for its doctrine to the OT, usually in a Gk. dress, though some writers appear to have used the Heb. text. Apocrypha such as *1 Enoch* were also used in some circles. Whether the term 'canonical' should be applied here is debatable, as the Jewish Canon was not yet fixed, at least *de jure*, and when it was it was moulded by anti-Christian controversy, in addition to other factors. In worship, the church already used some of its own peculiar traditions: in the Lord's Supper the Lord's death was 'proclaimed' (1 Cor. 11:26) probably in word (*sc.* the earliest Passion narrative) as well as in the symbols of the ordinance. The account of the Lord's Supper itself is regarded as derived 'from the Lord', a closely guarded tradition: we find this terminology too in places where ethical conduct is based on dominical utterance (*cf.* 1 Cor. 7:10, 12, 25; Acts 20:35). This is in the main oral material, a phrase which, as form criticism has shown, is by no means intended to suggest imprecision of outline or content. Written repositories of Christian tradition are at best hypothetical in the earliest apostolic age; for although it has been proposed to find in the phrase 'according to the scriptures' (1 Cor. 15:3–4) a reference to documents at this early date, this has met with but little favour. In this material, then, whether oral or written, we find at the earliest stage a church consciously preserving its traditions of the passion, resurrection, life (*cf.* Acts 10:36–40) and teaching of Jesus. Quite evidently, however, whatever was known and preserved by anyone did not exclude in his view the validity and value of traditions elsewhere preserved. The preservation is to a large extent unselfconscious in this 'prehistoric' stage of the development of Christian Scripture. It continues in the making of the Gospels, where two main streams are developed in independence of each other. It would appear that little escaped inclusion in these.

The epistolary material in the NT also possesses from the beginning a certain claim, if not to inspiration, at least to be an authoritative and adequate teaching on points of doctrine and conduct; yet it is as clear that no letter is written for other than specific recipients in a specific historical situation. The collection of a corpus of letters evidently post-dates the death of Paul: the Pauline corpus is textually homogeneous and there is more weighty evidence for the suggestion, most thoroughly developed by E. J. Goodspeed, that its collection was a single act at a specific date (probably about AD 80–85), than for the earlier view of Harnack that the corpus grew slowly. The corpus from the start would enjoy high status as a body of authoritative Christian literature. Its impact upon the church in the late 1st and early 2nd centuries is plain from the doctrine, language and literary form of the literature of the period. There is no corresponding evidence for any such corpora of non-Pauline writings at so early a date; nor does the Acts seem to have been produced primarily as a teaching document. The Revelation of John, on the contrary, makes the clearest claim to direct inspiration of any NT document, and is the sole example in this literature of the utterances and visions of the prophets of the NT church. Thus we have, in the NT itself, several clear instances of Christian material, even at the oral stage, viewed as authoritative and in some sense sacred: yet in no case does any writing explicitly claim that it alone preserves tradition. There is no sense, at this stage, of a Canon of Scripture, a closed list to which addition may not be made. This would appear to be due to two factors: the existence of an oral tradition and the presence of apostles, apostolic disciples, and prophets, who were the foci and the interpreters of the dominical traditions.

II. The Apostolic Fathers

The same factors are present in the age of the so-called Apostolic Fathers and are reflected in the data provided by them for Canon studies. As regards the Gospels, Clement (*First Epistle*, *c.* AD 90) quotes material akin to the Synoptics yet in a form not strictly identical with any particular Gospel; nor does he introduce the words with any formula of scriptural citation. John is unknown to him. Ignatius of Antioch (martyred *c.* AD 115) speaks frequently of 'the gospel': yet in all cases his words are patient of the interpretation that it is the message, not a document, of which he speaks. The frequent affinities with Matthew may indicate that this source was utilized, but other elucidations are possible. Whether John was known to him remains a matter of debate, in which the strongest case appears to be that it was not. Papias, fragmentarily preserved in Eusebius and elsewhere, gives us information on the Gospels, the precise import of which remains uncertain or controversial: he specifically asseverates his preference for the 'living and abiding voice', contrasted with the teaching of books. Polycarp of Smyrna's letter to the Philippians shows clear knowledge of Matthew and Luke. He is then the earliest unambiguous evidence for their use, but if, as is most likely, his letter is in fact the combination of two written at different times (*viz.* chs. 13–14 *c.* AD 115; the rest *c.* AD 135), this will not be so early as once was thought. The so-called *2 Clement* and the *Epistle of Barnabas* both date about AD 130. Both use much oral material, but attest the use of the Synoptics too; and each introduces one phrase from the Gospels with a formula of scriptural citation.

There is considerable and wide knowledge of the Pauline Corpus in the Apostolic Fathers: their language is strongly influenced by the apostle's words. Yet, highly valued as his letters evidently were, there is little introduction of quotations as scriptural. A number of passages suggest that a distinction was made in all Christian circles between the OT and writings of Christian provenance. The Philadelphians judged the 'gospel' by the 'archives' (Ignatius, *Philad.* 8. 2): *2 Clement* speaks of 'the

	Irenaeus of Lyons *c.* AD130-200	Muratorian Canon AD170-210	Eusebius' *EH* 3.25 *c.* AD260-340	Athanasius' 39th Paschal letter AD367	Present Canon
Matthew					
Mark					
Luke					
John					
Acts					
Romans					
1 Corinthians					
2 Corinthians					
Galatians					
Ephesians					
Philippians					
Colossians					
1 Thessalonians					
2 Thessalonians					
1 Timothy					
2 Timothy					
Titus					
Philemon					
Hebrews	Omitted	Omitted			
James		Omitted	D		
1 Peter		Omitted			
2 Peter	Omitted	Omitted	D		
1 John					
2 John			D		
3 John	Omitted	Omitted	D		
Jude			D		
Revelation					
Selected apocryphal works					
Wisdom of Solomon	Omitted		Omitted		Omitted
Apocalypse of Peter	Omitted		S	Omitted	Omitted
Shepherd of Hermas	Omitted	**	S	*	Omitted
Acts of Paul	Omitted	Omitted	S	Omitted	Omitted
Epistle of Barnabas	Omitted	Omitted	S	Omitted	Omitted
The Didache	Omitted	Omitted	S	*	Omitted
Gospel according to the Hebrews	Omitted	Omitted	S	Omitted	Omitted

D Disputed | S Spurious | Omitted (shaded)

* Permitted reading | ** Permitted reading but not for public worship

The Pauline Epistles were probably collected into a corpus *c.* AD 80-85

Some of the main stages in the acceptance of the Canon of the New Testament. The present Canon (right) was accepted in the West in AD 397.

books (*biblia*) and the apostles' (14. 2), a contrast which is probably equivalent to 'Old and New Testaments'. Even where the gospel was highly prized (*e.g.* Ignatius or Papias), it is apparently in an oral rather than a written form. Barnabas is chiefly concerned to expound the OT; the *Didache*, didactic and ethical material common to Jew and Christian. Along with material from the canonical Gospels or parallel to them, most of the Apostolic Fathers utilize what we anachronistically term 'apocryphal' or 'extra-canonical' material: it was evidently not so to them. We are still in a period when the NT writings are not clearly demarcated from other edifying material. This situation in fact continues yet further into the 2nd century, and may be seen in Justin Martyr and Tatian. Justin records that the 'memoirs of the apostles' called Gospels were read at Christian worship: his quotations and allusions, however, afford evidence that the extent of these was not identical with the four, but contained 'apocryphal' material. This same material was used by Tatian in his harmony of the Gospels known as the *Diatessaron*, or, as in one source, perhaps more accurately, as *Diapente*.

III. Influence of Marcion

It was towards the close of the 2nd century that awareness of the concept of a canon and scriptural status begins to reveal itself in the thought and activity of Christians. The challenge of heretical teachers was largely instrumental in stimulating this. One such was Marcion of Sinope who broke with the church in Rome in about AD 150, but was probably active in Asia Minor for some years previously. Believing himself the interpreter of Paul, he preached a doctrine of two Gods: the OT was the work of the Just God, the Creator, harsh judge of men: Jesus was the emissary of the Good (or Kind) God, higher than the Just, sent to free men from that God's bondage: crucified through malice of the Just God, he passed on his gospel, first to the Twelve, who failed to keep it from corruption, and then to Paul, the sole preacher of it. Since Marcion rejected the OT, according to this scheme, he felt the need of a distinctively Christian Scripture, and created a definite Canon of Scripture: *one* Gospel, which stood in some relation or other to our present Luke, and the ten Epistles of Paul (omitting Hebrews and the Pastorals), which constituted the *Apostolos*.

Certain features of the growth of the Catholic Canon, which supervenes upon the age of Justin and Tatian, appear due to the challenge which the Marcionite scriptures presented to the church, especially the dominant place occupied by Paul, in spite of his relative neglect in the mid-2nd century. Former generations, guided by the theories of Harnack, have seen this factor present also in two documentary sources, namely a series of prologues to the Pauline Epistles in some Latin manuscripts, which de Bruyne considered to show signs of Marcion's tendentious teaching, thus termed 'Marcionite prologues', and certain prologues to the Gospels of Mark, Luke and John (extant chiefly in Latin), which have been termed 'anti-Marcionite', on the assumption that they were prefaced to the components of the fourfold Gospel at the time of its creation as a unity. Lately, however, these hypotheses, which have often been received as facts, have been trenchantly criticized and no longer appear certainly acceptable.

The other main heretical teaching against which the emergent concept of the Canon was used was that of the various Gnostics. From the Nag-Hammadi (*CHENOBOSKION) discoveries we can now know these better than did previous generations. It seems clear that the majority of the books which later constituted the NT were known in Gnostic circles. For instance, some moving passages in the so-called *Gospel of Truth* draw upon Revelation, Hebrews, Acts and the Gospels. Again, the *Gospel of Thomas* contains much material akin to the Synoptics, either derived from these or from a parallel oral tradition. But what is significant is that the latter mingles these sayings common to the Synoptic tradition with others of which canonical Scripture bears no trace; while the title of the former shows how the doctrine of a Gnostic teacher is presented as on a par with other Gospel documents. The emergence is a crystallization of the awareness that there was a clear distinction between teaching transmitted in documents of known antiquity as of apostolic origin, and recent teaching which could not be thus validated even if it claimed esoteric tradition or revelation as its source.

IV. Irenaeus to Eusebius

In the second half of the 2nd century, as has been intimated, clear evidence of the concept of a canon appears, although not all the books now included in the Canon are decided upon in any one church. Irenaeus of Lyons, in his work *Against the Heresies*, gives plain evidence that by his time the fourfold Gospel was axiomatic, comparable with the four corners of the earth and the four winds of heaven. Acts is quoted by him, sometimes explicitly, as Scripture. The Pauline Epistles, the Revelation and some Catholic Epistles are regarded, although not often explicitly as Scripture, yet (especially in the two former cases) sufficiently highly to indicate that here is a primary source of doctrine and authority to which reference must be made in the context of controversy. Against the so-called esoteric knowledge of his opponents, Irenaeus stresses the traditions of the church as apostolically derived. In these traditions, the Scriptures of the NT have their place. We know, however, that he definitely rejected Hebrews as non-Pauline.

Hippolytus of Rome, contemporary of Irenaeus, is known to us through writings only partially extant. He cites most NT books, speaking explicitly of two testaments and of a fourfold Gospel. Many critics are willing to ascribe to him the fragmentary list of canonical Scriptures preserved in Latin in a MS at Milan, known as the Muratorian Canon (after its first editor Ludovico Muratori). This ascription should not be taken as proved, however: the Latin is not necessarily a translation. A reference to the recent origin of the *Shepherd* of Hermas places it within the approximate dates AD 170–210. The extant part of the document gives a list of NT writings with some account of their origin and scope. Here again we meet a fourfold Gospel, acknowledgment of the Pauline Epistles, knowledge of some Catholic Epistles, the Acts of the Apostles and the Revelation of John; also included as canonical are the *Apocalypse of Peter* (there is no reference to any Petrine Epistle) and, rather surprisingly, the *Wisdom of Solomon*. The *Shepherd* is mentioned, but is not regarded as fit for use in public worship. The date of this document makes it highly significant, not only as witness to the existence at that time of a wide-embracing concept of the Canon but also of the marginal uncertainties, the omissions and the inclusion of writings later rejected as apocryphal.

The state of affairs shown in these sources was widespread and continued into the 3rd century. Tertullian, Clement of Alexandria and Origen all make wide use of the NT Scriptures, either in controversy, in doctrinal discussion or in actual commentary upon the component books. The majority of books in the present Canon are known to them and given canonical status; but uncertainty remains in the case of Hebrews, some of the Catholic Epistles and the Revelation of John. Uncanonical Gospels are cited, *agrapha* quoted as authentic words of the Lord, and some works of the Apostolic Fathers such as the *Epistle of Barnabas*, the *Shepherd* and the *First Epistle of Clement* are cited as canonical or scriptural. We find great codices even of the 4th and 5th centuries which contain some of these latter: the Codex Sinaiticus includes Barnabas and Hermas; the Codex Alexandrinus includes the *First* and *Second Epistles of Clement*. Claromontanus contains a catalogue of canonical writings in which Hebrews is absent, and *Barnabas*, the *Shepherd*, the *Acts of Paul* and the *Apocalypse of Peter* are included. In brief, the idea of a definite canon is fully established, and its main outline firmly fixed: the issue now is which books out of a certain number of marginal cases belong to it. The position in the church in the 3rd century is well summarized by Eusebius (*EH* 3. 25). He distinguishes between acknowledged books (*homologoumena*), disputed books (*antilegomena*) and spurious books (*notha*). In the first class are placed the four Gospels, the Acts, the Epistles of Paul, 1 Peter, 1 John and (according to some) the Revelation of John; in the second class he places (as 'disputed, nevertheless known to most') James, Jude, 2 Peter, 2 and 3 John; in the third class the *Acts of Paul*, the *Shepherd*, the *Apocalypse of Peter*, the *Epistle of Barnabas*, the *Didache*, the *Gospel according to the Hebrews* and (according to others) the Revelation of John. These latter, Eusebius suggests, might well be in the second class were it not for the necessity of guarding against deliberate forgeries of Gospels and Acts under the name of apostles, made in a strictly heretical interest. As examples of these he names the *Gospels* of *Thomas*, *Peter* and *Matthias*, and the *Acts of Andrew* and *John*. These 'ought to be reckoned not even among the spurious books but shunned as altogether wicked and impious'.

V. Fixation of the Canon

The 4th century saw the fixation of the Canon within the limits to which we are accustomed, both in the W and E sectors of Christendom. In the E the definitive point is the Thirty-ninth Paschal Letter of Athanasius in AD 367. Here we find for the first time a NT of exact bounds as known to us. A clear line is drawn between works in the Canon which are described as the sole sources of religious instruction, and others which it is permitted to read, namely, the *Didache* and the *Shepherd*. Heretical apocrypha are said to be intentional forgeries for the purposes of deceit. In the W the Canon was fixed by conciliar decision at Carthage in 397, when a like list to that of Athanasius was agreed upon. About the same period a number of Latin authors showed interest in the bounds of the NT Canon: Priscillian in Spain, Rufinus of Aquileia in Gaul, Augustine in N Africa (whose views contributed to the decisions at Carthage), Innocent I, bishop of Rome, and the author of the pseudo-Gelasian Decree. All hold the same views.

VI. The Syriac Canon

The development of the Canon in the Syriac-speaking churches was strikingly different. It is probable that the first Scripture known in these circles was, in addition to the OT, the apocryphal *Gospel according to the Hebrews* which left its mark upon the *Diatessaron* when that took its place as the Gospel of Syriac Christianity. It is likely that Tatian introduced also the Pauline Epistles and perhaps even the Acts: these three are named as the Scriptures of the primitive Syriac church by the *Doctrine of Addai*, a 5th-century document which in its account of the beginnings of Christianity in Edessa mingles legend with trustworthy tradition. The next stage in the closer alignment of the Syriac Canon with the Greek was the production of the 'separated gospels' (*Evangelion da-Mepharreshe*) to take the place of the *Diatessaron*. This was by no means easily accomplished. The Peshitta (textually a partially corrected form of the *Evangelion da-Mepharreshe*) was produced at some time in the 4th century; it contains, in addition to the fourfold Gospel, the Paulines and the Acts, the Epistles of James, 1 Peter and 1 John, *i.e.* the equivalent of the basic Canon accepted in the Greek churches about a century before. Two versions of the remaining books of the eventually accepted Canon were produced among the Syriac Monophysites: that of Philoxenos is probably extant in the so-called 'Pococke Epistles' and 'Crawford Apocalypse', while the later version of Thomas of Harkel also contains 2 Peter, 2 and 3 John, and Jude, and the version of Revelation published by de Dieu is almost certainly from this translation. Both show in their slavish imitation of Greek text and language, as well as in the mere fact of their production, the ever-increasing assimilation of Syriac Christianity to a Greek mode.

VII. Recapitulation

We may recapitulate by tracing the canonical fortunes of the individual books of the NT. The four Gospels circulated in relative independence until the formation of the fourfold Canon. Mark was apparently eclipsed by its two 'expansions', but not submerged. Luke, in spite of Marcion's patronage, does not seem to have encountered opposition. Matthew very early achieved that predominant place which it occupied till the modern era of scholarship. John was in rather different case, since in the late 2nd century there was considerable opposition to it, of which the so-called Alogoi and the Roman presbyter Gaius may serve as examples; this was no doubt due to some of the obscurities which still surround some aspects of its background, origin and earliest circulation. Once accepted, its prestige continued to grow, and it proved of the highest value in the great doctrinal controversies and definitions. The Acts of the Apostles did not lend itself to liturgical or controversial use; it makes little appearance until after the time of Irenaeus; from then on it is firmly fixed as part of the Scriptures. The Pauline Corpus was securely established as Scripture from the earliest times. Marcion apparently rejected the Pastorals; otherwise we have no record of doubts concerning them, and already Polycarp holds them as authoritative. Hebrews, on the other hand, remained in dispute for several centuries. In the E, Pantaenus and Clement of Alexandria are known to have discussed the critical problems of its authorship; Origen solved the question by assuming that Pauline thought was here expressed by an anonymous author; Eusebius and some others report the doubts of the W, but after Origen the letter was accepted in the E. It is noteworthy that the letter takes pride of place after Romans in the 3rd-century Chester Beatty papyrus (p^{46}). In the W doubts persisted from the earliest days: Irenaeus did not accept it as Pauline, Tertullian and other African sources pay it little regard, 'Ambrosiaster' wrote no commentary upon it, and in this was followed by Pelagius. The councils of Hippo and Carthage separate Hebrews from the rest of the Pauline Epistles in their canonical enumerations, and Jerome reported that in his day the opinion in Rome was still against authenticity. The matter was not considered settled until a century or so later. The corpus of the Catholic Epistles is evidently a late creation, post-dating the establishment of the essential structure of the Canon at the end of the 2nd century. Its exact constitution varies from church to church, and Father to Father. The First Epistle of John has a certain place from the time of Irenaeus: the Second and Third are but little quoted, and sometimes (as in the Muratorian Canon) we are uncertain whether both are being referred to. This may, of course, be due to their slenderness or apparent lack of theological import. The First Epistle of Peter, too, has a place only less secure (note, however, the ambiguities of the Muratorian Canon); the Second is still among the 'disputed books' in Eusebius' day. The status of James and Jude fluctuates according to church, age and individual judgment. (We may note here how Jude and 2 Peter are grouped with a veritable pot-pourri of religious literature as one volume in a papyrus in the Bodmer collection.) For inclusion in this corpus there appear to have competed with all these such works as the *Shepherd, Barnabas*, the *Didache*, the Clementine 'correspondence', all of which seem to have been sporadically recognized and utilized as scriptural. The Revelation of John was twice opposed: once in the 2nd century because of its apparent support of the claims of Montanus to prophetic inspiration, once in the late 3rd century on critical grounds, by comparison with the Gospel of John, in the controversy of the Dionysii of Rome and Alexandria. Both kinds of doubt contributed to the continued mistrust with which it was viewed by the Gk. churches, and its very late acceptance in the Syriac and Armenian churches. In the W, on the contrary, it was very early accorded a high place; it was translated into Latin on at least three different occasions, and numerous commentaries were dedicated to it from the time of Victorinus of Pettau (martyred 304) onwards.

VIII. The present position

So the Canon of the NT grew and became fixed in that form in which we now know it. In the 16th century both Roman and Protestant Christianity, after debate, reaffirmed their adherence to the traditions, and the Roman church has yet more recently emphasized its continued adherence. Conservative Protestantism, too, continues to use the Canon received by tradition, and even the representatives of liberal theology generally abide by it. Doubtless, in the face of modern biblical research and the new acknowledgment of non-apostolic authorship which some scholars, at least, feel obliged to make concerning some of the NT documents, we need to understand afresh the factors and motives which underlie the historical processes here outlined. The inclusion of documents in the Canon is the Christian church's recognition of the authority of these documents. There is no Canon in the earliest times because of the presence of apostles or their disciples, and because of the living oral traditions. In the mid-2nd century, the apostles are dead, but their memoirs and other monuments attest their message: at the same time heresy has arisen, and by its appeal either to theological theory or to new inspiration has necessitated a fresh appeal to orthodoxy's authority, and a closer definition of authoritative books. Thus the fourfold Gospel and the Pauline Corpus, already widely used, are declared to be scriptural, together with some other works with claims to apostolic authorship. Both doctrinal and scholarly discussion and development continue the process of recognition until, in the great era of the intellectual and ecclesiastical crystallization of Christianity, the Canon is completed. Three criteria were utilized, whether in the 2nd or the 4th century, to establish that the written documents are the true record of the voice and message of apostolic witness. First, attribution to apostles: this does not meet all cases; such Gospels as Mark and Luke were accepted as the works of close associates of the apostles. Secondly, ecclesiastical usage: that is, recognition by a leading church or by a majority of churches. By this were rejected many apocrypha, some perhaps innocuous and even containing authentic traditions of the words of Jesus, many more mere fabrications, but none known to be acknowledged by the majority of churches. Thirdly, congruence with the standards of sound doctrine: on this ground the Fourth Gospel is at first in doubt and at length accepted; or, to give a contrary case, the *Gospel of Peter* is banned by Serapion of Antioch because of its Docetic tendencies in spite of its claim to apostolic title. Thus the history of the canonical development of the NT Scripture shows it to be a collection attributed to apostles or their disciples which in the view of the church in the first four Christian centuries was justly thus attributed because it adequately declared and defined apostolic doctrine, and so its components had been or were considered to be fit for public reading at divine worship. When this is understood, with the gradual growth and variegated nature of the Canon, we can see why there were, and still are, problems and doubts about particular works there included. But taking these three criteria as adequate, orthodox Protestant Christianity today finds no reasons to reject the decisions of earlier generations and accepts the NT as a full and authoritative record of divine revelation as declared from of old by men chosen, dedicated and inspired.

BIBLIOGRAPHY. Th. Zahn, *Geschichte des neutestamentlichen Kanons*, 1888–92; M.-J. Lagrange, *Histoire ancienne du Canon du Nouveau Testament*, 1933; A. Souter, *The Text and Canon of the New Testament*², 1954; J. Knox, *Marcion and the New Testament*, 1942; E. C. Blackman, *Marcion and His Influence*, 1948; *The New Testament in the Apostolic Fathers*, 1905; J. N. Sanders, *The Fourth*

Gospel in the Early Church, 1943; W. Bauer, *Rechtgläubigkeit und Ketzerei im ältesten Christen-tum*, 1934 (²rev., 1964; E.T. 1971); F. -M. Braun, *Jean le Théologien*, 1959; R. P. C. Hanson, *Tradition in the Early Church*, 1962; J. Regul, *Die antimarcionitischen Evangelienprologe*, 1969; R. M. Grant, 'The New Testament Canon' in *Cambridge History of the Bible*, 1, 1970, pp. 284–308 and 593f.; H. von Campenhausen, *The Formation of the Christian Bible*, 1972; H. Y. Gamble, *ABD* 1, pp. 852–861.

J.N.B.

CAPERNAUM.

I. Name

NT manuscripts mostly read *Kapharnaoum*, though *Kapernaoum* appears in minuscules dependent on codex Alexandrinus. Clearly Kapharnaoum is the original form, directly transcribing Semitic *kᵉp̄ar naḥûm*, 'village of Nahum'. This Semitic form is found at *Qohelet Rabbah* 1. 8 and 7. 26. Josephus (*BJ* 3. 517) refers to the spring *Kapharnaoum*, equivalent to Semitic *'en-kᵉp̄ar naḥûm*. His *Vita* 403 should probably be read *Kepharnakōn* (original of the MSS PRA, favoured by Thackeray). This is the same word with *nûnized* ending and *k* for *ḥ*.

II. Location

Evidence from the NT, Josephus, Christian pilgrim-texts, mediaeval Jewish itineraries, extant monumental remains and current excavations indicates that Capernaum was undoubtedly located at *Tell Hum*, and was inhabited continuously from the 2nd century BC to the 7th century AD. The Gospels are almost sufficient in themselves to fix the site, indicating that Capernaum was (*a*) by the lake-side (Mt. 4:13); (*b*) near a political border, so that a customs-post (Mk. 2:14) and military detachment were necessary (Mt. 8:5–13; Lk. 7:1–10); (*c*) near Gennesaret (Mk. 6:53; Jn. 6:22, 59), which is an area of highly productive land at the NW of the Lake. In short Capernaum was the nearest village to the river Jordan on the NW shores of the Sea of Galilee, a position occupied in fact by the ruins of *Tell Hum*. This is confirmed by Josephus *Vita* 403, which indicates a village close to Julias (*et-Tell*) in the direction of Magdala/Tarichaeae (*Mejdel*).

Capernaum was also near a most copious spring which watered Gennesaret (*BJ* 3. 519) and can only be the site *et-Tabgha*. But Arabic *et-Tabgha* is also undoubtedly a corruption of Gk. *Heptapēgōn* (place of seven springs). This 'Seven Springs' is mentioned by Egeria *c*. AD 383 (Lat. *septem fontes*), and by Theodosius (AD 530). Theodosius provides us with our only detailed early itinerary round the NW shores of the Sea of Galilee, moving N from Tiberias in Roman miles: 2 m Magdala, 2 m Heptapegon, 2 m Capernaum, 6 m Bethsaida. Thus Capernaum was 2 miles (3½km) N of Tabgha, which exactly locates *Tell Hum*. The name *Seven Springs* indicates a Semitic original denoting copious waters, but it was the Greek term that survived. In Arabic the succession is *Mejdel*, *et-Tabgha*, *Tell Hum*. The first two names correspond to the list of Theodosius, but *Hum* can hardly be a reduction of *Nahum*—which begins with a long syllable—nor is there in fact a *tell* (mound) at this site, but merely a *khirbe* or *rujm* (ruin or tumble of stones). Mediaeval Jewish itineraries provide the answer. The tomb of Rabbi Tanhum was thought to be here; by a natural progression the itineraries refer to the place baldly as 'Tanhum'. Degeneration from Tanhum to *tell hum* (dark mound) is readily comprehensible. The list of Theodosius locates Capernaum to the N of *et-Tabgha*. Note that the old rival site to *Tell Hum*, *Khirbet Munja* or *Minyeh*, is S of *et-Tabgha*. Its name has long been thought to be a survival of the *Munyat Hisham* or *el-Munya* of Arab sources. Excavation has now confirmed this by uncovering an Ummayad chateau, not a Jewish village (*IEJ* 10, 1960, pp.240–243).

Monuments are also important in confirming the site of Capernaum. Egeria saw a synagogue there of fine ashlars, approached 'by many steps'. Unusually, the synagogue remains at *Tell Hum* are set on a high platform, with a balcony at the front, reached by a flight of steps. Egeria was also shown a church (*ecclesia*) when she came to Capernaum (*c*. AD 383). She says that it had been made from the house of the apostle Peter, and the walls of this house were incorporated into it, still standing in their original form (*ita stant sicut fuerunt*). The pilgrim from Piacenza (AD 570) tells us that he entered Peter's house in Capernaum, but it had been replaced by a basilica.

III. History

Until the conversion of Constantine the Great (AD 306–337) Jewish communities flourished in Galilee under their rabbis and Patriarchs. About AD 335, a Jew of Tiberias, the Christian convert Joseph, informed Constantine that only Jews inhabited Tiberias, Sepphoris, Nazareth and Capernaum rigorously excluding Gentiles from their settlements. Joseph secured ready permission from the emperor to build 'churches for Christ' (*ekklēsiai*) in these places (Epiphanius, *Haer*. 30. 4. 1 = *PG* 41. 425), and managed to convert a derelict temple of Hadrian at Tiberias and erect a small church at Sepphoris. Yet it was not perhaps until the 5th century AD that Gentile Christians fully established themselves in this Jewish 'ghetto'. How far through all this time the 'Judeo-Christian' sect was established at Capernaum and elsewhere in Galilee is difficult to say. From stories in the rabbis one learns of *minîm* (heretics) at Tiberias, Sepphoris and Capernaum (2nd/3rd centuries AD). Only one tale is told about Capernaum, that R. Hananya was persuaded by *minîm* to break the sabbath-rule by riding a donkey (*c*. AD 110). These Jewish Christians held to the Law, attended synagogue and avoided contact with Gentiles; but they healed and spoke in the name of Jesus. Jerome says that the Pharisees called them 'Nazaraeans'; that they still flourished in his day (late 4th/early 5th centuries AD) 'in the synagogues of the East'; and that they were neither faithful Jews nor genuine Christians.

IV. Excavations

Excavations by the Franciscan *Custodia di Terra Santa*, directed by V. Corbo, began at Capernaum (*Tell Hum*) in 1968 and are still in progress. The synagogue had long before (1905) been cleared by Kohl and Watzinger to its flagstone pavement, and dated by comparison with Severan monuments in Syria to the late 2nd or early 3rd centuries AD. The plan which the Germans exposed was of a long, colonnaded assembly-hall divided into a central nave and side-aisles; this hall faced S and was connected on its E side to an impressive annexe, a colonnaded courtyard. Both the hall and annexe were raised up on a high platform (*podium*), and had a balcony in front of them reached by imposing flights of steps on either side. One would certainly suppose that this was the synagogue seen by Egeria (*c.* AD 383) at Capernaum, reached by an ascent of 'many steps'.

But if the dates argued for Egeria's pilgrimage by Devos and accepted by Wilkinson (AD 381–384) are correct, she must have seen the synagogue while it was being constructed. Eighteen trenches in and around the synagogue have yielded pottery (carefully studied by S. Loffreda) and coins establishing that work was begun *c.* AD 350 and completed *c.* AD 450. The rubble fill (stratum B) of the *podium* rests on destroyed houses (stratum A); it is sealed from above by a thick and unbroken mortar (stratum C) in which the flagstones of the hall and annexe were set. Excavations in the synagogue have not yet been completed and will be published in a separate volume when they are; the definitive publications so far are *Caf. 1* and *Stud. Hier.* (see bibliography). A further trench across the entire E/W width of the hall is planned (*Stud. Hier.*, p. 176). According to the material published so far, the earliest possible date for the pavement of the hall and its E colonnade is AD 383, since the latest coins from the sealed fill beneath the mortar are AD 352–360 (*Caf. 1*, pp. 121, 163) and AD 383–408 (*Stud. Hier.*, p. 164, under the stylobate for the E colonnade). The latest coin embedded within the thick mortar before it had set (trench 2, stratum C) is also from AD 383 (*LA* 22, 1972, pp. 15–16). These late dates for the synagogue were totally unexpected and have aroused great controversy (*IEJ* 21, 1971, pp. 207–211; 23, 1973, pp. 37–45, 184; *Ariel* 32, 1973, pp. 29–43).

Two successive shrines, totally different from each other, were excavated on the same site only one block of houses distant from the synagogue. The later shrine is the *basilica* seen by the Piacenza pilgrim; a small memorial completed by *c.* AD 450 in the unusual form of a double octagon. Its central ring is sited exactly over the main room of a house built in the 1st century BC. The basilica replaced a shrine of the early 4th century AD, possibly built by Joseph of Tiberias, which encapsulated the same early house, leaving its original walls standing, as Egeria was shown. The main room of this house had once again been marked out. In particular its walls were plastered and enlivened by painted designs in bold colours. On fallen pieces of plaster *graffiti* in Greek (a few Semitic) were found, including the words *amen*, *Lord* and *Jesus*. Clearly this was the traditional house of Peter, visited by pilgrims.

Excavation of these monuments and of five blocks (*insulae*) of houses indicates that Capernaum was inhabited continuously between the early 1st century BC and the 7th century AD. The houses are part of a village which was *c.* 800 by 250 m in extent, as sherds and remains indicate. Of the excavated area, *insulae* 1–3 are the older ones, begun in the 1st century BC; *insulae* 4–5 developed from the 4th century AD. The traditional house of Peter (*insula* 1) and the block between this and the synagogue (*insula* 2) are most fully studied by the excavators, and are reproduced as isometric drawings (*Caf. 1*, pl. X, XV). Corbo estimates that *insula* 2 could have housed fifteen families, about 130/150 people. It has only a few entries into the roads outside, and consists of small rooms opening on to a number of internal courtyards. Steps survive, and must have led up to terrace-roofs of earth and straw (as Mk. 2:4: healing of the paralytic), since the walls of basalt fieldstones and earth-mortar could not have supported an upper storey. The floors are of basalt cobbles covered by earth. *Insula* 2 was occupied from the beginning of the 1st century AD to the 7th century AD without a break; its original walls remained in use unchanged. A succession of floors provides sherds and coins for dating.

BIBLIOGRAPHY. E. W. G. Masterman, *PEQ* 1907, pp. 220–229; *idem, Studies in Galilee*, 1909; F.-M. Abel, *Capharnaum*, in *DBS*, 1, 1928; V. Corbo, *The House of St Peter at Capharnaum*, 1969; *idem, Cafarnao 1: Gli edifici della città*, 1975; *idem, Studia Hierosolymitana in honore di P. Bellarmino Bagatti*, 1976, pp. 159–176; S. Loffreda, *Cafarnao 2: La Ceramica*, 1974; A. Spijkerman, *Cafarnao 3: Catalogo delle monete della città*, 1975; E. Testa, *Cafarnao 4: I graffiti della casa di S. Pietro*, 1972; R. North, *Bib* 58, 1977, pp. 424–431; *NEAEHL*, pp. 291–296.

J.P.K.

CAPHTOR (*kaptôr*). The home of the *kaptōrîm* (Dt. 2:23), one of the peoples listed in the Table of *Nations as descended, with Casluhim, whence went forth the *Philistines, from Mizraim (Gn. 10:14; 1 Ch. 1:12). Caphtor was the land from which the Philistines came (Je. 47:4; Am. 9:7), and it is presumably the Philistines, as erstwhile sojourners in Caphtor, who are referred to as Caphtorim in Dt. 2:23. It is probable that the biblical name is to be identified with Ugaritic *kptr*, and *kap-ta-ra* in a school text from Assur which may well be a copy of one of 2nd-millennium date. It is likewise held by many scholars that Egyp. *kftyw* is also to be connected with this group, all of which refer in all probability to *Crete. At its height in the 2nd millennium, Minoan Crete controlled much of the Aegean area, and this would accord with the biblical description of Caphtor as an *'î*, a term which can mean both 'island' and 'coastland'. W Asia was influenced in art and other ways by the Aegean, and this may explain the occurrence in the Bible of the term *kaptôr* as applying to an architectural feature, evidently a column capital, rendered in the AV by 'knop' (Ex. 25:31–36; 37:17–22) and 'lintel' (Am. 9:1; Zp. 2:14).

BIBLIOGRAPHY. A. H. Gardiner, *Ancient Egyptian Onomastica*, Text, I, 1947, pp. 201*–203*; R. W. Hutchinson, *Prehistoric Crete*, 1962, pp. 106–112; T. C. Mitchell in *AOTS*, pp. 408, 413; K. A. Kitchen in *POTT*, p. 54.

T.C.M.

CAPITAL. 1. Heb. *kaptôr* (*a*) ornamental top of pillars, Am. 9:1; Zp. 2:14 (AV 'lintel'); (*b*) ornamental round protrusion (LXX *sphairōtēr*) in the *lampstand, Ex. 25:31–36; 37:17–22 (AV 'knop', whereas in 1 Ki. 6:18; 7:24 AV 'knop' represents *peqā'îm* = RSV 'gourds', Targ. 'eggs').

2. Heb. *'kōteret* (*a*) spherical capital 5 cubits high on each of the pillars, *Jachin and Boaz, in Solomon's *Temple, 1 Ki. 7:16–42; 2 Ch. 4:12; Je. 52:22 (AV 'chapiter'); (*b*) a circular lip projecting upwards round the edge of the hole in the top of the stand in which was placed the basin of each mobile laver, 1 Ki. 7:31 (RSV 'crown', AV 'chapiter').

3. Heb. *ṣepet*, 2 Ch. 3:15, same as **1.** (*b*) (AV 'chapiter').

4. Heb. *rô'š* (literally, 'head'), term used for the capitals (AV 'chapiters') on pillars in the tabernacle, Ex. 36:38; 38:17. D.W.G.

CAPPADOCIA. A highland province, much of it around 900 m, in the E of Asia Minor, bounded on the S by the chain of Mt Taurus, E by the Euphrates and N by Pontus, but its actual limits are vague. It was constituted a Roman province by Tiberius, AD 17, on the death of Archelaus. In AD 70 Vespasian united it with Armenia Minor as one of the great frontier bulwarks of the empire. Under later emperors, especially Trajan, the size and importance of the province greatly increased. It produced large numbers of sheep and horses. The trade route between Central Asia and the Black Sea ports passed through it, and it was easily accessible from Tarsus through the Cilician Gates. Jews from it were present at Jerusalem on the day of *Pentecost (Acts 2:9). Some of the Dispersion to whom Peter wrote lived in Cappadocia (1 Pet. 1:1). J.W.M.

CAPTAIN. The nearest Hebrew equivalent is *śar*, which can denote a leader of thousands, hundreds or fifties (Ex. 18:25; 1 Sa. 8:12). *rô'š* ('head') may occasionally be translated 'captain' as in Nu. 14:4. In Saul's reign the Israelite military machine was not yet at the peak of its efficiency, but the basis of organization had been established; the army consisted of companies headed by 'captains of thousands' (1 Sa. 17:18). David's standing army was led by 'The Thirty', commanders who had won their spurs while David was a fugitive from Saul. David also organized a militia and 1 Ch. 27:1–15 shows how it was divided into 12 battalions, each of which served for a month per year under the direction of its captain. 'Captain' is also used in connection with the chariot force of the N kingdom in the 9th century (1 Ki. 16:9, 'captain [*śar*] of half his chariots'). In the NT *chiliarchos*, lit. 'commander of a thousand men', is translated 'captain' at Jn. 18:12. It is also the term used for the Roman military tribune in Acts 21:31–33, 37, and can be used of any military officer (Mk. 6:21). *stratēgos*, originally referring to an army commander, is Luke's word for the captains of the Temple who would have been of levitical or priestly stock (Lk. 22:4, 52; Acts 4:1, *etc.*). *archēgos*, translated 'captain' in AV of Heb. 2:10, is better rendered 'pioneer' with RSV. *stratopedarchos* in some MSS of Acts 28:16 is translated 'captain of the guard' in AV; the operative clause is treated as secondary and therefore omitted by RSV. R.P.G.

CARCHEMISH. A city (mod. Jerablus) which guarded the main ford across the river Euphrates *c.* 100 km NE of Aleppo. It is first mentioned in a text of the 18th century BC as an independent trade-centre (Mari, Alalaḫ). As a Syrian city-state it had treaties with Ugarit and other states (Mitanni) during the 2nd millennium BC and continued as a neo-Hittite state after Inī-Teṣub (*c.* 1100) until Pisiris was defeated by Sargon II in 717 BC. Thereafter Carchemish was incorporated as an Assyr. province. The event is noted in Is. 10:9.

In 609 BC Neco II of Egypt moved *via* Megiddo to recapture the city (2 Ch. 35:20), which was made a base from which his army harassed the Babylonians. However, in May–June 605 BC Nebuchadrezzar II led the Babylonian forces who entered the city by surprise. The Egyptians were utterly defeated in hand-to-hand fighting in and around the city (Je. 46:2) and pursued to Hamath. Details of this battle, which resulted in the Babylonian control of the W, are given in the Babylonian Chronicle.

Excavations in 1912 and 1914 uncovered Hittite sculptures, a lower palace area with an open palace (*bît-ḫilani*), and evidence of the battle and later Babylonian occupation.

BIBLIOGRAPHY. C. L. Woolley, *Carchemish*, 1–3, 1914–52; D. J. Wiseman, *Chronicles of Chaldaean Kings*, 1956, pp. 20–27, 68–69; J. D. Hawkins, *Reallexikon der Assyriologie* 5, 1980, pp. 426–446; W. W. Hallo in C. F. Pfeiffer, *The Biblical World*, 1966, pp. 65–69. D.J.W.

CARMEL (Heb. *karmel*, 'garden-land', 'fruitful land'). The word is used as a common noun in Hebrew with this meaning; examples are Is. 16:10; Je. 4:26; 2 Ki. 19:23; 2 Ch. 26:10. It can even be used of fresh ears of grain, as in Lv. 2:14; 23:14. Thus, the limestone Carmel hills probably got their name from the luxuriant scrub and woodland that covered them. In the OT two places bear this name.

1. A range of hills, *c.* 50 km long, extending from NW to SE, from Mediterranean (S shore of Bay of Acre) to the plain of Dothan. Strictly, Mt Carmel is the main ridge (maximum height *c.* 530 m) at the NW end, running *c.* 19 km inland from the sea, forming a border of Asher (Jos. 19:26). This densely vegetated and little-inhabited region was a barrier pierced by two main passes, emerging at Jokneam and Megiddo, and a lesser one emerging at Taanach; between the first two, the hills are lower and more barren but have steep scarps. The main N–S road, however, passes by Carmel's hills through the plain of Dothan on the E. Carmel's luxuriant growth is reflected in Am. 1:2; 9:3; Mi. 7:14; Na. 1:4; also in Ct. 7:5 in an apt simile for thick, bushy hair. The forbidding figure of Nebuchadrezzar of Babylon marching against Egypt is once compared with the rocky eminences of Carmel and Tabor (Je. 46:18).

Joshua's vanquished foes included 'the king of Jokneam in Carmel' (Jos. 12:22). It was here that Elijah in the name of his God challenged the prophets of Baal and Asherah, the deities promoted by Jezebel, and won a notable victory against them (1 Ki. 18; 19:1–2). The text makes it obvious that it was Jezebel's gods that were thus discredited; as she came from Tyre, the Baal was almost certainly Baal-melqart the chief god there. This god also penetrated Aram; see *Ben-hadad for a stele to this deity. *Baal was still worshipped on Carmel as 'Zeus Heliopolitēs Carmel' in AD 200 (Ap-Thomas, *PEQ* 92, 1960, p. 146). Alt considered this Baal as purely local, a view refuted by the biblical text, and Eissfeldt preferred Baal-shamêm who is less appropriate than Baal-melqart (latter also advocated by de Vaux).

2. A town in Judah (Jos. 15:55), at present-day Khirbet el-Karmil (var. Kermel or Kurmul), some 12 km SSE of Hebron, in a rolling, pastoral region (Baly, p. 164) ideal for the flocks that Nabal grazed there in David's time (1 Sa. 25). His wife Abigail was a Carmelitess, and Hezro, one of David's warriors (2 Sa. 23:35; 1 Ch. 11:37) probably hailed from there. Saul passed that way on his return from the slaughter of the Amalekites (1 Sa. 15:12).

BIBLIOGRAPHY. D. Baly, *Geography of the Bible*, 1974, pp. 149 (map 51), 172f. K.A.K.

CART, WAGON (*ᵃgālâ*, from the 'rolling' of wheels). Originally in Babylonia (Early Dynastic period) sledges were devised for carrying light loads, and these were soon adopted in Egypt and other flat countries. With the advent of the wheel, and the consequent increased mobility, carts early came into common use throughout Babylonia (*ṣumbu*), Egypt (Gn. 45:19–21; 46:5), and Palestine, as a 2– or 4–wheeled vehicle used principally in the S and low-lying Shephelah. However, in the hills their use was restricted to the main tracks (1 Sa. 6:12), and they were not commonly used for long distances (Gn. 45). They could carry one or two drivers with a light load, despite a general instability (1 Ch. 13:7–9). The main use was transporting the more bulky harvest in country districts (Am. 2:13).

Such carts were made by carpenters of wood (1 Sa. 6:7), and could therefore be dismantled and burnt (v. 14; Ps. 46:9, see below). Some were covered wagons (Nu. 7:3). The two wheels, either solid or spoked, were sometimes equipped with a heavy metal tread (see Is. 28:27–28). Wagons were usually drawn by two oxen or milch-cows (Nu. 7:3–8; 2 Sa. 6:3–7) and are represented on Assyr. sculptures showing the fall of Lachish in 701 BC (British Museum). The 'covered wagon' of Nu. 7:3 may be a *chariot (as RSV; *cf.* Idrimi statue, Alalah, *ANET*, p. 557), though wagons were also used for military transport (Ps. 46:9, RSV 'chariot'). The wheeled vehicle may have preceded the threshing-sledge in Is. 28:27–28. The figurative reference to a cart-rope in Is. 5:18 is now obscure. D.J.W.

CASTLE. Five Hebrew words and one Greek word were thus translated in the AV. All have been differently translated in the RSV with the exception of *'armôn*. This appears as 'castle' (Pr. 18:19), but also as 'citadel' (1 Ki. 16:18) and 'tower' (Ps. 122:7), since it may be applied to any building of eminence. G.W.G.

CASTOR AND POLLUX (Gk. *dioskouroi*, lit. 'sons of Zeus'). The sign of the Alexandrian ship in which Paul sailed from Malta to Puteoli on his way to Rome (Acts 28:11, AV). RV and RSV render 'The Twin Brothers'. According to Gk. mythology they were the sons of Leda. They were worshipped especially at Sparta and were regarded as the special protectors of sailors. Their images were probably fastened one on either side of the bow of the vessel. J.W.M.

CATHOLIC EPISTLES. During the course of the formation of the *Canon of the NT the Epistles of James, 1 and 2 Peter, 1, 2 and 3 John and Jude came to be grouped together and known as 'Catholic' (AV 'General'), because, with the exception of 2 and 3 John, they were addressed to a wider audience than a local church or individual. Clement of Alexandria speaks of the epistle sent out by the Council at Jerusalem (Acts 15:23) as 'the catholic epistle of all the Apostles'; and Origen applies the term to the *Epistle of Barnabas*, as well as to the Epistles of John, Peter and Jude. Later the word 'Catholic' was applied to Epistles which were accepted by the universal church and were orthodox in doctrine; so it became synonymous with 'genuine' or 'canonical'. Thus with regard to other documents put forward in the name of Peter, Eusebius says 'we know nothing of them being handed down as catholic writings' (*EH* 3. 3). R.V.G.T.

CATTLE. Nomads and agriculturists alike counted their wealth and regulated their sacrificial worship by possessions in cattle. Heb. *bᵉhēmâ*, beast (sing. or collective), denotes the larger domestic animals—*cf.* Gk. *ktēnos.* The Gk. term frequently, the Heb. occasionally (Ne. 2:12, 14) indicates a mount. The plural may (Jb. 40:15), but need not (*cf.* Ps. 49:12, 20) describe the hippopotamus. *šôr* is an ox or cow—the stalled or fattened ox was a symbol of luxury (Pr. 15:17). *ᵃlāpîm* (plural only) is used for cattle in general. *bᵉʿîr* has a normal, though not exclusive, reference to beasts of burden. *bāqār* is a generic word incapable of pluralization denoting 'cattlehood', frequently accompanied by a defining word. *'ēḡel* is commonly used for calf or heifer. *par* is a bull, fem. *pārâ.* The latter is used for the spectacular red heifer ceremonial of Nu. 19. In Lk. 17:7; Jn. 4:12, Gk. suggests sheep or goats, rather than AV 'cattle'. Heb. *miqneh* (*e.g.* Gn. 13:2) means primarily wealth or possessions, derivatively cattle, the significant form of ancient E wealth, *cf.* Arab. *m'āl*, also Heb. *mᵉlā'ḵâ. 'anšê miqneh* are herdsmen or nomads.

BIBLIOGRAPHY. W. Bauder, C. Brown, *NIDNTT* 1, pp. 113–119; J. Gess, R. Tuente, *NIDNTT* 2, pp. 410–414; G. S. Cansdale, *Animals of Bible Lands*, 1970. R.A.S.

CAUDA, modern Gavdho (Gozzo), is an island off the S of Crete. Some ancient authorities call it Clauda (as in AV). Paul's ship was in the vicinity of Cape Matala when the wind changed from S to a strong ENE, and drove it some 40 km before it came under the lee of Cauda, where the crew were at last able to make preparations to face the storm (Acts 27:16; *SHIPS AND BOATS). K.L.McK.

CAVE. Except in Jb. 30:6, where *ḥôr*, 'hole', is used, the Heb. word usually rendered 'cave' is *mᵉʿārâ*. Natural caves are no rarity in Palestine, as nearly all the hill-country of Palestine W of the Jordan (except a basalt outcrop in S Galilee) is of limestone and chalk. Such caves were used as dwellings, hiding-places and tombs from the earliest times.

a. Use as dwellings

Remarkable cave-dwellings of 34th/33rd centuries BC have been excavated at Tell Abu Matar, just S of Beersheba. Great caverns had been hollowed out as homes of several chambers linked by galleries for a prosperous community of cultivators and copper-workers. In much later days (early 2nd millennium BC), Lot and his two daughters lodged in a cave after the fall of Sodom and Gomorrah (Gn. 19:30), and David and his band frequented the great cave at Adullam (1 Sa. 22:1; 24), and Elisha stayed in one at Horeb (1 Ki. 19:9–13).

b. Use as refuges

Joshua cornered 5 Canaanite kings who hid thus at Makkedah (Jos. 10:16ff.). Israelites also hid in this way from Midianite (Jdg. 6:2) and Philistine (1 Sa. 13:6) invaders. Elijah's friend Obadiah hid 100 prophets in caves 'by fifties' from the sword of Jezebel (1 Ki. 18:4, 13); *cf.* Is. 2:19; Heb. 11:38. Evidence of their use as refuges through the ages has been recovered from caves in the Jordan Valley and by the Dead Sea.

c. Use as tombs

This was a very common practice from prehistoric times onwards (*BURIAL AND MOURNING). Famous instances in Scripture are the cave at Machpelah used by Abraham and his family (Gn. 23, *etc.*), and that whence Jesus summoned Lazarus from the dead (Jn. 11:38).

BIBLIOGRAPHY. For the use of caves as dwellings, see K. M. Kenyon, *Archaeology in the Holy Land*, 1960, pp. 77–80, fig. 10; T. Abu Matar, *cf.* E. K. Vogel, *Bibliography of Holy Land Sites*, 1974, p. 15; as refuges, see P. Benoit, J. T. Milik, R. de Vaux, *Les Grottes de Murabba'at, Discoveries in the Judaean Desert*, 2, 1961; Y. Yadin, *The Finds from the Bar Kokhba Period in the 'Cave of Letters'*, 1963.

K.A.K.

CENCHREAE, the modern Kichries, a town near Corinth which served as outport for the city, handling its traffic with the Aegean and the Levant. Cenchreae had a church in which Phoebe served (Rom. 16:1–2); this was perhaps a fruit of Paul's long stay in Corinth. Here the apostle shaved his head, in observance of a vow he had taken (Acts 18:18), prior to leaving for Ephesus. J.H.P.

CENSER. In many rituals an *altar was specifically devoted to the burning of incense. Its form was usually either a bowl mounted on a pedestal, often conical in shape, *i.e.* 'incense-altar' (Heb. *miqṭereṯ*, LXX *thymiatērion*, 2 Ch. 26:19; Ezk. 8:11); so translate for censer (AV) in Heb. 9:4 (B. F. Westcott, *The Epistle to the Hebrews*, 1903, pp. 248–250). *libanotos* is used in Rev. 8:3, 5. On the altar perfumes such as frankincense or cedar-pine were piled or thrown to create a sweet-smelling smoke (*BASOR* 132, 1953, p. 46). Small stone incense-altars with concave bowls on legs are commonly found, or depicted in ancient art, *e.g.* the horned altar from Megiddo. For illustrations, see *ANEP*, pp. 575–581, 626.

Some censers were portable and made of bronze (*maḥtâ*, Lv. 10:1; 16:12; Nu. 16:6) or gold (1 Ki. 7:50), and used for carrying a few burning coals (so NIV; AV 'censer'; RSV 'firepan'). The 'censer' of Ezr. 1:9 (RSV, *maḥlāp̄*) may denote some other vessel (NIV 'silver dishes'; NEB 'of various kinds'; AV 'knife'). D.W.G.

D.J.W.

CENSUS (Lat. *census*, 'assessment', appearing as a loan-word in Gk. *kēnsos*, 'tribute money', in Mt. 17:25; 22:17, 19; Mk. 12:14).

I. In the Old Testament

The outstanding censuses in OT are those from which the book of Numbers receives its name, at the beginning (Nu. 1) and end (Nu. 26) of the wilderness wanderings; and that held by David (2 Sa. 24:1–9; 1 Ch. 21:1–6). In all these it was men of military age who were numbered. Two different sets of totals for David's census have been preserved—in 2 Sa., 800,000 men of Israel and 500,000 men of Judah; in 1 Ch., 1,100,000 men of Israel and 470,000 men of Judah. The plague which followed the census is recorded in both accounts as a divine judgment for David's sin in numbering the people. The censuses of Numbers have been regarded, especially by W. F. Albright ('The Administrative Divisions of Israel and Judah', *JPOS* 5, 1925, pp. 20ff.; *From the Stone Age to Christianity*, 1940, pp. 192, 222), as other variant accounts of David's census, but their totals are considerably less than those of 2 Sa. and 1 Ch. Nevertheless, the transmitted totals of the wilderness censuses—603,550 in Nu. 1 and 601,730 in Nu. 26—call for some interpretation. One suggestion is that *'elep̄* in the enumeration originally meant something like 'tent-group' rather than 'thousand', so that the figure of 'forty-six thousand five hundred' given for Reuben in Nu. 1:21 meant 46 tent-groups, amounting in all to 500 men (W. M. F. Petrie, *Egypt and Israel*, 1911, pp. 40ff.) (*NUMBER, 2).

A census of the Judaeans in Nehemiah's time (445–433 BC) is reproduced in Ezr. 2:1–65; Ne. 7:6–67. The total is given as 42,360, together with 7,582 servants and singers.

II. In the New Testament

Two Roman censuses are mentioned in NT, each being denoted by Gk. *apographē*, translated 'enrolment' in Lk. 2:2 and 'census' in Acts 5:37.

The census of Acts 5:37, which was marked by the insurrection led by *Judas of Galilee, was held in AD 6. In that year Judaea was incorporated into the Roman provincial system, and a census was held in order to assess the amount of tribute which the new province should pay to the imperial exchequer. The census was conducted by P. Sulpicius Quirinius, at that time imperial legate of Syria. The suggestion that Israel should pay tribute to a pagan overlord was deemed intolerable by Judas, and by the party of the *Zealots, whose formation has been dated from this time.

The census of Lk. 2:1ff., in the course of which Christ was born in Bethlehem, raises a number of problems. It is, however, widely agreed: (i) that such a census as Luke describes could have taken place in Judaea towards the end of Herod's reign (37–4 BC); (ii) that it could have formed part of an empire-wide enrolment, as Lk. 2:1 indicates; (iii) that it could have involved the return of each householder to his domicile of origin, as Lk. 2:3 states. (i) In Herod's later years Augustus treated him as a subject; all Judaea had to take an oath of loyalty to Augustus as well as to Herod (Jos., *Ant.* 16. 290; 17. 42). Compare the census imposed in AD 36 in the client-kingdom of Archelaus (Tacitus, *Annals* 6. 41). (ii) There is evidence of census activity in various parts of the Roman empire between 11 and 8 BC; that for a census in Egypt in 10–9 BC (first of a series held every 14 years) is specially persuasive. (iii) The custom described in Lk. 2:3 (evidently as something familiar) is attested from Egypt in AD 104. On the relation of Quirinius to this earlier census, *QUIRINIUS.

BIBLIOGRAPHY. W. M. Ramsay, 'The Augustan Census-System', in *BRD* pp. 255ff. F.F.B.

CHALDEA, CHALDEANS. The name of a land, and its inhabitants, in S Babylonia, later used to denote Babylonia as a whole, especially during the last dynasty of Babylonia (626–539 BC); a semi-nomadic tribe occupying the deserts between N Arabia and the Persian Gulf (*cf.,* Jb. 1:17) who early settled in this area occupying Ur 'of the Chaldees' (Gn. 11:28; Acts 7:4) and are distinct from the Aramaeans. The proposed derivation from Chesed (Gn. 22:22) is unsubstantiated but the Heb. *Kaśdîm* may reflect an earlier form of the name than the Assyr. From at least the 10th century BC the land of *Kaldu* is named in the Assyr. annals to designate the 'Sea-land' of the earlier inscriptions. Ashurnasirpal II (883–859 BC) distinguished its peoples from the more northerly Babylonians, and Adad-nirari III (*c.* 810 BC) names several chiefs of the Chaldeans among his vassals. When Marduk-apla-iddina II (*MERODACH-BALADAN), the chief of the Chaldean district of Bit-Yakin, seized the throne of Babylon in 721–710 and 703–702 BC he sought help from the W against Assyria (Is. 39). The prophet Isaiah warned of the danger to Judah of supporting the Chaldean rebels (Is. 23:13) and foresaw their defeat (43:14), perhaps after the initial invasion by Sargon in 710 BC. Since Babylon was at this time under a Chaldean king, 'Chaldean' is used as a synonym for Babylonian (Is. 13:19; 47:1, 5; 48:14, 20), a use later extended by Ezekiel to cover all the Babylonian dominions (23:23).

When Nabopolassar, a native Chaldean governor, came to the Babylonian throne in 626 BC, he inaugurated a dynasty which made the name of Chaldean famous. Among his successors were Nebuchadrezzar, Amēl-Marduk (*EVIL-MERODACH), Nabonidus and Belshazzar, 'king of the Chaldeans' (Dn. 5:30). The sturdy southerners provided strong contingents for the Babylonian army attacking Judah (2 Ki. 24–25).

In the time of Daniel the name was again used of Babylonia as a whole (Dn. 3:8), and Darius the Mede ruled the kingdom of the 'Chaldeans' (Dn. 9:1). The 'tongue of the Chaldeans' (Dn. 1:4) was, perhaps, a semitic Babylonian dialect, the name 'Chaldee' being, rarely in modern times, wrongly applied to Aramaic (*TARGUMS). The prominence of the classes of priests who, at Babylon and other centres, maintained the ancient traditions of astrology and philosophy in the classical Babylonian languages led to the designation 'Chaldean' being applied alike to priests (Dn. 3:8), astrologers and educated persons (Dn. 2:10; 4:7; 5:7, 11).

BIBLIOGRAPHY. D. J. Wiseman, *Chronicles of Chaldaean Kings*, 1956; A. R. Millard, *EQ* 49, 1977, pp. 69–71, on the use of the name and its origin. D.J.W.

CHALKSTONES. An expression which is used once in the OT (Is. 27:9) as a figure of what must be done to idolatrous altars if forgiveness and restoration are to come. They are to be 'pulverized' as if they were made of gypsum or limestone. T.C.M.

CHAMBERLAIN. The English word denotes the guardian of the (royal) chamber; in E antiquity men who performed this function were regularly eunuchs, and therefore words for 'chamberlain' and *'eunuch' are to a large extent interchangeable. This is true of Heb. *sārîs* and Gk. *eunouchos* (it is from the latter word, literally meaning 'bed-keeper', that 'eunuch' is derived).

In Acts 12:20 'the king's chamberlain' represents Gk. *ton epi tou koitōnos tou basileōs*, literally, 'him who was over the king's bed-chamber'. In Rom. 16:23 *Erastus, 'the chamberlain of the city' (AV), is 'the city treasurer' (Gk. *oikonomos tēs poleōs*, *cf.* RV, RSV); a Corinthian inscription mentions a man of that name as 'aedile'. F.F.B.

CHANGES OF RAIMENT. The Heb. *ḥalîpôt*, translated 'changes' in AV, suggests the meaning 'new clothes', particularly festival attire (RSV 'festal garments'). Such clothes were greatly prized, and were used as tangible evidence of royal wealth, both Egyptian and Syrian. When presented as gifts, the number of garments indicated the giver's status and generosity, while the recipient was honoured with special favour (Gn. 45:22; 2 Ki. 5:5, 22–23). The enormous amount (30) involved in Samson's wager reflects either their lower value in the Judges period or, more probably, Samson's overwhelming confidence (Jdg. 14:12–13). Clothes were used as a means of payment at *Alalaḫ, and it may be that the 'festal garments' of the OT had a similar function.

BIBLIOGRAPHY. D. J. Wiseman, *AOTS*, pp. 128–129, 134. M.J.S.

CHARIOT.

I. In the ancient Near East

Heavy wheeled vehicles drawn by asses were used for war and ceremonial in S Mesopotamia in the 3rd millennium BC, as is shown by discoveries from Ur, Kish and Tell Agrab. The true chariot, however, which was of light construction and was drawn by the swifter horse, did not appear until the 2nd millennium. It is probable that the horse (*ANIMALS OF THE BIBLE) was introduced by the peoples of the S Russian steppe who precipitated many folk movements in the 2nd millennium, and the likelihood that the word for horse in many ancient Near Eastern languages, including Heb. (*sûs*), was derived from an Indo-European original suggests that these people played an important part in its introduction. In the cuneiform inscriptions, 'horse' is commonly written with a logogram which signifies 'foreign ass', but the phonetic writing (*sisû*), which also occurs, is first found, significantly enough, in the 19th-century tablets from Kültepe in Asia Minor, indicating perhaps the linguistic influence of the forerunners of the N nomads, who not long after entered the Near East in large numbers. Perhaps as a result of these early contacts, the northerners developed the light horse-drawn war-chariot, and when in the first half of the 2nd millennium new peoples entered the ancient world, Hittites in Anatolia, Kassites in Mesopotamia and Hyksos in Syro-Palestine and Egypt, they brought the chariot with them.

The foreign character of the chariot is emphasized by the fact that in many of the Semitic languages of the ancient world the word for chariot was formed from the root *rkb*, 'to ride', resulting, for instance, in Akkad. *narkabtu*, Ugaritic *mrkbt*, Heb. *merkāḇâ*, and the form was even adopted in New Kingdom Egypt (*mrkb.t*). In the second half of the millennium, a class of society whose members were known as *maryanu* is attested at Alalaḫ, Ugarit, in the Amarna letters, and in New Kingdom Egypt. This indicated an individual of esteemed rank characterized particularly by the ownership of a chariot or wagon, and in many instances the best translation seems to be 'chariot warrior'. The word is usually considered of Indo-European origin (though some favour a Hurrian derivation), which would further illustrate the milieu of its introduction in the Near East. This is again emphasized by the treatise on horse-training by one Kikkuli of Mitanni, which was found in the cuneiform archives at Boghaz-Koi (*HITTITES). This work, written in Hurrian, contains a number of technical terms which are evidently Indo-European, the language-group of the rulers of Mitanni, who were among the newcomers with horses and chariots in the 2nd millennium.

By the second half of the 2nd millennium the two great powers, the Hittites and the Egyptians, were equipped with horse-drawn chariots, as indeed were many of the small Aramaean and Canaanite city states of Syro-Palestine, and it was in this milieu that the Israelites found themselves on their conquest of Palestine. In the 1st millennium the Assyrians developed this engine as the basis of one of their principal arms, and indeed it became an essential element in plains warfare.

In general, the chariot was of very light construction, wood and leather being extensively employed, and only the necessary fittings being of bronze or iron. The car was usually open at the back, and fitments for shields and receptacles for spears and archers' equipment were disposed on the outside of the front or side panels. The wheels were generally 6-spoked, but occasionally there were 4, and some of the later Assyrian ones had 8. While the wheels usually stood about waist-high, a bas-relief of Ashurbanipal shows an 8-spoked one as high as a man, with a nail-studded tyre, probably of iron. The practice of fixing scythes to the wheels was probably not introduced until Persian times. There were usually two horses—though in the time of Ashurnasirpal II the Assyrians had a third, running at the side as a reserve, a practice subsequently abandoned—and these were yoked on either side of the pole, which curved upwards from the floor level of the car. The yoke, which had been developed for harnessing oxen, was unsuitable for horses, but the more practical horse-collar did not come into use until well into the Christian era.

The crew consisted of from two to four men. The Egyptians favoured two, a driver and a warrior, but the Assyrians added a third, the *šalšu rakbu*, 'third rider', who manipulated a shield to protect the others. This was the most usual number, and was also employed by the Hittites, but in the time of Ashurbanipal a fourth man was sometimes placed in the Assyrian vehicles.

The chariot was obviously of main service in campaigns on flat country, and could be a handicap in irregular terrain, as is shown on the Bronze Gates of Shalmaneser III, which depict the difficulties encountered in a campaign to the source of the Tigris.

II. In the Old Testament

In company with the other Semitic-speaking peoples of antiquity, the Hebrews chiefly described the chariot by derivatives of *rkb*. The commonest form, used over 100 times, is *reḵeḇ*; *merkāḇâ* is used some 44 times; and *riḵbâ* (Ezk. 27:20) and *rᵉḵûḇ* (Ps. 104:3) once each. The word *merkāḇ*, while used of chariot in 1 Ki. 4:26, seems to have more the meaning of 'riding-seat' in Lv. 15:9 (AV 'saddle') and Ct. 3:10 (AV 'covering'). Also from *rkb* is formed *rakkāḇ*, 'charioteer', as used in 1 Ki. 22:34; 2 Ki. 9:17 (EVV 'horseman' on account of 'horse' in vv. 18–19, but he could be a 'charioteer' on horseback); and 2 Ch. 18:33. Of the terms not formed from *rkb*, the commonest, *ʿᵃgālâ*, probably usually signifies wagon or *cart, though in a poetic phrase in Ps. 46:9 it seems to mean chariot. In Ezk. 23:24 it is said of a warlike invasion that 'they shall come against thee with *hōṣen reḵeḇ* . . .' where *hōṣen* is a *hapax legomenon* of uncertain meaning. AV translates these terms as 'chariots, wagons', RV as 'weapons, chariots' and RSV as 'from the north with chariots'. The rendering of *reḵeḇ* as chariots rather than wagons is preferable. One other *hapax legomenon, 'appiryôn* in Ct. 3:9, is rendered 'chariot' by AV, but it is possible that this may mean 'palanquin' or 'litter', perhaps being an Iranian loan-word.

As one would expect, all the references to chariots in the Pentateuch concern the Egyptians. Joseph in his success came to own one (Gn. 41:43; 46:29; 50:9), and the fleeing Israelites were pursued by them (Ex. 14; *cf.* Ex. 15:4, 19; Dt. 11:4). The only exception is Dt. 20:1, and this looks forward to the things to be encountered during the conquest. While from the military point of view chariots were of little use in the hill country, and the Israelites who were without chariots seem to have taken this part of the land first, the 'chariots of iron' (*i.e.* with iron fittings) of the Canaanites of the plains (Jos. 17:16; Jdg. 1:19) and of the Philistines of the coast (1 Sa. 13:5) were a more formidable weapon. The excavations at Hazor have shown what a large number of chariots could have been accommodated in a city at this period (see Jos. 11 and Jdg. 4–5). Chariots were looked upon as symbols of the worldly splendour of a king (*cf.* 1 Sa. 8:11), but though David kept 100 captured chariot-horses after one battle (2 Sa. 8:4; *cf.* also 2 Sa. 15:1), it was not till the time of Solomon that they were incorporated into the Israelite forces as a main arm. At this time the best horses were bred in Cilicia and the best chariots manufactured in Egypt, and Solomon established himself as a middleman in trading these (1 Ki. 10:28–29). For his own army he established 'chariot cities' at *Hazor, *Megiddo, *Gezer and Jerusalem and reorganized his army to include 1,400 chariots (1 Ki. 9:15–19; 10:26). The Israelite chariot carried three men, the third man, like his Assyrian counterpart, the *šalšu rakbu*, being called the *šālîš* (*e.g.* 1 Ki. 9:22; AV renders variously as 'captain', 'lord', 'prince'). The division of the kingdom at Solomon's death was such that Israel kept most of the chariot forces, since Hazor, Megiddo and Gezer were all in its territory, and most of the territory of Judah was hill country where chariots were of less use. In Israel Ahab had a large chariot force, as is shown by the statement of Shalmaneser III that he brought 2,000 (read more probably '200') chariots to the battle of Qarqar (853 BC; Kurkh Stele 2. 91), and it is probable that the stables uncovered at *Megiddo, which have hitherto been ascribed to Solomon, are really due to him, Solomon's perhaps still lying buried in the mound. This large force was reduced by the setbacks suffered in the Aramaean wars, and indeed it is stated that Jehoahaz was left with no more than 10 chariots (2 Ki. 13:7). Samaria, as the capital, housed a chariot force, and it is illuminating that when the city fell to Sargon he took only 50 chariots (*Annals* 15), a clue to the declining forces of Israel. Judah was, of course, not entirely without chariots, as is shown by the fact that Josiah evidently had two personal ones at the battle of Megiddo (2 Ch. 35:24), but they may have been limited to those of high rank.

III. In the New Testament

Chariots do not figure greatly in the NT, the best-known reference being to that in which the Ethiopian eunuch was evangelized by Philip (Acts 8). The Gk. word used here, *harma*, the common word for 'chariot' in Homer, occurs in the LXX usually for *reḵeḇ*. In the Apocalypse chariots are twice referred to, Rev. 9:9 (*harma*); 18:13 (*rheda*).

BIBLIOGRAPHY I. V. G. Childe, in Singer, Holmyard and Hall (eds.), *A History of Technology*, 1954, pp. 724–728; S. Piggott, *Prehistoric India*, 1950, pp. 266–267, 273–281; Lefèvre des Noëttes, *L'Attelage, le Cheval de Selle à travers les ages*, 1931; O. R. Gurney, *The Hittites*, 1952, pp. 104–106, 124–125; T. G. E. Powell in *Culture and Environment. Essays in Honour of Sir Cyril Fox*, 1963, pp. 153–169; C. J. Gadd, *The Assyrian Sculptures*, 1934, pp. 27–28, 30–35; A. Salonen, *Die Landfahrzeuge des Alten Mesopotamien*, 1951; *Hippologica Accadica*, 1955, pp. 11–44.

II. R. de Vaux, *Ancient Israel*, 1961, pp. 222–225, 535; Y. Yadin, *The Art of Warfare in Biblical Lands*, 1963, pp. 4–5, 37–40, 74–75, 113, 284–287, 297–302; N. Na'aman, *Tel Aviv* 3, 1976, pp. 97–102 (Ahab's chariots). T.C.M.

CHEBAR. The name of a river in Babylonia, by which Jewish exiles were settled; the site of Ezekiel's visions (1:1, 3; 3:15, 23; 10:15, 20, 22; 43:3). The location is unknown, though Hilprecht proposed an identification with the *nāri kabari* ('great canal'), a name used in a Babylonian text from Nippur for the Shaṭṭ-en-Nil canal running E of that city.

BIBLIOGRAPHY. E. Vogt, *Biblica* 39, 1958, pp. 211–216; R. Zadok, *Israel Oriental Series* 8, 1978, pp. 266–332. D.J.W.

CHEDORLAOMER (Heb. *kᵉḏor lā'ōmer*; Gk. *Chodolla(o) gomor*). The king of Elam, leader of a coalition with *Amraphel, *Arioch and *Tidal, who marched against Sodom and Gomorrah, which had rebelled against him after 12 years as his vassals (Gn. 14:1–17). He was pursued by Abraham who slew him near Damascus (v. 15).

This ruler has not been certainly identified, but the name is unquestionably Elamite *kutir/kudur*, 'servant', usually followed by a divine name, *e.g.* Lagamar (used in Old Bab. names from Mari). Albright identifies Chedorlaomer with King Kitir-Nahhunti I, *c.* 1625 BC (*BASOR* 88, 1942, pp. 33ff.) but the equation of Nahhundi with La'omer is unproven as is the complex view, based on the so-called 'Chedorlaomer' tablets in the British Museum (7th century BC) in which Astour identifies KU.KU. KU.MAL as a king of Elam and representing the 'East', taking Gn. 14 as a late Midrash (in *Biblical Motifs*, 1966, pp. 65–112 (ed. A. Altmann)). The *Ebla texts, however, imply a possibility of early contact between Syria and Elam. D.J.W.

CHEEK (Heb. *lᵉḥî*, of cheek or jaw of man or animal, also of jawbone (Jdg. 15:15); Gk. *siagōn*). A blow on the cheek is indicative of ignominy or defeat (Jb. 16:10; Mt. 5:39), plucking or shaving off the beard more so (Is. 50:6; 1 Ch. 19:4). B.O.B.

CHEMOSH (*kᵉmôš*), the god of the Moabites, the people of Chemosh (Nu. 21:29; Je. 48:46). The sacrifice of children as a burnt-offering was part of his worship (2 Ki. 3:27). Solomon erected a high place for Chemosh in Jerusalem (1 Ki. 11:7), but Josiah destroyed this (2 Ki. 23:13). (*MOAB, *MOABITE STONE.) J.A.T.

CHENOBOSKION (lit. 'goose-pasture'; Coptic *Sheneset*), an ancient town in Egypt, E of the Nile, *c.* 48 km N of Luxor. Here one of the earliest Christian monasteries was founded by Pachomius, *c.* AD 320. Chenoboskion has acquired new fame because of the discovery at Jabal al-Ṭārif, in its vicinity, *c.* 1945, of a library of Gnostic literature (mainly Coptic translations from Gk.)—52 documents in 13 papyrus codices. They are commonly referred to as the Nag Hammadi documents, presumably because it was in Nag Hammadi, W of the river (the nearest modern town to the scene of the discovery), that the discovery was first reported. One of the codices was acquired by the Jung Institute in Zürich, whence it is called the Jung Codex; the others are the property of the Coptic Museum in Cairo. The two best-known of these documents are *The Gospel of Truth*, contained in the Jung Codex, and *The Gospel of Thomas*, contained in one of the codices at Cairo. *The Gospel of Truth* is a speculative meditation on the Christian message, coming from the Valentinian school of Gnosticism, and quite probably the work of Valentinus himself (*c.* AD 150). *The Gospel of Thomas* is a collection of 114 sayings ascribed to Jesus, 2nd-century fragments of which (in Gk.) were found at Oxyrhynchus at the end of the 19th century and beginning of the 20th. The whole collection is in course of publication and will make an invaluable contribution to our knowledge of *Gnosticism.

BIBLIOGRAPHY. F. L. Cross (ed.), *The Jung Codex*, 1955; K. Grobel, *The Gospel of Truth*, 1960; R. M. Grant and D. N. Freedman, *The Secret Sayings of Jesus*, 1960; R. McL. Wilson, *Studies in the Gospel of Thomas*, 1960, *The Gospel of Philip*, 1962; B. Gärtner, *The Theology of the Gospel of Thomas*, 1961; M. L. Peel, *The Epistle to Rheginos*, 1969; M. Krause in W. Foerster (ed.), *Gnosticism*, 2, 1974, pp. 3–120; J. D. M. Scholer, *Nag Hammadi Bibliography 1948–1969*, 1971, updated annually in *NovT*; J. M. Robinson (ed.) *The Facsimile Edition of the Nag Hammadi Codices*, 1972ff; *The Coptic Gnostic Library*, 1973ff; C. W. Hedrick and R. Hodgson (eds.), *Nag Hammadi, Gnosticism and Early Christianity*, 1986; J. M. Robinson and R. Smith (eds.), *The Nag Hammadi Library in English*, 1988. F.F.B.

CHEPHIRAH (*k*ᵉ*pîrâh*). A Hivite fortress on a spur 8 km W of Gibeon, Jos. 9:17. Modern Khirbet Kefireh, dominating the Wadi Qatneh, which leads down to Aijalon. It became Benjaminite territory, Jos. 18:26. The Gola-list (Ezr. 2:25; Ne. 7:29) associates it with *Kiriath-jearim. Described by K. Vriezen, *RB* 84, 1977, pp. 412–416.

J.P.U.L.

CHERETHITES (Heb. *k*ᵉ*rēṯî*). A people who were settled alongside the Philistines in S Palestine (1 Sa. 30:14; Ezk. 25:16; Zp.2:5). In the reign of David they formed, with the Pelethites, his private bodyguard under the command of Benaiah the son of Jehoiada (2 Sa. 8:18; 20:23; 1 Ch. 18:17). They remained loyal to him through the rebellions of Absalom (2 Sa. 15:18) and Sheba (2 Sa. 20:7), and were present when Solomon was anointed for kingship (1 Ki. 1:38, 44), though the fact that they are never again mentioned after this suggests that their loyalty to David depended on the personal factor which ended with his death.

It seems reasonable to suppose that the Cherethites were Cretans and the Pelethites *Philistines, the latter name being perhaps an analogic adaptation of *p*ᵉ*lištî* on the basis of *k*ᵉ*rēṯî*, together with assimilation of *š* to following *ṯ*, to form the easy phrase *hakk*ᵉ*rēṯî w*ᵉ*happ*ᵉ*lēṯî*, 'the Cherethites and the Pelethites'. This being so, the distinction between them was that though they both came from Crete, the Cherethites were native Cretans, whereas the Pelethites had only passed through the island in their travels from some other original homeland.

It seems that mercenaries from the Aegean were now, as in later times, not uncommon, for though Jehoiada no longer employed the Cherethites and Pelethites, he did have Carian troops (2 Ki. 11:4, 19; *kārî*, translated 'captains' in AV).

Bibliography. A. H. Gardiner, *Ancient Egyptian Onomastica*, Text, I, 1947, p. 202*; J. A. Montgomery, *The Books of Kings*, *ICC*, 1951, pp. 85–86; R. de Vaux, *Ancient Israel*, 1961, pp. 123, 219–221.

T.C.M.

CHERITH. A tributary of the river Jordan beside which Elijah was fed when he hid from Ahab at God's command (1 Ki. 17:3, 5). Locations S of Gilgal or E of the Jordan have been proposed.

D.W.B.

CHERUBIM (Heb. *k*ᵉ*rûḇîm*). The plural of 'cherub', represented in the OT as symbolic and celestial beings. In the book of Genesis they were assigned to guard the tree of life in Eden (Gn. 3:24). A similar symbolic function was credited to the golden cherubim, which were placed at either end of the cover ('mercy seat') of the ark of the covenant (Ex. 25:18–22; *cf.* Heb. 9:5), for they were thought of as protecting the sacred objects which the ark housed, and as providing, with their outstretched wings, a visible pedestal for the invisible throne of God (*cf.* 1 Sa. 4:4; 2 Sa. 6:2; 2 Ki. 19:15; Pss. 80:1; 99:1, *etc.*). In Ezk. 10 the chariot-throne of God, still upborne by cherubim, becomes mobile. Representations of those winged creatures were also embroidered on the curtains and veil of the tabernacle and on the walls of the Temple (Ex. 26:31; 2 Ch. 3:7).

Figures of cherubim formed part of the lavish decorations of Solomon's Temple (1 Ki. 6:26ff.). Two of these, carved in olivewood and overlaid with gold, dominated the inner sanctuary. They stood about 5 m in height, with a total wing-spread of similar dimensions, and when placed together they covered one entire wall. Cherubim were also carved in the form of a frieze around the wall of Solomon's Temple, and they appeared together with animal representations on decorative panels forming part of the base of the huge brass basin ('molten sea') which contained the water for ritual ablutions.

In other OT allusions, especially in the poetical books, they are symbolical representations of the storm-winds of heaven; thus in 2 Sa. 22:11 (Ps. 18:10) God was spoken of as riding upon a cherub (an expression which has as its parallel clause, 'he was seen upon the wings of the wind').

The OT does not describe the appearance and general nature of cherubim clearly. They were generally represented as winged creatures having feet and hands. In Ezekiel's vision of the restored Jerusalem the carved likenesses of cherubim had two faces, one of a man and the other of a young lion (Ezk. 41:18f.), whereas in those seen in his vision of the divine glory, each of the cherubim had 4 faces and 4 wings (Ezk. 10:21). To what extent they were thought to be possessed of moral and ethical qualities is unknown. They were invariably in close association with God, and were accorded an elevated, ethereal position.

Archaeological discoveries have brought to light some ancient representations of creatures which may be cherubim. At Samaria ivory panels depicted a composite figure with a human face, an animal body with 4 legs, and 2 elaborate and conspicuous wings. Excavations at the ancient Phoenician city of Gebal (the Gk. Byblos) have revealed a carved representation of two similar cherubim supporting the throne of Hiram king of Gebal, who reigned *c.* 1000 BC.

Symbolic winged creatures were a prominent feature alike of ancient Near Eastern mythology and architecture. Representations of this kind were a common feature of Egyptian animism, while in Mesopotamia, winged lions and bulls guarded buildings of importance. The Hittites popularized the griffin, a highly composite creature consisting of the body of a lion with the head and wings of an eagle, and in general appearance resembling a sphinx.

Bibliography. *ICC*, *Genesis*, pp. 89f., *Ezekiel*, pp. 112–*114*, *Revelation*, I, pp. 118–127; art. 'Cherub' in *JewE*; M. Horan, *Temples and Temple Services in Ancient Israel*, 1978.

R.K.H.

CHESULLOTH (Heb. *k*ᵉ*sullôṯ*), Jos. 19:18; Chisloth-tabor, Jos. 19:12. A town of Issachar in the plain W of Tabor; Zebulun occupied the hills to the NW. Modern Iksal preserves the name.

J.P.U.L.

CHINNERETH. A fortified city, Jos. 19:35 (probably mod. Khirbet el-Oreimah), also spelt Chinneroth (Jos. 11:2), which gave its name to the sea of Chinnereth (Nu. 34:11), known in NT as the lake of Gennesaret (Lk. 5:1), Sea of Galilee or Sea of Tiberias. Josephus uses the term Gennesar (*War* 2.573). The name could be derived from *kinnôr*, harp, from the shape of the lake. For excavations, see *NEAEHL*, pp. 299–301. N.H.

CHIOS. One of the larger Aegean islands off the W coast of Asia Minor, this was a free city-state under the Roman empire until Vespasian's day. Paul's ship on the way from Troas to Patara anchored for a night near the island (Acts 20:15). J.D.D.

CHLOE. Greek female name, signifying 'verdant', especially appropriated to Demeter.

'Chloe's people' told Paul of the Corinthians' schisms (1 Cor. 1:11) and perhaps other items in 1 Cor. 1–6. That the tactful Paul names his informants suggests they were not Corinthian. Possibly they were Christian slaves of an Ephesian lady visiting Corinth. Whether Chloe was herself a Christian is unknown.

F. R. M. Hitchcock (*JTS* 25, 1924, pp. 163ff.) argues that a pagan body, associated with the Demeter-cult, is intended. A.F.W.

CHORAZIN. A town on the Sea of Galilee associated with the Lord's preaching and miracles, but which he denounced because it did not repent (Mt. 11:21; Lk.10:13). Now identified with Kerazeh, 4 km N of Capernaum (Tell Hum?), the black basalt ruins of its synagogue can still be seen. For excavations, see *NEAEHL*, pp. 301–304. J.W.M.

CHRISTIAN. The 3 occurrences (Acts. 11:26; 26:28; 1 Pet. 4:16) all imply that it was a generally recognized title in the NT period, though it is evident that there were other names which Christians themselves used, and perhaps preferred (*cf.* H. J. Cadbury, *BC*, 5, 1933, pp. 375ff.).

a. Origin of the name

The formation seems to be Latin, where plural nouns ending in *-iani* may denote the soldiers of a particular general (*e.g.* *Galbiani*, Galba's men, Tacitus, *Hist.* 1. 51), and hence partisans of an individual. Both elements are combined in the quasi-military *Augustiani* (see below). In the late 1st century AD at least, *Caesariani* was used of Caesar's slaves and clients, and in the Gospels we meet the *Herodianoi*, who may have been partisans or clients of Herod (*HERODIANS).

Christian(o)i, therefore, may have originally been thought of as 'soldiers of Christus' (Souter), or 'the household of Christus' (Bickerman), or 'the partisans of Christus' (Peterson). H. B. Mattingly has recently given an ingenious turn to the latter interpretation by suggesting that *Christiani*, by an Antiochene joke, was modelled on *Augustiani*, the organized brigade of chanting devotees who led the public adulation of Nero Augustus; both the enthusiasm of the believers and the ludicrous homage of the imperial cheer-leaders being satirized by the implicit comparison with each other. But the name 'Christian' may well be older than the institution of the *Augustiani*.

b. Place and period of origin

Luke, who clearly knew the church there well, places the first use of the name at Syrian Antioch (Acts 11:26). The Latinizing form is no obstacle to this. The context describes events of the 40s of the 1st century AD, and Peterson has argued that the contemporary persecution by Herod Agrippa I (Acts 12:1) evoked the name *Christian(o)i* as a parallel to their foes, the *Herodian(o)i*. If *Augustiani* be the model, the title cannot have been coined before AD 59, and Acts 11:26 cannot be taken as implying any date for the title. There is, however, good reason to associate the occasion with what precedes, for Luke has just shown Antioch as the first church with a significant pure-Gentile, ex-pagan element: that is, the first place where pagans would see Christianity as something other than a Jewish sect. Appropriate names for the converts would not be long in coming.

At any rate, 'Christian' was well established in the 60s. The 'smart' Herod Agrippa II (Acts 26:28) uses it, doubtless satirically, to Paul (Mattingly: 'In a moment you'll be persuading me to enroll as a *Christianus*'). Peter, probably from Rome just before the Neronian persecution, warns 'the elect' in parts of Asia Minor that no-one should be ashamed if called on to suffer as a Christian (1 Pet. 4:16—this need not imply a formal charge in a law-court); and Nero, according to Tacitus (*Annals* 15. 44), trumped up a charge against a sect 'whom the common people *were calling* (*appellabat*—the tense is significant) Christians'.

c. The source of the name

The verb *chrēmatisai* (RSV 'were called') in Acts 11:26 is variously interpreted. Bickerman, translating it 'styled themselves', holds that 'Christian' was a name invented in the Antiochene church. His translation is possible, but not necessary, and it is more likely that Antiochene pagans coined the word. Certainly elsewhere, it is non-Christians who use the title—Agrippa, the accusers in 1 Peter, the 'common people' in Tacitus. The verb is frequently translated 'were publicly called' (*cf.* Rom. 7:3), referring to official action in registering the new sect under the name 'Christians'. (Registration would easily account for a Latin title.) But the verb could be used more loosely, and perhaps Luke means no more than that the name came into popular use in the first city where a distinctive name became necessary. From this it might early and easily pass into official and universal use.

d. Subsequent use

If 'Christian' was originally a nickname, it was, like 'Methodist' later on, adopted by the recipients. Increasingly, believers would have to answer the question 'Are you a Christian?', and there was no shame in accepting what was intended as a term of opprobrium when it contained the very name of the Redeemer (1 Pet. 4:16). And it had a certain appropriateness: it concentrated attention on the fact that the distinctive element in this new religion was that it was centred in the Person, Christ; and if the name *Christos* was unintelligible to most pagans, and they sometimes confused it with the common name *Chrēstos*, meaning 'good, kind', it was a *paronomasia* which could be turned to good effect. And so, in the earliest 2nd-century literature, the name is employed without question by the Christian bishop Ignatius (in Antioch) and the pagan governor Pliny (in the area addressed in 1 Peter).

BIBLIOGRAPHY. T. Zahn, *INT*, 2, 1909, pp. 191ff.; E. Peterson, *Frühkirche, Judentum und Gnosis*, 1959, pp. 64–87; E. J. Bickerman, *HTR* 42, 1949, pp. 109ff.; H. B. Mattingly, *JTS* n.s. 9, 1958, pp. 26ff. A.F.W.

CHRONICLES, BOOKS OF.

I. Outline of contents

Chronicles tells the story of Israel up to the return from exile, concentrating on matters of importance concerning her religious life.

a. Introduction (1 Ch. 1–9): genealogies tracing the line of descent from Adam through the patriarch (1) to the tribe of Judah (with its royal line) (2:1–4:23) and the other tribes (4:24–8:40), and on to those who returned from exile (9).

b. The acts of David (1 Ch. 10–29): his coming to power (10–12), his bringing the ark to Jerusalem and plans for a permanent Temple (13–17), his military victories (18–20) and his arrangements for the building of the Temple (21–29).

c. The acts of Solomon (2 Ch. 1–9): his building and dedication of the Temple and his other achievements.

d. The history of Judah from the rebellion of the N tribes to the exile (2 Ch. 10–36): the account of the S kingdom proceeds reign by reign, with special attention being paid to the religious reforms of Hezekiah and Josiah. The conclusion (36:22–23) introduces the return from exile.

II. Origin

The Talmud (*Baba Bathra* 15a) attributes Chronicles to Ezra. Like most OT books, however, Chronicles is of anonymous authorship, and no conclusions are possible as to who wrote it. Its interest in the Levites has been taken to indicate an origin among this group, but this is not a necessary inference. Little more precision is possible concerning its date. The last event alluded to is the return from exile (2 Ch. 36:22–23), and Chronicles could have been written soon after this in the Jerusalem community. On the other hand, the list of descendants of Jehoiachin (Jeconiah) (1 Ch. 3:17–24) seems to cover six generations from the exile, which takes us down to *c.* 400 BC as the earliest the book could have been finished. It could be, however, that the genealogies were supplemented later, and the main body of the work could still belong to a period soon after the exile. There is no certain reflection of the Greek period, and the beginning and end of the Persian empire (537–331 BC) thus probably mark the limits within which Chronicles must have been written.

The story of Chronicles is continued in Ezra, and the former's final verses are almost identical with the latter's opening. This has commonly been taken to suggest that at least Ezr. 1–6 is the original continuation of Chronicles. Alternatively, it may indicate that a later writer wanted to provide such a link (so H. G. M. Williamson, *Israel in the Books of Chronicles*, 1977).

III. Literary characteristics

The main bulk of the work, 1 Ch. 10–2 Ch. 36, parallels 1 Sa. 31–2 Ki. 25, and is frequently verbally identical with these earlier books. Although this might indicate that Chronicles and Samuel–Kings were independently utilizing material from an earlier work which is now lost, it seems more likely that Samuel–Kings itself is Chronicles' major source. Chronicles may thus be seen as essentially a revised edition of the earlier work, related to it rather in the way that (according to the usual theory) Matthew and Luke are to Mark's Gospel. (The 'Chronicles' to which Kings refers—*e.g.* 2 Ki. 20:20—are earlier royal annals and not the biblical books of Chronicles.)

Chronicles seems to have used a different edition of Samuel–Kings from the one which appears in the Hebrew Bible, and this makes it difficult with certainty to identify points at which it introduced changes to Samuel–Kings (see W. E. Lemke in *HTR* 58, 1965, pp. 349–363). But apparently earlier material was sometimes taken over virtually as it stood (*e.g.* 1 Ch. 19), or modified (*e.g.* 1 Ch. 21), or replaced by an alternative version (*e.g.* 2 Ch. 24). Sometimes extensive sections were omitted (*e.g.* those concerning the N kingdom) and other material inserted (*e.g.* concerning David's arrangements for the Temple). Old and new material is moulded into longer sections which offer a theological/historical exposition of a particular period (*e.g.* the reign of Hezekiah), and the various parts then take their place in the Chronicler's new total framework of a history of God's dealings with his people from creation to the return from exile.

The author's method suggests on the one hand that he regarded Samuel–Kings as an authoritative religious text, which he wished to apply to his own age. In this connection he has been described as an exegete of the earlier work (P. R. Ackroyd, 'The Chronicler as Exegete', *JSOT* 2, 1977), or his work has been spoken of as interpretative midrash (M. D. Goulder, *Midrash and Lection in Matthew*, 1974: with chapter on Chronicles). On the other hand, he did wish to bring a specific message from God applied to the people of his own day, and it is this that leads him to his extensive reworking of his text, omitting what was now irrelevant, adding material that was now newly relevant, changing what was now misleading, and so on.

Chronicles has been regarded as poorer history than Samuel–Kings, though for questionable reasons. Its greater concentration on ecclesiastical rather than political affairs has made it seem further from a modern historian's ideal than Samuel–Kings is. Some of its alterations to Samuel–Kings raise historical problems: notably, many of the financial and military figures are vastly increased. This may be the ancient equivalent to allowing for inflation, though textual corruption or misunderstanding has often been suspected (see R. K. Harrison, *IOT*, 1970, pp. 1163–1165). Religious practices (*e.g.* the offering of sacrifice) are made to conform clearly to the Pentateuchal law and the practice of the writer's own day here the author perhaps resembles an artist painting the figures of the past in the dress of his own age. Such characteristics have led to the questioning of the extra material Chronicles includes which does not appear in Samuel–Kings. But where this material can be checked (for instance, by archaeological discoveries) it has seemed to be of historical value (see J. M. Myers, *I Chronicles*, *AB*, 1965, p. lxiii and *passim* in Myers' two commentaries).

IV. Emphases

In its choice and treatment of its material, Chronicles manifests certain characteristic emphases, a concern with faithful worship, purity and trusting obedience (see J. E. Goldingay, *Biblical Theology Bulletin* 5, 1975, pp. 99–126).

a. Faithful worship. A comparison of the accounts of the reigns of David and Solomon in

Samuel–Kings and in Chronicles soon reveals that Chronicles is not very interested in their political or military achievement. They appear as the founders of the worship of the Temple, which is 'the hub of the Lord's kingdom on earth' (Myers, p. lxviii). Similarly, the ministry of the prophets whom Chronicles portrays centres on their concern for right worship and their involvement with the Temple, and the ministry of the Levites is the great privilege of leading the joyful worship of the Temple. Naturally the priests fulfil their sacrificial role in the Temple, too, and Chronicles often notes how the law was properly kept as regards the conducting of worship according to God's will.

b. Purity. A second reason for Chronicles' emphasis on David is that it supports his belief that David's tribe, Judah, is the true Israel. God chose Judah as leader of the tribes (as is reflected in its prominence in the genealogies) and out of Judah chose David to be king over Israel for ever. It was in Judah's capital that the Temple was located and the worship of Yahweh rightly offered. By their rebellion, the N tribes have cut themselves off from the sphere of God's grace and action. The Lord is not with them and Judah should dissociate herself from them—but only in as far as they persist in rebellion. The door is always open for them to return, and they still appear in the genealogies' roll-call of 'the complete kingdom of God' (M. D. Johnson, *The Purpose of the Biblical Genealogies*, 1969, p. 57).

c. Trusting obedience. Many of the stories the author adds to the Samuel–Kings framework emphasize the power of God, which his people are challenged to trust in the crises that confront them. Many of his other modifications to Samuel–Kings are designed to make even clearer than the earlier books do that God's justice, too, is at work in his people's history, so that men who are faithful to God (or who repent of their sin) find blessing, while trouble comes when men turn away from him (*cf.* the versions of the stories of Rehoboam, Joash, Manasseh and Josiah).

V. Context and implications of its thought

Chronicles is one of the later OT books, and it shows a knowledge of many parts of the OT. Its genealogies are dependent on Genesis, Joshua, *etc.*, and the main narratives, as we have noted, are substantially derived from Samuel–Kings. Chronicles also reflects the style and way of thinking of Deuteronomy as well as the emphases of the 'priestly' laws in Leviticus. It quotes extensively from Psalms which appear in the Psalter, and the homilies it includes often take up phrases in particular from the prophets (see G. von Rad, 'The Levitical sermon in *I* and *II Chronicles*', in *The Problem of the Hexateuch and other Essays*, 1966).

It represents an important stream of post-exilic thinking; but not, of course, the only such stream. Its outlook deserves to be compared with others, such as the wisdom tradition with its profound questionings and the prophetic/apocalyptic perspective with its eschatological orientation. The tension with these should not be exaggerated, but they do manifest differences in emphasis. Chronicles' contribution is to affirm that all is not an enigma (as Job and Ecclesiastes indicate some were inclined to believe); nor (as apocalyptic thinking might imply) has God absented himself from history until some hoped-for moment when he will break into it again. He can be known in the Temple and its worship, and he is to be trusted and obeyed in everyday life in the confident hope that his gracious lordship will be known in the community's experience. Again, if there were other circles that were either too inclined to assimilate to paganism around, or alternatively too ready to cut themselves off from anyone who was not of the purest Judaean blood, Chronicles urges a firm stand for the ways of Yahweh, but implies an openness to all who are prepared to share that commitment.

BIBLIOGRAPHY. P. R. Ackroyd, *I and II Chronicles, Ezra, Nehemiah*, *TBC*, 1973; H. G. M. Williamson, *1 and 2 Chronicles*, *NCB*, 1982; R. Braun, *1 Chronicles*, *WBC*, 1986; R. B. Dillard, *2 Chronicles*, *WBC*, 1987; M. J. Selman, *1 Chronicles, 2 Chronicles*, *TOTC*, 1994. J.E.G.

CHRONOLOGY OF THE OLD TESTAMENT.

The aim of such a chronology is to determine the correct dates of events and persons in the OT as precisely as possible, that we may better understand their significance.

I. Sources and methods of chronology

a. Older method

Until about a century ago OT dates were calculated almost entirely from the biblical statements (so Ussher). Two difficulties beset this approach. First, the OT does not provide all the details needed for this task, and some sequences of events may be concurrent rather than consecutive. Secondly, the ancient versions, *e.g.* the LXX, sometimes offer variant figures. Hence schemes of this kind are subject to much uncertainty.

b. Present methods

Modern scholars try to correlate data culled both from the Bible and from archaeological sources, in order to obtain absolute dates for the Hebrews and for their neighbours. From *c.* 620 BC, a framework is provided by the Canon of Ptolemy and other classical sources (*e.g.* Manetho, Berossus) which can be completed and corrected in detail from contemporary Babylonian tablets and Egyptian papyri, *etc.*, for the two great riverine states. The margin of error almost never exceeds a year, and in some cases is reduced to a week within a month, or even to nil.

Good dates from *c.* 1400 BC onwards are available, based on Mesopotamian data. The Assyrians each year appointed an official to be *limmu* or eponym, his name being given to his year of office. They kept lists of these names and often noted down events under each year, *e.g.* a king's accession or a campaign abroad. Thus, if any one year can be dated by our reckoning, the whole series is fixed. An eclipse of the sun in the year of the eponym Bur-Sagale is that of 15 June 763 BC, thus fixing a whole series of years and events from 892 to 648 BC, with material reaching back to 911 BC. Alongside these *limmu*-lists, king-lists giving names and reigns take Assyrian history back to nearly 2000 BC, with a maximum error of about a century then, which narrows to about a decade from *c.* 1400 BC until *c.* 1100 BC. Babylonian king-lists and 'synchronous histories' narrating contacts between Assyrian and Babylonian kings help to establish the history of the two kingdoms between *c.* 1400 BC and *c.* 800 BC. Finally, the scattered information from contemporary tablets and annals of various reigns provides first-hand evidence for some periods.

Good dates from *c.* 1200 BC back to *c.* 2100 BC can be obtained from Egyptian sources. These include king-lists, year-dates on contemporary monuments, cross-checks with Mesopotamia and elsewhere, and a few astronomical phenomena dated exactly in certain reigns. By this means, the 11th and 12th Dynasties can be dated to *c.* 2134–1786 BC, and the 18th to 20th Dynasties to *c.* 1552–1070 BC, each within a maximum error of some 10 years; the 13th to 17th Dynasties fit in between these two groups with a maximum error of about 15 or 20 years in their middle. Mesopotamian dates during 2000–1500 BC depend largely on the date assignable to Hammurapi of Babylon: at present it varies within the period 1850–1700 BC, the date 1792–1750 BC (S. Smith) being as good as any.

Between 3000 and 2000 BC all Near Eastern dates are subject to greater uncertainty, of up to two centuries, largely because they are inadequately linked to later dates. Before 3000 BC, all dates are reasoned estimates only, and are subject to several centuries' margin of error, increasing with distance in time. The 'Carbon-14' method of computing the dates of organic matter from antiquity is of most service for the period before 3000 BC, and such dates carry a margin of error of ±250 years. Hence this method is of little use to biblical chronology; the possible sources of error in the method require that 'Carbon-14' dates must still be treated with reserve.

Such a framework for Mesopotamia and Egypt helps to fix the dates of Palestinian discoveries and of events and people in the Bible; thus the story of the Heb. kingdoms affords cross-links with Assyria and Babylonia. The successive levels of human occupation discerned by archaeologists in the town-mounds ('tells') of ancient Palestine often contain datable objects which link a series of such levels to corresponding dates in Egyptian history down to the 12th century BC. Thereafter, the changes of occupation can sometimes be linked directly with Israelite history, as at *Samaria, *Hazor and *Lachish. Israelite dates can be fixed within a margin of error of about 10 years in Solomon's day, narrowing to almost nil by the time of the fall of Jerusalem in 587 BC. The margins of error alluded to arise from slight differences in names or figures in parallel king-lists, actual breakage in such lists, reigns of yet unknown duration and the limitations of certain astronomical data. They can be eliminated only by future discovery of more detailed data.

Further complications in chronology stem from the different modes of calendaric reckoning used by the ancients in counting the regnal years of their monarchs. By the accession-year system, that part of a civil year elapsing between a king's accession and the next New Year's day was reckoned not as his first year, but as an 'accession-year' (that year being credited to the previous ruler), and his first regnal year was counted from the first New Year's day. But by the non-accession-year system of reckoning, that part of the civil year between a king's accession and the next New Year's day was credited to him as his first regnal 'year', his second being counted from the first New Year's day. The type of reckoning used, by whom, of whom, and when, is especially important for right understanding of the chronological data in Kings and Chronicles.

II. Primeval antiquity before Abraham

The creation is sufficiently dated by that immortal phrase, 'in the beginning . . .', so distant is it. The period from Adam to Abraham is spanned by genealogies in the midst of which occurs the Flood. However, attempts to use this information to obtain dates for the period from Adam to Abraham are hindered by lack of certainty over the right interpretation. A literal Western interpretation of the figures as they stand yields too low a date for events recorded, *e.g.* the Flood. Thus, if, for example, Abraham's birth is set at about 2000 BC (the earliest likely period), the figures in Gn. 11:10–26 would then yield a date for the Flood just after 2300 BC—a date so late that it would fall some centuries *after* Sir Leonard Woolley's flood-level at Ur, itself of too late a date to be the flood of either the Heb. or Bab. records. Similar difficulties arise if Adam's date be further calculated in this way from Gn. 5 on the same basis.

Hence an attempted interpretation must be sought along other lines. Ancient Near Eastern documents must be understood in the first place as their writers and readers understood them. In the case of genealogies, this involves the possibility of abbreviation by omission of some names in a series. The main object of the genealogies in Gn. 5 and 11 is apparently not so much to provide a full chronology as to supply a link from earliest man to the great crisis of the Flood and then from the Flood down through the line of Shem to Abraham, forefather of the Hebrew nation. The abbreviation of a *genealogy by omission does not affect its value ideologically as a link, as could be readily demonstrated from analogous ancient Near Eastern sources. Hence genealogies, including those of Gn. 5 and 11, must always be used with great restraint whenever it appears that they are open to more than one interpretation.

III. Dates before the monarchy

a. The Patriarchs

Three lines of approach can be used for dating the Patriarchs: mention of external events in their time, statements of time elapsed between their day and some later point in history, and the evidence of period discernible in the social conditions in which they lived.

The only two striking external events recorded are the raid of the four kings against five in Gn. 14 (*AMRAPHEL, *ARIOCH, *CHEDORLAOMER) and the destruction of the cities of the plain in Gn. 19 (*PLAIN, CITIES OF THE), both falling in Abraham's lifetime.

None of the kings in Gn. 14 has yet been safely identified with a particular individual in the 2nd millennium BC, but the names can be identified with known names of that general period, especially 1900 to 1500 BC. Power-alliances formed by rival groups of kings in Mesopotamia and Syria are particularly typical of the period 2000–1700 BC: a famous letter from Mari on the middle Euphrates says of this period, 'there is no king who of himself is the strongest: ten or fifteen kings follow Hammurapi of Babylon, the same number follow Rim-Sin of Larsa, the same number follow Ibal-pi-El of Eshnunna, the same number follow Amut-pi-El of Qatna, and twenty

Chronological outline: Old Testament

The purpose of this chart is to set contemporary events alongside each other, not to show the development of nationhood or the progress of conquest.

All dates are best taken as '*about* BC', as the possible variation can run to a century or more in 2000 BC, down to a decade by 1000 BC. Most of the dates for the Hebrew monarchies are quoted in double form, *e.g.* Asa, 911/10-870/69 BC, because the Hebrew year does not coincide with the January to December of our civil year

For other Near Eastern rulers, space and scope forbid any explanation of the vast amount of documentation and reasoning which underlie the dates given in the tables below, but from *c.* 900 BC onward, Assyrian, Babylonian and Persian dates are nearly all very closely fixed.

Prophets are indicated by *

OLD TESTAMENT	EGYPT	MESOPOTAMIA
Before 2000 BC Events of Gn. 1–11	Middle Kingdom 2116–1973 *11th Dynasty*	
PATRIARCHS		
? 2000–1825 Abraham ? 1900–1720 Isaac ? 1800–1700 Jacob ? 1750–1640 Joseph	1973–1795 *12th Dynasty* New Kingdom 1638–1540 Hyksos rule	? 1894–1595: 1st Dynasty of Babylon ? 1792–1750 Hammurapi
ISRAEL IN EGYPT	1540–1295 (or 1294) *18th Dynasty*	*Kassite Dynasty* 1500 Burnaburiash I
? 1350–1230 Moses	1391–1353 Amenophis III	1350 Kurigalzu I 1345–1329 Kurigalzu II
ISRAEL IN CANAAN	1353–1337 Amenophis IV/ Akhenaten	
? 1300–1900 Joshua 1260 approx. The exodus	1295–1186 *19th Dynasty*	
1220 approx. Crossing of Jordan	1295–1294 Rameses I	ASSYRIA
1220 (or 1200)–1050 (or 1045) Period of the Judges	1294–1279 Sethos I 1279–1213 Rameses II	1274–1245 Shalmaneser I 1244–1208 Tukulti-Ninurta I 1224–1219 Adad-Shuma-iddina
? 1125 Deborah and Barak ? 1115–1075 Eli's judgeship	1213–1203 Merenptah	
? 1075–1035 Samuel, judge and prophet	1209 'Israel stele'	1124–1103 Nebuchadnezzar I (Babylonia)
UNITED MONARCHY	1186–1070 *20th Dynasty* *i.e.* Setnakht and Rameses III–XI	1115–1077 Tiglath-pileser 1
1045–1011/10 Saul 1011/10–971/70 David 971/70–931/30 Solomon	Late Period 1070–945 *21st Dynasty*	
DIVIDED MONARCHY	Psusennes I Amenemope Siamun Psusennes II	

ISRAEL	JUDAH	EGYPT	MESOPOTAMIA
931/30–910/09 Jeroboam I		945–715 *22nd Dynasty* 945–924 Sheshonq I (Shishak)	
910/09–909/08 Nadab	931/30–913 Rehoboam		
909/08–836/85 Baasha	925 Sheshonq invades Palestine	924–889 Osorkon I	933 Ashur-dan II
886/85–885/84 Elah	913–911/10 Abijam 911/10–870/69 Asa		
885/84 Zimri 885/84 Tibni 885/84–874/72 Omri 874/73–853 Ahab Elijah*		889–874 Takeloth I	
853–852 Ahaziah 852–841 Joram	870/69–848 Jehoshaphat (co-regent from 873/72)		
841–814/13 Jehu	848–841 Jehoram		
Elisha*			
814/13–798 Jehoahaz	848–841 Jehoram (co-regent from 853)	874–850 Osorkon II	883–859 Ashurnasirpal II
798–782/81 Jehoash	841 Ahaziah 841–835 Athaliah 835–796 Joash *c.* 810–750 Joel*		859–824 Shalmaneser III 853 Battle of Qarqar
782/81–753 Jeroboam II (co-regent from 793/92)	796–767 Amaziah		

c. 760 Amos*
c. 760 Jonah*
c. 755–722 Hosea*
753–752 Zechariah
752 Shallum
752–742/41 Menahem
742/41–740/39 Pekahiah
740/39–732/31 Pekah
732/31–723/22 Hoshea

722 Fall of Samaria

767–740/39 Azariah (Uzziah) (co-regent from 791/90)
c. 742–687 Micah*
c. 740–700 Isaiah*
740/39–732/31 Jotham (co-regent from 750)
732/31–716/15 Ahaz (co-regent from 744/43; senior partner from 735)
716/15–687/86 Hezekiah

JUDAH

687/86–642/41 Manasseh (co-regent from 696/95)
c. 664–612 Nahum*

c. 640 Zephaniah*
642/41–640/39 Amon
640/39–609 Josiah
c. 621–580 Jeremiah*
609 Jehoahaz

609–597 Jehoiakim
605 Battle of Carchemish (Daniel and his friends are taken to Babylon)
c. 605 Habakkuk*
597 Jehoiachin
597 2 Adar (15/16 March) Jerusalem taken by Nebuchadnezzar II. Many Jews exiled including Jehoiachin and Ezekiel
597–587 Zedekiah
c. Obadiah*
587 Fall of Jerusalem. More Jews into exile

THE RETURNED EXILES

538 Zerubbabel, Sheshbazzar and others return to Jerusalem
537 Rebuilding of the temple begun

c. 520 Haggai*
c. 520 Zechariah*
520 Temple-building resumed
516 Temple completed 3 Adar (10 March)

c. 460 Malachi*
458 Ezra goes to Jerusalem
445–433 Nehemiah at Jerusalem

Persian rule until 332

Alexander the Great 332–323

Egyptian rule 320–198

Syrian rule 198–63

EGYPT

767–730 Sheshonq V

730–715 Osorkon IV

716–664 *25th Dynasty*
716–702 Shabako ('Shabaka')
702–690 Shebitku ('Shabataka')

690–664 Taharqa ('Tirhakah')

664–525 *26th Dynasty*
664–656 Tanwetamani ('Tanutamen')

664–610 Psammeticus I

610–595 Neco II

595–589 Psammetichus II

589–570 Apries (Hophra)

570–526 Amasis (Ahmose II)

526–525 Psammetichus III

HELLENISTIC PERIOD

323/05–282 Ptolemy I Soter
320 Judea annexed by Ptolemy I

285/82–245 Ptolemy II Philadelphus

246–222 Ptolemy III Euergetes
222–205 Ptolemy IV Philopator
204–180 Ptomely V Epiphanes

ASSYRIA

745–727 Tiglath-pileser III

732 Fall of Damascus

727–722 Shalmaneser V
722–705 Sargon II

705–681 Sennacherib

681–669 Esarhaddon

669–627 Ashurbanipal

612 Fall of Nineveh
609–08 End of Assyria

BABYLON

626–605 Nabopolassar

605–562 Nebuchadnezzar II
c. 604–535 Daniel*

595–570 Ration-tablets of Jehoiachin at Babylon, 10th–35th years of Nebuchadnezzar II
c. 593–570 Ezekiel*

562–560 Amēl-Marduk (Evil-merodach)
562 Captive Jehoiachin favoured by Amēl-Marduk
560–556 Neriglissar
556 Labashi-Marduk
556–539 Nabonidus (Belshazzar usually acting in Babylon)
539 Fall of Babylon

PERSIAN EMPIRE

539–530 Cyrus
530–522 Cambyses
522–486 Darius I

486–465/64 Xerxes I (Ahasuerus)
464–423 Artaxerxes I
423–404 Darius II Nothus
404–359 Artaxerxes II Mnemon

359/58–338/37 Artaxerxes III Ochus

338/37–336/35 Arses
336/35–331 Darius III Codomanus
331–323 Alexander of Macedon

SYRIA

312–281 Seleucus I Nicator

281–261 Antiochus I Soter

261–246 Antiochus II Theos

246–226/25 Seleucus II

226/25 223 Seleucus III Soter
223–187 Antiochus III the Great
187–175 Seleucus IV

CHRONOLOGY OF THE OLD TESTAMENT

JUDEA	SYRIA
167 Mattathias inspires revolt at Modin	175–163 Antiochus IV Epiphanes
167–40 Maccabees/Hasmonaeans in Judea	163–162 Antiochus V
166–161 Judas Maccabaeus	162–150 Demetrius I
160–143 Jonathan Maccabaeus	139/8–129 Antiochus VII Sidetes
150 BC–AD 70 General period of the Dead Sea Scrolls	
143–135 Simon Maccabaeus	
135–104 John Hyrcanus I	
104/03 Aristobulus I	
103–76 Alexander Jannaeus	
76–67 Queen Salome Alexandra and Hyrcanus II	
67–40 Hyrcanus II and Aristobulus II	
63 Pompey establishes Roman protectorate	

kings follow Yarim-Lim of Yamkhad.' In this period also, Elam was one of several prominent kingdoms.

Glueck has endeavoured to date the campaign of Gn. 14 from its supposed archaeological results: he claims that the line of city-settlements along the later 'King's Highway' was clearly occupied at the start of the 2nd millennium (until the 19th century BC, on modern dating), but that soon thereafter the area suddenly ceased to be occupied, except for roving nomads, until about 1300 BC, when the Iron Age kingdoms of Edom, Moab and Ammon were effectually founded.

Similar reasoning has been applied to the date of the fall of the cities of the plain, although their actual remains appear now to be beyond recovery (probably being under the Dead Sea).

This picture of an occupational gap between the 19th and 13th centuries BC has been criticized by Lankester Harding in the light of certain recent finds in Transjordan, including Middle Bronze tombs and an important Middle and Late Bronze temple. However, the views of neither Glueck nor Harding need be pressed to extremes; in all probability the view of a reduced density of population between the 19th and 13th centuries is true in general and of the Highway cities in particular, while at certain isolated points occupation may have been continuous.

Two main statements link the day of the Patriarchs with later times. In Gn. 15:13–16 Abraham is forewarned that his descendants will dwell in a land not theirs for some four centuries. The 'fourth generation' of v. 16 is difficult; if a 'generation' be equated with a century (*cf.* Ex. 6:16–20), this usage would be unusual. A possible but dubious alternative is to see in v. 16 a prophetic allusion to Joseph's journey to Canaan to bury Jacob (Joseph being in the 'fourth generation' if Abraham is the first). The entry of Jacob into Egypt (Gn. 46:6–7) was the starting-point of the general four centuries of Gn. 15:13 as well as of the more specific 430 years of Ex. 12:40. The Hebrew *MT* form of Ex. 12:40, giving Israel 430 years in Egypt, is to be preferred to the LXX variant, which makes 430 years cover the sojournings in both Canaan and Egypt, because Ex. 12:41 clearly implies that 'on that very day', after 430 years, on which Israel went forth from Egypt was the anniversary of that distant day when the Patriarch Israel and his family had entered Egypt. Hence an interval of 430 years from Jacob's entry till Moses and Israel's departure seems assured. The genealogy of Ex. 6:16–20, which can hardly cover the 430 years if taken 'literally' Westernwise, is open to the same possibility of selectivity as those of Gn. 5 and 11, and so need raise no essential difficulty. Three points are worthy of reflection. First, although Moses is apparently in the fourth generation from the Patriarch Jacob through Levi, Kohath and Amram (Ex. 6:20; 1 Ch. 6:1–3), yet Moses' contemporary Bezalel is in the seventh generation from Jacob through Judah, Perez, Hezron, Caleb, Hur and Uri (1 Ch. 2:18–20), and his younger contemporary Joshua is in the twelfth generation from Jacob through Joseph, Ephraim, Beriah, Rephah, Resheph, Telah, Tahan, Laadan, Ammihud, Elishama and Nun (1 Ch. 7:23–27). Hence there is a possibility that Moses' genealogy is abbreviated by comparison with those of Joshua and even Bezalel. Secondly, Moses' 'father' Amram and his brothers gave rise to the clans of Amramites, Izharites, *etc.*, who already numbered 8,600 male members alone within a year of the Exodus (Nu. 3:27–28), an unlikely situation unless Amram and his brothers themselves flourished distinctly earlier than Moses. Thirdly, the wording that by Amram Jochebed 'bore' Moses, Aaron and Miriam (Ex. 6:20; Nu. 26:59), like 'became the father', AV 'begat', in Gn. 5 and 11, need not imply immediate parenthood but also simply descent. Compare Gn. 46:18, where the preceding verses show that great-grandsons of Zilpah are included among 'these she bore to Jacob'. On these three points, see also *WDB*, p.153. For the date of the Exodus occurring on independent grounds 430 years after a late-18th-century date for Jacob, see below.

The social conditions reflected in the patriarchal narratives afford no close dating, but fit in with the general date obtainable from Gn. 14 and 19 and from the use of the 430-year figure to the Exodus. Thus the social customs of adoption and inheritance in Gn. 15–16; 21; *etc.*, show close affinity with those observable in cuneiform documents from Ur, *etc.*, ranging in date from the 18th to 15th centuries BC.

The great freedom to travel long distances—witness Abraham's path including Ur and Egypt—is prominent in this general age: compare envoys from Babylon passing Mari to and from Hazor in Palestine. For power-alliances at this time, see above. In the 20th and 19th centuries BC in particular, the Negeb ('the South') of the later Judaea supported seasonal occupation, as illustrated by Abraham's periodic journeys into 'the South'. The general results, bearing in mind the traditional figures for the lives, births and deaths of the Patriarchs, is to put Abraham at about 2000–1850,

Isaac about 1900–1750, Jacob about 1800–1700 and Joseph about 1750–1650; these dates are deliberately given as round figures to allow for any later adjustment. They suit the limited but suggestive archaeological evidence, as well as a plausible interpretation of the biblical data.

A date for the entry of Jacob and his family into Egypt at roughly 1700 BC would put this event and *Joseph's ministry in the 13th Dynasty and Hyksos period of Egyptian history, during which rulers of Semitic stock posed as pharaohs of Egypt; the peculiar blend of Egyptian and Semitic elements in Gn. 37:1 would agree with this.

b. The Exodus and Conquest

(For alternative Egyptian dates in this section, see the Chronological Tables.) The next contact between Israel and her neighbours occurs in Ex. 1:11, when the Hebrews were building the cities Pithom and Ra'amses in Moses' time. Ra'amses was Egypt's Delta capital named after, and largely built by, Rameses II (*c.* 1279–1213 BC) superseding the work of his father Sethos I (*c.* 1294–1279 BC); this is true of Qantir, the likeliest site for Ra'amses. Rameses I (*c.* 1295–1294 BC) reigned for just over a year, and so does not come into consideration. Before Sethos I and Rameses II, no pharaoh had built a Delta capital since the Hyksos period (Joseph's day); the city Ra'amses is thus truly an original work of these two kings, and not merely renamed or appropriated by them from some earlier ruler, as is sometimes suggested. Hence, on this bit of evidence, the Exodus must fall after 1300 BC and preferably after 1279 BC (accession of Rameses II). A lower limit for the date of the Exodus is probably indicated by the so-called Israel Stele, a triumphal inscription of Merenptah dated to his fifth year (*c.* 1209 BC), which mentions the defeat of various cities and peoples in Palestine, including Israel. Some deny that Merenptah ever invaded Palestine; for Drioton, *La Bible et l'Orient*, 1955, pp. 43–46, the Palestinian peoples were merely overawed by Merenptah's great victory in Libya, which his stele principally commemorates; and the mention of Israel would be an allusion to the Hebrews disappearing into the wilderness to, as the Egyptians would think, certain death. See further, C. de Wit, *The Date and Route of the Exodus*, 1960. The Exodus would then fall in the first five years of Merenptah (*c.* 1213–1209 BC). However, this view is open to certain objections. An inscription of Merenptah in a temple at Amada in Nubia in strictly parallel clauses names him as 'Binder of Gezer' and 'Seizer of Libya'. 'Seizer of Libya' refers beyond all doubt to Merenptah's great Libyan victory in his 5th year, recounted at length in the Israel Stele. Hence the very specific, strictly parallel, title 'Binder of Gezer' must refer to successful intervention by Merenptah in Palestine, even if of limited scope. With this would agree the plain meaning of the Israel Stele's references to Ascalon, Gezer, Yenoam, Israel and Khuru as 'conquered', 'bound', 'annihilated', 'her crops are not' and 'widowed' respectively. Then, the reference to 'Israel, her crops (= lit. 'seed') are not' may reflect the Egyptians' practice of sometimes burning the growing crops of their foes—applicable to Israel beginning to settle in Palestine, but *not* to Israel going forth into the wilderness. Hence, on the likelier interpretation of the Israel Stele here upheld, Israel must have entered Palestine before 1209 BC, and the Exodus 40 years earlier would therefore fall before 1250 BC. The probable date of the Exodus is thus narrowed down to the period 1279–1250 BC. A good average date for the Exodus and wanderings would thus be roughly the period 1270–1230 BC. For views which postulate more than one Exodus, or that some tribes never entered Egypt, there is not a scrap of objective external evidence, and the biblical traditions are clearly against such suggestions.

The figure of 40 years for the wilderness travels of the Hebrews is often too easily dismissed as a round figure which might mean anything. This particular 40-year period is to be taken seriously as it stands, on the following evidence. Israel took a year and a fraction in going from Ra'amses to Kadesh-barnea (they left Ra'amses on the fifteenth day of the 'first month', Nu. 33:3) leaving Mt Sinai on the twentieth day of the second month of the second year, Nu. 10:11. To this period, add at least: 3 days, Nu. 10:33; perhaps a further month, Nu. 11:21; and 7 days, Nu. 12:15; total 1 year and 2½ months' travel; then the subsequent 38 years from Kadesh-barnea to crossing the brook Zered (Dt. 2:14 and Nu. 21:12), Moses addressing Israel in the plains of Moab in the eleventh month of the fortieth year (Dt. 1:3). The function of the 40 years in replacing one generation (rebellious) by another is clearly stated in Dt. 2:14.

The statement that Hebron was founded 7 years before Zoan in Egypt (Nu. 13:22) is sometimes linked with the contemporary Era of Pi-Ramesse in Egypt, covering 400 years from approximately 1720/1700 to about 1320/1300 BC. This Era would then run parallel to the 430 years of Hebrew tradition. This idea, however, is interesting rather than convincing.

The Palestinian evidence agrees in general terms with the Egyptian data.

Various Palestinian city-sites show evidence of clear destruction in the second half of the 13th century BC, which would agree with the onset of the Israelites placed at roughly 1240 BC onward. Such sites are Tell Beit Mirsim, Lachish, Bethel and Hazor. Two sites only have given rise to controversy: Jericho and Ai.

At Jericho the broad truth seems to be that Joshua and Israel did their work so well that Jericho's ruins lay open to the ravages of nature and of man for five centuries until Ahab's day (*cf.* 1 Ki. 16:34), so that the Late Bronze Age levels, lying uppermost, were almost entirely denuded, even earlier levels being distinctly affected. Thus on some parts of the mound the uppermost levels that remain date as far back as the Early Bronze Age (3rd millennium BC), but the evidence from other parts and the tombs demonstrates clearly the existence of a large Middle Bronze Age settlement subsequently much denuded by erosion. The exceedingly scanty relics of Late Bronze Age Jericho (*i.e.* of Joshua's age) are so few simply because they were exposed to erosion for an even longer period, from Joshua until Ahab's reign; and any areas not occupied by the Iron Age settlement of Ahab's time and after have been subject to erosion right down to the present day. Hence the nearly total loss of Late Bronze Jericho of the 14th century BC and the likelihood of the total loss of any settlement of the 13th century BC.

The walls attributed to the Late Bronze Age by Garstang prove, on fuller examination, to belong to the Early Bronze Age, *c.* 2300 BC, and so cease to be relevant to Joshua's victory. The apparent cessation of Egyptian kings' scarabs at Jericho with those of Amenophis III (died *c.* 1353 BC) does not of itself prove that Jericho fell then, but merely witnesses to the temporary eclipse of direct Egyptian influence in Palestine in the time of that king and his immediate successors, known also from other sources. Of Mycenaean pottery (commonly imported into Syria–Palestine in the 14th and 13th centuries BC), a paucity at Jericho likewise does not prove that Jericho fell earlier in the 14th century rather than well on in the 13th. The fact has been overlooked hitherto that these imported vessels are sometimes very rare on inland Syro-Palestinian sites at the same time as they are common in other settlements at, or readily accessible from, the coast. Thus the equally inland town of Hama in Syria is known to have been occupied during the 13th century BC, but it yielded only two late Mycenaean potsherds—which is less than even the few from Jericho; for Hama, see G. Hanfmann, review of P. J. Riis, 'Hama II', pt. 3, in *JNES* 12, 1953, pp. 206–207. The net result of all this is that a 13th-century Israelite conquest of *Jericho cannot be formally proven on the present archaeological evidence, but neither is it precluded thereby.

*Ai presents a problem demanding further field-research; the parts of the mound of Et-Tell so far excavated ceased to be occupied about 2300 BC. The answer may be that a Late Bronze settlement is still to be located in the neighbourhood, but certainty is at present unattainable.

At Hazor the destruction of city XIII probably reflects the attack under Joshua, but the date 1230 BC is too high (based on wrong Egyp. dates), and should read 'within 1220–1200 BC'. The proposed 1275 BC (P. Beck, M. Kochavi, *Tel Aviv* 12, 1985, pp. 33, 38), also fails for the same reason. At Lachish (Tell ed-Duweir), the partial burning in stratum VII might be Israelite, not stratum VI, too late (*cf.* D. Ussishkin, in J. N. Tubb, ed., *Palestine in the Bronze and Iron Ages*, 1985, p. 224). It is usually impossible to tell archaeologically *who* destroyed any particular settlement: The Habiru/Apiru of the Amarna Tablets (*c.* 1350 BC) are sometimes identified with the invading Israelites under Joshua. But the details in each case disagree; and the very equation of Habiru/Apiru with 'Hebrew' is now often discounted. For a defence of a 15th-century date of the Exodus and Entry, see J. J. Bimson, *Redating the Exodus and Conquest*, 1978; but new data (*e.g.* on history of Covenant) is not in favour.

c. From Joshua until David's accession

This period presents a problem in detail which cannot be finally solved without more information. If the 40 years of the Exodus journeyings, the 40 years of David's reign and the first 3 of Solomon's be subtracted from the total of 480 years from the Exodus to Solomon's 4th year (1 Ki. 6:1) a figure of about 397 years is obtained for Joshua, the elders, the judges and Saul. The archaeological evidence indicates roughly 1220 BC for the start of the conquest (see above), giving only some 210 years to 1010 BC, the probable date of David's accession. However, the actual total of recorded periods in Joshua, Judges and Samuel amounts neither to 397 nor to 210 years, but to $470 + x + y + z$ years, where x stands for the time of Joshua and the elders, y for the number of years beyond 20 that Samuel was judge and z for the reign of Saul, all unknown figures. But the main outline of the problem need not be difficult to handle in principle, if viewed against the background of normal ancient oriental modes of reckoning, which alone are relevant. It is nowhere explicitly stated that either the 397 years obtained from using 1 Ki. 6:1 or the 470 plus unknown years of Joshua–Samuel must all be reckoned consecutively, nor need this be assumed. Certain groups of judges and oppressions are clearly stated to be successive ('and after him . . .'), but this is not said of all: at least three main groups can be partly contemporary. So between the evidently consecutive 210 years obtained archaeologically and the possibly partly-concurrent 470–plus-unknown years recorded, the difference of some 230–plus-unknown years can readily be absorbed. The 397 years in turn would then be simply a selection on some principle not yet clear (such as omission of oppressions or something similar) from the greater number of the 470–plus-unknown total years available.

In Near Eastern works involving chronology, it is important to realize that ancient scribes did not draw up synchronistic lists as is done today. They simply listed each series of rulers and reigns separately, in succession on the papyrus or tablet. Synchronisms were to be derived from special historiographical works, not the king-lists or narratives serving other purposes. An excellent example of this is the Turin Papyrus of Kings from Egypt. It lists at great length all five Dynasties 13 to 17 in successive groups, totalling originally over 150 rulers and their reigns accounting for at least 450 years. However, it is known from other sources that all five Dynasties, the 150-odd rulers and 450-odd regnal years alike, must all fit inside the 234 years from *c.* 1786 to *c.* 1552 BC: rarely less than two series, and sometimes three series, of rulers are known to have reigned contemporaneously. The lack of cross-references between contemporaries (*e.g.* among the judges) is paralleled by similar lack of such references for most of the period of Egyptian history just cited.

A similar situation can be discerned in the king-lists and history of the Sumerian and Old Babylonian city-states of Mesopotamia. Hence, there is no reason why such methods should not apply in a work like the book of Judges. It must be stressed that in no case, biblical or extra-biblical, is it a question of inaccuracy, but of the methods current in antiquity. All the figures may be correct in themselves—it is their interpretation which needs care. Selective use of data by omission, as suggested above for the origin of the 397 (of 480) years, is known from both Egyptian lists and Mesopotamian annals, as well as elsewhere. The biblical figures and archaeological data together begin to make sense when the relevant ancient practices are borne in mind; any final solution in detail requires much fuller information.

IV. The Hebrew monarchies

a. The United Monarchy

That David's reign actually lasted 40 years is shown by its being a compound figure: 7 years at Hebron, 33 at Jerusalem (1 Ki. 2:11). Solomon's reign of 40 years began with a brief co-regency with his father of perhaps only a few months; *cf.* 1 Ki. 1:37–2:11; 1 Ch. 28:5; 29:20–23, 26–28. As Solomon's reign appears to have ended *c.* 931/30 BC, he acceded *c.* 971/70 BC, and David at *c.* 1011/10 BC.

The reign of Saul can only be estimated, as something has happened in the Hebrew text of 1 Sa. 13:1; but the 40 years of Acts 13:21 must be about right, because Saul's fourth son, Ishbosheth, was not less than 35 years old at Saul's death (dying at 42, not more than 7 years later, 2 Sa. 2:10). Hence if Jonathan the eldest was about 40 at death, Saul could not be much less than 60 at death. If he became king shortly after being anointed as a 'young man' (1 Sa. 9:2; 10:1, 17ff.), he probably would not be younger than 20 or much older than 30, so practically guaranteeing him a reign of 30 or 40 years. Thus if taken at a middle figure of about 25 years old at accession with a reign of at least 35 years, the biological data suit, and likewise Acts 13:21 as a figure either round or exact. Saul's accession is thus perhaps not far removed from about 1045 or 1050 BC.

b. The Divided Monarchy

(i) *To the fall of Samaria.* From comparison of the Assyrian *limmu* or eponym lists, king-lists and historical texts, the date 853 BC can be fixed for the battle of Qarqar, the death of Ahab and accession of Ahaziah in Israel; and likewise Jehu's accession at Joram's death in 841 BC. The intervening reigns of Ahaziah and Joram exactly fill this interval if reckoned according to the customary methods of regnal counting. Similar careful reckoning by ancient methods gives complete harmony of figures for the reigns of both kingdoms back to the accessions of Rehoboam in Judah and Jeroboam in Israel in the year 931/930 BC. Hence the dates given above for the United Monarchy.

Likewise the dates of both sets of kings can be worked out down to the fall of Samaria not later than 720 BC. This has been clearly shown by E. R. Thiele, *Mysterious Numbers of the Hebrew Kings*², 1965. It is possible to demonstrate, as he has done, co-regencies between Asa and Jehoshaphat, Jehoshaphat and Jehoram, Amaziah and Azariah (Uzziah), Azariah and Jotham, and Jotham and Ahaz. However, Thiele's objections to the synchronisms of 2 Ki. 17:1 (12th year of Ahaz equated with accession of Hoshea in Israel), 2 Ki. 18:1 (3rd year of Hoshea with accession of Hezekiah of Judah) and 2 Ki. 18:9–10 (equating Hezekiah's 4th and 6th years with Hoshea's 7th and 9th) are invalid. Thiele took these for years of sole reign, 12/13 years in error. However, the truth appears to be that in fact these four references simply continue the system of co-regencies: Ahaz was co-regent with Jotham 12 years, and Hezekiah with Ahaz. This practice of co-regencies in Judah must have contributed notably to the stability of that kingdom; David and Solomon had thus set a valuable precedent.

(ii) *Judah to the fall of Jerusalem.* From Hezekiah's reign until that of Jehoiachin, dates can still be worked out to the year, culminating in that of the Babylonian capture of Jerusalem in 597 BC, precisely dated to 15/16 March (2nd of Adar) 597 by the Babylonian Chronicle tablets covering this period. But from this point to the final fall of Jerusalem, some uncertainty reigns over the precise mode of reckoning of the Hebrew civil year and of the various regnal years of Zedekiah and Nebuchadrezzar in 2 Kings and Jeremiah. Consequently two different dates are current for the fall of Jerusalem: 587 and 586 BC. The date 587 is here preferred, with Wiseman and Albright (against Thiele for 586).

V. The Exile and after

Most of the dates in the reigns of Babylonian and Persian kings mentioned in biblical passages dealing with this period can be determined accurately. For over half a century, opinions have been divided over the relative order of Ezra and Nehemiah at Jerusalem. The biblical order of events which makes *Ezra reach Jerusalem in 458 BC and *Nehemiah arrive there in 445 is perfectly consistent under close scrutiny (*cf.* J. S. Wright).

The intertestamental period is reasonably clear; for the main dates, see the chronological table.

BIBLIOGRAPHY. *Near Eastern chronology:* W. C. Hayes, M. B. Rowton, F. Stubbings, *CAH*³, 1970, ch. VI: Chronology; T. Jacobsen, *The Sumerian King List*, 1939—deals with the early Mesopotamian rulers; R. A. Parker and W. H. Dubberstein, *Babylonian Chronology 626 BC–AD 75*, 1956—full dates for Babylonian, Persian and later kings for 626 BC–AD 75, with tables; K. A. Kitchen, in P. Åström (ed.), *High, Middle or Low? Acts of an International Colloquium on Absolute Chronology* 1–3, 1987–9; E. R. Thiele, *Mysterious Numbers of the Hebrew Kings*², 1965. A. Jepsen and A. Hanhart, *Untersuchungen zur Israelitisch-Jüdischen Chronologie*, 1964; J. Finegan, *Handbook of Biblical Chronology*, 1964; V. Pavlovsky, E. Vogt, *Bib.* 45, 1964, pp. 321–347, 348–354. A. Ungnad, *Eponymen*, in E. Ebeling and B. Meissner, *Reallexikon der Assyriologie*, 2, 1938, pp. 412–457—full statement and texts of the Assyrian eponym-lists.

Egypt: Sir A. H. Gardiner, in *JEA* 31, 1945, pp. 11–28—Egyptian regnal and civil years; R. A. Parker, *The Calendars of Ancient Egypt*, 1950—standard work; W. G. Waddell, *Manetho*, 1948—standard work; K. A. Kitchen, in Acta Archaeologica 67, 1996, I; *idem, World Archaeology* 23/2, 1991, pp. 201–208; W. A. Ward, *BASOR* 288, 1992, pp. 53–66.

Palestine: W. F. Albright, *Archaeology of Palestine*, 1956—a very convenient outline of its subject; N. Glueck, *Rivers in the Desert*, 1959—a popular summary of his work on 20th century BC seasonal occupation of the Negeb, continuing his reports in *BASOR*, Nos. 131, 137, 138, 142, 145, 149, 150, 152 and 155; N. Glueck, *The Other Side of the Jordan*, 1940, ²1970—on the question of Middle Bronze and Iron Age settlements in Transjordan, concerning the dates of Abraham and the Exodus; G. L. Harding in *PEQ* 90, 1958, pp. 10–12—against Glueck on Transjordanian settlement; H. H. Rowley, 'The Chronological Order of Ezra and Nehemiah', in *The Servant of the Lord and Other Essays on the Old Testament*, 1952, pp. 129ff.; J. S. Wright, *The Building of the Second Temple*, 1958—for the post-exilic dates; *idem, The Date of Ezra's Coming to Jerusalem*², 1958.

The fall of Judah: D. J. Wiseman, *Chronicles of Chaldaean Kings (626–556 BC)*, 1956—fundamental for its period; compare the following: W. F. Albright in *BASOR* 143, 1956, pp. 28–33; E. R. Thiele, *ibid.*, pp. 22–27; H. Tadmor, in *JNES* 15, 1956, pp. 226–230; D. J. A. Clines, 'Regnal Year Reckoning in the Last Years of the Kingdom of Judah', *AJBA* 2, 1972, pp. 9–34. K.A.K.

T.C.M.

CHRONOLOGY OF THE NEW TESTAMENT. An attempt to establish a firm chronology of the NT is difficult because the early Christians were more interested in the sayings and events of important personages than in the time when these occurred. This is not to say they were not interested in history but they did not live in a world where chronological precision was as possible as it is at present. Hence, in attempting to put events into a chronological framework, one must gather information from incidental time references.

I. Chronology of the life of Jesus

a. Birth of Jesus

The birth of Jesus occurred before the death of Herod the Great (Mt. 2:1; Lk. 1:5), hence before March/April 4 BC (*Ant* 17. 167, 191; 14. 487–490).

According to Lk. 2:1–5 the census of Quirinius was taken just before Jesus' birth but the date of this census is difficult to pinpoint because no Roman historian mentions it. While Quirinius was governor of Syria in AD 6/7, he was responsible for liquidating Archelaus of Judaea's estate and conducting a census to assess the amount of tribute the new province was to pay the imperial treasury. However, this census is not the same as the one mentioned in Lk. 2 unless Luke is mistaken, as some critics suppose – because it occurred after the deposition of Herod's son Archelaus, whereas the context of the birth narrative of Jesus in Lk. 2 was in the days of Herod the Great. In order to resolve the problem, some suggest that Quirinius was governor of Syria not only in AD 6/7 but also in 11/10 to 8/7 BC. Others suggest that this census was 'before' Quirinius was governor in AD 6/7. And some think that Quirinius had been proconsul of Syria and Cilicia during the last years of Herod the Great under the legates Saturninus and Varus. Of the various suggestions, it is not improbable that Quirinius conducted a census in the last years of Herod. Toward the end of his reign Herod fell out of favour with Rome (*c.* 8/7 BC). This was followed by an intense struggle by his sons for the throne at a time when Herod was extremely ill. This would allow the Roman government to take a census in Herod's land in order to assess the situation before his death. Although it is difficult to pinpoint the exact year of the census, it was probably sometime between 6 and 4 BC.

There has been much discussion regarding the historicity and identity of the star of Bethlehem. A triple conjunction of Saturn and Jupiter in the constellation Pisces in 7 BC, which occurs every 900 years, and the massing of Mars, Saturn and Jupiter in Pisces in 6 BC, which occurs every 800 years (much less frequently in Pisces), may have alerted the Magi of the birth of Israel's Messiah. Finally, in 5 BC a comet appeared in the E in the constellation of Capricornus that could well have caused the Magi to go to Bethlehem (Mt. 2:2) where it hovered (Mt. 2:9–10). Hence, Jesus may have been born sometime in the spring or summer of 5 BC. The account of Herod's murder of all the children under 2 years of age in Bethlehem may be because he thought that Jesus was born when the Magi had seen the first constellation in 7 BC, or perhaps simply because Herod wanted to be completely certain he had killed Jesus. This would not be unusual considering his paranoia in regard to a successor.

b. Commencement of Jesus' ministry

Except for the mention of Jesus' visit to the temple when he was 12 years old (Lk. 2:41–51), there are no chronological data until the beginning of his ministry. The first concrete clue for the commencement of Jesus' ministry is in Lk. 3:1–3, which states that John the Baptist's ministry began in the fifteenth year of Tiberius. Although there is debate, it is most likely that the fifteenth year of Tiberius is reckoned either on the basis of the Julian calendar, namely, 1 January to 31 December AD 29 or on the basis of Tiberius's reign, the normal Roman method, namely, 19 August AD 28 to 18 August AD 29. Combining these calendars, the fifteenth year of Tiberius would have occurred sometime between 19 August AD 28 and 31 December AD 29. Hence, John the Baptist's ministry began sometime during this period.

The impression given in the gospels is that shortly after the commencement of John the Baptist's ministry, Jesus was baptized and began his ministry. Luke indicates that when Jesus began his ministry, he was 'about thirty years of age' (Lk. 3:23). If Jesus was born in the spring or summer of 5 BC and was baptized in the summer or autumn of AD 29, he would have been around 33 years of age.

After his baptism, the first recorded visit of Jesus to Jerusalem is found in Jn. 2:13–3:21 where he celebrated the first Passover of his ministry, cleansing the temple. The Synoptic Gospels do not mention such a visit at the start of his ministry, and indeed they record the so-called 'cleansing' of the temple in the context of Jesus' visit to Jerusalem at the end of his ministry. This divergence has been variously explained: some scholars argued that there were two cleansings, one at the start and one at the end of his ministry; others concluded that John's gospel is theologically not chronologically arranged; and others argued that the synoptics have simplified the picture by having Jesus go to Jerusalem only once in his ministry and that John's account has great historical plausibility (see further below).

According to John, it was during Jesus' first Passover that the Jews mentioned that the Herodian temple had been constructed 46 years ago (Jn. 2:20). According to Josephus, the temple construction began in Herod's eighteenth year (*Ant.* 15. 380) which coincided with Augustus' arrival in Syria (*Ant.* 15. 354) and this occurred in the spring or summer of 20 BC (Dio Cassius 54. 7. 4–6). Herod's eighteenth year would have been from 1 Nisan 20 to 1 Nisan 19 BC. There were two parts in building the temple: the first was the inner sanctuary called the *naos* located within the priests' court which was completed by the priests in 18 months (*Ant.* 15. 421), and the second included the whole temple area including the three courts and was called the *hieron* which was completed in AD 63. This distinction is consistently maintained by Josephus and the NT. In discussing the temple with Jesus, the Jews were referring to the *naos* as having stood for 46 years. If the construction of the *naos* began in 20/19 BC and was completed in 18 months, *i.e.* in 18/17 BC, then 46 years later would bring the date to the year AD 29/30. This means, then, that Jesus' first Passover was the spring of AD 30. In conclusion, the commencement of Jesus' ministry was sometime in the summer or autumn of AD 29.

c. Duration of Jesus' ministry

Valentinus, an early Gnostic commentator (born *c.* AD 100), as well as many of the ante-Nicene period, suggested a 1-year ministry of Jesus based on the Lk. 4:19 quotation of Is. 61:2: 'To proclaim the acceptable year of the Lord.' However, Valentinus's contemporary, Irenaeus, refuted this view by indicating the three Passovers mentioned in John (2:13; 6:4; 11:55). Several present-century commentators suggest a 1-year ministry beginning with Jesus' disciples plucking the grain on the Sabbath in Mk. 2:23 (ripe grain at Passover time) and ending with the Passover (only one mentioned in the Synoptic Gospels) in Mk. 14:1. To propose a 1-year ministry on the basis of the Isaianic passage is dubious. Again, the mention of three Passovers in the Gospel of John makes shipwreck of a 1-year ministry. Furthermore, to compress 1 year between Mk. 2:23 and 14:1 is unlikely, for after the plucking of grain in 2:23, there is the mention of 'green grass' in the feeding of the 5,000 (6:39). This indicates that another year had elapsed and another year is required between this last incident and the passion Passover of 14:1.

A 2-year ministry based on the three Passovers mentioned in John was suggested by 4th-century bishops Apollinaris of Laodicea and Epiphanius of Salamis in Cyprus, and is held by a few scholars in the 20th century.

A 3-year ministry seems to be more viable. As mentioned above, the Gospel of John refers to three Passovers (2:13; 6:4; 11:55). Moreover, it seems that an additional year is needed between the Passovers of 2:13 and 6:4. The Passover of 6:4 is around the time Jesus fed the 5,000, the only miracle mentioned in all four gospels. Previous to this feeding, the Synoptic Gospels mention the disciples plucking grain in Galilee (Mt. 12:1; Mk. 2:23; Lk. 6:1) and this must have been after the Passover of John 2:13. The reason for this is that the Passover of John 2:13 occurred shortly after his baptism and he was ministering in Judaea, whereas the plucking of the grain occurred a considerable time after Jesus' baptism and the locale of his ministry was in Galilee. Therefore, the plucking of the grain would fit well with a Passover between the Passovers of John 2:13 and 6:4. John provides two additional chronological indicators which would support an additional year between these Passovers. First, after the Passover of Jn. 2:13, Jesus ministered in Judaea and then went to Samaria where he mentioned there were 4 months until harvest (Jn. 4:35), which would mean the following January/February. Although some consider it a proverbial statement, it seems best to take this as a literal chronological reference. The second chronological indicator is in Jn. 5:1 where there is mention of another unspecified feast. Some interpreters think it refers to another Passover, although it more likely refers to the Feast of Tabernacles. Thus, these two chronological notes would substantiate that there was another Passover between the Passovers of Jn. 2:13 and 6:4. This would make a total of four Passovers during Jesus' public ministry, and hence his ministry would have been 3½ to 3¾ years in length.

d. Death of Jesus

There is a need to discuss both the day of the week and the day of the month as well as the year of Jesus' death.

First, the day of the week on which Jesus died has been traditionally thought of as Friday of passion week. However because Jesus states in Mt. 12:40: 'For as Jonah was three days and three nights in the belly of the whale, so shall the Son of man be three days and three nights in the heart of the earth', some interpreters think that Jesus could not have died on Friday. They suggest that Jesus died either on Wednesday or Thursday, allowing for 3 days and 3 nights. But when one understands that the Jews reckoned a part of a day as a whole day, then Jesus' death on Friday does not present a serious problem. Furthermore, the NT repeatedly refers to Jesus' resurrection as having occurred on the third day (not on the fourth day, *e.g.* Mt. 16:21; 17:23; 20:19; Lk. 9:22; 18:33; 24:7, 46; Acts 10:40; 1 Cor. 15:4). Moreover, the gospels specifically mention the day before the Sabbath (Friday) as the day of his death (Mt. 27:62; Mk. 15:42; Lk. 23:54; Jn. 19:14, 31, 42). Therefore, both scripturally and traditionally, it seems best to accept Friday as the day of Jesus' death.

Second, there is a need to discuss the day of the Jewish month on which Jesus died. All the gospels state that Jesus ate the Last Supper the day before his crucifixion (Mt. 26:20; Mk. 14:17; Lk. 22:14; Jn. 13:2; *cf.* also 1 Cor. 11:23). On the one hand, the Synoptic Gospels (Mt. 26:17; Mk. 14:12; Lk. 22:7–8) portray that the Last Supper was the Passover meal celebrated on Thursday evening, 14 Nisan, and that Jesus was crucified the following day, Friday, 15 Nisan. On the other hand, John states that the Jews who took Jesus to the Praetorium did not enter it 'in order that they might not be defiled but might eat the Passover' (Jn. 18:28) and that Jesus' trial was on the 'day of preparation for the Passover' and not after the eating of the Passover (Jn. 19:14). This implies that Jesus' Last Supper (which occurred on Thursday night, 13 Nisan) was not a Passover and that Jesus was tried and crucified on Friday, 14 Nisan, just before the Jews ate their Passover.

In the attempt to reconcile the Synoptics and John, several theories have been proposed. Some suggest that the Last Supper was not a Passover meal but a meal the night before the Passover (Jn. 13:1, 29). However, the Synoptics explicitly state that the Last Supper was a Passover (Mt. 26:2, 17–19; Mk. 14:1, 12, 14, 16; Lk. 22:1, 7–8, 13, 15). Others suggest that the 'Passover' referred to in Jn 18:28 and 19:14 was not the Passover meal itself, but one of the other festal meals held in Passover week. All sorts of other harmonizations have been offered. Some have proposed that Jesus and his disciples had a private Passover. However, the Passover lamb had to be slaughtered within the temple precincts and the priests would not have allowed the slaughter of the Paschal lamb for a private Passover. Some think it was celebrated on two consecutive days, because it would have been impossible to slay all the Passover lambs on one day. Others think that different religious calendars were in operation in Palestine. So it has been suggested that Jesus and his followers followed the solar calendar used at Qumran, thus celebrating the Passover earlier in the week than the authorities who followed a lunar calendar. A different calendrical solution proposes that, on the one hand the Synoptic Gospels followed the method of the Galileans and the Pharisees in reckoning a day to be from sunrise to sunrise and thus Jesus and his disciples slaughtered the Paschal lamb in the late afternoon of Thursday, 14 Nisan, and later that evening they ate the Passover with the unleavened bread. On the other hand, John's Gospel followed the method of the Judaeans in reckoning a day to be from sunset to sunset and thus the Judaean Jews slaughtered the Paschal lamb in the late afternoon on Friday, 14 Nisan, and ate the Passover with the unleavened bread that night which had become 15 Nisan. Thus, Jesus had eaten the Passover meal when his enemies, who had not as yet had the Passover meal, arrested him.

Finally, the year of Jesus' death can be narrowed by several considerations. First, the three officials involved in the trial were Caiaphas the high priest (Mt. 26:3, 57; Jn. 11:49–53; 18:13–14, 24, 28) who began his office in AD 18 and was deposed at the Passover of AD 37 (*Ant.* 18. 35; 90–95); Pilate, prefect of Judaea (Mt. 27:2–26; Mk. 15:1–15; Lk. 23:1–25; Jn. 18:28–19:16; Acts 3:13; 4:27; 13:28; 1 Tim. 6:13) from AD 26 to 36 (*Ant.* 18. 89); and Herod Antipas, tetrarch of Galilee and Peraea (Lk. 23:6–12; Acts 4:27) from 4 BC until AD 39 (*Ant.* 18. 240–56; 19. 351). Thus Jesus' trial must have occurred between AD 26 and 36.

Second, evidence from astronomy helps us to identify which Passover took place on Thursdays/Fridays, and so to narrow the date of Jesus' crucifixion. Granted that Jesus' death occurred on Friday, 14 Nisan, and sometime between AD 26 and 36, only the years AD 27, 30, 33, and 36 qualify astronomically. Of these dates, AD 27 is the least likely astronomically and 36 is too late. Of the remaining dates, 30 has been debated as to whether or not 14 Nisan fell on a Friday, while the AD 33 date has the least problem astronomically. Those who maintain an AD 30 date need to begin John the Baptist's ministry 3 years earlier. They attempt it by reckoning the first year of Tiberius's reign when he became co-regent with Augustus. But this method must be rejected for there is no evidence, either from historical documents or coins, for its employment.

Third, history confirms the AD 33 date. Pilate is portrayed by his contemporary Philo (*Embassy to Gaius* 301–302) and later by Josephus (*Ant.* 18. 55–59; *BJ* 2. 167–77) as one who was greedy, inflexible and cruel, and who resorted to robbery and oppression, a portrait not out of keeping with Lk. 13:1. Yet, during Jesus' trial, Pilate is seen as one who was readily submissive to the pressures of the religious leaders who were demanding that Jesus be handed over to them.

How can such a change be explained? It must be understood that Pilate was probably appointed by Sejanus, a trusted friend of Tiberius, as well as the prefect of the Praetorian Guard, a dedicated anti-Semite who wanted to exterminate the Jewish race (Philo *In Flaccum*, 1; *Embassy to Gaius*, 159–161). When Pilate made trouble for the Jews in Palestine, Sejanus accepted this behaviour and did not report it to Tiberius. However, when Sejanus was deposed and executed by Tiberius on 18 October, AD 31, Pilate no longer had protection in Rome. In fact, it is most likely that Herod Antipas reported that he had caused a riot, probably at the Feast of Tabernacles in AD 32 (Philo *Embassy to Gaius* 299–305). Since Herod Antipas 'had one' on Pilate, it is understandable that in the midst of the trial, when there was the mention that Jesus stirred up trouble in Judaea and Galilee (Lk. 23:5), Pilate was eager to allow Herod Antipas to try Jesus (Lk. 23:6–12). In this context, the AD 33 date for the trial makes good sense for three reasons:

1. Pilate, on hearing that Jesus had caused trouble in Galilee, handed Jesus over to Herod Antipas. This was not required by Roman law but he did not want to make another wrong move that Herod could relate to the emperor;

2. the lack of progress in the trial in Lk. 23:6–12 makes sense because Herod Antipas did not want to make a bad judgment which would cause Pilate to take advantage of him;

3. Lk. 23:12 states that Pilate and Herod Antipas were friends from that day onward. This would be inaccurate if the crucifixion were in AD 30 because they were extremely at odds with each other in AD 32. Hence, the AD 33 date best fits the historical evidence.

Jesus' birth	summer 5 BC
Herod the Great's death	March/April, 4 BC
Jesus at the temple aged 12	Passover, 29 April, AD 9
Commencement of John the Baptist's ministry	AD 29
Commencement of Jesus' ministry	summer/autumn AD 29
Jesus' first Passover (Jn. 2:13)	7 April, AD 30
Jesus' second Passover	25 April, AD 31
Jesus at the Feast of Tabernacles (Jn. 5:1)	21–28 October, AD 31
Jesus' third Passover (Jn. 6:4)	13/14 April, AD 32
Jesus at the Feast of Tabernacles (Jn. 7:2, 10)	10–17 September, AD 32
Jesus at the Feast of Dedication (Jn. 10:22–39)	18 December, AD 32
Jesus' death	Friday, 3 April, AD 33
Jesus' resurrection	Sunday, 5 April, AD 33
Jesus' ascension (Acts 1)	Thursday, 14 May, AD 33
Day of Pentecost (Acts 2)	Sunday, 24 May, AD 33

II. Chronology of the apostolic age

a. Paul's ministry

The key figure in the apostolic age was the apostle Paul. Reconstructing the chronology of his life and ministry is complicated by scholarly questions (a) about the reliability of the Acts of the Apostles, being our most explicit source of information about Pauline chronology, and (b) about the authenticity of various of the Pauline letters, notably the Pastoral epistles. Some scholars have offered alternative Pauline chronologies to that suggested by Acts, basing their ideas primarily on selected Pauline letters. However, the evidence of Acts stands up remarkably well in the face of these challenges.

The date of Paul's conversion hinges primarily on two passages of Scripture. First, Gal. 1:17–18 states that he went from Damascus to Jerusalem 3 years after his conversion (*cf.* Acts 9:25–26). When he escaped from Damascus, the Nabataean Aretas IV was in power (*cf.* 2 Cor. 11:32) and since he reigned from AD 37–39, Paul's conversion must have been sometime between AD 34 and 36. Second, Gal. 2:1 indicates that Paul again went up to Jerusalem 14 years later. This probably refers to the famine visit he made with Barnabas, described in Acts 11 and 12, which can be dated around AD 47 to 49. It is likely that the 14 years are to be reckoned from his conversion rather than after the time of his first visit to Jerusalem, and thus his conversion would be sometime between AD 33 and 35. The overlap from these two primary passages would be AD 34 to 35 and probably the best time for his conversion would be in the summer of AD 35. Paul returned to Jerusalem in the summer of AD 37 – parts of years are equivalent to a whole year – (Acts 9:26–29; Gal. 1:18–20). Paul went to Tarsus and Syria-Cilicia around the autumn of AD 37 (Acts 9:30; Gal. 1:21) and then to Antioch around AD 41 (Acts 11:19–24). Paul visited Jerusalem during the time of famine, probably in the autumn of AD 47 (Acts 11:30; Gal. 2:1–10), and returned to Antioch from the autumn of AD 47 to the spring of 48 (Acts 12:25–13:1).

Paul, thereafter, embarked on his three missionary journeys. The first missionary journey (Acts 13–14) would have been from the spring of AD 48 to the autumn of 49. Probably, in the spring of AD 48 Paul and Barnabas sailed to Salamis in Cyprus and crossing the island to Paphos, met Sergius Paulus, the proconsul. In later summer/early autumn the missionaries crossed the sea to Perga of Pamphylia and in late summer arrived in Pisidian Antioch. They ministered in the cities of Iconium, Lystra and Derbe from approximately the autumn of AD 48 to the summer/autumn of 49 and then returned to Antioch of Syria around the autumn of 49.

Upon his return to Antioch, Paul may have written the book of Galatians, and then he and Barnabas went to the council meeting in Jerusalem in the autumn of AD 49 (Acts 15:1–29). A real chronological debate revolves around the identification of the conference in Gal. 2:1–10. Some interpreters think it is to be identified with Paul's attendance at the Jerusalem council of Acts 15 (his third visit to Jerusalem) because it would support the 14 years (Gal. 2:1) from the time of his conversion to the time of the Jerusalem council. However, it seems more likely that the conference in Gal. 2:1–10 refers to the famine relief visit of Acts 11:27–30; 12:25 (his second visit to Jerusalem) because to have suppressed the famine relief visit would have been fatal to his argument in Galatians that he was independent of human authority in his reception and proclamation of the gospel. Thus the 14 years covers the time of his conversion to the time of the famine relief visit (reckoning inclusively). This also means that Galatians was written before the Jerusalem council and the Galatians are those people in the area of Iconium, Lystra and Derbe of the first missionary journey.

After wintering in Antioch (Acts 15:33–35), Paul started on his second missionary journey (Acts 15:36 – 18:22) which would have been from the spring of AD 50 to the autumn of 52. On this missionary journey he retraced his steps by visiting Phrygia and Galatia (Iconium, Lystra and Derbe; Acts 16:6) and with the leading of the Spirit he entered Europe, stayed in Corinth for 18 months (Acts 18:11), and was tried before the proconsul Gallio (Acts 18:12–17) who ruled in Achaia probably from the summer of AD 51 to the summer of 52. Also, in Corinth Paul met Priscilla and Aquila, Jewish Christians who were forced out of Rome under the edict of Claudius, probably in AD 49 or 50 (Acts 18:2; Suetonius, *Claudius* 5. 25. 4; Orosius, *History* 7. 6). In the summer of AD 51, while in Corinth, Paul wrote 1 and 2 Thes. On his return to Antioch, Paul brought along Priscilla and Aquila and left them at Ephesus.

The third missionary journey (Acts 18:23–21:16) was from the spring of AD 53 to the spring of 57. Paul returned to Phrygia and Galatia and proceeded to Ephesus, where he remained for nearly 3 years (Acts 19:8, 10; 20:31), from the summer of AD 53 until May of 56 and in the spring of 56 he wrote 1 Cor. Paul is often thought to have paid a short 'painful' visit to Corinth during this Ephesian period (2 Cor. 2:1), and some scholars have speculated that he spent some time in prison in Ephesus, writing some or all of his 'Prison epistles' here (but see below).

When he finally left Ephesus, he went to Macedonia and Greece for three months (Acts 20:3). While in Macedonia he wrote 2 Cor. (which we take to be a unity, despite some critics' questions). In Corinth (Rom. 16:23) he wrote Rom. in the winter of AD 56/57. From Corinth Paul retraced his steps through Europe and then took ship from Troas, returning to Jerusalem by the Pentecost of AD 57 (Acts 20:16).

While in Jerusalem he was arrested and taken to Caesarea for a trial before Felix, who was probably procurator from the latter part of AD 52 to the summer of 59 (Acts 23:24; *Ant*. 20. 137; *BJ* 2. 247; *Ann*. 12. 54). Felix heard Paul (Acts 24) and Paul remained in the Caesarean prison for 2 years, at the end of which time Felix was succeeded by Festus (Acts 24:27; *Ant*. 20. 182; *BJ* 2. 271). Both Festus and Herod Agrippa II heard Paul in Caesarea (Acts 25:7–12; 26:1–32) in the late summer of AD 59. Paul was in prison in Caesarea from June of 57 until August of 59. He left Caesarea in August of 59 and arrived in Rome in February of 60 (Acts 27:1–28:29) and remained in prison for 2 years (Acts 28:30), from February 60 to March of 62. While in prison, he wrote the Prison epistles: Eph. in the autumn of 60, Col. and Ph. in the autumn of 61, and Phil. in the spring of 62. (Some scholars have speculated that some or all of the epistles were written earlier, either from Ephesus or from Caesarea.)

After the Roman imprisonment there are no recorded travels of Paul in Acts. From Paul's intentions, his travel notes in the Pastoral epistles, and from early church history, one can only attempt to reconstruct his itinerary after his release from the Roman prison in the spring of AD 62. It seems probable that he travelled E, possibly first in Ephesus and Colossae (spring–autumn 62), later in Macedonia (autumn 62–winter 62/63) from where he wrote 1 Tim. (1:3), and afterwards returned to Asia Minor (spring 63–spring 64). After Asia Minor Paul may well have gone to Spain (spring 64–spring 66) (Rom. 15:24, 28). After Spain it is possible that Paul, with Titus, returned to the E by going to Crete (early summer 66) and leaving Titus. Paul then returned to Asia Minor (summer–autumn 66) (2 Tim. 4:13–14) from where he wrote Tit. (Tit. 1:5). He went to Nicopolis for the winter of 66/67 (Tit. 3:12). It seems that Paul went to Macedonia and Greece (spring–autumn 67) (2 Tim. 4:20) and was possibly arrested when Nero was in Greece in the autumn of 67. It is probable that Paul was again imprisoned in Rome (2 Tim. 1:8; 2:9) from where he wrote 2 Tim. (autumn of 67). Paul's death may have come in the spring of 68.

b. Apostolic history

In the early part of Acts, Peter played a prominent role. Since it was concluded that Jesus died in AD 33 and that Paul's conversion was in the summer of 35, the ministry of Peter and the other apostles mentioned in the first 8 chapters of Acts would have taken place in the 2 years between AD 33 and

35. Peter plays a prominent part in the Jerusalem council in AD 49 (Acts 15). It is most likely that Peter did go to Rome towards the end of his life. Since Peter is neither mentioned by Paul when he wrote to the Romans in the winter of AD 56/57, when he wrote the Prison epistles in his first imprisonment in Rome in AD 60–62, nor when he wrote his second letter to Tim. in his second imprisonment in Rome in AD 67, nor by Luke when he narrates Paul's imprisonment in Acts 28:14–30, it seems that Peter was not in Rome before AD 62 or after 66. It is probable that Peter was in Rome when Paul was not there and thus he may well have come to Rome around AD 62 and been martyred in the Neronian persecution following the fire in the summer of 64.

In the persecution of Herod Agrippa I in AD 44, James, the brother of John, was killed and Peter was imprisoned (Acts 12:2–3). It was in that same year that Agrippa I died (Acts 12:20–23; *Ant.* 19. 343–53).

James, the brother of the Lord, was an important leader in the early church (Acts 15:13; Gal. 1:19; 2:9; 1 Cor. 15:7). Josephus speaks of his death as having occurred in the period of anarchy after the death of Festus in the winter of 61/62 and before the arrival of his successor, Albinus, in the summer of 62 (*Ant.* 20. 197–203). Hence, James was killed in the spring of 62.

The fall of Jerusalem was predicted by Christ (Mt. 24:15=Mk. 13:14=Lk. 21:20) and the first phase of the fulfilment was accomplished in AD 70. Many Christians are thought to have fled to Pella, E of the Sea of Galilee (Eusebius *EH* 3.5. 2–3).

Due to the destruction of Jerusalem, some have surmised that John fled to Asia Minor, possibly to Ephesus. Part of his time was spent on the island of Patmos (Rev. 1:9) and although there is no certainty regarding the time of his death, traditionally it is thought to have occurred in AD 100.

A proposed chronology for the whole apostolic period (with some dates more speculative and approximate than others) can be charted as follows:

Crucifixion	Friday, 3 April, AD 33
Pentecost (Acts 2)	Sunday, 24 May, 33
Peter's second sermon and brought before the Sanhedrin (Acts 3:1–4:31)	summer 33
Death of Ananias and Sapphira (Acts 4:32–5:11)	33–34
Peter brought before Sanhedrin (Acts 5:12–42)	34–35
Deacons selected (Acts 6:1–7)	late 34–early 35
Stephen martyred (Acts 6:8–7:60)	April 35
Paul's conversion (Acts 9:1–7)	summer 35
Paul in Damascus and Arabia (Acts 9:8–25; Gal. 1:16–17)	summer 35–early summer 37
Paul in Jerusalem, first visit (Acts 9:26–29; Gal. 1:18–20)	summer 37
Paul in Tarsus and Syria-Cilicia area (Acts 9:30; Gal. 1:21)	autumn 37
Peter ministers to the Gentiles (Acts 10:1–11:18)	40–41
Barnabas sent to Antioch (Acts 11:19–24)	41
Paul went to Antioch (Acts 11:25–26)	spring 43
Agabus predicts a famine (Acts 11:27–28)	spring 44
Agrippa's persecution, James martyred (Acts 12:1–23)	spring 44
Relief visit, Paul's second visit to Jerusalem (Acts 11:30; Gal. 2:1–10)	autumn 47
Paul in Antioch (Acts 12:25–13:1)	autumn 47–spring 48
First missionary journey (Acts 13–14)	April 48–September 49
Departure from Antioch	April 48
Cyprus	April–June 48
Pamphylia	beginning–middle of July 48
Pisidian Antioch	middle July–middle September 48
Iconium	October 48–end February 49
Lystra-Derbe	March–middle June 49
Return visit to churches	middle June–August 49
Return to Antioch of Syria	September 49
Peter at Antioch (Gal. 2:11–16)	autumn 49
Galatians written from Antioch	autumn 49
Jerusalem council, Paul's third visit (Acts 15)	autumn 49
Paul in Antioch (Acts 15:33–35)	winter 49/50
Second missionary journey (Acts 15:36- 18:22)	April 50–September 52
Departure from Antioch	April 50
Syria and Cilicia	April 50
Lystra-Derbe	May 50
Iconium	end May–middle June 50
Pisidian Antioch	middle June–beginning July 50
Antioch to Troas	July 50
Philippi	August–October 50
Thessalonica	November 50–January 51
Berea	February 51
Athens	end February–middle March 51
Arrival at Corinth	middle March 51
Silas and Timothy arrive from Berea	April/May 51
1 Thessalonians written	early summer 51
2 Thessalonians written	summer 51
Departure from Corinth	beginning September 52
Ephesus	middle September 52
Jerusalem, Paul's fourth visit	end September 52
Return to Antioch	beginning/middle November 52
Paul's stay at Antioch	winter 52/53
Third missionary journey (Acts 18:23–21:16)	spring 53–May 57
Departure from Antioch	spring 53
Visiting Galatian churches	spring–summer 53
Arrival at Ephesus	September 53
1 Corinthians written	early spring 56
Departure from Ephesus (riot)	beginning May 56
Troas	May 56
Arrival in Macedonia	beginning June 56
2 Corinthians written	September/October 56
Departure from Macedonia	middle November 56
Arrival in Corinth	end November 56

Romans written	winter 56/57
Departure from Corinth	end February 57
Philippi	6–14 April, 57
Troas	12–25 April, 57
Troas to Assos	Monday, 25 April, 57
Assos to Mitylene	26 April, 57
Mitylene to Chios	27 April, 57
Chios to Trogyllium	28 April, 57
Trogyllium to Miletus	29 April, 57
Ephesian elders see Paul	30 April–2 May 57
Miletus to Patara	2–4 May, 57
Patara to Tyre	5–9 May, 57
Stay at Tyre	10–16 May, 57
Tyre to Caesarea	17–19 May, 57
Stay at Caesarea	19–25 May, 57
Caesarea to Jerusalem	25–27 May, 57
Jerusalem, Paul's fifth visit	eve of Pentecost, 25 May, 57
Meeting with James (Acts 21:13–23)	28 May, 57
Paul's arrest and trial before Felix (Acts 21:26–24:22)	29 May–9 June, 57
First day of purification	Sunday, 29 May, 57
Second day of purification	30 May, 57
Third day of purification	31 May, 57
Fourth day of purification	1 June, 57
Fifth day of purification, riot, Paul's speech	2 June, 57
Paul before the Sanhedrin	3 June, 57
Appearance of the Lord (night) Conspiracy (day)	4 June, 57
Journey to Antipatris (night) Journey to Caesarea (day)	5 June, 57
Waiting in Caesarea for trial	5–9 June, 57
Trial before Felix	Thursday, 9 June, 57
Paul before Felix and Drusilla (Acts 24:24–26)	June 57
Caesarean imprisonment (Acts 24:27)	June 57–August 59
Trial before Festus (Acts 25:7–12)	July 59
Trial before Agrippa (Acts 26)	beginning August 59
Voyage to Rome (Acts 27:1–28:29)	August 59–February 60
Departure from Caesarea	middle August 59
Myra	beginning September 59
Fair Havens	October 5–10, 59
Shipwreck at Malta	end October 59
Departure from Malta	beginning February 60
Arrival in Rome	end February 60
First Roman imprisonment (Acts 28:30)	February 60–March 62
Ephesians written	autumn 60
Colossians and Philemon written	autumn 61
Philippians written	early spring 62
James, Lord's brother, martyred	spring 62
Paul in Ephesus and Colossae	spring–autumn 62
Peter goes to Rome	62
Paul in Macedonia (1 Tim. 1:3)	late summer 62–winter 62/63
1 Timothy written	autumn 62
Paul in Asia Minor	spring 63–spring 64
Paul in Spain (Rom. 15:24, 28)	spring 64–spring 66
Christians persecuted, Peter martyred	summer 64
Paul in Crete	early summer 66
Paul in Asia Minor (Tit. 1:5)	summer–autumn 66
Titus written	summer 66
Paul in Nicopolis (Tit. 3:12)	winter 66/67
Paul in Macedonia and Greece (2 Tim. 4:13, 20)	spring–autumn 67
Paul arrested and brought to Rome (2 Tim. 1:8; 2:9)	autumn 67
2 Timothy written	autumn 67
Paul's death	spring 68
Destruction of Jerusalem	2 September, 70

BIBLIOGRAPHY. J. van. Bruggen, *'Na veertien jaren' De datering van het in Galaten 2 genoemde overleg te Jeruzalem*, 1973; G. B. Caird, 'The Chronology of the NT', in *IDB* 1, 1962, pp. 599–607; S. Dockx, *Chronologies néotestamentaires et Vie l'Eglise primitive: Recherches exégétiques.* (rev. edn.), 1984; J. Finegan, *Handbook of Biblical Chronology*, 1964; J. K. Fotheringham, 'The Evidence of Astronomy and Technical Chronology for the Date of the Crucifixion', *JTS* 35, 1934, pp. 146–162; R. T. France, 'Chronological Aspects of "Gospel Harmony"', *Vox Evangelica* 16, 1986, pp. 33–59; J. J. Gunther, *Paul: Messenger and Exile. A Study in the Chronology of His Life and Letters*, 1972; H. W. Hoehner, *Chronological Aspects of the Life of Christ*, 1977; C. J. Humphreys, 'The Star of Bethlehem, a Comet in 5 BC and the Date of Christ's Birth', *TynB* 43.1, 1992, pp. 31–56; C. J. Humphreys and W. G. Waddington, 'The Jewish Calendar, a Lunar Eclipse and the Date of Christ's Crucifixion', *TynB* 43.2, 1992, pp. 331–351; N. Hyldahl, *Die Paulinische Chronologie*. Acta Theologica Danica 19, 1986; A. Jaubert, *The Date of the Last Supper*, 1965; R. Jewett, *A Chronology of Paul's Life*, 1979; 'Chronology and Methodology: Reflections on the Debate over Chapters in a Life of Paul', in *Colloquy on New Testament Studies: A Time for Reappraisal and Fresh Approaches*, 1983, pp. 271–287; J. Knox, *Chapters in Life of Paul* (rev. ed.), 1987; G. Luedemann, *Paul, Apostle to the Gentiles: Studies in Chronology*, F. Stanley Jones, 1984; G. Ogg, *The Chronology of the Life of Paul*, 1968. *The Chronology of the Public Ministry of Jesus*, 1940; D. Plooij, *De Chronologie van he Leven van Paulus*, 1918; J. Vardaman and E. M. Yamauchi (eds.), *Chronos, Kairos, Christos: Nativity and Chronological Studies Presented to Jack Finegan*, 1989. H.W.H.

CHURCH.

I. Meaning

The English word 'church' is derived from the Gk. adjective *kyriakos* as used in some such phrase as *kyriakon dōma* or *kyriakē oikia*, meaning 'the Lord's house', *i.e.* a Christian place of worship. 'Church' in the NT, however, renders Gk. *ekklēsia*, which mostly designates a local congregation of Christians and never a building. Although we often speak of these congregations collectively as the NT church or the early church, no NT writer uses *ekklēsia* in this collective way. An *ekklēsia* was a meeting or assembly. Its commonest use was for the public assembly of citizens duly summoned, which was a feature of all the cities outside Judaea where the gospel was planted (*e.g.* Acts 19:39); *ekklēsia* was also used among the Jews (LXX) for the *'congregation' of Israel which was constituted at Sinai and assembled before the Lord at the annual feasts in the persons of its representative males (Acts 7:38).

In Acts, James, 3 John, Revelation and the earlier Pauline letters, 'church' is always a particular local congregation. 'The church throughout all Judea and Galilee and Samaria' (Acts 9:31) may look like an exception, but the singular could be distributive (*cf.* Gal. 1:22) or, more likely, is due to the fact that the verse concludes a section about how 'the church in Jerusalem' (Acts 8:1) was persecuted and its members scattered. Although every local congregation is 'the church of God' (1 Cor. 1:2), Paul makes no use of the term in connection with his doctrine of justification and salvation, and it is conspicuously absent from his discussion of Israel and the Gentiles in Rom. 9–11. But in the later Colossians and Ephesians Paul generalizes his use of 'church' to indicate, not an ecumenical church, but the spiritual and heavenly significance of each and every local 'body' which has Christ as its 'head', and by which God demonstrates his manifold wisdom through the creation of 'one new man' out of all races and classes. In God's purpose there is only one church, one gathering of all under the headship of Christ. But on earth it is pluriform, seen wherever two or three gather in his name. There is no need to explain the relation between the one and the many. Like the believer, the church is both local and 'in heaven'. Heb. 12:23 also has a picture of a heavenly 'assembly' (*ekklēsia*), but this is based on the model of the 'congregation of Israel' at Sinai, and it is uncertain whether the 'first-born' who comprise it are human or heavenly beings. Likewise, Jesus' 'church' of Mt. 16:18 may not be identical with what Paul means by 'church'. Jesus may mean the gathering of his apostles to form, under him, the restored house of David (*cf.* Mt. 19:28; Acts 15:16), by means of which salvation would come to the Gentiles (Rom. 15:12). (In Mt. 18:17, 'the church' refers to the synagogue.) Paul likens the local church to a *body whose members are mutually dependent (1 Cor. 12:12ff.), and to a building being erected, especially a *temple for God's Spirit (1 Cor. 3:10ff.). Metaphors of growth are used, and also the image of a flock being fed (Acts 20:28; 1 Pet. 5:2). 'Church' is not a synonym for 'people of God'; it is rather an *activity* of the 'people of God'. Images such as 'aliens and exiles' (1 Pet. 2:11) apply to the people of God in the world, but do not describe the church, *i.e.* the people assembled with Christ in the midst (Mt. 18:20; Heb. 2:12).

II. The church at Jerusalem

The church in the Christian sense appeared first in Jerusalem after the ascension of Jesus. It was made up of the predominantly Galilean band of Jesus' disciples together with those who responded to the preaching of the apostles in Jerusalem. Its members saw themselves as the elect remnant of Israel destined to find salvation in Zion (Joel 2:32; Acts 2:17ff.) and as the restored tabernacle of David which Jesus himself had promised to build (Acts 15:16; Mt. 16:18). Jerusalem was thus the divinely-appointed locale for those who awaited the final fulfilment of all God's promises (Acts 3:21). Externally, the group of baptized believers had the character of a sect within Judaism. It was called 'the sect of the Nazarenes' by a professional orator (Acts 24:5, 14; *cf.* 28:22), while its own adherents called their distinctive faith 'the *Way'. It was more or less tolerated by Judaism throughout the 30–odd years of its life in Judaea, except when the Jewish authorities were disturbed by its fraternization with Gentile churches abroad. But the essentially Jewish character of the Jerusalem church should be noted. Its members accepted the obligations of the law and the worship of the Temple. Their distinctive belief was that Jesus of Nazareth was Israel's Messiah, that God himself had vindicated this by raising him from the dead after he had suffered for Israel's redemption, and that the 'great and manifest day' of the Lord was even now upon them and would culminate in a final appearance of Messiah in judgment and glory.

Their distinctive practices included a baptism in the name of Jesus, regular attendance at instruction given by the apostles, and 'fellowship' on a household basis, which Luke described as being 'the breaking of bread and the prayers' (Acts 2:41–46). The first leadership of the church was by the twelve (Galilean) apostles, especially *Peter and *John, but soon gave way to that of *elders in the regular Jewish manner, with *James the brother of Jesus as president (Gal. 2:9; Acts 15:6ff.). The latter's presidency extended through most of the life of the Jerusalem church, possibly from as early as the thirties (Gal. 1:19; *cf.* Acts 12:17) until his execution *c.* AD 62. It may well have been associated with the church's Messianic conceptions. 'The *throne of David' was a much more literal hope among believing Jews than we commonly realize, and James was also 'of the house and lineage of David'. Was he thought of as a legitimate Protector, or Prince Regent, pending the return of Messiah in person? Eusebius reports that a cousin of Jesus, Simeon son of Clopas, succeeded James as president, and that Vespasian, after the capture of Jerusalem in AD 70, is said to have ordered a search to be made for all who were of the family of David, that there might be left among the Jews no-one of the royal family (*EH* 3. 11–12).

The church became large (Acts 21:20) and included even priests and Pharisees in its membership (6:7; 15:5). At the outset it included also many *Hellenists, Greek-speaking Jews of the Dispersion who came as pilgrims to feasts or for various reasons were staying in Jerusalem. Such Jews were often more wealthy than those of Jerusalem, and displayed piety by bringing 'alms to their nation' (*cf.* Acts 24:17). When the church adopted the practice of mutual support, a typical benefactor was the Cypriot *Barnabas (Acts 4:34–37), and when a committee was needed to administer the relief the Seven appointed were, to judge by their names, Hellenists (6:5). It was apparently through this Hellenist element that the gospel overflowed the narrow limits of Judaistic Christianity and created fresh streams in alien territories. *Stephen, one of the Seven, came into debate in a Hellenist synagogue in Jerusalem (of which Saul of Tarsus was possibly a member) and was charged before the Sanhedrin with blaspheming the Temple and the Mosaic law. His defence certainly shows a liberal attitude towards the inviolability of the Temple, and the persecution which followed his death may have been directed against this sort of tendency among Hellenist believers rather than against the law-abiding Christianity of the apostles who remained in Jerusalem when others were 'scattered'. *Philip, another of the Seven, took the gospel to Samaria and, after baptizing a foreign eunuch near the old Philistine city of Gaza, went preaching up the coast till he came to the largely pagan Caesarea, where soon afterwards Peter found himself admitting uncircumcised Gentiles to baptism.

Significantly it was Hellenists who went from Jerusalem to Antioch and there preached to Gentiles without any stipulation about the Mosaic law. After Stephen, the Hellenistic element in the Jerusalem church seemed to disappear and its Judaic character to prevail. Some of its members disapproved of the gospel's being offered to Gentiles without obligation to keep the law and went off to press their point of view in the new churches (Acts 15:1; Gal. 2:12; 6:12f.). Officially, however, the Jerusalem church gave its approval not only to Philip's mission in Samaria and the baptism of Cornelius at Caesarea, but to the policy of the new church at Antioch and its missionaries. In *c.* AD 49 a *council of the Jerusalem church was formally asked what should be demanded of 'those of the Gentiles who turn to God'. It was determined that, while Jewish believers would, of course, continue to circumcise their children and keep the whole law, these requirements should not be laid on Gentile believers, although the latter should be asked to make certain concessions to Jewish scruples which would make table-fellowship between the two groups easier, and to keep the law concerning sexual purity (Acts 15:20, 29; 21:21–25). The proceedings reflect the primacy of Jerusalem in matters of faith and morals. Indeed, throughout the first generation it was 'the church' *par excellence* (see Acts 18:22, where the Jerusalem church is meant). This is noticeable in the attitude of Paul (Gal. 1:13; Phil. 3:6), who impressed it on his churches (Rom. 15:27). His final visit to Jerusalem *c.* AD 57 was in recognition of this spiritual primacy. He was greeted by 'James and all the elders' and reminded that the many members of the church were 'all zealous for the law'. Its scrupulosity, however, did not save it from suspicion of disloyalty to Jewish national hopes. James 'the Just' was judicially murdered at the instigation of the high priest *c.* AD 62.

When the war with Rome broke out in AD 66 the church came to an end. Its members betook themselves, says Eusebius, to Pella in Transjordan (*EH* 3. 5). Thereafter they divided into two groups: the Nazarenes, who keeping the law themselves, had a tolerant attitude towards their Gentile fellow-believers, and the Ebionites, who inherited the Judaizing view of obligation to the law. Later Christians listed the Ebionites among the heretics.

III. The church at Antioch

The Jerusalem believers had no exclusive claim on the term *ekklēsia*, despite its OT associations, and the mixed assemblage of Jewish and Gentile believers which was formed at Antioch on the Orontes was without ceremony also called 'the church' there (Acts 11:26; 13:1). Moreover *Antioch, not Jerusalem, was the model of the 'new church' which was to appear all over the world. It was founded by Hellenist Jews. Here believers were first dubbed *Christians, or 'Christites', by their Gentile neighbours (Acts 11:26). Antioch became the springboard for the expansion of the gospel throughout the Levant. The key figure at first was *Barnabas, himself perhaps a Hellenist but enjoying the full confidence of the Jerusalem leaders who sent him to investigate. He is first named among the 'prophets and teachers', who are the only functionaries we know to have been in this church. He brought Saul the converted Pharisee from Tarsus—an interesting solvent for the ferment! Barnabas also led two missionary expeditions to his own country of *Cyprus, and with Paul made the first incursions into Asia Minor. There were important links between Antioch and Jerusalem. Prophets from Jerusalem came up and ministered (Acts 11:27), as did Peter himself and delegates from James (Gal. 2:11–12), not to mention the Pharisaic visitors of Acts 15:1. In return, Antioch expressed its fellowship with Jerusalem by sending relief in time of famine (Acts 11:29) and later looked to the Jerusalem church to provide a solution to the legal controversy. The prophetic leadership of the church included an African called Symeon, Lucius of Cyrene and a member of Herod Antipas's entourage. The author of Acts has been claimed as a native of Antioch (Anti-Marcionite Prologues). But the greatest fame of the church at Antioch was that it 'commended' Barnabas and Saul 'to the grace of God for the work which they ... fulfilled' (Acts 14:26).

IV. Pauline churches

While *Paul and Barnabas were clearly not the only missionaries of the first generation, we know next to nothing about the labours of others, including the twelve apostles themselves. Paul, however, claimed to have preached the gospel 'from Jerusalem and as far round as Illyricum' (Rom. 15:19), and we know that he founded churches on the Antiochene pattern in the S provinces of Asia Minor, in Macedonia and Greece, in W Asia where he made *Ephesus his base, and, by inference from the Epistle to *Titus, in *Crete. Whether he founded churches in *Spain (Rom. 15:24) is unknown. Everywhere he made cities his centre, whence he (or his associates) reached other cities of the province (Acts 19:10; Col. 1:7). Where possible, the Jewish *synagogue was the jumping-off point, Paul preaching there as a rabbi as long as he was given opportunity. In time, however, a separate *ekklēsia*—the word must sometimes have had the flavour of *synagōgē* (*cf.* Jas. 2:2, RV)—of Jewish and Gentile converts came into being, each with its own elders appointed by the apostle or his delegate from among the responsible senior believers. The *family played an important role in the development of these churches. The OT in Greek was the sacred Scripture of all these churches, and the key to its interpretation was indicated in certain selected passages together with a clearly defined summary of the gospel itself (1 Cor. 15:1–4). Other 'traditions' concerning Jesus' ministry and teaching were laid on every church (1 Cor. 11:2, 23–25; 7:17; 11:16; 2 Thes. 2:15), with fixed patterns of ethical instruction in regard to social and political obligation. It is unknown who regularly administered *baptism or presided at the *Lord's Supper, though both ordinances are mentioned. How frequently or on what days the church assembled is also unknown. The meeting at Troas 'on the Saturday night' (Acts 20:7, NEB) may be a model, and if so would support the view that the use of 'the first day of the week' (or 'the first day after the sabbath') for Christian assembly began simply by using the night hours which followed the close of the sabbath (see H. Riesenfeld, 'The Sabbath and the Lord's Day in Judaism, the Preaching of Jesus and Early Christianity', *The Gospel Tradition*, 1970).

But it is not clear that there was a church at Troas; the occasion may merely have marked the parting of Paul's travelling companions, the time being dictated by travelling arrangements. The first day could not have been observed as a sabbath, however, since it was not a holiday for Gentiles, and Paul would have no binding rules about keeping days unto the Lord (Rom. 14:5). Jewish members must have observed many customs not joined in by their Gentile brethren. The fullest evidence for what took place when a church actually assembled is 1 Cor. 11–14. There was no organizational link between Paul's churches, though there were natural affinities between churches in the same province (Col. 4:15–16; 1 Thes. 4:10). All were expected to submit to Paul's authority in matters of the faith—hence the role of Paul's letters and of the visits of *Timothy—but this authority was spiritual and admonitory, not coercive (2 Cor. 10:8; 13:10). Local administration and discipline were autonomous (2 Cor. 2:5–10). No church had superiority over any other, though all acknowledged Jerusalem as the source of 'spiritual blessings' (Rom. 15:27), and the collection for the saints there was a token of this acknowledgment.

V. Other churches

The origin of the other churches mentioned in the NT is a matter of inference. There were Jewish and Gentile believers in Rome by *c.* AD 56 when Paul wrote his Epistle to them. 'Visitors from Rome, both Jews and proselytes' were present at Pentecost (Acts 2:10), and among greetings in Rom. 16 is one to two 'of note among the apostles', *Andronicus and Junias, kinsmen of Paul's who were converted before him. Is this a complimentary reference to their having brought the gospel to Rome? 'Brethren' came to meet Paul and his party when they went to *Rome, but our knowledge of the church there, its composition and its status, is problematical.

The address of *1 Peter shows that there was a group of churches scattered along the S coast of the Black Sea and its hinterland ('Pontus, Galatia, Cappadocia, Asia, and Bithynia') of either Jewish or Jewish–Gentile membership. These are the parts which Paul was prevented from entering (Acts 16:6–7), which may imply that they were the scene of another man's foundation, perhaps the work of Peter himself. But we learn nothing distinctive of these churches from the Epistle. Oversight and responsibility for 'feeding the flock' in each place was exercised by elders (1 Pet. 5:1–2).

This exhausts our knowledge of the founding of particular churches in NT times. A little more about the W Asian churches emerges from the Apocalypse. It is thought that churches must surely have been founded at least in Alexandria and in Mesopotamia, if not farther E, within the 1st century, but of this there is no certain evidence.

Of the life and organization of the churches generally, we know very little, except for Jerusalem, which was not typical. Yet what we know makes us confident that their unity lay in the gospel itself, acceptance of the OT Scriptures and acknowledgment of Jesus as 'Lord and Christ'. Differences of *church government, forms of *ministry, moulds of thought and levels of moral and spiritual achievement were probably greater than we commonly realize. No one NT church, nor all the churches together—though they formed no visible unity—exercises any authority over our faith today. This divine *authority belongs only to the apostolic gospel as contained in the whole of the Scriptures. (*POWER OF THE KEYS; *PETER, **IV**.)

BIBLIOGRAPHY. K. L. Schmidt, *TDNT* 3, pp. 501–536; R. Banks, *Paul's Idea of Community*, 1979; P. T. O'Brien in D. A. Carson (ed.), *The Church in the Bible and the World*, 1987, pp. 88ff.; J. Roloff, *EDNT* 1, pp. 410ff.; H. Merklein, 'Die Ekklesia Gottes. Der Kirchenbegriff bei Paulus und in Jerusalem', *Studien zu Jesus und Paulus*, 1987, pp. 296ff.; G. Cole, *Explorations* 2, 1987, pp. 3ff. D.W.B.R.

CHURCH GOVERNMENT. The NT provides no detailed code of regulations for the government of the church, and the very idea of such a code might seem repugnant to the liberty of the gospel dispensation; but Christ left behind him a body of leaders in the apostles whom he himself had chosen, and he also gave them a few general principles for the exercise of their ruling function.

I. The Twelve and Paul

The Twelve were chosen that they might be with Christ (Mk. 3:14), and this personal association qualified them to act as his witnesses (Acts 1:8); they were from the first endowed with power over unclean spirits and diseases (Mt. 10:1), and this power was renewed and increased, in a more general form, when the promise of the Father (Lk. 24:49) came upon them in the gift of the Holy Spirit (Acts 1:8); on their first mission they were sent forth to preach (Mk. 3:14), and in the great commission they were instructed to teach all nations (Mt. 28:19). They thus received Christ's authority to evangelize at large.

But they were also promised a more specific function as judges and rulers of God's people (Mt. 19:28; Lk. 22:29–30), with power to bind and to loose (Mt. 18:18), to remit and to retain sins (Jn. 20:23). Such language gave rise to the conception of the keys, traditionally defined in both mediaeval and Reformed theology as: (*a*) the key of doctrine, to teach what conduct is forbidden and what permitted (this is the technical meaning of binding and loosing in Jewish legal phraseology), and (*b*) the key of discipline, to exclude and excommunicate the unworthy, and to admit and reconcile the contrite, by declaring or praying for God's forgiveness, through the remission of sins in Christ alone.

Peter received these powers first (Mt. 16:18–19), as he also received the pastoral commission to feed Christ's flock (Jn. 21:15), but he did so in a representative, rather than in a personal, capacity; for when the commission is repeated in Mt. 18:18, authority to exercise the ministry of reconciliation is vested in the body of disciples as a whole, and it is the faithful congregation, rather than any individual, which acts in Christ's name to open the kingdom to believers and to close it against unbelief. None the less, this authoritative function is primarily exercised by preachers of the word, and the process of sifting, of conversion and rejection, is seen at work from Peter's first sermon onwards (Acts 2:37–41). When Peter confessed Christ, his faith was typical of the rock-like foundation on which the church is built (Mt. 16:18), but in fact the foundations of the heavenly Jerusalem contain the names of all of the apostles (Rev. 21:14; *cf.* Eph. 2:20); these acted as a body in the early days of the church, and, despite Peter's continued eminence (Acts 15:7; 1 Cor. 9:5; Gal. 1:18; 2:7–9), the idea that Peter exercised any constant primacy among them is refuted, partly by the leading position occupied by James in the Jerusalem *Council (Acts 15:13, 19), and partly by the fact that Paul withstood Peter to the face (Gal. 2:11). It was in a corporate capacity that the apostles provided leadership for the primitive church; and that leadership was effective both in mercy (Acts 2:42) and in judgment (Acts 5:1–11). They exercised a general authority over every congregation, sending two of their number to supervise new developments in Samaria (Acts 8:14), and deciding with the elders on a common policy for the admission of Gentiles (Acts 15), while Paul's 'care of all the churches' (2 Cor. 11:28) is illustrated both by the number of his missionary journeys and by the extent of his correspondence.

II. After the ascension

Their first step, immediately after Christ's ascension, was to fill the vacancy left by the defection of Judas, and this they did by means of a direct appeal to God (Acts 1:24–26). Others were later reckoned in the number of apostles (1 Cor. 9:5–6; Gal. 1:19), but the qualifications of being an eyewitness of the resurrection (Acts 1:22), and of having been in some way personally commissioned by Christ (Rom. 1:1, 5), were not such as could be extended indefinitely. When the pressure of work increased, they appointed seven assistants (Acts 6:1–6), elected by the people and ordained by the apostles, to administer the church's charity; these seven have been regarded as deacons from the time of Irenaeus onwards, but Philip, the only one whose later history is clearly known to us, became an evangelist (Acts 21:8) with an unrestricted mission to preach the gospel, and Stephen's activities were not dissimilar. Church-officers with a distinctive name are first found in the elders of Jerusalem, who received gifts (Acts 11:30) and took part in Council (Acts 15:6). This office (*PRESBYTER) was probably copied from the eldership of the Jewish synagogue; the church is itself called a synagogue in Jas. 2:2, and Jewish elders, who seem to have been ordained by imposition of hands, were responsible for maintaining the observance of God's law, with power to excommunicate law-breakers. But the Christian eldership, as a gospel ministry, acquired added pastoral (Jas. 5:14; 1 Pet. 5:1–3) and preaching (1 Tim. 5:17) duties. Elders were ordained for all the Asian churches by Paul and Barnabas (Acts 14:23), while Titus was enjoined to do the same for Crete (Tit. 1:5); and although the disturbances at Corinth may suggest that a more complete democracy prevailed in that congregation (*cf.* 1 Cor. 14:26), the general pattern of church government in the apostolic age would seem to be a board of elders or pastors, possibly augmented by prophets and teachers, ruling each of the local congregations, with deacons to help, and with a general superintendence of the entire church provided by apostles and evangelists. There is nothing in this system which corresponds exactly to the modern diocesan episcopate; *bishops, when they are mentioned (Phil. 1:1), form a board of local congregational officers, and the position occupied by Timothy and Titus is that of Paul's personal lieutenants in his missionary work. It seems most likely that one elder acquired a permanent chairmanship of the board, and that he was then specially designated with the title of bishop; but even when the monarchical bishop appears in the letters of Ignatius, he is still the pastor of a single congregation. NT terminology is much more fluid; instead of anything resembling a hierarchy, we meet with such vague descriptions as 'he who rules', those who 'are over you in the Lord' (*proïstamenoi*, 'presidents'; Rom. 12:8; 1 Thes. 5:12) or 'those who have the rule over you' or 'your leaders' (*hēgoumenoi*, 'guides'; Heb. 13:7, 17, 24). The *angels of the churches in Rev. 2:3 have sometimes been regarded as actual bishops, but they are more probably personifications of their respective communities. Those in responsible positions are entitled to honour (1 Thes. 5:12–13; 1 Tim. 5:17), maintenance (1 Cor. 9:14; Gal. 6:6) and freedom from trifling accusations (1 Tim. 5:19).

III. General principles

Five general principles can be deducted from the NT teaching as a whole: (*a*) all authority is derived from Christ and exercised in his name and Spirit; (*b*) Christ's humility provides the pattern for Christian service (Mt. 20:26–28); (*c*) government is collegiate rather than hierarchical (Mt. 18:19; 23:8; Acts 15:28); (*d*) teaching and ruling are closely associated functions (1 Thes. 5:12); (*e*) administrative assistants may be required to help the preachers of the word (Acts 6:2–3). See also *MINISTRY and bibliography there cited. G.S.M.W.

CILICIA. A region in SE Asia Minor. The W part, known as Tracheia, was a wild plateau of the Taurus range, the home of pirates and robbers from prehistoric to Roman times. The E part, known as Cilicia Pedias, was a fertile plain between Mt Amanus in the S, Mt Taurus in the N and the sea; and the vital trade route between Syria and Asia Minor lay through its twin majestic passes, the Syrian Gates and the Cilician Gates. Cilicia was officially made a province before 100 BC, but effective rule began only after Pompey's pirate drive in 67 BC. Cicero was governor here in 51 BC. The province apparently disappeared under the Early Empire, Augustus ceding Tracheia partly to the native dynasty and partly to the adjacent client kingdoms of Galatia and Cappadocia. Pedias, which consists of 16 semi-autonomous cities, of which Tarsus was the most outstanding, was administered by Syria until after Tracheia was taken from Antiochus IV of Commagene in AD 72. Then Vespasian re-combined both regions into the single province of Cilicia (Suetonius, *Vespasian* 8). Thus Paul, its most distinguished citizen, and Luke, both writing accurately of the earlier period, are strictly correct in combining Cilicia (*i.e.* Pedias) in one unit with Syria (Gal. 1:21 variant; Acts 15:23, 41; see E. M. B. Green, 'Syria and Cilicia', *ExpT* 71, 1959–60, pp. 50–53, and authorities quoted there). E.M.B.G.
C.J.H.

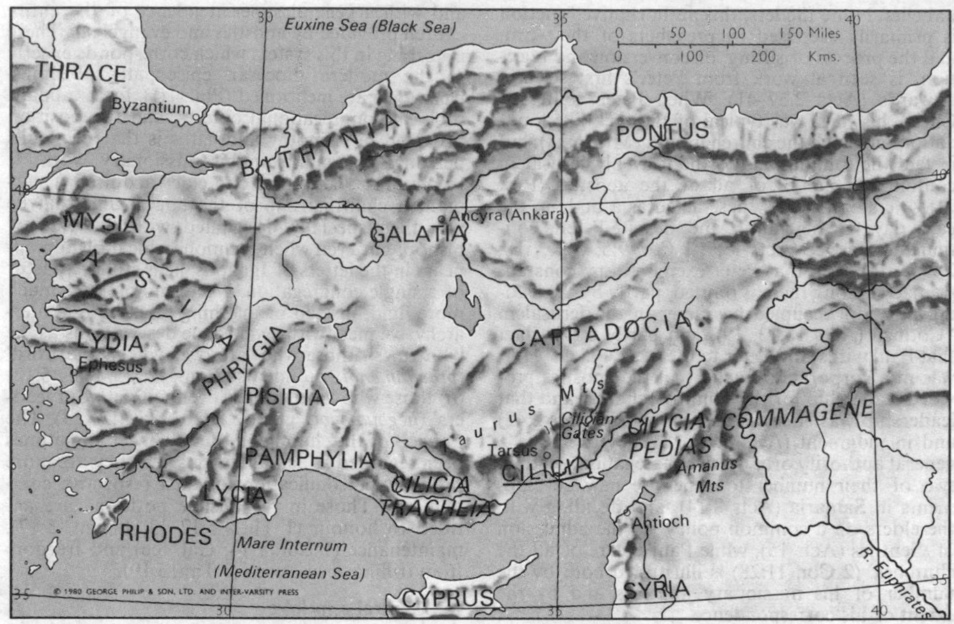

Cilicia, a Roman province important as controlling the vital trade route between Syria and Asia Minor, which ran through the Cilician Gates (see p. 203).

CIRCUMCISION.

I. In the Old Testament

The OT gives a coherent account of the origin and practice of circumcision in Israel.

a. Origin and occurrence

It is alleged that Ex. 4:24ff. and Jos. 5:2ff., along with Gn. 17, offer three different accounts of the origin of the rite, but, in fact, Ex. 4:24ff. can hardly be explained unless infant or child circumcision was already an established practice, and Jos. 5:2ff. states that those who left Egypt were circumcised. Gn. 17 remains as the sole biblical account of the origin of Israelite circumcision. It was integrated into the Mosaic system in connection with the Passover (Ex. 12:44), and apparently continued throughout the OT (*e.g.* Je. 9:25–26). It is a foundation feature of NT Judaism, and occasioned the Judaistic controversies of the apostolic period. The Jews in the NT had so associated circumcision with Moses that they had virtually forgotten its more fundamental association with Abraham (Acts 15:1, 5; 21:21; Gal. 5:2–3). Our Lord had to remind them that it antedated Moses (Jn. 7:22); Paul is emphatic that it was the current understanding of the Mosaic connection which was obnoxious to Christianity (Gal. 5:2–3, 11, *etc.*), and constantly brings his readers back to Abraham (Rom. 4:11; 15:8, *etc.*).

b. Significance of the practice

In Gn. 17 the divine covenant is set out first as a series of promises, personal (vv. 4b–5: Abram becomes the new man with new powers), national (v. 6, the predicted rise of monarchic nationhood), spiritual (v. 7, the pledged relationship of God with Abraham and his descendants). When the covenant is, secondly, expressed in a sign, circumcision (vv. 9–14), it is this totality of divine promise which is symbolized and applied to the divinely nominated recipients. This relationship of circumcision to foregoing promise shows that the rite signifies the gracious movement of God to man, and only derivatively, as we shall see, the consecration of man to God. This truth underlies Jos. 5:2ff.: while the nation walked in the wilderness under God's displeasure (*cf.* Nu. 14:34), the covenant was, as it were, in suspended animation, and circumcision lapsed. Or again, when Moses spoke of possessing 'uncircumcised lips' (Ex. 6:12, 30; *cf.* Je. 6:10), only the gift of God's word could remedy it. Further, the NT speaks of circumcision as a 'seal' (Rom. 4:11) upon God's gift of righteousness. Circumcision, therefore, is the token of that work of grace whereby God chooses out and marks men for his own.

The covenant of circumcision operates on the principle of the spiritual union of the household in its head. The covenant is 'between me and you and your descendants after you' (Gn. 17:7), and vv. 26–27 notably express the same truth: 'Abraham ... Ishmael ... and all the men of his house ... were circumcised with him.' Thus, from its inception, infant circumcision was the distinctive Israelite custom, not derived from Egyptian or other practice, and contrasting sharply with the puberty rites of other nations: the latter point to social acknowledgment of adult status, the former to a status before God and a prevenience of divine grace.

Those who thus became members of the covenant were expected to show it outwardly by obedience to God's law, expressed to Abram in its most general form, 'Walk before me, and be blameless' (Gn. 17:1). The relation between circumcision and obedience remains a biblical constant (Je. 4:4; Rom. 2:25–29; *cf.* Acts 15:5; Gal. 5:3). In this respect, circumcision involves the idea of consecration to God, but not as its essence. Circumcision embodies and applies covenant promises and summons to a life of covenant obedience. The blood which is shed in circumcision does not express the desperate lengths to which a man must go in self-consecration, but the costly demand which God makes of those whom he calls to himself and marks with the sign of his covenant.

This response of obedience was not always forthcoming, and, though sign and thing signified are identified in Gn. 17:10, 13–14, the Bible candidly allows that it is possible to possess the sign and nothing more, in which case it is spiritually defunct and, indeed, condemnatory (Rom. 2:27). The OT plainly teaches this, as it calls for the reality appropriate to the sign (Dt. 10:16; Je. 4:4), warns that in the absence of the reality the sign is nothing (Je. 9:25), and foresees the circumcising of the heart by God (Dt. 30:6).

II. In the New Testament

The NT is unequivocal: without obedience, circumcision becomes uncircumcision (Rom. 2:25–29); the outward sign fades into insignificance when compared with the realities of keeping the commandments (1 Cor. 7:18–19), faith working by love (Gal. 5:6) and a new creation (Gal. 6:15). Nevertheless, the Christian is not at liberty to scorn the sign. Although, in so far as it expressed salvation by works of law, the Christian must shun it (Gal. 5:2ff.), yet in its inner meaning he needs it (Col. 2:13; *cf.* Is. 52:1). Consequently, there is a 'circumcision of Christ', the 'putting off (of) the body (and not only part) of the . . . flesh', a spiritual transaction not made with hands, a relation to Christ in his death and resurrection, sealed by the initiatory ordinance of the new covenant (Col. 2:11–12).

In Phil. 3:2 Paul uses the deliberately offensive word *katatomē*, 'those who mutilate the flesh' (RSV), 'the concision' (AV). He is not defaming circumcision on Christians (*cf.* Gal. 5:12). The cognate verb (*katatemnō*) is used (Lv. 21:5, LXX) of forbidden heathen mutilations. To Christians, who are 'the circumcision' (Phil. 3:3), the enforcement of the outmoded sign is tantamount to a heathenish gashing of the body.

BIBLIOGRAPHY. L. Koehler, *Hebrew Man*, 1956, pp. 37ff.; G. A. F. Knight, *A Christian Theology of the Old Testament*, 1959, pp. 238f.; G. R. Beasley-Murray, *Baptism in the New Testament*, 1962; J. P. Hyatt, 'Circumcision', *IDB*; J. Sasson, *JBL* 85, 1966, pp. 473ff.; T. D. Alexander, 'Genesis 22 and the Covenant of Circumcision', *JSOT* 25, pp. 17–22; H. C. Hahn, 'Circumcision', *NIDNTT* 1, pp. 307–312.

J.A.M.

CISTERN (Heb. *bôr* or *bō'r*, from *bā'ar*, 'to dig or bore'), a subterranean reservoir for storing water which was collected from rainfall or from a spring. In contrast, the cylindrical well (*b*[e]*'ēr*) received water from percolation through its walls. However, the term *bôr* is translated *'well' or *'pit' many times and 'cistern' only 5 times in AV and 14 times in RSV. Many cisterns are found in Palestine, where rainfall is scarce from May to September. They are usually pear-shaped with a small opening at the top which can be sealed to prevent accidents (Ex. 21:33–34) and unauthorized use. Both Joseph (Gn. 37:22) and Jeremiah (Je. 38:6) nearly perished in such pits (*cf.* Zc. 9:11). Most homes in Jerusalem had private cisterns (2 Ki. 18:31; *cf.* Pr. 5:15); but there were also huge public cisterns, one in the Temple area having a capacity of over 2 million gallons. By *c.* 1500 BC cisterns were cemented (P. W. Lapp, *BASOR* 195, 1969, pp. 2–49), thus permitting large settlements in the barren Negeb region (*cf.* 2 Ch. 26:10), especially in Nabataean and Byzantine times. *Cf.* N. Glueck, *Rivers in the Desert*, 1959, p. 94; S. M. Paul and W. G. Dever, *Biblical Archaeology*, 1974, pp. 127–162; *EJ*, 5, pp. 578f.

J.C.W.

CITIES OF REFUGE. These were places of asylum mentioned principally in Nu. 35:9–34 and Jos. 20:1–9 (where they are named). They are also mentioned in Nu. 35:6; Jos. 21:13, 21, 27, 32, 38; 1 Ch. 6:57, 67. From these it appears that they were among the cities of the Levites. Dt. 4:41–43; 19:1–13 deal with the institution indicated by this name (*cf.* Ex. 21:12–14).

In Israel's public life the law of retribution was to be applied, and is, moreover, specified in the *lex talionis* (see Ex. 21:23–25, *etc.*) which particularly applied in cases of bloodshed (see Gn. 9:5f.; Ex. 21:12; Lv. 24:17, *etc.*; *cf.* also Dt. 21:1–9). In ancient Israel at least, the duty of punishing the slayer rested upon the *gō'ēl*, the nearest male relative (*AVENGER OF BLOOD). A distinction was made between slaying a man purposely or unawares. The wilful murderer was to be killed, while the unintentional murderer could find asylum in one of the cities of refuge. It may be said that the institution of the cities of refuge mainly served to prevent excesses which might develop from the execution of what is usually called the 'blood-feud'.

In 'the book of the covenant', Israel's oldest collection of laws, there is already a stipulation concerning this matter (Ex. 21:12–14). Perhaps the tendency of this regulation can be described as follows. Israel knew the ancient practice, which also prevailed among other nations, of regarding the altar or the sanctuary as an asylum. Here it is stipulated that the wilful slayer shall not find a refuge near the altar, though the unintentional slayer may do so. But the altar may be at a great distance, and, moreover, he cannot stay permanently near the altar, in the sanctuary. So the Lord announces that he will make further provisions for this matter. The curious expression 'God let him fall into his hand' has been interpreted in the sense that the unintentional murderer is an instrument of God, and accordingly it is only natural that God should look after his protection. Examples of the altar as an asylum in Israel occur in 1 Ki. 1:50–53; 2:28–34, while expressions such as those used in Pss. 27:4–6; 61:4; Ob. 17 show that this practice was well known in Israel.

There are characteristic differences between the two principal groups of regulations concerning the cities of refuge, Nu. 35:9ff.; Dt. 19:1ff. (*cf.* Dt. 4:41–43). As to the regulations of Nu. 35, which were also given in the plains of Moab (v. 1), we should note the following. The term 'cities of refuge, cities where a person is received (?)' is used. In due course Israel is to appoint three cities on the E side of Jordan, and three cities on the W side (vv. 13ff.), which cities are to be among the cities of the Levites (v. 6). The 'congregation' is to

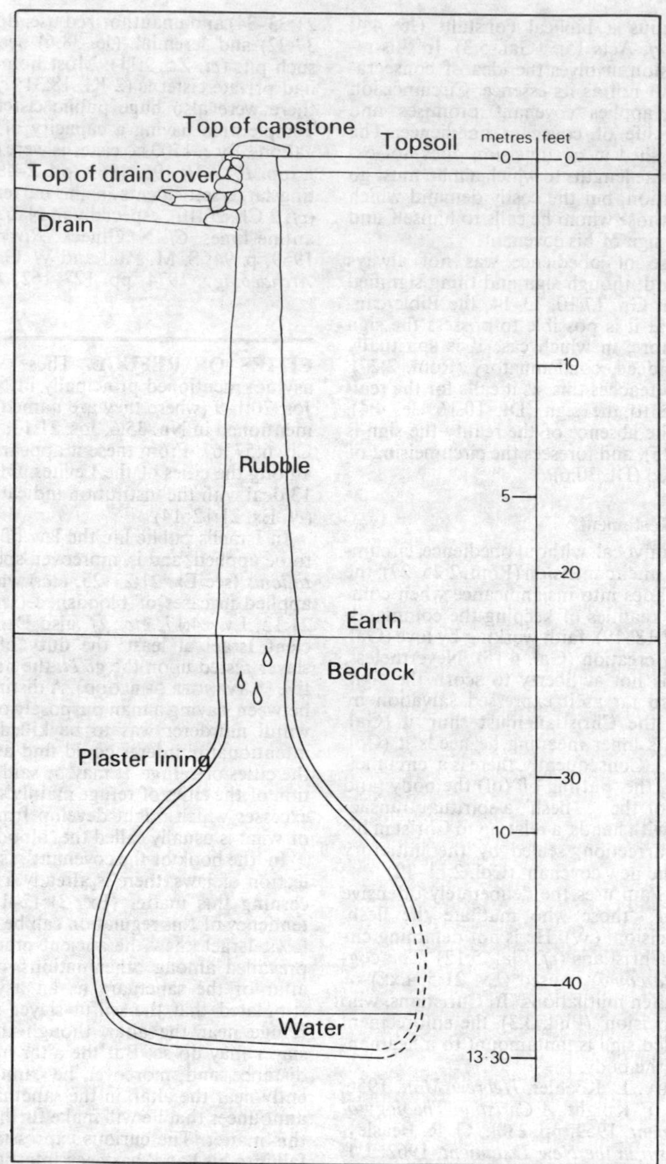

Sectional drawing of a cistern, fed by underground drain, excavated at Tell Ta'annek. Water would be drawn by using a bucket (see p. 205).

pronounce the final judgment (vv. 12, 24). (During the wanderings through the desert this body made decisions in such cases. Here no further stipulation is made as to what body is to act in a similar capacity once Israel had settled in Canaan.) In vv. 16–23 criteria are given to define accurately whether one has to do with intentional or unintentional murder. The unintentional slayer is to remain in the city until the death of the high priest (vv. 25, 28, 32). In this connection the stay receives the character of an exile, of penance (vv. 28, 32). Note also the stipulations of vv. 30–32, with the important motivation, given in vv. 33f.

Dt. 4:41–43 narrates how 'Moses set apart three cities in the east beyond the Jordan'. Dt. 19:1ff. stipulates that, after the conquest of Canaan, three cities of refuge shall be appointed on the W side of Jordan, and another three in case of a further extension of Israel's territory (the last regulation was apparently never carried out). It is emphasized that the Israelites should take care that a slayer who killed ignorantly was within easy reach of a city of refuge (vv. 3, 6ff.). To indicate the difference between a wilful and unintentional murder, an example is given in v. 5. The elders of the slayer's dwelling-place are to make the final decision (v. 12).

According to Jos. 20, the following cities of refuge were appointed during Joshua's lifetime:

Kedesh, Shechem, Kiriath-arba (= Hebron), Bezer, Ramoth and Golan. Jos. 20 assumes as known both the regulations of Nu. 35 and of Dt. 19. A new feature here is that the elders of the cities of refuge also have a responsibility (vv. 4–5).

Nothing is known about the putting into practice of the right of asylum. Except for 1 Ki. 1:50–53; 2:28–34, it is not mentioned, which *per se* need not surprise us. It is possible that, as the central authority established itself more firmly, the right of asylum decreased in significance.

Concerning the dating of these passages and the historicity of the facts they contain, Wellhausen and the scholars who follow him hold them to be the result of a development, as follows. Originally the sanctuary was the asylum. In the 7th century BC the authors of Deuteronomy aimed at the centralization of the cult. In this connection they secularized the right of asylum, and replaced the sanctuaries by a few cities and superseded the priests by the elders. Nu. 35 contains a project dating from the exilic or post-exilic time which was never carried out. Jos. 20 dates from an even later period. Nowadays many scholars are of the opinion that this institution dates from a much older time, *e.g.* from the time of David (Albright and others).

There seems to be no reason why we should not accept that the regulations in question date, at least in essence, from Moses' time. It is obvious that this cannot be discussed as an isolated question, for it is closely connected with the dating of sources. Suffice it to say here that only in ancient times did these six cities belong to Israel's territory, Golan already being lost shortly after Solomon's death, and Bezer about 850 BC (according to the *MOABITE STONE).

Two questions remain for discussion. First, why was the unintentional slayer to remain in the city of refuge till the death of the high priest? One answer given is that his guilt devolved upon the high priest and was atoned for by the (untimely) death of the high priest. A similar view occurs already in the Talmud (*Makkoth* 2b) and is still defended, among others by Nicolsky and Greenberg. This view has something attractive about it (*cf.* Ex. 28:36–38), but is still questionable. It is better to take the view that by the death of the high priest a definite period was concluded. Perhaps it is allowed, with van Oeveren, to work out this view in the following way: the cities of refuge were among the cities of the Levites; so the unintentional slayer, dwelling in a city of refuge, was linked up with the tribe of Levi; the death of the high priest, the chief of the tribe of Levi, unfastened this link.

Secondly, can it be stated with regard to the unintentional slayer that justice gave way to mercy? Probably the best thing to say is that the question cannot be answered, because the OT does not distinguish between mercy and justice in the way we do. But the pronouncement that the decrees which the Lord gave to Israel were good and just (Dt. 4:6ff., *etc.*) certainly applies to the regulations concerning the cities of refuge.

The answer to these two questions affects the extent to which we are to regard the regulations about the cities of refuge as Christological. It is undoubtedly legitimate to call Christ our Refuge. But to work out the parallel between Christ and the cities of refuge in further details is precarious.

For the opinions of later Judaism on these regulations, see the Mishnah tractate *Makkoth* 2, and the tractate in the Talmud associated with it (*cf.* also Löhr, p. 34).

BIBLIOGRAPHY. N. M. Nicolsky, 'Das Asylrecht in Israel', *ZAW* 48, 1930, pp. 146–175; M. Löhr, *Das Asylwesen im Alten Testament*, 1930; C. L. Feinberg, 'The Cities of Refuge', *BS* 103, 1946, pp. 411–416; 104, 1947, pp. 35–48; W. F. Albright, *Archaeology and the Religion of Israel*, 1956, pp. 120–125; R. de Vaux, *Ancient Israel*, 1961, pp. 160–163; M. Greenberg, 'The Biblical Conception of Asylum', *JBL* 78, 1959, pp. 125–132; B. van Oeveren, *De Vrijsteden in het Oude Testament*, 1968 (with a summary in German, pp. 257–260, and with an extensive bibliography). N.H.R.

CITY.

I. In the Old Testament

The word *'îr* occurs 1,090 times in the OT and describes a wide variety of permanent settlements. It does not appear to have regard to size or rights (*cf.* Gn. 4:17; 19:29; 24:10; Ex. 1:11; Lv. 25:29, 31; 1 Sa. 15:5; 20:6; 2 Ki. 17:6; Je. 51:42–43, 58; Jon. 3:3; Na. 3:1).

There are other words used in the Bible for city. Of the Hebrew words we note *qiryâ* (Ezr. 4:10), *qiryā'* (Ezr. 4:15, *etc.*), *qereṯ* (Jb. 29:7; Pr. 8:3; 9:3, *etc.*), *ša'ar*, literally 'gate', but used frequently for city or town in Deuteronomy (5:14; 12:15; 14:27–28).

Modern discussion about 'city' is based on recent archaeological excavations and on mature appreciation of sociological and anthropological issues so that a more comprehensive and authentic picture of the city in ancient times has become available. In particular, reference to biblical cities, the location, layout, size, architecture, building materials, provision of water and food as well as the economy, social organization, everyday life, administration and culture have been explored in some detail for many ancient cities of biblical interest (see V. Fritz, *The City in Ancient Israel*, 1994).

In the normal city there was a central area where commerce and law were transacted, and round about were the 'suburbs' (*migrāš*, 'pasture grounds'), where farming was carried on (Nu. 35:2; Jos. 14:4; 1 Ch. 5:16; 6:55; Ezk. 48:15, 17). There seem to have been villages as well in the general neighbourhood of the bigger towns, which were described as 'daughters', *bānôṯ*, and which were probably unwalled (Nu. 21:25; 32:42; 2 Ch. 28:18; Ne. 11:25–31). Where the central city was walled it was the place of shelter for the entire surrounding population in times of danger (*FORTIFICATION AND SIEGECRAFT). In pre-Israelite times many of these areas with their walled city were small city-states ruled by a 'king', *meleḵ*, and owing allegiance to some great power such as Egypt.

There are numerous references to non-Israelite cities in the OT, among the most famous being Pithom and Ra'amses, the store-cities of the pharaoh (Ex. 1:11), the cities of the Philistines, which were really city-states of the Greek type (1 Sa. 6:17–18), Damascus, the Syrian capital, *Nineveh, 'an exceedingly great city, three days' journey in breadth' (Jon. 3:3), *Babylon the great (Dn. 4:30; Je. 51:37, 43, 58), *Susa (Shushan), the capital of Persia (Est. 1:2). Excavation and general archaeological research have given us much significant information about some of these cities. Thus Nineveh was surrounded by walls of nearly 16 km circumference. In the neighbourhood were two other Assyrian cities, Khorsabad and Nimrud (*CALAH), both of some size. In addition, there were numerous villages in the area. The extent of the city that was in the mind of the writer of Jonah may not be quite clear today, but there is good reason to think of 'an exceedingly great city'. Again Babylon was a remarkable city with great fortifications and palaces.

Inside the walls of any of these ancient cities would be found the houses of the citizens, possibly the large houses of the nobles, and even a *palace. Excavations in Palestine have given a good idea of the lay-out of these cities. The gates of the city, of which many have now been excavated (*e.g.* Megiddo, Hazor, Gezer, Tell Sheba) were the place of commerce and law, and here the judges sat to give their decisions (Gn. 19:1; 2 Sa. 15:2–6; 1 Ki. 22:10; Am. 5:10, 12, 15). The number of gates varied. In Jericho there seems to have been only one gate, but in other cities there may have been several. The ideal city of Ezekiel had 12 gates (Ezk. 48:30–35; *cf.* Rev. 21:12–13). The area behind the walls was normally carefully planned with a ring-road all around the city and houses behind it, and other roads farther inside. Houses, public buildings, shrines or temples, and open spaces can be discerned on the excavators' plans.

Sometimes cities had a specific purpose. The Egyptian cities of Pithom and Ra'amses were store cities (Ex. 1:11) or 'treasure' cities. Solomon had cities for 'chariots and for horsemen' (1 Ki. 4:26; 9:19) as well as cities for stores. We judge that these were for defence and for grain storage. Excavations at Megiddo were particularly instructive in this regard, for they revealed that this town had at one time a huge grain storage-bin of some 500,000 litres capacity. A common picture brought to light by excavation is of a city gate with storehouses not far from the gate (*e.g.* Tell Sheba).

At times cities were used in bargaining between states, and when treaties were drawn up and boundaries were adjusted there was often a transfer of cities from one state to another (1 Ki. 9:10–14; 20:34). At times, also, cities formed part of a marriage dowry (1 Ki. 9:16). Again, people of neighbouring states were always anxious to gain access to the markets of their neighbours and to 'make streets' in their cities (1 Ki. 20:34), where trade could be carried on.

In any discussion of the term 'city' in reference to the Bible *Jerusalem should receive a special place, for among the cities of Israel Jerusalem predominated as the seat of the house of David and the centre of the religious life of the nation. It is termed the 'city of David' and the 'city of God', terms which have a close association with the pre-exilic worship of Israel and her king and which are reflected in many of the psalms. The character of Jerusalem in the last days of the kings has been greatly illuminated by the work of Kathleen Kenyon, whose excavations on the E slopes of the ancient city, where it overlooked the Kedron, showed terraces all along the slope which supported rows of houses. There was a massive collapse in the attack of Nebuchadrezzar. The W wall of the city of those days has recently been discovered.

Jerusalem lay in ruins for nearly a century before the new city was built. It was unwalled at first, but under Nehemiah was once again protected by a wall, traces of which are still to be seen.

When the OT was translated into Greek the Hebrew *'îr* became *polis* in the LXX. But whereas the Greek *polis* had political overtones and meant 'state' or 'body politic' rather than merely 'city', the term in its Hebrew setting was apolitical. Only Philo among the later Jewish writers used the term *polis* in a political sense.

BIBLIOGRAPHY. 'Cities' in S. M. Paul and W. G. Dever, *Biblical Archaeology*, 1973, pp. 3–26, V. Fritz, *The City in Ancient Isrrael*, 1994. J.A.T.

II. In the New Testament

In the NT *polis* is frequently found. In the Gospels it bears the extended and non-political sense of village, *etc.*, which is germane to the Jewish background of Jesus' ministry. In Acts it is used of various Hellenistic cities of Asia Minor and Europe but bears no reference to their political structure. In Rom. 16:23 we find the Corinth treasurer or steward (the term is known from inscriptions) in fellowship with the Christian church: apart from Paul's boast in Acts 21:39, this is practically the only place in the NT where we find even the most distant allusion to the political structure of the city. It may be tempting, however, to see in the words of Acts 15:28 *edoxen tō pneumati tō hagiō kai hēmin*, a phrase framed upon the civic formulary *edoxen tē boulē kai tō dēmō*. Even so, however attractive and suggestive the idea that here the Holy Spirit takes the place of the council and the apostles the assembly of citizens, it is quite clear that neither the apostles nor Luke are concerned to press the analogy. It may also be significant to note that the word *parrēsia* (the Christian's 'boldness' or 'freedom of speech') earlier has the specifically political connotation of the citizen's right to free speech in the assembly.

The verb *politeuomai* means in the NT simply 'to live one's life, to conduct oneself' (Acts 23:1; Phil. 1:27). The noun *politeia*, 'commonwealth' or 'body politic', is used with reference to the rights and privileges of Israel (Eph. 2:12). *politeuma* is used in Phil. 3:20, where some seek to find in it the technical use as 'colony', and to translate the verse 'we are a colony of heaven' (so appropriate to Philippi). To render it thus, however, involves turning the sentence about, and the suggestion must be rejected. We find here either the less specific 'citizenship' (*cf.* Philo, *Concerning the Confusion of Tongues* 78; *Epistle to Diognetus* 5. 9) or the very general 'way of life' (as AV 'conversation'), in which case *cf.* 2 Cor. 4:18.

Jerusalem still possesses for the NT writers the title 'holy city' and ranks high in the esteem of Jesus as the city of the great King (Mt. 5:35). It remained until AD 70 a centre of Christian influence and a focus of esteem. Yet it is spoken of also as a city of sinful men who have persecuted and slain the prophets, over which Jesus weeps as he sees the approach of its doom. This spiritual ambivalence strikes us in Revelation. Jerusalem is the beloved city (20:9), object of God's promises, centre of the millennial reign; but in ch. 11 the holy city is Sodom and Egypt where the Lord was crucified, and even the great city, a term normally reserved for the adversary of God (see chs. 16–18), of which Jerusalem in that hour was the locus and type. We may compare Paul's contrast of two Jerusalems in Gal. 4:24–26.

For the writer to the Hebrews and his addressees (whoever and however Hebrew either were), the emphasis lies upon the heavenly Jerusalem. It is their goal, the vision of which sustained the saints of old in their quest. In the coming of the Son it was given at length for a Man to sit down by God, to his brethren to come to the city of the living God, and to the just men to be at last made perfect (12:22–23; 11:40). But it is yet to come in its fullness, in that end which the writer so eagerly awaits. There are affinities here with Philo (*e.g. loc. cit. supra*), but Hebrews remains true to the kerygmatic points of crisis, the first and second comings of Jesus.

Heavenly Jerusalem, New Jerusalem, forms the subject of Rev. 21–22. As recent study of Revelation has revealed and emphasized, a number of sources are laid under contribution for the description. In the first place, for the plan of the city, Ezk. 40–48 is of predominant importance, and, for the benefits and blessings of that place and state, prophecies, especially of Isaiah and Zechariah, provide much of the language. Such hopes are also to be found widely in Jewish apocalyptic writing. Secondly, since the comparative work of the religio-historical school of exegetes, the relation of the description to the astronomy and astrology of antiquity has tended to be stressed. The twelve precious stones of the foundation are well-known counterparts of the twelve Zodiacal signs: the intermingled stones and pearls reflect the starry heavens above, and both street and stream the Milky Way: the cubic dimensions of the city and its vast size are patterned on the vastness of space. Even the heavenly wall has its origin in the pillars of the sky. Thirdly, numerous parallels may also be drawn between this description and that of Hellenistic cities (and Babylon, their possible pattern) in Greek geographers and orators. In these sources we find a tetragonal plan, a central street, praise of a river flanked by avenues or dotted with wooded islets, visions of cities adorned with fine trees and rendered salubrious by natural situation and flora. Yet there is one marked contrast. There were many temples in Hellenistic cities; there is none, nor any need of one, in the new Jerusalem. No one source necessarily excludes the others; the recognition of all brings out the spiritual meaning of this vision. In the appointed end, when God is All in all, we find the fulfilment of Israel's hopes, the realization of God's promises to her; the manifestation, in a city which has the glory of God, of the reality already declared by the heavens and the firmament; and the answer to all aesthetic yearnings and national aspirations in the place to which the kings of the earth bring their glory. Of this city the reborn are citizens, and to it all pilgrims of faith tend. The city is also described as the Lamb's bride; it is in another aspect his church for which he died, the pattern and goal of all human society. In the last analysis this chief of scriptural cities is men, not walls: just men made perfect, the city of the living God.

BIBLIOGRAPHY. R. de Vaux, *Ancient Israel*, 1961, pp. 229–240; M. du Buit, *Géographie de la Terre Sainte*, 1958; R. S. Lamon and G. M. Shipton, *Megiddo I*, 1939; G. Loud, *Megiddo II*, 1948, pp. 46–57; R. de Vaux, articles on excavations at Tell el-Far'a in *Revue Biblique* 1947–52; *TWBR*, *s.v.*; W. M. Ramsay, *The Cities of St Paul*, 1907; E. M. Blaiklock, *Cities of the NT*, 1965; D. H. McQueen, *The Expositor* (Ninth Series) 2, 1924, pp. 221–226; R. Knopf, *Festschrift für G. Heinrici*, 1914, pp. 213–219; W. Bousset, R. H. Charles, G. B. Caird, G. R. Beasley-Murray, commentaries on *Revelation* in *loc. cit*.

J.N.B.

CLAUDIA. A Roman Christian, greeting Timothy (2 Tim. 4:21); in some imaginative reconstructions the wife of *Pudens, and even, on the bad authority of *Apostolic Constitutions* 7. 2. 6, mother of *Linus. Alford, *in loc.*, identifies Timothy's friend with the British Claudia, whose marriage with one Pudens is celebrated by Martial (*cf. Epig*. 4. 13 with 11. 53), and with the hypothetical Claudia of a putative Pudens in a Chichester inscription (*CIL* 7. 11). Martial, however, came to Rome only in AD 66, and implies scarcely Christian proclivities of his Pudens. Another Pudens and Claudia appear in *CIL* 6. 15066; but Claudia is a very common contemporary name.

BIBLIOGRAPHY. J. B. Lightfoot, *Clement*, I, pp. 76ff.; G. Edmundson, *The Church in Rome*, 1913, pp. 244ff.

A.F.W.

CLAUDIUS. Roman Caesar from AD 41 to 54. He is supposed, on inconclusive grounds in each case, to have taken 3 different measures to deal with Christianity. (*a*) He expelled Jews from Rome for rioting at the instigation of Chrestus (Suetonius, *Claudius* 25). This is presumably the incident referred to in Acts 18:2. Chrestus is either a personal name or a variant of Christus. Suetonius assumes the former, and was, moreover, capable of recognizing Christianity. Even if he was wrong, it need not refer to *Christian* Messianism. Neither Paul's welcome in Rome nor the Epistle to the Romans suggests any history of conflict between Jews and Christians there. (*b*) Claudius reprimanded Jewish agitators imported into Alexandria from Syria (H. I. Bell, *Jews and Christians in Egypt*, 1924). Apollos's defective knowledge of Christianity, however, suggests that these were not Christians. (*c*) A Caesarian decree (*JRS* 22, 1932, pp. 184ff.), perhaps of Claudius, punished tomb robbery and was apparently published in Galilee. Whether or not this refers to the resurrection is likely to remain a moot point.

BIBLIOGRAPHY. A. Momigliano, *Claudius*², 1961.

E.A.J.

CLAUDIUS LYSIAS. In Acts 21:31ff. the military tribune (Gk. *chiliarchos*, 'captain of a thousand'; AV, RV 'chief captain'; RSV 'tribune of the cohort') in command of the Roman garrison of the Antonia Fortress in Jerusalem, who took Paul into custody. He had acquired his Roman citizenship by purchase (Acts 22:28); his *nomen* Claudius suggests that he had bought it in the principate of Claudius, when Roman citizenship became increasingly available for cash down. His *cognomen* Lysias implies that he was of Greek birth. His letter to Felix about Paul (Acts 23:26–30) subtly rearranges the facts so as to place his own behaviour in the most favourable light.

F.F.B.

CLEAN AND UNCLEAN. Heb. *ṭāhōr/ṭāmē'*. Gk. *katharos/ akathartos/ akatharsia.* According to Lv. 10:10–11 it was the duty of the priests 'to distinguish between the holy and the common, and between the unclean and the clean' and to teach the people about the differences. These fundamental categories of biblical thought are then expounded in the following chapters of Leviticus.

God is the supremely holy being, and anyone

who whishes to come into his presence must be holy too. But uncleanness is a bar to holiness: indeed if any unholy person comes into contact with the holy, he will die (*e.g.* 2 Sa. 6:6–7). Uncleanness has a variety of causes and cures.

Lv. 11 classifies living creatures into clean and unclean. Clean may be eaten, and some of the clean creatures may be sacrificed, but unclean may not. Cud-chewing animals with split hooves (*e.g.* cattle, sheep), are clean and may be eaten, but others (*e.g.* pigs) are unclean. Birds, except birds of prey, are clean and edible. Ordinary fish with fins and scales are also clean, but other aquatic creatures (*e.g.* shellfish) are unclean (Lv. 11:9–12).

All animals, whether clean or unclean when alive, when dead will make those who touch them unclean (Lv. 11:28, 31, 39). Even more polluting are human corpses. So holy people, like priests and Nazirites, are forbidden to mourn for the dead, in case they make themselves unclean (Lv. 21:1–12; Nu. 6:1–12). Laity who become unclean by touching a corpse remain so for a week.

Some bodily discharges also make people unclean. Mothers are polluted by the puerperal discharge for forty days after giving birth to a son, and for eighty days after bearing a daughter (Lv. 12). Sexual intercourse pollutes both parties for a day and menstruation makes a woman unclean for a week (Lv. 15:18–19). Long-term discharges from the sexual organs make people unclean for as long as the discharge continues. Skin diseases of various sorts may also make a person unclean. Lv. 13 distinguishes between unclean complaints (*e.g.* active, sore, peeling conditions) and stable conditions (*e.g.* baldness) classed as clean. Anyone suffering from a polluting skin condition remains unclean until it clears up. In general, short-term human uncleanness may be cleared by waiting a day and washing in water. When a condition causing long-term uncleanness clears up (*e.g.* skin disease), the sufferer has also to offer a sacrifice so as to become ritually clean again (Lv. 14).

Some sins pollute not just the sinner but the land and even the sanctuary itself. For example, sexual sins such as incest, adultery, homosexuality and bestiality, pollute those involved and the land (Lv. 18). They may lead to the loss of the land or the 'cutting-off', *i.e.* death by supernatural causes, of the offender (Lv. 18:25, 28–29). Idols and idolatry are also polluting. Worship of other gods, consulting the dead or possession of idols makes the perpetrators, the land and the sanctuary unclean (Lv. 18:21; 20:2–5; Ezk. 20:7, 18). Homicide is another sin that pollutes the land (Nu. 35:33–34). The uncleanness caused by these sins is so serious that only the death of the sinner suffices to cleanse it.

I. Theology of uncleanness

Modern readers tend to dismiss the uncleanness rules as unintelligible or irrelevant. Yet notions of uncleanness are found in most societies, including our own, and the biblical rules express one of its central theological convictions and served to teach it to Israel. Since Mary Douglas (1966) first looked at these rules from an anthropological perspective, there has emerged a broad consensus among biblical scholars about their significance.

Fundamental is the contrast between holiness and uncleanness. God is perfectly holy, whereas the unclean are those opposed to God, or who fall short of his perfection. But divine holiness does not merely demand total religious and moral commitment, it means life. God himself is full and perfect life, so that death is the very antithesis of holiness. Thus uncleanness is very often associated with death.

God	sin
life	death
holiness	uncleanness

Israel, the people of God, is called to be holy, 'because I the Lord am holy' (Lv. 20:26). This means shunning idolatry, murder and sexual immorality, but also avoiding the other conditions associated with death.

If the quintessence of uncleanness is death, it becomes clear why corpses are regarded as so polluting. Similarly, the loss of life liquids, such as blood or semen, means that the person has less life within and therefore may be moving towards death. So, too, people suffering from serious skin diseases are not enjoying the fullness of life, and they are therefore classified as unclean. Only the pure and clean may approach God. Handicapped priests may not officiate at the altar and blemished animals may not be sacrificed there (Lv. 21:17–23; 22:18–25). Lay people affected by uncleanness are barred from worship and sometimes forced to live outside the community until they recover (Nu. 5:1–4; 2 Ki. 7:3–4).

There are degrees of uncleanness in biblical thinking. So rather than regard holy and unclean, life and death, as mutually exclusive categories, it is better to see a spectrum of conditions ranging from the very holy to the very unclean.

holy (*cf.* God, life)	priests sacrificial animals
nearly holy	handicapped priests blemished sacrificial animals
clean	clean laity clean (edible) animals
unclean	unclean people unclean animals
very unclean (*cf.* death)	human corpses dead animals

These harsh regulations declared very loudly one aspect of God's character: he is life, perfect life, both morally and physically. He is opposed to death: those who embrace actions that lead to death separate themselves from God.

II. The food laws

The food laws (Lv. 11; Dt. 14) do not immediately seem to fit this understanding of uncleanness. Why are pigs, camels and crabs unclean and somehow closer to death than sheep, goats or salmon, which are clean? (However, that birds of prey are classified as unclean is suggestive, for they kill other creatures or live on carrion.)

The standard Jewish explanation is that the classification is arbitrary: they test obedience. Will you obey God, even if you cannot understand his reasons? Or is the aim to promote health? Pork, shellfish, and so on, often carry disease. There is nothing in the laws to suggest it. Some items classified as unclean are healthy foods, and *vice versa.* Nor does this explanation warrant Jesus' abolition of the food laws. Would he have wanted his disciples to eat unhealthy foods? Another scholarly explanation is that some of the unclean animals (*e.g.* pigs) were used in pagan worship. But the premier clean sacrificial beast in Israel, the bull,

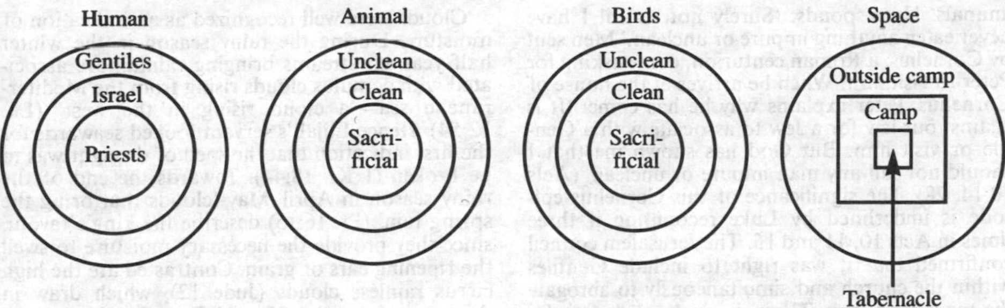

was also highly valued in Egyptian and Canaanite religion, so reaction to foreign practice does not explain these rules.

Once again Mary Douglas has put forward the most plausible type of explanation. She noted that the cleanness rules structure the bird, animal and human realms in a similar way (see above).

The realms of birds and beasts both contain a mixture of clean and unclean species. The clean may be eaten, the unclean may not. Within the clean group there is a subgroup of animals or birds that may also be sacrified (*e.g.* sheep, pigeons). This threefold division of the bird and animal kingdoms corresponds to the divisions among human beings. Mankind falls into two main groups, Israel and the Gentiles. Within Israel only one group, the priests may approach the altar to offer sacrifice. This matches the law's understanding of sacred space. Outside the camp is the abode of Gentiles and unclean Israelites. Ordinary Israelites dwell inside the camp, but only priests may approach the altar or enter the tabernacle tent.

These distinctions served to remind Israel of her special status as God's chosen people. The food laws not only reminded Israel of her distinctiveness, but they also served to enforce it. Jews faithful to these laws would tend to avoid Gentile company, in case they were offered unclean food to eat (*cf.* Dn. 1:8–16).

God is identified with life and holiness, and uncleanness is associated with death and opposition to God. The food laws symbolize that Israel is God's people, called to enjoy his life, while Gentile idolaters are by and large opposed to him and his people, and face death. The food laws also underline respect for life directly as well as symbolically. Eating meat is described as a concession in Gn. 9:1–4. And it may only be eaten if the blood is drained out first, 'for the life is . . . the blood' (Lv. 17:11). Therefore, consumption of the life liquid is banned. Wanton slaughter of living creatures is also discouraged by the limited number of animals classified as clean. In both ways, these food laws tended to promote respect for life.

III. Clean and unclean in the prophets

The prophets (*e.g.* Is. 6:3–5) focus on the worst types of uncleanness attributable to human sin, not only natural types of uncleanness. Thus Ho. 5:3 accuses Israel of contracting uncleanness (NIV corruption) through unfaithfulness to the Lord, which he calls spiritual harlotry. Ho. 6:7–10 associates uncleanness with murder and infidelity to the covenant. Is. 30:22 and Je. 2:7; 7:30 declare that idolatry defiles the land and the sanctuary.

But it is the priest/prophet Ezekiel, brought up strictly to avoid uncleanness (4:14), who makes most of the concept in his condemnation of Israel. Though he knows the laws on naturally occurring uncleanness (44:25; *cf.* 22:26 alluding to Lv. 10:10–11), he repeatedly focuses on the uncleanness caused by Israel's moral and spiritual apostasy, particularly bloodshed and idolatry, which he terms harlotry (*e.g.* 22:3–4, 11, 27; 33:25–26; 36:17–18).

IV. Clean and unclean in the NT

Like the prophets, the NT writers are most concerned with those sins which cause grave uncleanness, *e.g.* idolatry, sexual immorality and murder. According to Jesus, 'What comes out of a man makes him unclean . . . evil thoughts, sexual immorality, theft, murder, adultery, greed, . . .' (Mk. 7:16, 21–22). Frequently the demons cast out by Jesus are termed 'unclean spirits' (*e.g.* Mk. 1:23, 26–27). The essence of uncleanness is opposition to God. In the epistles, uncleanness is sometimes sandwiched between sexual immorality and greed, which is idolatry (*e.g.* Eph. 5:3; Col. 3:5), again reflecting the OT. However, as in the prophets, Mk. 7:21 and Mt. 15:19, uncleanness is most often associated with sexual sin (*e.g.* Rom. 1:24; Gal. 5:19; 1 Thes. 4:7), so that impurity is virtually identified with misuse of sex.

In these respects the NT teaching fully underlines the OT view of uncleanness, but in one important respect it transforms it. The natural types of uncleanness are either healed by Jesus or abolished by him. Thus he touches lepers, a woman suffering from a flow of blood, and even corpses, healing the former and bringing the dead back to life (*e.g.* Mk. 1:40–41; 5:21–43). The OT rarely offered healing for the unclean (*e.g.* 2 Ki. 5:14). But, in Christ, God drew near to the sufferers and healed them personally. His life-giving character is thus displayed even more vividly in the life of Jesus than in the OT era.

The OT food laws reminded the Jews of their special status as the one people chosen by God. The clean (edible) creatures symbolized Israel, whereas the unclean (prohibited) foods symbolized the Gentile nations. But the church is open to people of all nations, not just Jews, so it is inappropriate for the food laws to be maintained. In Mt. 15:16–17 and Mk. 7:18–19, Jesus' critique of the food laws is immediately followed by the story of the Syro-Phoenician woman (describing herself as a dog, *i.e.* unclean), whose daughter, possessed by an unclean spirit, was healed by Jesus (Mt. 15:21–28; Mk. 7:24–30).

Jesus' ministry and teaching thus laid the foundation for outreach to the Gentiles and the abolition of the food laws, but in Acts 10 the decisive step is taken. Peter has a vision in which a heavenly voice commands him to kill and eat unclean animals. He responds: 'Surely not, Lord! I have never eaten anything impure or unclean.' Men sent by Cornelius, a Roman centurion, come asking for Peter to visit him. When he arrives at the house of Cornelius, Peter explains why he has come: 'It is against our law for a Jew to associate with a Gentile or visit him. But God has shown me that I should not call any man impure or unclean' (Acts 10:14, 28). The significance of this Cornelius episode is underlined by Luke recounting it three times in Acts 10, 11 and 15. The Jerusalem council confirmed that it was right to include Gentiles within the church and simultaneously to abrogate the main food laws. The only uncleanness regulations they imposed concerned idolatry, sexual immorality and blood, which were the worst types of uncleanness in the OT (Acts 15:20). Paul takes it for granted that the other food laws no longer apply to Christians (*e.g.* 1 Cor. 8:8; 1 Tim. 4:3–5).

BIBLIOGRAPHY. M. Douglas, *Purity and Danger*, 1966; *idem. Implicit Meanings*, 1975; G. J. Wenham, *The Book of Leviticus*, 1979; P. P. Jenson, *Graded Holiness*, 1992; W. Houston, *Purity and Monotheism*, 1993; D. P. Wright, 'Unclean and Clean (OT)', *ABD* 6, pp. 729–41. G.J.W.

CLEMENT. A Philippian Christian mentioned in Phil. 4:3. It is uncertain whether the reference means that the 'true yokefellow' addressed by Paul is asked to assist Clement as well as Euodia and Syntyche; or that Clement as well as Euodia and Syntyche laboured with Paul in the work of the gospel. AV appears to adopt the former interpretation and RSV the latter. Some of the early Fathers identified him with Clement, the bishop of Rome at the close of the 1st century; but as the date of Clement of Rome's death is uncertain, and the name was a common one, this also must be regarded as uncertain. R.V.G.T.

CLEOPAS (a contracted form of *Cleopatros*). One of the two disciples accosted by the risen Jesus on the afternoon of the first Easter Day as they were returning to their home at Emmaus (Lk. 24:18). (*CLOPAS.) R.V.G.T.

CLOPAS ('Cleophas', AV) is mentioned in Jn. 19:25, where one of the women who stood near the cross is said to have been Mary *hē tou Klōpa*, an expression which could mean daughter, wife or mother of Clopas. The view that Clopas was the father of the apostle described in the lists of the apostles as 'James, the son of Alphaeus' rests on the assumption that Clopas and Alphaeus are renderings of the same Hebrew word—pronounced differently. In the early Latin and Syriac versions the Cleopas of Lk. 24:18 was confused with the Clopas of Jn. 19:25, but it is probable that they were two different people with two distinct names, as *eo* was usually contracted into *ou* and not into *ō*. R.V.G.T.

CLOUD. The regularity of the seasons in the Mediterranean area gives climatic significance to the appearance of clouds. But apart from the direction of wind influencing the weather and the colour of the evening sky, there is little evidence that the Hebrews understood the meteorological signs.

Clouds were well recognized as an indication of moisture. During the rainy season in the winter half-year, air-streams bringing rainfall are associated with cumulus clouds rising from the Mediterranean sea—'a cloud rising in the west' (Lk. 12:54). Hence Elijah's servant looked seawards for the first indication that the spell of drought was to be broken (1 Ki. 18:44). Towards the end of the rainy season in April–May 'clouds that bring the spring rain' (Pr. 16:15) describe the king's favour, since they provide the necessary moisture to swell the ripening ears of grain. Contrasted are the high cirrus rainless clouds (Jude 12), which draw in desert air from the SE and E, called Sirocco or Khamsīn, in association with depressions. The clouds and wind without rain (Pr. 25:14), the 'heat by the shade of a cloud' (Is. 25:5) and subsequently the 'sky of brass' (Dt. 28:23) vividly describe these dust-storms.

Clouds brought by sea-breezes readily dissolve as the hot, dry air of the interior is encountered. Thus the 'morning cloud' (Ho. 6:4) is symbolic of transitory things, of human prosperity (Jb. 30:15) and of human life (Jb. 7:9). It is also a text on the reality of divine forgiveness (Is. 44:22).

The usual luminosity of the Palestinian sky emphasizes that clouds cover and obscure (Ezk 32:7), and the joy of 'a cloudless morning' (2 Sa. 23:4) is vividly described. Like the cloud which hides the sun, divine favour or a supplication may be intercepted (La. 2:1; 3:44). Job prays that clouds may cover up the day of his birth (Jb. 3:5).

The cloud frequently means the whole circle of the sky; *cf.* 'the bow in the clouds' (Gn. 9:14). It represents the sphere of partial knowledge and hidden glory where God has a mysterious purpose in their motions (Jb. 36:29; 37:16; 38:37; Ps. 78:23). Thus too a cloud closes the scene of the incarnation (Acts 1:9), the transfiguration (Mt. 17:5; Mk. 9:7; Lk. 9:34), and clouds herald the second advent (Rev. 1:7). To the Israelites the cloud of God's presence was intimately related to their religious symbolism (Ex. 13:21; 40:34; 1 Ki. 8:10).

The clouds of Mk. 14:62, *etc.*, may refer to the ascension rather than the parousia. J.M.H.

CNIDUS. A city of Caria in SW Asia Minor, where Paul's ship changed course on its way to Rome (Acts 27:7). Cnidus had Jewish inhabitants as early as the 2nd century BC (1 Macc. 15:23), and had the status of free city. J.D.D.

COAL. In the OT (*MT*) there are 5 Heb. words rendered 'coal'. **1.** *gaḥeleṯ* (*e.g.* Pr. 26:21) means burning, as opposed to unlit, fuel; it is metaphorically employed in 2 Sa. 14:7; 22:9, 13. **2.** *peḥām* (*e.g.* Pr. 26:21; Is. 44:12) is used indifferently of unlit and burning fuel. **3.** *riṣpâ* (*e.g.* Is. 6:6; 1 Ki. 19:6) means a flat stone girdle (*cf.* Arab. *radf*, *radafa*). **4.** *rešep̄* (*e.g.* Ct. 8:6) means 'burning coals'; it should perhaps be rendered 'fiery pestilence' in Hab. 3:5. **5.** *šᵉḥôr* (*e.g.* La. 4:8) is literally 'blackness'.

In the NT the Gk. word *anthrax*, 'coal', occurs once (Rom. 12:20) as a metaphor for feelings of shame, but elsewhere *anthrakia*, 'a heap of burning *fuel', is used. R.J.W.

COELESYRIA (Gk. *koilē syria*, 'hollow Syria'), 1 Esdras 2:17, *etc.*; 2 Macc. 3:5, *etc.*, the valley lying between the Lebanon and Antilebanon ranges, modern El-Biqa‘ (*cf. biq‘at ’āwen*, ‘the Valley of Aven’, Am. 1:5). As a political region under the Ptolemaic and Seleucid empires it frequently embraces a wider area, sometimes stretching to Damascus in the N and including Phoenicia to the W or Judaea to the S. From 312 to 198 BC it formed part of the Ptolemaic empire, but fell to the Seleucids in consequence of the battle of Panion in the latter year. Coelesyria was an administrative division of the province of Syria after the Roman occupation (64 BC). Herod was appointed military prefect of Coelesyria by Sextus Caesar in 47 BC and again by Cassius in 43 BC. F.F.B.

COLLECTION (PAULINE CHURCHES). The collection (Gk. *logeia*) which Paul organized in his Gentile churches for the relief of the poverty of the Jerusalem church. In the 2 years preceding his last visit to Jerusalem (AD 57) it engaged his attention increasingly; it would, indeed, be difficult to exaggerate the important part which it played in his apostolic strategy.

I. Background

At the conference in Jerusalem (*c.* AD 46) at which it was agreed that he and Barnabas should continue to prosecute the work of Gentile evangelization, while the leaders of the Jerusalem church would concentrate on the Jewish mission (Gal. 2:1–10), the Jerusalem leaders added a special request that Barnabas and Paul should continue to remember ‘the poor’—a request which is best understood against the background of the famine relief which the church of Antioch had sent to the Jerusalem believers by the hand of Barnabas and Paul (Acts 11:30). In reporting this request Paul adds that this was a matter to which he himself paid special attention. It was in his mind throughout his evangelization of the provinces to E and W of the Aegean, and in the closing years of that period he applied himself energetically to the organizing of a relief fund for Jerusalem in the churches of Galatia, Asia, Macedonia and Achaia.

II. Evidence from Corinthian correspondence

We first learn about this fund from the instructions given to the Corinthian Christians in 1 Cor. 16:1–4; they had been told about it and wanted to know more. From what he says to them we learn that he had already given similar instructions to the churches of Galatia—presumably in the late summer of AD 52, when he passed through ‘the Galatic region and Phrygia’ on his way from Judaea and Syria to Ephesus (Acts 18:22f.). Thanks to Paul’s Corinthian correspondence, more details are known about the organizing of the fund in Corinth than in any of the other contributing churches.

If Paul’s instructions to his converts in Corinth had been carried out, then each householder among them would have set aside a proportion of his income week by week for some 12 months, so that the church’s contribution would have been ready to be taken to Jerusalem in the spring of the following year by the delegates appointed by the church for that purpose. The tension which developed soon afterwards between many of the Corinthian Christians and Paul perhaps occasioned a falling off in their enthusiasm for this good cause. Next time Paul wrote to them about it (in the aftermath of the reconciliation resulting from the severe letter which he sent to them by Titus) he expressed the assumption that they had been setting money aside for the fund systematically ever since they received his instructions, and told them how he had been holding up their promptness as an example to the Macedonian churches. But when one reads between the lines, it is plain that he had private misgivings on this score; hence he sent Titus back to Corinth with two companions to help the church to complete the gathering together of its contributions (2 Cor. 8:16–24). Some members of the church probably felt this was a subtle way of putting irresistible pressure on them: he was ‘crafty’, they said, and got the better of them ‘by guile’ (2 Cor. 12:16).

At the time when Paul sent Titus and his companions to Corinth to see about this matter, he himself was in Macedonia, helping the churches of that province to complete their share in it. Those churches had been passing through a period of unspecified trouble as a result of which they were living at bare subsistence level, if that; and Paul felt that he could hardly ask them to contribute to the relief of fellow-Christians who were no worse off than themselves. But they insisted on making a contribution, and Paul was greatly moved by this token of divine grace in their lives (2 Cor. 8:1–5). He pays them a warm tribute in writing to the Corinthians in order to encourage the latter to give as generously from their comparative affluence as the Macedonians gave from their destitution.

III. Evidence from Roman correspondence

Paul makes one further reference to this relief fund in his extant letters, and this reference is particularly informative, because it comes in a letter to a church which was not of Paul’s planting and which therefore was not involved in the scheme and indeed had no prior knowledge of it. Writing to the Roman Christians to prepare them for his intended visit to their city on the way to Spain, he tells them that the business of this relief fund must be completed before he can set out on his W journey (Rom. 15:25–28). From this reference we acquire some further insight into the motives behind the collection. The strengthening of fellowship between the church of Jerusalem and the Gentile mission was a major concern of Paul’s, and his organization of the relief fund was in large measure designed to promote this end. He knew that many members of the Jerusalem church looked with great suspicion on the independent direction taken by his Gentile mission: indeed, his mission-field was repeatedly invaded by men from Judaea who tried in one way or another to undermine his authority and impose the authority of Jerusalem. But in denouncing them Paul was careful not to give the impression that he was criticizing the church of Jerusalem or its leaders. On the other hand, many of his Gentile converts would be impatient of the idea that they were in any way indebted to the church of Jerusalem. Paul was anxious that they should recognize their substantial indebtedness to Jerusalem. He himself had never been a member of the Jerusalem church and denied emphatically that he derived his gospel or his commission from that church; yet in his eyes that church, as the mother-church of the people of God, occupied a unique place in the Christian order. If he himself were cut off from fellowship with the Jerusalem church, his apostolic activity, he felt, would be futile.

What could be better calculated to allay the suspicions entertained in the Jerusalem church about Paul and his Gentile mission than the manifest evidence of God's blessing on that mission with which Paul planned to confront the Jerusalem believers—not only the monetary gift which would betoken the Gentile churches' practical interest in Jerusalem but living representatives of those churches, deputed to convey their contributions? Writing to his friends in Corinth Paul holds out to them the prospect that their Jerusalem fellow-Christians will be moved to a deep feeling of brotherly affection for them 'because of the surpassing grace of God in you' (2 Cor. 9:14). That all suspicions would in fact be allayed was not a foregone conclusion—Paul asks the Roman Christians to join him in prayers that his 'service for Jerusalem may be acceptable to the saints' there (Rom. 15:31)—but if this would not allay them, nothing would.

Paul may have envisaged this appearance of Gentile believers with their gifts in Jerusalem as at least a token fulfilment of those Hebrew prophecies which spoke of the 'wealth of the nations' as coming to Jerusalem and of the brethren of its citizens as being brought 'from all the nations as an offering to the Lord' on his 'holy mountain' (Is. 60:5; 66:20). But if Paul had those prophecies in mind, perhaps the Jerusalem leaders had them in mind also, and drew different conclusions from them. In the original context, the wealth of the nations is a tribute which the Gentiles bring to Jerusalem in acknowledgment of her supremacy. In Paul's eyes the contributions made by his converts to the Jerusalem relief fund constituted a voluntary gift, an expression of Christian grace and gratitude, but it is conceivable that the recipients looked on them rather as a tribute due from the Gentile subjects of the Son of David.

Even the 'unbelievers in Judea', from whom Paul expected some opposition (Rom. 15:31), might nevertheless be impressed by the visible testimony of so many representative believers from the Gentile lands in their midst. We know that at the very time when Paul was preparing to sail for Judaea with his converts and their gifts, he was pondering the relation, in the divine programme, between his Gentile mission and the ultimate salvation of Israel: this also is a subject on which he lays bare his thought in his letter to the Romans. In this letter, indeed, he sets the collection for Jerusalem, with the problem of Jerusalem itself, in the context to which, in his judgment, they properly belong—the context of God's saving purpose for all mankind.

IV. Reticence of Acts

The delegates of the contributing churches probably included all those fellow-voyagers with Paul from Corinth or Philippi to Judaea who are named in Acts 20:4: Sopater of Beroea, Aristarchus and Secundus from Thessalonica, Gaius of Derbe and Timothy (originally from Lystra), and Tychicus and Trophimus from the province of Asia (the latter of whom we know from Acts 21:29 to have been a Gentile Christian from Ephesus). It would be unwise to attach sinister importance to the absence of a Corinthian name from Luke's list. The list may not be exhaustive; it may be confined to those who had travelled to Corinth from other places to join Paul. Paul had been spending several weeks with Gaius, his host, and other Corinthian friends; moreover, he had just told the Roman Christians how Macedonia and Achaia had resolved to contribute to the Jerusalem relief fund. Achaia, for Paul, meant Corinth and the places around it, and there is no breath of a suggestion in his letter to the Romans that 'Achaia' had not carried out its resolve. We should, indeed, consider the possibility that (in spite of some grumblings over Paul's 'craftiness' in sending Titus to help with the organizing of their contribution) the Corinthian church asked Titus to convey their gift to Jerusalem; if so, the omission of the name of Titus here is of a piece with its omission throughout the whole narrative of Acts. No delegate from the church of Philippi is listed; the narrator himself may have served in that capacity.

When Paul and his companions reached Jerusalem, they were received by James and the other elders of the mother-church, who welcomed them and presumably accepted gratefully the gifts which they brought. The saving adverb 'presumably' is necessary because the record of Acts is completely silent about the collection, except where Paul says, in his defence before Felix, that he had come to Jerusalem 'to bring to my nation alms and offerings' (Acts 24:17).

Luke's almost total silence on the subject may have been apologetically motivated. Apart from the insistence that no evidence was forthcoming to substantiate the allegation that he had violated the sanctity of the Temple, the contents of Paul's defence before Felix would have a greater relevance to his later appearance before the emperor's tribunal in Rome than to his appearance before the procurator of Judaea, and this might well be true of the allusion to 'alms and offerings'. If it can no longer be held that Acts was written to brief counsel for Paul's defence before Caesar, or otherwise to serve as a document in the case, the possibility remains that some material of this kind was used by Luke as source-material. The charge, expressed or implied, that Paul had diverted to a sectarian interest money which ought to have gone to the maintenance of the Temple or to the relief of the Judaeans as a whole, like the charge that, as 'a ringleader of the Nazarenes', he was stirring up subversion in Jewish communities throughout the Roman world, would have been more relevant to a trial before Caesar than to a case falling within the jurisdiction of Felix. A misrepresentation of the nature and purpose of the collection was probably included in the indictment prepared by Paul's prosecutors against the time when his appeal to Caesar came up for hearing; if so, this could account for Luke's reticence.

BIBLIOGRAPHY. C. H. Buck, 'The Collection for the Saints', *HTR* 43, 1950, pp. 1ff.; D. Georgi, *Die Geschichte der Kollekte des Paulus für Jerusalem*, 1965; K. Holl, 'Der Kirchenbegriff des Paulus in seinem Verhältnis zu dem der Urgemeinde', *Gesammelte Aufsätze zur Kirchengeschichte* 2, 1928, pp. 44ff.; A. J. Mattill, 'The Purpose of Acts: Schneckenburger Reconsidered', in *Apostolic History and the Gospel*, ed. W. W. Gasque and R. P. Martin, 1970, pp. 108ff.; K. F. Nickle, *The Collection: A Study in Paul's Strategy*, 1966. F.F.B.

COLONY. A corporation of Roman citizens settled in foreign parts and enjoying local self-government. The objective was sometimes strategic, more often the rehabilitation of veterans or the unemployed, probably never economic or cultural romanization. In the E colonies were rare, and often composed of Gk.-speaking citizens in any case. The practice even grew up of conferring colonial status on Gk. republics for honorific reasons. The self-conscious Romanism at Philippi (Acts 16:12) was probably therefore exceptional, and none of the other colonies mentioned in the NT is noticed as such (Corinth, Syracuse, Troas, Pisidian Antioch, Lystra, Ptolemais and possibly Iconium). Prominent in the affairs of most foreign states, however, was an association (*conventus*) of resident Roman citizens. The 'visitors from Rome' at Jerusalem (Acts 2:10) are an example of this.

BIBLIOGRAPHY. A. H. M. Jones, *The Greek City from Alexander to Justinian*, 1940, pp. 61–84; A. N. Sherwin-White, *The Roman Citizenship*², 1973; B. Levick, *Roman Colonies in Southern Asia Minor*, 1967; *BA1CS* 2. E.A.J.

COLOSSAE. A city in the Roman province of Asia, in the W of what is now Asiatic Turkey. It was situated about 15 km up the Lycus valley from *Laodicea, on the main road to the E. It was originally the point at which the great routes from Sardis and Ephesus joined, and at a defensible place with an abundant water-supply. It was an important city in the Lydian and Persian periods, but later it declined when the road through Sardis to Pergamum was resited farther W at the prosperous new foundation of Laodicea. The site is now uninhabited; it lies near Honaz, 16 km E of the town of Denizli.

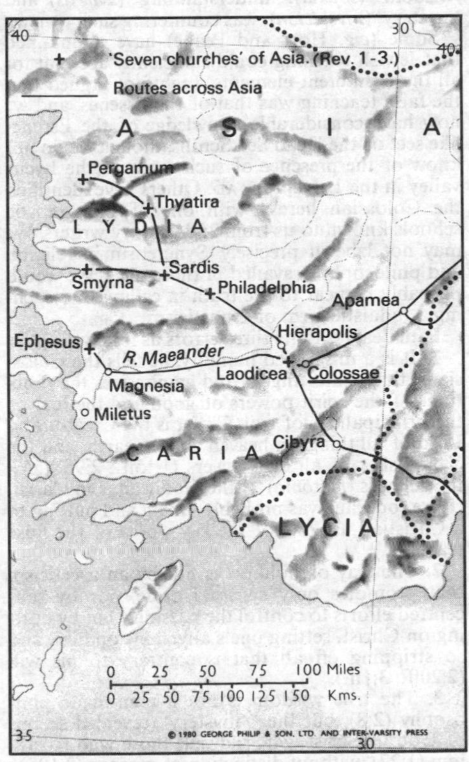

The location of Colossae.

The gospel probably reached the district while Paul was living at Ephesus (Acts 19:10), perhaps through Epaphras, who was a Colossian (Col. 1:7; 4:12–13). Paul had apparently not visited Colossae when he wrote his letter (Col. 2:1), though his desire to do so (Phm. 22) may have been met at a later date. Philemon (Phm. 1) and his slave Onesimus (Col. 4:9; Phm. 10) were members of the early Colossian church. The mixture of Jewish, Greek and Phrygian elements in the population of the city was probably found also in the church: it would have been fertile ground for the type of speculative heresy which Paul's letter was designed to counter.

The neighbourhood was devastated by an earthquake, dated by Tacitus (*Ann*. 14. 27) to AD 60. There is no hint of this in the Epistle, which we must suppose was written before news of the disaster had reached Rome. E.M.B.G.
C.J.H.

COLOSSIANS, EPISTLE TO THE.

I. Outline of contents

a. 1:1–2. Address.

b. 1:3–8. Thanksgiving for the faith and love of the Colossian Christians, and for the fruit of preaching the gospel among them.

c. 1:9–12. Prayer for their growth in understanding, and consequently in good works.

d. 1:13–23. The glory and greatness of Christ, the Image of God, his Agent in the creation of all things, the Head of the church, the One who by his cross reconciled all things to himself.

e. 1:24–2:3. Paul's labours and sufferings in making known the mystery of Christ, and in seeking to present every man perfect in Christ.

f. 2:4–3:4. The specific warning against false teaching, and the apostle's answer to it.

g. 3:5–17. The sins of the old life to be put off, and the virtues of the new to be put on with Christ.

h. 3:18–4:1. Instructions concerning conduct, to wives and husbands, children and parents, servants and masters.

i. 4:2–6. Exhortation to prayer and wisdom of speech.

j. 4:7–18. Personal messages.

II. Authorship

Doubts about the genuineness of Colossians were expressed first in the 19th century; in particular the Tübingen school rejected the Pauline authorship of this and other letters on the basis of 2nd-century Gnostic ideas supposed to be present in them. More seriously regarded today are arguments based on the vocabulary, style and doctrine of this letter as compared with other Pauline letters, but these are not sufficiently strong to have led many scholars to reject the Pauline authorship. The marked similarity to *Ephesians has led a few to argue for the genuineness of that letter and against that of Colossians (*e.g.* F. C. Synge, *Philippians and Colossians*, 1951), but the evidence has nearly always been taken overwhelmingly to indicate the priority of Colossians. A few scholars, like H. J. Holtzmann and C. Masson, have argued for a more complex relationship between the two letters.

The connection of Colossians with the little letter of *Philemon and the nature of that letter are such that it stands virtually as Paul's 'signature' to Colossians. The letter to Philemon concerns the runaway slave, Onesimus, who was returning to his master; this letter (4:9) says that along with Tychicus this Onesimus was being sent back to Colossae. Archippus is named as of the household of Philemon in that letter (v. 2); in this (4:17) there is a special message for the same man. There are greetings from Epaphras, Mark, Aristarchus, Demas and Luke in Philemon (vv. 23f.); the same people are specially mentioned in this letter (in 4:10–14). It is hard to imagine either or both of these references to particular people as inauthentic and fictitious. The only alternative is to see them as linking together the letters to Philemon and to the Colossians as having the same author and being written at the same time. As C. F. D. Moule puts it (*CGT*, p. 13), 'It seems ... impossible to doubt that Philemon was written by St Paul, or to doubt the close connection between Philemon and Colossians.'

III. Destination of the Epistle

*Colossae was a city of Phrygia in the Roman province of Asia, situated, like Hierapolis and Laodicea, in the valley of the river Lycus. Its former importance was diminished by NT times, and was further reduced by a disastrous earthquake in the year AD 60. Paul did not found the church there, nor had he visited it when he wrote this letter (1:4, 7–9; 2:1). On his second missionary journey he passed to the N of the Lycus valley (Acts 16:6–8). On his third missionary journey Ephesus was for 3 years the centre of his labours (Acts 19:1–20; 20:31), and it is most likely that at this time the gospel reached Colossae through the agency of the Colossian Epaphras (1:7; 4:12). Most of the Christians there were Gentiles (1:27; 2:13), but from the time of Antiochus the Great there had been considerable and influential settlements of Jews in the neighbourhood.

IV. Time and place of writing

That Colossians was written from prison is clear from the words of 4:3, 10 and 18. Serious consideration has been given to three places as possible sites of Paul's imprisonment when the letter was penned. **1.** Ephesus. The most specific argument in favour of this is the statement of the 2nd-century Marcionite prologue to Colossians. If, however, Colossians and *Ephesians were written at the same time (as indicated by 4:7f. and Eph. 6:21f.), this possibility is ruled out decisively. **2.** Caesarea. A number of arguments have been given in favour of Caesarea. Bo Reicke argues this way on the basis of the destructive earthquake referred to above, but the beginning of Paul's Roman imprisonment was probably earlier than the year that the earthquake took its toll in the Lycus valley. It is not likely that all of those named in ch. 4 were with the apostle when he was in prison in Caesarea. **3.** Rome. There is no difficulty urged against the Roman origin of the letter that has not been adequately met. There is no place more likely than Rome to which the fugitive Onesimus would go, and the contents and personal references of the letter would seem to be more suited to Paul's Roman imprisonment than to any other. A date of AD 60 thus seems likely.

V. Reason for the Epistle

Two matters brought the church in Colossae especially before Paul and occasioned the writing of this letter. First, he was writing to Philemon in Colossae sending back his runaway, but now converted, slave, Onesimus (Phm. 7–21). He could also take the opportunity of writing to the whole Colossian church. Secondly, Epaphras had brought to Paul a report of that church, which included many encouraging things (1:4–8), but apparently also disquieting news of the false teaching that threatened to lead its members away from the truth of Christ. This news pressed the apostle to write as he did.

VI. The false teaching

In his characteristic manner Paul meets the challenge confronting the Colossian church by positive teaching rather than point-by-point refutation. Thus we do not know fully what it involved, but we may infer three things:

1. It gave an important place to the powers of the spirit world to the detriment of the place given to Christ. In 2:18 he speaks of 'worship of angels', and other references to the relation of the spiritual creation to Christ (1:16, 20; 2:15) appear to have similar significance.

2. Great importance was attached to outward observances, such as feasts and fasts, new moons and sabbaths (2:16f.), and probably also circumcision (2:11). These were presented proudly as the true way of self-discipline and the subjection of the flesh (2:20ff.).

3. The teachers boasted that they possessed a higher philosophy. This is clear from 2:4, 8, 18; and we may assume also that Paul, in his frequent use of the terms 'knowledge' (*gnōsis* and *epignōsis*), 'wisdom' (*sophia*), 'understanding' (*synesis*) and 'mystery' (*mystērion*), was countering such a view.

Some (*e.g.* Hort and Peake) have maintained that Jewish teaching could sufficiently account for all these different elements. Lightfoot argued that the false teaching was that of the Essenes, and we now have considerable knowledge of the Essene-like sect of the Dead Sea Scrolls, though we do not know of the presence of such a sect in the Lycus valley in the 1st century AD. Others have identified the Colossian heresy with one of the Gnostic schools known to us from 2nd-century writers. We may not label it precisely. Syncretism in religion and philosophy prevailed in those days. We would probably be near to the truth in calling the teaching a Judaistic form of Gnosticism.

Paul deals with its three errors as follows:

1. It is a misguided humility, he tells the Colossians, that exalts angels, and emphasizes the functions of the spirit powers of good and the fear of the principalities of evil. Christ is the Creator and Lord of all things in heaven and on earth, and the Vanquisher of all evil powers (1:15ff.; 2:9ff.). All the fullness (*plērōma*) of the Godhead is in Christ. (Here too Paul was probably taking and putting to a Christian use one of the key words of the false teaching.)

2. The way of holiness is not by an asceticism that promotes only spiritual pride, nor by self-centred efforts to control the passions, but by putting on Christ, setting one's affections on him, and so stripping off all that is contrary to his will (2:20ff.; 3:1ff.).

3. The true wisdom is not a man-made philosophy (2:8), but the *'mystery' (revealed secret) of God in Christ, who indwells those who receive him (1:27), without distinction of persons (3:10f.).

BIBLIOGRAPHY. J. B. Lightfoot, *Saint Paul's*

Epistles to the Colossians and to Philemon, 1875; C. F. D. Moule, *The Epistles of Paul the Apostle to the Colossians and to Philemon*, *CGT*, 1957; R. P. Martin, *Colossians and Philemon*, *NCB*², 1982; E. Schweizer, *The Letter to the Colossians*, E.T. 1982; P. T. O'Brien, *Colossians, Philemon*, *WBC*, 1982; F. F. Bruce, *The Epistles to the Colossians, to Philemon, and to the Ephesians*, *NIC*, 1984; N. T. Wright, *Colossians and Philemon*, *TNTC*, 1986.

F.F.

COLOURS. Colour-adjectives appear but sparsely in OT and NT alike, for a variety of reasons. The first reason is specific: the Bible, being the account of God's dealings with a nation, and not the subjective record of a nation's aesthetic experience, is sparing in descriptive writing of the kind that involves extensive and precise use of adjectives of colour. Even where nature, animate or inanimate, is described in the OT (as frequently in the Pentateuch, Job and Pss.), it is in its more awe-inspiring aspects, as fitting reflection of its Creator.

The second reason is more general and linguistic: biblical Hebrew did not possess a complex and highly-developed colour vocabulary, such as exists in most modern Indo-European languages today. Thus, close definition of colour would have been difficult if not impossible, unless by the use of simile or metaphor. But this reason, which seems at first sight to be purely linguistic, turns out to be psychological, after all; for it is an axiom of linguistics that any culture, no matter how primitive, develops that vocabulary which is perfectly adequate to express its thought and desires. This linguistic paucity, then, corresponds to a lack of interest in colour as an aesthetic experience on the part of the Hebrew people; their practical concern was more with the nature of the material of which the article was made, by virtue of which it was a particular colour. Indeed, many of their colour-words were descriptive of origin rather than shade; *'argāmān*, for instance, generally translated 'purple' (*e.g.* Ex. 25:4), is reddish-purple cloth, usually woollen. It is a borrowed word, and probably means 'tribute'. Other similar words (*šānî*, *karmîl*, *tôlā'*) either contain a reference to the *murex*, the shellfish from whose juice the costly dye was obtained, or to the cochineal insect or shield-louse, which yielded a rich red. In consequence, one clothed in purple is not to the Hebrew primarily a beautiful object. He is a king, or wealthy man; just as one in sackcloth is not primarily an ugly object, but a beggar or a mourner. This approach makes easy the symbolic use of colour, which appears spasmodically in the OT and fully developed in the Apocalypse. However, even the RSV appears to have itself used 'crimson' and 'scarlet' quite indiscriminately, so little stress should be laid on the exact colour. *šāšar*, 'vermilion' (Je. 22:14 and Ezk. 23:14) is an exception. It was a lead or iron oxide, yielding a bright red pigment suitable for wall-painting, not for the dyeing of clothing.

The NT writers were, of course, fully equipped with the extensive and flexible Gk. colour-vocabulary; but they were, by virtue of their subject, concerned with colour as such even less than the writers of the OT. In any case, fixity of shade, and therefore exact precision of terminology, had to wait until the advent of purely chemical dyes, which are easier to control, and the consequent development of colour-charts. In common with other ancient peoples, the Greeks were much more impressed by the contrast between light and shade than that between different colours. In other words, they tended to see and describe all colours as graduations between black and white. To compensate, they had a remarkably rich vocabulary to describe degrees of refracted light. When this is realized, many imagined Bible problems disappear; the fields of Jn. 4:35, are not 'already white for harvest' but 'gleaming'; Ex. 25:4 groups 'blue and purple and scarlet' together, not only as all alike being symbols of richness, but because to the writer they were akin, perhaps scarcely differentiated, as being 'dark', not 'light', colours, similarly produced, and all alike being colours of textiles, *i.e.* artefacts and not natural objects. For Joseph's coat, see *JOSEPH.

BIBLIOGRAPHY. F. E. Wallace, *Colour in Homer and in Ancient Art*, 1927; A. E. Kober, *The Use of Color Terms in the Greek Poets*, 1932; I. Meyerson (ed.), *Problèmes de la Couleur*, 1957; G. T. D. Angel, *NIDNTT* 1, pp. 203–206; and see Index in *NIDNTT* 3.

A.C.

COMMUNION. In the NT the basic term, translated variously as 'communion', 'fellowship', 'communicate', 'partake', 'contribution', 'common' (in the sense of the Latin *communis*), stems from the Greek root *koin-*. There are two adjectives, *koinōnos* (found 10 times) and *synkoinōnos* (found 4 times), which are used as nouns also; and two verbs *koinōneō* (8 times) and *synkoinōneō* (3 times); and the noun *koinōnia* (20 times).

The fundamental connotation of the root *koin*-is that of sharing in something (genitive) with someone (dative); or the simple cases may be replaced by a prepositional phrase. In both constructions nouns may be replaced by prepositions. Very rarely it may mean 'to give a share in' something; the most characteristic NT usage is that which employs *koin-* with the genitive of the thing (or person) shared. There is also another NT use in which the term is found actively of a 'willingness to give a share'; hence the meaning 'generosity'. A third meaning emerges from the first use, with the sense of 'sharing' or 'fellowship' (which arises out of a common sharing of something). The results of the recent linguistic researches of such scholars as H. Seesemann and A. R. George may be stated in the latter's words: 'The important thing is that these words (belonging to the *koin-* family) refer primarily, though not invariably, to participation in something rather than to association with others: and there is often a genitive to indicate that in which one participates or shares' (A. R. George, *Communion with God in the New Testament*, p. 133). From this ground-plan of the word, the NT passages may be divided into three classes, according to whether the predominant idea is (*a*) having a share; (*b*) giving a share; or (*c*) sharing.

a. 'Having a share'

Under this heading we may classify, first of all, the adjectives which are used to describe partners in some common enterprise, *e.g.* Christian work (2 Cor. 8:23), or secular business (Lk. 5:10); also those who share in a common experience (*e.g.* persecution, Heb. 10:33; Rev. 1:9; suffering, 2 Cor. 1:7; worship, 1 Cor. 10:18; murder, Mt. 23:30; the compact with demons in pagan cult worship, 1 Cor. 10:20). Then it is used similarly of those who enjoy certain privileges in common, *e.g.* Rom. 11:17; 1 Cor. 9:23. References to a common sharing in direct spiritual realities are Phil. 1:7; 1 Pet. 5:1; and 2 Pet. 1:4, although in the first text the 'grace' in question may be that of apostleship in which both the apostle and church share, and of which Paul writes in Rom. 1:5; Eph. 3:2, 8.

The verb *koinōneō* and its cognate form, which adds the prefix *syn* meaning 'together with', occur in 11 passages in the NT; but some of these will fall more naturally under section *b*, *i.e.* they will lend themselves best to the translation 'generosity'. But under this heading we may note Rom. 15:27; Eph. 5:11; 1 Tim. 5:22; 2 Jn. 11; Rev. 18:4; Phil. 4:14; Heb. 2:14.

The noun is found to denote the corporate Christian life with the thought that believers share together in certain objective realities (*cf.* E. Lohmeyer, *Der Brief an die Philipper*, 1956, p. 17, who denies that it is ever found in Paul's writing in the sense of a bond joining Christians together, but always with the meaning of participation in an object outside the believer's subjective experience). These references are most notably: **1.** 1 Cor. 10:16 ('participation in the blood and body of Christ'); **2.** 1 Cor. 1:9, where Anderson Scott's view aims at seeing *koinōnia* as a designation of the church; but his interpretation here and elsewhere is being increasingly abandoned in favour of the objective sense of the genitive (or, with Deissmann, the 'mystical genitive' or 'genitive of fellowship'). So the best translation of a difficult verse is 'fellowship with his Son, Jesus Christ our Lord' whether in the sense of 'sharing in' or 'sharing with' him; **3.** Phil. 2:1, where the issue is to decide between a subjective genitive ('any fellowship wrought by the Spirit': so Anderson Scott, *Christianity According to St Paul*, 1927, pp. 160ff.), or an objective genitive ('fellowship with the Spirit', 'participation in the Spirit': so convincingly Seesemann); **4.** 2 Cor. 13:14, where again the choice is between *koinōnia* as fellowship which is created by the Holy Spirit and fellowship as participation in the Holy Spirit, a translation (*cf.* RSVmg.) which is much in favour since Seesemann's discussion in 1933; **5.** 2 Cor. 8:4, 'taking part in the relief of the saints'; and **6.** Phil. 3:10, where the genitive is clearly objective, meaning that Paul's 'own actual sufferings are a real participation in Christ's sufferings, suffered by virtue of his communion with Christ' (A. R. George, *op. cit.*, p. 184; *cf.* R. P. Martin, *Philippians*, *TNTC*, pp. 49–50; and *Philippians*, *NCB*, 1976, pp. 133ff. [biblio.]).

b. 'Giving a share'

The main texts which support the interpretation of *koinōnia* as 'giving a share' are 2 Cor. 9:13, 'the generosity of your contribution for them and for all others'. 'Your contribution' represents the Greek *tēs koinōnias*, for which Seesemann proposes the translation *Mitteilsamkeit*, *i.e.*, in this context, generosity. This same rendering may be suggested also for Phil. 1:5 in which case the object of Paul's gratitude to God is the generosity of the Philippian Christians in their support of the apostolic ministry for the progress of the gospel. Similarly, the same translation clarifies Phm. 6.

Another reference under this heading is Rom. 15:26, which indicates that *koinōnia* can take on a concrete form as a generosity which clothes itself in practical action, and is so applied to the collection for the saints of the Jerusalem church in their poverty-stricken condition (*cf.* 2 Cor. 8:4). In this light we may consider, finally, Acts 2:42, although A. R. George rules out the meaning of 'almsgiving', 'generosity'. Other views which have been offered to explain this reference are an allusion to the *Lord's Supper (*cf.* C. H. Dodd, *The Johannine Epistles*, 1946, p. 7); a technical expression for having a community of goods as in Acts 2:44; 4:32, as C. E. B. Cranfield takes it in *TWBR*, p. 82; Anderson Scott's view that the term *hē koinōnia* = the fellowship) is the translation of a special Heb. word *ḥᵃḇûrâ* meaning a religious society within Judaism; a recent proposal of J. Jeremias that Acts 2:42 lists, in its four notes of the church's corporate life, the liturgical sequence of early Christian worship, in which case *koinōnia* may be an allusion to the offering (*The Eucharistic Words of Jesus*, E.T. 1955, p. 83, n. 3, but in ²E.T. 1966, pp. 118–121 this view is withdrawn); and the view that *koinōnia* describes the inward spiritual bond which joined the early Jerusalem brotherhood and which expresses itself in the outward acts of a pooling of material resources (*cf.* L. S. Thornton, *The Common Life in the Body of Christ*, 1942, p. 451). See, further, R. N. Flew, *Jesus and His Church*², 1943, pp. 109–110.

c. 'Sharing'

Under this heading there are only three possible occurrences where *koinōnia* is used absolutely or with the preposition *meta* (with). These are Acts 2:42; Gal. 2:9 and 1 Jn. 1:3ff.

BIBLIOGRAPHY. The most important treatment of the *koin-* group of words in the NT is that by H. Seesemann, *Der Begriff KOINŌNIA im Neuen Testament*, *ZNW*, Beiheft 14, 1933. His conclusions are utilized by most subsequent writers on this theme, especially A. R. George, *Communion with God in the New Testament*, 1953, who provides a full discussion of most of the controverted passages mentioned above. He gives also a complete bibliography, to which may be added the most recent contribution to the subject, M. McDermott, 'The Biblical Doctrine of KOINONIA', *BZ* 19. 1–2, 1975, pp. 64–77, 219–233. G. F. Hawthorne, *Philippians*, *WBC*, 1983; P. T. O'Brien, *Philippians*, *NIGTC*, 1992. (*LORD'S SUPPER.) R.P.M.

COMPASSION. In the Bible it is a divine as well as a human quality. In RSV the word is often used to translate Heb. *ḥāmal* and *raḥᵃmîm*, which are, however, in AV more frequently rendered by 'pity' or 'spare' and 'mercy' or 'tender mercies' respectively. Thus compassion, pity and mercy can be regarded as synonyms. In the NT the most frequent words are *eleeō* (and cognate forms), translated by 'have compassion', 'have mercy' and 'have pity', and *eleos*, which is always translated 'mercy'. *oikteirō* is found twice and translated 'have compassion' and *oiktirmōn* three times with the meaning 'merciful' and 'of tender mercy'

The prophets and other men of God were deeply aware of the wonder of God's *mercy to sinful men. They taught that anyone who had experienced this would feel it his duty to have compassion on his fellows, especially 'the fatherless, the widow, and the foreigner' (frequently named together as in Dt. 10:18; 14:29; 16:11; 24:19; Je. 22:3, *etc.*) and also on those in *poverty and the afflicted (Ps. 146:9; Jb. 6:14; Pr. 19:17; Zc. 7:9–10; Mi. 6:8). There is no doubt from the frequent references in Deuteronomy that God expected his people to show compassion not only to each other but to foreigners who lived among them. Through the teaching of our Lord Jesus Christ, especially in the parable of the good Samaritan (Lk. 10), it is clear that compassion is to be shown by his disciples to anyone who needs their help. It is to be like his, not only in being without respect of persons, but also in that it is expressed in deeds (1 Jn. 3:17) which may involve personal sacrifice.

J.W.M.

CONCUBINE. The practice of concubinage was widespread in the biblical world. In Mesopotamia the husband was free to have legal sexual relations with slaves. In Assyria the husband was able to take several free-born concubines as well as his 'veiled' wife, although the 'concubine' was subject to the wife's authority. Her sons were entitled to share the inheritance. Concubines who bore children and who behaved arrogantly could be treated as slaves but not sold (*cf. Laws of Hammurapi* 146–147; 170–171). In Cappadocia (19th century BC) and Alalaḫ where a wife failed to produce a son within a specified time (3 or 7 years respectively) the husband was entitled to marry a second wife. In Ugarit a man who possessed a concubine was called a *b'l šślmt*, 'the possessor of a female who completes (the family)'. Sarah provided a slave concubine for Abraham (Gn. 16:2–3) and handmaidens given as a marriage gift to Leah and Rachel became Jacob's concubines (Gn. 29:24, Zilpah; Gn. 29:29, Bilhah). Concubines were protected under Mosaic law (Ex. 21:7–11; Dt. 21:10–14), although they were distinguished from wives (Jdg. 8:31; 2 Sa. 5:13; 1 Ki. 11:3; 2 Ch. 11:21) and were more easily divorced (Gn. 21:10–14). Kings such as Solomon went to excess in a plurality of wives and concubines. To lie with a monarch's concubine was tantamount to usurpation of the throne (2 Sa. 3:7; 16:21–22; 1 Ki. 2:21–24). Two terms are used in the OT, *pîlegeš*, a term of non-Semitic origin, and the Aram. *lᵉḥēnâ* (Dn. 5:2–3, 23), a 'temple servant'. The former term is used in the times of the Patriarchs, the Conquest and the early kingdom, with the most frequent use in the days of the Judges. The practice created tension with wives in all periods and later prophets encouraged monogamy (Mal. 2:14ff.). The ideal woman of Pr. 31 belonged to a monogamous society.

In the NT monogamy was enjoined by Jesus (Mt. 5:32; 19:3–12, *etc.*), and by NT writers (1 Tim. 3:2, 12). The contemporary Greek and Roman world still practised concubinage. Among the Greeks, *pallakai*, 'concubines', were regularly maintained for sexual pleasure and children born from such unions, although free, were bastards. It was the wives (*gynaikes*) who bore legitimate children. In the Roman world the state of *concubinatus*, or 'lying together', involved informal but more or less permanent unions without a marriage ceremony. Children of such unions took the legal status of their mother and were deprived of the status of citizens. Against such a background monogamy was the only form of marriage for Christians. Unmarried men who had a concubine were obliged to marry or be refused baptism; the believing woman could be baptized.

BIBLIOGRAPHY. A. F. Rainey, *EJ*, 5, col. 862f.; R. de Vaux, *Ancient Israel*, 1962, pp. 24–25, 29, 53–54, 83, 86, 115–117.

J.A.T.

CONFESSION. The word to 'confess' in both the Heb. and the Gk. (*yāḏâ* and *homologein*) has, as in English, a twofold reference. There is confession of faith and confession of sin. On the one hand, confession means to declare publicly a personal relationship with and allegiance to God. It is an act of open joyful commitment made to God in the presence of the world, by which a congregation or individuals bind themselves in loyalty to God or Jesus Christ. It is an avowal of faith which can have eternal eschatological consequences. On the other hand, it means to acknowledge sin and guilt in the light of God's revelation, and is thus generally an outward sign of repentance and faith. It may or may not be followed by forgiveness (Jos. 7:19; Lv. 26:40; Ps. 32:5; Mt. 27:4; 1 Jn. 1:9).

The biblical use of the word appears to reflect the language of ancient treaties where a vassal agrees to the terms of the *covenant made by his suzerain, and binds himself by an oath to be loyal. Likewise from the legal context of confession of guilt in a court of law, the term is transferred to the confession of sin to God.

I. In the Old Testament

In the OT confession frequently has the character of praise, where the believer in gratitude declares what God has done redemptively for Israel or his own soul. The noun (*tôḏâ*) may thus mean confession, thanksgiving, praise, or even be used for a company of people singing songs of praise. Such acknowledgment of God's mighty acts of mercy and deliverance is consequently closely related to the confession of sin. Both aspects of confession form an integral part of prayer and true worship (Gn. 32:9–11; 1 Ki. 8:35; 2 Ch. 6:26; Ne. 1:4–11; 9; Jb. 33:26–28; Pss. 22; 32; 51; 116; Dn. 9). Confession can lead the believer to pledge himself anew to God, to sing hymns of praise, to offer joyful sacrifice, and can give him a desire to tell others of God's mercy and to identify himself with the worshipping congregation in the house of God at Jerusalem.

Confession is not only personal and individual; it has a liturgical connotation where, as on the Day of *Atonement in the context of expiation and intercession, the high priest vicariously confesses the sins of the people, laying his hands on the head of a live goat which symbolically carries sin away from the covenant community (Lv. 16:21). In similar fashion Moses vicariously pleads for Israel (Ex. 32:32; *cf.* Ne. 1:6; Jb. 1:5; Dn. 9:4ff.).

Confession in the sense of joyful acknowledgment is prominent in the Qumran texts where frequently the psalms begin, 'I thank thee, Lord, because . . .', in a way similar to our Lord's prayer in Mt. 11:25 (1QH 2. 20, 31, *etc.*).

II. In the New Testament

In the NT the Gk. word to 'confess' has the generic meaning of acknowledging something to be the case in agreement with others; it is primarily used with reference to faith in Christ. It gathers up the OT aspects of thanksgiving and joyful praise, as well as of willing submission, as in Mt. 11:25; Rom. 15:9; Heb. 13:15. In this it follows the LXX usage of the word, as in Pss. 42:6; 43:4–5; Gn. 29:34. It means, however, more than mental assent. It implies a decision to pledge oneself in loyalty to Jesus Christ as Lord in response to the work of the Holy Spirit.

To confess Jesus Christ is to acknowledge him as the Messiah (Mt. 16:16; Mk. 4:29; Jn. 1:41; 9:22), as the Son of God (Mt. 8:29; Jn. 1:34, 49; 1 Jn. 4:15), that he came in the flesh (1 Jn. 4:2; 2 Jn. 7), and that he is Lord, primarily on the ground of the resurrection and ascension (Rom. 10:9; 1 Cor. 12:3; Phil. 2:11).

Confession of Jesus Christ is linked intimately with the confession of sins. To confess Christ is to confess that he 'died for our sins', and conversely to confess one's sins in real repentance is to look to Christ for forgiveness (1 Jn. 1:5–10). In preparation for the coming of Christ, John the Baptist summoned people to confess their sins, and confession was a constant element in the ministry both of our Lord and of the apostles (Mt. 3:6; 6:12; Lk. 5:8; 15:21; 18:13; 19:8; Jn. 20:23; Jas. 5:16).

Although addressed to God, confession of faith in Jesus Christ should be made openly 'before men' (Mt. 10:32; Lk. 12:8; 1 Tim. 6:12), by word of mouth (Rom. 10:9; Phil. 2:11), and may be costly (Mt. 10:32–39; Jn. 9:22; 12:42). It is the opposite of 'denying' the Lord. Confession of sin is likewise primarily addressed to God, but may also be made before men, for example, in corporate confession by a congregation or its representative in public prayer. Where the confession is for the benefit of the church or of others, an individual may openly confess sins in the presence of the church or of other believers (Acts 19:18; Jas. 5:16), but this should never be unedifying (Eph. 5:12). True repentance may require an acknowledgment of guilt to a brother (Mt. 5:23–24), but there is no suggestion that confession of private sin must be made to an individual presbyter.

Confession of Jesus Christ is the work of the Holy Spirit, and as such is the mark of the true church, the Body of Christ (Mt. 10:20; 16:16–19; 1 Cor. 12:3). For this reason it accompanies baptism (Acts 8:37; 10:44–48), out of which practice emerged some of the earliest creeds and confessions of the church, which acquired added significance with the rise of error and false doctrine (1 Jn. 4:2; 2 Jn. 7).

The perfect pattern of confession is given to us in Jesus Christ himself, who witnessed a good confession before Pontius Pilate (1 Tim. 6:12–13). He confessed that he is the Christ (Mk. 14:62) and that he is a King (Jn. 18:36). His confession was before men, over against the false witness of his enemies (Mk. 14:56) and the denial of a disciple (Mk. 14:68), and was infinitely costly, with eternal consequences for all men. The church in her confession identifies herself 'before many witnesses' with the 'good confession' of her crucified and risen Saviour. Her confession (of faith and of sin) is a sign that the old man is 'dead with Christ' and that she is possessed by her Lord, whom she is commissioned to serve. In her confession she is called to participate through the Spirit in the vicarious intercessions of Christ, 'the apostle and high priest of our confession' (Heb. 3:1), who has already confessed our sins on the cross and given praise to God (Heb. 2:12; Rom. 15:9, quoting Pss. 18:49; 22:22).

Confession in the NT (like denial of Christ) has an eschatological perspective, leading to either judgment or salvation, because it is the outward manifestation of faith or lack of it. Christ will one day confess before the Father those who confess him today, and deny those who deny him (Mt. 10:32–33; Lk. 12:8; 2 Tim. 2:11–13). Confession with the mouth is made to salvation (Rom. 10:9–10, 13; 2 Cor. 4:13–14), and our confessions today are a foretaste of the church's confessions of the last day, when every tongue shall confess that Jesus Christ is Lord (Rom. 14:11–12; Phil. 2:11; Rev. 4:11; 5:12; 7:10).

BIBLIOGRAPHY. V. Neufeld, *The Earliest Christian Confessions*, 1963; J. N. D. Kelly, *Early Christian Creeds*³, 1972; H. N. Ridderbos, in R. Banks (ed.), *Reconciliation and Hope*, 1974; O. Michel, *TDNT* 5, pp. 199–220; H. H. Rowden (ed.), *Christ the Lord*, 1982; M. Hengel, *Between Jesus and Paul*, 1983.

J.B.T.

CONFIRMATION. 1. Gk. *bebaiōsis* (Phil. 1:7; Heb. 6:16) is thus rendered, meaning 'a making firm' and 'a valid ratification', respectively. In the OT seven Heb. roots are translated by 'affirm', 'make firm', 'reaffirm', 'confirm' (*e.g.* Is. 35:3; Est. 9:32). In the NT four Gk. verbs are similarly used. 1. *bebaioun*; *e.g.* Rom. 15:8, 'confirm the promises'. 2. *kyroun*, used of a covenant (Gal. 3:15, 'ratified'), and of a personal attitude (2 Cor. 2:8—AV 'confirm your love'; RSV 'reaffirm your love'). 3. *mesiteuein*, *e.g.* Heb. 6:17 (AV 'confirm', RV, RSV 'interpose with an oath') where the meaning is that a promise is guaranteed because God is acting as Mediator. 4. *epistērizein* is Luke's word in Acts for the strengthening effect of an apostolic mission on fellow-Christians (11:2, Western Text), on the souls of the disciples (14:22), on the churches (15:41) and brethren (15:32).

2. The ecclesiastical rite known as 'confirmation', or 'laying on of hands', is not traced to these verses, where Luke speaks only of the consolidating effect on faith of the apostolic presence and preaching, but, presumably, to such passages as Acts 8:14–17; 19:1–6, where laying on of hands precedes a spectacular descent of the Holy Spirit upon previously baptized persons. Two observations may be made. In the first place, in these verses in Acts the gift of the Spirit is associated primarily with baptism, not with a subsequent and separate rite of 'laying on of hands' (*cf.* Heb. 6:2). Secondly, Acts shows no constant sequence. Thus, laying on of hands may precede baptism, and be performed by one not an apostle (9:17ff.); in Acts 6:6; 13:3 it is associated, not with baptism, but with special tasks to be done (*cf.* Nu. 27:18, 20, 23) in connection with the missionary activity of the church.

BIBLIOGRAPHY. G. W. H. Lampe, *The Seal of the Spirit*, 1951; H. Schönweiss *et al.*, *NIDNTT* 1, pp. 658–664; *ISBE* 1, p. 760; for the rite of 'confirmation', see *ODCC*.

M.R.W.F.

CONGREGATION, SOLEMN ASSEMBLY. The noun 'congregation' is used to render several Heb. words, one of which is also translated 'assembly'.

1. *mô'ēḏ* and *'ēḏâ* come from the root *yā'aḏ*, 'to appoint, assign, designate'. *mô'ēḏ* means an appointed time or place, or meeting, and occurs 223 times (*e.g.* Gn. 18:14; Ho. 9:5, 'appointed festival'). In its most frequent use *'ōhel mô'ēḏ* means the 'tent of meeting', AV 'tabernacle of the congregation'—a translation which fails to convey the sense of 'due appointment' (*e.g.* Ex. 27:21). In Is. 14:13 *mô'ēḏ* is used for 'mount of the congregation'. See *BDB*. *'ēḏâ* occurs 149 times (not in Dt.), and means a company of people assembled together by appointment (*e.g.* Ex. 16:1–2, where the congregation of Israel are assembled by God for the purpose of journeying from Egypt to Canaan).

2. *qāhāl* occurs 123 times, and comes from a root meaning 'assemble together', whether for war (*e.g.* 2 Sa. 20:14), rebellion (Nu. 16:3) or a religious purpose (*e.g.* Nu. 10:7). It is used in Dt. 5:22, where all Israel is assembled to hear the words of God, and in Dt. 23:3, where solemn statements of excommunication are being made. On the distinction between *'ēḏâ* and *qāhāl*, see *HDB*, *TWBR* and especially *TDNT* 3, pp. 487–536 (*ekklēsia*). It appears that *'ēḏâ*, the older word, is in frequent use in Ex. and Nu., and bears an almost technical sense of 'those gathered together' (for a specific purpose), but that *qāhāl*, preferred by Deuteronomy and later writers, came to mean 'all Israel gathered together by God as a theocratic state'.

3. The rare word *'ᵃṣeret*, from a root meaning 'restrain' or 'confine', is rendered 'solemn assembly' (*e.g.* Is. 1:13; Ne. 8:18; Am. 5:21) in connection with high festivals, *e.g.* Unleavened Bread, Tabernacles (Dt. 16:8; Lv. 23:36). This word, translated into Gk. as *panēgyris*, lies behind 'festal gathering and assembly' in Heb. 12:23, RSVmg.

4. In the LXX *ekklēsia* was usually employed to translate *qāhāl*, sometimes for *'ēḏâ*, for which *synagōgē* was also used. In the NT *ekklēsia* is normally rendered *'church', though Luke uses it in its classical sense in Acts 19:39, 41 of a summoned political assembly. In Acts 13:43 *synagōgē* is rendered 'congregation' by the AV (RV and RSV correctly 'synagogue'); its use in Jas. 2:2 indicates a Jewish–Christian meeting. Since *synagōgē*, like 'church' in Eng., had come to mean both the gathering and the building, and since the Christians no longer met in synagogues, they chose *ekklēsia* to describe themselves.

BIBLIOGRAPHY. L. Coenen, *NIDNTT* 1, pp. 291–307; G. L. Carey, *ZPEB* 1, pp. 939–941.

M.R.W.F.

CONSCIENCE.

I. Background

The OT has no word for 'conscience', and the Gk. term *syneidēsis* is virtually absent from the LXX. If the concept which it denotes is not to be regarded as an innovation by the NT writers, its origin must therefore be sought in a world of Gk. rather than Heb. ideas. Many scholars opt in fact for a Stoic origin of the term, including C. H. Dodd (*Romans* in *MNTC*, pp. 35–37), C. K. Barrett (*Romans* in *BNTC*, p. 53) and J. Moffatt (on 1 Cor. 8:7ff. in *MNTC*). But C. A. Pierce (*Conscience in the New Testament*, 1955, pp. 13ff.) suggests instead that the background to the word in the NT is to be found in non-philosophical, popular Gk. thought (see also J. Dupont, *Gnosis*, 1949, p. 267). Pierce further believes that the term came into the NT as a result of the troubles at Corinth, in which appeals to 'conscience' were being made in order to justify controversial actions, notably the eating of food offered to idols (Pierce, pp. 60ff.; *cf.* 1 Cor. 8:7–13). This would explain the absence of the term from the OT and Gospels, and its prevalence in Paul—especially in the Corinthian letters.

II. Meaning

The foundation-word of the group to which *syneidēsis* belongs is *synoida*, which occurs rarely in the NT and means 'I know in common with' (Acts 5:2; *cf.* the strict etymology of *conscientia*, the Lat. equivalent of *syneidēsis*), or—as it is used in the particular construction *hautō syneidenai*—something akin to the faculty of 'self-knowledge' (1 Cor. 4:4, which NEB translates as 'I have nothing on my conscience'). The chief meaning of *syneidēsis* in the NT is an extension of this idea, and implies more than simply 'consciousness', since it includes moral judgment on the quality (right or wrong) of a conscious act. To some extent the way for this meaning had already been prepared in Judaism.

In the OT, as in Gk. philosophy, the judgment of actions was normally referred to the state or to the law. But in 1 Sa. 24:5 'heart' (Heb. *lēḇ*), in the phrase 'David's heart smote him', plays the part of conscience, and conforms to the usual meaning of 'conscience' in popular Gk. as the pain suffered by man as man when by his actions begun or completed he 'transgresses the moral limits of his nature' (Pierce, p. 54; the effect of a 'bad conscience' in this sense is illustrated, although the term is not used, by the action of Adam and Eve in Gn. 3:8). The one occurrence of *syneidēsis* as such in the LXX (outside the Apocrypha) is Ec. 10:20, where RSV translates *en syneidēsei sou* as '(even) in your *thought* (the Heb. is literally "knowledge"), do not curse the king'. This obviously does not follow the pattern just noted, however; and it is only at Wisdom 17:11, the single certain Apocryphal appearance of the term (NEB, 'wickedness proves a cowardly thing when condemned by an inner witness, and in the grip of conscience gives way to forebodings of disaster') that we find a clear anticipation of the NT use and meaning of *syneidēsis*. (But *cf.* Jb. 27:6; also Ecclus. 14:2, and the variant reading at 42:18.)

III. New Testament usage

The NT use of 'conscience' must be considered against the background of 'the idea of God, holy and righteous, creator and judge, as well as redeemer and quickener' (Pierce, p. 106). The truth of this remark is evident from the fact that the NT writers see man's conscience negatively as the instrument of judgment, and positively as the means of guidance.

The term *syneidēsis* often occurs in the Pauline letters, as well as in Heb., 1 Pet. and two (Pauline) speeches in Acts (23:1; 24:16). In its Pauline setting the word describes first of all the pain suffered by man when he has done wrong (see Rom. 13:5, where Paul urges 'subjection' for the sake of *syneidēsis* as well as *orgē*—the personal and social manifestations of God's judgment). From this man is delivered by dying to sin through incorporation into Christ (*cf.* Rom. 7:15; 8:2). However, it is possible for man's conscience—the faculty by which he apprehends the moral demands of God, and which causes him pain when he falls short of those demands—to be inadequately disciplined (1 Cor. 8:7), to become weakened (v. 12) and even defiled (v. 7; *cf.* Tit. 1:15), and to grow seared and ultimately insensible (*cf.* 1 Tim. 4:2). Thus it is essential for the conscience to be properly educated, and indeed *informed*, by the Holy Spirit. That is why 'conscience' and 'faith' cannot be separated. By repentance and faith man is delivered from conscience as 'pain'; but faith is also the means whereby his conscience is quickened and instructed. To walk in 'newness of life' (Rom. 6:4) implies a living, growing faith, through which the Christian is open to the influence of the Spirit (Rom. 8:14); and this in turn is the guarantee of a 'good' or 'clear' conscience (1 Pet. 3:16; *cf.* Acts 23:1).

An important and developed use of *syneidēsis* in Paul occurs in Rom. 2:14f. The implication of this passage is that God's general revelation of himself as good and demanding goodness faces all men with moral responsibility. For the Jews the divine demands were made explicit in the Sinaitic Code, while the Gentiles perform 'by nature' what the law requires. But the recognition of holy obligations, whether by Jew or Gentile, is something individually apprehended (the law is 'written on their hearts', v. 15) and, according to personal response, morally judged (for 'their conscience also bears witness' with the understanding of their heart, *ibid.*). Thus 'conscience' belongs to all men, and through it God's character and will are actively appreciated. At the same time it may be regarded as a power 'apart' from man himself (*cf.* Rom. 9:1; and the echo of the Pauline doctrine of 'conscience' in Rom. at Jn. 8:9, in the phrase 'convicted by their own conscience'—although this is rejected as a gloss by RSV and NEB, and the whole *pericope de adultera* is omitted by the best MSS).

Like Paul, the writer of Heb. uses the term *syneidēsis* with both a negative and a positive reference. Under the terms of the old covenant, man's guilty conscience in relation to God could not be perfected (Heb. 9:9); but deliverance has been made possible by the work of Christ under the terms of the new covenant (9:14), and by the appropriation of the benefits of the death of Jesus through Christian initiation (10:22; *cf.* 1 Pet. 3:21). In terms of spiritual growth, therefore, a worshipper's conscience may be described as 'good' (Heb. 13:18).

To summarize, the NT significance of 'conscience' is twofold: it is the means of moral judgment, painful and absolute because the judgment is divine, upon the actions of an individual completed or begun; and it also acts as a witness and guide in all aspects of the believer's sanctification.

BIBLIOGRAPHY. J. Dupont, *Gnosis*, 1949; and *Studia Hellenistica*, pp. 119–153; O. Hallesby, *Conscience*, 1950; C. A. Pierce, *Conscience in the New Testament*, 1955; W. D. Stacey, *The Pauline View of Man*, 1956, pp. 206–210; J. N. Sevenster, *Paul and Seneca*, 1961, esp. pp. 84–102; R. Schnackenburg, *The Moral Teaching of the New Testament*, 1965, pp. 287–296; M. E. Thrall, *NTS* 14, 1967–8, pp. 118–125 (against Pierce); C. Brown in *NIDNTT* 1, pp. 348–353. S.S.S.

CONTENTMENT. The noun 'contentment' occurs only once in RSV (1 Tim. 6:6), but its Gk. equivalent *autarkeia* appears also in 2 Cor. 9:8 as 'enough'; the adjective *autarkēs* in Phil. 4:11 and the verb *arkeō* in Lk. 3:14; 1 Tim. 6:8; Heb. 13:5; 3 Jn. 10; see also 2 Cor. 12:9, 'is sufficient'. *autarkeia* denotes freedom from reliance upon others, whether other persons or other things; hence the satisfaction of one's needs (2 Cor. 9:8) or the control of one's desires (1 Tim. 6:6, 8). It is not a passive acceptance of the *status quo*, but the positive assurance that God has supplied one's needs, and the consequent release from unnecessary desire. The Christian can be 'self-contained' because he has been satisfied by the grace of God (2 Cor. 12:9). The Christian spirit of contentment follows the fundamental commandment of Ex. 20:17 against covetousness, the precept of Pr. 15:17; 17:1, the exhortations of the prophets against avarice (*e.g.* Mi. 2:2) and supremely the example and teaching of Jesus, who rebuked the discontent which grasps at material possessions to the neglect of God (Lk. 12:13–21) and who commended such confidence in our Father in heaven as will dispel all anxiety concerning physical supplies (Mt. 6:25–32). In the OT the phrase 'be content' (from Heb. *yā'al*) indicates pleasure or willingness to do a certain action, usually one which has been requested by another person, *e.g.* Ex. 2:21; Jdg. 17:11; 2 Ki. 5:23, AV. J.C.C.

CONVERSION.

I. Meaning of the word

A turning, or returning, to God. The chief words for expressing this idea are, in the OT, *šûḇ* (translated in EVV 'turn' or 'return'), and, in the NT, *strephomai* (Mt. 18:3; Jn. 12:40: the middle voice expresses the reflexive quality of the action, *cf.* the French 'se convertir'); *epistrephō* (regularly used in LXX to render *šûḇ*) and (in Acts 15:3 only) the cognate noun *epistrophē*. Despite the AV of Mt. 13:15; 18:3; Mk. 4:12; Lk. 22:32; Jn. 12:40; Acts 3:19; 28:27 (all changed to 'turn' or 'turn again' in RSV), *epistrephō* is not used in the NT in the passive voice. *šûḇ* and *epistrephō* can be used transitively as well as intransitively: in the OT God is said to turn men to himself (15 times); in the NT preachers are spoken of as turning men to God (Lk. 1:16f., echoing Mal. 4:5–6; Jas. 5:19f.; probably Acts 26:18). The basic meaning which the *strephō* word-group, like *šûḇ*, expresses is to turn *back* (*re*turn: so Lk. 2:39; Acts 7:39) or turn *round* (*about* turn: so Rev. 1:12). The theological meaning of these terms represents a transference of this idea into the realm of man's relationship with God.

II. Old Testament usage

The OT speaks mostly of national conversions, once of a pagan community (Nineveh: Jon. 3:7–10), otherwise of Israel; though there are also a few references to, and examples of, individual conversions (*cf.* Ps. 51:13, and the accounts of Naaman, 2 Ki. 5; Josiah, 2 Ki. 23:25; Manasseh, 2 Ch. 33:12f.), together with prophecies of world-wide conversions (*cf.* Ps. 22:27). Conversion in the OT means, simply, turning to Yahweh, Israel's covenant God. For Israelites, members of the covenant community by right of birth, conversion meant turning to 'Yahweh *your God*' (Dt. 4:30; 30:2, 10) in whole-hearted sincerity after a period of disloyalty to the terms of the covenant. Conversion in Israel was thus essentially the returning of backsliders to God. The reason why individuals, or the community, needed to '(re)turn to the Lord' was that they had turned away from him and strayed out of his paths. Hence national acts of returning to God were frequently marked by leader and people 'making a *covenant', *i.e.* making together a fresh solemn profession that henceforth they would be wholly loyal to God's covenant, to which they had sat loose in the past (so under Joshua, Jos. 24:25; Jehoiada, 2 Ki. 11:17; Asa, 2 Ch. 15:12; Hezekiah, 2 Ch. 29:10; Josiah, 2 Ch. 34:31). The theological basis for these public professions of conversion lay in the doctrine of the covenant. God's covenant with Israel was an abiding relationship; lapses into idolatry and sin exposed Israel to covenant chastisement (*cf.* Am. 3:2), but could not destroy the covenant; and if Israel turned again to Yahweh, he would return to them in blessing (*cf.* Zc. 1:3) and the nation would be restored and healed (Dt. 4:23–31; 29:1–30:10; Is. 6:10).

The OT stresses, however, that there is more to conversion than outward signs of sorrow and reformation of manners. A true turning to God under any circumstances will involve inward self-humbling, a real change of heart and a sincere seeking after the Lord (Dt. 4:29f.; 30:2, 10; Is. 6:9f.; Je. 24:7), and will be accompanied by a new clarity of knowledge of his being and his ways (Je. 24:7; *cf.* 2 Ki. 5:15; 2 Ch. 33:13).

III. New Testament usage

In the NT, *epistrephō* is only once used of the return to Christ of a Christian who has lapsed into sin (Peter: Lk. 22:32). Elsewhere, backsliders are exhorted, not to conversion, but to repentance (Rev. 2:5, 16, 21f.; 3:3, 19), and the conversion-words refer only to that decisive turning to God whereby, through faith in Christ, a sinner, Jew or Gentile, secures present entry into the eschatological kingdom of God and receives the eschatological blessing of forgiveness of sins (Mt. 18:3; Acts 3:19; 26:18). This conversion secures the salvation which Christ has brought. It is a once-for-all, unrepeatable event, as the habitual use of the aorist in the oblique moods of the verbs indicates. It is described as a turning from the darkness of idolatry, sin and the rule of Satan, to worship and serve the true God (Acts 14:15; 26:18; 1 Thes. 1:9) and his Son Jesus Christ (1 Pet. 2:25). It consists of an exercise of *repentance and *faith, which Christ and Paul link together as summing up between them the moral demand of the gospel (Mk. 1:15; Acts 20:21). Repentance means a change of mind and heart towards God; faith means belief of his word and trust in his Christ; conversion covers both. Thus we find both repentance and faith linked with conversion, as the narrower with the wider concept (repentance and conversion, Acts 3:19; 26:20; faith and conversion, Acts 11:21).

Though the NT records a number of conversion experiences, some more violent and dramatic (*e.g.* that of Paul, Acts 9:5ff.; of Cornelius, Acts 10:44ff.; *cf.* 15:7ff.; of the Philippian jailer, Acts 16:29ff.), some more quiet and unspectacular (*e.g.* that of the eunuch, Acts 8:30ff.; of Lydia, Acts 16:14), the writers show no interest in the psychology of conversion as such. Luke makes space for three accounts of the conversions of Paul and of Cornelius (Acts 10:5ff.; 22:6ff.; 26:12ff.; and 10:44ff.; 11:15ff.; 15:7ff.) because of the supreme significance of these events in early church history, not for any separate interest in the manifestations that accompanied them. The writers think of conversion dynamically—not as an experience, something one feels, but as an action, something one does—and they interpret it theologically, in terms of the gospel to which the convert assents and responds. Theologically, conversion means committing oneself to that union with Christ which baptism symbolizes: union with him in death, which brings freedom from the penalty and dominion of sin, and union with him in resurrection from death, to live to God through him and walk with him in newness of life through the power of the indwelling Holy Spirit. Christian conversion is commitment to Jesus Christ as divine Lord and Saviour, and this commitment means reckoning union with Christ to be a fact and living accordingly. (See Rom. 6:1–14; Col. 2:10–12, 20ff.; 3:1ff.)

IV. General conclusion

Turning to God under any circumstances is, psychologically regarded, man's own act, deliberately considered, freely chosen and spontaneously performed. Yet the Bible makes it clear that it is also, in a more fundamental sense, God's work in him. The OT says that sinners turn to God only when themselves turned by God (Je. 31:18f.; La. 5:21). The NT teaches that when men will and work for the furthering of God's will in regard to their salvation, it is God's working in them that makes them do so (Phil. 2:12f.). Also, it describes the initial conversion of unbelievers to God as the result of a divine work in them in which, by its very nature, they could play no part, since it is essentially a curing of the spiritual impotence which has precluded their turning to God hitherto: a raising from death (Eph. 2:1ff.), a new birth (Jn. 3:1ff.), an opening of the heart (Acts 16:14), an opening and enlightening of blinded eyes (2 Cor. 4:4–6), and the giving of an understanding (1 Jn. 5:20). Man responds to the gospel only because God has first worked in him in this way. Furthermore, the accounts of Paul's conversion and various references to the power and conviction imparted by the Spirit to the converting word (*cf.* Jn. 16:8; 1 Cor. 2:4f.; 1 Thes. 1:5) show that God draws men to himself under a strong, indeed overwhelming, sense of divine constraint. Thus, the AV's habit of rendering the active verb 'turn' by the interpretative passive, 'be converted', though bad translation, is good biblical theology. (*REGENERATION.)

BIBLIOGRAPHY. G. Bertram, *TDNT* 7, pp. 722–729; F. Laubach, J. Goetzmann, U. Becker, *NIDNTT* 1, pp. 354–362. J.I.P.

CORD, ROPE. A number of Heb. words and one Gk. word are thus rendered in the RSV. **1.** *ḥeḇel* is the most common and it is the usual word for rope, being translated 'rope' in Jos. 2:15, *etc.*, 'line' in Mi. 2:5, *etc.*, 'cord' in Est. 1:6, and 'tackle' in Is. 33:23. Some consider it is related etymologically to the English 'cable'. **2.** *ʿᵃḇōṯ*, lit. 'something intertwined', is also common and is rendered 'rope' in Jb. 39:10, *etc.*, 'branch' in Ps. 118:27, *etc.*, and 'cart rope' in Is. 5:18. **3.** *yeṯer*, the third general word, is variously rendered in Jdg. 16:7; Jb. 30:11 and Ps. 11:2. Rope was normally made of twisted hair or strips of skin. **4.** *mêṯār* (Ex. 35:18, *etc.*) is a tent-cord. **5.** *ḥûṭ* (Ec. 4:12) is thread.

6. The only word employed in the NT is *schoinion*, 'bulrush rope', which is rendered 'cord' in Jn. 2:15 and 'ropes' in Acts 27:32. G.W.G.

CORINTH. A city of Greece at the W end of the isthmus between central Greece and the Peloponnesus, in control of trade routes between N Greece and the Peloponnese and across the isthmus. The latter was particularly important because much trade was taken across the isthmus rather than round the stormy S promontories of the Peloponnese. There were two harbours, Lechaeum 2·5 km W on the Corinthian Gulf, connected with the city by long walls; and Cenchreae 14 km E on the Saronic Gulf. Corinth thus became a flourishing centre of trade, as well as of industry, particularly ceramics. The town is dominated by the Acrocorinth (566 m), a steep, flat-topped rock surmounted by the acropolis, which in ancient times contained, *inter alia*, a temple of Aphrodite, goddess of love, whose service gave rise to the city's proverbial immorality, notorious already by the time of Aristophanes (Strabo, 378; Athenaeus, 573).

From the late 4th century until 196 BC Corinth was held mainly by the Macedonians; but in that year it was liberated, with the rest of Greece, by T. Quinctius Flamininus, and joined the Achaean League. After a period of opposition to Rome, and social revolution under the dictator Critolaus, the city was, in 146 BC, razed to the ground by the consul L. Mummius, and its inhabitants sold into slavery.

In 46 BC Corinth was rebuilt by Caesar and began to recover its prosperity. Augustus made it the capital of the new province of Achaea, now detached from Macedonia and ruled by a separate proconsular governor.

Paul's 18-month stay in Corinth in his second missionary journey (Acts 18:1–18) has been dated by an inscription from Delphi which shows that Gallio came to Corinth as proconsul in AD 51 or 52 (Acts 18:12–17; *Paul, section **II**). His *bēma*, or judgment seat (Acts 18:12), has also been identified, as has the *macellum* or meat-market (1 Cor. 10:25). An inscription near the theatre mentions an aedile *Erastus, who possibly is the treasurer of Rom. 16:23.

BIBLIOGRAPHY. Strabo, 378–382; Pausanias, 2. 1–4; Athenaeus, 573; *Corinth I–VIII* (Princeton University Press), 1951 onwards; J. G. O'Neill, *Ancient Corinth*, 1930; H. G. Payne, *Necrocorinthia*, 1931; H. J. Cadbury, *JBL* 53, 1934, pp. 134ff.; O. Broneer, *BA* 14, 1951, pp. 78ff. Fine plates may be seen in A. A. M. van der Heyden and H. H. Scullard, *Atlas of the Classical World*, 1959, pp. 43f.; J. Murphy-O'Connor, *St. Paul's Corinth*, 1983; *BA* 47, 1984, pp. 147–159; J. B. Salmon, *Wealthy Corinth*, 1984.

J.H.H.

CORINTHIANS, EPISTLES TO THE.

I. Outline of contents

1 Corinthians

a. Greetings, and prayer for the recipients (1:1–9).

b. Christian wisdom and the unity of the church (1:10–4:21):

(i) The statement of the problem (1:10–16): the Corinthians are putting the unity of the church at risk by following a variety of leaders.

(ii) 'Wisdom' and the gospel (1:17–2:5): the world's wisdom is folly to God; the Corinthians were not chosen by God for their wisdom; Paul preached not wisdom but Christ crucified, in demonstration of the Spirit and of power.

(iii) True wisdom (2:6–13): God's true wisdom is imparted only to those in whom his Spirit works: they understand God's plans (2:9) and gifts (2:12).

(iv) The status of the Corinthians (2:14–3:4): But the Spirit is not being allowed to work in this way in the Corinthian church because of their unspiritual attitudes.

(v) The apostles and the church (3:5–4:5): Paul explains how the Corinthians ought to regard their apostles, and warns them to build aright on the foundation which he laid.

(vi) Conclusions (4:6–21): They must realize that they do not yet reign in the kingdom of the New Age, and learn humility.

c. Problems in Corinthian church life (5:1–6:20):

(i) A man and his father's wife (5:1–13): the church is conniving at a heinous sin, perhaps even boasting in this expression of 'Christian freedom'.

(ii) Lawsuits (6:1–11): Perhaps a comment on a *cause célèbre*.

(iii) Prostitution (6:12–20).

d. Answers to questions (7:1–14:40):

(i) Is celibacy the Christian ideal? (7:1–40): Paul's principles (7:1–7, 17–24); application to various cases (7:8–16, 25–40).

(ii) Meat offered to idols (8:1–11:1): the principles involved (8:1–13); the conflict with Christian liberty (9:1–27); an awesome example from Israel's history (10:1–13), and conclusions (10:14–11:1).

(iii) Behaviour in the Christian assembly (11:2–14:40): marital authority (11:2–16); attitudes to one another at the common meal (11:17–34); the principles governing the gifts of the Spirit: they do not contradict the gospel (12:1–3); they are all equally important (12:4–30); the most important thing is not which gift is possessed but whether it is used in love (12:31–13:13); practical considerations governing the use of these gifts: they should help the whole church (14:1–25); conclusions (14:26–40).

e. A fundamental problem tackled (15:1–58):

(i) The resurrection of Jesus an essential part of the gospel (15:1–11).

(ii) The implications of this: we too shall rise when the 'last enemy' is finally destroyed (15:12–34).

(iii) The relationship between the natural realm and the spiritual (15:35–50): there are different sorts of bodies (15:35–41); the resurrected body is very different from the present one (15:42–50).

(iv) The essence of *eschatology (15:51–58): we must yet 'put on' this new body (either through death and resurrection, or exceptionally through change) before we inherit the kingdom (*cf.* 4:8).

f. The collection, and closing remarks (16:1–24).

2 Corinthians

a. Greetings and prayer of thanksgiving (1:1–7).

b. Explanations for Paul's apparently inconsistent behaviour (1:8–2:13): Paul gives an account of what he has experienced of suffering and the accompanying comfort of God (1:8–11); and explains that his changes of plan were made in good faith and for the benefit of the Corinthians themselves (1:12–2:13).

c. Not our glory, but God's (2:14–4:12):

(i) A paean of praise for victory in Christ (2:14–17).

(ii) The glory of the new covenant (3:1–4:6): Paul is commending not himself (3:1–6) but the glorious covenant of the Spirit (3:7–11) which enables him boldly but in transparent honesty to proclaim the gospel (3:12–4:6).

(iii) A comparison between the treasure of the gospel and the vessel in which it is carried (4:7–12).

d. The basis of Paul's confidence (4:13–5:10): Paul's confidence is in the God who can raise the dead, so that even the prospect of death cannot diminish this confidence.

e. The motivation of the apostle (5:11–21):

(i) The love of Christ (5:11–15).

(ii) The good news of reconciliation (5:16–21).

f. An appeal for a response (6:1–7:4):

(i) For a positive response to Paul himself (6:1–13; 7:2–4).

(ii) For purity in the life of the church (6:14–7:1).

g. Paul's joy and confidence in his Corinthian church (7:5–16): his letter has had its effect (7:5–13) and Paul's trust in the church has been vindicated (7:14–16).

h. The collection (8:1–9:15):

(i) A tactful reminder that the Corinthians have not yet fulfilled their original offer of financial aid (8:1–7).

(ii) The basis of Christian giving (8:8–15).

(iii) Titus' zeal in this service (8:16–24).

(iv) Encouragement to the Corinthians to vindicate Paul's boast (9:1–15).

i. Warning against false apostles (10:1–13:10):

(i) An appeal for complete obedience (10:1–6).

(ii) Paul's challenge to the troublemakers (10:7–18): he does not really need to defend his authority in Corinth, since he was the first to bring the gospel there; but these men are boasting 'in other men's labours' (10:15).

(iii) Paul's own credentials (11:1–12:13): if the Corinthians are determined to have them, Paul's credentials are as good as any other man's (11:1–29); but he would rather boast in his weakness, not his strengths (11:30–12:10). Yet this is all folly; the only fact of any significance is that the church experienced the true signs of an apostle (12:11–13).

(iv) Paul's defence against the charge of defrauding the church (12:14–18): perhaps in the face of an accusation that the moneys for the collection had found their way into Paul's own pocket.

(v) Paul's ultimate concern (12:19–13:10): not that his own name might be cleared, but that his beloved church might improve and be built up.

j. Closing greetings (13:11–14).

II. The church at Corinth

a. Its milieu

The *Corinth which Paul evangelized *c.* AD 50 was a relatively new city. In ancient literature Corinth has a reputation for vice of every kind; but this was a reputation foisted upon Old Corinth by her trading-rival Athens. It is thus irrelevant for our understanding of the situation at the time of Paul. So also is the groundless tradition that the city was a centre of cult-prostitution in honour of the goddess Aphrodite. The morals of secular Corinth are likely to have been no better or worse than those of any other Mediterranean port. That there was a Jewish community in the city is attested by Acts 18:4.

b. Its foundation

Paul says little about the founding of the church, but a brief account will be found in Acts 18. Paul stayed with the Jewish couple *Aquila and Prisca, probably already Christians, and recently expelled from Rome. As was his custom, Paul preached in the synagogue and persuaded 'Jews and Greeks' (Acts 18:4); that is, Jews and proselytes or 'God-fearers' (a phrase which includes Jews, proselytes and Gentiles who had adopted most of the Jewish religion without taking the final step of circumcision). Perhaps as a result of the arrival of two more members of this unorthodox sect of the Nazarene (Acts 18:5), the Jewish authorities began to oppose Paul's use of the synagogue for his preaching. Paul withdrew, taking with him a number of Jewish converts, notably the ruler of the synagogue, and moved next door into the house of a (converted?) 'God-fearer', Titius *Justus. This group formed the nucleus of the Corinthian church, which grew rapidly (Acts 18:8, 10). The relationships between these two groups of neighbours must have remained tense, and the Jews took advantage of a change of proconsulship (*GALLIO) to make an attack upon Paul in the courts; but this was unsuccessful and the result was that the church was able to grow unmolested while Paul stayed the (for him) unusually long time of 18 months before sailing for Syria with Aquila and Prisca.

c. Its composition

As well as the Jews and proselytes who accompanied Paul on his move from the synagogue, the church consisted of subsequent converts, probably from both Jewish and pagan backgrounds. The debate still proceeds as to whether the church was predominantly Jewish-Christian or predominantly pagan-convert in constitution: there are no cogent reasons for it to have been either.

Socially the church embraced a wide range, including under its aegis the wealthy city-treasurer *Erastus; an erstwhile president of the synagogue; the refugee Jewish saddler Aquila, and the domestic slaves (if so they were) of *Chloe. Recent scholarship has used archaeological and sociological tools to shed much light on the social context of the Corinthian church. See the bibliography below.

d. Its intellectual background

To account for the surprisingly rapid development of so many errors so soon in a church where Paul had taught for so long, many scholars have suggested that we should look for one underlying cause, and a wide range of possible background influences have been suggested, from a predominantly Jewish situation (so J. M. Ford, 'The First Epistle to the Corinthians or the First Epistle to the Hebrews?', *CBQ* 28, 1966, pp. 402–416) to an influx of all-but full-blown *Gnosticism (so W. Schmithals, *Gnosticism in Corinth*, 1971). Before this question is discussed, a few comments about the thought-world of the time may be relevant.

There was certainly a significant Jewish group in the church. The Judaism of the *Dispersion was strongly influenced by many other currents of thought, including those from the Greek philosophical schools, and esoteric, 'proto-Gnostic' ideas; but still, of course, basing itself on the Torah, at least in so far as this was practicable. While sacrifice could be offered only in Jerusalem (involving a pilgrimage far beyond the means of most), Diaspora Jews were renowned in the Greek world for their adherence to circumcision and the sabbath, and for their refusal to eat swine's flesh. In many circles, however, the Torah was interpreted allegorically rather than literally (*PHILO). Jews often, though by no means exclusively, lived together in a 'Jewish quarter', and had certain civil rights, such as their own law-courts.

Gentile converts may have already been proselytes or 'God-fearers', or may have come directly from paganism. These latter would have been familiar with the usual Hellenistic pantheon and forms of worship, possibly including cult-prostitution. Ecstasy, including speaking in *tongues, was a common phenomenon in Graeco-Oriental religions, and this may help to account for the Corinthians' misuse of Christian *spiritual gifts, and possibly for the ecstatically-produced blasphemy of 1 Cor. 12:2f.

The pagan temples played a significant part in religious, and hence daily, life: they functioned as restaurants and social centres, as well as being significant (but not the only) sources of the butchers' meat-supply (*IDOLS, MEATS OFFERED TO; *MEAT MARKET).

As well as the emotional and cultic elements, Hellenistic religions also appealed to the intellect, and *Gnosticism found a fertile seedbed here. Many of these religions developed a strongly dualist outlook, for which matter was illusory and evil, whereas only the objects of thought, in the realm of the soul, were concrete and good. This easily led to a premium on knowledge; to a belief (also found in Hellenistic Judaism) in the immortality of the soul rather than the resurrection of the body; and, perhaps rather strangely, to both asceticism (in which the 'evil' world is simply rejected) and libertinism (in which the 'good' soul is held to be undefiled, no matter what the illusory body may do).

All of these factors no doubt contributed to the particular problems which arose in the church.

e. The source(s) of its problems

Several single factors have been suggested as the underlying cause for the Corinthians' errors:

(i) **Gnosticism*. Schmithals' suggestion that this is the source of the Corinthians' problems has already been noted. It suffers, however, from grave drawbacks, not least because there is no evidence that Gnosticism as a system can be dated so early. Also, Schmithals is forced to assume that Paul misunderstood the situation, since he does not effectively answer Gnostic teachings (see C. K. Barrett, 'Christianity at Corinth', *BJRL* 46, 1963–4, pp. 269–297).

(ii) *A change in Paul's own teaching.* J. C. Hurd, *The Origin of 1 Corinthians*, 1965, has developed the elaborate thesis that Paul was obliged in the face of the Jerusalem Council (Acts 15) to change his message radically, to the puzzlement of the Corinthians who remained faithful to his original preaching of freedom, *wisdom and enthusiasm. It is impossible to deal adequately with Hurd's thesis here, but three points are noteworthy. Hurd's reconstruction of events forces him to treat the chronology and history of the book of Acts in a cavalier fashion, and to postulate that within 2 years Paul preached at Corinth, underwent his *volte-face*, and then developed the 'mature' position expressed in 1 Cor. This seems far too short a time for such a development. Second, it is remarkable that Paul does not mention the Apostolic Decree, if he is now concerned to commend it to his churches. Third, Hurd's thesis fails to provide a satisfactory exegesis of the letter. For a more detailed critique, see J. W. Drane, *Paul: Libertine or Legalist?*, 1975, pp. 97f.

(iii) *An un-Pauline development of Paul's preaching*. A. C. Thiselton ('Realized Eschatology at Corinth', *NTS* 24, 1977–8, pp. 510–526) has recently suggested that the Corinthians developed Paul's own *eschatology far beyond his own position, and believed themselves to be already reigning in the kingdom of the New Age in which 'all things are lawful' (1 Cor. 4:8; 6:12; 10:23). Thiselton believes that he can interpret most of the letter on the basis of this view, though it makes heavy weather of some problems such as the lawsuits of ch. 6.

Other scholars have looked for the answer in a combination of factors: Drane (*op. cit.*), for instance, suggests that the Corinthians may have been influenced by gnostic ideas, if not by fully-developed Gnosticism, and by a misinterpretation of Paul's own letter to the *Galatians. This position is not incompatible with that of Thiselton, and some combination of these factors perhaps provides the best basis for an interpretation of the letter.

In 2 Cor. the problem seems to be rather different: here Paul is facing a personal attack on himself (2 Cor. 10:10) mounted by some people whom he in turn styles 'false apostles, deceitful workmen, servants of Satan and only disguised as apostles' (2 Cor. 11:13–15). Paul's stress on his own lack of oratorical ability, his refusal to assert his apostolic authority, and his weakness (11:6–7, 30), lead us to suppose that these people placed stress on their own great rhetoric, spiritual authority and strength. They are Hebrews (11:22) and presumably claim authority from the mother-church in Jerusalem. Indeed, it has been suggested on the basis of the phrase 'superlative apostles' (11:5; 12:11) that these men are none other than the Jerusalem apostles themselves, and that we have here a development of the split Paul mentions in Gal. 2:11f. But Paul would not be likely to compare himself on equal terms with men he regards as satanic, so it seems most reasonable to regard the 'superlative apostles' as a group distinct from the 'false apostles'. We then appear to be dealing with three groups:

(i) The 'superlative apostles' at Jerusalem, whose authority is being invoked over against Paul's, but to whom Paul regards himself as equal, not inferior.

(ii) The 'false apostles', perhaps sent by the Jerusalem apostles, but going beyond the bounds of the agreement of Gal. 2:9; and perhaps wilfully ignoring the wishes of the Jerusalem apostles.

(iii) The Corinthians themselves, in danger of being misled, but not as yet opposed to Paul (see C. K. Barrett, 'Paul's Opponents in II Corinthians', *NTS* 17, 1970–1, pp. 233–254).

III. The integrity of the letters

It is virtually certain that Paul had a greater correspondence with the Corinthian church than is preserved in Scripture. 1 Cor. 5:9–13 probably (though the verb in 5:9 could be translated 'I am writing') refers to a previous letter warning the church to separate from the immoral (that is, immoral Christians, but this was misinterpreted). We shall style this letter 'Cor. A'.

2 Cor. 2:3–11; 7:8–13a also refer to a previous letter. It is doubtful that this is 1 Cor., for the following reasons:

(i) the tone of this letter (see 2 Cor. 2:4; 7:8) is hardly the tone in which 1 Cor. is written.

(ii) this letter followed a 'painful visit' (2 Cor. 2:1–3; 12:14; 13:1–3), which does not seem to be true for 1 Cor.

(iii) despite the superficial similarity, 2 Cor. 2:5ff. does not seem to be referring to the same situation as 1 Cor. 5:5, since in 2 Cor. the wrongdoer appears to have offended against Paul personally.

So if we call our 1 Cor. 'Cor. B', there appears to

have been a 'Cor. C' (*i.e.* the letter referred to in 2 Cor.) before our 2 Cor. ('Cor. D'). Hence there appear to have been at least four epistles of Paul to the Corinthians. What happened to the others? There are two possibilities: either they have perished, or they survive as fragments in our 1 and 2 Cor. This second possibility is not just suggested on the assumption that we *must* possess all that Paul ever wrote: there is some evidence in the letters themselves that they may be composite.

(i) 2 Cor. 10–13 looks like 'Cor. E'. Even before anyone suggested that 2 Cor. may be composite, people had noted the sharp change of tone at ch. 10; and the contents also fit (see Barrett for details). It is further argued that these chapters are better understood as having been written *before* 1–9: *cf.* the references to Paul's visit in 10:6; 13:2 and 10 with those in 1:23; 2:3 and 9; or the references to boasting in 10:7f.; 11:18 and 12:1 with those in 3:1 and 5:12.

(ii) 2 Cor. 6:14–7:1 looks like 'Cor. A'. Again the contents fit, and if this section is removed from 2 Cor., the 'edges' match up quite remarkably.

(iii) It is also argued that 1 Cor. 8–10 is easier to understand as two (or even more) letters. Perhaps the most thorough attempt to analyse the Corinthian correspondence into several parts is that of W. Schmithals, 'Die Korintherbriefe als Briefsammlung', *ZNW* 64, 1973, pp. 263–288, where no fewer than nine separate letters are postulated. On this whole exercise, *cf.* C. K. Barrett, *1 Corinthians*, pp. 12–17 and *2 Corinthians*, pp. 11–21.

But at the very best partition-theories are counsels of despair: they raise as many problems as they solve, especially about the workings of the mind of the final editor. If it is possible to make sense of the letters as they stand, such theories should be rejected.

IV. Paul's dealings with the Corinthian church

The following attempts to present a reasonable reconstruction of the probable events in the history of the Corinthian church of which we have any knowledge.

a. Immediately after Paul's departure

Other preachers and teachers had come and gone: notably Apollos (Acts 19:1) and quite possibly Peter, or perhaps some emissaries from him (*cf.* 1 Cor. 1:12). Even at this stage there appears to have been something wrong, and Paul must have received reports of immorality, either actual or threatened, in the church.

b. 'Cor. A'

Paul responded to this problem with a letter warning the church to have nothing to do with the immoral (*cf.* 1 Cor. 5:9). We cannot say more about the letter than that, except that it may have been written in ignorance of the true gravity of the situation, and appears to have been misunderstood.

c. Corinthian news reaches Paul

Paul had news from three sources before writing 1 Cor.:

(i) *Chloe's people visited Paul, reporting that the church had split under various leaders. These may have simply been rallying-points for groups with basically the same beliefs, or have represented real differences of belief (though Paul gives no indication in his letter that he is addressing deeply divided groups). The splits may even, if Chloe's people brought the Corinthians' letter, have been caused by the writing of the letter itself, with the different groups wanting to send it to different authorities.

(ii) Stephanas, Fortunatus and Achaicus (1 Cor. 16:17) probably reported the situations which prompted Paul to write chs. 5 and 6 of his letter.

(iii) The Corinthians had also written a letter to Paul, raising a variety of questions, which he answers in 1 Cor. 7:1–16:4. In his reply Paul several times quotes from their letter to him; *cf.* 'It is good for a man not to touch a woman' (7:1); 'All of us possess knowledge' (8:1) and 'All things are lawful' (10:23). The letter appears to have asked, among other things, 'Is celibacy the Christian ideal?' (discussed in ch. 7 of Paul's reply); 'Why should Christians not feel free to join in idol sacrifices and eat sacrificed meat, since we know that the idols are nothing?' (discussed in chs. 8–10); 'Are our practices (presumably they described them in some detail) in our times of worship correct?' (discussed in chs. 11–14); 'Have we not already experienced the only *"resurrection" we are going to, in our new life in Christ?' (discussed in ch. 15); and 'What about the collection?' (discussed in ch. 16).

d. Paul replies: 'Cor. B'

Paul's response is our 1 Cor. Its length, and the emotion engendered by the issues raised, are more than adequate to account for the occasionally disjointed form of the letter. However, the letter appears to have failed in its intention: we read in 2 Cor. 2:1 and 13:2 of the necessity for further action.

e. The 'painful visit'

That further action took the form of another visit to Corinth, but this visit appears also to have been a failure: the church is still strife-torn, and Paul is rebuffed by one individual who personally offends him.

f. 'Cor. C'

Paul again attempts to achieve by letter what he was unable to achieve in the flesh: he delivers a stinging rebuke to his flock. This letter was delivered by Titus (2 Cor. 7:5–8) and is not now extant. Having written it, Paul went through agonies of regret, and was so upset that he could not complete his work, despite the opportunities: he finally left his work to go to meet Titus and learn how the letter had been received (2 Cor. 2:12f.). When he met Titus, however, he was overjoyed to learn that his letter had been just what was needed; the Corinthians had repented and were now solidly behind Paul, and Titus' report was thoroughly encouraging.

g. 'Cor. D'

Delighted with the restoration of good relationships between himself and his church, Paul immediately wrote again, this time a letter of praise and joy (our 2 Cor. 1–9).

h. Further news arrives

Before Paul had sent off his letter (or perhaps even immediately after) news appears to have arrived to the effect that this victory in Corinth had not after all been complete. Either Titus had been over-optimistic or else there had been a radical change: some outsiders, styling themselves 'apostles' and with the highest of credentials, were challenging

Paul's *authority and beginning to lead his flock astray.

Alternatively, we may assume that Paul knew of the existence of this 'pocket of resistance' all along, but reserved his strictures until the end. This view, however, makes heavier weather of the change in tone, and does not account for the fact that Paul gives no indication that he has moved on from addressing the whole church to addressing a minority within it.

i. 'Cor. E'

Paul responded with a blistering attack on these 'false apostles', and re-asserted his own authority in another letter or an appendix to 'Cor. D'. This is our 2 Cor. 10–13. Was this successful? We can only surmise. No further correspondence from Paul to the church survives, though in about AD 96 Clement, bishop of Rome, found it necessary to take up the cudgels once again against this wayward church. The church was again split, this time because some of the younger men had ousted their presbyters. Clement saw the problem as one of pride (an issue not wholly absent from Paul's letters) rather than doctrine. So on the major issues Paul may have won the day, though perhaps not as completely as he would have liked.

V. Authenticity and dates

Whatever is made of their integrity, there can be no doubt as to the authenticity of these two epistles: they have always been regarded as part of the undisputed Pauline Corpus. For the dating of the letters we may begin at the fixed point provided by the proconsulship of *Gallio which dates Acts 18:12 to the middle of AD 51 or 52 (proconsuls took up their posts in July). It is most reasonable to place the writing of 1 Cor. during the 2-year stay in Ephesus (Acts 19:10), so it may be dated somewhere in AD 53 or 54; and 2 Cor. soon after this, at the latest in AD 55.

BIBLIOGRAPHY. *Commentaries*: Among the best commentaries on the two letters are still those of C. K. Barrett in the *Black* series (1968 and 1973). Others include: *On* 1 *Cor*.: Calvin; F. Godet, 1886; J. Héring, 1962 (Fr. edn. 1948); H. Conzelmann, *Hermeneia*, 1975, L. Morris, *TNTC*², 1983; G. D. Fee, *NIC*, 1983 (Gk. text); E. E. Ellis, *ICC*, f.c. (Gk. text).

On 2 *Cor.*: Calvin; P. E. Hughes, *NIC*, 1962; V. P. Furnish, *AB*, 1984; R. P. Martin, *Word*, 1986; C. A. Kruse, *TNTC*, 1987; M. Thrall, *ICC*, 1 1994 (Gk. text).

Other studies: F. F. Bruce, *Paul*: *Apostle of the Free Spirit*, 1977, chs. 23 and 24; G. Theissen, *The Social Setting of Pauline Christianity*, 1982; A. J. Malherbe, *Social Aspects of Early Christianity*, 1983; J. Murphy-O'Connor, *St. Paul's Corinth*, 1983; B. J. Malina, *Christian Origins and Cultural Anthropology*, 1986; D. Georgi, *The Opponents of Paul in Second Corinthians*, 1987; P. Marshall, *Enmity in Corinth*, 1987; J. K. Chow, *Patronage and Power*, 1992; A. D. Clarke, *Secular and Christian Leadership in Corinth*, 1993. D.R. de L.

CORNELIUS. In Acts 10:1ff. a Roman centurion of Caesarea in Palestine, one of the class of Gentiles known as 'God-fearers' because of their attachment to Jewish religious practices, such as almsgiving and prayer, for which Cornelius receives special mention. Cornelius was a common *nomen* in the Roman world ever since Publius Cornelius Sulla in 82 BC emancipated 10,000 slaves and enrolled them in his own *gens Cornelia*. The Cornelius of Acts is specially notable as the first Gentile convert to Christianity. As he and his household and friends listened to Peter's preaching, they believed and received the Holy Spirit, whereupon they were baptized at Peter's command. The importance of this occasion in Luke's eyes is emphasized by repetition (*cf*. Acts 11:1–18; 15:7, 14). The 'Italian Cohort' to which Cornelius belonged was an auxiliary cohort of Roman citizens, whose presence in Syria in the 1st century AD is inscriptionally attested. F.F.B.

CORNERSTONE. The NT references draw their meaning from three passages in the OT. The first is Ps. 118:22 where the stone rejected by the builders has become 'the head of the corner' (Heb. *rô'š pinnâ*, LXX *kephalē gōnias*). In its original context this reflected the Psalmist's own jubilation at his vindication over the enemies who had rejected him, but in its liturgical setting in the Feast of Tabernacles the psalm came to refer more to national than to personal deliverance. In rabbinical exegesis it was accorded a Messianic interpretation and this prepared the way for its use by Christ of himself in Mt. 21:42; Mk. 12:10; Lk. 20:17. Peter also used the text in Acts 4:11 and 1 Pet. 2:7 to explain Christ's rejection by the Jews and his exaltation by God to be head of the church. The phrase 'head of the corner' can indicate one of the large stones near the foundations of a building which by their sheer size bind together two or more rows of stones, but it is more likely to refer to the final stone which completes an arch or is laid at the top corner of a building (so Jeremias). This idea underlies Eph. 2:20 (Gk. *akrogōniaios*, *sc. lithos*), where Paul pictures the stones of the new temple as joined together by Christ who as the cornerstone gives the building completeness and unity. Christ is elsewhere described as the church's *foundation, but Eph. 2:20 reverses the figure and regards the first-generation apostles and prophets as the foundation, with Christ as the summit and consummation.

The second passage (Is. 28:16) probably referred originally to the massive stonework of the Temple, symbolizing the Lord's abiding presence among his people, a feature which was firm, unshakeable, reliable. The juxtaposition in Isaiah of the words 'foundation' and 'cornerstone' suggests either identity or similarity of meaning, but the NT blending of this with the third passage (Is. 8:14) in Rom. 9:33 and in 1 Pet. 2:6 has effectively weakened the link and left the emphasis on Christ as a *stumbling-block to those without faith, but as security to those who believe.

BIBLIOGRAPHY. S. H. Hooke, 'The Corner-Stone of Scripture', in *The Siege Perilous*, 1956, pp. 235–249; F. F. Bruce, 'The Corner Stone', *ExpT* 84, 1972–3, pp. 231–235. J.B.Tr.

CORRUPTION (Gk. *phthora*, *diaphthora*) in EVV, and especially AV, usually connotes the transience of the present world order. In Rom. 8:21 it is used of the liability of the material universe to change and decay; contrast the 'imperishable' (Gk. *aphthartos*) inheritance reserved for believers (1 Pet. 1:4). In 1 Cor. 15:42ff. it denotes the liability of the 'natural' body to *death and dissolution; 'perishable' (Gk. *phthartos*) is practically equivalent to 'mortal' (Gk. *thnētos*), as 'imperishable' (Gk. *aphtharsia*), predicated of the 'spiritual' body, is a synonym of 'immortality' (Gk. *athanasia*). In Acts 2:27ff.; 13:35ff. 'corruption' (in the sense of decomposition) is the rendering of Gk. *diaphthora*, quoted from Ps. 16:10, LXX, for *MT šaḥaṯ* (RSV 'the *Pit'), parallel to Sheol. As a Messianic 'testimony' Ps. 16:10 in LXX lends itself even better than *MT* to the case of Jesus, whose body, being raised from death, 'saw no corruption' (Acts 13:37). (*HELL, *ESCHATOLOGY.)

BIBLIOGRAPHY. E. F. Sutcliffe, *The Old Testament and the Future Life*, 1946, pp. 76–81; J. Jeremias, 'Flesh and Blood cannot inherit the Kingdom of God', *NTS* 1, 1955–6, pp. 155ff. F.F.B.

COS (Acts 21:1). A massive and mountainous island, one of the Sporades group, off the SW coast of Asia Minor, near Halicarnassus. It was colonized at an early period by Dorian Greeks, and achieved fame as the site of the medical school founded in the 5th century BC by Hippocrates, and again as a literary centre, the home of Philetas and Theocritus, in the 3rd century BC. It was also noted for fine weaving.

The Romans made Cos a free state in the province of Asia, and the emperor Claudius, influenced by his Coan physician, conferred on it immunity from taxes. Herod the Great was a benefactor of the people of Cos. K.L.McK.

COSMETICS AND PERFUMERY.

I. Introductory

a. Scope

By cosmetics is here understood that wide range of concoctions from pulverized minerals, vegetable oils and extracts, and animal fats which has been used from earliest times to beautify, improve or restore personal appearance ('visual' cosmetics) or to produce pleasing fragrances ('odoriferous' cosmetics).

b. Cosmetic vessels and appliances

In Scripture, little is said of the boxes, phials, flasks, spoons and other cosmetic trinkets known from archaeology. Besides the 'perfume boxes' of Is. 3:20, a rendering the accuracy of which has been questioned, there is the well-known flask of precious ointment or spikenard with which the repentant woman anointed Christ's head (Lk. 7:37; *cf.* Mt. 26:7; Mk. 14:3). But Israelite town-sites in Palestine have produced many little patterned cosmetic-bowls; at most periods the tiny-handled pottery vessels probably served for scent-bottles, while from 14th/13th-century BC Lachish comes a superb ivory ointment-flask. Egyptian ladies of rank favoured elaborate ivory cosmetic-spoons featuring lotuses, maidens, ducks, *etc.*, in shape, and these were sometimes used in Palestine too. For eye-paint there were many little boxes and tubes, and the paint was commonly applied with a little stick (*spatula*) of wood or bronze. Egypt has yielded scores of such pots and spatulae. (*MIRROR.)

c. Hygiene

Throughout the biblical East, oil to anoint the body, with the object of soothing the sun-dried skin, was almost as essential as food and drink. This use of oil was customary except in mourning; see Dt. 28:40 (its loss, a curse); Ru. 3:3; 2 Sa. 12:20 (*cf.* Mt. 6:17). A striking example is the clothing, feeding and anointing of the repatriated troops of King Ahaz (*c.* 730 BC), described in 2 Ch. 28:15. Those with a passion for luxury, however, made free with expensive ointments (Am. 6:6), a sure way to empty one's purse (Pr. 21:17).

External sources corroborate the biblical picture. In Ramesside Egypt (13th century BC) one papyrus mentions 600 *hin* of 'anointing-oil' for a gang of workmen; other workmen are given 'ointment to anoint them, three times in the month', or 'their corn-ration and their ointment' (see R. A. Caminos, *Late Egyptian Miscellanies*, 1954, pp. 307–308, 312, 470). The same situation held true in Mesopotamia from at least the 18th century BC onwards. Oriental cosmetics, it must be remembered, were as much used for utilitarian as for decorative purposes. (See the oil-distribution texts from Mari, J. Bottéro, *Archives Royales de Mari*, 7, texts 5–85.)

II. Perfumers and perfume-making

In 1 Sa. 8:13 Samuel pictures a typical king 'like all the nations round about' as requiring the services of 'perfumers and cooks and bakers'. Three aspects of this passage find illumination in external sources: the existence of palace perfumeries, the association of cosmetics-manufacture and cooking, and the basic (Heb.) term *rqḥ*.

a. Royal perfumeries

The great palace at Mari on the middle Euphrates (18th century BC) had its own perfumery, the *bīt-raqqi*, which had to supply large quantities of various ointments for the king's dignitaries and soldiers, and the perfumes which were required for bodily use, for ritual, festivals and royal banquets. See J. Bottéro, *Archives Royales de Mari*, 7, 1957, *Textes Économiques et Administratifs*, pp. 3–27 (texts 5–85), 176–183 (the various oils), 183–184 (large quantities), 274, n. 2, and p. 360 (*bīt-raqqi*).

b. Methods of manufacture associated with cooking

The implication of 1 Sa. 8:13, which groups together perfumers (AV 'confectionaries'), cooks and bakers, also corresponds to ancient usage. The techniques of the perfumer were closely related to cooking. The perfume of flowers, *etc.*, could be extracted and 'fixed' by three processes. First is *enfleurage*: steeping the flowers in fat and continually changing them. Second is *maceration*: dipping the flowers, *etc.*, into hot fats or oils at 65° C (150° F). This was most widespread and closest to cooking. Third is *expressing*: squeezing out the scent-bearing juices by compressing flowers, *etc.*, in a bag. Oil of myrrh and other gum-resins were obtained by heating the substance concerned in a greasy-type 'fixative' oil/fat (plus water to avoid scent-evaporation); the perfume-essence of the myrrh or other 'resin' was thereby transferred to the greasy oil/fat which could then be strained off as liquid perfume. For these processes, see R. J. Forbes, *Studies in Ancient Technology*, 3, 1955, pp. 9–10, and references, and A. Lucas, *JEA* 23, 1937, pp. 29–30, 32–33. The N Canaanite texts of Ugarit mention 'oil of the perfumer' (*šmn rqḥ*; see Gordon, *Ugaritic Literature*, 1949, p. 130) and items such as '10 logs of oil', '3 logs of perfume' (*ṯlṯ lg rqḥ*; see Gordon, *Ugaritic Textbook*, 3, 1965, p. 427, No. 1354—14th/13th century BC; the same measure (log) is used in Lv. 14:10, 12, 15, 21, 24) (*WEIGHTS AND MEASURES).

These processes, so akin to cooking with fats, *etc*., are sometimes pictured in Egyptian tomb-paintings of the 15th century BC, showing people pouring and stirring the mixture in heated pans, or moulding incense into fancy shapes. Typical examples will be found in Davies, *JEA* 26, 1940, plate 22 with p. 133, and Forbes, *op. cit*., p. 13 and fig. 1. The cookery aspect of perfumery is also directly reflected in an Egyptian term for 'perfumer', *ps-sgnn*, lit. 'cooker of ointment', and by the use of fire in the elaborate cosmetics-recipes from Assyria (on which see E. Ebeling, *Parfümrezepte und Kultische Texte aus Assur*, 1950).

c. The rqḥ terminology

The ordinary participle *roqaḥ* is used for 'perfumer' in Ex. 30:25, 35 (AV 'compound', 'confection'); 37:29, and also in 1 Ch. 9:30, where it refers to priests commissioned by David and Saul to make perfumes for the tabernacle. It also occurs in Ec. 10:1, where it is identical with Ugaritic *šmn rqḥ* quoted above. *raqqāḥ*, fem. *raqqāḥâ*, is the noun-form for 'professional perfumer'; the latter is found in 1 Sa. 8:13 (AV 'confectionaries'), the former occurs in Ne. 3:8, 'Hananiah, a member (lit. 'son') of the perfumers' (guild)'. (*Cf*. Mendelsohn, *BASOR* 80, 1940, p. 18.) Of words for 'perfume' itself, *rōqaḥ* occurs in Ex. 30:25, 35; *riqqûaḥ*, 'unguents', in Is. 57:9; *reqaḥ*, of spiced wine in Ct. 8:2 (*FOOD); *merqaḥ*, 'perfume' or 'fragrance' (RSV), in Ct. 5:13; *meʿruqqāḥîm* is verbal passive in 'compounded with the perfumery of the artificer' in 2 Ch. 16:14; *mirqaḥaṯ* is 'ointment, perfumery' in 'makers of ointment', 1 Ch. 9:30, and in 'an ointment, a perfume of the perfumer's art', Ex. 30:25; finally, *merqāḥâ*, '(pot of) ointment' in Jb. 41:31, and perhaps in an imperative, 'spice the spicery', in a cooking context (?spiced meat), in Ezk. 24:10 (difficult).

III. 'Visual' cosmetics

a. 'Painting' of face and body

From the earliest times, ancient Oriental womenfolk used to paint round their eyes and darken their eyebrows with mineral pastes which were usually black. At first this was largely medicinal in aim (to protect the eyes from strong sun-glare), but it speedily became principally a feminine fashion, giving an enlarged and intense appearance to the eyes. This is attested in Egypt, Palestine and Mesopotamia.

In 841 BC Queen Jezebel is said to have used such cosmetics. 2 Ki. 9:30 indicates that she 'treated her eyes with eye-paint (*pûḵ*) and adorned her head' before going to the window whence she was thrown to her death at Jehu's word. Over two centuries later two Hebrew prophets pictured their idolatrous nation, faithless to God, as a woman made up for illegitimate lovers. Jeremiah (4:30) says 'you enlarge your eyes with eye-paint (*pûḵ*)', while Ezekiel (23:40) alleges 'you painted (*kāḥal*) your eyes . , .'. Note also Keren-happuch, the name of Job's third daughter (42:14), 'horn of eye-paint'—*i.e.* source of beauty. Such eye-paint was prepared by grinding the mineral concerned to a fine powder and mixing it with water or gum to form a paste that could be kept in a receptacle and applied to the face with the finger or a spatula (see **I.***b*, above).

The minerals used require some comment. In Roman times an antimony compound was used in eye-preparations; the Lat. for antimony sulphide and then antimony itself is *stibium*. Unfortunately this has led to ancient Oriental eye-paints being generally dubbed antimony or stibium—in large measure, wrongly so. In Egypt green malachite was quickly superseded by black eye-paint (Egyp. *msdmt*). Analysis of many excavated samples has shown that this consisted principally of *galena* (lead sulphide), never of antimony except as an accidental impurity. (See A. Lucas, *Ancient Egyptian Materials and Industries*[4], 1962, pp. 80–84 and *cf*. pp. 195–199.) In Mesopotamia the Babylonians called their black eye-paint *guḫlu*, alleged to be either galena or antimony/stibium. (For the former, see Forbes, *Studies in Ancient Technology*, 3, p. 18, who adduces no evidence for his case; for the latter, see R. C. Thompson, *Dictionary of Assyrian Chemistry and Geology*, 1936, pp. 49–51, where the evidence produced is irrelevant—but his 'needles of "lead"' would suit galena better than antimony.) *guḫlu* is same as Heb. *kāḥal*, 'to paint (eyes)', and passed into Arabic as *kohl*, 'eye-paint'. Modern Arab. *kohl* is often just moistened soot; it can include galena but not antimony (*cf*. Lucas, *op. cit*., p. 101). Hence Heb. *pûḵ*, 'eye-paint', was very likely galena rather than antimony. Thus, the *'aḇnê pûḵ* in the Temple treasures (1 Ch. 29:2) would be 'lumps of galena'. The use of *pûḵ* in Is. 54:11 (AV 'fair colours', RSV 'antimony') may presuppose the employment of (powdered) galena as part of an (dark-tinted) adhesive (*e.g.* resin) for setting gemstones. For resin plus powdered minerals in tinted adhesives for setting jewellery, *etc*., see Lucas, *op. cit*., pp. 12–13.

In Egypt red ochre (red oxide of iron), often found in tombs, may have served as a rouge for colouring the cheeks (Lucas, *op cit*., p. 104). Egyptian ladies also used powder-puffs (Forbes, *op cit*., p. 20 and fig. 4) and lipstick (see the lively picture reproduced in *ANEP*, p. 23, fig. 78). In antiquity the leaves of the fragrant henna-plant (see **IV**, below) were crushed to provide a red dye for feet, hands, nails and hair (Lucas, *op. cit*., p. 107). In Mesopotamia the Sumerians used for face-powder yellow ochre, quaintly called 'golden clay' or 'face bloom'; the Babylonians commonly used red ochre (Forbes, *op. cit*., p. 20). Similar fads doubtless pleased coquettish Hebrew ladies like those of Is. 3:18–26.

b. Hairdressing and restoratives

Hair-styles were part of ancient Near Eastern fashions. In Egypt skilled hairdressers attended to the coiffure (and wigs) of the great. For reproductions of these hairdressers and details of the hair-styles and the hair-pins used, see *ANEP*, p. 23, figs. 76–77, and refs. on p. 259, and also E. Riefstahl, *JNES* 15, 1956, pp. 10–17 with plates 8–14. Mesopotamia also had its fashions in hairdressing (*cf*. B. Meissner, *Babylonien und Assyrien*, 1, 1920, pp. 410–411; *RA* 48, 1954, pp. 113–129, 169–177; 49, pp. 9ff.). Canaan and Israel, too, provide examples of a variety of coiffures with curls long or short (see G. E. Wright, *Biblical Archaeology*, 1957, p. 191 and figs. 136–137, 72). In this connection notice Isaiah's jibe (3:24) and Jezebel's adorning her head (2 Ki. 9:30). Ornate combs were popular (see, *e.g.*, *ANEP*, p. 21, fig. 67). Men in the Semitic world (in contrast to Egypt) rejoiced in fine beards and took care over their hair—witness Samson's seven locks (Jdg. 16:13, 19). Barbers and razors are well known in the OT (*e.g.* Ezk. 5:1, *etc.*) and in the ancient Orient alike (*ANEP*, p. 24, figs. 80–83). Restoratives to repair the ravages of age were eagerly sought. Recipes found in the Egyptian medical papyri include one hopefully entitled 'Book of Transforming an Old Man into a Youth'; several were devoted to improving the complexion (see the renderings in Forbes, *op. cit.*, pp. 15–17).

IV. 'Odoriferous' cosmetics in personal use

a. Perfumery in the Song of Songs

'Ointment is simply *šemen* (*ṭôḇ*) (1:3; 4:10); *rēaḥ*, 'fragrance', applies to man-made ointments (1:3) and nature's scents (2:13) alike. Spikenard or nard (1:12; 4:13–14) is here very likely to be the same as the *lardu* of Assyro-Babylonian inscriptions, the root of the gingergrass *Cymbopogon schoenanthus* imported perhaps from Arabia (see R. C. Thompson, *Dictionary of Assyrian Botany*, 1949, p. 17). But the NT *nardos pistikē*, 'precious (spike)-nard' (Mk. 14:3; Jn. 12:3), is probably the *Nardostachys jatamansi* of India (Himalayas), a very expensive import for Roman Palestine. 'Bether' (Ct. 2:17, AV) is either a place-name or 'cleft mountains', rather than a spice. For myrrh (1:13; 3:6; 4:6; 5:1) and liquid myrrh, *mōr ōḇēr* (5:5, 13), see **V.***a, below; for frankincense, see* **V.***b*, below. The expressions 'mountain(s), hill, of myrrh, frankincense, spices' (4:6; 8:14) may perhaps allude to the terraces (mentioned also by Egyptian texts) on which the producing trees grew.

In 1:14; 4:13 *kōp̄er* may be the henna-plant with fragrant flowers whose leaves when crushed yield a red dye; see on henna, Lucas, *op cit.*, pp. 107, 355–357. 'Perfumed' in 3:6 is *mᵉquṭṭereṯ*, same root as *qᵉṭōreṯ*, 'incense'; as for 'powders of the merchant', see the powder-puff reference at the end of **III.***a*, above. In 4:14 *karkōm* is usually rendered as saffron; it could be either or both of saffron-crocus and turmeric, which yield a yellow dye (Thompson, *op cit.*, pp. 160–161, and refs. on Assyr. *azupiranu* and *kurkanu* for these). For calamus and cinnamon, see **V.***a*, below; on aloes, see *Herbs. The verses 5:13; 6:2 allude to beds of spices, *bōśem*, perhaps here specifically balm of Gilead, as opposed to its more general meaning of spices. For mandrakes (7:13), see *Plants. 'Spiced wine' (8:2) is known elsewhere in the ancient East (*Food).

b. Other references

bōśem, 'perfume', in Is. 3:24 is a general term in Scripture for spices; *cf.* the gifts of the Queen of Sheba (1 Ki. 10:2, 10), the treasures of Hezekiah (2 Ki. 20:13) and the references in the Song of Solomon (4:10, 14, 16; 8:14). Cleansing and beautifying of the body are apparently implied in the term *tamruq* used in Est. 2:3 (AV, RV 'purifications'; RSV 'ointments'), when Esther and others were preparing for King Ahasuerus. The perfume' of Pr. 27:9 is *qᵉṭōret* ('incense'). The 'precious ointment' of Ec. 7:1 (as of Ct. 1:3) is *šemen ṭôḇ*, exactly the term *šamnu ṭâbu* already used by a dignitary in a Mari tablet of the 18th century BC who requests it to rub himself with (C. F. Jean, *Archiv Orientálni* 17:1, 1949, p. 329, A179, 1. 6). Perfumes were put on clothes (Ps. 45:8), sprinkled on couches (Pr. 7:17), and precious oil (*šemen ṭôḇ* again) was poured upon the head, as in Aaron's anointing (Ps. 133). Perfumes or spices were burnt at the funerals of the great (2 Ch. 16:14). See M. Dayagi-Mendels, *Perfumes and Cosmetics in the Ancient World*, 1989.

V. Sacred perfumery

a. The holy anointing oil

For anointing the tabernacle and its furnishings, and the Aaronic priests at induction, not for profane use (Ex. 30:22–33). Several of its constituents can be identified. Myrrh, Heb. *mōr*, is a fragrant gum-resin of the tree-species *balsamo-dendron* and *commiphora* of S Arabia and Somaliland. Its fragrance resides in the 7–8% content of volatile oil. It is this essence that could be incorporated into a liquid perfume by heating with fixative oil/fat and straining off (see **II.***b*, above). Besides the 'liquid myrrh' of Ct. 5:5, 13, this liquid myrrh-perfume may be what is meant by 'flowing' or 'liquid myrrh' (*mor-dᵉrôr*) in Ex. 30:23, and is probably the *šmn mr* of 14th/13th-century BC Canaanite texts from Ugarit (Gordon, *Ugaritic Literature*, 1949, p. 130: texts 12 + 97, lines 2, 8, 15 and 120, line 15) and of the contemporary Amarna Letter No. 25, IV:51 (*šaman murri*); the Heb. word *mōr* is therefore early, not 'late' as is wrongly stated in *BDB*, p. 600b. Egyptian *'ntyw*, 'myrrh', was also used in this liquid form, for anointing and medicine (refs. Erman and Grapow, *Wörterbuch der Aegyptischen Sprache*, 1, p. 206: 7). It is this kind of liquid myrrh that is the true *stacte* (Lucas, *JEA* 23, 1937, pp. 29–33; Thompson, *Dictionary of Assyrian Botany*, p. 340).

The precise identity of the 'sweet cinnamon', *qinnmon bešem* (Ex. 30:23; *cf.* Pr. 7:17; Ct. 4:14) is uncertain. There is no formal evidence that this term represents the *Cinnamomum zeylanicum*, native to Ceylon; other plants with aromatic bark or wood in this cinnamon/cassia group are possible (*cf.* Thompson, *op. cit.*, pp. 189–190). That the Egyp. *ti-šps*-wood is cinnamon (Forbes, *Studies in Ancient Technology*, 3, p. 8, Table II, and Lucas, *op. cit.*, p. 354, by implication) is wholly uncertain. See also cassia, below. For fragrant cosmetic woods in Egypt (samples), see Lucas, p. 119; Shamshi-Adad I of Assyria also sought them (G. Dossin, *Archives Royales de Mari*, 1, No. 88, ll. 27–30—*iṣu riqu*).

The 'sweet calamus' (Ex. 30:23, AV, RV) or 'aromatic cane' (RSV) is Heb. *qᵉnēh-bōśem*, and its identity with the 'sweet cane from a far country' (Je. 6:20, and also the 'calamus' of Ezk. 27:19), *qāneh haṭṭôḇ*, is not certain. The latter, however, is very likely the *qanu tâbu* of Assyro-Babylonian texts, from 18th century BC onwards (for that of Mari, see C. F. Jean, *Archiv Orientálni* 17: 1, 1949, p. 328). And this is probably the *Acorus calamus* having an aromatic rhizome or stem-root; see Thompson, *op. cit.*, pp. 20–21. In New Kingdom Egypt, 15th–12th centuries BC, the scented *ḳnn*-plant is identified as *Acorus calamus* (G. Jéquier, *Bulletin de l'Institut Français d'Archéologie Orientale* 19, 1922, pp. 44–45, 259 and n. 3; Caminos, *Late-Egyptian Miscellanies*, 1954, p. 209—*ḳnni*-oil). Actual plant stalks in a pot labelled 'perfume' or similar were found in Tutankhamūn's tomb, *c.* 1340 BC (Lucas, p. 119). The '50 talents of reeds' in an Ugarit tablet (Gordon, *Ugaritic Literature*, p. 130, text 120: 9–10) among other aromatics might be sweet cane, but hardly cinnamon (Sukenik, *Tarbiz* 18, 1947, p. 126; see Gordon, *Ugaritic Textbook*, 3, 1965, p. 479, No. 2244).

Finally, there is cassia, which translates Heb. *qiddâ* in Ex. 30:24 and Ezk. 27:19. Whatever the real identity of this might be, it is very possible that *qiddâ* is the same as Egyp. *ḳdt* in Papyrus Harris I of *c.* 1160 BC (so Forbes, *op. cit.*, p. 8, Table II). The other Heb. term often rendered 'cassia'—*qᵉṣîʿāh*—is obscurer still. However, if in meaning this term is parallel to Arab. *salīḫāh*, 'peeled', and this in turn to Assyro-Bab. *kasi ṣîri* (as Thompson, *op. cit.*, p. 191, would suggest), then it might well be Assyr. *qulqullânu*, modern Arab. *qulqul*, the *Cassia tora* (Thompson, *op. cit.*, pp. 188–192). *Cf.* name of Job's second daughter (Jb. 42:14). (*HERBS, Cassia.)

b. The sacred incense

For the significance of incense, see *Incense. Only its make-up is dealt with here. The general Heb. word for incense (which also appears as 'smoke', and 'perfume' at times) is *qᵉṭoreṯ*, known as a loan-word in Egyp. from the 12th century BC (Erman and Grapow, *Wörterbuch d. Aeg. Sprache*, 5, p. 82: 3); other forms from the root *qṭr* occur. In the sacred incense of Ex. 30:34–38 the last two constituents are easiest to identify. One of these, Heb. *ḥelbᵉnāh*, is pretty certainly galbanum, *Ferula galbaniflua* Boiss., growing in Persia and known in Mesopotamia (Bab. *buluḫḫum*) from the 3rd millennium BC onwards. (See Thompson, *op. cit.*, pp. 342–344; W. von Soden, *Akkadisches Handwörterbuch*, Lieferung 2, 1959, p. 101 and refs.)

Frankincense, Heb. *lᵉḇônāh* ('white'), is named from its appearance as whitest of the gum-resins used for incense; it comes from the genus of trees *Boswellia* of S Arabia and Somaliland, and is the classical olibanum. The Egyptian queen Hatshepsut apparently had such trees brought to Egypt *c.* 1490 BC, and small balls of frankincense were found in Tutankhamūn's tomb (*c.* 1340 BC). See Lucas, *op. cit.*, pp. 111–113. *naṭāp̄*, 'drops', is given as *stacte* in LXX, but for true *stacte* see V.*a* above on myrrh. The name suggests a natural exudation and suitable for incense—perhaps a storax (*cf.* on these, Lucas, *op. cit.*, p. 116; Thompson, *op. cit.*, pp. 340–342) or else balm of Gilead, *opobalsamum*, *etc.*, on which see Thompson, pp. 363–364. The last term, *šᵉḥēleṯ*, is quite uncertain; LXX renders as *onyx*, hence EVV onycha—part of a mollusc giving an odour when burnt (Black and Cheyne, *EBi*, under Onycha). But it might just conceivably be a plant-product, *šiḫiltu* in Assyr. medicine (Aram. *šiḫlâ*), Thompson, *Dictionary of Assyrian Chemistry*, 1936, p. 73 and n. 1; but hardly Assyr. *saḫlê*, 'cress' (for which see Thompson, *Dictionary of Assyrian Botany*, 1949, pp. 55–61). But *šḫlt* in Ugarit-text 12 + 97 among aromatics and foodstuff (Gordon, *Ugaritic Literature*, p. 130, l. 4; *Ugaritic Textbook*, 3, p. 488, No. 2397) could very well be Heb. *šᵉḥēleṯ* and even Assyr. *šiḫiltu* and Aram. *šiḫlâ* already mentioned. None of these is Assyr. *saḫullatu*, because this latter must be read as *ḫullatu* (Thompson, *op. cit.*, p. 69). To attempt any closer solution would be too hazardous at present.

For an attempt to reconstitute the sacred incense of Ex. 30, see *Progress*, Vol. 47, No. 264, 1959–60, pp. 203–209 with specimen. K.A.K.

COUNCIL. In the OT (AV) the word appears once only, as a translation of Heb. *riḡmâ* (Ps. 68:27) in referring to 'the princes of Judah and their council', a general word which could be rendered 'company' (so AVmg.) or 'throng' (RSV). The similar word 'counsel' is used in Je. 23:18, 22, AV (RV, RSV 'council'), of the privy council (Heb. *sôḏ*) of Yahweh (*cf.* 1 Ki. 22:19ff.; Jb. 1:6ff.; 2:1ff.), where his decrees are announced; true prophets have access to this council and so have foreknowledge of those decrees.

In the NT two Gk. words are used. *symboulion* denotes a consultation of people (Mt. 12:14), or the provincial governor's advisory board (Acts 25:12). *synedrion*, a 'sitting together', is used most frequently with reference to the *Sanhedrin, the supreme court of the Jews, but sometimes also to lesser courts (*e.g.* Mt. 10:17; Mk. 13:9), of which Jerusalem had two and each Palestinian town one. J.D.D.

COUNCIL, JERUSALEM. The Council of Jerusalem is the name commonly given to the meeting convened between delegates from the church of Antioch (led by Paul and Barnabas) and the apostles and elders of the church of Jerusalem, to discuss problems arising from the large influx of Gentile converts into the church (Acts 15:2–29). Many commentators identify this meeting with the one described in Gal. 2:1–10; the view taken here, however, is that in Gal. 2:1–10 Paul refers to an earlier conference which he and Barnabas had with James the Just, Peter and John, at which the Jerusalem leaders recognized the vocation and status of Paul and Barnabas as apostles to the Gentiles. (For the view that one and the same occasion is referred to, see *CHRONOLOGY OF THE NEW TESTAMENT, section **II.*d*.**)

I. The occasion

The rapid progress of the gospel among Gentiles in Antioch (Acts 11:19ff.) and in Cyprus and Asia Minor (Acts 13:4–14:26) presented the conservative Jewish believers in Judaea with a serious problem. The apostles had acquiesced in Peter's evangelization of the household in Caesarea because it was attended by evident marks of divine approval (Acts 10:1–11:18), but if the spread of the gospel among Gentiles continued on the present scale there would soon be more Gentiles than Jews in the church, with a consequent threat to the maintenance of Christian moral standards. To this problem many Jewish Christians had a simple solution. Let the Gentile converts be admitted to the church in the same way as Gentile proselytes were admitted into the commonwealth of Israel: let them be circumcised and accept the obligation to keep the Jewish law.

Thus far these conditions had not been imposed on Gentile converts. No word appears to have been said about circumcision to Cornelius and his household, and when Titus, a Gentile Christian, visited Jerusalem with Paul and Barnabas on the earlier occasion the question of circumcising him was not even aired (Gal. 2:3). Now, however, some zealots for the law in the Jerusalem church decided to press upon the Gentile Christians of Antioch and her daughter-churches the necessity of taking on themselves the yoke of the law. Their pressure proved so persuasive in the recently-founded churches of Galatia that Paul had to send these churches the urgent protest which we know as his Epistle to the *Galatians. In Antioch itself they caused such controversy that the leaders of the church there decided to have the whole question ventilated and settled at the highest level. Accordingly, the Council of Jerusalem was convened (*c.* AD 48).

II. The main question settled

The debate was opened by the Pharisaic party in the Jerusalem church, who insisted that the Gentile converts must be circumcised and required to keep the law. After much disputing, Peter reminded the Council that God had already shown his will in the matter by giving the Holy Spirit to Cornelius and his household on the ground of their faith alone. Paul and Barnabas supported Peter's argument by telling how God had similarly blessed large numbers of believing Gentiles through their ministry. Then James the Just, leader of the Jerusalem church, summed up the debate and expressed his judgment that no conditions should be imposed on the Gentile converts beyond the condition of faith in Christ with which God had clearly shown himself to be satisfied. The Gentile cities, he said, had no lack of witnesses to the Mosaic law; but the entry of Gentiles into the church of the Messiah was the fulfilment of the promise that David's fallen tent would be set up again and his sovereignty be re-established over Gentile nations (Am. 9:11f.).

III. A practical issue decided

Once the main question of principle was settled in a way which must have given complete satisfaction to the Antiochene delegation, a practical matter remained to be dealt with, affecting the day-to-day fellowship between Jewish and Gentile converts where there were mixed communities. It would be a sign of grace and courtesy if Gentile Christians respected certain Jewish scruples. Hence, at James's suggestion, the letter in which the Jerusalem leaders conveyed their findings to the Gentile churches of Syria and Cilicia (including that of Antioch) ended with an admonition to them to abstain from certain kinds of food which their brethren of Jewish stock would find offensive, and to conform to the Jewish code of relations between the sexes. Without such concessions from Gentile Christians, there would have been grave practical difficulties in the way of their enjoying unrestrained table-fellowship with Jewish Christians. (When it is remembered that in those days the Lord's Supper was regularly taken in the course of a general fellowship meal, the importance of this consideration will be realized.) There is no real substance in the objection that Paul would not have agreed to communicate these conditions to his Gentile converts (as he is said to have done in Acts 16:4). Where basic principles were not compromised, Paul was the most conciliatory of men, and he repeatedly urges on Christians this very duty of respecting the scruples of others in such matters (*cf.* Rom. 14:1ff.; 1 Cor. 8:1ff.). Nevertheless, when the Corinthians asked Paul for a ruling on food offered to idols he appealed to first principles and not to the Jerusalem decree.

After a generation or two, the situation which called forth the Jerusalem Council and the apostolic letter of Acts 15:23–29 disappeared, and the Western Text of Acts adapts the letter to a new situation by altering its requirements in a more purely ethical direction—requiring abstention from idolatry, bloodshed and fornication. But the requirements in their original form were observed by Christians in Gaul and N Africa late in the 2nd century, and were incorporated by Alfred the Great in his English law-code towards the end of the 9th century.

BIBLIOGRAPHY. W. L. Knox, *The Acts of the Apostles*, 1948, pp. 40ff.; C. S. C. Williams, *The Acts of the Apostles*, 1957, pp. 177ff.; E. Haenchen, *The Acts of the Apostles*, 1971, pp. 440ff.; R. Bauckham, in *BA1CS* 2. F.F.B.

COUNSELLOR (Heb. *yô'ēṣ*, 'one who gives advice or counsel'). The basic idea appears in Pr. 24:6b. The word is used as a designation of the Messiah in Is. 9:6, where in respect to the giving of counsel he is said to be a wonder (*pele'*). RSV uses 'Counsellor' to translate *paraklētos* in Jn. but has 'advocate' in 1 Jn. 2:1.

The word *paraklētos* derived from the verb *parakaleō*, literally 'to call beside', has been interpreted both actively and passively; actively as meaning one who stands by and exhorts or encourages, whence the AV 'Comforter' in Jn. 14:16, 26; 15:26; 16:7; passively as meaning one called to stand by someone, particularly in a law-court (though as a friend of the accused rather than a professional pleader), whence 'advocate' in 1 Jn. 2:1. Many versions simply transliterate the Greek; hence the name 'Paraclete' for the Holy Spirit.

parakaleō is frequently used in the NT to mean 'exhort', 'encourage', and Acts 9:31 speaks expressly of the *paraklēsis* of the Holy Spirit, which probably means the 'exhortation' or 'encouragement' of the Spirit (though it may mean the invocation of the Spirit's aid).

There is little evidence for an active use of *paraklētos* outside the NT or the patristic commentators on the Gospel passages, who seem to derive the sense 'consoler' or 'encourager' simply from the general context, which speaks of the disciples' sense of desolation at Jesus' departure and of their need to be taught more about him. In Gk. translation of Jb. 16:2, Aquila and Theodotion used *paraklētoi* where LXX has *paraklētores*, the regular active noun for 'comforters'.

On the other hand, the help of the Spirit promised in Mt. 10:19–20; Mk. 13:11; Lk. 12:11–12 is precisely that of an advocate before the Jewish and secular authorities. Even Jn. 16:8–11 has a forensic tone, though admittedly rather of prosecution than defence. The translation 'advocate' is more appropriate in 1 Jn. 2:1, where the sinner is thought of as arraigned before God's justice. Even here, however, the more general sense is not impossible.

The evidence is nicely balanced, and since so many words in the fourth Gospel seem intended to suggest more than one meaning, an ambiguous rendering such as RSV 'Counsellor' is probably to be preferred.

Critics have argued that the application of the word *paraklētos* in the Gospel to the Spirit and in the Epistle to Jesus Christ indicates the different authorship of the two works. But: (i) the Spirit's *paraklēsis* is amid earthly dangers and difficulties; Jesus appears for us in heaven; (ii) these different but parallel offices are reflected also in Rom. 8:26, 34: the Spirit makes intercession in us and the risen Christ for us in heaven; (iii) the words *allos paraklētos* used in Jn. 14:16, though Greek usage permits the translation 'another, a Paraclete', may mean simply 'another Paraclete', implying that Jesus himself is a Paraclete. (*SPIRIT, HOLY.)

BIBLIOGRAPHY. C. K. Barrett, *JTS* n.s. 1, 1950, pp. 7–15; G. Johnston, *The Spirit-Paraclete in the Gospel of John*, 1970, pp. 80–118. M.H.C.

COURAGE. The Heb. word *ḥāzaq* means literally 'to show oneself strong'. Other words, *e.g.* *rûaḥ*, 'spirit' (Jos. 2:11), *lēḇāḇ*, 'heart' (Dn. 11:25) and *'āmaṣ*, 'to be quick' or 'alert', exhibit the basic attitude from which courage flows. Courage is, therefore, a quality of the mind, and, as such, finds a place among the cardinal virtues (Wisdom 8:7). Its opposite, cowardice, is found among the mortal sins (Ecclus. 2:12–13). The quality can be seen only in its manifestations and especially, in the OT, on the battlefield (Judges, Samuel, Chronicles). The moral idea is not entirely absent. Those who are objects of God's special care are to 'fear not' (Is. 41:13–14; Je. 1:8; Ezk. 2:6).

The absence of the word from the NT is striking. The noun *tharsos* occurs only once (Acts 28:15). The ideal for the Christian is not the Stoic *aretē* (virtue), but a quality of life based on faith in the present Christ. Here is no 'grin and bear it' attitude, but a more than natural one which sees an occasion for victory in every opposition (*cf.* 1 Cor. 16:9).

The verb *tharreō*, a form current from the time of Plato with the sense of 'to be confident, hopeful, of good courage', is found in Heb. 13:6; and in 2 Cor. 5:6, 8 ('good courage'); 7:16 ('perfect confidence'); 10:1–2 ('boldness'). The cognate term *tharseō* appears with more emotional overtones and is rendered 'take heart' in Mt. 9:2, 22; Mk. 10:49, but as 'take courage' in Acts 23:11. Courage is a Christian duty but also a constant possibility for one who places himself in the almighty hands of God. It shows itself in patient endurance, moral steadfastness and spiritual fidelity. H.D.McD.

COURT. 1. Heb. *ḥāṣēr* (*ḥāṣîr*, Is. 34:13, AV), 'an enclosure or court', as found in a private house (2 Sa. 17:18, AV) or a palace (1 Ki. 7:8), or in a garden (Est. 1:5). It is very commonly used of the court of the *tabernacle (*e.g.* Ex. 27; 35; 38); of the inner court (*heḥāṣēr happᵉnîmîṯ*, *e.g.* 1 Ki. 6:36) and the outer court (*heḥāṣēr haḥîṣônâ*, *e.g.* Ezk. 10:5) of the Temple of Solomon; and the courts of the *Temple in the vision of Ezekiel (Ezk. 40–46). See **4**, below.

2. *ᵃzārâ*, a word of rare occurrence, and therefore uncertain meaning, but evidently used in the sense of 'court' and so translated in 2 Ch. 4:9; 6:13. **3.** *bayiṯ*, 'house', rendered '(king's) court' in AV of Am. 7:13 (*bêṯ mamlāḵâ*), but RV and RSV give variant translations. **4.** *'îr*, 'city' in 2 Ki. 20:4, and so translated in RV, but AV and RSV follow some MSS, the *Qᵉrē*, and the ancient VSS in reading (*ḥa*)*ṣer*, 'court' (see **1**, above). **5.** Gk. *aulē*, an open enclosure, once (Rev. 11:2) translated 'court' (*PALACE).

In Herod's *Temple, which is not systematically described in the Bible, there were four courts, those of the Gentiles, the Women, the Men (Israel) and the Priests, in ascending order of exclusiveness (*ARCHITECTURE). T.C.M.

COUSIN. The AV rendering in Lk. 1:36 and 1:58 (plural) of Gk. *syngenēs*, 'one of the same family'. Because of the modern restricted use of the Eng. word 'cousin', a more accurate translation would be 'kinswoman' (so RV, RSV). (*KIN.) In Col. 4:10 *anepsios* ('sister's son' in AV) means 'cousin' (so RV, RSV). J.D.D.

COVENANT, ALLIANCE.

I. Terminology

The two key-words in the Bible for covenant or alliance are Heb. *bᵉrîṯ* and Gk. *diathēkē*. *bᵉrîṯ* usually refers to the act or rite of the making of a covenant and also to the standing contract between two partners. *diathēkē* is the Gk. translation (LXX) of the word *bᵉrîṯ* which is taken over in the NT. Its meaning is 'testament'. Along with *bᵉrîṯ* various other terms are used in a covenantal context. The most important are *'āhēḇ* 'to love', *ḥeseḏ* 'covenant love' or 'covenant solidarity', *ṭôḇâ* 'goodness' or 'friendship', *šālôm* 'covenantal peace' or 'covenantal prosperity' and *yāḏa'* 'to serve faithfully in accordance with the covenant'. With the exception of *ḥeseḏ* all the other terms can be somehow connected to terminology in ancient Near Eastern treaties.

Various verbs are used in connection with *bᵉrîṯ*. The technical term is *kāraṯ bᵉrîṯ*, lit. 'to cut a covenant', which points to the ancient rite of cutting an animal with the forming of a treaty or covenant. When the verb *kāraṯ* is used with the prepositions *lᵉ* or *'im*, it points in the direction of a covenant contracted by a superior. Many verbs are used in place of *kāraṯ*, *e.g.* *hēqîm*, 'to establish', *nāṯan* 'to give', *higgîḏ* 'to declare', *nišba'* 'to swear', *heᵉmîḏ* 'to confirm', *ṣiwwâ* 'to command' and *śām* 'to make'. Various verbs are also used to denote the participation of the people in the covenant, *e.g.* *bô'* 'to come into a covenant relationship with the Lord' (2 Ch. 15:12), *āḇar* 'to enter into such a relationship' (Dt. 29:12) and *āmaḏ* 'to stand in a covenant relationship'. Two verbs are used for keeping the covenant, *viz.* *nāṣar* and *šāmar*. A whole cluster of verbs are used for breaking the covenant: in the first place *lō'* with *nāṣar* and *šāmar*, then *e.g.* *šāḵaḥ* 'to forget', *āḇar* 'to transgress', *mā'as* 'to despise', *pārar* 'to break', *šāqar* 'to be false to', *ḥillēl* 'to profane' and *šāhaṯ* 'to corrupt'.

II. Covenantal rites

We are not well informed on covenantal rites, because of lack of material. There are, however, a few vestiges of these rites left in available material. The slaughtering of an animal (sheep, donkey, bull, *etc.*) is described in the Mari texts, the Alalaḫ tablets and in the OT. It was the custom to cut the animal in two or three parts (so lately advocated by Cazelles). Part of it was burnt in honour of the god and part of it was eaten at a covenantal meal. In Gn. 15 such a rite is described. In Ex. 24 the same rite is mentioned. In this case the sacrifice and the covenantal meal are clearly described. In certain ancient Near Eastern vassal treaties it is stated that the vassal is compelled to visit the great king annually to renew the treaty. Although the OT is not clear on this point, it is not unlikely that the same custom existed in Israel. It is possible that the Israelites gathered with a certain festival (New Year's festival) to renew the covenant.

III. Alliance or treaty

(*i*) *In the ancient Near East.* The idea of making a treaty pervades almost the whole history of the ancient Near East. It is only by chance that we are well informed on certain Near Eastern treaties, *e.g.* the Hittite treaties, the treaties of Esarhaddon and the Aramaean treaty of Sefire. A close study of, *e.g.*, the Mari tablets and those of Amarna shows that a treaty background existed between various of the nations and groups mentioned. The usage of, *e.g.*, father-son, or lord-servant (*abdu*) shows that in a friendly relationship the great king is usually called 'father' and the vassal king 'son', and in a more stern relationship the great king is called 'lord' and his vassal 'servant'. Two main types of treaties occurred: (1) a treaty of equals in which the two partners are called 'brothers', *e.g.* the treaty between Hattusilis III and Rameses II. The stipulations in this kind of treaty are restricted mainly to acknowledgment of borders and the return of runaway slaves. (2) a vassal-treaty was contracted between a great king (conqueror) and a minor king. These treaties were built up more or less around the following scheme: preamble or introduction, in which the great king is introduced with all his titles and attributes; the historical prologue, in which the history of the relationship between the great king and the vassal's forefathers and the vassal himself is sketched. It is not a stereotyped history, but actual historical occurrences which are described with strong emphasis on the benevolent deeds of the great king to the vassal and his country. Then the stipulations of the treaty are given. These consist, *e.g.*, of the following: prohibition of any relationship with a country outside the Hittite sphere; prohibition of hostility to other Hittite vassals; immediate help to the great king in times of war; the vassal must not listen to any slandering of the great king but immediately report it to the king; the vassal must not hide deserting slaves or refugees; the vassal must appear once a year before the king to pay his taxes and to renew the treaty. The stipulations are followed by the compulsion on the vassal to deposit the written treaty in the temple and to read it occasionally. This is followed by a list of gods as witnesses, in which the gods of the great king are prominently placed. Even certain natural phenomena such as heaven and earth, mountains, sea, rivers, *etc.*, are called in as witnesses. The vassal treaty is concluded by curses and blessings. Certain curses will come into effect when the treaty is broken. These curses are of a wide variety and it is clear that certain of them are reserved for the divine sphere and others could be executed by the army of the great king. When the treaty is kept, certain blessings will accrue to the vassal, *e.g.* the eternal reign of his descendants. Variations on this theme occur in later vassal treaties, *e.g.* in the vassal treaties of Esarhaddon heavy emphasis is laid on the curse motif. In the Sefire treaty the curse is illustrated by the melting of a wax figure, *etc.*, a kind of magic act.

(*ii*) *In the OT*. It is clear from the OT that the treaty relationship with foreign nations was not unknown to the Israelites. Both types of treaties, those between equals and vassal treaties, occur in the OT. Vestiges of a parity treaty between the Israelites and the Midianites (Ex. 18) are discernible, although many unsolved problems existed, *e.g.* the relationship between Midianites and Kenites and the later hostility between Midianites and Israelites. The best example of a parity treaty, however, is the one between the Israelites and the Phoenicians. It started probably between David and Hiram (note the word *'ōhēb*, 'loved', in expressing the relationship between David and Hiram, 1 Ki. 5:1) and was renewed on a more elaborate scale between Solomon and Hiram. They are called brothers, and one of their transactions, *viz.* the exchange of certain cities for timber, *etc.*, can be paralleled by the same kind of transaction in the Alalaḫ tablets, also in the treaty sphere. This treaty relationship is later inherited by N Israel after the division of the Israelite kingdom. The good relations between the Omrides and the Phoenicians were built on this treaty. We know, *e.g.*, that the parity treaty between Hattusilis III and Rameses II was concluded with a marriage between the daughter of Hattusilis and Rameses. The marriage between Jezebel and Ahab must be understood as a partial fulfilment of the conditions of the treaty.

The best example of a vassal treaty in the OT is the one contracted between the Israelites and Gibeonites (Jos. 9–10). The vassal character of the treaty is evident in the terminology. The Gibeonites came to the Israelites and told them that they wanted to become their slaves. The expression 'we are your slaves' (*'ᵃḇāḏeḵâ 'ᵃnāḥnû*) is definitely referring to vassalage. The treaty was contracted and then a covenantal peace (*šālôm*) between the two parties existed. Although most modern scholars regard Jos. 10 as a later addition, it is to be observed that the military assistance of the Israelites to the Gibeonites after the forming of the treaty was a well-known treaty obligation on the major partner (*e.g.* clearly stated in the vassal treaties discovered at Ugarit). It is thus abundantly clear that the Israelites were well aware of various forms of treaties as they were applied elsewhere in the ancient Near East.

IV. Biblical covenants

(*i*) *The covenant with the Lord*. The idea of a covenant relationship between a god and a king or his people is well attested through the history of the ancient Near East. It occurs in various forms with a great diversity of material. This is not always expressly stated, but can be deduced from terminology used. The idea of such a covenant was thus not at all foreign to the Israelites. At the same time the treaty relationship was well known to them, as we have seen above. It is thus not surprising that the Lord used this form of relationship to give expression to his relation with his people. This could have started early, because such an idea was well known in the ancient Near East from well back in the 3rd millennium BC.

(*ii*) *Early covenants*. Biblical tradition mentions two covenants contracted between God and Noah (Gn. 6:18; Gn. 9:8–17). It is clearly called a covenant, with a certain obligation on Noah and certain promises from the Lord. This is a prelude to biblical covenants where the promise plays an important role.

(*iii*) *The patriarchal covenant*. This is transmitted to us in two traditions, *viz.* Gn. 15 and 17. The Lord has contracted this covenant with Abraham with strong emphasis on the promise (especially in Gn. 17). Two promises were made, *viz.* the multiplication of Abraham's offspring and the inheritance of the *Promised Land. It is obvious, *e.g.* from the book of Exodus, that the promise of a large offspring is regarded as fulfilled (*cf.* Ex. 1:7–22). The description of the conquering of the Promised Land in Joshua points to the fulfilment of the promise of inheritance. The patriarchal covenant is thus mainly promissory. In this it is closely related to the Davidic covenant. The author of Exodus, although describing the forming of the new Sinaitic covenant, still emphasizes the importance of the patriarchal covenant. With the breaking of the Sinai covenant (Ex. 32) this author demonstrates that the patriarchal covenant was still in force (Ex. 33:1). It is thus to be noted that the Sinai covenant did not replace the patriarchal covenant, but co-existed with it.

(*iv*) *The Sinai covenant*. According to biblical tradition, this covenant was formed with Moses as mediator at Sinai after the Israelites were wonderfully saved by the Lord from their Egyptian bondage. In Ex. 24 the actual rite of the covenant-forming is described. This description has an ancient flavour. A sacrifice was made to the Lord. The blood of the sacrificial animals was divided in two parts, one of which was poured out against the altar. Mention is also made of the book of the covenant. Nothing is said of the contents of this book. Some scholars hold that this refers to the Decalogue and others that it refers to the preceding Covenant Code. We have here a new covenant in which the law is read, followed by the response of the people, sacrifice, sealing by oath and finally the covenant meal. It is clear that the author of Exodus has combined the covenant-forming with the stipulations of the Covenant Code. In Ex. 19 the theophany of the Lord is described; in Ex. 20 the policy of the Lord for his people is sketched (the Decalogue); in Ex. 21–23 the stipulations are given and in Ex. 24 the actual rite of the covenant is described. It is important to note that this covenant has a detailed description of stipulations. As we have seen from the Hittite vassal treaties, stipulations are part and parcel of the treaty form. But we must bear in mind that this is an Israelite covenant which could follow in certain aspects well-known treaty or covenant forms, but could deviate in other aspects from the restricted number of forms we know from the ancient Near East. The stipulations of the Covenant Code are totally different in content from what we know of treaty stipulations. Special circumstances and the different religious background should account for this. At the end of the Covenant Code as a kind of epilogue the promissory character is discernible. Here the reference to the Promised Land is again taken up.

(*v*) *The Davidic covenant*. This covenant is mainly promissory. We agree with various scholars who hold that this covenant is closely connected to the Sinai covenant. It is not to be regarded as a new covenant, but as a further extension of the Sinai covenant. The Davidic covenant became necessary with the development of a new historical situation. The Israelite king was now the mediator between the Lord and his people. A covenant with this king thus became a necessity. The latest research has shown that a close link also exists between the patriarchal and Davidic covenants. Both covenants are of the promissory type. The patriarchal promises were fulfilled with the growing of the Israelite population and with the inheritance of Palestine. It was thus necessary to make new promises in the new situation which developed. With the new promise to David of an eternal reign by his descendants, the patriarchal covenant was in a certain sense superseded by the new covenant. In 2 Sa. 7 the covenant is embedded in a narrative form, but certain terminology clearly points to the covenant background, *e.g.* God will be a father for David's son and the king will be a son for God. The eternal throne of David's descendants can be paralleled to the promise in the form of a blessing in the Hittite vassal treaties, *viz*. that the faithful vassal's sons would reign eternally on his throne. The Davidic covenant, as it is clear from Pss. 2 and 110, had profound influence on later expectations in the OT and even in the NT.

(*vi*) *Covenant in the NT*. In *c*. 600 BC a great upsurge of interest in the covenant occurred (*e.g.* in Jeremiah). The influence of the covenant idea was also strongly felt during the intertestamental period, as K. Baltzer and A. Jaubert have shown. The sect of Qumran can be regarded as a covenant community. It is to be expected that this would also be true in the NT. In the NT the word 'covenant' (*diathēkē* as a Gk. translation of *bᵉrîṯ*) is used in close connection with the *Lord's Supper (*cf*. Mk 14:22–25; 1 Cor. 11:23–25). With the institution of the Holy Communion Jesus refers to his body as the bread and his blood as the wine. This is obviously a reference to Jesus as the paschal lamb which must be slaughtered with Passover and be eaten by his disciples. The paschal lamb became the covenant animal and the Holy Communion a covenant meal. Interesting is Christ's reference to the new testament of his blood. Note the prominent role of blood in the covenant-forming at Sinai (Ex. 24:8). The killing of Jesus as the paschal lamb will take place at Golgotha the next day. Christ's sacrifice on the cross is the most important part of the forming of a new covenant. Paul correctly interpreted Christ's crucifixion as taking on him the curses of the law in order to redeem mankind (Gal. 3:13). With the new covenant the curse of the old Sinaitic covenant is removed by Christ. He became the new Davidic King on the eternal throne. At once two old covenants were superseded: the curses of the Sinai covenant were removed and the promise of the Davidic covenant fulfilled.

(*vii*) *Renewal and ratification of the covenant*. The renewal of the covenant means that the covenant is broken and must be renewed to come into force again. The best example of this is in Ex. 32–34, where the Sinai covenant is broken by Aaron and the Israelites by making a golden bull for worship. When Moses came back, the curses of breaking the covenant were applied by killing a number of Israelites (Ex. 32:26–28). Moses acted as mediator to renew the broken covenant. He went back on the mountain to receive once more the stipulations for the renewed covenant (Ex. 34). Jeremiah regarded the covenant as so totally broken that it could be replaced only by a new covenant (Je. 31:31).

The ratification of the covenant is when a covenant is renewed without necessarily being broken. The best example of this is in Jos. 23–24. In Jos. 23 a description is given of Joshua's final commandments to the Israelites in which they are requested to keep the covenant. According to Jos. 24, with a strong covenant background, the Israelites were gathered at Shechem to renew the covenant with the Lord. Some scholars think that the covenant communion was for the first time formed at Shechem because of the ancient tradition of covenant-forming at this place. We are following the biblical tradition and regard the meeting at Shechem as a ratification of the covenant.

V. The covenant and the prophets

The view of Wellhausen, still followed by many scholars, is that the covenant idea is foreign to the earlier prophets. The idea is only developed from the time of the Deuteronomist onwards (*cf.*, *e.g.*, the views of Kutsch and Perlitt). This view is mainly built on the assumption that nothing can be discovered of the covenant idea in the earlier prophets and that the usage of *bᵉrîṯ* is almost non-existent. It is true that *bᵉrîṯ* is scarce in these writings, but it is a question whether we could ascribe the scarcity of a term to the non-existence of an institution or not. There might have been a reason for the avoidance of *bᵉrîṯ*, *e.g.* a wrong conception could have existed amongst the readers and listeners of the real meaning of the term. Recent research has shown that the covenant idea pervades most of the writings of the prophets, if we use a wider approach and look for the different elements in the covenant, *e.g.* the curse and blessing and the breaking of the covenant by contravening the stipulations. What will happen when the stipulations are broken? Then a covenant lawsuit will follow. The connection between the prophetic office and law is clear from a close study of the prophetic writings. There is no difference in approach to the law between prophets like Hosea, Amos, Isaiah and Jeremiah. Why should Jeremiah be singled out as a protagonist of the covenant just because he has used *bᵉrîṯ* and the others not?

One of the main problems of the prophetic writings is the origin of the prophetic threat. Another problem is the combination of prophetic threat and blessing. A close study of the threats shows that many of them can be closely linked to roughly contemporary curses in vassal treaties, *e.g.* those of Esarhaddon and Sefire. The curse was, however, not only restricted to treaties, but used for a variety of purposes in the ancient Near East. It is to be observed that the treaty curse has certain characteristics which occur also in the prophetic threat. This makes it probable that the prophets regarded the covenant as broken and that as a result of this, certain curses would come into effect. This implies that the prophets were familiar with the covenant form. The fact that they have pronounced threats when the law (of the covenant) is broken, but blessing and prosperity when the law (of the covenant) is kept, shows their special knowledge of the covenant form. The whole problem of threat and blessing beside each other can then be explained by the breaking or the keeping of the covenant.

The covenant lawsuit, which is well attested in the ancient Near East, as Harvey has shown, can be traced from an early source like Dt. 32 to the early and later prophets, *e.g.* Is. 1:2–3, 10–20; Je. 2:4–13; Mi. 6:1–8. In the lawsuit the Israelites are accused of idolatry. It means that they have violated one of the conditions of the covenant, *viz.* not to worship any other god. On this, judgment is pronounced in the form of threats or curses. It is striking that in certain lawsuits heaven and earth are called in as witnesses. The parallel with the much earlier Hittite vassal treaties, where heaven and earth are also regarded as witnesses, is most illuminating. This points to a close link with the treaty or covenant form.

VI. The covenant and theology

Eichrodt in his *Theology of the Old Testament* takes covenant as the central idea of the OT. Israelite religious thought was built up around this concept. From the discussion above it is clear how pervading and important the covenant idea was for the Israelites. It does not, however, exclude other modes of expressing relationship between the Lord and his people. The covenant with its stipulations opens up the possibility of transgression and sin, with the consequence of judgment and punishment. This is one of the main themes of the OT. Another important feature of the covenant is promise and expectation. The Davidic covenant with the promise of an eternal throne gave rise to the expectation of the glorious coming of the Messiah, Son of David. This forms the important link between OT and NT. The covenant is thus the most important link between the Testaments. With the new covenant of the NT a fresh expectation is given of the *parousia* of the Messiah. This shows that the covenant and the expectations which it creates, are also responsible for the main theme of eschatological expectation.

Bibliography. For a good bibliography up to 1977, *cf.* D. J. McCarthy, *Old Testament Covenant*², 1978. The following is a selection from a vast literature: K. Baltzer, *The Covenant Formulary*, 1971; W. Beyerlin, *Origins and History of the Oldest Sinaitic Traditions*, 1965; P. J. Calderone, *Dynastic Oracle and Suzerainty Treaty*, 1966; H. Cazelles, *DBS*, 7, 1964, pp. 736–858; R. E. Clements, *Abraham and David*, 1967; W. J Dumbrell, *Covenant and Creation*, 1984; F. C. Fensham, 'Covenant, Promise and Expectation', *TZ* 23, 1967, pp. 305–322; *idem*, 'Common Trends in Curses of the Near Eastern Treaties and *Kudurru*-inscriptions compared with Maledictions of Amos and Isaiah', *ZAW* 75, 1963, pp. 155–175; *idem*, 'The Treaty between the Israelites and the Tyrians', *VT Supp* 17, 1969, pp. 78ff.; G. Fohrer, 'AT-Amphiktyonie und Bund', *ThL* 91, 1966, pp. 802–816, 893–904; J. Harvey, *Le plaidoyer prophétique contre Israël après la rupture de l'alliance*, 1967; D. R. Hillers, *Treaty-curses and the Old Testament Prophets*, 1964; *idem*, *Covenant: The History of a Biblical Idea*, 1968; H. B. Huffmon, 'The Covenant Lawsuit and the Prophets', *JBL* 78, 1959, pp. 286–295; A. Jaubert, *La notion d'alliance dans le judaïsme aux abords de l'ère chrétienne*, 1963; P. Kalluveettil, *Declaration and Covenant*, 1982; K. A. Kitchen, 'Egypt, Ugarit, Qatna and Covenant', *Ugarit Forschungen* 11 (1979), pp. 453–464; *BAR* (forthcoming); M. G. Kline, *Treaty of the Great King*, 1963; E. Kutsch, *Verheissung und Gesetz*, 1973; J. L'Hour, *La morale de l'alliance*, 1966; N. Lohfink, *Die Landverheissung als Eid*, 1967; D. J. McCarthy, *Treaty and Covenant*, 1963; G. E. Mendenhall, *Law and Covenant in Israel and the Ancient Near East*, 1955; J. Muilenburg, 'The Form and Structure of the Covenantal Formulations', *VT* 9, 1959, pp. 74–79; L. Perlitt, *Bundestheologie im Alten Testament*, 1969; A. Phillips, *Ancient Israel's Criminal Law*, 1970; H. Graf Reventlow, *Gebot und Predigt im Dekalog*, 1962; W. Schottroff, *Der Altisraelitische Fluchspruch*, 1969; R. Smend, *Die Bundesformel*, 1963; G. E. Wright, 'The Lawsuit of God: A Form-Critical Study of Deut. 32', *In Honour of J. Muilenburg*, 1962, pp. 26–27; W. Zimmerli, *The Law and the Prophets*, 1965.

F.C.F.

COVENANT, BOOK OF THE. In Ex. 24:7 'the book of the covenant' (*sēp̱er habbᵉrîṯ*) is read by Moses as the basis of Yahweh's covenant with Israel, at its ratification at the foot of Sinai. Probably this 'book' was the Decalogue of Ex. 20:2–17. It has, however, become customary to give the designation 'The Book of the Covenant' to Ex. 20:22–23:33 (which may at one time have occupied a later position in the record). In 2 Ki. 23:2, 21; 2 Ch.

34:30 'the book of the covenant' is the Deuteronomic law. (*DEUTERONOMY.)

Here we are concerned with Ex. 20:22–23:33, conventionally called 'The Book of the Covenant' and in any case the oldest extant codification of Israelite law. It comprises 'judgments' (*mišpāṭîm*, 'precedents') and 'statutes' (*dᵉḇārîm*, lit. 'words'). The 'judgments' take the form of case-laws: 'If a man do so-and-so, he shall pay so much.' The 'statutes' take the categorical or 'apodictic' form: 'You shall (not) do so-and-so.' Intermediate between those types are the participial laws (so called because they are expressed by means of the Hebrew participle), of the type: 'He that does so-and-so shall surely be put to death.' This type frequently replaces the 'If a man . . .' type when the death penalty is prescribed.

The principle on which the laws in this code are arranged does not lie on the surface, but it has been persuasively argued that each section falls within the scope of one of the Ten Commandments: the code could thus be described as 'a running midrash to the decalogue' (E. Robertson, *The Old Testament Problem*, 1950, p. 95; *cf.* A. E. Guilding, 'Notes on the Hebrew Law Codes', *JTS* 49, 1948, pp. 43ff.).

I. Cultic regulations

The code begins with two cultic regulations: the making of gods of silver or gold is forbidden (Ex. 20:22f.) and an 'altar of earth' is prescribed (20:24–26), neither manufactured of hewn stones nor approached by steps, like the more elaborate altars of Israel's neighbours.

II. Judgments

There follows a series of case-laws (21:1–22:17). These cover such civil and criminal cases as the treatment of Hebrew slaves (21:2–6), the sale of one's daughter into slavery (21:7–11), murder and manslaughter (21:12–14), injury to parents (21:15, 17), kidnapping (21:16), assault and battery (21:18–27, incorporating the *lex talionis*, 21:23–25), a goring ox (21:28–32), accidents to animals (21:33f.), killing of one ox by another (21:35f.), theft (22:1–4), damage to crops (22:5f.), deposits and loans (22:7–15), seduction (22:16f.).

It is this section of the code that presents affinities with the other ancient law-codes of the Near East—those of Ur-nammu of Ur, Lipitishtar of Isin, Bilalama (?) of Eshnunna and Hammurapi of Babylon, for example. These are constructed on the same general lines as the Israelite case-law. The Hittite code, too, in several points of detail and arrangement, shows resemblances to these Israelite laws, although the general outlook of the Hittite code differs from that of other Near Eastern codes, reflecting the Indo-European principle of compensation for injury done rather than the Semitic insistence on *talio* (retaliatory punishment).

While the Israelite case-laws are comparable to these other codes, they reflect a simpler way of life. A settled agricultural community is presumed, and people live in houses, but there is nothing of the rather elaborate urban organization or social stratification of Hammurapi's code. Full-grown men in the Israelite community are either citizens or serfs, whereas in Hammurapi's code the punishment for physical injury, for example, is graduated according as the injured person is a superior, an equal, a 'vassal' or a serf.

A life-setting in the early days of agricultural settlement in Israel suggests itself, and we may recall that such settlement began before the crossing of the Jordan—if not at Kadesh-barnea, then certainly in Transjordan, where the conquered kingdoms of Sihon and Og, with their cities, were occupied by Israelites (Nu. 21:25, 35).

In Ex. 18 we have a picture of Israelite case-law in formation; Moses and his assistants adjudicate on cases which are submitted to them. With this we may associate the alternative name of Kadesh given in Gn. 14:7, En-mishpat, *i.e.* the spring where judgment is given.

III. Statutes

The 'apodictic' laws which constitute the remaining part of the code have the form of directions (*tôrâ*) given by God through one of his spokesmen (*cf.* the function of the priest in Mal. 2:7), preferably at a sanctuary—in the first instance, through Moses at Sinai or Kadesh. They have no parallel in the ancient law-codes of W Asia, but it has been pointed out that they have close stylistic affinities with ancient Near Eastern treaties, especially treaties in which a superior imposes conditions on a vassal. The Decalogue, which is also couched in this apodictic style, is the constitution of the covenant established by Yahweh with Israel; the other apodictic laws are corollaries to the basic covenant-law. Many of the statutes of Ex. 22:18–23:33 are concerned with what we should call religious practice, *e.g.* the offering of firstfruits (22:29f.; 23:19a), sabbatical years and days (23:10–12), the three pilgrimage festivals (23:14–17). In 23:15 we find the beginning of a reinterpretation of these festivals to commemorate events in Israel's redemptive history. Ex. 23:10–19 has been regarded as a self-contained ritual code (compare the so-called 'Kenite' code of 34:17–26). But the statutes also include ethical and humanitarian injunctions, protecting those who have no natural protector (22:21–24), forbidding excessive severity to debtors (22:25–27), insisting on judicial impartiality, especially where one of the litigants is an alien who might feel himself at a disadvantage (23:6–9). We should remember that the Israelites knew no such clearcut distinction between civil and religious law as we take for granted today.

IV. Conclusion

The code ends with Yahweh's assurance of success and prosperity to Israel if his covenant-law is obeyed, accompanied by a solemn warning against fraternization with the Canaanites.

While the 'statutes' take the form of direct utterances of God, the 'judgments' also derive their authority from him (Ex. 18:19; 21:1).

BIBLIOGRAPHY. G. E. Mendenhall, *Law and Covenant in Israel and the Ancient Near East*, 1955; K. Baltzer, *The Covenant Formulary*, 1971; B. S. Childs, *Exodus*, 1974, pp. 440–496; C. M. Carmichael, *The Origins of Biblical Law*, 1992; J. W. Marshall, *Israel and the Book of the Covenant*, 1993; J. M. Sprinkle, *The Book of the Covenant*, 1994.

F.F.B.

COVETOUSNESS. The Hebrews visualized the soul as full of vigorous desires which urged it to extend its influence over other persons and things. There was *ḥāmaḏ*, to desire a neighbour's possessions (Dt. 5:21; Mi. 2:2), *beṣa'*, the desire for dishonest gain (Pr. 28:16; Je. 6:13) and *'āwâ*, selfish desire (Pr. 21:26). These are all rendered in AV by 'covetousness'. The OT places covetousness under a ban (Ex. 20:17), and Achan is stoned for the crime in Jos. 7:16–26.

Gk. *epithymia* expresses any intense desire, which if misdirected may be concentrated on money, as in Acts 20:33; 1 Tim. 6:9; Rom. 7:7. Gk. *pleonexia* generally expresses ruthless self-assertion, 2 Cor. 2:11; 7:2, which is applied to possessions in Lk. 12:15, and repudiated by Christ in Mk. 7:22. The word is often associated with immorality in lists of vices (Eph. 4:19; *cf.* Philo), and, being in essence the worship of self, is characterized as the ultimate idolatry in Eph. 5:5 and Col. 3:5. It can be rendered 'avarice' in 2 Cor. 9:5 and 2 Pet. 2:3. Gk. *zēlos* is used to inculcate an intense desire for spiritual gifts in 1 Cor. 12:31; but it describes a very sordid carnal strife in Jas. 4:2. D.H.T.

CREATION.

I. The biblical doctrine

This must not be confused or identified with any scientific theory of origins. The purpose of the biblical doctrine, in contrast to that of scientific investigation, is ethical and religious. Reference to the doctrine is widespread in both the OT and the NT, and is not confined to the opening chapters of Genesis. The following references may be noted: in the prophets, Is. 40:26, 28; 42:5; 45:18; Je. 10:12–16; Am. 4:13; in the Psalms, 33:6, 9; 90:2; 102:25; also Jb. 38:4ff.; Ne. 9:6; and in the NT, Jn. 1:1ff.; Acts 17:24; Rom. 1:20, 25; 11:36; Col. 1:16; Heb. 1:2; 11:3; Rev. 4:11; 10:6.

A necessary starting-point for any consideration of the doctrine is Heb. 11:3, 'By faith we understand that the world was created by the word of God.' This means that the biblical doctrine of creation is based on divine revelation and understood only from the standpoint of faith. It is this that sharply distinguishes the biblical approach from the scientific. The work of creation, no less than the mystery of redemption, is hidden from man and can be perceived only by faith.

The work of creation is variously attributed to all three persons of the Trinity: to the Father, as in Gn. 1:1; Is. 44:24; 45:12; Ps. 33:6; to the Son, as in Jn. 1:3, 10; Col. 1:16; to the Holy Spirit, as in Gn. 1:2; Jb. 26:13. This is not to be taken to mean that different parts of creation are attributed to different persons within the Trinity, but rather that the whole is the work of the triune God.

The words in Heb. 11:3, 'what is seen was made out of things which do not appear', taken with Gn. 1:1, 'in the beginning God created the heavens and the earth', indicate that the worlds were not made out of any pre-existent material, but out of nothing by the divine Word, in the sense that prior to the divine creative fiat there was no other kind of existence. This *creatio ex nihilo* has important theological implications, for among other things it precludes the idea that matter is eternal (Gn. 1:1 indicates that it had a beginning) or that there can be any kind of dualism in the universe in which another kind of existence or power stands over against God and outside his control. Likewise it indicates that God is distinct from his creation, and it is not, as pantheism maintains, a phenomenal, or external, manifestation of the Absolute.

At the same time, however, it is clear that the idea of primary creation contained in the formula *creatio ex nihilo* does not exhaust the biblical teaching on the subject. Man was not created *ex nihilo*, but out of the dust of the ground (Gn. 2:7) and the beasts of the field and the fowls of the air were formed out of the ground (Gn. 2:19). This has been called secondary creation, a creative activity making use of already created materials, and stands alongside primary creation as part of the biblical testimony.

Statements such as Eph. 4:6, 'One God . . . above all, and through all, and in all' indicate that God stands in a relationship of both transcendence and immanence to the created order. In that he is 'above all' and 'over all' (Rom. 9:5), he is the transcendent God, and independent of his creation, self-existent and self-sufficient. Thus creation must be understood as a free act of God determined only by his sovereign will, and in no way a necessary act. He did not need to create the universe (see Acts 17:25). He chose to do so. It is necessary to make this distinction, for only thus can he be God the Lord, the unconditioned, transcendent one. On the other hand, in that he is 'through all, and in all', he is immanent in his creation (though distinct from it), and it is entirely dependent on his power for its continued existence. 'In him *(en autō)* all things hold together' (Col. 1:17) and 'in him we live and move and have our being' (Acts 17:28).

The words 'by thy will they existed and were created' (Rev. 4:11), *cf.* 'created through him, and for him' (Col. 1:16), indicate the purpose and goal of creation. God created the world 'for the manifestation of the glory of his eternal power, wisdom and goodness' (*Westminster Confession*). Creation, in other words, is theocentric, and intended to display the glory of God; to be, as Calvin says, 'the theatre of his glory'. J.P.

II. The Genesis account

The opening chapter of Genesis is a majestic festive overture to the whole Bible. It introduces the reader to the two principal actors in the biblical drama, God and man (*i.e.* mankind, Heb. *'ādām*), and sketches the main elements in their relationship. We meet God, the almighty creator of all that exists, but also the triumphant climax of his work, man, made in the divine image to rule over God's world on his behalf. We sense God's concern for man's well-being as he assigns the plants for his food. This divine concern is even more apparent in Gn. 2, where the Lord God provides a garden for man to dwell in, animals as his companions, and a wife as his perfect counterpart.

These points are obvious to readers, naïve and sophisticated alike. But the latter often find great problems with the Genesis account, for it seems so out of tune with current scientific thinking. It is embarrassing to have such apparently mythical accounts opening the Christian Bible. But this is the fault of the reader who brings his anachronistic ideas to an ancient text. If the text is allowed to address the ideas and concerns of the age it was written for, some 3,000 years ago, it will be found to be a most revolutionary document, challenging some of the fond assumptions of its age and yet continuing to speak powerfully to all interested in fathoming the mystery of life.

To appreciate the uniqueness and originality of Genesis, its account of creation must be compared with other ancient accounts of about the same era from Babylon, Egypt and Canaan. We shall therefore begin by summarizing some of the main ancient Near Eastern beliefs about creation to illuminate the background to Genesis. Then we shall focus on the main assertions of Genesis about God, the world and man. A comparison with ancient Near Eastern creation stories also illuminates the nature of the genre of Gn. 1–3, and will allow us to elucidate the nature of the days of creation. We shall close by discussing the importance of these chapters to biblical theology and ethics and their relationship to modern scientific thought.

The ancient world was polytheistic: they believed in a multitude of gods and goddesses who varied in power and benevolence. Gn. 1 mentions only one God of supreme power: it goes out of its way to point out that the sun, moon and stars which were often regarded as divine were just created by God. The power of this one God is highlighted by the mode of creation: he just says 'Let there be' and there is, quite unlike the struggle of some Babylonian and Canaanite gods to create things.

The ancient world held that the gods were not wholly in favour of human existence. According to the Atrahasis epic, mankind was created as a divine strike-breaker: the minor gods had gone on strike, thus depriving the great gods of food, so the latter created seven human couples to supply them with food. Unfortunately, the human race turned out to be a mixed blessing: the population explosion spoiled the tranquillity of heaven, so the gods tried to annihilate mankind through famine, plague and flood.

Genesis paints a very different scenario. The creation of mankind is the climax of the creation story. God invites the angels 'Let us make man in our image' to witness the grand conclusion of his creative activity. He is not worried by the potential growth of the human race; he positively encourages it by creating mankind in two sexes and making their first duty, to 'Be fruitful and increase in number; fill the earth' (Gn. 1:28). Further analysis of Gn. 1 reveals that the creation of man is no afterthought: the previous five days' activity builds up to it. Those days on which things most essential to human existence, sun, land, plants, were created are described more fully than the others. The divine goodwill towards man is accentuated by his providing food for man, not *vice versa* as in the Babylonian account.

There thus runs through the opening chapters a critique of the theology of other oriental creation accounts. In some cases (*e.g.* the Atrahasis epic and the Sumerian flood story) a similar sequence of events may be observed to Gn. 1–9. But the theological emphases are quite different: the unity, the power of God, and his benevolence towards man are clear. Another difference is that whereas Mesopotamians tended to view human society as evolving upward, Genesis sees society as created perfect and then disintegrating as the result of human sin. Thus Genesis takes a story-line that was familiar in the ancient world, and in retelling it puts forward a quite new theology.

But how far does Genesis intend us to read its opening chapters as history? Would they, as many maintain, be better termed 'myth'? The first point to make is that Gn. 1:1–2:3 is quite different from all the following sections of the book. Each of these ten sections is headed 'This is the account of' (2:4; 6:9, *etc.*). 1:1, whether taken as title or first statement of chapter 1, is quite different: 'In the beginning God created the heavens and the earth'. Second, 1:1–2:3 is full of repetitive formulae and quasi-poetic language. It is not quite poetry, but rather high-flown prose. The division of the account into seven days is the most obvious repetition, but repeated commands, fulfilments, naming, blessing, and appreciation formulae, mostly in multiples of seven, show that is a very carefully-crafted opening to the book.

Furthermore, there is an interesting pattern in the arrangement of the creative acts by days. The first three days match the next three:

Day 1	Light	**Day 4**	Luminaries
Day 2	Sky	**Day 5**	Birds
Day 3	Seas and Land	**Day 6**	Animals and Man
Day 7	Sabbath		

The unique character of 1:1–2:3 *vis à vis* what follows needs to be borne in mind as we seek to determine the character of the opening chapters of Genesis. Not only does 2:4 begin with a formula that links it up to later sections of Genesis, suggesting that the author saw Adam and Eve in a similar way to the later patriarchs such as Abraham and Jacob, but he links the actors named in these opening chapters to those who lived later, by genealogies (*e.g.* chs. 5, 11). If he saw the stories of Jacob as describing real events and characters, it seems likely that he saw Gn. 2–3 in similar terms.

However, the absence of the usual opening formula and the distinctive style of 1:1–2:3 makes it likely that the author wants us to view this chapter differently. He gives us another clue, pointing in the same direction, by speaking of 'days' on days 1–3, before the creation of the sun on day 4 which he says marks the days and other seasons. 'What sort of days are those which are not defined by the sun and moon?' we should ask.

If 'myth' is defined as stories about God's action in the past which affect the present, it is clear that Genesis' accounts of the creation and the fall fit this definition. But as Jacobsen pointed out, in Genesis and many Near Eastern accounts there is a strong interest in cause and effect, the linkage of events over time, which give the narratives a historical cast. So he called them mytho-historical. If myth could be purged of its negative overtones of error and falsity, this might be acceptable. It is preferable to describe these chapters as proto-historical (German *Urgeschichte*) or theological history.

But there is more to Genesis 1ff. than a narrative making theological points about God and his relationship to man. Genesis is the first of the five books of the Torah, the Law. It is also teaching ethics as well as theology. We have already noted that God's first word to man was a command, 'Be fruitful'. But ch. 1 tells of six days of divine work, followed by one of divine rest. It leaves open how long God's days are from a human point of view. Ps. 90:4 compares a thousand human years to a day, or even a watch in the night, to God. Yet man was created in the divine image, hence it seems likely that he is meant to imitate his creator by working six days and resting on the seventh (*cf.* Ex. 20:8–11). Further models for human behaviour, especially between the sexes, are suggested by the Gn. 2 account of the creation of Adam and Eve.

Interpreted along these lines Gn. 1–2 conflicts with modern scientific discovery less than is often supposed. In its original BC context it was challenging the theology and ethics of ancient orientals, declaring that their notions of polytheism and the human situation were quite wrong. The world was not run by a set of capricious amoral deities for their own benefit, but was created by one sovereign holy God who controlled all things and desired the good of his supreme creature, man. Gn. 1 is not so much a scientific or historical explanation of how the world came to be, but a theological hymn of praise to the creator for his bounty bestowed on man. As the inspired writer of Genesis transformed the stories of origins well known in ancient times, to disclose the true nature of God to his contemporaries, so his achievement should provoke modern theologians to do the same. The character of the God revealed in Genesis, and his love for mankind, is now more fully revealed, especially through the incarnation, but new revelation has not so much as challenged Genesis so much as enriched its insights. The same surely is true of scientific discovery. The size and complexity of the universe as we know it is beyond the imaginings of the ancients, yet they worshipped and adored the creator of the little world they knew. How much more should modern man be awestruck by the wisdom and power of the God who can create and sustain the universe revealed by modern science, and be amazed by his love for mankind created in the divine image and redeemed by grace.

BIBLIOGRAPHY. T. Jacobsen, 'The Eridu Genesis', *JBL* 100, 1981, pp. 513–529; H. Blocher, *In the Beginning*, 1984; G. J. Wenham, *Genesis* 1–15, 1987; E. Beauchamp, *Création et séparation*, 1969; E. C. Lucas, *Genesis Today*, 1989. G.J.W.

CREATURES. Tr. of *ḥayyâ* and *nep̱eš ḥayyâ* in *OT, zōon, ktisma* and sometimes *ktisis* in NT, emphasizing mainly the aspect of being alive rather than createdness.

The term embraces 'all flesh that is upon the earth' (Gn. 9:16) which is under the all-seeing eye of God (Heb. 4:13) and within the scope of the gospel (Col. 1:23). Elsewhere man is distinguished from other creatures as having responsibility for them (Gn. 2:19), but abusing his position by idolatry (Rom. 1:25), yet in Christ being reborn as God intended him to be—'a kind of first fruits of his creatures' (Jas. 1:18).

The term also includes celestial beings (Ezk. 1; Rev. 5, *et passim*) where earthly imagery is taken up into the vision of the worship of heaven. P.A.B.

CREED. It is clear that a full-scale creed in the sense in which J. N. D. Kelly defines it ('a fixed formula summarizing the essential articles of the Christian religion and enjoying the sanction of ecclesiastical authority', *Early Christian Creeds*[3], 1972, p. 1) is not found in the NT. The so-called 'Apostles' Creed' does not go back to apostolic times. Yet recent investigation in the field of symbolic theology will not postpone the church's creed-making to the 2nd and subsequent centuries. There are clear indications that what appear as credal fragments, set in the context of the church's missionary preaching, cultic worship and defence against paganism, are already detectable in the NT. We shall examine some representative examples of these confessional forms. (A more extended discussion will be seen in V. H. Neufeld, *The Earliest Christian Confessions*, 1963, and R. P. Martin, *Worship in the Early Church*, 1974, ch. 5.)

a. Missionary preaching

There is evidence that in the primitive church there was a corpus of distinctive Christian teaching held as a sacred deposit from God (see Acts 2:42; Rom. 6:17; Eph. 4:5; Phil. 2:16; Col. 2:7; 2 Thes. 2:15; and especially in the Pastoral Epistles, 1 Tim. 4:6; 6:20; 2 Tim. 1:13–14; 4:3; Tit. 1:9). This body of doctrinal and catechetical instruction, variously known as 'the apostles' teaching', 'the word of life', 'the pattern of doctrine', the apostolic 'traditions', 'the deposit', the 'sound words', formed the basis of Christian ministry, and was to be held firm (Jude 3; and especially in Heb. 3:1; 4:14; 10:23), handed on to other believers as the apostolic men themselves had received it (see 1 Cor. 11:23ff.; 15:3, where the verbs, 'received', 'delivered', are technical terms for the transmission of authoritative teaching; *cf.* B. Gerhardsson, *Memory and Manuscript*, 1961), and utilized in the public proclamation of the gospel. In fact, the term 'gospel' designates the same web of truth, the *Heilsgeschichte*, which proclaims God's redeeming mercy in Christ to men (Rom. 2:16; 16:25; 1 Cor. 15:1ff.).

b. Cultic worship

Under this heading the cultic and liturgical acts of the church as a worshipping community may be shown to reveal credal elements, *e.g.* in baptism (Acts 8:37 according to the Western Text; Rom. 9:9: see J. Crehan, *Early Christian Baptism and the Creed*, 1950); in the worshipping life of the church, especially in the eucharist, with which are associated ceremonial declarations of faith, hymnic compositions, liturgical prayers and devotional exclamations (as in 1 Cor. 12:3; 16:22, which is probably the earliest example of corporate prayer, *Marānā thā*, 'Our Lord, come!' and Phil. 2:5–11, on which *cf.* R. P. Martin, *Carmen Christi: Philippians ii. 5–11 in Recent Interpretation and in the Setting of Early Christian Worship*, *NTS* Monograph series 4, 1967); and in exorcism for which formulae used in the casting out of evil spirits (*e.g.* Acts 16:18; 19:13) came into prominence, as in the Jewish practice.

c. Cullmann's theory of formulation

O. Cullmann, *The Earliest Christian Confessions*, E.T. 1949, pp. 25ff., has set forth the theory that the formulation of early creeds was controlled partly by the polemical needs of the church in the pagan world. When arraigned before the magistrates and required to attest their allegiance, the Christians' reply would be 'Jesus Christ is Lord'; and thus a credal form was shaped and systematized.

The NT 'creeds' range in scope from the simple confession, 'Jesus is Lord', to implicit Trinitarian formulations, as in the apostolic benediction of 2 Cor. 13:14 and such references as Mt. 28:19 (on which, see Martin, *Worship in the Early Church*, ch. 8; A. W. Wainwright, *The Trinity in the New Testament*, 1962); 1 Cor. 12:4ff.; 2 Cor. 1:21ff.; 1 Pet. 1:2; but excepting the interpolated 1 Jn. 5:7f. There are binitarian creeds which associate the Father and the Son, as in 1 Cor. 8:6 (which may be a Christianized version of the Jewish credo known as the *Shema'*, based on Dt. 6:4ff.); 1 Tim. 2:5f.;

6:13f.; 2 Tim. 4:1. The main type, however, is the Christological formula with such detailed summaries as in 1 Cor. 15:3ff.; Rom. 1:3; 8:34; Phil. 2:5–11; 2 Tim. 2:8; 1 Tim. 3:16 (on which, see R. H. Gundry in *Apostolic History and the Gospel*, ed. W. W. Gasque and R. P. Martin, 1970, pp. 203–222) and 1 Pet. 3:18ff. (on which, see R. Bultmann, *Coniectanea Neotestamentica* 11, 1949, pp. 1–14).

R.P.M.

CRESCENS. Companion of Paul (2 Tim. 4:10) on service in 'Galatia'. Elsewhere Paul uses this term of Anatolian Galatia, but here it could equally designate European Gaul, as most ancient commentators and some MSS interpret it. If so, with the contiguous references to Titus's Dalmatian mission, it may point to a concerted penetration of the W by associates of the imprisoned Paul. The name is Lat., and infrequent in Gk.

BIBLIOGRAPHY. Zahn, *INT*, 2, pp. 25f. A.F.W.

CRETE. A mainly mountainous island in the Mediterranean lying across the S end of the Aegean. It is about 250 km long, and its breadth varies from 56 km to 11 km. It is not mentioned by name in the OT, but it is probable that the *Cherethites, who formed part of David's bodyguard, came from it, and the place-name *Caphtor probably referred to the island and the adjacent coastlands which fell within its dominion during the 2nd millennium BC. In the NT Cretans (*Krētes*) are mentioned among those present at Pentecost (Acts 2:11), and later the island (*Krētē*) is named in the account of Paul's journey to Rome (Acts 27:7–13, 21). His ship sailed past Salmone at the E end and put into a port called Fair Havens near Lasea in the centre of the S coast, and Paul advised wintering there. He was overruled, however. The ship set out to coast round to a better wintering-berth at Phoenix in the SW, but a strong wind sprang up, driving them out to sea, and finally to Malta. After his imprisonment at Rome, Paul evidently revisited Crete, for he left *Titus there to carry on the work. The unflattering description of the Cretans in Tit. 1:12 is a quotation from Epimenides of Crete (quoted also in Acts 17:28a).

Our knowledge of the island's history is derived chiefly from archaeology. There were neolithic settlements on it in the 4th and 3rd millennia BC, but it was in the Bronze Age that a powerful civilization was achieved. This was centred upon Knossos, a site excavated over many years by Sir Arthur Evans. The Early Bronze Age (Early Minoan I–III,

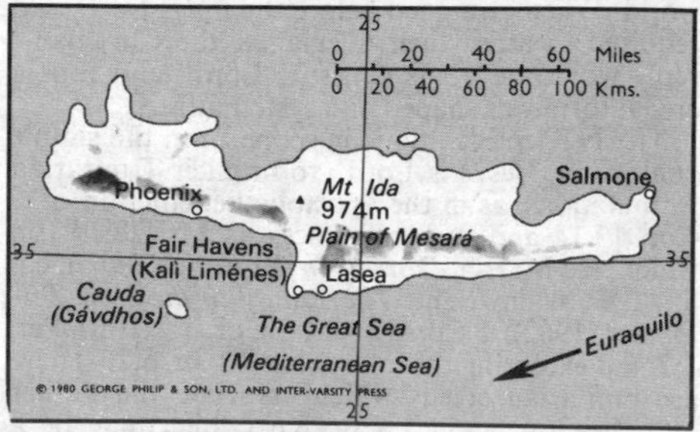

The island of Crete in NT times, showing the direction of the wind Euraquilo.

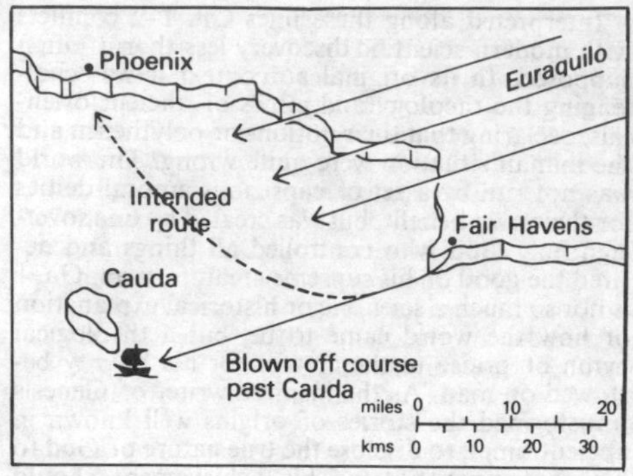

A diagrammatic representation of how Paul, sailing from Fair Havens, was blown off course past Cauda.

c. 2600–2000 BC) was a period of gradual commercial expansion, which was continued during the Middle Bronze Age (Middle Minoan I–III, *c.* 2000–1600 BC). In this latter period writing (on clay and copper tablets) was in use, first of all in the form of a pictographic script (*c.* 2000–1650 BC) and then in a simplified form, known as Linear A (*c.* 1750–1450 BC). Neither of these scripts has been positively deciphered (C. H. Gordon's suggestion that Linear A was used to write Akkadian has not been widely accepted).

The peak of Cretan civilization was reached in the early part of the Late Bronze Age (Late Minoan I(–II), *c.* 1600–1400 BC). The Linear A script continued in use during part of this period, but a third script, Linear B, appeared at Knossos (Late Minoan II, known only from Knossos). This was finally deciphered in 1953 by M. Ventris, and found to be couched in an archaic form of Gk. (Mycenaean), suggesting that the Late Minoan II period at Knossos was due to an enclave of Gk.-speaking invaders. Similar tablets have also been found at Mycenae and Pylos on the mainland of Greece, where the script continued to be used after the decline of Minoan civilization, a decline which was accelerated by the violent destruction, perhaps by pirates, of most of the towns in Crete, around 1400 BC. This decline continued through the last phases of the Bronze Age (Late Minoan III, *c.* 1400–1125 BC). Towards the end of this period Dorian Greeks came to the island and ushered in the Iron Age.

Discoveries in Egypt, and at such sites as Ras Shamra (*cf.* the name of king *krt* in the cuneiform tablets), Byblos and Atchana (Alalaḫ) in Syria, show that Cretan commerce had extended to W Asia by the Middle Minoan II period (1st quarter of the 2nd millennium), and from this time on the folk-movements, in which the *Philistines played a part and which culminated in the invasion of the 'Sea Peoples' in the 14th century, were taking place. Throughout the Iron Age the island was divided among a number of feuding city-states, until it was subdued by Rome in 67 BC.

BIBLIOGRAPHY. J. D. S. Pendlebury, *The Archaeology of Crete*, 1939; R. W. Hutchinson, *Prehistoric Crete*, 1962; H. J. Kantor, *The Aegean and the Orient in the Second Millennium BC*, 1947; J. Chadwick, *The Decipherment of Linear B*, 1958; A. Hopkins, *Crete: Its Past, Present and People*, 1978; C. H. Gordon, *HUCA* 26, 1955, pp. 43–108; *JNES* 17, 1958, pp. 245–255. T.C.M.

CRIME AND PUNISHMENT. Crime and punishment can be taken either in the juridical or in the religious sense, the latter in one way closely related to the former. We have thus to investigate the meaning of both to get a clear conception of our subject. The combination of crime and punishment in a strictly legal sense raises questions. The clear-cut distinction between criminal and civil offences of modern times is not present in OT and Near Eastern jurisprudence. Every offence was committed, in the first place, against a certain person or community, and the only way to put the wrong right was to compensate the injured or wronged person.

Jurisprudence was also connected all over the Near East with the divine. The god sanctioned the laws of a community. This is evident, *e.g.*, from the prologue of the laws of Ur-Nammu, where Nanna, the Sumerian moon god, is mentioned; there is the famous law code of Hammurapi with the well-known stele presenting the god Shamash and Hammurapi in front of him receiving the symbols of authority and justice. In a very special sense this is also true of the OT. The promulgation of laws is closely connected with the forming of the *covenant. This can now be paralleled by certain treaties like the treaty between Ir-IM of Tunip and Niqmepa of Alalaḫ, where a covenant is made, with certain mutual obligations couched in the typical form of Near Eastern jurisprudence. This is, however, only a formal parallel. The OT tradition takes the promulgation back to the covenant's origin at Sinai, giving every law the sanction of the Lord.

For our purpose it is preferable to sketch the meaning and background of crime and punishment separately.

I. Crime

a. Etymology

There is a close affinity between crime, guilt and punishment. This is evident from the Heb. word *'āwōn*, translated 55 times as 'offence' or 'crime', 159 times as 'guilt' and 7 times as 'punishment'. The basic meaning of crime is to act in a consciously crooked or wrong way. The word *reša'* means guilt and crime, and refers to the way of life of an irreligious person. The Heb. word in verb form, *šāgâ*, gives the meaning to act wrongly in ignorance. Another Heb. word, *peša'*, has the emphatic meaning rebellion or revolt. The common word for an offence, crime or sin is the verb *ḥāṭā'*, and noun *ḥēṭ'*. It has the double connotation of an offence against human beings (*e.g.* Gn. 41:9); and sin against God (*e.g.* Dt. 19:15). The basic meaning of the word was presumably 'to miss something', 'to err'; and this meaning was carried over to the sphere of offences against humanity and the deity. The whole idea of sin in OT and NT (Gk. *hamartia* is a direct translation of *ḥēṭ'*) is built up around this word.

In the Gk. NT the most important words connected with crime are *hamartia*, *hamartēma*, *asebeia*, *adikia*, *parakoē*, *anomia*, *paranomia*, *paraptōma*. *hamartia* and *hamartēma* mean to 'miss a mark', thus closely bound in meaning to the Heb. *ḥēṭ'*, denoting sin. *asebeia* and *adikia* mean to be actively irreligious and to be deliberately against God, a type of conduct usually regarded in the OT as the impious way of living, and described by *rāšā'*. *parakoē* means to be actively disobedient; the OT calls disobedience a refusing to hear (*lō' šāma'*, *e.g.* in Je. 9:13; 35:17). It denotes an action against the law, like *paranomia*. The nearest parallel in the OT is *'āwōn*. It is interesting to note that no technical terminology was used in biblical times to describe a transgression of law. Near Eastern jurisprudence has not developed a theoretical legal terminology. *parabasis* literally means to transgress, to transgress the existing laws with individual acts, *e.g.* Rom. 4:15. *paraptōma* is a less rigorous word than all those already discussed. It has the meaning of sin not of the worst enormity. 'Fault' comes nearest to the meaning, *e.g.* Gal. 6:1.

b. The treatment of offences

Legal decisions in Near Eastern civil and criminal law were made to protect individuals and the community against injustice. It is obvious from the general casuistic style of Near Eastern jurisprudence that the codified laws as found in the laws of Ur-Nammu, of the city of Eshnunna, of Hammurapi, of the Middle Assyrian times, as well as of certain laws from the Covenant Code and other parts of the Pentateuch, must be regarded as decisions by famous kings, officials, elders or heads of families, and not as a theoretical legal system built up by judges and sages. Every stipulation in the casuistic legal material is made to protect certain rights and to restore by compensation the damage done. For example, negligence in not properly looking after a goring ox was regarded as a crime when that ox gored a man, a slave or someone else's ox, *e.g.* Ex. 21:28–32, 35–36; Laws of Eshnunna §§53–55. According to Exodus, when negligence causes the death of a free person, the negligent person is punished by death. In all other cases fixed compensation in kind or in shekels must be paid. Even in criminal offences, such as rape or theft, the guilty person must compensate the victim. For the rape of a young girl, the OT prescribes fixed compensation to the amount of the normal bride-price. This shows that the value of the girl is diminished in a way which makes it impossible for her father, who has the legal right over her, to give her to another person for the usual bride-price. The guilty person, then, has to compensate the father for his loss, *e.g.* Ex. 22:16–17. This is true of all codified laws of the Near East, where in some cases further stipulations are inserted to cover various situations, *e.g.* in a special sense in the Middle Assyrian laws.

There is, however, one type of law, which A. Alt in 1934 considered as quite foreign to anything discovered outside the Israelite world, namely apodictic law, which is now called prohibitives and vetitives. The publication in 1958, however, of 'covenant' forms using a similar apodictic method in Assyr. times may show that such legal phraseology in the second person was not unknown elsewhere in the ancient Near East. What is unique in the OT legislation is that the laws in apodictic style are direct commands from the Lord to his people. The Ten Commandments, for example, are typical of this kind of law. 'You shall not kill' (Ex. 20:13) is given as a direct command by God to his people at Sinai, according to the reliable OT tradition. These laws originated in the sacred sphere of the Lord, and came as part of the Israelite religion right at the beginning of their nationhood when the covenant between God and his people was made. From the OT tradition it is also obvious that the casuistic laws were regarded as laws sanctioned by God. The whole corpus of legal material is immediately regarded as divinely inspired. These laws, promulgated with the covenant at Sinai, were there to bind the people to God and to unite the various tribes and individuals. Any transgression against a fellow-Israelite is a transgression against God.

c. Types of offences in Hebrew law

The more important types of offences are murder, assault, theft, negligence and transgressions of a moral and religious nature. In case of murder a distinction is made between an intentional act and unintentional manslaughter (*e.g.* Ex. 21:12–14). Murder was regarded all over the ancient Near East as a grave offence and, with a few exceptions, was punished by the death of the murderer. In the Bible human life, created by God, is regarded as precious. Assault which damaged the human body is also severely punished, but almost always with fixed compensation. Hebrew law is unique against Near Eastern legal practices in that a bodily injury inflicted by a master on his slave is punished by the release of the slave. Theft and negligence are usually punished by restitution or fixed compensation.

d. A distinction made

The OT as well as the NT makes a distinction between a mere transgression and a crooked and sinful life. The way of life was regarded as very important, especially in the Wisdom literature. The existence of the wicked is described in detail, *e.g.* in Ps. 1, which is closely connected with the Wisdom material of the OT. This psalm gives expression to wickedness and crime as the way of life of the ungodly, the sinners and the scornful. The life of these groups is a denial of the law of God. This kind of ungodly life means rebellion against God, and this is closely linked with all kinds of unrighteous deeds against other people. The clearest representation of this attitude is present in the writings of the prophets around 600 BC, and is especially stressed by Jeremiah. Crime against fellow-men is always regarded as crime against the Lord. A deep religious interpretation is thus attached to crime and transgression.

e. The New Testament interpretation

It is precisely this religious interpretation which predominates in the NT. Every transgression is taken as an offence against God. Paul's conception in Rom. 7 is that the law brings knowledge of sin, but cannot take it away; it even quickens the consciousness of sin and makes transgressions abound (7:7–11). Law is, however, not sin, but is intended to restrain transgression by ordaining penalties. By knowing the law, our sinful nature (*hamartia*) is provoked and entices us to individual sinful acts (*parabasis*). The sinful nature, the sinful way of life, is expressed by Paul in terms of the flesh (*sarx*); to describe the life saved by Christ, the word 'spiritual' (*pneuma*) is used. Every life which is not saved by Christ is sinful in nature, and thus culpable, and has to be punished by God.

II. Punishment

a. Etymology

Among the more important biblical words connected with punishment, the stem *šlm* has the meaning 'to compensate', or 'to restore the balance'. This word has a specific legal connotation, as is also evident from certain Amarna letters. The stem *ykḥ* has a legal meaning 'to punish', *e.g.* in Gn. 31:37; Jb. 9:33; 16:21, but in numerous other places has the more usual meaning 'to reprove'. The stem *ysr* is more widely used in the sense of punishment. It is interesting to note that in Ugaritic (Canaanite cuneiform) this word is present in the sense of instruction, as also in Heb. The noun *mûsār* is also used; this stem is thus linked up with an education background and not primarily with legal punishment. It is corrective punishment, as is the punishment inflicted by a father on his son. A strong word, used with the Lord as subject, is the stem *nqm*. Mendenhall pointed out that this, in the light of cuneiform material from Mari, means to vindicate. Vindication in the sense of punishment inflicted by God on the wicked is present, for example, in Nahum.

It is an interesting feature that in the NT, where the concept of divine punishment is fully realized, words with this connotation are used in only seven places. It is evident that *dikē*, the common word for judgment, may also have the secondary meaning 'punishment', much the same as the Heb. *mišpāṭ*. The only words with the clear meaning of punishment are *timōria* and *kolasis*. In classical Gk. the former has a vindicative character, very much like *nqm* in Heb. But in *koinē* and in NT Gk. this meaning is hardly found. The term became synonymous with *kolasis*, the ordinary word for punishment, *e.g.* Mt. 25:46; Acts 4:21; 22:5; 26:11; Heb. 10:29; 2 Pet. 2:9; 1 Jn. 4:18. In Matthew *kolasis* is used for the final punishment in contrast to eternal life. The same meaning for the final judgment is present in 2 Peter, where the punishment is connected with the eschatological day of judgment, a later development from the OT conception of the Day of the Lord.

b. The practice of blood revenge

Every crime or transgression must be punished, according to the common legal principles of the Near East. Primarily, this punishment was inflicted in the more primitive nomadic or semi-nomadic society by the victim or his relations, *e.g.* a common Semitic legal procedure is that a murderer must be punished by death by the dead person's nearest relations (*AVENGER OF BLOOD). This is still Islamic law. We have numerous examples of blood revenge in the OT, *e.g.* Ex. 21:23–25; 22:2–3. This is called *ius talionis*. The common formula of the *ius talionis* cannot only be traced back to the Old Babylonian Code of Hammurapi but is also present in a much later votive tablet discovered at Marseilles. It is the very basis of the Islamic law of 'deliberate homicide'.

c. The dispensing of justice

Decisions on various cases were made by judges or elders or the head of a family, usually in the city gate. Their activity is not to be confused with the modern conception of judge. These judges were arbitrators between two parties (the Heb. word *šāpaṭ* sometimes means 'to decide between two parties'). This role of arbitration was not only played by elders and officials but also by the king himself, *cf.*, *e.g.*, the decision made by David in favour of the woman of Tekoa (2 Sa. 14) and the wise decision of Solomon (1 Ki. 3:16ff.). But it is also clear that in nomadic and semi-nomadic society retribution was in some cases inflicted without the help of an arbitrator, *e.g.* in case of murder, where the common law of blood revenge took place. On the other hand, in modern bedouin society people travel long distances to a famous judge to get his decision on a case.

Both in civil and criminal offences the judge gave decisions designed to maintain 'social equilibrium'. When a bodily injury was inflicted, or damage done to a neighbour's property (which was taken in a much broader sense than our modern one, so that his wife, children and slaves, for example, were also included), the loss was restored by fixed compensation. It is, however, incorrect to suggest that in all cases only the value of the damage was paid; *e.g.* a thief had to compensate for stolen property such as cattle and sheep with five times its value in the former, and four times in the latter, case (*cf.* Ex. 22:1). This was probably used as a kind of deterrent against theft.

d. God as Judge

It is a fact that God is regarded in the Bible as the supreme Judge. This conception is not alien to the ancient Near East, *e.g.* in a very important cuneiform tablet of Mari, the god Shamash is described as judge of gods and men. Very early in the history of Israel God was regarded as Creator of all things. This makes him the Possessor of his creation. Any damage done to his creation is a direct act of rebellion against himself.

From a legal standpoint this gives him the right to punish. On the other hand, laws were made and sanctioned by God to protect his creation. His own commands put him under the compulsion to punish any transgression of them. Some places in the OT give the impression that the punishment decided on by the elders or officials was sufficient. On the other hand, it is evident that people who get away without human punishment are punished by God, some of them by a violent death, others by great damage (*cf.* Nu. 16). The idea shifted from punishment during a man's lifetime to the *Day of the Lord, with a final judgment where everybody shall be judged according to his deeds. The idea of a judgment after death is present also in the Egyptian conception of death. A deceased person is weighed over against the goddess Maat and receives his due according to his weight. The biblical conception does not only refer to judgment after death but also to a final judgment at the eschatological end of days. This idea is fully developed in the NT in the eschatological parts of the Gospels, in parts of Paul's Epistles, in 2 Peter and in Revelation (*e.g.* Mt. 24–25; Mk. 13; Lk. 21; 1 Thes. 5; 2 Thes. 2; 2 Pet. 3; Rev. 20–22). (*ESCHATOLOGY.)

III. Conclusion

It is evident that crime and punishment were not only bound up with ordinary jurisprudence but also with the divine. A crime against a human being or his property is a crime against God, and must be punished either by the authorities or by God. A transgression of religious stipulations must likewise be punished by God. A wicked way of life is rejected by God and punished.

BIBLIOGRAPHY. G. Mendenhall, *Law and Covenant in Israel and the Ancient Near East*, 1955; H. Cazelles, *Études sur le code de l'alliance*, 1946; M. Noth, *Die Gesetze im Pentateuch*, 1940; R. C. Trench, *The Synonyms of the New Testament*, 1901; D. J. Wiseman, 'The Laws of Hammurabi again', *JSS* 7, 1962, pp. 161–168; W. Eichrodt, *Theologie des Alten Testaments*, 1948; F. C. Fensham, *The mišpāṭîm in the Covenant Code* (typed dissertation), 1958; *idem*, 'Transgression and Penalty in the Book of the Covenant', *JNSL* 5, 1977, pp. 23–41; E. Gerstenberger, *Wesen und Herkunft des 'apodiktischen Rechts'*, 1965; G. Liedke, *Gestalt und Bezeichnung alttestamentlicher Rechtssätze*, 1971; H. J. Boecker, *Redeformen des Rechtsleben im Alten Testament*, 1964; *idem*, *Recht und Gesetz im Alten Testament und im Alten Orient*, 1976; A. Phillips, *Ancient Israel's Criminal Law*, 1970; B. S. Jackson, *Theft in Early Jewish Law*, 1972; J. A. Hoyles, *Punishment in the Bible*, 1986. F.C.F.

CRISPUS. He was *archisynagōgos* (*SYNAGOGUE) at Corinth. His conversion, with his family, was significant, most Corinthian Jews being bitterly hostile (Acts 18:5–8); hence, perhaps, his baptism by Paul himself (1 Cor. 1:14). *Acts of Pilate* 2. 4 probably intends him.

The name (meaning 'curly') is Lat., but is used elsewhere by Jews (*cf.* TJ *Yebhamoth* 2. 3; 12. 2; Lightfoot, *HHT* in 1 Cor. 1:14). Pesh., Goth. (*v.l.*) read 'Crispus' for 'Crescens' in 2 Tim. 4:10. A.F.W.

CROSS, CRUCIFIXION. The Gk. word for 'cross' (*stauros*; verb *stauroō*; Lat. *crux*, *crucifigo*, 'I fasten to a cross') means primarily an upright stake or beam, and secondarily a stake used as an instrument for punishment and execution. It is used in this latter sense in the NT. The noun occurs 28 times and the verb 46. The crucifixion of live criminals did not occur in the OT (*stauroō* in the LXX of Est. 7:10 is the Heb. *tālâ*, meaning 'to hang'). Execution was by stoning. However, dead bodies were occasionally hung on a tree as a warning (Dt. 21:22–23; Jos. 10:26). Such a body was regarded as accursed (hence Gal. 3:13) and had to be removed and buried before night came (*cf.* Jn. 19:31). This practice accounts for the NT reference to Christ's cross as a 'tree' (Acts 5:30; 10:39; 13:29; 1 Pet. 2:24), a symbol of humiliation.

Crucifixion was practised by the Phoenicians and Carthaginians and later used extensively by the Romans. Only slaves, provincials and the lowest types of criminals were crucified, but rarely Roman citizens. Thus tradition, which says that Peter, like Jesus, was crucified, but Paul beheaded, is in line with ancient practice.

Apart from the single upright post (*crux simplex*) on which the victim was tied or impaled, there were three types of cross. The *crux commissa* (St Anthony's cross) was shaped like a capital T, thought by some to be derived from the symbol of the god Tammuz, the letter *tau*; the *crux decussata* (St Andrew's cross) was shaped like the letter X; the *crux immissa* was the familiar two beams †, held by tradition to be the shape of the cross on which our Lord died (Irenaeus, *Haer.* 2. 24. 4). This is strengthened by the references in the four Gospels (Mt. 27:37; Mk. 15:26; Lk. 23:38; Jn. 19:19–22) to the title nailed to the cross of Christ over his head.

After a criminal's condemnation, it was the custom for a victim to be scourged with the *flagellum*, a whip with leather thongs, which in our Lord's case doubtless greatly weakened him and hastened eventual death. He was then made to carry the cross-beam (*patibulum*) like a slave to the scene of his torture and death, always outside the

Drawing showing the position of the body during crucifixion, based on a skeleton found near Jerusalem.

city, while a herald carried in front of him the 'title', the written accusation. It was this *patibulum*, not the whole cross, which Jesus was too weak to carry, and which was borne by Simon the Cyrenian. The condemned man was stripped naked, laid on the ground with the cross-beam under his shoulders, and his arms or his hands tied or nailed (Jn. 20:25) to it. This cross-bar was then lifted and secured to the upright post, so that the victim's feet, which were then tied or nailed, were just clear of the ground, not high up as so often depicted. The main weight of the body was usually borne by a projecting peg (*sedile*), astride which the victim sat. There the condemned man was left to die of hunger and exhaustion. Death was sometimes hastened by the *crurifragium*, breaking of the legs, as in the case of the two thieves, but not done in our Lord's case, because he was already dead. However, a spear was thrust into his side to make sure of death, so that the body could be removed, as the Jews demanded, before the sabbath (Jn. 19:31ff.).

The method of crucifixion seems to have varied in different parts of the Roman empire. Secular writers of the time shrink from giving detailed accounts of this most cruel and degrading of all forms of punishment. But new light has been thrown on the subject by archaeological work in Judaea. In the summer of 1968 a team of archaeologists under V. Tzaferis discovered four Jewish tombs at Giv'at ha-Mivtar (Ras el-Masaref), Ammunition Hill, near Jerusalem, where there was an ossuary containing the only extant bones of a (young) crucified man, dating from probably between AD 7 and AD 66, judging from Herodian pottery found there. The name Jehoḥanan is incised. Thorough research has been made into the causes and nature of his death and may throw considerable light on our Lord's form of death.

The young man's arms (not his hands) were nailed to the *patibulum*, the cross-beam, which might indicate that Lk. 24:39; Jn. 20:20, 25, 27 should be translated 'arms'. The weight of the body was probably borne by a plank (*sedecula*) nailed to the *simplex*, the upright beam, as a support for the buttocks. The legs had been bent at the knees and twisted back so that the calves were parallel to the *patibulum* or cross-bar, with the ankles under the buttocks. One iron nail (still *in situ*) had been driven through both his heels together, with his right foot above the left. A fragment shows that the cross was of olive wood. His legs had both been broken, presumably by a forcible blow, like those of Jesus' two companions in Jn. 19:32.

If Jesus died in similar fashion, then his legs were not fully extended as in traditional Christian art. His contorted leg muscles would then have probably caused severe pain with spasmodic contractions and rigid cramps. This could have contributed to the shortened time of his death in 6 hours, hastened doubtless by the earlier scourging.

Contemporary writers describe it as a most painful form of death. The Gospels, however, give no detailed description of our Lord's physical sufferings, but simply and reverently say 'they crucified him'. According to Mt. 27:34, our Lord refused any form of alleviation for his sufferings, doubtless that he might preserve clarity of mind to the end, in doing his Father's will. Hence the fact that he was able to comfort the dying thief, and pronounce the rest of the seven wonderful words from the cross.

The NT writers' interest in the cross is neither archaeological nor historical, but Christological. They are concerned with the eternal, cosmic, soteriological significance of what happened once for all in the death of Jesus Christ, the Son of God, on the cross. Theologically, the word 'cross' was used as a summary description of the gospel of salvation, that Jesus Christ 'died for our sins'. So the 'preaching of the gospel' is 'the word of the cross', 'the preaching of Christ crucified' (1 Cor. 1:17ff.). So the apostle glories 'in the cross of our Lord Jesus Christ', and speaks of suffering persecution 'for the cross of Christ'. Clearly the word 'cross' here stands for the whole glad announcement of our redemption through the atoning death of Jesus Christ.

'The word of the cross' is also 'the word of reconciliation' (2 Cor. 5:19). This theme emerges clearly in the Epistles to the Ephesians and Colossians. It is 'through the cross' that God has reconciled Jews and Gentiles, abolishing the middle wall of partition, the law of commandments (Eph. 2:14–16). It is 'by the blood of his cross' that God has made peace, in reconciling 'all things to himself' (Col. 1:20ff.). This reconciliation is at once personal and cosmic. It comes because Christ has set aside the bond which stood against us with its legal demands, 'nailing it to the cross' (Col. 2:14).

The cross, in the NT, is a symbol of shame and humiliation, as well as of God's wisdom and glory revealed through it. Rome used it not only as an instrument of torture and execution but also as a shameful pillory reserved for the worst and lowest. To the Jews it was a sign of being accursed (Dt. 21:23; Gal. 3:13). This was the death Jesus died, and for which the crowd clamoured. He 'endured the cross, despising the shame' (Heb. 12:2). The lowest rung in the ladder of our Lord's humiliation was that he endured 'even death on a cross' (Phil. 2:8). For this reason it was a 'stumbling block' to the Jews (1 Cor. 1:23; *cf.* Gal. 5:11). The shameful spectacle of a victim carrying a *patibulum* was so familiar to his hearers that Jesus three times spoke of the road of discipleship as that of cross-bearing (Mt. 10:38; Mk. 8:34; Lk. 14:27).

Further, the cross is the symbol of our union with Christ, not simply in virtue of our following his example, but in virtue of what he has done for us and in us. In his substitutionary death for us on the cross, we died 'in him' (*cf.* 2 Cor. 5:14), and 'our old man is crucified with him', that by his indwelling Spirit we might walk in newness of life (Rom. 6:4ff.; Gal. 2:20; 5:24ff.; 6:14), abiding 'in him'.

BIBLIOGRAPHY. M. Hengel, *Crucifixion*, 1977; J. H. Charlesworth, *ExpT* 84, 1972–3, pp. 147–150; B. Siede, *NIDNTT* 1, pp. 389–405; J. Schneider, *TDNT* 7, p. 572; L. Morris, *The Cross in the New Testament*, 1967; A. E. Harvey, *Jesus and the Constraints of History*, 1982; J. R. W. Stott, *The Cross of Christ*, 1986; J. B. Green, *The Death of Jesus*, 1988. J.B.T.

CROWN. A distinctive head-dress, often ornate, worn by kings and other exalted persons.

I. In the Old Testament

The high priest's crown was a gold plate inscribed 'Holy to the Lord', fastened to his mitre or turban by blue cord, this being an emblem of consecration (Ex. 29:6; 39:30; Lv. 8:9; 21:12). After the Exile, in 520 BC, Zechariah (6:11–14) was commanded by God to make gold and silver crowns and to place them on the head of Joshua the high priest, these being (later) laid up in the Temple as emblems of God's favour. They may have been combined in one double crown, uniting priestly and regal offices in one person.

Among royal crowns, David's gold crown was an emblem of his God-given kingship (Ps. 21:3; *cf.* 132:18; withdrawal of God's gift—and crown *cf.* Ps. 89:39; Ezk. 21:25–26). Joash's actual coronation is recorded (2 Ki. 11:12; 2 Ch. 23:11). David captured the gold, stone-inset crown of the king (or god Milcom) of Ammon, which weighed a talent (2 Sa. 12:30; 1 Ch. 20:2). Ammonite statues show kings or gods wearing large high crowns (see F. F. Bruce, *Israel and the Nations*, 1969, pl. I). For crown set with stones, *cf.* Zc. 9:16. The great royal crown of Vashti, Ahasuerus' queen (Est. 1:11), came to Esther's head (2:17), and the royal apparel with which Mordecai eventually was honoured included a gold crown (Est. 6:8; 8:15).

Besides being the mark of royalty (Pr. 27:24), a crown became metaphorical of glory (Jb. 19:9; Is. 28:5; 62:3; Je. 13:18; La. 5:16; Pr. 4:9; 12:4; 14:24; 16:31; 17:6), and sometimes, less happily, of pride (Jb. 31:36; Is. 28:1, 3).

The Bible world offers many examples of a variety of crowns. In Egypt the king and the gods wore a variety of tall and elaborate crowns of varying significance as well as a simple gold circlet or diadem. Most characteristic is the great Double Crown of Upper and Lower Egypt combined, incorporating the red crown of Lower Egypt (flat cap, with spiral at front and tall projection at rear) and above it the white crown of Upper Egypt (tall and conical with a knob at the top). Pharaoh's diadems were always fronted by the *uraeus* or royal cobra. In Mesopotamia the Assyr. kings wore a truncated conical cap adorned with bands of coloured embroidery or precious stones, or a simple diadem. The kings of Babylon wore a curving mitre ending in a point; see H. Frankfort, *Art and Architecture of the Ancient Orient*, 1954, plates 87–89, 95, 109–110, 114, 116, 120.

Palestinian excavations have yielded a series of circlets or diadems; for one of strip gold patterned with dots, see W. M. F. Petrie, *Ancient Gaza III*, 1933, plates 14: 6, 15. See also for further examples, K. Galling, *Biblisches Reallexikon*, 1937, cols. 125–128 and figures. K.A.K.

II. In the New Testament

There are two words to be considered. The more important is *stephanos*, which denotes properly a chaplet or a circlet. It is used of Christ's crown of thorns. 'Thorns' are no more specific in Gk. than in English, so that it is impossible to be sure just what plant was used. What is clear is that this 'crown' was a mocking symbol of royalty, perhaps also of divinity (see H. St J. Hart, *JTS* n.s. 3, pp. 66–75). But though the *stephanos* might denote a crown of royalty (Rev. 6:2, *etc.*), its more usual use was for the laurel wreath awarded to the victor at the Games or for a festive garland used on occasions of rejoicing. These uses underlie most of the NT references. Thus Paul reminds the Corinthians that athletes strive 'to receive a perishable wreath' and he adds, 'but we an imperishable' (1 Cor. 9:25). It is important that the seeker after the crown 'competes according to the rules' (2 Tim. 2:5). Sometimes the Christian's crown is here and now, as when Paul thinks of his converts as his crown (Phil. 4:1; 1 Thes. 2:19). More usually it is in the hereafter, as the 'crown of righteousness, which the Lord, the righteous judge, will award to me on that Day' (2 Tim. 4:8). There are references also to a 'crown of life' (Jas. 1:12; Rev. 2:10), and to 'an unfading crown of glory' (1 Pet. 5:4). The crown may be lost, for Christians are exhorted to hold fast lest it be taken from them (Rev. 3:11). God has crowned man 'with glory and honour' (Heb. 2:7), and Jesus was crowned likewise, 'so that by the grace of God he might taste death for every one' (Heb. 2:9).

diadēma is not frequent (Rev. 12:3; 13:1; 19:12). In the NT it is always a symbol of royalty or honour. L.M.

CUP. The ancient cup was a bowl, wider and shallower than the normal teacup. While usually made of pottery, it was sometimes of metal (Je. 51:7).

1. Heb. *kôs*, commonly used for a drinking-vessel, whether the pharaoh's (Gn. 40:11) or a poor man's (2 Sa. 12:3). This could be of a size to hold in the hand or might be larger (Ezk. 23:32), with a rim (1 Ki. 7:26). In Solomon's court they were made of gold. **2.** Heb. *gāḇîa'*. This is the name given to Joseph's silver divining cup (Gn. 44:2ff.) and to the bowls of the golden candlestick in the tabernacle, which were formed like almond blossom (Ex. 25:31ff.). In Je. 35:5 (AV 'pots') it is used for a pitcher. It may have been named as flower- or goblet-shaped. **3.** Heb. *sap̄*. At the Passover the blood was held in this bowl (Ex. 12:22, AV 'bason'). It was also a household vessel, appearing among equipment given to David (possibly of metal, contrasted with earthenware, 2 Sa. 17:28) and as a large wine bowl (Zc. 12:2). **4.** Heb. *qubba'aṯ* (Is. 51:17, 22) was evidently a large wine vessel, explained as *kôs*. **5.** Heb. *'aggān*. This was the common name for a large bowl in the ancient Semitic world used in sacred rites (Ex. 24:6) or for serving wine at a banquet (Ct. 7:2). With the storage jar, it could be hung from a peg (Is. 22:24). (*VESSELS.)

In the NT Gk. *potērion* denotes a drinking-vessel of any sort. Pottery continued in common use (Mk. 7:4), but the rich were now able to possess glass as well as metal cups, which were normally goblet-shaped, *cf.* the chalice depicted on coins of the first revolt (see *IBA*, p. 89). The cup used at the Last Supper was probably an earthenware bowl, sufficiently large for all to share (Mt. 26:27).

Throughout the Bible, cup is used figuratively as containing the share of blessings or disasters allotted to a man or nation or his divinely appointed fate (Pss. 16:5; 116:13; Is. 51:17; Mt. 26:39ff.; Jn. 18:11). (*LORD'S SUPPER.) A.R.M.

CUPBEARER (Heb. *mašqeh*, 'one giving to drink'). The 'butler' of Joseph's pharaoh (Gn. 40:1ff.) both in Heb. and by function was the king's cupbearer. His office as depicted in Gn. 40 corresponds in part to the (wider) Egyp. *wdpw* of early times and especially the Middle Kingdom period (broadly, *c.* 2000–1600 BC; *cf.* Joseph *c.* 1700 BC), and exactly to the later term *wb'*, 'cupbearer', of New Kingdom times (*c.* 1600–1100 BC), which includes Moses' day. See A. H. Gardiner, *Ancient Egyptian Onomastica*, 1, 1947, pp. 43*, 44* on No. 122 (*wb'*), and J. Vergote, *Joseph en Égypte*, 1959, pp. 35–40 (esp. p. 36). The Egyptian cupbearers, *wb'*, were often called *w'b-'wy*, 'pure of hands', and in the 13th century BC one such cupbearer is actually entitled *wb' dp írp*, 'cupbearer (or, butler) who tastes the wine' (R. A. Caminos, *Late-Egyptian Miscellanies*, 1954, p. 498). These officials (often foreigners) became in many cases confidants and favourites of the king and wielded political influence; this is very evident in 20th-Dynasty Egypt (12th century BC), and *cf.* Nehemiah. The (lesser) cupbearers of high Egyptian dignitaries are sometimes shown serving wine in the tomb-paintings.

Cupbearers were part of Solomon's glittering court that so impressed the queen of Sheba (1 Ki. 10:5; 2 Ch. 9:4); for a somewhat earlier cupbearer at a Palestinian court (Canaanite), see left end of the Megiddo ivory illustrated in E. W. Heaton, *Everyday Life in Old Testament Times*, 1956, p. 164, fig. 80, or W. F. Albright, *Archaeology of Palestine*, 1960, p. 123, fig. 31.

Nehemiah (1:11) was cupbearer to Artaxerxes I of Persia (*c.* 464–423 BC) and, like his earlier colleagues in Egypt, enjoyed royal trust and favour, and had access to the royal ear. For a picture of an Assyr. cupbearer, see H. Frankfort, *Art and Architecture of the Ancient Orient*, 1954, plate 89. K.A.K.

CURSE. The main biblical vocabulary of the curse consists of the Heb. synonyms *'ārar*, *qālal* and *'ālâ*, *corresponding to the Gk. kataraomai*, *katara* and *epikataratos*; and the Heb. *heḥerîm* and *ḥērem*, corresponding to the Gk. *anathematizō* and *anathema*.

The basic meaning of the first group is malediction. A man may utter a curse, desiring another's hurt (Jb. 31:30; Gn. 12:3); or in confirmation of his own promise (Gn. 24:41; 26:28; Ne. 10:29); or as a pledge of the truth of his testimony in law (1 Ki. 8:31; *cf.* Ex. 22:11). When God pronounces a curse, it is, *a.*, a denunciation of sin (Nu. 5:21, 23; Dt. 29:19–20), *b.* his judgment on sin (Nu. 5:22, 24, 27; Is. 24:6), and *c.*, the person who is suffering the consequences of sin by the judgment of God is called a curse (Nu. 5:21, 27; Je. 29:18).

However, for the Hebrew, just as a word was not a mere sound on the lips but an agent sent forth, so the spoken curse was an active agent for hurt. Behind the word stands the soul that created it. Thus, a word which is backed by no spiritual capacity of accomplishment is a mere 'word of the lip' (2 Ki. 18:20 RVmg.), but when the soul is powerful the word is clothed in that power (Ec. 8:4; 1 Ch. 21:4). The potency of the word is seen in some of our Lord's healing miracles (Mt. 8:8, 16; *cf.* Ps. 107:20), and in his cursing of the barren fig-tree (Mk. 11:14, 20–21). In Zc. 5:1–4 the curse, representing the law of God, itself flies through the land, discerns sinners and purges them out. A curse is as substantial a danger to the deaf man as is a stumbling-block to the blind, for he cannot take 'evasive action' by appeal to the more potent 'blessing' of Yahweh (Lv. 19:14; Ps. 109:28; contrast Rom. 12:14). The rehearsing of the blessings and curses on Mts Gerizim and Ebal (Dt. 27:11ff.; Jos. 8:33) reveals the same dynamic view of the curse. On the borders of Canaan, Moses set before the people 'life and death, the blessing and the curse' (see Dt. 30:19). The first national act on entering the land is to activate both: the blessing which will 'overtake' the obedient, and the curse which will 'overtake' the disobedient (Dt. 28:2, 15). Between these two poles the national life moves.

It is because of the relation between obedience and blessing, disobedience and cursing (Dt. 11:26–28; Is. 1:19–20) that Dt. 29:12, for example, can speak of God's covenant as his 'curse', and Zc. 5:3 can call the Decalogue the 'curse'. The word of God's grace and the word of God's wrath are the same word: the word which promises life is but a savour of death and judgment to the rebel, and therefore a curse. When God's curse falls on his disobedient people, it is not the abrogation but rather the implementation of his covenant (Lv. 25:14–45). Paul uses this truth to expound the doctrine of redemption. The law is a curse to those who fail to obey it (Gal. 3:10), but Christ redeemed us by becoming a curse for us (Gal. 3:13), and the very means of his death itself proves that he took our place, for 'cursed be every one that hangs on a tree'. This quotation from Dt. 21:23, where 'accursed of God' means 'under God's curse', displays the curse of God against sin falling on the Lord Jesus Christ, who thus became a curse for us.

The Heb. root *ḥāram* means 'to seclude from society' (Koehler, *Lexicon*, *s.v.*). This is borne out by OT usage. In general, the word applies to things open to human use but deliberately rendered unavailable to man. (*a*) Lv. 27:29 ('devoted') likely refers to capital punishment: the death penalty cannot be evaded. (*b*) In Ezk. 44:29; Nu. 18:14 offerings to God are called *ḥērem*, set apart for exclusively religious purposes. Lv. 27:21ff. parallels *ḥērem* with *qōḏeš* ('holiness') in order to express two sides of the same transaction: man sets something utterly apart for God (*ḥērem*), God accepts it and marks it as his own (*qōḏeš*), whereupon it becomes irredeemable by man. (*c*) Characteristically, the word is used of 'utter destruction'. Sometimes the implied reason is the wrath of God (*e.g.* Is. 34:5), but more often it is in order to remove a potential contagion for Israel's sake (Dt. 7:26; 20:17). Any contact with such a 'devoted thing' involved implication in its contagion, and share in its fate (Jos. 6:18; 7:1, 12; 22:20; 1 Sa. 15:23; 1 Ki. 20:42). However, while Achan involved himself and his house in the destruction of Jericho, Rahab, by identifying herself with Israel, escaped the curse and saved her house also (Jos. 6:21–24; 8:26–27; Jdg. 21:11). (*d*) Spiritually, *ḥērem* is the judgment of God against impenitent sinners (Mal. 4:6), and it is here that the impossibility of redeeming the *ḥērem* is clearly seen, *cf.* the NT, **anathema*, Gal. 1:8–9; 1 Cor. 16:22; Rom. 9:3.

BIBLIOGRAPHY. J. Pedersen, *Israel*, 1–2, 1926; 3–4, 1940, *passim*; D. Aust *et al.*, 'Curse', *NIDNTT* 1, pp. 413–418; H. C. Berichts, *JBL* 13, 1963; J. B. Payne, *The Theology of the Older Testament*, 1962, pp. 201ff., *etc.*; J. B. Lightfoot, *Galatians*, 1880, on 3:10, 13, and pp. 152–154. J.A.M.

CUSH. 1. Classed under Ham, and father of the hunter Nimrod (Gn. 10:6–8; 1 Ch. 1:8–10).

2. A region encompassed by the river Gihon (Gn. 2:13); probably in W Asia and unrelated to **4** below; see E. A. Speiser in *Festschrift Johannes Friedrich*, 1959, pp. 473–485.

3. A Benjaminite, some utterance of whom occasioned a psalm (7) of David seeking deliverance and justice.

4. The region S of Egypt, *i.e.* Nubia or N Sudan, the 'Ethiopia' of classical writers (not modern Abyssinia). The name Cush in both Heb. and Assyr. derives from Egyp. *Kš* (earlier *K's, K'š*), 'Kush'. Originally the name of a district somewhere between the second and third cataracts of the Nile *c.* 2000 BC, 'Kush' became also a general term for Nubia among the Egyptians, which wider use Hebrews, Assyrians and others took over (G. Posener, in *Kush* 6, 1958, pp. 39–68).

In 2 Ch. 21:16 Arabians are 'near' the Ethiopians —*i.e.* just across the Red Sea from them; *Syene or Seveneh (mod. Aswan) was the frontier of Egypt and Ethiopia in the 1st millennium BC (Ezk. 29:10). The far-removed location of Cush/Ethiopia gives point to Pss. 68:31; 87:4; Ezk. 29:10; Zp. 2:12; 3:10; and perhaps Am. 9:7; it is one limit of Ahasuerus' (Xerxes) vast Persian empire (Est. 1:1; 8:9 and texts of Xerxes' time). Ethiopian contingents featured in the armies of *Shishak against Rehoboam (2 Ch. 12:3) and of *Zerah against Asa (2 Ch. 14:9, 12–13; 16:8). Later, throughout Isaiah (11:11; 18:1ff. (preceding Egypt, 19:1ff.]; 20:3–5; and 43:3; 45:14), Egypt and Ethiopia are closely linked—for in the prophet Isaiah's time the 'Ethiopian' 25th Dynasty ruled over both; so, *e.g.*, King *Tirhakah, Is. 37:9 (= 2 Ki. 19:9), *cf.* 36:6, *etc.* Na. 3:9 also reflects this. But later still, from *c.* 660 BC onwards, the fortunes (and thrones) of Egypt and Ethiopia became separate again, and Ezekiel (30:4–5, 9) proclaims Egypt's impending fate as a warning to Ethiopia; in Je. 46:9, likewise, Ethiopians are merely mercenaries in the Egyptian forces again as in the days of Shishak. The 'topaz' came from this land (Jb. 28:19) of unchangeably dark skins (Je. 13:23), as did Ebed-melech at the Judaean court (Je. 38:7ff.; 39:15ff.), and Queen Candace's minister (Acts 8:27). The runner who bore news of Absalom's death to David was a 'Cushite' (2 Sa. 18:21, 23, 31–32). Ethiopia recurs in the prophecies of Ezk. 38:5 and Dn. 11:43. On Nu. 12:1, see *ETHIOPIAN WOMAN. K.A.K.

CUSHAN-RISHATHAIM. The king of Aram-Naharaim (E Syria–N Mesopotamia) who subjugated Israel for 8 years until their deliverance by Othniel (Jdg. 3:8–10). Both Heb. and Gk. versions take it as an unfamiliar composite personal name, otherwise unknown. Various attempts have been made to identify this name, which may be related to Cushan, an archaic term for the Midianites (Hab. 3:7) who, as nomads, reached Syria (*ARAM), where there is a place *Qsnrm* (Kushan-rōm). Some have tried to identify him with the Syrian Irsu, who ruled Egypt for 8 years about 1200 BC (*JNES* 13, 1954, pp. 231–242). An ancient interpretation of the name as 'Cushan of double wickedness' underlies the *MT* vocalization 'rishathaim'; *cf.* also the Kassite name Kašša-rišat, or the Ethiopian *Cush. D.J.W.

CUSHION. The only use of the word (Gk. *proskephalaion*) is in Mk. 4:38, where it refers to a pillow perhaps kept for the seat of honour in the stern of a boat. Cranfield defends the use of the Gk. *epi* (on, against), employed here with the 'accusative of place where'. Its rarity suggests the possibility that it is a graphic detail of eyewitness evidence. J.B.J.

CUTH, CUTHAH. An ancient city in Babylonia (Akkad. *kûtu* from Sumer. *gu-du-a*), the seat of the god Nergal, whose inhabitants were deported by Sargon to repopulate Samaria (2 Ki. 17:24, 30). The site, represented today by the mound called Tell Ibrahīm, was briefly excavated in 1881–2 by Hormuzd Rassam, who noted that it had at one time been a very extensive city.

BIBLIOGRAPHY. H. Rassam, *Asshur and the Land of Nimrod*, 1897, pp. 396, 409–411. T.C.M.

CYPRUS. The island of Cyprus, some 225 km long, and 100 km wide at its broadest, lies in the E Mediterranean some 100 km W of the coast of Syria and about the same distance from the Turkish coast.

Cyprus is not mentioned by that name in the OT, where it is probably referred to as *Elishah; the people called *Kittim in Gn. 10 may also have settled there at a later period. In the NT the island is named *Kypros* in Acts. Barnabas was a native of it (4:36), as were some of the other early disciples, and the church in the island was further augmented by refugees from the first persecution (Acts 11:19–20; 21:16). Paul and Barnabas travelled across the island from Salamis to Paphos at the beginning of their first missionary journey (Acts 13:4–13). It was at Paphos that they encountered *Bar-jesus, the sorcerer, and the proconsul (*anthypatos*) Sergius Paulus. Paul did not visit the island on his second missionary journey, but Barnabas went there separately with Mark (Acts 15:39). When returning from his third journey, Paul's ship passed it to the SW (Acts 21:3), and on the voyage to Rome contrary winds prevented him from landing (Acts 27:4). There is no other mention of the island in the Bible, but the church there continued to flourish, sending three bishops to the Council of Nicaea in AD 325.

There are traces of neolithic settlement on the island, and its Bronze Age culture shows evidence of contacts with Asia Minor and Syria. In the 15th century BC the Minoan civilization of *Crete extended to Cyprus, and in the following century there is evidence of colonization by the Mycenaeans, who were succeeding to the Cretan power on the Greek mainland. It was probably in this century that the copper mines, which in Roman times became famous enough for the metal to be named after the island (Lat. *cyprium*), first came into extensive use, and as a result of this Cyprus appears frequently in the records of the surrounding nations (*ELISHAH) at this period. In spite of outside influence, the basic Minoan–Mycenaean culture remained dominant, being evidenced particularly by the so-called Cypro-Minoan inscriptions (two early collections 15th and 12th centuries BC), which show close affinities with the Cretan Linear scripts. This script was still found in use in the late 1st millennium, together with the dialect of Gk. most closely related to that in the Minoan Linear B Tablets, Arcadian, which had presumably been superseded in S Greece and Crete by Doric.

Cyprus lay in the path of the 'Sea Peoples', and excavations at Enkomi and Sinda have revealed a late type of Mycenaean pottery from which the so-called *'Philistine' pottery of Palestine was clearly a development. In the 9th or 8th century BC Phoenicians settled on the island and later a number of bilingual inscriptions occur (*c.* 600–200 BC), of Phoenician and Greek severally with the Cypro-Minoan, now called classical Cypriot, script which was still in use at this time. That the Phoenicians did not gain much power is shown by an account of tribute to Esarhaddon in 672 BC, when only one Phoenician, as opposed to nine Greek kings, is mentioned (tribute had also been paid to Sargon in 709). In the 6th century Egypt dominated the island until it became part of the Persian empire under Cambyses in 525. In 333 BC it submitted to Alexander, and after a brief period under Antigonus it passed to the Ptolemies. It was made a Roman province in 58 BC, and after various changes it became a Senatorial province in 27 BC, from which time it was governed by a proconsul (Gk. *anthypatos*; *cf.* Acts 13:7).

BIBLIOGRAPHY. Sir G. F. Hill, *A History of Cyprus*, 1940; E. Gjerstad, *The Swedish Cyprus Expedition* 4, 2, 1948 (Geometric, Archaic and Classical periods); 4, 3, 1956 (Hellenistic and Roman periods); V. Karageorghis, *The Ancient Civilization of Cyprus*, 1969.
T.C.M.

CYRENE. A port in N Africa, of Dorian foundation, rich in corn, silphium, wool and dates. It became part of the Ptolemaic empire in the 3rd century BC, and was bequeathed to Rome in 96 BC, becoming a province in 74 BC. Josephus quotes Strabo as stating that Cyrene encouraged Jewish settlement, and that Jews formed one of the four recognized classes of the state (*Ant.* 14. 114). Josephus mentions also a Jewish rising there in Sulla's time, and Dio Cassius (68) another in Trajan's. To this Jewish community belonged Simon the cross-bearer (Mk. 15:21 and parallels), some of the missionaries to Antioch (Acts 11:20) and the Antiochene teacher *Lucius. It was also represented in the Pentecost crowd (Acts 2:10) and evidently had its own (or a shared) synagogue in Jerusalem (Acts 6:9).

BIBLIOGRAPHY. P. Romanelli, *La Cirenaica Romana*, 1943; A. Rowe, D. Buttle and J. Gray, *Cyrenaican Expeditions of the University of Manchester*, 1956; J. Reynolds, *JTS* n.s. 11, 1960, pp. 284ff.
J.H.H.

CYRUS (Heb./Aram. *kôreš*; Elam/Old Persian *kūruš*; Bab. *kuraš*). Persian king of the Achaemenid dynasty. Cyrus may have been an early dynastic name. Cyrus I was a contemporary of Ashurbanipal of Assyria, *c.* 668 BC, and therefore possibly known to Isaiah, who foresaw the restoration of the Jerusalem Temple through this new power which would free Jews from exile (Is. 44:28). Cyrus would be God's 'Messiah'-deliverer and an instrument of the divine plan (Is. 45:1).

Cyrus II (the Great), grandson of Cyrus I, came to the throne *c.* 559 BC. In 549 he conquered his mother's father, Astyages, the Median king, his overlord, founding the Persian (Achaemenid) empire. He took the titles 'king of the Medes' and 'king of Elam' (A. K. Grayson, *Babylonian Historical-Literary Texts*, 1975, p. 31). He conquered Croesus, and his kingdom of Lydia, and in 547 marched through Assyria. A few years later he was already threatening Babylonia, but it was not until 16 October 539 that the Persians with Gobryas entered Babylon, having diverted the river and thus been able to penetrate the city along the dried-up river bed to effect a surprise (Bab. Chronicle, *ANET*, p. 366; *DOTT*, p. 82; Herodotus, 1. 189–191; *cf.* Dn. 5:30). 17 days later Cyrus himself entered the city amid scenes of jubilation.

Cyrus' own inscriptions bear out the OT view of a sympathetic ruler. In his first year he issued a decree by which he 'gathered together all the inhabitants (who were exiles) and returned them to their homes' and in the same decree restored deities to their renovated temples (see Cyrus Cylinder, *ANET*, p. 316; *DOTT*, pp. 92–94; Ezr. 6:1ff.). The Jews, having no images, were allowed to restore their Temple and its fittings (Ezr. 6:3). During the first 3 years of the rule of Cyrus in Babylonia Daniel prospered (Dn. 1:21; 6:28; 10:1), but then, according to Josephus (*Ant.* 10. 249), was removed to Media or more probably to Susa the Persian capital (Dn. 8:2). For the theory that Cyrus might also have been called 'Darius the Mede', see *DARIUS. In Babylonia Cyrus was succeeded in 530 BC by his son Cambyses (II) who had been also for a while his co-regent.

BIBLIOGRAPHY. E. M. Yamauchi, *Persia and the Bible*, 1990, pp. 65–92.
D.J.W.

D

DABERATH. A levitical city of Issachar (1 Ch. 6:72; Jos. 21:28, where AV has 'Dabareh'), probably on the border of Zebulun (Jos. 19:12). It is usually identified with the ruins near the modern village of Debûriyeh, at the W foot of Mt Tabor. (*DEBORAH.) J.D.D.

DAGON. In the OT Dagon is a principal deity of the Philistines worshipped in Samson's time at Gaza (Jdg. 16:21–23), at Ashdod (to Maccabean days, 1 Macc. 10:83–85; 11:4) and at Beth-shan in the days of Saul and David (1 Sa. 5:2–7; 1 Ch. 10:10 with 1 Sa. 31:10). The true origin of this god's name is lost in antiquity, and even his precise nature is uncertain. The common idea that he was a fish-deity appears to have no foundation in fact, being adumbrated in Jerome (*BDB*, p. 1121) and first clearly expressed by Kimhi in the 13th century AD (Schmökel), influenced solely by the outward similarity between 'Dagon' and Heb. *dāḡ*, 'fish'. The fish-tailed divinity on coins from Arvad and Ascalon is linked with Atargatis and has no stated connection with Dagon (Dhorme and Dussaud). The common Heb. word *dāḡān*, 'grain, corn' (*BDB*, p. 186) may be derived from the name of the god Dagon or Dagan or be its origin; it is thus possible that he was a vegetation or grain god (*cf.* W. F. Albright, *Archaeology and the Religion of Israel*[3], 1953, pp. 74 and 220, n. 15).

From at least 2500 BC onwards, Dagon received worship throughout Mesopotamia, especially in the Middle-Euphrates region, in which, at Mari, he had a temple (18th century BC) adorned with bronze lions (see illustration in A. Champdor, *Babylon*, 1959). Many personal names were compounded with Dagon.

In the 14th century BC and earlier, Dagon had a temple at Ugarit in N Phoenicia, identified by two stelae in it dedicated to his name; these are pictured in *Syria* 16, 1935, plate 31: 1–2, opposite p. 156, and translated by Albright, *op. cit.*, p. 203, n. 30. This temple had a forecourt (?), an antechamber, and probably a tower (plan in C. F. A. Schaeffer, *The Cuneiform Texts of Ras Shamra-Ugarit*, 1939, plate 39), the whole probably taking the form of the ancient model illustrated by C. L. Woolley (*A Forgotten Kingdom*, 1953, p. 57, fig. 9). In the Ugaritic (N Canaanite) texts Dagon is father of Baal. At Bethshan, one temple discovered may be that of 1 Ch. 10:10 (see A. Rowe, *Four Canaanite Temples of Beth Shan*, 1, 1940, pp. 22–24). That Dagon had other shrines in Palestine is indicated by two settlements each called Bethdagon (Jos. 15:41; 19:27) in the territories of Judah and Asher. Rameses II mentions a B(e)th-D(a)g(o)n in his Palestinian lists (*c.* 1270 BC), and Sennacherib a Bit-Dagannu in 701 BC.

BIBLIOGRAPHY. H. Schmökel, *Der Gott Dagan*, 1928, and in Ebeling and Meissner (eds.), *Reallexikon der Assyriologie*, 2, 1938, pp. 99–101; E. Dhorme and R. Dussaud, *Les Religions de Babylonie et d'Assyrie . . . des Hittites . . . Phéniciens, etc.*, 1949, pp. 165–167, 173, 364f., 371, 395f.; M. Dahood, in S. Moscati (ed.), *Le antiche divinità semitiche*, 1958, pp. 77–80; M. Pope, in W. Haussing (ed.), *Wörterbuch der Mythologie*, 1, 1965, pp. 276–278. For Mari material, see J. R. Kupper, *Les Nomades en Mésopotamie au temps des Rois de Mari*, 1957, pp. 69–71. K.A.K.

DALMANUTHA. In Mk. 8:10 a district on the coast of the Lake of Galilee, to which Jesus and his disciples crossed after the feeding of the four thousand. It has never been satisfactorily identified. (Magadan in the parallel passage, Mt. 15:39, is equally unknown.) Various emendations have been proposed (including F. C. Burkitt's suggestion that it represents a corruption of Tiberias combined with its earlier name Amathus), but it is best to keep the attested reading and await further light. F.F.B.

DALMATIA. A Roman province in the mountainous region on the E of the Adriatic, formed by the emperor Tiberius. Its name was derived from an Illyrian tribe that inhabited it. It was bounded on the E by Moesia and the N by Pannonia. It is mentioned in 2 Tim. 4:10, and is identical with *Illyricum (Rom. 15:19). B.F.C.A.

DAMASCUS.

a. Location

The capital city of Syria (Is. 7:8) situated E of the Anti-Lebanon Mts and overshadowed in the SW by Mt Hermon (Ct. 7:4). It lies in the NW of the Ghuta plain 700 m above sea-level and W of the Syrian–Arabian desert. The district is famous for its orchards and gardens, being irrigated by the clear Abana (mod. Barada) and adjacent Pharpar rivers, which compared favourably with the slower, muddy Jordan (2 Ki. 5.12) and Euphrates rivers (Is. 8:5–8). It is a natural communications centre, linking the caravan route to the Mediterranean coast (*c.* 100 km to the W) through Tyre (Ezk. 27:18) to Egypt with the tracks E across the desert to Assyria and Babylonia, S to Arabia, and N to Aleppo. The city was of special importance as head of an *Aramaean state in the 10th–8th centuries BC.

The centre of the modern city lies beside the Barada river, part of it occupying the area of the old walled city. Some streets follow the lines of

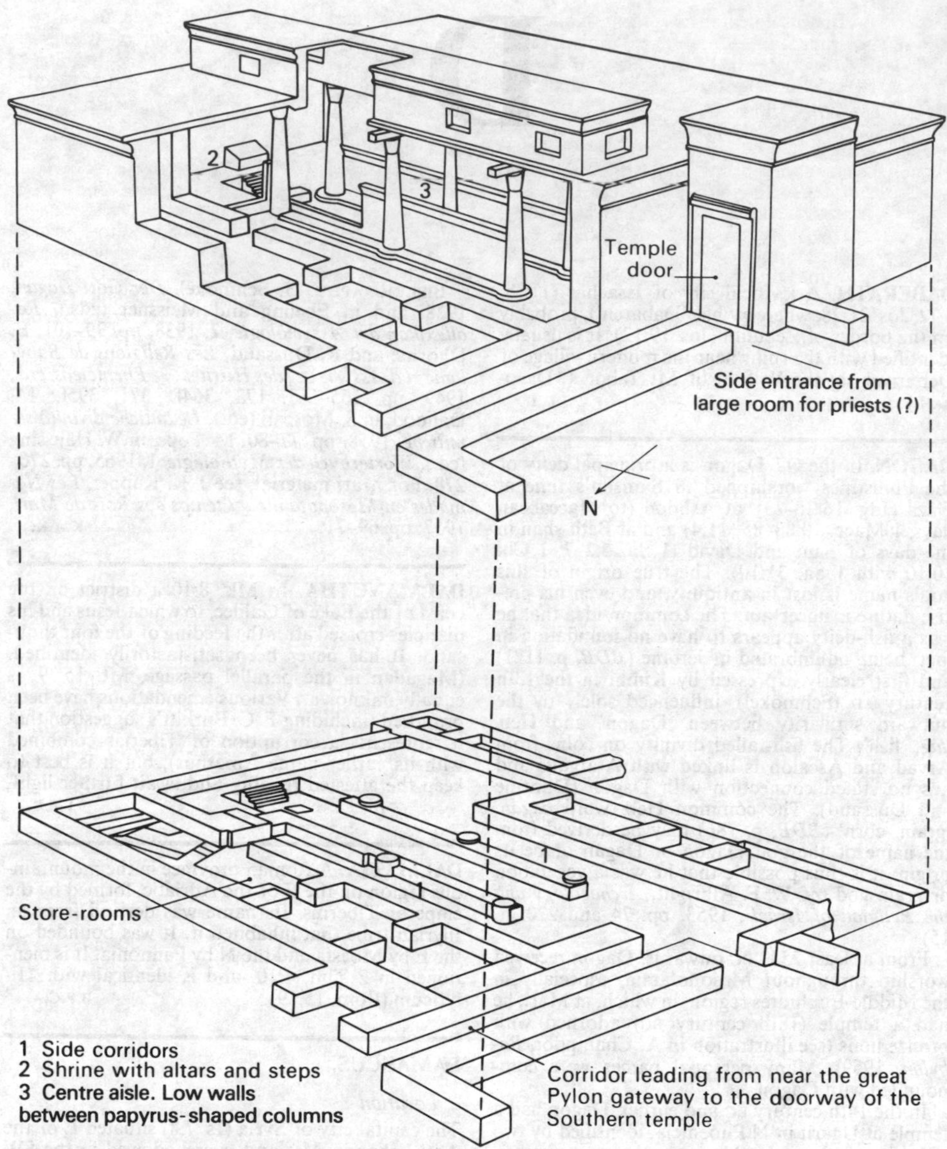

Plan and suggested reconstruction of the Canaanite temple of Dagan, built for Rameses III at Bethshean, possibly where the Philistines fastened Saul's head (1 Ch.10:10). 12th cent. BC.

Roman times, including Straight Street (*Darb al-mustaqim*) or Long Street (*Sūq al-Tawilēh*) as in Acts 9:11. The great mosque built in the 8th century AD is said to cover the site of the temple of *Rimmon (2 Ki. 5:18).

b. Name

The meaning of Damascus (Gk. *Damaskos*; Heb. *Dammeseq*; Aram. *Darmeseq*; 1 Ch. 18:5; 2 Ch. 28:5) is unknown. The *"ram darmeseq* of 1 Ch. 18:6 corresponds to the modern (*Dimašk-*)*eš-šām* as 'Damascus of the North (Syria)'. The name is found in Egyp. *Tjmšqw* (Tuthmosis III) and Amarna Letters (14th century) and cuneiform inscriptions as *Dimašqi*. Other names in the latter texts are *ša imerišu* (perhaps 'caravan city') and *Bīt-Haza'-ili* ('House of Hazael') in the 8th century BC (*DOTT*, p. 57). See *ANET*, p. 278, n. 8.

c. History

Damascus appears to have been occupied from prehistoric times. In the 2nd millennium BC it was a well-known city near which Abraham defeated a coalition of kings (Gn. 14:15). It is possible that his servant Eliezer was from this city (Gn. 15:2; Syr. and vss). David captured and garrisoned

Damascus after his defeat of the troops it had contributed in support of Hadadezer of Zobah (2 Sa. 8:5f.; 1 Ch. 18:5). Rezon of Zobah, who escaped from this battle, later entered the city which was made the capital of a newly formed Aramaean city-state of *Aram (Syria; 1 Ki. 11:24). The city increased its influence under Rezon's successors Hezion and his son Tabrimmon. By the time of the accession of the latter's son Benhadad I (*c.* 900–860 BC) Damascus was the dominant partner in the treaty made by Asa of Judah to offset the pressure brought against him by Baasha of Israel (2 Ch. 16:2). The same king (if not Benhadad II—see *CHRONOLOGY OF THE OLD TESTAMENT) made the provision of merchants' quarters in Damascus a term of a treaty made with Ahab (1 Ki. 20:34). The aim of this treaty was to gain the support of Israel for the coalition of city-states to oppose the Assyrians. Ben-hadad (Assyr. Adad-idri) of Damascus provided the largest contingent of 20,000 men at the indecisive battle of Qarqar in 853 BC. Benhadad may be the unnamed 'king of Aram', in fighting whom Ahab met his death (see 1 Ki. 22:29–36).

In the plain near Damascus the prophet Elijah anointed Hazael, a Damascene noble, as the future king of Syria (1 Ki. 19:15), and Elisha, who had healed the general Naaman of Damascus, was invited there by Hazael to advise on Benhadad's health (2 Ki. 8:7). In 841 BC Hazael had to face renewed attacks by the Assyrians under Shalmaneser III. For a time he held the pass leading through the Lebanon Mts, but having lost 16,000 men, 1,121 chariots and 470 cavalry was forced to retreat within Damascus, where he successfully withstood a siege. The Assyrians fired orchards and plantations round the city before they withdrew (*DOTT*, p. 48; *ANET*, p. 280). In 805–803 BC Adad-nirari III led fresh Assyrian attacks on Hazael and Damascus. A further campaign in 797 BC by Adad-nirari so weakened Damascus that J(eh)oash of Israel was able to recover towns on his N border previously lost to Hazael (2 Ki. 13:25).

Under Rezin (Assyr. *Raḫianu*) Aram again oppressed Judah (2 Ki. 16:6), and in 738 was, with Menahem of Israel, a vassal of Tiglath-pileser III of Assyria. Soon thereafter Rezin revolted, captured Elath and took many Judaeans captive to Damascus (2 Ch. 28:5). Ahaz of Judah thereupon appealed for help to Assyria who responded by launching a series of punitive raids in 734–732 BC, which culminated in the capture of Damascus, as prophesied by Isaiah (17:1) and Amos (1:4–5), and the death of Rezin. The spoiling of the city (Is. 8:4), the deportation of its inhabitants to Kir (2 Ki. 16:9), and its destruction were cited as an object-lesson to Judah (Is. 10:9f.). In return for this assistance Ahaz was summoned to pay tribute to the Assyrian king at Damascus, where he saw and copied the altar (2 Ki. 16:10–12) which led to the worship of Syrian deities within the Temple at Jerusalem (2 Ch. 28:23). Damascus was reduced to a subsidiary city within the Assyrian province of Hamath and henceforth lost its political, but not completely its economic, influence (*cf.* Ezk. 27:18). Judaean merchants continued to reside in the city, and the border of Damascus was considered the boundary of the ideal Jewish state (Ezk. 47:16–18; 48:1; Zc. 9:1).

In the Seleucid period Damascus lost its position as capital, and thus much trade, to Antioch, though it was restored as capital of Coelesyria under Antiochus IX in 111 BC. The Nabataean Aretas won the city in 85 BC, but lost control to Tigranes of Armenia. Damascus was a Roman city from 64 BC to AD 33.

By the time of Paul's conversion Aretas IV (9 BC–AD 40), who had defeated his son-in-law Herod Antipas, had an ethnarch in the city (2 Cor. 11: 32–33). The city had many synagogues (Acts 9:2; Jos., *BJ* 2. 20) and in these, after being led to the house of Judas in Straight Street (9:10–12) where he was visited by Ananias, Paul first preached. Opposition forced Paul to escape over the city wall (9:19–27) but he returned to the city after a period spent in nearby Arabia (Gal. 1:17). Damascus continued to be subsidiary to Antioch, both politically and economically, until its supremacy was restored by the Arab conquest of AD 634.

BIBILIOGRAPHY. M. F. Unger, *Israel and the Aramaeans of Damascus*, 1957; W. T. Pitard, *Ancient Damascus*, 1987. D.J.W.

DAN. 1. The ancestor of the tribe of Dan named after the son of Jacob, born to him by Rachel's servant Bilhah (Gn. 30:1–6).

2. The tribe of Dan first settled SW of Ephraim and W of Judah (Gn. 14:14; Jos. 19:40–48). Though pressed by Philistines and Amorites during the period of the Judges (Jdg. 1:34; 5:17; 13:2), some stayed until absorbed into Judah. The majority migrated to the N border of Israel and took over Laish (Leshem), renamed Dan (Jos. 19:47), at the foot of Mt. Hermon by the source of the River Jordan.

3. The tribal capital had been settled since *c.* 5,000 BC. Throughout the Early and Middle Bronze Ages the wealthy city covered 30 acres and was named in Egyptian Execration and Mari (texts *c.* 1825 *Lasi*) before its capture by Thutmose III in the 13th century. The site, Tel Dan (Arab. Tell el Qadi, 'the judges' mound') was then a prosperous urban centre with ramparts, an arched 3 m high gateway, found intact, and well-furnished tombs. In the Iron Age Jereboam developed it as a cult-centre, with golden calves. It was an alternative to distant Jerusalem (1 Ki. 12:29).

Israeli excavations over 25 years have traced the history. A fragment of an Aramaic stela, datable to the 9th century BC, has a reference to *byt dwd*, almost certainly to be read 'the House of David' and thus, with a possible similar reference in the Moabite Stone (Mesha') inscription, is the earliest note yet externally to that royal dynasty. In the Hellenistic levels a bilingual Gk. and Aramaic text reads 'to the god who is in Dan'. The biblical description of the extent of Hebrew territory as 'from Dan to Beersheba', *i.e.* N to S is apposite.

Dan remained occupied through the Roman and Persian periods. The omission of Dan from the list of tribes in Rev. 7:5–8 may be because the tribe was considered as antichrist on the basis of Je. 8:16 (LXX; Irenaeus, *Adv. Haer.* 5.30.2).

BIBLIOGRAPHY. A. Biran, *NEAEHL*, 1992, pp. 323–332; *idem.*, *Biblical Dan*, 1994; A. Biran and J. Naveh, 'An Aramaic stela fragment from Tel Dan', *IEJ* 43, 1993, pp. 81–99; *BAR* 20, 1994, pp. 26–38, 47. D.J.W.

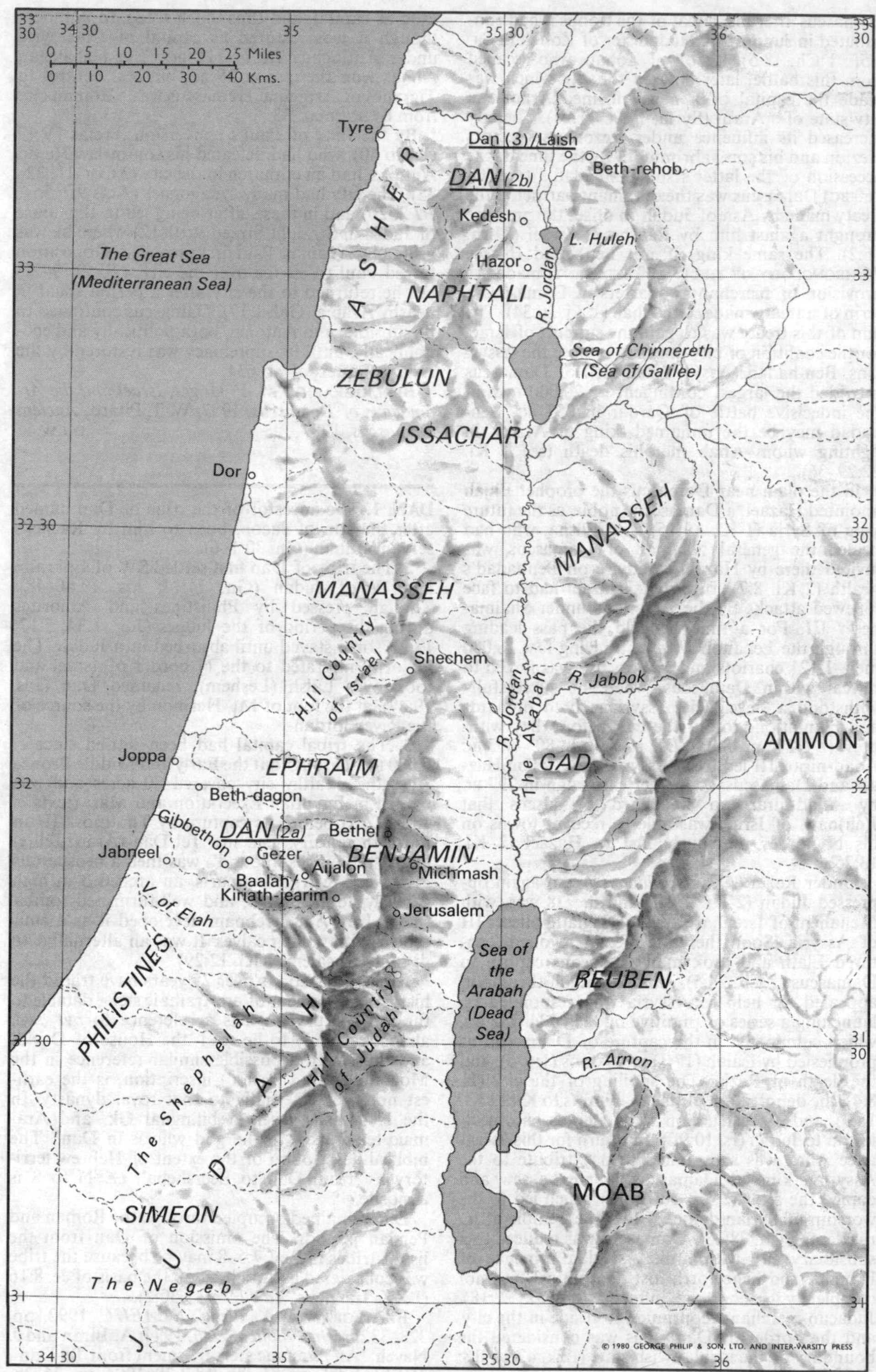

The two areas of settlement of the tribe of Dan and the city of Dan (see p. 253).

DANCE. The OT makes occasional reference to dancing as a source of amusement only (*e.g.* Ex. 32:19; Ec. 3:4), but usually behind the activity is some form of religious significance. Groups of women engaged in it on occasions of national celebration, such as after the crossing of the Red Sea (Ex. 15:20) after military victories (1 Sa. 18:6) and at religious festivals (Jdg. 21:19–21). Less frequently, men also are recorded as having danced (*e.g.* 2 Sa. 6:14).

In NT times the Greek custom of employing professional women dancers was followed in the case of Salome at Herod's birthday feast (Mk. 6:21–22); there was dancing at the prodigal son's homecoming festivities (Lk. 15:25); and it was such a common part of daily life that it entered into children's games (Mt. 11:17; Lk. 7:32; *cf.* Jb. 21:11).

For a comprehensive treatment, see the corresponding article in *EBi*. J.D.D.

DANIEL (Heb. *dāniyyē'l, dāni'ēl*, 'God is my judge'). **1.** Second son of David (1 Ch. 3:1) and Abigail, called also 'Chileab' (AVmg.). Although older than his brothers Absalom and Adonijah, nothing more is recorded of him, suggesting that he died young. **2.** A descendant of Ithamar, who accompanied Ezra (8:2) and was a signatory to the covenant (Ne. 10:1, 6). **3.** A man of extraordinary wisdom and righteousness whose name is coupled with Noah and Job (Ezk. 14:14, 20), and who is mentioned again in 28:3. Ezekiel need not be referring to the Ugaritic mythological *Dan'el* (*cf. ANET*[3], pp. 149–155) even though his spelling (*Dāni'ēl*) is slightly different from that of his contemporary (*Dānîy'ēl*), for in personal names the vowel letters were in free variation with one another, just as *Dō'ēg* the Edomite (1 Sa. 21:7; 22:9) is spelt *Dôyēg* in 1 Sa. 22:18, 22. Furthermore, Daniel's wisdom had become proverbial as early as 603 BC (Dn. 2:1), a number of years before Ezekiel spoke of it (Ezk. 28:3). Thus, he may be the same as the following.

4. The fourth of the so-called 'greater' prophets, of whose early career nothing is known except for what we are told in the book which bears his name. An Israelite of royal or noble descent (*cf.* Jos., *Ant.* 10. 188), he was carried captive to Babylon by Nebuchadrezzar in the third year of Jehoiakim, and with various companions trained for the king's service (Dn. 1:1–6). Following a custom of the time, he was given (v. 7) the Babylonian name of *Belteshazzar. He gained a reputation first as an interpreter of other men's visions (ch. 2–5), then of his own, in which he predicted the future triumph of the Messianic kingdom (ch. 7–12).

Renowned for sagacity, he successfully occupied leading governmental posts under Nebuchadrezzar, Belshazzar and Darius. His last recorded vision was on the banks of the Tigris in the third year of Cyrus.

There is a brief reference to 'the prophet Daniel' in Mt. 24:15 (= Mk. 13:14). (*DANIEL, BOOK OF.)

J.D.D.
J.C.W.

DANIEL, BOOK OF.

I. Outline of contents

The book covers the period of the exile from 605 BC, when Nebuchadrezzar first took captives from Judah to Babylon (1:1, 2), to 537 BC, 2 years after Cyrus of Persia defeated Babylon (10:1). For the captives, this was a time of painful reflection. Did loss of their land mean that history was no longer under God's control?

The book divides into two parts: chs. 1–6 relate six incidents from the years in Babylon; God working on behalf of his servants; chs. 7–12 record four visions, showing God's purpose for the nations, and the establishment of his kingdom. God had not abandoned his people. Chs. 2 and 7 are closely linked by their contents, so connecting the two parts. They also form a bracket round the intervening chapters, thus:

I. Daniel and his friends introduced (1:1–21)
II. God and the nations (2:1–7:28)
  A. Daniel interprets Nebuchadrezzar's dream (2:1–49)
    B. The nations see God's servants rescued (3:1–39)
      C. God's judgment on Nebuchadrezzar (4:1–37)
      C[1] God's judgment on Belshazzar (5:1–31)
    B[1] God rescues Daniel from the lions (6:1–28)
  A[1] An angel interprets Daniel's vision (7:1–28)
III. Two nations are identified (8:1–27)
IV. Daniel's prayer and its visionary answer (9:1–17)
V. A divine messenger gives an unprecedented revelation (10:1–12:13)

II. Date and authorship

Whereas the dates given in the text relate to the Babylonian empire, the visions introduce successive empires that stretch ahead into the 2nd century BC and beyond. Those who regard the visions as history rather than prophecy, date the last vision *c.* 167–165 BC, when Antiochus Epiphanes violated the temple (11:31). Some scholars would date the whole book from this period, while others regard the earlier chapters as having a much longer history. Extensive debate continues on the following topics:

1. *Historical accuracy*. Assuming that the author intended his stories to be accepted as events that actually happened, many commentators have questioned his accuracy (*cf.* H. H. Rowley, *Darius the Mede*, pp. 54–60). Some alleged discrepancies are easily accounted for, *e.g.* the difference between 1:1 and Je. 25:1. In Babylon it was usual to reckon the first months of a new reign as the accession year, hence *third year* in Daniel, whereas in Palestinian sources they would be reckoned as year 1, hence *fourth year* in Jeremiah (A. R. Millard, *EQ* 49, 2, 1977, p. 69). The author refers to Belshazzar as king (5:1; 7:1; 8:1), yet no such king was known in Babylon. He was in fact crown prince, and acted as regent for more than half his father's reign, during which time he was to all intents and purposes king (*BELSHAZZAR). A more intractable problem is the identity of Darius the Mede, who is said to have taken over the kingdom after the death of Belshazzar (5:31). At least seven different identifications have been suggested, though none has been verified from ancient sources (*cf.* J. E. Goldingay, *WBC*, p. 112). Perhaps Darius the Mede and Cyrus the Persian were titles of the same person (*DARIUS). It is unlikely, as some allege, that the author of Daniel, who was meticulous in other details, would have muddled Darius the Mede with Darius Hystaspes, whose reign began in 522 BC and was referred to as king of Persia in Ezr. 4:5.

The author of Daniel chs. 1–6 presents a detailed account of life at the Babylonian court, widely thought to have been recorded during, or soon after the exile, to encourage faith under persecution.

2. *Two languages*. The book opens and closes in Heb. but from 2:4b–7:28 the language is Aramaic, the *lingua franca* of the ancient Near East (*cf.* 2 Ki. 18:26). To account for the use of Aramaic in these chapters it has been suggested: (i) that they may have circulated separately because they were of interest to non-Jews; (ii) their message would have been equally encouraging to the Jewish resistance in the Maccabean struggle; (iii) the different languages may indicate different authors; (iv) 2:4 implies that the introduction of Aramaic was intentional. There are other examples in Near Eastern literature of an ABA structure, so the language changes do not necessarily indicate more than one author (J. G. Baldwin, *TOTC*, p. 69).

Attempts to date the Aramaic used in Daniel have failed, and we do not know whether it was written in Palestine or among the E dispersion. 'Several scholars today would consider an Eastern (Mesopotamian) origin for the Aramaic part of Daniel . . . as probable, in agreement with the subject matter, though absolute proof cannot be given within the relative unity of Imperial Aramaic (K. A. Kitchen, in D. J. Wiseman, *Some Problems*, pp. 78, 79). It has proved equally impossible to argue conclusively from the Heb. of Daniel.

3. *The prophecies*. Chs. 2 and 7–12 present stylized accounts of the course of future history as it concerned Israel and the world. Nebuchadrezzar of Babylon was the 'head of gold' (2:38) and the 'lion' of 7:4. The kings of Media and Persia were to take over from Babylon (8:20; the silver of 2:32 and the second beast of 7:5), while Greece would provide the next rulers (8:21; *cf.* the bronze of 2:39 and 7:6). Ch. 11 is a chronicle of contests for supremacy over the holy land after the death of Alexander the Great (11:3) until 165 BC. Though these events are presented as future, in vague terms, most commentators regard this chapter as history written after the event, in the 2nd century BC.

The simplest way to account for the Babylonian background of chs. 1–6 and the 2nd century Palestinian setting of chs. 7–12 is to postulate at least two authors. Against that, chs. 2 and 7 could reasonably be expected to have come from the same mind, and some recent scholars have assumed that there were a number of different authors, who drew on material handed down to them (Goldingay, *WBC*, pp. 326–329). Someone in the Maccabean period would then have acted as 'coordinating editor' to produce a book which several other scholars have regarded as demonstrably the work of one author (*cf.* Baldwin, *TOTC*, pp. 38–44).

Could the detail of ch. 11 possibly be regarded as prophecy? Babylon had long been familiar with a kind of predictive prophecy, centuries before Daniel's exile there (Baldwin, *TB*, 1979, pp. 77–99). It was appropriate, therefore, that Daniel's God should be seen to be in control of events, and of the climax of history (2:44) and judgment day (7:9, 10).

Since the discovery of the Dead Sea Scrolls in 1947, fragments of Daniel MSS have been available dating from the late-2nd century BC. No master text was in use at Qumran, for the fragments represent several different MSS. Evidently the book was already regarded as canonical, and the Qumran community looked for the fulfilment in their day of the 'unfulfilled' ending of Daniel 11. All this suggests the book was written before 165 BC.

The debate continues on both date and authorship, but the structure of the book favours unity of authorship, and there is no compelling argument that renders impossible a date in the late 6th or early 5th century BC.

III. Message

The introductory chapter, written after the return from exile (1:21), looked back over the events of a lifetime to show that youthful commitment to God's cause was abundantly vindicated. Already Daniel had stood out as leader of the young men from Judah, had undertaken a voluntary discipline over food and drink, and had received God's specific gifts for his future ministry (17). Even the king recognized that he and his friends were intellectually superior to their Babylonian contemporaries.

Ch. 2 shows God's sovereignty at work in Nebuchadrezzar's second year. The king's tantalizing dream became a test case for Daniel and a demonstration of the power of Daniel's God who reveals mysteries. The four sections of the towering statue represented four successive empires, Nebuchadrezzar's being the first. The fourth would be struck by a living stone that would shatter the whole structure. Human kingdoms are subject to the authority of the living God who will end them and set up his own kingdom. Daniel has a parallel vision of four beasts (ch. 7), but the empires are now characterized by brutality, while God's intervention is even more glorious. The climax of the vision and of the book is the coming of 'one like a son of man' to whom was given authority, glory and sovereign power (chs. 13, 14). To this mysterious title the gospels were to provide the commentary.

Nebuchadrezzar's image of gold (chs. 3, 4) was intended to bring all the representatives of his empire of nations into submission. But three of the king's administrators, who acknowledged a higher authority in the living God, refused to bow down to the image. Their deliverance from the furnace so impressed the king that he declared legal the worship of their God. Later, his building works completed (4:30), the king suffered from a terrifying mental illness which fulfilled a dream that Daniel had interpreted. Only after he had given due honour to the Most High God was his sanity restored. Then the king testified to the salutary effect of his illness in humbling his pride, and glorified God (4:37).

Belshazzar, by contrast, was totally irreligious (5:2), and desecrated vessels from the Jerusalem Temple at his feast. When writing mysteriously appeared on the wall he was horror-struck. The atheist is wrong-footed by the approach of death. In Belshazzar's case it came swiftly, but he had been warned (ch. 28). His empire was taken over by that of the Medes and Persians.

Daniel's outstanding courage was rewarded by high office in the new administration (6:1–3), but in his old age he was to be victimized by jealous rivals. By accusing him of breaking a law they had purposely devised, the nobles had Daniel thrown to the lions. That God rescued him from the lions is the best known incident in the book. King Darius recognized the living God who rescues and saves, and decreed that everyone in his empire should reverence Daniel's God. Thus persecution, though meant for evil, can result in God's glory.

The last five chapters, written like the first in Heb., return to God's future purposes (*cf.* chs. 2 and 7). The scope, however, is more limited, Babylon is not mentioned, and the emphasis is on the second and third kingdoms. The ram (8:3) is the Medo-Persian empire, and the he-goat the Gk. empire of Alexander the Great that was to split into four after his death (8:21–23). Later on, one 'master of intrigue' will take his stand against God himself, only to be defeated (8:25). In answer to Daniel's prayer pleading God's promise of restoration (9:4–19), Gabriel instructed Daniel more fully concerning future sufferings. Advance warning proves that God has not lost control, but will bring about his decreed end when the 'seventy sevens' have been fulfilled.

The final revelation (10:1–12:13), dated the 3rd year of Cyrus and fulfilling 1:21 (*cf.* use of the name Belteshazzar, given to Daniel in 1:7), was brought by a special divine messenger, seen only by Daniel. It concerned the holy land, sited between two power-seeking kingdoms (11:1–20). Under a particularly brutal usurper the era of persecution of God's people was to begin for political ends. This was unprecedented, hence the special revelation. The unmistakable message is the need to stand firm, to persevere and wait for God to bring in 'the end of days'. Jesus endorsed the message of Daniel, applying 9:27 to a time still future; he extended judgment for the persecutor to judgment for all the nations (Mt. 25:31–46). The NT, as a whole, endorses and completes the revelation to Daniel (Rev. 22:12–17).

BIBLIOGRAPHY. John Calvin, *Daniel I*, 1561, tr. T. H. L. Parker, 1993; J. A. Montgomery, *The Book of Daniel, ICC*, 1927; H. H. Rowley, *Darius the Mede and the Four World Empires in the Book of Daniel*, 1935; E. J. Young, *The Prophecy of Daniel*, 1949; J. C. Whitcomb Jr., *Darius the Mede*, 1959; *idem. Daniel*, 1985; D. J. Wiseman (ed.), *Notes on Some Problems in the Book of Daniel*, 1965; J. G. Baldwin, *Daniel, TOTC*, 1978; R. S. Wallace, *The Message of Daniel, BST*, 1979; A. Lacocque, *The Book of Daniel*, E. T. 1979; R. A. Anderson, *Daniel: Signs and Wonders, ITC*, 1984; J. J. Collins, *Daniel with an Introduction to Apocalyptic Literature*, 1984; P. R. Davies, *Daniel, OTG*, 1985; J. E. Goldingay, *Daniel, WBC*, 1989.

J.G.B

DAN-JAAN. Joab and his companions came to Dan-jaan in compiling the census ordered by David (2 Sa. 24:6–9). Starting from *Aroer, E of the Dead Sea, they camped S of the city in the valley of the Gadites (the Arnon basin), then went N to Jazer, through Gilead and other territory to Dan-jaan and its environs, and to Sidon (probably the territorial boundary is meant). Thence they moved S, past a Tyrian outpost, ending in Beersheba. As Beersheba is also mentioned in David's instructions along with Dan (v. 2), some scholars identify Dan-jaan with the well-known Dan. More probably it was a N town in the district of Dan, perhaps *Ijon of 1 Ki. 15:20 (*LOB*, p. 264). Among readings given by LXX is Dan-jaar, perhaps 'Dan of the Woods'. Another LXX reading, 'and from Dan they turned round to Sidon' seems indefensible. Jaan might be a personal name (*cf.* 1 Ch. 5:12 for a possible cognate); a place name *y'ny* is known in Ugaritic.

W.J.M.
A.R.M.

DARIUS (Heb. *Dārᵉyāweš*; Akkad. Elamite, *Dariawuš*; Old Persian, *Darayavauš*; Gk. *Dareios*).

1. Darius the Mede, the son of Ahasuerus (Xerxes; Dn. 9:1), received the government on the death of Belshazzar (5:30–31), being made king of the Chaldeans (9:1) at the age of 62 (5:31). He bore the title of 'king' (6:6, 9, 25) and the years were marked by his reign (11:1). He appointed 120 subordinate governors under three presidents, of whom one was Daniel (6:2), who prospered in his reign (6:28). According to Jos. (*Ant.* 10. 249), Daniel was removed by Darius to Media.

Since Darius the Mede is not mentioned by name outside the book of Daniel, and the contemporary cuneiform inscriptions reckon no king of Babylon between Nabonidus (and Belshazzar) and the accession of Cyrus, his historicity has been denied and the OT account of this reign considered a conflation of confused traditions (H. H. Rowley, *Darius the Mede*, 1935). On the other hand, the narrative has all the appearance of genuine historical writing, and in the absence of many historical records of this period there is no reason why the history should not be accepted.

There have been many attempts to identify Darius with persons mentioned in the Babylonian texts. The two most reasonable hypotheses identify Darius with (*a*) Gubaru, (*b*) *Cyrus. Gubaru was governor of Babylon and of the region beyond the river (Euphrates). There is, however, no specific evidence that he was a Mede, called king, named Darius, a son of Ahasuerus, or aged about 60. Cyrus, who was related to the Medes, was called 'king of the Medes' and is known to have been about 62 years old on becoming king of Babylon. According to the inscriptions, he appointed many subordinate officials, and documents were dated by his regnal years. This theory requires that Dn. 6:28 be translated '. . . in the reign of Darius, *even* in the reign of Cyrus the Persian' as an explanation by the writer of the use of sources using two names for the one person. The weakness of this theory lies in the fact that Cyrus is nowhere named son of Ahasuerus (but this might be a term used only of royal persons) or as 'of the seed of a Mede'.

2. Darius I, son of Hystaspes, who was king of Persia and of Babylon, where he succeeded Cambyses (after two usurpers had been displaced), and ruled 521–486 BC. He enabled the returned Jews to rebuild the Temple at Jerusalem with Jeshua and Zerubbabel (Ezr. 4:5; Hg. 1:1; Zc. 1:1).

3. Darius II (Nothus), who ruled Persia and Babylon (423–408 BC), called 'Darius the Persian' in Ne. 12:22, perhaps to distinguish him from 'Darius the Mede'. Since the father of Jaddua the high priest is mentioned in an Elephantine papyrus *c.* 400 BC, there is no need to assume that this Jaddua was the high priest who met Alexander in 332 BC and that the Darius here meant is Darius III (Codomanus), who reigned *c.* 336–331 BC.

BIBLIOGRAPHY. J. C. Whitcomb, *Darius the Mede*, 1959; D. J. Wiseman, *Notes on some Problems in the Book of Daniel*, 1970, pp. 9–16. D.J.W.

DATHAN (Heb. *dāṯān*, 'fount'?). A Reubenite, son of Eliab. Nu. 16:1–35 tells how, with his brother, Abiram, and *Korah, a Levite, he rebelled against Moses.

J.D.D.

DAVID (Heb. *dāwiḏ*, sometimes *dāwîḏ*; root and meaning doubtful, but see *BDB in loc.*; the equation with a supposed Old Bab. (Mari) *dawîdum*, 'chief', is now discounted (*JNES* 17, 1958, p. 130; *VT Supp* 7, 1960, pp. 165ff.); *cf.* Laesoe, *Shemsharah Tablets*, p. 56). The youngest son of Jesse, of the tribe of Judah, and second king of Israel. In Scripture the name is his alone, typifying the unique place he has as ancestor, forerunner and foreshadower of the Lord Jesus Christ—'great David's greater son'. There are 58 NT references to David, including the oft-repeated title given to Jesus—'Son of David'. Paul states that Jesus is 'descended from David according to the flesh' (Rom. 1:3), while Jesus himself is recorded by John as saying 'I am the root and the offspring of David' (Rev. 22:16).

When we return to the OT to find who this is who occupies a position of such prominence in the lineage of our Lord and the purposes of God, the material is abundant and rich. The story of David is found between 1 Sa. 16 and 1 Ki. 2, with much of the material paralleled in 1 Ch. 2–29.

I. Family background

Great-grandson of Ruth and Boaz, David was the youngest of eight brothers (1 Sa. 17:12ff.) and was brought up to be a shepherd. In this occupation he learnt the courage which was later to be evidenced in battle (1 Sa. 17:34–35) and the tenderness and care for his flock which he was later to sing of as the attributes of his God. Like Joseph, he suffered from the ill-will and jealousy of his older brothers, perhaps because of the talents with which God had endowed him (1 Sa. 18:28). Modest about his ancestry (1 Sa. 18:18), David was to father a line of notable descendants, as the genealogy of our Lord in Matthew's Gospel shows (Mt. 1:1–17).

II. Anointing and friendship with Saul

When God rejected Saul from the kingship of Israel, David was revealed to Samuel as his successor, who anointed him, without any ostentation, at Bethlehem (1 Sa. 16:1–13). One of the results of Saul's rejection was the departure of the Spirit of God from him, with a consequent depression of his own spirit, which at times seems to have approached madness. There is an awesome revelation of divine purpose in the providence by which David, who is to replace Saul in the favour and plan of God, is selected to minister to the fallen king's melancholy (1 Sa. 16:17–21). So the lives of these two men were brought together, the stricken giant and the rising stripling.

At first all went well. Saul was pleased with the youth, whose musical skill was to give us part of our richest devotional heritage, appointed him his armour-bearer. Then the well-known incident involving Goliath, the Philistine champion, changed everything (1 Sa. 17). David's agility and skill with the sling outdid the strength of the ponderous giant, whose slaughter was the signal for an Israelite repulsion of the Philistine force. The way was clear for David to reap the reward promised by Saul—the hand of the king's daughter in marriage, and freedom for his father's family from taxation; but a new factor changed the course of events—the king's jealousy of the new champion of Israel. As David returned from the slaying of Goliath, the

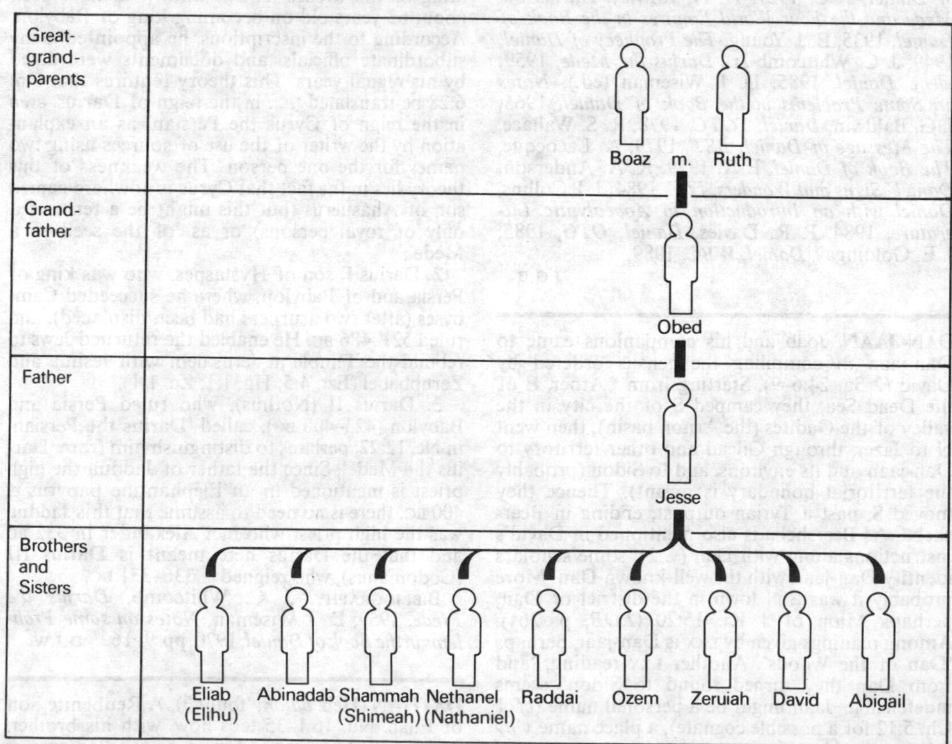

The ancestry of David of Judah.

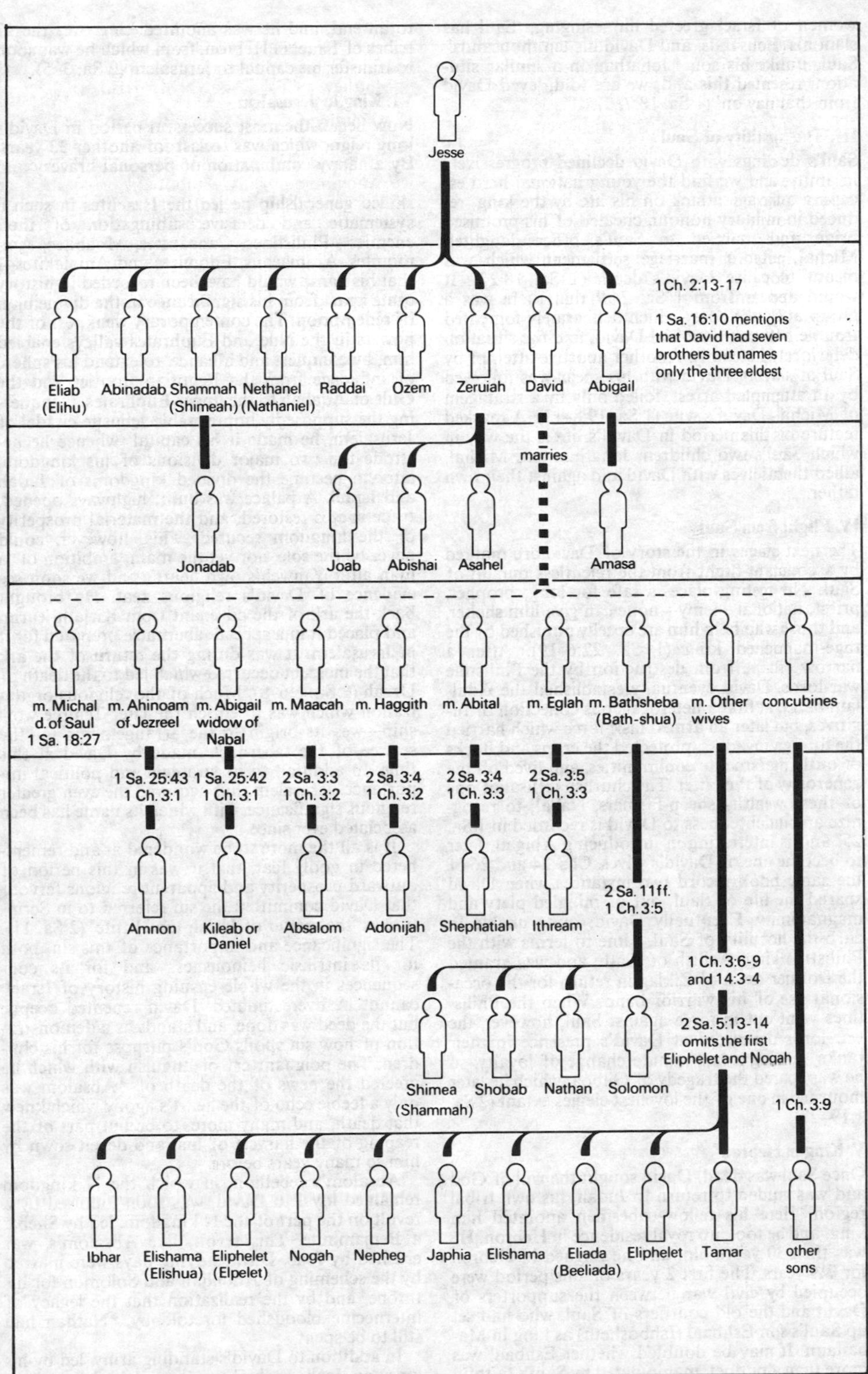

The family of David.

women of Israel greeted him, singing, 'Saul has slain his thousands, and David his ten thousands'. Saul, unlike his son *Jonathan in a similar situation, resented this and, we are told, 'eyed David from that day on' (1 Sa. 18:7, 9).

III. The hostility of Saul

Saul's dealings with David declined progressively in amity, and we find the young national hero escaping a savage attack on his life by the king, reduced in military honour, cheated of his promised bride and married to Saul's other daughter, Michal, after a marriage settlement which was meant to cause David's death (1 Sa. 18:25). It would appear from 1 Sa. 24:9 that there was a group at Saul's court which deliberately fomented trouble between Saul and David, and the situation deteriorated steadily. Another abortive attempt by Saul at slaying David with his spear was followed by an attempted arrest, foiled only by a stratagem of Michal, David's wife (1 Sa. 19:8–17). A marked feature of this period in David's life is the way in which Saul's two children, Jonathan and Michal, allied themselves with David and against their own father.

IV. Flight from Saul

The next stages in the story of David are marked by a constant flight from the relentless pursuit of Saul. No resting-place is safe for long; prophet, priest, national enemy—none can give him shelter, and those who help him are cruelly punished by the rage-maddened king (1 Sa. 22:6–19). After a narrow escape from destruction by the Philistine war-lords, David eventually established the Adullam band, at first a heterogeneous collection of fugitives, but later an armed task-force which harried the foreign invaders, protected the crops and flocks of outlying Israelite communities, and lived off the generosity of the latter. The churlish refusal of one of these wealthy sheep-farmers, Nabal, to recognize any indebtedness to David is recorded in 1 Sa. 25, and is interesting in introducing Abigail, later to become one of David's wives. Chs. 24 and 26 of the same book record two instances when David spared the life of Saul, out of mingled piety and magnanimity. Eventually David, quite unable to curb the hostility of Saul, came to terms with the Philistine king, Achish of Gath, and was granted the frontier town of Ziklag in return for the occasional use of his warrior band. When the Philistines went out in force against Saul, however, the war-lords demurred at David's presence in their ranks, fearing a last-minute change of loyalty, so he was spared the tragedy of Gilboa, which he later mourned in one of the loveliest elegies extant (2 Sa. 1:19–27).

V. King in Hebron

Once Saul was dead, David sought the will of God and was guided to return to Judah, his own tribal region. Here his fellow-tribesmen anointed him king, and he took up royal residence in Hebron. He was then 30 years old, and he reigned in Hebron for 7½ years. The first 2 years of this period were occupied by civil war between the supporters of David and the old courtiers of Saul, who had set up Saul's son Eshbaal (Ishbosheth) as king in Mahanaim. It may be doubted whether Eshbaal was more than a puppet, manipulated by Saul's faithful captain, Abner. With the death of these two by assassination, organized opposition to David came to an end, and he was anointed king over the 12 tribes of Israel in Hebron, from which he was soon to transfer his capital to Jerusalem (2 Sa. 3–5).

VI. King in Jerusalem

Now began the most successful period in David's long reign, which was to last for another 33 years. By a happy combination of personal bravery and skilled generalship he led the Israelites in such a systematic and decisive subjugation of their enemies—Philistines, Canaanites, Moabites, Ammonites, Aramaeans, Edomites and Amalekites—that his name would have been recorded in history quite apart from his significance in the divine plan of redemption. The contemporary weakness of the powers in the Nile and Euphrates valleys enabled him, by conquest and alliance, to extend his sphere of influence from the Egyptian frontier and the Gulf of Aqabah to the upper Euphrates. Conquering the supposedly impregnable Jebusite citadel of Jerusalem, he made it his capital, whence he bestrode the two major divisions of his kingdom, later to become the divided kingdoms of Judah and Israel. A palace was built, highways opened, trade routes restored, and the material prosperity of the kingdom secured. This, however, could never be the sole, nor yet the main, ambition of 'a man after Yahweh's own heart', and we soon see evidence of David's religious zeal. He brought back the ark of the covenant from Kiriath-jearim and placed it in a special tabernacle prepared for it in Jerusalem. It was during the return of the ark that the incident occurred which led to the death of Uzzah (2 Sa. 6:6–8). Much of the religious organization which was to enrich the later Temple worship owes its origin to the arrangements for the service of the tabernacle made by David at this time. In addition to its strategic and political importance, Jerusalem thus acquired the even greater religious significance, with which its name has been associated ever since.

It is all the more to be wondered at and remembered in godly fear, that it was in this period of outward prosperity and apparent religious fervour that David committed the sin referred to in Scripture as 'the matter of Uriah the Hittite' (2 Sa. 11). The significance and importance of this sin, both for its intrinsic heinousness and for its consequences in the whole ensuing history of Israel, cannot be overestimated. David repented deeply, but the deed was done, and stands as a demonstration of how sin spoils God's purpose for his children. The poignant cry of anguish with which he greeted the news of the death of *Absalom was only a feeble echo of the heart's agony which knew that death, and many more, to be but part of the reaping of the harvest of lust and deceit sown by him so many years before.

Absalom's rebellion, in which the N kingdom remained loyal to David, was soon followed by a revolt on the part of the N kingdom, led by Sheba, a Benjaminite. This revolt, like Absalom's, was crushed by Joab. David's dying days were marred by the scheming of Adonijah and Solomon for his throne, and by the realization that the legacy of internecine bloodshed foretold by *Nathan had still to be spent.

In addition to David's standing army, led by his kinsman Joab, he had a personal bodyguard recruited mainly from warriors of Philistine stock, whose loyalty to him never wavered. There is abundant evidence in the historical writings to which reference has already been made of David's skill in composing odes and elegies (see 2 Sa. 1:19–27; 3:33–34; 22; 23:1–7). An early tradition describes him as 'the sweet psalmist of Israel' (2 Sa. 23:1), while later OT writings refer to his direction of the musical worship of Israel, his invention of and skill in playing musical instruments, and his composition (Ne. 12:24, 36, 45–46; Am. 6:5). Seventy-three of the psalms in the Bible are recorded as 'David's', some of them in ways which clearly imply authorship. Most convincingly of all, our Lord himself spoke of David's authorship of at least one psalm (Lk. 20:42), using a quotation from it to make plain the nature of his Messiahship.

VII. Character

The Bible nowhere glosses over the sins or character defects of the children of God. 'Whatever was written in former days was written for our instruction' (Rom. 15:4). It is part of the task of Scripture to warn by example, as well as to encourage. The sin of David in the matter of Uriah the Hittite is a cardinal instance of this. Let this blot be seen for what it is – a stain on a character otherwise fair and wondrously to the glory of God. It is true that there are elements in the experience of David which seem foreign and even repugnant to the child of the new covenant. Yet 'he . . . served the counsel of God in his own generation' (Acts 13:36), and in that generation he stood out as a bright and shining light for the God of Israel. His accomplishments were many and varied; man of action, poet, tender lover, generous foe, stern dispenser of justice, loyal friend, he was all that men find wholesome and admirable in man, and this by the will of God, who made him and shaped him for his destiny. It is to David, not to Saul, that the Jews look back with pride and affection as the establisher of their kingdom, and it is in David that the more far-sighted of them saw the kingly ideal beyond which their minds could not reach, in the image of which they looked for a coming Messiah, who should deliver his people and sit upon the throne of David for ever. That this was not idealistic nonsense, still less idolatry, is indicated by the NT endorsement of the excellences of David, of whose seed Messiah indeed came, after the flesh.

BIBLIOGRAPHY. G. de S. Barrow, *David: Shepherd, Poet, Warrior, King*, 1946; A. C. Welch, *Kings and Prophets of Israel*, 1952, pp. 80ff. For a concise estimate of the 'Davidic' psalms, see N. H. Snaith, *The Psalms, A Short Introduction*, 1945, where Ewald's rearrangement is cited with approval. For an important and interesting appraisal of David's official role as divine representative and the significance of Jerusalem in the religious life of the monarchy, see A. R. Johnson, *Sacral Kingship in Ancient Israel*, 1955. T.H.J.

DAY OF THE LORD. This expression forms part of the *eschatology of the Bible. It has various equivalents, such as 'the day', 'in that day'.

In this article we consider the uses of the actual phrase. Am. 5:18–20, the earliest use, shows that the phrase was already a standard one in popular phraseology. To the people it meant the day when Yahweh would intervene to put Israel at the head of the nations, irrespective of Israel's faithfulness to him. Amos declares that the Day means judgment for Israel. So also in Is. 2:12f.; Ezk. 13:5; Joel 1:15; 2:1, 11; Zp. 1:7, 14; Zc. 14:1.

Other prophets, conscious of the sins of other nations as well as of Israel, declare that the Day will come on individual nations as a punishment for their brutalities, *e.g.* Babylon, Is. 13:6, 9; Egypt, Je. 46:10; Edom, Ob. 15; many nations, Joel 2:31; 3:14; Ob. 15.

The Day of the Lord is thus the occasion when Yahweh actively intervenes to punish sin that has come to a climax. This punishment may come through an invasion (Am. 5–6; Is. 13; Ezk. 13:5), or through some natural disaster, such as a locust invasion (Joel 1–2). All lesser interventions come to a head in the actual coming of the Lord himself. At this Day there are truly repentant believers who are saved (Joel 2:28–32), while those who remain enemies of the Lord, whether Jews or Gentiles, are punished. There are also physical effects on the world of nature (Is. 2).

In the NT the Day of the Lord (as in 2 Thes. 2:2) is the second coming of Christ, and the phrase 'the day of Jesus Christ', or an equivalent, occurs in 1 Cor. 1:8; 5:5; Phil. 1:6. 10; 2:16; 2 Thes. 2:2 (AV). The coming is unexpected (1 Thes. 5:2; 2 Pet. 3:10), yet certain signs must occur first, and these should be discerned by Christians (2 Thes. 2:2f.). Physical effects on the world of nature accompany the Day (2 Pet. 3:12f.). J.S.W.

DAY'S JOURNEY (Nu. 11:31; 1 Ki. 19:4; Jon. 3:4; Lk. 2:44). In the E distances were commonly considered in terms of hours and days. Thus a day's journey might be reckoned as 7–8 hours (perhaps 30–50 km), but it was a somewhat indefinite expression appropriate to a country where roads and other factors vary greatly. It should not be confused with a sabbath day's journey, for which see *WEIGHTS AND MEASURES. J.D.D.

DAYSPRING (Heb. *šahar*, 'dawn'; Gk. *anatolē*, 'uprising', elsewhere in AV 'east'). The 'place' of the dayspring (Jb. 38:12, RSV 'dawn') is the daily-changing point of the horizon at which the sun comes up. The Gk. (Lk. 1:78) presents difficulties of interpretation, but could intend a comparison of the Messiah with the rising of the sun. See A. R. C. Leaney, *The Gospel according to St Luke*, 1958, pp. 90–91. J.D.D.

DEACON. RSV renders 'deacon' only at Phil. 1:1 and 4 times in 1 Tim. 3; but the Gk. word thus represented, *diakonos* (generally in AV 'minister' or 'servant'), occurs some 30 times in NT, and the cognates *diakoneō* (to 'minister') and *diakonia* ('ministry') occur between them a further 70 times. In the majority of the 100 occurrences of the words there is no trace of a technical meaning relating to specialized functions in the church; in a few it is necessary to consider how far *diakonos* and its cognates have acquired such a connotation.

I. Derivation

Basically, *diakonos* is a servant, and often a table-servant, or waiter. In Hellenistic times it came also to represent certain cult and temple officials (see examples in *MM*), foreshadowing the Christian technical use. The more general sense is common in NT, whether for royal servants (Mt. 22:13) or for a servant of God (1 Thes. 3:2, TR). In a single passage Paul describes Epaphras as a 'deacon' of Christ and himself as a 'deacon' of the gospel and of the church (Col. 1:7, 23, 25). Others exercise a *diakonia* towards Paul (Acts 19:22; *cf.* Phm. 13 and perhaps Col. 4:7; Eph. 6:21), the context showing that they are his assistants in evangelistic work. To find here the origin of the later idea of the bishop with his deacon is straining language. In other words, *diakonia* is here being applied especially to preaching and pastoral work.

In NT, however, the word never quite loses its connection with the supply of material needs and service (*cf.*, *e.g.*, Rom. 15:25 in context; 2 Cor. 8:4). A waiter is a *diakonos* still (Jn. 2:5, 9); the table-waiting of Martha (Lk. 10:40) and of Peter's mother-in-law (Mk. 1:31) is *diakonia.* It is in this light that we are to see Christ's insistence that his coming was in order to minister (Mk. 10:45): significantly this claim is set in Lk. 22:26f. in the context of table-service. The Lord is the Deacon *par excellence*, the table-waiter of his people. And, as these passages show, 'deaconship' in this sense is a mark of his whole church.

II. The New Testament diaconate

As we have seen, there was contemporary analogy for 'deacons' as cult officials. When, therefore, we find the church greeted 'with the bishops and deacons' (Phil. 1:1) it is natural to see a reference to two particular classes within the church. It is true that Hort can see rather the 'ruling' and the 'serving' elements together making up the church, but it is doubtful if this could be applied to 1 Tim. 3, where a list of qualifications for bishops is immediately followed by a parallel list for deacons: sobriety, straightforwardness, freedom from excess and greed, probity. These would be particularly appropriate for those with responsibilities in finance and administration, and the prominence of social service in the early church would make *diakonos* an especially suitable word for such people—the more so since the love feast, involving literal table-service, was a regular agency of charity. While *diakonia* is a mark of the whole church, it is also a special gift—parallel with prophecy and government, but distinct from generous giving—to be exercised by those who possess it (Rom. 12:7; 1 Pet. 4:11). And while any servant of Christ is rightly called a 'deacon', the term may be particularly applied to those who minister, like Phoebe (Rom. 16:1), in the ways mentioned. But whether the diaconate existed universally under this name, or whether, for instance, the 'helps' at Corinth (1 Cor. 12:28) were equivalent to the 'deacons' at Philippi, remains uncertain. There is little to suggest that in NT times the term 'deacon' is ever more than semi-technical, or that it has any connection with the Jewish *ḥazzān* (*SYNAGOGUE). Significantly, immediately after listing the qualifications for deacons, Paul returns to the general sense of the word in exhorting Timothy himself (1 Tim. 4:6. *Cf.* also 1 Pet. 4:10 with 4:11).

The account in Acts 6 of the appointment by the Jerusalem church of seven approved men to supervise the administration of the widows' fund is commonly taken as the formal institution of the diaconate. It is doubtful if this has much basis in language. Leaving aside unprovable theories which see the Seven as but the Hellenistic counterpart of the Twelve, we may note, first, that the Seven are never called 'deacons', and secondly, that while the cognate words are used they apply equally to the *diakonia* of the Word exercised by the Twelve (v. 4) and to that of the tables (whether for meals or money) exercised by the Seven (v. 2). Laying on of hands is too common in Acts to be seen as a special milestone here (*ORDINATION), and the careers of Stephen and Philip show that the Seven were not confined to table-service.

There is, however, weight in Lightfoot's argument that the position Luke gives to the incident reflects his view of its high significance. It is 'one of those representative facts of which the earlier part of his narrative is almost wholly made up' (*Philippians*[5], p. 188). The significance lies, however, not in the institution of an order in the ministerial hierarchy, but as the first example of that delegation of administrative and social responsibilities to those of appropriate character and gifts, which was to become typical of the Gentile churches, and the recognition of such duties as part of the ministry of Christ.

Ecclesiastical usage institutionalized and narrowed the NT conception. Early non-canonical literature recognizes a class of deacons without specifying their functions (*cf. 1 Clement* 42; Ignatius, *Magnesians* 2. 1; *Trallians* 2. 3; 7. 3). Later literature shows the deacons undertaking functions such as attending the sick, which must have been part of Christian *diakonia* in apostolic times; but their duties in the Eucharist (*via* table-service at the communal meal?), and personal relationship with the monarchical bishop, become increasingly prominent. The occasional limitation of the diaconate to seven is probably due to deliberate archaizing.

BIBLIOGRAPHY. H. W. Beyer, *TDNT* 2, pp. 81–93; J. B. Lightfoot, *The Christian Ministry* (= *Philippians*[5], pp. 181ff.); F. J. A. Hort, *The Christian Ecclesia*, 1897, pp. 198ff.; A. M. Farrer in *The Apostolic Ministry*, ed. K. E. Kirk, 1946, especially pp. 142ff.; B. Reicke, *Diakonie, Festfreude und Zelos*, 1951, pp. 9ff.; K. Hess, *NIDNTT* 3, pp. 544–553.

A.F.W.

DEACONESS. There are a number of indications in the NT that women as well as men were appointed as deacons. *Phoebe was *diakonos* of the church at Cencreae (Rom. 16:1) and Paul recommends her as his messenger. Although sometimes translated 'servant' (AV), this is the word used for a deacon in 1 Tim. 3:8. It had no feminine form at this time. The Greek Fathers regularly read 1 Tim. 3:11, 'The women likewise must be serious' (RSV), as a reference to the qualities required for women deacons rather than deacons' wives (AV).

About AD 111 Pliny, governor of Bithynia, reported that he had questioned under torture two maidservants, who were called deaconesses (*ministrae*), concerning Christian rites (*Epistolae*, 10:96). After that there seems no clear literary notice of deaconesses before the 3rd century *Didascalia*. It portrays a culture where women were significantly enclosed. Women deacons had freedom to move within households, reaching women and children. They played an important role at the baptism of women and in continuing to teach the converts. Around this time the feminine term *diakonissa* was coined.

Some have doubted the existence of such an office in NT times, but the consensus today seems to be that women such as Phoebe held a recognized office as deacon in Paul's day. The emphasis in Luke 8:2f. on the involvement of women in Jesus' ministry may have been intended to be an encouragement to them. Deaconesses gradually disappeared in later centuries, with the tendency for women's ministry to be concentrated in celibate religious orders.

BIBLIOGRAPHY. B. Witherington, *Women in the Ministry of Jesus*, 1984; A Report to the House of Bishops of the General Synod of the Church of England, *Deacons in the Ministry of the Church*, 1981; C. Hall (ed.), *The Deacon's Ministry*, 1992.

V.M.S.

DEAD SEA. OT: 'Salt Sea' (Gn. 14:3), 'Eastern Sea' (Ezk. 47:18), 'Sea of the Arabah' (Dt. 4:49); classical: *Asphaltites*, later 'Dead Sea'; Arabic: 'Sea of Lot'.

The great rift valley reaches its deepest point at the Dead Sea basin. The surface of the water is on average 427 m below sea-level, and the deepest point of the bed some 433 m lower still. The Sea is about 77 km long and stretches from the sheer cliffs of Moab some 10 or 14 km across to the hills of Judah. On this W side is a narrow shore bounded by many terraces, the remains of earlier beaches. Except for a few springs (*e.g.* 'Ain Feshkha and Engedi, *cf.* Ct. 1:14), the Judaean coast is arid and bare. Four main streams feed the Sea from the E: the Mojin (Arnon), Zerqa Ma'in, Kerak and the Zered. The rate of evaporation is so great (temperature reaches 43°C in summer) that the inflow of these waters and the Jordan serves only to keep the sea-level constant. The annual rainfall is about 5 cm. Luxuriant vegetation is to be found where the rivers flow in or where there are fresh-water springs. The oases around the Kerak and the Zered delta show how fertile this basin could be (*cf.* Gn. 13:10), as Ezekiel saw in his vision of a river of pure water flowing from Jerusalem to sweeten the Salt Sea (Ezk. 47:8–12).

Until the mid-19th century it was possible to ford the sea from Lisan ('tongue'), a peninsula which projects from beside the Kerak to within 3 km of the opposite shore. Traces of a Roman road remain. Masada, an almost impregnable fortress built by the Maccabees and by Herod, guarded this road on the edge of Judaea. S of the Lisan, the sea is very shallow, gradually disappearing into the salty marsh (Zp. 2:9) called the Sebkha.

The concentrated chemical deposits (salt, potash, magnesium, and calcium chlorides and bromide, 25% of the water), which give the Dead Sea its buoyancy and its fatal effects on fish, may well have been ignited during an earthquake and caused the rain of brimstone and fire destroying Sodom and Gomorrah. Lot's wife, stopping to look back, was overwhelmed by the falling salt, while her family, hastening on, escaped (Gn. 19:15–28). Archaeological evidence suggests a break of several centuries in the sedentary occupation from early in the 2nd millennium BC. A hill of salt (*Jebel Usdum*, Mt Sodom) at the SW corner is eroded into strange forms, including pillars which are known as 'Lot's Wife' by local Arabs (*cf.* Wisdom 10:7). Salt was obtained from the shore (Ezk. 47:11), and the Nabataeans traded in the bitumen which floats on the surface (see P. C. Hammond, *BA* 22, 1959, pp. 40–48). Throughout the OT period the sea acted as a barrier between Judah and Moab and Edom (*cf.* 2 Ch. 20:1–30), although it may have been used by small trading boats, as it was in Roman times. (*PLAIN, CITIES OF THE; *PATRIARCHAL AGE; *ARCHAEOLOGY; *JORDAN; *ARABAH; *DEAD SEA SCROLLS.)

BIBLIOGRAPHY. G. A. Smith, *Historical Geography of the Holy Land*, 1931, pp. 499–516; D. Baly, *The Geography of the Bible*, 1974.

A.R.M.

DEAD SEA SCROLLS. Ancient manuscripts discovered in and around the cliffs along the W shore of the Dead Sea.

In the broadest usage, the expression Dead Sea Scrolls (DSS) embraces all epigraphic remains discovered since 1947 over a 75 km stretch from Wadi ed-Daliyeh 25 km N of the Dead Sea southward to Masada, mostly in caves. Strictly speaking, DSS designates only those manuscripts discovered in the vicinity of Khirbet Qumran. At present, this includes approximately 800 manuscripts from eleven caves, many extremely fragmentary. Almost certainly, the scrolls represent a 'library' for the community – probably Essenes – which inhabited the buildings at *QUMRAN (see also *ESSENES). One of the strongest pieces of evidence for this view of the DSS is the distribution of writings in the caves (Dimant).

Nevertheless, the recognition that the eleven caves contained parts of a large collection does not imply that all the works were composed by one group of people. This is obviously the case with the non-biblical texts. Of approximately 190 non-biblical compositions represented among the scrolls, nine were previously known: Ben Sira, Tobit, Epistle of Jeremiah, apocryphal psalms, Jubilees, 1 Enoch, Book of Giants, Testament of Levi and Testament of Naphtali. The tendency to regard the remaining non-biblical compositions as direct evidence for practices and beliefs of the Qumran community (*e.g.* 'the Qumran liturgy' and 'Qumran exegesis') has given way to much more circumspection in the use of DSS. Scholars now generally demand some concrete indication before labelling a piece as sectarian or of Qumran origin. They also find the use of sources, redactional layers and developments. It now appears possible that roughly one third of the total number of manuscripts and over one third of the non-biblical compositions are of non-Qumran provenance, many with no sectarian content whatsoever.

The biblical manuscripts are extremely valuable for textual criticism, since they predate by over a millennium the earliest Heb. biblical manuscripts previously known (the oldest DSS MSS date from the 3rd century BC: 4QSam[b], 4QEx[f], 4QJer[a]). These manuscripts confirm that three primary textual witnesses to the Heb. Bible were in existence prior to the Christian era: the MT 'type', the Heb. *Vorlage* of the LXX, and the Samaritan Pentateuch. But the DSS also hint at a greater diversity than previously imagined. Furthermore, the existence at Qumran of texts close to each of these, but also of a distinctive 'Qumran group' and many texts which share characteristics of several groups, without any decisive commitment to one, shows that a local text theory is not wholly adequate to explain the variations. It emerges that textual criticism of the Heb. Bible must not be pursued in isolation from literary criticism.

By the presence of every book of the Heb. canon (except Esther), the use of formulas to introduce quotations from Scripture and exegetical activity on biblical texts, the DSS give evidence of a distinct body of authoritative books headed by the Pentateuch, the prophets and the Psalms. Nevertheless, the divergent nature of the Psalter in 11QPs[a], the use of formulas to introduce quotations from the Apocryphon of Levi and Jubilees, and the implicit claim to inspiration in the Temple Scroll, imply that the boundaries of the corpus of authoritative writings were not rigid. Moreover, the existence of various forms of biblical texts side by side within one community, and especially expansive texts, imply that there was little or no concern for 'a canonical text'.

Several manuscripts consist only of excerpts of Scripture, some of which had a liturgical function (*tefillin* and *mezuzot*, probably 4QDeut[j,n]), and others whose purpose is less clear.

Biblical interpretation permeates most of the DSS, but there are some compositions whose central purpose is to explain, clarify, harmonize, systematize and extend the biblical text in different ways. Most distinctive to Qumran exegesis is the explicit commentary known as *pesher*, so named after the characteristic method of citing a brief biblical passage followed by the formula 'its interpretation concerns'. *Pesher* exegesis operates on the premise that hidden in Scripture is secret revelation pertaining to the last days, and only the sectarian community holds the key to the true interpretation. Consequently, it disregards the historical context of the biblical text but assumes that it concerns the history of the sect and its enemies. Continuous *pesharim* exist on the Psalms and several of the prophets (Isaiah, Hosea, Micah, Nahum, Zephaniah, Habakkuk). There are also thematic *pesharim* which assemble passages from different biblical books around a common subject, *e.g.* 4QFlorilegium, 4QCatena[a], and 11QMelchizedek treat eschatological themes while 4Q Ordinances (4Q159, 513–514) reinterprets various biblical laws. Examples of *pesher* exegesis also appear within non-biblical works, *e.g.* the Damascus Document.

Other types of exegesis are more subtle. Targums to Leviticus and Job interpret the text by means of Aramaic translation. Juxtaposition of biblical passages in 4QTestimonia points to an expectation of three eschatological figures: a prophet like Moses, a Davidic Messiah and a priestly Messiah. Various works follow the biblical text quite closely but with additions, omissions and reorderings for exegetical purpose, *e.g.* 4QReworked Pentateuch[a-c]; Temple Scroll. Others are more extensive in their exegetical retelling, rewording or paraphrasing the biblical text itself, *e.g.* Genesis (4QAges of Creation [4Q180–181], 4QGenesis Commentary [4Q252], 1QGenesis Apocryphon, Jubilees, 4QPseudo-Jubilees[a,b]), Exodus (4Q127), Joshua (4Q123) and the description of the eschatological city in Ezk. 40–48 (the Aramaic New Jerusalem texts). Among these examples of 'rewritten Bible', the Temple Scroll is unusual since it aims not only to restate and interpret Scripture, but to constitute a new revelation of law itself, perhaps as a sixth book of the Torah.

Numerous works are much more loosely related to the biblical text. Sometimes called 'para-biblical literature', these include a variety of works intended to supplement Scripture, often associated with important biblical characters such as Enoch, Noah, the patriarchs, Moses, Joshua, Samuel, Jeremiah and Ezekiel.

Among the most important of the non-biblical compositions are several which appear to be rule-books for a community: the Community Rule (S), the Damascus Document (D), the Eschatological Rule (Sa) and the War Rule (M). With the exception of Sa, which is appended to only one copy of S, these exist in multiple copies which attests to their popularity at Qumran. They incorporate a variety of literary forms and diverse content, are patently of composite origin and exhibit complex redactional histories perhaps related to developments in the community. S is usually regarded as the central source of information about the organization and life of the Qumran sect, its dualism, Messianism and eschatology. The close relationship between S and D probably reflects related communities. M and Sa provide rules for the eschatological community. All of the rules point to a highly structured organization and rigorous discipline, but this derives from theological rather than ascetical motivations. It is not certain, however, to what degree these might have been liturgical and/or utopian writing rather than purely practical rule-books.

The publication of the Temple Scroll in 1977 and 4QMMT in the early 1990s highlighted the central role of law at Qumran. The Temple Scroll is a collection of laws related to the Temple, sacrifices, priesthood and festivals, closely following but reinterpreting and supplementing biblical law. It is probable that it was a revered source at Qumran rather than a Qumran composition, since it lacks polemic and differs in some points from positions attested in the Rules. 4QMMT is a polemical collection of purity laws (and seemingly a calendar) with one group appealing to another on friendly but stern terms. Many of its legal positions resemble Sadducean *halakhah*, but this is a result of common Jewish tradition rather than identity or relationship of groups.

Liturgical works among the DSS include collections of prayers for days of the week with a hymn for the Sabbath, days of the month and festivals as well as grace at meals, purification ceremonies and possibly a wedding ceremony. It is unlikely that all of these were exclusive to the Qumran sect, and are therefore important evidence for the early development of Jewish liturgy. More certainly sectarian are blessing and cursing rituals, a collection of mystical Sabbath hymns, blessings for the last days and exorcism psalms. Numerous poetic texts could also have had some sort of liturgical use, such as the non-sectarian mixed psalter 11QPsalms[a], the sectarian Thanksgiving Hymns, collections of hymns beginning 'Bless, O my soul' and lamentations.

Only recently has the full scope of wisdom material among the DSS begun to be realized, and many texts remain unpublished. In 4QMysteries, wisdom and prophecy are linked: divine wisdom is hidden as mysteries discernible only by those specially gifted in interpreting signs.

Various calendrical texts coordinate the 364–day solar calendar, known from 1 Enoch and Jubilees, with both biblical and non-biblical festivals and/or the priestly courses. Some also synchronize these with the days of the lunar month.

The influence of apocalyptic writings, and interest in revelation of mysteries, visions and mystical communion with the angels, is apparent in many of the scrolls. Besides important fragments of previously known apocalypses such as 1 Enoch and the Book of Giants, there are several fragmentary works of an apocalyptic nature, mostly in Aramaic, *e.g.* part of a book of Noah, a visionary angel-guided tour of the New Jerusalem, a vision of Amram exhibiting a cosmic dualism, a Danielic vision about the four kingdoms, and another about a 'son of God' whose identity is still disputed. The Qumran sect emerges as a community which held in tension the apocalyptic impulse and concern for the law (*cf.* CD 1:5–7).

A few works might be termed magical texts. 4Q186 determines a person's spiritual nature by his physical features and the astrological conditions at his birth. Related to this, 4Q534 demonstrates the connection between physical features and the destiny of an individual. 4Q318 combines astrology with the interpretation of portents.

A scroll of copper lists the locations of hidden treasures, but scholars have not been able to agree on its significance or relationship to Qumran or the other scrolls.

Unanswered questions about the textual history of individual compositions and their relationship to one another, and about the library as a whole, render precarious broad claims about the history, beliefs and practices of the Qumran sect based on harmonization of various scrolls. Nevertheless, the priestly orientation of the community is prominent. A central element of their self-identity was the conviction that the community atoned for the land by the acceptance of discipline, enactment of judgments, right behaviour and prayer. Purity laws and calendar were issues of contention with the temple authorities. A founding leader, called the Teacher of Righteousness, had faced opposition from the high priest (the 'Wicked Priest') and was betrayed by a leader close to him (the 'Spouter of Lies'). Characteristic themes include a cosmic dualism between dark and light, eschatology, Messianism, predestination and election.

BIBLIOGRAPHY. G. J. Brooke, *Exegesis at Qumran*, 1985; G. J. Brooke (ed.), *Temple Scroll Studies*, 1989; J. J. Collins, 'Dead Sea Scrolls', in ABD 2, 1992, pp. 85–101; E. D. Cook, *Solving the Mysteries of the Dead Sea Scrolls*, 1994; D. Dimant, 'The Qumran Manuscripts: Contents and Significance', in *Time to Prepare the Way in the Wilderness*, 1995, pp. 23–58; *idem.*, 'Qumran Sectarian Literature', in *Jewish Writings of the Second Temple Period* 2, ed. by M. Stone, 1984, pp. 483–550; J. A. Fitzmyer, *The Dead Sea Scrolls: Major Publications and Tools for Study*, rev. edn., 1990; F. G. Martínez, *Qumran and Apocalyptic*, 1992; *idem.*, *The Dead Sea Scrolls Translated*, 1994; F. G. Martínez and J. Trebolle Barrera, *The People of the Dead Sea Scrolls*, 1995; J. Maier, 'The Judaic System of the Dead Sea Scrolls', in *Judaism in Late Antiquity* 2, ed. by J. Neusner, 1995, pp. 84–108; J. Murphy-O'Connor, 'The Judean Desert', in *Early Judaism and Its Modern Interpreters*, ed. by R. A. Kraft and G. W. E. Nickelsburg, 1986, pp. 119–156; B. Nitzan, *Qumran and Religious Poetry*, 1994; E. Schürer, *The History of the Jewish People in the Age of Jesus Christ. A New English Edition* 3, rev. and ed. by G. Vermes, *et al.*, 1986, pp. 380–469; H. Stegemann, *The Library of Qumran*, 1995; E. Tov (ed.), *Companion Volume to the Dead Sea Scrolls Microfiche Edition*, 1995; E. Tov, 'Hebrew Biblical Manuscripts from the Judaean Desert: Their Contribution to Textual Criticism', *JJS* 39, 1988, pp. 5–37; E. Ulrich and J. VanderKam (eds.), *The Community of the Renewed Covenant*, 1994; J. VanderKam, *The Dead Sea Scrolls Today*, 1994; G. Vermes, *The Dead Sea Scrolls in English*[4], 1995.

D.K.F.

DEATH. From one point of view death is the most natural of things: 'man is destined to die once' (Heb. 9:27). It may be accepted without rebellion: 'Let me die the death of the righteous' (Nu. 23:10). From another, it is most unnatural. It is the penalty for sin (Rom. 6:23), and is to be feared as such. Both points of view are found in the Bible; neither should be overlooked. Death is a biological necessity, but people do not die simply as the animals die.

I. Physical death

'Death' can have more than one meaning. Physical death seems inevitable for bodies like ours; decay and ultimate dissolution are inescapable. But the Bible speaks of death as the result of sin. God said to Adam, 'when you eat of it you will surely die' (Gn. 2:17). Paul tells us that 'sin entered the world through one man, and death through sin' (Rom. 5:12), and again that 'the wages of sin is death' (Rom. 6:23). But Adam did not die physically on the day that he disobeyed God. And in Rom. 5 and 6 Paul is contrasting the death that came about through Adam's sin with the life that Christ brings people. Now the possession of eternal life does not abolish physical death. It is opposed to a spiritual state, not to a physical event. The inference we draw from all this is that the death which is the result of sin is more than bodily death.

Suicide is rare in the OT, but there were people who took their lives in the face of military disaster, actual or expected (Jdg. 9:54; 1 Sa. 31:4; 2 Sa. 17:23; 1 Ki. 16:18). There is but one suicide in the NT, that of Judas (Mt. 27:5). We should see this as a sinful way of ending God's good gift of life, but the Bible does not discuss it.

The scriptural passages that connect death with sin do not qualify death. We would not realize from them anything other than the usual meaning attached to the word. Perhaps we should understand that mortality was the result of Adam's sin, and that the penalty of death includes both physical and spiritual aspects. But we do not know enough about Adam's pre-fallen condition to be dogmatic. If his body was like ours, then it was mortal. If it was not, we have no means of knowing whether it was mortal or not.

We should understand death as something that involves the whole person. We die, not as so many bodies, but as people, in the totality of our being. And the Bible does not put a sharp line of demarcation between the two aspects. Physical death, then, is a fit symbol and expression of, and unity with, the more serious death that sin inevitably brings.

II. Spiritual death

That more serious death is the divine penalty. We have already noticed that death is 'the wages' of sin (Rom. 6:23), *i.e.* the due reward for sin. Paul can speak of certain sinners who 'know God's righteous decree that those who do such things deserve death' (Rom. 1:32), and the thought of God's decree underlies John's reference to the 'sin that leads to death' (1 Jn. 5:16). This is a very important truth. It enables us to see the full horror of death. And at the same time, paradoxically, it gives us hope. We are not caught up in a web woven by blind fate, so that, once having sinned, nothing can ever be done about it. God is over the whole process, and, if he has decreed that death is the penalty of sin, he has also determined to give life eternal to those saved by Christ.

Sometimes the NT emphasizes the serious consequence of sin by referring to 'the second death' (Jude 12; Rev. 2:11, *etc*.). This is a rabbinic expression for eternal perdition. It is to be understood along with passages in which Jesus spoke of 'eternal fire prepared for the devil and his angels' (Mt. 25:41), 'eternal punishment' (set in contrast to 'eternal life', Mt. 25:46), and the like. The final state of the impenitent is variously described as death, punishment, being lost, *etc*. Obviously it would be unwise to equate it with any one description. But clearly it is a state to be regarded with horror.

Sometimes the objection is made that this is inconsistent with the truth that God is a loving God. There is a profound mystery here, but the objection, as commonly stated, overlooks the fact that death is a state as well as an event ('The mind of sinful man is death', Rom. 8:6). Paul does not say that the mind of the flesh causes death, but that it *is* death. He adds that 'the sinful mind is hostile to God. It does not submit to God's law, nor can it do so.' The same truth can be put in a different way: 'Anyone who does not love remains in death' (1 Jn. 3:14). When we have grasped the truth that death is a state, we see the impossibility of the impenitent being saved. Salvation for such is a contradiction in terms. For salvation, we must pass from death into life (Jn. 5:24).

III. Victory over death

An arresting feature of NT teaching on death is that the emphasis is on life. In most places *nekros* ('dead') is used of resurrection from the dead or the like. Scripture faces death, as it faces all reality. But its interest is in life. Death is treated more or less incidentally, as that from which people are

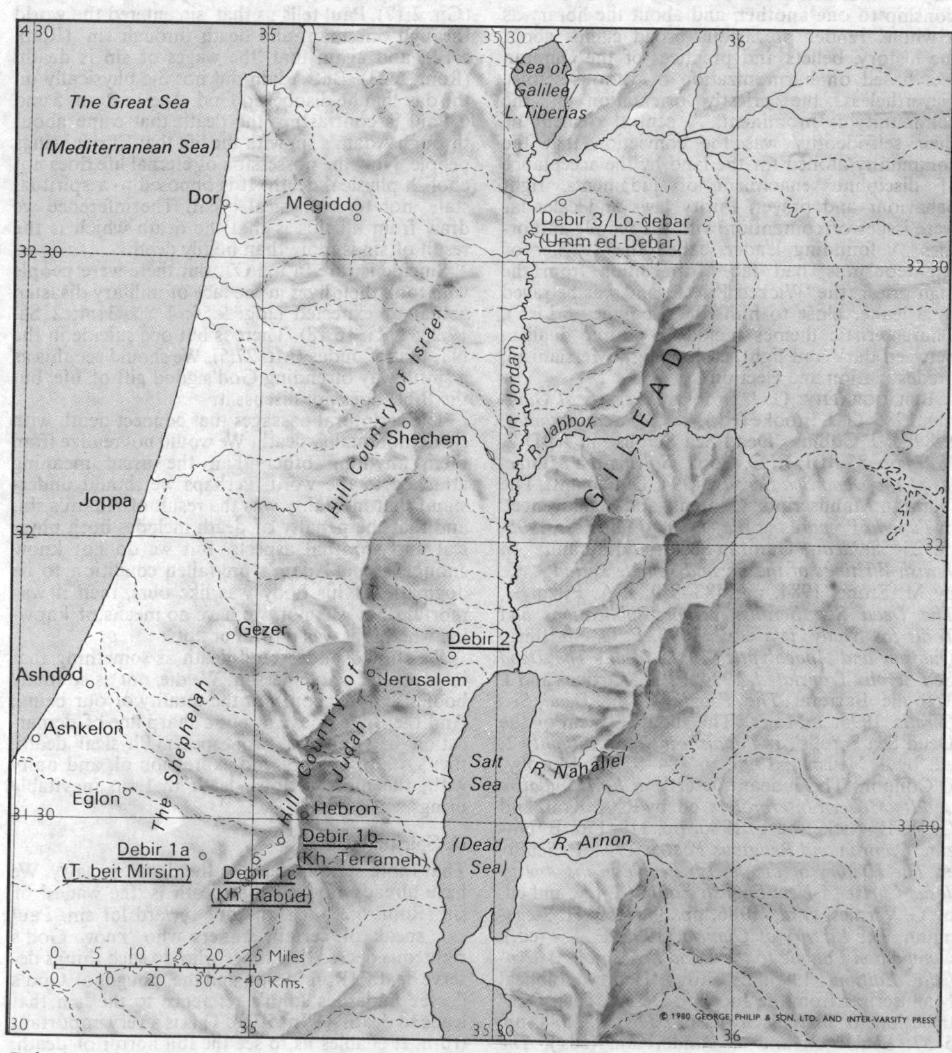

Debir: possible locations.

saved. Christ conquered death. He took upon himself our nature 'so that by his death he might destroy him who holds the power of death – that is, the devil' (Heb. 2:14). The devil's power is subject to God's overruling (Jb. 2:6; Lk. 12:5, *etc.*). Satan is no absolute disposer of death. Nevertheless death, the negation of life, is his proper sphere. And Christ came to put an end to death. It was through death, as the Hebrews passage indicates, that he defeated Satan. It was through death that he put away our sin: 'The death he died he died to sin, once for all' (Rom. 6:10). For those who are apart from Christ, death is the supreme enemy, the symbol of our alienation from God, the ultimate horror. But Christ has used death to deliver people from death. He died that believers may live. It is significant that the NT speaks of believers as 'sleeping' rather than as 'dying' (*e.g.* 1 Thes. 4:14). Jesus bore the full horror of death. Therefore, for those who are 'in Christ', death has been transformed so that it is no more than sleep. 'If a man keeps my word,' Jesus said, 'he will never see death' (Jn. 8:51).

The extent of Christ's victory over death is indicated by his resurrection. 'Since Christ was raised from the dead, he cannot die again; death no longer has mastery over him' (Rom. 6:9). The resurrection is the great triumphal event, and the whole of the NT note of victory originates here. Christ is 'the author of life' (Acts 3:15), 'the Lord of both the dead and living' (Rom. 14:9), 'the Word of life' (1 Jn. 1:1). His victory over death is complete. And his victory is made available to his people. Death's destruction is certain (1 Cor. 15:26, 54ff.; Rev. 21:4). The second death has no power over believers (Rev. 2:11; 20:6). In keeping with this the NT understands eternal life not as the immortality of the soul, but in terms of the resurrection of the body. Nothing could more graphically illustrate the finality and the completeness of death's defeat.

Not only is there a glorious future, there is a glorious present. Believers have already passed out of death and into life (Jn. 5:24; 1 Jn. 3:14). They are 'free from the law of sin and death' (Rom. 8:2). Death cannot separate them from God (Rom. 8:38f.). Jesus said, 'If a man keeps my word, he will never see death' (Jn. 8:51). Such words do not deny the reality of biological death. Rather, they point us to the truth that, because of the death of Jesus, believers have passed altogether out of the state which is death. They are brought into a new state, which is aptly characterized as life. They will in due course pass through the gateway we call death. But the sting has been drawn. The death of Jesus means victory over death for his followers.

BIBLIOGRAPHY. C. S. Lewis, *Miracles*, 1947, pp. 150ff.; C. Ryder Smith, *The Bible Doctrine of Salvation*, 1941, *passim.*; Leon Morris, *The Wages of Sin*, 1955; R. Bultmann, *TDNT* 2, pp. 856f., 4, pp. 892–895; L. Coenen and W. Schmithals, *NIDNTT* 1, pp. 429–446. L.M.

DEBIR (Heb. *d^e^bîr*). **1.** A city on the S side of the Judaean hills, held by Anakim before the Israelite invasion, then by Kenizzites (Jos. 10:38; 11:21; 15:15 = Jdg. 1:11). A levitical town (Jos. 21:15). In Jos. 15:49 it is equated with Kiriath-sanna; since the Achsah story recalls Kiriath-sepher as the Canaanite name, it has been argued that *sanna* is a mis-spelling or 'Debir' is an incorrect gloss (M. Noth, *Josua*[2], *ad loc.*, and *JPOS* 15, 1935, pp. 44–47; H. M. Orlinsky, *JBL* 58, 1939, p. 255). Debir was probably at Kh. Rabbud, 13 km SW of Hebron, a strong position overlooking the Nahal Hevron, occupied from Late Bronze Age to 586 BC (K. Galling, *ZDPV* 70, 1954, pp. 135ff.; excavated by M. Kochavi from 1969, *Tel Aviv* 1, 1974, pp. 2–33). The springs mentioned in Jos. 15:19, Jdg. 1:15 may be located 3 km to the N, up a side valley. Tell Beit Mirsim, 20 km WSW of Hebron, proposed by W. F. Albright, is not free of difficulties; it is hardly the southern site implied by Achsah's complaint, and authorities differ as to the duration and significance of occupational breaks. See K. M. Kenyon, *Archaeology in the Holy Land*, 1970, pp. 214, 306; *LOB*, p. 219; J. Bimson, *Redating the Exodus*, 1981, pp. 45–51, *etc.*

2. On the N border of Judah (Jos. 15:7); probably above the Wadi Debr, which is the lower part of the Wadi Mukallik, or near Tughret ed-Debr, S of the Ascent of *Adummim. See *GTT*, p. 137.

3. In the N of Gad (Jos. 13:26) (*MT Lidebir*); probably Umm ed-Debar, 16 km S of Lake Tiberias; *LOB* p. 252.

4. The Canaanite king of *Eglon who fought against Joshua (Jos. 10:3). The kings are named only in that text; there is no reason to see in it any evidence that the city of Debir was involved in the alliance. J.P.U.L.

DEBORAH (Heb. *d^e^bôrâ*, 'bee'). **1.** Rebekah's nurse, whose death at Bethel is recorded in Gn. 35:8; the tree beneath which she was buried was known as Allon-bacuth, 'the oak (or terebinth) of weeping'.

2. A prophetess who appears in the list of judges of Israel (*c.* 1125 BC). According to Jdg. 4:4ff., she had her headquarters under 'the palm tree of Deborah' between Ramah and Bethel, and was consulted there by Israelites from various tribes who wished to have their disputes settled—either disputes which proved too intractable for their local judges or intertribal disputes. She was thus a judge in the ordinary, non-military sense of the word, and it was probably because of her judicial and charismatic renown that the Israelites had recourse to her in the straits to which they were reduced under Sisera's oppression. She commanded *Barak to take the field as Israelite commander-in-chief against Sisera, and consented to accompany him at his insistence; the result was the crushing defeat of Sisera at the battle of Kishon (Jdg. 4:15; 5:19ff.).

She is called (Jdg. 4:4) the wife of Lappidoth (lit. 'torches'), and she is described (Jdg. 5:7) as 'a mother in Israel'. It has been argued that this last phrase means 'a metropolis in Israel' (*cf.* 2 Sa. 20:19), and that the reference is to the city of Daberath (Jos. 21:28; 1 Ch. 6:72), modern Debûriyeh at the W foot of Mt Tabor; but there is nothing in the narrative or in the poem to prepare us for the prominence which would thus suddenly be given to such an obscure place.

The song of Deborah (Jdg. 5:2–31a) has been preserved from the 12th century BC with its language practically unmodernized, and is thus one of the most archaic passages in the OT. It was evidently composed on the morrow of the victory which it celebrates, and is an important source of information on tribal relations in Israel at the time. It may be divided into eight sections: an exordium of praise (vv. 2–3); the invocation of Yahweh (4–5); the desolation under the oppressors (6–8); the mustering of the tribes (9–18); the battle of Kishon

(19–23); the death of Sisera (24–27); the description of Sisera's mother awaiting his return (28–30); and the epilogue (31a). It is from the song, rather than from the prose narrative of ch. 4, that we learn what precisely brought about Sisera's defeat: a cloudburst flooded the watercourse of Kishon and swept away the Canaanite chariotry (21), throwing the army into confusion and making it an easy prey for Barak's men.

The vivid and moving description of Sisera's mother (28ff.) has been felt to confirm the feminine authorship of the song; if it betrays sympathy of a sort, it is not a compassionate sympathy.

Deborah is apostrophized in the song not only in v. 12 but probably also in v. 7, where the repeated Heb. *qamtî* may be understood not as the normal first person singular ('I arose') but as an archaic second person singular ('thou didst arise'); *cf.* RSV (*JUDGES).

BIBLIOGRAPHY. A. D. H. Mayes, *Israel in the Period of the Judges*, 1974. F.F.B.

DEBT, DEBTOR.

a. Lending, loan

Loans in Israel were not commercial but charitable, granted not to enable a trader to set up or expand a business but to tide a peasant farmer over a period of poverty. Since the economy remained predominantly agricultural up to the end of the Monarchy, there developed no counterpart to the commercial loan system already existing in Babylonia in 2000 BC. Hence the legislation contains not mercantile regulations but exhortations to neighbourliness. The same outlook persists in Ecclus. 29. The background changes in the NT. The debtors in the parable of the unjust steward (Lk. 16:1–8) are either tenants who pay rent in kind or merchants who have goods on credit. The description of sins as debts (Mt. 6:12) is a Jewish commonplace which Jesus employs, not to characterize the relationship between God and man as one between creditor and debtor, but to proclaim the grace and enjoin the duty of forgiveness (Lk. 7:41f.; Mt. 18:21–27).

b. Interest, usury

The word 'usury' in the AV has not the modern sense of exorbitant interest. The complaint in the OT is not that interest is excessive but that it is charged at all. All three formulations of the law (Ex. 22:25, Dt. 23:19f., Lv. 25:35ff.,) forbid it as an exploitation of a fellow-Israelite's misfortune. Dt. 23:20 (*cf.* 15:1–8) allows that a foreigner may be charged. Interest is mentioned as an established practice in the Code of Hammurapi and earlier Babylonian laws. The word *nešek̲* (lit. 'something bitten off') probably denotes simply rapacious exaction from a debtor, though the play on the word *nôšᵉk̲îm* in Hab. 2:7 RVmg. (meaning both 'payers of interest' and 'biters') may imply a sum which eats away the savings set aside for repayment. The synonym *tarbîṯ* ('increase') and the Gk. *tokos* ('offspring') take the more modern view of interest as a growth upon principal. In keeping with a changed economy, Jesus approves of investment to earn income (Mt. 25:27; Lk. 19:23) but retains the traditional distrust of any charge on a private loan (Lk. 6:31ff.).

c. Pledge, surety

Security took the form of a pledge of some personal effect for a small temporary loan (Dt. 24:10; Jb. 24:3), the mortgage of real estate (Ne. 5) or the surety of a guarantor (Pr. 6:1–5; Ecclus. 8:13; 29:14–20). Where there was no security to forfeit debtors could be sold into slavery (Ex. 22:3; 2 Ki. 4:1; Am. 2:6; 8:6, *etc.*). The laws are framed to mitigate the severity of custom. Restrictions are laid on the range of pledgeable items and conditions of borrowing (Dt. 24). By a sort of 'Statute of Limitations' all debts were to be cancelled every seventh year (Dt. 15:1ff., only Dt. mentions debts in connection with the year of Jubilee), and Israelites giving service in discharge of debts to be released (Lv. 25:39–55). This legislation seems not to have been observed historically. Elisha helps the widow in 2 Ki. 4:1–7 not by invoking the law but by working a miracle. Ne. 5 makes no appeal to Dt. 15 (though *cf.* Ne. 10:31 and Je. 34:13f.). In the Judaistic period Hillel invented a system for legal evasion of Dt.15, the purpose of which was not to frustrate or circumvent the law but to adapt it to a commercial economy.

BIBLIOGRAPHY. R. de Vaux, *Ancient Israel*, 1961; J. D. M. Derrett, *Law in the New Testament*, 1970. A.E.W.

DECAPOLIS. A large territory S of the Sea of Galilee, mainly to the E of Jordan, but including Beth-shean to the W. The Greeks had occupied towns like Gadara and Philadelphia as early as 200 BC. In 63 BC Pompey liberated Hippos, Scythopolis and Pella from the Jews. He annexed the cities to the province of Syria, but gave them municipal freedom. About AD 1 they formed a league for trade and mutual defence against Semitic tribes. Pliny named the ten original members as Scythopolis, Pella, Dion, Gerasa, Philadelphia, Gadara, Raphana, Kanatha, Hippos and Damascus. Ptolemy included other towns S of Damascus in a list of 18 cities in the 2nd century AD.

Inhabitants of Decapolis joined the great crowds which followed Christ in Mt. 4:25. He landed in the territory at Gerasa (Mk. 5:1; Origen reads Gergesa, a site on the cliff). The presence of so many swine suggests a predominantly Gentile population who, on suffering economic loss through the miracle, requested Christ's departure, despite the demoniac's testimony. Christ revisited Decapolis when making an unusual detour through the Hippos area on a journey from Sidon to the E shore of Galilee (Mk. 7:31). The Jewish church retired to Pella before the war of AD 70.

BIBLIOGRAPHY. *DCG*; G. A. Smith, *Historical Geography of the Holy Land*, 1931, pp. 595–608; H. Bietenhard, 'Die Dekapolis von Pompeius bis Traian', *ZDPV* 79, 1963, pp. 24–58; Pliny, *NH* 5. 18. 74. D.H.T.

DECEIT. From Heb. root *rāmâ*, meaning treachery or guile (Ps. 34:13). It is used of a witness, of *balances and of a bow (Ps. 78:57). It is expressed by several Gk. words, e.g. planē*, 'error' (Eph. 4:14); *dolos*, 'cunning', 'treachery' (Rom. 1:29; Mk. 7:22); *apatē*, 'beguiling pleasure' (Mt. 13:22; Heb. 3:13; Col. 2:8). Since the devil is the arch-deceiver (Rev. 20:10) his children are described as 'full of deceit', *e.g.* Elymas (Acts 13:10). Conversely, in Christ's mouth there is no deceit (1 Pet. 2:22) and in the true Israelite Nathanael no guile (Jn. 1:47).

BIBLIOGRAPHY. *BAGD*; *MM*; *HDB*; W. Günther, *NIDNTT* 2, pp. 457–461. D.H.T.

DECISION, VALLEY OF. Mentioned in Joel 3:14 as the place of God's judgment on the nations, the 'valley of decision' is also called (vv. 2, 12) 'the valley of Jehoshaphat'. V. 16 suggests proximity to Zion, but, as Am. 1:2 shows, this wording may be a prophetic formula rather than an indication of location. 'Jehoshaphat', meaning 'Yahweh judges', may be symbolic rather than topographic. 2 Ch. 20 would explain the symbolism: in the valley of Beracah, 24 km S of Jerusalem, King Jehoshaphat observed Yahweh's victory over heathen nations, a microcosm of the Day of Yahweh. However, from the 4th century AD onwards the name 'valley of Jehoshaphat' has been given to the valley between the Temple Hill and the Mount of Olives. J.A.M.

DECREE. In the AV the term occurs frequently in Esther, Ezra and Daniel as a translation of various Heb. and Aram. words for royal decrees. RSV often differentiates between them, using 'interdict' in Dn. 6:8, 'sentence' (RV 'law') in Dn. 2:9 and 'decree' in Ezr. 5:13. God, as King of the earth, is said in the OT to make decrees (Dn. 4:24; Ps. 2:7), and the world is controlled by them: there is one for the rain, Jb. 28:26, and one for the sea, Pr. 8:29 (RSV 'command'), where we should speak of laws of nature. The Heb. *ḥōq*, 'statute' (Ps. 119:5, 8, 12, *etc.*), is the nearest biblical approach to the 'decrees of God' spoken of by theologians.

In the NT the Gk. *dogma* describes special decrees of the Roman emperor in Lk. 2:1 and Acts 17:7 (*cf.* E. A. Judge, 'The Decrees of Caesar at Thessalonica', *RTR* 30, 1971, pp.1–7). In Acts 16:4 it is used of the findings of the Jerusalem Council: *cf.* Gk. usage for authoritative decisions of groups of philosophers. In Eph. 2:15 and Col. 2:14, 20 it refers to Jewish enactments.

BIBLIOGRAPHY. *BAGD*; *HDB*; *MM*. D.H.T.

DEDAN. A city and people of NW *Arabia, famous for its role in the caravan trade (Is. 21:13; Ezk. 27:20—the reference in *MT* of v. 20 is probably due to a textual error—*cf.* RSV), since it lay on the well-known 'incense route' from S Arabia to Syria and the Mediterranean. It is mentioned in close association with Sheba in the Table of *Nations (Gn. 10:7—*cf.* 1 Ch. 1:9) and elsewhere (Gn. 25:3; 1 Ch. 1:32; Ezk. 38:13), and probably played a part in the trading relations established by Solomon with the queen of Sheba (1 Ki. 10). But it only comes into prominence in OT texts in the 7th century BC (Je. 25:23; 49:8; Ezk. 25:13; 27:20), when it may have been a Sabaean trading colony (von Wissman); this would help to explain why, in the biblical genealogies, it is associated with both N and S Arabian peoples. It is mentioned by Nabonidus in one of his inscriptions (*ANET*, p. 562), and seems to have been at least temporarily conquered by him (mid-6th century BC): some Arabian inscriptions found near Taima', which mention Dedan, may refer to his wars (*POTT*, p. 293). The site of the city of Dedan is that now known as al--'Ula, some 110 km SW of Taima'. A number of Dedanite inscriptions are known, and give the names of one king and several gods of the Dedanites (*POTT*, p. 294). Subsequently the kingdom seems to have fallen into Persian hands, and later still (3rd–2nd centuries BC?) came under Lihyanite rule. With the arrival of the Nabataeans Dedan gave place to the neighbouring city of Hegra (Medain Salih) as the main centre in the area.

BIBLIOGRAPHY. *POTT*, pp. 287–311, esp. 293–296, with bibliography, to which add W. F. Albright, *Geschichte und Altes Testament* (*Festschrift* A. Alt), 1953, pp. 1–12; H. von Wissmann, *RE* Supp. Bd. 12, cols. 947–969; I. Eph'al, *The Ancient Arabs*, 1982. G.I.D.

DEDICATION. The term is used in the OT almost exclusively of the consecration of things, *e.g.* the altar (Nu. 7:10), silver and gold (2 Sa. 8:11). Three Heb. words are used: *ḥ*[a]*nukkâ*, 'consecration'; *qōḏeš*, 'a thing separated, hallowed'; *ḥērem*, 'a thing devoted to God'. (*CURSE, *BAN.) D.G.S.

DEDICATION, FEAST OF (Gk. *ho enkainismos tou thysiastēriou*, 1 Macc. 4:47–59; *ta enkainia*, Jn. 10:22, rendering Heb. *ḥ*[a]*nukkâ*, from *ḥānaḵ*, 'dedicate'). Held on 25 Kislew, and lasting 8 days, it originally celebrated the winter solstice, but later commemorated the cleansing of the Temple and altar by Judas Maccabaeus in 164 BC, 3 years to the day after their defilement by Antiochus Epiphanes. Its resemblance in mode of celebration to the Feast of Tabernacles (2 Macc. 10:6) was deliberate, though, unlike the great feasts, it might be celebrated outside Jerusalem. The prominent feature of illuminations gave it the name Feast of Lights (Jn. 9:5; Jos., *Ant.* 12. 325). The sole NT reference (Jn. 10:22) indicates the season of the year.

BIBLIOGRAPHY. O. S. Rankin, *The Origins of the Festival of Hanukkah*, 1930. T.H.J.

DEHAVITES, DEHAITES. A name occurring in an Aramaic list (Ezr. 4:9, AV) prepared for Artaxerxes, which enumerates the various peoples who had been settled in Samaria by *Ashurbanipal. The name (*K*[e]*ṯîḇ*: *dehāwē*; *Q*[e]*rē*: *dehāyē*) falls in the list between the 'Susanchites' and the Elamites, and from the facts that *Susa was in Elam, and that no satisfactory identification for *dehāwē* has been found in extra-biblical sources, it has been plausibly suggested that it be read *dĕhû* (for *dî-hû'*), 'that is' (with Codex Vaticanus *hoi eisin*), which would result in the rendering, 'the Susians, that is the Elamites' (so RSV).

BIBLIOGRAPHY. G. Hoffmann, *ZA* 2, 1887, p. 54; F. Rosenthal, *A Grammar of Biblical Aramaic*, 1961, §35. T.C.M.

DEMAS. A co-worker with Paul in the first imprisonment, sending greetings in Phm. 24 and Col. 4:14. In the latter he alone is mentioned without commendation. There follows the pathetic notice of his desertion in the second imprisonment (2 Tim. 4:10; Parry neatly renders 'left me in the lurch'). Paul's words, 'in love with (*agapēsas*) this present world', suggest that personal interest, not cowardice, took Demas to Thessalonica: perhaps he was a Thessalonian. The name is not uncommon; it may be a pet-form of Demetrius. John Chapman (*JTS* 5, 1904, pp. 364ff.) argued that Demas, restored, is the Demetrius of 3 Jn. 12; but this is as conjectural as is the ugly portrait of Demas in the *Acts of Paul and Thecla*. A.F.W.

DEMETRIUS was a common Gk. name, and two people bearing it are mentioned in the NT.

1. A Christian whose witness is commended in 3 Jn. 12.

2. The silversmith of Ephesus, who stirred up a riot against Paul (Acts 19:24, 38).

Conjectures have been made identifying the two (J. V. Bartlet, *JTS* 6, 1905, pp. 208f., 215), while J. Chapman (*JTS* 5, 1904, pp. 364ff.) would identify **1** above with Demas, the companion of Paul (Col. 4:14; Phm. 24; 2 Tim. 4:10).

The name also occurs in the Apocrypha, where it refers to three kings of the Seleucid dynasty. Demetrius I Soter was king of Syria 162–150 BC. Son of Seleucus IV, he obtained the throne on the death of his uncle *Antiochus Epiphanes IV by killing Antiochus' son, Eupator, and his general Lysias. He continued his predecessor's persecution of the Maccabees, and was killed by Alexander Balas (1 Macc. 10:50). His son, Demetrius II Nicator, avenged his father's death by overcoming Balas in 145 BC and, after a reign characterized by intrigue and duplicity, he was taken captive in 138 BC by Mithradates I of Persia. Demetrius III Eucaerus, the son of Antiochus Grypos, appears briefly on the stage of history in 88 BC to aid in the defeat of Jannaeus, but quickly fell from favour. See R. H. Pfeiffer, *History of New Testament Times*, 1949. D.H.W.

DEMON.

I. In the Old Testament

In the OT there are references to demons under the names *śā'îr* (RSV 'satyrs', Lv. 17:7; 2 Ch. 11:15) and *šēḏ* (Dt. 32:17; Ps. 106:37). The former term means 'hairy one', and points to the demon as a satyr. The latter is of uncertain meaning, though it is evidently connected with a similar Assyr. word. In such passages there is the thought that the deities who were served from time to time by Israel are no true gods, but are really demons (*cf.* 1 Cor. 10:19f.). But the subject is not one of great interest in the OT, and the relevant passages are few.

II. In the Gospels

It is otherwise when we turn to the Gospels. There are many references there to demons. The usual designation is *daimonion*, a diminutive of *daimōn*, which is found in Mt. 8:31, but apparently with no difference of meaning (the parallel accounts use *daimonion*). In the classics *daimōn* is frequently used in a good sense, of a god or of the divine power. But in the NT *daimōn* and *daimonion* always refer to spiritual beings hostile to God and men. Beelzebul (*BAAL-ZEBUB) is their 'prince' (Mk. 3:22), so that they may be regarded as his agents. This is the sting behind the accusation that Jesus had 'a demon' (Jn. 7:20; 10:20). Those who opposed his ministry tried to link him with the very forces of evil, instead of recognizing his divine origin.

In the Gospels there are many references to people possessed by demons. A variety of effects results, such as dumbness (Lk. 11:14), epilepsy (Mk. 9:17f.), a refusal to wear clothing and a living among the tombs (Lk. 8:27). It is often said in modern times that demon-possession was simply the way people had in the 1st century of referring to conditions that we today would call sickness or madness. The Gospel accounts, however, distinguish between sickness and possession by demons. For example, in Mt. 4:24 we read of 'the sick, those afflicted with various diseases and pains, demoniacs, epileptics (*selēniazomenous*, which may mean 'lunatics' as AV), and paralytics'. None of these classes appears to be identical with the others.

Neither in the OT nor in the Acts and Epistles do we find many references to demon-possession. (The incident of Acts 19:13ff. is exceptional.) Apparently it was a phenomenon especially associated with the earthly ministry of our Lord. It should surely be interpreted as an outburst of demoniacal opposition to the work of Jesus.

The Gospels picture Jesus as in continual conflict with *evil spirits. To cast out such beings from men was not easy. His opponents recognized both that he did this, and also that it required a power greater than human. Therefore they attributed his success to the indwelling of *Satan (Lk. 11:15), exposing themselves to the counter that this would spell ruin in the kingdom of the evil one (Lk. 11:17f.). Jesus' power was that of 'the Spirit of God' (Mt. 12:28) or, as Luke expresses it, 'if it is by the finger of God that I cast out demons . . .' (Lk. 11:20).

The victory that Jesus won over demons he shared with his followers. When he sent out the Twelve he 'gave them power and authority over all demons and to cure diseases' (Lk. 9:1). Again, the seventy could report when they returned from their mission, 'Lord, even the demons are subject to us in your name' (Lk. 10:17). Others than Jesus' immediate disciples might use his name to cast out demons, a fact which caused perturbation to some of the inner circle, but not to the Master (Mk. 9:38f.).

III. Other New Testament references

After the Gospels there are few references to demons. In 1 Cor. 10:20f. Paul is concerned with idol worship, and regards idols as in reality demons, a use we see again in Rev. 9:20. There is an interesting passage in Jas. 2:19, 'the demons believe—and shudder'. It reminds us of Gospel passages in which the demons recognized Jesus for what he was (Mk. 1:24; 3:11, *etc.*).

There seems no reason *a priori* why we should reject the whole concept of *demon-possession. When the Gospels give us good evidence that it did take place it is best to accept this.

BIBLIOGRAPHY. J. M. Ross, *ExpT* 66, 1954–5, pp. 58–61; E. Langton, *Essentials of Demonology*, 1949; G. H. Twelftree, *Jesus the Exorcist*, 1993.
L.M.

DEMON-POSSESSION. Apparent possession by spirits is a world-wide phenomenon. It may be sought deliberately, as by the shaman and witch-doctor among primitive peoples, and by the medium among both primitive and civilized men and women. It may come upon individuals suddenly, as with watchers at the Voodoo rites, or in the form of what is generally known as demon-possession. In each case the possessed person behaves in a way that is not normal for him or her, speaks in a voice totally different from normal, and often shows powers of telepathy and clairvoyance.

In the Bible the pagan prophets probably sought possession. The prophets of Baal in 1 Ki. 18 would come in this category. Mediums, who were banned in Israel, must have deliberately cultivated possession, since the law regards them as guilty people, not as sick (*e.g.* Lv. 20:6, 27). In the OT *Saul is an outstanding example of unsought possession. The Spirit of the Lord leaves him, and 'an evil spirit from the Lord tormented him' (1 Sa. 16:14; 19:9). We may fairly interpret this by saying that, if a person has been powerfully open to the Holy Spirit in a charismatic way, disobedience is liable to be followed by the entry into his life of an evil spirit allowed by God. On the other hand, we may simply say that 'evil' has no moral connotation here, but signifies depression. The spirit is driven away by David's playing: since playing was normally accompanied by singing, it was probably David's psalm-singing that drove away the spirit, as Robert Browning implies in his poem *Saul.*

The NT records many cases of possession. It is as though Satan had concentrated his forces in a special way to challenge Christ and his followers. The Gospel records show that Christ distinguished between ordinary illness and those that accompanied demon-possession. The former were healed by laying on of hands or anointing, the latter by commanding the demon to depart (*e.g.* Mt. 10:8; Mk. 6:13; Lk. 13:32; also Acts 8:7; 19:12). Possession was apparently not always continuous, but when it came it produced effects that were often violent (Mk. 9:18). Blindness and dumbness, when caused by possession, would presumably have been persistent (*e.g.* Mt. 9:32–33; 12:22).

Most psychologists dismiss the idea of demon-possession. A good representative writer is T. K. Oesterreich, whose German work is published in English as *Possession, Demoniacal and Other, among Primitive Races, in Antiquity, the Middle Ages, and Modern Times*, 1930. He maintains that the equivalents of possession today are 'a particularly extensive complex of compulsive phenomena'. So also W. Sargant in *Battle for the Mind* (1957) and *The Mind Possessed* (1973). On the other hand, there is the classic by J. L. Nevius, a missionary doctor in China, *Demon Possession and Allied Themes*, 1892. This book takes demon-possession as a genuine phenomenon, and most missionaries would probably agree.

It is possible to take an intermediate position, and to hold that a demon can seize on a repressed facet of the personality, and from this centre influence a person's actions. The demon may produce hysterical blindness or dumbness, or symptoms of other illnesses, such as epilepsy. Among many peoples an epileptic fit has been regarded as a sign of possession by a spirit or a god, and indeed epileptics are often psychically sensitive. The Bible does not link epilepsy with demon-possession, and even the description of the fits of the possessed boy in Mt. 17:14f.; Mk. 9:14f.; Lk. 9:37f., seem to indicate something more than mere epilepsy. The nature of epilepsy is still unknown, but it can be artificially induced in apparently normal people (W. G. Walter, *The Living Brain*, 1953, pp. 60f.). Students of personality disorders know that it is often impossible to say just how these are triggered off. We are not saying that all, or even the majority, are due to demon-possession, but some may be.

The Bible does not say what conditions predispose to demon-possession, though Christ's words in Mt. 12:44–45 indicate that an 'empty house' can be reoccupied. The early church cast out demons in the name of Jesus Christ (Acts 16:18), but it would seem that there were also non-Christian exorcists who met with some success (Lk. 11:19; though note Acts 19:13–16).

The command to 'try the spirits' in 1 Jn. 4:1–3 shows that there were false prophets in the church who spoke under possession. Since the spiritualists make much of this verse, it should be noted that the Bible never speaks of possession by any good departed spirit or by an angel. The alternatives are either the Holy Spirit or an evil spirit. See also 1 Cor. 12:1–3.

BIBLIOGRAPHY. M. F. Unger, *Demons in the World Today*, 1971; V. White, *God and the Unconscious*, 1952, chapter 10; J. S. Wright, *Mind, Man, and the Spirits* (formerly *What is Man?*), 1972, pp. 108ff.; J. Richards, *But deliver us from evil*, 1974; G. H. Twelftree, *Jesus the Exorcist*, 1993.

J.S.W.

DEPUTY. In the OT, two words are used: Heb. *niṣṣāḇ*, 'one set up', used in 1 Ki. 22:47 of the viceroy or regent who administered Edom when it was tributary to Judah in Jehoshaphat's reign; and Heb. *peḥâ*, in Est. 8:9; 9:3 (AV; RSV *'governor').

In the NT, AV rendering of Gk. *anthypatos* (Acts 13:7–8, 12; 19:38) and *anthypateuō* ('was the *deputy'*, Acts 18:12), RSV *'proconsul'. F.F.B.

DERBE (Lycaonian *delbeia*, 'juniper'). In Acts 14:6ff. a city of Lycaonia, the most easterly place visited by Paul and Barnabas when they founded the churches of S Galatia. Paul and Silas visited it on their westward journey through Asia Minor (Acts 16:1). Paul's fellow-traveller Gaius came from Derbe (Acts 20:4; the Western Text brings him from Doberus in Macedonia). The site of Derbe was identified in 1956 by M. Ballance at Kerti Hüyük, 21 km NNE of Karaman (Laranda), some 100 km from Lystra (whence Acts 14:20b must evidently be translated: 'and on the morrow he set out with Barnabas for Derbe'). In 1964 M. Ballance attempted to identify the site even more precisely at Devri Şehri, 4 km SSE of Kerti Hüyük. It may have lain beyond the E frontier of Roman Galatia, in the client kingdom of Commagene.

BIBLIOGRAPHY. M. Ballance, 'The Site of Derbe: A New Inscription', *AS* 7, 1957, pp. 147ff.; and 'Derbe and Faustinopolis', *AS* 14, 1964, pp. 139ff.; B. Van Elderen, 'Some Archaeological Observations on Paul's First Missionary Journey', in W. W. Gasque and R. P. Martin (eds.), *Apostolic History and the Gospel*, 1970, pp. 156ff. F.F.B.

DESCENT INTO HADES. Although the doctrine of the descent of Christ into hell is firmly embedded in the early Christian creeds (it first appears in 4th-century Arian formularies), its place in Scripture is in fact circumferential. It receives explicit mention possibly twice (1 Pet. 3:19; 4:6), and is indirectly referred to in only two other places (Acts 2:27 and Rom. 10:7), where it is hinted at by the reinterpretation of OT passages—Ps. 16 in the case of Acts, and Dt. 30. It is doubtful whether we are right to press for a reference to the *descensus ad inferos* in Eph. 4:9f., since the comprehensive movement in these verses is best understood as forming a parallel to that in the 'kenotic' passage Phil. 2:5–11.

The references in the two Petrine passages are more direct, but by no means clear. The context of the first (1 Pet. 3:19) is the congruent suffering of Christ (the climax of which was his death) and of the Christian. It was after his passion and 'in the spirit' (*pneumati*) that the Lord 'preached' (the technical term *ekēryxen*) to the *'spirits in prison'. As victor, and no longer victim, Christ proclaimed his triumph (*kēryssein* is to be distinguished from *euangelizein*, 4:6) inclusively.

In 1 Pet. 4:6 the thought of preaching the good news to the 'dead' arises from a consideration of the painfulness as well as the glory of being dead to sin. This, says Peter, may well involve suffering for Christ's sake, as Christ suffered for ours (4:1f.). It was this gospel that judged the 'dead', and gave them the opportunity of sharing God's eternal life (v. 6). This may well refer to Christians who have heard the gospel while alive, and died before the Lord's return (so Selwyn, Stibbs and Dalton). Others interpret 'the dead' as meaning those who are spiritually dead; and a third view connects this verse with 3:19, and sees in it a further reference to the 'spirits in prison'. In this case the thought of judgment (= death, here) is subordinate to that of life (the fullness of God's life, denoted by *zōsi*, as opposed to the transitoriness of man's life, implied in 4:2 by the verb *bioō*, similarly translated).

The interval between the death and the resurrection of Jesus cannot be regarded as without significance. But the event claimed by Christians as taking place then, whether or not Peter has it in mind in these two passages, is more a matter of theology than chronology. Then the *meaning* becomes more important than the manner, and we can understand the *descensus* as a part of the triumphant activity of Christ, who is Lord of hell as well as of heaven (*cf.* Rev. 1:18 and Phil. 2:10), and who thus completes his involvement in every conceivable area of experience.

BIBLIOGRAPHY. See the commentaries on 1 Pet., esp. those by E. G. Selwyn, 1946; A. M. Stibbs, 1959; J. N. D. Kelly, 1969; E. Best, 1971. See also C. E. B. Cranfield, *ExpT* 69, 1957–8, pp. 369–372; W. J. Dalton, *Christ's Proclamation to the Spirits*, 1965. S.S.S.

DESIRE. In their numerous references to 'desire' the OT and NT provide many acute and incisive psychological insights. Indeed both by the diversity of the vocabulary of 'desire', and the manner of handling it, the Bible makes plain an important part of its doctrine of man.

In the OT 'desire' means much more than merely 'to long for', 'to ask for' or 'to demand'. In Heb. psychology the whole personality was involved in desire. Hence 'desire' could easily become 'covetousness', leading to 'envy' and 'jealousy', *etc.* Among the Hebrews 'desire' was the request which the *nep̄eš* (the 'soul' or 'self') made of the personality (Dt. 14:26, RV). 'Desire' was the inclination of the *nep̄eš* (2 Sa. 3:21). And when the whole 'soul' lay behind an inclination or desire that was sinful then the soul, it was said, 'lusted a lust' (see Nu. 11:4, 6). It was against this kind of covetousness that the tenth commandment was directed (Ex. 20:17), because when such sinful desire was given free rein the well-being of the whole community was endangered (Je. 6:13–15).

In the NT sinful desire is stimulated by the will to get rich (1 Tim. 6:9); so much so that it is equated with 'the love of money' (v. 10). But it may also manifest itself in illicit sexual desire (Mt. 5:28), or in what Paul describes as 'the desires of the flesh and of the thoughts' (Eph. 2:3, RVmg.). The NT testifies also to what is an observable fact in human experience: that if these sinful desires are gratified instead of crucified they become a consuming fire (Col. 3:5f.). On the other hand, where God is the object of the soul's desire (Rom. 10:2a), and his best gifts (1 Cor. 12:31), the body becomes the instrument of righteousness (Rom. 6:12f.).

J.G.S.S.T.

DESOLATING SACRILEGE ('abomination of desolation', AV). The phrase (Heb. *šiqqûṣ šômēm*) occurs first in Dn. 12:11, with variants in Dn. 9:27; 11:31. *šiqqûṣ* = an offensive object, due to uncleanness, then an idol as offensive to God; *šiqqûṣ šomēm* probably represents a contemptuous equivalent for *Baal šamēm*, 'lord of heaven': the 'lord' is a mere 'idol', and he is not 'of heaven' (*šamēm*) but he 'desolates' (*šomēm*). The name appears to have in view the action of Antiochus Epiphanes, who placed on the altar in the Jerusalem Temple a small idolatrous altar, described in 1 Macc. 1:54ff. as the 'desolating sacrilege' (Gk. *bdelygma erēmōseōs*). With it, according to Jewish tradition, went an image—almost certainly of Zeus, the lord of heaven, bearing the emperor's likeness. The sacrilege creates 'desolation': *i.e.* both desolating horror and destruction (for the combination of the two concepts see Je. 4:1–8; 7:30–34; 44:22; Ezk. 5:11–15; Dan. 9:27–29). In Mk. 13:14; Mt. 24:15 a related sacrilege may be in view—a sign of the impending destruction of the Temple. The sacrilege has been interpreted as the appearance of the Antichrist (*cf.* 2 Thes. 2:3f., and note that in Mark 'standing' is masculine in gender), or of the Roman army under a sacrilegious leader. Luke's version is best viewed as a translation for Gentile readers, to whom the Danielic phrase would be largely incomprehensible). The precise interpretation of Mk. 13:14 is uncertain. D. Ford pointed out, 'Daniel's presentation of the *shiqqutz shomem* is a welding of elements already existing in the historical and prophetic books . . . What Daniel did with motifs from his prececessors Christ did with Daniel' (*Abomination of Desolation*, 309).

BIBLIOGRAPHY. G. Kittel, *TDNT* 2, p. 660; G. R. Beasley-Murray, *A Commentary on Mark 13*, 1957, pp. 54–72; *idem. Jesus and the Last Days*, 1993, pp. 408–416; W. G. Kummel, *Prophecy and Fulfilment*, 1957, pp. 95–103; C. H. Dodd, *More New Testament Studies*, 1968; D. Ford, *The Abomination of Desolation in Biblical Eschatology*, 1979; R. T. France, *Jesus and the Old Testament*, 1971. G.R.B.-M.

DEUTERONOMY, BOOK OF. The name Deuteronomy derives from the LXX rendering of a phrase in 17:18. The king was to prepare 'a copy of this law'. The phrase is rendered in Greek as *to deuteronomion touto*, *lit.* this second law. Subsequently the Vulgate rendered the Greek as *deuteronomium.* The contents of the book were regarded as a second law, the first having been given on Mt Horeb (Sinai) and the second (repetition) on the plains of Moab.

Early 2nd millennium BC law-codes (1st column) normally begin with title and prologue glorifying the king who had proclaimed the laws that follow, then there are blessings and curses for those who keep or break the laws. Column two shows the more complex, but very consistent pattern of late 2nd millennium treaties: the title identifies the chief partner; then comes a historical prologue to show how past benefits from the chief partner should inspire the vassal to grateful obedience to the stipulations that follow. There are provisions for the text to be preserved in the vassal's chief temple, for regular reading to his people as reminder of its terms. The gods of both parties are witnesses and guarantors of the pact, enacting the curses and blessings on those who disobey or obey its terms. A treaty or covenant was ratified by an oath and solemn ceremony, and mention of sanctions against one who breaks it.

After *c.* 1200 BC, this elaborate arrangement disappears. During the 1st millennium, treaties had only four elements, the title plus the terms, curses for infringement and gods of witness in no fixed order. Strikingly, the biblical covenants in Sinai, Moab and Shechem (Ex.; Dt.; Jos. 24) agree in content and form with the late 2nd millennium treaties, and not those of the 1st millennium. This suggests a date of origin *c.* 1400–1200 BC, the probable period of Moses and Joshua, the leaders traditionally associated with those covenants.

2nd Millennium BC

Laws	Treaties	OT Covenant (Deuteronomy)	
Title	Title	Title	Identifies the chief partner
Prologue	Historical Prologue	Historical Prologue	To show how past benefits from the chief partner should inspire the vassal to grateful obedience to the stipulations that follow
	Stipulations/Laws	Stipulations/Laws	
Blessings and curses	Deposition	Deposition	There are provisions for the text to be preserved in the vassal's chief temple.
	Reading	Reading	
	Witnesses	Witnesses	The gods of both parties are witnesses and guarantors of the pact.
		Blessings and curses	Curses and blessings on those who disobey or obey its terms.
	Blessings and curses		
	Oath Ceremony Sanctions	Oath Ceremony Sanctions	A treaty or covenant was ratified by an oath and solemn ceremony and mention of sanctions against one who breaks it.

A diagram showing the changes in form and contents of laws, treaties and covenants in OT times.

I. Outline of contents

The book falls naturally into three sections.

a. 1:1–4:43. First address of Moses. A historical retrospect describing God's mighty acts between Horeb and Beth-peor (1:6–3:29) is followed by an appeal to Israel to hearken and obey as God's chosen people.

b. 4:44–28:68. Moses' second address. The section is lengthy. The nature of the covenant faith with its fundamental demand for total allegiance to Yahweh is presented to Israel (5:1–11:32). Lessons are drawn from the past (8:1–10:11) and Israel is called to commitment (10:12–11:32). In 12:1–26:19 the law of God with its detailed covenant stipulations is presented. The section deals with aspects of worship (12:1–16:17), the character of Israel's leaders (16:18–18:22), criminal law (19:1–21), the Holy War (20:1–20), a range of miscellaneous laws (21:1–25:19) and two rituals (26:1–19). The need to undertake a covenant renewal in the land, and to respond to the covenant challenge is given in 27:1–26. Finally, the *covenant sanctions, that is, the curses and blessings of the covenant, are set out in 28:1–68.

c. 29:1–30:20. Moses' third address. A recapitulation of the covenant demand including, among other things, a historical review (29:1–9), an exhortation to commitment (29:10–15), a warning of punishment for disobedience (29:16–28) and a solemn appeal to choose life (30:11–20).

Finally, the last acts of Moses, his parting words and his call for a covenant-renewal ceremony every seventh year (31:1–13). Moses' charge to Joshua (31:14–23), his song of witness (31:30–32:47), final blessing and his death (32:48–34:12) bring the book to a close.

II. A covenant manifesto

Probably no book in the OT gives such profound and continuous expression to the covenant idea. Yahweh, the Lord of the Covenant, who performed unprecedented saving acts to redeem his people Israel, made a covenant with them (4:23, 31; 5:2–3; 9:9; 29:1, 12) which he would remember and keep (7:9, 12) and display 'covenant faithfulness' or 'steadfast loyalty' (*ḥeseḏ*, 5:10; 7:9, 12) towards them. For their part, loyalty to Yahweh and to his covenant would find expression in their obedience to the covenant stipulations, the 'law' (*tôrâ*). Reference is made to 'this book of the law' (28:61; 29:21; 30:10; 31:26) and 'this law' (1:5; 4:18; 17:18–19; 27:3, 8, 26). More precisely the law is defined as 'testimonies' (*'ēḏûṯ*), 'statutes' (*mišpāṭîm*) and 'ordinances' (*ḥuqqîm*). Sometimes only two of these terms appear, 'testimonies and statutes' (6:17), or 'statutes and judgments' (AV)/ 'statutes and ordinances' (RSV) (4:1; 12:1). All these constituted a body of teaching which provided Israel with guidance for living in fellowship with Yahweh and with one another. Such a life would enable Israel to enjoy to the full all the blessings of the covenant. To live any other life was tantamount to a rejection of Yahweh's gracious intention for his people.

III. The theology of Deuteronomy

Both the literary shape of Deuteronomy and its underlying central concept provide clues to the basic theology of the book. In summary the book expounds:

a. Yahweh, as the Lord of the covenant, Israel's sovereign Lord, King, Judge and Warrior who undertook mighty saving acts for Israel and demanded their obedience.

b. Yahweh, as the God of history, able to perform saving acts in Egypt, in the wilderness, in Canaan, the leader of Israel's armies, able to fulfil his purposes for Israel in the face of every enemy.

c. Israel, as the people of the covenant, obligated to love, to obey, to worship and to serve Yahweh exclusively. That way lay peace (*šālôm*) and life (*ḥayyîm*).

d. The worship of the God of the covenant, based on love and gratitude and finding expression both in personal devotion and in a carefully defined range of festivals and rituals.

IV. The structure of Deuteronomy

Even a cursory reading of the book suggests that a more complex plan lies behind the book. Several attempts have been made to define the structure. M. Noth, 1948, proposed that chs. 1–4 were the introduction to a great historical work stretching from Joshua to 2 Kings, while the rest of Deuteronomy was a great prologue to this history. G. von Rad, 1932, regarded the book as a cultic celebration, perhaps a feast of covenant-renewal, arranged in four segments, (1) Historical (1–11), (2) The Law (12:1–26:15), (3) The Sealing of the Covenant (26:16–19), (4) The Blessings and Curses (27f.).

When G. E. Mendenhall, 1955, drew attention to the many parallels between the Hittite treaties of the 2nd millennium and the *covenant of Yahweh with Israel, a new turn was given to the study of the structure of Deuteronomy. The Hittite treaties comprised (1) a preamble; (2) a historical prologue; (3) the treaty stipulations: (*a*) general, (*b*) specific; (4) the treaty sanctions, curses and blessings; (5) the witnesses, plus clauses requiring the treaty document to be deposited in the Temple and the periodic public reading of the treaty.

M. G. Kline, 1963, proposed that Deuteronomy was a unity, and held it to be an authentic Mosaic document cast in the form of the ancient Near Eastern treaty, as follows: (1) preamble (1:1–5); (2) historical prologue (1:6–4:45); (3) the covenant stipulations (5:1–26:19); (4) the covenant sanctions and oath (27:1–30:20); (5) dynastic disposition, covenant continuity (31:1–34:12).

D. J. McCarthy, 1963, accepted the view that the basic structure of Deuteronomy was that of an ancient Near Eastern treaty, but argued that chs. 1–3 should be set apart as a piece of historical writing, chs. 4, 29 and 30 should be seen as formal units in themselves comprising all the elements of the covenant scheme. He held that chs. 5–28 comprised the kernel framed between two speeches in covenant form.

G. J. Wenham, 1970, has argued that Deuteronomy constitutes a distinctive OT covenant form resembling both the Law Codes and the Near Eastern treaties, but assuming a shape somewhere between them as follows: (1) historical prologue (1:6–3:29); (2a) basic stipulations (4:1–40; 5:1–11:32); (2b) detailed stipulations (12:1–26:19); (3) document clause requiring the recording and renewal of the covenant (27:1–26); (4) blessings (28:1–14); (5) curses (28:15–68); (6) recapitulation (29:1–30:20), concluding with an appeal. The later chs. 31–34 do not belong to the covenant form but represent a covenant-renewal.

M. Weinfeld, 1972, allows that Deuteronomy follows a literary tradition of covenant writing rather than imitating a periodic cultic ceremony (von Rad). But while the book preserves the motifs of the old covenant tradition, he argues that these were re-worked and adapted to the covenant literary pattern by scribes/wise men of the Hezekiah–Josiah period under the strong influence of Assyrian treaty models.

It seems beyond question that the structure of Deuteronomy is related in some way to the political treaties of the ancient Near East, although it appears to be a particular adaptation of the model in a form that was distinctive for Israel.

V. The basic social and religious background of Deuteronomy

It is widely recognized today that a great deal of Deuteronomy is ancient, although the exact age of such parts is not easy to define. It is almost a refrain in the commentary of G. von Rad, 1966, that such and such a law is 'early' or 'earlier'. In his view Deuteronomy is firmly rooted in the sacred and cultic traditions of the old Israelite tribal system of the pre-monarchical period, even though its present form may represent a modification to suit a later stage in Israel's history.

A. C. Welch, 1924, considered that the cultic laws of chs. 12, 14, 16 and 27 all point to the primitive conditions of the age of settlement probably about the 10th century. E. Robertson, 1949, 1950, argued strenuously that Deuteronomy was drawn up under the guidance of Samuel as the standard law book, both civil and religious, for the emerging monarchy and therefore represents a period of about the 11th century.

Certainly the society portrayed in Deuteronomy is an early one. Israel's neighbours are Canaanites (7:1–5; 20:16f.), Amalekites (25:17–19), Ammonites and Edomites (23:3–6). There are laws about the discharge of the Holy War (20:1–20; 21:10–14; 23:10–14; 25:17–19). There is no Temple. The only reference to a king (17:14–20) is to the king that shall arise. Many of the laws have close parallels to the Laws of Hammurapi. Some reflect a background of Canaanite religion (14:21b); others reflect an agricultural society of a simple kind and deal with such items as standing crops (23:24–25), millstones (24:6), oxen treading corn (25:4), landmarks (19:14), *etc.* Although some of these features were applicable over a long period, there are good grounds for arguing that behind the present Deuteronomy lies an ancient and authentic period of national existence which pre-dated the Monarchy. It has been argued that there is a deliberate 'archaizing' on the part of the writer. But archaizing is based on a knowledge of the past and much in Deuteronomy would have been quite meaningful in a simple rural economy in pre-monarchical times in Israel.

VI. Deuteronomy and the central sanctuary

The central sanctuary plays an important part in Deuteronomy. There is a 'place which the Lord your God shall choose' (12:5, 11, 18; 18:6–8; 31:10–13, *etc.*). There is no indication that this place is specifically Jerusalem, although it became so eventually. The central sanctuary seems to have moved from place to place in earlier years. Thus the Ark rested at Gilgal (Jos. 4:19; 5:9; 9:6), Shechem (Jos. 8:33), Bethel (Jdg. 20:18, 26–28; 21:2), Shiloh (Jos. 18:1; Jdg. 18:31; 1 Sa. 1:7, 24; 4:3, *etc.*). It is extremely difficult to decide whether the relevant texts specify one particular place at a particular time, a permanent place for all time or even a variety of places at a particular time, each of which was approved. Certainly the books of Kings and excavations at Arad, Dan and Beersheba suggest that, in practice, several places existed. The reforming kings of later centuries like Asa, Hezekiah and Josiah sought to regularize the 'high places' where there were irregular practices, or even to centralize worship in Jerusalem.

What seems evident is that Deuteronomy presents the ideal, feasible and capable of operation in the days of Moses, impossible to maintain from the days of the Conquest onwards though not forgotten by reformers, but never realized till post-exilic times. There was a central sanctuary in Moses' day in the first half of the 13th century BC. The ideal place it was intended to occupy in Israel's national and religious life is set out in Deuteronomy.

VII. The date and authorship of Deuteronomy

Few questions have proved more difficult to answer than this. On the surface the NT seems to imply Mosaic authorship of the Pentateuch and hence of Deuteronomy (Mt. 19:8; Mk. 12:26; Lk. 24:27, 44; Jn. 7:19, 23; Acts 13:39; 15:5; 1 Cor. 9:9; 2 Cor. 3:15; Heb. 9:19; 10:28). The difficulty with all these references is that the exact meaning of the term *Moses* is not clear. It may refer simply to the Pentateuch scroll and not to authorship. Deuteronomy itself refers to Moses speaking (1:6, 9; 5:1; 27:1, 9; 29:2; 31:1, 30; 33:1, *etc.*) and to writing (31:9, 24).

But none of these statements permits the conclusion that Deuteronomy as we have it today came completely, or even in large measure, from Moses himself. One has to allow for editorial activity and adaptations of original Mosaic material to a later age. Even if it could be shown that much of the geography, the legal background and the society would suit a generally Mosaic age, this falls short of a complete Mosaic authorship. Four main views have been proposed about the authorship and date of the book:

a. A substantially Mosaic date and authorship with a certain amount of post-Mosaic material;

b. A date in the period Samuel–Solomon. Much of the material is held to go back to the time of Moses, but the book as we have it was compiled 300–400 years after Moses' death.

c. A date in the Hezekiah–Josiah period during the 7th century BC. It is not denied that there may well be a considerable stratum of Mosaic material and that Mosaic principles underlie much of the work. But the book represents a gathering together of ancient material preserved in religious and prophetic circles in a time of profound apostasy when the nation needed to be recalled to its ancient covenant obligations. These were set out in terms of addresses given by Moses at the time of Israel's entry into the land. The publication of this collection of material lent support to Josiah in his reform.

d. A post-exilic date and authorship. The book was not a programme of reform but the wishful thinking of unrealistic post-exilic dreamers.

Increasingly scholars are recognizing that although any investigation of the origin of Deuteronomy will lead ultimately to the figure of Moses himself, it is quite impossible to decide on the date at which Deuteronomy reached its final form. There are two aspects to the problem: (1) the age of the original data, and (2) the period at which those data were drawn together. There are grounds for thinking that much in Deuteronomy goes back to Moses' time and much to be said for the view that Moses himself provided Israel with the heart of Deuteronomy. However, it became necessary in new situations to represent the words of Moses and to show their relevance for a new day. There are several key points in Israel's history when this might have happened—in the days when the kingdom was newly established under Saul, or David, or Solomon; in the critical period following the break-up of the kingdom on Solomon's death; or again at a number of critical points in the centuries that followed. We have to allow both for the powerful influence of Moses and for editorial processes which brought the book to its present shape. While there seems little reason to deny that a substantial part of Deuteronomy was in existence some centuries before the 7th century BC, it is not possible to say how much of it comprises the *ipsissima verba* of Moses himself.

BIBLIOGRAPHY. P. Buis and J. Leclerq, *Le Deutéronome*, 1963; R. E. Clements, *God's Chosen People*, 1968; P. C. Craigie, *Deuteronomy*, 1977; S. R. Driver, *Deuteronomy*, *ICC*, 1902; G. H. Davies, 'Deuteronomy', in *Peake's Commentary on the Bible*, rev. 1962; M. G. Kline, *Treaty of the Great King*, 1963; G. T. Manley, *The Book of the Law*, 1957; D. J. McCarthy, *Treaty and Covenant*, 1963; G. E. Mendenhall, *Law and Covenant in Israel and the Ancient Near East*, 1955; E. W. Nicholson, *Deuteronomy and Tradition*, 1967; E. Robertson, *The Old Testament Problem*, 1950; G. von Rad, *Deuteronomy*, 1966; *idem*, *Studies in Deuteronomy*, 1953; G. A. Smith, *The Book of Deuteronomy*, 1918; J. A. Thompson, *Deuteronomy*, *TOTC*, 1974; *idem*, *The Ancient Near Eastern Treaties and the Old Testament*, 1964; M. Weinfeld, *Deuteronomy and the Deuteronomic School*, 1972; *idem*., *Deuteronomy 1–11*, *AB*, 1991; A. C. Welch, *The Code of Deuteronomy*, 1924; *idem*, *Deuteronomy and the Framework to the Code*, 1932; G. J. Wenham, *The Structure and Date of Deuteronomy* (unpublished Ph.D. thesis, London, 1970); *idem*, 'Deuteronomy and the Central Sanctuary', *TynB* 22, 1971, pp.103–118; G. E. Wright, 'Deuteronomy', in *IB*, 2; *idem*, *The Old Testament and Theology*, 1965.

J.A.T.

DEW. The Heb. *ṭal*, 'sprinkled moisture', is referred to indiscriminately for dew and night mist. As the effects upon plants of dew (*i.e.* condensation of water vapour on a cooled surface), and of mist (*i.e.* condensation in the air), are not yet understood, the difference is perhaps irrelevant. Moist air drawn in from the sea is largely responsible for dew-fall in W Palestine, especially in the districts near the coast and on the W slopes of the mountains, though it does not occur in summer in the Jordan valley S of Beisan and on the W uplands of Transjordan. According to Ashbel, the number of yearly dew-nights varies from 250 on the sandy soil of Gaza and the high slopes of Mt Carmel to 100–150 days in the Judaean Highlands, dropping rapidly E in the Jordan trough. The maximum dew occurs in the beneficial summer months when the plants need moisture most. Duvdevani has experimented with two types of condensation. 'Downward dew' is characteristic of summer in areas of loose soil, *i.e.* with good soil-cooling conditions. 'Upward dew' results from the condensation of water vapour from damp soil, and is therefore more frequent in the winter season. This may be the explanation of Gideon's signs (Jdg. 6:36–40). In his first experience so heavy was the night mist or dew, that he wrung out from the fleece a bowl full of water, while the hard-baked earth of the threshing-floor was dry. In the second experience the fleece was dry, while the earth, perhaps the disturbed soil in the edge of the threshing-floor, produced conditions for 'upward dew' from the soil, inadequate to moisten the fleece.

Scriptural references show that, though dew-fall is mysterious, its incidence is well known. 'Who has begotten the drops of dew?' says the Lord as he answers Job (38:28), and its origin is considered heavenly (Gn. 27:28; Dt. 33:28; Hg. 1:10; Zc. 8:12). It falls suddenly (2 Sa. 17:12), gently (Dt. 32:2), lies all night (Jb. 29:19), and exposure to it is discomforting (Ct. 5:2; Dn. 4:15, 23, 25, 33), but it quickly evaporates in the morning (Jb. 7:9; Ho. 6:4). Dew is to be expected in the hot summer weather of harvest (Is. 18:4; *cf.* Ho. 14:5; Mi. 5:7).

Dew is beneficial to summer crops. This has been proved conclusively by agronomical field-studies made since 1937. The ancients therefore were not exaggerating it as a source of blessing. Dew is sufficiently copious to permit dry-farming in the absence of rain (Ecclus. 18:16; 43:22). It allows geophytes to be cultivated in the Negeb and aids the vine harvest; hence the prayer, 'May God give you of the dew of heaven, and of the fatness of the earth, and plenty of grain and wine' (Gn. 27:28; *cf.* Dt. 33:28). The absence of dew was therefore a cause of severe plight (Hg. 1:10; *cf.* Jb. 29:19; Zc. 8:12), intensifying the drought in the absence of rain (1 Ki. 17:1; *cf.* 2 Sa. 1:21). Its preciousness is therefore taken up as an emblem of resurrection; 'thy dew is a dew of light, and on the land of the shades thou wilt let it fall' (Is. 26:19). From this prophecy was based the talmudic phrase 'the dew of resurrection'.

The passage in Ps. 133:3 appears to state that the dew of Hermon comes down on the mountain of Zion. This is incapable of a geographical interpretation. It may be a proverbial expression for plentiful dew, since Hermon receives a maximum amount. In consequence of the heavy dew on Hermon and Mt Carmel, the soft, friable limestone rapidly disintegrates and the soil is frequently replenished. Thus, these mountains have been symbolic of fertility.

BIBLIOGRAPHY. D. Ashbel, *Bioclimatic Atlas of Israel*, 1950, pp. 51–55; S. Duvdevani, 'Dew observations and their significances', *Proc. United Nations Scientific Conference in the Conservation and Utilization of Resources*, 1949, 4. J.M.H.

DIBLATH, DIBLAH. Occurring only in Ezk. 6:14, no place of this name has been identified, and it is probably an ancient scribal error for *Riblah as RSV text; LXX already read Diblah. J.D.D.

DIBON. 1. A town in Judah, occupied after the Exile (Ne. 11:25) but not identifiable today.

2. Dibon (Heb. *dîḇôn*) of Moab, marked by the modern village of Dhiban, to the E of the Dead Sea and 6 km N of the river Arnon. The city is mentioned by Rameses II, who claimed its capture (K. A. Kitchen, *JEA* 50, 1964, pp. 63–70). Originally it belonged to Moab, but it was captured by

Sihon, king of the Amorites, in pre-Israelite times (Nu. 21:26). The Israelites took it at the time of the Exodus (Nu. 21:30), and it was given to the tribes of Reuben and Gad (Nu. 32:2–3). Gad built Dibon, however (Nu. 32:34), and hence it is called Dibon-gad (Nu. 33:45), although in Jos. 13:15ff. it is reckoned to Reuben. It is probably one of the halting-places on the Exodus journey and is referred to in Nu. 33:45–46. Israel lost it later, it was regained by Omri and lost again to Mesha, king of Moab, who speaks of it on the *Moabite Stone, lines 21 and 28. Isaiah and Jeremiah knew it as a Moabite town (Is. 15:2; Je. 48:18, 22).

Archaeological excavations were carried out by the American Schools of Oriental Research in 1950–5 in the SE, NW and NE corners of the mound. There is some evidence for Early Bronze Age occupation, some levels at bedrock, a wall and pottery from Early Bronze III. The Moabite occupation proper dates from Iron I and is represented by several large buildings. In the SE corner the remains are from Iron II extending from the mid-9th century to the destruction by Nebuchadrezzar in 582 BC. Here lay a royal quarter, possibly built by Mesha. Later remains come from the Nabataean, Byzantine and Arab periods.

BIBLIOGRAPHY. N. Glueck, *Exploration in Eastern Palestine*, 3, *AASOR* 18–19, 1937–8, pp. 115, 224ff.; *AASOR* 40, 1972; F. V. Winnett & W. L. Reid, *AASOR* 36–37, 1961; J. C. L. Gibson, *Textbook of Syrian Semitic Inscriptions*, I, 1971, pp. 71–83; *NEAEHL*, pp. 350–352. J.A.T.

DINAH (Heb. *dînâ*, 'judgment' or 'judged'). Daughter of Jacob by Leah (Gn. 30:21; 46:15). While Jacob was encamped near Shechem, Dinah went out to visit the local womenfolk (Gn. 34); however, Shechem, son of Hamor, Hivite prince of Shechem, was attracted to her, apparently forced himself upon her, and then sought her in marriage from Jacob. But Jacob's sons were indignant; they stipulated circumcision of the Shechemites before any marriage could be agreed to. Then Simeon and Levi (obviously with their retainers) caught the Shechemites off guard and slaughtered them treacherously. This deed was disapproved of (Gn. 34:30) and denounced (Gn. 49:5–7) by Jacob. The recording of sad incidents of this kind involving womenfolk is noted as a mark of early (pre-Solomonic) date for such narratives by C. H. Gordon, *HUCA* 26, 1955, p. 80. K.A.K.

DIONYSIUS THE AREOPAGITE. A member of the aristocratic council of Athens (*AREOPAGUS); one of Paul's few Athenian converts (Acts 17:34). A 2nd-century tradition (Dionysius of Corinth in Eusebius, *EH* 3. 4; 4. 23), that he was the first bishop of Athens may rest only on this passage. A body of much later mystical writings was long accepted as his and exercised a very strong influence in the Middle Ages (see partial English tr. by C. E. Rolt; R. Roques, 'Dionysius Areopagitica' in *RAC* for recent study). Other speculations about Dionysius, possibly related to the pagan Dionysos cult, are traced by Rendel Harris, *Annotators of the Codex Bezae*, 1901, pp. 76ff. A.F.W.

DIOTREPHES. A refractory person of overweening ambition who would not recognize John the Elder, publicly attacked him, forbade the reception of his adherents, and, whether by formal excommunication or physical violence, excluded those who did receive them. Though the Elder's personal intervention would eventually be decisive, the effect of his letters could be annulled by the present influence of Diotrephes (3 Jn. 9–10). It is not clear whether this was in virtue of a regular office (*e.g.* as an early monarchical bishop—*cf.* T. Zahn, *INT*, 3, pp. 374ff.) or by dominance of personality among his peers (*cf.* J. V. Bartlet, *JTS* 6, 1905, pp. 204ff.). For other imaginative reconstructions, *cf.* J. Chapman, *JTS* 5, 1904, pp. 357ff., 517ff.; B. H. Streeter, *The Primitive Church*, 1929, pp. 83ff.; C. H. Dodd, *The Johannine Epistles*, 1945, pp. 161ff. A.F.W.

DISCIPLE. A disciple (from Lat. *discipulus*, 'pupil, learner', corresponding to Gk. *mathētēs*, from *manthanō*, 'to learn') is basically the pupil of a teacher. The corresponding Heb. term *limmûḏ* is somewhat rare in the OT (Is. 8:16; 50:4; 54:13; *cf.* Je. 13:23), but in the rabbinical writings the *talmîḏ* (*cf.* 1 Ch. 25:8) is a familiar figure as the pupil of a rabbi from whom he learned traditional lore. In the Gk. world philosophers were likewise surrounded by their pupils. Since pupils often adopted the distinctive teaching of their masters, the word came to signify the adherent of a particular outlook in religion or philosophy.

Jewish usage is seen in the NT references to the disciples of the Pharisees (Mk. 2:18). The Jews considered themselves to be ultimately disciples of Moses (Jn. 9:28), since his teaching formed the basis of rabbinic instruction. The followers of John the Baptist were known as his disciples (Mk. 2:18; Jn. 1:35). The term was probably applied to his close associates. They practised prayer and fasting in accordance with his instructions (Mk. 2:18; Lk. 11:1), and some of them cared for him in prison and saw to his burial (Mt. 11:2–7; Mk. 6:29).

Although Jesus (like John) was not an officially recognized teacher (Jn. 7:14f.), he was popularly known as a teacher or rabbi (Mk. 9:5; 11:21; Jn. 3:2), and his associates were known as disciples. The word can be used of all who responded to his message (Mt. 5:1; Lk. 6:17; 19:37), but it can also refer more narrowly to those who accompanied him on his travels (Mk. 6:45; Lk. 8:2f.; 10:1), and especially to the twelve apostles (Mk. 3:14). Discipleship was based on a call by Jesus (Mk. 1:16–20; 2:13f.; Lk. 9:59–62; even Lk. 9:57f. presupposes Jesus' invitation in general terms). It involved personal allegiance to him, expressed in following him and giving him an exclusive loyalty (Mk. 8:34–38; Lk. 14:26–33). In at least some cases it meant literal abandonment of home, business ties and possessions (Mk. 10:21, 28), but in every case readiness to put the claims of Jesus first, whatever the cost, was demanded. Such an attitude went well beyond the normal pupil–teacher relationship and gave the word 'disciple' a new sense. Faith in Jesus and allegiance to him are what determine the fate of men at the last judgment (Lk. 12:8f.).

Those who became disciples were taught by Jesus and appointed as his representatives to preach his message, cast out demons and heal the sick (Mk. 3:14f.); although these responsibilities were primarily delegated to the Twelve, they were not confined to them (Mk. 5:19; 9:38–41; Lk. 10:1–16).

According to Luke, the members of the early church were known as disciples (Acts 6:1f., and frequently thereafter). This makes it clear that the earthly disciples of Jesus formed the nucleus of the church and that the pattern of the relationship between Jesus and his earthly disciples was constitutive for the relationship between the risen Lord and the members of his church. The word, however, is not found outside the Gospels and Acts, and other NT writers used a variety of terms (believers, saints, brothers) to express more fully the characteristics of discipleship after Easter.

Bibliography. K. H. Rengstorf, *TDNT* 4, pp. 415–460; *NIDNTT* 1, pp. 480–494; M. Hengel, *The Charismatic Leader and His Followers*, 1981; M. J. Wilkins, *DJG*, pp. 176–182. I.H.M.

DISPERSION. The term 'Dispersion' (Gk. *diaspora*) can denote either Jews scattered in the non-Jewish world (as in Jn. 7:35; 1 Pet. 1:1) or the places in which they reside (as in Jas. 1:1; Judith 5:19).

I. Origins

It is difficult to know how early the voluntary dispersion of Israel began; there are hints of an early 'colony' in Damascus (1 Ki. 20:34), and Solomon's expansionist policies may well have led to earlier commercial outposts. But the conquering kings of Assyria and Babylonia introduced a new factor, the compulsory transplantation of sections of the population to other parts of their empire (2 Ki. 15:29; 17:6; 24:14ff.; 25:11ff.). Involved in this policy was the removal of the classes providing the natural leadership and the skilled craftsmen. Many of these transplanted groups, especially from the N kingdom, probably lost their national and religious identity, but the Judaean community in Babylon had a rich prophetic ministry, learnt to retain the worship of the God of Israel without Temple or sacrifice, and produced the purposeful men who returned to rebuild Jerusalem. Only a portion, however, returned under Cyrus; a sizeable and intensely self-conscious Jewish community remained in mediaeval times, with its own recension of the Talmud.

II. Extent

The Israelites abroad were not forgotten at home, and prophetic pictures of God's gracious intervention in the last times include the happy restoration of 'the dispersed of Israel' (*e.g.* Is. 11:12; Zp. 3:10; *cf.* also Ps. 147:2, where LXX significantly renders 'the *diasporai* of Israel'). The area of the prophets' visions is often much wider than the Assyrian and Babylonian empires. In other words, another dispersion—probably originally voluntary, but reinforced, as Je. 43:7; 44:1 show, by refugees—had already begun. Jews were settling in Egypt and beyond, and in less-known areas. Some rather lurid light is cast on what the communities in Egypt could be like by the Aramaic papyri found at Elephantine (*Papyri, *Seveneh) as distant as the First Cataract, from a Jewish trading-community with its own altar and idiosyncrasies.

With Alexander the Great's conquests a new era of the Dispersion begins: a steadily increasing stream of Jewish immigrants is noticed in the most diverse places. In the 1st century AD Philo numbered the Jews in Egypt at a million (*In Flaccum* 43). Strabo the geographer, somewhat earlier, notes the number and status of the Jews in Cyrene, adding: 'This people has already made its way into every city, and it is not easy to find any place in the habitable world which has not received this nation, and in which it has not made its power felt' (quoted by Jos., *Ant.* 14. 115, Loeb edition).

Of the general truth of Strabo's estimate there is abundant evidence. Syria had large Jewish 'colonies'. Juster (1914) listed 71 cities in Asia Minor which the Dispersion affected: the list could doubtless be augmented today. Roman writers such as Horace testify in no friendly fashion to the presence and habits of Jews in the capital. As early as 139 BC there was an expulsion of the Jews from Rome: the edict mentioned in Acts 18:2 had several precedents. But somehow the Jews always came back. For all their unpopularity—barely concealed in the speeches of the governors Pilate and Gallio, quite evident in the mob-cries of Philippi (Acts 16:20) and Ephesus (Acts 19:34)—the Jews established themselves as a kind of universal exception. Their social exclusiveness, their incomprehensible taboos and their uncompromising religion were all tolerated. They alone might be exempted from 'official' sacrifices, and (since they would not march on the sabbath) from military service. Under Seleucids, Ptolemies and Romans alike, the Dispersion, with much patent dislike to face, and occasionally outbreaks of savage violence, enjoyed, in the main, peace and prosperity.

The spread of the Dispersion was not confined to the Roman empire: it was prominent in the Persian sphere of influence too, as the account of the Pentecost crowd illustrates (Acts 2:9–11). Josephus has revealing stories of Jewish free-booters of Fra Diavolo stature in Parthia (*Ant.* 18. 310ff.), and of the conversion and circumcision of the king of the buffer state of Adiabene (*Ant.* 20. 17ff.).

III. Characteristics

The oddities of Elephantine are not typical of later Dispersion Judaism. The life of most of these communities lay in the law and the synagogue, though it may be noted that the refugee Zadokite high priest Onias set up a temple at Leontopolis in Egypt, in the 2nd century BC, on the basis of Is. 19:18ff., and said that most of the Egyptian Jews had temples 'contrary to what is proper' (*Ant.* 13. 66). But in the nature of things they could not live exactly as the Jews in Palestine. The westward Dispersion had to live in the Greek world, and it had to speak Greek. One major result of this was the translation of the sacred books into Greek, the Septuagint (*Texts and Versions). The legends about its origin at least bear witness to the missionary spirit of Hellenistic Judaism. Although it may be misleading to generalize from Alexandria, we can see there a prosperous and educated Jewish community seeking to make intellectual contact with an established Greek culture. The 'de-Messianized' but otherwise orthodox Judaism of the book of Wisdom and of Philo are characteristic products. There is evidence also of Jewish missionary apologetic directed to pagans of Greek education, and of codes of instruction for pagan converts. There is perhaps a slightly satirical commentary on Diaspora Judaism's understanding of its mission in Rom. 2:17–24.

Hellenistic Jewish culture was faithful to law and nation (*cf.* Phil. 3:5–6—the confession of a Jew of the Dispersion). The communities paid the half-shekel Temple tax, and maintained contact with each other and with Jerusalem (*cf.* Acts 28:21f.). The devout visited Jerusalem for the great feasts when possible (Acts 2:5ff.; 8:27) and often had closer ties with the mother-country. But so different had the cultural atmosphere become that the Dispersion communities had their own synagogues there (*cf.* Acts 6:9). It is possible that Stephen learnt some of his radicalism about the Temple from Diaspora Judaism in pre-conversion days.

Notwithstanding Jewish unpopularity, it is clear that Judaism strongly attracted many Gentiles. The simple but majestic worship of one God, the lofty ethics, the generally high standards of family life, brought many, including people of rank, to the synagogues. The necessity of circumcision probably held back many men from becoming full *proselytes, but numbers remained in attendance as 'God-fearers'. Thus we regularly find Gentiles in the synagogues during Paul's missionary journeys (*cf.* Acts 13:43ff.; 14:1; 17:4; 18:4ff.).

A less happy aspect of the attraction of Judaism was the widespread belief, to which many sources testify, that Jews possessed special magical powers and that their sacred words were particularly efficacious in incantations. Undoubtedly unscrupulous Jews traded on this reputation, and we meet one such in Acts 13:6ff. It is likely, too, that there was a fringe of Jewish syncretistic and sectarian teaching which dealt in the mystery and occult so fascinating to the Hellenistic world. Some pagan cults—such as the Sabazios cult in Phrygia—eagerly scattered Judaic ingredients into their exotically flavoured religious pot-pourri; but, however important these may be for the history of Christian heresy (*GNOSTICISM), there is little evidence that they were in themselves representative of and significant for Dispersion Judaism as a whole. As might be expected, archaeological study reveals considerable formal differences, and differing degrees of cultural exclusiveness, at various times and places; but nothing indicates that there was any major indecision in Diaspora Judaism as to the uniqueness of Israel's God, his revelation in the Torah, and his people.

IV. Relation to Christianity

The influence of the Dispersion in preparing the way for the gospel is beyond doubt. The synagogues stretched over the greater part of the known world were the stepping-stones of the early missionaries. Acts shows Paul, the self-confessed apostle to the Gentiles, regularly opening his evangelistic work by synagogue preaching. Almost as regularly a division follows, the majority of Israelites by birth refusing the proffered Messiah, the Gentiles (*i.e.* the proselytes and God-fearers) receiving him joyfully. Representative converts, such as Cornelius and the Ethiopian eunuch, had first been proselytes or God-fearers. Clearly the God-fearers—children of the Dispersion—are a vital factor in early church history. They came to faith with some previous knowledge of God and the Scriptures, and already watchful of idolatry and immorality.

The LXX also performed a missionary service beyond its effect on those Gentiles in contact with synagogues; and more than one Christian Father testifies that the reading of the LXX played a vital part in his conversion.

An apparent confusion in some pagan writers makes it difficult to tell whether Judaism or Christianity is alluded to. This may be due to the fact that so often a Christian community arose within the bosom of Diaspora Judaism: and to an ignorant or indifferent pagan, even if he believed the horror stories about Christian arson and cannibalism, the attitude of converts towards many traditional practices might seem to be Jewish. On the other hand, Jewish influence on many leading converts helps to explain why 'Judaizing' was such a peril in the apostolic church.

It is interesting that Peter and James, both Palestinian Jews, address Christians as 'the Dispersion' (Jas. 1:1; 1 Pet. 1:1). Like the members of the old dispersion, they are 'sojourners' where they live; they enjoy a solidarity unknown to the heathen; and they owe a transcendent loyalty to the Jerusalem which is above.

BIBLIOGRAPHY. J. Juster, *Les Juifs dans l'Empire Romain*, 1914; A. Causse, *Les Dispersés d'Israel*, 1929; E. Schürer, *History of the Jewish People*, 2, 1978; *BC*, 1, pp. 137ff.; E. R. Goodenough, *Jewish Symbols in the Greco-Roman period*, 1953–68 (relation to pagan symbolism); R. McL. Wilson, *The Gnostic Problem*, 1958; V. Tcherikover, *Hellenistic Civilization and the Jews*, 1959; H. J. Leon, *The Jews of Ancient Rome*, 1960; M. Grant, *The Jews in the Roman World*, 1973; E. M. Smallwood, *The Jews under Roman Rule*, 1977. A.F.W.

DIVINATION. The usual Heb. word translated 'divination' and 'diviner' is the root *qsm*. The root *nḥš* is used in Gn. 44:5, 15, and elsewhere this is translated 'enchanter', 'enchantment', 'use enchantments'. The root *'nn* is sometimes coupled with the former words, and is translated 'observe times' (RV 'practise augury'), and twice 'soothsayings'.

Divination is roughly the attempt to discern events that are distant in time or space, and that consequently cannot be perceived by normal means. A similar definition could be given for the seership aspect of prophecy, as exercised in, *e.g.*, 1 Sa. 9:6–10. Hence the term could be used occasionally in a good sense, as we might speak of a prophet having clairvoyant gifts without thereby approving all forms of clairvoyance. Thus Balaam is a diviner as well as being inspired of God (Nu. 22:7; 24:1). The divination condemned in Ezk. 13:6–7 is specified as 'lying'. In Mi. 3:6–7, 11, divining is a function of the prophets, though here also they have prostituted their gift; *cf.* Zc. 10:2. In Pr. 16:10 *qesem* ('inspired decisions') is used of the divine guidance given through the king.

Apart from these general uses, divination is condemned, except for two passages noted below. God's people are forbidden to use divination and enchantments as the pagan world did (Lv. 19:26; Dt. 18:9–14), and 2 Ki. 17:17; 21:6 record their disobedience. Pagan diviners are mentioned in 1 Sa. 6:2, Is. 44:25, Ezk. 21:22.

Divination may take many forms. One can make two broad divisions, namely, internal and mechanical: the former is either the trance inspiration of the shaman type, or direct second sight; the latter makes use of technical means, such as sand, entrails of a sacrifice, or in modern times tea-leaves. These divisions cannot be pressed, since the objects may release the clairvoyant faculty, as with crystal-gazing. Balaam may have released his powers in this way (Nu. 24:1).

The following forms are mentioned in the Bible.

a. Rhabdomancy. Ezk. 21:21. Sticks or arrows were thrown into the air, and omens were deduced from their position when they fell. Ho. 4:12 could also be a reference to this.

b. Hepatoscopy. Ezk. 21:21. Examination of the liver or other entrails of a sacrifice was supposed to give guidance. Probably shapes and markings were classified, and the priest interpreted them.

c. *Teraphim. Associated with divination in 1 Sa. 15:23 ('idolatry', RSV); Ezk. 21:21; Zc. 10:2. If the teraphim were images of dead ancestors, the divination was probably a form of spiritualism.

d. Necromancy, or the consultation of the departed. This is associated with divination in Dt. 18:11; 1 Sa. 28:8; 2 Ki. 21:6, and is condemned in the Law (Lv. 19:31; 20:6), the Prophets (Is. 8:19–20) and the historical books (1 Ch. 10:13). The medium was spoken of as having an *'ôḇ*, translated 'a familiar spirit', or in modern terms 'a control'. An associated term, translated 'wizard', is *yid'ônî*, probably from the root *yāḏa'*, 'know', and presumably refers to the supernatural knowledge claimed by the spirit and in a secondary sense by its owner.

e. Astrology draws conclusions from the position of the sun, moon and planets in relation to the zodiac and to one another. While not condemned, astrology is belittled in Is. 47:13 and Je. 10:2. The wise men (*MAGI) who came to the infant Jesus (Mt. 2:9) were probably trained in Bab. tradition which mixed astronomy with astrology.

f. Hydromancy, or divination through water. Here forms and pictures appear in the water in a bowl, as also in crystal-gazing. The gleam of the water induces a state of light trance, and the visions are subjective. The only reference to this in the Bible is Gn. 44:5, 15, where it might appear that Joseph used his silver cup for this purpose. But one cannot say how much credence to give to a statement that comes in a section where Joseph and his steward are deliberately deceiving his brothers.

g. Lots. In the OT the lot was cast to discover God's will for the allocation of territory (Jos. 18–19, *etc.*), the choice of the goat to be sacrificed on the Day of Atonement (Lv. 16), the detection of a guilty person (Jos. 7:14; Jon. 1:7), the allocation of Temple duties (1 Ch. 24:5), the discovery of a lucky day by Haman (Est. 3:7). In the NT Christ's clothes were allocated by lot (Mt. 27:35). The last occasion in the Bible on which the lot is used to divine the will of God is in the choice of Matthias (Acts 1:15–26), and there may be a significance in that this is before Pentecost. (See also *URIM AND THUMMIM.)

h. **Dreams* are often counted as a means of divination, but in the Bible there is no instance of a person's deliberately asking for guidance or supernatural knowledge through dreams, except perhaps the false prophets in Je. 23:25–27. The spontaneous dream, however, is often a means of divine guidance.

In Acts 16:16 a girl has a spirit of divination. The Gk. here is *pythōn*. The famous Delphic oracle was in the district of Pytho, and the term evidently was used loosely for anyone supernaturally inspired, as was the priestess at Delphi. (*MAGIC AND SORCERY.)

BIBLIOGRAPHY. C. Brown, J. S. Wright, *NIDNTT* 2, pp. 552–562. J.S.W.

DIZAHAB. One of the places named in Dt. 1:1 to define the site of the speeches which follow. It has often been identified with Ḍahab on the E coast of the Sinai peninsula (*e.g.* Rothenberg and Aharoni), but this is not easily reconciled with the other data given (*cf.* v. 5). A location in N Moab is required, and eḏ-Ḍheibe (30 km E of Ḥesbân/Heshbon) seems the most probable suggestion so far.

BIBLIOGRAPHY. F. M. Abel, *Géographie de la Palestine*, 2, 1937, p. 307 and map 4; B. Rothenberg and Y. Aharoni, *God's Wilderness*, 1961, pp. 144, 161. G.I.D.

DOCTRINE. In the OT the word occurs chiefly as a translation of *leqaḥ*, meaning 'what is received' (Dt. 32:2; Jb. 11:4; Pr. 4:2; Is. 29:24). The idea of a body of revealed teaching is chiefly expressed by *tôrâ*, which occurs 216 times and is rendered as 'law'.

In the NT two words are used. *didaskalia* means both the act and the content of teaching. It is used of the Pharisees' teaching (Mt. 15:9; Mk. 7:7). Apart from one instance in Colossians and one in Ephesians, it is otherwise confined to the Pastoral Epistles (and seems to refer often to some body of teaching used as a standard of orthodoxy). *didachē* is used in more parts of the NT. It too can mean either the act or the content of teaching. It occurs of the teaching of Jesus (Mt. 7:28, *etc.*) which he claimed to be divine (Jn. 7:16–17). After Pentecost Christian doctrine began to be formulated (Acts 2:42) as the instruction given to those who had responded to the *kērygma* (Rom. 6:17). There were some in the church whose official function was to teach this to new converts (*e.g.* 1 Cor. 12:28–29). For the content of the *didachē*, see E. G. Selwyn, *The First Epistle of St Peter*, 1946, Essay II.

R.E.N.

DODANIM. The name of a people descended from Javan, son of Japheth, mentioned twice in the OT (Gn. 10:4: Heb. *dōḏānîm*, LXX *Rhodioi*; 1 Ch. 1:7: Heb. *rôḏānîm*, LXX *Rhodioi*). The Genesis reference is probably to be read (with the Samaritan Pentateuch) *rôḏānîm* (*d* and *r* are readily confused in both the old and the 'square' Heb. scripts), referring to the inhabitants of the island of Rhodes. See E. Dhorme, *Syria* 13, 1932, pp. 48–49. T.C.M.

DOOR-POST, GATE-POST, POST. 1. Heb. *mᵉzûzôṯ* were the wooden planks which framed a doorway and which supported the lintel, *mašqôp̄*, and on which an *amulet was later fixed. Blood was sprinkled on them at the first Passover (Ex. 12:7, 22–23), a slave's ear was pierced against one when he chose to remain with his master (Ex. 21:6), and the posts were to be written upon (Dt. 6:9; 11:20). The term is also used of temples (1 Sa. 1:9; 1 Ki. 6:33; Ezk. 41:21) and gates (Jdg. 16:3).

2. *'ayil.* Used mainly of Ezekiel's temple (40:9–10, *etc.*) where it is translated 'post' AV and 'jamb' RSV. It is thought to be a projection from the wall, such as a pilaster. **3.** *sap̄*, 'post' AV, see *THRESHOLD.

C.J.D.

DOR. A sea-port on the Mediterranean coast, S of Carmel, occupied from *c.* 1900 BC to Gk. times. Mentioned by Ramesses II and as the city Sikil ruled by Beder of the Tjeker (sea-peoples) in the 11th century Wen-Amon story (*ANET*, p. 26). It opposed the Israelites and was defeated (Jos. 11:1–2; 12:23; 17:11–13, *cf.* Ch. 7:29). Its Canaanite inhabitants were not conquered (Jdg. 1:27) until the reign of David and it remained essentially Phoenician. Solomon developed it (1 Ki. 4:11). The four-room gatehouse and temple belong to this period or Ahab's restorations. The Assyrians in 722 BC took Dor into their provincial system (*Duru*). It was rebuilt on a Gk. model by Ptolemy II. The port was later overshadowed by Herod's Caesarea Maritima. For excavations, see *NEAEHL*, pp. 357–372.

BIBLIOGRAPHY. E. Stern, *BAR* 19, 1993, pp. 13–44; *idem. Dor, Ruler of the Seas*, 1994. D.J.W.

DORCAS, or Tabitha ('gazelle'), was renowned for charity in the church at Joppa (Acts 9:36). When she died they sent two members to Lydda for the apostle Peter. He came immediately, and following Jesus' example, excluded the mourners. Then he knelt and prayed, and fulfilled his divine commission (Mt. 10:8). She is the only woman disciple so called (*mathētria*) in the NT. M.B.

DOTHAN. The fertile plain of Dothan separates the hills of Samaria from the Carmel range. It provides an easy pass for travellers from Bethshan and Gilead on their way to Egypt. This was the route of the Ishmaelites who carried Joseph into Egypt. The good pasturage had attracted Jacob's sons from Shechem, 32 km to the S. Near the town (now *tell dōṯā*) are rectangular cisterns about 3 m deep similar to the pit into which Joseph was put (Gn. 37:17ff.). Elisha led the Syrian force, which had been sent to capture him, along the hill road to Samaria, 16 km S. His servant was encouraged by a vision of heavenly forces arrayed on the hill to the E of the town (2 Ki. 6:13–23).

Excavations (1953–60) revealed a walled city of the Early and Middle Bronze Ages, and a Late Bronze Age settlement apparently using the older city wall. Thothmes III lists Dothan among his conquests (*c.* 1480 BC). It was probably one of the towns which was absorbed by the Israelites, but not actually conquered (*cf.* Jdg. 1:27). Areas of the Iron Age town which have been cleared show the narrow streets and small houses with storage-pits and bread-ovens of Elisha's day. Among the finds are fifteen pieces of silver in a pottery box representing an individual's savings. There was also settlement in the Assyrian and Hellenistic periods (*cf.* Judith 4:6; 7:3).

BIBLIOGRAPHY. Excavation reports by J. P. Free, *BA* 19, 1956, pp. 43–48, 1953–5 seasons; *BASOR* 131, 1953, pp. 16–29; 135, 1954, pp. 14–20; 139, 1955, pp. 3–9; 143, 1956, pp. 11–17; 147, 1957, pp. 36–37; 152, 1958, pp. 10–18; 156, 1959, pp. 22–29; 160, 1960, pp. 6–15; *NEAEHL* pp. 372–374. A.R.M.

DRAGON. In the OT two Heb. words are so translated by the AV.

1. *tan*, 'jackal' (so RSV). It always occurs in the plural, usually masculine (*tannîm*: Jb. 30:29; Ps. 44:19; Is. 13:22; 34:13; 35:7; 43:20; Je. 9:11; 10:22; 14:6; 49:33; 51:37; Ezk. 29:3; Mi. 1:8), but once in the feminine (*tannôṯ*: Mal. 1:3). In La. 4:3 the form *tannîn* occurs, but this is probably *tan* with the rare plural ending *-în* (nunation, as found in the Moabite Stone), and not a member of **2** below.

2. *tannîn*. A word of uncertain meaning, probably unrelated to *tan*. It is translated in AV 'dragon', 'whale' (Gn. 1:21; Jb. 7:12; RSV 'sea monster') and 'serpent' (Ex. 7:9–10, 12), the last being a satisfactory rendering in the Exodus passage, and it also seems to be the sense in Dt. 32:33 and Ps. 91:13; and possibly in Ne. 2:13. The other occurrences are less easy to define. In Gn. 1:21 evidently large sea-creatures such as the whale are intended, and this may be the meaning of Jb. 7:12 and Ps. 148:7, though, on the basis of an Arabic cognate, 'water spout' is suggested by some (*e.g.* RVmg. for the latter). In Ps. 74:13; Is. 27:1 and 51:9, the crocodile may be intended, and the association with Egypt suggests the same possibility in Ezk. 29:3; 32:2, and even Je. 51:34. None of these meanings can be certain, and the term may in some contexts refer to an apocalyptic creature of some kind, as in NT *drakōn*, 'dragon', used figuratively of Satan in Rev. 12–13; 16 and 20. The word occurs in the LXX chiefly for *tannîn*.

BIBLIOGRAPHY. G. R. Driver in Z. V. Togan (ed.), *Proceedings of the Twenty-Second Congress of Orientalists . . . Istanbul . . ., 1951*, 2, 1957, pp. 114–115; A. Heidel, *The Babylonian Genesis*², 1951, pp. 102–105. T.C.M.

DREAM. If comparing the 'dream' literature of the Babylonians and the Egyptians with the references to dreams in the OT, one is impressed by the Hebrews' lack of preoccupation with this phenomenon. Nor is the religious significance of the dreams that are recorded in the OT at all prominent. Indeed, dreams are said to derive from the activities in which the dreamer has been immersed during the day (Ec. 5:3). However, the OT recognizes that, whatever the origin of a dream, it may become a means by which God communicates with men, be they Israelites (1 Ki. 3:5) or non-Israelites (Gn. 20:3ff.).

Dreams recorded in Scripture are of two kinds. First, there are those consisting of the ordinary dream phenomena in which the sleeper 'sees' a connected series of images which correspond to events in everyday life (Gn. 40:9–17; 41:1–7). Secondly, there are dreams which communicate to the sleeper a message from God (Gn. 20:3–7; 1 Ki. 3:5–15; Mt. 1:20–24). On occasions there is virtually no distinction between a dream and a *vision during the night (Jb. 4:12f.; Acts 16:9; 18:9f.)

In interpreting dreams the Bible distinguishes between the dream-phenomena reported by non-Israelites and by Israelites. Gentiles such as pharaoh (Gn. 41:15ff.) and his high-ranking officers (40:12f., 18f.) require Joseph to explain their dreams, and Nebuchadrezzar needs Daniel (Dn. 2:17ff.). On occasion God himself speaks and so renders human intervention unnecessary (Gn. 20:3ff.; 31:24; Mt. 2:12). But when the members of the covenant community dream, the interpretation accompanies the dream (Gn. 37:5–10; Acts 16:9f.).

This subject is important for the OT view of prophecy. Among the Hebrews there was a close association between dreams and the function of the prophet. The *locus classicus* is Dt. 13:1–5, where the prophet is mentioned along with the dreamer without betraying any sense of incongruity. The close connection in Heb. thought between dreaming and prophesying is again revealed in Je. 23:25–32. It is also clear that in the days of Samuel and Saul it was commonly believed that the Lord spoke through dreams as well as by Urim and prophets (1 Sa. 28:6). Joel 2:28 (quoted Acts 2:17) links prophecy, dreams and visions with the outpouring of the Spirit.

Moses is described as the only prophet to whom the Lord spoke 'mouth to mouth, clearly, and not in dark speech' (Nu. 12:6–8; *cf.* Dt. 34:10), but the context shows that vision and dream are equally valid means of prophetic revelation (Nu. 12:6). Jeremiah censures the false prophets for treating the dreams of their own subconscious as revelations from God (Je. 23:16, 25–27, 32), but he admits that a true prophet can have a genuine prophetic dream (v. 28), the proof being the hammerlike message it contained (v. 29). Jeremiah himself certainly knew the dream form of prophetic inspiration (31:26).

In the NT Matthew records five dreams in connection with the birth and infancy of Jesus, in three of which an angel appeared with God's message (Mt. 1:20; 2:12–13, 19, 22). Later he records the troubled dream of Pilate's wife (27:19). Other passages speak of * visions rather than dreams, but the borderline is thin.

BIBLIOGRAPHY. *EBT*, 1, pp. 214ff.; P. J. Budd, *NIDNTT* 1, pp. 511–513; *ZPEB*, 2, p. 162; E. D. Ehrlich, *Der Traum im Alten Testament*, *BZAW* 73, 1953; *DBT*, pp. 127–128.

J.G.S.S.T.
J.S.W.

DRESS. The OT does not give us a detailed description of the various kinds of dress which were worn in Palestine. However, the Egyp., Bab. and Hittite monuments enable us to get a good idea of the general dress. In the tomb of Khnumhotep at Beni-hasan (Egypt) we find a procession of Asiatics who arrive in Egypt with eyepaint (*ANEP*, fig. 3). They are all dressed in vividly coloured garments, and this gives a clue as to how Abraham and other nomads were clad in about the 12th Egyptian Dynasty.

According to Gn. 3:7, 21 the origin of dress is associated with the sense of shame. It is a shame to be naked (Gn. 9:22–23) and this is especially the fate of prisoners and fugitives (Is. 20:4; Am. 2:16; Mk. 14:52). Children, however, used to run naked up to puberty.

The most important garments seem to have been a kind of loin- or waist-cloth, a long or short shirt or robe, an upper garment and a cloak, not to speak of the belt, headdress, veil and sandals.

a. Men's dress

We find but few mentions of a loin- or waist-cloth (*'ēzôr*) reaching from the waist to the knee. This was a common dress during the Bronze II and III ages, but it disappears as a civilian dress during Bronze III, although remaining as a military dress (Ezk. 23:15; Is. 5:27). Almost as primitive is an animal skin and the hairy cloak or mantle (Zc. 13:4; 2 Ki. 1:8; Mt. 3:4), which was worn only by prophets and poor people (Ecclus. 40:4) or for penitence. Covering of the hips and thighs was required only of priests (Ex. 28:42; 39:28). Otherwise these breeches were unknown in the OT and in the ancient Near East, except among the Persians, who knew the *šalwâr*, probably the *sarbâl* of Dn. 3:21, 27.

The ordinary shirt, which becomes predominant in Bronze III and is the normal dress in the Iron Age, is mentioned in the Bible as *kuttōneṯ* (Gk. *chitôn*), which seems to have been made of linen or wool. It is worn next to the skin and reaches down to the knees or to the ankles. It is made with or without sleeves, short or long (see Benzinger, *Hebr. Arch.*, figs. 59–60; Marston, *The Bible Comes Alive*, plate 15, bottom). For work or while running, this shirt was pulled up (Ex. 12:11; 2 Ki. 4:29). The Bible also mentions a *kuttōneṯ passîm*, which was a special kind of garment (Gn. 37:3, 23, 32), and was worn also by princes (2 Sa. 13:18–19). It was possibly a highly coloured garment, a kind of plaid twisted round the body, as is shown by the Syrian ambassadors to Tutankhamūn (*ANEP*, fig. 52). The shirt, presumably worn underneath it, is possibly the *sāḏin* (Jdg. 14:12; Pr. 31:24; Is. 3:23; LXX *sindōn*), but might include in this class of garments the *meʻîl*, regularly torn as a sign of mourning (Ezr. 9:3; Jb. 1:20; 2:12), and worn by men of importance, *e.g.* Jonathan (1 Sa. 18:4), Samuel (1 Sa. 2:19; 15:27; 28:14), Saul (1 Sa. 24:4, 11), Job and his friends (Jb. 1:20; 2:12) and Ezra (Ezr. 9:3).

The ordinary mantle is generally called *śimlâ*. It can be identified with the *'abâye* of the modern *fellahin* (Benzinger, *Hebr. Arch.*, fig. 73). This is a more or less square piece of cloth, which is sometimes thrown over one shoulder or, as now, over both shoulders. There are openings for the arms at the sides. This cloak, which everybody possessed, could not be given in loan, as it was used at night as a covering (Ex. 22:25–26; Dt. 24:13). It was generally taken off for work (Mt. 24:18; Mk. 10:50). It was also used to carry all kinds of objects (see Ex. 12:34; Jdg. 8:25; 2 Ki. 4:39; Hg. 2:12).

Another cloak was called *'addereṯ*, which it is not easy to describe. It was sometimes made of a costly material (Jos. 7:21, 24) and was worn by the king (Jon. 3:6) and by prophets (1 Ki. 19:13, 19; 2 Ki. 2:13–14), where it was possibly made from animal's skin. It was not in general use, and the word does not appear in late Hebrew.

For a head-covering Israelites probably wore a folded square of cloth as a veil for protection against the sun, or wrapped it as a turban around the head. RSV translates *miḡbā'ôṯ* as 'caps' (Ex. 28:40; Lv. 8:13) and *peʼēr* as 'headdress' (Is. 3:20) and 'linen turbans' (Ezk. 44:18); AV 'bonnet'. Notable men and women wore in later times the *ṣānîp̄* (Is. 3:23; 62:3), which was a piece of cloth twisted round the head.

The poor people generally went about barefoot, but the sandal was known (Dt. 25:10; Am. 2:6; 8:6). The soles (*neʻālîm*) were of leather or wood and tied with thongs (*śerôḵ*) (Gn. 14:23; Is. 5:27; Mk. 1:7; Lk. 3:16, AV 'latchet'). These were not worn inside the house.

b. Women's dress

The dress of women was very much the same as that for men. But the difference must have been sufficiently noticeable, because it was forbidden for men to wear women's clothes, and vice versa (Dt. 22:5). The difference has to be sought in finer material, more colours and the use of a veil and a kind of headcloth (*mitpaḥaṯ*: Is. 3:22, AV 'wimple'; translated 'mantle' in Ru. 3:15), which could be used to carry loads (Benzinger, *Hebr. Arch.*, fig. 59; Marston, *loc. cit.*). The most common dresses for the Israelite women are the *kuttōneṯ* and the *śimlâ*. The fine underwear *saḏîn* is also worn by women (Pr. 31:24; Is. 3:23). For feasts, women wore a more costly attire (1 Tim. 2:9). Hip and thigh clothing was not worn. A long train or veil was used by ladies of rank (Is. 47:2; Na. 3:5). Articles mentioned in the catalogue of Is. 3:18ff. cannot now be more particularly identified.

c. Dress for special occasions

Festive attire was distinctive from ordinary dress only in that the material was more costly (Gn. 27:15; Mt. 22:11–12; Lk. 15:22). The colour was preferably white (Ec. 9:8; Mk. 9:3; Rev. 3:4). Tissues of byssus, scarlet and purple were much appreciated (Pr. 31:22; Ecclus. 6:30; Je. 4:30). Women liked to adorn their clothes with gold and silver (2 Sa. 1:24; Ps. 45:9, 14–15; Ezk. 16:10, 13; 27:7).

Dress for mourning and penitence (*śaq*) was probably some kind of haircloth similar to the mantle of the prophets. This was worn with a belt and sometimes on the naked body (Gn. 37:34; 2 Sa. 3:31; 1 Ki. 21:27; 2 Ki. 6:30).

d. Dress of priests

The oldest sacred dress seems to have been the *'ēpôḏ baḏ*, probably a simple loin-cloth (2 Sa. 6:14, 20). The priests of Nob were known as men who wore the 'linen ephod' (1 Sa. 22:18). Samuel (1 Sa. 2:18) and David (2 Sa. 6:14) wore a simple linen ephod. This ordinary ephod has to be distinguished from the ephod of the high priest made of costly material (byssus = *šēš*), worked with gold, purple, scarlet or the like. This part of the dress reached from the breast down to the hips. It was held in place by two shoulder-bands and was tied round the waist (Ex. 39:1–26). There is also mention of an ephod which was used for the oracles. This was hung in the Temple (1 Sa. 21:9). The ordinary priests wore during the liturgical service a cloth which covered the hips and thighs (Ex. 28:42–43; Lv. 16:4) and a long embroidered linen tunic with sleeves (Ex. 28:40; 39:27), also an elaborately worked belt of twined linen, blue, purple and scarlet stuff (Ex. 28:40; 39:29) (Nötscher, *Bibl. Alterumskunde*, 1940). They had also a kind of turban called *miṣnep̄eṯ* (Ex. 28:4, 37, 39; 29:6; 39:28). As in Egypt and Babylon, it was forbidden for priests to wear woollen clothes (Ezk. 44:17). They were not allowed to wear sandals in the Temple (Ex. 3:5; 29:20).

BIBLIOGRAPHY. In general: M. G. Houston, *Ancient Egyptian and Persian Costume and Decoration*[2], 1954; *ANEP*, figs. 1–66 and *passim*; H. F. Lutz, *Textiles and Customs among the People of the Ancient Near East*, 1923. Near East with special reference to the OT: I. Benzinger, *Hebräische Archäologie*[3], 1927, pp. 72–89. Egyptian material in A. Erman, *Life in Ancient Egypt*, 1894 (old but useful), pp. 200–233; *BA* 24, 1961, pp. 119–128 (for tasselled garments). All these works are profusely illustrated.

C.D.W.

DRUSILLA. Born in AD 38 (Jos., *Ant*. 19. 354), the youngest daughter of *Herod Agrippa I, and sister of Agrippa II, who gave her in marriage to a Syrian petty king, Azizus of Emesa. The procurator *Felix, abetted by the Cypriot magician Atomos (whom some, following an inferior text of Josephus (*Ant*. 20. 142), connect with the 'Elymas' of Acts 13:8), persuaded her to desert Azizus and to marry him.

The Western Text records that it was Drusilla, not her husband, who wanted to meet Paul (AD 57), but it seems doubtful whether in this sophisticated Jewish teenager the apostle would find a receptive listener to his discourse on 'justice and self-control and future judgment' (Acts 24:24–25).

J.D.D.

DUALISM. Several characteristic themes of biblical doctrine can be better understood if considered against their background of dualistic thought. The word 'dualism' has been variously used in the history of theology and philosophy, but the basic conception is that of a distinction between two principles as independent of one another and in some instances opposed to one another. Thus in theology God is set over against some spiritual principle of evil or the material world, in philosophy spirit over against matter, in psychology soul or mind over against body.

I. God and the powers of evil

The first use of the term 'dualism' was in Hyde's *Historia Religionis Veterum Persarum*, published in 1700. Although it is a matter for dispute among experts whether Persian religion as a whole should be described as dualistic, it is clear that at some periods of Mazdaeism there existed a belief in a being evil by his own nature and the author of evil, who does not owe his origin to the creator of good but exists independently of him. This being brought into existence creatures opposed to those created by the good spirit.

With these views the Israelites certainly came in contact through Persian influences on them, but any such belief in the existence of evil from eternity and its creative power, even if modified by a belief in the ultimate victory of good, was unacceptable to the biblical writers. Satan and all the powers of evil are subordinated to God, not only in his final victory but also in their present activity and in their very being as fallen creatures of his (*cf.* especially Jb. 1–2; Col. 1:16–17).

II. God and the world

Many ancient cosmogonies picture God or the gods as imposing order and form on a formless but pre-existent matter. However malleable to the divine hand, matter which is not itself created by God necessarily imposes a limit on the divine operation, assimilating it to the creative activity of man, who always has to deal with a given material.

In the biblical conception of creation, although God and the world are kept very clearly distinct and Pantheism is rigorously avoided, the world is regarded as owing not only its form but also its very being to God (Heb. 11:3; *cf.* 2 Macc. 7:28).

III. Spirit and matter

Dualism finds more philosophical expression in the making of an absolute distinction between spirit and matter, coupled with a considerable tendency to regard spirit as good and matter as positively evil or at best an encumbrance to spirit.

This moral depreciation of matter as contrasted with spirit is contrary to the Christian doctrine of creation and the biblical understanding of sin. The situation is both better and worse than dualism portrays it. On the one hand, matter is not inherently evil; the Creator saw all that he had made as good (Gn. 1:31); on the other hand, the evil consequences of rebellion against God affect not only the material but also the spiritual realm. There are spiritual hosts of wickedness in the heavenly places (Eph. 6:12) and the most heinous sins are spiritual.

Nor does the Bible altogether accept the metaphysical distinction of spirit and matter. Hebrew dynamism sees the world less in terms of static substance than of a constant activity of divine providence which as readily uses material agencies as it does purely spiritual powers. Thus modern scientific concepts of the inter-relation of energy and matter are more akin to the biblical outlook than is a Platonist or idealist dualism. 'God is spirit' (Jn. 4:24); but 'the Word became flesh' (Jn. 1:14).

IV. Soul and body

A particular instance of the Heb. avoidance of dualism is the biblical doctrine of man. Greek thought, and in consequence many Hellenizing Jewish and Christian sages, regarded the body as a prison-house of the soul: *sōma sēma*, 'the body is a tomb'. The aim of the sage was to achieve deliverance from all that is bodily and thus liberate the soul. But to the Bible man is not a soul in a body but a body/soul unity; so true is this that even in the resurrection, although flesh and blood cannot inherit the kingdom of God, we shall still have bodies (1 Cor. 15:35ff.). M.H.C.

DUKE (Heb. *'allûp̄*, ? leader of an *'elep̄*, 'thousand'). AV title (RSV 'chief') of the sons of Seir the Horite (Gn. 36:20–30), of Esau's grandsons by Adah and Basemath and his sons by Aholibamah (Gn. 36:1–19), and of Esau's later(?) descendants (Gn. 36:40–43; 1 Ch. 1:51–54). Characteristic title of tribal chiefs of Edom down to Moses' time (Ex. 15:15), and known also in Ugaritic about then. In Jos. 13:21, 'dukes' of AV represents Heb. *nāsîḵ*, *i.e.* 'princes' of Sihon. K.A.K.

DUMAH. 1. Son of Ishmael and founder of an Arab community (Gn. 25:14; 1 Ch. 1:30). These descendants gave their name to Dumah, capital of a district known as the Jawf, about halfway across N Arabia between Palestine and S Babylonia. Dumah is modern Arabic Dûmat-al-Jandal, and the Adummatu of Assyrian and Babylonian royal inscriptions in the 7th to 6th centuries BC (references in Ebeling and Meissner, *Reallexikon der Assyriologie*, 1, 1932, pp. 39–40).

2. The name is apparently used figuratively of that nearer semi-desert land, Edom (Seir), in a brief oracle of Isaiah (21:11–12).

3. A township in Judah (Jos. 15:52), usually identified with the present ed-Dômeh or ed-Dûmah, *c.* 18 km SW of Hebron. The name Rumah in 2 Ki. 23:36 might conceivably be for Dumah in Judah; see *GTT*, §963, p. 368. K.A.K.

DUNG. The word is used in the AV to translate various Heb. terms. Heb. *'aśpōṯ*, usually rendered 'dunghill', is probably a refuse-tip, rubbish-dump or ash-heap, and is used as a simile to convey the haunt of the destitute (1 Sa. 2:8; Ps. 113:7; La. 4:5); *cf.* also Lk. 14:35. Jerusalem's Dung Gate (the same word) in Ne. 2:13; 3:13–14; 12:31, may be the gate by which refuse was taken out of the city. A grimmer comparison was of unburied corpses (perishing) as dung (*dōmen*) in the fields (2 Ki. 9:37, Jezebel; Je. 8:2; 9:22; 16:4; 25:33; *cf.* Jb. 20:7; Zp. 1:17). Disobedient priests are once threatened that the dung of their sacrifices (*i.e.* that which is unclean, *cf.* Ex. 29:14; Lv. 4:11; 8:17, *etc.*) will be spread upon their faces and they removed with it (Mal. 2:3). Jehu turned a temple of Baal into a latrine (2 Ki. 10:27). Utter privation under siege was pictured as eating dung (2 Ki. 18:27). The 'dunghills' (*nᵉwālîlû*) of Ezr. 6:11; Dn. 2:5; 3:29, should probably be 'ruin-heaps'.

Animal-dung had of old two main uses: for fuel and for manure. As fuel, it would often be mixed with straw (*cf.* Is. 25:10) and dried; it was then suitable for heating the simple 'bread ovens' of clay or stones used in Palestine, human dung being so used only exceptionally (Ezk. 4:12–15) and often burnt up (*cf.* the simile of 1 Ki. 14:10). When Ben-hadad II closely besieged Samaria, poor food and fuel (doves' dung) sold at inflated prices (2 Ki. 6:25). For dung as fuel into modern times, see Doughty, *Travels in Arabia Deserta*.

Ps. 83:10 may refer to manuring the ground, while Lk. 13:8 with reference to the fig-tree certainly does. In a powerful metaphor Paul counted all things as dung (AV) or refuse, in comparison with the 'surpassing worth' of knowing Christ (Phil. 3:8). K.A.K.

DURA (Aram. *Dûrā'*; LXX *Deeira*). The place in the administrative district of Babylon where King Nebuchadrezzar set up an image for all to worship (Dn. 3:1). Possibly Tell Dēr (27 km SW of Baghdad), though there are several Bab. places named Dūru. Oppert reported structures SSE of Babylon at 'Doura' (*Expédition scientifique en Mésopotamie*, 1, 1862, pp. 238–240). Pinches (*ISBE*) proposed the general interpretation of the plain of the 'Wall' (Bab. *dūru*), part of the outer defences of the city. For the name Dura, *cf.* Dura (Europos); Old Bab. *Da-mara* (*Orientalia* 21, 1952, p. 275, n. 1). D.J.W.

DUST. Heb. *'āḇāq*, *'āpār*, dust of the earth, is used literally and in similes to express: multitude (Gn. 13:16; Is. 29:5); smallness (Dt. 9:21; 2 Ki. 13:7); poverty (1 Sa. 2:8); abasement (Gn. 18:27) (*ASHES); dust on the head as a sign of sorrow (Jb. 2:12; Rev. 18:19); contrition (Jos. 7:6).

Man's lowliness is emphasized by his being taken from the dust (Gn. 2:7; Jb. 4:19; Ps. 103:14) and by his ultimate return to dust (Gn. 3:19; Jb. 17:16). Paul distinguishes the present mortal body as 'the image of the man of dust', inherited from Adam, from the immortal or 'spiritual' body to be put on at the resurrection, as 'the image of the man of heaven' (1 Cor. 15:44–49). The serpent is sentenced to 'eat dust' (Gn. 3:14) and warning of judgment is conveyed by shaking the dust off the feet (Mt. 10:14–15; Acts 13:51). P.A.B. F.F.B.

DWARF (Heb. *daq*, 'thin', 'small'). Used to denote one of the physical disabilities which precluded a man from officiating as a priest (Lv. 21:20), the exact meaning of the Heb. word is not clear. The same word is used of the lean kine and blasted ears in Pharaoh's dream (Gn. 41:3, 23), and the reference may simply be to a withered person. Dwarfs in the ancient Near East were always thought to be possessed of special (frequently magical) powers. See *IEJ* 4, 1954, pp. 1ff.; *HUCA* 26, 1955, p. 96. J.D.D.

EAR. 1. In the OT Heb. *'ōzen*, possibly derived from a root meaning 'pointed', is used of the ears of animals (Am. 3:12), and more frequently of man. There are parallels to this word in other Near Eastern languages. The denominative verb *'āzan* (in the Hiphʻîl) means 'to give ear', 'to hear'. In the NT Gk. *ous* is commonly used. Occasionally (*e.g.* Acts 17:20) *akoē*, from *akouō*, 'to hear', is also found. In the incident of the cutting off of the ear (Mt. 26:51) the word is *ōtion*, meaning particularly the external lobe.

While NT concepts envisage the interdependence of the members of the *body (1 Cor. 12:16), the OT views them more as semi-independent organs. This is clear in the case of the ear, which God planted (Ps. 94:9), or dug (Ps. 40:6 mg.), and which not only hears but attends (Ne. 1:6), tests words (Jb. 34:3), and can be stopped from hearing (Is. 33:15) or made heavy, rendering hearing difficult (Is. 6:10). God is spoken of also as having ears in the same way (Is. 59:1), different from the unhearing ears of the idols (Ps. 135:17). The ears must be used aright to get the true meaning of words (Mt. 11:15).

There are two OT customs which focus attention especially on the ear. The one was the rite of confirming a Hebrew slave in perpetual, voluntary service, by nailing his ear to his master's door (Ex. 21:6). The other was the putting of the blood of the sacrifice upon the right ear, thumb and toe of the priest (Lv. 8:23–24). Both probably have reference to securing obedience. To 'open the ear' is used in Heb. as a figurative expression for revealing (*e.g.* Is. 50:5).

2. An ear of grain. This would be of barley in the OT, of corn in the NT (Ex. 9:31; Mk. 4:28). The Heb. word *'āḇîḇ* gives rise to the name for the first month, the month of the Passover, at the time of the barley harvest (Ex. 23:15). B.O.B.

EARNEST (Gk. *arrabōn*, a Semitic loan-word; Heb. *'ērāḇôn*; Lat. *arrha*, *arr(h)abo*). AV translation of a commercial term, probably brought W by Phoenician traders. It means, strictly, the first instalment of a gift or payment, put down as a pledge that the rest will follow later (*cf.* the down-payment in modern hire-purchase). Paying the earnest makes obligatory payment of the remainder.

In this sense Paul calls the gift of the Spirit an earnest of the Christian's inheritance (Eph. 1:14; 2 Cor. 1:22; 5:5)—a guarantee (RSV), foretaste and first instalment of coming glory.

More generally, an *arrabōn* is any pledge or deposit, of whatever sort, given in token that a larger payment will later be made; so in LXX, Gn. 38:17–18, 20, rendering *'ērāḇôn*.

BIBLIOGRAPHY. O. Becker, *NIDNTT* 2, pp. 39f.; J. Behm, *TDNT* 1, p. 475. J.I.P.

EARTH. 1. The physical *world in which man lives, as opposed to the heavens, *e.g.* Gn. 1:1; Dt. 31:28; Ps. 68:8; Dn. 6:27, *etc.* (Heb. *'ereṣ* or Aram. *'ᵃra'*). This word is ambiguous in so far as it sometimes expresses this wider meaning of 'earth' (*i.e.* so far as the Hebrews knew it) and sometimes only 'land', a more restricted area. In the accounts of the Flood (Gn. 6–9) and of the division of speech (Gn. 11:1) each meaning has its advocates. This ambivalence is not peculiar to Hebrew; suffice it to mention the Egyptian word *ta'*, which likewise means land (as in 'conqueror of all lands') and earth ('you who are upon earth', *i.e.* the living).

2. Dry land as opposed to the sea, Gn. 1:10, *etc.* (Heb. *'ereṣ*; also *yabbešeṯ*, 'dry land' in Dn. 2:10). Phrases such as 'pillars of the earth', 'foundation of the earth' (1 Sa. 2:8; Jb. 9:6; Ps. 102:25; Is. 48:13) are simply poetic expressions from early Semitic which do not imply a doctrine of a table-like surface upon supports. The 'water under the earth' (Ex. 20:4) probably refers to subterranean springs and pools which, as the main source of water in Palestine, are referred to in poetic passages such as Pss. 24:2; 136:6; *cf.* Gn. 8:2.

3. The ground-surface, the soil which supports vegetation and so all life, *e.g.* Gn. 1:11–12; Dt. 26:2 (both *'ereṣ* and *'ᵃḏāmâ* are so used). Soil served for temporary altars (Ex. 20:24); the Aramaean Naaman took Israelite soil on which to worship Israel's God (2 Ki. 5:17). Torn clothes and the placing of earth on the head were tokens of mourning (2 Sa. 1:2; 15:32).

4. In passages such as Gn. 11:1; Ps. 98:9; La. 2:15, the word comes to mean, by transference, the inhabitants of the earth or part of it. In the NT Gk. *gē* is variously translated, generally 'earth', and appears with all these four meanings. For **1** see, *e.g.*, Mt. 6:10 and note the restricted use in Jn. 3:22, 'land of Judea'; for **2** see Acts 4:24 and *cf.* Mk. 4:1; for **3** see Mt. 25:18, 25 and *cf.* Mt. 10:29; for **4** see Rev. 13:3 (AV 'world'). K.A.K.

EARTHQUAKE. Earthquakes have been the *alter ego* of *Palestine consequent on its geological structure. In the biblical record earthquakes or their associated phenomena are recorded at various periods and attested in some excavations (*e.g.* Y. Yadin, *Hazor*, 1975, pp.150–151), at Mt Sinai on the giving of the law (Ex. 19:18), in the days of Saul (1 Sa. 14:15), Elijah (1 Ki. 19:11), Uzziah (Am. 1:1; Zc. 14:5) and Paul and Silas (Acts 16:26). An earthquake associated with crustal fissures destroyed Korah and his companions (Nu. 16:31), and a similar event may have been associated with the destruction of Sodom and Gomorrah (see Am. 4:11). The earthquake at the crucifixion is described in Mt. 27:51f. with miraculous manifestations.

There are many references to this terrible form of natural calamity: Jdg. 5:4; Pss. 18:7; 29:6; 97:4; 114:4; Joel 2:10; 3:16; Am. 8:8; Na. 1:5; Hab. 3:6; Zc. 14:4; Rev. 6:12; 8:5; 11:13; 16:18. The earthquake was figurative of divine judgment (Is. 29:6; Ezk. 38:19ff.). Earthquakes (*rību*) are also attested in Assyr. texts (*Iraq* 4, 1927, pp. 186–189).

BIBLIOGRAPHY. *IEJ* 1, 1951, pp. 223–246; D. P. McKenzie, *Nature* 226, 1970, pp. 237–243.

J.M.H.
D.J.W.

EAST. A bearing indicated in the OT by the phrase *mizraḥ-šemeš*, 'rising of the sun' (*e.g.* Nu. 21:11; Jdg. 11:18), or more frequently by *mizrāḥ*, 'rising', alone (*e.g.* Jos. 4:19), and once (Ps. 75:6) by *môṣā'*, 'going forth', alone. In the NT the same usage is found with *anatolē*, 'rising' (*e.g.* in Mt. 2:1). The rising of the luminaries gave the ancient peoples their standard of direction, so the term *qeḏem*, 'front', or some variation of the root *qdm*, was thus frequently employed to designate the E. The word *qdm* is attested from *c.* 2000 BC as a loan-word in the Egyptian 'Story of Sinuhe' and from the 14th century in the Ugaritic texts. The wisdom of the East (probably *Babylonia rather than Moab, 1 Ki. 4:30; *cf.* Mt. 2:1–12) was proverbial, and comparable to that of *Egypt. T.C.M.

EAST, CHILDREN OF THE (Heb. *bᵉnê-qeḏem*). A general term applied to various peoples living to the E (and NE, Gn. 29:1) of Canaan, and used in association with such neighbours as the Midianites, Amalekites (Jdg. 6:3), Moabites, Ammonites (Ezk. 25:10) and Kedarites (Je. 49:28). Sometimes *nomads are indicated (Ezk. 25:4), but the term could evidently also apply to the inhabitants of Mesopotamia (1 Ki. 4:30), and the patriarch Job is described (1:3) as one of the *bᵉnê-qeḏem*. (*EAST, *KADMONITES.)

BIBLIOGRAPHY. A. Musil, *Arabia Deserta*, 1927, pp. 494ff.; P. K. Hitti, *History of the Arabs*, 1956, p. 43. T.C.M.

EASTER, a word used in the Germanic languages to denote the festival of the vernal equinox, and subsequently, with the coming of Christianity, to denote the anniversary of the resurrection of Christ (which in Gk. and Romance tongues is denoted by *pascha*, 'Passover', and its derivatives). Tyndale, Coverdale and others give 'Easter' as a rendering of *pascha*, and one example survives in AV, at Acts 12:4 ('after Easter', where RV and RSV have 'after the Passover'; similarly NEB).

In the 2nd century AD and later there was considerable diversity and debate over the dating of the Christian Easter; the churches of Asia Minor for long followed the 'quartodeciman' reckoning, by which it was observed regularly on the 14th of Nisan, while those of Rome and elsewhere followed a calendar which commemorated the passion year by year on a Friday and the resurrection on a Sunday. The latter mode prevailed. F.F.B.

EBAL (OBAL). 1. A 'son' of *Joktan (Gn. 10:28; 1 Ch. 1:22); one of the Semitic families which inhabited S Arabia. **2.** A descendant of Esau (Gn. 36:23).

BIBLIOGRAPHY. *IDB*, 3, p. 579 (art. 'Obal').

J.D.D.

EBAL, MOUNT. The northern, and higher, of two mountains which overshadowed Shechem, the modern Nablus. It lies N of the Vale of Shechem, 427 m above the valley and 938 m above sea-level. The space between Ebal and its neighbour Gerizim, S of the vale, provides a natural amphitheatre with wonderful acoustic properties. At the close of his discourse in Dt. 5–11 Moses points to the two mountains on the W horizon beyond Gilgal and Moreh (Shechem) and announces that when they have entered the land a blessing shall be set on Gerizim and a curse on Ebal.

After the laws of Dt. 12–26 the narrative is resumed, and Moses gives detailed instructions. First, great stones were to be set up on Mt Ebal, covered with cement, and the law inscribed on them. The practice of writing on plaster laid on stones, previously known from Egypt, is now attested in Palestine itself, in the 8th century BC wall-inscriptions from Tell Deir Alla (J. Hoftijzer, *BA* 39, 1976, p. 11; for the date, *cf.* p. 87). After this an altar of unhewn stones was to be erected and sacrifices offered (Dt. 27:1–8). The Samaritan Pentateuch (*TEXTS AND VERSIONS, **1. V**) reads 'Gerizim' for 'Ebal' in v. 4; the textual variation seems to be connected in some way with the existence of a Samaritan temple on Mt Gerizim, but it is not certain which reading is the more original. Another possibility is that the Samaritan reading is due to the uneasiness felt in a late period at sacrifice (vv. 6–7) being offered on 'the mountain of the curse' (*cf.* 11:29).

In a further address (Dt. 27:9–28:68) Moses ordered six tribes to stand on Gerizim to bless obedience and six on Ebal to curse disobedience (27:9–13). Then the Levites should curse any who sin (27:15–26). By their response of 'Amen' the people are to condemn such practices openly. After victories in the centre of Palestine, Joshua gathered the people at Shechem, where these ceremonies were duly performed (Jos. 8:30–35). Remains of a small stone building, dated 1240–1140 BC, containing pottery and bones of cattle, sheep and goats, may indicate a cult place, see *NEAEHL*, pp. 375–377.

The rituals described have been seen as evidence for regarding Deuteronomy as a document in treaty-form (M. G. Kline, *The Treaty of the Great King*, 1963, ch. 2, esp. pp. 33–34) and for supposing that in early times there was a recurring festival for the renewal of the covenant at Shechem (G. von Rad, *The Problem of the Hexateuch and Other Essays*, E.T. 1966, pp. 37–38). Whatever the merits of these particular theories, Dt. 27 certainly contains early material of great importance for the early history of Israelite religion.

BIBLIOGRAPHY. G. Adam Smith, *The Historical Geography of the Holy Land*[25], 1931, ch. 6 ('The View from Mt Ebal'); R. J. Coggins, *Samaritans and Jews*, 1975, pp. 73, 155. G.T.M.
G.I.D.

EBED-MELECH (Heb. *eḇed-meleḵ*, a common name = 'servant of the king'). Ethiopian servant of Zedekiah who rescued Jeremiah from a dungeon

(Je. 38:7–13), and for this his life was to be spared at the sack of Jerusalem (Je. 39:15–18). D.J.W.

EBENEZER (Heb. *'eḇen 'ēzer*, 'stone of help').

1. The site of the dual defeat of Israel at the hands of the Philistines near Aphek in the N of Sharon. The sons of Eli were slain, the ark taken (1 Sa. 4:1–22), and a period of Philistine overlordship begun which continued until the days of national reinvigoration under the Monarchy.

2. The name of the stone which Samuel erected between Mizpah and Shen some years after this battle, to commemorate his victory over the Philistines (1 Sa. 7:12). The stone was probably given the same name as the site of Israel's earlier defeat in order to encourage the impression that that defeat had now been reversed. The exact site of the stone is unknown. R.J.W.

EBER. 1. The son of Salah or Shelah (1 Ch. 1:18–19, 25) and great-grandson of Shem who, when aged 34, became father of Peleg (Gn. 11:16) and later of other sons and daughters, one of whom was Joktan (Gn. 10:21, 25). He lived 464 years according to Gn. 11:16–17. Some identify him with Ebru(m), king of *Ebla, Syria, *c.* 2300 BC.

Eber (Heb. *'ēḇer*), meaning 'one who emigrates', is the same as the name Hebrew (Ḥabiru). His sons lived at a time when there was a 'division' as at *Babel, perhaps between those who were 'Arabs' (probably by metathesis the same as, or a dialectal variant for, *'ēḇer*) under *Joktan and those who lived semi-sedentary lives on irrigated land (Akkad. *palgu*) under *Peleg. The name Eber appears to be used as a poetic description of Israel in Nu. 24:24.

2. A Gadite family (1 Ch. 5:13). **3.** Two Benjaminites (1 Ch. 8:12, 22). **4.** The head of a priestly family of Amok who returned to Jerusalem from Babylonia with Zerubbabel (Ne. 12:20). D.J.W.

EBLA is modern Tell Mardikh, located 70 km S of Aleppo. The city-state flourished in the mid-third millennium BC. P. Matthiae has excavated it since 1964, finding second millennium BC occupation, as attested in texts from Mari and Alalakh. However, excavation of the third millennium palace in 1975 revealed an archive of about 8,000 cuneiform tablets. The texts are 80% administrative, but lexical texts, letters and a few literary compositions also occur.

A variety of claims have been made about the Ebla texts and their relationship to the Bible that now appear unfounded (Biggs, 1992). We must treat with caution great biblical parallels suggested in earlier studies of the Ebla texts. No certain identification exists for the names of biblical places and persons in these texts. The Ebla texts attest an age centuries before that of Abram and the patriarchs of Genesis. They probably cover a period of 40 years. Scholars now reject claims that Ebla was the centre of a far-flung empire. They identify all the place names attested in the texts with sites in N Syria. Even the identification of Ebrium, king of Ebla, with the name Eber in Gn. 10:24, raises questions. Ebrium was more likely an official than the king, and his name may have a different root than that of Eber (Krebernik, 1988, 39).

Research suggests a language closely related to that used at contemporary Mari and N Babylonia (Gelb, 1992). Linked to Amorite and Old Akkadian, these languages provide the earliest examples of the family of languages where Heb. finds its home. Thus some linguistic structures and vocabulary similar to Heb. occur. For example, officials at Ebla use the titles *malikum* and *šapiṭum* that resemble Heb. *melek* ('king') and *šōpeṭ* ('judge'). We also find similar customs, such as a law that forbids cursing both the king and the deity, found in a treaty at Ebla (Lambert, 1987, 359) and in Ex. 22:28. Parallels like these also occur in other W Semitic archives, *e.g.* 'Alalakh and Ugarit. The evidence from Ebla shows how the biblical patriarchs of the second millennium BC inherited a sophisticated N Syrian culture already present for 500 years.

A special study shows that forms and structures of the many personal names at Ebla resemble those of ancient Israel. Thus theophoric elements appear in most names and many describe the deity (or deities) with similar attributes (Millard, 1988). Although the names refer to different people, some possess similarities of elements and structure with those found in the genealogies of Gn. 1–11 (Hess, 1993). Adam, Eve, Noah, Jabal, Jubal, and Haran all bear similarities with names at Ebla. Especially interesting is Adam. It occurs as a personal name only at Ebla and in early second millennium BC Amorite sources, but not later.

Temples and palatial buildings of the Middle Bronze Age show the town flourished in the age of the biblical Patriarchs, having architectural styles, defensive ramparts and gates of patterns common throughout Syria and Canaan. Richly furnished tombs contained fine pottery, ivory carving and gold jewellery in the same fashions as found in Babylonia and S Canaan, including a gold nose-ring (*cf.* Gn. 24:22, 30) (Millard, 1992).

BIBLIOGRAPHY. A. Archi, 'The Archives of Ebla' in *Cuneiform Archives and Libraries*, 1986, pp. 72–86; W. G. Lambert, 'The Treaty of Ebla' in *Ebla 1975–1985. Dieci anni di studi linguistici e filologici*, 1987, pp. 353–364; A. R. Millard, 'Ebla Personal Names and Personal Names of the First Millennium BC in Syria and Palestine' in *Eblaite Personal Names and Semitic Name-giving. Papers of a Symposium Held in Rome July 15–17, 1985*, 1988, pp. 159–164; *idem*. 'Ebla and the Bible. What's Left (If Anything)?' in *BRev* 8, 1992, pp. 19–31, 60, 62; R. Biggs, 'Ebla Texts' in *ABD* 2, 1992, pp. 263–270; I. J. Gelb, 'Mari and the Kish Civilization' in *Mari in Retrospect*, 1992, pp. 121–202; R. S. Hess, *Studies in the Personal Names of Genesis 1–11*, 1993.

R.S.H.

ECBATANA (AV ACHMETHA), mod. Hamadan. The former capital of the Median empire, it became the summer residence of the Persian kings after *Cyrus had founded the *Persian empire (*c.* 540 BC). Herodotus (1. 98) and Judith 1:1–4 describe the magnificence of the city. The decree of Cyrus (Ezr. 6:3–5), authorizing the rebuilding of the Temple under *Zerubbabel (Ezr. 1:2; 3:8–13), was filed here in the royal archives, and re-issued with additions by *Darius (Ezr. 6:6–12).

D.J.A.C.

ECCLESIASTES, BOOK OF. The writer calls himself *qōheleṯ*. The fem. ending probably denotes an office that is held, in this instance the office of a caller of assemblies. Hence 'Preacher' or 'Teacher' is a reasonable translation.

I. Outline of contents

The theme of the book is a search for the key to the meaning of life. The Preacher examines life from all angles to see where satisfaction can be found. He finds that God alone holds the key, and he must be trusted. Meanwhile we are to take life day by day from his hand, and glorify him in the ordinary things.

Within this general framework Ecclesiastes falls into two main divisions of thought, (*a*) 'the futility of life', and (*b*) 'the answer of practical faith'. These run concurrently through its chapters. In the outline below, those passages belonging to the first category are printed in roman type, and those belonging to the second in italic.

1:1–2. The theme stated.

1:3–1. Nature is a closed system, and history a mere succession of events.

1:12–18. Wisdom discourages man.

2:1–11. Pleasure leaves him unsatisfied.

2:12–23. Wisdom is to be rated above such things, but death defeats the wise and foolish alike.

2:24–26. *Take life day by day from God, and glorify him in ordinary things.*

3:1–15. *Live step by step and remember that God alone knows the whole plan.*

3:16. The problem of injustice.

3:17. *God will judge all.*

3:18–21. Man dies like the beasts.

3:22. *God must therefore be glorified in this life.*

4:1–5. The problems of oppression and envy.

4:6. *Quietness of spirit is therefore to be sought.*

4:7–8. The lonely miser.

4:9–12. *The blessing of friendship.*

4:13–16. The failure of kings.

5:1–7. *The nature of the true worshipper.*

5:8–9. Oppressive officialdom.

5:10–17; 6:1–12. Money brings many evils.

5:18–20. *Be content with what God gives.*

7:1–29. *Practical wisdom, involving the fear of God, is a guide for life.*

8:1–7. *Man must submit to God's commands even though the future is hidden.*

8:8–9:3. The problem of death, which comes to good and bad alike.

9:4–10. *Since death is universal, use life energetically while its powers remain.*

9:11–12. *But do not be proud of natural talents.*

9:13–10:20. *More proverbs for practical living.*

11:1–8. *Since the future cannot be known, man must co-operate sensibly with the natural laws that are known.*

11:9–12:8. *Remember God in youth, for old age weakens the faculties.*

12:9–12. *Listen to wise words.*

To summarize its contents, the book constitutes an exhortation to live a God-fearing life, realizing that one day account must be rendered to him.

II. Authorship and date

Although the writer says that he was king over Israel (1:12), and speaks as though he were Solomon, he nowhere says that he is Solomon. The style of the Heb. is later than Solomon's time. If Solomon was the author, the book underwent a later modernization of language. Otherwise a later writer may have taken up a comment on life that had been made by Solomon, 'Vanity of vanities, all is vanity,' and used this as a text to show why even a wise and wealthy king should say such a thing. We cannot tell at what date the book received its present form, since there are no clear historical allusions in it. About 200 BC is commonly suggested.

III. Interpretation

(See the outline of contents above.) The interpretation is partially bound up with the question of the unity of the book. Those who reject the unity hold that there is an original nucleus by a sceptical writer who queried God's hand in the world. This was worked over by one or more writers, one at least trying to redress the balance on the side of orthodoxy (*e.g.* 2:26; 3:14, *etc.*), and another possibly inserting the Epicurean passages (*e.g.* 2:24–26; 3:12–15, *etc.*). It would, however, be strange if an orthodox writer thought it worth while to salvage what was fundamentally a book of scepticism. Moreover, why should a sceptic be commended as wise (12:9)?

If the book is a unity, some take it as the musings of the natural man. The Preacher gives up the problems of God and man, but holds that it is best to live a quiet and normal life, avoiding dangerous extremes (*e.g.* A. Bentzen, *IOT*, 2, p. 191). The closing summary in 12:13–14 suggests that the book is not primarily sceptical, and that the so-called Epicurean passages are not intended in the Epicurean sense. Life is a riddle, for which the Preacher tries to find the key. The meaning of life is not to be found in the acquisition of knowledge, money, sensual pleasures, oppression, religious profession or folly. Either these things prove empty or something happens against which they are helpless. Even God's hand at times is inscrutable. Man is so made that he must always try to make sense of the universe, since God has set eternity in his heart; yet God alone knows the whole pattern (3:11, RVmg.).

Therefore the plan for man is to take his life each day from the hand of God, and enjoy it from him and for him. This theme should be compared with what Paul says about the vanity of the world in Rom. 8:20–25, 28.

BIBLIOGRAPHY. F. D. Kidner, *The Message of Ecclesiastes, BST*, 1976; R. E. Murphy (ed.), *FOTL XIII: Wisdom Literature*, 1983; J. Crenshaw, *Ecclesiastes*, 1987; G. Ogden, *Qoheleth*, 1987; R. N. Whybray, *Ecclesiastes*, 1989; R. Murphy, *Ecclesiastes*, 1992.

J.S.W.

ED. It is related in Jos. 22 that when the two and a half tribes left Shiloh to take up their possessions E of Jordan, they set up 'an altar of great size' (v. 10) on the banks of the river, not for sacrifice, but as a 'witness' (Heb. *'ēḏ*). Fearing a schism, their brethren sent Phinehas and ten princes to protest (vv. 13–14), but they were satisfied that, on the contrary, it was to bear witness to their loyalty to Yahweh (v. 28). In v. 34 *MT* the word *'ēḏ* occurs only once, in the phrase 'it is a witness', but its earlier occurrence after 'they called the altar' is presupposed by AV, RV ('*Ed*'), and RSV, NEB ('Witness').

G.T.M.
F.F.B.

EDEN. 1. The name of the Levite(s) who shared in Hezekiah's reforms (2 Ch. 29:12; 31:15).

2. A place that traded with Tyre, associated with Harran and Canneh (Ezk. 27:23). This Eden and its people are identical with the Beth-eden (House of Eden) of Am. 1:5 and the 'children' of Eden of 2 Ki. 19:12; Is. 37:12—and these comprise the Assyrian province (and former kingdom) of Bit-Adini between Harran and the Euphrates at Carchemish. See further on *TELASSAR, *EDEN, HOUSE OF, and literature there cited. K.A.K.

EDEN, GARDEN OF. The place which God made for Adam to live in, and from which Adam and Eve were driven after the Fall.

I. The name

The *MT* states that God planted a garden in Eden (*gan-bᵉʿēḏen*; Gn. 2:8), which indicates that the garden was not co-extensive with Eden, but must have been an enclosed area within it. Of possible origins of the name: *a.* direct from the Sumerian *edin*, 'plain, steppe'; *b.* from the Sumerian *edin* via Akkadian *edinu*; or *c.* from the Common West Semitic, *ʿdn*, 'pleasure, luxury', the last, already long noted by commentators as a 'homophonous' root, seems most plausible, with a possible derived meaning of 'place with abundance of water' or the like. The question must remain open, however, since the name might go back to some quite unknown earlier language. From its situation in Eden the garden came to be called the 'garden of Eden' (*gan-ʿēḏen*; Gn. 2:15; 3:23–24; Ezk. 36:35; Joel 2:3), but it was also referred to as the 'garden of God' (*gan-ᵉlōhîm*, Ezk. 28:13; 31:9) and the 'garden of the Lord' (*gan-YHWH*, Is. 51:3). In Gn. 2:8ff. the word *gan*, 'garden', and in Is. 51:3 *ʿēḏen* itself, is rendered *paradeisos* by the LXX, this being a loan-word from Old Persian (Avestan) *pairidaēza*, 'enclosure', which came to mean 'park, pleasure ground', and from this usage came English *'paradise' for the garden of Eden.

II. The rivers

A river came from Eden, or the plain, and watered the garden, and from thence it was parted and became four heads (*rā'šîm*, Gn. 2:10). The word *rō'š*, 'head, top, beginning', is interpreted variously by scholars to mean either the beginning of a branch, as in a delta, going downstream, or the beginning or junction of a tributary, going upstream. Either interpretation is possible, though the latter is perhaps the more probable. The names of the four tributaries or mouths, which were evidently outside the garden, are given as *pîšôn* (Gn. 2:11), *gîḥôn* (2:13), *ḥiddeqel* (2:14) and *pᵉrāṯ* (2:14). (see under V. below).

Genesis 2:6 states that 'an *'ēḏ* went up from the earth, and watered the whole face of the ground'. The etymology of *'ēḏ* has been much debated, the main suggestions being: *a.* from the Sumerian *id*, 'river'; *b.* from the Sumerian *id* via Akkadian *id* (though the more usual Akkadian reading of the ideogram is *naru*); *c.* from the Sumerian *e-de* (strictly e(4)-de(2); *i.e.* written respectively with the fourth and second homonymous cunieform signs representing those sounds) 'high water'; and *d.* from the Sumerian *e* 4 *de*(*-a*) via Akkadian *edû*, 'flood'.

Of these the third, from the Sumerian *e-de* possibly via another language such as Hurrian, is perhaps the most plausible, but the possibility of an origin in an unknown earlier language must leave the question open. The sense seems to be of some form of natural irrigation. It seems reasonable to understand this as relating to the inside of the garden.

III. The contents of the garden

If the statement in Gn. 2:5–6 may be taken to indicate what did subsequently take place within the garden, an area of arable land (*śāḏeh*, AV 'field') to be tilled by Adam may be postulated. On this were to grow plants (*śîᵃḥ*) and herbs (*ʿēśeḇ*), perhaps to be understood as shrubs and cereals respectively. There were also trees of every kind, both beautiful and fruit-bearing (Gn. 2:9), and two in particular in the middle of the garden, the tree of life, to eat from which would make a man live for ever (Gn. 3:22), and the tree of knowledge of good and evil, from which man was specifically forbidden to eat (Gn. 2:17; 3:3). Many views of the meaning of 'the knowledge of good and evil' in this context have been put forward. One of the most common would see it as the knowledge of right and wrong, but it is difficult to suppose that Adam did not already possess this, and that, if he did not, he was forbidden to acquire it. Others would connect it with the worldly knowledge that comes to man with maturity, and which can be put to either a good or bad use. Another view would take the expression 'good and evil' as an example of a figure of speech whereby an antonymic pair signifies totality, meaning therefore 'everything' and in the context universal knowledge. Against this is the fact that Adam, having eaten of the tree, did not gain universal knowledge. Yet another view would see this as a quite ordinary tree, which was selected by God to provide an ethical test for the man, who 'would acquire an experiential knowledge of good or evil according as he was stedfast in obedience or fell away into disobedience' (*NBC*, pp. 78f.). (*FALL, *TEMPTATION.) There were also animals in the garden, cattle (*bᵉhēmâ*, *BEAST), and beasts of the field (Gn. 2:19–20), and birds.

IV. The neighbouring territories

Three territories are named in connection with the rivers. The Tigris is said to have gone 'east of Assyria' (*qiḏmaṯ 'aššûr*, literally 'in front of *'aššûr*'; Gn. 2:14), an expression which could also mean 'between *'aššûr* and the spectator'. The name *'aššûr* could refer either to the state of Assyria, which first began to emerge in the early 2nd millennium BC, or the city of Assur, mod. Qal'at Sharqât on the W bank of the Tigris, the earliest capital of Assyria, which was flourishing, as excavations have shown, in the early 3rd millennium BC. Since even at its smallest extent Assyria probably lay on both sides of the Tigris, it is probable that the city is meant and that the phrase correctly states that the Tigris ran to the E of Assur. Secondly, the river Gihon is described as winding through (*sāḇaḇ*) 'the whole land of Cush' (*kûš*, Gn. 2:13). *Cush in the Bible usually signifies Ethiopia, and has commonly been taken in this passage (*e.g.* AV) to have that meaning; but there was also a region to the E of the Tigris, from which the Kassites descended in the 2nd millennium, which had this name, and this may be the meaning in this passage. Thirdly, the Pishon is described as winding through the whole land of *Havilah (Gn. 2:11). Various products of this place are named: gold, *bdellium and *šōham*-stone (Gn. 2:11–12), the latter being translated 'onyx' in the EVV, but being of uncertain meaning.

Since bdellium is usually taken to indicate an aromatic gum, a characteristic product of Arabia, and the two other biblical usages of the name Havilah also refer to parts of Arabia, it is most often taken in this context to refer to some part of that peninsula.

V. The location of the garden of Eden

Theories as to the location of the garden of Eden are numerous. That most commonly held, by Calvin, for instance, and in more recent times by F. Delitzsch and others, is the view that the garden lay somewhere in S Mesopotamia, the Pishon and Gihon being either canals connecting the Tigris and Euphrates, tributaries joining these, or in one theory the Pishon being the body of water from the Persian Gulf to the Red Sea, compassing the Arabian peninsula. These theories assume that the four 'heads' (AV) of Gn. 2:10 are tributaries which unite in one main stream, which then joins the Persian Gulf; but another group of theories takes 'heads' to refer to branches spreading out from a supposed original common source, and seeks to locate the garden in the region of Armenia, where both the Tigris and Euphrates take their rise. The Pishon and Gihon are then identified with various smaller rivers of Armenia and Trans-Caucasia, and in some theories by extension, assuming an ignorance of true geography in the author, with such other rivers as the Indus and even Ganges.

The expression 'in Eden, in the east' (Gn. 2:8), literally 'in Eden from in front', could mean either that the garden was in the E part of Eden or that Eden was in the E from the narrator's point of view, and some commentators have taken it as 'in Eden in old times', but in either case, in the absence of certainty as to the meaning of the other indications of locality, this information cannot narrow it down further.

In view of the possibility that, if the Deluge was universal (*FLOOD), geographical features have been altered, the site of Eden remains unknown.

VI. Dilmun

Among the Sumerian literary texts discovered early this century at Nippur in S Babylonia, one was discovered which described a place called Dilmun, a pleasant place, in which neither sickness nor death were known. At first it had no fresh water, but Enki the water-god ordered the sun-god to remedy this, and, this being done, various other events took place, in the course of which the goddess Ninti (*EVE) is mentioned. In later times the Babylonians adopted the name and idea of Dilmun and called it the 'land of the living', the home of their immortals. Certain similarities between this Sumerian notion of an earthly paradise and the biblical Eden emerge, and some scholars therefore conclude that the Genesis account is dependent upon the Sumerian. But an equally possible explanation is that both accounts refer to a real place, the Sumerian version having collected mythological accretions in the course of transmission.

BIBLIOGRAPHY. C. Westermann, *Genesis* 1–11, 1984, pp. 208–219; D. T. Tsamura, *The Earth and the Waters in Genesis 1 and 2*, 1989; W. F. Albright, 'The Location of the Garden of Eden', *AJSL* 39, 1922, pp. 15–31; E. A. Speiser, 'The Rivers of Paradise', *Festschrift Johannes Friedrich*, 1959, pp. 473–485; M. G. Kline, 'Because It Had Not Rained', *WTJ* 20, 1957–8, pp. 146ff. On **VI**, S. N. Kramer, *History Begins at Sumer*, 3rd ed., 1981, pp. 141–147; N. M. Sarna, *Understanding Genesis*, 1966, pp. 23–28.

T.C.M.

EDEN, HOUSE OF (Heb. *bêṯ 'eḏen*, Am. 1:5; sometimes written *bᵉnê 'eḏen*, 2 Ki. 19:12; Is. 37:12, which may be a contraction of *bᵉnê bêṯ 'eḏen*, 'children of the house of Eden'), and its association with Gozan and Harran suggests a location in N Syria.

It is very probably to be identified with the Aramaean state of Bît-Adini which lay between the river Baliḫ and the Euphrates, and blocked the path of the Assyrian expansion to N Syria. Under these circumstances it could not last long, and its main city Til Barsip, modern Tell Aḥmar, on the E bank of the Euphrates, was taken by Shalmaneser III, and in 855 BC the state became an Assyrian province. It is presumably to this conquest that both Amos and Rabshakeh referred over a century later (*BASOR* 129, 1953, p. 25). The Eden referred to in Ezk. 27:23 (without *bêṯ*, 'house of'), among the far-flung places trading with Tyre, has been connected, plausibly, with cuneiform Hindanu, original 'Iddan/Giddan on the middle Euphrates.

T.C.M.

EDER, EDAR (Heb. *'ēḏer*, 'flock'). **1.** The place of Israel's encampment between Bethlehem and Hebron (Gn. 35:21). In Mi. 4:8 'tower of the flock' (RVmg. 'of Eder') was probably the site of a watch-tower erected against sheep thieves. **2.** A town to the S of Judah near to the Edomite border; perhaps mod. Khirbet el-'Adar 8 km S of Gaza (Jos. 15:21). Y. Aharoni proposed to emend this name to *Arad (*LOB*, pp. 105, 298). **3.** A Levite of David's time. A member of the house of Merari and a son of Mushi (1 Ch. 23:23; 24:30). **4.** A Benjaminite, and son of Beriah (1 Ch. 8:15).

R.J.W.

EDOM, EDOMITES.

I. Biblical

The term Edom (*'ᵉḏôm*) denotes either the name of Esau, given in memory of the red pottage for which he exchanged his birthright (Gn. 25:30; 36:1, 8, 19), or the Edomites collectively (Nu. 20:18, 20–21; Am. 1:6, 11; 9:12; Mal. 1:4), or the land occupied by Esau's descendants, formerly the land of Seir (Gn. 32:3; 36:20–21, 30; Nu. 24:18). It stretched from the Wadi Zered to the Gulf of Aqabah for *c.* 160 km, and extended to both sides of the Arabah or wilderness of Edom (2 Ki. 3:8, 20), the great depression connecting the Dead Sea to the Red Sea (Gn. 14:6; Dt. 2:1, 12; Jos. 15:1; Jdg. 11:17–18; 1 Ki. 9:26, *etc.*). It is a rugged, mountainous area, with peaks rising to 1,067 m. While not a fertile land, there are good cultivable areas (Nu. 20:17, 19). In Bible times the king's highway passed along the E plateau (Nu. 20:14–18). The capital, *Sela, lay on a small plateau behind Petra. Other important towns were Bozrah and Teman.

The Edomites (*'ᵉḏôm*, *'ᵃḏômîm*) were descendants of Edom (Esau, Gn. 36:1–17). Modern archaeology has shown that the land was occupied before Esau's time. We conclude that Esau's descendants migrated to that land and in time became

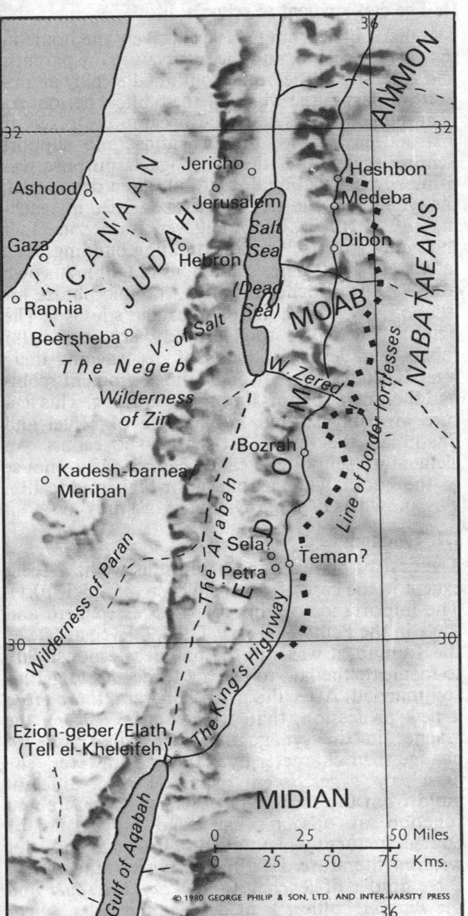

The land of the Edomites between the Dead Sea and the Gulf of Aqabah.

the dominant group incorporating the original Horites (Gn. 14:6) and others into their number. After *c.* 1850 BC there was a break in the culture of Edom till just before *c.* 1300 BC and the land was occupied by nomads.

Esau had already occupied Edom when Jacob returned from Harran (Gn. 32:3, 36:6–8; Dt. 2:4–5; Jos. 24:4). Tribal chiefs (AV 'dukes') emerged here quite early (Gn. 36:15–19, 40–43; 1 Ch. 1:51–54), and the Edomites had kings 'before any king reigned over the Israelites' (Gn. 36:31–39; 1 Ch. 1:43–51).

At the time of the Exodus, Israel sought permission to travel by the king's highway, but the request was refused (Nu. 20:14–21; 21:4; Jdg. 11:17–18). Notwithstanding this discourtesy, Israel was forbidden to abhor his Edomite brother (Dt. 23:7–8). In those days Balaam predicted the conquest of Edom (Nu. 24:18).

Joshua allotted the territory of Judah up to the borders of Edom (Jos. 15:1, 21), but did not encroach on their lands. Two centuries later King Saul was fighting the Edomites (1 Sa. 14:47) although some of them were in his service (1 Sa. 21:7; 22:9, 18). David conquered Edom and put garrisons throughout the land (2 Sa. 8:13–14. Emend *'ᵃrām* in v. 13 to *'ᵉdôm* because of a scribal confusion of *resh* 'r' and *daleth* 'd'. *Cf.* 1 Ch. 18:13). There was considerable slaughter of the Edomites at this time (2 Sa. 8:13), and 1 Ki. 11:15–16 speaks of Joab, David's commander, remaining in Edom for six months 'until he had cut off every male in Edom'. Some must have escaped, for Hadad, a royal prince, fled to Egypt and later became a trouble to Solomon (1 Ki. 11:14–22). This conquest of Edom enabled Solomon to build a port at Ezion-geber, and to exploit the copper-mines in the region, as excavation clearly shows (1 Ki. 9:26–28).

In Jehoshaphat's time the Edomites joined the Ammonites and Moabites in a raid on Judah (2 Ch. 20:1), but the allies fell to fighting one another (vv. 22–23). Jehoshaphat endeavoured to use the port at Ezion-geber, but his ships were wrecked (1 Ki. 22:48). At this time Edom was ruled by a deputy, who acted as king (1 Ki. 22:47). This 'king' acknowledged the supremacy of Judah and joined the Judah–Israel coalition in an attack on Mesha, king of Moab (2 Ki. 3:4–27).

Under Joram (Jehoram), Edom rebelled, but, although Joram defeated them in battle, he could not reduce them to subjection (2 Ki. 8:20–22; 2 Ch. 21:8–10), and Edom had a respite of some 40 years.

Amaziah later invaded Edom, slew 10,000 Edomites in the Valley of Salt, captured Sela their capital and sent 10,000 more to their death by casting them from the top of Sela (2 Ki. 14:7; 2 Ch. 25:11–12). Uzziah, his successor, restored the port at Elath (2 Ki. 14:22), but under Ahaz, when Judah was being attacked by Pekah and Rezin, the Edomites invaded Judah and carried off captives (2 Ch. 28:17). The port of Elath was lost once again. (Read 'Edom' for 'Aram' in 2 Ki. 16:6, as RSV.) Judah never again recovered Edom. Assyr. inscriptions show that Edom became a vassal-state of Assyria after *c.* 736 BC.

After the fall of Judah, Edom rejoiced (Ps. 137:7). The prophets foretold judgment on Edom for her bitter hatred (Je. 49:7–22; La. 4:21–22; Ezk. 25:12–14; 35:15; Joel 3:19; Am. 9:12; Ob. 10ff.). Some Edomites pressed into S Judah and settled to the S of Hebron (*IDUMAEA). Edom proper fell into Arab hands during the 5th century BC, and in the 3rd century BC was overrun by the Nabataeans. Through these centuries yet other Edomites fled to Judah. Judas Maccabaeus later subdued them (1 Macc. 5:65), and John Hyrcanus compelled them to be circumcised and incorporated into the Jewish people. The Herods were of general Edomite stock.

II. Archaeological

If we date the emergence of the Edomites proper from the end of the Late Bronze Age and the beginning of the Iron Age, there is a limited range of archaeological evidence throughout the centuries until Roman times. A few important sites have been excavated—Tawilân was occupied from the 8th to the 6th centuries BC. Tell el-Kheleifeh on the Gulf of Aqabah was occupied throughout the period of Israel's kings, and later. Umm el-Biyāra (behind Petra) has been investigated. A variety of small Iron Age fortresses on the borders of Edom is known. Important data are preserved on Assyrian records from about 733 BC to the end of the Assyrian empire in 612 BC. Some aspects of the general culture are beginning to emerge, *e.g.* several important seals and ostraca reveal names and deities and throw light on commercial transactions. The name of the deity *Qaus* appears in personal names. But, in general, the archaeological information is comparatively sparse at present.

BIBLIOGRAPHY. J. R. Bartlett, *Edom and the Edomites*, 1989; *ABD* 2, 1992, pp. 287–295 (history); A. MacDonald, *ABD* 2, 1992, pp. 295–301 (archaeology); K. G. Hoglund, *Peoples of the Old Testament World*, 1994, pp. 335–347.

J.A.T.

EDREI (Heb. *'eḏre'î*). **1.** A chief city of the Amorite kingdom of Og, where Israel defeated the Amorites in a pitched battle (Nu. 21:33; Dt. 1:4; 3:1; Jos. 12:4; 13:12, 31). Probably modern Der'a, 24 km ENE of Irbid (so Eusebius); this occupies a key point for communications in the Bashan area, and has remains dating from the Early Bronze Age. See F. M. Abel, *Géographie de la Palestine*, 2, 1937, p. 310; R. Hill, *VT* 16, 1966, pp. 412ff.

2. A town in Naphtali (Jos. 19:37); near Abel-beth-Maacah (list of Tuthmosis III, *LOB*, p. 162).

J.P.U.L.

EDUCATION. The child has always been of paramount importance in Judaism, as the Mishnah and Talmud clearly show in several passages. For that matter, Jesus certainly taught the value of children, in his kindly treatment of them as well as in his instruction regarding them. Because of this, there are a number of source-books for the study of education in the biblical period to be found in the OT, the Apocrypha and the Mishnah; *viz.* Proverbs, Ecclesiasticus, Wisdom of Solomon and *Pirqe Aboth*, quite apart from useful allusions in other books. On the other hand, actual details of schooling are few; the word 'school' occurs but once in AV, and then refers merely to a lecture-room borrowed by Paul (Acts 19:9), not to any Jewish or Christian school.

I. Early links with religion

Three events stand out in the history of Jewish education. They centre on three persons, Ezra, Simon ben-Shetaḥ and Joshua ben-Gamala. It was Ezra who established Scripture (such as it was at the time) as the basis for schooling; and his successors went on to make the synagogue a place of instruction as well as a place of worship. Simon ben-Shetaḥ enacted, about 75 BC, that elementary schooling should be compulsory. Joshua ben-Gamala improved existing organization, appointing teachers in every province and town, a century later. But otherwise it is not easy to date innovations. Even the origins of the synagogue are obscure, though the Exile is a likely time for their rise. Schürer doubts the historicity of Simon ben-Shetaḥ's enactment, though most scholars accept it. In any case, Simon did not institute the elementary school, but merely extended its use. Simon and Joshua in no way interfered with existing trends and methods, and indeed Ezra only made more definite the previous linking of religion with everyday life. So it will prove better to divide the topic by subject rather than date, since none of the three men made sweeping changes.

II. The development of schools

The place of learning was exclusively the home in the earliest period, and the tutors were the parents; and teaching in the home continued to play an important part in the whole of the biblical period. As it developed, the synagogue became the place of instruction. Indeed, the NT and Philo support Schürer's view that the synagogue's purpose was primarily instructional, and only then devotional; the synagogue ministry of Jesus consisted in 'teaching' (*cf.* Mt. 4:23). The young were trained in either the synagogue itself or an adjoining building. At a later stage the teacher sometimes taught in his own house, as is evidenced by the Aramaic phrase for 'school', *bêṯ sāp̄ᵉrâ*, literally 'teacher's house'. The Temple porticoes, too, proved very useful for rabbis, and Jesus did much of his teaching there (*cf.* Mt. 26:55). By Mishnaic times, eminent rabbis had their own schools for higher learning. This feature probably started in the time of Hillel and Shammai, the famed 1st-century BC rabbis. An elementary school was called *bêṯ has-sēp̄er*, 'house of the book', while a college for higher education was known as *bêṯ midrāš*, 'house of study'.

III. Teaching as a profession

The first tutors were the parents, as we have seen, except in the case of royal children (*cf.* 2 Ki. 10:1). The importance of this role is stressed here and there in the Pentateuch, *e.g.* Dt. 4:9. Even as late as the Talmud, it was still the parent's responsibility to inculcate the law, to teach a trade and to get his son married. After the period of Ezra, there arose a new profession, that of the scribe (*sōp̄ēr*), the teacher in the synagogue. The scribes were to change their character by NT times, however. The 'wise', or 'sages', seem to have been a different guild from the scribes, but their exact nature and function are obscure. The 'sage' (*ḥāḵām*) is, of course, frequently mentioned in Proverbs and later wisdom literature. By the NT period, there were three grades of teacher, the *ḥāḵām*, the *sōp̄ēr* and the *ḥazzān* ('officer'), in descending order. Nicodemus was presumably of the highest grade, the 'teachers of the law' (Lk. 5:17, where the Gk. term is *nomodidaskalos*) of the lowest. The generic term 'teacher' (Heb. *mᵉlammēḏ*; Aram. *sāp̄ᵉrâ*) was usually applied to the lowest grade. But the honorific titles given to teachers (rabbi, *etc.*) indicate the respect in which they were held. Ideally, they were not to be paid for teaching, but frequently a polite fiction granted them remuneration for time spent instead of services rendered. Ecclus. 38:24f. considers manual labour beneath a teacher's dignity; besides, leisure is a necessary adjunct to his task. But later on there were many rabbis who learnt a trade. Paul's views can be seen in 1 Cor. 9:3ff. The Talmud gives stringent rulings about the qualifications of teachers; it is interesting that none of them is academic—they are all moral, except those that prescribe that he must be male and married.

IV. The scope of education

This was not wide in the early period. The boy would learn ordinary moral instruction from his mother, and a trade, usually agricultural, plus some religious and ritual knowledge, from his father. The interplay of religion and agricultural life would have been self-evident at every festival (*cf.* Lv. 23, *passim*). The festivals also taught religious history (*cf.* Ex. 13:8). So even at the earliest period everyday life and religious belief and practice were inseparable. This was the more so in the synagogue, where Scripture became the sole authority for both belief and daily conduct. Life, indeed, was itself considered a 'discipline' (Heb. *mûsār*, a frequent word in Proverbs). Education, then, was and remained religious and ethical, with Pr. 1:7 its motto. To read was essential for the study of Scripture; writing was perhaps less important, although it was known as early as Jdg. 8:14. Basic arithmetic was taught. Languages were not taught *per se*, but note that, as Aramaic became the vernacular, study of the Heb. Scriptures became a linguistic exercise.

Girls' education was wholly in their mothers' hands. They learnt the domestic arts, simple moral and ethical instruction, and they were taught to read in order to become acquainted with the law. Their education was considered important, however, and they were even encouraged to learn a foreign language. King Lemuel's mother apparently proved an able teacher to him (Pr. 31:1); this chapter also shows the character of the ideal woman.

V. Methods and aims

Methods of instruction were largely by repetition; the Heb. verb *šānâ*, 'repeat', came to mean both 'learn' and 'teach'. Mnemonic devices such as acrostics were therefore employed. Scripture was the textbook, but that other books were not unknown is evidenced by Ec. 12:12. The value of rebuke was known (Pr. 17:10), but an emphasis on corporal chastisement is to be found in Proverbs and Ecclesiasticus. But discipline was much milder in Mishnaic times.

Until comparatively late times, it was customary for the pupil to sit on the ground at his teacher's feet, as did Paul at Gamaliel's (Acts 22:3). The bench (*sap̄sāl*) was a later invention.

Jewish education's whole function was to make the Jew holy, and separate from his neighbours, and to transform the religious into the practical. Such, then, was normal Jewish education; but undoubtedly there were schools after a Gk. pattern, especially in the closing centuries BC, and indeed Ecclesiasticus may have been written to combat deficiencies in such non-Jewish instruction. Hellenistic schools were found even in Palestine, but of course more frequently among Jewish communities elsewhere, notably in Alexandria.

In the infant church child and parent were told how to behave towards one another (Eph. 6:1, 4). Church officers had to know how to rule their own children. There were no Christian schools in early days; for one thing, the church was too poor to finance them. But the children were included in the church fellowship, and doubtless received their training there as well as in the home.

BIBLIOGRAPHY. W. Barclay, *Educational Ideals in the Ancient World*, 1959, chs. I, VI; E. B. Castle, *Ancient Education and Today*, 1961, ch. V; *TDNT* 5, pp. 596–625; entries *s.v.* 'Education' in *EJ* and *ISBE*; R. N. Whybray, *Intellectual Tradition in the OT*, 1974. (*WISDOM; *WISDOM LITERATURE; *WRITING.)

D.F.P.

EGLON (Heb. *'eglôn*). **1.** A city near Lachish, in the S confederacy against Joshua; eventually occupied by Judah (Jos. 10:3; 15:39). W. F. Albright's identification with Tell el-Hesi (*BASOR* 17, 1925, p. 7) has been widely accepted (J. Simons, *GTT*, p. 147; *LOB*, p. 219) and is not inconsistent with the sequence in Jos. 10:34; the position and stratigraphy present problems, however, and M. Noth's choice of Tell Eitun (20 km ESE), may be right. See V. Fargo, K. O'Connell, *BA* 41, 1978, pp. 165–182; L. Toombs, *IEJ* 32, 1982, pp. 67ff., E. Ayalon, *Tel Aviv* 12, 1985, pp. 54–62.

2. The king of Moab who occupied territory W of the Jordan early in the period of the Judges, and was assassinated by Ehud (Jdg. 3:12ff.).

J.P.U.L.

EGYPT. The ancient kingdom and modern republic in the NE corner of Africa and linked with W Asia by the Sinai isthmus.

I. Name

a. Egypt

The word 'Egypt' derives from the Gk. *Aigyptos*, Lat. *Aegyptus*. This term itself is probably a transcript of the Egyp. *Ḥ(wt)-k'-Pt(ḥ)*, pronounced roughly Ha-ku-ptah, as is shown by the cuneiform transcript *Ḫikuptaḫ* in the Amarna letters, *c.* 1360 BC. 'Hakuptah' is one of the names of Memphis, the old Egyptian capital on the W bank of the Nile just above Cairo (which eventually replaced it). If this explanation is correct, then the name of the city must have been used *pars pro toto* for Egypt generally besides Memphis by the Greeks, rather as today Cairo and Egypt are both *Miṣr* in Arabic.

b. Mizraim

The regular Heb. (and common Sem.) word for Egypt is *miṣrayim*. The word first occurs in external sources in the 14th century BC: as *mṣrm* in the Ugaritic (N Canaanite) texts and as *miṣri* in the Amarna letters. In the 1st millennium BC, the Assyr.-Bab. texts refer to *Muṣur* or *Muṣri*; unfortunately they use this term ambiguously: for Egypt on the one hand, for a region in N Syria/S Asia Minor on the other, and (very doubtfully) for part of N Arabia (see literature cited by Oppenheim in *ANET*, p. 279, n. 9). For the doubtful possibility of the N Syrian *Muṣri* being intended in 1 Ki. 10:28, see *MIZRAIM. The term *Muṣri* is thought to mean 'march(es)', borderlands, and so to be applicable to any fringe-land (Egyptian, Syrian or Arabian; *cf.* Oppenheim, *loc. cit.*). However true from an Assyr. military point of view, this explanation is hardly adequate to account for the Heb./Canaanite form *miṣrayim*/*mṣrm* of the 2nd millennium, or for its use. That *miṣrayim* is a dual form reflecting the duality of Egypt (see **II**, below) is possible but quite uncertain. Spiegelberg, in *Recueil de Travaux* 21, 1899, pp. 39–41, sought to derive *mṣr* from Egyp. *(i')mḏr*, '(fortification-) walls', referring to the guard-forts on Egypt's Asiatic frontier from *c.* 2000 BC onwards, the first feature of the country to be encountered by visiting Semites from that time. The fact that the term might be assimilated to Semitic *māṣôr*, 'fortress', adds weight to this. However, a final and complete explanation of *miṣrayim* cannot be offered at present.

II. Natural features and geography

a. General

The present political unit 'Egypt' is roughly a square, extending from the Mediterranean coast of Africa in the N to the line of 22° N latitude (1100

Prehistory	Down to *c.* 3100 BC.
4th millennium BC	Three successive predynastic cultures. *Tasian and Badarian*: first agriculturalists. *Naqada I*: merges into *Naqada II*: emergence of separate kingdoms of Upper and Lower Egypt by end of this period.
3rd millennium BC	*Archaic Period (Protodynastic)*: Dynasties 1–2, *c.* 3100–2680 BC. *Old Kingdom, or pyramid age*: Dynasties 3–6, *c.* 2680–2180 BC. First great flowering of Egyptian culture. *First Intermediate Period*: Dynasties 7–11, *c.* 2180–2040 BC.
2nd millennium BC	*Middle Kingdom*: Dynasties 11–12, *c.* 2134–1786 BC. Second great age of Egyptian culture. *Second Intermediate Period*: Dynasties 13–17, includes the Hyksos, *c.* 1786–1540 BC. *New Kingdom or Empire*: Dynasties 18–20, *c.* 1552–1069 BC. Third great period in Egyptian civilization.
1st millennium BC	*Late Period*: Dynasties 21–31, *c.* 1069–332 BC. Long period of decay interspersed with occasional brief periods of recovery. *Hellenistic Egypt*: Alexander the Great and the Ptolemies, *c.* 332–30 BC.
1st millennium AD	*Roman and Byzantine Epochs*: Egypt (Coptic) becomes part of Christendom, *c.* 30 BC–AD 641. This is followed by the Islamic epoch lasting to the present day.

Chart outlining the principal periods in the chronology of Egypt from prehistoric times until AD 641.

km from N to S), and from the Red Sea in the E across to the line of 25° E longitude in the W, with a total surface-area of roughly 1,000,250 sq. km. However, of this whole area, 96% is desert and only 4% usable land; and 99% of Egypt's population live in that 4% of viable land.

The real Egypt is the land reached by the Nile, being Herodotus' oft-quoted 'gift of the Nile'. Egypt is in a 'temperate zone' desert-belt having a warm, rainless climate: in a year Alexandria has barely 19 cm of rain, Cairo 3 cm and Aswan virtually nil. For life-giving water, Egypt depends wholly on the Nile.

b. The two Egypts

Historically ancient Egypt consists of the long, narrow Nile valley from the first cataract at Aswan (not from the second, as today) to the Memphis /Cairo district, plus the broad, flat triangle (hence its name) of the Delta from Cairo to the sea. The contrast of valley and delta enforce a dual nature upon Egypt.

(i) *Upper Egypt*. Bounded on either side by cliffs (limestone to the N and sandstone to the S of Esna some 530 km S of Cairo), the valley is never more than *c.* 19 km wide and sometimes narrows to a few hundred metres (as at Gebel Silsileh). At its annual inundation the *Nile deposited fresh silt upon the land beyond its banks each year until the Aswan barrages halted deposition in modern times. As far as the waters reach, green plants can grow; immediately beyond, all is desert up to the cliffs.

(ii) *Lower Egypt*. Some 20 km N of Cairo, the Nile divides into two main branches. The N branch reaches the sea at Rosetta, and the E at Damietta about 145 km away; from Cairo to the sea is roughly 160 km. Between the two great arms of the Nile, and over a considerable area beyond them to the E and W, stretches the flat, swampy Delta-land, entirely composed of river-borne alluvium and intersected by canals and drainage-channels. Lower Egypt has, from antiquity, always included the northernmost part of the Nile valley from just S of Memphis/Cairo, in addition to the Delta proper. In ancient times tradition held that the Nile had seven mouths on the Delta coast (Herodotus), but only three are recognized as important in ancient Egyptian sources.

c. The Egypt of antiquity

To the W of the Nile valley stretches the Sahara, a flat, rocky desert of drifted sand, and parallel with the valley a series of oases—great natural depressions, where cultivation and habitation are made possible by a supply of artesian water. Between the Nile valley and Red Sea on the E is the Arabian desert, a mountainous terrain with some mineral wealth: gold, ornamental stone, including alabaster, breccia and diorite. Across the Gulf of Suez is the rocky peninsula of Sinai.

Egypt was thus sufficiently isolated between her deserts to develop her own individual culture; but, at the same time, access from the E by either the Sinai isthmus or Red Sea and Wadi Hammamat, and from the N and S by way of the Nile was direct enough for her to receive (and give) external stimulus.

The ancient geography of pharaonic Egypt is a subject of considerable complexity. The historic nomes or provinces first clearly emerge in the Old Kingdom (4th Dynasty) in the 3rd millennium BC, but some probably originated earlier as territories of what were originally separate little communities in prehistory. There were reckoned 22 of these nomes for Upper Egypt and 20 for Lower Egypt in the enumeration that was traditional by Graeco-Roman times, when geographical records are fullest.

III. People and language

a. People

The earliest evidences of human activity in Egypt are flint tools of the Palaeolithic age from the Nile terraces. But the first real Egyptians who settled as agriculturists in the Nile valley (and of whom physical remains survive) are those labelled as Taso-Badarians, the first predynastic (prehistoric) culture. They appear to be of African origin, together with the two successive prehistoric culture-phases, best called Naqada I and II, ending about 3000 BC or shortly thereafter. Modern Egyptians are in direct descent from the people of ancient Egypt.

b. Language

The ancient Egyptian language is of mixed origin and has had a very long history. It is usually called 'Hamito-Semitic', and was basically a Hamitic tongue (*i.e.* related to the Libyco-Berber languages of N Africa) swamped at an early epoch (in prehistory) by a Semitic language. Much Egyptian vocabulary is directly cognate with Semitic, and there are analogies in syntax. Lack of early written matter hinders proper comparison with Hamitic. On the affinities of the Egyptian language, see A. H. Gardiner, *Egyptian Grammar*, § 3, and (in more detail) G. Lefebvre, *Chronique d'Égypte*, 11, No. 22, 1936, pp. 266–292.

In the history of the Egyptian language, five main stages may conveniently be distinguished in the written documents. *Old Egyptian* was an archaic and terse form, used in the 3rd millennium BC. *Middle Egyptian* was perhaps the vernacular of Dynasties 9–11 (2200–2000 BC) and was used universally for written records during the Middle Kingdom and early New Kingdom (to *c.* 1300 BC), and continued in use in official texts, in a slightly modified form, as late as Graeco-Roman days. *Late Egyptian* was the popular speech of the New Kingdom and after (16th–8th centuries BC), but was already coming into popular use two centuries before this time (1800–1600). It is also the language of documents and New Kingdom literature and official texts from Dynasty 19 onwards. Old, Middle and Late Egyptian were written in hieroglyphic and hieratic scripts (*WRITING). *Demotic* is really the name of a script, applied to the still more evolved form of Egyptian current in documents dating from the 8th century BC to Roman times. *Coptic*, the last stage of Egyptian, and the native language of Roman-Byzantine Egypt, has several dialect forms and was turned into a literary medium by Egyptian Christians or Copts. It was written, not in Egyptian script, but in the Coptic alphabet, which is composed of the Greek alphabet plus seven extra characters taken over from the old Demotic script. Coptic has survived as the purely liturgical language of the Coptic (Egyptian) Church down to modern times, its use being equivalent to that of Latin in the Roman Catholic Church.

IV. History

Of Egypt's long history only the salient features and those periods of direct relevance to biblical studies are discussed below. For further detail, see the classified Bibliography at the end of the article.

a. Egypt before 2000 BC

(i) *Predynastic Egypt*. During the three successive phases of predynastic settlement the foundations for historic Egypt were laid. Communities grew up having villages, local shrines and belief in an after-life (evidenced by burial-customs). Late in the final prehistoric phase (Naqada II) definite contact with Sumerian Mesopotamia existed, and Mesopotamian influences and ideas were so strong as to leave their mark on formative Egyptian culture (*cf.* H. Frankfort, *Birth of Civilisation in the Near East*, 1951, pp. 100–111). It is at this point that hieroglyphic writing appears, Egyptian art assumes its characteristic forms and monumental architecture begins.

(ii) *Archaic Egypt*. The first pharaoh of all Egypt was apparently Narmer of Upper Egypt, who conquered the rival Delta kingdom; he was perhaps the Menes of later tradition, and certainly the founder of Dynasty 1. Egyptian culture advanced and matured rapidly during the first two Dynasties.

(iii) *Old Kingdom*. In Dynasties 3–6, Egypt reached a peak of prosperity, splendour and cultural achievement. King Djoser's step-pyramid and its attendant buildings is the first major structure of cut stone in history (*c.* 2650 BC). In Dynasty 4 the pharaoh was absolute master, not in theory only (as was always the case) but also in fact, as never occurred before or after. Next in authority to the divine king stood the vizier, and beneath him the heads of the various branches of administration. At first members of the royal family held such offices. During this period material culture reached high levels in architecture (culminating in the Great Pyramid of Kheops, Dynasty 4), sculpture and painted relief, as well as in furnishings and jewellery. In Dynasty 5 the power of the kings weakened economically, and the priesthood of the sun-god Rē' stood behind the throne. In Dynasty 6 the Egyptians were actively exploring and trading in Nubia (later Cush). Meanwhile the decline in the king's power continued. This situation reached its climax late in the 94 years' reign of Pepi II. The literature of the time included several wisdom-books: those of Imhotep, Hardidief, (?Kairos) to Kagemni, and, of especial note, that of Ptah-hotep.

(iv) *First Intermediate Period*. In the Delta, where the established order was overthrown, this was a time of social upheaval (revolution) and of Asiatic infiltration. New kings in Middle-Egypt (Dynasties 9 and 10) then took over and sought to restore order in the Delta. But eventually they quarrelled with the princes of Thebes in Upper Egypt, and these then declared their independence (Dynasty 11) and eventually vanquished their northern rivals, reuniting Egypt under one strong sceptre (that of the Intef and Mentuhotep kings). The disturbances of this troubled epoch shattered the bland self-confidence of Old Kingdom Egypt and called forth a series of pessimistic writings that are among the finest and the most remarkable in Egyptian literature.

b. The Middle Kingdom and Second Intermediate Period

(i) *Middle Kingdom*. Eventually the 11th Dynasty was followed by Amenemhat I, founder of Dynasty 12, the strong man of his time. He and his Dynasty (*c.* 1991 BC) were alike remarkable. Elected to an unstable throne by fellow-nobles jealous for their local autonomy, Amenemhat I sought to rehabilitate the kingship by a programme of material reform announced and justified in literary works produced as royal propaganda (see G. Posener, *Littérature et Politique dans l'Égypte de la XIIe Dynastie*, 1956). He therein proclaimed himself the (political) saviour of Egypt. He accordingly rebuilt the administration, promoted agricultural prosperity and secured the frontiers, placing a series of forts on the Asiatic border. The administration was no longer at 11th-Dynasty

Thebes, which was too far S, but moved back to the strategically far superior area of Memphis, to Ithet-Tawy, a centre specifically built for the purpose. Sesostris III raided into Palestine, as far as Shechem ('Sekmem'). The extent of Egyptian influence in Palestine, Phoenicia and S Syria in Dynasty 12 is indicated by the execration texts (19th century BC) which record the names for magical cursing of possibly-hostile Semitic princes and their districts, besides Nubians and Egyptians. (See W. F. Albright, *JPOS* 8, 1928, pp. 223–256; *BASOR* 81, 1941, pp. 16–21 and *BASOR* 83, 1941, pp. 30–36.)

This was the golden age of Egypt's classical literature, especially short stories. This well-organized 12th-Dynasty Egypt, careful of its Asiatic frontier, was in all probability the Egypt of Abraham. The charge which pharaoh gave to his men concerning Abraham (Gn. 12:20) when he left Egypt is exactly paralleled (in reverse) by that given with regard to the returning Egyptian exile Sinuhe (*ANET*, p. 21, lines 240–250) and, pictorially, by the group of 37 Asiatics visiting Egypt, shown in a famous tomb-scene at Beni-hasan (see, *e.g.*, *IBA*, fig. 25, pp. 28–29). Amūn of Thebes, fused with the sun-god as Amen-Rē', had become chief national god; but in Osiris resided most of the Egyptians' hopes of the afterlife.

(ii) *Second Intermediate Period and Hyksos*. For barely a century after 1786 BC, a new line of kings, the 13th Dynasty, held sway over most of Egypt, still ruling from Ithet-Tawy. Their reigns were mostly brief so that a vizier might thus serve several kings. Deprived of settled, firm, personal royal control, the machinery of state inevitably began to run down. At this time many Semitic slaves were to be found in Egypt, even as far as Thebes (*JOSEPH), and eventually Semitic chiefs (Egyp. 'chiefs of foreign lands' *ḥḳ'w-ḫ'swt* = Hyksos) gained prominence in Lower Egypt and then (perhaps by a swift *coup d'état*) took over the kingship of Egypt at Ithet-Tawy itself (forming the 15th–16th 'Hyksos' Dynasties), where they ruled for about 100 years. They established also an E Delta capital, Avaris (on S of modern Qantir). These Semitic pharaohs assumed the full rank and style of traditional royalty. The Hyksos at first took over the Egyptian state administration as a going concern, but as time passed, Semitic officials were appointed to high office; of these the chancellor Ḥūr is the best-known.

Into this background, Joseph (Gn. 37–50) fits perfectly. Like so many others, he was a Semitic servant in the household of an important Egyptian. The royal court is punctiliously Egyptian in etiquette (Gn. 41:14; 43:32; *JOSEPH), yet the Semite Joseph is readily appointed to high office (as in the case of Ḥūr, perhaps, a little later). The peculiar and ready blend of Egyptian and Semitic elements mirrored in the Joseph-narrative (independent of its being a Heb. story set in Egypt) fits the Hyksos period perfectly. Furthermore, the E Delta is prominent under the Hyksos (Avaris), but not again in Egyptian history until Moses' day (*i.e.* the 19th Dynasty, or, at the earliest, the very end of the 18th).

Eventually princes at Thebes clashed with the Hyksos in the N; King Kamose took all Egypt from Apopi III ('Awoserrē) except for Avaris in NE Delta, according to his recently discovered historical stele (see L. Habachi, *The Second Stela of Kamose*, 1972). Finally, Kamose's successor Ahmose I (founder of the 18th Dynasty and the New Kingdom) expelled the Hyksos regime and its immediate adherents (Egyp. as well as Asiatic) from Egypt and worsted them in Palestine. An outline of this period's culture (illustrated) is in W. C. Hayes, *Scepter of Egypt*, 2, 1959, pp. 3–41.

c. New Kingdom—the Empire

The next five centuries, from *c.* 1552 to *c.* 1069 BC, witnessed the pinnacle of Egypt's political power and influence and the age of her greatest outward grandeur and luxury, but also, by their end, the breakdown of the old Egyptian spirit and eventual dissolution of Egyptian life and civilization which came about during the Late Period.

(i) *Dynasty 18*. The first kings of this line (except Tuthmosis I) were apparently content to expel the Hyksos and to rule Egypt and Nubia in the old 12th-Dynasty tradition. But the energetic Tuthmosis III took up the embryo policy of his grandfather Tuthmosis I, aiming to conquer Palestine–Syria and set the national boundary as far from Egypt proper as possible, in order to avoid any repetition of the Hyksos dominion. The princes of the Canaanite/Amorite city-states were reduced to tribute-paying vassals. This structure lasted almost a century till late into the reign of Amenophis III (*c.* 1360 BC); for this brief spell, Egypt was the paramount power in the ancient Near East.

Thebes was not sole capital at this time: Memphis in the N was more convenient administratively (especially for Asia). Amenophis III showed particular predilection for Aten, the sun-god manifest in the solar disc, while seeking to curb priestly ambition and still officially honouring Amūn. But his son Amenophis IV broke completely with Amūn and then with almost all the old gods, proscribing their worship and excising their very names from the monuments. Amenophis IV proclaimed the sole worship of Aten, changed his own name to Akhenaten and moved to his own newly-created capital-city in Middle Egypt (Akhet-Aten, the modern Tell el-Amarna). Only he and the royal family worshipped Aten directly; ordinary men worshipped Aten in the person of the divine pharaoh Akhenaten himself.

Meantime, Egypt's hold on Syria–Palestine slackened somewhat. The petty princes there were free to fight each other in pursuit of personal ambition, denouncing each other to the pharaoh and seeking military aid from him to further their own designs. This information comes from the famous Amarna letters. At home, Akhenaten eventually had to compromise with the opposing forces, and within 2 or 3 years of his death Amūn's worship, wealth and renown were fully restored.

General Haremhab now assumed control and began to set the affairs of Egypt to rights again. At his death the throne passed to his colleague Paramessu, who, as Rameses I, founded Dynasty 19 and reigned for 1 year.

(ii) *Dynasty 19*. Roughly 1300–1200 BC. Following Haremhab's internal restoration of Egypt, Sethos I (son of Rameses I) felt able to reassert Egyptian authority in Syria. His clash with the Hittites was not unsuccessful and the two powers made a treaty. Sethos began a large building programme in the NE Delta (the first since Hyksos times) and had a residence there. He may have founded the Delta capital so largely built by his son Rameses II, who named it after himself, 'Pi-Ramessē', 'House of Rameses' (the Raamses of

Ex. 1:11). Rameses II posed as the imperial pharaoh *par excellence*, dazzling later generations to such an extent that nine later kings took his name (Rameses III–XI). Besides the Delta residence, this king undertook extensive building throughout all Egypt and Nubia during his long reign of 66 years. In Syria he campaigned (usually against the Hittites) for 20 years (including the battle of Qadesh) until, wearied of the struggle, and with other foes to face, he and his Hittite contemporary Hattusil III finally signed a treaty of lasting peace between them. His successor Merenptah made one brief raid into Palestine (his capture of Gezer is attested by an inscription at Amada independent of the famous Israel Stele), apparently brushing with a few Israelites among others, and had to beat off a dangerous invasion (that of the 'Sea Peoples') from Libya; his successors were ineffective.

The first half of Dynasty 19 apparently witnessed the Israelite oppression and Exodus (*CHRONOLOGY OF THE OLD TESTAMENT). The restoration of firm order under Haremhab and the great impetus given to building activity in the E Delta by both Sethos I and Rameses II, with the consequent need of a large and economic labour-force, set the background for the Heb. oppression which culminated in the work on Pithom and Ra'amses described in Ex. 1:8–11. *Ra'amses was the great Delta-residence of the pharaoh, and *Pithom a township in the Wadi Tumilat. Ex. 1:12–22 gives some details of the conditions of this slavery, and for background to the Hebrews' brick-making, see *BRICK; *MOSES.

As for the early life of Moses, there is nothing either exceptional or incredible in a W Semite's being brought up in Egyptian court circles, perhaps in a *harim* in a Delta pleasure-residence, the pharaohs having several such scattered *harims* (*cf.* J. Yoyotte in G. Posener, *Dictionary of Egyptian Civilization*, 1962). At least from the reign of Rameses II onwards, Asiatics were brought up in royal *harims*, with the purpose of holding office (see S. Sauneron and J. Yoyotte, *Revue d'Égyptologie* 7, 1950, pp. 67–70). The thoroughly Semitic Ben'Ozen from Ṣûr-Bāšān ('Rock of Bashan') was royal cupbearer (*wb'-nṣw*) to Merenptah (J. M. A. Janssen, *Chronique d'Égypte* 26, No. 51, 1951, pp. 54–57 and fig. 11), and another Semitic cupbearer of his was called Pen-Ḥaṣu[ri], ('he of Hazor') (*cf.* Sauneron and Yoyotte, *op. cit.*, p. 68, n. 6). On a lower level, an Egyptian of *c.* 1170 BC scolds his son for joining in blood-brotherhood with Asiatics in the Delta (J. Černý, *JNES* 14, 1955, pp. 161ff.). Hence the Egyptian training and upbringing of Moses in Ex. 2 is entirely credible; the onus of proof lies upon any who would discredit the account. A further implication is that Moses would have an Egyptian education, one of the best available in his day. See further *MOSES. For the magicians, *MAGIC AND SORCERY; and for the plagues, *PLAGUES OF EGYPT. For the flight of fugitives (comparable to that of Moses in Ex. 2:15), *cf.* the flight of two runaway slaves in Papyrus Anastasi V (*ANET*, p. 259) and clauses on the extradition of fugitives in the treaty between Rameses II and the Hittites (*ANET*, pp. 200–203). For movements of peoples or large groups, see the Hittite example quoted in the article *EXODUS, and for the number of Israelites at the Exodus, *WILDERNESS OF WANDERING. Between Egypt and Canaan at this period there was constant coming and going (*cf.* the frontier-reports in *ANET*, pp. 258–259). The age of the 19th Dynasty was the most cosmopolitan in Egyptian history. More than in Dynasty 18, Hebrew–Canaanitic loan-words penetrated Egyptian language and literature by the score, and Egyptian officials proudly showed off their knowledge of the Canaanite tongue (Papyrus Anastasi I, see *ANET*, p. 477b). Semitic deities (Baal, Anath, Resheph, Astarte or Ashtaroth) were accepted in Egypt and even had temples there. Thus the Hebrews could hardly fail to hear something of the land of Canaan, and Canaanites with their customs were before their eyes, before they had even stirred from Egypt; the knowledge of such matters displayed in the Pentateuch does not imply a date of writing after the Israelite invasion of Canaan, as is so often erroneously surmised.

(iii) *Dynasty 20*. In due course, a prince Setnakht restored order. His son Rameses III was Egypt's last great imperial pharaoh. In the first decade of his reign (*c.* 1190–1180 BC) great folk-movements in the E Mediterranean basin swept away the Hittite empire in Asia Minor, entirely disrupted the traditional Canaanite–Amorite city-states of Syria–Palestine and threatened Egypt with invasion from both Libya and Palestine. These attacks Rameses III beat off in three desperate campaigns, and he even briefly carried Egyptian arms into Palestine. Since his successors Rameses IV–XI were for the most part ineffective personally, the machinery of state became increasingly inefficient and corrupt, and chronic inflation upset the economy, causing great hardship for the common people. The famous robberies of the royal tombs at Thebes reached their peak at this time.

d. Late-Period Egypt and Israelite History

From now on, Egypt's story is one of a decline, halted at intervals, but then only briefly, by occasional kings of outstanding character. But the memory of Egypt's past greatness lingered on far beyond her own borders, and served Israel and Judah ill when they were foolish enough to depend on the 'bruised reed'.

(i) *Dynasty 21 and the united monarchy*. Late in the reign of Rameses XI the general Herihor (now also high priest of Amūn) ruled Upper Egypt and the prince Nesubanebded I (Smendes) ruled Lower Egypt; this was styled, politically, as a 'renaissance' (*wḥm-mswt*). At the death of Rameses XI (*c.* 1069 BC), Smendes at Tanis became pharaoh, the succession being secured for his descendants (Dynasty 21), while, in return, Herihor's successors at Thebes were confirmed in the hereditary high-priesthood of Amūn, and in the rule of Upper Egypt under the Tanite pharaohs. So in Dynasty 21, one half of Egypt ruled the whole only by gracious permission of the other half!

These peculiar circumstances help to explain the modest foreign policy of this Dynasty in Asia: a policy of friendship and alliance with neighbouring Palestinian states, military action being restricted to 'police' action to safeguard the frontier in the SW corner of Palestine nearest the Egyptian border. Commercial motives would also be strong, as Tanis was a great port. All this links up with contemporary OT references.

When King David conquered Edom, Hadad the infant Edomite heir was taken to Egypt for safety. There he found a welcome so favourable that, when he was grown up, he gained a royal wife (1 Ki. 11:18–22). A clear example of 21st Dynasty foreign policy occurs early in Solomon's reign. A *pharaoh 'smote Gezer' and gave it as dowry with his daughter's hand in marriage-alliance with Solomon (1 Ki. 9:16; *cf.* 3:1; 7:8; 9:24; 11:1). The combination of 'police' action in SW Palestine (Gezer) and alliance with the powerful Israelite state gave Egypt security on her Asiatic frontier and doubtless brought economic gain to both states. At Tanis was found a damaged triumphal relief-scene of the pharaoh Siamūn smiting a foreigner—apparently a Philistine, to judge by the Aegean-type axe in his hand. This very specific detail strongly suggests that it was Siamūn who conducted a 'police' action in Philistia (reaching Canaanite Gezer) and became Solomon's ally. (For this scene, see P. Montet, *L'Égypte et la Bible*, 1959, p. 40, fig. 5.)

(ii) *The Libyan Dynasties and the divided monarchy.* 1. *Shishak. When the last Tanite king died in 945 BC a powerful Libyan tribal chief (? of Bubastis/Pi-beseth) acceded to the throne peacefully as Sheshonq I (biblical Shishak), thereby founding Dynasty 22. While consolidating Egypt internally under his rule, Sheshonq I began a new and aggressive Asiatic foreign policy. He viewed Solomon's Israel not as an ally but as a political and commercial rival on his NE frontier, and therefore worked for the break-up of the Hebrew kingdom. While Solomon lived, Sheshonq shrewdly took no action apart from harbouring political refugees, notably Jeroboam son of Nebat (1 Ki. 11:29–40). At Solomon's death Jeroboam's return to Palestine precipitated the division of the kingdom into the two lesser realms of Rehoboam and Jeroboam. Soon after, in Rehoboam's 'fifth year', 925 BC (1 Ki. 14:25–26; 2 Ch. 12:2–12), and apparently on pretext of a bedouin border incident (stele-fragment, Grdseloff, *Revue de l'Histoire Juive en Égypte*, 1, 1947, pp. 95–97), Shishak invaded Palestine, subduing Israel as well as Judah, as is shown by the discovery of a stele of his at Megiddo (C. S. Fisher, *The Excavation of Armageddon*, 1929, p. 13 and fig.). Many biblical placenames occur in the list attached to the triumphal relief subsequently sculptured by Shishak on the temple of Amūn (Karnak) in Thebes (see *ANEP*, p. 118 and fig. 349). (See also *SUKKIIM.) Sheshonq's purpose was limited and definite: to gain political and commercial security by subduing his immediate neighbour. He made no attempt to revive the empire of Tuthmosis or Rameses.

2. *Zerah. It would appear from 2 Ch. 14:9–15; 16:8, that Sheshonq's successor Osorkon I sought to emulate his father's Palestinian success but was too lazy to go himself. Instead, he apparently sent as general Zerah the Ethiopian, who was soundly defeated by Asa of Judah *c.* 897 BC. This defeat spelt the end of Egypt's aggressive policy in Asia. However, again like Sheshonq I, Osorkon I maintained relations with Byblos in Phoenicia, where statues of both pharaohs were found (*Syria* 5, 1924, pp. 145–147 and plate 42; *Syria* 6, 1925, pp. 101–117 and plate 25).

3. Egypt and Ahab's dynasty. Osorkon I's successor, Takeloth I, was apparently a nonentity who allowed the royal power to slip through his incompetent fingers. Thus the next king, Osorkon II, inherited an Egypt whose unity was already menaced: the local Libyan provincial governors were becoming increasingly independent, and separatist tendencies appeared in Thebes. Hence, he apparently returned to the old 'modest' foreign policy of (similarly-weak) Dynasty 21, that of alliance with his Palestinian neighbours. This is hinted at by the discovery, in Omri and Ahab's palace at Samaria, of an alabaster vase of Osorkon II, such as the pharaohs included in their diplomatic presents to fellow-rulers (illustrated in Reisner, *etc.*, *Harvard Excavations at Samaria*, 1, 1924, fig. on p. 247). This suggests that Omri or Ahab had links with Egypt as well as Tyre (*cf.* Ahab's marriage with Jezebel). Osorkon II also presented a statue at Byblos (M. Dunand, *Fouilles de Byblos*, 1, pp. 115–116 and plate 43).

4. Hoshea and 'So king of Egypt'. The 'modest' policy revived by Osorkon II was doubtless continued by his ever-weaker successors, under whom Egypt progressively fell apart into its constituent local provinces with kings reigning elsewhere (Dynasty 23) alongside the main, parent 22nd Dynasty at Tanis/Zoan. Prior to a dual rule (perhaps mutually agreed), the Egyptian state was rocked by bitter civil wars centred on Thebes (*cf.* R. A. Caminos, *The Chronicle of Prince Osorkon*, 1958), and could hardly have supported any different external policy.

All this indicates why Israel's last king, Hoshea, turned so readily for help against Assyria to *So king of Egypt' in 725/4 BC (2 Ki. 17:4), and how very misplaced was his trust in an Egypt so weak and divided. No help came to save Samaria from its fall. The identity of 'So' has long been obscure. He is probably Osorkon IV, last pharaoh of Dynasty 22, *c.* 730–715 BC. The real power in Lower Egypt was wielded by Tafnekht and his successor Bekenrenef (Dynasty 24) from Sais in the W Delta; so powerless was Osorkon IV that in 716 BC he bought off Sargon of Assyria at the borders of Egypt with a gift of twelve horses (H. Tadmor, *JCS* 12, 1958, pp. 77–78).

(iii) *Ethiopia—the 'bruised reed'.* In Nubia (Cush) there had meantime arisen a kingdom ruled by princes who were thoroughly Egyptian in culture. Of these, Kashta and Piankhy laid claim to a protectorate over Upper Egypt, being worshippers of Amūn of Thebes. In one campaign, Piankhy subdued Tafnekht of Lower Egypt to keep Thebes safe, but promptly returned to Nubia.

However, his successor Shabaka (*c.* 716–702 BC) promptly reconquered Egypt, eliminating Bekenrenef by 715 BC. Shabaka was a friendly neutral towards Assyria; in 712 he extradited a fugitive at Sargon II's request, and sealings of Shabaka (possibly from diplomatic documents) were found at Nineveh. Doubtless, Shabaka had enough to do inside Egypt without meddling abroad; but unfortunately his successors in this Dynasty (the 25th) were less wise. When *Sennacherib of Assyria attacked Hezekiah of Judah in 701 BC the rash new Ethiopian pharaoh Shebitku sent his equally young and inexperienced brother *Tirhakah to oppose Assyria (2 Ki. 19:9; Is. 37:9), resulting in dire defeat for Egypt. The Ethiopian pharaohs had no appreciation of Assyria's superior strength—after this setback, Tirhakah was defeated twice more by Assyria (*c.* 671 and 666/5, as king) and Tanutamen once—and their incompetent interference in Palestinian affairs was disastrous for Egypt and Palestine alike. They were most certainly the 'bruised reed' of the Assyrian king's jibe (2 Ki. 18:21; Is. 36:6). Exasperated by this stubborn meddling, Ashurbanipal in 664/3 BC finally sacked the ancient holy city Thebes, pillaging fourteen centuries of temple treasures. No more vivid comparison than the downfall of this city could the prophet Nahum find (3:8–10) when proclaiming the oncoming ruin of Nineveh in its turn. However, Assyria could not occupy Egypt, and left only key garrisons.

(iv) *Egypt, Judah and Babylon*. In a now disorganized Egypt, the astute local prince of Sais (W Delta) managed with great skill to unite all Egypt under his sceptre. This was Psammetichus I, who thereby established the 26th (or Saite) Dynasty. He and his successors restored Egypt's internal unity and prosperity. They built up an effective army round a hard core of Greek mercenaries, greatly enhanced trade by encouraging Greek merchants and founded strong fleets on the Mediterranean and Red Seas. But, as if in compensation for the lack of real, inner vitality, inspiration was sought in Egypt's past glories; ancient art was copied and archaic titles were artificially brought back into fashion.

Externally, this dynasty (except for the headstrong Hophra) practised as far as possible a policy of the balance of powers in W Asia. Thus, Psammetichus I did not attack Assyria but remained her ally against the reviving power of Babylon. So, too, Neco II (610–595 BC) was marching to help a reduced Assyria (2 Ki. 23:29) against Babylon, when Josiah of Judah sealed Assyria's fate by delaying Neco at Megiddo at the cost of his own life. Egypt considered herself heir to Assyria's Palestinian possessions, but her forces were signally defeated at Carchemish in 605 BC so that all Syria–Palestine fell to Babylon (Je. 46:2). Jehoiakim of Judah thus exchanged Egyp. for Bab. vassalage for 3 years. But as the Bab. chronicle-tablets reveal, Egypt and Babylon clashed in open conflict in 601 BC with heavy losses on both sides; Nebuchadrezzar then remained 18 months in Babylonia to refit his army. At this point Jehoiakim of Judah rebelled (2 Ki. 24:1f.), doubtless hoping for Egyptian aid. None came; Neco now wisely kept neutral. So Nebuchadrezzar was not molested in his capture of Jerusalem in 597 BC. Psammetichus II maintained the peace; his state visit to Byblos was linked rather with Egypt's acknowledged commercial than other interests in Phoenicia. He fought only in Nubia. But Hophra (589–570 BC; the Apries of the Greeks) foolishly cast dynastic restraint aside, and marched to support Zedekiah in his revolt against Babylon (Ezk. 17:11–21; Je. 37:5), but returned in haste to Egypt when Nebuchadrezzar temporarily raised his (second) siege of Jerusalem to repulse him—leaving Jerusalem to perish at the Babylonian's hand in 587 BC. After other disasters, *Hophra was finally supplanted in 570 BC by Ahmose II (Amasis, 570–526 BC). As earlier prophesied by Jeremiah (46:13 ff.), Nebuchadrezzar now marched against Egypt (as referred to in a damaged Bab. tablet), doubtless to prevent any recurrence of interference from that direction. He and Ahmose must have reached some understanding, for henceforth, till both were swallowed up by Medo-Persia, Egypt and Babylon were allies against the growing menace of Media. But in 525 BC Egypt followed her allies into Persian dominion, under Cambyses. On this period, see further, *BABYLONIA and *PERSIA.

(v) *The base kingdom*. At first Persian rule in Egypt (Darius I) was fair and firm; but repeated Egyptian rebellions brought about a harshening of Persian policy. The Egyptians manufactured anti-Persian propaganda that went down well in Greece (*cf.* Herodotus); they shared a common foe. Briefly, during *c.* 400–341 BC, Egypt's last native pharaohs (Dynasties 28–30) regained a precarious independence until they were overwhelmed by Persia to whom they remained subject for just 9 years, until Alexander entered Egypt as 'liberator' in 332 BC. (See F. K. Kienitz, in Bibliography, and G. Posener, *La Première Domination Perse en Égypte*, 1936). Thereafter, Egypt was first a Hellenistic monarchy under the *Ptolemies and then fell under the heel of Rome and Byzantium. From the 3rd century AD, Egypt was a predominantly Christian land with its own, eventually schismatic (Coptic) church. In AD 641/2 the Islamic conquest heralded the mediaeval and modern epochs.

V. Literature

a. Scope of Egyptian literature

(i) *3rd millennium BC*. Religious and wisdom-literature are the best-known products of the Old Kingdom and 1st Intermediate Period. The great sages Imhotep, Hardidief [?Kairos] to Kagemni, and Ptahhotep produced 'Instructions' or 'Teachings' (Egyp. *sb'yt*, written collections of shrewd maxims for wise conduct of everyday life, especially for young men hopeful of high office, so beginning a very long tradition in Egypt. The best-preserved is that of Ptahhotep; see Z. Žába, *Les Maxims de Ptahhotep*, 1956. For the Pyramid Texts and Memphite Theology, see **VI**, below.

In the 1st Intermediate Period, the collapse of Egyptian society and the old order may be pictured in the *Admonitions of Ipuwer*, while the *Dispute of a Man Tired of Life with his Soul* reflects the agony of this period in terms of a personal conflict which brings man to the brink of suicide. The *Instruction for King Merikarē* shows remarkable regard for right dealing in matters of state, while the *Eloquent Peasant*'s nine rhetorical speeches within a narrative prose prologue and epilogue (*cf.* Job) call for social justice.

(ii) *Early 2nd millennium BC*. In the Middle Kingdom, stories and propaganda-works are outstanding. Finest of the narratives is the *Biography of Sinuhē*, an Egyptian who spent long years of exile in Palestine. The *Shipwrecked Sailor* is a nautical fantasy. Among the propaganda, the *Prophecy of Neferty* ('*Neferrohu*' of older books) is a pseudo-prophecy to announce Amenemhat I as saviour of Egypt. On prediction in Egypt, see Kitchen, *Tyndale House Bulletin* 5/6, 1960, pp. 6–7 and refs. Two loyalist 'Instructions', *Sehetepibrē* and *A Man to his Son*, were intended to identify the good life with loyalty to the throne in the minds of the ruling and labouring classes respectively. The poetry of the *Hymns to Sesostris III* apparently also expresses that loyalty. For administrators in training, the *Instruction of Khety son of Duauf* or *Satire of the Trades* points out the advantages of the scribal profession over all other (manual) occupations by painting these in dark colours. For tales of magicians, *MAGIC AND SORCERY (Egyptian).

(iii) *Late 2nd millennium BC*. During this period the Empire produced further stories, including delightful fairy-tales (*e.g. The Foredoomed Prince*; *Tale of the Two Brothers*), historical adventure (*The Capture of Joppa*, a precursor of *Alibaba and the Forty Thieves*) and biographical reports such as the *Misadventures of Wenamūn*, who was sent to Lebanon for cedarwood in the ill-starred days of Rameses XI. Poetry excelled in three forms: lyric, royal and religious. Under the first head come some charming love-poems, in general style heralding the tender cadences of the Song of Songs. The Empire pharaohs commemorated their victories with triumph-hymns, the finest being those of Tuthmosis III, Amenophis III, Rameses II and Merenptah (Israel Stele). Though less prominent, wisdom is still well represented; beside the 'Instructions' of Ani and Amennakhte, there is a remarkable ode on the Immortality of Writing. For Amenemope's wisdom see *b.* (i) 2, below.

(iv) *1st millennium* BC. Less new literature is known from this epoch so far. In Demotic the 'Instruction' of 'Onchsheshonqy dates to the last centuries BC, and the *Stories of the High Priests of Memphis* (magicians) to the 1st centuries AD. Most Coptic (Christian) literature is translated from Gk. church literature, Shenoute being the only outstanding native Christian writer.

b. Egyptian literature and the OT

The very incomplete survey given above will serve to emphasize the quantity, richness and variety of early Egyptian literature; besides the additional matter under Religion below, there is a whole body of historical, business and formal texts. Egypt is but one of the Bible lands; the neighbouring countries, too, offer a wealth of writings (*ASSYRIA; *CANAAN; *HITTITES.) The relevance of such literatures is twofold: firstly, with regard to questions of direct contact with the Heb. writings; and secondly, in so far as they provide dated, first-hand comparative and contemporary material for objective control of OT literary forms and types of literary criticism.

(i) *Questions of direct contact.* 1. Gn. 39; Ps. 104. In times past the incident of Potiphar's unfaithful wife in Gn. 39 has occasionally been stated to be based on a similar incident in the mythical *Tale of Two Brothers*. But an unfaithful wife is the only common point; the *Tale* is designedly a work of pure fantasy (the hero is changed into a bull, a persea-tree, *etc.*), whereas the Joseph-narrative is biography, touching actuality at every point. Unfortunately, unfaithful wives are not mere myth, either in Egypt or elsewhere (see an incidental Egyptian instance in *JNES* 14, 1955, p. 163).

Egyptologists today do not usually consider that Akhenaten's 'Hymn to Aten' inspired parts of Ps. 104 as Breasted once thought (*cf.* J. H. Breasted, *Dawn of Conscience*, 1933, pp. 366–370). The same universalism and adoration of the deity as creator and sustainer occur in hymns to Amūn both before and after the Aten hymn in date, which could carry these concepts down to the age of Heb. psalmody (so, *e.g.*, J. A. Wilson, *Burden of Egypt/Culture of Ancient Egypt*, pp. 224–229). But even this tenuous link-up can carry no weight, for the same universalism occurs just as early in W Asia (*cf.* the examples given in W. F. Albright, *From Stone Age to Christianity*, 1957 ed., pp. 12–13, 213–223) and is therefore too generally diffused to allow of its being made a criterion to prove direct relationship. The same point might be made with regard to the so-called penitential psalms of the Theban necropolis-workers of Dynasty 19. A sense of shortcoming or sin is not peculiar to Egypt (and is even, in fact, quite atypical there); and the Egyp. psalms should be compared with the confession of man's sinfulness made by the Hittite king, Mursil II (*ANET*, p. 395b) and with the Babylonian penitential odes. The latter again show the wide diffusion of a general concept (although it may have different local emphases); and they cannot be used to establish direct relationship (*cf.* G. R. Driver, *The Psalmists*, ed. D. C. Simpson, 1926, pp. 109–175, especially 171–175).

2. The Wisdom of Amenemope and Proverbs. Impressed by the close verbal resemblances between various passages in the Egyptian 'Instruction' of Amenemope (*c.* 1100 BC, see below) and the 'words of the wise' (Pr. 22:17–24:22) quoted by Solomon (equating the 'my knowledge' of 22:17 with that of Solomon from 10:1), many have assumed, following Erman, that Proverbs was debtor to Amenemope; only Kevin and McGlinchey ventured to take the opposite view. Others, with W. O. E. Oesterley, *Wisdom of Egypt and the Old Testament*, 1927, doubted the justice of a view at either extreme, considering that perhaps both Amenemope and Proverbs had drawn upon a common fund of Ancient Oriental proverbial lore, and specifically upon an older Heb. work. The alleged dependence of Proverbs upon Amenemope is still the common view (*e.g.* P. Montet, *L'Égypte et la Bible*, 1959, pp. 113, 127), but is undoubtedly too simple. By a thoroughgoing examination of both Amenemope and Proverbs against the entire realm of ancient Near Eastern Wisdom, recent research has shown that in fact there is *no* adequate basis for assuming a special relationship either way between Amenemope and Proverbs. Two other points require note. First, with regard to date, Plumley (*DOTT*, p. 173) mentions a Cairo ostracon of Amenemope that 'can be dated with some certainty to the latter half of the Twenty-first Dynasty'. Therefore the Egyp. Amenemope cannot be any later than 945 BC (= end of Dynasty 21), and Egyptologists now tend to favour a date in Dynasties 18–20. In any case, there is no objective reason why the Hebrew Words of the Wise should not be as old as Solomon's reign, *i.e.* the 10th century BC. The second point concerns the word *šilšôm*, found in Pr. 22:20, which Erman and others render as 'thirty', making Proverbs imitate the 'thirty chapters' of Amenemope. But Pr. 22:17–24:22 contains not 30 but 33 admonitions, and the simplest interpretation of *šlšwm* is to take it as elliptical for *'eṯmôl šilšôm*, 'formerly', 'already', and to render the clause simply as, 'Have I not written for thee, already, in/with counsels of knowledge?'

(ii) *Literary usage and OT criticism.* It is singularly unfortunate that the conventional methods of OT literary criticism (see also *BIBLICAL CRITICISM) have been formulated and developed, over the last century in particular, without any but the most superficial reference to the actual characteristics of the contemporary literature of the Bible world, alongside which the Hebrew writings came into existence and with the literary phenomena of which they present very considerable external, formal similarities. The application of such external and tangibly objective controls cannot fail to have drastic consequences for these methods of literary criticism. While Egyp. texts are a specially fruitful source of such external control-data, Mesopotamian, N Canaanite (Ugaritic), Hittite and other literatures provide valuable confirmation. See for preliminary survey, K. A. Kitchen, *Ancient Orient and Old Testament*, 1966, chs. 6–7.

VI. Religion

a. The gods and theology

Egyptian religion was never a unitary whole. There

were always local gods up and down the land, among whom were Ptah, artificer-god of Memphis; Thoth, god of learning and the moon at Hermopolis; Amūn 'the hidden', god of Thebes, who overshadowed the war-god Mentu there and became state god of 2nd-millennium Egypt; Hathor, goddess of joy at Dendera; and many more. Then there were the cosmic gods: first and foremost Rē' or Atum the sun-god, whose daughter Ma'et personified Truth, Justice, Right and the cosmic order; then Nūt the sky-goddess and Shu, Geb and Nu, the gods of air, earth and the primordial waters respectively. The nearest thing to a truly national religion was the cult of Osiris and his cycle (with his wife, Isis, and son, Horus). The story of Osiris had great human appeal: the good king, murdered by his wicked brother Seth, becoming ruler of the realm of the dead and triumphing in the person of his posthumous son and avenger Horus, who, with the support of his mother Isis, gained his father's kingship on earth. The Egyptian could identify himself with Osiris the revivified in his kingdom of the hereafter; Osiris's other aspect, as a god of vegetation, linking with the annual rise of the Nile and consequent rebirth of life, combined powerfully with his funerary aspect in Egyptian aspirations.

b. Egyptian worship

Egyptian worship was a complete contrast to Hebrew worship in particular, and to Semitic in general. The temple was isolated within its own high-walled estate. Only the officiating priesthood worshipped in such temples; and it was only when the god went forth in glittering procession on great festivals that the populace actively shared in honouring the great gods. Apart from this, they sought their solace in household and lesser gods. The cult of the great gods followed one general pattern, the god being treated just like an earthly king. He was awakened from sleep each morning with a hymn, was washed and dressed (*i.e.* his image), and breakfasted (morning offering), did a morning's business, and had midday and evening meals (corresponding offerings) before retiring for the night. The contrast could hardly be greater between the ever-vigilant, self-sufficient God of Israel with his didactic sacrificial system, symbolizing the need and means of atonement to deal with human sin, and of peace-offerings in fellowship at tabernacle or Temple, and those earthly Egyp. deities of nature. For Egyp. temple-worship, *cf.* H. W. Fairman, *BJRL* 37, 1954, pp. 165–203.

c. Religious literature

To the 3rd millennium BC belong the Pyramid Texts (so-called from their being inscribed in 6th-Dynasty pyramids), a large body of 'spells', apparently forming incredibly intricate royal funerary rituals, and also the Memphite Theology, which glorifies the god Ptah as first cause, conceiving in the mind ('heart') and creating by the word of power ('tongue') (a distant herald of the *logos*-concept of John's Gospel (1:1ff.) transformed through Christ). At all times there are hymns and prayers to the gods, usually full of mythological allusions. In the Empire certain hymns to Amūn, and Akhenaten's famous Aten-hymn, remarkably illustrate the universalism of the day; see V. Literature, *b* (i) 1, above. Epics of the gods which at present remain to us exist only in excerpts. A ribald part of the Osiris-cycle survives in the *Contendings of Horus and Seth*. The Coffin Texts of the Middle Kingdom (usually painted inside coffins at that time) and the 'Book of the Dead' of the Empire and Late Period are nothing more than collections of magical spells to protect and benefit the deceased in the after-life; special guide-books to 'infernal' geography were inscribed on the tomb-walls of Empire pharaohs. On magical literature, *MAGIC AND SORCERY. See *ANET* for translations from religious texts.

d. Funerary beliefs

The Egyptians' elaborate beliefs about the afterlife found expression in the concrete, material terms of a more-glorious, other-worldly Egypt ruled by Osiris. Alternative hereafters included accompanying the sun-god Rē' on his daily voyage across the sky and through the underworld, or dwelling with the stars. The body was a material attachment for the soul; mummification was simply an artificial means of preserving the body to this end, when tombs early became too elaborate for the sun's rays to desiccate the body naturally, as it did in prehistory's shallow graves. Objects in tombs left for the use of the dead usually attracted robbers. Egyptian concern over death was not morbid; this cheerful, pragmatic, materialistic people simply sought to take the good things of this world with them, using magical means so to do. The tomb was the deceased's eternal physical dwelling. The pyramids were simply royal tombs whose shape was modelled on that of the sacred stone of the sun-god Rē' at Heliopolis (see I. E. S. Edwards, *The Pyramids of Egypt*, 1961). The Empire pharaohs' secret rock-hewn tombs in the Valley of Kings at Thebes were planned to foil the robbers, but failed, like the pyramids they replaced.

BIBLIOGRAPHY. *General*. Very useful is S. R. K. Glanville (ed.), *The Legacy of Egypt*, 1942 (new edn., 1965); well illustrated is W. C. Hayes, *Sceptre of Egypt*, 1, 1953; 2, 1959. Likewise, G. Posener, S. Sauneron and J. Yoyotte, *Dictionary of Egyptian Civilization*, 1962. On Egypt and Asia, W. Helck, *Die Beziehungen Ägyptens zum Vorderasien im 3. und 2. Jahrtausend v. Chr.*, 1962. H. Kees, *Ancient Egypt, a Cultural Topography*, 1961, is useful and reliable. W. Helck *et al.*, *Lexikon der Agyptologie*, 1–7, 1972–92; B. J. Kemp, *Ancient Egypt, Anatomy of a Civilisation*, 1989. Full bibliography is obtainable from: I. A. Pratt, *Ancient Egypt*, 1925, and her *Ancient Egypt* (*1925–41*), 1942, for nearly everything pre-war; W. Federn, eight lists in *Orientalia* 17, 1948; 18, 1949; and 19, 1950, for the years 1939–47; and J. M. A. Janssen, *Annual Egyptological Bibliography*, 1948ff., for 1947 onwards. Also Porter-Moss, *Topographical Bibliography*, 7 vols.

Origin of name. Brugsch, *Geographische Inschriften*, 1, 1857, p. 83; A. H. Gardiner, *Ancient Egyptian Onomastica*, 2, 1947, pp. 124*, 211*.

Geography. Very valuable for the physical structure and geography of Egypt is J. Ball, *Contributions to the Geography of Egypt*, 1939. See also J. Bainbes and J. Malek, *Atlas of Ancient Egypt*, 1980. The deserts find some description in A. E. P. Weigall, *Travels in the Upper Egyptian Deserts*, 1909. On the early state and settlement of the Nile valley, W. C. Hayes, 'Most Ancient Egypt' = *JNES* 22, 1964. For ancient Egyptian geography, a mine of information is (Sir) Alan Gardiner's *Ancient Egyptian Onomastica*, 3 vols., 1947, with good discussions and references to literature. See also *EGYPT, RIVER OF, *HANES, *MEMPHIS,

* NAPHTUHIM, * NILE, * ON, PATHROS, * PI-BESETH, * RA'AMSES, * THEBES, * ZOAN, *etc.*

Language. For details of, and bibliography on, the Egyp. language, see Sir A. H. Gardiner, *Egyptian Grammar*[3], 1957. For Coptic, see W. C. Till, *Koptische Grammatik*, 1955, and A. Mallon, *Grammaire Copte*, 1956, for full bibliography; in English, *cf.* C. C. Walters, *An Elementary Coptic Grammar*, 1972.

History. The standard work is É. Drioton and J. Vandier, *L'Égypte* (Collection '*Clio*')[4], 1962, with full discussions and bibliography. Valuable is J. A. Wilson, *The Burden of Egypt*, 1951, reprinted as a paperback, *The Culture of Ancient Egypt*, 1956. J. H. Breasted's *History of Egypt*, various dates, is now out of date, as is H. R. Hall's *Ancient History of the Near East*. See also A. H. Gardiner, *Egypt of the Pharaohs*, 1961; and esp. *CAH*[3], Vols. 1–3, 1970ff.

On Egyp. historical writings, see L. Bull in R. C. Dentan (ed.), *The Idea of History in the Ancient Near East*, 1955, pp. 3–34; C. de Wit, *EQ* 28, 1956, pp. 158–169.

On rival Egyp. priesthoods, see H. Kees, *Das Priestertum im Ägyptischen Staat*, 1953, pp. 78–88 and 62–69, also *Nachträge*, 1958; see also J. A. Wilson, *Burden of Egypt/Culture of Ancient Egypt*, ch. ix. Late Period, see K. A. Kitchen, *The Third Intermediate Period in Egypt (1100–650 BC)*[2], 1986, esp. Part IV.

On Egypt under Persian dominion, see F. K. Kienitz, *Die Politische Geschichte Ägyptens, vom 7. bis zum 4. Jahrhundert vor der Zeitwende*, 1953. For the Babylonian chronicle-tablets, see D. J. Wiseman, *Chronicles of Chaldaean Kings*, 1956. For a small but very important correction of Egyptian 26th Dynasty dates, see R. A. Parker, *Mitteilungen des Deutschen Archäologischen Instituts, Kairo Abteilung*, 15, 1957, pp. 208–212.

For Graeco-Roman Egypt, see *CAH*, later volumes; Sir H. I. Bell, *Egypt from Alexander the Great to the Arab Conquest*, 1948, and his *Cults and Creeds in Graeco-Roman Egypt*, 1953 and later edns.; W. H. Worrell, *A Short Account of the Copts*, 1945.

Literature. For literary works, *cf.* W. K. Simpson (ed.), *The Literature of Ancient Egypt*, 1972, and M. Lichtheim, *Ancient Egyptian Literature*, 1–3, 1973–80; many historical texts in J. H. Breasted, *Ancient Records of Egypt*, 5 vols., 1906/ 7. Considerable but abbreviated selections appear in *ANET*. Brilliant work in listing, identifying and restoring Egyp. literature is Posener's *Recherches Littéraires*, 1–7, in the *Revue d'Égyptologie* 6–12 (1949–60). Still valuable in its field is T. E. Peet, *A Comparative Study of the Literatures of Egypt, Palestine and Mesopotamia*, 1931.

Religion. For Egyptian religion, a convenient outline in English is J. Černý, *Ancient Egyptian Religion*, 1952; fuller detail and bibliography in J. Vandier, *La Religion Égyptienne*, 1949; *cf.* also S. Morenz, *Egyptian Religion*, 1973; G. Hart, *A Dictionary of Egyptian Gods and Goddesses*, 1986.

K.A.K.

EGYPT, RIVER OF. The correct identification of 'River of Egypt' is still uncertain; several distinct Heb. terms must be carefully distinguished. *y*e*'ôr miṣrayim*, 'river (= *Nile) of Egypt', refers exclusively to the Nile proper: its seasonal rise and fall being mentioned in Am. 8:8, and its upper Egyptian reaches in Is. 7:18 (plural). The term *n*e*har miṣrayim*, '(flowing) river of Egypt', occurs once only (Gn. 15:18), where by general definition the promised land lies between the two great rivers, Nile and Euphrates. These two terms (*y*e*'ôr/n*e*har miṣrayim*) are wholly separate from, and irrelevant to, the so-called 'river of Egypt' proper, the *naḥal miṣrayim* or 'torrent-wadi of Egypt'. The identification of this term, however, is bound up with that of Shihor, as will be evident from what now follows.

In the OT it is clearly seen that Shihor is a part of the Nile; see the parallelism of Shihor and *y*e*'ôr* (Nile) in Is. 23:3, and Shihor as Egypt's Nile corresponding to Assyria's great river (Euphrates) in Je. 2:18. Shihor is the extreme SW limit of territory yet to be occupied in Jos. 13:3 and from which Israelites could come to welcome the ark into Jerusalem in 1 Ch. 13:5, and Jos 13:3 specifies it as east of Egypt'. Hence Shihor is the lowest reaches of the easternmost of the Nile's ancient branches (the Pelusiac), flowing into the Mediterranean just W of Pelusium (Tell Farameh). This term Shihor is by origin Egyp. *š-ḥr*, 'waters of Horus'; the Egyptian references agree with the biblical location in so far as they mention Shihor's producing salt and rushes for the not-distant Delta-capital Pi-Ramessē (Tanis or Qantir) and as the 'river' of the 14th Lower-Egyptian nome (province); see R. A. Caminos, *Late-Egyptian Miscellanies*, 1954, pp. 74, 78 (his Menzalah-identification is erroneous), and especially A. H. Gardiner, *JEA* 5, 1918, pp. 251–252.

The real question is whether or not the *naḥal miṣrayim*, 'river (torrent-wadi) of Egypt', is the same as the Shihor, easternmost branch of the Nile.

Against the identification stands the fact that elsewhere in Scripture the Nile is never referred to as a *naḥal*. The river of Is. 11:15 is often taken to be the Euphrates (note the Assyro-Egyp. context here, especially v. 16), and the threat to smite it into seven *n*e*ḥālîm*, wadis traversable on foot, represents a transformation of (not the normal description for) the river concerned, whether Nile or Euphrates.

If the 'wadi of Egypt' is not the Nile, the best alternative is the Wadi el-'Arish, which runs N out of Sinai to the Mediterranean 145 km E of Egypt proper (Suez Canal) and 80 km W of Gaza in Palestine. In defence of this identification can be argued a perceptible change of terrain W and E from el-'Arish. Westward to Egypt there is only barren desert and slight scrub; eastward there are meadows and arable land (A. H. Gardiner, *JEA* 6, 1920, p. 115). Hence Wadi el-'Arish would be a practical boundary, including the usable land and excluding mere desert, in the specific delimitations of Nu. 34:5 and Jos. 15:4, 47 (*cf.* also Ezk. 47:19; 48:28). This is then simply echoed in 1 Ki. 8:65 (= 2 Ch. 7:8); 2 Ki. 24:7 and Is. 27:12. Jos. 13:3 and 1 Ch. 13:5 would then indicate the uttermost SW limit (Shihor) of Israelite activity (*cf.* above). Sargon II and Esarhaddon of Assyria also mention the Wadi or Brook of Egypt in their texts. In 716 BC Sargon reached the 'Brook (or Wadi) of Egypt' (*naḥal muṣur*), 'opened the sealed harbour of Egypt' mingling Assyrians and Egyptians for trade purposes, and mentioning 'the border of the City of the Brook of Egypt', where he appointed a governor. Alarmed by the Assyr. activity, the shadow-pharaoh Osorkon IV sent a diplomatic present of '12 big horses' to Sargon (H. Tadmor, *JCS* 12, 1958, pp. 34, 78). All this fits well with *naḥal muṣur*

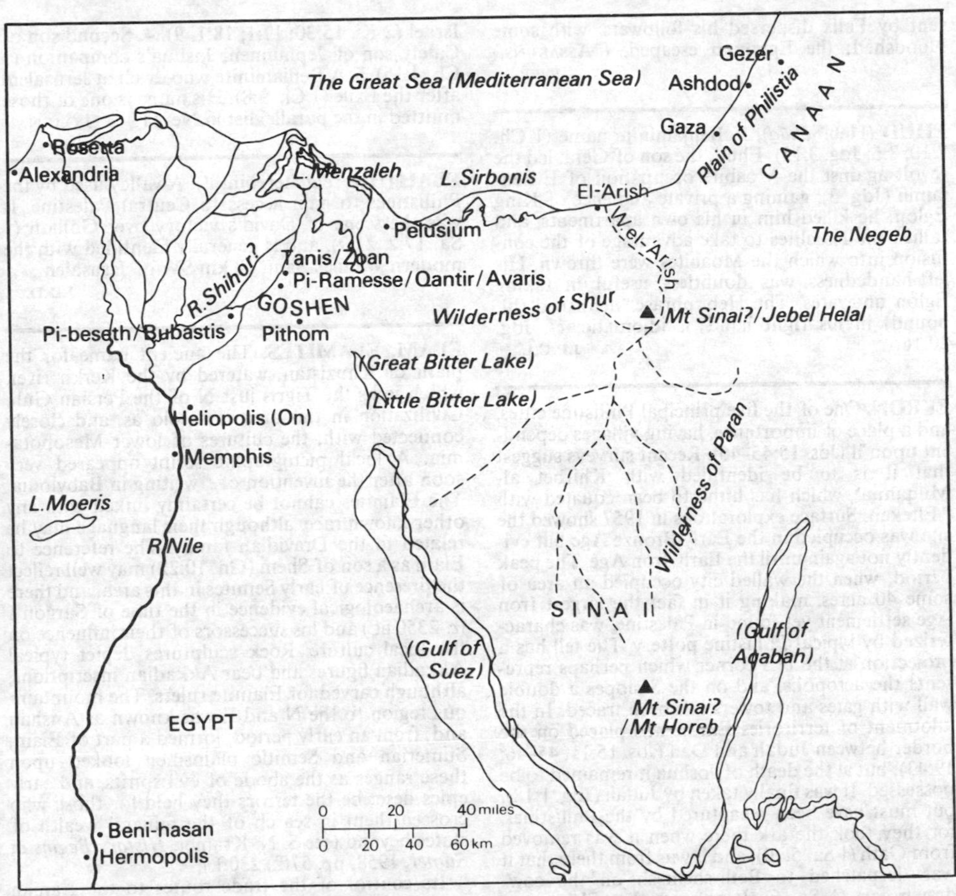

Egypt, showing the Wadi el-'Arish and the river Shihor, both possible identifications with the 'River of Egypt'.

being Wadi el-'Arish and the 'City' there being the settlement El-'Arish, Assyr. *Arzâ* (Tadmor, *art. cit.*, p. 78, note 194, with further bibliography on 'River of Egypt').

One or two points apparently favouring the alternative view, *viz.* that the 'Wadi of Egypt' is the Shihor/Pelusiac Nile-arm, must, however, not be overlooked. Many are inclined to equate precisely the terms of Jos. 13:3, Shihor, and Nu. 34:5, Jos. 15:4, 47 (likewise 1 Ki. 8:65 and 1 Ch. 13:5), *naḥal miṣrayim*, making Wadi of Egypt another name of the Shihor-Nile. But this would make no allowance for different nuances in the Scripture texts concerned as outlined above. Further, it is true that Sargon II could well have reached the Pelusiac (easternmost) arm of the Nile; his 'City' there would then be Pelusium—which would most decidedly alarm Osorkon IV. But the 'City' is certainly the Arza(ni) of Esarhaddon's inscriptions (*ANET*, pp. 290–292, *passim*) which corresponds well to 'Arish but not Pelusium (Egyp. *sinw*, *swn*). Finally, Egyptians and the 19th Dynasty evidently regarded the Pelusiac area as *de facto* the edge of Egypt proper: in Papyrus Anastasi III, 1: 10, Ḥuru (Palestine generally) extends 'from Silē to 'Upa (= Damascus)'; Silē ('Thel') is modern Qantara a few km S and E of the former Pelusiac Nile-arm (R. A. Caminos, *Late-Egyptian Miscellanies*, pp. 69, 73 and refs.). But this proves nothing about Israel's boundaries; as already mentioned, from Qantara to 'Arish is a desolate no-man's-land. In any case, 19th-Dynasty Egypt did assert authority and maintain wells across the entire coast-strip, Qantara–'Arish–Gaza (see A. H. Gardiner, *JEA* 6, 1920, pp. 99–116, on the military road here). The Shihor/Nile identification of the Wadi of Egypt has been advocated by H. Bar-Deroma, *PEQ* 92, 1960, pp. 37–56, but he takes no account of the contemporary Egyp. and Assyr. sources, the post-biblical matter cited being imprecise and of too late a date. The subject is not closed, but Wadi el- 'Arish is more likely to be the 'River (Wadi) of Egypt' than is the E Nile on present evidence. K.A.K.

EGYPTIAN, THE. In Acts 21:38 an agitator for whom the Roman officer commanding the Antonia fortress mistook Paul when the latter was set upon in the Temple precincts. According to Josephus (*BJ* 2. 261–263; *Ant*. 20. 169–172), this Egyptian came to Jerusalem *c.* AD 54, claiming to be a prophet, and led a great multitude to the Mount of Olives, promising that, at his command, the city walls would collapse before them. Soldiers sent by Felix dispersed his followers, with some bloodshed; the Egyptian escaped. (*ASSASSINS.)

F.F.B.

EHUD (Heb. *'ēhûḏ*). A Benjaminite name (1 Ch. 7:10; 8:6; Jdg. 3:15). Ehud, the son of Gera, led the revolt against the Moabite occupation of E Benjamin (Jdg. 3); gaining a private audience of King Eglon, he killed him in his own apartments, and rallied the Israelites to take advantage of the confusion into which the Moabites were thrown. His left-handedness was doubtless useful in taking Eglon unawares. The Heb. phrase 'deformed (lit. bound) in his right hand' is idiomatic; *cf.* Jdg. 20:16.

J.P.U.L.

EKRON. One of the five principal Philistine cities, and a place of importance, having villages dependent upon it (Jos. 15:45–46). Recent surveys suggest that it is to be identified with Khirbet al-Muqanna', which has hitherto been equated with *Eltekeh. Surface explorations in 1957 showed the site was occupied in the Early Bronze Age but evidently not again until the Early Iron Age. The peak period, when the walled city occupied an area of some 40 acres, making it in fact the largest Iron Age settlement yet found in Palestine, was characterized by typical Philistine pottery. The tell has a projection at the NE corner which perhaps represents the acropolis, and on the S slopes a double wall with gates and towers has been traced. In the allotment of territories Ekron was placed on the border between Judah and Dan (Jos. 15:11, 45–46; 19:43), but at the death of Joshua it remained to be possessed. It was finally taken by Judah (Jdg. 1:18), but must have been recaptured by the Philistines, for they took the ark there when it was removed from Gath (1 Sa. 5:10), and it was from there that it was despatched to Beth-shemesh on the cow-drawn cart (1 Sa. 6). It appears that Ekron was again temporarily in Israelite hands in the time of Samuel (1 Sa. 7:14), but the Philistines had retaken it by Saul's time (1 Sa. 17:52), and it was still held by them in the time of Amos (1:8). In 701 BC Padi the ruler of Ekron, a vassal of the Assyrians, was expelled by certain Ekronites and held captive by Hezekiah in Jerusalem, but Sennacherib, in his campaign of the year, retook Ekron (*am-qar-ru-na*) and restored Padi (*ANET*, pp. 287–288; *DOTT*, pp. 66–67). The city is mentioned in the Annals of Esarhaddon as tributary (*ANET*, p. 291; *DOTT*, p. 74), but was still at that time regarded as a Philistine city from the ethnic point of view (Je. 25:20; Zp. 2:4; Zc. 9:5, 7). The Bible is not concerned with the subsequent history of the city, though the name of the city god, *Baal-zebub (2 Ki. 1:2–3), is familiar from the NT.

BIBLIOGRAPHY. *NEAEHL*, pp. 1051–1059; Y. Aharoni, *PEQ* 90, 1958, pp. 27–31; Honigmann, *Reallexikon der Assyriologie*, 1, 1932, p. 99; T. C. Mitchell in *AOTS*, pp. 405–406.

T.C.M.

ELAH (Heb. *'ēlâ*, 'terebinth'). **1.** A tribal prince of Edom (Gn. 36:41; 1 Ch. 1:52), perhaps the chief of the district of Elah, possibly the seaport of *Elath. **2.** Son of Baasha, and king of Israel for 2 years until he was assassinated by Zimri during a drunken orgy in the house of Arza, his steward (1 Ki. 16:6–14). **3.** Father of Hoshea, the last king of Israel (2 Ki. 15:30; 17:1; 18:1, 9). **4.** Second son of Caleb, son of Jephunneh, Joshua's companion (1 Ch. 4:15). **5.** A Benjaminite who dwelt at Jerusalem after the Exile (1 Ch. 9:8). His name is one of those omitted in the parallel list in Ne. 11.

J.G.G.N.

ELAH (Heb. *'ēlâ*, 'terebinth'). A valley used by the Philistines to gain access to Central Palestine. It was the scene of David's victory over Goliath (1 Sa. 17:2; 21:9), and is generally identified with the modern Wadi es-Sant, 18 km SW of Jerusalem.

J.D.D.

ELAM, ELAMITES. The ancient name for the plain of Khuzistan, watered by the Kerkh river, which joins the Tigris just N of the Persian Gulf. Civilization in this area is as old as, and closely connected with, the cultures of lower Mesopotamia. A local pictographic script appeared very soon after the invention of *writing in Babylonia. The Elamites cannot be certainly linked with any other known race, although their language may be related to the Dravidian family. The reference to Elam as a son of Shem (Gn. 10:22) may well reflect the presence of early Semites in this area, and there is archaeological evidence in the time of Sargon I (*c.* 2350 BC) and his successors of their influence on the local culture. Rock sculptures depict typical Akkadian figures and bear Akkadian inscriptions, although carved for Elamite rulers. The mountainous region to the N and E was known as Anshan and, from an early period, formed a part of Elam. Sumerian and Semitic plainsmen looked upon these ranges as the abode of evil spirits, and early epics describe the terrors they held for those who crossed them in search of the mineral wealth of states beyond (see S. N. Kramer, *History Begins at Sumer*, 1958, pp. 57ff., 230ff.).

Its control of the trade routes to the Iranian plateau, and to the SE, made Elam the object of constant attacks from the plains of Mesopotamia. These in turn offered great wealth to any conqueror. A strong Elamite dynasty, a king being succeeded by his brother, then his son, arose about 2000 BC and gained control of several cities in Babylonia, destroying the power of the Sumerian rulers of Ur and sacking it (see *ANET*, pp. 455ff., 480f.). To this period of Elamite supremacy should *Chedorlaomer probably be assigned (Gn. 14:1). Hammurapi of Babylon drove the Elamites out *c.* 1760 BC, but the 'Amorite' dynasty, to which he belonged, fell before Hittite and Elamite attacks *c.* 1595 BC. Invasions of Kassites coming from the central Zagros mountains (*BABYLONIA) drove the Elamites back to Susa, until a resurgence of power enabled them to conquer and rule Babylon for several centuries (*c.* 1300–1120 BC). Among trophies taken to Susa at this time was the famous Law stele of Hammurapi. Elamite history is obscure from *c.* 1000 BC until the campaigns of Sargon of Assyria (*c.* 721–705 BC). Sennacherib and Ashurbanipal subjected the Elamites and deported some of them to Samaria, taking Israelites to Elam (Ezr. 4:9; Is. 11:11).

After the collapse of *Assyria, Elam was annexed by the Indo-Europeans, who had gradually gained power in Iran following their invasions *c.* 1000 BC. Teispes (*c.* 675–640 BC), ancestor of Cyrus, bore the title 'king of Anshan' and Susa eventually became one of the three chief cities of the Medo-Persian empire.

Elam is called upon by Isaiah to crush Babylon (Is. 21:2) and this was carried out (*cf.* Dn. 8:2). Yet Elam will be crushed in turn, even the famous archers defeated (Je. 25:25; 49:34–39; *cf.* Is. 22:6; Ezk. 32:24). The crowd at Pentecost (Acts 2:9) contained men from as far away as Elam, presumably members of Jewish communities who had remained in exile in the semi-autonomous state of Elymais, though using Aramaic, the last flicker of Elamite independence. (*ARCHAEOLOGY, *MEDES, *PERSIA, *SUSA.)

BIBLIOGRAPHY. W. Hinz, *The Lost World of Elam*, 1972; E. Porada, *Ancient Iran*, 1965.

A.R.M.

ELATH (ELOTH), EZION-GEBER. In the biblical sources there are three phases in the history of these places. First, as stations along the route of the Israelites moving from the Sinai wilderness (its E side) up to Qadesh-Barnea (Nu. 33:35–36; Dt. 2:8). Ezion-Geber *and* Elath are mentioned as two entities. Second, Ezion-Geber appears alone in the 10th–9th centuries BC as the port from which Solomon, in alliance with Hiram of Tyre, sent fleets out to Ophir and elsewhere (1 Ki. 9:22; 2 Ch. 8:17), and at which the ships of Jehoshaphat's planned expedition were wrecked (1 Ki. 22:48; 2 Ch. 20:36–37). Third, Elath/Eloth reappears in the 8th century BC, when Azariah (Uzziah) of Judah captured it and rebuilt it (2 Ki. 14:22), only for Ahaz to lose it to the Edomites up to 40 years later, under Aramean pressure (2 Ki. 16:6). The main site of Elath was placed at later Aila (about 1 km NE of Aqaba) by Robinson (*Bibilical Researches in Palestine* I, 1841, 241).

Some 4 km further W, Frank noted and Nelson Glueck dug an ancient site, Tell el-Kheleifeh, which both identified as Ezion-Geber. Glueck went further by identifying the main building within the fortress as a copper-smelting station, and assumed the sea had once been further N than now (*cf.* his *Other Side of the Jordan*, 1970, pp. 103–137), but, under later criticism, he modified his views somewhat (*BASOR* 179, 1965, pp. 15–17), but still identified as one site what the Bible gave as two.

Recent work leads to much more radical conclusions. Tell el-Kheleifeh may never have been a port. Some 20 km to the SW, along the Sinai side of the Gulf of Aqaba, study of the little island, Jazirat Faraun, suggests that it would be a better location for Ezion-Geber. The island itself has an inner harbour. The strait between it is a suitably sheltered mooring for ancient shipping and there are traces of ancient quays running out from the shore (*cf.* A. Flinder, *BAR* 15/4, 1989, pp. 30–43). This would provide a suitable starting-point for the enterprises of Solomon and (failed) Jehoshaphat.

A re-study of the excavations of Tell Kheleifeh was made by G. Pratico (initially *BA* 45, 1982, pp. 120–121; *BASOR* 259, 1985, pp. 1–32; *cf. BAR* 12/5, 1986, pp. 24–35; full report, G. D. Pratico, *Nelson Glueck's* 1938–1940 *Excavations at Tell el-Kheleifeh: A Reappraisal*, 1993). As a result, the history of the site extends only to the 8th–4th centuries BC, not back to the 10th (as Glueck had thought). It had two main phases: an official building within a rectangular casemate-wall precinct, and then a fort and buildings within a larger precinct with offsets in the wall. It is conceivable that this site represented the Elath captured and rebuilt by Azariah (casemate level I), then lost to the Edomites and rebuilt by them (fort, levels II-IV). But if the real Elath was just further E, then this site would have been a satellite of Elath proper, whoever built it. Certainly it later belonged to the Edomites, witness the seal-impressions of an official Quas-anal. Phase V belonged to the Persian period (5th–4th centuries BC). K.A.K.

ELDAD (Heb. 'God has loved'). An Israelite elder, associated with Medad in Nu. 11:26–30; perhaps to be identified with Elidad (Nu. 34:21). He and Medad failed to appear at the tabernacle of the congregation when summoned there with the seventy elders by Moses. They nevertheless shared in the gift of prophecy which the elders received from the Lord. Far from forbidding this apparently irregular display of divine power, Moses rejoiced and wished that all the Lord's people might become prophets. Such ecstatic behaviour was a significant feature of early OT *prophecy.

J.B.Tr.

ELDER. In most civilizations authority has been vested in those who by reason of age or experience have been thought best qualified to rule. It is not surprising therefore that the leaders in many ancient communities have borne a title derived from a root meaning 'old age'. In this respect the Heb. 'elder' (*zāqēn*) stands side by side with the Homeric *gerontes*, the Spartan *presbys*, the Roman *senatus* and the Arab *sheikh*.

In thc Pentateuch elders are referred to among the Egyptians (Gn. 50:7) and the Moabites and Midianites (Nu. 22:7), as well as among the Israelites. In Ex. 3:16 the Israelites are represented as having had elders from the time of the Egyptian captivity, and it is with them that Moses is commanded to collaborate in his bid for freedom. They were probably the heads of families in the first instance, but Ex. 24:1 gives a fixed number of seventy. It was upon this inner circle of seventy elders that the Lord poured out the spirit in order that they should share the government of the people with Moses (Nu. 11:25).

After the wilderness period every city seems to have had its own ruling body of elders whose duties, according to Deuteronomic legislation, included acting as judges in apprehending murderers (Dt. 19:12), conducting inquests (Dt. 21:2) and settling matrimonial disputes (Dt. 22:15; 25:7). If theirs was a city of refuge they also heard pleas for asylum (Jos. 20:4; but see also Nu. 35:24). Their numbers varied, Succoth having seventy-seven (Jdg. 8:14), and they are associated with other civil officials, *e.g.* heads of tribes (Dt. 5:23; 29:10) and officers and judges (Jos. 8:33). Maybe the term 'elders' was a general word for the ruling body and included some of these officials.

The national body of 'elders of Israel' still exercised considerable influence under the Monarchy as the chieftains of the people, having first agitated for the appointment of a king (1 Sa. 8:4f.) and having finally accepted David (2 Sa. 5:3). Their position and influence were recognized by Solomon (1 Ki. 8:1, 3), Ahab (1 Ki. 20:7), Jezebel (1 Ki. 21:8), Jehu (2 Ki. 10:1), Hezekiah (2 Ki. 19:2) and Josiah (2 Ki. 23:1). Ezekiel in captivity dealt with them (Ezk. 8:1; 14:1; 20:1), and they appear also in Ezra's time and in the Gk. period. While their authority was originally civil, by NT times the 'elders of the people' (*presbyteroi tou laou*) shared with the chief priests the power of determining religious affairs and, if necessary, of expulsion from the *synagogue. See also *Sanhedrin and (for NT use) *Presbyter. J.B.Tr.

ELEALEH (Heb. *'el'ālēh*, 'God is exalted'). A town E of Jordan always mentioned in conjunction with Heshbon. Conquered by Gad and Reuben (Nu. 32:3), rebuilt by the latter tribe (32:37), and later Moabite, it was the subject of prophetic warnings (Is. 15:4; 16:9; Je. 48:34). Identified with the modern el-'Al, 4 km NE of Heshbon. J.D.D.

ELEAZAR. The name (meaning 'God has helped') of a number of OT figures. In all but a few cases (1 Sa. 7:1; 2 Sa. 23:9–10 *(*1 Ch. 11:12*)*; 1 Ch. 23:21–22; 24:28; Ezr. 8:33; 10:25; Ne. 12:42; Mt. 1:15) Eleazar the third son of *Aaron, whom he succeeded as chief priest (Nu. 20:25–28; Dt. 10:6), is meant. Even before his father's death he is represented as having an important position in the priestly hierarchy (Nu. 3:32; 4:16; 16:37–40; 19:3–4), which resulted from the punishment of his elder brothers Nadab and Abihu (Lv. 10:1–2). As chief priest he is frequently mentioned alongside Moses or Joshua as a leader of the Israelites (*e.g.* Nu. 26:1; Jos. 14:1).

Most references in the OT are either in what some scholars call the 'priestly' sections of the Pentateuch (see below) or in the work of the Chronicler. In post-exilic times 'the sons of Eleazar' formed one of the two main divisions of the full priesthood, 'the sons of Aaron' (1 Ch. 24:4–6; in Ezr. 8:2 his son Phinehas appears as the ancestor of the group). Since Zadok was at this time regarded as a descendant of Eleazar (1 Ch. 6:1–8, 50–53; 24:3), it appears that the high priesthood was held by members of this division. Ezra was an important member of it (Ezr. 7:5). It is widely thought that the tradition about Eleazar was developed in priestly circles to safeguard the exclusive privileges of this group, who have been the descendants of the priests who officiated in Jerusalem before the Exile (*cf.* Cody). If this were correct, it would affect the way in which the relevant texts are understood. But that Aaron did have a son Eleazar who followed him in his priestly office and had a son called Phinehas is firmly established on the basis of older texts (Dt. 10:6; Jos. 24:33 and (?) Jdg. 20:28). According to Jos. 24:33 he was buried at Gibeah in the land of Ephraim.

BIBLIOGRAPHY. *IDB*, 2, pp. 75–76; A. Cody, *A History of Old Testament Priesthood*, 1969, pp. 171–174. G.I.D.

ELECTION. The act of choice whereby God picks an individual or group out of a larger company for a purpose or destiny of his own appointment. The main OT word for this is the verb *bāḥar*, which expresses the idea of deliberately selecting someone or something after carefully considering the alternatives (*e.g.* sling-stones, 1 Sa. 17:40; a place of refuge, Dt. 23:16; a wife, Gn. 6:2; good rather than evil, Is. 7:15f.; life rather than death, Dt. 30:19f.; the service of God rather than of idols, Jos. 24:22). The word implies a decided preference for, sometimes positive pleasure in, the object chosen (*cf.*, *e.g.*, Is. 1:29). In LXX and the NT the corresponding verb is *eklegomai. eklegō* is commonly active in classical Gk., but the biblical writers always use it in the middle voice, with reflexive overtones: it thus means 'choose out for oneself'. *haireomai* is used synonymously of God's choice in 2 Thes. 2:13, as in Dt. 26:18, LXX. The cognate adjectives are Heb. *bāḥîr* and Gk. *eklektos*, translated 'elect' or 'chosen'; the NT also uses the noun *eklogē*, 'election'. The Heb. verb *yāḏa'*, 'know', which is used of various acts of knowing that, in idea at least, imply and express affection (*e.g.* relations between the sexes, and the believer's acknowledgment of God), is used to denote God's election (*i.e.* his taking cognizance of persons in love) in Gn. 18:19 (see RV); Am. 3:2; Ho. 13:5. The Gk. *proginōskō*, 'foreknow', is similarly used in Rom. 8:29; 11:2 to mean 'forelove' (*cf.* also the use of *ginōskō* in 1 Cor. 8:3 and Gal. 4:9).

I. Old Testament usage

Israelite faith was founded on the belief that Israel was God's chosen people. His choice of her had been made by means of two connected and complementary acts. (*a*) He chose Abraham and his seed, by taking Abraham out of Ur and bringing him to the promised land of Canaan, making there an everlasting covenant with him and his descendants, and promising him that his seed should be a blessing to all the earth (Gn. 11:31–12:7; 15; 17; 22:15–18; Ne. 9:7; Is. 41:8). (*b*) He chose Abraham's seed by redeeming them from slavery in Egypt, bringing them out of bondage under Moses, renewing the Abrahamic covenant with them in an amplified form at Sinai and setting them in the promised land as their national home (Ex. 3:6–10; Dt. 6:21–23; Ps. 105). Each of these acts of choice is also described as God's call, *i.e.* a sovereign utterance of words and disposal of events by which God summoned, in the one case, Abraham, and in the other, Abraham's seed, to acknowledge him as their God and live to him as his people (Is. 51:2; Ho. 11:1; *CALL). Israelite faith looked back to these two acts as having created the nation (*cf.* Is. 43:1; Acts 13:17).

The meaning of Israel's election appears from the following facts:

a. Its *source* was God's free omnipotent love. Moses' speeches in Deuteronomy stress this. When he chose Israel, God 'set his love on' Israel (Dt. 7:7; 23:5): why? Not because Israel first chose him, nor because Israel deserved his favour. Israel was in fact the reverse of attractive, being neither numerous nor righteous, but feeble, small and rebellious (Dt. 7:7; 9:4–6). God's love to Israel was spontaneous and free, exercised in defiance of demerit, having no cause save his own good pleasure. He made it his delight and satisfaction to do Israel good (Dt. 28:63; *cf.* 30:9) simply because he resolved to do so. It was true that in delivering Israel from Egypt he was keeping a promise made to the Patriarchs (Dt. 7:8), and there was a necessity of the divine character in that, for it is God's nature always to be faithful to his promises (*cf.* Nu. 23:19; 2 Tim. 2:13); but the making of this promise had itself been an act of free unmerited love, for the Patriarchs were themselves sinners (as Gn. is at pains to show), and God chose Abraham, the first recipient of the promise, out of idolatry (Jos. 24:2f.). Here too, therefore, the cause of election must be sought, not in man, but in God.

God is King in his world, and his love is omnipotent. Accordingly, he implemented his choice of

Israel by means of a miraculous deliverance (by 'a mighty hand', Dt. 7:8, *etc*.) out of a state of helpless captivity. Ezk. 16:3–6 dwells on Israel's pitiable condition when God chose her; Ps. 135:4–12 extols his display of sovereignty in bringing his chosen people out of bondage into the promised land.

b. The *goal* of Israel's election was, proximately, the blessing and salvation of the people through God's separating them for himself (Ps. 33:12), and, ultimately, God's own glory through Israel's showing forth his praise to the world (Is. 43:20f.; *cf.* Pss. 79:13; 96:1–10), and bearing witness of the great things he had done (Is. 43:10–12; 44:8). Israel's election involved separation. By it, God made Israel a holy people, *i.e.* one set apart for himself (Dt. 7:6; Lv. 20:26b). He took them as his inheritance (Dt. 4:20; 32:9–12) and treasure (Ex. 19:5; Ps. 135:4), promising to protect and prosper them (Dt. 28:1–14), and to dwell with them (Lv. 26:11f.). Election made them his people, and him their God, in covenant together. It had in view living communion between them and him. Their destiny, as his chosen people, was to enjoy his manifested presence in their midst and to receive the multitude of good gifts which he promised to shower upon them. Their election was thus an act of blessing which was the fount of all other blessings. Hence the prophets express the hope that God would restore his people and presence to Jerusalem after the Exile, and re-establish conditions of blessing there, by saying that God will again 'choose' Israel and Jerusalem (Is. 14:1; Zc. 1:17; 2:12; *cf.* 3:2).

c. The *religious and ethical obligations* created by Israel's election were far-reaching. Election, and the covenant relationship based on it, which distinguished Israel from all other nations, was a motive to grateful praise (Ps. 147:19f.), loyal keeping of God's law (Lv. 18:4f.) and resolute nonconformity to the idolatry and wrongdoing of the unelected world (Lv. 18:2f.; 20:22f.; Dt. 14:1f.; Ezk. 20:5–7, *etc.*). Also, it gave Israel grounds for unfaltering hope and trust in God in times of distress and discouragement (*cf.* Is. 41:8–14; 44:1f.; Hg. 2:23; Ps. 106:4f.). Irreligious Israelites, however, were betrayed by the thought of the national election into complacently despising other nations, and assuming that they could always rely on God for protection and preferential treatment, no matter what their own lives were like (*cf.* Mi. 3:11; Je. 5:12). It was this delusion, and in particular the idea that Jerusalem, as the city of God, was inviolable, that the false prophets fostered in the days before the Exile (Je. 7:1–15; 23:9f.; Ezk. 13). In fact, however, as God had made plain from the first (Lv. 26:14ff.; Dt. 28:15ff.), national election implied a strict judgment of national sins (Am. 3:2). The Exile proved that God's threats had not been idle.

d. Within the chosen people, *God chose individuals for specific tasks* designed to further the purpose of the national election—*i.e.* Israel's own enjoyment of God's blessing, and, ultimately, the blessing of the world. God chose Moses (Ps. 106:23), Aaron (Ps. 105:26), the priests (Dt. 18:5), the prophets (*cf.* Je. 1:5), the kings (1 Sa. 10:24; 2 Sa. 6:21; 1 Ch. 28:5), and the Servant-Saviour of Isaiah's prophecy ('my elect', Is. 42:1; *cf.* 49:1, 5), who suffers persecution (Is. 50:5ff.), dies for sins (Is. 53) and brings the Gentiles light (Is. 42:1–7; 49:6). God's use of Assyria and 'my servant' Nebuchadrezzar as his scourges (Is. 7:18ff.; 10:5ff.; Je. 25:9; 27:6; 43:10), and of Cyrus, a man ignorant of God, as a benefactor to the chosen people (Is. 45:4), is termed by H. H. Rowley 'election without covenant' (*The Biblical Doctrine of Election*, 1950, ch. 5), but the phrase is improper; the Bible always reserves the vocabulary of election for the covenant people and covenant functionaries drawn from Israel's own ranks.

e. The promised blessings of election were *forfeited through unbelief and disobedience.* The prophets, facing widespread hypocrisy, insisted that God would reject the ungodly among his people (Je. 6:30; 7:29). Isaiah foretold that only a faithful remnant would live to enjoy the golden age that was to follow the inevitable judgment on Israel's sins (Is. 10:20–22; 4:3; 27:6; 37:31f.). Jeremiah and Ezekiel, living in the time of that judgment, looked for a day when God, as part of his work of restoration, would regenerate such of his people as he had spared, and ensure their covenant faithfulness for the future by giving each of them a new heart (Je. 31:31ff.; 32:39f.; Ezk. 11:19f.; 36:25ff.). These prophecies, with their focus on individual piety, pointed to an individualizing of the concept of election (*cf.* Ps. 65:4): they gave grounds for distinguishing between election to privilege and election to life, and for concluding that, while God had chosen the whole nation for the privilege of living under the covenant, he had chosen only some of them (those made faithful by regeneration) to inherit the riches of the relationship to himself which the covenant held out, while the rest forfeited those riches by their unbelief. The NT teaching about election assumes these distinctions; see especially Rom. 9.

II. New Testament usage

The NT announces the extension of God's covenant-promises to the Gentile world and the transference of covenant-privileges from the lineal seed of Abraham to a predominantly Gentile body (*cf.* Mt. 21:43) consisting of all who had become Abraham's true seed and God's true Israel through faith in Christ (Rom. 4:9–18; 9:6f.; Gal. 3:14ff., 29; 6:16; Eph. 2:11ff.; 3:6–8). The unbelieving natural branches were broken off from God's olive-tree (the elect community, sprung from the Patriarchs), and wild olive branches (believing Gentiles) were ingrafted in their place (Rom. 11:16–24). Faithless Israel was rejected and judged, and the international Christian church took Israel's place as God's chosen nation, living in the world as his people and worshipping and proclaiming him as their God.

The NT presents the idea of election in the following forms:

a. Jesus is hailed as God's elect one by the Father himself (Lk. 9:35, reading *eklelegmenos*, an echo of Is. 42:1), and probably by John the Baptist (Jn. 1:34, if *eklektos* is the right reading; see Barrett *ad loc.*). The sneer of Lk. 23:35 shows that 'the elect one' was used as a Messianic designation in Christ's day (as it is in the book of *Enoch*, 40:5; 45:3–5, *etc.*). In 1 Pet. 2:4, 6 Christ is called God's elect corner-stone; this echoes Is. 28:16, LXX. In reference to Christ, the designation 'points to the unique and distinctive office with which he is invested and to the peculiar delight which God the Father takes in him' (J. Murray in *Baker's Dictionary of Theology*, 1960, p. 179).

b. The adjective 'elect' denotes the Christian community in its character as the chosen people of God, in contrast with the rest of mankind. This usage simply echoes the OT. The church is 'an elect race' (1 Pet. 2:9, quoting Is. 43:20; *cf.* also 2 Jn. 1, 13), having the privileges of access to God and the responsibilities of praising and proclaiming him, and faithfully guarding his truth, which Israel had had before. As in the case of Israel, God had magnified his mercy by choosing poor and undistinguished persons for this momentous destiny (1 Cor. 1:27ff.; Jas. 2:5; *cf.* Dt. 7:7; 9:6); and, as before, God's gracious choice and call had created a people—his people—which had no existence as a people before (1 Pet. 2:10; Rom. 9:25f., citing Ho. 1:10; 2:23).

In the Synoptics Christ refers to the *eklektoi* (pl.) in various eschatological contexts. They are those whom God accepts, and will accept, because they have responded to the gospel invitation and come to the wedding-feast stripped of self-righteousness and clad in the wedding-garment provided by the host, *i.e.* trusting in God's mercy (Mt. 22:14). God will vindicate them (Lk. 18:7) and keep them through coming tribulation and peril (Mk. 13:20, 22), for they are the objects of his special care.

c. eklegomai is used of Christ's choice of his apostles (Lk. 6:13; *cf.* Acts 1:24; 9:15) and the church's choice of deacons (Acts 6:5) and delegates (Acts 15:22, 25). This is election to special service from among the ranks of the elect community, as in the OT. Christ's choosing of the Twelve for apostolic office involved the choosing of them out of the world to enjoy salvation (*cf.* Jn. 15:16, 19), except in the case of Judas (*cf.* Jn. 13:18).

III. Theological development in NT

The complete theological development of the idea of election is found in Paul's Epistles (see especially Rom. 8:28–11:36; Eph. 1:3–14; 1 Thes. 1:2–10; 2 Thes. 2:13–14; 2 Tim. 1:9–10). Paul presents divine election as a gracious, sovereign, eternal choice of individual sinners to be saved and glorified in and through Christ.

a. Election is a *gracious* choice. Election 'by grace' (Rom. 11:5; *cf.* 2 Tim. 1:9) is an act of undeserved favour freely shown towards members of a fallen race to which God owed nothing but wrath (Rom. 1:18ff.). And not only does God choose sinners to save (*cf.* Rom. 4:5; 5:6–8; Eph. 2:1–9); he chooses to save them in a way which exalts his grace by magnifying their sinfulness. He shuts up his elect, both Jew and Gentile, in a state of disobedience and unbelief, so that they display their true character as sinners, and stand out in history confessed as unbelievers, before he shows them his mercy (Rom. 11:30–32; the Gentiles, 9:30; 10:20; the Jews, 10:19, 21; 11:11, 25f. ['so' in v. 26 means 'through the coming in of the Gentiles']). Thus the outworking of election further exhibits the gratuitousness of grace.

b. Election is a *sovereign* choice, prompted by God's own good pleasure alone (Eph. 1:5, 9), and not by any works of man, accomplished or foreseen (Rom. 9:11), or any human efforts to win God's favour (Rom. 9:15–18). Such efforts would in any case be vain, for however high sinners aspire and however fast they run, they still in reality only sin (Rom. 8:7f.). God in sovereign freedom treats some sinners as they deserve, hardening (Rom. 9:18; 11:7–10, *cf.* 1:28; 1 Thes. 2:15f.) and destroying them (Rom. 9:21f.); but he selects others to be 'vessels of mercy', receiving 'the riches of his glory' (Rom. 9:23). This discrimination involves no injustice, for the Creator owes mercy to none, and has a right to do as he pleases with his rebellious creatures (Rom. 9:14–21). The wonder is not that he withholds mercy from some, but that he should be gracious to any. God's purpose of sovereign discrimination between sinner and sinner appeared as early as his limitation of the Abrahamic promise to Isaac's line and his setting of Jacob over Esau (Rom. 9:7–13). It was true from the first that 'not all who are descended from Israel belong to Israel' (Rom. 9:6), and that those Israelites who actually enjoyed the salvation promised to the chosen people were only 'a remnant, chosen by grace' (Rom. 11:5; 9:27–29). And it remains true, according to Paul, that it is God's sovereign election alone that explains why, when the gospel is preached, some do in fact respond to it. The unbelief of the rest requires no special explanation, for no sinner, left to himself, can believe (1 Cor. 2:14); but the phenomenon of faith needs explaining. Paul's explanation is that God by his Spirit causes the elect to believe, so that when men come to a true and active faith in Christ it proves their election to be a reality (1 Thes. 1:4ff.; Tit. 1:1; *cf.* Acts 13:48).

c. Election is an *eternal* choice. God chose us, says Paul, 'before the foundation of the world' (Eph. 1:4; 2 Thes. 2:13; 2 Tim. 1:9). This choice was an act of *predestination (Eph. 1:5, 11), a part of God's eternal purpose (Eph. 1:9), an exercise of loving foreknowledge whereby God determined to save those whom he foreknew (Rom. 8:29f.; *cf.* 1 Pet. 1:2). Whereas the OT, dealing with the national election to privilege, equates God's choosing with his calling, Paul, dealing with personal election to salvation, distinguishes the choice from the call, and speaks of God's calling (by which he means a summons to faith which effectively evokes a response) as a stage in the temporal execution of an eternal purpose of love (Rom. 8:30; 9:23f.; 2 Thes. 2:13f.; 2 Tim. 1:9). Paul stresses that election is eternal in order to assure his readers that it is immutable, and nothing that happens in time can shake God's resolve to save them.

d. Election is a choice of individual sinners to be saved *in and through Christ.* Election is 'in Christ' (see Eph. 1:4), the incarnate Son, whose historical appearing and mediation were themselves included in God's eternal plan (1 Pet. 1:20; Acts 2:23). Election in Christ means, first, that the goal of election is that God's chosen should bear Christ's image and share his glory (Rom. 8:29, *cf.* v. 17; 2 Thes. 2:14). They are chosen for holiness (which means Christlikeness in all their conduct) in this life (Eph. 1:4), and glorification (which means Christlikeness in all their being, *cf.* 2 Cor. 3:18; Phil. 3:21) in the life to come. Election in Christ means, second, that the elect are to be redeemed from the guilt and stain of sin by Christ, through his atoning death and the gift of his Spirit (Eph. 5:25–27; 2 Thes. 2:13; *cf.* 1 Pet. 1:2). As he himself said, the Father has given him a certain number of persons to save, and he has undertaken to do everything necessary to bring them all to eternal glory (Jn. 6:37–45; 10:14–16, 27–30; 17:2, 6, 9ff., 24). Election in Christ means, third, that the means whereby the blessings of election are brought to the elect is union with Christ—his union with them representatively, as the last Adam, and vitally, as the life-giver, indwelling them by his Spirit, and their union with him by faith.

IV. Significance of election for the believer

Paul finds in the believer's knowledge of his election a threefold religious significance.

a. It shows him that his salvation, first to last, is all of God, a fruit of sovereign discriminating mercy. The redemption which he finds in Christ alone and receives by faith alone has its source, not in any personal qualification, but in grace alone—the grace of election. Every spiritual blessing flows to him from God's electing decree (Eph. 1:3ff.). The knowledge of his election, therefore, should teach him to glory in God, and God only (1 Cor. 1:31), and to give him the praise that is his due (Rom. 11:36). The ultimate end of election is that God should be praised (Eph. 1:6, 12, 14), and the thought of election should drive ransomed sinners to incessant doxologies and thanksgivings, as it does Paul (Rom. 11:33f.; Eph. 1:3ff.; 1 Thes. 1:3ff.; 2 Thes. 2:13ff.). What God has revealed about election is to Paul a theme, not for argument, but for worship.

b. It assures the believer of his eternal security, and removes all grounds for fear and despondency. If he is in grace now he is in grace for ever. Nothing can affect his justified status (Rom. 8:33f.); nothing can cut him off from God's love in Christ (Rom. 8:35–39). He will never be safer than he is, for he is already as safe as he can be. This is precious knowledge; hence the desirability of making sure that one's election is a fact (*cf.* 2 Pet. 1:10).

c. It spurs the believer to ethical endeavour. So far from sanctioning licence (*cf.* Eph. 5:5f.) or presumption (*cf.* Rom. 11:19–22), the knowledge of one's election and the benefits that flow from it is the supreme incentive to humble, joyful, thankful love, the mainspring of sanctifying gratitude (Col. 3:12–17)

BIBLIOGRAPHY. *BAGD*; T. Nicol in *DAC*; J. Orr in *HDB* (1 vol.); C. Hodge, *Systematic Theology*, 2, pp. 331–353; H. H. Rowley, *The Biblical Doctrine of Election*, 1950; G. C. Berkouwer, *Divine Election*, 1960; *TDNT* 4, pp. 144–192; *NIDNTT* 1, pp. 533–543.

J.I.P.

ELECT LADY. 2 John is addressed to 'the elect lady' (*eklektē kyria*). This may signify an individual, either unnamed, or named Electa, or Kyria, or Electa Kyria. There are fairly convincing objections to each of these suggestions. Further, the absence of personal allusions, the almost unvarying use of the plural, the contents of the letter and the concluding 'The children of your elect sister greet you' combine to make it likely that the Epistle is addressed to a church. No parallel is known, but this seems to be the least difficult explanation.

L.M.

ELEMENTS. Gk. *stoicheia*, translated 'elements' in 2 Pet. 3:10, 12; 'elemental spirits' in Gal. 4:3, 9; Col. 2:8, 20 (AV 'rudiments'), is the neuter plural of the adjective *stoicheios*, which means 'standing in a row', 'an element in a series'. Hence *stoicheia* is used: **1.** for the letters of the alphabet when written out in series. From this use comes the meaning 'first principles', 'the ABC' of any subject, as in Heb. 5:12. **2.** It may also mean the component parts of physical bodies. In particular, the Stoics used the term for the four elements: earth, water, air, fire. **3.** There is evidence in Christian writers from the middle of the 2nd century AD for the use of *stoicheia* in an astronomical sense for the heavenly bodies (*cf.* Justin Martyr, *Apol.* 2. 5. 2). **4.** Evidence from the Orphic hymns and the *Hermetica*, coupled with modern Gk. usage, shows that *stoicheia* later came to mean 'angels', 'spirits' ('elemental spirits'). But it is not established that it was thus used as early as the 1st century AD; alleged early instances are either of doubtful meaning or of doubtful date. Jewish writers associate spirits or angels with various physical objects (*cf. 1 Enoch* 40:11–21; *Jubilees* 2:2) but do not call them *stoicheia* (of *2 Enoch* 16:7, sometimes cited for this, we do not have the Gk. text).

Critics have suggested all four senses for the Pauline passages. **2** agrees with the preoccupation with regulations about material things in Col. 2:21, and the reference to philosophy in 2:8. **3** agrees with the mention of calendar observances in Gal. 4:10. **4** agrees with the reference to false gods in Gal. 4:8 and to angels in Col. 2:18. Paul seems to apply his remarks equally to the Jewish and Gentile worlds, but this offers no criterion for his meaning. The Jews paid great attention to physical things and astronomy in the law and believed in the mediation of angels (*cf.* Gal. 3:19; 1:8); the Gentiles concerned themselves with the elements and with astronomy in their philosophy and worshipped false gods, whom Paul identifies with demons (1 Cor. 10:20). Perhaps the best interpretation on these lines combines senses **2** and **3** in the fashion of the *Sibylline Oracles* (2. 206; 8. 337). Sense **1**, 'the ABC of religion', accords well with the general context in Galatians, with its insistence that Paul's converts should not turn back to a system meant for the 'childhood' of religion, but this gives a strained sense to the genitive 'of the world', which must be taken to mean 'favoured by the world' or 'characteristic of the world'. The question has been in dispute since the Patristic period, and must be left open unless more evidence comes to light.

In 2 Pet. 3 the mention of *stoicheia* between 'heaven' and 'earth' in v. 10 strongly suggests sense **2**. Those who favour sense **4** in Paul have argued for it here also, pointing to the *Testament of Levi* 4:1; *1 Enoch* 68:2 for references to spirits being dissolved in fire.

BIBLIOGRAPHY. G. Delling, *TDNT* 7, pp. 670–687; P. T. O'Brien, *Colossians, Philemon*, *WBC*, 1982, pp. 129–134.

M.H.C.

ELHANAN. 1. In 2 Sa. 21:19, RV, RSV, we read that Elhanan the son of Jaare-oregim slew Goliath the Gittite. When this is compared with 1 Ch. 20:5, where we read, 'Elhanan the son of Jair slew Lahmi the brother of Goliath the Gittite', it is apparent from the setting and the names used that the two verses refer to the same event.

One solution is to conclude that in 2 Samuel we have an interesting example of how easily corruption may slip into the text. Jaare is the same as Jair with the two final Heb. letters reversed. The word *'ōr^egîm* is the Heb. for 'weavers' and has slipped in by careless copying, duplicating the place where EVV translate 'weavers'. The Heb. words for 'Bethlehemite' and 'Lahmi the brother' are so similar as to make it almost certain that one is the corruption of the other. We should therefore regard 1 Ch. 20:5 as the original and true reading. An alternative solution is to conclude that in 1 Ch. 20:5 we have a harmonistic midrash, designed to get rid of the apparent discrepancy between 2 Sa. 21:19 and 1 Sa. 17:12ff., where Goliath the Gittite is killed by

David. But Elhanan may have been David's original name.

2. In 2 Sa. 23:24 and 1 Ch. 11:26 Elhanan, the son of Dodo, is named as one of David's mighty men. This is a different person.

BIBLIOGRAPHY. J. Weingreen, *From Bible to Mishna*, 1976, pp. 16f., 139. G.T.M.
F.F.B.

ELI. The story of Eli is told in 1 Sa. 1–4. He was 'the priest' in 'the house of the Lord' at Shiloh (1 Sa. 1:3, 7, 9). This 'house' must have been the intertribal sanctuary, incorporating the tabernacle (Jos. 18:1; Jdg. 18:31), with some additional structure; and here was the ark (1 Sa. 4:3). Eli's ancestry is not given, but by comparing 1 Ki. 2:27 with 1 Ch. 24:3 we deduce that Phinehas, his son, and therefore Eli himself, was a descendant of Ithamar, the youngest son of Aaron. We have no information as to how the priesthood passed from the line of Eleazar (1 Ch. 6:4–15); but the Samaritan tradition that it was seized from Uzzi when a child must be rejected as due to racial bias. (See E. Robertson, *The Old Testament Problem*, 1950, p. 176.)

From 1 Sa. 14:3 and 22:9ff. it appears that Eli's descendants, through Phinehas and his son Ahitub, continued to exercise the priesthood for a time at Nob.

Because of the scandalous conduct of Eli's sons, ineffectively rebuked by their father, a man of God came to pronounce a doom upon them and their descendants (1 Sa. 2:27–36). This was confirmed by a revelation to the child Samuel (1 Sa. 3:11–14). It was partially fulfilled in the death of Hophni and Phinehas (1 Sa. 4:11) and the ruthless murder of the priests in Nob (1 Sa. 22:9–20). But Abiathar escaped and shared with Zadok the priesthood under David (2 Sa. 19:11). But from this he was degraded by Solomon, in further fulfilment of the ancient prophecy (1 Ki. 2:26f.).

Eli 'had judged Israel forty years' (1 Sa. 4:18), a testimony to the service he rendered to his people. But it was marred by the sinful sacrilege of his sons, and by his failure to eject them from their sacred office. G.T.M.

ELIAB. 'God is father', a common OT name. **1.** A son of Helon, prince and representative of Zebulun (Nu. 1:9; 2:7, *etc.*). **2.** A Reubenite, the son of Pallu and father of Dathan, Abiram and Nemuel (Nu. 26:8–9). **3.** The eldest son of Jesse and brother of David (1 Sa. 16:5ff., *etc.*), father of Abihail (2 Ch. 11:18), and called 'Elihu' in 1 Ch. 27:18. **4.** A Gadite warrior and companion of David (1 Ch. 12:9). **5.** A levitical musician of the time of David (1 Ch. 15:18ff.). **6.** An ancestor of Samuel (1 Ch. 6:27), also called Eliel (1 Ch. 6:34) and Elihu (1 Sa. 1:1). G.W.G.

ELIAKIM (Heb. *'el-yāqîm*, 'God establishes'?; Gk. *Eliakeim*). The name of at least five different individuals. Two were ancestors of our Lord (Mt. 1:13; Lk. 3:30); one was a priest, a contemporary of Nehemiah (Ne. 12:41). Eliakim was also the one whom Pharaoh-neco made king after Josiah and whose name he changed to Jehoiakim (2 Ki. 23:34; 2 Ch. 36:4).

The most prominent individual to bear this name was the son of Hilkiah, who was appointed

Seal inscribed 'belonging to Eliakim, assistant of Jehoiachin' (l'lyqm n'r ywkn). *Impressions of this seal have been found on jar-handles at Tell beit Mirsim. Beth-shemesh and Ramat Rahel. Perhaps this was the seal of Eliakim (6th cent.* BC*), but it may be of earlier date.*

steward in place of the deposed Shebna (Is. 22: 20ff.). Since the time of Solomon (1 Ki. 4:6) this office had existed both in the N and S kingdoms (1 Ki. 16:9; 18:3; 2 Ki. 10:5), and was apparently even exercised by Jotham after Uzziah's leprosy (2 Ki. 15:5). When Sennacherib besieged Jerusalem Eliakim went to talk with the Rabshakeh (2 Ki. 18:18, 26–27; Is. 36:3, 11, 22), and Hezekiah then sent him to bear the news to Isaiah (2 Ki. 19:2; Is. 37:2). An Eliakim servant of Jokin (*ywkn*) appears on seal-impressions of Hezekiah's time. E.J.Y.

ELIASHIB. There are several people with this name in the OT: a descendant of David (1 Ch. 3:24); a priest in the time of David (1 Ch. 24:12); a singer (Ezr. 10:24); a son of Zattu (Ezr. 10:27); a son of Bani (Ezr. 10:36). The name is also found on seals and ostraca at *Arad.

The most important was the high priest in the time of Nehemiah. He is first mentioned in Ezr. 10:6 as the father of Johanan, but is not called high priest at this time. Josephus says that Eliashib's father, Joiakim, was high priest when Ezra came to Jerusalem in 458 BC (*Ant.* 11. 154). When Nehemiah came in 445 BC Eliashib was high priest, and took part in the building of the city walls (Ne. 3:1, 20–21). Later he compromised, and formed a marriage alliance with Tobiah (Ne. 13:4) and gave him a room in the Temple precincts (Ne. 13:5). One of his grandsons married Sanballat's daughter (Ne. 13:28). His genealogy is given in Ne. 12:10–11.

J.S.W.

ELIEZER (Heb. *'ᵉlî'ezer*, 'God is [my?] help'). A name scattered right through biblical history.

1. Eliezer the Damascene, Abraham's chief servant, and his adopted heir before the birth of Ishmael and Isaac (Gn. 15:2–3). The custom whereby a childless couple could adopt someone from outside as an heir is very well attested during *c.* 2000–1500 BC; such an adoptive heir had to take second place to any subsequent first-born son. See also, D. J. Wiseman, *IBA*, 1959, pp. 25–26. For these customs in Ur, *c.* 1800 BC, see Wiseman, *JTVI* 88, 1956, p. 124. For similar customs in the *Nuzi tablets, see Speiser, *AASOR* 10, 1930, texts H 60, H 67, pp. 30, 32, *etc.*

2. Second son of Moses, named Eliezer in allusion to Moses' escaping the sword of Pharaoh (Ex.

18:4; 1 Ch. 23:15). Eliezer had only one son, Rehabiah, but the latter had many descendants, of whom one (Shelomith) became treasurer of David's dedicated things (1 Ch. 23:17–18; 26:25–26).

3. Grandson of Benjamin, and progenitor of a later Benjaminite clan (1 Ch. 7:8).

4. One of the seven priests who sounded the trumpets before the ark when David brought it into Jerusalem (1 Ch. 15:24). **5.** Eliezer son of Zichri, tribal ruler of Reuben under David (1 Ch. 27:16). **6.** The prophet who prophesied to King Jehoshaphat of Judah that his fleet of vessels at Ezion-geber would be wrecked in punishment for his alliance with the wicked King Ahaziah of Israel (2 Ch. 20:35–37).

7. One of eleven men commissioned by Ezra to seek out Levites for the return to Jerusalem in 458 BC (Ezr. 8:16ff.). **8–10.** Three men, including a priest and a Levite, who had taken alien wives (Ezr. 10:18, 23, 31). **11.** An Eliezer appears in Christ's earthly lineage as given by Luke (3:29). K.A.K.

ELIHU (Heb. *'ᵉlihû*, 'My God is he'). **1.** An Ephraimite, Samuel's paternal great-grandfather (1 Sa. 1:1), whose name seems to occur as Eliab in 1 Ch. 6:27 and as Eliel in 1 Ch. 6:34. **2.** One of the captains of Manasseh, who deserted to David just before the battle of Ziklag (1 Ch. 12:20). **3.** A Korahite, member of the gatekeepers, grandson of Obed-edom, and son of Shemaiah (1 Ch. 26:7). **4.** A chief officer of Judah, brother (or near relative) of David (1 Ch. 27:18), perhaps identical with Eliab (1 Sa. 16:6). **5.** Job's young friend, son of Barachel, a Buzite of the family of Ram (Jb. 32:2, 4–6; 34:1; 35:1; 36:1). His appearance at the end of the story is somewhat of a puzzle, since he was not included in the list of friends whose debate with *Job forms the bulk of the book. Elihu's speeches, with their strong stress on divine sovereignty, serve both to prepare for the revelation of God (Jb. 38) and to promote suspense by delaying it. D.A.H.

ELIJAH. The 9th-century prophet of Israel. His name appears in the Heb. OT as *'ēlîyyâhû* and *'ēlîyyâ*, in the Gk. OT as *Ēleiou*, and in the NT as *Ēleias*. The name means 'Yah is El' or 'Yahweh is God'.

Apart from the reference to Elijah in 1 Ki. 17:1 as 'the Tishbite, of Tishbe in Gilead', no information about his background is available. Even this reference is obscure. The *MT* suggests that while Elijah resided in Gilead (*mittōšāḇê gilᵉʿāḏ*) his birthplace was elsewhere (perhaps Tishbe of Naphtali). The LXX reads *ek thesbōn tēs galaad*, thus indicating a Tishbe of *Gilead. Josephus seems to concur (*Ant.* 8. 319). This has traditionally been identified with a site about 13 km N of the Jabbok.

Elijah's prophetic ministry is recorded in 1 Ki. 17–19; 21; 2 Ki. 1–2. These narratives are written in the purest classical Heb. 'of a type which can hardly be later than the 8th century' (W. F. Albright, *From the Stone Age to Christianity*, p. 307). They could not have enjoyed an existence for long in oral form. They describe his ministry to the N kingdom during the Omrid Dynasty (*OMRI). Elijah was contemporary with Ahab and Ahaziah, and from the position of the translation narrative (2 Ki. 2) and the answer to Jehoshaphat's question in 2 Ki. 3:11, we conclude that his translation probably occurred about the time of the accession to the throne of Jehoram of Israel. The difficulty presented to this conclusion by 2 Ch. 21:12–15 can possibly be resolved either by interpreting the much-controverted 2 Ki. 8:16 to teach a co-regency of Jehoshaphat and Jehoram, kings of Judah (*CHRONOLOGY OF THE OT) or by regarding the letter as a prophetic oracle written prior to his translation.

The Elijah cycle presents six episodes in the life of the prophet: his prediction of drought and his subsequent flight, the Mt Carmel contest, the flight to Horeb, the Naboth incident, the oracle about Ahaziah, and his translation. Except for the last, they are all basically concerned with the clash between the worship of Yahweh and *Baal. The Baal in these stories is Baal-melqart, the official protective deity of Tyre. Ahab fostered this Phoenician variant of the nature-religion of Canaan after his marriage with the Tyrian princess *Jezebel (1 Ki. 16:30–33), but it was Jezebel who was chiefly responsible for the systematic extermination of Yahweh worship and the propagation of the Baal cult in Israel (1 Ki. 18:4, 13, 19; 19:10, 14).

Elijah appears in the first episode (1 Ki. 17) without introduction, and after the delivery of the oracle to Ahab announcing a drought, he retires beyond Ahab's jurisdiction first to the wadi Cherith, E of Jordan, and then to Zarephath (modern Sarafend below Sidon still preserves the name and overlooks what remains of this ancient Mediterranean sea-port). Elijah was miraculously sustained in both places, and while at Zarephath he performed a miracle of healing (1 Ki. 17:17–24).

The second episode, 3 years later (1 Ki. 18:1; *cf.* Lk. 4:25; Jas. 5:17, which follow Jewish tradition), recounts the break in the drought following the overthrow of organized Baal worship on Mt Carmel. The drought imposed and withdrawn at Yahweh's word was a challenge to Baal's sovereignty over nature. 1 Ki. 17 had depicted Elijah in the very stronghold of Baal-melqart sustained by Yahweh while the country languishes (1 Ki. 17:12; *cf.* Jos., *Ant.* 8. 320–4). 1 Ki. 18 brings the challenge into the open, and Yahweh's supremacy is spectacularly demonstrated. That Baal worship in Israel was certainly not exterminated at Mt Carmel is seen from later references (*e.g.* 2 Ki. 10:18–21). For the presence of an altar of Yahweh on Mt Carmel, see *Altar. Keil suggests that this was probably built by pious Yahweh-worshippers after the division in the kingdom. Some commentators omit 1 Ki. 18:30b altogether, while others omit vv. 31–32a.

The third episode (1 Ki. 19) describing Elijah's flight to Horeb to avoid Jezebel's wrath is particularly significant. Horeb was the sacred mountain where the covenant God of Moses had made himself known, and Elijah's return to this place represents the return of a loyal but disheartened prophet to the very source of the faith for which he had contended. The closing commission in 1 Ki. 19:15–18 seems to have been only partially discharged by Elijah. The accession of Hazael and Jehu to the thrones of Syria and Israel respectively is recorded in the *Elisha cycle.

The Naboth incident (1 Ki. 21) illustrates and vindicates the principle embedded in the religious consciousness of Israel, that land owned by an Israelite family or clan was understood as a gift from

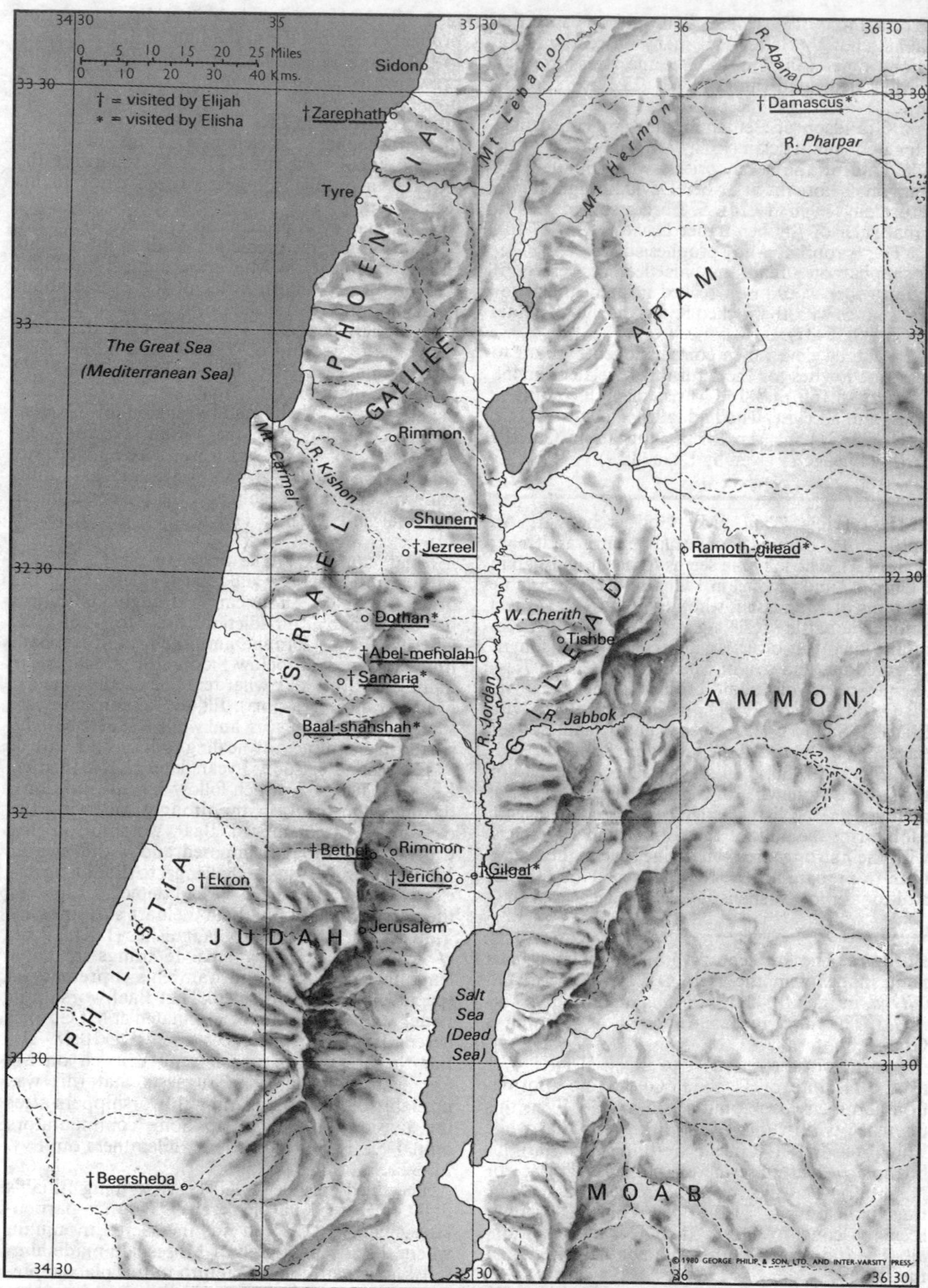

Places associated with Elijah and Elisha.

Yahweh, and that failure to recognize this and respect the rights of the individual and family within the covenant community would issue in judgment. Elijah emerges as a champion of the strong ethical demands of the Mosaic faith so significantly lacking in the Baal cult.

The fifth episode in 2 Ki. 1 continues to illustrate the Yahweh–Baal clash. Ahaziah's dependence upon the life-god of Syria, Baalzebub (Baal-zebul of Ras Shamra texts, *cf.* Mt. 10:25 RVmg.; Baalzebub, meaning 'Lord of Flies', was probably a way of ridiculing the Syrian deity), evokes the judgment of God (2 Ki. 1:6, 16). A judgment of fire also falls on those who endeavoured to resist the word of Yahweh by harming his prophet (2 Ki. 1:9–15). The translation of Elijah in a whirlwind (*sᶜārâ*) brings to a dramatic close his spectacular prophetic career. The exclamation of Elisha (2 Ki.

2:12) is repeated in 2 Ki. 13:14 with reference to Elisha himself.

Two observations may be made about the importance of Elijah. First, he stands in the OT tradition of ecstatic prophecy coming through from the days of Samuel and he is also a forerunner of the 8th-century rhapsodists or writing *prophets. His link with the earlier tradition is seen in that he is first of all a man of action and his Spirit-determined movements defy human anticipation (1 Ki. 18:12). In the background of the Elijah pericope the prophetic schools of Samuel's day continue to exist (1 Ki. 18:4, 13; 2 Ki. 2:3, 5, 7). His link with the later prophets lies in his constant endeavour to recall his people to the religion of Moses, both in worshipping Yahweh alone as well as in proclaiming Mosaic standards of righteousness in the community. In both these respects he anticipates the more fully developed oracles of Amos and Hosea. This advocacy of the Mosaic faith by Elijah is supported by several details which suggest a parallel between Elijah and Moses. Elijah's return to Horeb is obvious enough, but there is also the fact that Elijah is accompanied and succeeded by Elisha as Moses was by Joshua. This parallel is quite striking. Not only has the death of Moses an air of mystery attaching to it (Dt. 34:6) but his successor secured the allegiance of Israel by participating in the same spirit as Moses and demonstrated his fitness for office by a miraculous river crossing (Dt. 34:9; Jos. 4:14). The translation narrative (2 Ki. 2) reproduces this pattern fairly precisely. The fact also that God answers Elijah by fire on two occasions (1 Ki. 18:38; 2 Ki. 1:10, 12) seems to look back to the exhibition of God's presence and judgment in fire in the Exodus narratives (*e.g.* Ex. 13:21; 19:18; 24:17; Nu. 11:1; 16:35). Little wonder that in Jewish Haggadic thought Elijah was viewed as the counterpart to Moses.

Second, his ministry is spoken of as being revived 'before the coming of the great and dreadful day of the Lord' (Mal. 4:5–6). This theme is a popular one in the Jewish Mishnah (*TALMUD AND MIDRASH), and was a common topic of discussion during the ministry of Jesus (Mk. 8:28). Jesus indicated that the Malachi prophecy had reference to the ministry of *John the Baptist (Mt. 11:14; 17:12f.). Elijah reappears in person on the mount of transfiguration (Mk. 9:4) and he is referred to elsewhere in the NT in Lk. 4:25–26; Rom. 11:2–4; Jas. 5:17–18.

Three other men of the same name appear in the OT, the first a Benjaminite priest (1 Ch. 8:27; Heb. *'ēlîyyâ*), and the second and third a priest and a layman respectively, who married foreign wives (Ezr. 10:21, 26; Heb. *'ēlîyyâ*).

BIBLIOGRAPHY. E. Fohrer, *Elia*², 1968; H. H. Rowley, *Men of God*, 1963; J. Lindblom, *Prophecy in Ancient Israel*, 1963; L. Bronner, *The Stories of Elijah and Elisha*, 1968; M. B. Van't Veer, *My God as Yahweh*, 1980; commentaries on the books of Kings by G. H. Jones, *NCB*, 1984; B. O. Long, *FOTL* 91, 1984; S. J. De Vries and T. R. Hobbs, *WBC*, 1985; D. J. Wiseman, *TOTC*, 1993.

B.L.S.

ELIM (Heb. 'terebinths' or 'oaks'). Second stopping-place of the Israelites after their crossing of the Re(e)d Sea from Egypt. Beyond the wilderness of *Shur, E of the modern Suez canal, they first encamped at Marah in the wilderness of Etham not far away (because named after Etham in E Delta), and thence reached Elim with its twelve springs and seventy palm-trees. After this the Israelites went on 'and pitched by the Red Sea', before eventually reaching the wilderness of *Sin, Ex. 15:27; 16:1; Nu. 33:9–10.

By putting the stop at Elim shortly after the escape from Egypt and passage of its desert edge (Shur), and before a stop by the Red Sea prior to reaching the wilderness of Sin, the biblical references suggest that Elim is situated on the W side of the Sinai peninsula, facing on to the Gulf of Suez. Any closer location is still not certain, but a plausible suggestion of long standing is Wadi Gharandel (or, Ghurundel), a well-known watering-place with tamarisks and palms, *c.* 60 km SSE of Suez along the W side of *Sinai. (*WILDERNESS OF WANDERING.)

BIBLIOGRAPHY. E. Robinson, *Biblical Researches in Palestine*, 1, 1841, pp. 99–100, 105–106, and map at end; A. P. Stanley, *Sinai and Palestine*, 1887, pp. 37–38; Wright and Filson, *Westminster Historical Atlas to the Bible*, 1956, pp. 38–39 and plate V.

K.A.K.

ELISHA. The 9th-century prophet of Israel. His name appears in the Heb. OT as *'ᵉlîšā'*, in the Gk. OT as *Eleisaie*, in Josephus as *Elissaios* and in the NT as *Elisaios*. The name means 'God is salvation'. His father's name was Shaphat.

All that can be known about Elisha's background is found in 1 Ki. 19:16, 19–21. We are not told his age or his birthplace, but we may assume that he was a native of Abel-meholah (Tell Abū Sifri?) in the Jordan valley and was still only young when Elijah sought him out. That he was the son of a family of some means also seems clear.

His ministry, if we date it from his call, extended through the reigns of Ahab, Ahaziah, Jehoram, Jehu, Jehoahaz and Jehoash, a period of more than 50 years. The narratives of Elisha's ministry are recorded in 1 Ki. 19; 2 Ki. 2–9; 13, and comprise a series of some eighteen episodes. It is not possible to be certain of their chronological order throughout because of obvious breaks in the sequence of events (*e.g.*, *cf.* 2 Ki. 6:23 with 6:24; 5:27 with 8:4–5; 13:13 with 13:14ff.). These episodes do not betray the same tension between Yahweh and Baal worship as those of the *Elijah cycle. It is a ministry conducted at the head of the prophetic schools which consists of a display of signs and wonders both at a personal as well as a national level. Elisha emerges as a kind of seer in the tradition of Samuel to whom peasants and kings alike turn for help.

Examining these episodes in their biblical order, we make the following observations. (1) Elisha's call (1 Ki. 19:19–21) was not so much an anointing (*cf.* 1 Ki. 19:16) as an ordination by investiture with Elijah's prophetic mantle. Until Elijah's translation Elisha remained his servant (1 Ki. 19:21; 2 Ki. 3:11). (2) 2 Ki. 2:1–18 recounts Elisha's assumption of the role of his master. The double portion of the spirit upon Elisha recalls the language and thought of Dt. 21:17 while the whole episode is reminiscent of the replacement of Moses by Joshua as leader of Israel. (3) The healing of the injurious waters in 2 Ki. 2:19–22 also finds a parallel in the events of the Exodus (Ex. 15:22–25). (4) The incident in 2 Ki. 2:23–25 must be understood as a judgment upon the deliberate mockery of the new head of the school of Yahweh's prophets. Some scholars incline to the view that Elisha's baldness was a prophetic tonsure.

(5) The story of Elisha's part in the campaign of the three kings against *Moab (2 Ki. 3:1–27) records his request for music when receiving an oracle from Yahweh (v. 15). There is a strong suggestion of ecstatic prophecy here as in 1 Sa. 10:5–13 (*cf.* 1 Ch. 25:1). (6) 2 Ki. 4:1–7 is parallel to Elijah's miracle in 1 Ki. 17:8–16 and introduces (7) the longer story of Elisha's dealings with the Shunammite woman (2 Ki. 4:8–37), which has many points of similarity with 1 Ki. 17:8–24. (8) 2 Ki. 4:38–41 and (9) 4:42–44 occur at sessions with the fraternity of prophets at Gilgal, probably during the famine referred to in 2 Ki. 8:1. The second of these miracles anticipates the miracle of Jesus which is recorded in Mk. 6:35–44.

(10) The Naaman story (2 Ki. 5:1–27) cannot be dated with accuracy. It must have occurred during one of the temporary lulls in hostilities between Israel and Syria. The editorial comment in v. 1 ascribing the Syrian's victories to Yahweh should be compared with Am. 9:7. This cosmic view of Yahweh is recognized by Naaman (v. 15), and his request for Israelite soil (v. 17) need not necessarily be taken to imply that he believed Yahweh's influence to be confined to Israelite territory. Elisha makes no comment on this, but sends Naaman on his way (v. 19). Since most Israelites saw nothing wrong in including other gods in their debased worship of Yahweh, a Syrian who did not at once accept monotheism could hardly be blamed. (*RIMMON).

(11) 2 Ki. 6:1–7 recounts a miraculous feat of Elisha and incidentally casts light on the size and habitations of prophetic fraternities (*cf.* 2 Ki. 4:38–44). (12) 2 Ki. 6:8–23 and (13) 6:24–7:20 depict Elisha as a counsellor of kings and a deliverer of the nation from national disaster (*cf.* 2 Ki. 3:1–27). The second of these episodes is said to involve *Ben-hadad of Aram and 'the king of Israel'. This is unfortunately obscure. (14) 2 Ki. 8:1–6 clearly belongs before 5:1–27. It is a continuation of the Shunammite story (2 Ki. 4:8–37).

(15) 2 Ki. 8:7–15, (16) 9:1–13, and (17) 13:14–19 all depict Elisha involved in affairs of state. The first of these describes the ascent of *Hazael to the throne of Damascus (*cf.* 1 Ki. 19:15). Elisha's reply (v. 10) may be understood to mean that the king would recover from his sickness but would die for other reasons, or it may have been the prophet's spontaneous reply that had to be corrected by a vision from Yahweh (*cf.* 2 Sa. 7:1–17; 2 Ki. 4:26–36). The anointing of Jehu discharged the last of the tasks committed to Elijah (1 Ki. 19:15–16) and precipitated the predicted overthrow of the Omrid Dynasty (1 Ki. 21:21–24). This prophetic-inspired revolt is in contrast to the corresponding priestly revolt in the S that removed Athaliah from the throne (2 Ki. 11). If he lived into the reign of Jehoash of Israel, he must have been about 80 years old at the time of his death. He appears as a favourite of the king, who realizes his political value (v. 14). Sympathetic or mimetic actions accompanying prophetic oracles are not uncommon in the OT.

Although Elisha is a prophet of the 9th century and belongs to the prophetic tradition which produced the 8th-century rhapsodists or writing prophets, he has more affinities with the ecstatic prophets of the 11th century. He is very like Samuel, with gifts of knowledge and foresight and a capacity to work miracles. He figures at the head of the prophetic schools and is in frequent demand because of his singular gifts. Although he is spoken of as having a home in Samaria (2 Ki. 6:32), he is, like Samuel, constantly moving about the land and enjoys an easy access into royal courts and peasant dwellings. While his relation to *Elijah is certainly suggestive of the relationship between Joshua and Moses, the fact that Elijah's ministry is reproduced in John the Baptist and Elisha's directly anticipates the miracle-aspect of the ministry of Jesus is even more significant. Elisha is referred to only once in the NT (Lk. 4:27).

BIBLIOGRAPHY. L. Bronner, *The Stories of Elijah and Elisha*, 1968; commentaries on the books of Kings by G. H. Jones, *NCB*, 1984; B. O. Long, *FOTL* 91, 1984; S. J. De Vries and T. R. Hobbs, *WBC*, 1985; D. J. Wiseman, *TOTC*, 1993.

B.L.S.

ELISHAH. The eldest son of *Javan (Gn. 10:4 = 1 Ch. 1:7), whose name was later applied to his descendants, who inhabited a maritime region (*'iyyê*, 'isles' or 'coastlands') which traded purple to Tyre (Ezk. 27:7). It is very probable that the biblical name *'ᵉlîšâ* (LXX *Elisa*) is to be equated with Alašia of the extra-biblical sources. This name occurs in the Egyptian and cuneiform (Boghaz-Koi, Alalaḫ, Ugarit) inscriptions, and it was the source of eight of the Amarna letters, in which it usually occurs in the form *a-la-ši-ia.* These texts indicate that Alašia was an exporter of copper, and it is possible, though not universally accepted, that it is to be identified with the site of Enkomi on the E coast of Cyprus, where excavations under C. F. A. Schaeffer have revealed an important trading-centre of the Late Bronze Age. The name Alašia would also apply to the area under the political domination of the city, and may at times have included outposts on the Phoenician coast.

BIBLIOGRAPHY. R. Dussaud in C. F. A. Schaeffer, *Enkomi-Alasia*, 1952, pp. 1–10; *AS* 6, 1956, pp. 63–65; *KB*³, p. 55.

T.C.M.

ELIZABETH (from Heb. *'ᵉlîšeḇa'*, 'God is [my] oath'). The wife of Zechariah the priest, and mother of John the Baptist (Lk. 1:5ff.). Herself of priestly descent, Elizabeth is described in the AV as a 'cousin' (more accurately, 'kinswoman', RSV) of the Virgin Mary (Lk. 1:36), to whom she addressed the remarkable words of Lk. 1:42–45. J.D.D.

ELLASAR. The city or kingdom ruled by Arioch, an ally of *Chedorlaomer king of Elam, who attacked Sodom and captured Lot, Abraham's nephew (Gn. 14:1, 9). Identifications suggested depend on those proposed for the kings involved. These include: (*i*) *āl Aššur* —Ashur/Assyria (so Dhorme, Böhl, Dossin); (*ii*) Ilânsura—in the Mari texts, between Harran and Carchemish (Yeivin); (*iii*) Telassar—(2 Ki. 19:12; Is. 37:12) in N Mesopotamia as a parallel to *Shinar = Singara, but the name is to be read Til-Bašeri; (*iv*) Larsa—in S Babylonia. This depends on the outmoded equation *Amraphel = Hammurapi (of Babylon).

BIBLIOGRAPHY. E. Lipiński, *Studies in Aramaic Inscriptions and Onomastica* 1, 1975. D.J.W.

ELOI, ELOI, LAMA SABACHTHANI. Occurs in Mk. 15:34 and in a slightly different form in Mt. 27:46. It is one of the Lord's sayings on the cross, and is a quotation from Ps. 22:1. The form 'Eli' would be more likely to give rise to the confusion with Elijah, and the form in Matthew is thus more likely to be original. Our Lord uses the Aramaic, almost exactly the form of the Targum.

The difficulty of accounting for this saying is the strongest argument for its authenticity. Inadequate explanations are that it reflects the intensity of the Lord's human feeling, that it reveals the disappointment of his hope that in his extremity the Father would usher in the new age, or that he was merely reciting the Psalm as an act of devotion. It can be understood only in the light of the NT doctrine of the atonement, according to which Christ identified himself with sinful man and endured separation from God (*cf.* Phil. 2:8; 2 Cor. 5:21). It is a mystery we cannot fathom.

BIBLIOGRAPHY. D. H. C. Read, 'The Cry of Dereliction', *ExpT* 68, 1956–7, pp. 260ff. A.G.

ELON (Heb. *'êlôn*, *'êlôn*). **1.** A Hittite of Canaan (Gn. 26:34; 36:2). **2.** Head of a family in Zebulun (Gn. 46:14; Nu. 26:26) ('Helon', Nu. 1:9; 2:7 *etc.*). **3.** A Zebulunite judge of Israel (Jdg. 12:11–12). **4.** A S Danite town (Jos. 19:43); possibly Kh. W. Alin, 2 km E of Beth-shemesh (*GTT*, p. 349). Elon-beth-hanan (1 Ki. 4:9) may be this Elon (Mazar, *IEJ* 10, 1960, p. 67), or Aijalon (*LOB*, pp. 311f.). The name, like *Elah, means 'terebinth' (RSV 'oak', Jos. 19:33). J.P.U.L.

ELTEKEH. A city in Palestine allotted to the tribe of Dan (Jos. 19:44) and later made a levitical city (Elteke, Jos. 21:23). Sennacherib mentions it (Altakū) together with Timnā among his conquests in his annals for 701/700 BC (Chicago Cylinder 3. 6; Taylor Cylinder 2. 82–83). Some identify it with Khirbet el-Muqanna' *c.* 40 km W of Jerusalem (so Albright) but this may be *Ekron; Tell-esh-Shalaf, 16 km NNE of Ashdod, is an alternative (Mazar).

BIBLIOGPHAPHY. D. D. Luckenbill, *The Annals of Sennacherib*, 1924, p. 32; W. F. Albright, *BASOR* 15, 1924, p. 8; B. Mazar, *IEJ* 10, 1960, pp. 72–77. T.C.M.

ELZAPHAN (Heb. *'elṣāphān*, 'God has hidden'). **1.** Also called Elizaphan. A son of Uzziel, a Levite (Ex. 6:22) who, with his brother *Mishael, disposed of the bodies of Nadab and Abihu, who had been killed for desecrating the altar (Lv. 10:1–5). A leader of the Kohathites in the wilderness (Nu. 3:30), he also was the father of a house of priests (1 Ch. 15:8, 2 Ch. 29.13).

2. A son of Parosh who, representing the tribe of Zebulun, was to assist in the division of Canaan (Nu. 34:25). D.W.B.

EMBROIDERY. The ornamentation of cloth was of two main types: **1.** chequer work (*tašbēṣ*); **2.** coloured embroidery (*riqmâ*). RSV (Ex. 28:39) describes the former as weaving (*cf.* AV 'embroider'), the latter as needlework, though the methods used are not specified in the Hebrew (*cf.* NEB). Chequer work decorated the high priest's tunic (Ex. 28:4) and, worked in gold thread, a princess's wedding dress (Ps. 45:13). Such thread was cut from thin plates of beaten gold (Ex. 39:3). Some idea of the pattern produced is suggested by the use of the same term for the gold filigree work in which gems were set (Ex. 28:11).

Coloured embroidery decorated the high priest's girdle (Ex. 28:39), the screens for the tabernacle door (Ex. 26:36) and the gate of the court (Ex. 27:16). A distinction may be intended between this type of ornamentation and the equally intricate and richly coloured work of the ephod and breastpiece (Ex. 28:6, 15), the tabernacle curtains and veil (Ex. 26:1, 31), and the garments of those who ministered in the sanctuary (Ex. 39:1), since only the former is designated 'the work of the embroiderer' (*ma'ᵃśēh rōqēm*; Ex. 26:36).

Its value is evident from its importance for trade (Ezk. 27:16, 24) and as the spoils of war (Jdg. 5:30). It decorated not only clothing for men (Ezk. 16:18; 26:16) and women (Ezk. 16:10, 13; Ps. 45:14), but could be used for other ornamentation, *e.g.* a ship's sail (Ezk. 27:7). By an extended use the word is applied to the plumage of an eagle (Ezk. 17:3) and to the variegated stones prepared by David for the Temple (1 Ch. 29:2). Its intricacy made it a suitable figure to describe the human embryo (Ps. 139:15).

Appliqué work may have been used for the coloured pomegranates which, with golden bells, decorated the skirt of the high priest's robe (Ex. 28:33). (*ARTS AND CRAFTS.) G.I.E.

EMIM. Early inhabitants of Moab, who were smitten in the plain of *Kiriathaim by Chedorlaomer in the time of Abraham (Gn. 14:5). They were described by Moses as a great and numerous people, to be compared in stature to the *Anakim (Dt. 2:10). They were evidently considered to belong to the peoples known as *Rephaim, but were called *'êmîm*, 'terrifying beings', by the Moabites who followed them in the area (Dt. 2:11). They are unknown outside the Bible. (*GIANT). T.C.M.

EMMAUS. A village, said to be 60 furlongs (11 km) from Jerusalem, to which *Cleopas and another disciple were journeying when Jesus appeared to them after his resurrection (Lk. 24:13). The site cannot be certainly identified. One possibility is the town still known as 'Amwas, 32 km WNW of Jerusalem, where Judas Maccabeus defeated Gorgias in 166 BC (1 Macc. 3:40, 57; 4:3). But this is at the wrong distance from Jerusalem, as given by Luke (unless the variant reading of 160 furlongs found in Codex Sinaiticus and other MSS preserves the original text); it also demands a long, though by no means impossible, walk by the travellers.

Of places within about 11 km from Jerusalem two have been suggested. There was a village at El-qubeibeh in the 1st century, and Crusaders found a fort here named Castellum Emmaus; unfortunately the name cannot be traced back to the 1st century. Josephus (*BJ* 7. 217) refers to a military colony of Vespasian at Ammaous, some 6 km W of Jerusalem. This has been identified with Kaloniye (Lat. *colonia*) or with Kh. Beit Mizza (ancient Mozah); here again the distance is wrong, unless we suppose that Luke's 60 furlongs was meant as the total length of the outward and return journeys.

BIBLIOGRAPHY. J. Finegan, *The Archaeology of the New Testament*, 1969, pp. 177–180; *ZPEB*, 2, pp. 299f.; *NEAEHL*, pp. 385–389. I.H.M.

ENCAMPMENT BY THE SEA. The place where the Israelites camped by the sea and made the crossing (Ex. 13:18; 14:2) has been the subject of much controversy during the last 100 years. The question is inseparable from that of the location of such places as Baal-zephon, Etham, Migdol, Pihahiroth, Sea of Reeds and Succoth.

Two main traditions have grown up around the route of the Exodus out of Egypt: the 'Southern' theory favouring a route from the Wadi Tumilat region SE to the Suez area, and the 'Northern' theory advocating a crossing near Lake Menzaleh to S of Port Said.

The S theory was foreshadowed by Josephus (*Ant.* 2. 315), who considered the Israelites to have started from Latopolis (= Egyp. Babylon, Old Cairo) to a Baal-zephon on the Red Sea; Pierre Diacre and Antonin de Plaisance had a tradition of the Hebrews passing Clysma near the present-day Suez. Among moderns, Lepsius, Mallon, Bourdon (with a crossing at Clysma), Cazelles and Montet favoured this view.

The N route was championed by Brugsch, identifying the Sea of Reeds, *yam-sûp̄*, with Egyp. *p'-ṯwf* and placing it in Lake Serbonis on the Mediterranean shore with Baal-zephon at Ras Qasrun there. But this hardly agrees with the biblical account, in which God forbade Israel to go by 'the way of the land of the Philistines' (Ex. 13:17–18). Gardiner was the next to espouse the N route (*JEA* 5, 1918, pp. 261–269; *Recueil Champollion*, 1922, pp. 203–215), likewise O. Eissfeldt and N. Aimé-Giron, the former identifying Casios and Baal-zephon on the Mediterranean shore and the latter equating Baal-zephon with Tahpanhes (Phoenician papyrus). For Albright, see below.

H. Cazelles summed up the whole problem. He considers that later tradition from the LXX onward (note the LXX's *thalassa erythra*, 'Red Sea') speaks for a S route, but that study of the names in the Heb. text suggests that this latter indicates a N route by the Mediterranean; according to Cazelles, these N locations were due to an editor of J and E documents who (like Manetho and Josephus) associated the Hebrew Exodus with the expulsion of the Hyksos from Egypt. However, this is speculative.

Finally, there is an entirely different suggestion by W. F. Albright (*BASOR* 109, 1948, pp. 15–16). He placed Ra'amses at Tanis in the N, brought the Israelites SE past the places in the Wadi Tumilat (Pithom at Retabeh, Succoth at Tell el-Maskhutah) and then sharply back up N again (*cf.* 'that they turn back', Ex. 14:2) by the Bitter Lakes to the region of a Baal-zephon located at later Tahpanhes (Defneh); Migdol is then Tell el-Her just S of Pelusium, with the Sea of Reeds (*yam-sûp̄*) in this general area. Having thus left Egypt proper, the Israelites would then flee to the SE into the Sinai peninsula, so that Albright's route in its end-result becomes a 'southern' one (*i.e.* he does not take Israel by the forbidden way of the Philistines). Noth's reserves (*Festschrift Otto Eissfeldt*, 1947, pp. 181–190) are largely based on literary-critical considerations of doubtful relevance. As will be evident, the route of the Exodus is still a very live issue.

BIBLIOGRAPHY. N. Aimé-Giron, *Annales du Service des Antiquités de l'Égypte* 40, 1940–1, pp. 433–460; Bourdon, *RB* 41, 1932, pp. 370–382, 538–549; H. Cazelles, *RB* 62, 1955, pp. 321–364; O. Eissfeldt, *Baal-Zaphon, Zeus Casios und der Durchzug der Israeliten durch das Meer*, 1932; Lepsius, *Zeitschrift für Aegyptische Sprache* 21, 1883, pp. 41–53; Mallon, 'Les Hébreux en Égypte', *Orientalia* 3, 1921; Montet, *Géographie de l'Égypte Ancienne*, 1, 1957, pp. 218–219, and *L'Égypte et la Bible*, 1959, pp. 59–63; E. Uphill, *Pithom and Raamses*; *JNES* 27, 1968, pp. 291–316, and 28, 1969, pp. 15–39.

See also H. H. Rowley, *From Joseph to Joshua*, 1950, for much older bibliography, and C. de Wit, *The Date and Route of the Exodus*, 1960, for more specifically Egyptian aspects. M. Bietak, *Tell El-Dab'a II*, Vienna, 1975, is invaluable for E Delta topography and conditions. C.D.W.

ENDOR. Modern 'En-dûr, 6 km S of Mt Tabor. The town was assigned to Manasseh, but was never wrested from Canaanite possession (Jos. 17:11–12). The medium of Endor, of whom Saul inquired before his last battle (1 Sa. 28:7), was probably from this Canaanite stock, for an attempt had been made to do away with such practices among the Hebrews (1 Sa. 28:3). R.J.W.

EN-EGLAIM (Heb. *'ên-'eḡlayim*, 'spring of the two calves'). A place mentioned once only (Ezk. 47:10) as lying on the shore of the Dead Sea. Though the site is unknown, the reference to *En-gedi suggests a location somewhere in the NW sector. This site is distinct from Eglaim (*'eḡlayim*, Is. 15:8), a town in Moab.

BIBLIOGRAPHY. *GTT*, pp. 459–460; W. R. Farmer, *BA* 19, 1956, pp. 19–21. T.C.M.

EN-GANNIM (Heb. *'ên-gannîm*, 'spring of gardens'). **1.** A town in Judah's inheritance in the Shephelah (Jos. 15:34); perhaps modern Beit Jamal, 3 km S of Beth-shemesh.

2. A levitical city in Issachar's territory (Jos. 19:21; 21:29; called Anem, 1 Ch. 6:73). Variously identified with Jenin, Olam and Khirbet Beit Jann, SW of Tiberias. G.G.G.

EN-GEDI (Heb. *'ên-geḏî*, 'spring of the kid'). Important oasis and fresh water spring W of the Dead Sea, allotted to Judah at the conquest (Jos. 15:62). David hid there (1 Sa. 23:29; 24:1ff.), its rugged terrain and fertility making it an ideal refuge. Famous for aromatic plants and perfume (Ct. 1:14). Excavations 1949 and 1961–5 revealed several fortresses and a late synagogue. Hazazon-tamar = En-gedi (Gn. 14:7; 2 Ch. 20:2). See *NEAEHL*, pp. 399–409. G.G.G.

ENGLISH VERSIONS OF THE BIBLE. The main justification for an article on English (rather than Latin or Spanish) versions of the Bible is that, although English has far fewer mother-tongue speakers than Chinese, more Bibles are distributed in English than in any other of the over 2,000 languages into which at least one of its books has been translated.

I. Old English versions

The history of versions of the Bible in English has its beginnings in the Old English (Anglo-Saxon) period of the language. The Venerable Bede has supplied a fascinating account (*Ecclesiastical History* 4, ch. 24) of a heavenly gift granted to the herdsman Caedmon in the latter part of the 7th century AD, which enabled him to sing in English verse the substance and the themes of the Scriptures. Bede does not quote any of Caedmon's poetry verbatim. Surviving Old English metrical treatments or paraphrases of biblical materials, whether or not they are to be connected with Caedmon, witness to an important means of disseminating knowledge of the Scriptures in that period.

To Bede himself has been attributed the translation of the Gospel according to John. His follower Cuthbert, in a letter on the death of his 'father and master', relates that Bede completed his translation of the fourth Gospel on the day of his death at the virtual moment of his departure. Bede's work has regrettably not survived.

Aldhelm (640–709) has been credited with a translation of the Psalms and indeed of much, if not all, of the Bible into English; but no extant MS can with certainty be said to represent his work. The Vespasian Psalter, the oldest surviving Latin text of the Psalms with a gloss or interlinear translation of the individual words into Old English, cannot with any assurance be held to contain Aldhelm's work. This MS of the Psalter was succeeded by a considerable number of others with Old English glosses.

King Alfred the Great (849–899) introduced his *Code of Saxon Laws* with an abbreviated and rearranged English rendering of the Ten Commandments and portions in English of Ex. 21–23 and Acts 15. William of Malmesbury says that Alfred was at work on an English translation of the Psalms at the time of his death. There has been disagreement as to whether Alfred's work is represented by the prose rendering in English of the first 50 psalms in the Paris Psalter. His translation of Gregory's *De cura pastolari* involved, of course, translation of the Scripture references in the text.

Ælfric, an abbot at about the beginning of the 11th century, made translations or paraphrases of extensive parts of the OT text.

Two MSS of the Gospels in Latin with an Old English gloss have survived. One of them is the famous Lindisfarne Gospels *c.* 700 with a gloss made *c.* 950. The other MS is the Rushworth Gospels, whose gloss is very much dependent on that of the Lindisfarne MS in Mark, Luke and John.

A noteworthy development in the Old English period was the competent translation of the four Gospels into a continuous English text, a text which is represented by six extant MSS.

II. Middle English versions

The development of a literature in Middle English begins in the closing part of the 12th century. In about 1300 a metrical version of the Psalter appeared; it was followed by prose translations, one of which was the work of Richard Rolle of Hampole. Portions of the NT were also translated. The distinguishing achievement of the Middle English period, however, was the translation work associated with John Wyclif (*c.* 1320–84) and the movement he represented. An earlier Wyclifite version was produced *c.* 1380–3. A substantial portion of it was made by Nicholas of Hereford (from Genesis to Baruch 3:20). Whatever may have been Wyclif's personal contribution to the actual work of translation, his zeal for the Scriptures and for making them accessible to the people in the English language must be credited with giving the impetus to this highly influential version. It was made from a Latin base and it clung to the original with some damage to English idiom and clarity, but it was a commendable new effort. It was soon followed by a translation in smoother style which was probably made by John Purvey, a follower of Wyclif, with the assistance of others. The principles and procedures followed by Purvey were in many respects exemplary, and his revision was very influential. It was indeed finally superseded by the work of William Tyndale and Miles Coverdale in the 16th century, but its influence has been perpetuated through its successors.

III. William Tyndale (*c.* 1494–1536)

William Tyndale was the first to translate the NT directly from Greek into English. He received his MA degree at Oxford in 1515, the year before the appearance of Erasmus' Greek NT, the first printed NT in Greek actually to be published. Tyndale may have studied Greek at Cambridge. His zeal for making the Scriptures available in the vernacular is indicated in the story of his encounter with a 'learned man' who expressed the judgment that we might better be without the laws of God than without those of the Pope. To him Tyndale expressed defiance of the Pope and his laws and said that if God would spare his life he would cause a ploughboy to know more of the Scripture than his learned adversary did. Finding England uncongenial to his desire to lay the NT plainly before the eyes of the people in their native language, he went to Hamburg and later travelled widely in continental Europe. He was never to return to the land which was to enter into his labours and to be enriched by his dedication.

In completing his translation of the NT, Tyndale made use of the 1519 and 1522 editions of Erasmus' Greek NT. He also consulted Erasmus' Latin translation, Luther's German text and the Latin Vulgate. The printing of his NT was begun in 1525 in Cologne, but opposition forced him to flee to Worms with the sheets that had been printed. There before long (in 1525 or 1526) two editions were completed (one quarto, the other octavo) of 3,000 copies each. Virulent official opposition in England was so successful in destroying copies of early issues of Tyndale's NT that there are only minimal remains today. Revised editions appeared in 1534 and 1535. Tyndale's NT, despite the opposition to it, could not be destroyed. The first printed English NT, the first made from the Greek, opened a new period in the history of the English Bible and made an ineradicable contribution to the English Bibles yet to come. The influence of the wording and structure of Tyndale's NT on the AV is immense; the AV is a continuing witness to the simplicity, freshness, vitality and felicity of his work. Tyndale also published translations of the Pentateuch in 1530, Jonah in 1531 and selections from the OT (published with his edition of the NT in 1534). An edition of the Pentateuch with a revised translation of Genesis was printed in 1534. There is good authority for believing that Tyndale translated much more of the OT, but before he could complete his translation of the Bible he suffered a

CHRONOLOGICAL TABLE OF THE PRINCIPAL ENGLISH VERSIONS OF THE BIBLE

Date AD	Version (*italics* = Catholic version)	Translator
ANGLO-SAXON VERSIONS		
Late 7th cent.	English verse (oral)	Caedmon
	John's Gospel, +?	Bede
	Psalms; entire Bible?	Aldheim (640–709)
	Anglo-Saxon Psalter glosses	
Late 9th cent.	Ten Commandments	Alfred the Great (849–901)
	Ex. 21–23	
	Acts 15	
	Scripture refs. in Gregory's 'De Cura Pastorali'	
c. 950	Anglo-Saxon gloss of the Lindisfarne Gospels	
	Anglo-Saxon gloss of the Rushworth Gospels	
11th cent.	Parts of the OT	Aelfric
	Four Gospels into continuous English text	
MIDDLE ENGLISH VERSIONS		
c. 1300	Metrical Psalter	
	Prose Psalter	Richard Rolle of Hampole
c. 1380–1383	Wyclif Bible	Nicholas of Hereford and Wyclif (?)
	Revision of Wyclif's Bible	John Purvey
SIXTEENTH-CENTURY VERSIONS		
1525/6	NT	William Tyndale
1530	Pentateuch	Tyndale
1531	Jonah	Tyndale
	Isaiah	George Joye
1534	OT selections	Tyndale
	NT revision	
	Psalms, Lamentations, Jeremiah	Joye
	Song of Moses at the Red Sea	
	Revision (unauthorized) of Tyndale's NT	
1535	NT revision	Tyndale
	First complete Bible in English	Miles Coverdale
1537	The Matthew Bible	John Rogers? ('Thomas Matthew')
1538	Parallel English–Latin NT (Vulgate)	Coverdale
1539	Revision of the Matthew Bible	Richard Taverner
	The Great Bible	Coverdale, for Thomas Cromwell
1540	2nd edition of the Great Bible	Preface by Archbp. Cranmer
1545	Revised Primer ('Primer of Henry VIII')	
1557	Geneva NT	William Whittingham
1560	Geneva Bible	Various (including Whittingham)
1568	The Bishops' Bible	Matthew Parker and others
1572	Revised folio edition of the Bishops' Bible	
1582	*Rheims NT*	*Gregory Martin, William Allen and others*
SEVENTEENTH-CENTURY VERSIONS		
1609–1610	*Douay OT*	*Gregory Martin and others*
1611	Authorized (King James) Version	Fifty-four translators
1613	Revision of AV	
1616–1623	Pentateuch, Song of Solomon, Psalms	Henry Ainsworth
EIGHTEENTH-CENTURY VERSIONS		
1718–1719	*NT*	*Cornelius Nary*
1729	Greek and English NT	William Mace
1730	*NT*	*Robert Witham*
1745	The Primitive NT	William Whiston
1749–1772	*Two revisions of Douay OT, five revisions of Rheims NT*	*Richard Challoner*
1755	Revision of AV	John Wesley
1764	NT	Richard Wynne
	Bible	Anthony Purver
1768	Liberal translation of the NT	E. Harwood
1770	NT	John Worsley
1783–1810	*Revisions of Rheims and Douay texts*	*Bernard MacMahon*
NINETEENTH-CENTURY VERSIONS		
1822	Paul's Epistles	Thomas Belsham (Unitarian)
1832	Paul's Epistles	Charles Eyre (Unitarian)
1833	NT	Rodolphus Dickinson
1840	NT	Samuel Sharpe (Unitarian)

NINETEENTH-CENTURY VERSIONS—*continued*		
1849–1860	*Annotated revision of Douay-Rheims text*	*Bishop Francis Patrick Kenrick*
1855	Gospels	Andrew Norton
1858	NT	Leicester Ambrose Sawyer
1862	OT & NT	Robert Young
1863	Gospels	G. W. Braineld
1869	NT	Henry Alford
	OT & NT	Robert Ainslie
1871	NT	J. N. Darby
1872	NT	J. B. Rotherham
1875	NT	Samuel Davidson
1881	Revised Version (RV) NT	British & American companies
1882	Romans	Ferrar Fenton
1883	Paul's Epistles	Fenton
1885	RV complete Bible	British & American companies
1890	Bible	J. N. Darby
1895	Current English NT	Fenton

TWENTIETH-CENTURY VERSIONS		
1898–1901	The Twentieth Century NT	Twenty lay scholars
1901	American Standard Edition (of RV)	American scholars
1903	Bible in Modern English	Fenton
	NT in Modern Sspeech	R. F. Weymouth
1913	NT	James Moffatt
1923	American translation of the NT	E. J. Goodspeed
	Riverside NT	W. G. Ballantine
1924	OT	Mofatt
	Centenary translation of the NT	Helen B. Montgomery
1927	American translation of the OT	A. R. Gordon, T. J. Meek, Leroy Waterman, J. M. Powis Smith
1935	*Westminster Version of the Sacred Scriptures, NT*	*Various Catholic scholars*
1937	NT	C. B. Williams
	NT	*F. A. Spencer*
1941	The NT in Basic English	S. H. Hooke
1945	Berkeley Version of the NT	Gerrit Verkuyl
	NT (trans. from Vulgate)	*Monsignor R. A. Knox*
1946	Revision of American RV NT (RSV)	International Council of Religious Education
1947–1957	NT	J. B. Phillips
1948	The Letchworth Version (NT) in Modern English	T. F. & R. E. Ford
1949	Bible in Basic English	S. H. Hooke
	OT	*R. A. Knox*
1952	Entire RSV Bible	
	Plain English NT	C. K. Williams
1954	*NT*	*J. A. Kleist & J. L. Lilly*
1955	Authentic NT	H. J. Schonfield
	Revision of Knox's OT	
1956–1959	Expanded Translation of the Greek NT	K. S. Wuest
1958	The Amplified NT	Lockman Foundation
1959	The Berkeley Bible	Gerrit Verkuyl
1961	The New English Bible NT	Representatives of major British churches & Bible Societies
1962–1971	The Living Bible	K. N. Taylor
1963	The NT in the Language of Today	W. F. Beck
	New American Standard Bible (revision of the American RV)	Evangelical scholars
1966	Today's English Version (Good News for Modern Man), NT	American Bible Society
	Jerusalem Bible	*Catholic scholars*
1968–9	New translation, NT	William Barclay
1969	The New Berkeley (Modern Language) Bible	Verkuyl
1970	The New English Bible OT	Representatives of major British churches, etc.
	The New American Bible	*Bishops' Committee of the Confraternity of Christian Doctrine*
1972	New International Version (NT)	Evangelical scholars
1973	The Translator's NT	British & Foreign Bible Society
1976	Complete Good News Bible	American Bible Society
1979	New International Version Holy Bible	Evangelical scholars
	New King James Version NT	
1982	New King James Version	
1985	*New Jerusalem Bible*	*General editor: Henry Wansbrough*
1989	Revised English Bible	Director of Revision: W. D. McHardy
1990	New Revised Standard Version, international edition	General editor: Bruce M. Metzger
1994	Good News Bible, second edition	
1995	New Revised Standard Version, anglicized edition	

martyr's death. In his OT work he used the Hebrew text. Among other works available to him were Luther's German translation, the Latin Vulgate and a Latin rendering by Pagninus. Like his version of the NT, Tyndale's faithful and vivid translations of books of the OT has been exceedingly influential. His dying prayer was that the Lord would open the eyes of the king of England.

George Joye also had a significant part in the development of the English Bible in Tyndale's day. He graduated from Cambridge in 1513, was later influenced by Lutheran doctrine and found it necessary to seek refuge abroad *c.* 1527. He may have published a version of the Psalter in 1530, different from that which he published in 1534. He also published English translations of Isaiah (1531), Jeremiah, Lamentations, and the Song of Moses at the Red Sea (1534), and a revision of Tyndale's NT (1534) without Tyndale's authorization and with changes of which Tyndale did not approve. After Tyndale had issued his own revision of his NT in 1534, with selections from the OT, Joye published another edition of his NT, together with selections from the OT. He may also have published translations of Proverbs and Ecclesiastes.

IV. Miles Coverdale (1488–1568)

The first really notable name in the history of English Bible translation and revision between Tyndale and the AV is that of Miles Coverdale, whose work benefited from an altered royal and ecclesiastical attitude. In 1535 Coverdale published a translation (which he had prepared on the Continent) of the entire Bible, the first full Bible to be printed in English. This version was dedicated to Henry VIII. It was made from German and Latin versions and with the aid of translations made by Tyndale. A folio edition and a quarto edition appeared in 1537. The quarto edition asserts on its title-page that it was set forth with the king's most gracious licence. In 1538 Coverdale published an edition of the Latin Vulgate NT with an English translation in parallel columns. His capacity for beautiful rhythm and phrasing have made an enduring contribution to the great tradition of English Bible translation.

V. The Matthew Bible

In 1537 there appeared a Bible whose title-page asserts that it was truly and purely translated into English by Thomas Matthew. This Bible has often been regarded as the work of one of Tyndale's followers, John Rogers, who regarded it as inexpedient to issue under his own name. It was virtually a compilation of Tyndale's and Coverdale's work with minor alterations and some 2,000 notes. It was a fact of remarkable irony that a Bible which was substantially the work of Tyndale, who had been opposed by Henry VIII and the church, could now be dedicated to Henry and set forth with his most gracious licence! On the solicitation of Cranmer, the Archbishop of Canterbury, Thomas Cromwell secured Henry's authorization that this Bible would be allowed by his authority to be bought and read within the realm.

VI. Taverner's Bible

Richard Taverner (*c.* 1505–75) published in 1539 a revision of Matthew's Bible which introduced a number of improvements indicating some scholarly competence. It was not without influence on future versions, but has not generally been regarded as occupying a place in the main line of English versions of the Bible.

VII. The Great Bible

In 1539 there appeared a Bible which was to exercise enormous influence on England and on the subsequent history of the English Bible. It was prepared by Coverdale on the invitation of Thomas Cromwell, and has therefore been called Cromwell's Bible. Because of its large size it is commonly called the Great Bible. The second edition of April 1540 and later editions had a preface by Archbishop Cranmer, and consequently the version has frequently been referred to as Cranmer's Bible. But regardless of its multiple designations, it is really a revision of Matthew's Bible. It was authorized for distribution among the people and for the use of every church. Copies were obtained for the churches; people collected around them, and even disturbed church services with their reading and discussions. Three editions appeared in 1540 and three more in 1541. The Psalter of the Great Bible has been perpetuated in the Book of Common Prayer.

VIII. The Geneva Bible

In the last years of Henry VIII no new editions of the English Bible were produced, and the official attitude towards the use of vernacular Scriptures changed. The Great Bible was not banned, as were Tyndale's and Coverdale's Bibles, but its use was limited. The new attitude was carried over into the field of Primers, which contained selections from the Scriptures. In 1545 a revised Primer, frequently referred to as the Primer of Henry VIII, was published, and the use of any other was forbidden. In the reign of Edward VI the climate again became favourable to the development and use of the Bible in English. Many editions of the older translations were published, but practically no new work was done. Sir John Cheke prepared independent translations of Matthew and the beginning of Mark made from the Greek in a style designed to be intelligible to the less cultured, and trying to avoid words of non-English origin, but his work was not in fact published until 1843.

The reign of Mary Tudor was of a quite different character from that of Edward. Bibles were taken from churches, and many Protestants suffered martyrdom. Some fled to the Continent. A group of such men in Geneva was responsible for the production of the Geneva Bible. First, however, a Geneva NT was published in 1557, prepared chiefly, it would seem, by William Whittingham. This NT employed the verse divisions which Stephanus had introduced into the fourth edition of his Greek NT in 1551. Italics were used to distinguish words introduced by the translator to clarify the meaning. Whittingham seems to have used as the foundation text for his praiseworthy revision a recently published edition of Tyndale's NT.

In 1558 Elizabeth's reign began, and the official attitude towards the use of the Bible and towards its translators changed again. Whittingham and others nevertheless continued in Geneva until they had completed the version of the Bible on which they had been working. This Geneva Bible, dedicated to Elizabeth, was published in 1560. It made an enormous contribution to the Authorized Version, and achieved a dominant popularity in the period 1570–1620. A very scholarly work, it drew upon the unique competence and assistance of the great and devoted men who were in Geneva at the time, and upon works in different languages which were available there. The OT section was a painstaking revision of that of the Great Bible with careful attention to the Hebrew; and for the NT it drew upon the Whittingham 1557 edition. Because of its use of 'breeches' in Genesis 3:7 (a reading which, however, was not new), it became known as the 'Breeches Bible'. Verse divisions were employed throughout the entire Bible.

IX. The Bishops' Bible

The Geneva Bible was more accurate than the Great Bible, but official endorsement was not transferred to it. Instead, the Archbishop of Canterbury, Matthew Parker, promoted a revision of the Great Bible, with much of the work done by bishops. This revision, of varying merit and at points considerably influenced by the Geneva Bible, was published in a folio edition in 1568. It came to be known as the Bishops' Bible, and received ecclesiastical authorization. A slightly revised quarto edition appeared in 1569. A folio edition with an extensive revision of the NT section was published in 1572. The Prayer Book version of the Psalms and the Bishops' Bible Psalter were printed in this edition in parallel columns. In following editions, except for that of 1585, only the Prayer Book Psalter was included. The 1572 revision had a substantial influence on the AV.

X. The Rheims–Douay Version

Roman Catholics, who during the reign of Elizabeth I had found refuge on the Continent, in 1582 published in Rheims a NT which they hoped would counteract the influence of Protestant translations. This was the work of Gregory Martin, William Allen and others of the English College in Rheims. Their reason for addressing themselves to this task was not that which actuated Protestant translators (*i.e.*, a zealous desire to make the Word of God generally accessible in the vernacular), for in their preface they held that, on the contrary, the translation of the Bible into the 'vulgar tongues' was not an absolute necessity, or even necessarily profitable. They based their translation on a Latin Vulgate text, but did give attention to the Greek, as is evidenced by their treatment of the definite article. They gave some attention also to previous translations in English. Of set purpose they retained certain Latin words and followed their basic text closely, even, at times, to the point of sacrifice of intelligibility. They did, however, provide a glossary to assist the English reader, and their work served to broaden the word-base on which the AV was constructed. The OT was not published until 1609–10 at Douai, which was too late to exert much, if any, influence on the AV. In style it was similar to the Rheims NT.

XI. The Authorized Version

At the Hampton Court Conference in 1604 a proposal was made by Dr John Reynolds, a Puritan and president of Corpus Christi College, Oxford, that a new translation of the Bible be made. This proposal, although not favoured by a majority of those present, appealed to King James I, and resulted ultimately in the production of the AV. The king wished to have a uniform translation made by the finest scholars in the two English universities, a translation to be reviewed by the bishops and the most learned men in the church, afterwards presented to the Privy Council, and finally ratified by his authority.

James appointed fifty-four learned men for the work of translation, and the translators were divided into six companies. Among other things, the revisers were to follow the Bishops' Bible, and were to modify it as slightly as the 'truth of the original' or emphasis required; they were to retain the old ecclesiastical terms such as 'church', and marginal notes were to be avoided except for certain non-controversial uses.

Further information about the principles and practices which were followed by the revisers is given in the preface, 'The Translators to the Reader'. The Scriptures are there acknowledged to be high and divine, full and perfect; and their translation into the vernacular is shown to be necessary. The revisers appreciated the excellent translation work that had been done in previous years. They never designed to make a new translation or to change a bad one into a good one, but their aim was 'to make a good one better, or out of many good ones, one principal good one, not justly to be excepted against'. They sought not praise, but the truth; their trust was in him who has the key of David.

They worked from the Hebrew text of the OT and the Greek text of the NT. They did not labour with undue haste or hesitate to revise what they had done; but brought back to the anvil that which they had hammered. They consulted translators or commentators in various languages. When the text was not clear, they gave alternative translations in the margin. They did not bind themselves to translate a given Heb. or Gk. expression by the same English expression in all cases, but responded sensitively to the context. They avoided the obscurity of the Douay Bible with its Latinate element. Their desire was that the Bible speak like itself, that it be understood 'euen of the very vulgar'.

When the various companies had completed their work, twelve representatives chosen from among them revised the entire translation. After some further modifications of detail the version was ready for publication. There is no extant record of official ecclesiastical or royal authorization, but the words 'appointed to be read in churches' appeared on the title-page of the first edition. The version immediately displaced the Bishops' Bible in the churches and in time gained a victory over the Geneva Bible in popular favour, although the latter continued in use privately for a long while, especially in Scotland. The AV gathered to itself the virtues of the long and brilliant line of English Bible translations; it united high scholarship with Christian devotion and piety. It came into being at a time of vigorous literary activity, and its scholars had a remarkable mastery of the instrument which Providence had prepared for them. Their version has justifiably been called 'the noblest monument of English prose'. It has been estimated that the AV is indebted to the earlier English translations of the Bible for about 60% of its text. The chief contributors were the Geneva Bible (about 19%), and Tyndale's translations, including the Matthew Bible (about 18%).

XII. From the Authorized to the Revised Version

Even in the years following its first publication, the AV underwent significant though unofficial revision. More than 300 changes are found in the 1613 edition. Extensive modifications were introduced in editions published in the 18th century. Other English versions continued to be made. Henry Ainsworth from 1616 to 1623 published translations of the Pentateuch and the Song of Solomon, and his translation of these books and of the Psalms was published after his death. His work was animated by a desire for accurate rendering. Paraphrases became fairly numerous. Several significant contributions were made in the 18th century. William Mace published in 1729 a NT in Greek and English in which he attempted to take into account 'the most Authentic Manuscripts' and to use the accepted colloquial style of his day. Translations made in the 18th century by Philip Doddridge (*Family Expositor, or, a Paraphrase and Version of the New Testament*), George Campbell (*Translation of the Gospels*) and James Macknight (*A New Literal Translations of all the Apostolical Epistles*) were used in a NT published in 1818. In 1745 William Whiston published his *Primitive New Testament*, which uses the text of the AV, but modifies it in the interest of readings found in Codex Bezae, Codex Claromontanus and Codex Alexandrinus. John Wesley published in 1755 a revision of the AV NT.

Richard Wynne issued in 1764 *The New Testament, carefully collated with the Greek, corrected, divided and printed according to the subjects treated of*. Wynne sought to find a middle course between a literal rendering and loose paraphrase. Anthony Purver, a member of the Society of Friends, worked for 30 years on the translation of the Bible which he published in 1764. One of the most noteworthy of 18th-century efforts was that of E. Harwood, who published in 1768 his *Liberal Translation of the New Testament*. His use of an 'elegant', literary, paraphrastic 18th-century style dates his work.

John Worsley made an effort to translate the NT from the Greek into the 'Present Idiom of the English Tongue'. He wished to remove from the text obsolete and hardly intelligible words, and to bring the translation closer to the original. His translation was published posthumously in 1770. Other versions which were published (or printed) in the late 18th century were those of Gilbert Wakefield, W. H. Roberts, Thomas Haweis, William Newcome, who utilized Griesbach's Greek text of 1774–5, Nathaniel Scarlett, assisted by certain other 'men of piety and literature' (whose translation allows itself the freedom of arranging material in the form of a drama), and 'J. M. Ray'.

The Philadelphia publisher R. Aitken, who in 1782 had produced the first edition of the AV published in America, issued in 1808 the first printed translation of the Septuagint, by Charles Thomson.

The 19th century saw the appearance of translations of the Epistles of Paul by the Unitarians Thomas Belsham (1822) and Charles Eyre (1832), and of the entire NT by the Unitarian Samuel Sharpe (1840) from J. J. Griesbach's Greek text. In 1865 Sharpe published a revised text of the AV of the OT. In 1833 the American, Rodolphus Dickinson, published with indifferent success a NT in which he attempted to improve on the style of the AV. Among the literal translations of the 19th century, mention should be made of that of Robert Young in 1863. New textual information continued to be reflected in the English versions. 'Herman Heinfetter' made use of the Codex Vaticanus: G. W. Braineld took into account the texts of Griesbach, Lachmann, Tischendorf, Alford and Tregelles in his translation of the Gospels (1863); Robert Ainslie used the AV in 1869, but modified it in the interest of readings favoured by Tischendorf; Samuel Davidson published in 1875 a translation of the NT from the text of Tischendorf; and J. B. Rotherham translated the NT from the text of Tregelles (1872).

Andrew Norton's new translation of the Gospels (1855) and Leicester Ambrose Sawyer's translation of the NT (1858) were efforts to use the style of their day. They have been credited with introducing the succession of 20th-century versions in modern speech. Various private revisions of the AV were published in the 19th century, in both Britain and the United States.

XIII. Roman Catholic versions in the 18th and 19th centuries

In the 18th century a number of Roman Catholic efforts were made to provide an improved English version. Cornelius Nary published in 1718 and 1719 a NT translated from the Latin Vulgate with attention given to the Greek and Hebrew idiom, in which he attempted to use intelligible, idiomatic English. Robert Witham also desired to make the text of the English NT intelligible to the contemporary reader. His version, translated from the Latin Vulgate, was published in 1730. In 1738 the fifth, lightly revised, edition of the Rheims-Douay NT appeared, more than a century after the fourth edition (1633). Richard Challoner, who has been credited with some of the work on this fifth edition, later published two revisions of the Douay OT and five of the NT (1749–72), providing a simpler, more idiomatic type of text which continued in general use among English-speaking Roman Catholics until at least 1941. He was not averse to following the AV when he approved its readings. The revisions made by Bernard MacMahon 1783–1810 had a considerable influence, especially in Ireland. Bishop Francis Patrick Kenrick from 1849 to 1860 published a revised text of the Rheims-Douay version with annotations.

XIV. The Revised Version

Conviction that a revision of the AV had become necessary came to formal ecclesiastical expression in 1870, and a revision of the AV was undertaken by the Convocation of Canterbury of the Church of England. Distinguished scholars, not all of whom were members of the Church of England, participated in the project. Among the general principles adopted, it was agreed that as few changes as possible were to be made in the text of the AV consistent with faithfulness, and that such changes as were introduced should be expressed in the language of the AV and its predecessors.

The initial meeting of the NT Company was held on 22 June 1870, in the Jerusalem Chamber of Westminster Abbey. This opening session was preceded by a communion service conducted by the Dean of Westminster in the Henry VII Chapel. Among those who were admitted to the Lord's table was a Unitarian member of the company. Strong protest was naturally aroused. From this inauspicious beginning the company began more than 10 years of labour. The assistance of American biblical scholars was sought; and two American companies, one for the OT and one for the NT, were formed. Exclusive copyright was given to the

University Presses of Oxford and Cambridge. The American companies agreed not to publish an edition embodying their distinctive readings for 14 years after the publication of the English RV. The University Presses promised to publish during that period an appendix listing readings preferred by the American companies which had not been accepted by the British revisers. On 17 May 1881 the RV of the NT was published in England, and the whole Bible on 19 May 1885. The textual theories of Westcott and Hort were manifest in the NT; the OT characteristically followed the Massoretic Text, and much effort was made to represent the original faithfully and accurately even in details. Where possible, unlike the AV translators, the revisers attempted consistently to represent a given word in the original by a given English word. Because of its accuracy the RV has proved very valuable for study purposes. Its style, however, has not generally been approved by those who have been captivated by the rhythm and the music of the AV.

In 1901 the preferences of the American companies and other preferences of the surviving members of the committee were embodied in the text of an 'American Standard Edition' of the Revised Bible. Among the changes which were introduced, the substitution of 'Jehovah' for 'LORD' and 'GOD' (in small capitals) was unwelcome to many.

XV. Since the Revised Version

The RV did not succeed in displacing the AV in the affections of the majority of Bible-readers, and was unable to satisfy all of those who were persuaded of the need for a revision. They did, however, open a remarkably prolific period of Bible translation. Since 1881 there has been an unceasing flow of translations, or revisions of translations, of the NT, or the entire Bible, or of parts of the Bible. The Bible Society's Library in Cambridge, UK, listed fifteen new English translations between 1980 and 1984 alone. Among them there has been a diversity in basic texts employed, in methods of translation, in language and style, and in theological viewpoint. The influence of the Greek text and of the principles of textual criticism advocated by Westcott and Hort has been strongly felt. The view that the Greek of the NT was in the main the popular, vernacular Greek of the 1st century and not the literary Greek of that time has encouraged translators to undertake versions in 'everyday English'. There has been a generally successful effort to achieve intelligibility and contemporaneity of expression. However, in the realm of felicity and grace of style the accomplishment has often been undistinguished.

A number of the versions or revisions which have appeared since the time of the English RV might be given brief mention. Among the pioneers in the translation of the Scriptures into modern English was Ferrar Fenton, who published a translation of Romans 'direct from the original Greek into modern English' in 1882 and a translation of the Epistles of Paul in 1883. His NT translated into 'current English' appeared in 1895 and his *Bible in Modern English* in 1903. *The Twentieth Century New Testament*, the work of about twenty persons, was published from 1898 to 1901, and was subsequently issued in revised form. The *New Testament in Modern Speech*, R. F. Weymouth's much-used translation from the text of his *Resultant Greek Testament*, was posthumously published in 1903, with Ernest Hampden-Cook as editor. James Moffatt issued *The Historical New Testament* in 1901, in which he attempted to arrange the writings of the NT in a conjectured order of 'literary growth' and date of composition. In 1913 his new translation of the NT appeared. Its textual basis was mainly von Soden's Greek text. The singular reading of the Sinaitic Syriac is followed at Mt. 1:16, and the reader is not assisted by any textual note. Moffatt's translation of the OT was published in 1924. E. J. Goodspeed's 'American' translation of the NT, based on the Greek text of Westcott and Hort and intended to be expressed in popular American idiom, appeared in 1923, and the 'American' translation of the OT, prepared by A. R. Gordon, T. J. Meek, Leroy Waterman and J. M. Powis Smith, appeared in 1927. Attention should also be called to W. G. Ballantine's *Riverside New Testament* (1923); Helen B. Montgomery's *Centenary Translation of the New Testament* (1924); C. B. Williams' translation of the New Testament 'in the language of the people' (1937), a version which attempts a precise rendering of Gk. verb forms; *The New Testament in Basic English* (1941) and *The Bible in Basic English* (1949); Gerrit Verkuyl's *Berkeley Version of the New Testament* (1945), the Berkeley Version of the entire Bible (1959), the OT section of which was prepared by a sizeable staff of translators, with Gerrit Verkuyl as editor-in-chief, and the *New Berkeley* or *Modern Language Bible* (1969); J. B. Phillips' translation of the NT (1947–57; one-volume edition, 1958), in vigorous and contemporary but not always common language; *The Letchworth Version* (of the NT) *in Modern English*, by T. F. Ford and R. E. Ford (1948), a remarkably successful light revision of the AV which conserves much of stylistic beauty of its original; *The New World Translation of the Christian Greek Scriptures* (1950 revised 1984), a version prepared by the Jehovah's Witnesses; C. K. Williams' translation of the NT into a limited-vocabulary 'Plain English' (1952); H. J. Schonfield's *Authentic New Testament* (1955); Kenneth S. Wuest's *Expanded Translation of the Greek New Testament* (1956–9); the *Amplified New Testament* (1958); W. F. Beck's New Testament in the Language of Today (1963); William Barclay's *New Translation* of the New Testament (1968–9); and *The Translator's New Testament* (1973).

Several Roman Catholic translations of special interest have appeared in this period. The NT section of *The Westminster Version of the Sacred Scriptures*, (1913–35), was translated from the Greek by various men working on individual assignments under general editors. It employs a solemn or 'biblical' style with archaic forms. J. A. Carey issued a revision of the Challoner–Rheims NT in 1935. F. A. Spencer's translation of the NT from the Greek was published in 1937. In 1941 a revision of the Challoner–Rheims NT appeared in USA, prepared under the supervision of the Confraternity of Christian Doctrine by a large number of scholars. It was not bound by the official Clementine text of the Latin Vulgate, but its revisers were free to take account of critical editions. They succeeded in commendable measure in producing a version of clarity, simplicity and contemporary style.

Monsignor R. A. Knox published in 1944 a trial edition of a translation of the NT from the Vulgate and a slightly modified definitive edition in 1945, which was 'authorized by the Archbishops and Bishops of England and Wales'. It was accorded an official status along with the Rheims-Douay version. Knox's translation of the OT from the Latin Vulgate was published in 1949 in two volumes 'for private use only'. A revision appeared in 1955 with hierarchical authorization. The translation of the NT by James A. Kleist and Joseph L. Lilly (1954) was made from the Greek. Kleist translated the Gospels from the text of Bover; Lilly translated the rest of the NT. The *Jerusalem Bible* (1966) is related to the French version *La Bible de Jérusalem*, though is not simply a translation of it. *The New American Bible* (1970), sponsored by the Bishops' Committee of the Confraternity of Christian Doctrine, represented a major translation effort. It was based on the original languages of Scripture or on what was held to be the oldest form of the text extant.

Several of the most widely used and most influential of recent versions remain to be mentioned. A committee-revision of the American RV, authorized by the International Council of Religious Education, was published in 1946 (NT; [2]1971), 1952 (entire Bible), 1965 (Catholic edition). This *Revised Standard Version* (RSV) was a more flexible, less concordant translation than the RV. It made significant use of conjectural emendations in the OT, and its translation 'expiation' in Rom 3:25 was criticized by evangelicals. Its successor *The New Revised Standard Version* (NRSV, 1989) did much to meet such criticisms.

Another revision of the American RV, *The New American Standard Bible* (1963), prepared by evangelical scholars, is a close and faithful translation in a clear and readable style, which is admirable for study purposes. Also by evangelicals is the *New International Version* (1978). It is a completely new translation into contemporary English, somewhat freer than is NASB. The very successful *Good News Bible*: *Today's English Version* (GNB or TEV; NT 1966 by Robert G. Bratcher, Bible 1976, 2nd edn. USA 1992, UK 1994), first published by the American Bible Society and later in a British usage edition, is based on faithfulness to the semantic content rather than to the grammatical structure of the original, and on the use of common rather than literary or church language; the Contemporary English Version (USA 1995, UK NT 1996) also seeks oral readability. The first but not the second of these principles also marks the *New English Bible* (NEB; NT 1961, Bible 1970), in which all the main British non-Roman Catholic churches and the British Bible Societies participated, and its successor the *Revised English Bible* (REB; 1989), in which British Roman Catholic churches also participated. REB addressed charges of excessive OT conjectural emendation in NEB, and also somewhat lowered NEB's language level.

The Living Bible (NT 1962, Bible 1971) describes itself as a paraphrase, and is not based directly on the original texts.

It may reasonably be claimed that there are enough English translations in print to satisfy the needs, beliefs and tastes of every kind of reader. Yet changes in the language, greater understanding of how language works and communication takes place, and new discoveries about the languages and the world of the Bible, mean that no translation, in English or any other language, is likely to prove definitive.

BIBLIOGRAPHY. F. F. Bruce, *History of the Bible in English*[4], 1985; C. C. Butterworth, *The Literary Lineage of the King James Bible*, 1941; D. A. Carson, *The King James Version Debate*, 1979; A. S. Herbert, *A Historical Catalogue of Printed Editions of the English Bible*, 1525–1961, 1968; M. T. Hills, *The English Bible in America*, 1961; G. W. H. Lampe (ed.), *The Cambridge History of the Bible*, vol. 2, 1969, pp. 362–415; vol. 3, 1970, pp. 141–174; S. Kubo and W. F. Specht, *So Many Versions?*[2], 1983; J. P. Lewis, *The English Bible from KJV to NIV*[2], 1991; W. F. Moulton, *The History of the English Bible*[5], 1911; H. Pope, *English Versions of the Bible*, revised and amplified by Sebastian Bullough, 1952; E. H. Robertson, *The New Translations of the Bible*, 1959; P. M. Simms, *The Bible in America*, 1936; B. F. Westcott, *A General View of the History of the English Bible*[3], revised W. A. Wright, 1927.

J.H.S.
P.E.

EN-HADDAH. 'Sharp spring', the name of a place which fell to the lot of Issachar (Jos. 19:21). Suggested identifications have been made (see *GTT*, p. 185), but the site has not been definitely identified.

T.C.M.

EN-HAKKORE (Heb. *'ên-haqqôrē'*). The spring in Lehi from which Samson refreshed himself after slaughtering the Philistines with the jawbone of an ass (Jdg. 15:19). None of the places mentioned in the story has been identified. En-hakkore could mean 'the spring of the partridge' (*cf.* En-gedi, 'the spring of the goat'), but Jdg. 15 gives a coherent account of the origin of the name, indicating that it means 'the spring of him who called'. J.A.M.

EN-HAZOR. The name of a place which fell to the lot of Naphtali (Jos. 19:37). The site is unknown, though suggestions have been made (see *GTT*, p. 198). It is distinct from *Hazor.

T.C.M.

ENOCH. 1. Son of Cain (Gn. 4:17) after whom a city was named.

2. Son of Jared and father of Methuselah (Gn. 5:18, 21). Enoch was a man of outstanding sanctity who enjoyed close fellowship with God (Gn. 5:22, 24: for the expression 'walked with God', *cf.* Gn. 6:9; Mi. 6:8; Mal. 2:6). Like Elijah (2 Ki. 2:11), he was received into the presence of God without dying (Gn. 5:24).

It is probable that the language of Pss. 49:15; 73:24 reflects the story of Enoch. In that case the example of Enoch's assumption played a part in the origin of Jewish hope for life with God beyond death. (In the Apocrypha, Wisdom 4:10–14 also treats Enoch as the outstanding example of the righteous man's hope of eternal life.)

In the NT, Heb. 11:5f. attributes Enoch's assumption to his faith; the expression 'pleased God' is the LXX translation of 'walked with God' (Gn. 5:24). Jude 14f. quotes a prophecy attributed to Enoch in *1 Enoch* 1:9.

In the intertestamental period Enoch became a popular figure: see Ecclus. 44:16; 49:14, 16 (Heb.); *Jubilees* 4:14–26; 10:17; and *1 Enoch.* Probably the legend of Enoch was elaborated in the Babylonian diaspora as a counterpart to the antediluvian sages of Mesopotamian legend. So Enoch became the initiator of the art of writing and the first wise man, who received heavenly revelations of the secrets of the universe and transmitted them in writing to later generations.

In the earlier tradition his scientific wisdom is prominent, acquired on journeys through the heavens with angelic guides, and including astronomical, cosmographical and meteorological lore, as well as the solar calendar used at Qumran. He was also God's prophet against the fallen angels. Later tradition (2nd century BC) emphasizes his ethical teaching and especially his apocalyptic revelations of the course of world history down to the last judgment. In the Similitudes (*1 Enoch* 37–71) he is identified with the Messianic Son of man (71:14–17), and some later Jewish traditions identified him with the nearly divine figure Metatron (*Targum of Pseudo-Jonathan*, Gn. 5:24; *3 Enoch*). Early Christian apocalyptic writings frequently expect his return to earth with Elijah before the End.

1 Enoch (*Ethiopic Enoch*) is among the most important intertestamental works. The complete text survives only in Ethiopic, but sections are extant in Greek and important fragments of the original Aramaic are now available from Qumran. *1 Enoch* comprises five books: the Book of Watchers (1–36), the Similitudes (37–71), the Astronomical Book (72–82), the Book of Dreams (83–90) and the Epistle of Enoch (91–105). The Qumran MSS include fragments of all these except the Similitudes, which are therefore now generally dated no earlier than the 1st century AD. Also from Qumran there are fragments of a hitherto almost unknown Book of Giants, which was probably the original fifth book of the Enoch Pentateuch, for which the Similitudes were later substituted.

The Qumran MSS help clarify the dates of these works. The oldest sections are the Astronomical Book and 6–19: these date from no later than the beginning of the 2nd century BC and may be as early as the 5th century. The Book of Watchers (incorporating 6–19) cannot be later than the mid-1st and is probably from the mid-3rd century BC. The Book of Dreams is from 165 or 164 BC. The Epistle of Enoch and Book of Giants may date from the end of the 2nd century BC.

Other works under the name of Enoch are from the Christian era. The Similitudes (*1 Enoch* 37–71) (important as perhaps illustrating the background to the use of 'Son of man' in the Gospels) seem to be a Jewish work, though some argue for Christian origin. *3 Enoch* (*Hebrew Enoch*) is a Jewish work of disputed date. *2 Enoch* (*Slavonic Enoch*) is a late Christian work which may incorporate Jewish material.

BIBLIOGRAPHY. J. T. Milik, *The Books of Enoch: Aramaic Fragments from Qumrân Cave 4*, 1976; J. C. VanderKam, *Enoch and the Growth of an Apocalyptic Tradition*, 1984; M. Black, *The Book of Enoch or 1 Enoch*, 1985.

R.J.B.

ENOSH. Son of Seth and father of Kenan (Gn. 4:26; 5:6–11; 1 Ch. 1:1; Lk. 3:38). His life-span is recorded as 905 years. In his time men began to call upon the covenant name of Yahweh. The Heb. word *'enôš*, 'man', occurs some 42 times in OT, and often suggests the aspect of frailty and mortality (Jb. 4:17); the corresponding verb *'ānaš* means 'to be weak' (*cf.* *ADAM). N.H.

EN-RIMMON (Heb. *'ên-rimmôn*, 'spring of the pomegranate'). A village in Judah reoccupied after the Exile (Ne. 11:29). Either it was formed by the coalescing of two separate villages Ain and Rimmon, or more probably, reading Jos. 15:32; 19:7; 1 Ch. 4:32 all as En-rimmon, it was always a single town, originally in Judah's inheritance (Jos. 15:32), but soon transferred to Simeon (Jos. 19:7). It has been identified with Umm er-Ramāmîn, 15 km N of Beersheba. M.A.M.

EN-ROGEL (Heb. *'ên-rōgēl*, 'well of the fuller'). A water source just outside Jerusalem, some 200 m S of the confluence of the Valley of Hinnom and the Kidron valley. It is known today as Job's well. The well marked a point on the N boundary of Judah (Jos. 15:7) before David captured Jerusalem (2 Sa. 5:6ff.).

The narrative of Adonijah's abortive attempt to gain the throne in David's old age suggests the site had cultic associations (1 Ki. 1:9ff.). R.J.W.

EN-SHEMESH (Heb. *'ên-šemeš*, 'spring of the sun'). A point on the Judah–Benjamin border 4 km E of Jerusalem, below Olivet, and just S of the Jericho road, and now sometimes called the 'Spring of the Apostles'; modern 'Ain Haud.

J.D.D.

ENVY. A grudging regard for the advantages seen to be enjoyed by others—*cf.* Lat. *invidia* from *invideo*, 'to look closely at', then 'to look with malicious intent' (see 1 Sa. 18:9). The Heb. *qin'â* means originally a burning, then the colour produced in the face by a deep emotion, thus ardour, zeal, jealousy. RSV substitutes 'jealousy' for 'envy' in Jb. 5:2; Pr. 27:4; Acts 7:9; 1 Cor. 3:3, *etc.* But they are not synonymous. Jealousy makes us fear to lose what we possess; envy creates sorrow that others have what we have not. The word *qin'â* is used to express Rachel's envy for her sister (Gn. 30:1, *cf.* Gn. 37:11; Nu. 25:11, *etc.*). Its evils are depicted especially in the book of Proverbs: thus the question in 27:4: 'Who can stand before jealousy?' The NT *zēlos* is usually translated in a good sense as *'zeal' as well as in a bad sense as 'envy' (Jn. 2:17; *cf.* Col. 4:13 where it is translated 'worked hard' [AV 'great zeal']; note also its reference to God, 2 Ki. 19:31; Is. 9:7; 37:32, *etc.*). The word *phthonos* always appears in a bad sense except in the difficult verse Jas. 4:5, which should be translated as in RVmg. (A comparable sentiment is expressed in the Qumran *Manual of Discipline*, 4. 16–18.) *phthonos* is characteristic of the unredeemed life (Rom. 1:29; Gal. 5:21; 1 Tim. 6:4; Tit. 3:3). It was the spirit which crucified our Lord (Mt. 27:18; Mk. 15:10). Envy, *zēlos*, as inconsiderate zeal, is to be avoided by Christians (Rom. 13:13; 2 Cor. 12:20; Jas. 3:14, 16). See *NIDNTT* 1, pp. 557f.; *TDNT* 2, pp. 877–882.

H.D.McD.

EPAPHRAS. In Col. 1:7; 4:12; Phm. 23, one of Paul's friends and associates, called by him his 'fellow slave' and 'fellow prisoner'. The name is abbreviated from Epaphroditus, but Epaphras is probably not to be identified with the Epaphroditus of Phil. 2:25; 4:18 (as he is by T. R. Glover, *Paul* *of Tarsus*, 1925, p. 179). We gather that Epaphras evangelized the cities of the Lycus valley in Phrygia under Paul's direction during the latter's Ephesian ministry, and founded the churches of Colossae, Hierapolis and Laodicea. Later he visited Paul during his Roman captivity, and it was his news of conditions in the churches of the Lycus valley that moved Paul to write the Epistle to the Colossians.

BIBLIOGRAPHY. P. T. O'Brien, *Colossians, Philemon, WBC*, 1982. F.F.B.

EPAPHRODITUS. A Macedonian Christian from Philippi. There are no grounds for identifying him with Epaphras of Col. 1:7; 4:12, or Phm. 23. His name means 'comely' or 'charming'. Paul calls him 'your messenger' (*hymōn apostolon*, Phil. 2:25), where the word used is one more frequently translated elsewhere as 'apostle'. This does not mean that Epaphroditus held any office in the Philippian church; he was simply a messenger (*cf.* 2 Cor. 8:23) who brought the gift from the church to Paul in prison at Rome. He became seriously ill, possibly as a result of over-exerting himself in journeying from Philippi to Rome, or in serving Paul at Rome. The AV says 'he regarded not his life' (see Phil. 2:30), but RSV more correctly 'risking his life'. The word used is *paraboleusamenos*, 'having gambled with his life', from *paraboleuesthai* 'to throw down a stake, to make a venture'.

BIBLIOGRAPHY. J. Agar Beet, 'Epaphroditus and the gift from Philippi', *The Expositor*, 3rd Series, 9, 1889, pp. 64ff.; C. O. Buchanan, 'Epaphroditus' Sickness and the Letter to the Philippians', *EQ* 36, 1964, pp. 157ff. D.O.S.

EPHESIANS, EPISTLE TO THE.

I. Outline of contents

This letter, in its form less restricted by particular controversial or pastoral needs than any other NT letter, stands as a wonderful declaration of the eternal purpose of God in Christ wrought out in his church (chs. 1–3), and of the practical consequences of that purpose (4–6).

a. God's eternal purposes for man in Christ, 1:1–3:21

1:1–2. Greeting.

1:3–14. Praise for all the spiritual blessings that come to men in Christ.

1:15–23. Thanksgiving for the readers' faith, and prayer for their experience of the wisdom and power of God.

2:1–10. God's purpose to raise men from the death of sin to new life in Christ.

2:11–22. His purpose to reconcile men not only to himself, but to one another—in particular to bring Jews and Gentiles together into the one people of God.

3:1–13. The privilege of the apostle's calling to preach the gospel to the Gentiles.

3:14–21. A second prayer, for the knowledge of the love of Christ, and his indwelling fullness; and a doxology.

b. Practical consequences, 4:1–6:24

4:1–16. Exhortation to walk worthily, and to work to build up the one body of Christ.

4:17–32. The old life of ignorance, lust and unrighteousness must be put off, and the new life of holiness put on.

5:1–21. A further call to live in love and purity, as children of light, full of praise and usefulness.

5:22–33. Instructions to wives and husbands, based on the analogy of the relationship between Christ and his church.

6:1–9. Instructions to children and parents, servants and masters.

6:10–20. Summons to Christian conflict in the armour of God and in his strength.

6:21–24. Concluding personal message.

II. Destination

Although the great majority of MSS and all the early vss have the words 'at Ephesus' in 1:1, the 4th-century codices Vaticanus and Sinaiticus, the important corrector of the cursive 424, the cursive 1739, the papyrus 46 (dated AD 200) omit these words. Tertullian probably, Origen certainly, did not have them. Basil said they were lacking in the oldest MSS known to him. The heretic Marcion called this letter 'to the Laodiceans'. This small but very weighty evidence is supported by the evidence of the contents of the letter. It is difficult to explain such verses as 1:15; 3:2; 4:21, and the complete absence of personal greetings, if this were a letter addressed by Paul to Christians among whom he had laboured for 3 years (Acts 19:1–20 and 20:31). Yet it seems to have been addressed to a specific circle of Christians (1:15ff.; 6:21). The most likely interpretation of all the evidence is that the letter, if genuinely Paul's, was sent to a group of churches in Asia Minor (of which Ephesus was the greatest). Either one copy was sent to each in turn, the place-name being inserted in reading; or there may have been several copies with different addresses.

III. Authorship

There is abundant early evidence (perhaps going back to AD 95) of the use of this letter and from the end of the 2nd century we read of its unquestioned acceptance as the letter of Paul that it claims to be (1:1; 3:1). Since the end of the 18th century, however, the traditional authorship has been questioned. It is impossible here to do justice to the arguments for and against it. (They are set forward very fully, with opposite conclusions, in C. L. Mitton, *The Epistle to the Ephesians*, 1951, and A. van Roon, *The Authenticity of Ephesians*, 1974.) Very briefly the most important arguments against the genuineness of Ephesians are as follows:

1. Ephesians is not a real letter addressed to a particular situation like all the others we know as Paul's. It is more lyrical in style, full of participles and relatives, distinctive in its piling up of similar or related expressions. For the Pauline authorship it is argued that the absence of controversy accounts for the difference. We have here not the reasoned argument necessary in the other letters, but a 'prophetic declaration of incontrovertible, patent facts' (Dodd).

2. There are 42 words not otherwise used in the NT, and 44 more not used elsewhere by Paul. This argument can be assessed only by comparison with other Epistles, and by examining the words themselves. In the view of many the nature of the subject-matter sufficiently accounts for them.

3. It is urged that nowhere in Paul's writings have we such stress on the church and so little eschatology. Yet satisfying reasons can be given for the difference of emphasis, and in particular for

the great exposition here of the part of the church in the eternal purpose of God.

4. Certain features and expressions are taken as indicative of a later date or another hand than that of the apostle, *e.g.* the reference to the 'holy apostles and prophets' (3:5; *cf.* 2:20), the treatment of the Gentile question and the self-abasement of 3:8. Each individual objection may be answered, though those who oppose the Pauline authorship urge the cumulative force of all the objections.

5. Other arguments are based on a comparison of Ephesians with other NT writings. This letter has more in common with non-Pauline writings (especially Luke and Acts, 1 Peter and the Johannine writings) than any other letter of the Pauline Corpus. Sometimes the resemblances in thought and expression are very striking, but rarely such as make literary dependence probable. They witness rather to a large common vocabulary, and perhaps also to a similar formalizing of teaching and belief in the early church in different places. (See E. G. Selwyn, *The First Epistle of St Peter*, 1946, pp. 363–466.) Most significant, however, is the extensive similarity in content, expression and even order of subject-matter between this letter and Colossians. It is almost universally accepted that Colossians is prior to Ephesians. Ephesians has the doctrine and exhortation of Colossians, only developed further. With the exception of 6:21f. and Col. 4:7f., there is no evidence of direct copying, but in Ephesians the same expressions are often used with a slightly different connotation; one passage in one letter resembles two in the other; one passage in Ephesians has a parallel in Colossians and also in another Pauline letter. To some these phenomena are the strongest arguments for the work of an imitator; in the view of others they make the apostolic authorship more sure.

IV. Purpose

Many scholars have opposed the Pauline authorship without giving any positive suggestion as to how the letter came to be written. Others have been more specific.

1. Some have seen it as 'an attempt to sum up and to recommend to a later generation the apostle's teaching' (M. Barth, *AB*, p. 57). E. J. Goodspeed, for example, sees it as written to introduce the collection of Paul's letters, the quintessence of Paul presented by one (Onesimus, he suggests) who was saturated in Paul's writings and Colossians most of all.

2. Others have seen a historical crisis in the life of the early church—the threat of Gnosticism, the threat to Christian unity, or the danger of a turning aside from the great Pauline doctrines—as calling forth this work, written in the name of the great apostle.

3. J. C. Kirby (*Ephesians: Baptism and Pentecost*, 1968) partly follows the views of others in drawing attention to a great deal of liturgical and didactic material in the Epistle, but goes further and gives reasons for thinking of Ephesians as the transformation into a letter of what basically was an annual covenant renewal service, held at the time of Pentecost, recalling to Christians the meaning of their baptism.

To many the arguments against the Pauline authorship appear strong. To some, one or another of the views of the suggested purposes seems attractive. Yet, as E. F. Scott puts it, the Epistle 'is everywhere marked by a grandeur and originality of thought which seems utterly beyond the reach of any mere imitator' (*MNTC*, p. 136). It is not easy to imagine a writer trying in Paul's name to present the essence of his theology and then turning to Colossians and quoting exactly the words of 4:7f. to give the impression that Ephesians was written at the same time as the letter to Colossae. It seems better to return to the Pauline authorship and reconstruct the situation that called forth Ephesians as follows.

Paul was a prisoner in Rome *c.* the year AD 61 (see *COLOSSIANS for other possibilities of the place of Paul's imprisonment at the time of writing). Onesimus, Philemon's runaway slave, had come to the apostle, been brought to faith in Christ and, with a letter from Paul, was being sent back to his master 'no longer as a slave, but more than a slave, as a beloved brother' (Phm. 16). At the same time the apostle had heard from Epaphras of the difficulties being faced, especially through false teaching, by the Colossian church. Thus when Onesimus was returning to Colossae, Paul also sent Tychicus with a letter to that church, answering their problems and giving practical instructions concerning Christian living to Christians whom he had never met or taught personally. Writing thus to the Colossians, the apostle's mind was filled with the theme of the glory of Christ and his perfect provision for the life of men. Paul's thoughts turned to the other churches in the whole neighbourhood of Colossae, and, no longer having to deal with particular pastoral problems or doctrinal difficulties, he fulfilled his desire to express, in teaching and exhortation, in praise and prayer, the glory of the purpose of God in Christ and the responsibility of the church to make known that purpose by proclamation and by living in unity, love and purity. This letter was despatched with Philemon and Colossians, but sent to the various churches of the Roman province of Asia, of which Ephesus was one and indeed the most significant. In all probability this is the very letter that Paul in Col. 4:16 says that the Colossian Christians should receive 'from Laodicea'.

BIBLIOGRAPHY. J. A. Robinson, *St Paul's Epistle to the Ephesians*, 1904; Markus Barth, *Ephesians*, *AB*, 1974; J. R. W. Stott, *The Message of Ephesians*, *BST*, 1979; C. L. Mitton, *Ephesians*, *NCB*, 1982; F. F. Bruce, *The Epistles to the Colossians, to Philemon, and to the Ephesians*, *NIC*, 1984: F. Foulkes, *The Letter of Paul to the Ephesians*, *TNTC*[2], 1989; A. T. Lincoln, *Ephesians, WBC*, 1990; A. G. Patzia, *Ephesians*, *Colossians*, *Philemon*, *NIBC*, 1991.

F.F.

EPHESUS. The most important city in the Roman province of Asia, on the W coast of what is now Asiatic Turkey. It was situated at the mouth of the Caÿster River between the mountain range of Coressus and the sea. A magnificent road 11 m wide and lined with columns ran down through the city to the fine harbour, which served both as a great export centre at the end of the Asiatic caravan-route and also as a natural landing-point from Rome. The city, now uninhabited, has been undergoing excavation for many years, and is probably the most extensive and impressive ruined site of Asia Minor. The sea is now some 10 km away, owing to the silting process which has been at work for centuries. The harbour had to undergo extensive clearing operations at various times from the 2nd century BC; is that, perhaps, why Paul had to stop at Miletus (Acts 20:15–16)? The main part of the city, with its theatre, baths, library, agora and paved streets, lay between the Coressus ridge and the Caÿster, but the temple for which it was famed lay over 2 km to the NE. This site was originally sacred to the worship of the Anatolian fertility goddess, later identified with Greek Artemis and Latin Diana. Justinian built a church to St John on the hill nearby (hence the later name Ayasoluk—a corruption of *hagios theologos*), which was itself succeeded by a Seljuk mosque. The neighbouring settlement is now called Selçuk.

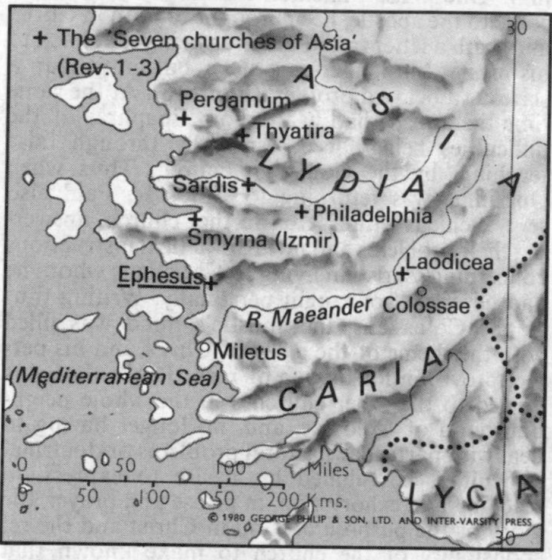

Ephesus, one of the 'seven churches of Asia' (Rev. 1–3).

The original Anatolian settlement was augmented before the 10th century BC by Ionian colonists, and a joint city was set up. The goddess of Ephesus took a Greek name, but clearly retained her earlier characteristics, for she was repeatedly represented at later periods as a many-breasted figure. Ephesus was conquered by Croesus shortly after his accession in *c.* 560 BC, and owed some of its artistic glories to his munificence. After his fall in 546 it came under Persian rule. Croesus shifted the site of the archaic city to focus upon the temple of *Artemis: Lysimachus, one of the successors of Alexander, forcibly replanted it about the harbour early in the 3rd century BC. Ephesus later formed part of the kingdom of Pergamum, which Attalus III bequeathed to Rome in 133 BC. It became the greatest commercial city of the Roman province of Asia. It then occupied a vast area, and its population may have numbered a third of a million. It is estimated that the great theatre built into Mt Pion in the centre of the city had a capacity of about 25,000.

Ephesus also maintained its religious importance under Roman rule. It became a centre of the emperor cult, and eventually possessed three official temples, thus qualifying thrice over for the proud title *neōkoros* ('temple-warden') of the emperors, as well as being *neōkoros* of Artemis (Acts 19:35). It is remarkable that Paul had friends among the *Asiarchs (*Asiarchai*, Acts 19:31), who were officers of the 'commune' of Asia, whose primary function was actually to foster the imperial cult.

The temple of Artemis itself had been rebuilt after a great fire in 356 BC, and ranked as one of the seven wonders of the world until its destruction by the Goths in AD 263. After years of patient search J. T. Wood in 1870 uncovered its remains in the marsh at the foot of Mt Ayasoluk. It had been the largest building in the Greek world. It contained an image of the goddess which, it was claimed, had fallen from heaven (*cf.* Acts 19:35). Indeed, it may well have been a meteorite originally. Silver coins from many places show the validity of the claim that the goddess of Ephesus was revered all over the world (Acts 19:27). They bear the inscription *Diana Ephesia* (*cf.* Acts 19:34).

There was a large colony of Jews at Ephesus, and they had long enjoyed a privileged position under Roman rule (Jos., *Ant.* 14. 225ff.; 14. 262ff.). The earliest reference to the coming of Christianity there is in *c.* AD 52, when Paul made a short visit and left Aquila and Priscilla there (Acts 18:18–21). Paul's third missionary journey had Ephesus as its goal, and he stayed there for over 2 years (Acts 19:8, 10), attracted, no doubt, by its strategic importance as a commercial, political and religious centre. His work was at first based on the synagogue: later he debated in the lecture-hall of Tyrannus, making of Ephesus a base for the evangelization of the whole province of Asia. The spread of Christianity, which refused syncretism, began to incur the hostility of vested religious interests. It affected not only the magic cults which flourished there (Acts 19:13ff.—one kind of magic formula was actually called *Ephesia grammata*) but also the worship of Artemis (Acts 19:27), causing damage to the trade in cult objects which was one source of the prosperity of Ephesus. There followed the celebrated riot described in Acts 19. Inscriptions show that the *grammateus* ('town clerk') who gained control of the assembly on this occasion was the leading civic official, directly responsible to the Romans for such breaches of the peace as illicit assembly (Acts 19:40). It has been suggested that his assertion 'there are proconsuls' (19:38), if it is not a generalizing plural, may fix the date with some precision. On Nero's accession in AD 54, M. Junius Silvanus, the proconsul of Asia, was poisoned by his subordinates Helius and Celer, who acted as proconsuls until the arrival of a regular successor.

Christianity evidently spread to *Colossae and the other cities of the Lycus valley at the period of Paul's stay in Ephesus (*cf.* Col. 1:6–7; 2:1). It was Paul's headquarters for most of the time of the Corinthian controversy and correspondence (1 Cor. 16:8), and the experience which he describes as 'fighting with wild beasts' happened there (1 Cor. 15:32). This seems to be a metaphorical allusion to something already known to the Corinthians, perhaps mob violence. (There was no amphitheatre at Ephesus, though the stadium was later adapted to accommodate beast-fighting.) G. S. Duncan (*St Paul's Ephesian Ministry*, 1929) has maintained that Paul was imprisoned two or three times at Ephesus, and that all the captivity Epistles were written from there and not from Rome. E. J. Goodspeed (*INT*, 1937), followed by C. L. Mitton and J. Knox, have located at Ephesus the collection of the Pauline Corpus of letters. There are difficulties in the hypothesis of an Ephesian imprisonment which suits the case, and although B. Reicke and J. A. T. Robinson have recently revived the idea that some or all of the captivity Epistles were written from Caesarea, it remains preferable to place them in Rome (see C. H. Dodd, *BJRL* 18, 1934, pp. 72–92).

After Paul's departure Timothy was left at Ephesus (1 Tim. 1:3). The Pastorals give a glimpse of the period of consolidation there. It is thought by many that Rom. 16 was originally addressed by Paul to Ephesus.

The city was later the headquarters of the John who had jurisdiction over the seven leading churches of Asia addressed in the Apocalypse. The church in Ephesus is addressed first of the seven (Rev. 2:1–7), as being the most important church in the *de facto* capital, and as being the landing-place for a messenger from Patmos and standing at the head of a circular road joining the seven cities in order. This church is flourishing, but is troubled by false teachers, and has lost its 'first love'. The false apostles (2:2) are most probably like the *Nicolaitans, who seem to have advocated compromise with the power of paganism for the Christian under pressure. The Ephesians were steadfast, but deficient in love. Ramsay characterized Ephesus as the 'city of change'. Its problems were the problems of a successful church coping with changing circumstances: the city too had had a long history of shifting sites (*cf.* 2:5b). The promise of eating of the tree of life is here probably set against the background of the sacred date-palm of Artemis, which figures on Ephesian coins.

According to Irenaeus and Eusebius, Ephesus became the home of John the apostle. A generation after his time Ignatius wrote of the continuing fame and faithfulness of the Ephesian church (*Ephesians* 8–9). The third General Council took place here in AD 431 to condemn Nestorian Christology, and sat in the double church of St Mary, the ruins of which are still to be seen. The city declined, and the progressive silting of its gulf finally severed it wholly from the sea.

BIBLIOGRAPHY. G. E. Bean, *Aegean Turkey. An Archaeological Guide*, 1966; E. Akurgal, *The Ancient Ruins and Civilisations of Turkey*, 1973; C. J. Hemer, *The Letters to the Seven Churches of Asia in Their Local Setting*, 1986; E. M. Yamauchi, *New Testament Cities in Western Asia Minor*, 1980.

E.M.B.G.
C.J.H.

EPHPHATHA. The actual word addressed by Jesus to the deaf man (Mk. 7:34). It is probably an Aramaic imperative transliterated into Greek, and the Evangelist adds the translation (in Greek), 'be opened'. The Aramaic verb used is *p^eṯaḥ*, 'to open'; it is not certain whether the simple passive (ethpeel) or intensive passive (ethpaal) was employed. The former form would be *'eṯp^eṯaḥ*, the latter *'eṯpattaḥ*. It seems that in either case the *ṯ* was assimilated to the *p̄*; this is a regular feature of later Aramaic and its dialects (*e.g.* Syriac). An alternative possibility is that the word is Hebrew (niphal conjugation).

BIBLIOGRAPHY. J. A. Emerton, *JTS* 24, 1973, pp. 1–23.

D.F.P.

EPHRAIM. The second son of Joseph, born to him by Asenath, the daughter of Potipherah, before the years of famine came (Gn. 41:50–52). The sick Jacob acknowledged the two sons of Joseph (Gn. 48:5), blessing Ephraim with his right hand and Manasseh with his left (vv. 13–14), thus signifying that Ephraim would become the greater people (v. 19).

In the order of the tribes in the wilderness encampment the standard of Ephraim's camp was on the W side (Nu. 2:18). From the tribe of Ephraim Elishama was to stand with Moses (Nu. 1:10), and Joshua the son of Nun, one of the spies, was descended from Ephraim (Nu. 13:8). He was chosen with Eleazar the priest to divide the land (Nu. 34:17). Ephraim is also included in the blessing of Moses.

Under the valiant leadership of Joshua, Ephraim with the other tribes received its inheritance, which is described in Jos. 16. The territory may be roughly identified as follows. Proceeding W from Gilgal we come to Bethel, then to lower Beth-horon, W to Gezer, then N to Lod and W towards the sea, N to the Qanah river and then E to Tappuah, Janobah, Taanath-shiloh to Ataroth, then S to Nasrath and Gilgal.

From the beginning the tribe of Ephraim occupied a position of prestige and significance. It complained to Gideon that he had not called it to fight against the Midianites. His reply reveals the superior position of Ephraim. 'Is not the gleaning of the grapes of Ephraim better than the vintage of Abiezer?' (Jdg. 8:2). The men of Ephraim complained again in similar terms to Jephthah, and this led to war between the Ephraimites and the Gileadites.

The prestige of Ephraim kept it from looking with favour upon Judah. After the death of Saul, Abner, Saul's captain, made Eshbaal king over the N tribes, including Ephraim. Because of the Philistine domination, however, Eshbaal's authority was effectively limited to Transjordan. He reigned for 2 years, but Judah followed David (2 Sa. 2:8ff.). After Eshbaal's death the N tribes invited David to become their king.

Later David learnt that Israel followed after Absalom. The N tribes never did desire to yield to David's reign, but David grew continually greater and stronger. Under Solomon the S kingdom reached the pinnacle of splendour and prosperity. Nevertheless, even at this time, there was discontent in the N (1 Ki. 11:26ff.).

Rehoboam's folly provided the necessary pretext, and the N revolted, renouncing all claim to the promises made to David (1 Ki. 12:16). Nevertheless, God continued to send his prophets to the N kingdom, and one of the characteristics of the Messianic kingdom is to be the healing of the tragic schism introduced by Jeroboam the son of Nebat (*cf.* Ho. 1:11; Is. 11:13). Even when exile has overtaken the S as well as the N kingdom, Ephraim retains a special place: 'I am a father to Israel, and Ephraim is my first-born' (Je. 31:9).

E.J.Y.
F.F.B.

EPHRAIM (geographical). The boundaries of Ephraim are recorded in Jos. 16, and with Manasseh in Jos. 17. Only some of the main topographical features of these boundaries have so far been determined beyond dispute; most of the places mentioned cannot be precisely located at present.

The S boundary of Ephraim is most clearly expressed in Jos. 16:1–3, where, however, it is given as the (S) boundary of 'the children of Joseph', *i.e.* Ephraim-Manasseh. But as Manasseh was situated wholly to the N and NE of Ephraim, this boundary is, in practice, that of Ephraim. It ran (E to W) up from the Jordan and Jericho inland to Bethel (Beitin, *c.* 16 km N of Jerusalem), Luz (?near by) and Ataroth (site uncertain), then *via* the border of Lower Beth-horon to Gezer—well-known site—and the Mediterranean sea-coast (Jos. 16:1–3). V. 5 is difficult, but may perhaps further define part of this S boundary.

The N boundary from a point Michmetha(t)h (16:6) 'before Shechem' (17:7) turned W; its course in that direction ran from Tappuah (location still disputed) to and along the brook of Qanah (perhaps the present Wadi Qānah, which joins Wadi Aujah, and reaches the Mediterranean *c.* 6½ km N of Joppa) to the sea (16:8). E from Michmetha(t)h, the border turned by Taanath-shiloh (S) along the E of Janoah to (another) Ataroth, Naarah, and back to Jericho and the Jordan (16:6–7). On the N, Shechem apparently was within Ephraim's share, to judge from the levitical city-lists (Jos. 21:20–21; 1 Ch. 6:67).

The region in central W Palestine that fell to Ephraim is mainly relatively high hill-country with better rainfall than Judaea and some good soils; hence some biblical references to the fruitfulness of the Ephraim district. The Ephraimites had direct but not over-easy access to the great N–S trunk road through the W plain.

BIBLIOGRAPHY. D. Baly, *The Geography of the Bible*², 1974, pp. 164–176; Y. Kaufmann, *The Biblical Account of the Conquest of Palestine*, 1953, pp. 28–36. Also F. M. Abel, *Géographie de la Palestine*, 1–2, 1933–8. With reserve, Z. Kallai, *Historical Geography of the Bible*, 1986; N. Na'aman, *Borders and Districts in Biblical Historiography*, 1986.

K.A.K.

EPHRATH, EPHRATHAH. 1. The ancient name of *Bethlehem Judah, which occurs in all cases but one (Gn. 48:7, *'ep̄rāṯ*) in the form *'ep̄rāṯâ*. Rachel was buried on the route there from Bethel (Gn. 35:16, 19; 48:7; *cf.* 1 Sa. 10:2); it was the home of Naomi's family (Ru. 4:11), who are described as Ephrathites (*'ep̄rāṯî*, Ru. 1:2), of Ruth's descendant David (1 Sa. 17:12; *cf.* Ps. 132:6), and of the Messiah, as foretold in Mi. 5:2.

2. The gentilic *'ep̄rāṯî* is applied three times to Ephraimites (Jdg. 12:5; 1 Sa. 1:1; 1 Ki. 11:26).

3. The second wife of Caleb the son of Hezron (1 Ch. 2:19, 50; 4:4; *cf.* 2:24).

T.C.M.

EPHRON. 1. Name of a 'son of Heth' (Hittite or Syrian), a son of Zohar from whom Abraham bought the cave of Machpelah as a burial-place for Sarah (Gn. 23:8; 25:9; 49:30). A similar type name (Apran) is known from *Alalaḫ, Syria. **2.** A hill area between Nephtoah and *Kiriath-jearim which marked the border of Judah (Jos. 15:9; 18:15, RSV amended text). **3.** A place near *Bethel taken by Abijah from Jeroboam I (2 Ch. 13:19). RSV 'Ephron'; *MT* 'Ephrain', AV 'Ephraim'; *cf.* 2 Sa. 13:23) to be identified with Ophrah (Jos. 18:23). Perhaps a word meaning 'province' (*VT* 12, 1962, p. 339). Generally identified as et-Taiyibeh *c.* 7 km NE of Bethel. **4.** A fort between Ashtoreth-karnaim (Carmion) and Beth-shan (Scythopolis) captured by Judas Maccabaeus (1 Macc. 5:46–52; 2 Macc. 12:27–29; Jos., *Ant.* 12. 346). Possibly the modern et-Taiybeh SE of Galilee.

D.J.W.

EPICUREANS. Some of the philosophers whom Paul encountered at Athens (Acts 17:18) were of this school, whose best-known disciple is the Roman poet Lucretius. The founder, Epicurus, was born in 341 BC on the island of Samos. His early studies under Nausiphanes, a disciple of Democritus, taught him to regard the world as the result of the random motion and combination of atomic particles. He lived for a time in exile and poverty. Gradually he gathered round him a circle of friends and began to teach his distinctive doctrines. In 306 he established himself in Athens at the famous 'Garden' which became the headquarters of the school. He died in 270 after great suffering from an internal complaint, but in peace of mind.

The founder's experiences, coupled with the general uncertainty of life in the last centuries before Christ, gave a special stamp to the Epicurean teachings. The whole system had a practical end in view, the achievement of happiness by serene detachment. Democritean atomism banished all fear of divine intervention in life or punishment after death; the gods follow to perfection the life of serene detachment and will have nothing to do with human existence, and death brings a final dispersion of our constituent atoms.

The Epicureans found contentment in limiting desire and in the joys and solaces of friendship. The pursuit of extravagant pleasure which gives to 'epicure' its modern connotation was a late perversion of their quest for happiness.

It is easy to see why the Epicureans found Paul's teaching about the resurrection strange and unpalatable. Jewish rabbis use the word *apiqôrôs* to mean one who denies life after death, and later as a synonym for 'infidel'.

BIBLIOGRAPHY. Usener, *Epicurea*, 1887; A. J. Festugière, *Epicurus and his Gods*, E.T. 1955; N. W. de Witt, *Epicurus and his Philosophy*, 1954.

M.H.C.

EPISTLE. Gk. *epistolē* and Lat. *epistula* represent a letter of any kind: originally simply a written communication between persons apart, whether personal and private or official. In this sense epistles are a part of the heritage of all literate peoples, and examples are to be found in the OT (2 Sa. 11; 1 Ki. 21; 2 Ki. 5; 10; 20; 2 Ch. 30; 32; Ezr. 4–5; 7; Ne. 2; 6; Est. 1; 3; 8–9; Is. 37; 39; Je. 29) and in the Greek papyri from Egypt (*cf.* all the large published collections of papyri, *passim*, and especially the Zenon correspondence). Such a letter was described by Demetrius, *Typoi epistolikoi* (1st century BC), as a written conversation, while Demetrius, *On Style* 3. 223ff., quotes Artemon, the ancient collector of Aristotle's letters, as calling it half a dialogue.

But the earliest collections of Greek letters generally regarded as genuine, in part at least, those of Isocrates and Plato, already show a tendency to use letters, or the letter-form, for larger purposes than mere private or official communication; so that among Isocrates' letters (368–338 BC) some are set speeches, or introductions to speeches, and Plato's Seventh Letter (*c.* 354 BC) is a refutation of popular misconceptions about his philosophy and conduct. In both cases the letters aim at other readers than those addressed, and are thus a form of publication. Compare here present-day letters 'to the Editor of *The Times*'.

Despite a feeling often hinted at, and sometimes

Three places bearing the name Ephron: on the border of Judah, near Bethel and near Bethshan.

expressed, that such letters have neither the size nor the subject-matter of true letters, but are rather 'writings with "greetings" added' (Demetrius, *On Style*, *loc. cit.*), the epistolary form continued to be used for philosophical, scientific and literary publication (*e.g.* Epicurus, *Epistles*, and the three literary letters of Dionysius of Halicarnassus). The theory and practice of letter-writing came to be treated by the teachers of rhetoric (*e.g.* Demetrius, *On Style*; *idem*, *Typoi epistolikoi*), and letter-writing in the characters of famous men formed part of the rhetorical school exercise of *prosōpopoeia*. The growth in Hellenistic and Roman times of collections of fictitious letters may be attributed to such exercises, and to the eagerness of the great libraries to buy additional works, especially of famous men.

G. A. Deissmann, confronted by the simplicity of most letters in the papyri, maintained a sharp distinction between 'genuine letters' as personal, direct, transient and un-literary, and 'epistles' as impersonal, aimed at a reading public and permanence, and literary. Feeling an undeniable similarity between certain elements in the NT Epistles and the papyri, he classed most of Paul's Epistles and 2 and 3 John as letters, Hebrews, James, 1 and 2 Peter, Jude and Revelation as epistles, and 1 John as a *diatribē* (*LAE*[3], ch. 3, pp. 148–251). But the distinction cannot be so sharply maintained, as there are different degrees of 'literariness', sorts and sizes of 'public', and kinds of publication.

Of the Pauline letters to churches, those to the Corinthians, Galatians, Philippians and Thessalonians contain most personal elements, Romans fewer, and Ephesians and Colossians least of all. Galatians and Ephesians are composed on a rhetorical plan, and all of them have considerable rhetorical elements. In the Pastoral Epistles the personal references are fairly numerous and rhetorical elements comparatively few. Philemon, rightly regarded by Deissmann as the most personal letter in the NT, and compared to British Museum Papyrus 417, is nevertheless very cleverly written and contains rhetorical elements noticeable especially when considered beside Isocrates, *Ep.* 8, and Demetrius, *Typoi epistolikoi* 12. Hebrews is the most artistic literary writing in the NT, being composed from beginning to end on the pattern of *proem, thesis, diēgēsis, apodeixis, epilogue,* laid down by Greek rhetoricians, and is written in rhythmic, periodic prose. In James, 1 and 2 Peter and Jude there are very few personal references; all are literary, especially 1 Peter; and 2 Peter and Jude are definitely rhetorical. 2 and 3 John appear as private communications, while 1 John is not, as we have it, in letter-form at all. Thus most of the NT Epistles show a greater or smaller affinity with preaching; some may be classed as sent sermons, while in others the letter-elements are a more literary form.

BIBLIOGRAPHY. *LAE*, pp. 146ff.; J. Sykutris, *Epistolographie*, in *RE*, Supp. 5, pp. 185–220; V. Weichert (ed.), *Demetrii et Libanii qui feruntur Typoi Epistolikoi et Epistolimaioi Characteres* (Teubner), 1910; O. Roller, *Das Formular der Paulinischen Briefe*, 1933; M. Dibelius, *A Fresh Approach to the New Testament and Early Christian Literature*, E. T. 1936, pp. 137–171, 185–189, 194–197, 205–213, 226–234; A. J. Malherbe, *Ancient Epistolary Theorists*, 1988.

J.H.H.

ERASTUS. 1. An assistant of Paul, who shared Timothy's mission to Macedonia to allow Paul to continue working from Ephesus (Acts 19:22). The mission may have been directed ultimately to Corinth (*cf.* 1 Cor. 4:17), and Erastus been one of the 'brethren' of 2 Cor. 8; but certainty is impossible. Undoubtedly, however, he is the Erastus mentioned as staying at Corinth in 2 Tim. 4:20.

2. City-treasurer (not 'chamberlain' as AV) of Corinth, sending greetings in Rom. 16:23 (*QUARTUS). A Lat. inscription found at Corinth states, 'Erastus laid this pavement at his own expense, in appreciation of his appointment as aedile.' Many (*e.g.* Broneer) accept the identification with the Christian city treasurer.

Some further identify **1** and **2**: G. S. Duncan, for example, suggests that 2 Tim. 4:20 indicates that Erastus, unlike Timothy, completed the journey to Corinth, where he became treasurer a year or so later (*St Paul's Ephesian Ministry*, pp. 79ff.); but such a rapid rise to power is most unlikely, and the name is quite common.

BIBLIOGRAPHY. H. J. Cadbury, *JBL* 50, 1931, pp. 42ff.; O. Broneer, *BA* 14, 1951, pp. 78ff., especially p. 94; P. N. Harrison, *Paulines and Pastorals*, 1964, pp. 100–105.

A.F.W.

ERECH. An ancient city of Mesopotamia mentioned in the Table of Nations (Gn. 10:10) as one of the possessions of Nimrod in the land of *Shinar. Known to the Sumerians as *Unu(g)* and to the Akkadians as *Uruk*, it was one of the great cities of Sumerian times. It is named in the Sumerian king list as the seat of the 2nd Dynasty after the Flood, one of whose kings was Gilgamesh, who later became one of the great heroes of Sumerian legend. Though the city continued in occupation during later periods (Gk. *Orchoē*), it never surpassed its early importance. Uruk is represented today by the group of mounds known to the Arabs as *Warka*, which lies in S Babylonia some 64 km NW of Ur and 6 km E of the present course of the *Euphrates. While the site was investigated over a century ago by W. K. Loftus (*Travels and Researches in Chaldaea and Susiana*, 1857), the principal excavations have been conducted by a series of German expeditions in 1912, 1928–39 and 1954–60. The results are of outstanding importance for the early history of Mesopotamia. Prehistoric remains of the Ubaid Period (*SUMER) were followed by monumental architecture and stone sculpture of the Late Prehistoric Period which richly illustrate the material culture of Mesopotamia at the beginning of history. It was in these levels, dating from the 4th millennium BC, that the earliest inscriptions so far known were found. These are in the form of clay tablets, and, though the signs are only pictographic, it is probable that the language behind them was Sumerian.

BIBLIOGRAPHY. R. North, 'Status of the Warka Excavations', *Orientalia* n.s. 26, 1957, pp. 185–256.

T.C.M.

ESARHADDON (Heb. *'ēsarhaddōn*; Assyr. *Aššur-aḫ-iddin*, 'Ashur has given a brother') was king of Assyria and Babylonia 681–669 BC. He succeeded his father Sennacherib who was murdered in Tebet in 681 BC (2 Ki. 19:37; Is. 37:38). His first act was to pursue the murderers as far as Hanigalbat (S Armenia) and to quash the rebellion in Nineveh, which lasted 6 weeks. There is little support for the theory that Esarhaddon was the head of a pro-Babylonian faction or 'the son' mentioned in the Bab. Chronicle as the murderer (*DOTT*, pp. 70–73). His own inscriptions tell how he had been made crown-prince by his father earlier in the year, and though he had been viceroy in Babylon his attention to the religious centre was merely in keeping with his care for all the ancient shrines. His early military operations were designed to safeguard the N frontier and trade-routes against the warlike Ṭeušpa and the incursions of the Cimmerians (*GOMER), whom he defeated. In the S the Elamites, who had been defeated by his father, once more stirred up the tribes of S Babylonia, and Esarhaddon was forced to campaign against the 'sea-lands' where he installed Na'id-Marduk, son of *Merodach-baladan, as the local sheikh in 678 BC. His clashes with Elam and the Babylonians resulted in the deportation of many captives, some of whom were settled in Samaria (Ezr. 4:2).

In the W Esarhaddon continued his father's policy. He exacted heavy tribute from the vassal kings of Syria and Palestine, listing Manasseh (*Menasī*) of Judah (*Yaudi*) after Ba'ali of Tyre, with whom he concluded a treaty, having failed to isolate and thus subdue the port. The rulers of Edom, Moab and Ammon were made vassals after a series of raids on their territory in which he sought to counter the influence of Tirhakah of Egypt, who had incited a number of the Philistine cities to revolt. Esarhaddon sacked Sidon in 676 BC, after a 3-year siege, and incorporated part of its territory into an extended Assyrian province (probably including Samaria). Some of the refugees from the city were housed in a new town, Kār-Esarhaddon, built nearby. About this time Gaza and Ashkelon were counted among his vassals.

The subordinate kingdoms in Syria and Palestine were called upon to provide materials for Esarhaddon's building operations in Assyria and in Babylon, which he now sought to revive after earlier changes of fortune. This may explain the temporary detention of Manasseh in Babylon (2 Ch. 33:11). Assyrian letters referring to tribute in silver received from Judah, Moab and Edom may be assigned to this time.

In May 672 BC Esarhaddon brought all the vassal-kings together to acknowledge his arrangements to ensure that the succession to the throne was less disturbed than his own. *Ashurbanipal was declared to be crown-prince or heir to Assyria and Šamaš-šum-ukin to Babylonia. Copies of the treaty imposed on the Median city-chiefs on this occasion, found at Calah (Nimrud), show the provisions to which all, including Manasseh, would have had to assent. They declared their loyalty to the Assyrian national god Ashur and their willingness to serve Assyria for ever. History tells how soon all the client kings broke their oaths.

Having gained control of the W, Esarhaddon subdued Egypt, defeated Tirhakah, besieged Memphis and counted the land as an Assyrian dependency under Neco. When the victorious army was withdrawn, local intrigues developed into open revolt. While Esarhaddon was on his way to deal with this in 669 BC he died at Harran, leaving five surviving sons and one daughter. His mother, the forceful wife of Sennacherib (Naqi'a-Zakutu), also survived him.

BIBLIOGRAPHY. D. J. Wiseman, *The Vassal-Treaties of Esarhaddon*, 1958; A. K. Grayson, *CAH* 3/2, 1991, pp. 122–141. D.J.W.

ESAU. Esau was the elder of Isaac's twin sons (Gn. 25:21–26). His relations with Jacob his brother are the subject of the well-known stories in Gn. 25:27–34; 27:1ff.; 32:3–12; 33:1–16. Esau was his father's favourite son, and it was Isaac's intention to impart to him the blessing that was the eldest son's right (Gn. 27:1ff.). However, the supremacy of Jacob over his older brother, foreshadowed before, and at the moment of, their birth (Gn. 25:21–26), and eventually confirmed unwittingly by the aged Isaac (Gn. 27:22–29, 33–37), was finally established.

It was from this duplicity on the part of Jacob, the ancestor of the Israelites, that there stemmed the deep-rooted animosity that dominated Israel's relations with Edom, of whom Esau was the ancestor. Instances of this antagonism between the Israelites and the Edomites occur in the OT (*e.g.* Nu. 20:18–21; 1 Ki. 11:14ff.; Ps. 137:7).

The chief importance of the biblical references to Esau lies in the theological significance given to his rejection, in spite of the right of succession being his by virtue of primogeniture. The biblical explanation is that the Lord hated Esau and loved Jacob (Mal. 1:2f.; Rom. 9:13). Esau symbolizes those whom God has not elected; Jacob typifies those whom God has chosen.

But the ground of this election was not any difference in the lives and characters of Jacob and Esau. Jacob was chosen before he and his brother were born. And even God's 'hate' and 'love' could not be the ground of divine election, otherwise God's choice would depend on caprice or whim. God has exercised his sovereign will in the free exercise of his elective grace, the moral purpose of which he was the sole Originator. (*ELECTION.)

In Heb. 12:16f. Esau symbolizes those who abandon their hope of glory for the sake of the things that are seen and not eternal. J.G.S.S.T.

ESCHATOLOGY. From Gk. *eschatos*, 'last', the term refers to the 'doctrine of the last things'.

In contrast to cyclical conceptions of history, the biblical writings understand history as a linear movement towards a goal. God is driving history towards the ultimate fulfilment of his purposes for his creation. So biblical eschatology is not limited to the destiny of the individual; it concerns the consummation of the whole history of the world, towards which all God's redemptive acts in history are directed.

I. The OT perspective

The forward-looking character of Israelite faith dates from the call of Abraham (Gn. 12:1–3) and the promise of the land, but it is in the message of the prophets that it becomes fully eschatological, looking towards a final and permanent goal of God's purpose in history. The prophetic term 'the Day of the Lord' (with a variety of similar expressions such as 'on that day') refers to the coming event of God's decisive action in judgment and salvation in the historical realm. For the prophets it is always immediately related to their present historical context, and by no means necessarily refers to the end of history. Increasingly, however, there emerges the concept of a final resolution of history: a day of judgment beyond which God establishes a permanent age of salvation. A fully transcendent eschatology, which expects a direct and universal act of God, beyond the possibilities of ordinary history, issuing in a radically transformed world, is characteristic of *apocalyptic, which is already to be found in several parts of the prophetic books.

The prophets frequently depict the eschatological age of salvation which lies on the far side of judgment. Fundamentally it is the age in which God's will is to prevail. The nations will serve the God of Israel and learn his will (Is. 2:2f. = Mi. 4:1f.; Je. 3:17; Zp. 3:9f.; Zc. 8:20–23). There will be international peace and justice (Is. 2:4 = Mi. 4:3) and peace in nature (Is. 11:6; 65:25). God's people will have security (Mi. 4:4; Is. 65:21–23) and prosperity (Zc. 8:12). The law of God will be written on their hearts (Je. 31:31–34; Ezk. 36:26f.).

Frequently associated with the eschatological age is the Davidic king who will rule Israel (and, sometimes, the nations) as God's representative (Is. 9:6f.; 11:1–10; Je. 23:5f.; Ezk. 34:23f., 37.24f.; Mi. 5:2–4; Zc. 9:9f.). A principal feature of these prophecies is that the Messiah will rule in *righteousness.* (In the OT itself 'Messiah' [Christ] is not yet used as a technical term for the eschatological king.) Other 'Messianic' figures in the OT hope are the 'one like a son of man' (Dn. 7:13), the heavenly representative of Israel who receives universal dominion, the suffering Servant (Is. 53), and the eschatological prophet (Is. 61:1–3). Commonly the eschatological act of judgment and salvation is accomplished by the personal coming of God himself (Is. 26:21; Zc. 14:5; Mal. 3:1–5).

II. The NT perspective

The distinctive character of NT eschatology is determined by the conviction that in the history of Jesus Christ God's decisive eschatological act has already taken place, though in such a way that the consummation remains still future. There is in NT eschatology both an 'already' of accomplished fulfilment and a 'not yet' of still outstanding promise. There is both a 'realized' and a 'future' aspect to NT eschatology, which is therefore probably best described by the term *'inaugurated eschatology'*.

The note of eschatological fulfilment already under way means that OT eschatology has become, in a measure, present reality for the NT. The 'last days' of the prophets have arrived: for Christ 'was made manifest at the end of the times' (1 Pet. 1:20); God 'in these last days ... has spoken to us by a Son' (Heb. 1:2); Christians are those 'upon whom the end of the ages has come' (1 Cor. 10:11); 'it is the last hour' (1 Jn. 2:18); *cf.* also Acts 2:17; Heb. 6:5. On the other hand, NT writers oppose the fantasy that fulfilment is already complete (2 Tim. 2:18).

It is important to preserve the theological unity of God's redemptive work, past, present and future, 'already' and 'not yet'. Too often traditional theology has kept these aspects apart, as the finished work of Christ on the one hand, and the 'last things' on the other. In the NT perspective the 'last things' began with the ministry of Jesus. The historical work of Christ ensures, requires and points us forward to the future consummation of God's kingdom. The Christian hope for the future arises out of the historical work of Christ. The Christian church lives between the 'already' and the 'not yet', caught up in the ongoing process of eschatological fulfilment.

Inaugurated eschatology is found already in Jesus' proclamation of the kingdom of God. Jesus modifies the purely future expectation of Jewish apocalyptic by his message that the eschatological rule of God has already drawn near (Mt. 4:17). Its power is already at work in Jesus' deeds of victory over the realm of evil (Mt. 12:28f.). In Jesus' own person and mission the kingdom of God is present (Lk. 17:20f.), demanding response, so that a man's participation in the future of the kingdom is determined by his response to Jesus in the present (Mt. 10:32f.). Thus Jesus makes the kingdom a present reality which nevertheless remains future (Mk. 9:1; 14:25).

The eschatological character of Jesus' mission was confirmed by his resurrection. Resurrection is an eschatological event, belonging to the OT expectation of man's final destiny. So the unexpected resurrection of the one man Jesus ahead of all others determined the church's conviction that the End had already begun. He is risen already as the 'first fruits' of the dead (1 Cor. 15:20). On behalf of his people, Jesus has already entered upon the eternal life of the eschatological age; he has pioneered the way (Heb. 12:2) so that others may follow. In Paul's terms, he is the 'last Adam' (1 Cor. 15:45), the eschatological Man. For all other men eschatological salvation now means sharing *his* eschatological humanity, *his* resurrection life.

So for NT writers, the death and resurrection of Jesus are the absolutely decisive eschatological event which determines the Christian hope for the future: see, *e.g.*, Acts 17:31; Rom. 8:11; 2 Cor. 4:14; 1 Thes. 4:14. This accounts for the second distinctive feature of NT eschatology. As well as its characteristic tension of 'already' and 'not yet', NT eschatology is distinctive in being wholly *Christ-centred*. The role of Jesus in NT eschatology goes far beyond the role of the Messiah in OT or later Jewish expectation. Certainly he is the heavenly Son of man (Dn. 7), the eschatological prophet (Is. 61; *cf.* Lk. 4:18–21), the suffering Servant (Is. 53), and even the Davidic king, though not in the way his contemporaries expected. But the NT's concentration of eschatological fulfilment in Jesus reflects not only his fulfilment of these particular eschatological roles. For NT theology, Jesus embodies both God's own work of eschatological salvation and also man's eschatological destiny. So he is, on the one hand, the Saviour and the Judge, the Conqueror of evil, the Agent of God's rule and the Mediator of God's eschatological presence to men: he is himself the fulfilment of the OT expectations of God's own eschatological coming (*cf.* Mal. 3:1 with Lk. 1:76; 7:27). On the other hand, he is also the eschatological Man: he has achieved and defines in his own risen humanity the eschatological destiny of all men. So now the most adequate statement of our destiny is that we shall be like him (Rom. 8:29; 1 Cor. 15:49; Phil. 3:21; 1 Jn. 3:2). For both these reasons the Christian hope is focused on the coming of Jesus Christ.

In all the NT writings, eschatology has these two distinctive characteristics: it is inaugurated and Christ-centred. There are, however, differences of emphasis, especially in the balance of 'already' and 'not yet'. The Fourth Gospel lays a heavy weight of emphasis both on realized eschatology and on the identification of eschatological salvation with Jesus himself (see, *e.g.*, 11:23–26), but does not eliminate the future expectation (5:28f.; 6:39, *etc.*).

III. Christian life in hope

The Christian lives between the 'already' and the 'not yet', between the resurrection of Christ and the future general resurrection at the coming of Christ. This accounts for the distinctive structure of Christian existence, founded on the finished work of Christ in the historical past and at the same time living in the hope of the future which is kindled and guaranteed by that past history itself. The structure is seen, *e.g.*, in the Lord's Supper, where the risen Lord is present with his people in an act of 'remembrance' of his death, which is at the same time a symbolic anticipation of the eschatological banquet of the future, witnessing therefore to the hope of his coming.

The time between the 'already' and the 'not yet' is the time of the Spirit and the time of the church. The Spirit is the eschatological gift promised by the prophets (Acts 2:16–18), by which Christians already participate in the eternal life of the age to come. The Spirit creates the church, the eschatological people of God, who have already been transferred from the dominion of darkness to the kingdom of Christ (Col. 1:13). Through the Spirit in the church the life of the age to come is already being lived in the midst of the history of this present evil age (Gal. 1:4). Thus, in a sense, the new age and the old age overlap; the new humanity of the last Adam co-exists with the old humanity of the first Adam. By faith we know that the old is passing and under judgment, and the future lies with the new reality of Christ.

The process of eschatological fulfilment in the overlap of the ages involves the mission of the church, which fulfils the universalism of the OT hope. The death and resurrection of Christ are an eschatological event of universal significance which must, however, be universally realized in history, through the church's world-wide proclamation of the gospel (Mt. 28:18–20; Mk. 13:10; Col. 1:23).

The line between the new age and the old does not, however, run simply between the church and the world; it runs through the church and through the individual Christian life. We are always in transition from the old to the new, living in the eschatological tension of the 'already' and the 'not yet'. We are saved and yet we still await salvation. God has justified us, *i.e.* he has anticipated the verdict of the last judgment by declaring us acquitted through Christ. Yet we still 'wait for the hope of righteousness' (Gal. 5:5). God has given us the Spirit by which we share Christ's resurrection life. But the Spirit is still only the first instalment (2 Cor. 1:22; 5:5; Eph. 1:14) of the eschatological inheritance, the down-payment which guarantees the full payment. The Spirit is the first fruits (Rom. 8:23) of the full harvest. Therefore in present Christian existence we still know the warfare of flesh and Spirit (Gal. 5:13–26), the struggle within us between the nature we owe to the first Adam and the new nature we owe to the last Adam. We still await the redemption of our bodies at the resurrection (Rom. 8:23; 1 Cor. 15:44–50), and perfection is still the goal towards which we strive (Phil. 3:10–14). The tension of 'already' and 'not yet' is an existential reality of Christian life.

For the same reason the Christian life involves suffering. In this age Christians must share Christ's sufferings, so that in the age to come they may share his glory (Acts 14:22; Rom. 8:17; 2 Cor. 4:17; 2 Thes. 1:4f.; Heb. 12:2; 1 Pet. 4:13; 5:10; Rev. 2:10), *i.e.* 'glory' belongs to the 'not yet' of Christian existence. This is both because we are still in this mortal body, and also because the church is still in the world of Satan's dominion. Its mission is therefore inseparable from persecution, as Christ's was (Jn. 15:18–20).

It is important to notice that NT eschatology is never mere information about the future. The future hope is always relevant to Christian life in the present. It is therefore repeatedly made the basis of exhortations to Christian living appropriate to the Christian hope (Mt. 5:3–10, 24f.; Rom. 13:11–14; 1 Cor. 7:26–31; 15:58; 1 Thes. 5:1–11; Heb. 10:32–39; 1 Pet. 1:13; 4:7; 2 Pet. 3:14; Rev. 2f.). Christian life is characterized by its orientation towards the time when God's rule will finally prevail universally (Mt. 6:10), and Christians will therefore stand for that reality against all the apparent dominance of evil in this age. They will *wait* for that day in solidarity with the eager longing of the whole creation (Rom. 8:18–25; 1 Cor. 1:7; Jude 21), and they will suffer with *patient endurance* the contradictions of the present. Steadfast endurance is the virtue which the NT most often associates with Christian hope (Mt. 10:22; 24:13; Rom. 8:25; 1 Thes. 1:3; 2 Tim. 2:12; Heb. 6:11f.; 10:36; Jas. 5:7–11; Rev. 1:9; 13:10; 14:12). Through the tribulation of the present age, Christians endure, even rejoicing (Rom. 12:12), in the strength of their hope which, founded on the resurrection of the crucified Christ, assures them that the way of the cross is the way to the kingdom. Christians whose hope is focused on the permanent values of God's coming kingdom will be freed from the bondage of this world's materialistic values (Mt. 6:33; 1 Cor. 7:29–31; Phil. 3:18–21; Col. 3:1–4). Christians whose hope is that Christ will finally present them perfect before his Father (1 Cor. 1:8; 1 Thes. 3:13; Jude 24) will strive towards that perfection in the present (Phil. 3:12–15; Heb. 12:14; 2 Pet. 3:11–14; 1 Jn. 3:3). They will live *vigilantly* (Mt. 24:42–44; 25:1–13; Mk. 13:33–37; Lk. 21:34–36; 1 Thes. 5:1–11; 1 Pet. 5:8; Rev. 16:15), like servants who daily expect the return of their master (Lk. 12:35–48).

The Christian hope is not utopian. The kingdom of God will not be built by human effort; it is God's own act. Nevertheless, because the kingdom represents the perfect realization of God's will for human society, it will also be the motive for Christian social action in the present. The kingdom is anticipated now primarily in the church, the community of those who acknowledge the King, but Christian social action for the realization of God's will in society at large will also be a sign of the coming kingdom. Those who pray for the coming of the kingdom (Mt. 6:10) cannot fail to act out that prayer so far as it is possible. They will do so, however, with that eschatological realism which recognizes that all anticipations of the kingdom in this age will be provisional and imperfect, that the coming kingdom must never be confused with the social and political structures of this age (Lk. 22:25–27; Jn. 18:36), and the latter will not infrequently embody satanic opposition to the kingdom (Rev. 13:17). In this way Christians will not be disillusioned by human failure but continue to trust the promise of God. Human utopianism must rediscover its true goal in Christian hope, not vice versa.

IV. Signs of the times

The NT consistently represents the coming of Christ as imminent (Mt. 16:28; 24:33; Rom. 13:11f.; 1 Cor. 7:29; Jas. 5:8f.; 1 Pet. 4:7; Rev. 1:1; 22:7, 10, 12, 20). This temporal imminence is, however, qualified by the expectation that certain events must happen 'first' (Mt. 24:14; 2 Thes. 2:2–8), and especially by clear teaching that the date of the end cannot be known in advance (Mt. 24:36, 42; 25:13; Mk. 13:32f.; Acts 1:7). All calculation is ruled out, and Christians live in daily expectation precisely because the date cannot be known. Imminence has less to do with dates than with the *theological* relationship of future fulfilment to the past history of Christ and the present situation of Christians. The 'already' promises, guarantees, demands the 'not yet', and so the coming of Christ exercises a continuous pressure on the present, motivating Christian life towards it. This theological relationship accounts for the characteristic foreshortening of perspective in Jesus' prophecy of the judgment of Jerusalem (Mt. 24; Mk. 13; Lk. 21) and John's prophecy of the judgment of pagan Rome (Rev.); both these judgments are foreseen as events of the final triumph of God's kingdom, because theologically they are such, whatever the chronological gap between them and the end. It is because God's kingdom is coming that the powers of this world are judged even within the history of this age. All such judgments anticipate the final judgment.

As the church's future, the coming of Christ must inspire the church's present, however near or distant in time it may be. In this sense, therefore, the Christian hope in the NT is unaffected by the so-called 'delay of the *parousia*' which some scholars have conjectured as a major feature in early Christian theological development. The 'delay' is explicitly reflected only in 2 Pet. 3:1–10 (*cf.* also Jn. 21:22f.): there it is shown to have its own theological rationale in God's merciful forbearance (*cf.* Rom. 2:4).

Some exegetes think the NT provides 'signs' by which the church will be warned of the approach of the end (*cf.* Mt. 24:3). The strongest support for this idea comes from Jesus' parable of the fig tree, with its lesson (Mt. 24:32f.; Mk. 13:28f.; Lk. 21:28–31). Yet the signs in question seem to be either the fall of Jerusalem (Lk. 21:5–7, 20–24), which, while it signals the coming of the end, provides no *temporal* indication, or characteristics of the whole of this age from the resurrection of Christ to the end: false teachers (Mt. 24:4f., 11, 24f.; *cf.* 1 Tim. 4:1; 2 Tim. 3:1–9; 2 Pet. 1–3; 1 Jn. 2:18f.; 4:3); wars (Mt. 24:6f.; *cf.* Rev. 6:4); natural disasters (Mt. 24:7; *cf.* Rev. 6:5–8); persecution of the church (Mt. 24:9f.; *cf.* Rev. 6:9–11), and the world-wide preaching of the gospel (Mt. 24:14). All these are signs by which the church at every period of history knows that it lives in the end-time, but they do not provide an eschatological timetable. Only the coming of Christ itself is unmistakably the end (Mt. 24:27–30).

The NT does, however, expect the time of the church's witness to reach a final climax in the appearance of *Antichrist and a period of unparalleled tribulation (Mt. 24:21f.; Rev. 3:10; 7:14). Paul certainly treats the non-appearance of Antichrist as an indication that the end is not yet (2 Thes. 2:3–12).

Antichrist represents the principle of satanic opposition to God's rule active throughout history (*e.g.* in the persecution of Jewish believers under Antiochus Epiphanes: Dn. 8:9–12, 23–25; 11:21ff.), but especially in the last times, the age of the church (1 Jn. 2:18). Christ's victory over evil, already achieved in principle, is manifest in this age primarily in the suffering witness of the church; only at the end will his victory be complete in the elimination of the powers of evil. Therefore in this age the success of the church's witness is always accompanied by the mounting violence of satanic opposition (*cf.* Rev. 12).

Evil will reach its final crescendo in the final Antichrist, who is both a false Messiah or prophet, inspired by Satan to perform false miracles (2 Thes. 2:9; *cf.* Mt. 24:24; Rev. 13:11–15), and a persecuting political power blasphemously claiming divine honours (2 Thes. 2:4; *cf.* Dn. 8:9–12, 23–25; 11:30–39; Mt. 24: 15; Rev. 13:5–8). It is noteworthy that, while Paul provides a sketch of this human embodiment of evil (2 Thes. 2:3–12), other NT references find Antichrist already present in heretical teachers (1 Jn. 2:18f., 22; 4:3) or in the religio-political pretensions of the persecuting Roman empire (Rev. 13). The climax is anticipated in every great crisis of the church's history.

V. The coming of Christ

Christian hope is focused on the coming of Christ, which may be called his 'second' coming (Heb. 9:28). Thus the OT term, 'the *day of the Lord', which the NT uses for the event of final fulfilment (1 Thes. 5:2; 2 Thes. 2:2; 2 Pet. 3:10; *cf.* 'the day of God', 2 Pet. 3:12; 'the great day of God the Almighty', Rev. 16:14), is characteristically 'the day of the Lord Jesus' (1 Cor. 5:5; 2 Cor. 1:14; *cf.* 1 Cor. 1:8; Phil. 1:6, 10; 2:16).

The coming of Christ is called his *parousia* ('coming'), his *apokalypsis* ('revelation') and his *epiphaneia* ('appearing'). The word *parousia* means 'presence' or 'arrival', and was used in Hellenistic Greek of the visits of gods and rulers. Christ's *parousia* will be a personal coming of the same Jesus of Nazareth who ascended into heaven (Acts 1:11); but it will be a universally evident event (Mt. 24:27), a coming in power and glory (Mt. 24:30), to destroy Antichrist and evil (2 Thes. 2:8), to gather his people, living and dead (Mt. 24:31; 1 Cor. 15:23; 1 Thes. 4:14–17; 2 Thes. 2:1), and to judge the world (Mt. 25:31; Jas. 5:9).

His coming will also be an *apokalypsis*, an 'unveiling' or 'disclosure', when the power and glory which are now his by virtue of his exaltation and heavenly session (Phil. 2:9; Eph. 1:20–23; Heb. 2:9) will be disclosed to the world. Christ's reign as Lord, now invisible to the world, will then be made visible by his *apokalypsis.*

VI. The * resurrection

At the coming of Christ, the Christian dead will be raised (1 Cor. 15:23; 1 Thes. 4:16) and those who are alive at the time will be transformed (1 Cor. 15:52; *cf.* 1 Thes. 4:17), *i.e.* they will pass into the same resurrection existence without dying.

Belief in the resurrection of the dead is found already in a few OT texts (Is. 25:8; 26:19; Dn. 12:2) and is common in the intertestamental literature. Both Jesus (Mk. 12:18–27) and Paul (Acts 23:6–8) agreed on this point with the Pharisees against the Sadducees, who denied resurrection. The Christian expectation of resurrection, however, is based decisively on the resurrection of Jesus, from which God is known as 'God who raises the dead' (2 Cor. 1:9). Jesus, in his resurrection, 'abolished death and brought life and immortality to light' (2 Tim. 1:10). He is 'the living one', who died and is now alive for ever, who has 'the keys of death' (Rev. 1:18).

Jesus' resurrection was no mere re-animation of a corpse. It was entry into eschatological life, a transformed existence beyond the reach of death. As such it was the beginning of the eschatological resurrection (1 Cor. 15:23). The fact of Jesus' resurrection already guarantees the future resurrection of Christians at his coming (Rom. 8:11; 1 Cor. 6:14; 15:20–23; 2 Cor. 4:14; 1 Thes. 4:14).

Eschatological life, the risen life of Christ, is already communicated to Christians in this age by his Spirit (Jn. 5:24; Rom. 8:11; Eph. 2:5f.; Col. 2:12; 3:1), and this too is a guarantee of their future resurrection (Jn. 11:26; Rom. 8:11; 2 Cor. 1:22; 3:18; 5:4f.). But the Spirit's transformation of Christians into the glorious image of Christ is incomplete in this age because their bodies remain mortal. The future resurrection will be the completion of their transformation into Christ's image, characterized by incorruption, glory and power (1 Cor. 15:42–44). The resurrection existence is not 'flesh and blood' (1 Cor. 15:20) but a 'spiritual body' (15:44), *i.e.* a body wholly vitalized and transformed by the Spirit of the risen Christ. From 1 Cor. 15:35–54 it is clear that the continuity between this present existence and resurrection life is the continuity of the personal self, independent of physical identity.

In NT thought, immortality belongs intrinsically to God alone (1 Tim. 6:16), while men by their descent from Adam are naturally mortal (Rom. 5:12). Eternal life is the gift of God to men through the resurrection of Christ. Only in Christ and by means of their future resurrection will men attain that full eschatological life which is beyond the reach of death. Resurrection is therefore equivalent to man's final attainment of eschatological salvation.

It follows that the damned will not be raised in this full sense of resurrection to eternal life. The resurrection of the damned is mentioned only occasionally in Scripture (Dn. 12:2; Jn. 5:28f.; Acts 24:15; Rev. 20:5, 12f.; *cf.* Mt. 12:41f.), as the means of their condemnation at the judgment.

VII. The state of the dead

The Christian hope for life beyond death is not based on the belief that part of man survives death. All men, through their descent from Adam, are naturally mortal. Immortality is the gift of God, which will be attained through the resurrection of the whole person.

The Bible therefore takes death seriously. It is not an illusion. It is the consequence of sin (Rom. 5:12; 6:23), an evil (Dt. 30:15, 19) from which men shrink in terror (Ps. 55:4f.). It is an enemy of God and man, and resurrection is therefore God's great victory over death (1 Cor. 15:54–57). Death is 'the last enemy to be destroyed' (1 Cor. 15:26), abolished in principle at Christ's resurrection (2 Tim. 1:10), to be finally abolished at the end (Rev. 20:14; *cf.* Is. 25:8). Only because Christ's resurrection guarantees their future resurrection are Christians delivered from the fear of death (Heb. 2:14f.) and able to see it as a sleep from which they will awaken (1 Thes. 4:13f.; 5:10) or even a departing to be with Christ (Phil. 1:23).

The OT pictures the state of the dead as existence in Sheol, the grave or the underworld. But existence in Sheol is not life. It is a land of darkness (Jb. 10:21f.) and silence (Ps. 115:17), in which God is not remembered (Pss. 6:5; 30:9; 88:11; Is. 38:18). The dead in Sheol are cut off from God (Ps. 88:5), the source of life. Only occasionally does the OT attain a hope of real life beyond death, *i.e.* life out of reach of Sheol in the presence of God (Pss. 16:10f.; 49:15; 73:24; perhaps Jb. 19:25f.). Probably the example of *Enoch (Gn. 5:24; *cf.* Elijah, 2 Ki. 2:11) helped stimulate this hope. A clear doctrine of resurrection is found only in Is. 26:19; Dn. 12:2.

'Hades' is the NT equivalent of Sheol (Mt. 11:23; 16:18; Lk. 10:15; Acts 2:27, 31; Rev. 1:18; 6:8; 20:13f.), in most cases referring to death or the power of death. In Lk. 16:23 it is the place of torment for the wicked after death, in accordance with some contemporary Jewish thinking, but it is doubtful whether this parabolic use of current ideas can be treated as teaching about the state of the dead. 1 Pet. 3:19 calls the dead who perished in the Flood 'the spirits in prison' (*cf.* 4:6).

The NT hope for the Christian dead is concentrated on their participation in the resurrection (1 Thes. 4:13–18), and there is therefore little evidence of belief about the 'intermediate state'. Passages which indicate, or may indicate, that the Christian dead are with Christ are Lk. 23:43; Rom. 8:38f.; 2 Cor. 5:8; Phil. 1:23; *cf.* Heb. 12:23. The difficult passage 2 Cor. 5:2–8 may mean that Paul conceives existence between death and resurrection as a bodiless existence in Christ's presence.

VIII. The judgment

The NT insists on the prospect of divine judgment as, besides death, the single unavoidable fact of a man's future: 'It is appointed for men to die once, and after that comes judgment' (Heb. 9:27). This fact expresses the holiness of the biblical God, whose moral will must prevail, and before whom all responsible creatures must therefore in the end be judged obedient or rebellious. When God's will finally prevails at the coming of Christ, there must be a separation between the finally obedient and the finally rebellious, so that the kingdom of God will include the one and exclude the other for ever. No such final judgment occurs within history, though there are provisional judgments in history, while God in his forbearance gives all men time to repent (Acts 17:30f.; Rom. 2:4; 2 Pet. 3:9). But at the end the truth of every man's position before God must come to light.

The Judge is God (Rom. 2:6; Heb. 12:23; Jas. 4:12; 1 Pet. 1:17; Rev. 20:11) or Christ (Mt. 16:27; 25:31; Jn. 5:22; Acts 10:42; 2 Tim. 4:1, 8; 1 Pet. 4:5; Rev. 22:12). It is God who judges through his eschatological agent Christ (Jn. 5:22, 27, 30; Acts 17:31; Rom. 2:16). The judgment seat of God (Rom. 14:10) and the judgment seat of Christ (2 Cor. 5:10) are therefore equivalent. (The judgment committed to the saints, according to Mt. 19:28; Lk. 22:30; 1 Cor. 6:2f.; Rev. 20:4, means their authority to rule with Christ in his kingdom, not to officiate at the last judgment.)

The standard of judgment is God's impartial righteousness according to men's works (Mt. 16:27; Rom. 2:6, 11: 2 Tim. 4:14; 1 Pet. 1:17; Rev. 2:23; 20:12; 22:12). This is true even for Christians: 'We must all appear before the judgment seat of Christ, so that each one may receive good or evil, according to what he has done in the body' (2 Cor. 5:10). The judgment will be according to men's lights (*cf.* Jn. 9:41); according to whether they have the law of Moses (Rom. 2:12) or the natural knowledge of God's moral standards (Rom. 2:12–16), but by these standards no man can be declared righteous before God according to his works (Rom. 3:19f.). There is no hope for the man who seeks to justify himself at the judgment.

There is hope, however, for the man who seeks his justification from God (Rom. 2:7). The gospel reveals that righteousness which is not required of men but given to men through Christ. In the death and resurrection of Christ, God in his merciful love has already made his eschatological judgment in favour of sinners, acquitting them for the sake of Christ, offering them in Christ that righteousness which they could never achieve. Thus the man who has faith in Christ is free from all condemnation (Jn. 5:24; Rom. 8:33f.). The final criterion of judgment is therefore a man's relation to Christ (*cf.* Mt. 10:32f.). This is the meaning of the 'book of life' (Rev. 20:12, 15; *i.e.* the *Lamb*'s book of life, Rev. 13:8).

The meaning of Paul's doctrine of justification is that in Christ God has anticipated the verdict of the last judgment, and pronounced an acquittal of sinners who trust in Christ. Very similar is John's doctrine that judgment takes place already in men's belief or disbelief in Christ (Jn. 3:17–21; 5:24).

The last judgment remains an eschatological fact, even for believers (Rom. 14:10), though they may face it without fear (1 Jn. 4:17). We hope for acquittal in the final judgment (Gal. 5:5), 'the crown of righteousness' (2 Tim. 4:8), on the ground of the same mercy of God through which we have already been acquitted (2 Tim. 1:16). But, even for the Christian, works are not irrelevant

(Mt. 7:1f., 21, 24–27; 25:31–46; Jn. 3:21; 2 Cor. 5:10; Jas. 2:13), since justification does not abrogate the need for obedience, but precisely makes it possible for the first time. Justification is the foundation, but what men build on it is exposed to judgment (1 Cor. 3:10–15): 'If any man's work is burned up, he will suffer loss, though he himself will be saved, but only as through fire' (3:15).

IX. *Hell

The final destiny of the wicked is 'hell', which translates Gk. *Gehenna*, derived from the Heb. *gê-hinnōm*, 'the valley of Hinnom'. This originally denoted a valley outside Jerusalem, where child sacrifices were offered to Molech (2 Ch. 28:3; 33:6). It became a symbol of judgment in Je. 7:31–33; 19:6f., and in the intertestamental literature the term for the eschatological hell of fire.

In the NT, hell is pictured as a place of unquenchable or eternal fire (Mk. 9:43, 48; Mt. 18:8; 25:30) and the undying worm (Mk. 9:48), a place of weeping and gnashing of teeth (Mt. 8:12; 13:42, 50; 22:13; 25:30), the outer darkness (Mt. 8:12; 22:13; 25:30; *cf.* 2 Pet. 2:17; Jude 13) and the lake of fire and brimstone (Rev. 19:20; 20:10, 14f.; 21:8; *cf.* 14:10). Revelation identifies it as 'the second death' (2:11; 20:14; 21:8). It is the place of the destruction of both body and soul (Mt. 10:28).

The NT pictures of hell are markedly restrained by comparison with Jewish apocalyptic and with later Christian writings. The imagery used derives especially from Is. 66:24 (*cf.* Mk. 9:48) and Gn. 19:24, 28; Is. 34:9f. (*cf.* Rev. 14:10f.; also Jude 7; Rev. 19:3). It is clearly not intended literally but indicates the terror and finality of condemnation to hell, which is less metaphorically described as exclusion from the presence of Christ (Mt. 7:23; 25:41; 2 Thes. 1:9). The imagery of Rev. 14:10f.; 20:10 (*cf.* 19:3) should probably not be pressed to prove eternal torment, but the NT clearly teaches eternal destruction (2 Thes. 1:9) or punishment (Mt. 25:46), from which there can be no release.

Hell is the destiny of all the powers of evil: Satan (Rev. 20:10), the demons (Mt. 8:29; 25:41), the beast and the false prophet (Rev. 19:20), death and Hades (Rev. 20:14). It is the destiny of men only because they have identified themselves with evil. It is important to notice that there is no symmetry about the two destinies of men: the kingdom of God has been prepared for the redeemed (Mt. 25:34), but hell has been prepared for the devil and his angels (Mt. 25:41) and becomes the fate of men only because they have refused their true destiny which God offers them in Christ. The NT doctrine of hell, like all NT eschatology, is never mere information; it is a warning given in the context of the gospel's call to repentance and faith in Christ.

The NT teaching about hell cannot be reconciled with an absolute universalism, the doctrine of the final salvation of all men. The element of truth in this doctrine is that God desires the salvation of all men (1 Tim. 2:4) and gave his Son for the salvation of the world (Jn. 3:16). Accordingly, the cosmic goal of God's eschatological action in Christ can be described in universalistic terms (Eph. 1:10; Col. 1:20; Rev. 5:13). The error of dogmatic universalism is the same as that of a symmetrical doctrine of double predestination: that they abstract eschatological doctrine from its proper NT context in the proclamation of the gospel. They rob the gospel of its eschatological urgency and challenge. The gospel sets before men their true destiny in Christ and warns them in all seriousness of the consequence of missing this destiny.

X. The millennium

The interpretation of the passage Rev. 20:1–10, which describes a period of a thousand years (known as the 'millennium') in which Satan is bound and the saints reign with Christ before the last judgment, has long been a subject of disagreement between Christians. 'Amillennialism' is the view which regards the millennium as a symbol of the age of the church and identifies the binding of Satan with Christ's work in the past (Mt. 12:29). 'Postmillennialism' regards it as a future period of success for the gospel in history before the coming of Christ. 'Premillennialism' regards it as a period between the coming of Christ and the last judgment. (The term 'chiliasm' is also used for this view, especially in forms which emphasize the materialistic aspect of the millennium.) 'Premillennialism' may be further subdivided. There is what is sometimes called 'historic premillennialism', which regards the millennium as a further stage in the achievement of Christ's kingdom, an interim stage between the church age and the age to come. (Sometimes 1 Cor. 15:23–28 is interpreted as supporting this idea of three stages in the fulfilment of Christ's redemptive work.) 'Dispensationalism', on the other hand, teaches that the millennium is not a stage in God's single universal redemptive action in Christ, but specifically a period in which the OT promises to the nation of Israel will be fulfilled in strictly literal form.

It should be emphasized that no other passage of Scripture clearly refers to the millennium. To apply OT prophecies of the age of salvation specifically to the millennium runs counter to the general NT interpretation of such prophecies, which find their fulfilment in the salvation already achieved by Christ and to be consummated in the age to come. This is also how Rev. itself interprets such prophecies in chs. 21f. Within the structure of Rev., the millennium has a limited role, as a demonstration of the final victory of Christ and his saints over the powers of evil. The principal object of Christian hope is not the millennium but the new creation of Rev. 21f.

Some Jewish apocalyptic writings look forward to a preliminary kingdom of the Messiah on this earth prior to the age to come, and John has very probably adapted that expectation. There are strong exegetical reasons for regarding the millennium as the consequence of the coming of Christ depicted in Rev. 19:11–21. (See G. R. Beasley-Murray, *The Book of Revelation*, *NCB*, 1974, pp. 284–298.) This favours 'historic premillennialism', but it is also possible that the image of the millennium is taken too literally when it is understood as a precise period of time. Whether it is a period of time or a comprehensive symbol of the significance of the coming of Christ, the theological meaning of the millennium is the same: it expresses the hope of Christ's final triumph over evil and the vindication with him of his people who have suffered under the tyranny of evil in the present age.

XI. The new creation

The final goal of God's purposes for the world includes, negatively, the destruction of all God's enemies: Satan, sin and death, and the elimination of all forms of suffering (Rev. 20:10, 14–15; 7:16f.;

21:4; Is. 25:8; 27:1; Rom. 16:20; 1 Cor. 15:26, 54). Positively, God's rule will finally prevail entirely (Zc. 14:9; 1 Cor. 15:24–28; Rev. 11:15), so that in Christ all things will be united (Eph. 1:10) and God will be all in all (1 Cor. 15:28, AV).

With the final achievement of human salvation there will come also the liberation of the whole material creation from its share in the curse of sin (Rom. 8:19–23). The Christian hope is not for redemption from the world, but for the redemption of the world. Out of judgment (Heb. 12:26; 2 Pet. 3:10) will emerge a recreated universe (Rev. 21:1; *cf.* Is. 65:17; 66:22; Mt. 19:28), 'a new heaven and a new earth in which righteousness dwells' (2 Pet. 3:13).

The destiny of the redeemed is to be like Christ (Rom. 8:29; 1 Cor. 15:49; Phil. 3:21; 1 Jn. 3:2), to be with Christ (Jn. 14:3; 2 Cor. 5:8; Phil. 1:23; Col. 3:4; 1 Thes. 4:17), to share his glory (Rom. 8:18, 30; 2 Cor. 3:18; 4:17; Col. 3:4; Heb. 2:10; 1 Pet. 5:1) and his kingdom (1 Tim. 2:12; Rev. 2:26f.; 3:21; 4:10; 20:4, 6); to be sons of God in perfect fellowship with God (Rev. 21:3, 7), to worship God (Rev. 7:15; 22:3), to see God (Mt. 5:8; Rev. 22:4), to know him face to face (1 Cor. 13:12). Faith, hope and especially love are the permanent characteristics of Christian existence which abide even in the perfection of the age to come (1 Cor. 13:13), while 'righteousness and peace and joy in the Holy Spirit' are similarly abiding qualities of man's enjoyment of God (Rom. 14:17).

The corporate life of the redeemed with God is described in a number of pictures: the eschatological banquet (Mt. 8:11; Mk. 14:25; Lk. 14:15–24; 22:30) or wedding feast (Mt. 25:10; Rev. 19:9), paradise restored (Lk. 23:43; Rev. 2:7; 22:1f.), the new Jerusalem (Heb. 12:22; Rev. 21). All these are only pictures, since 'no eye has seen, nor ear heard, nor the heart of man conceived, what God has prepared for those who love him' (1 Cor. 2:9).

BIBLIOGRAPHY. W. G. Kümmel, *Promise and Fulfilment*, 1961; R. Schnackenburg, *God's Rule and Kingdom*, 1963; G. E. Ladd, *The Eschatology of Biblical Realism*, 1964; A. L. Moore, *The Parousia in the New Testament*, 1966; G. C. Berkouwer, *The Return of Christ*, 1972; J. Bright, *Covenant and Promise*, 1976; R. G. Clouse (ed.), *The Meaning of the Millennium: Four Views*, 1977; A. J. Mattill, *Luke and the Last Things*, 1979; P. S. Minear, *New Testament Apocalyptic*, 1981; J. C. Beker, *Paul's Apocalyptic Gospel*, 1982; S. H. Travis, *I Believe in the Second Coming of Jesus*, 1982; M. J. Harris, *Raised Immortal*, 1983; A. van der Walle, *From Darkness to the Dawn*, 1984; G. R. Beasley-Murray, *Jesus and the Kingdom of God*, 1986; D. Gowan, *Eschatology and the Old Testament*, 1986; S. H. Travis, *Christ and the Judgment of God*, 1986; Z. Hayes, *Visions of a Future*, 1989; J. H. Charlesworth (ed.), *The Messiah: Developments in Early Judaism and Christianity*, 1992. R.J.B.

ESDRAELON. The Greek form of the name *Jezreel. However, the Greek and Hebrew names really apply to two distinct but adjacent lowlands, even though in some modern works the term Jezreel is loosely extended to cover both regions. The vale of Jezreel proper is the valley that slopes down from the town of Jezreel to Beth-shan overlooking the Jordan rift-valley, with Galilee to the N and Mt Gilboa to the S.

Esdraelon is the triangular alluvial plain bounded along its SW side by the Carmel range from Jokneam to Ibleam and Engannim (modern Jenin), along its N side by a line from Jokneam to the hills of Nazareth, and on the E by a line thence back down to Ibleam and Engannim. On the E, Jezreel guards the entry to its own valley, while in the W the SW spur of hills from Galilee leaves only a small gap by which the river Kishon flows out into the plain of Acre after crossing the Esdraelon plain. At the foot of the NE-facing slopes of Carmel the important towns of *Jokneam, *Megiddo, *Taanach and *Ibleam controlled the main passes and N–S routes through W Palestine, while these and Jezreel (town) also controlled the important route running E–W from the Jordan valley to the Mediterranean coast, the only one unimpeded by ranges of hills. Esdraelon was a marshy region, important mainly for these roads; the vale of Jezreel was agriculturally valuable as well as being strategically placed. For geographical background, see D. Baly, *Geography of the Bible*, 1974, pp. 39, 144–151. K.A.K.

ESHCOL. 1. Brother of Mamre and Aner, who were 'confederates' with Abraham when in Hebron, and joined with his company in the rescue of Lot (Gn. 14:13–24).

2. The valley where the spies sent forth by Moses gathered a huge cluster (Heb. *'eškōl*) of grapes, typical of the fruitfulness of the land (Nu. 13:23–24; 32:9; Dt. 1:24). Traditionally thought to be located a few km N of Hebron (already Jerome, *Ep.* 108. 11 = *PL* 22. 886), where the vineyards are still famous for the quality of their grapes.

Some scholars prefer a location S of Hebron (Gray; Noth), but although the texts are not explicit about the direction, it does seem to be implied that the spies continued N from Hebron to the Valley of Eshcol (Nu. 13:22–23).

BIBLIOGRAPHY. G. B. Gray, *Numbers, ICC*, 1903, pp. 142–143; P. Thomsen, *Loca Sancta*, 1907, p. 62; *IDB*, 2, p. 142. G.T.M.
G.I.D.

ESHTAOL (*'eštā'ōl*, from the verb *šā'al*, 'to ask'), **ESHTAOLITES.** A lowland city, W of Jerusalem, tentatively identified with the modern Eshwa', it was included in the territory of both Judah (Jos. 15:33) and Dan (Jos. 19:41), an anomaly which is partially explained by the fluidity of the border, a fact attributable to Amorite (Jdg. 1:34) and then Philistine pressure. The Eshtaolites are numbered amongst the Calebites, traditionally associated with Judah (1 Ch. 2:53).

It was at Eshtaol that the Danite Samson was first moved by the Spirit of the Lord (Jdg. 13:25) and where he was finally buried in the tomb of his father (Jdg. 16:31). From Eshtaol and neighbouring Zorah originated the Danite quest for a settled habitation (Jdg. 18:2, 11). A.E.C.

ESSENES. The name given in classical sources to a major Jewish sect which existed in Judaea at least from the middle of the 2nd century BC until the Jewish revolt in AD 66–70.

The etymology of the name (Gk. *Essēnoi*, *Essaioi*; Lat. *Esseni*) remains a puzzle. Of the numerous proposals, the three with the most to commend them are derivations from:

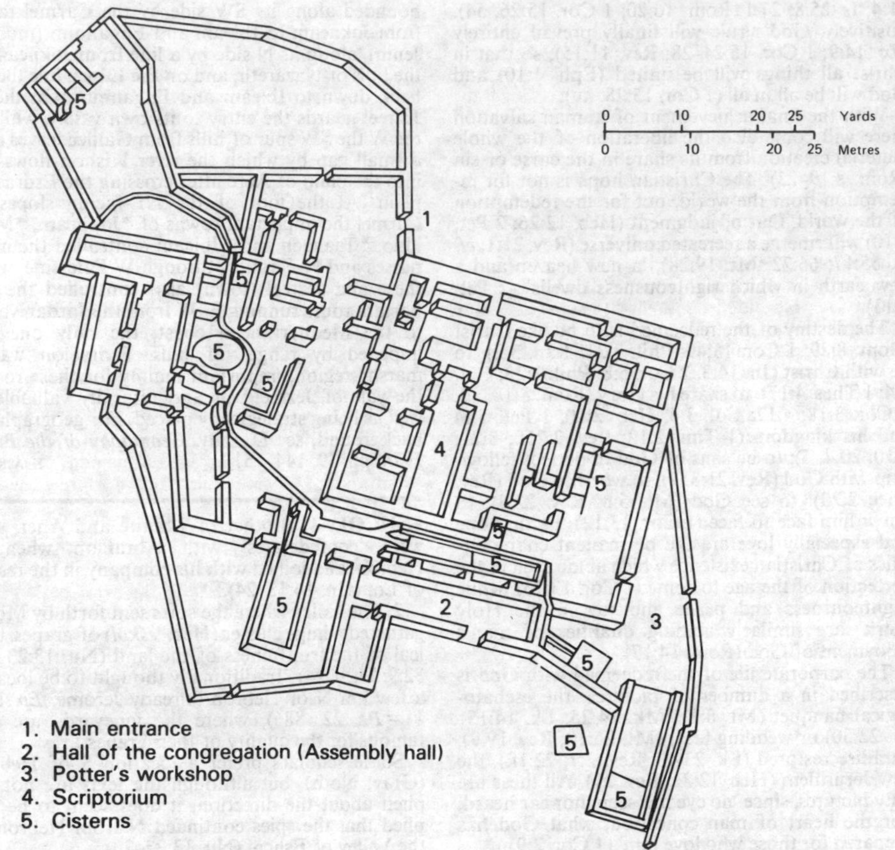

Plan of the buildings at Khirbet Qumran, believed to have been occupied by an Essene community. 2nd cent. BC*–1st cent.* AD*.*

1. Aramaic 'asayya' 'healers';

2. Syriac *ḥassayyâ* 'pious' [= Heb. *ḥasîdîm*/Gk. *asidaioi*];

3. the Gk. name for priests of Artemis (*essēnas*).

In any case, there is no evidence that 'Essene' was a self-designation.

Our main outside observations come from Philo (*Quod omnis Probus Liber sit* 75–91; *Apology*, preserved by Eusebius *Praep. Ev.* 8.11.1–18), Josephus (*BJ* 2.119–161 and *Ant.* 18.18–22; anecdotal comments in *BJ* 1.78–80; 2.113; 2.567; 3.11; 5.145; *Ant.* 13.171–172; 15.371–379; *Vit. Mos.* 10–11), Pliny (*NH* 5.73) and Hippolytus of Rome (*Refutation of All Heresies* 9.18–28). All of these require caution in interpretation (see *PHARISEES).

It is believed that the Jews who inhabited Qumran, and whose views are reflected in some of the DSS, were Essenes because of:

1. similarities of the classical descriptions with practices and community organization expressed in the DSS;

2. the agreement of Pliny's geographical comments with the location of Qumran;

3. the agreement of Josephus' chronological framework for the Essenes (*c.* 150 BC–AD 70) with the archaeological data of Qumran, the dating of the manuscripts (palaeography and C-14) and historical references in the texts. Consequently, we have a considerable body of direct textual sources for the Essenes, unparalleled for any other Jewish group of the Second Temple period. Nevertheless, one must be cautious when reading the DSS for the history of Essenes. Several factors reveal a complex relationship among the DSS, Qumran and the Essenes: more than one community is represented among the DSS (see *DEAD SEA SCROLLS); the relationship between Qumran and these other communities is not yet clear; there is no solid evidence that Qumran was the focus for Essene life (some have even posited that the Qumran settlement was a break from the Essenes); the classical sources indicate diversity among the Essenes (*e.g.* marrying and celibate).

Generally it is safe to accept as Essene characteristics those elements in which the DSS evidence reinforces and corrects the picture derived from the classical sources. They lived in various communities throughout Palestine, but had a large settlement at Qumran. An initiation regime was required of all potential members: a preparatory period of study and examination was followed by 2 years of training, during which they were accepted in stages to share in the common property and the pure foods and drink. At some point a solemn oath of loyalty was taken. A strict hierarchy, dominated by priests and elders, ordered their communities, led by individual fiscal and spiritual overseers, but judicial functions were carried out democractically by large bodies of full members. They held property in common but retained some personal discretion. Regularly (twice daily according to Jos.), they shared a common meal over which a priest had to pray. Their purification baths were unique in that access was restricted to members of the sect alone after a probationary year, and purification was required before common meals as well as for the usual cases of impurity. They differed from the temple authorities with regard to cultic purity, and therefore seem to have restricted or renounced participation in sacrifices. Because of their stringent purity, they avoided contact with oil, isolated excrement away from the community, and prohibited spitting into the middle of a group. Sabbath regulations among the Essenes were especially strict. Josephus's report that they prayed to the sun is unlikely to mean that the Essenes worshipped the sun, but refers rather to the practice of daily communal prayer at sunrise (Jos.; DSS) and sunset (DSS). Also, Josephus's statements that they believed in 'fate' and the immortality of the soul, express to a Gk. audience the determinism and (probably) life beyond death witnessed in the DSS. Essenes carefully guarded certain esoteric knowledge, including the names of angels. Wealth was despised as a corrupting influence. They devoted themselves to the study of sacred writings. Transgressions of Mosaic laws and community rules were strictly punished by fines and expulsion. It is not certain that the majority of Essenes were celibate or that they completely withdrew from all participation in the temple cult as is commonly believed.

Even though they are not mentioned in the NT, study of the Essenes is important for understanding early Christianity because of numerous similarities between the two groups (*e.g.* organization and offices, common meals, common property, purification baths restricted to those who have undergone instruction and repentance). Attempts to identify Essenes and early Christians have failed, however, and suggestions that the two groups inhabited a common quarter in Jerusalem remain highly speculative.

BIBLIOGRAPHY. T. S. Beall, *Josephus' Description of the Essenes Illustrated by the DSS*, 1988; J. J. Collins, 'Essenes', *ABD* 2, 1992, pp. 619–626; P. R. Davies, *Behind the Essenes*, 1987; L. B. Elder, 'The Woman Question and Female Ascetics among Essenes', *BA* 57, 1994, pp. 220–234; F. García Martínez and A. S. Van der Woude, 'A "Gröningen" Hypothesis of Qumran Origins and Early History', *RQ* 14, 1990, pp. 521–541; E. Schürer, *The History of the Jewish People in the Age of Jesus Christ. A New English Edition*, rev. and ed. by G. Vermes, *et al.*, 2, 1979, pp. 555–597; H. Stegemann, 'The Qumran Essenes – Local Members of the Main Jewish Union in Late Second Temple Times', in *The Madrid Proceedings of the International Congress on the DSS* 1, ed. by J. Trebolle Barrera and L. Vegas Montaner, 1992, pp. 83–166; G. Vermes and M. D. Goodman, (eds.), *The Essenes According to the Classical Sources*, 1989. D.K.F.

ESTHER. According to Est. 2:7, Esther's Jewish name was Hadassah (Myrtle). The name Esther may be the equivalent of the Persian *stara* ('star'), though some find a link with the Babylonian goddess Ishtar.

Esther married Ahasuerus (Xerxes, 486–465 BC). Herodotus and Ctesias say that the wife of Xerxes was Amestris (who is probably Vashti), and that she went with Xerxes on his expedition to Greece, which happened after the events of Est. 1. On the way home she incurred Xerxes' anger by mutilating the mother of one of his mistresses and nearly starting a revolution (Her. 9. 108f.). Small wonder that Xerxes remembered his original plan to divorce her, and now looked for a successor, which he found in Esther. Amestris came into power again as queen mother during the reign of her son, Artaxerxes I, and may indeed be the 'queen' of Ne. 2:6. If we assume that Esther died within a few years of the events recorded in the book that bears her name, there is no difficulty in harmonizing the two queens.

Although Esther was a brave woman, who risked her life to save the Jews (4:11–17), the Bible does not commend her encouragement of the Jews to massacre their enemies in ch. 9. Here she was the child of her age. J.S.W.

ESTHER, BOOK OF. This book tells how *Esther, a Jewess, became the wife of a Persian king, and was able to prevent the wholesale massacre of the Jewish race within the Persian empire.

I. Outline of contents

a. 1:1–22. Ahasuerus deposes his wife, Vashti, for refusing to appear at his banquet.

b. 2:1–18. Esther, the cousin of Mordecai, a Jew, is chosen in Vashti's place.

c. 2:19–23. Mordecai tells Esther of a plot to kill the king.

d. 3:1–15. Mordecai refuses to bow to Haman, the king's favourite, who thereupon plans to massacre the Jews on a fixed date.

e. 4:1–17. Mordecai persuades Esther to intercede with the king.

f. 5:1–14. Esther invites the king and Haman to a banquet.

g. 6:1–14. The king makes Haman honour Mordecai publicly as a reward for revealing the plot against him.

h. 7:1–10. At a second banquet Esther reveals Haman's plan to massacre the Jews, and Haman is hanged on the gallows that he had prepared for Mordecai.

i. 8:1–17. Since the edict for the massacre cannot be revoked, the king sends a second edict allowing the Jews to defend themselves.

j. 9:1–19. The Jews take advantage of this to kill their enemies.

k. 9:20–32. The deliverance is commemorated at the feast of Purim.

l. 10:1–3. Mordecai is put in a position of authority.

II. Authorship and date

The book was written some time after the death of Ahasuerus (1:1), which would be after 465 BC if Ahasuerus is identified with Xerxes. Some Jews regarded Mordecai as the author, and the references in 9:20, 32 could suggest this. Much of the contents may have been inserted in the annals of the king, as mentioned in 10:2 and perhaps 6:1, and this would account for the omission of the name of God, although the reference to fasting for

Esther in 4:16 certainly implies prayer, and the doctrine of providence is stated in 4:14.

It should be noted that the Gk. versions of Esther contain 107 extra verses, which do include references to God by name. These are collected together in the Apocrypha of our English Version, and are numbered as though they followed 10:3. In fact, their order in the Gk. is as follows: 9:2–12:6; 1:1–3:13; 13:1–7; 3:14–4:17; 13:8–15:16; 5:1–8:12; 16:1–24; 8:13–10:3; 10:4–11:1. The date given in 11:1 is 114 BC, and could be the date when the Gk. translation or expanded version was made.

III. Authenticity

Although some, such as R. H. Pfeiffer, regard the book as entire fiction, other commentators would agree with the verdict of H. H. Rowley that the author 'seems to have had access to some good sources of information on things Persian, and the nucleus of his story may be older than his book' (*Growth of the Old Testament*, p. 155). The story as such has not been confirmed by any Persian records, and it is often supposed that it cannot be fitted into what is known of Persian history.

King Ahasuerus is usually identified with Xerxes (486–465 BC), though a few, *e.g.* J. Hoschander and A. T. Olmstead, have identified him with Artaxerxes II (404–359 BC). If he is Xerxes we have an explanation of the strange gap between the third year in 1:3 and the seventh year of 2:16, since between 483 and 480 BC he was planning and carrying out his disastrous invasion of Greece. Herodotus (7. 114; 9. 108f.) gives the name of Xerxes' wife as Amestris, but we do not know from secular historians whether or not he had more than one wife. Although, according to Herodotus (3. 84), the Persian king was supposed to choose his wife from one of seven noble families (*cf.* Est. 1:14), rules of this kind could generally be evaded. Xerxes had no scruples about taking any women that he chose.

The author is alleged to be hopelessly in error in 2:5–6, when he describes *Mordecai as having been taken captive in 597 BC. By this time he would have been over 120. On the principle that a translation that makes sense is preferable to one that makes nonsense, we may refer the word 'who' in v. 6 to Mordecai's great-grandfather, Kish, as the Heb. allows us to do.

Other supposed improbabilities are largely a matter of subjective opinion. Thus, would *Haman have attempted the massacre of all the Jewish race simply because one man defied him, and would the king have permitted it? And would Haman have fixed a date for the massacre so far ahead? Such criticism shows a strange ignorance of human nature. Massacres and wars have been sparked off many times through the injured pride of one or two individuals. Persian kings also were easily swayed by their favourites, and in this case Haman represents the Jews as traitors (3:8). Haman is depicted as a thoroughly superstitious man, and the day of the massacre was chosen because the casting of lots indicated that it would be a lucky day (3:7). The gallows 25 m high (7:9) would be the typically extravagant display of a thwarted man in power, while the £2½ million offered as a bribe to the king in 3:9 is hardly to be taken seriously; what the king would understand was that a large proportion of Jewish property would be put in the royal treasuries, and with Oriental politeness he replies that Haman may keep it for himself (3:11): both parties would understand that, so long as the king received a substantial share of the spoil, he would turn a blind eye to whatever Haman took for himself.

One strange interpretation of the book demands brief notice. This is the mythological origin postulated by Zimmern and Jensen. Esther is the goddess Ishtar; Mordecai is Marduk; Haman is the Elamite deity Humman; Vashti is Mashti, an Elamite goddess. The story may have concerned a conflict between Babylonian and Elamite gods. It would be strange if the Jews had made use of a polytheistic tale, or cultic ceremony, to account for a Jewish festival; and even if *Purim could be shown to have been originally a pagan ceremony, a whole new story must have been written round it, and in this story it is unlikely that the names of gods and goddesses would have been retained. It might still be true that the names of the characters in the book of Esther have some connection with the names of gods and goddesses, since there are other examples of Jews being given extra names that probably contain the names of some god or goddess, *e.g.* Dn. 1:7; Ezr. 1:8. Moreover there is another Mordecai mentioned in Ezr. 2:2. Esther is said to be a second name in Est. 2:7.

BIBLIOGRAPHY. L. B. Paton, *Esther*, *ICC*, 1908; B. W. Anderson, *The Book of Esther*, Introduction and Exegesis, in *IB*, 3, 1951; J. S. Wright, 'The Historicity of the Book of Esther', in *New Perspectives on the Old Testament*, ed. J. B. Payne; C. A. Moore, *Esther*, *AB*, 1971; J. G. Baldwin, *TOTC*, 1984; C. F. Keil, *Chronik, Esra, Nehemia und Esther*, 1990; D. J. A. Clines, *Ezra, Nehemiah, Esther NCB*², 1985.

J.S.W.

ETAM. **1.** A place in the hill-country of Judah, rebuilt by Rehoboam (2 Ch. 11:6), probably referred to in 1 Ch. 4:3, and in the LXX of Jos. 15:59 (*Aitan*). The site is usually identified with modern Khirbet el-Ḥoḫ, some 10½km SSW of Jerusalem. **2.** A village in the territory of Simeon (1 Ch. 4:32). The site is unknown, though some scholars would equate the place with **1** above. **3.** The cave (*sᵉʿîp̄ selaʿ*, 'cleft of rock') where Samson took refuge from the Philistines (Jdg. 15:8, 11). The site is unknown, but must be in W Judah.

BIBLIOGRAPHY. *KB*, p. 699; F. M. Abel, *Géographie de la Palestine*, 2, 1938, p. 321. T.C.M.

ETHAM. Camp of the Israelites somewhere on the isthmus of Suez (Ex. 13:20; Nu. 33:6–7), about whose precise location scholars differ. Müller suggested a connection with the name of the Egyp. god Atum; Naville proposed Edom; Clédat, Gauthier, Bourdon, Lagrange, Abel and Montet would connect it with the Old Egyp. word for 'fort' (*ḫtm*), a name which was given to several places; but none of these suggestions seems very likely. The Old Egyp. *ḫtm* seems rather to designate the frontier-city of Sile. (*ENCAMPMENT BY THE SEA.)

C.D.W.

ETHAN (Heb. *'êṯān*, 'enduring', 'ancient'). A wise man in the time of Solomon, known as 'the Ezrahite', of the line of Judah, referred to in 1 Ki. 4:31, in the title of Ps. 89, and perhaps in 1 Ch. 2:6, if 'Zerah' is regarded as a form of 'Ezrah'.

Two other men called Ethan are mentioned

briefly—in 1 Ch. 6:42 (perhaps identical with *Jeduthun), and 1 Ch. 6:44; 15:17. J.D.D.

ETHICS, BIBLICAL.

I. The distinctive principle

The distinctiveness of the Bible's ethical teaching is well illustrated by the derivation of the words 'ethics' and 'morals' themselves. Both come from roots (Greek and Latin) which mean 'custom'. The implication is that we behave in an ethically correct manner when we do what custom dictates. We discover the things that are usually done, and conclude that these are the things we ought to do.

In sharp contrast to this approach, biblical ethics are Godcentred. Instead of following majority opinion or conforming to customary behaviour, the Scriptures encourage us to start with God and his requirements—not with man and his habits—when we look for moral guidelines. This central, unifying principle is expressed in many ways in the Bible:

(*a*) *The standard of goodness is personal.* If we want to discover the nature of goodness, the Bible directs us to the person of God himself. He alone is good (Mk. 10:18), and it is his will that expresses 'what is good and acceptable and perfect' (Rom. 12:2). Out in the Sinai desert, Yahweh promised Moses 'I will make all my goodness pass before you' (Ex. 33:19), and the promise was honoured with a special revelation of the Lord's character (Ex. 34:6f.). Unlike any other moral teacher, God is utterly consistent. What he wills, he is.

(*b*) *The source of moral knowledge is revelation.* According to the Bible, knowledge of right and wrong is not so much an object of philosophical enquiry as an acceptance of divine revelation. As Paul puts it, knowing God's will (which is equivalent to discovering what is right) comes through instruction in his law (Rom. 2:18). So while the moral philosopher investigates his data in order to draw judicious conclusions, the biblical writers are content to declare God's revealed will without feeling the need to justify their judgments.

(*c*) *Moral teaching is phrased as command, not statement.* Outwardly, the most striking difference between the Bible and a secular textbook on ethics is the way its moral teaching is communicated. To find reasoned-out arguments for ethical demands in the Bible, one has to look almost exclusively in the OT Wisdom literature (*cf.* Pr. 5:1ff.). Elsewhere, moral judgments are laid down flatly, not argued out reasonably. A philosopher who does not back his opinions with a well-argued case cannot expect people to take him seriously. But the biblical writers, inasmuch as they believed themselves to be conveying God's will, felt no need for logical argument to support their moral commands.

(*d*) *The basic ethical demand is to imitate God.* As God sums up goodness in his own person, man's supreme ideal, according to the Bible, is to imitate him. This is reflected in the OT refrain 'Be holy, for I am holy' (Lv. 11:44f., *etc.*); and in the way great old covenant words like *ḥeseḏ* ('steadfast love') and *'emûnâh* ('faithfulness') are used to describe both God's character and his moral requirements of man. In the NT, too, the same note is struck. Christians must display their heavenly Father's mercy, said Jesus, and even his moral perfection (Lk. 6:36; Mt. 5:48). And because Jesus 'bears the very stamp of his nature' (Heb. 1:3), the call to imitate him comes with equal force (*cf.* 1 Cor. 11:1). We become imitators of the Father as we live out the Son's love (Eph. 5:1f.).

(*e*) *Religion and ethics are inseparable.* All attempts to drive a wedge between the Bible's moral precepts and its religious teaching fail. Because the biblical ethic is theocentric, the moral teaching of Scripture loses its credibility once the religious undergirding is removed (*cf.*, *e.g.*, the Beatitudes, Mt. 5:3ff.). Religion and ethics are related as foundation to building. The moral demands of the Decalogue, for example, are founded on the fact of God's redemptive activity (Ex. 20:2); and much of Jesus' moral teaching is presented as deduction from religious premises (*cf.* Mt. 5:43ff.). The same principle is well illustrated by the literary structure of Paul's Epistles. As well as providing specific examples of moral teaching built on religious foundations (*e.g.* 1 Cor. 6:18ff.; 2 Cor. 8:7ff.; Phil. 2:4ff.), Paul shapes his letters to follow the same pattern. A carefully presented theological main section is made the springboard for a clear-cut ethical tail-piece (*cf.*, especially, Rom., Eph., Phil.). Christian ethics spring from Christian doctrine, and the two are inseparable.

II. The Old Testament

(*a*) *The covenant.* The covenant God made with Israel through Moses (Ex. 24) had direct and far-reaching ethical significance. In particular, the keynote of grace, first struck in the Lord's choice of covenant partner (Dt. 7:7f.; 9:4), sets the theme for the whole of the OT's moral teaching.

God's grace supplies the chief motive for obedience to his commandments. Appeals to godly fear are by no means absent from the OT (*cf.* Ex. 22:22ff.), but far more often grace provides the main stimulus to good behaviour. Men, as God's covenant partners, are invited to respond gratefully to his prior acts of undeserved love; they are summoned to do his will in gratitude for his grace, rather than submit in terror to threats of punishment. So slaves must be treated generously because God treated Hebrew slaves with generosity in Egypt (Dt. 15:12ff.). Businessmen are not to weight their scales unfairly, remembering that it was the God of justice who redeemed their ancestors (Lv. 19:36). Strangers are to be treated with the same kindness that the Lord of grace showed to his people—'for you were strangers in the land of Egypt' (Lv. 19:33f.). In a word, God's covenant demand is 'you shall keep my commandments and do them', because 'I am the Lord . . . who brought you out of the land of Egypt to be your God' (Lv. 22:31ff.).

The covenant also encouraged an intense awareness of corporate solidarity in Israel. Its effect was not only to unite the individual to God, but also to bind all covenant members into a single community (*cf.* the language Paul uses to describe the effect of the new covenant in Eph. 2:11ff.). The recurrence of 'flesh and bone' language in the Bible illustrates this principle vividly; first used of a one-to-one relationship in Gn. 2:23, it could be applied by an individual to his extended family (Jdg. 9:1f.), by the nation declaring its loyalty to its leader (2 Sa. 5:1), and even—in later days—by one Jew describing his relationship to his race (Rom. 11:14, AV). So it was that when a man transgressed one of God's commandments, the whole community was implicated in his sin (Jos. 7:1ff.); and when an individual fell on hard times, everyone felt the obligation to go to his aid.

Hence the very strong emphasis the OT lays on social ethics. Corporate solidarity led straight to neighbour-concern. In the one close community unit, every individual was important. The poor had the same rights as the rich because they both came under the one covenant umbrella. Weaker members of society were specially protected (*cf.* the specific regulations of Ex. 22 and 23, with their safeguards for the widow, the orphan, the stranger and the poor).

(*b*) *The law.* The covenant provided the context for God's law-giving. Consequently, a distinctive feature of OT law was its stress on the maintenance of right relationships. Its main concern was not to set a fence round abstract ethical ideals, but to cement good relationships between people, and between people and God. So the majority of its specific precepts are couched in the second person rather than the third. Hence, too, the strongly positive and warm attitude adopted by those under the law towards law-keeping (*cf.* Pss. 19:7ff.; 119:33ff., 72); and the recognition that the most serious consequence of law-breaking was not any material punishment but the resulting breakdown in relationships (*cf.* Ho. 1:2).

At the heart of the law lie the Ten Commandments (Ex. 20:3ff.; Dt. 5:7ff.), concerned as they are with the most fundamental of relationships. No summary could be more inclusive. They set out the basic sanctities governing belief, worship and life—the sanctity of God's being, his worship, his name and his day; and the sanctity of marriage and family, life, property and truth. The context in which they are given is one of redemption (Ex. 20:2), and their relevance is not exhausted with the coming of Christ (Mt. 5:17ff.; Rom. 13:9; Jas. 2:10f.).

As well as being the fruit of God's redemptive work, the Decalogue has deep roots in the creation ordinances of Gn. 1 and 2. These are the ordinances of procreation and managerial responsibility for the rest of creation (Gn. 1:28); of the sabbath (Gn. 2:2f.); of work (Gn. 2:15) and of marriage (Gn. 2:24). Together (like the Decalogue), they touch upon all the main areas of human life and behaviour, and provide basic guidelines for those seeking a life-style that is in line with the Creator's ideal.

Man's fall into sin did nothing to abrogate these ordinances. Their lasting relevance is upheld in the rest of Scripture (*cf.* Gn. 3:16, 19; 4:1–2, 17, 25; 5:1ff.; 9:7). But the Fall did materially affect the specific content of the OT law. As well as penal sanctions, new provisions were necessary to deal with the radically different situation sin had created. Moses' permission of divorce (Dt. 24:1ff.) is a good case in point. This provision was God's concession to severely sin-torn marriage relationships, not an annulment of his creation marriage ordinance (Gn. 2:24; *cf.* Mt. 19:3ff.). Here, as elsewhere, we must be careful not to confuse God's tolerance with his approval; just as we must always clearly distinguish between the biblical ethic and some of the equivocal behaviour of God's people recorded in the Bible.

(*c*) *The prophets.* The 8th-century prophets have been aptly called 'the politicians of the covenant'. Social conditions had changed dramatically since Moses' times. Amos' contemporaries had summer-houses as well as winter-houses. Big business flourished. There was financial speculation and money-lending on a large scale. Alliances and cultural exchanges were arranged with foreign powers. On the face of it, the covenant law had little help to offer to those struggling with the moral dilemmas of so vastly different an environment. But the prophets made it their business to interpret the law by digging down to its basic principles and applying these to the concrete moral problems of their day.

In particular, they echoed the law's deep concern for social justice. Accurately reflecting the spirit of the covenant's concern for the weak, Amos and Hosea flay those who sell the needy for a pair of shoes, accept bribes, use false weights and measures, or generally oppress the poor (Am. 2:6; 5:12; Mi. 6:11). With Isaiah and Hosea, they are particularly savage on those who try to hide their moral failures behind a façade of religious observance (Is. 1:10ff.; Ho. 6:6). God finds feast-days and hymn-singing nauseating, they thundered, while injustice and unrighteousness flourish (Am. 5:21ff.). A humble walk with him involves doing justice and loving kindness (Mi. 6:8).

The prophets also corrected any imbalance that may have resulted from observance of the covenant law. The covenant's stress on corporate solidarity, for example, may have blurred, in some minds, the concept of personal responsibility. So Ezekiel, especially, is at pains to point out that in God's sight every individual is morally responsible for what he does; no-one can simply shelve the blame for wrong-doing on his heredity and environment (Ezk. 18:20ff.). Again, God's special covenant concern for Israel had fostered in some people an unhealthy, narrow brand of nationalism which led them to depise foreigners. The prophets administered the necessary corrective by insisting that God's moral standards are applied evenly. His love embraces Ethiopians as well as Israelites (Am. 9:7). And Israel will not escape his judgment for sin by pleading her special position as the Lord's chosen people; in fact, says Amos, a privileged knowledge of God brings with it extra responsibilities and greater risk (Am. 1:1–3:2).

The enormity of sin, and the vastness of the gulf between the holy God and sinful men, impressed the prophets deeply (*cf.* Hab. 1:13; Is. 6:3ff.). Without a special act of divine grace, they knew no bridge could be built across this gap (*cf.* Je. 13:23). Man's renewal depended on the activity of God's Spirit (Ezk. 37:1ff.) and on a new kind of covenant law which God himself would write on his people's hearts (Je. 31:31ff.).

III. The New Testament

(*a*) *The Gospels.* Jesus showed great respect for the OT moral law; he came not to abolish but to fulfil it (Mt. 5:17ff.). But he did not teach as a legislator himself. Though he phrased much of his moral teaching in imperatives (*e.g.* Mt. 5:39ff.; Mk. 10:9), and taught with a law-giver's authority (*cf.* Mt. 7:24ff.; Mk. 1:22), it was not his purpose to lay down a comprehensive code of rules for moral living. Law prescribes or forbids specific things; Jesus was more concerned to set out and illustrate the general character of God's will. Law deals in actions; Jesus dealt far more in character and in the motives that inspire action.

Jesus' internalizing of the law's demands is well illustrated in the Sermon on the Mount. The law forbade murder and adultery. Jesus (while not, of course, condoning either) put his finger on the thoughts and attitudes behind the actions. The man who nursed a private hatred towards his neighbour, or mentally undressed the latter's wife in lust, could not (he taught) evade moral blame by pleading that he had not broken the letter of the law (Mt. 5:21f., 27f.). The Beatitudes, with which the Sermon begins (vv. 3ff.), underline the same point. They comprise not a list of rules, but a set of congratulations directed at those whose lives exemplify godly attitudes. Conversely, the sins Jesus condemns are mainly those of the spirit, not those of the flesh. He has surprisingly little to say (*e.g.*) about sexual misconduct. On two occasions when sexual sin was brought to his notice (Lk. 7:37ff.; Jn. 8:3ff.), he deliberately turned the spotlight on to the bad motives of the critics. He reserved his most stinging rebukes for wrong attitudes of mind and heart—like moral blindness, callousness and pride (Mt. 7:3ff.; Mk. 3:5; Lk. 18:9ff.).

Jesus' approach to love provides a further illustration of the way he reinforced and developed OT moral teaching. Both parts of his well-known love-summary of the law (Mk. 12:28ff.) are taken straight from the pages of the OT (Dt. 6:4; Lv. 19:18). But he cut across the racial convictions of many of his contemporaries in his radical interpretation of the second of these commandments. Too often 'love your neighbour' was taken to mean 'love your covenant-neighbour—and him only'. Through (especially) the parable of the Good Samaritan (Lk. 10:29ff.), Jesus taught that neighbour-love must extend to anyone in need, irrespective of race, creed or culture. He universalized love's demands.

In expounding neighbour-love, Jesus identified grace as its distinctive feature. Other kinds of loving—all of them treated positively in the NT—are either a response to something attractive in the one loved (as with physical desire and friendship), or the kind of love that is limited to the members of a group (like family devotion). True neighbour-love, Jesus taught, operates quite independently of any lovableness. It is evoked by need, not merit, and does not look for returns (Lk. 6:32ff.; 14:12ff.). It has no group limits either. And in all these ways it mirrors the love of God (Jn. 3:16; 13:34; Lk. 15:11ff.; *cf.* Gal. 2:20; 1 Jn. 4:7ff.).

When the rich young ruler responded enthusiastically to Jesus' summary of the law, the Lord's rejoinder was 'You are not far from the kingdom of God' (Mk. 12:34). So as well as being the kingpin of God's law, love is the gateway to his kingdom, and Jesus' kingdom teaching is packed with ethical significance. Those who enter the kingdom are those who submit themselves to God's rule; when his kingdom comes, his will is done. And God provides those in his kingdom with royal guidance and power to carry right ethical decisions into practice.

It is this availability of supernatural moral power that makes sense of some of Jesus' otherwise impossible demands (*cf.* Mt. 5:48). He was no triumphalist (repentance is associated with the kingdom too—Mk. 1:15), but most of his moral imperatives were addressed to those already in the kingdom, with the implied assurance that all who submit to God's rule can share his strength to convert their ethical convictions into action.

Because the kingdom is a present reality in Christ, the King's guidance and power are available here and now. But because there is also a sense in which the fullness of the kingdom's coming is still imminent, there is a consistent note of urgency in Jesus' moral teaching too. When God's rule over men is fully revealed there will be a judgment, and only a fool would ignore the warning note the kingdom sounds (*cf.* Lk. 12:20). Hence the gospel-call to repentance (Mt. 4:17).

(*b*) *The rest of the New Testament.* As is to be expected, the Epistles provide clear parallels with the moral teaching of the Gospels, even though they quote Jesus' words surprisingly rarely (*cf.* 1 Cor. 7:10; 9:14). But because they were written as practical answers to urgent questions from living churches, the tone of their moral teaching is slightly different. From the Gospels it would seem that Jesus taught mainly in broad general principles, leaving his hearers to make their own applications. In the Epistles, on the other hand, the applications are often spelt out in very specific terms. Sexual sin, for example, is analysed in considerable detail (*cf.* 1 Cor. 6:9; 2 Cor. 12:21), and sins of speech come in for similarly detailed treatment (*cf.* Rom. 1:29f.; Eph. 4:29; 5:4; Col. 3:8; Jas. 3:5ff.).

Another distinctive feature of the Epistles' ethical teaching is the recurrence of the so-called household codes (Eph. 5:22ff.; Col. 3:18f.; 1 Tim. 2:8ff.; Tit. 2:2ff.; 1 Pet. 2:18ff.). These are small sections of teaching on right relationships, especially in marriage, in the home and at work. They are notably conservative in tone, as are parallel sections on the relationship between believers and the secular authorities (*cf.* Rom. 13:1ff.; Tit. 3:1; 1 Pet. 2:13f.). However eagerly the early Christian community looked forward to the consummation of God's kingdom, their keenness clearly did not lead them to reject the basic authority structures on which the life of society was founded. Even in the book of Revelation, where the veil of apocalyptic language covering John's condemnation of the secular government at Rome is transparently thin, the saints are called to martyrdom, not revolution. Nevertheless, seeds of social change are to be found in the NT, notably in the relationships Christians are encouraged to foster with one another in the church (*cf.* Gal. 3:28).

The theme of the kingdom is not nearly so prominent in the Epistles as in the Gospels, but there is the same emphasis on man's need for God's guidance and power in moral living. In Paul's language, union with Christ (2 Cor. 5:17) and the indwelling Spirit (Phil. 2:13) raise the Christian's moral life to a new plane. Fed by God's Word (Heb. 5:14), the redeemed believer is given sharper insight into distinctions between good and bad (*cf.* Rom. 12:2); and indwelt by the Spirit, he has new power to do what he knows to be right.

It is sometimes said that in his revolt against Jewish legalism, and boosted by his confidence in the Spirit's power to inform and transform the Christian believer, Paul (especially) held that the OT moral law had become obsolete in Christ. There are certainly passages in the Epistles which, taken alone, might suggest such a view (*e.g.* Gal. 3:23ff.; Rom. 7:6; 10:4; 2 Cor. 3:6), but it is important to recognize that Paul uses the word 'law' in different ways. Where he uses it as shorthand for 'justification by law' (*e.g.* Rom. 10:4), he clearly regards living by law as both obsolete and dangerous for Christians. But where he uses the word simply to mean the expression of God's will (*e.g.* Rom. 7:12), he is far more positive. He quotes the Decalogue without embarrassment (*e.g.* Eph. 6:2f.), and writes freely about a law principle which is operative in the Christian life (Rom. 8:2; 1 Cor. 9:21; Gal. 6:2; *cf.* Jas. 1:25; 2:12). Here, as elsewhere, the teaching of the NT dovetails into that of the OT. So far as it contains God's basic moral demands the law retains its validity, because he alone expresses in his person and will all that is good and right.

BIBLIOGRAPHY. H. Thielicke, *Theological Ethics*, 2 vols., E.T. 1968–69, repr. 1978; R. C. Birch and L. L. Rasmussen, *The Bible and Ethics in the Christian Life*, 1976; L. B. Smedes, *Mere Morality*, 1983; C. J. H. Wright, *Living as the People of God*, 1983; A. Verhey, *The Great Reversal*, 1984; R. Higginson, *Dilemmas*, 1988; R. Bauckham, *The Bible in Politics*, 1989; E. D. Cook, *Dilemmas of Life*, 1990; N. L. Geisler, *Christian Ethics*, 1990; J. R. W. Stott, *Issues Facing Christians Today*[2], 1990; E. D. Cook, *Living in the Kingdom*, 1992; O. O'Donovan, *Resurrection and Moral Order*[2], 1993; D. J. Atkinson and D. H. Field (eds.), *New Dictionary of Christian Ethics and Pastoral Theology*, 1995. D.H.F.

ETHIOPIA. Settled by the descendants of *Cush (Gn. 10:6), biblical Ethiopia (Gk. *Aithiōps*, 'burnt face', *cf.* Je. 13:23) is part of the kingdom of Nubia stretching from Aswan (*SEVENEH) S to the junction of the Nile near modern Khartoum. Invaded in prehistoric times by Hamites from Arabia and Asia, Ethiopia was dominated by Egypt for nearly 500 years beginning with Dynasty 18 (*c.* 1500 BC) and was governed by a viceroy ('King's Son of Kush') who ruled the African empire, controlled the army in Africa and managed the Nubian gold mines.

During the 9th century the Ethiopians, whose capital was Napata near the fourth cataract, engaged in at least one foray into Palestine, only to suffer defeat at Asa's hand (2 Ch. 14:9–15). Ethiopia's heyday began about 720 BC when Pi-ankhi took advantage of Egypt's internal strife and became the first conqueror of that land in a millennium. For about 60 years Ethiopian rulers (Dynasty 25) controlled the Nile Valley. One of them, Tirhakah, seems to have been Hezekiah's ally and attempted to forestall Sennacherib's invasion (2 Ki. 19:9; Is. 37:9; J. Bright, *History of Israel*[2], 1972, pp. 296ff., discusses the chronological problems in this narrative). Na. 3:9 alludes to the glory of this period: 'Ethiopia was her (Egypt's) strength.' Invasions by Esarhaddon and Ashurbanipal reduced the Ethiopian–Egyptian kingdom to tributary status; the destruction of Thebes (*c.* 663 BC; Na. 3:8–10) brought a total eclipse, fulfilling Isaiah's prophetic symbolism (20:2–6).

Ethiopian troops fought vainly in Pharaoh Neco's army at Carchemish (605 BC; Je. 46:2, 9). Cambyses' conquest of Egypt brought Ethiopia under Persian sway; Est. 1:1; 8:9 name Ethiopia as the most remote Persian province to the SW, while biblical writers sometimes use her to symbolize the unlimited extent of God's sovereignty (Ps. 87:4; Ezk. 30:4ff.; Am. 9:7; Zp. 2:12). 'Beyond the rivers of Ethiopia' (Is. 18:1; Zp. 3:10) may refer to N Abyssinia, where Jewish colonists had apparently settled along with other Semites from S Arabia. The Chronicler is cognizant of this close relationship between Ethiopia and S Arabia (2 Ch. 21:16).

In Acts 8:27 Ethiopia refers to the Nilotic kingdom of *Candace, who ruled at Meroë, where the capital had been moved during the Persian period. Modern Ethiopians (Abyssinians) have appropriated biblical references to Ethiopia and consider the *Ethiopian eunuch's conversion to be a fulfilment of Ps. 68:31.

BIBLIOGRAPHY. E. A. W. Budge, *History of Ethiopia*, 1928; E. Ullendorff, *The Ethiopians*, 1960; *idem*, *Ethiopia and the Bible*, 1968; J. Wilson, *The Burden of Egypt*, 1951. D.A.H.

ETHIOPIAN EUNUCH. A high official (*dynastēs*), royal treasurer in the court of *Ethiopia's Queen *Candace, converted under Philip's ministry (Acts 8:26–40). It was not unusual in antiquity for *eunuchs, who were customarily harem attendants, to rise to positions of influence.

Barred from active participation in the Jewish rites by his race and his emasculation (Dt. 23:1), he was most probably a 'God-fearer'. His acquaintance with Judaism and the OT (the quotation from Is. 53 seems to be from the LXX) is not completely unexpected in light of Jewish settlements in Upper Egypt and the considerable impact made by Jewish life and thought on the Ethiopians. His zeal in studying the Scriptures, his ready reception of the gospel and baptism mark him as one of the outstanding converts in Acts, even if his confession (Acts 8:37) is not supported in the better MSS. Ethiopian tradition claims him as his country's first evangelist. D.A.H.

ETHIOPIAN WOMAN. Married by Moses, whom Aaron and Miriam then criticized (Nu. 12:1). As the last mention of Zipporah is just after the defeat of Amalek (Ex. 17) when Jethro returned her to Moses (Ex. 18), it is possible that she subsequently died, Moses then taking this 'Cushite woman' as his second wife, unless Moses then had two wives. 'Cushite' is usually taken as 'Ethiopian' (*cf.* *CUSH, *ETHIOPIA); if so, she probably left Egypt among the Israelites and their sympathizers. It is also, perhaps, possible to derive 'Cushite' from Kushu and Heb. Cushan, associated with Midian (Hab. 3:7); if so, this woman might be of allied stock to Jethro and Zipporah. K.A.K.

ETHNARCH (Gk. *ethnarchēs*, 'governor', 2 Cor. 11:32). An officer in charge of Damascus with a garrison under *Aretas IV, king of Arabia Petraea (9 BC–AD 39), who was encouraged by the Jews to arrest Paul after his conversion (*cf.* Acts 9:24–25). Damascus in 64 BC became part of the Rom. province of Syria. At this time (*c.* AD 33) it was temporarily under Aretas.

The title is used by Josephus for subordinate rulers, particularly of peoples under foreign control, *e.g.* the Jews in Alexandria (*Ant.* 14. 117); *cf.* Simon, ethnarch of Judaea under Demetrius II (1 Macc. 14:47). B.F.H.

EUNICE. Timothy's mother, a woman of notable faith (2 Tim. 1:5). She was Jewish (Acts 16:1) and pious, for Timothy's biblical instruction had begun early (2 Tim. 3:15), but her husband was a Gentile and her son uncircumcised (Acts 16:3). In view of Jewish intermarriage with leading Phrygian families (Ramsay, *BRD*, p. 357; *cf.* *CBP*, 2, pp. 667ff.), such things may represent her family's social climbing, not personal declension. Some Lat. MSS of Acts 16:1, and Origen on Rom. 16:21, call her a widow, and *hypērchen* in Acts 16:3 might support this. She lived at Derbe or Lystra: linguistically a case can be made for either (*cf. BC*, 4, pp. 184, 254). Her name is Greek, and does not seem common.

It is sometimes suggested that Paul refers to Jewish faith, but the most natural interpretation of 2 Tim. 1:5 (and of Acts 16:1) is that Christian faith 'dwelt' (aorist, perhaps alluding to the event of conversion, doubtless in Paul's first missionary journey) 'first' in * Lois and herself (*i.e.* antecedent to Timothy's conversion). A.F.W.

EUNUCH (Heb. *sārîs*). The derivation of the OT word is uncertain, but is thought to come from an Assyr. term meaning, 'He who is head (to the king)'. (So Jensen (*ZA* 7, 1892, 174A.1), and Zimmern (*ZDMG* 53, 1899, 116 A.2); accepted by S. R. Driver and L. Koehler in their lexicons; see further note by the latter in his *Supplement*, p. 219.) The primary meaning is 'court officer'. In Hebrew a secondary meaning is found, namely, a 'castrate' or 'eunuch'. From Herodotus we learn that 'in eastern countries eunuchs are valued as being specially trustworthy in every way' (8. 105, tr. Selingcourt). Such persons were frequently employed by eastern rulers as officers of the household. Hence, in the E it is sometimes difficult to know which of the two meanings is intended or whether both are implied. Potiphar (Gn. 39:1), who was married (v. 7), is called a *sārîs* (LXX *eunouchos*): the meaning 'court officer' may be best here. In Is. 56:3 the meaning 'castrate' is obvious. In Ne. 1:11, 'I was the king's cupbearer', some copies of the LXX have *eunouchos*; but this is probably a slip for *oinochoos*, as Rahlfs in *Septuaginta* (1, p. 923) has seen. The 'castrate' was to be excluded from the assembly of the Lord (Dt. 23:1). There is no necessity to assume, as Josephus seems to do (*Ant.* 10. 186), that Daniel and his companions were 'castrates', for they were 'without blemish' (see Dn. 1:4).

In the NT the word *eunouchos* is used, and may be derived from *eunēn echō* ('to keep the bed'). Like its counterpart *sārîs*, it need not denote strictly a castrate. In Acts 8:27 both meanings may be intended; in Mt. 19:12 the meaning 'castrate' is beyond doubt. In this last passage three classes of eunuch are mentioned, namely, born eunuchs, man-made eunuchs and spiritual eunuchs. The last class includes all those who sacrificed legitimate, natural desires for the sake of the kingdom of heaven. Report in the early church had it that Origen, misinterpreting in a literal sense the above passage, mutilated himself.

Judaism knew only two classes of eunuch: man-made (*sārîs 'āḏām*) and natural (*sārîs ḥammâ*), thus the Mishnah (*Zabim* 2. 1). This last term *sārîs ḥammâ* or 'eunuch of the sun' is explained by Jastrow, *Dictionary of Babylonian Talmud*, etc., 1, p. 476, to mean 'a eunuch from the time of seeing the sun', in other words, a eunuch who is born so. (* CHAMBERLAIN.) R.J.A.S.

EUODIA. This RSV rendering is to be preferred to the AV's 'Euodias' (Phil. 4:2), for the reference is to a woman rather than a man. Paul begs her and Syntyche to be reconciled. Probably, as Lightfoot suggests, they were deaconesses at Philippi. J.D.D.

EUPHRATES. The largest river in W Asia, and on this account generally referred to as *hannāhār*, 'the river', in the OT (*e.g.* Dt. 11:24). It is sometimes mentioned by name, however, the Heb. form being *pᵉrāṯ* (*e.g.* Gn. 2:14; 15:18) derived from Akkadian *purattu*, which represents Sumerian *buranun*, and the NT form *Euphratēs* (Rev. 9:14; 16:12). The Euphrates takes its source in two main affluents in E Turkey, the Murad-Su, which rises near Lake Van, and the Kara-Su, which rises near Erzerum, and runs, joined only by the Ḫâbûr (* HABOR) for 2,000 km to the Persian Gulf. From low water in September it rises by degrees throughout the winter to some 3 m higher by May, and then declines again until September, thus enjoying a milder régime than the * Tigris. In the alluvial plain of Babylonia (* MESOPOTAMIA) its course has shifted to the W since ancient times, when most of the important cities, now some km to the E of it, lay on or near its banks. This is illustrated by the fact that the Sumerians wrote its name ideographically as 'river of Sippar', a city whose ruins lie today some 6 km to the E (* SEPHARVAIM). In addition to the many important cities, including Babylon, which lay on its banks in the S plain, the city of Mari was situated on its middle course, not far from the junction with the Ḫâbûr, and the strategic crossing-place from N Mesopotamia to N Syria was commanded by the fortress city of * Carchemish.

BIBLIOGRAPHY. S. A. Pallis, *The Antiquity of Iraq*, 1956, pp. 4–7. T.C.M.

EUTYCHUS ('Lucky', a common Gk. name). A young man from Troas who fell from an upstairs window-seat during Paul's protracted nocturnal address there (Acts 20:7–12). H. J. Cadbury (*Book of Acts in History*, pp. 8ff.) points out a similar fatal accident in *Oxyrhynchus Papyri*, 3. 475. Luke's words suggest an increasing and eventually irresistible drowsiness, perhaps—since v. 8 seems related to the incident—induced by the numerous lamps rather than in spite of them.

The miraculous nature of the outcome has been questioned, Paul's words in v. 10 being applied to diagnosis, not healing. However, v. 9 shows that Luke was himself sure that Eutychus died. 'His life' would then be 'in him' from the moment of Paul's embrace (*cf.* 2 Ki. 4:34). On Paul's departure next morning, Eutychus was recovered (v. 12: according to the Western Text he joined the farewell party). Seen as an eyewitness account by Luke, the story is vivid and the broken sequence intelligible. The assumption that 'a current anecdote had come to be applied to Paul, that Luke found it in this form and introduced it into his narrative' (Dibelius) creates obscurities.

BIBLIOGRAPHY. W. M. Ramsay, *SPT*, pp. 290f.; M. Dibelius, *Studies in the Acts of the Apostles*, E.T. 1956, pp. 17ff. A.F.W.

EVANGELIST. The word translated in the NT 'evangelist' is a noun from the verb *euangelizomai* 'to announce news', and usually rendered in EVV as 'preach the gospel'. (The NT term echoes Heb. *mᵉḇaśśēr*, *mᵉḇaśśereṯ*, in Is. 40:9; 52:7.) The verb is very common in the NT, and is applied to God (Gal. 3:8), to our Lord (Lk. 20:1), and to ordinary church members (Acts 8:4), as well as to apostles on their missionary journeys. The noun 'evangelist' occurs three times only in the NT. Timothy (2 Tim. 4:5) is exhorted by Paul to do the work of an evangelist; that is to say, make known the facts of the gospel. Timothy had accompanied the apostle on his missionary journeys. But it is plain from the injunctions in the two letters addressed to him that his work when the apostle wrote was very largely local and pastoral. That he is enjoined to do the work of an evangelist shows that a man who was an evangelist could also be a pastor and teacher.

In Acts 21:8 Philip is described as 'the evangelist'. Philip had been chosen as one of the Seven in Acts 6, and after the persecution of Stephen he was prominent in preaching the gospel in unevangelized parts (*e.g.* Acts 8:5, 12, 35, 40). Though an evangelist, he was not included among the apostles (Acts 8:14). A similar distinction is made between Timothy and the apostles in 2 Cor. 1:1 and Col. 1:1. It will be seen, then, that though apostles were evangelists, not all evangelists were apostles. This distinction is confirmed in Eph. 4:11, where the office of 'evangelist' is mentioned after 'apostle' and 'prophet', and before 'pastor' and 'teacher'. From this passage it is plain that the gift of evangelist was a distinct gift within the Christian church; and although all Christians doubtless performed this sacred task, as opportunity was given to them, there were some who were pre-eminently called and endowed by the Holy Spirit for this work.

Later in the history of the church the term 'evangelist' was used for a writer of one of the four Gospels.

BIBLIOGRAPHY. L. Coenen, *NIDNTT* 2, pp. 107–115. D.B.K.

EVE. The first woman, wife of *Adam and mother of Cain, Abel and Seth (Gn. 4:1–2, 25). When he had made Adam, God resolved to provide 'a helper fit for him' (*'ēzer k^e negdô*, Gn. 2:18, 20, lit. 'a helper as in front of him', *i.e.* 'a helper corresponding to him'), so he caused him to sleep and, taking one of his ribs (*ṣēlā'*, Gn. 2:21), made (*bānâ*, Gn. 2:22, a word normally meaning 'to build') it into a woman (*l^e'iššâ*). (*CREATION.) Adam, recognizing his close relationship, declared that she should be called 'Woman (*'iššâ*), because she was taken out of (*min*; *cf.* 1 Cor. 11:8, *ek*) Man (*'îš*)' (Gn. 2:23). Some scholars consider that *'îš* and *'iššâ* are etymologically distinct, but this need not be significant, since the context requires only that there should be formal similarity between the words, as indeed is the case with EVV 'man' and '*wo*man'.

Eve was the instrument of the serpent in causing Adam to eat the forbidden fruit (*FALL), and as a result God condemned her to bear children in pain, and to be ruled over (*māšal b^e*) by Adam (Gn. 3:16). Adam then called her 'Eve (*ḥawwâ*, Gn. 3:20); because she was the mother of all living (*ḥay*)'. Many theories have been put forward as to the name *ḥawwâ*. Some would see it as an archaic form of *ḥayyâ*, 'living thing' (the LXX takes this view, translating it in Gn. 3:20 by *zōē*, 'life'), others note a similarity with Aramaic *ḥiwyā'*, 'serpent', with which is connected a Phoenician (possibly serpent) deity *ḥwt*, but as with *'îš* and *'iššâ* nothing beyond a formal assonance appears to be required by the text. The name *ḥawwâ* occurs twice only in the OT (Gn. 3:20; 4:1), the word 'woman' being more commonly used. In the LXX and NT it appears as *Heua* (*Eua* in some MSS), which passes to *Heva* in the Vulgate, and thence to *Eve* in the EVV.

A sidelight on the biblical statements about Eve is found in a Sumerian myth concerning the god Enki. In this Enki finds himself suffering from a series of ailments, to deal with each of which the goddess Ninḫursag produces a special goddess. Thus, when he says 'My rib (*ti*; written with a logogram, one of whose Akkadian values was *ṣîlu*, 'side, rib') hurts me', she replies that she has caused a goddess *Nin-ti* ('Lady of the rib') to be born for him. But Sumerian *Nin-ti* can equally mean 'Lady who makes live'. It may be that this reflects in some way a common original narrative with the Genesis account.

BIBLIOGRAPHY. *KB*[3], p. 284; G. J. Spurrell, *Notes on the Text of the Book of Genesis*[2], 1896, p. 45; S. N. Kramer, *Enki and Ninḫursag. A Sumerian Paradise Myth* (*BASOR* Supplementary Studies 1), 1945, pp. 8–9; *From the Tablets of Sumer*, 1956, pp. 170–171 = *History Begins at Sumer*, 1958, pp. 195–196; I. M. Kikawada, 'Two Notes on Eve', *JBL* 91, 1972, pp. 33–37. T.C.M.

EVIL (Heb. *ra'*; Gk. *kakos, ponēros, phaulos*). Evil has a broader meaning than *sin. The Heb. word comes from a root meaning 'to spoil', 'to break in pieces': being broken and so made worthless. It is essentially what is unpleasant, disagreeable, offensive. The word binds together the evil deed and its consequences. In the NT *kakos* and *ponēros* mean respectively the quality of evil in its essential character, and its hurtful effects or influence. It is used in both physical and moral senses. While these aspects are different, there is frequently a close relationship between them. Much physical evil is due to moral evil: suffering and sin are not necessarily connected in individual cases, but human selfishness and sin explain much of the world's ills. Though all evil must be punished, not all physical ill is a punishment of wrongdoing (Lk. 13:2, 4; Jn. 9:3; *cf.* Job).

I. Physical evil

The prophets regarded God as the ultimate Cause of evil, as expressed in pain, suffering or disaster. In his sovereignty he tolerates evil in the universe, though he overrules and uses it in his administration of the world. It is used to punish individual and national wickedness (Is. 45:7; La. 3:38; Am. 3:6). The world must be marked by regulation and order to be the scene of man's moral life; otherwise there would be chaos. When men violate the basic laws of God they experience the repercussions of their actions, which may be in penal or retributive affliction (Mt. 9:2; 23:35; Jn. 5:14; Acts 5:5; 13:11). Divine 'vengeance' in the form of pain or sorrow does not imply evil passions in God. Pain may awaken an evil man to reality; till then 'he is enclosed in illusion' (C. S. Lewis, *The Problem of Pain*, p. 83). Nature's present 'vanity' (profitlessness, Rom. 8:19–23) is its mark of evil, the earth being under a curse (Gn. 3:17–18). Christian suffering, whether trouble or persecution, is divinely permitted for purposes of spiritual blessing (Jas. 1:2–4; 1 Pet. 1:7; *etc.*). It is chastening, not penal; nor can it separate from the love of God (Rom. 8:38–39); it prepares for glory (Rom. 8:18; 2 Cor. 4:16–18; Eph. 3:13; Rev. 7:14). Suffering and sorrow create sympathy and kindness in men, bringing them into fellowship with God's purpose to overcome evil.

II. Moral evil

God is separate from all evil and is in no way responsible for it. Moral evil arises from man's sinful inclinations (Jas. 1:13–15). Israel repeatedly 'did evil' and suffered its consequences (Jdg. 2:11; 1 Ki. 11:6, *etc.*). Behind all history is a spiritual conflict with evil powers (Eph. 6:10–17; Rev. 12:7–12), 'the evil one' being the very embodiment of wickedness (Mt. 5:37; 6:13; 13:19, 38; Jn. 17:15; Eph. 6:16; 2 Thes. 3:3; 1 Jn. 2:13–14; 3:12; 5:18–19). Satan's power is under divine control (*cf.* Jb. 1–2), and will finally be broken (Heb. 2:14; Rev. 12:9–11).

God is against evil, but its existence is often a stumbling-block to belief in a God of love. It can only be attributed to the abuse of free-will on the part of created beings, angelic and human. God's whole saving activity is directed to deal with evil. In his life, Christ combated its manifestations of pain and sorrow (Mt. 8:16–17); but the cross is God's final answer to the problem of evil. His love was supremely demonstrated there (Rom. 5:8; 8:32) in the identification of the Lord with the suffering world as the Sin-bearer. The moral change effected in men by the gospel is evidence of the reality of Christ's triumph over all evil powers (Col. 2:15; 1 Jn. 3:8), and therefore of the final victory of God. Evil will be eliminated from the universe, and the creation will share redeemed man's glorious destiny. Both physical and moral evil will be banished eternally (Rev. 21:1–8).

BIBLIOGRAPHY. James Orr, *The Christian View of God and the World*, 1897; A. M. Farrer, *Love Almighty and Ills Unlimited*, 1962; O. F. Clarke, *God and Suffering*, 1964; J. Hick, *Evil and the God of Love*, 1966; J. W. Wenham, *The Goodness of God*, 1974; *TDNT* 3, pp. 469–484; 6, pp. 546–566; *NIDNTT* 1, pp. 561–567; W. C. Kaiser, *A Biblical Approach to Personal Suffering*, 1982; D. A. Carson, *How Long O Lord?: Reflections on Suffering and Evil*, 1990; E. S. Gerstenberger and W. Schrage, *Suffering*, 1982. G.C.D.H.

EVIL-MERODACH. The king of *Babylon who released Jehoiachin of Judah from imprisonment in the first year of his reign (Je. 52:31; 2 Ki. 25:27–30). Amēl-Marduk ('man of Marduk') succeeded his father Nebuchadrezzar II in the early days of October 562 BC. According to Josephus (from Berossus), he ruled 'lawlessly and wantonly' (*Ap.* 1. 146), but the only allusions to him extant are in administrative tablets. He was killed *c.* 7–13 August 560 BC in a plot led by his brother-in-law *Nergal-sharezer (Neriglissar).

BIBLIOGRAPHY. R. H. Sack, *Amēl-Marduk: 562–560 B.C.*, 1972. D.J.W.

EVIL SPEAKING may be defined as slander, calumny, defamation or deceit. This may be done by spreading false reports (Pr. 12:17; 14:5, 25) or by reporting truth maliciously, *i.e.* tale-bearing (Lv. 19:16; Pr. 26:20).

Evil speaking is prohibited in Ps. 34:13; Pr. 24:28; Eph. 4:31; Jas. 4:11; 1 Pet. 3:10. It disqualifies a person from God's favour (Ps. 15:3) and from office in the church (1 Tim. 3:8; Tit. 2:3). When a Christian is slandered he must patiently bear it (1 Pet. 3:9) even as Christ did (1 Pet. 2:23).

The ninth commandment forbids false witness (Ex. 20:16; Dt. 5:20; *cf.* Ex. 23:1). To avoid the evil of false accusation more than one witness was required in courts of law (Nu. 35:30; Dt. 17:6; 19:15–21). M.R.G.

EVIL SPIRITS. The term 'evil (*ponēra*) spirit(s)' is found in but 6 passages (Matthew, Luke, Acts). There are 23 references to 'unclean (*akatharta*) spirits' (Gospels, Acts, Revelation), and these appear to be much the same. Thus in Lk. 11:24 'the unclean spirit' goes out of a man, but when he returns it is with 'seven other spirits more evil than himself' (v. 26). Similarly, 'unclean spirits' and 'demons' are interchangeable terms, for both are applied to the Gadarene demoniac (Lk. 8:27, 29).

These beings appear to have been regarded in more than one light. They might cause physical disability (Mk. 1:23; 7:25). Indeed, on most occasions in the NT when they are mentioned it is in such cases. There appears to have been nothing moral involved, for the sufferer was not excluded from places of worship, such as the synagogue. The idea would appear to be that the spirit was evil (or unclean) in that it produced baleful effects. But the sufferer was not regarded as especially evil or as polluted in any way. Yet the spirit itself was not to be regarded in neutral fashion. Everywhere it was to be resisted and defeated. Sometimes we read of Jesus as doing this in person (Mk. 5:8; Lk.6:18), sometimes of such power being delegated to his followers (Mt. 10:1) or being exercised by them (Acts 5:16; 8:7). The spirits are apparently part of Satan's forces, and thus are reckoned as enemies of God and of men.

Sometimes it is clear that the spirits are concerned with moral evil. This is so in the case of the 'unclean spirit' who goes out of a man and returns with others more wicked than himself (Mt. 12:43–45). The story indicates the impossibility of a man's bringing about a moral reformation by expelling the demons within. There must also be the entry of the Spirit of God. But for our present purpose it is sufficient to notice that the spirits are evil and may bring about evil. The evil spirits 'like frogs' of Rev. 16:13 are also thought of as working evil as they gather the forces of wickedness for the great final battle.

Such passages indicate that on the biblical view evil is not merely impersonal. It is led by Satan, and, just as there are subordinate powers of good, the angels, so there are subordinate powers of evil. Their appearance is mostly concerned with the incarnation (with a resurgence in the last days) as they oppose the work of Christ. See further *SATAN, *DEMON POSSESSION. L.M.

EXCOMMUNICATION. Mt. 18:15–18; 1 Cor. 5; 2 Cor. 2:5–11; Tit. 3:10. The exclusion of a member from the church due to a serious (or aggravation, through stubbornness, of a less serious) offence. It is the final step in the negative side of normal discipline—there is also *Anathema and delivering over to *Satan. When educative discipline (*disciplina*) fails to prevent offences, repressive discipline is used to remove them. The *gradus admonitionis* leading up to excommunication are private remonstrance (incumbent on all, Lv. 19:17), then, if that proves ineffective, remonstrance with the aid of witnesses; finally, the offender should be dealt with by the church, presumably through its duly-elected representatives, following the Jewish pattern. The apostle puts this responsibility upon the local church (1 Cor. 5:4–13). If the offender still shows no repentance he is to be excommunicated. 'Let him be to you as a Gentile and a tax collector' (Mt. 18:17).

Some critics (*e.g.* Bultmann, T. W. Manson) make this 'quasi-legal' procedure a later development of the church, from rabbinic sources. But then it is hard to see why Paul reproved the Corinthians so sharply for neglecting it. And our Lord's condemnation of these sources would be fresh in their minds (Mt. 23:13ff.). The opprobrious sense of 'Gentile and tax collector' has been said to show a Jewish–Christian origin, *c.* AD 50. This is, at the least, doubtful. Ultimately, it is a question of 'the historical validity of the Gospel record and of the origins of Christianity itself, and this question it is impossible to ignore' (W. Manson, *Jesus the Messiah*, 1952, p. 26). The mind of the early church is the mind of the Lord.

Public, notorious faults are to be rebuked publicly (1 Tim. 5:20; Gal. 2:11, 14). Very serious offences merit immediate excommunication (1 Cor. 5:3). It is also noteworthy, however, that no amount of excommunication will produce a perfect church, for it has to ignore secret sins and hypocrisy. Also, the oil of leniency has to be mixed with the vinegar of severity: 'We judge that it pertains unto sound doctrine ... to attemper our life and opinion, so that we both endure dogs in the church, for the sake of the peace of the church, and, where the peace of the church is safe, give not what is holy unto dogs . . . that we neither grow listless under the name of patience, nor be cruel under the pretext of diligence' (Augustine, *Short Treatises*, 1884, p. 43).

The aims involved are, first, to promote the glory of God, that his name be not blasphemed owing to manifest evil in the church; second, to prevent the evil from spreading to other members (1 Cor. 5:6); and third, to bring about true repentance in the offender. Here the ultimate aim is seen to be redemptive (Calvin, *Institutes*, 4. 12. 5).

Excommunication implies that we suspend convivial intercourse with the offender, though not ceasing to pray for his recovery; and though he is excluded from the benefits of the sacraments, he will be encouraged to attend the preaching of the Word. R.N.C.

EXODUS. This event marked the birth of Israel as a nation and—through the immediately-following covenant at Sinai—as a theocracy.

I. The event itself

After the Hebrews' residence in the Egyptian E Delta for 430 years (Ex. 12:40–41) culminating in enslavement in Egyptian state-corvée in the 18th and 19th Dynasties, God commissioned Moses, with Aaron as his mouthpiece, to lead out the Hebrew slaves, tribal descendants of Abraham, Isaac and Jacob, from Egypt to become a nation in Palestine, the land of promise (Ex. 3–4). Despite the hostility and temporal power of the pharaoh and, later, Israel's own faithlessness, this duly came to pass (Jos. 24).

That a large group of subject people should go out from a major state is neither impossible nor unparalleled in antiquity. In the late 15th century BC people of some fourteen 'lands', 'mountain-regions' and townships apparently decamped from their habitats within the Hittite kingdom, and transferred themselves to the land of Isuwa (Treaty-prologue of Suppiluliuma and 'Mattiwaza', Weidner, *Politische Dokumente aus Kleinasien*, 1923, p. 5), only later to be brought back by the powerful Hittite King Suppiluliuma. However, Pharaoh's attempts to retain, and then to recapture, the Hebrews were rendered utterly futile by God's marshalling against him the powers of nature in nine plagues and a supernatural punishment in the tenth, and by swamping his pursuing chariotry in the Re(e)d Sea. The calling-out of a nation in this way specifically to serve a God, and live out a covenant directly with their God, is unique. The peoples who fled to Isuwa doubtless also considered themselves oppressed, but had no positive commission or divine calling to some high destiny. There went out with Israel a motley crowd, mixed in motives as in origins ('mixed multitude', Ex. 12:38, Heb. *'ēreḇraḇ*, *cf.* Eng. 'riff-raff'). This element preferred meat to manna (Nu. 11:4, Heb. *'ᵃsap̄sup̄*, 'rabble').

Other specific aspects of the Exodus are more appropriately dealt with in other articles as follows: for *date* of the Exodus, see *CHRONOLOGY OF THE OLD TESTAMENT. For *route* of the Exodus, see also on Egyptian sites *ENCAMPMENT BY THE SEA, *BAAL-ZEPHON, *PITHOM, *RA'AMSES, *SUCCOTH, *MIGDOL, *etc.*, and on the Sinaitic journeyings, *WILDERNESS OF THE WANDERING, *SINAI and individual palaces—*ELIM, *REPHIDIM, *etc.* For the Egyptian background to the oppression and conditions attending on the Exodus, see *EGYPT **(IV)**, *MOSES and *PLAGUES OF EGYPT.

II. The Exodus in later history

Repeatedly in later generations, the prophets in exhorting Israel to return to her God and the psalmists in their meditations hark back to this Exodus—to God's redeeming grace in summoning a nation from Egyptian bondage in fulfilment of promises to the Patriarchs, to serve himself and exemplify his truth. For them, the great redemption is ever to be remembered with gratitude and response in obedience. See such passages as the following: historical books, Jdg. 6:8–9, 13; 1 Sa. 12:6, 8; 1 Ki. 8:51; 2 Ch. 7:22; Ne. 9:9ff. For Psalms, *cf.* Pss. 77:14–20; 78:12–55; 80:8; 106:7–12; 114. Among the prophets, see Ho. 11:1; Je. 7:21–24; 11:1–8; 34:13; Dn. 9:15. In the NT Christ accomplished the final 'Exodus', the full redemption (*cf.* Heb. 13:13 and elsewhere generally).

BIBLIOGRAPHY. J. J. Bimson, *Redating the Exodus and Conquest*, 1978 (includes archaeological and other evidence for a 15th-century BC date for the Exodus); D. Daube, *The Exodus Pattern in the Bible*, 1963; R. E. Nixon, *The Exodus in the New Testament*, 1963; background data, K. A. Kitchen, *ABD* 2, pp. 700–708. K.A.K.

EXODUS, BOOK OF.

I. Outline of contents

Exodus (the latinized form of LXX *exodos*, 'a going out') is the second section of the Pentateuch, and deals with the fortunes of Israel subsequent to the

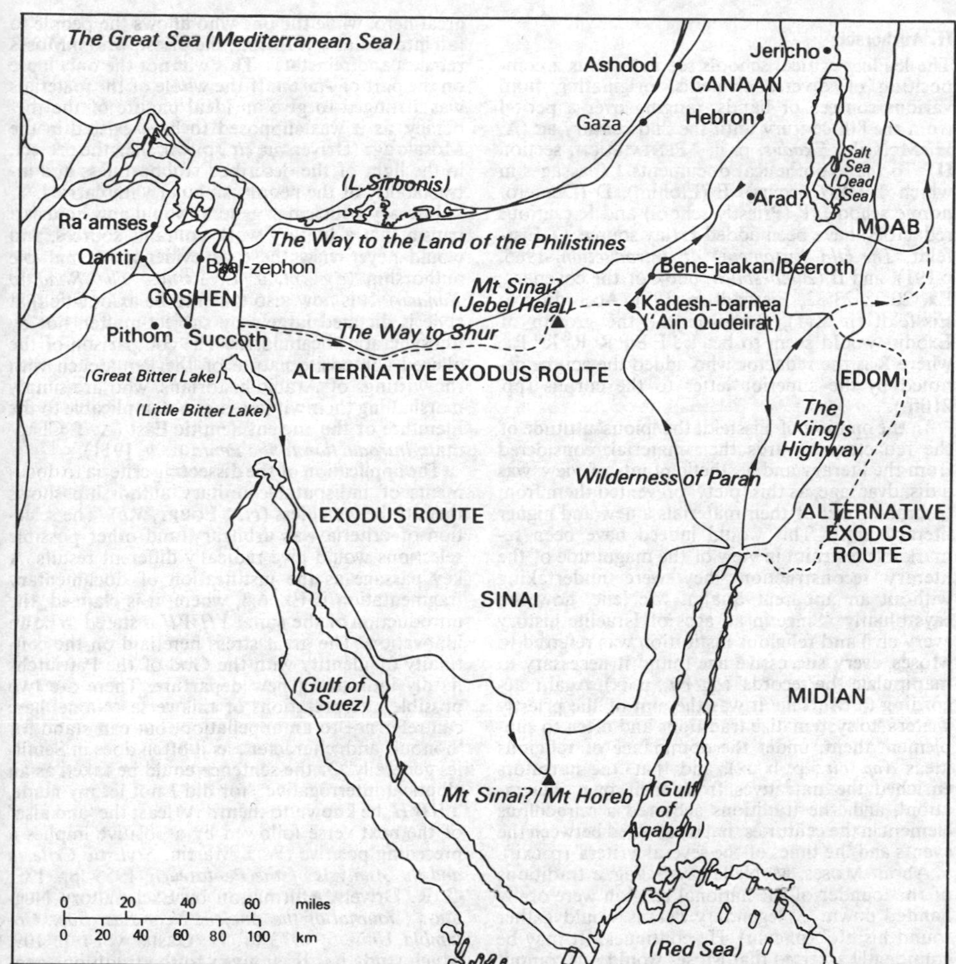

Possible routes of the Exodus.

propitious times of Joseph's governorship. It records the two great culminating points in Israel's history: the deliverance from Egypt and the giving of the law. Henceforth the events of Exodus hold a central place in God's revelation of himself to his people, not only in the old but also in the new covenant, in which the Passover lamb provides the type for our Lord's sacrifice, and the Passover Feast is adapted to serve as the commemoration of our redemption.

The events leading up to and following Israel's flight from Egypt form the main theme of the book. The chronological setting is given only in general terms, consistent with the Hebrew treatment of history as series of events and not as a sequence of dates.

The book, after giving a short genealogical note to effect the transition from Genesis, begins with an account of the disquiet on the part of the Egyptians at the great numerical increase of the Israelites. To counteract what was considered to be a growing menace, the Israelites were first subjected to forced labour under Egyptian task-masters, probably both to meet a current need for a large labour force and to keep them under strict observation. Then their labour was intensified, probably to reduce their leisure, and thus their opportunities for mischief, to a minimum. Finally an attempt was made to check any further increase in the population by the extermination of all new-born male infants. The boys rather than the girls would be chosen, as they would be regarded as potential instigators of revolt. This final step furnishes the background of the account of the birth and upbringing of Moses, the second great figure in Jewish history, at the Egyptian court. His early life, encounter with God and rise to leadership occupy chs. 2–4. In chs. 5–13 are related the attempts to gain release for Israel, ending in the *Plagues of Egypt and the institution of the *Passover. After the crossing of the *Red Sea and its celebration in song (14:1–15:21) follows a journal of the march to Sinai (15:22–18:27). The remainder of the book tells of the Covenant at Sinai (19–31), its breach (32–33), renewal (34) and the construction of the *tabernacle according to the instructions given (35–40).

II. Authorship

The leading critical schools see in Exodus a composition of diverse elements, originating from various sources or hands, ranging over a period from the 8th century until the 2nd century BC (A. H. McNeile, *Exodus*, p. ii; * PENTATEUCH, section II). To the hypothetical documents J (passages in which *YHWH* occurs), E (Elohim), D (Deuteronomic school), P (Priestly school) and R (various redactors) have been added L (lay source, O. Eissfeldt, *The Old Testament: An Introduction*, 1965, p.191), and B (*Bundesbuch*, book of the covenant, Ex. 20:22–23:33, Eissfeldt, p. 191). According to Eissfeldt (p. 211), the order of the growth of Exodus would seem to be: L J E B P R^J R^E R^B R^P, where R is the redactor who added the source denoted by the superior letter to the corpus (pp. 210ff.).

In the opinion of Eissfeldt the 'pious' attitude of the redactors towards their material, considered from the literary and aesthetic points of view, was a disadvantage, as this 'piety' prevented them from fashioning out of their materials a new and higher literary unity. This would indeed have been remarkable restraint in view of the magnitude of the literary reconstruction they were undertaking without an apparent qualm. McNeile, however, says bluntly: 'Since in all ages of Israelite history every civil and religious institution was referred to Moses, every successive age found it necessary to manipulate the records' (*op. cit.*, p. ix). Again, according to McNeile it was the aim of the priestly writers 'to systematize traditions and often to supplement them, under the dominance of religious ideas' (*op. cit.*, p. lxxix), and that 'the narrators enriched the narratives from their own imagination', and 'the traditions acquired a miraculous element in the centuries that intervened between the events and the times of the several writers' (p. cxii).

About Moses, McNeile says: 'Vague traditions of the founder of the national religion were orally handed down ... legendary details would gather round his life' (p. cviii). He continues: 'It may be confidently asserted that Moses would not commit to writing a series of moral precepts'; and 'It is impossible to say of any particular detail that it derived from Moses himself' (p. cxvii). About the tabernacle this same author says: 'the historicity is unhesitatingly denied by all who accept the main principles of historical and literary criticism' (p. cxviii). The reason given for this last piece of scepticism is the mention of the tent of audience in 33:7, alleged to be identical with the tabernacle. It is, however, clear that the reference here is to the practice obtaining in the period preceding the erection of the tabernacle, the purpose of which was to be a sanctuary, symbolizing God's presence in their midst (25:8). S. R. Driver thinks that customs and rites 'are antedated and represented as having been already propounded and put in force in the Mosiac age' (*Exodus*, p. lxv).

If these views had any objective validity the narratives in Exodus would cease to be of historical value. The theories are in the nature of the case not amenable to proof. As Eissfeldt says: '. . . the whole of Pentateuchal criticism is a hypothesis, though admittedly one that rests upon very significant arguments' (*op. cit.*, p. 240).

It is strange that P, written from a priestly point of view, does so little to enhance the priesthood. It is Moses, the political leader, who remains the great hero, while the one who allows the people to fall into idolatry is Aaron, the priest, whom Moses rebukes and reinstates. This was not the only lapse on the part of Aaron. If the whole of the materials was arranged to give an ideal picture of the theocracy, as it was supposed to have existed in the Mosaic age (Driver, *op. cit.*, p. xii), then the project, in the light of the described stubbornness and intractability of the people, singularly miscarried.

Literary criticism in general would now hold as a truism that a literary work contains sources, and would never view these as evidence of multiple authorship (*e.g.*, *cf.* J. L. Lowes, *The Road to Xanadu*). It is now also taken to be axiomatic that style is dictated largely by subject-matter, not by idiosyncratic vocabularies. The comparison of the alleged composite nature of the Pentateuch with the writings of Arabic historians, who are simply marshalling their witnesses, is not applicable to the literature of the ancient Semitic East (A. T. Chapman, *Introduction to the Pentateuch*, 1911).

The application of the dissecting criteria to documents of indisputable unitary authorship shows them to be worthless (*cf.* * EGYPT, V.*b*). The selection of criteria was arbitrary, and other possible selections would give radically different results. A key passage as the justification of documentary fragmentation is Ex. 6:3, where, it is claimed, the introduction of the name *YHWH* is stated to be an innovation. The great stress here laid on the continuity of identity with the God of the Patriarchs hardly indicates a new departure. There are two possible interpretations of this verse. 'Name' here can refer not to an appellation, but can stand for 'honour' and 'character', as it often does in Semitics generally. Or the sentence could be taken as an elliptical interrogative: 'for did I not let my name, *YHWH*, be known to them?' At least the 'and also' of the next verse followed by a positive implies a preceding positive (W. J. Martin, *Stylistic Criteria and the Analysis of the Pentateuch*, 1955, pp. 17f.; G. R. Driver, 'Affirmation by Exclamatory Negation', *Journal of the Ancient Near East Soc.*, *Columbia Univ.* 5, 1973 (T. H. Gaster vol.), p. 109. Much study has been given to the traditions contained in Exodus, particularly by G. von Rad and M. Noth. All work like theirs is purely conjectural, so long as it is based upon the subjective literary criticism described above, and doctrinaire views of Israelite religious history. However, there is an advance in that the traditions are regarded in many cases as much older than the literary sources.

The Jewish view from the time of Joshua (8:34f.), subscribed to by our Lord, and accepted by the Christian church, held that Exodus was the work of Moses. From internal evidence this is also the impression given by the book itself. No objective philological evidence has been produced for the rejection of this view. If editing took place, one would expect it to be confined to such things as the modernization of geographical names. This done honestly in the interests of clarity would be far removed from inserting into documents extensive interpolations, and representing them as compositions of the Mosaic age.

III. The text

The text of Exodus is remarkably free from transcriptional errors. Letters on occasion have dropped out. There are a few examples of dittography (*e.g.* possibly of *sammîm*, 'spices', in 30:34). Haplography (writing only once that which occurs twice) appears, *e.g.*, in 19:12, where an *m* (= 'from') has been omitted. In 11:1 a marginal note may have found its way into the text: 'when his sending away is final'. In 20:18, apparently through the omission of Heb. *y*, 'fear' has become 'saw'. In 34:19 the Heb. definite article *h* has become *t*. In 23:3, through the misreading of *g* as *w*, 'great' has become 'poor' (*cf.* Lv. 19:15). In 17:16 the letters *k* and *n* have apparently been confused: read probably: 'For he said: power is with the banner of the Lord'. In 23:5 *b* seems to have replaced *r*, changing 'help' into 'forsake'; the reading is possibly: 'and thou shalt refrain from abandoning it, thou shalt surely give him your help'. One could read the text as it stands: 'and thou shalt refrain from abandoning it, thou shalt surely along with him free it'.

The magnitude of the *numbers seems to some to present difficulties. The transmission of numbers is especially exposed to error. In any consideration of the large number of people involved and the problem of providing for them, it should be borne in mind that these were not an urbanized people, but men and women whose manner of life made them well able to fend for themselves.

BIBLIOGRAPHY. A. H. McNeile, *The Book of Exodus*, *WC*, 1917; E. J. Young, *IOT*, 1954; M. Noth, *Exodus*, 1962; B. P. Napier, *Exodus*, 1963; D. W. Gooding, *The Account of the Tabernacle*, 1959; U. Cassuto, *Commentary on the Book of Exodus*, 1967; B. S. Childs, *Exodus*, 1974 (thorough survey of recent studies); R. A. Cole, *Exodus*, *TOTC*, 1973; J. Finegan, *Let My People Go*, 1963; E. W. Nicholson, *Exodus and Sinai in History and Tradition*, 1973.

W.J.M.
A.R.M.

EXPIATION. This term does not occur in AV, but it is found in some modern translations in place of 'propitiation', *e.g.* 1 Jn. 4:10, RSV. Objection is made to 'propitiation' on the ground that it means the appeasement of an angry God, an idea not found in Scripture. Therefore expiation is substituted for it. But the matter is not so simple. Expiation properly has a thing as its object. We may expiate a crime, or a sin. Propitiation is a personal word. We propitiate a person rather than a sin (though we should not overlook the fact that in the Bible 'propitiate' is occasionally found with sin as the object, the meaning being 'to make propitiation with respect to sin'). If we are to think of our relationship to God as basically personal we cannot afford to dispense with the concept of propitiation. Those who advocate the use of expiation must face questions like: Why should sin be expiated? What are the consequences if no expiation takes place? Is the hand of God in those consequences? Expiation is a valuable word only if we can confidently answer 'No' to the last question. If sin is a thing, and can be dealt with as a thing, blotted out, cast from us, and the like, then we may properly talk of expiation. But if sin affects man's relationship with God, if the relationship with God is the primary thing, then it is difficult to see how expiation is adequate. Once we bring in the category of the personal we need some such term as propitiation.

It seems, then, that, despite the confident claims of some, expiation is not the solution to our difficulties. The ideas expressed in the words usually translated *'propitiation' are not adequately safeguarded by the use of the term 'expiation'.

BIBLIOGRAPHY. C. Brown, *NIDNTT* 3, pp. 151–160.

L.M.

EYE. The Heb. word for eye, *'ayin*, with parallels in other Near Eastern languages, is used of the physical organ of man (Gn. 3:6) or beast (30:41), of God anthropomorphically (Ps. 33:18), and also of objects (Ezk. 1:18; *cf.* Rev. 4:6). The Gk. word *ophthalmos* has familiar derivations in English.

In Hebrew the physical organs are construed as acting semi-independently and possessing also psychical and moral qualities. Thus the eye not only has sight but is proud (Is. 5:15), has pity (Dt. 7:16), sleep (Gn. 31:40), delight (Ezk. 24:16), *etc.*, and, while Paul emphasizes the interdependence of the physical organs (1 Cor. 12:16ff.), Mt. 5:29 preserves the Hebraic notion of the almost self-contained function of the organ.

The practice of putting out the eyes of a defeated enemy was common in the E (Jdg. 16:21; 2 Ki. 25:7).

The phrase 'the eye of the Lord is on those who fear him' (Ps. 33:18) is significant of God's watchful care (*cf.* Ps. 1:6).

Other phrases are: 'eye for eye' (Lv. 24:20); 'face to face', literally 'eye to eye' (Nu. 14:14); 'before their eyes', *i.e.*, in full view (Gn. 42:24; *cf.* Je. 32:12); and 'between your eyes', *i.e.*, on the forehead (Ex. 13:9), of the phylactery.

Derived usages are: 'face of the land' (Heb. *'ayin*) (Ex. 10:5), and 'gleaming' or 'sparkling' (Ezk. 1:4; Pr. 23:31). B.O.B.

EYE OF A NEEDLE. In Mt. 19:24; Mk. 10:25; Lk. 18:25 we find the statement of Jesus: 'It is easier for a camel to go through the eye of a needle than for a rich man to enter the kingdom of God.' This form of words, familiar in rabbinic writings, signifies something both very unusual and very difficult—*e.g.* in the Talmud an elephant passing through the eye of a needle is twice used of what is impossible, and a camel is portrayed as dancing in a very small corn measure (*cf.* also J. Lightfoot, *Horae Hebraicae*, 2, 1859, pp. 264f.). Some scholars interpret 'needle's eye' as a reference to a narrow gateway for pedestrians, but there is no historical evidence to support this. See F. W. Farrar, 'The Camel and the Needle's Eye', *The Expositor* 3, 1876, pp. 369–380. J.D.D.

EZEKIEL (Heb. *y^eḥezqē'l*, 'God strengthens'). The name is found in approximately its Heb. form in 1 Ch. 24:16 for the head of one of the priestly orders.

Ezekiel, the son of *Buzi, was deported to Babylonia, almost certainly with Jehoiachin in 597 BC (2 Ki. 24:14–17). He was settled in the village of Tel-abib by the river *Chebar. Five years later he received his call as prophet (Ezk. 1:2), possibly at the age of 30 (1:1), though this interpretation is denied by many without offering a more satisfactory one. He lived for at least another 22 years (29:17).

We have little information about his life. Though he possessed detailed knowledge of the Jerusalem Temple and its cultus, there is no evidence he had served in it. Even those, *e.g.* Cooke (*ICC*), who suggest that the bulk of chs. 1–24 were pronounced in Jerusalem, do not suggest Temple service. His thought, more than that of any other prophet, is influenced by priestly symbolism. His prophecies were badly received (3:25), but we soon find him in an honoured position (8:1; 14:1; 20:1), due possibly to his family rank; the majority hardly took his message very seriously (33:30–32—AV is misleading in v. 30). His wife died suddenly the day Nebuchadrezzar invested Jerusalem (24:1–2, 15–18); there is no mention of children.

H. Klostermann, *Theologische Studien und Kritiken*, 1877, tried on the basis of such passages as 3:23–4:8 to show that he suffered from an organic nervous disease, which he called catalepsy. Though popular for a time, the view is today accepted by few. Considerable controversy exists as to how Ezekiel's symbolic actions are to be interpreted. Some, *e.g.* A. B. Davidson, *Ezekiel* (*CBSC*), p. xxx, and J. Skinner, *HDB*, 1, p. 817a, have held they took place purely in the prophet's mind. More usual is the conception that, though they were carried out, in our understanding of them we must allow for a metaphorical element inconsistent with a purely literal interpretation. See also the following article. H.L.E.

EZEKIEL, BOOK OF.

I. Structure and contents

The indications of date (1:2; 3:16; 8:1; 20:1; 24:1; 26:1; 29:1, 17; 30:20; 31:1; 32:1, 17; 33:21; 40:1) apart from those in chs. 25–32 form a coherent series marking major developments in Ezekiel's message (see previous article). It is reasonable to infer that chs. 25–32 were inserted in their present position on analogy with Is. 13–27 to mark the division between the two main phases of Ezekiel's activity; *cf.* also the probably original position of the prophecies against the nations in Jeremiah (so LXX). In chs. 1–24 he is the prophet of inexorable doom, interpreting coming events to the remnant in exile (not to Jerusalem!) to prepare them for their future role. Chs. 33–39 give an outline of the message by which he tried to build up the exiles as the people of God. The long interval between 33:21 and 40:1 (some 13 years), the striking change in style and the fact that Josephus writes of Ezekiel's *two* books (*Ant.* 10. 79) suggest that chs. 40–48 represent a separate, though allied, group of prophecies beside chs. 33–39.

II. Authorship and date

Ezekiel has an unquestioned place in Ben Sira's list at the beginning of the 2nd century BC (Ecclus. 49:8), but there was a move in the 1st century AD to have the book withdrawn from public use. For this there were three reasons. Some felt ch. 16 too repugnant for public reading; ch. 1 and parallels were used in dangerous theosophical speculations (the students of *Merkabhah* ['chariot'] mysticism thought they were the key to the mysteries of creation); above all, numerous details in chs. 40–48 were considered contradictory to the law of Moses, already considered immutable. The labours of Hananiah ben Hezekiah, which resolved the apparent discrepancies, guaranteed for Ezekiel a public position in the Pharisaic canon.

This position was seldom challenged, and J. Skinner could say in 1898 (*HDB*, 1, p. 817a), 'The Book of Ezekiel (save for a somewhat corrupt text) exists in the form in which it left the hand of its author. . . . Neither the unity nor the authenticity of Ezekiel has been questioned by more than a very small minority of scholars. Not only does it bear the stamp of a single mind in its phraseology, its imagery, and its mode of thought, but it is arranged on a plan so perspicuous and so comprehensive that the evidence of literary design in the composition becomes altogether irresistible.'

In spite of the cogency of these arguments the position began to change in 1924; attacks on the unity and authenticity of Ezekiel may be divided into three groups, which tend to overlap.

a. The date of composition

C. C. Torrey saw in it a pseudepigraph, written about 230 BC, describing the abominations of Manasseh's reign; an editor gave it its present form not later than 200 BC. M. Burrows reached a similar date by linguistic evidence. L. E. Browne advocated a date during the time of Alexander the Great. J. Smith, on the other hand, regarded Ezekiel as a N Israelite deported in 734 BC, who prophesied to his fellow exiles until he returned to Jerusalem in 691 BC, where he gave the bulk of his oracles. Such views have won very little favour.

b. The place of prophecy

Though Torrey's dating has had little acceptance, many have followed him in seeing the bulk of the book as Palestinian. It is widely believed that, whether or not Ezekiel was deported in 597 BC, he was prophesying in or near Jerusalem until its destruction in 586 BC. Perhaps the best presentation of this view is by Pfeiffer, *IOT*, 1948, pp. 535–543. The main justification for this interpretation is the traditional misinterpretation of Ezekiel's oracles before 586 BC as addressed to doomed Jerusalem. Its great weakness is the very extensive rearrangement of the text involved, and the absence of any adequate motivation for the distortion of Ezekiel's actual activity.

c. The unity of the book

Basing himself mainly on the contrast between Ezekiel's poetry and prose, G. Hölscher attributed to him only 170 verses (mostly poetry) of the total 1,273, the rest coming from a levitical editor between 500 and 450 BC. W. A. Irwin reached similar results by other methods, attributing some 250 verses to Ezekiel. Many deny chs. 40–48 to him. Their arguments are a challenge to profounder exegesis, but they have failed to carry conviction with the majority, though editorial insertions are increasingly recognized.

It seems fair to say that these intensive critical studies have largely cancelled themselves out. They have led to a deeper understanding of many aspects of the book, but have left the general position much as it was before 1924. Since the work of C. G. Howie there has been a general swing back to a more conservative position. Few now deny that it is an Exilic production by Ezekiel himself. In the first 39 chapters, G. Fohrer, mainly on subjective grounds, denies only just over 100 verses to the prophet, and that without impairing any major section of his message. About the same number of verses from the last 9 chapters are denied to the prophet but here the motivation seems to be more subjective.

There has also been a general swing away from the idea that Ezekiel must have prophesied in Jerusalem during the earlier part of his activity. The latest major commentary, that of W. Zimmerli, takes up a mainly conservative position, but does not attribute the composition of the book to Ezekiel himself.

III. The text

Many *hapax legomena* and technical expressions and obscurity in the symbolical language have led scribes into frequent error. The LXX can often be used to correct the Hebrew, but only with extreme care. There is an interesting comparison of the Hebrew and Greek in Cooke, *Ezekiel, ICC*, pp. xl–xlvii.

IV. The religious teaching of the book

To understand the book correctly we must grasp that, like all the writings of the prophets, it is not a manual of theology; it is the word of God to a battered remnant in exile experiencing what the theologians of the time had considered impossible. If Ezekiel by his symbolism seems to stress the transcendence of God, it is to make clear that his omnipotence cannot be limited by the failure of his people. This leads to the most unsparing exposure of Israel's history and religion in the OT (16; 20; 23). The promise of restoration is no longer bound to the prior repentance of the people, but is an act of God's grace which leads to repentance (36:16–32). The restoration is above all to vindicate God's honour and not for Israel's sake. Because all is of God's grace, the relationship of the individual to God depends neither on his heredity nor his own past (18; 33:10–20). Many have deduced from 40–48 a picture of Ezekiel as a narrow, priestly ritualist, but this comes from failure to recognize the essentially eschatological character of these chapters. Witness to this is borne by the apparent lack of interest of the returned exiles in these chapters. They did not even try to enforce those points that lay in their power, such as confirming the priesthood to the Zadokites (44:15–16), or the apparent duplication of a Day of Atonement (45:18, 20; *cf.* RVmg. for LXX correctly). In the symbolism of exact conformity to divine plan and law we are shown God's people ultimately conforming perfectly to his purposes.

BIBLIOGRAPHY. G. A. Cooke, *The Book of Ezekiel, ICC*, 1936; W. A. Irwin, *The Problem of Ezekiel*, 1943, 'Ezekiel Research since 1943', *VT* 3, 1953, pp. 54–66; C. G. Howie, *The Date and Composition of Ezekiel*, 1950; G. Fohrer and K. Galling, *Ezechiel*, 1955; J. B. Taylor, *Ezekiel, TOTC*, 1969; W. Zimmerli, *Ezechiel*, 1969; W. H. Brownlee, *Ezekiel 1–19*, 1986; R. M. Halls, *Ezekiel*, 1989; L. C. Allen, *Ezekiel 20–48*, 1990; I. M. Duguid, *Ezekiel and the Leaders of Israel*, 1994. H.L.E.

EZEL. The agreed rendezvous of David and Jonathan, occurring in 1 Sa. 20:19 (AV, RV, RSVmg.). It is sometimes taken to mean 'departure', but the RVmg. and the RSV, following the LXX, read 'this mound' and 'yonder stone heap' respectively, and assume corruption in the Heb. text. See also the mg. of 1 Sa. 20:41. G.W.G.

EZRA. According to the record in Ezr. 7, Ezra was sent to Jerusalem by Artaxerxes I in 458 BC. It would seem probable that he held a position in Persia comparable to Secretary of State for Jewish affairs. His task was to enforce the uniform observance of the Jewish law, and to this end he had authority to make appointments within the Jewish state. A large company of exiles came with him, and he brought valuable gifts for the Temple from the king and the exiled Jews. He was asked to deal with the problem of mixed marriages, and, after fasting and prayer, he and a chosen committee blacklisted the guilty and induced some at least to put away their pagan wives (10:19).

After this we do not hear of Ezra until he reads the law publicly in Ne. 8. This was in 444 BC. Since he had been sent by the king on a temporary mission, he presumably returned with his report, but was sent back again on a similar mission when the walls of the city were completed. Nehemiah, in part of his memoirs in Ne. 12:36ff., records that he himself led one party round the walls on the occasion of their dedication, while Ezra led the other.

Largely on the strength of three passages, many have held that Ezra did not come to Jerusalem until the time of Artaxerxes II, *i.e.* in 398 BC, long after the time of Nehemiah.

a. Ezr. 9:9 speaks of a city wall, whereas the wall was not built until Nehemiah's time. But Ezr. 4:12 shows that a wall of some sort was being built in the reign of Artaxerxes I, and its destruction is probably referred to in 4:23 and Ne. 1:3. Ezra is rejoicing in faith at the work which has progressed so far.

b. Ezr. 10:1 speaks of a very great congregation in Jerusalem, whereas Ne. 7:4 says that only a few people lived in the city. But the context of Ezr. 10 shows that the congregation was drawn from all around Jerusalem, *e.g.* 10:7, whereas Ne. 7 is concerned with actual dwelling-houses in the city.

c. Ezr. 10:6 speaks of Jehohanan (or Johanan) the son of Eliashib as Ezra's contemporary. We know from Ne. 12:22–23 that Johanan was the grandson of Eliashib, and from the Elephantine papyri that Johanan was high priest in 408 BC. But Johanan was a common name, and it is reasonable to think that Eliashib had a son named Johanan, and also another son, Joiada, who in turn had a son, Johanan, who became high priest. Ezr. 10:6 does not say that Johanan was high priest in Ezra's day.

As against the idea that the writer of Ezra and Nehemiah confused Artaxerxes I and II (which this theory of the priority of Nehemiah demands), a writer even as late as 330 BC could not have confused the order of the two men. If Ezra really came in 398 BC, a few of the writer's contemporaries would have remembered him, and many would have been told of him by their parents; whereas no-one would have remembered Nehemiah. Thus the writer could not have put Ezra back before Nehemiah by accident, and no-one has suggested any reason for his doing so deliberately. (See J. Stafford Wright, *The Date of Ezra's Coming to Jerusalem*, 1958; H. H. Rowley, 'The Chronological Order of Ezra and Nehemiah' in *The Servant of the Lord and Other Essays*, 1952, pp. 129ff.)

It should be noted that Ezra attained a great reputation among the Jews in post-biblical times. In 2 Esdras 14 he is said to have been inspired of God to re-write the law, which had been destroyed in the Exile, and a number of other books. See also the following article.

BIBLIOGRAPHY. H. H. Schaeder, *Esra der Schreiber*, 1930; W. F. Albright, 'The Date and Personality of the Chronicler', *JBL* 40, 1921, pp. 104ff. J.S.W.

EZRA, BOOK OF.

I. Outline of contents

a. 1:1–11. Cyrus permits the Jews to return from exile under Sheshbazzar. 537 BC.

b. 2:1–70. The register of those who returned.

c. 3:1–13. The altar is set up and the Temple foundations laid. 536 BC.

d. 4:1–5, 24. Enemies hinder the work until the time of Darius.

e. 4:6–23. Further opposition to the building of the city walls in the reign of Ahasuerus (Xerxes, 485–465 BC) and Artaxerxes (464–424 BC), resulting in a decree to stop the building altogether.

f. 5:1–6:22. Renewal of the Temple building through the prophecies of Haggai and Zechariah. In spite of protests to Darius the work is completed. 520–516 BC.

g. 7:1–28. Ezra is sent from Persia to enforce the law. 458 BC.

h. 8:1–36. Ezra's journey and safe arrival.

i. 9:1–10:44. Ezra and the Jews deal with the problem of mixed marriages.

In this outline it is assumed that the author has collected examples of opposition together in 4:6–23. There are those who think that Ahasuerus in v. 6 is Cambyses (529–522 BC) and Artaxerxes in v. 7 is the usurper Gaumata, or Pseudo-Smerdis, who reigned for a few months in 522–521 BC. But the subject-matter of vv. 7–23 is the walls and not the Temple, and it is probable that the damage referred to in v. 23 is that referred to in Ne. 1:3.

II. Authorship and date

See the general note under *CHRONICLES, of which it is probable that Ezra and Nehemiah formed part. Traditionally the author is Ezra himself, but some bring the date down to about 330 BC. Whether or not Ezra was the final compiler, chs. 7–9 would appear to be from his hand, much of this section being in the first person singular. The account in chs. 1–6 is compiled from records, including decrees (1:2–4; 6:3–12), genealogies and name lists (2), and letters (4:7–22; 5:6–17). There are two sections which have been preserved in Aramaic (4:8–6:18; 7:12–26). Aramaic was the diplomatic language of the day, and was suitable for the section dealing with the coming and going of letters and decrees between Palestine and Persia.

III. Credibility

The documents that are found in Ezra present no great difficulties of harmonization with one another and with what is known from secular history. We may note the following.

a. The decree of Cyrus (1), acknowledging Jehovah, is in harmony with Cyrus's favourable references to Babylonian deities in contemporary records. This is a public decree, written in terms that would appeal to the Jews. The formal decree in 6:3–5 is filed in the records, and gives the maximum size of the Temple for which the king was prepared to give a grant.

b. It is pointed out that from Hg. 2:18 we learn that the foundation of the Temple was laid in 520 BC, whereas Ezr. 3:10 indicates that it was laid in 536 BC. In actual fact so little was done in the intervening period that it is likely that the revival would begin with a fresh foundation ceremony. Records show that in important buildings there was more than one official foundation stone.

c. The date of the coming of Ezra is bound up with the book of Nehemiah, and is considered separately under the entry *EZRA, above. See also *NEHEMIAH, *SHESHBAZZAR, *ZERUBBABEL.

IV. The book of Ezra and 1 Esdras

Esdras is the Gk. equivalent of Ezra, and our Apocrypha contains in 1 Esdras a book that is very similar to Ezra, though with certain striking differences. It runs from 2 Ch. 35:1 to the end of Ezra, after which it adds Ne. 8:1–12. Its history is confused. Thus Cyrus permits the return under Sheshbazzar, while Darius commissions Zerubbabel to go and build the Temple and the city; yet 5:70–73 says that Zerubbabel was working in Judah 'as long as King Cyrus lived'. Thus, while it may be useful to compare the two versions, Ezra is undoubtedly the more reliable. The famous story of the three guardsmen comes in 1 Esdras 3.

BIBLIOGRAPHY. J. M. Myers, *Ezra, Nehemiah*, *AB*, 1965; A. C. Welch, *Post-Exilic Judaism*, 1935; L. E. Browne, *Early Judaism*, 1920; K. Galling, 'The Gola-list in Ezra ii/Neh. vii', *JBL* 70, 1951, pp. 149ff.; F. D. Kidner, *Ezra and Nehemiah*, *TOTC*, 1979; *Ezra, Nehemiah*, 1985; H. G. M. Williamson, *Ezra and Nehemiah*, 1987; M. Roberts, *Ezra–Nehemiah*, 1992. J.S.W.

Dates BC	Persian Kings	Dates BC	Events in Jerusalem
539–530	Cyrus	537	First attempts to rebuild the Temple
530–522	Cambyses		
522–486	Darius I Hystaspes	520–516	The Temple rebuilt
486–465	Xerxes I		
465–424	Artaxerxes I Longimanus	458	Ezra sent to Jerusalem by Artaxerxes
		445–433	Nehemiah governor of Judah
423–404	Darius II Nothus	410 and 407	Letters from Jews at Elephantine – to Johanan, High Priest in Jerusalem and Bagaos, Governor of Judah
404–359	Artaxerxes II Mnemon		
359/8–338/7	Artaxerxes III Ochus		
338/7–336/5	Arses		
336/5–331	Darius III Codomanus		

Chronology for the book of Ezra.

FACE. The Eng. word usually translates Heb. *pānîm* or Gk. *prosōpon*. The Heb. word is used in many Eng. senses—of the faces of people and animals, and metaphorically of the sky; it could refer to the front of something, or its outward appearance. Then the 'face' of a person became synonymous with his 'presence', and the Heb. *lip̄ᵉnê* (lit. 'to the face of', and so 'to the presence of', and 'in front of') is a very common preposition.

The face, of course, gives visible indication of inward emotions, and a variety of adjectives accompany the word in Scripture, such as 'sad', 'tearful', 'ashamed' or 'pale'. The face could change colour, darkening or blushing.

Modesty or reverence demanded the veiling of the face, as did Rebekah before Isaac. God's face might not be seen by man for fear of death (Ex. 33:20); in Isaiah's visions, seraphim veiled the Almighty's face. It was a sign of humility to bow the face to the ground; and falling on the face betokened great fear. Utter contempt, on the other hand, could be shown by spitting in somebody's face. Metaphorically, determination could be shown by 'setting' one's face—note the graphic phrase of Is. 50:7, denoting unswerving purpose. Determined opposition was made by withstanding someone to his face. Intimacy and understanding were conveyed by the phrase 'face to face'. This phrase has, of course, passed into English, as has also 'his face fell' (Gn. 4:5).

The face of the dead was covered (Jn. 11:44), and so this action to Haman made it clear that he was doomed (Est. 7:8).

When a man prostrated himself to make a request, his superior would raise the supplicant's head as a sign that the favour would be granted. To lift someone's face thus meant primarily to grant a favour (*cf.* Gn. 19:21), and then to make a favourite of (Dt. 10:17). This concept is also found in NT Greek, in the words *prosōpolēptēs* ('respecter of persons'; literally, 'face-taker') and *prosōpolēpsia*, the abstract noun (*cf.* Acts 10:34; Rom. 2:11).

The 'face of God', *i.e.*, his gracious presence, is an important OT theme, as, *e.g.*, in the *showbread.

BIBLIOGRAPHY. *THAT*, *s.v. pānîm*; E. Tiedke, *NIDNTT* 1, pp. 585–587; E. Lohse, *TDNT* 6, pp. 768–780.

D.F.P.

FAIR HAVENS, modern Kaloi Limenes, a small bay on the S coast of Crete, a few km E of Cape Matala. Although protected by small islands, it is too open to be an ideal winter harbour (Acts 27:8), but it would be the last place where Paul's ship could stay to avoid the NW wind, as the coast swings N beyond Cape Matala.

K.L.McK.

FAITH.

I. In the Old Testament

In the OT the word 'faith' is found twice only in AV (Dt. 32:20; Hab. 2:4), but RSV has it eighteen times. Twelve times it is used of breaking faith (*e.g.* Lv. 5:15; Dt. 32:51) or acting in good faith (Jdg. 9:15f.), while the other six passages speak rather of trust. We should not, however, conclude from the rarity of the word that faith is unimportant in the OT, for the idea, if not the word, is frequent. It is usually expressed by verbs such as 'believe', 'trust' or 'hope', and such abound.

We may begin with such a passage as Ps. 26:1, 'Vindicate me, O Lord, for I have walked in my integrity, and I have trusted in the Lord without wavering.' It is often said that the OT looks for men to be saved on the basis of their deeds, but this passage puts the matter in its right perspective. The Psalmist does indeed appeal to his 'integrity', but this does not mean that he trusts in himself or his deeds. His trust is in God, and his 'integrity' is the evidence of that trust. The OT is a long book, and the truths about salvation are stated in various ways. The writers do not always make the distinctions that we, with the NT in our hands, might wish. But close examination will reveal that in the OT, as in the NT, the basic demand is for a right attitude to God, *i.e.* for faith. *Cf.* Ps. 37:3ff., 'Trust in the Lord, and do good . . . Take delight in the Lord, and he will give you the desires of your heart. Commit your way to the Lord; trust in him, and he will act.' Here there is no question but that the Psalmist is looking for an upright life. But there is no question, either, that basically he is advocating an attitude. He calls on men to put their trust in the Lord, which is only another way of telling them to live by faith. Sometimes men are urged to trust the Word of God (Ps. 119:42), but more usually it is faith in God himself that is sought. 'Trust in the Lord with all your heart; and do not rely on your own insight' (Pr. 3:5).

The latter part of this verse frowns upon trust in one's own powers, and this thought is frequent. 'He who trusts in his own mind is a fool' (Pr. 28:26). A man may not trust to his own righteousness (Ezk. 33:13). Ephraim is castigated for trusting 'in your chariots (Heb. 'way') and in the multitude of your warriors' (Ho. 10:13). Trust in idols is often denounced (Is. 42:17; Hab. 2:18). Jeremiah warns against confidence in anything human, 'Cursed is the man who trusts in man, and makes flesh his arm, and whose heart turns away from the Lord' (Je. 17:5). The list of things not to be trusted in might be multiplied, and it is the more impressive alongside the even more lengthy list of passages urging trust in the Lord. It is clear that the men of the OT thought of the Lord as the one worthy object of trust. They put not their trust in anything they did, or that other men did, or that the gods did. Their trust was in the Lord alone. Sometimes this is picturesquely expressed. Thus he is 'my rock, and my fortress, and my deliverer, my God, my rock, in whom I take refuge, my shield, and the horn of my salvation, my stronghold' (Ps. 18:2). Faith may be confidently rested in a God like that.

Special mention must be made of Abraham. His whole life gives evidence of a spirit of trustfulness, of a deep faith. Of him it is recorded that 'he believed the Lord; and he reckoned it to him as righteousness' (Gn. 15:6). This text is taken up by NT writers, and the fundamental truth it expresses developed more fully.

II. In the New Testament

a. General use of the word

In the NT faith is exceedingly prominent. The Gk. noun *pistis* and the verb *pisteuō* both occur more than 240 times, while the adjective *pistos* is found 67 times. This stress on faith is to be seen against the background of the saving work of God in Christ. Central to the NT is the thought that God sent his Son to be the Saviour of the world. Christ accomplished man's salvation by dying an atoning death on Calvary's cross. Faith is the attitude whereby a man abandons all reliance in his own efforts to obtain salvation, be they deeds of piety, of ethical goodness or anything else. It is the attitude of complete trust in Christ, of reliance on him alone for all that salvation means. When the Philippian jailer asked, 'Men, what must I do to be saved?', Paul and Silas answered without hesitation, 'Believe in the Lord Jesus, and you will be saved' (Acts 16:30f.). It is 'whoever believes in him' that does not perish, but has everlasting life (Jn. 3:16). Faith is the one way by which men receive salvation.

The verb *pisteuō* is often followed by 'that', indicating that faith is concerned with facts, though there is more to it than that. James tells us that the devils believe 'that God is one', but this 'faith' does not profit them (Jas. 2:19). *pisteuō* may be followed by the simple dative, when the meaning is that of giving credence to, of accepting as true, what someone says. Thus Jesus reminds the Jews that 'John came . . . in the way of righteousness, and you did not believe him' (Mt. 21:32). There is no question here of faith in the sense of trust. The Jews simply did not believe what John said. This may be so also with respect to Jesus, as in Jn. 8:45, 'you do not believe me', or the next verse, 'if I tell the truth, why do you not believe me?' Yet it must not be forgotten that there is an intellectual content to faith. Consequently this construction is sometimes used where saving faith is in mind, as in Jn. 5:24, 'he who hears my word and believes him who sent me, has eternal life'. The man who really believes God will, of course, act on that belief. In other words, a genuine belief that what God has revealed is true will issue in a true faith.

The characteristic construction for saving faith is that wherein the verb *pisteuō* is followed by the preposition *eis*. Literally this means to believe 'into'. It denotes a faith which, so to speak, takes a man out of himself, and puts him into Christ (*cf.* the NT expression frequently used of Christians, being 'in Christ'). This experience may also be referred to with the term 'faith-union with Christ'. It denotes not simply a belief that carries an intellectual assent, but one wherein the believer cleaves to his Saviour with all his heart. The man who believes in this sense abides in Christ and Christ in him (Jn. 15:4). Faith is not accepting certain things as true, but trusting a Person, and that Person Christ.

Sometimes *pisteuō* is followed by *epi*, 'upon'. Faith has a firm basis. We see this construction in Acts 9:42, where, when the raising of Tabitha was known, 'many believed in the Lord'. The people had seen what Christ could do, and they rested their faith 'on' him. Sometimes faith rests on the Father, as when Paul speaks of believing 'in him that raised from the dead Jesus our Lord' (Rom. 4:24).

Very characteristic of the NT is the absolute use of the verb. When Jesus stayed with the Samaritans many of them 'believed because of his word' (Jn. 4:41). There is no need to add what they believed, or in whom they believed. Faith is so central to Christianity that one may speak of 'believing' without the necessity for further clarification. Christians are simply 'believers'. This use extends throughout the NT, and is not confined to any particular writer. We may fairly conclude that faith is fundamental.

The tenses of the verb *pisteuō* are also instructive. The aorist tense points to a single act in past time and indicates the determinative character of faith. When a man comes to believe he commits himself decisively to Christ. The present tense has the idea of continuity. Faith is not a passing phase. It is a continuing attitude. The perfect tense combines both ideas. It speaks of a present faith which is continuous with a past act of belief. The man who believes enters a permanent state. Perhaps we should notice here that the noun 'faith' sometimes has the article 'the faith', *i.e.* the whole body of Christian teaching, as when Paul speaks of the Colossians as being 'established in the faith', adding 'just as you were taught' (Col. 2:7).

b. Particular uses of the word

(i) In the Synoptic Gospels faith is often connected with healing, as when Jesus said to the woman who touched his garment in the crowd, 'Take heart, daughter; your faith has made you well' (Mt. 9:22). But these Gospels are also concerned with faith in a wider sense. Mark, for example, records the words of the Lord Jesus, 'All things are possible to him who believes' (Mk. 9:23). Similarly, the Lord speaks of the great results of having 'faith as a grain of mustard seed' (Mt. 17:20; Lk. 17:6). It is clear that our Lord called for faith in himself personally. The characteristic Christian demand for faith in Christ rests ultimately on Christ's own requirement.

(ii) In the Fourth Gospel faith occupies a very prominent place, the verb *pisteuō* being found 98 times. Curiously the noun *pistis*, 'faith', is never employed. This is possibly due to its use in circles of a Gnostic type. There are indications that John had such opponents in mind, and it may be that he wanted to avoid using a term of which they were very fond. Or he may have preferred the more dynamic meaning conveyed by the verb. Whatever his reason, he uses the verb *pisteuō* more often than any other writer in the NT, three times as often, in fact, as the first three Gospels put together. His characteristic construction is that with the preposition *eis*, 'to believe into', 'to believe on'. The important thing is the connection between the believer and the Christ. Accordingly, John speaks again and again of believing in him or of believing 'in the name' of Christ (*e.g.* Jn. 3:18). The 'name', for men of antiquity, was a way of summing up the whole personality. It stood for all that the man was. Believing on the name of Christ, then, means believing in all that he is essentially in himself. Jn. 3:18 also says, 'He who believes in him is not condemned: but he who does not believe is condemned already.' It is characteristic of Johannine teaching that eternal issues are decided here and now. Faith does not simply give men assurance of everlasting life at some unspecified time in the future. It gives them everlasting life here and now. He that believes on the Son 'has' everlasting life (3:36; *cf.* 5:24, *etc.*).

(iii) In Acts, with its story of vigorous missionary advance, it is not surprising that the characteristic expression is the use of the aorist tense, to indicate the act of decision. Luke records many occasions wherein people came to put their trust in Christ. Other constructions are found, and both the continuing state and the permanent results of belief find mention. But decision is the characteristic thing.

(iv) For Paul, faith is the typical Christian attitude. He does not share John's antipathy to the noun, but uses it more than twice as often as he uses the verb. It occurs in connection with some of his leading ideas. Thus in Rom. 1:16 he speaks of the gospel as 'the power of God for salvation to every one who has faith'. It means a great deal to Paul that Christianity is more than a system of good advice. It not only tells men what they ought to do, but gives them power to do it. Again and again Paul contrasts mere words with power, always with a view to emphasizing that the power of the Holy Spirit of God is seen in the lives of Christians. This power becomes available to a man only when he believes. There is no substitute for faith.

Much of Paul's controversial writing centres round the dispute with the Judaizers. These men insisted that it was not enough for Christians to be baptized. They must also be circumcised, and, being thus admitted to Judaism, endeavour to keep the whole of the Mosaic law. They made obedience to the law a necessary pre-condition of salvation, at least in the fullest sense of that term. Paul will have none of this. He insists that men can do nothing, nothing at all, to bring about their salvation. All has been done by Christ, and no man can add anything to the perfection of Christ's finished work. So it is that Paul insists that men are justified 'by faith' (Rom. 5:1). The doctrine of *justification by faith lies at the very heart of Paul's message. Whether with this terminology or not, he is always putting the idea forward. He vigorously combats any idea of the efficacy of good deeds. 'A man is not justified by works of the law but through faith in Jesus Christ,' he writes to the Galatians and proceeds, 'even we have believed in Christ Jesus, in order to be justified by faith in Christ, and not by works of the law.' He adds resoundingly 'because by works of the law shall no one be justified' (Gal. 2:16). Clearly, for Paul, faith means the abandonment of all reliance on one's ability to merit salvation. It is a trustful acceptance of God's gift in Christ, a reliance on Christ, Christ alone, for all that salvation means.

Another outstanding feature of Pauline theology is the very large place the apostle gives to the work of the Holy Spirit. He thinks of all Christians as indwelt by the Spirit (Rom. 8:9, 14), and he connects this too with faith. Thus he writes to the Ephesians concerning Christ, 'you also, who . . . have believed in him, were sealed with the promised Holy Spirit, which is the guarantee of our inheritance' (Eph. 1:13f.). Sealing represented the mark of ownership, a metaphor readily understood in an age when many could not read. The Spirit within believers is God's mark of ownership, and this mark is put on men only as they believe. The apostle goes on to speak of the Spirit as 'the guarantee (Gk. *arrabōn*) of our inheritance'. Paul employs here a word which in the 1st century meant a down-payment, *i.e.* a payment which at one and the same time was part of the agreed price and the guarantee that the remainder would be forthcoming. Thus when a man believes he receives the Holy Spirit as part of the life in the age to come, and as an assurance that the remainder will infallibly follow. (*Earnest.)

(v) The writer of the Epistle to the Hebrews sees that faith has always been a characteristic of the people of God. In his great portrait gallery in Heb. 11 he reviews the worthies of the past, showing how one by one they illustrate the great theme that 'without faith it is impossible to please' God (Heb. 11:6). He is particularly interested in the opposition of faith to sight. Faith is 'the assurance of things hoped for, the conviction of things not seen' (Heb. 11:1). He emphasizes the point that men who had nothing in the way of outward evidence to support them nevertheless retained a firm hold on the promises of God. In other words, they walked by faith, not by sight.

(vi) Of the other writers in the NT we must notice James, for he has often been held to be in opposition to Paul in this matter. Where Paul insists that a man is justified by faith and not by works James maintains 'that a man is justified by works, and not by faith alone' (Jas. 2:24). There is no more than a verbal contradiction, however. The kind of 'faith' that James is opposing is not that warm personal trust in a living Saviour of which Paul speaks. It is a faith which James himself describes: 'You believe that God is one; you do well. Even the demons believe—and shudder' (Jas. 2:19). He has in mind an intellectual assent to certain truths, an assent which is not backed up by a life lived in accordance with those truths (Jas. 2:15f.). So far is James from opposing faith in the full sense that he everywhere presupposes it. Right at the beginning of his Epistle he speaks naturally of 'the testing of your faith' (Jas. 1:3), and he exhorts his readers, 'show no partiality as you hold the faith of our Lord Jesus Christ, the Lord of glory' (Jas. 2:1). He criticizes a wrong faith but assumes that everyone will recognize the need for a right faith. Moreover, by 'works' James does not mean what Paul means by that term. Paul thinks of obedience to the commands of the law regarded as a system whereby a man may merit salvation. For James the law is 'the law of liberty' (Jas. 2:12). His 'works' look uncommonly like 'the fruit of the Spirit' of which Paul speaks. They are warm deeds of love springing from a right attitude to God. They are the fruits of faith. What James objects to is the claim that faith is there when there is no fruit to attest it.

Faith is clearly one of the most important concepts in the whole NT. Everywhere it is required and its importance insisted upon. Faith means abandoning all trust in one's own resources. Faith means casting oneself unreservedly on the mercy of God. Faith means laying hold on the promises of God in Christ, relying entirely on the finished work of Christ for salvation, and on the power of the indwelling Holy Spirit of God for daily strength. Faith implies complete reliance on God and full obedience to God.

BIBLIOGRAPHY. D. M. Baillie, *Faith in God*, 1964; G. C. Berkouwer, *Faith and Justification*², 1954; J. Hick, *Faith and Knowledge*², 1966; O. Becker, O. Michel, *NIDNTT* 1, pp. 587–606; A. Weiser *et al.*, *TDNT* 6, pp. 174–228; T. Söding, *Glaube bei Markus*, 1985; *Die Trias Glaube, Hoffnung, Liebe bei Paulus* 1992.

L.M.

FALL.

I. The biblical account

The story of the Fall of man, given in Gn. 3, describes how mankind's first parents, when tempted by the serpent, disobeyed God's express command by eating of the fruit of the tree of the knowledge of good and evil. The essence of all sin is displayed in this first sin: having been tempted to doubt God's word ('Did God say . . . ?'), man is led on to disbelieve it ('You will not die'), and then to disobey it (they 'ate'). Sin is man's rebellion against the authority of God, and pride in his own supposed self-adequacy ('You will be like God'). The consequences of sin are twofold: first, awareness of guilt and immediate separation from God (they 'hid themselves'), with whom hitherto there had been unimpaired daily fellowship; and secondly, the sentence of the curse, decreeing toil, sorrow and death for man himself, and in addition inevitably involving the whole of the created order, of which man is the crown.

II. The effect on man

Man henceforth is a perverted creature. In revolting against the purpose of his being, which is to live and act entirely to the glory of his sovereign and beneficent Creator and to fulfil his will, he ceases to be truly man. His true manhood consists in conformity to the image of God in which he was created. This image of God is manifested in man's original capacity for communion with his Creator; in his enjoyment exclusively of what is good; in his rationality which makes it possible for him alone of all creatures to hear and respond to the Word of God; in his knowledge of the truth and in the freedom which that knowledge ensures; and in government, as the head of God's creation, in obedience to the mandate to have dominion over every living thing and to subdue the earth.

Yet, rebel as he will against the image of God with which he has been stamped, man cannot efface it, because it is part of his very constitution as man. It is evident, for example, in his pursuit of scientific knowledge, in his harnessing of the forces of nature and in his development of culture, art and civilization. But at the same time the efforts of fallen man are cursed with frustration. This frustration is itself a proof of the perversity of the human heart. Thus history shows that the very discoveries and advances which have promised most good to mankind have through misuse brought great evils in their train. The man who does not love God does not love his fellow men. He is driven by selfish motives. The image of Satan, the great hater of God and man, is superimposed upon him. The result of the Fall is that man now knows good *and evil*.

The psychological and ethical effects of the Fall are nowhere more graphically described than by Paul in Rom. 1:18ff. All men, however ungodly and unrighteous they may be, *know* the truth about God and themselves; but they wickedly *suppress* this truth (v. 18). It is, however, an inescapable truth, for the fact of the 'eternal power and Godhead' of the Creator is both manifested within them, by their very constitution as God's creatures made in his image, and also manifested all around them in the whole created order of the universe which bears eloquent testimony to its origin as God's handiwork (vv. 19f.; *cf.* Ps. 19:1ff.). Basically, therefore, man's state is not one of ignorance but of knowledge. His condemnation is that he loves darkness rather than light. His refusal to glorify God as God and his ingratitude lead him into intellectual vanity and futility. Arrogantly professing himself to be wise, he in fact becomes a fool (Rom. 1:21f.). Having wilfully cut himself adrift from the Creator in whom alone the meaning of his existence is to be found, he must seek that meaning elsewhere, for his creaturely finitude makes it impossible for him to cease from being a religious creature. And his search becomes ever more foolish and degrading. It carries him into the gross irrationality of superstition and idolatry, into vileness and unnatural vice, and into all those evils, social and international, which give rise to the hatreds and miseries that disfigure our world. The Fall has, in brief, overthrown the true dignity of man (Rom. 1:23ff.).

III. The biblical doctrine

It will be seen that the scriptural doctrine of the Fall altogether contradicts the popular modern view of man as a being who, by a slow evolutionary development, has succeeded in rising from the primeval fear and groping ignorance of a humble origin to proud heights of religious sensitivity and insight. The Bible does not portray man as risen, but as fallen, and in the most desperate of situations. It is only against this background that God's saving action in Christ takes on its proper significance. Through the grateful appropriation by faith of Christ's atoning work, what was forfeited by the fall is restored to man: his true and intended dignity is recovered, the purpose of life recaptured, the image of God restored, and the way into the paradise of intimate communion with God reopened.

IV. Its historical development

In the history of the church the classic controversy concerning the nature of the Fall and its effects is that waged by Augustine at the beginning of the 5th century against the advocates of the Pelagian heresy. The latter taught that Adam's sin affected only himself and not the human race as a whole, that every individual is born free from sin and capable in his own power of living a sinless life, and that there had even been persons who had succeeded in doing so. The controversy and its implications may be studied with profit in Augustine's anti-Pelagian writings. Pelagianism, with its affirmation of the total ability of man, came to the fore again in the Socinianism of the 16th and 17th centuries, and continues under the guise of modern humanistic religion.

A halfway position is taken by the Roman Catholic Church, which teaches that what man lost through the Fall was a supernatural gift of original righteousness that did not belong properly to his being as man but was something extra added by God (*donum superadditum*), with the consequence that the Fall left man in his natural state as created (*in puris naturalibus*): he has suffered a negative rather than a positive evil; deprivation rather than depravation. This teaching opens the door for the affirmation of the ability and indeed necessity of unregenerate man to contribute by his works towards the achievement of his salvation (semi-Pelagianism, synergism), which is characteristic of the Roman Catholic theology of man and grace. For a Roman Catholic view, see H. J. Richards, 'The Creation and Fall', in *Scripture* 8, 1956, pp. 109–115.

Although retaining the conception of man as a fallen being, contemporary liberal theology denies the historicity of the event of the Fall. Every man, it is said, is his own Adam. Similarly, certain forms of modern existentialist philosophy, which is essentially a repudiation of historical objectivism, are willing to make use of the term 'fallenness' to describe the subjective state in which man pessimistically finds himself. A floating concept, however, which is unrelated to historical event explains nothing. But the NT certainly understands the Fall as a definite event in human history—an event, moreover, of such critical consequences for the whole human race that it stands side by side with and explains the other great crucial event of history, namely the coming of Christ to save the world (see Rom. 5:12ff.; 1 Cor. 15:21f.). Mankind, together with the rest of the created order, awaits a third and conclusive event of history, namely the second advent of Christ at the end of this age, when the effects of the Fall will be finally abolished, unbelievers eternally judged, and the renewed creation, the new heavens and new earth wherein righteousness dwells, be established in accordance with almighty God's immutable purposes (see Acts 3:20f.; Rom. 8:19ff.; 2 Pet. 3:13; Rev. 21–22). Thus by God's grace all that was lost in Adam, and much more than that, is restored in Christ. (*SIN.)

BIBLIOGRAPHY. N. P. Williams, *The Ideas of the Fall and of Original Sin*, 1927; J. G. Machen, *The Christian View of Man*, 1937, ch. 14; J. Murray, *The Imputation of Adam's Sin*, 1959. P.E.H.

FAMILY, HOUSEHOLD.

I. In the Old Testament

There is no word in the OT which corresponds precisely to modern English 'family', as consisting of father, mother and children. The closest approximation is found in the word *bayiṯ* ('house'), which, from signifying the group of people, probably came to refer to the dwelling (AV translates as 'family' in 1 Ch. 13:14; 2 Ch. 35:5, 12; Ps. 68:6). In the Bible the term could be used not only of those sheltering under the same roof (Ex. 12:4) but also of much larger groups, as for instance the 'house of Israel' (Is. 5:7), which included the whole nation. Perhaps a closer equivalent to English 'family' is found in the phrase *bêṯ 'āḇ*, 'father's house'. The term most frequently translated 'family' in the EVV is *mišpāḥâ*, which had more the meaning of 'clan' than the smaller 'family', being applied for instance to 600 Danites from two villages (Jdg. 18:11).

Some idea of the relation of these two terms can be gained from the account in Jos. 7:16–18 of the detection of Achan after the failure to capture Ai. The search was first narrowed to the 'tribe' (*šēḇeṭ*) of Judah, then to the clan (*mišpāḥâ*, AV 'family') of the Zarhites, and finally to the 'household' (*bayiṯ*) of Zabdi. The fact that Achan was a married man with children of his own (7:24), but was still counted as a member of the *bayiṯ* of his grandfather Zabdi, shows the extent of this term. Conceptually the members of a tribe can be pictured as a cone, with the founding ancestor at the apex and the living generation at the base. The term *šēḇeṭ*, 'staff', perhaps in reference to the staff, signifying the authority, of the founding ancestor, applied to the whole tribe; *mišpāḥâ* referred to a smaller division lower down in the cone; and the term *bayiṯ* could apply to a yet smaller division, though its application depended upon its context, for if qualified by the name of the founding ancestor it could refer to the whole tribe. In each case the terms could indicate simply the base of the relevant cone, *i.e.* the living members of the group; or the entire volume of the cone, *i.e.* the members past and present, living and dead.

a. Determination of mates

In the choice of mates certain close relatives both by blood and *marriage were excluded (Lv. 18:6–18; Dt. 27:20–23), but outside these prohibited degrees marriage with kin was preferred, as is shown by the marriages of Isaac with Rebekah (Gn. 24:4), Jacob with Rachel and Leah (Gn. 28:2; 29:19), and Manoah's wish concerning Samson (Jdg. 14:3). On the other hand, marriages with foreigners, Hittite (Gn. 26:34), Egyptian (Gn. 41:45), Midianite (Ex. 2:21), Moabite (Ru. 1:4), Zidonian (1 Ki. 16:31) and others, did take place. A special case where the mate is determined is found in the levirate marriage law, whereby if a married man died childless his next brother was obliged to marry the widow, and raise up children to perpetuate the name of the deceased.

b. Methods of acquiring a wife

In most cases the choice of a mate and subsequent arrangements for marriage were made by the parents concerned, as is shown by the fact that, though Samson was attracted by the Timnathite, he applied to his parents to make the arrangements. The usual method of acquiring a wife was by purchase, though this is not an altogether satisfactory term, since the 'bride-price' (*mōhar*; Gn. 34:12; Ex. 22:16; 1 Sa. 18:25), though it was a payment made by the man to the bride's father, was more in the nature of a compensation to the family for the loss of a valued member than an outright cash purchase. Service could be given instead of payment, as with Jacob, who served Laban 14 years for Rachel and Leah, but this practice was not common during the Monarchy. Unorthodox means of acquiring a wife, which did not always involve the parents, included capture in war (Dt. 21:10–14) or in raids (Jdg. 21), or seduction, in which case the seducer was obliged to marry the violated maiden (Ex. 22:16; *cf.* Gn. 34:1–4).

c. Residence

Israelite marriage was patrilocal: the woman left her father's house and went to live with her husband. In patriarchal times this would often have involved going to live in the same group, *bayiṯ* or *mišpāḥâ*, as her husband's father and brothers, but in the time of the Monarchy the son on marriage probably left home to set up his own *bayiṯ*, as is suggested by the smallness of many of the private houses uncovered in excavations. Three cases are sometimes quoted as evidence for matrilocal residence, Jacob, Gideon (Jdg. 8:31; 9:1–2) and Samson, but such an interpretation is not necessary. Jacob lived in Laban's 'house' only while he was working in return for his wives, and it was the manner rather than the fact of his departure which aroused Laban's ill-will (Gn. 31:26–28). Gideon did not himself live with the woman in question, and she was in any case no more than a concubine. The same is true of Samson and the Timnathite, whom he only visited, and did not live with.

d. Number of mates

While at the creation monogamy seemed to have been intended, by the time of the patriarchal age polygamy (polygyny not polyandry) is found. At first Abraham had but one wife, Sarah, but when she proved barren he followed the custom of the time in having children by her handmaid Hagar (Gn. 16:1–2), and he took Keturah as a wife after the death of Sarah (Gn. 25:1). In subsequent generations more wives were taken, Jacob having two and their two handmaids. The possession of two wives was evidently assumed in the Mosaic legislation (Dt. 21:15), and under the Judges and the Monarchy there was still less restraint, and the economic factor imposed the only limit. That this was not God's plan is shown by the prophetic representation of Israel as the sole bride of God (Is. 50:1; 54:6–7; 62:4–5; Je. 2:2; Ezk. 16; Ho. 2:4f.). In addition to wives and the maidservants of wives, those who could afford them had *concubines, and children born by these could be accorded equal status with true sons, if the father was so minded.

e. Husband and wife

In addition to the terms *'îš* and *'iššâ*, 'man' and 'woman', which also served for 'husband' and 'wife', the husband was the *ba'al*, 'master', and *'āḏôn*, 'lord', of the wife, which illustrates the legal and normally practical relative positions of the two. Until her marriage a *woman was subject to her father, and after marriage to her husband, and to each she was a chattel. A man could divorce his wife, but probably not she him; she did not inherit his property, which went to his sons; and she might have to get along with other wives. On the other hand, in practice there was great variation in accordance with personality and strength of character, and that some women came to public prominence is shown by the cases of Deborah (Jdg. 4–5), Athaliah (2 Ki. 11), Huldah (2 Ki. 22:14f.) and Esther. The duties of the wife included first of all the bearing and care of children, and such household tasks as cooking, in addition to helping the husband in the fields when opportunity offered. Fidelity was important in both parties, and there was strict provision in the law for the punishment of adultery. The most important function of the wife was the bearing of children, and *barrenness was a source of shame.

f. Parents and children

The four terms, 'father' (*'āḇ*), 'mother' (*'ēm*), 'son' (*bēn*) and 'daughter' (*baṯ*), have cognates in most Semitic languages and were in such frequent use in OT times that they are irregular in grammatical inflexion. The greatest wish of man and wife was for many children (Ps. 127:3–5), but especially for sons, as is clearly shown in the history of Abraham and his dealings with God, from whom they came. The eldest son occupied a special position, and on his father's death he inherited a double portion and became head of the family. Sometimes, however, a father would show special favour to his youngest son, as did Jacob for Joseph and then Benjamin. A daughter did not inherit from her father unless there were no sons (*cf.*, however, Jb. 42:13–15; see also *INHERITANCE).

In ancient Mesopotamia, particularly as evidenced in the Nuzi documents, the practice of adoption by childless people of someone to take the place of a son is well attested (*NUZI, *PATRIARCHAL AGE), and it was in keeping with this practice that *Abraham considered making one of his servants his heir (Gn. 15:3). There is, however, no specific legislation concerning this matter of *adoption in the OT. Such cases as are reported are either in a foreign setting (as for instance the case quoted above, Moses by Pharaoh's daughter (Ex. 2:10) and Esther by Mordecai (Est. 2:7, 15)) or else are not cases of full adoption, as the adoptees were already descendants of the adopters, as in the cases of Jacob and Joseph's sons (Gn. 48:5, 12), and Naomi and the child of Ruth (Ru. 4:16–17). When they were very small all children were looked after by the mother, but as the boys grew older they were taught to share their father's work, so that in general the father governed the *education of the son, and the mother that of the daughter. That to the children the mother was as worthy of honour as the father is shown by the fifth commandment (Ex. 20:12).

g. Other kinsfolk

The terms 'brother' (*'āḥ*) and 'sister' (*'āḥôṯ*) could be applied not only to children of the same parents but to half siblings by either a different father or mother, and the restrictions on sexual intercourse between full siblings applied also to these (Lv. 18:9, 11; Dt. 27:22). Often of particular importance to children were their uncles and aunts, especially the mother's brother to the son, and the father's sister to the daughter. These are usually designated by the appropriate combination of terms such as *'ᵃḥôṯ-'āḇ*, 'father's sister', but sometimes described by the words *dôḏ*, 'uncle', and *dôḏâ*, 'aunt'. A woman would refer to her husband's father and mother by the special terms *ḥām* (*e.g.* Gn. 38:13, 25; 1 Sa. 4:19, 21) and *ḥāmôṯ* (*e.g.* Ru. 1:14), and it may be that *ḥōṯēn* (*e.g.* Ex. 3:1; 4:18) and *ḥōṯeneṯ* (Dt. 27:23) were corresponding terms used by the man of his wife's mother and father, though the limited contexts in which these terms occur make this uncertain.

h. Solidarity of kin

Two main factors made for solidarity in patriarchal times, common blood or descent, and common habitation and legal obligations according to customs and law. Though after the settlement in the land the tendency for families to divide weakened these, they continued to be of importance throughout OT times. The community of interests among the members of the household, clan and tribe was also a source of unity within these groups, and under their heads. One of the outgrowths of this unity was the right of each member of a group to protection by that group, and indeed the obligations on the group to provide certain services. Outstanding among these was that of the *gō'ēl*, whose obligations might extend from marrying the widow of a kinsman (Ru. 2:20; 3:12; 4) to redeeming a kinsman from slavery into which he had sold himself to pay a debt (see also *AVENGER OF BLOOD).

BIBLIOGRAPHY. R. de Vaux, *Ancient Israel*, 1961, pp. 19–55, 520–523; E. A. Speiser, 'The Wife-Sister Motif in the Patriarchal Narratives' in A. Altmann (ed.), *Biblical and other Studies*, 1963, pp. 15–28.

T.C.M.

II. In the New Testament

Family (Gk. *patria*) is mentioned as such only three times, although the related idea of 'house' or 'household' (Gk. *oikos*, *oikia*) is more frequent. *patria* ('lineage, descent', *LSJ*) signifies the historical origin of a household, *i.e.* its 'patriarch', rather than its present head. A family might be a tribe or even a nation. In Acts 3:25 the promise to Abraham is quoted in the form, 'in your posterity shall all the families (*patriai*) of the earth be blessed'. The LXX has 'tribes' (*phylai*) in the original promise (Gn. 12:3) and 'nations' (*ethnē*) when the promise is recalled in Gn. 18:18 and 22:18. Joseph was 'of the house and lineage (*patria*) of David' (Lk. 2:4), where the patronymic is the vital point. As this verse shows, 'house' (*oikos*) can be used in the same sense (*cf.* Lk. 1:27); *cf.* also 'the house of Israel' (Mt. 10:6; 15:24; Acts 2:36; 7:42, *etc.*), 'the house of Jacob' (Lk. 1:33).

The prominence of paternity is well seen in the third occurrence of *patria*, Eph. 3:14–15: 'I bow my knees before the Father, from whom every family in heaven and on earth is named.' This means that, just as every *patria* implies a *patēr* ('father'), so behind them all stands the universal fatherhood of God whence the whole scheme of ordered relationships is derived. Elsewhere we meet the more restricted concept of the fatherhood of God in relation to the household of the faithful.

The word 'household', where it is not simply a synonym for 'family', is a unit of society which meets us everywhere in the Roman and Hellenistic, as well as the Jewish, world of the 1st century. It consisted not only of the lord (Gk. *kyrios*), master (Gk. *despotēs*) or paterfamilias, his wife, children and slaves, but also of various dependants, such as servants, employees and even 'clients' (*e.g.* freedmen or friends) who voluntarily joined themselves to a household for the sake of mutual benefits (*CAESAR'S HOUSEHOLD). The Gospels abound with allusions to the household and its character (*e.g.* Mt. 21:33ff.). The household was an important factor in the growth and stability of the church. Already among the Jews the household was the context of such religious exercises as the Passover, a weekly sacred meal, prayers and instruction (*EDUCATION). Luke states that 'the breaking of the bread' took place in the Jerusalem church 'by households' (Acts 2:46). This phrase, *kat' oikon*, occurs in papyri in contrast to the phrase 'by individuals' (*kata prosōpon*—see *MM*).

In Hellenistic cities the role of the household in the establishment of churches was no less important. The first accession of Gentiles was the entire household of Cornelius at Caesarea, comprising household servants, a batman, kinsmen and near friends (Acts 10:7, 24). When Paul crossed to Europe, the church was planted at Philippi with the baptism of Lydia's household and that of the jailer (Acts 16:15, 31–34). At Corinth 'the first converts in Achaia' were the household of Stephanas (1 Cor. 16:15), which, in common, probably, with the households of Crispus the ruler of the synagogue and the hospitable Gaius (Acts 18:8; 1 Cor. 1:14–16; Rom. 16:23), was baptized by Paul himself. Other Christian households mentioned by name are those of Prisca and Aquila (at Ephesus, 1 Cor. 16:19; and perhaps Rome, Rom. 16:5), Onesiphorus (at Ephesus, 2 Tim. 1:16; 4:19), Philemon (at Colossae, Phm. 1–2), Nymphas or Nympha (at Laodicea, Col. 4:15), Asyncritus and Philologus (at Rome [?], Rom. 16:14–15).

In the Jerusalem church households were apparently instructed as units (Acts 5:42), and this was also Paul's custom, as he reminded the Ephesian elders (Acts 20:20). A regular catechesis existed setting forth the mutual duties of members of a Christian household: wives and husbands, children and fathers, servants and masters. See Col. 3:18–4:1; Eph. 5:22–6:9; 1 Pet. 2:18–3:7.

Reference is made to the church in the house of Prisca and Aquila (Rom. 16:5 and 1 Cor. 16:19), of Nymphas or Nympha (Col. 4:15) and of Philemon (or was it Archippus?) (Phm. 2). This means either that the household was regarded as a *church in itself, or that the church in a given locality met within the scope of one household's hospitality (see above, 'by households'). When Gaius is spoken of as host of 'the whole church' (Rom. 16:23), the existence of other household churches in Corinth is perhaps implied, with the suggestion that on occasion, presumably for the Lord's Supper (1 Cor. 11:18–22), they all came together 'as a church'. It is, however, not unimportant to note that both baptism and the Lord's Supper in certain situations took place within a household, not to mention instruction of wife and children (1 Cor. 14:35; Eph. 6:4), and that it was from the ranks of proved heads of households that overseers (bishops) as well as deacons for the church were drawn (1 Tim. 3:2–7, 12).

It is not surprising that the church itself should be thought of as the household of God (Eph. 2:19, where the figure is combined with that of the sacred republic) or the household of faith (Gal. 6:10). The description of believers as adopted sons (Rom. 8:15–17) or as servants and stewards (1 Pet. 4:10) implies this figure. Paul sees himself as a servant of Jesus Christ, a steward set to perform a particular ministry (Rom. 1:1; 1 Cor. 4:1; 9:17, RV). In a related picture the writer to the Hebrews depicts Moses as a faithful head steward in God's household, foreshadowing Christ as the son and heir (*cf.* Gal. 3:23–4:7) of the household of God; 'and we are his house', says the writer, 'if we hold fast our confidence and pride in our hope' (Heb. 3:1–6).

BIBLIOGRAPHY. E. A. Judge, *The Social Pattern of Christian Groups in the First Century*, 1960; R. P. Martin, *The Family and the Fellowship*, 1979; P. T. O'Brien, *Colossians, Philemon, WBC*, 1982, pp. 214ff.

D.W.B.R.

FAMINE. The Bible does not always indicate the moral and spiritual significance of the famines it records. Those, for example, of Gn. 12:10; 26:1; Acts 11:28, *etc*., are simply stated as historical facts. But famines, like every other event in nature or history, are elsewhere integrated into the characteristic biblical doctrine of divine providence, *e.g.* Am. 4:6; Rev. 6:8. Canaanite religion deified natural processes, and sought to control them by the practice of sympathetic magic, but Israel possessed a different key to prosperity. Yahweh, as Creator, possessed and controlled the 'forces' of nature, the seasons in their order, and the material foundation of man's life on earth (*e.g.* Ps. 104). The exercise of this power by the holy God directly corresponds to the relationship existing between him and man at any given time. Thus, at the one end of the scale the 'Messianic day', when perfect accord between God and his people exists, is marked by unprecedented fertility of the earth (*e.g.* Is. 4:2; 41:19; Ho. 2:21–22; Am. 9:13). On the other hand, the fruits of nature are withdrawn in times of disobedience, when the relationship of God and man is dislocated. Thus the curse on the soil was one of the foremost and immediate results of the Fall (Gn. 3:17–18), and God used famines throughout history as indications of his displeasure, and as warnings to repent (*e.g.* 1 Ki. 17:1; 18:17–18; Hg. 1:6, 9–11; 2:16–17). This view persists in Revelation (*e.g.* 6:5–8), where famine is a direct visitation on human sin. Obedience and prosperity (Ps. 1:1–3; Pr. 3:7–10; Is. 1:19), disobedience and want (Lv. 26:14–16) are biblical inseparables. This law is given classic expression in Dt. 28, and poetic illustration in Je. 14.

The famine (Gk. *limos*) which severely affected Judaea in the principate of Claudius (*c*. AD 46–47) is attested in other records: thus Josephus tells how Queen Helena of Adiabene bought grain in Egypt and figs in Cyprus for the relief of hard-pressed Judaeans (*Ant.* 20. 51f.). This famine figures in Acts as the occasion for the first instance of interchurch aid: when it was foretold by Agabus in the church of Syrian Antioch, that church collected a sum of money for the relief of the Jerusalem church (Acts 11:27–30).

The proclamation of Rev. 6:6 indicates that food prices would be up to ten times as high as in normal times.

In 2 Cor. 11:27 'hunger' (*limos*) is due to absence of food; 'without food' (*nēsteia*) implies voluntary fasting. J.A.M.

F.F.B.

FAN (AV; RSV 'fork'; Heb. *mizreh*, 'fan'; Heb. *zārâ*, 'to scatter', 'to winnow'; Gk. *ptyon*, 'fan'). A long wooden fork used by threshers to toss grain into the air so that the chaff is blown away (*e.g.* Is. 30:24; Je. 15:7), a method still found in some remote areas of the Middle East. Thus John the Baptist employed an easily understood figure of speech in depicting Christ as the great Winnower who would separate evil from good (Mt. 3:12; Lk. 3:17). (*AGRICULTURE.) J.D.D.

FASTING. Fasting in the Bible generally means going without all food and drink for a period (*e.g.* Est. 4:16), and not merely refraining from certain foods.

I. In the Old Testament

The Heb. words are *ṣûm* (verb) and *ṣôm* (noun). The phrase *'innâ napšô* ('to afflict the soul') also refers to fasting. First, there were certain annual fasts. Thus the Hebrews fasted on the Day of Atonement (Lv. 16:29, 31; 23:27–32; Nu. 29:7). After the Exile, four other annual fasts were observed (Zc. 8:19), all of them, according to the Talmud, marking disasters in Jewish history. Est. 9:31 can be interpreted as implying the establishment of yet another regular fast.

In addition to these there were occasional fasts. These were sometimes individual (*e.g.* 2 Sa. 12:22) and sometimes corporate (*e.g.* Jdg. 20:26; Joel 1:14). Fasting gave expression to grief (1 Sa. 31:13; 2 Sa. 1:12; 3:35; Ne. 1:4; Est. 4:3; Ps. 35:13–14) and penitence (1 Sa. 7:6; 1 Ki. 21:27; Ne. 9:1–2; Dn. 9:3–4; Jon. 3:5–8). It was a way by which men might humble themselves (Ezr. 8:21; Ps. 69:10). Sometimes it may have been thought of as a self- inflicted punishment (*cf.* the phrase 'to afflict the soul'). Fasting was often directed towards securing the guidance and help of God (Ex. 34:28; Dt. 9:9; 2 Sa. 12:16–23; 2 Ch. 20:3–4; Ezr. 8:21–23). Fasting could be vicarious (Ezr. 10:6; Est. 4:15–17). Some came to think that fasting would automatically gain man a hearing from God (Is. 58:3–4). Against this the prophets declared that without right conduct fasting was in vain (Is. 58:5–12; Je. 14:11–12; Zc. 7).

II. In the New Testament

The usual Gk. words are *nēsteuō* (verb), and *nēsteia* and *nēstis* (nouns). In Acts 27:21, 33 the words *asitia* and *asitos* ('without food') are also used.

As far as general Jewish practice is concerned, the Day of Atonement is the only annual fast referred to in the NT (Acts 27:9). Some strict Pharisees fasted every Monday and Thursday (Lk. 18:12). Other devout Jews, like Anna, might fast often (Lk. 2:37).

The only occasion when Jesus is recorded as fasting is at the time of his temptations in the wilderness. Then, however, he was not necessarily fasting from choice. The first temptation implies that there was no food available in the place he had selected for his weeks of preparation for his ministry (Mt. 4:1–4). *Cf.* the 40 days' fasts of Moses (Ex. 34:28) and Elijah (1 Ki. 19:8).

Jesus assumed that his hearers would fast, but taught them when they did so to face Godward, not manward (Mt. 6:16–18). When asked why his disciples did not fast as did those of John the Baptist and of the Pharisees, Jesus did not repudiate fasting, but declared it to be inappropriate for his disciples 'as long as the bridegroom is with them' (Mt. 9:14–17; Mk. 2:18–22; Lk. 5:33–39). Later they would fast like others.

In Acts leaders of the church fast when choosing missionaries (13:2–3) and elders (14:23). Paul twice refers to his fasting (2 Cor. 6:5; 11:27). In the former passage voluntary fasting, by way of self-discipline, appears to be meant (*nēsteia*); the latter passage mentions both involuntary 'hunger' (*limos*) and voluntary going 'without food' (*nēsteia*).

The weight of textual evidence is against the inclusion of references to fasting in Mt. 17:21; Mk. 9:29; Acts 10:30; 1 Cor. 7:5, though the presence of these references in many MSS in itself indicates that there was a growing belief in the value of fasting in the early church. H.A.G.B.

FEAR. The Bible uses numerous words to denote fear. The most common of these (giving the noun forms) are Heb. *yir'â*, 'reverence'; Heb. *paḥaḏ*, 'dread', 'fear'; Gk. *phobos*, 'fear', 'terror'. Theologically, four main categories can be suggested.

a. Holy fear

This comes from the believer's apprehension of the living God. According to Luther, the natural man cannot fear God perfectly; according to Rudolf Otto, he is 'quite unable even to shudder (*grauen*) or feel horror in the real sense of the word'. Holy fear, on the other hand, is God-given, enabling men to reverence God's authority, obey his commandments and hate and shun all form of evil (Je. 32:40; *cf.* Gn. 22:12; Heb. 5:7). It is, moreover, the beginning (or principle) of wisdom (Ps. 111:10); the secret of uprightness (Pr. 8:13); a feature of the people in whom God delights (Ps. 147:11); and the whole duty of man (Ec. 12:13). It is also one of the divine qualifications of the Messiah (Is. 11:2–3).

In the OT, largely because of the law's legal sanctions, true religion is often regarded as synonymous with the fear of God (*cf.* Je. 2:19; Ps. 34:11, Moffatt), and even in NT times the term 'walking in the fear of the Lord' was used in connection with the early Christians. Gentile adherents of the synagogue were called 'God-fearers' (Acts 10:2, *etc.*; *cf.* Phil. 2:12).

In the NT generally, however, emphasis is laid on God as loving and forgiving, the One who through Christ gives to men the spirit of sonship (Rom. 8:15), and enables them boldly to face up to life (2 Tim. 1:6–7) and death (Heb. 2:15) without fear. Nevertheless, a reverent fear remains; for the awesomeness of God has not changed, and there is a day of judgment to be met (2 Cor. 5:10f.). Godly fear stimulates the believer to seek holiness (2 Cor. 7:1), and is reflected in his attitude towards his fellow-Christians (Eph. 5:21).

b. Slavish fear

This is strictly a natural consequence of sin (Gn. 3:10; Pr. 28:1), and can come as a punishment (Dt. 28:28). It was felt by Felix when he heard Paul preach (Acts 24:25); it is felt by Christ-rejecters, for whom remains only 'a fearful expectation of judgment' (Heb. 10:27, RV, 31; *cf.* Rev. 21:8). Though not of itself good, this fear is often used by the Holy Spirit for the conversion of men (Acts 16:29ff., *etc.*).

c. Fear of men

This can be expressed as: (i) a reverential awe and regard of men, as of masters and magistrates (1 Pet. 2:18; Rom. 13:7); (ii) a blind dread of them and what they can do (Nu. 14:9; Is. 8:12; Pr. 29:25); and (iii) in a peculiar sense a Christian concern for them lest they be ruined by sin (1 Cor. 2:3; 2 Cor. 11:3; Col. 2:1). This kind of fear, and also the slavish fear mentioned in (*b*) above, can be cast out by true love to God (1 Jn. 4:18).

d. 'Fear' as the object of fear

Fear is used in another sense, as in Gn. 31:42, 53, where God is called the 'Fear' of *Isaac—*i.e.* the God whom Isaac feared and worshipped. Their 'fear', the thing that terrifies them, comes upon the wicked (Pr. 1:26–27; 10:24; *cf.* Is. 66:4). When the Hebrews entered the promised land God sent his fear before them, destroying and scattering the Canaanites, or so impressing them with his fear as to render them spiritless and unable to withstand the invaders (Ex. 23:27–28). Fear in this sense is found also in Jb. 4:6 (*cf.* 9:34; 13:21): 'Is not your fear of God your confidence, and the integrity of your ways your hope?'

BIBLIOGRAPHY. R. Otto, *The Idea of the Holy*, 1929; J. Murray, *Principles of Conduct*, 1957, pp. 229ff.; J.-J. von Allmen, *Vocabulary of the Bible*, 1958, pp. 113–119; R. H. Pfeiffer, 'The Fear of God', *IEJ* 5, 1955, pp. 43–48 (a valuable survey of the idea of fear in the non-biblical literatures of the ancient Near East); W. Mundle, *NIDNTT* 1, pp. 621–624; H. Balz, G. Wanke, *TDNT* 9, pp. 189–219; W. Foerster, *TDNT* 7, pp. 168–196; R. Bultmann, *TDNT* 2, pp. 751–754.

J.D.D.

FEASTS. Heb. *ḥaḡ*, 'feast' (Lv. 23:6; Dt. 16:16), *mô'ᵃḏê Yahweh*, 'feasts of the Lord' (Lv. 23:2, 4; Nu. 15:3). The terms are expressive of a day or season of religious joy. While some of these feasts coincide with the seasons, it does not follow that they have their origin in the seasonal ritual of the religions of the ancient Near East. These are associated with the gods of the pantheon who banquet together or feast with men. (See C. H. Gordon, *Ugaritic Literature*, 1949, pp. 57–103; T. Gaster, *Thespis*, 1950, pp. 6–108.) Biblical feasts differ in origin, purpose and content. To the Israelite the seasons were the work of the Creator for the benefit of man. They manifested the beneficence of God towards his creatures. By these feasts man not only acknowledged God as his Provider but recorded the Lord's unbounded and free favour to a chosen people whom he delivered, by personal intervention, in this world (Ex. 10:2; 12:8–9, 11, 14; Lv. 23:5; Dt. 16:6, 12). The joy expressed was heartfelt. Religious commitment was not incompatible with pleasure in temporal things conceived as gifts of God (Lv. 23:40; Dt. 16:14). The response of the participant was religiously ethical. Acknowledgment of sin and devotion to the law of God was involved (Ex. 13:9; Zc. 8:9). The sacrifices offered bespoke forgiveness of sin and reconciliation with God (Lv. 17:11; Nu. 28:22; 29:7–11; 2 Ch. 30:22; Ezk. 45:17, 20). To be withheld from the feast was considered a loss and a bar from privilege (Nu. 9:7). Not only did the Israelite appear at the feast as a beneficiary of the divine favour, but he made return to the Lord as he had been blessed (Dt. 16:10). Only in unauthorized feasts did unbelieving Israelites eat, drink and play (Ex. 32:6; 1 Ki. 12:32–33).

The feasts of the OT do not follow the ancient Near Eastern pattern of a period of joy preceded by rites of mortification and purgation (T. Gaster, *op. cit.*, pp. 6, 12). The Bible festival itself contained the element of mourning, for this is involved in sacrifice for sin (Lv. 23:27; Nu. 29:7). There is no sharp line of demarcation between sorrow for sin and the joy of the Lord.

Prophetical displeasure with the feasts as observed by the Jews (Is. 1:13–20) was not because they were in themselves on a lower plane of piety, but because many Israelites had departed from their spiritual purpose. They made the sum of religion consist in external observance, which was never the divine intent for the feasts from the time of their promulgation (Na. 1:15). In the NT this was well understood by our

	Month	Modern equivalent	Feasts
1	Nisan	Mar.–Apr.	14–21 Passover (*pesaḥ*): Feast of Unleavened Bread (*ḥaḡ hammaṣṣôṯ*) ● (Ex. 12:3–20; Lv. 23:6; Dt.16:1–8)
2	Iyyar	Apr.–May	
3	Sivan	May–June	6 Pentecost: Feast of Weeks, Day of Firstfruits, Feast of Harvest (*ḥaḡ šāḇû'ōṯ*) ● (Ex. 23:16; 34:22; Nu.28:26; Lv. 23:16)
4	Tammuz	June–July	17 Fast of Seventeenth of Tammuz □
5	Ab	July–Aug.	9 Fast of Tishah Be-ab □ 15 Fifteenth of Ab (Mishnaic) □
6	Elul	Aug.–Sept.	
7	Tishri	Sept.–Oct.	1 Day of blowing trumpets (Rosh ha-shanah) ● (Nu. 29:1; Lv. 23:24) 3 Fast of Gedaliah □ 10 Day of Atonement (Yom Kippur) ● (Lv. 23:26–31; Ex. 30:10) 15–21 Feast of Tabernacles/Booths (*hag hassukkôt*) ● (Lv. 23:34; Nu. 29:12–38; Ex. 23:16; 34:22; Dt. 16:13) 21 Hoshanah Rabba □ 22 Shemini Azeret □ 23 Simhat Torah □
8	Marchesvan	Oct.–Nov.	
9	Chislev	Nov.–Dec.	25–30 Festival of Lights (*ḥᵃnukkâ*) □
10	Tebeth	Dec.–Jan.	1–2 Festival of Lights □ 10 Fast of Tenth of Tebet □
11	Shebat	Jan.–Feb.	
12	Adar	Feb.–Mar.	13 Fast of Esther ● 14 Purim ● (Est. 9) 15 Shushan Purim □
● Biblical	□ Extra-biblical		

Chart showing the major biblical and extra-biblical Jewish feasts.

Lord and devout believers who diligently and spiritually observed the prescribed feasts of the old economy (Lk. 2:41; 22:8; Jn. 4:45; 5:1; 7:2, 11; 12:20).

The feasts to which reference is made in the OT are as follows:

1. The Feast of Unleavened Bread, Heb. *ḥaḡ hammaṣṣôṯ* (Ex. 23:15), or *Passover, Heb. *pesaḥ* (Lv. 23:5), was established to commemorate the historical deliverance from Egypt (Ex. 10:2; 12:8, 14). It was one of the three annual festivals, and was observed on the fourteenth day of the first month. For 7 days unleavened bread was eaten and no servile work done. The first and the last day being 'holy convocations', sacrifices were offered (Nu. 28:16–25; Dt. 16:1–8).

2. The Feast of Weeks, Heb. *ḥag̱ šāḇû'ōṯ*. It is also called the 'feast of harvest' and 'the day of first fruits' (Ex. 23:16; 34:22; Nu. 28:26). Later it was known as *Pentecost because it was celebrated on the fiftieth day from the sabbath beginning the Passover. It was marked by a holy convocation and the offering of sacrifices.

3. The Feast of *Tabernacles, Heb. *ḥag̱ has-sukkôṯ*, or 'the feast of booths', is also called the 'feast of ingathering', Heb. *ḥag̱ hā'āsîp̄* (Ex. 23:16; 34:22; Lv. 23:34; Dt. 16:13). It lasted 7 days, the first and last days being holy convocations. Fruit was gathered in and people dwelt in booths made of branches and boughs of trees (Lv. 23:39–43; Nu. 29:12–38).

4. The *Sabbath. This is regarded as a feast in Lv. 23:2–3, and called a 'sabbath of rest'. It was marked by a solemn assembly (Is. 1:13), and cessation from all labour. It was also a day of joy (Is. 58:13).

5. The Day of Blowing of Trumpets (Nu. 29:1). In Lv. 23:24 it is called 'a memorial of blowing of trumpets' and 'a sabbath'. Sacrifices were offered and hard labour ceased.

6. The Day of *Atonement (Lv. 23:26–31). It was observed on the tenth day of the seventh month, and was a day of a 'holy convocation' in which souls were afflicted and an atonement made for sin. It was observed but once in the year (Ex. 30:10).

7. The Feast of Purim, described in Est. 9. Established by Mordecai in the time of Ahasuerus to commemorate the remarkable deliverance from the intrigues of Haman, this was a day of feasting and gladness.

The extra-biblical feast of *ḥ^{a}nukkâ* is the celebration of the recovery and cleansing of the Jerusalem Temple by Judas Maccabaeus in 164 BC, after its desecration by Antiochus Epiphanes. It is also called the 'festival of lights'. See Jn. 10:22, where it is called by its Gk. name *enkainia* ('dedication').

BIBLIOGRAPHY. *EJ*, 6, cols. 1189–1196, 1237–1246. D.F.

FELIX. Brother of Claudius' favourite, the *freedman Pallas, through whose influence he was appointed procurator of Judaea. His name is usually taken to have been Antonius Felix (Tacitus, *Hist.* 5. 9), but the MSS of Josephus (*Ant.* 20. 137), as of Suidas, read 'Claudius Felix', though this is usually emended out. It is suggested, however, that reference in a new inscription to a procurator named Claudius must be to Felix, though the cognomen is not preserved (*IEJ* 16, 1966, pp. 259–264). This name would indicate that he was a freedman of Claudius himself, not, like Pallas, of Claudius' mother Antonia.

Tacitus (*Annals* 12. 54) and Josephus (*BJ* 2. 247ff.) also disagree as to the time and circumstances of his arrival in Palestine: Tacitus has him in Samaria before the trial of the procurator Ventidius Cumanus (is the 'many years' of Acts 24:10 some corroboration of this?), but in any case he seems to have held the procuratorship of Judaea from *c.* AD 52. Unrest increased under his rule, for 'with savagery and lust he exercised the powers of a king with the disposition of a slave' (Tacitus, *Hist.* 5. 9), and he was utterly merciless in crushing opposition. In *c.* AD 55 he put down the followers of a Messianic pretender of Egyptian origin, but the man himself escaped (Jos., *BJ* 2. 261ff.). When the riot recorded in Acts 21:27ff. broke out the tribune Claudius Lysias initially mistook Paul for this *Egyptian (Acts 21:38).

After his arrest Paul was conveyed to Caesarea, the Roman capital of Palestine, and was tried before Felix. Two well-attested characteristics of the governor stand out in the subsequent narrative: his disregard for justice and his avarice. He kept Paul in prison for 2 years, hoping he would be paid a fat bribe (Acts 24:26). Disappointed of this hope, he deferred judgment in a case where there was ample evidence of the prisoner's innocence (23:29), and upon his recall he left Paul in prison in order to please the Jews (24:27) or, according to the Western Text, to please his wife *Drusilla.

He was recalled by Nero, probably in AD 59 (*FESTUS), and was saved from proceedings instigated by the Jews only through the influence of Pallas. Of Felix' later history nothing is known.

E.M.B.G.
C.J.H.

FESTUS. Porcius Festus succeeded *Felix as procurator of Judaea. Nothing is known of his life before his appointment, and he died in office after about 2 years. In Josephus (*Ant.* 20. 182ff. and *BJ* 2. 271) he makes an agreeable contrast with his predecessor Felix and his successor Albinus. In Acts (24:27–26:32) he appears in a less favourable light. Though he tried Paul's case with commendable alacrity (25:6) and was convinced of his innocence (26:31), he was prepared to sacrifice Paul to do the Jews a pleasure (25:9). Hence the scandalous suggestion of retrial at Jerusalem. Paul was constrained to appeal to Caesar in the face of an arrangement which would have put him in the power of his enemies. Yet Festus was apparently baffled by Paul, and brought the case before Agrippa II and *Bernice. Paul's innocence emerges clearly in the sequel, but the appeal proceeds to Rome.

Festus was later involved when the Jewish leaders brought to Nero a successful suit against Agrippa's violation of the privacy of the Temple area (Jos., *Ant.* 20. 189ff.).

The date of Festus' arrival in Judaea is a major crux of Pauline chronology. W. M. Ramsay in *Pauline Studies*, pp. 348ff., argued that Eusebius' evidence, when rightly understood, points to AD 59, and some support for this date is found in the sudden change of procuratorial coinage in that year, an event most plausibly attributed to the arrival of a new governor (see H. J. Cadbury, *The Book of Acts in History*, 1955, pp. 9f).

E.M.B.G.
C.J.H.

FIELD. A word used in the EVV for several biblical terms. **1.** Heb. *śāḏeh* (and its poetical form *śāḏay*) is the most common term (*e.g.* Gn. 2:5) with the simple meaning of 'field', 'plain', 'open space'. **2.** *š^{e}ḏēmâ* is used six times only (*e.g.* Dt. 32:32) with much the same meaning. **3.** *bar* (Aram.) is used only in Dn. 2 and 4 with the same meaning. **4.** *ḥûṣ*, 'the outside', is frequently translated 'abroad' (*e.g.* Dt. 23:13), but twice rendered 'field' (Jb. 5:10; Pr. 8:26). **5.** *ḥelqâ*, in fact, means 'portion of ground' but is translated 'field' in 2 Sa. 14:30. **6.** *'ereṣ*, the common word for 'earth, land', is translated 'field' in Ezk. 29:5 (AV). **7.** *yᵉgēḇîm*, a word which occurs once only in the OT, is there translated 'field' (Je. 39:10). **8.** Gk. *agros*, 'field' (*e.g.* Mt. 6:28), in LXX is used mainly to render *śāḏeh*. **9.** Gk. *chōra* usually refers to a large region (Acts 16:6), but is twice rendered 'field' (Jn. 4:35; Jas. 5:4), and its diminutive *chōrion* is translated 'field' in Acts 1:18–19.

T.C.M.

FIG, FIG-TREE (Heb. *tᵉ'ēnâ*, 'fig', 'fig-tree'; Heb. *paḡ*, 'unripe first fig', Ct. 2:13 only; Gk. *olynthoi*, 'unripe fig', unspecified season, Rev. 6:13 only; Gk. *sykon*, 'fig', Gk. *sykē*, 'fig-tree').

Indigenous to Asia Minor and the E Mediterranean region, the fig-tree (*Ficus carica*) makes a tree up to 11 m high, although it often grows as a several-stemmed shrub in rocky places. It was brought into cultivation early in Palestine, like the vine and the olive (*e.g.* Jdg. 9:7ff.), with which it is associated in God's promises of prosperity and in prophetic warnings (Je. 5:17; Ho. 2:12; Joel 1:7, 12; Hab. 3:17). The fig is often planted with the vine (Lk. 13:6), so that its branches and the vine's foliage led to the well-known expression 'to sit down under one's own vine and fig-tree' as a symbol of long-continued well-being and prosperity (1 Ki. 4:25; Mi. 4:4; Zc. 3:10; *cf.* 2 Ki. 18:31; Is. 36:16—though some cases may refer merely to a rural preference for the cultivation of fig-trees overlooking houses).

The failure or destruction of these slow-growing trees, which demand years of patient labour (Pr. 27:18; Lk. 13:7), was a national calamity (Je. 5:17; Hab. 3:17; *cf.* Ps. 105:33), while productiveness was a token of peace and of divine favour. Figs are frequently mentioned in conjunction with the vine, palm and pomegranate (*e.g.* Dt. 8:8), and their absence formed part of the Israelites' complaint in Nu. 20:5.

Adam and Eve are said to have been clothed with girdles made from the fig-tree's broad leaves (Gn. 3:7), and fig leaves are still sewn together in the E and used as wrappings for fresh fruit sent to the markets, where they are a valuable item of commerce. Lumps or cakes of dried figs (from Heb. *dᵉḇēlâ*, 'pressed together') made an excellent food, were easy to carry and constituted an acceptable gift (1 Sa. 25:18; 1 Ch. 12:40). Such a mass of figs was prescribed by Isaiah as a poultice for Hezekiah's boil (2 Ki. 20:7; Is. 38:21).

The complicated biology of the fig has confused authors who are unfamiliar with it. The primitive fig-tree needs to be pollinated by a fig-wasp which creeps into the apical hole of the young fig. The insect has its life history inside inedible male caprifigs which are borne several times a year on the branchlets. The edible female figs are pollinated by these insects, but the commonly cultivated varieties of fig develop the fruit without the need of insect pollinators. Thus the figs mentioned in Je. 8:13; Rev. 6:13 do not belong to a definite crop, while the bad figs could be inedible caprifigs (Je. 24:2b; 29:17). Edible good figs of the first crop are referred to in Ct. 2:13 (Heb. *paḡ*, still unripe, green); Is. 28:4; Je. 24:2a; Ho. 9:10; Mi. 7:1; Na. 3:12. The curious incident when Jesus cursed the fig-tree (Mt. 21:18–22; Mk. 11:12–14) may be explained by the out-of-season leafiness of the tree well before the fruits normally mature.

The fig has inspired numerous similes, metaphors and proverbs (*e.g.* Je. 24:1ff.; Mi. 7:1; Mt. 7:16; Jas. 3:12). In Hellenistic times figs were considered so important to the national economy that the Greeks made special laws to regulate their export.

The sycamore tree (Gk. *sykomōraia*; Lat. *Ficus sycomorus*) associated with Zacchaeus in Lk. 19:4 is often known as the mulberry-fig because it possesses the habit of the mulberry.

BIBLIOGRAPHY. A. Goor and M. Nurock, *Fruits of the Holy Land*, 1968, pp. 54–69; F. N. Hepper, *IEBP*, pp. 110–114.

J.D.D.
F.N.H.

FIRE. A word usually represented in the OT by Heb. *'ēš* and in the NT by Gk. *pyr*, the term generally used in the LXX for *'ēš*. These signify the state of combustion, and the visible aspects of it, such as the flame. The production of fire by artificial means was a skill known to man from Stone Age times, but then and in later times great care was taken to preserve a burning fire to avoid the necessity for rekindling. Abraham apparently carried a piece of burning fire with him when he went to offer Isaac (Gn. 22:6), and Is. 30:14 indicates that this was a usual domestic practice. Probably the commonest methods of kindling a flame in biblical times were by means of the fire-drill, attested in the Egyptian hieroglyphic *d'* (18th Dynasty), and the striking of flint on iron pyrites, a practice attested from Neolithic times and therefore assumed to be in use later. It may be that this latter method is referred to in 2 Macc. 10:3.

Fire was used in the normal course for such purposes as cooking (Ex. 12:8; Jn. 21:9), providing warmth (Is. 44:16; Lk. 22:55) and refining metals (Ex. 32:24; Je. 6:29), but also for destroying such things as idols (Ex. 32:20; Dt. 7:5, 25), Asherim (Dt. 12:3), chariots (Jos. 11:6, 9) and cities (Jos. 6:24; Jdg. 18:27), and the culprits in two cases of sexual breach (Lv. 20:14; 21:9). It also played an important part in the worship of the tabernacle and Temple, where the altars of incense and of burnt offering constantly required it. The fire on the latter having been started by God (Lv. 9:24; 2 Ch. 7:1–3), it was kept burning continuously (Lv. 6:13). This fire was special, and offerings by means of 'strange fire' were not acceptable (Lv. 10:1; Nu. 3:4; 26:61). The heathen practice of making children 'pass through the fire' was occasionally practised by the Israelites (2 Ki. 3:27; 16:3; 17:17, 31; 21:6; 23:10; 2 Ch. 28:3; 33:6), was included in the condemnations of the prophets (Mi. 6:7). This practice does not necessarily denote human *sacrifice so much as a dedication to *Moloch or Milcam. It may also have involved fire incantations similar to those practised in Mesopotamia (*AfO* 23, 1970, pp. 39–45).

Theophanies of God were sometimes accompanied by fire (Ex. 3:2; 13:21–22; 19:18; Dt. 4:11) and the image of fire is used to symbolize God's glory (Ezk. 1:4, 13), protective presence (2 Ki. 6:17), holiness (Dt. 4:24), righteous judgment (Zc. 13:9) and wrath against sin (Is. 66:15–16). It is also used of the Holy Spirit (Mt. 3:11; *cf.* Acts 2:3), of prophetic inspiration (Je. 5:14; 20:9; 23:29) and religious feeling (Ps. 39:3). In other contexts fire is used as a literary symbol of sin (Is. 9:18), lust (Ho. 7:6) and affliction (Ps. 46:12).

BIBLIOGRAPHY. R. J. Forbes, *Studies in Ancient Technology*, 6, 1958, pp. 4ff.; *Le Feu dans le Proche-Orient antique*, 1973.

T.C.M.

FIREPAN (Heb. *maḥtâ*, from *ḥatâ*, 'to snatch up'). A bowl-shaped utensil with a handle used in connection with the tabernacle and Temple services for three different purposes. **1.** In some passages it refers to the *snuffdish* made of gold, which held the pieces of burnt lamp-wick removed by the tongs or *snuffers (Ex. 25:38; 37:23; Nu. 4:9; 1 Ki. 7:50; 2 Ki. 25:15; 2 Ch. 4:22; Je. 52:19, the last four of these references being wrongly translated 'censer' and 'firepan' in AV). **2.** Elsewhere it refers to the bronze *firepan* which was used to carry coals away from the altar of burnt offering (Ex. 27:3; Nu. 4:14, the second of these references being wrongly translated 'censer' in AV). **3.** In other passages it is used of the ***censer**, also made of bronze, in which incense was burnt (Lv. 10:1; 16:12; Nu. 16:6, 17–18, 37–39, 46). J.C.W.

FIRST-BORN.

I. In the Old Testament

The Heb. root *bkr*, found in many Semitic languages, has the general meaning '(to be) early'. *bᵉḵôr*, 'first-born' (fem. *bᵉḵîrâ*), is used of people and animals, cognate terms being employed for firstfruits, and the first-born son's privileges and responsibilities are known as his 'birthright' (*bᵉḵōrāh*). In Gn. 25:23, the eldest son is called *raḇ*, a description occurring elsewhere only in 2nd-millennium cuneiform texts.

The first-born was regarded as 'the beginning of (his) strength' (*rē'šîṯ 'ôn*—Gn. 49:3; Dt. 21:17; *cf.* Ps. 78:51; 105:36) and 'the opener of the womb' (*peṭer reḥem*—Ex. 13:2, 12, 15; Nu. 18:15; *etc.*), emphasizing both paternal and maternal lines. The pre-eminent status of first-born was also accorded to Israel (Ex. 4:22) and the Davidic line (Ps. 89:27).

The eldest son's special position was widely recognized in the ancient Near East, though it was not usually extended to sons of concubines or slave-girls (*cf.* Gn. 21:9–13; Jdg. 11:1–2). The accompanying privileges were highly valued, and in the OT included a larger inheritance, a special paternal blessing, family leadership and an honoured place at mealtimes (Gn. 25:5–6; 27:35–36; 37:21ff.; 42:37; 43:33; Dt. 21:15–17). The double inheritance of Dt. 21:15–17, though apparently unknown to the Patriarchs (Gn. 25:5–6), is mentioned in several Old Babylonian, Middle Assyrian and Nuzi documents, and is alluded to elsewhere in the OT (2 Ki. 2:9; Is. 61:7).

These privileges could normally be forfeited only by committing a serious offence (Gn. 35:22, 49:4; 1 Ch. 5:1–2) or by sale (Gn. 25:29–34), though paternal preference occasionally overruled in the matter of royal succession (1 Ki. 1–2; 2 Ch. 11:22–23; *cf.* 1 Ch. 26:10). There is also a marked interest, especially in Genesis, in the youngest son (Jacob, Ephraim, David; *cf.* Isaac, Joseph), but such cases were certainly contrary to expectation (Gn. 48:17ff.; 1 Sa. 16:6ff.).

Where no sons existed, the eldest daughter took responsibility for her younger sisters (Gn. 19:30ff.). It was an Aramaean custom (Gn. 29:26), and perhaps also an Israelite one (1 Sa. 18:17–27), for the eldest daughter to be married first. A Ugaritic text mentions the transfer of birthright from the eldest to the youngest daughter.

In Israelite ritual, the first-born of man and beast had a special place. The male first-born belonged to Yahweh (Ex. 13:2; 22:29b–30; Nu. 3:13), and this was underlined by Israel's deliverance in the final plague. Children were redeemed in the Exodus generation by the Levites (Nu. 3:40–41), and later, at a month old, by a payment of five shekels (Nu. 18:16; *cf.* 3:42–51). Sacrifice of human first-born is occasionally mentioned, following Canaanite practice (2 Ki. 3:27; Ezk. 20:25–26; Mi. 6:7; *cf.* 1 Ki. 16:34), but this was a misinterpretation of Ex. 22:29. Clean male firstlings were sacrificed (Nu. 18:17–18; Dt. 12:6, 17), while imperfect animals were eaten in the towns (Dt. 15:21–23). Male firstlings of unclean animals were redeemed (Nu. 18:15), though an ass was redeemed with a lamb or had its neck broken (Ex. 13:13; 34:20).

BIBLIOGRAPHY. I. Mendelsohn, *BASOR* 156, 1959, pp. 38–40; R. de Vaux, *Ancient Israel*[2], 1965, pp. 41–42, 442–445, 488–489; *idem, Studies in OT Sacrifice*, 1964, pp. 70–73; J. Henninger, in E. Gräf (ed.), *Festschrift W. Caskel*, 1968, pp. 162–183; M. Tsevat, *TDOT* 2, pp. 121–127. M.J.S.

II. In the New Testament

Jesus was the first-born (*prōtotokos*) of his mother (Mt. 1:25; Lk. 2:7), a phrase which allows, but does not demand, that Mary had other, later children (*cf.* Mk. 6:3; *BRETHREN OF THE LORD). As such, Jesus was taken to the Temple by Mary and Joseph to be offered to God (Lk. 2:22–24); since Luke omits mention of a price being paid to redeem the child, he may have intended the incident to be regarded as the dedication of the first-born to the service of God (*cf.* 1 Sa. 1:11, 22, 28). Jesus is also the first-born of his heavenly Father. He is the first-born of all creation, not in the sense that he himself is a created being, but rather that as God's Son he was his agent in creation and hence has authority over all created things (Col. 1:15–17). Similarly, he is the first-born in the new creation by being raised first from the dead, and is thus Lord over the church (Col. 1:18; Rev. 1:5). He is thus the first-born in a whole family of children of God who are destined to bear his image (Rom. 8:29). There may be an echo of Ps. 89:27 in Heb. 1:6, where God's Son is the object of worship by the angels at his coming into the world (whether the incarnation, resurrection or second advent is meant is debatable). Finally, God's people, both living and dead, can be described as the first-born who are enrolled in heaven, since they share the privileges of the Son (Heb. 12:23).

BIBLIOGRAPHY. O. Eissfeldt, *Erstlinge und Zehnten im Alten Testament*, 1917; W. Michaelis, *TDNT* 6, pp. 871–881; K. H. Bartels, *NIDNTT* 1, pp. 667–670. I.H.M.

FISH, FISHING.

I. Kinds of fish and sources of supply

The general Heb. words for water-creatures are *dāḡ* and *dāḡâ*. According to the Mosaic law (Lv. 11:9–12; Dt. 14:9–10) water-creatures having fins and scales were 'clean', but those without fins and scales (*e.g.* shellfish) were 'unclean'. The creature which swallowed Jonah is called 'a great fish' in Jon. 1:17. Mt. 12:40 carefully adopts the same designation (Gk. *kētos*, 'a large sea-monster', translated and interpreted by AV, RV and RSV as 'whale'). According to Tobit 6:2 a large fish in the Tigris river threatened to swallow Tobias. The fisherman of the parable of the drag-net (Mt. 13:48) discarded some fish because they were too small, inedible or 'unclean'. The fish in whose mouth Peter found the stater (Mt. 17:27) must have had a large mouth, like the fish of the Sea of Galilee called *Chromis simonis* after the apostle. In addition to the common Gk. word for fish, *ichthys* (*e.g.* Mt. 7:10), the NT uses the diminutive *ichthydion*, 'small fish' (Mt. 15:34; Mk. 8:7, both passages which describe the feeding of the four thousand), and *opsarion*, small fish eaten with bread (Jn. 6:11; 21:9). In the Sea of Galilee today at least twenty-four species of fish are found, sometimes in large shoals.

The Bible mentions Egypt as a place where fish are plentiful (Nu. 11:5), and the Sea of Galilee (Lk. 5:6) and Tyre (Ne. 13:16) are also noted as ample sources of supply. Fish cannot live in the salty waters of the Dead Sea, but Ezk. 47:10 foresees that this lake will be stocked with fish as one of the blessings of the kingdom of glory.

II. Fishermen and their methods

The strenuous life of fishermen required a strong physique (Lk. 5:2), and their speech was sometimes rough (Mk. 14:70f.). At least seven of Jesus' disciples were fishermen: Peter, Andrew, probably Philip, who also came from Bethsaida (Aram. for 'house of fishing') on the Sea of Galilee, James, John, Thomas and Nathanael (Mt. 4:18, 21; Jn. 1:44; 21:2). Some of these were partners in fishing and were used to working together (Lk. 5:7, 10).

The Bible mentions fishing by *net, specifically the casting-net (Mt. 4:18) and the large drag-net (Mt. 13:47).

On the Sea of Galilee the fishermen used small boats, which were propelled by oars (Jn. 6:19). The statement that the wind was contrary (Mt. 14:24) may indicate the use of a sail as in the present-day fishing-boats on this lake. (*SHIPS AND BOATS.) Often on the Sea of Galilee fishing was done at night (Lk. 5:5; Jn. 21:3). During the day the fisherman on the shore or wading in the water could throw the casting-net (Mt. 4:18). Larger nets were let down by several men from boats (Lk. 5:4). The fish were either emptied into the boat (Lk. 5:7) or the nets were dragged to the shore (Mt. 13:48; Jn. 21:8). Then the fish were sorted, the saleable ones being put in baskets and the useless ones thrown away (Mt. 13:48). The Bible does not refer to fishing as a recreation.

III. Marketing and preparation

In Jerusalem there was a Fish Gate (perhaps on the N side of the city), through which traders brought their fish to sell to the populace (Zp. 1:10). From Ne. 13:16 we know that Tyrian fish merchants lived in the city after the Exile. In Bible times common methods of preparing fish for eating were roasting (Jn. 21:9; Tobit 6:5), and salting and drying (Tobit 6:5, Sinaitic Text). The fish which Tyrians sold in Jerusalem and the small fish which were used in the miraculous feeding of the 5,000 and of the 4,000 (Mt. 14:17; 15:36) were probably prepared in the latter way. (*FOOD.)

IV. Fish worship

Dt. 4:18 forbids making images of fish for worship. The pagan fish-goddess Atargatis was worshipped at Ascalon and among the Nabataeans. The oxyrhynchus was worshipped in a nome in Egypt named after that fish.

V. Figurative and symbolic uses

People suffering misfortune (Ec. 9:12) or captured by enemies (Hab. 1:15) are compared to fish caught in a net. Fishing is used in the OT as a figure of God's judgment on nations or individuals (*e.g.* Je. 16:16; Ezk. 32:3). Jesus called disciples to become fishers of men (Mt. 4:19). The kingdom of heaven is likened to a drag-net (Mt. 13:47).

The fish was one of the earliest symbols of Christian art, because the letters of Gk. *ichthys* were taken as an acronym for *Iēsous Christos Theou Hyios Sōtēr*, 'Jesus Christ, of God the Son, Saviour' (see F. J. Dölger, ΙΧΘΥΣ, 1928).

BIBLIOGRAPHY. G. Dalman, *Arbeit und Sitte*, 6, 1939, pp. 343–370; G. S. Cansdale, *Animals of Bible Lands*, 1970; J. D. M. Derrett, 'Peter's Penny', in *Law in the New Testament*, 1970, pp. 247–265; M. Nun, *The Sea of Galilee and its Fisherman in the New Testament*, 1989. J.T.

FLAGON. Heb. *nēḇel*, Is. 22:24, a large, two-handled jar for storing wine (*GLASS). AV translates Heb. *ᵃšîšâ* as 'flagon', following the interpretation of Qimchi. However, Ho. 3:1 (Heb. *ᵃšîšê ᵃnāḇîm* ... of grapes) and Ct. 2:5 (parallel to 'refresh me with apples', RSV) suggest a derivation from the root *'šš*, 'be firm', 'compress'. LXX preserves the meaning by translating 'cake from a pan' (*laganon apo tēganou*, 2 Sa. 6:19); 'raisin cake' (*pemmata meta staphidōn*, Ho. 3:1); 'sweet cake' (*amoritēn*, 1 Ch. 16:3; *amorais*, Ct. 2:5). Heb. *ᵃšîšâ* denotes, therefore, a cake of compressed, dried grapes, possibly used as an offering in pagan worship (Ho. 3:1). (*VINE.) A.R.M.

FLAX (Heb. *pištâ* in Ex. 9:31 and Is. 42:3; *pišteh* elsewhere in the OT; Gk. *linon* in Mt. 12:20). Used chiefly in making *linen, flax (*Linum usitatissimum*) is the oldest of the textile fibres. The plant grows often to a height of 1 m, and produces beautiful blue flowers. From the shiny seeds comes linseed oil.

Flax was cultivated by the Egyptians before the Exodus (Ex. 9:31) and, before the Conquest, by the Canaanites, who dried the stalks on the housetops (Jos. 2:6). Among God's judgments in Hosea's day was the taking away of the flax (Ho. 2:9).

In the single NT reference (Mt. 12:20), an allusion to flax as being slow-burning, Matthew is quoting from Is. 42:3. J.D.D.

FLESH.

I. In the Old Testament

In the OT the principal word is *bāśār* (found 269 times), though *šᵉ'ēr* (16 times, 4 times translated 'flesh' in RSV) also occurs. *bāśār* denotes the principal constituent of the body, human (Gn. 40:19) or animal (Lv. 6:27). The latter use leads on to the thought of meat as used for food and to that of the flesh of the animal sacrifices, whether eaten or not. From the former usage 'flesh' comes to mean the whole body (Pr. 14:30), and by a natural extension of meaning the whole man, as when the

Psalmist says, 'my body (Heb. flesh) also dwells secure' (Ps. 16:9). This leads to the concept of the union of one person with another. Man and wife are 'one flesh' (Gn. 2:24), and a man can say of his relatives, 'I am your bone and your flesh' (Jdg. 9:2).

Again, the notion of flesh as the whole man gives rise to the expression 'all flesh', which denotes the totality of human existence, sometimes also including the animal creation. There is sometimes the sense that flesh is weak: 'in God I trust without a fear. What can flesh do to me?' (Ps. 56:4). This is not the thought of moral weakness (perhaps the nearest we get to this is Ps. 78:39). It is the physical frailty of man that is meant.

II. In the New Testament

In the NT the Gk. word for 'flesh' is *sarx*. This term reproduces most of the OT meaning of *bāśār*. It denotes the fleshy part of the body, as in references to eating flesh (Rev. 19:18, *etc.*), or to the whole body (Gal. 4:13f.). It may mean the whole man, 'our bodies (lit. our flesh) had no rest . . . fighting without and fear within' (2 Cor. 7:5), or 'within me, that is, in my flesh' (Rom. 7:18). As in the OT, man and wife are 'one flesh' (Mt. 19:5f.), and there are passages referring to 'all flesh' (Jn. 17:2). The weakness of the flesh is spoken of in connection with the apostles' failure to watch in Gethsemane (Mt. 26:41; Mk. 14:38).

But the NT has also some distinctive meanings. Akin to the 'my bone and my flesh' passages of the OT (though not quite the same) are those which refer to physical descent and the like. Thus Christ 'was descended from David according to the flesh' (Rom. 1:3). Paul can speak of 'Israel according to the flesh' (1 Cor. 10:18; see RSVmg.), and the Israelites as his 'kinsmen by race' (Gk. 'according to the flesh') (Rom. 9:3).

'The flesh' may stand for the whole of this physical existence, and there are references to being 'in the flesh' (Col. 2:1; RSV omits). There is no blame attached to this, and, indeed, Christ is said more than once to have been 'in the flesh' (Eph. 2:15; 1 Pet. 3:18; 1 Jn. 4:2, *etc.*). To be 'in the flesh' is not incompatible with being 'in the Lord' (Phm. 16). The flesh may be defiled (Jude 8) or purified (Heb. 9:13). The life that Paul the Christian now lived was 'in the flesh' (Gal. 2:20).

But, by definition, the flesh is the earthly part of man. It has its 'lusts' and its 'desires' (Eph. 2:3). If men concentrate on these they may be said to 'set their minds on the things of the flesh' (Rom. 8:5). And to set the mind on the flesh 'is death' (Rom. 8:6). This is explained as 'enmity against God' (Rom. 8:7). The man whose horizon is limited by the flesh is by that very fact opposed to God. He lives 'according to the flesh' (Rom. 8:13), that flesh that 'lusteth against the Spirit' (Gal. 5:17, AV; RSV has 'the desires of the flesh are against the Spirit' but AV is more literal). For a dreadful list of 'the works of the flesh', see Gal. 5:19–21. The flesh in this sense denotes the whole personality of man as organized in the wrong direction, as directed to earthly pursuits rather than the service of God.

BIBLIOGRAPHY. K. Grayston in *TWBR*; D. E. H. Whiteley, *The Theology of St. Paul*, 1964; J. A. T. Robinson, *The Body*, 1952; E. Schweizer, F. Baumgärtel and R. Meyer in *TDNT* 7, pp. 98–151; H. Seebass, A. C. Thiselton, in *NIDNTT* 1, pp. 671–682. L.M.

FLESH-HOOK (AV; RSV 'fork'). A bronze implement associated like others with the altar of burnt offering at the tabernacle (Ex. 27:3; 38:3; Nu. 4:14) and Solomon's Temple (1 Ch. 28:17; 2 Ch. 4:16). Seen in use at Shiloh (1 Sa. 2:13–14) as a three-pronged fork. K.A.K.

FLESHPOTS (Heb. *sîr*, probably a foreign loanword; *cf.* Arab. *sîr*, 'a large waterjar', and later Gk. *siras*). A large household utensil usually made of metal for placing over a fire (Ex.16:3; Ec. 7:6, 'pot'; 2 Ki. 4:38, 'great pot'). It is used symbolically of Jerusalem (Ezk. 11:3, 'cauldron'), in similes for avarice (Mi. 3:3), and figuratively for speedy vengeance (Ps. 58:9). Such pots were in use in the sanctuary (Ex. 27:3; 2 Ki. 25:14, *etc.*) and were probably deep bronze cauldrons (so Je. 1:13, RV). They were also used as *washbasins (Ps. 108:9). Their shape was that adopted for the excavation of cisterns (2 Sa. 3:26). (*POTTER, *VESSELS.) J.D.D.

FLOOD. A deluge of water sent by God in the time of Noah to destroy all but a selected few from the earth (Gn. 6–8). The word used in the OT to describe this phenomenon is *mabbûl*, probably derived from *ybl*, 'to bring', the counterpart of Akkadian *wâbālum*, 'to bring', which has the meaning, among others, 'to sweep away' (of water, wind, *etc.*) and from which are derived *biblum*, 'devastating flood', and *bubbulum*, 'flood'. A different word, *abūbum*, is used in the Akkadian flood stories. In the OT, *mabbûl* is otherwise found only in Ps. 29:10, also meaning 'flood'. In the LXX, *mabbûl* is translated by *kataklysmos*, and this is the word used in NT (Mt. 24:38–39; Lk. 17:27; 2 Pet. 2:5) to describe the same event.

In the EVV various other terms are translated by the word 'flood', most of them referring to rivers, either in normal flow or in spate, which was one of the meanings of 'flood' in AV English. Thus in OT *nāhār* (*e.g.* Jos. 24:2), *yᵉ'ōr* (*e.g.* Je. 46:7; the form *'ōr* occurs in Am. 8:8), *naḥal* (*e.g.* 2 Sa. 22:5), and *šibbōleṯ* (Ps. 69:2, 15; Jdg. 12:6), and in NT *potamos* (*e.g.* Mt. 7:25), all bear roughly this meaning. Other words translated 'flood' are *šeṭep̄*, 'an overflowing' (*e.g.* Ps. 32:6), and the verb *nāzal*, 'to flow', in its participial form 'flower' (*e.g.* Ex. 15:8) in OT, and *plēmmyra*, 'high water' (Lk. 6:48), in NT.

a. The reason for the Flood

When God saw that man was constantly planning and doing evil (Gn. 6:5), he resolved to bring a just destruction upon him (6:1–7). But *Noah was a righteous man, so he and his immediate family were to be spared to make a new start.

b. The preparation

Gn. 6:3 and 1 Pet. 3:20 indicate that through the longsuffering of God there would be 120 years' respite before the coming of the Flood. In this period God commanded Noah to build an *ark and gave him careful instructions for it. He also announced that he would make a covenant with Noah (6:18; see *g*, below).

c. The occupants of the ark

Eight people, Noah, his three sons, Shem, Ham and Japeth, and their four wives were preserved in the ark (Gn. 6.18; 7:7, 13; 2 Pet. 2:5). There were also two members, a male and a female, of each division (after their kind, *mîn*, not necessarily 'species'; *CREATION, II.*d*) of the animal kingdom, including the birds, on board (6:19–20; 7:8–9, 14–15) and in addition to these there were twelve extra creatures, six male and six female, of each clean species, presumably for food and sacrifice (7:2–3; some commentators interpret the numbers as seven, rather than fourteen altogether of each). Vegetable food for all these occupants was also stowed aboard. No mention is made of sea creatures, but these may have been included in 'every living thing of all flesh' (6:19), and could have been accommodated outside the ark.

d. The Flood

When Noah and his companions had entered the ark God secured it behind him (7:16) and loosed the waters. These came in the form of rain (7:4, 12), and of such force that the Bible says 'the windows of heaven were opened' (7:11), a very telling metaphor. The level of the waters was also raised from below, 'all the fountains of the great deep (*t*ᵉ*hôm*) were broken up' (7:11), but this may be a metaphorical statement, as is suggested by the use of the word *t*ᵉ*hôm*, which is usually found in poetic passages, so it is inappropriate to seek references to geological phenomena in it.

e. The chronology of the Flood

Noah entered the ark on the 17th day of the 2nd month of his 600th year (7:11), and the earth was dry on the 27th day of the 2nd month of his 601st year, so, counting 30 days to a month, the Flood lasted 371 days. The rain fell for 40 days (7:12) and the waters continued to rise for another 110 (7:24) = 150; the waters then fell for 74 days (8:5) = 224; 40 days later the raven was sent out (8:6–7) = 264; 7 days later Noah sent out the dove (8:8, with implication of 'other 7 days' in 8:10) = 271; he sent it out again 7 days later (8:10) = 278; and for the third time 7 days later (8:12) = 285; Noah removed the covering of the ark 29 days later (8:13 with 7:11) = 314; and the earth was finally dry 57 days later (8:14) = 371 days altogether.

f. The extent of the Flood

That everything (6:17), including man (6:7; 7:21) and beast (6:7, 13, 17; 7:21–22), was to be blotted out by the Flood is clearly stated, but it can be argued that these categories are qualified by the statements of locality: upon the earth (*'ereṣ*; 6:17; 7:17, 23); under heaven (*šāmayim*; 6:17; 7:19); and upon the ground (*'ᵃdāmâ*; 7:4, 23). *'ereṣ* can mean 'land' (*e.g.* Gn. 10:10), *šāmayim* can mean 'sky', or the visible part of heaven within the horizon (*e.g.* 1

BC	Kish	Ur	Shuruppak (Farah)
2600	*c.***2600** Most violent of the Kish floods observable in the city streets (Early Dynastic III)	*c.***2600** Royal Cemetery	*c.***2600** Fara Tablets
	*c.***2700** Kish Palace built	*c.***2700** Traces of flood levels preserved in Pit F, Stratum B (Early Dynastic III)	
2800			
	*c.***2900** First and second floods in city streets (End of Early Dynastic I, beginning of Early Dynastic II)		*c.***2850** Stratum containing traces of a flood, between Jamdat Nasr and Early Dynastic strata
3000			
3200			
3400			
		*c.***3500** Flood stratum (between 3.72 and 0.72 m. thick) in several places e.g. beneath the Royal Cemetery (End of ''Ubaid Period')	
3600			

Archaeological indications of major floods in various Mesopotamian cities in the 4th–3rd millennia BC.

Ki. 18:45), and the extent of *ʾᵃḏāmâ* would be determined by these other two words; thus it is possible that a flood of unexampled severity might meet these conditions without covering the entire surface of the globe. The argument that such a flood would make the preservation of animals unnecessary might be countered with the suggestion that if a whole environmental zone with its own individual fauna were involved, such a measure would be necessary. The statement that all the high mountains (*harê*) under the whole heaven were covered (7:19–20) and that near the end of the Flood they began to be seen (8:5) is interpreted in this scheme as a phenomenon due to the cloud and mist that must have accompanied the cataclysm. This interpretation favours a limited Flood, but the text is also capable of bearing the interpretation of a universal Flood, and dogmatism is not reasonable, either way. The theological teaching of the Bible has traditionally been interpreted in the sense that all men except Noah and his family were destroyed.

g. The end of the Flood

God remembered Noah in the ark, and caused the waters steadily to decrease until the ark came to rest on the mountains of Urarṭu (*ARARAT). The *MT* here, *hārê ʾarārāṭ*, consonantal *hry'rrṭ*, is unequivocally in the plural (*-êl-y*) and refers, therefore, to the mountains of Urartu (*ARARAT), a retrospective use of the name, but referring to the whole mountainous area of modern Armenia and not specifically to Mount Ararat. To find out whether it was safe to disembark Noah sent out a raven first, which was perhaps able to feed on carrion, and perch on the roof of the ark (8:7), and then a dove, which on the second attempt brought back an olive leaf, indicating perhaps that the waters had fallen enough for the foothills, where the olive trees grow, to be dry, and therefore sufficient food to be now available for the animals (8:8–11). The third time he sent out the dove it did not return (8:12), so he deemed it time to leave the ark, and this he was commanded by God to do. Noah then made burnt offerings of every clean beast and bird (see *c*, above), and God swore not to bring another flood (8:21–22; Is. 54:9), blessed Noah and his sons (9:1), and confirmed it in a covenant (9:11), whose sign was a bow in the clouds (9:13–17).

h. Cuneiform parallels

Stories of a flood have been found among the cuneiform documents excavated in the Near East. A Sumerian tablet from Nippur in S Babylonia relates how king Ziusudra was warned that the gods had decreed a deluge to destroy mankind and told to build a great boat in which to escape. This tablet was written *c.* 1600 BC, but the story had probably been known in Mesopotamia for many centuries before this. The fact of a devastating flood is a part of Sumerian historical and literary tradition. An Akkadian story is contained in incomplete copies of the *Atrahasis Epic* made *c.* 1630 BC and circulated widely during later centuries (it was known at *Ugarit). This describes a flood sent by the gods to destroy man after earlier attempts to control him had failed. The pious Atrahasis is warned by the creator-god Enki (or Ea) to build a boat and escape with his family, treasure and animals. Then the flood comes, lasting for 7 days, and, after a missing passage, Atrahasis offers a sacrifice to the gods who gather like flies around it. They regret their act, and reinstitute society with the rule of individual guilt and punishment. The famous Babylonian *Story of the Flood*, which forms part of Tablet XI of the longer *Epic of Gilgamesh* (*BABYLONIA), derives largely from this work. It was a copy of this, which had been excavated from Nineveh some 20 years before, that was identified in the BM in 1872 by George Smith. In this version the hero, named Uta-napishtim (once Atrahasis, line 187) describes to Gilgamesh how he was given immortality after surviving the Flood. He tells the same story as the *Atrahasis Epic* with some details not preserved in that account. Notable among them is the boat's coming to rest on Mt Niṣir (in NW Persia) and the despatch in succession of a dove, a swallow and a raven, the occupants of the boat disembarking when the raven did not return. These cuneiform accounts show similarities with Gn. 6–9, a fact which is possibly to be explained by common reference to an actual historical event. The many crude elements in the cuneiform versions suggest that these are the less reliable of the two accounts.

i. Sources

Many scholars consider that the narrative of the Flood in Gn. 6–9 is composed of two sources, J (Yahwist) and P (Priestly), woven together by a late editor, working after the return from the Exile. According to this theory, oral traditions from early times were brought together, and were committed to writing in the 'document' called J over a period of centuries, beginning in the time of the early monarchy. The other source (P) was the result of centuries of the traditions of the priests from the time of David, which were written down in the period from perhaps 500 BC to the time of Ezra, drawing, in the case of such sections as that dealing with the Flood, upon the Babylonian traditions as learnt during the Exile. Evidence for the two sources is found in such criteria as the use of the two divine names, *YHWH* in J and *ʾᵉlōhîm* in P, and in such observations as that Noah is bidden to take seven (or fourteen) of every clean creature and two of every unclean creature into the ark (Gn. 7:2–3 = J), and that he is bidden to take one pair of every species (Gn. 6:19 = P; see *c*, above).

These matters are susceptible of other explanations, however (see Bibliography), and the unity of the Flood account is suggested by the consistent statements as to the cause of the Flood (Gn. 6:5–7, J, 11–13, P), the purpose of it (Gn. 6:7, J, 13, 17, P; 7:4, J, 21, P, 22–23, J; 8:21, J), and the saving of a representative remnant (Gn. 6:8, J, 18–20, P; 7:1–3, 7–9, J, 13–16a, P, 16b, J; 8:16–19, P).

j. Other Flood stories

A large number of Flood stories, principally from Europe, Asia and America have been recorded.

k. Archaeology and the Flood

Excavations at Ur, Kish, and Farah in Mesopotamia have uncovered evidence of serious floods. The excavators of the first two sites, Sir Leonard Woolley and S. H. Langdon, believed these remains were connected with the biblical Flood. This is unlikely, however, since the flood levels at the three sites do not all date from the same period, and in each case they are most readily explained as due to a river inundation of unusual severity. Moreover, the earliest, that at Ur, is unlikely to have taken place much before 4000 BC, a date which comes well on in the continuous sequence of prehistoric cultures in the Near East, and one at which there is no sign of a break in other areas. If a serious local flood in the Mesopotamian plain is considered to be all that is implied by the biblical account, one or other of the flood deposits at these sites may be thought to be evidence of it, but if, as seems probable, a far more serious event is recorded in Genesis, the evidence from Mesopotamia must be considered irrelevant.

l. Geology and the Flood

No certain geological evidence of the biblical Flood is known. Many phenomena have been noted, however, which in the past, and particularly the 19th century, were cited as evidence of a serious flood. The majority of these are today most plausibly explained as vestiges of the glacial action of the Quaternary Ice Age, or as the result of much earlier geological occurrences. Associated with the ice age, however, were certain changes, such as varying sea-levels through locking up and release of water in the glaciers, and depression and rising of land masses in concord with the increase and decrease in the weight of ice on them, which might well have produced effects in keeping with the biblical account. The effective end of the last glaciation may be dated around 10,000 BC, so it may be that Noah and his contemporaries are to be given an antiquity of this magnitude (*GENEALOGY).

No certain evidence is, however, available, and any scheme to place the events described in Genesis in their actual historical setting can be no more than tentative.

BIBLIOGRAPHY. *General:* A. Parrot, *The Flood and Noah's Ark*, 1955; A. Heidel, *The Gilgamesh Epic and Old Testament Parallels*², 1949, ch. IV. *Section h*: W. G. Lambert and A. R. Millard, *Atraḫasīs. The Babylonian Story of the Flood*, 1969; J. H. Tigay, *The Evolution of the Gilgamesh Epic*, 1982, pp. 214–240; *ANET*, pp. 72–99, 104–106; *DOTT*, pp. 17–26. *Section i:* O. T. Allis, *The Five Books of Moses*, 1943, pp. 95–99; G. Ch. Aalders, *A Short Introduction to the Pentateuch*, 1949, pp. 45–47. *Section j*: J. G. Frazer, *Folk-lore in the Old Testament*, 1919, pp. 146–332 (pp. 107–125 for Mesopotamian versions in Gk. and Akkadian. *Section k*: M. E. L. Mallowan, *Iraq* 26, 1964, pp. 62–82; R. L. Raikes, *Iraq* 28, 1966, pp. 52–63. *Section l*: J. K. Charlesworth, *The Quaternary Era* 2, 1957, pp. 614–619.

T.C.M.

FOLLY. While folly in the OT is sometimes plain silliness (*e.g.* Pr. 10:14; 14:15; 18:13), it is usually culpable: a disdain for God's truth and discipline (Pr. 1:7). Hence even the 'simple' or gullible man (*peṯî*) is not merely 'without sense' (Pr. 7:7ff.) but fatally wayward (Pr. 1:32). He must make a moral and spiritual choice, not only a mental effort (Pr. 9:1–6, 13–18; Ps. 19:7). Likewise the 'fool' (known by various, virtually interchangeable terms, chiefly *kᵉsîl*, *'ᵉwîl*, *sāḵāl*) is typically one who, like Saul, has 'played the fool' (1 Sa. 26:21) and closed his mind to God (*e.g.* Ps. 94:8ff.; Pr. 27:22; Je. 5:21). The most hardened folly is that of the 'scoffer' (*lēṣ*, *e.g.* Pr. 1:22; 14:6; 24:9) and of the aggressive unbeliever called the *nāḇāl* (1 Sa. 25:25; Ps. 14:1; Is. 32:5f.).

Christ's warning against branding anybody 'fool' (*mōros*, Mt. 5:22) presupposes these spiritual and moral connotations (see Arndt for other explanations). In 1 Cor. 1:25, 27 Paul takes up the term (*mōros*, 'foolishness') used by unbelievers in their faulty evaluation of God's purposes. A man's folly may sometimes lie in his being unable to perceive the issues (*e.g.* Lk. 11:40; 1 Cor. 15:36, *aphrōn*), but more likely in the fact that he has made an unworthy choice (*e.g.* Lk. 12:20, *aphrōn*; Rom. 1:21, *asynetos*; Gal. 3:1, 3, *anoētos*; Mt. 7:26, *mōros*).

D.A.H.
F.D.K.

FOOD. Within this general term are included all the vegetable and animal products used by man to maintain the physical life of his body.

I. In the Old Testament

a. Earliest periods

From the beginning (Gn. 1:29–30; 2:16) all seed-bearing plants (mainly grains and vegetables, presumably) and fruit-bearing trees served as food for man, and natural greenstuffs as food for animals. The Fall brought with it the necessity for hard toil in food gathering and production (Gn. 3:18, 23; 4:2–3). Food in the ark was evidently representative of that in common use at the time, but no details of it are given (Gn. 6:21). After the Flood, God promised that seedtime and harvest should not cease while the earth endured, and all living things (besides vegetation) might be used for food, but not their blood (Gn. 8:22–9:4). At the time of Noah's resettlement of the earth after the Flood, grape-growing (and, in consequence, drunkenness) first appears (Gn. 9:20–21).

b. The patriarchal age

In Egypt, Palestine and Mesopotamia in the early 2nd millennium BC, grain and various breads were a staple diet, along with milk, butter, cheeses, water, wine and beer. Doubtless the semi-nomadic Patriarchs lived mainly on the milk-products of their cattle and flocks, but also had bread (see the supply given to Hagar, Gn. 21:14) and sometimes cultivated grain seasonally as did Isaac (Gn. 26:12) and presumably Jacob (*cf.* Gn. 37:7), since he needed to buy Egyptian grain in time of famine (Gn. 42:2, 25f.; 43:2; 44:1–2). Lentil soup (a red soup) was probably a common dish in the days when Esau traded his birthright for a meal of it (Gn. 25:29–34), as it certainly was later on (*e.g.* 2 Sa. 17:28). Honoured guests were treated to the fatted calf accompanied by curds and milk (Gn. 18:6–8). With Abraham's action we may compare the references in the N Canaanite texts from Ugarit which mention slaughter and preparation of 'a lamb from the flock' or 'the sleekest of . . . fatlings' (*ANET*, pp. 146, 149, 151). Although meat was not an everyday dish, desert-game was popular in patriarchal Syria–Palestine. Isaac liked his tasty meat from the hunt (Gn. 27:3–4), just as did the Egyp. Sinuhe in Palestine a little earlier (*ANET*, p. 20). Presents to dignitaries might include nuts and honey as delicacies (Gn. 43:11). The tablets from the 18th-century BC palace at Mari indicate that large amounts of honey were provided at banquets for visiting royalty, and during the same period King Ishme-Dagan of Assyria sent pistachio-nuts to his brother ruling at Mari. In Egypt, too, honey was first and foremost the prerogative of royalty and high society, but was also occasionally enjoyed by their inferiors. Finally, the common meal was a recognized token of amity between the two contracting parties of an agreement, *e.g.* Isaac and the Philistines in Gn. 26:30, and Jacob and Laban in Gn. 31:54. No details are given of the meal to which Joseph treated his brothers in Egypt (Gn. 43:31–34).

c. Israel in Egypt

In Egypt, despite their hard life, the captive Israelites had had a variety of food that they remembered with nostalgia in the wilderness journeyings: fish in plenty, cucumbers, melons, leeks, onions, garlic (Nu. 11:5). This list corresponds quite closely with known ancient Egyp. foods, not least in the E Delta (Goshen area) in the 13th century BC. Thus, in praising the region of Ra'amses, a scribe extols its wealth of foods: onions and leeks, seven kinds of fish in its waters, and various fruits and vegetables (*ANET*, p. 471; better, R. A. Caminos, *Late-Egyptian Miscellanies*, 1954, p. 74).

d. Food in Israel

(i) *Vegetable foods.* Grain, wine and olive-oil were the three staple commodities (Dt. 7:13; Ne. 5:11; Ho. 2:8). The grain was mainly barley, wheat and sometimes spelt, an inferior wheat; see Ex. 9:32 (Egypt); Dt. 8:8; and Is. 28:25 (note order of grains). For preparation and baking of bread, see *BREAD; this basic food was the most appropriate word-picture for Christ himself, the Bread of Life (*cf.* Jn. 6:33, 35).

The *vine was the second great provider; not only of fresh grapes as a fruit (Nu. 6:3; Dt. 23:24) but also of dried grapes as raisins (1 Sa. 25:18; 30:12); of the sweet grape-juice, *'asîs* (Is. 49:26; Am. 9:13; Joel 1:5; 3:18, AV, 'sweet wine', 'new wine'); of the half-fermented must or new wine (Jdg. 9:13; Ho. 4:11; Pr. 3:10; *etc.*); and of the fully fermented wine (*yayin*). These red juices of the grape were often called 'the blood of the grape' (Gn. 49:11; Dt. 32:14). *Wine in its various forms was the general drink in ancient Palestine. Various wines in ancient Egypt, Palestine (*cf.* that of Helbon, in Ezk. 27:18 and Assyr. texts) and Asia Minor were celebrated in antiquity. Vinegar (wine gone acid), diluted with water, helped to refresh field-workers (Ru. 2:14).

Besides being a general word for fermented drinks, *šēḵār*, 'strong drink', appears to have been applied specifically to beverages brewed from grain (*i.e.* beer; Herodotus, 2. 77) or dates (*ibid.*, 1. 193) or perhaps even honey. Beer was the more popular drink in Mesopotamia, but wine in Palestine; both were common in Egypt, where date-wine and other drinks are mentioned. For spiced wine, see (iv) *Seasoning*, below.

The third basic commodity, olive-oil, was used both as food and for cooking-fat. With flour, *oil went into breads and cakes, or these could be cooked in oil (Ex. 29:2); its use was universal, *cf.* the widow of Zarephath (1 Ki. 17.12).

For vegetables, see sections *b* and *c*, above, *Patriarchal age* (lentils) and *Israel in Egypt* (Nu. 11:5); beans, *pôl*, were also used (2 Sa. 17:28; Ezk. 4:9). The word occurs also in Egypt from the 13th century BC. Besides the grapes and olives already mentioned, fruits included *figs proper, sometimes pressed into fig-cakes (*cf.* Is. 38:21 for a medicinal use; also used medically at Ugarit, for horses), and also sycomore-figs, as in Egypt, that had to be notched to swell to edible size (which was Amos's occupation; Am. 7:14). Pomegranates were eaten and their juice drunk (Ct. 8:2). The various nuts available included almonds (Je. 1:11) and pistachio-nuts (see under *Patriarchal age* above). In Pr. 25:11; Ct. 2:3, 5; 7:8; 8:5; Joel 1:12, the term *tappûaḥ* probably means 'apple', although this interpretation is often questioned. Outside of Egypt and Palestine, Bab. texts indicate a long knowledge of the apple (*ḫašḫûru*) in Mesopotamia, as well as in SE Asia Minor (Purušḫanda, near modern Topada). (See also *TREES.)

(ii) *Animal products.* These include honey, fats and meat. The honey of wild bees found in rocks, trees, *etc.*, was widely used (Dt. 32:13; Jdg. 14:8; 1 Sa. 14:25; 2 Sa. 17:29). The OT writers do not say whether the Hebrews (like the Egyptians) practised bee-keeping. *Honey was a delicacy much enjoyed (Ps. 19:10; Pr. 24:13). Palestine was indeed a land of 'milk and honey' (Ex. 3:8)—in the 15th century BC the Egyptian pharaoh Tuthmosis III brought back hundreds of jars of honey from Syria–Palestine as tribute (7th and 14th campaigns). See the ecstatic description of Palestine's wealth of grain, wine, oil, honey, fruits and cattle by Sinuhe (*ANET*, pp. 19–20).

Milk was another staple item of diet, along with its products butter and cheese. For milk, *cf.* Pr. 27:27; Is. 7:22; Ezk. 25:4; for butter, Pr. 30:33; and for cheese, see Jb. 10:10; 1 Sa. 17:18; 2 Sa. 17:29 (as a gift). Milk was often offered to the unexpected visitor or guest, as it was to Sisera in Jdg. 4:19; 5:25, and as it had been centuries earlier to the Egyptian fugitive Sinuhe (*ANET*, p. 19).

Meat was eaten only occasionally, except perhaps for the rich, who may have had it regularly. As with Abraham, guests were entertained to calf, kid or lamb (*cf.* Jdg. 6:19ff.; 2 Sa. 12:4), and these were acceptable gifts alive or already dressed (1 Sa. 16:20; 25:18). The fatted ox in the stall sometimes provided a princely repast (Pr. 15:17), just as in Egypt (picture in N. M. Davies, *Egyptian Paintings*, 1955, plate 4) or in Mesopotamia—witness the official, charged with banqueting arrangements for visiting royalty, who reports on a fatted ox so heavy with flesh that 'when he stands up, the blood rushes to his feet and he cannot stand . . .' Eli's renegade sons preferred roast to boiled meat (1 Sa. 2:13–15), and meat boiled in a pot of water provided Ezekiel with a text (24:3–5). But a kid was not to be boiled in its mother's milk (Ex. 23:19), perhaps because this appears to have been associated with Canaanite sacrificial practice, and hence would carry similar implications to the 'food offered to idols' of NT times. Lv. 11:1–23, 29ff. (*cf.* 41ff.) and Dt. 14:3–21 record the law on animals allowed or forbidden as food. In addition to the ox, sheep and goat, it was permissible to eat seven kinds of venison (Dt. 14:5), and all other cloven-hoofed animals that chewed the cud. Those *animals which failed to fulfil both demands were forbidden as food and listed as 'unclean', together with more than a score of different kinds of birds. With regard to fish, *etc.*, only those with both fins and scales might be eaten. A very few specified insects might be consumed (the locust-family). Some of the creatures forbidden were simply unfit for human consumption; others (*e.g.* swine) were unsafe in a hot climate; still others may have been too closely identified with surrounding idolatry. For fish, see section *c*, above, on *Israel in Egypt*, and *FISH, FISHING.

(iii) *Solomon's palace food-supplies.* In 1 Ki. 4:7, 22–23, 27–28, it is recorded that the governors of

ENGLISH	LATIN	SELECTED BIBLICAL REFERENCES	HEBREW ARABIC	EGYPTIAN	SUMERIAN	AKKADIAN
CEREALS						
GRAIN (General)		Gn. 42:2. 25; 43:2; 44:1–2; Dt. 7:13; Ne. 5:11	*zêr'oîm (H)* *kishné (A)*		ŠE ÚŠE. ŠEŠ	*še'u* *sigušu*
EMMER	*Triticum dicoccum*		*kussèmeth (H)*	*bd.t*	ZÍZ.ÀM	*kunašu*
DURUM WHEAT	*Triticum durum*	Ex. 9:32 Dt. 8:8		*hrnt* *bd.t*	ŠE.IR.ZI	*qutru*
BREAD WHEAT	*Triticum vulgare*	1 Cor. 15:37	*ḥiṭṭā (H)*	*sw.t*	ŠE.GIG	*kibtu*
SPELT	*Triticum spelta*	Ex. 9:32; Is. 28:25; Ezk. 4:9				
BARLEY	*Hordeum vulgare*	Ex. 9:31; Dt. 8:8 (Barley loaves, Jdg. 7:13)	*śe'ôra (H)* *shaeir (A)*	*'it* *'nḥ.t*	ŠE.BAR	*uṭṭaṭu*
SIX-ROWED BARLEY	*Hordeum hexastichon*	2 Ki. 4:42 Jn. 6:9, 13		*sm'j* *šr.t*	ŠE.IN.NU.ḪA	*inninu*
MALT					MUNU ŠE	*buglu*
MILLET	*Andropogon Sorghum* *(Paniceum milioceum)*	Ezk. 4:9	*dôḫan (H)* *dúra, duḫn (A)*		ŠE.AR.ZÍB	*duḫnu*
VEGETABLES						
RICE	*Oryza sativa*		*ōrez (H)*		ÚŠE. LI.A	*šam kurangu (?)*
LENTILS	*Lens culinaris* *(Ervum lens)*	Gn. 25:34 2 Sa. 17:28; 23:11	*'ădāšîm (H)* *addes (A)*	*'ršn*	GÚG, KUKKA	
BEANS	*Vicia faba* *Phaseolus maximus* *Phaseolus vulgare*	2 Sa. 17:28 Ezk. 4:9	*pôl (H)* *túl (A)* *lūbā (A)*	*iwrj.t* *pr*	LU.ÚB.ŠAR	*lubbu (luppu)*
CHICK PEAS	*Cicer arietanum*		*hummes (A)*		ZID.MAD.MAL	*upuntu, maṣḫâti*
VETCH	*Vicia nissoliana*		*kursenni (H)*		GÚ.NIG.HAR.RA	*kiššenu (?)*
CRESS CAROB (POD HUSK)	*Lapidium sativum* *Ceratoria siliqua*	Lk. 15:16		*(ḫlin)* *nḏm*	ZAG.ḪI.LI.ŠAR ᵁURU.TÌL.LA	*šam saḫlû* *šam ḫarubu*
LEEK GARLIC	*Allium kurrat* *Allium sativum*	Nu. 11:5 Nu. 11:5	*ḥāṣîr (H)* *shûm (H)* *ṯûm(A)*	*iz kt* *ḥḏt* *ḥḏw*	GA.RAŠ SUM	*karašu* *šūmu*

ENGLISH	LATIN	SELECTED BIBLICAL REFERENCES	HEBREW ARABIC	EGYPTIAN	SUMERIAN	AKKADIAN
VEGETABLES (*continued*)						
ONIONS	*Allium cepa*	Nu. 11:5	*b^{e}ṣālîm* (*H*) *baṣal* (*A*)	*ḥḏw*		^{šam} *andahšum* ^{šam} *amu(š)šu*
CUCUMBER	*Cucumis melo*	Nu. 11:5; Is. 1:8	*qiššu'â* (*H*) *qiṯṯā'* (*A*)	*šspt*	UKÚŠ	*qiššû*
FRUIT						
FIG	*Ficus carica*	Dt. 8:8; Is. 36:16; Je. 5:17; Ho. 2:12; Joel 1:7, 12; Hab. 3:17; Mt. 7:16; Mk. 11:12–14; Lk. 13:6	*tĕ'ēnâ* (*H*)	*dzb*	^{iṣ}MA	*tittu*
DATE	*Phoenix dactylifera*		*dĕbaš* (*H*)	*bnr*	ZÚ.LUM.MA	*suluppu*
APPLE	*Pyrus malus*	Pr. 25:11; Ct. 2:3, 5; 7:8; 8:5; Joel 1:12	*tappûaḥ?* (*H*)	*tpḥ* *ḏpḥ*	^{iṣ}ḪAŠḪUR	*hašhûru* *arsappu*
APRICOT	*Prunus Armeniaca*		*tappûaḥ* (*H*)		^{iṣ}ḪAŠḪUR. KUR.RA	*armânu?*
PEAR	*Pyrus communis*				^{iṣ}ḪAŠḪUR. GIŠ.DA	*kameššarû*
QUINCE	*Cydonia vulgaris*		*tappûaḥ?* (*H*) *safarjal* (*A*)		^{iṣ}ḪAŠḪUR. ^{iṣ}PĚŠ ^{iṣ}ḪAŠḪUR. KUR.RA	*tîtânû* *supurgillu*
MEDLAR	*Mespilus germanica*				ŠENNUR	*šalluru*
PEACH	*Prunus Persica*				^{iṣ}DAR.RU.UG	*darruqu*
POMEGRANATE	*Punica granatum*	Dt. 8:8; Ct. 8:2; Joel 1:12	*rimmôn* (*H*)	*inhmn*	NU.ÚR.MA	*nurmû*
GRAPES	*Vitis vinifera*	Nu. 6:3; Dt. 23:24; Is. 5:2; Mt. 7:16	*eśqōl* (*H*)	*ízzrt*	^{iṣ}KIN.GEŠTIN ^{iṣ}GEŠTIN	*isḫunnatu* *karānu*
MELON	*Citrullus vulgaris*	Nu. 11:5	*'^{a}ḇaṭṭiḥîm* (*H*)	*bddw-ks*		

Some of the principal food plants of the ancient Near East the twelve administrative provinces in Israel had each to supply a month's food in the year for Solomon's court: one day's provision being 30 *kōr* of fine flour, 60 *kōr* of meal, 30 cattle, 100 sheep, venison and fowls, and provender for the royal stables. Similarly, Solomon paid Hiram I of Tyre for his timber and woodcutters with 20,000 *kōr* of wheat per annum, and a corresponding quantity of oil. This palatial catering was typical of ancient Oriental courts, as is shown by Egyptian and Mesopotamian court-accounts. The courts of Nebuchadrezzar II of Babylon and Cyrus of Persia were apparently supplied by district-officials on a monthly basis, similar to the system in operation in Solomon's court; see R. P. Dougherty, *AASOR* 5, 1925, pp. 23–31, 40–46. Presumably Solomon's monthly supplies were levied either from, or in addition to, the local taxes in kind (grain for flour, livestock) paid by the twelve districts.

Not only the system but also the amount and the probable distribution of Solomon's court-provisions will bear some comparison with the consumption at other royal courts. The court-personnel of the ancient Orient may be divided conveniently into three classes: first, the king, the royal family and all the chief ministers of the realm; second, the main body of courtiers and subordinate officials attached to the 'departments' of the chief ministers; and third, the (probably) still greater number of domestic employees of every conceivable kind. The ancient Near Eastern palace was not just a royal residence but also the practical focus of the entire central government of the state. Partial statistics are available for comparison from Egypt and Mesopotamia. In the 18th century BC royal archives from Mari and Chagar Bazar in NW Mesopotamia record the daily food-supply for the king and his chief officials (*i.e.* the first class); the amounts ran into hundreds of litres (*qa*) of grain, bread, pastries, honey and syrups each day, averaging 945 litres daily at Chagar Bazar for the 'royal repast' (J. Bottéro, *Archives Royales de Mari*, 7, 1957, pp. 270–273). *Cf.* the great quantities of barley alone which were consumed in the Mari palace itself (see Birot, *ibid.*, 9, 1960, pp. 264–265). Similar accounts from the Egyptian court of the 13th Dynasty (same period) have also survived. Directly comparable is the vast supply for the court of Sethos I: K. A. Kitchen, *Ramesside Inscriptions*: *Translations* I, 1993, pp. 208ff., *Notes and Comments*, 1993, pp. 163ff. Preparations for a pharaoh's arrival in the late 13th century BC included the furnishing of 9,200 loaves (eight varieties), 20,000 biscuits (two kinds) and vast quantities of other victuals (R. A. Caminos, *Late-Egyptian Miscellanies*, 1954, pp. 198–201). All these figures also apply principally to 'class 1' consumers (and possibly 'class 2' in the last example), but take no account of the numerous domestics ('class 3')—*e.g.* the 400 palace-women at Mari. Ration-tablets from Babylon in the 10th to 35th years (595–570 BC) of Nebuchadrezzar II give detailed accounts of grain and oil for royal captives, including King Jehoiachin of Judah and his sons, as well as numerous artisans from Egypt, Philistia, Phoenicia, Ionia, Lydia, Cilicia, Elam, Media and Persia. (For details, see *ANET*, p. 308; *DOTT*, pp. 84–86; basic source is E. F. Weidner, *Mélanges R. Dussaud*, 2, 1939, pp. 923–935; for useful background, see W. F. Albright, *BA* 5, 1942, pp. 49–55.)

In Solomon's case, if the *kōr* ('measure') be taken as 220 litres (R. B. Y. Scott, *BA* 22, 1959, p. 31; *cf.* *WEIGHTS AND MEASURES), then his 30 plus 60 *kōr* of flour and meal per day would be some 6,600 plus 13,200 litres respectively, totalling 19,800 litres or 594,000 litres per monthly quota. Bearing in mind the comparative figures given above, 600 litres a day would go to Solomon, his family and chief ministers (*cf.* 726 and 945 litres, Egypt and Chagar Bazar, above), *i.e.* 'class 1'; the other 6,000 litres of fine flour would perhaps go to the main body of courtiers and officials ('class 2'), and the 13,200 litres of ordinary meal to the crowd of domestic employees ('class 3'). Evidence from Mari indicates that 1 *iku* of land (3,600 square metres) produced 1 *ugar* of grain (1,200 litres). If Israelite crop-yields were at all similar, and if a litre of grain made about a litre of wholemeal flour, then it is possible to suggest that each month's flour-supply to Solomon's court (594,000 litres) would be roughly equivalent to the grain grown on 495 *iku* or about 424 acres. This represents an area of land about 1·7 sq. km—surely no impossible annual burden on each of Israel's twelve administrative districts. As for Hiram's 20,000 *kōr* of wheat per annum, this amount by the same reckoning would take up the crop-yield of about 305 *iku* or 262 acres for each month, *i.e.* from land about 1·06 sq. km, again a reasonable kind of figure.

(iv) *Seasoning and cooking.* Cooking included the baking of bread and cakes (with or without leaven), making of soups and stews, and the roasting or boiling of meat (see above). *Salt was a prime necessity with a meal (Jb. 6:6). As already mentioned, sharing a meal marked agreement (Gn. 26:30; 31:54), and the phrases 'covenant of salt' (Nu. 18:19), or 'eating someone's salt' (Ezr. 4:14), were idioms of the same kind (*i.e.* indicating agreement or loyalty). *Herbs for seasonings included dill and cummin (Is. 28:25, 27) and coriander (Ex. 16:31; Nu. 11:7). Common use of these in antiquity is exemplified by actual finds of plants and seeds in Egyptian tombs from the 18th Dynasty onwards, and the mention of them in Egyp. and Bab. texts (*cf.* L. Keimer, *Die Gartenpflanzen im Alten Ägypten*, 1, 1924, Nos. 24, 29–30, pp. 37–38, 40–42 and refs., 147–149).

In Mycenaean Greek tablets from Crete and Greece, written in the 'Linear B' script and dated to the 15th–13th centuries BC, occur the spices cummin (*ku-mi-no*), coriander (*ko-ri-a-da-na/do-no*) and sesame (*sa-sa-ma*) among others. These names (and probably some of the spices too) were imports from the Near East, *via* Syria–Palestine and Cyprus, and so witness to the antiquity of the use of both spices and names in the Bible lands. Details are given in M. Ventris and J. Chadwick, *Documents in Mycenaean Greek*, 1956, pp. 131, 135–136, 221–231; and Chadwick, *The Decipherment of Linear B*, 1958, pp. 64, 120, contains a brief treatment. Sesame is attested at this same period in Syria itself, at Ugarit (Gordon, *Ugaritic Textbook*, 3, 1965, p. 495, No. 2496, as *ššmn*).

Honey could be used in baking (*cf.* Ex. 16:31), but not in sacrifice to God (Lv. 2:11), although the Egyptians offered it to their gods. Sweetened and spiced wines (Ct. 8:2) and beers are also known from Egyptian and Mesopotamian texts, honey or herbs being used for this purpose. With the rather doubtful 'spice the spicery' in a cooking context in Ezk. 24:10 (meaning spiced meat?), one might compare 'spiced (lit. "sweetened") meat' in Egypt (*iwf sndm*), Gardiner, *Ancient Egyptian Onomastica*, 2, 1947, pp. 255*–256*, A. 610.

The AV phrase 'white of an egg' (*rîr ḥallāmûṯ*, Jb. 6:6, RVmg. 'the juice of purslain'), used as a symbol of something tasteless, was perhaps the sap of some vegetable. D. J. Wiseman (*The Alalakh Tablets*, 1953, p. 87), in outlining 18th-century BC ration lists from Alalaḫ, notes a possible connection between *ḫilimitu*, classed among the grains, and Syr. *ḥallâmûṯ* (*cf.* Heb. form above); *cf.* A. R. Millard, *Ugarit-Forschungen* 1, 1969, p. 210.

BIBLIOGRAPHY. For modern sidelights *cf.* H. Carey, *The Art of Syrian Cookery*, 1960. On ancient food generally, see R. J. Forbes, *Studies in Ancient Technology*, 3, 1955, pp. 50–105, and on honey and sugars, Forbes, *op. cit.*, 5, 1957, pp. 78–88, 97f; H. A. Hoffner, *Alimenta Hethaeorum*, 1974; *Reallexikon der Assyriologie*, 3, 1957–71, pp. 211ff., 302ff., 308ff. K.A.K.

II. In the New Testament

a. Vegetable foods

(i) *Cereals*. The staple human diet in the Bible is bread, made either from wheat flour (Mt. 13:33; Lk. 13:21) or barley flour (Jn. 6:9, 13; *cf.* Jdg. 7:13; 2 Ki. 4:42). The latter was the usual ingredient of bread for the poorer people (*cf.* Jos., *BJ* 5. 427; and, for the relative value of wheat and barley, Rev. 6:6). The NT witnesses to the primitive method of using corn by plucking the fresh ears (Lv. 23:14) and removing the husk by rubbing them in the hands (Dt. 23:25; Mt. 12:1; Mk. 2:23; Lk. 6:1). When this was done in another person's field it was accounted by the rabbis as equivalent to reaping, and therefore forbidden on the sabbath (Mishnah, *Shabbath* 7. 2). Other methods of dealing with the corn are referred to in Mt. 3:12 = Lk. 3:17; Lk. 22:31. Special mention should be made of the *maṣṣôṯ* or cakes of unleavened pastry, which alone were permitted in Jewish households during the days of the Passover festival (Ex. 12:19; 13:7, *etc.*; 1 Cor. 5:7f.).

(ii) *Fruits and oil.* From the garden came grapes (Mt. 7:16) and thereby 'the fruit of the vine' (Mt. 26:29, *etc.*); and olives, although the latter (*cf.* Rom. 11:17ff.; Jas. 3:12) are never expressly recorded as an article of food. The olive, however, provided a most useful oil which was used in the preparation of food, and the olive berry itself was preserved by a process of pickling it in brine. Pickled olives were eaten with bread as a relish. A sauce compounded of dates, figs, raisins and vinegar and called *ḥᵃrōseṯ* was a feature of the Paschal feast (Mk. 14:20; Jn. 13:26; in the Mishnah, *Pesaḥim*, 2. 8; 10. 3).

The fruit of the fig-tree is spoken of in Mt. 7:16 in the same context as the grape. These two fruits were much prized in Palestine, whereas at the extreme end of the social scale the fruit or pods of the carob-tree provided the frugal 'husks' which the prodigal would have been glad to eat in his plight (Lk. 15:16), though they were properly swine-food.

b. Animal products

(i) ***Animals* (popularly speaking). The Jewish world of NT times was one in which dietary laws were strictly enforced, especially in regard to the distinction between* clean and unclean animals and birds (Lv. 11:1–23; Dt. 14:4–20; Acts 10:9ff.; the Mishnaic tractate *'Abodah Zarah*). The eventual breakdown of these dietary regulations is a notable theme of the NT (Mk. 7:18–20; Acts 15:20, 29; Rom. 14; 1 Cor. 8; 10. *IDOLS, MEATS OFFERED TO). See W. L. Willis, *Idol Meat in Corinth*, *SBLDS* 68, 1985. Among the clean animals which were eaten as food (provided that they had been slaughtered in legitimate fashion and the blood drained away, thereby making them *kosher*) we may note the kid (Lk. 15:29), and the calf (Lk. 15:23) which had been specially fattened for a festive occasion.

(ii) *Fish. Fish were similarly classified as clean and unclean according to the rubric of Dt. 14:9f. (*cf.* Lv. 11:9–12); and the reader of the Gospel story will be familiar with the names of the Galilean towns which were the centre of the fishing industry on the shores of the lake. The earliest disciples are called 'fishermen' (Mk. 1:16ff. and parallels). Apart from the reference in Lk. 11:11 there is the well-known mention of fish in the miraculous feedings of the multitude (Mk. 6:41ff. and parallels and Mk. 8:7ff. and parallels) as well as in the meals which the risen Lord shared with his own followers (Lk. 24:42–43; Jn. 21:9ff.). The popularity of the fish-symbol in early Christianity (*cf.* the definitive study of F. J. Dölger, ΙΧΘΥΣ, 1928) and the use of fish at some observances of the Eucharist in early Christian circles are probably derived from these Gospel incidents.

(iii) *Birds.* Birds as items of food are not mentioned in the NT, apart from the general reference in Acts 10:12 and the implication of the sale of sparrows in Mt. 10:29 and Lk. 12:6; but eggs are alluded to in Lk. 11:12.

(iv) *Insects*. Edible insects include the locust, which, along with wild honey, formed the diet of the Baptist in the Judaean wilderness Mk. 1:6). See R. L. Webb, *John the Baptizer and Prophet*, 1992.

c. Seasoning

To increase the pleasure of eating, various condiments were employed. The chief of these was salt, which has the property of adding savour to a dish of food (Jb. 6:6). This fact is made the central feature of some ethical instruction in the Gospels (Mt. 5:13; Mk. 9:50; Lk. 14:34) and Epistles (Col. 4:6). Compare, for the Jewish background here, W. Nauck, 'Salt as a Metaphor in Instructions for Discipleship', *Studia Theologica* 6, 1952, pp. 165–178. 'The Torah is like salt' is a common comparison among the Rabbis. Mint, dill, cummin and rue (conflating Mt. 23:23 and Lk. 11:42 which adds 'every herb': *cf. ExpT* 15, 1903–4, p. 528) continue the list of spices and *herbs used for flavouring; and in Mt. 13:31f. there is a reference to the mustard plant, the leaves of which were cut up and used to give extra flavour. The tiny mustard seed must be sown in the field, according to Jewish practice, and not in the garden; and in Palestine the plant could reach a height of 3 m. On the various issues raised by the mustard seed simile, see C.-H. Hunzinger, *TDNT* 7, pp. 287–291 (bibliography).

BIBLIOGRAPHY. D. E. Smith, 'Meal Customs', *ABD* 4, 1992, pp. 650–655. R.P.M.

FOOT. Heb. *reḡel*, with parallels in other Near Eastern languages, is used occasionally of objects (Ex. 25:26), but mainly of animal or human feet, or legs, and anthropomorphically, of God's feet. Derivatively it is used of the pace (Gn. 33:14). Gk. *pous* is used of the feet of man or beast.

Both in Heb. and Gk. the foot frequently indicates the position, destination or inclination of the person (Pr. 6:18; 7:11; Acts 5:9), and then further in reference to guidance of, and watchful care over, a person, principally by God (1 Sa. 2:9; Ps. 66:9; Lk. 1:79).

Figuratively the word is often used to symbolize defeat of an enemy, with the picture of putting one's foot on his neck (Jos. 10:24; 1 Cor. 15:25).

Falling at a person's feet indicates homage or supplication (1 Sa. 25:24; 2 Ki. 4:27), sitting there implies discipleship or learning (Acts 22:3), and casting something at a person's feet indicates an offering (Acts 4:35). The figure of the foot taken in a snare, or slipping, is used of calamity (Ps. 73:2; Je. 18:22).

The necessity to wash the feet, for comfort and cleanliness, resulted from the dusty roads, and foot-washing was a sign of *hospitality, generally performed by the meanest slave (1 Sa. 25:41; Lk. 7:44; Jn. 13:5ff.; *cf.* Acts 13:25). Removing one's dusty sandals was a sign of respect (Ex. 3:5) and of mourning (Ezk. 24:17). Shaking off the dust from one's feet was a *gesture of scorn, probably based on the idea that to take so much as dust from a place implied a bond (Mk. 6:11; *cf.* 2 Ki. 5:17).

B.O.B.

FOOTMAN. Heb. *raḡlî* from *reḡel*, 'foot'. The word is used of masculine persons only. Footmen are distinguished from children (Ex. 12:37; *cf.* Nu. 11:21). The word is a military term (Jdg. 20:2), and often denotes soldiers in general (1 Sa. 4:10; 15:4; 2 Sa. 10:6; 1 Ki. 20:29). It is used to distinguish infantry from chariot-fighters (2 Sa. 8:4; 2 Ki. 13:17; Je. 12:5; 1 Ch. 18:4; 19:18). AV uses 'footmen' in 1 Sa. 22:17 as a translation for *rāṣîm*, *'runners' (RSV 'guard'), *i.e.* the fifty men who ran before the king's chariot (1 Sa. 8:11; 2 Sa. 15:1; 1 Ki. 1:5). They also acted as a guard (1 Ki. 14:27–28; 2 Ki. 10:25; 11:4 *etc.*; 2 Ch. 12:10–11) and as royal messengers (2 Ch. 30:6, 10). Elijah once acted as a runner before Ahab (1 Ki. 18:46). The royal posts of the Persian empire are called 'runners' (RSV 'couriers') in Est. 3:13, 15, and retain the name even when mounted (Est. 8:10, 14). The word is used as a simile in Jb. 9:25.

A. van S.

FOOTSTOOL. The word occurs seven times in the OT, but on only one occasion is it used in a literal sense (2 Ch. 9:18), and there a different word (*keḇeš*) is used; on the other six occasions *hᵃḏōm raḡlayim*, 'stool of the feet', is used. The equivalent in the NT (*hypopodion tōn podōn*, 'footstool of the feet') occurs eight times, again only once used literally (where the word is simply *hypopodion*, Jas. 2:3), and apart from this reference all are quotations from the OT. In its metaphorical sense it has reference to God and applies to the ark of the covenant (1 Ch. 28:2) the Temple (which contains the ark) (Pss. 99:5; 132:7; La. 2:1); the earth (Is. 66:1; Mt. 5:35; Acts 7:49); and the enemies of his Messiah King (Ps. 110:1, referred to six times in the NT). The footstool of Tutankhamun of Egypt is carved with pictures of his enemies, and other Egyptian kings are shown resting their feet on their enemies' heads.

M.A.M.

FOREHEAD (Heb. *mēṣaḥ*; Gk. *metōpon*, literally 'between the eyes'). The set of the forehead can indicate opposition, defiance or rebellion (Je. 3:3, 'brow' in RSV), and hardness of the forehead indicates the determination or power to persevere in that attitude (Is. 48:4; Ezk. 3:8–9).

The forehead, being open and fully visible, was the most obvious place for a badge or mark (Ezk. 9:4; Ex. 28:38; Rev. 7:3; 13:16, *etc.*). In Ezekiel this mark was made with ink, but in the book of Revelation it is a seal, and in Exodus a plaque. Note also the *phylactery which was worn on the forehead (*EYE).

B.O.B.

FOREIGNER. The rather arbitrary fluctuation in EVV between alien, foreigner, sojourner and stranger tends to obscure the fact that different groups of people are in view. In the classification which follows this inconsistency of translation should be kept in mind.

a. The stranger or alien

A stranger is essentially one who does not belong to the house or community in which he finds himself. The word *zār* is from the root *zûr*, 'to turn aside' or 'to depart'. Thus it can be used simply of an outsider (1 Ki. 3:18). It can therefore mean one who usurps a position to which he has no right. The 'loose woman' in Proverbs is such an interloper. A further extension of the word makes it equivalent to alien or foreigner, *i.e.* one who does not belong to the nation, and so virtually equates it with an enemy (Is. 1:7; Je. 5:19; 51:51; Ezk. 7:21; 28:7, 10; Ob. 11).

b. The foreigner

The word *noḵrî* can refer simply to one of another race; but it also acquires a religious connotation because of the association of other nations with idolatry. It was for this reason that the Israelites were forbidden to intermarry with the Canaanites (Dt. 7:1–6). One of the indictments of Solomon is that he loved many foreign women who turned him aside from Yahweh (1 Ki. 11:1ff.). The Exile in Babylon was seen as a judgment on this decline, which was widespread in the nation. As a result the return from the Exile is marked by a vigorous enforcement of the prohibitions of mixed marriages. This emphasis by Ezra on national purity (Ezr. 9–10) was perverted in later Judaism into the hard exclusiveness which in the Judaizing movement in the early church proved such a hindrance to the free access of Gentile converts.

c. The sojourner

A sojourner is one whose permanent residence is in another nation, in contrast with the foreigner whose stay is only temporary. The word thus rendered is *gēr* from the root *gûr*, 'to sojourn', though the alternative *tôšāḇ* is sometimes used in the simple sense of a settler. The Israelites themselves were sojourners in Egypt (Gn. 15:13; Ex. 22:21; Dt. 10:19; 23:7). Indeed, this fact was to govern their attitude to the sojourners in Israel. These might comprise a whole tribe such as the Gibeonites (Jos. 9) or the remnants of the Canaanite tribes after the Conquest. Their number was quite considerable, as may be seen in Solomon's census of them (2 Ch. 2:17).

The sojourner had many privileges. The Israelites must not oppress him (Ex. 22:21; 23:9; Lv. 19:33–34). Indeed they are to go further and to love him (Dt. 10:19). One reason given for the observance of the sabbath is that the sojourner may be refreshed (Ex. 23:12). The gleanings of the vineyard and the harvest field are to be left for him (Lv. 19:10; 23:22; Dt. 24:19–21). He is included in the provision made in the cities of refuge (Nu. 35:15; Jos. 20:9). He is ranked with the fatherless and widow as being defenceless; and so God is his defence and will judge his oppressor (Pss. 94:6; 146:9; Je. 7:6; 22:3; Ezk. 22:7, 29; Zc. 7:10; Mal. 3:5). The chief drawback of his position is that, if he is a bond-servant, he is not included in the general liberation in the year of Jubilee (Lv. 25:45–46).

As far as religious life is concerned, he is bound by the law which forbids leaven during the Feast of Unleavened Bread (Ex.12:19). He must abstain from work on the sabbath and on the Day of Atonement (Ex. 20:10; Lv. 16:29). He shares the prohibitions on eating blood (Lv. 17:10, 13), immorality (Lv. 18:26), idolatry (Lv. 20:2) and blasphemy (Lv. 24:16). He might, however, eat unclean meat (Dt. 14:21). He is not compelled to keep the Passover, but if he wishes to do so he must be circumcised (Ex. 12:48). He is indeed virtually on a level with the Israelite (Lv. 24:22), and in Ezekiel's vision of the Messianic age he is to share the inheritance of Israel (Ezk. 47:22–23).

In the NT the great feature of the gospel is that those who were aliens from Israel, and so were 'strangers and sojourners' (Eph. 2:12, 19–20), have been made fellow heirs in the Israel of God. Now Christians are the aliens in this world and must live as pilgrims (1 Pet. 2:11).

BIBLIOGRAPHY. *EBi* and *DAC* (*s.v.* 'stranger'); J. Pedersen, *Israel*, 3–4, 1940, 272ff., 585; H. Bietenhard *et al.*, *NIDNTT* 1, pp. 683–692; 2, pp. 788–790. H.M.C.

FORERUNNER. This word is often used by Christians to describe John the Baptist, because in him the words of Mal. 3:1 found their fulfilment (Mk. 1:2 and Mt. 11:10), and also because his father Zechariah prophesied that he would 'go before the face of the Lord to prepare his ways' (Lk. 1:76). The actual word, however, is found only once in the NT, with reference to the ascended Christ (Heb. 6:20). It translates *prodromos*, a military term used of scouts sent on ahead to prepare the way for an advancing army.

Usually a 'forerunner' is of less importance than the person or persons for whose coming he is paving the way. This was true of the runners who preceded the chariots of kings (1 Sa. 8:11; *FOOTMAN); it was also true of John the Baptist, and of the messengers sent by Jesus to make ready his entrance into the villages of Samaria (Lk. 9:52). But in the case of Jesus himself, who entered for us within the veil into the holy of holies, having become our High Priest, the reverse is true. As the supreme Head of the church he has gone on ahead that his brethren may follow him in due course. Jesus made it clear to his followers that this was one of the main purposes of his departure to the Father, when he told them in the upper room that he was going to prepare a place for them in the many dwelling-places of his Father's house (Jn. 14:2–3). It is true that *already* Christians have boldness to enter heaven through the blood of Jesus (Heb. 10:19), and that God has already raised them up with Christ and made them to sit with him in the heavenly places (Eph. 2:6). They can through prayer and sacrament ascend in heart and mind to their Lord, and with him continually dwell. But, because Jesus is their Forerunner, they have the assurance that one day they will themselves enter heaven as he has done and enjoy the glory which is now his. Christ will receive them unto himself, that where he is there they may be also (Jn. 14:3). 'The Forerunner is also the Way by which, after long following, the whole Church will reach at last the Father's House.' (See H. B. Swete, *The Ascended Christ*, 1911.) R.V.G.T.

FOREST. 1. Heb. *ḥōreš*, 'thicket', 'wood, wooded height', occurs in a number of passages (*e.g.* Ezk. 31:3), though in one of them (2 Ch. 27:4) the text is possibly corrupt and a proper name intended.

2. Heb. *pardēs*, 'park', a loan-word from Persian *pari-daeza*, 'enclosure', used of a preserve or park containing trees (Ne. 2:8), fruit-trees (Ct. 4:13) and laid-out *gardens (Ec. 2:5).

3. Heb. *ya'ar*, 'outspread place', the most common word, is found thirty-five times in the OT. In biblical times much of the hill-country was covered with forests. Apart altogether from general uses of the word, the Bible mentions several of the woods and forests by name, *e.g.* 'forest of Lebanon' (1 Ki. 7:2f.). (*Articles under such place-names.)

BIBLIOGRAPHY. D. Baly, *The Geography of the Bible*[2], 1974, pp. 105–110. J.D.D.

FORGIVENESS.

I. In the Old Testament

In the OT the idea of forgiveness is conveyed principally by words from three roots. *kpr* more usually carries the idea of atonement, and its use in connection with the sacrifices is frequent. Its use for 'forgive' implies that atonement is made. The verb *nś'* means basically 'lift', 'carry', and presents us with a vivid picture of sin being lifted from the sinner and carried right away. The third root is *slḥ*, of unknown derivation, but which corresponds in use pretty closely to our 'forgive'. The first and the last are used always of God's forgiveness, but *nś'* is applied to human forgiveness as well.

Forgiveness is not regarded as a truism, as something in the nature of things. Passages which speak of the Lord as not pardoning certain offences abound (Dt. 29:20; 2 Ki. 24:4; Je. 5:7; La. 3:42). Where forgiveness is obtained it is something to be received with gratitude and regarded with awe and wonder. Sin merits punishment. Pardon is astounding grace. 'There is forgiveness with thee,' says the Psalmist, and then (perhaps surprisingly to us) he adds, 'that thou mayest be feared' (Ps. 130:4).

Forgiveness is sometimes connected with atonement. *slḥ* is repeatedly connected with the sacrifices and, as we have seen, the verb from the root *kpr* has the essential meaning 'to make atonement'. Again, it may not be coincidence that *nś'*, besides being used of the forgiveness of sin, is also used of bearing the penalty of sin (Nu. 14:33f.; Ezk. 14:10). The two seem to be connected. This does not mean that God is a stern Being who will not forgive without a *quid pro quo*. He is a God of grace, and the very means of bearing sin are instituted by him. The sacrifices avail only because he has given the blood as the means of making atonement (Lv. 17:11). The OT knows nothing of a forgiveness wrung from an unwilling God or purchased by a bribe.

Forgiveness, then, is possible only because God is a God of grace, or in the beautiful expression in Ne. 9:17 'a God of pardons' (RSV, 'a God ready to forgive'). 'To the Lord our God belong mercy and forgiveness' (Dn. 9:9). A very instructive passage for the whole OT understanding of forgiveness is Ex. 34:6f., 'The Lord, the Lord, a God merciful and gracious, slow to anger, and abounding in steadfast love and faithfulness, keeping steadfast love for thousands, forgiving iniquity and transgression and sin, but who will by no means clear the guilty.' Forgiveness is rooted in the nature of God as gracious. But his forgiveness is not indiscriminate. He will 'by no means clear the guilty'. On man's side there is the need for penitence if he is to be forgiven. While this is not put into a formal demand, it is everywhere implied. Penitent sinners are forgiven. Impenitent men, who still go on in their wicked way, are not.

It remains to be noticed that the thought of pardon is conveyed in a most graphic way by other imagery than the use of our three basic forgiveness words. Thus the Psalmist tells us that, 'As far as the east is from the west, so far does he remove our transgressions from us' (Ps. 103:12). Isaiah speaks of God as casting all the prophet's sins behind his back (Is. 38:17), and as 'blotting out' the people's transgressions (Is. 43:25; *cf.* Ps. 51:1, 9). In Je. 31:34 the Lord says, 'I will remember their sin no more,' and Micah speaks of him as casting sins 'into the depths of the sea' (Mi. 7:19). Such vivid language emphasizes the completeness of God's forgiveness. When he forgives, men's sins are dealt with thoroughly. God sees them no more.

II. In the New Testament

In the NT there are two main verbs to consider, *charizomai* (which means 'to deal graciously with') and *aphiēmi* ('to send away', 'to loose'). The noun *aphesis*, 'remission', is also found with some frequency. There are also two other words, *apolyō*, 'to release', which is used in Lk. 6:37, 'forgive, and you will be forgiven', and *paresis*, 'a passing by', used in Rom. 3:25 of God's passing over of sins done in earlier days.

In the NT several points are made clear. One is that the forgiven sinner must forgive others. This is manifest in Lk. 6:37, cited above, in the Lord's Prayer, and in other places. A readiness to forgive others is part of the indication that we have truly repented. Moreover, it is to be whole-hearted. It springs from Christ's forgiveness of us, and it is to be like Christ's forgiveness: 'as the Lord has forgiven you, so you also must forgive' (Col. 3:13). Several times Christ insists on the same thing, as in his parable of the unmerciful servant (Mt. 18:23–35).

Forgiveness is not often linked directly with the cross, though sometimes this is done, as in Eph. 1:7, 'In him we have redemption through his blood, the forgiveness of our trespasses.' Similarly, from Mt. 26:28 we find that Christ's blood was shed 'for many for the forgiveness of sins'. More usual is it to find it linked directly with Christ himself. God 'in Christ forgave you' (Eph. 4:32). 'God exalted him ... to give repentance to Israel and forgiveness of sins' (Acts 5:31). 'Through this man forgiveness of sins is proclaimed to you' (Acts 13:38). With these we should place passages wherein Jesus, during the days of his flesh, declared that men were forgiven. Indeed, in the incident of the healing of the paralysed man lowered through the roof, he worked the miracle expressly 'that you may know that the Son of man has authority on earth to forgive sins' (Mk. 2:10). But the Person of Christ is not to be separated from his work. Forgiveness by or through Jesus Christ means forgiveness arising from all that he is and all that he does. In particular, it is not to be understood apart from the cross, all the more so since his death is often said to be a death 'for sin' (*ATONEMENT). In addition to the specific passages which link forgiveness and the death of Christ, there is the whole thrust of the NT passages dealing with the atoning death of the Saviour.

Forgiveness rests basically, then, on the atoning work of Christ. That is to say, it is an act of sheer grace. 'He is faithful and just, and will forgive our sins' (1 Jn. 1:9). On man's side repentance is insisted upon again and again. John the Baptist preached 'a baptism of repentance for the forgiveness of sins' (Mk. 1:4), a theme which is taken up by Peter with reference to Christian baptism (Acts 2:38). Christ himself directed that 'repentance and forgiveness of sins should be preached in his name' (Lk. 24:47). Forgiveness is similarly linked with faith (Acts 10:43; Jas. 5:15). Faith and repentance are not to be thought of as merits whereby we deserve forgiveness. Rather they are the means whereby we appropriate the grace of God.

Two difficulties must be mentioned. One is that of the sin against the Holy Spirit which can never be forgiven (Mt. 12:31f.; Mk. 3:28f.; Lk. 12:10; *cf.* 1 Jn. 5:16). This sin is never defined. But in the light of NT teaching generally it is impossible to think of it as any specific act of sin. The reference is rather to the continuing blasphemy against the Spirit of God by one who consistently rejects God's gracious call. This is blasphemy indeed.

The other is Jn. 20:23, 'If you forgive the sins of any, they are forgiven'. It is more than difficult to think of Christ as leaving in men's hands the determination of whether the sins of other men are to be forgiven or not. The important points are the plural ('any' is plural in the Gk.; it points to categories, not individuals), and the perfect tense rendered 'are forgiven' (it means 'have been forgiven', not 'will be forgiven'). The meaning of the passage then seems to be that as they are inspired by the Holy Spirit (v. 22) the followers of Jesus will be able to say with accuracy which categories of men have sins forgiven, and which not.

BIBLIOGRAPHY. V. Taylor, *Forgiveness and Reconciliation*, 1941; H. R. Mackintosh, *The Christian Experience of Forgiveness*, 1947; *TDNT* 1, pp. 509–512; 3, pp. 300–301; 4, pp. 295–307; 9, pp. 372–402; H. Vorländer, *NIDNTT* 1, pp. 697–703; M Hengel, *The Atonement*, 1981. L.M.

FORTIFICATION AND SIEGECRAFT.

I. Defence in the ancient world

a. Site and size of the fortress

Throughout most of the biblical period the words 'city' and 'fortress' (*miḇṣār*, *et al.*) were virtually synonyms in Palestine. Sometimes 'walled city' emphasizes this normal defensive aspect of a town in contrast to unwalled villages. The account of the rebuilding of Jerusalem under Nehemiah clearly demonstrates that walls make a city.

Whenever possible a natural defensible site was chosen for the city's location, although a water-source was also essential. A steep isolated hill, such as Samaria, or an impregnable spur of a hill, such as Ophel, the site of David's Jerusalem, made excellent sites. Some cities, however, were selected because of regional strategical planning, protecting highways and communications, or like Bethel because of a readily available water-supply. These sites, and lower cities established when the population outgrew the upper city on a hill, required an artificial system of defence.

Usually the term 'fortress' implies a limited defence perimeter. In Palestine the average city or town covered about 2–4 hectares (5–10 acres). Some were half that area, others greater. For example, Jerusalem of David's day and Megiddo occupied 4·5–5·3 hectares (11–13 acres), whilst Canaanite Hazor covered some 81 hectares (200 acres). The capitals of Egypt, Assyria, Babylonia, Persia and Rome were exceptional in size and differed from normal cities in other features as well (*e.g.*, *NINEVEH, *CALAH, *BABYLON).

City walls varied considerably in width, height and design. Solid walls averaged 3 m in width, but could be two to three times this at base. Casemate walls, a double wall system, averaged about 1·5 m each. In height walls ranged from about 6 m to at least 9 m. Usually the foundations were of stone and the walls proper of stone, mud-brick or brick above a varying number of stone courses. Defences could be strengthened by adding an outer wall within bow-shot of the main wall.

b. The development of city defences

Although open warfare was preferred, a defending army could retire to its city if necessary. Walls and associated fortifications were required both to prevent the enemy entering and to provide a protected firing-platform for the defenders. Walls and ramparts, free-standing or attached to the wall, bastions, towers and a battlement or crenellated parapet were all used at various times.

Excavations have revealed remains of city walls in Syria–Palestine from the 3rd millennium BC, probably developed under Mesopotamian influence. A long time-gap separates these from the earliest known fortifications. In pre-pottery Neolithic Jericho several walls of undressed stone were found as well as a circular tower 13 m in diameter with an interior shaft containing 22 steps. These and a 9 m wide moat cut from solid rock date to 7000–6000 BC, over 4000 years before Abraham. Open villages without fortifications were succeeded about 3000 BC by some fortified cities—Jericho, Megiddo, Gezer, Ai, *etc.* A variety of stone and/or brick walls were used, some with bastions and ramparts. Semi-circular and square corner towers have also been discovered.

During the next period, the Middle Bronze Age (Patriarchs to Joseph), some important changes were made to walls and gates, connected in part with the use of chariots and possibly the battering ram. About 1700 BC when the Hyksos entered Egypt (*CHRONOLOGY OF THE OT) a massive *terra piseé* or beaten earth bank was added to the existing walls or free-standing ramparts were built. Sometimes a wall was erected on top of the embankment. Massive stone walls also occur later (*SHECHEM). The rampart or 'glacis'—a special consolidated facing on a rampart or tell slope—often surfaced with plaster or chalk as waterproofing, may have been introduced to counter the arrival of the battering ram (*EAEHL*, p. 113). It enclosed, not a camp for chariots and their warriors, but extended lower cities (*HAZOR). The Hyksos were apparently responsible for this new defence system, although the Canaanite inhabitants still occupied the cities. Finally a ditch or moat often fronted the rampart, the excavated material forming the embankment (*CAH*, 2, 1, pp. 77–116).

Joshua entered the land of Canaan in the Late Bronze Age, in the 13th century BC. Excavations have revealed little evidence of the defences of this era. There were few new developments and the Middle Bronze defence systems continued to be used or were reconstructed on the same lines. This could account for the apparent lack of walls at *Jericho attributable to Joshua's time. To date no Israelite fortifications are known before the days of Saul and David.

In the days of the united kingdom casemate walls were built at a number of cities. These consist of two thin parallel walls (1·5 m thick on average) separated by about 2 m, joined at regular intervals by transverse walls. The long narrow rooms formed within the wall could be used for living (Jos. 2:15), storage, or filled for added strength. Such a wall was cheaper to build yet provided reasonable solidity. Casemate walls were used from *c.* 1600 BC down to the 2nd century BC. Saul's capital at Gibeah was a fortress, 52 m by 35 m, with corner towers and casemate walls. Other walls were also used. At Beersheba two thin parallel walls, followed by a solid wall 4 m thick, are attributable to the Davidic–Solomonic era. Solomon's cities used different types of fortifications, although a hallmark of his fortifications, as seen at *Megiddo, *Hazor and *Gezer, is the use of casemate walls and a gate with three sets of piers and two towers. Throughout the rest of the OT period both solid and casemate walls were used, and at times an outer and inner wall (*LACHISH).

Royal fortresses, such as Gibeah of Saul, were built during the Iron Age. A series of forts, rectangular or irregular in shape, built in the Negeb between the 10th and 6th centuries BC mark the S extension of the Israelites. The citadel of *Arad was an important royal border fortress. Roman forts were also built in the Negeb, Arabah and Transjordan.

Excavations at *Jerusalem have revealed some of its defences throughout the ages. Kathleen Kenyon exposed sections of two walls well down in the Kidron Valley which were respectively the walls used down to the 7th century BC and a new wall built that century, destroyed by Nebuchadrezzar in 586 BC. A wall on the E crest of Ophel well above these would appear to be that built by Nehemiah, as he could not clear the debris left by the Babylonian destruction. On the W, 275 m from the Temple platform, over 40 m of wall 7 m thick built of large stones is probably the extension to Jerusalem's walls added by Hezekiah (2 Ch. 32:5).

In intertestamental and NT times one or two solid stone walls usually surrounded a city. At Mareshah the nearly square town wall had buttresses and corner towers. The excellent Roman wall at Samaria, apparently built by Herod, enclosed 69 hectares (170 acres). Herod the Great was the most prolific builder in all Palestine's history. His work at Jerusalem may be seen in the massive retaining wall of the Temple platform, especially in the areas excavated under B. Mazar and at the SE corner. Sections of Hasmonaean defences and the three walls of *Jerusalem in NT times are being discovered in current excavations.

At the citadel by the Jaffa gate part of the 'first wall', a massive Hasmonaean tower base, and the Phasael Tower of Herod's palace (David's Tower) are typical of the defence systems being recovered.

c. The city gate

The weakest point of a city's fortifications was the gate. A number of ways were developed to make this more secure. These included towers, angled approaches and inner gates with several sets of piers. Towers were used in the walls to protect the dead area at the foot of the wall, as was the 'glacis'. Most cities built on tells had one main gate, or one inner and outer gate. Large cities, such as Jerusalem, would have a number of gates. Up to about 1000 BC a number of posterns, small gates easily defended, allowed soldiers to leave or enter the city quickly because open battle was preferred.

Before the need for a straight entrance for chariots, angled gates with two doors hampered the enemy's assault. With the advent of chariots *c.* 1700 BC, towers and a complex gate with several piers or pilasters provided greater security. The towers and upper rooms enabled the defenders to fire down on the advancing foe. One upper room possibly was a special royal chamber, as reliefs in the Great Gate room at Medinet Habu suggest (*cf.* 2 Sa. 18:33). In the patriarchal age gates had two sets of three piers; so did the Solomonic gates, although with the entrance towers and walls this created three guardrooms. Two guardroom designs were used both before and after Solomon's day. At Dan and Tell en-Nasbeh an overlap in the walls formed a hollow square at the rear of which the gate was located. At en-Nasbeh a large tower on the right (outer wall) could handle attackers on three sides. Stone benches before the gate, and between the outer and inner gates at Dan, where there is also a probable throne base and canopy, mark the place of judgment (Ru. 4:1–2; 2 Sa. 19:8). The city gate was closed by massive wooden double doors. These doors were supported by posts sunk into the ground where they pivoted on specially hollowed-out stones. Discovery of these stones shows that only one set of doors was erected for each gate. When closed against the threshold stone the door was barred by a large beam held in position by sockets in both doorposts. Since an enemy would try to set fire to the doors they were often covered with metal sheets.

d. Citadels and small forts

The towered gateway was a virtual fortress or citadel in itself. The term 'tower' (*miğdāl, et al.*) may also mean an inner citadel, a palace or temple (*BAAL-BERITH in Shechem), which provided an inner fortress for a secondary stand should the walls be breached. Sometimes a city was divided into sections for similar defensive reasons. 'Tower' may also refer to a small fortress or what we should call a blockhouse. The chain of forts in the Negeb and Transjordan are examples (above).

e. The problem of water-supply

Second only in importance to the walls and gates of a city was its water-supply. Until the invention of waterproof plaster to seal cisterns, every city needed a spring or stream nearby. Cisterns did enable fortresses to withstand long sieges, as Masada illustrates. Cities on tells, however, needed access to the springs at the base of the hill. In the 10th century and later, tunnels and shafts were dug from within the city, giving access to the water, whilst outside entrances were blocked off. Such shafts were used at Megiddo, Hazor, Gezer, Gibeon and Jerusalem (*SILOAM tunnel). These water-supply systems display advanced engineering knowledge and skills. Defenders tried to deny the invader water-supplies by filling cisterns, draining pools and concealing springs wherever possible. Food-supplies were also vital to withstand sieges, so that granaries and storehouses are found within cities.

II. Methods of attack

The least costly method of taking a city was, of course, to persuade it to surrender without fighting. The Assyrian Sennacherib used this technique in vain against Jerusalem. Other methods were to capture a city by some ruse or by surprise, as David secured Jerusalem. Joab entered the city probably by its water-tunnel. Usually, however, large cities had to be captured by assault or by long siege.

a. The assault

In a direct assault the invader could try to scale the wall by ladders, break through the walls by digging with tools or the battering-ram, penetrate the gate by firing it or battering it open, or tunnel under the wall. Where ramparts, moats or the side of a tell made direct attack difficult, an assault ramp was used. Part of the moat was filled with earth or rubble and an inclined ramp built up to the city wall proper. An Assyrian ramp investigated at Lachish in 1977 was made up entirely of large field stones. Assyrian reliefs from Nineveh depicting Sennacherib's assault on *Lachish (Is. 37:33) show the ramps were surfaced with wood. Assault troops behind large shields and the shield-covered battering-rams moved up the ramps, the latter protected by archers and slingers. The wooden beam of the ram had an iron axe-shaped head. When this penetrated the brick-work it was levered sideways to dislodge the bricks. A tower at the front of the ram was used by archers to fire at defenders on the walls. Mobile towers could also be brought against the walls, and catapults throwing large stones were used against the upper sections of the walls and the defenders. To prevent the escape of the besieged a mound or bank of earth was constructed around the city (Je. 6:6; Ezk. 17:17). From the walls the defenders would rain down arrows, javelins, stones, boiling water and also burning torches to set fire to the battering-rams. They also might make occasional sorties out of the city to destroy assault equipment and attack its protecting troops.

b. The siege

The protracted process of siege was used when a city was too powerful for a direct assault or when for other reasons the invader preferred to wait. By encircling the city the attackers sought to cut off its supplies and outside assistance, until the defenders were forced to surrender. An encircling mound and fortified camps were necessary to protect the more passive invading army. Sieges could last up to several years, such as the Assyrian siege of Samaria (2 Ki. 17:5).

c. Capture and destruction

After a city was captured it was normally plundered and burnt. Most cities, however, were rebuilt and used again. The surviving defenders might be deported, enslaved or placed under tribute, and their leaders tortured, killed or taken as hostages. The most famous destruction of OT times was Nebuchadrezzar's devastation of all the Judaean cities, including Jerusalem, in 588–587 BC. Titus' destruction of Jerusalem in AD 70 was equally complete, although under the Romans lesser cities fared far better.

BIBLIOGRAPHY. Y. Yadin, *The Art of Warfare in Biblical Lands in the Light of Archaeological Study*, 1963; S. M. Paul and W. G. Dever, *Biblical Archaeology*, 1973; *NEAEHL*; A. Negev, *Archaeological Encyclopaedia of the Holy Land*, 1972. G.G.G.

FORTUNATUS. A member of the Corinthian party which was a blessing to Paul at Ephesus (1 Cor. 16:17f.). Nothing else is certainly known of him. The name is Latin and a common one, and here the man is probably a slave. It has been needlessly assumed that he and *Achaicus belonged to the household of *Stephanas (*cf.* 1 Cor. 16:15) or even of Chloe (1 Cor. 1:11). It is attractive to find Fortunatus 'forty years on' in *1 Clement* 65, but, *pace* Lightfoot (*St Clement of Rome*, 1, p. 62; 2, p. 187), it is not certain that Clement's Fortunatus was a Corinthian. A.F.W.

FORUM OF APPIUS. A market town and staging-post in Latium, a foundation of Appius Claudius Caecus, the builder of the Via Appia, on which the town stands. It is 63 km from Rome, a place 'packed with bargees and extortionate innkeepers', if the poet Horace is to be believed. The town was the N terminus of the canal through the Pontine Marshes. This was one of the places where the Roman Christians met Paul (Acts 28:15); see also *TAVERNS, THE THREE. E.M.B.

FOUNDATION.

I. In the Old Testament

The Heb. *yāsad̠* and compounds mean 'to fix firmly, found' and is thus used both literally and metaphorically of all types of foundations whether of buildings (Jb. 4:19) and objects such as altars (Ex. 29:12) or of the earth (Ps. 24:2; Is. 24:18), the inhabited world (Ps. 18:15) and the vault of heaven (Am. 9:6). In this way the future Israel (Is. 54:11), Zion (Is. 14:32) and the righteous (Pr. 10:25) are described.

The 'laying down' of foundations (Is. 28:16), especially of a temple (1 Ki. 6:37; Ezr. 5:16) was a matter of religious ritual. There is, however, no sure archaeological evidence that human sacrifice (or 'threshold covenant') was involved. The loss of Hiel's sons (1 Ki. 16:34) at the rebuilding of Jericho is interpreted as a punishment (Jos. 6:26) rather than as an offering. The choice and preparation were important and sometimes the foundations were laid on bed-rock or pure sand. Usually the site was levelled by filling within a retaining wall of stones either to support the whole structure or the corners. The foundations of Solomon's Temple consisted of large and expensively trimmed blocks of stone (1 Ki. 5:17; 6:37; 7:10; *cf.* 1 Ch. 22:2). It has been suggested that different parts of the foundation of the second Temple are referred to; that a retaining wall (Aram. *'uššа*; Akkad. *'uššu*, Ezr. 5:16) was first built to retain the foundation platform (*temenos*; Akkad. *timēnu*), then later the returnees filled this in with earth and relaid foundations upon it (Ezr. 3:10; Zc. 4:9), but there is no archaeological or linguistic support for this theory. The foundations are often the only feature of ancient *architecture remaining today.

The 'gate of the foundation' in Jerusalem (2 Ch. 23:5, AV) may be the Horse-gate or 'Gate of Sur', while the 'rod of foundation' (*mûsāḏâ*, Is. 30:32, AV 'grounded staff') is probably for 'staff of punishment' (RSV; reading *mūsar*).

BIBLIOGRAPHY. R. S. Ellis, *Foundation-Deposits in Ancient Mesopotamia*, 1968; G. Turner, *Iraq* 32, 1970, pp. 69–71. D.J.W.

II. In the New Testament

Two Gk. words are thus translated.

1. *katabolē*, 'a casting or laying down'. All ten occurrences of this word are bound up with the phrase 'the foundation of the world' (*e.g.* Mt. 13:35; Lk. 11:50).

2. *themelios*, 'anything laid', appears sixteen times. Generally this word is found in a figurative sense, but it is used literally in speaking of the wise man who builds his foundation upon a rock (Lk. 6:48). Christ is spoken of as the foundation of the church, *i.e.*, the true and only basis of our salvation (1 Cor. 3:11). He is the chief *Cornerstone, and the apostles, who are the trustees and publishers of his gospel, are referred to as the foundation on which Christians are built (Eph. 2:20; *cf.* Rev. 21:14, 19). 'Foundation' is used also of one's ministry (Rom. 15:20; 1 Cor. 3:10), and in referring to the security of God's seal (2 Tim. 2:19). The first principles of divine truth are a foundation on which the rest depend (Heb. 6:1–2).

In a slightly different use of the word Timothy is instructed to urge those who are 'rich in this world' to lay up a good foundation (1 Tim. 6:19; *cf.* Heb. 11:10; Mt. 6:19–20) by trusting all to God—perhaps in contrast to the Ephesian merchants who deposited their earthly treasures in the temple of 'the great goddess Artemis'.

BIBLIOGRAPHY. K. L. Schmidt, *TDNT* 3, pp. 63f.; H. H. Esser, *NIDNTT* 1, pp. 376–378; J. Blunck, *idem*, pp. 660–662. J.D.D.
J.B.Tr.

FOUNTAIN. Palestine, owing to its geological structure, is a land of many springs, as was forecast to the Israelites before they settled there (Dt. 8:7). As a result of this, several Heb. words were in use which are commonly rendered 'fountain' or 'spring' in the EVV.

1. *'ayin*, 'spring, fountain', the commonest word (*e.g.* Gn. 16:7), is well known from the fact that in its construct form, *'ên*-(EVV 'En-'), it is a common element in place-names. Its Arabic cognate is familiar today, as in 'Ain es-Sulṭân, the spring by which the city of *Jericho stood. The word occurs in a modified form as the place-name Ainōn or Aenōn, where John baptized (Jn. 3:23). Sometimes translated *'well' in AV (*e.g.* Gn. 24:13).

2. *ma'yān*, 'place of springs', is a variant of **1** and rendered in the AV by both 'fountain' (*e.g.* Gn. 7:11) and 'spring' (*e.g.* Ps. 87:7).

3. *mabbûa'*, 'spring', from *nāḇa'*, 'to flow, bubble up', is rendered in the EVV by both 'fountain' (*e.g.* Ec. 12:6) and 'spring' (*e.g.* Is. 35:7).

4. *māqôr.* This is sometimes used in a figurative sense of, *e.g.*, 'life' (Ps. 36:9) or in a physiological sense (*e.g.* Lv. 20:18) and rendered in the EVV by both 'fountain' (*e.g.* Ps. 36:9) and 'spring' (*e.g.* Pr. 25:26).

5. *môṣā'*, 'place of going forth', comes from *yāṣā'*, 'to go out', and is sometimes rendered 'spring' (*e.g.* 2 Ki. 2:21). **6.** *gal* is usually 'heap' (*e.g.* Gn. 31:46), but in Ct. 4:12 it is translated 'spring' (RSV, however, reads *gan*, 'garden'). **7.** *gullâ*, 'basin, bowl', is rendered 'spring' in EVV of Jos. 15:19 and Jdg. 1:15.

8. *'ašēḏâ*, 'foundation', '(mountain-)slope', which occurs only in the plural, is in the AV sometimes rendered 'spring' (Dt. 4:49; Jos. 10:40; 12:8) and thrice treated as part of a place-name, Ashdoth-pisgah (Dt. 3:17; Jos. 12:3; 13:20). The other EVV give 'slopes of Pisgah'.

9. *bôr*, 'cistern, 'well'. In Je. 6:7, where the *Keṯîḇ* gives *bawir* and the *Q'rē bayir*, the AV renders 'fountain' but RV and RSV give 'well'. **10.** *ḥay*, 'living'. In Gn. 26:19 'living waters' is rendered 'springing water' in the EVV. **11.** *nēḇeḵ* is a word which occurs once only, in the plural construct *niḇ'ḵê-yām*, in Jb. 38:16, and rendered 'springs of the sea' in the EVV.

In NT the principal Gk. word for 'spring', 'fountain' is *pēgē* (*e.g.* Rev. 7:17, *etc.*; *cf.* Mk. 5:29; Jn. 4:6), a word which is, in the LXX, used chiefly for Heb. *'ayin*. T.C.M.

FREEDMEN (AV 'Libertines'), **SYNAGOGUE OF THE.** The Gk. of Acts 6:9 makes it difficult to determine whether the *Libertinoi*, the members of a Jewish synagogue at Jerusalem, worshipped by themselves, or with the Cyrenians, the Alexandrians, the Cilicians and the Asiatics. The meaning of the name is equally uncertain, and this has given rise to a number of variants for this verse (notably the reading 'Libyans' for 'Libertines', which appears in the Armenian vss and the Syriac). Schürer suggests that the Libertines were Rom. freedmen descended from Jews who had been prisoners of war under Pompey (63 BC) and subsequently released. Possibly only one synagogue is referred to here (then *kai Kyrēnaiōn . . . Asias* is epexegetic of *Libertinōn*), which was attended by Jewish freedmen or their descendants from the places mentioned (so F. F. Bruce, *The Acts of the Apostles*[2], 1952, p. 156). S.S.S.

FREEMAN, FREEWOMAN. Two Gk. words are used. **1.** *apeleutheros*, 'one fully freed', applies to a man who, born a slave, has been freed. In 1 Cor. 7:22a the reference is to one freed by the Lord from the bondage of sin (*cf.* 1 Cor. 12:13; Col. 3:11; Rev. 13:16, *etc.*). **2.** *eleutheros*, 'free man', occurs in 1 Cor. 7:21, 22b; also in Rev. 6:15; *eleuthera*, 'free woman' (Gal. 4:22–23, 30) contrasts Sarah, Abraham's wife, with Hagar, his concubine, the Egyp. slave-girl. A metaphorical application of this is made in Gal. 4:31. J.D.D.

FRIEND OF THE BRIDEGROOM. The Heb. words *rēa'*, *rē'eh* and *mērēa'*, though often meaning 'friend' in general, sometimes have the special meaning of 'friend of the bridegroom', 'best man'. The ancient versions sometimes show this special meaning. In the case of an abortive marriage Mesopotamian law forbade any marriage between the 'friend' and the forsaken bride. This explains the reaction of the Philistines and of Samson on the marriage of his former fiancée with his best man (Jdg. 14; 15:1–6). Jdg. 14:20 should be rendered 'to his best man, who had performed for him the offices of a best man'. A metaphorical use of the position of the best man is to be found in Jn. 3:29 (*cf.* 2 Cor. 11:2).

BIBLIOGRAPHY. A. van Selms, 'The best man and bride—from Sumer to St John', *JNES* 9, 1950, pp. 65–75. A.VAN S.

FRIEND OF THE KING. A phrase which was applied to various individuals. Ahuzzath was the 'friend' (*mērēa'*) of Abimelech the king of Gerar (Gn. 26:26); Saul had a 'friend' (*mērēa'*) (unnamed, 2 Sa. 3:8); Hushai the Archite was David's 'friend' (*rē'eh*, 2 Sa. 15:37); Solomon's 'friend' (*rē'eh*) was Zabud the priest (1 Ki. 4:5); and Baasha of Israel had a 'friend' (*rēa'*) (unnamed, 1 Ki. 16:11). *rēa'* is the common OT word for 'friend', and *mērēa'* and *rē'eh* are generally taken as variant forms of it. It has been suggested, however, that *rē'eh* is to be connected with Egyp. *rḫ nsw.t*, which came in the Middle Kingdom to mean 'acquaintance of the king', or with *ruḫi šarri* in the Amarna letters, which has much the same meaning. The title does not seem to have implied any specific function, though marriage arrangements were a special concern, but the importance of the 'friend' is shown by the fact that there was never more than one at a time. A similar title was found later in Persian times, Themistocles, for example, being named a 'King's Friend' by Xerxes.

BIBLIOGRAPHY. R. de Vaux, *Ancient Israel*, 1961, pp. 122–123, 528; H. Donner, *ZATW* 73, 1961, pp. 269ff.; T. N. D. Mettinger, *Solomonic State Officials*, 1971, pp. 63–69; A. van Selms, 'The origin of the title "the king's friend"', *JNES* 16, 1957, pp. 118–123. T.C.M.

FRINGES. A border of tassels along the edges of a garment (Dt. 22:12). This was bound by a blue cord, and served to remind the wearer of God's commands and of the need to obey them (Nu. 15:38–39). Various monuments show Hebrews and others wearing fringed garments. In NT times those who delighted in an outward show of piety put noticeably wide fringed borders on their garments (Mt. 23:5). K.A.K.

FRUIT, FRUITS. The AV translation of the following Heb. and Gk. words, some of which are used interchangeably: Heb. *'ēḇ*, 'budding' (Ct. 6:11; Dn. 4:12, 14, 21); *y'ḇûl*, 'increase' (Dt. 11:17; Hab. 3:17; Hg. 1:10); *t'nûḇâ*, 'increase' (Jdg. 9:11; Is. 27:6; La. 4:9); *yeleḏ*, 'child' (Ex. 21:22); *leḥem* 'bread, food' (Je. 11:19); *nîḇ*, 'utterance' (Is. 57:19; Mal. 1:12); *ma'ᵃḵāl*, 'eating' (Ne. 9:25); *m'lē'â*, 'fullness' (Dt. 22:9; also 'ripe fruits' in Ex. 22:29); *p'rî*, 'fruit' (107 times); *t'ḇû'â*, 'incoming' (13 times); *kōaḥ*, 'strength' (Jb. 31:39). Gk. *gennēma*, 'produce' (Mt. 26:29; Mk. 14:25; Lk. 12:18; 22:18; 2 Cor. 9:10); *karpos*, 'fruit' (64 times; *akarpos*, 'without fruit', in Jude 12); *opōra*, 'ripe or full fruits' (Rev. 18:14).

a. Literal use

Mosaic law decreed that fruit-bearing trees be regarded as unclean for 3 years after planting, as the Lord's in the fourth year, and to be eaten by the people only in the fifth year. This preserved the health of the tree against premature plucking, gave

God his due place, perhaps commemorated the entrance of sin by forbidden fruit and certainly inculcated self-discipline. Fruit-trees were so highly valued that for many centuries thereafter, even during the bitterest wars, special efforts were made to protect them (*cf.* Dt. 20:19–20). See *AGRICULTURE, *FIG, *FOOD, *VINE, *TREES.

Children are sometimes spoken of as the fruit of the body or womb (Dt. 28:4; Ps. 127:3).

b. Metaphorical use

The term has inspired a large number of metaphorical uses, involving such phrases as the fruit of the Spirit (Gal. 5:22); fruit for God (Rom. 7:4) and for death (Rom. 7:5; *cf.* Jas. 1:15); fruit of the lips (*i.e.* speaking, Is. 57:19; Heb. 13:15); fruit unto holiness and life (Rom. 6:22); fruit of the wicked (Mt. 7:16) and of self-centredness (Ho. 10:1; *cf.* Zc. 7:5–6); fruit in season (*i.e.* true prosperity, Ps. 1:3; Je. 17:8); fruits of the gospel (Rom. 1:13; Col. 1:6); of righteousness (Phil. 1:11; Jas. 3:18); fruits which demonstrate repentance (Mt. 3:8; *cf.* Am. 6:12). The unfruitful works of darkness are contrasted with the fruit of light (Eph. 5:9–11).

'The tree of life with its twelve kinds of fruit' (Rev. 22:2) some regard as 'a sacrament of the covenant of works, and analogous to the bread and wine used by Melchizedek (Gn. 14:18) and to the Christian Eucharist (Mt. 26:29) in the covenant of grace' (*Baker's Dictionary of Theology*, 1960, p. 231). More probably it is a symbol of abundant life (Jn. 10:10).

BIBLIOGRAPHY. A. Goor and M. Nurock, *The Fruits of the Holy Land*, 1968; R. Hensel, *NIDNTT* 1, pp. 721–723; F. N. Hepper, *IEBP: Flowers and trees, Fruits and Vegetables, Ecology*, 1992.

J.D.D.

FUEL. *Coal was unknown to the Hebrews. Charcoal was used by the wealthy (Je. 36:22; Jn. 18:18) and by smiths, while the poor gathered their own sticks (1 Ki. 17:10). Ezekiel refers to the use of dried *dung as a fuel (4:12ff.), a practice which obtains today among the poor. Is. 44:14–16 lists some of the trees used as fuel, while shrubs (especially 'broom', Ps. 120:4), briars and thorns (Ec. 7:6), chaff (Mt. 3:12) and hay (Mt. 6:30) were used to obtain a quick, fierce, but evanescent heat. Fuel appears to have been common property among the Hebrews, and to be charged for it was a great hardship (La. 5:4).

R.J.W.

FULLNESS. The Gk. word *plērōma*, translated 'fullness', carries three possible connotations: 'that which is filled'; 'that which fills or fills up', *i.e.* 'completes'; 'that which is brought to fullness or completion'.

The first does not seem to be relevant in the Scriptures, but the other two possibilities are important for the interpretation of certain crucial biblical texts. For the second we may cite Ps. 24:1, LXX (= 1 Cor. 10:26); Mt. 9:16; Mk. 6:43; 8:20. The Matthew reference may have the meaning 'that which makes something full or complete', as it refers to a patch which fills up the hole in a torn garment.

Under the third meaning should be placed Rom. 11:25, 'the full number, the totality of the Gentiles', and Rom. 15:29, 'the full measure of Christ's blessing'. Rom. 13:10 describes love as the *plērōma* of the law. This has been construed as 'the sum total of the law's prescriptions and demands'; but it is possible that the correct meaning here is 'fulfilment'. Love, like the Lord Jesus, is the end of the law (Rom. 10:4; *cf.* Gal. 5:14; 6:2) in that it brings the law to its full realization and perfect completion in the sense of Mt. 5:17; 26:56; Mk. 1:15. This nuance leads on to those verses where the precise meaning of the word is disputed. It is convenient to divide them into two groups.

1. Col. 1:19 and 2:9 are best taken together. See J. Ernst, *Pleroma und Pleroma Christi*, 1970. The exegesis of the use of *plērōma* in 2:9 is undoubtedly 'the fullness of deity, the totality of the Godhead' which dwells in Christ; and this meaning may be decisive in settling the correct interpretation of 1:19. In this text the choice is between taking it as a quasi-technical term of early gnostic speculation, which used the word *plērōma* to denote the region inhabited by the 'full number' of intermediary beings which were thought to exist between the Creator God and the created world; and taking it in the sense 'God in his fullness', 'the entirety of God's attributes, his full divinity' which was pleased to dwell in Christ. On the former view, Paul is combating speculative teachers at Colossae, who reduced Christ to a member of the celestial hierarchy. The apostle asserts in reply to this teaching that Christ is the fullness of these intermediary beings. They are subsumed in him, for he is the *plērōma* of them all. See R. P. Martin, *Colossians and Philemon, NCB*, 1974, pp. 59f., 79f.

This view, however, which assumes that Paul and the Colossian heretics are using a common term, although supported by many scholars, among whom are J. B. Lightfoot, E. F. Scott, and R. Bultmann (*Theology of the New Testament*, 2, E.T. 1955, pp. 149ff.), is open to serious objection. Apart from the lack of convincing evidence for an early gnostic creed in the 1st century, the most obvious consideration which tells against this proposal is that stated by E. Percy, that there is no trace in 1:19 and 2:9 of a polemic against the use which the supposed heretical teachers were making of the term *plērōma*, and in any case it is very unlikely that Paul would have borrowed so important a term from such a source. J. A. T. Robinson's suggestion (*The Body*, 1952, p. 67), that the apostle deliberately took over for apologetic use this word which he found in Hellenistic circles, lacks plausibility.

With C. F. D. Moule and C. Masson we may accept the second view and interpret *plērōma* in its OT light, where the Heb. equivalent is *m*ᵉ*lō'*; this reading sees the word as conveying the thought somewhat parallel to the Logos Christology of John, *i.e.* in Christ the sum-total of the divine attributes dwells and is revealed and communicated to men (Jn. 1:14, 16).

2. In Ephesians the term is taken by some commentators as applying to the church as well as to Christ; and this would confirm the view expressed above that *plērōma* is not being used in any technical 'gnostic' sense. In Eph. 1:10 there is a meaning similar to that in Mt. 5:17; Mk. 1:15; Gal. 4:4 with the thought that God's pre-ordained plan is now about to be consummated.

Eph. 1:22–23 may be taken in a number of ways, listed with admirable clarity by R. Yates, 'A Re-examination of Eph. 1:23', *ExpT* 83, 1971–2, pp. 146–151. The real crux is whether, on the one hand, *plērōma* refers to the church, which is then to be taken actively as that which completes Christ who is filling all things (corresponding to Eph. 4:10: so J. Dupont, *Gnosis: la connaissance religieuse dans les épîtres de Saint Paul*, 1949, p. 424, n. 1), or, in a passive sense, as that which is filled by Christ: or whether, on the other hand, *plērōma* should be treated as in apposition to 'him' in v. 22 and so taken to apply to the Lord himself as the One who has been designated by God the Father as the fullness of the Godhead who fills all in all (as in 1 Cor. 15:28). This latter interpretation has the advantage of harmonizing with the rest of the Epistle (4:10) and with the teaching of *plērōma* in Colossians noted above. See Moule for a defence of this view, and F. C. Synge, who also takes *plērōma* as a reference to Christ.

Eph. 3:19 requires no comment, except that it confirms the understanding of *plērōma* as a Christological title. This verse is another way of expressing the hope that 'Christ may dwell in your hearts by faith' (3:17); Eph. 4:12–13 holds out the prospect of the whole body of believers coming into such an experience.

Another interpretation takes more seriously the voice of the verb (passive or middle) in the earlier texts. Christ is being fulfilled or is filling himself: but by or with whom? The answer to this question is that he is fulfilled either by the Christians who, as members of his Body, 'complement' the Head, and together form the 'whole Christ' (so A. Robinson, F. W. Beare); or with W. L. Knox, L. S. Thornton and J. A. T. Robinson, who propose the translation 'that which is filled by him who is always being filled (by God)', so that the meaning of the whole phrase is that the church is constantly receiving from Christ its Head the complete fullness which Christ receives from the Father.

Bibliography. C. F. D. Moule, *The Epistles to the Colossians and to Philemon, CGT*, 1957, Appendix IV; *idem*, '"Fulness" and "Fill" in the New Testament', *SJT* 4, 1951, pp. 79–86; J. A. T. Robinson, *The Body*, 1952, p. 65, n. 3. See also J. B. Lightfoot, *St Paul's Epistles to the Colossians and to Philemon*, 1897, pp. 255, 271; J. Ernst, *Pleroma and Pleroma Christi*, 1970; M. Barth, *Ephesians, AB*, 1974; T. Brandt *et al.*, *NIDNTT* 1, pp. 728–744; G. Delling, *TDNT* 6, pp. 283–311; P. Benoit, *Jesus and the Gospel*, vol. 2, 1974, pp. 51–92; P. D. Overfield, '*Pleroma*: A study in Content and Context', *NTS* 25, 1979, pp. 384–396; P. T. O'Brien, *Colossians, Philemon, WBC* 1982; A. T. Lincoln, *Ephesians, WBC* 1990; G. L. O. R. Yorke, *The Church as the Body of Christ in the Pauline Corpus*, 1991. R.P.M.

FURNACE. A word used to translate five Heb. terms and one Gk.

1. *'attûn*. An Aram. word which is used in Dn. 3 of the furnace into which Shadrach, Meshach and Abednego were cast by Nebuchadrezzar. It was probably a loan-word from Akkad. *utūnu*, 'oven', as used for baking bricks or smelting metals.

2. *kiḇšān*. A word occurring four times in the Bible, as a simile to describe the smoke of Sodom and Gomorrah (Gn. 19:28) and of Mt Sinai (Ex. 9:8, 10). In post-biblical Heb. it was understood to mean a kiln as used for firing pottery or burning lime.

3. *kûr*. A pot or crucible for smelting metals. The word always occurs in the Bible as a metaphor or simile of God's punishment or tempering of man. Egypt was a crucible of iron (Dt. 4:20; Je. 11:4; 1 Ki. 8:51); God will put Israel in the crucible and melt it with his fury (Ezk. 22:18, 20, 22); and Israel is passed through the crucible of affliction (Is. 48:10).

4. *'ᵃlîl*. Used only in Ps. 12:6 in a simile of the words of God which are as silver tried in a furnace. The usage suggests a crucible.

5. *tannûr*. 'Portable stove' or 'oven' (*Bread), the latter probably being a preferable translation in Ne. 3:11; 12:38; Is. 31:9; and perhaps Gn. 15:17, where AV gives 'furnace'.

6. *kaminos*. 'Oven, furnace', a word used in LXX to translate *'attûn*, *kiḇšān* and *kûr*, and in Mt. 13:42, 50 and Rev. 9:2 as a figure of the fires of hell (*cf.* also Rev. 1:15).

Copper-refining furnaces have been excavated in Palestine at Beth-shemesh, Ai and Ezion-geber, the last lying at the S end of the Wadi Arabah, which forms a funnel down which powerful winds blow. Well-preserved furnaces for iron refining built below the level of the ground have been found at Tell Jemmeh (?Gerar). (*Arts and Crafts.)

Bibliography. A. G. Barrois, *Manuel d'Archéologie biblique*, 1, 1939, pp. 372–373; R. J. Forbes, *Studies in Ancient Technology*, 6, 1958, pp. 66ff. T.C.M.

G

GAAL (Heb. *ga'al*). Son of Ebed; LXX(B) *Iobel* suggests Heb. *'ōḇēḏ* = 'servant' (*cf.* Moore, *ICC, Judges*, p. 256, and Jdg. 9:28). Leader of a roving band, who came to Shechem in the reign of Abimelech to take advantage of disaffection in the city. His activity forced Abimelech to attack Shechem; Gaal and his men were expelled by Abimelech's governor, but Abimelech took vengeance on the city for supporting him (Jdg. 9:22–45). J.P.U.L.

GABBATHA. An Aramaic word meaning 'height', 'eminence'; the local, native word for the area. It must have been on a height.

Gabbatha identifies the same location as the other term, 'the Pavement' (*lithostrōton*), but does not describe exactly the same thing. As Jn. 19:13 specifies, it is a 'place' called either the Height or the Pavement. One may suppose that the Pavement was laid by Herod in front of his palace in the Upper City (at the NW angle of the first N wall). This palace was the official residence of the Roman governors, including Pilate, as is clear from incidents described by Josephus.

The Greek word *lithostrōton* was adopted by the Romans to describe a paved area, either of marquetry (*opus sectile*) or of flagstones. Both types of work are known to have been used by Herod; marquetry at Jericho (inlaid stones, some coloured, set in a pattern) and flags at Jerusalem, notably for the streets and terraces outside the immense walls of the Temple Mount (now excavated by Mazar). The foundations of this palace in the Upper City have been excavated, but the superstructures were missing. Nor has the Pavement been found as yet.

The site for 'the Pavement' favoured by Christian pilgrims at the Convent of the Sisters of Zion is to be rejected. Its adherents err in claiming that Jesus was brought to trial at the Antonia fortress on the Temple Mount; as stated above, the palace in the Upper City was Pilate's headquarters. Moreover the location of this pavement is slightly wrong even for the Antonia; it is probably part of the public square at the E gate of Hadrian's Aelia Capitolina. The pools beneath it were filled in and had siege-engines erected on them when the Romans under Titus attacked the Antonia (1st Revolt). At the time of Jesus they were open pools *outside* the walls of the Antonia. The pavement set over them, now shown as the *lithostrōton*, had not been laid. J.P.K.

GABRIEL (Heb. *Gaḇrî'ēl*, 'man of God' or 'strength of God'). One of the two angels whom the Bible names: the other is *Michael. He is sent to interpret Daniel's vision (Dn. 8:16) and to give him the prophecy of the 70 weeks (Dn. 9:21). Some commentators identify the angel of Dn. 10:5ff. as Gabriel.

In intertestamental Jewish literature, Gabriel is one of the archangels, the 'angels of the presence' who stand before God's throne praising him and interceding for men (Tobit 12:15; *Jubilees* 2:2; 1QH 6:13; 1QSb 4; *Testament of Levi* 3:5, 7; *cf.* Lk. 1:19; Rev. 8:2). He is named either as one of four archangels, with Michael, Sariel (or Uriel) and Raphael (*1 Enoch* 9:1; 1QM 9:15f.; *cf. 1 Enoch* 40:6; 54:6; *Sibylline Oracles* 2:215 (some MSS); *Numbers Rabbah* 2:10), or as one of seven, with Uriel, Raphael, Raguel, Michael, Sariel (or Saraqael) and Remiel (*1 Enoch* 20). Gabriel's special responsibility is paradise (*1 Enoch* 20:7). He destroyed the antediluvian giants (*1 Enoch* 10:9). With the other archangels, he will officiate at the last judgment (*1 Enoch* 90:21f.; *cf.* 54:6; *Sibylline Oracles* 2:214–219; 1 Thes. 4:16; Rev. 8:2). The Targums and rabbinic literature often identify anonymous angels in the OT as Gabriel or Michael.

In the NT, Gabriel is sent to Zechariah to announce the birth of John the Baptist (Lk. 1:11–20) and to Mary to announce the birth of Jesus (Lk. 1:26–38). His self-description, 'I am Gabriel, who stand in the presence of God' (Lk. 1:19) identifies him as one of the archangels (*cf. Tobit* 12:15). R.J.B.

GAD ('good fortune'). **1.** The seventh son of Jacob, his first by Leah's maid Zilpah (Gn. 30:10–11). Gad himself already had seven sons when Jacob and his family entered Egypt (Gn. 46:16); Jacob promised Gad's descendants a troubled life, but foretold that they would hit back (Gn. 49:19). They recur later in Moses' blessing (Dt. 33:20–21).

2. An Israelite tribe descended from Gad, and the territory they occupied. The tribe in Moses' time had seven clans (Nu. 26:15–18), was commanded and represented by one Eliasaph (Nu. 1:14; 2:14; 7:42; 10:20), and supplied a spy for exploration of Canaan (Nu. 13:15). When Israel reached the plains of Moab, Reuben, Gad and half-Manasseh sought permission to settle in Transjordan, which they desired as their share in the promised land, because *Gilead was so suitable for their considerable livestock. To this Moses agreed, on condition that they first help their fellow-Israelites to establish themselves in W Palestine (Nu. 32). The Gadites and Reubenites then hastily repaired cities (including Ataroth) and sheepfolds to safeguard their families and livestock (Nu. 32:34–38, *cf.* 26–27) while preparing to help their brethren, a promise of help duly kept (Jos. 22:1–8). Then came the incident of the altar of witness (Jos. 22:9–34). As tribal territory, Reuben and Gad received the Amorite kingdom of Sihon: Reuben had the land from *Aroer on the Arnon river, N to a line running from the Jordan's mouth E to the region of Heshbon (Jos. 13:15–23). N of this line, Gad had all S Gilead, from the Jordan valley E as far as the S-to-N course of the upper Jabbok (the border with Ammon), and N generally as far as the E-to-W course of the lower Jabbok, but with two extensions beyond this: first, all the Jordan valley on the E side of Jordan river (formerly Sihon's) between the Dead Sea and the Sea of Galilee (or Chinneroth), and second, across the NE angle of the river Jabbok to include the district of *Mahanaim and a fertile tract flanking the E side of N Gilead N over Jebel Kafkafa to strategic Ramoth-gilead at modern Tell Ramith, 32 km NE of Jerash (*cf.* Jos. 13:24–28). Heshbon was assigned as a levitical city out of the territory of Gad (Jos. 21:38–39); hence perhaps read Jos. 13:16–17 as (Reuben's) 'border was from Aroer ... and all the plain by Medeba, [unto] Heshbon ...' (emending only by the addition of one letter, locative-*h*). Dibon, *etc.*, are then cities between these limits, and Heshbon would be the southernmost territory of Gad.

The Gadites doubtless shared the troubles of Transjordanian Israel generally in the judges' period (*e.g.* Jdg. 10–12). In Saul's day the wooded Gileadite hills of Gad offered a place of refuge (1 Sa. 13:7), and Gadites among others joined the fugitive David and supported his becoming king (1 Ch. 12:1, 8–15, 37–38). Gadites likewise shared in, and were subject to, David's administration (2 Sa. 23:36; 24:5; 1 Ch. 26:32). On his Moabite Stone, roughly 840/830 BC, King Mesha mentions that the Gadites had long dwelt in the land of Ataroth. Just after this, within Jehu of Israel's reign, Hazael of Damascus smote all Gilead, Gad included (2 Ki. 10:32–33). In the 8th century BC Gadite settlement apparently extended NE into Bashan (1 Ch. 5:11–17), until Tiglath-pileser III carried the Transjordanians into exile (2 Ki. 15:29; 1 Ch. 5:25–26). Then the Ammonites again invaded Gad (Je. 49: 1–6). Gad is assigned the southernmost zone in Ezekiel's vision of the tribal portions (48:27–28). Geographical background, in D. Baly, *Geography of the Bible*[2], 1974, pp. 210ff., 221ff., 227–232.

3. A prophet or seer, the contemporary of Saul and David; he advised David to leave Moab for Judah (1 Sa. 22:5). Later, God through Gad offered a choice of three possible punishments to David after his census, and then commanded that David build an altar on Araunah's threshing-floor (2 Sa. 24:10ff.; 1 Ch. 21). Gad helped David and Nathan in organizing music for eventual use in the Temple (2 Ch. 29:25), and wrote a history of David's reign (1 Ch. 29:29).

4. A pagan deity worshipped by the Canaanites as the god of Fortune for whom they 'prepare a table' (Is. 65:11, RV, AVmg.). (*GAD, VALLEY OF.) K.A.K.

GAD, VALLEY OF. The place where the census ordered by David was begun is given as 'Aroer, on the right side of the city that is in the middle of the valley (Heb. *naḥal*) of Gad' (2 Sa. 24:5, RV). In Dt. 2:36 Aroer is described as 'on the edge of the valley (*naḥal*) of the Arnon'. Since the census would naturally begin at the S border of the Transjordan territory, this is probably the place intended. Various MSS of the LXX indicate corruptions in the text of 2 Sa. 24:5, which should read 'toward Gad and Jazer' (so RSV). G.T.M.

GADARENES, GADARA. The only biblical references to the Gadarene area concern the story of the miracle of Legion and the swine. The word 'Gadarenes' is found in some texts or versions of Mt. 8:28; Mk. 5:1; and Lk. 8:26. The probability is, however, that it is the original reading only in Mt. (Compare these vv. in AV and modern EVV.) The actual site of the miracle is in little doubt, at the edge of the Sea of Galilee. It would have been in a sub-district of Gadara, which lay 10 km SE of the Sea, near the gorge of the Yarmuk (or Hieromax). The Mishnah claims that Gadara dates from the OT period. It was held variously by Ptolemies, Seleucids, Jews and Romans between the 3rd century BC and the Jewish War. It was one of the Decapolis cities. The ruins at Umm Qays now mark the site. (*GERASA.) D.F.P.

GAIUS. A Latin praenomen, used without addition several times in the NT.

1. A Macedonian involved in the Ephesian riot (Acts 19:29; *ARISTARCHUS).

2. A companion of Paul's to Jerusalem, a member of the party which awaited the apostle at Troas (Acts 20:4f.), perhaps an official delegate of his church, which on the usual reading was Derbe. It is attractive, however, to follow the Western reading, 'of Doubērus' (a Macedonian town), and also possible to attach 'of Derbe' to Timothy (in which case Gaius would be a Thessalonian). Either way he would be a Macedonian, and thus conceivably the same as **1**. Proof is impossible: Luke may rather be interposing two Galatians (Timothy representing Lystra) between two Thessalonians and two Asians.

3. A Corinthian, baptized by Paul (1 Cor. 1:14). The church met in his house, and Paul stayed with him on his third Corinthian visit (Rom. 16:23). A suggestion of Ramsay's has been revived that Gaius was the praenomen of Titius *Justus (Acts 18:7). Origen (on Rom. 16) refers to a tradition that he became first bishop of Thessalonica.

4. The addressee of 3 John: the Elder commends his rectitude and hospitality (of which he asks a renewal), and expects to see him shortly. J. Chapman (*JTS* 5, 1904, pp. 366ff.) would identify him with any of the preceding, especially **1** and **3**, but his reconstruction is highly conjectural. The name was very common; the four references may well represent four different people. A.F.W.

GALATIA. 1. The ancient ethnic kingdom of Galatia located in the N of the great inner plateau of Asia Minor, including a large portion of the valley of the Halys river. A great population explosion in central Europe brought Gauls into this area during the 3rd century BC. Although never in the majority, the Gauls gained the upper hand and ruled over the more numerous tribes of Phrygians and Cappadocians. Ultimately the Gauls separated into three tribes, each inhabiting a separate area: the Trokmi settled in the E which bordered on Cappadocia and Pontus, with Tavium as their capital; the Tolistobogii inhabited the W bordering on Phrygia and Bithynia, with Pessinus as their chief town; and the Tektosages settled in the central area with Ancyra as their principal city.

2. The Roman province of Galatia. In 64 BC Galatia became a client of the Romans and, after

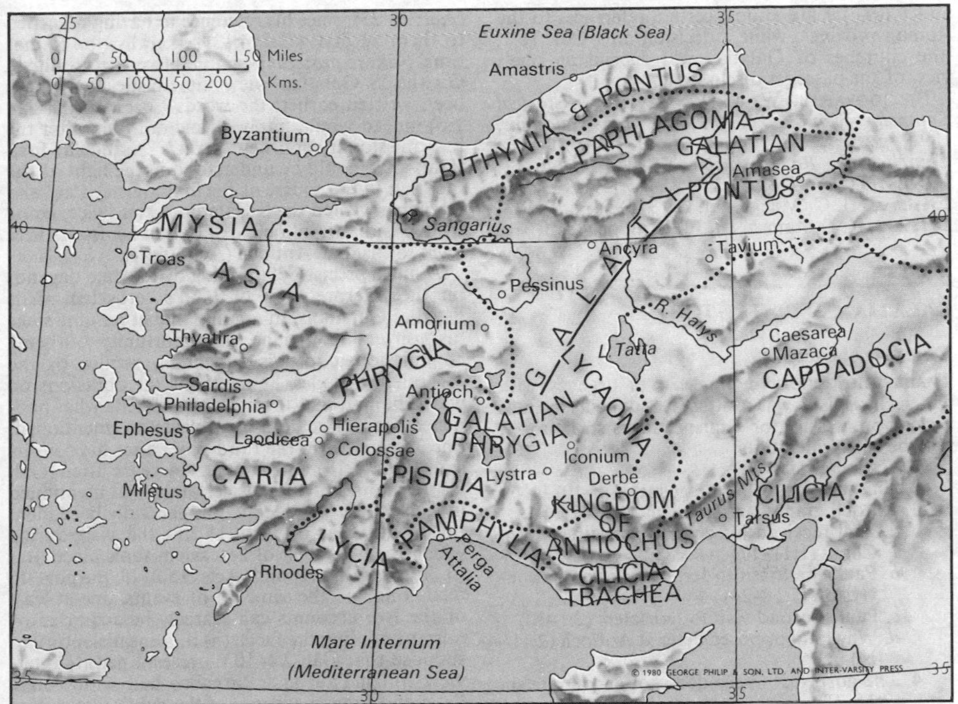

Galatia, an ancient ethnic kingdom which, as a new Roman province, also included parts of Pontus, Phrygia, Lycaonia, Pisidia, Paphlagonia and Isauria.

the death of Amyntas, its last king, was given full status as a Roman province (25 BC). The new province of Galatia included not only the old ethnic territory but also parts of Pontus, Phrygia, Lycaonia, Pisidia, Paphlagonia and Isauria. Within the provincial Galatia were the towns which the apostle Paul evangelized on his first missionary journey, *viz*. Antioch, Iconium, Lystra and Derbe (Acts 13–14). The latter two cities were Roman colonies, and the former two had been Romanized by the emperor Claudius. Large numbers of Romans, Greeks and Jews were attracted to these population centres because of their strategic geographical location.

A particularly difficult question arises out of Paul's use of the word 'Galatia' in the Epistle to the Galatians (1:2). Does Paul use the term in its geographical sense, *i.e.*, to denote the ancient ethnic kingdom of Galatia, or in its political sense, to denote the Roman province by that name? NT scholars are almost evenly divided on this question (* CHRONOLOGY OF THE NEW TESTAMENT).

It is clear from the account in Acts 13–14 that Paul visited S Galatia and established churches there. Did he ever conduct a mission in N Galatia? Two texts especially have been used to support such a ministry. The first (Acts 16:6) reads: 'And they went through the region of Phrygia and Galatia. . . .' N Galatian proponents understand 'Phrygia' here to be the territory in which Antioch and Iconium were located, whereas 'Galatia' refers to the geographical or ethnic kingdom by that name. Ramsay, however, takes the phrase *tēn Phrygian kai Galatikēn chōran* to be a composite term describing a single area—the Phrygian–Galatic region. The word *chōra*, 'territory', was the official word used to describe one of the *regiones* into which Roman provinces were divided. Part of the old kingdom of Phrygia belonged to the Roman province of Galatia and another part belonged to the province of Asia. Thus Acts 16:6 refers to the parts of Phrygia which had been incorporated into the Roman province of Galatia. This interpretation is supported by the following statement in the Acts account, 'having been forbidden by the Holy Spirit to speak the word in Asia'. The plan of the missionary party apparently was to strike out directly in a W direction from Antioch of Pisidia, which would have taken them into the province of Asia. Instead they went N towards Bithynia, crossing only a part of Asia.

The other passage is Acts 18:23. Here the order of the words is reversed: '. . . and went from place to place through the region of Galatia and Phrygia, strengthening all the disciples'. The 'region of Galatia' here is probably 'Galatic Lycaonia, so called to distinguish it from eastern Lycaonia, which lay, not in the province of Galatia, but in the territory of King Antiochus' (F. F. Bruce, *The Book of the Acts*, 1954, p. 380). 'Phrygia' then would probably include both Galatic and Asiatic Phrygia, since on this occasion there was no prohibition to prevent Paul preaching the word in Asia. In neither of these passages in Acts does there seem to be any good reason to suppose that Galatia means N Galatia. It is doubtful that Paul ever visited the ancient kingdom to the N, much less that he conducted an extensive mission there. (* GALATIANS, IV).

There are three other occurrences of 'Galatia' in the NT. 2 Tim. 4:10 (which has the variant 'Gaul') and 1 Pet. 1:1 are almost certain references to the Roman province, while a decision on 1 Cor. 16:1, 'the churches of Galatia', will depend on one's view of the passages discussed above.

BIBLIOGRAPHY. W. M. Ramsay, *An Historical Commentary on St. Paul's Epistle to the Galatians*, 1899, *passim*; *SPT*, pp. 89–151, 178–193; *The Church in the Roman Empire*[3], 1894, pp. 74–111; *HDB*; *HDAC*; *IDB*; K. Lake, *BC*, 5, 1933, pp. 231ff.; G. H. C. Macgregor, *IB*, 9, 1954, pp. 213f., 247, 252; R. T. Stamm, *IB*, 10, 1953, pp. 435ff.

W.W.W.

GALATIANS, EPISTLE TO THE.

I. Outline of contents

Thanks, no doubt, to the sense of urgency with which the Epistle was written, it is difficult to trace a clear progression or sequence in its structure. It may be subdivided thus:

1. Greetings (1:1–5)
2. This new 'gospel' is no gospel (1:6–10)
3. Autobiography and apologia (1:11–2:14)
   a. Paul received his commission direct from Christ (1:11–17)
   b. Paul's first visit to Jerusalem after his conversion (1:18–24)
   c. Paul's second visit to Jerusalem (2:1–10)
   d. Why Paul opposed Peter at Antioch (2:11–14)
4. The gospel of grace does not encourage sin (2:15–21)
5. An appeal to the Galatians' personal experience (3:1–6)
6. The gospel covenant with Abraham is prior to Moses' law (3:7–22)
7. Christian maturity (3:23–4:11)
   a. We are full-grown sons now (3:23–29)
   b. Going back to infancy (4:1–7)
   c. Going back to slavery (4:8–11)
8. A further personal appeal (4:12–20)
9. Christian freedom: the two Jerusalems (4:21–5:1)
10. Faith, not works (5:2–12)
11. Liberty, not licence (5:13–26)
12. A call to mutual aid (6:1–5)
13. Sowing and reaping (6:6–10)
14. Postscript in Paul's hand (6:11–18)
   a. Paul takes up the pen (6:11)
   b. False and true boasting (6:12–16)
   c. The true marks of a servant of Christ (6:17)
   d. Benediction (6:18)

II. Authorship and date

Except in such extreme and unrepresentative circles as the Van Manen school (whose views received publicity in *EBi*), the Pauline authorship of Galatians has been an axiom of NT criticism. Galatians has traditionally been recognized as one of the four 'capital epistles' of Paul (the other three being Romans and 1 and 2 Corinthians); indeed, it has been regarded as a standard by which other documents' claims to Pauline authorship could safely be measured.

On the 'N Galatian' view of its destination (see section IV, below) the Epistle could not have been written before AD 49/50, when Paul's second missionary journey began (Acts 16:6), and was more probably written after AD 52, when the third journey began and Paul visited 'Galatia' a second time (Acts 18:23), since his reference to having preached to them 'at first' (Gal. 4:13)—literally 'the former time' (Gk. *to proteron*)—implies two visits to them. On the 'S Galatian' view the Epistle could have been written earlier; the words 'so quickly' (Gal. 1:6) indeed would imply a time not long after the first missionary journey (AD 47–8), and 'at first' (Gal. 4:13) could be understood in the light of the fact that in the course of the first journey Paul and Barnabas visited the S Galatian cities twice, going from Pisidian Antioch to Derbe and from there back to Pisidian Antioch (Acts 14:21).

A more precise determining of the date depends on the interpretation of Paul's Jerusalem visits listed in Galatians. In arguing that at no time since his conversion had he an opportunity of being commissioned for his missionary service by the Jerusalem apostles, he mentions the occasions on which he had met them since, and tells what happened then. Two Jerusalem visits are mentioned: one 3 years (or in the third year) after his conversion (Gal. 1:18) and another 14 years after (Gal. 2:1). The first of these is certainly that mentioned in Acts 9:26ff. The second has generally been identified with that of Acts 15:2ff., the visit during which the *Council of Jerusalem took place. But (i) if Gal. 2:1–10 and Acts 15:2–29 purport to relate one and the same set of events, one at least of the two accounts can scarcely be acquitted of misrepresenting the facts; (ii) it is unsatisfactory to suppose that Gal. 2:1–10 narrates a private interview which Paul and Barnabas had with James, Peter and John in advance of the public Council; in that case Paul's suppression of the findings of the Council is inexplicable, for they were directly relevant to the Galatian controversy; (iii) the fact that the findings of the Council are not mentioned in Galatians can best be explained if in fact the Council had not yet been held when the Epistle was written; (iv) if the Jerusalem visit of Gal. 2:1 is that of Acts 15, Paul's critics would have pointed out immediately that he had failed to mention the earlier visit mentioned in Acts 11:30; 12:25. (The view that the visit of Acts 11:30; 12:25 is a duplicate of that recorded in Acts 15 is unacceptable; and the high estimate of the accuracy of the narrative of *Acts, which underlies the present discussion, can be defended by strong arguments.) There are weighty reasons for identifying the visit of Gal. 2:1 with that of Acts 11:30, and for dating the Epistle shortly before the Council of Jerusalem, *c.* AD 48/49. The incident of Gal. 2:12 is probably to be correlated with Acts 15:1.

III. Occasion of writing

Galatians was plainly written to converts of Paul's who were in imminent danger of adulterating the gospel of Christian freedom which he had taught them with elements of Jewish legalism. Among these elements circumcision took a chief place; they also included the observance of the Jewish calendar (Gal. 4:10) and possibly Jewish food-laws. The 'churches of Galatia' had evidently been visited by Judaizers who cast doubt on Paul's apostolic status and insisted that, in addition to the faith in Christ which he inculcated, it was necessary to be circumcised and to conform in other respects to the Jewish law in order to attain salvation. When news of this reached Paul he wrote this letter in white-hot urgency, denouncing this teaching which mingled grace and law as a different gospel from that which he had preached to them in Christ's name—in fact, no gospel at all—and entreating his readers to stand fast in their new-found liberty and not place their necks again under a yoke of bondage.

IV. Destination

The letter is addressed to 'the churches of Galatia' (1:2). To us this is a not unambiguous designation, for 'Galatia' was used in two distinct senses in the 1st century AD: it might denote ethnic Galatia in central Asia Minor, or the much larger Roman province of *Galatia. If the letter was sent to people in ethnic Galatia (the view of J. B. Lightfoot and most of the older commentators), we must suppose that that is the region visited by Paul in Acts 16:6 and 18:23 (or at least in one of these passages). But these two passages should probably be interpreted otherwise. There is, in fact, little evidence that Paul ever visited ethnic Galatia, whereas there is ample evidence that he visited the S area of the province of Galatia and planted churches there. The view that this Epistle is addressed to ethnic Galatia is commonly called the 'N Galatian' theory; the 'S Galatian' theory, on the other hand, supposes that the Epistle was sent to the churches of Pisidian Antioch, Iconium, Lystra and Derbe, all in the S of the Roman province, and all planted by Paul and Barnabas in the course of their first missionary journey (Acts 13:14–14:23).

Against the 'S Galatian' theory it has been argued that it would be psychologically inept for Paul to address his readers as 'Galatians' (Gal. 3:1) if in fact they were not ethnically Galatian. But if they belonged to different ethnic groups (Phrygian and Lycaonian) what common appellation could he have chosen to cover them all except their common political denominator, 'Galatians'? (So a modern writer, addressing a mixed group of English, Welsh and Scots, would probably address them as 'Britons' or 'British' in the political sense, although in its ethnic sense it would be applicable only to the Welsh members of the group.)

V. Principal arguments

If a logical analysis of the Epistle as a whole defies us, we can at least recognize the leading arguments which Paul uses in defence of true gospel liberty. Nine of them may be briefly stated as follows.

1. The gospel which Paul preached was the gospel which he received by direct commission from Christ; it came to his hearers with Christ's authority, not with Paul's (1:11ff.).

2. Against Paul's claim to unmediated commission from Christ, some argued that all valid apostolic authority must be mediated through Jerusalem, and that Paul's teaching or practice therefore was invalid if it deviated from the Jerusalem pattern. Paul replies by describing his visits to Jerusalem between his conversion and the time of writing, showing that the Jerusalem leaders had no opportunity of commissioning him but that, on the contrary, they acknowledged the apostolic commission (to the Gentiles) which he had already received from Christ (1:15–2:10).

3. If acceptance with God could have been obtained through circumcision and the other observances of the Jewish law, Christ's death was pointless and vain (2:21).

4. Christian life, as the Galatian converts knew from their own experience, is a gift of the Spirit of God; when they received it they received at the same time unmistakable proofs of the Spirit's presence and power in their midst. But if they began their Christian life on that high plane it was preposterous to imagine that they should continue it on the lower plane of legal works (3:2ff.).

5. The Judaizers justified their insistence on circumcision by appealing to the example of Abraham: since circumcision was the seal of God's covenant with him, they argued, no uncircumcised person could have a share in that covenant with all the blessings which went with it. But the true children of Abraham are those who are justified by faith in God, as Abraham was; it is they who enjoy the blessings promised to Abraham. God's promise to Abraham was fulfilled in Christ, not in the law; therefore the blessings bestowed by that promise are to be enjoyed not through keeping the law (which came long after the promise and could not affect its terms) but through faith in Christ (3:6–9, 15–22).

6. The law pronounces a curse on those who fail to keep it in every detail; those who place their trust in the law therefore put themselves in danger of that curse. But Christ, by his death on the cross, bore the divine curse in his people's place and delivered them from the curse which the law pronounces; his people therefore ought not to go back and put themselves under the law with its attendant curse (3:10–14).

7. The principle of law-keeping belongs to the age of spiritual immaturity; now that Christ has come, those who believe in him have attained their spiritual majority as responsible sons of God. To accept the arguments of the Judaizers would be to revert to infancy (3:23–4:7).

8. The law imposed a yoke of slavery; faith in Christ brings liberation. Those whom Christ has emancipated are foolish indeed if they give up their freedom and submit afresh to the dictation of those elemental powers through which the law was mediated (4:8–11; 5:1; 3:19).

9. This freedom which the gospel of grace proclaims has nothing to do with anarchy or licence; faith in Christ is a faith which works by love and thus fulfils the law of Christ (5:6; 5:13–6:10).

These arguments are presented in a more systematic form in the Epistle to the Romans, written 8 or 9 years later. The basic understanding of the gospel which underlies all these arguments took shape in Paul's mind very probably quite soon after his conversion, although the way in which it finds expression in Galatians is due to the special situation to which Paul addresses himself here. But perhaps for that very reason Galatians has to this day been cherished by Christians as a great charter of gospel liberty.

BIBLIOGRAPHY. J. H. Ropes, *The Singular Problem of the Epistle to the Galatians*, 1929; C. H. Buck, Jr., 'The Date of Galatians', *JBL* 70, 1951, pp. 113ff.; F. F. Bruce, 'Galatian Problems, 1–5', *BJRL* 51, 1968–9, to 55, 1972–3; D. Guthrie, *Galatians, NCB*, 1969; F. F. Bruce, *The Epistle to the Galatians, NIGTC*, 1982; R. Y. K. Fung, *The Epistle to the Galatians, NIC*, 1988; R. A. Cole, *Galatians, TNTC*², 1989; R. N. Longenecker, *Galatians, WBC*, 1990; G. W. Hansen, *Galatians, IVPNTC*, 1994; P. H. Kern, *Rhetoric, Scholarship and Galatians: Assessing an Approach to Paul's Epistle* (diss. Sheffield, forthcoming). F.F.B.

GALEED (Heb. *gal'ēḏ*, 'witness pile'). Name given to the cairn erected by Jacob and Laban as a memorial to their covenant made in N Transjordan (Gn. 31:47–48; *PILLAR). By Laban it was given the equivalent Aramaic name *Yegar-sahadutha*. Documents of the earlier 2nd millennium BC reveal a great mixture of ethnic groups in N Mesopotamia. It is quite possible that some Aramaeans were included among them and that their dialect had been adopted by other Semitic groups. Specific evidence of Aramaeans in this area at this date is not yet available (*ARAM). A.R.M.

GALILEE (Heb. *gālîl*, 'ring, circle', hence a 'district, region'). The regional name of part of N Palestine, which was the scene of Christ's boyhood and early ministry. The origin of the name as applied here is uncertain. It occurs occasionally in the OT (*e.g.* Jos. 20:7; 1 Ki. 9:11), and notably in Is. 9:1. The latter reference probably recalls the region's history: it originally formed part of the lands allocated to the twelve tribes, but, owing to the pressure from peoples farther north, its Jewish population found themselves in a kind of N salient, surrounded on three sides by non-Jewish populations—'the nations'. Under the Maccabees, the Gentile influence upon the Jews became so strong that the latter were actually withdrawn S for half a century. Thus Galilee had to be recolonized, and this fact, together with its diversity of population, contributed to the contempt felt for the Galileans by the S Jews (Jn. 7:52).

Exact demarcation of the Galilee region is difficult, except in terms of the provincial boundaries of the Roman empire. The name was evidently applied to the N marchlands of Israel, the location of which varied from time to time. In the time of Christ, however, the province of Galilee formed a rectangular territory some 70 km from N to S, and 40 km from E to W, bordered on the E by the Jordan and the Sea of *Galilee, and cut off from the Mediterranean by the S extension of Syro-Phoenicia down the coastal plain.

Thus defined, Galilee consists essentially of an upland area, bordered on all sides save the N by plains—the coastlands, the plain of Esdraelon and the Jordan Rift. It is, in fact, the S end of the mountains of Lebanon, and the land surface falls, in two steps, from N to S across the area. The higher 'step' forms Upper Galilee, much of which is at 1,000 m above sea-level; in NT times it was a forested and thinly inhabited hill-country. The lower 'step' forms Lower Galilee, 450–600 m above sea-level, but falling steeply to more than 180 m below sea-level at the Sea of Galilee.

It is to this area of Lower Galilee that most of the Gospel narrative refers. Well watered by streams flowing from the N mountains, and possessing considerable stretches of fertile land in the limestone basins among its hills, it was an area of

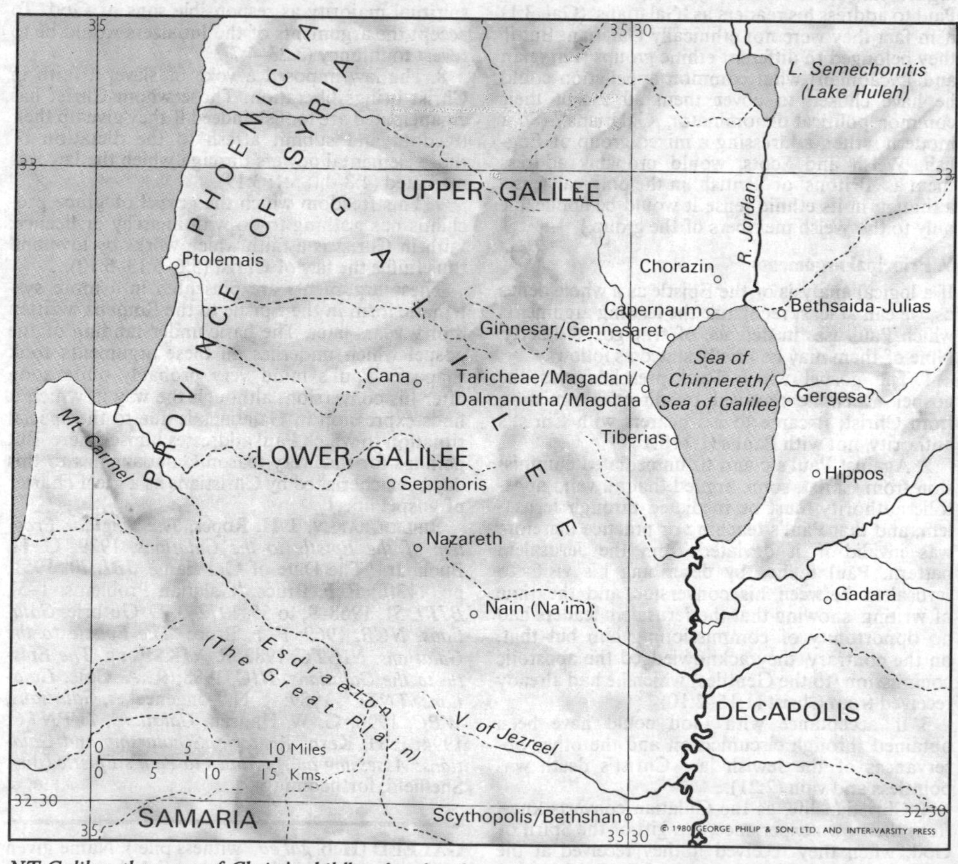

NT Galilee: the scene of Christ's childhood and early ministry.

dense and prosperous settlement. It exported olive oil and cereals, and fish from the lake.

'Outside the main stream of Israelite life in OT times, Galilee came into its own in the NT' (D. Baly, *The Geography of the Bible*, 1957, p. 190). The Roman region was governed successively by Herod the Great (died 4 BC), Herod Antipas and Herod Agrippa. Cut off from Judaea—at least in Jewish eyes—by the territory of Samaria, Galilee nevertheless formed an integral part of 'the land', and the Galileans had, in fact, resisted the Romans even more doggedly than the S Jews. In the time of Christ the relationship between the two groups is well described as having been that of 'England and Scotland soon after the Union' (G. A. Smith, *Historical Geography of the Holy Land*[25], 1931, p. 425).

This, then, was the region in which Christ grew up—at Nazareth, in the limestone hills of Lower Galilee. Thanks to its position, it was traversed by several major routeways of the empire, and was therefore far from being a rural backwater. Its agriculture, fisheries and commerce provided him with his cultural background, and are reflected in his parables and teaching. Its people provided him with his first disciples, and its dense scattering of settlements formed their first mission field.

Today, Galilee and the plain of Esdraelon form the core area of N Israel, but its modern inhabitants have the task of rehabilitating an area which has lost much of the prosperity it enjoyed in NT days. Its forests have been largely replaced by *maquis*, the characteristic scrub of the Mediterranean, and many of its towns and villages, places which Christ knew and visited, have disappeared from the map, leaving hardly a trace behind them.

BIBLIOGRAPHY. G. A. Smith, *The Historical Geography of the Holy Land*[25], 1931, pp. 413–436; D. Baly, *The Geography of the Bible*, 1957.

J.H.P.

GALILEE, SEA OF. A lake in the region of Galilee, also referred to, in the OT, as the 'sea of *Chinnereth' (Nu. 34:11) or Chinneroth (Jos. 12:3), and in the NT as the 'lake of Gennesaret' (Lk. 5:1) and the 'Sea of Tiberias' (Jn. 21:1). Its modern Heb. name is Yam Kinneret.

The lake is some 21 km long and up to 11 km broad, and it lies at 211 m below sea-level. The river Jordan flows through it from N to S; its waters are therefore sweet—unlike those of the Dead Sea—and its fisheries (*FISH), so prominent in the NT narrative, were famous throughout the Roman empire and produced a flourishing export trade. On the other hand, the position of the lake, in the depths of the Jordan Rift and surrounded by hills, renders it liable to atmospheric down-draughts and sudden storms.

The lake is bordered by a plain of varying width; in general, the slopes on the E side are abrupt (Mk. 5:13), and are somewhat gentler on the W. To the N and S are the river plains of the Jordan as it enters and leaves the lake.

The shores of the lake were the site of towns—Capernaum, Bethsaida, *etc.*—where much of Christ's ministry was carried out. In his time they formed a flourishing, and almost continuous, belt of settlement around the lake, and communicated and traded across it with each other. Today, only *Tiberias remains as a town—even the sites of several other former towns are uncertain—and changed patterns of commerce have robbed the lake of its focal importance in the life of the region.

BIBLIOGRAPHY. G. A. Smith, *The Historical Geography of the Holy Land*[25], 1931, pp. 437–463.

J.H.P.

GALL. The Hebrews used *rôš* and *m*ᵉ*rôrâ* to describe a *plant and its fruit which were extremely bitter. Variously translated as 'hemlock' AV, 'poisonous weeds' RSV, NEB (Ho. 10:4), 'poison' (Jb. 20:16; Je. 8:14) and 'venom' (*cf.* Dt. 32:33), it is frequently associated with the bitter herb wormwood (*Artemisia*) (Dt. 29:18; Je. 9:15; La. 3:19; Am. 6:12). Gall is referred to literally as the yellowish-brown secretion of the liver in Jb. 16:13; 20:14, 25. As a plant it probably refers to the extract of the colocynth gourd fruit (*Citrullus colocynthis*).

Metaphorically it denoted travail (La. 3:5) or any bitter experience (Acts 8:23). The anodyne offered to Christ during his crucifixion (Mt. 27:34; *cf.* Mk. 15:23) was a diluted wine containing stupefying drugs.

R.K.H.
F.N.H.

GALLIO. Lucius Junius Annaeus (or Annaeanus) Gallio was the son of Seneca the rhetorician and brother of Seneca the philosopher. An inscription at Delphi (*SIG*, 2[3], 801; *cf.* text and discussion by K. Lake, *BC*, 5, pp. 460ff.) makes it virtually certain that he was proconsul of Achaia in AD 52–53, in which office we meet him in Acts 18:12ff. A fixed point for Pauline chronology is thus afforded, even though the precise dates of office are unknown. His brother Seneca writes of him (*Ep. Mor.* 104. 1: *Quaest.* 4a, pref. 11), as do several other ancient writers (*e.g.* Pliny, *NH* 21. 33; Tacitus, *Ann.* 15. 73; Dio Cassius, 61. 35; 62. 25), with little to his discredit. Luke depicts his vigorous refusal to hear a Jewish-sponsored prosecution of Paul, on the ground that no criminal charge was brought. The now proverbial 'Gallio cared for none of those things' (Acts 18:17, AV) denotes less his religious indifference than his connivance at the subsequent outburst of anti-Semitism. The Western text conveys the sense: 'Gallio pretended not to see'. Gallio was executed by Nero's order in AD 65. J.H.H.

GALLOWS (Heb. *'ēṣ*, 'tree'). Found only in the book of Esther (nine times). Haman had a gallows (AVmg. 'tree') made on which to execute Mordecai, but the mode of the intended execution has been much debated. Hanging was not usual in Persia, where the events took place; it is suggested that the Heb. word means 'pole' or 'stake' (which seems likely), and that, following Persian custom, the victim was to be impaled. (*CROSS.) J.D.D.

GAMALIEL (Heb. *gamlî'ēl*, 'reward of God'; Gk. *Gamaliēl*). **1.** Son of Pedahzur, and a 'prince of the children of Manasseh' chosen to help Moses in taking the census in the wilderness (Nu. 1:10; 2:20; 7:54, 59; 10:23).

2. Son of Simon and grandson of Hillel (according to later, but doubtful, tradition), Gamaliel was a doctor of the law and a member of the Sanhedrin. Representing the liberal wing of the *Pharisees, the school of Hillel, as opposed to that of Shammai, he intervened with a reasoned and persuasive speech at the trial of the apostles (Acts 5:33–40).

Paul acknowledged him as his teacher (Acts 22:3), and he was held in such high honour that he was designated 'Rabban' ('our teacher'), a higher title than 'Rabbi' ('my teacher'). See J. Neusner, *The Rabbinic Traditions about the Pharisees before 70*, 1, 1971, pp. 341ff.

The Mishnah (*Soṭa* 9. 15) says, 'Since Rabban Gamaliel the Elder died there has been no more reverence for the Law, and purity and abstinence died out at the same time.' As we might expect from this reputation among the Jews, there is no evidence, despite early suggestions (*e.g. Clementine Recognitions* 1. 65), that he ever became a Christian. J.D.D.

GAMES.

I. In the Old Testament

a. Physical sport

In common with their Near Eastern neighbours, the life of the majority of Hebrews left little time or inclination for physical sport. When introduced by Hellenizing Jews in the time of Antiochus Epiphanes (1 Macc. 1:10–14; Jos., *Ant.* 15. 268) and patronized by Jason, the high priest (2 Macc. 4:7–17), the Greek love of sport was considered irreligious. Nevertheless, there can be little doubt that, despite the absence of explicit references, running, throwing and hunting were undertaken on occasions when they were not a necessity. Like the Egyptians and Babylonians, the people of Palestine would have enjoyed contests at weight-lifting and wrestling. Jacob's long wrestling-match may reflect both practised ability at the sport and the recognition of rules precluding holds below the belt (Gn. 32:24–26). The expression 'hip and thigh' (Jdg. 15:8) may be a technical wrestling term, like English 'cross-buttock'. It has been suggested that the group combat at Gibeon was initiated as a wrestling-match (2 Sa. 2:14), wrestling by grasping an opponent's belt being an ancient form of this sport. Archery could be a game of skill aiming at fixed marks (1 Sa. 20:20; Jb. 16:12; La. 3:12), as is shown on Assyrian reliefs, as well as a warlike art.

b. Games of chance

Gaming-boards have been discovered at a number of sites, including Tell el 'Ajjul and Beth-shemesh. Some made of ivory (Megiddo, *c.* 1350–1150 BC), stone (Gezer, *c.* 1200 BC) or wood were in 'human' or 'violin' shape pierced with peg-holes for a game of '55 Holes' commonly found in Egypt and Mesopotamia. Draughts was played on boards of twenty or thirty squares made of stone, clay, ebony or ivory and sometimes hollowed at the back to contain the men. Unlike modern western methods of play in these games, moves were made as a result of the throw of a dice (of which an ivory example of the 17th century BC was found at Tell Beit Mirsim), knuckle-bones or casting-sticks. Pyramidal or conical game places and counters have been found, also 'halma' men at Lachish. 'Chinese-type' chess was known in Elam and Babylonia from the 3rd millennium BC and may well have been played in Palestine. Unusual board-games, like those discovered at *Ur, Nineveh and Tell Halaf, Syria (8th century), were played, though the method of play is at present obscure. The Hebrews, with their neighbours, considered that the lot (*pûr*; *DIVINATION) was a means of determining the divine will, and in this way some board-games also had religious significance.

c. Children's games

The young played in the streets (Zc. 8:5), imitating their elders in daily life or at marriages and funerals. The boys may have imitated the Egyptian team-games shown in paintings and a form of tug-of-war, while the girls practised juggling or ball-games, including catch played by teams with one mounted on another's back. Leather-covered balls have been found. Whistles, rattles, model pots, chariots and animals (some with wheels) have been recovered and betray an unchanging taste for toys by the youngest. It is unlikely that all the slings found were used only in the serious business of driving birds from the crops or guarding the flocks from straying. There is no evidence that the figurines or small statues with movable joints found at a number of sites were dolls. It is more likely that they were cult objects. People of all ages were amused by miming, skipping-ropes, whipped tops and hoops.

d. Diversion

Feasting, songs, music, and especially dancing, were the commonest form of relaxation. Opportunity was taken for this at every domestic rejoicing (Je. 31:4), including merry-making at harvest (Jdg. 9:27; 21:21) as well as at such public and state functions as the royal accession (1 Ki. 1:40) or celebration of victory (Ex. 15:20; Jdg. 11:34; 1 Sa. 18:6). Story-telling and the art of propounding riddles was also a highly-esteemed practice (Jdg. 14:12; Ezk. 17:2; 1 Ki. 10:1). (*DANCE.)

BIBLIOGRAPHY. H. J. C. Murray, *A History of Board Games other than Chess*, 1952; P. Montet, *Everyday Life in Egypt*, 1958; *Iraq* 1, 1935, pp. 45–50; 4, 1938, pp. 11ff.; 8, 1946, pp. 166ff.; *ANEP*, 1976, pp. 212–219 (illustrations); U. Hubner, *Spiele un Speilzeug im antiken Palästina*, 1992. D.J.W.

II. In the New Testament

Apart from one obscure reference to a children's game (Mt. 11:16–17), and a possible allusion to a chariot race (Phil. 3:13f.), the games mentioned in the NT are the Greek athletic contests. Reference to 1 Macc. 1:10–14; 2 Macc. 4:13–14 will emphasize the Hellenic outlook of the writers who found metaphor in this worthy subject. The festivals were religious in origin and flavour, encouraged discipline, art, health and fair play, and were not without diplomatic usefulness (see Lysias, 33). Surviving odes of Pindar reveal the honour paid the victor in the Pythian, Nemean, Isthmian and above all the Olympic Games.

In the Epistles metaphors are drawn from the Games generally, and from the foot-race and from the chariot race in particular.

In 1 Cor. 9: 24–27 Paul calls attention to the vigorous training of the athlete (a metaphor also used by Epictetus). The athlete is preoccupied not with the immediate token prize of the wreath of wild olive, parsley, pine or laurel, but with the later reward. The Christian is likewise exhorted to strive 'for the mastery', for his reward is, by contrast, an 'incorruptible' crown (*cf.* 2 Tim. 2:5; 4:8; 1 Pet. 1:4; 5:4). 1 Cor. 9:26 depicts a boxing contest. Here the arms and hands were bound with studded leather, which inflicted grave injury, and the combatant therefore sought to evade rather than to parry—

hence the phrase 'beating the air'. Having begun with the scene of victory, Paul concludes with a picture of failure. He sees himself as the herald calling others to the contest, but himself disqualified from competing. 'Preached' and 'castaway' (1 Cor. 9:27, AV) are unhappy renderings (see RV, RSV). Metaphors drawn from the Games would carry particular weight with the readers of this Epistle, since the Isthmian Games were a Corinthian festival.

In Gal. 2:2; 5:7; Phil. 2:16; Heb. 12:1–2 the reference is to the foot-race, for which a minimum of clothing was worn. 'Every weight' probably refers to weight shed in preparatory training in order to bring the runner to peak condition for the race. 'The sin which clings so closely' is more clearly a reference to clothing. The 'cloud' is a common metaphor for multitudes. It suggests the runner's blurred vision of the spectators as his eyes are focused on the goal.

The reference in Phil. 3:13–14 is probably to a chariot race. Horse-racing with light chariots was well known to the Greeks, and references go back to Homer and Sophocles. They were also a spectacular feature of the festivals. At the time Paul wrote, they were especially in fashion with the Romans, and Philippi was a Roman colony. We may translate these verses: 'I do not count myself to have done this, but this one thing I do, forgetting those things which are behind, and stretching out to those which lie before, I make for the mark, towards the prize of the upward calling of God in Jesus his Anointed.' Paul pictures himself in the chariot, bent over the curved rail against which the charioteer's knees were pressed, and, with the reins round his body, stretching out over the horses' backs and leaning his weight on the reins. In such intense preoccupation a glance at 'the things behind' would have been fatal. E.M.B.

GARDEN. It was promised that the lives of God's redeemed people would be like a watered garden, ordered and fruitful (Is. 58:11; Je. 31:12; *cf.* Nu. 24:6).

In Egypt the Hebrews had known richly productive vegetable-gardens (Dt. 11:10; *cf.* Nu 11:5; *FOOD). Fed from an irrigation-ditch, or from vessels by hand, a network of little earth channels criss-crossed the vegetable-beds like a chessboard. In New-Kingdom Egypt, M.-F. Moens, *Orientalia Lovanensia Periodica* 15, 1984, pp. 11–53.

In Palestine people cultivated gardens for vegetables ('garden of *herbs', 1 Ki. 21:2; 'what is sown', Is. 61:11), and fruit (Am. 9:14; Je. 29:5, 28; Ct. 4:16). Gardens might be associated with, or even part of, vineyards, olive-groves or orchards (Ec. 2:5; Am. 4:9; *cf.* 1 Ki. 21:2). Spices and choice plants featured in the gardens of royalty and of the nobility (Ct. 5:1; 6:2, 11 (walnuts); *cf.* 4:12–16 generally; Ec. 2:5). These and other gardens were walled round (*cf.* Ct. 4:12) and had to be kept watered, *e.g.* from a spring or pool (Ct. 4:15; *cf.* Ec. 2:5–6; contrast Is. 1:30). They may also have sometimes contained a summerhouse (2 Ki. 9:27). The 'king's garden' at Jerusalem was a well-known landmark (2 Ki. 25:4; Je. 39:4; 52:7; Ne. 3:15); and the Persian royal palace is mentioned as having a pleasure-garden (Est. 1:5; 7:7–8). Similarly, Egyptian and Mesopotamian kings kept fine gardens; and a garden once occupied a large court inside the sumptuous palace of the kings of Canaanite Ugarit (14th–13th century BC). For full references to gardens in Assyria and Babylonia, see in Ebeling, Meissner and Weidner, *Reallexikon der Assyriologie*, 3, 1959, pp. 147–150. For 'Hanging Gardens' of Babylon see D. J. Wiseman, *Nebuchadrezzar and Babylon*, 1991, pp. 55–60, plates I–II.

Tombs were sometimes situated in gardens (2 Ki. 21:18, 26; Jn. 18:1, 26; 19:41; *GETHSEMANE). A less happy use of gardens was for pagan rites, perhaps linked with the fertility cults of Canaan (Is. 1:29; 65:3; 66:17).

The Garden of *Eden was a symbol of God-created fertility (Gn. 13:10; Is. 51:3, *etc.*). K.A.K.

GATH. One of the five principal Philistine cities, and formerly occupied by the Anakim (*ANAK; Jos. 11:22). The gentilic from the name *gaṯ* was *gittî* or *gittîm* (Jos. 13:3), and this accounts for the 'Gittite' of the EVV. When the Philistines captured the ark and it brought ill fortune to Ashdod it was moved to Gath, where the people were struck with bubonic plague, so it was moved on to Ekron (1 Sa. 5:6–10; 6:17). Gath was famous as the home of *Goliath (1 Sa. 17), whom David killed. David later feigned madness to avoid retribution at the hands of Achish, king of Gath, when fleeing from Saul (1 Sa. 21:10–15), but subsequently took service under Achish, and lived for more than a year in his territory (1 Sa. 27). When David's fortunes revived, and later during Absalom's rebellion, after he had added Gath to his dominions (1 Ch. 18:1), he had Gittite friends in his retinue (2 Sa. 6:10–11; 15:19–21; 18:2) and a Gittite contingent among his mercenaries (2 Sa. 15:18). Another interesting Gittite is mentioned in 2 Sa. 21:20 (= 1 Ch. 20:6). He was very tall and had six digits on each extremity. Though Achish is still spoken of as king of Gath (1 Ki. 2:39–41), the city was probably subservient to David, and evidently continued subject to Judah in the time of Rehoboam, who fortified it (2 Ch. 11:8). It was captured by Hazael of Damascus in the late 9th century (2 Ki. 12:17), and may have regained its independence by the time Uzziah broke down its wall when he campaigned in Philistia (2 Ch. 26:6); soon afterwards Amos describes it as belonging to the Philistines (6:2), so it may have been a Philistine enclave, in loose vassalage, in the territory of Judah. Gath was besieged and conquered by Sargon of Assyria in the late 8th century.

The site has not been identified with certainty. Excavations at Tell el-'Areini some 30 km NE of Gaza failed to support its candidature. Tell esh-Sheri'ah and Tell eṣ-Ṣafi are other possibilities. So too is the adjacent Tell en Nagila or 'Araq el-Menshîyeh, but certainty must await further investigation.

BIBLIOGRAPHY. E. K. Vogel, *HUCA* 42, 1971, p. 88; K. A. Kitchen, *POTT*, pp. 62ff.; *NEAEHL*, pp. 418, 1329, 1522–1523; G. E. Wright, *BA* 29, 1966, pp. 78–86; *LOB*, p. 250. T.C.M.

GATH-HEPHER (Heb. *gaṯ-haḥēper*, 'winepress of digging'). The rendering Gittah-hepher of Jos. 19:13 in the AV arose through a misunderstanding of the *he locale*. A town on the border of Zebulun and Naphtali (Jos. 19:13), the birthplace of the prophet Jonah (2 Ki. 14:25). Identified with Khirbet ez-Zurra' and nearby el-Meshhed, 5 km NE of Nazareth. Ancient and continuous tradition indicated this as the birthplace and tomb of the prophet. Jerome in the 4th century AD said that his tomb was about 3 km from Sepphoris, which would coincide with Gath-hepher. M.A.M.

GAZA (Heb. *'azzâ*, LXX *Gaza*). One of the five principal Philistine cities. Originally inhabited by the Avvim, driven out by the Caphtorim (*CAPHTOR; Dt. 2:23), it was considered to mark the S limit of Canaan at the point on the coast where it was situated (Gn. 10:19). Joshua conquered it (Jos. 10:41) and found that some Anakim remained there (Jos. 11:21–22); the city was lost to Israel during his lifetime (Jos. 13:3). Judah, to whom it was allotted (Jos. 15:47), recaptured the town (Jdg. 1:18; though some hold that this refers to the same campaign as Jos. 10:41). In the period of the Judges Samson consorted with a harlot of Gaza in connection with which a description of the city gate is given (Jdg. 16:1–3). Israel's hold over Gaza must have been lost again at this period, for when the Philistines finally captured Samson they imprisoned him there, and it was there that he 'made sport' for them, and dislodged the pillars of the house, killing many of them (Jdg. 16:21–31). It has been pointed out that the description of Samson 'making sport' in front of a pillared building with spectators on the roof is reminiscent of some of the features of Cretan civilization, and this is to be expected in view of the origins of the *Philistines. At the time of the Philistine capture of the ark, Gaza with the other cities suffered from bubonic plague and made an offering of an emerod and a mouse of gold to avert it (1 Sa. 6:17).

The city occupied an important position on the trade routes from Egypt to W Asia, and from the 8th century it is frequently mentioned among Assyr. conquests. Tiglath-pileser III captured it (*Ḫa-az-zu-tu*) in 734 BC, perhaps at the request of Jehoahaz of Judah, the ruler, Hanno, fleeing to Egypt, and Tiglath-pileser set up an image of himself in the palace. Sargon had to repeat the action in 722 BC, for Hanno had returned to Gaza in support of a rebellion led by Hamath. Hanno was taken prisoner to Assyria. The city remained faithful to Assyria, for Sennacherib, when he proceeded against Hezekiah in Jerusalem, gave some of the territory taken from Judah to Ṣillibel, king of Gaza, and Esarhaddon put a strain on this loyalty when he laid heavy tribute on him and twenty other kings of the Hittite country. In the time of Jeremiah the city was captured by Egypt (Je. 47:1). Gaza was taken by Alexander the Great in 332 BC after a 5-month siege, and finally desolated—as prophesied by Amos (1:6–7), Zephaniah (2:4) and Zechariah (9:5)—by Alexander Jannaeus in 96 BC.

The site of ancient Gaza, Tell Kharubeh (Ḥarube), lies in the modern city. Small excavations showed that it was occupied in the Late Bronze and Iron Ages, and pieces of Philistine pottery were found. Various remains show the importance of the place in Hellenistic and Roman times. Gabinius, the proconsul, rebuilt it in 57 BC on a new site to the S of the old, nearer the sea. It was presumably to distinguish the old abandoned site from this that the angel, who wanted Philip to go to the old site, qualified the name Gaza with the phrase 'this is a desert road' (*hautē estin erēmos*, Acts 8:26).

At Tell el-'Aijjul, 6 km SW, Flinders Petrie found extensive cemeteries and a town that flourished during the 2nd millennium BC. Numerous pieces of gold jewellery were discovered in tombs and buildings of *c.* 1400 BC. Nearby later burials have been uncovered containing so-called *Philistine clay-coffins.

BIBLIOGRAPHY. J. Garstang, *Joshua–Judges*, 1931, pp. 375f.; *NEAEHL*, pp. 49–53, 464–467.

T.C.M.
A.R.M.

GEBA (Heb. *geḇa'*, 'a hill'). A town belonging to Benjamin, 11 km N of Jerusalem and 5 km from Gibeah, from which it is to be distinguished; *cf.* Jos 18:24 and 28; Is. 10:29. It was assigned to the Levites under Joshua (Jos. 21:17; 1 Ch. 6:60). It was in the descent from here that Jonathan and his armour-bearer revealed themselves to the Philistines during their daring attack (1 Sa. 14:1ff.). In the days of Asa, king of Judah, it was fortified, and then regarded as the N limit of Judah; it replaced the name of Dan in the saying 'from Dan to Beersheba' (2 Ki. 23:8). It remained prominent after the Exile (Ne. 11:31; 12:29). The modern town of Jeba stands on the same site. M.A.M.

GEBAL. 1. A Canaanite and Phoenician port whose ruins lie at Jebeil, 40 km N of Beirut. Its name, W Semitic *gᵉḇal*, Akkad. *gubla*, Egyp. *kpn*, means 'hill, bluff'. The Gk. name Byblos may involve a phonetic shift *g-b*, or imply that it was the place where Greeks first saw papyrus (Gk. *byblos*) imported from Egypt as writing material.

Excavations, begun in 1919 by M. Dunand, have revealed a city that flourished from Neolithic times to the Crusades. By the mid-3rd millennium BC it was a centre for exporting cedar wood to Egypt, receiving Egyp. luxury goods in exchange. Strong stone ramparts guarded the city. Inside were temples, houses and tombs. At the end of the 3rd millennium it was sacked, but soon recovered. One temple was devoted to the city's patron goddess (Baalat Gebal), another was a memorial shrine filled with obelisks commemorating the dead, originally probably plastered and inscribed. Dozens of jars containing bronze weapons, jewellery and figures of gods were buried around the temples as offerings. Tombs of Byblian kings were furnished with Egyptian and stone vessels of about 1800 BC. From this time scribes at Byblos, trained to write in Egyptian, seem to have invented a simpler script, the Byblos hieroglyphic, a syllabary of about eighty signs known from texts engraved on stone slabs and copper plates. It may have been here that the alphabet arose (*WRITING). Certainly it was used here fully developed by about 1000 BC, the date of the stone coffin of King Ahiram which bears the longest early alphabetic inscription. Other texts from *c.* 900 BC show continuing links with Egypt. Byblos declined as the power of Tyre and Sidon grew.

Jos. 13:5 includes Gebal as part of the Promised Land then unconquered, and in fact Israel never ruled it. Solomon hired masons there (1 Ki. 5:18), and its skilled shipbuilders are mentioned in Ezk. 27:9. The Egyptian story of Wen-amun describes the city about 1100 BC (*ANET*, pp. 25–29).

2. A mountain region in Transjordan whose inhabitants allied with Israel's other neighbours against her (Ps. 83:7).

BIBLIOGRAPHY. M. Dunand, *Fouilles de Byblos*, 1937– ; N. Jidejian, *Byblos through the Ages*, 1968.
A.R.M.

GEBER. An Israelite prince, the son of Uri, who is mentioned, in what is perhaps a historical note to the list of Solomon's administrative districts, as the prefect of the whole of Transjordan ('the land of Gilead'; 1 Ki. 4:19) before Solomon divided it between his 6th and 7th districts, over the former of which he set Ben-geber (1 Ki. 4:13), possibly Geber's son.

BIBLIOGRAPHY. T. N. D. Mettinger, *Solomonic State Officials*, 1971, pp. 121–122. T.C.M.

GEDALIAH (Heb. *gᵉḏalyâ* or *gᵉḏalyāhû*, 'Yahweh is great'). **1.** Son of Ahikam, grandson of Shaphan, he was appointed chief minister and governor of Judah by Nebuchadrezzar II in 587 BC (2 Ki. 25:22). With Jeremiah the prophet he was entrusted with the care of some royal princesses and those persons remaining after the Babylonian war (Je. 41:16; 43:6). He made Mizpah his residence, and there he was joined by Jeremiah (40:6) and by many officers and men who had escaped from the enemy. These were granted asylum on condition that they maintained the peace (Je. 40:7–12). However, Baalis, king of Ammon, plotted against him and provoked a refugee officer, Ishmael, to assassinate Gedaliah (2 Ki. 25:25; Je. 41:1–3). Fear of possible Babylonian reprisals led more Jews to emigrate to Egypt, despite Jeremiah's warning (Je. 42). The Jewish fast on the third of Tishri commemorates the death of Gedaliah (Zc. 7:5; 8:19). A seal impression inscribed 'Belonging to Gedaliah who is over the House' found at Lachish almost certainly refers to this person.

Scarab-shaped seal impression, inscribed lgdlyhw 'šr 'l hbyt, *'belonging to Gedaliah who is over the house'. This may well be the Gedaliah who was made governor of Judah by the Babylonians in 587 BC* (2 Ki. 25:22). *Lachish. 6th cent. BC.*

2. Son of Jeduthun, instrumentalist leader of the levitical choir (1 Ch. 25:3, 9). **3.** A priest married to a foreign woman in the time of Ezra (Ezr. 10:18). **4.** Son of Pashhur, a leading citizen of Jerusalem and opponent of Jeremiah (Je. 38:1, 4–6). **5.** Grandfather of the prophet Zephaniah and grandson of Hezekiah (Zp. 1:1). D.J.W.

GEDER. S Canaanite town (Jos. 12:13). LXX (B) reads *asei*, and other minuscules suggest 's' as second letter; *Goshen* may be the correct reading. Y. Aharoni, *LOB*, p. 231, suggests Gerar. J.D.D.

GEDERAH (Heb. *gᵉḏērâh*). **1.** In the Shephelah, Jos. 15:36; probably Kh. Judraya (M. Noth, *Josua*, *ad loc.*) on the N side of the Vale of Elah, opposite Soco. Kh. Jedireh, W of Latrun (L. Grollenberg), does not suit the context. **2.** The 'Potteries' of the Monarchy, 1 Ch. 4:23 (AV 'hedges'); perhaps Tell ej-Judeideh N of the Mareshah valley (W. F. Albright, *JPOS* 5, 1925, pp. 50ff.), where a large quantity of stamped jar-handles has been found. **3.** In Benjamin, 1 Ch. 12:4; possibly Judeira, NE of Gibeon, or Kh. Judeira, 10 km farther W. J.P.U.L.

GEDEROTH (Heb. *gᵉḏērôṯ*). A town in the Lachish district of Judah, Jos. 15:41; 2 Ch. 28:18. The area of Qatra and modern Gedera, SE of Jabneel (F.-M. Abel, L. Grollenberg) is too far W and out of context (*GTT*, p. 147; M. Noth, *Josua*², p. 95). J.P.U.L.

GEDEROTHAIM (Heb. *gᵉḏērōṯaim*). May be a variant of *Gederah, Jos. 15:36; the count is correct without it; LXX ('its penfolds') read *giḏrōṯêhâh*. J.P.U.L.

GEDOR (Heb. *gᵉḏôr*). **1.** A town in the hills of Judah (Jos. 15:58, and perhaps 1 Ch. 4:4); Kh. Jedur, 2 km W of Beit Ummar and just off the central ridge; possibly the Beth-gader of 1 Ch. 2:51 (*GTT*, p. 155). **2.** In the Negeb, near Soco and Zanoah. The 'entrance of Gedor' (1 Ch. 4:39) may be the Nahal Hevron, though LXX has 'Gerar' (*LOB*, p. 388), while the context may indicate an area further SE. **3.** In Benjamin, 1 Ch. 12:7; perhaps *Gederah (3). **4.** A personal Benjaminite name, 1 Ch. 8:31 = 9:37. J.P.U.L.

GEHAZI. The servant of Elisha. He may be the unnamed 'servitor' of 2 Ki. 4:43 and the 'servant' of 2 Ki. 6:15, but he is specifically named on only three occasions.

In 2 Ki. 4 he suggests to Elisha that the Shunammite should be rewarded with the promise of a son, and later takes Elisha's staff and lays it upon the dead child in the vain hope of restoring his life.

In 2 Ki. 5, after Elisha has refused to take a present from Naaman when his leprosy had been cured, Gehazi obtains gifts for himself under false pretences. As a punishment he himself is struck down with leprosy. 2 Ki. 5:27 should be compared with the leprosy regulations of Lv. 13:12–13. When this particular form of skin disease, whatever it may have been, turned the whole skin white, the victim was 'clean', and was not segregated. Hence Gehazi was able to continue as Elisha's servant.

In 2 Ki. 8:1–6 Gehazi relates to King Jehoram the story of how the Shunammite's son was restored to life. While he is talking the woman herself comes in to appeal to the king for the restoration of her property. J.S.W.

GELILOTH. Perhaps means 'circuit, circle' (of stones), *cf.* *Gilgal. Only named in Jos. 18:17, as on the border of Judah and Benjamin, in terms almost identical with those used of Gilgal (Jos. 15:7). As Geliloth and Gilgal have more or less the same meaning, both derived from Heb. *gālal*, 'to roll', they may be variant-names for one and the same place. J. Simons, *GTT*, p. 173, § 326, thinks of Geliloth as a small region near Jericho. Y. Aharoni, *LOB*, p. 235, sought it near Tal'at ed-Damm, S of the Wadi Qilt. K.A.K.

GENEALOGY.

I. In the Old Testament

a. General

A genealogy in the OT sense is a list of names indicating the ancestors or descendants of an individual or individuals, or simply a registration of the names of people concerned in some situation. The word 'genealogy' in EVV renders Heb. *yaḥaś*, which occurs only in Ne. 7:5, *sēp̄er hayyaḥaś*, 'book of the genealogy', referring to a register of those who returned to Jerusalem with Sheshbazzar. Clearly 'genealogy' here is not used so strictly as in modern English where it is an account of descent from an ancestor by the enumeration of intermediate persons, though this is frequently what is intended. The genealogies of OT are found chiefly in the Pentateuch, and in Ezra–Nehemiah and Chronicles, and it is exclusively in the latter three books that the verbal form of *yaḥaś* occurs, always in the intensive reflexive stem (*hiṯyaḥēś*), 'enrol oneself by genealogy' (Ezr. 2:62; 8:1, 3; Ne. 7:5, 64; 1 Ch. 4:33; 5:1, 7, 17; 7:5, 7, 9, 40; 9:1, 22; 2 Ch. 12:15; 31:16–19). The term *tôlēḏôṯ*, 'generations', is used in Genesis more or less in the sense of 'genealogical history' (*GENERATION).

(i) *Types of genealogies*. The genealogies given in the scriptural record range from a bare list of names as in 1 Ch. 1:1, through the most common type which links the names by means of a standard formula and inserts additional information under some but not all (*e.g.* Gn. 5 and *cf.* v. 24), to the fully expanded historical account which is based on a framework of names, as in the books of Kings.

Genealogies of two forms are found in the OT. 'Ascending' genealogies commonly have a linking formula, '*x* the son (*bēn*) of *y*' (1 Ch. 6:33–43; Ezr. 7:1–5); 'descending' genealogies often have '*x* begat (*yālaḏ*) *y*' (Gn. 5; Ru. 4:18–23; RSV translates 'became the father of'). The descending type of genealogy may include much information as to the age and actions of the individual links, whereas the ascending type is more commonly used to trace the ancestry of an individual back to some important figure of the past, when the doings of the intermediate figures do not affect the issue.

(ii) *Genealogies as sources for chronology*. That some genealogies in the Bible omit some generations is demonstrable (compare Mt. 1:1 with 1:2–17). For instance, the list of Aaron's descendants in Ezr. 7:1–5 omits six names which are given in 1Ch. 6:3–14. (See also *CHRONOLOGY OF THE OLD TESTAMENT, III.*a.*) This is readily understandable from the formulae, for the word *bēn* could mean not only son but also 'grandson' and 'descendant', and in like manner it is probable that the verb *yālaḏ* could mean not only 'bear' in the immediate physical sense but also 'become the ancestor of' (the noun *yeleḏ* from this verb has the meaning of descendant in Is. 29:23). Factors such as the inclusion of the age of each member at the birth of his descendant and the number of years he lived after this (Gn. 5:6), need not militate against an interpretation of these genealogies as being abridgments. As Green and Warfield have suggested, the purpose of mentioning the years of age may have been to emphasize the mortality in spite of vigorous longevity of these Patriarchs, thus bearing out one result of the Fall.

(iii) *Ancient Near Eastern usage*. Genealogies were a standard feature of ancient historical tradition. Naturally, royal family trees furnish our principal examples, but records of lawsuits over land ownership show that many other people maintained such knowledge. Assyrian scribes of the 1st millennium BC listed kings of Assyria from remote times, with a line almost unbroken spanning 1,000 years (*ANET*[3], pp. 564–566). The relationship of one to another was noted, and the length of reign of each. Heading the list are the names of 'seventeen kings who lived in tents'; long considered legendary, personifications of tribes, or fictitious, they now seem to have an historical basis with the discovery at *Ebla of a treaty naming the first of them. From the 17th century BC survives a list of kings of Babylon, their ancestors and predecessors, sharing some names with the early part of the Assyrian King List. Earlier still is the Sumerian King List, completed about 1800 BC, which names kings of S Babylonia reaching back to the Flood, and before (*ANET*, pp. 265–266). Hittite, Ugaritic and Egyptian scribes have also left us king lists of varying lengths and purposes.

Some of the particular characteristics of biblical genealogies may also be observed in the texts. The lists of names are interspersed with historical or personal notes, comparable with those in Gn. 4:21, 23; 36:24; 1 Ch. 5:9–10, *etc.* The Sumerian King List has one Mes-kiaga-nuna, king of Ur, as son of Mes-ane-pada, but contemporary records suggest he was in fact the grandson of Mes-ane-pada, his father being one A-ane-pada. Either a scribe has omitted the father's name by error because it was so like the grandfather's, or 'son' is used in a wider sense than in English. The wider usage was common in Babylonian, as in all Semitic languages, for 'member of a specific group', and from 1500 BC onwards, *māru* ('son') was used in the sense 'descendant of'. An interesting case is found in the Black Obelisk of Shalmaneser III which refers to *Jehu as 'son (*mār*) of Omri' when in fact he was not related, but simply ruled the same state. A remarkable Egyptian example is a brief text in which King Tirhakah (*c.* 670 BC) honours his 'father' Sesostris III (*c.* 1870 BC) who lived some 1200 years before him. Similarly, King Abdul Aziz of Saudi Arabia was called Ibn (son of) Saud, though he was really the son of AbderRahman, and the Saud whose name he bore died in 1724. The use of relationship words, of family and dynastic names, and many other factors have to be borne in mind when interpreting any ancient genealogies.

There is thus no reason to suppose that all the genealogies in the Bible purport to be complete, since their purpose was more the establishment of descent from some particular ancestor or ancestors, a purpose unaffected by the omission of names, than the reckoning of exact chronologies (*CHRONOLOGY). It is wrong, too, to dismiss any part of them as legendary, personifications of tribes or deities, or pure fiction in the light of growing evidence that other similar records have factual bases.

b. Old Testament genealogies

The principal genealogical lists of the OT are:

(i) Adam to Noah (Gn. 5; 1 Ch. 1:1–4). Ten names, each given in the formula 'A lived *x* years and begat (*yālaḏ*) B, and A lived after he begat B *y* years and begat sons and daughters, and all the days of A were *z* years, and he died'. The figures for *x* and *y* vary to some extent between the *MT*, the Samaritan Pentateuch (SP) and the LXX, though there is a considerable measure of agreement in the totals (*z*), as follows: Adam, 930; Seth, 912; Enos, 905; Cainan, 910; Mahalaleel, 895; Jared, 962 (*MT*, LXX), 847 (SP); Enoch, 365; Methuselah, 969 (*MT*, LXX), 720 (SP); Lamech, 777 (*MT*), 635 (SP), 753 (LXX); Noah's age at the Flood, 600. It is probable that this list is abridged, so that it cannot safely be used as a basis for *chronology. Reminiscent of this genealogy is the first part of the Sumerian King List, which names ten 'great men' who ruled before the Flood. The years of reign for these range in one recension as high as 43,200.

(ii) The descendants of Cain (Gn. 4:17–22).

(iii) The descendants of Noah (Gn. 10; 1 Ch. 1:1–23). The list of the nations who were descended from Shem, Ham and Japheth (*NATIONS, TABLE OF).

(iv) Shem to Abraham (Gn. 11:10–26; 1 Ch. 1:24–27). Ten names. A genealogy couched in the same terms as (i) above, except that, while the Samaritan Pentateuch gives the total years (*z*), *MT* and LXX give only the figures *x* and *y*. The totals given by the Samaritan Pentateuch and worked out for *MT* and LXX are as follows, the *MT* and Samaritan Pentateuch agreeing in most cases against the LXX. Shem, 600; Arpachshad, 438 (*MT*, SP), 565 (LXX); LXX here inserts Kainan, 460, omitted in *MT* and SP; Shelah, 433 (*MT*, SP), 460 (LXX); Eber, 464 (*MT*), 404 (SP), 504 (LXX); Peleg, 239 (*MT*, SP), 339 (LXX); Reu, 239 (*MT*, SP), 339 (LXX); Serug, 230 (*MT*, SP), 330 (LXX); Nahor, 148 (*MT*, SP), 208 (LXX); Terah, 205 (*MT*, LXX), 145 (SP); Abraham.

(v) The descendants of Abraham by Keturah (Gn. 25:1–4; 1 Ch. 1:32–33). (*ARABIA.)

(vi) The descendants of Nahor (Gn. 22:20–24).

(vii) The descendants of Lot (Gn. 19:37–38).

(viii) The descendants of Ishmael (Gn. 25:12–18; 1 Ch. 1:29–31).

(ix) The descendants of Esau (Gn. 36; 1 Ch. 1:35–54).

(x) The descendants of Israel (Jacob; Gn. 46), 1–6 by Leah; 7–8 by Bilhah; 9–10 by Zilpah; and 11–12 by Rachel.

1. Reuben (Gn. 46:9; Ex. 6:14; Nu. 26:5–11; 1 Ch. 5:1–10).

2. Simeon (Gn. 46:10; Ex. 6:15; Nu. 26:12–14; 1 Ch. 4:24–43).

3. Levi (Gn. 46:11; Ex. 6:16–26; 1 Ch. 6:1–53). This was an important genealogy, since the hereditary priesthood resided in this lineage and the high priests were descended from Aaron, whose own genealogy is given in condensed form in Ex. 6:16–22. The descent of Samuel from Levi is given in 1 Ch. 6 and that of Ezra from Aaron in Ezr. 7:1–5. See also (xi) below.

4. Judah (Gn. 46:12; Nu. 26:19–22; 1 Ch. 2:3–4:22; 9:4). This was the lineage of David (1 Ch. 2–3), from whom the line of kings from Solomon to Josiah was descended (1 Ch. 3:10–15).

5. Issachar (Gn. 46:13; Nu. 26:23–25; 1 Ch. 7:1–5).

6. Zebulun (Gn. 46:14; Nu. 26:26–27).

7. Dan (Gn. 46:23; Nu. 26:42–43).

8. Naphtali (Gn. 46:24; Nu. 26:48–50; 1 Ch. 7:13).

9. Gad (Gn. 46:16; Nu. 26:15–18; 1 Ch. 5:11–17).

10. Asher (Gn. 46:17; Nu. 26:44–47; 1 Ch. 7:30–40).

11. Joseph (Gn. 46:20; Nu. 26:28–37; 1 Ch. 7:14–27), through his two sons, Ephraim and Manasseh, who were accepted by Jacob as equivalent to his own sons (Gn. 48:5, 12; *ADOPTION).

12. Benjamin (Gn. 46:21; Nu. 26:38–41; 1 Ch. 7:6–12; 8:1–40; 9:7, 35–44). This was the lineage of Saul (1 Ch. 8–9).

In addition to these lists, which establish genealogical relationships, there are a number of other registers of individuals in one context or another, mentioned in connection with certain periods of OT history.

(xi) Registers of Levites (see also (x) 3 above). Of the time of David (1 Ch. 15:5–24), Jehoshaphat (2 Ch. 17:8), Hezekiah (2 Ch. 29:12–14; 31:12–17), Josiah (2 Ch. 34:8–13; 35:8–9), Zerubbabel and Joiakim (Ne. 12:1–24), Nehemiah (Ne. 10:2–13).

(xii) Registers of the reign of David. His recruits at Ziklag (1 Ch. 12:3–13, 20), his mighty men (2 Sa. 23:8–39; 1 Ch. 11:11–47), his officers over the tribes (1 Ch. 27:16–22) and his other administrative officers (1 Ch. 27:25–31).

(xiii) Registers of families and individuals of the time of the return and the labours of Ezra and Nehemiah. Those who returned with Zerubbabel (Ne. 7:7–63; Ezr. 2:2–61), those who returned with Ezra (Ezr. 8:2–14), the builders of the wall of Jerusalem (Ne. 3:1–32), those who had foreign wives (Ezr. 10:18–43), those who signed the covenant (Ne. 10:1–27), those resident in Jerusalem (Ne. 11:4–19; 1 Ch. 9:3–17).

II. In the New Testament

There are two genealogies in the NT (Mt. 1:1–17; Lk. 3:23–38), both of which give the human ancestry of Jesus the Messiah (*GENEALOGY OF JESUS CHRIST).

Apart from the word *genesis* in Mt. 1:1, which is rendered 'genealogy' by RSV, the EVV translate the term *genealogia* thus in 1 Tim. 1:4 and Tit. 3:9. The corresponding verb, *genealogeō*, 'to trace ancestry', occurs in Heb. 7:6 in reference to Melchizedek, who did not count his ancestry from Levi. In the passages in Timothy and Titus the word 'genealogies' is used in a depreciatory sense, in Timothy in conjunction with the word *mythos*, 'fable', and in Titus together with 'foolish questions'. It is possible that in speaking of these Paul had in mind either the sort of mythical histories based on the OT which are found in Jewish apocryphal books such as the book of *Jubilees*, or else the family-trees of aeons found in Gnostic literature. They obviously do not refer to the genealogies of the OT.

BIBLIOGRAPHY. E. L. Curtis, *HDB*, 2, pp. 121–137; P. W. Crannel, *ISBE*, 2, pp. 1183–1196; W. H. Green, 'Primeval Chronology', *Bibliotheca Sacra* 1890, pp. 285–303; B. B. Warfield, 'On the Antiquity . . . of the Human Race', *PTR* 9, 1911, pp. 1–17; E. J. Young, *WTJ* 12–13, 1949–51, pp. 189–193; W. G. Lambert, *JCS* 11, 1957, pp. 1–14, 112; A. Malamat, *JAOS* 88, 1968, pp. 163–73; R. R. Wilson, *Genealogy and History in the Biblical World*, 1977; M. D. Johnson, *The Purpose of*

Biblical Genealogies, 1969. For New Testament, see D. Guthrie, *The Pastoral Epistles*, 1957, pp. 58, 208. T.C.M.
A.R.M.

GENEALOGY OF JESUS CHRIST. Twice in the NT we are presented with the detailed genealogy of Christ. The first Evangelist introduces his record, in language which echoes Genesis, as 'the book of the genealogy of Jesus Christ, the son of David, the son of Abraham', and then traces the line of descent through forty-two generations from Abraham to Christ (Mt. 1:1–17). The third Evangelist, immediately after his account of the baptism of Christ, says that 'Jesus, when he began his ministry, was about thirty years of age, being the son (as was supposed) of Joseph', and then goes back from Joseph through more than seventy generations to 'Adam, the son of God' (Lk. 3:23–38).

We need not examine the genealogy from Adam to Abraham, which is not given in Matthew, and which Luke patently derived—perhaps *via* 1 Ch. 1:1–4, 24–27—from Gn. 5:3–32; 11:10–26 (following LXX, since in v. 36 he inserts Cainan between Arphaxad and Shelah). From Abraham to David the two lists are practically identical; the line from Judah to David is based on 1 Ch. 2:4–15 (*cf.* Ru. 4:18–22). Mt. 1:5 adds the information that the mother of Boaz was Rahab (presumably Rahab of Jericho). From David to Joseph the lists diverge, for Matthew traces the line through David's son Solomon and the successive kings of Judah as far as Jehoiachin (Jeconiah), whereas Luke traces it through Nathan, another son of David by Bathsheba (1 Ch. 3:5, where she is called Bathshua), and not through the royal line. In Matthew Jehoiachin is followed by Shealtiel and his son Zerubbabel, and these two names appear also in Luke (3:27), but after this momentary convergence there is no further agreement between the lists until we reach Joseph.

It is most improbable that the names in either list which have no OT attestation were simply invented by the Evangelists or their sources. But if we take the lists seriously, the relation between them constitutes a problem. Both make Jesus a descendant of David; his Davidic descent was a matter of common repute during his ministry (Mk. 10:47f.) and is attested by the apostolic witness (Rom. 1:3; so Heb. 7:14 assumes that everyone knows that Jesus belonged to the tribe of Judah). But both lists trace his Davidic descent through Joseph, although they appear in the two Gospels which make it plain that Joseph, while Jesus' father *de iure*, was not his father *de facto*. The Lucan genealogy acknowledges this by the parenthetic clause 'as was supposed' in Lk. 3:23; similarly, the best attested text of Mt. 1:16 says that Joseph was 'the husband of Mary, of whom Jesus was born, who is called Christ'. Even with the Sinaitic Syr. reading of Mt. 1:16 ('Joseph ... begat Jesus ...') the biological sense of 'begat' is excluded by the following narrative (vv. 18–25), and it is in any case probable that in other parts of this genealogy too 'begat' implies legal succession rather than actual parentage. Matthew's line is probably intended to trace the succession to David's throne, even where it did not run through the direct line from father to son.

In that case it might be expected that Luke, on the contrary, would endeavour to present the line of biological descent. It has accordingly been held by several commentators that the Lucan genealogy traces Jesus' lineage actually, though not explicitly, through Mary, his mother. It is possible to infer from Gabriel's words in Lk. 1:32 that Mary was a descendant of David; although these words may be explained by the reference to 'Joseph, of the house of David' in v. 27, while Mary in v. 36 is a kinswoman of Elizabeth, said to be 'of the daughters of Aaron' (v. 5). No help should be looked for in the Talmudic reference (TJ *Hagigah* 77d) to one Miriam, a daughter of Eli (*cf.* Heli, Lk. 3:23), for this Miriam has no connection with the mother of Jesus. In any case, it is strange that, if the Lucan list intended to trace the genealogy through Mary, this was not stated expressly. More probably both lists intend to trace the genealogy through Joseph. If Matthan, Joseph's grandfather in Mt. 1:15, is the same as Matthat, his grandfather in Lk. 3:24, then 'we should need only to suppose that Jacob [Joseph's father in Mt.] died without issue, so that his nephew, the son of his brother Heli [Joseph's father in Lk.] would become his heir' (J. G. Machen, *The Virgin Birth of Christ*, 1932, p. 208). As for the propriety of tracing Jesus' lineage through Joseph, 'Joseph was the heir of David, and the child, though born without his agency, was born in a real sense "to him"' (*ibid.*, p. 187). A more complicated account, involving levirate marriage, was given by Julius Africanus (*c.* AD 230), on the basis of a tradition allegedly preserved in the holy family (Eus., *EH* 1. 7).

If Nathan in Zc. 12:12 is David's son of that name, his house evidently had some special standing in Israel, and there might then be more significance than meets the eye in the fact that Jesus is made a descendant of his in Lk. 3:31.

The Lucan list enumerates twenty or twenty-one generations between David and the Babylonian Exile, and as many between the Exile and Jesus, whereas the Matthaean list enumerates only fourteen generations for each of these periods. But several generations are demonstrably omitted from the Matthaean list in the period from David to the Exile, and others may be omitted in the later period. 'Rhesa' in Lk. 3:27 may originally have been not an individual name, but Aram. *rēšâ* ('prince'), the title of Zerubbabel (in which case the post-exilic section of the Lucan list may be derived from an Aramaic document).

The main purpose of the two lists is to establish Jesus' claim to be the Son of David, and more generally to emphasize his solidarity with mankind and his close relation with all that had gone before. Christ and the new covenant are securely linked to the age of the old covenant. Marcion, who wished to sever all the links binding Christianity to the OT, knew what he was about when he cut the genealogy out of his edition of Luke.

BIBLIOGRAPHY. J. G. Machen, *The Virgin Birth of Christ*[2], 1932, pp. 173ff., 203ff.; M. D. Johnson, *The Purpose of the Biblical Genealogies*, 1988; N. Hillyer, *NIDNTT* 3, pp. 653–660. F.F.B.

GENERATION. A word used in the EVV to translate various biblical terms.

1. Heb. *tôlᵉḏôṯ*. A word occurring ten times in Genesis (2:4; 5:1; 6:9; 10:1; 11:10, 27; 25:12, 19; 36:1; 37:2) in such a way as to divide it into eleven sections, each being styled 'the generations of ...' It also occurs in Gn. 10:32; 25:13; 36:9; Ex. 6:16, 19; Nu. 1 many times; 3:1; Ru. 4:18; 1 Ch. 1:29; 5:7;

7:2, 4, 9; 8:28; 9:9, 34; 26:31. In Ex. 28:10 the EVV translate it 'birth'. The word is formed from *yālaḏ*, 'to bear, beget', and this probably accounts for the E.T. 'generation'. From its OT usage, however, it is apparent that the word means 'history' or 'genealogical history', of a family or the like. In the LXX the word is often rendered by Gk. *genesis* (see **3**, below), and the expression *biblos geneseōs Iēsou Christou*, 'book of the genealogy of Jesus Christ' in Mt. 1:1, closely reflects *sēp̄er tôlᵉḏôṯ 'āḏām*, 'book of the genealogy of Adam', in Gn. 5:1.

2. Heb. *dôr*. A word occurring frequently, which corresponds in general to the word 'generation' as commonly understood in Eng. It can refer to a generation, as a period in the past (Is. 51:9) or future (Ex. 3:15), or to the men of a generation (Ex. 1:6). It is the word used in Gn. 17:7, 9, where God's covenant with Abraham and his descendants is announced. The word is also used to refer to a class of men, as in 'crooked generations' (Dt. 32:5) or 'generation of the righteous' (Ps. 14:5). The Aram. cognate, *dār*, occurs in Dn. 4:3, 34. Akkad. *duru* is used of a generation as grandfather to grandson spanning about 70 years.

3. Gk. *genesis*. Used chiefly in the LXX for *tôlᵉḏôṯ*, and employed in the same sense in Mt. 1:1 (see **1**, above). In the other NT occurrences, however, it is used in the sense of 'birth' (Mt. 1:18; Lk. 1:14; Jas. 1:23, 'his natural face', lit. 'face of his birth'; Jas. 3:6, 'cycle of nature', lit. 'course of birth').

4. Gk. *genea*. Used chiefly in the LXX to translate *dôr*, and like it including among its meanings much the same range as Eng. 'generation'. It is used of the people living at a given time (Mt. 11:16), and, by extension, of the time itself (Lk. 1:50). It is also evidently used to designate the components of a genealogy (Mt. 1:17).

5. Gk. *gennēma*, 'child' and 'offspring', occurring in Mt. 3:7; 12:34; 23:33; Lk. 3:7, in each case in the phrase 'brood of vipers', AV 'generation of vipers'.

6. Gk. *genos*, 'race'. AV translates the phrase *genos eklekton* in 1 Pet. 2:9 'chosen generation', but RV 'elect race' or RSV 'chosen race' is to be preferred.

It is sometimes held that a period of 40 years, the duration, for instance, of the wilderness wanderings, is to be taken as a round *number indicating a generation.

BIBLIOGRAPHY. P. J. Wiseman, *Clues to Creation in Genesis*, 1977, pp. 34–45; F. Büchsel, *TDNT* 1, pp. 662–663, 672, 682–685; R. R. Wilson, *Genealogy and History in the Biblical World*, 1977, pp. 158–159, n. 57; R. Morgenthaler, C. Brown, *NIDNTT* 2, pp. 35–39. T.C.M.

GENESIS, BOOK OF.

I. Outline of contents

a. Pre-history: the creation record (1:1–2:3)
b. The story of man (2:4–11:26)

His creation and Fall (2:4–3:24); his increasing numbers (4:1–6:8); the judgment of the Flood (6:9–9:29); the rise of nations (10:1–11:26).

c. The story of Abraham (11:27–23:20)

His entry into the promised land (11:27–14:24); the covenant and the promise (15:1–18:15); Sodom and Gomorrah (18:16–19:38); Sarah, Isaac and Ishmael (20:1–23:20).

d. The story of Isaac (24:1–26:35)

His marriage with Rebekah (24:1–67); death of his father and birth of his children (25:1–34); the promise renewed at Gerar (26:1–35).

e. The story of Jacob (27:1–36:43)

His obtaining of the blessing by deceit (27:1–46); his flight to Harran, and renewal of the promise at Bethel (28:1–22); his life and marriages in Harran (29:1–31:16); his return to the promised land, and renewal of the promise at Bethel (31:17–35:29); Esau's line (36:1–43).

f. The story of Joseph (37:1–50:26)

Joseph sold into Egypt (37:1–36); Judah and his daughter-in-law (38:1–30); Joseph in Egypt (39:1–45:28); Joseph's father and brothers in Egypt (46:1–47:31); Jacob's blessing gives priority to Ephraim and to Judah (48:1–49:28); deaths of Jacob and Joseph (49:29–50:26).

The book of Genesis closes with the people of Israel already in Egypt. They were the elect family among all mankind for whom God purposed to display the mighty acts of redemption outlined in Exodus. Among this people the tribe of Judah has already emerged as of special significance (49:9–12).

A technical analysis may also be based on the 10 occurrences of the phrase (or its equivalent), 'These are the generations of ...'. *'Generations' (Heb. *tôlᵉḏôṯ*) means 'begettings' or 'genealogical records'. This phrase is used with reference to the heavens and the earth (2:4); Adam (5:1); Noah (6:9); the sons of Noah (10:1); Shem (11:10); Terah (11:27); Ishmael (25:12); Isaac (25:19); Esau (36:1); Jacob (37:2).

II. Authorship

For a discussion of the authorship of the Pentateuch, see *PENTATEUCH. Concerning the authorship of Genesis in particular, there is nothing in the book to indicate its author. There are two opinions, though there are variants of each: (*a*) Mosaic authorship, (*b*) non-Mosaic authorship.

a. Mosaic authorship

The education that Moses received at pharaoh's court would have enabled him to read and write (Ex. 24:4; Dt. 31:9, *etc.*), and he would obviously be anxious to preserve the records that had come down. This means that Moses was not so much the author as the editor and compiler of Genesis. Family records had been handed down either orally or in written form, and Moses brought these together, editing and translating where necessary. The creation story in Gn. 1 may have been received as a direct revelation from God, since Moses certainly had the experience of immediate contact with God (*e.g.* Ex. 33:11; Dt. 34:10). Accordingly, we may legitimately look for documents or for orally transmitted stories in Genesis, and, if we use some recent terminology, we may speak of Moses as the one who faithfully set down what had come to him from past generations.

If we allow for a few later 'footnotes' added by copyists up to the time of the Monarchy to explain points for contemporary readers (*e.g.* 12:6; 13:7; 14:17, and parts of 36:9–43), there is nothing that need be dated after the time of Moses. While the proper interpretation of Ex. 6:3 does not exclude some use of the name Yahweh in Genesis, it would be perfectly understandable if Moses sometimes substituted the covenant name of his own day for the covenant name 'El Shaddai (God Almighty) of patriarchal times, in order to remind his readers that this was the same God as the God of Sinai.

For this section, see E. J. Young, *IOT*,1949, pp. 51ff.

b. Non-Mosaic authorship

There is no one theory here that commands general acceptance. Since the days of Jean Astruc, in the 18th century, scholars have looked for various 'documents' in the Pentateuch. These for Genesis are J (which uses Yahweh for the divine name), E (which uses Elohim for the divine name) and P (which is concerned chiefly with religious matters). Early forms of this theory were extremely radical and denied historicity to a great deal in Genesis. More recently it has been argued that the 'documents' grew by the collection of ancient material until they reached their final shape; J in about the 10th or 9th century BC, E a little later and P in post-exilic times. Historicity is not necessarily denied in the more moderate forms of this theory.

More recently the 'documentary' theory has been abandoned by some who deny that formal documents ever existed. Scholars of this school speak of 'cycles of tradition' which grew up in various areas, chiefly with a religious interest, *e.g.* Ex. 1–12 is quoted as a 'cycle of tradition' that has the Passover event as its focal point. Some time later editors collected these materials and cast them into their present shape. For the most part the material was in oral form before collection. Again there is no necessary denial of historicity in this view, although some writers do deny exact historicity, but admit a 'general historicity'. This 'tradition history' school thinks in terms of the development of the traditions around central events which had significance for the religious life of Israel and found expression in their religious rituals and liturgies.

It is not possible to say in general conclusion that any one school today has acceptance by all scholars. The exact origin of Genesis remains something of a mystery.

III. The place of Genesis in the Bible

Genesis is the Book of Beginnings, the great introduction to the drama of redemption. Gn. 1–11 may be regarded as the prologue to the drama, whose first act begins at ch. 12 with the introduction of Abraham. At the other end of the drama the book of Revelation is the epilogue.

The prologue is cast in universal terms. God made all things (ch. 1). In particular, he made man, who became a rebel and a sinner (chs. 2–3). Sin became universal (ch. 4), and being rebellion against God is always under divine judgment, exemplified in the story of the Flood (chs. 6–9). Even after God had demonstrated his displeasure by an act of judgment in the Flood, man returned to his rebellion (ch. 11). Yet always God gave evidences of grace and mercy. Adam and Eve were cast out, but not destroyed (ch. 3); Cain was driven out but 'marked' by God (ch. 4); mankind was overwhelmed by the Flood but not obliterated, for a remnant was saved (chs. 6–9); man was scattered but allowed to live on (ch. 11).

That is the prologue which paints the background for the drama which is about to develop. What was God's answer to the universal, persistent sin of man? As the drama proper opens in Gn. 12 we meet Abraham, the first stage in God's answer. He would call out an elect people, from whom in due course would come the Redeemer. That people would proclaim the message of redemption to men everywhere. Genesis tells only the beginning of the story up to the time of Joseph, giving the setting for God's mighty act of deliverance from Egypt, pattern of the greater deliverance yet to be achieved.

IV. Genesis and historicity

It is extremely difficult to obtain independent evidence as to the historicity of Genesis, since many of the narratives have no parallel in non-biblical literature. This is especially difficult for Gn. 1–11, though easier for Gn. 12–50. It should always be remembered that much in the Bible is beyond scientific investigation, but notably those areas which touch on faith and personal relations. The areas on which one might ask for evidence in Genesis may be summarized as follows:

a. The creation (*CREATION)

b. The origin of man

The Bible asserts that God made man. It does not allow that there was any other source for man's origin. It is not possible, however, to discover from Genesis precisely how God did this. Scientifically, the origin of man is still obscure, and neither archaeology nor anthropology can give a final answer as to the time, place or means of man's origin. It is safest for the Christian to be cautious about the subject, to be content to assert with Genesis that, however it happened, God lay behind the process, and to be content to await further evidence before rushing to hasty conclusions (*MAN).

c. The Flood

There is no final evidence here either as to the time, the extent or the cause. There were certainly extensive floods in the area from which the Patriarchs came, and the ancient Sumerians had a detailed account of a great flood in the ancient world. There are no serious reasons, however, for accepting the suggestion of Sir Leonard Woolley that the flood at Ur, which left a deep deposit of silt revealed by his excavation, was in fact the result of the Bible *Flood.

d. Patriarchal narratives

It is possible today to read the patriarchal narratives against the background of the social, political and cultural state of the ancient Near East in the period 2000–1500 BC. While it is not possible to date the events in Genesis, it is true to say that the Bible reflects the life of certain areas of Mesopotamia during these centuries. (*PATRIARCHAL AGE.) H. H. Rowley, 'Recent Discoveries in the Patriarchal Age', *BJRL* 32, 1949–50, pp. 76ff. (reprinted in *The Servant of the Lord and Other Essays on the Old Testament*, 1952); J. Bright, *A History of Israel*[2], 1972, pp. 67–102.

V. Genesis and theology

It cannot be emphasized too strongly that the primary value of Genesis, as indeed of all Scripture, is theological. It is possible to devote a great deal of time and energy to all kinds of incidental details and to miss the great theological issues. For example, the story of the Flood speaks of sin, judgment, redemption, new life. To be occupied with details about the size of the ark, and with problems of feeding or of the disposal of refuse, is to be concerned with side-issues. While God's revelation was largely in historical events, and while history is of tremendous significance for the biblical revelation, it is the theological significance of events that is finally important. Where corroborative evidence of the Genesis narratives is lacking, the theological significance may still be discerned.

BIBLIOGRAPHY. B. Vawter, *A Path through Genesis*, 1955; E. A. Speiser, *Genesis*, 1956; G. von Rad, *Genesis*, 1961; D. Kidner, *Genesis*, *TOTC*, 1967; C. Westermann, *Genesis, 1–11*, 1974; G. J. Wenham, *Genesis, 1–15*, *WBC*, 1987. J.S.W.

J.A.T.

GENTILES (Heb. *gôyîm*; Gk. *ethnē* (or *Hellēnes*) *via* Vulg. *gentiles*). This was originally a general term for 'nations', but acquired a restricted sense by usage. In the OT the affinity of all nations is stressed in the tradition of Noah's descendants (Gn. 10). In God's covenant with Abraham his descendants are distinguished from other nations, but not in any narrowly exclusive sense (Gn. 12:2; 18:18; 22:18; 26:4). Israel became conscious of being a nation uniquely distinct from others by being separated to God after the Exodus (Dt. 26:5), and the covenant of Sinai (Ex. 19:6). From then on this dedication dominated all her relations with other nations (Ex. 34:10; Lv. 18:24–25; Dt. 15:6).

The Israelites were constantly tempted to compromise with the idolatry and immorality practised by other nations (1 Ki. 14:24), so bringing God's judgment on themselves (2 Ki. 17:7ff.; Ezk. 5:5ff.). On their return from the Exile the danger was still more insidious because of the corruptness of the Jews who had remained in Canaan (*cf.* Ezr. 6:21). This continual struggle against contamination from their neighbours led to so hard and exclusive an attitude to other nations that by the time of Christ for a Jew to stigmatize his fellow as 'Gentile' (*ethnikos*, Mt. 18:17) was a term of scorn equal in opprobrium to 'tax-collector', and they earned for themselves from Tacitus the censure that 'they regard the rest of mankind with all the hatred of enemies' (*Histories* 5. 5).

Yet the Gentiles were assigned a place in prophecies of the kingdom, merely as the vanquished who would enhance the glory of Israel (Is. 60:5–6), or as themselves seeking the Lord (Is. 11:10), and offering worship (Mal. 1:11) when the Messiah should come to be their Light (Is. 42:6), and to bring salvation to the ends of the earth (Is. 49:6). In this tradition Simeon hailed Jesus (Lk. 2:32), and Jesus began his ministry (Mt. 12:18, 21), and the Jews themselves could question whether he would go to the Gentiles (Jn. 7:35). Though hesitant and astonished when Cornelius was converted (Acts 10:45; 11:18), the church quickly accepted the equality of Jew and Gentile before God (Rom. 1:16; Col. 3:11), thus revealing the full scope of the gospel and its glorious hope for all (Gal. 2:14ff.; Rev. 21:24; 22:2). P.A.B.

GENTLENESS. In Gal. 5:23 'gentleness' (*praÿtēs*) is part of the ninefold 'fruit of the Spirit'. In 2 Cor. 10:1 Paul beseeches his readers by the 'gentleness' (*epieikeia*) of Christ, coupled with his 'meekness' (*praÿtēs*). *epieikeia* suggests the yielding of a judge, who, instead of demanding the exact penalty required by strict justice, gives way to circumstances which call for mercy. Thus the concession of a legal right may avoid the perpetration of a moral wrong (see R. C. Trench, *Synonyms of the New Testament*, pp. 153–157). Similarly in the OT the Heb. *'ānâ*, 'to be humble', and its cognate noun are used of God: 'Thy gentleness (RSVmg.) made me great' (2 Sa. 22:36; Ps. 18:35). Although the word itself is rarely used, it expresses the typical condescension of the divine Judge, whose refusal to exact the full demands of the law lifts up those who would otherwise be crushed under its condemnation. The adjective *epieikēs* describes one of the qualities of the Christlike believer. Note the other qualities with which it is associated in 1 Tim. 3:3; Tit. 3:2; Jas. 3:17; 1 Pet. 2:18. *epieikeia* is used in a formal rhetorical sense in Acts 24:4. J.C.C.

GERAR (Heb. *g*ᵉ*rār*, 'circle'). An ancient city S of Gaza (Gn. 10:19) in the foothills of the Judaean mountains. Both Abraham (Gn. 20–21) and Isaac (Gn. 26) stayed there, digging wells, and had cordial relations with Abimelech its king, though Isaac quarrelled with him at one stage. The city lay in the 'land of the *Philistines' (*'ereṣ p*ᵉ*lištîm*, Gn. 21:32, 34; see also 26:1, 8), not necessarily an anachronistic designation. In the early 9th century BC it was the scene of a great victory by Asa of Judah over the invading Ethiopian army of Zerah (2 Ch. 14:13–14).

The site of Gerar was identified with modern Tell Jemmeh by W. M. Flinders Petrie, but following a survey by D. Alon, the site of Tell Abu Hureira, a mound about 18 km SE of Gaza, in the Wadi Eš-Šari'ah has been proposed as more likely. As no pre-Iron-Age remains had been found near it, this site had hitherto been believed to be a natural hill, but Alon's survey has shown that it was first inhabited in Chalcolithic times, and continued in occupation through every period of the Bronze and Iron Ages. The evidence of surface potsherds indicated that the city had a prosperous period in Middle Bronze Age, the age of the Patriarchs.

BIBLIOGRAPHY. Y. Aharoni, 'The Land of Gerar', *IEJ* 6, 1956, pp. 26–32; *cf.* F. M. Cross Jr. and G. E. Wright, *JBL* 75, 1956, pp. 212–213; W. F. Albright, *BASOR* 163, 1961, p. 48. T.C.M.

GERASA. An important city of the classical period, ranking in importance with Palmyra and Petra. Lying in Transjordan, mid-way between the Dead Sea and the Sea of Galilee, and some 30 km E of the Jordan, the site today, still preserving the name in the form *Jaraš*, is one of the best preserved examples of a Roman provincial town in the Middle East. It is only indirectly mentioned in the Bible in the passages describing our Lord's visit to the E side of the Sea of Galilee, where the territory is described as the country of the Gerasenes (RV, Mk. 5:1; Lk. 8:26, 37, AV 'Gadarenes'; in Mt. 8:28, AV gives Gergesenes, RV, RSV *Gadarenes. In all three passages variant MSS give *Gerasēnos*, *Gergesēnos* and *Gadarēnos*. The town lies in a well-watered valley with a perennial stream running through the middle of it, and its wealth was probably derived from the cultivation of the fertile corn lands to the E of it. First noted in 1806 by the German traveller Seetzen, it was subsequently visited by many Europeans. In 1867 Charles Warren made many plans and photographs of the ruins. In 1878 a modern village was founded at the site, and the resulting destruction of the buildings led to considerable conservation, reconstruction and excavation under the auspices of the Department of Antiquities between the wars, a work that still goes on. The extent of the Roman remains makes research into the earlier periods difficult, but Gerasa probably emerged from a village to a Hellenistic town under the name of Antioch, some time after the 4th century BC, when increasing security made prosperity possible. It is first mentioned historically in the writings of Josephus, who states that Theodorus of Gadara took refuge there at the end of the 2nd century BC, but it was soon afterward taken by Alexander Jannaeus, and remained in Jewish hands until Pompey's conquest of 63 BC, when it became part of the province of Syria. The Hellenistic practice of allowing a measure of self-government was continued by Rome, and Gerasa, now one of the cities of the *Decapolis, flourished, carrying on a lively trade with the Nabataeans to the S. This prosperity was such that in the 1st century AD the city was largely rebuilt on a typical Roman plan with a straight main street flanked by columns leading to a forum. There were temples to Artemis and Zeus and two theatres and an enclosing wall round the whole. The 2nd century AD was, however, a period of greater prosperity, and the surviving remains, including a triumphal arch commemorating a personal visit by the emperor Hadrian in AD 129–130, date largely from that time. In the early 3rd century the city became a colony, but soon thereafter declined, and by the time of the Crusades it had been long deserted.

BIBLIOGRAPHY. C. C. McCown, *The Ladder of Progress in Palestine*, 1943, pp. 309–325; G. Lankester Harding, *The Antiquities of Jordan*, 1959, pp. 78–104; E. G. Kraeling, *Gerasa, City of the Decapolis*, 1938; *NEAEHL*, pp. 470–479.

T.C.M.

GERIZIM. The more southerly of the two mountains which overshadow the modern town of Nablus, 4 km NW of ancient Shechem, called Jebel eṭ-Ṭôr in Arabic. It has been called the mount of blessing, because here the blessings for obedience were pronounced at the solemn assembly of Israel described in Jos. 8:30–35 (*EBAL, MOUNT).

A ledge halfway to the top is popularly called 'Jotham's pulpit', from which he once addressed the men of Shechem (Jdg. 9:7). On the summit are the bare ruins of a Christian church of the 5th century. Still earlier there stood there a temple of Jupiter, to which a staircase of 300 steps led up, as shown on ancient coins found in Nablus.

Gerizim remains the sacred mount of the Samaritans; for they have 'worshipped on this mountain' (Jn. 4:20) for countless generations, ascending it to keep the feasts of Passover, Pentecost and Tabernacles. According to Samaritan tradition, Gerizim is Mt Moriah (Gn. 22:2) and the place where God chose to place his name (Dt. 12:5). Accordingly it was here that the Samaritan temple was built with Persian authorization in the 4th century BC—the temple which was demolished by John Hyrcanus when he captured Shechem and the surrounding area *c.* 128 BC. See further E. Robertson, *The Old Testament Problem*, 1950, pp. 157–171; G. E. Wright, *Shechem*, 1965, pp. 170–184; *NEAEHL*, pp. 484–492.

G.T.M.
F.F.B.

GERSHOM, GERSHON. The form Gershom is used of the following people.

1. The elder son of Moses, born in Midian (Ex. 2:22; 18:3). The name (construed as 'banishment' or 'a stranger there') commemorated Moses' exile. Gershom's sons counted as Levites (1 Ch. 23:14–15).

2. A descendant of Phinehas the priest (Ezr. 8:2).

3. Levi's son (1 Ch. 6:1, 16–17; elsewhere the allied forms, 'Gershon' and 'Gershonite', are used). In the wilderness the Gershonites carried the tabernacle, tent, coverings, hangings and cords for the door, court and gate; they received two wagons and four oxen to help in the task. They encamped W of the tabernacle. Their males, over a month old, numbered 7,500; those who served (age-group 30–50) 2,630 (Nu. 3:17–26; 4:38–41; 7:7). In the land they obtained thirteen cities (Jos. 21:6). Under David the Asaphites and Ladanites, both Gershonite families, had special singing and treasury duties (1 Ch. 6:39; 23:1–11; 26:21–22). Gershonites are mentioned at the bringing up of the ark (1 Ch. 15:7), at the cleansings of the Temple under Hezekiah and Josiah (2 Ch. 29:12; 35:15), and as serving under Ezra (Ezr. 3:10) and Nehemiah (Ne. 11:17).

D.W.G.

GESHEM. Mentioned in Ne. 2:19; 6:1–2 as one of the chief opponents of Nehemiah, and almost certainly the Gashmu of Ne. 6:6. In these passages he is called simply 'the Arabian', but is evidently an influential person. Two inscriptions throw a vivid light on this man. One is a memorial in ancient Dedan (modern el-'Ula) dated 'in the days of Jasm (dialect-form of Geshem) son of Shahru', testifying to Geshem's fame in N Arabia. The other is an Aramaic dedication on a silver bowl from an Arabian shrine in the Egyptian E Delta. It reads, 'What Qaynu son of Geshem, king of Kedar, brought (as offering) to (the goddess) Han-'Ilat.' This text of his successor shows that Geshem was none other than king (paramount chief) of the tribesfolk and desert traders of biblically attested *Kedar in N Arabia. The Persian kings maintained good relations with the Arabs from the time they invaded Egypt in 525 BC (*cf.* Herodotus, 3. 4ff., 88), which lends point to Ne. 6:6, for a complaint by Gashmu to the Persian king would not go unheard. For the silver bowl and full background on Geshem, see I. Rabinowitz, *JNES* 15, 1956, pp. 2, 5–9, and pls. 6–7. *Cf.* also W. F. Albright, 'Dedan' (also in English) in the Alt anniversary volume, *Geschichte und Altes Testament*, 1953, pp. 4, 6 (Dedan inscription).

K.A.K.

GESHUR, GESHURITES. **1.** In the list of David's sons in 2 Sa. 3:3 the third is 'Absalom the son of Maacah the daughter of Talmai king of Geshur', a city in Syria (2 Sa. 15:8; 1 Ch. 3:2), NE of Bashan (Jos. 12:5; 13:11, 13).

It was this city to which Absalom fled after the murder of his brother Amnon (2 Sa. 13:37) and to which David sent Joab to bring him back (14:23). The young man returned to Jerusalem, but only to plot rebellion against his father (2 Sa. 14:32; 15:8).

2. Another group called 'Geshurites' is attested in Jos. 13:2 and 1 Sa. 27:8 as resident in the Negeb, near the Egyptian border.

F.F.B.

GESTURES. The Oriental is much more given to physical gestures than is the Westerner. As might be expected, then, the Bible records numerous gestures. These may be roughly divided into three categories: first, natural physical reactions to certain circumstances; second, conventional or customary gestures; third, deliberate symbolic actions. Gestures of the first type are involuntary, and those of the second often tend to become so, through long habit.

Not many gestures of the first category are recorded; the Bible does not mention, for instance, shrugs and movements of the head by the story-teller. Signs with the hands, for different purposes, are recorded in Mt. 12:49 and Acts 12:17. The circumstances of the people around him also caused Jesus to sigh (Mk. 7:34) and to weep (Jn. 11:35).

A great number of conventional actions are to be found in Scripture. When greeting a superior one would bow low, and perhaps kiss his hand. Friends greeting each other would grasp the other's chin or beard, and kiss. Lk. 7:44–46 records the customary gestures of hospitality. Scorn was expressed by wagging the head and grimacing with the mouth (Ps. 22:7). In commerce, a bargain was sealed by 'striking' hands (Pr. 6:1—the gesture is lost in the RSV paraphrase). Extreme grief was expressed by tearing the garments and placing dust upon the head. This category also includes the physical attitudes adopted for prayer and benediction. Notice also Ex. 6:6 and Is. 65:2.

Symbolic action was a method of prophetic instruction; Ezekiel in particular made great use of it, and many of Jesus' actions were of a symbolic nature. He frequently touched those he meant to heal; he breathed on the disciples, as he imparted the Holy Spirit (Jn. 20:22). Notice, too, Pilate's eloquent gesture in Mt. 27:24. See also *FOOT, *HAND, *HEAD, *etc.* D.F.P.

GETHSEMANE (from Aram. *gaṯ šemen,* 'an oil press'). A garden (*kēpos*, Jn. 18:1), E of Jerusalem beyond the Kidron valley and near the Mount of Olives (Mt. 26:30). It was a favourite retreat frequented by Christ and his disciples, which became the scene of the agony, Judas' betrayal and the arrest (Mk. 14:32–52). It should probably be contrasted with Eden, as the garden where the second Adam prevailed over temptation. Christ's action in Gethsemane (Lk. 22:41) gave rise to the Christian custom of kneeling for prayer. The traditional Latin site lies E of the Jericho road-bridge over the Kidron, and contains olive trees said to date back to the 7th century AD. It measures 50 m square, and was enclosed with a wall by the Franciscans in 1848. It corresponds to the position located by Eusebius and Jerome, but is regarded by Thomson, Robinson and Barclay as too small and too near the road. The Greeks enclosed an adjacent site to the N. There is a broad area of land NE of the Church of St Mary where larger, more secluded gardens were put at the disposal of pilgrims, and Thomson locates the genuine site here. The original trees were cut down by Titus (Jos., *BJ* 5. 523).

BIBLIOGRAPHY. W. M. Thomson, *The Land and the Book*, 1888, p. 634; G. Dalman, *Sacred Sites and Ways*, 1935, pp. 321ff. D.H.T.

GEZER. One of the chief cities of pre-Roman Palestine from at least 1800 BC. It is strategically located on the road from Jerusalem to Joppa, on the most N ridge of the Shephelah overlooking the

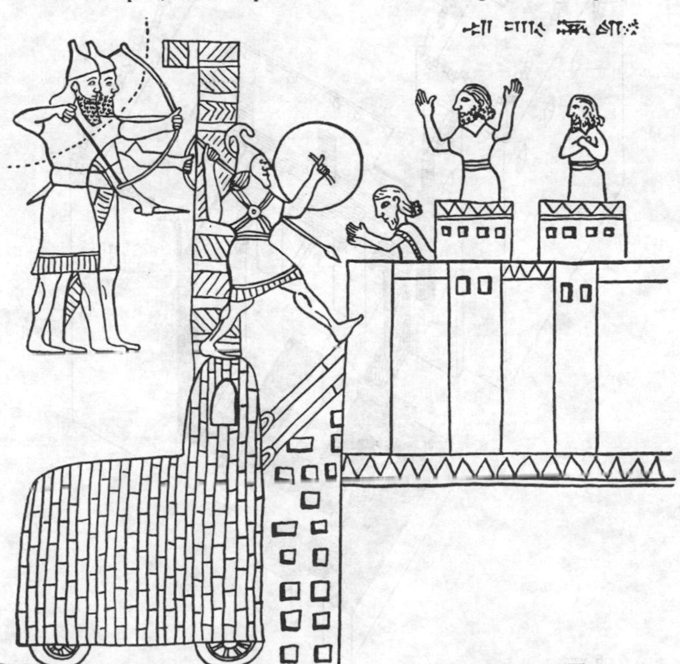

The assault of the city of Gezer by the army of Tiglath-pileser III. A relief from the SW palace at Nimrud. 744–727 BC.

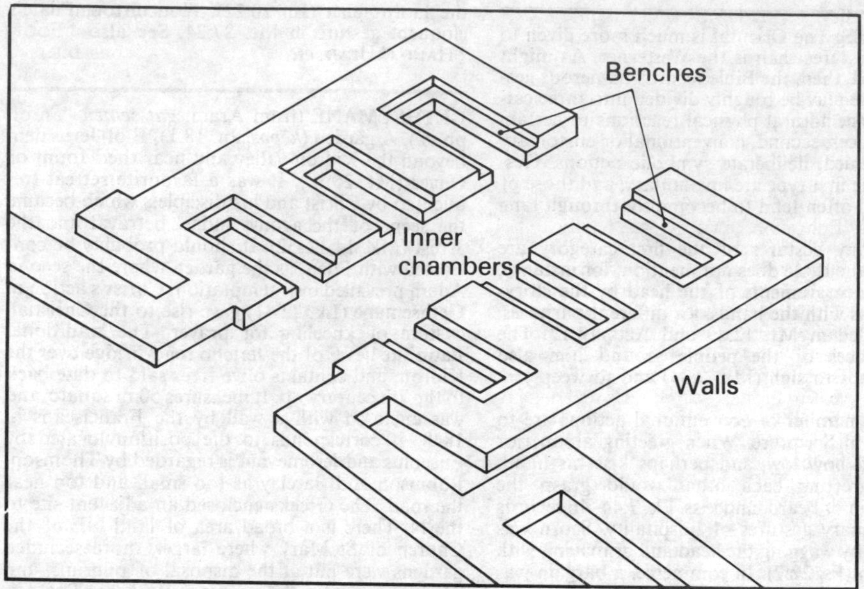

Plan of the gate built by Solomon as part of the fortifications of Gezer.

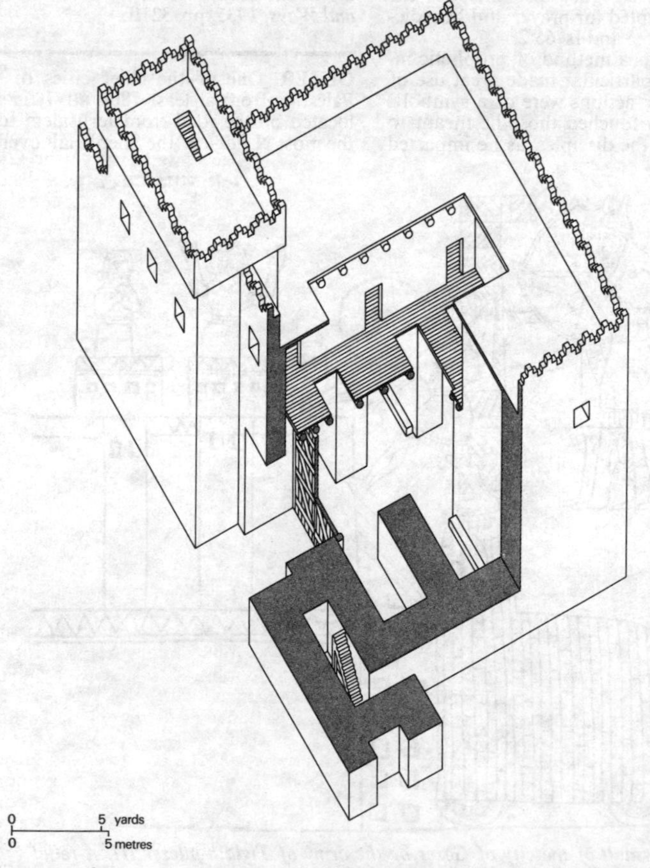

A suggested reconstruction of Solomon's gate at Gezer.

Ayyalon valley, and 12 km from the main highway between Egypt and Mesopotamia. Pharaoh Thutmosis III captured the Canaanite city in *c.* 1468 BC. Ten el-*Amarna letters from Gezer show the city vacillated but finally remained loyal to Egypt in the 14th century BC. At the time of the Hebrew conquest its Canaanite king, Horam, tried to help Lachish but was defeated (Jos. 10:33; 12:12). Gezer, however, was not taken by the Israelites (Jos. 16:10; Jdg. 1:29). Even so the city was included in Ephraim's territory as a Levitical city (Jos. 21:21). Soon after the conquest Pharaoh Merenptah claims, on his stele, to have recaptured it. Archaeological evidence indicates that after 1200 BC the Philistines controlled the city, possibly with Egyptian approval, which may explain David's battles in this region (2 Sa. 5:25). Gezer became an Israelite possession when the Egyptian pharaoh gave it to his daughter on her marriage to Solomon, who rebuilt the city and its defences (1 Ki. 9:15–17). Excavations (1964–73) have uncovered a six-chambered gate and defences. This area has also yielded great quantities of calcined stone, probably of Pharaoh Shishak's assault on Judah *c.* 925 BC (1 Ki. 14:25ff.). The city was rebuilt and remained an Israelite city until the end of the Assyrian occupation *c.* 630 BC. There was an Assyrian administrative centre in the city in which two contracts for the sale of land by an Israelite to an Assyrian were discovered. Settlement continued under the Persians, Selucids and Maccabeans. Gezer (Gazara) figures frequently in the Maccabean struggle. Two interesting archaeological finds are the Gezer *Calendar and a ten monolith *'High Place' (*c.* 1600 BC onwards).

BIBLIOGRAPHY. R. A. S. Macalister, *The Excavations of Gezer*, 1912; W. G. Dever *et al.* (eds.), *Gezer* 1–8, 1970ff.; *NEAEHL*, pp. 496–506.

G.G.G.
J.W.

GIANT. A man of great stature. The word is used in EVV, sometimes following LXX, to render various Heb. words. **1.** *nᵉpīlîm* (Gn. 6:4; Nu. 13:33, AV) following LXX *gigas.* RV, RSV 'Nephilim' in both verses.

2. *rāpā'*, *rāpâ*, perhaps variant forms derived from the proper name *rᵉpā'îm* (*REPHAIM), and so rendered by RV, RSV in Dt. 2:11, 20; 3:11, 13; Jos. 12:4; 13:12; 15:8; 17:15; 18:16 where AV gives 'giant'. In 2 Sa. 21:16, 18, 20, 22 and 1 Ch. 20:4, 6, 8, which speak of certain Philistines as 'sons of the giant', a man of great stature may be meant (*cf.* 2 Sa. 21:19–20); it may be noted here that *Goliath is never described as a 'giant' in the Bible, but some scholars hold that these verses indicate descent from the Rephaim. The LXX translates these terms with *gigas* in such passages as Gn. 14:5; Jos. 12:4; 13:12; 1 Ch. 11:15; 14:9; 20:4, 6.

3. *gibbôr*, 'mighty man', and frequently so translated in EVV (*e.g.* Gn. 6:4; Jos. 1:14; 1 Sa. 9:1, *etc.*) but rendered 'giant' in Jb. 16:14 (AV, RV; RSV 'warrior'). The word corresponds very much with English 'hero' in meaning. The LXX gives *gigas* for this term in Gn. 6:4; 10:8–9; 1 Ch. 1:10; Pss. 19:5; 33:16; Is. 3:2; 13:3; 49:24–25; Ezk. 32:12, 21, 27; 39:18, 20.

One other word is translated by *gigas* in the LXX, *'anāq* (*ANAK) in Dt. 1:28, though the EVV do not so take it.

No archaeological remains have been recovered which throw any light on this question, unless the presence of Neanderthal skeletons of Palaeolithic date in the caves of Mt Carmel are considered to do so (*EMIM; *ZUZIM). T.C.M.

GIBBETHON (Heb. *gibbᵉṯôn*, 'mound'). A city in Dan (Jos. 19: 44), given to the Kohathite Levites (Jos. 21:23). For some time it was in Philistine hands and was the scene of battles between them and N Israel. Here Baasha slew Nadab (1 Ki. 15:27) and, about 26 years later, Omri was acclaimed king (1 Ki. 16:17). Sargon of Assyria depicted the conquest of the city on the walls of his palace, amongst the triumphs of his 712 BC campaign (see P. E. Botta, *Monument de Ninive*, 1849, 2, pl. 89). Probably modern Tell el-Melât, W of Gezer. G.W.G.

GIBEAH (Heb. *giḇᵉ'â, giḇᵉ'aṯ*). A noun meaning 'hill', and often so used in the Bible (*e.g.* 2 Sa. 2:25 and probably in 2 Sa. 6:3 with RV and RSV), but also used as a place-name. Owing to its similarity in form with the place-name *geḇa'* (*GEBA), these two are sometimes confused (*e.g.* Jdg. 20:10).

1. A city in the hill country of Judah (Jos. 15:57), possibly to be identified with modern el-Jeba' near Bethlehem.

2. A city in Benjamin (Jos. 18:28), evidently N of Jerusalem (Is. 10:29). As a result of a crime committed by the inhabitants, the city was destroyed in the period of the Judges (Jdg. 19–20; *cf.* Ho. 9:9; 10:9). It was famous as the birthplace of Saul (1 Sa. 10:26), *giḇᵉ'aṯ šā'ûl*, 'Gibeah of Saul' (1 Sa. 11:4), and it served as his residence while he was king (1 Sa. 13–15), and after David was anointed in his place (1 Sa. 22:6; 23:19; 26:1). When David was king it was necessary to allow the Gibeonites to hang up the bodies of seven of Saul's descendants on the walls of Gibeah to make amends for his slaughter of them (2 Sa. 21:6; LXX 'Gibeon').

Biblical Gibeah of Saul is almost certainly to be identified with the mound of Tell el-Ful, about 5 km N of Jerusalem. The site was excavated by W. F. Albright in 1922–3 and 1933, with results that agreed with this identification. Further excavations were made by P. W. Lapp in 1964, bringing some changes to Albright's conclusions. The situation of the place away from running water meant that it was not permanently occupied until the Iron Age, when rain-water cisterns came into common use in the hill country. The first small settlement belonged to the 12th century BC, perhaps being destroyed in the episode which Jdg. 19–20 relate. After an interval, a small fortress was erected and manned about 1025–950 BC, the time of Saul. Albright had restored its plan as a rectangle with a tower at each corner, but only one tower has been uncovered, and Lapp's work has shown that the plan is uncertain. An iron plough-tip from this period was found, indicating the introduction of iron, monopolized up to now by the Philistines. There are signs that the fortress was pillaged and then abandoned for a few years, presumably at the death of Saul, but the site was soon reoccupied, possibly as an outpost in David's war with Ishbosheth. It must have lost its importance with David's conquest of the whole kingdom, however, and the excavations indicate that it lay deserted for about 2 centuries. The fortress was rebuilt with a watchtower, possibly by Hezekiah, and destroyed soon after (*cf.* Is. 10:29), to be re-fortified in the 7th century BC with a casemate wall (*FORTIFICATION). After a destruction attributed to Nebuchadrezzar's forces, there was quite an extensive village on the site until about 500 BC. A further period of abandonment ensued until the spread of a new village across the site in the Maccabean age. Thereafter there was sporadic occupation until the expulsion of all Jews from Jerusalem, when Gibeah presumably fell under the same ban because of its proximity to the city.

BIBLIOGRAPHY. W. F. Albright, *AASOR* 4, 1924; L. A. Sinclair, 'An Archaeological Study of Gibeah', *AASOR* 34, 1960; P. W. Lapp, *BA* 28, 1965, pp. 2–10; N. W. Lapp, *BASOR* 223, 1976, pp. 25–42; *NEAEHL*, 2, pp. 445–448. T.C.M.
A.R.M.

GIBEON. At the time of the Israelite invasion of Canaan this was an important city inhabited by Hivites (Jos. 9:17; LXX *'Horites' is perhaps preferable) and apparently governed by a council of elders (Jos. 9:11; *cf.* 10:2). Following the fall of Jericho and Ai, the Gibeonites tricked Joshua into making a treaty with them as vassals. They were reduced to menial service and cursed when their deceit was discovered. The Amorite kings of the S hill-country attacked Gibeon for its defection to the Israelites, but Joshua led a force to aid his allies and, by means of a hailstorm and a miraculous extension of the daylight, routed the Amorites (Jos. 9–10; 11:19). The city was allotted to Benjamin and set apart for the Levites (Jos. 18:25; 21:17). During the struggle between David and the adherents of Ishbosheth the two sides met at Gibeon. Twelve warriors from either side were chosen for a contest, but each killed his opposite number and only after a general mêlée were David's men victorious (2 Sa. 2:12–17). At 'the great stone which is in Gibeon' Joab killed the dilatory Amasa (2 Sa. 20:8). This may have been merely a notable landmark, or it may have had some religious significance connected with the high place where the tabernacle and the altar of burnt-offering were, and where Solomon worshipped after his accession (1 Ch. 16:39; 21:29; 2 Ch. 1:3, 13; 1 Ki. 3:4–5). The 'Geba' of 2 Sa. 5:25 should probably be altered to 'Gibeon' in view of 1 Ch. 14:16; Is. 28:21 and LXX. The Gibeonites still retained their treaty rights in David's time, so that the only way of removing the guilt incurred by Saul's slaughter of Gibeonites was to hand over seven of his descendants for execution (2 Sa. 21:1–11). The close connection of Saul's family with Gibeon (1 Ch. 8:29–30; 9:35–39) may well have made his deed appear all the worse. Shishak of Egypt numbers Gibeon among the cities he captured (*ANET*, p. 242; *cf.* 1 Ki. 14:25). The assassins of Gedaliah, the governor of Judah appointed by Nebuchadrezzar, were overtaken by the 'great waters' of Gibeon and the prisoners they had taken set free (Je. 41:11–14). Gibeonites helped Nehemiah to rebuild the walls of Jerusalem (Ne. 3:7).

Excavations at el-Jib, some 9 km N of Jerusalem, between 1956 and 1962 have revealed remains of cities of the Early and Middle II Bronze Age, and of the Iron Age from its beginning to the Persian period. There was also a large town during Roman times. No remains of a Late Bronze Age settlement, which might be considered contemporary with Joshua, have been discovered, but burials of the time showed there had been life there. Some time in the Early Iron Age a large pit with a stairway descending around it was dug to a depth of 11 m in the rock. Steps led down a tunnel a further 12 m to a water-chamber, perhaps the 'pool' of 2 Sa. 2 and the 'waters' of Je. 41. It seems that this pit was often almost full of water. Later another tunnel was cut leading from the city to a spring outside the walls. The filling of the great pit contained the handles of many storage jars, stamped with a royal *seal or inscribed with the owners' names and the name Gibeon. Examination of the area around the pit has shown that it was the site of an extensive wine-making industry in the 7th century BC. Sealed jars of wine were stored in cool rock-cut cellars. The evidence suggests that the inscriptions relate to this site and so identify it.

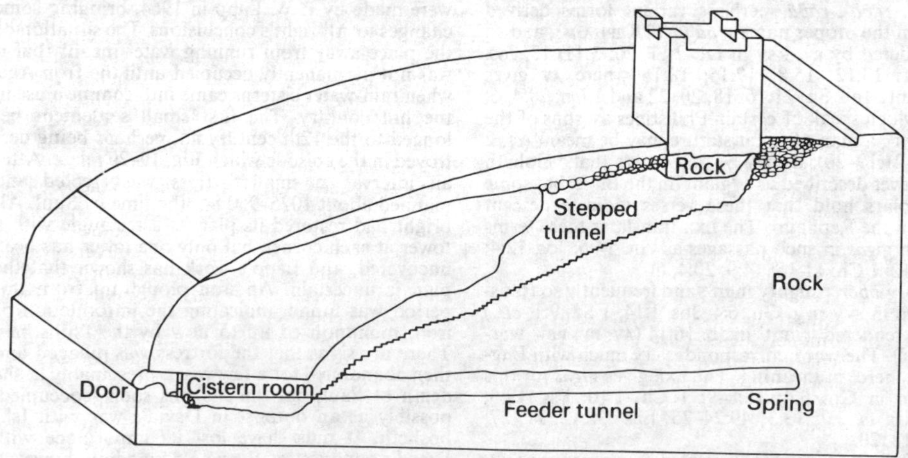

The water-system at Gibeon consisted of a water-chamber cut into the rock, reached by a spiral staircase, and an Iron Age tunnel of 93 steps leading to the spring outside the city wall. Section through E side of hill, showing the stepped tunnel and spring.

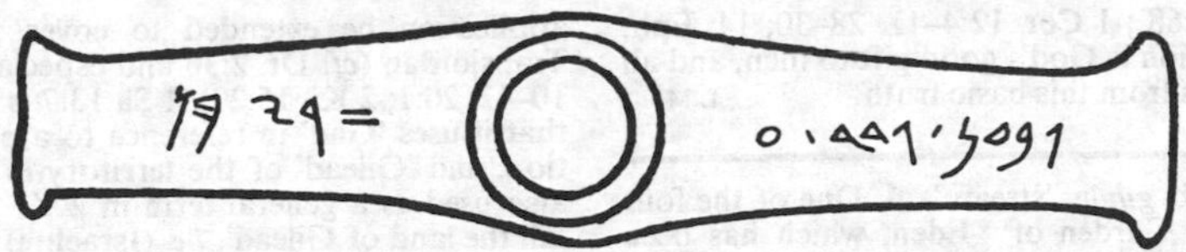

Handles and mouth of a storage jar from el-Jib, inscribed in Old Hebrew gb'n gdr 'zrhyw, *'Gibeon-Gedor, Azariah'*.

BIBLIOGRAPHY. J. B. Pritchard, *Hebrew Inscriptions and Stamps from Gibeon*, 1959; *idem*, *The Water System of Gibeon*, 1961; *idem*, *Gibeon where the Sun stood still*, 1962; *idem*, *The Bronze Age Cemetery at Gibeon*, and *Winery, Defences and Soundings at Gibeon*, 1964; *NEAEHL*, pp. 511–514.

A.R.M.

GIDEON (Heb. *gid*ᵉ*'ôn*, 'hewer, smiter'), the judge who delivered Israel from the Midianites, a bedouin people then dominating the central area of Palestine (Jdg. 6:1–8:35). He was the son of Joash, of the clan of Abiezer, of the tribe of Manasseh, and he was also called Jerubbaal. Some scholars hold that the narrative is composite, made up of at least two accounts (see the commentaries).

Gideon was called to deliver his people while threshing wheat secretly for fear of Midianite depredations. There followed an act of defiance in which he destroyed his father's Baal-altar and Asherah, from the consequences of which he was saved by Joash's quick-wittedness. The gesture of defiance seems to signify a protest against the assimilation of the worship of Yahweh with the Baal-cult. This act is associated with the giving to Gideon of the name Jerubbaal (*y*ᵉ*rubba'al*), which is variously interpreted as 'Baal strives', 'Baal founds' or 'may Baal give increase'. Some suggest that this may have been Gideon's earliest name, reflecting the prevailing syncretism, receiving, however, a new significance in view of this act of iconoclasm (*cf.* R. Kittel, *Great Men and Movements in Israel*, 1929, p. 65; F. F. Bruce, *NBCR*, *ad loc.*). In 2 Sa. 11:21 it appears as Jerubbesheth (*y*ᵉ*rubbešeṯ*), replacing the abhorred name Baal with the word for 'shame'.

The defeat of the Midianites is graphically described in Jdg. 7, when at God's command Gideon reduced his army from 32,000 to 300, and received personal reassurance during a secret reconnaissance when he heard a Midianite warrior's dream of defeat. He made a sudden night attack which demoralized the enemy and led to a thorough rout. Jdg. 8 records the completion of the victory with the slaying of Zebah and Zalmunna, despite the hostility of the towns of Succoth and Penuel, for which Gideon exacted punishment.

After the deliverance Gideon was asked to set up a hereditary monarchy, but he refused. He did, however, accept the golden earrings taken as spoil in battle, with which he made an 'ephod' (probably an image of Yahweh). This he set up in his own city, where it later became a source of apostasy.

The defeat of Midian was decisive, and Israel had peace during the remainder of Gideon's life. The final picture of Gideon is of a peaceful old age, with many wives and sons, among the latter being the notorious Abimelech (Jdg. 9).

Heb. 11:32 gives Gideon a place among the heroes of faith. He trusted in God rather than in a large army, gaining a victory with a handful of men which made it clear it was wholly of God. 'The day of Midian' seems to have become proverbial for deliverance by God without the aid of man (Is. 9:4). Gideon is portrayed as a humble man, and his refusal of the kingship establishes the fact that Israel's ideal government was a theocracy (Jdg. 8:23).

BIBLIOGRAPHY. See *JUDGES. *Commentaries* by G. A. Cooke (*CBSC*), 1918, C. F. Burney, 1930, H. W. Hertzberg (*Das Alte Testament Deutsch*), 1953. Fleming James, *Personalities of the Old Testament*, 1947.

J.G.G.N.

GIFT. In the OT a dozen words are used of gifts of one kind or other. The sacrifices and other offerings were gifts to God (Ex. 28:38; Nu. 18:11, *etc.*). The Levites were also, in a way, a gift to the Lord (Nu. 18:6). Occasionally there is the thought of God's gifts to men, as health and food and wealth and enjoyment (Ec. 3:13; 5:19). Men gave gifts on festive occasions (Ps. 45:12; Est. 9:22), or in association with a dowry (Gn. 34:12). Gifts might be tokens of royal bounty (Dn. 2:6). But there was little goodwill in the 'gifts' (RSV, 'tribute') the Moabites brought David (2 Sa. 8:2). Gifts might be the expression of shrewd policy, as when 'a man's gift makes room for him' (Pr. 18:16). Indeed, a gift might be offered with altogether improper motives, so that the word comes to mean much the same as 'bribe'. The Israelites were commanded, 'thou shalt take no gift: for the gift blindeth the wise' (Ex. 23:8, AV).

In the NT there is a marked change of emphasis. Some of the 9 Gk. words for 'gift' refer to men's gifts to God, as *anathēma* (Lk. 21:5), and especially *dōron* (Mt. 5:23f.; 23:18f., *etc.*). Some refer also to men's gifts to one another, *e.g.* *dōron* (Rev. 11:10), *doma* (Mt. 7:11; Phil. 4:17). But the characteristic thing is the use of several words to denote entirely or primarily the gifts that God gives to men. *dōrea* (the word expresses freeness, bounty) is found 11 times, always of a divine gift. Sometimes this is salvation (Rom. 5:15, 17), or it may be undefined ('his inexpressible gift', 2 Cor. 9:15), or it is the Holy Spirit (Acts 2:38). James reminds us that 'Every good endowment (*dosis*) and every perfect gift (*dōrēma*) is from above' (Jas. 1:17). A most important word is *charisma*. This may be used of God's good gift of eternal life (Rom. 6:23), but its characteristic use is for the *'spiritual gifts', *i.e.* the gifts which the Holy Spirit imparts to certain people. Everyone has such a gift (1 Pet. 4:10), but specific gifts are reserved for individuals (1 Cor. 12:30), and individuals endowed with these gifts are themselves 'gifts' from the ascended Christ to the church (Eph. 4:7ff.). The important passages are Rom. 12:6ff.; 1 Cor. 12:4–11, 28–30; 14; Eph. 4:11ff. Salvation is God's good gift to men, and all the rest arises from this basic truth. L.M.

GIHON (Heb. *gîḥôn*, 'stream'). **1.** One of the four rivers of the Garden of *Eden, which has been identified variously with the Oxus, Araxes, Ganges, Nile and many other rivers. The Nile identification arises from the statement that it wound through (*sāḇaḇ*) the land of *Cush (Gn. 2:13), which is identified with Ethiopia, but it is more probable that the Cush here referred to is the area to the E of Mesopotamia from which the Kassites later descended. If this is so, some river descending to Mesopotamia from the E mountains, perhaps the Diyala or the Kerkha, is possible, though the possibility of changed geographical features makes any identification uncertain.

2. The name of a spring to the E of Jerusalem, where Solomon was anointed king (1 Ki. 1:33, 38, 45). It was from this spring that Hezekiah cut a conduit to take the water to the pool of Siloam (2 Ch. 32:30) inside the city walls, and it was still outside the outer wall built by Manasseh (2 Ch. 33:14). It is probably to be identified with modern 'Ain Sitti Maryām.

BIBLIOGRAPHY. On **1** see E. A. Speiser, 'The Rivers of Paradise', *Festschrift Johannes Friedrich*, 1959, pp. 473–485; on **2** see J. Simons, *Jerusalem in the Old Testament*, 1952, pp. 162–188. T.C.M.

GILBOA (Heb. *gilbōa'*, probably 'bubbling fountain', although there is some doubt about this). Sometimes the name is anarthrous, while 'Mt Gilboa' also occurs. It was a range of mountains in the territory of Issachar, and so, in 2 Sa. 1:21, David apostrophizes 'ye mountains of Gilboa'. It was the scene of Saul's final clash with the Philistines and of his death (1 Sa. 28:4; 31). It may seem surprising to find the Philistines so far N, but the route from Philistia to Esdraelon was an easy one for armies on the march. The hills are now called Jebel Fuḳû'a, but the ancient name is perpetuated in the village of Jelbôn on the hillside. G.W.G.

GILEAD. 1. The son of Machir, son of Manasseh and progenitor of the Gileadite clan which was a major part of the tribe of Manasseh (Nu. 26:29–30; 27:1; 36:1; Jos. 17:1, 3; 1 Ch. 2:21, 23; 7:14–17). **2.** A descendant of Gad and ancestor of some later Gadites (1 Ch. 5:14). **3.** Jephthah's father (Jdg. 11:1–2).

4. The name applied to the whole or part of the Transjordanian lands occupied by the tribes of Reuben, Gad and half-Manasseh. Geographically, Gilead proper was the hilly, wooded country N of a line from Heshbon W to the N end of the Dead Sea, and extending N towards the present-day river and Wadi Yarmuk but flattening out into plains from *c.* 29 km S of Yarmuk. The N extension of these plains forms the territory of Bashan. Gilead thus defined is divided into N and S halves by the E–W course of the lower Jabbok river. S of Gilead proper (*i.e.* S of the Heshbon–Dead Sea line) and reaching to the Arnon river, there is a rolling plateau suitable for grain-growing, cattle and flocks. This tract, too, was sometimes included under 'Gilead'. But the term Gilead could in its widest application be extended to cover all (Israelite) Transjordan (*cf.* Dt. 2:36 and especially 34:1; Jdg. 10–12; 20:1; 2 Ki. 15:29). 1 Sa 13:7 is interesting in that it uses 'Gad' in reference to a particular section, and 'Gilead' of the territory in general. It is also used as a general term in 2 Ki. 10:33, where 'all the land of Gilead', *i.e.* (Israelite) Transjordan, includes 'Gilead (*i.e.* Gilead proper, plus the land to the Arnon) and Bashan'. For Gilead in the narrower sense, as the wooded hill-country stretching to the N and S of the Jabbok, see Dt. 3:10, where it is described as lying between the cities of the plain or tableland S of Heshbon and Bashan in the N, and Jos. 13:11 (in context). Either half of Gilead proper could be called simply 'Gilead' (referring to the N, see Dt. 3:15; Jos. 17:1, 5–6). Where fuller designations were used, Gilead S of the Jabbok (which fell to Gad) was sometimes called 'half the hill-country of Gilead' (RV, Dt. 3:12, *cf.* 16; Jos. 12:2, 5; *cf.* 13:25), a name also used of Gilead N of the Jabbok (Jos. 13:31). The N half was also known as 'the rest of Gilead' (Dt. 3:13). In Dt. 3:12 with 16, and 13 with 15, the sequence of full and abbreviated terms is particularly noteworthy. The simultaneous use of a term or title in both wide and restricted senses, or in both full and abbreviated forms, is a common phenomenon in antiquity and modern times alike. In most OT references to Gilead study of context usually shows the nuance intended.

The balm of Gilead was proverbial (Je. 8:22; 46:11; *cf.* Gn. 37:25). The rich woodland covering its hills is cited with Lebanon and Carmel as a symbol of luxury (Je. 22:6; 50:19; Zc. 10:10). It was the grazing-ground of goats (Ct. 4:1; 6:5), and also provided refuge for fugitives. Among those who sought refuge in Gilead were Jacob when he fled before Laban (Gn. 31:21–55), the Israelites who feared the Philistines in Saul's time (1 Sa. 13:7), Ishbosheth (2 Sa. 2:8–9) and David during Absalom's revolt (2 Sa. 17:22ff.).

BIBLIOGRAPHY. On natural geography, *cf.* D. Baly, *The Geography of the Bible*, 1974, pp. 219–225. On archaeology, *cf.* N. Glueck, *Explorations in Eastern Palestine*, 3; *AASOR* 18/19, 1939, pp. 151–153, 242–251 (extent and history), and pp. 153–242, 251ff. (archaeology). In general, M. Ottoson, *Gilead*, 1969; speculative is M. Wüst, *Untersuchungen zu den siedlungsgeographischen Texten des Alten Testaments*, 1. *Ostjordanland*, 1975. See also *REUBEN, *GAD, *MANASSEH, *RAMOTH-GILEAD and *MAHANAIM. K.A.K.

GILGAL. The name can mean 'circle (of stones)', or 'rolling', from Heb. *gālal*, 'to roll'. In its latter meaning the name Gilgal was used by God through Joshua to serve as a reminder to Israel of their deliverance from Egypt when they were circumcised there: 'This day I have rolled away (*gallôṯî*) the reproach of Egypt from you' (Jos. 5:9).

1. Gilgal to the E of Jericho, between it and the Jordan. The exact site of Gilgal within this area is still uncertain. J. Muilenburg (*BASOR* 140, 1955, pp. 11–27) very tentatively suggests a site just N of Khirbet el-Mefjir, about 2 km NE of OT Jericho (Tell es-Sulṭan). In support of this approximate location, Muilenburg adduces the combined testimony of the OT references and of later writers (Josephus, Eusebius, *etc.*), and a trial excavation revealed Early Iron Age remains there. J. Simons (*GTT*, pp. 269–270, §464) criticized Muilenburg's view on the ground that Khirbet el-Mefjir is more fairly N than E of Jericho; but this is not a very strong objection because Khirbet el-Mefjir is as much E as it is N (see Muilenburg's map, *op. cit.*, fig. I, p. 17).

Gilgal became Israel's base of operations after the crossing of Jordan (Jos. 4:19), and was the focus of a series of events during the conquest: twelve commemorative stones were set up when Israel pitched camp there (Jos. 4:20); the new generation grown up in the wilderness were circumcised there; the first Passover in Canaan was held there (Jos. 5:9–10) and the manna ceased (Jos. 5:11–12). From Gilgal, Joshua led forth Israel against Jericho (Jos. 6:11, 14ff.), and conducted his S campaign (Jos. 10) after receiving the artful Gibeonite envoys (Jos. 9:6), and there began to allot tribal territories (Jos. 14:6). Gilgal thus became at once a reminder of God's past deliverance from Egypt, a token of present victory under his guidance, and saw the promise of inheritance yet to be gained. On the camp at Gilgal in Joshua's strategy, compare Y. Kaufmann, *The Biblical Account of the Conquest of Palestine*, 1953, pp. 91–97, especially 92, 95f. Kaufmann also incisively refutes Alt's and Noth's erroneous views about Gilgal as an early shrine of Benjaminite tradition (pp. 67–69).

In later days God's angel went up from Gilgal to Bochim in judgment against forgetful Israel (Jdg. 2:1); thence Ehud returned to slay a Moabite king for Israel's deliverance (Jdg. 3:19). Samuel used to visit Gilgal on circuit (1 Sa. 7:16); there Saul's kingship was confirmed after the Ammonite emergency with joyful sacrifices (1 Sa. 11:14–15; *cf.* 10:8). But thereafter, Saul offered precipitate sacrifice (1 Sa. 13:8–14), and it was at Gilgal that Samuel and Saul parted for ever after Saul's disobedience in the Amalekite war (1 Sa. 15:12–35). After Absalom's abortive revolt, the Judaeans welcomed David back at Gilgal (2 Sa. 19:15, 40). In the days of Ahab and Joram, Elijah and Elisha passed that way just before Elijah's translation to heaven (2 Ki. 2:1) (although some, quite unnecessarily it would seem, consider this place to be distinct from the historic Gilgal), and there Elisha sweetened the wild gourds in the cooking-pot of a group of prophets who feared poison (2 Ki. 4:38).

But during the 8th century BC, at least under the kings Uzziah to Hezekiah, Gilgal became a centre of formal and unspiritual worship which like Bethel drew condemnation from Amos (4:4; 5:5) and Hosea (4:15; 9:15; 12:11). The association of Bethel and Gilgal (reflected also in 2 Ki. 2:1–2) was strengthened by an important road that connected them (Muilenburg, *op. cit.*, p. 13). Finally, Micah (6:5) reminds his people of Gilgal's first role in their spiritual pilgrimage, witnessing to God's righteousness and saving power, 'from Shittim to Gilgal', *i.e.* across Jordan into the promised land.

2. In Jos. 15:7, the N boundary of Judah at least came in view of a Gilgal that was 'opposite the ascent of Adummim'; in the parallel description of this line, as also the S boundary of Benjamin (Jos. 18:17), Geliloth is so described. But whether *this* Gilgal/Geliloth is the same as the famous Gilgal E of Jericho remains quite uncertain though just possible. Otherwise, it must be some other local 'circle' farther W. Suggestions about this boundary will be found in Simons (*GTT*, pp. 139–140, § 314, 173, § 326), who, however, makes too free a use of emendation.

3. In Dt. 11:30, the phrase 'opposite Gilgal' may refer to the Canaanites dwelling in the Arabah (Jordan rift valley), rather than to the mountains Ebal and Gerizim. If so, then this is simply the historic Gilgal, see **1** above. Compare *GTT*, p. 35, §§ 87–88.

4. Among Joshua's defeated enemies occurs the king of Goyyim belonging to Gilgal (Jos. 12:23) between the kings of Dor and Tirzah. This Gilgal might be the capital of a king ruling over a mixed population on the edge of the maritime plain of Sharon, if—as is sometimes suggested—it is to be placed at Jiljūliyeh, about 5 km N of Aphek or about 22 km NE of the coast at Joppa.

5. The Beth-gilgal from which singers came to the dedication of the walls of Jerusalem by Nehemiah and Ezra is either the famous Gilgal (**1** above) or else remains unidentified (Ne 12:29).

K.A.K.

GIRDLE. In AV this word covers several Hebrew terms and body-garments. The word *'aḇnēṭ* is used of the ceremonial sash, especially as worn by the high priest and his associates, made of embroidered linen in blue, purple and scarlet (Ex. 28:4, 39–40; 29:9; 39:29; Lv. 8:7, 13; 16:4), but worn also by other high dignitaries (Is. 22:21). In Ex. 28:8, 27–28, *etc.*, the 'curious girdle' of AV is *ḥēšeḇ*, 'device', of gold, blue, purple, scarlet, and fine linen, apparently an elaborately worked belt for the ephod (*DRESS, *d*). The term *'ēzôr* usually means 'waistcloth', 'loincloth'. A rough leather one characterized the prophet Elijah (2 Ki. 1:8) and his NT counterpart John the Baptist (Mt. 3:4; Mk. 1:6, RV).

Jeremiah (13:1–11) was bidden to use a spoilt linen loincloth as a symbol that spoilt Judah was good-for-nothing. Centuries later, Agabus bound himself with Paul's girdle in token of Paul's coming captivity (Acts 21:11). Besides picturing the onset of Assyrian troops with well-girt loincloths (Is. 5:27; *cf. ANEP*, fig. 236), Isaiah envisaged (11:5) righteousness and faithfulness as clothing the son of David like a loincloth. Ezekiel (23:15) alludes to Babylonians arrayed in vermilion, waistbands and turbans(?); *cf. ANEP*, fig. 454.

*ḥ*ᵃ*gôr*, *ḥ*ᵃ*gôrâ* means belt, waistband or girdle proper. Such belts were often ornate and valuable, including, doubtless, those for sale in Pr. 31:24 and belonging to fashionable women in Is. 3:24; *cf.* Dn. 10:5; Rev. 1:13; 15:6. They were used by warriors to support a sword in its sheath (2 Sa. 20:8; *cf.* 1 Ki. 2:5 and Heb. of 2 Ki. 3:21; *cf. ANEP*, figs. 173–174), and could be part of presents and rewards (1 Sa. 18:4; 2 Sa. 18:11). People at work commonly tucked up their clothes into their girdle, as is done in the East today.

The word *mēzaḥ*, 'girdle', occurs in Ps. 109:19; it and *'aḇnēṭ* may perhaps be connected with the Egyp. words *mḏḥ* and *bnd* respectively (T. O. Lambdin, *JAOS* 73, 1953, pp. 146, 152). K.A.K.

GIRGASHITES. A tribe listed among the descendants of Canaan in Gn. 10:16; 1 Ch. 1:14, and part of the very mixed population of Canaan as described in the original promise to Abraham (Gn. 15:21; *cf.* Ne. 9:8). In due course they were overcome by Israel (Dt. 7:1; Jos. 3:10; 24:11). In N Canaanite Ugarit (14th/13th centuries BC), the Girgashites are indirectly attested by two personal names: *grgš* and *bn-grgš*, *i.e.* Girgash and Ben-Girgash (references in Gordon, *Ugaritic Textbook*, 3, 1965, p. 381, No. 619). The biblical and Ugaritic Girgash(ites) are probably different from a people in Asia Minor called Karkisa in Hittite annals and *ḳrḳš* in similar Egyp. records. K.A.K.

GIRZITES. In AV 'Gezrites'; either form is possible. Little-known semi-nomadic clans, associated with *Geshurites and *Amalekites in the NW of the *Negeb, and extirpated by David (1 Sa. 27:8) while he governed Ziklag under the Philistine Achish. K.A.K.

GLASS. Seldom mentioned in the Bible, glass was a rare luxury until Roman times. It was considered something precious like gold (Jb. 28:17, AV 'crystal'; Heb. *zᵉḵûḵîṯ*). Several passages translated 'glass' (AV) refer to reflecting metal surfaces used as mirrors. Glazing was early known and used on beads and brickwork from *c.* 4000 BC, but glass itself is first attested in the Early Bronze Age (*c.* 2600 BC).

By the 18th Egyptian Dynasty (*c.* 1546–1316 BC) a glass factory at el-Amarna in Egypt imitated stone and pottery types and made small unguent vessels by casting, or by winding drawn glass rods round a sand core and re-heating.

Early core-formed decorated goblets, bottles and bowls have been found in N Mesopotamia (Rimah, Nuzi), Babylonia, N Syria (Alalaḫ) and Palestine (Megiddo). Other imported and local products have been discovered at Gezer, Lachish (Late Iron Age), Achzib and Hazor. From the 13th century BC glazes are mentioned in contemporary Hittite and Assyr. texts. A reference in a Ras Shamra text to *spsg*, 'glaze', makes it probable that this word is found in Pr. 26:23—'like glaze crusted over pottery are smooth lips and an evil heart' (*BASOR* 98, 1945, pp. 21, 24; now disputed, *Ugarit-Forschungen* 8, 1976, pp. 37–40). Cobalt and manganese were used as colouring agents, but early glass was not very transparent because of impurities in the basic materials. The iridescence common on ancient glass is due to decomposition and weathering.

In the late Iron and Israelite periods Egyp. glass vessels, now imitating alabaster vessels (hence Gk. *alabastron*), were imported into Syria and Palestine. Phoenician products found at Samaria and elsewhere show that glass amphorae, juglets and aryballoi were in use.

The Hellenistic period brought the additional technique which resulted in gold glass, millefiore and coloured glasses found at many Palestinian sites. The *alabastron* broken open as a gift for our Lord was probably a long-necked glass ointment bottle, the so-called tear-bottle (Mt. 26:7; Mk. 14:3; Lk. 7:37; AV 'alabaster box').

By the Roman period the invention of glass-blowing methods (at Sidon?) resulted in mass-produced table services which rivalled pottery and metal for ease and cheapness of manufacture. Much of this was translucent, and much like a highly-polished glaze. The latter may be the allusion in the *'sea of glass' (Rev. 4:6; 15:2) and in the city and street of the New Jerusalem made of pure gold likened to glass (Rev. 21:18, 21).

BIBLIOGRAPHY. D. B. Harden, *Journal of Glass Studies* 12, 1970, pp. 17–27, 35–63; 13, 1971, pp. 45–63; A. L. Oppenheim *et al.*, *Glass and Glass-making in Ancient Mesopotamia*, 1970. D.J.W.

GLEANING (*lāqaṭ*, 'to gather, glean'; *ʿālal*, 'to roll, glean, suck', usually of grapes). Amid the rejoicing of harvest-time a kindly Israelitish law upheld the custom whereby the poor, orphans and strangers were allowed to glean grain, grapes and olives (Lv. 19:9–10; 23:22; Dt. 24:19). *Ruth took full advantage of the practice (Ru. 2:2ff.); Gideon used it in striking illustration of the superiority of Ephraim (Jdg. 8:2); and Jeremiah made of it a metaphor to express the complete annihilation of backsliding Israel (Je. 6:9; 49:9–10). The custom of gleaning still persists in certain eastern countries. (*AGRICULTURE). J.D.D.

GLORIA IN EXCELSIS. This term refers primarily to a liturgical hymn originating in the patristic church (*cf. SHERK*, 6, 501; *ODCC*) and inspired by the angelic hymn in Lk. 2:14. As in the visions to Zechariah and Mary (Lk. 1:13, 30), the reassurance of the angel in Lk. 2:10 is an intimation of the good news which he brings. The previous angelic proclamations were directed particularly to the persons to whom the visions came. The joy of this message is for all the people of God; the shepherds are only representative of the larger group who anticipate and long for the deliverance Messiah brings. The benediction of praise expresses not merely the hope for the future but the reality that has become actual in Messiah's birth:

> To God in the highest, glory!
> To his people on earth, peace!

'Men of God's good will' is the better-attested reading and is parallel to 'the people' in v. 10. It refers to those upon whom God's redemptive mercy has been bestowed and with whom he is well pleased (*cf.* Lk. 3:22). The peace which the angels announce is not the external and transient *pax Romana*; it is the peace which heals the estrangement between sinful men and a holy God (*cf.* Is. 9:6f.; Rom. 10:15). (*BENEDICTUS.) E.E.E.

GLORY.

I. In the Old Testament

'Glory' generally represents Heb. *kāḇôḏ*, with the root idea of 'heaviness' and so of 'weight' or 'worthiness'. It is used of men to describe their wealth, splendour or reputation (though in the last sense *kāḇôḏ* is often rendered 'honour'). The glory of Israel was not her armies but Yahweh (Je. 2:11). The word could also mean the self or soul (Gn. 49:6).

The most important concept is that of the glory of Yahweh. This denotes the revelation of God's being, nature and presence to mankind, sometimes with physical phenomena.

In the Pentateuch the glory of Yahweh went with his people out of Egypt and was shown in the cloud which led them through the wilderness (Ex. 16:7, 10). The cloud rested on Mt Sinai, where Moses saw his glory (Ex. 24:15–18). No man could see God's face and live (Ex. 33:20), but some vision of his glory was granted (Ex. 34:5–8).

The glory of Yahweh filled the tabernacle (Ex. 40:34–35) and appeared especially at the hour of sacrifice (Lv. 9:6, 23). These passages seem all to be connected with a 'thunderstorm-theophany', but there are also passages which suggest more the character of Yahweh which is to be made known throughout the earth (Nu. 14:21–22).

The historical books tell of the Temple's becoming the place where the glory of Yahweh was especially to be located (1 Ki. 8:11; 2 Ch. 7:1–3).

In the prophets there are both the quasi-physical conception of Yahweh's glory as seen in the visions of Ezekiel (Ezk. 1:28, *etc.*) and also a more spiritualized doctrine (Is. 40:4–5; 60:1–3, *etc.*). The vision of Isaiah in the Temple seems to combine both ideas (Is. 6:1–4).

There can be found, likewise, in the psalms all the imagery of the storm (Pss. 18; 29) and also the idea of the future display of God's character to the world (Pss. 57:11; 96:3).

II. In the New Testament

Here the LXX is followed in translating *kāḇôḏ* by *doxa*. In secular Greek this means 'opinion' or 'reputation'. The former idea disappears entirely in the LXX and NT, and words akin to *kāḇôḏ* are also rendered by *doxa*.

In certain places in the NT *doxa* refers to human honour (Mt. 4:8; 6:29), but its chief use is to describe the revelation of the character and the presence of God in the Person and work of Jesus Christ. He is the outshining of the divine glory (Heb. 1:3).

The glory of God was seen by the shepherds at the birth of Christ (Lk. 2:9, 14) and by his disciples during his incarnate life (Jn. 1:14). Particularly was it revealed in his *sēmeia* (Jn. 2:11) and at his transfiguration (Mt. 17:1–8; Mk. 9:2–8; Lk. 9:28–36). This recalls the ascent of Moses to Sinai (Ex. 24:15) and of Elijah to Horeb (1 Ki. 19:8) and their visions of the glory of God. Now Christ both sees and reflects the divine glory, but no tabernacle needs to be built because the Word of God has pitched his tent in the human flesh of Jesus (Jn. 1:14) and his glory is to be more fully revealed at the coming exodus at Jerusalem (Lk. 9:31) and finally at his parousia.

In the Fourth Gospel it is the hour of dedication to death which is essentially the hour of glory (Jn. 7:39; 12:23–28; 13:31; 17:5; *cf.* Heb. 2:9).

The resurrection and ascension are also seen as manifestations of the glory of God in Christ (Lk. 24:26; Acts 3:13; 7:55; Rom. 6:4; 1 Tim. 3:16; 1 Pet. 1:21). But above all it is to be revealed in its fullness at the parousia (Mk. 8:38; 13:26, *etc.*).

Man, who was made as the image and glory of God (1 Cor. 11:7) for relationship with him, has fallen short of his destiny (Rom. 3:23), which has been fulfilled only by Christ, the second Adam (Heb. 2:6–9).

The glory of God in the face of Jesus Christ is still to be seen and reflected by the church (2 Cor. 4:3–6). It is the glory of the new covenant (2 Cor. 3:7–11), and it is especially shared both now (1 Pet. 4:14) and hereafter (Rom. 8:18) by those who suffer with Christ. The object of the church is to see that the world acknowledges the glory which is God's (Rom. 15:9) and is shown in his deeds (Acts 4:21), in his disciples (1 Cor. 6:20) and above all in his Son, the Lord of glory (Rom. 16:27).

BIBLIOGRAPHY. A. Richardson, *An Introduction to the Theology of the New Testament*, 1958, pp. 64ff.; S. Aalen, *NIDNTT* 2, pp. 44–52; G. Kittel, G. von Rad, *TDNT* 2, pp. 233–255; C. C. Newman, *Paul's Glory-Christology: Tradition and Rhetoric*, 1992; L. D. Hurst & N. T. Wright, *The Glory of Christ in the New Testament*, 1987. R.E.N.

GNOSTICISM. A term derived from Gk. *gnōsis*, 'knowledge'. Until modern times it was applied exclusively to a body of heretical teaching denounced by the church Fathers in the early Christian centuries. But in 20th-century scholarship it has often been applied more loosely to any form of religious belief which emphasizes any kind of dualism and/or the possession of secret knowledge. So, for example, Zoroastrianism, Mandaeism, the Hermetic literature, the Dead Sea scrolls and even the NT itself have all been described as 'gnostic'.

I. Definition

This is one of the most hotly debated issues today, and there are two main schools of thought: one, represented by conservative British scholars such as R. McL. Wilson, which supports a 'narrow' definition (*i.e.* restricting the term to the 2nd-century Christian heresies); and the other, popularized especially by German scholars like R. Bultmann and K. Rudolf, which supports a 'wide' definition (*i.e.* including other groups with a similar outlook).

There are difficulties with the 'wide' definition of the term, for under this usage the word 'Gnosticism' comes to have such a broad connotation that it almost ceases to have any specific reference at all, and simply denotes the lowest common denominator of Hellenistic thought, in which dualism of one sort or another was often a prominent feature.

At the same time, however, there are also difficulties in defining more precisely what Gnosticism is. Some groups in the early church (*e.g.* Valentinians, Naassenes) actually called themselves Gnostics. But the church Fathers are far from unanimous in their attempts to define what was common even to these groups. Indeed Irenaeus went so far as to comment that 'there are as many systems of redemption as there are teachers of these mystical doctrines' (*Adv. Haer.* 1. 21. 1).

But in spite of such obstacles to comprehensive definition, these 2nd-century groups had enough in common for us to be able to form some idea of a basic Gnostic belief.

The foundation-stone of this belief was a radical cosmological dualism, *i.e.* the belief that the created world was evil, and was totally separate from and in opposition to the world of spirit. The supreme God dwelt in unapproachable splendour in this spiritual world, and had no dealings with the world of matter. Matter was the creation of an inferior being, the *Demiurge*. He, along with his aides the *archōns*, kept mankind imprisoned within their material existence, and barred the path of individual souls trying to ascend to the spirit world after death. Not even this possibility was open to everyone, however. For only those who possessed a divine spark (*pneuma*) could hope to escape from their corporeal existence. And even those possessing such a spark did not have an automatic escape, for they needed to receive the enlightenment of *gnōsis* before they could become aware of their own spiritual condition: '. . . it is not only the washing that is liberty, but the knowledge of who we were, and what we have become, where we were or where we were placed, whither we hasten, from what we are redeemed, what birth is, and what rebirth' (*Exc. Theod.* 78. 2). In most of the Gnostic systems reported by the church Fathers, this enlightenment is the work of a divine redeemer, who descends from the spiritual world in disguise and is often equated with the Christian Jesus. Salvation for the Gnostic, therefore, is to be alerted to the existence of his divine *pneuma* and then, as a result of this knowledge, to escape on death from the material world to the spiritual.

The Gnostics themselves conceptualized all this in a highly mythological form, but the realities to which it corresponded were undoubtedly of a more existential nature. The Gnostic was trying to discover his own identity, and the appreciation of this fact led the eminent psychiatrist Carl Gustav Jung, for example, to base many of his observations about human nature on an understanding of ancient Gnosticism.

From the standpoint of traditional Christianity, Gnostic thinking is quite alien. Its mythological setting of redemption leads to a depreciation of the historical events of the life, death and resurrection of Jesus. Its view of man's relationship to God leads to a denial of the importance of the person and work of Christ, while, in a Gnostic context, 'salvation' is not understood in terms of deliverance from sin, but as a form of existential self-realization.

II. Sources

We know of the Gnostic sects from two different sources:

a. The church Fathers

The most important work here is Irenaeus, *Against Heresies*, though Tertullian, Clement of Alexandria and Hippolytus of Rome all wrote extensively on the same subjects. Some of these writings are interdependent, and they all have a similar outlook. They were all written from the standpoint of orthodox Catholic Christianity, to refute what the Fathers saw as a corruption of that 'original' apostolic Christianity of which they believed themselves to be the true upholders. This means that they are tendentious works, rather than impartial accounts of Gnostic beliefs. They were also written on the basis of secondhand knowledge. This, of course, was inevitable, since *gnōsis* by its very nature was esoteric and was not therefore readily accessible to anyone who was not an initiate. Nevertheless, when compared with the writings of the Gnostics themselves, the accounts of the church Fathers can be seen to be fair and reliable, at least in their general outlines, if not always in specific details.

b. Gnostic texts

These are by far the most important sources of our modern knowledge of Gnosticism, for they suffer from none of the disadvantages of the patristic accounts, and give us a direct insight into the workings of the Gnostic mind.

A number of isolated Gnostic texts have been known for some time, including important ones like the *Pistis Sophia*, the *Books of Jeû* and the *Apocryphon of John*, as well as a number of lesser works. But most of our direct knowledge of Gnostic writings comes from a remarkable find of 13 codices discovered about 1945 near Nag Hammadi in upper Egypt (*CHENOBOSKION). These were written in Coptic, though they are all translations of Gk. originals. They formed part of a library collected by an early Christian sect, and were eventually abandoned about AD 400. They comprise some 52 separate works. Publication of these texts has been a long and arduous business, and a complete facsimile edition of the original text did not become fully available until 1978. An Eng. translation of the texts had been published the previous year, though some of them had been made known much earlier through various scholarly articles and monographs. Nevertheless, the real task of interpreting these texts is only just beginning, and any assessment of them made now can only be provisional and tentative.

Some of the better-known works found at Nag Hammadi include a number of so-called 'gospels'. Like the Synoptic Gospel source Q, the *Gospel of Thomas* is a collection of sayings of Jesus, some of which parallel those found in the NT Gospels. Others are quite different, though some of them may well be genuine sayings of Jesus. But the collection as a whole has obviously been edited from a distinctively sectarian viewpoint. The *Gospel of Philip*, the *Gospel of Truth*, the Coptic *Gospel of the Egyptians* and the *Gospel of Mary* have less in common with the NT Gospels, and are more explicitly Gnostic in character.

The other Nag Hammadi texts include various collections of prayers, works with the title of *Apocryphon* ('secret book'—of James and of John), a number of others with the title of *Apocalypse* (of Paul, of James, of Adam, of Peter), together with heterogeneous examples of Gnostic speculative literature. Not all the works in this library represent the same type of Gnosticism. Many seem to be of Valentinian origin, but this does not apply to them all. Indeed some are not Gnostic at all. Codex VI, for example, contains a Coptic version of part of Plato's *Republic*, while two examples of early Christian wisdom writing are preserved in the *Teachings of Silvanus* (Codex VII) and the *Sentences of Sextus* (Codex XII).

An important question raised by these texts is the nature of Gnosticism itself *vis-à-vis* Christianity. Was it really a Christian heresy, as the Fathers supposed—or was it a non-Christian form of belief which in certain circles became overlaid with Christian ideas? So far as the evidence has been assessed, the Nag Hammadi texts do seem to show that there were non-Christian forms of Gnosticism. This can be seen most clearly in a comparison of *Eugnostos the Blessed* with the *Sophia of Jesus Christ*. For the two are so closely parallel that it is obvious that they must be different versions of the same text, though the former is cast in the form of a religio-philosophical tractate written by a teacher to his pupils, whereas the latter has the form of a post-resurrection discourse delivered by the risen Christ to his disciples. Detailed study of these two texts has so far tended to confirm that *Eugnostos the Blessed* is the original version, which was subsequently Christianized as the *Sophia of Jesus Christ*. Other texts, such as the *Apocalypse of Adam* and the *Paraphrase of Shem*, also seem to represent a non-Christian form of Gnosticism.

III. Origins

Where did Gnosticism come from? According to

the church Fathers, it was a perversion of Christianity. But that idea is now all but universally discounted, for it does not square with the evidence. There is, however, no consensus on the question of Gnostic origins. It is easy to recognize this or that Gnostic idea as having affinity with the concepts of some other religion, but it is very difficult to pin down more precisely the actual origin of Gnostic thought.

Some believe that Gnosticism was in some way connected with Judaism in one of its various forms, and it is undoubtedly true that OT ideas feature prominently in Gnostic speculations, though always in a context that tears them from the fabric of authentic OT thought. Others point to the similarities between Gnosticism and the kind of dualism often found in the writings of the Gk. philosophers. The discovery of part of Plato's *Republic* at Nag Hammadi certainly demonstrates that his ideas were not uncongenial to the Gnostics, though at the same time it is hardly proof that there was some intrinsic connection between them.

A different origin for Gnosticism has been sought in Iranian religion. Here again the evidence is scarcely conclusive, though it cannot be denied that Gnosticism is much closer in outlook to the cyclical concepts of those eastern religions which stem from Zoroastrianism than it is to traditional Christianity.

It is impossible to pinpoint accurately the origins of Gnosticism. Indeed it is unlikely that it had a single origin, for by nature Gnostic thinking was extremely syncretistic, and its adherents were always ready, even eager, to utilize religious ideas from many diverse sources to serve their own ends.

IV. Issues in New Testament interpretation

Two major issues for the student of the NT stem from the study of Gnosticism:

a. Pre-Christian Gnosticism

According to Reitzenstein (followed by Bultmann and many other German scholars), when Christianity first made its appearance in the Hellenistic world, its apostles found already in existence a comprehensive world-view that combined Greek and Oriental thought, and included the descent of a divine redeemer who saved the souls of mankind. This 'Gnostic' view was taken over *in toto* by the first Christians and applied to their experience of Jesus, so that he became the heavenly redeemer figure. Thus, the NT itself can be viewed as a form of Christianized Gnosticism.

There are many difficulties with the view that Gnosticism antedated Christianity. For one thing, there is no evidence for it, either in the texts known to Reitzenstein or in those now known to us. The Nag Hammadi texts have shown that there were non-Christian forms of Gnosticism, but that does not provide evidence for pre-Christian Gnosticism.

The idea that the NT is a form of Gnosticism is in any case unlikely, for there are serious and fundamental differences between the outlook of the Gnostics and that of the NT writers. The Gnostics held a cyclical concept of time, and the notion of history was meaningless to them. Gnostic redemption could never have any meaning in this life, but only in an escape from temporal existence to the world of spirit. By contrast, both OT and NT emphasize that time and history are important and both have a divine significance. God has acted in the course of the historical process as both Creator and Redeemer to provide salvation for his people. Whereas, for the Gnostic, God can be known only by an escape from history, to the Christian he can be supremely known because of his involvement in history, specifically in the life, death and resurrection of Jesus Christ. And Christian salvation is something to be enjoyed here and now in this world, rather than in some ethereal, 'spiritual' world.

b. Heresy and orthodoxy

Gnosticism is not, however, irrelevant for NT study. For traces of 'Gnostic' belief can be found in a number of NT writings, most strikingly in the beliefs of the Corinthian church as reflected in 1 Cor. These people claimed that because of their possession of special 'knowledge' they were released from the normal rules of society, and they claimed to be living an elevated, 'spiritual' existence even in their present material state. For them the resurrection was already a past event—past because they understood it spiritually, as did many Gnostics. And, like other Gnostics, they laid considerable emphasis on the supposed magical properties of the Christian sacraments.

Colossians has often been supposed to indicate the existence of a similar, though not identical, view in the church at Colossae, while the letters to the seven churches in Rev. 1–3 confirm the presence of similar 'Gnostic' ideas in other churches in the same area of Asia Minor. The Pastoral Epistles go so far as to denounce explicitly 'what is falsely called *gnōsis*' (1 Tim. 6:20), and 1 Jn. likewise seems to be written against some kind of 'Gnostic' background.

The NT writers themselves condemn these ideas. Though they often use Gnostic terminology in doing so, they make it clear that they do not accept its Gnostic connotations. But at the same time, the fact that such ideas seem to have been current, perhaps even widespread, in churches in different parts of the Roman empire, does give some credence to the hypothesis of W. Bauer, that the difference between heresy and orthodoxy was not so neatly defined in the 1st century as it later came to be by the anti-Gnostic Fathers of the Catholic Church.

BIBLIOGRAPHY. A. Logan and A. J. M. Wedderburn (eds.), *The New Testament and Gnosis*, 1983; K. Rudolph, *Gnosis*, 1983; E. M. Yamauchi, *Pre-Christian Gnosticism*[2], 1983; S. Pétrement, *A Separate God: the Christian Origins of Gnosticism*, 1984; C. W. Hedrick and R. Hodgson, Jr. (eds.), *Nag Hammadi, Gnosticism, and Early Christianity*, 1986; B. Layton, *The Gnostic Scriptures*, 1987; J. M. Robinson, *The Nag Hammadi Library in English*[3], 1988, G. Filoramo, *A History of Gnosticism*, 1990; J. E. Goehring (ed.), *Gnosticism and the Early Christian World*, 2 vols., 1990; I. P. Couliano, *The Tree of Gnosis*, 1992. J.W.D.

GOAD. A long-handled, pointed instrument used to urge on the oxen when ploughing. Shamgar used one as a weapon and slew 600 Philistines (Jdg. 3:31). The term is employed metaphorically in Ec. 12:11 to describe the words of the wise, and in Acts 26:14 where Paul is warned that for him to resist the new heavenly directive will be as fruitless as for a stubborn ox to resist the goad. J.D.D.

GOD. God is and he may be known. These two affirmations form the foundation and inspiration of all true religion. The first is an affirmation of faith, the second of experience. Since the existence of God is not subject to scientific proof, it must be a postulate of faith; and since God transcends all his creation, he can be known only in his self-revelation.

The Christian religion is distinctive in that it claims that God can be known as a personal God only in his self-revelation in the Scriptures. The Bible is written not to prove that God is, but to reveal him in his activities. For that reason, the biblical revelation of God is, in its nature, progressive, reaching its fullness in Jesus Christ his Son.

In the light of his self-revelation in the Scriptures, there are several fundamental affirmations that can be made about God.

I. His Being

In his being God is self-existing. While his creation is dependent on him, he is utterly independent of the creation. He not only has life, but he is life to his universe, and has the source of that life within himself. God is utterly independent of every environment in which he wills to make himself known. This quality of God's being probably finds expression in his personal name, Yahweh, and in his self-affirmation: 'I am who I am', *i.e.* 'I am the one that has being within himself' (Ex. 3:14).

This perception was implied in Isaiah's vision of God: 'The Lord is the everlasting God, the Creator of the ends of the earth. He will not grow tired or weary . . . He gives strength to the weary, and increases the power of the weak' (Is. 40:28–29). He is the Giver, and all his creatures are receivers. Christ gave this mystery its clearest expression when he said: 'For as the Father has life in himself, so he has granted the Son also to have life in himself' (Jn. 5:26). This makes independence of life a distinctive quality of deity. Throughout the whole of Scripture God is revealed as the Fountainhead of all there is, animate and inanimate, the Creator and life-giver, who alone has life within himself.

II. His nature

In his nature God is pure spirit, which means intelligent energy. Christ made this disclosure about the God who is the object of our worship to the woman of Samaria: 'God is spirit, and those who worship him must worship in spirit and truth' (Jn. 4:24). In this respect we must distinguish between God and those of his creatures that are spiritual. When we say that God is pure spirit, it is to emphasize that he is not part spirit and part body as man is. He is simple spirit without form or parts, and for that reason he has no physical presence. When the Bible writers speak of God as having eyes, ears, hands and feet, they are ascribing to God powers that correspond to what these physical parts enable us humans to do. If we did not speak of God in physical terms in this way we could hardly speak of him at all. This, of course, does not imply any imperfection in God, since his life as Spirit is not a limited or restricted form of existence.

When we say that God is infinite spirit, we pass completely out of the reach of our experience. We are limited as to time and place, as to knowledge and power. God is essentially unlimited, and every element of his nature is infinite. His infinity in relation to time we call his *eternity*, in relation to space his *omnipresence*, in relation to knowledge his *omniscience*, and in relation to power his *omnipotence*. God is eternal, all-present, all-knowing and all-powerful.

His infinity likewise means that God is *transcendent* over his universe. It emphasizes his distinctness as self-existing spirit, from all his creatures. He is not shut in by what we call nature, but infinitely exalted above it. Even those passages of Scripture which stress his local and temporal manifestation, lay emphasis also on his exaltation and omnipotence as a being external to the world, its sovereign Creator and Judge (*cf.* Is. 40:12–17).

At the same time God's infinity implies his *immanence*. By this we mean his all-pervading presence and power within his creation (*cf.* Ps. 139). He does not stand apart from the world, a mere spectator of the work of his hands. He pervades everything, organic and inorganic, acting from within outwards, from the centre of every atom, and from the innermost springs of thought and life and feeling, in a continuous sequence of energizing effect.

In such passages as Is. 57 and Acts 17 we have an expression of both God's transcendence and his immanence. In the first of these passages his transcendence finds expression as 'the high and lofty One who lives for ever, whose name is holy', and his immanence as the one who dwells 'with him who is contrite and lowly in spirit' (Is. 57:15, NIV). In the second passage, Paul, in addressing the men of Athens, affirmed of the transcendent God that 'the God who made the world and everything in it, is the Lord of heaven and earth, and does not live in temples built by hands. And he is not served by human hands, as if he needed anything, because he himself gives all men life and breath and everything else', and then affirms his immanence as the one who 'is not far from each one of us, for "In him we live and move and have our being"' (Acts 17:24, 28).

III. His character

God is personal. When we say this we assert that God is rational, self-conscious and self-determining, an intelligent moral agent. As supreme mind he is the source of all rationality in the universe. Since God's rational creatures possess independent characters, God must be in possession of a character that is divine in both its transcendence and immanence.

The OT reveals a God who is personal, both in terms of his own self-disclosure and of his people's relations with him, and the NT clearly shows that Christ spoke to God in terms that were meaningful only in a person-to-person relationship. For that reason we can predicate specific mental and moral qualities of God, such as we do of human character. Attempts have been made to classify the divine attributes, *i.e.* character qualities, under such headings as 'Mental and Moral', 'Communicable and Incommunicable' or 'Related and Unrelated'. Scripture would seem to give no support to any of these classifications. *God's names are to us the designation of his attributes, and it is significant that, historically, God's names were given in the context of his people's needs.

It would seem, therefore, more true to the biblical revelation to treat each attribute as a manifestation of God in the human situation that called it forth, compassion in the presence of misery, long-suffering in the presence of ill-desert, grace in the presence of guilt, mercy in the presence of penitence, and so forth, suggesting that the attributes of God designate a relation which he establishes with those who feel their need of him. That bears with it the undoubted truth that God, in the full plenitude of his nature, is in each of his attributes, so that there is never more of one attribute than of another, never more love than justice, or more mercy than righteousness, but that God is unchanging, undiminished and wholly involved in all that he does. If there is one attribute of God that can be recognized as all-comprehensive and all-pervading, it is his *holiness, which must be predicated of all his attributes, holy love, holy compassion, holy wisdom, *etc*.

IV. His will

God is sovereign. That means that he makes his own plans and carries them out in his own time and way. His sovereignty in willing and working is simply an expression of his supreme intelligence, power and wisdom. God's will is not arbitrary, but acts in complete harmony with his character. It is the forth-putting of his power and goodness, and is thus the final determinant of all existence for the divine glory.

There is, however, a distinction between God's will which prescribes what *we* shall do, and his will which determines what *he* will do. So theologians distinguish between the *decretive will* of God by which he ordains whatsoever comes to pass, and his *preceptive will* by which he enjoins upon his creatures the duties that belong to them. The decretive will of God is thus always accomplished, while his preceptive will is often disobeyed.

When we conceive of the sovereign sway of the divine will as the ultimate ground of all that happens, either actively bringing it to pass (*cf*. Ps. 135:5–12), or passively permitting it to come to pass (*cf*. Acts 14:16), we need to recognize the distinction between the active will of God and his permissive will. The entrance of sin into the world, and its continued prevalence, must be attributed to the permissive will of God, since sin is a contradiction of his holiness and goodness. There is, therefore, a realm in which God's will to act is dominant, and a realm in which man's liberty appears in exercise against God. The Bible presents both in operation. The note which rings through the OT is that struck by Nebuchadrezzar: 'He does what he pleases with the powers of heaven and the peoples of the earth. No one can hold back his hand or say to him: "What have you done?"' (Dn. 4:35). In the NT we come across an impressive example of the divine will resisted by human unbelief, when Christ uttered his agonizing cry over Jerusalem: 'How often I have longed to gather your children together, as a hen gathers her chicks under her wings, but you were not willing!' (Mt. 23:37). Nevertheless, the sovereignty of God ensures that all will be overruled to serve his eternal purpose, and that ultimately Christ's petition, which his followers echo, 'Your will be done on earth as it is in heaven' (Mt. 6:10; 26:39–42) shall be answered.

It is true that we are not able to reconcile God's sovereignty and man's responsibility within a single logical frame. That is because we do not understand the full range of divine knowledge and comprehension of all the laws that govern human conduct. The Bible teaches us that all life is lived in the sustaining will of God 'in whom we live and move and have our being', and that as a bird is free in the air, and a fish in the sea, so we humans have our own real freedom in the will of God who created us for himself. God sustains us all in the responsible freedom of being accountable to him for what we choose to do, and without this the deeper freedom of living for him in faith and love, and enjoying him as our supreme good, could not be.

V. His essential life

In his essential life God is a fellowship. The supreme revelation of God given in the Scriptures is that God's life is eternally within himself a loving fellowship of three equal and distinct persons, Father, Son and Spirit, and that in his relationship to his moral creatures God is extending to them the followship that is essentially his own. This truth might perhaps be read into the dictum that expressed God's deliberate will to create man: 'Let us make man in our image, after our likeness.' That form of words stands as an expression of the will of God, not only to reveal himself as a fellowship, but to open the divine life of fellowship to moral creatures made in his image and so fitted to enjoy it. While it is true that through sinning man lost his fitness for that holy fellowship, it is also true that God willed to restore it to him. This was the grand end of redemption: here we see God in Three Persons acting for our restoration, in electing love that claimed us, in redeeming love that emancipated us, and in regenerating love that recreated us for his fellowship (*TRINITY). It is the fitting climax of the biblical revelation that John affirms on the basis of Christ's redeeming work, linked with the divine plurality and fellowship of which he had spoken earlier (1 Jn. 1:3–2:2; 3:24–4:6), 'God is love' (1 Jn. 4:8–10, 16).

VI. His Fatherhood

The personal God can enter into personal relationships, and the closest and tenderest that the Bible knows is that of Father. This was Christ's most common designation for the One to whom he prayed and of whom he taught, and in theology the name of Father is reserved specially for the first Person of the Trinity. There are four types of relationship in which the word 'Father' is applied to God in Scripture.

1. There is his *Creational Fatherhood*. The fundamental relationship of God to man, whom he made in his own image, finds its most full and fitting illustration in the natural relationship which involves the gift of life. It is, more particularly, for man's spiritual nature that this relationship is claimed. In Heb. God is called 'the Father of our spirits' (12:9), and in Nu. 'the God of the spirits of all mankind' (16:22). Paul, when he preached in the Areopagus, used this consideration to drive home the irrationality of rational man worshipping idols of wood and stone, quoting the poet Aratus ('For we are his offspring') to indicate that man is a creature of God. The creaturehood of man is thus the counterpart of the general Fatherhood of God. Without the Creator-Father there would be no human race, no family of mankind at all.

2. There is the *Theocratic Fatherhood*. This is God's relationship to his covenant-people, Israel. In this, since it is a collective relationship that is indicated rather than a personal one, Israel, as covenant-people, was the child of God (Ex. 4:22–23), and she was challenged to recognize and respond to this filial relationship: 'If I am a father, where is the honour due me?' (Mal. 1:6, *cf.* 2:10; Is. 64:8). But since the covenant relationship was redemptive in its spiritual significance, this may be regarded as a foreshadowing of the NT revelation of the divine Fatherhood.

3. There is *Generative Fatherhood*. This belongs exclusively to the second Person of the Trinity, designated the Son of God, and the only begotten Son. It is, therefore, unique, and not to be applied to any mere creature. Christ, while on earth, spoke most frequently of this relationship which was peculiarly his. God was his Father by eternal generation, expressive of an essential and timeless relationship that transcends our comprehension. It is significant that Jesus, in his teaching of the Twelve, never used the term 'Our Father' as embracing himself and them. In the resurrection message through Mary he indicated two distinct relationships: 'My Father, and your Father' (Jn. 20:17), but the two are so linked together that the one becomes the ground of the other. His Sonship, though on a level altogether unique, was the basis of their sonship, by virtue of the faith-communion and Holy Spirit-union that bound them to him.

4. There is also the *Adoptive Fatherhood*. This is the redeeming relationship that belongs to all believers, and in the context of redemption it is viewed from two aspects: that of their standing in Christ, and that of the regenerating work of the Holy Spirit in them. This relationship to God is basic for all believers, as Paul reminds the Galatians: 'For in Christ Jesus you are all sons of God, through faith' (Gal. 3:26). In this living union with Christ they are adopted into the family of God, and they become subjects of the regenerative work of the Spirit that bestows upon them the nature of children: one is the objective aspect, the other the subjective. Because of their new standing (justification) and their relationship (adoption) to God the Father in Christ, they become partakers of the divine nature and are born into the family of God. John made this clear in the opening chapter of his gospel: 'To all who received him, to those who believed in his name, he gave the right (authority) to become children of God – children born, not of natural descent, nor of human decision or a husband's will, but born of God' (Jn. 1:12, 13). And so they are granted all the privileges that belong to that filial relationship: 'if children, then heirs' is the sequence (Rom. 8:17).

It is clear that Christ's teaching on the Fatherhood of God restricts the relationship to his believing people. Nowhere is he reported as assuming this relationship to exist between God and unbelievers. Not only does he not give any hint of a redeeming Fatherhood of God towards all men, but he said pointedly to his cavilling opponents: 'You belong to your father, the devil' (Jn. 8:44).

While it is under this relationship of Father that the NT brings out the tenderest aspects of God's character, his love, his faithfulness and his watchful care, it also brings out the responsibility of our having to show God the reverence, the trust and the loving obedience that children owe to a father. Christ has taught us to pray not simply 'Our Father', but 'Our Father who art in heaven', thus inculcating reverence and humility. However intimate, rich and warm-hearted his love, God remains God, majestic, amazing and awesome.

BIBLIOGRAPHY. J. Orr, *The Christian View of God and the World*, 1908; G. Vos, *Biblical Theology*, 1948; H. Bavinck, *The Doctrine of God*, 1951; J. I. Packer, *Knowing God*, 1973; G. Bray, *The Doctrine of God*, 1993; P. Helm, *The Providence of God*, 1993; J. Schneider, C. Brown, J. Stafford Wright, in *NIDNTT* 2, pp. 66–90; H. Kleinknecht *et al.*, in *TDNT* 3, pp. 65–123. R.A.F.
P.F.J.

GOD, NAMES OF. In considering the various names, titles or descriptions of God in the OT there are three words of basic importance—*'ēl*, *'ᵉlōhîm* and *Yahweh* (Jehovah). It is necessary at the outset to realize the meaning of these severally, and their relationship one to another.

I. Basic names

a. El

El (*'ēl*), EVV 'God' or 'god', has cognate forms in other Semitic tongues, and means a god in the widest sense, true or false, or even an image treated as a god (Gn. 35:2). Because of this general character it is frequently associated with a defining adjective or predicate. For example, in Dt. 5:9 we read, 'I the LORD (*Yahweh*) your God (*'ᵉlohîm*) am a jealous God (*'ēl*)', or in Gn. 31:13, 'the God (*'ēl*) of Bethel'. In the Ras Shamra tablets, however, El is a proper noun, the name of the Canaanite 'high God' whose son was Ba'al. The plural of *'ēl* is *'ᵉlōhîm*, and when used as a plural is translated 'gods' (but see below). These may be mere images, 'wood and stone' (Dt. 4:28), or the imaginary beings which they represent (Dt. 12:2).

b. Elyon, El Elyon

'El 'elyôn, 'the most high God', was the title of God as worshipped by Melchizedek (see below). *'Elyôn* is found in Nu. 24:16 and elsewhere. In Ps. 7:17 it is found in combination with *Yahweh*, and in Ps. 18:13 in parallel. See also Dn. 7:22, 25 for the Aram. plural *'elyônîn*; elsewhere in the Aram. of Daniel the equivalent of Heb. *'elyôn* is *'illāyâ* (*e.g.* 4:17; 7:25).

c. Elohim

Though a plural form (*'ᵉlōhîm*), Elohim can be treated as a singular, in which case it means the one supreme deity, and in EVV is rendered 'God'. Like its English equivalent, it is, grammatically considered, a common noun, and conveys the notion of all that belongs to the concept of deity, in contrast with man (Nu. 23:19) and other created beings. It is appropriate to cosmic and world-wide relationships (Gn. 1:1), because there is only one supreme and true God, and he is a Person; it approaches the character of a proper noun, while not losing its abstract and conceptual quality.

d. Eloah

This word (*'ᵉlōah*) is a singular form of *'ᵉlōhîm*, and has the same meaning as *'ēl*. In the OT it is chiefly found in poetry (*e.g.* Dt. 32:15, 17; it is most frequent in Job). The corresponding Aramaic form is *'ᵉlāh*.

e. Jehovah

The Heb. word *Yahweh* is in EVV usually translated 'the LORD' (note the capitals) and sometimes 'Jehovah'. The latter name originated as follows. The original Heb. text was not vocalized; in time the 'tetragrammaton' YHWH was considered too sacred to pronounce; so *'ᵃḏōnāy* ('my Lord') was substituted in reading, and the vowels of this word were combined with the consonants YHWH to give 'Jehovah', a form first attested at the start of the 12th century AD.

The pronunciation Yahweh is indicated by transliterations of the name into Greek in early Christian literature, in the form *iaoue* (Clement of Alexandria) or *iabe* (Theodoret; by this time Gk. *b* had the pronunciation of *v*). The name is certainly connected with Heb. *hāyâ*, 'to be', or rather with a variant and earlier form of the root, *hāwâ*. It is not, however, to be regarded as an imperfective aspect of the verb; the Hiph'îl conjugation, to which alone such a form could be assigned, is not forthcoming for this verb; and the imperfective of the Qal conjugation could not have the vowel *a* in the first syllable. Yahweh should be regarded as a straightforward substantive, in which the root *hwh* is preceded by the preformative *y*. See L. Koehler and W. Baumgartner, *Lexicon in Veteris Testamenti Libros*, 1958, pp. 368f.; also L. Koehler, *Vom Hebräischen Lexikon*, 1950, pp. 17f.

Strictly speaking, Yahweh is the only 'name' of God. In Genesis wherever the word *šēm* ('name') is associated with the divine being that name is Yahweh. When Abraham or Isaac built an altar 'he called on the name of Yahweh' (Gn. 12:8; 13:4; 26:25).

In particular, Yahweh was the God of the Patriarchs, and we read of 'Yahweh the God (Elohim) of Abraham' and then of Isaac and finally 'Yahweh, the God of Abraham, and the God of Isaac, and the God of Jacob', concerning which Elohim says, 'this is my name for ever' (Ex. 3:15). Yahweh, therefore, in contrast with Elohim, is a proper noun, the name of a Person, though that Person is divine. As such, it has its own ideological setting; it presents God as a Person, and so brings him into relationship with other, human, personalities. It brings God near to man, and he speaks to the Patriarchs as one friend to another.

A study of the word *'name' in the OT reveals how much it means in Hebrew. The name is no mere label, but is significant of the real personality of him to whom it belongs. It may derive from the circumstances of his birth (Gn. 5:29), or reflect his character (Gn. 27:36), and when a person puts his 'name' upon a thing or another person the latter comes under his influence and protection.

f. Yahweh Elohim

These two words are combined in the narrative of Gn. 2:4–3:24, though 'Elohim' alone is used in the colloquy between Eve and the serpent. If the narrative concerning Eden was related to a Sumerian original it could have been brought by Abraham from Ur, and it would thus be possible to account for the different use in these two chapters from those which precede and follow it.

g. How El, Elohim and Yahweh are related

We are now in a position to consider how these three words agree or differ in their use. While there are occasions on which any one of them could be used of God, they are by no means identical or interchangeable. In the account of Gn. 14, now regarded by many as giving a true picture of the situation in the early 2nd millennium BC, we read how Abraham met with Melchizedek, the priest of *'ēl 'elyôn*, 'the most high God'. Here we have Melchizedek's 'name' or title for the deity he worshipped. It would be clearly wrong to substitute either 'Elohim' or 'Yahweh' for *'ēl 'elyôn* (Gn. 14:18). Melchizedek blesses Abraham in the name of *'ēl 'elyôn*, 'maker of heaven and earth', so identifying *'ēl 'elyôn* as the supreme God (14:19–20).

The king of Sodom offers Abraham a gift, which he refuses, lifting up his hand to *Yahweh*, *'ēl 'elyôn*, 'maker of heaven and earth' (14:22). He means that he also worships the supreme God, the same God (for there is only one), but knows him by the name of 'Yahweh'. (LXX and SP omit *Yahweh* in Gn. 14:22.)

To cite a second example, in Gn. 27:20 Jacob deceives his father with the words, 'Because Yahweh your God (Elohim) granted me success.' To interchange 'Yahweh' and 'Elohim' would not make sense. Yahweh is the name by which his father worships the supreme God (Elohim).

II. The revelation to Moses

The revelation made to Moses at the burning bush is one of the most striking and convincing incidents in the Bible story. After the opening words God introduces himself thus, 'I am the God (Elohim) of your father' (Ex. 3:6). This at once assumes that Moses would know the name of his father's God. When God announces his purpose of delivering Israel by the hand of Moses the latter shows reluctance and begins to make excuse.

He inquires, 'If . . . the people of Israel . . . ask me, "What (*mah*) is his name?" what shall I say to them?' (Ex. 3:13). The normal way to ask a name is to use the pronoun *mî*; to use *mah* invites an answer which goes further, and gives the meaning (*'what?'*) or substance of the name.

This helps to explain the reply, namely, 'I AM WHO I AM' (*'ehyeh 'ᵃšer 'ehyeh*). And he said, 'Say this to the people of Israel, "I AM has sent me to you"' (Ex. 3:14). By this Moses would not think that God was announcing a *new name*, nor is it called a 'name'; it is just the inner meaning of the name Moses knew. We have here a play upon words; 'Yahweh' is interpreted by *'ehyeh*. M. Buber translates 'I will be as I will be', and expounds it as a promise of God's power and enduring presence with them in the process of deliverance (*Moses*, pp. 39–55). That something like this is the purport of these words, which in English sound enigmatical, is shown by what follows, '"Yahweh, the God of your fathers, the God of Abraham, the God of Isaac, and the God of Jacob, has sent me to you": this is my name for ever' (v. 15). The full content of the name comes first; the name itself follows.

III. The interpretation of Exodus 6:2–3

After Moses' return to Egypt Yahweh further instructs him how to deal with Pharaoh and with his own people: 'I am the LORD (Yahweh),' he says. 'I appeared to Abraham, to Isaac, and to Jacob, as God Almighty (*'ēl šadday*), but by my name the LORD (Yahweh) I did not make myself known to them' (Ex. 6:3).

The former revelation, to the Patriarchs, concerned promises belonging to a distant future; it supposed that they should be assured that he, Yahweh, was such a God (*'ēl*) as was competent (one possible meaning of *šadday*) to fulfil them. The revelation at the bush was greater and more intimate, God's power and immediate and continuing presence with them being all wrapped up in the familiar name of Yahweh. Henceforth, 'I am Yahweh, your God' (Ex. 6:7) gives them all the assurance they need of his purpose, his presence and his power.

For God's self-revelation to the Patriarchs as God Almighty (*'ēl šadday*), initiating or reaffirming his covenant with them, *cf.* Gn. 17:1; 35:11; 48:3—passages which, like Ex. 6:1–6, are assigned to the priestly narrator in the prevalent documentary hypothesis.

IV. Particular names containing El or Jehovah

a. 'El 'Olām

At Beersheba Abraham planted a tamarisk, and 'called there on the name of *Yahweh*', *'ēl 'ôlām* (Gn. 21:33). Here 'Yahweh' is the name, and the description follows, 'the Everlasting God'. F. M. Cross has drawn attention to the original form of this name—*'El dhū-'Ôlami,* 'God of Eternity' (*cf.* W. F. Albright in *BO* 17, 1960, p. 242).

b. 'Ēl-'Elōhê-Israel

Jacob, reaching Shechem, bought a piece of land, reared an altar and called it *'ēl-'ᵉlōhê-Yiśrā'ēl* (Gn. 33:20), 'God (*'ēl*) is the God (*'ᵉlōhîm*) of Israel'. In this manner he commemorates the recent encounter with the angel at the place he had called Peniel (*pᵉnî-'ēl*, 'the face of God', Gn. 32:30). He thus accepts Israel as his name and so renders worship to God.

c. Jehovah-jireh

In Gn. 22, when the angel of the Lord had pointed to a ram as a substitute for Isaac, Abraham named the place *Yahweh yir'eh*, 'the LORD provides' (vv. 8, 14).

d. Jehovah-nissi

In somewhat similar fashion, after the defeat of the Amalekites, Moses erected an altar and called it *Yahweh nissî*, 'the LORD is my banner' (Ex. 17:15). These, however, are not the names of God, but are commemorative of events.

e. Jehovah-shalom

This is the name given by Gideon to the altar he erected in Ophrah, *Yahweh šālôm*, 'the LORD is peace' (Jdg. 6:24).

f. Jehovah-tsidkenu

This is the name by which Messiah shall be known, *Yahweh ṣiḏqēnû*, 'the LORD is our righteousness' (Je. 23:6; 33:16), in contrast to the last king of Judah, who was an unworthy bearer of the name Zedekiah (*ṣiḏqiyāhû*, 'Yahweh is righteousness').

g. Jehovah-shammah

This is the name given to the city of Ezekiel's vision, *Yahweh šāmmâ*, 'the LORD is there' (Ezk. 48:35).

h. The LORD of hosts

Differing from the preceding names, *Yahweh ṣᵉḇā'ôṯ*, 'the LORD of hosts', is a divine title. It does not occur in the Pentateuch; it appears first in 1 Sa. 1:3 as the title by which God was worshipped at Shiloh. It was used by David in defying the Philistine (1 Sa. 17:45); and David again makes use of it as the climax to a glorious song of victory (Ps. 24:10). It is common in the prophets (88 times in Jeremiah), and is used to exhibit Yahweh as at all times the Saviour and Protector of his people (Ps. 46:7, 11). The 'hosts' may originally have been the armies of Israel, as in 1 Sa. 17:45, but at an early date came to comprise all the heavenly powers, ready to do the LORD's command.

i. LORD God of Israel

This title (*Yahweh 'ᵉlōhê Yiśrā'ēl*) is found as early as Deborah's song (Jdg. 5:3), and is frequently used by the prophets (*e.g.* Is. 17:6; Zp. 2:9). It follows in the series 'the God of Abraham, of Isaac, and of Jacob'. In Ps. 59:5 ('Thou, LORD God of hosts, art God of Israel') it is combined with the preceding title.

j. The Holy One of Israel

This title (*qᵉḏôš Yiśrā'ēl*) is a favourite in Isaiah (29 times—1:4, *etc.*) in both the earlier and later parts of the book, and also in Jeremiah and the Psalms. Somewhat similar to this is 'the Mighty One of Israel' (*'ᵃḇîr Yiśrā'ēl*, Is. 1:24, *etc.*); also 'the Glory (victory) of Israel' (*nēṣaḥ Yiśrā'ēl*, 1 Sa. 15:29) used by Samuel.

k. Ancient of days

This is the description (Aram. *'attîq yômîn*) given by Daniel, who pictures God on his throne of judgment, judging the great world-empires (Dn. 7:9, 13, 22). It alternates with the title 'most High' (Aram. *'illāyâ*, *'elyônîn*, vv. 18, 22, 25, 27).

BIBLIOGRAPHY. W. F. Albright, *Yahweh and the Gods of Canaan*, 1968; A. Alt, 'The God of the Fathers', in *Essays on OT History and Religion*, 1966, pp. 1–77; F. M. Cross, 'Yahweh and the God of the Patriarchs', *HTR* 55, 1962, pp. 225–259; O. Eissfeldt, 'El and Yahweh', *JSS* 1, 1956, pp. 25–37; G. T. Manley, *The Book of the Law*, 1957, pp. 37–47; J. A. Motyer, *The Revelation of the Divine Name*, 1959; A. Murtonen, *A Philological and Literary Treatise on the Divine Names* 'ēl, 'elōah, 'ᵉlōhîm *and* Yahweh, 1952.

G.T.M.
F.F.B.

GODLINESS. In pagan literature, godliness (Gk. *eusebeia*, *eulabeia* and related terms) meant showing proper caution, fear or reverence towards the gods. Such piety involved the offering of sacrifices and other cultic activities. It also meant honouring the gods by respecting elders, masters, rulers, and all the orders of life thought to be under the protection of the gods. When this terminology was used in the Bible, a different notion of fear or respect was intended. The one true God, as creator and redeemer, requires an active obedience to his revealed will and a personal devotion that surpasses lip-service, mere trepidation, or bare admiration (*e.g.* Pr. 1:7; Is. 11:2; 33:6; Lk. 2:25; Acts 10:2; 22:12). Pre-eminently, Jesus is the godly One, whose prayers were heard because of his 'godly fear' or 'reverent submission' to the Father (Heb. 5:7). His death and heavenly exaltation makes it possible for others to offer to God, through him, acceptable worship or service, 'with reverence and awe' (Heb. 12:28).

Ungodliness (Gk. *asebeia*) brings the wrath of God, because it involves suppressing the truth about God, worshipping created things rather than the Creator, and pursuing unrighteous relationships and behaviour (Rom. 1:18–25; 1 Tim. 1:9–11). It is a condition from which we can only be rescued by trusting 'him who justifies the ungodly'

(Rom. 4:5; *cf.* 5:6; Tit. 2:11–14). Godliness is most frequently mentioned in the Pastoral Epistles, where Paul uses the terminology to counter its misapplication by false teachers (1 Tim. 6:3–10; 2 Tim. 3:4–5). Positively, it is a God-honouring manner of life, issuing from a true knowledge of God and his grace in Jesus Christ (1 Tim. 3:16; 4:7–10; 2 Tim. 3:10–12; Tit. 1:1; 2:11–12). A genuine devotion to God transforms relationships and behaviour in every context. See *FEAR, *HOLINESS.

BIBLIOGRAPHY. C. Brown (ed.), *NIDNTT* 2, 1976, pp. 90–95; P. H. Towner, 'The Goal of our Instruction', *JSOT*, 1989, pp. 147–154; J. J. Wainwright, '*Eusebeia*: Syncretism or Conservative Contextualization?' *EQ* 65:3, 1993, pp. 211–224.

D.G.P.

GOG AND MAGOG. In Ezk. 38:2 we are introduced to 'Gog, of the land of Magog, the chief prince (AV, RVmg., RSV; RV 'prince of *Rosh'), of *Meshech and Tubal'. LXX understood Magog as a people, not a country. The only reasonable identification of Gog is with Gyges, king of Lydia (*c.* 660 BC)—Assyr. Gugu; Magog could be Assyr. *mā(t) gugu*, 'land of Gog'. The linkage with peoples at the extremities of the then known world (Ezk. 38:5–6; *cf.* Rev. 20:8) suggests that we are to regard them as eschatological figures rather than as a historically identifiable king, *etc.* This is the interpretation in Rev. 20:8 and rabbinic literature. The popular identification of Rosh with Russia, Meshech with Moscow and Tubal with Tobolsk in Siberia has nothing to commend it from the standpoint of hermeneutics, though some of the wilder Russian tribes would fit into the explanation given.

Since we need not interpret Ezk. 38–39 as earlier in time than Ezk. 40–48, and rabbinic tradition places Gog after the days of the Messiah, we need see no contradiction between Ezekiel and Revelation, provided we understand the millennium in the sense the rabbis gave to 'the days of the Messiah'. H.L.E.

GOLAN. The N city of refuge in Transjordan, in Manasseh's territory of Bashan (Dt. 4:43), and a levitical city (Jos. 21:27). Location uncertain, but may be identified with Sahm el-Jolan, 22 km E of Aphek (Hippos). The district of Gaulanitis was later named after it.

BIBLIOGRAPHY. *LOB*, p. 377. N.H.

GOLIATH. A *giant of Gath serving in the Philistine army (1 Sa. 17:4), Goliath may have descended from that remnant of the Rephaim which, after having been scattered by the Ammonites (Dt. 2:20–21; 2 Sa. 21:22), took refuge with the Philistines. For discussion of his origin, see G. A. Wainwright, 'Early Philistine History', *VT* 9, 1959, pp. 79f. His height is given as 'six cubits and a span', *i.e.* 3·2 m, if the cubit is understood as 52·5 cm (*WEIGHTS AND MEASURES). That this, though unusual, is not an impossible phenomenon, is confirmed by the discovery in Palestine of human skeletons of similar stature and of roughly the same period.

Goliath was slain by *David at Ephes-dammim in a duel whose religious character is attested by 1 Sa. 17:43, 45; and perhaps also by the Philistines' flight, if this is directly attributed to their conviction that the God of Israel had overcome their god (*cf.* 2 Sa. 23:9–12; 1 Ch. 11:12ff.). Goliath's sword, which had been kept in the sanctuary at Nob, was given by the priest Ahimelech to David when the latter was fleeing from Saul to the king of Gath, for whom the weapon was likely to be an acceptable present.

Two later appearances of the name have puzzled scholars. Elhanan is recorded as having slain '(the brother of) Goliath the Gittite'—so AV of 2 Sa. 21:19, and again (without parentheses) in 1 Ch. 20:5, where the victim's name is given as Lahmi. It may be that *Elhanan was David's original name. On the other hand, some have suggested that this second Goliath could have been the son of David's adversary. For full discussion of the problem and possible emendation, see S. R. Driver, *Notes on the Hebrew Text of the Books of Samuel*, 1913; and E. J. Young, *IOT*, 1949, pp. 181f. J.D.D.

GOMER (*gōmer*, 'completion'). **1.** The eldest son of Japheth and the father of Ashkenaz, Riphath and Togarmah (Gn. 10:2–3). In Ezk. 38 the people of Gomer are closely associated with the house of Togarmah in the army of Gog, and are probably to be identified with the ancient Gimirrai (Cimmerians), an Aryan group who conquered Urarṭu (Armenia) from their Ukrainian homeland some time before the 8th cent. BC, when they appear as enemies of Assyria.

2. The daughter of Diblaim and wife of *Hosea (Ho. 1:3). She bore Jezreel, Lo-ruhamah and Lo-ammi (Ho. 1). G.W.G.

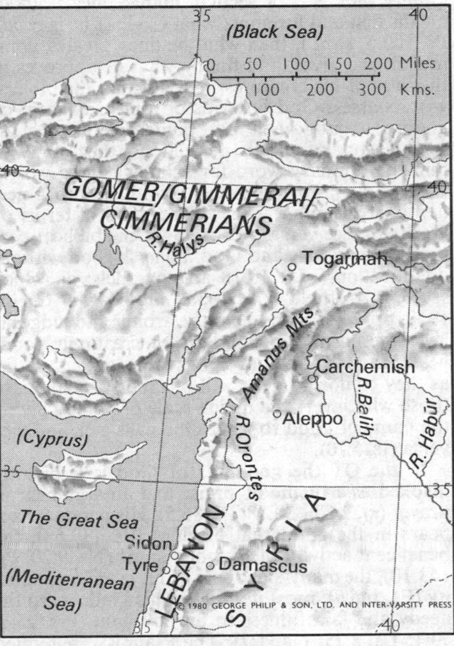

The region occupied by Gomer, known also as Gimirrai (Gimmerai), the territory of the 'Cimmerians'.

GOOD. The Hebrew word is *ṭôḇ* ('pleasant', 'joyful', 'agreeable'), signifying primarily that which gratifies the senses and derivatively that which gives aesthetic or moral satisfaction. The LXX renders *ṭôḇ* by *agathos*, the regular Greek word for good as a physical or moral quality, and sometimes by *kalos* (lit. 'beautiful'; hence, in classical as well as biblical Greek, 'noble', 'honourable', 'admirable', 'worthy'). The NT reproduces this usage, employing the two adjectives interchangeably (*cf.*, *e.g.*, Rom. 7:12–21). Paul, following the LXX, uses the noun *agathosynē* for the Christian's goodness, with the accent especially on his beneficence (Rom. 15:14; Gal. 5:22; Eph. 5:9; 2 Thes. 1:11, RV: for the translation, see the commentaries). He also uses *chrēstotēs* ('goodness', AV, RV; 'kindness', RSV) for the merciful beneficence of God (Rom. 2:4; 11:22).

The common element of meaning in the many applications which the word 'good' has in every language is that of approbation, either for inherent value, or for beneficent effect, or both. There is nothing distinctive about the various non-moral senses in which the Bible speaks of things as 'good' (*e.g.* 'useful', as salt, Mt. 5:13; Lk. 14:34; 'of high quality', as gold, Gn. 2:12, or cattle, Gn. 41:26; 'productive', as trees, Mt. 7:17, ground, Lk. 8:8; *etc.*). But the biblical concept of moral and spiritual good is thoroughly theological, and stands in sharp contrast with the anthropocentric view of goodness developed by the Greeks and later thinkers in the Greek tradition. This biblical view may be analysed as follows.

a. God is good: for he is morally perfect, and gloriously generous.

The acknowledgment of God as good is the foundation of all biblical thinking about moral goodness. 'Good' in Scripture is not an abstract quality, nor is it a secular human ideal; 'good' means first and foremost what God is ('he is *good*', Ps. 100:5, *et al.*), then what he does, creates, commands and gives, and finally what he approves in the lives of his creatures. It is not that the biblical writers assess God in terms of a prior concept of goodness, but rather that, contemplating the supreme glory of God's perfections, they apply to him the ordinary word for acknowledging worth. By so doing, however, they give that word a new depth of meaning. They define good in terms of God; not vice versa. Accordingly, the biblical position is that God, and God alone, is good without qualification (Mk. 10:18 and parallels: on which see B. B. Warfield, *The Person and Work of Christ*, 1950, pp. 149ff.); and he is the arbiter and judge, as he is the norm and standard, of creaturely goodness. Man is good, and things are good, just so far as they conform to the will of God. Woe, then, to those who invert the divine scale of values, giving the name of good to what God calls evil, and vice versa (Is. 5:20).

In the OT the goodness of God is frequently invoked as a theme of praise and an argument in prayer (*cf.* 2 Ch. 30:18; Ps. 86:5). His goodness appears in the good that he does (Ps. 119:68), the beneficent activity of his good spirit (Ne. 9:20; Ps. 143:10), the many-sidedness of his cosmic generosity (Ps. 145:9); most notably, in his kindness to the needy and faithfulness to his covenant (Pss. 25:8; 73:1; La. 3:25; Na. 1:7). The Psalmists' reiterated exhortation to praise and give thanks to God, 'for he is good: for his steadfast love endures for ever' (Pss. 106:1; 107:1; 118:1; 136:1; *cf.* 100:4f.; also 1 Ch. 16:34; 2 Ch. 5:13; 7:3), is quoted by Jeremiah as the characteristic motto theme of Israel's worship (Je. 33:11).

b. The works of God are good: for they reveal his attributes of wisdom and power (see Ps. 104:24–31), and are the objects of his own approval.

When creation was done, 'God saw every thing that he had made, and behold, it was very good' (Gn. 1:31, *cf.* vv. 4, 10, 12, 18, 21, 25). The whole material order, as such, being God's handiwork, is good (1 Tim. 4:4; *cf.* Rom. 14:14). There is no room for Manichaean dualism in the Bible.

c. The gifts of God are good: for they express his generosity, and make for the welfare of their recipients.

'Beneficial', 'advantageous', is one of the standard secular meanings of 'good' as an adjective; as 'prosperity', 'well-being', is of 'good' as a noun. The Bible integrates this usage into its theology by teaching, not merely that all God's gifts are good, both in intention and in effect, but also that all good is in fact God's gift (Jas. 1:17; *cf.* Ps. 4:6). It is characteristic of God to do good to the needy, as it was of Jesus, God's anointed (Acts 10:38; Mk. 3:4). God does good to all men in his ordinary providence, showering on them the blessings of nature (Acts 14:17; Ps. 145:9; Lk. 6:35); and, as a perfect Father, he knows how to give good gifts to those who are his children through Christ (Mt. 7:11). God's promise to 'do good' to his people is a comprehensive promise of blessing (Je. 32:40, *cf.* 24:6f.), as the plea that God will 'do good' to them is a comprehensive prayer for it (Pss. 51:18; 125:4). In such passages the 'good' in question is the pledged blessing of the covenant; it is virtually 'salvation' (*cf.* Is. 52:7). 'Good' on the material level was the promised blessing of the old covenant (with 'evil', the state of blessing withdrawn, as its alternative: Dt. 30:15), and 'good' in the realm of spiritual privilege, 'good' not enjoyed under the old covenant, is the gift of the new (Heb. 9:11; 10:1). Both testaments, however, authorize God's faithful people to rest assured that in God's good time everything that is truly good for them will be made theirs (Pss. 84:11; 34:10, *cf.* 85:12; Rom. 8:32; Eph. 1:3).

'Good', as an adjective, is used in various instrumental senses in connection with God's gracious activity of doing good to men. It is used of the word of God that announces blessing, of the hand and work of God that conveys it, of the course of action that leads to enjoyment of it, and of the days in which that enjoyment is experienced (see 1 Ki. 8:56; Is. 39:8; Je. 29:10; Heb. 6:5; Ezr. 7:9; 8:18; Phil. 1:6; 1 Ki. 8:36; Je. 6:16; Ps. 73:28; 1 Pet. 3:10; *cf.* Ps. 34:12).

Even when God withdraws the 'good' of outward prosperity from his people and brings upon them 'evil' (hardship) in its place (*cf.* Jb. 2:10), there is still a sense in which he is doing them good. 'It is good' for a man to be thus afflicted; hereby he receives correction, for his own subsequent benefit (*cf.* Heb. 12:10), and is exercised and strengthened in faith, patience and obedience (Ps. 119:67, 71; *cf.* La. 3:26f.). Anything that drives a man closer to God is for his good, and the Christian's temporary distresses, under God, work for him an eternal weight of glory (2 Cor. 4:17). Paul is therefore fully entitled to insist that 'in *everything* (afflictions included) God works for good with those who love him' (Rom. 8:28). The Christian should regard every circumstance, however ungratifying, as among God's good gifts to him, the expression of a beneficent purpose and, if rightly used, a sure means to his lasting profit.

d. The commands of God are good: for they

express the moral perfection of his character and, by showing us how to please him, mark out for us the path of blessing (Ps. 119:39; Rom. 7:12; 12:2).

The moral ideal in the Bible is to do the will of God, as revealed in his law. When the rich ruler asked Christ what good thing he should do to gain life, Christ immediately directed him to the Decalogue (Mt. 19:17ff.). In a lawless and unloving world, Christians must resist the temptation to do as they are done by, and in face of evil must seek out and hold fast in their conduct that 'good' which the law prescribes (Rom. 12:9, 21; 1 Thes. 5:15, 21).

e. Obedience to God's commands is good: for God approves and accepts it (1 Tim. 2:3), and those who yield it profit by it (Tit. 3:8).

Unredeemed men do not and cannot obey God's law, for they are in bondage 'under sin' (Rom. 3:9ff.; 8:7f.). The evil tree (man as he is in Adam) must be made good before its fruit can be good (*cf.* Mt. 12:33–35). But those who are in Christ have been freed from sin's bondage precisely in order that they may practise the righteousness which the law prescribes (Rom. 6:12–22). The characteristic NT phrase for this obligatory Christian obedience is 'good works'. The performance of good works is to be the Christian's life's work; it was for this that God saved him (Eph. 2:10; Col. 1:10; 2 Cor. 9:8; Tit. 2:14; Mt. 5:14–16). The Christian is called to be ready for every good work that his circumstances admit of (2 Tim. 2:21; Tit. 3:1), so that it is a damning indictment of a man's Christian profession when he is 'unfit for any good deed' (Tit. 1:16; *cf.* Jas. 2:14–26). Good works are the Christian's adornment (1 Tim. 2:10); God takes pleasure in them, and will reward them (Eph. 6:8).

Good works are good from three standpoints: they are done (i) in accordance with a right standard (the biblical law: 2 Tim. 3:16f.); (ii) from a right motive (love and gratitude for redemption: 1 Thes. 1:3; Heb. 6:10; *cf.* Rom. 12:1ff.); (iii) with a right aim (God's glory: 1 Cor. 10:31; *cf.* 1 Cor. 6:20; Mt. 5:16; 1 Pet. 2:12). They take the form of works of love towards God and men, since 'love is the fulfilling of the law' (Rom. 13:8–10; *cf.* Mt. 22:36–40). This does not, of course, mean that no more is required of a Christian than a right motive; the point is, rather, that the particular acts which the commandments prescribe are to be understood as so many expressions of love, so that without a loving heart the commandments cannot be fulfilled. It is not that a right spirit excuses lapses from the letter of the law, but that rectitude in the letter is no fulfilling of the law where an attitude of love is lacking. The truly good man is no less than the truly righteous man; for, as the truly righteous man observes the spirit as well as the letter of the law (*cf.* Mt. 5:18–20), so the truly good man observes its letter as well as its spirit. Nor is the truly good man any more than the truly righteous man. In Rom. 5:7, where Paul for a moment sets the good man above the righteous man in value, he is speaking popularly, not theologically. The world thinks of righteousness as a merely negative rectitude, and of the kindness and generosity that mark the good man as something more than righteousness; but biblical theology effectively identifies righteousness with goodness, and goodness with righteousness, by insisting that what the law requires is, in fact, love.

Good works, then, are works of love, and the nature of love is to give to the beloved. Love to God is expressed in the gift of personal devotion, however costly (*cf.* Mary's 'good work', Mk. 14:3–6). Love to men is expressed by doing them 'good', laying out one's own resources to relieve their need, and seeking their welfare in every possible way (Gal. 6:9f.; Eph. 4:29; *cf.* Pss. 34:14; 37:3, 27). The Jerusalem church's poor-relief system (Acts 2:44f.; 4:34ff.), and Paul's collection for the saints (*cf.* 2 Cor. 7–9) illustrate this. 'Kind', 'generous' are among the ordinary secular meanings of 'good' as a description of persons (*cf.* 1 Sa. 25:15; 1 Pet. 2:18); the Bible comprehends them in the Christian ethic, making the love of God and Christ the model and standard for the kindness and generosity required of Christians (*cf.* Eph. 5:1f.; Jn. 13:14, 34).

The believer who seeks thus to fulfil the law has a 'good conscience' (Acts 23:1; 1 Tim. 1:5, 19; Heb. 13:18; 1 Pet. 3:16, 21)—not because he thinks himself sinlessly perfect, but because he knows that his relationship with God is right, being founded on true faith and repentance. Such a Christian will appear to his fellows as a 'good man' (so Barnabas, Acts 11:24).

BIBLIOGRAPHY. *BAGD*, *s.v. agathos*, *kalos*; E. Beyreuther, *NIDNTT* 2, pp. 98–107; G. Vos in *DAC*, 2, 470f.; C. F. H. Henry, *Christian Personal Ethics*, 1957, pp. 209–218. J.I.P.

GOPHER WOOD (Heb. *'aṣê-gōp̄er*), the wood of which Noah's ark was constructed (Gn. 6:14). Many commentators favour an identification with cypress wood, on the ground of the similarity in name (Gk. *kyparissos*). Others, noting the similarity with Heb. *kōp̄er* (* BITUMEN), suggest a resinous * tree. It may be that the word is connected in some way with Akkad. *gubru/gudru*, '(shepherd's) reed hut', and such a cuneiform parallel is further suggested by the construct *'aṣê* which might correspond to the determinative *giš*, which precedes the names of trees and objects of wood, and which is read *iṣu* or *iṣ* in Akkadian. See *The Chicago Assyrian Dictionary*, 5, 1956, p. 118. T.C.M.

GOSHEN. 1. The territory assigned to Israel and his descendants during their Egyp. sojourn. Its exact location and extent remain uncertain, but it was certainly in Egypt (Gn. 47:6, 27), and in the E Nile Delta: Gn. 47:6 with 11 clearly equate Goshen with 'the land of Rameses', so named from the residence-city Pi-Ramessē, biblical * Ra'amses, in the NE Delta. The LXX's topographical interpretations are of uncertain authenticity. The E Delta would be suitably 'near' the court (Gn. 45:10) for Joseph serving his (probably Hyksos) pharaoh at * Memphis (near Cairo) or Avaris (NE Delta), *cf.* also Gn. 46:28–29; likewise for Moses interviewing his pharaoh at Pi-Ramesse (Ex. 7–12). Goshen was a well-favoured region suited to flocks and herds (Gn. 46:34; 47:1, 4, 6, 27; 50:8). It remained the habitat of the Hebrews until the Exodus, being therefore largely shielded from the plagues (Ex. 8:22; 9:26); nevertheless, contact was close with Egyptians living in the same general region (*e.g. cf.* Ex. 11:2–3; 12:35–36). The name *Gsmt* occurring in certain Egyp. texts, once equated with Heb. Goshen through LXX Gesem, should be read *Šsmt* and is therefore irrelevant.

2. A district in the S of Palestine (Jos. 10:41;

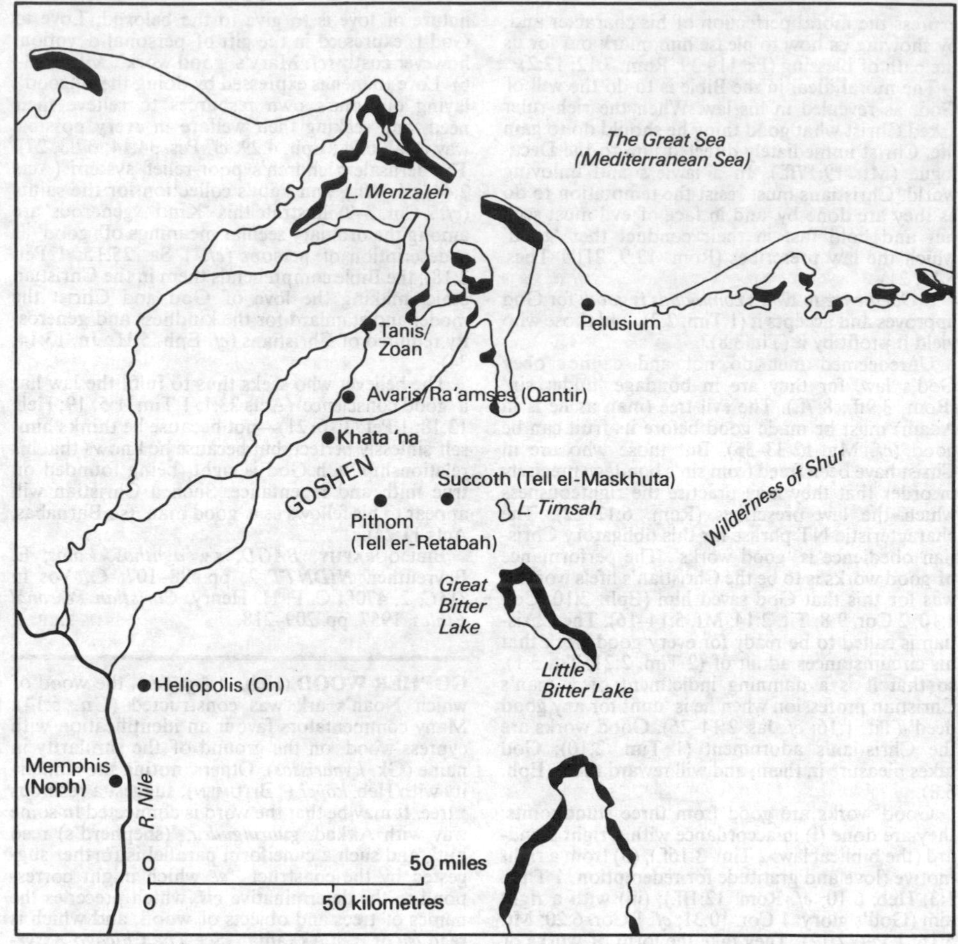

Goshen and the delta area of the river Nile.

11:16), probably named after 3, a town in the hills of S Palestine (Jos. 15:51), possibly near Ẓāhiriyeh, *c.* 19 km SW of Hebron (so Abel) or else somewhat farther E (*GTT*, 1959, §§ 285–287, 497). (*GEDER.)

K.A.K.

GOSPEL (Gk. *euangelion*, 'good news'). In classical literature the word designated the reward given for good tidings. It also indicated the message itself, originally the announcement of victory, but later applied to other messages bringing joy. That it is found more than 75 times in the NT indicates a distinctly Christian connotation. The gospel is the good news that God in Jesus Christ has fulfilled his promises to Israel, and that a way of salvation has been opened to all. The gospel is not to be set over against the OT as if God had changed his way of dealing with man, but is the fulfilment of OT promise (Mt. 11:2–5). Jesus himself saw in the prophecies of Isaiah a description of his own ministry (Lk. 4:16–21).

Mark defines the 'gospel of God' in 1:14 (AV, following the Byzantine text, adds 'of the kingdom') as 'The time is fulfilled, and the kingdom of God is at hand'. To believe means salvation: to reject is damnation (Mk. 16:15–16). This same gospel is proclaimed by the first heralds of Christianity, but now the essential message is made more explicit by the death and resurrection of Jesus the Christ. While the gospel came with Jesus (the Christ-event *is* the gospel), it was anticipated in God's promise of blessing to Abraham (Gal. 3:8) and promised in prophetic Scripture (Rom. 1:2).

The gospel not only comes in power (1 Thes. 1:5) but *is* the power of God (Rom. 1:16). It reveals the righteousness of God and leads to salvation all who believe (Rom. 1:16–17). Paul regards the gospel as a sacred trust (1 Tim. 1:11). Thus he is under divine compulsion to proclaim it (1 Cor. 9:16), and requests prayer that he may carry out his task with boldness (Eph. 6:19), even though this involves opposition (1 Thes. 2:2) and affliction (2 Tim. 1:8). The gospel is 'the word of truth' (Eph. 1:13), but it is hidden to unbelieving men (2 Cor. 4:3–4) who demand supernatural verification or rational proof (1 Cor. 1:21–23). Even as it was by revelation that the full theological impact of the gospel came to Paul (Gal. 1:11–12), so also it is by the response of faith that the gospel comes with saving power (Heb. 4:2).

The use of 'Gospels' as a designation of the first four books of the NT is post-biblical (2nd cent. AD).

BIBLIOGRAPHY. U. Becker, *NIDNTT* 2, pp. 107–115; C. H. Dodd, *The Apostolic Preaching and its Developments*, 1936; R. H. Mounce, *The Essential Nature of New Testament Preaching*, 1960; G. Friedrich in *TDNT* 2, pp. 705–735. R.H.M.

GOSPELS. The plural form 'Gospels' (Gk. *euangelia*) would not have been understood in the apostolic age, nor yet for two generations following; it is of the essence of the apostolic witness that there is only one true *euangelion*; whoever proclaims another, says Paul, is anathema (Gal. 1:8f.). The four records which traditionally stand in the forefront of the NT are, properly speaking, four records of the one gospel—'the gospel of God ... concerning his Son' (Rom. 1:1–3). It was not until the middle of the 2nd century AD that the plural form came to be used; thus Justin Martyr says that the 'memoirs composed by the apostles' are called 'Gospels' (*First Apology* 66). Earlier writers use the singular, whether they are referring to a single gospel-writing or to a set of such writings (*cf. Didache* 8. 2; Ignatius, *Philadelphians* 8. 2). The traditional titles of the four records imply that in them we have the gospel or good news about Christ according to each of the four Evangelists. And the usage of the singular form to denote the fourfold record continued for long after the earliest attested instance of the plural.

I. The oral stage

Most of the material in our Gospels existed for a considerable time in an oral stage before it was given the written form with which we are familiar.

a. The words of Jesus

Jesus began his Galilean ministry by 'preaching the gospel of God'; the content of this gospel was that the time appointed had arrived and the kingdom of God had drawn near; he urged his hearers to repent and believe the good news (Mk. 1:14f.; *cf.* Lk. 4:18–21). His preaching was no bolt from the blue; it was the fulfilment of the promise of God communicated in earlier days through the prophets. Now, at length, God had visited his people; this was the burden not only of Jesus' preaching but of his mighty works (Lk. 7:16), which were signs that the domain of evil was crumbling before the onset of the kingdom of God (Mt. 12:22–29; Lk. 11:14–22). The same theme runs through the parables of Jesus, which call his hearers to decision and watchfulness in view of the advent of the kingdom.

In addition to his public ministry, Jesus took care to give his disciples systematic instruction in a form that they could easily commit to memory. His debates with the Pharisees and other opponents, too, led to pronouncements which, once heard, would not be readily forgotten, and which in fact stood his disciples in good stead later on when they were confronted with controversial issues in which it was helpful to recall their Master's ruling.

b. The apostolic tradition

There are several references in the NT Epistles to the 'tradition' (Gk. *paradosis*) received by the apostles from their Lord and delivered by them in turn to their converts. This tradition, in the fullest sense, comprises the apostles' witness to 'all that Jesus began to do and teach, until the day when he was taken up' (Acts 1:1f., *cf.* 1:21f.). This witness was borne and perpetuated in various ways—principally in missionary preaching, in the teaching of converts and in Christian worship. An outline of the basic facts of the missionary preaching is given by Paul in 1 Cor. 15:3ff.—'that Christ died for our sins in accordance with the scriptures, that he was buried, that he was raised on the third day in accordance with the scriptures, and that he appeared' to a large number of eyewitnesses, some of whom are named, and most of whom were still alive when Paul was writing. Paul adds that whether the gospel was preached by himself or by the original apostles, the basic facts of the message were the same (1 Cor. 15:11). This is confirmed by the evidence of the non-Pauline Epistles, and by the extracts from early Christian preaching summarized in Acts. In the preaching the saving events were announced; Jesus was proclaimed as Lord and Christ; men were summoned to repent and receive forgiveness through him.

Some occasional samples of the teaching of converts appear in the Epistles, from which it is plain that the basis of this teaching was what Jesus himself had taught. Thus, in giving instruction about marriage Paul quotes Jesus' commandment forbidding divorce (1 Cor. 7:10), and similarly quotes his ruling about the maintenance of gospel preachers (1 Cor. 9:14). But there is evidence of more systematic instruction by the catechetical method; and as the number of converts increased, especially in the course of the Gentile mission, 'schools' for the training of instructors would have become almost a necessity, and digests of the teaching of Jesus would inevitably have been drawn up, orally if not in writing. We may envisage such a life-setting for the 'sayings collection' on which Matthew and Luke drew, and at a later date the Matthaean Gospel itself has been viewed as taking shape in such a school; *cf.* K. Stendahl, *The School of St Matthew*[2], 1968.

In worship too the works and words of Jesus were bound to be recalled. In the earliest days of the faith those who had known Jesus could scarcely avoid saying to one another, when they met informally or at the stated occasions of fellowship and worship, 'Do you remember how our Master ...?' In particular, the Lord's Supper provided a regular opportunity for retelling the story of his death, with the events immediately preceding and following it (1 Cor. 11:26).

The passion narrative, indeed, being told and retold both in Christian worship and in missionary preaching (*cf.* 1 Cor. 2:2; Gal. 3:1), took shape as a connected whole at an early date—a conclusion which is otherwise established by the form criticism of our existing Gospels. By the form-critical method an attempt is made to isolate and classify the various self-contained units which have been brought together in the written Gospels and to envisage the living situations in which they originated and were preserved in the oral stage of transmission. (*BIBLICAL CRITICISM, III.)

II. The written Gospels

The beginning of gospel writing, as we might expect, coincides with the end of the first Christian generation. As those who 'from the beginning were eyewitnesses and ministers of the word' (Lk. 1:2) were removed by death, the necessity of a permanent written record of their witness would be more acutely felt than before. It is just at this point that 2nd-century tradition places the beginnings of gospel writing, and rightly so: all four of our canonical Gospels are probably to be dated within the four decades AD 60–100. We need not suppose that the transmission of the apostolic witness had been exclusively oral before AD 60—some at least of the 'many' who, according to Lk. 1:1, had undertaken to draw up an orderly account of the evangelic events may have done so in writing before AD 60—but no document of an earlier date has survived except in so far as it has been incorporated in our written Gospels.

Several strands of tradition can be distinguished in the four Gospels. In this respect, as in some others, John stands apart from the other Gospels and is best considered independently. The other three Gospels are inter-related to the point where they lend themselves excellently to 'synoptic' study—*e.g.* as when their text is arranged in three parallel columns, so that their coincidences and divergences can be conveniently examined. For this reason they are commonly known as the 'Synoptic Gospels'—a designation apparently first given to them by J. J. Griesbach in 1774.

a. The Synoptic Gospels

A comparative study of Matthew, Mark and Luke leads to the recognition that there is a considerable body of material common to all three, or to two of the three. The substance of 606 out of the 661 verses of Mark (leaving Mk. 16:9–20 out of the reckoning) reappears in abridged form in Matthew; some 380 of the 661 verses of Mark reappear in Luke. This may be stated otherwise by saying that, out of the 1,068 verses of Matthew, about 500 contain the substance of 606 verses of Mark, while out of the 1,149 verses of Luke some 380 are paralleled in Mark. Only 31 verses of Mark have no parallel in either Matthew or Luke. Matthew and Luke have each up to 250 verses containing common material not paralleled in Mark; sometimes this common material appears in Matthew and Luke in practically identical language, while sometimes the verbal divergence is considerable. About 300 verses of Matthew have no parallel in any of the other Gospels; the same is true of about 520 verses in Luke.

There is no short cut to a satisfactory account of this distribution of common and special material in the Synoptic Gospels. There is no *a priori* reason for holding one Gospel to be earlier and another later, for holding one to be a source of another and the latter to be dependent on the former. Nor will the objectivity of statistical analysis guarantee a solution. A solution can be attained only by the exercise of critical judgment after all the relevant data have been marshalled and the alternative possibilities assessed. If unanimity has not been reached after a century and a half of intensive Synoptic study, it may be because the data are insufficient for the purpose, or because the field of inquiry has been unduly restricted. Yet certain findings command a much greater area of agreement than others.

One of these is the priority of Mark and its use as a principal source by the other two Synoptic Evangelists. This finding, which is commonly said to have been placed on a stable basis by C. Lachmann in 1835, depends not merely on the formal evidence that Matthew and Mark sometimes agree in order against Luke; Mark and Luke more frequently against Matthew; but Matthew and Luke never against Mark (which could be explained otherwise), but rather on the detailed comparative examination of the way in which common material is reproduced in the three Gospels, section by section. In the overwhelming majority of sections the situation can best be understood if Mark's account was used as a source by one or both of the others. Few have ever considered Luke as a possible source of the other two, but the view that Mark is an abridgment of Matthew was held for a long time, largely through the influence of Augustine. But where Matthew and Mark have material in common Mark is fuller than Matthew, and by no means an abridgment; and time after time the two parallel accounts can be much better explained by supposing that Matthew condenses Mark than by supposing that Mark amplifies Matthew. While Matthew and Luke never agree in order against Mark, they do occasionally exhibit verbal agreement against him, but such instances mainly represent grammatical or stylistic improvements of Mark, and are neither numerous nor significant enough to be offset against the general weight of the evidence for Mark's priority.

The common Marcan element in the Synoptic tradition is the more important because of the close relation between the framework of Mark and the apostolic preaching. This relation does not depend so much on the tradition which sees in Peter the authority behind the Marcan narrative (a tradition borne out by internal evidence in certain sections of the narrative) as on the fact (demonstrated by C. H. Dodd) that an outline of the primitive preaching, comparable to those outlines which can be discerned in a few passages in the NT Epistles and in the reports of speeches in Acts, supplies the thread on which Mark has strung his several units of gospel material.

The material common to Mark and one or both of the other Synoptic Gospels consists mainly of narrative. (The principal exceptions to this are the parables of Mk. 4 and the eschatological discourse of Mk. 13.) On the other hand, the non-Marcan material common to Matthew and Luke consists mainly of sayings of Jesus. One might almost say that the Marcan material relates what Jesus did; the non-Marcan material, what Jesus taught. We have here a distinction comparable to that commonly made (albeit to an exaggerated degree) between apostolic 'preaching' (*kērygma*) and 'teaching' (*didachē*). The non-Marcan material common to Matthew and Luke may conveniently, and without prejudice, be labelled 'Q', in accordance with a custom dating from the beginning of the 20th century.

This body of material, extending to between 200 and 250 verses, might have been derived by the one Evangelist from the other, or by both from a common source. Few, if any, can be found to suggest that Matthew derived it from Luke, although some would find it easier to suppose this than to suppose that Luke derived it from Matthew. This latter supposition continues to receive widespread support, but it is specially vulnerable because it implies that Luke reduced to relative disorder the orderly arrangement in which the 'Q' material appears in Matthew, without giving any plausible reason why this should have been done.

The supposition that the 'Q' material was

derived from a common source by Matthew and Luke involves fewer difficulties than any alternative supposition.

When we attempt to reconstruct this postulated common source we must beware of thinking that we can do so in anything like a complete form. Yet what we can reconstruct of it reminds us forcibly of the general pattern of the prophetical books of the OT. These books commonly contain an account of the prophet's call, with a record of his oracles set in a narrative framework, but with no mention of his death. So the 'Q' material appears to have come from a compilation which began with an account of Jesus' baptism by John and his wilderness temptations; this forms the prelude to his ministry, and is followed by groups of his sayings set in a minimum of narrative framework; but there is no trace of a passion narrative. There are four main groups of teaching, which may be entitled: (i) Jesus and John the Baptist; (ii) Jesus and his disciples; (iii) Jesus and his opponents; (iv) Jesus and the future.

Since our only means of reconstructing this source is provided by the non-Marcan material common to Matthew and Luke, the question whether Mark also made some use of it cannot be satisfactorily answered. That it is earlier than Mark is probable; it may well have been used for catechetical purposes in the Gentile mission based on Antioch. The fact that some of the 'Q' material in Matthew and Luke is almost verbally identical, while elsewhere there are divergences of language, has sometimes been explained in terms of there being two distinct strands of tradition in 'Q', but a much more probable account is that 'Q' was translated into Greek from Aramaic and that Matthew and Luke sometimes use the same translation and sometimes different ones. In this regard it is apposite to recall the statement of Papias (*apud* Eus., *EH* 3. 39) that 'Matthew compiled the *logia* in the Hebrew [Aramaic] speech, and everyone translated them as best he could'. *Logia* ('oracles') would be a specially appropriate term for the contents of such a compilation as we have tried to recognize behind the 'Q' material.

What other sources were utilized by Matthew and Luke is an even more uncertain question than the reconstruction of the 'Q' source. Matthew appears to have incorporated material from another sayings-collection, parallel to 'Q' but preserved in Judaea rather than in Antioch—the collection conveniently labelled 'M'. Luke has embodied a block of quite distinctive material (found largely between chs. 9 and 18) which may have been derived from Caesarea—the material labelled 'L'. Whether these 'sources' had a written form before they were taken over by the Evangelists is doubtful. Luke has been pictured as amplifying his copy of the 'Q' source by means of the information acquired in Caesarea and elsewhere, thus producing the preliminary draft of his Gospel sometimes called 'Proto-Luke', into which at a later date blocks of Marcan material were inserted. For an evaluation of the 'Proto-Luke' hypothesis see D. Guthrie, *New Testament Introduction*[3], 1970, pp. 175–183. In general, it may be agreed that Matthew conflates his sources while Luke combines his. The nativity narratives which introduce Matthew and Luke lie outside the general scheme of Synoptic criticism; with regard to them some dependence on Semitic documents cannot be excluded. But it must be emphasized that, fascinating and instructive as Gospel source criticism is, the Gospels themselves are much more important than their putative sources. It is good to consider what sources the Evangelists may have used; it is better to consider what use they made of their sources. In recent years it has been increasingly recognized that redaction criticism has as important a place in Gospel study as tradition criticism—the latter tracing the history of the traditions which in due course the Evangelists received, the former concentrating on the contribution of the individual Evangelists in their treatment and presentation of the traditions. Each of the Synoptic Gospels is an independent whole, no mere scissors-and-paste compilation; each has its own view of Jesus and his ministry, and each has its special contribution to make to the full-orbed picture of Jesus with which the NT presents us.

b. The Fourth Gospel

John represents a good primitive tradition which was preserved independently of the Synoptic lines of tradition, not only in the memory of the beloved disciple but in a living Christian community, quite probably in the milieu from which at a rather later date came the *Odes of Solomon*. The large area of common background which John shares with the Qumran texts, and the links binding its structure to the Palestinian synagogue lectionary, have in recent times helped to impress upon us that the Johannine tradition has its roots in Jewish Palestine, however much the requirements of a wider Hellenistic audience were borne in mind when this Gospel was given its literary form at the end of the first Christian century. And the fixed outline of the apostolic preaching can be discerned in the Fourth Gospel 'no less clearly than in Mark' (C. H. Dodd, *The Apostolic Preaching and its Developments*, 1950, p. 69). (*JOHN, GOSPEL OF.)

III. The fourfold Gospel

At an early date after the publication of the Fourth Gospel the four canonical Gospels began to circulate as a collection, and have continued to do so ever since. Who first gathered them together to form a fourfold corpus we do not know, and it is quite uncertain where the fourfold corpus first became known—claims have been made for both Ephesus and Rome. Catholic and Gnostic writers alike show not only acquaintance with the fourfold Gospel but recognition of its authority. The Valentinian *Gospel of Truth* (*c.* AD 140–150), recently brought to light among the Gnostic writings from *Chenoboskion, was not intended to supplement or supersede the canonical four, whose authority it presupposes; it is rather a series of meditations on the 'true gospel' which is enshrined in the four (and in other NT books). Marcion stands out as an exception in his repudiation of Matthew, Mark and John, and his promulgation of Luke (edited by himself) as the only authentic *euangelion*. The documents of the anti-Marcionite reaction (*e.g.* the anti-Marcionite prologues to the Gospels and, later, the Muratorian Canon) do not introduce the fourfold Gospel as something new, but reaffirm its authority in reply to Marcion's criticisms.

In the half-century following AD 95 Theodor Zahn could find only four Gospel citations in surviving Christian literature which demonstrably do not come from the canonical four. That the 'memoirs of the apostles' which Justin says were read in church along with the writings of the prophets were the four Gospels is rendered the more probable by the fact that such traces of gospel material in his works as may come from the pseudonymous *Gospel of Peter* or *Gospel of Thomas* are slight indeed compared with traces of the canonical four.

The situation is clearer when we come to Justin's disciple Tatian, whose Gospel harmony or *Diatessaron* (compiled *c.* AD 170) remained for long the favourite (if not the 'authorized') edition of the Gospels in the Assyr. church. Apart from a small fragment of a Gk. edition of the *Diatessaron* discovered at Dura-Europos on the Euphrates and published in 1935, our knowledge of the work has until recently been indirect, being based on translations (some of them secondary or tertiary) from the Syr. text. But in 1957 a considerable portion of the Syr. original of Ephraem's commentary on the *Diatessaron* (written about the middle of the 4th century) was identified in a parchment manuscript in A. Chester Beatty's collection; this text was edited with a Latin translation by L. Leloir in 1963 and throws valuable light on the early history of the *Diatessaron.*

Tatian began his compilation with Jn. 1:1–5, and perhaps ended it with Jn. 21:25. It was the fourfold Gospel that supplied him with the material for his harmony; such occasional intrusions of extra-canonical material as can be detected (possibly from the *Gospel according to the Hebrews*) do not affect this basic fact any more than do the occasional modifications of the Gospel wording which reflect Tatian's Encratite outlook. (*CANON OF THE NEW TESTAMENT.)

The supremacy of the fourfold Gospel which Tatian's work attests is confirmed a decade or so later by Irenaeus. To him the fourfold character of the Gospel is one of the accepted facts of Christianity, as axiomatic as the four quarters of the world or the four winds of heaven (*Adv. Haer.* 3. 11. 8). His contemporary Clement of Alexandria is careful to distinguish 'the four Gospels that have been handed down to us' from uncanonical writings on which he draws from time to time, such as the *Gospel according to the Egyptians* (*Miscellanies* 3. 13). Tertullian does not even draw upon such uncanonical writings, restricting himself to the canonical four, to which he accords unique authority because their authors were either apostles or men in close association with apostles. (Like other western Christian writers, he arranges the four so as to make the two 'apostolic' Gospels, Matthew and John, precede Luke and Mark.) Origen (*c.* AD 230) sums up the long-established catholic attitude when he speaks of 'the four Gospels, which alone are undisputed in the church of God beneath the whole heaven' (*Commentary on Matthew* in Eus., *EH* 6. 25. 4). (Like Irenaeus, Origen arranges them in the order with which we are familiar.)

All four of the Gospels are anonymous in the sense that none of them includes its author's name. The first reference to Matthew and Mark as Evangelists is found in Papias, bishop of Hierapolis in Phrygia in the first half of the 2nd century AD. His statement, made on the authority of 'the elder', that 'Mark, the interpreter of Peter, wrote down accurately all the words or deeds of the Lord of which he [Peter] made mention, but not in order . . .', is certainly a reference to our second Gospel. His statement about Matthew's compilation of *logia* (quoted above, under **II**) is more problematic, and it is still disputed whether it refers to our first Gospel, or to a collection of the sayings of Jesus (as has been suggested in this article), or to a catena of Messianic prophecies, or to something else. The earliest explicit references to Luke and John as Evangelists come in the anti-Marcionite Gospel prologues (which to some extent at least draw upon Papias's lost work) and Irenaeus. The latter sums up the account which he had received as follows: 'Matthew put forth a Gospel writing among the Hebrews in their own speech while Peter and Paul were preaching the gospel in Rome and founding the church there. After their departure, Mark, Peter's disciple and interpreter, has likewise delivered to us in writing the substance of Peter's preaching. Luke, the companion of Paul, set down in a book the gospel proclaimed by that apostle. Then John, the disciple of the Lord, who reclined on his bosom, in turn published his Gospel while he was staying in Ephesus in Asia' (*Adv. Haer.* 3. 1. 1).

Without endorsing all that Irenaeus says, we may heartily agree that in the canonical Gospels we have the apostolic witness to the redemptive revelation of God in Christ preserved in a fourfold form. (See articles on the four Gospels.)

BIBLIOGRAPHY. K. Aland and others, *Studia Evangelica*, 1959; C. Blomberg, *The Historical Reliability of the Gospels*, 1987; W. R. Farmer, *The Synoptic Problem*, 1976; R. T. France and D. Wenham (eds.), *Gospel Perspectives*, 1–6, 1980–85; *DJG;* E. Linnemann, *Is There a Synoptic Problem?*, 1992; T. W. Manson, *Studies in the Gospels and Epistles*, 1961; D. E. Nineham (ed.), *Studies in the Gospels*, 1955; B. Orchard and T. R. W. Longstaff (eds.), *J. J. Griesbach: Synoptic and Text-critical Studies*, 1978; N. Perrin, *Rediscovering the Teaching of Jesus*, 1967; J. Rohde, *Rediscovering the Teaching of the Evangelists*, 1968; E. P. Sanders and M. Davies, *Studying the Synoptic Gospels*, 1989; B. de Solages, *A Greek Synopsis of the Gospels*, 1959; G. N. Stanton, *The Gospels and Jesus*, 1989; B. H. Streeter, *The Four Gospels*, 1924; V. Taylor, *The Gospels*[9], 1960.

F.F.B.

GOVERNMENT.

I. In the Old Testament.

During the OT period the people of God lived under various types of government. The Patriarchs might be called semi-nomads. The father was the head of the family and its priest. His jurisdiction extended not only over the members of the immediate family but also over all who were in his employ or subject to him. This type of government was similar to that of the bedouin nomads of Arabia. In the head of the family (*i.e.* of the clan) there resided even the power of life and death as well as that of making various decisions (*cf.* Jdg. 11:11ff.).

In Egypt the descendants of Jacob were in bondage until they were brought forth from the land by Moses. Moses acted as the representative of God, and the people listened to him. At this time also there were officers of the people, although it is difficult to say just how the Israelites were organized in relationship to Egypt. The organization of Sinai was unique in that it consisted in the formation of the tribes into a theocracy (*i.e.* 'the rule of God'—*theos*, 'god'; *kratos*, 'power', 'rule'). The essence of this type of government is set forth by divine revelation in Ex.

19:5–6. Primarily it was a rule of God over a nation that was to be holy and a kingdom of priests.

In the wilderness there were elders of the people who assisted Moses in his tasks. The plan of the theocracy was presented to them and they accepted it. God was to rule and he would rule through the agency of a human judge or king. This man should 'reign in righteousness', in that he should give decisions in accordance with strict justice and manifest in his rule the righteousness of God. The people were to be separate from the rest of the world, for they were holy, belonging unto God himself.

For a time the nation was not ready to accept the full implications of the theocracy. Under Joshua it was necessary that they should obtain possession of the land that had been promised to them. For a time there were rulers or judges over them, but there was no central organization. This condition led them to realize that they must have a king. Their request for a king, however, was made in an untheocratic spirit, for they merely wanted to be like the nations round about them. For this reason Samuel reproached them with having rejected Yahweh himself (1 Sa. 8:7).

The nation therefore needed not merely to learn that it must have a king but also that it must have the right kind of king. The first king chosen was a man who did not follow Yahweh, and for that reason was rejected. In David there was found the man after God's own heart. David rendered the decisions of a more important kind, but minor decisions were left to under-officers. Some of these officers are mentioned in the Scriptures, *e.g.* the priests, officers of the household, the cup-bearer, the officer in charge of the palace (1 Ki. 4:6), scribes, recorders, counsellors, chief of the army and chief of the king's guard (2 Sa. 8:18). The ministers of the king served in the administration of the affairs of the state (1 Ki. 4:2ff.).

Solomon divided the kingdom into twelve districts, over each of which he placed a prefect to provide victuals for the king and his house (1 Ki. 4:7ff.). The Exile brought about an interruption of the theocracy, which had long before ceased to be a theocracy in actual fact. After the Exile the Jews were subject to Persia, and Judaea was reconstituted as a temple-state, with the high priest at its head. The Persian king was represented by a provincial governor, who might occasionally be himself a Jew (*e.g.* Nehemiah). This same arrangement continued under the Greek period, although at this time a council of elders is introduced. The Temple constitution was abolished by Antiochus IV in 168 BC, but restored by the Hasmonaeans who, however, combined the high-priesthood and the civil and military sovereignty in their own family. Their secular power was terminated by the Roman conquest of 63 BC but (except for the special circumstances of the rule of Herod the Great and Archelaus) the high priest was recognized by the Romans as head of the internal Jewish administration.

The central point of the theocracy was the Temple, which symbolized the dwelling-place of God in the midst of his people. Thus, Jerusalem, the city in which the Temple was located, became known as the holy city. The formal destruction of the theocracy occurred when the Temple was burned in AD 70.

E.J.Y.
F.F.B.

II. In the New Testament.

1. The situation in Palestine

The land was largely partitioned among a number of republican states (*e.g.* Caesarea and the cities of the Decapolis). This was a device used by the successive supervisory powers, and especially the Romans, to hellenize the population and thus contain Jewish nationalism. The less tractable areas (*e.g.* Galilee) were entrusted to Herodian princes, while Jerusalem itself and its neighbourhood were under the Sanhedrin, a council drawn from the religious aristocracy. The whole complex of governments was supervised in the interests of Roman frontier security by the Caesars, acting at different stages either through a Herodian client king or through a personal deputy, the prefect or procurator. Jewish nationalism found institutional expression in a series of religious sects, whose attitudes to the government ranged from terrorism (the Zealots) to detachment (the Essenes), on the one hand, and collaboration (the Sadducees), on the other. All were dedicated in their own way to the restoration of the kingdom.

a. The career of Jesus

Jesus was inextricably involved in this confusion of government. He was attacked at birth (Mt. 2:16) as a threat to Herod's throne, and denounced in death as a pretender to royal power (Jn. 19:21). He was dogged on all sides by pressures to avow this goal. The devil's advances (Mt. 4:9) were mirrored in popular enthusiasm (Jn. 6:15), the obtuse arrogance of the disciples (Mt. 16:22f.) and the fears of those who precipitated the arrest (Jn. 11:50). Faced with such a consensus of misconstruction, Jesus generally avoided the claim to kingship, but did not conceal it from the disciples (Lk. 22:29–30) and in the end owned it publicly (Jn. 18:36–37).

b. The teaching of Jesus

Three main assertions about the relation of the kingdom of heaven to temporal government may be singled out. (i) The kingdom of Jesus is not of the same order as the temporal powers. It is not established by political action (Jn. 18:36). (ii) Temporal power is not autonomous: it is enjoyed only by permission of God (Jn. 19:11). (iii) The temporal power therefore has its rights, as does God (Lk. 20:25): both must be conceded.

c. The church in Jerusalem

After the resurrection the disciples were again instructed in the nature of the kingdom (Acts 1:3). Their view of it was still narrowly political, however (Acts 1:6), and even after the ascension the preaching of Jesus' exaltation at God's right hand (*e.g.* Acts 2:32–36) was capable of political overtones (Acts 5:31), and certainly taken as politically provocative by the Sanhedrin (Acts 5:33ff.). The apostles defied a court order restraining their preaching on the grounds of their prior duty to God (Acts 5:29). The prosecution of Peter and James (Acts 12:2–3) may have been political, but in the cases of Stephen (Acts 6:11) and Paul (Acts 21:28) the offences were religious, and reflect the transformation of the Nazarenes into a regular sect of the Jewish religion, differentiated perhaps chiefly by the added sanction that the kingship of Jesus had lent to the law (Jas. 2:5, 8).

2. The Hellenistic states

All the places outside Palestine where churches were established were, along with Rome itself, republican states, either satellites of the Romans or actual Roman colonies. Christians might thus become involved either with the local administration (*e.g.* Acts 16:19–21; 17:6, 22) or with the superintendent Roman governors (*e.g.* Acts 13:7; 18:12). The tendency to refer difficult cases to the Roman authority, however, meant that the attitude of that government became the major concern.

a. Support for the government

The only case where Christians were accused of direct opposition to the Caesars (Acts 17:7) was fobbed off by the authorities responsible. In all other known cases the charges were not political, and the various governments showed a reluctance to pursue them. Christian writers reciprocated this respectful *laissez-faire* (Rom. 13:1–7; 1 Tim. 2:2; Tit. 3:1): the teaching of Jesus was elaborated to show that the 'governing authorities' (*exousiai*) not only had their authority allowed by God but that they were positively 'ministers of God' for the punishment of evil; to oppose them was to oppose God. This attitude was sustained even (as happened under Nero) when the courts were being used for fabricated charges; the legitimacy of government was studiously defended, while its victims were solaced with the innocent sufferings of Christ (1 Pet. 2:11–25). Some have held that the restrainer of antichrist (2 Thes. 2:6–8) is meant to be the Roman government.

b. Criticism of the government

Even Paul had some reservations, however. The responsibility for the crucifixion rests on 'the rulers of this age' (1 Cor. 2:8). Saints must not settle their disputes in civil courts, because their destiny is to 'judge the world' (1 Cor. 6:2). Attention is repeatedly drawn to the rule of the 'only Sovereign, the King of kings' (1 Tim. 6:15), and the citizenship of the republic that transcends all the barriers of earthly states (*e.g.* Eph 2:19). The demonic powers (*archai* or *exousiai*) over whom Christ has triumphed (Col. 2:15) and with whom we now struggle (Eph. 6:12) may well be conceived of as the forces behind human government. This is certainly the theme taken up in detail in the Revelation, which envisages a struggle for world government between God and satanic powers. The allusions to the ruler cult (Rev. 13:15) seem sufficiently plain to identify the enemy as the Roman Caesars. We know from Pliny (*Ep.* 10. 96) that attempts to induce Christians to escape condemnation by making the formal offering to the ruler met with incorrigible obstinacy. They had presumably decided that they were being asked to render to Caesar the things that were God's.

BIBLIOGRAPHY. A. H. M. Jones, *The Greek City from Alexander to Justinian*, 1940; A. N. Sherwin-White, *Roman Society and Roman Law in the New Testament*, 1963; O. Cullmann, *The State in the New Testament*, 1957; E. A. Judge, *The Social Pattern of the Christian Groups in the First Century*, 1960; M. Avi-Yonah, *The Holy Land from the Persian to the Arab Conquest; a Historical Geography*, 1966; D. R. Griffiths, *The New Testament and the Roman State*, 1970; A. Richardson, *The Political Christ*, 1973; E. M. Smallwood, *The Jews under Roman Rule*, 1976; *BA1CS* 2. E.A.J.

GOVERNOR.

I. In the Old Testament

Since Israel through her history was involved directly or indirectly with various civilizations, each of which had its own distinctive constitutional system and titles for those in authority, it is not surprising to find a variety of Hebrew terms, and of English translations in RSV, *e.g.* 'governor', 'ruler', 'captain'. They may be classed as follows.

a. Technical words

Of these Heb. *peḥâ* (*cf.* Assyr. *paḫatu*) is the most frequent, meaning the ruler of a district under a king, *e.g.* an Assyrian provincial governor (Is. 36:9), Chaldean and Persian governors (Ezk. 23:6, 23; Est. 3:12; 8:9), the Persian Tattenai (Ezr. 5:3; 6:6), whose satrapy included Palestine, Phoenicia and Egypt; and Nehemiah and Zerubbabel as governors of Judah (Ne. 5:14; Ezr. 6:7). The latter are also called 'Tirshatha' (Ezr. 2:63; Ne. 7:65, 70), the Heb. form of a Persian title (from Avestan *tarshta*, 'reverenced').

b. General words

Nine other Heb. terms indicate authority in various spheres. *'allûp* (*e.g.* Zc. 9:7, of governors of Judah), *môšēl* (Gn. 45:26, of Joseph in Egypt) and *šallîṭ* (Gn. 42:6, also of Joseph) are wider terms; the others have more particular references: *pāqîḏ* ('overseer', Je. 20:1, of a priest; *cf.* Gn. 41:34, of Egyptian officers), *ḥôqēq* (of lawgivers, Jdg. 5:9, 14), *sāḡān* ('deputy', 'lieutenant', *e.g.* Dn. 3:2, RSV 'governors'), *nāśî'* (indicating social rank, 2 Ch. 1:2), *śar* ('governor of a city', 1 Ki. 22:26) and *nāḡîḏ* ('commander of a palace', 2 Ch. 28:7).

II. In the New Testament

Fewer Gk. words are used, and these sometimes imprecisely, sometimes with technical accuracy.

a. hēgoumai ('lead') and its derivatives occur most frequently. The term *hēgemōn* is used for governors in the general sense (Mk. 13:9; 1 Pet. 2:14) but more often describes Roman subordinate rulers, such as Pilate (Mt. 27:2; 28:14), Felix (Acts 23:26) and Festus (Acts 26:30), who were 'procurators' (or, in the case of Pilate, 'prefect') under the legate of the province Syria (the official Gk. equivalent was *epitropoi*).

b. Other terms appear at Jn. 2:8 (*architriklinos*, 'steward of the feast'), 2 Cor. 11:32 (*ethnarchēs*, *'ethnarch'), Gal. 4:2 (*oikonomos*, RSV 'trustees', *cf.* Lk. 12:42; 1 Cor. 4:2) and Jas. 3:4 (*euthynōn*, 'pilot'). B.F.H.

GOZAN is identified with ancient Guzana, modern Tell Halaf, on the Upper Habur river. Israelites from Samaria were deported here in 722 BC (2 Ki. 17:6; 18:11). Sennacherib, in his letter to Hezekiah (2 Ki. 19:12 = Is. 37:12), refers to the heavy punishment inflicted on this Assyr. provincial capital when it rebelled in 759 BC. Excavations in 1899, 1911–13 and 1927 (M. von Oppenheim, *Tell Halaf*, 1933) produced tablets of the 8th–7th centuries BC, in which W Semitic names may attest, or explain, the presence of the Israelite exiles (*AfO* Beiheft 6). D.J.W.

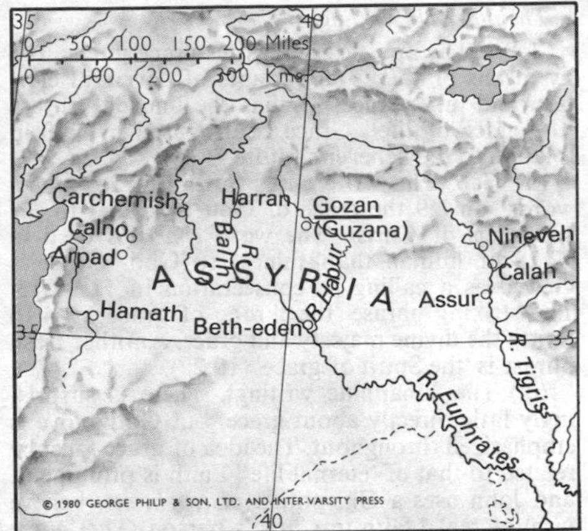

The location of Gozan.

GRACE, FAVOUR.

I. In the Old Testament

a. Vocabulary

Grace involves such other subjects as forgiveness, salvation, regeneration, repentance and the love of God. 'There are "grace-words" which do not contain the word "grace"' (Moffatt); see Dt. 7:7; 9:4–6. The OT 'grace-words' are:

(i) *ḥesed*, in RSV usually 'steadfast love', occasionally 'loyalty'. This is translated in AV as 'mercy' (149 times), 'kindness' (38), 'lovingkindness' (30) and 'goodness' (12). Luther translates it by *Gnade*, the German word for 'grace'. Despite that, it is not quite the equivalent of grace. It is a two-way word, and can be used of God and man. Of God, it certainly implies grace. Of man, it implies steadfast love to another human being or to God. It is often found in association with the word 'covenant', and denotes the attitude of faithfulness which both parties to a covenant should observe. For God's *ḥesed*, see La. 3:22; for man's, Ho. 6:6. Snaith suggests 'covenant love' as the nearest Eng. equivalent.

(ii) *ḥēn*, 'favour' (RSV). This is not a covenant word and not two-way. It is used of the action of a superior, human or divine, to an inferior. It speaks of undeserved favour; in AV it is translated 'grace' (38) and 'favour' (26). Examples of man's *ḥēn* are found in Gn. 33:8, 10, 15; 39:4; Ru. 2:2, 10. God's *ḥēn* is found in Je. 31:2 (RSV 'faithfulness', AV 'lovingkindness'). No-one can show *ḥēn* to God (as one can show *ḥesed*), for no-one can do him a favour.

b. The law

(i) Jn. 1:17 puts the law into sharp antithesis with grace. See Tit. 2:11, which also states that grace came into the world with Christ. That does not mean that grace was non-existent in the OT, but merely that it is not in the foreground, and that it is concerned chiefly with Israel. The Bible often uses antithesis where we would use comparison.

(ii) The idea of promise is developed in the NT in Gal. (3:16–22) and in Hebrews. It shows that grace is prior to law. God dealt with the Patriarchs as individuals by way of promise, and with the nation as a whole by way of law. The law was not primary, but it clarified and emphasized the kind of *ḥesed* that God expected of his covenant people.

(iii) Grace is found, however, in the law itself. The election of Israel to be God's people is attributed in the law to God's free choice, and not to Israel's righteousness (Dt. 7:7–8; *cf.* 8:18). The initiative in the Sinai covenant comes from God, just as much as did the covenant of grace with Abraham. Then there is the statement in Ps. 19 of the converting or restoring power of the law.

c. The prophets

Repentance is the chief point of interest in the prophetic writings. Typical passages are Am. 5:14; Ho. 2:7; 6:1; 14:1; Is. 1:16–18; Je. 3:1, 7, 12–14. The prophets are often accused of a doctrine of repentance which lays stress on human willpower, as did the Pelagian heresy. But the prophets regarded repentance as inward (Joel 2:13). Ezekiel, who demanded that the individual should make himself a new heart (18:31), also recognized that a new heart can only be a gift of God's grace (36:26). With this agrees the 'new covenant' passage in Je. 31:31–34.

d. The Psalms

The word *ḥēn* is almost absent from the Psalms, though its cognates appear. *ḥesed* is very often found, *e.g.* Pss. 5:7; 57:3 ('steadfast love', AV 'mercy'); 89:33 (AV 'lovingkindness'). In the Psalms also is found the increasing use of the cognate word *ḥāsîḏ*, which is found in, *e.g.*, Pss. 12:1; 86:2 ('godly man'); 79:2 ('saints'). The plural of this word (*ḥ^a^sîḏîm*) appears as 'Hasidaeans' in 1 Macc. 2:42; 7:13; 2 Macc. 14:6; it really meant those who were loyal to the covenant, the rigorous, devout, law-keeping party in Judaism, from whose ranks came the *Pharisees.

II. In the New Testament

a. Vocabulary

Gk. *charis* was the normal word used to translate Heb. *ḥēn*. The nearest corresponding verb, *charizesthai*, was used to denote forgiveness, human as well as divine (Col. 2:13; 3:13; Eph. 4:32). *eleos* represents the Heb. *ḥesed* and has the meaning of 'mercy'. It is not used very often, and occurs largely in passages based on the OT, such as Rom. 9:15–18, 23; 11:30–32. 'Grace' is preferred to 'mercy', because it includes the idea of the divine power which equips a man to live a moral life.

b. The Synoptic Gospels

Quite apart from the word *charis*, which is never placed on the lips of Jesus, the idea of grace is very prominent. Jesus says that he came to seek and save the lost. Many of his parables teach the doctrine of grace. The parable of the labourers in the vineyard (Mt. 20:1–16) teaches that God is answerable to no-one for his gifts of grace. The parable of the great supper (Lk. 14:16–24) shows that spiritual privilege does not ensure final bliss, and that the gospel invitation is to all. The prodigal son was welcomed by his father in a way he did not deserve (Lk. 15:20–24). Repentance is stressed as a condition of salvation (Mk. 1:15; 6:12; Lk. 24:47). Faith also has its place (*e.g.* Mk. 1:15; Lk. 7:50), although there is no theological statement on Pauline lines.

c. The writings of Luke

Both the Gospel and the Acts need special attention. Luke shows flexibility in dealing with the subject. Even the non-religious sense of the noun, of a favour done by one man to another, appears (Acts 24:27; 25:3, 9). The OT sense of 'favour' is seen in Lk. 1:30; 2:52; Acts 2:47; 7:10, 46. The dynamic sense of grace resulting in fearless courage and effective witness is seen in Acts 4:33; 11:23; 13:43 and is used in the context of the universal appeal of the gospel. Luke also brings together, in a way that even Paul does not, the terms 'gospel' ('word') and 'grace' (Lk. 4:22; Acts 14:3; 20:24).

d. The Pauline Epistles

The word 'grace' has a prominent place in the opening greetings and the closing benedictions of the Epistles, being added to the conventional Jewish greeting of 'peace'. The basis of Paul's doctrine is found in Rom. 1:16–3:20. Man is shown as a sinner, but by grace he is justified (Rom. 3:21–4:25), *i.e.* God in his grace treats him, though guilty, as if he had never sinned.

*Faith is the human response to divine grace (Rom. 5:2; 10:9; Eph. 2:8). This faith is the gift of God (Eph. 2:8); the words 'not your own doing' may refer to *sesōsmenoi* ('saved'), but Paul is seeking to point out that the word 'faith' must not be thought to imply some independent action on the part of the believer. See also 2 Cor. 4:13; Phil. 1:29. This faith, although it implies that there is no salvation through the law, is not unethical. Faith is morally vital by itself. It works 'through love' (Gal. 5:6). C. A. Anderson Scott (*Christianity according to St Paul*, 1927, p. 111) says that from the moment that faith was active a transformation of ethical outlook was ideally there.

The believer's position in grace is explained, not by anything in himself, but by the will of God. The doctrine of *election has two functions: it checks human independence and self-righteousness, and shows that in bestowing favour God is perfectly free (Eph. 1:1–6; 2 Tim. 1:9; Tit. 3:5). Every step in the process of the Christian life is due to grace—Gal. 1:15 (call); 2 Tim. 2:25 (repentance); Eph. 2:8–9 (faith).

In Rom. 8:28–30 Paul surveys the divine agency from the call to the final glory of the redeemed. He does not, however, overlook man's responsibility. Obedience (Rom. 1:5; 6:17) is a moral attitude, and cannot be made anything else. A man of himself turns to the Lord (2 Cor. 3:16). A. Stewart in *HDB* suggests that 1 Thes. 3:5 teaches that even perseverance is doubted. The two sides are brought together in Rom. 9–10. Ch. 9 contains the strongest possible statements of double predestination, while ch. 10 states that rejection by God is due to unbelief and disobedience. It must be remembered, however, that the primary subject of these chapters is not personal salvation, but the collective functions of those chosen by God to carry out his purpose.

Rom. 6 uses the figure of baptism to teach the conquest of sin by grace. See also 1 Cor. 6:11; 12:13; Eph. 5:26; Col. 2:12; Tit. 3:5. H. Wheeler Robinson (*The Christian Doctrine of Man*, 1926, pp. 124–125) holds that believers' baptism is not merely illustrative symbolism but the objective aspect of what is subjectively faith. Others would argue that infant baptism is a means of grace, because the child is a symbol of human inability and helplessness. These views seem to contradict the unvarying Pauline emphasis on faith.

e. The other NT writings

(i) 1 Pet. The apostle emphasizes grace in chs. 1–2 by means of the usual variants of covenant election and inheritance; 3:7 has the unusual phrase 'the grace of life'. Grace is also used in 5:10 in relation to the believer's future glory.

(ii) Heb. The writer uses most of the 'grace-words'. In 2:9 the grace of God is related to the sufferings of Christ. The word *charis* is used in 12:28 of human thankfulness to God. Grace is viewed as a calling to consecration in 12:14–15. The striking phrase 'the throne of grace' in 4:16 unites the divine majesty and grace. Another fresh phrase is 'the Spirit of grace' (10:29).

(iii) The Johannine writings. There is surprisingly little directly about grace, but God's love is emphasized throughout. The idea of grace must be related to that of 'eternal life'. Faith is prominent, and John uses a Gk. phrase *pisteuein eis* (believe *into*) of real *faith in Christ's person. The 'grace and truth' which characterize the glory of the incarnate Word in Jn. 1:14 (*cf.* v. 17) echo the 'mercy and truth' (*ḥeseḏ we'ᵉmeṯ*) of Ex. 34:6.

We conclude with Moffatt that the religion of the Bible 'is a religion of grace or it is nothing ... no grace, no gospel' (*Grace in the New Testament*, p. xv).

BIBLIOGRAPHY. H. Wheeler Robinson, *The Christian Doctrine of Man*, 1926; N. H. Snaith, *The Distinctive Ideas of the Old Testament*, 1944, pp. 94–130; J. Moffatt, *Grace in the New Testament*, 1931; N. P. Williams, *The Grace of God*, 1930; C. Ryder Smith, *The Bible Doctrine of Grace*, 1956; H.-H. Esser, *NIDNTT* 2, pp. 115–124; H. Conzelmann, W. Zimmerli, *TDNT* 9, pp. 372–402; H. D. McDonald, *ZPEB*, 2, pp. 799–804. J.H.Sr.

GRAIN. The commonest OT Heb. words are **1.** *dāḡān*, wheat (fully-developed grain). **2.** *bar*, grain of any kind standing in the open field (hence *bar* means also 'open country'). **3.** *šeḇer*, grain, cereal, victuals, *i.e.* broken crushed grain.

'Parched grain' (*qālî*, *qālâ*, 'roasted') were ears or grains of wheat (Lv. 23:14; Ru. 2:14; 1 Sa. 17:17; 25:18; 2 Sa. 17:28) roasted over a blazing fire, usually on an iron pan or flat stone.

kussemeṯ (Ex. 9:32; Is. 28:25; Ezk. 4:9), rendered 'spelt' (RSV) and 'rie', 'rye' or 'fitches' (AV), denotes the false spelt or einkorn wheat (*Triticum monoccum*) and not true spelt (*Triticum spelta*) which has not been recorded from Egypt of that time.

The Gk. word *kokkos* ('kernel', Mt. 13:31, *etc.*) denotes the singular form, *e.g.* 'a grain of mustard seed'.

By 'grain' in the Bible the cereal crops barley and wheat are usually intended. (*AGRICULTURE, *FOOD.) F.N.H.

Barley (Heb. *śᵉʻōrâ*, Gk. *krithē*). An edible grain of the genus *Hordeum*. The grass *H. spontaneum*, which still grows wild in Palestine, gave rise to the primitive cultivated 'two-row' barley (*H. distichon*), and later to the 'six-row' barley (*H. vulgare*), which was the barley of biblical times and continues today.

Barley formed the major part of the staple food of Palestine (Dt. 8:8), particularly of the poorer classes (Ru. 2:17; Ezk. 4:9; Jn. 6:9). It has a shorter growing season than wheat and can flourish on poorer soil. Barley was also used as fodder for horses and cattle (1 Ki. 4:28), and for brewing, judging from evidence of Philistine drinking vessels. In Jdg. 7:13 it apparently symbolizes a reformed Israel. Barley meal as a jealousy offering (Nu. 5:15) seems to show that basic integrity had been disrupted. F.N.H.

Chaff. 1. Heb. *mōṣ*, the most common word, denotes worthless husks and broken straw blown away by the wind during the winnowing of grain (Jb. 21:18; Pss. 1:4; 35:5; Is. 17:13; 29:5; 41:15; Ho. 13:3; Zp. 2:2). **2.** Heb. *ḥᵃšaš*, 'hay', 'dry grass' (Is. 5:24; 33:11). **3.** Aram. *'ûr*, 'skin', 'chaff' (Dn. 2:35). **4.** Gk. *achyron*, 'chaff' (Mt. 3:12; Lk. 3:17).

In some of the above references it is applied figuratively in connection with superficial or wrong teaching, and with the inevitable fate of wrongdoers. J.D.D.

Straw (Heb. *teḇen*; Arab. *tibn*). The stalk of wheat or barley, while chaff is the wind-scattered husk of the threshed grain, and stubble remains after harvesting. Chopped straw mixed with more solid foodstuffs contributed to the provender of horses, asses and camels (Gn. 24:32; Jdg. 19:19; 1 Ki. 4:28). In Egypt straw was and is mixed with clay to make the familiar mud bricks of the poorer houses. When the Israelite brickmakers, already overworked, had to collect their own straw, their burdens were almost intolerably increased (Ex. 5).

Straw is also still used in certain kinds of hand-moulded pottery, later burnt by fire. Such was the strength of leviathan that he could bend iron like straw (Jb. 41:27). In the peace of the Messianic age the lion will cease to devour flesh, and eat straw (Is. 11:7; 65:25). The final fate of Moab is pictured as straw trampled down among dung (Is. 25:10). In the Bible, stubble (Heb. *qaš*, 'dried up') is used to typify worthless inflammable substances, since chaff and straw were often thrown on to fires to give instant heat (Ex. 15:7; Jb. 13:25; 41:28–29; Ps. 83:13; Is. 5:24; so Gk. *kalamē* in 1 Cor. 3:12). See C. F. Nims, 'Bricks without Straw', *BA* 13, 1950, pp. 22ff. R.A.S.

Wheat (Heb. *dāḡān*, Gk. *sitos*). A cereal grass of great antiquity and importance as a food of mankind. The typical wheat of OT times in the Mediterranean region was the 'emmer' wheat (*Triticum dicoccum*), which gave rise to the 'hard' wheat (*T. durum*) that was immensely important from Hellenistic times onward, thus including the NT period. Modern cultivated varieties are of the 'bread' wheat (*T. vulgare*). Owing to its physical and chemical qualities, wheat makes more palatable and better *bread than any other cereal.

Wheat formed an important part of the diet of the Israelites (Jdg. 6:11; Ru. 2:23; 2 Sa. 4:6), and the wheat harvest is used as a *calendar reference (Gn. 30:14; 1 Sa. 6:13; 12:17). Because of its importance as a food, it is a symbol of God's goodness and provision (Pss. 81:16; 147:14). It was used as a cereal offering in the Temple (Ezr. 6:9; 7:22) and forms part of the sacrifice made by David on Ornan's threshing-floor (1 Ch. 21:23).

Its botanical nature whereby one grain gives rise to several new ears of wheat, while the original grain is used up, is taken by Christ to show that spiritual fruitfulness has its origin in the death of self (Jn. 12:24; *cf.* 1 Cor. 15:36ff.). As symbolic of the children of God, it is contrasted with the valueless chaff (Mt. 3:12). Similarly, in Mt. 13:24–30 the darnel or tares (*Lolium temulentum*) in their early stages of growth appear as grass-like as wheat, but can easily be distinguished at harvest-time.

BIBLIOGRAPHY. H. Helbaek, 'Ancient Egyptian wheats', *Proceedings of Prehistory Society* 11, 1955, pp. 93–95; D. Zohary and M. Hopf, *Domestication of Plants in the Old World*, 1988, pp. 13–82; F. N. Hepper, *IEBP*, pp. 84–95.

F.N.H. *et al.*

GRASS (Heb. *ḥāṣîr*, *deše'*, *yereq*, *'ēśeḇ*; Gk. *chortos*).

Gn. 1:11 records that the earth brought forth vegetation (literally 'grass', as AV) on the 'third day' of the creation narrative. In the promised land it provided food for cattle; it would be given to the land by God in response to the people's obedience (Dt. 11:15). It was the portion of Nebuchadrezzar during his madness (Dn. 4:15, 25).

Green pastures are not of permanent occurrence in Palestine, but last only for a while after the rains, withering in the dry season. As a result, grass is a fitting symbol of the transitoriness of human life (*e.g.* Ps. 103:15; Is. 40:6–7), of the brief sway of the rich man (Jas. 1:10–11), and is a figure of weakness, of perishing enemies (Is. 37:27 = 2 Ki. 19:26), of the wicked soon to be cut down (Ps. 37:2) and of haters of Zion (Ps. 129:6).

The multitude of blades is likened to a multitude of people (Jb. 5:25; Is. 44:4) and to a flourishing people (Ps. 72:16), and the luxuriance of green pastures is likened to serenity in the spiritual life (Ps. 23:2). In tender grass can be seen a quality of the just ruler (2 Sa. 23:4), and a benevolent ruler is as refreshing and productive of good as rain upon mown meadows (Ps. 72:6).

In contrast, a barren locality without grass can indicate God's wrath (Dt. 29:23). R.A.H.G.

GREECE. Who the Greeks were is a famous crux. Their language is Indo-European and its earliest known location is in the Mycenaean states of the Peloponnesus (as established by the decipherment of the Linear B script) in the 2nd millennium BC. When they emerge into history well into the 1st millennium they belong indifferently to either side of the Aegean.

The first flowering of the two institutions that became the hallmarks of Hellenism, speculative philosophy and republican government, apparently occurred on the Ionian coast of Asia Minor. Ionia is perhaps the OT Javan (Is. 66:19). The area of Greek settlement was never static. The republics were early established throughout the Black Sea, Sicily and S Italy, and as far W as Marseilles and Spain. After Alexander there were Greek states as far E as India. Under Seleucid and more especially Roman control the wealthy and ancient nations of Asia Minor and the Levant were systematically broken up into many hundreds of Greek republics, leaving only the most backward regions under the indigenous royal or priestly governments. This political fragmentation was always characteristic of the Greeks, as was the consequent subordination to foreign powers. Greece was never a political entity. 'The king of Greece' (*yāwān*, Dn. 8:21) must be one of the *Macedonian rulers, Alexander or a Seleucid, who controlled the affairs of many but by no means all Greek states. 'Greece' (*Hellas*) in Acts 20:2 must refer to the Roman province of *Achaia, which, while it contained many ancient Greek states, was now almost a backwater of Hellenism.

On the other hand, the ever-increasing diffusion

of Greek institutions brought unification at a different level. The whole of the E Mediterranean and much beyond was raised to the common norm of civilization that Hellenism supplied. Both the opulence of the states and the degree of standardization are attested by the splendid ruins that indiscriminately litter these parts today. The ideal of a free and cultivated life in a small autonomous community, once the boast of a few Aegean states, was now almost universally accepted. *Athens was still a home of learning, but Pergamum, Antioch and Alexandria, and many others in the new world, rivalled or eclipsed her.

The states provided not only education but brilliant entertainment and a wider range of health and welfare services than most modern communities. It was membership in such a republic and use of the Greek language that marked a man as civilized (Acts 21:37–39). Such a person might be called a Greek, whatever his race (Mk. 7:26); all others were 'barbarians' (Rom. 1:14). The term 'Hellenists' in Acts 6:1; 9:29 presumably shows that this distinction applied even within the Jewish ethnic community. The term 'Greek' (*hellēn*, Acts 11:20; 19:17; Rom. 1:16, *etc.*) is, however, the regular NT usage for non-Jews, being virtually equivalent to 'Gentile'. *Greeks were frequently associated with the synagogues as observers (Jn. 12:20; Acts 14:1; 17:4; 18:4), but the exclusiveness of Israel as a nation was jealously preserved. It was the agonizing delivery of the gospel from this constricting matrix that marked the birth of the Christian religion in its universal form. The translation from Hebrew into Greek opened the gospel to all civilized men. It also produced the NT.

BIBLIOGRAPHY. M. I. Finley, *The Ancient Greeks*, 1963; A. Andrewes, *The Greeks*, 1967; M. Hengel, *Judaism and Hellenism*, 1974; W. R. Biers, *The Archaeology of Greece: An Introduction*, 1980.

E.A.J.

GREEKS. Two words are used in the NT: *Hellēnes* and *Hellēnistai*. The term *Hellēnes* refers to the inhabitants of Greece or their descendants (*cf.* Acts 16:1; Rom. 1:14). It is also used, as a virtual equivalent of 'Gentile', to describe those who are not of Jewish origin (*cf.* Rom. 10:12; Gal. 3:28).

The term *Hellēnistai* is a crux. It is confined to Acts 6:1; 9:29 (where A reads *Hellēnas*); and 11:20 (as a variant reading, although *Hellēnas* is probably to be preferred). The objection to the traditional interpretation of *Hellēnistai* as 'Gk.-speaking Jews' is that Paul, who spoke Gk., called himself *Hebraios* (Phil. 3:5), which in Acts 6:1 forms the contrast to *Hellēnistai* (*cf.* C. F. D. Moule, *ExpT* 70, 1958–9, p. 100). Various alternatives have been offered: *e.g.* Jews who spoke *only* Gk. (Moule, *loc. cit.*); Gk.-speaking diaspora Jews living in Palestine (J. A. T. Robinson, *Twelve New Testament Studies*, 1962, pp. 116f.); 'nonconformist' Jews influenced by Hellenism and noted for their opposition to the Temple (O. Cullmann, *ExpT* 71, 1959–60, pp. 8–12, 39–43; also *The Johannine Circle*, 1976).

S.S.S.

GREETING. Following modern idiom, RSV changes AV 'salutation' invariably to 'greeting', the verb 'salute' to 'greet' or some equivalent. The social courtesies intended have six main biblical forms:

1. An epistolary message of greeting, involving no personal encounter. Paul occasionally uses the noun *aspasmos*, more frequently the cognate verb *aspazomai*, a customary formula in contemporary Gk. correspondence, as the papyri prove (see *MM*). The greeting may be in the name of the writer, or of some other person specified by him (*cf.* Rom. 16, *etc.*).

2. A formal greeting with obeisance from subject to monarch, invoking, with oriental exaggeration, eternal life for him (*cf.* Ne. 2:3, *etc.*, Heb.; Dn. 2:4, *etc.*, Aram.).

3. A face-to-face greeting, formal, verbal, perhaps with hand gesture, but without physical contact. The Gk. descriptive terms are the same as Paul's (Mt. 10:12; Mk. 12:38, *etc.*). Note the mock homage to Jesus in Mk. 15:18. The uttered word was frequently the imperative *chaire*, plural *chairete*, 'rejoice', AV 'Hail!' (Mt. 27:29, *etc.*). The infinitive *chairein* is also used (*cf.* 2 Jn. 11; 1 Macc. 10:18, 25). The commonest Heb. terms are connected with blessing (root *bārak̠*, 2 Ki. 4:29, *etc.*), or with the invoking of peace (*šā'al lᵉ šālôm*, 1 Sa. 17:22, *etc.*). Modern Heb. and Arab. greetings are based on the same vocabulary stock (*cf. šālôm*, *salaam*).

4. A formal cheek kiss, Heb. *nāšaq* and cognate noun; Gk. *philēma* (*cf.* 1 Sa. 10:1; Rom. 16:16, *etc.*). The double-cheek kiss is still daily exchanged between males in the Orient. **5.** The affectionate kiss, normally on the mouth, implying greater intimacy (same words, Gn. 29:11; Ct. 1:2). **6.** The deceitful kiss (same words, Pr. 27:6; the kiss of Judas, Mt. 26:48, *etc.*).

Greetings might be forbidden through urgency (2 Ki. 4:29; Lk. 10:4) or to prevent association with error (2 Jn. 11).

BIBLIOGRAPHY. G. Finkenrath, *NIDNTT* 2, pp. 356–358; H. Windisch, *TDNT* 1, pp. 496–502.

R.A.S.

GRINDER (from Heb. *ṭāḥan*, 'to grind'). Grinding in the E is usually done by women (*cf.* Mt. 24:41). In Ec. 12:3 the word is used in a metaphorical sense to denote the teeth. For a full discussion of the Jewish poetic imagery employed here, see *ICC*, *Ecclesiastes*, pp. 186ff.

J.D.D.

GRUDGE. Frequently found in the earliest translations, this word was altered to 'murmur' in most of the AV occurrences, then similarly changed in all but two of the RV passages. Where it is retained in AV several words are thus rendered, *viz.* Heb. *nāṭar*, 'to keep anger' (Lv. 19:18, so RSV); Heb. *lûn*, *lîn*, 'to murmur' (Ps. 59:15, RSV 'growl'); Gk. *stenazō*, 'to groan, sigh' (Jas. 5:9, RSV 'grumble'); Gk. *gongysmos*, 'grudging' (1 Pet. 4:9, so RSV); Gk. *ek lypēs*, 'grudgingly', 'out of grief' (2 Cor. 9:7, RSV 'reluctantly'). RSV translates 'grudge' at Dt. 28:54, 56; Mk. 6:19, *enechō* (AV quarrel); 'grudging' at Dt. 15:10, *rā'a'* (AV 'grieve').

J.D.D.

GUARD. In the OT the word translates four Heb. terms. **1.** *ṭabbāḥ*. The word originally signified royal 'slaughterers' (*BDB*), but later came to mean guardsmen or bodyguard, being used of Pharaoh's bodyguard (Gn. 37:36; 39:1) and of Nebuchadrezzar's bodyguard (2 Ki. 25:8–10). (In Israel Aegean mercenaries [Cherethites and Pelethites] formed

David's bodyguard, while Carian troops seem to have had a similar appointment in the time of Athaliah [2 Ki. 11:4, 19].) **2.** *mišma'aṯ*, from *šāma'*, 'hear', 'respond', the attitude of an obedient body of subjects, was sometimes the name given to the bodyguard (2 Sa. 23:23; *cf.* 1 Sa. 22:14). **3.** *mišmār* denotes 'guard', 'watch' or 'guardhouse' in a camp (Lv. 24:12; Nu. 15:34), or 'guard-post' (Ne. 7:3). **4.** *rāṣîm*, lit. 'runners', were the runners of the king who acted also as the royal bodyguard (1 Sa. 22:17; *cf.* 1 Ki. 1:5; 14:27). (*FOOTMAN.)

'Guard' occurs once in the AV of the NT (Acts 28:16), but the text is disputed (*CAPTAIN). The Temple had its own police department known as the Temple Guard, who were mostly Levites and whose task, among other things, was to keep out the forbidden Gentiles (*cf.* Mt. 27:65, RSV). The *spekoulatōr*, a Latinism found in Mk. 6:27, was one of ten such officers attached to a legion who acted mostly as couriers but sometimes as executioners; one such was in the employ of Herod Antipas.

R.P.G.

GUDGODAH. One of the Israelite encampments in the wilderness according to Dt. 10:7. Hor-haggidgad in Nu. 33:32–33 is probably another form of the same name. Its location is not known, although its proximity to *Bene-jaakan and *Jotbathah suggests that it was somewhere in the mountains W of Wadi Arabah. The suggestion that the name survives in Wadi Ḫadaḫid, in this area, is unlikely from a linguistic point of view. Baumgartner, comparing an Arab. word, has suggested that it may be an animal name, 'a cricket': the first element of the longer form, Hor, appears to mean 'cave'.

BIBLIOGRAPHY. *KB*, pp. 169, 335 (bibl.).

G.I.D.

GULF (Gk. *chasma*, 'chasm' (RSV), from *chainō*, 'to gape' or 'yawn'). Found only in the parable of Lazarus and Dives (Lk. 16:19–31, AV), this word is sometimes connected with an ill-defined rabbinical belief that the souls of righteous and wicked exist after death in different compartments of Hades (see J. M. Creed, *The Gospel according to St Luke*, 1942, pp. 212–213), with no road between them, but so situated as to allow the inhabitants of each to see those of the other. There is, however, insufficient evidence for this application of the word. Any interpretation, moreover, must take into account the oriental love of imagery, for which full scope is provided by a subject such as this (which in various forms was a common feature of the writings of classical antiquity).

The passage seems to imply also that the gulf is seen in this earthly life, in which the respective conditions of Lazarus and Dives are reversed. Abraham, after outlining this aspect, is made to say, 'In all these things' (v. 26 RVmg.) '... there is a great gulf fixed.' It seems clear that the gulf is in character as well as in condition, otherwise the false impression would be given that some stigma attaches to riches in themselves. The story reminds us that it is of the very essence of the gospel that there is between believers and unbelievers a fundamental difference in this world and in the next. (*LAZARUS AND DIVES, *ABRAHAM'S BOSOM.)

J.D.D.

HABAKKUK, BOOK OF.

I. Outline of contents

The prophecy attributed to Habakkuk consists of six sections.

a. 1:1–4. The prophet cries to God because of the lawlessness he sees around him and asks how long it will go unpunished.

b. 1:5–11. As if in reply, God announces that he is raising up the Chaldeans and describes the fierceness of their armies and their contempt for all who stand in their way.

c. 1:12–17. But if God is holy, how can he allow the brutal inhumanity and idolatry of the Chaldeans, whose atrocities are worse than the evils that they are sent to punish?

d. 2:1–5. The prophet waits in imagination upon his watchtower to see if God will resolve his dilemma. The answer comes in the asseveration of the principle that the pride of the Chaldean will be his downfall and the faithfulness of the righteous will be his salvation.

e. 2:6–20. A taunt-song (*māšāl*) addressed to the Chaldeans, consisting of a series of five woes predicting dire consequences upon them for the acts of inhumanity for which they are responsible.

f. 3:1–19. If this psalm of Habakkuk has any connection with the theme of the earlier chapters it describes a revelation of God coming in his awful majesty to bring judgment upon the nations and salvation to his people.

II. Authorship

So little is known of the prophet Habaḳkuk that anything that is written about him must be conjectural and based on internal evidence. His name may be connected with a Heb. root meaning 'embrace' (*ḥbq*) or with an Assyr. plant name, *ḥambaḳuḳu*. The Gk. form of his name is *Hambakoum*. The suggestions that he was the son of the Shunammite woman of 2 Ki. 4:16, or the watchman of Is. 21:6, have as little evidence to support them as the tradition associating him with Daniel in the lions' den (so Bel and the Dragon, verses 33ff.).

III. Date and background

There has been considerable discussion among scholars about which if any of these sections are original to Habakkuk, and there is no agreement with regard to unity, authorship and date. The only clear historical reference is to the Chaldeans in 1:6 and so the prophecy is usually dated at the close of the 7th century BC shortly after the battle of Carchemish (605 BC) when the Chaldeans routed the Egyptians under Pharaoh Neco on the fords of the Euphrates and marched W to subjugate King Jehoiakim of Judah.

The theory of Duhm and C. C. Torrey that 'Chaldeans' (Heb. *kaśdîm*) should read 'Kittim' in the sense of 'Greeks' was based on the problematical 1:9 (Heb. lit. 'the eagerness of their faces is *eastwards*'). This would fit in better with Alexander's invasion from the W (and a 4th-century date) than with Nebuchadrezzar's from the N or E. But the text of 1:9 is extremely difficult; there is no textual evidence for the reading 'Kittim' in 1:6; and the traditional dating is to be preferred.

IV. The prophet's message

A unity of theme may be observed throughout the book, though whether this is due to 'the molding influence of liturgical use' (Irwin) or to unity of authorship cannot be known. Habakkuk deals with the moral problem of God's raising up of the Chaldeans to inflict his judgment upon Judah, when their cruelty and barbarity are a denial of his righteousness. The answer given in 2:4 is that a man's arrogance carries within it the seed of his ruin, whereas the faithful man is assured of living in the light of God's favour. Clearly the full Pauline meaning of faith is not to be found in this oft-quoted scripture (*cf.* Rom. 1:17; Gal. 3:11; Heb. 10:38); indeed, it is doubtful whether Pauline faith could have been expressed by any Heb. word. But the NT gives a legitimate development of the prophet's thought through the medium of the LXX translation, *pistis*.

The Commentary on Habakkuk of the Dead Sea Scrolls interprets 1:4–2:20 only in the light of the history of the Qumran sect and gives no clue to the meaning of the prophecy. Although on 1:6 and elsewhere it reads 'This means the Kittim', there is no suggestion that the original 'Kasdim' was in need of emendation.

BIBLIOGRAPHY. Commentaries: S. R. Driver, A. B. Davidson, J. H. Eaton, standard series. C. C. Torrey, 'The Prophecy of Habakkuk', in *Jewish Studies in Memory of George A. Kohut*, 1935; W. A. Irwin, 'The Psalm of Habakkuk', *JNES* 1, 1942, pp. 10–40; W. F. Albright, 'The Psalm of Habakkuk', in H. H. Rowley (ed.), *Studies in OT Prophecy*, 1950, pp. 1–18; D. W. Baker, *Nahum, Habakkuk and Zephaniah*, 1988. J.B.Tr.

HABOR. A river (the modern Ḫâbûr) which carries the waters of several streams draining the Mardin area SW to the middle Euphrates. It ran through the Assyr. province of *Gozan (*nᵉhar gôzān*, 'river of Gozan') and was one of the locations to which the Israelites were deported by the Assyrians (2 Ki. 17:6; 18:11; 1 Ch. 5:26). T.C.M.

HACHILAH (Heb. *ḥᵃḵîlâ*, 'drought'). A hill in the wilderness of Judah where David was hidden when the Ziphites plotted to betray him to Saul (1 Sa. 23:19; 26:1, 3). The site is uncertain, but generally regarded as being near Dahret el-Kôlâ, between Ziph and *En-gedi. J.D.D.

HADAD. The name of a Syrian deity meaning 'the Thunderer' (Heb. *h^{a}ḏaḏ*; Akkad. *(H)ad(d)u* or Adad) the storm-god, also named in Ras Shamra texts as *Baal. A Hadad temple at Aleppo is known. The personal names Hadad, and their dialectal variant Hadar, are probably abbreviations of names compounded with this divine element, *e.g.*, *Hadadezer,*Ben-hadad, *Hadad-rimmon. There is as yet no evidence to support the view that Hadad was a specifically Edomite name, although it was borne by four rulers of that country.

1. The grandson of Abraham, being the son of Ishmael (Gn. 25:15 = 1 Ch. 1:30). The *MT* Hadad is supported by LXX readings, while the AV 'Hadar' follows the Syr. and other MSS.

2. A son of Bedad who came from Avith and defeated the Midianites in the plain of Moab. He was succeeded as king of Edom by Samlah (Gn. 36:35–36; 1 Ch. 1:46).

3. A later king of Edom, named Hadar in 1 Ch. 1:50, whose native village was Pau.

4. An Edomite of the ruling family who lived in the time of Solomon. He was a young child and fled to Paran when Joab murdered his family after Judah's conquest of Edom. He took refuge in Egypt, where he married the pharaoh's daughter, his son Genubath being brought up at the Egyptian court. When Hadad heard of the death of David and Joab he returned to Edom and plotted against Solomon (1 Ki. 11:14–22, 25).

BIBLIOGRAPHY. A. LeMaire, 'Hadad l'Édomite ou Hadad l'Araméen', *Biblische Notizen* 43, 1988, pp. 14–15. D.J.W.

HADADEZER. This Aramaean personal name, meaning '(the god) *Hadad is (my) helper', was borne by at least two kings of the Damascus region. It is sometimes written 'Hadarezer', perhaps reflecting an Aramaic dialectal variant, in 2 Sa. 10:16–19; 1 Ch. 18:3–8 (AV).

Hadadezer, son of Rehob, was king of Zobah, E of Hamath, whose territory at one time included part of the bank of the river Euphrates (2 Sa. 8:3). He was defeated by David and the gilded shields of his bodyguard taken as trophies to Jerusalem together with booty from the towns of Betah and Berothai in his territory, despite the advance of reinforcements from Damascus. Following this reversal his old enemy, Toi of Hamath, sent gifts to David (v. 10). However, Hadadezer continued to rule his territory and later supported the Ammonites in force in their war with David (2 Sa. 10:16–19; 1 Ch. 18:3–8). When the Israelites again defeated the Syrian forces *Rezon, a refugee from the court of Hadadezer, became king in Damascus and plotted against Solomon (1 Ki. 11:23).

A Hadadezer (Assyr. *Adad-'idri*), king of Damascus, is named as one of the allies who, with Ahab of Israel, opposed Shalmaneser III at Qarqar in 853 BC (*DOTT*, pp. 47–48). These kings are sometimes identified with *Ben-hadad I–II. See *Or* 34, 1965, pp. 472–473 for name. D.J.W.

HADAD-RIMMON. The mourning in Jerusalem on the death of Josiah in battle with Neco II of Egypt in 609 BC is compared with that 'of Hadad-rimmon in the plain of Megiddo' (Zc. 12:11). It is commonly supposed to be the name of a place near Megiddo and thus to be identified with modern Rummaneh, S of that city. However, the form of the name meaning '(the god) *Hadad is (the god) Rimmon', and the context, may show that it is a composite name. Both elements mean 'the thunderer' and are local names or epithets for Baal, and such a name can be compared with the deity Rashap-shalmon. The allusion would then be to the great mourning normally associated with this deity personifying the elements in ceremonies at Megiddo, and perhaps a counterpart to that described in Jdg. 11:37–40 (*DOTT*, p. 133). D.J.W.

HADRACH. A place on the N boundaries of Syria (Zc. 9:1). Mentioned in the Aram. inscription of Zakur of Hamath, *c.* 780 BC, it is the Hatarikka of Assyr. inscriptions, once the seat of a district governor, near Qinneṣrin, 25 km S of Aleppo (*HUCA* 18, 1944, p. 449, n. 108). A.R.M.

HAGAR. A Semitic, not an Egyptian, name and thus perhaps given to the woman by Abraham when he left Egypt. It may mean 'flight' or something similar, *cf.* Arab. *hegira.* Hagar was an Egyp. bondservant in Abraham's household, handmaid to Sarah; Abraham probably acquired her during his visit to Egypt. With the passing years Abraham felt keenly the lack of a son and heir, and, after the war of the kings (Gn. 14), with magnificent faith believed God's promise that he would indeed have a son (Gn. 15:2–6). But as time still passed, Abraham and Sarah had doubts, and sought to gain an heir by their own unsanctioned efforts: in accordance with the customary law of the period (attested in tablets from Ur and Nuzi), the childless Sarah urged Abraham to have a son by her servant Hagar—so Ishmael was born, the son of a slave-woman (Gn. 16). In conception, Hagar despised the barren Sarah, and fled into the desert from Sarah's wrath. At a well, God commanded her to return to her mistress and promised her numerous descendants. Awed by this experience of God, Hagar called the well 'the well of him who lives and sees me' (Beer-lahai-roi). In due course (Gn. 21:1–7) the promised son, Isaac, was born, the gift of God's initiative and supernatural grace. At Isaac's weaning the half-slave Ishmael mocked; God then commanded Abraham (against the custom of the day) to expel Hagar and her son (Gordon, *BA* 3, 1940, p. 3), for the line of promise was in Isaac, and God had another destiny for Ishmael (Gn. 21:9–14). In the wilderness the fugitive pair soon ran out of water, and Hagar sat apart from Ishmael to avoid witnessing his death. God then showed her a well of water. Ishmael grew up in Paran (in NE Sinai) as a hunter with the bow, and Hagar procured him a wife from her Egyp. homeland (Gn. 21:15–21).

Two millennia later, Paul had to rebuke his Galatian converts for hankering after a deceptive 'righteousness' gained by self-exertion in obeying the stipulations of the law, instead of continuing in

Christ by faith (Gal. 3–5). He used the story of Hagar and Ishmael, Sarah and Isaac, as an allegory. Ishmael was the son, by earthly effort, of Hagar the slave. Similarly, the Jews (*i.e.* 'the present Jerusalem') were 'sons' of the Sinai covenant (pictured as Hagar); their failure to keep it faultlessly demonstrated the power of sin and the futility of seeking justification by self-effort. Isaac was the son of a promise received by faith, the gift of God's grace: Sarah typified the covenant of promise and grace (*cf.* Gn. 15) and all reborn spiritually in saving faith are numbered with Isaac. As Isaac was the true heir and Hagar and Ishmael were expelled, so the law as a limited phase in God's plan of redemption was in due time supplanted by the covenant of faith established finally and eternally in Christ (Gal. 4:21–5:1). K.A.K.

HAGGAI, BOOK OF. This little book, as we know from the dates it contains, records messages given between August and December 520 BC. Some 18 years had elapsed since the return from Babylon permitted by Cyrus, but work on restoring the Temple had long since ceased (Ezr. 4:24). Haggai's main task was to rouse his contemporaries to action once more and in this he was assisted by the prophet Zechariah (Ezr. 5:1).

I. Contents and structure

Despite the internal evidence of chronological sequence the order of the text has been questioned and its rearrangement suggested (*cf.* NEB). The biblical order is attested by the *Scroll of the Twelve* from the caves of Murabba'at, the earliest known Heb. MS, and follows a recognizable pattern. The structure is a twofold accusation, response, assurance:

Accusation	1:1–11	2:10–17
Response	1:12–15	2:18–19
Assurance	2:1–9	2:20–23

Though there may well have been editorial arrangement of the prophecies, the immediacy of the message and the absence of comment upon it suggest that little time elapsed between the prophet's preaching and the publication of his words.

II. Development of theme

The twofold presentation serves a specific purpose. In the first half the prophet starts with the present and looks back over the previous 18 years, whereas in the second half he works from the present to the future, though in each case the assurance section contains references to promised blessing.

Part I. 1:1–11. Catching the current mood of lethargy Haggai intersperses accusation with diagnostic comment on the economic situation. One directive (v. 8) provides a goal for the community and a test of their willingness to accept correction.

1:12–15. The response is unprecedented. Zerubbabel the prince and Joshua the priest lead their people into unanimous acknowledgment of Haggai's authority as God's spokesman. With the promise of God's Spirit among them they make a start 3 weeks later on rebuilding the Temple.

2:1–9. After a further 4 weeks discouragement was again hindering progress. Because of their poverty the new building was necessarily basic, lacking the splendour of Solomon's Temple. Nevertheless it would one day be beautified with silver and gold contributed by the nations, and would then surpass even that of Solomon.

Part II. 2:10–17. It was one thing to reconstruct the Temple but quite another to remove the contamination caused by its desecration under heathen armies. The mere offering of sacrificial meat in their ritual could not ensure acceptance by the Lord. Far from being a place of cleansing, the Temple-skeleton had been a defilement. Repentance was all-important, and of that obedience to the prophet was a tangible proof. God would acknowledge this change of heart by changing shortage into abundance.

2:18–19. The people had responded and the Lord would once again give his blessing. That very December day, when no farmer could predict what next year's harvest would be, God promised prosperity as a sign of his approval.

2:20–23. There are echoes here of the imagery used in 2:1–9. In 520 BC there was little in the political scene to cheer the returned exiles. The great powers were entrenched, but the day of their overthrow was imminent. Then the Davidic prince, Zerubbabel, God's chosen servant, would be the Lord's executive, like the signet ring which was used to seal royal documents (*cf.* Je. 22:24), and would perform all his will.

According to Haggai, there is a strict correlation between commitment to God's cause and the enjoyment of his good gifts. There are priorities too. When these are observed and God has pride of place, he will see that the needs of his work and of his people are met. For the fulfilment of the promise to Zerubbabel, see Mt. 1:12; Lk. 3:27.

BIBLIOGRAPHY. J. G. Baldwin, *Haggai, Zechariah, Malachi*, *TOTC*, 1972; R. L. Smith, *Micah–Malachi*, *WBC*, 1984; P. A. Verhoef, *The Books of Haggai and Malachi*, *NIC*, 1987. J.G.B.

HAGRITES. A prosperous tribe or confederation living E of Gilead which was attacked by Israelites in the time of Saul (1 Ch. 5:10, 18–22); in Ps. 83:6–8 they are listed among the enemies of Israel. They are mentioned in association with Aramaean tribes in an inscription of Tiglath-pileser III and the name also occurs in inscriptions in Nabataean, Sabaean, *etc.* They are probably the *Agraioi* mentioned by Strabo, Ptolemy and Pliny. The resemblance to the name Hagar has inclined some to consider them as her descendants (Ishmaelites), but this is improbable. R.P.G.

HAIR. The normal Israelite custom, for both sexes, seems to have been to let the hair grow to considerable length. Absalom's luxuriant growth is recorded with apparent admiration (2 Sa. 14:26). It was only the weight of it that forced him to have it cut annually. Barbers are mentioned (Ezk. 5:1), but their function was to trim rather than to crop the hair. But by the NT period long hair was a 'shame' to a man (1 Cor. 11:14), although Paul made that statement to a church in Greece. Women, on the other hand, wore the hair long and practically uncut in both periods. The Talmud does mention women's hairdressers, but the root of the word (*mᵉḡaddᵉlâ*) is 'to plait' rather than 'to cut'. Baldness was disliked, perhaps because of its possible connection with leprosy (*cf.* Lv. 13), and evidently the youths' reference to Elisha's baldness was a studied insult. In Egypt the head and face were shaved, however, and Joseph had to comply with the local customs (Gn. 41:14). Dark hair was admired in both sexes; but grey hair was very honourable, and revered accordingly (*AGE, OLD AGE). Indeed, we find God himself portrayed as having grey (or white) hair (Dn. 7:9; *cf.* Rev. 1:14). But Herod the Great apparently preferred a youthful appearance, for he dyed his hair when it began to go grey.

The hair was treated in various ways. Samson had seven plaits, and women frequently braided or plaited their hair. Soldiers proceeding to battle let it hang loose, but to leave it unkempt was a sign of mourning; tearing it betokened fear and distress. The trimming of it had to be done in special ways; the forelock must never be cut (Lv. 19:27), since this was a feature of some idolatrous cults (*cf.* Dt. 14:1). To this day orthodox Jews observe this custom; small boys can be seen with the whole head cropped close, except for the ringlets hanging at the ears. The priests were given instructions about their hair by Ezekiel (44:20). The Nazirite had to leave his hair untrimmed so long as his vow lasted, and then shave it completely. This shaving signified purification (Lv. 14:8). Another special case was that of Samson, the secret of whose strength was his untrimmed hair.

It was a sign of hospitality to anoint a guest's head (Lk. 7:46). The hair was frequently anointed on festive occasions (*cf.* Ps. 45:7). Swearing by the hair (or head) was a custom which Jesus could not commend (Mt. 5:36).

In metaphor and simile the hair was used to denote multitude, insignificance and fineness (Ps. 40:12; Mt. 10:29f.; Jdg. 20:16).

BIBLIOGRAPHY. L. Köhler, *Hebrew Man*, E.T. 1956, pp. 26ff. D.F.P.

HALAH. A place in Assyria to which Israelites were deported from Samaria (2 Ki. 17:6; 18:11; 1 Ch. 5:26; *cf.* Ob. 20, RSV 'exiles in Halah' by small emendation). There is no doubt this was Assyr. Halahhu, a town and district NE of Nineveh, giving its name to one of the gates of that city. Other proposed locations are far less likely. A.R.M.

HALAK (Heb. *ḥālāq*, 'smooth, bald'). A mountain (lit. 'the bald mountain') in Judaea which marked the S limit of Joshua's conquests (Jos. 11:17; 12:7). Its locality is described as 'going up to Seir'. Probably the modern Jebel Ḫalàq, W of the Ascent of Akrabbim. J.G.G.N.

HALLELUJAH. This is a transliteration of the Heb. liturgical call *hal^e lû-yâh* = 'praise ye Yah', the shortened form of Yahweh (see *GOD, NAMES OF), which occurs 24 times in the Psalter. Though it is merely one variant of several calls to praise, the fact that with one exception (Ps. 135:3) it is always found at the beginning or end of psalms, and these all anonymous and so presumably among the later ones, suggests that it had become a standardized call to praise in the post-exilic Temple worship.

The psalms where it is found fall into groups: (1) Pss. 104–105 (at the end), 106 (at the beginning and end, the latter being part of the doxology to the Fourth Book of Psalter). (2) Pss. 111–113 (at the beginning), 115–117 (at the end), LXX is almost certainly correct in placing the repetition at the end of Ps. 113 at the beginning of Ps. 114, thus completing the series. (3) Ps. 135, at the beginning and end, but LXX correctly places the latter at the beginning of Ps. 136. (4) Pss. 146–150, at the beginning and end of each.

From the NT ('Alleluia', Rev. 19:1, 3–4, 6) the call has been taken over into Christian worship. Most of the Hallelujah psalms play a special role in synagogue worship. Pss. 113–118, the Egyp. Hallel, are sung at the feasts of *Passover, *Pentecost, *Tabernacles and *Dedication, at the first Pss. 113–114 being sung before the meal, Pss. 115–118 after the third cup (*cf.* Mk. 14:26). Pss. 135–136 are sung on the sabbath, and the Great Hallel (Pss. 146–150), with Ps. 145, at all morning services. H.L.E.

HAM. 1. (Heb. *ḥām*, LXX *cham*; etymology uncertain). One of the sons of Noah, probably the second (Gn. 5:32; 6:10; 7:13; 9:18; 1 Ch. 1:4, 8; though *cf.* Gn. 9:20–24), and ancestor of many descendants (*NATIONS, TABLE OF). In 1 Ch. 4:40 and Pss. 78:51; 105:23, 27; 106:22 the name is used to indicate one section of his descent: Egypt (*MIZRAIM). From its biblical usage the term 'Hamitic' is applied by modern authors to a group of languages of which Egyptian is one, and for precision it is limited to this linguistic sense, a Hamitic 'race' not being recognized by modern anthropological classifications. In the biblical sense, however, genetic descent is all that is implied, and with the movement and intermarriage of peoples and the changes of language which took place in ancient times common descent from Ham would not necessarily imply common habitat, language, or even race in a recognizable form. At the end of the Flood when Noah was drunk Ham saw him naked and informed his two brothers, who covered up their father. In consequence of this, Noah put a curse upon Canaan (Gn. 9:20–27). Many explanations of this apparent cursing of Canaan for what Ham had done have been put forward, perhaps the most plausible being that Canaan did something not recorded which was worthy of cursing and that the phrase 'his younger son' (*b^e nô haqqāṭān*, lit. 'his son/grandson, the little [one]') in v. 24 might refer to Canaan. This would be consistent with the twice-repeated statement (vv. 18, 22) that Ham was the father of Canaan.

2. *Hām*. The name of a city whose inhabitants, the Zuzim, were smitten by Chedorlaomer in the time of Abraham (Gn. 14:5). The site, though probably somewhere in Transjordan, is unknown. LXX (*hama autois*) interprets the Heb. *b^e hām* 'in Ham' as *bāhem*, 'with them'. T.C.M.

HAMAN. The villain of the book of *Esther, who plots to massacre the Jews when his vanity is hurt by Mordecai's refusal to bow to him. He is eventually hanged on the gallows that he has prepared for Mordecai. He is called an *Agagite. His name may be derived from the Elamite god, Hum(b)an. J.S.W.

HAMATH (Heb. *ḥ^a maṯ*, 'fortress, citadel'). City on the E bank of the Orontes, lying on one of the

'Hamath' (hmt) *inscribed in Aramaic letters on an ivory label, probably captured by Sargon II and taken to Nimrud* (*Calah*). *9·2 cm × 6·5 cm. 8th cent.* BC.

main trade-routes to the S from Asia Minor. Gn. 10:18 describes it as Canaanite. In David's time, under King Toi (or Tou), it was friendly towards Israel (2 Sa. 8:9–10; 1 Ch. 18:9–10). Toi's son is named Joram in 2 Sa. 8:10. This is probably not a Yahweh name ('Yah is exalted'), but an abbreviation of Hadoram as given in 1 Ch. 18:10. Connection of a Hamathite rebel called *Ya'u-bidi* by Sargon of Assyria with Yahweh is also unlikely (*cf. ANET*, p. 285; *DOTT*, p. 59). Solomon controlled it (2 Ch. 8:4), and it was conquered by Jeroboam II (*c.* 780 BC, 2 Ki. 14:28) and Sargon (*c.* 721 BC, *cf.* 2 Ki. 18:33f.; Is. 36:18f.; 37:13, 18f.), some of its inhabitants being settled by the Assyrians in *Samaria worshipping their deity *Ashima there (2 Ki. 17:24ff.). Palace buildings of the 9th and 8th centuries BC were excavated by a Danish team, 1931–8 (see E. Fugmann, *Hama, l'Architecture des périodes préhellénistiques*, 1958). Inscriptions in Hittite hieroglyphs, cuneiforms and Aramaic were found. According to the Babylonian Chronicle, it was at Hamath that Nebuchadrezzar overtook the Egyptians fleeing from Carchemish in 605 BC (*cf.* D. J. Wiseman, *Chronicles of Chaldaean Kings*, 1956, p. 69). The city was known in Greek and Roman times as Epiphaneia; today it is *Ḥamāh*. The ideal N boundary of Israel reached 'Labo of Hamath', formerly rendered 'the entering in of Hamath', *e.g.* Nu. 34:8; Jos. 13:5; Am. 6:14, but probably modern Lebweh, NNE of Baalbek, at the watershed of the Beqa' valley, near one source of the Orontes, so at the head of the road N to Hamath, Assyrian Laba'u in the province of Supite (*ZOBAH). For discussion see R. North, *Mélanges de l'Université S. Joseph* 46, 1970–1, pp. 71–103.

J.G.G.N.
A.R.M.

HAMMURAPI. (Akkad. [Amorite] Hammu-rapi, '(the god) Hammu heals'). **1.** King of Babylon *c.* 1792–1750 BC, sixth in line of First Amorite Dynasty. **2.** Name of two kings of Yamhad (Aleppo), the first *c.* 1760 BC. **3.** King of Kurda, mid-2nd millennium BC. **4.** Common 2nd millennium BC personal name especially in Upper Mesopotamia. Formerly **1** was identified with *Amraphel (Gn. 14:1).

Hammurapi (more correct than Hammurabi) as 'Governor of Babylon' was stated as having ten or fifteen kings 'going with him' as had his contemporary Rim-Sin of Larsa, while Ibal-piel of Eshnunna had twenty. The same Mari letter shows that all these were less powerful than the ruler of Yamhad.

Initially Hammurapi devoted himself to gaining control of *Babylonia and of the Euphrates waters. By 1764 BC he had defeated a coalition of Ashur, Eshnunna and Elam and the next year defeated Rim-Sin and by 1761 BC Zimrilim of *Mari. His reign was marked by a distinctive personal style which sought to unify Mesopotamia under a single ruler. He is now adjudged a weak administrator. A selection of his legal judgments (not a 'code' of laws, *e.g.* omission of homicide laws) survives on a diorite stele found at Susa in AD 1902. In this he reports to the national god Marduk on his role as 'king of justice' towards the end of his reign. The 282 sections of the Laws of Hammurapi (= LH) are roughly arranged to cover cases of theft and miscellaneous decisions (LH 1–25), property (26–49), commercial law (100–126), marriage (127–161), priestesses (178–184), adoption (185–194), assault (195–240), agricultural cases (241–267), rates and wages (268–277) and an appendix on slaves (278–282). Some of the cases and decisions are similar to earlier collections of laws (Ur-Nammu, Lipit-Ishtar, Eshnunna). A few are worded similarly to OT cases, *e.g.* false witness (LH 1, 3–4; *cf.* Ex. 23:1–3; Dt. 19:16–20), kidnapping (LH 14; *cf.* Ex. 21:16.), loss of animals on deposit (LH 266–7; *cf.* Ex. 22:10–13), just as warning to the owner of goring ox (Ex. 21:35–36) compares with Eshnunna Law 53. Many of the specific cases concerning marriage, divorce and sexual offences, *e.g.* the death penalty for both parties in adultery with a married woman (Dt. 22:22; LH 129), have a similar approach. In other cases the offences are the same but the penalty differs, the Hebrew being seemingly the more consistently humane. In most cases the legal treatment differs, but precise comparison with OT is difficult since only the established fact (without supporting evidence) is given, followed by the oral judicial decision. These laws therefore represent a local Babylonian manifestation of the attitude to law and order common throughout much of the ancient Near East.

BIBLIOGRAPHY. C. J. Gadd, *CAH*, 2/1, 1973, pp. 176–227; D. J. Wiseman, *Vox Evangelica* 8, 1973, pp. 5–21; W. F. Leemans, 'Hammurapi's Babylon', *Sumer* 41, 1985, pp. 91–96. D.J.W.

HAMOR. '(He-)ass', see below. The ruler of Shechem in the time of Jacob (Gn. 33:19–34:31), from whose citizens (lit. 'sons', a common Sem. usage, *cf.* below) Jacob bought a plot of land (Gn. as cited; Jos. 24:32). Both Hamor and his son Shechem fell in Simeon and Levi's slaughter of the Shechemite menfolk and despoliation of the city in revenge for the humiliation of their sister *Dinah. In the period of the judges Hamor's name was still attached to Shechem (Jdg. 9:28). In the NT, in his dramatic speech to the council, Stephen telescopes Abraham's purchase of the Machpelah cave with Jacob's acquisition of the plot at Shechem—a realistic mark of the rapid flow of Stephen's impromptu, lightning exposition of Israel's history, not an error by Luke (Acts 7:16).

Animal personal names such as Hamor, 'ass', were common in biblical lands and times. *Cf.* Merānum ('pup'), the name of a doctor in the Mari tablets of patriarchal date (Bottéro and Finet, *Archives Royales de Mari*, 15, 1954, p. 152, refs.; compare Mendenhall, *BASOR* 133, 1954, p. 26, n. 3). Egypt also affords many examples.

Killing an ass was sometimes part of covenant-making (Mendenhall, *op. cit.*), but to interpret the phrase 'sons of Hamor' as 'members of a confederacy'—as suggested by Albright, *Archaeology and the Religion of Israel*, 1953, p. 113—is unnecessary. 'Son' of a place or person often means simply a citizen of that place or member of that person's tribal group. *Cf.* the common phrase 'children (sons) of Israel', 'daughter of Jerusalem', as well as Assyr. usage. K.A.K.

HANANEL. In Ne. 3:1, a *Jerusalem tower, lying between the Sheep and Fish Gates, at the NE corner of the city. It is closely connected with the Tower of the *Hundred, and some scholars would equate the two, or else make them two parts of the same fortress. AV spells the name 'Hananeel'; Heb. is *ḥ*ª*nan'ēl*, 'God is gracious'.

The Targum of Zc. 14:10 seems to place the tower on the W of the city, by identifying it with the later Hippicus; this cannot be correct. D.F.P.

HANANIAH (Heb. 'Yahweh has been gracious'). A Heb. name occurring frequently in the OT and, under its Gk. form *Ananias, in later times also.

1. A cult-prophet, son of Azur, whom Jeremiah denounced (Je. 28) for publicly declaring in the Temple that in 2 years' time, in opposition to Jeremiah's prophecy of 70 years (25:12), the booty taken from Jerusalem by Nebuchadrezzar would be restored, the captives returned and the power of Babylon broken. He confirmed his words by the symbolic action of removing from Jeremiah's neck the yoke worn as a symbol of Jeremiah's policy of submission to Babylon (27:2–3, 12), and breaking it. Jeremiah's denunciation, 'Yahweh has not sent you' (28:15), was shown to be true by the death of Hananiah 2 months later.

2. Father of a prince under Jehoiakim, king of Judah (Je. 36:12). **3.** Grandfather of Irijah, the officer of the guard who arrested Jeremiah as a traitor (Je. 37:13). **4.** One of Daniel's companions in captivity, renamed Shadrach (Dn. 1:6–7, 11, 19). **5.** Son of Zerubbabel (1 Ch. 3:19, 21). **6.** A Benjaminite (1 Ch. 8:24). **7.** Leader of one of the groups of musicians set up by David for the service of the Temple (1 Ch. 25:4, 23). **8.** A captain in Uzziah's army (2 Ch. 26:11). **9.** Commandant of the citadel whom Nehemiah put in charge of Jerusalem (Ne. 7:2). **10.** Various persons figuring in the lists of Ezra-Nehemiah (Ezr. 10:28; Ne. 3:8, 30; 10:23; 12:12, 41). J.B.Tr.

HAND. In comparison with the Gk. word *cheir* (which is translated only by 'hand', with some composite words such as *cheiropoiētos*, 'made with hands'), the two main Heb. words translated 'hand' in RSV have very wide meanings. *yāḏ* has many variant translations in RSV, and *kap̄* several, all of which are related to the primary meaning, 'hollow' or 'palm', from a root meaning 'curved' or 'bent'. *kap̄* is also the name of one of the letters of the Heb. alphabet, probably descriptive of its shape, which is somewhat like a reversed C.

In common with other parts of the body in Heb. thought, the hand is described as having apparently almost autonomous functions (1 Sa. 24:11). But the balancing of the phrases 'my power' and 'the might of my hand' in Dt. 8:17, and other examples of parallelism, indicate that this is far from absolute autonomy, the primary reference being to the action of the whole individual, although, at the same time, attention is specifically focused on the relevant functioning part (*cf.* Mt. 5:30).

Like the *arm, the hand (especially the right hand) is used as a symbol of might and power. In the case of 'hand', however, the figurative meaning has gone a step further than with 'arm'. See, *e.g.*, Jos. 8:20, where *yāḏ* is translated 'power'. There are several very common phrases in which the hand is used as a symbol of power, *e.g.*, in or out of 'the hand of one's enemies' (Ps. 31:15; Mk. 14:41). Conversely, the dropping of the hands symbolizes weakness or lack of resolution, and to strengthen them is to remedy that (Is. 35:3; Jdg. 9:24). Left-handed persons are specially noted (Jdg. 3:15).

Lifting the hand is symbolic of violence (1 Ki. 11:26) as well as of supplication (Ex. 9:33; 17:11; Ps. 28:2), the *gesture being indicative of the attitude or action. The word *kap̄*, indicating the open palm, is more frequently used in the latter sense.

Clasping hands (Jb. 17:3; AV, RSV 'give surety') ratified an agreement, as did also the placing of one's hand under another's *thigh (Gn. 24:9) or raising one's hand, as in a law court today (Gn. 14:22 [RSV 'I have sworn', lit. 'I have lifted my hand'] Ex. 17:16).

The touch of a person's hands was held to communicate authority, power or blessing, the right hand being more significant in this respect than the left, but both hands were often used (Gn.

48:13–14; Dt. 34:9). Notice especially the laying of the hands of the worshipper on the head of his sacrificial beast, where the communication of authority probably signified identity with the offering (Lv. 1:4); and the NT communication of the Holy Spirit or performance of miracles by the laying on of hands (Mk. 6:5; Acts 8:17–19; 19:11). This is but another indication that in Heb. thought, and to a certain extent in the NT as well, there was a close relation between what much Gk. and modern thought would designate separately as 'body' and 'spirit'.

'Absalom's monument' (2 Sa. 18:18) is literally 'Absalom's hand'.

BIBLIOGRAPHY. C. Ryder Smith, *The Bible Doctrine of Man*, 1951; D. P. Wright, 'The Gesture of Hand Placement in the Hebrew Bible and in Hittite Literature', *JAOS* 106, pp. 433–436. B.O.B.

HANDKERCHIEF (Gk. *soudarion*, in Acts 19:12; rendered as 'napkin' in Lk. 19:20; Jn. 11:44; 20:7). It transliterates Lat. *sudarium* defined etymologically (*sudor*, 'sweat') as a cloth for wiping perspiration. Catullus, however, uses the word for 'table-napkin' (12. 14), and Nero (Suetonius, *Nero* 25) undoubtedly used *sudarium* with the meaning of 'handkerchief'. E.M.B.

HANES. Is often identified with Egyp. *Ḥ(wt-nni-)-nsw*, Gk.-Lat. Heracleopolis magna, modern Ihnâsyeh el-Medîneh or Ahnâs, about 80 km upstream (*i.e.* S) of Cairo, and an important city in Middle Egypt. However, this does not really suit Is. 30:4, in the two parallel clauses: 'His officials are at Zoan, and his envoys reach Hanes.' *Zoan is Tanis in the NE Delta, the seat of the 22nd–23rd Dynasty pharaohs, and Lower Egypt advanced-headquarters of the Ethiopian 25th Dynasty, for Asiatic affairs. Hence the parallelism of the verse seems to demand that Hanes be closely linked with E Delta Tanis, not Upper Egypt Heracleopolis, far distant and irrelevant.

Two solutions are possible. W. Spiegelberg, *Aegyptologische Randglossen zum Alten Testament*, 1904, pp. 36–38, postulated a 'Heracleopolis parva' in the E Delta, arguing from Herodotus' mention of a province and city of Anysis there (2. 166, 137); this would then be Egyp. *Ḥ(wt-nni'-)nsw* of Lower Egypt, Heb. *Ḥanes*, and Assyr. *Ḫininsi. Cf.* Caminos, *JEA* 50, 1964, p. 94. Or Hanes may merely be a Heb. transcription of an Egyp. *ḥ(wt)-nsw*, 'mansion of the king', as the name of the pharaoh's palace in Zoan/Tanis itself. Either interpretation is plausible; neither is proven. Some refer the 'his' (princes, envoys) of Is. 30:4 to the Judaean king; but the natural antecedent is pharaoh in v. 3. Hence, with É. Naville, *Ahnas el Medineh*, 1894, p. 3, these are pharaoh's officials at Zoan and his envoys who come to treat with the Jewish emissaries, either at Hanes as an advance-post for Zoan (Naville, Spiegelberg), or summoned to the 'Ha-nesu', the king's palace, in Zoan itself. K.A.K.

HANNAH (Heb. *ḥannâ*, 'grace'). The favourite of the two wives of Elkanah, an Ephraimite who lived at Ramathaim-zophim (1 Sa. 1). The other wife, Peninnah, tormented her because she had no family. She vowed that if she bore a son she would devote him to God as a *Nazirite. This she did, and named him *Samuel. Her song of thanksgiving (1 Sa. 2:1–10) suggests that she was a prophetess. It contains the first mention of the king as Yahweh's Messiah ('his anointed'). There are many echoes of it in Mary's song when Christ's birth was announced (Lk. 1:46–55; *MAGNIFICAT). She brought Samuel a robe every year when she came to Shiloh to worship. She later became the mother of three sons and two daughters (1 Sa. 2:19, 21). J.W.M.

HARA. With *Halah, *Habor and *Gozan, a place to which Tiglath-pileser III removed rebellious Israelites in 734–732 BC (1 Ch. 5:26). An Assyr. site of this name is not known. 2 Ki. 17:6; 18:11, however, interpret *hārā'* as '*cities* of the Medes' and LXX 'mountains' may represent Heb. *hārê*, 'hill-country'. D.J.W.

HARAN (Heb. *ḥar(r)an*; Akkad. *ḫarrānu*, 'cross-roads'; Gk. *charrhan*, Acts 7:4). **1.** The city *c.* 32 km SE of Urfa (Edessa), Turkey, on the river Baliḫ, lies on the main route from Nineveh to Aleppo. Terah lived there with Abram (Gn. 11:31; *cf.* Acts 7:2, 4) before the latter migrated to Canaan (Gn. 12:1). It was the home of Isaac's bride *Rebekah. Jacob fled there to escape Esau (Gn. 29:4), married Leah and Rachel, daughters of Laban, and all his children (except Benjamin) were born there (Gn. 29:32–30:24).

Harran is referred to in texts from the Ur III period *c.* 2000 BC as a temple (*é.ḫul.ḫul*) for the worship of *Sin the moon-god, and its occupation is confirmed by archaeological evidence. Its strategic position made it a focus for Amorite tribes according to *Mari texts of the 2nd millennium BC, and later an Assyrian centre fortified by Adad-nirari I (*c.* 1310 BC) with a temple embellished by Tiglath-pileser I (*c.* 1115 BC). Harran rebelled and was sacked in 763 BC, an event used by Sennacherib's officials to intimidate Jerusalem (2 Ki. 19:12 = Is. 37:12). The city was restored by Sargon II, and the temple repaired and refurnished by Esarhaddon (675 BC) and by Ashurbanipal. After the fall of Nineveh (612 BC) Harran became the last capital of Assyria until its capture by the Babylonians in 609 BC. The Chaldean Dynasty's interest in the Babylonian temples led to the restoration of the Sin temples at Harran and at Ur. At the former the mother of Nabonidus (who lived to 104), and at the latter his daughter, were made the high priestesses. It was a thriving commercial city in contact with Tyre (Ezk. 27:23).

The site, excavated 1951–3, 1959, indicates clearly an occupation before the Assyrian period. The existing ruins are mainly from the Roman city near which the Parthians slew Crassus (53 BC) and from the later occupation by Sabaean and Islamic rulers in Harran, then called Carrhae. In AV of Acts 7:4 the city is named Charran.

2. Haran is also a personal name. (*a*) The son of Terah, brother of Abraham and Terah, father of Lot, Milcah and Iscah, who died at *Ur (Gn. 11:26–31); (*b*) A man of Judah, son of Caleb and his concubine Ephah (1 Ch. 2:46); (*c*) A Levite; son of Shimei, of Gershon (1 Ch. 23:9).

BIBLIOGRAPHY. S. Lloyd and W. Brice, *AS* 1, 1951, pp. 77–112; D. S. Rice, *AS* 2, 1952, pp. 36–84;

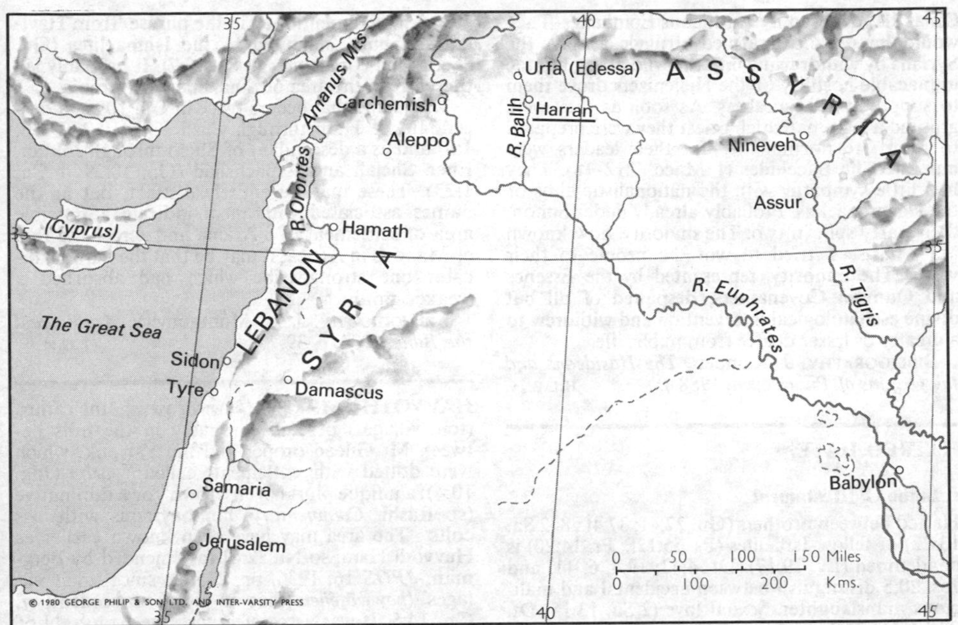

Harran ('Crossroads' or 'Highways') lies at a strategic point between Mesopotamia and the West.

C. J. Gadd, *AS* 8, 1958, pp. 35–92; K. Prag, *Levant* 2, 1970, pp. 63–94. D.J.W.

HARARITE. A designation applied to some of David's heroes: Shammah (*šammā'*) son of Agee, who was possibly the same as Shammah (*Šammâ*) (2 Sa. 23:11, 33); Jonathan son of Shage (1 Ch. 11:34); and Ahiam son of Sacar (1 Ch. 11:35). The name is unknown outside the Bible, and may be that of a tribe or city, or may simply mean 'mountain dweller' from *har*, 'mountain, hill'. T.C.M.

HARMON. A place (RSV, Am. 4:3) otherwise not mentioned in OT (AV interprets as 'the palace', from VSS. LXX has 'the mountains of Rimmon', possibly the hill of *Rimmon (Jdg. 20:45, 47). Various emendations, 'naked' (*'armôṯ*), 'devoted to destruction', have been suggested. More plausible is the suggestion, on the basis of Ugaritic *hrmn*, that this may be Harmel (S of *Kadesh on the Orontes).

BIBLIOGRAPHY. *BASOR* 198, 1970, p. 41. D.J.W.

HAROD (Heb. *ḥ^{a}rōḏ*, 'trembling'). A copious and beautiful spring at the foot of Mt Gilboa, E of Jezreel, which flows E into the Beth-shean valley. Here Gideon, confronting the Midianite hordes, reduced his army in two stages from 32,000 to 300 (Jdg. 7:1–8). Probably Saul and his army camped here prior to the fatal battle on Mt Gilboa (1 Sa. 29:1; *cf.* 31:1). Two of David's 'mighty men', Shammah and Elika (2 Sa. 23:25; 1 Ch. 11:27), came from Harod, possibly to be identified with the modern 'Ain Jalud. A.E.C.

HAROSHETH. Always occurs as 'Harosheth of the Nations' (*ḥ^{a}rōšeṯ hagôyīm*). It is found only in connection with *Sisera, a Canaanite commander who fought against Barak, and whose base it was (Jdg. 4:2, 13, 16). The battle is located in NW Palestine near the river Kishon. Mazar has suggested that a region rather than a city is implied, but v.16 would strongly suggest the latter (*cf.* Targum). Tell 'Amr NW of Megiddo and Tell el-Harbaj SE of Haifa have been suggested as possible sites, but of these the former appears to be disqualified by soundings indicating an absence of habitation before the 10th century BC. The city is not mentioned in extra-biblical documents, and the exact location remains uncertain.

BIBLIOGRAPHY. *LOB*, pp. 201, 203; B. Mazar, *HUCA* 24, 1952–3; pp. 80ff.; *GTT*, p. 288. W.O.

HARROW. A toothed implement dragged along the ground to break clods of earth after ploughing. The verb (Heb. *śāḏaḏ*) always occurs parallel to verbs of ploughing or breaking the soil (Jb. 39:10; Is. 28:24; Hos. 10:11, AV 'break'). The actual form of the implement used is uncertain; it was drawn by a led ox (Jb. 39:10), but there is no known representation of anything corresponding to a modern harrow in form. Heb. *ḥārîṣ* (2 Sa. 12:31) denotes a sharp or pointed implement, RSV 'picks' rather than AV 'harrows'. A.R.M.

HASIDAEANS. This is a transliteration of *Hasidaioi* in 1 Macc. 2:42; 7:13; 2 Macc. 14:6, though 'Hasmonaeans' may be the correct reading in the last case. RVmg. and modern literature prefer the underlying Heb. *ḥ^{a}sîdîm*. This term, meaning fundamentally 'loyal ones', is used frequently in the Psalms (usually 'saints' in EVV). It seems to have been adopted by the zealots for the law, when Hellenistic ideas came flooding in early in the 2nd century BC.

Their leader seems to have been the high priest

Onias III, deposed by Antiochus Epiphanes. They would have avoided armed struggle against the Syrians by withdrawing into the wilderness, but the implacable hostility of the Hellenizers drove them to support the Maccabees. As soon as they were granted a legitimate high priest they were prepared to return to normal life, but their leaders were murdered by Bacchides (1 Macc. 7:12–18). They had little sympathy with the nationalistic aims of the Hasmonaeans. Probably already under Simon, their party split in two. The majority, now known as *Pharisees, tried to win the people to their views. The minority, represented by the Essenes and Qumran Covenanters, despaired of all but divine eschatological intervention and withdrew to a greater or lesser degree from public life.

BIBLIOGRAPHY. J. Kampen, *The Hasideans and the Origins of Pharisaism*, 1988. H.L.E.

HATRED, HATE.

I. In the Old Testament

Hatred between brothers (Gn. 27:41; 37:4f., 8; 2 Sa. 13:22) or fellow-Israelites (Ps. 55:12f.; Pr. 14:20) is condemned (Lv. 19:17). Dt. 4:42; 19:4, 6, 11, and Jos. 20:5 distinguish between accidental and malicious manslaughter. Sexual love (2 Sa. 13:15; Dt. 22:13–16; 24:3; *cf.* Jdg. 14:16, see **III**, below) may turn to hatred. Personal enmity is sometimes tempered with mercy (Ex. 23:5; Jb. 31:29), but the enemies of Israel (2 Sa. 22:41; Ps. 129:5; Ezk. 23:28) or of the godly (Ps. 34:21; Pr. 29:10) are God's enemies too (Nu. 10:35; *cf.* Ex. 20:5; Dt. 5:9; 7:10). God hates both evil (Pr. 6:16; Am. 6:8) and evildoers (Dt. 32:41): so therefore do the righteous (Pss. 101:3; 139:21f.; 119:104, 113). God hates idolatry (Dt. 12:31; 16:22), injustice (Is. 61:8), worship that is inconsistent with conduct (Is. 1:14), and even sinful Israel herself (Ho. 9:15; *cf.* Je. 12:8).

II. In the New Testament

The Father (Jn. 15:24), Jesus (Jn. 7:7; 15:18, 24f.), and all Christians (Mk. 13:13; Lk. 6:22; Jn. 15:18–20; 17:14; 1 Jn. 3:13) are hated by the world; but believers must not hate either fellow-Christians (1 Jn. 4:20) or enemies (Mt. 5:43f.). Hatred of evil (Heb. 1:9 = Ps. 45:7; Rev. 2:6; *cf.* Mk. 3:5), though not of persons, is attributed to Christ. (*WRATH.)

III. Contrasted with love

'Hate' as opposed to 'love' in Gn. 29:31, 33 (*cf.* 30, 'loved . . . more'); Dt. 21:15–17; Mt. 6:24 = Lk. 16:13, implies the choice or preference of another rather than active hatred of what is not chosen or preferred. *Cf.* Mal. 1:2f. = Rom. 9:13 of God's election of Israel; Lk. 14:26 (*cf.* Mt. 10:37, 'loves . . . more'); Jn. 12:25 of the overriding claims of discipleship.

BIBLIOGRAPHY. J. Denney, *ExpT* 21, 1909–10, pp. 41f.; W. Foerster, *TDNT* 2, pp. 811–816; O. Michel, *TDNT* 4, pp. 683–694; H. Bietenhard, H. Seebass, *NIDNTT* 1, pp. 553–557. P.E.

HAVILAH (Heb. *ḥ*ᵃ*wîlâ*, 'circle', 'district'). **1.** A land (*'ereṣ*) in the neighbourhood of *Eden, through which meandered (*sābab*) the river Pishon, and in which was found gold, *bdellium and *shoham*-stone (Gn. 2:11–12). The location of the place is unknown.

2. An area mentioned in the phrase 'from Havilah to Shur'; inhabited by the Ishmaelites (Gn. 25:18) and Amalekites (1 Sa. 15:7). It probably lay therefore in the area of Sinai and NW Arabia.

3. A name that occurs twice in Gn. 10; as a descendant of Ham through Cush (Gn. 10:7; 1 Ch. 1:9) and as a descendant of Shem through Joktan, Eber, Shelah and Arpachshad (Gn. 10:29; 1 Ch. 1:23). These may be entirely distinct, but as the names associated with them indicate a possible area of settlement in S Arabia and across the Bab el-Mandeb in Africa, it may be that the name indicates one strong tribe which had absorbed a weaker group.

BIBLIOGRAPHY. J. A. Montgomery, *Arabia and the Bible*, 1934, p. 39. T.C.M.

HAVVOTH-JAIR (Heb. *ḥawwōṯ yā'îr*), 'the camps (tent-villages) of Jair', probably in the hills between Mt Gilead proper and the Yarmuk, which were dotted with settlements called *'*ᵃ*yārîm* (Jdg. 10:4); a unique plural of *'îr*, 'town', or a diminutive (so Rashi, *Commentary*) homonymous with 'ass colts'. The area may have been known earlier as Havvoth Ham; so Nu.32:41 (as emended by Bergman, *JPOS* 16, 1936, pp. 235ff.), since 'their villages' (*ḥawwōṯêhem*) has no plural antecedent; *cf.* Gn. 14:5. It was associated with the Argob, N of the Yarmuk, as part of Bashan, of which Og was the last king. Jair was credited with the conquest of the whole region (Dt. 3:14; 1 Ch. 2:23f.), including the Argob, to which the 'sixty cities' of Jos. 13:30; 1 Ch. 2:23 refer; *cf.* 1 Ki. 4:13. J.P.U.L.

HAZAEL (Heb. *ḥ*ᵃ*zā'ēl*, *ḥ*ᵃ*zâh'ēl*, 'El sees' or 'whom God beholds'). A powerful king of Syria (Aram), God's scourge to Israel during the reigns of Jehoram, Jehu and Jehoahaz. Elijah was commissioned to anoint him as one of the three ordained to complete the extirpation of Baal-worship that he had begun (1 Ki. 19:15–17). Later, Hazael, as the emissary of Ben-hadad II to Elisha, learnt that he was to be king and would become an oppressor of Israel, a prophecy speedily put into effect by his murder of Ben-hadad and assumption of the throne (2 Ki. 8:7–15). He fought against Jehoram at Ramoth-gilead (2 Ki. 8:28–29; 9:14–15), and frequently defeated Jehu, devastating the country E of Jordan as far S as the Arnon valley (2 Ki. 10:32–33). He continued his attacks in the reign of Jehoahaz, and Israel was preserved from complete destruction only by God's mercy (2 Ki. 13:3, 22f.). 2 Ki. 12:17–18 reveals a Syrian incursion into SW Palestine, probably with the aim of securing the trade-routes. Gath was taken, and Jerusalem threatened, and Hazael was bought off only with a tribute from the Temple treasures. Syria's ascendancy was checked only after Hazael's death, when his son, Ben-hadad III, was thrice defeated by Jehoash of Israel (2 Ki. 13:24–25). As one of the chief Syrian oppressors of Israel, the memory of Hazael's might lingered, so that half a century later Amos recalled his name as symbolizing the height of Syria's power which would yet feel the fire of God's judgment (Am. 1:4).

Hazael's name also occurs in Assyr. cuneiform inscriptions as an opponent of Shalmaneser III from 841 BC onwards. The wording of one text shows that the Assyrians not only knew Hazael to be a usurper ('son of a nobody', *ANET*, p. 280,

Ivory plaque inscribed '. . . son of Amma, for our lord Hazael, in the year of . . .'. Perhaps part of a tribute brought to Hazael, king of Damascus. From Arslan Tash, Syria. 9th century BC.

text (c), 14–2:1) but that they also knew that his predecessor was the victim of foul play (Weidner, *AfO* 13, 1940, pp. 233f.).

Hazael must have attained his throne before 841 BC, as his and the Israelite Joram's forces fought in 842 at Ramoth-gilead; 843 BC, as suggested by Unger (*Israel and the Arameans of Damascus*, 1957, p. 75), is an early enough date. Shalmaneser III and Hazael fought again in 837 BC. Thereafter for 30 years no further collision of the two kingdoms is known, until Adad-nirari III in *c.* 805–802 BC cowed the now ageing Hazael into submission (*ANET*, pp. 281–282; *DOTT*, pp. 51–52), referring to him as *Marī*, Aramaic for 'lord'. In Syria the earlier redoubtable Hazael had evidently become known as 'the lord' *par excellence*, and this current epithet was simply taken over by the Assyrian analists. Hazael 'oppressed Israel all the days of Jehoahaz' (2 Ki. 13:22), who reigned *c.* 814/813–798 BC, and hence, at least briefly, outlived him, surviving to perhaps *c.* 797 or 796 BC.

Assyrian spoils from Hazael's Damascus included ivory-work, two pieces inscribed *l-mr'n Ḥz'l*, 'belonging to our lord Hazael', and another bearing the figure of a prince, just possibly a representation of Hazael himself.

BIBLIOGRAPHY. F. Bron and A. Lemaire, *Reallexikon der Assyriologie* 83, 1989, pp. 35–44; I. Eph'al and J. Naveh, *IEJ* 39, 1989, pp. 192–200; E. Puech, *RB* 88, 1981, pp. 544–562; W. T. Pitard, *Ancient Damascus*, 1987. See also *ARAM, *BEN-HADAD. J.G.G.N. K.A.K.

HAZARMAVETH (*ḥᵃṣarmāweṯ*). The third son of *Joktan (Gn. 10:26; 1 Ch. 1:20), probably to be identified with the kingdom of Ḥaḍramaut in S *Arabia, written *ḥḍrmt* and later *ḥḍrmwt* in the native inscriptions. The latter form corresponds closely to the unvocalized Heb. *ḥṣrmwt*, Heb. *ṣ* often corresponding to S Semitic *ḍ*.

BIBLIOGRAPHY. G. Ryckmans, *Les Noms propres sud-sémitiques*, 1, 1934, p. 338; C. Brockelmann, *Grundriss der vergleichenden Grammatik der semitischen Sprachen*, 1, 1908, § 46. T.C.M.

HAZEROTH. A stopping-place on the desert journey of the Israelites (Nu. 11:35; 33:17–18), where Miriam became a leper (Nu. 12:1–16; *cf.* Dt. 1:1). Generally identified with 'Ayin Khodara, an oasis with a well on the way from Sinai to Aqabah. (*ENCAMPMENT BY THE SEA.) C.D.W.

HAZOR (Heb. *ḥāṣôr*). A place-name, probably meaning 'settlement' or 'village', and therefore used of several places in the OT, of which the most important was a fortified city in the territory of Naphtali (Jos. 19:36).

I. In the Old Testament

This city lay in N Palestine, and at the conquest it was the royal seat of Jabin (called 'king of Hazor', *meleḵ-ḥāṣôr*, Jos. 11:1), who organized a coalition against Joshua. The Israelites defeated this, however, Jabin was killed, and Hazor was destroyed and burnt (Jos. 11:1–13; 12:19). Hazor was the only city thus burnt, perhaps because of its former importance (Jos. 11:10), but in spite of this destruction a later king of the same name, who this time was styled 'king of Canaan' (*meleḵ-kᵉna'an*, Jdg. 4:2, 24) threatened Israel in the time of Deborah. Though his general, Sisera, had 900 *chariots at his disposal, the Israelites under Barak were able to defeat him, and crush Jabin (Jdg. 4; 1 Sa. 12:9). Some two centuries later Hazor was fortified, together with Jerusalem, Megiddo and Gezer, by Solomon when he was organizing his kingdom (1 Ki. 9:15), but in the 8th century, in the time of Pekah of Israel, Tiglath-pileser III of Assyria came and destroyed the city and carried off its remaining inhabitants to Assyria (2 Ki. 15:29).

II. Excavation

The site of Hazor was identified in 1875 by J. L. Porter with the abandoned mound of Tell el-Qedah some 8 km SW of Lake Huleh in Galilee. J. Garstang made some trial soundings in 1928, but the first major excavations were carried out from 1955 to 1958 and 1968 to 1969 by an Israeli expedition under Yigael Yadin. The site lies on a NE facing slope, and consists of the city tell of some 100,000 sq.m extent at the S end, and adjoining this to the N a much larger area of about 0·6 sq.km with an earthen rampart on the W or uphill side. The main tell was founded in the 3rd millennium, and the lower city added to it in the early part of the 2nd millennium, probably by the Hyksos. Though Garstang assumed this lower city to be a camping enclosure for horses and chariots, excavation revealed that the whole of this area had been occupied by a built city, which at its height must, with the tell proper, have accommodated up to 40,000 souls. A further indication of the importance of the city at this time is given by the discovery of a pottery jug with an Akkadian inscription (the earliest known in Palestine) scratched on it. Though crudely done, the inscription has been read as *Iš-me-ilam*, an Akkadian personal name, perhaps that of a Mesopotamian merchant. This lower city was occupied for only about five centuries, having been destroyed in the 13th century (Level 13). This destruction is attributed by the excavators to Joshua. Among the remains in this destroyed city were found a Canaanite temple and a small shrine. While the lower city lay barren, the tell was reoccupied by the Canaanites, and then by the Israelites. A city gate and casemate wall from the time of Solomon, almost exactly matching those found at *Megiddo and *Gezer (*cf.* 1 Ki. 9:15), were uncovered. Evidence from the later Israelite period included a pillared public building of the time of Ahab (taken by Garstang to be stables), and a fortress containing a thick layer of ash, in which was a fragment of a wine jar bearing the name Pekah (*pqḥ*), and other signs of violent destruction, probably due to Tiglath-pileser III, who took the city in 732 BC (2 Ki. 15:29).

III. In extra-biblical texts

Hazor is first mentioned in the Egyp. Execration Texts of the 19th century BC, as a Canaanite city likely to be a danger to the empire. It figures (*ḫa-ṣu-ra*) in the Mari archives of the first quarter of the 2nd millennium, and in a slightly later Bab. text, as an important political centre on the route from Mesopotamia, perhaps to Egypt. In one tablet the ruler is spoken of as a 'king' (*šarrum*), a title not usually applied to city rulers (*cf.* Jos. 11:1), and his importance is further indicated by the mention of ambassadors from Babylon travelling to see him. One king's name is given as Ibni-Adad, an Akkadian form suggesting Bab. influence, but there was also contact with the N and W, as is manifested in gifts from the king to Ugarit and Crete (*Kaptara*). Hazor is mentioned in the lists of their dominions made by the Egyp. kings Tuthmosis III, Amenhotep II and Seti I in the 15th and 14th centuries BC. The city is later mentioned in the Amarna letters, of the 14th century, the ruler still being spoken of as a king (*Šar ḫa-zu-ra*). Finally, from the next century, the city is mentioned in an Egyp. papyrus (Anastasi I) in a military context. Thus the texts and excavations amply bear out the biblical testimony to the importance of the site.

IV. Other places of the same name

1. A place in the S of Judah (Jos. 15:23) whose site is unknown. **2.** (*ḥāṣôr ḥᵃdattâ*) 'New Hazor' (Jos. 15:25), a place in S Judah whose site is unknown. **3.** Another name for Kerioth-hezron (Jos. 15:25) in S Judah, site unknown, perhaps the same as **2.** **4.** A place in Benjamin (Ne. 11:33) probably modern Khirbet Hazzur. **5.** An area occupied by semi-nomadic Arabs, mentioned by Jeremiah (49:28, 30, 33).

BIBLIOGRAPHY. Y. Yadin *et al.*, *Hazor I*, 1958, *Hazor II*, 1960, *Hazor III–IV*, 1961, 1989; Y. Yadin, *Hazor* (Schweich Lectures, 1970), 1972; see also A. Malamat, *JBL* 79, 1960, pp. 12–19; *NEAEHL*, pp. 594–606. T.C.M.

HEAD. The head (Heb. *rō'š*; Gk. *kephalē*) is not regarded as the seat of the intellect, but as the source of life (Mt. 14:8, 11; Jn. 19:30). Thus to lift up the head is to grant life in the sense of success (Jdg. 8:28; Ps. 27:6; Gn. 40:13, but *cf.* the pun in v. 19), or to expect it in God himself (Ps. 24:7, 9; Lk. 21:28). To cover the head by the hand or with dust and ashes is to mourn the loss of life (2 Sa. 13:19; La. 2:10). Figuratively, headship denotes superiority of rank and authority over another (Jdg. 11:11; 2 Sa. 22:44); though when Christ is spoken of as head of his body the church (Eph. 5:23; Col. 2:19), of every man (1 Cor. 11:3), of the entire universe (*hyper panta*, Eph. 1:22), and of every cosmic power (Col. 2:10), and when man is spoken of as the head of the woman (1 Cor. 11:3; Eph. 5:23; *cf.* Gn. 2:21f.), the basic meaning of head as the source of all life and energy is predominant.

The church is Christ's body and he is her head (Eph. 4:15f.): the two cannot be severed. In this unity of head and body, Christ the head directs the growth of the body to himself: he is not merely the source of being of the body (1 Cor. 10:16f.) but also the consummation of its life (Eph. 4:15f.); *cf.* *CORNERSTONE. Hence to give allegiance to any other spiritual mediator, as was being done at Colossae, cuts the vital link between the limbs and Christ the head who is the source of all their being (Col. 2:18f.).

BIBLIOGRAPHY. F. Foulkes, *Ephesians*, *TNTC*, 1963, pp. 65f., 124, 155ff.; K. Munzer and C. Brown, *NIDNTT* 2, pp. 156–163; H. Schlier, *TDNT* 3, pp. 673–681; D. W. Baker, *Idiomatic Expressions in Hebrew and Akkadian Relating to the Head* (diss. London, 1976). F.H.P.

HEALTH, DISEASE AND HEALING.

I. Introduction

The biblical descriptions of health, disease, healing and death are limited by:

a. The purpose of Scripture, which is theological rather than medical. Only those details which are relevant to the over-all purpose, revealing God to man, are included. Thus, for example, it is sufficient to record that a boy was 'paralysed' and 'in terrible distress' (Mt. 8:6). The object was to indicate the severity of the illness and the gravity of the prognosis against which to contrast the greatness of the cure and the divine power of Christ. This illness may have been an example of poliomyelitis with respiratory paralysis. Like most of the diseases of the Bible it was unnecessary to say so even if that had been known. There is no evidence to suggest exactly what caused that boy's illness in medical terms (the proximal cause), although some instances of disease in OT and NT do have a spiritual explanation given (the ultimate cause), *e.g.* Lk. 13:11–16.

b. Contemporary medical knowledge. Descriptions of disease were simple and were mostly confined to what could be seen (*e.g.* ulcer, swelling, haemorrhage) and/or felt by an observer (fever) or by the patient himself (dysentery, paralysis).

c. Contemporary public knowledge was even more restricted. Even if the medical knowledge of the day had been advanced, it would not have been understood by the readers.

d. Patterns of disease are constantly changing. This is particularly true of diseases of microbiological origin. 'Plague' refers to any epidemic disease and is not the equivalent of the modern infection with *Yersinia pestis*. Others may be unchanged for centuries, *e.g.* blindness from trachoma is still very common in the Middle East and was probably even more common in biblical times. In addition, the terms used to describe disease have also been greatly altered, even in the last few hundred years. No longer do doctors report that their patients suffer from the botch, the blain or the emerods, mentioned in the AV.

None the less, the biblical accounts of disease are based on observed facts. Sincere and honest men, mostly with no medical knowledge, wrote of what they saw as they understood best. The facts that they describe, therefore, can and should be treated as facts. Moreover, the standard of medical treatment (such as it was) and public hygiene (see **VII**, below) were superior to those of contemporary adjacent cultures.

II. Medical terms

a. Some general (non-medical) terms used to describe disease, healing and health

(*i*) OT. Heb. *ḥālâ* is used for 'to be sick' (nouns *ḥºlî* and *maḥᵃlâ*), and also *maḏweh* (Dt. 7:15; 28:61) and *dāḇār* (Ps. 41:8) meaning 'a matter' (*i.e.* evil matter). *rāpā'* (to heal) is most commonly used for healing, and is also used for 'physician' in Gn. 50:2 (twice); 2 Ch. 16:12; Jb. 13:4; Je. 8:22. Other OT terms include *ḥāyâ* (revive) and *šûḇ* (restore).

The words for health are infrequently used in the OT, and then always figuratively (*e.g.* Je. 30:17; 33:6; Ps. 42:11; Pr. 12:18).

(*ii*) NT. Disease is normally described by the Gk. nouns *astheneia* (weakness), *malakia* (misfortune)—used three times in Mt. only, or the verbs *astheneō* (to weaken) or *kakōs echein* (lit. 'to have badly') and once (Jas. 5:15) *kamnō* (to be ill, to ail). The adjective *arrhōstos* ('not robust') is used four times (*e.g.* Mk. 6:13); *mastix* (a whip) is used not only literally but metaphorically of disease—see *Plague*, below.

The commonest non-technical words for healing and health are *ischyō* (be strong) and *hygiainō* (be healthy), while *sōzō* and *diasōzō* (save) are used both of physical and spiritual healing (see *Leprosy*, below). *stereoō* (set up, make strong) is used in Acts 3:16, where *holoklēria*, 'perfect health', also occurs, possibly indicating active rehabilitation to normal life as well as to physical well-being.

b. Some more technical terms describing disease and healing in the New Testament

nosos (disease), while a specific term, was used only of disease in general rather than of any individual case. Luke and the other Evangelists employ the word in the same way (*e.g.* Mt. 4:23; 8:17; Lk. 4:40; 6:17; Acts 19:12, *etc.*). For other yet more specific words, see below.

Verbs for healing are *therapeuō*, *iaomai* and *apokathistēmi*.

The medical terminology used by Luke, as well as his discreet silence about the failures of his colleagues in treating the woman with an issue of blood (see *Menstruation*, below), indicate his medical training. Only Luke quotes 'Physician, heal yourself' (4:23). In Lk. 4:35 *ripsan*, 'thrown him down', is a medical term describing epileptic convulsions and *blaptein*, 'harm', is similarly a technical medical term (J. R. W. Stott, *Men with a Message*). In Lk. 24:11 *lēros*, 'idle tale', is a medical term used to describe the babblings of a feverish or insane patient (W. Barclay, *Commentary on Luke*).

c. Further medical terms

Barrenness. To be a wife without bearing children has always been regarded in the East, not only as a matter of regret, but as a reproach which could lead to divorce. This is the cause of Sarah's despairing laughter (Gn. 18:12), Hannah's silent prayer (1 Sa. 1:10ff.), Rachel's passionate alternative of children or death (Gn. 30:1) and Elizabeth's cry that God had taken away her reproach (Lk. 1:25). The awfulness of the coming judgment on Jerusalem is emphasized by the incredible statement, 'Blessed are the barren . . .' (Lk. 23:29). It was believed that the gift of children or the withholding of them indicated God's blessing or curse (Ex. 23:26; Dt 7:14), as also did the barrenness or fruitfulness of the land (Ps. 107:33–34).

Blindness. Heb. *'iwwēr*, 'closed' or 'contracted', and its cognate *'iwwārôn*, *'awwereṯ* and *sanwērîm*, 'blindness'; Gk. *typhlos*. Blindness was common throughout the Middle East in biblical times. It is probable that several different diseases were responsible. Trachoma may have been common then, as it still is in some parts, causing blindness in infancy. Gonorrhoea in the mother can infect the eyes of children during their birth and lead to blindness. Blindness was sometimes seen as a punishment from God, as Dt. 28:28–29 indicates (also describing the pathetic groping gait of the blind and their propensity for being robbed).

There is one fascinating instance of a two stage or double miracle of Jesus on a blind man (Mk. 8:22–25) in the Gentile town of Bethsaida. In the first miracle the blind man was led by Jesus out of the village, saliva was applied to his eyes and he was enabled to 'see'. However, presumably because he had never remembered seeing, his mind could not interpret the images he saw (v. 24). 'Men' looked like 'trees'; this is a well recognized phenomenon in those who have never seen and who have sight made possible by corneal grafting or cataract surgery—see a fascinating article by R. E. D. Clark on 'Men as trees walking' (*FR* 93), 1963, pp. 88ff.) in which the subject is reviewed in depth. Jesus therefore performed a further miracle. Again a simple sign, a touch, was given and then he 'saw everything clearly' (v. 25). If the man had once learnt to 'see' and then become blind the second miracle would not have been necessary (*cf.* Mt. 9:27–31; 12:22; 20:29–34; 21:14). The sign applied for each miracle, an aid to faith, may have been the more necessary for him if he was a Gentile. See V, below.

Boil, botch. Heb. *šᵉḥîn*, 'burning'; *cf.* root in Arab., Aram., Eth., 'to be hot'. A generic term which the OT uses to denote different kinds of localized inflammation. For the 'boils breaking out in sores' of the sixth plague (Ex. 9:9) see *PLAGUES OF EGYPT. In Lv. 13:18–24 boils are mentioned in association with what is there termed leprosy, while the 'boils' (AV) or 'loathsome sores' (RSV) which afflicted Job (2:7), of which various diagnoses have been made, may have been tuberculous leprosy. 'The boils of Egypt', which extended from head to toe (Dt. 28:27, 35), was probably one of the cutaneous diseases peculiar to Egypt (*cf.* Pliny, *NH* 26.5) such as an endemic boil or malignant pustule. Hezekiah's boil (2 Ki. 20:7; Is. 38:21) was probably a carbuncle.

Burn. Heb. *ṣāreḇeṯ*, a 'burning' or 'scorching'. Used twice of a skin disorder (Lv. 13:24, 28) and once metaphorically (Pr. 16:27). It is not clear whether the word means a literal burn from fire or simply a skin disorder producing a burning sensation.

Childbirth. See *Midwifery*, below.

Consumption. Heb. *šaḥepeṯ*, 'wasting away'. Occurs in Lv. 26:16; Dt. 28:22. In neither case is the exact medical meaning at all clear. It could mean tuberculosis, cancer or a host of other diseases producing wasting. Tuberculosis existed in Egypt when the children of Israel were there (D. Morse *et al.*, *Tuberculosis in Ancient Egypt*).

Deafness. Heb. *ḥērēš* 'silent', Gk. *kōphos*, 'blunted, dull, dumb'. The Israelites were to be kind to the deaf (Lv. 19:14). Isaiah foretold that the deaf would be made to hear (29:18; 35:5; 42:18), a prophecy fulfilled by Jesus (Mt. 11:5; Mk. 7:37).

One man whom Jesus healed was deaf and had 'an impediment in his speech' (*mogilalos*, 'speaking with difficulty', Mk. 7:32) which was probably caused by his deafness (but obviously might have been due to a separate mechanical defect, as AV 'the string', lit. bond, 'of his tongue was loosed' might suggest). It is surely significant that his hearing was healed first. Some authorities consider that the man was deaf and dumb but the Greek does not suggest this. It is more likely that he could make noises but, because he could not hear them (or other people's words), they did not form normal speech. Zechariah was temporarily dumb and deaf (Lk. 1:20, 22, 64). (*EAR.)

Dropsy. Gk. *hydrōpikos*, 'full of water' (Lk. 14:2). Dropsy (ascites) is strictly not a disease in itself but rather a sign of disease of the heart, kidneys or liver, *etc.*

Dumbness. Heb. *'illēm*, 'dumb', 'bound', 'tied', *dûmān*, 'silent', *'ālam*, to be dumb, bound, tied'. Gk. *alalos*, 'speechless', *aphōnos*, 'voiceless', and most commonly *kōphos*, 'blunted', 'dumb' or 'deaf'. This disorder occurred throughout biblical history. It can be attributed to no specific cause. Sometimes it was a feature of *demon-possession (*e.g.* Mt. 9:32–35; 12:22). Zechariah was temporarily dumb and deaf (Lk. 1:20, 22, 64) through an act of God because of his unbelief. The deaf man of Mk. 7:32 was almost certainly not dumb even though he is called the 'deaf-mute'.

Dysentery. The RSV rendering of Gk. *dysenteria* (AV 'bloody flux'), a technical medical term used by Herodotus, Plato, Aristotle, *et al.*, the infectious disease of which Paul healed the father of Publius (Acts 28:8). It has been suggested that the 'incurable disease' of the bowels with which the Lord afflicted Jehoram was a chronic amoebic dysentery (2 Ch. 21:15, 18–19). See also *Prolapsed rectum*, below.

Emerods. (AV). See *Tumours*, below.

Epilepsy. Gk. *selēniazomai*, 'to be moon-struck', a concept from which the English word 'lunatic' is derived, occurs twice (Mt. 4:24; 17:15), translated 'lunatick' in AV, 'epileptic' in RSV. Epilepsy was thought to vary in its severity in cycle with the visible size of the moon. The boy described in Mt. 17:15 appears to have had typical *grandmal* epilepsy (*cf.* Mk. 9:17–29; Lk. 9:38–42) as well as being *demon-possessed, a condition from which epilepsy was distinguished (Mt. 4:24).

Fever. Heb. *qaddaḥaṯ*, 'burning heat' (Dt. 28:22); Gk. *pyretos*, 'fiery heat' (Lk. 4:38; Jn. 4:52; Acts 28:8, *etc.*). A generic term which in EVV covers various ailments, all of them suggesting the presence of a high temperature. Luke describes (4:38) Peter's wife's mother as having 'a great fever', indicating that he recognized degrees of fever and, probably, that he saw the grave prognosis indicated by the severity of the fever which Mt. (8:14) and Mk. (1:30) did not.

Inflammation. Heb. *dalleqeṯ* (only Dt. 28:22). The physical afflictions of consumption, fever and inflammation, and the climatic ones—heat and drought—would have combined to form an awful prospect. The terms are too vague to allow specific interpretation.

Issue; issue of blood. Apart from the more usual meanings of 'issue', the word is also used biblically in connection with disease. In Lv. 15:2ff. Heb. *zôḇ* denotes a discharge which rendered its victims ritually unclean. In Lv. 12:7; Mt. 9:20; Mk. 52:25; Lk. 8:43f.; Heb. *māqôr* and Gk. *rhysis* and *haimorrhoeō* (the latter of which is used in Lv. 15:33, LXX) refer to an issue of blood, translated by NEB as 'haemorrhages'. It is possible that the woman of Lk. 8:43, *etc*, had menorrhagia. See *Menstruation*, below.

Itch. 1. Heb. *ḥeres*, 'heat, sun, itch'. A skin condition, probably akin to eczema, included among the scourges ('which cannot be healed') which would overtake the disobedient (Dt. 28:27). No data are available for precise identification.

2. Heb. *neṯeq* (Lv. 13:30–37; 14:54). A general term, apparently meaning an irritating skin rash, sometimes regarded then as a sign of 'leprosy'. See also *Scab*.

Leprosy. The common OT word translated thus is *ṣāra'aṯ* (Lv. 13–14) which in the LXX was rendered *lepra*, the same Greek word being used in the NT. Both terms were simple, non-specific, imprecise, 'lay' ones and lacked the precision of the modern word leprosy which indicates an infection by *Mycobacterium leprae*. *ṣāra'aṯ* is primarily a word describing ritualistic uncleanness or defilement characterized by the presence of coloured patches. The same word was used to describe human skin disease (Lv. 13:1–46), discolouration of wool, leather, linen (vv. 47–59), and even the walls of houses (14:33–57), thus indicating that *ṣāra'aṯ* cannot have been (but it might possibly have included) true leprosy. The word *lepra* in the NT occurs only in the Gospels and was used only of human disease. The evidence for uncleanness, on which the diagnosis was based, depended on the presence of depigmented (pale) patches on the human skin or discoloured or dark patches on the surface of inanimate objects. Some of the features described in Lv. 13–14 do not occur in leprosy and some suggest other conditions such as erysipelas adjacent to a boil (Lv. 13:18), infection following a burn (v. 24), ringworm, or sycosis of the scalp or beard (v. 29), pustular dermatitis (v. 36), *etc*. Leprosy is such a slowly-changing process it could not possibly have recovered in the 7 days of Lv. 13:4–6. It is significant that in Lk. 17:11–19, ten lepers were *cleansed* (*katharizō*) (v. 14), while only the one who was grateful was *cured* (*iaomai*) (v. 15) and he was told his faith had (lit.) saved him (*sōzō*) (v. 19) which may refer to his spiritual state or simply mean 'made well' (RSV). There is no clue as to the nature of their 'leprosy'—it is possible that more than one disease process was present among them.

Undoubted leprosy existed in India by *c.* 600 BC and in Europe by 400 BC. There is no definite evidence that it is referred to in the OT or that it even existed at the time of the Exodus, although it certainly did in NT times. For a detailed study of the subject, see S. G. Browne, *Leprosy in the Bible* (good bibliography).

Madness, mental disorder. Several different words are used, all non-specific. The more important are:

1. Heb. *hōlēlâ*, *hōlēlûṯ*, 'foolishness', 'madness' or 'boasting' (Ec. 1:17; 2:12; 7:25; 9:3; 10:13).

2. Heb. *šiggā'ôn*, 'madness', 'erring', madness inflicted as a judgment from God (Dt. 28:28; Zc. 12:4).

3. Gk. *anoia*, 'mindlessness', leading to folly (2 Tim. 3:9) or rage (Lk. 6:11). In neither case is mental disease implied but rather unbalanced behaviour.

4. Gk. *paraphronia*, 'madness' (2 Cor. 11:23; 2 Pet. 2:16).

5. Gk. *mania* (Acts 26:25). Paul said he had not got (lit.) mania after Festus had accused him of raving (*mainomai*) madly (*cf.* Jn. 10:20).

The recurrent episodes of madness of *Saul and the single severe attack suffered by *Nebuchadrezzar are described in some detail. Saul (1 Sa., *passim*) was a man who was gifted but in some respects inadequate, *e.g.* he was much at the mercy of other people's opinions; he was subject to moods of recurrent depression; and, in later life, he had the paranoid ideas and irritability characteristic of depression in older patients, though homicidal tendencies such as he had are uncommon. His suicide is probably medically unimportant and that of a defeated warrior rather than a depressed neurotic. Nebuchadrezzar, active and irascible, had a hypomanic personality, *i.e.* an inherited liability to develop a manic-depressive psychosis. His illness (Dn. 4:28–37) was long-lasting and occurred when he was perhaps in his fifties. Though he remained conscious he was totally incapable of government. There was no evidence of organic disorder. There was some perversion of appetite. He recovered from it completely (v. 36) in the end, and it would be described today as involutional melancholia.

Menstruation. Heb. *dāwā* or *dāweh*, 'sick', 'menstruous' (Lv. 12:2, 5; 15:33; 18:19; 20:18). Both RSV and AV translate the words rather inconsistently, although AV uses such expressions as 'sick of her flowers' (Lv. 15:33). This normal, physiological feature of the life of women in the reproductive phase of their lives rendered them ritually unclean.

It is probable that the woman with an issue of blood (Mk. 5:25; Lk. 8:43 *rhysei haimatos*, 'a flow of blood'; Mt. 9:20 *haimorrhoeō*, 'to suffer from a flow of blood'; the latter word was used in Greek medical writings and in LXX for Lv. 15:33 meaning 'menstruous') had menorrhagia, a disease in which the menstrual flow is abnormally prolonged—in her case continuous for 12 years—and may produce anaemia.

Midwifery. While childbirth is a normal and healthy phenomenon, it seems appropriate to include it in this 'medical' section. Midwifery was in the hands of women, who had probably considerable experience, perhaps little skill and training (Gn. 38:27–30; Ex. 1:15–21; Ezk. 16:4–5). A birthstool (Ex. 1:16, Heb. *'oḇnayim*, lit. 'double stones', probably indicating its origin) of the type used in Egypt at the time of the Exodus is described in the article *MIDWIFE.

Palsy, paralysis. The Gk. terms for a paralytic, *paralytikos* (*e.g.* Mt. 4:24; 9:2; Mk. 2:3) and to be paralysed, *paralyomai* (*e.g.* Lk. 5:18, 24; Acts 8:7; 9:33) are similar and non-specific. Some types of paralysis in biblical times were clearly non-fatal because patients managed to survive for many years in spite of being paralysed. The centurion's boy servant (Mt. 8:6) was paralysed and 'in terrible distress'. This could be a description of the frightening respiratory paralysis that is a feature of some cases of poliomyelitis.

Plague, pestilence. The AV rendering of five Heb. and three Gk. words connected with disease, death or destruction. None is to be interpreted as necessarily indicating infection with *Yersinia pestis* (the modern 'plague').

1. Heb. *deḇer*, 'pestilence, plague'. Originally meaning 'destruction', this word is used comprehensively for all sorts of disasters, and is often linked with the sword and famine (which three evils generally go hand in hand; *cf.* Je. 14:12; Ezk. 6:11, *etc.*), and with divine visitation. It describes also the virulent epidemic which, after David's numbering of the people, cut off 70,000 Israelites (2 Sa. 24:15; *cf.* Jos., *Ant.* 7. 326), and is probably the same affliction as destroyed 185,000 of *Sennacherib's men (2 Ki. 19:35; Is. 37:36). The same word is found in Solomon's dedication prayer (1 Ki. 8:37; 2 Ch. 6:28); is employed in an unusual sense to describe God's effect on death (Ho. 13:14); and, translated 'murrain', is connected with a disease of cattle (Ex. 9:3, AV; *cf.* Ps. 78:50, AVmg.).

2. Heb. *maggēp̄â*, 'plague, smiting' (Ex. 9:14; Zc. 14:12, *etc.*). **3.** Heb. *makkâ*, 'a smiting, beating' (Lv. 26:21; Je. 19:8, *etc.*). **4.** Heb. *neḡa'*, 'a touch, smiting'. This word, associated most often with leprosy (Lv. 13–14), also denotes any great distress or calamity (Ps. 91:10, *etc.*), or inward corruption (1 Ki. 8:38). **5.** Heb. *neḡep̄*, 'a stumbling, plague' (Ex. 12:13; Jos. 22:17, *etc.*). **6.** Gk. *mastix*, 'a scourge, whip, plague' (Mk. 3:10; 5:29, 34; Lk. 7:21). This is used as a synonym for disease in general. **7.** Gk. *loimos*, 'a plague, pestilence' (Mt. 24:7; Lk. 21:11; *cf.* Jos., *BJ* 6. 421). In both biblical references it is coupled with famine, but RV and RSV follow some older MSS in omitting 'pestilence' in Mt. 24:7–8. **8.** Gk. *plēgē*, 'a stroke, plague'. This word is thus translated only in Rev. (9:20; 11:6, *etc.*), in connection with the judgment that will overtake the wicked.

Prolapsed rectum. Jehoram (2 Ch. 21:15, 18–19) was smitten 'with an incurable disease' in his bowels. After 2 years of this 'his bowels came out' and he died 'in great agony' (*taḥ^a lû'îm*—a plural noun not translated thus in any other place in RSV; it is translated 'deadly diseases' in Je. 16:4, and 'diseases' in Ps. 103:3). This was almost certainly chronic dysentery which, when very severe and prolonged, occasionally may be complicated by prolapse of the rectum or more of the large intestine, producing *intussusception* which itself produces intestinal obstruction. This could have been the cause of his painful death.

Scab, spot. Skin diseases are rife in the East, and it is often difficult both to identify precisely those mentioned in Scripture and to distinguish one from another. 'Scab', for example, represents four different Heb. words.

1. *gārāḇ*, Dt. 28:27 ('scurvy', AV, Lv. 21:20; 22:22; LXX *psora*; Vulg. *scabies*). Included among the curses that should overtake the disobedient, this was evidently not the true scurvy, but a chronic disease which formed a thick crust on the head and sometimes spread over the whole body. It was regarded as incurable.

2. *yallep̄eṯ*, 'scabbed' (LXX *leichēn*). One of the afflictions that rendered men unfit for the priesthood (Lv. 21:20) and animals unsuitable for sacrifices (Lv. 22:22), it may be another form of **1**, above.

3. *sappaḥaṯ* ('spot'), Lv. 13:2; 14:56.

4. *mispaḥaṯ*, Lv. 13:6–8. A verbal form (*śippaḥ*) is employed in Is. 3:17, 'smite with a scab'.

Tumours (RSV), **Emerods** (AV). The Philistines in Ashdod captured the *ark and the Lord 'afflicted them with tumours' (Heb. *'opālîm*, 'tumours' or 'boils'), 1 Sa. 5:6. The root meaning of the Heb. word means 'to swell, bump up', hence the name of Mt Ophel at Jerusalem. The word may be a technical 'medical' one. When the ark was taken to Gath 'tumours broke out on them', 'both young and old' (5:9), and many died (5:11–12). After 7 months the ark was returned to Israel with golden models of five tumours and five 'mice' (Heb. *'akbār*), an inexact word meaning 'rodent' and including mice, rats and gerbils which were common in the Middle East (G. S. Cansdale, *Animals of Bible Lands*). Both rats and gerbils are known vectors of infected fleas which transmit bubonic plague. The description of a plague spreading along lines of communication and breaking out in successive communities, producing multiple boil-like swellings or tumours and an illness that was sometimes fatal and that was associated with numerous 'mice' ruining the crops (6:5), is consistent with (though not proof of) a diagnosis of bubonic plague. It is possible that the same plague caused the seventy deaths in Beth-shemesh 'because they looked into the ark of the Lord' (6:19). The explanation for the number five (mice and tumours) models is 6:16–18.

Wen (AV) (Heb. *yabbeleṯ*, Lv. 22:22; *cf.* LXX *myrmēkiōnta*). Included in a list of blemishes which made animals an unacceptable sacrifice to the Lord. According to Jewish tradition, the Heb. word applies to 'one suffering from warts'. RVmg. reads 'having sores'; RSV 'having a discharge'.

Withered hand. Gk. *xēros* (Mt. 12:10; Lk. 6:6, 8), 'dry', 'withered', denotes a hand in which the muscles are paralysed and shrunken, leaving the affected limb shorter and thinner than normal—a chronic condition in biblical times regarded as incurable. Some identify with a late complication of infantile paralysis (poliomyelitis). Luke records that it was the man's right hand.

III. The treatment of disease

The therapeutics of the Bible are those of the time, and are described in general terms, *e.g.* Pr. 17:22; Je. 46:11. Local applications are frequently referred to for sores (Is. 1:6; Je. 8:22; 51:8), and a 'cake of figs' is recommended by Isaiah for Hezekiah's boil (Is. 38:21). The good Samaritan used wine and oil as a local treatment (Lk. 10:34). Such treatment is often ineffective, however, as in the case of the woman with the issue of blood (Mk. 5:26), or conditions are apparently intrinsically incurable, as in the case of Mephibosheth (2 Sa. 4:4). In Dt. 28:27 there is a note of despair about some illnesses. It is not surprising that treatment is sometimes bound up with superstition, such as the attempt by Leah and Rachel to use mandrakes to increase sexual desire in infertility (Gn. 30:14–16). Wine is twice mentioned as a medicament and stimulant (Pr. 31:6; 1 Tim. 5:23).

The word physician is rarely used, but implies much the same as 'doctor' in English today (Heb. *rāpā'*, *e.g.* Ex. 15:26; Je. 8:22; Gk. *iatros*, Mk. 5:26; Lk. 8:43). Asa is condemned (2 Ch. 16:12) for consulting 'physicians', but these may have been pagan, magically minded and worthless, and not really deserving the name of physician. The point of the condemnation is that he 'did not seek the Lord'. Job condemns his comforters as 'worthless physicians' (Jb. 13:4). In the NT physicians are twice mentioned proverbially by Christ (Lk. 4:23; 5:31). They are mentioned in the incident of the woman who had an issue of blood (Lk. 8:43). Luke is referred to by Paul as 'the beloved physician' (Col. 4:14).

The Jewish religion differed from many pagan ones in that there was almost no confusion between the offices of priest and physician. Declaration of diagnosis of, and freedom from, leprosy is an exception (Lv. 13:9–17; Lk. 17:14). Prophets were consulted about prognosis (see, *e.g.*, 1 Ki. 14:1–13; 2 Ki. 1:1–4; 8:9; Is. 38:1, 21). A primitive form of bone-setting is mentioned in Ezk. 30:21. It is remarkable that medical practice changed so little in its essentials over the centuries during which the events described in the Bible occurred that it is possible to speak of the whole time as though it were a relatively circumscribed period, and there was scarcely any element in it which could be dignified with the name of science.

IV. Demon possession

The singular phenomenon of *demon possession, rarely paralleled since apostolic times, is clearly something *sui generis*. It is recorded as having occurred at the time of Christ more frequently than at any other time. (The account of Saul—'an evil spirit from the Lord troubled him', in 1 Sa. 16:14–15—is probably to be regarded as a statement of his mental disorder rather than as a theological explanation of its origin.) It seems likely that Satan was particularly active at this time in an attempt to counter the effect of the *miracles of Christ and his apostles. Demon possession was real and cannot be 'explained' simply as the current interpretation of purely physical or mental disorders by ignorant (but sincere) people. Jesus himself made this diagnosis and accepted it when made by others. He was never deceived by contemporary error.

Those who were 'demon possessed' (Gk. *daimonizomenos* = 'demonized') could be used as a mouthpiece by the possessing spirit; they often had accompanying physical manifestations such as dumbness (Mt. 9:32), blindness (Mt. 12:22), epilepsy (Lk. 9:37–43) or mental disorder (Mk. 5:1–20). Particularly they were able to recognize the divinity of Jesus and knew they were subject to his authority. However, demon possession is definitely *not* synonymous either with epilepsy or with mental disorder in general, and is clearly distinguished by the Synoptists and in Acts (5:16) from the general run of disease. The disciples were commanded by Jesus to 'heal' (*therapeuō*) the sick but to 'cast out' (*ekballō*) demons and unclean spirits (Mt. 10:1, 8). Luke (9:37–43) describes how Jesus 'rebuked' (*epitimaō*) the unclean spirit and 'healed' (*iaomai*) the boy, suggesting that the presence of the unclean spirit (which was 'rebuked') was associated with, but distinct from, any medical or mental disease—probably epilepsy—which was 'healed'.

Different degrees of involvement were recognized as is shown (Mt. 15:22) by a girl 'severely possessed by a demon' (*kakōs daimonizetai*).

There is no significant difference between the 'man with an unclean spirit' (Mk. 5:2), 'the demoniac' (*daimonizomenos*) (Mk. 5:15–16) or the man who had been 'possessed with demons' (v. 18) as the same man was variously described.

The best authenticated modern cases seem to be those described by missionaries in China from about 1850 onwards. There is no good reason to doubt the biblical view of it as a 'possession' by an evil spiritual being of the personality and body of the person concerned. For present-day examples, see D. Basham, *Deliver us from evil*, 1972.

V. Miracles and healing

a. Healing—its meaning

Healing means the restoration of one to full health who had been ill—in body or mind (or both). This includes recovery resulting from medical treatment and spontaneous remission of a disease. It includes the improvement in a patient's outlook on his condition even if no physical amelioration is possible, and even a correction of a patient's misconception of the nature of his illness. In psychological disorders the term is used to describe an improved mental state. It is important that these different facets of the meaning of the word be realized, because the biblical miracles of healing (apart from cases of demon possession) show healing in its primary medical sense of the restoration to normal in cases of organic disease. Any cases claimed as present-day miracles must show comparably outstanding cases of the healing of organic disorders. Changes in spiritual outlook, an improved acceptance of an organically incurable condition, or the natural and spontaneous remission of disease, are all continually occurring, but do not partake of the miraculous, in the strict theological sense. There are, of course, natural recoveries from illness, as well as miracles, recorded in the Bible, and in fact probably most recoveries other than the miraculous ones were natural, because of the almost complete ineffectiveness of therapy in ancient times.

b. Healing—its Author

God is the one who heals all our diseases (Ps. 103:3; Acts 3:12–16). Even today when medical and surgical skill is so developed, God is the healer, using men (trained or untrained) to do his work for him in the same way that he uses the governing authorities to maintain order and execute justice in the world (Rom. 13:1–5).

c. Healing—the use of means

Even in biblical times, when so few treatments for disease existed (see **III**, above), men were encouraged and expected to use the means that were available, both in OT times (*e.g.* the fig poultice for Hezekiah's boil, Is. 38:21) and in NT times (Paul's advice to Timothy, 1 Tim. 5:23). True faith in God gladly and gratefully uses such means as are available, whether medicines, blood transfusions or surgical operations to prevent death, as much as life-jackets to prevent drowning.

d. Faith healing

Various terms are currently used to describe healing that occurs without the use of means and in response to faith. Because all true healing comes from God the term 'divine healing' is not helpful to distinguish this especial form. 'Spiritual' healing suggests more the restoration of health to the spirit than the body and moreover may be confused with the work of spiritists who, in the name of the devil, can produce spurious healing. Faith healing is a helpful term so long as the object of faith is clear (it is by no means always God).

e. Miraculous healing

A *miracle essentially consists of 'a striking interposition of divine power by which the operations of the ordinary course of nature are overruled, suspended or modified' (*Chambers's Encyclopaedia*, 'Miracle'). So far as miraculous healing in Scripture is concerned, the essential features are that the cure is instantaneous (the incident of Mk. 8:22–26 being a notable exception), complete and permanent, and usually without the use of means (the saliva of Mk. 7:33; 8:23; Jn. 9:6 is an exception; *cf.* also Mk. 5:27–29; Acts 5:15; 19:12). Divine miracles of healing show no relapses, which typify spurious miracles, except, of course, when dead persons were raised to life who, sooner or later, subsequently died again (*e.g.* Jairus' daughter, Mk. 5:21–24, 35–43; the widow of Nain's son, Lk. 7:11–15; Lazarus in Jn. 11:1–44, *etc.*).

1. *The purpose of miraculous healing.* Like the other miracles in Scripture, they were dramatized signs and enacted parables intended to teach a double lesson. They were to *authenticate* the word of the person who performed them (*e.g.* Ex. 7:9; Lk. 5:20–24; Jn. 7:19–22; 10:37–38; Acts 2:22) and to *illustrate* the word. Thus what happened to the body of the paralytic in Lk. 5:18–26 was a proof and picture of what happened in his soul. It is important to see, therefore, that the purpose of the healing miracles was theological, not medical. The many who were healed at the beginning of the ministry of Jesus, of the early church and of individual Christians (*e.g.* Philip, Acts 8:5–8) gradually became fewer as the essential lesson was learnt. Many lay ill at the pool of Bethesda (Jn. 5:3) but Jesus healed only one because one was enough to teach the spiritual truth. If Christ's purpose had been the healing of the sick, he would have healed them all.

Thus a miracle of healing today should not be expected simply when it is medically desirable but rather where the Word of God and his servant needs to be authenticated and illustrated, and such evidence is not already available in the Bible. The fringe of an area of new evangelization on the mission field would therefore seem to be the most likely place for miraculous healing to occur today, the very place where miracles can least scientifically be proven! (But the church in general is now recovering her healing ministry as an integral part of the total gospel of wholeness, and such healings sometimes include the instantaneous as well as the more usual gradual recoveries. See J. C. Peddie, *The Forgotten Talent*, 1961; G. Bennett, *The Heart of Healing*, 1971; F. MacNutt, *Healing*, 1974; *The Power to Heal*, 1977.—N.H.)

2. *Miraculous healing in the Old Testament*. Even if medical means were also used, recovery in the OT is generally attributed to the intervention of God, *e.g.* the recovery of Moses (Ex. 4:24–26) from the illness associated with his disobedience over his son's circumcision is given an entirely spiritual significance. The healing of Miriam's leprosy (Nu. 12:1–15) and of Naaman, through Elisha (2 Ki. 5:8–14), appear to be miraculous. The healing of Jeroboam's suddenly paralysed hand (1 Ki. 13:4–6) and the raising from the dead of the son of the widow of Zarephath by Elijah (1 Ki. 17:17–24) and of the son of the Shunammite woman by Elisha (2 Ki. 4:1–37) are clearly miraculous. This boy's illness has been attributed to sunstroke; but it could equally well have been a fulminating encephalitis or a subarachnoid haemorrhage. (The Jews were conscious of the effects of the sun [see Ps. 121:6], and a case of sunstroke is reported in the Apocrypha [Judith 8:2–3].) The recovery of the Israelites bitten by the serpents when they looked on the bronze serpent is miraculous also, though individuals are not specified (Nu. 21:6–9). The salvation of the Israelites from the later plagues in Egypt is a curious example of what might be termed a 'prophylactic miracle', *i.e.* for them disease was miraculously prevented rather than miraculously healed. The recovery of Hezekiah (2 Ki. 20:1–11) was probably natural, though it is attributed directly to God (v. 8) and is accompanied by a nature miracle (vv. 9–11); the illness was probably a severe carbuncle.

Miraculous healing, even counting raising from the dead, is unusual in the OT, and the few cases seem to cluster about the two critical times of the Exodus and the ministry of Elijah and Elisha. See

Ex. 7:10–12 for nature miracles performed by Moses and Aaron. The miracles performed by the Egyptian sorcerers (Ex. 7:11, 22; 8:7) mimicked the first three miraculous signs wrought by Moses and Aaron (even though their second and third attempts only added to the sufferings of their people), but they were unable to counterfeit the power of God in the subsequent signs (8:18). Thus the miracles wrought by Moses achieved their purpose (7:9) of authenticating his word of authority and finally led to the escape of the children of Israel.

3. *Miraculous healing in the Gospels.* Our Lord's miracles of healing are reported by the Synoptists as groups (*e.g.* Lk. 4:40–41) and, in greater detail and more specifically, as individual cases. *Demon possession is clearly distinguished from other forms of disease (*e.g.* Mk. 1:32–34, where *kakōs echōn* is separate from *daimonizomenos*). People came to him in large numbers (Mt. 4:23–24) and were all healed (Lk. 4:40). Doubtless cases of mental as well as of physical illness were included, and on one occasion our Lord even restored a severed part of the body (Lk. 22:50–51). At the same time, these recorded instances can represent only a small fraction of those ill in the country at this time.

In the combined narrative of the four Gospels there are over twenty stories of the healing of individuals or of small groups. Some were healed at a distance, some with a word but without physical contact, some with physical contact, and some with both physical contact and 'means', *i.e.* the use of clay made from spittle, which was a popular remedy of the time for blindness (Mk. 8:23; Jn. 9:6) and deafness (Mk. 7:32–35). This may have been to aid the patient's faith, or to demonstrate that God does not exclude the use of means, or both. In one unique instance Jesus performed two successive miracles on the same man—see *Blindness*, above.

Luke's Gospel is the only one to give the story of the good Samaritan. It also includes five miracles of healing not recorded by the other Evangelists. These are the raising of the son of the widow of Nain (7:11–16), the healing of the woman 'bowed together' (13:11–16), the man with dropsy (ascites) (14:1–4), the ten lepers (17:12–19) and the healing of Malchus' ear (22:51). More details of cases are given and the writer uses the more technical *iaomai* for healing, rather than the non-technical words.

The Fourth Evangelist, unlike the Synoptists, never refers to healing of people in large numbers, nor to demon possession (though demons are referred to, and the word *daimonizomenos* is used, Jn. 10:21). In addition to the raising of Lazarus from the dead, only three cases are described. These are the healing of the nobleman's son of a serious febrile condition (4:46–54), the man paralysed 38 years (5:1–16), and the man born blind (9:1–14). These miracles of healing in John's Gospel are not only mighty works (*dynameis*) but also signs (*sēmeia*). They demonstrate that Christ's miracles of healing have not only an individual, local, contemporary physical significance but a general, eternal and spiritual meaning also. For example, in the case of the man born blind, the point is made that individual sickness is not necessarily attributable to individual sin.

4. *Miraculous healing in apostolic times.* While the promise of healing powers in Mk. 16:18 is probably to be dismissed as being no part of the true text, Christ had commissioned the Twelve (Mt. 10:1) and the Seventy (Lk. 10:9). The Twelve were evidently commissioned for life, while the mission of the Seventy seems to have ended when they reported back (Lk. 10:17–20). In Acts there are several accounts of individual miracles, which have much the same character as those performed by Christ. The lame man in Jerusalem (3:1–11) and the one at Lystra (14:8–10), the paralytic (9:33–34), and Publius' father's dysentery ('bloody flux', AV, 28:8) are individual cases, and there are a few reports of multiple healings, including that in 5:15–16 and the unique case of the use of clothing taken from Paul (19:11–12). Two people were raised from the dead (Dorcas, 9:36–41, and Eutychus, 20:9f.) and demons were cast out on two occasions (5:16 and 16:16–18). The author distinguishes between demon possession and other illness (5:16).

Cases of illness among Christians in apostolic times are mentioned. The fact that they occur indicates that the apostolic commission to heal could not be used indiscriminately to keep themselves or their friends free from illness. Timothy had a gastric complaint (1 Tim. 5:23). Trophimus was too ill to accompany Paul from Miletus (2 Tim. 4:20). Epaphroditus was gravely ill (Phil. 2:30), and his recovery is attributed to the mercy of God (Phil. 2:27). Most striking of all is Paul's enigmatic 'thorn in the flesh' (*skolops tē sarki*), which has been variously identified (most often as a chronic eye disease), but by few convincingly and by none conclusively. Its spiritual significance far exceeds its importance as an exercise in diagnosis. Paul gives three reasons (2 Cor. 12:7–10) for it; 'to keep his feet on the ground' (v. 7), to enable him to be spiritually powerful (v. 9) and as a personal service to Christ (v. 10, 'for Christ's sake'). There is perhaps more resemblance between this 'thorn' and Jacob's shrunken sinew than has been realized (Gn. 32:24–32).

The classical passage on prayer for the sick (Jas. 5:13–20) has suffered from two misinterpretations: that which finds in it authority for the institution of anointing those who are *in extremis*, and that which regards it as a promise that all who are sick and who are prayed over in faith will recover. The oil may have been used as was Christ's clay or spittle (see above) to reinforce faith, and may in some cases even have been medicinal. Or oil may be taken as a symbol of separating the sickness from the patient on to Christ (*cf.* Mt. 8:17), after the pattern of kings, *etc.* being *anointed to separate them from others for their office. For a full discussion, see R. V. G. Tasker's commentary on James (*TNTC*). The important points are that the outlook in the passage is spiritual (*i.e.* the matter is referred to God), the distress of the individual is made the concern of the church, and what is said neither excludes nor condemns the use by doctors of the normal means of healing available at any particular time and place. The whole of this passage is really concerned with the power of prayer.

5. *Miraculous healing after apostolic times.* This is, strictly, outside the scope of this article, but is relevant in that certain texts are quoted in favour of there being a possibility, and more, of miraculous healing mediated by Christians at the present day (*cf.* Jn. 14:12, above). However, there must be considerable caution in equating personal commands by Christ to the apostles with those which are generally binding upon Christians today. Such views are out of keeping with the general view of miracles as instruments and accompaniments of

revelation. Great care must be exercised in avoiding the magical in a search for the miraculous. The ecclesiastical miracles of patristic times, often posthumously attributed, sometimes became absurd. It has also been shown that the frequently quoted passages in Irenaeus, Tertullian and Justin Martyr, which purport to show that miracles of healing continued well into the 3rd century, will not in fact bear that interpretation. Post-apostolic claims should therefore be treated with extreme care. But this cautious attitude should not be confused with modern materialistic unbelief and scepticism. See also 1. *The purpose of miraculous healing*, above.

VI. The biblical outlook on disease

The topics of suffering and disease, in the Bible, are closely bound up with the questions of the nature and origin of evil itself. Suffering is a human experience, with diverse causes, and is one of the results of human sin. In the case of suffering from disease, the link is not usually obvious, though sometimes the illness is directly connected. From the account of the Fall of man in Genesis it is clear that soon afterwards man knew insecurity, fear and pain (Gn. 3:16:17). Here *'iṣṣāḇôn* (AV 'sorrow') is better rendered 'pain', and then mental anguish (Gn. 4:13). The direct connection between sin and suffering becomes rapidly more complex, but nations which obeyed God were, in general, promised freedom from disease (Ex. 15:25–26; Lv. 26:14–16; Dt. 7:12–16 and ch. 28, especially vv. 22, 27, 58–61). On the other hand, pestilence is one of the three sore judgments on the people of God (Je. 24:10; 32:24; Ezk. 14:21) and on other nations, *e.g.* Philistines (1 Sa. 5:6) and Assyrians (2 Ki. 19:35). There are passages such as Ps. 119:67, where the sinner himself is involved, and the case of the impotent man healed (Jn. 5:1–16), where his own fault is perhaps implied (v. 14). David's sin involved the afflictions of others (2 Sa. 24:15–17). On the whole, human suffering, from disease or from any other cause, is the effect on the individual of the spiritual malaise of the human society of which he is an integral part. In Job 1 something is seen of the activity of Satan. This is also apparent in Acts 10:38, where the sick are spoken of as 'all that were oppressed by the devil' and in the suggestive parable of the wheat and tares ('An enemy has done this', Mt. 13:28). Again, Christ himself spoke of 'this woman, whom Satan bound . . .' (Lk. 13:16).

God does not stand by helplessly, however. Suffering is sometimes used punitively. This may be on a national scale. Or it may be applied to individuals, as in the cases of Moses (Ex. 4:24), Miriam (Nu. 12:10), Uzziah (2 Ch. 26:16–21), Jeroboam (2 Ch. 13:20), Gehazi (2 Ki. 5:25–27), Ananias and Sapphira (Acts 5:5, 10), Herod (Acts 12:21–23) and Elymas (Acts 13:11). Much more detail is given when suffering is used constructively (Heb. 12:6–11), as in the case of Jacob, who, after a real physical injury miraculously inflicted, learnt to depend upon God, and matured spiritually to fulfil his new name of Israel (Gn. 32:24–32). Hezekiah's illness demonstrated his faith in God, and is probably in this category (2 Ki. 20:1–7). The book of Job shows that the real issue is a man's relationship to God rather than his attitude to his own suffering. It is the principal OT refutation of the view, put forward with great skill by Job's 'comforters', that there is an inevitable link between individual sin and individual suffering. After disposing of the view, which is only partially true, that the reason for the existence of suffering is disciplinary, it leads to the sublime picture of Job both comforted, vindicated and blessed. It is important to realize that the biblical picture is not a mere *dualism. Rather, suffering is presented in the light of eternity and in relation to a God who is sovereign, but who is nevertheless forbearing in his dealings with the world because of his love for men (2 Pet. 3:9). Conscious of the sorrow and pain round about them, the NT writers look forward to the final consummation when suffering shall be no more (Rom. 8:18; Rev. 21:4).

This conception is different from the Gk. notion of the body as something inherently evil, and the spirit as something inherently good. The biblical conception of the transience yet nobility of the body is best seen in 2 Cor., especially in 5:1–10 (*cf.* also 1 Cor. 6:15). It is an integral part of the complex of the individual through which the personality is expressed.

VII. Hygiene and sanitation

One respect in which Jewish medicine was better than that of contemporary peoples was the remarkable sanitary code of the Israelites in Moses' time (*e.g.* Lv. 15). A. Rendle Short gives an excellent short account of this (*The Bible and Modern Medicine*, pp. 37–46). Although generally referred to as a code, the details are, in fact, scattered through the Pentateuch. The Jews, as a nation, might not have survived their time in the wilderness, or the many other vicissitudes through which they passed, without their sanitary 'code'. It deals with public hygiene, water supply, sewage disposal, inspection and selection of food, and control of infectious disease. The most interesting thing about it is that it implies a knowledge which in the circumstances of the Exodus and the wilderness wanderings they could scarcely have discovered for themselves, *e.g.* the prohibition, as food, of pigs and of *animals which had died natural deaths, the burial or burning of excreta, *etc.*, and the contagious nature of some diseases. Burning of excreta (Ex. 29:14) was a particularly wise practice for a wandering people, since there was no time for dung to do good as manure. The spread of disease was thus effectively prevented. The origin of the word 'quarantine' is the Jewish use of the period of 40 days of segregation from patients with certain diseases (Lv. 12:1–4) adopted by the Italians in the 14th century because of the relative immunity of Jews from certain plagues. In a number of respects the biblical outlook on the sick, and on health in general, has a bearing on modern medical practice, and is perhaps more up-to-date than is generally realized. The story of the good Samaritan (Lk. 10:30–37) presents an ideal of care which has always inspired the medical and para-medical professions and typifies selflessness and after-care. There is more than a little in the Bible about what might be called 'the medicine of the family', the ideal of marriage among the Jews being a high one.

BIBLIOGRAPHY. W. Barclay, *The Gospel of Luke*, 1958; G. Bennett, *The Heart of Healing*, 1971; M. Botting, *Christian Healing in the Parish*, 1976; S. G. Browne, *Leprosy in the Bible*, 1974; G. S. Cansdale, *Animals of Bible Lands*, 1970; R. E. D. Clark, 'Men as Trees Walking', *FT* 93, 1963, pp. 88–94; R. A. Cole, *Mark*, *TNTC*, 1961; V. Edmunds and C. G. Scorer, *Some Thoughts on Faith Healing*, 1956; J. N. Geldenhuys, *Commentary on the Gospel of*

Luke, *NIC*, 1950; H. C. Kee, *Medicine, Miracle and Magic in the NT*, 1986; J. S. McEwen, *SJT* 7, 1954, pp. 133–152 (miracles in patristic times); F. MacNutt, *Healing*, 1974; *idem*, *The Power to Heal*, 1977; D. Morse *et al.*, 'Tuberculosis in Ancient Egypt', *American Review of Respiratory Diseases* 90, 1964, pp. 524–541; B. Palmer (ed.), *Medicine and the Bible*, 1986; J. C. Peddie, *The Forgotten Talent*, 1961; J. R. W. Stott, *Men with a Message*, 1954; M. Sussman, 'Diseases in the Bible and the Talmud', in *Diseases in Antiquity*, ed. D. Brothwell and A. T. Sandison, 1967; B. B. Warfield, *Miracles: Yesterday and Today*, 1965 (reprint of *Counterfeit Miracles*, 1918); F. Graber, D. Müller, *NIDNTT* 2, pp. 163–172; on Paul's thorn in the flesh, see C. Brown, *NIDNTT* 1, pp. 726f. D.T.

HEART (Heb. *lēḇ* or *lēḇāḇ*; Gk. *kardia*). The term is used of the centre of things (Dt. 4:11; Jon. 2:3; Mt. 12:40); the root of the Heb. word, which is obscure, may mean centre.

The references to the physical organ as such are few and by no means specific. The clearest is 1 Sa. 25:37. In 2 Sa. 18:14 and 2 Ki. 9:24 the meaning seems to be wider, indicating the internal organs generally, especially since, in the former passage, Absalom remained alive after three darts had pierced his 'heart'. But this lack of accurate physiological definition is typical of Hebrew thought, particularly in respect of the internal organs. In Ps. 104:15, for instance, the 'heart' is affected by food and drink, and though this may not be true in a direct way physiologically, it certainly is true in experience, if one takes the 'heart' to mean, as outlined below, the inner man, in a wide sense.

The Hebrews thought in terms of subjective experience rather than objective, scientific observation, and thereby avoided the modern error of over-departmentalization. It was essentially the whole man, with all his attributes, physical, intellectual and psychological, of which the Hebrew thought and spoke, and the heart was conceived of as the governing centre for all of these. It is the heart which makes a man, or a beast, what he is, and governs all his actions (Pr. 4:23). Character, personality, will, mind are modern terms which all reflect something of the meaning of 'heart' in its biblical usage. (But *cf.* *BODY where mention is made of synecdoche.)

H. Wheeler Robinson gives the following classification of the various senses in which the words *lēḇ* and *lēḇāḇ* are used.

a. Physical or figurative ('midst'; 29 times).

b. Personality, inner life or character in general (257 times, *e.g.* Ex. 9:14; 1 Sa. 16:7; Gn. 20:5).

c. Emotional states of consciousness, found in widest range (166 times); intoxication (1 Sa. 25:36); joy or sorrow (Jdg. 18:20; 1 Sa. 1:8); anxiety (1 Sa. 4:13); courage and fear (Gn. 42:28); love (2 Sa. 14:1).

d. Intellectual activities (204 times); attention (Ex. 7:23); reflection (Dt. 7:17); memory (Dt. 4:9); understanding (1 Ki. 3:9); technical skill (Ex. 28:3) (latter two = 'mind' in RSV).

e. Volition or purpose (195 times; 1 Sa. 2:35), this being one of the most characteristic usages of the term in the OT.

The NT usage is very similar, and C. Ryder Smith writes of it as follows: 'It (the heart) does not altogether lose its physical reference, for it is made of "flesh" (2 Cor. 3:3), but it is the seat of the will (*e.g.* Mk. 3:5), of the intellect (*e.g.* Mk. 2:6, 8), and of feeling (*e.g.* Lk. 24:32). This means that "heart" comes the nearest of the NT terms to mean "person".'

There is no suggestion in the Bible that the brain is the centre of consciousness, thought or will. It is the heart which is so regarded, and, though it is used of emotions also, it is more frequently the lower organs (*BOWELS, *etc.*), in so far as they are distinguished, that are connected with the emotions. As a broad general statement, it is true that the Bible places the psychological focus one step lower in the anatomy than most popular modern speech, which uses 'mind' for consciousness, thought and will, and 'heart' for emotions.

'Mind' is perhaps the closest modern term to the biblical usage of 'heart', and many passages in RSV are so translated (*e.g.* Ec. 1:17; Pr. 16:23). The 'heart' is, however, a wider term, and the Bible does not distinguish the rational or mental processes in the way that Gk. philosophy does.

C. Ryder Smith suggests that: 'The First great Commandment probably means "You shall love (*agapān*) the Lord your God with all your heart—that is with all your soul and with all your mind and with all your strength" (*e.g.* Mk. 12:30, 33).'

The heart of man does not always do that, however. It is not what it should be (Gn. 6:5; Je. 17:9), and the OT reaches its highest point in the realization that a change of heart is needed (Je. 24:7; Ezk. 11:19), and that, of course, is fulfilled in the NT (Eph. 3:17).

There are the exceptional people whose hearts are right with God (1 Ki. 15:14; Ps. 37:31; Acts 13:22), though it is obvious from what we know of David, the example referred to in the last passage, that this is not true in an absolute sense, but that repentance and conversion are still necessary (2 Ki. 23:25, of Josiah).

The right attitude of heart begins with its being broken or crushed (Ps. 51:17), symbolic of humility and penitence, and synonymous with 'a broken spirit' (*rûaḥ*). This brokenness is necessary because it is the hard or stony heart which does not submit to the will of God (Ezk. 11:19). Alternatively, it is the 'fat' or 'uncircumcised' heart which fails to respond to Yahweh's will (Is. 6:10; Ezk. 44:7).

Yahweh knows the heart of each one and is not deceived by outward appearance (1 Sa. 16:7), but a worthy prayer is, nevertheless, that he should search and know the heart (Ps. 139:23), and make it clean (Ps. 51:10). A 'new heart' must be the aim of the wicked (Ezk. 18:31), and that will mean that God's law has to become no longer merely external but 'written on the heart' and make it clean (Je. 31:33).

Thus it is that the heart, the spring of all desires, must be guarded (Pr. 4:23), and the teacher aims to win his pupil's heart to the right way (Pr. 23:26).

It is the pure in heart who shall see God (Mt. 5:8), and it is through Christ's dwelling in the heart by faith that the saints can comprehend the love of God (Eph. 3:17).

BIBLIOGRAPHY. A. R. Johnson, *The Vitality of the Individual in the Thought of Ancient Israel*, 1949, pp. 77ff.; C. Ryder Smith, *The Bible Doctrine of Man*, 1951; H. Wheeler Robinson, *The Christian Doctrine of Man*, 1911; F. Baumgärtel, J. Behm, *TDNT* 3, pp. 605–613; H. Köster, *TDNT* 7, pp. 548–559; T. Sorg, *NIDNTT* 2, pp. 180–184; H.-H. Esser, *NIDNTT* 2, pp. 599f. B.O.B.

HEAVEN. Several words are translated 'heaven', but the only important ones are the Heb. *šāmayim* and the Gk. *ouranos*. The former is plural, and the latter often occurs in the plural. But, just as in Eng., there does not seem to be any great difference between 'heaven' and 'the heavens'. The term is used of the physical heaven, especially in the expression 'heaven and earth' (Gn. 14:19; Mt. 5:18). Some suggest that the Bible writers thought of heaven in this aspect as solid, and rather like an inverted bowl (the 'firmament', Gn. 1:8). The sun makes his daily pilgrimage across it (Ps. 19:4–6), and there are windows through which the rain might descend (Gn. 7:11). Some Hebrews may well have held this idea, but it must not be forgotten that the men of the OT were capable of vivid imagery. It will never do to treat them as wooden literalists. The theological meaning of their language about heaven can be understood without recourse to such hypotheses.

Heaven is the abode of God, and of those closely associated with him. The Israelite is to pray, 'Look down from thy holy habitation, from heaven' (Dt. 26:15). God is 'the God of heaven' (Jon. 1:9), or 'the Lord, the God of heaven' (Ezr. 1:2), or the 'Father who is in heaven' (Mt. 5:45; 7:21, *etc.*). God is not alone there, for we read of 'the host of heaven' which worships him (Ne. 9:6), and of 'the angels in heaven' (Mk. 13:32). Believers also may look forward to 'an inheritance . . . kept in heaven' for them (1 Pet. 1:4). Heaven is thus the present abode of God and his angels, and the ultimate destination of his saints on earth.

Among many ancient peoples there was the thought of a multiplicity of heavens. It has been suggested that the NT bears witness to the rabbinic idea of seven heavens, for there are references to Paradise (Lk. 23:43), and to 'the third heaven' (2 Cor. 12:2; this was called Paradise on the rabbinic reckoning, *cf.* 2 Cor. 12:3). Jesus also is said to have passed 'through the heavens' (Heb. 4:14). These, however, are slender bases on which to erect such a structure. All the NT language is perfectly capable of being understood along the lines of heaven as the place of perfection.

Heaven comes to be used as a reverent periphrasis for God. Thus when the prodigal says 'I have sinned against heaven' (Lk. 15:18, 21), he means 'I have sinned against God'. So with Jn. 3:27, 'what is given him from heaven'. The most important example of this is Matthew's use of the expression 'the kingdom of heaven', which seems to be identical with 'the kingdom of God'.

Finally, we must notice an eschatological use of the term. In both OT and NT it is recognized that the present physical universe is not eternal, but will vanish away and be replaced by 'new heavens and a new earth' (Is. 65:17; 66:22; 2 Pet. 3:10–13; Rev. 21:1). We should understand such passages as indicating that the final condition of things will be such as fully expresses the will of God.

BIBLIOGRAPHY. P. Toon, *Heaven and Hell*, 1986; *TDNT* 5, pp. 497–543; *NIDNTT* 2, pp. 184–196; *ZPEB*, 3, pp. 60–64. L.M.

HEBER. 1. An Asherite, the son of Beriah (Gn. 46:17; Nu. 26:45; 1 Ch. 7:31–32; Lk. 3:35). **2.** The husband of *Jael, known as Heber the Kenite (Jdg. 4:11, 17; 5:24), though he lived apart from the rest of the Kenites or nomad smiths. The context suggests him to be a man of some importance. **3.** A Judahite, the father of Soco (1 Ch. 4:18). **4.** A son of Elpaal, a Benjaminite (1 Ch. 8:17). J.D.D.

HEBREWS. In the OT *'iḇrî* is confined to the narrative of the sons of Israel in Egypt (Gn. 39–Ex. 10), the legislation concerning the manumission of Heb. servants (Ex. 21; Dt. 15; *cf.* Je. 34), the record of Israelite–Philistine encounter during the days of Samuel and Saul (1 Sa. 4; 13–14; 29), plus Gn. 14:13 and Jon. 1:9.

The patronymic 'Hebrew', *'iḇrî*, used for Abraham and his descendants, can be traced to his ancestor Aber (Gn. 10:21ff.; 11:14ff.). Accordingly, this designation serves to tie the Abrahamic revelation to the covenant promise to Shem. The Noahic doxology in praise of the covenantal union of Yahweh with the family of Shem (Gn. 9:26) is echoed in Gn. 14 in the doxology of Melchizedek (vv. 19–20) celebrating God's covenantal blessing on Abraham the Hebrew, *i.e.* of the lineage of Shem. That the divine favour is shown to Abraham the Hebrew in a conflict which finds him in military alliance with the 'sons of Canaan' against the forces of an Elamite 'son of Shem' (*cf.* Gn. 10:15ff., 22) is indicative that the covenantal election of Shem announced by Noah was being more particularly realized through the Eberite (Hebrew) Semites (*cf.* Gn. 11:10–26).

The broad significance of *'iḇrî* in Gn. 14:13 might also be plausibly assumed in the Gn. 39–Ex. 10 context (*cf.* especially Gn. 40:15; 43:32; Ex. 2:11). However, the usage there is perhaps not uniform, since there seems to be a simple equation of Hebrews and Israelites in Ex. 5:1–3 (*cf.* 3:18), for example, though in speaking of 'the God of the Hebrews' Moses possibly designates his brethren 'Hebrews' as being the Hebrews *par excellence*.

In view of this broader application of *'iḇrî*, the appearance of non-Israelite or even non-Abrahamite *'iḇrîm* need not come unexpectedly in non-biblical texts of the patriarchal and Mosaic ages. According to a popular theory, the *ḫa-BI-ru*, who figure in numerous texts of the 2nd millennium BC, are such *'iḇrîm*. The term *ḫa-BI-ru* is usually regarded as an appellative denoting a social or professional group, but some find an ethnic component in their identity. However, the phonetic equation of *'iḇrî* and *ḫa-BI-ru* is highly debatable. The *ḫa-BI-ru* presence in Canaan attested in the Amarna letters cannot be successfully identified with the Hebrew conquest.

On the basis of the interpretation of the term *ḫa-BI-ru* in Nuzi servant contracts as an appellative meaning 'foreign-servant', it has been contended that *'iḇrî* in the legislation of Ex. 21:2 and Dt. 15:12, whose terms correspond closely to the stipulations of the *ḫa-BI-ru* contracts, denotes not a specific ethnic identity but the status of an alien and, therefore, that the *'eḇed 'iḇrî* is like the Nuzi *ḫa-BI-ru* a foreign servant. But that interpretation of *ḫa-BI-ru* in the Nuzi texts seems to be inaccurate, and certainly the biblical legislation is concerned with Israelite servants. Dt. 15:12 identifies the Heb. servant as 'your brother' (*cf.* v. 3; Je. 34:9, 14). It is objected that what Ex. 21 allows for an *'eḇed 'iḇrî*, Lv. 25 forbids for an Israelite; but what Ex. 21:2ff. allows is a voluntary perpetuation of an agreeable type of service, while Lv. 25:43–44 forbids compulsorily permanent, rigorous slavery. The Jubilee stipulation of Lv. 25 is a supplementary privilege granted the Heb. servant, which apparently yielded precedence to the servant's further right of voluntary lifelong service (Ex. 21:5–6).

It has been maintained that the *'iḇrîm* in 1 Sa. 13 and 14 are non-Israelite mercenaries (a role characteristic of the *ḫa-BI-ru*). But in 13:3–4 'the Hebrews' are obviously the same as 'all Israel'. Moreover, it is apparently the 'men of Israel' described in 13:6 to whom the Philistines refer in 14:11, designating them 'Hebrews'. There is similar identification of the *'iḇrîm* in 13:19–20 (*cf.* also 4:5–9). In 13:6–7 the *'iḇrîm* are not, as alleged, distinguished from the 'men of Israel'; rather, two groups of Israelites are described. V. 6 refers to those who had been excused from military service (2b) and later hid in the hills W of Jordan. V. 7 refers to certain Israelites, here called 'Hebrews', who had been selected by Saul (2a) but afterwards, deserting, sought refuge E of the Jordan (note the reduction in Saul's army: 13:2, 11, 15; 14:2). As for 14:21, even if, following EVV, the *'iḇrîm* are regarded as having fought for the enemy, they might have been Israelite traitors. The original text of v. 21, however, supports the exegesis that certain Hebrews after a lapse of courage resumed their former active hostility against the Philistines by rejoining Saul. These *'iḇrîm* are those mentioned in 13:7a. Along with the men of Israel who had hidden in the hill-country of Ephraim (14:22; *cf.* 13:6) they returned to swell the ranks of Saul's unexpectedly triumphant army.

The OT usage of *'iḇrî* is thus consistently ethnic. Most occurrences being in discourse spoken by or addressed to non-Israelites, many would see a derogatory nuance in *'iḇrî.* The suggestion that *'iḇrî* is an alternative for 'Israelite' in situations where the person is not a free citizen on free soil is perhaps not unsuitable to any of the OT passages. But even if such a connotation were intended it would be neither primary nor permanent. In the NT, 'Hebrew' is found as an exclusivist term for Jews not decisively influenced by Hellenization (Acts 6:1), but also as a term distinguishing Jews in general from Gentiles (2 Cor. 11:22; Phil. 3:5).

BIBLIOGRAPHY. M. G. Kline, 'The Ḫa-BI-ru—Kin or Foe of Israel?', *WTJ* 20, 1957, pp. 46ff.; F. F. Bruce in *AOTS*, pp. 3ff.; R. Mayer and T. McComiskey, *NIDNTT* 2, pp. 304–323; N. Na'aman, 'Habiru and Hebrews', *JNES* 45, pp. 271–288.

M.G.K.

HEBREWS, EPISTLE TO THE.

I. Outline of contents

The doctrinal theme: the superiority of Christ. 1:1–10:18

a. The Person of Christ, 1:1–4:13

(i) *Christ is superior to the Prophets* (1:1–4). The Prophets are here representative of OT revelation generally.

(ii) *Christ is superior to angels* (1:5–2:18). This is demonstrated by an appeal to various Scriptures, and Christ's apparent inferiority through suffering is then explained.

(iii) *Parenthesis* (2:1–4). Solemn warnings are given to those who neglect God's revelation.

(iv) *Christ is superior to Moses* (3:1–19). Since Moses was no more than a servant, Christ's Sonship establishes his superiority over the great lawgiver. This superiority is also seen by the fact that Moses, unlike Christ, could not lead his people into rest.

(v) *Christ is superior to Joshua* (4:1–13). Although Joshua led the Israelites into their inheritance, a better rest, still future, remains for God's people.

b. The work of Christ, 4:14–10:18

This is particularly exemplified in his office as Priest.

(i) *His priesthood is divinely appointed* (4:14–5:10). In this section the sympathy of Christ as an essential qualification for the high-priestly office is emphasized.

(ii) *His priesthood is after the order of Melchizedek* (5:11–7:28). This section begins with a long digression consisting of rebuke, solemn warning and exhortation (5:11–6:8). Then the order of Melchizedek is explained. His priesthood is perpetual (7:1–3); it is anterior to, and therefore greater than, the levitical (7:4–10); it shows the imperfections of the levitical priesthood (7:11–19). Christ's priesthood is seen to be the perfect fulfilment of the order of Melchizedek because it was established by oath, is unaffected by death and unmarred by sin (7:20–28).

(iii) *His work is within the new covenant* (8:1–9:10). Every aspect of the old order has its counterpart in the new. There is a new sanctuary in which the Mediator of a new covenant has entered to minister.

(iv) *His work is centred in a perfect atonement* (9:11–10:18). Our High Priest offered a unique sacrifice (himself), and because this offering was made 'through the eternal Spirit' it is superior to the levitical offerings (9:11–15). The necessity of Christ's death is demonstrated by an illustration from a legal testament (9:16–22). His perfect sacrifice shows up the blemishes of the levitical system (10:1–10). His ministry, unlike the Aaronic, is complete and effective (10:11–18).

The practical application of the doctrinal theme. 10:19–13:25

a. Exhortations to hold fast, 10:19–25

b. Parenthesis, 10:26–37

(i) A serious warning against apostasy (10:26–31).

(ii) Encouragement based on the readers' former experiences (10:32–37).

c. Examples from the past, 11:1–40

The writer appeals to the heroes of faith in order to inspire his readers into heroic action.

d. Advice concerning present sufferings, 12:1–29

(i) Present trials to be regarded as chastisements (12:1–13).

(ii) Warnings based on the story of Esau (12:14–17).

(iii) A final contrast between the old and the greater glory of the new (12:18–29).

e. Christian responsibilities, 13:1–25

(i) Various exhortations affecting the social and personal life of the believer (13:1–8).

(ii) A concluding warning to the readers to go forth from the camp (of Judaism) and some final personal references (13:9–25).

II. Authorship and date

The question of authorship was of greater importance in the early church than it is today, for upon it depended the canonicity of the Epistle. Ancient tradition regarding authorship consisted of various opinions. Tertullian (*De Pudicitia* 20) attributed it to Barnabas, while Origen reports that many ancients held it to be by Paul, a view shared by Clement of Alexandria. The latter seems to have regarded it as written in the Heb. dialect but translated by Luke, and he appears to have received the tradition from his predecessor Pantaenus (the blessed presbyter). Origen mentions that some in his day ascribed it to Clement of Rome and others to Luke, but he himself regarded the thoughts as the apostle's though not the words. His own conclusion regarding authorship was that God alone knew for certain who wrote the Epistle, but this reserve was not followed by the later Alexandrians, who adhered so strongly to Pauline authorship that it became accepted as canonical not only in the E but also in the W, where earlier doubts concerning it had been strong. It was not, however, until the time of Jerome and Augustine that canonicity was settled in the W. The tradition of Pauline authorship was not again seriously challenged until the time of the Reformation, when Erasmus, Luther and Calvin all disputed it. Luther's idea that Apollos was the author has commended itself to many modern scholars, although none would regard it as any more than speculative. Grotius revived the early idea that Luke was the author, and many other suggestions have been offered by modern criticism. But it is significant that few modern scholars have attempted to support the theory of Pauline authorship. It falls down on difference of style, as Origen noted when he recognized the language as 'more Greek'; on different modes of composition, such as the absence of greetings, the manner of introducing exhortations, the method of argument, and the lack of Pauline signature; on the different historical situation in which the author places himself, for whereas Paul never tired of stating that he had received the gospel by revelation, this author makes clear his personal indebtedness to second-hand information (2:3–4); and on the difference of background clearly evident in the absence from this Epistle of any past spiritual crisis dominating the author's thought and in the absence of the familiar Pauline antitheses.

Two interesting alternative suggestions are those of Ramsay, who suggested that Philip wrote the Epistle from Caesarea after contact with Paul and sent it to the Jerusalem church, and of Harnack, who made out a case for Priscilla and Aquila as joint-authors. But at best these are only ingenious guesses, and modern criticism would do well to abide by Origen's caution and let the author remain incognito.

Although the information available for dating purposes is scanty, there is enough to enable the most probable period to be ascertained. Since it was cited by Clement of Rome (*c.* AD 95) it must have been produced some while before his time. In all probability it was written before AD 70, as no mention is made of the fall of Jerusalem and as the ecclesiastical situation suits an earlier date (*cf.* 13:7,17, where those in charge are vaguely called 'leaders'). Yet some interval is required after the foundation of the church addressed to allow for the 'former days' of persecution to be regarded in retrospect. If the persecution was that under Nero a date about AD 67–8 would be required, but probably only general opposition is meant, in which case a date before AD 64 would be possible. Some scholars date the Epistle *c.* AD 80–90 on the strength of the author's use of the Pauline Epistles, but since the date of the collection of these Epistles is shrouded in mystery, and since the author does not show the influence of them all, little importance can be attached to this line of evidence.

III. Destination and purpose

The opening sentences of the Epistle give no indication of the location or identity of the readers, but the traditional title ascribes it simply 'To the Hebrews'. Although this was not part of the original text, it cannot be entirely ignored, since it may preserve genuine tradition. If that is so it must be Jewish Christians and not simply Jews who are intended. Yet a theory which has gained some support in modern times is that the title is no more than an inference from the substance of the Epistle and that it was really sent to Gentiles. Support for this notion is claimed from the consistent citations from LXX rather than the Heb. text of the OT and from the supposed Hellenistic background to which the writer appeals. The Epistle would then set forth the absolute character of Christianity to the Gentile world, showing it to supersede all other faiths, especially the mystery cults. But there is nothing in the Epistle which corresponds to mystery religions or to unbelief in religion as a whole.

Akin to this latter theory is the suggestion that the Epistle was an answer to a pre-Gnostic heresy of a type similar to that combated in Colossians. The passage showing Christ's superiority to angels (Heb. 1:4–14) would certainly give an effective answer to the tendency to angel-worship (*cf.* Col. 2:18). T. W. Manson went so far as to suggest that Apollos wrote this Epistle to the Colossian church to answer the two main tendencies of reliance on intermediaries (answered in chs. 1–4) and on ritual practices (chs. 5–10). Yet there are no evidences of pre-Gnostic tendencies in the situation underlying Hebrews such as clearly existed at Colossae.

The more widely-held view is that the Epistle was addressed to Jewish Christians to warn them against apostasy to Judaism. This is based on the serious exhortations in chs. 6 and 10, which presuppose that there is danger of a definite falling away which would amount to nothing short of crucifying the Son of God afresh (6:6) and of profanation of the blood of the covenant (10:29). Since the author is addressing those who have once tasted the goodness of God (6:4–5) and who are therefore in danger of forsaking Christianity for their old faith, and since the Epistle sets forth the superiority of Christianity to OT ritual, it is natural to suppose that Jewish Christians are in mind. The question then arises as to whether these Jewish Christians can be any more specifically defined, and various answers have been given to this inquiry: (*a*) that the Epistle was designed generally for all Jewish Christians; (*b*) that it was designed for a small house-community of Christians who had the capacity to be teachers (*cf.* 5:12) but who were not exercising it; and (*c*) that the readers were converted Jewish priests. The first view is difficult because of the personal notes in the conclusion (13:22–25) and the direct personal approach in many places in the body of the Epistle. The second view is for this reason preferable, since a particular historic situation seems to be in mind, and the readers were evidently a group apart from the main body of the church, since 5:12 could not well apply to the whole community. Moreover, the language and concepts of the Epistle presuppose an educated group, and this lends support to the idea of an intellectual clique within the local church. As to the location of these Jewish Christians, various suggestions have been made, depending partially on theories of authorship. Palestine and Alexandria have both found supporters, the former particularly by those regarding Barnabas as the author, but Rome is more favoured, supported by the somewhat ambiguous allusion in 13:24 ('They who come from Italy send you greetings'). It is not without significance in this connection that the earliest evidence for the use of the Epistle is the writing of Clement of Rome. The third alternative mentioned above, *i.e.* that the readers were converted priests, has gained support from those who claim that the argument of the Epistle would be of great relevance to those who had just recently turned from Jewish ritual practices, and especially to those who had been connected with the Jerusalem Temple (Acts records that a great many of these people were converted through Stephen's ministry). It has been objected that no evidence of separate priestly communities exists from the primitive period, but nevertheless this Epistle may provide such evidence. There seems to be no conclusive reason against this theory, and it must remain an interesting conjecture.

Yet another view, a modification of the last, sees in the Epistle a challenge to restricted Jewish Christians to embrace the world mission. This is based on certain similarities between this Epistle and Stephen's speech, such as the conception of Christianity as superseding Judaism, and the definite call to the people addressed to leave their present position. But the resemblances must not be pressed too far, since Stephen's audience did not consist of Jewish Christians. But nevertheless it is possible that the apostasy danger was the forsaking of the divine world mission purpose. A group of Jewish Christians who regarded Christianity as little more than a sect of official Judaism would certainly have benefited from the arguments of this Epistle, and it seems possible that this view will gain more support.

IV. Canonicity

The Epistle had an interesting early history, with the West generally more reluctant to accept it than the East. Through the influence of Origen the eastern churches came to accept it, mostly on the strength of Pauline authorship. But although certain of the early western Fathers used it (Clement of Rome and Tertullian), it suffered a period of eclipse, until the time of Jerome and Augustine by whom it was fully accepted, and their opinion settled the matter for the western churches.

V. Background

An understanding of the author's milieu is essential for a right appreciation of his thought, and there has been a great deal of discussion on this subject. It may be dealt with under five headings.

a. Old Testament

Since the whole argument of the Epistle revolves around OT history and ritual, it goes without saying that the author was deeply influenced by biblical teaching. In fact, it is to be noted that the basis of his approach is biblical and not Judaistic. His reverence for the sacred text is seen in the care with which he cites it, though always from LXX, in the manner in which he introduces his citations (*e.g.* the repetitive 'he says' in ch. 1) and in the strictly historical approach to OT history as contrasted with the contemporary allegorical tendencies. The author, well versed as he is in OT concepts, has clearly thought through the problem of the Christian approach to the OT, and his major emphasis is on the fulfilment in Christ of all that was adumbrated in the old order. This subject is further elaborated in the section on the theology of the Epistle, but for the present it should be noted that the author not only himself accepts the full authority of the Scriptures but clearly expects his readers to do the same.

b. Philonism

At the end of the 19th century a strong movement existed which assumed that the author's mind was so steeped in Philonic thought that it was only possible to understand his Epistle against the background of Philo's philosophical and allegorical expositions. The leading exponent of this view was E. Ménégoz, and one of his presuppositions was that a gap existed between this author's theology and that of Paul, and any similarities were clutched at to prove his indebtedness to Philo rather than to Paul. Yet some similarities cannot be denied. The notion of heaven as real and earth as only a place of shadows and the corresponding antitheses between the old covenant and the new show a similar tendency to Philo. Moreover, many words and phrases may be paralleled in the two authors, some of which occur nowhere else in the NT. C. Spicq finds the similarities reaching even to matters of style, schemes of thought, and psychology, and concludes that the author was a converted Philonist. Yet this opinion must be received with reserve, for the author differs from Philo on a number of important issues. His biblical exegesis is more akin to rabbinic methods than Philonic, his understanding of history is not, as Philo's, allegorical, and his idea of Christ as High Priest is far removed from Philo's abstract ideas of the Logos. A Christian Philonist would certainly transform his master's conceptions, but it is questionable whether the Christology of Hebrews stands in direct line of succession from Philo. The author may echo Philonic language and ideas, but his roots are without doubt elsewhere.

c. Primitive tradition

The question arises whether or not this Epistle is to be regarded as being a natural development from primitive Christian theology and whether it has any close connections with Pauline and Johannine theology, or even whether it stands as an unrelated attempt of an author to deal with the OT outside the main stream of development. Increasing interest is being shown in the early roots of the Epistle. The attempt to connect it with the catechesis of Stephen focuses attention on this, but further features from the primitive tradition may also be mentioned by way of illustration. The idea of the continuity between the old and new covenants, the interest in the earthly life of Jesus, the realization that his death must be interpreted, and the mixture of present and eschatological appeals, are all basic to the primitive Christian tradition. The main theme of this Epistle, with its predominant interest in man's approach to God, could not fail to find roots in the earliest preaching and teaching. The author introduces many new features, such as Christ's enthronement and heavenly high priesthood, but he brings in nothing alien to that primitive tradition.

d. Paulinism

It was inevitable under the hypothesis of Pauline authorship which held the field for so long that the Epistle should be regarded as an aspect of Pauline theology, yet with the rejection of Pauline authorship an unfortunate reaction set in against any Pauline influence. Support for this extreme position has declined; but it is undeniable that there are some differences from Paul which would support the theory of the author's belonging to an independent stream of tradition, as, for instance, the different treatment of Christ's relation to the law, for there is an absence of that wrestling with the law which is so evident in Paul's experience. Yet the differences must not be stretched into contrasts, and it remains possible to conceive of the author as having been under Pauline influence while at the same time acknowledging his debt to other influences. Thus he becomes an independent witness, in the truest sense, of early Christian reflection upon the great themes of the gospel.

e. Johannine thought

Whether there are any close connections between the Johannine literature and this Epistle will clearly depend on the dating of each. It has been argued that Hebrews stands midway between Paul and John in the line of theological development (as, for instance, by R. H. Strachan, *The Historic Jesus in the New Testament*, 1931), but in view of the increasing emphasis which is being placed on the primitive character of the Johannine catechesis, to which the evidence of the Dead Sea Scrolls has lent some support, this notion of theological development must be modified. The main points of contact between Hebrews and the Johannine theology are the common use of antithetic parallelism, the similar conception of Christ's high-priestly work, the description of Christ as Shepherd, the allusion to the propitiatory work of Christ, and the attention given to the perfect character of that work.

To sum up, the author is no antiquary whose researches into the biblical revelation possess no relevance for Christians generally, whether ancient or modern, but a writer who presents a vital aspect of Christian thought, complementary to other streams of primitive tradition.

VI. Theology

All that precedes has prepared the way for the most important consideration, the theological contribution of the Epistle. The standpoint of the author is to regard Christianity as the perfect revelation of God. This meant that Christianity not only superseded all other faiths, including Judaism, but that it could not itself be superseded. Its salvation is eternal (5:9), so is its redemption, inheritance and covenant (9:12, 15; 13:20), while Christ's offering is described as being 'through the eternal Spirit' (9:14). This idea of the perfection and abiding character of Christianity pervades the whole Epistle and furnishes the key for the understanding of all its major themes.

a. Christology

The first part of the Epistle is devoted to demonstrating Christ's superiority to all other intermediaries, to prophets, angels, Moses, Joshua and Aaron, but the opening chapter strikes the positive and exalted note of his divine Sonship. This Sonship is conceived of as unique, for Christ is heir of all and agent of creation (1:2). He is even more closely related to God in 1:3, where he is described as the bursting forth of his glory and the express stamp of his nature, and these two statements taken together exclude the twin errors of difference of nature and lack of distinct personality. The pre-existence of Christ seems to be clearly in the author's mind. The further statement in 1:3 that after effecting purification the Son sat down on the right hand of the majesty on high links this opening Christological statement with the later theme of the Epistle, *i.e.* the processes of redemption. Although some have sought, mistakenly, to trace influences of the currently held enthronement ritual of a king who becomes a god, the idea of Christ's exaltation is firmly rooted in the primitive Christian tradition and is a close corollary to the ascension of Christ. When he comes to his later high priest theme the writer clearly intends to introduce his readers to an exalted Christ who no longer needs liturgical means for the purgation of sins.

The incarnation of the Son is many times mentioned. He was made lower than the angels (2:9) in order to taste death for everyone, he partook of the same nature as man (2:14), he was made like his brethren in every respect (2:17) and is capable of sympathizing with our weaknesses because he was in all points tempted as we are (4:15). These statements are a necessary prelude to the high priest theme, since he must be shown to be truly representative (*cf.* 5:1). The earthly life of Jesus comes into focus not only in his temptations (2:18; 4:15) but also in his agony of prayer (5:7), in his perfect obedience (5:8), in his teaching ministry (2:3) and in his endurance of hostility (12:3).

But it is the priestly office of Christ which dominates the author's thought. The Aaronic order was good as far as it went, but its inadequacy is brought out strikingly in contrast to the perfect priesthood of Christ. This leads the author to introduce the mysterious * Melchizedek theme before his expositions of the weakness of the levitical economy (5:6, 10; 6:20–7:19). There is no means of ascertaining whether the writer himself innovated this theme or received it from primitive tradition, as it is nowhere else elaborated in the NT. But Ps. 110 in which the theme occurs exerted a powerful influence on primitive Christian thought, mainly through our Lord's own use of it, and it is reasonable to suppose that this Psalm provided the author with his conception of a superior order of priesthood. Philo, it is true, had already identified Melchizedek with the Logos, but there is no need to appeal to Philo to account for the usage of this Epistle. Nor is it just to maintain that the Melchizedek exposition is entirely speculative and without any modern relevance, for although the method of argument in 7:1ff. borders on the allegorical, the author is clear on the fundamental Christian position that Christ must belong to a higher order than that of Aaron, and in introducing the Melchizedek motive he justifies his contention that, although Christ is not a Priest according to the Aaronic order, he still is a Priest, and not only a Priest but a King.

b. The work of Christ

Against the background of the weaknesses of the Aaronic order the author brings out the positive superiority of Christ's atoning work, and the major factors involved are: (i) the finality of Christ's offering (7:27; 9:12, 28; 10:10); (ii) the personal character of his offering in that he offered himself (9:14); (iii) the spiritual character of the offering (9:14); and (iv) the abiding results of his priestly work achieving as it did *eternal* redemption (9:12). The Aaronic order, with its constantly repeated ritual, could offer no comparison with this. Even the arrangement of furniture in the holy place and the holiest place is brought into the argument (9:1ff.) in order to contrast this with the greater and more perfect sanctuary into which Christ entered once for all by virtue of his own blood. The climax of the soteriological argument is essentially reached at 9:14, where Christ is said to have offered himself 'through the eternal Spirit', which brings into striking contrast the helpless and hapless victims of the Aaronic ritual and the deliberate self-offering of our High Priest. The practical application of all this is found in 10:19, where confidence of approach on the basis of Christ's high-priestly work is urged upon the readers, and this leads on to the mainly practical conclusion of the Epistle.

c. Other theological concepts

One of the great words of the Epistle is 'faith', but it has a different meaning from the Pauline concept. For this writer there is little of the dynamic concept of faith which accepts God's provision of salvation (though 10:22 approximates to this and requires to be so understood). In the use of the concept in the great gallery of heroes in ch. 11, the writer does not give a formal definition of faith but rather gives a description of some of its active qualities. It is essentially practical, comprising rather an approach to life than a mystical appropriation. In various ways the author makes clear the meaning of Christian *salvation*, which has deeply impressed him with its greatness (2:3). He makes use of Ps. 8 to introduce the fact that it is through humiliation that Christ gained the right to bring 'many sons to glory' (2:5–10); he conceives of salvation as deliverance from the power of the devil (2:14–15) and also depicts it as a rest into which believers enter as an inheritance (3:1–4:13). The processes of salvation are described as sanctification (*hagiasmos*, 12:14; *cf.* 2:11; 10:10, 29; 13:12) and perfection (*teleiōsis*, 7:11; *cf.* 11:40; 12:23).

BIBLIOGRAPHY. A. Nairne, *The Epistle to the Hebrews, CGT*, 1922; J. Moffatt, *The Epistle to the Hebrews, ICC*, 1924; F. D. V. Narborough, *The Epistle to the Hebrews, Clarendon Bible*, 1930; F. J. Badcock, *The Pauline Epistles and the Epistle to the Hebrews*, 1937; E. Käsemann, *Das wandernde Gottesvolk*, 1939; O. Michel, *Der Brief an die Hebräer, Kritisch-Exegetischer Kommentar*, 1949; W. Manson, *The Epistle to the Hebrews*, 1951; C. Spicq, *L'Épître aux Hébreux, Études Bibliques*, 1952; T. Hewitt, *The Epistle to the Hebrews, TNTC*, 1960; J. Héring, *The Epistle to the Hebrews*, E.T. 1970; R. Williamson, *Philo and the Epistle to the Hebrews*, 1970; F. L. Horton, *The Melchizedek Tradition*, 1976; P. E. Hughes, *A Commentary on the Epistle to the Hebrews*, 1977; R. Brown, *The Message of Hebrews, BST*, 1982; D. Guthrie, *Hebrews, TNTC*², 1983; F. F. Bruce, *The Epistle to the Hebrews, NIC*², 1990; W. L. Lane, *Hebrews 1–8, WBC*, 1991; *Hebrews 9–13, WBC*, 1991. D.G.

HEBRON (Heb. *ḥeḇrôn*, 'confederacy'; *cf.* its alternative and older name Kiriath-arba, 'tetrapolis'), the highest town in Palestine, 927 m above the level of the Mediterranean, 30 km SSW of Jerusalem. The statement that it 'was built seven years before Zoan in Egypt' (Nu. 13:22) probably relates its foundation to the 'Era of Tanis' (*c.* 1720 BC). Abraham lived in its vicinity for considerable periods (*MAMRE); in his days the resident population ('the people of the land') were 'sons of Heth' (*HITTITES), from whom Abraham bought the field of Machpelah with its cave to be a family burying-ground (Gn. 23). There he and Sarah, Isaac and Rebekah, Jacob and Leah were buried (Gn. 49:31; 50:13). According to Josephus (*Ant.* 2. 199; 3. 305), the sons of Jacob, with the exception of Joseph, were buried there too. The traditional site of the Patriarchs' sepulchre lies within the great *Ḥaram el-Ḥalîl*, the 'Enclosure of the Friend' (*i.e.* Abraham; *cf.* Is. 41:8), with its Herodian masonry. During the Israelites' wilderness wandering the twelve spies sent out to report on the land of Canaan explored the region of Hebron; at that time it was populated by the 'descendants of Anak' (Nu. 13:22, 28, 33) (*NEAEHL*, pp. 606–609). After Israel's entry into Canaan, Hoham, king of Hebron, joined the anti-Gibeonite coalition led by Adonizedek, king of Jerusalem, and was killed by Joshua (Jos. 10:1–27). Hebron itself and the surrounding territory were conquered from the Anakim by Caleb and given to him as a family possession (Jos. 14:12ff.; 15:13f.; Jdg. 1:10, 20). In Hebron David was anointed king of Judah (2 Sa. 2:4) and 2 years later king of Israel also (2 Sa. 5:3); it remained his capital for 7½ years. It was here too, later in his reign, that Absalom raised the standard of rebellion against him (2 Sa. 15:7ff.). It was fortified by Rehoboam (2 Ch. 11:10).

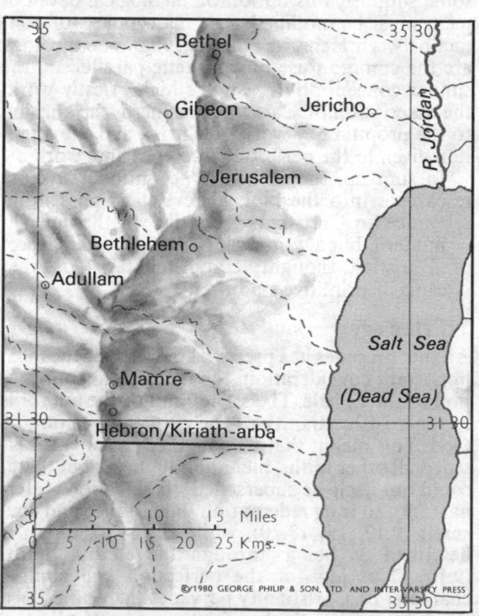

Hebron, burial-place of Abraham.

Hebron is one of the four cities named on royal jar-handle stamps found at * Lachish and other sites, which probably points to its importance as a major Judaean administrative centre in the reign of Hezekiah. After the Babylonian captivity it was one of the places where returning exiles settled (Ne. 11:25; Kiriath-arba = Hebron). Later it was occupied by the Idumaeans, from whom Judas Maccabaeus captured it (1 Macc. 5:65). During the war of AD 66–70 it was occupied by Simon bar-Giora, but was stormed and burnt by the Romans (Jos., *BJ* 4. 529, 554).

Under the name of el-Ḫalîl it is one of the four sacred cities of the Muslims.

Bibliography. L. H. Vincent and E. J. H. Mackay, *Hébron, le Ḥaram el-Khalil, sépulture des patriarches*, 2 vols., 1923; D. Baly, *Geography of the Bible*², 1974. F.F.B.

HEIFER (Heb. *'eglâ*, 12 times; Heb. *pārâ*, 'young cow', 6 times; Gk. *damalis*, 'tamed heifer', Heb. 9:13 only). Mixed with water, the ashes of an unblemished red heifer, burnt in its entirety 'outside the camp', imparted levitical purification (Nu. 19; Heb. 9:13). A heifer with a broken neck cleansed the nearest city from the blood-guiltiness of a corpse slain by unknown hands (Dt. 21:1–9). Jdg. 14:18; Je. 46:20; Ho. 4:16, *etc.*, give interesting metaphorical usages.

Bibliography. F. F. Bruce, *The Epistle to the Hebrews*², *NIC*, 1988; C. Brown, *NIDNTT* 1, pp. 115f.; R. A. Stewart, *Rabbinic Theology*, 1961, p. 138. R.A.S.

HELAM. A city in Transjordan, probably the modern 'Alma, the location of the defeat of Hadadezer's Syrian forces, reinforced by Syrian troops from beyond the Euphrates, by David (2 Sa. 10:16f.), following the defeat of an Ammonite–Syrian alliance by David's captain Joab. The mention of the Gk. form, Eliam, constituting part of a place-name in LXX of Ezk. 47:16, has led to a proposed alternative location on the border between Damascus and Hamath. Connection with Alema (1 Macc. 5:26) has also been suggested. R.A.H.G.

HELBON (Heb. *ḥelbôn*, 'fat', 'fruitful'). A town mentioned in Ezk. 27:18 as trading wine to Tyre. This has been identified with the village of Khalbun, 25 km N of Damascus. The author of the Genesis Apocryphon from Qumran wrote Helbon for the place-name *Hobah of Gn. 14:15, described as 'on the left hand of' or 'north of' Damascus, and this gives interesting evidence for thus identifying an otherwise unknown site. J.B.Tr.

HELDAI. *Cf.* Heled. (Heb. *ḥeleḏ* means 'duration of life'; *cf.* Arab. *ḫalada* and *ḫuludun*.)

1. In 1 Ch. 27:15, one of David's famous soldiers who was appointed over 24,000 in the 12th month. He was a Netophathite, and thus from Judah, from the stock of Othniel (*cf.* Jdg. 1:12–15). The 'Heled' of 1 Ch. 11:30 is doubtless the same person. He is called a free man (Heb. *gibbôr ḥayil*, v. 26), one of the commanders of the army. We must probably read 'Heled' and not 'Heleb' in 2 Sa. 23:29, and he may have been the same person as the above mentioned.

2. A Heldai is mentioned in Zc. 6:10 with Tobijah and Jedaiah. After they returned from the Exile, silver and gold was taken from them to make a crown for Joshua, the high priest. Heldai is called Helem in v. 14 (Heb.); this may have been a nickname or may be due to a scribal error. F.C.F.

HELEZ. The Heb. *ḥeleṣ* may mean 'loins' or perhaps 'strength'.

1. One of David's heroes. The Helez of 2 Sa. 23:26 is probably the same as the one of 1 Ch. 11:27 and 27:10. The problem is that in 2 Sa. he is described as the Paltite (Heb. *palṭî*, a man of *bêṯ peleṭ*, a place in Judah) and in 1 Ch. as the Pelonite (Heb. *pᵉlōnî* means 'any one'). We may have to change 'Pelonite' to 'Paltite' or to accept that Helez of 2 Sa. is not to be identified with the one of 1 Ch. 11 and 27. In 1 Ch. 27:10 he is called one 'of the sons of Ephraim'. It may be that as a descendant of Ephraim he was regarded as a Pelonite, 'one without any connection to Judah', but lived in Beth Pelet.

2. The son of Azariah, a descendant of Judah (1 Ch. 2:39). F.C.F.

HELKATH. In the border-territory of Asher (Jos. 19:25) and a levitical city (Jos. 21:31). 1 Ch. 6:75 gives Hukok as a variant for Helkath. The exact location in the Kishon valley is disputed: a likely site for it is Tell el-Harbaj nearly 10 km SE of Haifa (A. Alt, *Palästinajahrbuch* 25, 1929, pp. 38ff.), or perhaps even better, Tell el-Qasis (or Kussis) 8 km SSE of Tell el-Harbaj (Y. Aharoni, *IEJ* 9, 1959, pp. 119–120). Helkath is probably the *ḥrḳt* in topographical lists of the pharaoh Tuthmosis III, *c.* 1460 BC. K.A.K.

HELKATH-HAZZURIM (Heb. *ḥelqaṯ haṣṣurîm*, 'field of flints' or 'field of (sword)-edges'). This is the name given to the place in Gibeon where there was a tournament between the champions of Joab and Abner, which led on to a battle (2 Sa. 2:16). Other meanings conjectured include 'field of plotters', based on the LXX *meris tōn epiboulōn*, 'field of sides' and 'field of adversaries'. (*Cf.* S. R. Driver, *Notes on the Hebrew Text of the Books of Samuel*, 1913.) J.G.G.N.

HELL. 'Hell' in the NT renders the Gk. word transliterated as 'Gehenna' (Mt. 5:22, 29–30; 10:28; 18:9; 23:15, 33; Mk. 9:43, 45, 47; Lk. 12:5; Jas. 3:6). The name is derived from the Heb. *gê(ben)(bᵉnê) hinnōm*, the valley of (the son[s] of) Hinnom, a valley near Jerusalem (Jos. 15:8; 18:16) where children were sacrificed by fire in connection with pagan rites (2 Ki. 23:10; 2 Ch. 28:3; 33:6; Je. 7:31; 32:35). Its original derivation is obscure, but Hinnom is almost certainly the name of a person. In later Jewish writings Gehenna came to mean the place of punishment for sinners (*Assumption of Moses* 10:10; 2 Esdras 7:36). It was depicted as a place of unquenchable fire—the general idea of fire to express the divine judgment is found in the OT (Dt. 32:22; Dn. 7:10). The rabbinic literature contains various opinions as to who would suffer eternal punishment. The ideas were widespread that the sufferings of some would be terminated by annihilation, or that the fires of Gehenna were in some cases purgatorial (*Rosh Hashanah* 16b–17a;

Baba Mezi'a 58b; Mishnah *Eduyoth* 2. 10). But those who held these doctrines also taught the reality of eternal punishment for certain classes of sinners. Both this literature and the Apocryphal books affirm belief in an eternal retribution (*cf.* Judith 16:17; *Psalms of Solomon* 3:13).

The teaching of the NT endorses this past belief. The fire of hell is unquenchable (Mk. 9:43), eternal (Mt. 18:8), its punishment is the converse of eternal life (Mt. 25:46). There is no suggestion that those who enter hell ever emerge from it. However, the NT leaves the door open for the belief that while hell as a manifestation of God's implacable wrath against sin is unending, the existence of those who suffer in it may not be. It is difficult to reconcile the ultimate fulfilment of the whole universe in Christ (Eph. 1:10; Col. 1:20) with the continued existence of those who reject him. Some scholars have contended that an eternal punishment is one which is eternal in its effects; in any case eternal does not necessarily mean never-ending, but implies 'long duration extending to the writer's mental horizon' (J. A. Beet). On the other hand Rev. 20:10 does indicate conscious, never-ending torment for the devil and his agents, albeit in a highly symbolic passage, and some would affirm that a similar end awaits human beings who ultimately refuse to repent. In any case, nothing should be allowed to detract from the seriousness of our Lord's warnings about the terrible reality of God's judgment in the world to come.

In Jas. 3:6 Gehenna, like the bottomless pit in Rev. 9:1ff.; 11:7, appears to be the source of evil on the earth.

NT imagery concerning eternal punishment is not uniform. As well as fire it is described as darkness (Mt. 25:30; 2 Pet. 2:17), death (Rev. 2:11), destruction and exclusion from the presence of the Lord (2 Thes. 1:9; Mt. 7:21–23), and a debt to pay (Mt. 5:25–26).

In 2 Pet. 2:4 only, we find the verb *tartaroō*, translated in RSV 'cast into hell', and rendered by the Pesh. 'cast down to the lower regions'. *Tartaros* is the classical word for the place of eternal punishment but is here applied to the intermediate sphere of punishment for fallen angels.

BIBLIOGRAPHY. J. A. Beet, *The Last Things*, 1905; S. D. F. Salmond, *The Christian Doctrine of Immortality*, 1907; J. W. Wenham, *The Enigma of Evil*[2], 1994; H. Bietenhard, *NIDNTT* 2, pp. 205–210; J. Jeremias, *TDNT* 1, pp. 9f., 146–149, 657f.

D.K.I.

HELLENISTS. Gk. *hellēnistai*, people, not themselves Greeks (*hellēnes*), who 'hellenized', *i.e.* spoke the Greek language (*hellēnisti*, Acts 21:37, *etc.*) and otherwise adopted the Greek way of life (*hellēnismos*, 2 Macc. 4:10).

The earliest occurrence of the word in Greek literature is in Acts 6:1, where it denotes a group of Jewish Christians in the primitive church of Jerusalem, distinguished from the 'Hebrews' (*hebraioi*), who were probably Aramaic-speaking. The seven almoners, including Stephen and Philip, appointed in response to the Hellenists' complaint that the 'Hebrew' widows were being favoured over theirs in the distribution of charity from the common fund, all appear by their names to have been Hellenists (Acts 6:5). Many of the Hellenists would have connections with the Diaspora, whereas most of the Hebrews would be Palestinian Jews. The line of demarcation between Hebrews and Hellenists cannot have been hard and fast, for many Jews were bilingual. Paul, for example, who spoke Greek habitually (as might be expected in a native of Tarsus), nevertheless calls himself 'a Hebrew born of Hebrews' (Phil. 3:5; *cf.* 2 Cor. 11:22). Perhaps the determinant factor with such a person was whether the services in the synagogue which he attended were conducted in Greek (*cf.* Acts 6:9) or in Hebrew.

To judge from Stephen and Philip, the Hellenists in the Jerusalem church were more forward-looking than the Hebrews, in teaching and practice alike. In the persecution which broke out after Stephen's death, it was mainly the Hellenists who were scattered, propagating the gospel wherever they went. Attempts to link these Hellenists with Essenes or with Samaritans have not been successful (apart from their antecedent improbability).

The Hellenists of Acts 9:29 were members of one or more Greek-speaking synagogues in Jerusalem.

In Acts 11:20 the MSS are divided between 'Hellenists' (*hellēnistas*) and 'Greeks' (*hellēnas*), with the weight of evidence favouring the former. Whichever reading be preferred, the context makes it plain that the reference is to Gentile residents of Antioch, to whom Christian visitors, 'men of Cyprus and Cyrene', took the initiative in preaching the gospel, whereas their associates on first coming to Antioch had preached it 'to none except Jews' (Acts 11:19). If they were not Greeks (*hellēnes*) by origin, they could have belonged to other ethnic groups in Antioch which had adopted Greek language and culture.

BIBLIOGRAPHY. H. J. Cadbury, 'The Hellenists', *BC* 5, pp. 59ff.; H. Windisch, *TDNT* 2, pp. 511f. (*s.v. Hellēnistēs*); E. C. Blackman, 'The Hellenists of Acts vi.1', *ExpT* 48, 1936–7, pp. 524f.; O. Cullmann, 'The Significance of the Qumran Texts for Research into the Beginnings of Christianity', *JBL* 74, 1955, pp. 213ff.; M. Simon, *St. Stephen and the Hellenists in the Primitive Church*, 1958; C. F. D. Moule, 'Once More, Who Were the Hellenists?', *ExpT* 70, 1958–9, pp. 100ff.; C. S. Mann, ' "Hellenists" and "Hebrews" in Acts VI 1', in J. Munck, *The Acts of the Apostles*, 1967, pp. 301ff.; I. H. Marshall, 'Palestinian and Hellenistic Christianity', *NTS* 19, 1972–3, pp. 271ff.; M. Hengel, *Judaism and Hellenism*, 1974; M. Hengel, 'Between Jesus and Paul: The "Hellenists", the "Seven" and Stephen', *Between Jesus and Paul*, 1983.

F.F.B.

HEMAN (Heb. *hêmān*, 'faithful'). **1.** One of the sages whom Solomon excelled in wisdom (1 Ki. 4:31). Said to be a son of *Mahol; but 1 Ch. 2:6 calls him a son of Zerah, a Judahite.

2. A Kohathite Levite, son of Joel, one of David's leading singers (1 Ch. 6:33; 15:17, 19; 16:41–42; 25:1, 4–6; 2 Ch. 5:12; 35:15). Probably the 'sons of Heman' in 1 Ch. 25:4 are really the titles of parts of a prayer or anthem, the singers receiving names from their parts (*cf.* H. L. Ellison in *NBCR*, 1970, pp. 281f.; W. R. Smith, *The Old Testament in the Jewish Church*[2], p. 143 n.).

3. The Ezrahite named in the title of Ps. 88. Probably the same as **1**.

J.G.G.N.

HEN (Heb. *ḥēn*, 'favour'). One of the men who were to receive a symbolical crown (Zc. 6:14), this may be a figurative name for Josiah who had earlier (6:10) been similarly described as 'the son of Zephaniah'. J.D.D.

HENA. A city whose god, the Assyrians boasted, could not save it (2 Ki. 18:34). It is identified by LXX with Ana on the Euphrates. Hena and Ivvah have been identified as Arab. star names, and consequently taken as the names of deities. This is, however, unlikely, as the latter is almost certainly a place-name identical with Avva (2 Ki. 17:24, 31). M.A.M.

HERALD. 1. Aram. *kārôz* occurs only in Dn. 3:4 with reference to the official who relayed Nebuchadrezzar's commands. *kārôz* may be derived from Old Persian *xrausa* (*KB*), 'caller', or is related to Hurrian *kirezzi*, 'proclamation'. The causative form of the associated verb *krz*, 'made a proclamation', occurs in Dn. 5:29 (see A. Shaffer, *Orientalia* 34, 1965, pp. 32–34). **2.** Heb. *m^e baśśereṯ* (Is. 40:9; masculine. Is. 41:27), 'bringing good news', is rendered in RSV as 'herald of good tidings'. The verbal form is used elsewhere in Is. in the same sense of preaching the deliverance of Yahweh (Is. 52:7; 61:1).

3. Gk. *kēryx* is translated 'herald' by RSV in 2 Pet. 2:5, but 'preacher' in 1 Tim. 2:7; 2 Tim. 1:11. W.O. A.R.M.

HERBS AND SPICES. Here considered in the popular sense of edible culinary, or sometimes medicinal, plants, although strictly a herb is a non-woody plant with seasonal foliage and varying expectation of life in the root. This selection of species mentioned in the Bible is complementary to the articles on *plants, *trees, *cosmetics and individual subjects.

In the OT *deše'* normally denotes grass, *ḥāṣîr*, *'ēśeḇ*, and the less common *yārāq* (Dt. 11:10; 1 Ki. 21:2; Pr. 15:17) may mean grass, and also herbs or vegetables. *'ōrōṯ* (2 Ki. 4:39) is talmudically rendered 'garden-rocket' or 'colewort' (*Eruca*), precision perhaps exceeding the evidence (*Yoma* 18b). Is. 26:19 may speak of the dew of light (RSV) rather than the dew of herbs (AV). The NT uses *chortos* for pasturage, *lachanon* for herbs in the popular sense.

Spices are aromatic vegetable substances, highly esteemed by ancient Near Eastern peoples. Spice caravans pioneered the trading routes from N India to Sumeria, Akkad and Egypt at a very early period, and subsequently these routes became an important factor in cultural exchanges. While many spices were brought to Palestine from Mesopotamia and India, a number of those in common use were the product of the country itself. In OT times the Palestinian spice trade was carefully protected. Solomon derived considerable revenue by exacting tolls of the caravans passing through his realm.

Herbs and spices such as cummin, dill, cinnamon and mint were employed in the preparation of food (Ezk. 24:10) and the flavouring of wines (Ct. 8:2). The manufacture of the sacred *incense necessitated the use of frankincense, stacte, galbanum, onycha and sweet cane (Ex. 30:34), while substances such as cassia, aloes and spikenard were used as unguents for cosmetic purposes (Est. 2:12; Ct. 4:14; Mk. 14:3; Jn. 12:3).

When bodies were being prepared for burial it was customary for spices to be placed in the graveclothes as a form of embalming. They included mixtures of myrrh and aloes (Jn. 19:39), or, more generally, 'spices and ointments' (Lk. 23:56). While they did not significantly inhibit putrefaction, they served as deodorants and disinfectants.

Aloes (Heb. *'^a hālîm* in Pr. 7:17; Nu. 24:6, 'lign aloes'; *'^a hālôṯ* in Ps. 45:8; Ct. 4:14). Probably the modern eaglewood (*Aquilaria agallocha*) found today in E Bengal, Malaya and parts of China. From it was derived a precious spice used in biblical times for perfuming garments and beds. The perplexing question of the reference in Nu. 24:6 may suggest that the tree (or one similar) grew in the Jordan valley, but Balaam need not have actually seen the tree of which he spoke.

Aloes in Jn. 19:39 refers to a totally different liliaceous plant *Aloe barbadense*, also known as *A. vera*, wild in the Yemen and now widely naturalized. The juice of its fleshy, sword-like leaves is bitter and was used for embalming.

Balm (Heb. *ṣ^e rî, ṣ^o rî*; LXX *rhētinē*). This product of *Gilead, a somewhat vague geographical area, was exported to Egypt (Gn. 37:25; 43:11) and to Tyre (Ezk. 27:17). Celebrated for healing properties (Je. 46:11) and often used for cosmetic purposes, it was used also to symbolize deliverance from national distress (Je. 8:22; 51:8). It was probably an aromatic gum or spice, but the original meaning of the word is not clear and it cannot now be identified with any plant in Gilead, despite the claims made for a similarly-named substance prepared by the monks of Jericho from the fruit of the *zaqqûm* (*Balanites aegyptiaca*). Some understand the *ṣ^o rî* of Gn. 37:25 to be gum mastic, a product of the shrub *Pistacia lentiscus* which, common in Palestine for healing purposes, is used by the Arabs in flavouring coffee and sweets, and as a chewing-gum. Classical authors applied the name 'balm of Gilead' to what is now known as Mecca balsam or stacte (*Commiphora gileadensis*), still imported into Egypt from Arabia. The gum (Heb. *n^e kō'ṯ*, 'spicery' AV) of Gn. 37:25; 43:11 could have been the exudate from the stems of the small prickly shrub *Astragalus gummifer.* It grows on the arid slopes of Iran and Turkey and belongs to the pea family.

Bitter herbs (Heb. *m^e rôrîm*; Gk. *pikrides*). A salad composed of herbs constituted part of the Passover ordinance (Ex. 12:8; Nu. 9:11), and ordinarily was eaten after the Passover lamb had been tasted. The bitter herbs were not named individually, but are identified in the Mishna as lettuce, chicory, eryngo, horseradish and sow-thistle, although all these may not have been available in biblical times. Though *m^e rôrîm* was used elsewhere of 'bitterness' (*cf.* La. 3:15), the Passover herbs, being easily prepared, reminded the Israelites of their haste in leaving Egypt, not their bitter persecution there.

Black cummin (Heb. *qeṣaḥ*: 'fitches' AV, 'dill' RSV). *Nigella sativa*, or nut-meg flower, is an annual closely related to the ornamental love-in-the-mist, but with greenish-blue flowers and black seeds. Its dry fruits were beaten with light sticks (Is. 28:27) to avoid damaging the aromatic, oily seeds, which were a favourite condiment of the ancient Greeks and Romans and are still used for seasoning bread and as a carminative. See also **Dill** below.

Cassia (Heb. *qiddâ*, Ex. 30:24; Ezk. 27:19; *qᵉṣîʿōṯ*, Ps. 45:8). These two words, identified as similar in the Pesh. and the Targ., have traditionally been considered to refer to the bark of *Cinnamomum cassia*. But, since this is a Far Eastern tree, it is unlikely to have been the fragrant aromatic substance used in the anointing oil of Ex. 30:24. The word 'cassia', like other plant products (*e.g.* ebony), was probably applied in ancient times to one substance and the application later transferred to another more easily obtainable product having properties similar to or better than the original. Cassia and cinnamon were perfumes used at Roman funerals by which time the E trade routes were established and they used the products at present known by these names.

Cinnamon (Heb. *qinnāmôn*; Gk. *kinnamōmon*). Traditionally considered to be the product of *Cinnamomum zeylanicum*, a plant of the laurel family cultivated in Ceylon and Java, but possibly cinnamon, like cassia, was obtained from an as yet uncertainly identified plant more readily available to the Israelites in Sinai. Used as one of the perfumes of the 'holy anointing oil' (Ex. 30:23), and for beds (Pr. 7:17), it was highly prized in Solomon's day (Ct. 4:14), and was listed as one of the valuable commodities of 'Babylon the Great' (Rev. 18:13).

Coriander (Heb. *gaḏ*, Ex. 16:31; Nu. 11:7). Indigenous to the Mediterranean area, this small umbelliferous annual (*Coriandrum sativum*) is known to have been used as early as 1550 BC for culinary and medicinal purposes. Its aromatic seed, to which the wandering Israelites likened *manna, is grey-yellow in colour, enclosed in a spherical fruit 4 mm in diameter.

Cummin (Heb. *kammōn*; Gk. *kyminon*). An aromatic seed from *Cuminum cyminum*, a plant indigenous to W Asia and cultivated from the earliest times. Resembling the caraway in taste and appearance, it is used to flavour dishes, particularly during fasts, and is said to have medicinal properties. The plant is still threshed with sticks to preserve the small brittle seeds which would be crushed by a wheel (Is. 28:27). The scribes and Pharisees, scrupulously paying tithes of cummin, were charged by Jesus with neglecting weightier matters (Mt. 23:23).

Dill (Gk. *anēthon*, 'anise' AV, Mt. 23:23). An annual umbelliferous plant (*Anethum graveolens*) with finely divided leaves and small greenish yellow flowers. The seeds and leaves were widely used for culinary and medicinal purposes in antiquity. See **Black cummin** above for 'dill' of Is. 28:27.

Henna. A cultivated shrub (*Lawsonia inermis*; Heb. *kōp̄er*, Ct. 1:14; 4:13, 'camphire' AV) which favours warm conditions such as prevail at Ein Gedi where Solomon had vineyards. Its fragrant white blossoms were given between friends; its pulverized leaves were made into a paste as a cosmetic by women in ancient times to impart a yellow dye to skin, especially the palms of the hands, and the men's beards, even the manes and tails of horses. Any women thus adorned who fell captive to the Hebrews were required to remove all traces of the dye (Dt. 21:11–12). The orange or bright yellow colour probably had pagan associations.

Mint (Gk. *hēdyosmon*, Mt. 23:23; Lk. 11:42). Many species of the mint family (Labiatae) are fragrant, but the most likely one to be used was a species of *Mentha*, probably the horse-mint (*M. longifolia*). It is a perennial about 40 cm high with mauve flowers in whorls. The characteristic essential oils present in mints make the herbs a useful condiment. NT references, however, merely point out the scrupulosity of the Pharisees, who tithed even the commonest garden herbs.

Myrrh (Akkad. *murru*; Heb. *mōr*). The resinous exudate from incisions on the stems and branches of a low shrubby tree, either *Commiphora myrrha* (formerly *Balsamodendron myrrha*) or the closely related *Commiphora kataf*. Both species are native to S Arabia and adjacent parts of Africa. The gum oozes from the wounds as 'tears' which harden to form an oily yellowish-brown resin.

Myrrh was an ingredient of the holy anointing oil (Ex. 30:23–33). It was prized for its aromatic qualities (Ps. 45:8; Pr. 7:17; Ct. 3:6; 4:14; 5:5, 13), and used in female purification rites (Est. 2:12), as well as in cosmetic preparations. Myrrh was presented to the infant Jesus by the magi (Mt. 2:11); it formed part of an anodyne offered to him on Calvary (Mk. 15:23), and was one of the spices employed at his burial, together with aloes, as a form of embalming (Jn. 19:39).

The 'myrrh' of Gn. 37:25; 43:11 (Heb. *lōṭ*) carried by Ishmaelite traders to Egypt was probably a ladanum resin obtained from the rock roses *Cistus laurifolius* or *C. creticus* (= *C. villosus*). They are rounded evergreen bushes sticky to the touch, with large white or pink rose-like flowers.

Rue (Gk. *pēganon*, Lk. 11:42). A perennial herb up to 80 cm high, shrubby at the base, with grey-green leaves emitting a strong odour. *Ruta chalepensis* grows in rocky places in Palestine, and the similar *R. graveolens* is S European, having been in cultivation since ancient times. Rue was highly prized for its medicinal values, having alleged disinfectant and antiseptic properties, and for flavouring food. Christ criticized the Pharisees for their meticulous legalism in tithing it while neglecting more important matters.

Saffron (Heb. *karkōm*, LXX *krokos*, Ct. 4:14). This expensive substance is produced from the flowers of *Crocus sativus*, a native of Greece and flowers of *Crocus sativus*, a native of Greece and Asia Minor. Only the orange styles and stigmas are collected, dried and packed. In antiquity saffron was used for dyeing and colouring foodstuffs. It was also a therapeutic agent, being used as an emmenagogue, stimulant and antispasmodic. The ancient Egyptians employed a different plant, safflower (*Carthamus tinctorius*), which yields a yellow dye similar to saffron for colouring the grave-clothes of mummies.

Spikenard (Heb. *nērd*; Gk. *nardos*). The fragrant essential oil referred to as a perfume in Ct. 1:12; 4:13f. is very likely to be the same as the *lardu* of Assyro-Babylonian inscriptions, which was obtained from the camel-grass, *Cymbopogon schoenanthus*, common in the deserts of Arabia and N Africa.

Spikenard of the NT (Mk. 14:3; Jn. 12:3) was described as 'pistic', an obscure term probably meaning 'genuine'. This perfume is considered to have been obtained from the essential oil in the roots of *Nardostachys jatamansi*, a more pleasantly scented relative of the valerian. It is native of the Himalayas and is still used for the hair.

Stacte (Hebb. *nāṭāp̄*; Gk. *staktē*). One of the ingredients of the sacred incense (Ex. 30:34). The Heb. name indicates 'dropping', from which is implied its origin as an exudate in the form of drops.

Two plants are possibilities: the balm-of-Gilead (*Commiphora gileadensis*), a native of S Arabia in spite of its name, and storax (*Styrax officinale*) of the Palestinian hills. The balm-of-Gilead is also known as opobalsam and is a much-branched bush less than the height of a man, with small, three-foliolate leaves. The storax is a small tree with white flowers. The resin is obtained from both by making incisions in the branches. Another suggestion, *Liquidambar orientalis*, also known as storax, is not as likely since it is a tree of Cyprus, Rhodes and Turkey.

Sweet cane (Heb. *qāneh*, Is. 43:24; Je. 6:20). Whole dry rhizomes of sweet flag (*Acorus calamus*), a marsh plant of the arum family, were traded as sweet cane in ancient times for use as a tonic and stimulant. Native of temperate Asia, it has been introduced into a wider area. The sugar cane, with which sweet-cane has also been identified, actually spread E after OT times.

BIBLIOGRAPHY. See *PLANTS. F.N.H. *et al.*

HERESY. The Gk. word *hairesis* properly denotes 'choice', and this is the meaning which it always bears in the LXX; in classical authors, however, it can refer to a philosophical school which the individual chooses to follow. Similarly, the NT uses the word to denote a 'party', with the suggestion of self-will or sectarian spirit; but it must be noted that none of the parties thus described is in a state of schism from its parent body. The Sadducees (Acts 5:17) and the Pharisees (Acts 15:5; 26:5) form sects within the fold of Judaism; and the same word is used to describe Christianity as seen from outside (Acts 24:5, 14; 28:22). Josephus, however, uses the same term to describe the Essenes as well, who were in schism (*Ant.* 13. 171; 18. 18–22). When parties appear within the church they are called 'heresies' (1 Cor. 11:19, where Paul seems to imply that, though bad, they have the good result of making it clear who are the true Christians). Such divisions are regarded as a work of the flesh (Gal. 5:20), and primarily as a breach of mutual charity, so that the heretic, *i.e.* the man who stubbornly chooses to form or follow his own group, is to be rejected after two admonitions (Tit. 3:10).

The only NT use of 'heresy' in the sense of opinion or doctrinal error occurs in 2 Pet. 2:1, where it includes a denial of the Redeemer. Among incipient heresies mentioned in the NT, the most prominent are: Gnosticism of a Jewish type (Col. 2:8–23) and Docetism (1 Jn. 4:2–3; 2 Jn. 7).

BIBLIOGRAPHY. G. Forkman, *The Limits of the Religious Community*, 1972; W. Elert, *Eucharist and Church Fellowship in the First Four Centuries*, E.T. 1966; H. Schlier, *TDNT* 1, pp. 180–184.

G.S.M.W.
R.T.B.

HERMAS. One of a group of Christians greeted, some by name, in Rom. 16:14. They apparently belonged to a single community, perhaps a house-church. The name is a fairly common diminutive for a number of compound names. Origen's suggestion that the author of *The Shepherd* of Hermas (*PATRISTIC LITERATURE) is indicated here has nothing to commend it. A.F.W.

HERMENEUTICS. This term, from Gk. *hermēneuō* ('interpret'), is used to denote (*a*) the study and statement of the principles on which a text—for present purposes, the biblical text—is to be understood, or (*b*) the interpretation of the text in such a way that its message comes home to the reader or hearer. In our own day this aim has been pursued by means of an existential interpretation of the text. For example, while the understanding of the parables of Jesus is greatly aided at one level by an examination of the local and contemporary setting (as in J. Jeremias, *The Parables of Jesus*, 1954), their relevance to readers today has been brought out by existential interpretation (as in G. V. Jones, *The Art and Truth of the Parables*, 1964, or E. Linnemann, *The Parables of Jesus*, 1966). There is a place for both levels of interpretation, but without the prior historical exegesis the existential hermeneutic lacks any anchorage. The task of existential hermeneutics has been seen as the re-establishment, for today's reader of (say) the parables, of that common understanding with his hearers which Jesus established when he first told them. (*INTERPRETATION, BIBLICAL.)

BIBLIOGRAPHY. J. D. Smart, *The Strange Silence of the Bible in the Church*, 1970; H. G. Gadamer, *Truth and Method*, 1975; N. Perrin, *Jesus and the Language of the Kingdom*, 1976; I. H. Marshall (ed.), *New Testament Interpretation*, 1977; R. Lundin, A. C. Thistleton and C. Walhout, *The Responsibility of Hermeneutics*, 1985; D. A. Carson and J. D. Woodbridge (eds.), *Hermeneutics, Authority and Canon*, 1986. F.F.B.

HERMES. Originally the spirit inhabiting the *herma* or cairn, set up as a guide-mark or boundary. Hence the doorside *herms*, roughly carved phallic stones of Athens, and the god's function as guide of living and dead, as patron of road-users (including footpads), and as Zeus' attendant and spokesman (Acts 14:12). (The cultic association of Zeus and Hermes at Lystra is illustrated in that part of Asia Minor by the legend of Philemon and Baucis, preserved by Ovid, and by inscriptions in which the two deities appear together. The description of Hermes as 'the chief speaker' in Acts 14:12 is paralleled by Iamblichus' description of him as 'the leader of the utterances'.) Anthropomorphic myth made him the son of Zeus and Maia, heaven's swift messenger, patron of commerce, eloquence, literature and youth. Latinized as Mercurius (Mercury).

E.M.B.
F.F.B.

HERMETIC LITERATURE. A collection of writings associated with the name of 'Hermes Trismegistos' ('Thrice-great Hermes').

I. Origin and character

The writings represent a coalescence of Egyptian and Greek modes of thought, often transfused with mystical personal religion. Hellenistic syncretism identified Thoth, the Egyptian scribe of the gods, with the Greek Hermes, whose functions were not dissimilar. In this way the name of the ancient and wise 'Hermes Trismegistos' became attached to much of the magical and astrological lore of the Egyptian temples, which was now seasoned with Greek science and presented in a revelatory form. The surviving literature of this type may go back to the early 2nd century BC.

More permanent interest attaches, however, to the more recognizably philosophical and religious treatises in Greek, of diverse but unknown authorship, in which Hermes, Tat (really a by-form of Thoth, but regarded as distinct), Asclepius and others appear as teacher and disciples. The treatises are usually dated in the 2nd and 3rd centuries AD: some may be slightly earlier. The main extant items are a body of eighteen treatises (of which one has been artificially constructed from fragments) preserved in Christian manuscript tradition, and a long tractate dedicated to Asclepius, surviving in a Latin translation, and in a Coptic version in the Nag Hammadi library (*CHENOBOSKION). In addition there are some thirty Hermetic fragments in the *Anthology* of Stobaeus, and others in other early writers. Three other tractates included in Codex 6 of the Nag Hammadi library in addition to the Coptic version of *Asclepius* 21–29 are *Authoritative Teaching*, *The Discourse on the Eighth and Ninth*, and *The Prayer of Thanksgiving. Asclepius* and *The Discourse* both specifically mention Hermes, but all contain similarities with the previously known Hermetic documents. *The Prayer*, although very short, is valuable for the light it sheds on Hermetic cultic practices.

Some of the tractates are in the form of epistolary discourses: others are Socratic dialogues. The most famous, the *Poimandres*, is a vision reminiscent of that of Hermas (*PATRISTIC LITERATURE).

II. Contents

In some ways the *Poimandres* may be taken as a typical Hermetic work. In it Poimandres (perhaps from the Coptic *p-emi-n-re*, 'knowledge of the [sun] god'), described as 'the Mind (*Nous*) of the Sovereignty', offers to reveal to Hermes what he longs to know: 'the things that are, and to understand their nature, and to know God'. There follows the story of the creation of the universe and the fall of man. The former has elements drawn from Gn. 1; the latter describes how archetypal man, God's image, entered into a fatal embrace with Nature, and accordingly became a mixed being, both mortal and immortal. Escape from the dead hand of Nature is, however, possible for those who repent and abandon corruption, till the ascent of the soul is completed at death, when body, passion, feeling are utterly surrendered, and man enters into God.

Not all the Hermetica are as coherent, but the aim expressed and the outlook reflected in the *Poimandres* are generally dominant. Knowledge is the goal; the mortal body the curse; regeneration (enthusiastically described in Treatise 13), the purification of the soul from the taint of matter, the *summum bonum* the soul's final liberation and absorption into God. There is a warm strain of devotion: the appeal to heedless humanity in the *Poimandres* and the still more impassioned cry of Treatise 7 are moving; and the occasional hymns are fervent and rapturous.

To this mystical piety is added rather shopsoiled philosophy, partly Platonic, partly Stoic in origin, with a free use of cosmogonic myth. Judaic sources are under tribute, and there are echoes of the language of the LXX. Indeed, it is arguable that Jewish influences originally stimulated religion of this type. The various elements do not always cohere: there are inconsistencies and contradictions of thought within the corpus. The whole tendency is monotheistic, though not polemically so. Of ceremony or sacrament little is said. Although there is no evidence of a Hermetic 'church', there is a reference in the Nag Hammadi tractate, *On the Eighth and the Ninth*, to a brotherhood consisting of Hermetic saints, and in the *Prayer* to cultic kissing and eating of food without blood.

III. The Hermetica and the Bible

The Hermetic use of the OT, as already noted, is undoubted. The relationship between Hermetic religion and the NT is more variously assessed. The Christian father Lactantius, who thought of 'Hermes' as writing in remote antiquity, delightedly notes his monotheism and his address of God as 'Father' (*Divine Institutes* 1. 6). More recent writers point to subtler parallels of thought and language with the NT, though not all of equal significance. The Logos in Hermetic thought, for instance, is both cosmic and an activity of the soul: but not personal. A statement like 'Thou who by a word hast constituted all things that are' (*Poimandres* 21) need have no other background than Gn. 1; there is no definite article in the original. More striking are phrases like 'No one can be saved before rebirth' (*Treat.* 13. 1), 'He that loveth the body, the same abideth in darkness' (*Poimandres* 19), and the 'Johannine' vocabulary of light and darkness, life and death, belief and witness. Direct influence by the NT on later Hermetica is not impossible, but unproven: direct influence of the Hermetic literature on the NT would be even harder to substantiate. However, while our extant religious Hermetica are almost certainly later than most of the NT, they clearly derive from a well-established tradition; and those may be right who suggest that John has partly in view a public with this *kind* of education and devotion. We must remember, however, that the Hermetica are but one example of contemporary piety; and the language of the Johannine writings can be paralleled also in the Judaic, and essentially biblical, dualism of Qumran.

As to content, it will be seen that the Hermetic parallels are closest with what might be called the accidentals of the NT: with the process of redemption rather than with its essential nature and the means by which it is effected. Concerned with sin as ignorance or passion to be sloughed off, rather than as rebellion requiring reconciliation, and with desire set on a salvation which involved deification through union with God, the motive forces of the Hermetists maintained a pagan, not a biblical, direction. And, while the ethical teaching of the Hermetica is insistent and lofty, its other-worldly nature does not allow for the concreteness of biblical ethics. As C. H. Dodd says, the Hermetists share the second, but not the first half of the description of 'pure religion' in Jas. 1:27. (*GNOSTICISM.)

BIBLIOGRAPHY. Best edn. by A. D. Nock and A. J. Festugière, *Corpus Hermeticum*[2], 4 vols., 1960 (with French translation); *cf.* also W. Scott, *Hermetica*, 4 vols., 1924–36; A. J. Festugière, *La Révélation d'Hermès Trismégiste*, 4 vols., 1944–9; C. H. Dodd, *The Bible and the Greeks*, 1935; For the new Hermetica see J. Doresse, *The Secret Books of the Egyptian Gnostics*, E.T. 1960, pp. 275ff.; L. S. Keizer, *The Eighth Reveals the Ninth*, 1974; *The Nag Hammadi Library in English*, ed. J. M. Robinson, 1977; W. Grese, *JCSBR* 28, pp. 37–54.

A.F.W.

HERMOGENES. Mentioned with Phygelus as representative of Asian Christians who once repudiated Paul (2 Tim. 1:15). The language indicates Roman Asia (not, as some suggest, an Asian community in Rome), and a specific action (*cf.* RV)—perhaps breaking off relations (through fear of involvement?) when Paul had a right to expect their support. For the meaning of 'turned away', *cf.* Mt. 5:42: total apostasy is not in question. The occasion, which is unlikely to have been very remote, was known to Timothy, but it is not to us (*ONESIPHORUS). A.F.W.

HERMON (Heb. *ḥermôn*, 'sanctuary'). A mountain in the Anti-Lebanon Range, and easily the highest (2,814 m) in the neighbourhood of Palestine. It is called also Mt Sirion (Heb. Sion, Dt. 4:48), and known to the Amorites as S(h)enir (Dt. 3:9). Note, however, that Ct. 4:8 and 1 Ch. 5:23 explicitly distinguish between Hermon and *Senir (*cf. GTT*, p. 41; *DOTT*, p. 49).

Regarded as a sacred place by the original inhabitants of Canaan (*cf.* 'Baal-hermon', Jdg. 3:3; 'Baal-gad', Jos. 13:5, *etc.*), it formed the N boundary of Israel's conquests from the Amorites (Dt. 3:8; Jos. 11:17, *etc.*). Snow usually lies on the top all year round, causing plentiful dews in stark contrast to the parched land of that region (hence probably the Psalmist's allusion in Ps. 133:3), and the melting ice forms a major source of the Jordan. Hermon is identified with the modern Jebel es-Sheik, 'the Sheik's mountain', 48 km SW of Damascus (but on this point see *GTT*, p. 83). Its proximity to Caesarea Philippi has made some suggest Hermon as the 'high mountain' (Mk. 9:2, *etc.*) of the *transfiguration.

A misleading reference to 'the Hermonites' (Ps. 42:6, AV) should probably be amended to RV 'the Hermons', signifying the three summits of Mt Hermon. J.D.D.

HEROD. 1. Herod the Great, king of the Jews 40–4 BC, born *c.* 73 BC. His father Antipater, a Jew of Idumaean descent, attained a position of great influence in Judaea after the Roman conquest and was appointed procurator of Judaea by Julius Caesar in 47 BC. He in turn appointed his son Herod military prefect of Galilee, and Herod showed his qualities by the vigour with which he suppressed brigandage in that region; the Roman governor of Syria was so impressed by his energy that he made him military prefect of Coele-Syria. After the assassination of Caesar and subsequent civil war Herod enjoyed the goodwill of Antony. When the Parthians invaded Syria and Palestine and set the Hasmonaean Antigonus on the throne of Judaea (40–37 BC) the Roman senate, advised by Antony and Octavian, gave Herod the title 'king of the Jews'. It took him 3 years of fighting to make his title effective, but when he had done so he governed Judaea for 33 years as a loyal 'friend and ally' of Rome.

Until 31 BC, despite Antony's goodwill, Herod's position was rendered precarious by the machinations of Cleopatra, who hoped to see Judaea and Coele-Syria reunited to the Ptolemaic kingdom. This peril was removed by the battle of Actium, after which Herod was confirmed in his kingdom by Octavian (Augustus), the new master of the Roman world. Another source of anxiety for Herod was the Hasmonaean family, who resented being displaced on the throne by one whom they regarded as an upstart. Although he married into this family by taking to wife Mariamne, granddaughter of the former high priest Hyrcanus II, Herod's suspicions led him to get rid of the leading Hasmonaean survivors one by one, including Mariamne herself (29 BC).

Herod pacified the territories on his NE frontier in the interests of Rome, and Augustus added them to his kingdom. He furthered the emperor's cultural policy by lavish building projects, not only in his own realm but in foreign cities (*e.g.* Athens). In his own realm he rebuilt Samaria and renamed it Sebaste after the emperor (Gk. *Sebastos* = Lat. *Augustus*); he rebuilt Strato's Tower on the Mediterranean coast, equipped it with a splendid artificial harbour, and called it Caesarea, also in honour of the emperor. Other settlements and strongholds were founded throughout the land. In Jerusalem he built a palace for himself on the W wall; he had already rebuilt the Antonia fortress (called after Antony) NW of the Temple area. The greatest of all his building enterprises was the reconstruction of the Jerusalem Temple, begun early in 19 BC.

Nothing that Herod could do, not even the expenditure lavished on the Temple, endeared him to his Jewish subjects. His Edomite descent was never forgotten; if he was a Jew by religion and rebuilt the Temple of the God of Israel in Jerusalem, that did not deter him from erecting temples to pagan deities elsewhere. Above all, his wiping out of the Hasmonaean family could not be forgiven.

This drastic action did not in fact put an end to his domestic troubles. There was friction between his own female relatives and his wives, and between the children of his respective wives. His two sons by Mariamne, Alexander and Aristobulus, were brought up at Rome and were his designated heirs. Their Hasmonaean descent (through their mother) made them acceptable to the Jewish people. But their privileged position stirred the envy of their half-brothers, and especially of Herod's eldest son Antipater, who set himself to poison his father's mind against them. At last (7 BC) they were found guilty of plotting against their father, and executed. Antipater derived no advantage from their death, for 3 years later he too fell victim to Herod's suspicions, and was executed only a few days before Herod's own death (4 BC).

Herod's suspicious nature is well illustrated by the story of the visit of the Magi and the slaughter of the infants of Bethlehem (Mt. 2); although this story does not appear elsewhere, any rumour of a rival king of the Jews was bound to rouse his worst fears. This suspicion latterly grew to insane proportions, and in consequence Herod has been remembered more for his murderous outbursts than for his administrative ability.

In his will he bequeathed his kingdom to three of his sons—Judaea and Samaria to Archelaus (Mt. 2:22), Galilee and Peraea to Antipas, and his NE territories to Philip (Lk. 3:1). These bequests were ratified by Augustus.

2. Archelaus ('Herod the Ethnarch' on his coins). He reigned in Judaea 'in place of his father Herod' (Mt. 2:22) from 4 BC to AD 6, but without the title of king. He was Herod's elder son by his

Samaritan wife Malthace, and has the worst reputation of all the sons of Herod. He offended Jewish religious susceptibilities by marrying Glaphyra, the widow of his half-brother Alexander. He continued his father's building policy, but his repressive rule became intolerable; a deputation of the Judaean and Samaritan aristocracy at last went to Rome to warn Augustus that, unless Archelaus were removed, there would be a full-scale revolt. Archelaus was accordingly deposed and banished, and Judaea became a Roman province, administered by prefects appointed by the emperor.

3. 'Herod the tetrarch' (Lk. 3:19, *etc.*), who bore the distinctive name of Antipas. He was Herod's younger son by Malthace, and inherited the Galilean and Peraean portions of his father's kingdom. In the Gospels he is conspicuous chiefly for his part in the imprisonment and execution of John the Baptist (Mk. 6:14–28) and for his brief encounter with Jesus when the latter was sent to him by Pilate

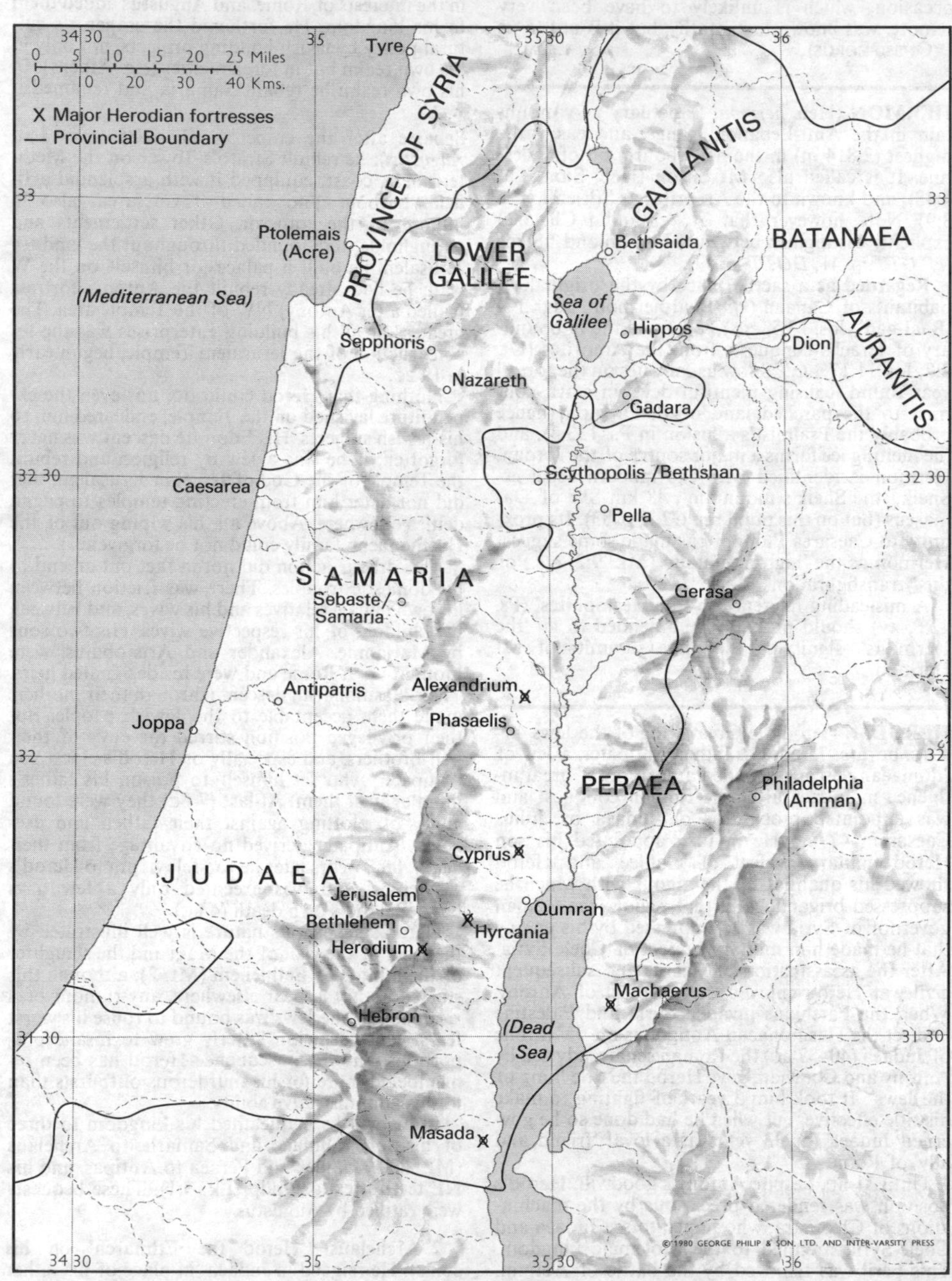

The kingdom of Herod the Great.

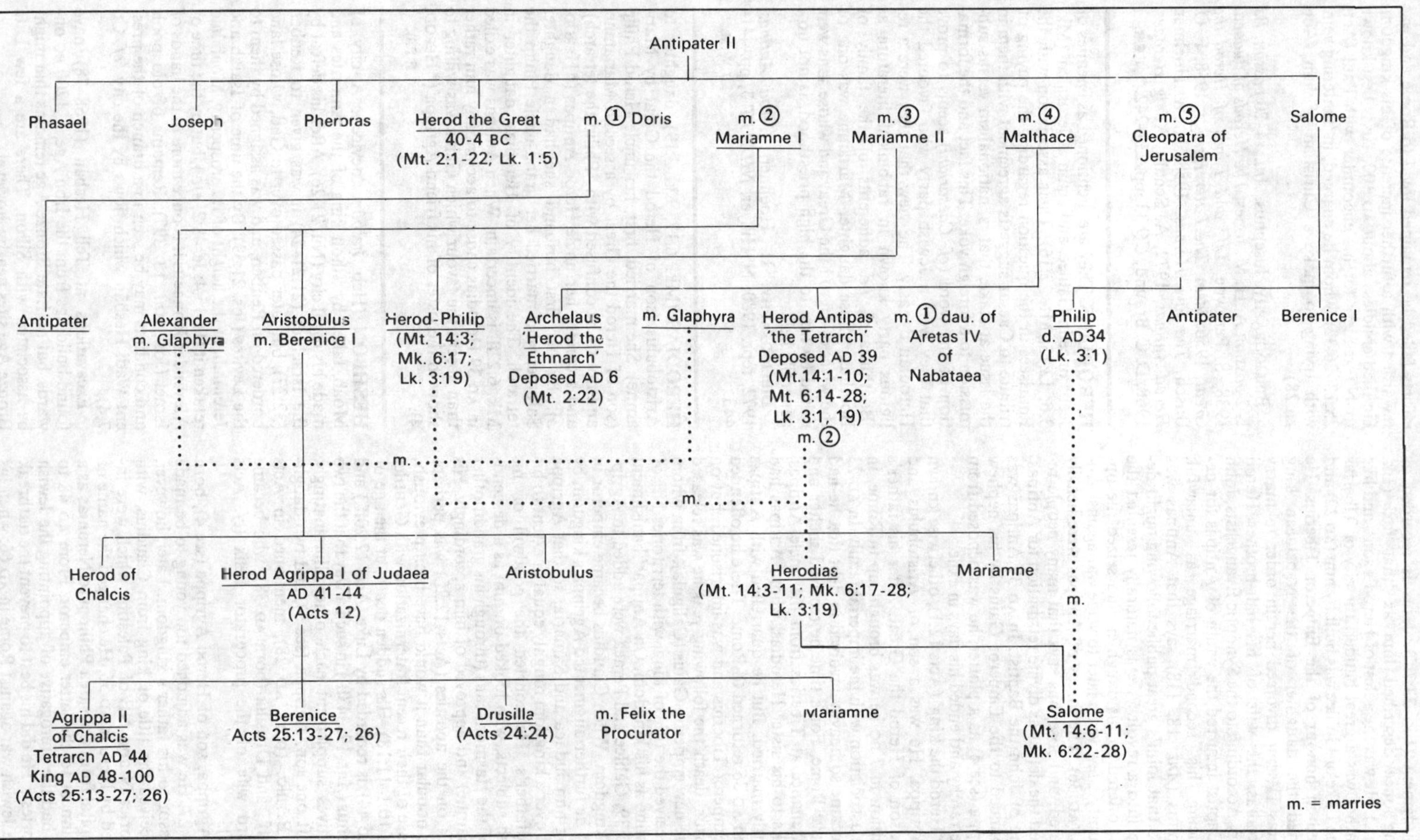

Herod's family tree simplified. The names underlined are those principally discussed in the article Herod.

for judgment (Lk. 23:7ff.). Jesus is recorded as having once described him as 'that fox' (Lk. 13:31f.). He was the ablest of Herod's sons, and like his father was a great builder; the city of Tiberias on the Lake of Galilee was built by him (AD 22) and named in honour of the Emperor Tiberius. He married the daughter of the Nabataean king *Aretas IV, but divorced her in order to marry *Herodias, the wife of his half-brother Herod Philip. According to the Synoptic Evangelists, John the Baptist incurred the wrath of Antipas for denouncing his second marriage as unlawful; Josephus (*Ant.* 18. 118) says that Antipas was afraid that John's great public following might develop into a revolt. Aretas naturally resented the insult offered to his daughter, and seized the opportunity a few years later to wage war against Antipas (AD 36). The forces of Antipas were heavily defeated, and Josephus says that many people regarded the defeat as divine retribution for Antipas' killing of John the Baptist. In AD 39 Antipas was denounced to the Emperor Gaius by his nephew Agrippa (see **4**) as a plotter; he was deposed from his tetrarchy and ended his days in exile.

4. 'Herod the king' (Acts 12:1), otherwise known as Agrippa. He was a son of Aristobulus and grandson of Herod the Great. After his father's execution in 7 BC he was brought up in Rome, in close association with the imperial family. In AD 23 he became so heavily involved in debt that he had to leave Rome. For a time he received shelter and maintenance at Tiberias from his uncle Antipas, thanks to his sister Herodias, whom Antipas had recently married. But he quarrelled with Antipas and in AD 36 returned to Rome. There he offended the Emperor Tiberius and was imprisoned, but on Tiberius' death the following year he was released by the new emperor, Gaius (Caligula), from whom he received the title of king, with territories NE of Palestine as his kingdom. On Antipas' banishment in AD 39, Galilee and Peraea were added to Agrippa's kingdom. When Claudius became emperor in AD 41 he further augmented Agrippa's kingdom by giving him Judaea and Samaria, so that Agrippa ruled over a kingdom roughly equal in extent to his grandfather's. He courted the goodwill of his Jewish subjects, who looked on him as a descendant of the Hasmonaeans (through his grandmother Mariamne) and approved of him accordingly. His attack on the apostles (Acts 12:2f.) was perhaps more popular than it would have been previously, because of their recent fraternization with Gentiles (Acts 10:1–11:18). His sudden death, at the age of 54 (AD 44), is recorded by Luke (Acts 12:20ff.) and Josephus (*Ant.* 19. 343ff.) in such a way that the two narratives supplement each other illuminatingly. He left one son, Agrippa (see **5**), and two daughters: Bernice (born AD 28), mentioned in Acts 25:13ff., and Drusilla (born AD 38), who became the 3rd wife of the procurator Felix (*cf.* Acts 24:24).

5. Agrippa, son of Herod Agrippa (see **4**), born in AD 27. He was adjudged too young to be made successor to his father's kingdom. Later, however, he received the title of king from Claudius, with territories N and NE of Palestine which were increased by Nero in AD 56. He changed the name of his capital from Caesarea Philippi to Neronias as a compliment to the latter emperor. From AD 48 to 66 he had the prerogative of appointing the Jewish high priests. He did his best to prevent the outbreak of the Jewish war against Rome in AD 66; when his efforts failed he remained loyal to Rome and was rewarded with a further increase of his kingdom. He died childless about AD 100. He is best known to NT readers for his encounter with Paul (Acts 25:13–26:32), whom he charged, in bantering vein, with trying to make a Christian of him (Acts 26:28).

BIBLIOGRAPHY. Josephus, *Ant.* 14–20 *passim*, *BJ* 1–2 *passim*; A. H. M. Jones, *The Herods of Judaea*, 1938; S. Perowne, *Life and Times of Herod the Great*, 1956; *idem*, *The Later Herods*, 1958; F. O. Busch, *The Five Herods*, 1958; H. W. Hoehner, *Herod Antipas*, 1972; A. Schalit, *König Herodes*, 1968; D. C. Braund, *CQ* 33, pp. 239–242. F.F.B.

HERODIANS. They are mentioned as enemies of Jesus once in Galilee, and again at Jerusalem (Mk. 3:6; 12:13; Mt. 22:16). Their association with the Pharisees in the question regarding the paying of tribute to Caesar suggests agreement with them in the issue at stake, that is, nationalism versus submission to a foreign yoke. This fact and the formation of the word (*cf. Caesariani*) seems to prove that they were a Jewish party who favoured the Herodian dynasty. The view that they were a religious party known in rabbinical literature as 'Boethusians', *i.e.* adherents of the family of Boethus, whose daughter Mariamne was one of the wives of Herod the Great and whose sons were raised by him to the high priesthood, is not now generally held.

BIBLIOGRAPHY. H. Hoehner, *Herod Antipas*, 1972, repr. 1980; N. Hillyer, *NIDNTT* 3, pp. 441–443. J.W.M.

HERODIAS (Mk. 6:17; Lk. 3:19), daughter to Aristobulus (son of Herod the Great by Mariamne). She married, first, her uncle Herod Philip (son of Herod the Great by a second Mariamne, and not to be confused with *Philip the tetrarch), and secondly, her uncle Herod Antipas (*HEROD, 3). By her first husband she had a daughter Salome, who married her grand-uncle Philip the tetrarch. The identity of Herodias' daughter in Mk. 6:22ff. is uncertain. When Antipas was exiled in AD 39 Herodias chose to accompany him rather than accept the favour which Gaius was willing to show to the sister of his friend Agrippa (*HEROD, 4). F.F.B.

HESHBON (Heb. *ḥešbôn*, 'device'). A city of Moab, taken by Sihon king of the Amorites and made his royal city (Nu. 21:26). After his defeat by the Israelites (21:21–24) it was given to Reuben (32:37), but later passed over to Gad, whose land bordered on Reuben, and was assigned by them to the Levites (Jos. 21:39). By the time of Isaiah and Jeremiah, at the height of its prosperity, Moab had retaken it (Is. 15:4; Je. 48:2, *etc.*), but by the time of Alexander Jannaeus it is once more in the hands of Israel (Jos., *Ant.* 13. 397). Remains of old pools and conduits may be seen in a branch of the present Wadi Hesbān which flows by the city (*cf.* Ct. 7:4).

Excavations at Tell Hesban (1968–78) have found buildings from the Iron Age, *c.* 1200 BC onwards, but no Late Bronze Age remains that might be associated with Sihon. There are a few Late Bronze Age sites nearby, however.

BIBLIOGRAPHY. L. T. Geraty, *Ann. Department of Antiquities of Jordan* 20, 1975, pp. 47–56; *NEAEHL*, pp. 986–989. M.A.M.
A.R.M.

HETHLON. (Heb. *ḥeṯlôn*). A city on the ideal N boundary of Palestine as seen by Ezekiel, near Hamath and Zedad and referred to only by him (Ezk. 47:15; 48:1). Identified with the modern Heitela, NE of Tripoli, Syria. J.D.D.

HEZEKIAH (Heb. *ḥizqîyâ* or *ḥizqîyāhû*, 'Yahweh is [my] strength').

1. The 14th king of Judah. Son of Ahaz who was 25 at the start of his reign and reigned for 29 years (2 Ki. 18:2; 2 Ch. 29:1). He was outstanding for his own piety (2 Ki. 18:5) and also cared for previous traditions and teaching (Pr. 25:1). His importance is reflected by the three accounts of his reign (2 Ki. 17–20; Is. 36–39; 2 Ch. 29–32).

There are difficulties surrounding the chronology of Hezekiah's reign, but he appears to have assumed a co-regency with Ahaz *c.* 729 BC and became king *c.* 716 BC. Thus the fall of Samaria (722 BC) occurred in the 6th year of his reign (as co-regent; 2 Ki. 18:10), while Sennacherib invaded Judah (701 BC) in the 14th year of his reign (as sole monarch; 2 Ki. 18:13). The king's illness and recovery appear to have occurred just before Sennacherib's invasion, when Hezekiah was promised an extra 15 years of rule (2 Ki. 20) (*STEPS).

After the pagan practices introduced during the period of Ahaz's submission to the Assyrians (*cf.* Is. 2:6ff.; 8:16ff.), Hezekiah undertook a major reform of religious practice in the 1st year of his sole reign (2 Ch. 29:3ff.). He re-established the true worship of Yahweh in the purified and renovated Temple, reaffirmed the covenant between Yahweh and his people, and reinstituted the Passover on a grand scale (2 Ch. 30:26), even inviting Israelites from the N to participate (2 Ch. 30:5ff.). He also destroyed the *high places in the surrounding area (2 Ki. 18:4; 2 Ch. 31:1) as well as breaking up the bronze *serpent which Moses had made in the wilderness but which had come to be regarded as an idol (2 Ki. 18:4).

Politically, Hezekiah was restive under Assyrian domination and he allied Judah with an anti-Assyrian revolt instigated by Egypt and led by *Ashdod. Judah must have listened to Isaiah's warnings (Is. 20), for although Sargon II claimed to have subdued *ia-u-di*, 'Judah' (*cf. DOTT*, p. 61; also N. Na'aman, *BASOR* 214, 1974, p. 27), no evidence of an invasion at this time is found in the OT. When Sargon died (705 BC) Hezekiah, seeing an opportunity to rebel against his son, Sennacherib, entertained envoys of the rebel Chaldean, *Merodach-baladan (2 Ki. 20:12–19; Is. 39) and received promises of support from Egypt. He also strengthened his own defences in Jerusalem, including digging the *Siloam tunnel to safeguard the water-supply (2 Ki. 20:20; Is. 22:9ff.).

Sennacherib's own records of his campaign in the W picture Hezekiah as leader of rebellion (*ANET*, pp. 287–288; *DOTT*, pp. 64–69). He claims to have taken forty-six fortified towns and imprisoned Hezekiah 'like a bird in a cage in Jerusalem, his royal city'. He does not claim to have conquered the city and the OT tells of Yahweh's intervention by destroying the Assyrian army (2 Ki. 19:32–36).

The mention of *Tirhakah, king of Ethiopia, in 2 Ki. 19:9, has led some to propose a second campaign by Sennacherib into Judah, *c.* 688 BC, since Tirhakah would have been too young in 701 BC to have taken part and also was not then called 'king'. It has, however, been shown that he was 20–21 at this time and that the title is in terms of the time of writing rather than of the events themselves (*cf.* K. A. Kitchen, *The Third Intermediate Period in Egypt*, 1972, pp. 385–386 and nn. 823–824).

2. The father of a clan which returned from Babylonian exile with Ezra (Ezr. 2:16; Ne. 7:21), and among those who sealed the new covenant with Yahweh (Ne. 10:17). His name is given in two forms, Ater being Akkadian. Ne. 10:17 lists the names as separate people. D.W.B.

HIDDEKEL. The ancient name of the river *Tigris used in the account of the Garden of Eden (Gn. 2:14) and in Daniel's description of his visions (Dn. 10:4) in the 3rd year of Cyrus. The name comes from Akkadian *idiqlat*, which is equivalent to Sumerian *idigna*, *i.e.* always flowing river.

BIBLIOGRAPHY. D. O. Edzard *et al.*, *Répertoire Géographique des Textes Cunéiformes*, 1, 1977, pp. 216–217. T.C.M.

HIEL (Heb. *ḥî'ēl*, 'El lives'; but *cf.* LXX 'brother of God', from *'ᵃḥî'ēl*). A Bethelite whose sons were (accidentally?) killed during his rebuilding of Jericho *c.* 870 BC, fulfilling Joshua's curse (1 Ki. 16:34; *cf.* Jos. 6:26). D.W.B.

HIERAPOLIS. A city in the Roman province of Asia, in the W of what is now Asiatic Turkey. It was situated about 10 km N of *Laodicea, on the opposite side of the broad valley of the Lycus. The city was built around copious hot springs, which were famed for their medicinal powers. There was also a subterranean vent of poisonous gases (the Plutonium), which was later filled in by the Christians in about the 4th century AD. When the hot water flows over the edge of the city terrace it forms spectacular pools and cascades encrusted with lime. The resulting white cliffs give the site its modern name Pamuk-kale ('cotton castle'). These natural features made Hierapolis ('sacred city', for earlier 'Hieropolis', 'city of the sanctuary') an ancient centre of pagan cults, from which its importance and prosperity mainly derived.

The church in Hierapolis was probably founded while Paul was living at Ephesus (Acts 19:10), perhaps by Epaphras. It is mentioned only in conjunction with its close neighbours, *Colossae and *Laodicea (Col. 4:13). There may be a reminiscence of its famous hot waters in Rev. 3:15–16, in contrast with the cold waters of Colossae and the tepid of Laodicea.

According to Polycrates, bishop of Ephesus *c.* AD 190, as quoted by Eusebius (*HE* 3. 31), the apostle Philip was buried at Hierapolis, though the authorities show confusion between apostle and evangelist. Papias and the Stoic philosopher Epictetus were also connected with the city.

M.J.S.R.
C.J.H.

HIGH PLACE. The Heb. word *bāmâ*, rendered 'high place' by AV, RSV and JB, is used over 100 times in *MT* and in two distinct ways: of heights in a literal sense and of shrines. NEB renders 'heights' and 'hill shrine'.

The 20 non-cultic uses are all in the plural form and in poetic passages. In contrast to other height words, the plural *bāmôṯ* always carries overtones of dominance and control. Battles often took place on hill slopes; possession of heights therefore gave lordship over the land (Nu. 21:28; 2 Sa. 1:19, 25). Thus Israel asserted that God 'rides' or 'walks' on the heights (Am. 4:13; Mi. 1:3) or that he sets Israel (Dt. 32:13; Is. 58:14) or an individual (2 Sa. 22:34; Ps. 18:33; Hab. 3:19) 'upon the heights of the earth'. Cylinder seals portray *Baal astride mountains and in the Ras Shamra texts he is called *rkb rpt*, 'rider of the clouds'. Both Akkadian and Ugaritic had closely related words denoting heights or the middle region of the body (*cf.* Jb. 9:8).

The association of heights with lordship may account for their choice as locations of shrines. It has been suggested that, despite the warnings of Moses (Dt. 12, *etc.*), Israel took over the Canaanites' shrines after the conquest. Certainly loyal worshippers of God used *bāmôṯ* in the early Monarchy period. Samuel officiated at a special sacrifice when Saul was anointed before invited guests (1 Sa. 9) and later Saul went with a group of prophets coming down from a *bāmâ* led by lute, fife and drum (1 Sa. 10:5). By the time of Solomon Gibeon had risen to unique status and was known as 'the Great High Place'. The *tabernacle and the altar of bronze 'which Bezalel, son of Uri, son of Hur' had made was kept there and it was at Gibeon that God challenged Solomon in a dream about the character of his reign (1 Ki. 3; 2 Ch. 1).

After the disruption of the kingdom in 922 BC the *bāmôṯ* posed a new threat to the purity of Israel's faith. In the N kingdom Jeroboam built 'houses of the high places' as part of his campaign to distract his subjects' attention away from Jerusalem (1 Ki. 12). Thus 'he made Israel to sin' for the *bāmôṯ*, though often nominally dedicated to God, clearly included many Canaanite features, such as images, standing stones, Asherah poles, sacred prostitution and other fertility rites. Bloodshed, instability and apostasy characterized the two centuries of the N kingdom's existence and, as the biblical historians saw, the *bāmôṯ* were a major source of the moral and religious collapse (2 Ki. 17:9). In the S kingdom the situation was little better. *bāmôṯ* revived under Rehoboam. Attempts to suppress them by Asa and Jehoshaphat had no lasting results. Hezekiah conducted a more thorough reformation (2 Ki. 18:1–8), but his son Manasseh 'who did more evil than all the kings that were before him' again revived *bāmôṯ*. Under Josiah a far-reaching purge was undertaken (2 Ki. 23), but his successors were not of his calibre and the shrines were again reviving when the Babylonian army put an end to the Judaean kingdom. Little is known of the *bāmôṯ* thereafter.

Early study of the *bāmôṯ* reveals the embarrassment felt at the use of these shrines by Israel's heroes. The Talmud and the rabbis sharply distinguished between 'great' and 'small' *bāmôṯ* or maintained that the ban was lifted periodically. J. Wellhausen solved the problem by suggesting that the single sanctuary law was not operative until the time of Josiah; the book of Deuteronomy was but a 'pious fraud'. It seems more likely that Samuel, Saul and Solomon simply wished to claim these shrines for God without realizing the syncretistic dangers which had been plain to Moses and were all too accurately vindicated by history.

W. F. Albright proposed that the *bāmôṯ* were basically tomb-shrines, but no excavated shrine or unamended biblical reference has clear mortuary associations. P. H. Vaughan suggests that *bāmôṯ* were round or flat cult platforms on which worship was celebrated. However, although some *bāmôṯ* may have contained a platform, the term seems more naturally taken as embracing the whole cult area including altar, stones, houses, *etc.*

A gradual development in the location of *bāmôṯ* is discernible. Shrines on heights were typical of the early period (Nu. 22:41; 1 Sa. 9), whereas later they are to be found in the towns (2 Ki. 17:9) or, in one instance, in a valley (Je. 7:31). By the end of the Monarchy period, the term was applied to many types of local shrine. Thus 2 Ki. 23 refers to a small gate shrine, royal centres to foreign gods, large public shrines and local rustic shrines all as *bāmôṯ*.

Widely publicized discoveries at Gezer and the 'Conway High Place at Petra' have now been discounted as *bāmôṯ*. Despite a 'wishful thinking' phase, archaeology has now revealed examples of the main types of biblical *bāmôṯ*. Shrines outside settlements are known from Naharijah, Samaria, Jerusalem and 'the Great High Place at Petra'. *bāmôṯ* in towns on heights are known from Megiddo and Arad. Shrines on lower ground in towns are known from Hazor, Dan and Jerusalem. Small gate shrines are known from Tirzah and Dan. Biblical evidence about the structures, cult and tendency of a shrine to change its status can all be illustrated from archaeological discoveries, so revealing a detailed picture of the period when Israel 'had as many gods as towns' (Je. 2:28).

BIBLIOGRAPHY. W. F. Albright, *Supplement to VT* 4, 1957, pp. 242–258; P. H. Vaughan, *The meaning of 'bāmâ' in the Old Testament*, 1974; J. T. Whitney, *The Israelite bamah*, unpublished thesis, University of Nottingham, 1975; M. D. Fowler, *ZAW* 94, pp. 203–213.

J.T.W.

HILKIAH (Heb. *ḥilqîyâhû*, *ḥilqîyâ*, 'my portion is Yahweh').

1. The father of Eliakim, Hezekiah's chamberlain (2 Ki. 18:18, 26, 37; Is. 22:20; 36:3, 22).

2. The high priest in Josiah's reign. During the repairs on the Temple, he found the book of the law, and brought it to the notice of Shaphan the scribe. Subsequently he was a member of the king's deputation to Huldah the prophetess to learn God's will in the matter, and later he helped to put Josiah's reformation into effect (2 Ki. 22–23; 2 Ch. 34; 35:8).

3, 4. Levites of the family of Merari (1 Ch. 6:45; 26:11). **5.** One who stood with Ezra the scribe when he read the law of God from a wooden pulpit (Ne. 8:4). **6.** A chief of the priests who went up to Judaea with Zerubbabel (Ne. 12:7, 21). Possibly identical with **5**.

7. The father of Jeremiah the prophet, and member of the priestly family of Anathoth (Je. 1:1). Probably a descendant of Abiathar, David's high priest who was expelled by Solomon for supporting Adonijah (1 Ki. 2:26). Hilkiah was possibly the officiating priest to the rural community at Anathoth.

8. The father of Gemariah, one of Zedekiah's ambassadors to Nebuchadrezzar (Je. 29:3).

J.G.G.N.

HILL, HILL-COUNTRY. These terms translate the Heb. words *giḇ'â* and *har*. The root-meaning of the former is convexity; bare hills, like an inverted basin, are a common feature of Palestine, notably the area of Judah. But *giḇ'â* is often a proper name (Gibeah) to indicate towns built on such eminences, coupled with a distinguishing 'surname' (*e.g.* 'of Saul', 1 Sa. 11:4).

The second word, *har*, may indicate a single eminence or a range of hills; this led to some confusion in AV, but recent EVV make it clear when a range of hills is meant. The mountainous backbone of Palestine is so styled sometimes divided into the N and S parts of it, respectively called the hill-country 'of Ephraim' and 'of Judah'. It should, however, be noted that it is not always possible to decide whether a single hill or a hilly region is meant.

D.F.P.

HINNOM, VALLEY OF. A valley to the S of Jerusalem, also styled 'the valley of the son (or sons) of Hinnom'. It was associated in Jeremiah's time with the worship of Molech. Josiah defiled this shrine, and put an end to the sacrifices offered there. Later the valley seems to have been used for burning the corpses of criminals and animals, and indeed refuse of any sort. Hence the name came to be used as a synonym for *hell, the Hebrew phrase *gê* ('valley of') *hinnōm* becoming *geenna* in Greek, whence Gehenna in Latin and English. Jewish tradition at one time held that the mouth of hell was in the valley.

The identification of the valley presents problems. It formed part of the boundary between the territories of Judah and Benjamin, and lay between the 'south side of the Jebusite; the same is Jerusalem' and Enrogel (Jos. 15:7f., AV). So clearly the identification of these two localities will affect our identification of the Valley of Hinnom. If *En-rogel was the Virgin's Fountain, the Valley of Hinnom can be equated with the Kidron valley, which runs from the E to the SE of Jerusalem. But if it was what is now called Bir Eyyub, two possibilities remain: the valley was either the Tyropoeon valley, running from the centre of Jerusalem to the SE, or the valley encircling the city on the W and S, now called the Wadi al-Rababi. Each of these three valleys, at its SE extremity, terminates near Siloam. Muslim tradition supports the Kidron valley identification, but that is the least likely; the great majority of scholars accept the Wadi al-Rababi as the correct identification.

D.F.P.

HIRAM. The king of *Tyre, contemporary with David and Solomon; he reigned 979/8–945/4 BC (according to Albright, 969–936 BC).

a. Name

Heb. *Ḥîrām* (Sa. and Ki.); *Ḥîrōm* (1 Ki. 5:10, 18; LXX, *Ḥ(e)iram*); *Ḥûrām* (Ch.) is a Phoenician name possibly equivalent to, or an abbreviation for, Aḥiram (Nu. 26:38), meaning 'my brother is the exalted (god)', as Ḥiel stands for Aḥiel (1 Ki. 16:34). Hiram, or Huram-(abi), was also the name of the chief technician from Tyre, married to a woman of Naphtali (1 Ki. 7:13f.) or Dan (2 Ch. 2:13) sent by King Hiram to help Solomon.

b. Relations with Judah

Hiram was a great admirer of David (1 Ki. 5:1) and sent materials and craftsmen to aid the building of his palace at Jerusalem (2 Sa. 5:11; 1 Ch. 14:1). On Solomon's accession Hiram sent ambassadors to make fresh contacts which led to a trade-treaty whereby he supplied wood from Lebanon and skilled craftsmen for the construction of the new Temple at Jerusalem, in return for an annual payment by Solomon of wheat and fine oil (1 Ki. 5:2–11) which the Phoenician cities lacked. Additional payments of barley and wine seem to have been required for the maintenance of the Tyrian workmen, who included technicians acquainted with fabric design and dyes, sent to instruct the Israelites (2 Ch. 2:3–7).

Twenty years later, on the completion of the Temple, Solomon gave Hiram twenty villages in Galilee, presumably near Tyre, and received in exchange 120 talents of gold (1 Ki. 9:10–14). Such treaties to adjust the borders between states are known from early Syrian agreements (*e.g.* Alalaḫ). These treaties, which were planned for the economic advantage of both parties, were supplemented by trading operations in which Solomon's ocean-going *ships joined the fleet of Hiram to import gold, silver and various kinds of rarities, including monkeys (1 Ki. 10:22; 2 Ch. 9:21). The vessels sailing from Ezion-geber for *Ophir were accompanied by experienced pilots provided by Hiram (1 Ki. 9:26–28; 2 Ch. 8:17–18). The trade expansion of *Phoenicia in Hiram's time included colonies in N Africa and Spain.

c. The reign of Hiram

Apart from the OT, Hiram's rule is chronicled by Josephus (*Ant.* 8. 50–54; *Contra Apionem* 1. 17f.), based on the historians Menander and Dius. According to this source, Hiram (LXX *Chiram*, Gk. *Heiramos, Heirōmos*) was the son of Abi-baal and reigned 34 years before dying at the age of 53. The building of the Temple at Jerusalem began in his 11th year, *i.e.* the 4th year of Solomon (1 Ki. 6:1). Hiram warred against Cyprus to enforce the payment of tribute and fortified the island of Tyre, where he built temples to Astarte-Melqart (later Hercules) and enriched the older temples.

Josephus, like Eupolemos and Alexander Polyhistor, recounts the letters, said to have been preserved in the state archives at Tyre, which passed between Hiram and Solomon concerning the building of the Temple. Josephus states also that the two kings engaged in an exchange of riddles until Solomon was defeated by a young Tyrian named Abdemon. Clement of Alexandria and Tatian say that a daughter of Hiram was married to Solomon; *cf.* 1 Ki. 11:1–2.

BIBLIOGRAPHY. *CAH* 3/2, 1991, pp. 466–467; H. J. Katzenstein, *The History of Tyre*, 1973.

D.J.W.

HIRE, HIRELING. The two main classes of *wage-earner in Israel were the foreign mercenary and the agricultural labourer, typifying respectively dereliction of duty (Je. 46:21) and stinting service (Jb. 7:1f.) under exploitation (Mal. 3:5). Hence the pejoratives in Jn. 10:12–13 and Lk. 15:19. David introduced foreign mercenaries to buttress the newly adopted monarchy (2 Sa. 8:18). The agricultural labourer was debased by an enclosure movement in the 8th century (Is. 5:8) which dispossessed many freehold farmers of their patrimony and left them in *debt. By custom the ultimate discharge of debt was perpetual *slavery (2 Ki. 4:1). The law provided that an Israelite who, through poverty, had to sell himself to a fellow-Israelite should be allowed the status of an employee and be manumitted in the year of Jubilee (Lv. 25:39–55). Other laws also protected him (*e.g.* Lv. 19:13; *cf.* Dt. 24:14–15). Jacob's two contracts (Gn. 29) disclose a background of nomadic kinship and recall the great national codes of the 2nd millennium BC.

BIBLIOGRAPHY. J. D. M. Derrett, *Law in the New Testament*, 1961, ch. 1; J. Jeremias, *Jerusalem in the Time of Jesus*, 1969, ch. 6; R. de Vaux, *Ancient Israel*, 1961, p. 76. A.E.W.

HITTITES (Heb. *ḥittîm, bᵉnê ḥēṯ*). In the OT the Hittites are, firstly, a great nation which gave its name to the whole region of Syria, 'from the wilderness and this Lebanon as far as the great river, the river Euphrates, all the land of the Hittites to the Great Sea toward the going down of the sun' (Jos. 1:4); and secondly, an ethnic group living in Canaan from patriarchal times until after the Israelite settlement (Gn. 15:20; Dt. 7:1; Jdg. 3:5), called literally 'the children of Heth' (Gn. 23:3, *etc.*) after their eponymous ancestor Heth, a son of Canaan (Gn. 10:15).

I. The Hittite empire

The Hittite empire was founded *c.* 1800 BC by an Indo-European nation which had settled in Asia Minor in city-states some two centuries before. They derived the name 'Hittite' from the Hatti, the earlier inhabitants of the area where they settled, whose legacy is clearly traceable in Hittite art and religion and in divine and royal names and titles. With the spread of the Hittite empire the designation 'Hittites' was extended to the peoples and lands which it incorporated.

An early Hittite king, Tudhaliyas I (*c.* 1720 BC), has been identified (precariously) with 'Tidal king of nations' of Gn. 14:1. About 1600 BC Hattusilis I extended his rule over parts of N Syria. His successor Mursilis I established a new capital at Hattusas (modern Boğaz-köy), E of the Halys; it is largely to the archives uncovered there since 1906 that we owe our knowledge of Hittite history and literature. Mursilis I captured Aleppo and subsequently (*c.* 1560 BC) raided Babylon—an event which precipitated the fall of the 1st Babylonian Dynasty.

King Telepinus (*c.* 1480 BC) was the great Hittite legislator. There are some striking affinities between the Hittite law-codes and those of the Pentateuch, although affinities are found in matters of detail and arrangement rather than in general conception. Whereas the Pentateuchal codes resemble the great Semitic law-codes of the ancient Near East in employing the *lex talionis* as a basic principle, the Hittite laws are dominated by the distinctively Indo-European principle of compensation (*Wergeld*). Some analogy has also been discerned between Hittite treaty forms and OT covenant terms. Other notable points of contact are found in the levirate marriage and in the procedures for ascertaining the divine will or the unknown future by means of teraphim and *'ōḇôṯ* ('familiar spirits').

The Hittite empire reached the peak of its power under Suppiluliumas I (*c.* 1380–1350 BC). It was in his province of Kizzuwatna, in SE Asia Minor, that iron was first smelted in the Near East on a scale which justifies one in speaking of the beginning of the Iron Age. He extended his empire over Upper Mesopotamia and over Syria as far S as the Lebanon. The Hittites thus collided with the N thrust of the Egyptian empire in Asia, and hostilities continued between the two powers until 1284 BC, when a non-aggression pact between Hattusilis III and Rameses II recognized the Orontes as their common frontier.

The Hittite empire collapsed around 1200 BC as the result of blows from western enemies.

II. The Hittite kingdoms

With the fall of the Hittite empire, 24 city-states of the Tabali ('Tubal' in the OT) became heirs to the Hittite home territory N of the Taurus range. In Syria seven city-states which had belonged to the Hittite empire perpetuated the name 'Hittite' for several centuries; their rulers were called 'the kings of the Hittites'. Hamath on the Orontes and Carchemish on the Euphrates were among the most important of the seven. Hamath was allied with David (2 Sa. 8:9ff.), whose kingdom bordered on 'Kadesh in the land of the Hittites' (2 Sa. 24:6; *TAHTIM-HODSHI). Solomon traded and intermarried with these 'kings of the Hittites' (1 Ki. 10:28f.; 11:1). In the 9th century BC their military reputation could throw the army of Damascus into panic (2 Ki. 7:6). But in the following century they were reduced one by one by the Assyrians; Hamath fell in 720 BC and Carchemish in 717 (*cf.* 2 Ki. 18:34; 19:13; Is. 10:9).

The Assyrian and Babylonian records of the period (as late as the Chaldean dynasty) regularly refer to the whole of Syria (including Palestine) as the 'Hatti-land'; Sargon II in 711 BC can speak of the people of Ashdod as 'the faithless Hatti'.

The language of the seven Hittite kingdoms is known from hieroglyphic texts which have been deciphered in recent years; bilingual inscriptions in hieroglyphic Hittite and Phoenician, discovered at Karatepe in Cilicia (1946–7), have helped considerably in their decipherment. The language of these texts is not identical with the official language of the earlier Hittite empire, which was written in cuneiform script and identified as an Indo-European language in 1917; it resembles rather a neighbouring Indo-European language called Luvian.

III. The Hittites of Canaan

The Hittites of Canaan in patriarchal times appear as inhabiting the central ridge of Judah, especially the Hebron district. It has been surmised that they were a branch of the pre-Indo-European Hatti, or early migrants from some part of the Hittite empire; the Hittite empire itself never extended so far S. They may, on the other hand, have had nothing in common with the N Hittites but their similar (though not completely identical) name. In Gn. 23 the Hittites are the resident population of Hebron ('the people of the land') among whom Abraham lives as 'a stranger and a sojourner' and from whom he buys the field of Machpelah, with its cave, as a family burying-ground. The record of the purchase is said to be 'permeated with intricate subtleties of Hittite laws and customs, correctly corresponding to the time of Abraham' (M. R. Lehmann, *BASOR* 129, 1953, p. 18; but see for another opinion G. M. Tucker, *JBL* 85, 1966, pp. 77ff.). Esau grieved his parents by marrying two 'Hittite women . . . women of the land' (Gn. 27:46; *cf.* 26:34f.)—apparently in the Beersheba region. Jerusalem, according to Ezk. 16:3, 45, had a mixed Hittite and Amorite foundation. The name of *Araunah the Jebusite (2 Sa. 24:16ff.) has been thought to be Hittite, and Uriah the Hittite, evidently a Jerusalemite, was one of David's mighty men (2 Sa. 23:39). Ahimelech, one of David's companions in the days of his outlawry, is called a Hittite (1 Sa. 26:6).

The last reference to the Hittites of Canaan is in Solomon's reign (2 Ch. 8:7); thereafter they were merged in the general population of the land.

Bibliography. O. R. Gurney, *The Hittites*, 2nd rev. edn., 1981; *idem*, *Some Aspects of Hittite religion*, 1976; O. R. Gurney and J. Garstang, *The Geography of the Hittite Empire*, 1959; S. Lloyd, *Early Anatolia*, 1956; E. Akurgal, *The Art of the Hittites*, 1962; G. Walser (ed.), *Neuere Hethiterforschung*, 1964; H. A. Hoffner, 'Some Contributions of Hittitology to OT Study', *TynB* 20, 1969, pp. 29ff.; *idem*, 'The Hittites and Hurrians' in *POTT*, pp. 197ff.; J. G. MacQueen, *The Hittites and Their Contemporaries in Asia Minor*, rev. edn., 1986; J. Lehmann, *The Hittites*, 1977. F.F.B.

HIVITE. One of the sons of Canaan (Gn. 10:17; 1 Ch. 1:15); an early inhabitant of Syria and Palestine, named as distinct from the Canaanites, Jebusites, Perizzites, Girgashites and Amorites (Ex. 3:8; 23:28; Dt. 7:1), and in association with the *Arkites known to have dwelt in Lebanon (Gn. 10:17). This accords with their principal location in the Lebanon hills (Jdg. 3:3) and the Hermon range as far as the valley leading to Hamath (Jos. 11:3), where they still lived in the time of David, who lists them after Sidon and Tyre (2 Sa. 24:7). Hivites were conscripted as labourers for Solomon's building projects (1 Ki. 9:20; 2 Ch. 8:7). Others were settled in Shechem, whose founder is described as son of Hamor, a Hivite, in the time of Jacob (Gn. 34:2) and near Gibeon (Jos. 9:7; 11:19).

Many equate the Hivites (Heb. *Hiwwî*; Gk. *Heuaios*) with the *Horites (*Ḥorri[m]*, assuming a scribal confusion between the Heb. *w* and *r*. In Gn. 36:20–30 Zibeon is called a Horite as opposed to a Hivite in v. 2. Similarly, the LXX of Gn. 34:2 and Jos. 9:7 renders 'Horite' for 'Hivite', and some read 'Hittite' (*ḥittî*) for 'Hivite' in Jos. 11:3; Jdg. 3:3. The derivation from *ḥawwâ*, 'tent-village', is uncertain, as is the identification of the Hivites, otherwise unattested.

Bibliography. H. A. Hoffner, *TynB* 20, 1969, pp. 27–37. D.J.W.

HOBAB (Heb. *ḥōḇāḇ*, 'beloved'). Nu. 10:29 speaks of 'Hobab, the son of Raguel the Midianite, Moses' father in law'—ambiguous wording which leaves unclear whether Moses' father-in-law was Hobab or Raguel (Reuel). Jdg. 4:11 (*cf.* Jdg. 1:16) says Hobab; Ex. 2:18 says Reuel; but evidence is too slight to choose between the two accounts. Islamic tradition identifies Hobab with Jethro, but others suggest an identification between Reuel and *Jethro (Ex. 2:18; 3:1). The latter would make Hobab the brother-in-law of Moses; but such an interpretation of the Heb. word (*ḥōṯēn*) is questionable. J.D.D.

HOBAH. The name of the place to which Abraham pursued the four kings who had pillaged Sodom and Gomorrah and carried off Lot (Gn. 14:15). It lay 'on the left hand of', that is (to one facing E) to the N of Damascus. Though modern sites have been suggested, the place is unknown. A district Ube is mentioned in the *Amarna letters and identified by some with Tell el-Salihiye *c.* 20 km E of Damascus. T.C.M.

HOLINESS

a. Meaning

In the OT, the main Heb. root denoting holiness or the holy is *qdš*. It appears as a noun, verb and adjective over 850 times. In the LXX, the *qdš* group is translated primarily by the *hagios* group, the usage which forms the semantic background of *hagios* and cognates in the NT. Etymological studies suggest for *qdš* at least two associations, namely, 'separation' and 'brightness' (Muilenberg, 617) but the result of such studies are of limited value. More fruitful is a consideration of the term as the focal point of an idea which emerges by reference to its context and the wider semantic field.

b. Old Testament

The idea of the holy is at the heart of God's self-revelation and his call of Israel (Ex. 19:6; Lv. 19:2). This highlights the two dimensions of holiness. With respect to God, holiness is his quintessential nature (Hartley, 56), his very selfhood (Ex. 15:11; Is. 6:3; Am. 4:2). With respect to humans, objects, places, times and miscellaneous items like war and the covenant (Dn. 11:28), holiness is always derived and dependent upon proximity or relationship to the holy God. Holiness may also be predicated of lesser celestial beings (Ps. 89:5–7; Zc. 14:5) but the context implies that they are holy by proximity to God.

God's holiness is associated with other biblical and post-biblical words: power, glory, transcendence, uniqueness, exclusiveness, pureness, dangerousness. Earlier studies (*e.g.* that by Otto) stressed transcendence but the fundamental biblical picture is of God as the Holy One in the midst of his people (Ho. 11:9), a picture which emerges from the earliest chapters of Gn. (3:8). God's holiness does not make him unapproachable (Is. 57:15). On the contrary, he is a seeking God, whose holiness is expressed in his saving activity (Is. 40–55). At the same time, any approach to God can only be made under the provisions which God has himself established. The entire cultus has to do with making it safe for God's people to encounter the holy God who dwells in their midst. Any approach to God made under other conditions is dangerous (Ex. 19:12, 21, 24).

The holy God created a people by making his covenant with them (Ex. 19:5, 6; 20:1ff.). The lives of God's people were now to reflect his own holiness: 'You shall be holy for I am holy' (Lv. 19:2). This key verse is at the centre of the so-called

Holiness Code (Lv. 17–26), which shows the standards of holy living: in worship, in love for the neighbour, and in promoting justice and rooting out injustice. These foci are expressed in a variety of ethical commands which apply in cultic, sexual and social relationships. These mandates are to be followed by the forgiven people of God, not only for their own sake but for the sake of all peoples (Ex. 19:5–6).

The awesomeness of God's holiness, with a corresponding sense of personal unworthiness and the need for cleanness in God's sight, is seen clearly in Is. 6. The 8th century prophets are critical of the abuse of the sacrificial system, arguing that God's means of grace must be matched by righteous living and inward cleansing (Is. 1:10–20; Je. 7:1–27). The prophet tradition further develops the priestly belief that the holiness of God demands justice (Is. 5:16; Je. 31:31–34; Ezk. 28:22; 38:23). God manifests his holiness by moving humans to righteous living by which they model his values in their communal life and mediate a true knowledge of the Holy One to the nations (Is. 42:1, 6).

God abhors sin and injustice among his people; his holiness brings judgment upon it. The purpose of such judgment, however, is not destructive but redemptive. The supreme manifestation of God's holiness is his love. When God acts to save, it is to vindicate his holiness before all people (Ezk. 36:22–32). When Isaiah preaches forgiveness and redemption, he calls the God of mercy the Holy One of Israel (Is. 10:20; 12:6; 29:19). Hosea in particular demonstrates how holiness 'finds deeper expression in the conquering holy love rooted in the covenantal bond of grace' (Muilenburg, 621).

If corporate holy living by the people of God was the primary concern of the priestly and prophetic traditions, the primary concern of the wisdom tradition was individual holy living. Particularly noteworthy is Ps. 24:2–3.

Who shall ascend the hill of the Lord?
 And who shall stand in his holy place?
He who has clean hands and a pure heart,
 who does not lift up his soul to what is false,
 and does not swear deceitfully.

This passage builds on the priestly view that purity is a prerequisite for holiness of life. It calls for cultic cleanness but also shows that holiness demands individual integrity and single-minded devotion to God.

c. New Testament

Holiness in the NT exhibits remarkable continuity with the OT. The Lord's Prayer (Mt. 6:2 = Lk. 11:2) hallows the name of the Father in a manner reminiscent of Ezekiel. The trisagion of Rev. 4:6b–10 presupposes Is. 6:3 while the Song of Moses and the Lamb (Rev. 15:4–7) reflects Ps. 99. God's call of a holy people (1 Pet. 2:9–10) reflects Ex. 19:2 and Ho. 2:23, while the command and response of holy living (1 Pet. 1:15) mirrors Lv. 11:44; 19:2.

Few passages refer to God's holiness, though the NT always assumes the holiness of God the Father. Likewise, the term 'holy' is not often applied to Jesus, but when it is, it carries great weight. Luke emphasizes that Jesus, who will be called holy from his birth (Lk. 1:35), is full of the Holy Spirit (Lk. 3:22; 4:1) and his ministry as a whole is exercised in the power of the Holy Spirit (Lk. 3:22; 4:1, 14, 18; Acts 3:14; 4:27, 30). His life is holy in character (Heb. 1:9; 4:15, 1 Pet. 2:22). In conflict with evil he is recognized as the Holy One (Mk. 1:24). Peter confesses that Jesus is the Holy One of God (Jn. 6:69) while Rev. 3:7 gives Jesus the same ascription ('holy and true') as is given to God in Rev. 6:10. Jesus, designated Son of God in power by the Spirit of holiness through the resurrection from the dead (Rom. 1:4), incarnates holiness for us (1 Cor. 1:30).

The most frequent ascription of holiness to a divine person is to the *Holy* Spirit, who is the Spirit of God and of Christ (Rom. 8:9). All NT writers saw the coming of Jesus as God's Messiah who was to give the Spirit (Jn. 1:33; 20:22), and who poured the Spirit out at Pentecost on all flesh (Acts 2:17ff.), as the inauguration of the new age. The inextricable links between Father, Son and Spirit (Mt. 28:19) support the later doctrine of the Holy Trinity.

The Spirit is designated the Holy Spirit to distinguish him from other spirits (Mk. 3:28–30) and to show that he shares the holiness of God (Mt. 12:28 = Lk. 11:20). In the OT, God's holiness is displayed in awesome power; in the NT, God's powerful presence in the midst of his people is first through the words and deeds of Jesus the Messiah (Mt. 4:23–9:23; Jn. 5:19–29; 14:8–11), then through the Holy Spirit (Jn. 7:39; 14:25–26).

As is the case in the OT, a holy God calls a holy people (1 Pet. 1:15–16) so that they might proclaim his wonderful deeds (1 Pet. 2:9–10). Holiness continues to be permanently required of God's people. The adjective *hagios* is often used substantivally to refer to Christians in the relationship to God. Consecrated to him in obedience to his call, and accepted by him in the greatness of his grace, these persons are designated the *hagioi*. Through the sanctifying presence of the indwelling Spirit, on the basis of the atoning work of Christ, people who believe are made holy, children of God (Rom. 8:14–17). See *SANCTIFICATION. They live their lives through 'God's empowering presence' (see Fee) by the Spirit (Gal 5:16: Rom. 8:12–13), producing the active Christlikeness which is the fruit of the Spirit (Gal. 5:22). These holy people, born of the Spirit (Jn. 3:5–8), are made one through the Spirit (1 Cor. 12:12–13; Eph. 4:3–4) who empowers them for the proclamation of the gospel (Acts 1:8) and whose gifts are always given to be used for the upbuilding of the community of faith (1 Cor. 12:27).

BIBLIOGRAPHY. R. Otto, *The Idea of the Holy*, 1946; J. G. Gammie, *Holiness in Israel. Overtures to Biblical Theology*, 1989; J. E. Hartley, 'Leviticus', *WBC* 4, 1992, pp. 56–63; D. Peterson, *Possessed by God*, 1995; D. P. Wright, 'Holiness (OT)', *ABD* 3, pp. 237–249; R. Hodgson, Jr., 'Holiness (NT)', *ABD* 3, pp. 249–254; H. Seebass, 'Holy, Consecrate, Sanctify, Saints, Devout', *NIDNTT* 2, pp. 223–238; A. S. Wood, 'Holiness', *ZPEB* 2, pp. 173–183; G. D. Fee, *God's Empowering Presence*, 1994.

K.E.B.

HOMOSEXUALITY. The Bible says nothing specifically about the homosexual condition (despite the rather misleading RSV translation of 1 Cor. 6:9), but its condemnations of homosexual conduct are explicit. The scope of these strictures must, however, be carefully determined. Too often they have been used as tools of a homophobic polemic which has claimed too much.

The exegesis of the Sodom and Gibeah stories (Gn. 19:1–25; Jdg. 19:13–20:48) is a good case in point. We must resist D. S. Bailey's widely-quoted claim that the sin God punished on these occasions was a breach of hospitality etiquette without sexual overtones (it fails to explain adequately both the double usage of the word 'know' (*yāḏa‘*) and the reason behind the substitutionary offer of Lot's daughters and the Levite's concubine); but neither account amounts to a wholesale condemnation of all homosexual acts. On both occasions the sin condemned was attempted homosexual rape, not a caring homosexual relationship between consenting partners.

The force of the other OT references to homosexuality is similarly limited by the context in which they are set. Historically, homosexual behaviour was linked with idolatrous cult prostitution (1 Ki. 14:24; 15:12; 22:46). The stern warnings of the levitical law (Lv. 18:22; 20:13) are primarily aimed at idolatry too; the word 'abomination' (*tô‘ēḇâ*), for example, which features in both these references, is a religious term often used for idolatrous practices. Viewed strictly within their context, then, these OT condemnations apply to homosexual activity conducted in the course of idolatry, but not necessarily more widely than that.

In Rom. 1 Paul condemns homosexual acts, lesbian as well as male, in the same breath as idolatry (vv. 23–27), but his theological canvas is broader than that of Lv. Instead of treating homosexual behaviour as an expression of idolatrous worship, he traces both to the bad 'exchange' fallen man has made in departing from his Creator's intention (vv. 25f.). Seen from this angle, every homosexual act is unnatural (*para physin*, v. 26), not because it cuts across the individual's natural sexual orientation (which, of course, it may not) or infringes OT law (*contra* McNeill), but because it flies in the face of God's creation scheme for human sexual expression.

Paul makes two more references to homosexual practice in other Epistles. Both occur in lists of banned activities and strike the same condemnatory note. In 1 Cor. 6:9f. practising homosexuals are included among the unrighteous who will not inherit the kingdom of God (but with the redemptive note added, 'such *were* some of you'); and in 1 Tim. 1:9f. they feature in a list of 'the lawless and disobedient'. The latter is especially important because the whole list represents an updated version of the *Ten Commandments. Paul parallels the 7th commandment (on adultery) with a reference to 'immoral persons' (*pornoi*) and 'sodomites' (*arsenokoitai*), words which cover all sexual intercourse outside marriage, whether heterosexual or homosexual. If the Decalogue is permanently valid, the significance of this application is heightened still further.

It has been suggested that the meaning of *arsenikoitēs* in 1 Cor. 6:9 and 1 Tim. 1:10 may be restricted to that of 'male prostitute' (*cf.* Vulg. *masculi concubitores*). Linguistic evidence to support this view is lacking, however, though the word itself is certainly rare in literature of the NT period. It seems beyond reasonable doubt that Paul intended to condemn homosexual conduct (but not homosexual people) in the most general and theologically broad terms he knew. His three scattered references fit together in an impressive way as an expression of God's will as he saw it. As Creator, Law-Giver and King, the Lord's condemnation of such behaviour was absolutely plain.

BIBLIOGRAPHY. D. J. Atkinson, *Homosexuals in the Christian Fellowship*, 1979; E. Moberly, *Homosexuality: A New Christian Ethic*, 1983; P. Coleman, *Gay Christians*, 1989. D.H.F.

HONEY, HONEYCOMB (Heb. *dᵉḇaš*, 'honey', the usual word; *nōp̄eṯ*, 'juice', 'dropping'; *ya‘ar*, 'comb'; *ya‘raṯ had-dᵉḇaš*, 'comb of honey'; *ṣûp̄ dᵉḇaš*, 'a flowing of honey'; Gk. *meli*, 'honey'; *melission kērion*, 'honeycomb'). A favourite *food in biblical times (Pr. 24:13; *cf.* Ecclus. 11:3), honey was found in hollows of the rocks (Dt. 32:13; Ps. 81:16); in trees (1 Sa. 14:25–26, though the Heb. text here is obscure); in the wilderness of Judaea (Mt. 3:4; Mk. 1:6); and in animal carcasses (Jdg. 14:8).

Honey was used in cake-making (Ex. 16:31), and was regarded as having medicinal properties (Pr. 16:24). It was as acceptable gift (2 Sa. 17:29; 1 Ki. 14:3); a valuable resource (Je. 41:8); and was evidently plentiful enough to be exported (Ezk. 27:17, but some suggest that in this verse and in Gn. 43:11 grape or date syrup (Arab. *dibs*) may be intended; *cf.* Jos., *BJ* 4. 469). It was forbidden as an ingredient of any meal-offering to Yahweh (Lv. 2:11) because of its liability to fermentation (so Pliny, *NH* 11. 15), but included in tithes and first-fruits (2 Ch. 31:5), which incidentally suggests domesticated bees (*ANIMALS). In later times bee-keeping may have been practised by the Jews.

Canaan is spoken of as a land 'flowing with milk and honey' (Ex. 3:8, *etc.*; *cf.* *ANET*, pp. 19–20), for a discussion of which see T. K. Cheyne's note (*EBi*, 2104). Goshen is similarly described (Nu. 16:13).

Honey as the 'chief of sweet things' has inspired many figurative allusions—*e.g.* Ps. 19:9–10; Pr. 5:3 (*cf.* Ct. 4:11); Pr. 24:13–14 (*cf.* Ecclus. 39:26); Ezk. 3:2–3; Rev. 10:9. J.D.D.

HOOK. 1. Heb. *ḥāḥ* (Ezk. 29:4; 38:4), *ḥāḥî* (Ex. 35:22; 2 Ki. 19:28; Is. 37:29; Ezk. 19:4, 9). A hook put in the nose of a tamed beast to lead it about, or of a wild one to bring it under control. **2.** *ḥōḥîm* (2 Ch. 33:11), nose rings. Assyr. monuments show this method of treating captives. NEB has 'spiked weapons'. **3.** *šᵉp̄attayim* (Ezk. 40:43); possibly a double-pronged hook used in flaying a carcase, but the meaning is uncertain. RVmg., NEB render as 'ledges'. **4.** *mazmērôṯ*, 'pruning hooks' (Is. 2:4; 18:5; Joel 3:10; Mi. 4:3). Small sickle-shaped knives employed by vinedressers, easily convertible to, and probably used as, a weapon of war. **5.** *wāw* (Ex. 26:32, *etc.*) is used only in connection with the hangings of the *tabernacle. **6.** *’agmôn* (Jb. 41:1), *ḥakkâ* (Jb. 41:2; Is. 19:8; Hab. 1:15), *ṣinnâ* and *sîrôṯ dûḡâ* (Am. 4:2) and Gk. *ankistron* (Mt. 17:27) all mean 'fish hook'. N.H.

HOPE. Hope, it would seem, is a psychological necessity, if man is to envisage the future at all. Even if there are no rational grounds for it, man still continues to hope. Very naturally such hope, even when it appears to be justified, is transient and illusory; and it is remarkable how often it is qualified by poets and other writers by such epithets as 'faint', 'trembling', 'feeble', 'desperate', 'phantom'. The Bible sometimes uses hope in the conventional sense. The ploughman, for example, should plough in hope (1 Cor. 9:10), for it is the hope of reward that sweetens labour. But for the most part the hope with which the Bible is concerned is something very different; and in comparison with it other hope is scarcely recognized as hope. The majority of secular thinkers in the ancient world did not regard hope as a virtue, but merely as a temporary illusion; and Paul was giving an accurate description of pagans when he said they had no hope (Eph. 2:12; *cf.* 1 Thes. 4:13), the fundamental reason for this being that they were 'without God'.

Where there is a belief in the living God, who acts and intervenes in human life and who can be trusted to implement his promises, hope in the specifically biblical sense becomes possible. Such hope is not a matter of temperament, nor is it conditioned by prevailing circumstances or any human possibilities. It does not depend upon what a man possesses, upon what he may be able to do for himself, nor upon what any other human being may do for him. There was, for example, nothing in the situation in which Abraham found himself to justify his hope that Sarah would give birth to a son, but because he believed in God, he could 'in hope' believe 'against hope' (Rom. 4:18). Biblical hope is inseparable therefore from faith in God. Because of what God has done in the past, particularly in preparing for the coming of Christ, and because of what God has done and is now doing through Christ, the Christian dares to expect future blessings at present invisible (2 Cor. 1:10). The goodness of God is for him never exhausted. The best is still to be. His hope is increased as he reflects on the activities of God in the Scriptures (Rom. 12:12; 15:4). Christ in him is the hope of future glory (Col. 1:27). His final salvation rests on such hope (Rom. 8:24); and this hope of salvation is a 'helmet', an essential part of his defensive armour in the struggle against evil (1 Thes. 5:8). Hope, to be sure, is not a kite at the mercy of the changing winds, but 'a sure and steadfast anchor of the soul', penetrating deep into the invisible eternal world (Heb. 6:19). Because of his faith the Christian has an assurance that the things he hopes for are real (Heb. 11:1); and his hope never disappoints him (Rom. 5:5).

There are no explicit references to hope in the teaching of Jesus. He teaches his disciples, however, not to be anxious about the future, because that future is in the hands of a loving Father. He also leads them to expect that after his resurrection renewed spiritual power will be available for them, enabling them to do even greater works than he did, to overcome sin and death, and to look forward to sharing his own eternal glory. The resurrection of Jesus revitalized their hope. It was the mightiest act of God wrought in history. Before it 'panic, despair flee away'. Christian faith is essentially faith in God who raised Jesus from the dead (1 Pet. 1:21). This God towards whom the Christian directs his faith is called 'the God of hope', who can fill the believer with joy and peace, and enable him to abound in hope (Rom. 15:13). Because of the resurrection, the Christian is saved from the miserable condition of having his hope in Christ limited to this world only (1 Cor. 15:19). Christ Jesus is his Hope for time and eternity (1 Tim. 1:1). His call to be Christ's disciple carries with it the hope of finally sharing his glory (Eph. 1:18). His hope is laid up for him in heaven (Col. 1:5) and will be realized when his Lord is revealed (1 Pet. 1:13).

The existence of this hope makes it impossible for the Christian to be satisfied with transient joys (Heb. 13:14); it also acts as a stimulus to purity of life (1 Jn. 3:2–3) and enables him to suffer cheerfully. It is noticeable how often hope is associated in the NT with 'patience' or 'steadfastness'. This virtue is vastly different from Stoic endurance, precisely because it is bound up with a hope unknown to the Stoic (see 1 Thes. 1:3; Rom. 5:3–5).

In the light of what has been said it is not surprising that hope should so often be mentioned as a concomitant of faith. The heroes of faith in Heb. 11 are also beacons of hope. What is perhaps more remarkable is the frequent association of hope with love as well as with faith. This threefold combination of faith, hope and love is found in 1 Thes. 1:3; 5:8; Gal. 5:5–6; 1 Cor. 13:13; Heb. 6:10–12; 1 Pet. 1:21–22. By its connection with love, Christian hope is freed from all selfishness. The Christian does not hope for blessings for himself which he does not desire others to share. When he loves his fellow-men he hopes that they will be the recipients of the good things that he knows God longs to give them. Paul gave evidence of his hope just as much as his love and his faith when he returned the runaway slave Onesimus to his master Philemon. Faith, hope and love are thus inseparable. Hope cannot exist apart from faith, and love cannot be exercised without hope. These three are the things that abide (1 Cor. 13:13) and together they comprise the Christian way of life.

BIBLIOGRAPHY. E. J. Bicknell, *The First and Second Epistles to the Thessalonians, WC*, 1932; *RB* 61, 1954, pp. 481–532; J-J. von Allmen, *Vocabulary of the Bible*, 1958; R. Bultmann, K. H. Rengstorf, *TDNT* 2, pp. 517–535; E. Hoffmann, *NIDNTT* 2, pp. 238–246. R.V.G.T.

HOPHNI AND PHINEHAS. The two sons of *Eli, 'priests of the Lord' at Shiloh (1 Sa. 1:3). Both names are Egyptian, meaning 'tadpole' and 'the Nubian' respectively. They are described as 'worthless men; they had no regard for the Lord' (1 Sa. 2:12). They abused their privileges as priests, claiming more than their proper share of the sacrifices and insisting on having it when and as they pleased on threat of force, so that men treated the offerings of the Lord with contempt. Because of this and their licentiousness, a curse was pronounced against the house of Eli, first by an unknown prophet (1 Sa. 2:27–36) and later by Samuel (1 Sa. 3:11–14). They died in the battle against the Philistines at Aphek (1 Sa. 4:11). J.W.M.

HOPHRA. The pharaoh Ḥa'a'ibrē' Waḥibrē; Gk. Apries, 4th king of the 26th Dynasty, who reigned for 19 years, from 589 to 570 BC. He was an impetuous king, over-ambitious to meddle in Palestinian affairs. The Heb. form *ḥôp̄ra'* is best derived from his personal name, (Wa)ḥibrē', precisely as with Shishak, Tirhakah and Neco. 'Pharaoh-hophra' is explicitly mentioned only in Je. 44:30, but several other references to 'Pharaoh' in the prophets concern him. Shortly after Hophra's accession, Zedekiah requested forces from him, presumably against Nebuchadrezzar (Ezk. 17:11–21).

Hophra duly invaded Palestine during Nebuchadrezzar's siege of Jerusalem (Je. 37:5; perhaps also Je. 47:1?), accompanied by his fleet (Herodotus, 2. 161). In 588 Ezekiel prophesied against the Egyptians (Ezk. 29:1–16) and Jeremiah prophesied Hophra's retreat (Je. 37:7). The Babylonians raised the siege of Jerusalem (Je. 37:11) just long enough to repulse Hophra; whether a battle actually occurred is uncertain. After a disastrous Libyan campaign and a revolt which resulted in Ahmose becoming co-regent, Hophra was slain in conflict with Ahmose (*cf.* Je. 44:30). K.A.K.

HOR. 1. A mountain on the border of Edom where Aaron was buried (Nu. 20:22–29; 33:37–39; Dt. 32:50), possibly Moserah (Dt. 10:6), although Nu. 33:30, 39 distinguishes them. The place was in the region of Kadesh (Nu. 20:22; 33:37). More accurately it is 'Hor, the mountain', suggesting that it was a prominent feature.

Josephus (*Ant.* 4. 82) thought it was near Petra, and tradition has identified it with Jebel Nebi Harun, a lofty peak 1,460 m high, to the W of Edom. This, however, is far from Kadesh.

Jebel Madeira, NE of Kadesh, on the NW border of Edom has been suggested, for Israel began the detour round Edom at Mt Hor (Nu. 21:4), and Aaron could well have been buried here 'in the sight of all the congregation' (Nu. 20:22–29). However the site should be sought on 'the way of Atharim' from Kadesh-barnea to the vicinity of Arad, because it is always mentioned on the line of this journey (see references above).

2. A mountain on the N border of Israel, probably one of the N summits of the Lebanese range in the vicinity of the coast. From Jos. 13:4 the N border of 'the land that remains' included the region of Byblos and extended to Aphek on the Amorite border. Mt Hor was thus probably one of the NW peaks of the Lebanese range N of Byblos, such as Ras Shaqqah. J.A.T.

HORESH. A place in the wilderness of Ziph (1 Sa. 23:15–19), possibly to be identified with Khirbet Khoreisa some 9–10 km S of Hebron. AV, RV 'wood' is grammatically possible but topographically unlikely; trees could scarcely have grown in this region. R.P.G.

HORITES, HORIM. The ancient inhabitants of Edom, defeated by Chedorlaomer (Gn. 14:6), said to be the descendants of Seir the Horite (Gn. 36:20) and an ethnic group distinct from Rephaim. They were driven out by the sons of Esau (Dt. 2:12, 22). Esau himself seems to have married the daughter of a Horite chief, Anah (Gn. 36:25). The Horites (Heb. *ḥōrî*, Gk. *chorraios*) also occupied some places in central Palestine, including Shechem (Gn. 34:2) and Gilgal (Jos. 9:6–7), the LXX reading 'Horite' in both passages (AV; RSV, 'Hivite').

The E Horites cannot be identified as Hurrians either archaeologically or linguistically (Semitic personal names in Gn. 36:20–30). Some think the pre-Edomites to have been cave-dwellers (*ḥôr*) and equate this with the Egyp. name for Palestine (*ḫr* = *hurru*) cited with Israel on the Merenptah stele *c.* 1225 BC.

The pre-Israelite Jebusites ruled by Abdi-hepa during the *Amarna period seem to be Hurrians, as was *Araunah (Ornan, *'rwnh*, *'wrnh*, 2 Sa. 24:16; *'rnn* (1 Ch. 21:18), the Hurrian word for 'the king[sl]lord' (*ewirne*).

Hurrian, a non-Semitic (Caucasian?) language was spoken by a people who formed part of the indigenous population of N Syria and Upper Mesopotamia from *c.* 2300 BC. From the 18th century they are well attested at Mari and Alalaḫ as well as in the Hittite archives where from *c.* 1500 to 1380 BC Hurrian myths and literature are found.

At this time the Hurrian kingdom of Mitanni, ruled by kings with Indo-Aryan names, corresponded with Egypt (*e.g.* Tušratta–Amenophis IV) and influenced Assyria (*e.g.* *NUZI). Hurrian personal names are found throughout Syro-Palestine (*ALALAH, *TAANACH, *SHECHEM) and some biblical names may best be considered of Hurrian origin: Anah, Ajah, Dishon, *Shamgar, Toi and Eliahba (D. J. Wiseman, *JTVI* 72, 1950, p. 6).

Hori was also the personal name both of an Edomite (Gn. 36:22; 1 Ch. 1:39) and of a Simeonite (Nu. 13:5).

BIBLIOGRAPHY. I. J. Gelb, *Hurrians and Subarians*, 1944; E. A. Speiser, *Introduction to Hurrian*, 1941; E. A. Speiser, *JWH* 1, 1953, pp. 311–327; H. A. Hoffner, *POTT*, 1973, pp. 221–226; G. Wilhelm, *The Hurrians*, 1989. D.J.W.

HORMAH (Heb. *ḥormâh*). An important town in the Negeb, formerly Canaanite Zephath (destroyed by Judahites and Simeonites, Jdg. 1:17); its king is listed as defeated by Joshua (Jos. 12:14). The Israelite name 'sacred' recalled the sacrifice of the captured town under a national vow made after a previous defeat (Nu. 21:1–3); there is no clear link with Nu. 14:45, though AV follows Symmachus, Vulg., *et al.*, in emending 'way of Atharim' to 'way of the spies' (see *BDB*, *s.v.* Atharim).

Hormah was certainly linked with *Arad, but is not identical; *cf.* Jos. 12:14; Jdg. 1:16f. The sequence in Jos. 15:30f.; 19:4f. suggests that it was in the N of Simeon, towards Ziklag; W. F. Albright proposed Tell es-Sheri'ah as the only site in this area with extensive Late Bronze remains (*BASOR* 15, 1924). A more S location, at the limit of Canaanite pursuit towards Kadesh, is indicated by Nu. 14:45; Dt. 1:44. J. Garstang suggested Tell el-Milh (Tel Malhata), 22 km E of Beersheba, but it now seems likely that this was Canaanite *Arad and that Middle Bronze fortifications S of Tel Masos, 6 km to the W, represent Hormah.

BIBLIOGRAPHY. S. Talmon, *IEJ* 15, 1965, p. 239; M. Kochavi, *RB* 79, 1972, pp. 543ff.; Y. Aharoni, *IEJ* 22, 1972, p. 243; *BA* 39, 1976, pp. 55–76; *LOB*, pp. 201, 215ff.; J. Bimson, *Redating the Exodus*, 1981, pp. 190, 217f.; V. Fritz, *BASOR* 241, 1981, pp. 61–74; *NEAEHL*, pp. 986–989. J.P.U.L

HORN (Heb. *qeren*; Gk. *keras*). **1.** Used literally of the horns of the ram (Gn. 22:13; Dn. 8:3), the goat (Dn. 8:5), and the wild ox (Heb. *rᵉ'ēm*, Dt. 33:17; Pss. 22:21; 92:10; AV 'unicorn'). It was used as a receptacle for oil for ceremonial anointing (1 Sa. 16:1, 13; 1 Ki. 1:39). The ram's horn (*qeren hayyôḇēl*) was also used as a *musical instrument (Jos. 6:5; *cf.* 1 Ch. 25:5).

2. The horn-shaped protuberances on the four corners of the *altars in the tabernacle and Temple, an example of which has been found at

Megiddo. The sacrificial blood was smeared on these (Ex. 29:12; Lv. 4:7, 18, *etc.*) and they were regarded as places of refuge (*cf.* the respective fates of Adonijah and Joab, 1 Ki. 1:50ff.; 2:28ff.).

3. Horns symbolized power, in Zedekiah's prophetic action (1 Ki. 22:11) and in Zechariah's vision (Zc. 1:18ff.), and often the word is metaphorically used in poetic writings. God exalts the horn of the righteous and cuts off the horn of the wicked (Ps. 75:10, *etc.*). He causes the horn of David to sprout (Ps. 132:17; *cf.* Ezk. 29:21). He is spoken of as 'the horn of my salvation' (2 Sa. 22:3; Ps. 18:2; *cf.* Lk. 1:69), but this may be a metaphor based on the horns of the *altar as the place of atonement. Am. 6:13 'horns' (AV) should be read as a place-name, Karnaim (so RSV).

4. In the peculiar apocalyptic usage of Dn. 7 and 8 and Rev. 13 and 17 the horns on the creatures in the visons represent individual rulers of each world-empire.

5. For 'ink-horn', see *WRITING. J.B.TR.

HORONAIM. A town of Moab (Is. 15:5; Je. 48:3, 5, 34) which lay at the foot of a plateau close to Zoar. The *Moabite Stone refers to it in line 32. Some would identify it with el-'Araq, 500 m below the plateau, where there are springs, gardens and caves. It may, however, be Oronae, taken from the Arabs and restored to the Nabataean king by Alexander Jannaeus (Jos., *Ant.* 13. 397; 14. 18). J.A.T.

HOSANNA. The Gk. form of a Heb. term, used at the triumphal entry of Jesus into Jerusalem (Mt. 21:9, 15; Mk. 11:9; Jn. 12:13). The Heb. consists of the hiphil imperative *hôšaʿ*, 'save', followed by the enclitic particle of entreaty *nāʾ*, sometimes translated 'pray', 'we beseech thee'. It does not occur in the OT except in the longer imperative form *hôšîʿâ nāʾ* in Ps. 118:25, where it is followed by the words, also quoted at the triumphal entry, 'Blessed be he who enters in the name of the Lord.' Ps. 118 was used in connection with the Feast of Tabernacles, and v. 25 had special significance as a cue for the waving of the branches (*lûlāḇ*); see Mishnah, *Sukkah* 3. 9; 4. 5. But similar expressions of religious enthusiasm were not restricted to the Feast of Tabernacles: 2 Macc. 10:6–7 implies that psalm-singing and branch-waving were part of the festivities at the Feast of Dedication also. We may reasonably assume that the waving of palm-branches and the cries of Hosanna which welcomed Jesus were a spontaneous gesture of religious exuberance, without any reference to a particular festival and without the supplicatory meaning of the original phrase in Ps. 118. J.B.TR.

HOSEA, BOOK OF. This first book in the collection of twelve small prophetic writings which conclude our OT comes from the 8th century BC and, along with Amos, is addressed to the N kingdom Israel, often called by Hosea Ephraim. There is every indication that the prophet had his home in the N and loved the land and its people. It was therefore all the more painful for him to have to issue rebukes and threats when appeals went unheeded. The intensity of his emotion may be gauged from his vivid use of language. He packs metaphors and similes into allusions which in his day were no doubt extremely telling, though their exact meaning sometimes escapes the modern reader. Changes of subject-matter are abrupt and, in the absence of introductory phrases, it is by no means self-evident where one passage ends and another begins. The material appears to have been arranged in roughly chronological order, and to recognize historical situations behind the prophet's words is to find an important aid to understanding.

I. Outline of contents

1:1 Title
1:2–9 The prophet's family before 752 BC
1:10–2:1 A sermon on his children's names
2:2–15 Unfaithful Israel, prosperous now but not for long
2:16–23 The Lord's new covenant
3:1–5 The Lord's love will have its way
4:1–5:7 Sweeping condemnations of pagan worship and its consequences
5:8–7:16 Panic at the encroachment of Assyria *c.* 733 BC
8:1–14 Religious and political disintegration
9:1–9 The despised prophet warns of exile
9:10–17 Their population will decline
10:1–8 Their altars will be in ruins
10:9–15 They will reap as they have sown
11:1–11 The Lord's love recoils from punishment
11:12–12:14 A sermon on Jacob the deceiver
13:1–16 Death is inevitable, exile is imminent *c.* 724 BC
14:1–8 The Lord's pledge to forgive those who return to him
14:9 Concluding exhortation

II. Historical setting

Though Hosea prophesied in Israel the opening verse mentions only one king, Jeroboam II, who reigned in Israel. His successors were deemed unworthy of mention and the period of Hosea's ministry is marked instead by the reigns of the corresponding kings in Judah. The period covered by the prophecy is the last 30 years of the N kingdom. After years of prosperity, reflected in the prophecy of Amos but seen by him as a gross abuse of God-given resources, decline set in suddenly after the death of Jeroboam II (753 BC). The highly confident, rollicking behaviour depicted in Hosea 4 and 5 suggests the earlier period of the prophet's ministry, when politically everything seemed set fair and there was a booming economy. At that time a prophecy of destruction must have seemed incredible.

As time went on the sequence of events should have reinforced the truth of the prophet's words, but habitual attitudes were not easily changed, even under threat of invasion. The armies of Assyria marched nearer and nearer to Israel during the reign of Tiglath-pileser III (745–727 BC), until in 743 Damascus was forced to pay tribute. Before the death of Menahem of Israel in 742/1 this same king records having received tribute from Israel. On a later occasion each man paid the price of a slave to avoid deportation (2 Ki. 15:19–20).

An attempt at revolt against Assyria was made by Pekah of Israel (740–732 BC) in alliance with Syria (Is. 7); even if Judah had joined the coalition the cause would still have been hopeless. Assyrian power was too great and in 732 Damascus fell to the enemy. At the same time Israel was invaded, her Galilean territory annexed, and many of her subjects taken captive (Ho. 7:8–9). It was during Hoshea's reign (732–723/2) that an appeal was made to Egypt (2 Ki. 17:4) in an attempt to find liberation from the Assyrian yoke (Ho. 9:3; 11:5; 12:1). The attempt was abortive, Hoshea was taken captive and in 722 Samaria fell after a siege of 3 years.

Despite the worsening political situation there was no change for the better in Israel's way of life, nor was there any desire to listen to the word of the prophet.

III. Israel's way of life

Unlike his contemporary Amos, Hosea laid much of the blame for Israel's collapse on the adoption of an alien life-style borrowed from Canaanite neighbours. By going after 'Baal', the prophet's shorthand for the pagan deity and all that he stood for, Israel committed herself to a system which affected not only worship. Every part of life, from work in the fields, the use of leisure and the presuppositions of social duties and commitments to political decisions and relationships, was bound up with it. The Baals were regarded as the source of fertility (2:5; 4:10) and of financial prosperity (2:8). To worship them demanded neither selfdiscipline nor high moral standards. Instead, orgiastic ritual at the shrines appealed to the sensual in human nature and militated against everything that the ancient covenant morality had stood for.

The leaders of the nation, kings, priests and merchants, were the major offenders in promoting this way of life (5:1–7). It had become the norm, whereas the prophet's passion for the right was regarded as slightly mad (9:7). If the powerful in the land were to take rebuke and initiate reform, the prophet had an unenviable task ahead of him. There is evidence that at the first sign of Assyria's encroachment there was some attempt at repentance (6:1–3), but it was superficial and did not begin to result in a reformed society.

Socially lawlessness and injustice reigned. Burglary and highway robbery, murder, drunkenness, intrigue (6:7–7:7) and all the consequent evils are noted by the prophet; but his concern is not merely to list sins and point an accusing finger. What grieves him and drives him to protest is the choice Israel has made, rejecting the Lord, to whom Israel was 'betrothed', for worthless gods which, far from bestowing prosperity, could bring only ruin to the land and its people.

IV. The involvement of the prophet

To Hosea's mind it was no accident that his own personal experience had prepared him to understand the profound truth of the Lord's undying love for Israel, despite the fact that Israel had rejected him. The way Hosea expresses this (1:2) raises problems for the modern reader. Whatever explanation a biographer might have revealed, looking back Hosea could see that his experience was no accident. The Lord was in it, preparing his servant for a ministry which he could not have exercised without that particular form of suffering.

His wife Gomer bore three children whose names spoke of the Lord's judgment: 'Jezreel', the place where Jehu's sword ended the dynasty of Omri (2 Ki. 9:23–10:17), 'Not pitied' and 'Not my people' (1:4–9). It seems that subsequently Gomer left her husband for the promiscuous life that came most easily to her, and that eventually, worn and no longer attractive, she found herself forsaken, only to be bought back by the husband she had deserted. After keeping her for a while in seclusion he would restore her to her place as his wife. The story is not told explicitly, for the point is not to intrigue us with human heart-break but to demonstrate the consistency of God's love. There are therefore differences of interpretation as to the prophet's action, but as regards Israel the Lord would provide a way back to himself after the discipline of exile, and 'Not my people' would again become 'Sons of the living God' (1:10).

To help him understand the situation Hosea drew on his knowledge of God's dealings with the Patriarchs, in particular with Jacob, who strove to get his own way, even to the extent of striving with God (12:2–14). Yet the Lord had his way even with this cunning man from whom the nation was descended. Just as Jacob brought exile upon himself, so Ephraim was preparing his own destruction. As in the case of Jacob this was not the end of the story, so the prophet saw that exile would not be the last word on Israel's guilt.

Hosea also knew the Exodus story and meditated on its significance for his own time (11:1–4). Like a father with wayward sons, the Lord went on making provision for his people, though they did not realize the source of their health and progress. The Lord's love, like that of a caring parent, continued despite his son's rebellion and rejection. Still he called Ephraim 'my people' (11:7). Conflict between the Lord's love and his need to chastise and destroy tore the very heart of God (11:8). Here the prophet comes very close to the NT revelation of God's love as seen in the cross.

Opposition from the authorities is hinted at in 9:7. Not surprisingly, in the light of the treatment of earlier prophets (1 Ki. 19:2; 22:8; Am. 7:12–13), Hosea was regarded as an interfering fool, who could be passed off as a madman, to be shut away if necessary. He identified with and shared the Lord's suffering to the extent that he shared his love.

V. Hosea's theology

Whereas Amos had a message for Israel's neighbours as well as for God's people, Hosea concentrates on the relationship between the Lord and Israel, bound together as they were by a covenant of which the name Yahweh was a pledge and token (12:9). The terms of the covenant are referred to in 13:4, where reference is made to the first commandment. Evidently the Ten Commandments were known. The name Yahweh occurs most frequently, and when Elohim is used it is almost always with the possessive, 'your God' or 'our God'. Four times Hosea uses El, the Holy One (11:9, 12), the living God (1:10), the Lord of hosts (12:5). Here the emphasis is on the incomparability of Israel's God.

On another level Hosea sees that Israel has brought trouble on her own head. The natural disasters and military defeats Israel had suffered resulted from the outworking of a providential law of cause and effect, though Hosea never spoke of this as operating in any mechanical way. It is the Lord himself who is at work in circumstances, secretly eating 'like a moth' ('festering sore', JB, NEB) to destroy, or 'like dry rot' to cause collapse (5:12). This law will operate till full judgment has been worked out. Harvests will fail (9:2), riches will prove useless to save (9:6), conception will not take place and even if it does children will be born only to become war fodder (9:11–14). Men must learn that the mysterious generative powers they possess and the reproductive life of plants and animals are not ultimately under human control. There is a built-in retribution which comes into play to check abuse.

Hosea uses outrageous similes in likening the Lord to a lion, a leopard and a she-bear robbed of her cubs (13:7–8). In each case the animal is doing no more and no less than by nature it was intended to do. Such was the Lord's love that he could do no less than roar and destroy and devour. He too had been robbed of the love of his people and raging Assyrian armies would literally tear and devour and carry away their prey. Thus historical events as well as the world of nature were seen to be directed according to the Lord's will.

Did Hosea's contemporaries regard the prophet's accusations as exaggerated, so that the punishment appeared altogether out of proportion to the crime? This may well have been so, hence Hosea's insistence that throughout their history, with the possible exception of the first flush of the Exodus deliverance (2:15; 11:1). Israel had been rebellious. As soon as they encountered Baal-worship in the wilderness their true nature became apparent (9:10; 13:16). King-making had been another sign of apostasy (13:10; *cf.* 9:15), and the prophet commented on the collapse of the monarchy as kings were murdered and replaced by usurpers (7:7; 8:4). History again proved to be working out the Lord's purpose, and its meaning could be discerned by the man in tune with God's word. The apostasy of Hosea's contemporaries was the culmination of a long history of such rebellion and now the time had come for the Lord to call a halt. Israel did not in fact know the Lord, though they claimed to know him (8:2). For this reason they misunderstood his dealings with them. Such estrangement could not be resolved, largely because no estrangement was admitted on Israel's side. Neither appeals nor threats made any impression and therefore punishment had to come.

Undoubtedly Israel had set much store by public worship. The repentance formula (6:1–3) may have been a well-known 'general confession', and there was no lack of worshippers at the shrines (4:13; 8:11). Sacrifices were offered and the ritual was observed, but there was only the most fleeting consciousness of any need of forgiveness, and therefore worship bore no fruit in changed lives (6:4–6). Knowledge of God would have brought home the enormity of the people's need of forgiveness and of positive response to the Lord's steadfast love. Without these there would never be justice and right dealing between men.

In the light of all this, what hope could Hosea hold out for his own time or for the future? He knew that the next stage would be exile and the destruction of all that Israel had held dear. Then access to their idols would no longer be open (2:6), they would not be able to hold their festivals, and poverty would bring home to them their desperate need (2:9f.). This experience would drive them back to the Lord (2:7) and cause the 'wayward wife' to listen once more to his words of love (2:14). The result would be true repentance (3:5) and an enduring betrothal relationship (2:19–20).

Later in the book, when Assyria's sword was about to complete its work, the prophet found hope in meditation on the Exodus (12:13). Israel at that time had in no way merited deliverance, yet the Lord had worked through his prophet Moses to bring it about. They still had the same Lord (13:4) in whom alone was their hope (14:4). The anguish which the prophet saw so clearly to be involved in God's love was ultimately to issue in the incarnation and the cross. Jesus Christ would bear the penalty of estrangement on behalf of men and so open up the way back to communion with God. The confession of 14:1–3 would then become meaningful for men and promised blessing would become a reality (14:4–8). After that the Lord would find his lovingkindness returned.

BIBLIOGRAPHY. J. L. Mays, *Hosea*, 1969; H. W. Wolff, *Hosea*, E.T. 1974; F. I. Anderson and D. N. Freedman, *Hosea*, *AB*, 1980; L. J. Wood, *Hosea*, *EBC*, 1985; D. Stuart, *Hosea–Jonah*, *WBC*, 1987; T. E. McComiskey, 'Hosea', in *The Minor Prophets* 1, 1992. J.G.B.

HOSHEA (Heb. *hôšēa'*). **1.** The original name of Joshua (Nu. 13:8; *cf.* Dt. 32:44) which was changed by Moses (Nu. 13:16).

2. An official placed by David over the Ephraimites (1 Ch. 27:20).

3. The son of Elah; the 20th and last king of the N kingdom of Israel, who wrested the throne from Pekah by assassinating him (2 Ki. 15:30) and reigned for 9 years (2 Ki. 17:1). During Pekah's reign (*c.* 733 BC), Tiglath-pileser III had overrun much of Israel and claims to have established Hoshea as a vassal on his throne (*ANET*, p. 284). Expecting support from the pharaoh So, Hoshea stopped paying tribute, leading to an advance by Shalmaneser V (724 BC). When Hoshea asked him for peace, Shalmaneser arrested him and occupied the land, finally capturing Samaria in 722 BC, bringing the N kingdom to an end (2 Ki. 17:3–6). Hoshea, whose death is not recorded, apparently sought to change the religious policies of his predecessors since he receives only a qualified censure of his reign (2 Ki. 17:2).

4. A witness to the people's covenant with Yahweh after the exile (Ne. 10:23). D.W.B.

HOSPITALITY. Throughout Scripture, the responsibility of caring for the traveller and those in need is largely taken for granted. Although examples are found right through the Bible, the only specific commands about providing hospitality concern the Christian's responsibility towards his fellow believer.

I. In the Old Testament

Comparison with modern bedouin tribes, among whom hospitality is very highly regarded, suggests that the prominence of hospitality in the OT is partly due to Israel's nomadic origins. Abraham's generosity towards the three strangers (Gn. 18:1–8) provides an excellent illustration of nomadic practice, and was often remembered in later Jewish writings for its exemplary character, though settled communities were no less welcoming to the stranger (Jdg. 13:15; 2 Ki. 4:8ff.)

Hospitality in the OT was more than just a custom, however. It was also a demonstration of faithfulness to God (Jb. 31:32; Is. 58:7). One might even entertain Yahweh (Gn. 18:1–8) or his angels (Jdg. 6:17–23; 13:15–21; *cf.* Heb. 13:2), while God in his turn held a feast on the day of the Lord to which guests were invited (Zp. 1:7). The divine provision of *cities of refuge (Nu. 35:9–34; Jos. 20:1–9) and concern for the sojourner (Ex. 22:21; Lv. 19:10; Dt. 10:19) indicate the extent of OT hospitality.

Failure to provide for the traveller's needs was a serious offence, liable to punishment by God (Dt. 23:3–4) and man (1 Sa. 25:2–38; Jdg. 8:5–17). The use of *peša'* (1 Sa. 25:28), a term employed for transgression of covenants, indicates the importance attached to such obligations. The unique breach of hospitality by Jael (Jdg. 4:11–21; 5:24–27) could be commended only because of her unwavering loyalty to old family ties and to Yahweh. Some invitations were better refused, however, since they might result in spiritual ruin (Pr. 9:18).

Though hospitality was extended to all, a particular responsibility existed to provide for one's own family (Gn. 29:1–14; Jdg. 19:10–12; Is. 58:7) and for God's servants (2 Sa. 17:27–29; 1 Ki. 17:10ff.; 2 Ki. 4:8ff.). A future son-in-law might be entertained as a guest, though this is known only as a Midianite custom (Ex. 2:20). The peace agreement between Heber the Kenite and Jabin of Hazor seems to have included a mutual obligation to provide hospitality (Jdg. 4:11–21).

That a host was responsible for the safety and welfare of his guests is vividly illustrated by Lot and by the old man of Gibeah (Gn. 19:8; Jdg. 19:24–25). The immorality of the communities in which both lived suggests that their disregard for their daughters was due more to the prevailing moral climate than to the requirements of the hospitality oath.

A stranger would wait at the city-gate for an offer of hospitality (Gn. 19:1; Jdg. 19:15), though the well also formed a suitable meeting-place (Gn. 24:14ff.; Ex. 2:20). Sometimes hospitality might be given in return for an earlier kindness (Ex. 2:20; 2 Sa. 19:32–40). Bread and water was the minimum provision (Dt. 23:4; 1 Ki. 17:10–11), though such meagre fare was often exceeded. A guest's feet were washed from the dust of travel (Gn. 18:4; 19:2; 24:32; Jdg. 19:21), and his head sometimes anointed with oil (Ps. 23:5; Am. 6:6; *cf.* Lk. 7:46). The best *food might be presented (Gn. 18:5; 1 Sa. 25:18), and meat, rarely eaten in the E, specially procured (Gn. 18:7; Jdg. 6:19; 13:15; *cf.* Lk. 15:23). Curds and milk also particularly refreshed the traveller (Gn. 18:8; Jdg. 5:25). Animal fodder was supplied when required (Gn. 24:14, 32; Jdg. 19:21), while Elisha even received furnished accommodation (2 Ki. 4:10).

II. In the New Testament

The Gk. terms used are *philoxenia* (lit. 'love of strangers'), *cf. xenizō*, 'to receive as a guest', also *synagō* (Mt. 25:35ff.) and *lambanō* (3 Jn. 8).

Many aspects of OT hospitality reappear in the NT. The courtesies of providing water for a guest's feet and oil for his head continue, though the NT also mentions a kiss of welcome and guests reclining at a meal (Lk. 7:44ff.). In fact, Simon the Pharisee's home appears to have been an open house, judging by the way in which the presence of the woman who anointed Jesus was unconsciously accepted (Lk. 7:37ff.).

A special responsibility towards God's servants is also evident, and Jesus' earthly ministry (Mk. 1:29ff.; 2:15ff.; Lk. 7:36ff.; 10:38–41) and the apostles' missionary labours (Acts 10:6ff.; 16:15; 17:7) were greatly dependent on the hospitality they received. The NT develops this by regarding the giving or refusing of hospitality to Jesus and his followers as an indication of one's acceptance or rejection of the gospel (Mt. 10:9; Lk. 10:4), even at the final judgment (Mt. 25:34–46). These Christian responsibilities, however, are no more than a pale reflection of divine generosity. Jesus both spoke of the parable of the Great Supper (Mt. 22:2ff.; Lk. 14:16ff.) and gave the disciples an example to follow (Jn. 13:1ff.). Above all, he took the obligations of hospitality to the extreme by laying down his life to redeem his guests (Mk. 10:45; 14:22ff.).

The NT letters specifically command the provision of hospitality for fellow believers (*e.g.* Gal. 6:10). The existence of certain special factors in the 1st century AD emphasized the importance of these instructions. Persecution led to Christians being scattered and driven from their homes, and in many cases there was doubtless very real material need (Acts 8:1; 11:19). Itinerant preachers were also a charge upon the church. They received nothing from the pagan world (3 Jn. 7), and therefore became the responsibility of local Christians (Acts 9:43; 16:15; 18:3, 7), even though risks might be involved (Acts 17:5–9). Sometimes the hosts would be the evangelists' own converts (3 Jn. 5–7). False teachers, however, were to be turned away (2 Jn. 10), and letters of recommendation served to identify genuine cases (Rom. 16:1; 2 Cor. 3:1). Many inns of the time were also of low standard, both materially and morally, and the Christian traveller would often have found them unattractive.

The 'pursuit' of hospitality (Rom. 12:13) was obligatory for the Christian, who must ensure that the needs of fellow believers were properly met, though hospitality was to be offered to all (Rom. 12:13–14; Gal. 6:10). Thus Paul instructs the Colossian church to receive Mark (Col. 4:10), and assumes that Philemon will prepare a room for Paul when he is released from prison (Phm. 22). The duty of providing hospitality was also one of the special qualifications of a *bishop (1 Tim. 3:2; Tit. 1:8), and of a *widow requiring support from the church (1 Tim. 5:10).

Although hospitality was a mark of civilization for the Greeks, and the NT contains an excellent example of non-Christian generosity (Acts 28:7), hospitality in the NT had a specifically Christian character. It was to be offered freely, without grudging (1 Pet. 4:9) and in a spirit of brotherly love (Heb. 13:1). Such love (*agapē*: 1 Pet. 4:8; *cf.* Rom. 12:9) is essentially outward-looking, issuing in a readiness to provide for the needs of others, and could be demonstrated only because the giver had received a gift (*charisma*) from God (1 Pet. 4:10–11). The care of others was therefore the discharge of a debt of gratitude.

III. The biblical inn

OT references to a 'lodging place' (*mālôn*) are rare (Gn. 42:27; 43:21; Ex. 4:24; Je. 9:2) and specific locations are confined to routes linking Egypt and Palestine or Midian. Nothing is known of these places, though one of them was large enough to accommodate a sudden influx of nine travellers (Gn. 42:27). The LXX equivalent *katalyma* and the cognate verb *katalyō* suggest the idea of unharnessing the animals, though it usually conveyed the general sense of lodging. Bethlehem's inn (*katalyma*) may have been a fairly simple lodging-place. It was probably not a guest-room in a private house, as no name is given, and may have been the village's common responsibility. Elsewhere *katalyma* describes a room in a private residence borrowed for the Passover meal (Mk. 14:14; Lk. 22:11; *cf.* Lk. 19:7). The *pandocheion* of Lk. 10:34 is more developed, being open to anyone and providing overnight shelter, food and attention for a recognized charge, while *xenia* is used both for Philemon's guest-room and the place of Paul's house-arrest in Rome (Phm. 22; Acts 28:23).

BIBLIOGRAPHY. G. Stählin, *TDNT* 5, pp. 17–25; A. D. Kilmer, *UF* 3, 1971, pp. 299–309; J. H. Elliott, *A Home for the Homeless*, 1981; J. Koenig, *New Testament Hospitality*, 1985; J. J. Glassner, *ZA* 80, 1990, pp. 60–75. M.J.S.

HOST, HOST OF HEAVEN. In RSV, the word most commonly translated 'host' is *ṣāḇā'*, used nearly 400 times. *ḥayil* is also translated 'host' a number of times (but see *ARMY), while *maḥ^a^neh* ('host' in AV) is translated 'camp' or 'encampment'. Each of these words, with due regard to its special emphasis, may be used quite neutrally, for example of pharaoh's 'host' but equally of the 'host' of Israel. However, when used of the host of Israel, there are usually religious overtones, and there are two exclusively religious uses of *ṣāḇā* which ought to be noted.

a. Host of heaven

This phrase (*ṣ^e^ḇā' haššāmayim*) occurs about 15 times, in most cases implying the object of heathen worship (Dt. 4:19, *etc.*). The two meanings 'celestial bodies' and 'angelic beings' are inextricably intertwined. The LXX translation, using *kosmos*, *stratia* or *dynamis*, does not help to resolve this. No doubt to the Heb. mind the distinction was superficial, and the celestial bodies were thought to be closely associated with heavenly beings. In fact, the implied angelology of C. S. Lewis' novels (*Out of the Silent Planet*, *etc.*) would probably have commended itself with some force to the biblical writers. The Bible certainly suggests that angels of different ranks have charge of individuals and of nations; no doubt in the light of modern cosmology this concept, if retained at all (as biblically it must be), ought properly to be extended, as the dual sense of the phrase 'host of heaven' suggests, to the oversight of the elements of the physical universe—planets, stars and nebulae.

b. Lord of hosts (*Yahweh ṣ^e^ḇā'ôṯ*)

This expression is used nearly 300 times in the OT and is especially common in Isaiah, Jeremiah, Zechariah and Malachi. It is a title of might and power, used frequently in a military or apocalyptic context. It is significant that the first occurrence is 1 Sa. 1:3 in association with the sanctuary at Shiloh. 'Of hosts' is rendered in LXX either by transliteration as *sabaōth* (*cf.* Rom. 9:29; Jas. 5:4) or by use of *pantokratōr* ('almighty'). It is thought by some to have arisen as a title of God associated with his lordship over the 'host' of Israel; but its usage, especially in the prophets, clearly implies also a relationship to the 'host of heaven' in its angelic sense; and this could well be the original connotation. (*GOD, NAMES OF.) M.T.F.

HOUR (Heb., Aram. *šā'â*; Gk. *hōra*) is used in Scripture in a precise sense and in a more general sense.

1. In its more precise sense (which is probably later than the more general sense), an hour is one-twelfth of the period of daylight: 'Are there not twelve hours in the day?' (Jn. 11:9). They were reckoned from sunrise to sunset, just as the three (Jewish) or four (Roman) watches into which the period of darkness was divided were reckoned from sunset to sunrise. As sunrise and sunset varied according to the time of the year, biblical hours cannot be translated exactly into modern clock-hours; and in any case the absence of accurate chronometers meant that the time of day was indicated in more general terms than with us. It is not surprising that the hours most frequently mentioned are the third, sixth and ninth hours. All three are mentioned in the parable of the labourers in the vineyard (Mt. 20:3, 5), as is also the eleventh hour (vv. 6, 9), which has become proverbial for the last opportunity. The two disciples of Jn. 1:35ff. stayed with Jesus for the remainder of the day after going home with him, 'for it was about the tenth hour' (v. 39), *i.e.* about 4 p.m., and darkness would have fallen before they concluded their conversation with him. The third, sixth and ninth hours are mentioned in the Synoptic record of the crucifixion (Mk. 15:25, 33f.). The difficulty of reconciling the 'sixth hour' of Jn. 19:14 with the 'third hour' of Mk. 15:25 has led some to suppose that in John the hours are counted from midnight, not from sunrise. The one concrete piece of evidence in this connection—the statement in the *Martyrdom of Polycarp* (21) that Polycarp was martyred 'at the eighth hour', where 8 a.m. is regarded by some as more probable than 2 p.m.—is insufficient to set against the well-attested fact that Romans and Jews alike counted their hours from sunrise. (The fact that the Romans reckoned their civil day as starting at midnight, while the Jews reckoned theirs as starting at sunset, has nothing to do with the numbering of the hours.) The 'seventh hour' of Jn. 4:52 is 1 p.m.; such difficulty as is felt about the reference to 'yesterday' in that verse is not removed by interpreting the hour differently. In Rev. 8:1 'half an hour' represents Gk. *hēmiōrion*.

2. More generally, 'hour' indicates a fairly well-defined point of time. 'In the same hour' (Dn. 5:5, AV, RV; 'immediately', RSV) means 'while the king and his guests were at the height of their sacrilegious revelry'. 'In the selfsame hour' (Mt. 8:13, AV) means 'at that very moment (RSV) when Jesus assured the centurion that his plea to have his servant healed was granted'. Frequently some specially critical occasion is referred to as an 'hour' *e.g.* the hour of Jesus' betrayal (Mk. 14:41; *cf.* Lk. 22:53, 'your hour', *i.e.* 'your brief season of power'); the hour of his parousia, with the attendant resurrection and judgment (Mt. 25:13; Jn. 5:28f.). In John the appointed time for Jesus' passion and glorification is repeatedly spoken of as his

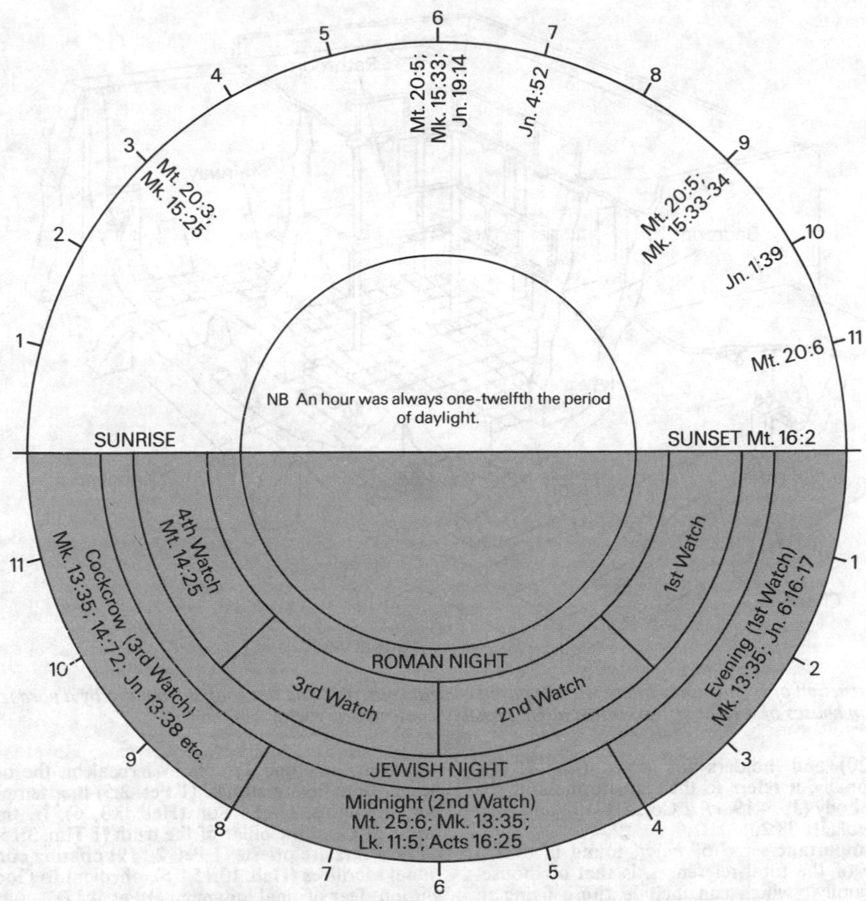

Biblical divisions of time, showing the night-watches. The hours (around the perimeter) will vary in length as they are calculated according to the times of sunrise and sunset.

'hour' (*cf.* Jn. 2:4; 7:30; 8:20; also 12:23; 17:1). The present situation between the times is 'the last hour' (1 Jn. 2:18); the rise of many antichrists indicates that Christ is soon to appear.

BIBLIOGRAPHY. W. M. O'Neil, *Time and the Calendars*, 1975; H.-C. Hahn, *NIDNTT* 3, pp. 845–850. F.F.B.

HOUSE (Heb. *bayit*; Gk. *oikos*, *oikia*). The Heb. and Gk. words are used with reference to various kinds of buildings and also in the sense of 'household, family'. Particularly in the NT, the 'house of God' is developed into an important theological concept. Architectural information in the Bible has been supplemented considerably by the results of archaeological excavation, though a complete picture of the houses people lived in is still not available for every period.

I. Old Testament

Heb. *bayit*, which occurs over 2,000 times, is cognate with a nominal form occurring in many Semitic languages. It has a wide use in the OT for all kinds of dwellings, from palaces (*e.g.* Je. 39:8) and temples (*e.g.* 1 Ki. 8:13) to private houses (*e.g.* Ex. 12:7; Dt. 6:7) and possibly even tents (Gn. 33:17). Houses were usually constructed of solid materials, stone, timber and plaster (Lv. 14:37, 39, 45; Am. 5:11), and were often built into the city wall (Jos. 2:15). Some were of excellent quality (Dt. 8:12; Hg. 1:4), such as David's cedar palace (2 Sa. 7:2, 7; *cf.* 1 Ki. 7:2; Is. 22:8) or the luxurious ivory-decorated houses of Samaria (1 Ki. 22:39; Am. 3:15). *bayit* is often combined with other nouns to indicate either a specialized building or part of a building, *e.g.* winter and summer houses (Je. 36:22; Am. 3:15), prisons (Gn. 39:20ff.; 2 Ki. 25:27), the Persian king's harem (Est. 2:9ff.) and above all the Jerusalem Temple ('house of God', 1 Ch. 9:11, 13, 26; 'house of Yahweh', 1 Ki. 7:12, 40–41). It is also used in other combinations to describe the quality or character of life in a house or building, *e.g.* pleasantness, mirth (Ezk. 26:12; Mi. 2:9; Ec. 7:4), mourning (Je. 16:5; Ec. 7:2, 4) and rebelliousness (Ezk. 2:5–6). By extension, *bayit* can sometimes signify the 'homes' of various animals (sparrow, Ps. 84:3–4; stork, Ps. 104:17; spider's web, Jb. 8:14; moth, Jb. 27:18; wild ass, Jb. 39:5–6; calf, 1 Sa. 6:7, 10), and is also used for various receptacles such as an altar trench (1 Ki. 18:32), perfume containers

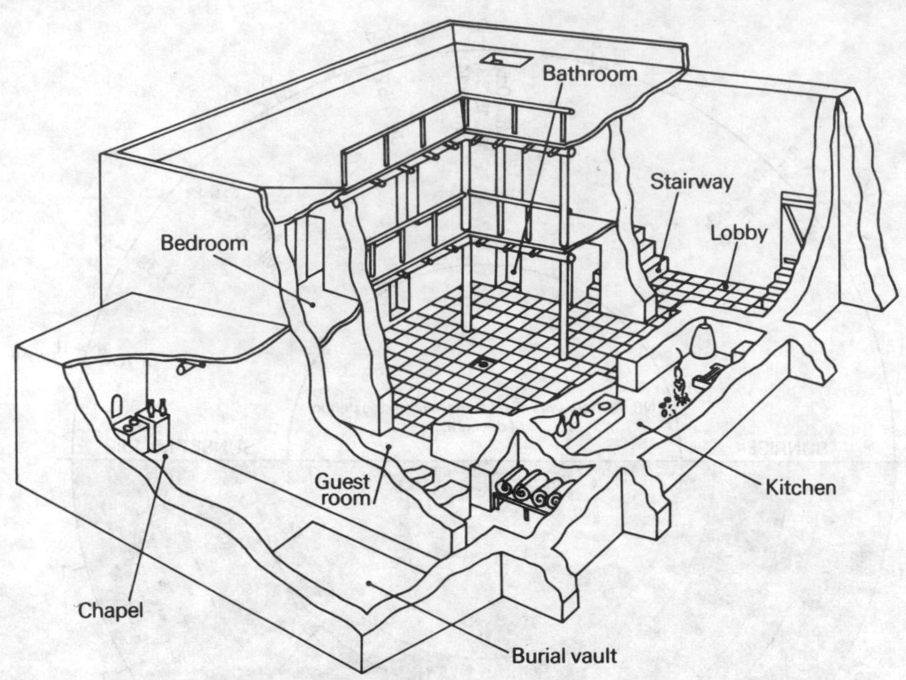

Reconstruction of a two-storey house with its paved central courtyard and flat roof surrounded by a parapet. Based on houses of c.1800 BC*, excavated at Ur, possibly contemporary with Abraham.*

(Is. 3:20) and holders for poles (Ex. 25:27). Occasionally, it refers to the transitoriness of the human body (Jb. 4:19; *cf.* 2 Cor. 5:1–10), and even to *Sheol (Jb. 38:20).

An important sense of *bayiṯ*, found in over a quarter of the total references, is that of 'household, family', which can include those living in tents (Nu. 16:32; Dt. 11:6). The frequent phrases 'father's house' and 'house of Israel' are both associated with the biblical concept by which a family, tribe or nation derives its name from an ancestor or leader. Finally, 'house' can designate both persons (including slaves) and property (Gn. 39:1–2; Ex. 20:17; 1 Ki. 13:8) belonging to a household.

II. New Testament

Much of the OT usage is continued in the NT. *oikos* has both literal and figurative meanings, with 'household, family, race' in addition to 'house'. The rarer *oikia* is largely synonymous with *oikos* in the NT, though it sometimes has the specialized meaning 'possession', notably in the distinctive phrase 'devour widows' houses' (Mk. 12:40). 'House' often occurs in the NT with reference to the Temple, both in its earthly and heavenly forms. For example, Jesus spoke in both senses of 'my Father's house' (*cf.* Jn. 2:16; 14:2), which was to be an international prayer-house (Mk. 11:15–17; *cf.* Is. 56:7; 60:7, LXX) rather than a 'house of trade' (Jn. 2:16; *cf.* Zc. 14:21).

A most important development of the idea of 'God's house' was its application to the church (*e.g.* Eph. 2:19–22; Heb. 3:1–6), whose communal character was emphasized in the concepts of the 'spiritual house' (1 Pet. 2:5) and God's temple (1 Cor. 3:16; 6:19). In contrast to the pagan temples and even the stone Temple in Jerusalem, the believers were 'living stones' (1 Pet. 2:5) in a temple built by Jesus, God's Son (Heb. 3:3, 6). In this house of God, the pillar of the truth (1 Tim. 3:15), all believers are priests (1 Pet. 2:5, 9) offering continual sacrifices (Heb. 13:15–16), obedient to God, without fear of final judgment (1 Pet. 4:17).

The theme of the 'household of God' undoubtedly owed much to the function of the house in early Christianity as a place of meeting and fellowship (*e.g.* 2 Tim. 4:19; Phm. 2; 2 Jn. 10). Whole households turned to the Lord (*e.g.* Acts 16:34; 1 Cor. 1:16), and the breaking of bread (Acts 2:46), evangelism (Acts 5:42) and teaching (Acts 20:20) were conducted 'from house to house'.

III. Archaeology

a. General

The large majority of houses in ancient Palestine were built in fortified cities, though there were also many dependent villages. Even the farmer often lived in the city, although he might camp out at harvest-time, and threshing-floors were always near the city. Large cities might cover an area of 20 acres, though most towns or villages probably did not average more than about 6 acres. Houses were usually packed closely together, particularly if the city was built on a hill, so that space was used economically. Town planning is known as early as the mid-3rd millennium BC, and during the Israelite period towns were often arranged with a central complex of houses encircled by a street and a wall with houses attached (*e.g.* Tell beit Mirsim, Tell en-Nasbeh). Larger houses were often on the W side of a city, to escape from smoke and dirt carried by the prevailing W winds.

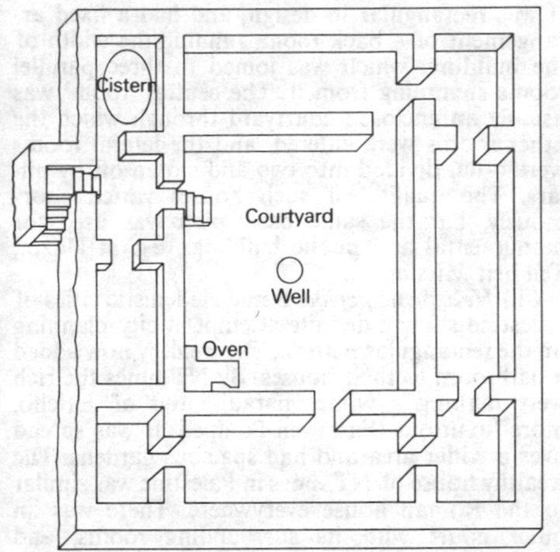

Ground plan of a villa of the early 2nd millennium BC *in Palestine. Stairs lead to the upper floor and main living-rooms from the central courtyard.*

Foundations varied according to the size and importance of the house, though they were important both because of the severe effects of heavy rain (*cf.* Mt. 7:24–27) and because Palestine is an earthquake area. The foundations sometimes went down into virgin soil, or even to the bedrock in the case of large houses, though in many instances remains of earlier walls and foundations were used in the building of new houses. If the ground was sloping, foundation layers were set on level terraces. The foundation layer often provided a ground plan for the house. The laying of foundations might be accompanied by human sacrifice (Jos. 6:26; 1 Ki. 16:34), but there is no widespread evidence of this horrific practice.

The walls of private houses were usually built of rough stone and mud-brick; where stone was scarce, the entire house was of mud-brick on stone foundations. The mud-bricks were coated with waterproof plaster on the inner faces of the wall, sometimes up to only half the height of the wall, while floors were made of marly clay, which can withstand hard use from bare feet. In the case of richer houses, the floor was sometimes paved, even in the courtyard. Strengthening of walls was sometimes achieved by placing hewn-stone pilasters at the corners and at regular intervals along the walls, or during the Divided Monarchy by stone pilasters laid horizontally, particularly in the upper parts of the wall. Walls could be up to 1 m thick, though interior walls were often thinner.

Doors were fixed in a frame of two doorposts, lintel, and sill or threshold. The doorway was usually lower than a man's height, and the door usually opened inwards, being prevented from swinging outwards by ridges on the lintel and threshold. The latter also served to keep out water and dirt. Doorposts were of wood (Ex. 21:6; Dt. 15:17) or stone (Is. 6:4), and the door could be locked or bolted (*cf.* 2 Sa. 13:17–18).

Windows are known from the 4th millennium BC onwards in Palestine. They were rarely on the ground floor, as the open door furnished plenty of light during most of the year, and were usually placed in the wall opposite the entrance. Window-space was kept to a minimum to keep the temperature down in summer and up in winter. Assyrian wall-reliefs of the Israelite city Lachish show windows high in the towers of the outer wall, and such windows in city walls provided a means of escape more than once (Jos. 2:15; 1 Sa. 19:12). Ivory carvings from various sites portraying a woman's face at a balustraded window may be related to the lattice windows of the OT which were located in outside walls (Jdg. 5:28; 2 Ki. 1:2; Pr. 7:6; Ct. 2:9).

Many houses had two storeys, though, since no building in ancient Israel has yet been preserved with a complete roofed ground floor or ceiling, the original height of a building is not always certain. Upper rooms were reached by stairs or ladders. These rooms provided the main living and sleeping accommodation (*cf.* 2 Ki. 9:13, 17), and guests could also be looked after there (1 Ki. 17:19; 2 Ki. 4:10–11). Roofs were constructed from beams covered with branches and a thick layer of mud plaster, though the rafters were sometimes supported by a row of pillars along the middle of the room. Cylindrical stone rollers about 60 cm long were used to keep the roofs flat and waterproof, though roofs needed to be replastered annually prior to the rainy season to seal cracks which had developed during the summer heat. The family would often sleep on the roof in summer or use it to dry raisins, figs, flax, *etc.*, in the sun. A parapet was to be built as a safety precaution according to Dt. 22:8. Vaulted roofs were certainly in use in Palestine by the Persian period, while the tiled roof also appeared before NT times. The rooftop was also a place of worship, either for Baal and especially the host of heaven (Je. 19:13; Zp. 1:5), or for the true God (Acts 10:9).

b. Life in the house

The house during most of the biblical period was usually a dwelling-place, store-room, and even had industrial and commercial purposes. There is evidence of dyeing, weaving and corn-grinding in houses, while at Jericho there is some indication that grain was sold from narrow booths attached to exterior house-walls. The farmer lived in the house, with everything he owned. Foods sufficient for the winter, fodder for the animals, storage jars and farm tools were all kept in the house. Archaeologists have been surprised by the amount of carbonaceous matter found in these houses, especially in those destroyed by Joshua's troops. In very cold, wet weather and in times of war, the family would also have to share the house, or at least the courtyard, with the most valuable of the animals. Religious objects have also been found in many houses, such as horned altars, incense stands, braziers and figurines. Many inhabitants undoubtedly followed local practices in contrast to the official worship of Yahweh.

The furniture in the house varied with the wealth of the inhabitants. The poor could afford only kitchen equipment and bedding. The furniture in the guest-room given to Elisha would be typical of that used in the average family (2 Ki. 4:10). It consisted of a bed, table, chair and a lamp. The rich used a high bed, others a cot, while the poorest used a reed mat on the floor. Plenty of bedding was necessary, for Palestine's winters are cold and damp. There would be chests to hold clothes and bedding. The furniture of the wealthy was inlaid with ivory, and others sometimes imitated this in common bone inlay. The ivory inlays in turn were sometimes inlaid with gold and precious stones. The hand-loom would also be found in many homes.

In winter, to keep the house warm, the cooking was often done indoors, and in the coldest weather a pottery or copper brazier filled with burning charcoal was used, though this was not very efficient. An oven was usually built in the courtyard of the house. Hollow at the top, it could be about 60 cm in diameter at the base and about 30 cms in height, and was often shaped of alternate layers of clay and potsherds. Inside the house were stone or clay storage-silos. Large jars were employed for keeping the winter's supplies, and there was a mill for grinding the grain. Flour was kept in a wide-mouthed jar, and olive oil was stored in a specially designed vessel. Often there was a large stone mortar set in the floor, where various foods could be prepared by grinding with a pestle. If there was no cistern in the house, a large jar for storing water was at hand, with smaller jars to carry water from the spring. Wide-mouthed cooking-pots for stirring food and narrow-mouthed ones for heating liquids have been found, along with a wide variety of bowls used in serving foods. The rich used gold and silver tableware, and copper kitchen kettles. Am. 6:4–6 describes the luxurious life of Israel at its worst.

c. Developments in architecture

(i) *Pre-Israelite period*. The oldest houses in Palestine were sturdy one-room structures mainly of circular or rectangular design. Two-room houses appear *c.* 5000 BC at Jericho, while some Chalcolithic houses with artistic representations on the walls have been preserved. By the 3rd millennium BC, two-room houses, usually rectangular, were much commoner, though the largest known house of this period is at et-Tell (Ai?), being *c.* 18 m long and containing three equal rectangular rooms. Apsidal houses are also found at several sites in the early 3rd millennium, and may have been a native Canaanite type of house.

During the resurgence of urban life in the Middle Bronze Age, the courtyard-based house became widespread in Palestine, though the poor continued to live in single-room hovels. Rooms were built on one or more sides of the courtyard, though rooms on all four sides are rare in Palestine. A large house dating to *c.* 1600 BC has been uncovered at Tell beit Mirsim (Debir?), where the courtyard alone measured 11 × 6 m and the six roofed rooms on two floors covered a floor-space of *c.* 140 sq. m. A more complex example of a century earlier from Ta'anach had good-quality walls 1 m thick, neatly-plastered floors, an internal staircase, and the ground floor measured *c.* 210 sq. m.

(ii) *Israelite period.* Where the Israelites replaced Canaanite towns, the quality of housing was noticeably poorer, though standards improved rapidly in the days of David and Solomon, partly through Phoenician influence. The most striking difference of all is the absence of Canaanite cult-objects in the period immediately following the Conquest. The poorest houses comprised a single room with a courtyard, of which many examples were found at Tell Qasile. The commonest-type house, however, of the pre-exilic period is what has become known generally as the four-room house, which appears to be an original Israelite concept. It was rectangular in design, and had a fixed arrangement of a back room, running the width of the building, which was joined to three parallel rooms stemming from it. The central 'room' was usually an enclosed courtyard through which the other rooms were entered, and the lateral rooms were often divided into two and closed off by pillars. The quality of such houses varied enormously, but the same basic plan was used for monumental and public buildings, *e.g.* at Hazor, Tell beit Mirsim.

(iii) *Hellenistic period.* Some Hellenistic cities of Palestine show a definite attempt at city planning on the rectangular pattern. The wealthy now added a bathroom to their houses. By NT times the rich were making a winter paradise out of Jericho, more luxurious than even Pompeii. It was spread over a wider area and had spacious gardens. The wealthy house of NT times in Palestine was similar to the Roman house everywhere. There was an outer court with its surrounding rooms, and behind it a second court with its adjacent rooms. In this latter area there was the utmost privacy.

(iv) *Royal palaces*. The OT gives only a brief description of Solomon's palace, but the detailed account of the building of the Temple enables us to conjecture what the palace looked like, for it was designed by the same architects and constructed by the same craftsmen. The masonry was of fine dressed stone laid in headers and stretchers. Fine woods, finished to show off their textures, were used for interior decoration. The excavation of the governor's palace at Megiddo has thrown light on Solomon's building programme. The palace of the Omri dynasty at Samaria was also built by Phoenician workmen. Here the king lived apart from his people in a citadel, built with very strong walls, and at least partially insulated from the poverty of much of his population. The beautiful ivory inlays are an indication of the luxurious style of living (*cf.* Am. 6:4–6), in marked contrast to the poorer areas of the city. Herod's palace in Jerusalem, with its extensive gardens, was the last word in luxury, as was also his winter palace at Jericho.

BIBLIOGRAPHY. S. M. Paul and W. G. Dever (eds.), *Biblical Archaeology*, 1973; L. Stager, *BASOR* 260, 1985, pp. 1–35; G. R. H. Wright, *Ancient Building in South Syria and Palestine*, 2 vols., 1985; K. W. Schaar, *SJOT* 2, 1991, pp. 75–98; A. Kempinski and R. Reich (eds.), *The Architecture of Ancient Israel*, 1992.

M.J.S.

HOZAI. The name of a history, translated in RSV as 'the Seers', quoted in 2 Ch. 33:19, RV, which recorded certain of the deeds of King Manasseh, and his prayer. The translation 'the Seers' for 'Hozai' follows LXX, which presupposes a Heb. text *ḥōzim*. The *MT ḥôzai* means 'my seers'.

R.A.H.G.

HUKKOK. A town on the S border of Naphtali, listed with Aznoth-tabor (Jos. 19:34). Generally identified with Yakuk, 8 km W of the suggested site of Capernaum. 1 Ch. 6:75 gives it as a Levitical city in Asher, but this may be a mistake for Helkath as in the parallel passage, Jos. 21:31. Y. Aharoni, *LOB*, p. 378, proposed Khirbet el-Jemeijmeh.

J.D.D.
A.R.M.

HULDAH. This prophetess, wife of Shallum, keeper of the wardrobe (either of priestly vestments or royal robes), lived in the second (western?) quarter of Jerusalem. She was consulted (*c.* 621 BC), on behalf of King Josiah, by Hilkiah the chief priest, Shaphan the scribe and others, following the discovery of 'the book of the law in the house of the Lord' (2 Ki. 22:14; 2 Ch. 34:22). She accepted the book as the word of Yahweh, and with his authority prophesied judgment against Jerusalem and Judah after Josiah's death. It is noteworthy that, although both Jeremiah and Zephaniah were prophesying at this time, it is she who was approached on this matter of the cultus.
M.B.

HUMILITY. The importance of this virtue springs from the fact that it is found as part of the character of God. In Ps. 113:5–6 God is represented as being incomparably high and great, and yet he humbles himself to take note of the things which are created, while in Ps. 18:35 (*cf.* 2 Sa. 22:36) the greatness of God's servant is attributed to the humility (gentleness) which God has displayed towards him.

Wherever the quality is found in the OT it is praised (*e.g.* Pr. 15:33; 18:12) and God's blessing is frequently poured upon those who possess it. Moses is vindicated because of it (Nu. 12:3), while Belshazzar is reproved by Daniel (5:22) because he has not profited by the experience of Nebuchadrezzar before him, which might have brought him into an attitude of humility. 2 Ch. in particular makes it the criterion by which the rule of successive kings is to be judged.

The term is closely connected in derivation with affliction, which is sometimes brought upon men by their fellows, and sometimes attributed directly to the purpose of God, but is always calculated to produce humility of spirit.

Similarly, in the NT, at Mt. 23:12 and parallels, the same word is used to express the penalty for arrogance (abasement) and the prerequisite of preferment (humility). In the first case it is a condition of low estate which will be brought about through the judgment of God. In the second it is a spirit of lowliness which enables God to bring the blessing of advancement. Paul too, in Phil. 4:12, uses it to describe his affliction, but goes on to make clear that the virtue lies in the acceptance of the experience, so that a condition imposed from without becomes the occasion for the development of the corresponding attitude within. In the same Epistle (2:8) he cites as an example to be emulated the humility of Christ, who deliberately set aside his divine prerogative and progressively humbled himself, receiving in due time the exaltation which must inevitably follow.

Like all virtues, humility is capable of being simulated, and the danger of this is particularly plain in Paul's letter to the Colossians. Whatever may be the true rendering of the difficult passage in Col. 2:18, it is clear that here and in 2:23 the reference is to a sham. In spite of all the appearances of humility, these false teachers are really puffed up with a sense of their own importance. Setting their own speculative system over against the revelation of God, they deny the very thing which by their asceticism they seem to proclaim. Paul warns his readers against this pseudo-humility and goes on in 3:12 to exhort them to the genuine thing.

BIBLIOGRAPHY. W. Baudel, H.-H. Esser, *NIDNTT* 2, pp. 256–264; *TDNT* 5, p. 939; 6, pp. 37–40, 865–882; 8, pp. 1–26.
F.S.F.

HUNDRED, TOWER OF THE. In Ne. 3:1, a Jerusalem tower which stood between the Sheep and Fish Gates, probably near the NE corner of the city. The Hebrew is *ham-mē'â*, meaning 'the hundred'; AV reads 'Meah', omitting the definite article, while RSV translates it literally. The name may refer to its height—perhaps 100 cubits; or to the number of its steps; or to the number of the garrison it housed. (*JERUSALEM.)
D.F.P.

HUNTING, HUNTER. The narratives of the patriarchal period depict the Hebrews as occupied chiefly with the raising of flocks and other semi-sedentary agricultural activities. Hunting was seldom engaged in as a pastime, and was generally resorted to only either at the promptings of hunger or when the wild *animals with which Palestine abounded in antiquity (Ex. 23:29) threatened the security of the Hebrews and their flocks (Jdg. 14:5; 1 Sa. 17:34). Certain individuals, however, were renowned for their hunting prowess, including Ishmael (Gn. 21:20) and Esau (Gn. 25:27).

By contrast the ancient Mesopotamians and Egyptians spent considerably more time in the pursuit of game. Many Assyrian monuments and bas-reliefs depict hunting-scenes, indicating a long tradition of sporting activity which may well go back as far as Nimrod, the mighty hunter of antiquity (Gn. 10:8) who colonized Assyria (Gn. 10:11). Whereas the Mesopotamians hunted lions and other ferocious beasts, the Egyptians preferred to catch game and predatory birds. In this pursuit dogs and cats frequently participated.

The austerity of the Hebrew diet in ancient times was occasionally relieved by such delicacies as partridge (*cf.* 1 Sa. 26:20), gazelle and hart meat (Dt. 12:15). The provision for Solomon's table also included roebuck (1 Ki. 4:23). Such is the general nature of OT references to hunting that few of the animals are named, and virtually nothing is said of the methods employed or of the accoutrements of the hunter. At Hassuna in Iraq the camp of a hunter was unearthed and found to contain weapons, storage jars and tools dating back to *c.* 5000 BC. Biblical references allude to bows and arrows (Gn. 27:3), clubs (Jb. 41:29, RV), slingstones (1 Sa. 17:40), nets (Jb. 19:6), the *snares of fowlers (Ps. 91:3) and pits for larger animals such as bears (Ezk. 19:8).

While hunting was not a common occupation in ancient Palestine, its procedures were sufficiently familiar to be enshrined in figurative speech (Jb. 18:10; Je. 5:26). The NT employs few hunting metaphors (Lk. 11:54; Rom. 11:9; Mt. 22:15).

BIBLIOGRAPHY. A. Van Selms, *ISBE* 2, pp. 782–784.
R.K.H.

HUR (*hûr*, 'child'? or *HORITE). **1.** A prominent Israelite who with Aaron held up the arms of Moses at Rephidim in the battle against Amalek (Ex. 17:10, 12), and who also helped Aaron to judge the people while Moses went up into Mt Sinai (Ex. 24:14).

2. A descendant through Caleb and Hezron of Perez (1 Ch. 2:19–20) and grandfather of *Bezalel (Ex. 31:2; 35:30; 38:22; 1 Ch. 4:1; 2 Ch. 1:5). **3.** A son of Ephratah and father of Caleb (1 Ch. 2:50; 4:4).

4. One of the five kings of Midian who were killed with Balaam by the Israelites (Nu. 31:8; Jos. 13:21). **5.** The father of one of Solomon's twelve commissariat officers (1 Ki. 4:8). The son, who was over the district of Mt Ephraim, is not named, so RSV transliterates the Heb. 'son of' and names him Ben-hur. **6.** The father of Rephaiah, who helped to rebuild the walls and was ruler over half of Jerusalem in Nehemiah's time (Ne. 3:9). T.C.M.

HUSHAI. The story of Hushai the Archite (*cf.* Jos. 16:2), his devotion to his king and his readiness to undertake a dangerous errand for him, affords a model for the Christian to study and to follow (2 Sa. 15:32ff.). Hushai's arrival at the heights E of Jerusalem where David halted, and his successful mission, defeated the advice of Ahithophel and came as an answer to David's prayer (v. 31). In a list of David's officers the Chronicler includes Hushai as 'the king's friend' (1 Ch. 27:33; *cf.* 2 Sa. 15:37). Baanah, Hushai's son, appears in the list of Solomon's local officers (1 Ki. 4:7, 16). G.T.M.

HUSHIM. 'Those who hasten'. **1.** A son of Dan (Gn. 46:23), called Shuham in Nu. 26:42. **2.** A son of Aher the Benjaminite (1 Ch. 7:12). **3.** One of the two wives of Shaharaim and the mother of Abitub and Elpaal (1 Ch. 8:8, 11). G.W.G.

HUZZAB (Heb. *huṣṣaḇ*, uncertain meaning, possibly from *nāṣaḇ*, 'it is decreed'). Occurring only in Na. 2:7. LXX gives *hē hypostasis* = Heb. *maṣṣāḇ* = 'standing-place'. AV, RV read as a proper name, but no such name is known in the cuneiform texts. RSV renders 'its mistress', referring to the Assyrian queen, but J. M. P. Smith (*ICC*) thought a reference to the goddess of Nineveh more likely. W. Gesenius derived it from *ṣāḇaḇ* and put it at the end of v. 6, reading 'the palace is dissolved and *made to flow away*'. NEB renders 'the train of captives goes into exile'. J.G.G.N.

HYMENAEUS. A pernicious teacher associated with *Alexander (1 Tim. 1:19–20) and *Philetus (2 Tim. 2:17). Paul's delivery of Hymenaeus and Alexander to Satan recalls 1 Cor. 5:5; both passages have been interpreted of excommunication (*i.e.* surrender to Satan's sphere) and of the infliction of bodily punishment. These are not, of course, incompatible, but the verbal similarity with Jb. 2:6, LXX, and various other disciplinary transactions in the apostolic church (*cf.* Acts 5:3–11; 8:20–24; 13:9–11; 1 Cor. 11:30) suggest that physical effects were at least included. There are also parallels in execration texts (*cf. LAE*, p. 302). At all events the discipline, though drastic, was merciful and remedial in intention.

It had not, however, evoked repentance when 2 Tim. 2:17 was written. The error of Hymenaeus and others, described in clinical terms as 'feeding like gangrene', was still much in Paul's mind. It involved a 'spiritualization' of the resurrection (including, doubtless, the judgment), doctrine always repugnant to the Greek mind: there were similar misunderstandings at Corinth earlier (1 Cor. 15:12). Such ideas took various forms in Gnostic religion: *cf.* the claim of the false teachers in the *Acts of Paul and Thecla* 14 (combining two ideas): 'We will teach thee of that resurrection which he asserteth, that it is already come to pass in the children which we have, and we rise again when we have come to the knowledge of the true God' (tr. M. R. James, *Apocryphal New Testament*, p. 275).

The name (that of the marriage-god) is not noticeably frequent. A.F.W.

HYMN. The Gk. *hymnos* was used by the classical writers to signify any ode or song written in praise of gods or heroes, and occasionally by LXX translators of praise to God, *e.g.* Pss. 40:3; 65:1; Is. 42:10. In the NT the word occurs only in Eph. 5:19 and Col. 3:16, with the verbal form (*hymneō*) in Mt. 26:30 and the parallel Mk. 14:26 (which refer to the singing of the second part of the Hallel, Pss. 115–118); Acts 16:25 (of Paul and Silas singing in prison); and Heb. 2:12 (a quotation from Ps. 22:22, LXX). It is clear, however, that the singing of spiritual songs was a feature of the life of the apostolic church, as is witnessed by 1 Cor. 14:15, 26; Jas. 5:13, the Christian canticles recorded by Luke, and the many doxologies found elsewhere in the NT. They were used as a spontaneous expression of Christian joy, as a means of instruction in the faith (Col. 3:16), and, on the basis of synagogue practice, as an integral part of the worship of the church.

The threefold division of psalms, hymns and spiritual songs (*ōdai*) must not be pressed too closely, as the terms overlap, but two distinct styles of composition can be observed. The first followed the form and style of the OT psalm and was a Christian counterpart of the psalmodic writing exemplified by the 1st-century BC *Psalms of Solomon* or the *Hymns of Thanksgiving* (*Hôḏāyôṯ*) of the Qumran sect. In this category may be included the canticles: Lk. 1:46–55 (*MAGNIFICAT); 1:68–79 (*BENEDICTUS); 2:29–32 (*NUNC DIMITTIS). The second group consists of doxologies (as Lk. 2:14; 1 Tim. 1:17; 6:15–16; Rev. 4:8, 11; 5:9, 12–13; 7:12, *etc.*), many of which were doubtless used in corporate worship. Some other passages have been loosely described by commentators as hymns, where the majesty of the subject-matter has driven the writer to poetical language, *e.g.* 1 Cor. 13; Rom. 8:31–39; Eph. 1:3–14; Phil. 2:5–11; but there is no certainty that they were ever set to music or recited liturgically. Fragments of liturgical or credal formulae have been detected in Eph. 5:14; 1 Tim. 3:16; 2 Tim. 2:11–13; Tit. 3:4–7.

BIBLIOGRAPHY. R. P. Martin, *Worship in the Early Church*², 1974; S. Farris, *The Hymns of Luke's Infancy Narratives*, 1985; M. Hengel, in W. Baier *et al.* (eds.), *Weisheit Gottes, Weisheit der Welt*, 1987. J.B.TR.

HYPOCRITE. In English a hypocrite is one who deliberately and as a habit professes to be good when he is aware that he is not. But the word itself is a transliteration of Gk. *hypokritēs*, which mostly meant play-actor. Though it was soon in ecclesiastical Greek to take on its modern meaning, it seems impossible to prove that it bore this meaning in the 1st century AD. In LXX it is twice used to translate Heb. *ḥānēp̄*, 'godless'.

In the NT, hypocrite is used only in the Synoptic accounts of Christ's judgments on the scribes and Pharisees. Though 'Pharisaic' sources (*Soṭah* 22b) acknowledge and condemn hypocrisy in their ranks, the general tenor of the NT, the 1st-century evidences for the teaching of the Pharisees in Talmud and Midrash and their support by the mass of the people (Jos., *Ant*. 13. 298), all make it hard to accept a general charge of hypocrisy against them. A study of the actual charges against them will show that only in the rarest cases can we possibly interpret them as hypocrisy. We find blindness to their faults (Mt. 7:5), to God's workings (Lk. 12:56), to a true sense of values (Lk. 13:15), an over-valuation of human tradition (Mt. 15:7; Mk. 7:6), sheer ignorance of God's demands (Mt. 23:14–15, 25, 29), and love of display (Mt. 6:2, 5, 16). It was only Christ, the sole perfect reader of inward realities (Mt. 23:27–28), who dared pass this judgment.

BIBLIOGRAPHY. J. Jocz, *The Jewish People and Jesus Christ*, 1949; H. L. Ellison, 'Jesus and the Pharisees' in *JTVI* 85, 1953; *BAGD*, under *hypokritēs*; U. Wilckens, *TDNT* 8, pp. 559–570; W. Günther *et al.*, *NIDNTT* 2, pp. 467–474. H.L.E.

I

IBLEAM. A Canaanite town in the N borderland of Manasseh, whose territory extended to (not 'in') Issachar (Jos. 17:11; Y. Kaufmann, *The Biblical Account of the Conquest of Palestine*, 1953, p. 38). During the Israelite settlement, its Canaanite inhabitants were subdued, not expelled (Jdg. 1:27). The site of Ibleam is now Khirbet Bil'ameh, *c.* 16 km SE of Megiddo on the road from Beth-shean (2 Ki. 9:27). It is probably the Bileam of 1 Ch. 6:70, a levitical city. Ibleam occurs in Egyp. lists as *Ybr'm*.
K.A.K.

IBZAN (Heb. *'ibṣān*). Known only from Jdg. 12:8–10; a national judge for 7 years, following Jephthah; apparently a person of consequence, who raised a large family and arranged marriages for thirty sons. His home and burial-place was Bethlehem, probably of Zebulun (Jos. 19:15), 11 km WNW of Nazareth; Jewish commentators, assuming it was Bethlehem-judah, identified him with * Boaz.
J.P.U.L.

ICHABOD (Heb. *'īḵāḇôḏ*). The name given by the wife of Phinehas to her child, on hearing that the Philistines had captured the ark (1 Sa. 4:19–22, *cf.* 14:3). There are several possible explanations: (1) that *'ī* is interrogative ('where is the glory?'); (2) *'ī* is the negative particle ('no glory', *cf.* Josephus, *Ant.* 5. 360); (3) that the name stands for *'āḇî-ḵāḇôḏ* ('my father is glory').
R.P.G.

ICONIUM. A city of Asia Minor mentioned in Acts 13:51; 14:1, *etc.* and 2 Tim. 3:11 as the scene of Paul's trials, and in Acts 16:2 as a place where Timothy was commended. Standing on the edge of the plateau, it was well watered, a productive and wealthy region. It was originally Phrygian, its

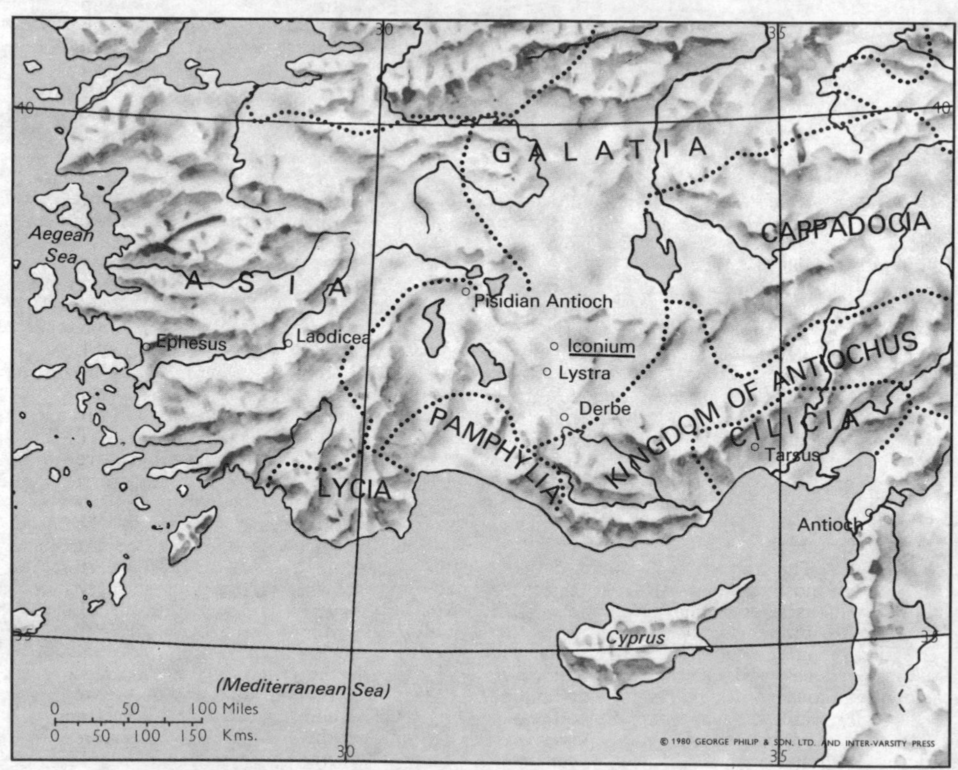

Iconium in the Roman province of Galatia, Asia Minor.

name Kawania: its religion remained Phrygian into Roman times, the worship of a mother goddess with eunuch priests. After being for a time the chief city of Lycaonia, and passing through various political fortunes, it was at length included in the kingdom of Galatia and a little later in the Roman province of Galatia. Its fame and prestige grew greatly under Roman rule: Claudius honoured it with the title of Claudiconium, and under Hadrian it became a colony in an honorary sense (since no Italians were settled there). In NT times, then, it maintained the polity of a Hellenistic city, the juridical powers of the assembly being vested in the two magistrates annually appointed.

The passage in Acts 14, though brief, gives occasion for differing interpretations. The so-called Western Text implies two attacks on Paul, one open, the second more subtle, after which the apostles flee. Two classes of Jewish leaders are mentioned, 'chief men of the synagogue' and 'rulers', a distinction epigraphically defensible. The text of Codex Vaticanus and its allies has a more difficult text with only one attack of fairly long duration implied. Here the rulers of v. 5 may plausibly be identified with the magistrates of the city, as Ramsay suggests, but whether the Old Uncial text is a bad abbreviation, or the Western Text an attempt at correction of a text perhaps corrupt, has not yet been finally decided.

Iconium is the scene of the well-known apocryphal story of Paul and Thecla, contained in the longer *Acts of Paul*. Apart from the scarcely doubtful existence of an early martyr of the name, there is no ascertainable historical content to be found in the story.

BIBLIOGRAPHY. Commentaries on Acts *in loc.*, especially *BC*, 3, pp. 129–132; 4, pp. 160–162; W. M. Ramsay, *Cities of St Paul*, 1907, part iv.

J.N.B.

IDDO. The name represents seven variant spellings in the Heb. and its derivations and meanings are uncertain. **1.** The father of Ahinadab, one of Solomon's officers, 1 Ki. 4:14 (*'iddō'*). **2.** A Levite of the line of Gershon, 1 Ch. 6:21 (*MT* 6:6 *'iddô*), but called Adaiah in 6:41 (*MT* 6:16). **3.** A tribal chief of the E section of Manasseh, 1 Ch. 27:21 (*yiddô*). **4.** A seer and prophet cited as one of the sources of the Chronicler in 2 Ch. 9:29 (*ye'dî* but *Q'rē' ye'dô*); 12:15 and 2 Ch. 13:22 (*'iddô*). **5.** The grandfather ('father' in Ezra) of Zechariah the prophet, Zc. 1:1, 7 (*'iddô*); Ezr. 5:1; 6:14 (*'iddô'*). **6.** One of those guilty of a mixed marriage; EVV Jaddai (AV Jadau), Ezr. 10:43 (*yiddô* or *yadday*). **7.** Head of one of the priestly families which returned to Jerusalem with Zerubbabel, Ne. 12:4 (*'iddô'*); 12:16 (*'iddoy'*).

J.G.B.

IDOLATRY. The story of OT religion could be told for the most part in terms of a tension between a spiritual conception of God and worship, the hallmark of the genuine faith of Israel, and various pressures, such as idolatry, which attempted to debase and materialize the national religious consciousness and practice. We do not find, in the OT, an ascending from idolatry to the pure worship of God, but rather a people possessing a pure worship and a spiritual theology, constantly fighting, through the medium of divinely-raised spiritual leaders, religious seductions which, nevertheless, often claimed the mass of the people. Idolatry is a declension from the norm, not an earlier stage gradually and with difficulty superseded.

If we consider the broad sweep of evidence for patriarchal religion we find it to be a religion of the altar and of prayer, but not of idols. There are certain events, all associated with Jacob, which might appear to show patriarchal idolatry. For example, Rachel stole her father's *teraphim (Gn. 31:19). By itself, this, of course, need prove nothing more than that Jacob's wife had failed to free herself from her Mesopotamian religious environment (*cf.* Jos. 24:15). If these objects were of legal as well as religious significance, the possessor of them would hold the right of succession to the family property (*NUZI). This accords well with the anxiety of Laban, who does not appear otherwise as a religious man, to recover them, and his care, when he fails to find them, to exclude Jacob from Mesopotamia by a carefully-worded treaty (Gn. 31:45ff.). Again, it is urged that Jacob's pillars (Gn. 28:18; 31:13, 45; 35:14, 20) are the same as the idolatrous stones with which Canaan was familiar. The interpretation is not inescapable. The pillar at Bethel is associated with Jacob's vow (see Gn. 31:13), and could more easily belong to the category of memorial pillars (*e.g.* Gn. 35:20; Jos. 24:27; 1 Sa. 7:12; 2 Sa. 18:18). Finally, the evidence of Gn. 35:4, often used to show patriarchal idolatry, actually points to the recognized incompatibility of idols with the God of Bethel. Jacob must dispose of the unacceptable objects before he stands before this God. That Jacob 'hid' them is surely not to be construed as indicating that he feared to destroy them for reasons of superstitious reverence. It is allowing suspicion to govern exegesis if we do more than assume that this was the simplest as well as the most effective way of disposing of non-combustible objects.

The weight of evidence for the Mosaic period is the same. The whole narrative of the golden calf (Ex. 32) reveals the extent of the contrast between the religion which stemmed from Mt Sinai and the form of religion congenial to the unregenerate heart. These religions, we learn, are incompatible. The religion of Sinai is emphatically aniconic. Moses warned the people (Dt. 4:12) that the revelation of God vouchsafed to them there contained no 'form', lest they corrupt themselves with images. This is the essential Mosaic position, as recorded in the Decalogue (Ex. 20:4; *cf.* Ex. 34:17). The prohibition in Dt. 4:12 is in the realm of religion, it should be noted, not of theology. It is correct to speak of a 'form' of the Lord and Dt. 4:12 and Nu. 12:8 have the word *t'mûnâ* ('form') in common. But for Israel to carry this over into religious practice could only involve corruption of truth and life. This is a striking testimony to the aniconic nature of Israel's worship. The second commandment was unique in the world of its day, and the failure of archaeology to unearth a figure of Yahweh (while idols abounded in every other religion) shows its fundamental place in Israel's religion from Mosaic days.

The historical record of Judges, Samuel and Kings tells the same story of the lapse of the nation from the spiritual forms proper to their religion. The book of Judges, at least from ch. 17 onwards, deliberately sets out to picture for us a time of general lawlessness (*cf.* 17:6; 18:1; 19:1; 21:25). We should not dream of seeing in the events of ch. 19 the norm of Israelite morality. It is candidly a story of a degraded society and we have as little reason for seeing the story of Micah (Jdg. 17–18) as displaying a lawful but primitive stage in Israel's religion. The same comment from the author of Judges points in turn to the religious corruption (17:1–13; see v. 6), social unrest and lawlessness (18:1–31; see v. 1) and moral declension (19:1ff.) of the day.

We are not told in what form the images of Micah were made. It has been suggested that, since they subsequently found a home in the N Danite sanctuary, they were in the calf or bull form. This is likely enough, for it is a most significant thing that when Israel turned to idolatry it was always necessary to borrow the outward trappings from the pagan environment, thus suggesting that there was something in the very nature of Yahwism which prevented the growth of indigenous idolatrous forms. The golden calves made by Jeroboam (1 Ki. 12:28) were well-known Canaanite symbols, and in the same way, whenever the kings of Israel and Judah lapsed into idolatry, it was by means of borrowing and syncretism. H. H. Rowley (*Faith of Israel*, pp. 77f.) urges that such evidences of idolatry as exist after Moses are to be explained either by the impulse to syncretism or by the tendency for customs eradicated in one generation to reappear in the next (*cf.* Je. 44). We might add to these the tendency to corrupt the use of something which in itself was lawful: the superstitious use of the ephod (Jdg. 8:27) and the cult of the serpent (2 Ki. 18:4).

The main forms of idolatry into which Israel fell were the use of graven and molten *images, pillars, the *asherah and *teraphim. The *massēḵâ*, or molten image, was made by casting metal in a mould and shaping it with a tool (Ex. 32:4, 24). There is some doubt whether this figure, and the later calves made by Jeroboam, were intended to represent Yahweh, or were thought of as a pedestal over which he was enthroned. The analogy of the cherubim (*cf.* 2 Sa. 6:2) suggests the latter, which also receives the support of archaeology (*cf.* G. E. Wright, *Biblical Archaeology*, p. 148, for an illustration of the god Hadad riding upon a bull). The cherubim were, however, concealed from view and were at any rate 'unearthly' in appearance. They could not point to any unacceptable affiliation of the enthroned God with earthly parallels. The bulls, on the contrary, were not (as far as the narrative suggests) concealed from view and could not but point to an involvement of Yahweh in fertility religion and theology.

The pillars and the asherah were both forbidden to Israel (*cf.* Dt. 12:3; 16:21–22). In Baal sanctuaries the pillar of Baal (*cf.* 2 Ki. 10:27) and the pole of the Asherah stood beside the altar. The pillar was thought of as a stylized representation of the presence of the god at the shrine. It was the object of great veneration: sometimes it was hollowed in part so as to receive the blood of sacrifice, and sometimes, as appears from its polished surface, it was kissed by its devotees. The asherah was wooden, as we learn from its usual destruction by burning (Dt. 12:3; 2 Ki. 23:6), and probably originated from the sacred evergreen, the symbol of life. The association of these with Canaanite fertility practice sufficed to make them abominable to Yahweh.

The OT polemic against idolatry, carried on chiefly by prophets and psalmists, recognizes the same two truths which Paul was later to affirm: that the idol was nothing, but that nevertheless there was a demonic spiritual force to be reckoned with, and that the idol therefore constituted a positive spiritual menace (Is. 44:6–20; 1 Cor. 8:4; 10:19–20). Thus, the idol is nothing at all: man made it (Is. 2:8); its very composition and construction proclaims its futility (Is. 40:18–20; 41:6–7; 44:9–20); its helpless bulk invites derision (Is. 46:1–2); it has nothing but the bare appearance of life (Ps. 115:4–7). The prophets derisively named them *gillûlîm* (Ezk. 6:4, and at least 38 other times in Ezekiel) or 'dung pellets' (Koehler's *Lexicon*), and *'elîlîm*, 'godlets'.

But, though entirely subject to Yahweh (*e.g.* Ps. 95:3), there are spiritual forces of evil, and the practice of idolatry brings men into deadly contact with these 'gods'. Isaiah, who is usually said to bring the ironic scorning of idols to its peak, is well aware of this spiritual evil. He knows that there is only one God (44:8), but even so no-one can touch an idol, though it be 'nothing', and come away unscathed. Man's contact with the false god infects him with a deadly spiritual blindness of heart and mind (44:18). Though what he worships is mere 'ashes', yet it is full of the poison of spiritual delusion (44:20). Those who worship idols become like them (Ps. 115:8; Je. 2:5; Ho. 9:10). Because of the reality of evil power behind the idol, it is an *abomination (*tô'ēḇâ*) to Yahweh (Dt. 7:25), a detested thing (*šiqqûṣ*) (Dt. 29:17), and it is the gravest sin, spiritual adultery, to follow idols (Dt. 31:16; Jdg. 2:17; Ho. 1:2). Nevertheless, there is only one God, and the contrast between Yahweh and idols is to be drawn in terms of life, activity and government. The idol cannot predict and bring to pass, but Yahweh can (Is. 41:26–27; 44:7); the idol is a helpless piece of flotsam on the river of history, only wise after the event and helpless in the face of it (Is. 41:5–7; 46:1–2), but Yahweh is Lord and controller of history (Is. 40:22–25; 41:1–2, 25; 43:14–15, *etc.*).

The NT reinforces and amplifies the OT teaching. Its recognition that idols are both nonentities and dangerous spiritual potencies has been noted above. In addition, Rom. 1 expresses the OT view that idolatry is a decline from true spirituality, and not a stage on the way to a pure knowledge of God. The NT recognizes, however, that the peril of idolatry exists even where material idols are not fashioned: the association of idolatry with sexual sins in Gal. 5:19–20 ought to be linked with the equating of covetousness with idolatry (1 Cor. 5:11; Eph. 5:5; Col. 3:5), for by covetousness Paul certainly includes and stresses sexual covetousness (*cf.* Eph. 4:19; 5:3; 1 Thes. 4:6, Gk.; 1 Cor. 10:7, 14). John, having urged the finality and fullness of revelation in Christ, warns that any deviation is idolatry (1 Jn. 5:19–21). The idol is whatever claims that loyalty which belongs to God alone (Is. 42:8).

The bearing of the biblical teaching on idols on its monotheistic doctrine of God cannot be overlooked. In its recognition of the magnetism of idolatrous religion for Israel and also in such seeming recognition of 'other gods' as, *e.g.*, Ps. 95:3, the OT acknowledges not the real existence of the 'gods' but the real existence of the threat to Israel, the menace of alternative cults and claims. It thus constantly holds its monotheism (as indeed the NT also does) in the setting of the religion and religious environment of the people of God.

BIBLIOGRAPHY. J. Tigay, *You Shall Have No Other Gods Before Me*, 1986; T. Jacobsen, 'The

Graven Image', in *Ancient Israelite Religion*, 1987, pp. 23–32. J.A.M.

IDOLS, MEATS OFFERED TO. Among the questions submitted by the Corinthians for the apostle's ruling was the matter of 'food offered to idols', a phrase which represents one Gk. term, *eidōlothyta.* Paul handles this subject in 1 Cor. 8:1–13 and 10:14–33. The background of the Corinthians' query may first be sketched.

I. The background

In the ancient system of sacrifice, which was the centre not only of the religious life of the Graeco-Roman world in the 1st century but also of the domestic and social life, only part of the sacrifice was presented to the god in the temple. The sacrifice was followed by a cultic meal, when the remainder of the consecrated food was eaten either in the precincts of the temple or at home. Sometimes the remaining food was sent to the market to be sold (1 Cor. 10:25).

Evidence for the practice of a meal in the temple is found in the following well-known Oxyrhynchus papyrus which Lietzmann regards as 'a striking parallel' to the reference in 1 Cor. 10:27: 'Chaeremon invites you to dinner at the table of the lord Serapis (the name of the deity) in the Serapeum tomorrow the 15th at the 9th hour' (= 3 p.m.) (quoted and discussed in Chan-Hie Kim's essay, 'The Papyrus Invitation', *JBL* 94, 1975, pp. 391–402). An invitation to a meal of this character, whether in the temple or in a private house, would be commonplace in the social life of the city of Corinth, and would pose a thorny question for the believer who was so invited. Other aspects of life in such a cosmopolitan centre would be affected by the Christian's attitude to idol-meats. Attendance at the public festivals, which opened with pagan adoration and sacrifice, would have to be considered. Membership of a trade guild, and therefore one's commercial standing, and public-spiritedness were also involved, as such membership would entail sitting 'at table in an idol's temple' (1 Cor. 8:10). Even daily shopping in the market would present a problem to the thoughtful Christian in Corinth. As much of the meat would be passed on from the temple-officials to the meat-dealers and by them exposed for sale, the question arose: was the Christian housewife at liberty to purchase this meat which, coming from sacrificial animals which had to be free from blemish, might well be the best meat in the market? Moreover, there were gratuitous banquets in the temple precincts which were a real boon to the poor. If 1 Cor. 1:26 means that some of the Corinthian church members belonged to the poorer classes, the question of whether they were free or not to avail themselves of such meals would have been a practical issue.

II. Different reactions

Conviction in the church was sharply divided. One group, in the name of Christian liberty (6:12; 10:23; *cf.* 8:9) and on the basis of a supposed superior knowledge (*gnōsis*, 8:1–2), could see no harm in accepting an invitation to a cultic meal and no possible reason why food, formerly dedicated in the temple, should not be bought and eaten.

The justification for such an attitude of religious syncretism was, first, that the meal in the temple precincts was just a social occasion. They claimed that it had no religious significance at all. And, secondly, they appear to have stated that in any case the pagan gods are nonentities. 'An idol has no real existence' and 'there is no God but one' was their plea of defence (8:4; cited probably from the Corinthians' own letter to Paul).

On the other hand, the 'weak' group (8:9; *cf.* Rom. 15:1) viewed the situation differently. With abhorrence of the least suspicion of idolatry, they believed that the demons behind the idols still exerted malign influence on the food and 'contaminated' it, thus rendering it unfit for consumption by believers (8:7; *cf.* Acts 10:14).

III. Paul's answer

Paul begins his answer to the church's inquiry by expressing agreement with the proposition, 'There is no God but one' (8:4). But he immediately qualifies this explicit confession of his monotheism by reminding his readers that there are so-called gods and lords which exert demonic influence in the world. He concedes the point, however, that 'for us' who acknowledge one God and one Lord, the power of these demons has been overcome by the cross, so that the Corinthians ought no longer to be in bondage to them (*cf.* Col. 2:15–16; Gal. 4:3, 8–9). Not all the Corinthian believers have found that freedom in Christ, and their case must be remembered and their weak conscience not outraged by indiscreet action (8:7–13). The apostle has a more serious word to say on this matter, which he takes up after a digression in ch. 9.

He comes to grips with the menace of idolatry in 10:14ff. These verses are an exposition of the inner meaning of the Lord's Table in the light of communion in the body and blood of Christ (10:16); the unity of the church as the body of Christ (10:17); the spell cast by demons over their worshippers at idol-feasts which led actually to a compact with the demons (10:20); and the impossibility of a double allegiance represented by trying to share both the table of the Lord and the table of demons (10:21–22). (*LORD'S SUPPER.)

The apostle in this section, therefore, takes a serious attitude to the implications of attendance at idolatrous banquets (*cf.* 10:14). In line with rabbinical teaching which was later codified in the Mishnah tractate *'Abodah Zarah* ('Strange Worship'), he forbids absolutely the use of food and drink in an idol-temple (10:19–20; *cf.* Rev. 2:14) on the ground no doubt that, as the rabbis said, 'as a dead body defiles by overshadowing, so also an idolatrous sacrifice causes defilement by overshadowing', *i.e.* by having been brought under a pagan roof, and by this contact becomes ritually unclean. See the Mishnah in Danby's edition, p. 649, n. 3.

But, in regard to food which has formerly been offered in the temple and is afterwards made available for consumption, Paul says that it is permitted on the basis of Ps. 24:1 (1 Cor. 10:25ff.). Although such food has been dedicated in the temple and is exposed for sale in the meat-market, it may be eaten by virtue of being God's creation (1 Tim. 4:4–5). This is a distinct departure from the rabbinical ceremonial rules (and, indeed, from the apostolic decree of Acts 15:28–29), and is the practical application of the Lord's word in Mk. 7:19, '*Thus he declared* all foods clean'; *cf.* Acts 10:15). The only qualification is that the 'law of love' (*TDNT* 2, p. 379) must be observed, and a Christian's own freedom to eat such food must be waived if the conscience of the 'weaker' believer is likely to be damaged and he is thereby caused to stumble (10:28–32), or if a Gentile is scandalized by this practice (10:32). The situation envisaged by these verses is a Christian's acceptance of an invitation to a meal in a private house (10:27). In such a circumstance the believer is free to eat the food set before him, making no inquiries as to its 'past history', *i.e.* where it comes from or whether it has been dedicated in an idol shrine. If, however, a pagan, at the meal, draws attention to the food and says, 'This has been offered in sacrifice'—using the pagan term *hierothyton*—then the food must be refused, not because it is 'infected' or unfit for consumption, but because it 'places the eater in a false position, and confuses the conscience of others' (Robertson–Plummer, *I Corinthians*, p. 219), notably his heathen neighbour (10:29). This reading differs from the suggestion of Robertson–Plummer, where they take the speaker in v. 28 to be a Gentile Christian using the terminology of his pre-Christian days; it is better, however, to regard this speaker as 'one of them that believe not' in v. 27; and then the apostle's word links up with the altruism of the rabbis, who taught that a devout Jew will not countenance idolatry lest he should encourage his Gentile neighbour in error, for which he would then be responsible (*Aboth* 5. 18; *Sanhedrin* 7. 4, 10).

BIBLIOGRAPHY. A. Ehrhardt, *The Framework of the New Testament Stories*, 1964, pp. 275–290; C. K. Barrett, *NTS* 11, 1964–5, pp. 138ff.; W. L. Willis, *Idol Meat in Corinth*, 1985; G. D. Fee, *The First Epistle to the Corinthians*, *NIC* 1987; H. Hübner, 'eidōlothyon', *EDNT* 1, pp. 386–388. R.P.M.

IDUMAEA. The Gk. form (*idoumaia*) of the Heb. *'ᵉḏôm* refers to an area in W Palestine, rather than to Edom proper. At the time of the Exodus, Edom extended to both sides of the Arabah, and the W portion reached close to Kadesh (Nu. 20:16). David subdued Edom, but there was continual conflict between *Edom and Judah. After the fall of Jerusalem in 587 BC the Edomites took advantage of the calamity to migrate into the heart of S Judah, S of Hebron. Several prophets inveighed against Edom for this (Je. 49:7–22; La. 4:21–22; Ezk. 25:12–14; 35:3; Ob. 10ff.).

Later, as various Arab groups, notably the Nabataeans, pressed into old Edom, more migrants settled in Judah, and the area they occupied became known as Idumaea (1 Macc. 4:29; 5:65). Judas Maccabaeus had successful campaigns against these people, and John Hyrcanus subdued them *c.* 126 BC, placed them under Antipater as governor and compelled them to be circumcised (Jos., *Ant.* 13. 258). Antipater was the grandfather of *Herod the Great. The word Idumaea occurs in the NT only in Mk. 3:8. J.A.T.

IGNORANCE. As is the case with *knowledge, ignorance has in Scripture a moral rather than a purely intellectual connotation, except in such casual uses as the Pauline 'I would not have you ignorant, brethren. . .' (Rom. 1:13, AV), which simply means 'I want you to know. . .' (RSV).

In the books of the Law ignorance is regarded as a palliating feature of sinful acts. For sins done in ignorance (*šᵉḡāḡâ*) expiation could be made by sacrifice (*cf.* particularly Lv. 4–5; Nu. 15:22–29). This idea of ignorance as an excuse is reflected in the NT uses of the verb *agnoeō*, 'to be ignorant', and its derivatives. Paul declares that he received mercy for his persecution of the church because he acted ignorantly in unbelief (1 Tim. 1:13); and at Athens he tells his Gentile audience that God overlooked the times of ignorance (Acts 17:30; *cf.* 3:17).

Nevertheless, although ignorance partly excuses the sins which result from it, ignorance itself is often culpable. It may be linked with hardness of heart (Eph. 4:18; *cf.* 2 Cor. 4:4) or even be deliberate (2 Pet. 3:5; *cf.* Rom. 1:18ff.; 10:3).

Ignorance is used absolutely to refer to the condition of the Gentile world which had not received the revelation of God (Acts 17:23, 30; Eph. 4:18; 1 Pet. 1:14; 2:15). This usage is found in LXX; *e.g.* Wisdom 14:22.

The word *idiōtēs*, translated 'ignorant' in AV of Acts 4:13 (RSV 'uneducated'), implies the want of special training rather than of knowledge in general; *cf.* the modern somewhat derogatory use of 'layman'.

BIBLIOGRAPHY. R. Bultmann, *TDNT* 1, pp. 689–719; E. Schütz, *NIDNTT* 2, pp. 406–408.

M.H.C.

IJON. A town in N Naphtali taken by the Syrians under *Ben-hadad along with *Dan and *Abel of Beth-maacah (1 Ki. 15:20 = 2 Ch. 16:4). Subsequently captured by Tiglath-pileser III in 733 BC (2 Ki. 15:29). Possibly the Dan-jaan of 2 Sa. 24:6. Generally identified with Tell Dibbin, 30 km N of Lake Huleh. D.W.B.

ILLYRICUM. The name of the large mountainous region on the E of the Adriatic, extending to the central Balkans in the E and reaching from NE Italy and the Celtic tribes in the N to Macedonia in the S. Its name was derived from that of one of the first tribes within its boundaries that the Greeks came across. Its inhabitants spoke dialects which were probably the linguistic ancestors of modern Albanian. The Romans had first come into conflict with some of its tribes in the 3rd century BC, but it was not finally conquered till the 1st century AD, when it was divided into the provinces of Pannonia and Dalmatia. Paul says at the time of writing the Epistle to the Romans (15:19) that it was the limit of his evangelistic activity. His reference to it appears to be inclusive, but it is not known when, or from what direction, he had entered it (possibly from Macedonia when he revisited that province after his Ephesian ministry, Acts 20:1). It was the first Latin-speaking province which he visited in the course of his apostolic ministry, and could have prepared him for his projected mission in Latin-speaking Spain (Rom. 15:24, 28). B.F.C.A.

IMAGE. The term denotes a material representation, usually of a deity. Unlike the term 'idol', which has a pejorative overtone, 'image' is objectively descriptive. Throughout the ancient Near East numerous images of various deities were to be found in temples and other holy places, such as open-air shrines; many private houses also contained a niche where the image of the protective deity of the household stood. Images were commonly anthropomorphic (in human form), though theriomorphic images (in animal form) were also widely used, especially in Egypt.

The region of Illyricum in the time of Paul.

The form of the image, especially of the theriomorphic examples, frequently represented some prominent characteristic of the particular deity; thus an image of a bull (*e.g.* of El in Canaan) portrayed the god's power and fertility. The image was not primarily intended as a visual representation of the deity, but as a dwelling-place of the spirit of the deity enabling the god to be physically present in many different places simultaneously. A worshipper praying before an image would not necessarily accept that his prayers were being offered to the figure of wood or metal itself, but would probably have regarded the image as a 'projection' or embodiment of the deity. Of course, those in Israel who denied any reality to the deity represented by the image maintained that the worshippers of foreign deities were paying homage to mere wood and stone (*IDOLATRY).

Images were made in various ways. A molten image (*massēkâ*) was cast in a mould from copper, silver or gold. A graven image (*pesel*) was carved from stone or wood; wooden images could be overlaid with precious metals (*cf.* Is. 40:19, NEB). See Is. 41:6–7; 44:12–17.

I. In the Old Testament

a. Images of foreign gods. Though the making and worshipping of images is forbidden by Pentateuchal law (Ex. 20:4–5) and condemned by the prophets (*e.g.* Je. 10:3–5; Ho. 11:2), their use in Israel throughout pre-exilic times was common (Jdg. 6:25; 1 Ki. 11:5–8; 16:31–33), even at times within the Temple itself (2 Ki. 21:3–5, 7).

b. Images of Yahweh. Standing stones (*maṣṣēḇôṯ*) erected by the Patriarchs (*e.g.* Gn. 28:18, 22; 35:14) were perhaps originally regarded as images (similarly the sacred trees; *cf.* Gn. 21:33), but were later forbidden (Asherah, Dt. 16:21) or re-interpreted as merely commemorative objects (*cf.* Gn. 31:45–50; Jos. 4:4–9). Later, images of Yahweh were denounced by pure Yahwists: the golden calf at Sinai (Ex. 32:1–8), the image (*EPHOD) made by Gideon (Jdg. 8:26–27), the golden calves at Dan and Bethel (1 Ki. 12:28–30), the calf of Samaria (Ho. 8:6).

c. Man as the image of God. In a few texts in Genesis (1:26–27; 5:2; 9:6) man is said to have been created 'in' or 'as' the image of God, 'according to his likeness'. Though many interpreters have thought to locate the 'image' of God in man's reason, creativity, speech, or spiritual nature, it is more likely that it is the whole of man, rather than some part or aspect of him, that is the image of God. The whole man, body and soul, is the image of God; man is the corporeal image of the incorporeal God. As in the ancient Near East, man as the image of God represents him through his participation in the divine breath or spirit (*cf.* Gn. 2:7; perhaps also the spirit of God is included in the 'us' of 1:26; *cf.* the reference to the spirit of God in 1:2). Man's role as ruler of the earth is established by his creation as God's image (1:27). Elsewhere in the ancient Near East it is usually the king who is said to be the image of God, but in Gn. 1 it is mankind as a whole that is God's vizier and representative. Significantly, man is still spoken of as the image of God after the Fall: the force of Gn.

9:6 depends on the belief that man represents God, so that an injury done to a man is an injury done to God himself (*cf*. also Jas. 3:9).

BIBLIOGRAPHY. K. H. Bernhardt, *Gott und Bild*, 1956; A. L. Oppenheim, *Ancient Mesopotamia*, 1964, pp. 171–227; D. Cairns, *The Image of God in Man*, 1953; G. C. Berkouwer, *Man: The Image of God*, 1962; D. J. A. Clines, *TynB* 19, 1968, pp. 53–103; J. Barr, *BJRL* 51, 1968–9, pp. 11–26; J. M. Miller, *JBL* 91, 1972, pp. 289–304; T. N. D. Mettinger, *ZAW* 86, 1974, pp. 403–424; J. F. A. Sawyer, *JTS* 25, 1974, pp. 418–426; E. M. Curtis, *Man as the Image of God in Genesis in the Light of Ancient Near Eastern Parallels* (diss.), 1984. D.J.A.C.

II. In the New Testament

The NT teaching builds on the foundation laid in the OT. There man is described (in the seminal passage of Gn. 1:26f.) as made to be God's representative on earth and to act as God's vicegerent and steward of creation. The term is best thought of as functional, and man's destiny as man is in view (see, in particular, D. J. A. Clines' essay for details and exegetical support).

The two passages of 1 Cor. 11:7 and Jas. 3:9 re-echo this teaching, and both assert the continuance of man's position in the created order and as reflecting the divine 'glory', in spite of human sinfulness. The emphasis in the NT, however, falls more on the person of Jesus Christ who is called the 'image of God' (2 Cor. 4:4; Col. 1:15; both are creed-like passages, set on a polemical background, to oppose current false or inadequate notions). Christ's rank as the 'image' of the Father derives from his unique relationship as pre-existent. He is the Logos from all eternity (Jn. 1:1–18), and so he is able to reflect faithfully and fully the glory of the invisible God. See too Heb. 1:1–3 and Phil. 2:6–11 where parallel expressions are used to clarify the unique relationship of Jesus Christ to God. 'Image' (or its equivalent terms, 'form', 'stamp', 'glory') does not suggest a mere likeness to God or a paradigm of his person. Rather it connotes a sharing in the divine life and indeed an 'objectivization' of the essence of God, so that the One who is by nature invisible comes to visible expression in the figure of his Son (see the evidence in R. P. Martin, *op. cit*., pp. 112f.).

He is thus the 'ultimate Adam' (1 Cor. 15:45) who stands at the head of a new humanity that draws its life from him. So Jesus Christ is both the unique 'Image' and the prototype of those who owe their knowledge of God and life in God to him (Rom. 8:29; 1 Cor. 15:49; 2 Cor. 3:18; 1 Jn. 3:2).

The term 'image of God' is closely connected with 'the new man' (Eph. 4:24; Col. 3:10f.; *cf*. Gal. 3:28). This is a reminder that there are important social aspects to what the 'image' means as it is reproduced in human lives, both in the fellowship of the church and in man's custodianship of nature (Heb. 2:8, referring to Ps. 8).

There is an eschatological dimension also to be recognized. The fulfilment of God's plan for humanity-in-Christ awaits the parousia when Christians' mortal existence will be transformed to a perfect likeness to their Lord (1 Cor. 15:49; Phil. 3:20–21), and in this way the image of God in man will be fully restored.

BIBLIOGRAPHY. D. J. A. Clines, *TynB* 19, 1968, pp. 53–103 (bibliography); J. Jervell, *Imago Dei. Gen. 1, 26f. im Spätjudentum, in der Gnosis und in den paulinischen Briefen*, 1960; F.-W. Eltester, *Eikon im Neuen Testament*, 1958; R. Scroggs, *The Last Adam*, 1966; and R. P. Martin, *Carmen Christi. Philippians 2:5–11*[2], 1983; *idem*, *NIDNTT* 2, pp. 284–293; H. Kuhli, *EDNT* 1, pp. 388–391.

On the dogmatic issues, see G. C. Berkouwer, *Man: The Image of God*, 1962. R.P.M.

IMMANUEL (Heb. *'immānû'ēl*, 'with us is God'). The word is found twice in OT (Is. 7:14; 8:8) and once in NT (Mt. 1:23, RSV 'Emmanuel'). It may be employed also in Is. 8:10.

To understand the significance of the word, which in itself means 'God with us', we must note the context in which it appears. Syria and Israel had desired to form a coalition with Judah in order to oppose the increasing power of Assyria. Judah had vacillated, and Syria and Israel determined to punish her. Upon hearing this news, Ahaz trembled. Isaiah was sent to him to inform him that he had nothing to fear. The power of his enemies was about played out, and they could do him no harm. Isaiah even commanded him to ask for a sign in confirmation of the divine message. This Ahaz refused to do. Hence, in reply to the hypocritical king, Isaiah announces that the Lord will give to the people of Judah a sign. In vision the prophet beholds a virgin (*'almâ, i.e.* an unmarried woman), who is with child and about to bear a son and she will call his name Immanuel.

In any interpretation of this prophecy there are three factors which must be kept in mind.

a. The birth of the child is to be a sign. It is true that in itself a sign need not be a miracle, but in this particular context, after the command issued to Ahaz to ask for a sign deep or high, one would be justified in expecting a sign such as the recession of the shadow on the sundial. There should be something unusual in the birth; a birth in the ordinary course of nature would not seem to meet the requirements of the sign. In this connection it must be noted that the question is made more difficult by the fact that there cannot be a local reference of the prophecy to Hezekiah, because Hezekiah had already been born.

b. The mother of the child is an unmarried woman. Why did Isaiah designate her by this particular word *'almâ*? It is sometimes said that had he wished to teach a virgin birth there was a good word at his disposal, namely, *bᵉṯûlâ*. But an examination of the usage of the latter word in OT reveals that it was very unsatisfactory, in that it would have been ambiguous. The word *bᵉṯûlâ* may designate a virgin, but when it does the explanatory phrase 'and a man had not known her' is often added (*cf*. Gn. 24:16). The word may also designate a betrothed virgin (*cf*. Dt. 22:23ff.). In this latter case the virgin is known as the wife (*'iššâ*) of the man, and he as her husband (*'îš*). But the word *bᵉṯûlâ* may also indicate a married woman (Joel 1:8). On the basis of this latter passage a tradition arose among the Jews in which the word could clearly refer to a married woman. Had Isaiah employed this word, therefore, it would not have been clear what type of woman he had in mind, whether virgin or married. Other Heb. words which were at his disposal would not be satisfactory. Had he wished to designate the mother as a young woman he would most likely have employed the common term *naʿᵃrâ* ('girl'). In using the word *'almâ*, however, Isaiah employs the one word which is never applied (either in the Bible or in the other Near

Eastern sources) to anyone but an unmarried woman. This unmarried woman might have been immoral, in which case the birth could hardly have been a sign. We are left then with the conclusion that the mother was a good woman and yet unmarried; in other words, the birth was supernatural. It is the presence of this word *'almâ* which makes an application of the passage to some local birth difficult, if not impossible.

c. We must note the force of the term Immanuel. A natural reading of the passage would lead us to expect that the presence of God is to be seen in the birth of the child himself. This interpretation, however, is seriously disputed, and vigorously rejected by most modern writers on the passage. The presence of God is found, rather, so we are told, in the deliverance of Judah from her two northern enemies. The infancy of the child is made the measure of time that would elapse until the two enemies are removed. Such a period of time would be short—a child learns the difference between good and evil at a tender age. Hence, within, say, 2 years, or possibly even less, Judah would have nothing to fear from Syria and Israel. In this deliverance the presence of God would be manifested, and as a token or pledge of this deliverance some mother would call her child Immanuel.

This interpretation poses tremendous problems which it does not answer. What warrant would a mother have for naming her particular child Immanuel? How could she know that her own child and no other would be a sign that in 2 years or so the presence of God would be manifested in the deliverance of Judah from Syria and Israel? Furthermore, how would Israel itself know that a particular child had been born in answer to the prophecy and that the birth of this particular child would be the promised sign? It would seem that, if the prophecy refers to a local birth, the child to be born must be someone prominent. The most prominent person, namely Hezekiah, is ruled out, and therefore we must assume that it is a child of Isaiah or some other child of Ahaz. But this is also ruled out by the word *'almâ*. Neither the wife of Ahaz nor the wife of Isaiah could properly be designated an *'almâ*, for the obvious reason that both were married women.

It seems best, then, to apply the name Immanuel to the Child himself. In his birth the presence of God is to be found. God has come to his people in a little Child, that very Child whom Isaiah later names 'Mighty God' (*'ēl gibbôr*). This interpretation is strengthened by the fact that Isaiah is seeking to dissuade men from trusting the Assyrian king. The nation's help rests not in Assyria but in God. In this dark moment God is with his people. He is found in the birth of a Child.

The infancy of the divine Child is a measure of the time that will elapse until Ahaz is freed from the fear of his two northern enemies (Is. 7:15–16). Ahaz rejects the sign of Immanuel, and turns to the king of Assyria. That king and his successors caused Judah's downfall, but for the remnant there was given the promise of Immanuel, and in Immanuel they would find their hope and salvation.

BIBLIOGRAPHY. E. J. Young, *The Book of Isaiah*, 1, 1964; E. W. Hengstenberg, *Christology of the Old Testament*, 1856, 2, pp. 26–66; J. G. Machen, *The Virgin Birth of Christ*, 1930; J. Lindblom, *A Study on the Immanuel Section in Isaiah*, 1957/8; J. S. Wright, C. Brown, *NIDNTT* 2, pp. 86f.

E.J.Y.

INCARNATION.

I. Meaning of the word

Neither the noun 'incarnation' nor the adjective 'incarnate' is biblical, but the Gk. equivalent of Lat. *in carne* (*en sarki*, 'in flesh') is found in some important NT statements about the person and work of Jesus Christ. Thus the hymn quoted in 1 Tim. 3:16 speaks of 'he was manifested in the flesh' (so RSV, following the true text). John ascribes to the spirit of antichrist any denial that Jesus Christ has 'come in the flesh' (1 Jn. 4:2; 2 Jn. 7). Paul says that Christ did his reconciling work 'in his body of flesh' (Col. 1:22; *cf.* Eph. 2:15), and that by sending his Son 'in the likeness of sinful flesh' God 'condemned sin in the flesh' (Rom. 8:3). Peter speaks of Christ dying for us 'in the flesh' (*sarki*, dative of reference: 1 Pet. 3:18; 4:1). All these texts are enforcing from different angles the same truth: that it was precisely by coming and dying 'in the flesh' that Christ secured our salvation. Theology calls his coming the incarnation, and his dying the atonement.

What does *'flesh' mean in these texts? In the Bible this word (Heb. *bāśār*, *š^e'ēr*; Gk. *sarx*) has fundamentally a physiological meaning: 'flesh' is the solid stuff which, together with blood and bones, makes up the physical organism of a man or animal (*cf.* Gn. 2:21; Lk. 24:39; 1 Cor. 15:50). Since Heb. thought associates bodily organs with psychical functions, we find that in the OT 'flesh' can cover the psychological as well as the physical aspects of man's personal life (*cf.* the parallelism between 'flesh' and 'heart', Ps. 73:26, and between 'flesh' and 'soul', Ps. 63:1). The word, however, bears more than a merely anthropological significance. The Bible sees physical flesh as a theologically significant symbol—a symbol, namely, of the created and dependent sort of life which men and animals share, a sort of life which is derived from God and which, unlike God's own life, requires a physical organism to sustain it in its characteristic activity. Hence 'flesh' becomes a generic term for men, or animals, or men and animals together (*cf.* Gn. 6:12; 7:15, 21f.), viewed as creatures of God, whose life on earth lasts only for the comparatively short period during which God supplies the breath of life in their nostrils. 'Flesh' in this theologically developed sense is thus not something that a man *has*, but something that he *is*. Its mark is creaturely weakness and frailty (Is. 40:6), and in this respect it stands in contrast with 'spirit', the eternal and unflagging energy that is of God, and is God (Is. 31:3; *cf.* 40:6–31).

To say, therefore, that Jesus Christ came and died 'in the flesh' is to say that he came and died in the state and under the conditions of created physical and psychical life: in other words, that he who died was man. But the NT also affirms that he who died eternally was, and continues to be, God. The formula which enshrines the incarnation therefore is that in some sense God, without ceasing to be God, was made man. This is what John asserts in the prologue of his Gospel: 'the Word' (God's agent in creation, who 'in the beginning', before the creation, not only 'was with God', but himself 'was God', Jn. 1:1–3) 'became flesh' (Jn. 1:14).

II. Origin of the belief

Such an assertion, considered abstractly against the background of OT monotheism, might seem blasphemous or nonsensical—as, indeed, orthodox Judaism has always held it to be. It appears to mean that the divine Maker became one of his own creatures, which is a *prima facie* contradiction in theological terms. Whence came the conviction that inspired John's strange statement? How did the early church's belief that Jesus of Nazareth was God incarnate arise? On the assumption that it was not occasioned by what Jesus himself said and did, but grew up later, attempts have been made to trace its origin to Jewish speculations about a pre-existent superhuman Messiah, or to the polytheistic myths about redeemer-gods which were characteristic of Hellenistic mystery-religions and Gnostic cults. But it is now widely recognized that these attempts have failed: partly because the differences between these Jewish and Gentile fancies and NT Christology have invariably proved to be more substantial and deep-rooted than their surface similarities are; partly because it has been shown that a virtual claim to deity is embedded in the most undoubted sayings of the historical Jesus, as reported in the Synoptic Gospels, and that a virtual acceptance of this claim was fundamental to the faith and worship of the primitive Palestinian church, as pictured in the first chapters of Acts (the substantial historicity of which is now rarely disputed). The only explanation that covers the facts is that the impact of Jesus' own life, ministry, death and resurrection convinced his disciples of his personal deity even before he ascended. This, of course, is precisely the account of the matter which the Fourth Gospel itself gives (see especially Jn. 20:28ff.). In line with this, Acts tells us that the first Christians prayed to Jesus as Lord (7:59), even before Pentecost (1:21: the 'Lord' who chooses apostles is surely 'the Lord Jesus' of v. 21, *cf.* v. 3); that, beginning on the day of Pentecost, they baptized in his name (2:38; 8:16; 19:5); that they invoked and put faith in his name (*i.e.* in himself: 3:16; 9:14; 22:16; *cf.* 16:31); and that they proclaimed him as the One who gives repentance and remission of sins (5:31). All this shows that, even if the deity of Jesus was not at first clearly stated in words (and Acts gives no hint that it was), it was nevertheless part of the faith by which the first Christians lived and prayed. *Lex orandi lex credendi*. The theological formulation of belief in the incarnation came later, but the belief itself, however incoherently expressed, was there in the church from the beginning.

III. Standpoint of the New Testament writers

It is important to note the nature and limits of the interest which motivates NT thinking about the incarnation, particularly that of Paul, John and the author of Hebrews, who deal with the subject comparatively fully. The NT writers nowhere notice, much less handle, the metaphysical questions about the mode of the incarnation, and the psychological questions about the incarnate state, which have been so prominent in Christological discussion since the 4th century. Their interest in Christ's person is not philosophical and speculative, but religious and evangelical. They speak of Christ, not as a metaphysical problem, but as a divine Saviour; and all that they say about his person is prompted by their desire to glorify him through exhibiting his work and vindicating his centrality in the redemptive purpose of God. They never attempt to dissect the mystery of his person; it is enough for them to proclaim the incarnation as a fact, one of the sequence of mighty works whereby God has wrought salvation for sinners. The only sense in which the NT writers ever attempt to explain the incarnation is by showing how it fits into God's over-all plan for redeeming mankind (see, *e.g.*, Rom. 8:3; Phil. 2:6–11; Col. 1:13–22; Jn. 1:18; 1 Jn. 1:1–2:2; and the main argument of Hebrews, 1–2; 4:14–5:10; 7:1–10:18).

The exclusiveness of this evangelical interest throws light on the otherwise puzzling fact that the NT nowhere reflects on the *virgin birth of Jesus as witnessing to the conjunction of deity and manhood in his person—a line of thought much canvassed by later theology. This silence need not mean that any of the NT writers were ignorant of the virgin birth, as some have supposed. It is sufficiently explained by the fact that NT interest in Jesus centres elsewhere, upon his relation to the saving purposes of God. Proof of this is given by the way in which the virgin birth story is itself told by Matthew and Luke, the two Evangelists who recount it. Each lays all his stress, not on the unique constitution of the Person thus miraculously born, but on the fact that by this miraculous birth God began to fulfil his long-foretold intention of visiting and redeeming his people (*cf.* Mt. 1:21ff.; Lk. 1:31ff., 68–75; 2:10f., 29–32). The only significance which they, or any NT writers, see in the incarnation is directly soteriological. The Scotist speculation, popularized by Westcott, that the incarnation was primarily for the perfecting of creation, and only secondarily and incidentally for the redeeming of sinners, finds not the least support in the NT.

The apostolic writers clearly see that both the deity and the manhood of Jesus are fundamental to his saving work. They see that it is just because Jesus is God the Son that they are to regard his disclosure of the Father's mind and heart as perfect and final (*cf.* Jn. 1:18; 14:7–10; Heb. 1:1f.), and his death as the supreme evidence of God's love for sinners and his will to bless believers (*cf.* Jn. 3:16; Rom. 5:5–10; 8:32; 1 Jn. 4:8–10). They realize that it is Jesus' divine Sonship that guarantees the endless duration, sinless perfection and limitless efficacy, of his high-priestly service (Heb. 7:3, 16, 24–28). They are aware that it was in virtue of his deity that he was able to defeat and dispossess the devil, the 'strong man armed' who kept sinners in a state of helpless thraldom (Heb. 2:14f.; Rev. 20:1f.; *cf.* Mk. 3:27; Lk. 10:17f.; Jn. 12:31f.; 16:11). Equally, they see that it was necessary for the Son of God to 'become flesh', for only so could he take his place as the 'second man' through whom God deals with the race (1 Cor. 15:21f., 47ff.; Rom. 5:15–19); only so could he mediate between God and men (1 Tim. 2:5); and only so could he die for sins, for only flesh can die. (Indeed, the thought of 'flesh' is so bound up with death that the NT will not apply the term to Christ's manhood in its glorified and incorruptible state: 'the days of his flesh' (Heb. 5:7) means Christ's time on earth up to the cross.)

We should, therefore, expect the NT to treat any denial that Jesus Christ was both truly divine and truly human as a damning heresy, destructive of the gospel; and so it does. The only such denial that it knows is the docetic Christology (traditionally, that of Cerinthus) which denied the reality of Christ's 'flesh' (1 Jn. 4:2f.), and hence of his physical death ('blood', 1 Jn. 5:6). John denounces this in his first two Epistles as a deadly error inspired by the spirit of antichrist, a lying denial of both the Father and the Son (1 Jn. 2:22–25; 4:1–6; 5:5–12; 2 Jn. 7, 9ff.). It is usually thought that the emphasis in John's Gospel on the reality of Jesus' experience of human frailty (his weariness, 4:6; thirst, 4:7; 19:28; tears, 11:33ff.) is intended to cut at the root of the same docetic error.

IV. Elements of the New Testament doctrine

The meaning of the NT claim that 'Jesus Christ has come in the flesh' may be drawn out under three heads.

a. The Person incarnate

The NT uniformly defines the identity of Jesus in terms of his relation to the one God of OT monotheism (*cf.* 1 Cor. 8:4, 6; 1 Tim. 2:5; with Is. 43:10f.; 44:6). The basic definition is that Jesus is God's *Son*. This identification is rooted in Jesus' own thought and teaching. His sense of being 'the Son' in a unique sense that set him apart from the rest of men went back at least to his 13th year (Lk. 2:49), and was confirmed to him by his Father's voice from heaven at his baptism: 'Thou art my beloved Son' (Mk. 1:11; *cf.* Mt. 3:17; Lk. 3:22; *agapētos*, which appears in all three reports of the heavenly utterance, carries the implication of '*only* beloved': so again in the parable, Mk. 12:6; *cf.* the similar words from heaven at the transfiguration, Mk. 9:7; Mt. 17:5). At his trial, when asked under oath whether he was 'the Son of God' (a phrase which on the high priest's lips probably signified no more than 'Davidic Messiah'), Mark and Luke report Jesus as making an affirmative reply which was in effect a claim to personal deity: *egō eimi* (so Mk. 14:62; Lk. 22:70 has: 'you say *(sc.* rightly*)* that *egō eimi*'). *egō eimi*, the emphatic 'I am', were words that no Jew would take on his lips, for they expressed the self-identification of God (Ex. 3:14). Jesus, who according to Mark had used these words before in a similar suggestive way (Mk. 6:50; *cf.* 13:6; and *cf.* the long series of *egō eimi* sayings in John's Gospel: Jn. 4:26; 6:35; 8:12; 10:7, 11; 11:25; 14:6; 15:1; 18:5ff.), evidently wished to make it perfectly clear that the divine Sonship to which he laid claim was nothing less than personal deity. It was for this 'blasphemy' that he was condemned.

Jesus' references to himself as 'the Son' are always in contexts which mark him out as uniquely close to God and uniquely favoured by God. There are comparatively few in the Synoptic Gospels (Mt. 11:27 = Lk. 10:22; Mk. 13:32 = Mt. 24:36; *cf.* Mk. 12:1–11), but many in John, both in Jesus' own words and in the Evangelist's commentary. According to John, Jesus is God's 'only' Son (*monogenēs*: 1:14, 18; 3:16, 18). He exists eternally (8:58; *cf.* 1:1f.). He stands in an unchanging relation of perfect love, union and communion, with the Father (1:18; 8:16, 29; 10:30; 16:32). As Son, he has no independent initiative (5:19); he lives to glorify his Father (17:1, 4), by doing his Father's will (4:34; 5:30; 8:28f.). He came into the world because the Father 'sent' him (42 references), and gave him a task to fulfil there (4:34; 17:4; *cf.* 19:30). He came in his Father's name, *i.e.* as his Father's representative (5:43), and, because all that he said and did was according to the Father's command (7:16ff.; 8:26ff.; 12:49f.; 14:10), his life on earth revealed his Father perfectly (14:7ff.). When he speaks of the Father as greater than himself (14:28; *cf.* 10:29) he is evidently referring, not to any essential or circumstantial inferiority, but to the fact that subordination to the Father's will and initiative is natural and necessary to him. The Father is greater than he because in relation to the Father it is always his nature freely and joyfully to act as a Son. But this does not mean that he is to be subordinated to the Father in men's esteem and worship. Just the reverse; for the Father seeks the Son's glory no less than the Son seeks the Father's glory. The Father has committed to the Son his two great works of giving life and executing judgment, 'that all may honour the Son, even as they honour the Father' (5:21ff.). This amounts to saying that the Father directs all men to do as Thomas did (20:28), and acknowledge the Son in the same terms in which they ought to acknowledge the Father himself—namely, as 'my Lord and my God'.

The NT contains other lines of thought, subsidiary to that of divine Sonship, which also proclaim the deity of Jesus of Nazareth. We may mention the more important of these: (i) John identifies the eternal divine *Word* with God's personal Son, Jesus Christ (Jn. 1:1–18; *cf.* 1 Jn. 1:1–3; Rev. 19:13; *LOGOS). (ii) Paul speaks of the Son as 'the *image* of God', both as incarnate (2 Cor. 4:4) and in his pre-incarnate state (Col. 1:15), and in Phil. 2:6 says that prior to the incarnation Jesus Christ was in the 'form' (*morphē*) of God: a phrase the exact exegesis of which is disputed, but which J. B. Phillips is almost certainly right to render: 'always . . . God by nature'. Heb. 1:3 (RV) calls the Son 'the effulgence of his (God's) glory, and the *very image of his substance*'. These statements, made as they are within a monotheistic frame of reference which excludes any thought of two Gods, are clearly meant to imply: (1) that the Son is personally divine, and ontologically one with the Father; (2) that the Son perfectly embodies all that is in the Father, or, putting it negatively, that there is no aspect or constituent of deity or character which the Father has and the Son lacks. (iii) Paul can apply an OT prophecy concerning the invocation of 'the Lord' (Yahweh) to the Lord Jesus, thus indicating that it finds its true fulfilment in him (Rom. 10:13, quoting Joel 2:32; *cf.* Phil. 2:10f., echoing Is. 45:23). Similarly, the writer to the Hebrews quotes Moses' exhortation to the angels to worship God (Dt. 32:43, LXX), and the psalmist's declaration: 'Thy throne, O God, is for ever and ever' (Ps. 45:6), as words spoken by the Father with reference to his Son (Heb. 1:6, 8). This shows that both writers regard Jesus as divine. (iv) The regular NT habit of referring to Jesus as 'Lord'—the title given to the gods of Hellenistic religion (*cf.* 1 Cor. 8:5), and invariably used in LXX to render the divine name—would seem to be an implicit ascription of deity.

b. The nature of the incarnation

When the Word 'became flesh' his deity was not abandoned, or reduced, or contracted, nor did he cease to exercise the divine functions which had been his before. It is he, we are told, who sustains the creation in ordered existence, and who gives and upholds all life (Col. 1:17; Heb. 1:3; Jn. 1:4), and these functions were certainly not in abeyance during his time on earth. When he came into the world he 'emptied himself' of outward glory (Phil. 2:7; Jn. 17:5), and in that sense he 'became poor' (2 Cor. 8:9), but this does not at all imply a curtailing of his divine powers, such as the so-called kenosis theories would suggest. The NT stresses rather that the Son's deity was not reduced through the incarnation. In the man Christ Jesus, says Paul, 'dwelleth *all the fullness of the Godhead* bodily' (Col. 2:9; *cf.* 1:19).

The incarnation of the Son of God, then, was not a diminishing of deity, but an acquiring of manhood. It was not that God the Son came to indwell a human being, as the Spirit was later to do. (To assimilate incarnation to indwelling is the essence of the Nestorian heresy.) It was rather that the Son in person began to live a fully human life. He did not simply clothe himself in a human body, taking the place of its soul, as Apollinaris maintained; he took to himself a human soul as well as a human body, *i.e.* he entered into the experience of human psychical life as well as of human physical life. His manhood was complete; he became 'the *man* Christ Jesus' (1 Tim. 2:5; *cf.* Gal. 4:4; Heb. 2:14, 17). And his manhood is permanent. Though now exalted, he 'continueth to be, God and man in two distinct natures, and one person, for ever' (*Westminster Shorter Catechism*, Q. 21; *cf.* Heb. 7:24).

c. The incarnate state

(i) It was a state of *dependence* and *obedience*, because the incarnation did not change the relationship between the Son and the Father. They continued in unbroken fellowship, the Son saying and doing what the Father gave him to say and do, and not going beyond the Father's known will at any single moment (*cf.* the first temptation, Mt. 4:2ff.). His confessed ignorance of the time of his return (Mk. 13:32) should no doubt be explained, not as edifying pretence (Aquinas), nor as evidence of his having laid aside his divine knowledge for the purpose of the incarnation (the kenosis theories), but simply as showing that it was not the Father's will for him to have this knowledge in his mind at that time. As the Son, he did not wish or seek to know more than the Father wished him to know.

(ii) It was a state of *sinlessness* and *impeccability*, because the incarnation did not change the nature and character of the Son. That his whole life was sinless is several times asserted (2 Cor. 5:21; 1 Pet. 2:22; Heb. 4:15; *cf.* Mt. 3:14–17; Jn. 8:46; 1 Jn. 2:1f.). That he was exempt from the entail of original sin in Adam is evident from the fact that he was not bound to die for sins of his own (*cf.* Heb. 7:26), and hence could die vicariously and representatively, the righteous taking the place of the unrighteous (*cf.* 2 Cor. 5:21; Rom. 5:16ff.; Gal. 3:13; 1 Pet. 3:18). That he was impeccable, and could not sin, follows from the fact that he remained God the Son (*cf.* Jn. 5:19, 30). Deviation from the Father's will was no more possible for him in the incarnate state than before. His deity was the guarantee that he would achieve in the flesh that sinlessness which was prerequisite if he were to die as 'a lamb without blemish or spot' (1 Pet. 1:19).

(iii) It was a state of *temptation* and *moral conflict*, because the incarnation was a true entry into the conditions of man's moral life. Though, being God, it was not in him to yield to temptation, yet, being man, it was necessary for him to fight temptation in order to overcome it. What his deity ensured was not that he would not be tempted to stray from his Father's will, nor that he would be exempt from the strain and distress that repeated insidious temptations create in the soul, but that, when tempted, he would fight and win; as he did in the initial temptations of his Messianic ministry (Mt. 4:1ff.). The writer to the Hebrews stresses that in virtue of his firsthand experience of temptation and the costliness of obedience he is able to extend effective sympathy and help to tempted and distraught Christians (Heb. 2:18; 4:14ff.; 5:2, 7ff.). (*JESUS CHRIST, LIFE AND TEACHING OF.)

BIBLIOGRAPHY. J. Denney, *Jesus and the Gospel*, 1908; P. T. Forsyth, *The Person and Place of Jesus Christ*, 1909; H. R. Mackintosh, *The Doctrine of the Person of Jesus Christ*, 1912; A. E. J. Rawlinson, *The New Testament Doctrine of the Christ*, 1926; L. Hodgson, *And was made Man*, 1928; E. Brunner, *The Mediator*, E.T. 1934; D. M. Baillie, *God was in Christ*, 1948; L. Berkhof, *Systematic Theology*[4], 1949, pp. 305–330; G. C. Berkouwer, *The Person of Christ*, 1954; K. Barth, *Church Dogmatics*, I, 2, 1956, pp. 122–202; V. Taylor, *The Person of Christ in New Testament Teaching*, 1958; O. Cullmann, *The Christology of the New Testament*, E.T. 1960; W. Pannenberg, *Jesus—God and Man*, E.T. 1968; C. F. D. Moule, *The Origin of Christology*, 1977.

J.I.P.

INCENSE. A common feature of OT ritual, incense was a costly offering and a sign essentially of the acknowledgment of deity (*cf.* Mal. 1:11). The word has a double application: it refers both to the substance used for burning and to the aromatic odour which is produced. Two Heb. words are thus rendered: (1) *l^ebônâ*, 'frankincense'; and (2) *q^eṭōreṯ*, the 'sweet smoke' (EVV 'incense') of Is. 1:13. Among the Israelites only priests were allowed to offer incense. When the Lord gave Moses instructions for Aaron, these included strict regulations concerning the use of incense in the holy place (Lv. 16:12f.). Incense is also used in Scripture as a symbol for prayer (*e.g.* Ps. 141:2; Rev. 8:3f., Gk. *thymiama*).

Frankincense (Heb. *l^ebônâ*). This substance consisted of the resinous exudate of certain *Boswellia* trees, the principal species being *B. frereana*, *B. carteri* and *B. papyrifera* in NE Africa, *B. sacra* in Dhofar, S. Arabia, and *B. serrata* in NW India, where they grow in semi-desert mountains. They furnished much of the wealth acquired by traders who followed the old spice-routes from S Arabia to Gaza and Damascus (Is. 60:6).

The whitish-yellow aromatic resin was obtained by incising the bark, and, although acrid to the taste, frankincense was extremely odoriferous. It comprised one ingredient of the holy anointing oil (Ex. 30:34), and was also burnt with other substances during the cereal-offering (Lv. 6:15). Frankincense was placed in purified form on the showbread in the tabernacle (Lv. 24:7). While it gratified the senses (Ct. 3:6; 4:6, 14), it was also symbolic of religious fervour (*cf.* Mal. 1:11). The gift of frankincense presented to Christ by the wise men (Mt. 2:11) has been interpreted as symbolizing his priestly office.

See F. N. Hepper, 'Arabian and African Frankincense', *JEA* 55, 1969, pp. 66–72.

Galbanum (Heb. *ḥelb^enâ*; etymology uncertain). A strong-smelling spice (Ex. 30:34), usually regarded as the gum of an umbelliferous plant, *Ferula galbaniflua*, native to Persia.

The other constituents of the sacred incense were stacte and onycha (*HERBS AND SPICES).

See also *SACRIFICE AND OFFERING (OT), **IV**, *a*;

*Cosmetics and Perfumery, V. *b* (which includes bibliography). F.N.H.

INCREASE.

INCREASE. A noun or verb meaning multiplication or growth, translating sundry Heb. and Gk. words. Primarily the term involved the natural reproduction and germination of cattle and harvest, but always under God's direction and control (Lv. 26:4; Dt. 7:13; Ps. 67:6), as acknowledged by the tithe (Dt. 14:22; *cf.* Pr. 3:9). Hence prosperity is a sign of God's favour (Dt. 6:3), adversity of his displeasure (Je. 15:8), and man's exacting gain from possessions is condemned in the same manner as usury (Lv. 25:37; Ezk. 18:8ff.; *cf.* Ps. 62:10). The term is used symbolically of Israel's relationship with God (Je. 2:3) and of the spiritual blessings God imparts (Is. 29:19; 40:29), especially by the coming of the Messiah (Is. 9:3, 7).

In the NT the term is applied to the growth of the church in numbers (Acts 6:7; 16:5; 1 Cor. 3:6) and in depth (Eph. 4:16; Col. 2:19). It is also applied to individuals generally (Lk. 2:52; Jn. 3:30; Acts 9:22), and specifically with regard to faith (Lk. 17:5; 2 Cor. 10:15), love (1 Thes. 3:12; 4:10), knowledge (Col. 1:10), or ungodliness (2 Tim. 2:16). P.A.B.

INDIA.

I. Early period

Heb. *hōddû*, from Old Persian *hindu* (*cf.* Sanskrit *sindhu*), in inscriptions of Darius I and Xerxes I of Persia. The area so designated was that part of the Indus valley and plains E of the Afghan mountains incorporated into the Persian empire by Darius I, who made it his E boundary (Herodotus, 3. 94; 4. 40, 44). In Est. 1:1; 8:9 the limits of the dominion of Ahasuerus (Xerxes I) are 'from India unto Ethiopia', *hōddû* and *kûš*; this corresponds with Xerxes I's own Old Persian inscriptions, *cf.* the list of countries including 'Sind' or India (*Hiduš*) and Ethiopia (*Kušiya*) in R. G. Kent, *Old Persian: Grammar, Texts, Lexicon*, 1953 ed., p. 151, ll. 25, 29 and § 3. But long before this, trade between India and Mesopotamia is known as early as *c.* 2100 BC (Ur III period), both in texts and by the presence of Indus Valley seals in Mesopotamia. Some think that *Ophir might be Indian (S)upāra. India was the source of the war-elephants used by Alexander and his Seleucid successors in Syria, and in the Graeco-Roman period many exotic products came from India, usually through S Arabia, either up the Red Sea or overland up the W side of Arabia. On routes and navigation, *cf.* van Beek and Hourani, *JAOS* 78, 1958, pp. 146–147; and 80, 1960, pp. 135–139. Greek principalities maintained themselves for some time in parts of NW India; *cf.* W. W. Tarn, *The Greeks in Bactria and India*, 1938. For Indians in Egypt in the Graeco-Roman period, *cf.* Sir H. I. Bell, *Cults and Creeds in Graeco-Roman Egypt*, 1953, p. 48; E. Bevan, *History of Egypt under the Ptolemaic Dynasty*, 1927, p. 155; models from Memphis: Petrie, *Memphis I*, 1909, pp. 16–17, plate 39.

II. Later period

Between the 1st century BC and *c.* AD 200, India and the Mediterranean lands entered into closer commercial and cultural relations, stimulated by the Roman market for Eastern luxuries and facilitated by the discovery of the nature of the monsoons, with the subsequent opening of a regular sea-route to the Tamil towns (mod. Cranganore and Kottayam) and even to Madras (*Sopatma*) and beyond. Against this background we must view the stories of the first introduction of Christianity to India. The unanimous tradition of the old S India church traces its foundation to Thomas the apostle. The narrative of the gnosticizing *Acts of* (Judas) *Thomas* (*New Testament Apocrypha) also sets Thomas' activities in India. In itself it is the wildest legend, but J. N. Farquhar argued that it reflects accurate knowledge of 1st-century India and postulated that Thomas worked first in the Punjab and later in the S (*BJRL* 11, 1926; 12, 1927). There seems, however, no other early account of Thomas in India clearly independent of these *Acts* (A. Mingana, *BJRL* 11, 1926; 12, 1927). The peripatetic Pantaenus is said to have been a missionary in India some time before AD 180, and to have found Christians there with Matthew's Gospel in Hebrew left by Bartholomew (Eusebius, *EH* 5. 10); but a loose designation of Aden or some other part of Arabia may be involved. That the Syriac S India church is very ancient is undeniable: the question of apostolic or subapostolic foundation remains open.

Bibliography. E. H. Warmington, *Indian Commerce*, 1928; L. W. Browne, *The Indian Christians of St Thomas*, 1956. K.A.K.

INHERITANCE.

I. In the Old Testament

In the OT there are two basic roots for inheritance, *nāḥal* and *yāraš*. In each case the emphasis was much more upon possession generally than upon the process of succession, though this idea is not altogether absent. The words occur only rarely in Gn. and Ex. and are most frequent in Nu and Dt., which look forward to the allotment of land in Canaan, and in Jos. which records how it was put into effect. The law of inheritance was as follows. Land belonged to the family rather than to the individual. There was therefore a strict entail. The eldest son received a double portion and the others equal shares. If a man died leaving no sons the inheritance went to his daughters; if no daughters, to his brothers; if no brothers, to his father's brothers; if no father's brothers, to the next of kin (Nu. 27:8–11). If daughters inherited they had to marry in their own tribe (Nu. 36:6). The emphasis of the word *yāraš* is on possession, for the heir succeeded by right and not by disposition. Wills were unknown in Israel before the time of Herod. Before the giving of the law the Patriarchs were free to pass over the *first-born in favour of a younger son. Abraham, Isaac and Jacob were all younger sons. Joseph was preferred to Reuben (1 Ch. 5:1–2) and Ephraim to Manasseh (Gn. 48:8–20). The giving of the rights of the first-born to the first-born of a second and favourite wife was forbidden in Dt. 21:15–17. However, in the case of the royal succession David was preferred to his older brothers (1 Sa. 16:11) and Solomon to Adonijah (1 Ki. 2:15), though the normal custom was for the first-born to succeed (2 Ch. 21:3).

If a man died childless his brother had to marry his widow (Gn. 38:8–9; Dt. 25:5–10; Mt. 22:23–25). The first son of that union was regarded as the first-born of the deceased brother, and therefore if there were only one son the surviving brother would have no heir. It was accordingly possible for the brother not to marry his brother's wife, and then the right went to the nearest kinsman (Ru. 2:20; 3:9–13; 4:1–12). In the book of Ruth, Ruth plays the part of Naomi, who was past the age of marriage (Ru. 4:17). Land could not be sold in perpetuity (Lv. 25:23–24). If it was sold it could be redeemed by the next of kin (Lv. 25:25). Naboth knew Ahab's offer was against the law (1 Ki. 21:3).

The land of Canaan was regarded as the inheritance of Yahweh in a particular way (Ex. 15:17; *cf.* Jos. 22:19; Ps. 79:1), though he was God of all the earth (Ps. 47:2, *etc.*). It was for that reason that Israel was able to enjoy it as their inheritance.

The promises made to Abraham concerned a land as well as descendants (Gn. 12:7; 15:18–21, *etc.*). Abraham's faith was shown in believing that he would have descendants when he was childless and his wife was past child-bearing age, and in believing that he would have a land, though during his lifetime he was a nomad with no settled possession (Acts 7:5). The children of Israel were brought out of Egypt not only to escape from bondage but also to inherit a land (Ex. 6:6–8). This land was conquered by them, but it was the gift of Yahweh (Jos. 21:43–45). He allotted them in it an inheritance which was to last for ever (Gn. 13:15, *etc.*).

Lots were cast to discover Yahweh's disposal of portions to individual tribes (Jos. 18:2–10). Eventually it was to be a remnant who returned from exile to inherit the land (Is. 10:20–21, *etc.*). Those who formed that faithful remnant were to inherit the nations as well (Ps. 2:8).

The Levites were to have no territory because Yahweh was their inheritance (Dt. 18:1–2). Materially this meant that their portion consisted of the dues and firstfruits given by the people to Yahweh (Dt. 18:3–5). Spiritually the idea was extended to the whole of Israel (Ps. 16:5–6, *etc.*). Also Israel was to be his inheritance as the people which belonged specially to him (Dt. 7:6; 32:9). (*PROMISED LAND.)

II. In the New Testament

In the NT 'inheritance' renders Gk. *klēronomos* and its cognates, derived from *klēros*, meaning a 'lot'. The inheritance is narrowed down to the true Israel, Christ himself, who is 'the heir' (Mk. 12:7). As heir of God he enters into a possession given to him because of his relationship. He has been made heir of everything (Heb. 1:2). Believers in a sense share the divine sonship by adoption and therefore also the divine heirship (Rom. 8:17). They follow in the footsteps of faithful Abraham as heirs of the promise (Rom. 4:13–14) and like Isaac they are his children, heirs according to promise (Gal. 3:29). Their inheritance is something which is given by God's grace because of their status in his sight, and it is in no sense earned.

The object of the Christian inheritance is all that was symbolized by the land of Canaan, and more. Believers inherit the kingdom of God (Mt. 25:34; 1 Cor. 6:9–10; 15:50; Gal. 5:21; Eph. 5:5; Jas. 2:5). They inherit the earth or 'the land' (Mt. 5:5; *cf.* Ps. 37:29). They inherit salvation (Heb. 1:14), a blessing (1 Pet. 3:9), glory (Rom. 8:17–18), and incorruption (1 Cor. 15:50). These are all 'the promises' (Heb. 6:12), not received in their fulfilment by the believers of the OT (Heb. 11:39–40). In Hebrews stress is laid upon the new 'covenant' or 'testament'. It is on this that the promised inheritance is based, especially as it required the death of the testator (Heb. 9:15–17). Two men asked Jesus what they should do in order to inherit eternal life (Lk. 10:25; 18:18), and Christ spoke of that as being part of the blessing of the new world (Mt. 19:29). A Christian man and wife are joint heirs of the grace of life (1 Pet. 3:7).

The consummation of the blessings promised will not take place until the parousia. The inheritance is reserved in heaven (1 Pet. 1:4). He who overcomes is to have the inheritance of God (Rev. 21:7). However, that does not alter the fact that many of the blessings of heirship may be enjoyed in advance. The Holy Spirit is the agent who makes our position as heirs real (Rom. 8:16–17), and he is given to us 'as the guarantee of our inheritance until we acquire possession of it' (Eph. 1:14). He was sent to the church after Christ's own entry into his inheritance at his ascension.

In the NT we still see God's people as his inheritance (Eph. 1:18), and all the blessings mentioned above show that he himself is still their inheritance.

But that inheritance is not of right, it is by the free disposition of God, who is able in his sovereign pleasure to dispossess those who seem to have most title to it and give it to others of his choice.

BIBLIOGRAPHY. *TWBR*, pp. 112–114; J. Herrmann, W. Foerster, *TDNT* 3, pp. 758–785; J. Eichler, W. Mundle, *NIDNTT* 2, pp. 295–304; James D. Hester, *Paul's Concept of Inheritance*, 1968; F. Lyall, *Tynbul* 32, 1981, pp. 90–95; D. R. Denton, *EQ* 54, 1982, pp. 157–162. R.E.N.

INNER MAN. Paul uses this phrase (*ho esō anthrōpos*, in Rom. 7:22; 2 Cor. 4:16; Eph. 3:16) to denote the Christian's true self, as seen by God and known (partially) in consciousness. (For a vindication of the view that Rom. 7:14–26 pictures Paul the Christian, see A. Nygren, *Romans*, 1952, pp. 284ff.) The contrast, implicit if not explicit, is with *ho exō anthrōpos*, 'the outward man' (2 Cor. 4:16), the same individual as seen by his fellow-men, a being physically alive and active, known (so far as he is known) through his behaviour.

This contrast differs both from that which Paul drew between the new and old man (*i.e.* between man's status, condition and affinities in Christ and apart from Christ), and from that which Platonists drew between the immaterial, immortal soul (the real man) and his material, mortal body (his lodging), or, again, between the soul's rational (higher) and sensual (lower) impulses. The contrast in view is rather that between the 'outward appearance' and the 'heart' drawn in 1 Sa. 16:7: 'inner man' and *'heart' are, indeed, almost synonymous. This contrast reflects two facts. First, God, the searcher of hearts, sees things in a man that are hidden from his fellows, who see only his exterior (*cf.* 1 Sa. 16:7; Mt. 23:27f., and Peter's assertion that meekness and quietness adorn 'the *hidden* person of the heart', which God notices, if men do not, 1 Pet. 3:3f.). Secondly, God's renewal of sinners in Christ is a hidden work (Col. 3:3f.), of which human observers see only certain of the effects (*cf.* Jn. 3:8). The sphere of character, and of the Spirit's transforming work, is not the outward, but the inner man. The exact point of the contrast differs in each of the three texts.

1. In 2 Cor. 4:16 it is between the outward Paul,

the Paul whom men saw, worn down by constant work, ill health, anxiety, strain and persecution, and the Paul whom God knew and who knew God, the Paul who had been recreated, and was now indwelt, by the Spirit (2 Cor. 5:5, 17), and who after physical dissolution would be 'further clothed' with a resurrection body (2 Cor. 5:1ff.). The outward Paul was going to pieces; the real Paul was daily renewed.

2. In Rom. 7:22f. the contrast is between the 'law (active principle) of sin' in Paul's 'members', influencing his outward actions, and the 'law of my mind', Paul's heart's delight in God's law and heart's desire to keep it, which desire sin constantly frustrated.

3. In Eph. 3:16–19 the contrast is only implicit. The inward man, the heart, the temple in which Christ dwells and the sphere of his strengthening operation, is the real, abiding self, the self that knows Christ's love and will be filled into God's fullness; but this self is hidden from men. Hence Paul has need to exhort his readers to show the world what God has wrought in them by the quality of their outward conduct (Eph. 4–6).

BIBLIOGRAPHY. *BAGD*, *s.v. anthrōpos*; R. Bultmann, *Theology of the New Testament*, 1, p. 203.

J.I.P.

INSPIRATION. Noun formed from Latin and English translations of *theopneustos* in 2 Tim. 3:16, which AV rendered: 'All Scripture is given by inspiration of God, and is profitable for doctrine, for reproof, for correction, for instruction in righteousness.' 'Inspired of God' in RSV is no improvement on AV, for *theopneustos* means *out*-breathed rather than *in*-breathed by God—divinely *ex*-spired, rather than *in*-spired. In the last century Ewald and Cremer argued that the adjective bore an active sense, 'breathing the Spirit', and Barth appears to agree (he glosses it as meaning not only 'given and filled and ruled by the Spirit of God', but also 'actively out-breathing and spreading abroad and making known the Spirit of God' (*Church Dogmatics*, I. 2, E.T. 1956, p. 504)); but B. B. Warfield showed decisively in 1900 that the sense of the word can only be passive. The thought is not of God as breathing through Scripture, or of Scripture as breathing out God, but of God as having breathed out Scripture. Paul's words mean, not that Scripture is inspiring (true though this is), but that Scripture is a divine product, and must be approached and estimated as such.

The 'breath' or 'spirit' of God in the OT (Heb. *rûaḥ*, *nᵉšāmâ*) denotes the active outgoing of divine power, whether in creation (Ps. 33:6; Jb. 33:4; *cf.* Gn. 1:2; 2:7), preservation (Jb. 34:14), revelation to and through prophets (Is. 48:16; 61:1; Mi. 3:8; Joel 2:28f.), regeneration (Ezk. 36:27), or judgment (Is. 30:28, 33). The NT reveals this divine 'breath' (Gk. *pneuma*) to be a Person of the Godhead. God's 'breath' (*i.e.* the Holy Spirit) produced Scripture, as a means to the conveyance of spiritual understanding. Whether we render *pasa graphē* as 'the whole Scripture' or 'every text', and whether we follow RSV or RV in construing the sentence (RV has 'Every scripture inspired of God is also profitable . . .', which is a possible translation), Paul's meaning is clear beyond all doubt. He is affirming that all that comes in the category of Scripture, all that has a place among the 'sacred writings' (*hiera grammata*, v. 15, RV), just because it is God-breathed, is profitable for the guiding of both faith and life.

On the basis of this Pauline text, English theology regularly uses the word 'inspiration' to express the thought of the divine origin and quality of Holy Scripture. Actively, the noun denotes God's out-breathing operation which produced Scripture: passively, the inspiredness of the Scriptures so produced. The word is also used more generally of the divine influence which enabled the human organs of revelation—prophets, psalmists, wise men and apostles—to speak, as well as to write, the words of God.

I. The idea of biblical inspiration

According to 2 Tim. 3:16, what is inspired is precisely the biblical writings. Inspiration is a work of God terminating, not in the men who were to write Scripture (as if, having given them an idea of what to say, God left them to themselves to find a way of saying it), but in the actual written product. It is Scripture—*graphē*, the written text—that is God-breathed. The essential idea here is that all Scripture has the same character as the prophets' sermons had, both when preached and when written (*cf.* 2 Pet. 1:19–21, on the divine origin of every 'prophecy of the scripture'; see also Je. 36; Is. 8:16–20). That is to say, Scripture is not only man's word, the fruit of human thought, premeditation and art, but also, and equally, God's word, spoken through man's lips or written with man's pen. In other words, Scripture has a double authorship, and man is only the secondary author; the primary author, through whose initiative, prompting and enlightenment, and under whose superintendence, each human writer did his work, is God the Holy Spirit.

Revelation to the prophets was essentially verbal; often it had a visionary aspect, but even 'revelation in visions is also verbal revelation' L. Koehler, *Old Testament Theology*, E.T. 1957, p. 103). Brunner has observed that in 'the words of God which the Prophets proclaim as those which they have received directly from God, and have been commissioned to repeat, as they have received them . . . perhaps we may find the closest analogy to the meaning of the theory of verbal inspiration' (*Revelation and Reason*, 1946, p. 122, n. 9). Indeed we do; we find not merely an analogy to it, but the paradigm of it; and 'theory' is the wrong word to use, for this is just the biblical doctrine itself. Biblical inspiration should be defined in the same theological terms as prophetic inspiration: namely, as the whole process (manifold, no doubt, in its psychological forms, as prophetic inspiration was) whereby God moved those men whom he had chosen and prepared (*cf.* Je. 1:5; Gal. 1:15) to write exactly what he wanted written for the communication of saving knowledge to his people, and through them to the world. Biblical inspiration is thus verbal by its very nature; for it is of God-given words that the God-breathed Scriptures consist.

Thus, inspired Scripture is written revelation, just as the prophets' sermons were spoken revelation. The biblical record of God's self-disclosure in redemptive history is not merely human testimony to revelation, but is itself revelation. The inspiring of Scripture was an integral part in the revelatory process, for in Scripture God gave the church his saving work in history, and his own authoritative interpretation of its place in his eternal plan. 'Thus saith the Lord' could be prefixed to each book of

Scripture with no less propriety than it is (359 times, according to Koehler, *op. cit.*, p. 245) to individual prophetic utterances which Scripture contains. Inspiration, therefore, guarantees the truth of all that the Bible asserts, just as the inspiration of the prophets guaranteed the truth of their representation of the mind of God. ('Truth' here denotes correspondence between the words of man and the thoughts of God, whether in the realm of fact or of meaning.) As truth from God, man's Creator and rightful King, biblical instruction, like prophetic oracles, carries divine authority.

II. Biblical presentation

The idea of canonical Scripture, *i.e.* of a document or corpus of documents containing a permanent authoritative record of divine revelation, goes back to Moses' writing of God's law in the wilderness (Ex. 34:27f.; Dt. 31:9ff., 24ff.). The truth of all statements, historical or theological, which Scripture makes, and their authority as words of God, are assumed without question or discussion in both Testaments. The Canon grew, but the concept of inspiration, which the idea of canonicity presupposes, was fully developed from the first, and is unchanged throughout the Bible. As there presented, it comprises two convictions.

1. *The words of Scripture are God's own words.* OT passages identify the Mosaic law and the words of the prophets, both spoken and written, with God's own speech (*cf.* 1 Ki. 22:8–16; Ne. 8; Ps. 119; Je. 25:1–13; 36, *etc.*). NT writers view the OT as a whole as 'the oracles of God' (Rom. 3:2), prophetic in character (Rom. 16:26; *cf.* 1:2; 3:21), written by men who were moved and taught by the Holy Spirit (2 Pet. 1:20f.; *cf.* 1 Pet. 1:10–12). Christ and his apostles quote OT texts, not merely as what, *e.g.*, Moses, David or Isaiah said (see Mk. 7:10; 12:36; 7:6; Rom. 10:5; 11:9; 10:20, *etc.*), but also as what God said through these men (see Acts 4:25; 28:25, *etc.*), or sometimes simply as what 'he' (God) says (*e.g.* 1 Cor. 6:16; Heb. 8:5, 8), or what the Holy Spirit says (Heb. 3:7; 10:15). Furthermore, OT statements, not made by God in their contexts, are quoted as utterances of God (Mt. 19:4f.; Heb. 3:7; Acts 13:34f., citing Gn. 2:24; Ps. 95:7; Is. 55:2 respectively). Also, Paul refers to God's promise to Abraham and his threat to Pharaoh, both spoken long before the biblical record of them was written, as words which *Scripture* spoke to these two men (Gal. 3:8; Rom. 9:17); which shows how completely he equated the statements of Scripture with the utterance of God.

2. *Man's part in the producing of Scripture was merely to transmit what he had received.* Psychologically, from the standpoint of form, it is clear that the human writers contributed much to the making of Scripture—historical research, theological meditation, linguistic style, *etc.* Each biblical book is in one sense the literary creation of its author. But theologically, from the standpoint of content, the Bible regards the human writers as having contributed nothing, and Scripture as being entirely the creation of God. This conviction is rooted in the self-consciousness of the founders of biblical religion, all of whom claimed to utter—and, in the case of the prophets and apostles, to write—what were, in the most literal sense, the words of another: God himself. The prophets (among whom Moses must be numbered: Dt. 18:15; 34:10) professed that they spoke the words of Yahweh, setting before Israel what Yahweh had shown them (Je. 1:7; Ezk. 2:7; Am. 3:7f.; *cf.* 1 Ki. 22). Jesus of Nazareth professed that he spoke words given him by his Father (Jn. 7:16; 12:49f.). The apostles taught and issued commands in Christ's name (2 Thes. 3:6), so claiming his authority and sanction (1 Cor. 14:37), and they maintained that both their matter and their words had been taught them by God's Spirit (1 Cor. 2:9–13; *cf.* Christ's promises, Jn. 14:26; 15:26f.; 16:13ff.). These are claims to inspiration. In the light of these claims, the evaluation of prophetic and apostolic writings as wholly God's word, in just the same way in which the two tables of the law, 'written with the finger of God' (Ex. 24:12; 31:18; 32:16), were wholly God's word, naturally became part of the biblical faith.

Christ and the apostles bore striking witness to the fact of inspiration by their appeal to the authority of the OT. In effect, they claimed the Jewish Scriptures as the Christian Bible: a body of literature bearing prophetic witness to Christ (Jn. 5:39f.; Lk. 24:25ff., 44f.; 2 Cor. 3:14ff.) and designed by God specially for the instruction of Christian believers (Rom. 15:4; 1 Cor. 10:11; 2 Tim. 3:14ff.; *cf.* the exposition of Ps. 95:7–11 in Heb. 3–4, and indeed the whole of Hebrews, in which every major point is made by appeal to OT texts). Christ insisted that what was written in the OT 'cannot be broken' (Jn. 10:35). He had not come, he told the Jews, to annul the law or the prophets (Mt. 5:17); if they thought he was doing that, they were mistaken; he had come to do the opposite—to bear witness to the divine authority of both by fulfilling them. The law stands for ever, because it is God's word (Mt. 5:18; Lk. 16:17); the prophecies, particularly those concerning himself, must be fulfilled, for the same reason (Mt. 26:54; Lk. 22:37; *cf.* Mk. 8:31; Lk. 18:31). To Christ and his apostles, the appeal to Scripture was always decisive (*cf.* Mt. 4:4, 7, 10; Rom. 12:19; 1 Pet. 1:16, *etc.*).

The freedom with which NT writers quote the OT (following LXX, Targums, or an *ad hoc* rendering of the Hebrew, as best suits them) has been held to show that they did not believe in the inspiredness of the original words. But their interest was not in the words, as such, but in their meaning; and recent study has made it appear that these quotations are interpretative and expository—a mode of quotation well known among the Jews. The writers seek to indicate the true (*i.e.* Christian) meaning and application of their text by the form in which they cite it. In most cases this meaning has evidently been reached by a strict application of clear-cut theological principles about the relation of Christ and the church to the OT. (See C. H. Dodd, *According to the Scriptures*, 1952; K. Stendahl, *The School of St Matthew*, 1954; R. V. G. Tasker, *The Old Testament in the New Testament*[2], 1954; E. E. Ellis, *Paul's Use of the Old Testament*[5], 1991.)

III. Theological statement

In formulating the biblical idea of inspiration, it is desirable that four negative points be made.

1. The idea is not of mechanical dictation, or automatic writing, or any process which involved the suspending of the action of the human writer's mind. Such concepts of inspiration are found in the Talmud, Philo and the Fathers, but not in the Bible. The divine direction and control under which the biblical authors wrote was not a physical or psychological force, and it did not detract from,

but rather heightened, the freedom, spontaneity and creativeness of their writing.

2. The fact that in inspiration God did not obliterate the personality, style, outlook and cultural conditioning of his penmen does not mean that his control of them was imperfect, or that they inevitably distorted the truth they had been given to convey in the process of writing it down. B. B. Warfield gently mocks the notion that when God wanted Paul's letters written 'He was reduced to the necessity of going down to earth and painfully scrutinizing the men He found there, seeking anxiously for the one who, on the whole, promised best for His purpose; and then violently forcing the material He wished expressed through him, against his natural bent, and with as little loss from his recalcitrant characteristics as possible. Of course, nothing of the sort took place. If God wished to give His people a series of letters like Paul's, He prepared a Paul to write them, and the Paul He brought to the task was a Paul who spontaneously would write just such letters' (*The Inspiration and Authority of the Bible*, 1951, p. 155).

3. Inspiredness is not a quality attaching to corruptions which intrude in the course of the transmission of the text, but only to the text as originally produced by the inspired writers. The acknowledgment of biblical inspiration thus makes more urgent the task of meticulous textual criticism, in order to eliminate such corruptions and ascertain what that original text was.

4. The inspiredness of biblical writing is not to be equated with the inspiredness of great literature, not even when (as often) the biblical writing is in fact great literature. The biblical idea of inspiration relates, not to the literary quality of what is written, but to its character as divine revelation in writing.

(*SPIRIT, HOLY SPIRIT; *PROPHECY; *SCRIPTURE; *AUTHORITY; *CANON OF THE OLD TESTAMENT; *CANON OF THE NEW TESTAMENT; *INTERPRETATION, BIBLICAL.)

BIBLIOGRAPHY. B. B. Warfield, *op. cit.* (much of the relevant material is also in his *Biblical Foundations*, 1958, chs. 1 and 2); A. Kuyper, *Encyclopaedia of Sacred Theology*, E.T. 1899; J. Orr, *Revelation and Inspiration*, 1910; C. F. H. Henry (ed.), *Revelation and the Bible*, 1958; K. Barth, *Church Dogmatics*, I, 1, 2 (*The Doctrine of the Word of God*), E.T. 1936, 1956; W. Sanday, *Inspiration*, 1893; R. Abba, *The Nature and Authority of the Bible*, 1958; J. W. Wenham, *Christ and the Bible*, 1972; G. C. Berkouwer, *Holy Scripture*, 1975; *TDNT* I, pp. 742–773 (*s.v. graphō*), and 4, pp. 1022–1091 (*s.v. nomos*).

J.I.P.

INTERPRETATION, BIBLICAL. The purpose of biblical interpretation is to make the meaning and message of the biblical writings plain to their readers. Some principles of interpretation are common to the Bible and other literature, especially other ancient literature; other principles of interpretation are bound up with the unique place of the Bible in the revelation of God and in the life of his people.

I. General interpretation

Each part of the Bible must be interpreted in its context, and that means not only its immediate verbal context but the wider context of time, place and human situation to which it belongs. Thus there are a number of considerations to be kept in mind if the meaning of the text is to be grasped as fully as is desirable.

a. Language and style

The idioms and constructions of the biblical languages can differ quite widely from those with which we are familiar today, and some acquaintance with these is necessary for a proper interpretation (*LANGUAGE OF THE APOCRYPHA; *LANGUAGE OF THE OT; *LANGUAGE OF THE NT). The literary categories represented in the Bible should also be noted; this will save us, for example, from interpreting poetry according to the canons of prose narration, or vice versa. Most of the literary categories in the Bible are well known from other literature, but biblical prophecy, and still more biblical apocalyptic, have features peculiar to themselves which call for special interpretative procedures.

b. Historical background

The biblical narrative covers the whole span of Near Eastern civilization until AD 100, a period of several millennia within which a succession of sweeping changes took place. It is therefore important to relate the various phases of the biblical revelation to their proper historical context if we are to understand them aright; otherwise we may find ourselves, for example, assessing people's conduct in the Middle Bronze Age by the ethical standards of the Gospels. And we can discern the permanent principles in a biblical document only when we first of all relate that document to the conditions of its own times; we shall then be better able to reapply to our times those features of its teaching which are valid for all time.

c. Geographical setting

We should not underestimate the influence exercised by climate and terrain on a people's outlook and way of life, including its religion. The religious conflicts of the OT are interwoven with the conditions of Palestinian geography. Baal-worship, for example, arose in a land where life depended on rain. To the Canaanites Baal was the storm-god who fertilized the earth, and Baal-worship was a magical ritual calculated to ensure regular rainfall and plentiful harvests. Indeed, to such an extent have geographical conditions entered into the biblical language, literal and figurative, that some acquaintance with these conditions is necessary for an understanding of the language. This is especially true of the OT, but even in the NT it has long been recognized, for instance, that the historical geography of Asia Minor makes an important contribution to the interpretation of Acts and the Epistles.

d. The human situation

Even more important than questions of time, place and language are questions about the everyday life of the people whom we meet in the Bible, their loves and hates, their hopes and fears, their social relations, and so forth. To read the Bible without regard to this living environment is to read it in a vacuum and to put constructions upon it which it was never intended to bear. Thanks largely to archaeological discovery, we are able to reconstruct in fair measure the private and public conditions in which the people of the Bible lived, in age after age; while a sympathetic reading of the text itself enables us in some degree to get under their skins and look at the world through their eyes. It is not unimportant to try to envisage what it must have felt like to be a servant in Abraham's household, an Israelite slave in Egypt, a citizen of Jericho when Joshua's men were marching round the city or a citizen of Jerusalem in face of Sennacherib's threats, a soldier in David's army, a captive maid waiting on Naaman's wife or a builder of the wall under Nehemiah. We may then realize that part of the Bible's perennial appeal is due to its concentration on those features of human life that remain basically the same in all times and places.

II. Special interpretation

Biblical interpretation involves not only the interpretation of the several documents but their interpretation as part of the Bible, having regard to the way in which each part contributes to the purpose of the Bible as a whole. Since the Bible records God's word to man and man's response to God, since it contains 'all things necessary to salvation' and constitutes the church's 'rule of faith and life', we may look for such a unity throughout the volume that each part can be interpreted in the light of the whole. We may look, indeed, for some unifying principle of interpretation.

In traditional Jewish interpretation of the Heb. Scriptures this unifying principle was found in the Law, understood in accordance with the teaching of the great rabbinical schools. The Prophets and the Writings were treated largely as commentaries on the Law. In addition to the surface meaning of the text, the *pᵉšaṭ*, there was the more extended application, the *dᵉraš*, derived by the use of various well-defined principles of exegesis, but sometimes appearing far-fetched by the exegetical standards of today.

In the NT and early Christian literature the OT oracles are viewed as a unity, instructing the reader 'for salvation' and equipping him with all that he needs for the service of God (2 Tim. 3:15ff.). The prophets, speaking in the power of the Holy Spirit, bear witness to Christ as the One in whom the promises of God find their fulfilment. The NT writers—whose diversity of personality, style and thought must be taken into account in the interpretation of their works—are agreed on this. In Heb. 1:1f. the 'many and various ways' in which God spoke in earlier days are contrasted with the perfect and final word which he has spoken in his Son; in the Pauline writings God's dealings with the world are traced through successive stages associated with Adam, Abraham, Moses and Christ. Biblical interpretation in the NT has Christ as its unifying principle, but this principle is not applied mechanically but in such a way as to bring out the historical and progressive nature of the biblical revelation. This creative principle of interpretation was certainly derived by the apostolic church from Christ himself.

In post-apostolic times biblical interpretation was influenced by a Gk. concept of inspiration which called for large-scale allegorization of the text. This influence was most apparent in Alexandria, where in the pre-Christian period it is found in the biblical interpretation of Philo. By allegorization, it was believed, the mind of the inspiring Spirit could be ascertained; by allegorization much in the Bible that was intellectually or ethically unacceptable in its literal sense could be made acceptable. This method, developed by the Alexandrian Fathers and taken over from them by many of the Western Fathers, in fact obscured the mind of the Spirit and obliterated the historical character of biblical revelation. In contrast to the Alexandrians the school of Antioch, while not rejecting allegorization entirely, did more justice to the historical sense of the text.

The distinction between the literal sense of Scripture and the higher or spiritual sense was elaborated in mediaeval times, and three varieties of spiritual sense were distinguished—the allegorical, which deduced doctrine from the narrative; the moral, which drew lessons for life and behaviour; and the anagogical, which derived heavenly meanings from earthly things. Yet the early Middle Ages also saw good work done in the field of literal interpretation, notably by the 12th-century school of St Victor in France.

The Reformers laid fresh emphasis on the literal sense of Scripture and on the grammatico-historical method of exegesis as the way to establish its literal sense. Grammatico-historical exegesis is fundamental, but when the foundation has been laid by its means theological exegesis and practical application are also called for. Moreover, the use of the Bible in the life of the people of God throughout the centuries continually brings fresh aspects of its meaning to light, although these fresh aspects have general validity only as they are rooted in the true and original sense. Thus, we may understand the Epistle to the Romans better because of the part it played in the lives of Augustine, Luther and Wesley; but the part it played in their lives owes its significance to the fact that these men had a rare grasp of what Paul really meant when he wrote the Epistle.

Typological interpretation, revived in our own day, must be used (if at all) with caution and restraint. Its most acceptable form is that which discerns in the biblical recital of God's acts of mercy and judgment a recurring rhythm, by virtue of which earlier stages in the recital can be viewed as foreshadowings and illustrations of later stages (*cf.* Paul's use of the wilderness experiences of Israel in 1 Cor. 10:1ff.).

Christians have an abiding standard and pattern in their Lord's use of the OT, and part of the Holy Spirit's present work for them is to open the Scriptures as the risen Christ opened them for two disciples on the Emmaus road (Lk. 24:25ff.).

BIBLIOGRAPHY. J. D. Smart, *The Interpretation of Scripture*, 1962; *Cambridge History of the Bible*, 1–3, 1963–70; J. Barr, *Old and New in Interpretation*, 1966; I. H. Marshall (ed.), *New Testament Interpretation*, 1977; G. W. Anderson (ed.), *Tradition and Interpretation*, 1979; G. L. Bray, *Biblical Interpretation Past and Present*, 1996. F.F.B.

IRA (Heb. *'îrā'*). **1.** A Jairite, described as 'David's priest' (2 Sa. 20:26), a difficult description to understand, as he was not of the tribe of Levi. However, Pesh. reads 'of Jattir', which was a city of Levi. Alternatively, 'priest' here may mean a chief official (*cf.* 2 Sa. 8:18, AV; 1 Ch. 18:17, AV).

2. An Ithrite, one of David's mighty men (2 Sa. 23:38). May be same as **1** if Pesh. reading is correct.

3. Another of David's heroes, son of Ikkesh the Tekoite (2 Sa. 23:26). M.A.M.

ISAAC (Heb. *yiṣḥāq*, 'he laughs' or 'laughter'). At the announcement of Isaac's birth Abraham laughed (Gn. 17:17), and later Sarah herself laughed at the thought that she who was so old should bear a son (Gn. 18:12–15). At Isaac's birth, when Abraham was 100 years old, Sarah declares that God has made her to laugh (Gn. 21:6). On the day of Isaac's weaning Ishmael laughed (Gn. 21:9). It is difficult to discover a precise subject for the verb, and possibly it is best to take the form impersonally. Some scholars render 'God laughs', but there is little warrant for this interpretation.

The two great features of Isaac's life centre upon his birth and marriage, and the reason for this is that he was the seed through whom the line of promise was to be continued. Abraham had been sorely tested with respect to the promise of a seed, and now, at an advanced age, when he was as good as dead, that seed came. Thus, it is seen that God is carrying out his purposes in fulfilment of the promises made to Abraham (Gn. 12:1–3), even though those promises seem to man to be incapable of fulfilment.

At the feast of Isaac's weaning the sight of Ishmael 'playing with her son Isaac' aroused Sarah's resentment. Hagar and her son Ishmael were therefore driven from the household (Gn. 21). God then put Abraham to the test, commanding him to slay his son Isaac. Abraham obeyed God and the Lord intervened, providing a ram for the sacrifice. The promise is then renewed, that Abraham shall have much seed (Gn. 22).

The second feature of Isaac's life which is of significance is his marriage. That Isaac should be born was a miracle, and soon afterwards it seemed that he must die. How, then, could he be the promised seed? He lives, however, and attention is centred upon his marriage, for it is to be through him that the line of promise is to be continued. Abraham is concerned that the promised seed be continued and sends his eldest servant to take a wife for Isaac from his own country, Harran. Rebekah, the daughter of Bethuel, Abraham's nephew, is indicated as the intended bride and willingly leaves her home to accompany the servant. Isaac receives her and brings her into his mother's tent. Isaac and Rebekah are married, with love developing as a result of Isaac's considerate and courteous actions (Gn. 24).

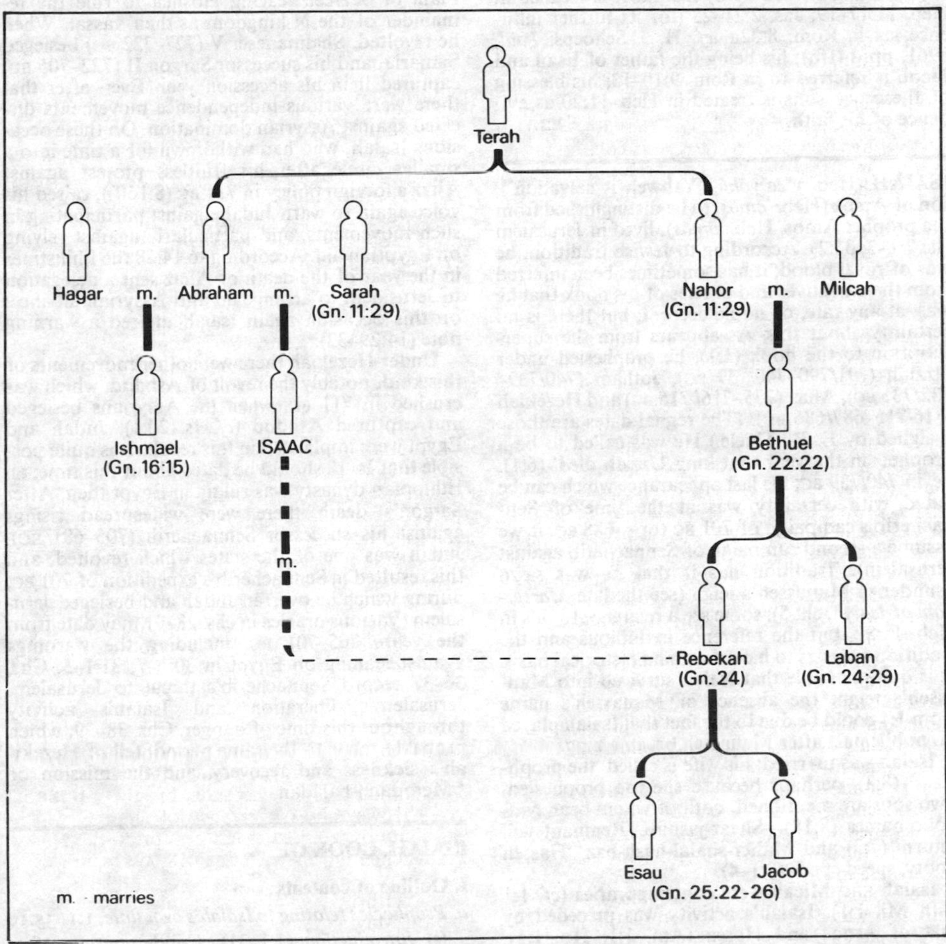

The family of Isaac.

For 20 years Rebekah was barren, and so it is again seen that the promised seed is not to come merely through the natural means of ordinary fatherhood, but through God's supernatural creative power. Rebekah's barrenness causes Isaac to entreat the Lord, and the announcement is made to Rebekah that two children are struggling in her womb (Gn. 25:22–26). These two children, representing two nations, will follow mutually hostile courses. Isaac himself is to remain a sojourner in the land and, instead of going to Egypt in time of famine, remains at Gerar. At the sign of crisis he, like Abraham, seeks to protect his wife by introducing her as his sister. After quarrels with the herdsmen at Gerar he goes to Beersheba and finally makes an agreement with Abimelech. Mutual antagonism appears between Isaac and Rebekah, occasioned by Jacob's actions. Being deceived, Isaac pronounces the paternal blessing upon Jacob and utters a devout prophetical wish upon Esau. Isaac died at the age of 180 years, and was buried by his sons, Esau and Jacob.

In the NT his birth as the son of promise is mentioned in Rom. 4:16–21; 9:7–9; the separation between him and Ishmael is allegorized in Gal. 4:22–31; his being offered up by his father is recalled in Heb. 11:17–19; Jas. 2:21–23 (for its further influence, as in Rom. 8:32a, *cf.* H. J. Schoeps, *Paul*, 1961, pp. 141ff.); his being the father of Esau and Jacob is referred to in Rom. 9:10–13; his blessing of these two sons is treated in Heb. 11:20 as evidence of his faith. E.J.Y.

ISAIAH (Heb. *yᵉšaʿyāhû*, 'Yahweh is salvation'), son of Amoz (Heb. *'āmôṣ*, to be distinguished from the prophet Amos, Heb. *'āmôs*), lived in Jerusalem (Is. 7:1–3; 37:2). According to Jewish tradition, he was of royal blood; it has sometimes been inferred from the narratives and oracles of his book that he was, at any rate, of noble descent; but there is no certainty about this. As appears from the superscription to the book (1:1), he prophesied under Uzziah (791/790–740/739 BC), Jotham (740/739–732/731 BC), Ahaz (735–716/ 715 BC) and Hezekiah (716/715–687/686 BC). (The regnal dates are those assigned by E. R. Thiele.) He was called to be a prophet 'in the year that king Uzziah died' (6:1), *i.e.* in 740/739 BC; his last appearance which can be dated with certainty was at the time of Sennacherib's campaign of 701 BC (or *c.* 688 BC, if we assume a second campaign of Sennacherib against Jerusalem). Tradition has it that he was sawn asunder in Manasseh's reign (see the late *Martyrdom of Isaiah*, ch. 5); some see a reference to this in Heb. 11:37, but the reference is dubious and the tradition appears to have no sound historical basis. It is quite possible that Isaiah survived into Manasseh's reign; the absence of Manasseh's name from 1:1 could be due to the fact that Isaiah played no public part after Manasseh became king.

Isaiah was married; his wife is called 'the prophetess' (8:3), perhaps because she too prophesied. Two sons are mentioned, both of whom bear symbolic names (8:18)—Shear-jashub, 'Remnant will return' (7:3) and Maher-shalal-hash-baz, 'Hasten booty, speed spoil' (8:1–4).

Isaiah and Micah were contemporaries (*cf.* 1:1 with Mi. 1:1). Isaiah's activity was preceded by that of Amos and Hosea (Am. 1:1; Ho. 1:1). Amos and Hosea prophesied mainly against the N tribes; Isaiah and Micah concentrated their prophecies mainly on Judah and Jerusalem (Is. 1:1).

In the first half of the 8th century both Israel, under Jeroboam II (*c.* 782–753 BC), and Judah, under Uzziah, enjoyed a time of great prosperity. This was due in large measure to the weakness of the kingdom of Aram and to Assyria's non-intervention in the W for considerable periods. Uzziah's reign may be described as the most prosperous time that Judah had known since the disruption of the Monarchy after Solomon's death. Under Uzziah and Jotham prosperity and luxury abounded in Judah; we have this state of affairs reflected in Is. 2–4. But with the accession to power of Tiglath-pileser III (745–727 BC), Assyria began once more to impose her yoke on the W lands. Pekah of Israel and Rezin of Damascus formed an anti-Assyrian coalition and tried to compel Ahaz of Judah to join them. When Ahaz refused, they threatened to depose him and place a puppet of their own on his throne (734 BC). Isaiah's action at this time is recorded in ch. 7. Ahaz committed the sinful folly of asking the Assyrian king for aid; the result was that Judah became a satellite state of Assyria. In 732 BC the Assyrians captured Damascus and annexed the territory of Israel N of the Plain of Jezreel, leaving Hoshea to rule the remainder of the N kingdom as their vassal. When he revolted, Shalmaneser V (727–722 BC) besieged Samaria, and his successor Sargon II (722–705 BC) captured it in his accession year. Even after that there were various independence movements directed against Assyrian domination. On these occasions Isaiah, who had withdrawn for a time into a smaller circle after his fruitless protest against Ahaz's foreign policy in 734 BC (8:16ff.), raised his voice again to warn Judah against participating in such movements, and particularly against relying on Egyptian aid. According to 14:28 the Philistines in the year of the death of Ahaz sent a delegation to Jerusalem to arrange an anti-Assyrian alliance; on this occasion again Isaiah uttered a warning note (14:29–32).

Under Hezekiah there were other movements of this kind, notably the revolt of Ashdod, which was crushed in 711 BC, when the Assyrians besieged and captured Ashdod (*cf.* Is. 20:1). Judah and Egypt were implicated in this revolt. It is quite possible that Is. 18 should be dated about this time; an Ethiopian dynasty was ruling in Egypt then. After Sargon's death there were widespread risings against his successor Sennacherib (705–681 BC). Judah was one of the states which revolted, and this resulted in Sennacherib's expedition of 701 BC, during which he overran Judah and besieged Jerusalem. Various oracles in chs. 28–31 may date from the years 705–701 BC, including the warnings against leaning on Egypt in 30:1–7; 31:1–3. Chs. 36–37 record Sennacherib's threat to Jerusalem, Jerusalem's liberation and Isaiah's activity throughout this time of danger. Chs. 38–39, which probably relate to the same period, tell of Hezekiah's sickness and recovery, and the mission of *Merodach-baladan. N.H.R.

ISAIAH, BOOK OF.

I. Outline of contents

a. Prophecies relating to Isaiah's own time, 1:1–35:10

(i) *Introduction* (1:1–31). Condemnation of a merely external form of worship, *etc*. Date uncertain.

(ii) *Prophecies from Isaiah's earliest period* (for the greater part) (2:1–5:30). Prophecy of the coming kingdom of peace (2:2–5; *cf.* Mi. 4:1ff.). The Day of the Lord which is to bring down everyone who is proud and exalted (2:6–22). The haughty women of Jerusalem ('Isaiah's fashion-journal') (3:16–4:1). The song of the vineyard (5:1–7).

(iii) *Isaiah's inaugural vision* (6:1–13).

(iv) *The present world-empire and the coming kingdom of God* (7:1–12:6). Chs. 7:1–9:7 originate chiefly from the time of the Syro-Ephraimite war. Rebuke of Ahaz and prophecy of Immanuel (7:1–25). Isaiah's temporary withdrawal from the public eye (8:11–22). The birth of the Messiah (9:1–7). The hand stretched out to smite Ephraim (probably one of Isaiah's earliest oracles) (9:8–10:4). Assyria brought low by the Holy One of Israel (10:5–34). The Messiah and the kingdom of God (11:1–12:6); especially here a sharp contrast is drawn between the violent world-empire and the peacefulness of the coming kingdom. Ch. 12 contains a song of thanksgiving; it forms a conclusion to this section.

(v) *Mainly prophecies regarding foreign nations* (13:1–23:18). Babylon (13:1–14:23) (incorporating the impressive taunt-song in 14:4–23). Assyria (14:24–27). The Philistines (14:28–32). Moab (15:1–16:14). Aram and Ephraim (17:1–14; probably not long before ch. 7). Ethiopia and Egypt (18:1–20:6; 20, and probably 18, are to be dated *c.* 715 BC; the date of 19 is uncertain). Babylon (21:1–10). Edom ('Watchman, what of the night?') (21:11f.). Arabia (21:13–17). Jerusalem (22:1–14). Shebna and Eliakim (22:15–25). Phoenicia (23:1–18).

(vi) *The consummation: the 'Isaianic apocalypse'* (24:1–27:13). See below, under **III.***a* (iv).

(vii) *Zion's sin, oppression and deliverance; Assyria's downfall; Egypt's vain help* (28:1–33:24). Several of the prophecies in these chapters are to be dated between 705 and 701 BC. The parable of the ploughman (28:23–29). The Messianic kingdom (32:1–8).

(viii) *A twofold future* (34:1–35:10). The judgment of Edom and the world (34:1–17). Salvation for 'the ransomed of the Lord' (35:1–10).

b. Historical chapters, 36:1–39:8

Sennacherib's invasion (36:1–37:38). Hezekiah's sickness and recovery (38:1–22). Mission of Merodach-baladan (39:1–8).

c. Prophecies which presuppose the Babylonian Exile, 40:1–55:13

These chs. foretell Israel's liberation from exile and the restoration of Zion, and in doing so they proclaim the majesty of Yahweh. They may be divided as follows:

(i) *Introduction* (40:1–31). The substance of the following chs. is presented; it consists of four parts: vv. 1–2, vv. 3–5, vv. 6–11, vv. 12–31.

(ii) *Prophecies in which those concerning Cyrus are conspicuous* (41:1–48:22). He is mentioned by name in 44:28; 45:1. *Cf.* 41:1–16 (Cyrus' activity will make the nations tremble, but there is no need for Israel to fear), 41:21–29 (Cyrus' activity will cause Zion to rejoice), 43:9–15 (Cyrus overthrows Babylon), 44:24–45:13 (Cyrus' victory leads to the rebuilding of Zion), 46:8–13 (amidst prophecies of Babylon's downfall), 48:12–16. *Cf.* also the prophecies of Babylon's downfall, especially 46:1–47:15. There is a marked contrast drawn between the 'daughter of Babylon' (ch. 47) and the 'daughter of Zion' (49:14ff., *etc.*). Throughout these chs. Israel is comforted in her distress, her deliverance from Babylon is promised (*cf.* 41:8–20; 42:8–43:8; 43:16–44:5; 48, *passim*), Yahweh's majesty is proclaimed, and the contrast between him and the idols is emphasized (*cf.* 42:8–17; 44:6–20; 45:9–25, *passim*). In 42:1–7, the first of the 'Servant Songs', the Servant of the Lord is introduced.

(iii) *Chapters in which the restoration of Zion is prominent* (49:1–54:17). *Cf.* 49:14–50:3; 51:17–52:12; 54. We hear no more of the conquests of Cyrus or the ruin of Babylon; there is consequently less emphasis on the contrast between Yahweh and the idols. In 49:1–9a; 50:4–11 and 52:13–53:12, the second, third and fourth 'Servant Songs', there are further prophecies concerning the Servant of the Lord, his mission to Israel and the nations, his obedience and suffering, his death and vindication.

(iv) *Exhortation to accept these promises in faith* (55:1–13).

d. Various prophecies, 56:1–66:24

It is not easy to summarize the contents of these chs. The prophecies which they contain are diverse in nature and may even refer to different times. In some places Israel appears to be in exile (57:14; 58:12; 60:10ff.; 63:18; 64:10f.), in others the nation seems settled in Canaan (*e.g.* 57:3–7). Many of the ideas which are expressed in these chs. have already appeared in the preceding sections of the book.

(i) *Law-abiding proselytes and even eunuchs have a share in God's salvation* (56:1–8; see especially v. 7).

(ii) *Leaders and people alike are rebuked for their sins, particularly for idolatry* (56:9–57:13a). This section may refer to the reign of Manasseh.

(iii) *Comfort for the contrite* (57:13b–21; see especially v. 15); an affinity can be traced here with chs. 40–55.

(iv) *False and true religion* (58:1–14). Special mention is made of fasting and sabbath-observance.

(v) *Deliverance is conditional upon repentance* (59:1–21). Rebuke of sins (vv. 1–8); complaint and confession of sin (vv. 9–15a); judgment and deliverance (vv. 15b–20); Yahweh's covenant (v. 21).

(vi) *Zion's deliverance* (60:1–62:12; note again the close affinity with chs. 40–55). The glorious prospect of salvation for Zion involves blessing for the nations as well (60:1–3). The appearance of the messenger of joyful news in 61:1ff. (*cf.* 40:9; 41:27; 52:7) becomes the programme of Jesus' ministry in Lk. 4:17ff.

(vii) *Yahweh's vengeance against Edom* (63:1–6).

(viii) *Penitence and supplication.* God who wrought such wonderful deliverances for his people in the past is entreated to intervene on their behalf again (63:7–64:12).

(ix) *Rebels against God and obedient servants* (65:1–25). Idolatry rebuked (vv. 3ff., 11); new heavens and a new earth promised (v. 17).

(x) *Ch. 66:1–24.* Yahweh's repudiation of forbidden forms of sacrificial worship (vv. 1–4), Zion glorified and sinners punished (vv. 5–24).

II. Origin, construction, authorship

a. Isaiah's literary activity

We are given but little information about Isaiah's own literary activity. In 8:1 only a short inscription is involved ('Maher-shalal-hash-baz'); 8:16 should be understood in a figurative sense; 30:8 may relate to the writing down of the brief utterance of v. 7, 'Rahab who sits still', although it is possible that a more extensive passage was to be recorded. The reference to 'the book of the Lord' in 34:16 implies that the preceding prophecy of ch. 34 was written down. The 'I' style in chs. 6 and 8 tells in favour of the assumption that these chs. were written by Isaiah himself; it is noteworthy, however, that ch. 7 speaks of him in the third person (*cf.* ch. 20).

It is very likely, indeed, that more prophecies were written by Isaiah himself than the above-mentioned passages indicate. In favour of this conclusion the high standard and unity of language and style may be taken into consideration. But if Isaiah himself had had a substantial part in the composition of his book, its structure would presumably have been more straightforward than is now the case.

Chs. 36–39 are essentially parallel to 2 Ki. 18:13–20:19. In this connection it should be borne in mind that, according to 2 Ch. 26:22; 32:32, Isaiah also figured as a historical writer. The question whether Isaiah was the author of chs. 36–39 cannot be answered with certainty.

b. Construction

The book of Isaiah is decidedly not an arbitrary string of disconnected prophecies. There is a certain chronological arrangement. Chs. 2–5 consist to a large extent of prophecies from Isaiah's earliest activity. 7:1–9:7 originate mostly from the period of the Syro-Ephraimite war (734 BC). Chs. 18–20 take us to the period 715–711 BC, and various prophecies of chs. 28–37 belong to the years between 705 and 701 BC. The greater part of chs. 40–66 consists of prophecies uttered from an exilic, or perhaps even post-exilic, standpoint.

There is also a certain arrangement according to subject-matter (see **I**, Outline of contents). In this regard an outstanding feature is the group of oracles concerning foreign nations in chs. 13–23; it should also be noted here that most of the prophecies in these chapters are introduced by the words 'The oracle concerning...' Chs. 40–55 also, to a considerable degree, form a unity. One further point: in 39:6ff. there is clearly a transition from chs. 1–39 to chs. 40–66.

On the other hand, chronological order has certainly not been followed throughout. For example, 9:8–10:4 contains what is perhaps one of Isaiah's oldest prophecies; ch. 17 may date from the period shortly before 734 BC, *i.e.* close in time to ch. 7; 28:1–6 contains an early prophecy. It should also be noted that, while prophecies from an exilic standpoint occur chiefly in chs. 40ff., ch. 35 also presupposes the period of the Exile; and we may even be forced to the conclusion that chs. 56–66 set alongside one another prophecies whose respective standpoints are pre-exilic (*e.g.* 56:9–57:13), exilic (*e.g.* chs. 60–62) and post-exilic (*e.g.* ch. 58).

Again, it is equally plain that arrangement according to subject-matter has not been carried through with entire consistency. As we have seen, chs. 13–23 consist mainly of prophecies about foreign nations, but ch. 22 forms an exception, and elsewhere there are other prophecies against foreign nations (for example, the oracle against Assyria in 10:5–34 is similar to that in 14:24–27):

It should be noted, too, that there are superscriptions in 1:1; 2:1 and 13:1; and further, the account of the vision in which Isaiah received his call to be a prophet does not come until ch. 6.

The situation is involved—more involved, indeed, than might be gathered from the considerations which have been briefly outlined above. It may be taken as certain that our book of Isaiah has been constructed on the basis of shorter collections. But in the end we can only say that the history of its composition can no longer be reconstructed. Scholars have made various attempts to trace the stages of its composition, but have not reached convincing conclusions. Thus, some have supposed that chs. 1–12, 13–23, 24–27, 28–35 originally formed separate collections. Admittedly these divisions, lying before us in their present arrangement, do form more or less self-contained units. The song of ch. 12 or the promise of salvation in ch. 35 would form an appropriate conclusion to a collection. But we should reckon with the possibility that this is due to the work of the latest redactor.

As for chs. 40–55, they probably contain a collection of originally independent prophecies: it is hardly to be assumed that they formed a unity from the beginning. On the other hand, in these chs. the same subjects recur time and again. Their arrangement is by no means completely arbitrary; *i.e.* a certain chronological order can be observed (see **I**, Outline of contents). Many critics are of the opinion that these chs., in essence at least, come from one author.

c. Authorship

Many scholars nowadays deny great portions of the book to Isaiah—not only in the sense that he did not write them down, but in the sense that their subject-matter does not come from him at all. Even chs. 1–35 are believed by some to contain much non-Isaianic material. Some scholars go farther than others, but there is a wide measure of agreement that Isaiah cannot be credited with chs. 13:1–14:23; 21; 24–27; 34–35. In addition, critical scholars are practically unanimous in the view that chs. 40–66 do not come from Isaiah.

Chs. 40–55 are believed to be mainly the work of a prophet to whom the name Deutero-Isaiah ('Second Isaiah') has been given. It is held that his prophecies must be dated between the first victories of the Persian king, Cyrus (*c.* 550 BC), and Cyrus' conquest of Babylon, which was followed by his decree permitting the Jewish exiles to return to their own country (538 BC). Some defend the view that part of Deutero-Isaiah's prophecies should be assigned to the period after 538 BC. Babylon is mostly envisaged as this prophet's field of activity; others think of Palestine, Egypt and other lands.

As for chs. 56–66, some scholars credit Deutero-Isaiah with them too, while others ascribe them to a separate author, called Trito-Isaiah ('Third Isaiah'), who is dated either *c.* 450 BC, in the time of Malachi (*e.g.* by B. Duhm), or *c.* 520 BC, in the time of Haggai and Zechariah (*e.g.* by E. Sellin and K. Elliger). Others, again, take the view that the prophecies of chs. 56–66 do not all come from the same time; it has even been held that some come from the 8th century BC, some from the 2nd.

The following considerations are relevant to the Deutero-Isaiah question:

1. The unanimous testimony of tradition credits Isaiah with the authorship of the whole book. Chs. 1–39 and 40–66 have come down to us as a unity;

ch. 39:6–8 may certainly be regarded as a planned transition from the first to the second part of the book. From Ecclus. 48:24f. it is plain that Jesus ben Sira (*c*. 200 BC) considered Isaiah to be the author of chs. 40–66 as well as of chs. 1–39. The Qumran MSS of Isaiah indicate that, at the time when they were copied (2nd or 1st century BC), the book was regarded as a unity. It is true that the testimony of extra-biblical tradition is not decisive; and in the judgment of the present author it cannot be said that the OT itself points unequivocally to Isaiah as author of the entire book. Even so, two things should be borne in mind.

First, Deutero-Isaiah is taken to be one of the greatest prophets, if not *the* greatest prophet, of Israel; it would be surprising indeed if every trace of this great prophet had been so thoroughly effaced from tradition that his very name is unknown to us. Secondly, the evidence of the NT naturally takes a special place in the testimony of tradition. The following passages from chs. 40–66 are introduced in the NT by some such words as 'that which was spoken by the prophet Isaiah': 40:3 (in Mt. 3:3); 42:1–4 (in Mt. 12:17–21); 53:1 (in Jn. 12:38 and Rom. 10:16); 53:4 (in Mt. 8:17); 65:1f. (in Rom. 10:20f.). To this it may be added that those who deny chs. 40ff. to Isaiah usually deny him ch. 13 on similar grounds; but the superscription of this chapter ascribes it to 'Isaiah the son of Amoz'.

2. The weightiest argument for ascribing chs. 40ff. to Deutero-Isaiah is no doubt the fact that these chapters have as their background the period of the Babylonian Exile—more precisely, the closing years of the Exile, from 550 BC onwards. At the very outset it is stated that Israel 'has received double for all her sins' (40:2). Babylon is the oppressing power (46–47), not Assyria, as we should expect in Isaiah's time. The Persian king, Cyrus (559–529 BC), is mentioned by name. While his conquest of Babylon is predicted in 43:14; 48:14, *etc*., it is suggested by 41:1–7, 25, *etc*., that he has already achieved his first successes.

It may be said in reply that the Spirit of prophecy can reveal the future to the prophets; and it is true that this fact has not always been taken sufficiently into account by adherents of the Deutero-Isaiah theory. But even those who are prepared to make full allowance for it find themselves faced with difficulties here. It is certainly inconceivable that Isaiah stood in the Temple court, comforting his people in view of a calamity which was not to come upon them until more than a century had elapsed. We may indeed suppose that Isaiah communicated these prophecies to the circle of his disciples (*cf*. 8:16)—or rather that he did not speak them but only committed them to writing. Even so, the question arises: if we credit Isaiah with these chs., must we not assume that his inspiration took a very 'mechanical' form, bearing no relation to the concepts existing in the prophet's conscious mind? The following suggestion may help in some degree to meet these objections.

Isaiah wrote down these prophecies in Manasseh's reign. He found it impossible to appear in public in those years (*cf*. 2 Ki. 21:16). Iniquity had reached such a pitch that Isaiah recognized that the divine judgment was bound to come (*cf*. 2 Ki. 21:10–15); indeed, before his mind's eye it had already come. Then the Spirit of prophecy showed him that this judgment in its turn would come to an end (see under **III.** *a* (ii), 'Judgment and salvation'). It can be said further that the judgment which Isaiah saw as already fulfilled before his mind's eye was 'delayed' by Manasseh's repentance (2 Ch. 33:12ff.) and Josiah's reformation (2 Ki. 22–23). It is, besides, important to observe that, according to Is. 39:5–7, Isaiah knew that a deportation to Babylon would take place.

And while it is true that these prophecies presuppose as their background the closing phase of the Babylonian Exile, and Cyrus is represented as having already entered upon the stage of history, yet in other respects the author expresses himself much less concretely on conditions during the Exile than might have been expected from someone who lived in the midst of it.

3. Attention has been drawn to the differences between chs. 1–39 and 40–66 in matters of language, style and conceptions. It may indeed be said that in 1–39 the language is suggestive and full of illustrations, while in 40–66 it is often more verbose; that in 40–66 the cosmological aspect of the Kingship of God is more prominent than in 1–39; that while 1–39 speak of the Messiah-King, this figure is displaced in 40–66 by the suffering Servant of Yahweh. Yet these divergences do not make it necessary to abandon belief in the unity of the book. For over against these divergences there are striking points of similarity. As examples of these it may be pointed out, first, that as chs. 1–39 do not describe only Messiah's glory (*cf*. 11:1 with 53:2), so chs. 40–66 do not describe only the Servant's suffering (*cf*. 42:1–7; 53:11f.); and secondly, that the divine appellation 'the Holy One of Israel' occurs 12 times in chs. 1–39, 13 times in chs. 40–66 and only five times in the rest of the OT. *Cf*. further J. H. Eaton, *VT* 9, 1959, pp. 138–157.

The preceding paragraphs are intended to give some idea of the lines along which the discussion of these problems proceeds and of the arguments which are adduced on either side. The conclusion is that it is both unnecessary and open to objection to deny to Isaiah any share in the composition of chs. 40–66. On the other hand, even those who desire to submit unconditionally to the testimony of Scripture may come to the conclusion that the book of Isaiah contains some parts which are not of Isaianic origin. This is perhaps the situation already in chs. 1–39. And especially with regard to chs. 40–66 there are reasons for accepting this suggestion. In the opinion of the present writer it is acceptable to hold that chs. 40–66 contain an Isaianic core, upon which the prophet's disciples (men who felt themselves closely bound to him) later worked in the spirit of the original author. It is, however, impossible for us to assess how much belongs to the Isaianic core and how much to the later elaborations.

Two final remarks will close this section.

1. There is a prevalent trend of thought nowadays which lays great emphasis on the significance of oral tradition. According to this trend of thought, a prophet's utterances were handed down orally by the circle of his disciples; in this process they were repeatedly adapted to the changing circumstances of the time. If there is an element of truth in this view it should certainly be taken into account in any attempt to explain the origin of Is. 40–66. It might lead to the conclusion that chs. 40–66 contain an Isaianic core but that the extent of this core can no longer be ascertained.

2. It should be remembered that those who deny to Isaiah the whole of chs. 40–66 frequently assume that the author or authors of these chs.

belonged to the school of Isaiah. It is admitted that, alongside all the arguments for diversity of authorship, there is a close affinity between chs. 1–39 and 40–66. See, *e.g.*, what was said above about the appellation 'the Holy One of Israel'.

III. The message of the book

From ancient times Isaiah has been considered the greatest of OT prophets. He has been called 'the eagle among the prophets', 'the Evangelist of the Old Covenant', and the like. His book is not only lofty in style and conception, but rich in spiritual meaning.

a. Chs. 1–39

In endeavouring to outline the message of these chapters we may start with the divine appellation 'the Holy One of Israel' (which, as we have seen, is characteristic of Isaiah), and with the name of one of his sons, Shear-jashub, 'Remnant will return'.

That God was the Holy One was inscribed indelibly on Isaiah's heart as a result of his inaugural vision (6:3). As Amos has been called the prophet of righteousness and Hosea the prophet of loving-kindness, so Isaiah has been called the prophet of holiness (*cf.* 1:4; 5:16, 24; 8:14; 10:17, 20; 12:6; 17:7; 29:23; 30:11f.; 31:1; 37:23, *etc.*). God is the Holy One; that means he is so highly exalted above his creatures as to be totally different from them, not only in his moral perfection (*cf.* 6:5) but also in his power, his wrath, his love, his faithfulness and all his virtues (*cf.* also 29:16; 31:3). Yahweh's holiness is the very essence of his divine being, which causes men to tremble before him as they worship him.

This holy God has associated himself in a special way with Israel (1:2; 5:1ff., *etc.*), and in a pre-eminent degree with the house of David (8:13; 11:1, *etc.*). He dwells in the midst of Israel, on Mt Zion (8:18; 11:9, *etc.*).

The fact that God is 'the Holy One of Israel' involves an abiding tension in his relation to his people. On the one hand, he fulminates in a violent way against Israel's sin; on the other hand, he does not break his covenant with Israel. Hence the assurance: 'Remnant will return'. This means, first: judgment will come, only a remnant will be left. But it also means: at least a remnant will be left, a remnant will indeed return (*i.e.* to its homeland). In his wrath God remembers mercy. It is also possible to translate: 'Remnant returns to God, changes its mind'; its return and deliverance come along the path of conversion. This remnant-doctrine figures prominently in Isaiah's preaching, from the very first (6:13). And he may have seen the beginnings of the remnant in the circle of his disciples, among whom he withdrew himself from public life for a considerable time at an early stage in his ministry (8:16–18).

Some of the implications of the outlined teaching of Isaiah may now be elaborated.

(i) *God's requirements and Israel's sin.* The Holy One of Israel requires his people to sanctify him (8:13) by putting their trust in him alone, by keeping his commandments, by paying heed to the words of his prophets. Because Yahweh has entered into a covenant with Israel, Israel's sin is essentially apostasy (1:2–4; 30:1–9, *etc.*). Instead of preserving due humility in the presence of the Holy One of Israel, they are haughty and frivolous (2:6ff.; 3:8; 5:15f., 19ff.; 22:1ff.; 28:15; 29:14ff.; 32:9ff., *etc.*). Isaiah repeatedly insists that sin, in whatever sphere it may be committed, is first and foremost sin against God.

Isaiah denounces sinful worship (although this is not so prominent a feature of his preaching as of Hosea's); he inveighs against a ritual which confines itself to external matters (1:10ff.; 29:13), against the offering of sacrifices on the high places (1:29), against heathen worship (2:6–8; 17:7f.; 30:22; 31:7, *etc.*; see also 8:19).

Especially during the early years of his ministry he also spoke out sternly against sins in the social realm—oppression of the defenceless, immoderate luxury, drunkenness, *etc.* (*cf.*, *e.g.*, 1:15–17, 21–23; 3:14f., 16ff.; 5:7–8, 11ff., 14, 22f.; 10:1f.; 28:7ff.; 32:9ff.). In this connection we may think of a possible influence of Amos.

In the political domain, Isaiah's governing demand is trust in the Holy One of Israel (7:9ff.; 8:12f.; 10:20; 17:7; 28:16; 30:15, *etc.*). What did this involve in practical politics? Isaiah never advocated defencelessness, but he uttered repeated warnings against joining in coalitions, especially with Egypt (14:28–32; 18; 20; 30:1–7; 31:1–3). This abstention from active participation in world-politics would, in the circumstances, also have been a requirement of statecraft (*cf.*, *e.g.*, 36:5f.), but Isaiah's warnings should not be attributed to keen political vision, but to divine revelation (see also 30:1). Isaiah's warnings may sometimes have been heeded; we do not hear of any open conflict between Assyria and Judah during the years 714–711 BC. But often people would not listen to him. Ahaz's attitude, for example, is made quite clear in ch. 7 (*cf.* 2 Ki. 16:7ff.); and as for the time of Hezekiah, see 29:15; 30:1ff.; 31:1ff.; 36:4ff. (*cf.* 2 Ki. 18:7).

(ii) *Judgment and salvation.* It is often objected that the preaching of judgment and salvation in Is. 1–39 contains inherent contradictions. From this it is concluded that various parts of these chapters do not come from Isaiah, or else that Isaiah's views underwent a change; for example, a distinction is drawn between a pro- and an anti-Assyrian period in his ministry. But it has already been said that an inevitable tension is involved in the title 'the Holy One of Israel'. As the situation requires, this may mean that he protects Israel and Jerusalem, the Temple city, the royal city; it may mean that he enters into judgment expressly against Israel and Jerusalem. Therefore there is no need for surprise if Isaiah, in his preaching of judgment and salvation, does not always lay the emphasis in the same place (*cf.* 28:23–29; it is rightly said that this parable has a central place in the preaching of Isaiah). The persistent emphasis in his preaching is what was revealed to him at the outset, in his inaugural vision (6:11–13). A thoroughgoing judgment is to come upon Judah and upon Jerusalem as well (3:1–4:1; 5:1–7, 8–24; 32:9–14, *etc.*); in this connection the Assyrians are mentioned (5:26–30; 7:17ff.; 8:5–8, *etc.*); but through and beyond this judgment, which is consequently sometimes portrayed as a purifying judgment (1:24ff.; 4:2ff.), a remnant is saved, and for this remnant a triumphant future breaks (4:2ff.; 10:20ff., *etc.*). But this is not all that should be mentioned here. This thoroughgoing judgment on Jerusalem does not fall immediately. Isaiah is allowed to prophesy that Pekah and Rezin's attack on Jerusalem will fail (7:1–8:4), that the Assyrians will overflow Judah and cause great distress to Jerusalem, but will in their turn be struck by divine judgment and not be permitted to capture Jerusalem (8:9f.; 10:5–34; 14:24–32; 18; 29:1–8; 31:4ff.; 37:6f., 21–35). One statement does not contradict another. (It is to be noted too that before the reassuring prophecies of 37:6f., 21–35, Sennacherib has dealt treacherously, 30:1ff.; *cf.* 2 Ki. 18:14ff., and blasphemed the Holy One of Israel.) That Isaiah's prophecies on this subject are not inherently contradictory is also shown by their fulfilment. The Assyrians did cause much distress to Jerusalem in 701 BC, but were not able to capture it; later on a thoroughgoing judgment did fall on Jerusalem, at the hand of the Babylonians. Isaiah nowhere specifies the Assyrians as the executors of the thoroughgoing judgment of Jerusalem; in a later time he foretold that the Babylonians would come (39:5ff.). Finally, some prophecies, like those of 5:14ff., have their complete fulfilment only in the eschatological judgment (see below, under subsection (iv)).

The prophet's summons to repentance should also be mentioned in this connection. In a sense his announcement of judgment and salvation is conditional; if they harden their hearts, judgment will follow; if they repent, forgiveness and salvation will be theirs (1:16ff.; 30:15ff., *etc.*). But this announcement is conditional only in a sense; for as early as Isaiah's inaugural vision it was revealed to him that Yahweh was determined to execute judgment on Judah; the broad masses of the people were sunk so deep in their sins that Isaiah's preaching would have no effect save to harden their hearts still more (6:9ff.). Equally, there is no uncertainty about the coming salvation. And, just as Isaiah's preaching, by hardening his hearers' hearts, contributed to Israel's ripening for judgment, so too it contributed to the postponement of the judgment, the rescue of Jerusalem and the formation of the remnant on which Yahweh purposed to bestow his salvation.

The salvation proclaimed by Isaiah includes the deliverance of Jerusalem from great distress, but this deliverance is not the full salvation. The promised salvation in its fullest sense is based on the remission of sins (*cf.* 1:18; 6:5f., *etc.*), and it consists further in a renewal of the heart (*cf.*, *e.g.*, 32:15ff.), a life lived in accordance with God's commandments, a life crowned with prosperity and glory. In this salvation Zion would take a central place, but the other nations would participate in it too (*cf.* 1:19, 26f.; 2:2–5; 4:2–6; 33:13ff.). Special mention should also be made here of the Messianic prophecies, which are of paramount importance (*cf.* 9:1–7; 11:1–10, where there is a marked contrast with the Assyrian empire described in 10:5ff., *cf.* also 16:5; 28:16f.; 32:1ff.; 33:17; the Immanuel prophecy of 7:14 is also Messianic, as its quotation in Mt. 1:22f. shows, but indirectly so, as v. 16 indicates). In these prophecies Isaiah naturally employs OT terms—the Messiah is portrayed as king of Israel, and the idea is raised that he will liberate his people from the Assyrians (9.3, *cf.* 11:1ff., with the preceding oracle)—but by means of these terms he gives a glorious portrayal of the coming salvation, which Christians recognize as having been inaugurated with the first advent of Christ, and as coming to its complete fulfilment with his second advent (*cf.* 11:9, *etc.*).

(iii) *The Holy One of Israel and the nations.* That Yahweh is the only true God is stated more emphatically in chs. 40ff. than in 1–39, yet it is stressed plainly enough in the first part of the book (*cf.* 2:8; 30:22; 37:16, *etc.*). Yahweh is Lord of the whole earth (6:3). All that happens is his doing, the execution of his decree (5:12, 19; 14:24, 26; 37:26, *etc.*). He directs the history of Israel and of the other nations too. Assyria is the rod of his anger (10:5ff.; *cf.* 5:26; 7:17ff.; 8:7f., *etc.*); but because of the Assyrians' pursuit of their own ambitions (10:7ff.), their haughtiness, their violence, their cruelty, their faithlessness and their blasphemy of Yahweh, they too will have to undergo his judgment (8:9.; 10:5ff.; 14:24–27; 18:4–6; 29:1–8; 30:27–33; 31:8f.; 33:1ff.; 36–37, *etc.*). See further the prophecies concerning Babylon (13–14; 21:1–10), Moab (15–16; *cf.* also 25:10ff.), Ethiopia and Egypt (18–20), Edom (21:11f.; 34), and other nations. We should observe, too, that Isaiah predicts not only disaster but also blessing for the nations—*e.g.* in the great prophecy of 19:18–25, with its promise that Egypt, Assyria and Israel will be joint witnesses for Yahweh (*cf.* 16:1ff.; 18:7; 23:15–18, and also 2:2–5; 11:10, *etc.*).

(iv) *Chs. 24–27.* These chapters, which form an epilogue to chs. 13–23, call for a special mention, because of their eloquent portrayal of world judgment (24) and the great salvation which God will accomplish (all nations will have a share in this salvation: 'He will swallow up death for ever'; *cf.* 25:6ff.) and because of their reference to the resurrection of the just (26:19).

b. Chs. 40–55

Jerusalem lies in ruins, Israel is in exile in Babylonia and the Exile has lasted a long time. The people of Israel are in great distress (42:22; 51:18ff.), Yahweh's anger lies heavily upon them because of their sins (40:2; 42:24f.; 51:17, *etc.*); they think that he has forgotten them (40:27; 49:14). Some of them have come to regard the place of their exile as their homeland (55:2). But the prophet promises that Yahweh is about to liberate his people, and he urges them to believe this promise.

(i) *The Holy One of Israel* (41:14, 16, 20; 43:3, 14f.; 45:11; 47:4; 48:17; 49:7; 55:5) *is able to help*. In view of what is said above, it is not surprising that nowhere in the OT is it asserted so emphatically as in these chs. that Yahweh is the one true God, that he alone can help (*cf.* 41:1ff., 21ff.; 43:10f.; 44:6, 8; 45:5, 14, 18, 21f.; 46:9, *etc.*) Trust in other gods is vain, image-worship is sinful folly (40:18ff.; 41:7, 29; 42:8, 17; 44:6–20, 25; 45:20; 46:1ff.; 47:9ff.). He far transcends all his creatures; he has created all things (this has more stress in chs. 40–55 than in chs. 1–39) and directs the course of all things (*cf.* 40:12–26, which forms the introduction to vv. 27–31; 41:4; 43:13; 44:7; 48:13, *etc.*). He is the eternal God (40:28; 41:4; 43:10; 44:6; 48:12); he acts in accordance with his own good pleasure (45:9ff.), and his decree is certain of accomplishment (44:28; 46:10, *etc.*). His word, spoken by the mouth of his prophets, will not return to him 'empty'—without fulfilling its mission (40:6–8; 55:10f.). Even a world-conqueror such as Cyrus is but a tool in his hand for the performance of his purpose (41:1ff., 21–29; 43:9–15; 44:24–45:13; 46:8–13; 48:12–16).

(ii) *The Holy One of Israel is willing to help.* Israel has not deserved his help; she has shown herself unworthy of it (43:22ff., *etc.*). But Israel is his people (40:1, *etc.*; *cf.* too, *e.g.*, 43:15; 44:2), and his name, his reputation, is involved in Israel's deliverance (48:1–11, *etc.*). His relation to Israel, to Zion, is compared to the marriage bond (50:1; 54:5ff.). He has chosen Israel out of all the nations (41:8f.; 48:10, *etc.*) and Israel is his servant—a title which implies both a privilege (41:8f., *etc.*) and a mission (43:10, *etc*.). His love is unchangeably set upon Israel, upon Zion (40:11; 43:3f.; 46:3f.; 49:15ff., *etc*.), and his righteousness is the guarantee of her liberation (*e.g.* 41:10; 45:24).

(iii) *The Holy One of Israel will certainly help.* The coming salvation is painted in bright colours. The basis of this salvation, and at the same time its very essence, consists in his turning away his anger, his remission of Israel's sin (40:2; 43:25; 44:22; 51:21ff., *etc*.). He uses Cyrus as his instrument to inaugurate his salvation; Cyrus is described in quite remarkable terms as Yahweh's 'anointed' (45:1), and the man whom he 'loves' (48:14, *etc*.). Babylon is overthrown by him (46–47; *cf.* 43:14; 48:14); Israel is set free, her exiled children are gathered from all the lands of their dispersion, and return to Canaan (43:1–8, 18–21; 48:20f.; 49:24–26; 52:11f., *etc*.). Yahweh returns to Zion (40:9–11; 52:7f.), Zion is once again inhabited (49:17–23; 54:1ff.), rebuilt (44:28; 45:13; 54:11f.), and protected (54:14–17).

Note especially the following points. 1. This work of deliverance is described as a new creation (41:20; 45:8; *cf.* 45:18). The miracles which marked the Exodus from Egypt are now to be repeated on a grander scale (43:16ff.; 48:21; 51:9f., *etc*.). 2. The prophet sees the whole future as a unity. Israel's liberation from exile is viewed as the beginning of the great era of salvation, in which all things will be made new. Here it can be mentioned that Israel's homeward progress is attended by a series of nature-miracles (41:17ff.; 43:18–21; 48:21; 49:9bf.; 55:12f.; *cf.* 54:13). 3. It is repeatedly emphasized that the grand aim of all this is the praise and glory of God (41:20; 43:21; 44:23; 48:9–11, *etc*.).

The prophet bends all his energies to persuade the people to accept and believe this assurance of blessing; see especially the closing ch. 55. He tries to convince them by pointing to Yahweh's majesty in nature and history. He propounds pointed questions, and challenges them to enter into debate (*cf.*, *e.g.*, 40:12–31; 49:14ff.). He also challenges the Gentile nations and their gods: can *these* gods do what the God of Israel does? It is the God of Israel who has called Cyrus into being and raised him up, in order that he may be the instrument to set Israel free. The God of Israel is therefore the only One who can foretell the result of Cyrus' actions. As certainly as Yahweh made the 'former things' come to pass—that is to say, as certainly as he fulfilled what he foretold in earlier days—so certainly will he bring the 'new things' to pass by the fulfilment of the promises which he now makes through his prophet (41:1ff., 21–29; 43:9–15; 44:6–45:25; 46:8–13; 48:12–16; *cf.* 42:9; 48:1–11). With all this the prophet does not furnish proofs in the strict sense of the word, but he makes a strong appeal to mind, heart and conscience.

All this underlines the outspoken universalism of these chapters. Yahweh, the Creator of the universe, directs world-events, including the victorious career of Cyrus. He rebukes the nations, particularly Babylon, because of their hostility to Israel and also because of their idolatry (41:11–16; 42:13, 17; 46; 47). The goal to which he is directing the course of the world is summed up in the words, 'to me every knee shall bow, every tongue shall swear' (45:23); in this serving of Yahweh lies also the salvation of the nations of the earth; *cf.*, *e.g.*, 42:10–12; 45:6, 22–24; 51:4f.

(iv) On the 'Servant Songs' (42:1–7; 49:1–9a; 50:4–11; 52:13–53:12), see *SERVANT OF THE LORD.

c. Chs. 56–66

The following features are specially noteworthy in these concluding chapters:

1. Yahweh is presented as the living God. He is fearful in his anger (59:16ff.; 63:1–6), but he bends down in kindness to his people, he shows them mercy and restores their comfort, he delights in Zion (57:15ff.; 60:10; 61:1ff.; 62:4f.; 63:7, 15; 65:1f., 8, 19; 66:2, 13). That he is no inflexible or inexorable power is movingly shown in the review of his dealings with Israel in earlier days (63:8ff.).

2. A sharp contrast is drawn between those in Israel who love God and those who disobey him (*e.g.* 57:1; 65:13ff.; 66:5; *cf.* 65:8).

3. It is frequently said, but without justification, that in some parts at least of this section of the book a legalist and nationalist spirit is manifested. True, it is clearly laid down that it is necessary to practise righteousness if one is to share in the coming salvation, and occasionally the importance of keeping the sabbath is stressed (*cf.*, *e.g.*, 56:1–8). But this is not intended to inculcate a spirit of ceremonialism and legalism; on the contrary, this very spirit is roundly condemned (*cf.* 58; 66:1, 5), and an attitude of humility is repeatedly commended (*cf.*, *e.g.*, 57:15; 61:2f.; 66:2). As to the glorifying of Zion (*cf.*, *e.g.*, 60:4ff.; 61:5ff.; 66:20), this is no mere outburst of nationalist feeling. Zion is not only the capital of Judah but the dwelling-place of God; and the Gentiles who turn to him participate in his salvation (*e.g.* 56:1–8; 60:3).

BIBLIOGRAPHY. See the Introductions to the OT and the Commentaries – *e.g.* J. Mauchline, *Isaiah 1–39*, *TBC*, 1962; C. R. North, *Isaiah 40–55*, *TBC*, 1964; D. R. Jones, *Isaiah 56–66 and Joel*, *TBC*, 1964; C. R. North, *The Second Isaiah*, 1964; E. J. Young, *The Book of Isaiah*, *NIC* 1, 1965, 2, 1969, 3, 1972; H. C. Leupold, *Exposition of Isaiah I* (chs. 1–39), 1968; J. L. McKenzie, *Second Isaiah*, *AB*, 1968; O. Kaiser, *Isaiah 1–12*, *OTL*, 1972, *Isaiah 13–39*, *OTL*, 1974; C. Westermann, *Isaiah 40–66*, *OTL*, 1969; A. S. Herbert, *Isaiah 1–39*, CBC, 1973. *Cf.*, too: O. T. Allis, *The Unity of Isaiah*, 1950; J. D. W. Watts, *Isaiah*, 1989; *Isaiah 1–33*, 1985; *Isaiah 34–66*, 1987; J. A. Motyer, *The Prophecy of Isaiah*, 1993; D. Carr, *JSOT* 57, 1993, pp. 61–80; H. G. M. Williamson, *The Book Called Isaiah*, 1994.

N.H.R.

ISHBOSHETH. The name (2 Sa. 2–4) is commonly thought to have been Eshbaal originally, altered by scribes who wrote *bōšeṯ* ('shame') instead of the apparently pagan divine name *Baal. In 1 Ch. 8:33; 9:39 the form Eshbaal is written. Recently a strong case has been argued against this view, *bōšeṯ* being understood as a divine attribute, 'pride, strength'. Ishbosheth and Eshbaal would be alternative names for one man (so, too, Mephibosheth and Meribbaal; see M. Tsevat, *HUCA* 46, 1975, pp. 71–87). A son of Saul, the Ishvi of 1 Sa. 14:49 (a corruption of Ishiah, *i.e.* Ishbaal), he was made king of Israel at *Mahanaim, out of reach of the Philistines, by Abner, his father's commander. As David's power grew, Abner began an intrigue with him but was murdered. Ishbosheth's supporters lost heart, and two of his cavalry officers, Rechab and Baanah, assassinated him during his midday rest (2 Sa. 2–4). The LXX account of this crime is more explicit than *MT* (2 Sa. 4:6, *cf.* AV with RVmg. or RSV), which may be emended to agree with the Greek. The death of Ishbosheth enabled David to gain control of all Israel from the house of Saul. A.R.M.

ISHI (Heb. *'îšî*, 'my husband'). In Ho. 2:16 the name which the Israelites were to use for God, to supersede 'Baali' with its pagan associations. J.D.D.

ISHMAEL (Heb. *yišmā'ē'l*, 'God hears'). **1.** The son of Abraham by Hagar the Egyptian handmaid of Sarah. When Sarah realized that she was barren, she gave her handmaid to Abraham to conceive seed for her (Gn. 16:2). An example of this ancient custom has been discovered in the *Nuzi tablets (*ANET*, p. 220). After conceiving by Abraham, Hagar began to despise Sarah, who then drove her out of the home with Abraham's reluctant consent. On her way to Egypt she was met by the angel of Yahweh, who told her to return and submit to Sarah. He also gave her the promise of a multiplied seed through her son Ishmael, who would be 'a wild ass of a man' (16:12; *cf.* Jb. 39:5–8). Ishmael was born when Abraham was 86, 11 years after his arrival in Canaan (16:15–16; *cf.* 12:4). 13 years later, both Ishmael and his father were circumcised in obedience to God's command (17:25–26). But on that same day, God had also promised Abraham a son by Sarah. The fact that he had long since centred his hopes on Ishmael caused him to cry out, 'O that Ishmael might live in thy sight!' (17:18). God then assured him that Ishmael would beget twelve princes and ultimately a great nation (17:20; *cf.* 16:10; 25:13–16). When Ishmael was about 16, a great celebration was held at the weaning of the child Isaac (21:8). Ishmael gave vent to his jealousy of 'the child of the promise' (Rom. 9:7–9) by 'mocking' him. The apostle Paul employs the verb 'persecuted' (*ediōke*) to describe this act (Gal. 4:29) and builds upon it an extended allegory of the opposition of legalistic religionists to those 'born according to the Spirit' (Gal. 4:21–31). Sarah insisted that both Ishmael and Hagar be expelled from the home, and Abraham consented only after the Lord revealed to him that 'through Isaac shall your descendants be named' (Gn. 21:12). Hagar and her son nearly perished from thirst in the desert of Beersheba, until the angel of Yahweh pointed her to a well of water in response to Ishmael's cry. He grew to be an archer, married an Egyptian and fathered twelve princes (25:12–16). Esau married one of his daughters (28:9; 36:3, 10). He joined Isaac in the burial of their father and died at the age of 137 (25:9, 17).

2. A descendant of Saul and Jonathan, and the son of Azel (1 Ch. 8:38; *cf.* 9:44). **3.** A man of Judah, father of the Zebadiah who was a high official under King Jehoshaphat (2 Ch. 19:11). **4.** The son of Jehohanan, and a captain of hundreds who took part in the conspiracy against Athaliah (2 Ch. 23:1). **5.** A son of Pashhur the priest. He was one of those whom Ezra compelled to put away their foreign wives (Ezr. 10:22).

6. The son of Nethaniah, of the seed royal of Judah, who murdered Gedaliah 2 months after the destruction of Jerusalem in 586 BC. When Gedaliah was appointed by Nebuchadrezzar to be the governor of Judah, many Jews gathered themselves to him at Mizpah for security. Among these, however, was Ishmael, who was jealous of Gedaliah and permitted himself to be hired by Baalis the king of Ammon to plot the governor's death. In spite of Johanan's warnings, Gedaliah trusted Ishmael and invited him and ten of his men to a banquet. They used the occasion to murder Gedaliah and all the others in Mizpah. Two days later they killed a group of Jewish pilgrims and set off for Ammon with many hostages, including Jeremiah and the king's daughters. They were pursued by Johanan and other captains and were overtaken at Gibeon. The hostages were rescued, but Ishmael and eight of his men escaped to Ammon (2 Ki. 25:25; Je. 40:7–41:18).

BIBLIOGRAPHY. H. C. Leupold, *Exposition of Genesis*, 1942; C. F. Keil, *Biblical Commentary on the Old Testament*, I, *The Pentateuch*, 1949; J. J. Davis, *Paradise to Prison*, 1975; H. C. White, *ZAW* 87, 1975, pp. 267–306. J.C.W.

ISLAND, ISLE (Heb. *'î*, pl. *'iyyîm*; Gk. *nēsos*, *nēsion*). Etymologically, the Heb. term is frequently supposed to mean 'habitable land', through a cognate Arab. word, but 'coastlands' is a better translation, as usually in RSV. The general OT usage is to denote the islands and coastlands of the Mediterranean. The idea of distance is also included, *e.g.* Is. 66:19; Je. 31:10. Occasionally it appears to have the strict meaning, *e.g.* 'Kittim' or 'Cyprus' (RSV) in Je. 2:10, 'Caphtor' in Je. 47:4 (see RSV: probably Crete). Isaiah's usage is interesting. In 42:15 it denotes 'dry land' as opposed to water. In 40:15 it is parallel to 'nations'; in 41:1; 49:1 to 'peoples'; and in 41:5 to 'the ends of the earth'.

NT usage is unambiguous. Several islands are named, *e.g.* Cyprus (Acts 4:36; 13:4; 15:39), Crete and Cauda (Acts 27), Malta (Acts 28:1) and Patmos (Rev. 1:9). J.G.G.N.

ISRAEL (Heb. *yiśrā'ēl*, 'God strives'). **1.** The new name given to Jacob after his night of wrestling at Penuel: 'Your name', said his supernatural antagonist, 'shall no more be called Jacob, but Israel, for you have striven [*śārîṯā*, from *śārâ*, 'strive'] with God and with men, and have prevailed' (Gn. 32:28). With this account, assigned to J in the four-document hypothesis, *cf.* Ho. 12:3f., 'in his manhood he [Jacob] strove [*śārâ*] with God. He strove [*wayyāśar*, from the same verb] with the angel and prevailed'. The re-naming is confirmed at Bethel in Gn. 35:10 (assigned to P), where God Almighty appears to Jacob and says: 'Your name is Jacob; no longer shall your name be called Jacob, but Israel shall be your name.' 'So', adds the narrator, 'his name was called Israel.' Thenceforward Israel appears throughout the OT as an occasional synonym for Jacob; it is used most frequently when the Patriarch's descendants are called 'the children (or people) of Israel' (Heb. *bᵉnê yiśrā'ēl*).

2. The nation which traced its ancestry back to the 12 sons of Jacob, referred to variously as 'Israel' (Gn. 34:7, *etc.*), 'the people of Israel' (Ex. 1:8, *etc.*), 'the (twelve) tribes of Israel' (Gn. 49:16, 28,), 'the Israelites' (Gn. 32:32, *etc.*). The earliest reference to the nation of Israel in a non-Israelite record appears in an inscription of Merenptah, king of Egypt, *c.* 1230 BC, 'Israel is desolate; it has no seed left' (*DOTT*, p. 139). The next non-Israelite references come in inscriptions of Shalmaneser III of Assyria, *c.* 853 BC, mentioning 'Ahab the Israelite' (*DOTT*, p. 47), and of Mesha

Jeroboam I 931/30–910/09	
Nadab 910/09–909/08	
Baasha 909/08–886/85	
Elah 886/85–885/84	
Zimri 885/84	
Tibni 885/84–880	overlapping reign 885/84–880
Omri 880–874/73	
Ahab 874/73–853	
Ahaziah 853–852	
Joram 852–841	
Jehu 841–814/13	
Jehoahaz 814/13–798	
Jehoash 798–782/81	overlapping reign 793/92–782/81
Jeroboam II 782/81–753	
Zachariah 753–752	
Shallum 752	
Menahem 752–742/41	overlapping reign 752–740/39
Pekahiah 742/41–740/39	
Pekah 740/39–732/31	
Hoshea 732/31–723/22	
Hasmonaean dynasty	Re-dedication of the Temple 164 BC
	Jonathan 160–143
	Simeon 143–135
	John Hyrcanus 135–104
	Aristobulus 104–103
	Alexander Jannaeus 103–76
	Salome 76–67
	Aristobulus II 67–63
	Hyrcanus II 63–40
	Matthias Antigonus 40–37
Herodian dynasty	Herod (the Great) 37–4 BC
	Archelaus 4 BC–AD 6
	Herod Antipas 4 BC–AD 39
	Philip 4 BC–AD 34
	Herod Agrippa I AD 37–44

Chronological table of the rulers of Israel down to the reign of Herod Agrippa I.

of Moab, whose victory-inscription (*c.* 830 BC) makes repeated mention of Israel, including the boast, 'Israel perished utterly for ever' (*DOTT*, pp. 196f.; *MOABITE STONE. For illustrations see *IBA*, figs. 40, 48, 50–51).

I. Israel's beginnings

Merenptah's reference practically coincides with the beginning of Israel's national history, for it is the Exodus from Egypt, which took place in his reign or his father's, that marks Israel's birth as a nation. Some generations previously their ancestors, members of a pastoral clan, went down from Canaan to Egypt in time of famine and settled in the Wadi Tumilat. The early kings of Dynasty 19 drafted them in large numbers into forced labour gangs for the building of fortified cities on Egypt's NE frontier. In these circumstances they might have been completely assimilated to their fellow-serfs had not their ancestral faith been reawakened by Moses, who came to them in the name of the God of their fathers and led them out of Egypt amid a series of phenomena in which he taught them to recognize the power of that God, put forth for their deliverance.

Under Moses' leadership they trekked E by 'the way of the wilderness of the Yam Suph' until they reached the place where the God of their fathers had previously revealed himself to Moses by his covenant-name Yahweh and commissioned him to bring them out of Egypt. There, at the foot of Mt Sinai, they were brought into special covenant-relationship with Yahweh. He had already shown himself to be their God by rescuing them from bondage in Egypt; they now undertook to be his people. This undertaking involved their obedience to the 'Ten Words' in which Yahweh made his will known to them. They were to worship him alone; they were not to represent him by means of any image; they were to treat his name with due reverence; they were to reserve every seventh day for him; and in thought, word and deed they were to behave one towards another in a manner befitting the covenant which bound them together. They were to be a people set apart for Yahweh, and were therefore to have something of his righteousness, mercy and truth reproduced in their lives.

This attitude we may call practical monotheism. Whether the gods of neighbouring peoples had any sort of existence or not was a question about which neither Moses nor his followers were likely to trouble their minds; their business was to acknowledge Yahweh as supreme and sole God.

Moses was not only Israel's first and greatest legislator; in his own person he combined the functions of prophet, priest and king. He judged their lawsuits and taught them the principles of religious duty; he led them from Egypt to the Jordan, and when he died, a generation after the Exodus, he left behind him no undisciplined body of slave-labourers, such as had followed him out of Egypt, but a formidable host ready to invade Canaan as conquerors and settlers.

This host, even before its settlement in Canaan, was organized as a confederacy of twelve tribes, united in part by a common ancestry but even more so by common participation in the covenant with Yahweh. The visible token of their covenant unity was the sacred ark, housed in a tent-shrine which was located in the centre of their encampment when they were stationary, but which preceded them on the march or in battle. They formed close alliances with other nomad groups such as the Kenites (to whom Moses was related by marriage), the Kenizzites and the Jerahmeelites, who in due course appear to have been incorporated into the tribe of Judah. It was probably a breach of alliance on the part of another nomad group, the Amalekites, that was responsible for the bitter feud which Israel pursued against them from generation to generation. Alliance with such pastoral communities was very different from alliance with the settled agricultural population of Canaan, with its fertility cults so inimical to pure Yahweh-worship. Their covenant with Yahweh strictly prohibited the Israelites from making common cause with the Canaanites.

The principal centre of the tribes of Israel in their wilderness period was Kadesh-barnea, evidently (from its name) a sanctuary and also (from its alternative name En-mishpat) a place where causes were heard and judgment pronounced. When they left Kadesh-barnea some of them infiltrated N into the central Negeb, but the main body advanced S and E of the Dead Sea, skirting the territories of their Edomite, Ammonite and Moabite kinsfolk, who had very recently organized themselves as settled kingdoms. Farther N in Transjordan lay the Amorite kingdoms of Sihon and Og, which they entered as hostile invaders. The resisting forces of Sihon and Og were crushed, and their territories were occupied—these are the territories later known as Reuben, Gad and E Manasseh. Part at least of the Israelite community thus settled down to an agricultural way of life even before the crossing of the Jordan.

II. The settlement in Canaan

The crossing of the Jordan was followed quickly by the capture and destruction of the fortress of *Jericho. From Jericho they pressed into the heart of the land, taking one fortress after another. Egypt was no longer in a position to send help to her former Canaanite vassals; only along the W coastal road did she now exercise some control, as far N as the pass of Megiddo, and even in that region the Philistine settlement (*c.* 1190 BC) was soon to present a barrier to the extension of Egyptian power.

A coalition of five military governors of Canaanite fortresses attempted to prevent the Israelites from turning S from the central hill-country, where Gibeon and the associated cities of the Hivite tetrapolis had submitted to them as subject-allies. The coalition was completely defeated in the pass of Beth-horon and the road to the S lay open to the invaders. Although the chariot-forces of Canaanite citadels prevented them from operating in more level country, they soon dominated and occupied the central and S highlands, and also the Galilean uplands, N of the Plain of Jezreel.

The tribes which settled in the N were cut off from their fellows in central Canaan by a chain of Canaanite fortifications in the Plain of Jezreel, stretching from the Mediterranean to the Jordan. Judah, in the S, was even more effectively cut off from the central tribes by the stronghold of Jerusalem, which remained a Canaanite enclave for 200 years.

On one notable occasion the N and central tribes joined forces in an uprising against the military governors of the Plain of Jezreel, who were steadily reducing them to serfdom. Their united rising was crowned with success at the battle of Kishon (*c.* 1125 BC), when a sudden storm flooded the watercourse and put the Canaanite chariotry out of action, so that the light-armed Israelites easily routed them. But even on this occasion, while the call to action went out to all the N and central tribes, and to those in Transjordan, Judah appears to have received no summons, being too completely cut off from the other tribes.

On an occasion like this, when the tribes of Israel remembered their covenant-bond, their united strength enabled them to resist their enemies. But such united action was rare. The recession of danger was regularly followed by a period of assimilation to Canaanite ways. This assimilation involved intermarriage and the imitation of Canaanite fertility rites, so that Yahweh was thought of rather in terms of Baal, the fructifying rain-god, than as the God of their fathers who had redeemed them from Egypt to be his peculiar people. The covenant-bond was thus weakened and they became an easy prey to their enemies. Not only did Canaanite city-states try to reduce them to servitude; from time to time they suffered incursions from beyond Jordan, by their own kinsmen the Moabites and Ammonites, and much more disastrously at the hands of raiding bedouin. The leaders who rallied them in such periods of distress were the charismatic 'judges' after whom this whole settlement period is commonly named; these men not only led them forward to victory against their enemies but back to loyalty to Yahweh.

The greatest and most recalcitrant menace to Israelite independence, however, came from the W. Not long after the Israelites crossed the Jordan, bands of sea-rovers from the Aegean islands and coastlands settled on the W seaboard of Canaan and organized themselves in the five city-states of Ashdod, Ashkelon, Ekron, Gaza and Gath, each of which was governed by a *seren*—one of the 'five lords of the Philistines'. These *Philistines intermarried with the Canaanites and soon became Canaanite in language and religion, but they retained the political and military traditions of their homelands. Once they had established themselves in their pentapolis they began to extend control over other parts of Canaan, including those parts occupied by the Israelites. Militarily the Israelites were no match for them. The Philistines had mastered the art of iron-working, and kept it as a monopoly in their own hands. When the Israelites began to use iron implements in their agriculture the Philistines insisted that they must come to Philistine smiths to have them sharpened. This was a means of ensuring that the Israelites would not be able to forge iron implements of war with which they might rise against their overlords.

At last the Philistines extended their domination over the Plain of Jezreel as far as the Jordan. While their suzerainty did not menace Israelite existence, it did menace Israelite national identity. The covenant shrine in those days was established at *Shiloh, in the territory of Ephraim, where the sacred ark was tended by a priesthood tracing its lineage back to Aaron, the brother of Moses. This priesthood took a leading part in an inter-tribal revolt against the Philistines which was an utter failure. The ark was captured, Shiloh and the

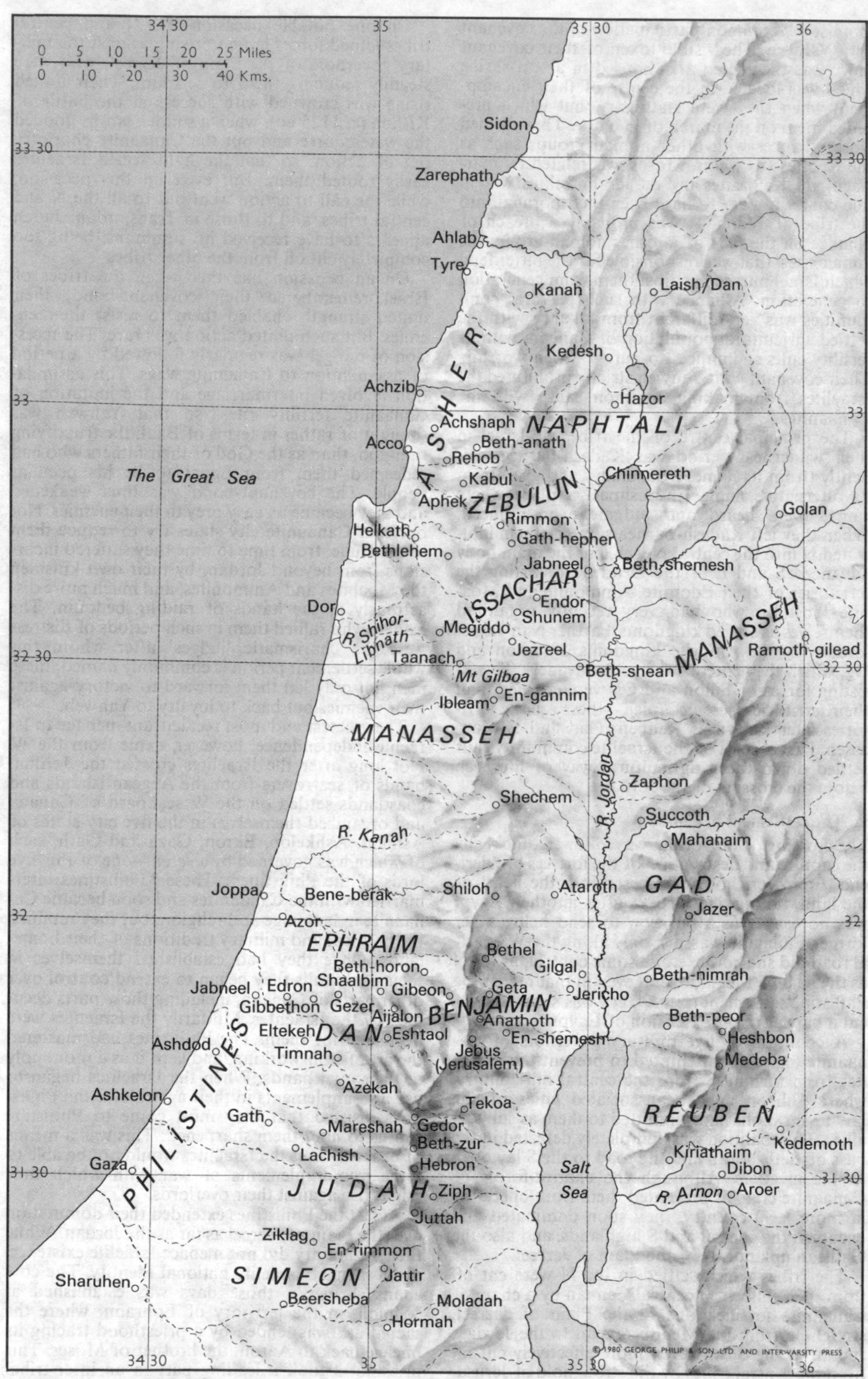

The tribes of Israel.

sanctuary were destroyed and the central priesthood was practically wiped out (*c.* 1050 BC). All the visible bonds which united the tribes of Israel had disappeared, and Israel's national identity seemed likely to disappear with them.

That it did not disappear, but rather became more vigorous, was due to the character and enterprise of *Samuel, the greatest of Israel's charismatic leaders between Moses and David. Samuel, like Moses, combined the functions of prophet, priest and judge; and in his own person he provided a rallying-centre for the national life. Under his guidance Israel returned to its covenant loyalty, and with the return of religious devotion came a resurgence of national spirit; after some years the Israelites were able to defeat the Philistines on the very battlefield where they had been so shamefully routed.

As Samuel grew old, the question of the succession became acute. There arose a widespread demand for a king, and at last Samuel consented to this demand and anointed the Benjaminite *Saul to reign over them. Saul's reign began auspiciously with a prompt retort to a hostile show of force by the Ammonites, and this was followed by successful action against the Philistines in the central highlands. So long as Saul accepted Samuel's direction in the religious sphere all went well, but Saul's fortunes began to decline when a breach came about between them. He met his death in battle against the Philistine at Mt Gilboa, in a bold but vain attempt to bring the N tribes, beyond the Plain of Jezreel, into the unity of Israel. The Philistine grip on Israel was now firmer than ever (*c.* 1010 BC).

III. David and Solomon

The man who enabled Israel to throw off the Philistine yoke was *David, a member of the tribe of Judah, at one time a military commander under Saul and later a mercenary warrior with the Philistines. On Saul's death he was immediately acclaimed as king of Judah, and 2 years later the tribes of Israel as a whole also invited him to be their king. In a series of brilliant military actions he inflicted decisive defeats on the Philistines, who thereafter had to live as David's vassals. The capture of Jerusalem by David in the 7th year of his reign provided his kingdom with a strong and strategically situated capital and also with a new religious centre. The ark was brought back from exile and solemnly installed in a tent-shrine on Mt Zion, later superseded by Solomon's Temple.

After establishing Israelite independence and supremacy in Canaan, David went on by conquest and diplomacy to build up an empire stretching from the Egyptian border and the Gulf of Aqaba to the Upper Euphrates. This empire he bequeathed to his son Solomon, who overtaxed its resources by a grandiose building programme and the maintenance of a splendid court. For the more efficient exploitation of his kingdom's revenue, he divided it into twelve new administrative districts, which took the place of the old tribal divisions, and exacted not only heavy taxes but compulsory labour on public works, ultimately even from his Israelite subjects. The burden at last became intolerable. Towards the end of his reign most of the subject nations had regained their independence, and after his death (*c.* 930 BC) the tribes of Israel themselves split into two kingdoms—the N kingdom of Israel, which renounced its allegiance to the throne of David, and the S Kingdom of Judah, consisting of the tribal territories of Judah and Benjamin, over which the descendants of David and Solomon continued to reign in their capital at Jerusalem (*JUDAH, IV).

IV. The kingdom of Israel

Jeroboam, founder of the separate monarchy in the N, elevated the two ancient sanctuaries of Dan (in the far N) and Bethel (near the frontier with Judah) to the status of national shrines. In both of these golden bull-calves provided the visible pedestals for Yahweh's invisible throne (the function fulfilled by golden cherubs in the Jerusalem Temple). Early in his reign both Hebrew kingdoms were invaded by the Egyptians under Shishak, but the S kingdom appears to have suffered the more, so that later the N kingdom had no need to fear an attempt by the Davidic dynasty to regain control of its lost territories.

A more serious threat, however, presented itself from the N. The Aramaean kingdom of Damascus, founded in Solomon's reign, began to encroach on Israelite territory about 900 BC, and this was the beginning of 100 years of intermittent war which at times reduced Israel to desperate straits.

The security of the kingdom of Israel was also impaired by frequent palace-revolts and dynastic changes. Only two dynasties—those founded by Omri (*c.* 880 BC) and Jehu (*c.* 841 BC)—lasted for more than two generations. Jeroboam's son was assassinated by Baasha, one of his army commanders, in the year after he succeeded to the kingdom; when Baasha had reigned for 20 years his son too fell victim to a similar fate. A few years of civil war followed, from which Omri emerged as the victor.

Omri founded a new capital for his kingdom at *Samaria. Externally he strengthened his position by subduing Moab, E of the Dead Sea, and entering into an economic alliance with Phoenicia. His son Ahab married a Phoenician princess, Jezebel, and also brought the hostility between his kingdom and Judah to an end by means of an alliance which lasted until the dynasty of Omri was overthrown.

The commercial benefits of the Phoenician alliance were great, but in the religious realm it led to a revival of Baal-worship, in which Jezebel played a leading part. The principal champion of pure Yahweh-worship was the prophet *Elijah, who also denounced the royal departure from the old covenant-loyalty in the social sphere (notably in the case of Naboth the Jezreelite) and proclaimed the impending doom of the dynasty of Omri.

The war with Damascus continued throughout the reigns of Omri and his descendants, apart from 3 years during the reign of Ahab, when the kings of Israel and Damascus and neighbouring states formed a military coalition to resist the invading king of Assyria, Shalmaneser III. They gave him battle at Qarqar on the Orontes (853 BC), and he did not invade the W lands again for 12 years. His withdrawal was the signal for the break-up of the coalition and the resumption of hostilities between Israel and Damascus.

The extermination of the house of Omri in Jehu's revolt (841 BC) was followed by the suppression of official Baal-worship. The revolt was supported by the prophetic guilds, who had no reason to love the house of Omri. But it gravely weakened the kingdom of Israel in face of the Aramaean assaults, and the first 40 years of the dynasty of

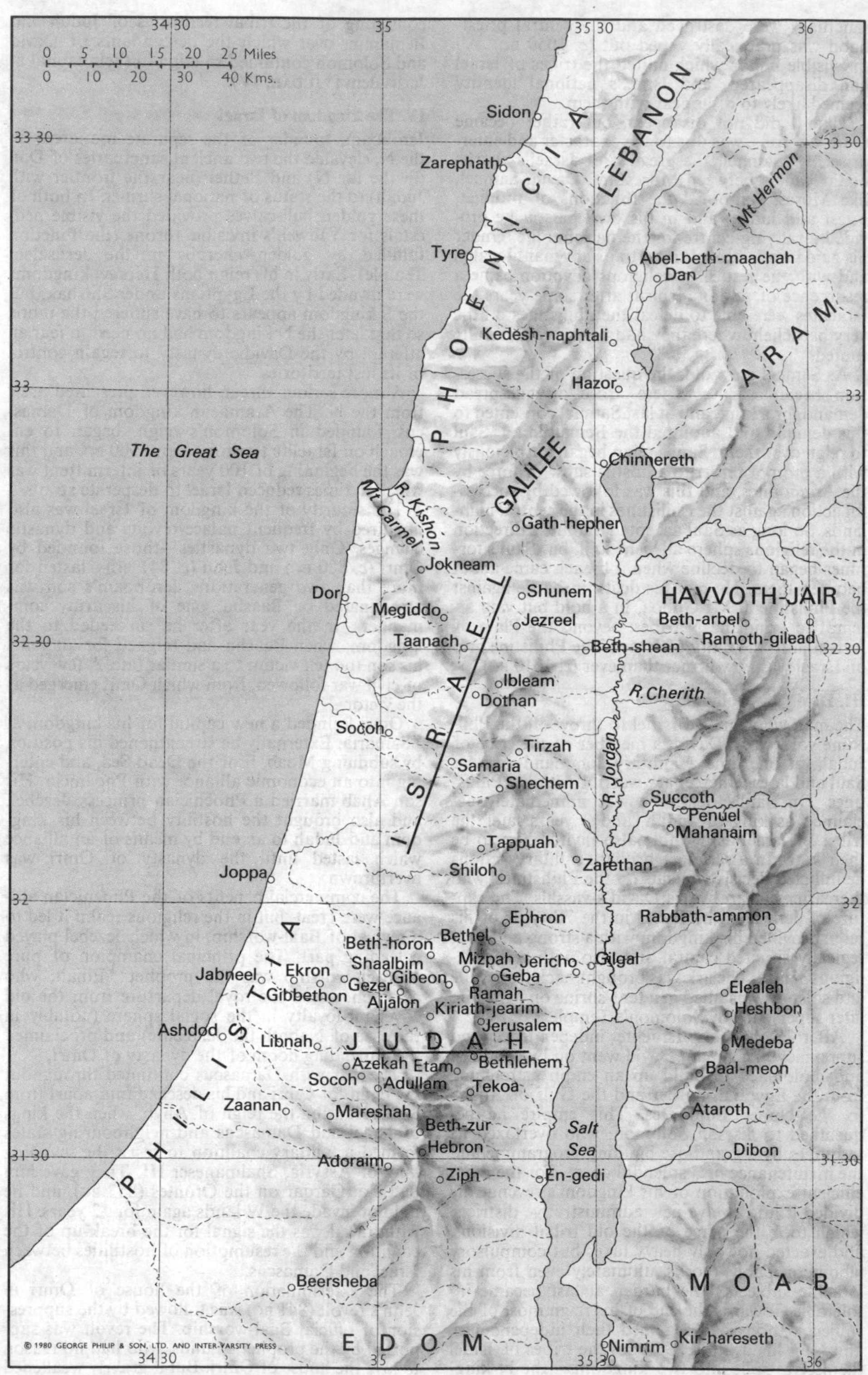

The kingdoms of Israel and Judah.

Jehu were years of continual tribulation for Israel. Not only were Israel's Transjordanian territories overrun by the enemy but her N provinces too; the Aramaeans invaded the Plain of Jezreel and made their way along the Mediterranean seaboard as far S as Gath. Israel had been reduced to desperate straits when in 803 BC the Assyrian king Adad-nirari III invaded Syria, raided Damascus and imposed tribute on it. Damascene pressure on Israel was relaxed; and the Israelites were able to take advantage of this turn of fortune and regain many of the cities which the Aramaeans had taken from them.

Throughout the years of tribulation there was one man in Israel whose morale and confidence in Yahweh never wavered—the prophet *Elisha. Well might the king of Israel address him on his deathbed as 'the chariots of Israel and its horsemen' (2 Ki. 13:14). Elisha died with a prediction of victory over the Aramaeans on his lips.

The first half of the 8th century BC witnessed a return of prosperity to Israel, especially under Jeroboam II, the 4th king of Jehu's dynasty. Both Hebrew kingdoms were free from external molestation; Damascus was too weak after her rough handling by Assyria to renew her aggression. Jeroboam extended his kingdom's frontiers and the national wealth increased greatly.

But this increase of national wealth was concentrated in the hands of a relatively small section of the population—the well-to-do merchants and landowners, who enriched themselves at the expense of the peasantry. The smallholders who had formerly tilled their own fields were now obliged in large numbers to become serfs on the growing estates of their wealthy neighbours, cultivating the land which they had once cultivated as independent owners. This increasing disparity between two sections of Israel's freeborn citizens called forth the denunciation of such prophets as Amos and Hosea, the more so as the rich expropriators of their poorer neighbours were punctilious in the performance of what they considered their religious duties. The prophets insisted tirelessly that what Yahweh required from his people was not sacrifices of fatted beasts but righteousness and covenant-loyalty, for lack of which the nation faced disaster greater than anything it had hitherto known.

About 745 BC the dynasty of Jehu ended as it had begun, by assassination and revolt. In that year Tiglath-pileser III became king of Assyria and inaugurated a campaign of imperial conquest which in less than a quarter of a century brought an end to the existence of the kingdom of Israel and to the independence of the kingdom of Judah. Menahem of Israel (*c.* 745–737 BC) paid tribute to Tiglath-pileser, but an anti-Assyrian policy was pursued by Pekah (*c.* 736–732 BC), who allied himself for this purpose with Damascus. Tiglath-pileser took Damascus, abolished the monarchy and transformed the territory into an Assyrian province; the N and Transjordanian regions of Israel were detached and made into Assyrian provinces. The upper strata of the populations of these areas were deported and replaced by immigrants from other parts of the Assyrian empire. When Hoshea, the last king of Israel, withheld payment of tribute from Assyria at the instance of Egypt, he was imprisoned. Samaria, his capital, was stormed in 722 BC after a 3-years' siege, and became the seat of government of the Assyrian province of Samaria. A further deportation took place—according to Assyrian records 27,290 people were taken captive—and foreign settlers were sent to take their place.

V. The province of Samaria

The deportation of Israelites from the N and Transjordanian territories was so thorough that these territories quite lost their Israelite character. In the province of Samaria it was different; the immigrants in due course adopted Israelite religion—'the law of the god of the land' (2 Ki. 17:26ff.)—and were completely assimilated to the Israelites who had not been carried away; but the *Samaritans, as the population of the province of Samaria were later called, came to be despised as racial and religious half-breeds by the people of Judah farther S, especially from the end of the 6th century BC onward.

King Hezekiah of Judah attempted (*c.* 705 BC) to revive the religious unity of Israel by inviting the people of Samaria to come to Jerusalem to worship, but his attempt was rendered ineffective by Sennacherib's invasion of Judah (701 BC). Greater success attended the action of Hezekiah's great-grandson Josiah, who took advantage of the recession of Assyrian power to extend his political sovereignty and religious reformation into the regions formerly belonging to the kingdom of Israel (621 BC). The fact that he tried to bar Pharaoh Neco's advance at Megiddo is evidence enough of the expansion of his kingdom, but his death there (609 BC) brought an end to such hopes as might have been cherished of the reunion of all Israel under a prince of the house of David. The land of Israel passed under the hegemony of Egypt, and a few years later under that of Babylonia.

The Babylonians appear to have perpetuated the Assyrian provincial organization in the W. After the assassination of Gedaliah, governor of Judah under the Babylonians, the land of Judah with the exception of the Negeb (now being occupied by the Edomites) was added to the province of Samaria (*c.* 582 BC). No great change in this respect resulted from the Persian conquest (539 BC), except that the men of Judah exiled under Nebuchadrezzar were allowed to return and settle in Jerusalem and the surrounding area, which now became the separate, if tiny, province of Judaea under a governor appointed by the Persian king (*JUDAH, V).

The Samaritans made friendly overtures to the restored exiles and offered to co-operate in rebuilding the Jerusalem Temple, but these overtures were not welcomed by the Judaeans, who no doubt feared that they would be swamped by the much greater numbers of the Samaritans, and also had serious doubts of the Samaritans' racial and religious purity. In consequence, a long-standing breach which might have been healed at this time became more bitter than ever, and the Samaritans seized every opportunity to represent the Judaeans to the Persian authorities in an unfavourable light. They were unable to prevent the rebuilding of the Jerusalem Temple, which had been authorized by Cyrus in 538 BC, but they had better success for a time in obstructing the Judaeans' attempts to fortify Jerusalem. When, however, Artaxerxes I sent *Nehemiah to Judah as governor in 445 BC, with express directions to rebuild the walls of Jerusalem, the Samaritans and other neighbours of Judah might betray their chagrin in various ways but could take no effective action in face of the royal edict.

The governor of Samaria at this time was *Sanballat, who continued in office for many years. In 408 BC he is mentioned in a letter from the Jewish community of Elephantine (*PAPYRI, **II.** *c*) in Egypt, who seek the good offices of Sanballat's sons in procuring permission from the Persian court for the rebuilding of their temple, which had been destroyed in an anti-Jewish riot 2 or 3 years previously. This temple had been built more than a century before to serve the religious needs of a Jewish community which the Egyptian kings of Dynasty 26 had settled on their S frontier as an insurance against Ethiopian inroads. Before writing to Sanballat's sons, the Elephantine Jews had tried to enlist the aid of the high priest in Jerusalem, but he had paid no attention to their plea; no doubt he disapproved of the existence of a rival temple to that in Jerusalem. Sanballat's sons—not unnaturally, in view of the relations between Samaria and Jerusalem—showed greater alacrity, and procured the necessary permission for the rebuilding of the Elephantine temple.

The fact that it was Sanballat's sons and not their father whom the Elephantine Jews approached suggests that, while Sanballat was still nominally governor, his sons were discharging many of his duties on his behalf, probably because of his age.

The Elephantine papyri which supply us with our information about this Jewish community in Egypt are particularly interesting because they portray a group of Jews who show no signs of having been influenced by the reformation of Josiah's days. In this they form a strong contrast to the Jews who returned from exile to Jerusalem and the surrounding territory. The latter, together with their brethren in Babylonia, had learnt the lesson of exile, and were increasingly marked by strict adherence to the Torah, including especially those features of it which were calculated to mark off the people of the law from all other communities. The emergence of the Jews as the people of the law in the most particularist sense is associated above all with the work of *Ezra, under whom the Pentateuchal law became the recognized constitution of the Judaean temple-state, subject to the overriding authority of the Persian court.

The work of Ezra (which had the whole-hearted backing of Nehemiah as governor) meant that the cleavage between the Samaritans and Judaeans was less likely than ever to be mended. Some time before 400 BC a scion of the Jerusalem high-priestly family, Manasseh by name, who had married a daughter of Sanballat, was installed by his father-in-law as high priest of the ancient holy place on Mt Gerizim, near Shechem, where a temple was built by royal permission. The rival cult thus established to that of Jerusalem has survived to the present day—based, remarkably enough, on the same law-book as that recognized by the Jews.

VI. Under the Macedonians

The conquest of the Persian empire by Alexander the Great brought no constitutional changes either to Samaria or to Judah. These provinces were now administered by Graeco-Macedonian governors in place of the former Persian governors, and tribute had to be paid to the new overlord in place of the old one. The Jewish *diaspora*, which had been widespread under the Persian empire—Haman did not exaggerate when he described them to Xerxes as 'dispersed among the peoples in all the provinces of your kingdom' (Est. 3:8)—now found new centres to settle in, especially Alexandria and Cyrene. Hellenistic influences inevitably began to give evidence of their presence among them. These influences in some directions were good; we may think in particular of the situation among the Greek-speaking Jews of Alexandria which necessitated the translation of the Pentateuch and other OT writings into Greek in the 3rd and 2nd centuries BC, and thus made the knowledge of Israel's God accessible to the Gentile world (*TEXTS AND VERSIONS, OT). On the other hand, there was a tendency to imitate features of Hellenistic culture which were inextricably interwoven with paganism and which otherwise blurred the distinction between Yahweh's 'peculiar people' and their neighbours. How far a prominent Jewish family could go in unscrupulous assimilation to the unworthier aspects of life under the Hellenistic monarchies is illustrated by Josephus's account of the fortunes of the Tobiads, who enriched themselves as tax-collectors on behalf first of the Ptolemies and then of the Seleucids.

Among the dynasties which inherited Alexander's empire, the two which chiefly affect the history of Israel are those of the Ptolemies in Egypt and of the Seleucids who dominated Syria and the lands beyond the Euphrates. From 320 to 198 BC the Ptolemies' rule extended from Egypt into Asia as far as the Lebanon range and the Phoenician coast, including Judaea and Samaria. In 198 BC the Seleucid victory at Panion, near the sources of Jordan, meant that Judaea and Samaria were now tributary to Antioch instead of Alexandria. The defeat which the Seleucid king Antiochus III suffered at the hands of the Romans at Magnesia in 190 BC, and the heavy indemnity which they imposed on him, involved an enormous increase of taxation for his subjects, including the Jews. When his son, Antiochus IV, attempted to redress the situation by imposing his sovereignty over Egypt (in the two campaigns of 169 and 168 BC), the Romans forced him to relinquish these ambitions. Judaea, on the SW frontier of his kingdom, now became a region of strategic importance, and he felt that there was grave reason for suspecting the loyalty of his Jewish subjects. On the advice of unwise counsellors, he decided to abolish their distinctive nationhood and religion, and the climax of this policy was the installation of a pagan cult—the worship of Zeus Olympios (a name metamorphosed by the Jews into 'the abomination of desolation')—in the Temple at Jerusalem in December 167 BC. The Samaritan temple on Gerizim was similarly diverted to the worship of Zeus Xenios.

Many pious Jews endured martyrdom at this time sooner than forswear their religion. Others took up arms against their overlord. Among the latter were members of the priestly family of the Hasmonaeans, headed by Mattathias of Modin and his five sons. The outstanding son, Judas Maccabaeus, was a born leader of men, who excelled in guerrilla warfare. His initial successes against the royal forces brought many of his fellow-countrymen under his leadership, including a large number of the pious people in Israel, the *ḥᵃsîḏîm* (*HASIDAEANS) who realized that passive resistance was not enough in face of the present threat to their national and religious existence. Larger armies were sent against them by the king, but they too were routed by the unexpected tactics of Judas and his men.

It became clear to the king that his policy had misfired, and Judas was invited to send ambassadors to Antioch to discuss conditions of peace. Antiochus had military plans for the reconquest of seceding territories in the E part of his kingdom, and it was important to reach a settlement on his Egyptian frontier. The basic Jewish condition was, naturally, the complete rescission of the ban on Jewish religious practice. This was conceded; the Jews became free to practise their ancestral religion. The concession was followed at once by the purification of the Temple from the idolatrous cult which had been installed in it, and its rededication to the age-long worship of the God of Israel. The dedication of the Temple at the end of 164 BC (ever afterwards commemorated in the festival of Hanukkah; *cf.* Jn. 10:22) was probably not envisaged in the terms of peace, but in itself it might have been accepted as a *fait accompli*.

It speedily became clear, however, that Judas, with his brothers and followers, was not content with the regaining of religious liberty. Having won that success by force of arms, they continued their struggle in order to win political independence. The dedication of the Temple was followed by the fortification of the Temple hill, over against the citadel or Akra (*JERUSALEM, IV) which was manned by a royal garrison. Judas sent armed bands to Galilee, Transjordan and other regions where there were isolated Jewish communities and brought them back to the safety of those parts of Judaea which were controlled by his forces.

Such a succession of hostile acts could not be overlooked by the Seleucid government, and further armies were sent against Judas. Judas fell in battle in the spring of 160 BC, and for a time the cause which he had led seemed lost. But events played into the hands of his successors. In particular, the death of Antiochus IV in 164 BC was followed by a lengthy period of intermittent civil war in the Seleucid empire, between rival claimants to the throne and their respective partisans. Jonathan, the brother of Judas who took his place as leader of the insurgent party, lay low until times were propitious, and then by diplomatic dealing won rapid and astounding advancement. In 152 BC Alexander Balas, who claimed the Seleucid throne on the ground that he was the son of Antiochus IV (the validity of this claim is difficult to assess), authorized Jonathan to maintain his own military force in Judaea and recognized him as high priest of the Jews, in return for Jonathan's promise to support him.

Antiochus IV had begun his intervention in Jewish religious affairs, which ultimately brought about the Hasmonaean rising, by deposing and appointing Jewish high priests at his own discretion, in defiance of ancient custom. Now a Hasmonaean accepted the high-priesthood from a man whose title to bestow it was based on his claim to be son and successor to Antiochus IV. So much for the high ideals with which the struggle had begun!

The pious groups who had lent their aid to the Hasmonaeans, at a time when it seemed that only by Hasmonaean might could religious freedom be regained, were disposed to be content when that goal was attained, and grew increasingly critical of the Hasmonaeans' dynastic ambitions. But no feature of these ambitions displeased them more than the Hasmonaean assumption of the high-priesthood. Some of them refused to recognize any high-priesthood other than the Zadokite one as legitimate, and looked forward to a day when the sons of Zadok would once more officiate in a purified Temple (*DEAD SEA SCROLLS). One branch of the Zadokite family was permitted to found a Jewish temple at Leontopolis in Egypt and function in the high-priestly office there; but a temple outside the land of Israel could not be countenanced by those *ḥ^a^sîḏîm* who had any regard for the law.

In 143 BC Jonathan was trapped and put to death by one of the rival claimants for mastery of the Seleucid kingdom, but he was succeeded by his brother Simon, under whom the Jews achieved complete independence from the Gentile yoke. This independence was granted in a rescript from the Seleucid king Demetrius II in May 142 BC, by which the Jews were released from the obligation to pay tribute. Simon followed up this diplomatic success by reducing the last vestiges of Seleucid ascendancy in Judaea—the fortress of Gazara (Gezer) and the citadel in Jerusalem. Demetrius had embarked on an expedition against the Parthians, and could take no action against Simon, even had he so wished. Simon received signal honours from his grateful fellow-Jews for the freedom and peace which he had secured for them. At a meeting of the popular assembly of the Jews in September 140 BC, it was decreed, in consideration of the patriotic achievements of himself and his brothers before him, that he should be appointed ethnarch or governor of the nation, commander-in-chief of the army and hereditary high priest. This triple authority he bequeathed to his descendants and successors.

Simon was assassinated at Jericho in 134 BC by his son-in-law Ptolemy, son of Abubus, who hoped to seize supreme power in Judaea. But Simon's son, John Hyrcanus, thwarted the assassin's plans and secured his position as successor to his father.

The Seleucid king Antiochus VII, who had tried to reassert his authority over Judaea during Simon's later years, succeeded in imposing tribute on John Hyrcanus for the first few years of his rule. But the death of Antiochus VII in battle with the Parthians in 128 BC brought Seleucid overlordship over Judaea to a decisive end.

VII. The Hasmonaean Dynasty

In the 7th year of John Hyrcanus, then, the independent state of Judaea was firmly established, 40 years after Antiochus IV had abolished its old constitution as an autonomous temple-state within the empire. The devotion of the *ḥ^a^sîḏîm*, the military genius of Judas and the statesmanship of Simon, together with increasing division and weakness in the Seleucid government, had won for the Jews more (to all outward appearance) than they had lost at the hands of Antiochus IV. No wonder, then, that the early years of independence under John Hyrcanus were looked back to by later generations as a kind of golden age.

It was in the time of John Hyrcanus that the final breach between the majority of the *ḥ^a^sîḏîm* and the Hasmonaean family came about. John was offended by their objections to his tenure of the high-priesthood, and broke with them. From this time onward they appear in history as the party of the *Pharisees, although it is not certain that they

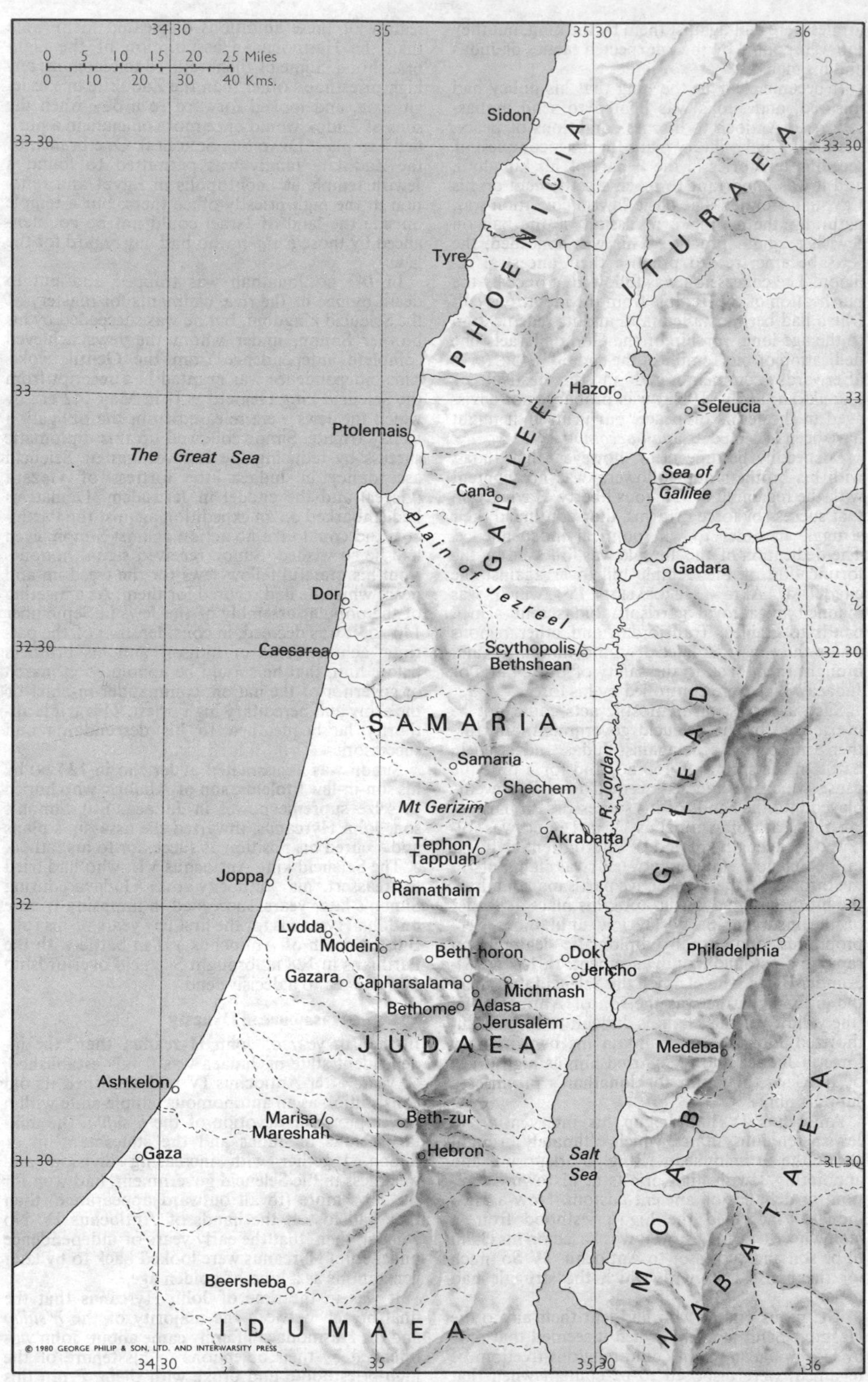

Israel in the inter-testamental period.

owed that name (Heb. *pᵉrûšîm*, 'separated ones') to the fact of their withdrawal from their former alliance with the Hasmonaeans, as has frequently been supposed. They remained in opposition to the regime for 50 years. Those religious leaders who supported the regime and manned the national council appear about the same time with the name *Sadducees.

John Hyrcanus profited by the growing weakness of the Seleucid kingdom to extend his own power. One of his earliest actions after the establishment of Jewish independence was to invade Samaritan territory and besiege Samaria, which held out for a year but was then stormed and destroyed. Shechem was also captured and the Samaritan shrine on Mt Gerizim was demolished. The Samaritans appealed to the Seleucid king for help, but the Romans warned him not to interfere. The Hasmonaeans, at an early stage in their struggle, had secured a treaty of alliance with the Romans, and this treaty was renewed by John.

To the S of his kingdom John warred against the Idumaeans, conquered them and forced them to accept circumcision and adopt the Jewish religion. He reduced Greek cities in Transjordan and invaded Galilee.

His work in Galilee was continued by his son and successor Aristobulus I (104–103 BC), who forced the subjected Galileans to accept Judaism, as his father had done with the Idumaeans.

According to Josephus, Aristobulus assumed the title 'king' instead of that of 'ethnarch' with which his grandfather and (so far as we know) his father had been content, and wore a diadem in token of his royal estate. No doubt he hoped in this way to enjoy greater prestige among his Gentile neighbours, although his coins designate him, in language more congenial to his Jewish subjects, as 'Judah the high priest'.

Aristobulus died (perhaps of phthisis) after a year's reign and was succeeded by his brother Alexander Jannaeus (103–76 BC), who married his widow Salome Alexandra. A more inappropriate high priest than Jannaeus could hardly be imagined. He did go through the motions of his sacred office on occasions of high ceremony—and did so in a way that deliberately offended the sentiments of many of his most religiously minded subjects (especially the Pharisees). But the master-ambition of his reign was military conquest. His pursuit of this policy brought him many reverses, but by the end of his reign he had brought under his control practically all the territory that had been Israelite in the great days of the nation's history—at a ruinous cost to all that was of value in his people's spiritual heritage.

Greek cities on the Mediterranean seaboard and in Transjordan were his special targets for attack; one after another he besieged and conquered them, showing by his ruthless vandalism how little he cared for the true values of Hellenistic civilization. He modelled his way of life on that of the cruder Hellenistic princelings of W Asia. Feeling against him on the part of many of his Jewish subjects reached such a pitch that, when he suffered a disastrous defeat at the hands of a Nabataean force in Transjordan in 94 BC, they revolted against him and even enlisted the aid of the Seleucid king Demetrius III. But other Jewish subjects of Jannaeus, however much they disliked him, found the spectacle of a Seleucid king being called in to help a revolt against a member of the Hasmonaean family too much for their patriotism; they volunteered to support the cause of their hard-pressed king and enabled him to put down the revolt and send the Seleucid contingents packing. The barbarity of the revenge which Jannaeus took against the leaders of the revolt (who evidently included some outstanding Pharisees) was long remembered with horror.

Jannaeus bequeathed his kingdom to his widow, Salome Alexandra, who ruled it as queen regnant for 9 years. She bestowed the high-priesthood on her elder son, Hyrcanus II. In one important respect she reversed the policy of her predecessors; she befriended the Pharisees and paid attention to their counsel throughout her reign.

Her death in 67 BC was followed by civil war between the supporters of the claims of her two sons, Hyrcanus II and Aristobulus II, to succeed to supreme power in Judaea. Aristobulus was a typical Hasmonaean prince, ambitious and aggressive; Hyrcanus was a nonentity, but was easily manipulated by those who supported his claims in their own interests, among whom the dominating personality was the Idumaean Antipater, whose father had been governor of Idumaea under Jannaeus.

The civil strife between the two brothers and their respective partisans was halted by the Romans in 63 BC, in circumstances which brought Judaea's short-lived independence under the Hasmonaeans to an end.

VIII. The Roman supremacy

In 66 BC the Roman senate and people sent their most brilliant general at that time, Pompey, to bring to a successful conclusion the war which they had been waging intermittently for over 20 years with Mithridates, king of Pontus, who had carved out an empire for himself in W Asia from the lands of the decadent Seleucid kingdom and neighbouring states. Pompey was not long in defeating Mithridates (who fled to Crimea and committed suicide there); but having done that, he found himself faced with the necessity of reorganizing the political life of W Asia. In 64 BC he annexed Syria as a province of Rome, and was invited by various parties in the Jewish state to intervene in its affairs too and put an end to the civil war between the sons of Jannaeus.

Thanks to Antipater's shrewd appraisal of the situation, the party favouring Hyrcanus showed itself willing to co-operate with Rome, and Jerusalem opened its gates to Pompey in the spring of 63 BC. The Temple, however, which was separately fortified and was held by the partisans of Aristobulus, sustained a siege of 3 months before it was taken by Pompey's forces.

Judaea now became tributary to Rome. She was deprived of the Greek cities which the Hasmonaean kings had conquered and annexed, and the Samaritans were liberated from Jewish control. Hyrcanus was confirmed in the high-priesthood and leadership of the nation; but he had to be content with the title of 'ethnarch', for the Romans refused to recognize him as king. Antipater continued to support him, determined to exploit this new turn of events to his own advantage, which (it must be conceded) coincided largely with the advantage of Judaea.

Aristobulus and his family endeavoured time after time to foment rebellion against Rome so as to secure power in Judaea for themselves. For many years, however, these attempts proved abortive. Successive Roman governors kept a firm grip on Judaea and Syria, because these provinces now lay on the E frontier of the Roman empire, beyond which was the rival empire of Parthia. The strategic importance of this area may be gauged by the number of dominant figures in Roman history who play a part in the history of Judaea in these years—Pompey, who annexed it to the empire; Crassus, who as governor of Syria in 54–53 BC plundered the Jerusalem Temple and many other temples in Syria while collecting resources for a war against the Parthians, but was defeated and killed by them at Carrhae in 53 BC; Julius Caesar, who became master of the Roman world after defeating Pompey at Pharsalus in 48 BC; Cassius, a leader of Caesar's assassins, who as proconsul of Syria from 44 BC proved financially oppressive to Judaea; Antony, who dominated the E provinces of the empire after he and Octavian had defeated Caesar's assassins and their followers at Philippi in 42 BC; and then Octavian himself, who defeated Antony and Cleopatra at Actium in 31 BC and thereafter ruled the Roman world alone as the emperor Augustus. Throughout the vicissitudes of Roman civil and external war Antipater and his family made it their settled policy to support the chief representative of Roman power in the E at any one time, whoever he might be and whichever party in the Roman state he might belong to. Julius Caesar in particular had reason to be grateful for Antipater's support when he was besieged in Alexandria during the winter of 48–47 BC, and he conferred special privileges not only on Antipater himself but on the Jews as well.

This confidence which the Romans learnt to place in Antipater's family was manifested outstandingly in 40 BC, when the Parthians invaded Syria and Palestine and enabled Antigonus, the last surviving son of Aristobulus II, to regain the Hasmonaean throne and reign as king and high priest of the Jews. Hyrcanus II was mutilated so as to be disqualified from ever becoming high priest again. Antipater was now dead, but an attempt was made to seize and liquidate his family. One son, Phasael, was captured and killed, but Herod, the ablest of Antipater's sons, escaped to Rome, where the senate nominated him king of the Jews, at the instance of Antony and Octavian. It was his task now to recover Judaea from Antigonus (who was left in peace by the Roman commander in Syria when the Parthian invaders were driven out) and to rule his kingdom in the interests of the Romans, as their 'friend and ally'. The task was not easy, and its successful completion in 37 BC, with the storming of Jerusalem after a siege of 3 months, secured for Herod a bitter ill-will on the part of his new subjects which no effort of his could remove. Antigonus was sent in chains to Antony, who ordered him to be executed. Herod tried to legitimate his position in Jewish eyes by marrying Mariamne, a Hasmonaean princess, but this marriage brought him more trouble, not less.

Herod's position was precarious for the first 6 years of his reign. Although Antony was his friend and patron, Cleopatra longed to incorporate Judaea in her kingdom, as her earlier Ptolemaic ancestors had done, and tried to exploit her ascendancy over Antony to this end. The overthrow of Antony and Cleopatra in 31 BC, and Herod's confirmation in his kingdom by the conqueror, Augustus, brought him some relief externally, but domestic peace was denied him both in his family circle and in his relations with the Jewish people. Yet he governed Judaea with a firm hand, serving the interests of Rome even better than a Roman governor could have done. (For further details of his reign, *HEROD, **1**.)

When Herod died in 4 BC his kingdom was divided among three of his surviving sons. Archelaus governed Judaea and Samaria as ethnarch until AD 6; Antipas governed Galilee and Peraea as tetrarch until AD 39; Philip received as a tetrarchy the territory E and NE of the Sea of Galilee which his father had pacified in the emperor's interests, and ruled it until his death in AD 34. (*HEROD, **2**, **3**; *PHILIP, **2**.)

Antipas inherited a full share of his father's political acumen, and continued the thankless task of promoting the Roman cause in his tetrarchy and the surrounding regions. Archelaus, however, had all his father's brutality without his genius, and soon drove his subjects to the point where they petitioned the Roman emperor to remove him so as to prevent a revolt from breaking out. Archelaus was accordingly deposed and banished, and his ethnarchy was reconstituted as a Roman province of the third grade. In order that its annual yield of tribute to the imperial exchequer might be assessed, the governor of Syria, *Quirinius, held a census in Judaea and Samaria. This census provoked the rising of *Judas the Galilean, and, while the rising was crushed, its ideals lived on in the party of the *Zealots, who maintained that the payment of tribute to Caesar, or to any other pagan ruler, was an act of treason to Israel's God.

After the census, Judaea (as the province of Judaea and Samaria was called) received a prefect as governor. These prefects were appointed by the emperor and were subject to the general supervision of the governors of Syria. The early Roman prefects exercised the privilege of appointing the high priest of Israel—a privilege which, since the end of the Hasmonaean dynasty, had been exercised by Herod and Archelaus after him. The prefects sold the sacred office to the highest bidder, and its religious prestige was naturally very low. By virtue of his office the high priest presided over the *Sanhedrin, which administered the internal affairs of the nation.

Of the earlier prefects the only one whose name is well known is Pontius *Pilate, whose harsh and stubborn character is recorded in the pages of Josephus and Philo—not to mention the part he plays in the NT narrative. His construction of a new aqueduct to provide Jerusalem and the Temple with a better water-supply illustrates the material benefits of Roman rule; his flouting the religious scruples of the Jews by insisting on defraying the expense of it from the sacred Temple-fund illustrates an aspect of Roman rule which was largely responsible for the revolt of AD 66—the insensitivity of many of the governors to local feeling.

For a short time, between the years 41 and 44, Judaea enjoyed a welcome relief from administration by Roman prefects. Herod Agrippa I, a grandson of Herod the Great and Mariamne, to whom the emperor Gaius had given Philip's former tetrarchy as a kingdom in AD 37 (augmenting it by the addition of Galilee and Peraea in AD 39, after the deposition and banishment of Antipas), received Judaea and Samaria as further extensions of his kingdom from the emperor Claudius in AD 41 (*HEROD, **4**). Because of his descent from the Hasmonaeans (through Mariamne) he was popular with his Jewish subjects. But his sudden death in AD 44, at the age of 54, meant that the province of Judaea (now including Galilee as well as Samaria) reverted to rule by Roman governors, now called procurators, since Agrippa's son, Agrippa the Younger (*HEROD, 5), was too young to be entrusted with his father's royal responsibility. One concession was made to Jewish sentiment, however: the privilege of appointing the high priest, which Agrippa had inherited from the prefects who preceded him, did not go back to the procurators who followed him, but was given first to his brother Herod of Chalcis, and then (after the death of that Herod in AD 48) to Agrippa the Younger.

IX. End of the second commonwealth

During the 20 years or so that followed the death of Herod Agrippa I, troubles multiplied in Judaea. The people in general found the re-imposition of procurators all the more irksome after their brief spell of government by a Jewish king; and the procurators themselves did little to conciliate the sentiments of their Jewish subjects. There was a succession of risings stirred up by pseudo-Messiahs such as *Theudas, who was killed by a cavalry detachment sent against him by the procurator Fadus (AD 44–46), or by Zealot leaders such as James and Simon (two sons of Judas the Galilean), crucified by the next procurator Tiberius Julius Alexander (AD 46–48). The fact that Alexander was a renegade Jew, scion of an illustrious Jewish family of Alexandria, did nothing to ingratiate him with the Jews of Judaea.

It was during the procuratorships of Fadus and Alexander that Judaea was hard hit by the famine of Acts 11:28. Josephus records how Helena, the queen-mother of Adiabene, E of the Tigris, bought grain in Egypt and figs in Cyprus at this time for the relief of the famine-stricken people of Judaea. The royal family of Adiabene were the most distinguished Jewish proselytes of the period; some of them actually fought on the Jewish side in the war against Rome which broke out in AD 66.

Under the procuratorship of *Felix disaffection increased in Judaea. Felix set himself energetically to rid the province of insurgent bands, and his severe measures against them were attended by temporary success, but they alienated large numbers of the population, in whose eyes the insurgents were not criminals but patriots.

The closing years of Felix's procuratorship were attended by fierce riots between the Gentile and Jewish inhabitants of Caesarea, arising out of a dispute about civic privileges. Felix sent the leaders of both parties to Rome to have the matter decided by the emperor, but was himself recalled and replaced in the procuratorship by Festus (AD 59). The Caesarean dispute was decided in favour of the Gentiles, and Jewish resentment at the decision, coupled with the Gentiles' malicious exploitation of their victory, was one of the factors in the explosion of AD 66.

*Festus was a relatively just and mild governor, but he died in office in AD 62, and his two successors, Albinus and Florus, by their persistent offending of Jewish national and religious sentiment, played into the hands of the anti-Roman extremists. The last straw was Florus' sacrilegious seizure of 17 talents from the Temple treasury. This provoked a riot which was put down with much bloodshed. The moderate elements in the nation, aided by the younger Agrippa, counselled restraint, but the people were in no mood to listen to them. They cut the communications between the fortress of Antonia and the Temple courts, and the captain of the Temple, who was leader of the war-party in Jerusalem, formally renounced the imperial authority by putting an end to the daily sacrifice for the emperor's welfare.

Matters had now escaped Florus' control, and even the intervention of Cestius Gallus, governor of Syria, with stronger military forces than Florus had at his disposal, proved ineffective. Gallus had to withdraw, and his army suffered heavy losses on its retreat through the pass of Beth-horon (November AD 66).

This success, as it seemed to the insurgent Jews, filled them with false optimism. The extremists' policy appeared to have been vindicated: Rome could not stand before them. The whole of Palestine was placed on a war footing.

But Vespasian, who was entrusted with the putting down of the revolt, set about his task methodically. In 67 he crushed the rebellion in Galilee. Some of the leaders of the Galilean revolt, however, escaped to Jerusalem, and their arrival there added to the internal strife which racked the city during its last years and months. In the summer of 68 Vespasian was approaching Jerusalem itself when news came of Nero's deposition and death at Rome. The ensuing civil war at the heart of the empire nerved the defenders of Jerusalem with fresh hope; it looked from their standpoint as though Rome and the empire were on the verge of dissolution and Daniel's 5th monarchy was about to be established on their ruins.

From Caesarea, Vespasian watched the progress of events at Rome. On 1 July, AD 69, he himself was proclaimed emperor at Alexandria by the governor of Egypt (the same apostate Jew, Alexander, who had earlier been procurator of Judaea); the example of Alexandria was swiftly followed in Caesarea and Antioch and by the armies in most of the E provinces. Vespasian returned to Rome to occupy the imperial throne, leaving his son Titus to complete the suppression of the revolt in Judaea. By the end of AD 69 all Judaea had been subdued except Jerusalem and three strongholds overlooking the Dead Sea.

Jerusalem was invested in the spring of AD 70. By May half the city was in the hands of the Romans, but the defenders refused to accept terms of submission. On 24 July the fortress of Antonia was stormed; 12 days later the daily sacrifices ceased in the Temple, and on 29 August the sanctuary itself was set on fire and destroyed. Four weeks later the whole city was in Titus' hands. It was razed to the ground, except for part of the W wall, with three towers of Herod's palace on that wall, which provided headquarters for a Roman garrison. The last centre of revolt to be crushed was the almost impregnable fortress of Masada, SW of the Dead Sea, where a Zealot force held out until the spring of AD 74 and then committed mass-suicide in preference to being captured.

Judaea was reconstituted as a province under its own imperial legate, directly responsible to the emperor and in no way subordinate to the imperial legate of Syria; unlike the procurators, the imperial legates of Judaea had legionary forces under their command. The former Temple tax, which Jews throughout the world had paid for the maintenance of the house of God at Jerusalem, was still exacted, but it was now diverted to the maintenance of the temple of Jupiter on the Capitoline hill in Rome.

With the disappearance of the Temple hierarchy and the Sanhedrin as formerly organized, the chief internal authority in the Jewish nation passed to a new Sanhedrin of rabbis, led at first by Yohanan ben Zakkai, a teacher of the school of Hillel. This religious court exercised its control through the synagogues and began the work of codifying the traditional body of oral law which was in due course committed to writing in the Mishnah towards the end of the 2nd century AD. It was in large measure due to the action of Yohanan ben Zakkai and his colleagues and their successors that Israel's national and religious identity survived the downfall of the Temple and the Second Jewish Commonwealth in AD 70 (*TALMUD AND MIDRASH.)

See also *JUDAH; *ARCHAEOLOGY; *SACRIFICE; *LAW, *etc.* and entries on individual kings and places.

BIBLIOGRAPHY. R. de Vaux, *The Early History of Israel*, 2 vols., 1977; G. W. Ahlström, *Who were the Israelites?*, 1986; J. A. Soggin, *A History of Israel*, 1984; J. M. Miller and J. H. Hayes, *A History of Ancient Israel and Judah*, 1986; B. Halpern, *The Emergence of Israel in Canaan*, 1983; N. P. Lemche, *Ancient Israel*, 1988; *Early Israel*, 1985.

F.F.B.

ISRAEL OF GOD. Paul's statement that 'not all who are descended from Israel belong to Israel' (Rom. 9:6) is in line with the prophetic insistence that the true people of God, those who are worthy of the name of Israel, may be but a relatively small 'remnant' of faithful souls within the nation of Israel. In the NT the concept of such a remnant appears in the preaching of John the Baptist, who insists that descent from Abraham is valueless in itself (Mt. 3:9 = Lk. 3:8). Jesus' calling of disciples around himself to form the 'little flock' who were to receive the kingdom (Lk. 12:32; *cf.* Dn. 7:22, 27) marks him out as the founder of the new Israel; he explicitly designated the twelve apostles as judges of 'the twelve tribes of Israel' in the new age (Mt. 19:28; Lk. 22:30). The 'little flock' was to be augmented by the accession of 'other sheep' who had never belonged to the Jewish fold (Jn. 10:16).

Whether the expression 'the Israel of God' in its one appearance in the NT (Gal. 6:16) denotes believing Jews only, or believing Jews and Gentiles without distinction, is disputed; the latter is more probable, especially if the expression is to be construed in apposition to 'all who walk by this rule'. But that the community of believers in Jesus, irrespective of their natural origin, is looked upon as the new Israel throughout the NT is clear. They are 'the twelve tribes in the dispersion' (Jas. 1:1), 'the exiles of the dispersion' (1 Pet. 1:1), who are further designated, in language borrowed from OT descriptions of Israel, as 'a chosen race, a royal priesthood, a holy nation, God's own people' (1 Pet. 2:9).

But the nucleus of this new Israel is Jewish (Rom. 11:18). And while the greater proportion of 'Israel according to the flesh' is at present prevented, by a partial and temporary blindness, from recognizing their ancestral hope in Jesus, the time is coming when the veil will be removed from their eyes (2 Cor. 3:16) and they will be re-established by faith as members of the beloved community: their present estrangement will last only 'until the full number of the Gentiles come in, and so all Israel will be saved' (Rom. 11:25ff.).

BIBLIOGRAPHY. L. Gillet, *Communion in the Messiah*, 1942; M. Simon, *Verus Israel*, 1948; R. Campbell, *Israel and the New Covenant*, 1954; J. Munck, *Paul and the Salvation of Mankind*, E.T. 1959; *idem, Christ and Israel*, 1967; P. Richardson, *Israel in the Apostolic Church*, 1970; *BAICS* 6, f.c.

F.F.B.

ISSACHAR. 1. The fifth son of Jacob and Leah and the ninth son of Jacob (Gn. 30:18; 35:23). The name may derive from a compound of Heb. *'îš*, 'man', and *śāḵār*, 'wages', hence 'a hired worker', although others suggest a less likely connection with a verbal form, meaning, 'May (God) show mercy'. Issachar's tribal portion fell between Mt Gilboa and the hills of Lower Galilee, at the E end of the Valley of Jezreel, but the boundaries cannot be drawn precisely. In some of the lists (*e.g.*, Jdg. 1:30) Issachar is not mentioned and may have been included with Zebulun (as Simeon was incorporated with Judah). Manasseh also seems to have expanded N into the territory of Issachar. Sixteen cities and their associated villages were assigned to Issachar (Jos. 19:17–23; *cf.* 17:10–11).

The close connection between Zebulun and Issachar is shown in their inclusion in a common blessing (Dt. 33:18–19). The mountain mentioned is undoubtedly Tabor, where there was a common sanctuary.

Issachar was involved in the campaign led by Deborah, who probably came from this tribe (Jdg. 5:15), although it is not mentioned in the prose account (ch. 4). The battle began in Issachar's territory and completely broke the Canaanite domination of the low-lying areas. The minor judge, Tola, was a man of Issachar (Jdg. 10:1) as was also the usurper, Baasha (1 Ki. 15:27). Issachar was one of the twelve administrative districts set up by Solomon (1 Ki. 4:17).

The blessing of Jacob (Gn. 49:14–15) has been viewed as evidence that part of Issachar was resident in the land in the Amarna period, maintaining its position by giving a certain amount of compulsory labour to its Canaanite overlords. But the implied reproach may be merely a statement of the fact that Issachar's material prosperity made it submissive and effete. At the time of David, however, the tribe had gained a reputation for wisdom (1 Ch. 12:32), a fact which re-emerges in the Talmudic statement that the wisest members of the Sanhedrin came from Issachar.

2. The seventh son of Obed-edom, a Levitical gatekeeper in the Davidic period (1 Ch. 26:5).

BIBLIOGRAPHY. *LOB*, pp. 200, 212, 223, 232f.; A. Alt, *PJB* 24, 1928, pp. 47ff.; W. F. Albright, *JAOS* 74, 1954, pp. 222f.; S. Yeivin, *Mélanges A. Robert*, 1957, pp. 100ff.

A.E.C.

ITALY (Gk. *Italia*). By the middle of the 1st century this name had come to have substantially its modern geographical meaning. 'All roads led to *Rome', and even before the time of Christ many Jews had resorted to Italy, especially to the metropolis. It was because the emperor Claudius had carried out a purge against the Jews that Paul met

*Aquila and Priscilla (Acts 18:2). Italy was the apostle's destination when after his appeal to Caesar he and other prisoners embarked at Caesarea on what was to be his most famous journey (Acts 27:1, 6). In Heb. 13:24 'those who come from Italy' greet the addressees. J.D.D.

ITHAMAR (Heb. *'îṯāmār*). The meaning of the name is uncertain, but may possibly be 'land of palms'. The youngest of Aaron and Elisheba's four sons (Ex. 6:23), Ithamar was ordained to the priesthood (Ex. 28:1) and directed the building of the tabernacle (Ex. 38:21). In the apostasy of Nadab and Abihu he remained faithful in all but the matter of the sin-offering (Lv. 10). He was placed over the Gershonites and Merarites (Nu. 4:28, 33). For evidence that Eli was a descendant of Ithamar, see 1 Sa. 14:3; 22:9; 1 Ch. 24:3. A man called Daniel, one of his descendants, is named among the returning exiles (Ezr. 8:2). G.W.G.

ITHIEL. Probably 'God is with me' (correcting Heb. pointing to *'ittî'ēl*). **1.** A Benjaminite ancestor of Sallu who resided in Jerusalem in Nehemiah's time (Ne. 11:7). **2.** A man mentioned with Ucal in Pr. 30:1. An altering of the word-divisions results in the more satisfactory rendering: 'I have wearied myself, O God (*lā'îṯî 'ēl*), and am consumed' (RVmg.; NEB; *BDB*). D.A.H.

ITHRA (Heb. *yiṯrā'*, 'abundance'). Husband of Abigail, David's sister, and father of Amasa, one of David's generals. Though called an Israelite in 2 Sa. 17:25, the marginal reading and 1 Ch. 2:17 describe him as an Ishmaelite and give his name as 'Jether' (*cf.* 1 Ki. 2:5). J.D.D.

ITHRITE. 'Ithrites' was the name given to one of the families descended from Kiriath-jearim (1 Ch. 2:53). Two members of David's bodyguard, Ira and Gareb, came from this family (2 Sa. 23:38; 1 Ch. 11:40) and may have originated from the town of *Jattir (1 Sa. 30:27). R.A.H.G.

ITTAI (Heb. *'ittay*, ? '(God) is with me'. **1.** The leader of 600 men from Gath, who joined David shortly before Absalom's rebellion. His fidelity was such that he refused to leave the king when he advised him to return (2 Sa. 15:19–22). 'Gittite' indicates that he was a Philistine; he was probably a soldier of fortune who found in David a leader worthy of his loyalty. With Joab and Abishai, he was subsequently one of David's 3 generals (2 Sa. 18:2).

2. A Benjaminite. One of the 'thirty' of David's mighty men (2 Sa. 23:29; 'Ithai' in 1 Ch. 11:31). J.G.G.N.

ITURAEA (Gk. *Itouraia*, Lk. 3:1). The name, mentioned in conjunction with *Trachonitis, almost certainly comes from Heb. *y^eṭûr* (AV 'Jetur'), a son of Ishmael (Gn. 25:15–16; 1 Ch. 1:31), mentioned also as a tribe at war with the Israelites E of the Jordan (1 Ch. 5:19). Little or nothing is known of them thereafter until the time of the Jewish king Aristobulus I (105–104 BC), who is recorded as having fought against the Ituraeans and taken from them a portion of their land (Jos., *Ant.* 13. 318). Thereafter frequent allusion is made to them by classical writers (Josephus, Strabo, Pliny, Dio Cassius, *etc.*). Sometimes they are called Syrians, sometimes Arabians.

At the time of the Roman conquest they were known as a wild robber tribe especially proficient in the use of the bow, but not associated with any precisely defined geographical location. It was part of the territory ruled by Herod the Great, after whose death in 4 BC the kingdom was partitioned, and certain lands including Trachonitis and what was called 'the house of Zeno (or Zenodorus) about Paneas' formed the tetrarchy of Philip (*TETRARCH). If, as seems likely, this latter section was inhabited by Ituraeans, it may have been known as Ituraea, for migratory tribes frequently gave their name to their new home. Josephus, in defining the limits of Philip's sovereignty, does not specifically mention Ituraea—some would say because it was indistinguishable from Trachonitis (*Ant.* 17. 189).

Is Luke's reference, then, to be understood as a noun or as an adjectival form? Does he intend the place or the people? No certainty is possible. Place-names of this region and time are notoriously elastic and liable to corruption, and overlapping is frequently found. The most we can safely say is that it was, in W. Manson's words (*Luke* in *MNTC*), 'a hilly country in the Anti-Lebanon range, inhabited by roving Arabs'.

Caligula gave it to Herod Agrippa I. When the latter died it was incorporated into the province of Syria under procurators.

BIBLIOGRAPHY. A. H. M. Jones, *The Herods of Judaea*, 1938, pp. 9–11, *passim*; E. Schurer, *HJP* 1, 1973, pp. 561–573; W. Schottroff, *ZDPV* 98, 1982, pp. 125–152. J.D.D.

IVA. A town conquered by the Assyrians in Isaiah's time, illustrating the certain defeat of Samaria (2 Ki. 18:34; 19:13; Is. 37:13). Probably Ava of 2 Ki. 17:24. Imm ('Aya) on the Orontes and 'Ama in Elam are among suggested locations. D.J.W. D.W.B.

IVAH. A foreign town conquered by the Assyrians during the time of Isaiah and used as an illustration of the inevitability of the defeat of Samaria (2 Ki. 18:34; 19:13; Is. 37:13). Probably the Ava of 2 Ki. 17:24. The location is unknown. D.W.B.

IVORY (Heb. *šēn*, 'tooth', or *šenhabbîm* (1 Ki. 10:22; 2 Ch. 9:21) thought by some to be 'tooth of elephant' (so LXX), but possibly meaning 'ivory (and) ebony' as in Ezk. 27:15; *cf.* Akkad. *šin piri*).

Ivory was a form of wealth and a mark of luxurious and fine goods (1 Ki. 10:18–22; Rev. 18:12, Gk. *elephantinos*). It was used for thrones and sometimes overlaid with gold (1 Ki. 10:18), for couches (Am. 6:4), and for furnishing and panelling rooms or palaces, hence Ahab's 'house of ivory' in *Samaria (1 Ki. 22:39; *cf.* Ps. 45:8) condemned by Amos (3:15). Its commonest use was in the manufacture of small objects and in composite models, where it simulated human flesh and thus was employed figuratively in poetry (Ct. 5:14; 7:4;

in the latter, 'tower of ivory' may, however, be a reference to a specific locality).

Most ivory in use in Syria and Palestine came from Syrian (so-called 'Asiatic') elephants (*Elephas maximus*) which inhabited the upper Euphrates until hunted to extinction in the late 1st millennium BC. Other sources were India, from which tusks (*qarnôṯ šēn*) were imported by ocean-going ships (2 Ch. 9:17, 21) to Babylonia (Ur) by Phoenicians who decorated their vessels with plaques of ivory (Ezk. 27:6), or overland from the Nilotic Sudan *via* Dedan in central Arabia (v. 15). Five tusks were found in the excavations at *Alalaḫ (Syria).

In the early 3rd millennium ivory was used for carving small figurines (Beersheba area), animal heads (Jericho), or for silhouettes for inlay, in the early Mesopotamian fashion, in wooden objects (El-Jisr). By the following millennium the trade flourished. Tusks are shown on Egyp. paintings and Assyr. sculpture as valued trophies of war. The Syro-Phoenician trade and guilds of ivory-workers under Egyptian influence sought to meet a growing export market to Assyria, making use of inlay, appliqué, ajouré, veneer and fretwork techniques. Furniture, especially chairs, beds, caskets and round boxes (pyxides), are found, some showing foreign influences in design. Remarkable caches of ivories have been recovered from Ras Shamra and Megiddo (*c.* 1200 BC) and Nimrud (*CALAH) in Assyria (*c.* 700 BC). In the Israelite period ivories from Samaria and Hazor attest its use for ladies' hair combs, unguent vases, flasks and elaborate spoons supported by figures of maidens as well as furniture. See also *PHOENICIA, *ARTS AND CRAFTS.

BIBLIOGRAPHY. J. V. and G. M. Crowfoot, *Early Ivories from Samaria*, 1938; I. J. Winter, 'Phoenician and North Syrian Ivory Carving in Historical Context', *Iraq* 38, 1976, pp. 1–22; M. E. L. Mallowan and G. Hermann, *Ivories from Nimrud*, 1–5, 1967–92. D.J.W.

IYE-ABARIM, a stopping-place on the Exodus journey on the borders of Moab (Nu. 21:11; 33:44–45). Iye-abarim (Heb. *'iyyê hā'ᵃḇārîm*, ruins of Abarim, or of the regions beyond) is abbreviated in Nu. 33:45 AV to Iim. Abel identifies it with the ancient site of Maḥaiy to the SE of Moab, Glueck places it farther W, and du Buit chooses a site near the river Arnon. Its position is still debatable. J.A.T.

J

JAAR (Heb. *ya'ar*, 'forest') in the OT usually means 'forest', but once only it may be a proper name (Ps. 132:6) as a poetical abbreviation for *Kiriath-jearim (city of forests). The allusion in this psalm is to the bringing of the ark to Jerusalem from Kiriath-jearim, where it had lain for 20 years or more after it was recovered from the Philistines (1 Sa. 7:1–2; 1 Ch. 13:5). Some take the word here, as elsewhere, to mean forest and refer 'it' to the oath in the preceding verses. M.A.M.

JAAZANIAH (Heb. *ya'ᵃzanyah(u)*, 'Yahweh hears'). **1.** The Judaean army-commander, son of Hoshaiah, who supported Gedaliah at Mizpah (2 Ki. 25:23; Je. 40:8). Jezaniah (Je. 40:8) may be the same as the brother of Azariah (Je. 43:2, LXX). A seal found at Mizpah (Tell en-Nasbeh) inscribed 'Ja'azaniah, servant of the king' may be ascribed to this man, but the name was common, occurring on ostraca from Lachish (1) and Arad (39).

The imprint of an onyx scaraboid seal inscribed in Old Hebrew script (as described in the accompanying article). c. 600 BC.

2. Son of Jeremiah, a Rechabite leader (Je. 35:3). **3.** Son of Shaphan, an Israelite elder, seen in a vision by Ezekiel (8:11) offering incense to idols in Jerusalem. **4.** Son of Azur, seen by Ezekiel at the E gate of the Temple (Ezk. 11:1). D.J.W.

JABAL. A son of Adah, wife of Lamech, and ancestor of those 'who dwell in tents and have cattle (*ûmiqneh*)', or perhaps better 'who dwell in tents and places of reeds' (*m* [local] + *qāneh*, 'reed'). See Gn. 4:20. J.D.D.

JABBOK. A river flowing W into the river Jordan, some 32 km N of the Dead Sea. It rises near Amman (*RABBAH) in Jordan and in all is over 96 km long. It is today called the Wadi Zerqa. It marked a boundary line between Ammonite and Gadite territory (Dt. 3:16), once the Israelites had defeated the Amorite king Sihon S of the Jabbok (Nu. 21:21ff.). It was also the river forded by Jacob (Gn. 32:22) on the occasion of his wrestling with the angel and subsequent change of name. There may well be a play on words here: 'Jabbok' is in Heb. *yabbōq*, while '[and] .. wrestled' is [way] *yē'āḇēq*. In the unvowelled text there is just an extra letter, an aleph, in the latterword. D.F.P.

JABESH-GILEAD (Heb. *yāḇēš gil'āḏ*). An Israelite town E of the Jordan which kept out of the war against Benjamin and suffered severe reprisals (Jdg. 21). Here Saul proved his kingship, routing the Ammonites who were besieging it (1 Sa. 11). The citizens rescued Saul's body from the walls of Beth-shan after the battle of Gilboa (1 Sa. 31; 1 Ch. 10).

Tell abu-Kharaz, on the N side of the Wadi Yabis where it reaches the plain, is the probable site (N. Glueck, *BASOR* 89, 91, 1943; *The River Jordan*, 1946, pp. 159–166). This isolated hill, 3 km from the Jordan and 15 km from Beth-shan, dominates the area and was heavily fortified in Israelite times. Earlier writers located Jabesh smaller sites upstream, but only Tell el-Maqlub is pre-Roman; this Glueck identifies with Abel-meholah. M. Noth (*ZDPV* 69, 1953, p. 28) disputes some of Glueck's arguments, but the fact that Tell abu-Kharaz exists makes Maqlub an unlikely location for Jabesh. J.P.U.L.

JABEZ (Heb. *ya'bēṣ*, 'he makes sorrowful'). **1.** A city, evidently in Judah, inhabited by 'the families of the scribes' (1 Ch. 2:55). **2.** The head of a family of the tribe of Judah (1 Ch. 4:9–10), an 'honourable' man whose prayer God answered. For discussion of a play on the Heb. words here, see C. F. Keil, *Chronicles*, p. 88; J. M. Myers, *I Chronicles*, 1965, pp. 28f. J.D.D.

JABIN (Heb. *yāḇîn*, possibly '[God] perceives'). **1.** A king of *Hazor, leader of an alliance of N princes defeated in battle by Joshua, who afterwards slew Jabin (Jos. 11:1–14). **2.** Another king of Hazor (called 'king of Canaan' in Jdg. 4:2) who for 20 years 'cruelly oppressed' the Israelites, who had been reduced thus to vassalage because of idolatry. Liberation came when Barak and Deborah defeated Jabin's general *Sisera (Jdg. 4:3–16), a notable victory immortalized in the Song of Deborah (Jdg. 5) and leading to the destruction of Jabin (Jdg. 4:23–24), which is briefly referred to also in Ps. 83:9. J.D.D.

JABNEEL (Heb. *yaḇneʾēl,* 'God (El) causes to build'), a name, of which a comparable form *Jabni-ilu* occurs in the Amarna letters, which is used of two places in the Bible.

1. A city on the SW boundary of Judah (Jos. 15:11) and probably to be identified with Jabneh, a Philistine city which was captured by Uzziah (2 Ch. 26:6). Jabneh was called Jamnia in the Gk. and Rom. periods, and it was at this city that the Sanhedrin was re-formed after the destruction of Jerusalem in AD 70.

2. A town of Naphtali (Jos. 19:33), possibly to be identified with modern Khirbet Yamma (see *NEAEHL*, pp. 1515–1516).

BIBLIOGRAPHY. M. Avi-Yonah, *Gazetteer of Roman Palestine* (Qedem, 5), 1976, p. 67; S. Z. Leiman, *The Canonization of Hebrew Scripture*, 1976, pp. 120–124. T.C.M.

JACHIN and BOAZ. The names of the decorated bronze pillars or columns which flanked the entrance to the *Temple of Solomon in Jerusalem (1 Ki. 7:21; 2 Ch. 3:15–17). When Nebuchadrezzar captured Jerusalem in 587 BC, they were broken up and taken to Babylon (2 Ki. 25:13).

I. Description and construction

The columns were 18 cubits high (*c.* 9 m) and 12 cubits in circumference (*c.* 1 m diameter) and were topped with capitals which were 5 cubits high (*c.* 2·5 m) (1 Ki. 7:15–16). The Chronicler gives the height as 35 cubits (2 Ch. 3:15) which is thought to indicate the combined height of both columns allowing 1 cubit for inserting the columns into their bases and capitals. At the time of the destruction of the Temple the capitals are said to be 3 cubits high (2 Ki. 25:17); this reduction in height may have occurred when Jehoash (2 Ki. 12:6ff.) or Josiah (2 Ki. 22:3ff.) undertook renovations in the Temple (*cf.* Je. 52:22). This is preferable to the view that the earlier figure was mis-read or that there has been an error in the transmission of the text.

Various attempts have been made to visualize the decoration as it is described (1 Ki. 7:17–22, 41–42; Je. 52:22–23). It would appear that the capital had four opened and inverted lotus petals (*šušān*, RSV 'lily-work') 4 cubits in width (*bāʾûlām*, 1 Ki. 7:19, RSV 'in the vestibule', so Yeivin) and above this an inverted bowl (*gullā*). This bowl or pommel was encircled by a network (*śᵉḇāḵâ*) fringed with two rows of pomegranates.

The columns and capitals were cast by Hiram, a craftsman from Tyre (1 Ki. 7:13–14), who worked in the ground between Succoth and Zarethan (1 Ki. 7:46). They were hollow (Je. 52:21) and may have been cast with a technique similar to that used by Sennacherib when he had large mythical beasts cast in bronze (*ARAB*, 2, 1927, p. 169; also see Underwood, *Man* 58, 1958, p. 42), or some method akin to the casting of mediaeval cannon barrels may well have been adopted for this immense task.

II. Purpose

Although it has been suggested that the columns supported the roof of the porch, the OT description includes them with the furnishings of the Temple rather than with the architectural element and says that they were placed 'at' or 'near' (1 Ki. 7:21) and 'before' (2 Ch. 3:17) the porch. There is considerable evidence for free-standing columns at the entrances of temple sanctuaries. Bases for columns have been found in 13th-century BC temples at *Hazor, and Kamid el-Loz in a Phoenician temple at Kition and an Israelite temple at *Arad, but whether these were free-standing is impossible to determine. The appearance of the columns can be gauged from clay model shrines found in Palestine and Cyprus (13th–9th centuries BC) and from ivories found at Arslan Tash and Nimrud. Impressions of temples on Greek and Roman coins from Cyprus and Phoenicia and descriptions made by Herodotus (2. 44), Strabo (3. 4. 170) and Lucian (*de dea Syria* 15. 27) reveal that pairs of columns continued to be placed at the entrances of temples until at least the 2nd century AD.

While it is clear that the columns did not serve an architectural function, any religious significance that they may have had is obscure. They may indicate the divine presence, as did the pillars of fire and smoke during the desert wanderings (Ex. 33:9; Dt. 31:15). Various stones and pillars in use from prehistoric times to the present seem to have a similar portent.

III. Names

The names of the columns may enshrine the memory of David's ancestry through his mother (Jachin occurs as a Simeonite name [Nu. 26:12] and in a priestly family [1 Ch. 24:1]) and through the paternal line (*BOAZ). However, a more likely theory is that the names may be the first words of oracles giving power to the Davidic dynasty: perhaps 'Yahweh will establish (*yaḵîn*) thy throne for ever' and 'In the strength (*bᵉʿōz*) of Yahweh shall the king rejoice' or something similar.

BIBLIOGRAPHY. R. B. Y. Scott, *JBL* 57, 1939, pp. 143ff.; S. Yeivin, *PEQ* 91, 1959, pp. 6–22; J. Ouellette, in E. Gutmann (ed.), *The Temple of Solomon*, 1976, pp.1–20. D.J.W.
C.J.D.

JACOB. It is fitting that almost a quarter of the book of Genesis should be devoted to the biography of Jacob, the father of the chosen people. Written documents of the 2nd millennium BC have provided extensive material corroborating the background to the stories of Gn. 26–50. While this does not prove the existence of the Patriarch or the historicity of the narrative, it does show that they are not late compositions from the time of the Exile with imaginative and anachronistic details. Rather it suggests that the stories were recorded in writing at an early date (*PATRIARCHAL AGE). A collection of stories with details apparently discrediting the hero is unlikely to be centred on a mythical figure.

I. Date

The exact limits of the lifetime of Jacob cannot be fixed because of a lack of explicit correlations between the biblical accounts and the surviving secular records (*CHRONOLOGY OF THE OLD TESTAMENT). Evidence at present available suggests approximately the 18th century BC. Such a date would place his settlement in Goshen, not far from the Egyptian court, early in the period of the Hyksos domination, centred on Tanis (*EGYPT, *ZOAN). This date also allows *Abraham's life to be placed in the 20th and 19th centuries BC, as suggested by biblical and archaeological evidence.

Palestine and Syria in the time of Jacob.

II. Biography

Jacob was born clutching the heel (Heb. *'ēqēḇ*) of his elder twin Esau (Gn. 25:26), so the name given to him was 'he clutches' or, on another plausible interpretation, 'he clutched' (Heb. *ya'ᵃqōḇ*). This may have been intentional punning on a current name *ya'ᵃqōḇ-il*, 'may God protect' or 'God has protected'. Cuneiform and Egyptian documents of the period contain personal names from the same root (*'qb*), including some of parallel form, in use among people of the W Semitic group (*AMORITES).

Jacob 'supplanted' (this is a nuance developed from 'to take by the heel, to overtake', Heb. root *'qb*) his brother, first obtaining the birthright of the elder son by taking advantage of his brother's hunger and then beguiling Isaac into giving to him the blessing which was by custom that of the first-born. The first-born son normally inherited more of the paternal estate than each of the other children (twice as much later, *cf.* Dt. 21:16). As well as the special legacy, it seems that the chief heir was marked out for a social and religious position as

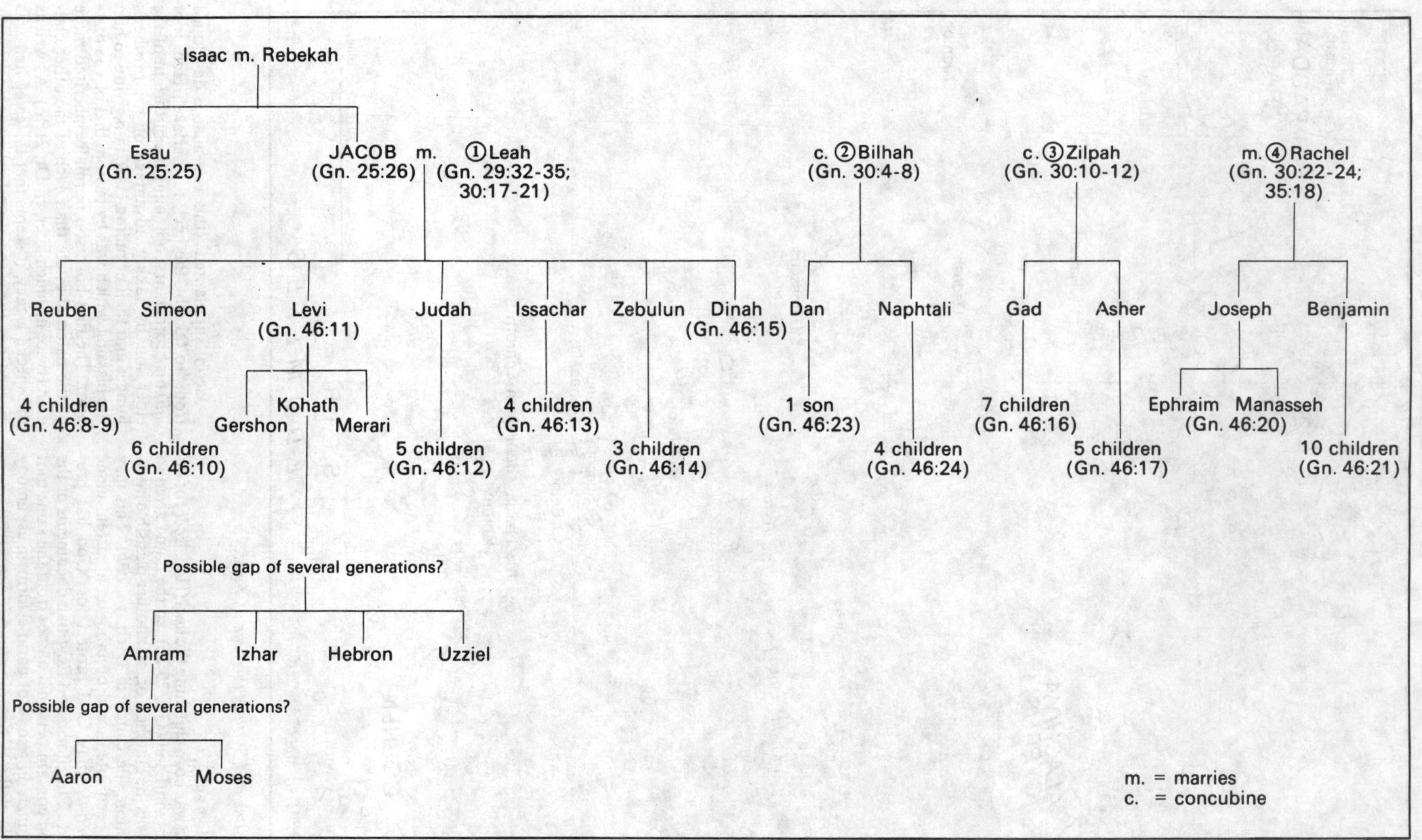

Jacob and his descendants.

head of the family. The bestowal of a blessing by the father, and the possession of the household gods, probably symbolized this. These customs may be deduced from contemporary deeds of adoption and legal records as well as from the biblical accounts. The brief narrative of the sale of Esau's birthright for a meal does not tell how the exchange was confirmed or whether it was recorded officially. A document of the 15th century BC records the sale of the patrimony of a man in Assyria. A document from the same milieu shows that the oral promise of a man to his son could be upheld in a court of law (see *ANET*, p. 220). So Isaac's blessing was irrevocable, as the text emphasizes (Gn. 27:33f.). Thus Jacob became the bearer of God's promise and the inheritor of Canaan (*cf.* Rom. 9:10–13). Esau received the less fertile region, which became known as *Edom. Rebekah, the mother, obtained Isaac's permission for Jacob to flee from Esau's anger to her home in *Paddan-aram (Gn. 28:1ff.). She used as excuse the need for Jacob to marry a member of the same clan and so avoid mixed marriages such as Esau had contracted with the local people.

The central event of Jacob's life took place during his flight N. At the end of a day's journey, perhaps the first, he had arrived in the hill-country near *Bethel, some 100 km from Beersheba. This is a reasonable distance for a fast camel to cover in one day. The first stage of the flight would obviously finish as far from home as possible. There is no indication that Jacob had any knowledge of a particular sanctity attaching to the area, although he may have known of the site of his grandfather's altar (Gn. 12:8). As he slept he was granted the vision of a ladder between heaven and earth and of the God of his family standing above it. The promise given to Abraham was confirmed to him and he was given a promise of divine protection. Jacob commemorated his dream by setting up the stone on which he had rested his head and pouring a libation of oil over it (Gn. 28:11ff.). Such simple monuments were often erected in sacred places (*PILLAR). This one marked the place where, for Jacob, God was known to be present.

The narrative leaps from Bethel to the district of Harran at the time of Jacob's arrival. As had Eliezer (Gn. 24:11), so Jacob came first to the well outside the city. Here he was met by his cousin Rachel and taken to Laban, his uncle, who accepted him as his kinsman. When a month had elapsed, Jacob agreed to work for his uncle and, after 7 years, to take Rachel as his wife (Gn. 29:1ff.). The wedding was duly celebrated in the presence of witnesses to the oral or written marriage contract, legally required in Babylonia to give a woman the status of wife. Laban claimed a local custom as his excuse for actually giving his elder daughter Leah to Jacob. That the elder daughter should be married first is a custom not otherwise known. Jacob acquiesced in Laban's action and a new agreement was made allowing Jacob to marry Rachel after the week (presumably of celebrations) was completed. Seven more years' service were required in place of the money given by a man to his father-in-law (*MARRIAGE).

Eleven sons and one daughter were born to Jacob in Laban's house during the 20 years he stayed there. Leah bore four sons while Rachel remained barren. Her chagrin was partly overcome by giving her maid Bilhah to Jacob and adopting her two sons (*NUZI). Leah did likewise with her maid Zilpah, who also bore two sons. The knowledge that adoption might lead to conception by the adoptive mother may have prompted this (*cf.* Sarah and Hagar, Gn. 16:2). Two more sons and a daughter were borne by Leah before Rachel bore Joseph. Several of the names given to Jacob's children also occur in contemporary texts, although there is no mention of the biblical characters known.

Harran was an important trading centre as well as a fertile agricultural and pastoral district. Laban, it may be assumed, had a town house where he lived during the summer harvest season, taking his flocks to pasture on the hills during the winter. As head of what was evidently a fairly wealthy family, he would have had authority over his own household and perhaps in the city council. Jacob's request to be allowed to return to his home was, perhaps, made at the end of the 14 years' service for his two wives, and after Rachel had borne her first son, Joseph. His management of Laban's flocks had been so successful that Laban was unwilling to let him go (Gn. 30:25ff.). An agreement was made whereby Jacob should continue to work for Laban in return for all the beasts of Laban's flocks and herds which were of impure colour. In this way Jacob would build up a capital from which to support his family. Laban, again breaking his agreement, removed all the animals to which Jacob might lay claim, but Jacob, following advice received in a dream, ingeniously turned his father-in-law's trickery to his own advantage without infringing the agreement. His prosperity aroused the envy of Laban's sons, who felt that he was robbing them of their lawful inheritance (Gn. 31:1). A divine command overcame any reluctance Jacob may have had at leaving Harran without Laban's approval. Rachel and Leah supported his plan, since, they claimed, their father had spent the dowry they should have received (*MARRIAGE). The flight was accomplished while Laban was away from home for sheep-shearing. A 2-day start enabled Jacob and his flocks to travel as far as Gilead in N Transjordan before he was overtaken by Laban (Gn. 31:22ff.). Seven days for Laban's pursuit, covering about 400 miles, is well within the reach of a riding camel. Laban complained of Jacob's furtive departure but his particular concern was for the theft of his gods (*TERAPHIM, *NUZI). If possession of these images did mark the head of the family, then Rachel's deed was intended to exalt Jacob. She managed to retain them by a ruse. Jacob in turn reminded Laban of how well he had served him, complying with all the current requirements of a good herdsman, and how ill he had been rewarded. A pact was made, Laban using his authoritative position to dictate the terms: his daughters were not to be maltreated, nor should Jacob take another wife. A pillar was erected to commemorate the covenant and a cairn was built. These also served as points of demarcation beyond which neither party should go; possibly a recognition of the extent of Jacob's territorial rights under the promise. Each party called upon God to be witness and punish whoever might break the covenant. A sacrifice was made and the two parties shared a meal as a sign of their goodwill.

Jacob proceeded to *Mahanaim, where an angelic host met him, and then he sent scouts to discover Esau's attitude (Gn. 32:1ff.). At his approach, Jacob took care to safeguard half of his possessions and also sent a large gift to his brother. After he had asked for divine protection, and as he was about to ford the river Jabbok at *Penuel, he was engaged in a struggle with a stranger who prevailed only by dislocating Jacob's thigh. This incident was regarded as Jacob's redemption 'from all evil' (Gn. 48:16), the new name Israel showing that he was able to contend with God (*cf.* Ho. 12:4), his disability displaying his subordination. Esau's friendly greeting did not overcome Jacob's qualms. He turned down to *Succoth instead of following Esau. From Succoth he moved up to a town in the territory of Shechem and purchased a piece of land. The rape of Dinah and the vengeance taken by her brothers made the area hostile to him (Gn. 34:1ff.). God instructed him to go to Bethel, presumably outside the jurisdiction of Shechem, to worship. The various pagan symbols brought from Paddan-aram were buried before the family could proceed. As before, Jacob erected a pillar to commemorate his communion with God and poured a libation. He did the same to mark Rachel's tomb at *Ephrath but without a libation (Gn. 35:1–20). After Isaac's death (Gn. 35:28–29) he settled in the region of Hebron and there lived as he had in Harran, by herding and by cultivation. When the famine struck and he was invited to Egypt, he first sought assurance that it was right for him to go S of Beersheba (Gn. 46:1ff.).

Before his death he adopted the two sons of Joseph and gave them a special blessing, preferring the younger over the elder (Gn. 48). The blessings of the twelve sons are recorded in a poetic composition that plays upon the meanings of their names (Gn. 49:1–27). Jacob died, over 130 years old, and was buried in the family tomb at *Machpelah near Hebron (Gn. 50:13).

His descendants called themselves by his name *Israel (paralleled by Jacob in poetry). As the chosen people they had the privilege of striving with God. A.R.M.

III. New Testament references

Jacob the son of Isaac is listed in the genealogies (Mt. 1:2; Lk. 3:34). More significant is the recurring conjunction, Abraham, Isaac and Jacob, where Jacob stands with the other two as a type of the eternally blessed (Mt. 8:11; Lk. 13:28). All three Synoptists record Jesus' quotation of Ex. 3:6, 'I am the God of Abraham, and the God of Isaac, and the God of Jacob' (Mt. 22:32; Mk. 12:26; Lk. 20:37; also Acts 7:32). This sonorous formula (taken up in the Jewish liturgy, *cf.* the Eighteen Benedictions) gives emphasis and solemnity to the character of God as the one who entered into covenant relation with the Patriarchs of old, and who honours his promises. Peter uses nearly the same formula to heighten his declaration of what God has done in Christ (Acts 3:13). Stephen mentions Jacob several times (Acts 7:12, 14–15, 46). The last time he speaks of 'the God of Jacob', thus giving this Patriarch central importance in the history of religion. Paul refers to Jacob twice, the first time to bring out God's purposes in election (he chose Jacob before the two children were even born, Rom. 9:11–13), and the second time as a way of symbolizing the nation (Rom. 11:26). Finally, this Patriarch figures in Hebrews as one of the heroes of faith (Heb. 11:9, 20f.).

A Jacob also occurs as the name of the father of Joseph in the Matthean genealogy of our Lord (Mt. 1:15–16). L.M.

JAEL (Heb. *yā'ēl*, 'wild goat'). The wife of Heber the Kenite and murderess of Sisera (Jdg. 4:17–21). At that time the Canaanites, under the leadership of Jabin, king of Hazor, and Sisera dominated Israel. In a parenthetical note (Jdg. 4:11) the presence of the Kenites as far N as Zaanannim, on the border of Naphtali (Jos. 19:33), is explained; normally they were associated with the tribe of Judah. Their skills in metal-working would make them useful allies to the Canaanites (Jdg. 4:17).

After the Israelites, under Deborah and Barak, had inflicted a crushing defeat upon the Canaanites, the main part of the defeated army fled W. Sisera, however, evidently having abandoned his command, headed N, probably to seek sanctuary at Hazor. Jael, appreciating his vital importance (*cf.* Jdg. 4:22), offered him hospitality, which, according to contemporary custom, guaranteed protection. Her treachery was increased by her attempt to convey a sense of security (Jdg. 4:18). Since the erection of tents was women's work, Jael was able to despatch Sisera efficiently by driving a tent peg into his temple. To be killed by a woman would be considered a disgrace (*cf.* Jdg. 9:54). So Deborah's prophecy, that the principal honour of slaying Sisera would be a woman's, was fulfilled (Jdg. 4:9).

This victory gave permanent relief from Canaanite oppression and allowed Israel control of the strategic Esdraelon valley. It was immortalized in the Song of Deborah (Jdg. 5), reckoned to be contemporary, which shows a barbaric exultation in Jael's vicious act (Jdg. 5:24–27). But, whilst not approving, we must not overlook the natural human reaction of these long-oppressed Israelites at the death of their arch-enemy.

Various unlikely emendations have been suggested to remove the surprising reference to Jael in Jdg. 5:6. The point made is probably that, although Shamgar and Jael were living when Israel was persecuted, neither was able to effect deliverance. Deborah gains full credit for this.

BIBLIOGRAPHY. A. E. Cundall, *Judges and Ruth*, 1968, pp. 81–101. A.E.C.

JAHAZ (Heb. *yahaṣ*). A site in the plains of Moab where Israel defeated Sihon, the Amorite king (Nu. 21:23; Dt. 2:32; Jdg. 11:20). The name occurs in several forms—Jahzah, Jahaza (Jos. 13:18), and Jahazah (Jos. 21:36; Je. 48:21). It fell in the portion of Reuben, and was assigned to the Merarite Levites (Jos. 13:18; 21:34, 36). The area was later lost to Israel, but Omri reconquered the land as far as Jahaz. The *Moabite Stone (lines 18–20) states that the Israelites dwelt there while they fought Mesha. Finally, Mesha drove them out and added Jahaz to his domains.

M. du Buit would place the site just off the central highlands road on the right of the Wadi Wali. Y. Aharoni has proposed Khirbet el-Medeiyineh on the fringe of the desert (*LOB*). The city was still in Moabite hands in the days of Isaiah and Jeremiah (Is. 15:4; Je. 48:21, 34). J.A.T.

JAHZEIAH (Heb. *yaḥ'yâ*, 'Yahweh sees, reveals'; AV 'Jahaziah', Ezr. 10:15). One of four men mentioned in connection with the controversy over foreign wives. AV regards the four as supporting Ezra, 'being employed about this matter'; but the same Heb. phrase can be translated also as 'opposed this' (so RSV, *BDB*, *etc*.). The context would seem to support the AV rendering. J.D.D.

JAIR (Heb. *yā'îr*, 'he enlightens'). **1.** Descendant of Manasseh who, during the conquest E of the Jordan under Moses, took several villages on the border of Bashan and Gilead (Nu. 32:41) and named them *Havvoth-jair. **2.** A judge who judged Israel for 22 years (Jdg. 10:3, 5). His thirty sons had thirty cities in Gilead, the name Havvoth-jair being associated with them. **3.** Father of Mordecai (Est. 2:5).

4. (*yā'îr*, 'he arouses'.) Father of *Elhanan (1 Ch. 20:5), one of David's heroes; he is called Jaare-oregim (2 Sa. 21:19) by a scribal error. M.A.M.

JAIRUS. A ruler of the synagogue whose daughter was healed by Christ (Mk. 5:21–43; Lk. 8:41–56; *cf*. Mt. 9:18–26). The name may be derived from Heb. *yā'îr*, 'Yahweh enlightens' (*cf*. Jair, Jdg. 10:3). He is named by Mark and Luke but not by Matthew. His duties included the conducting of the synagogue worship and the selection of those who were to lead the prayer, read the Scriptures, and preach in it. There was generally only one *archisynagōgos* to each synagogue (Matthew describes him simply as *archōn*, which here has the same significance).

Jairus came to Jesus after he had crossed the sea of Galilee from the Decapolis and landed near Capernaum. His daughter, aged 12, was at the point of death, and he asked him to come and heal her. On the way to his home Jesus healed the woman with a haemorrhage. Then the news came that the girl was dead. Most of those present felt it unnecessary to trouble Christ any further, and they were scornful of his statement that the girl was not dead but asleep. When all but Peter, James, John, Jairus and his wife had been dismissed, Jesus took her by the hand and she came back to life. He ordered her to be fed and enjoined strict secrecy upon them.

From a literary point of view it is interesting to see how Matthew compresses the story, so much so as to give the impression that the child was dead when Jairus first approached Jesus. It is also noteworthy that the Aramaic phrase *ṭ^elîṯâ qûm(î)* is retained by Mark. R.E.N.

JAMES (Gk. *Iakōbos*, Heb. *ya^a qōḇ*, 'heel-catcher', 'supplanter').

1. The son of Zebedee, a Galilean fisherman who was called with his brother John to be one of the twelve apostles (Mt. 4:21). These two along with Peter formed the inner core of three among the twelve, being present at the raising of Jairus' daughter (Mk. 5:37), the transfiguration (Mk. 9:2), and the agony in Gethsemane (Mk. 14:33) to the exclusion of the others. James and John, whom Jesus nicknamed 'Boanerges, that is, sons of thunder' (Mk. 3:17), were rebuked by Jesus when they suggested that they should 'bid fire come down from heaven' to destroy a Samaritan village which had refused to receive the Jerusalem-bound Jesus (Lk. 9:54). The pair also caused envy among the disciples by requesting a place of honour in Christ's kingdom; while not promised this advantage, they were told they would drink the cup their Master was to drink (Mk. 10:39), a prophecy which was fulfilled for James when he was 'killed . . . with the sword' by Herod Agrippa I, *c*. AD 44 (Acts 12:2).

2. The son of Alphaeus, another of the twelve apostles (Mt. 10:3; Acts 1:13). He is usually identified with 'James the younger', the son of Mary (Mk. 15:40). The description 'the younger' (Gk. *ho mikros*, 'the little') distinguishes him from the sons of Zebedee as either younger or smaller in stature.

3. An otherwise unknown James who was the father of the apostle Judas (not Iscariot) in the Lucan writings (Lk. 6:16; Acts 1:13; the other Gospels have Thaddaeus instead of Judas).

4. The brother of Jesus who, along with his brothers Joses, Simon and Judas (Mt. 13:55), apparently did not accept the authority of Jesus before the resurrection (see Mk. 3:21 and Jn. 7:5). After the risen Jesus had appeared to him (1 Cor. 15:7), he became a leader of the Jewish-Christian church at Jerusalem (Gal. 1:19; 2:9; Acts 12:17). Tradition stated that he was appointed first bishop of Jerusalem by the Lord himself (Eusebius, *EH* 7. 19). He presided at the first Council of Jerusalem, which considered the terms of admission of Gentiles into the church, formulated the decree which was promulgated to the churches of Antioch, Syria and Cilicia (Acts 15:19–23), and remained as sole leader of the Jerusalem church, working to maintain its unity with Paul and his mission when Paul visited Jerusalem for the last time (Acts 21:18ff.). A few years later James suffered martyrdom by stoning at the instigation of the high priest Ananus during the interregnum after the death of the procurator Festus in AD 61 (Josephus, *Ant*. 20. 9). Hegesippus' largely legendary tradition claims that James was known as 'the Just' because of his (Jewish) piety (Eusebius, *EH* 2. 23). Jerome (*De viris illustribus* 2) records a fragment from the lost apocryphal *Gospel according to the Hebrews* (*NEW TESTAMENT APOCRYPHA) containing a brief and probably unhistorical account of the appearance of the risen Jesus to James. James is the traditional author of the canonical Epistle of James, where he describes himself as 'a servant of God and of the Lord Jesus Christ' (Jas. 1:1).

BIBLIOGRAPHY. R. Bauckham, *Jude and the Relatives of Jesus*, 1980. P.H.D.

JAMES, EPISTLE OF.

I. Outline of contents

a. Introduction
  Greeting 1:1
  Statement and restatement of themes 1:2–27
  (Test of faith, speech and spirit, piety and poverty)

b. Development
  Piety and poverty 2:1–26
  Speech and spirit (Wisdom) 3:1–4:12
  Test and result 4:13–5:6

c. Conclusion (with restatement of themes) 5:7–20

II. Authorship and date

Due to uncertainty about the identity of the author, who describes himself as 'James, a servant of God and of the Lord Jesus Christ' (1:1), this Epistle did not receive general acceptance in the W until the 4th century. Most Christians recognized that James the son of Zebedee was martyred too early to have been the author, and there is no evidence that the early church ever attributed the Epistle to any other James, *e.g.* 'James the younger', Mk. 3:18; 15:40; Luther's attribution to some unknown James was the result of his dogmatic devaluation of the work as 'a right strawy epistle', since it apparently contradicted Paul on the matter of justification and did not set forth the central doctrines of salvation.

Some modern scholars, noticing the almost complete lack of references to distinctively Christian doctrines, the apparently disjointed nature of the moral axioms in which the Epistle abounds, and the fact that Jesus Christ is explicitly mentioned only twice, have rejected the idea that it was composed by any Christian, suggesting instead that an originally pre-Christian Jewish homily was adapted for Jewish-Christian use by the insertion of 'Jesus Christ' at 1:1 and 2:1. Other scholars, noticing doctrinal and church situations which could point to a date later than the life of the Lord's brother, regard the Epistle as a late Christian homily written to meet the needs of the more settled Christian communities after early evangelistic fervour had subsided (AD 70–130).

The first theory, which sometimes attributes the work to an unknown James or pseudonymously to the patriarch Jacob, might account for such expressions as 'Abraham our father' (2:21) and 'the Lord of hosts' (5:4), and the emphasis laid upon works in justification (2:14–26). It could also explain the phenomena that the writer speaks like a second Amos when he denounces the rich (5:1–6), and cites Abraham (2:21), Rahab (2:25), Job (5:11) and Elijah (5:17) as examples of virtue, but not Jesus. Yet these and similar features do not *demand* such an explanation, especially if the Epistle were written before the wide circulation of the Gospels, for the OT was the Bible of the early Christians. As has been pointed out, 'there is no sentence in the Epistle, which a Jew could have written and a Christian could not'. Moreover, the Christianity of the Epistle is much more extensive than it appears on the surface, and it is difficult to suppose that the imaginary Christian interpolator would have been capable of exercising such great restraint!

The second theory, which normally assumes that the work was pseudonymously attributed to the Lord's brother to give it authority, gains credence from the quality of Greek in the Epistle and the argument that 2:14–26 was written to counteract an antinomian perversion of Paul's doctrine of justification by faith. But it fails to account for the primitive features of the Epistle (*e.g.* the mention of elders and not bishops in 5:14) and the Palestinian colouring (*e.g.* 'the early and the late rain' in 5:7). Furthermore, were the Epistle pseudepigraphic, it is hard to explain why the author did not use a clearer and more exalted title (*e.g.* 'James the apostle' or 'James the brother of the Lord').

The address 'to the twelve tribes in the Dispersion' (1:1), probably referring to scattered Jewish-Christian congregations (it is the reason why the letter is included among the general or catholic Epistles), the homiletic character of the work, its Jewish-Christian flavour, its concern with a communal ethic and community solidarity, its echoes of the later Jewish Wisdom literature ('wisdom', probably meaning the Spirit, is one of its keywords, see 1:5; 3:17), of nonconformist Jewish theology (it contains striking parallels to the *DEAD SEA SCROLLS), and of the sayings of Jesus which became embodied in the Sermon on the Mount (*cf.* 2:13 and Mt. 5:7; 3:12 and Mt. 7:16; 3:18 and Mt. 7:20; 5:2 and Mt. 6:19; 5:12 and Mt. 5:34–37), and the note of authority with which the author speaks are all consistent with the tradition that he was James the Lord's brother, first 'bishop' of the church in Jerusalem. Moreover, although the Epistle contains some curious non-biblical literary phrases (*e.g.* 1:17, 23; 3:6), its Hebraic features coupled with the frequent use of rhetorical questions, vivid similes, imaginary dialogues, telling aphorisms and picturesque illustrations make it reasonable to suppose that we are listening to the completely bilingual Palestinian Jewish-Christian James, who resided at Jerusalem, a cosmopolitan centre for both Jews and Christians, for some 30 years after the resurrection of Jesus. The resemblances in Greek words and phrases between the Epistle and James' speech at the Council of Jerusalem (*cf.* 1:1 and Acts 15:23; 1:27 and Acts 15:14; 2:5 and Acts 15:13; 2:7 and Acts 15:17) may afford possible supporting evidence. It seems logical to suppose that either James himself composed the work, or else a secretary or later redactor compiled it from James' sermons. The situation of the church in the Epistle fits an early date of origin for much, if not all, of the contents: a date before the Council of Jerusalem (AD 48/49) would best explain the data, including the seeming conflict with Paul in 2:14–26.

III. Teaching

The Epistle concerns itself with the need for Christians to resist the pressure to compromise with the world, especially with respect to the use of wealth. It supplements and in no way contradicts the teaching of Gal. and Rom. on the matter of justification. James does not use the word 'justified' in 2:21 with reference to the occasion in the Abraham narrative to which Paul refers, *viz.* Gn. 15:6, but with reference to Gn. 22, a declaration of justification on the occasion of the binding of Isaac, itself the crown of a life of charity and faithfulness *flowing from* the faith of Gn. 15:6.

Roman Catholics have always valued the Epistle highly as affording evidence for the doctrines of justification by works, auricular confession (5:16), and extreme unction (5:14). On the other hand, Protestants—unduly influenced by Luther—have tended to regard it as somewhat sub-Christian. But Calvin pointed out that this Epistle contains nothing unworthy of an apostle of Christ, but on the contrary gives instruction on numerous subjects, all of which are important for Christian living, such as 'patience, prayer to God, the excellency and fruit of heavenly truth, humility, holy duties, the restraining of the tongue, the cultivation of peace, the repression of lusts, the contempt of the world, and the like'. Many modern evangelicals have begun to see the folly of underemphasizing the ethical implications of justification and the place which good works should occupy in the Christian life. As R. V. G. Tasker has said in *TNTC*, 'Whenever faith does not issue in love, and dogma, however orthodox, is unrelated to life; whenever Christians are tempted to settle down to a self-centred religion, and become oblivious of the social and material needs of others; or whenever they deny by their manner of living the creed they profess, and seem more anxious to be friends of the world than friends of God, then the Epistle of James has something to say to them which they reject at their peril.'

In an age when evangelicals are again concerned about social righteousness, the use of wealth and communal life, this Epistle calls for special study, for it draws attention to community-building virtues and to the destructive social force of improperly used wealth. In an age when the severity of the divine nature and the transcendence of God tend to be forgotten, the balance needs to be redressed by the emphasis laid in this Epistle on the unchangeable God (1:17), the Creator (1:18), the Father (1:27; 3:9), the Sovereign (4:15), the Righteous One (1:20), who must not be tested by evil men (1:13), to whom humanity must submit in humility (4:7, 10), the Lawgiver, the Judge, the Saviour and Destroyer (4:11–12), who will brook no rivals (4:4–5), the Giver of wisdom (1:5) and grace (4:6), who promises a crown of life to those who stand the test of faith and love him alone (1:12).

BIBLIOGRAPHY. Commentaries by M. Dibelius, 1975; S. Laws, *BNTC*, 1980; P. H. Davids, *NIGTC*, 1980; *NIBC*, 1989; R. P. Martin, *WBC*, 1988.

P.H.D.

JANNES AND JAMBRES. Paul speaks of certain false and morally dangerous teachers as resisting the truth as 'Jannes and Jambres' resisted Moses (2 Tim. 3:6–8). These names do not occur in OT, but extra-biblical allusions show that the Egyp. magicians of Ex. 7–8 are intended. Like them, the teachers played on superstitious susceptibilities with a plausibly presented parody of the truth.

The names, of unknown age, occur in various forms. The so-called 'Zadokite Work', now known to belong with the Qumran literature, has Belial raising up 'Yoḥaneh and his brother' against Moses and Aaron (7.19 in R. H. Charles, *Pseudepigrapha*, 1913; 5.19 in C. Rabin, *The Zadokite Documents*², 1958, p. 21); the Babylonian Talmud 'Yoḥanē and Mamre' (*Menaḥoth* 85a; *cf.* the spelling 'Mambres' in most Lat. and some Gk. MSS of 2 Tim. 3:8). Jewish legend made much of them, even attributing their paternity to Balaam. Pagan sources refer, not always perspicuously, to one or both (*cf.* Pliny, *NH* 30. 1. 11; Apuleius, *Apology* 90; Numenius of Apamea in Eusebius, *Praep. Ev.* 9. 8. 1), reflecting the story's celebrity. Origen knew a book on the subject (*Comm. in Mt.* 23:37; 27:9), and the Gelasian Decree a *Penitence of Jannes and Jambres*, of which M. R. James identified a fragment in a Saxon MS (*JTS* 2, 1901, pp. 572ff.). It is improbable, however, that Paul is alluding to the book: he would employ the names simply as being then in common use, with Ex. 7–8 alone in mind.

BIBLIOGRAPHY. *HJP*, 2. 3, pp. 149ff.; *SB*, 3, pp. 660ff. A.F.W.

JANOAH (Heb. *yānôaḥ*, *yānôḥâ*, 'rest'). **1.** A town (see *NEAEHL*, p. 860) of Naphtali seized by Tiglath-pileser during Pekah's reign (2 Ki. 15:29). Possibly modern Yanūḥ, NW of Acco (*LOB*, p. 379). **2.** A town of Ephraim, SE from Shechem, used in defining Ephraim's border with Manasseh (Jos. 16:6–70; AV 'Janohah'). Modern Khirbet Yānun. J.G.G.N.

JAPHETH (Heb. *yep̄eṯ*). One of the sons of Noah, usually mentioned last of the three (Gn. 5:32; 6:10; 7:13; 9:18, 23, 27; 1 Ch. 1:4), but his descendants are recorded first in Gn. 10 (and 1 Ch. 1:5–7). He was the ancestor of a number of tribes and peoples, most of whom had names which in historical times are associated with the regions to the N and W of the Middle East, especially Anatolia, and the Aegean (*NATIONS, TABLE OF). Japheth and his wife were among the eight people who escaped the Flood, and in a later incident he and Shem covered the nakedness of their father, Noah. In Noah's prophetic declaration after this episode he prayed that God might enlarge Japheth, and that *he* might dwell in the tents of Shem, and have Canaan as a servant (Gn. 9:27). Many commentators take *he* to refer to God rather than Japheth, though either interpretation is possible.

If the latter alternative is followed the reference may be to the benefits of the gospel which, coming first to the descendants of Shem, were later extended to the N peoples. In the above verse the word used for 'may he enlarge' is *yap̄t*, but this is probably only a play on words and does not have anything else to do with the name Japheth (*yep̄eṯ*), which does not occur elsewhere in the Bible or in the ancient inscriptions. Some have connected Japheth, however, with the Gk. mythological figure *Iapetos*, a son of earth and heaven, who had many descendants. The name is not Gk., so may be a form of the biblical name.

BIBLIOGRAPHY. P. Dhorme, 'Les Peuples issus de Japhet, d'après le Chapître X de la Genèse', *Syria* 13, 1932, pp. 28–49; D. J. Wiseman, Genesis 10: Some Archaeological Considerations', *JTVI* 87, 1955, pp. 14ff.; D. Neisman, 'The Two Genealogies of Japheth', in H. A. Hoffner (ed.), *Orient & Occident*, 1973, pp. 119ff.

T.C.M.

JAREB. The AV name or epithet of a king of Assyria who received tribute from Israel (Ho. 5:13; 10:6). If taken as a personal name it is assumed that the reference is to Tiglath-pileser III and Menahem's attempt to buy off the Assyrians in 738 BC (2 Ki. 15:19) or to the plea by Ahaz for his help against Rezin of Syria and Pekah of Israel (2 Ki. 16:7–10). Sayce's suggestion that it is Sargon II, conqueror of Samaria in 722 BC, is unlikely because of the date and circumstances.

It is more probable, since the customary definite article is here omitted, that *meleḵ yārēḇ* is a title to be translated 'warlike (or contending) king' or, taking *malki raḇ* as an old form for *meleḵ raḇ*, the usual Assyr. royal title of 'great king'. *Cf.* RVmg., RSVmg., 'a king that contends'; AVmg., 'the king that should plead'. On either interpretation the historical reference would be that quoted above.

D.J.W.

JARMUTH (Heb. *yarmûṯ*). **1.** Tel Yarmut (Khirbet Yarmuk), in a commanding position above the Wadi Surar 5 km S of Beth-shemesh. Late Bronze walls and pottery indicate occupation of 6–8 acres by a population of 1,500–2,000 before the Israelite invasion, when Jarmuth was a leading Amorite city. See Jos. 10:3; 15:35; Ne. 11:29.

BIBLIOGRAPHY. A. Ben-Tor, *IEJ* 35, 1985, pp. 71–73; *NEAEHL*, pp. 661–665.

2. A levitical town in Issachar, Jos. 21:29, otherwise Remeth (Jos. 19:21; *cf.* LXX(B) Jos. 21:29), Ramoth (1 Ch. 6:73); but the Egyptians called the district 'the hills of Yarmuta'. Aharoni (*LOB*, p. 28) suggests Khokav-hayyarden, the Crusader Belvoir, 10 km N of Bethshan. J.P.U.L.

JASHAR, BOOK OF. In Jos. 10:13 and 2 Sa. 1:18 the book of *yāšār* ('the upright one') is mentioned. Solomon's words in 1 Ki. 8:12–13, according to LXX, who put them after 8:53, are to be found in 'the book of the song'. As 'song', *šyr*, closely resembles *yšr*, perhaps the same book is meant here. All three quotations are in poetic style. It is possible that more quotations from ancient poetry came from this lost book. Some scholars identify it with 'the book of the wars of the Lord' (Nu. 21:14). As the quotations differ in metre, style and general contents, and date from different times, it is not probable that the book was a 'national epic'; it was rather a collection of songs with short historical introductions, *cf.* Arab. anthologies as, *e.g.*, Ḥamāsa. It must have been composed under Solomon's reign or later. The name *yāšār* is probably related to *Jeshurun. Printed books of Jashar are modern fabrications.

BIBLIOGRAPHY. S. Mowinckel, 'Hat es ein israelitisches Nationalepos gegeben?', *ZAW* n.f. 12, 1935, pp. 130–152; R. K. Harrison, *IOT*, 1970, pp. 669f. A. vanS.

JASHOBEAM. 1. '. . . a Hachmonite, was chief of the three', 1. Ch. 11:11; 'son of Zabdiel', 1 Ch. 27:2. He is to be identified with 'Josheb-basshebeth, a Tah-chemonite' (2 Sa. 23:8), which might be read 'Josheb-bashebeth the Hachmonite' (*hahakmōnî* for *taḥkᵉmōnî*, meaning unclear). LXX *Iebosthe*, *Iesebada*, Lucian *Iesbaal* imply a form 'Ishbaal'. David's leading warrior, who slew 'three hundred' (1 Ch.) or 'eight hundred' (2 Sa.), which is more likely, as it gives him superiority over Abishai (2 Sa. 23:18). (*CAPTAIN.)

2. Another warrior, who joined David at Ziklag (1 Ch. 12:6). A.R.M.

JASON. 1. Paul's host at Thessalonica (Acts 17:5–9). A rabble instigated by Jews raided his house, and, not finding Paul and Silas, seized Jason with some converts, and accused him before the politarchs (local magistrates) of harbouring seditious agitators. The prisoners were released on giving security for good behaviour. Luke does not say whether this involved a promise not to shelter the missionaries (*cf.* T. W. Manson, *BJRL* 35, 1952–3, p. 432), or simply to keep the peace. In either case the effect was the hasty departure of Paul (Acts 17:10) in circumstances which precluded an early return (*cf.* 1 Thes. 2:18). Jason was no doubt a Jew (*cf.* Acts 17:2 with 18:2–4) and probably a Christian (*cf.* Acts 17:7).

2. A Christian at Corinth, sending greetings in Rom. 16:21. 'Kinsman' here probably means 'fellow Jew' (*cf.* vv. 7, 11 and Rom. 9:3). Jason may be identical with **1**; if Sosipater is the *Sopater of Acts 20:4, Paul may be linking two fellow-Macedonians.

The name—that of the leader of the Argonauts—was very widespread, and Greek-speaking Jews seem to have sometimes used it instead of the similar-sounding, but conspicuously Jewish, name Jesus, *i.e.* Joshua (Deissmann, *Bible Studies*, p. 315n.). A.F.W.

JATTIR (Heb. *yattir*). Hurvat Yatir (Khirbet Attir) on the SW escarpment of the Hills of Judah, 21 km from Hebron; assigned to the priests (Jos. 21:14). David shared the spoils of the Amalekites with its inhabitants (1 Sa. 30:27). J.P.U.L.

JAVAN. One of the sons of Japheth (Gn. 10:2; 1 Ch. 1:5) and father of a group of peoples, *Elishah, *Tarshish, *Kittim and *Dodanim (Gn. 10:4; 1 Ch. 1:7), whose associations are with the regions to the N and W of the Middle East. It is generally accepted that this name (Heb. *yāwān*) is to be identified with Gk. *Iōnes*, which occurs as *Iaones*, probably for *Iawones*, in Homer (*Iliad* 13. 685), and refers to the people who later gave their name to Ionia. The name also occurs in Assyr. and Achaemenian inscriptions (*Iâmanu* and *Yauna* respectively). Isaiah mentions the descendants of Javan (LXX *Hellas*) beside Tubal as one of the nations (*gôyīm*) inhabiting distant islands and coastlands (*'iyyîm*, Is. 66:19). In the time of Ezekiel the descendants of Javan (LXX *Hellas*) were known as traders in men, bronze vessels and yarn, with Tyre (Ezk. 27:13, 19; in v. 19 RSV prefers to read *mē'ûzāl*, 'from Uzal', for *mᵉ'ûzzāl*, 'that which is spun, yarn'). The name Javan (EVV Greece) is used in the prophecies of Daniel to refer to the kingdom of Alexander of Macedon, and in Zc. 9:13 the term (EVV Greece, LXX Hellēnes) is probably used of the Seleucid Greeks.

BIBLIOGRAPHY. P. Dhorme, *Syria* 13, 1932, pp. 35–36; W. Brandenstein and M. Mayrhofer, *Handbuch des Altpersischen*, 1964, p. 156. T.C.M.

JAZER. A town of the Amorite kingdom of Sihon captured by Israel (Nu. 21:32) and part of the pasture-lands allotted to the tribe of Gad. It was later given to the Merarite families of the tribe of Levi. During David's reign, Jazer furnished 'mighty men of valour' (1 Ch. 26:31) and was one of the towns on the route of the census-takers (2 Sa. 24:5). The Moabites gained control of it, probably a little before the fall of Samaria (Is. 16:8–9; Je. 48:32, where 'sea of' has been considered a scribal error). Judas Maccabaeus captured and sacked the town *c.* 164 BC (1 Macc. 5:7–8). The site may be Khirbet Gazzir on the Wadi Šza'īb near es-Salt. A.R.M.

JEALOUSY. The principal OT term rendered as jealousy in the English Bible is *qin'â* from the verb *qānā'*, root meaning 'become dark red' (Nu. 5:14; Pr. 6:34; Ezk. 16:42; *etc.*). The normal LXX translation of *qinâ* and its cognates is *zēloō* or the cognate *parazēloō* (Dt. 32:21; *cf.* Rom. 10:19), and these are the principal terms used in the NT (Acts 7:9; Rom. 11:11; 1 Cor. 10:22; 13:4). Both Heb. and Gk. words refer to an exclusive single-mindedness of emotion which may be morally blameworthy or praiseworthy depending on whether the object of the jealousy is the self or some cause beyond the self. In the former case the result is envy, or hatred of others (Gn. 30:1; Pr. 3:31; Ezk. 31:9), which for the NT is the antithesis of love and hence the enemy of true Christian fellowship (1 Cor. 13:4; 2 Cor. 12:20; Jas. 3:14). The Bible however also represents the other possibility, of a '*divine* jealousy' (2 Cor. 11:2), a consuming single-minded pursuit of a good end (1 Ki. 19:10; Ex. 20:5; 1 Cor. 12:31). This positive usage is frequently associated with the marriage relationship where a jealousy for the exclusiveness of the relationship is the necessary condition of its permanence (Nu. 5:11ff.; Ezk.

16:38; 2 Cor. 11:2). Jealousy is referred to God as well as men (Ex. 20:5; 34:14; Na. 1:2). Difficulty is sometimes felt with this, due principally to the way in which the negative connotations of the term have come to predominate in common English usage. Scripture however also witnesses to a positive application of jealousy and finds in this idea a highly relevant term to denote God's holy zeal for the honour of his name and the good of his people who are bound to him in the marriage of the covenant (Dt. 32:16, 21; 2 Ki. 19:31; Ezk. 36:5f.; Zc. 1:14f.; Jn. 2:17). In this sense the jealousy of God is of the essence of his moral character, a major cause for worship and confidence on the part of his people and a ground for fear on the part of his enemies. B.A.M.

JEBUSITE. The ethnic name of a people dwelling in the hills (Nu. 13:29; Jos. 11:3) round about Jerusalem (Jos. 15:8; 18:16). Descended from the third son of Canaan (Gn. 10:16; 1 Ch. 1:14), they are, however, listed as a distinct, but minority, group of people living alongside such peoples as Amorites and Heth. Jebus was a name given to *Jerusalem, the principal city in their territory (Jdg. 19:10–11; 1 Ch. 11:4–5; called Jebusi in Jos. 18:16, 28, RSV), and 'Jebusite' described the inhabitants of the city (Gn. 15:21; Ex. 3:8). Later the term is used of the former inhabitants (Ezk. 16:3, 45; Zc. 9:7).

Unless Melchizedek was ruler of Jerusalem (*SALEM), its earliest king named in the OT is Adoni-zedek (Jos. 10:1), who raised his local Amorite allies (v. 5) to protect the city from the Israelites entering the area. He met his death at Beth-horon (vv. 10–11). According to the *Amarna tablets (*c.* 1400 BC), *Urusa-limmu* was under Abdi-ḫepa, whose name, like that of a later Jebusite ruler *Araunah (2 Sa. 24:24) or Ornan (1 Ch. 21:15), is non-Semite, probably Hurrian or *Horite. Jebus was burnt after its capture by the men of Judah (Jdg. 1:8), but its original inhabitants regained control at least until the attack by David (2 Sa. 5:6). The Jebusites were allowed to remain on the temple hill until their ground was bought over or the Jebusite minority absorbed by the Judaeans who built a new quarter on Zion (Jdg. 1:21; 19:11). D.J.W.

JEDUTHUN (Heb. *y^e^dûṯûn*). A Levite appointed by David to conduct the music of the Temple along with Heman and Asaph (1 Ch. 25:1, 3, 6, *etc.*). He is also known as *Ethan (1 Ch. 6:44, *etc.*), which was possibly his name before his appointment. A variation of the name, Jedithun (*y^e^diṯûn*), appears several times in the *K^e^ṯîḇ* (Ps. 39, *etc.*). The name appears in the titles of three psalms: 39, 62, 77. In the first of these the title is simply 'to (*l^e^*) Jeduthun', but in the other two it is '*'al* Jeduthun', which may mean 'according to' or 'over'; if the latter, Jeduthun there means the family or guild of singers called after him. The family continued to officiate after the Exile (Ne. 11:17). M.A.M.

JEHOAHAZ (Heb. *y^e^hô'āḥāz*, 'Yahweh has grasped').

1. A variant of the name of *Ahaziah, Jehoram's son, 6th king of Judah (*c.* 848–841 BC; 2 Ch. 21:17; 25:23) in which the divine element comes first rather than last.

2. Son of Jehu; the 11th king of the N kingdom of Israel, who reigned for 17 years after his father's death (*c.* 814–798 BC; 2 Ki. 13:1). His reign saw the repeated advances of Syria under *Hazael and *Ben-hadad II, recorded as a result of his misdeeds (13:2–3). These included toleration of pagan worship (v. 6). His forces were so depleted (v. 7) that finally he had to call on Yahweh for aid (v. 4; *cf.* v. 22).

3. An inscription of *Tiglath-pileser III records tribute being received from *ia-u-ḫa-zi* (*māt*)*ia-u-da-a*, 'Jehoahaz of Judah' (*DOTT*, p. 57). This is the full form of the abbreviated name *Ahaz, 13th king of Judah, who sent gifts to the Assyrian king (2 Ki. 16:7–8).

4. 4th son of Josiah (1 Ch. 3:15) who became the 18th king of Judah upon his father's death at Megiddo (*c.* 609 BC; 2 Ki. 23:30). After reigning 3 months, he was deported by the pharaoh Neco to his headquarters at Riblah in Hamath and then to Egypt, where he died (23:33–34). Jeremiah called him *Shallum (Je. 22:11–12), an indication that Jehoahaz was his throne name (*cf.* A. M. Honeyman, *JBL* 67, 1948, p. 20). D.W.B.

JEHOIACHIN (Heb. *y^e^hôyāḵîn*, 'Yahweh will establish'; 'Jeconiah' in 1 Ch. 3:16; *cf.* Mt. 1:11–12; 'Coniah' in Je. 22:24, 28).

Jehoiachin was appointed king of Judah by the Babylonians following the revolt and death of his father Jehoiakim (6 December 598 BC). His brief reign of 3 months and 10 days (2 Ch. 36:9; Jos., *Ant.* 10. 98) is described in 2 Ki. 24:8–6; 2 Ch. 36:9–10. It was marked by evil, and the prophet Jeremiah foretold the end of both his rule and dynasty (Je. 22:24–30). According to Josephus (*Ant.* 10. 99) Nebuchadrezzar changed his mind about the appointment and returned to besiege Jerusalem and carried off the 18-year-old king, with his mother Nehushta, his family, and fellow Jews, to exile in Babylon. This famous historical event is also described in the OT and in the Bab. Chronicle. The city fell on 16 March 597, and Jehoiachin's young uncle Mattaniah (Zedekiah) was appointed to succeed him (2 Ki. 24:17; Je. 37:1).

In Babylon Jehoiachin was treated as a royal hostage. He is named (*Ya'u-kîn*) in Bab. tablets, dated between 595 and 570 BC, as receiving rations at the court in company with his five sons (E. F. Weidner, *Mélanges Syriens offerts à M. René Dussaud*, 2, 1939, pp. 923ff.; *DOTT*, pp. 84–86). Impressions of a seal, thought to belong to his steward Eliakim (*DOTT*, p. 224), were actually made a century earlier (see *BA* 53, 1990, pp. 74–79). The Jews in Babylonia reckoned the years by those of Jehoiachin's captivity (Ezk. 1:2). After Nebuchadrezzar's death his successor Amel-Marduk (*EVIL-MERODACH) in 561 BC showed Jehoiachin special favour and removed him from prison to the royal palace (2 Ki. 25:27–30; Je. 52:31–34). Jehoiachin's eldest son Shealtiel, the father of Zerubbabel, was born in 598 BC. Another son Shenazar is named in 1 Ch. 3:18.

BIBLIOGRAPHY. D. J. Wiseman, *Nebuchadrezzar and Babylon*, 1985, pp. 81ff. D.J.W.

JEHOIADA (Heb. *y^e^hôyāḏā'*, 'Yahweh knows') was a popular name in OT times. **1.** The father of Benaiah (2 Sa. 8:18), a valiant man from Kabzeel in the Negeb (1 Ch. 11:22); the son was one of David's officers. **2.** The leader of the Aaronites, who supported David at Ziklag (1 Ch. 12:27). **3.** The son of Benaiah, and grandson of Jehoiada, one of David's counsellors (1 Ch. 27:34).

4. The chief priest of the Temple in Jerusalem during the reigns of Ahaziah, Athaliah and Joash was also named Jehoiada. He married Jehoshabeath, sister of King Ahaziah, and played a prominent part in political affairs. On the death of Ahaziah he frustrated the queen-mother Athaliah's attempt to destroy all 'the seed royal'. He and his wife hid their nephew, Joash, for 6 years in the Temple precincts, while Athaliah usurped the throne. Then in a *coup d'état* he brought him out of hiding as the rightful ruler of Judah. A covenant was made for his protection, and another on his proclamation as king (2 Ki. 11:17). During Joash's minority, Jehoiada virtually ruled on his behalf. He destroyed the shrines of Baal and organized the Levites. He helped in the selection of Joash's two wives to ensure the royal succession (2 Ch. 24:3). After a rebuke from Joash himself he repaired the Temple (2 Ki. 12:7). When he died at the age of 130, he was buried in the royal tomb, in recognition of his service to the community.

5. A priest in Jerusalem before the Exile, during the lifetime of Jeremiah, who was replaced by Zephaniah (Je. 29:26). **6.** The son of Paseah who returned from the Exile with Nehemiah and played his part in the rebuilding programme (Ne. 3:6). M.B.

JEHOIAKIM (Heb. *y^e^hôyāqîm*, 'Ya(h)w has established'; *cf.* Joakim, 1 Esdras 1:37–39). King of Judah (609–598 BC), a son of *Josiah and elder brother of *Jehoahaz, whose place he took at the command of Neco II of Egypt. His name was

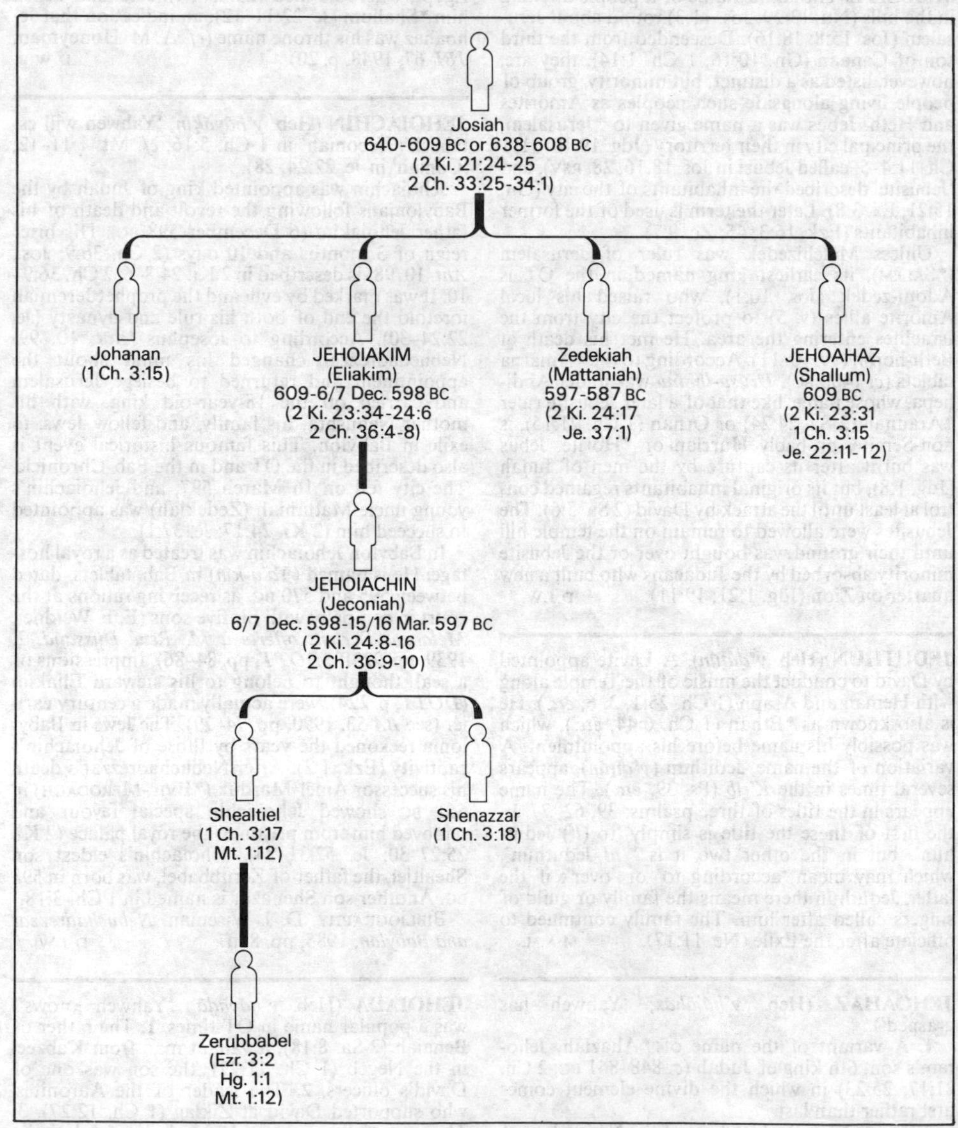

Chart showing how Jehoahaz, Jehoiachin and Jehoiakim were related.

changed from Eliakim as a mark of vassalage. The reign is recorded in 2 Ki. 23:34–24:6; 2 Ch. 36:4–8, and as the last-named entry in the 'book of the Chronicle of the Kings of Judah' (2 Ki. 24:5). To pay the Egyp. dues Jehoiakim imposed heavy land taxes (2 Ki. 23:35). He built costly royal buildings, using forced labour (Je. 22:13–17), and is described as an oppressive and covetous ruler. The religious decay during his reign is noted by the contemporary prophets Jeremiah and Habakkuk. Josiah's reforms were forgotten in the reversion to idolatry and introduction of Egyp. rites (Ezk. 8:5–17). Jehoiakim shed much innocent blood (2 Ki. 24:4) and had the prophet Uriah murdered for opposing him (Je. 26:20–21). He opposed Jeremiah (36:26) and personally burnt the scroll from which Jehudi read the words of the prophet to him (v. 22). He was 'unjust and wicked by nature, and was neither reverent toward God, nor kind to man' (Josephus, *Ant*. 10. 83), that is, he followed in the tradition of Manasseh's sin (2 Ki. 24:3).

In Jehoiakim's fourth year (605 BC) Nebuchadrezzar defeated the Egyptians at *Carchemish and won control of Palestine as far as the Egyp. border (Je. 25:1; 46:2), but it was not until the following year that Jehoiakim, with other rulers, went before Nebuchadrezzar to submit to him as vassal (Je. 36:9–29; Bab. Chronicle). Three years later, doubtless encouraged by the Egyptian defeat of the Babylonians in 601 BC, but against the advice of Jeremiah, Jehoiakim rebelled (2 Ki. 24:1). Nebuchadrezzar did not at first intervene but sent local Babylonian garrison troops with Syrians, Moabites and Ammonites to raid Judah (v. 2). At length, 3 months and 10 days before Jerusalem fell to the Bab. besiegers Jehoiakim died, aged 36 (*i.e.* 6 December 598 BC). His death occurred on the way to captivity (2 Ch. 36:6), apparently at the instigation of Nebuchadrezzar, who, according to Josephus (*Ant*. 10. 97), had his body thrown outside the city wall as prophesied by Jeremiah (22:18f.). 2 Ki. 24:6 is silent as to his burial. Jehoiakim was succeeded by his son Jehoiachin.

BIBLIOGRAPHY. D. J. Wiseman, *Chronicles of Chaldean Kings*, 1956, pp. 20–32, 65–75; *AUSS* 20, 1982, pp. 103–109. D.J.W.

JEHONADAB (Heb. *yᵉhônāḏāḇ*, 'Yahweh is liberal'). Jonadab is an alternative form of this name. **1.** Son of Shimeah, David's brother. His cunning enabled his friend Amnon, David's son, to obtain his foul desire on Tamar, Amnon's half-sister (2 Sa. 13:3–5). His knowledge of the death of Amnon would seem to indicate complicity in it, although he was his professed friend (2 Sa. 13:30–33). **2.** A son of Rechab, a Kenite (1 Ch. 2:55; Je. 35:6). He prohibited his clan from engaging in agriculture, possessing vineyards and using their produce, and dwelling in settled communities (Je. 35:6–10). But this may have been codifying what was already general practice. He was a zealous worshipper of Yahweh and assisted Jehu in suppressing the worship of Baal Melqart (2 Ki. 10:15, 23). M.A.M.

JEHORAM (Heb. *yᵉhôrām*, 'Yahweh is exalted'). Sometimes abbreviated to Joram. **1.** A Levite in the

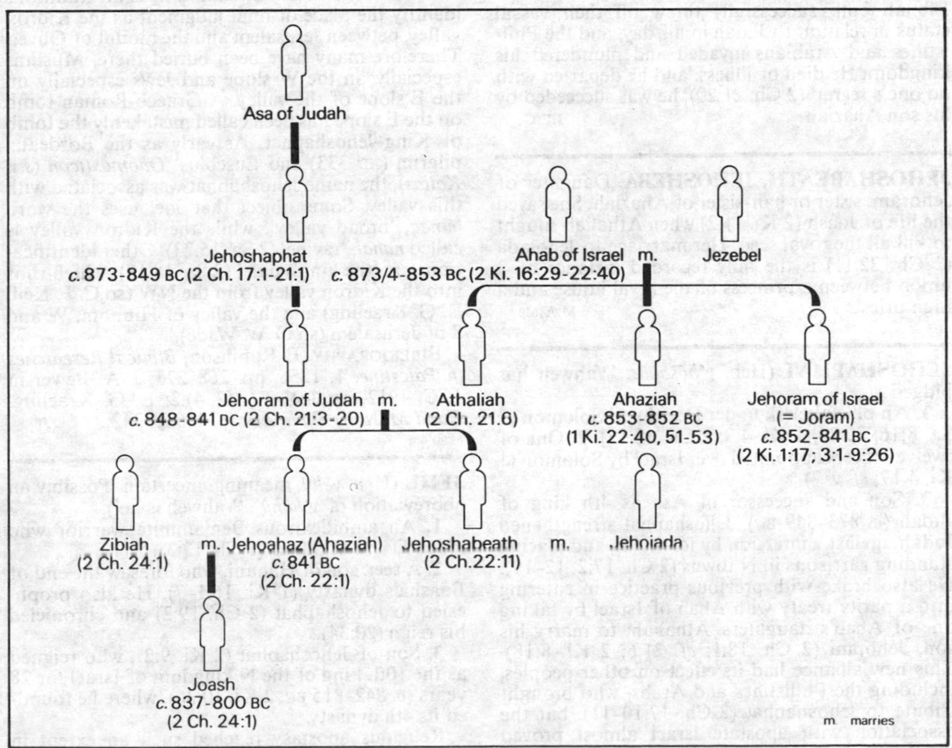

Family tree of Jehoram and Jehoshaphat.

time of David (1 Ch. 26:25). **2.** A prince of Hamath (2 Sa. 8:9–12). 1 Ch. 18:9–11 suggests his real name was Hadoram. **3.** A priest in the time of Jehoshaphat (2 Ch. 17:8).

4. King of (N) Israel, 852–841 BC; the last ruler of the dynasty of Omri (2 Ki. 1–9). Jehoram was a son of King Ahab and Jezebel, and although he is said to have removed one pagan feature of Israel's worship, in general he followed the unorthodox ways of other N kings (2 Ki. 3:1–3). He had to deal with the Moabites' rebellion against their position as vassals of Israel (*MOABITE STONE) and won a spectacular, though not conclusive, victory over the Moabites (3:4–27). He was later wounded in battle with the Syrians (8:28–29). Some of the other Elisha stories also have as their background the conflict between Israel and Syria, and refer to 'the king of Israel' (5:1–8; 6:8–23; 6:24–7:20; *cf.* 8:1–6), but we cannot be sure whether or not this king was Jehoram. Jehoram was killed and succeeded by *Jehu when recovering from injury in his capital, Jezreel (9:1–37). It was Elisha who instigated this deed; he saw it as a beginning to God's final act of judgment on Ahab and Jezebel, who were still alive and active for evil in Jezreel (9:7–10, 22). It was thus also the further fulfilment of Elijah's prophecy concerning Ahab and Jezebel (9:24–26, 30–36; *cf.* 1 Ki. 21:17–29).

5. King of Judah, 848–841 BC (2 Ki. 8:16–24; 2 Ch. 21). He was son of and successor to Jehoshaphat, but reversed his father's Yahwist policies. He married Athaliah, who was a daughter of King Ahab of Israel and thus a sister of King Jehoram of Israel, and led Israel in the pagan and bloody ways of Ahab and Jezebel. Edom and Libnah both successfully threw off their vassal status in relation to Judah in his day, and the Philistines and Arabians invaded and plundered his kingdom. He died of illness 'and he departed with no one's regret' (2 Ch. 21:20); he was succeeded by his son Ahaziah. J.E.G.

JEHOSHABEATH, JEHOSHEBA. Daughter of Jehoram, sister or half-sister of Ahaziah. She saved the life of Joash (2 Ki. 11:2) when Athaliah sought to kill all the royal seed. Her marriage to Jehoiada (2 Ch. 22:11) is the only recorded instance of a union between a princess of the royal house and a high priest. M.A.M.

JEHOSHAPHAT (Heb. *yᵉhôšāpāṭ*, 'Yahweh has judged').

1. An official clerk under David and Solomon (2 Sa. 8:16; 20:24; 1 Ki. 4:3; 1 Ch. 18:15). **2.** One of twelve officers appointed over Israel by Solomon (1 Ki. 4:17; *cf.* v. 7).

3. Son and successor of Asa as 4th king of Judah (*c.* 873–849 BC). Jehoshaphat strengthened Judah against aggression by fortifying and placing standing garrisons in N towns (2 Ch. 17:2, 12–19). He also broke with previous practice in entering into a parity treaty with Ahab of Israel by taking one of Ahab's daughters, Athaliah, to marry his son, Jehoram (2 Ch. 18:1; *cf.* 21:6; 2 Ki. 8:18). This new alliance had its effect on other peoples, including the Philistines and Arabs, who brought tribute to Jehoshaphat (2 Ch. 17:10–11), but the association with apostate Israel almost proved Judah's undoing after Jehoshaphat's death (2 Ki. 11:1–3).

Jehoshaphat's reign is noted for its adherence to Yahweh's instructions (1 Ki. 22:42; 2 Ch. 20:32). He eradicated much of the pagan worship (1 Ki. 22:43, 46) and provided itinerant teachers of Mosaic law (2 Ch. 17:7–9). He reorganized the legal system by appointing judges in key cities, with an appeal court in Jerusalem (2 Ch. 19:4–11).

4. Father of *Jehu, 10th king of Israel (2 Ki. 9:2; 14:20). D.W.B.

JEHOSHAPHAT, VALLEY OF. The name which Joel gives to the place of the final judgment in Joel 3:2, 12. In both of these verses 'Jehoshaphat' (meaning 'Yahweh has judged') is associated with statements that God will judge (Heb. *šāpaṭ*). Therefore it is probable that 'the valley of Jehoshaphat', like 'the valley of decision' in v. 14, is a term symbolic of the judgment, not a current geographical name.

The valley of Jehoshaphat has been variously identified. Some have thought that Joel had no definite place in mind; *e.g.* Targum Jonathan translates this name 'the plain of the decision of judgment', and Theodotion renders 'the place of judgment'. Since Joel uses the geographical term 'valley', most students have thought that some location was intended. Ibn Ezra suggests the valley of Berachah S of Bethlehem, where Jehoshaphat's forces gathered after the destruction of enemies (2 Ch. 20:26), but Zc. 14 locates the judgment near Jerusalem, and according to *1 Enoch* 53:1 all people gather for judgment in a deep valley near the valley of Hinnom. Jewish, Christian and Muslim traditions identify the place of final judgment as the Kidron valley, between Jerusalem and the mount of Olives. Therefore many have been buried there, Muslims especially on the W slope and Jews especially on the E slope of the valley. A Graeco-Roman tomb on the E slope has been called mistakenly the tomb of King Jehoshaphat. As early as the Bordeaux pilgrim (AD 333) and Eusebius' *Onomasticon* (*s.v. Koilas*), the name Jehoshaphat was associated with this valley. Some object that Joel uses the word *'ēmeq*, 'broad valley', while the Kidron valley is called *naḥal*, 'ravine' (2 Sa. 15:23). Other identifications are 'the king's dale' (2 Sa. 18:18), which runs into the Kidron valley from the NW (so C. F. Keil, E. G. Kraeling) and the valley of Hinnom, W and S of Jerusalem (so G. W. Wade).

BIBLIOGRAPHY. E. Robinson, *Biblical Researches in Palestine*, 1, 1856, pp. 268–273; J. A. Bewer in *ICC*, 1912, on Joel 3 (*MT* 4):2; E. G. Kraeling, *Rand McNally Bible Atlas*, 1956, p. 342. J.T.

JEHU (Heb. *yēhû*, meaning uncertain. Possibly an abbreviation of *yᵉhôhû'*, 'Yahweh is he').

1. An ambidextrous Benjaminite warrior who aided David at Ziklag (1 Ch. 12:3).

2. A seer, son of Hanani, who foresaw the end of Baasha's dynasty (1 Ki. 16:1–7). He also prophesied to Jehoshaphat (2 Ch. 19:2) and chronicled his reign (20:34).

3. Son of Jehoshaphat (2 Ki. 9:2), who reigned as the 10th king of the N kingdom of Israel for 28 years (*c.* 842–815 BC; 2 Ki. 10:36), where he founded its 4th dynasty.

Religious apostasy reached such an extent in Israel during the reigns of Ahab and Jehoram (2 Ki. 8:27) that a revolt was instigated by Elisha's appointing a prophet to anoint Jehu king (9:1–13). This rebellion was also supported by elements among the people, *e.g.*, the Rechabites (10:15–16). Jehu, receiving the acclamation of the army of Jehoram which he commanded, went to Jezreel, where the king lay wounded following a battle at Ramoth-gilead (8:28–29). He there killed both Jehoram and Ahaziah, king of Judah, who came out to meet him (9:21–27; *cf.* 2 Ch. 22:9). The new king entered Jezreel and had Jezebel put to death. He then eradicated all opposition by executing Ahab's family and followers (2 Ki. 10:1–11) as well as 42 visiting members of Ahaziah's family (vv. 12–17; 2 Ch. 22:8). He then proceeded to stamp out worship of Baal by tricking the god's followers into meeting together and then slaughtering them, also destroying their temple (2 Ki. 10:18–28).

Jehu himself continued in apostasy by worshipping golden calves at Bethel and Dan (vv. 29–31), for which he was punished by the Syrians, under *Hazael, annexing parts of his territory (vv. 32–33).

The Black Obelisk of *Shalmaneser III mentions tribute paid by *'ia-ú-a mar ḫu-um-ri*, '*Yâw*, son of *Omri' (*DOTT*, pp. 48–49). This is generally taken to refer to an action of Jehu of Israel not mentioned by the OT. He, or his representative, is pictured bowing before the king. *Yâw* might also be an abbreviated form of the name Jehoram (P. K. McCarter, *BASOR* 216, 1974, pp. 5–7). In either case the date would be 841 BC (E. R. Thiele, *BASOR* 222, 1976, pp. 19–23). D.W.B.

JEHUDI (Heb. *yᵉhûḏî*). Normally means 'a Jew', as in Zc. 8:23, but in Je. 36:14, 21, 23 it is the name of an officer of Jehoiakim's court, who commanded Baruch to read the roll of Jeremiah's prophecies to the princes, and later himself read it to the king, until Jehoiakim personally destroyed it. J.G.G.N.

JEPHTHAH. One of the later (*c.* 1100 BC) Hebrew judges (Jdg. 11:1–12:7), whose name *yip̄tāḥ* is 'probably shortened from *yip̄taḥ-'ēl*, "God opens (*sc.* the womb)", which is cited as a proper name in Sabean' (*NBCR*, p. 267). The son of a common heathen prostitute (*zônâ*) and the then childless Gilead, Jephthah felt he had been illegally disinherited by the younger legitimate sons of Gilead. He fled to the land of *Tob. From there he and the renegades he gathered raided settlements and caravans and, like David's gang (1 Sa. 22:2; 27:8–9; 30), may have protected Israelite villages from marauding tribes, perhaps including the Ammonites.

Thus when the Israelites in Transjordan were threatened by a full-scale invasion of the Ammonites, the elders of Gilead invited Jephthah to be their commander. He consented only when they promised he would continue as their head (*i.e.* judge) after fighting ceased. This pact was confirmed with oaths taken at Mizpeh (Gn. 31:48–49). Jephthah's attempted diplomacy to dissuade the Ammonites failed (Jdg. 11:12–28).

Given courage and ingenuity for his task by the Spirit of God, Jephthah passed through Gilead and Manasseh to raise additional troops. He then passed over the Jabbok to Israelite headquarters at Mizpeh. There, before moving against the Ammonites, he vowed a vow (*neḏer*) unto his God, a common practice before battle among ancient peoples. Jephthah intentionally promised Yahweh a human sacrifice, probably intending a slave, because a single animal would have been as nothing from a people's leader. The LXX translation of *hayyôṣē'*, *ho emporeuomenos*, 'whoever comes by the way', long ago indicated that this is the proper interpretation. V. 31 should read: 'Then whoever comes forth . . . shall be the Lord's, and I will offer him up for a burnt offering.' Jephthah was living among heathen who offered human sacrifices to pagan deities (*cf.* 2 Ki. 3:27) and in a day when the law of Moses was little known or practised. Jephthah might sincerely (although wrongly—Lv. 18:21; Dt. 12:31) suppose 'that Jehovah would need to be propitiated by some offering as costly as those which bled on the altars of Chemosh and Moloch' (F. W. Farrar).

After subduing the Ammonites by faith (Heb. 11:32) Jephthah returned triumphantly to his headquarters house, only to meet his daughter, his only child, leading a victory procession (*cf.* 1 Sa. 18:6; Ex. 15:20). With utter grief, Jephthah felt he must fulfil his vow by offering her as a burnt-offering (*'ôlâ*, which always was burnt). He did not devote her to a life of celibacy (a view not introduced until Rabbi Kimchi), for there is no record that female attendants in tabernacle or Temple had to be virgins (Anna had been married, Lk. 2:36).

Jephthah showed himself as stern with his brethren the Ephraimites as he was with his enemies the Ammonites and with himself concerning his daughter. Offended because they had no share in his victory, the Ephraimites threatened his life. Jephthah answered harshly and slaughtered them relentlessly at the Jordan (Jdg. 12:1–6). J.R.

JERAH. One of the sons of *Joktan (Gn. 10:26; 1 Ch. 1:20), some of whom can be connected with tribes of S Arabia. The name (*yeraḥ*) is identical in form with the Heb. for 'month' or *'moon', and the word occurs in the S Arabian inscriptions (*yrḥ*) with this meaning, so it may be concluded that the descendants of Jerah had likewise settled in S Arabia. The site of Beth-Yerah (Khirbet Kerak) on the Sea of Galilee is probably unrelated.

BIBLIOGRAPHY. J. A. Montgomery, *Arabia and the Bible*, 1934, p. 40. T.C.M.

JERAHMEEL (Heb. *yᵉraḥmᵉ'ēl*, 'may God have compassion'). **1.** The ancestor of the Jerahmeelites, a clan on the S frontier of Judah, 'the Negeb of the Jerahmeelites' (1 Sa. 27:10; *cf.* 30:29), related to the Calebites (*cf.* 1 Sa. 25:3) and bordering on the

'Jerahmeel, the king's son' (lyrhm'l bn hmlk) *named on a seal impression in clay dating from the late 7th cent.* BC. *He may be identified with the Jerahmeel who burnt Jeremiah's scroll* (*Je.* 36:26). *12 mm × 10 10 mm.*

Kenites. Like the Calebites, they were absorbed into the tribe of Judah; their adoptive relationship to other branches of that tribe is given in 1 Ch. 2:9ff., together with the sub-divisions of the Jerahmeelite clan itself. They play a very minor part in the OT record, but by dint of large-scale textual emendation T. K. Cheyne concluded that they occupy a position of major importance in the narrative—a theory which retains interest only as a notable aberration in the history of biblical criticism (*cf. EBi, s. v.* 'Jerahmeel', *etc.*)

2. In 1 Ch. 24:29 the son of one Kish, a member of the Merarite clan of the tribe of Levi. **3.** In Je. 36:26 a member of the royal family of Judah who occupied an official position at the court of Jehoiakim. F.F.B.

JEREMIAH.

I. His background

Jeremiah's history covered a span of 40 years—from his call in the 13th year of King Josiah (626 BC) until the fall of Jerusalem in 587 BC. In those 4 decades he prophesied under the last five kings of Judah—Josiah, Jehoahaz, Jehoiakim, Jehoiachin and Zedekiah. While he was preaching, important personalities and events were shaping history beyond his native Judah. It was one of the most fateful periods in the history of the ancient Near East and it affected Judah's history too.

The Assyrian empire disintegrated and Babylon and Egypt were left to struggle against each other for the leadership of the E. The chronology of the last quarter of the 7th century BC has been greatly clarified by the publication of some tablets which were excavated years ago but which had lain in obscurity in the vaults of the British Museum in London. In 1956 D. J. Wiseman made these Chaldean documents available to students of the ancient Near East, thus making possible a reappraisal of the chronology of the last quarter of the 7th century BC. Further light has also been shed by the discovery of ostraca (letters on jar fragments) and bullae (seals), in some cases naming personalities known from the book of Jeremiah. The most interesting seal reads: 'belonging to Berekyahu (Baruch) son of Neriyahu (Neriah) the scribe'. This is probably the very Baruch who helped Jeremiah record his prophecies (Je. 36:4), and who may indeed have written the third-person accounts of Jeremiah's life. Other seals name Gemariah, the son of Shaphan (Je. 36:11) and 'Jerahmeel, the son of the king' (Je 36:26; see P. J. King, *Jeremiah: An Archaeological Companion*, pp. 93–99). For the ostraca, see **II*e*** below.

Jeremiah's life and times which fall within this all-important period are remarkably well documented, and the intimacies of his personality are more vividly portrayed than those of the more spectral Minor Prophets or even of Isaiah and Ezekiel.

When Jeremiah was called to the prophetic office he was still 'a child' (*na'ar*, 1:6), an ambiguous term descriptive of infancy (Ex. 2:6) and advanced adolescence (1 Sa. 30:17). If the demure Jeremiah simply meant he was spiritually and socially immature the word might indicate that he was not the average age of a prophet, say between 20 and 30, if we may argue from the rules laid down for Levites (Nu. 8:24; 1 Ch. 23:24). Assuming, then, that at his call Jeremiah was in his early 20s his boyhood was spent in the reigns of Manasseh and Amon. When the call came to Jeremiah nearly a century had passed since the N kingdom of Israel (Samaria) had fallen to the Assyrians. Judah in the S, however, contrived to survive. By a miracle it weathered the storm of Sennacherib's invasion as Isaiah had predicted. King Hezekiah initiated reforms in Judah's religion and morals (2 Ki. 18:1ff.), but these had been nullified by the long apostasy of his son Manasseh (2 Ki. 21:1ff.) and the short idolatrous reign of Amon (2 Ki. 21:19ff.). While Judah was wallowing in the slough of idolatry the Assyrians under Esarhaddon and Ashurbanipal conquered Egypt. Under Psammetichus (664–610 BC) Egypt reasserted herself and began afresh to intimidate Judah, who found herself vacillating between now the blandishments, now the menaces of the two world powers, Egypt and Babylon. In this atmosphere of international political tension and national religious declension Jeremiah grew up into boyhood.

Doubtless many in Judah yearned for the dawn that would end the night of 60 years' moral degeneracy. Jeremiah grew up in a pious priestly home (1:1). His name, 'Yahweh exalts' or 'Yahweh throws down', might well symbolize both his parents' prayers for the disconsolate nation and their aspirations for young Jeremiah. They would communicate to him their anxiety over the religious persecutions and apostasies of Manasseh and Amon, educate him in Israel's laws, and fill his fertile mind with the teachings of Isaiah and other prophets of the previous century.

II. The five reigns

a. Josiah

When God called Jeremiah, Josiah (640–609 BC), who had been on the throne of Judah for 12 years, had already introduced religious reforms (2 Ch. 34:4–7). But it was not until 621 BC, the 18th year of his reign, that he initiated a systematic reformation in Judah's religion and morals (2 Ki. 23).

The impulse to reform was generated by the momentous discovery in the Temple of 'the book of the law' by Hilkiah. Jeremiah had already been a prophet for 5 years. Probably chs. 1–6 describe conditions in Judah before Josiah's main reforms in 622–621 BC. The nation is incorrigibly corrupt, insensible to God's offer of pardon, and oblivious to the menace of an invincible enemy. Apart from 11:1–8, which may contain hints of Jeremiah's enthusiasm for Josiah's reforms, the prophet has left no reference to the last 12 years of Josiah's reign. In 609 BC the king was killed at Megiddo (2 Ki. 23:29) in an abortive attempt to resist Pharaoh Neco (610–594 BC), successor to Psammetichus. Naturally Jeremiah mourned the early death of Josiah (22:10a) of whom he thought kindly (22:15f.).

b. Jehoahaz

Neco continued to meddle in the affairs of Judah. Jehoahaz (or Shallum, Je. 22:11) succeeded Josiah (609 BC) but 3 months later was deposed by Neco, who imposed on Judah a heavy tribute (2 Ki. 23:31–33) and appointed Jehoiakim (or Eliakim), brother of Jehoahaz, to the throne (2 Ki. 23:34; 2 Ch. 36:2, 5). Jeremiah lamented Jehoahaz's deposition and exile to Egypt (22:10–12).

c. Jehoiakim

In this reign (609–597 BC) an event of great political significance occurred—the battle of

Carchemish (Je. 46) in 605 BC. The Egyptians under Neco were crushed by the Chaldeans under Nebuchadrezzar at the battle of Carchemish, on the right-hand bank of the Euphrates NW of Aleppo, and at Hamath. Politically this event was pivotal because it marked the transference of the hegemony of the Middle East to Babylon. Therefore Carchemish also had considerable significance for Judah. Since all routes to the Egyptian border were now under Nebuchadrezzar's control, it was inevitable that the whole Middle East should come under his rule (Je. 25:15ff.). From that moment, therefore, the prophet advocated Judah's submission to Babylonian suzerainty. In 604 BC Nebuchadrezzar sacked the city of Ashkelon, against which Jeremiah (47:5–7) and Zephaniah (2:4–7) prophesy judgment. In Je. 36:9ff. a fast in Judah is proclaimed. This undoubtedly points to an approaching national calamity; and indeed the date of Nebuchadrezzar's campaign against Ashkelon coincides with the date of this fast in Judah. Jeremiah anticipates that from Ashkelon Nebuchadrezzar will come against Judah; hence the fast and the proclamation of Jeremiah's message in Jerusalem. But Jeremiah's policy opposed Jehoiakim's domestic and foreign strategy. The king favoured idolatrous usages (2 Ki. 23:37), and his selfishness and vanity aggravated Judah's misfortunes (Je. 22:13–19). Jehoiakim had scant respect for the prophet's person (26:20–23) or message (26:9). His vacillating policy of alliance with Egypt, then with Babylon, was probably due to the fact that the outcome of the fighting between Babylon and Egypt in the year 601/600 BC was inconclusive. Three years later he rebelled against Babylon, but failure only brought him under the Babylonian yoke more completely, and this exacerbated Judah's anguish (2 Ki. 24:1f.). Jeremiah reprimanded the king, the prophets and the priests, and the hostility which this rebuke engendered is mirrored in his oracles. He was persecuted (12:6; 15:15–18), plotted against (11:18–23; 18:18), imprisoned (20:2), declared worthy of death (26:10f., 24; *cf.* vv. 20–23; 36:26). His prophecies in written form were destroyed (36:27). But in these depressing circumstances Jeremiah persisted in his ministry—interceding for Judah (11:14; 14:11; 17:16), expostulating with God (17:14–18; 18:18–23; 20:7–18), unmasking the time-serving prophets (23:9–40), predicting the destruction of the Temple (7:1–15) and nation (chs. 18f.), and lamenting the doom of his people (9:1; 13:17; 14:17). Eventually Jehoiakim's life ended violently in Jerusalem at the close of 598 BC, the 11th year of his reign, as Jeremiah had foretold (22:18; *cf.* 2 Ki. 24:1ff.). On the other hand, 2 Ch. 36:6f. speaks of Nebuchadrezzar's binding Jehoiakim in fetters to take him to Babylon. Dn. 1:1f. also speaks of Jehoiakim's exile in the 3rd year of his reign.

d. Jehoiachin

Jehoiachin (or Coniah, 22:24, 28, or Jeconiah, 24:1) succeeded Jehoiakim in 597 BC and reaped what his father had sown. This immature youth of 18 reigned only 3 months (2 Ki. 24:8). The rebellion of Jehoiachin's father compelled Nebuchadrezzar in the 7th year of his reign to besiege Jerusalem, and the youthful king of Judah 'went out' (2 Ki. 24:12), *i.e.* gave himself up. He, along with the majority of Judah's aristocracy, artisans and soldiers, was exiled to Babylon (as Je. 22:18f. implies) and the Temple was plundered (2 Ki. 24:10–16). In the Babylonian Chronicle we now find for the first time confirmation of this information from an extra-biblical contemporary source. Jeremiah had already predicted Jehoiachin's fate (22:24–30). 36 years later, however, he was released by the son and successor of Nebuchadrezzar (2 Ki. 25:27–30).

e. Zedekiah

Zedekiah, the new appointee of Nebuchadrezzar to the throne of Judah, was Josiah's youngest son (Je. 1:3) and uncle of Jehoiachin (2 Ki. 24:17; 2 Ch. 36:10). This OT account of Zedekiah's appointment by Nebuchadrezzar to succeed Jehoiachin is fully verified by the Babylonian Chronicle. His reign (597–587 BC) sealed Judah's doom (2 Ki. 24:19f.). He was weak and vacillating, and his officers of state were men of humble station. Having superseded the exiled aristocracy, they now looked upon them with contempt, but Jeremiah had his own convictions concerning the 'bad' and the 'good' figs (24:1ff.). It was to the latter that the prophet sent his famous letter (29:1ff.). But both in Babylon and Judah false prophets sought to have Jeremiah executed (28:1ff.; 29:24ff.). The main point at issue between them was the length of the captivity. Jeremiah foretold an exile of 70 years, while the false prophets argued that it would last only 2 years.

Jeremiah's main conflict with Zedekiah was over the question of rebellion against Nebuchadrezzar. A revolt was planned in the 4th year of the reign in conspiracy with neighbouring states which the prophet violently opposed (chs. 27f.). However, Zedekiah seems to have succeeded in allaying Nebuchadrezzar's suspicions by visiting Babylon the same year (51:59).

Finally, however, in the 7th or 8th year of his reign Zedekiah compromised himself irrevocably in the eyes of Nebuchadrezzar by entering into treasonable negotiations with Pharaoh Hophra. The die was cast, and the Babylonians marched again into Judah. As the Assyrians had done in Hezekiah's reign they reduced first the cities of Judah. Je. 34:7 comes from a point in proceedings when only the S outposts of Lachish and Azekah still held out, a moment that has been illuminated by the so-called Lachish ostraca, one of which records the lament of an officer in a remote station that the lights of Azekah have now gone out, and he looks in hope for the lights of Lachish (Ostracon 4; see P. J. King, *Jeremiah: An Archaeological Companion*, p. 82f.). In Zedekiah's 9th year (589) the Babylonians besieged Jerusalem for the second time. But before (21:1–10) and during the siege (34:1ff., 8ff.; 37:3ff., 17ff.; 38:14ff.) Jeremiah had only one message for Zedekiah—surrender to the Babylonians, for Jerusalem must fall into their hands. Jeremiah's interpretation of the battle of Carchemish 17 years earlier (605) was being fully vindicated. At one point during the siege, the Egyptian army's advance compelled the Babylonians to withdraw, but hopes that Jeremiah was mistaken were quickly disillusioned. His warning that the Babylonians would annihilate the Egyptians was soon fulfilled and the siege was immediately resumed (37:1–10). The perfidy of some Jews towards their slaves at this juncture roused Jeremiah's withering scorn and severest condemnation (34:8–22). Thanks to the cowardly vacillations of Zedekiah, the prophet was so rigorously maltreated by his enemies during the siege that he despaired of his life. Arrested on the charge of deserting to the enemy, he was thrown into a dungeon (37:11–16), but was later removed to a prison in the guard-court close to the palace (37:17–21). He was then accused of treason and thrown into a disused cistern, where he would have died but for the timely intervention of Ebed-melech. He was later transferred to the prison court (38:1–13), where the king secretly conferred with him (vv. 14–28).

During the last stages of the siege Jeremiah, in a great act of faith, bought the land belonging to his cousin in Anathoth (32:1–15). At this moment too he proclaimed promises of restoration (32:36–44; 33:1–26). To this period may be assigned his great prophecy of a new covenant (31:31ff.), ultimately fulfilled in Christ the Mediator of that covenant. But Judah's cup of iniquity was now full and in 587 judgment engulfed the doomed city of Jerusalem (ch. 39). Here also it is instructive to notice that the account of the captivity of Jerusalem in the Bab. Chronicle agrees in general with the OT account in 2 Ki. 24:10–17; 2 Ch. 36:17; Je. 52:28. The destruction of Jerusalem is now to be dated 587 BC, not 586, calculating the new year from the spring rather than the autumn, according to the Babylonian calendar.

Nebuchadrezzar treated Jeremiah kindly, and when he appointed Gedaliah governor of Judah Jeremiah joined him at Mizpah (40:1–6). The murder of Gedaliah soon followed (41:1ff.), and the remnant in Mizpah resolved to flee into Egypt in spite of the earnest protestations of Jeremiah, who, along with Baruch his secretary, was compelled to accompany them (42:1–43:7). The last scene in the aged Jeremiah's stormy ministry shows him at Tahpanhes in Egypt still unbowed. He prophesies the conquest of Egypt by Nebuchadrezzar (43:8–13) and rebukes the idolatrous worship of the Jews then residing in Egypt (44:1ff.). Of subsequent events in his life or the circumstances of his death nothing is known.

III. Jeremiah's personality

Jeremiah's personality is the most sharply etched of any of the OT prophets. Indeed, it is no exaggeration to say that in order to understand what the OT means by the term 'prophet' it is necessary to study the book of Jeremiah. Jeremiah's call, his vocation as a bearer of the word of God, the authority which this communicated to him, the manner in which the word was revealed to him, his clear-cut distinctions between the true prophet and the false, his message and the agonizing dilemmas in which his fidelity to it entangled him—all are delineated in Jeremiah's oracles with an authority that is irresistible. This is because of the correlation between the prophet's spiritual and emotional experience and his prophetic ministry. For interpretations of Jeremiah's inner life, especially in his so-called Confessions or prayers of lamentation, see Skinner and McConville (ch. 3).

It is impossible to plumb the depths of grief into which Jeremiah was plunged. Despairing of comfort (8:18, 21), he desired to dissolve in tears for doomed Judah (9:1; 13:17) and abandon her to her self-inflicted fate (9:2). Convinced of ultimate failure, he cursed the day he was born (15:10; 20:14–18), accused God of having wronged him (20:7a), complained of the ignominy that had befallen him (20:7b–10), invoked imprecations upon his tormentors (18:18, 21–23). It is in this sense that the emotional, highly-strung Jeremiah was a tragic figure. The tragedy of his life springs from the conflicts which raged within and around him—his higher self wrestling with the lower, courage conflicting with cowardice, certain triumph struggling with apparent defeat, a determination to abandon his calling defeated by an inability to evade it (*cf.* 5:14; 15:16, 19–21 with 6:11; 20:9, 11; 23:29). But these fierce internal conflicts and the ignominy in which his calling involved him (15:17f.; 16:2, 5, 8) compelled him to find in God a refuge. Thus the OT ideal of communion with God comes to its finest expression in Jeremiah. And it was in this fellowship with God that Jeremiah was able finally to withstand the erosive effects of timidity, anguish, helplessness, hostility, loneliness, despair, misunderstanding and failure.

IV. His message

a. Jeremiah's concept of God

God is Creator and sovereign Lord who governs all things in heaven and earth (27:5; 28:23f.; 5:22, 24; 10:12f.). While the gods of the nations are non-entities (10:14f.; 14:22), Israel's God disposes all things according to his will (18:5–10; 25:15–38; 27:6–8). He knows the hearts of men (17:5–10) and is the fountain of life to all who trust in him (2:13; 17:13). He loves his people tenderly (2:2; 31:1–3), but demands their obedience and allegiance (7:1–15). Sacrifices to pagan gods (7:30f.; 19:5) and oblations offered to him by a disobedient people (6:20; 7:21f.; 14:12) are alike abominations to him.

b. Jeremiah and idolatry

From the outset the prophet was a proclaimer of judgment. The sinfulness of Judah made this inevitable. The particular evil against which Jeremiah inveighed was idolatry. His many references to the worship of heathen deities confirm that the practice was widespread and diverse. Baal, Moloch and the queen of heaven are mentioned. Idols were found in the Temple (32:34), and in the vicinity of Jerusalem children were sacrificed to Baal and Moloch (*cf.* 7:31; 19:5; 32:35). Josiah had suppressed the idolatrous practices which his grandfather Manasseh had promoted, but the nation had apostatized after Josiah's death.

c. Jeremiah and immorality

Throughout the OT immorality was a concomitant of idolatry. This principle is powerfully exemplified in Jeremiah's idolatrous generation (5:1–9; 7:3–11; 23:10–14). Inescapably moral corruption followed the elimination of the fear of God and reverence for his law. Profligacy and improbity were common even among the priests and prophets (5:30f.; 6:13–15; 14:14). Instead of arresting immorality, they contributed to its spread. Ironically, idolatrous and immoral Judah was still zealously religious! This explains Jeremiah's oft-reiterated contention that before God the moral law takes precedence over the ceremonial. This principle Jeremiah applies to Judah's reverence for the ark (3:16), the tablets of the Torah (31:31f.), the covenant sign of circumcision (4:4; 6:10; 9:26), the Temple (7:4, 10f.; 11:15; 17:3; 26:6, 9, 12; 27:16) and the sacrificial system (6:20; 7:21f.; 11:15; 14:12).

d. Jeremiah and judgment

Naturally, then, the inevitability of judgment was prominent in Jeremiah's message. Judah's punishment at the hands of God took many forms, such as drought and famine (5:24; 14:1–6) and invasion by a foreign power (1:13–16; 4:11–22; 5:15–19; 6:1–15, *etc.*). And inexorably the great day of doom dawned when God's instrument for punishing apostate Judah appeared (25:9; 52:1–30). The history of the background against which these oracles of judgment should be set has become much clearer with the publication of *Chronicles of Chaldaean Kings* (*626–556 BC*), to which reference has already been made. It describes a number of international events which took place in Jeremiah's lifetime, and hints of these are found in his oracles against the foreign nations. Doubtless his oracles against the nations in ch. 25 were written under the influence of Nebuchadrezzar's first advance W (Je. 25:1; *cf.* v. 9). Ch. 46 opens with a reference to the battle of Carchemish in 605. Then comes an oracle relating to Nebuchadrezzar's campaign against Egypt (46:13–26). The Bab. Chronicle also provides a factual basis for Jeremiah's oracles against Kedar and Hazor (49:28–33) and Elam (49:34–39). It also relates how Nebuchadrezzar in 599 made raids against the Arab tribes (*cf.* Je. 49:29, 32), while in 596 he campaigned against Elam. Hitherto this oracle has had no historical basis. See further for the light shed by the Bab. Chronicle on the dating and authenticity of the oracles in Jeremiah 46–51 in *JBL* 75, 1956, pp. 282f.

e. Jeremiah and the false prophets

Jeremiah's elevated conception of, and total commitment to, his call evoked within him an uncompromising antagonism towards the professional prophets and priests, and they in turn were his sworn enemies. Jeremiah's major polemic with the priests was over their policy of making gain of their office and their contention that the Jerusalem Temple would never fall to the Babylonians (6:13; 18:18; 29:25–32, *etc.*). The false prophets confirmed the duped people of Judah in this facile optimism (8:10–17; 14:14–18; 23:9–40, *etc.*).

f. Jeremiah's hope

By contrast Jeremiah was an uncompromising preacher of judgment. However, his announcement of judgment was shot through and through with hope. Judah's exile in Babylon would not last for ever (25:11; 29:10). Indeed, Babylon herself would be overthrown (50f.). This word of hope concerning Judah's survival of judgment was present in Jeremiah's message from the start (3:14–25; 12:14–17), but as the situation became more ominous Jeremiah's confidence shone brighter (23:1–8; 30–33). And it was this hope that gave birth to his great act of faith in the darkest days (32:1–15).

g. Jeremiah and Judah's religion

Jeremiah could therefore anticipate the destruction of the Temple, the fall of the Davidic dynasty, the cessation of the sacrificial system and the ministry of the priesthood with perfect equanimity. He even proclaimed that the covenant sign of circumcision was largely meaningless without the circumcision of the heart (4:4; 9:26, *cf.* 6:10). Confidence in Temple, sacrifice, priesthood, was vain unless accompanied by a change of heart (7:4–15, 21–26). Even the ark of the covenant would be dispensed with (3:16). Knowledge of the law without obedience to the law was valueless (2:8; 5:13, 30f.; 8:8). Jeremiah therefore sees the necessity of having the law written not on stone but on the heart, thus prompting all to spontaneous and perfect obedience (31:31–34; 32:40). The passing away of the outward symbols of the covenant signified not the end of the covenant but its renewal in a more glorious form (33:14–26).

h. Jeremiah and the ideal future

Thus Jeremiah looks far beyond Judah's return from exile and the resumption of life in Palestine (30:17–22; 32:15, 44; 33:9–13). In the ideal future Samaria will have a part (3:18; 31:4–9), abundance will prevail (31:12–14), Jerusalem will be holy unto the Lord (31:23, 38–40), and be named 'the Lord is our righteousness' (33:16). Its inhabitants will return to the Lord penitently (3:22–25; 31:18–20) and with their whole heart (24:7). God will forgive them (31:34b), put his fear within them (32:37–40), establish the rule of the Messianic Prince over them (23:5f.) and admit the Gentile nations to a share of the blessing (16:19; 3:17; 30:9).

V. His oracles

The oracles in Jeremiah's book are not presented to the reader in chronological sequence. His ministry was spread over five reigns, and the oracles emanate from all periods. For example, much of chs. 2–6 may come from Josiah's reign; chs. 26, 35–36 are from Jehoiakim's; and chs. 21, 24, 29, 37–39 come from the time of Zedekiah. Some commentators have attempted to date all the oracles (Bright, Holladay), but there are many uncertainties.

Since, then, the chapters are not arranged chronologically, probably their subject-matter has determined their present order. Ch. 36 would seem to confirm this suggestion. When Jeremiah's oracles were first committed to writing in the 4th year of Jehoiakim (604 BC) they covered a period of 23 years—from the 13th year of Josiah (626 BC) until 604 BC. These oracles Jehoiakim destroyed in the 5th year of his reign, but Baruch rewrote them at Jeremiah's dictation, and 'many similar words were added to them' (36:32). What these additions were is uncertain, as are also the contents of the original roll which Jehoiakim destroyed. But clearly the original oracles and the additions formed the nucleus of the book of Jeremiah as it has come down to us, although how the whole was given its final form can only be conjectured. But the disorderly arrangement of the oracles strengthens the conviction that they are the words Jeremiah's inspired lips uttered and were then put together during days of danger and turmoil.

The question of the order of Jeremiah's oracles is also bound up with the relation between the *MT* and LXX text of his book. The Gk. translation deviates from the Heb. text in two respects. (i) It is shorter than the Heb. text by approximately one-eighth (*i.e.* about 2,700 words). This is the more remarkable when it is recalled that on the whole the text of the LXX corresponds fairly closely to the *MT*. The main exceptions are Jeremiah, Job and Daniel. (ii) In the LXX the oracles against the foreign nations (46–51) are placed after 25:13, and their sequence is also altered. These divergences go back to Origen's time, but it is difficult to believe that the Heb. and Gk. texts represent two different recensions of the book of Jeremiah. Because of Jeremiah's prophetic stature and spiritual calibre, these two texts of his book must have existed from a very early date, since no text which differed so radically from the received text as the Gk. differs from the Heb. would have been able to gain a foothold if it had been produced centuries after Jeremiah's death.

In the debate on the superiority of one text to the other those who favour the LXX version argue that it gives the oracles against the foreign nations a more natural context, and that some of the omissions (*e.g.* 29:16–20; 33:14–26; 39:4–13; 52; 28–33, *etc.*) could not have been accidental. But the foregoing references to the Bab. Chronicle have shown how it now enables us to re-create the historical background against which some of these oracles have to be set, especially those against Kedar, Hazor, Elam and the Arabs. Those who support the claims of the Heb. text emphasize 'the arbitrary character of the renderings' (Streane), which according to Graf makes it 'altogether impossible to give to this new edition—for one can scarcely call it a translation—any critical authority'. The impression too is that the omissions are not motivated by scholarly interests. And the fact remains that the men of the 'great synagogue' who did so much in determining the Canon of the OT preferred the Heb. text to the Gk. version.

VI. Conclusion

In summarizing the greatness of Jeremiah, several things should be stressed. He recognized that Josiah's reforms were in reality a retrograde movement because they threatened to undo the work of the prophets. Reformation in worship without reformation of heart was useless. He also perceived that religion in Judah would continue even though the Temple and Jerusalem were destroyed. In his famous letter to the exiles in Babylon (ch. 29) he affirmed that in a pagan land Jews could still worship God although denied the ministry of priesthood and the service of sacrifice. Indeed, they could be closer to God in Babylon than were their brethren in Jerusalem, who made the outward trappings of religion a substitute for inward faith.

He saw too that, since religion was essentially a moral and spiritual relation with God (31:31–34), its demands must also be moral and spiritual. The essence of the new covenant was inwardness. This is not the same as 'individualism'. Rather, Jeremiah's rejection of the 'sour grapes' proverb (Je. 31:29–30) was intended to relieve a new generation of the burden of inherited guilt, while affirming its own responsibility for its standing before God. The new covenant people of God remains the 'house of Israel and the house of Judah' (Je. 31:31), *i.e.* a community.

In Christian terms this new community is to be understood as those who belong together in Christ. The new covenant is established by his death and resurrection, and by the dwelling of his Spirit among his people (Heb. 8:8–13; 10:16–17). In the life which he gives, enabling them to live in the Spirit, lies the way through the old impasse of a covenant which could not be kept (Je. 31:32).

BIBLIOGRAPHY. J. Skinner, *Prophecy and Religion*, 1922; J. P. Hyatt, *IB* 5, 1956; D. J. Wiseman, *Chronicles of Chaldaean Kings (625–556 BC)*, 1956; J. G. S. S. Thomson, *The Old Testament View of Revelation*, 1960, ch. 4; Commentaries by J. Bright, *AB*, 1965; J. A. Thompson, *NICOT*, 1980; W. L. Holladay, *Jeremiah 1, 2, Hermeneia*, 1986, 1989; D. R. Jones, *Jeremiah*, *NCB*, 1992; P. J. King, *Jeremiah: An Archaeological Companion*, 1993; J. G. McConville, *Judgment and Promise*, 1993.

J.G.S.S.T.
J.G.McC.

JERICHO.

I. Name

The original meaning of the name Jericho is open to doubt. It is simplest to take Heb. *yᵉrîḥô* as from the same root as *yārēaḥ*, 'moon', and to connect it with the early W Semitic moon-god *Yariḥ* or *Yeraḥ*. *Cf.* remarks by Albright in *Archaeology and the Religion of Israel*, 1953 edn., pp. 83, 91–92, 197 note 36, and in *AASOR* 6, 1926, pp. 73–74. Some suggest *rwḥ*, 'fragrant place' (*BDB*, p. 437b, after Gesenius), or as 'founded by (deity) Ḥô' (*PEQ* 77, 1945, p. 13), but this is improbable.

II. Sites

OT Jericho is generally identified with the present mound of Tell es-Sultan *c.* 16 km NW of the pres-

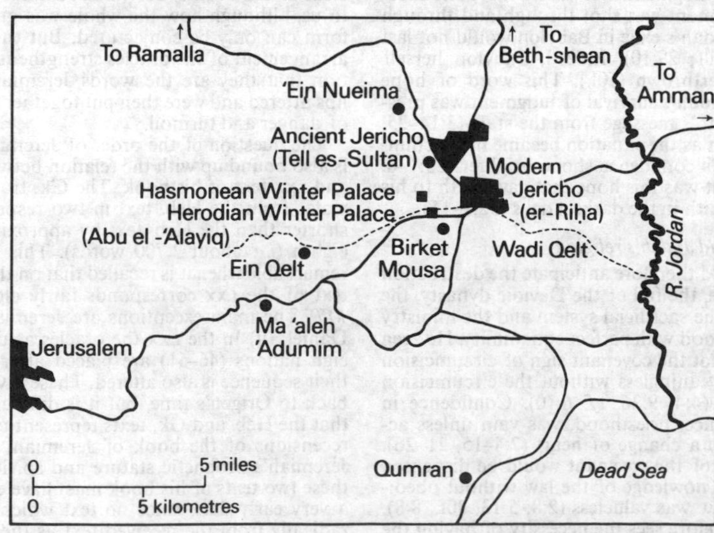

Jericho and adjacent ancient sites.

ent mouth of the Jordan at the Dead Sea, 2 km NW of er-Riḥa village (modern Jericho), and about 27 km ENE of Jerusalem. The imposing, pear-shaped mound is about 400 m long from N to S and roughly 200 m wide at the broad N end, and some 20 m thick. Herodian and NT Jericho is represented by the mounds of Tulul Abu el-'Alayiq, 2 km W of modern er-Riḥa, and so is S of OT Jericho. The mountains of Judaea rise abruptly from the plains of Jericho a little distance to the W.

III. History

a. Before Joshua

(i) *Beginnings.* The story of Jericho is virtually a précis of the whole archaeological history of Palestine between *c.* 8000 and *c.* 1200 BC. (For the special abbreviations used here, see bibliography at the end of this article.) Every settlement at Jericho has owed its existence to the fine perennial spring there and the 'oasis' which it waters (*DUJ*, pl. 1); in the OT Jericho is sometimes called 'the city of palm trees' (Dt. 34:3). Already *c.* 9600/7700 BC, food-gathering hunters may have had a shrine there, and Palestine's earliest-known agriculturists built huts by the spring (*AHL*, pp. 41–43; pl. 5A). Early in the 8th millennium BC (Carbon-14 date), the oldest *town* of Jericho was built with a stone revetment-wall that included at least one tower (with built-in stairway) and round houses. Subsequently, spacious rectangular houses became fashionable and skulls of venerated ancestors (?) were embodied in clay-moulded portrait heads of remarkable realism (*DUJ*, pp. 67–73 and pls. 25, 29–30, or *AHL*, pp. 43–47 and pl. 7, for 'prepottery Neolithic, phase A'; *DUJ*, pp. 51–67 and pls. 20–22, or *AHL*, pp. 47–57, 60 and pls. 13ff., for 'phase B'). In the 5th and 4th millennia BC later Jericho citizens learnt to make pottery, but eventually abandoned the place ('Pottery Neolithic A and B', 'Jericho IX and VIII' of older books, *DUJ*, pp. 79–94, *AHL*, pp. 60–70). Ancient Jericho is currently the primary source of information on the earliest settled life of Palestine; *cf.* also *W*, chs. 2–4 and *GSJ*, pp. 55–72.

(ii) *Early historical period.* From *c.* 3200 BC Jericho was again inhabited as a walled and towered town of the Early Bronze Age, when towns famous later (*e.g.* Megiddo) were first founded, contemporary with Egypt's Pyramid Age and the Sumerian civilization in Mesopotamia (*DUJ*, pp. 167–185; *AHL*, pp. 101–134; *W*, ch. 5; *GSJ*, pp. 75–88, cities I and II). But *c.* 2300 BC Jericho perished violently at the hands of uncultured newcomers who eventually resettled the site (Albright's Middle Bronze Age I; K. M. Kenyon's Intermediate Early/Middle Bronze Age, *cf. DUJ*, pp. 186–209; *AHL*, pp. 135–161). These coalesced with the Canaanites of the Middle Bronze Age proper (*c.* 1900–1600/1550 BC). Biblically this was the period of Abraham, Isaac and Jacob; the remains from contemporary Jericho throw a vivid light on the daily life of Abraham's Canaanite/ Amorite town-dwelling neighbours. The tombs have preserved more than the badly-denuded town buildings. Splendid pottery, wooden three- and four-legged tables, stools and beds, trinket-boxes of bone inlay, basketry, platters of fruit and joints of meat, metal daggers and circlets—all have been preserved by peculiar atmospheric conditions (*DUJ*, pp. 210–232 [city], 233–255 [tombs]; *AHL*, pp. 162–194; *GSJ*, pp. 91–108). For restoration of a Jericho house-interior, see *DUJ*, endpapers. For reconstructions of the walled city on its mound, see *Illustrated London News*, 19 May 1956, pp. 554–555; *cf. AHL*, p. 188, fig. 45.

b. Jericho and the Old Testament

(i) *Joshua's invasion.* After *c.* 1600 BC Jericho was violently destroyed, probably by Egypt's 18th Dynasty imperial pharaohs. After this the only (Late Bronze) occupation found at Jericho dates mainly between *c.* 1400 and 1325 BC; from the 13th century BC, the date of the Israelite conquest (*CHRONOLOGY OF OT), virtually nothing is known (*DUJ*, pp. 259–263; *AHL*, pp. 197–198, 209–211). Garstang's 'Late Bronze Age' walls (*GSJ*, ch. 7) actually date from the Early Bronze Age, over 1,000 years before Joshua, because of the associated Early Bronze remains, and they are overlaid by Middle Bronze material, only subsequently identified in Miss Kenyon's excavations (*e.g. DUJ*, pp. 170–171, 176–177, and especially 181). It is possible that in Joshua's day (13th century BC) there was a small town on the E part of the mound, later wholly eroded away. Such a possibility is not just a 'harmonistic' or heuristic view, but one suggested by the evidence of considerable erosion of the older settlements at Jericho. The tombs conclusively prove the importance of Middle Bronze Age Jericho (patriarchal period), although on the city mound most of the Middle Bronze town—and even much of the Early Bronze one before it—was eroded away between *c.* 1600 and *c.* 1400 BC (*cf. DUJ*, pp. 170–171, and also 45, 93, 259–260, 262–263). When so much damage was done by the elements in barely 200 years it is easy to see how much havoc natural erosion must have wrought on the deserted mound in the 400 years that separated Joshua from Jericho's refounding by Hiel the Bethelite (1 Ki. 16:34) in Ahab's reign. It seems highly likely that the washed-out remains of the last Late Bronze Age city are now lost under the modern road and cultivated land along the E side of the town mound, as the main slope of the mound is from W down to E. It remains highly doubtful whether excavation here (even if allowed) would yield much now. The narrative of Jos. 3–8 within which the fall of Jericho is recounted is known to reflect faithfully conditions in, and topography of, the area, while Joshua's generalship is recounted in a realistic manner. On terrain, *cf.* J. Garstang, *Joshua-Judges*, 1931, pp. 135–148 (his earth-tremors, providentially sent, remain a valid suggestion, even though his 'Late Bronze' (actually Early Bronze) walls do not now count as direct evidence for Joshua's day). On Joshua's generalship, *cf.* Garstang, *op. cit.*, pp. 149–161, and Y. Kaufmann, *The Biblical Account of the Conquest of Palestine*, 1953, pp. 91–97.

(ii) *From Joshua to Nehemiah.* For centuries no attempt was made to rebuild the town-mound of Jericho in awe of Joshua's curse (Jos. 6:26), but the spring and oasis were still frequented, perhaps supporting a hamlet there. In the time of the judges, Eglon king of Moab temporarily occupied the oasis (Jdg. 3:13) and David's envoys tarried there after being outraged by Hanun of Ammon (2 Sa. 10:5; 1 Ch. 19:5); the 'blockhouse' may have been a guard-post in this period (10th century BC: so Albright and Wright, cited by Tushingham, *BA* 16, 1953, p. 67). Then in Ahab's reign (*c.* 874/3–853 BC) Hiel the Bethelite refounded Jericho proper and finally fulfilled the ancient curse in the loss of his eldest and youngest sons (1 Ki. 16:34). This humble Iron Age Jericho was that of Elijah and Elisha (2 Ki. 2:4–5, 18–22), and it was in the plains of Jericho that the Babylonians captured Zedekiah, last king of Judah (2 Ki. 25:5; 2 Ch. 28:15; Je. 39:5; 52:8). The remains of this Jericho (9th–6th centuries BC) are very fragmentary (erosion again to blame), but quite definite: buildings, pottery and tombs; probably the Babylonians destroyed the place in 587 BC (see *BA* 16, 1953, pp. 66–67; *PEQ* 85, 1953, pp. 91, 95; *DUJ*, pp. 263–264). After the Exile, a modest Jericho still existed in Persian times. Some 345 Jerichoans returned to Judaea with Zerubbabel (Ezr. 2:34; Ne. 7:36), and their descendants in Jericho helped with repairing Jerusalem's walls in 445 BC under Nehemiah (Ne. 3:2); a pottery jar-stamp (*c.* 4th century BC) 'belonging to Hagar (daughter of) Uriah' is the last memento of OT Jericho (Hammond, *PEQ* 89, 1957, pp. 68–69, with pl. 16, corrected in *BASOR* 147, 1957, pp. 37–39; *cf.* also Albright, *BASOR* 148, 1957, pp. 28–30).

c. New Testament Jericho

In NT times, the town of Jericho was sited S of the old mound. In that region, Herod the Great (40/37–4 BC) and his successors built a winter palace with ornamental gardens, near the famous palm and balsam groves that yielded lucrative revenues. Fragmentary ruins that may be connected with these great buildings have been excavated See Kelso and Baramki, 'Excavations at New Testament Jericho' in *AASOR* 29/30, 1955, and *BA* 14, 1951, pp. 33–43; Pritchard, *The Excavation at Herodian Jericho* in *AASOR* 32/33, 1958, and *BASOR* 123, 1951, pp. 8–17. Herod brought water by aqueduct from the Wadi Qilt (Perowne, *Life and Times of Herod the Great*, 1956, plates opposite pp. 96–97).

The environs of NT Jericho witnessed Christ's healing of blind men, including Bartimaeus (Mt. 20:29; Mk. 10:46; Lk. 18:35). Zacchaeus (Lk. 19:1) was not the only wealthy Jew who had his home in this fashionable district. The immortal story of the good Samaritan is set on the narrow, bandit-infested road from Jerusalem down to Jericho (Lk. 10:30–37).

IV. Bibliography

Sir Charles Warren sank shafts at Jericho in about 1868 with little result. The first scientific excavation there (1907–9) was by Sellin and Watzinger (*Jericho*, 1913), but they could not date their finds properly. Apart from his errors over 'Joshua's Jericho' (see above), Garstang in 1930–6 put the archaeology of the site on a sound basis. See J. and J. B. E. Garstang, *The Story of Jericho*, 1948 (*GSJ*). Detailed preliminary reports are in *Liverpool Annals of Archaeology and Anthropology* 19, 1932, to 23, 1936, and in *PEQ* for the same years. Miss Kenyon reviewed Garstang's results in *PEQ* 83, 1951, pp. 101–138. Further older bibliography is in Barrois, *Manuel d'Archéologie Biblique*, 1, 1939, pp. 61, 63.

Detailed preliminary reports of Miss Kenyon's excavations from 1952 to 1958 are in *PEQ* 84, 1952, to 92, 1960; *BASOR* 127, 1952, pp. 5–16; *BA* 16, 1953, pp. 45–67, and 17, 1954, pp. 98–104. For an instructive (and humorous) general account, see *W* = M. Wheeler, *The Walls of Jericho*, 1956 (paperback, 1960). Best detailed over-all account is *DUJ* = K. M. Kenyon, *Digging Up Jericho*, 1957 (fully illustrated), supplemented for the earliest periods by *AHL* = K. M. Kenyon, *Archaeology in the Holy Land*, 1960. The definitive publication is K. M. Kenyon and others, *Jericho* I–V, 1960–83. General background and a summary in P. Bienkowski, *Jericho in the Late Bronze Age*, 1986. For NT Jericho, see above (**III.** c) and good background by L. Mowry, *BA* 15, 1952, pp. 25–42. Overall bibliography, *cf.* E. K. Vogel, *Bibliography of Holy Land Sites*, 1974, pp. 42–44; survey, *cf. NEAEHL*, 2, pp. 674–695. K.A.K.

JEROBOAM (probably 'may the people increase'; possibly 'may he contend for the people', *i.e.* against Rehoboam's oppressions).

1. First king of Israel (*c.* 931–910 BC; 1 Ki. 11:26–14:20; 2 Ch. 10:2–13:20), Jeroboam, son of Nebat, seems to have been a wealthy land owner (*gibbôr ḥayil*, 1 Ki. 11:28), able to equip himself and others for war, despite the fact that his mother was a widow. *Solomon, building the Millo, placed Jeroboam, an Ephraimite, in charge of the workforce of the N tribes. The king's oppressive practices led Jeroboam to foment a revolt, resulting in his exile to Egypt until Solomon's death. The LXX contains an unreliable midrash (based partly on Hadad's experiences, 1 Ki. 11:14–22) which attempts to complete the sketchy biblical picture of Jeroboam's flight. His friendship with *Shishak was short-lived, for the pharaoh's subsequent invasion (*c.* 925 BC) proved costly to both Judah and Israel (including the destruction, as archaeological evidence indicates, of Gezer, Taanach, Megiddo, Beth-shean, *et al.*). Rehoboam's rash refusal to initiate a more clement policy than his father's brought the fulfilment of Ahijah's prophecy (1 Ki. 12:29ff.): the kingdom was rent asunder. Benjamin alone remained loyal to Judah and became a battleground for a series of border skirmishes between the two kings (1 Ki. 14:30). The conflict with Judah (1 Ki. 15:6–7; 2 Ch. 13:2–20) along with repeated pressures from Damascus and the Philistine cities, prompted Jeroboam to fortify key cities like Shechem, Penuel and Tirzah, which had served in turn as his capitals (1 Ki. 12:25; 14:17).

Jeroboam incurred divine wrath by building, in Dan and Bethel, shrines that rivalled the Jerusalem Temple and were staffed by a newly formed, non-levitical priesthood. The date of the Feast of Tabernacles was changed in the process (1 Ki. 12:31–32). The infamous calves were probably not representations of deity but pedestals on which the invisible Yahweh was supposed to stand (*cf.* W. F. Albright, *From the Stone Age to Christianity*[2], 1957, pp. 299–301). They threatened the covenant faith by encouraging a syncretism of Yahweh worship with the fertility cult of Baal and thus drew prophetic rebuke (*e.g.* the man of God, 1 Ki. 13:1ff.; Ahijah, 1 Ki. 14:14–16). Jeroboam's ascent to the throne by popular choice rather than hereditary right doomed the N kingdom to dynastic instability from the beginning. His royal cult set the pattern for his successors, who are customarily evaluated as perpetuating his sins (*e.g.* 1 Ki. 16:26).

BIBLIOGRAPHY. M. Aberbach, L. Smolar, in *IDBS*, 1976, pp. 473–475; J. Bright, *A History of Israel*[2], 1972, pp. 226–235; J. Gray, *1 and 2 Kings*[2], 1970; *EJ*, 9, cols. 1371–1374; M. Noth, *The History*

A seal inscribed 'belonging to Shema, servant of Jeroboam' (lšm' 'bd yrbm), *probably Jeroboam II (793–753* BC). *The roaring lion was used as a symbol for Judah. Length 3·8 cm. Megiddo.*

of Israel[2], 1960, pp. 225ff.; M. Haran, *VT* 17, 1967, pp. 266ff., 325ff.

2. Jeroboam II (*c.* 793–753 BC) was the 4th king of Jehu's dynasty and one of Israel's most illustrious rulers (2 Ki. 14:23–29). Co-regent with his father for a decade, Jeroboam II carried on Jehoash's policies of aggressive expansion. Aided by Adad-nirari's campaigns (805–802 BC) which broke the back of the Aramaean kingdom and by the Assyr. preoccupation with Armenia, he was able to restore Israel's boundaries virtually to their Solomonic scope and thus fulfil Jonah's prophecy (2 Ki. 14:25).

Jeroboam's administrative skills combined with comparative freedom from foreign attack to bring unparalleled economic prosperity. Excavations in *Samaria, including the discovery of the Samaritan ostraca, have demonstrated the grandeur of Jeroboam's fortress city together with the luxury and false worship which vexed Amos' righteous soul (*e.g.* Am. 6:1–7; 5:26; 8:14). Extreme wealth and poverty (Am. 2:6–7), empty religious ritual (Am. 5:21–24; 7:10–17) and false security (Am. 6:1–8) are among the characteristics of Jeroboam's lengthy reign. Amos' gloomy prophecy (7:9) was verified when Shallum's successful *coup* against Zechariah (whose name shows that Jeroboam retained some regard for Yahweh, 2 Ki. 15:8–12) wrote *finis* to Jehu's house. See J. Bright, *op. cit.*, pp. 254–256; *EJ*, 9, cols. 1374–1375; M. F. Unger, *Israel and the Arameans of Damascus*, 1957, pp. 89–95. D.A.H.

JERUEL (Heb. *yᵉrû'ēl*, 'founded by El'; LXX 'Jeriel'). Mentioned by the prophet Jahaziel as the wilderness where Jehoshaphat would meet and conquer the Moabites and Ammonites (2 Ch. 20:16). Possibly identical with, or a part of, the wilderness of *Tekoa, the country extending from the W shores of the Dead Sea N of En-gedi. J.D.D.

JERUSALEM.

I. Introduction and general description

Jerusalem is one of the world's famous cities. Under that name, it dates from at least the 3rd millennium BC; and today is considered sacred by the adherents of the three great monotheistic faiths, Judaism, Christianity and Islam. The city is set high in the hills of Judah, about 50 km from the Mediterranean, and over 30 km W of the N end of the Dead Sea. It rests on a none-too-level plateau, which slopes noticeably towards the SE. To the E lies the ridge of Olivet. Access to the city on all sides except the N is hampered by three deep ravines, which join in the Siloam Valley, near the well Bir Eyyub, SE of the city. The E valley is Kidron; the W is now called the Wadi al-Rababi, and is probably to be equated with the Valley of Hinnom; and the third cuts the city in half before it runs S, and slightly E, to meet the other two. This latter ravine is not mentioned or named in Scripture (although Maktesh, Zp. 1:11, may well have been the name of part of it), so it is usually referred to as the Tyropoeon Valley, *i.e.*, the Valley of the Cheesemakers, after Josephus.

Eminences rise each side of the Tyropoeon Valley, and the city can at once be divided into W and E halves. Ignoring lesser heights, we may subdivide each of these two sections into N and S hills. When considering the growth and development of the city (see **IV**) it will be important to visualize these details. In discussing the respective heights and depths of these hills and valleys, it must be realized that they have changed considerably over the centuries. This is inevitable in any city continuously inhabited for centuries, and particularly when periodic destructions have taken place. Layer after layer of rubble and debris piles up, amounting here and there to more than 30 m in parts of Jerusalem. In the case of Jerusalem there is also the factor that deliberate attempts have been made at various periods to fill in valleys (especially the Tyropoeon) and diminish hills.

Jerusalem's water-supply has always presented problems. Apart from Bir Eyyub, the well mentioned above, there is only the Virgin's Spring, which is connected by an aqueduct with the Pool of Siloam. There are, and have been, other reservoirs, of course, such as Bethesda in NT times and Mamilla Pool today, but they all depend on the rains or else on aqueducts to fill them. Bir Eyyub and the Virgin's Spring are in all probability the biblical En-rogel and Gihon respectively. Bir Eyyub lies SE of the city, at the junction of the three ravines mentioned above. The Virgin's Spring is due N of Bir Eyyub, E and a little S of the Temple area. Thus it is evident that only the SE part of Jerusalem has a reliable water-supply. (See A. Mazar, 'The Aqueducts of Jerusalem', in Y. Yadin, *Jerusalem Revealed*, pp. 79–84.)

II. Name

The meaning of the name is not certain. The Heb. word is usually written *yᵉrûšālaim* in the OT, but this is an anomalous form, since Heb. cannot have two consecutive vowels. The anomaly was resolved in later Heb. by inserting the letter 'y', thus giving *yᵉrûšālayim*; this form does in fact occur a few times in the OT, *e.g.*, Je. 26:18. This may well have been understood to be a dual (for the ending *-ayim* is dual), viewing the city as twofold. (Similarly, the Heb. name for 'Egypt', *miṣrayim*, appears to be dual.) But there can be little doubt that the original form of the word in Heb. was *yᵉrušālēm*; this is evidenced by the abbreviation *šālēm* (Eng. 'Salem') in Ps. 76:2, and by the Aramaic form of the name *yᵉrûšlēm*, found in Ezr. 5:14, *etc.*

The name is pre-Israelite, appearing in the Egyp. Execration Texts (19th–18th century; the form appears to be Rushalimum) and in later Assyrian documents (as *Urusalim* or *Urisalimmu*). The first part of the name is usually thought to mean 'foundation'; the second element, though cognate with the Heb. word for 'peace', probably originally referred to a Canaanite deity Shalem. Thus 'foundation of Shalem' is probably the original sense of the name; in course of time, however, the second element will have been associated with 'peace' (Heb. *šālôm*) in Jewish minds; *cf*. Heb. 7:2.

In NT Greek the name is transliterated in two different ways, *Hierosolyma* (as in Mt. 2:1) and *Hierousalēm* (as in Mt. 23:37). The latter is evidently a close approximation to the Heb. pronunciation, and incidentally an additional evidence for an '*e*' as the original final vowel in Hebrew. The former is deliberately Hellenized, to make a Greek-sounding word; the first part of the word at once recalls the Greek word *hieros*, 'holy', and probably the whole

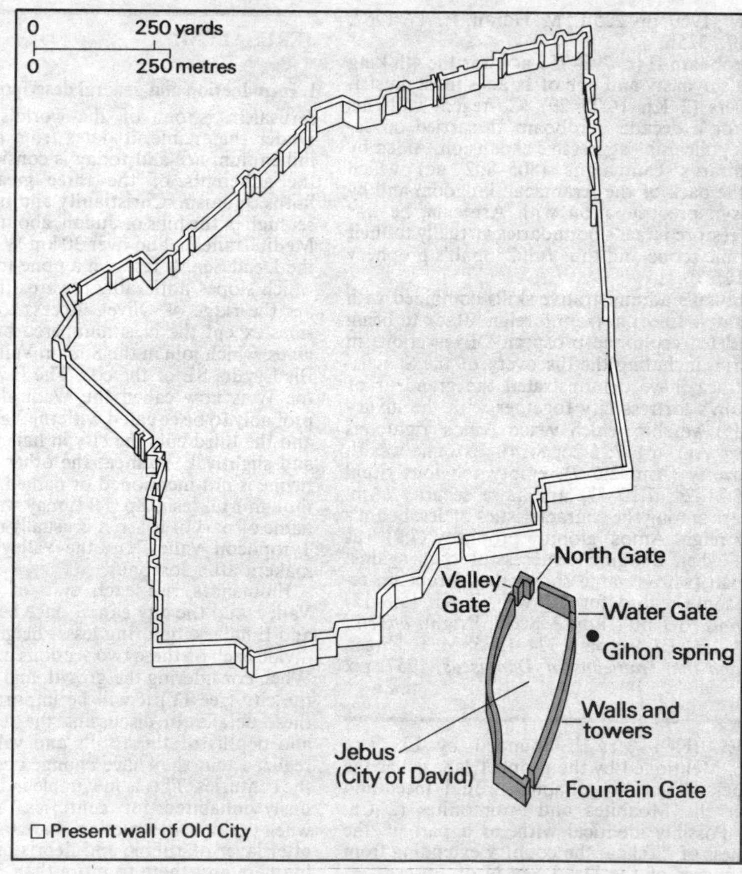

Jebus, the site of the City of David, Jerusalem, on the SE hill, Mt Zion.

was understood to mean something like 'sacred Salem'. LXX has only the form *Hierousalēm*, whereas Greek classical writers use *Hierosolyma* (*e.g.* Polybius; so too Latin, *e.g.* Pliny).

Jerusalem is described in Is. 52:1 as the holy city, and to this day it often receives this title. The Heb. phrase is *'îr haq-qōdeš*, literally 'the city of holiness'. Probably the reason for this title was that Jerusalem contained the Temple, the shrine where God deigned to meet his people. Hence, the word *qōdeš* came to mean 'sanctuary' as well as 'holiness'. To Judaism, then, Jerusalem was the holy city without a rival. It was natural for Paul and John, seeing that the earthly city was far from perfect, to designate the place where God dwells in true holiness as 'Jerusalem which is above' (Gal. 4:26) and 'new Jerusalem' (Rev. 21:2).

For other names the city has borne, see **III**, in historical sequence.

III. History

Traces of prehistoric settlement at Jerusalem have been found, but its early history cannot be traced. After a bare mention in the Egyp. Execration Texts early in the 2nd millennium, it reappears in the 14th-century el-Amarna letters, ruled by a king named Abdi-Khepa. At that time it was under the suzerainty of Egypt, and was probably little more than a mountain fortress. Possible pentateuchal references to it are as Salem (Gn. 14:18) and the mountain in the 'land of Moriah' of Gn. 22:2. According to very ancient tradition, the latter was the place where later the Temple was built, but there is no possible proof of this. As for Salem, it is almost certainly to be identified with Jerusalem (*cf.* Ps. 76:2); if so, it was ruled in Abraham's day by an earlier king, Melchizedek, who was also 'priest of God Most High' (*'ēl 'elyôn*).

When the Israelites entered Canaan they found Jerusalem in the hands of an indigenous Semitic tribe, the Jebusites, ruled over by a king named Adoni-zedek. This ruler formed an alliance of kings against Joshua, who soundly defeated them; but Joshua did not take the city, owing, doubtless, to its natural strength of position. It remained in Jebusite hands, bearing the name Jebus. Comparing Jdg. 1:8 with Jdg. 1:21, it appears that Judah overcame the part of the city outside the fortress walls, and that Benjamin occupied this part, living peaceably alongside the Jebusites in the fortress.

This was the situation when David became king. His first capital was Hebron, but he soon saw the value of Jerusalem, and set about its capture. This was not only a tactical move but also a diplomatic

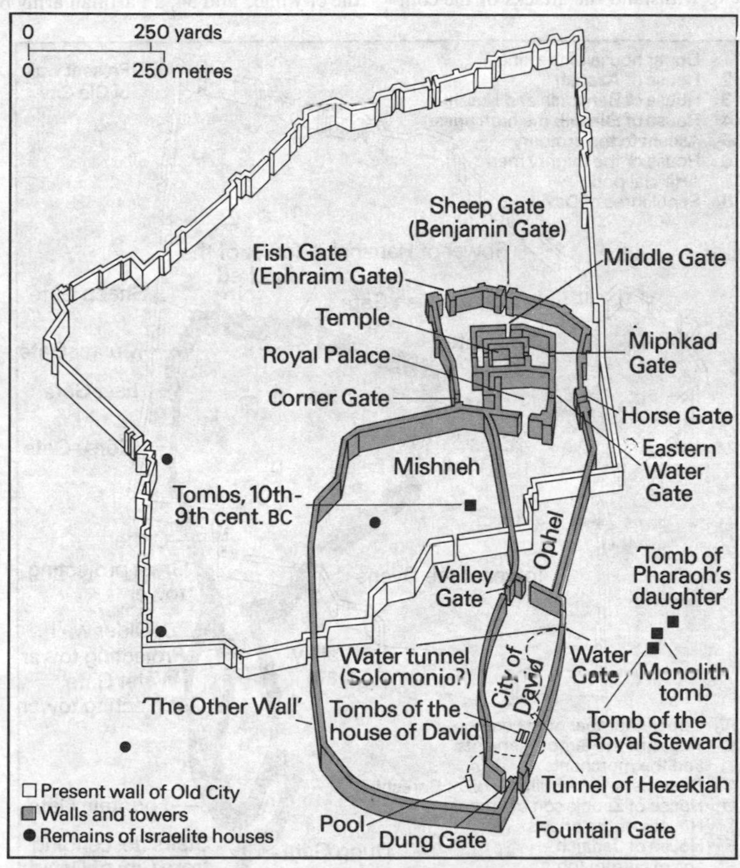

Jerusalem from Solomon to Hezekiah, showing extensions to the N and W, including the Temple area.

one, for his use of a city on the Benjamin–Judah border would help to diminish the jealousy between the two tribes. The Jebusites felt confident of their safety behind the fortress walls, but David's men used an unexpected mode of entry, and took the citadel by surprise (2 Sa. 5:6ff.). In this passage we meet a third name, 'Zion'. This was probably the name of the hill on which the citadel stood; Vincent, however, thinks the name originally applied rather to the fortress building than to the ground it occupied.

Having taken the city, David improved the fortifications and built himself a palace; he also installed the ark in his new capital. Solomon carried the work of fortification further, but his great achievement was the construction of the Temple. After his death and the subsequent division of the kingdom, Jerusalem naturally declined somewhat, being now capital only of Judah. As early as the 5th year of Solomon's successor, Rehoboam, the Temple and royal palace were plundered by Egyp. troops (1 Ki. 14:25f.). Philistine and Arab marauders again plundered the palace in Jehoram's reign. In Amaziah's reign a quarrel with the king of the N kingdom, Jehoash, resulted in part of the city walls being broken down, and fresh looting of Temple and palace. Uzziah repaired this damage to the fortifications, so that in the reign of Ahaz the city was able to withstand the attacks of the combined armies of Syria and Israel. Soon after this the N kingdom fell to the Assyrians. Hezekiah of Judah had good reason to fear Assyria too, but Jerusalem providentially escaped. In case of siege, he made a conduit to improve the city's water-supply.

Nebuchadrezzar of Babylon captured Jerusalem in 597 and in 587 BC destroyed the city and Temple. At the end of that century the Jews, now under Persian rule, were allowed to return to their land and city, and they rebuilt the Temple, but the city walls remained in ruins until Nehemiah restored them in the middle of the 5th century BC. Alexander the Great ended the power of Persia at the end of the 4th century, and after his death his general Ptolemy, founder of the Ptolemaic dynasty in Egypt, entered Jerusalem and included it in his realm. In 198 BC Palestine fell to Antiochus II, the Seleucid king of Syria. About 30 years later, Antiochus IV entered Jerusalem, destroying its walls and plundering and desecrating the Temple; and he installed a Syrian garrison in the city, on the Akra. Judas the Maccabee led a Jewish revolt, and in 165 BC the Temple was rededicated. He and his successors gradually won independence for Judaea, and the Hasmonaean dynasty ruled a free Jerusalem until the middle of the 1st century BC when Rome intervened. Roman generals forced their way into the city in 63 and 54; a Parthian army plundered it

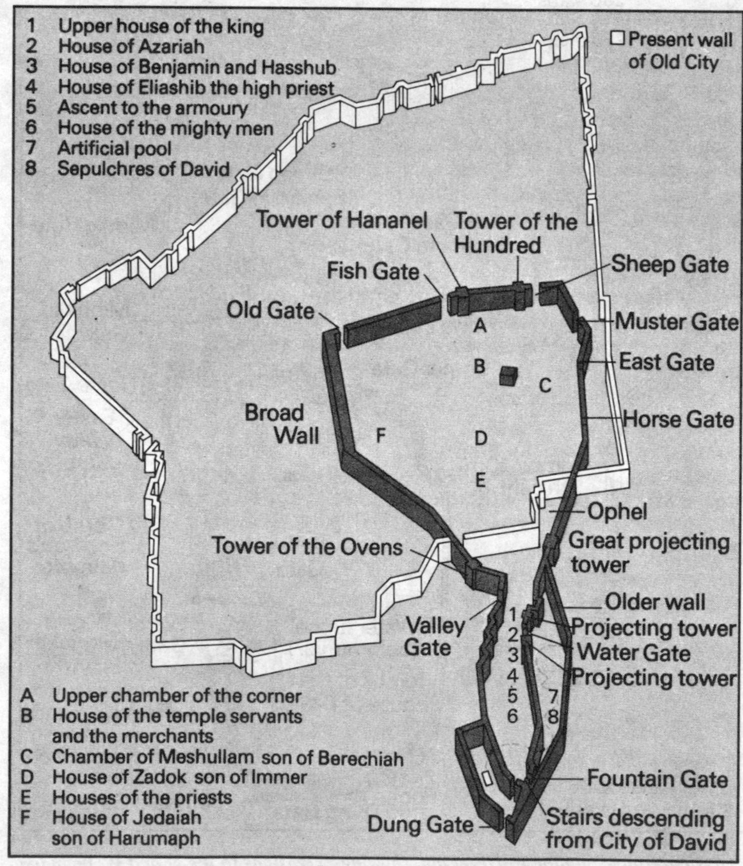

Probable reconstruction of Jerusalem as rebuilt by Nehemiah in the 5th cent. BC

in 40; and 3 years after that Herod the Great had to fight his way into it, to take control. He first had to repair the damage created by these various incursions; then he launched a big building programme, erecting some notable towers. His most renowned work was the rebuilding of the Temple on a much grander scale, although this was not finished within his lifetime. One of his towers was Antonia, commanding the Temple area (it housed the Roman garrison which came to Paul's aid, Acts 21:34).

The Jewish revolt against the Romans in AD 66 could have but one conclusion; in AD 70 the Roman general Titus systematically forced his way into Jerusalem, and destroyed the fortifications and the Temple. He left three towers standing; one of them, Phasael, still remains, incorporated in the so-called 'Tower of David'. But further disaster awaited the Jews: another revolt in AD 132 led to the rebuilding of Jerusalem (on a much smaller scale) as a pagan city, dedicated to Jupiter Capitolinus, from which all Jews were excluded. This was the work of the emperor Hadrian; he called the newly constructed city Aelia Capitolina (the name even found its way into Arabic, as Iliya). It was not until the reign of Constantine (early 4th century) that the Jews were again permitted to enter the city. From his reign on, the city became Christian instead of pagan, and many churches and monasteries were built, notably the Church of the Holy Sepulchre.

Jerusalem has suffered many vicissitudes since the 2nd century, and has been captured and held at various times by Persian, Arab, Turkish, Crusader, British and Israeli troops and administrations. The most important building developments in the Old City (as opposed to the rapidly growing modern suburbs) were due to the early Muslims, the Crusaders and finally the Turkish sultan Suleiman the Magnificent who in 1542 rebuilt the city walls as they can be seen today. The Israelis give the city its ancient Heb. name, *yᵉrûšālayim*; the Arabs usually call it *al-Quds* (*al-Sharîf*), 'the (noble) Sanctuary'.

IV. Growth and extent

It must be stated at the outset that there is a good deal of uncertainty about the physical history of Jerusalem. This is, of course, partly due to the periodic disasters and destructions, and to the layers upon layers of rubble that have piled up over the centuries. These factors have caused difficulty elsewhere, of course, but archaeologists have often been able to surmount them to a large extent. The particular problem with Jerusalem is that it has been continuously inhabited and still is, so that excavations can be made only with difficulty.

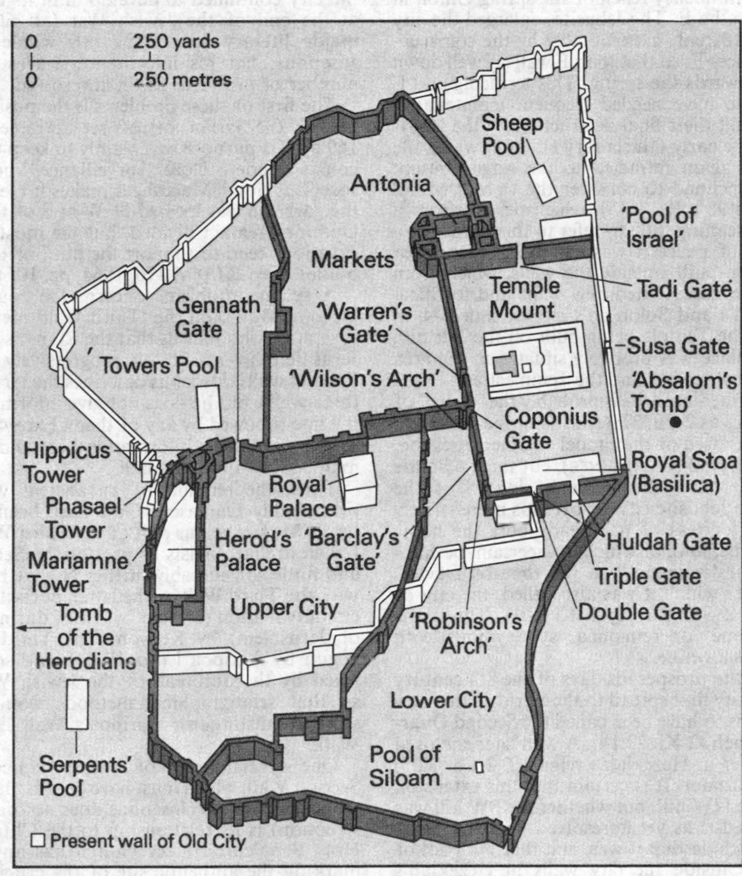

Jerusalem in the time of Herod the Great.

Archaeologists here have to dig where they can, not where they think it might be profitable. On the other hand, there is an abundance of traditions, Christian, Jewish and Muslim; but in many cases it is not easy to evaluate them. So uncertainty and controversy remain; however, much valuable archaeological work has been done during the last century, and it has solved some problems.

Scripture nowhere gives a systematic description of the city. The nearest approach to such a description is the account of the rebuilding of the walls by Nehemiah. But there are a great number of references giving some information. These have to be pieced together, and fitted in with the picture we get from archaeology. Our earliest description of the city is that of Josephus (*BJ* 5. 136–141); Josephus is here laying a background for his account of the gradual capture of the city by Titus and the Roman armies. This too has to be fitted into the picture.

Excavations have conclusively shown that the earliest city was on the SE hill, an area now wholly outside the city walls (the S wall was retracted N in the 2nd century AD). It must be clearly borne in mind that the original Zion lay on the E ridge; the name was by the time of Josephus already erroneously attached to the SW hill.

Few traces remain from the pre-Jebusite period, but it may be inferred that a small town grew on the SE ridge, within easy reach of the spring Gihon in the valley to the E. The Jebusites enlarged the city to a limited extent, most notably by the construction of terraces E, so that their E wall lay well down the slope towards the spring. This terracing and E wall seem to have needed frequent maintenance and repair till their final destruction by the Babylonians in the early 6th century BC, after which the E wall was again retracted to the ridge. Present opinion is inclined to consider the word *'Millo' (*e.g.* 2 Sa. 5:9; 1 Ki. 9:15), which derives from a Heb. root meaning 'fill', to refer to this terracing.

In times of peace it was common practice for houses to be built outside the walls, which from time to time necessitated new walls and fortifications. David's and Solomon's city extended N, in particular, the Temple being built on the NE hill; the royal palace was probably situated in the area between the older city and the Temple area.

This intermediate area is probably the 'Ophel' of such passages as 2 Ch. 27:3 (the name means 'swelling', and was used of the citadel of other cities too, *e.g.* Samaria, *cf.* 2 Ki. 5:24, NEB); but some scholars apply the term to the whole E ridge S of the Temple. The Jebusite city, or perhaps more strictly the central fortress of it, already bore the name 'Zion' (the meaning of which is uncertain, perhaps 'dry area' or 'eminence') at the time of David's capture, after which it was also called 'the city of David' (*cf.* 2 Sa. 5:6–10; 1 Ki. 8:1). The name 'Zion' became, or remained, synonymous with Jerusalem as a whole.

It was in the prosperous days of the 8th century BC that the city first spread to the W ridge; this new suburb seems to have been called the Second Quarter or Mishneh (2 Ki. 22:14). A wall later enclosed it, built either in Hezekiah's reign (*cf.* 2 Ch. 32:5) or somewhat later. It is certain that this extension included the NW hill, but whether the SW hill was now occupied is as yet unresolved. Israeli archaeologists conclude that it was, and that the Pool of Siloam was inside the city walls in Hezekiah's reign.

When Nebuchadrezzar's troops sacked Jerusalem in 587 BC, they destroyed most of the buildings and demolished the city walls. The Temple was rebuilt at the end of the century, and the city had a small population once again. In the mid-5th century the Persian authorities permitted Nehemiah to rebuild the city walls. No doubt he restored earlier walls where possible, but it is clear from excavations that he retracted the E wall on the E side to the crest of the hill because the ancient terraces were broken beyond repair and no doubt the W ridge was abandoned. Persian period deposits occur principally on the top of the E hill. Nehemiah's description of Jerusalem presents several problems. It is not clear which gates were in the city wall and which led into the Temple. Names of gates changed from time to time, and there are difficulties in the Heb. text. Earlier attempts to interpret Nehemiah's data require revision in the light of recent excavations. Although Nehemiah gives no indication of direction or changes of direction, it is fairly clear that the circuit he described in ch. 3 began N of the city and took an anti-clockwise direction.

There is little evidence that the city spread to the W ridge again until the 2nd century BC. After the Maccabaean revolt, the city began to grow once more. Herod the Great was responsible for a major building programme in the late 1st century BC, and the city continued to develop until its destruction at the end of the Jewish War (AD 66–70). Our major literary source for this whole period is Josephus; but his information leaves us with a number of problems as yet unresolved.

The first of these problems is the position of the 'Akra', the Syrian fortress set up in Jerusalem in 169 BC. Its purpose was plainly to keep the Temple courts under close surveillance, but neither Josephus nor 1 Maccabees makes it clear whether the garrison was located N, W or S of the Temple. Opinions remain divided, but the most recent excavations tend to support the third of these possibilities. (See *BASOR* 176, 1964, pp. 10f.)

A second problem concerns the course of the 'Second Wall' and the 'Third Wall' mentioned by Josephus, who tells us that the Romans penetrated Jerusalem in AD 70 by progressively breaching three N walls. Josephus describes the termini of the three walls, but he does not give information as to the line followed by any of them. Excavations have supplemented his information here and there, but many uncertainties remain.

Thus, the remains of an ancient wall at the present-day Damascus Gate have been identified by K. M. Kenyon as part of the Third Wall, but by Israeli archaeologists as part of the Second Wall; and finds considerably further N have been linked with the Third Wall by the latter, but with a wall of circumvallation (erected by Titus, during the siege of Jerusalem) by Kenyon. The Third Wall was begun by Agrippa I (AD 41–44), and scarcely finished by the outbreak of the Jewish War AD 66, so that stratigraphical methods would scarcely serve to distinguish Agrippa's Wall from Titus' Wall.

One special point of interest concerning the Second Wall, which must have been built in the 2nd or 1st century BC (Josephus does not date its construction) is its relationship to the Church of the Holy Sepulchre. If the church has any claim to marking the authentic site of the crucifixion and burial of Christ, its site must have lain outside the city walls; but for many years it was considered doubtful whether the site lay inside or outside the line of the Second Wall (the Third Wall was not then in existence). It has now been established that this area lay to the N of the wall; the site may therefore be authentic.

The city lay in ruins between AD 70 and the Bar-Kokhba revolt 60 years later. The emperor Hadrian then rebuilt the city, naming it Aelia Capitolina; his city was much smaller than its predecessor, with the permanent retraction of the S wall. During the Christian era, the size of Jerusalem has been by no means constant. The present-day walled area ('the Old City') was given its definitive shape by Suleiman the Magnificent in the 16th century.

V. Theological significance

By natural metonymy, the names 'Zion' and 'Jerusalem' frequently stand for the body of citizens (even when far away in exile), the whole of Judah, the whole of Israel, or the entire people of God.

Jerusalem plays an important theological role in both Testaments; in this respect too it is not readily distinguishable from the wider perspective of the whole land. Two motifs predominate: Jerusalem is at the same time the place of Jewish infidelity and disobedience, and also the place of God's election and presence, protection, and glory. The process of history demonstrated the former, which inevitably provoked divine anger and punishment; the glories of the city can only lie in the future. (See especially Is. 1:21; 29:1–4; Mt. 23:37f.; and Ps. 78:68f.; Is. 37:35; 54:11–17.) The contrast between the actual and the ideal naturally gave rise to the concept of a heavenly Jerusalem (*cf.* Gal. 4:25f.; Heb. 12:22; Rev. 21).

BIBLIOGRAPHY. On history and archaeology, see especially K. M. Kenyon, *Digging up Jerusalem*, 1974, and bibliography there listed; Y. Yadin (ed.), *Jerusalem Revealed*, 1975; B. Mazar, *The Mountain of the Lord*, 1975; H. Geva, *Ancient Jerusalem Revealed*, 1994; *NEAEHL* 2, pp. 698–804. On economic and social conditions, see J. Jeremias, *Jerusalem in the Time of Jesus*, 1969. On theology see *TDNT* 7, pp. 292–338; W. D. Davies, *The Gospel and the Land*, 1974. D.F.P.

JESHIMON (Heb. *yᵉšîmōn*, 'waste', 'desert'). Apparently used as a proper noun in Nu. 21:20; 23:28; 1 Sa. 23:19, 24; 26:1, 3. G. A. Smith, followed by G. E. Wright and F. V. Filson, identifies the name simply with the Wilderness of Judaea, but there is reason to think that in the Nu. references a location NE of the Dead Sea is indicated. See *GTT*, pp. 22f. R.P.G.

JESHUA. This is a late form of the name Joshua (the same individual is called Jeshua in Nehemiah and Ezra, and Joshua in Haggai and Zechariah). There is doubt about how many Jeshuas there are, but the following may perhaps be distinguished.

1. The head of a course of priests (1 Ch. 24:11, AV 'Jeshuah'). **2.** A Levite mentioned in Hezekiah's reorganization (2 Ch. 31:15). **3.** The high priest also called Joshua (Ezr. 2:2, *etc.*). **4.** A man of Pahath-moab who returned from the Exile with Zerubbabel (Ezr. 2:6). **5.** A head of a house of priests associated with 'the sons of Jedaiah' (Ezr. 2:36). **6.** A Levite, Jeshua son of Azaniah (Ne. 10:9). **7.** One of the chief of the Levites, the son of Kadmiel (Ne. 12:24; the text here may be corrupt). **8.** The father of Ezer, ruler of Mizpah (Ne. 3:19). **9.** The son of Nun (Ne. 8:17) (*JOSHUA).

It is clear that the name was a common one at the time of the return from the Exile. But little is told us of the various bearers of the name, and it is possible that some of those in the list ought to be identified with others.

Jeshua is also the name of a place in Judah (Ne. 11:26), usually taken as identical with Shema (Jos. 15:26), and Sheba (Jos. 19:2). The original form would be Shema, *m* becomes *b*, then *w*, and finally *j* is prefixed. L.M.

JESHURUN (Heb. *yᵉšurûn*, 'the upright one'; LXX 'the beloved one'). A poetic variant of the name Israel (Dt. 32:15; 33:5, 26, AV 'Jesurun'). Used of the chosen Servant (Is. 44:2), the same Gk. word of LXX is used of Jesus (Eph. 1:6) and the church (Col. 3:12; 1 Thes. 1:4; 2 Thes. 2:3; Jude 1). Possibly to be interpreted 'People of the Law' (*cf.* D. J. Wiseman, *Vox Evangelica* 8, 1973, p. 14). D.W.B.

JESSE (Heb. *yišay*). Grandson of Boaz and father of David. He lived in Bethlehem and is commonly termed 'the Bethlehemite', but once the 'Ephrathite of Bethlehem-Judah'. He was the father of eight sons (1 Sa. 16:10–11), but the names of only seven are known (1 Ch. 2:13–15). The eighth is omitted, probably as he had no issue, unless the Elihu of 1 Ch. 27:18 is other than Eliab.

Ancient Jewish tradition (Targ. Ruth 4:22) followed by later interpreters (*cf.* AVmg.) identifies Nahash (2 Sa. 17:25) with Jesse. Two other solutions are more probable. Either Abigail and Zeruiah were daughters of Jesse's wife by a former marriage to a Nahash (*cf.* A. P. Stanley, *Jewish Church*, Lect. 22) or Nahash may be a feminine name and taken as the mother of the daughters. Jesse's last appearance is at the cave of Adullam, whence David sent his parents for safety to Moab (1 Sa. 22:3–4). M.A.M.

JESUS CHRIST, LIFE AND TEACHING OF. A general article on the life and teaching of Jesus can touch only briefly on individual incidents and issues. Full use should therefore be made of the numerous references (at the end of sections and by asterisks in the text) to articles on specific points.

I. Sources

a. Non-Christian sources

Very few early references to Jesus with any claim to be independent of Christian sources have survived. The only direct mention by a Roman historian is a bare record of his execution by order of Pontius Pilatus in Judaea in the reign of Tiberius (Tacitus, *Annals* 15. 44). Other early Roman references to Christians do not refer to Jesus as a historical figure. The Jewish historian *Josephus has one brief account of Jesus, which is generally agreed to have been rewritten by Christians; it is likely that the original text referred to him as a reputed miracle-worker and teacher who attracted a considerable following and was executed by crucifixion under Pilate, though even this content is disputed (*Ant.* 18. 64). A number of rather obscure passages in the Talmud, whose reference to Jesus is in most

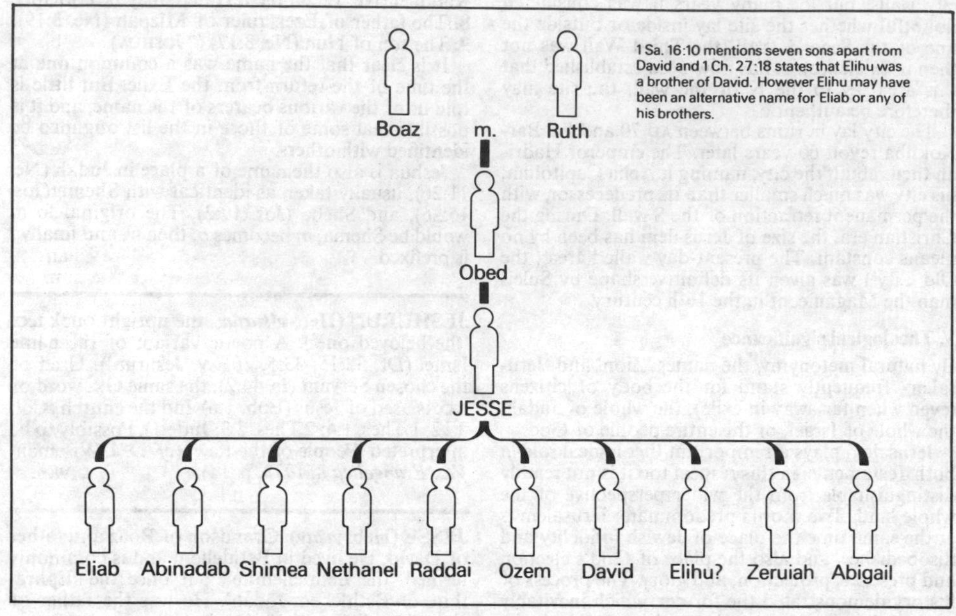

Jesse's family tree according to 1 Ch. 2:13–17 (see p. 563).

cases only conjectural, add no clear historical detail, beyond the statement that he was hanged on Passover Eve, after due trial, as a sorcerer and one who 'led Israel astray' (*Sanhedrin* 43a). Non-Christian evidence therefore substantiates the fact of Jesus' existence, his popular following, his execution and the rough date (Pilate was in office in Judaea AD 26–36).

b. Christian sources

1. Outside the NT there are numerous accounts of the life and teaching of Jesus in early Christian writings (*NEW TESTAMENT APOCRYPHA). Some are clearly legendary, aiming to fill the gaps in the narratives of the canonical Gospels or to heighten the miraculous element. Others are apparently written to propagate Gnostic and other deviant views. While some of these works are quite early (early 2nd century), most of their historically credible material is clearly based on the canonical Gospels; only the *Gospel of Thomas* is generally treated seriously as possibly preserving independent authentic tradition, and many even of its sayings are influenced by Gnosticism, while many of the rest are paralleled in the canonical Gospels.

2. Thus in practice we are almost entirely restricted to the four canonical Gospels for evidence about Jesus. The rest of the NT contributes only a few isolated sayings and traditions (*e.g.* Acts 20:35; 1 Cor. 11:23–25).

The reliability of the Gospels as historical sources is hotly debated. Their primary purpose is clearly more than a mere recounting of facts, but it is not so clear that their avowedly 'propagandist' purpose necessarily calls in question their historical accuracy. If the Gospels are studied in the light of comparable literature of the period, and particularly of what is known of Jewish ideas of tradition, it appears that, while there was considerable freedom in the selection and wording of sayings and narratives, so that each writer's individual thought and purpose come out in the way he presents his material, they were essentially concerned to pass on a carefully preserved tradition of the words and deeds of Jesus. See further *Gospels, and the articles on the Gospels individually; also *Tradition.

BIBLIOGRAPHY. F. F. Bruce, *Jesus and Christian Origins outside the New Testament*[2], 1984, R. T. France, *The Evidence for Jesus*, 1986. On *b.* 2: C. L. Blomberg, *The Historical Reliability of the Gospels*, 1987; G. N. Stanton, *The Gospels and Jesus*, 1989.

II. Setting

A. Time

Jesus was born shortly before the death of *Herod the Great in 4 BC (Mt. 2:1, 13–15); the exact date cannot be determined. His public ministry began when he was 'about thirty years of age' (Lk. 3:23); this was some time after the beginning of John the Baptist's mission in, probably, AD 28 (Lk. 3:1ff.). The length of his ministry is again impossible to determine exactly, but a period of roughly 3 years is generally agreed (based on the two springtimes indicated in Mark before the final Passover, Mk. 2:23; 6:39, and the three Passovers of Jn. 2:13; 6:4; 12:1). This would suggest a date of about AD 33 for the crucifixion, and if the Gospels indicate that the Passover (Nisan 14/15) fell on a Friday in the year of the crucifixion (though this too is disputed: see *LORD'S SUPPER), the astronomical data for AD 33 would support this date. But certainty on the precise dates is impossible. (*CHRONOLOGY OF THE NEW TESTAMENT.)

BIBLIOGRAPHY. H. Hoehner, *Chronological Aspects of the Life of Christ*, 1977; J. P. Meir, *A Marginal Jew* 1, 1991, pp. 372–433.

b. Place

Practically the whole of Jesus' public ministry took place within Palestine. Only a few journeys outside Palestine are recorded, *e.g.* into Phoenicia and Decapolis (Mk. 7:24, 31), and to Caesarea Philippi on the slopes of Mt Hermon (Mk. 8:27). Jesus first came to the notice of John the Baptist in the Jordan valley, and John's Gospel records some early ministry in that area and in Judaea (Jn. 1:28–42; 2:13–4:3, dated before John's imprisonment, 3:24; 4:1–3, after which the Galilean ministry began, Mk. 1:14). Thereafter the main scene of ministry was Galilee, punctuated by visits to Jerusalem recorded by John in connection with festivals, until the final Passover visit.

c. Historical situation

1. Palestine had been under *Roman rule* for some 60 years when Jesus was born. It was indirect rule, through local princes, of whom *Herod the Great was the most famous. The division of his kingdom among his sons resulted in three regional rulers, of whom *Herod Antipas, tetrarch of Galilee and Peraea, held office throughout the period of Jesus' ministry; he is the Herod whom we meet in the Gospels outside the infancy stories. Archelaus, who took over Judaea and Samaria, was deposed after 10 years of misrule, and here direct rule was imposed, in the person of a Roman prefect, responsible to the governor of the province of Syria. The prefect during the period of Jesus' ministry was Pontius *Pilate.

Roman rule brought real benefits to the subject nation, but it was not popular. A special grievance was the system of taxation under which the already high official taxes were swollen by the unofficial rake-off of the *tax-collectors (AV 'publicans') who thus became a feared and hated group, both as extortioners and as collaborators with the occupying power. But the chief cause of resentment was the mere fact of political subjection, a position felt by many to be incompatible with Israel's status as the people of God.

2. The varying *Jewish reactions* to this situation may be seen in the attitudes of the 'parties' which had by this time emerged within Judaism. The priestly *Sadducees, who with the lay 'elders' exercised the effective leadership of the Jews under Roman rule (*SANHEDRIN) seem to have been more concerned with the maintenance of the *status quo* and the proper observance of the Temple ritual than with any ideological resistance to Roman rule. The *Pharisees, though in some cases willing to support insurrectionary movements, busied themselves with the law and the complex business of its rigorous application to everyday life. The *Essenes went further and opted out of all political and social involvement in favour of a monastic withdrawal. (The *DEAD SEA SCROLLS provide vivid documentation of such a separatist group at Qumran.) But there was a strong and popular movement towards political activism (*'ZEALOT', the name of one such group later in the century, is often used loosely to denote the various groups who took this stance), particularly since the abortive revolt of Judas of Galilee, provoked by the *census of AD 6. Sporadic outbreaks of insurrectionary activity, particularly in Galilee, led up eventually to the devastating Jewish War AD 66–70.

3. **Galilee*, Jesus' home province, stood to some extent apart from the Jewish heartland of Judaea. Its population, until quite recently largely Gentile, and geographically separated from Judaea by the hostile territory of Samaria, was despised by Judaean Jews as of questionable religious orthodoxy, if not still half-pagan. The pronounced N accent made a Galilean conspicuous in Jerusalem society. This difference of background may be a significant factor in Jesus' dealings with the Jewish authorities. It is also relevant to his reputation with the Romans, to whom 'Galilean' was almost tantamount to 'revolutionary'.

4. The *languages* of Palestine in the 1st century AD are a complex problem. It seems clear that Aram., Heb. and Gk. were all spoken. Aram. was most probably Jesus' vernacular, but a Galilean would almost certainly also have a working knowledge of Gk., and Heb. (in a form akin to the later Mishnaic) may well have been the medium for his debates with the religious authorities in Jerusalem.

BIBLIOGRAPHY. F. F. Bruce, *New Testament History*, 1982, chs. 1–9; C. Rowland, *Christian Origins*, 1985, pp. 25–108; J. Stambaugh and D. Balch, *The Social World of the First Christians*, 1986; S. Freyne, *Galilee, Jesus and the Gospels*, 1988.

III. Birth and childhood

The details of the birth of Jesus are recorded only in the Gospels of Matthew and Luke, each Gospel clearly using different sources, that of Matthew concentrating more on Joseph's side of the story, while Luke shows an intimate knowledge of Mary's experiences (and of those of her relative Elizabeth, mother of John the Baptist) which it is generally agreed could only have been derived, directly or indirectly, from Mary herself. It is therefore the more remarkable that on the crucial fact of the supernatural origin of Jesus' birth, without a human father, the two Gospels with their independent sources are agreed (*VIRGIN BIRTH).

The circumstances of Jesus' birth and childhood were in striking contrast to the supernatural mode of his conception. He was born in the animal quarters of a crowded village inn, and brought up in a very ordinary home in the obscure Galilean village of *Nazareth, which had achieved no mention in earlier literature. His family may have been what we would call 'middle class', the 'carpenter' (actually more a building contractor) being a skilled craftsman, perhaps employing labour, and a respected figure in village life (*ARTS AND CRAFTS, **III.** *c*). But the Gospel records make it clear that they were not affluent (Lk. 2:24; *cf.* Lv. 12:8), and Jesus' parables sometimes reflect experience of a home where comfort and money were limited (*e.g.* Lk. 11:5–7; 15:8–10). The fact that Joseph is not mentioned after the birth and childhood stories, and that Jesus was referred to in the village as 'Mary's son' (Mk. 6:3), is often taken to mean that Joseph died while Jesus was young, leaving Jesus as the oldest son to run the family business and provide for his four younger brothers and unknown number of sisters (Mk. 6:3).

In such circumstances Jesus could not aspire to a higher education. His full knowledge of the OT Scriptures attests to his having received the normal Jewish child's education at the village *synagogue-school, and the one story of his childhood preserved in the Gospels indicates an abnormal aptitude in matters of religious debate (Lk. 2:42–50). Beyond this we know nothing of his childhood, though his later teaching shows a mind well stocked with the incidents and characters of daily life in a country village.

IV. The beginning of public ministry

a. John the Baptist

The occasion of Jesus' emergence from obscurity was the mission of *John the Baptist, a Judaean relative of Jesus who had grown up as an ascetic in the Judaean desert, and whose call for repentance in the light of God's imminent judgment attracted large crowds to be baptized by him in the Jordan. It was among these followers of John that Jesus found his first disciples, with John's active encouragement (Jn. 1:35–42). John recognized in Jesus the judge whose coming he had predicted (Mt. 3:11f., *etc.*), and while the later style of Jesus' mission apparently caused him some doubts (Mt. 11:2–3), he does not seem to have withdrawn that recognition, even though some of his disciples maintained a separate existence throughout the NT period (Acts 18:24f.; 19:1–5).

b. The baptism of Jesus

Jesus' baptism by John was the event which most clearly inaugurated his mission. Why Jesus chose to submit to a baptism whose explicit significance was of repentance with a view to the forgiveness of sin has been much debated. Christians have agreed, following the lead of the NT (*e.g.* Jn. 8:46; Heb. 4:15; 1 Pet. 2:22), that it was not consciousness of personal sin which prompted him. More plausible is the suggestion that his intention was to identify himself with what John stood for, a 'vote' for the purified and reformed Israel which John demanded, and whose ideals were to form an important element in Jesus' own preaching. Further, in identifying himself with those who responded to John's call for repentance, he put himself in a position to be their representative. His own enigmatic explanation, 'thus it is fitting for us to fulfil all righteousness' (Mt. 3:15), may reflect an understanding of his role in line with that of the Servant of the Lord, who by his suffering on behalf of his people was to 'make many to be accounted righteous' (Is. 53:11).

Whatever Jesus' own intention, his baptism in fact led to a decisive revelation of his future role (Mk. 1:10f.). A visible descent of the Holy Spirit upon him marked him as the promised deliverer of, *e.g.*, Is. 11:2; 42:1 and 61:1, while a voice from heaven addressed him in terms reminiscent of Ps. 2:7 and Is. 42:1, the former greeting the Lord's anointed as his Son, and the latter introducing the Servant, chosen by God to deliver his people. Thus several important strands in OT Messianic hope are woven together, and the decisive role of Jesus in God's redemptive purpose is marked out.

c. The temptation of Jesus

The 'temptation' (Mt. 4:1–11; Lk. 4:1–13), which followed quickly, was essentially an exploration of what it meant to be 'Son of God', as he had just been proclaimed at his baptism. 'If you are the Son of God . . .' is the theme of the challenges, and a study of Jesus' replies to them shows that their focus was not primarily on the way his mission should be accomplished, but on his own relationship with God. The temptation to turn stones into bread was to doubt his Father's care and wisdom in providing this period of abstinence. The temptation to leap from the Temple wall was to force his Father's hand to prove that he would protect his Son, rather than accept his care on trust. The third temptation was to compromise the Son's necessarily absolute loyalty to his Father. Jesus' three replies are drawn from verses in Dt. 6–8, and refer to the lessons the nation Israel was intended to learn from its experiences in the wilderness, suggesting that Jesus now takes up the nation's role as son of God, and by his success where Israel failed proves to be the true Son.

The encounter with Satan, concluding a long period of withdrawal in the desert area around the Jordan valley, thus served to strengthen Jesus' understanding of his unique status as Son of God which was to be the key to his mission. There is no suggestion that these were the whole of the temptations Jesus ever faced (*cf.* Heb. 4:15), or even that they were typical. They were the focal point of a vital period of preparation.

Bibliography. G. H. P. Thompson, *JTS* n.s. 11, 1960, pp. 1–12; J. A. T. Robinson, *Twelve New Testament Studies*, 1962, pp. 53–60; R. T. France, *Jesus and the Old Testament*, 1971, pp. 50ff.

d. The move to Galilee

Jesus' public ministry now began, apparently at first in the Jordan valley with a focus on baptism parallel to that of John (Jn. 3:22f.; 4:1f.). Jesus appeared to many as a second Baptist, and a certain amount of rivalry soon arose between the two groups of disciples, though John refused to countenance this (Jn. 3:26–30). But this style of activity was soon brought to an end both by Jesus' increasing popularity coming to the notice of the authorities, and especially by the arrest of John the Baptist by Antipas, partly, as the gospels record, due to his criticism of Antipas' marriage, but also, according to Josephus, on suspicion of arousing political unrest, a charge which could easily affect the parallel ministry of Jesus. In this situation Jesus withdrew into his own region of Galilee, and his style of ministry changed to an itinerant preaching and healing mission. We do not hear of him baptizing again. (See **II.** *b* for the geographical location of the ministry.)

V. Features of Jesus' public ministry

a. Life-style

Despite Jesus' 'middle-class' background (above, **III**), his chosen style of life from this point was one of no financial security. He and his disciples lived on the contributions and hospitality of those who supported his mission (Mt. 10:8–11; Lk. 8:3; 10:38–42). He taught them to rely on God for all material needs (Mt. 6:24–34), and demanded that one would-be disciple should give away all his possessions (Mk. 10:17–22). Their money was held in common (Jn. 12:6; 13:29), but it sufficed only for their basic needs. Poverty, for Jesus, was not a disaster (Lk. 6:20f., 24f.; Mk. 10:23–31). Unmarried, and with no settled home (Lk. 9:58) or material ties, he was free to travel around Palestine preaching and healing.

In the early part of his ministry he was invited to speak in *synagogues as a visiting teacher (Mk. 1:21, 39; Mt. 9:35; Lk. 4:16–27), but later synagogue teaching is not mentioned (because his radical teaching was unacceptable?), and Jesus is found teaching the crowds in the open air, and devoting an increasing proportion of time to the instruction of his closest disciples.

b. Disciples

Like other Jewish teachers, Jesus gathered a group of *disciples. The 'crowds' came and went, listening to Jesus eagerly, but not committed to follow him; the 'disciples' were those who to a greater or lesser degree threw in their lot with him, and accompanied him on his travels. From among these disciples, an inner circle of 'the twelve' (often called the 'apostles', though the term 'apostle' is not confined to them in the NT) was selected by Jesus; and within the Twelve the special group of Peter, James and John were selected as Jesus' most intimate companions on a number of significant occasions.

To be a disciple involved an unreserved and exclusive commitment to Jesus. It involved, at least for the inner circle, the acceptance of his style of life (though not the permanent abandonment of home and family, as the case of Peter illustrates, Mk. 1:29–31; 1 Cor. 9:5), and a readiness to suffer persecution and ostracism for his sake (Mt. 10:16–39). It is an indication of the authority and attractiveness of Jesus and his teaching that he could nonetheless call people to follow him and expect to be taken seriously.

The majority of his disciples were Galileans. Of the inner circle it is probable that all except *Judas Iscariot (if his name means 'man of Kerioth') were from Galilee. But in character and background they varied from *Thomas the pessimist to *Peter the extrovert, and from *Matthew the tax-collector (and therefore in the employment of the pro-Roman government) to *Simon 'the Zealot'. To have held together such a group, and made them the foundation of the world's greatest religion, is no mean part of the achievement of Jesus.

c. Social attitudes

One of the most persistent objections to Jesus on the part of the Jewish establishment was his habit of keeping doubtful company, particularly that of 'tax-collectors and sinners', the outcasts of respectable society. That he even took meals with them was especially scandalous. But Jesus defended his actions as essential to his mission, which was to those in need, whatever their social standing (Mk. 2:17; *cf.* Lk. 15:1–2 and the sequel). He would welcome and talk with women of doubtful morals whom others shunned (Lk. 7:36–50; Jn. 4:7ff.), and even found a welcome among *Samaritans, the traditional enemies of the Jews (Jn. 4:39–42; Lk. 17:11–19). His story of the Good Samaritan (Lk. 10:29–37) is a daring challenge to the traditional Jewish taboo. His direct contacts with Gentiles were few but positive (Mt. 8:5–13; 15:22–28), and his teaching made it clear that he did not regard Gentiles as an inferior category, but gave them a place alongside Jews in God's purpose (*e.g.* Mt. 8:11–12; Lk. 4:25–27).

This unwillingness to be restricted by conventional social barriers is seen also in his relations with rich and poor. Most of his closest disciples seem to have been from the same social class as himself (particularly fishermen, owning boats and employing men, Mk. 1:20), but his preaching met with a favourable response among the poor (*e.g.* Mt. 11:5), while he also had rich and influential followers (*e.g.* Nicodemus and Joseph of Arimathaea, Jn. 19:38–42), and was at home in more affluent company (Lk. 7:36; 14:1ff.). He was apparently unimpressed by wealth or poverty as such: it was the attitude to wealth which mattered (Mk. 12:41–44; Lk. 12:13–21). He required of his followers a similar unconcern for artificial barriers (Lk. 14:7–14), and sternly condemned a callous neglect of the less fortunate (Lk. 16:19ff.).

In all this Jesus' concern was with the real needs of those he met, physical and spiritual, and in meeting those needs he cared little if conventions and taboos were overridden.

Bibliography. M. Hengel, *Property and Riches in the Early Church*, 1974; R. T. France, *EQ* 51, 1979, pp. 3ff.

d. Disputes about the law

Debates with the Jewish religious leaders, especially the *scribes and *Pharisees, take up a good part of the Gospel narratives. Jesus lacked a formal scribal education (Jn. 7:15), but his style of teaching and his group of disciples cast him in the role of a *rabbi, and he was sometimes so addressed. The content of his teaching at many points, however, inevitably set him apart from scribal orthodoxy, and was a major factor in the hostility which eventually led to his death.

Central was the issue of authority. The authority of the OT *law itself was not in question, but rather the authority to interpret it. Scribal *tradition had evolved a complex and constantly growing body of oral teaching on the precise application of the law to the most minute areas of everyday life, and this tradition too was regarded as authoritative. Points of dispute were settled by appeal to previous teachers. In contrast, Jesus paid little attention to traditional rules not clearly found in the OT, and never quoted an authority other than himself (and, of course, the OT); note his formula, 'You have heard . . . but *I* say to you . . .' (Mt. 5:21f., 27f., 31f., *etc.*).

The issues are seen most clearly in the debate on defilement (Mk. 7:1–23), where Jesus explicitly accuses the Pharisees and scribes of evading OT requirements on the basis of man-made rules, and dismisses the issue of ritual defilement as relatively trivial; and in the numerous clashes on the observance of the *sabbath (*e.g.* Mk. 2:23–3:6; Lk. 13:10–17), one of the most elaborately legislated areas in scribal tradition, where Jesus cut through the tangle of legislation to the original intention of the sabbath, and asserted his own right to determine its proper observance.

The series of six 'antitheses' in the Sermon on the Mount (Mt. 5:21–48) further illustrates Jesus' radical approach to the law, going beyond the literal rule to the thought behind the act, and putting principles before precepts even to the extent of apparently setting aside the latter (Mt. 5:38f.). This radical attitude to legal questions made Jesus a danger to the scribal establishment, and the popularity of his views made it essential to get rid of him. The conflict was apparently heated, with very strong language being used by both sides (Mk. 3:22; Mt. 23:1–36). It was the legalistic attitude of the scribal authorities, more than their actual traditions, which Jesus found necessary to denounce.

Bibliography. D. J. Moo, *JSNT* 20, 1984, pp. 3–49.

e. Miracles

Christian and non-Christian sources attest that Jesus was known to his contemporaries as a worker of *miracles. The vast majority of those recorded are cases of miraculous healing, and the Gospels present healing, often of large number of people, as a regular feature of Jesus' ministry (Mk. 1:32–34; 3:7–12; 6:55f.; Lk. 7:21f.). Often coupled with his healing miracles (though usually carefully differentiated from them, *e.g.* Mk. 1:32–34; Lk. 13:32) are his exorcisms (*DEMON POSSESSION). Both of these activities were expected also of his disciples when they went out in his name (Mk. 6:13; Mt. 10:8), and they are integrally related with his preaching, as aspects of a total onslaught on the powers of evil, in their physical as well as their spiritual manifestation.

Healing and exorcism were an accepted part of the activity of godly men within 1st-century Judaism, but nothing approaching the intensity of Jesus' healing ministry is recorded of any contemporary figure (*HEALTH, **V**). The range of complaints he healed is very wide, from paralysis to blindness, and from leprosy to a severed ear. Three cases of restoring to life those who had recently died are also recorded. Unlike some contemporary exorcists, he used little or no ritual, a mere word of command being often the only means employed (Mt. 8:8f., 16). The overwhelming impression was of his simple authority over physical and spiritual evil, and his compassion for those in need. His healing ministry was not a bid for recognition, nor was it primarily designed to prove anything, but it was the automatic response of his compassion to human need when he met it.

Jesus' other ('nature') miracles are comparatively few, but again the same pattern of an automatic and unselfconscious response to a pressing need can be seen in most of them, feeding hungry crowds, supplying wine in an emergency, providing fish after a night of fishing in vain, and calming a storm on the lake. That Jesus solved such problems by miraculous means was not so much a deliberate display of power as a natural result of who he was. Only the walking on water and the sudden withering of the fig-tree seem to have been performed more to teach the nature of his person and mission than to meet a definite need.

The miracles, then, are not *the* proof of Jesus' divine nature, though they imply it. They are an inevitable part of a total ministry of deliverance and of the conquest of evil.

f. Political stance

The charge on which Jesus was finally condemned was of political sedition (Lk. 23:2): he had claimed to be 'king of the Jews'. While the title never occurs in his sayings, he did often speak about the *'kingdom of God' as the object of his mission (see below, **VII.** *d*), and such language, particularly in Galilee, was open to nationalistic interpretation. Much of his early support was probably due to hopes that he would lead a revolt against Rome, culminating in the unsuccessful attempt to force him to accept the title of 'king' (Jn. 6:14f.). After this episode his support seems to have decreased, and more of his time was spent instructing his disciples on the true nature of his mission.

Some modern writers (especially S. G. F. Brandon, *Jesus and the Zealots*, 1967) have tried to show that Jesus' intentions were in fact political, and that the spiritual nature of his kingship is a later invention in the gospels to gloss over his real revolutionary aim. While Jesus was certainly not as blind to political and social problems as more pietistic Christians have suggested, Brandon's view involves a wholesale rewriting of the Gospels on very flimsy grounds. The Jesus of the Gospels was at pains to correct misunderstandings of the nature of his mission (Mk. 8:27–38; 12:35–37; 14:61f.), avoided publicity and popular demonstrations until the last week of his ministry, refused to affirm the nationalist position when asked about the validity of Roman taxation (Mk. 12:13–17), and was declared innocent of sedition by the Roman prefect (Lk. 23:13–16). His declared attitude to the Jewish nation of his day, which he regarded as approaching its final punishment for its rejection of God's messengers in the imminent destruction of Jerusalem (Lk. 11:47–51; 13:25–35, *etc.*), is quite incompatible with nationalist sympathies. The circumstances of his ministry inevitably laid him open to political suspicion, but there is ample evidence that his own intentions were otherwise, even though some of his followers undoubtedly expected him to adopt a nationalist role. (*MESSIAH, **II.** *a.*)

BIBLIOGRAPHY. M. Hengel, *Victory over Violence*, 1972; M. Langley, *NIDNTT* 3, pp. 967–981; E. Bammel and C. F. D. Moule (eds.), *Jesus and the Politics of his Day*, 1984.

g. Jesus' authority

The Gospels tell us that the dominant impression of Jesus' ministry was that of authority. This is true both of his boldly self-authenticating teaching (Mk. 1:22) and of his miraculous activity (Mk. 1:27; Mt. 9:8). It was his personal authority which impressed the Gentile centurion (Mt. 8:8f.), which caused his disciples to leave their homes and jobs to follow him, and which carried all before him when he strode into the Temple court and threw out the traders (Mk. 11:15–17). While Jesus himself refused to state openly the source of this authority (Mk. 11:27–33), the implication is clear that it derived from God, and his own claim to be Son of God carried the same implication. After his resurrection he declared openly his universal authority (Mt. 28:18; *cf.* Jn. 17:2).

VI. The close of the ministry

a. The last week in Jerusalem

Jesus' last visit to Jerusalem was deliberately undertaken with the knowledge that it would lead to the final confrontation with the authorities, culminating in his own death (Lk. 13:33; 18:31–33). It was made at *Passover time, when Jerusalem would be crowded with pilgrims, and when the themes of death and redemption were in mind. Certain incidents are of special importance.

1. *The entry.* Jesus' arrival in Jerusalem was deliberately dramatic. Instead of arriving unnoticed among the thousands of other pilgrims, he staged a conspicuous ride into the city on a donkey, while his disciples and other pilgrims greeted him with shouts of *'Hosanna' (Mk. 11:1–10). It was a visible allusion to Zc. 9:9–10, the prophecy of the king coming to Jerusalem on a donkey. Its intention was clearly to make a Messianic claim, and it was so interpreted by the crowds, who would include many of his former supporters from Galilee. The prophecy is of a king of peace, but many probably interpreted the gesture in a more militantly nationalistic sense.

2. *Cleansing the Temple.* One of Jesus' first acts on arrival was equally deliberately symbolic. He threw out from the Temple precincts the traders in sacrificial animals and in the special Temple coin-

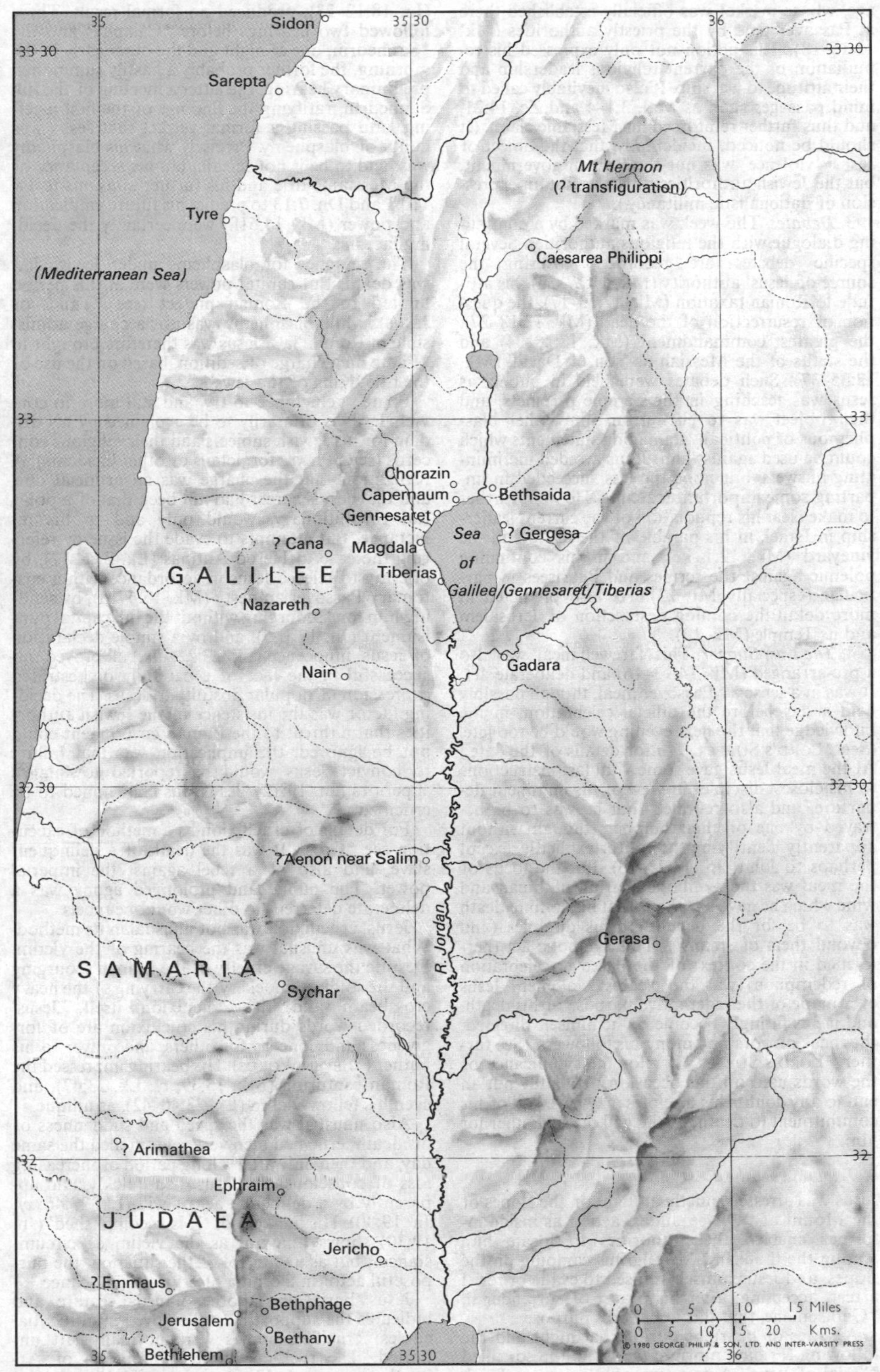

Map showing the places prominent in the ministry of Jesus Christ.

age, whose market was officially established there at Passover time by the priestly authorities (Mk. 11:15–18). This action not only expressed his repudiation of the current religious leadership and their attitude to worship. It also inevitably called to mind passages such as Mal. 3:1–4 and Zc. 14:21, and thus further reinforced his Messianic claim. (It should be noticed, incidentally, that the object of Jesus' 'violence' was not the Roman government, but the Jewish authorities; this was not an expression of nationalistic militancy.)

3. *Debates.* The week was marked by a continuing dialogue with the religious authorities. Several specific debates are recorded, covering the source of Jesus' authority (Mk. 11:27–33), his attitude to Roman taxation (Mk. 12:13–17), the question of resurrection of the dead (Mk. 12:18–27), the greatest commandment (Mk. 12:28–34) and the status of the Messiah as 'son of David' (Mk. 12:35–37). Such debates were held in public, as Jesus was teaching in the Temple precincts, and their object was to elicit from him either blasphemous or politically damaging statements which could be used against him. Jesus avoided incriminating answers, but none the less succeeded in imparting some important teaching. He went further to make clear his repudiation of the current leadership in Israel, in his parable of the tenants in the vineyard (Mk. 12:1–12), and in his continuing polemic against the scribes and Pharisees in particular (especially Mt. 23). He also predicted in more detail the coming destruction of Jerusalem and its Temple (Mk. 13).

4. *The Last Supper.* This 'farewell meal' was also a pre-arranged (Mk. 14:13–16) and deliberate act. It was in a sense a *Passover meal, though possibly held a day before the official celebration, in the knowledge that the next evening would be too late. (See *LORD'S SUPPER, **I.** *a* for details of the date.) At the meal Jesus gave some vital last instructions to his closest disciples in view of his imminent departure, and also revealed that he was to be betrayed by one of their number (though without apparently identifying the traitor explicitly, except perhaps to John, Jn. 13:23–26). But the focus of the meal was the symbolic sharing of bread and wine which he gave as tokens that his coming death was to be for the benefit of his disciples (and beyond them of 'many'). This symbolic act (performed in the context of the Passover celebration of redemption) was the clearest statement Jesus ever made of the redemptive purpose of his death, and it has fittingly become, as he himself directed, the focus of worship among his followers. (See further *LORD'S SUPPER, **I.** *b* for the significance of the words used on this occasion.) It finally put an end to any doubts his disciples may have had of his commitment to death, as the will of the Father for him.

b. Trial and death

Jesus was arrested quietly at night on the slopes of the Mount of *Olives. Judas' action as inside informer enabled the authorities to locate him among the thousands of pilgrims camping on the slopes, and Jesus himself refused to evade or resist arrest, accepting, after his prayer of surrender in *Gethsemane, that this was God's purpose.

A series of hearings during that night and the following (Friday) morning make up the so-called *'Trial of Jesus'. A first, probably quite unofficial, hearing before *Annas, the deposed high priest (Jn. 18:12–23), produced no formal result. There followed two hearings before *Caiaphas and the *Sanhedrin, one at night and the other early in the morning, the former probably a hastily summoned preliminary hearing, the latter a meeting of the full Sanhedrin, ratifying the findings of the first meeting, and passing a formal verdict that Jesus was guilty of blasphemy. Precisely what his blasphemy was held to be is not certain, but his acceptance of the Messianic title and his further allusions to Ps. 110:1 and Dn. 7:13 to predict his future vindication and power (Mk. 14:61f.) were certainly the deciding factors.

The sentence for blasphemy under Jewish law was death. But capital powers were at this period limited to the Roman prefect (see *TRIAL OF JESUS), while blasphemy was not a charge admissible in Roman law. Jesus was therefore brought to *Pilate on a charge of sedition, based on the use of the title 'King of the Jews'.

Pilate's reluctance to try, and still more to convict, Jesus is primarily to be explained by his disdain for his Jewish subjects and their religious concerns (see *PILATE for details of other incidents). A realization that the charge was an artificial one, and that Jesus' career had not been that of a political revolutionary, would only add to his reluctance. But attempts to evade the issue by referring the case to Herod Antipas (Lk. 23:6–12), by offering to release Jesus in accordance with a customary Passover amnesty (Mk. 15:6–15), by sending him for *scourging without the full capital punishment (Jn. 19:1–5), and by a simple declaration of Jesus' innocence (Lk. 23:22, *etc.*) all proved unsuccessful in the face of a carefully orchestrated expression of popular hostility to Jesus. The deciding factor was the insistence of the Jewish authorities that a threat to the Roman government could not be ignored; the implication was that failure to convict Jesus would be reported to Pilate's superiors (Jn. 19:12). Jesus was condemned to be crucified.

For details of crucifixion as a method of execution see *Cross. It was the death of a delinquent slave, and also of a rebel against the imperial power. The public and prolonged agony was a deliberate deterrent to other would-be rebels.

Jesus' crucifixion was not unusual in its method. What was unusual was the bearing of the victim. Despite the savage cruelty of the Roman scourging and the soldiers' mockery, the carrying of the heavy crossbeam and the crucifixion itself, Jesus' recorded words during his crucifixion are of forgiveness and concern for others, and prayer to his Father (*SEVEN WORDS). His bearing impressed the Roman centurion (Mk. 15:39; *cf.* Lk. 23:47), and even his fellow-victim (Lk. 23:40–42), as unique.

Also unusual was the speed and suddenness of his death; crucified men very seldom died the same day, and then only after a long period of increasing loss of consciousness. Jesus died quickly, and apparently by a deliberate act of will (Lk. 23:46; *cf.* Jn. 19:30). His final cry of 'It is accomplished' (Jn. 19:30) shows him not as the victim of circumstances, but as in control of the situation, the purposeful actor in a drama of crucial significance.

Jesus' burial was another unusual feature, and indicates the support he still enjoyed in influential circles; crucified bodies were normally left unburied. The rock-cut tomb of *Joseph of Arimathea was probably one of many in the vicinity (*BURIAL AND MOURNING).

BIBLIOGRAPHY. J. Blinzler, *The Trial of Jesus*, 1960; A. N. Sherwin-White, *Roman Society and Roman Law in the NT*, 1963; E. Bammel (ed.), *The Trial of Jesus*, 1970; D. R. Catchpole, *The Trial of Jesus*, 1971; M. Hengel, *Crucifixion*, 1977.

c. Resurrection and ascension

That Jesus' tomb was found to be empty on the Sunday morning following his crucifixion is asserted in different ways by all four Gospels, and cannot be seriously disputed on historical grounds. Explanations of this fact which dispense with a literal *resurrection of his body are entirely speculative, and open to more palpable objections than the fact they aim to discredit.

The Gospels and Paul (in 1 Cor. 15) together attest also to probably eleven separate encounters with the risen Jesus in the period immediately following that Sunday morning. Their varied and generally quite unexpected character, and the different groups involved (from single individuals to a group of more than 500), make it impossible to dismiss them as hallucinations, and the difficulty of fitting them all together (as with the accounts of finding the empty tomb) only makes it the more unlikely that there was any deliberate collusion in perpetrating a well-intentioned deception.

On these grounds, Christians have concluded that Jesus rose bodily from the tomb, with a body which, while set free from some of the limitations of time and space (he could pass through closed doors, and appear and disappear suddenly), was solidly physical, able to break bread and to eat, and to be mistaken for a gardener or a fellow traveller.

For some weeks Jesus continued to appear in this way to his disciples, not living or travelling with them, but in single encounters. Having thus convinced them of his victory over death, and assured them that they could continue to rely on his presence and help even when he was physically removed, he left them in a way which showed clearly that his bodily presence was no longer necessary (Acts 1:9–11; *ASCENSION). It was for them in future to continue the mission which he had begun, and in which he would always be spiritually present with them (Mt. 28:18–20).

BIBLIOGRAPHY. J. N. D. Anderson, *A Lawyer among the Theologians*, 1973, chs. 3–4; G. R. Osborne, *The Resurrection Narratives*, 1984; J. W. Wenham, *Easter Enigma*, 1984.

VII. The teaching of Jesus

The teaching of Jesus is not easily set out in systematic form; it was not delivered as an ordered treatise, but in a wide variety of real-life situations and encounters. In an article of this nature we can only pick out certain key themes and emphases of his teaching, concentrating on those which were most distinctive and unexpected in the environment of 1st-century Judaism.

a. Forms of teaching

Formally, Jesus' teaching has much in common with the methods traditionally employed by Jewish teachers. His arguments from and about scriptural texts, his ethical exhortations, his rules of conduct, his parables and his eschatological predictions can all be paralleled, in terms of teaching method, in rabbinic or sectarian Judaism of the period. So also can the rhythmic and sometimes poetic form in which much of his teaching is cast, and which was an aid to memorization. It is in the tone and content of his teaching that its uniqueness lies. For instance, while *parable was a known and accepted teaching form, there is nothing in Jewish literature to match the vividness, the variety and the sheer quantity of Jesus' parables, still less the doctrinal and ethical emphases which they convey.

It is a characteristic of Jesus' teaching that it was not delivered in an academic lecture-type setting. It arose out of personal encounters, questions from enquirers, debates with the religious authorities (usually initiated by them), and the need to instruct his disciples in the light of his own imminent suffering and death, and of their role in continuing his ministry afterwards. While Jesus did 'lecture' to the crowds, often for long periods (*e.g.* Mk. 6:34f.), such carefully structured discourses as we find in the Gospels (*e.g.* the *SERMON ON THE MOUNT and the discourses in the GOSPEL OF *JOHN) bear the marks of a later compilation of sayings of Jesus rather than of verbatim transcripts of actual addresses.

Particularly characteristic of Jesus' teaching are epigrams, striking expressions often using deliberate exaggeration and paradox to drive home his point (*e.g.* Mk. 10:25; 12:17; Lk. 9:24, 58, 60, 62). Illustrations are frequent and graphic. Sometimes he used visual aids or acted parables (*e.g.* Mt. 18:2; Jn. 13:1–15). Jesus' teaching can never have been dull, and it is consequently far more memorable than more formal or stylized teaching. Above all, it is not merely theoretical, but life-related.

b. Use of the Old Testament

Jesus based his teaching firmly on the OT. His recorded words in the Gospels contain more than 40 verbatim quotations, about 60 clear verbal allusions or other references to OT passages and well over 100 other possible allusions, where it is hard to say whether a specific allusion is intended or Jesus' mind was so full of OT words and ideas that he inevitably expressed himself in ways reminiscent of the OT.

He used the OT in every aspect of his teaching. He discussed its legal and ethical requirements, and used these as the basis for his own moral teaching (*e.g.* Mt. 5:17–48; Mk. 10:2–9; 12:28–31). He used its historical narratives to illustrate aspects of his own teaching (*e.g.* Mk. 2:25f.; Mt. 12:40–42; 24:37–39). In debate with the religious leaders he normally turned to the OT as the final authority, and sometimes chided them over their failure to grasp its basic principles (*e.g.* Mk. 7:6–13; 12:24; Mt. 12:3–7). But it is especially in his teaching about the nature of his own person and mission that Jesus uses the OT, and that in a variety of ways.

Sometimes he simply quotes clear OT predictions as finding their fulfilment in him. Many of these are predictions of the coming *Messiah, and these cause no surprise to the Christian (for details see *g*, below). But many of the passages he alluded to in this connection make no mention of a Messiah, but only of God himself coming to judge and save (*e.g.* Mt. 11:5, alluding to Is. 35:5f.; Lk. 19:10 to Ezk. 34:16, 22; Lk. 22:20 to Je. 31:31); these also Jesus sees as fulfilled in his coming. Even more remarkably, many passages which are not predictive at all, but are simply accounts of historical persons, events, *etc.*, are none the less taken up as patterns which are 'fulfilled' in Jesus' mission (*e.g.* Mt. 12:40–42 referring to Jonah and Solomon; Mt. 4:4, 7, 10 referring to Israel's wilderness experience in

Dt. 8:3; 6:16, 13; Mk. 12:10f. quoting Ps. 118:22f.). This last method of using the OT is more fully developed in the rest of the NT (especially Heb.), and is generally known as *'typology'. Numerous incidental allusions throughout Jesus' teaching show that he saw his ministry as 'fulfilling' not only the explicit predictions of the OT, but the whole pattern of God's working in the history of Israel which it records.

BIBLIOGRAPHY. R. T. France, *Jesus and the Old Testament*, 1971; J. W. Wenham, *Christ and the Bible*, 1973.

c. The time of fulfilment

Jesus' first recorded words in his Galilean ministry are a concise statement of the basic presupposition of all his teaching: 'The time is fulfilled, and the kingdom of God is at hand' (Mk. 1:15). In Luke's Gospel Jesus' first public appearance focuses on the claim, 'Today this scripture (Is. 61:1f.) has been fulfilled in your hearing' (Lk. 4:21). Throughout his ministry this note of present fulfilment is of central importance. This was the arrival of the Messiah, the coming of the Day of Yahweh long expected by the Jews, the fulfilment of all the hopes of the OT (see *b*, above). While he did not openly use the title 'Messiah' (see *g*, below, and *MESSIAH, **II.** *a*), he never denied that this was his role, and when John the Baptist asked him directly, he replied with a clear affirmative (Mt. 11:2–6, alluding to Is. 35:5f.; 61:1).

The coming of Jesus thus introduces, according to his own teaching, a new era. The many centuries of expectation now give way to fulfilment. Jesus' use of typology (see *b* above) does not simply see his ministry as a *repetition* of the previous patterns of God's working, but as their *climax*. This is now the final and definitive act of God which brings in the promised days of salvation (and of judgment). It is in Jesus himself, his teaching, and especially his saving ministry of suffering, death and vindication, that God's dealings with men are henceforward focused.

A recognition of this emphasis is vital to a grasp of the significance of much of Jesus' teaching. He is not simply reaffirming what was already there in the OT, but bringing that to which the OT pointed forward, and in which it finds its role fulfilled. From now on the OT itself can only truly be understood *Christologically.*

Thus Jesus gives no sanction to a search for the fulfilment of prophecy in world events unrelated to his ministry. He himself is the focus of fulfilment, and that fulfilment has already arrived in his coming.

This emphasis is summed up in his announcement at the Last Supper of a 'new *covenant' (Lk. 22:20; 1 Cor. 11:25). The covenant made with Israel at Sinai (Ex. 24, *etc.*) is now, as Jeremiah had predicted (Je. 31:31–34), replaced by a new covenant, established by the sacrificial death of Jesus. A new era has begun.

d. The kingdom of God

This idea of present fulfilment and of a new age comes out particularly in the teaching of Jesus about the *kingdom of God, one of his central themes. He used the term in a wide variety of contexts, so that its essential meaning needs careful definition. It means the *sovereignty* of God, the situation in which God is in control, his rule or reign. Now while in one sense God is always in control, it is also a fact that man rejects his sovereignty and rebels. The 'coming of the kingdom' therefore denotes the practical implementation of God's rule in human affairs, and it was this coming of the kingdom which Jesus announced as he began his ministry (Mk. 1:15). Other sayings reinforce the message that his coming already brought into operation the rule of God (*e.g.* Mt. 12:28; Lk. 17:20f.). Thus he could already speak of people 'entering' or 'receiving' the kingdom (Mk. 10:15, 23–25; Lk. 12:31; 16:16), and assure his disciples that 'Yours is the kingdom of God' (Lk. 6:20; *cf.* Mt. 5:3, 10).

At the same time, there is an important sense in which the kingdom is still future, when it will 'come with power' (Mk. 9:1; *cf.* Mt. 6:10; Lk. 19:11; 22:18); for the acceptance of God's sovereignty which was open to all men in Jesus' ministry, and which was realized in the experience of those who followed him (in that sense the kingdom was already present), would one day become a universal fact, when all men everywhere would recognize the rule of God.

That future consummation is the ultimate horizon of Jesus' proclamation of the kingdom, but it is the final completion of a process already begun in his earthly ministry. The new era which Jesus came to bring is the era of the rule of God. As individuals respond to his message, that rule is progressively established. The 'already' and the 'not yet' combine in a grand panorama of history, of which we have yet to see the culmination. But at the centre of it stands Jesus himself, for it is in response to his teaching and through faith in his saving work that a man can be restored to a true relationship with God, and so 'enter the kingdom of God'.

BIBLIOGRAPHY. G. E. Ladd, *The Presence of the Future*, 1973; R. T. France, *Divine Government*, 1990.

e. God the Father

To enter the kingdom of God, then, is essentially to accept God's rule. And as such it involves a new relationship with God. So Jesus taught his followers, those who through his ministry entered the kingdom of God, to regard God as their Father. This very personal image of the disciple's relationship with God occurs very frequently in the Gospels, and is one of the most distinctive and novel features of Jesus' teaching. He taught them to address God as 'Our Father who art in heaven' (Mt. 6:9; *LORD'S PRAYER), and to rely on his fatherly care and provision in the very practical matters of food and clothing, because 'your heavenly Father knows that you need them all' (Mt. 6:25–34). Their Father could be relied on to protect them (Mt. 10:28–31) and to provide them with all good things (Mt. 7:7–11). As sons of their Father they must try to be like him, perfect (Mt. 5:43–48).

Jesus' teaching of the Fatherhood of God is not, therefore, a general statement of God's benevolence to his creation, but a specific relationship of love and trust open only to those who have entered the kingdom. It is totally opposed to either a vague universalism or a formal religiosity. It is an exclusive and intimate relationship.

But if Jesus' teaching on God as the Father of his disciples was novel, even more remarkable was his claim to be, in a still more exclusive sense, himself the Son of God. He regularly addressed God as 'Father' or 'my Father', assuming an intimacy never before heard in Jewish religion. (See J. Jeremias, 'Abba', in *The Prayers of Jesus*, 1967, pp. 11–65.) In the Gospel of John the overwhelming majority of references to God as Father (and there are well over 100) are specifically to him as the Father of *Jesus*. The exclusiveness of this relationship is shown by the fact that Jesus never coupled himself with even his disciples as being *in the same sense* sons of God; he never referred to God as 'our Father', including himself in the 'our'. Mt. 11:27 sums up the relationship: 'All things have been delivered to me by my Father; and no one knows the Son except the Father, and no one knows the Father except the Son and any one to whom the Son chooses to reveal him.'

Thus there are two distinct ways of being related to God as Father. There is the essential Father/Son unity which is exclusively the prerogative of Jesus; and there is the disciple's privilege, into which Jesus alone can introduce him, of knowing and depending on God as his Father in heaven. There is no suggestion in Jesus' teaching of a more general Fatherhood of *God embracing all men.

BIBLIOGRAPHY. J. Jeremias, *New Testament Theology* 1, 1971, pp. 56–68, 178–203.

f. Ethics of the kingdom

Jesus' attack on legalism and his tendency to place personal need before conventional rules (see above, **V.** *c*, *d*) are reflected in the ethics he laid down for his disciples. There is no weakening of the moral demand; the standard is perfection (Mt. 5:48). The righteousness he requires is greater than that of the most scrupulous legalists (Mt. 5:20). But its greatness consists not in a further proliferation of rules of conduct (in fact Jesus made no attempt to lay down a complete ethic for all areas of life), but in a more searching critique of motives and attitudes. There are still rules (the *SERMON ON THE MOUNT contains many of them), but Jesus' demand focuses on the thought behind the act (*e.g.* Mt. 5:21–28; Mk. 7:14–23). Most striking in his teaching is the focal place given to *love* (Mk. 12:28–34; *cf.* Lk. 6:27–35; Mt. 7:12; Jn. 13:34f.; 15:12–17, *etc.*); and lest this demand should be weakened into sentimentality, the Good Samaritan is held up as an example of how love works (Lk. 10:25ff.), and unselfish service is made the criterion of true greatness (Mk. 10:42–45).

Such a practical love must inevitably have its effect on social attitudes and action. Jesus did not, as far as the Gospels record, make specific proposals for the reform of society, any more than he engaged in political agitation (see above, **V.** *f*). But both his life (see above, **V.** *a*, *c*) and teaching tend to undermine a comfortable acceptance of the socio-economic *status quo*. In particular his recommendation of poverty (Lk. 6:20–25; Mk. 10:17–31; Mt. 6:19–24) and his call for unstinting generosity (Lk. 6:34f.; 12:33; 14:12–14; Mk. 10:21) provide the foundation, if not the framework, for a quite radical social ethic. (See R. T. France, 'God and Mammon: the practical relevance of the teaching of Jesus', *EQ* 51, 1979, pp. 3ff.)

Discipleship is, then, a serious and total commitment, which may demand drastic renunciation not only of material possessions but of reputation and relationships (Mk. 10:28–31; Mt. 10:34–39). It is not for the dilettante (Lk. 9:62). It requires a complete reorientation whereby God and not man becomes the point of reference for a man's life and thought (Mt. 6:33, and the whole thrust of Mt. 6), and the ruling motive is not the prospect of reward from man or even from God but gratitude for the forgiving grace of God (Mt. 18:23–35; Lk. 7:36–47).

It is this reorientation rather than specific ethical rules which marks out the ethic of Jesus as radical in comparison with either the legalism or the humanitarianism which marked the best religious systems of his day.

g. The mission of Jesus

We have seen that Jesus regarded himself as playing the central role in bringing in the kingdom of God. It was in his ministry that the hopes of the OT were to find their fulfilment. In other words, he was the *Messiah.

Yet Jesus hardly ever claimed to be Messiah, using that term. The only occasion when he took the initiative in making this claim was outside Jewish territory (Jn. 4:25f.). When others referred to him as Messiah ('Christ') he accepted the idea, but was clearly anxious to avoid the title itself, and substituted his regular title 'Son of man' (Mk. 8:29–33; 14:61f.; *MESSIAH, **II.** *a*). Popular Jewish Messianic hope was firmly committed to a political and nationalistic understanding of the coming day of liberation, and Jesus had no such political intentions (see above, **V.** *f*). His own conception of his mission as Messiah was such that popular Judaism would not have recognized it under that name, and so the title itself was an embarrassment.

But if Jesus avoided the *title* 'Messiah' (and with it the still more politically loaded 'Son of David', which others used of him but which he never used of himself), he did refer specifically to several figures of OT prediction as fulfilled in his ministry. Four or five such figures stand out in his teaching, and the selection is instructive. He was David's lord, as portrayed in Ps. 110:1 (Mk. 12:35–37; 14:62); the humble and rejected shepherd/king who recurs several times in Zc. 9–13 (Mt. 21:1–11; 24:30; 26:31); the suffering Servant of the Lord in Isaiah 53 (Mk. 10:45; 14:24; Lk. 22:37; *SERVANT OF THE LORD, **II.** *a*), with the related figure of the Lord's anointed in Is. 61:1 (Lk. 4:18ff.; Mt. 11:4f.); and the vindicated and enthroned 'son of man' in Dn. 7:13f. (Mk. 8:38; 13:26; 14:62; Mt. 19:28; 25:31; 28:18). The emphasis, therefore, except in the case of Dn. 7:13f. (on which see below, *i*), is strongly on a role of suffering, rejection and death, and a humble rather than a commanding status. Even the discussion of Ps. 110:1 in Mk. 12:35–37 is specifically designed to dissociate Jesus from the title 'Son of David' with its political implications; the dominant figure of OT Messianism, a king like David, does not otherwise appear in Jesus' selection, but is superseded by the picture of suffering and humiliation.

It is for this reason, probably, that Jesus regularly referred to himself as the 'Son of man'. Other titles already had a clearly defined, and usually nationalistic, content, but 'Son of man' was not current as a Messianic *title* in mainstream Judaism (though Dn. 7:13f. was widely referred to as a Messianic prophecy, without use of the title as such), and this rather enigmatic phrase (*cf.* Jn. 12:34) enabled Jesus to define his own conception of his Messianic role. (See further *MESSIAH, **II.** *a*; *JESUS CHRIST, TITLES OF.)

The necessity of his suffering and death is a constant theme of Jesus' teaching (especially Mk. 8:31; 9:31; 10:33f.; but also Mk. 9:12; 10:38, 45; 12:6–8;

14:8, 21–25; Mt. 26:54; Lk. 9:31; 12:50; 13:32f.; 17:25; 22:37; Jn. 10:11–15; 12:23–25; *etc.*), and it is frequently stressed that this *must* be so, because it is written.

The purpose of this suffering and death is most clearly spelt out in some of the references to Isaiah 53, which speaks of the Servant's role of suffering for the sins of his people, dying on their behalf, and thus 'making many to be accounted righteous'; thus Jesus would 'give his life as a ransom for many' (Mk. 10:45), and his 'blood of the covenant' would be 'poured out for many for the forgiveness of sins' (Mt. 26:28). This is sacrificial language, and the goal of Jesus' death is to be the final sacrifice which would make possible the forgiveness of sins and the restoration of fellowship between man and God, thus ending man's rebellion and bringing in the kingdom of God. This redemptive theology appears seldom and allusively in Jesus' teaching, but its direction is unmistakable, and is subsequently taken up into the more developed theology of Paul and the other NT writers. (*ATONEMENT; *REDEMPTION.)

BIBLIOGRAPHY. V. Taylor, *Jesus and his Sacrifice*, 1937; J. Jeremias, *The Eucharistic Words of Jesus*, 1966; R. T. France, *Jesus and the Old Testament*, 1971, ch. 4.

h. The people of God

It is often asserted that Jesus did not intend to found a church. If by 'church' is understood a formal, hierarchical organization, this is no doubt true. But the conception of his mission outlined above inevitably involved the creation of a new community of those who through his redemptive sacrifice entered the kingdom of God. This community, focused at first in his immediate group of disciples but destined to embrace all who responded to his teaching of whatever racial or social background, figures significantly in his teaching.

The word 'church' (*ekklēsia*) occurs only twice in the Gospels. In Mt. 18:17 it refers to the local group of followers of Jesus gathered together to settle disputes among its members, while in Mt. 16:18 it foreshadows the NT view of the universal church as Jesus' continuing representative on earth. But other terms imply the same idea of a defined community: they are, *e.g.*, God's 'little flock' (Lk. 12:32; *cf.* Mk. 14:27; Jn. 10:16), his family (Mk. 3:34f.; 10:29f.; Mt. 10:25), and the guests at his banquet (Mk. 2:19; Mt. 8:11f.; 22:1–14).

Hitherto Israel, the nation, had been the special people of God. Now, Jesus taught, the true people of God will be both wider and narrower than Israel: Gentiles will find a place at the banquet, while some Jews will not (Mt. 8:11f.; *cf.* Mt. 22:12–10). John the Baptist had warned that to be Jewish was not in itself a guarantee of salvation (Mt. 3:8–10), and Jesus took up the same theme. In numerous metaphors and allusions the impression is given that the true Israel is now focused in himself (see above, *c*; also **IV.** *c*) and in those who respond to his call to repentance. This conviction, symbolized in his choice of twelve disciples as his foundation group (see especially Mt. 19:28), and expressed in his establishment of a 'new covenant' (Lk. 22:20, *etc.*), explains why, while his own ministry was deliberately limited to Israel (Mt. 10:5f.; 15:24), he could send out his disciples after his resurrection to make disciples of all nations (Mt. 28:19; Lk. 24:47; Acts 1:8), to form a people of God drawn from all corners of the earth (Mk. 13:27). (*ISRAEL OF GOD.)

BIBLIOGRAPHY. J. Jeremias, *Jesus' Promise to the Nations*, 1958; G. B. Caird, *Jesus and the Jewish Nation*, 1965; C. H. Dodd, *The Founder of Christianity*, 1970, ch. 5; R. T. France, *TynB* 26, 1975, pp. 53–78.

i. The future

Jesus looked for a future 'coming of the kingdom' (see above, *d*). But precisely how and when he expected it to come is not systematically spelt out, and a number of different interpretations are possible. The following stages in this consummation seem, however, to be clearly taught.

1. Jesus several times predicted that after his suffering he would receive the power and dominion of the 'son of man' of Dn. 7:13f. (see above, *g*). When this vindication is expected is not always clear, but in Mt. 28:18, after the resurrection, he claimed that it was already accomplished. Mk. 14:62 also seems to envisage an imminent vindication, which his judges will themselves witness.

2. One future event which is clearly and repeatedly predicted by Jesus is the destruction of Jerusalem and its Temple (Mk. 13:2 and the following discourse; Lk. 21:20ff.; *cf.* also Mt. 23:37–39; Lk. 23:28–31). This is presented as the inevitable result of the Jewish rejection of God's final appeal (Lk. 13:34f.; 19:41–44; *cf.* Mt. 22:7), and it will come upon that generation (Mt. 23:36; Mk. 13:30). It is likely that some of Jesus' sayings about the 'coming of the Son of man' (again echoing Dn. 7:13f.) relate at least in part to this event rather than to his second coming, particularly as they too envisage a fulfilment within the living generation (Mk. 8:38–9:1; Mt. 10:23; Mk. 13:26, 30). This act of judgment would then be a further manifestation of his vindication. It is not agreed how much of the *Olivet Discourse refers to the question about the destruction of the Temple with which it opens and how much to a more ultimate future, but certainly the fate of Jerusalem holds a prominent place in Jesus' expectations for the future, and is viewed in relation to his own ministry.

3. A further application of Dn. 7:13f. is to the final judgment (Mt. 25:31–34; *cf.* Mt. 19:28). Most fully portrayed in Mt. 25:31ff., this 'day of judgment' is mentioned frequently in Jesus' teaching, applying both to individuals and to communities or nations (*e.g.* Mt. 10:15, 32f.; 11:22–24; 12:36, 41f.). In this final judgment too Jesus plays a central role.

4. Jesus also predicted his own second coming, or *parousia* (the term occurs in the Gospels only in Mt. 24:3, 27, 37, 39), sometimes called the 'day of the Son of man'. It will be as unmistakable and as universally visible as a flash of lightning (Lk. 17:24). It will be sudden and quite unexpected (Mt. 24:37–44; Lk. 17:26–35), demanding constant readiness (Mt. 24:42–51; 25:1–13). Its date cannot be calculated; indeed Jesus himself disclaimed any knowledge of when it would be (Mk. 13:32).

These four aspects of Jesus' teaching about the future merge into one another, so that it is not always possible to be sure which is referred to. In general, while 1 represents a constant state of affairs from the resurrection on, 2 relates to a specific future event expected within the generation, and 3 and 4 are two aspects of the final consummation when the kingdom is fully established; but all are related to Jesus' continuing role as the vindicated and enthroned 'Son of man'. Exegetical disagreement over the reference of specific passages should not be allowed to obscure this over-all pattern in Jesus' vision of the coming of the kingdom of God. Such an understanding of his teaching gives no support to the allegation that Jesus expected the end of the world in the very near future; and it ensures that his call for constant readiness is as binding on us today as on those who first heard him. (*ESCHATOLOGY.)

GENERAL BIBLIOGRAPHY. In addition to the works listed under individual sections above, the following more general works on the life and teaching of Jesus are of value.

J. Jeremias, *The Parables of Jesus*², 1963; *idem*, *New Testament Theology 1: The Proclamation of Jesus*, 1971; C. H. Dodd, *The Founder of Christianity*, 1970; G. Bornkamm, *Jesus of Nazareth*², 1973; G. Vermes, *Jesus the Jew*, 1973; G. N. Stanton, *Jesus of Nazareth in New Testament Preaching*, 1974; B. F. Meyer, *The Aims of Jesus*, 1979; J. Riches, *Jesus and the Transformation of Judaism*, 1980; A. E. Harvey, *Jesus and the Constraints of History*, 1982; M. J. Borg, *Conflict, Holiness and Politics in the Teachings of Jesus*, 1984; E. P. Sanders, *Jesus and Judaism*, 1985; G. R. Beasley-Murray, *Jesus and the Kingdom of God*, 1986; R. Leivestad, *Jesus in His Own Perspective*, 1987; G. Theissen, *The Shadow of the Galilean*, 1987; J. H. Charlesworth, *Jesus Within Judaism*, 1989; C. A. Evans, *Life of Jesus Research: An Annotated Bibliography*, 1989; R. T. France, *Jesus the Radical*, 1989; D. Wenham, *The Parables of Jesus*, 1989; J. D. Crossan, *The Historical Jesus: The Life of a Mediterranean Jewish Peasant*, 1991; J. P. Meir, *A Marginal Jew* 1, 1991; N. T. Wright, *Who Was Jesus?*, 1992; G. E. Ladd, *A Theology of the New Testament*², 1993, part 1. R.T.F.

JESUS CHRIST, TITLES OF. A title is a designation which describes or refers to some particular function or status of a person and hence may indicate the honour which is to be ascribed to him. For example, John was known as 'the Baptist' because this term described his characteristic function. Such a function need not be a unique one; there were many people who could be designated by such formulae as 'Z the prophet' or 'Y the king'.

Names and titles are closely related. Sometimes what began as a name could become a title, and vice versa. This is well illustrated in the case of the Roman emperors. Originally Caesar was the family name of Julius Caesar and his adopted nephew Octavian who became the first Roman emperor; after that it became a title meaning 'the Emperor' (Phil. 4:22; although it is mostly used without the article in the NT, *e.g.* Mk. 12:14–17, it still remains a title). Octavian himself was given the title 'Augustus' by the Roman senate in 27 BC; it means 'worthy of reverence' and was translated into Gk. as *sebastos*. As such it could be used of later emperors (Acts 25:21, 25), but to most people today it is the name of the first emperor, since it was the name by which he was known from the time of its presentation.

The meaning of a title can be altered by the character and deeds of a particular person who holds it and gives it a new stamp. The functions of a king in the UK have been drastically altered over many centuries, so that the title no longer conveys the same meaning as it did when it was first used. The simple title of 'the Leader' (*der Führer*) has been so much coloured by the particular character of Adolf Hitler who used it as a political title in Germany as to render it quite unsuitable for further use in politics.

Finally, there may be cases where a person can be described in such a way that it is clear that he holds the status, or performs the functions, associated with a particular title even though the title itself is not applied to him in that context. Thus we might say 'Z was king in all but name' of somebody who usurped a throne.

These rather general considerations are relevant to a consideration of the titles given to Jesus in the NT, and will help us to avoid some of the pitfalls in the study of this topic.

I. Titles used for Jesus during his lifetime

The name *Jesus* is not strictly a title for the person who bore it. It is, however, a name with a meaning, being a Greek form of 'Joshua', *i.e.* 'Yahweh is salvation'. The NT writers were well aware of this meaning (Mt. 1:21). The name thus indicated the function which was ascribed to Jesus, and this later found expression in the title *Saviour*, which was at first simply a *description* of the function of Jesus (Acts 5:31; 13:23; Phil. 3:20) but then became part of his solemn title (2 Tim. 1:10; Tit. 1:4; 2 Pet. 1:11). Jesus was the personal name of the Saviour, and while its titular significance remains present for informed hearers, it is probable that to many people it is now no more than a name (compare how the fact that 'John' means 'gift of God' is not usually in mind when the name is used).

Jesus was a common enough name in the first half of the 1st century AD, although it is significant that by the end of that century it was beginning to drop completely out of use: it was too sacred for use as a personal name by Christians, and it was abhorrent to Jews. To distinguish Jesus (Christ) from other bearers of the name he was known as *Jesus from Nazareth* or *Jesus the *Nazarene*. The use of this phrase may have acquired some theological significance in view of the similarity of the word 'Nazirite'.

As a result of his characteristic activity Jesus was known as a *Teacher*, and addressed by this title just like any other Jewish teacher (Mk. 4:38; 9:17, 38; 10:17; *et al.*). Occasionally, when there was no danger of confusion with other teachers, he could be called simply 'the Teacher' (Mk. 5:35; 14:14; Jn. 11:28). Jewish teachers were regularly addressed as *Rabbi* (literally, 'my great one'), a mark of respect which came to mean 'the revered (*sc.* teacher)'. This form of address was used by the disciples for Jesus (Mk. 9:5; 11:21; 14:45), although it was not used to refer to him in the third person. In Luke Jesus is sometimes addressed as *Master* (*epistatēs*; Lk. 5:5; 8:24; *et al.*), a term which suggests respect for Jesus by his disciples and sympathizers, and which perhaps was used of his relationship to groups of people rather than to individuals. A further respectful term was *Lord* (*kyrie*, the vocative form of *kyrios*). In the Gospels this probably represents an original Aramaic *rabbī* or *mārī* ('my lord') used as a respectful title (Mk. 7:28; Mt. 8:2, 6, 8; *et al.*). Although this form of address may simply refer to Jesus as a teacher worthy of respect (Lk. 6:46; Jn. 13:13f.), there is a case that Jesus was sometimes addressed in this way in his capacity as a person with miraculous powers (G. Vermes, *Jesus the Jew*, pp. 122–137). The term is not used in Mt. and Mk. as a means of referring to Jesus by a third person (except Mt. 21:3; Mk. 11:3), but Luke calls Jesus 'the Lord' not infrequently in narrative passages (Lk. 7:13; 10:1, 39, 41; *et al.*). This usage suggests that Luke was well aware that the full significance of the title was not realized until after the resurrection, but that he wanted to show that Jesus acted during his lifetime with something of the same authority which he possessed in full measure after the resurrection.

The fact that Jesus was regarded as more than an ordinary Jewish teacher is expressed in the term *Prophet* (Mt. 21:11, 46; Mk. 6:15; 8:28; Lk. 7:16, 39; 24:19; Jn. 4:19; 6:14; 7:40; 9:17). This understanding of his own position was recognized and expressed by Jesus (Mk. 6:4; Lk. 4:24; 13:33f.). In themselves neither of the titles, 'teacher' and 'prophet', distinguished Jesus from other teachers and prophets of his time, whether from Jewish religious leaders or from some groups of early church leaders (*e.g.* Acts 13:1), although naturally the early church would have claimed that Jesus was *the* Teacher and Prophet *par excellence*.

It is probable, however, that in some cases the term *The Prophet* was used in a unique sense. Jewish thought expected the coming of Elijah, or a person like him, to usher in the End, and there was some speculation whether John the Baptist or Jesus was to be identified as this so-called eschatological or final prophet (*cf.* Jn. 1:21, 25). There is some apparent confusion on the matter, since John denied that he was the prophet, while Jesus claimed that John was in fact Elijah (Mt. 17:12f.). The confusion would disappear if the reference in Jn. 1:21, 25 was to the coming of a final prophet like Moses (Dt. 18:15–19); Peter identified Jesus as this 'Mosaic' prophet (Acts 3:22–26), and this would leave the way clear for John to be regarded as a separate forerunner of the End, a prophet like Elijah. The difficulty may have arisen because Jewish thought did not keep the two figures quite separate. It is probable that Jesus himself saw his role as that of the Mosaic prophet. He did not use the title in this connection, but he regarded himself as re-enacting the work of Moses and as fulfilling the role of the prophet who speaks in Is. 61:1–3. He used passages from Is. 29:18f.; 35:5f. and 61:1 to describe his own work (Lk. 4:18f.; 7:22) in terms of a new creation of the paradisial conditions of the Exodus period and the wilderness wanderings, *i.e.* in terms of the work of Moses. From this point of view the teaching of Jesus in which he reinterpreted the law of Moses may also be significant.

Just as Jesus saw his work in terms of the lawgiver and the prophets (Moses and Elijah/Elisha; *cf.* Lk. 4:25–27), so it is probable that the Jewish concept of wisdom affected his thinking, although the actual title of *Wisdom* is not applied to him in the Gospels (see, however, 1 Cor. 1:24, 30). In the OT and the intertestamental literature we find the personified concept of Wisdom as the assistant of God at creation and (in the form of the law) as the guide of God's people (Pr. 8:22–36). The wise man *par excellence* was Solomon, and it is no accident that Jesus claimed that in his ministry something greater than Solomon was present (Mt. 12:42). Wisdom was regarded as sending her emissaries to men to reveal God's ways (Pr. 9:3–6). At times Jesus spoke as if he were such an emissary (Lk. 11:49–51) or as if he himself were to be identified with Wisdom (Lk. 13:34; *cf.* Mt. 23:34–37).

Jewish hopes were centred on the establishment of God's rule or kingdom, and this hope was often associated with the coming of an agent of God to exercise his rule. Such a person would be a king, anointed by God and belonging to the line of David. The term *Anointed One*, which could be used to describe a king, priest or prophet, came to be used as a technical term in the intertestamental period for this expected agent of God. The Heb. word was *māšîaḥ*, from which was derived the *transliterated* Gk. form *Messias*, anglicized as *Messiah; the corresponding Gk. word *meaning* 'anointed' was *Christos*, from which comes the alternative English form *Christ*. Since the expected ruler was expected to be a *King* and a *Son* (*i.e.* descendant) *of David*, these two terms were also used as titles or designations for him.

It stands beyond all doubt that Jesus was put to death by the Romans on a charge of claiming to be the king of the Jews (Mk. 15:26). The question is whether he explicitly claimed this office and implicitly acted in this role. The actual term 'Messiah' is only rarely found on the lips of Jesus. In Mk. 12:35 and 13:21 (*cf.* Mt. 24:5) he speaks about the Messiah and claimants to Messiahship without directly identifying himself as Messiah. In Mt. 23:10 and Mk. 9:41 he is represented as teaching his disciples, apparently with reference primarily to the situation in the early church. Mt. 16:20 merely echoes v. 16. It follows that Jesus did not refer to himself as Messiah in his public teaching to the crowds and that at best he used the title rarely in speaking to his disciples (*cf.* Jn. 4:25f.). The situation is the same with regard to 'Son of David'; the question in Mk. 12:35–37 does not explicitly identify Jesus as the Son of David. Nor did Jesus publicly claim the title of 'King' (Mt. 25:34, 40 is addressed to the disciples). On the other hand, many of Jesus' actions could be regarded as those of the Messiah. His baptism with the Spirit was regarded by both himself (Lk. 4:18) and the early church (Acts 4:27; 10:38) as an anointing. He proclaimed the coming rule of God, associated its coming with his own activity (Mt. 12:28), and acted with an authority that suggested that he stood in the place of God (Mk. 2:7). It is not surprising that the question whether he was the expected king was in the air (*cf.* Jn. 4:29; 7:25–31) and that the people would have made him king (Jn. 6:15). At his trial he was asked whether he was the Messiah, and on this occasion he did publicly admit the fact (Mk. 14:61f.; *cf.* Jn. 18:33–38). At an earlier point Peter named him as the Messiah, and Jesus did not reject the identification (Mk. 8:29f.); people who hoped that he would mercifully help them in their need addressed him as 'Son of David' (Mk. 10:47f.).

The evidence shows that while Jesus implicitly acted as Messiah he was reticent on the matter and indeed tried to hush down suggestions that he was the Messiah (Mk. 8:30). Various explanations have been offered for his attitude. We can dismiss the view that the Gospels have misrepresented the situation, and that Jesus was not recognized by himself or anybody else to be the Messiah; only after the resurrection did the church give this title to him (so W. Wrede, *The Messianic Secret*, E.T. 1971; *contra*: J. D. G. Dunn, *TynB* 21, 1970, pp. 92–117). One important element in explanation is certainly that Jesus' concept of Messiahship was markedly different from that of many Jews who expected the Messiah to inaugurate a political upheaval and liberate the country from the Romans;

even if there were Jews with a more spiritual ideal of the Messiah's work, Jesus had to guard against this misrepresentation. (It should go without saying that Jesus in no way associated himself with the advocacy of violence by the political revolutionaries of his day; on this subject the last word has been spoken by M. Hengel, *Was Jesus a Revolutionist?*, 1971.) Another element may be that Jesus did not wish to claim Messiahship until he had shown himself to be Messiah by what he did, or until people recognized the real significance of his ministry. In so doing he freed Messiahship from its this-worldly political associations and reinterpreted it in terms of the OT concept of God's mighty act of salvation.

Undoubtedly, however, the Gospels give the impression that Jesus preferred to use another description, *Son of man* (note the shift in terminology in Mk. 8:29f./31 and 14:61/62). This unusual Gk. expression can have arisen only as a translation of an idiomatic Semitic phrase (Heb. *ben 'āḏām*; Aram. *bar 'ᵉnāš(â)*) which means either a particular member of the species 'man' (*e.g.* Ezk. 2:1) or mankind in general (*e.g.* Ps. 8:4). In Dn. 7:13f. the phrase describes 'one like a man' (NEB) or 'what looked like a human being' (TEV) who comes with the clouds to the Ancient of Days and receives everlasting dominion over all peoples from him. In the language of Jesus' time it appears to have been possible to use the phrase as a modest way of referring to oneself in certain situations, although opinions differ whether it was used to make a statement true of mankind in general and hence of the speaker in particular or to make a statement applying only to the speaker.

The phrase occurs quite often on the lips of Jesus, and its occurrences in the Synoptic Gospels have led to much debate.

1. On the one hand, it has been assumed that the significance of the phrase is derived from Dn. 7:13f., in which case it refers to the future coming of a heavenly being described with apocalyptic symbolism (Mk. 13:26; 14:62) and to the role played by this figure at the last judgment (Mk. 8:38; Mt. 10:23; 19:28; 25:31; Lk. 12:8f.; 17:22–30; 18:8). Some scholars think that the early church was the first to use this concept to describe the future role of Jesus (so N. Perrin, *A Modern Pilgrimage in New Testament Christology*, 1974); others argue, on the basis of Lk. 12:8f., that Jesus looked forward to the coming of an apocalyptic figure *other than himself* who would vindicate his work, and that it was the early church which later identified Jesus himself with this coming figure (so H. E. Tödt, *The Son of Man in the Synoptic Tradition*, 1965); others again argue that Jesus looked forward to his own future coming as the Son of man (so O. Cullmann, *The Christology of the New Testament*², 1963).

Alongside these 'future' statements there are others which speak of the present authority and humiliation of the Son of man (Mk. 2:10, 27f.; Lk. 6:22; 7:34; 9:58; 12:10; 19:10) and prophesy his suffering, death and resurrection (Mk. 8:31; 9:9, 12, 31; 10:33f., 45; 14:21, 41; *cf.* Lk. 24:7). It is hard (but not impossible: see below) to see how statements like these could be made about the Son of man described in Dn. 7, and accordingly many scholars think that the use of Son of man in such sayings derives from the early church which, having identified Jesus as the coming Son of man, proceeded to use the same title with reference to his earthly ministry and his passion. Other scholars hold that Jesus produced his own creative reinterpretation of the role of the Son of man under the influence of the prophecy of the suffering Servant of Yahweh (Is. 52:13–53:12).

2. On the other hand, various scholars take the use of *bar 'ᵉnāš(â)* as a self-designation in Aram. as their starting-point, and hold that Jesus used it simply as a means of referring to himself. On this view, the statements in the Gospels which are non-apocalyptic in content and refer to Jesus simply as a man are most likely to be authentic. Later, the use of the term by Jesus led the church back to Dn. 7, and it proceeded to reinterpret the teaching of Jesus in apocalyptic terms (G. Vermes, *op. cit.*, pp. 160–191).

3. It is probable that scholars have been led astray by insisting on one basic origin for all the sayings and not taking the ambiguity of the term sufficiently seriously. Clearly it could be used as a self-designation, even although the precise circumstances in which this was felt to be proper remain uncertain. At the same time it cannot be denied that the term could have a titular force. C. F. D. Moule rightly observes that the use of the article in the phrase may give the force of '*the* human figure' (*sc.* the one mentioned in Dn. 7:13f.; 'Neglected Features in the Problem of "the Son of Man"', in J. Gnilka (ed.), *Neues Testament und Kirche*, 1974, pp. 413–428). The fact that this figure played a role in some areas of Jewish thought is shown by the allusions in *1 Enoch* and *4 Ezra* (although the dating of the crucial portions in *1 Enoch* is notoriously insecure). The most probable approach, therefore, is still that which takes Dn. 7:13f. as its starting-point and sees there a figure, perhaps the leader and representative of Israel, with whom Jesus identifies himself. This figure is one possessing authority and destined to rule the world, but the way to that rule is by humility, suffering and rejection. It is not too difficult to understand Jesus speaking in this way, provided that he can be assumed to have looked forward to his own rejection and subsequent vindication by God. This assumption is wholly probable when we take account of: (a) Jesus' recognition of the realities of the situation in which he carried on a ministry that brought him into collision with the hostile Jewish authorities; and (b) Jesus' acceptance of the way of life of the godly man described in the OT, according to which the godly can expect rejection and persecution and must put their trust in God to deliver them. This pattern can be traced in certain of the Psalms (especially Pss. 22; 69), in the prophecies of the suffering Servant and in the career of 'the saints of the Most High' in Dn. It is also to be found in the book of Wisdom (although it is doubtful whether this book could have influenced Jesus himself) and in the popular legends in which the Jews glorified the fate of the Maccabean martyrs. Against this considerable background it would be strange if Jesus had not understood his career in such terms. At the same time, his manner of speaking certainly mystified his hearers: 'Who is this Son of man?' (Jn. 12:34). It was probably a deliberate means of concealing his own claims to some extent so as not to lead to false expectations. It laid claim to authority but an authority which was largely rejected by men. Thus by his use of this phrase Jesus laid claim to being the final representative of God to men, destined to rule but rejected by Israel, condemned to suffer but vindicated by God.

One of the elements which contributed to Jesus' understanding of his role as Son of man was the figure of the *Servant of Yahweh*. The actual title was not used by Jesus, and the nearest approach to its use is when it occurs in a quotation from Is. 42:1–4 in Mt. 12:18–21. Nevertheless, there is good evidence that Jesus saw himself as fulfilling the role of one who came to serve and give himself as a ransom for many (Mk. 10:45; *cf.* 14:24; Is. 53:10–12) and who therefore 'shared the fate of criminals' (Lk. 22:37, TEV; *cf.* Is. 53:12; R. T. France, *TynB* 19, 1968, pp. 26–52).

If the above titles express the role of Jesus, his status and relationship to God find expression in the title of *Son of God*. The use of this title for angels and other heavenly beings does not seem to be of central significance for its application to Jesus. More important is the way in which it was used in the OT to refer to the people of Israel as a whole and to their king in particular and to express the relationship which they had to God in terms of divine care and protection on the one hand and human service and obedience on the other. It is possible that by NT times the Messiah was beginning to be regarded as in some special sense the Son of God, and the thought that godly individuals were the special objects of God's fatherly care and concern had also developed.

Jesus himself was undoubtedly conscious of a particular relationship to *God whom he addressed in prayer by the intimate name of *Abba (Mk. 14:36). It is against this background that we should understand his use of the term 'Son' to express his relationship to God as his Father (Mt. 11:27; Lk. 10:22). Here he claims that the same intimacy exists between himself and God as between a son and his father, so that he alone is qualified to reveal God to men. Yet there are secrets of the Father's purpose hidden even from the Son (Mk. 13:32). Although the allusion may well not have been clear to the crowds, it is likely that the reference to the owner's son in the parable of the vineyard (Mk. 12:6) was a veiled way of pointing to Jesus himself and to his fate. This sense of a unique Sonship goes beyond the general sense of a filial relationship to God which might have been held by a pious Jew. It is further to be seen in the way in which God himself addresses Jesus as his Son in the stories of the baptism and the transfiguration (Mk. 1:11; 9:7), and also in the manner of address used by Satan and the demons (Mt. 4:3, 6; Mk. 3:11; 5:7). The evidence shows that Jesus himself was extremely reticent to express his sense of unique personal relationship to God; nevertheless it is clear that the Jewish authorities suspected that he was making claims of this kind (Mk. 14:61; Lk. 22:70), claims which were perhaps made more openly on occasion than the Synoptic Gospels suggest (in Jn. Jesus' self-revelation is more public, but this may be due to the way in which John has deliberately brought out more clearly the full implications of Jesus' teaching for his readers). It is in this title that the fullest expression of who Jesus was is to be found (see I. H. Marshall, *Int* 21, 1967, pp. 87–103).

II. The use of titles in the earliest period of the church

A period of some 20 years separates the death and resurrection of Jesus from the earliest NT documents (the earliest letters of Paul) which can be reliably dated. By Paul's time the use of various titles to refer to Jesus was well established; he manifestly used an existing, fully developed terminology which he could take for granted and which he had no need to explain to his readers. It is, however, difficult to trace the use of the various titles and the associated theological understanding of Jesus during this pre-literary period. We have to proceed by attempting to recognize occurrences of the titles in the NT writings which can plausibly be regarded as reflecting traditional usage; this is a subjective process and leads to hypotheses of varying credibility. We can also make use of the account of the early church given to us in Acts, but it has to be recognized that Luke wrote some years after the events which he described, and that there would be an inevitable tendency to adopt the terminology with which his readers were familiar. We may compare how a well-known public figure tends to be described by his later title even when his earlier career is being discussed; there is a temptation to say 'Queen Victoria spent her earlier years in Kensington Palace' rather than more pedantically 'Princess Victoria (who later became Queen) spent her earlier years . . .'. Nevertheless, with due caution we can make some progress in tracing the early development of titles to describe Jesus.

Some scholars have admittedly shown considerable boldness in postulating a series of stages in the Christological thinking of the early church on the assumption that an original understanding of Jesus in purely Jewish terms was succeeded by an understanding that was increasingly affected by Hellenistic ways of thinking mediated to the church first by Diaspora Judaism and then more directly by the Gentile world (F. Hahn; R. H. Fuller). While some *broad* developments of this kind no doubt occurred, the hypothesis cannot be used to trace stages of development with any precision, since it is clear that influences of all kinds affected the church from its earliest days and also that we have to do with the Christological thinking of a number of different semi-independent churches. There is no possibility of tracing a simple evolutionary line of development through the complex thought-processes of the first 20 years or so of the Christian church. What we can say is that this period was one of unparalleled creative thinking in the development of Christology (I. H. Marshall, *NTS* 19, 1972–3, pp. 271–287).

It is sometimes suggested that the early church's interest in Jesus was originally purely functional rather than ontological (O. Cullmann). It was concerned with what Jesus did rather than who he was, and did not ask metaphysical questions about his status. But to put the alternatives so sharply is probably to separate what originally belonged together: function and status cannot be so easily separated. The early church was no doubt concerned with what Jesus had accomplished, but the very nature of what he had accomplished inevitably raised the question of his relationship to God from the very start, and this is reflected in the titles used to describe him.

During this period most of the ordinary 'human' terms used to describe Jesus during his ministry fell out of use, except in so far as they were preserved in narrative material about his career. Terms such as *Rabbi* and *Teacher* were no longer appropriate. The term *Prophet* which had represented a higher level of popular insight into the function of Jesus likewise dropped out of use; although the term was still applied to him (Acts

3:22f.; *cf.* 7:37), it does not occur as an actual title of Jesus. What is surprising is the virtually complete disappearance of *Son of man* from circulation. The phrase is found as a title only on the lips of the dying Stephen (Acts 7:56). Elsewhere it has survived only in a citation from the OT (Heb. 2:6; quoting Ps. 8:5) and in a description of Jesus in Rev. 1:13; 14:14 (*cf.* Dn. 7:13f.). But the thought was probably still alive. One the one hand, it is possible that we have a translation of 'Son of man' into more intelligible Gk. as 'the Man' in one or two passages where Jesus is placed over against Adam, the first man (Rom. 5:15; 1 Cor. 15:21, 47; *cf.* 1 Tim. 2:5). On the other hand, the Gospels have preserved the use of the term on the lips of Jesus. As we observed, there are scholars who claim that the use of the term originated in the early church, or that at least the majority of examples of its use were developed by the early church on the basis of a small number of actual sayings of Jesus. While these suggestions are highly unlikely, we cannot exclude the possibility that the inclusion of the title in a few sayings may be due to the early church; this is most probably the case in Jn. where the teaching of Jesus has come down to us in a form where it is impossible to disentangle the actual words of Jesus from the Evangelist's interpretative commentary. But it is important that John's fuller expression of the implicit significance of the title takes place within the confines of a Gospel, and as teaching which is ascribed to Jesus himself and which ultimately rests on his own words (see **IV**, below). There is no indication that the early church used the title independently. Clearly it was regarded as a term that was appropriate only on the lips of Jesus as a self-designation, with the one exception of Acts 7:56. It never became a term for use in confessional statements (with the possible exception of Jn. 9:35).

Although the title of *Servant* did not occur in the Gospels, we saw that the associated motifs were present in the description of the work of Jesus as service for 'the many'. This same motif reappears in the thinking of the early church. It is most obvious in 1 Pet. 2:21–25, where the passion and death of Jesus are described in language drawn from Is. 53; it is not quite so clearly present in a number of traditional formulae in Paul which express the significance of the death of Jesus (Rom. 4:25; 8:34; 1 Cor. 11:23–25; 15:3–5; Phil. 2:6–11; 1 Tim. 2:6; J. Jeremias, *TDNT* 5, pp. 705–712). The title itself (*pais*) is to be found in Acts 3:13, 26; 4:27, 30 where Jesus is declared to be God's Servant who was delivered up by the Jews to death, but raised and glorified by God to be the source of blessing for his people. If Jesus is designated here by a title also borne by David (Acts 4:25, *pais*) and the prophets (Rev. 11:18; 22:9, *doulos*), here it is above all the thought of Is. 42:1–4; 52:13f. which has influenced the early church. Although the title does not reappear until the Apostolic Fathers and has therefore been suspected to be a Lucan rather than a primitive designation for Jesus, it is more likely that the term was used in the Palestinian church and then fell out of use because of its ambiguity in the form *pais* (which can mean 'child' or 'servant') and its subordinationist colouring in the form *doulos* ('slave').

According to the speech attributed to Peter on the day of Pentecost the significance of the resurrection was that God had made the Jesus whom the Jews crucified to be both Lord and *Christ* (Acts 2:36). This text gives the key to the development of the Christological titles. The resurrection was the decisive event which led the followers of Jesus to a new evaluation of his person, and this was confirmed for them by the gift of the Spirit coming from the exalted Jesus (Acts 2:33). Jesus' claims to be a 'Messianic' figure of some kind had now been vindicated by God in raising him from the dead and thereby attesting the truth of these claims. The One who died under Pilate's sarcastic placard as 'The King of the Jews' had now been shown to be king in a deeper sense. The actual title of 'king' does not seem to have been used overmuch. It is true that the king replaced the 'kingdom' in the apostolic preaching, but the word was perhaps politically dangerous (Acts 17:7) and use of it was restrained (Rev. 17:14; 19:16); note, however, that the title of 'Lord' which was equally dangerous politically was in frequent use. 'Messiah'—a word meaningless outside Heb.-speaking circles—was replaced not so much by 'king' as by 'Christ'. In this form the title tended to lose its original meaning of 'anointed one' (see, however, 2 Cor. 1:21) and to take on more the sense of 'Saviour'. It was particularly used in statements about the death and resurrection of Jesus (Rom. 5:6, 8; 6:3–9; 8:34; 14:9; 1 Cor. 15:3–5; 1 Pet. 3:18; W. Kramer, *Christ, Lord, Son of God*, 1966). It was as the One who died and rose again that Jesus was the Christ. Although 'Christ' tended to become more and more a name for Jesus, rather than a title, it continued to have a sense of dignity about it, so that it was scarcely ever used alone with the title 'Lord' (*i.e.* in the combination 'the Lord Christ'; Rom. 16:18; Col. 3:24) but rather in the form 'the Lord Jesus Christ'.

In Acts 3:20f. Jesus is represented as the One who is designated to appear as the Christ at the end of time. Accordingly it has been claimed (especially by F. Hahn) that the earliest Christology of the church was concerned with the future coming of Jesus, and that the various titles of Son of man, Christ and Lord were originally used to indicate what his function would be at the end of time; only later (though still within this pre-literary period) was it realized that the One who would come as Christ and Lord at the end was *already* Christ and Lord by virtue of his resurrection and exaltation (and that the resurrection and exaltation confirmed an existing status). This theory lacks substantiation. Acts 3:20f. can only mean that the One who has already been ordained as the Christ will return at the end of time. Jesus is not the Messiah-designate, but is already the Messiah. It was indeed only because of the resurrection and what it implied concerning the person of Jesus that the early church could look forward with confidence to his parousia as the Son of man. It was, accordingly, the death and resurrection which established the meaning of the term Christ: the Christian message in Paul's view was exclusively oriented to 'Christ crucified' (1 Cor. 1:23; 2:5).

The other title which figures in Acts 2:36 is *Lord*. By the resurrection God had demonstrated that Jesus was indeed the Lord, and the early church applied the words of Ps. 110:1 to him in virtue of this event: 'The Lord said to my Lord, Sit at my right hand, till I make thy enemies a stool for thy feet' (Acts 2:34f.). This text had already been used by Jesus when he taught that the Messiah was David's Lord (Mk. 12:36) and in his reply to the high priest at his trial (Mk. 14:62). If Jesus was now Lord, it followed that the task of the early church was to lead people to recognize the status of Jesus. New converts became members of the church by acknowledging Jesus as Lord: 'If you confess with your lips that Jesus is Lord and believe in your heart that God raised him from the dead, you will be saved' (Rom. 10:9; *cf.* 1 Cor. 12:3). The great significance of this confession is seen in Phil. 2:11 where the climax of God's purpose is that all creation will acknowledge Jesus Christ as Lord. In this confession there may well be a polemical note, since it places Jesus over against other 'lords' recognized by worshippers in the Hellenistic world. Certainly Jews recognized only one God and Lord, but pagans worshipped 'gods many and lords many'; over against them both Christians acknowledged 'one God, the Father, . . . and one Lord, Jesus Christ' (1 Cor. 8:6). The Roman emperor too was acclaimed as lord (*dominus*) by his subjects and successive emperors increasingly claimed their total allegiance; this was to lead to keen conflicts of conscience for Christians at a later stage.

An important piece of evidence for the early Christian use of the title for Jesus is the phrase preserved in Aramaic in 1 Cor. 16:22: *'*Maranatha*'. This is a combination of two words and means 'Our Lord, come' or 'Our Lord has/will come'. Scholars debate whether it was originally a prayer for the parousia of Jesus as Lord (*cf.* Rev. 22:20) or a promise that his coming was at hand (*cf.* Phil. 4:5). The fact that the phrase was preserved in a Gk.-speaking church in Aram. indicates that it was originally used in an Aram.-speaking church, *i.e.* it most probably arose in the earliest days of the church in Palestine. Evidence from Qumran has helped to confirm the possibility of this development in an Aram.-speaking environment (J. A. Fitzmyer, *NTS* 20, 1973–4, pp. 386–391).

The final term to be discussed in this section is *Son of God*. It may well have been especially associated with the preaching of Paul: it is significant that Acts 9:20 links the title with his preaching, and that it appears only once elsewhere in Acts, namely in a citation of Ps. 2:7 in Paul's sermon in Pisidian Antioch (Acts 13:33). Here the promise, 'Thou art my Son, today I have begotten thee', is applied by Paul to the resurrection which is regarded as the begetting of Jesus to new life. The thought, however, is not that Jesus became God's Son by being raised from the dead, but rather that *because* he was his Son, God raised him from the dead (*cf.* Wisdom 2:18). The same thought reappears in Rom. 1:3f., generally regarded as a pre-Pauline formula, where Jesus is said to have been declared to be Son of God with power by the resurrection from the dead. In 1 Thes. 1:9f. the sonship of Jesus is again connected with the resurrection, and this fact is made the basis for the hope of his parousia.

Two further elements appear to be associated with the title of 'Son' in this early period. One is the thought of the pre-existence of the Son; a number of texts speak of God sending his Son (Jn. 3:17; Rom. 8:3; Gal. 4:4f.; 1 Jn. 4:9f., 14), and clearly presuppose that the Son came from being with the Father into the world. This line of thought is expressed quite explicitly without the actual use of the term 'Son' in the pre-Pauline hymn in Phil. 2:6–11 (R. P. Martin, *Carmen Christi*, 1967). Here Jesus is a divine figure, existing in the image of God and equal with God, who exchanged his heavenly mode of existence for a human, earthly form of existence in humility. Although the hymn speaks of his 'emptying himself*' so that he exchanged the form of God for that of a slave, the fact that Paul regarded Jesus as God's Son during his life and death indicates that he did not interpret the hymn to mean that Jesus surrendered his divine nature in order to become incarnate. Rather, 'He emptied Himself in that He took the servant's form . . . ; and this necessarily involved an eclipsing of His glory as the divine Image in order that He might come, in human flesh, as the Image of God incarnate' (R. P. Martin, p. 194).

The other element associated with the title of Son is that God gave him up to suffer and die (Rom. 4:25; 8:32; Gal. 2:20; *cf.* Jn. 3:16). There may be some connection here with the OT example of Abraham who was prepared to give up his son, Isaac, to show his faith and obedience (Gn. 22:12, 16). Nor did God withhold his only Son, but gave him up freely to take away our sins. By the use of the title 'Son' the greatness of the divine sacrifice is made all the more plain.

It is not certain at what point the tradition of the virgin birth of Jesus began to influence the Christological thinking of the church. The implication of both the birth stories is that the circumstances of Jesus' birth were kept quiet (*cf.* Mt. 1:19; Lk. 2:19, 51), and there is very little evidence that the tradition influenced the church before it was given expression in the Gospels. In both accounts Jesus is presented as the Son of God (Mt. 2:15; Lk. 1:32, 35) whose birth as the son of Mary is due to the influence of the Holy Spirit; it is as the Son of God that he is qualified for the office and task of the Messiah (Lk. 1:32f.). Not only so, but as the Son of God he can be designated *Emmanuel*, 'God with us'; his presence on earth is tantamount to that of God himself. The two accounts do not take up the question of the relation between the Spirit-conception of Jesus and his identity with the pre-existent Son of God; their concern is exclusively with the way in which the son of Mary could be born as the Son of God.

III. Paul's use of Christological titles

In the preceding section we have seen that the essential stages in the development of the Christological vocabulary of the church had already taken place before the writing of Paul's letters. He uses an existing vocabulary in them, and he can assume that the terms which he uses are generally familiar to his Christian readers. Consequently, there is little to be said about the use of the titles which is distinctive of Paul. This may well be because he himself was closely involved in the development of the theology of the early church and had already made his own contribution to the common store of Christological thinking before he came to write his letters. In conscious opposition, therefore, to the scheme adopted by R. Bultmann (*Theology of the New Testament*, 1, 1952, ch. 3), L. Goppelt rightly refuses to discuss 'The kerygma of the Hellenistic Church aside from Paul' because this simply leads to 'unhistorical abstractions'; while recognizing that there were many currents of thought in the early church, he prefers to discuss the theology of Paul in the light of the traditions which he received and the situations in which he worked (*Theologie des Neuen Testaments*, 2, 1976, pp. 360f.).

Two titles which we might have expected to find

in Paul's letters are conspicuously absent or rare. Paul never uses *Servant* with respect to Jesus, and he uses the motifs associated with the title only when alluding to traditional material. He does, however, think of himself and his fellow workers as slaves of God (*doulos*), and just once he can speak of Jesus as a *minister* (*diakonos*; Rom. 15:8) for the circumcision (*i.e.* for the Jews). He also sees the role of the Servant as being fulfilled in the missionary witness of the church (Rom. 10:16; 15:21; *cf.* Acts 13:47).

The actual name *Jesus*, used by itself, is quite rare in Paul (about 16 occurrences), although it is of course common in combinations. Half of these occurrences are in 2 Cor. 4:10–14 and 1 Thes. 4:14 where Paul is discussing how the death and resurrection of Jesus are repeated in the lives of believers. Otherwise he mainly uses 'Jesus' when he is discussing what other titles should be predicated of its bearer (1 Cor. 12:3; *cf.* 2 Cor. 11:4; Phil. 2:10).

For Paul *Christ* has become the main designation by which he refers to Jesus. His message was the 'gospel of Christ' (*e.g.* Gal. 1:7), and a study of the occurrences of 'Christ' produces a Pauline theology in miniature (see the excellent treatment by W. Grundmann, *TDNT* 9, pp. 543–551). He takes over the traditional uses of the title with respect especially to the death and resurrection of Jesus, but he also uses it in many other ways. The distinctively Pauline element comes out in the use of the phrase 'in Christ', by which Christ is described as the determining circumstance which conditions the life of the believer (J. K. S. Reid, *Our Life in Christ*, 1963, ch. 1). This means that the phrase does not refer so much to a mystical union with a heavenly figure but rather to the historical facts of the crucifixion and resurrection which condition our existence. Thus justification takes place 'in Christ' (Gal. 2:17); the individual Christian is 'a man in Christ' (2 Cor. 12:2), and the churches are 'in Christ' (Gal. 1:22, Gk.); Christian witness takes place 'in Christ' (1 Cor. 4:15; Phil. 1:13, Gk.; 2 Cor. 2:17). At every point the Christian life is determined by the new situation brought about by the fact of Christ.

Paul frequently uses the combination 'Jesus Christ' as a title. Sometimes the words occur in the reverse order 'Christ Jesus', but a satisfying explanation for the variations in word order has not been discovered: grammatical reasons may contribute to the variation, and it has also been suggested that Paul wished to emphasize the human Jesus or the heavenly, pre-existent Christ by placing one or the other first. In any case, there does not appear to be any difference in the use of the compound title from that of the simple 'Christ', except that the compound title was felt to be more emphatic and dignified.

Paul's usage of *Lord* is essentially the same as that of the pre-Pauline church. Here especially there is no need to invoke the influence of pagan worship of cult deities in order to account for the distinctive features of Pauline usage. This thesis—along with the associated claim that much of Paul's theology was derived from transfer of originally pagan ideas to Christianity—has been increasingly shown to be unnecessary and untenable (O. Cullmann, *op. cit.*, ch. 7). Of course Christians who already acknowledged Jesus as Lord had to define more closely what they meant by this title over against pagan worship of other lords (1 Cor. 8:6), but this is quite different from saying that the Christian usage was derived from the pagan.

Since confession of Jesus as Lord was the mark of the Christian, and since for Christians there was no other Lord, it was natural for Paul to speak simply of 'the Lord' when he wished to refer to Jesus. It is true that the same title was used to refer to God the Father, and that this can lead to a certain ambiguity as to whether God or Jesus is meant (this is especially the case in Acts; J. C. O'Neill, *SJT* 8, 1955, pp. 155–174); generally, however, 'Lord' is used for God by Paul almost exclusively in quotations from the OT, so that there is little risk of confusion.

If the title 'Christ' had come to have the connotation of 'Saviour', that of 'Lord' primarily expresses the exalted position of Jesus and his rule over the universe and especially over believers who accept his Lordship. It is thus especially used when the responsibility of Christians to obey Jesus is being expressed (*e.g.* Rom. 12:11; 1 Cor. 4:4f.). But Paul also uses it quite freely to refer to the earthly Jesus (1 Cor. 9:5), especially with reference to what came to be known as 'the supper of the Lord' (1 Cor. 10:21; 11:23, 26f.) and also when referring to instructions given by the earthly Jesus (1 Cor. 7:10, 25; 9:14; *et al.*). It is not surprising that the formula 'in Christ' is altered to 'in the Lord' when it occurs in the context of exhortations and commands (Eph. 6:1; Phil. 4:2; Col. 4:17; *et al.*). Nevertheless, the use of the two titles is quite fluid, and sometimes Paul uses the one where we might have expected him to use the other.

Compound titles including the title of Lord are frequent in Paul, and are evidently used in order to exalt the person thus designated. The early Christian confession 'Jesus (Christ) is Lord' lies behind the development of 'the Lord Jesus (Christ)' (2 Cor. 4:5), and Paul often speaks of *our* Lord, thereby emphasizing both the need for personal commitment to Jesus and also the saving care and concern of Jesus for his people. This formula is found in the introductory salutations of Paul's letters where 'God our Father and the Lord Jesus Christ' are associated together as the source of spiritual blessings. W. Grundmann (*TDNT* 9, p. 554) has suggested that behind this formula there lies the OT phrase 'the Lord God' which was transformed in Christian worship into 'God the Father' and the co-ordinated 'Lord Jesus Christ', indicating that the person who has Jesus as his Lord also has God as his Father. Whether or not this explanation is correct, two facts are noteworthy. The one is that here God the Father and Jesus are placed quite naturally alongside each other in a way that indicates an equality of status; to be sure, the subordination of Jesus to the Father is always carefully preserved (1 Cor. 15:28; Phil. 2:11), but no other being is ever placed alongside the Father in this way. The second fact is that the OT usage of 'Lord' as a title for God has undoubtedly influenced Christian usage. This is clear from Phil. 2:10f. which takes up the language of Is. 45:22–25 and applies what is said there about God to Jesus. Similarly, in Rom. 10:9, 13 a citation from Joel 2:32 about calling on the name of the Lord (*i.e.* Yahweh) has been applied to Jesus. This usage is by no means peculiar to Paul (*cf.* Jn. 12:38; Heb. 1:10; 1 Pet. 3:14f.; Jude 24f.; Rev. 17:14; 19:16). When, finally, Paul refers to 'the day of the Lord', he undoubtedly understands the Lord here to be no longer Yahweh but Jesus (1 Cor. 1:8; 2 Cor. 1:14).

If statistics were our guide, it would appear that *Son of God* (15 occurrences) was much less important for Paul than *Lord*, which appears at least ten times more frequently in his writings. Nevertheless, as M. Hengel (*The Son of God*, 1976, ch. 3) has shown, Paul uses this title for Jesus when he is summing up the content of his gospel (Rom. 1:3–4, 9; Gal. 1:15f.), and tends to reserve it for important statements. He uses it when the question of the relationship between God and Jesus is particularly in his mind, and, as we saw earlier, took up the traditional statements which spoke of God sending his pre-existent Son into the world and giving him up to die for us. He brings out especially the fact that it is through the work of the Son that we can be adopted as God's sons (Rom. 8:29; Gal. 4:4–6).

A number of other expressions are used by Paul in this connection. Jesus is described as the **Image* of the invisible God (Col. 1:15; *cf.* 2 Cor. 4:4); he is the **Firstborn* of all creation (Rom. 8:29; Col. 1:15–18) and the *Beloved* (Son) of God (Eph. 1:6). These, however, should be regarded more as descriptions of Jesus than as titles. The same is true of other phrases which describe various functions of Jesus, such as **Head* (Eph. 1:22) and even *Saviour* (Eph. 5:23; Phil. 3:20).

It is a moot point whether the title *God* is applied to Jesus by Paul. The interpretation of Rom. 9:5 (see RSV and mg.) is debatable, but the text should probably be understood as a doxology to the Christ as God (B. M. Metzger, in B. Lindars and S. S. Smalley (ed.), *Christ and Spirit in the New Testament*, 1973, pp. 95–112). Equally ambiguous is 2 Thes. 1:12 (see TEV and mg.; NIV and mg.).

By the time that we reach the Pastoral Epistles the rich diversity of titular usage characteristic of the earlier Pauline writings is beginning to disappear. *Son of God* is not used at all. Neither *Jesus* nor *Christ* is used independently (except in 1 Tim. 5:11) but only in combination, usually in the order *Christ Jesus*. *Lord* is, however, used as an independent title and also in combinations. In several cases we probably have examples of formal, credal statements expressed in a dignified style and based on traditional material (1 Tim. 1:15; 2:5f.; 6:13; 2 Tim. 1:9f.; 2:8; Tit. 2:11–14; 3:6). There is no doubt that here Jesus is given the title of God (Tit. 2:13), and he shares with God the title of *Saviour* (2 Tim. 1:10; Tit. 1:4; 2:13; 3:6).

IV. The titles of Jesus in the Johannine literature

In Jn. the pattern of usage is similar to that in the other Gospels. The Gospel is concerned with the activities of the human person *Jesus*, and the compound form *Jesus Christ* is used only a couple of times when the total significance of Jesus is viewed from a post-resurrection standpoint (Jn. 1:17; 17:3—the latter passage being uttered from the perspective of one who has 'accomplished the work' which the Father gave him to do). Although the term *Lord* is frequently used in the vocative to address Jesus, it is scarcely used in narrative to refer to Jesus (only in Jn. 4:1; 6:23; 11:2) until after the resurrection which established the new status of Jesus. Nevertheless, it is significant that Jesus himself describes his status as that of a 'master' (Jn. 13:13f., 16; 15:15, 20) who can give commands to his slaves—although he regards his disciples as friends rather than slaves.

One of the key questions in Jn. is whether Jesus is the *Messiah* of both Jewish and Samaritan expectation; the purpose of the Gospel is to lead to belief that this is the case (Jn. 20:31). Despite the rarity of its use in the other Gospels, Jesus is confessed as Messiah in Jn. (Jn. 1:41; 4:29; 11:27), but it is interesting that the word never appears on the lips of Jesus himself. Other quasi-titular descriptions of Jesus which are used in Jn. include the *Coming One* (Jn. 11:27; 12:13; *cf.* Mt. 11:3); the *Holy One of God* (Jn. 6:69; *cf.* Mk. 1:24), the *Saviour* (Jn. 4:42), the *Lamb of God* (Jn. 1:29, 36), the *Prophet* (Jn. 6:14; 7:40) and the *King of Israel* (Jn. 1:49; 12:13; 18:33–38; 19:3, 14–22). Several of these are also found in the Synoptic Gospels.

Jesus' characteristic self-designation of *Son of man* also figures prominently in Jn., but here there is a new stress on the heavenly origin of the Son of man, his descent into this world, his glorification on the cross and his significance as the giver of life (Jn. 3:13; 5:27; 6:27, 53, 62; 12:23, 34; 13:31) which is absent from the Synoptic Gospels. While it is unnecessary to assume that foreign influences have contributed to the use of the title in Jn., the language used is sufficiently different from that in the Synoptic Gospels to suggest that, although the sayings in Jn. ultimately rest on the actual teaching of Jesus, they have been to some extent rewritten by the Evangelist or his sources (S. S. Smalley, *NTS* 15, 1968–9, pp. 278–301).

The most fundamental title for Jesus in Jn. is undoubtedly *Son of God*. It indicates the closeness of the relationship between the Father and his pre-existent, only Son (Jn. 3:16–18); this relationship is one of mutual love (Jn. 3:35; 5:20), and it is expressed in the way in which the Son obeys the Father (Jn. 5:19) and is entrusted by him with his functions as the judge and the bringer of life (Jn. 5:17–30). The unique filial relationship of Jesus to God which we find in the Synoptic Gospels is here most clearly expressed (Jn. 11:41; 12:27f.; 17:1). Essentially the same ideas are conveyed by the title **Logos* (or *Word*) which figures in the prologue to the Gospel. So closely is the Logos identified with God, that it is not surprising to find that Jesus is actually given the title of *God*; this is clearly the case in Thomas' confession in Jn. 20:28, where it is the appearance of the resurrected Jesus which leads to recognition of his divine status, but it is also probable that Jesus is described as 'the only Son, who is the same as God and is at the Father's side' (TEV) in Jn. 1:18 (the text, however, is uncertain).

Finally, it should be noted that there are various 'I am' sayings in Jn. which apply such descriptions as 'the Good Shepherd' and 'the true Vine' to Jesus. Sometimes we simply have the words 'I am he' (Jn. 4:26; 6:20; 8:24, 28, 58; 13:19). Since these words echo the self-affirmation of Yahweh found in Is. 43:10; 48:12, it is likely that we should see them as a veiled indication of the deity of Jesus.

The use of titles in the Johannine Epistles is similar to that in the Gospel, although of course there is a difference between the way in which the earthly Jesus is described in a Gospel and that in which the risen Lord is described in an Epistle. It is a curious but no doubt unimportant fact that 3 Jn. is the only NT book which never refers to Jesus. In 1 Jn. *Jesus* is often the subject of statements in which his significance as *Christ* or *Son of God* is expressed (1 Jn. 2:22; 4:15; 5:1, 5). While the question raised here may be simply whether Jesus was indeed the Messiah of Jewish expectation, scholars generally agree that the issue was rather whether there had been a true and lasting incarnation of God in Jesus. The opponents of John appear to have denied that there was a true and lasting union between the Messiah or Son of God and Jesus (1 Jn. 4:2; 2 Jn. 7), and John had to emphasize that *Jesus Christ* had truly come in both water and blood, *i.e.* in his baptism and his death. He therefore uses the full title 'his Son Jesus Christ' (1 Jn. 1:3; 3:23; 5:20) to indicate the object of Christian belief. Only the Son of God can be the *Saviour* of the world (1 Jn. 4:14). The term *Lord* is absent from the Epistles of John.

In Rev. *Jesus* figures prominently as a designation, in the same way as in Heb. The fuller title *Jesus Christ* is used only as a solemn designation in the introduction to the book (Rev. 1:1f., 5), but there are four references to (the) *Christ* or to *his* Christ (Rev. 20:4, 6; 11:15; 12:10), which show that the thought of the Messiah as God's agent in the establishment of his rule was very much alive for John. This idea is further seen in the way in which the divine titles of *King* and *Lord* are used of both God and Jesus (Rev. 15:3; 17:14; 19:16). But undoubtedly the most distinctive title of Jesus in Rev. is that of **Lamb* which is used 28 times here and nowhere else (the Gk. word used in Jn. 1:29, 36; Acts 8:32; 1 Pet. 1:19 is different). The Lamb combines the paradoxical features of being slain or sacrificed (Rev. 5:6) and yet being the Lord who is worthy of worship (Rev. 5:8). He displays his wrath against evil (Rev. 6:16) and leads the people of God in battle (Rev. 17:14), and yet it is his blood which acts as a sacrifice for sin (Rev. 7:14) and through which his martyred people emerge victorious (Rev. 12:11).

V. The titles of Jesus in the rest of the New Testament

Of the remaining books of the NT, Heb. is perhaps the most distinctive in its use of titles. Thus it reverts to the use of the simple *Jesus* to designate the One who suffered humiliation and death and yet has been exalted by God (Heb. 2:9; 13:12). It can also refer to him simply as the *Lord* (Heb. 2:3; 7:14) or as *Christ* (Heb. 3:6, 14; *et al.*). But although the writer is no doubt conscious that Christ means 'anointed' (Heb. 1:9), he uses it more as a name which needs to be explained by other titles. He describes Jesus as a *Pioneer* of salvation and faith (Heb. 2:10; 12:2), using a phrase which may have had a wider currency as a Christological title (Acts 3:15; 5:31). But above all he thinks of Jesus as the *High Priest* and expounds his work in terms of this category drawn from the OT sacrificial legislation. If this term is more a description than a title of Jesus, the term *Son* is the significant title which underlies it. It is only after he has established the identity of Jesus as the Son of God, exalted above the angels and Moses, that the writer goes on to demonstrate how this position qualified Jesus to be the high priest and mediator between God and man. The writer makes careful use of Pss. 2:7 (Heb. 1:5; 5:5) and 110:4 to define the status of Jesus. He stresses the enormity of rejecting the salvation achieved by so exalted a Saviour (Heb. 6:6; 10:29).

Jas. is remarkable for referring only twice to the *Lord Jesus Christ* (Jas. 1:1; 2:1), but when he speaks of the coming of the Lord (Jas. 5:7f.) he is no doubt thinking of Jesus.

In 1 Pet. the use of *Jesus* as an independent name is missing, and the writer prefers *Jesus Christ*. He uses *Lord Jesus Christ* once (1 Pet. 1:3) in a traditional phrase. But he refers frequently to *Christ*, and it is interesting that he does so particularly in the context of suffering and death (1 Pet. 1:11, 19; 2:21; 3:18; *et al.*) which we saw to be characteristic of the primitive use of the title. He also speaks of confessing Christ as *Lord* (1 Pet. 3:15; *cf.* 2:13) in a way which is again reminiscent of early usage.

2 Pet. is characterized by the use of *Lord Jesus Christ*. The title of *Saviour* is also frequent here (2 Pet. 1:1, 11; 2:20; 3:2, 18), and in 2 Pet. 1:1 Jesus is described as 'our *God* and Saviour'. The usage of Jude is generally similar; both writers use the unusual form *despotēs*, 'Lord', for Jesus (2 Pet. 2:1; Jude 4), possibly because the background thought is that of the redemption of slaves; the term was not a popular one because it suggested arbitrary despotism.

VI. Conclusion

The teaching of the NT about the person of Jesus is not confined to what is expressed by the titles whose use has been rapidly sketched above. We should also need to take into account what is said about the character and activity of Jesus both during his earthly life and in his heavenly state; it is also important to consider the kinds of credal statement and literary works which were created to express his significance. Nevertheless, the titles themselves sum up much of the NT teaching. Study of them enables us to see how the thinking of the disciples was moulded by their first contact with Jesus during his lifetime, and then decisively fixed by their experience of him as the risen Lord, and finally elaborated in the course of their evangelism and teaching in the Jewish and Hellenistic world. In differing ways the titles express the supreme worth of Jesus as the Son of God, his saving function as Messiah and Saviour, and his honourable position as the Lord. The early church drew on a rich source of material to explain who Jesus was; basically it took its material from the OT, which it saw as the divinely given prophecy of the coming of Jesus, but at the same time it did not shrink from using titles which would be meaningful in the wider world. Some titles proved less adequate than others, but collectively they all bear testimony to the fact that in Jesus God has acted decisively to judge and save the world, and they summon all to acknowledge that this Jesus is indeed one with God and worthy of the worship that is fitting for God himself.

BIBLIOGRAPHY. See the relevant articles in *DBS*; *DJG*; *NIDNTT*; *TDNT*; F. H. Borsch, *The Son of Man in Myth and History*, 1967; W. Bousset, *Kyrios Christos*, 1970; M. Casey, *From Jewish Prophet to Gentile God*, 1991; O. Cullmann, *The Christology of the New Testament*[2], 1963; J. D. G. Dunn, *Christology in the Making*[2], 1989; R. H. Fuller, *The Foundations of New Testament Christology*, 1965; F. Hahn, *The Titles of Jesus in Christology*, 1969; M. Hengel, *The Son of God*, 1976; M. D. Hooker, *Jesus and the Servant*, 1959; *idem*, *The Son of Man in Mark*, 1967; W. Kramer, *Christ Lord, Son of God*, 1966; I. H. Marshall, *The Origins of New Testament Christology*, 1977; V. Taylor, *The Names of Jesus*, 1953; *idem*, *The Person of Christ in New Testament Teaching*, 1958; H. E. Tödt, *The Son of Man in the Synoptic Tradition*, 1965; G. Vermes, *Jesus the Jew*, 1973; B. Witherington III, *The Christology of Jesus*, 1990.

I.H.M.

JETHRO. Moses' father-in-law *Reuel, called Jethro in Ex. 3:1; 4:18. He brought Zipporah and her sons to meet Moses at Mt Horeb, and held a sacrifice to Yahweh in thanksgiving for the deliverance of Israel. Here he also advised Moses to delegate the administration of justice (Ex. 18). Moses persuaded Jethro's son Hobab to join the Israelites. In Jdg. 4:11 'Hobab the Kenite' is called Moses' *ḥōṯēn*, perhaps a broad term for 'in-law'; this, with Jdg. 1:16, is the only evidence for Jethro's Kenite descent. The name may mean 'pre-eminence'.

J.P.U.L.

JEW (Heb. *yᵉhûḏî*; Aram. *yᵉhûḏai*; Gk. *joudaios*; Lat. *judaeus*). Originally a member of the state of *Judah (2 Ki. 16:6; Ne. 1:2; Je. 32:12) and so used by foreigners from the 8th century BC onwards (*e.g.* Assyr. *Yaudaia*, *ANET*, pp. 287, 301). Non-Jews used this term of the former inhabitants of the province of Judah as opposed to other nations in post-exilic times (Est. 9:15; Dn. 3:8; Zc. 8:23) or of proselytes to *Judaism (Est. 8:17). 'Jewess' occurs in 1 Ch. 4:18; Acts 16:1; 24:24 and 'Jewish' in Gal. 2:14 (Gk.); Tit. 1:14. The 'Jew's language' describes the local Semitic dialect spoken in Judah which, like 'Jew' (Je. 34:9), becomes synonymous with 'Hebrew'. AV 'Jewry' (Dn. 5:13; Lk. 23:5; Jn. 7:1) stands for Judah.

In the NT, 'Jews' is used of members of the Jewish faith or their representative leaders (especially Jn.), but in modern times, and especially in the state of Israel, this is sometimes extended to denote ethnic birth but not necessarily religion. Its precise connotation is therefore now often a matter of debate.

BIBLIOGRAPHY. *EJ*, 10, 1971, pp. 22–26.

D.J.W.

JEWELS AND PRECIOUS STONES. In biblical times as nowadays various forms of jewellery were worn and highly esteemed by both men and women (Ex. 11:2; Is. 3:18–21). They were given as presents (Gn. 24:22, 53), and were an important item of spoil in war (2 Ch. 20:25). They were a form of wealth, especially before the use of coins (2 Ch. 21:3), and were used as a standard of value (Jb. 28:16; Pr. 3:15; Rev. 21:11). Among the various types of jewellery used we find mention of bracelets for the arm (Gn. 24:22, 30, 47; Ezk. 16:11), ornaments for the ankles (Is. 3:18, 20), necklaces (Gn. 41:42; *cf.* Lk. 15:8, where the ten pieces of silver may have been coins strung together to form a necklace), crowns (Zc. 9:16; here the Lord's people are likened to shining jewels in a crown), ear-rings (Gn. 24:22), nose-rings (Is. 3:21) and rings for the fingers (Gn. 41:42; Est. 3:10; Lk. 15:22). These might be made of gold, silver or other metals (Ex. 3:22).

A considerable number of precious and semi-precious stones were known and used in jewellery. Inscribed seals have been found in cornelian, chalcedony, jasper, agate, onyx, rock crystal, haematite, jade, opal and amethyst (D. Diringer, 'Seals', in *DOTT*, pp. 218–226). The stones were valued for their rarity, beauty and durability. The modern method of faceting was not employed; instead the stones were rounded and polished, and often engraved and carved.

In general, the ancients were more familiar with semi-precious than with precious stones. Since many species of stone occur in a variety of colours and since a scientific terminology had not been developed, the identification of the various stones mentioned in the Bible is not always easy, and in some cases we can only guess at the meaning of the terms used. Etymology is not much help, since many of the roots simply mean 'sparkle', 'gleam' or the like. The following list is geared to the RSV translation.

Agate (*šᵉḇô*, Ex. 28:19; 39:12) was probably modern agate, a type of translucent quartz with layers of different colours, or the very similar onyx. In Is. 54:12; Ezk. 27:16 (*kaḏkōḏ*), a red stone, possibly carbuncle, red jasper (NEB) or ruby (JB), may be meant (*cf.* Ezk. 27:16, where Symmachus has *karchēdonion*, *i.e.* carbuncle). For Rev. 21:19, RSV, TEV, see **Chalcedony**.

The word **Alabaster** (*alabastron*, Mk. 14:3 = Mt. 26:7; Lk. 7:37), originally the neuter form of the adjective *alabastros*, was used to mean an alabaster flask with a long neck for storing perfume, the neck being broken off when the contents were used; but the word was also used for flasks of this shape of *any* material. Ancient alabaster was a banded variety of calcium carbonate produced by gradual deposition from solution in water, as in stalactites; modern alabaster is a softer stone, a variety of gypsum (calcium sulphate).

Amethyst (*'aḥlāmâ*, Ex. 28:19; 39:12) was the well-known stone of that name, a purple variety of transparent, crystalline quartz. (NEB 'jasper' identifies it as an Egyp. stone.) So also in Rev. 21:20 (*amethystos*, so called because it was supposed to prevent intoxication).

Beryl (*taršîš*, Ex. 28:20; 39:13; Ct. 5:14; Ezk. 1:16; 10:9; 28:13; Dn. 10:6) was associated with Spain (Tarshish), and was probably Spanish gold topaz, known to the ancient world as chrysolith. In Rev. 21:20 (*bēryllos*) ordinary green beryl is meant.

Carbuncle (*bāreqeṯ*, Ex. 28:17; 39:10; *bārᵉqaṯ*, Ezk. 28:13) was probably a green stone in view of the LXX translation as 'emerald' (*smaragdos*) in the Ex. references; possibly green felspar (NEB) is meant. (The modern carbuncle is a red stone.) In Is. 54:12 (*'eqdaḥ*) a red stone is meant in view of the derivation from *qāḏaḥ*, 'to kindle', possibly garnet (NEB).

For **Carnelian** (better spelt 'cornelian', the common form being due to confusion with Latin *caro*), see **Sardius**, below.

Chalcedony (*chalkēdōn*, Rev. 21:19, NEB; RSV 'agate') is usually taken to have been a green stone, since Pliny refers to a kind of emerald and jasper as Chalcedonian (from Chalcedon in Asia Minor). (The word is used in modern writers for various types of translucent quartz, including agate, onyx, cornelian and chrysoprase.)

Chrysolite (*chrysolithos*, Rev. 21:20) is the ancient term for yellow topaz (alminium fluo-silicate) or yellow quartz. (Note that ancient chrysolite is modern topaz, and vice versa.) For Ezk. 1:16; 10:9; 28:13, RSV, see **Beryl**, above. For Ex. 28:17 NEB see **Topaz**.

Chrysoprase (*chrysoprasos*, Rev. 21:20) is in modern usage an apple-green form of chalcedony, but the identification here is uncertain. The name suggests a golden-tinted variety.

Coral (*rā'môṯ*, Jb. 28:18; Ezk. 27:16) may be either black or red coral. It is, of course, not strictly a precious stone, being the skeleton of innumerable small marine polyps. *rā'môṯ* also occurs in Pr. 24:7, *MT*, but this is probably to be read as *rāmôṯ*, 'high'. The RSV translates *pᵉnînîm* as coral

References in the Old Testament (jewels in the High Priest's breastplate). Ex. 28:17–20 = 39:10–13 = Ezk. 28:13 (omitting nos. 7–9)						
MT	LXX	RSV	NEB	JB	GNB	NIV
1. *ʼōdem*	*sardion*	sardius	sardin	sard	ruby	ruby
2. *piṭeḏâ*	*topazion*	topaz	chrysolite	topaz	topaz	topaz
3. *bāreqeṯ*	*smaragdos*	carbuncle	green felspar	carbuncle	garnet	beryl
4. *nōp̄eḵ*	*anthrax*	emerald	purple garnet	emerald	emerald	turquoise
5. *sappîr*	*sappheiros*	sapphire	lapis lazuli	sapphire	sapphire	sapphire
6. *yāhalōm*	*iaspis*	diamond	jade	diamond	diamond	emerald
7. *lešem*	*ligyrion*	jacinth	turquoise	hyacinth	turquoise	jacinth
8. *šeḇô*	*achatēs*	agate	agate	ruby	agate	agate
9. *ʼaḥlāmâ*	*amethystos*	amethyst	jasper	amethyst	amethyst	amethyst
10. *taršîš*	*chrysolithos*	beryl	topaz	beryl	beryl	chrysolite
11. *šōham*	*beryllion*	onyx	carnelian	beryl	carnelian	onyx
12. *yašep̄eh*	*onychion*	jasper	green jasper	jasper	jasper	jasper

Other Old Testament references						
		RSV	NEB	JB	GNB	NIV
zekôkîṯ	Jb. 28:17	glass	crystal	glass	crystal	crystal
rāʼmôṯ	Jb. 28:18	coral	black coral	coral	coral	coral
	Pr. 24:7 *MT*					
	Ezk. 27:16					
gāḇîš	Jb. 28:18	crystal	alabaster	crystal	crystal	jasper
penînîm	Jb. 28:18	pearls	red coral	pearls	rubies	rubies
	La. 4:7	coral	branching coral	coral	–	rubies
	Pr. 3:15 *et al.*	jewels	red coral	pearls	jewels	rubies
kaḏkōḏ	Is. 54:12	agate	red jasper (*mg.* carbuncle)	rubies	rubies	rubies
	Ezk. 27:16	agate	red jasper	rubies	rubies	rubies
ʼeqdaḥ	Is. 54:12	carbuncle	garnet (*mg.* firestone)	crystal	–	sparkling jewels
qeraḥ	Ezk. 1:22	crystal	ice	crystal	crystal	ice

References in the New Testament Rev. 21:19–20 (Gk.)	
1. *iaspis*	jasper (RSV, NEB, GNB, NIV, TNT); diamond (JB)
2. *sappheiros*	sapphire (RSV, GNB, NIV, TNT); lapis lazuli (NEB, JB)
3. *chalkedōn*	agate (RSV, GNB); chalcedony (NEB, NIV, TNT); turquoise (JB)
4. *smaragdos*	emerald (RSV, NEB, GNB, NIV, TNT); crystal (JB)
5. *sardonyx*	onyx (RSV, GNB); sardonyx (NEB, NIV, TNT); agate (JB)
6. *sardion*	carnelian (RSV, GNB, NIV); carnelian (NEB); ruby (JB); sardius (TNT)
7. *chrysolithos*	chrysolite (RSV, NEB, NIV, TNT); gold quartz (JB); yellow quartz (GNB)
8. *bēryllos*	beryl (RSV, NEB, GNB, NIV, TNT); malachite (JB)
9. *topazion*	topaz (RSV, NEB, JB, GNB, NIV, TNT)
10. *chrysoprasos*	chrysoprase (RSV, NEB, NIV, TNT); emerald (JB); chalcedony (GNB)
11. *hyakinthos*	jacinth (RSV, NIV, TNT); turquoise (NEB, GNB); sapphire (JB)
12. *amethystos*	amethyst (RSV, NEB, JB, GNB, NIV, TNT)

Jewels, precious and semi-precious stones as translated in some versions of the Bible.

in La. 4:7, where some red stone is meant (see **Pearl**, below).

Crystal (*gābîš*; Jb. 28:18a) is a translucent substance (*cf.* *'elgābîš*, 'hail') but G. R. Driver thinks that gypsum is meant (*cf.* NEB 'alabaster'). The word *zᵉkôkîṯ* ('crystal', Jb. 28:17, AV) was applied in the ancient world not simply to rock crystal (pure transparent crystalline quartz) but to any hard, transparent, colourless substance. Glass may be meant (RSV). *qeraḥ* (Ezk. 1:22) is elsewhere translated 'frost' or 'ice'. In Rev. 4:6; 21:11; 22:1 (*krystallon*, *krystallizō*), either ice or rock crystal may be the rendering.

Diamond (*yāhᵃlôm*, Ex. 28:18; 39:11; Ezk. 28:13) is of uncertain identification. The modern diamond was probably unknown in OT times, the first certain reference to it apparently being in Manilius (1st century AD). Probably a white, opaque stone is meant (possibly moonstone); G. R. Driver suggests jadeite or nephrite (*cf.* NEB). In Je. 17:1 (*šāmîr*) adamant or emery, a form of corundum (the hardest substance known except for diamond), is meant (*cf.* Ezk. 3:9; Zc. 7:12).

Emerald (*nōpeḵ*, Ex. 28:18; 39:11; also Ezk. 27:16, where various scholars consider the text uncertain) may have been a green stone like the modern emerald, but in view of the LXX translation (*anthrax*, 'a burning coal'), some authorities prefer the purple almandine garnet (NEB). In Rev. 4:3 (*smaragdinos*) and 21:19 (*smaragdos*), the green emerald is meant.

For **Glass**, see **Crystal**.

For **Hyacinth**, see **Jacinth**.

Jacinth (*lešem*, Ex. 28:19; 39:12; AV 'ligure') is usually thought to have been a yellow stone; G. R. Driver prefers a blue stone such as turquoise (NEB). In the NT jacinth (*hyakinthos*, Rev. 21:20) is a blue stone, aquamarine (the blue variety of beryl), sapphire or turquoise. (Modern jacinth is quite different.) The name was used to indicate a blue colour (in classical Greek as a noun it means the hyacinth or bluebell), as in Rev. 9:17 (*hyakinthinos*), where RSVmg. has 'hyacinth' and RSV has 'sapphire'.

Jasper (*yāšᵉpeh*, Ex. 28:20; 39:13; Ezk. 28:13) is a translucent, green stone. In Rev. 4:3; 21:11, 18–19 (*iaspis*), green quartz may be meant. In 21:11 the reference to crystal suggests that a transparent stone may be intended.

For **Lapis lazuli**, see **Sapphire**.

Onyx (*šōham*, Gn. 2:12; Ex. 25:7; 28:8, 20; 35:9, 27; 39:6, 13; 1 Ch. 29:2; Jb. 28:16; Ezk. 28:13) has been identified as a green stone (*cf.* LXX 'beryl' in some of these verses) or as onyx (translucent agate with layers of black and white). The word means finger-nail, the stone being so called because of its appearance. S. R. Driver prefers red carnelian. For Rev. 21:20, see **Sardonyx**, below.

Pearl is found in the OT in Jb. 28:18a (*gābîš*) AV, where RSV has 'crystal'. In the RSV 'pearl' is found as the translation of *pᵉnînîm* in Jb. 28:18b (AV, 'rubies'). The same Heb. word occurs in Pr. 3:15; 8:11; 20:15; 31:10 and La. 4:7 (it is also accepted by some scholars as an emendation in Ps. 45:14). In all these references AV has 'rubies'; RSV has 'jewels' or 'costly stones', except in La. 4:7, where it has 'coral'. *BDB* prefer 'corals' (*cf.* NEB), but E. Burrows (*JTS* 42, 1941, pp. 53–64) argues that the word properly means 'pearls' but also has the generic sense of 'jewels'. *Unger's Bible Dictionary* (1957, p. 742) suggests that the pink pearls found in the Red Sea are meant, and this would solve the difficulty of La. 4:7, where a reddish stone is indicated.

There is no doubt that in the NT *margaritēs* means 'pearl'. Pearls are noted as articles of feminine ornament (1 Tim. 2:9, where they are frowned upon; Rev. 17:4) and of merchandise (Mt. 13:45f.; Rev. 18:12, 16). The gates of the New Jerusalem are each made of a single large pearl or possibly of mother-of-pearl (Rev. 21:21). The kingdom of heaven is like a fine pearl which a man will seek to obtain at the cost of all that he has (Mt. 13:45f. In view of the context it is unlikely that this parable refers primarily to Christ giving his life for men, although in fact Christ himself is the supreme example of giving up all for the sake of the kingdom). On the other hand, it is as foolish to put the Christian message before men who refuse to appreciate it as to cast pearls before swine (Mt. 7:6; *cf.* *Didache* 9. 5, where Christ's saying is used to justify exclusion of the unbaptized from the Lord's Supper).

Ruby is found in AV as a translation of *pᵉnînîm* in six places (see **Pearl**, above). RV also has 'ruby' in Is. 54:12 and Ezk. 27:16 for *kaḏkōḏ* (see **Agate**, above).

Sapphire (*sappîr*, Ex. 24:10; 28:18; 39:11; Jb. 28:6, 16; Ct. 5:14; Is. 54:11; La. 4:7; Ezk. 1:26; 10:1; 28:13) was the ancient name for lapis lazuli (*cf.* RSVmg.), a deep blue stone with golden flecks of iron pyrites (*cf.* 'dust of gold', Jb. 28:6). Lapis lazuli is also meant in Rev. 21:19 (*sappheiros*). The modern sapphire (blue corundum) was scarcely known to the ancients. For Rev. 9:17, RSV, see **Jacinth**, above.

Sardius (*'ōḏem*, Ex. 28:17; 29:10; Ezk. 28:13) was certainly a red stone (from *'āḏam*, 'to be red'), probably modern sard (a form of cornelian; *cf.* Ezk. 28:13, RSV), *i.e.* a deep brown or red form of quartz. It is also mentioned in Rev. 21:20 (*sardios*) and is the sardine stone of Rev. 4:3 (*sardinos*): RSV and NEB have carnelian/cornelian in both places.

Sardonyx (*sardonyx*, Rev. 21:20, RV, NEB; RSV 'onyx') is in modern usage a form of agate with layers of brown and white; but, according to *LSJ*, in ancient usage a stone was called 'onyx' when the dark ground was simply streaked or spotted with white, and 'sardonyx' when the different colours were arranged in layers.

Topaz (*piṭᵉḏâ*, Ex. 28:17; 39:10; Jb. 28:19; Ezk. 28:13) was a yellow stone, probably yellow rock crystal or chrysolite (a pale yellow variety of peridot); *cf.* Ezk. 1:16; 10:9; 28:13, NEB (*taršîš*). So also in Rev. 22:20 (*topazion*).

The fullest list of stones in the OT is given in the description of the high priest's breastpiece (Ex. 28:17–20, repeated in 39:10–13). This contained four rows of three stones, each stone engraved with the name of one of the twelve tribes of Israel. Later authors commenting on the OT regarded these twelve stones as symbolic of the months of the year or the signs of the zodiac (Philo, *Vit. Mos.* 2. 124ff.; Jos., *Ant.* 3. 186), but it is impossible to work out any correlations. Some scholars have rearranged the order of the stones in the *MT* on the basis of the LXX translation, but this is a dubious procedure.

An abbreviated version of the same list of stones is found in Ezk. 28:13 as a description of the covering of the king of Tyre when, according to the poetic imagery used here, he was in Eden, the garden of God. Nine of the stones are mentioned, the jacinth, agate and amethyst being omitted. In the LXX version of this verse, however, the full list of twelve stones is substituted.

A list of twelve stones is given in Rev. 21:19f. as decorations of the foundations of the New Jerusalem. The basis of this description is clearly Is. 54:11f. (*cf.* also Tobit 13:16–18). The number twelve is clearly significant for John, and various attempts have been made to ascertain whether the twelve stones have any special meaning. It is likely that the form of the vision has been influenced by the description of the twelve stones of the high priest's breastpiece; scholars have attempted to relate the two lists of stones more closely to each other, but in view of the difficulties of translation from Heb. to Gk. and the fact that John was probably not quoting verbatim from Ex., it is very doubtful whether we can say more than that he was generally influenced by the description in Ex. R. H. Charles (*ICC*, *ad loc.*) has taken up the symbolism of the signs of the zodiac mentioned above and holds that the stones represent these signs arranged in precisely the opposite order to that in which the sun travels through the zodiac, thus portraying the truth that the New Jerusalem and Christianity bear no relation to those religions in which men worship the sun; this theory is implausible (T. F. Glasson, *JTS* n.s. 26, 1975, pp. 95–100). It is further possible that the stones, like the twelve gates of the city, are symbolical of the tribes of Israel (A. M. Farrer, *A Rebirth of Images*, 1949, pp. 216ff.), but again it is impossible to work out convincing identifications of individual stones with individual tribes. In the light of 21:14 there is perhaps more to be said for the suggestion that the stones represent the twelve apostles, in which case individual identifications are clearly not to be attempted. What is beyond dispute in the symbolism is that in the New Jerusalem we see the fulfilment of the OT prophecy of the perfect city of God in which the saints of the old and new covenants find a place. (*MINING AND METALS, *ORNAMENTS.)

BIBLIOGRAPHY. G. R. Driver, *HDB*², pp. 497–500; J. S. Harris, *ALUOS* 4, 1962–3, pp. 49–83; 5, 1963–5, pp. 40–62; U. Jart, *ST* 24, 1970, pp. 150–181; *RAC*, 4, pp. 505–535; C. Aldred, *Jewels of the Pharaohs*, 1971; N. Hillyer, *NIDNTT* 3, pp. 395–398; W. W. Reader, *JBL* 100, 1981, pp. 433–457; E. E. Platt, *ABD* 3, pp. 823–834. I.H.M.

JEZANIAH (Heb. *yᵉzanyāhû*). One of the Judaean military commanders who joined Gedaliah at Mizpah (Je. 40:8). He was among those who sought counsel from Jeremiah concerning going down to Egypt (Je. 42:1—LXX here has 'Azariah', *cf.* 43:2). In 2 Ki. 25:23 his name appears as *'Jaazaniah'. J.C.J.W.

JEZEBEL. 1. The daughter of Ethbaal, priest-king of Tyre and Sidon. She was married to Ahab, to ratify an alliance between Tyre and Israel, by which Omri, Ahab's father, sought to offset the hostility of Damascus towards Israel (*c.* 880 BC). Provision was made for her to continue to worship her native god Baal in Samaria, her new home (1 Ki. 16:31–33).

She had a strong, domineering character, and was self-willed and forceful. A fanatical devotee of Melqart, the Tyrian Baal, her staff numbered 450 of his prophets, and 400 prophets of the goddess Asherah, by the time Ahab was king (1 Ki. 18:19). She clamoured for her god to have at least equal rights with Yahweh, God of Israel. This brought her into conflict with the prophet Elijah. A battle between Yahweh and Baal was fought on Mt Carmel, when Yahweh triumphed gloriously (1 Ki. 18:17–40). Even so, this and the massacre of her prophets, instead of diminishing her zeal, augmented it.

Her conception of an absolute monarchy was at variance with the Heb. covenant-relationship between Yahweh, the king and the people. She took the lead in the incident of Naboth's vineyard with high-handed, unscrupulous action, affecting the whole community as well as undermining the throne of Ahab. It resulted in the prophetic revolution and the extermination of the house of Ahab. She had written letters and used her husband's seal (1 Ki. 21:8), but that she had a seal of her own is suggested and illustrated by N. Avigad, *IEJ* 14, 1964, pp. 274–276.

After Ahab's death, Jezebel continued as a power in Israel for 10 years, in her role as queen-mother, throughout the reign of Ahaziah, then during Jehoram's lifetime. When Jehoram was killed by Jehu she attired herself regally (2 Ki. 9:30), and awaited him. She mocked Jehu, and went to her fate with courage and dignity (842 BC).

It is remarkable that Yahweh was honoured in the naming of her three children, Ahaziah, Jehoram and Athaliah (if indeed she was Athaliah's mother), but they may have been born before her ascendancy over Ahab became so absolute.

2. In the letter to the church at Thyatira (Rev. 2:20), 'that Jezebel of a woman' is the designation given to a seductive prophetess who encouraged immorality and idolatry under the cloak of religion (*NICOLAS). This could refer to an individual, or to a group within the church. It indicates that the name had become a byword for apostasy. M.B.

JEZREEL (Heb. *Yizra'el*, 'God sows'). **1.** The town in Judah (Jos. 15:56), home of Ahinoam, one of David's wives (1 Sa. 25:43). **2.** A city of Issachar in the Jezreel plain (*ESDRAELON), about 90 km N of Jerusalem, identified with Zer'in (Jos. 19:18). The city and surroundings are associated with several notable events. The Israelites assembled by its spring before engaging the Philistines at Gilboa (1 Sa. 29:1; 31). It was part of Ishbosheth's short-lived kingdom (2 Sa. 2:8ff.) and an administrative district of Solomon (1 Ki. 4:12). Recent excavations have revealed a fortified site from the time of Ahab, 300 × 150 m, with fortifications, including a moat, 36 m wide. It is thought to have been Ahab's chariot centre, and the scene of the tragedy of Naboth and his vineyard (1 Ki. 21). Here Joram was slain by Jehu, and his body significantly cast into the vineyard so appropriated by Ahab (2 Ki. 8:29; 9:14–29). At Jehu's instigation Jezebel (2 Ki. 9:30–37) and the remnant of Ahab's household (2 Ki. 10:1–11) were also slain. Parts of Israelite buildings have been found (*Levant* 26, 1994, pp. 1–50). **3.** The name symbolically given to Hosea's eldest son (Ho. 1:4–5) and to Israel (Ho. 2:22). **4.** A Judahite (1 Ch. 4:3). J.W.
J.D.D.

JOAB (Heb. *yô'āḇ*, 'Yahweh is father'). **1.** Son of Zeruiah, half-sister of David (2 Sa. 2:18). His father's name is not recorded here, but Josephus (*Ant.* 7. 11) gives it as Suri, whose sepulchre was in Bethlehem (2 Sa. 2:32).

Joab is first heard of when, with his brothers Asahel and Abishai, he led David's army to victory at Helkath-hazzurim against Ishbosheth's rebel forces under Abner (2 Sa. 2:12–17). In fleeing, *Abner reluctantly killed *Asahel in self-defence and was himself later treacherously slain by Joab, ostensibly in blood-revenge (2 Sa. 2:23; 3:27, 30), but probably also because Abner's new-found loyalty to David confronted Joab with a potential rival for the king's favour.

David was angry with his nephew for this murder, greatly mourned Abner as 'a prince and a great man', and prophesied that God would punish the killer (2 Sa. 3:31–39). Nevertheless, after taking the Jebusite stronghold, Joab was made commander-in-chief of all Israel (2 Sa. 5:8; 1 Ch. 11:6, 8), of which David was by this time king.

Joab proved himself a skilful general who greatly helped the establishment of the monarchy, but his character was a strange mixture. Apart from his personal deeds of violence and his opportunism, his cruelty can be seen in the way he swiftly comprehended and carried out David's plan to kill Uriah (2 Sa. 11:6–26). Yet he could be magnanimous also, as when he gave David the credit after the capture of Rabboth-ammon (2 Sa. 12:26–31). Perhaps most notably and surprisingly, he tried to dissuade David from numbering the people (2 Sa. 24:2–4).

Joab is found in the role of peacemaker, reconciling David and Absalom on one occasion (2 Sa. 14:23, 31–33), but later when Absalom's guilt was clearly seen he had a hand in his death (2 Sa. 18:14–33), despite David's injunction that the young man's life should be spared. After this David superseded Joab by Amasa as commander (2 Sa. 19:13), but the resourceful Joab subdued Sheba's revolt and seized the first opportunity to slay the new commander, who had proved inefficient (2 Sa. 20:3–23). Thereafter for a time Joab seems to have been restored to favour (2 Sa. 24:2).

In David's last days Joab's loyalty to the king faltered, and with Abiathar and others he supported Adonijah as claimant to the throne (1 Ki. 1:5–53), in defiance of David, who had resolved that Solomon should succeed him (1 Ki. 2:28). For once Joab supported the wrong side, and it eventually cost him his life (1 Ki. 2:34), when with the connivance of Solomon he was slain by Benaiah before the altar at Gibeon, where he had fled for sanctuary.

2. Son of Seraiah (1 Ch. 4:14; *cf.* Ne. 11:35), a Judahite. **3.** A family which returned with Zerubbabel (Ezr. 2:6; Ne. 7:11). Probably the 'Joab' of Ezr. 8:9 is the same person. J.D.D.

JOANNA. One of several women, healed by Jesus, who assisted in maintaining the Lord's itinerant company. Her husband, Chuza, was a responsible official of Herod Antipas: whether in the household ('a steward of Herod's', NEB) or in government ('the chancellor', Moffatt) is uncertain (Lk. 8:1–3). She sought also to share in the last offices to the Lord's body, and became instead one of those who announced the resurrection to the Twelve (Lk. 24:1–10). Luke's notes may indicate personal acquaintance with, and possibly indebtedness for information to, these women. A.F.W.

JOASH, JEHOASH (Heb. *yô'āš*, *yᵉhô'āš*, 'Yahweh has given'). **1.** Father of *Gideon; member of the Abiezrite branch of the tribe of Manasseh living at Ophrah (Jdg. 6:11–32). A Baal worshipper who had his own altar and *Asherah, which Gideon replaced by an altar to Yahweh (vv. 25–27). He told those who would defend him that Baal could take care of himself (v. 31). It was possibly he who renamed Gideon Jerubbaal (v. 32).

2. An ambidextrous Benjaminite warrior who, although a relative of Saul, aided David in his revolt (1 Ch. 12:1–3).

3. A 'son' of King *Ahab to whom the prophet Micaiah was to be taken in order to be imprisoned after angering Ahab by prophesying unfavourably (1 Ki. 22:26; 2 Ch. 18:25f.). Possibly 'son of the king' was an official's title rather than a kinship form.

4. Son of *Ahaziah and 8th king of Judah (*c.* 837–800 BC). When Athaliah annihilated the royal line at the death of her son Ahaziah, his aunt Jehosheba hid him in the Temple for 6 years under the protection of her husband *Jehoiada, the high priest (2 Ki. 11:1–6; 2 Ch. 22:10–12). At 7 years of age he was proclaimed king by Jehoiada and Athaliah was executed (2 Ki. 11:7–20; 2 Ch. 23:1–15).

Joash's reign lasted 40 years (2 Ki. 12:1), although the 6 years of Athaliah's reign might be included in this number. He rebuilt the *Temple with the help of Jehoiada (2 Ki. 12:5–16; 2 Ch. 24:4–14) but allowed the re-emergence of pagan practices upon Jehoiada's death (2 Ch. 24:17–18). When reprimanded for this by Zechariah, son of Jehoiada, he killed him (2 Ch. 24:20–22). In order to forestall a Syrian invasion under *Hazael, Joash bribed him with the Temple's treasure (2 Ki. 12:18–19). Joash was killed in a plot by his officers to replace him (2 Ki. 12:21–22; 2 Ch. 24:25–26).

5. Son of *Jehoahaz; 12th king of Israel who reigned 16 years (*c.* 801–786 BC; 2 Ki. 13:10). Israel was under external pressure from three sources during his reign. A stele of Adad-nirari III from Rimah records him receiving tribute from 'Iu'usu the Samaritan' in 796 BC (S. Page, *Iraq* 30, 1968, pp. 139ff.; *cf.* A. Malamat, *BASOR* 204, 1971, 37ff., concerning the reading of the name). The Aramaeans were oppressing them, but he was able to regain territory from them which had previously been lost (2 Ki. 13:22–25). Joash was helped in this by the ageing Elishah (vv. 14–19). He was also challenged by *Amaziah, king of Judah, whom he defeated. He sacked Jerusalem, taking hostages to ensure good conduct (2 Ki. 14:8–14; 2 Ch. 25:17–24).

BIBLIOGRAPHY. W. H. Shea, *JCS* 30, 1978, pp. 101–113. D.W.B.

JOB (Heb. *'iyyôḇ*). Apart from the book bearing his name and the passing references to him in Ezk. 14:14, 20; Jas. 5:11 we have no reliable information about Job. It is impossible to show that the Jewish, Christian and Muslim legends about Job (the latter summarized in W. B. Stevenson, *The Poem of Job*, 1947, ch. 6) have any firm roots in a pre-biblical form of the story. Apart from the tradition of the location of Job's home (see below), which may be no more than intelligent deduction from the Bible, we have the impression of popular or pious fancy.

If we identify the Daniel (*dānī'ēl*) of Ezk. 14:14 not with the Daniel (*dāniyyē'l*) of the Exile but with the person mentioned in Ugaritic inscriptions, we can with some confidence give all three names in Ezk. 14:14 a very early date. If we do not accept this clue we have no indication of his date. The location of the land of Uz, where he lived, is uncertain. The modern tendency is to regard it as on the borders of Edom, certain indications in the book being regarded as Edomite; but the traditions placing it in the Hauran (Bashan) are far more probable. Job was a man of great wealth and high social position, but the book is so concerned with stressing his position among the Wise that it avoids precise details; we can, however, unhesitatingly reject the legends that make him a king.

As a result of divine permission Satan robbed him of his wealth, his ten children and finally his health. There is no agreement on what disease he was smitten with, the main suggestions being elephantiasis, erythema and smallpox. This wide disagreeement is due to the symptoms being given in highly poetic language. His relations and fellow-townsmen interpreted his misfortunes as a divine punishment for gross sin and threw him out of the town, the rabble taking a particular pleasure in this. His wife accepted the common opinion and urged him to expedite the inevitable end by cursing God.

Job was visited by three friends, Eliphaz, Bildad and Zophar, also members of the Wise, and rich and affluent, as he had been. When they saw his plight they shared popular opinion and could only sit in silence with Job on the dunghill outside the city gate for the 7 days of mourning for a man as good as dead. Job's outburst of agony led to a long, vehement discussion, ending with a wordy intrusion by a younger man, Elihu. All this only revealed the bankruptcy of traditional wisdom and theology when faced with an exceptional case like Job's. Though his friends' lack of comprehension drove Job almost to distraction, it also turned him to God and prepared him for the revelation of divine sovereignty, which brought him peace. The mob was confounded by his healing, the doubling of his wealth, and the gift of ten children.

H.L.E.

JOB, BOOK OF.

I. Outline of contents

Ch. 1 and 2 (in prose) introduce us to the encounter in heaven between God and Satan and its effects on earth. Ch. 3 is Job's great 'Why?'; Eliphaz gives his views in chs. 4–5 and Job replies in chs. 6–7. Bildad continues in ch. 8, Job replying in chs. 9–10. The first round of the discussion is completed by Zophar's contribution in ch. 11 and Job's reply in chs. 12–14. In the second round we hear Eliphaz (15), Bildad (18) and Zophar (20), with Job's replies in chs. 16–17, 19, 21. As the text stands (see **III**, below), the third round is incomplete, only Eliphaz (22) and Bildad (25) speaking, with Job's replies in chs. 23–24, 26–27. After an interlude in praise of wisdom (28), Job sums up the debate (29–31). Elihu's intervention follows in chs. 32–37, and then God replies to Job in chs. 38–42:6. The book ends with a prose epilogue telling of Job's restored prosperity (42:7–17).

II. Authorship and date

The book is anonymous. The 'official' Talmudic tradition, followed by many earlier Christian writers, is that the book was written by Moses (*Baba Bathra* 14b, *seq.*), but the continuation of the passage and other statements show that this is merely a pious pronouncement, based presumably on a feeling of fitness, and not to be taken seriously. The simple fact is that we have no purely objective evidence to guide us either in the question of authorship or of date. The evidence for a very early date lies mostly in the non-mention of any of the details of Israelite history, but this is sufficiently explained by the author's wish to discuss the central problem outside the framework of the covenant. Other evidence, such as the mention of the Chaldeans as nomadic raiders (1:17) and of the archaic *qᵉśîṭâ* (42:11), point merely to the antiquity of the story and not to that of its present written form. Moderns have varied in their dating from the time of Solomon to about 250 BC, dates between 600 and 400 BC being most popular, though there is a growing tendency to favour later dates. A Solomonic date, accepted by Franz Delitzsch and E. J. Young, is the earliest we can reasonably adopt. The arguments from subject, language and theology probably favour a somewhat later date, but since the book is *sui generis* in Heb. literature, and the language is so distinctive (some even regard it as a translation from Aramaic, or consider the author lived outside Israel), while the theology is timeless, any dogmatism derives from subjectivism or preconceptions.

III. Text

The fact that we are dealing with some of the most difficult poetry in the OT, and that in the vocabulary we have some 110 words (W. B. Stevenson, *The Poem of Job*, p. 71) not found elsewhere, has made the scribe's task very difficult. Unfortunately the versions are no great help in checking the Heb. text. The LXX must be used with great caution. In its earlier form about 17–25% of the Heb. is missing, probably because the translators were daunted by their task; the rendering is often free and periphrastic, and not seldom incorrect.

The main textual problem concerns chs. 26–27. As they stand they are Job's answer to Bildad's third speech. No objection can be raised to Zophar's failure to speak a third time; it is in keeping with his character, and would be the most obvious proof of Job's verbal triumph over his friends. Indubitably we hear Job speaking in 27:2–6, but in its context it is virtually impossible to ascribe 27:7–23 to him. It is probably part of Zophar's third speech or possibly of Bildad's. If that is so, no entirely satisfactory reconstruction of the text has been suggested and it may be that part of the original MS has been lost, which could easily happen with a brittle papyrus roll.

IV. Integrity

Most scholars separate the prose prologue and epilogue from the poetry of 3:1–42:6. Where this is interpreted as meaning that they are older than the poem, and that the author transformed the heart of the old story into magnificent verse, the theory is unobjectionable and quite possibly correct. There are no objective proofs for the suggestion that the prose was added later to the verse by another hand, whether it is earlier or later in composition. In the hands of W. B. Stevenson (*op. cit.*) this theory has been used to impose a non-natural interpretation on the book.

Very many scholars regard certain portions as later insertions. In descending order of importance the chief are: Elihu's speeches (32–37), the praise of divine wisdom (28) and certain parts of God's answer (39:13–18; 40:15–24; 41:1–34). In every case the linguistic arguments are very tenuous. The argument from their contents is liable to take the passages in isolation. A very reasonable defence of them in their actual setting can be made.

V. As Wisdom literature

R. H. Pfeiffer, *IOT*, 1948, pp. 683f., says very well: 'If our poet ranks with the greatest writers of mankind, as can hardly be doubted, his creative genius did not of necessity rely on earlier models for the general structure of his work. . . . We may regard it as one of the most original works in the poetry of mankind. So original in fact that it does not fit into any of the standard categories devised by literary criticism . . . it is not exclusively lyric . . . nor epic . . . . nor dramatic . . . nor didactic nor reflective . . . . unless the poem is cut down to fit a particular category.' The convention that calls Job part of Heb. Wisdom literature and aligns it with Proverbs and Ecclesiastes and compares it with certain Egyp. and Bab. 'Wisdom' writings is justified only if we are careful to keep Pfeiffer's warning in mind. For all that, it is clear that Job and his friends are depicted as, and speak primarily as, members of the Wise, and they are so addressed by Elihu (34:2).

The Wise in Israel sought to understand God and his ways by studying the great uniformities of human experience by reason illuminated by 'the fear of the Lord'. Proverbs is a typical example of their understanding of life. Job is a flaming protest, less against the basic concept of Proverbs that a God-fearing life brings prosperity, godlessness suffering and destruction, than against the idea that thereby the ways of God are fully grasped. Job is not a type; he is the exception that makes folly of the assumption that through normal experience the depths of God's wisdom and working can be fully grasped.

VI. The problem of Job

The poem is so rich in its thought, so wide in its sweep, that much in human experience and its mysteries has been found mirrored there. Mostly, however, it has been regarded as concerned with the problem of human suffering. Though he has overstated his case, W. B. Stevenson (*op. cit.*, pp. 34ff.) makes it clear that in the poem there is far less allusion to Job's physical sufferings than has often been assumed. Job is concerned less with his physical pain than with his treatment by his relations, his fellow-townsmen, the mob and finally his friends. But these are merely evidence that God has forsaken him. In other words, Job's problem is not that of pain, nor even suffering in a wider sense, but the theological one, why God had not acted as all theory and his earlier experiences demanded he should. Being a child of his age, he had naturally built up his life on the theory that God's justice implied the equation of goodness and prosperity.

Taken out of their context, the words of his friends and Elihu are more acceptable than many of the rasher utterances of Job. They are rejected by God (42:7), not because they are untrue, but because they are too narrow. This is made especially clear by the discussion on the fate of the wicked. With all Job's exaggeration we recognize at once that his friends are in fact producing an *a priori* picture of what the fate of the wicked should be. They create their picture of God only by a careful selection of evidence. Job's agony is caused by the breakdown of his theological world-picture.

This explains the apparently unsatisfactory climax in which God does not answer Job's questions or charges, but though he proclaims the greatness of his all-might, not of his ethical rule, Job is satisfied. He realizes that his concept of God collapsed because it was too small; his problems evaporate when he realizes the greatness of God. The book does not set out to answer the problem of suffering but to proclaim a God so great that no answer is needed, for it would transcend the finite mind if given; the same applies to the problems incidentally raised.

BIBLIOGRAPHY. W. B. Stevenson, *The Poem of Job*, 1947; H. L. Ellison, *From Tragedy to Triumph*, 1958; E. Dhorme, *The Book of Job*, 1967; H. H. Rowley, *Job, NCB*, 1970; F. I. Andersen, *Job, TOTC*, 1976; R. E. Murphy, *The Forms of the Old Testament Literature*, 13, 1981; D. Kidner, *Wisdom to Live By*, 1985; D. J. A. Clines, *Job 1–20*, 1989.

H.L.E.

JOCHEBED (Heb. *yôḵeḇeḏ*, probably 'Yahweh is glory', though M. Noth [*Die israelitschen Personennamen*, 1928, p. 111] thinks it may be of foreign origin.) The mother of Moses, Aaron and Miriam (Ex. 6:20; Nu. 26:59). She was a daughter of Levi, and married her nephew Amram. However, according to the LXX of Ex. 6:20 they were cousins, though S. R. Driver (*CBSC*, 1918) thinks that *MT* preserves a genuine ancient tradition. J.G.G.N.

JOEL, BOOK OF.

I. Outline of contents

Joel discusses four main topics: (*a*) the appalling devastations of successive plagues of locusts, literal enough, yet symbolizing deeper meanings; (*b*) the renewed fruitfulness of the land on the repentance of Israel; (*c*) the gifts of the Spirit; (*d*) final judgment on the nations which have wronged Israel, and the blessedness-to-be of the land of Judah. In all these, primary and eschatological references intertwine.

a. The locust plague, 1:1–12

For locusts in the OT, *cf.* also Ex. 10:12–15 *et passim*, with Pss. 78:46; 105:34; also Pr. 30:27; Na. 3:15, 17, *etc.* (*ANIMALS.)

(i) Joel claims in customary prophetic manner that he has received the word of the Lord, giving his own name and that of his father, both otherwise unknown (1:1).

(ii) The burden of his message is prodigious—a locust plague in successive swarms, of frightening dimensions (1:2–4; *cf.* Ex. 10:14). Full etymological, entomological and figurative discussion of v. 4 will be found in commentaries.

(iii) The effects of the plague are vividly described (1:5–12). The first to be mentioned, perhaps in derision, is the loss to the drunkard of his solace. The teeth of the locust host are fearsome (*cf.* Pr. 30:14, *etc.*)—the very fig-bark is devoured, the white, sappy interior uncovered to the world. Temple priests should mourn with the bitterness of an aged virgin whose betrothed died in her youth before marriage, for the very materials of sacrifice are cut off (*cf.* Dn. 8:11; 11:31; 12:11; contrast Is. 1:11–15; Mi. 6:6; *etc.*). The devastation in cornfield, vineyard and orchard is vividly described.

b. The fruits of repentance, 1:13–2:27

(i) The priests in sackcloth are to lament, with fasting and prayer, the day of God's wrath, the 'conquest from the Conqueror', to reflect palely the striking Heb. assonance (1:13–15; see Ne. 9:1; Est. 4:3, 16; Dn. 9:3, *etc.*, contrasted with Is. 58:4ff.; Je. 14:12; Zc. 7:5; *etc.*). The OT views on sacrifice and fasting are not contradictory; much depended on circumstance and particular usage. Joel need not stand condemned because he is more ritualistic than Amos or Isaiah.

(ii) It seems reasonable to regard the next section (1:16–20) as a prayer, despite the vivid initial delineation of locust ravage. V. 18 should read 'What shall we put in them?'—*i.e.* the flimsy barns not rebuilt through lack of need. The fire and flame of v. 19 may be heat and drought, or even the vivid red colouring in the locust bodies.

(iii) The prophet now reverts from the devastation of the locusts to their initial onslaught, likening it to the Day of the Lord (2:1–11). V. 2b is typical oriental idiom (*cf.* Ex. 10:14). Vividly accurate is the likening of the swarm to an advancing fire. The fruitful earth before them becomes a black desolation as they pass over it (v. 3). First-hand experience is reflected also in the likening of the separate locusts to horsemen, and the parallel drawn between the noise of their advance and the sound of a rapidly spreading bush fire (vv. 4–5). People are horror-stricken before the unswerving, unjostling, accurate advance of myriads of myriads of these insects, invincible through sheer numbers (vv. 6–9). The real locusts could be symbols of the Gentiles in the valley of decision, before their judgment.

(iv) In the hour of horror it is not too late to repent, with mortification of the flesh (2:12–14). Official rending of the garments may be hypocritical; real repentance is in the heart. This may even make God 'repent' of his recently appropriate judgment, and provide sacrificial materials again. This is oriental symbolism, implying no 'sinful' deity.

(v) A fresh call to special temple worship is given (2:15–17). This embraces priests and people, with specific mention of suckling babes, tottering greybeards and newly-weds, who normally enjoyed far-reaching exemptions from public duties. J. A. Bewer (*ICC*, 1911) ingeniously points the imperatives as perfects, without consonantal change, making v. 15, not v. 18, the turning-point of the book, and the beginning of continuous narrative.

(vi) The devastation of the locust will be surpassed by the plenty that the Lord will grant on repentance (2:18–25). V. 20 means that the physical bodies of the locusts in Judaea will be wind-driven into the Dead Sea and the Mediterranean Sea, and this will be followed by a stench of decay (18–25).

c. The gifts of the Spirit, 2:28–32

The outpouring of the Spirit described in this passage is the apex of prophetic utterance. Vv. 28–29, and 32 were clearly fulfilled at Pentecost; aspects of vv. 30 and 31 were fulfilled in the passion of our Lord. Ecstatic prophesying might include the gift of tongues. The pillars of smoke might be sand columns raised by desert whirlwinds, or the conflagration of doomed cities. A solar eclipse can make a blood-red moon. What more saving name could be foreshadowed in v. 32 than that of Jesus? Everything here has a meaning—yet there is a deeper meaning belonging to the days when the last sands of human time will sink for evermore.

d. God's enemies judged, 3:1–21

The surface meaning of this section is the prediction of divine vengeance on the nations which have scattered and persecuted the Jews. The references of vv. 3–8 are clearly historical. The locusts might foreshadow these armies of Gentiles in their brief hour of victory. Vv. 9–11 are biting in their sarcasm as the prophet urges the heathen to make war on God. God alone will judge the assembled nations in the valley of decision (vv. 12, 14; *JEHOSHAPHAT, VALLEY OF). The full horror of vv. 15ff., 19a, and the full benediction of v. 18, are both alike as yet unrealized. Earthly prophecy and eschatology are wedded in a chapter of rich prefiguring. The Christian church is the heir of the OT, and the sure word of prophecy, be it about Egypt or anything else, will come to pass in God's good time.

II. Authorship and date

This is superb extrovert literature, betraying a Judaean flavour, but intrinsically concerned with bigger issues than contemporary politics. This makes dating exceptionally difficult. Most scholars maintain (*cf.* W. Nowack, 1922; K. Marti, 1904), some deny (*cf.* Bewer, *ICC*) that Joel is a literary unity. Older conservatives dated the book in the 8th century BC, the time of Amos and Hosea. Oesterley and Robinson adopt the extreme late dating of 200 BC, others assign between these limits. R. K. Harrison (*IOT*, 1970, pp. 874–882) discusses the issues thoroughly, but, stressing the book's timelessness, will not commit his dating beyond 'in advance of 400 BC'. Were the early dating to be taken as correct, certain familiar prophetic battle-cries would then find their first known utterance in Joel. Ploughshares might have been considered the fathers of swords before the hope of the reverse transformation was born (Joel 3:10; Is. 2:4).

III. Special characteristics

Joel was the vehicle of a divine revelation which has a significance perhaps beyond his full understanding. In his book the impinging of the eternal on the temporal, which is the hallmark of genuine inspiration, is undeniably in evidence. This is especially true in his arresting description of locust-plague havoc, symbolic of God's wrath and punitive visitation of sin. Vividly portrayed also is God's gracious restoration of his people following upon repentance. There are factual prophecies linked with our Lord's death, with the coming of the Holy Spirit, with both the horror and the hope of the end-times. This is one of the briefest and yet one of the most disturbing and heart-searching books of the OT.

BIBLIOGRAPHY. A. S. Kapelrud, *Joel Studies*, 1948; J. A. Thompson, *JNES* 14, 1955, pp. 52ff.; *IB*, 6, pp. 727–760; L. C. Allen, *Joel, Obadiah, Jonah and Micah*, *NICOT*, 1976; D. Stuart, *Hosea–*

Jonah, 1987; D. A. Hubbard, *Joel and Amos*, *TOTC*, 1989. R.A.S.

JOGBEHAH (Heb. *yoḡb ᵉhâ*, 'height'). A town in Gilead assigned to Gad (Nu 32:35), named also in Gideon's pursuit of the Midianites (Jdg. 8:11). It is the modern Jubeihât, about 10 km NW of Amman and 1057 m above sea-level. J.D.D.

JOHANAN (Heb. *yôḥānān*, 'Yahweh is gracious'). A number of men are so called in the OT, the most notable being the son of Kareah. A Jewish leader who supported Gedaliah on the latter's appointment as governor of Judah (2 Ki. 25:23; Je. 40:8) after the fall of Jerusalem, Johanan offered to kill Ishmael, who was plotting Gedaliah's assassination (Je. 40:13–16). The offer rejected and the warning ignored, Ishmael succeeded in his purpose. Johanan pursued him, rescued the people captured by him (Je. 41:11–16), and took them and the protesting Jeremiah to Tahpanhes in Egypt (Je. 43:1–7).

Others possessing the same name include the eldest son of Josiah, king of Judah (1 Ch. 3:15); a son of Elioenai (1 Ch. 3:24); a grandson of Ahimaaz (1 Ch. 6:9–10); a Benjaminite recruit of David at Ziklag (1 Ch. 12:4); a Gadite who likewise joined David (1 Ch. 12:12); an Ephraimite chief (2 Ch. 28:12, where Hebrew has 'Jehohanan'); a returned exile in Artaxerxes' time (Ezr. 8:12); and a priest in the days of Joiakim (Ne. 12:22–23).

J.D.D.

JOHN, THE APOSTLE. Our information about John comes from two sources: NT and Patristic.

I. New Testament evidence

a. In the Gospels

John was the son of Zebedee, probably the younger son, for except in Luke–Acts he is mentioned after his brother James. Luke gives the order Peter, John and James, probably because in the early days of the church John was closely associated with Peter (Lk. 8:51; 9:28; Acts 1:13). That John's mother's name was Salome is an inference from Mk. 16:1 and Mt. 27:56; for the third woman who is said to have accompanied the two Marys to the tomb is designated Salome by Mark, and 'the mother of Zebedee's children' by Matthew. Salome is usually regarded as the sister of Mary the mother of Jesus, because in Jn. 19:25 four women are said to have stood near the cross, the two Marys mentioned in Mark and Matthew, the mother of Jesus, and his mother's sister. If this identification is correct, John was a cousin of Jesus on his mother's side. His parents would appear to have been well-to-do, for his father, a fisherman, had 'hired servants' (Mk. 1:20); and Salome was one of the women who 'provided for Jesus out of their means' (Lk. 8:3; Mk. 15:40). John has often been identified with the unnamed disciple of John the Baptist, who with Andrew was directed by the Baptist to Jesus as the Lamb of God (Jn. 1:35–37); and if *prōtos* is read in Jn. 1:41, it is possible that Andrew was the first of these two disciples to bring his brother Simon to Jesus, and that the unnamed disciple (John) subsequently brought his own brother James. This is not certain, however, as there are textual variants (see *TNTC*). After their subsequent call by Jesus to leave their father and their fishing (Mk. 1:19–20), James and John were nicknamed by him *Boanērges*, 'sons of thunder' (Mk. 3:17), probably because they were high-spirited, impetuous Galileans, whose zeal was undisciplined and sometimes misdirected (Lk. 9:49). This aspect of their character is shown by their outburst after a Samaritan village had refused their Master entrance (Lk. 9:54). Moreover, their personal ambition was, it would seem, untempered by a true insight into the nature of his kingship; and this lingering trait of selfishness, together with their readiness to suffer for Jesus regardless of self, is illustrated in the request they made to him (a request encouraged by their mother [Mt. 20:20]) that they should be allowed to sit in places of special privilege when Jesus entered into his kingdom (Mk. 10:37).

On three important occasions in the earthly ministry of Jesus, John is mentioned in company with his brother James and Simon Peter, to the exclusion of the other apostles: at the raising of Jairus' daughter (Mk. 5:37), at the transfiguration (Mk. 9:2) and in the garden of Gethsemane (Mk. 14:33); and, according to Luke, Peter and John were the two disciples sent by Jesus to make preparations for the final Passover meal (Lk. 22:8).

John is not mentioned by name in the Fourth Gospel (though the sons of Zebedee are referred to in 21:2), but he is almost certainly the disciple called 'the disciple whom Jesus loved', who lay close to the breast of Jesus at the Last Supper (13:23); who was entrusted with the care of his mother at the time of his death (19:26–27); who ran with Peter to the tomb on the first Easter morning and was the first to see the full significance of the undisturbed grave-clothes with no body inside them (20:2, 8); and who was present when the risen Christ revealed himself to seven of his disciples by the sea of Tiberias. In the account of that last incident in ch. 21, support is given to the later tradition that John lived on to a great age (21:23). The evidence of Jn. 21:24 for the Johannine authorship of this Gospel is capable of different interpretations (see *TNTC*).

b. In the Acts

According to the early narratives of Acts, John, together with Peter, with whom he remained closely associated, had to bear the main brunt of Jewish hostility to the early Christian church (Acts 4:13; 5:33, 40). Both men showed a boldness of speech and action which astounded the Jewish authorities, who regarded them as 'uneducated, common men' (Acts 4:13). John, it would seem, continued for some years to play a leading part in the church at Jerusalem. On behalf of the other apostles he and Peter laid hands on the Samaritans who had been converted through the ministry of Philip (Acts 8:14); and he could be described as a reputed 'pillar' of the Jerusalem church at the time when Paul visited the city some 14 years after his conversion (Gal. 2:9). We do not know when John left Jerusalem, nor where he went after his departure. Assuming that he is the seer of the book of Revelation, he was presumably at Ephesus when he was banished to Patmos 'on account of the word of God, and the testimony of Jesus' (Rev. 1:9), though the date of this exile is uncertain. There is no other mention of John in the NT, though some think that he refers to himself as 'the elder' in 2 Jn. 1; 3 Jn. 1.

II. Patristic evidence

There is a certain amount of late but probably unreliable evidence, that John the apostle died as a martyr early in his career, perhaps at the time his brother James was slain by Herod (Acts 12:2). A 9th-century chronicler, George Hamartolos, reproduces, as we can now see, a statement contained in the history of Philip of Side (*c.* 450), a relevant fragment of which was discovered by de Boor in 1889, to the effect that Papias, bishop of Hierapolis in the middle of the 2nd century, in the second book of his *Expositions* asserted that *both* the sons of Zebedee met a violent death in fulfilment of the Lord's prediction (Mk. 10:39). Though some scholars accept this testimony as genuine, most regard Philip of Side as an unreliable witness to Papias, and are impressed by the absence from Eusebius of any reference to the early martyrdom of John, and also by the failure of Acts to mention it, if both the sons of Zebedee in fact suffered in the same way at approximately the same time. It is true that some support for Philip of Side's statement seems to be obtainable from a Syr. martyrology written about AD 400, in which the entry for 27 December is 'John and James the apostles at Jerusalem'; and also from a calendar of the church at Carthage, dated AD 505, in which the entry for the same date reads 'John the Baptist and James the apostle whom Herod killed', for it is pointed out by those who accept this evidence that, as the Baptist is commemorated in this calendar on 24 June, the probability is that the entry for 27 December is a mistake for 'John the Apostle'. It is, however, very doubtful whether the Syr. martyrology preserves an ancient tradition independent of the Gk.-speaking church; nor does it follow that, because the two brothers were commemorated on the same day, they were commemorated as being both martyrs in *death* who had been slain at the same time. Nor again does the reference to the sons of Zebedee as 'drinking the cup' and 'being baptized with the baptism of Christ' necessarily imply that both were destined to come to a violent end.

Against this partial and weakly attested tradition must be set the much stronger tradition reflected in the statement of Polycrates, bishop of Ephesus (AD 190), that John 'who reclined on the Lord's breast', after being 'a witness and a teacher' (note the order of the words), 'fell asleep at Ephesus'. According to Irenaeus, it was at Ephesus that John 'gave out' the Gospel, and confuted the heretics, refusing to remain under the same roof as Cerinthus, 'the enemy of truth'; at Ephesus that he lingered on 'till the days of Trajan', who reigned AD 98–117. Jerome also repeats the tradition that John tarried at Ephesus to extreme old age, and records that, when John had to be carried to the Christian meetings, he used to repeat again and again 'Little children, love one another'. The only evidence that might seemingly conflict with this tradition of John the apostle's residence at Ephesus is negative in character. It is alleged that if, as the writers at the end of the 2nd century assert, John resided long at Ephesus and exercised such influence, it is remarkable that there should be an entire absence of any reference to John in the extant Christian literature which emanated from Asia during the first half of the century, particularly in the letters of Ignatius and the Epistle of Polycarp. But, even if the absence of allusions to John in these documents is significant, it may merely be an indication that 'there was a difference between his reputation and influence at the beginning and at the close of the century' (so V. H. Stanton, *The Gospels as Historical Documents*, 1, p. 236). On any score the objection, it would seem, is insufficient to overthrow the tradition which later became so firmly established. Westcott concluded that 'nothing is better attested in early church history than the residence and work of St John at Ephesus'. It is true that Westcott wrote before the evidence for John's early martyrdom had accumulated, but as we have seen, that evidence is not adequate enough or reliable enough to confute the definite statements of the man who occupied the see of Ephesus at the close of the century, and of the man who at the same period made it his primary aim to investigate the traditions of the apostolic sees.

(*JOHN, EPISTLES OF; *JOHN, GOSPEL OF; *REVELATION, BOOK OF).

BIBLIOGRAPHY. S. S. Smalley, *John: Evangelist and Interpreter*, 1978; K. B. Quast, *Peter and the Beloved Disciple*, 1989; R. A. Culpepper, *John, the Son of Zebedee*, 1994. See also under *JOHN, GOSPEL OF.

R.V.G.T.

JOHN THE BAPTIST. Born (*c.* 7 BC) to an elderly couple, Zechariah a priest and his wife Elizabeth, he grew to manhood in the wilderness of Judaea (Lk. 1:80), where he received his prophetic call, *c.* AD 27 (Lk. 3:2). The view that his wilderness period was spent in association with the Qumran community or a similar Essene group must be treated with caution; even if it could be substantiated, it was a new impulse which sent him forth 'to make ready for the Lord a people prepared' (Lk. 1:17), and his prophetic ministry must have involved a break with any Essene or similar group with which he may previously have been connected. After the Spirit of prophecy came upon him, he quickly gained widespread fame as a preacher calling for national repentance. Crowds flocked to hear him, and many of his hearers were baptized by him in the Jordan, confessing their sins.

His attitude to the established order in Israel was one of radical condemnation; 'the axe', he said, 'is laid to the root of the trees' (Mt. 3:10; Lk. 3:9). He denounced the religious leaders of the people as a brood of vipers, and denied that there was any value in the bare fact of descent from Abraham. A new beginning was necessary; the time had come to call out from the nation as a whole a loyal remnant who would be ready for the imminent arrival of the Coming One and the judgment which he would execute. John thought and spoke of himself as a mere preparer of the way for this Coming One, for whom he was unworthy, he said, to perform the lowliest service. Whereas John's own ministry was characterized by baptism with water, the Coming One's ministry would be a baptism with the Holy Spirit and fire.

That John aimed at giving the loyal remnant a distinct and recognizable existence is suggested by the statement in Josephus (*Ant.* 18. 117) that John was 'a good man who bade the Jews practise virtue, be just one to another, and pious toward God, and come together by means of baptism'; these last words seem to envisage the formation of a religious community which was entered by baptism. This is probably an accurate assessment of the situation. But when Josephus goes on to say that John 'taught that baptism was acceptable to God provided that they underwent it not to procure remission of sins but for the purification of the body, if the soul had first been purified by righteousness', he differs from the NT account. The Evangelists say quite plainly that John preached a 'baptism of repentance for the remission of sins'. Josephus is probably transferring to John's baptism what he knew to be the significance of Essene washings; the Qumran *Rule of the Community* gives an account of the significance of such washings almost identical with that which Josephus gives of John's baptism. But John's baptism, like his preaching, may well represent a deliberate turning away from Essene beliefs and practices.

Among those who came to John for baptism was Jesus, whom John apparently hailed as the Coming One of whom he had spoken—although later, in prison, he had doubts about this identification and had to be reassured by being told that Jesus' ministry was marked by precisely those features which the prophets had foretold as characteristic of the age of restoration.

John's ministry was not confined to the Jordan valley. The statement in John 3:23 that he left the Jordan valley for a time and conducted a baptismal campaign (presumably of brief duration) 'at Aenon near Salim', where there was abundance of water, has implications which are easily overlooked. For W. F. Albright (*The Archaeology of Palestine*, 1956, p. 247) is probably right in locating this place NE of Nablus, near the sources of the Wadi Far'ah—that is to say, in territory which was then Samaritan. This could explain certain features of Samaritan religion attested for the early Christian centuries, but it also illuminates the words of Jesus to his disciples in John 4:35–38, spoken with regard to the people in this very area, and ending with the statement: 'others have laboured, and you have entered into their labour'. The harvest which they reaped (Jn. 4:39, 41) had been sown by John.

After this period of ministry in Samaria John must have returned to the territory of Herod Antipas (*HEROD, 3), probably Peraea. He aroused Antipas' suspicion as the leader of a mass movement which might have unforeseen results; he also incurred his hostility, and still more that of Herod's second wife *Herodias, by denouncing their marriage as illicit. He was accordingly imprisoned in the Peraean fortress of *Machaerus and there, some months later, put to death.

In the NT John is presented chiefly as the forerunner of Christ. His imprisonment was the signal for the start of Jesus' Galilean ministry (Mk. 1:14f.); his baptismal activity provided a starting-point for the apostolic preaching (Acts 10:37; 13:24f.; *cf.* 1:22 and Mk.1:1–4). In Jesus' estimation, John was the promised Elijah of Mal. 4:5f., who was to come and complete his ministry of restoration on the eve of 'the great and terrible day of the Lord' (Mk. 9:13; Mt. 11:14; *cf.* Lk. 1:17). Jesus also regarded him as the last and greatest member of the prophetic succession: 'the law and the prophets were until John: since then the good news of the kingdom of God is preached' (Lk. 16:16). Therefore, while unsurpassed in personal stature, he was (in respect of privilege) less than the least in the kingdom of God; he stood on the threshold of the new order as its herald (as Moses viewed the promised land from Pisgah) without entering in. His disciples preserved their corporate existence for a considerable time after his death.

BIBLIOGRAPHY. C. H. Kraeling, *John the Baptist*, 1951; J. Steinmann, *Saint John the Baptist and the Desert Tradition*, 1958; A. S. Geyser, 'The Youth of John the Baptist', *NovT* 1, 1956, pp. 70ff.; W. H. Brownlee, 'John the Baptist in the New Light of Ancient Scrolls', in *The Scrolls and the New Testament*, ed. K. Stendahl, 1958, pp. 33ff.; C. H. H. Scobie, *John the Baptist*, 1964; R. A. Horsley, *CBQ* 47, pp. 435–463.

F.F.B.

JOHN, EPISTLES OF.

I. Background and circumstances of 1 John

1 John is headed as an Epistle, but there is nothing 'epistolary' in the strict sense about it (contrast 2 and 3 John), and it is more like a tract addressed to a particular situation.

It was called forth by the activities of false teachers who had seceded from the church (or churches) to which John is writing, and who were attempting to seduce the faithful (2:18f., 26). They formed an esoteric group, believing that they had superior knowledge to ordinary Christians (cf. 2:20, 27; 2 Jn. 9) and showing little love to them (*cf.* 4:20).

They were forerunners of the later heretics generally known as 'Gnostics' (from Gk. *gnōsis*, meaning 'knowledge') and claimed a special knowledge of God and of theology. On the basis of their new doctrine they appear to have denied that Jesus was the Christ (2:22), the pre-existent (1:1) Son of God (4:15; 5:5, 10) come in the flesh (4:2; 2 Jn. 7) to provide salvation for men (4:9f., 14). But the precise form which this heresy took is uncertain. It is generally regarded as having had some affinity with the views held by Cerinthus in Asia Minor at the end of the 1st century, although it was not fully identical with what we know of his teaching. According to Cerinthus, Jesus was a good man who was indwelt by the heavenly Christ from the time of his baptism until just before his crucifixion (Irenaeus, *Adv. Haer.* 1. 26. 1, in J. Stevenson, *A New Eusebius*, 1957, No. 70)—a view which is apparently contradicted in 5:6 and in various verses where belief that Jesus *is* (not simply *was*) the Christ, the Son of God, is emphasized (2:22; 5:1, 5). Such teaching was probably bound up with the common gnostic distinction between spirit and matter, according to which a real incarnation of God in man was impossible and was only apparent (as in Docetism) or temporary (as in Cerinthianism).

The false teachers further claimed that they were 'sinless' (1:8, 10) and possibly also that they did not need redemption through the death of Jesus Christ, while they were in fact morally indifferent, following the ways of the world (*cf.* 2:15), ignoring the commandments of Christ (2:4), and freely doing what they pleased (without, however, indulging in gross sin). They did not realize that sin is a moral category, *i.e.* lawlessness (3:4, 7f.), and consequently they felt quite consistent in claiming sinlessness while indulging in selfishness and lack of love. Probably we are to see here also the influence of the gnostic distinction between spirit and matter: since the body (matter) was evil anyhow and only the (divinely implanted) spirit or soul mattered, their bodily behaviour was irrelevant to their Christian belief.

John writes to provide an antidote to this teaching, and the progress of the argument in his tract is best understood when this is kept in mind. Attempts to explain its difficult structure in terms of source criticism (R. Bultmann; W. Nauck; J. C. O'Neill) have met with little favour.

II. Outline of contents of 1 John

John begins by stating that his purpose is to explain to his readers what he has heard and seen as regards the word of life manifested in Jesus Christ, so that there may be joyful fellowship between himself, his readers and God (1:1–4).

He then states the fundamental proposition, *God is light*, and on the basis of this universally acceptable truth proceeds to take up certain erroneous slogans of his opponents (1:6a, 8a, 10a; 2:4a). In opposition to them he asserts that only those who walk in the light can have fellowship with God and cleansing through the blood of Jesus. To deny that one is a sinner in need of cleansing is to commit self-deceit, but sinners can be sure of forgiveness from a faithful God through the righteous Advocate, Jesus Christ. To claim a true knowledge of God without obeying his commandments is to be a liar (1:5–2:6).

Christians, then, are called to obey God's new commandment. Although it is really an old one, yet it is now presented anew as the law of the new era of light which has already begun to shine in the darkness of the old, sinful world. John feels able to address his readers in this way because they have already entered into this new era and enjoy the privileges of forgiveness, knowledge and power, and he further exhorts them not to cling to the sinful world which is doomed to pass away (2:7–17).

One of the marks of the arrival of the new era is the rise of these false teachers who have now left their temporary home in the church. Their teaching is a denial that Jesus is the Christ, the Son of God, and this really means that they are denying God the Father himself. They claim special knowledge, to be sure, but John assures his readers that in view of their anointing by God (*i.e.* with the Spirit or perhaps with the Word of God) all Christians have true knowledge (2:18–27).

He now counsels them to abide in Christ, the holy and righteous One, and to test themselves and their teachers by their likeness to him. This leads to the thought of the great privilege of Christians as children of God, and the even greater privilege that at the advent of Christ they will become altogether like him—all of which constitutes a powerful incentive to holy living (2:28–3:3).

What, then, is the character of children of God in contrast with those who are the children of the devil? Since Christ came to take away sin, it follows that God's children do not, and in fact cannot, sin, while the children of the devil neither do what is right nor show love. By this uncompromising statement, which must be considered in the light of 1:8, John means that the Christian *as a Christian* cannot sin: he is speaking of the ideal character of the Christian, in contrast with the false teachers who made no attempt to emulate this ideal (3:4–10).

In fact, Christians can expect to be hated by children of the devil, just as Abel was murdered by Cain; by contrast, the mark of the true Christian is love, seen not in murder but in self-sacrifice and practical charity (3:11–18).

Through such deeds of love a man knows that he is a Christian, so that, even if his conscience at times condemns him, he can still have perfect confidence before his Judge, the God who knows his desire to love and serve him (*cf.* Jn. 21:17); indeed, armed with this confidence, he can be bold in prayer, since he knows that he is pleasing God by keeping his commandment of love, and, further, he will receive inward assurance from the Spirit of God (3:19–24).

But how can a Christian be sure that he has the Spirit of *God*? For the false teachers also claim to have the Spirit. John replies that correct belief about Jesus Christ come in the flesh is the sure sign of true inspiration. The false teachers, however, are motivated by the spirit of antichrist (4:1–6).

After this digression, John returns to the theme of love. Love, he repeats, is the token that a man is born of God, for, as was shown in the sacrifice of Christ, *God is love*. (This is John's second great declaration about the nature of God.) Even if men cannot see God, they can know that he dwells in them if they show love (4:7–12).

John now summarizes the grounds of Christian assurance—possession of the Spirit, confession of Jesus Christ and the practice of love. These are signs that God dwells in us and give us confidence for the day of judgment, since there can be no fear where there is love. Yet, to avoid any antinomian or 'spiritualistic' misunderstanding, John emphasizes that such love for God is inevitably accompanied by love for the brethren. All who truly confess Jesus Christ love God and their fellow-men. Nor is it difficult to keep this commandment, for by faith those who are born of God can overcome the forces arrayed against them (4:13–5:4).

This leads John back to the theme of faith. True Christian faith is centred on Jesus Christ, who not only submitted to the water of baptism but also shed his blood on the cross, and to whom the Spirit bears witness (Jn. 15:26). These three—the Spirit, water and blood—are God's sure testimony to confirm faith in Christ. John possibly also means that the saving activity of the Spirit in the church (or the individual believer) and the sacraments of baptism and the Lord's supper continue this testimony. To disbelieve this testimony is to make God a liar and to reject the eternal life which he has given to men in his Son (5:5–12).

In conclusion, John states that his purpose has been to assure his readers of their salvation. Since they can be sure of divine response to their prayers, they are to win back erring brethren through prayer (although prayer is of no avail in the case of mortal sin, whatever that may be). Finally come three great declarations—that Christians have power not to sin, that they belong to God, and that they are in Jesus Christ who is their great instructor—and a final admonition to avoid idolatry (*i.e.* worship of pagan gods, but the meaning is not certain) (5:13–21).

III. Background and contents of 2 and 3 John

2 and 3 John are real letters, each long enough to be accommodated on a standard size sheet of papyrus (25 by 20 cm) and conforming to the pattern of letter-writing of the time. (For a remarkably close parallel to the structure of 3 John, see C. K. Barrett, *The New Testament Background: Selected Documents*, 1956, No. 22.)

2 John is addressed from 'the elder' to 'the elect lady and her children'. This is in all likelihood a symbolic manner of addressing a church (*cf.* 1 Pet. 5:13), perhaps intended to baffle any hostile people into whose hands the letter might fall (1–3). The occasion of the letter is similar to that of 1 John (*cf.* 2 Jn. 7 with 1 Jn. 4:3); false teachers were travelling from church to church and denying that the Son of God had really been incarnate. The elder issues a warning against such teaching; those who 'go on' to accept this new or higher teaching are abandoning their faith in God, the Father of Jesus Christ. He cautions his friends not to extend hospitality to the false teachers, and he encourages them to follow after the truth which already abides in them and to fulfil the command of love (4–11). Finally, he expresses the hope of seeing them soon and adds greetings from his own church (12f.).

3 John is a private letter (like Philemon) addressed to the elder's friend Gaius, who was a leading member in another church. He is commended for his attachment to the truth and for showing practical love to travelling preachers who depended on the churches for their keep (1–8). His attitude is the reverse of that of Diotrephes, who was seeking to be the leader in his church (probably a neighbouring church to that of Gaius), resisting the advice of John and perhaps withholding a previous letter of his from the church, refusing to welcome the travelling preachers and excommunicating those who did welcome them. It is likely that we see here the difficulties caused by the development of a settled local church leadership alongside the existence of apostolic overseers and travelling teachers, and that Diotrephes was aspiring to the position of 'bishop' in his own church and resented any interference from outside. Such difficulties were no doubt bound to arise as the apostles passed on, but it is clear that Diotrephes was not handling matters in a Christian manner. The elder warns that he will come and deal personally with Diotrephes if necessary (9–11). Finally, a word of commendation is added for Demetrius (probably the bearer of the letter and a travelling teacher), and the letter concludes with warm greetings (12–14).

IV. External attestation of the Epistles

1 John was used by Papias (*c.* 140) according to Eusebius, and is quoted by Polycarp (*c.* 110–120) and very probably by Justin (*c.* 150–160). It was accepted as the work of the fourth Evangelist, John the apostle, by Irenaeus (*c.* 180), the Muratorian Canon (*c.* 180–200), and Clement of Alexandria (*c.* 200). According to Eusebius, there was never any questioning of its authenticity. 2 and 3 John are probably listed in the Muratorian Canon (J. Stevenson, *op. cit.*, No. 124 and note); 2 John is quoted by Irenaeus, and both Epistles were probably commented on by Clement of Alexandria. Lack of mention and doubts about their canonicity, reflected in Eusebius, who quotes Origen (J. Stevenson, *op. cit.*, No. 289), were due to their slight nature.

V. Provenance, authorship and date

The Asian provenance of all five Johannine writings is still the most likely. For the Epistles this is supported by the Cerinthian teaching which is opposed and by the traditions which connect their author with Ephesus.

The authorship of the Epistles and of the Johannine writings presents problems which are not yet fully solved.

First, it is certain that one author is responsible for the three Epistles, although this was denied by Jerome and more recently doubted by R. Bultmann (*op. cit.*, pp. 1f.). 1 John is anonymous, but we may now assert that its author was also 'the elder'.

Second, it is reasonably certain that John's Gospel and 1 John are by the same author. This is disputed by C. H. Dodd (pp. xlvii–lvi; more fully in 'The First Epistle of John and the Fourth Gospel', *BJRL* 21, 1937, pp. 129–156) and C. K. Barrett (*The Gospel according to St. John*, 1955, pp. 49–52), but convincing proof is given by A. E. Brooke (pp. i–xix), W. F. Howard (*The Fourth Gospel in Recent Criticism and Interpretation*[4], 1955, pp. 281–296), and W. G. Wilson (*JTS* 49, 1948, pp. 147–156). There can really be no doubt that John and 1 John represent the same mind at work in two different situations. John is a profound study of the incarnation of Christ addressed primarily as an apologetic to the outside world; 1 John is a tract called forth by a particular situation in the church. The differences between the two can largely be explained by this difference of audience and purpose. Logically John precedes 1 John, but whether this was the order of composition is hardly possible to determine; John is obviously the work of many years of meditation, and 1 John may have been written in that period.

Third, the relation of Revelation (which is ascribed to John the apostle by strong external evidence) to John and 1–3 John must be considered. The theory of common authorship of all five books is very difficult to maintain, as was seen quite early by Dionysius of Alexandria (J. Stevenson, *op. cit.*, No. 237). There are considerable theological differences between Revelation and the other Johannine writings, although there are also close similarities. Further, the Greek of Revelation is unlike that of any other book in the NT; despite suggestions that it was originally written in *Aramaic*, and so possibly by the same person who wrote John and 1–3 John in *Greek*, the theory of common authorship must remain doubtful.

In view of these facts, various theories of authorship have been put forward, of which three deserve attention.

First, the traditional theory, which is supported by D. Guthrie (*New Testament Introduction*), attributes all five books to John the apostle. He was known as 'the elder' *par excellence* in Asia Minor on account of his age and authority (*cf.* 1 Pet. 5:1 for a similar title). Against this theory must be reckoned the problems raised by Revelation and the uncertainty which some scholars find in the external evidence for the apostolic authorship of John's Gospel.

A second solution, which avoids the first of these difficulties, is that John's Gospel and 1–3 John are by John the apostle and Revelation by another John who is otherwise unknown to us. This was essentially the theory of Dionysius of Alexandria, and is supported today by A. Wikenhauser (*New Testament Introduction*, E.T. 1958, pp. 547–553). On this view, some connection between the two Johns must be presupposed to account for the theological similarities between the writings.

A third solution, which avoids the second of the difficulties in the traditional theory, sees a close disciple of John the apostle as the author of John's Gospel and 1–3 John and John himself as possibly the author of Revelation. (There are various forms of this theory.) On this view, it was John's disciple who was known as 'the elder'.

Support for this third solution has often been sought in a well-known passage in Papias (J. Stevenson, *op. cit.*, No. 31); Papias refers to certain of the apostles, including John, who are apparently dead, as 'elders' and then to two living disciples of the Lord, Aristion and the elder John. Some scholars think that this elder John was a disciple of John the apostle and was the author of John's Gospel and 1–3 John. But this is extremely conjectural. It is not certain whether Papias is here referring to one John (the apostle) twice or to two separate Johns, and weighty names can be quoted for both interpretations. Further, Papias clearly applied the title of 'elder' to more than one person (including John the apostle in any case), and it is not certain that he used the title in the same sense as the author of 2 and 3 John. Finally, Papias does not state that the hypothetical 'elder John' was a disciple of John the apostle. We cannot, therefore, be certain on this theory that the elder of 2 and 3 John was called John or that he was the 'elder John' of Papias.

On the whole, it still remains most plausible that the Gospel and the three letters are the work of John the apostle or of a close disciple of his.

The date of 1–3 John cannot be rigidly determined. The evidence from Qumran *allows* the possibility of an earlier development of the kind of theology found in the Johannine literature than was formerly believed possible. The chief clue, however, is the nature of the heresy attacked and the church situation, both of which suggest a date between the 60s and 90s of the 1st century; our knowledge of the church in this period is so meagre that a closer dating is impossible.

BIBLIOGRAPHY. Commentaries by B. F. Westcott, 1883, reprinted 1966; A. E. Brooke, *ICC*, 1912; C. H. Dodd, *MNTC*, 1946; R. Bultmann, *Hermeneia*, 1973; J. L. Houlden, *BNTC*, 1973; I. H. Marshall, *NIC/NLC*, 1978; R. E. Brown, *AB*, 1982; K. Grayston, *NCB*, 1984; S. S. Smalley, *WBC*, 1984; J. R. W. Stott, *TNTC*², 1988; M. M. Thompson, *IVPNTC*, 1992. Studies: J. Lieu, *The Second and Third Epistles of John*, 1986; *idem*, *The Theology of the Johannine Epistles*, 1991. I.H.M.

JOHN, GOSPEL OF.

I. Outline of contents

a. The revelation of Jesus to the world, 1:1–12:50

(i) Prologue (1:1–18).
(ii) The manifestation of Jesus (1:19–2:11).
(iii) The new message (2:12–4:54).
(iv) Jesus, the Son of God (5:1–47).
(v) The bread of life (6:1–71).
(vi) Conflict with the Jews (7:1–8:59).
(vii) The light of the world (9:1–41).
(viii) The good shepherd (10:1–42).
(ix) The resurrection and the life (11:1–57).
(x) The shadow of the cross (12:1–36a).
(xi) Epilogue (12:36b–50).

b. The revelation of Jesus to his disciples, 13:1–17:26

(i) The Last Supper (13:1–30).
(ii) The farewell discourses (13:31–16:33).
(iii) Jesus' prayer for his disciples (17:1–26).

c. The glorification of Jesus, 18:1–21:25

(i) The passion of Jesus (18:1–19:42).
(ii) The resurrection of Jesus (20:1–31).
(iii) The commission to the disciples (21:1–25).

II. Purpose

A clear statement of the purpose of John is given in Jn. 20:30f. (*Cf.* W. C. van Unnik, *TU* 73, 1959, pp. 382–411.) John has made a selection out of a large number of available 'signs', and his purpose in narrating them is to bring his readers to the belief that Jesus is the Christ (*i.e.* the Messiah) and the Son of God, and thus to bring them into an experience of eternal life.

From this statement we can draw certain conclusions which are amply attested by the substance of the Gospel. First, it is basically an evangelistic document. Second, its explicit method is to present the work and words of Jesus in such a way as to show the nature of his person. Third, the description of this person as Messiah indicates that a Jewish audience is probably in mind. Since, however, John appears to be writing for an audience outside Palestine and in part ignorant of Jewish customs, it is an attractive hypothesis that he wrote especially for Jews of the Diaspora and proselytes in Hellenistic synagogues. (*Cf.* J. A. T. Robinson, *Twelve NT Studies*, 1962, pp. 107–125.) This naturally does not exclude a Gentile audience from his purview, although the view that the Gospel was written primarily to convert the thoughtful Gentile (*cf.* C. H. Dodd, *The Interpretation of the Fourth Gospel*, 1953) is unlikely.

This main purpose does not exclude other, subordinate aims. Thus, first, John consciously stresses points which would refute the false or antagonistic views about Jesus held by Jews in his time. There may also be an attempt to correct an over-zealous veneration for John the Baptist. Second, particularly in 13–17, John addresses Christians and gives teaching about life in the church. But the view that a principal aim of John was to correct the church's eschatology (so C. K. Barrett) is not tenable, although this is not to deny that the Gospel contains eschatological teaching. Third, it is often alleged that John was written as a polemic against Gnosticism. This view gains some plausibility from the purpose of 1 John, but is not so self-evident as is sometimes supposed; nevertheless, John was no doubt aware of the danger of Gnosticism while he wrote, and his Gospel is in fact an excellent weapon against Gnosticism.

III. Structure and theological content

a. The historical structure

As a historical work, John is selective. It begins with the incarnation of the pre-existent Word of God in Jesus (1:1–18), and then passes straight to the early days of Jesus' ministry—his baptism by John and the call of his first disciples (1:19–51), and his return from the Jordan to Galilee (1:43). But the scene of his work is not confined in the main to Galilee, as in the Synoptic narrative. Only a few of the incidents related take place there (1:43–2:12; 4:43–54; 6:1–7:9). Once the scene is Samaria (4:1–42), but most frequently it is Jerusalem, usually at the time of a Jewish feast (2:13; 5:1; 6:4; 7:2; 10:22; 11:55; *cf.* A. Guilding, *The Fourth Gospel and Jewish Worship*, 1960). The last of these incidents is the raising of Lazarus, which provoked the Jewish leaders to do away with Jesus (11:45ff.), although, as in the Synoptic Gospels, their enmity had been mounting for some time (*e.g.* 7:1). From this point the narrative follows lines familiar to us from the Synoptic Gospels—the anointing at Bethany (12:1–11), the triumphal entry (12:12–19), the Last Supper (13), recorded with no reference to its sacramental features, the arrest (18:1–12), trials and Peter's denial (18:13–19:16), the crucifixion and resurrection (20–21). Yet in this section also there is much material not found in the Synoptic Gospels, especially the last discourses and prayer (14–16; 17), the details of the trial before Pilate (18:28–19:16), and the resurrection appearances.

There is no need to doubt that this historical outline corresponds broadly to the actual order of events, although it must be remembered that John has recorded only a few incidents and arranged them from the standpoint of his presentation of Jesus as the Messiah.

b. The theological content

(i) *John as revelation.* This historical outline is the vehicle of a theological presentation of Jesus. John's purpose is to reveal the *glory* of Jesus as the Son of God. As the pre-existent Son he shared the glory of the Father (17:5, 24), and in his earthly life his glory was demonstrated to the world—or rather to those who had eyes to see (1:14)—in the series of signs which he wrought (2:11). Yet in these signs Jesus was seeking not his own glory but that of the Father (5:41; 7:18). This revelation of Jesus before the world is the theme of chs. 1–12, which concludes with a summarizing passage and a clear break in thought (12:36b–50). Since the world had largely not believed in him (12:37), Jesus turned to his disciples, and in chs. 13–17 we have a revelation of his glory, seen in humble service, to the disciples, who were themselves also called to a life in which God is glorified (15:8; 21:19). But a theme which had been hinted at earlier also finds expression here, namely that Jesus is supremely glorified in his passion and death. Thus the third section of the Gospel (chs. 18–21) shows us that the hour has come in which Jesus is glorified as the Son of God and glorifies God.

At the same time the Gospel may be regarded as a revelation of *truth* (1:14, 17). In the Gospel the world is characterized by error, imperfection and sin, because it has lost contact with God who is the true One (7:28); to it Jesus brings the truth of God (18:37). He himself is the incarnation of truth (14:6) and will be succeeded by the Spirit of truth (14:17). He leads men to a true worship of God (4:23f.) and frees them from the errors of the devil (8:44) through knowledge of the truth (8:32). In contrast to the empty satisfactions of the world he brings true, real bread for the souls of men (6:32, 55).

(ii) *Signs and witnesses.* The way in which this revelation is brought to men is twofold. First, there are the *signs* or *works* performed by Jesus, seven of which (excluding the resurrection) are related at length. They are signs not simply because they are evidence of a miraculous, supernatural power (4:48) but rather because by their character they show that their author is sent by God (9:16) as the Messiah and Son of God (3:2; 6:14; 7:31); they thus authenticate his person to those who have eyes to see (2:23; 12:37).

Usually these signs are the basis of a discourse or dialogue in which their spiritual significance is brought out. There is, however, what may be regarded as a further series of signs in words. Seven times (6:35; 8:12; 10:7, 11; 11:25; 14:6; 15:1; to which 8:24 is perhaps to be added) Jesus says, 'I am . . .'. A number of concepts, all of them already current in religious language, are here taken over by Jesus and used to explain who he is and what he has come to do. What is especially significant is that this use of 'I am' contains a veiled claim to deity.

Second, the glory of Jesus is attested by *witnesses.* Jesus himself came to bear witness to the truth (18:37), and witness is borne to him by John the Baptist, the woman of Samaria, the crowd who saw his signs (12:17), the disciples (15:27), the witness at the cross (19:35), and the Evangelist himself (21:24). Witness is also given by the Scriptures (5:39), by the Father (5:37), and by Jesus' signs (10:25). Such witness was meant to lead men to faith (4:39; 5:34).

(iii) *The Person of Jesus.* These signs and witnesses are thus meant to show that Jesus is the Son of God who offers life to men. Right at the beginning of the Gospel he is affirmed to be the *Word* (*LOGOS) of God (1:14, 17). Although this technical term does not recur in John, it is plain that the rest of the Gospel is an exposition and justification of the doctrine that the Word became flesh. The use of 'Word' is singularly happy, for by it John was able to speak to Jews who had already taken some steps towards regarding God's creative Word (Ps. 33:6) as in some sense a separate being from God (*cf.* the figurative description of Wisdom in Pr. 8:22ff.), to Christians who preached the Word of God and virtually identified it with Jesus (*cf.* Col. 4:3 with Eph. 6:19), and to educated pagans who saw the Word as the principle of order and rationality in the universe (popular Stoicism). But what John says goes far beyond anything that had previously been said.

Second, Jesus is the *Messiah* from the house of David awaited by the Jews (7:42). In fact, the great question for the Jews is whether Jesus is the Messiah (7:26ff.; 10:24), and the confession of the disciples is that this is precisely who he is (1:41; 4:29; 11:27; 20:31).

Third, he is the *Son of man.* This term is the key to Jesus' understanding of himself in the Synoptic Gospels, where it is connected with three ideas, the 'hiddenness' of his Messiahship, the necessity of his suffering, and his function as judge at the parousia. These ideas are latent in John (*cf.* 12:34; 3:14; 5:27), but the emphasis falls on the two ideas that the Son of man has been sent from heaven as the revealer of God and the Saviour of men (3:13; 9:35) and that he is glorified by being 'lifted up' to die (12:23–34).

Fourth, he is the *Son of God.* This is probably Jesus' most important title in John. Since the heart of the gospel is that God sent his Son as Saviour (3:16), John's purpose is to lead the reader to recognize the claim of Jesus (19:7) and make the confession of the disciples (1:34, 49; 11:27) that he is the Son of God. As Son, he reveals the Father (1:18), whose activities of life-giving and judgment he shares (5:19–29). Through belief in him men receive salvation (3:36) and freedom (8:36).

But to say that Jesus is the Son of God is, fifth, to ascribe full deity to him. Thus he who as the Word of God is himself *God* (1:1), is also confessed by men on earth as Lord and God (20:28, which is the climax of the Gospel; *cf.* also 1:18, RSVmg.).

(iv) *The work of Jesus.* A further set of titles expresses what Jesus came to do for men and what he offers them. These are summed up in 14:6, where Jesus claims to be the way, the truth, and the life. The last of these words, *life*, is the favourite word in John for salvation. The world of men is in a state of death (5:24f.) and is destined for judgment (3:18, 36). What Jesus offers to men is life, defined by John as knowledge of God and Jesus Christ (17:3). Jesus himself can thus be called the life (1:4; 11:25; 14:6), the giver of *living water* (*i.e.* life-bestowing water, 4:14), and *living bread* (6:33f.). To receive Jesus by believing in him (3:36; 6:29) is to receive the bread of life, and to eat the flesh and drink the blood of Jesus (an expression in which many scholars see an allusion to the Lord's Supper) is to partake of eternal life (6:54).

This same truth is presented in the picture of Jesus as the *light* of the world (8:12), developed especially in ch. 9. The state of men is now regarded as blindness (9:39–41) or darkness (3:19; 12:46), and Jesus is the one who cures blindness and gives the light of life to those who walk in darkness. He is also depicted as the *way* to God (14:1–7). This idea is hinted at in 10:9, where he is the *door* of the sheepfold, but here another idea becomes prominent—that Jesus is the *good shepherd* who gives his life for the sheep and gathers them into his sheepfold. Three vital ideas are contained in this description. First, Jesus is the true fulfilment of the OT promise of a shepherd for the people of God. (Note that life and light are Jewish descriptions of the Law which finds its fulfilment in Jesus.) Second, his death is not simply due to the opposition of his enemies, but is a saving death on behalf of men (10:11) by which they are drawn to God (12:32). Only through a sacrificial death can sin be removed (1:29) and life be given to the world (6:51b). Third, the picture of a flock introduces the idea of the church.

(v) *The new life*. Jesus is thus portrayed as the *Saviour* of the world (4:42). In his presence men face the decisive moment in which they either accept him and pass from death to life (5:24) or remain in darkness until the day of judgment (12:46–48).

Such acceptance of Jesus occurs when the Father draws men to his Son (6:44). Through the work of the Spirit of God, whose movement is beyond human comprehension, there then takes place the radical change known as the *new birth* (3:1–21) by which a man becomes a son of God (1:12).

From the human side this change is the product of *faith*, which is centred on the Son of God who was lifted up on the cross to save the world (3:14–18). A distinction is drawn between two kinds of faith—intellectual acceptance of the claims of Jesus (11:42; 8:24; 11:27; 20:31), which by itself is not sufficient, and full self-committal to him (3:16; 4:42; 9:35–38; 14:1).

Such faith is closely related to *knowledge*. Whereas ordinary men have no real knowledge of God (1:10; 16:3), through knowledge of Jesus men can know the Father (8:19; 14:7). The content of this knowledge is not stated in John; there is no place here for the esoteric revelations characteristic of the mystery religions. Our only clue is that the way in which men know God and are known by him is analogous to the way in which Jesus knows God and is known by him (10:14f.).

One thing, however, can be said. This new relationship is characterized by *love*. Disciples share in a relationship of mutual love with God like that which exists between the Father and the Son (3:35; 14:31), though it is to be noted that their love is directed towards the Son rather than towards the Father (14:23; 15:9; 17:26; 21:15–17; *cf.* 5:42; 1 Jn. 4:20f.).

Other expressions are also used to express this communion of disciples with Jesus. They are said to *abide* in him (6:56; 15:4–10), and he abides in them (6:56; *cf.* 14:17). The preposition *in* is also important in describing the close relationship of mutual indwelling between God and Jesus and between Jesus and his disciples (14:20, 23; 17:21, 23, 26).

(vi) *The people of God.* Although the word 'church' is not found in John, the idea is most certainly present. To be a disciple is automatically to be a member of the *flock* whose shepherd is Jesus. Jesus also uses the concept of the *vine* (15:1–8). A new vine is to replace the old vine (*i.e.* the earthly people of Israel); Jesus himself is the stem, and from him life flows to the branches and enables them to bear fruit.

The life of disciples is characterized by a *love* which follows the example of Jesus, who humbly washed his disciples' feet (13:1–20, 34f.). Such love is in contrast with the attitude of the world which *hates* and *persecutes* the disciples (15:18–16:4, 32f.), and its result is that the church shows that *unity* for which Jesus prays in ch. 17.

But the church is no closed fellowship; others are to come to belief through the word of the disciples (17:20). This is confirmed in ch. 21, where the idea of *mission* or sending (20:21) is developed. The 153 fish are symbolic of the spread of the gospel to all men, and the task of the good shepherd is handed on from the Master to the disciples.

(vii) *Eschatology.* Jesus thus looks forward to the continuing life of the church after his glorification (14:12). In anticipation of his second advent he promises to come to the church (14:18) in the person of the *Spirit*. The Spirit comes to the individual disciple (7:37–39) and to the church (14:16f., 26; 15:26; 16:7–11, 13–15), and his function is to take the place of Jesus (as '*another* Counsellor') and glorify him.

It may thus be said that in John the future is 'realized' in the present; Jesus comes again through the Spirit to his disciples, they already partake of eternal life, and already the process of judgment is at work. Yet it would be wrong to conclude that in John the future activity of God is replaced by his present activity. No less than in the rest of the NT is the future coming of Jesus (14:3; 21:23) and the future judgment of all men (5:25–29) taught.

IV. Textual problems and source criticism

Two passages found in the AV of John do not belong to the original text and have been removed to the margin in modern VSS. These are the *Pericope de Adulteria* (7:53–8:11), a genuine story about Jesus which has been preserved outside the canonical Gospels and found its way into certain late MSS of John, and the explanation of the moving of the water (5:3b–4), which is omitted in the best MSS.

A special problem is raised by ch. 21. While E. C. Hoskyns held that it was an integral part of the original Gospel, the majority of scholars think that it was either a later addition of the author or (less probably) that it was added by another hand. The main argument is that 20:31 reads like the conclusion of a book; some scholars also find stylistic differences between ch. 21 and chs. 1–20, but in the opinion of C. K. Barrett these are not in themselves decisive.

Some scholars (*e.g.* R. Bultmann) believe that the present order of the material in John is not that of the author but has been seriously altered, perhaps by loose sheets of papyrus being combined in the wrong order. There is, however, no objective textual evidence for this, although the phenomenon is not unknown in ancient literature. The displacements found in ch. 18 in certain MSS are clearly secondary, and Tatian (*c.* 170), who made some alterations in order when he was combining the Gospels in a single narrative, does not support modern reconstructions. Most recent commentators find that the Gospel makes good sense as it stands.

Attempts have also been made, most comprehensively by R. Bultmann, to trace the use of written sources and editorial activity in John. While the use of sources is probable, there is little unanimity regarding their extent. It is likely that the Gospel went through several stages of composition, a fact which makes analysis extremely difficult.

V. The background of thought

After a period in which John was regarded as a Hellenistic book, to which the closest parallels were to be found in a strongly Hellenized Judaism, mystery religions and even Greek philosophy, there is at present a rediscovery of the essentially Jewish background of the Gospel.

Much evidence has been found of Aramaic traditions behind the Synoptic Gospels and John (M. Black, *An Aramaic Approach to the Gospels and Acts*[3], 1967). An Aramaic sayings source may lie behind John—Aramaic being, of course, the mother tongue of Jesus. The thought in John is often expressed with the parataxis and parallelism which are well-known features of Semitic writing. All the indications are that the linguistic background of John is Aramaic, although the theory that it was originally written in Aramaic is unconvincing.

This naturally means that the thought of John is likely to be Jewish, which is in fact the case. Although there are comparatively few quotations, most of the key ideas in John are taken from the OT (*e.g.* word, life, light, shepherd, Spirit, bread, vine, love, witness) and Jesus is portrayed as the fulfilment of the OT.

Parallels with contemporary Jewish thought, especially with orthodox rabbinic Judaism, may also be found, it being only natural that Jesus and his followers should often have agreed with the OT scholars of their time and been influenced—both positively and negatively—by them (*cf.* 5:39; 7:42). Since Palestinian Judaism had been subject to Hellenistic influences for about two centuries, there is no need to look wider for Hellenistic influence upon John. The degree of resemblance between ideas found in John and in Philo of Alexandria is variously estimated.

The Jewish sectarian texts from Qumran also help to fill in the background of John, although their importance for the understanding of the NT tends to be exaggerated. Attention is usually drawn to the dualism of light and darkness and to the Messianic hopes found in the texts, but the roots of these ideas lie in the OT, and it is doubtful whether a direct influence from Qumran upon John requires to be postulated. (See F. M. Braun, *RB* 62, 1955, pp. 5–44); J. H. Charlesworth (ed.), *John and Qumran*, 1972).

Other possible formative influences are discussed in detail by C. H. Dodd. He rightly rejects Mandaism, a pagan-Christian syncretism whose earliest literature is considerably later than John. But he devotes considerable attention to Hellenistic mystery religion, especially as depicted in the *Corpus Hermeticum* (*HERMETIC LITERATURE), a series of tracts probably emanating from Egypt in the 3rd century in their present form. But, while there are interesting parallels of thought which demonstrate that John would be intelligible to pagans and not merely to Jews, a close affiliation of thought is unlikely. (*Cf.* G. D. Kilpatrick in *Studies in the Fourth Gospel*, ed. F. L. Cross, 1957.)

In the 2nd century there was a developed Christian *Gnosticism, and we must certainly think of some kind of 'pre-Gnosticism' in the 1st century, reflected in the polemic in Col. and 1 Jn. The theory that John was influenced by the Gnostic heretics whom he opposes (*cf.* **II**, above) was propounded by E. F. Scott (*The Fourth Gospel*[2], 1908, pp. 86–103); more recently than this R. Bultmann and E. Käsemann have argued that in John Jesus is presented in terms of Gnostic myths. The view of C. H. Dodd that Johannine Christianity is entirely different from Gnosticism in spite of a common background (*op. cit.*, p. 114) does much greater justice to facts.

Within the early Christian world the Johannine literature occupies a unique place and represents an independently developed strand of thought. Nevertheless, its teaching is that of the Christian church generally, and the differences from, say, Paul are more of form than of content. (*Cf.* A. M. Hunter, *The Unity of the New Testament*, 1943.)

VI. External attestation

The existence of John's Gospel is attested in Egypt before AD 150 by the Rylands Papyrus 457, the earliest known fragment of a NT MS.

The use of John as an authoritative Gospel alongside the other three is attested by the Egerton Papyrus 2, also dated before 150 (C. H. Dodd, *New Testament Studies*, 1953, pp. 12–52). It was also used by Tatian in his *Diatessaron*, and Irenaeus (*c.* 180) speaks of a four-Gospel canon. John was certainly also known and used in heretical Gnostic circles—*e.g.* by Ptolemaeus, a disciple of Valentinus, by the *Gospel of Peter* (*c.* 150), and (fairly certainly) by the author of the Valentinian *Gospel of Truth.* Knowledge of John by other writers in this period is difficult to attest. There are traces of Johannine language in Ignatius (*c.* 115) and Justin (*c.* 150–160), but it is questionable whether literary dependence is indicated.

Traditions about the authorship of John are given by Irenaeus, who states that John, the disciple of the Lord, gave out the Gospel at Ephesus. This tradition is repeated by Clement of Alexandria (*c.* 200) and the anti-Marcionite prologue to John; the 2nd-century date of the latter is, however, suspect. The Muratorian Canon (*c.* 180–200) gives a legend in which John the apostle is the author, and the apostolic authorship was accepted by Ptolemaeus. But Papias, who had close access to apostolic traditions, is silent on the matter, and Polycarp, who was an associate of John according to Irenaeus, quotes the Epistles but not the Gospel. Nor do the apocryphal *Acts of John* say anything about the Gospel. At the beginning of the 3rd century there was some opposition to the apostolic authorship of John, possibly because of the use made of it by the Gnostics.

VII. Authorship

At the end of the 19th century the view that John the apostle wrote the Fourth Gospel was widely accepted on the basis of the external evidence set out above and the internal evidence. The latter received its classical formulation from B. F. Westcott and from J. B. Lightfoot (*Biblical Essays*, 1893, pp. 1–198), who demonstrated that the Gospel was written by a Jew, by a Palestinian Jew, by an eyewitness of the events recorded, by an apostle, and, in particular, by the apostle John, who is referred to as the 'beloved disciple'.

A number of arguments have been raised against this chain of reasoning. First, there is the theory that *John died as a martyr at an early age, but this is rightly rejected by the majority of scholars.

Second, the alleged geographical and historical inaccuracy of John is held to militate against authorship by an eyewitness. The most recent archaeology has, however, confirmed the geographical accuracy of John in a striking way (*cf.* R. D. Potter, *TU* 73, 1959, pp. 329–337). For the historical problem, see below.

Third, it is alleged that the apostle John was incapable of writing such a Gospel. He was an unlearned man—a view which finds its only and inadequate basis in a questionable exegesis of Acts 4:13 and ignores such analogies as Bunyan, the Bedford tinker. As an apostle he could not have written a Gospel so different from the other three—a view which does not take into account the special purpose of John and the fact that we have no other Gospel directly written by an apostle for comparison. As a Jew he could not have the mastery of Hellenistic thought seen in the Gospel—see, however, V, above. Finally, nobody would presume to call himself the 'beloved disciple'—which is, however, no more than a subjective argument (those who find it weighty can attribute the use of the title to John's scribe).

Fourth, the weightiest argument is the slowness of the church to accept John's Gospel. The reliability of Irenaeus has been called in question (but with uncertain justification), and it has been observed that the people who might be expected to know John and quote from it fail to do so. Against this must be pointed out the general weakness of arguments from silence (*cf.* W. F. Howard, *The Fourth Gospel in Recent Criticism and Interpretation*[4], 1955, p. 273) and the fact that the evidence for the acceptance and use of the other three Gospels is almost equally scanty before the period in which we find all four Gospels accepted together. Further, we are completely ignorant of the circumstances of publication of John except for the brief note in 21:24.

It may be taken as quite certain that we can safely disregard any theory which denies a connection between John the apostle and the Gospel. Three possibilities then arise. First, John may have composed it himself with the aid of an amanuensis. Second, a disciple of John may have used the memoirs of John or a Johannine tradition as the basis for the Gospel. A third possibility, which is a variant of the second, is that there was a Johannine 'school', possibly to be linked with S Palestine, in which the characteristic Johannine theology was developed and whose members produced the Johannine literature. It is, however, difficult to bring forward decisive evidence for or against such a theory. (One may compare K. Stendahl's hypothesis of a Matthean school, the evidence for which is still flimsy.)

It is difficult to decide between these theories. But the tradition that John dictated the Gospel is widespread (*cf.* R. V. G. Tasker, *TNTC*, 1960, pp. 17–20) and bears the marks of genuineness. There are still good grounds for maintaining a close association of John the apostle with the actual writing of the Gospel.

(See also *John, Epistles of.)

VIII. Provenance and date

Early tradition connects John the apostle with Asia Minor and in particular with Ephesus. A connection with Asia Minor is most suitable for 1–3 Jn. and is demanded by Rev.; whether the author of the latter be the Evangelist or an associate of his, this strengthens the case for Asia.

The claims of other places cannot, however, be ignored. The apparent lack of knowledge of John in Asia gives weight to the claims of Alexandria: here John was certainly used very early by the gnostics (*cf.* also the papyri), the climate of thought (Hellenistic Judaism) could be regarded as suitable, and the general remoteness of Alexandria would explain the Gospel's slow circulation. There is, however, no tradition connecting John with Alexandria. The claims of Antioch have also been pressed, but they are hardly strong. Some would connect the Gospel of John with S Palestine in view of its background of thought, but this only confirms that for part of his life the author was resident in Palestine.

John is usually dated in the 90s. This view is based on the assumed dependence of John on the Synoptic Gospels (but see **IX**, below) and the alleged post-Pauline character of its theology. While there is no need to regard John as dependent on Paulinism, it is difficult to avoid the impression that it is not an early writing. If it is connected with Ephesus it must be placed after the activity of Paul there; this is confirmed by the date of 1–3 Jn., which is hardly earlier than the 60s. If John is connected with some other place of composition, *e.g.* Palestine, an earlier date is possible but remains unlikely. The real point of the 'Palestinian background' argument is that the date no longer needs to be put extremely late in order to account for the development of thought. (*Cf.* J. A. T. Robinson, *op. cit.*, pp. 94–106.)

IX. Relation to the Synoptic Gospels

a. Knowledge of the Synoptic tradition

The accepted opinion until about 40 years ago was that John knew the Synoptic Gospels, or at least Mark and Luke, and that he wrote in order to correct, supplement or replace them. Sharp criticism of this view came from P. Gardner-Smith (*St. John and the Synoptic Gospels*, 1938), B. Noack (*Zur Johanneischen Tradition*, 1954) and C. H. Dodd (*Historical Tradition in the Fourth Gospel*, 1963), who argued that John was dependent on the oral tradition behind the Synoptics, and wrote independently of them. The closest contacts are between John and Luke, especially in the passion narrative, but it is doubtful whether these prove literary dependence; Luke may well have had access to the traditions recorded in John or even had personal acquaintance with its author (*cf.* G. W. Broomfield, *John, Peter and the Fourth Gospel*, 1934).

The external evidence must also be taken into account. Papias' information about Mark and the Logia came from [John] 'the elder', who *may* be connected with the composition of the Gospel of John. Clement of Alexandria wrote, 'Last of all, John, perceiving that the external facts had been made plain in the Gospel, being urged by his friends, and inspired by the Spirit, composed a spiritual Gospel.' We can, of course, accept this description of John as the spiritual Gospel without believing that John wrote out of a knowledge of the other Gospels, but it is difficult to believe that he did not have some idea of their contents, even if he did not have copies of them before him as he wrote. The question, then, must be regarded as still open.

b. Comparison of the narratives

Two problems arise here. The first is whether the Synoptic and Johannine narratives are compatible with each other and can be worked into a single account. It is a fact that attempts can be made to fit the two together in a reasonably convincing manner and thus to shed new light on both. (E. Stauffer, *Jesus and His Story*, 1960.) This is possible because the two accounts describe the activity of Jesus at different periods and in different localities; the old-fashioned idea that the Synoptic Gospels leave no room for a ministry in Jerusalem (other than in the passion narrative) is now quite discredited. It must be remembered, of course, that none of the Gospels pretends to give an exact chronological narrative, so that a detailed reconstruction of the order of events is impossible.

The second problem concerns the cases where historical contradictions appear to arise between the Gospels, including cases where it is held that John is consciously correcting data given in the Synoptic Gospels. Examples of this are the reason for Jesus' arrest (in particular, the question why the raising of Lazarus is omitted in the Synoptic narrative; see a possible answer in J. N. Sanders, *NTS* 1, 1954–5, p. 34); the date of the cleansing of the Temple; and the date of the last supper and crucifixion (see N. Geldenhuys, *Commentary on the Gospel of Luke*, 1950, pp. 649–670). The extent of such difficulties can be exaggerated, but it must be admitted that some real problems exist to which answers have yet to be found. In any case the substance of the Gospel records is not affected by these differences.

c. The discourses in John

The teaching ascribed to Jesus in John differs markedly in content and style from that in the Synoptic Gospels. Such familiar ideas as the kingdom of God, demons, repentance and prayer are missing, and new topics appear, such as truth, life, the world, abiding and witness. At the same time there are close and intricate connections between the two traditions, and common themes appear, *e.g.* Father, Son of man, faith, love and sending. The style and vocabulary also differ. There are no parables in John, and Jesus often speaks in long discourses or dialogues which are unparalleled in the Synoptic Gospels.

Many scholars, therefore, believe that John gives us his own thoughts or his own meditations upon the words of Jesus rather than his *ipsissima verba.* This conclusion is strongly supported by the fact that a very similar style and content is found in 1 Jn. Nevertheless, it must be carefully qualified. First of all, the Gospel of John contains many sayings which are similar in form and content to Synoptic sayings (*cf.* B. Noack, *op. cit.*, pp. 89–109; C. H. Dodd, *op. cit.*, pp. 335–349) and which have equal right to be regarded as authentic. Second, there is, on the other hand, at least one famous 'bolt from the Johannine blue' in the Synoptic Gospels (Mt. 11:25–27) which is a standing warning against the facile assumption that the Synoptic Jesus did not speak the language of the Johannine Jesus. Third, the same traces of Aramaic speech and the same conformity to Jewish methods of discussion are to be found in John as in the Synoptic Gospels.

Thus we can say with considerable confidence that the sayings recorded in John have a firm historical basis in the actual words of Jesus. They have, however, been preserved in a Johannine commentary from which they can be separated only with great difficulty. (*Cf.* the problem of Gal. 2:14ff.; where does Paul's speech to Peter end and his meditation upon it begin?) This is no radical conclusion. So conservative a scholar as Westcott saw, for example, the words of John rather than of Jesus in 3:16–21.

X. History and interpretation in John

The purpose of John (see **II**, above) demands that, in broad outline at least, the contents of John be regarded as history; it completely fails of attainment if John gives us a legendary construction devised to substantiate the church's preaching of Jesus as the Messiah instead of the historical facts which lie behind and authenticate that preaching. (See C. F. D. Moule, *The Phenomenon of the NT*, 1967, pp. 100–114.)

It has already been suggested that many of the difficulties commonly raised against the historicity of John are by no means so serious as they are often made out to be. There is in fact a growing tendency to recognize that John contains important historical traditions about Jesus and that an adequate understanding of his earthly life cannot be obtained from the Synoptic Gospels alone (*cf.* T. W. Manson, *BJRL* 30, 1947, pp. 312–329; A. M. Hunter, *According to John*, 1968).

On the other hand, the total impression given by John after a reading of the Synoptic Gospels is that here we have an interpretation of Jesus rather than a strictly literal account of his life. The teaching which he gives is different and the picture of his person is also different, particularly as regards his Messianic and filial self-consciousness. Yet it would be unwise to over-emphasize these differences. Jesus is no less human in John than in the other Gospels, and even the 'Messianic secrecy' of the Synoptic Gospels is not altogether absent from John. F. F. Bruce can go so far as to say that there is no fundamental discrepancy between the Jesus of the Synoptic Gospels and of John (*The New Testament Documents*[5], 1960, pp. 60f.).

What this amounts to is that John does not contradict the other Gospels but interprets the Person who is depicted in them. While the other Evangelists have given us a photograph of Jesus, John has given us a portrait (W. Temple, *op. cit.* below, p. xvi). Consequently, in the light of what has been said, John can be used as a source for the life of Jesus and for John's interpretation of that life, even if it is impossible to separate these two rigidly from each other. The earthly life of Jesus cannot be completely understood in isolation from his revelation of himself as the risen Lord to his church. Under the inspiration of the Spirit (*cf.* 14:26; 16:14) John has brought out the meaning of the earthly life of Jesus; he interprets the story of Jesus, and in doing so he gives us, in the words of A. M. Hunter, 'the true meaning of the earthly story' (*Introducing New Testament Theology*, 1957, p. 129).

BIBLIOGRAPHY. *Commentaries on the English text*: B. F. Westcott, 1882 and later (also on the Gk. text, 1908); E. C. Hoskyns and F. N. Davey, [2]1947; R. V. G. Tasker, *TNTC*, 1960; J. Marsh, *Pelican*, 1968; J. N. Sanders and B. A. Mastin, *BNTC*, 1968 reprinted 1985; R. E. Brown, *AB*, 1971; L. Morris, *NIC/NLC*, 1971; B. Lindars, *NCB*, 1972; F. F. Bruce, 1983; J. A. Michaels, *NIBC*, 1983; D. A. Carson, 1991; *on the Greek text*: J. H. Bernard, *ICC*, 1928; C. K. Barrett, 1955, [2]1978; R. Schnackenburg, 1–3, 1968–82 (vol. 4 only available in Ger., *HTKNT*, 1984); R. Bultmann, 1971; G. R. Beasley-Murray, *WBC*, 1987.

W. F. Howard, *The Fourth Gospel in Recent Criticism and Interpretation*[4], 1955; C. H. Dodd, *The Interpretation of the Fourth Gospel*, 1953; *idem*, *Historical Tradition in the Fourth Gospel*, 1963; J. L. Martyn, *History and Theology in the Fourth Gospel*, 1968; A. M. Hunter, *According to John*, 1968; R. T. Fortna, *The Gospel of Signs*, 1970; C. K. Barrett, *The Gospel of John and Judaism*, 1975; S. S. Smalley, *John: Evangelist and Interpreter*, 1978; J. A. T. Robinson, *The Priority of John*, 1985; G. M. Burge, *The Anointed Community*, 1987; J Ashton, *Understanding the Fourth Gospel*, 1991.

I.H.M.

JOKNEAM, JOKMEAM (Heb. *yoqn'am*, *yoqm'am*). **1.** A Canaanite city (Jos 12:22), no. 113 in the list of Tuthmosis III; modern Tel Yoqneam (Tell Qeimun), 12 km NW of Megiddo. 'The brook east of (*'al p'né*, facing) Jokneam' (Jos. 19:11), which bounded Zebulun, was probably not the Kishon (*GTT*) but a tributary (*LOB*). As a levitical city, Jokneam was in Zebulun (Jos. 21:34), so the boundary may have run S of the Kishon here.

BIBLIOGRAPHY. *GTT*, pp. 306, 350; *LOB*, pp. 152, 257; M. Noth, *Josua*[2] (German), 1953, p. 115; J. Drinkard, *JBL* 98, 1979, pp. 285f.; A. Ben-Tor, *IEJ* 33, 1983, pp. 30–54; *NEAEHL*, pp. 805–811.

2. A levitical city in Ephraim (1 Ch. 6:68, perhaps Kibzaim, Jos. 21:22); in the Jordan valley, 1 Ki. 4.12, but Noth and Gray regard this as Jokneam (1). Perhaps Tell el-Mazar (B. Mazar, *VT Supp.* 7, 1960, p. 198; *LOB*, p. 313). J.P.U.L.

JOKSHAN. A son of Abraham and Keturah, and father of Sheba and Dedan (Gn. 25:2–3; 1 Ch. 1:32). The name is sometimes assumed to be another form of *Joktan (Gn. 10:25–29; 1 Ch.1:19–23), but bearers of these names are kept distinct in the genealogical lists. R.J.W.

JOKTAN. A son of Eber of the family of Shem, and father of Almodad, Sheleph, Hazarmaveth, Jerah, Hadoram, Uzal, Diklah, Obal, Abimael, Sheba, Ophir, Havilah and Jobab (Gn. 10:25–26, 29; 1 Ch. 1:19–20, 23), many of whom have been connected with tribes in S Arabia. The name is unknown outside the Bible, but on the basis of the descendants a region of occupation in S or SW Arabia may be postulated. The modern tribes of S Arabia claim that the pure Arabs are descended from Joktan.

BIBLIOGRAPHY. J. A. Montgomery, *Arabia and the Bible*, 1934, pp. 37–42; W. Thesiger, *Arabian Sands*, 1960, p. 77. T.C.M.

JONAH. Hebrew personal name, meaning 'dove'. The NT form of the name in AV is normally Jonas, twice Jona. **1.** A Heb. prophet of the reign of Jeroboam II of Israel, in the 8th century BC. He came from Gath-hepher, a Zebulunite town, located in the vicinity of Nazareth. His father's name was Amittai. He predicted the territorial expansion achieved by Jeroboam at the expense of Syria (2 Ki. 14:25). This Jonah is also the hero of the book that bears his name, the fifth of the twelve Minor Prophets. The book differs considerably from the other OT Prophets in that it is almost entirely narrative and contains no long prophetic oracles. (See the following article.)

2. The father of Simon Peter, according to Mt. 16:17. Some MSS of Jn. 1:42; 21:15ff. also call him Jonah (*cf.* AV rendering), but the best attested reading here is 'John'. D.F.P.

JONAH, BOOK OF.

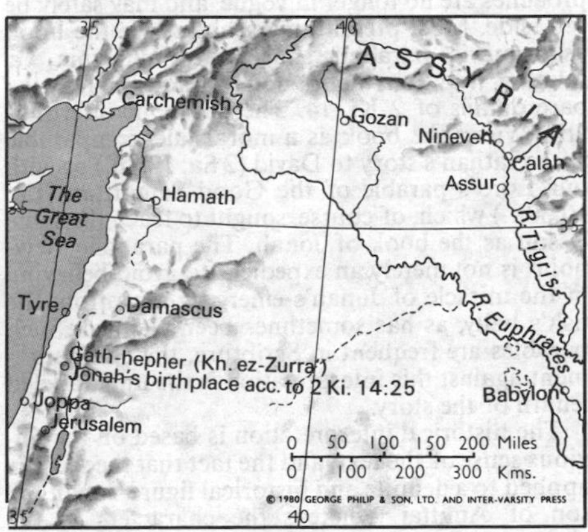

Map showing the area covered by the mission of Jonah.

I. Outline of contents

The book is divided into four chapters, which neatly divide the subject-matter. The first chapter relates that Jonah, bidden by God to go to Nineveh and protest against its wickedness, rebelled and took ship in the opposite direction. A storm arose, and the sailors eventually threw Jonah overboard, at his own suggestion. A great fish then swallowed the prophet. Ch. 2 gives the text of his prayer, or rather psalm of thanksgiving, from the fish's belly. The fish presently disgorged Jonah on to the shore. Ch. 3 shows Jonah going to Nineveh, after all. His preaching of doom led the citizens to repent of their evil ways. In ch. 4 we find Jonah angry at their repentance and subsequent escape from destruction; whereupon God, by inducing Jonah's pity on a plant, taught him that he must have compassion for all men.

II. Authorship and date

The book gives no indication who its author was. Jonah himself may have written it, but the book nowhere uses the first person (contrast, for example, Ho. 3:1); and the probability of a date later than the 8th century is indicated by the implication of Jon. 3:3 that Nineveh was no more (it was destroyed in 612 BC). If Jonah was not the author, nobody can say who did write it. The date of writing, then, may have been in the 8th century, but was more probably not earlier than the 6th century. The twelve Minor Prophets were known and venerated by the end of the 3rd century (*cf.* Ecclus. 40:10), so a 3rd-century date for the book is the latest it can possibly be allowed. The universalistic emphasis of the book is frequently considered to be a protest against the ultra-nationalistic spirit of the Jews after the time of Ezra; however, universalistic passages occur as early as the 8th century (*cf.* Is. 2:2ff.). Various features of the Heb. of Jonah constitute the strongest argument for post-exilic date; but the brevity of the book permits no certainty. (See also D. W. B. Robinson in *NBCR* on this issue.)

III. Interpretations

The nature of the book is a very controversial topic. It has been variously explained as mythology, allegory, commentary (or Midrash), parable and history. The mythological and allegorical approaches are no longer in vogue, and may safely be set aside. Most present-day scholars see the book as primarily parabolic, but partly midrashic, *i.e.* relating traditions about Jonah additional to the bare details of 2 Ki. 14. The parabolic interpretation views the book as a moral tale, comparable with Nathan's story to David (2 Sa. 12:1ff.) or with our Lord's parable of the Good Samaritan (Lk. 10:30ff.) which, of course, sought to teach the same lesson as the book of Jonah. The parabolic viewpoint is not merely an expedient to avoid believing in the miracle of Jonah's emerging alive from the fish's belly, as has sometimes been claimed. Such parables are frequent in Scripture; the chief argument against this interpretation is the unparalleled length of the story.

The historical interpretation is based on the obvious sense of the text, and the fact that the story is applied to a definite and historical figure, Jonah the son of Amittai (whereas the characters in the above-mentioned parables are anonymous). Certainly Jewish tradition accepted the book as history, and our Lord's references to it (Mt. 12; Lk. 11) probably, though not necessarily, imply that he did so too. The historical interpretation is, however, challenged on several points, notably the miracle of the fish, the vast size attributed to Nineveh, the statement that its king and citizens not only listened to a Heb. prophet but without hesitation or exception repented, and lastly, the unnaturally fast rate of growth of the gourd. However, it may be that the first was a genuine miracle; in any case the story may have modern parallels (see A. J. Wilson). The growth of the gourd might again be miraculous; or, more simply, one can claim that Jon. 4:10 is not intended to be strictly literal. As for the size of Nineveh (Jon. 3:3), it is possible that the author intended a much bigger area than the city itself; confirmation of this may be seen in the fact that he refers to a 'king of Nineveh' (3:6), whereas other OT writers speak of kings of Assyria, of which country Nineveh was the last capital. (But see *NINEVEH.) It can also be asserted that in the low fortunes of Assyria prior to the accession of Tiglath-pileser III (745 BC) the Ninevites would readily have listened to a prophet who forecast disaster unless they repented. Theirs was a polytheistic religion, so they might well have sought to avoid offending even a foreign unknown deity.

It is fair to say that none of the objections to the historical interpretation is insuperable. The same might be said about the parabolic interpretation. The choice seems to rest, therefore, between these two.

IV. Purpose

It is generally agreed that the purpose of Jonah is didactic; it ends with a challenging question (*cf.* Lk. 10:36). It is disputed whether the intention was a protest against a narrow, exclusivistic Judaism; a challenge to missionary endeavour; or an explanation for the apparent non-fulfilment of earlier prophetic oracles against foreign nations. Without knowing the exact circumstances in which the book was issued, we cannot easily decide the question; in any case, these possibilities are not mutually exclusive. The book undeniably stresses the universal powers of God, over individuals and nations east and west, and over life and death; and also the universal mercy and love of God, towards disobedient Jews and cruel Gentiles alike.

V. Composition

The book is widely accepted as a unity, apart from the psalm (2:2–9), which many scholars have held to be an interpolation. The present trend may be towards its acceptance, however (*cf.* Kaiser, *IOT*, p. 196). The psalm is not so inapposite as has often been claimed; Jonah had been rescued from a watery grave—even if he had yet to be released from the fish's belly—and the use of traditional language depicting death in marine metaphors is therefore remarkably fitting. At the same time, it is noteworthy that the more usual frame of reference of such a psalm lays the basis for the NT interpretation of its significance (*cf.* Mt. 12:39ff.).

BIBLIOGRAPHY. A. J. Wilson, *PTR* 25, 1927, pp. 636ff.; G. Ch. Aalders, *The Problem of the Book of Jonah*, 1948; L. C. Allen, *The Books of Joel, Obadiah, Jonah and Micah*, *NICOT*, 1976, pp. 173–235; D. W. B. Robinson, in *NBCR*; F. D. Kidner, 'The Distribution of Divine Names in Jonah', *TynB* 21, 1970, pp. 126ff.; J. Magonet, *Form and Meaning . . . in . . . Jonah*, 1983; D. Stuart, *Hosea-Jonah*, *WBC*, 1987; T. D. Alexander in D. W. Baker, *et al.*, *Obadiah, Jonah and Micah*, *TOTC*, 1988; and entries in standard dictionaries and introductions.

D.F.P.

JONATHAN (Heb *yᵉhônāṯān* or *yônāṯān*, 'Yahweh has given').

1. Son of Gershom, descendant of Moses (AV 'Manasseh'). He was hired by Micah to officiate as priest before an idol in Ephraim, then became priest and progenitor of a line of priests to the Danites 'until the day of the captivity of the land' (Jdg. 17; 18:30–31).

2. Eldest son of King Saul by his only wife (1 Sa. 14:49–50), he was his father's heir, which makes his loyalty and affection for David, who succeeded Saul, the more wonderful (1 Sa. 20:31). Jonathan first appears in the biblical record as the victor at Geba, a Philistine stronghold, though his father's strategy at that time suggests by analogy that he may have taken part in the relief of Jabesh-gilead (1 Sa. 11:11; 13:2). His prowess and courage as a warrior, recalled in David's elegy (2 Sa. 1:22), are clearly seen in his lone attack on another Philistine garrison, an incident which also shows his ability to inspire loyalty as well as to offer it (1 Sa. 14:7). It is for his own loyalty to David, however, that he is chiefly remembered; a loyalty made more difficult because it conflicted with his filial duty to and affection for Saul, his father and sovereign. As the king, deserted by the Spirit of God and a victim to increasing fears and passions, showed ever greater hatred to 'the man after God's own heart' who was to succeed him, so Jonathan, in fealty to the brotherhood pact sworn with David after the death of Goliath (1 Sa. 18:1–4), was driven into defiance and deception of his father, even to the jeopardizing of his own life (1 Sa. 19:1–7; 20). The parting scene between the two friends is most moving. It does not appear that Jonathan accompanied his father on the two expeditions against David, to En-gedi and Hachilah, and he disappears finally in the tragic Philistine victory at Mt Gilboa, along with his father and brothers (1 Sa. 31:2). Gifted physically and morally, he is a model to those of a more favoured dispensation of loyalty to truth and friendship, as well as of that peacemaking which is the role of the sons of God.

3. Others who bore this name are an uncle of David, a counsellor and scribe, perhaps to be identified with the nephew of David who slew a giant (1 Ch. 27:32; 2 Sa. 21:21–22); a son of the high priest Abiathar, who was involved in the attempts on David's throne by Absalom and Adonijah, though not as a rebel (2 Sa. 15:36; 17:15–22; 1 Ki. 1:41–49); one of David's 'mighty men' (2 Sa. 23:32; 1 Ch. 11:34); a son of Kareah associated with Gedaliah during the domination of Jerusalem by Nebuchadrezzar (Je. 40:8); and a scribe in whose house Jeremiah was imprisoned (Je. 37:20). The same name occurs at the time of the restoration (Ezr. 8:6; 10:15; Ne. 12:11, 14, 35). T.H.J.

JOPPA. The ancient seaport, now part of Tel Aviv-Jaffa (Heb. *yāfō*), was the only major harbour between Acco (Haifa) and the Egypt. border (see also *DOR, *CAESAREA). It served Jerusalem 50 km away. Tuthmosis III captured it by stratagem in the 15th century BC, and after the entry of the Israelites it marked the border of Dan's territory (Jos. 19:46). Liberated from Philistine control by David, it was used as a port to bring in Lebanon cedars sent by Hiram for Solomon's temple (2 Ch. 2:15, 16) and by Cyrus for the second temple (Ezr. 3:7). Jonah embarked here for Tarshish (1:3). Sennacherib captured the town in 701 BC. It was given to the Sidonians under Eshmunazzar and they occupied the port until it was colonized by the Gks. Under the Hasmoneans it became part of Judaea until destroyed by Vespasian in AD 67. Peter stayed in Simon the tanner's house (Acts 9:43) and had the vision of God embracing Jew and Gentile (Acts 10:5, 11f.). Excavation shows occupation from the 17th century BC onwards. A pre-Philistine temple of the 13th century shows the existence of a lion cult and also wooden columns on stone bases to support the ceiling (*cf.* Jdg. 16:25–27).

BIBLIOGRAPHY. J. and H. Kaplan, *NEAEHL*, 1992, pp. 655–659. D.F.P.
D.J.W.

JORDAN. The Jordan depression is unique among the features of physical geography. Formed as a result of a rift valley, it is the lowest depression on earth. The headwaters of the river Jordan, fed by springs, collect into Lake Huleh, 70 m above sea-level. Ten km S at Lake Tiberias the river is already nearly 200 m below the Mediterranean, while at the N end of the Dead Sea the floor of the trench has dropped a further 177 m and the river has plunged to 393 m below sea-level. Thus the name 'Jordan' (Heb. *yardēn*) aptly means 'the descender'. The river is the largest perennial course in Palestine, and its distance of some 120 km from Lake Huleh to the Dead Sea is more than doubled by its meander. No other river has more biblical allusions and significance.

I. Archaeological sites

Archaeological sites in the Jordan valley have revealed it to be one of the earliest loci of urban settlement in the world. The Natufian transition from hunting to urban life at Jericho may be as old as 7000 BC. A pottery-making people arrived about 5000 BC, and with the later pottery (Neolithic B culture) the first evidence occurs of links with other Jordan valley sites and the N Fertile Crescent. Copper was introduced in the Chalcolithic period (4500–3200 BC), such as at Teleilat Ghassul, just N of the Dead Sea. At Ghassul, three city levels existed from the 4th millennium onwards, with evidence of irrigation farming. This Ghassulian culture is identified widely in Palestine, but it was especially prevalent in the Jordan valley, at Mefjar, Abu Habil, Jiftlik Beth-shan, En-gedi and Tell esh-Shuneh, S of the Sea of Galilee.

At the end of the 4th millennium at least three groups of peoples entered the Jordan valley from the N, to settle in unwalled villages in the plains of Esdraelon, or from the E via Jericho. This period K. M. Kenyon has called proto-urban. City-states then began to appear in the Jordan valley, such as Jericho in the S, Beth-shan in the centre and Beth-yerah (Khirbet Kerak) in the N, and these traded with Egypt and Mesopotamia.

About 2200 BC Amorite nomads invaded the valley and destroyed many of the urban centres. They may have been part of a vast general eruption of peoples that went on from 2300 to 1900 BC, that is, to the beginning of the Middle Bronze Age. Abraham may have come into the Jordan valley in association with this period of nomadic unrest. This was followed by the N invasion of the Hyksos culture, when elaborate urban defences in depth were built at such towns as Jericho. Following the defeat of the Hyksos by the Egyptians, the great fortress towns of the Jordan valley, such as Beth-shan and Hazor, were rebuilt and equipped with Egyptian garrisons. Then later in the Bronze Age, at least by 1220 BC, the Israelites entered Palestine through the Jordan valley. There is evidence of the destruction of the cities of Hazor, Debir and Lachish. But the archaeological evidence for Joshua's capture of Jericho is obscure.

II. Topographical features

a. The Huleh basin

The Jordan valley begins below Mt Hermon (2,814

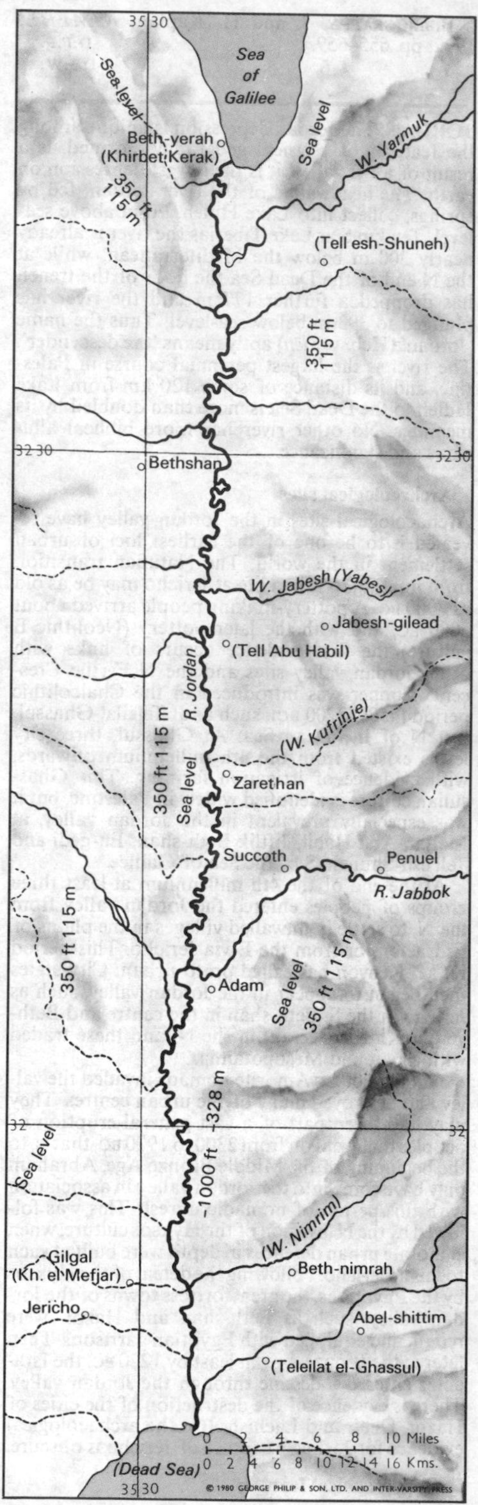

The Jordan valley in OT times

m) out of whose limestone springs issue the headwaters of the Jordan. Banias, later called Caesarea Philippi, may have been the centre of Baal-gad in the valley 'of Lebanon' (Jos. 12:7). It was the territory of Dan, the N limit of Israel, whose inhabitants controlled the vital trade route into Syria and were likened to a nest of vipers (Gn. 49:17). Moving down the upper valley is the Huleh area, a depression some 5 × 15 km, where ancient lava flows blocked the valley, so that the Jordan plunges 280 m in 15 km of gorges. On the plateau overlooking the Huleh plain stands the site of Hazor, the great Canaanite town.

b. The Tiberias district

Beyond the Huleh gorges, at about 213 m below sea-level, the Jordan enters the Sea of Galilee, a harp-shaped lake, 21 km long, and about 13 km across. Fed by numerous thermal springs, its fresh waters are well stocked with fish, the maximum depth of 50 km permitting vertical migrations of the fish with the seasonal temperatures. It was, therefore, probably in the hot summer season when the normal winter temperature of 13° C. lies 37 m below the surface of the lake, that Jesus advised the fishermen to 'cast into the deep' (Lk. 5:4). The methods of catching *fish referred to in the Gospels are still practised: the single-hook line (Mt. 17:27); the circular fishing net (Mt. 4:18; Mk. 1:16); the draw-net cast out by a boat (Mt. 13:47f.); deep-sea nets (Mt. 4:18f.; Mk. 1:19f.); and deep-sea fishing undertaken with two boats (Lk. 5:10).

A dense population clustered round the lake in our Lord's day, and it was the sophisticated city folk of Chorazin, Bethsaida and Capernaum that he condemned (Mt. 11:20–24). 'There is no spot in the whole of Palestine where memories heap themselves up to such an extent as in Capernaum' (G. Dalman). Jewish life throbbed in its synagogues (Mt. 12:9; Mk. 1:21; 3:1; 5:22; Lk. 4:31; 6:6; 8:41). There lived Jairus, the chief of the synagogue (Mk. 5:22), the centurion who built a synagogue (Lk. 7:5) and Levi the customs official (Mt. 9:9; Mk. 2:14; Lk. 5:27). E of Capernaum was Bethsaida from which Philip, Andrew and Peter came (Jn. 1:44), and beyond that the less populous district of the Gadarenes, where the heathen reared their pigs (Lk. 8:32). The lake, plains and steep rocky slopes, interspersed with boulders and thistle-fields, provide the setting for the parable of the sower (Mk. 4:2–8), while in spring the flowered carpets of asphodels, anemones and irises are also telling sermons.

Dominating this lake environment are the surrounding mountains, especially those of the NW, which played so vital a part in the prayer-life of our Lord, where he taught his disciples (Mt. 5:1) and from which he appeared as the risen Lord (Mt. 28:16). The NE corner of the lake is supposedly the scene of the miracle of the feeding of the five thousand (Lk. 9:10–17).

c. The 'Ghor' or Jordan valley

This runs for over 105 km between Lake Tiberias and the Dead Sea. The Yarmuk, entering the left bank of the Jordan 8 km downstream from the lake, doubles the volume of flow, and the valley is progressively deepened to as much as 50 m below the floor of the trough. In this sector, three physical zones are distinguishable: the broad upper terrace of the Pliocene trough, the Ghor proper; the

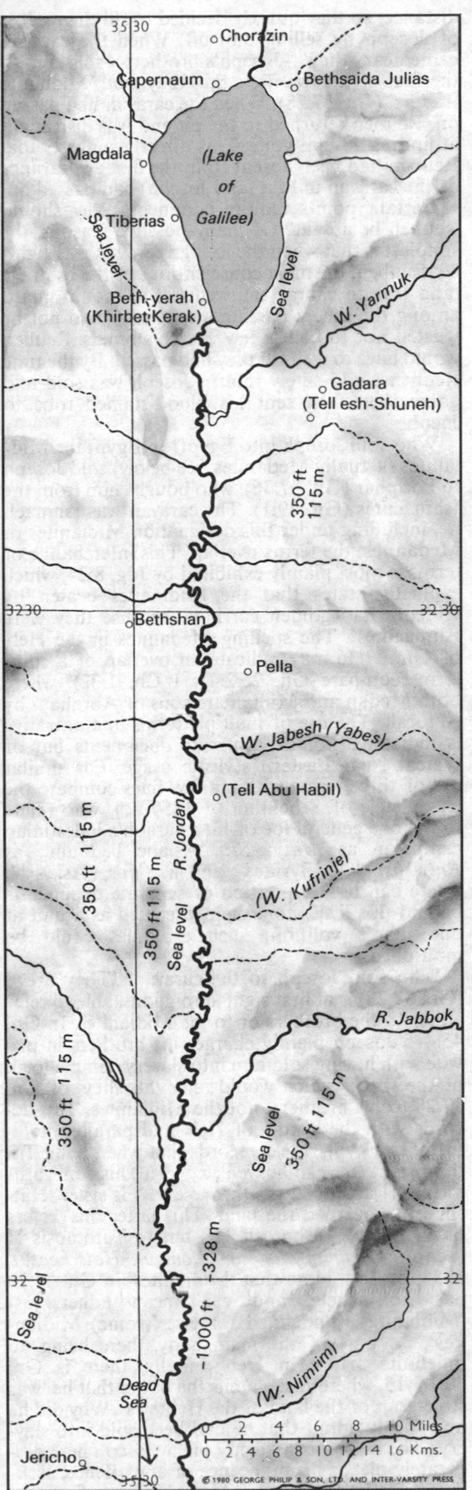

The Jordan valley in NT times.

lower Quaternary terrace and the flood plain of the river, the Zor; and between them the deeply dissected slopes and badlands of the Qattara. It is the Qattara and the Zor together, rather than the river Jordan, which have created the frontier character of this obstacle (Jos. 22:25). The N half of the Ghor is a broad, well-cultivated tract, but the Judaean–Gilead dome, crossing the trough, narrows the valley S of Gilead. Beyond it, the trough becomes increasingly more arid, until at the head of the Dead Sea there is scarcely more than 5 cm mean annual rainfall. The Qattara badlands, carved grotesquely in soft marls and clays, create a steep, desolate descent to the valley floor. The Zor, making its way in vivid green vegetation cover, stands out in sharp contrast below, hence its name *gā'ôn* ('luxuriant growth') of Jordan (Je. 12:5; 49:19; 50:44; Zc. 11:3; *cf.* Pss. 47:4; 59:12; Pr. 16:18). The haunt of wild animals (Je. 49:19), it is partly flooded in spring (Jos. 3:15). Thus the question can be understood, 'And if in a safe land you fall down, how will you do in the jungle of the Jordan?' (Je. 12:5).

Between the Yarmuk in the N and the Jabbok are nine other perennial streams entering the left bank of the Jordan, and their water-supply explains why all the important settlements were located on the E side of the Ghor, towns such as Succoth, Zaphon, Zaretan, Jabesh-gilead and Pella. With the aid of irrigation, this was probably the view Lot saw 'like the garden of the Lord' (Gn. 13:10). The brook Cherith may well have been a seasonal tributary of the Jabesh farther N, where Elijah, a native of Jabesh-gilead, hid himself from Ahab (1 Ki. 17:1–7). Between Succoth and Zarthan (identified by Glueck as Tell es-Saidiyeh) Solomon had his copper cast in earthen moulds, using local clay and fuel (1 Ki. 7:46; 2 Ch. 4:17). In this section of the valley, there are a number of fords, though the river was not bridged until Roman times. Near the mouth of the Jabbok, both Abraham and Jacob crossed it (Gn. 32:10). Somewhere here, the Midianites crossed pursued by Gideon (Jdg. 7:24; 8:4–5). Twice David crossed it in the rebellion of Absalom (2 Sa. 17:22–24; 19:15–18). But between the Jabbok confluence and the Dead Sea, crossings are more difficult, owing to the swift current. The miraculous crossing of the Israelites appears to have taken place at Adam (modern Tell Dâmiyeh), 26 km N of Jericho (Jos. 3:1–17; 4:1–24; Ps. 114:3, 5).

Between the Jabbok and Beth-nimrah for 26 km (Is. 15:6) there are no streams entering the Jordan, and little settlement. Oasis towns occur near springs, such as Jericho W of the Jordan, and in the plains of Moab (Nu. 20:1) to the E was Shittim, where the spies were sent (Jos. 2:1–7).

BIBLIOGRAPHY. D. Baly, *The Geography of the Bible*[2], 1974; G. Dalman, *Sacred Sites and Ways*, trans. by P. P. Levertoff, 1935; J. and J. B. E. Garstang, *The Story of Jericho*, 1948; N. Glueck, *The River Jordan*, 1946; K. M. Kenyon, *Jericho I*, 1960; E. B. Smick, *Archaeology of the Jordan Valley*, 1973.

J.M.H.

JOSEPH.

1. In the Old Testament

I. Name

Joseph is a jussive form of the verb *yāsap̄*, 'to add'; the name *yôsēp̄* means 'may he (God) add (sons)';

cf. Gn. 30:24. A Palestinian place-name *yšp-ir* (*i.e. y-š-p-'El*) in Egyp. topographical lists of the 15th and 14th centuries BC has been compared with Heb. *yôsēp̄*. But the 's'-sounds are different and the two names are almost certainly not related (so W. F. Albright, *JPOS* 8, 1928, p, 249). For the Egyp. *y-š-pEl*, compare biblical place-names such as Iphtahel (Jos. 19:14, 27).

II. History

a. Background

Joseph was the eleventh son of Jacob, his first by Rachel (Gn. 30:24; 35:24), and his favourite son (Gn. 37:3; *cf.* 33:2, 7). The story of Joseph is one of the most graphic and attractive in the OT: a spoilt boy sold into Egyp. slavery by jealous brothers, who makes good in adversity, and from an unjust imprisonment rises to the highest offices of state. By wise planning he averts the scourge of famine, thereby saving Egypt, Canaan and his own family from starvation. Reconciliation with his brothers follows and the family settles in the pastures of Goshen in the NE Delta. After burying Jacob in Canaan, Joseph commands that his bones too should be carried there when Israel's descendants eventually leave Egypt for the land of promise. The story as told in Genesis cannot be bettered; the following paragraphs will therefore merely present some Egyp. and related background material and deal with some textual points.

b. Date

The most likely date for Joseph is the period of the Hyksos pharaohs, *c.* 1720–1550 BC (*CHRONOLOGY OF THE OLD TESTAMENT). These were Semitic rulers who had infiltrated from Canaan, but scrupulously observed Egyp. conventions. At first they took over the existing Egyp. bureaucratic administration, but later appointed naturalized Semites to high office. For the historical background, see *EGYPT: History.

c. The 'coat of many colours'

Jacob's partiality for Joseph was marked by the 'coat of many colours' (AV, RV) or 'long robe with sleeves' (*cf.* RVmg., RSV). Archaeologically either rendering of the Heb. *k^e^tōneṯ passîm* is possible. For Semites in multicoloured garb, see *IBA*, p. 29, fig. 25, right, or in colour, E. W. Heaton, *Everyday Life in Old Testament Times*, 1956, dust-jacket; later examples in *IBA*, p. 35, fig. 29, or *ANEP*, p. 17, fig. 52. These same garments, especially the last cited examples, are also often long and sleeved. In favour of the meaning 'varicoloured', *passîm* has been compared with Assyr. *paspasu*, 'brightly coloured bird' and Arabic *fasafisa*, 'mosaic' (Eisler, *Orientalistische Literaturzeitung* 11, 1908, pp. 368–371, and *cf. ibid.*, 14, 1911, p. 509). The rendering 'long robe with sleeves' is attained by taking *pas* as flat of hand or foot, hence *k^e^tōneṯ passîm* is a 'tunic of (= reaching to) palms and soles' (*BDB*, p. 821a). On dreams, see below.

d. Joseph sold into Egypt

The text records that, when Joseph was sent to visit his brothers pasturing the flocks, they at first planned to kill him, but instead put him in a cistern at the suggestion of the more scrupulous Reuben, who secretly hoped to rescue him. After the brothers had sat down to a meal, a caravan of Ishmaelite merchants from Gilead appeared in the distance; so they quickly decided to rid themselves of Joseph by selling him off. When the caravan came near, 'they'—Joseph's brothers—sold him to the first of the travellers that they met: 'Midianite traders' (Gn. 37:28). When the caravan had passed on, Reuben returned to the pit and was distraught at finding Joseph gone. This directly suggests that Reuben had been absent from the first appearance of the caravan until it (and Joseph) had passed on.

Certain points require comment. Why should Reuben be absent? Of many possible reasons, the simplest is that when the foreign caravan was sighted, Reuben, the most conscientious of the brothers (and true to character), went off to mount guard among the sheep: passing foreigners could not be trusted not to filch a few choice animals. Reuben would have to wait till they had passed. By the time Reuben could safely return, Joseph was sold and gone; they then sent his blood-stained robe to Jacob.

Who sold Joseph into Egypt? In Egypt the Midianites (actually Medanites, see below) sold Joseph to Potiphar (Gn. 37:36), who bought him from the Ishmaelites (Gn. 39:1). The caravan was Ishmaelite, including under this designation Midianites or Medanites; the terms overlap. This interchange of terms is most plainly exhibited by Jdg. 8:24, which explicitly states that the Midianites beaten by Gideon 'had golden earrings, because they were Ishmaelites'. The spelling Medanites in the Heb. of Gn. 37:36 may indicate an overlap of a third term; compare Gn. 25:2 (= 1 Ch. 1:32), where both Medan and Midian are sons of Abraham by Keturah. The use of multiple terms in a narrative is indicative not of disparate documents but of typical Near Eastern stylistic usage. For similar use of three terms within a few lines compare the Egyp. stele of Sebekkhu (*c.* 1850 BC), who refers to the one general foe of his pharaoh's Palestinian campaign as *Mntyw-Stt*, 'Asiatic bedouin'; as *Rntw ẖst*, 'vile Syrians'; and as *''mw*, 'Asiatics'. There can be no question of separate documents behind this little stone stele, executed as a unit at one man's volition; such examples could be multiplied.

Who sold Joseph to the caravan? 'They drew' (Gn. 37:28) is at first sight ambiguous, able to refer either to the brothers or to the Midianites. In Gn. 45:4–5 Joseph plainly charges his brothers in private with having sold him into slavery (simple form of the verb), which would refer the 'they' of Gn. 37:28 to his brothers, not the Midianites. This accords with the syntax of Heb. and parallel literatures. In Egypt, a text records that when King Tuthmosis II 'flew to heaven', *i.e.* died, his son Tuthmosis III ascended the throne and 'his sister' Hatshepsut governed the land. This latter 'his' refers back, not to Tuthmosis III, but to Tuthmosis II (Schott, *Krönungstag d. Königin Hatschepsut*, 1955, p. 197). Note that 'Midianites' in Gn. 37:28 has no article, and can mean either just 'Midianites' (undefined) or else '(some) Midianites', *i.e.* part of the main body, there being no indefinite article in Heb. Finally, there is Gn. 40:14–15, where Joseph tells the butler that he 'was stolen out of the land of the Hebrews'. Why did he not openly admit that he had been sold into slavery? The reason is perfectly plain. Joseph here desperately pleads his innocence of any offence, seeking to persuade the butler to get him out of prison; it would have wrecked his plea to have revealed the humiliating fact that he had been sold into slavery by his own blood brothers. With his brothers in private (Gn. 45) Joseph could be frank; but the butler would be bound to think they had had some good reason to rid themselves of him, and Joseph's appeal would be in vain. Joseph therefore said vaguely that he was 'stolen', which was true in so far as his brothers had no right to sell him for gain. This is not a question of harmonization at any price, but of common sense and practical psychology. The truth is that Gn. 37; 39–40; 45 read plainly when put in their proper setting of exact exegesis, Heb. and other Near Eastern syntax and literary usage, and the motivated actions of individuals.

e. Joseph in Egypt

Joseph was but one of many young Semites who became servants in Egyp. households between 1900 and 1600 BC. Papyrus Brooklyn 35.1446, part of a prison-register (see below), bears on its reverse a list of 79 servants in an Egyp. household *c.* 1740 BC, of whom at least 45 were not Egyptians but 'Asiatics', *i.e.* Semites like Joseph. Many of these have good NW Semitic names linguistically related to those of Jacob, Issachar, Asher, Job (Ayyabum) and Menahem. Some were 'domestics' (*hry-pr*) just like Joseph in Gn. 39:2 ('in the house'). See Hayes, *A Papyrus of the Late Middle Kingdom*, 1955, and Albright, *JAOS* 74, 1954, pp. 222–233.

There are ample scattered indications of numbers of Asiatics in Egypt at this period, some of whom reached high and trusted positions under their masters (Posener, *Syria* 34, 1957, pp. 145–163), rather like Joseph, who became Potiphar's steward (*imy-r pr*, a common Egyp. title). Potiphar's title (*śar-haṭṭabbāḥim*) 'captain of the guard', *i.e.* of Pharaoh's bodyguard, would render the Egyp. *sḥḏ-šmsw*, 'Instructor of Retainers'. However, Vergote (*Joseph en Égypte*, 1959, pp. 31–35) has put up a plausible case for interpreting his title as actually 'butler'. For the Egyp. original of Potiphar's name, see *POTIPHAR, *POTIPHERA. Both Potiphar and the 'butler' and 'baker' of Gn. 40 are termed *sārîs*, usually rendered 'officer', but in Semitic it often means 'eunuch'. However, eunuchs are not prominent in Egypt, and *sārîs* in early times meant generally 'courtier, dignitary' as much as 'eunuch' (though this was the main meaning later). See *JEA* 47, 1961, p. 160.

The incident of Potiphar's covetous wife, who turned the tables on Joseph by asserting the opposite of the truth, is often compared with a very similar incident in the Egyp. *Tales of Two Brothers.* However, there is no other point of contact at all between these two narratives: Joseph's is pure biography, while everything else in the *Two Brothers* is pure fantasy. For a full translation see, *e.g.*, Erman-Blackman, *Literature of the Ancient Egyptians*, 1927, pp. 150–161, as the extracts in *ANET*, pp. 23–25, are abbreviated. More prosaic Egyp. documents reveal that Potiphar's wife was not unique in her sin.

Egyp. prisons served a threefold purpose: as local lock-ups like modern prisons, as forced-labour reserves for state corvée and as centres for remanded prisoners awaiting trial (*cf.* Joseph). Trials were sometimes conducted in the prisons, whose administration was highly organized, as the Papyrus Brooklyn (Hayes, *op cit.*) vividly shows; each prisoner's record was filed under seven

Joseph was invested with high office by Pharaoh in the traditional Egyptian manner (Gn. 41:42). The ceremony is illustrated by the investiture of Paser as vizier of Sethos I. Drawing after a carving in the tomb of Paser, Thebes, c. 1300 BC.

separate headings, from initial arrest to completion of the sentence. The 'keeper of the prison' (Gn. 39:21–23, *etc.*) probably represents the Egyp. title *s'wty n ḫnrt* which has the same meaning.

The 'butler' of Gn. 40 should be rendered *'cup-bearer', Heb. *mašqeh* being the exact equivalent of Egyp. *wdpw*, later *wb'*, 'cup-bearer' (*cf.* Gn. 40:11, 13). Bakers, too, are well known in Egypt, but chief bakers apparently were not explicitly so called. Perhaps the Egyp. title *sš wdḥw nsw*, 'Royal Table-scribe', is the nearest equivalent. For bread-baskets carried on the head, see *IBA*, p. 33, fig. 28. *Dreams (Gn. 37; 40–41) were considered important also in the non-biblical East. The 'magicians of Egypt' (*ḥarṭummîm*, an Egyp. word) were familiar figures, and special manuals were used for interpreting dreams. For details, see under *MAGIC AND SORCERY, **2. II.**

Joseph had to be properly shaved and robed in linen to appear at court (Gn. 41:14). His practical approach to the threat of famine impressed the pharaoh, who invested him with high office in traditional Egyp. manner, bestowing signet, fine linen and gold necklace. Joseph's exact rank is disputed; it seems most probable that he was actually vizier, second only to the pharaoh (so Vergote); but some would make him a minister for agriculture directly responsible to the king in person (Ward, *JSS* 5, 1960, pp. 144–150). The mention of chariots (Gn. 41:43) and horses (Gn. 47:17) fits the Hyksos period and decades immediately preceding, but not earlier. Remains of horses from the period just before the Hyksos have been excavated near Wadi Halfa (Faulkner, *JEA* 45, 1959, pp. 1–2). For the Egyp. names of Joseph and his wife, see *ZAPHENATH-PANEAH and *ASENATH.

Egypt was famed for her great agricultural wealth; *cf.* reckoning of grain, *IBA*, p. 32, fig. 27. But Egypt also suffered periodic famines; one oft-quoted biographical text reads: 'When famine came for many years, I gave grain to my town in each famine' (Vandier, *La Famine dans l'Égypte ancienne*, 1936, p. 115). The Egyptians would not eat with the Hebrews (Gn. 43:32) for fear of transgressing various ritual taboos on food (Montet, *L'Égypte et la Bible*, 1959, pp. 99–101). It is possible that Gn. 44:5 on divination should be rendered 'is it not from this (= the silver cup) that my lord drinks and *concerning* which he will assuredly divine?' (*cf.* Gn. 44:15); for possible cup-divination, see *MAGIC AND SORCERY, **2. II.**

When pharaoh invited Joseph's family to settle in Egypt (Gn. 45:17–21; 46:5), he sent wagons and told them to leave all, for they would have sufficiency in Egypt. Judging from Egyp. scenes 200 years later, such wagons were probably large, two-wheeled ox-carts. (For an excellent picture and discussion of these, see Aldred, *JNES* 15, 1956, pp. 150–153, pl. 17.) Sinuhe, a fugitive Egyptian in Syria *c.* 1900 BC, was also told to leave all by the pharaoh who recalled him to Egypt. Different customs again explain an allusion in Gn. 46:34b; by this means Joseph's family could be settled in secluded security in Goshen. Joseph's economic policy in Gn. 47:16–19 simply made Egypt in fact what it always was in theory: the land became pharaoh's property and its inhabitants his tenants. The priests were exempt not from taxation but only from Joseph's one-fifth levy, and the temple estates were separately managed (Gn. 47:22, 26). Gn. 47:21 merely indicates that throughout Egypt Joseph brought the people of each district into their nearest cities where the granaries were, the better to feed them; the unsavoury emendation in RSV ('he made slaves of them') is unnecessary. Gn. 48–49 reflects purely Asiatic usage within the patriarchal family; such oral blessings as Jacob's were legally binding in W Asia in the first half of the 2nd millennium BC (*cf.* Gordon, *BA* 3, 1940, p. 8).

f. Death of Joseph

Both Joseph and his father were embalmed in the Egyp. manner (Gn. 50:2–3, 26), and Joseph was 'put in a coffin in Egypt'. Coffins at this period were anthropoid, wooden ones with a conventional portrait-face at the head-end. The period of embalming varied in length; 40 days is one possibility among many. But 70 days' mourning was characteristic. Joseph's age at death, 110 years, is also significant: this was the ideal life-span in Egyp. eyes, and to them would signify divine blessing upon him.

For background, detailed discussion, and full source references, see J. Vergote, *Joseph en Égypte*, 1959; on D. B. Redford, *A Study of the Biblical Story of Joseph*, 1970, see K. A. Kitchen, *Oriens Antiquus* 12, 1973, pp. 233–242.

III. Joseph's descendants

The tribes of Ephraim and Manasseh, descended from Joseph's two sons, were sometimes termed '(the tribe of) Joseph', or house of Joseph; 'sons of Joseph' is common (Nu.; Jos.). So, Joseph is blessed as progenitor of the two future tribes by Jacob (Gn. 49:22–26; *cf.* Gn. 48), and Moses also blesses 'Joseph', meaning Ephraim and Manasseh (Dt. 33:13, 16). Compare also Nu. 13:11; Dt. 27:12; Jdg. 1:22–23, 35; Ps. 80:1 (poetic); and Ezk. 47:13. K.A.K.

2. In the New Testament

The husband of Mary. He is not mentioned in Mark and the references in Jn. 1:45 and 6:42 are indirect. According to Matthew, he was a descendant of David (Mt. 1:20). It seems that the genealogy in Lk. 3 is not that of Joseph but of Mary (but see *GENEALOGY OF JESUS CHRIST). Luke had already shown that Jesus was not the son of Joseph. Matthew is tracing the legal relationship back to David and Abraham.

Matthew and Luke both record that Jesus was conceived by the Holy Spirit at a time when Joseph was betrothed to Mary, but before he had intercourse with her (Mt. 1:18; Lk. 1:27, 35). Luke records the revelation by an angel to Mary, Matthew that to Joseph. It seems that Matthew drew his information from Joseph (possibly *via* James, the Lord's brother) and that Luke obtained his from Mary.

Joseph acted as a father towards Jesus, taking him to Jerusalem for the purification (Lk. 2:22) and fleeing with him to Egypt to escape Herod. He returned to Nazareth and settled there (Mt. 2). He took the boy Jesus to Jerusalem each year for the Passover (Lk. 2:41). Perhaps his words in Lk. 2:49 indicate that Jesus knew when he was 12 years old that he was not Joseph's son.

It is almost certain that Joseph was not alive during the ministry of Jesus. There is no direct mention of him, and it is hard to explain otherwise the word to John from the cross (Jn. 19:26–27) and the reference to Mary and his brothers seeking

Jesus (Mt. 12:46; Mk. 3:31; Lk. 8:19). It is natural to assume that the brothers of Jesus were subsequent children of Joseph and Mary.

Others mentioned in the NT who bear this name are three ancestors of Joseph the husband of Mary (or ancestors of Mary?) (Lk. 3:24, 26, 30); Joseph called Barsabbas, surnamed Justus, the unsuccessful candidate for the apostleship of Judas (Acts 1:23); and one of the brothers of the Lord (Mt. 13:55). It was also the natal name of *Barnabas (Acts 4:36). R.E.N.

JOSEPH OF ARIMATHEA. A Jew of *Arimathea, 'a good and righteous man, . . . and he was looking for the kingdom of God' (Lk. 23:50–51), 'a disciple of Jesus, but secretly, for fear of the Jews' (Jn. 19:38), and a member of the Sanhedrin who had not voted for Jesus' death. He was rich and, having asked Pilate for Jesus' body, provided fine linen for the burial, laying it in his own, unused, rock tomb (Mt. 27:57–60). (In this Matthew perhaps sees the fulfilment of Is. 53:9.) In a legend which first appears in William of Malmesbury he is sent by Philip from Gaul to Britain in AD 63 and founded the first Christian settlement in this country, afterwards the site of Glastonbury. There is no reference to this story in Gildas and Bede. J. A. Robinson, in his *Two Glastonbury Legends*, 1926, says that the passages are interpolations. A still later legend, probably composed by Walter Map in 1200, tells how Joseph brought the Holy Grail to England. J.W.M.

JOSEPHUS, FLAVIUS. A Jewish historian, who was born AD 37/38, and died early in the 2nd century. He was the son of a priest named Matthias, of the order of Jehoiarib (1 Ch. 24:7), and claimed kinship with the Hasmonaeans, who belonged to that order. After a brief period of association with the Essenes, and with an ascetic wilderness-dweller named Banus, he joined the party of the Pharisees at the age of 19. On a visit to Rome in AD 63 he was impressed by the power of the empire. He was strongly opposed to the Jewish revolt against Rome in AD 66, and although he was given a command in Galilee in which he manifested considerable energy and ability, he had no confidence in the insurgent cause. After the Roman seizure of the stronghold of Jotapata, which he had defended until further resistance was useless, he escaped with forty others to a cave. When this refuge in turn was about to be stormed the defenders entered into a suicide pact, and Josephus found himself one of the last two survivors. He persuaded his fellow-survivor that they might as well surrender to the Romans, and then he contrived to win the favour of Vespasian, the Roman commander, by predicting his elevation to the imperial purple. This prediction came true in AD 69. Next year Josephus was attached to the Roman general headquarters during the siege of Jerusalem, acting as interpreter for Titus (Vespasian's son and successor in the Palestinian command), when he wished to offer terms to the defenders of the city. After the fall of Jerusalem Josephus went to Rome, where he settled down as a client and pensioner of the emperor, whose family name, Flavius, he adopted.

Not unnaturally, Josephus' behaviour during the war won for him the indelible stigma of treason in the eyes of his nation. Yet he employed the years of his leisure in Rome in such a way as to establish some claim on their gratitude. These years were devoted to literary activity in which he shows himself to be a true patriot according to his lights, jealous for the good name of his people. His first work was a *History of the Jewish War*, written first in Aramaic for the benefit of Jews in Mesopotamia and then published in a Gk. edition. The account of the outbreak of the war is here preceded by a summary of Jewish history from 168 BC to AD 66. His two books *Against Apion* constitute a defence of his people against the anti-Jewish calumnies of an Alexandrian schoolmaster named Apion; in them, too, he endeavours to show that the Jews can boast a greater antiquity than the Greeks, and in the course of this argument he has preserved for us a number of valuable extracts from ancient writers not otherwise extant. His longest work is his *Jewish Antiquities*, in twenty books, relating the history of his people from earliest times (in fact, he begins his narrative with the creation of the world) down to his own day. This work was completed in AD 93. Finally, he wrote his *Autobiography* largely as a defence of his war record, which had been represented in unflattering terms by another Jewish writer, Justus of Tiberias. It is impossible to reconcile the account of his war activities given in his *Autobiography* with that given earlier in his *History of the Jewish War.*

For the history of the Jews between the reign of Antiochus Epiphanes (175–164 BC) and the war of AD 66–74, and especially for the period beginning with the Roman occupation of 63 BC, the works of Josephus are of incomparable value. He had access to first-rate sources, both published and unpublished: the work of Nicolas of Damascus, historiographer to Herod the Great, supplied a detailed record of that monarch's career; official Roman records were placed at his disposal; he consulted the younger Agrippa (*HEROD, 5) on various details concerning the origin of the Jewish war, and of course could rely on his own immediate knowledge of many phases of it. He can indeed be thoroughly tendentious in his portrayal of personalities and presentation of events, but his 'tendency' is so obvious that the reader can easily detect it and make necessary allowances for it.

The works of Josephus provide indispensable background material for the student of late intertestamental and NT history. In them we meet many figures, both Jewish and Gentile, who are well known to us from the NT. Sometimes his writings supply a direct commentary on NT references, *e.g.* on the mention of Judas of Galilee in Acts 5:37 and of the *'Egyptian' in Acts 21:38. It is unlikely, however, that his works were known to any NT writer. Of special interest are his references to John the Baptist (*Ant.* 18. 116ff.), to James the Lord's brother (*Ant.* 20. 200), and to our Lord (*Ant.* 18. 63f.)—a passage which, while it has been subjected to some Christian editing, is basically authentic.

BIBLIOGRAPHY. The standard edition of Josephus' works in Greek is that by B. Niese (1887–95). The Loeb edition (1926–65), in Greek and English, begun by H. St J. Thackeray and completed by R. Marcus and L. H. Feldman, comprises 10 volumes. The best-known English translation is that by W. Whiston (1736); revisions by Shilleto (1890) and Margoliouth (1906) are supplanted by the Loeb edition. *The Jewish War*, translated by G. A. Williamson was revised by E.

M. Smallwood, 1981. See also H. St J. Thackeray, *Josephus, the Man and the Historian*, 1929; J. M. Creed, 'The Slavonic Version of Josephus' History of the Jewish War', *HTR* 25, 1932, pp. 277ff.; F. F. Bruce, *Jesus and Christian Origins outside the NT*, 1974, pp. 32–53; T. Rajak, *Josephus: The Historian and his Society*, 1983; L. H. Feldman, *Josephus and Modern Scholarship (1937–1980)*, 1984; *idem* and G. Hata (eds.), *Josephus, Judaism and Christianity*, 1987; *Josephus, the Bible and History*, 1989.

F.F.B.

JOSHUA, 1. Joshua ben Nun, grandson of Elishama chief of Ephraim (1 Ch. 7:27; Nu. 1:10), was called by his family *hôšea'*, 'salvation', Nu. 13:8 (AV 'Oshea'); Dt. 32:44 Heb.; this name recurs in the tribe of Ephraim (1 Ch. 27:20; 2 Ki. 17:1; Ho. 1:1). Moses added the divine name, and called him *yᵉhôšua'*, normally rendered in Eng. 'Joshua'. The Gk. *Iēsous* reflects the Aram. contraction *yešu'* (*cf.* Ne. 3:19, *etc.*).

At the Exodus Joshua was a young man (Ex. 33:11). Moses chose him as personal assistant, and gave him command of a detachment from the as yet unorganized tribes to repel the raiding Amalekites (Ex. 17). As the Ephraimite representative on the reconnaissance from Kadesh (Nu. 13–14) he backed Caleb's recommendation to go ahead with invasion. *Caleb, the senior and leading figure, sometimes is mentioned alone in this connection; but it is unlikely that there was a version of the episode excluding Joshua, or that any later historian denied, or was unaware, that he too escaped the curse on the unbelieving people.

While Moses was alone before God at Sinai, Joshua kept watch; in the Tent of Meeting also he learnt to wait on the Lord; and in the years following, something of Moses' patience and meekness was doubtless added to his valour (Ex. 24:13; 32:17; 33:11; Nu. 11:28). In the plains by the Jordan he was formally consecrated as Moses' successor to the military leadership, co-ordinate with *Eleazar the priest (Nu. 27:18ff.; 34:17; *cf.* Dt. 3 and 31, where Joshua's position is naturally emphasized). He was then probably about 70 years old; Caleb was a remarkably vigorous 85 when he began to occupy the Judaean hills (Jos. 15:13–15).

Joshua occupied and consolidated the area of Gilgal, fought successful campaigns against Canaanite confederacies and directed further operations as long as the united efforts of Israel were required. Settlement of the land depended on tribal initiative; Joshua sought to encourage this by a formal allocation at Shiloh, where the national sanctuary was established. The time had come for him to dissolve his command and set an example by retiring to his land at Timnath-serah in Mt Ephraim. It was perhaps at this time that he called Israel to the national covenant at Shechem (Jos. 24). Ch. 23, his farewell, may refer to the same occasion; but the substance is different, and seems to imply a later period. Joshua died aged 110, and was buried near his home at Timnath-serah.

For *JOSHUA, BOOK OF, see the following article, which also discusses some modern theories of the invasion of Canaan and of Joshua's role.

2. Joshua ben Josedech was high priest of the restoration in 537 BC. Under him the altar was rebuilt and the Temple dedicated. Progress was hindered by opposition, however, until in 520 BC he was strengthened by the prophecies of Haggai and Zechariah, including a remarkable pattern of justification by the grace of God (Zc. 3). He was named prophetically the 'Branch' (or, 'shoot'; *ṣemaḥ*, Zc. 6:12). See J. Stafford Wright, *The Building of the Second Temple*, 1958, for a review of the problems in Ezra and Haggai.

3. Joshua of Beth-shemesh, owner of the field to which the ark was brought when the Philistines sent it back to Israel (1 Sa. 6:14). J.P.U.L.

JOSHUA, BOOK OF. The book of Joshua records the invasion of Canaan by Israel and its partition among the tribes. It tells in detail how they crossed the Jordan and secured a bridgehead, describes more briefly two campaigns which broke the power of the Canaanites and summarizes Israel's further military progress. The account of the partition includes a full description of Judahite territory, and notes on the Kenite settlement of Hebron and the difficulties experienced in N Manasseh. After referring to the levitical settlements and the problem of the Transjordanian tribes, the book closes with an account of Joshua's spiritual testament, the climax being the national covenant at Shechem.

I. Outline of contents

a. The invasion of Canaan (1:1–11:23)

(i) *Change of command* (1:1–4:24). Commission; reconnaissance; the river crossing.

(ii) *The bridgehead* (5:1–8:35). Gilgal to Ai.

(iii) *Campaign in the south* (9:1–10:43). The Hivite cities; defeat of the Jerusalem confederacy; cities captured.

(iv) *Campaign in the north, and further progress* (11:1–23).

b. The settlement in Canaan (12:1–24:33)

(i) *List of defeated enemies* (12:1–24).

(ii) *The early settlements* (13:1–17:18). Unfinished tasks; Transjordan; Caleb; the land of Judah; allotments for Ephraim and Manasseh.

(iii) *Later settlements* (18:1–21:45). Shiloh conference; cities of refuge; levitical towns.

(iv) *The way ahead* (22:1–24:33). The Witness Altar; Joshua's charge; the covenant at Shechem.

II. Composition and purpose

In the Heb. Bible, Jos. heads the 'Former Prophets', which cover Israelite history from the invasion to the Exile. In immediate and natural sequence to Dt., the book extends from Joshua's assumption of command to his passing and the death of Eleazar. Chs. 1–11 form a continuous narrative, though the treatment is progressively more summary, ending with a general evaluation of Joshua's achievement (11:15–23). In whatever form the author found his material, he has made of it a story of the highest dramatic quality, alike in treatment of the subject and in narrative technique. This is no mere editing of pre-existing work; but much is omitted or generalized to get the broad picture, in due proportions, into a limited space.

A climax is reached at the end of ch. 11, but the story is not finished. The book is about Joshua's work, and about the fulfilment of God's promises in that Israel was in possession of the land 'which I swore to their fathers to give them' (1:6, *cf.* 23:14; 24:13). For both purposes it must give an account of the settlement, and show the position of

Joshua	Numbers	Dt.	Subject	Notes
1:1–9		31	Joshua commissioned	Especially Dt. 31:6, 7f., 12b, 23.
1:3–4		11:24	Extent of promises	Slight differences in phrasing.
1:12–15	32	3:18f.	Eastern tribes	Phrasing echoes Dt., with variations.
8:30–35		11:29–32; 27	Reading the Law at Shechem	Jos. abbreviates, but also mentions ark and foreigners.
12:1–16	21:21–35	2:26–3:17; 4:45–49	Conquests in Transjordan	Dt. 3:1f. = Nu. 21:33f.; Jos. phrases occur in various places in Dt.
13:6–7	34:13, 17		'divide this land'	Verbs differ.
13:8–12, 15–31	32:33–42	2:36; 3:8ff.	Settlement in Transjordan	Distinctive description of Aroer in Jos. and Dt.
13:14, 33	18:24	14:27	No territory for Levi	*Cf.* Dt. 18:1f.
14:1	34:17		Joshua and Eleazar	*Cf.* Jos. 19:51.
14:6ff.	14:24	1:28–36	Caleb's inheritance	
15:1–4	34:3–5		South frontier	'Your,' Jos. 15:4; as Nu. 34:3.
17:3–6	27:1–11		Women's inheritance	
18:4–10	34:13–29		Commission for the partition	10 supervisors nominated in Nu., 21 scribes in Jos.
20	35:9–29	19:1–13	Sanctuary towns	Joshua expands on acceptance procedure, but is otherwise brief.
20		4:41–43	Transjordan towns	
21	35:2–8		Levitical towns	
23:3		1:30	'God fights for you'	*Cf.* Ex. 14:14.
23:6		5:32	'turn not . . .'	
23:8		10:20 *etc.*	'cleave to him'	v. 7 'make mention' *cf.* Ex. 23:13.
23:13	33:55		'thorns in your side'	*s^enīnim* only here.

Passages in Numbers and Deuteronomy recalled in Joshua.

strength in which Joshua left the nation. In this part there is much use of sources, some of which reappear elsewhere (Nu., Jdg., Ch.), The author keeps firm control of his material, editing heavily in places (*e.g.* ch. 20, and probably in most of the boundary lists). Joshua's 'farewell to the nation' is recorded in ch. 23; but from the prophetic viewpoint his work was really crowned by the Shechem Covenant, though this may have been much earlier (24:28; RSV 'then', v. 1, is intrusive).

III. Authorship, sources, date

Dt. echoes strongly in Jos., both in its purpose and its language. There is also much (especially in the second part) of quite another stamp. It was therefore natural that Pentateuchal source-analysis was projected into Jos., and the concept of a 'Hexateuch' has been promoted. The theory has been largely unsuccessful because (*a*) insecure criteria have bred disagreement and increasing confusion in the analysis; (*b*) the 'priestly source' (P) is especially difficult to identify, and Jos. raises in an acute form the disputed question whether such a source was ever an independent narrative (see C. R. North, *The Old Testament and Modern Study*, 1951); (*c*) in its general form and concept, Jos. is much more one of the Former Prophets than part of the Law.

A fresh approach was made by M. Noth, stressing the importance of traditions and trying to see how they were developed. Noth concluded that an author belonging to a 'deuteronomic school' had edited old compilations of sanctuary traditions and settlement records to form the 'Joshua' part of a complete deuteronomic history, subsequently retouched by P. This lead has been widely taken, and is accepted in the main by Gray and Soggin (latest commentaries in English). Implications for dating depend on the view taken of Dt. itself. The term 'deuteronomistic' becomes assimilated to 'prophetic', and the theory fails to explain why there is so little 'deuteronomic style' in Jdg. (*cf.* S. R. Driver, *LOT* [9], pp. 112, 126ff.; C. F. Burney, *Judges*, 1920, pp. xliff.).

Noth emphasized the extent of aetiology (stories explaining names and monuments) in the traditions, and took an extremely sceptical view of its value (criticized by J. Bright, *Early Israel in Recent History Writing*, 1956). Others have explored the role of religious festivals in tradition-history, but the reconstructions are largely speculative.

IV. Historical evaluation

The account of the invasion has often been criticized as 'unrealistic', presenting a 'total reduction' of Canaan in contrast to the 'more sober account' in Jdg. 1 (Gray, p. 43). This assessment misinterprets both books. Jos. does not say that all was over in two campaigns (11:18), and it preserves hints of trouble (15:63; 17:12–18) which could easily have been omitted; but it is primarily concerned with the great measure of success in the invasion, and with the reasons for it. On the other hand, Jdg. 1 is not an account of the invasion; it highlights the beginnings of failure, but the whole book would be pointless if there had not been great success.

Many scholars have imagined an invasion by independent tribes (see H. H. Rowley, *From Joseph to Joshua*, 1948). Noth went so far as to claim that Israel was formed in Canaan as an 'amphictyony' (holy alliance, on the Gk. analogy); *cf.* Bright, *op. cit.*, pp. 83ff., for criticism; and B. D. Rathjen, *JNES* 24, 1965, pp. 100–104. Archaeological evidence is still very incomplete, and its interpretation often uncertain, but there is enough proof of the destruction of Canaanite society (*e.g.* Hazor, Tell Beit Mirsim) to demand that the invasion be taken seriously. Theories of a piecemeal invasion must restrict Joshua's role to that of a local leader, or at most an arbitrator (Soggin, pp. 14–18). The ground of such theories lies not so much in any analysis of Joshua–Judges as in the devaluation of Moses' work.

The crux of the biblical account is that the 'Sinai tradition' is the authentic tap-root of Israel's faith and hence of her political being (see Jos. 24). G. E. Mendenhall (*BA* 25, 1962, pp. 66–87) sees it as precipitating a liberation movement in Canaan, but he overstates the case. Biblical evidence of the absorption of non-Israelite elements into the tribal system presupposes the system itself, based ultimately on kinship.

V. Spiritual content

The importance of Joshua for Christians lies chiefly in that it (*a*) shows God's faithfulness to his covenant (*cf.* Dt. 7:7; 9:5f.); (*b*) records the development of his purpose for the nation; (*c*) gives reasons for a failure, already foreshadowed (17:13; 18:3), to carry out the divine plan; (*d*) provides analogies for discipleship, since the spiritual issues of faith, obedience and purity were clearly at stake in the invasion.

Israel under Joshua showed better morale than their fathers, but were no less susceptible to polytheism and nature-religion (Nu. 25; Dt. 4:3, 23). Determination to extirpate the Canaanites and their religion was therefore of prime importance (*cf.* Gn. 15:16; Ex. 20:2–6; 23:23–33; 34:10–17; Nu. 31:15ff.; Dt. 7). The Israelites could not understand or give effect to a redemptive approach, while daily contact with Canaanite culture would jeopardize their own faith in a unique, all-powerful God, as well as their moral standards, as the sequel showed. Moreover, salvation by grace could not be generally offered (as under the NT) before its necessary judicial ground had been publicly set out in Christ's death; but we see a pattern of it in God's dealing with Rahab (*cf.* Heb. 11:31). God's purpose at the time was not to teach Christianity, but to prepare the way for Christ through Israel.

The experiences of Israel in Canaan, as in the deserts, were 'written for our admonition' (1 Cor. 10:11). The chief theme of the book is that God gave Israel rest, which their unbelieving fathers had failed to obtain (Ps. 95:11). In Heb. 4:1–11 it is shown that this is a 'type'; the principle, which the Psalmist applied in his own generation, is equally valid for the Christian, while the promise is completely fulfilled (v. 8) only in the rest which God has provided for us in Christ (*cf.* J. N. Darby, *Synopsis*, 1, p. 328). If this is the primary application of the invasion story, there is also much to be learnt from the successes and failures, and from Joshua's leadership.

VI. Text and translations

Apart from topographical problems, the Heb. text contains few obscurities. The LXX maintains an average standard; its Heb. original does not appear materially different from the *MT*.

BIBLIOGRAPHY. *Text*: L. Greenspoon, *Textual Studies in Joshua*, 1983; A. G. Auld, *VT Suppl.* 30, 1979, pp. 1–14. *Commentaries*: M. Woudstra (*NICS*), 1981; T. Butler (*WBC*), 1983; J. Gray, *Joshua–Judges–Ruth*[3], 1986. *Historical*: S. Yeivin, *Israelite Conquest of Canaan*, 1971; Y. Aharoni, *BA* 39, 1976, pp. 55–76; *LOB*, pp. 191–285; J. J. Bimson, *Redating the Exodus*, *JSOT Suppl.* 5, 1981.

J.P.U.L.

JOSIAH (Heb. *yō'šiyyāhû*, **2** as *yō'šiyyâ*, 'May Yahweh give'). **1.** The 17th king of Judah. As son of Amon and grandson of Manasseh, the 'people of the land' enthroned him at the age of 8 upon the assassination of his father. He reigned for 31 years (*c.* 640–609 BC; 2 Ki. 21:24–25:1; 2 Ch. 33:25–34:1).

Assyria, while still Judah's overlord, was weak enough for the vassal to take cautious steps towards freedom. In 633/2 BC, Josiah, in turning back to Yahweh (2 Ch. 34:32), was turning away from an imposed dependence on Assyria and its gods. By 629/8 BC, Ashurbanipal being aged, Josiah was able to free the country of Assyrian as well as residual native cultic practices (2 Ch. 34:3b–5). Not only was this carried out in Judah, which Josiah must have taken from the control of the weakening Assyrians, but also extended into Israel (2 Ch. 34:6–7). This period of religious reform and political emancipation also produced the great prophet Jeremiah a year later (Je. 1:2).

In 622/1 BC, the 'book of the law' was found during the course of Temple repairs (2 Ki. 22:8–10; 2 Ch. 34:8–18). It is commonly accepted that this scroll was, or contained, the book of Deuteronomy, although this is not proven. This collection of ancient law, fanning the already burning feeling of nationalism, led to further political and religious reform. On the basis of this book, Josiah obliterated pagan worship (2 Ki. 23:4–14), including the false priests (*kᵉmārîm*, Akk. *kumru*; 2 Ki. 23:5) and the altar at Bethel (2 Ki. 23:15; *cf.* 1 Ki. 13:2). He and the people made a new covenant with Yahweh (2 Ki. 23:1–3; 2 Ch. 34:29–33) which would make this book the law of the land. He also celebrated the Passover in such a grand style as had not been seen since the days of Samuel (2 Ki. 23:21–23; 2 Ch. 35:1–19).

In 609 BC, *Neco II of Egypt went from the Egyp. outpost in Megiddo to Harran in aid of the Assyrians (A. K. Grayson, *Assyrian and Babylonian Chronicles*, 1975, p. 96, ll. 66–69), whose king had been driven out of his capital by Babylonia and the Medes. Seeing Egypt as a threat to his own kingdom, in spite of Neco's denial, Josiah met him in Esdraelon, and was severely wounded, dying in Jerusalem (2 Ki. 23:29–30; 2 Ch. 35:20–24).

2. An Israelite during the time of Zechariah who had not been exiled to Babylon (Zc. 6:10).

BIBLIOGRAPHY: A. Malamat, *Journal of the Ancient Near Eastern Society of Columbia University* 5, 1973, pp. 167–179; John McKay, *Religion in Judah under the Assyrians*, 1973, pp. 28–44; H. G. M. Williamson, *VT* 32, 1982, pp. 242–248; 37, 1987, pp. 9–15.

D.W.B.

JOT AND TITTLE. In Mt. 5:18 (AV) 'jot' is a transliteration of *iōta* (RSV), the name of the Gk. *i*; here, however, it stands for the corresponding Heb. *yôḏ*, the smallest letter of the alphabet, the use of which is frequently optional. 'Tittle' is a variant spelling for 'title', which in older Eng. meant a stroke above an abridged word, and then any minor stroke. Here and in Lk. 16:17 it represents *keraia*, meaning a horn, and refers to the minor strokes which distinguish one letter from another, *e.g.* in Heb. *bêṯ* and *kap̄*, *dāleṯ* and *rêš*. H.L.E.

Left: the smallest letter in the Hebrew alphabet, y (*Heb.* yôḏ, AV *'jot'*). *Centre and right: the letters* r (*Heb.* rêš) *and* d (*Heb.* dāleṯ), *distinguished from each other by the addition of a 'tittle' to the latter. Hebrew script of the 1st cent.* AD.

JOTBAH. Birthplace of Manasseh's wife (2 Ki. 21:19). Conquered by Tiglath-pileser III (*ANET*, p. 283). Called Jotapata during the Roman period (Jos., *BJ* 2. 573). Tentatively identified with Khirbet Jefat (W. F. Albright, *JBL* 58, 1939, pp. 184f.), *c.* 20 km E of Sea of Galilee. D.W.B.

JOTBATHAH. A stopping-place in the Israelites' wilderness wanderings (Nu. 33:33–34; Dt. 10:7). Described in Dt. as 'a land of brooks of water', it is identified with either 'Ain Ṭābah in the Arabah N of Elath or perhaps more accurately with Ṭabeh, about 11 km S of Elath on the W shore of the Gulf of Aqabah (*LOB*, p. 183). W.O.

JOTHAM (Heb. *yôṯām*, 'Yahweh is perfect'). **1.** The youngest of the 70 legitimate sons of Jerubbaal (Gideon), and sole survivor of Abimelech's massacre of the other brothers. Through the parable of the trees selecting the bramble to be their king (an honour previously declined by the cedar, the olive and the vine), Jotham warned the Shechemites against Abimelech (Jdg. 9:5ff.). The warning was ignored, and the curse that he uttered was fulfilled 3 years later (v. 57).

2. Son of Uzziah (Mt. 1:9), and 12th king of Judah. He began his reign as co-regent *c.* 750 BC when his father was found to be a leper (2 Ki. 15:5), and was sole monarch *c.* 740–*c.* 732 BC (*CHRONOLOGY OF THE OLD TESTAMENT). A man who feared God, Jotham built the high gate of the Temple, fortified and extended the land of Judah and subdued the Ammonites (2 Ch. 27:3–6). **3.** A son of Jahdai and descendant from Caleb (1 Ch. 2:47). J.D.D.

JOY. The biblical words are: Heb. *śimḥâ*, verb *śāmēaḥ*, which imply also its outward expression (*cf.* the Arab. cognate, meaning 'to be excited'), and less usually *gîl* (verb and noun); Gk. *chara* (verb *chairō*), and *agalliasis* (frequently used in LXX, and corresponding to *śimḥâ*), meaning intense joy.

In both OT and NT joy is consistently the mark both individually of the believer and corporately of the church. It is a quality, and not simply an emotion, grounded upon God himself and indeed derived from him (Ps. 16:11; Phil. 4:4; Rom. 15:13), which characterizes the Christian's life on earth (1 Pet. 1:8), and also anticipates eschatologically the joy of being with Christ for ever in the kingdom of heaven (*cf.* Rev. 19:7).

I. In the Old Testament

Joy is related to the total national and religious life of Israel, and is particularly expressed in terms of noisy, tumultuous excitement at festivals, sacrifices and enthronements (Dt. 12:6f.; 1 Sa. 18:6; 1 Ki. 1:39f.). Spontaneous joy is a prevailing feature of the Psalter, where it is a mark both of corporate worship (largely centred on the Temple, Pss. 42:4; 81:1–3) and of personal adoration (Pss. 16:8f., 43:4). Isaiah conceives of joy in other than simply ritual terms (*cf.* Ps. 126), and he associates it with the fullness of God's salvation, and therefore (in terms of a cosmic rejoicing) with the anticipation of a future state (Is. 49:13; 61:10f.). In later Judaism, as a result, joy is a characteristic of the last days.

II. In the New Testament

The Synoptic Gospels record the note of joy in connection with the proclamation, in its varied forms, of the good news of the kingdom: for example, at the Saviour's birth (Lk. 2:10), at the triumphal entry (Mk. 11:9f.; Lk. 19:37), and after the resurrection (Mt. 28:8). In the Fourth Gospel it is Jesus himself who communicates this joy (Jn. 15:11; 16:24), and it now becomes the result of a deep fellowship between the church and himself (*cf.* 16:22).

In Acts joy marks the life of the early church. It accompanies the gift of the Holy Spirit to the disciples (Acts 13:52), the miracles performed in the name of Christ (8:8), and the fact and report of the conversion of the Gentiles (15:3); it also characterizes the eucharistic meal (2:46).

Paul uses the term *chara* in three ways. First, progress in the faith on the part of the members of the body of Christ, and particularly those he has led to Christ, is a cause for joy—he describes them, indeed, as *hē chara hēmōin*, 'our joy' (1 Thes. 2:19f.; *cf.* Phil. 2:2). Secondly, Christian joy may paradoxically be the outcome of suffering and even sorrow for Christ's sake (Col. 1:24; 2 Cor. 6:10; *cf.* 1 Pet. 4:13; Heb. 10:34, *etc.*), since it is produced by the Lord and not by ourselves. Joy is in fact, finally, a gift of the Holy Spirit (Gal. 5:22), and is therefore something dynamic and not static. Moreover, it derives from love—God's and ours—and is therefore closely associated with love in Paul's list of the fruit of the Spirit. But since it is a gift which may be interrupted by sin, every believer is called upon to share in the joy of Christ by a daily walk with him and a daily practice of rejoicing in the knowledge of him and his salvation (1 Thes. 5:16; Phil. 3:1; 4:4; 1 Pet. 1:8).

BIBLIOGRAPHY. The standard work on the subject is E. G. Gulin, *Die Freude im Neuen Testament*, 1932; see also J. Moffatt, *Grace in the New Testament*, 1931, p. 168, for the relation between *chara* and *charis*; E. Beyreuther, G. Finkenrath, *NIDNTT* 2, pp. 352–361; *TDNT* 1, pp. 19–21; 2, pp. 772–775; 9, pp. 359–372. S.S.S.

JOZACHAR (Heb. *yôzāḵār*, 'Yahweh has remembered'). A servant of Joash who took part in his assassination (2 Ki. 12:21–22) but was subsequently executed by Amaziah (2 Ki. 14:5). Some MSS read 'Jozabad' in 2 Ki. 12:22, abbreviated to 'Zabad' in 2 Ch. 24:26, by confusion with the similar name of the other assassin, Jehozabad. D.W.B.

JUBAL. A son of Adah, wife of Lamech, and ancestor of those who 'handle the harp (*kinnôr*) and pipe (*'ûgāḇ*)' (Gn. 4:21). (*MUSIC AND MUSICAL INSTRUMENTS.) T.C.M.

JUBILEES, BOOK OF. A Jewish intertestamental work, extant completely only in Ethiopic and partly in Latin, though fragments in the original Heb. have now been found at Qumran. It was probably written in the late 2nd century BC in (proto-) Essene circles shortly before the Qumran sect came into existence. It was popular at Qumran, where its special legal precepts and calendar were observed. (It is cited by name in CD 16. 13f.)

Jubilees is a midrash or legendary rewriting of Genesis and the early chapters of Exodus. It gives the biblical history a detailed chronology, calculated in jubilee periods of 49 years, each divided into 7 weeks of years, each year a solar year of 364 days. The revelation at Sinai occurs in the 50th jubilee since the Creation. (Several texts from Qumran employ jubilee periods in historical and eschatological speculation.)

Jubilees supplements the biblical narrative with legends about the Patriarchs, passages of eschatological prophecy and legal material endorsing a strict sectarian interpretation of the Law. In opposition to hellenizing influences, the author glorifies the Law as distinguishing Israel from the Gentiles. The solar calendar has the same effect of setting Israel apart from the Gentiles, and faithful Israel from apostate Israel: only this calendar ensures the observance of the festivals on the correct dates.

The *Jubilees* *calendar derives from *1 Enoch* and was observed at Qumran. A day of the month falls on the same day of the week every year; *e.g.* New Year's day always falls on a Wednesday. Some scholars have suggested, as a solution to the problem of the date of the Last Supper, that Jesus celebrated the Passover according to this calendar, *i.e.* on a Tuesday evening.

BIBLIOGRAPHY. G. L. Davenport, *The Eschatology of the Book of Jubilees*, 1971; J. C. VanderKam, *Textual and Historical Studies in the Book of Jubilees*, 1977. R.J.B.

JUDAEA. The Gk. and Rom. designation of the land of *Judah. The word is actually an adjective

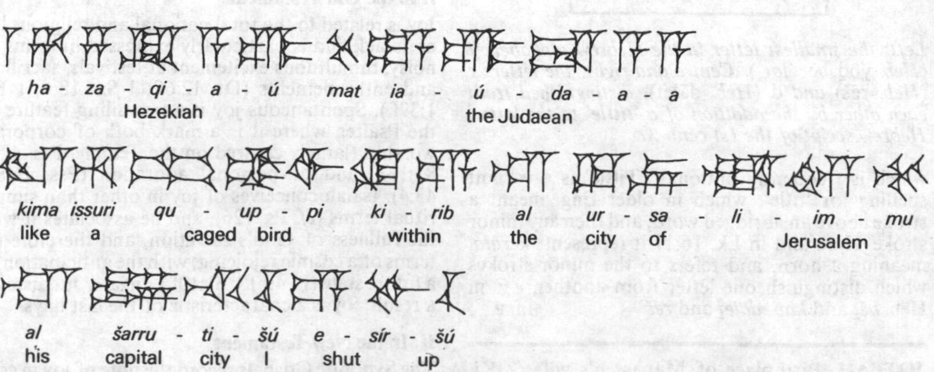

Hezekiah 'the Judaean' (ḫazaqiau māt Yaudaya) *named on the clay prism which describes the early campaign of Sennacherib of Assyria, including the siege of Jerusalem in 701 BC.*

('Jewish') with *gē* ('land') or *chōra* ('country') understood. After the Roman conquest (63 BC) it appears both in a wider sense, denoting all Palestine, including Galilee and Samaria, and in the narrower sense, which excludes these two regions. Herod's kingdom of Judaea (37–4 BC) included all Palestine and some districts E of the Jordan. Archelaus' ethnarchy of Judaea (4 BC–AD 6 embraced Judaea in the narrower sense and Samaria, and the same is true of the Rom. province of Judaea from AD 6 to 41. After the death of Herod Agrippa I in AD 44 the Rom. province of Judaea included Galilee also. (*ISRAEL.)

The 'wilderness of Judaea' (Mt. 3:1), associated with John the Baptist, is probably identical with the 'wilderness of Judah' (Jdg. 1:16, *etc.*), *i.e.* the desert to the W of the Dead Sea. J.D.D.

JUDAH.

I. The son of Jacob

The 4th son of Jacob by Leah (Gn. 29:35) was called Judah (*yᵉhûḏâ*); the name is there explained as meaning 'praised', as derived from the root *ydh*, 'to praise'. Gn. 49:8 contains a play on this meaning. The derivation is widely rejected, but no other suggested etymology has been generally accepted (for literature, see *KB*). Judah early took a leading role among his brothers, as is shown by the story of Joseph (Gn. 37:26–27; 43:3–10; 44:16–34; 46:28). Gn. 38, though throwing light on the beginnings of the tribe of Judah, clearly stands in its present position to contrast Judah's character with that of Joseph. Though Gn. 49:8–12 is not strictly a promise to Judah of kingship, but rather of leadership, victory and tribal stability, the promise of *Shiloh involves kingship ultimately. The genealogies of Judah's descendants are found in 1 Ch. 2–4.

II. Other individuals of the same name

After the Babylonian Exile Judah became increasingly one of the favourite names among the Jews. Five men of this name are mentioned in the OT, *viz.* a Levite, ancestor of Kadmiel (Ezr. 3:9), possibly the father or son of Hodaviah (Ezr. 2:40); a Levite of the return under Zerubbabel (Ne. 12:8); a levitical contemporary of Ezra (Ezr. 10:23); a leading Benjaminite under Nehemiah (Ne. 11:9); a priest under Nehemiah (Ne. 12:36). In Ne. 12:34 probably members of the tribe in general are meant by 'Judah'. In the NT the name is represented by its Hellenized form *Judas (shortened to Jude in Jude 1).

III. The tribe of Judah

a. From the Exodus till Saul

Judah plays no special role in the story of the Exodus and of the wilderness wanderings, though it is to be noted that he was the leader of the vanguard (Nu. 2:9). There is no significant change in the two census figures from this period (Nu. 1:27; 26:22).

Achan, a member of the tribe, was the cause of the defeat of Israel before Ai (Jos. 7). This may be the reason for the special task laid on Judah to lead an independent attack on the Canaanites (Jdg. 1:1–2). No explanation is given, but it is clear that Judah's portion was allocated not by lot in Shiloh (Jos. 18:1–10) but before its conquest (Jdg. 1:3); *cf.* the similar treatment of Ephraim and half Manasseh (Jos. 16–17). It was bounded on the N by the portions of Dan and Benjamin, and ran approximately E and W from the N end of the Dead Sea, S of Jerusalem and the Gibeonite tetrapolis to the Mediterranean. Its W and E frontiers were the Mediterranean and the Dead Sea, and it extended S as far as cultivation permitted (*cf.* Jos. 15).

Judah first overran most of the coastal plain, soon to be occupied by the Philistines (Jdg. 1:18), but evidently quickly withdrew from the struggle (Jdg. 1:19; 3:3; Jos. 11:22; 13:2–3). Since it was the best of the land apportioned to him that Judah voluntarily abandoned to Simeon (Jos. 19:1, 9), it is reasonable to suppose that he hoped to have Simeon as a buffer between him and the unconquered coastal plain.

The story of the conquest of the S in Jdg. 1:1–17 has been very widely interpreted to mean that Judah (and other tribes) entered the land from the S *before* the invasion under Joshua (*cf.* H. H. Rowley, *From Joseph to Joshua*, 1950, pp. 4f., 101f., 110ff., with literature), but the whole trend of modern archaeological discovery seems to be unfavourable to the theory, which is unacceptable on other, general grounds.

The failure to maintain a hold on Jerusalem (Jdg. 1:8, 21), combined with the existence of the semi-independent Gibeonite tetrapolis (Jos. 9; 2 Sa. 21:1–2), created a psychological frontier between Judah and the central tribes. Though there was no barrier to communications (*cf.* Jdg. 19:10–13), Judah will increasingly have looked S to Hebron rather than to the sanctuary at Shiloh. While Judah provided the first of the judges, Othniel (Jdg. 3:9–11), and shared in the early action against Benjamin (Jdg. 20:18), he does not seem even to have been expected to join against Jabin and Sisera (Jdg. 5). As a result, when Judah became tributary to the Philistines (Jdg. 15:11), he appears not to have appealed to the other tribes, nor do they seem to have been concerned.

The fact of this division seems to have been generally recognized, for by Saul's time we find the contingent from Judah separately enumerated (1 Sa. 11:8; 15:4; 17:52; 18:16).

b. Under David and Solomon

After Saul's death this growing split was perpetuated by David's being crowned as king in Hebron over Judah (2 Sa. 2:4). A. Alt is probably correct in maintaining ('The Formation of the Israelite State in Palestine', in *Essays on Old Testament History and Religion*, 1966, pp. 216ff.) that the crowning of David as king over 'all Israel' (2 Sa. 5:1–5) made him king of a dual kingdom in which Judah kept its separate identity. Certainly during Absalom's rebellion Judah seems to have maintained its neutrality, while the N followed the rebel.

There is no evidence that Solomon showed any favouritism to Judah compared with the other tribes, for 'and one officer, which was in the land' (1 Ki. 4:19, RVmg.) will refer to Judah (RSV).

IV. The kingdom of Judah

a. Its relations with Israel

If A. Alt's view is correct, Judah and Israel in accepting different kings were acting in accordance with their rights as separate political entities. Apart from Jeroboam himself, the kings of Israel do not seem to have sought the destruction of Judah (*cf.* 2 Ki. 14:13–14), and the prophets never questioned

Judah's family tree according to 1 Ch. 2:3–6.

931/30–913 Rehoboam

913–911/10 Abijam

911/10–870/69 Asa

Co-regency 873/72–870/69

870/69–848 Jehoshaphat

Co-regency 853–848

848–841 Jehoram

841 Ahaziah

841–835 Athaliah

835–796 Joash

796–767 Amaziah

Co-regency 791/90–767

767–740/39 Azariah

Co-regency 750–740/39

740/39–732/31 Jotham

Co-regency 735–732/31

732/31–716/15 Ahaz

Co-regency 729–716/15

716/15–687/86 Hezekiah

Co-regency 696/95–687/86

687/86–643/42 Manasseh

643/42–641/40 Amon

640/39–609 Josiah

609 Jehoahaz

609–597 Jehoiakim

597 Jehoiachin

597–587 Zedekiah

Dates of the kings of Judah.

the right of Israel to exist, though they foresaw the time when it would return to its allegiance to 'David'.

The heritage of Solomon's riches seemed to give Judah the advantage at the disruption, despite its less fertile land and smaller population compared with the N. In spite of claims to the contrary, there is no evidence that Rehoboam later disregarded the command of Shemaiah (1 Ki. 12:22–24) and attacked Jeroboam. The suggestion that Shishak's attack on Judah (1 Ki. 14:25–26) was in support of his ally Jeroboam lacks positive evidence in its support. The resultant loss of the wealth Solomon had amassed, even though Israel seems to have suffered from Shishak's attack as well, meant that Judah now stood permanently in a position of material inferiority compared with Israel. The evidence suggests that Judah needed a prosperous Israel for its own prosperity.

One effective test of the absolute, rather than relative, prosperity of Judah was its ability to control Edom, or as much of it as was necessary for the safeguarding of the trade-route to the Gulf of Aqabah. Rehoboam made no effort to maintain his father's precarious hold on the area. Jehoshaphat evidently completely subdued the country (1 Ki. 22:47), but later he had to install a vassal king (2 Ki. 3:9). Edom regained its independence under his son Jehoram (2 Ki. 8:20–22). Amaziah, about half a century later, reconquered Edom (2 Ki. 14:7). This time the conquest was more effective, and not until the troubles of Ahaz' reign 60 years later was Edom finally able to free itself (2 Ki. 16:6). After this Judah does not seem even to have attempted conquest.

It was only a decisive victory by Abijah (or Abijam) that restored a measure of parity between the kingdoms (2 Ch. 13). Asa, faced with the capable Baasha, could maintain it only by allying himself with Ben-hadad, king of Damascus (1 Ki. 15:18–20). The dynasty of Omri, disturbed both by the increasing power of Damascus, and even more by the threat from *Assyria, made peace with Judah, which was later sealed by the marriage of Athaliah, Ahab's daughter, or perhaps sister (2 Ki. 8:26), with Jehoram. It is widely held that at this time Judah was Israel's vassal. So far from this being true, the evidence suggests that Jehoshaphat used Israel as a buffer between him and Assyria. This is the most likely explanation why Judah does not figure on Shalmaneser's list of his enemies at the battle of Qarqar, nor for that matter on the 'Black Obelisk'. He seems to have looked on, with the sole exception of the battle of Ramoth-gilead (1 Ki. 22:1–38), while Israel and Damascus tore at one another's vitals. Hence, by the end of his long reign, he felt himself strong enough to refuse Ahaziah's request for a joint venture to Ophir after the first had failed (1 Ki. 22:48–49 compared with 2 Ch. 20:35–37). The relative equality between the kingdoms at this time is seen in the fact that Jehu, though he had killed Ahaziah of Judah (2 Ki. 9:27), did not venture to carry his anti-Baal campaign into Judah, nor, on the other hand, did Athaliah try to avenge her son's death.

In the century between the accession of Jehu and the deaths of Jeroboam II and Uzziah the fortunes of Judah seem to have kept pace with those of Israel both in affliction and prosperity. Probably the latter came more slowly to the S, even as the hollowness of its prosperity was revealed somewhat later than in Israel.

b. Earlier foreign enemies

Until the collapse of Israel the history of Judah is singularly uninfluenced by foreign threats. Shishak's invasion was a last stirring of Egypt's ancient power until the Assyr. advance forced it to measures of self-defence. The Philistines had been so weakened that we find them as aggressors only when Judah was weakest, *viz.* under Jehoram (2 Ch. 21:16) and Ahaz (2 Ch. 28:18). At the height of Hazael's power, when he had almost destroyed Israel, Jehoash was forced to become tributary to Damascus, but this cannot have lasted long. In fact, the only two major threats of this period were from those sudden movements that the nomads and semi-nomads of the desert have periodically thrown up. Zerah 'the Cushite' (2 Ch. 14:9) is more likely to have been an Arabian (*cf.* Gn. 10:7) than an Ethiopian, *i.e.* a Sudanese. The second was from a sudden movement of the inhabitants of the Transjordan steppe-land (2 Ch. 20:1, 10).

c. Judah and Assyria

As stated above, the earlier advances of Assyria do not seem to have affected Judah. When Damascus and Israel attacked Ahaz (2 Ki. 16:5), it was a last desperate attempt to unite the remnants of the West against the advance of Tiglath-pileser III. There are no grounds for thinking that Judah was threatened by the Assyrians, for until they wanted to challenge Egypt they would hardly alarm it by advancing prematurely to its desert frontier. By accepting the suzerainty of Assyria Ahaz virtually sealed the fate of Judah. On the one hand, it remained a vassal until the approaching doom of Assyria (612 BC) could be foreseen; on the other, it was caught up in the intrigues stirred up by Egypt, for which it duly suffered. Hezekiah's revolt in 705 BC, crushed by Sennacherib 4 years later, reduced Judah to a shadow of its former self, at least two-thirds of the population perishing or being carried away captive, and a large portion of its territory being lost. For details, see J. Bright, *A History of Israel*[2], 1972, pp. 282–286, 296–308; *DOTT*, pp. 64–70.

d. Revival and downfall

A revival of religious and nationalistic feeling under the young Josiah began just after Ashurbanipal's death (631 BC), when the weakness of Assyria was already becoming manifest. The steps in reform indicated in 2 Ch. 34:3, 8 suggest how closely interwoven religion and politics had become, for each step was in itself also a rejection of Assyr. religious and therefore political control. By the height of the reform in 621 BC Josiah, though probably still nominally tributary to Assyria, was in fact independent. With or without the approval of his nominal overlord he took over the Assyr. provinces of Samaria and E Galilee (2 Ch. 34:6) and doubtless recovered the territory that Hezekiah had lost as a punishment for his rebellion. There is no reliable evidence that the Scythian inroad, which did so much to give Assyria its mortal wound, affected or even reached Judah.

There is no indication that Josiah offered any opposition to Pharaoh Psammetichus' expedition in aid of Assyria in 616 BC, but when Pharaoh Neco repeated the expedition in 609 BC Josiah evidently felt that in the new international position his only chance of maintaining Judah's independence was to fight, but in the ensuing battle at Megiddo he met his death. There is no evidence for the suggestion that he was acting in alliance with the rising star of *Babylon, though the possibility must not be rejected.

Egypt marked its victory by deposing Josiah's son Jehoahaz and replacing him by his brother Jehoiakim, who had, however, to accept Babylonian overlordship soon after Nebuchadrezzar's victory at Carchemish (605 BC) (Dn. 1:1; 2 Ki. 24:1). In 601 BC Nebuchadrezzar was checked by Neco in a battle near the Egyp. frontier, and on his withdrawal to Babylon Jehoiakim rebelled. Judah was ravaged by Bab. troops and auxiliary levies (2 Ki. 24:2). Jehoiakim died an obscure death in December 598 BC, before he could suffer the full penalty of rebellion, and Jehoiachin, his 18-year-old son, surrendered Jerusalem to Nebuchadrezzar on 16 March 597 BC.

His uncle Zedekiah became the last king of Judah, but revolted in 589 BC. By January 588 BC the Bab. armies were before the walls of Jerusalem. In July 587 BC the walls were breached and Zedekiah was captured to meet a traitor's fate (2 Ki. 25:6–7); a month later the city was burnt down and the walls razed.

e. Religion under the Monarchy

Popular religion in Judah was probably as degraded by concepts of nature-religion as in Israel, but its relative isolation and openness to the desert will have made it less influenced by its Canaanite forms. Its lack of major sanctuaries—only Hebron and Beersheba are known to us, with Gibeon in Benjamin—increased the influence of Jerusalem and its Solomonic Temple. It is questionable whether any king of Israel could even have attempted the centralizing reforms of Hezekiah and Josiah. The Davidic covenant (2 Sa. 7:8–16), far more than the general atmosphere of the 'Fertile Crescent', made the king the undisputed leader of the national religion, even though cultic functions were denied him (2 Ch. 26:16–21).

The power of the king might be used for good, as in the reformations, but where national policy seemed to demand an acceptance of Baal-worship, as under Jehoram, Ahaziah and Athaliah, or a recognition of the Assyr. astral deities, as under Ahaz and Manasseh, there was no effective power that could resist the royal will. The royal authority in matters of religion will also have helped to make the official cult for many merely an external and official matter.

f. Exile (597–538 BC)

Apart from an unspecified number of ordinary captives destined to slavery, Nebuchadrezzar deported the cream of the population in 597 BC (2 Ki. 24:14; Je. 52:28—the difference in figures is doubtless due to different categories of captives being envisaged). A few, including the royal family, became 'guests' of Nebuchadrezzar in Babylon; others, *e.g.* Ezekiel, were settled in communities in Babylonia, where they had apparently full freedom apart from the right to change their domicile; the skilled artisans became part of a mobile labour force used by Nebuchadrezzar in his building operations. The destruction of Jerusalem added to the general total of captives (2 Ki. 25:11), and Je. 52:29 shows there was another group of designated deportees. The murder of Gedaliah, whom Nebuchadrezzar had made governor of Judah, led to a large-scale flight to Egypt (2 Ki. 25:25–26; Je. 41:1–43:7). This, in turn, was followed in 582 BC by another, obviously punitive, deportation to Babylonia (Je. 52:30).

As the result of deportation and flight Judah was left, and remained, virtually empty (see W. F. Albright, *The Archaeology of Palestine*², 1954, pp. 140–142). The land S of a line between Beth-zur and Hebron seems to have been detached from Judah in 597 BC; into it the Edomites gradually moved. As a result, this area was lost to Judah until its capture by John Hyrcanus after 129 BC and the forcible Judaizing of its population. The remainder was placed under the governor of Samaria and deliberately kept virtually empty; there is no evidence for the infiltration of other peoples. It may be presumed that Nebuchadrezzar intended to follow the normal Assyr.–Bab. practice of bringing in settlers from other conquered areas (*cf.* 2 Ki. 17:24), but for some reason refrained.

V. Post-exilic Judah

a. Restoration

Babylon fell to Cyrus in 539 BC, and the next year he ordered the rebuilding of the Jerusalem Temple (Ezr. 6:3–5); he accompanied this with permission for the deportees and their descendants to return (Ezr. 1:2–4). The list of names, involving a total of some 43,000 persons, in Ezr. 2 may well cover the period 538–522 BC, but there are no solid grounds for doubting that there was an immediate and considerable response to Cyrus' decree.

Sheshbazzar, a member of the Davidic royal family, seems to have been Cyrus' commissioner to oversee the rebuilding of the Temple; he will have returned (or died?) after the laying of the foundations (Ezr. 5:14, 16). There is no evidence that Judah was detached politically from the district of Samaria until the time of Nehemiah; the title 'governor' given Sheshbazzar is too specific a rendering for *pēḥâ*. Zerubbabel, probably heir-apparent of the royal house, does not seem to have held any official position, the title of *pēḥâ* in Hg. 1:1; 2:21 being probably honorific —note his non-appearance in Ezr. 5:3–17. Other Jewish leaders bore the title *pēḥâ* in the following decades, appointed by the Persians.

By the time of Ezra in the second half of the 4th century it had become apparent to most that political independence and the restoration of the Davidic monarchy were no more than a hope for the more distant future. Ezra transformed the Jews from a national state into a 'church', making the keeping of the Torah the purpose of their existence. The political insignificance of Judaea under the Persians and the relatively peaceful conditions of the country favoured the steady instruction of the mass of the people in the Torah. The only political upheaval of the period may have been a deportation to Babylonia and Hyrcania, though many doubt it (*cf.* Jos., *Contra Apionem* 1. 194).

b. The end of Judah

The campaigns of Alexander the Great will hardly have affected Judaea, but his founding of Alexandria provided a centre for a western, and for the most part voluntary, dispersion, which soon rivalled that of Babylonia and Persia in numbers and surpassed it in wealth and influence. The division of Alexander's empire among his generals meant that Palestine became a debatable land between Syria and Egypt. Till 198 BC it was normally in the hands of the Egyp. Ptolemies, but then it became part of the Syrian Seleucid empire.

The extravagances of the rich Hellenized upper classes of Jerusalem, in large proportion priests, and the unbalanced efforts of Antiochus Epiphanes (175–163 BC) to Hellenize his empire, which led him to forbid circumcision and Sabbath-keeping and to demand the worship of Greek deities, created an alliance between religious zeal and dormant nationalism. The Jews achieved first religious autonomy and then political freedom (140 BC) for the first time since Josiah. By 76 BC their boundaries extended virtually from the traditional Dan to Beersheba. For the history of this meteoric rise and sudden collapse, see *ISRAEL.

When the Romans destroyed the last vestiges of political independence in AD 70, and especially after the crushing of Bar-Kokhba's revolt in AD 135, Judaea ceased to be a Jewish land, but the name of Judah in its form of Jew became the title of all dispersed through the world who clung to the Mosiac law, irrespective of tribal or national origin.

BIBLIOGRAPHY. Archaeological discovery has put all earlier treatments of the subject to a greater or less degree out of date. John Bright, *A History of Israel**², 1972, gives an up-to-date and balanced presentation with a mention of the most important literature. See A. R. Millard, 'The Meaning of the Name Judah', *ZAW* 86, 1974, pp. 246f. For the text of *Kings*, see J. A. Montgomery and H. S. Gehman, *The Books of Kings*, *ICC*, 1951. For extra-biblical texts naming Judah, see J. B. Pritchard, *ANET*³, 1969; and *DOTT*. For the post-exilic period, see W. O. E. Oesterley, *A History of Israel*, 2, 1932; F. F. Bruce, *Israel and the Nations*, 1963. See *ISRAEL. H.L.E.

JUDAISM. When one defines Judaism as 'the religion of the Jews', *i.e.* their faith and their practice, one must ask which historical era is in view, for the religion of the Jews has changed through the centuries. The religion of the Patriarchs in the book of Genesis, that of the era of the Sinaitic Covenant and Mosaic Law, and that of the post-exilic period and the rabbinic Judaism that followed the destruction of the second Temple (of which the modern forms of Orthodox and Conservative Judaism are direct descendants), are all different.

Here we are concerned primarily with the Judaism of the Greco-Roman period, the later post-exilic period up to the end of the 1st century when rabbinic Judaism began to consolidate itself in order to survive without nation and Temple. This therefore is the Judaism of the second Temple, the time of Jesus and the emergence of Christianity. Twentieth-century study of this Judaism has resulted in two momentous conclusions that will determine much of what is discussed below. First, it has become increasingly clear that even this Judaism was very diverse. The once fashionable talk of 'normative' Judaism in this period (*e.g.* as in G. F. Moore) has given way to the reference to Judaisms in the plural. Second, the all too common Christian portrayal of this Judaism as a legalistic religion, wherein one established righteousness before God on the basis of good works, is now seen to be a caricature. Understood correctly, this Judaism embodies a 'covenantal nomism', *i.e.* a law-centredness within the covenantal framework (thus E. P. Sanders) that rests as squarely upon the grace of God as does Christianity. The implications of these important conclusions will be made clear in what follows.

I. The fundamental elements of all Judaisms

Despite its diversity, we may note constant elements that serve as the *sine qua non* of anything that bears the name Judaism. The importance of these basic, constitutive elements can hardly be exaggerated. In every case they derive from the scriptures that came to be canonized by the end of the 1st century as the Heb. Bible.

a. Election and covenant

The origin and basis of Judaism is to be found already in the Abrahamic Covenant (Gn. 12:1–3). Abram is chosen by God – the one true God, as Israel's monotheism insisted – to be the recipient of wonderful blessings that will involve the emergence of a great nation and ultimately blessing for all the families of the earth. These covenant promises that brought Abram into a special relationship with Yahweh required no special merit or righteousness on his part. The election of Abraham, and the promises bestowed upon him, rest solely upon God's gracious initiative. Further statements of the Abrahamic Covenant add references to the gift of the land (13:14–17) and many descendants (15:5) who will have power over their enemies (22:17). The covenant is renewed with Abraham's son Isaac (26:3–4) and his grandson Jacob (28:13–15), who in turn articulates it to Joseph (48:3–4, 21). It is 'an everlasting covenant' (17:7). This promise, confirmed and extended with new metaphors in the covenants at Sinai (Ex. 19:3–6; Dt. 7:6–9) and with David (2 Sa. 7:8–16), is foundational to all Judaisms and a fixed point that henceforward separates Jew from non-Jew.

b. Torah

Of nearly equal importance to election and covenant is the gift of the Torah, in the sense of the commandments given to Israel at Sinai through the mediation of Moses (Ex. 20–40; Lv. 1–27). Although the Torah does not establish Israel, it is nevertheless her supreme calling. The Sinaitic statements link the covenantal promises with obedience to the Law. Moses is instructed to tell the people: 'Now therefore, if you will obey my voice and keep my covenant, you shall be my own possession among all the peoples' (Ex. 19:5) and similarly: 'If you obey the commandments of the Lord your God which I command you this day, by loving the Lord your God, by walking in his ways, and by keeping his commandments and his statutes and his ordinances, then you shall live and multiply, and the Lord your God will bless you in the land which you are entering to take possession of it' (Dt. 30:16). This still does not mean, however, that Israel must keep the commandments in order to enter into relationship with God. Her election remains prior to the call to obedience, yet now the maintenance of that elect status, and the realization of the covenant promises, are made contingent upon obedience to the commandments. From this time on Judaism in principle becomes what has been called a 'covenantal nomism', *i.e.* a religion focused on the obedience to the Law, but within the larger and prior framework provided by election and covenant. Judaism of necessity becomes nomistic, 'law-centred', but within a context of grace (hence, not 'legalistic').

c. Temple

The focal point of the religious praxis of the Jews became first the wilderness tent-shrine and then the Solomonic Temple. Through the several aspects of the tent-shrine/Temple, *i.e.* its structure (with the ark of the covenant in the holy of holies, and the various courts of approach), its cultus (the sacrificial ritual) and its mediatorial priesthood and regulations, the Jews learned about the holiness of God, the sinfulness of humanity, and the necessity of atonement for the experience of forgiveness. The Temple, housing the presence of God in Israel's midst, furthermore became the symbolic centre of Israel's identity as God's people, its centre of authority, not only religiously but economically, nationally and politically. After the destruction of Solomon's Temple in 586 BC, when the Jews returned from the exile, it became an immediate priority to build a second temple (Ezr. 1:3; 3:2–3, 10–13).

In principle all Jews and all Judaisms were committed to the Temple. There was not, however, always agreement concerning the morality or the legitimacy of the priesthood in charge of the Temple. With the deposition of Onias III in 174 BC the Temple fell into the control of a succession of high priests not of the Zadokite lineage. The Qumran sect rejected not the Temple itself but the illegitimate reigning priesthood, and looked for the day when the Temple would be purged and Zadokite priests would once more gain control.

d. Land

As we have seen, the land was a part of the covenantal promises from the very beginning. The land became inextricably connected with the hope of the Jews in the covenant loyalty of Yahweh. The future that God had promised to Israel was inconceivable apart from the reality of the secure possession of the land. Thus the land, like the Temple, came to have a highly symbolic significance for the Jews.

II. The emergence of Second Temple Judaisms

a. The crucial significance of the exile

The Babylonian exile was a catastrophe of immeasurable significance for the subsequent shape of Judaism. The defeat of Judah and the destruction of the Temple represented the boldest possible contradiction of Israel's election and covenant promises. The tension in post-exilic perspectives is everywhere apparent (*e.g.* La. 5:19–22; Ps. 137:1–4; Hg. 2:3; Zc. 1:12; 2 Baruch 10:6–11:7). The dominant explanation of the tragedy, leaning on the rationale of such Torah passages as Dt. 4:25–28; 30; 31:27–29, focused on Israel's failure to obey the commandments of the Lord (see esp. La. 1:8, 18, 22; 4:6; Ezr. 5:12; 9:6–7, 13; Ne. 9:26–31; Zc. 7:12; Testament of Moses 3:13; Testament of Judah 23; Testament of Zebulun 9; Testament of Naphtali 4:1–3; Psalms of Solomon 9:1–3). The other side of the coin was that Israel had not yet experienced the fulfilment of the promises given to her, because she had not been obedient to the Law.

Even after the actual return from the exile many Jews probably believed that because of the lack of the fulfilment of the promises, Israel still remained in exile. Therefore post-exilic Judaism turned to the Law with a new, burning intensity.

This has led to the commonly encountered, yet simplistic, contrast between the religion of the OT and 'Judaism'. Therefore many speak of the birth of Judaism in the new reading of the Law of Moses by Ezra the scribe (law scholar) recorded in Ne. 8:1–12, followed by the study of 'the words of the Law' in 8:13–18. The balance with the covenant has now clearly shifted towards nomism.

b. The attempted destruction of Judaism by Antiochus IV Epiphanes

In 168–167 BC an event occurred that was in many respects analogous to the experience of exile and also of very great importance in shaping the mind-set of the Second Temple Judaisms of the time of Jesus. Antiochus defiled the Temple, prohibited the practice of Judaism, and attempted to Hellenize the Jews thoroughly. Although this disaster was effectively counteracted by the heroic deeds of the Maccabees, it left its indelible mark on the psyche of 2nd-century Judaism. The importance of maintaining the distinctives of the Law burned more deeply in the Jewish mind.

c. The development of apocalyptic

Apocalyptic flourished in the soil of post-exilic Judaism. It provided a way to cope with the apparent failure of God to fulfil the promises made to Israel, and thus eased the tension referred to above. The goal that God had in mind, the age to come, could not be reached by evolution within ordinary history. The future was indeed in God's hands, but the fulfilment of the promises would come only through a radical divine intervention. The time for this was unchangeably fixed in the will of God and indications of its nearness had been revealed (Gk. *apokalyptō*), so it was claimed, to certain individuals who published their views commonly under the pseudonyms of past heroes of the scriptures. All Israel had to do was to wait patiently and in readiness.

III. Sects and varying aspects of Second Temple Judaisms

a. Pharisees

Pride of place must go to the Pharisees, because it is they who served as the fountain-head of all later (post 70) Judaism. They are logically, if not in fact, the descendants of the Torah movement begun by Ezra and the 2nd-century BC Hasidim who, like the Maccabees, so valiantly resisted the Hellenization of the Jews. The Pharisees' programme for the post-exilic situation was to adhere to the commandments more faithfully by spelling out their meaning in great detail, thus building a fence around the Torah (*'Aboth* 3:14). This they did by developing an oral tradition that elaborated the commandments. This tradition was later claimed to have been derived from Moses on Sinai (*'Aboth* 1:1), where two laws, written and oral, were supposedly given. The Pharisees appear in the gospels as arch-opponents of Jesus and are described by him as those who 'sit on Moses' seat', *i.e.* those who are known for their expertise in the interpretation of the law of Moses (Mt. 23:2; *cf.* Josephus, *War* 1.110; *Ant.* 17.41; 13.297). The Pharisees' quest for righteousness is approved by Jesus in principle and yet he severely criticises their oral tradition (*e.g.* Mk. 7:8–9; Mt. 23:4, 13–28). The Pharisees focused on matters of ritual purity, calling for the standards of purity observed by the priests in the Temple to be applied to ordinary households. They were most concerned with table fellowship including the dietary restrictions, although Sabbath observance and tithing were also important, as was circumcision.

It is well known that the Pharisees, unlike the Sadducees, believed in the resurrection of the dead as well as in angels and demons (*cf.* Acts 23:8 and the Josephus references mentioned above). They also differed from the Sadducees in believing in reward and retribution after death and that the promises made to Israel would find a future fulfilment through the coming of a Messiah. (Many, if not all, Pharisees accepted the apocalyptic perspective on the future.) The Pharisees held the sovereignty of God and human free will in unresolved tension. See also *PHARISEES.

b. Essenes

Already known from Josephus and the Damascus Document (but surprisingly not mentioned in the NT), the Essenes have now become much more familiar to us, thanks to the discovery of the Dead Sea Scrolls. These Scrolls probably reflect a monastic community of Essenes living at Qumran on the NW shore of the Dead Sea (Essene communities existed elsewhere as well) from the 2nd century BC to AD 70. The agenda of the Essenes was also the intensive quest for achieving the righteousness of the Torah. The most distinctive belief held by the Essenes, however, was that they themselves were the community of the new covenant living in the last days immediately prior to the eschatological realization of Israel's hope. The leader of the community, the Teacher of Righteousness, interpreted the prophetic writings so as to show that the community members were what the prophets were talking about as they spoke of the end of the present age. See also *ESSENES.

c. Sadducees

The Sadducees were a priestly group who held the authority of the high priesthood and thus had power over the Temple cultus. As aristocratic opportunists who catered to the Romans in the administration of Palestine, the Sadducees reflected their lack of belief in the eschatological fulfilment of Israel's promises. As we have seen, they did not accept the resurrection of the dead, nor therefore did they believe in reward or retribution after death. They appeared to want to make the most of the present *status quo* and they firmly rejected the partial determinism of the Pharisees, believing in the full freedom of the individual. They refused to accept the authority of the Pharisees' oral law and accepted the final authority of the Pentateuch alone. There is some rabbinic evidence that the Sadducees disagreed with the Pharisees over certain purity issues. See also *SADDUCEES.

d. Zealots

Although possessing little if any distinctiveness as a Jewish sect (in most respects they agreed with the Pharisees; Josephus, *Ant.* 18.23), the 'fourth philosophy' described by Josephus deserves mention here. With Maccabean successes in their minds, this group believed that God would honour violent tactics against the Romans. If the Sicarii ('daggermen'), political assassins, are not to be identified with the Zealots, they at least shared a similar perspective. Such a viewpoint obviously differed dramatically from the Pharisees' idea of determinism and the apocalyptists' notion of a fixed time for the realization of the promises. Yet their hope was not dissimilar to that of the apocalyptic perspective, despite the fact that they would not wait passively for God to act, but took political action themselves. The ambitions of the Zealots came to a tragic end with the capture of Masada in AD 74, although the zealotic spirit surfaced for a while again in the Second Jewish Revolt of AD 132–135. See also *ZEALOTS.

IV. The emergence of rabbinic Judaism

The catastrophe of the fall of Jerusalem and the destruction of the Temple in AD 70 confronted Judaism with yet another pivotal crisis, as significant as the Babylonian exile and Antiochus' desecration of the Temple and persecution of Judaism, yet possessing a finality not contradicted by the Second Jewish Revolt of AD 132–135. Of all the varieties of Judaism existing in the Second Temple Period, only one emerged from the ashes: Pharisaic Judaism. As G. E. Moore put it, 'Judaism is the monument of the Pharisees' (*Judaism* 2, p. 193). In the last decades of the 1st century, rabbinic Judaism began to consolidate itself at Yavneh under the leadership of Johanan ben Zakkai. In Jacob Neusner's phrase, Pharisaic Judaism moved 'from politics to piety'. Without abandoning the basic belief structure of Judaism outlined above, rabbinic Judaism focused persistently on personal obedience of the law as stipulated in the growing oral tradition. Although the rabbis undoubtedly prayed for the fulfilment of the promises and the realization of Israel's hope (*e.g.* in the Qaddish), in the rabbinic world of Torah piety, it was as though time had stopped. Without the Temple and without a nation, the focus of piety became the individual, his table, his prayer, his study of the Torah, and particularly the study of the commandments. Through the work of the Tannaim ('repeaters') the oral law was maintained and further developed until it was edited and put into final form, in what is known as the Mishnah, by Judah the Patriarch, *c.* AD 200. Other Tannaitic materials (*Baraitoth*) were gathered into the Tosephta ('supplement') and their work can also be seen in the Midrashim (commentaries on Scripture). Further custodians of rabbinic tradition, the Amoraim ('speakers') continued work that eventually came to fruition in the commentaries on the Mishnah, represented by the Babylonian and Palestinian Talmuds. And thus the course and tone of Judaism was set down to its present manifestations.

BIBLIOGRAPHY. J. H. Charlesworth (ed.), *The Old Testament Pseudepigrapha*, 1983, 1985; S. J. D. Cohen, *From the Maccabees to the Mishnah*, 1987; W. D. Davies and L. Finkelstein (eds.), *The Cambridge History of Judaism*, 2, 1989; J. D. G. Dunn, *The Partings of the Ways Between Christianity and Judaism and their Significance for the Character of Christianity*, 1991; C. A. Evans and D. A. Hagner (eds.), *Anti-Semitism and Early Christianity. Issues of Polemic and Faith*, 1993; S. Freyne, *Galilee from Alexander the Great to Hadrian. A Study of Second Temple Judaism*, 1980; L. L. Grabbe, *Judaism from Cyrus to Hadrian*, 1992; R. A. Kraft and G. W. E. Nickelsburg (eds.), *Early Judaism and its Modern Interpreters*, 1986; F. G. Martínez, *The Dead Sea Scrolls Translated*, 1994; G. F. Moore, *Judaism in the First Centuries of the Christian Era: The Age of the Tannaim*, 1927–1930; J. Neusner, *From Politics to Piety. The Emergence of Pharisaic Judaism*, 1973; J. Neusner, *Judaism. The Evidence of the Mishnah*, 1981; G. W. E. Nickelburg, *Jewish Literature Between the Bible and the Mishnah*, 1981; S. Safrai, *Compendia. Rerum Iudaicarum ad Novum Testamentum*, 3:2, *The Literature of the Sages. First part: Oral Torah, Halakha, Mishnah, Tosefta, Talmud, External Tractates*, 1987; S. Safrai and M. Stern, *Compendia. Rerum Iudaicarum ad Novum Testamentum*, Section 1. *The Jewish People in the First Century: Historical Geography, Political History, Social, Cultural and Religious Life and Institutions*, 2 vols., 1974–76; A. J. Saldarini, *Pharisees, Scribes and Sadducees in Palestinian Society*, 1988; E. P. Sanders, *Judaism: Practice and Belief 63BCE–66CE*, 1992; E. Schürer, *The History of the Jewish People in the Age of Jesus Christ* (175 BC–AD 135), rev. edn. G. Vermes, F. Millar and M. Black, 1973–1987; M. E. Stone, *Compendia*, 2:2, *Jewish Writings of the Second Temple Period: Apocrypha, Pseudepigrapha, Qumran Sectarian Writings, Philo, Josephus*, 1984; H. L. Strack and G. Stemberger, *Introduction to the Talmud and Midrash* (tr. M. Bockmuehl), 1991; J. C. VanderKam, *The Dead Sea Scrolls Today*, 1994; N. T. Wright, *The New Testament and the People of God*, 1992, pp. 145–338. D.A.Ha.

JUDAS. 1. The Lord's brother (Mt. 13:55 = Mk. 6:3). Perhaps the author of the Epistle of *Jude, who styles himself 'brother of James' (*BRETHREN OF THE LORD).

2. The son of James, and one of the Twelve (Lk. 6:16), called also Lebbaeus (Mt. 10:3, AV) and Thaddaeus (Mk. 3:18), who asked Jesus a question in the upper room (Jn. 14:22). Some regard him as the author of the Epistle of Jude.

3. For Judas Iscariot, see next article.

4. The Galilean who stirred up a rebellion against the Romans (Acts 5:37). Josephus says he was born in Gamala (*Ant.* 18. 3), and places the rebellion in AD 6. *Quirinius defeated the rebels and Judas was slain. **5.** A Jew at whose house in Damascus Paul lodged (Acts 9:11). **6.** A prophet surnamed Barsabbas, who with Silas was chosen by the Jerusalem Christian leaders to accompany Paul and Barnabas to Antioch to convey the apostles' decision regarding circumcision (Acts 15:22–33). J.D.D.

JUDAS ISCARIOT.

I. Name and origin

In the Synoptic lists of the Twelve whom Jesus called 'to be with him' (Mk. 3:14) the name of Judas always appears last, and usually with some description which brands him with an infamous stigma (*e.g.* 'who betrayed him', Mk. 3:19; Mt. 10:4; Lk. 6:16; *cf.* Jn. 18:2, 5). We may compare the case of Jeroboam I, in the OT, who is mentioned with horror as the one 'who made Israel to sin'.

The term 'Iscariot' is applied to his name, in the Synoptic texts and in Jn. 12:4; while in the other Johannine references the textual tradition shows considerable variation, with the name of Simon being given as Judas' father (Jn.6:71; 13:2, 26), and Iscariot being further explained by the addition *apo Karyotou* (in certain readings of 6:71; 12:4; 13:2, 26; 14:22). These additional facts supplied by John would confirm the derivation of 'Iscariot' from Heb *'îs q^erîyot*, 'a man of Kerioth'. Kerioth is located in Moab, according to Je. 48:24, 41; Am. 2:2; but there is another possible identification, Kerioth-hezron (Jos. 15:25), which is 19 km S of Hebron. This geographical explanation of 'Iscarioth' is preferable to the view which traces the word to *sikarios*, by way of an Aramaicized *'isqaryā'ā*, 'an assassin' (*cf.* Acts 21:38), as suggested by Schulthess and O. Cullmann, *The State in the New Testament*, E.T. 1957, pp. 15f. But see, to the contrary, M. Hengel, *Die Zeloten*, 1961, p. 49.

II. Career

In the apostolic band Judas was treasurer (Jn. 13:29), while another Johannine text speaks of him as a thief (12:6), mainly, we may suppose, on the ground that he 'pilfered' the money which was entrusted to him. For this sense of the verb translated 'used to take' in 12:6, as attested in the papyri, see A. Deissmann, *Bible Studies*, E.T. 1901, p. 257.

The closing scenes of the Gospel story are shadowed by the treachery of this 'one of the twelve', as he is repeatedly called (Mk. 14:10, *cf.* 14:20; Jn. 6:71; 12:4). He raises the voice of criticism against the action of Mary, who anointed the Master's feet with the precious ointment (Jn. 12:3–5). The comment of the Evangelist is intended to stress the avarice of Judas, who saw in the price of the ointment nothing of the beautiful deed which Jesus praised (Mk. 14:6) but only a means by which the apostolic fund would be increased, and thereby his own pocket lined. And even this motive was cloaked under a specious plea that the money could be given away to relieve the poor. Thus to covetousness there is added the trait of deceit. Immediately following this incident at Bethany he goes to the chief priests to betray the Lord (Mt. 26:14–16; Mk. 14:10–11; Lk. 22:3–6). Mark records simply the fact of the treachery, adding that money was promised by the priests.

Matthew supplies the detail of the amount, which may have been a part-payment of the agreed sum (with an implicit allusion to Zc. 11:12, and possibly Ex. 21:32; *cf.* Mt. 27:9). Luke gives the deep significance of the act when he records that Satan entered into the traitor and inspired his nefarious sin (*cf.* Jn. 13:2, 27). All Synoptists agree that Judas determined to await a favourable opportunity when he might deliver Jesus up to his enemies 'privately', *i.e.* secretly, by craft (for this rendering in Lk. 22:6; Mk. 14:1–2, see J. Jeremias, *The Eucharistic Words of Jesus*[2], E.T. 1966, p. 72).

That opportunity came on the evening when Jesus gathered in the upper room for the last meal with the Twelve (Mk. 14:17ff. and parallels), and this fact is perpetuated in the church's eucharistic tradition which dates from the time of St Paul (1 Cor. 11:23: 'on the night when he was betrayed'). The Lord, with prophetic insight, foresees the action of the traitor whose presence is known at the table. In the Marcan account Judas is not mentioned by name, and there seems to be a general air of bewilderment as to the traitor's identity. The conversation of Mt. 26:25 with the question-and-answer dialogue is best understood as spoken in whispered undertones, while the Johannine account preserves the first-hand tradition of the beloved disciple's question and Jesus' action with the Paschal sop, both of which may have been said and done in a secretive fashion. At all events, this is the Lord's final appeal to Judas—and the traitor's final refusal. (See F. C. Fensham, 'Judas' Hand in the Bowl and Qumran', *RQ* 5, 1965, pp. 259–261, for Judas' rejection of Jesus.) Thereafter Satan takes control of one who has become his captive; and he goes out into the night (Jn. 13:27–30).

The pre-arranged plan for Jesus' arrest was carried through. The secret which Judas betrayed was evidently the meeting-place in Gethsemane later that night; and to our Lord at prayer there came the band of soldiery, led by Judas (Mk. 14:43). The sign of identification was the last touch of irony. 'The one I shall kiss is the man' ; and with that the traitor's work was completed.

The last chapters of Judas' life are beset with much difficulty. Of his pathetic remorse the Scripture bears witness, yet the only Evangelist to record this is Matthew (27:3–10). To this account of his agony of remorse and suicide, the account of Acts 1:18–19 must be added; and also, to complete the evidence, the grotesque testimony of Papias, *Frag.* 3, preserved by Apollinarius of Laodicea. This last-named text may be conveniently consulted in the series *Ancient Christian Writers*, 6, translated and annotated by J. A. Kleist, 1957 edn., p. 119. Papias relates how Judas' body swelled (this may be a possible meaning of Acts 1:18 for the EVV 'falling headlong'; see Arndt, *s.v. prēnēs*), and dies on his own land. There have been various attempts at harmonization (*e.g.* Augustine's suggestion that the rope broke and Judas was killed by the fall, in the manner of Acts 1:18, thus conflating the Matthean and Acts accounts). But even more terrifying than the gruesome details of these accounts is the plain, stark verdict of Acts 1:25: 'this ministry and apostleship, from which Judas turned aside, to go to his own place'. The apostle had become an apostate; and had gone to the destiny reserved for such a man.

III. Character

This reference invites the question of the true character of Judas. If 'his own place' is the place he chose for himself, what motives led him to his awful destiny and fate? How can we reconcile this statement with those scriptures which give the impression that he was predetermined to fulfil the role of traitor, that Jesus chose him, knowing that he would betray him, that he had stamped on him from the beginning the inexorable character of 'the son of perdition' (Jn. 17:12)? Psychological studies are indecisive and not very profitable. Love of money; jealousy of the other disciples; fear of the inevitable outcome of the Master's ministry which made him turn state's evidence in order to save his own skin; an enthusiastic intention to force Christ's hand and make him declare himself as Messiah—de Quincey's famous reconstruction; a bitter, revengeful spirit which arose when his worldly hopes were crushed and this disappointment turned to spite and spite became hate—all these motives have been suggested. Three guiding principles ought perhaps to be stated as a preliminary to all such considerations. 1. We ought not to doubt the sincerity of the Lord's call. Jesus, at the beginning, viewed him as a potential follower and disciple. No other presupposition does justice to the Lord's character, and his repeated appeals to Judas. 2. The Lord's foreknowledge of him does not imply fore-ordination that Judas must inexorably become the traitor. 3. Judas was never really Christ's man. He fell from apostleship, but never (so far as we can tell) had a genuine relationship to the Lord Jesus. So he remained 'the son of perdition' who was lost because he was never 'saved'. His highest title for Christ was 'Rabbi' (Mt. 26:25), never 'Lord'. He lives on the stage of Scripture as an awful warning to the uncommitted follower of Jesus who is in his company but does not share his spirit (*cf.* Rom. 8:9b); he leaves the Gospel story 'a doomed and damned man' because he chose it so, and God confirmed him in that dreadful choice.

BIBLIOGRAPHY. The difficulties associated with the variant details of the death of Judas are discussed in *BC*, 1.5, pp. 22–30; J. S. Stewart, *The Life and Teaching of Jesus Christ*, 1933, pp. 166–170; P. Benoit, art. 'La mort de Judas' in *Exégèse et Théologie*, 1961; B. Gärtner, *Iscariot*, E.T. 1971; H.-J. Klauck, *Judas–Ein Jünger des Herrn*, 1987; G. Schwarz, *Jesus und Judas*, 1988; W. Klassen, *ABD* 3, pp. 1091–1096. R.P.M.

JUDE, EPISTLE OF. One of the *'Catholic Epistles'.

I. Outline of contents

The Epistle falls into five parts:

a. Salutation (vv. 1–2).

b. Jude's purpose in writing (vv. 3–4).

c. False teachers denounced and their doom foretold (vv. 5–16).

d. Exhortation to Christians (vv. 17–23).

e. Doxology (vv. 24–25).

II. Authorship, date and canonicity

The author of this little tract identifies himself as 'Jude, a servant of Jesus Christ and brother of James'. In the early church there was only one James who could be referred to in this way without further specification—'James the Lord's brother' (as he is called in Gal. 1:19). This points to an identification of the author with the Judas who is numbered among the brothers of Jesus in Mt. 13:55 and Mk. 6:3, the Judas whose two grandsons, according to Hegesippus, were examined and dismissed by Domitian when he was informed that they belonged to the house of David (Eusebius, *EH* 3. 19–20). Its date cannot be fixed with certainty; it may be tentatively assigned to the second half of the 1st century AD, after the fall of Jerusalem (v. 17 refers to the apostles in the past). We have express references to it towards the end of the 2nd century, in the Muratorian list and elsewhere; but there are probable allusions to it earlier in that century, in the *Didache* and the *Shepherd* of Hermas. Although its canonicity was long disputed, we may be glad that it was finally established, for (as Origen says) 'while it consists of but a few lines, yet it is full of mighty words of heavenly grace'.

III. Occasion and purpose

Jude had projected another treatise, concerning 'our common salvation', when he found himself obliged to take up a more controversial line, in vigorous defence of the apostolic faith. This defence was made necessary by the alarming advances made by an incipient gnosticism in the circle of Christians to which Jude addresses himself—not in this case an ascetic form of teaching like that attacked by Paul in Colossians, but an antinomian form which may have appealed to Paul's teaching about Christian liberty, misinterpreting that liberty as licence and using it 'as an opportunity for the flesh' (*cf.* Gal. 5:13). This is suggested by Jude's description of the false teachers in question as 'perverting the grace of our God into licentiousness' as well as 'denying our only Master and Lord, Jesus Christ' (v. 4).

IV. Argument of the Epistle

False teaching requires to be exposed; it is not enough to set the truth alongside it in the expectation that everyone will recognize which is which. The refutation of error is an essential correlative to the defence of the faith 'once for all delivered to the saints' (v. 3).

The doom of these false teachers has been pronounced of old. God's judgment, if slow, is sure, and once executed it abides for ever. This appears from the examples of the disobedient Israelites who died in the wilderness (*cf.* 1 Cor. 10:5; Heb. 3:17; this was evidently a commonplace of primitive Christian 'typology'), of the rebellious angels of Gn. 6:1–4, and of the cities of the plain (*cf.* Gn. 19). Like those prototypes, the false teachers defy divinely constituted authority, unlike the archangel Michael, who would not use insulting language even to the devil (vv. 8–10). (Clement and Origen tell us that the incident of Michael's dispute with the devil was related in the *Assumption of Moses*, but the part of this work containing the incident is no longer extant.) The examples of Cain, Balaam and Korah also point the lesson of doom for these latter-day followers of theirs (v. 11).

These false teachers introduce trouble and disgrace into the church's fellowship, into its very love-feasts; they are shepherds who feed themselves and not the flock ('blind mouths', in Milton's phrase), clouds which blot out the sun but send down no refreshing rain, trees which produce only Dead Sea fruit (v. 12). They are ineffectual as roaring waves whose rage expends itself in froth and foam; they are stars wandering out of their orbits into eternal night (v. 13). The judgment which awaits them at the parousia was foretold by Enoch (vv. 14f.; *cf.* *1 Enoch* 1. 9).

True believers, however, need not be alarmed at the activity of such people, of whose rise and fall the apostles had given them warning in advance. Let them safeguard themselves by being built up in faith, praying in the power of the Spirit, continuing steadfastly in the fellowship of divine love, and looking forward to the consummation of mercy and life at the appearing of Christ (vv. 17–21). While they must abhor and avoid all false teachers, they should pity and rescue those who are led astray by them (vv. 22–23).

The Epistle ends with an ascription of praise to God as the One who is able to guard his people from stumbling until they stand without blemish 'before the presence of his glory with rejoicing'.

BIBLIOGRAPHY. E. M. Sidebottom, *James, Jude and 2 Peter, NCB*, 1967; R. J. Bauckham, *ANRW* II. 25.5, 1988, pp. 3791–3826; *Jude and the Relatives of Jesus*, 1990; *Jude, II Peter*, WBC, 1983; E. M. B. Green, *2 Peter and Jude*[2], *TNTC*, 1987. F.F.B.

JUDGES. The Heb. word (*šōpēṭ*) means one who dispenses justice, punishing the evil-doer and vindicating the righteous. The corresponding word for 'judgment' is used to describe a rule by which he must be guided (Ex. 21:1).

I. The Mosaic institution

In the wilderness period Moses wore himself out by sitting to judge the cases brought to him (Ex. 18:13–27, and *cf.* Ex. 2:14). On Jethro's advice he appointed deputies to judge ordinary cases, bringing to him only the most important (see also Dt. 1:9–18).

The Deuteronomic law provides for the appointment of judges, and *officers to assist them (Dt. 16:18); 'in all your towns'. So the more primitive rule of the nomadic period is adapted to the future settlement.

There is insistence upon the need for scrupulous fairness, and impartial justice (Dt. 1:16f.; 16:19f.; 24:17f.; 25:13–16). Since the book of the law was in the charge of the priests, the more important cases were to be tried by a judge with priests as assessors (Dt. 17:8–13). During the period of the conquest we find judges taking part in assemblies of the nation (Jos. 8:33; 24:1).

II. The period of the Judges

After the death of Joshua there followed the period of disorganization, tribal discord and defeat, which is described in the book of Jdg. But when the people cried to the Lord, the author tells us, he 'raised up judges, who saved them' (Jdg. 2:16). These national heroes are sometimes called 'deliverers' (AV 'saviours') (3:9, 15), and of most of them it is said that they 'judged Israel' for a stated period of years, Othniel being the first (3:9) and Samson the last (16:31).

It is clear that this imparts a new meaning into the word 'judge', namely, that of a leader in battle and a ruler in peace. We may see in them a type of Christ, who came to be our Saviour, is with us as our Leader, and will come to be our Judge.

In 1 Sa. there is a transition to the time of the monarchy. Eli 'had judged Israel forty years' (1 Sa. 4:18), and 'Samuel judged Israel all the days of his life', going in circuit to Bethel and Gilgal and Mizpeh; and appointed his sons also as judges (7:15–8:1).

Texts from *Mari (*c.* 1800 BC) describe the activities of leaders termed *šāpiṭum*, generally similar to the work of Israelite 'judges'. These acted as local provincial 'governors' working with other neighbouring 'governors' under the Great King (A. Marzal, *JNES* 30, 1971, pp. 186–217). Their responsibilities included the exercise of justice, maintenance of order, collection of taxes and tribute, and provision of information and hospitality. Thus the Heb. *šōpēṭ* should probably be better translated 'governor' than 'judge' since the latter describes only part of his function. Similar officials are named in the earlier tablets from *Ebla.

III. Under the Monarchy

Under the kings we find judges engaged in both judiciary and other administration. Among David's officers 'Chenaniah and his sons were appointed to outside duties for Israel, as officers and judges' (1 Ch. 26:29).

After the disruption, Jehoshaphat displayed zeal for 'the book of the law of the Lord' (2 Ch. 17:9), appointed judges and officers city by city (19:5), and charged them to deal faithfully (2 Ch. 19:9f.; *cf.* Dt. 16:19f.).

Finally, on the return from exile, the decree of Artaxerxes bade Ezra set magistrates and judges to administer justice and to teach the people (Ezr. 7:25).

Later rulers of Phoenician cities took the title *šōpēṭ*; *cf.* the Carthaginian *suffetes*, mentioned by Roman writers (*PHOENICIA).

BIBLIOGRAPHY. W. Richter, *ZAW* 77, 1965, pp. 40–72; D. J. Wiseman, *BS* 134, 1977, pp. 233–237; *JBL* 8, 1988, pp. 130–136.

G.T.M.
D.J.W.

JUDGES, BOOK OF. Judges follows chronologically upon the Pentateuch and Joshua and describes the history of Israel from Joshua's death to the rise of Samuel. It takes its name from its leading characters, the *šôp̄ᵉṭîm* (Jdg. 2:16). These *'judges', however, were more than judicial arbiters; they were 'deliverers' (AV 'saviours') (3:9), charismatically empowered by God's Holy Spirit for the deliverance and preservation of Israel (6:34) up to the establishment of the kingdom (*cf.* the use of this same word for the chief magistrates of Carthage, and as a synonym for 'king' in ancient Canaanitish Ugarit, *Anat* 5. 40). Yahweh himself is the chief *šôpēṭ* (Jdg. 11:27).

I. Outline of contents

a. Events following the death of Joshua (1:1–2:5)

With initial obedience the tribes of Judah and Simeon advanced S to the conquest of Bezek, Jerusalem (not held, 1:21), Hebron and Debir (reoccupied since their devastation in Jos. 10:36, 39), Hormah, and three of the Philistine cities (not held, Jdg. 1:19). The Joseph tribes likewise captured Bethel (1:22–26), which had revolted (*cf.* Jos. 8:17; 12:9). But then came failure: Israel ceased to remove the Canaanites, no more cities were taken (Jdg. 1:27–36), and the tribe of Dan actually suffered eviction from its allotted territory (1:34). Such tolerance of evil necessitated the extended period of chastening that followed (2:1–5).

b. Israel's history under the judges (2:6–16:31)

(i) *The writer's prophetic understanding of history* (2:6–3:6). This book teaches divine retribution: that God in his providence recompenses a nation in direct correspondence to the faithfulness of its people. Israel at this time suffered under constant temptation to adopt the fertility rites of their Canaanitish neighbours, along with their confessedly superior agriculture. Many recognized that Yahweh had guided Israel in the wilderness, but Baal seemed better able to make the crops come out of the ground! Jdg. thus exhibits a repeated cycle of sin (Baal-worship), servitude (to foreign aggressors), supplication (to the merciful God, for relief) and salvation (through divinely raised up judges).

(ii) *Six successive periods of oppression and the careers of twelve deliverer-judges* (3:7–16:31).

1. *Invasions of Cushan-rishathaim* (3:7–11). After adopting the ways of Canaan, Israel suffered for 8 years under the depredations of Cushan-rishathaim, an invader who came from Hittite-controlled Mesopotamia (Jdg. 3:8). The cause, however, lay in Israel's sin (3:7) (see below, part *c*).

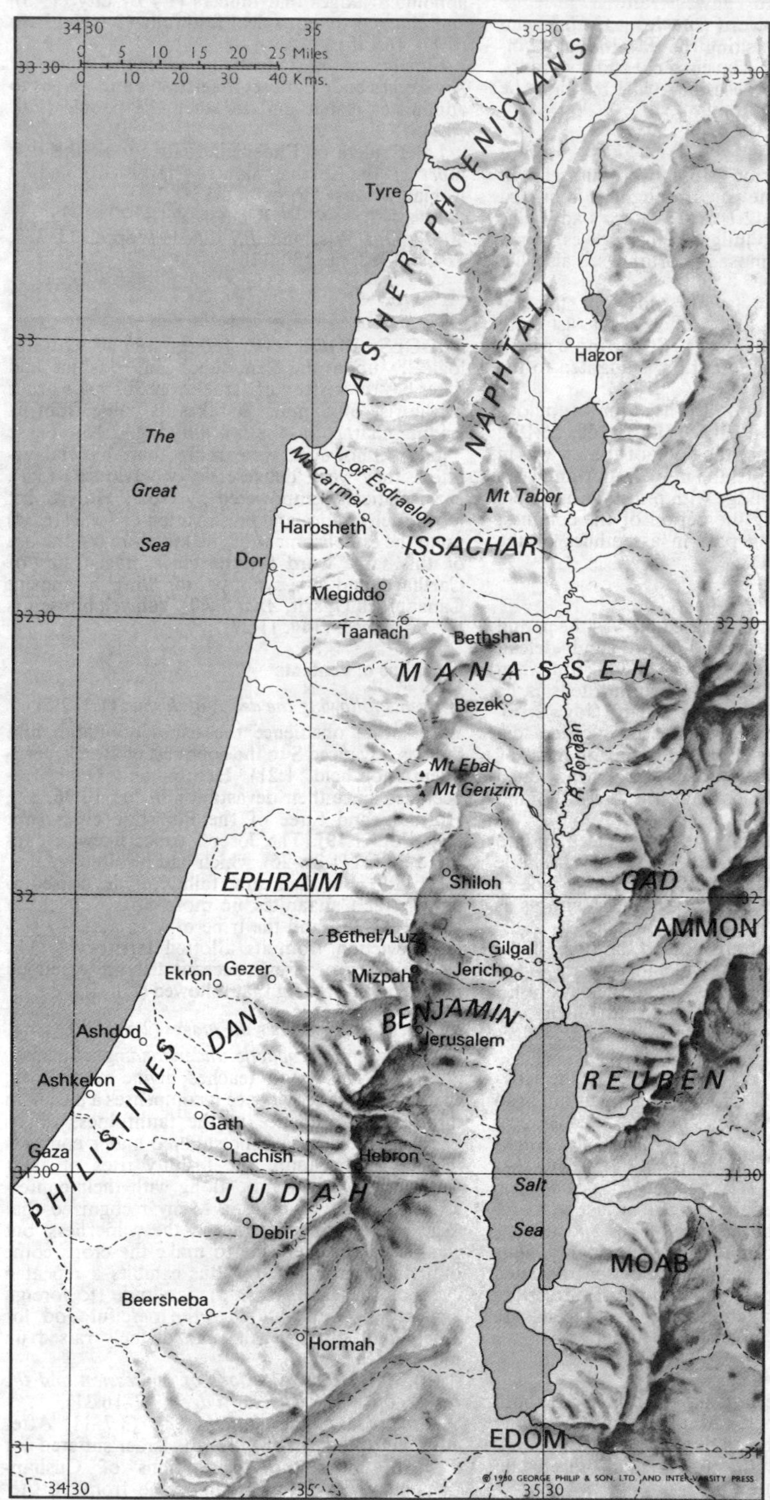

Palestine in the time of the Judges.

But when they 'cried to Yahweh, Yahweh raised up a deliverer for the people of Israel, . . . Othniel, . . . Caleb's younger brother' (3:9). The 40 years of peace that followed may correspond to the parallel period of Hittite overlordship, until some years after the death of Suppiluliuma in 1346 BC (*CAH*, 2, 2:19).

2. *Oppression under Eglon* (3:12–31). Just prior to the days of international confusion coincident with the rise of Egypt's aggressive 19th Dynasty, 'Israel again did what was evil . . .; and Yahweh strengthened Eglon the king of Moab against Israel' (3:12). 'But when (they) cried to Yahweh, (he) raised up for them a deliverer, Ehud, . . . the Benjaminite' (3:15), and granted them 80 years of peace, perhaps dating from the time of the treaty of 1315, between Seti and Mursil, *cf.* its renewel in 1284 by Rameses II. Neither Egypt nor the Hittites seem to have comprehended their providential function, but the years in which either succeeded in bringing peace to Palestine do seem to correspond to the very periods that God had ordained for granting 'rest' to his people (*cf.* J. Garstang, *Joshua–Judges*, 1931, pp. 51–66). Shamgar next achieved a limited success against early Philistines, who were better equipped than he (3:31).

3. *Deliverance by Deborah* (4:1–5:31). With the decay of the empires and the rise of local Canaanitish oppression under Jabin II of Hazor (4:2–3), God raised up the fourth of the judges, the woman Deborah. Her military commander, Barak, proceeded to muster the N-central tribes to the Valley of Esdraelon for war with Jabin's troops led by Sisera. But, 'From heaven fought the stars, from their courses they fought against Sisera' (5:20): a divinely sent cloudburst immobilized the Canaanitish chariotry, and Sisera was slain in flight by a Kenite woman. The 40 years of peace that followed upon Deborah's victory may parallel the strong rule of Rameses III, the last great pharaoh (1199–1168 BC).

4. *Deliverance by Gideon* (6:1–8:32). Next there appeared out of the E desert, Midianites and Amalekites to plunder sinful Israel (Jdg. 6:2–6; *cf.* Ru. 1:1). But Israel was cleared of the nomadic raiders (7:19–25; 8:10–12; *cf.* the peaceful background of Ru. 2–4, some 20 years later).

5. *The rise and fall of Abimelech* (8:33–10:5). The turmoil that resulted from the attempt of Gideon's son Abimelech to make himself king over Israel (Jdg. 9) was rectified by the sixth and seventh judges, Tola and Jair (10:1–5).

6. *Oppression under Ammon and the Philistines* (10:6–16:31). But with the apostasy that subsequently arose, God gave up his land to simultaneous oppressions by the Ammonites in the E and the Philistines in the W (10:7). After 18 years E Israel was freed by Jephthah, the eighth judge (ch. 11), who was succeeded by the three minor judges. W Israel, however, remained subject to the rising power of the Philistines, despite the spectacular exploits of Samson, the twelfth and last judge of the book of Judges (chs. 13–16).

c. An appendix (17:1–21:25)

This provides details on two events from Israel's very first period of apostasy (before Othniel; *cf.* the appearance of Phinehas in 20:28 and the mention of the events of ch. 18 in Jos. 19:47, the author of which seems contemporary with the conquest, Jos. 5:1; 6:25, though see *JOSHUA, II). The purpose of the appendix is to illustrate the depth of Israel's sin, whereby almost every standard of the Decalogue was transgressed. The section on Micah and the Danites (chs. 17–18) relates, *e.g.*, how Micah stole from his mother and then converted the proceeds into an idol for his house of gods (17:5). God's Levite, meanwhile, wandered unsupported, until hired by Micah. But he in turn proved false to his employer when offered a position of leadership by the covetous, idolatrous and murderous Danites (18:25). Yet this Levite was Jonathan, a direct descendant of Moses (18:30). Nothing, admittedly, is said respecting the seventh commandment (on purity); but the following chapters (19–21, the Benjaminite outrage) describe not simply civil war and the harbouring of criminals but also harlotry and marital desertion by a Levite's concubine (19:2), homosexuality, rape and adultery (19:22–24), and finally mass abduction (21:23). Such were the results when 'every man did what was right in his own eyes'.

II. Authorship and date

The book of Jdg. makes no direct statement about the date of its writing. The song of Deborah (5:2–31) does claim contemporary composition (5:1), and its authenticity is generally accepted. But the book as a whole could not have been compiled for another 2 centuries. It refers to the destruction and captivity of Shiloh (18:30–31) during the youth of Samuel (1 Sa. 4; *c.* 1080 BC); and the last event that it records is the death of Samson (Jdg. 16:30–31), which occurred a few years before Samuel's inauguration as judge (*c.* 1063). Furthermore, the repeated explanation that 'in those days there was no king in Israel' (17:6; 18:1; 21:25) suggests that the book was written *after* the accession of Saul as king in 1043 BC. Yet the popular appreciation for the kingship is still fresh; and the book seems to have been composed before the sack of Gezer in 970 BC (1 Ki. 9:16; *cf.* Jdg. 1:29) or David's capture of Jerusalem in 1003 (2 Sa. 5:6–7; *cf.* Jdg. 1:21).

The writer of Jdg. must therefore have been a man who was active during the early reign of Saul (before 1020 BC). He must also have been a prophet; for in the Heb. Bible, Jdg. takes its place in the prophetic division of the canon (the 'former' prophets: in Josephus, *Against Apion* 1. 8, the historical books, Jos.–Jb.), *cf.* the sermonic tone of 2:10–14; 3:7–8, *etc.* The most likely possibility is Samuel the prophet, who is indeed identified as the author of Jdg.–Ru. according to the Jewish Talmud (*Baba Bathra* 14b). But since this traditional account goes on to make the improbable assertion that Samuel also wrote 'the book which bears his name', we seem justified in concluding only that the author must, at least, have been one of Samuel's prophetic associates.

III. Sources of the book

The writer of Jdg. may have relied upon oral and written sources that are now lost, *e.g.* hero anthologies, such as 'the book of the *yāšār* [upright]' (Jos. 10:13). Modern critics are accustomed to assert that the writer's sources consisted of largely independent materials (later perhaps a 'J' and 'E' document) and edited by an exilic Deuteronomist ('D') and post-exilic Priestly ('P') redactors; but this analysis runs counter to the evidence of the book itself and unnecessarily discredits the unity and authenticity of its contents. It seeks, for example, to equate God's call to Gideon at the winepress and his resulting sacrifice (Jdg. 6:11–24,

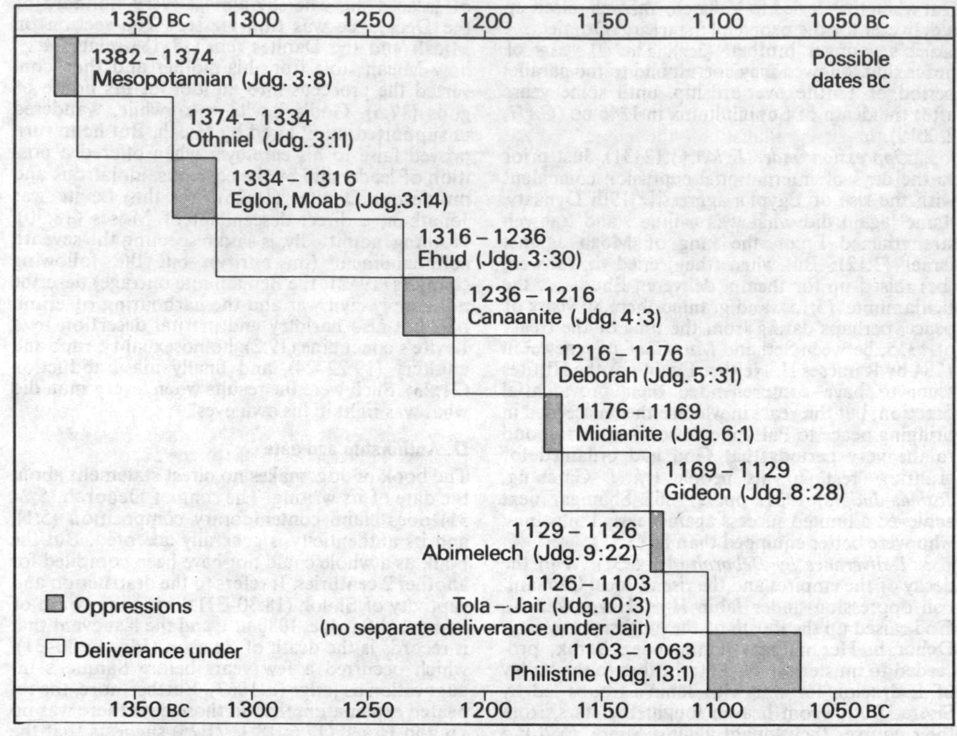

A chronology of the Judges period based on the years of oppression and peace. (*For a different interpretation see* CHRONOLOGY OF THE OT.)

said to be 'J') with his subsequent command to Gideon to destroy the Baal altar and to replace it with one to Yahweh (6:25–32, said to be 'E'), as if these were two conflicting versions of one call. Or again, it confuses Gideon's taking of the Midianite princes Oreb and Zeeb at the fords of the Jordan (7:24–25, 'E') with his final capture of the *kings*, Zeba and Zalmunna, farther east (8:10–11, 'J'), though it must then eliminate the words in 8:10, 'all who *were left* of the army', as being an attempt by some later editor to harmonize the supposedly conflicting stories. (*PENTATEUCH.)

The Heb. text of the book of Jdg. is better preserved than that of any of the other Former Prophets and is generally free from errors of scribal transmission. Its ancient LXX translation, however, exhibits inner-Greek variations to the extent that Rahlfs' edition of the LXX now presents on each page two divergent forms of Gk. text, according to codices A and B.

IV. Historical background

The historical background to the period of Jdg. concerns, locally, the presence of the Canaanites. Prior to the Heb. conquest, Moses had ordered their 'destruction' (Dt. 7:2; *cf.* Jos. 6:17), both because of long-standing immorality (Dt. 9:5; *cf.* Gn. 9:22, 25; 15:16) and because of their debasing religious influence upon God's people (Dt. 7:4); for on countless 'high places' the Canaanites worshipped local gods of fertility, Baalim, with rites that included sacred prostitution and even child sacrifice (11:31). Joshua had thus subdued the whole of Canaan (Jos. 11:16; *cf.* 21:43). But its native inhabitants had not yet lost their potential for resistance. Indeed, Moses himself had anticipated a gradual occupation of the land (Ex. 23:28–30; Dt. 7:22); and much still remained to be possessed (Jos. 13:1). On the international scene, the relevant facts may be outlined as follows: (1) At the time of Joshua's death, perhaps soon after 1400 BC, 18th Dynasty Egyptian imperial control over Palestine had become ephemeral: Amenhotep III was content to rule in decadent luxury; and his successor, Amenhotep IV (Akhenaten, *c.* 1379–1362 BC; *CAH*, 2. 2, p. 1038), devoted his exclusive attention to monotheistic religious reforms. The contemporary *Amarna letters from the Canaanitish city-states contain futile pleas for help against the plundering Habiru. This designation embraces the biblical *Hebrews, though it was also used for various Hurrian (?) aggressors from the N (descendants of Eber, Gn. 10:21, 25; *cf.* M. G. Kline, *WTJ* 19, May 1957, p. 184; 20, November 1957, p. 68). For this era was marked, at the same time, by revived Hittite activity from beyond Syria. King Suppiluliuma (*c.* 1385–1346 BC), the greatest of the Hittites, at the first encouraged anarchy among the states farther S and later achieved their practical domination for himself and his son Mursil II.

(2) But Egypt, under the new 19th Dynasty (1320–1200 BC), in turn experienced revival. Seti I retook Galilee and Phoenicia in 1318, defeated the Hittites, and 3 years later concluded a treaty with Mursil, by which Syria was assigned to Hittite control and Palestine and Phoenicia to Egyptian. Young Rameses II (1304–1237) indeed broke the treaty and invaded the Hittite territory. But after

years of costly fighting the former division of power was re-established by the treaty of 1284; and peace was kept until the decline of the Hittite empire, due to the barbarian invasions in the latter part of the century.

(3) With the fall of Crete to the barbarians in 1200 BC the ousted Philistines, 'the remnant of the coastland of Caphtor' (Je. 47:4) fled E to reinforce their older settlements on the coast of Palestine (*cf.* Gn. 21:32; Dt. 2:23). Driven back from Egypt in about 1191 by Rameses III of the 20th Dynasty, they proceeded to consolidate their position in Canaan. Before the end of the century they were thus able to mount the first of their great offensives against Israel, with which event the history of the book of Judges comes to a close.

V. Chronology

The over-all chronology of Jdg. is indicated by the statement of Jephthah, near the conclusion of the period, that Israel had by his time been occupying Palestinian territory for some 300 years (Jdg. 11:26; *cf.* the similar figure drawn from 1 Ki. 6:1). The calculation of a more precise chronology, however, depends upon two other facts that appear in the biblical record. First, since the lapse of time from the termination of the conquest to the commencement of the first (Mesopotamian) oppression is not stated, one must count backward from the accession of Samuel, *c.* 1063 BC (reckoning, from the probable date of 930 for the division of the kingdom, with 113 years for Solomon, David (over all Israel), and Saul and his successors [1 Ki. 11:42; 2:11; Acts 13:21], plus 20 years for Samuel [1 Sa. 7:2; *cf. HDB*, 1, p. 399]. Second, since some of the judges overlapped each other (*cf.* Ehud and Shamgar, Jdg. 3:30–4:1), the chronology is best gathered from the dated oppressions and subsequent deliverances. Of particular significance is the fact that the 40-year Philistine oppression (13:1) in W. Palestine continued uninterruptedly from the deaths of Tola and Jair (10:7), through the judgeships of Jephthah, the three minor judges, Eli and Samson, down to the victorious advent of Samuel. (See the chart on p. 641.)

Confirmation of 1216 for Deborah's victory now arises from pottery types found in the last Canaanite city at Hazor, so that 'Barak is to be dated in the second half of the 13th century' (*CAH*, 1, 1:239). 319 years (1382–1063) would thus seem to elapse between the first oppression and Samuel's rise, which suggests a conquest dating 1406–1400 BC. An alternative date *c.* 1240 would require greater compression of the Judges' data. (*CHRONOLOGY OF THE OLD TESTAMENT.)

VI. Teaching

From the principles stated in Jdg. 2:6–3:6 and the concrete historical examples furnished by the remainder of the book, its teaching may be summarized as follows.

a. God's wrath at sin (2:11, 14). Israel's hope for survival was dependent upon their intertribal unity, yet such co-operative effort arose only from a common dedication to their God (*cf.* 5:8–9, 16–18). Loss of faith meant extinction.

b. God's mercy upon repentance (2:16). Even foreign oppression served as a medium of divine grace, for Israel's edification (3:1–4).

c. Man's total depravity. For after each deliverance, 'whenever the judge died, they turned back and behaved worse than their fathers' (2:19). Individualistic society had demonstrated its inherent inadequacy, for man on his own inevitably goes wrong (17:6). Israel needed a king, though indeed only such a king as should accomplish the ultimate will of God (*cf.* 8:23; 9:6, 56). The author of Jdg. was thus one of civilization's first true historians, not simply recording events, but then interpreting the facts on the basis of an explicit philosophy of history. As to the permanent validity of his deuteronomic philosophy of retribution, one must grant that in those early days, when revelation was more limited, providence operated more obviously than at present. But his basic principles remain eternally sound: the sinning nation shall be punished, the repentant shall be saved, and all man-created systems must ultimately fail. The only valid hope of history lies in the coming of Christ, the King.

BIBLIOGRAPHY. G. L. Archer, Jr., *A Survey of Old Testament Introduction*, 1974, pp. 274–279; A. E. Cundall and L. Morris, *Judges–Ruth*, *TOTC*, 1968; G. Fohrer, (Sellin's) *IOT*, 1968, pp. 196–215; R. K. Harrison, *IOT*, 1968, pp. 680–694; J. D. Martin, *The Book of Judges, CBC*, 1975; A. D. H. Mayes, *Judges*, 1985; J. B. Payne, *ZPEB*, 1, pp. 833–836; *idem*, *An Outline of Hebrew History*, 1954, pp. 78–91; J. A. Soggin, *Judges*, 1987; B. G. Webb, *The Book of Judges: An Integrated Reading*, 1987; M. Wilcock, *The Message of Judges*, *BST*, 1992; L. T. Wood, pp. 66–87 in J. B. Payne (ed.), *New Perspectives on the Old Testament*, 1970.

J.B.P.

JUDGMENT (Heb. *šāp̄aṭ*; Gk. *krima*, *krisis*).

I. Biblical teaching

God appears in the OT very commonly in the role of 'Judge of all the earth' (Gn. 18:25), or more generally as a 'God of justice' (Mal. 2:17; *cf.* Dt. 1:17; 32:4; Pss. 9:8; 94:2; 97:2; Is. 30:18; 41:1; 61:8; Je. 12:1; Ezk. 7:27; Mi. 6:1f.; *etc.*). Judgment does not simply imply an impartial and detached weighing up of good and evil but rather the thought of vigorous action against evil. It is on this understanding that the people of God are summoned to exercise judgment in turn (Is. 1:17; Mi. 6:8; Zc. 8:16). The judgment of God is not impersonal, the operation of some undeviating principle, it is a strongly personal notion. It is closely linked to the thought of God's character of mercy, lovingkindness, righteousness, truth, *etc.* (Ps. 36:5f.; Ezk. 39:21; Ho. 2:19). It is the working out of the mercy and wrath of God in history and in human life and experience. Thus the judgment of God can bring deliverance for the righteous (Dt. 10:18; Ps. 25:9–10) as well as doom for the wicked (Ex. 6:6; Nu. 33:4; Dt. 32:41; Is. 4:4; Je. 1:10; 4:12; Ezk. 5:10; 23:10; 28:22). Judgment is a particularly rich idea in the OT and a variety of other terms are used with this meaning (*cf. dîn*, Gn. 30:6; Jb. 36:17; *pll*, 1 Sa. 2:25; Ps. 106:30; *pqd*, Je. 14:10; 51:47; *ykḥ*, Is. 1:18; Mi. 6:2; *rîḇ*, Ex. 23:2f.; Ps. 43:1). As the OT draws towards its close the thought of God's judgment becomes increasingly bound up with the eschatological expectation of the coming Day of the Lord (Joel 2:1f.; Am. 5:18f.; 8:9f.; Ob. 15 and *passim*; Zp. 1:7, 14f.; Mal. 4:1f.).

The NT, as we should expect, continues the OT stress upon judgment as belonging to the nature of God and as part of his essential activity (Rom. 1:18; Heb. 12:23; 1 Pet. 1:17; 2:23; Rev. 16:5f.;). As in the OT, God's judgments are not confined to the future but are already at work in man's life in the present age (Jn. 8:50; Rom. 1:18, 22, 24, 26, 28; Rev. 18:8). Judgment is associated even now with Christ who exercises the Father's judgments (Mt. 3:11f.; 10:34; Jn. 3:19; 5:30; 8:12, 16; 9:39). The light of God's word is already shining into the world through his self-revelation in man's moral experience, and supremely in the incarnate Word, Jesus Christ. The judgment of men is therefore already in operation, for they show by their evil deeds that they 'love darkness rather than light' (Jn. 3:19).

The spotlight in the NT, however, falls upon the 'judgment to come', a future and final judgment which will accompany the return of Christ (Mt. 25:31–46; Jn. 5:22, 27f.; Rom. 3:5f.; 1 Cor. 4:3–5; Heb. 6:1f.). This is the coming Day of judgement (Jn. 6:39; Rom. 2:15f.; 1 Cor. 1:8; 5:5; Eph. 4:30; Phil. 2:16; 2 Thes. 1:10; 1 Pet. 2:12; 2 Pet. 3:12; 1 Jn. 4:17; Jude 6; Rev. 6:17; 16:14). Christ himself will judge (Jn. 5:22; 12:47f.; Acts 10:42; 17:31; 2 Tim. 4:8). All men will be judged; none will be absent (2 Tim. 4:1; Heb. 12:23; 1 Pet. 4:5). Even the angels will be passed under judgement (2 Pet 2:4; Jude 6). Every aspect of life will come into account, including the 'secrets of men' (Rom. 2:16), 'the purposes of the heart' (1 Cor. 4:5; *cf.* Mk. 4:22; Lk. 12:2f.), and 'every careless word' (Mt. 12:36). The judgement will not be confined to unbelievers. Christians too (see **III**, below) will face a judgment (Mt. 7:22f.; 25:14–30; Lk. 19:12–28; 1 Cor. 3:12–15; 2 Cor. 5:10; Heb. 10:30; Jas. 3:1; 1 Pet. 1:17; 4:17; Rev. 20:12f.). There can be no avoiding this coming judgment (Heb. 9:27); it is as certain as death (Rom. 2:3; Heb. 10:27). Nowhere is this fact more clearly asserted than in the teaching of the parables of Jesus (Mt. 13:24–30, 36–43, 47–50; 21:33–41; 22:1–14; 25:1–13, 31–46; *etc.*).

II. The basis of judgment

The basis of judgment will be man's response to the revealed will of God. It will therefore include the entire range of human experience, thoughts, words and deeds, and will be such as to allow account to be taken of different degrees of knowledge of God's will, and hence of different degrees of ability to fulfil it (Mt. 11:21–24; Rom. 2:12–16). It will be utterly just and completely convincing (Gn. 18:25; Rom. 3:19). The judge of all the earth will do right and every mouth will be stopped in acknowledgment of the justice of his judgments (*cf.* Jb. 40:1–5; 42:1–6). Like Job we can cling to the justice of God (Jb. 13:13f.; 16:18f.; 19:23f.; 23:1–17; 31:1–40). In face of the frequent injustices of life in the present age we can rest in the certainty that God knows all, that he is not mocked and that he has appointed a day in which he will judge the world in righteousness (Acts 17:31). We can trust him to act in his future work of judgment with the same perfection and triumph which he manifests in the present in his works of grace and sovereignty.

Sometimes a difficulty is alleged as far as the basis of judgment is concerned in that Scripture appears to speak with two voices at points. On the one hand our *justification before God is said to rest on faith alone apart from our good works (Rom. 5:1f.; 3:28), and yet judgment is elsewhere declared to be on the basis of human works (Mt. 16:27; 25:31–46; Rom. 2:6; 1 Cor. 3:8; Rev. 22:12). The difficulty is more apparent than real. The following points need to be borne in mind.

i. Justification is an eschatological idea; *i.e.* it means that we are declared righteous before God at his judgment seat. It anticipates precisely the issue under discussion here, the final judgment of God. The man of faith who is trusting in the perfect merit and finished work of Christ has a guarantee of acquittal at the last day (Rom. 5:1; 8:1; 1 Cor. 1:30). The meaning of faith in Christ is nothing less than the truth that Christ's 'good works', *i.e.* his perfect obedience in life and death, are imputed to us here and now and will stand to our account on the judgment day. In this fundamental sense there can be no justification for anyone apart from 'works', *i.e.* the obedience of Christ in life and death which represents the only basis for human standing before God.

ii. This relationship to the perfect character and works of Christ is not merely judicial. We are not simply declared to be righteous. Our union with Christ implies a real incorporation into his death and resurrection (Rom. 6:1ff.; Gal. 2:20; Eph. 2:5f.; Col. 2:20; 3:1f.). Hence the character of Christ will inevitably be reproduced in a measure in the lives of his people. This is the insistence of James (*cf.* 2:18ff.). Faith without works is spurious because there is no such thing as a faith in Christ which does not incorporate us into union with him in his whole redeeming mission, including his death and resurrection, with all the radical implications of that for subsequent moral character. Putting this point more technically, justification which does not lead to sanctification is shown to have been no justification at all. In the words of a Puritan writer we must 'prove our pedigree by daring to be holy' (W. Gurnall). *Cf.* Rom. 6:1f.; Heb. 2:10f.; 1 Jn. 3:5f. Of course the Christian will remain a sinner to the end as far as his moral practice is concerned. Indeed it is only 'in Christ' that he begins to see sin in its true proportion and discover the depth of his moral depravity (1 Jn. 1:8–2:1f.). Yet alongside this he is 'being changed into his likeness from one degree of glory to another' (2 Cor. 3:18). Thus if a person is truly reborn by the Spirit (Jn. 3:1ff.) the scrutiny of God will certainly uncover evidences of this in their 'works'. But these works are the direct fruit of the Christian's having been regenerated by the Holy Spirit. They are in no sense a human ground of self-justification, but are simply elements of God's gift and grace towards us in Jesus Christ.

iii. When Jesus was asked 'What must we do, to be doing the works of God?' he replied, 'This is the work of God, that you believe in him whom he has sent' (Jn. 6:28f.). It is a mistake at this point to distinguish between Father and Son. God's supreme work and claim upon man, and his perfect will for his creature are expressed in Jesus Christ. God's will for us is therefore that we recognize and make response to the person and mission of Jesus. To believe in him is accordingly to work the works which God requires.

iv. Particular difficulty has been found with respect to the parable in Mt. 25:31–46, and recent interpreters have made all sorts of points on the basis of this parable, *e.g.* the idea of the so-called 'anonymous Christian' (J. A. T. Robinson, K. Rahner). This expresses the notion that some people, including atheists who have spurned God and his witness to them, agnostics who aspire to sit on the fence with respect to God's witness to them, and men and women of other faiths who have repudiated to a greater or lesser degree Christian claims for Christ, because they feed the hungry, visit the prisoners, minister to the needy, even fight in wars of liberation from political oppression, are unconsciously followers of Christ and will be acquitted at the end because in ministering to the needy in this way they have actually ministered to Christ. Such interpretations, however, suffer from a crucial weakness; they require us to interpret one parable (which is not a straightforward piece of Scripture teaching anyway since it *is* a parable) in a manner which yields conclusions at plain variance with many other clear sections of the Bible in general and the teaching of Jesus in particular. Conversely, if we are able to interpret this parable in a manner which does not involve any basic contradictions but which enables it to be integrated harmoniously into Jesus' other teaching, then clearly that ought to be the course to follow on any sound hermeneutic. This second course is entirely possible if we keep before us Jesus' statement that the acts of mercy which are in question in the parable are done to his 'brethren' (25:40). Here is a reflection of a truth which he states elsewhere that the church as the instrument of his mission to the world is so identified with him that men's response to the disciples of Jesus and their testimony becomes their response to him (Mt. 10:9–14, 40; 12:48–50; 18:18; Mk. 9:37; Jn. 20:21ff.) 'He who receives you receives me.' 'The deeds of the righteous are not just casual acts of benevolence. They are acts by which the mission of Jesus and his followers was helped, and helped at some cost to the doers, even at some risk' (T. W. Manson, *The Sayings of Jesus*, 1949, p. 251; *cf.* G. E. Ladd, *A Theology of the New Testament*, 1974, pp. 116–119). All this is not to deny the fact that many non-Christians perform deeds of love and mercy, or even that Christians are sometimes put to shame by their 'good works'. These works however need to be evaluated biblically. They are evidences of God's 'common grace' operating within fallen society restraining evil and promoting goodness. We ought to give thanks for this to God, and identify our Christian compassion where possible with all such efforts for the well-being of our human neighbours. Such action, however, even when carried to the limits of self-sacrifice, cannot claim to be atoning or justifying. These people too are fallen sinners who at many points in their lives are resisting God's will and claim, and these too can have hope at the coming judgment only in the righteousness of Christ. There are no 'anonymous Christians'. 'There is salvation in no one else (than Jesus Christ), for there is no other name under heaven given among men by which we must be saved' (Acts 4:12). The basis of judgment remains our response to God's will as embodied in his general and special revelation focused in Jesus Christ.

There is one further view of the basis of judgment which requires comment. This is the notion that the *only* basis upon which a man or woman may be exposed to the final judgment and condemnation of God is their explicit rejection of the gospel of Christ. In support of this, scriptures such as Mk. 16:15f.; Jn. 3:18, 36; Rom. 10:9–12; Eph. 4:18; 2 Pet. 2:3f.; 1 Jn. 4:3 are cited which represent *unbelief* as the ground of condemnation. However, we note the following: (*a*) these passages only prove that faith in Christ is the one way of salvation, which is not the same as proving that conscious rejection of Christ is the only ground of condemnation. No doubt unbelief is a great and serious matter and the form in which sin expresses itself when men spurn the one hope of their redemption, but it is not the only form of man's revolt against God, and hence it is certainly not the only possible ground on which man stands condemned before God. (*b*) In fact the Bible represents men as already under condemnation before the gospel is preached to them, and it is precisely this prior condemnation which represents the need of man to which the gospel comes as God's gracious answer. The effect of the gospel is not first to create and then to remove man's condemnation, but to deal with the condemnation which already hangs over man's head (*cf.* Rom. 1:18; 2:12; 5:16, 18; Eph. 2:4; 5:3–6; Col. 3:5f.). (*c*) The view that the gospel creates the possibility of man's condemnation as well as of his deliverance cannot but have a most debilitating effect upon evangelistic and missionary zeal, since, if it is only by rejecting the gospel men are finally condemned, and if, as statistics show, the majority of those who hear the gospel do not accept it, then on purely utilitarian grounds it is in the interests of the greatest happiness of the greatest number not to preach the gospel at all, and indeed to do all in our power to stop its being preached. This ludicrous and patently unbiblical conclusion shows how mistaken is the original premise.

The germ of truth in this position is that increased knowledge and increased opportunity do imply increased responsibility. Scripture certainly does recognize that men are not equal as far as their opportunity to know God is concerned, and this factor will be taken into account when God exercises his judgment (Mt. 11:20–24; Rom. 2:1–24; 2 Pet. 2:21). The principle of Lk. 12:48, 'to whom much is given, of him will much be required', is applicable at this point. Thus the general comment that those who have never heard the gospel will be judged by the light they have is correct. However, we need to add that the light they have had has not been followed by them. Only in Jesus Christ is there hope of salvation (Jn. 14:6; Acts 4:12; Eph. 2:12).

Scripture witnesses to a division at the final judgment between the 'righteous' and the 'wicked', the 'elect' and the 'non-elect', *i.e.* 'those whose names were found written in the book of life' and those whose names were 'not found written in the book of life' (Dn. 12:1–3; Mal. 3:18; Mt. 13:30, 39–43, 49f.; 25:32f., 41, 46; Mk. 13:27; Jn. 5:28f.; 1 Cor. 1:18f.; 2 Cor. 2:15f.; Rev. 20:11–15). The future existence of those who are acquitted at the final judgment is referred to in the Bible as *heaven; that of those not acquitted as *hell.

III. The judgment of Christians

Scripture speaks also of a judgment of Christians. Christ at his coming will judge his people (Mt. 25:14–30, 31–46; Lk. 19:12–28; 1 Cor. 3:12–15; 2 Cor. 5:10; 1 Pet. 1:17; Rev. 20:12f.). Christians will be judged by their Lord in respect of their stewardship of the talents, gifts, opportunities and responsibilities granted to them during the course of their lives. The reference to this judgment in 1 Pet. 1:17 is particularly significant in conveying its character. The divine judgment of the people of God will be a fatherly judgment. It will not be such as to place in peril the Christian's standing within the family of God; it will have all of a father's understanding and compassion; and yet it is not therefore to be lightly or carelessly regarded. This fatherly judgment will be exercised by Christ at his coming.

IV. Human judgment

Here as elsewhere man is called upon to imitate God. Just as God is a righteous judge, so men are called upon to judge righteously (Lk. 12:57; Jn. 7:24) in the constant recognition that ultimately the judgment is God's (Dt. 1:17). The Christian is expected to show discrimination and judgment in moral matters, and the ability to do so is a sign of true maturity (Lk. 12:57; Jn. 7:24; Rom. 15:14; 1 Cor. 2:15; 6:1–6; 10:15; 2 Cor. 13:5; Phil. 1:9f.; Col. 1:9; 1 Jn. 4:1). However, the Christian is also given frequent warnings against the danger of passing judgment on others in a way which attempts to anticipate the final divine judgment (Mt. 7:1; Lk. 6:41f.; Jn. 8:7; Rom. 2:1; 14:4; Jas. 4:1). All human judgments are provisional in the light of the coming judgment (1 Cor. 4:3–5). When the new age is fully manifest at the return of Christ, Christians, according to 1 Cor. 6:2f., will be called upon to exercise judgment with respect to the world (v. 2), and angels in particular (v. 3).

V. Present attitudes

There are few points at which the teaching of the Bible is more sharply in conflict with the assumptions of our age than in its teaching concerning God's future judgment of all men. It is correspondingly one of the most serious contemporary expressions of Christian intellectual and spiritual capitulation that this particular truth should be so little reflected in current preaching and writing. The world has been permitted at this point only too clearly to squeeze the church into its own mould (Rom. 12:1f., Phillips). Thus a theological commentator can complain with full justice that today the notion of final judgment 'figures so little in the theology and preaching of the Church' (T. Preiss, *Life in Christ*, 1954, p. 79). This theological neglect is the more inexcusable in that this century has witnessed an unprecedented recovery of the biblical eschatological perspective. This particular aspect of eschatology, however, *viz.* future divine judgment, quite unwarrantedly, has been largely left on one side.

Man today rejects out of hand the idea that he must one day render account for his life and its decisions. His loss of conviction concerning an after-life, combined with the erosion of the notion of moral responsibility on the basis of popular understanding of psychological and psychoanalytical theories, has contributed to the moral indifference and pragmatism of our times. Moral issues, in so far as they matter at all, relate only to the present moment and to considerations of personal happiness. The thought that they might relate to some transcendent divine dimension, or that all men will one day be inescapably summoned to accept responsibility for these very moral decisions in the all-seeing presence of their Creator, is anathema. Unfortunately for modern man it happens to be true. Judgment is inevitable and awaits us all. In face of this modern tendency to dismiss future judgment there is the greater and more urgent responsibility placed upon the Christian church tenaciously to maintain the biblical perspective.

Bibliography. L. Morris, *The Biblical Doctrine of Judgment*, 1960; F. Büchsel, V. Herntrich, *TDNT* 3, pp. 921–954; W. Schneider, H. Beck, T. McComiskey, *NIDNTT* 2, pp. 361–371; S. H. Travis, *NDT*, p. 358. B.A.M.

JUDGMENT SEAT. In Greek states the assembly met in front of a dais (*bēma*) from which all official business was conducted. Thus Herod Agrippa I sits on the dais (RSV 'throne') to address the republics of Tyre and Sidon (Acts 12:21). The Gk. term is otherwise used in the NT for the *tribunal* (Acts 18:12, *etc.*), the platform on which a Roman magistrate sat, flanked by his counsellors, to administer justice. It was traditionally erected in some public place, as apparently in the case of Pilate (Jn. 19:13), or alternatively in an auditorium (Acts 25:23). That it was the solemn integrity of Roman justice that prompted the image of the judgment seat of God (Rom. 14:10) or Christ (2 Cor. 5:10) seems likely from the fact that Paul is in either case addressing an audience familiar with direct Roman government.

Bibliography. E. Weiss, *RE*, 6.A.2. 2428–30, *s.v. tribunal.* E.A.J.

JULIUS. The family name of the Caesars, which must have become widespread since their rise to power due to the custom of conferring on new citizens the name of the magistrate under whose auspices they were enfranchised. The centurion who escorted Paul to Rome (Acts 27:1) presumably belongs to this class of Julii, since no aristocratic member of the house would serve in that rank. His unit (the 'Augustan Cohort', see *ARMY) has been thought (by Mommsen and Ramsay) to be the Caesar's regular staff of couriers. The term corresponds exactly, however, to the *cohors Augusta* known from epigraphic evidence. That this was an auxiliary (*i.e.* non-citizen) force, and therefore not likely to supply the escort for a Roman, is not a serious objection, since the centurion himself is manifestly a citizen. Whether enfranchised on promotion, or seconded to the *auxilia* from the legions, he belongs with Paul to the proud and growing body of new citizen families that Roman statesmanship created in the East.

Bibliography. T. R. S. Broughton, *BC*, 1.5, pp. 427–445. E.A.J.

JUSTICE. The word 'justice' occurs 115 times in RSV OT, usually for *mišpāṭ*, 'judgment', the rule that should guide *judges. In the AV, however, it represents *mišpāṭ* only once (Jb. 36:17); elsewhere it translates *ṣeḏeq* or *ṣᵉḏāqâ*. The more frequent rendering of these latter nouns is 'righteousness'; but when *mišpāṭ* and *ṣᵉḏāqâ* appear together AV translates the whole phrase as 'judgment and justice' (*e.g.* 2 Sa. 8:15; *cf.* Gn. 18:19), though RSV renders the same combination as 'justice and righteousness'. In AV, therefore, 'justice' must be understood as being the same word as *'righteousness', and seldom as denoting the specialized concept of 'fair play', or legal equity, with which the term justice is presently associated. The expression, 'to do (someone) justice', occurs twice, being taken from the corresponding Heb. verbal root, *ṣāḏaq*, causative, which means 'to declare one right' (2 Sa. 15:4; Ps. 82:3). Similarly, the adjective *ṣaddîq*, 'righteous', is over 40 times rendered by the adjective 'just', in both vss. In RSV NT, the noun 'justice' represents both *krisis*, 'judgment', and *dikaiosynē*, 'righteousness'. In AV it does not appear; but at over 30 points the adjective *dikaios*, 'righteous', is likewise translated by the English term 'just'.

This biblical concept of justice exhibits development through nine, generally chronological stages.

1. Etymologically, it appears that the root of *ṣᵉḏāqa^*, like that of its kindred noun *yōšer*, 'uprightness' (Dt. 9:5), signifies 'straightness', in a physical sense (*BDB*, p. 841).

2. But already in the patriarchal age *ṣᵉḏāqa^* has the abstract meaning of conformity, by a given object or action, to an accepted standard of values, *e.g.* Jacob's 'honest' living up to the terms of his sheep-contract with Laban (Gn. 30:33). Moses thus speaks of just balances, weights and measures (Lv. 19:36; Dt. 25:15) and insists that Israel's *judges pronounce 'just (AV; righteous, RSV) judgment' (Dt. 16:18, 20). Arguments that are actually questionable may seem, at first glance, to be 'just' (Pr. 18:17; RSV, 'right'); and Christian masters are cautioned to treat their slaves 'justly and fairly' (Col. 4:1). Even inanimate objects may be described as *ṣeḏeq*, if they measure up to the appropriate standards. The phrase, 'paths of *ṣeḏeq*' (Ps. 23:3), for example, designates walkable paths.

3. Since life's highest standard is derived from the character of deity, 'justice', from the time of Moses and onwards (*cf.* Dt. 32:4), comes to distinguish that which is God's will and those activities which result from it. Heavenly choirs proclaim, 'Just and true are thy ways' (Rev. 15:3). Recognizing the ultimacy of the will of the Lord, Job therefore asks, 'How can a man be just before God?' (Jb. 9:2; *cf.* 4:17; 33:12). But even though God stands answerable to no man, still 'to justice . . . he doeth no violence' (37:23, RVmg.); for the actions of the God who acts in harmony with his own standard are always perfect and right (Zp. 3:5; Ps. 89:14). *ṣᵉḏāqâ* may thus describe Yahweh's preservation of both human and animal life (Ps. 36:6) or his dissociation from vain enterprise (Is. 45:19). In both of the latter verses the EVV translate *ṣᵉḏāqâ* as 'righteousness'; but it might with greater accuracy be rendered 'regularity' or 'reliability'.

4. By a natural transition, 'justice' then comes to identify that moral standard by which God measures human conduct (Is. 26:7). Men too must 'do justice' (Gn. 18:19) as they walk with deity (Gn. 6:9; Mt. 5:48); for not the hearers, but the doers of the law, are 'just (AV; righteous, RSV) before God' (Rom. 2:13). The attribute of justice is to be anticipated only in the hearts of those who fear God (Lk. 18:2), because justice in the biblical sense begins with holiness (Mi. 6:8; Mk. 6:20; 1 Thes. 2:10) and with sincere devotion (Lk. 2:25; Acts 10:22). Positively, however, the wholehearted participation of the Gadites in the divinely ordered conquest of Canaan is described as 'executing the just decrees of the Lord' (Dt. 33:21; *cf.* S. R. Driver, *ICC*). The need for earnest conformity to the moral will of God lies especially incumbent upon kings (2 Sa. 8:15; Je. 22:15), princes (Pr. 8.15), and judges (Ec. 5:8); but every true believer is expected to 'do justice' (Ps. 119:121, AV; Pr. 1:3; *cf.* its personification in Is. 59:14). Justice constitutes the opposite of sin (Ec. 7:20) and serves as a marked characteristic of Jesus the Messiah (Is. 9:7; Zc. 9:9; Mt. 27:19; Acts 3:14). In the poetry of the OT there do arise affirmations of self-righteousness by men like David ('Judge me according to my righteousness, and establish the just', Ps. 7:8–9, AV; *cf.* 18:20–24) or Job ('I am . . . just and blameless' Jb. 12:4; *cf.* 1:1), that might appear incongruous when considered in the light of their acknowledged iniquity (*cf.* Jb. 7:21; 13:26). The poets' aims, however, are either to exonerate themselves from particular crimes that enemies have laid to their charge (*cf.* Ps. 7:4) or to profess a genuine purity of purpose and single-hearted devotion to God (Ps. 17:1). 'They breathe the spirit of simple faith and childlike trust, which throws itself unreservedly on God . . . and they disclaim all fellowship with the wicked, from whom they may expect to be distinguished in the course of His Providence' (A. F. Kirkpatrick, *The Book of Psalms*, 1906, 1, p. lxxxvii). As Ezekiel described such a man, 'He walks in my statutes . . . he is righteous (AV, just), he shall surely live, says the Lord God' (Ezk. 18:9).

5. In reference to divine government, justice becomes descriptive in a particular way of punishment for moral infraction. Under the lash of heaven-sent plagues, Pharaoh confessed, 'The Lord is *ṣaddîq*, and I and my people are wicked' (Ex. 9:27; *cf.* Ne. 9:33); and the one thief cried to the other as they were crucified, 'We indeed justly . . .' (Lk. 23:41). For God cannot remain indifferent to evil (Hab. 1:13; *cf.* Zp. 1:12), nor will the Almighty pervert justice (Jb. 8:3; *cf.* 8:4; 36:17). Even the pagans of Malta believed in a divine nemesis, so that when they saw Paul bitten by a viper they concluded, 'This man is a murderer . . . justice has not allowed him to live' (Acts 28:4). God's punitive righteousness is as a consuming fire (Dt. 32:22; Heb. 12:29; *WRATH), and condemnation is just (Rom. 3:8).

6. From the time of the judges and onward, however, *ṣᵉḏāqâ* comes also to describe his deeds of vindication for the deserving, 'the triumph of the Lord' (Jdg. 5:11). Absalom thus promised a petitioner he 'would give him justice' (2 Sa. 15:4; *cf.* Ps. 82:3), and Solomon proclaimed that God 'blesses the abode of the righteous (AV, just)' (Pr. 3:33; *cf.* Ps. 94:15). Divine vindication became also the plea of Isaiah's contemporaries, 'They ask of me the ordinances of justice' (Is. 58:2–3, AV); for though God's intervention might have been delayed (Ec. 7:15; 8:14; *cf.* Is. 40:27), he yet 'became jealous for his land, and had pity on his people' (Joel 2:18).

7. Such words, however, introduce another aspect, in which divine justice ceases to constitute an expression of precise moral desert and partakes rather of divine pity, love and grace. This connotation appears first in David's prayer for the forgiveness of his crimes over Bathsheba, when he implored, 'Deliver me from bloodguiltiness, O God, thou God of my salvation, and my tongue will sing aloud of thy *ṣᵉḏāqâ'* (deliverance)' (Ps. 51:14). But what David sought was not vindication; for he had just acknowledged his heinous sin and, indeed, his depravity from birth (Ps. 51:5). His petition sought rather for undeserved pardon; and *ṣᵉḏāqa^* may be translated by simple repetition—O God of my salvation: my tongue shall sing of thy 'salvation'. *ṣᵉḏāqa^*, in other words, has become redemptive; it is God's fulfilling of his own graciously promised salvation, irrespective of the merits of men (*cf.* David's same usage in Pss. 31:1; 103:17; 143:1). David's counsellor Ethan thus moves, in the space of two verses, from a reference to God's 'justice [*ṣeḏeq*, according to sense **4** above] and judgment' (Ps. 89:14, AV) to the joyful testimony, 'In thy *ṣᵉḏāqâ* [promised grace] shall Israel be exalted' (Ps. 89:16, AV; *cf.* a similar contrast within Is. 56:1). When Isaiah, therefore, speaks of 'a just [AV;

righteous, RSV; *ṣaddîq*] God and a Saviour' (Is. 45:21), his thought is not, 'A just God, and yet at the same time a Saviour', but rather, 'A *ṣaddîq* God, and therefore a Saviour' (*cf.* the parallelism of *'righteousness' with salvation in Is. 45:8; 46:13). Correspondingly, we read in the NT that 'if we confess our sins, he is faithful and just [*dikaios* = faithful to his gracious promise, not, demanding justice] and will forgive our sins' (1 Jn. 1:9). Such concepts of non-judicial 'justice', however, must be limited to those passages in which this usage is specifically intended. In Rom. 3, on the contrary, with its contextual emphasis upon the wrath of God against sin and upon the propitiatory sacrifice of Christ for the satisfaction of the Father's justice, we must continue to understand *dikaios* (Rom. 3:26) in its traditional sense: 'That he [God] might be just [exacting punishment, according to sense **5** above], and [yet at the same time] the justifier of him which believeth in Jesus' (AV; see Sanday and Headlam, *ICC*; *JUSTIFICATION).

8. As a condition that arises out of God's forgiving 'justice', there next appears in Scripture a humanly possessed *ṣᵉḏāqâ*, which is simultaneously declared to have been God's own moral attribute (*ṣᵉḏāqâ* in sense **4** above), but which has now been imparted to those who believe on his grace. Moses thus describes how Abraham's faith served as a medium for imputed righteousness (Gn. 15:6), though one must, of course, observe that his faith did not constitute in itself the meritorious righteousness but was merely 'reckoned' so. He was justified *through* faith, not *because of* it (*cf.* John Murray, *Redemption, Accomplished and Applied*, 1955, p. 155). Habakkuk likewise declared, 'The just shall live by his faith' (Hab. 2:4, AV), though here too the justification derives, not from man's own, rugged 'faithfulness' (RSVmg.), but from his humble dependence upon God's mercy (contrast the self-reliance of the Babylonians, which the same context condemns; and *cf.* Rom. 1:17; Gal. 3:11). It was God's prophet Isaiah, however, who first spoke directly of 'the heritage of the servants of the Lord . . . their *ṣᵉḏāqâ* from me' (Is. 54:17). Of this 'righteousness', A. B. Davidson accurately observed, 'It is not a Divine attribute. It is a Divine effect . . . produced in the world by God' (*The Theology of the Old Testament*, 1925, p. 143). That is to say, there exists within Yahweh a righteousness which, by his grace, becomes the possession of the believer (Is. 45:24). Our own righteousness is totally inadequate (Is. 64:6); but 'in Yahweh' we 'are righteous' (*ṣāḏaq*) (Is. 45:25), having been made just by the imputed merit of Christ (Phil. 3:9). A century later, Jeremiah thus speaks both of Judah and of God himself as a 'habitation of justice' (Je. 31:23; 50:7, AV), *i.e.* a source of justification for the faithful (*cf.* Je. 23:6; 33:16, 'Yahweh our righteousness', Theo. Laetsch, *Biblical Commentary, Jeremiah*, 1952, pp. 191–192, 254).

9. But even as God in his grace bestows righteousness upon the unworthy, so the people of God are called upon to 'seek justice' (Is. 1:17) in the sense of pleading for the widow and 'judging the cause of the poor and needy' (Je. 22:16). 'Justice' has thus come to connote goodness (Lk. 23:50) and loving consideration (Mt. 1:19). Further, from the days of the Exile onward, Aram. *ṣiḏqâ*, 'righteousness', becomes specialized into a designation for alms or charity (Dn. 4:27), an equivalent expression for 'giving to the poor' (Ps. 112:9; *cf.* Mt. 6:1) One might therefore be led to conceive of biblical 'justice', particularly in these last three, supra-judicial senses, as involving a certain tension or even contradiction: *e.g.* *ṣᵉḏāqâ* in its 7th, gracious sense seems to forgive the very crimes that it condemns in its 5th, punitive sense. The ultimate solution, however, appears in the person and work of the Lord Jesus Christ. The ethical example furnished by his sinless life (Heb. 4:15) constitutes the climax of biblical revelation on the moral will of God and far exceeds the perverted though seemingly lofty justice of the scribes and Pharisees (Mt. 5:20). Yet he who commanded men to be perfect, even as their heavenly Father is perfect (Mt. 5:48), exhibited at the same time that love which has no equal, as he laid down his life for his undeserving friends (Jn. 15:13). Here was revealed *ṣᵉḏāqâ*, 'justice', in its ethical stage **5**, in its redemptive stage **7**, and in its imputed stage **8**, all united in one. He came that God might be just and yet the justifier of him that believeth in Jesus (Rom. 3:26) and that we might be found in him, who is made our righteousness and sanctification and redemption (1 Cor. 1:30).

BIBLIOGRAPHY. H. Conzelmann, in R. Batey (ed.), *New Testament Issues*, 1970, pp. 130–147; P. Bovati, *Re-establishing Justice*, 1994; W. Eichrodt, *Theology of the Old Testament*, 1, 1961, pp. 239–249; L. Epsztein, *Social Justice in the Ancient Near East and the People of the Bible*, 1986; D. Hill, *Greek Words and Hebrew Meanings*, 1967, pp. 82–162; J. Jeremias, *The Central Message of the New Testament*, 1965, pp. 51–70; G. E. Ladd, *A Theology of the New Testament*, 1975, pp. 437–450; J. B. Payne, *Theology of the Older Testament*, 1962, pp. 155–161, 165f.; G. Quell and G. Schrenk, *TDNT* 2, pp. 174–225); H. G. Reventlow, *Justice and Righteousness*, 1992; J. A. Ziesler, *The Meaning of Righteousness in Paul*, 1972; H. Seebass, C. Brown, *NIDNTT* 3, pp. 352–377. J.B.P.

JUSTIFICATION.

I. Meaning of the word

'Justify' (Heb. *ṣāḏaq*; Gk. [LXX and NT], *dikaioō*) is a forensic term meaning 'acquit', 'declare righteous', the opposite of 'condemn' (*cf.* Dt. 25:1; Pr. 17:15; Rom. 8:33). Justifying is the judge's act. From the litigant's standpoint, therefore, 'be justified' means 'get the verdict' (Is. 43:9, 26).

In Scripture, God is 'the Judge of all the earth' (Gn. 18:25), and his dealings with men are constantly described in forensic terms. God's Law is a complex of moral goals and standards by which his rational creatures should live. Righteousness, *i.e.* conformity with his law, is what he requires of his human creatures, and he shows his own righteousness as Judge in taking vengeance, *i.e.* inflicting punitive retribution ('wrath') on those who fall short of it (*cf.* Ps. 7:11, RV; Is. 5:16; 10:22; Acts 17:31; Rom. 2:5; 3:5f.). There is no hope for anyone if God's verdict goes against him.

Because God is King, the thought of him as justifying may have an executive as well as a judicial aspect. Like the ideal royal judge in Israel, he will not only pass a verdict in favour of the accused, but actively implement it by showing favour towards him and publicly reinstating him. The verb 'justify' may focus on either aspect of God's action. For instance, the justifying of Israel and the Servant, envisaged in Is. 45:25; 50:8, is a public vindication through a change in their fortunes. The justification of sinners that Jesus illustrates by his shock-ending story of the Pharisee and the publican (Lk. 18:9–14) and that Paul expounds in Rom. 3–5, Gal. 2–4 and 2 Cor. 5:14–21 is, however, simply the passing and sustaining of a favourable verdict. Jesus and Paul certainly believe that God shows favour to those whom he has acquitted, but they use other terms to describe this (chiefly, the family language of adoption, inheritance, and paternal care).

'Justify' is also used for ascriptions of righteousness in non-forensic contexts. Men are said to justify God by confessing him just (Lk. 7:29; *cf.* Rom. 3:4, quoting Ps. 51:4), and themselves by claiming to be just (Jb. 32:2; Lk. 10:29; 16:15). Jerusalem is ironically said to have 'justified' Sodom and Samaria by outdoing them in sin! (Ezk. 16:51). The passive can denote being vindicated by events against suspicion, criticism and mistrust (Mt. 11:19; Lk. 7:35; 1 Tim. 3:16; *cf.* Jas. 2:21, 24f., for which see below).

Lexical support is wanting for the view of Chrysostom, Augustine and the Council of Trent that when Paul and James speak of present justification they refer to God's work of *making* righteous by inner renewal, as well as of *counting* righteous through remission of sins. James seems to mean neither, Paul only the latter. His synonyms for 'justify' are 'reckon righteousness', 'remit sins', 'not reckon sin' (see Rom. 4:5–8, RV)—phrases expressing the idea, not of inner transformation, but of conferring a legal status and cancelling a legal liability. Justification, to Paul, is a judgment passed on man, not a work wrought within man. The two things go together, no doubt, but they are distinct.

II. Justification in Paul

Out of the 39 occurrences of the verb 'justify' in the NT, 29 come in the Epistles or recorded words of Paul; so do the two occurrences of the corresponding noun, *dikaiōsis* (Rom. 4:25; 5:18). This reflects the fact that Paul alone of NT writers left us letters (Romans and Galatians in particular) that make the reality of justification by grace, bringing freedom from the dominion of sin and death, the focus for his exposition of salvation in and through Christ.

Justification means to Paul *God's act of remitting the sins of guilty men, and accounting them righteous, freely, by his grace, through faith in Christ, on the ground, not of their own works, but of the representative law-keeping and redemptive blood-shedding of the Lord Jesus Christ on their behalf.* (For the parts of this definition, see Rom. 3:23–26; 4:5–8; 5:18f.) Paul's doctrine of justification is his characteristic way of formulating the central gospel truth, that God forgives believing sinners. Theologically, it is the most highly developed expression of this truth in the NT.

In Romans, Paul introduces the gospel as disclosing 'the righteousness of God' (1:17). The most natural of the many views canvassed is that this phrase expresses the single, complex, dynamic idea of God's morally glorious and eternally worship-worthy display of mercy and justice in bestowing on guilty transgressors the status of perfect lawkeepers. Within this frame, the phrase has two points of reference. **1.** It refers to this status, which God through Christ freely confers upon believing sinners ('the *gift* of righteousness' as opposed to condemnation and death, Rom. 5:17; *cf.* 3:21f.; 9:30; 10:3–10; 2 Cor. 5:21; Phil. 3:9). It has been argued that the essence of this gift is covenant status in the new Israel that is constituted by faith-union with the risen Christ, and certainly the justified are henceforth in covenant with God in just this way. But justification, as such, for Paul is pardon and acceptance, not covenant involvement, and the hinge-question throughout Romans is not who is in covenant with God, but how may sinners find eternal life. **2.** Also, and indeed primarily, the phrase refers to the way in which the gospel reveals God as doing what is right—not only judging transgressors as they deserve (2:5; 3:5f.) but also keeping his promise to send salvation to Israel (3:4f.), and justifying sinners in such a way that his own judicial claims upon them are met (3:25f.). 'The righteousness of God' is thus a predominantly forensic concept, denoting God's gracious work of bestowing upon guilty sinners a justified justification, acquitting them in the court of heaven without prejudice to his justice as their Judge.

Many scholars today find the background of this phrase in a few passages from Is. 40ff. and the psalms in which God's 'righteousness' and 'salvation' appear as equivalents (Is. 45:8, *cf.* vv. 19–25; 46:13; 51:3–6; Ps. 98:2; *etc.*). This may be right, but since Paul nowhere quotes these verses, it cannot be proved. It must also be remembered that the reason why these texts call God's vindication of his oppressed people his 'righteousness' is that it is an act of faithfulness to his covenant promise to them; whereas Romans deals principally with God's justifying of Gentiles, who previously were not his people and to whom he had promised nothing (*cf.* 9:24f.; 10:19f.)—quite a different situation.

E. Käsemann and others construe God's righteousness in Paul as a gracious exertion of power whereby God keeps faith with both his covenant people (by fulfilling his promise to save them) and his captive creation (by restoring his dominion over it). Both thoughts are Pauline, but it is doubtful whether (as is argued) 'righteousness' in Rom. 3:25–26 and 'just' in v. 26 point only to gracious faithfulness saving the needy and not to judicial retribution (*cf.* 2:5; 3:5) saving the guilty by being diverted upon the One set forth to be a *propitiation. The latter exegesis fits the flow of thought better; the former cannot explain why 'and' appears in the phrase 'just *and* the justifier' (AV), for it finds in these words only one thought, not two.

It has been questioned whether Paul's doctrine of justification by faith without works is any more than a controversial device, developed simply as a weapon against the Judaizers. But the following facts indicate that it was more than this.

1. The Epistle to the *Romans is evidently to be read as a full-dress statement of Paul's gospel, and the doctrine of justification is its backbone.

2. In three places Paul writes in personal terms of the convictions that had made him the man and the missionary that he was, and all three are couched in terms of justification (Gal. 2:15–21; 2 Cor. 5:16–21; Phil. 3:4–14). In Rom. 7:7ff. Paul describes his personal need of Christ in terms of the law's condemnation—a need which only God's justifying sentence in Christ could relieve (*cf.* Rom. 8:1f.; Gal. 3:19–4:7). Paul's personal religion was evidently rooted in the knowledge of his justification.

3. Justification is to Paul God's fundamental act

of blessing, for it both saves from the past and secures for the future. On the one hand, it means pardon, and the end of hostility between God and ourselves (Acts 13:39; Rom. 4:6f.; 5:9f.). On the other hand, it means acceptance and a title to all blessings promised to the just, a thought which Paul develops by linking justification with adoption and heirship (Gal. 4:4ff.; Rom. 8:14ff.). Both aspects appear in Rom. 5:1–2, where Paul says that justification brings both peace with God (because sins are remitted) and hope of God's glory (because the sinner is accepted as righteous). This hope is a certainty; for justification has an eschatological significance. It is the judgment of the last day brought into the present, a final, irreversible verdict. The justified person can accordingly be sure that nothing will ever separate him from the love of his God (Rom. 8:33–39; *cf.* 5:9). His glorification is certain (Rom. 8:30). The coming inquisition before Christ's judgment-seat (Rom. 14:10ff.; 2 Cor. 5:10) may deprive him of particular rewards (1 Cor. 3:15), but not of his justified status.

4. Paul's doctrine of salvation has justification as its basic reference-point. His belief about justification is the source from which flows his view of Christianity as a world-religion of grace and faith, in which Gentiles and Jews stand on an equal footing (Rom. 1:16; 3:29ff.; Gal. 3:8–14, 28f., *etc.*). It is in terms of justification that he explains grace (Rom. 3:24; 4:4f., 16), the saving significance of Christ's obedience and death (Rom. 3:24f.; 5:16ff.), the revelation of God's love at the cross (Rom. 5:5–9), the meaning of redemption (Rom. 3:24; Gal. 3:13; Eph. 1:7) and reconciliation (2 Cor. 5:18f.), the covenant relationship (Gal. 3:15f.), faith (Rom. 4:23ff.; 10:8ff.), union with Christ (Rom. 8:1; Gal. 2:17, RV), adoption and the gift of the Spirit (Gal. 4:6–8; Rom. 8:10, *cf.* v. 15), and Christian assurance (Rom. 5:1–11; 8:33ff.). It is in terms of justification that Paul explains all hints, prophecies and instances of salvation in the OT (Rom. 1:17; Gal. 3:11, quoting Hab. 2:4; Rom. 3:21; 4:3–8, quoting Gn. 15:6; Ps. 32:1f.; Rom. 9:22–10:21, quoting Ho. 2:23; 1:10; Is. 8:14; Joel 2:32; Is. 65:1, *etc.*; Rom. 11:26f., quoting Is. 59:20f.; Gal. 3:8, quoting Gn. 12:3; Gal. 4:21ff., quoting Gn. 21:10; *etc.*).

5. Justification is the key to Paul's philosophy of history. He holds that God's central overarching purpose in his ordering of world-history since the Fall has been to lead sinners to justifying faith.

God deals with mankind, Paul tells us, through two representative men: 'the first man Adam', and 'the second man', who is 'the last Adam', Jesus Christ (1 Cor. 15:45ff.; Rom. 5:12ff.). The first man, by disobeying, brought condemnation and death upon the whole race; the second man, by his obedience, has become the author of justification and life for all who have faith (Rom. 5:16ff.).

From the time of Adam's fall, death reigned universally, though sin was not yet clearly known (Rom. 5:12ff.). But God took Abraham and his family into covenant, justifying Abraham through his faith, and promising that in Abraham's seed (*i.e.* through one of his descendants) all nations should be blessed (*i.e.* justified) (Gal. 3:6–9, 16; Rom. 4:3, 9–22). Then through Moses God revealed his law to Abraham's family. The law was meant to give, not salvation, but knowledge of sin. By detecting and provoking transgressions, it was to teach Israelites their need of justification, thus acting as a *paidagōgos* (the household slave who took children to school) to lead them to Christ (Gal. 3:19–24; Rom. 3:20; 5:20; 7:5, 7–13). This epoch of divine preparatory education lasted till the coming of Christ (Gal. 3:23–25; 4:1–5).

The effect of Christ's work was to abolish the barrier of exclusivism which Israel's possession of the law and promise had erected between Jew and Gentile (Eph. 2:14ff.). Through Christ, justification by faith could now be preached to Jew and Gentile without distinction, for in Christ all believers were made Abraham's seed, and became sons of God and heirs of the covenant (Gal. 3:26–29). Unhappily, in this situation most Jews proved to be legalists; they sought to establish a righteousness of their own by works of law, and would not believe that faith in Christ was the God-given way to righteousness (Rom. 9:30–10:21). So many 'natural branches' had been cut off from the olive-tree of the historic covenant community (Rom. 11:16ff.), and the church was for the present predominantly Gentile; but there was hope that an elect remnant from fallen Israel, provoked by the mercy shown to undeserving Gentiles, would itself come to faith and find remission of sins in the end (Rom. 11:23–32). Thus both Jew and Gentile would be saved, not through their own works and effort, but through the free grace of God justifying the disobedient and ungodly; and all the glory of salvation will be God's alone (Rom. 11:30–36).

These considerations point to the fundamental place of justification in Paul's apprehension and analysis of what was always his central theme, namely salvation in and through Jesus Christ.

III. The ground of justification

As stated by Paul in Romans, the doctrine of justification seems to raise a problem of theodicy. Its background, set out in 1:18–3:20, is the solidarity of humankind in sin, and the inevitability of judgment. In 2:5–16 Paul states his doctrine of the judgment day. The principle of judgment, he says, will be 'to every man according to his works' (v. 6, RSV). The standard of judgment will be God's law, in the highest form in which men know it (if not the Mosaic law, then the law of conscience, vv. 12–15). The evidence will be 'the secrets of men' (v. 16). Only law-keepers can hope to be justified (vv. 7, 10, 12f.). And there are no law-keepers. None is righteous; all have sinned (3:9ff.). So the prospect is of universal condemnation, for Jew as well as Gentile, for a law-breaking Jew is no more acceptable to God than anyone else (2:17–27). All, it seems, are doomed. 'No human being will be justified in his sight by works of the law' (3:20, echoing Ps. 143:2).

But now Paul proclaims the present justification of believing sinners (3:21ff.). God reckons righteousness to the unrighteous and justifies the ungodly (3:23f.; 4:5f.). The (deliberately?) paradoxical quality of the last phrase is heightened by the fact that these very Greek words are used in the LXX of Ex. 23:7 ('I will not justify the wicked') and Is. 5:22f. ('Woe unto them . . . which justify the wicked . . .'). The question arises: on what grounds can God justify the ungodly without compromising his own justice as the Judge?

Paul maintains that God justifies sinners on a just ground: namely, that Jesus Christ, acting on their behalf, has satisfied the claims of God's law upon them. He was 'born under the law' (Gal. 4:4) in order to fulfil the precept and bear the penalty of the law in their stead. By his *'blood' (*i.e.* his death) he put away their sins (Rom. 3:25; 5:9). By his obedience to God he won for all his people the status of law-keepers (Rom. 5:19). He became 'obedient unto death' (Phil. 2:8); his life of righteousness culminated in his dying the death of the unrighteous, bearing the law's penal curse (Gal. 3:13; *cf.* Is. 53:4–12). In his person on the cross, the sins of his people were judged and expiated. Through this 'one act of righteousness'—his sinless life and death—'the free gift came unto all men to justification of life' (Rom. 5:18, RV). Thus believers become 'the righteousness of God' in and through him who 'knew no sin' personally, but was representatively 'made sin' (treated as a sinner, and judged) in their place (2 Cor. 5:21). Thus Paul speaks of 'Christ Jesus, whom God made . . . our righteousness' (1 Cor. 1:30). This was the thought expressed in older Protestant theology by the phrase 'the imputation of Christ's righteousness'. The phrase is not in Paul, but its meaning is. The point that it makes is that believers are made righteous before God (Rom. 5:19) through his admitting them to share Christ's status of acceptance. In other words, God treats them according to Christ's desert. There is nothing arbitrary or artificial in this, for God recognizes the existence of a real union of covenantal solidarity between them and Christ. For Paul, union with Christ is not fiction, but fact—the basic fact, indeed, of Christianity; and his doctrine of justification is simply his first step in analysing its meaning. So it is 'in Christ' (Gal. 2:17; 2 Cor. 5:21) that sinners are justified. God accounts them righteous, not because he accounts them to have kept his law personally (which would be a false judgment), but because he accounts them to be 'in' the One who kept God's law representatively (which is a true judgment).

So, when God justifies sinners on the ground of Christ's obedience and death, he acts justly. So far from compromising his judicial righteousness, this method of justification actually exhibits it. It is designed 'to show God's righteousness, because in his divine forbearance he had passed over former sins [*i.e.* in OT times]; it was to prove at the present time that he himself is righteous and that he justifies him who has faith in Jesus' (Rom. 3:25f.). The key words are repeated for emphasis, for the point is crucial. The gospel which proclaims God's apparent violation of his justice really reveals his justice. By his method of justifying sinners, God (in another sense) justified himself; for by setting forth Christ as a propitiation for sins, in whom human sin was actually judged and punished as it deserved, he revealed the just ground on which he was able to pardon and accept believing sinners in OT times (as in fact he did: *cf.* Ps. 130:3f.), no less than in the Christian era.

IV. The means of justification

Faith in Christ, says Paul, is the means whereby righteousness is received and justification bestowed. Sinners are justified 'by' or 'through' faith (Gk. *pistei, dia* or *ek pisteōs*). Paul does not regard faith as the ground of justification. If it were, it would be a meritorious work, and Paul would not be able to term the believer, as such, 'one who does not work' (Rom. 4:5); nor could he go on to say that salvation by faith rests on grace (v. 16), for grace absolutely excludes works (Rom. 11:6). Paul quotes the case of Abraham, who 'believed God, and it was reckoned to him as righteousness', to prove that a person is justified through faith without works (Rom. 4:3ff.; Gal. 3:6; quoting Gn. 15:6). In Rom. 4:5, 9 (*cf.* vv. 22, 24) Paul refers to the Genesis text as teaching that Abraham's faith was 'reckoned . . . as righteousness'. All he means, however, as the context shows, is that Abraham's faith—whole-hearted reliance on God's promise (vv. 18ff.)—was the occasion and means of his being justified. The phrase 'reckoned *eis* righteousness' could either mean 'as' (by real equivalence, or some arbitrary method of calculation), or else 'with a view to', 'leading to', 'issuing in'. The latter alternative is clearly right. Paul is not suggesting that faith, viewed either as righteousness, actual or inchoate, or as a substitute for righteousness, is the *ground* of justification; Rom. 4 does not deal with the ground of justification at all, only with the means of securing it.

V. Paul and James

On the assumption that Jas. 2:14–26 teaches that God accepts men on the double ground of faith and works, some have thought that James deliberately contradicts Paul's teaching of justification by faith without works, supposing it to be antinomian (*cf.* Rom. 3:8). But this seems to misconceive James' point. It must be remembered that Paul is the only NT writer to use 'justify' as a technical term for God's act of accepting sinners when they believe. When James speaks of 'being justified', he appears to be using the word in its more general sense of being vindicated, or proved genuine and right before God and men, in face of possible doubt as to whether one was all that one professed, or was said, to be (*cf.* the usage in Mt. 11:19). For someone to be justified in this sense is for him to be shown a genuine believer, one who will demonstrate his faith by action. This justification is, in effect, a manifesting of the justification that concerns Paul. James quotes Gn. 15:6 for the same purpose as Paul does—to show that it was faith that secured Abraham's acceptance. But now, he argues, this statement was 'fulfilled' (confirmed, shown to be true, and brought to its appointed completion by events) 30 years later, when 'Abraham (was) justified by works, when he offered his son Isaac upon the altar' (v. 21). By this his faith was 'made perfect', *i.e.* brought to due expression in appropriate actions; thus he was shown to be a true believer. The case of Rahab is parallel (v. 25). James' point in this paragraph is simply that 'faith', *i.e.* a bare orthodoxy, such as the devils have (v. 19), unaccompanied by good works, provides no sufficient grounds for inferring that a man is saved. Paul would have agreed heartily (*cf.* 1 Cor. 6:9; Eph. 5:5f.; Tit. 1:16).

BIBLIOGRAPHY. *BAGD*; G. Quell and G. Schrenk in *TDNT* 2, pp. 174–225; Klein in *IDBS*, pp. 750–752; commentaries on Romans: especially C. Hodge[2], 1864; C. E. B. Cranfield, *ICC*, 1, 1976; A. Nygren, E.T. 1952; and on Galatians: especially J. B. Lightfoot[10], 1890, E. D. Burton, *ICC*, 1921; J. Buchanan, *The Doctrine of Justification*, 1867; C. Hodge, *Systematic Theology*, 1874, 3, pp. 114–212; V. Taylor, *Forgiveness and Reconciliation*, 1946; L. Morris, *The Apostolic Preaching of the Cross*, 1955; K. Barth, *Church Dogmatics*, 4. 1, E.T. 1956, pp. 514–642; A. Richardson, *Introduction to the Theology of the New Testament*, 1958, pp. 232ff.; J. Murray, *Romans 1–8*, 1959, pp. 336–362; J. A. Ziesler, *The Meaning of Righteousness in Paul*, 1972; H. Seebass, C. Brown, *NIDNTT* 3, pp. 352–377; E. Käsemann, *Perspectives on Paul*, 1971, pp.

60–78; N. T. Wright, *The Climax of the Covenant*, 1991. J.I.P.

JUSTUS. A Latin name. Lightfoot (on Col. 4:11) notes its frequency among Jews and proselytes, often combined with a Jewish name (*cf.* 1 and 3 below, and see Deissmann, *Bible Studies*, pp. 315f.), and suggests that it was meant to denote obedience and devotion to the Law.

1. A name of Joseph Barsabbas, one of the two conceived as the possible apostolic successor to Judas Iscariot (Acts 1:23). By the context he was thus a consistent disciple from John the Baptist's time. Papias had a story of his survival of a heathen ordeal by poison (Eusebius, *EH* 3. 39. 9; *cf.* Lightfoot, *Apostolic Fathers*, 1891, p. 531, for another authority). On the name 'Barsabbas' ('son of—*i.e.* born on—a Sabbath'?), see H. J. Cadbury in *Amicitiae Corolla*, ed. H. G. Wood, 1933, pp. 48ff. If it is a true patronymic, Judas Barsabbas (Acts 15:22) could be a brother.

2. Gentile adherent and neighbour of the synagogue in Corinth. When Christian preaching split the synagogue, the house of Justus became Paul's centre (Acts 18:7). The MSS variously render his other name as Titus or Titius, or omit it altogether (accepted as the original reading by Ropes, *BC*, 3, p. 173). Following the hint of Rom. 16:23, Ramsay, and, more fully, E. J. Goodspeed (*JBL* 69, 1950, pp. 382ff.) identify him with * Gaius of Corinth, rendering his name 'Gaius Titius Justus'. The guess that he was the Titus of Paul's letters has nothing but its antiquity to commend it.

3. Alias Jesus, a valued Jewish co-worker of Paul (Col. 4:11). Nothing more is known of him. It has been conjectured that his name has accidently dropped out from Phm. 24 (*cf.* E. Amling, *ZNW* 10, 1909, p. 261). A.F.W.

JUTTAH (Heb. *yuṭṭâh*). A walled town on a hill 8 km due S of Hebron, 5 km SW of Ziph, assigned to the priests (Jos. 15:55; 21:16; *cf.* 1 Ch. 6:59, where Juttah appears in LXX as *Atta*, and is required to make the count); modern Yatta. In Lk. 1:39 some commentators would read Juttah, in apposition to *polin*, for 'Judah'; F.-M. Abel emphatically disagrees (*Géographie de la Palestine* 2, 1938, p. 367). J.P.U.L.

K

KABZEEL. A town in S Judah; birthplace of Benaiah ben-Jehoiada (2 Sa. 23:20); resettled in Nehemiah's time (called Jekabzeel in Ne. 11:25). Khirbet Hora, site of an Israelite fortress 13 km E of Beer-sheba, is a possible identification. See F.-M. Abel, *Géographie de la Palestine*, 2, 1938, pp. 89, 353; Y. Aharoni, *IEJ* 8, 1958, pp. 36–38.

R.P.G.

KADESH. 1. Kadesh Barne'a. The site has been identified with 'Ain Qudeis, about 80 km SW of Beer Sheva, but this depends on the similarity of the ancient and modern names. The spring produces an insignificant amount of water. 'Ain Qudeirat, roughly 8 km NW of 'Ain Qudeis, has much more water and vegetation and is a more suitable location for Kadesh Barne'a.

Chadarlaomer and his allies came to En Mishpat (*i.e.* Kadesh) and subdued the Amalekites before returning to defeat the kings of the Cities of the (Dead Sea) Plain (Gn. 14:5–9). In the narrative of the fugitive Hagar's experience of God, the well Be'er-le Hai-Ro'i is 'between Kadesh and Bered', on the way to Shur (Gn. 16:7, 14); Kadesh is also associated with the way to Shur in Gn. 20:1.

Journeying through the Sinai wilderness, the Israelites stayed in the region of Kadesh on the edges of the wilderness of Paran and Zin more than once (Nu. 13:26; 20:1; Dt. 1:19, 46); from here Moses sent his spies into Canaan. From Horeb or Sinai to Kadesh was 11 days' journey via Mt. Seir (Dt. 1:2). From the traditional Mt. Sinai to Dahab on the E coast of Sinai and up the coast and across to Kadesh (Qudeirat) is indeed 11 days' travel. At Kadesh, after doubting God's ability to give them the promised land, Israel was condemned to wander for 40 years until a new generation should arise (Nu. 14:32–35; *cf.* Dt. 2:14). After some time, Israel returned to Kadesh (Nu. 33:36–37), Miriam being buried there (Nu. 20:1). At this time, too, for failing to glorify God when striking water from the rock (Nu. 20:10–13; 27:14; Dt. 32:51), Moses was denied entry to the promised land; from there, too, he sent messengers in vain to the king of Edom, to grant Israel permission to pass through his territory (Nu. 20:14–21; Jdg. 11:16–17). Kadesh Barne'a was to be the S corner of the SW boundary of Judah, turning W then NW to reach the Mediterranean along the 'Brook of Egypt' (Nu. 34:4; Jos. 15:3). It was also included as a boundary-point by Ezekiel (47:19; 48:28). The SE to SW limits of Joshua's S Canaanite campaign were marked by Kadesh Barne'a and Gaza respectively (Jos. 10:41). Kedesh in Jos. 15:23, in the southernmost territory of Judah, may either be Kadesh Barne'a or an otherwise unknown site.

The site of Tell el-Qudeirat was first surveyed by Woolley and Lawrence in 1914. The fortress they identified was excavated by M. Dothan in 1956, and by Cohen in 1976–82. Cohen identified three superimposed fortresses, but Ussishkin has shown that there were only two. The lower fortlet was small and elliptical in shape, fortified by a casemate wall with a courtyard in the centre. To the W of it was a small unfortified settlement. The fortlet is dated to the 10th century BC and is one of many such fortlets known from the Negev. Today they are thought to have served as focal points for local desert clans. The daily utensil pots were made of the local 'Negbite' ware, whereas the storage jars had been imported with their contents from Judah. The later and larger fortress is rectangular with casemate walls and eight protruding towers, one in each corner, and one along each side. The fortress was constructed on a raised platform of earth with a shallow moat around it. On the inside were a number of buildings and a cistern. Around the fortress and the spring was a small unfortified settlement. The fortress is one of a number known from the Negev from the end of the Judaean kingdom. Its construction was probably the initiative of the Assyrians, as part of their efforts to control the trade routes to Arabia, but following Assyria's collapse it came under the control of the Egyptians before finally being destroyed in 586 BC by Nebuchadrezzar. It is from this final phase that a number of ostraca (potsherds with writing on them) were found. One ostracon contained three columns of Heb. script and hieratic numerals, and is thought to have been part of a student's exercise.

2. Kadesh (on the Orontes). The site was excavated by M. Pezard and later P. Parr at Tell Nebi Merd and flourished in the late Bronze Age; renowned for the battle when Rameses II defeated the Hittites.

See also *KEDESH.

J.W.

KADMIEL (Heb. *qaḏmî'ēl*, 'God/El is the first/ ancient one'). A Levite who returned with Zerubbabel (Ezr. 2:40; Ne. 7:43; 12:8, 24), and was concerned with the commencement of the Temple rebuilding (Ezr. 3:9), with the day of national repentance (Ne. 9:4–5) and with the sealing of the covenant (Ne. 10:9). L. H. Brockington (*Ezra, Nehemiah and Esther*, *NCB*, 1969) suggests that the name appears mainly, if not entirely, limited to the designation of a levitical family.

J.G.G.N.

KADMONITES. A people whose name, *qaḏmōnî*, is identical in form with the adjective *qaḏmōnî*, 'eastern' (*e.g.* Ezk. 47:18), and for this reason may simply mean 'Easterners' and be another designation for the *bᵉnê-qedem* *'(children of the) East'. The word occurs but once as a name however (Gn. 15:19, with the article), in the list of peoples to be given to Abraham's seed. It may therefore well be the name of a tribe. T.C.M.

KAIN. A town to the S of Hebron (Jos. 15:57). Khirbet Yaqin has been suggested, but its antiquity is uncertain. LXX takes as one name with Zanoah, altering the count (* ZANOAH, **2**).

J.D.D.

KAIWAN (Heb. *kiyyûn*), AV **CHIUN** (Am. 5:26). Earlier scholars thought it meant 'pedestal' or 'image-stand' (see W. R. Harper, *Amos, ICC*, 1910, pp. 139f.). Vulg. has *imaginem*, RVmg. 'shrine'. Most now believe that it represents Assyr. *kaiwanu*, a name of Ninurta, god of the planet Saturn, but that the Massoretes have changed the original vowel-points of *kaiwan* to those of *šiqqûṣ* (= 'abomination'). LXX *Rhaiphan* (* REPHAN, AV Remphan) seems to support this view. D.W.G.

KANAH (Heb. *qānâh*). **1.** A wadi running W from the watershed at the head of the Michmethath valley, 8 km SW of Shechem; its lower course was the boundary of Ephraim with Manasseh (Jos. 16:8).

2. A town in the Lebanon foothills, assigned to Asher (Jos. 19:28); probably modern Qana, 10 km SE of Tyre. J.P.U.L.

KEDAR (Heb. *qēḏār*, probably 'black', 'swarthy'). **1.** A son of Ishmael (Gn. 25:13; 1 Ch. 1:29), forebear of like-named tribe.

2. Nomadic tribesfolk of the Syro-Arabian desert from Palestine to Mesopotamia. In 8th century BC, known in S Babylonia (I. Eph'al, *JAOS* 94, 1974, p. 112), Isaiah prophesying their downfall (Is. 21:16–17). They developed 'villages' (Is. 42:11), possibly simple encampments (H. M. Orlinsky, *JAOS* 59, 1939, pp. 22ff.), living in black tents (Ct. 1:5). As keepers of large flocks (Is. 60:7), they traded over to Tyre (Ezk. 27:21). Geographically, Kittim (Cyprus) W in the Mediterranean and Kedar E into the desert were like opposite poles (Je. 2:10). Dwelling with the Kedarites was like a barbaric exile to one psalmist (Ps. 120:5).

Alongside Arabian tribes, Nebaioth, *etc.*, Kedarites clashed with Ashurbanipal in the 7th century BC (M. Weippert, *Welt des Orients* 7, 1973–74, p. 67). Likewise they suffered attack by Nebuchadrezzar II of Babylon in 599 BC (*cf.* D. J. Wiseman, *Chronicles of Chaldaean Kings*, 1956, p. 32), as announced by Jeremiah (Je. 49:28). By the Persian period, a regular succession of kings of Kedar controlled a realm astride the vital land-route from Palestine to Egypt, regarded as its guardians by the Persian emperors. Such was * Geshem (Gashmu)—opponent of Nehemiah (Ne. 6:1–2, 6)—whose son Qaynu is entitled 'King of Kedar' on a silver bowl from a shrine in the Egyp. E Delta. On this and these kings, see I. Rabinowitz, *JNES* 15, 1956, pp. 1–9, pl. 7; W. J. Dumbrell, *BASOR* 203, 1971, pp. 33–44; A. Lemaire, *RB* 81, 1974, pp. 63–72.

J.D.D.
K.A.K.

KEDEMOTH. Probably present-day ez-Za'ferān, *c.* 16 km N of the Arnon, just inside Sihon's territory and near the Amorites' E border. A levitical city (Jos. 21:37; 1 Ch. 6:79) from the inheritance of Reuben (Jos. 13:18), giving its name to a nearby desert area (Dt. 2:26).

BIBLIOGRAPHY. F. M. Abel, *Géographie de la Bible*, 1938, p. 69; *LOB*, p. 186. N.H.

KEDESH, KEDESH IN NAPHTALI. 1. A former Canaanite royal city (Jos. 12:22) which became a principal town in Naphtali (Jos. 19:37). It was sometimes designated 'of Naphtali' (Jdg. 4:6) to distinguish it from **2.** It was assigned to the Levites (Jos. 21:32) and made a city of refuge (20:7). Kedesh was also marked by its location in Galilee (Jos. 20:7; 1 Ch. 6:76).

This Kedesh may well be the home of Barak where he collected his forces from Naphtali and Zebulun for war against Sisera (Jdg. 4:9–11). When Tiglath-pileser III of Assyria invaded N Israel in 734–732 BC Kedesh, being on the route S from Hazor, was one of the first cities to fall to him (2 Ki. 15:29). It was the scene of the great battle fought between the Maccabees and Demetrius (1 Macc. 11:63, 73). Kedesh is the modern Tell Kudeish, NW of Lake Huleh, where soundings and surface finds show it to have been occupied during the early and late Bronze Ages.

2. A town of Issachar given to Gershonite Levites (1 Ch. 6:72). Its place is taken by Kishion in the list of Jos. 21:28. It is identified with the modern Tell Abu Qedes, SSW of Megiddo. See *NEAEHL*, p. 860.

3. A town in S Judah near the Edomite border (Jos. 15:23), probably to be identified with Kadesh Barne'a, so * Kadesh.

BIBLIOGRAPHY. *Excavations and Researches*, 1973 (Tell Aviv), pp. 93–122. D.J.W.

KEILAH (Heb. *qᵉʿîlâh*). A town in the Shephelah (Jos. 15:43), probably Kelti of Amarna Letters 279–280, 290 (*ANET*, pp. 289, 487). In Saul's time, David relieved it from a Philistine attack, but found Saul's influence too strong for his safety (1 Sa. 23). At the Restoration its territory formed two districts (Ne. 3:17f.). Khirbet Qila, on a hill 10 km E of Beit Guvrin, commands the ascent to Hebron S from Socoh, in the valley between the Shephelah and the hills. J.P.U.L.

KENATH (Heb. *qᵉnāṯ*, 'possession'). A city in N Transjordan taken from the Amorites by * Nobah, who gave it his name (Nu. 32:42), and later taken by * Geshur and Aram (1 Ch. 2:23). The name appears in several Egyp. texts of the 2nd millennium (*cf. LOB*, index). It is usually identified with the extensive ruins at Qanawât, some 25 km NE of Bozrah; but see F.-M. Abel, *Géographie de la Palestine*, 2, p. 417, and M. Noth, *Numbers*, p. 241 (*cf. PJB* 37, 1941, pp. 80–81), who prefers a location W or NW of modern Amman, comparing Jdg. 8:11.

J.D.D.
G.I.D.

KENAZ. 1. A grandson of * Esau and an * Edomite chief (Gn. 36:11, 15, 42). Some commentators consider these vv. indicate Kenaz was the ancestor of the * Kenizzites. **2.** The brother of * Caleb and father of * Othniel and * Seraiah (Jos.

15:17; Jdg. 1:13; 3:9, 11; 1 Ch. 4:13). **3.** A grandson of Caleb (1 Ch. 4:15). Uknaz (AVmg.) results from Heb. word for 'and' being read as part of the name of Kenaz. R.A.H.G.

KENITES. The Kenites were a Midianite tribe (Nu. 10:29; Jdg. 1:16; 4:11). The name means 'smith', and the presence of copper SE of the Gulf of Aqabah, the Kenite–Midianite region, confirms this interpretation. The Kenites first appear as inhabitants of patriarchal Canaan (Gn. 15:19). Subsequently Moses becomes son-in-law of Reuel (Ex. 2:18), and invites Hobab his son to accompany the Israelites, coveting his nomadic skill (Nu. 10:29). Kenites accompanied Judah into their inheritance (Jdg. 1:16; 1 Sa. 27:10). They were spared by Saul in his Amalekite war (1 Sa. 15:6), and David cultivated their friendship (1 Sa. 30:29). The Rechabites were of Kenite stock (1 Ch. 2:55), and were prominent in post-exilic times (Ne. 3:14).

The 'Kenite hypothesis' gives this Midianite clan importance in the religion of Israel. It purports to answer the question: Where did Moses learn the name Yahweh? Rejecting pre-Mosaic knowledge of the name in Israel, some reply that he learnt the name from Jethro, the Kenite–Midianite. The later Yahwistic zeal of the Rechabite–Kenites cannot support this theory: it is not unknown for converts to be more zealous than traditional believers! Nor does Jethro's sacrifice (Ex. 18:12) bear the weight placed upon it, that Jethro was instructing Moses how Yahweh should be worshipped, for the chapter shows him as the learner, led to faith by Moses' testimony (v. 11). Apart, therefore, from the unconvincing observation that 'the Kenites were the smiths of the ancient nomad tribes, ... and undoubtedly Yahweh is a fire-god' (Oesterley and Robinson, *History of Israel*, 1, p. 92), the sole support of the Kenite hypothesis is that their ancestor Cain bore the mark of Yahweh (Gn. 4:15). This hypothesis is advocated, *e.g.*, by L. Koehler, *Old Testament Theology*, p. 45; contested by M. Buber, *Moses*, p. 94. The testimony of Genesis is that the name Yahweh was known to the Patriarchs, and indeed from the earliest times (Gn. 4:1, 26). The hypothesis is a fruit of the application of documentary analysis, and well merits being called 'the acme of liberal inventiveness' (U. E. Simon, *A Theology of Salvation*, 1953, p. 88).

BIBLIOGRAPHY. H. H. Rowley, *From Moses to Qumran*, 1963, pp. 48ff.; *Joseph to Joshua*, 1950, pp. 149ff.; Y. Kaufmann, *The Religion of Israel*, 1961, pp. 242ff. J.A.M.

KENIZZITES (Heb. *qᵉnizzî*). A leading Edomite family, tracing descent from Eliphaz, Esau's eldest son (Gn. 36:11, 15, 42; 1 Ch. 1:36, 53). Part of them joined the Judahites; their contribution to Israel's history is indicated in 1 Ch. 4:13ff. V. 15 is difficult; perhaps it read originally '... *(names lost)*; these were the sons of Kenaz'. Caleb's Kenizzite descent is always expressed through Jephunneh (Nu. 32:12, Jos. 14:6, 14). 'Othniel, son of Kenaz' may simply mean 'Othniel, the Kenizzite'; otherwise, this Kenaz would have been Caleb's younger brother, and Othniel his nephew. Caleb's history implies that his family was well established in Judah before the Exodus (*cf.* Nu. 13:6); so it may have been Jephunneh's ancestors who first joined the tribe.

The Kenizzites are mentioned in Gn. 15:19 with nine other nations as occupying the land promised to Abraham; this, apparently defined in terms of settlements made after his time, included the Negeb but no part of Edom proper (*cf.* Dt. 2:5). J.P.U.L.

KENOSIS. This Gk. term is formed from the verb *heauton ekenōsen*, 'he emptied himself', which the AV of Phil. 2:7 renders 'he made himself of no reputation'. As a substantive it is used, in the technical sense, of the Christological theory which sets out 'to show how the Second Person of the Trinity could so enter into human life as that there resulted the genuinely human experience which is described by the evangelists' (H. R. Mackintosh). In its classic form this Christology goes back no farther than the middle of the last century, to Thomasius of Erlangen in Germany.

The essence of the original kenotic view is stated clearly by J. M. Creed. 'The Divine Logos by His Incarnation divested Himself of His divine attributes of omniscience and omnipotence, so that in His incarnate life the Divine Person is revealed and solely revealed through a human consciousness' (art. 'Recent Tendencies in English Christology' in *Mysterium Christi*, ed. Bell and Deissmann, 1930, p. 133). This Christological statement is open to damaging theological objections; and, on exegetical grounds too, there is little support for it.

The verb *kenoun* means simply 'to empty'. In the literal sense it is used, for example, of Rebekah's emptying the water from her pitcher into the trough (Gn. 24:20, LXX: the verb is *exekenōsen*). In Je. 14:2; 15:9 the LXX uses the verb *kenoun* to render the *pu'al* of *'āmal*, which the RV translates as 'languish'; and this translation points to a metaphorical usage which prepares the way for the interpretation of the Philippians text. The use of *kenoun* there in the active voice is unique in the NT, and the whole phrase with the reflexive is not only un-Pauline but un-Greek too. This fact supports the suggestion that the phrase is a rendering into Gk. of a Sem. original, the linguistic solecism being explained by the literal translation from one language into another. Recent scholars (H. W. Robinson, J. Jeremias) have found this original in Is. 53:12: 'He poured out his soul to death'. On this reading of Phil. 2:7, the 'kenosis' is not that of his incarnation but the final surrender of his life, in utter self-giving and sacrifice, on the cross. Even if this novel interpretation is regarded as somewhat forced (for a critique, see R. P. Martin, *Carmen Christi*, 1967, ch. 7) it puts us on the right track. The words 'he emptied himself' in the Pauline context say nothing about the abandonment of the divine attributes, and to that extent the kenotic theory is an entire misunderstanding of the scriptural words. Linguistically the self-emptying is to be interpreted in the light of the words which immediately follow. It refers to the 'pre-incarnate renunciation coincident with the act of "taking the form of a servant"' (V. Taylor, *The Person of Christ in New Testament Teaching*, 1958, p. 77). His taking of the servant's form involved the necessary limitation of the glory which he laid aside that he might be born 'in the likeness of men'. That glory of his pre-existent oneness with the Father (see Jn. 17:5, 24) was his because from all eternity he existed 'in the form of God' (Phil. 2:6). It was concealed in the 'form of a servant' which he took when he assumed our nature and appeared in our likeness; and with the acceptance of our humanity he took also his destiny as the Servant of the Lord who humbled himself to the sacrifice of himself at Calvary. The 'kenosis' then began in his Father's presence with his preincarnate choice to assume our nature; it led inevitably to the final obedience of the cross when he did, to the fullest extent, pour out his soul unto death (see Rom. 8:3; 2 Cor. 8:9; Gal. 4:4–5; Heb. 2:14–16; 10:5ff.).

BIBLIOGRAPHY. The fullest modern treatment of the kenosis doctrine, both historically and theologically, is that by P. Henry, art. 'Kénose' in *DBS*, Fasc. 24, 1950, cols. 7–161; D. G. Dawe, *The Form of a Servant*, 1964; T. A. Thomas, *EQ* 42, 1970, pp. 142–151. For a modern theological discussion, see R. S. Anderson, *Historical Transcendence and the Reality of God*, 1975.

R.P.M.

KERCHIEFS (AV trans. of Heb. *mispāḥôṯ*, only in plur. Ezk. 13:18, 21, RSV 'veils'). A word associated with the practice of divination, and found in this obscure passage. Some understand the word as denoting long drapes or coverings put over the heads of those who consulted false prophetesses. These coverings for 'persons of every stature' reached down to the feet, and were connected with the introduction of the wearer into the magical circle. Others suggest that the word means a close-fitting cap (*cf.* Heb. *sāp̄aḥ*, 'to join'), which also fulfuls the condition of certain forms of divination or sorcery that the head should be covered. See also *AMULETS, *MAGIC AND SORCERY, **II.** *b*; and, for full discussion of the context and possible interpretations, G. A. Cooke, *Ezekiel*, *ICC*, 1936, pp. 144ff.

J.D.D.

KEREN-HAPPUCH (Heb. *qeren happûḵ* 'painthorn', *i.e.* 'beautifier'; LXX *Amaltheias keras*). The name given to the third and youngest daughter of Job after his prosperity had been restored (Jb. 42:14). For discussion of the name, *COSMETICS AND PERFUMERY, **III.** *a*.

J.D.D.

KERIOTH. 1. A town in the extreme S of Judah, known also as Kerioth-hezron or Hazor, possibly the modern Khirbet el-Qaryatein (Jos. 15:25). **2.** A city of Moab (Je. 48:24), formerly fortified (Je. 48:41), and possessing palaces (Am. 2:2). Probably El-Qereiyat, S of Ataroth. Some writers identify it with Ar, the ancient capital of Moab, because when Ar is listed among Moabite towns Kerioth is omitted (Is. 15–16), and *vice versa* (Je. 48). There was a sanctuary there for Chemosh, to which Mesha dragged Arel the chief of Ataroth. (*MOABITE STONE.)

J.A.T.

KESITAH (Heb. *qᵉśîṭâ*, probably 'that which is weighed', 'a fixed weight', from an Arab. word meaning 'to divide, fix'). A unit of unknown value, evidently uncoined money used by the Patriarchs. LXX, Onkelos and Jerome render as 'lambs', early weights often being modelled in animal-forms (*WEIGHTS AND MEASURES). Possibly it may represent the value of a sheep in silver. It occurs only in Gn. 33:19 and Jos. 24:32 of Jacob's land-purchase at Shechem, and in Jb. 42:11 of a congratulatory present. RSV translates as 'piece of money', but NEB as 'sheep'.

J.G.G.N.

KETURAH (Heb. *qᵉṭûrâ*, 'perfumed one'). Abraham's second wife after the death of Sarah who bore him Zimran, Jokshan, Medan, Midian, Ishbak and Shuah, who in their turn became the ancestors of a number of N Arabian peoples (Gn. 25:1–4; 1 Ch. 1:32–33). (*ARABIA.)

BIBLIOGRAPHY. J. A. Montgomery, *Arabia and the Bible*, 1934, pp. 42–45.

T.C.M.

KEY (Heb. *map̄tēaḥ*, 'opener'; Gk. *kleis*, 'key'). In its literal sense the word is found only in Jdg. 3:25; the key was 'a flat piece of wood furnished with pins corresponding to holes in a hollow bolt. The bolt was on the inside, shot into a socket in the doorpost and fastened by pins which fell into the holes in the bolt from an upright piece of wood (the lock) attached to the inside of the door. To unlock the door one put one's hand in by a hole in the door (*cf.* Ct. 5:4) and raised the pins in the bolt by means of the corresponding pins in the key' (F. F. Bruce in *NBCR*, p. 260). The more usual biblical sense of the word is a symbol of power and authority (*e.g.* Mt. 16:19; Rev. 1:18; Is. 22:22).

See also *POWER OF THE KEYS.

J.D.D.

KIBROTH-HATTAAVAH (Heb. *qiḇrôṯ hatta'ᵃwâ*, 'graves of craving'). A camp of the Israelites a day's journey from the wilderness of Sinai. There the people, having craved flesh to eat and been sent quails by the Lord, were overtaken by plague, which caused many fatalities (Nu. 11:31–34; 33:16; Dt. 9:22; *cf.* Ps. 78:27–31). Some have suggested that the incident at Taberah (Nu. 11:1–3) had the same location as that at Kibroth-hattaavah, but Dt. 9:22 seems to argue against this. Grollenberg makes an identification with Ruweis el-Ebeirig, NE of Mt Sinai.

J.D.D.

KIDNEYS. In the RSV the Heb. word *kᵉlāyôṯ* is translated by 'kidneys' when it refers to the physical organ of sacrificial beasts, principally in Leviticus (3:4; 4:9; 7:4; *etc.*). The practice was that the two kidneys, together with the fat and part of the liver, were burnt on the altar as Yahweh's portion, while the worshippers no doubt consumed the rest. The kidneys along with the blood and other internal organs were held to contain the life, and the kidneys were regarded as a choice portion, perhaps because of their coating of fat; *cf.* Dt. 32:14, where the RSV translates *ḥēleḇ kᵉlayôṯ*, lit. 'fat of the kidneys of', as 'the finest of' (the wheat).

The same Heb. word is translated variously where it refers, generally figuratively, to the human organs, which were held to possess psychical functions. RSV renders it as 'the heart' which is 'troubled' (Jb. 19:27; Ps. 73:21), and 'tried' by God (Je. 11:20). In Pr. 23:16 RSV uses 'soul', which 'rejoices'. In NT Gk. *nephros* (lit. kidneys) occurs once, but RSV renders 'mind' (Rev. 2:23).

The parallelism reveals how the heart and the other internal organs (*BOWELS, *HEART) were held to be the centre of the personality and will, without clear distinction between them.

The reference to the *kᵉlayôṯ* (RSV 'heart') instructing one (Ps. 16:7) (with a parallel in the Ras

Shamra texts, 'his inwards instruct him') is a further similar usage, with which compare the late Jewish concept that one kidney prompts a man to do good and the other prompts him to do evil (TJ, *Berakhoth* 61a). B.O.B.

KIDRON. The brook Kidron, the modern Wadi en-Nar, is a torrent-bed, which begins to the N of Jerusalem, passes the Temple mount and the Mount of Olives *en route* to the Dead Sea, which it reaches by way of the wilderness of Judaea. Its modern name means 'the Fire wadi', and this bears witness to the fact that it is dry and sun-baked for most of the year. Only for short periods during the rainy seasons is it filled with water. It was also called 'the Valley of *Jehoshaphat'

On the W side of the Kidron there is a spring known as the Gihon ('Gusher') or 'Virgin's Fountain', the flow of which was artificially diverted under Hezekiah's orders to serve the needs of Jerusalem and to protect its water-supply from the enemy. This was the latest of several tunnels and shafts connected with the spring.

As its name would suggest, the water does not come through in a steady flow, but accumulates underground in a reservoir and breaks out from time to time. In 1880 a Heb. inscription was found in which information was recorded about the making of Hezekiah's tunnel (*SILOAM). For the archaeology, see K. M. Kenyon, *Digging up Jerusalem*, 1974, pp. 84–89, 151–159.

David passed over the brook Kidron on his way out of Jerusalem during Absalom's revolt (2 Sa. 15:23). The reforming kings, such as Asa, Hezekiah and Josiah, used the valley as a place of destruction where heathen idols, altars, *etc.*, were burnt or ground to powder (1 Ki. 15:13, *etc.*). It seems to be taken as one of the boundaries of Jerusalem in 1 Ki. 2:37 and Je. 31:40.

Some suggest a reference to the Kidron in Ezk. 47, where the prophet sees a stream of water issuing from the threshold of the Temple and pursuing its way towards the Dead Sea, making the land fertile in the process. See especially G. Adam Smith, *The Historical Geography of the Holy Land*, 1931, pp. 510ff.; W. R. Farmer, 'The Geography of Ezekiel's River of Life', *BA* 19, 1956, pp. 17ff. That Ezekiel was thinking of the filling-up of the dry bed of the Kidron by the healing stream of water seems probable, but cannot be maintained with any degree of certainty. G.W.G.

KIN, KINSMAN. Israel was originally tribal in nature. The idea was never entirely lost, although as the centuries passed the distinctions became less well marked, until today they have all but disappeared (*cf.* Scots' clans). Many of Israel's family relationships are to be understood in terms of tribal customs known all over the world. Kinship consisted basically in the possession of a common blood and was strongest nearest to its origin in the father's house, but it was not lost in the further reaches of family relationship. At the head of the family (*mišpāḥâ*) stood the father (*'āḇ*), a word which expressed kinship and authority. The father founded a father's house (*bêṯ 'āḇ*), which was the smallest unit of a tribe. But the strong cohesion of the family extended upwards from the father to the fathers, and downwards from the father to the sons and daughters. Hence the term family could mean the father's house (*bêṯ 'āḇ*), and also the house of the fathers (*bêṯ 'āḇôṯ*). Indeed, at times the whole of Israel was called a family.

A picture of tribal relationships which is more or less contemporary with the patriarchs comes from the Middle Bronze Age society at *Mari on the Euphrates. Here semi-nomadic and urban peoples of the same general stock lived side by side in a dimorphic society. The village-pastoral group were not marauding peoples but sheep-breeders who moved their encampments periodically in search of water and pastures, living in tents but settling at times. These peoples were tribally organized into 'paternal houses' or 'families' (*bit abim*; *cf.* *bêṯ 'āḇ* in Gn. 12:1, *etc.*). Recent studies provide several detailed comparisons between Mari and the patriarchal society. The texts from Mari provide literary evidence for such a comparison.

The word brother (*'āḥ*) also connoted various things. In its simplest meaning it referred to those who had common parents. In polygamous Israel there were many brothers who had only a common father. These too were brothers, though the brotherhood was not the same as that of men who had a common mother. Thus in Gn. 42:4 there are two kinds of brothers, full and half. The full brother was defined by the phrase 'his brother, Benjamin, his mother's son' (Gn. 43:29). However, the term extended as far as the feeling of consanguinity extended. Wherever there was a family there were brothers, for all were bearers of kinship (Gn. 24:4, 27, 38; Jdg. 14:3). At times all Israelites were called brothers (Ex. 2:11; Lv. 10:6; 2 Sa. 19:41–42).

There were limits to the closeness of relationship permitted when a man came to seek a wife. Abraham would seek a wife for his son Isaac from his kindred (*mišpāḥâ*) and from his father's house (*bêṯ 'āḇ*), not from the daughters of Canaan (Gn. 24:38, 40). She had to be someone of the same flesh and blood. But she could not be of such close relationship as a sister, mother, child's daughter, *etc.* The forbidden areas are defined in Lv. 18.

There were significant obligations laid on kinsmen. Among the more important we may mention the following.

Since a woman, married to a man, would normally have the privilege of bearing his son and heir, in the case of the untimely death of the husband without a son, the law of levirate (Lat. *levir*, 'husband's brother') *marriage came into force, and progeny was raised up to the dead man who had died 'without a name in Israel' by his next of kin (Dt. 25:5–10). There is a good illustration of this in the book of Ruth.

Then in the matter of inheritance, a man's property was normally passed on to his son or sons. Failing these, it went to his daughters, and then in order to his brethren, to his father's brethren, and finally to his kinsman who was nearest to him (Nu. 27:1–11).

Again it was obligatory on a kinsman to redeem the property of a fellow-kinsman who had fallen into the hands of creditors (Lv. 25:25ff.).

In the special circumstances where a man's life was taken by another, since this was part of the life of the family, an obligation rested on the son, or the brother, or the next of kin in order, to take vengeance (*cf.* Gn. 9:5–6). Where kinship ends, there is no longer any *avenger (*gō'ēl*).

BIBLIOGRAPHY. W. G. Dever, 'Palestine in the

Second Millennium BC: The Archaeological Picture', in J. H. Hayes and J. Maxwell Miller (eds.), *Israelite and Judaean History*, pp. 70–120, with a good bibliography; D. Jacobson, *The Social Background of the Old Testament*, 1942; L. Kohler, *Hebrew Man*, 1956, pp. 75ff.; A. Malamat, 'Mari and the Bible: Some Patterns of Tribal Organization and Institutions', *JAOS* 82, 1962, pp. 143–150; *idem*, 'Aspects of Tribal Societies in Mari and Israel', in J. R. Kupper (ed.), *La civilization de Mari*, XV[e] Rencontre Assyriologique Internationale, Paris, 1967; J. Pedersen, *Israel I–II*, 1926, pp. 49, 52, 58ff., 284ff., *etc.*; C. R. Taber, 'Kinship and Family', *IDBS*; F. I. Andersen, 'Israelite Kinship Terminology and Social Structure', *Bible Translator* 29, 1969, pp. 29–39. J.A.T.

KING, KINGSHIP. Heb. *meleḵ*; Gk. *basileus.* Both words are of obscure origin; the former, common to all Semitic languages, is possibly connected either with an Arab. root meaning 'possess' or an Assyr. and Aram. word meaning 'counsel'. The latter is probably taken over from an early Aegean language.

The office was common in the Middle East from the earliest times, the general pattern apparently being of a ruler who held sway over a settled region, often centred on a city (Gn. 14:1–2; 20:1ff.). His authority seems to have been hereditary (but *cf.* Gn. 36:31ff.), and to have derived from the divine-king or god of the land (see J. A. Soggin, *Protestantismo* 17, 1962, pp. 85–89), often spoken of as the ancestor or father of the ruling king (*e.g.* Ras Shamra—Legend of King Keret). In Egypt the tendency was for the king or pharaoh to be regarded as identical with the god; in Assyria, rather as representing the god.

In classical Greek *basileus* denotes the legal hereditary ruler, guiding the life of the people by his justice or injustice, but contrasted with the tyrant or usurper. The king's power is traced back to Zeus. Later, under Plato, we find a movement towards the idea of the king as 'benefactor', whose will is law, leading up to the idea of 'divine-king' in Alexander and the Caesars.

I. Early ideas in Israel

In the history of Israel the early nomadic tribes were ruled by the clan Patriarch. During the Exodus from Egypt rule was exercised by Moses, succeeded by Joshua, in what was a virtual theocracy, with the non-hereditary leader elected by divine call and acknowledged by the people, though not without some protest (Ex. 4:29ff.; Nu. 16:1ff.). When Israel first settled in Palestine the tribes were ruled largely by village fathers (Jdg. 11:5), who would call on a certain man to lead the militia against an enemy. Jephthah (Jdg. 11:9) demanded that he be made 'head' if he took the lead in this way, but his son did not succeed him. Gideon was asked to rule (*mālaḵ*) over Israel (8:22) and refused, but his son Abimelech seized a temporary and local kingship after him (9:6ff.). The book of Judges ends on a note of social chaos (chs. 19–21), and this is attributed to the lack of a king (19:1; 21:25).

II. From Eli and Samuel

The following period was one of improvement under the religio-judicial lead of Eli and Samuel. Eli was chief priest at the central sanctuary in Shiloh (1 Sa. 1:3; 4:13); Samuel was a non-hereditary leader (after the style of Moses and Joshua) who, after the destruction of Shiloh, judged Israel from several places which he visited in circuit (7:15f.). Finally, Samuel became the king-maker of Israel, though at the insistence of the people (1 Sa. 8:4ff.). This seems to have been regarded as a measure of apostasy from the theocracy (1 Sa. 8:7). The request was probably made largely in view of the continual Philistine threat, necessitating a sustained army (8:20), and Saul's success as a warrior was his main qualification for the role as the first king of Israel. Under his reign, however, Samuel, while he lived, preserved the religious leadership (1 Sa. 13:9ff.), and Saul never quite established his position, nor his dynasty.

III. Development under David

David, however, was eminently successful, and was ever afterwards regarded as the ideal king. He established a dynasty that lasted for over 400 years, until the break-up of the state in 587 BC. The security of David's dynasty seems to have been based largely on what has been called the Davidic covenant (Ps. 132:11f.). The capital city, centrally situated between what became later the N and S states, was Jerusalem (2 Sa. 5:5ff.). It may be that David assumed something of the role of priest-king after the style of the Jebusite kings, whose priesthood apparently dated back to the time of Abraham (Gn. 14:17ff.; Ps. 110), since he seems to have taken a lead in the cult (2 Sa. 6:13ff.; *cf.* also 1 Ki. 8:5).

The Davidic covenant may have been an extension of the Mosaic covenant, particularly if G. E. Mendenhall is right in suggesting that the form of the Mosaic covenant was analogous to Hittite treaty patterns. Under these a Hittite overlord granted an enduring dynasty to his vassal, if the vassal king was a relation, but otherwise he was always personally responsible for the appointment of a successor. The reference to the king as the son of God (Ps. 2:6–7) and the promise to maintain the dynasty in terms of the covenant (1 Ki. 9:4–5) make the suggestion easily credible.

The main responsibility of the king was the maintenance of righteousness (Is. 11:1–4; Je. 33:15), possibly signified by the possession of the testimonies or law or *tôrâ* (Dt. 17:18ff.; 1 Sa. 10:25; 1 Ki. 9:4ff.; 2 Ki. 11:12), with the duty not only to act as judge (1 Ki. 3:28) but to preserve justice and proclaim the law (2 Ki. 23:2; *cf.* 2 Ch. 17:7ff.; *cf.* also Jdg. 17:6).

But many of the kings were wicked themselves and encouraged injustice and wickedness to flourish, not only in the schismatic N kingdom but in the S too (1 Ki. 14:16; 2 Ki. 21:16). The reform under Josaiah (2 Ki. 22–23) may have been an attempt to revive the Mosaic precepts in connection with the Davidic covenant, but it was above all the prophetic movement which povided a check upon the waywardness of the kings (2 Sa. 12:1ff.; 1 Ki. 18:17–18; Je. 26:1ff.) (*PROPHECY; see also **IV**, below).

It will be noticed that several so-called Messianic passages have been applied above to the Davidic dynasty (Pss. 2; 110; 132; Is. 11:1–4; Je. 33:15), and it is the considered view of many modern scholars that this is their primary reference, the psalms referred to being, among others, probably coronation psalms used in the Jerusalem Temple. The failure of the kings to live up to the ideal, however, tended to cast the hope for a righteous ruler more and more into the future. With the fall of the S kingdom, and later the failure of the Davidic prince, Zerubbabel (1 Ch. 3:19; Hg. 2:23; Mt. 1:12) to restore the dynasty on the throne of the post-exilic state, the expectation crystallized into what is technically known as the Messianic hope, though many scholars believe it began earlier. (*Messiah.)

IV. The king's ministers

But it should be noted that the prophets were not apparently appointed by the king, though the priests were (1 Ki. 2:27). Both officiated in the installation of a king (1:34), but the prophet sometimes took the greater initiative, especially with a change of dynasty, as in the N kingdom (1 Ki. 19:16). Other servants of the king were the commander of the army (2 Sa. 19:13); the secretary (2 Sa. 8:17; 2 Ki. 12:10), and the recorder, plus sundry others (1 Ki. 4:3ff.). The recorder (*mazkîr*, literally one who causes to remember) was perhaps connected with the chronicling of state events (*cf.* 2 Ki. 21:25), or the term may signify the advisory and executive position of a prime minister or grand vizier. Another possibility is that it was a vocal office, parallel to the Egyp. *whm.w*, 'court announcer' or 'king's herald'.

V. Later developments

During the period 104–37 BC certain of the Maccabean high priests assumed the title of king, and some were proclaimed as the fulfilment of the Messianic hope, but it is essentially the message of the NT that this hope was fulfilled only in Jesus Christ (Mt. 1:1–17; 21:5, with which compare Zc. 9:9 and the coronation procedure in the case of Solomon, 1 Ki. 1:33; also Jn. 1:49). Jesus' message began with the proclamation, 'The kingdom of God is at hand' (Mk. 1:15), and announced to the Pharisees that the kingdom was in their midst (Lk. 17:21). He pointed out that it was not a kingdom of this world (Jn. 18:36), and so was not on the same plane as that of the Roman governor, Pilate, or of Herod, the Idumaean king of Judah and vassal of Rome (*cf.* Mt. 2:16).

Though the word translated 'kingdom' (*basileia*) is used in the sense of realm or domain (Mt. 12:25), the dominant sense is 'sovereignty' or 'kingly rule'. The sovereignty of God is absolute, but not recognized by sinful man, who thus merits destruction. The 'gospel of the kingdom of God' means that men are given an opportunity to receive the kingdom by repentance and faith (Mk. 1:15). This is achieved through Christ the Messiah-King, to whom every knee must bow, whether in willing loyalty or under judgment (Rom. 14:10–11; Phil. 2:9–11).

The rule of earthly kings is limited, and Christ claims the first allegiance (Mt. 6:33). His subjects are delivered from the power of darkness (Col. 1:13), and thus are set free to live righteously (Rom. 14:17). Christ's kingdom is an everlasting kingdom (2 Pet. 1:11), but yet to be consummated (Lk. 22:16; 1 Cor. 15:24–28). (*Kingdom of God.)

Bibliography. S. Mowinckel, *He that Cometh*, 1956; A. R. Johnson, *Sacral Kingship in Ancient Israel*, 1955; G. E. Mendenhall, *Law and Covenant in Israel and the Ancient Near East*, 1955; K. L. Schmidt *et al.*, *TDNT* 1, pp. 564–593; B. Klappert, *NIDNTT* 2, pp. 372–390; R. de Vaux, *Ancient Israel*, 1961; J. Bright, *A History of Israel*², 1972; G. W. Ahlström, *Royal Administration and National Religion in Ancient Palestine*, 1982.

B.O.B.

KINGDOM OF GOD, KINGDOM OF HEAVEN. The kingdom of heaven or kingdom of God is the central theme of Jesus' preaching, according to the Synoptic Gospels. While Matthew, who addresses himself to the Jews, speaks for the most part of the 'kingdom of heaven', Mark and Luke speak of the 'kingdom of God', which has the same meaning as the 'kingdom of heaven', but was more intelligible to non-Jews. The use of 'kingdom of heaven' in Matthew is certainly due to the tendency in Judaism to avoid the direct use of the name of God. In any case no distinction in sense is to be assumed between the two expressions (*cf.*, *e.g.*, Mt. 5:3 with Lk. 6:20).

I. In John the Baptist

John the Baptist first comes forward with the announcement that the kingdom of heaven is at hand (Mt. 3:2) and Jesus takes this message over from him (Mt. 4:17). The expression 'kingdom of heaven' (Heb. *malᵉḵûṯ šāmayim*) originates with the late-Jewish expectation of the future in which it denoted the decisive intervention of God, ardently expected by Israel, to restore his people's fortunes and liberate them from the power of their enemies. The coming of the kingdom is the great perspective of the future, prepared by the coming of the *Messiah, which paves the way for the kingdom of God.

By the time of Jesus the development of this eschatological hope in Judaism had taken a great variety of forms, in which now the national element and now the cosmic and apocalyptic element is prominent. This hope goes back to the proclamation in OT prophecy concerning both the restoration of David's throne and the coming of God to renew the world. Although the OT has nothing to say of the eschatological kingdom of heaven in so many words, yet in the Psalms and prophets the future manifestation of God's royal sovereignty belongs to the most central concepts of OT faith and hope. Here too various elements achieve prominence, as may be clearly seen from a comparison of the earlier prophets with the prophecies regarding universal world-sovereignty and the emergence of the Son of man in the book of *Daniel.

When John the Baptist and, after him, Jesus himself proclaimed that the kingdom was at hand, this proclamation involved an awakening cry of sensational and universal significance. The long-expected divine turning-point in history, the great restoration, however it was conceived at the time, is proclaimed as being at hand. It is therefore of all the greater importance to survey the content of the NT preaching with regard to the coming of the kingdom.

In the preaching of John the Baptist prominence is given to the announcement of divine judgment as a reality which is immediately at hand. The axe is already laid to the root of the trees. God's coming as King is above all else a coming to purify, to sift, to judge. No-one can evade it. No privilege can buy exemption from it, not even the ability to claim Abraham as one's father. At the same time John the Baptist points to the coming One who is to follow him, whose forerunner he himself is. The coming One comes with the winnowing-fan in his hand. In view of his coming the people must repent and submit to baptism for the washing away of sins, so as to escape the coming wrath and participate in the salvation of the kingdom and the baptism with the Holy Spirit which will be poured out when it comes (Mt. 3:1–12).

II. In the teaching of Jesus

a. Present aspect

Jesus' proclamation of the kingdom follows word for word on John's, yet it bears a much more comprehensive character. After John the Baptist had watched Jesus' appearance for a considerable time, he began to be in doubt whether Jesus was, after all, the coming One whom he had announced (Mt. 11:2f.). Jesus' proclamation of the kingdom differs in two respects from that of the Baptist. In the first place, while it retains without qualification the announcement of judgment and the call to repentance, it is the saving significance of the kingdom that stands in the foreground. In the second place—and here is the pith and core of the matter—he announced the kingdom not just as a reality which was at hand, something which would appear in the immediate future, but as a reality which was already present, manifested in his own person and ministry. Although the places where Jesus speaks explicitly of the kingdom as being present are not numerous (see especially Mt. 12:28 and parallels), his whole preaching and ministry are marked by this dominant reality. In him the great future has already become 'present time'.

This present aspect of the kingdom manifests itself in all sorts of ways in the person and deeds of Christ. It appears palpably and visibly in the casting out of demons (*cf.* Lk. 11:20) and generally in Jesus' miraculous power. In the healing of those who are demon-possessed it becomes evident that Jesus has invaded the house of 'the strong man', has bound him fast and so is in a position to plunder his goods (Mt. 12:29). The kingdom of heaven breaks into the domain of the evil one. The power of Satan is broken. Jesus sees him fall like lightning from heaven. He possesses and bestows power to trample on the dominion of the enemy. Nothing can be impossible for those who go forth into the world, invested with Jesus' power, as witnesses of the kingdom (Lk. 10:18f.). The whole of Jesus' miraculous activity is the proof of the coming of the kingdom. What many prophets and righteous men desired in vain to see—the breaking in of the great epoch of salvation—the disciples can now see and hear (Mt. 13:16; Lk. 10:23). When John the Baptist sent his disciples to ask, 'Are you he who is to come, or shall we look for another?' they were shown the wonderful works done by Jesus, in which, according to the promise of prophecy, the kingdom was already being manifested: the blind were enabled to see, the lame to walk, the deaf to hear; lepers were being cleansed and dead people raised to life, and the gospel was being proclaimed to the poor (Mt. 11:2ff.; Lk. 7:18ff.). Also in the last of these—the proclamation of the gospel—the breaking through of the kingdom is seen. Since salvation is announced and offered as a gift already available to the poor in spirit, the hungry and the mourners, the kingdom is theirs. So too the forgiveness of sins is proclaimed, not merely as a future reality to be accomplished in heaven, nor merely as a present possibility, but as a dispensation offered today, on earth, through Jesus himself; 'Son, daughter, your sins are forgiven; for the Son of man has power on earth to forgive sins' (see Mk. 2:1–12, *et passim*).

As appears clearly from this last-quoted word of power, all this is founded on the fact that Jesus is the Christ, the Son of God. The kingdom has come in him and with him; he is the *auto-basileia.* Jesus' self-revelation as the Messiah, the Son of man and Servant of the Lord, constitutes both the mystery and the unfolding of the whole gospel.

It is impossible to explain these sayings of Jesus about himself in a future sense, as some have wished to do, as though he referred to himself only as the future *Messiah, the Son of man who was to be expected on a coming day on the clouds of heaven. For however much this future revelation of the kingdom remains an essential element in the content of the gospel, we cannot mistake the fact that in the Gospels Jesus' Messiahship is present here and now. Not only is he proclaimed as such at his baptism and on the Mount of Transfiguration—as the beloved and elect One of God (plain Messianic designations)—but he is also endowed with the Holy Spirit (Mt. 3:16) and invested with full divine authority (Mt. 21:27); the Gospel is full of his declarations of absolute authority, he is presented as the One sent by the Father, the One who has come to fulfil what the prophets foretold. In his coming and teaching the Scripture is fulfilled in the ears of those who listen to him (Lk. 4:21). He came not to destroy but to fulfil (Mt. 5:17ff.), to announce the kingdom (Mk. 1:38), to seek and to save the lost (Lk. 19:10), to serve others, and to give his life a ransom for many (Mk. 10:45). The secret of belonging to the kingdom lies in belonging to him (Mt. 7:23; 25:41). In brief, the person of Jesus as the Messiah is the centre of all that is announced in the gospel concerning the kingdom. The kingdom is concentrated in him in its present and future aspects alike.

b. Future aspect

There is a future aspect as well. For although it is clearly stated that the kingdom is manifested here and now in the gospel, so also is it shown that as yet it is manifested in this world only in a provisional manner. That is why the proclamation of its present activity in the words, 'The blind receive their sight; the dead are raised; the poor have good news preached to them', is followed by the warning: 'Blessed is he who takes no offence at me' (Mt. 11:6; Lk. 7:23). The 'offence' lies in the hidden character of the kingdom in this epoch. The miracles are still tokens of another order of reality than the present one; it is not yet the time when the demons will be delivered to eternal darkness (Mt. 8:29). The gospel of the kingdom is still revealed only as a seed which is being sown. In the parables of the sower, the seed growing secretly, the tares among the wheat, the mustard seed, the leaven, it is about this hidden aspect of the kingdom that Jesus instructs his disciples. The Son of man himself, invested with all power by God, the One who is to come on the clouds of heaven, is the Sower who sows the Word of God. He is depicted as a man dependent upon others: the birds, the thorns, human beings, can partially frustrate his work. He has to wait and see what will come of his seed. Indeed, the hiddenness of the kingdom is deeper still: the King himself comes in the form of a slave. The birds of the air have nests, but the Son of man (Dn. 7:13) has no place to lay his head. In order to receive everything, he must first of all give up everything. He must give his life as a ransom; as the suffering Servant of the Lord of Is. 53, he must be numbered with the transgressors. The kingdom has come; the kingdom will come. But it comes by the way of the cross, and before the Son of man exercises his authority over all the kingdoms of the earth (Mt. 4:8; 28:18) he must tread the path of obedience to his Father in order thus to fulfil all righteousness (Mt. 3:15). The manifestation of the kingdom has therefore a history in this world. It must be proclaimed to every creature. Like the wonderful seed, it must sprout and grow, no man knows how (Mk. 4:27). It has an inward power by which it makes its way through all sorts of obstacles and advances over all; for the field in which the seed is sown is the world (Mt. 13:38). The gospel of the kingdom goes forth to all nations (Mt. 28:19), for the King of the kingdom is also Lord of the Spirit. His resurrection brings in a new aeon; the preaching of the kingdom *and* the King reaches out to the ends of the earth. The decision has already come to pass; but the fulfilment still recedes into the future. What at first appears to be one and the same coming of the kingdom, what is announced as one indivisible reality, at hand and at close quarters, extends itself to cover new periods of time and far distances. For the frontiers of this kingdom are not coterminous with Israel's boundaries or history: the kingdom embraces all nations and fills all ages until the end of the world comes.

III. Kingdom and church

The kingdom is thus related to the history of the church and of the world alike. A connection exists between kingdom and church, but they are not identical, even in the present age. The kingdom is the whole of God's redeeming activity in Christ in this world; the church is the assembly of those who belong to Jesus Christ. Perhaps one could speak in terms of two concentric circles, of which the church is the smaller and the kingdom the larger, while Christ is the centre of both. This relation of the church to the kingdom can be formulated in all kinds of ways. The church is the assembly of those who have accepted the gospel of the kingdom in faith, who participate in the salvation of the kingdom, which includes the forgiveness of sins, adoption by God, the indwelling of the Holy Spirit, the possession of eternal life. They are also those in whose life the kingdom takes visible form, the light of the world, the salt of the earth; those who have taken on themselves the yoke of the kingdom, who live by their King's commandments and learn from him (Mt. 11:28–30). The church, as the organ of the kingdom, is called to confess Jesus as the Christ, to the missionary task of preaching the gospel in the world; she is also the community of those who wait for the coming of the kingdom in glory, the servants who have received their Lord's talents in prospect of his return. The church receives her whole constitution from the kingdom, on all sides she is beset and directed by the revelation, the progress, the future coming of the kingdom of God, without at any time being the kingdom herself or even being identified with it.

Therefore the kingdom is not confined within the frontiers of the church. Christ's Kingship is supreme above all. Where it prevails and is acknowledged, not only is the individual human being set free, but the whole pattern of life is changed: the curse of the demons and fear of hostile powers disappears. The change which Christianity brings about among peoples dominated by nature-religions is a proof of the comprehensive, all-embracing significance of the kingdom. It works not only outwardly like a mustard seed but inwardly like leaven. It makes its way into the world with its redeeming power. The last book of the Bible, which portrays Christ's Kingship in the history of the world and its advancing momentum right to the end, especially illuminates the antithesis between the triumphant Christ-King (*cf.*, *e.g.*, Rev. 5:1ff.) and the power of Satan and antichrist, which still survives on earth and contends against Christ and his church. However much the kingdom invades world-history with its blessing and deliverance, however much it presents itself as a saving power against the tyranny of gods and forces inimical to mankind, it is only through a final and universal crisis that the kingdom, as a visible and all-conquering reign of peace and salvation, will bring to full fruition the new heaven and the new earth.

IV. In the rest of the New Testament

The expression 'kingdom of heaven' or 'kingdom of God' does not appear so frequently in the NT outside the Synoptic Gospels. This is, however, simply a matter of terminology. As the indication of the great revolution in the history of salvation which has already been inaugurated by Christ's coming, and as the expected consummation of all the acts of God, it is the central theme of the whole NT revelation of God.

V. In theological thought

As regards the conception of the kingdom of heaven in theology, this has been powerfully subjected to all kinds of influences and viewpoints during the various periods and trends of theological thought. In Roman Catholic theology a distinctive feature is the identification of the kingdom of God and the church in the earthly dispensation, an identification which is principally due to Augustine's influence. Through the ecclesiastical hierarchy Christ is actualized as King of the kingdom of God. The area of the kingdom is coterminous with the frontiers of the church's power and authority. The kingdom of heaven is extended by the mission and advance of the church in the world.

In their resistance to the Roman Catholic hierarchy, the Reformers laid chief emphasis on the spiritual and invisible significance of the kingdom and readily (and wrongly) invoked Lk. 17:20f. in support of this. The kingdom of heaven, that is to say, is a spiritual sovereignty which Christ exercises through the preaching of his word and the operation of the Holy Spirit. While the Reformation in its earliest days did not lose sight of the kingdom's great dimensions of saving history, the kingdom of God, under the influence of the Enlightenment and pietism, came to be increasingly conceived in an individualistic sense; it is the sovereignty of grace and peace in the hearts of men. In later liberal theology this conception developed in a moralistic direction (especially under the influence of Kant): the kingdom of God is the kingdom of peace, love and righteousness. At first, even in pietism and sectarian circles, the expectation of the coming kingdom of God was maintained, without, however, making allowance for a positive significance of the kingdom for life in this world. Over against this more or less dualistic understanding of the kingdom we must distinguish the social conception of the kingdom which lays all the stress on its visible and communal significance. This conception is distinguished in some writers by a social radicalism (the 'Sermon on the Mount' Christianity of Tolstoy and others, or the 'religious-social' interpretation of, *e.g.*, Kutter and Ragaz in Switzerland), in others by the evolutionary belief in progress (the 'social gospel' in America). The coming of the kingdom consists in the forward march of social righteousness and communal development.

In contrast to these spiritualizing, moralistic and evolutionary interpretations of the kingdom, NT scholarship is rightly laying stress again on the original significance of the kingdom in Jesus' preaching—a significance bound up with the history of salvation and eschatology. While the founders of this newer eschatological direction gave an extreme interpretation to the idea of the kingdom of heaven, so that there was no room left for the kingdom's penetration of the present world-order (Johannes Weiss, Albert Schweitzer, the so-called 'thoroughgoing' eschatology), more attention has been paid latterly to the unmistakable present significance of the kingdom, while this significance has been brought within the perspective of the history of salvation, the perspective of the progress of God's dynamic activity in history, which has the final consummation as its goal.

BIBLIOGRAPHY. The literature on the kingdom of God is immense. For the use of the term in the New Testament, see G. Dalman, *The Words of Jesus*, 1902; *SBI*, pp. 172–184; G. Gloege, RGG, pp. 916–929; K. L. Schmidt *et al.*, *TDNT* 1, pp. 564–593; B. Klappert, *NIDNTT* 2, pp. 372–390; for the newer interpretation, see among others H. D. Wendland, *Die Eschatologie des Reiches Gottes bei Jesus*, 1931; J. Jeremias, *New Testament Theology*, 1, 1970; C. H. Dodd, *The Parables of the Kingdom*, 1935; W. G. Kümmel, *Die Eschatologie der Evangelien*, 1936; *idem*, *Promise and Fulfilment*, 1957; G. Vos, *The Teaching of Jesus concerning the Kingdom and the Church*, 1951; J. Héring, *Le royaume de Dieu et sa venue*, 1959; H. Ridderbos, *The Coming of the Kingdom*, 1962; G. E. Ladd, *Jesus and the Kingdom*, 1962; H. Flender, *Die Botschaft Jesu von der Herrschaft Gottes*, 1968; J. Gray, *The Biblical Teaching of the Reign of God*, 1979; B. Chilton *et al.*, *The Kingdom of God*, 1984; H. Merklein, *Jesu Botschaft von der Gottesherrschaft*, 1989; M. de Jonge, *Jesus' Message About the Kingdom of God*, 1991; H. Baarlink, *Christologische Perspectiven*, 1992, pp. 28–88. H.R.

KINGS, BOOKS OF. The closing part of the narrative which begins in Genesis and focuses on the story of Israel from her origins in Egypt to the ending of her political independence by the Babylonians. The division of the books of Kings from the books of Samuel is an artificial one, as is the further division of Kings itself into two books, which was introduced by the LXX.

I. Outline of contents

Kings consists of an account of the Israelite monarchy written from a theological perspective and taking the history from its high point in the united monarchy to its low point in the Exile.

(*a*) The reign of Solomon (1 Ki. 1–11): his accession (1–2), his successes (3–10), his failures (11).

(*b*) The divided kingdom (1 Ki. 12–2 Ki. 17): Judah under Rehoboam, and the majority N tribes under Jeroboam who retain the title Israel, separate from each other. Israel comes under considerable pagan influence from the beginning and experiences many bloody coups before finally being exiled. Judah is less paganized, though only preserved because of Yahweh's faithfulness to his promise to David. The prophets Elijah and Elisha are heavily involved, especially in the story of Israel.

(*c*) The kingdom of Judah (2 Ki. 18–25): despite the reforms of Hezekiah and Josiah, the paganizing policy of Manasseh finally bears fruit in the fall of Judah too. But the conclusion of the books sounds a possible note of hope (25:27–30).

II. Origin

The last event to which Kings refers is the exiled king Jehoiachin's release from prison in Babylon in 561 (2 Ki. 25:27), and clearly the books in their final form must come from after this time. There may be elsewhere hints of even later situations: notably, the dating of the building of the Temple (1 Ki. 6:1) perhaps reflects a chronological scheme which places that event midway between the Exodus and the rebuilding of the Temple after the Exile.

The main composition of the work is to be dated earlier, however. This may have been in the early years of the Exile (P. R. Ackroyd, *Exile and Restoration*, *OTL*, 1968, ch. 5). Alternatively, it may have been after the release of Jehoiachin in 561 (R. K. Harrison, *IOT*, 1970, pp. 730f., following M. Noth). Another view dates the 'first edition' of Kings in the reign of Josiah (J. Gray, *I and II Kings*², *OTL*, 1970). But while much of the material in Kings dates from long before the Exile, and some reflects its pre-exilic perspective, the evidence for an actual 'first edition' of Kings in the reign of Josiah, or for a pre-Deuteronomistic earlier version of the history, is scant.

Any pre- or post-exilic work on the books must have taken place in Palestine. Work during the exilic period itself might have taken place in Babylon or Palestine (the arguments for each location are discussed by Ackroyd, pp. 65–68, and by E. W. Nicholson, *Preaching to the Exiles: A Study of the Prose Tradition in the Book of Jeremiah*, 1970, pp. 117–122).

We do not know the name of the author(s) of Kings, though the group which was responsible for the work is often described as the 'Deuteronomists'. This description reflects the view that Kings is not merely the last part of the story begun in Genesis; it is more specifically the last part of the 'Deuteronomistic history', which begins with the book of Deuteronomy. On this view, the story from Joshua to Kings, known in the Hebrew Bible as the 'Former Prophets', has been written or edited as a whole to show how principles declared in Deuteronomy worked out in Israel's history from the conquest, via the period of the judges and the united monarchy, to the Exile. The view usually presupposes a belief that Deuteronomy itself was written in the late pre-exilic period, though it need not involve this. It is to be noted, however, that the emphases of the Deuteronomic law by no means coincide with those of Kings. On the one side, the humanitarian, social and moral concerns of Deuteronomy are not reflected in Kings. Conversely, while Deuteronomy stresses the central sanctuary

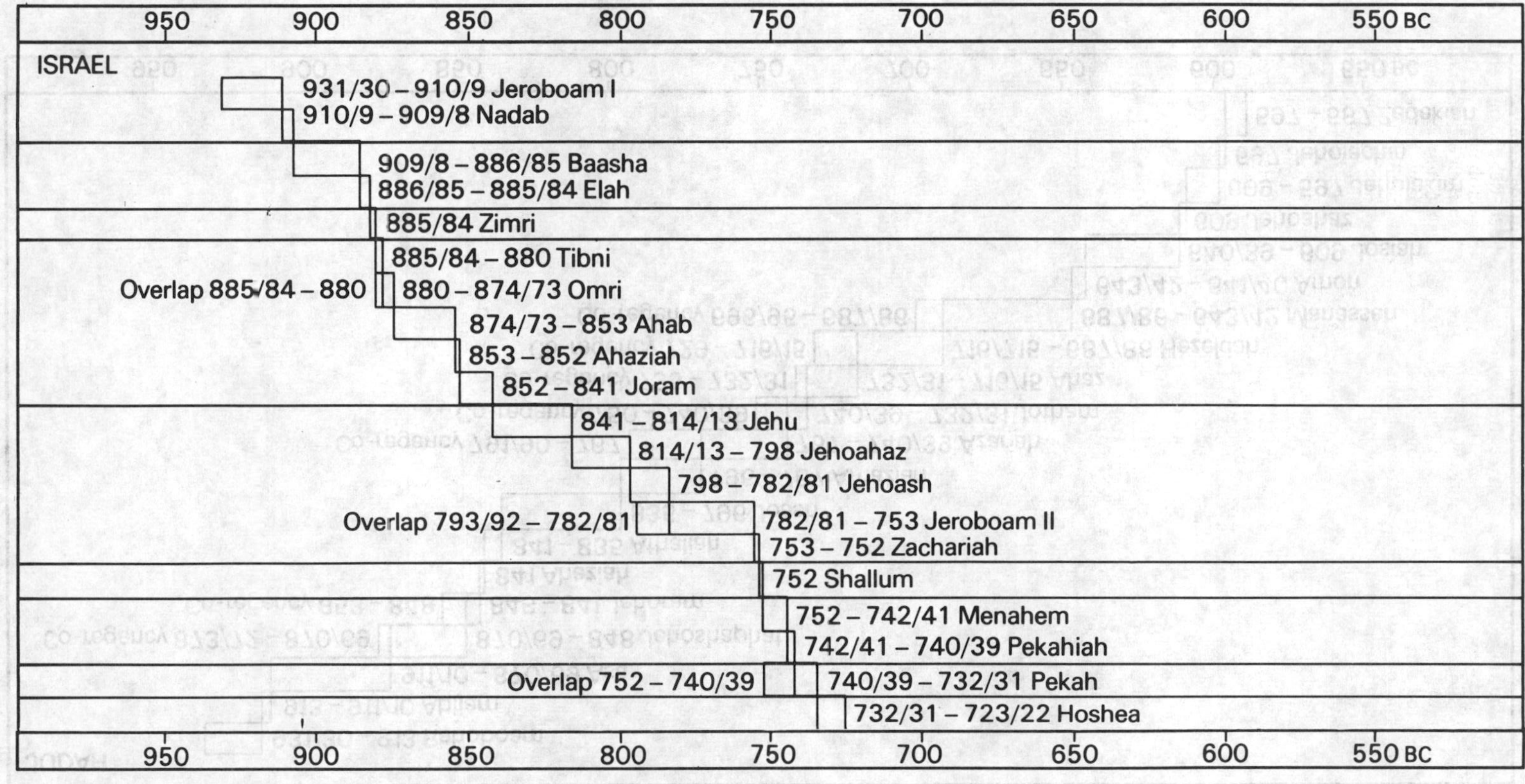

Chronological table of the kings of Israel.

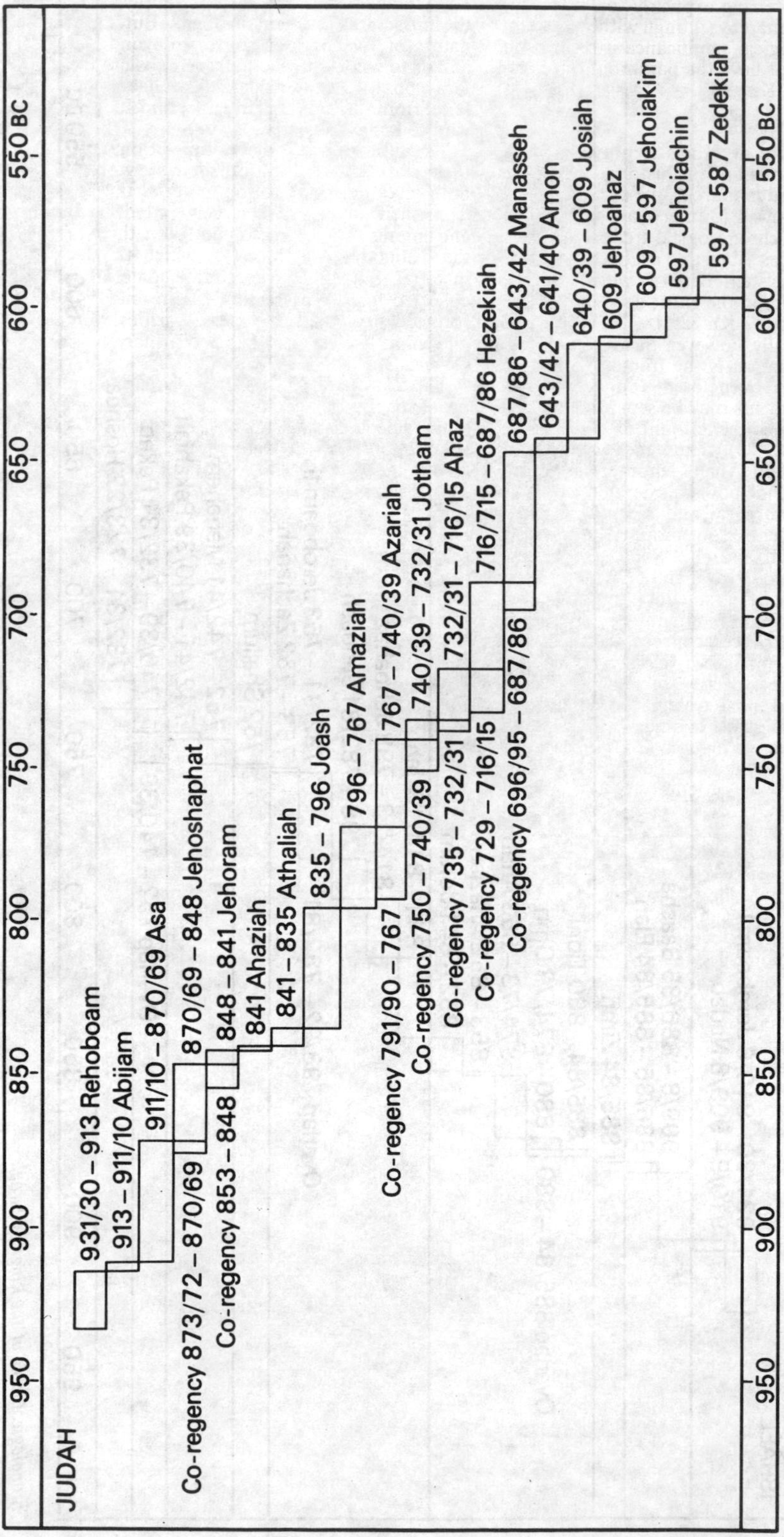

JUDAH

950 900 850 800 750 700 650 600 550 BC

931/30 – 913 Rehoboam
913 – 911/10 Abijam
911/10 – 870/69 Asa
Co-regency 873/72 – 870/69 870/69 – 848 Jehoshaphat
Co-regency 853 – 848 848 – 841 Jehoram
841 Ahaziah
841 – 835 Athaliah
835 – 796 Joash
796 – 767 Amaziah
Co-regency 791/90 – 767 767 – 740/39 Azariah
Co-regency 750 – 740/39 740/39 – 732/31 Jotham
Co-regency 735 – 732/31 732/31 – 716/15 Ahaz
Co-regency 729 – 716/15 716/715 – 687/86 Hezekiah
Co-regency 696/95 – 687/86 687/86 – 643/42 Manasseh
643/42 – 641/40 Amon
640/39 – 609 Josiah
609 Jehoahaz
609 – 597 Jehoiakim
597 Jehoiachin
597 – 587 Zedekiah

950 900 850 800 750 700 650 600 550 BC

Chronological table of the kings of Judah.

(though without referring explicitly to Jerusalem) and refers to the monarchy (though without ascribing to it the theological significance it receives in Judah), these do not have the paramount importance they receive in Kings.

III. Literary characteristics

The formal structure of Kings is provided by a reign-by-reign treatment of the history. During the period of the divided monarchy, the accounts of N and S kings are allowed to interweave in order to preserve a broadly chronological treatment. Each king is summarily described and evaluated according to a fairly consistent pattern, which may be perceived by examining the short accounts of the reign of Jehoshaphat (1 Ki. 22:41–50) or Amon (2 Ki. 21:19–26). Usually, however, this summary description and evaluation is the framework within which other material is enclosed, so that its opening and closing elements may be separated by several chapters (see, *e.g.*, the account of the reign of Hezekiah, 2 Ki. 18–20). Thus the accounts of Solomon, Rehoboam, Ahab, Jehoram, Jehu and Joash, for instance, include considerable narrative material centring on royal and political matters. Other narratives centre on prophets, especially Elijah, Elisha and Isaiah. Sometimes these prophets are involved in royal and political matters (revealingly, however, the Israelite king is not even named in 2 Ki. 5–7: he is not the real centre of interest). Other narratives concern the prophets' personal lives and ministries (*e.g.* 2 Ki. 4). The 'Deuteronomistic' perspective of the work as a whole is expounded most systematically in Kings in an extensive theological comment which closes off the history of the N kingdom (2 Ki. 17).

Various views are held as to the historical value of Kings. Clearly it is no attempt to write 'objective' or 'critical' history of a post-Enlightenment kind. It is history with a message, and the events it relates are chosen in accordance with their relevance to the message. It is thus not a political history, and some periods of great political significance (such as the reign of Omri) are passed over relatively briefly because they are of little significance in relation to the writer's concern with the history of Israel's relationship with Yahweh.

Within the Deuteronomistic framework, however, material of recognized historical value is included. The summary frameworks refer the reader to 'the book of the acts of Solomon' and to the annals of the kings of Judah and of Israel for further information on the various reigns, and it seems likely that these were the sources of many of the bare historical facts passed on by Kings (such as the name of a king's mother and the brief references to specific events). Complex chronological problems are raised by the dates provided for the kings (one basic solution for these is provided by E. Thiele, *The Mysterious Numbers of the Hebrew Kings*², 1965; *cf.* *CHRONOLOGY OF THE OT). Beyond these royal annals, it is widely accepted that 1 Ki. 1–2 forms the original ending of an account of how Solomon came to the throne, which extends back at least to 2 Sa. 9. As for the other narratives incorporated into Kings, Gray (for instance) accepts the fundamental historical value both of the material more concerned with political and military events and that concerned with the prophets, though he regards the more personal stories about Elijah and Elisha in 1 Ki. 17 and 2 Ki. 1–6 as folk-loristic, in part simply because of the miraculous element in them. But the precise nature of the author's sources, beyond the royal annals to which they actually refer, is not clear (*cf.* Gray, pp. 14–35). Considerable archaeological material from the Iron Age in Israel and Judah is relevant to Kings (*ARCHAEOLOGY).

The authors' method of composition means that their work is not a smooth literary whole, but it both gives us access to the material they pass on from their sources in a largely unredacted form, and impresses a degree of unity on the whole by the distinctive framework in which they set this material. Sometimes the source material, or the collected form of a section of the material, may fruitfully be treated by a literary critical approach, and this is likely to be a subject of increasing study (*Semeia* 3, 1975; 8, 1977).

The text of Kings in *MT* presents relatively few problems. But the Qumran discoveries (combined with evidence from Chronicles and the LXX) have implications for the state of the pre-*MT* textual traditions of Kings, as of other books (*TEXTS AND VERSIONS).

IV. Emphases

(*a*) We have noted that Kings begins at the high point of the period covered by the Deuteronomistic history, the united monarchy. The fact that this is the high point reflects the importance of the Davidic monarchy and the Temple of Solomon. Yahweh's commitment to David (2 Sa. 7:11–16) is often referred to by Yahweh and by the narrator as the explanation for Yahweh's faithfulness to Judah and to David's successors (1 Ki. 6:12; 11:12–13, 36; 2 Ki. 8:19; 19:34), and David's loyalty to Yahweh is frequently (and slightly surprisingly) a standard by which later kings are judged (*e.g.* 1 Ki. 9:4; 2 Ki. 22:2). But the repercussions of one king's reign in later times can also be negative: the sins of Manasseh are ultimately the cause of the Exile (2 Ki. 24:3–4). Thus the well-being of the people as a whole is tied up with the behaviour of the king (2 Ki. 21:11–15).

The building of the Temple is the climax of the opening chapters of Kings. 1 Ki. 8 focuses the Kings' theology of the Temple, which is the dwelling-place of Yahweh's name. W. Eichrodt (*Theology of the OT*, 2, 1967, pp. 23–45) sees Yahweh's name as the most sophisticated OT form of 'the spiritualization of the theophany'—a way of talking of the real revelatory presence of God without compromising his transcendence. The importance of the Temple makes it a crucial touchstone for the evaluation of the kings. Jeroboam I is condemned for devising alternative places and forms of worship for the N kingdom (1 Ki. 12–13), and his successors are condemned for continuing to have recourse to these. Josiah, the antitype to Jeroboam, appearing near the end of the story as Jeroboam appears near its beginning, is commended for his reform of temple worship and for his destruction of high places generally and of the shrine at Bethel in particular (2 Ki. 22–23).

(*b*) Kings' attitude to the monarchy and to the Temple, however, shows that these are not to be seen as absolutes. They are subject, first of all, to the Torah. 'The Deuteronomist sees the main problem of the history of Israel as lying in the question of the correct correlation of Moses and David' (G. von Rad, *Old Testament Theology*, 1, 1968, p. 339).

The Davidic promise can be relied on only as long as the Mosaic covenant demand is accepted. Thus the great villain of the story of Judah in Kings is Manasseh; the list of his acts corresponds closely to what Deuteronomy says Israel should not do (*cf.* 2 Ki. 21:2–9 with Dt. 17:2–4; 18:9–12). Conversely in the story of its great hero Josiah, Kings emphasizes the significance of his discovery of the 'book of the covenant' by giving it first mention in its account of his reign (contrast the account in 2 Ch. 34), and the list of his acts corresponds closely to what Deuteronomy says Israel should do. Thus the requirements and the sanctions of the Torah (specifically of Deuteronomy) provide the principles for understanding Israel's history. When kings obeyed the Torah (especially its demand for faithful worship at the central shrine), they generally prospered. When they ignored it, they did not.

But the spoken word of the prophet is thought of as succeeding and supporting the written word of Moses (*cf.* the role of Huldah after the discovery of the lawbook in 2 Ki. 22:13–20), and also demanding the attention of king and people. 'What fascinated (the Deuteronomist) was, we might say, the functioning of the divine word in history' (*cf.* 1 Ki. 8:24) (G. von Rad, 'The Deuteronomistic theology of history in the books of Kings', in 'Studies in Deuteronomy', *SBT* 9, 1961, p. 91). Thus Kings pictures 'a course of history which was shaped and led to a fulfilment by a word of judgment and salvation continually injected into it' (von Rad, *Old Testament Theology*, 1, p. 344). This point is made by including lengthy stories about various prophets, especially as regards their involvement in the nation's political life. 'In the decisive political events the initiative stems from prophets, who change the gears of history with a word of God' (*ibid.*, p. 342). It is also made by criss-crossing the story with prophecies and their fulfilment (*e.g.* 1 Ki. 11:29–39 and 12:15; 1 Ki. 13:1–10 and 2 Ki. 23:15–18; 2 Ki. 20:16–17 and 24:13). The stress on how true prophecies were fulfilled may reflect concern with the problem of false prophecy during the Exile. Thus a king's attitude to the prophet's word forms another index of his attitude to God (Hezekiah, Josiah).

(*c*) One of the characteristic emphases of the covenant as expounded in Deuteronomy is that God blesses those who are faithful to him but brings trouble to those who disobey him (Dt. 28–30). Thus in Kings the material concerning Solomon's reign is arranged so that Solomon's setbacks are seen as consequences of his association with foreign women (1 Ki. 11). On the other hand, Kings recognizes that God's justice does not work out in this way in every reign. Manasseh enjoys a long reign, and his apostasy only brings its fruit decades later (2 Ki. 21; 24:3–4). Josiah is responsive to Yahweh's word, but dies an early and tragic death (2 Ki. 23:29).

V. Message and purpose

The function of Kings' review of the history which led up to the Exile is to explain why the Exile came about and to express an admission that there was ample cause for God to judge Israel. It is a form of confession, or 'an act of praise at the justice of the judgment of God'; 'this statement with its apparent lack of hope for the future lays the only possible foundation for the future' (Ackroyd, p. 78, following von Rad) because it throws the people of God totally back on the grace of God.

The possibility of hope for the future is hinted at in the way the theological emphases of Kings, described above, remain open to the future. Perhaps God's commitment to David still holds: it may be that the release of Jehoiachin, related in the final paragraph of Kings, makes this hope explicit. Although the Temple has been pillaged and burnt, prayer is still possible in the Temple, or towards it on the part of people who are cut off from it, and God has undertaken to hear such prayer (see 1 Ki. 8–9). Although judgment has come in accordance with the sanctions of the covenant, the same covenant allows for the possibility of repentance and restoration after judgment (see 1 Ki. 8:46–53; *cf.* Dt. 30). Although the prophetic words which Israel ignored form a further reason for her punishment, the fact that those prophetic words of judgment have come true may encourage the hope that the prophetic promises of restoration (*e.g.* those of Jeremiah) may come true, too.

Thus the aim of Kings is in part didactic, 'to present the divine view of Israelite history' (R. K. Harrison, p. 722). Beyond this, there are at least hints of the kerygmatic (*cf.* E. W. Nicholson, p. 75). Kings does open up the possibility of there being a future. On the basis of this possibility it further seeks to be paraenetic, in that it implicitly challenges the generation of the Exile to turn back to Yahweh in repentance, faith and commitment to obedience (*cf.* 1 Ki. 8:46–50). For 'the judgment of 587 did not mean the end of the people of God; nothing but refusal to turn would be the end' (von Rad, *Old Testament Theology*, 1, p. 346).

VI. Context and implications

Kings is thus one of the several responses to the fall of Judah and the Exile. It bears comparison especially with *Lamentations (five psalms which express the feelings and tentative hopes of people in Judah after the fall of Jerusalem) and with the book of Jeremiah (whose material was collected and assembled in this same period and manifests many literary and theological points of contact with Kings; see E. W. Nicholson, *op. cit.*). Kings may also be studied in the light of parallel treatments of events it narrates as these appear in Chronicles, Isaiah and Jeremiah (see, *e.g.*, B. S. Childs, 'Isaiah and the Assyrian Crisis', *SBT* 2. 3, 1967).

In a volume of expositions of passages from 2 Kings, *The Politics of God and the Politics of Man* (1972, pp. 13–21), J. Ellul suggests that Kings makes a twofold distinctive contribution to the Canon of Scripture. First, it pictures God's involvement in political life, and thus warns both against undervaluing the importance of politics, and against absolutizing this realm (since it shows how God brings judgment on politics). Secondly, it displays the interplay of the free determination of man (who in various political situations makes his decisions and puts his policies into effect) and the free decision of God (who nevertheless effects his will through or despite these deliberate human acts).

In reaction to an overstress in recent biblical study on the idea of God as the one who acts in history, the importance of this motif in the Bible is in danger of being understressed. Kings is a book which itself particularly emphasizes this motif (see J. E. Goldingay, '"That you may know that Yahweh is God": A study in the relationship between theology and historical truth in the Old

Testament', *TynB* 23, 1972, pp. 58–93; and on the application of this idea today, see D. N. Freedman, 'The biblical idea of history', *Int* 21, 1967, pp. 32–49). God *is* one who works out a purpose in history, and his people may use the marks of his footsteps in past history to see what he may be doing in the present.

BIBLIOGRAPHY. W. Brueggemann, *1 Kings and 2 Kings*, 1982; G. H. Jones, *1 and 2 Kings*, *NCB*, 2 vols., 1984; R. Nelson, *First and Second Kings*, 1987; D. J. Wiseman, *1 and 2 Kings*, *TOTC*, 1993.

J.E.G.

KING'S GARDEN. An open space in Jerusalem near 'the gate between the two walls' (2 Ki. 25:4; Je. 39:4; 52:7) and close to the Pool of *Siloam (Ne. 3:15). The 'two walls' (*cf.* Is. 22:11) were probably those below the 'Fountain Gate', SE of Ophel, running along the W side of the E hill of Jerusalem, and along the E side of the W hill (S. R. Driver, *Jeremiah*, 1918, p. 239; N. Grollenberg, *Atlas*, Maps 24B & C).

J.D.D.

KING'S HIGHWAY. The name given to the direct road running from the Gulf of Aqabah to Damascus in Syria, E of the Dead Sea and Jordan valley. The route was in use between the 23rd and 20th centuries BC, being marked along its length by Early Bronze Age settlements and fortresses. It was, therefore, likely that Chedorlaomer and his allies approached Sodom and Gomorrah by this way and were pursued up it by Abraham (Gn. 14). Its further use in the 13th–6th centuries BC is also marked by datable ruins showing that the road was occupied at the time that the Edomites and the Ammonites prevented Moses and the Israelites from using it (Nu. 20:17; 21:22; *cf.* Dt. 2:27). In Solomon's reign the highway played an important part as a trade-link between Ezion-geber, Judah and Syria. Roman milestones show that it was incorporated into Trajan's road built in the 2nd century AD and was used by the Nabataeans. The modern motorway follows part of the old track, which is still called Ṭarīq es-Sulṭan.

BIBLIOGRAPHY. N. Glueck, *The Other Side of the Jordan*, 1945, pp. 10–16; J. A. Thompson, *Archaeology and the Old Testament*, 1957, pp. 57–58; Y. Aharoni, *LOB*, pp. 54–57.

D.J.W.

KIR. In the Heb. text the name of the place of exile of the Syrians (2 Ki. 16:9; Am. 1:5), and a country, not necessarily the same, from which Yahweh brought them (Am. 9:7). This is perhaps not their original home, but a land occupied at some earlier stage in their history, parallel to Israel in Egypt and the *Philistines in *Caphtor (*ARAM). In Is. 22:6 Kir is parallel to Elam. No ancient place of this name is known; however, as it simply means 'city', it need not be specific. The LXX does not use a proper name in any of these passages, but translates 'from a pit' (Am. 9:7, Gk. *ek bothrou*), 'called as an ally' (Am. 1:5, Gk. *epiklētos*) and 'congregation' (Is. 22:6, Gk. *synagōgē*), feasible translations of an unpointed Heb. text. Vulg. follows the mistaken identification with Cyrene made by Symmachus. Kir has been altered to read Koa' (by Cheyne), and said to be Gutium in the Kurdish hills (*cf.* Ezk. 23:23; Is. 22:5–6). The problem is not yet solved.

A.R.M.

Map showing the route of the ancient 'King's Highway'.

KIRIATHAIM. The dual form of Heb. *qiryâ*, 'city, town', and meaning therefore 'double city', a name applied to two cities in the Bible.

1. A place in the territory allotted to Reuben (Jos. 13:19) which had already been conquered and rebuilt by the Reubenites (Nu. 32:37). It is possible that Shaveh Kiriathaim, which is mentioned in the account of the invasion of Chedorlaomer in the time of Abraham (Gn. 14:5), refers to this locality, as the 'plain' of Kiriathaim (RVmg.), though *šāwēh* is a rare word of uncertain meaning. The city was later in the hands of the Moabites (Je. 48:1, 23; Ezk. 25:9), and is mentioned in the 9th-century inscription of King Mesha of Moab (*qrytn*, line 10) as having been rebuilt by him, so it cannot have remained under Israelite control for more than about 3 centuries. The site is possibly near to modern El Quraiyāt about 10 km NW of Dibon in Jordan, but the place has not yet been located (*cf.* H. Douner and W. Röllig, *Kanaanäische und aramäische Inschriften*, 1962–4, pp. 74–175).

2. A levitical city in Naphtali (1 Ch. 6:76), possibly to be identified with Kartan (*qartān*) of Jos. 21:32. The site is unknown, though various suggestions have been made (see *GTT*, §§ 298, 337, 357). T.C.M.

KIRIATH-ARBA (Heb. *qiryaṯ 'arba'*, 'city of four', *i.e.* 'tetrapolis'), an earlier name of *Hebron. According to Jos. 14:15, it was 'the metropolis of the Anakim' (so LXX; *MT* makes the numeral *'arba'*, 'four', into a personal name). The name Kiriath-arba occurs once in the story of Abraham (Gn. 23:2) and a few times in the narrative of the Conquest (Jos. 14:15; 15:54; 20:7; Jdg. 1:10); thereafter it evidently fell into disuse. Some attempt may have been made to revive it in the post-exilic age (Ne. 11:25), but with the Idumaean occupation of the place soon afterwards the old name was completely discontinued. F.F.B.

KIRIATH-JEARIM (Heb. *qiryaṯ-yᵉʿārîm*, 'city of forests'). A chief city of the Gibeonites (Jos. 9:17), on the Judah–Benjamin border (Jos. 18:14–15; *cf.* Jdg. 18:12), assigned first to Judah (Jos. 15:60), then, assuming an identification with 'Kiriath', to Benjamin (Jos. 18:28). It is called also Kiriath-baal (Jos. 15:60, suggesting that it was an old Canaanite high place), Baalah (Jos. 15:9–10), Baale-judah (2 Sa. 6:2) and Kiriath-arim (Ezr. 2:25).

Here the ark was brought from Beth-shemesh and entrusted to the keeping of Eleazar (1 Sa. 7:1), whence after 20 years David took it to Jerusalem (2 Sa. 6:2; 1 Ch. 13:5; 2 Ch. 1:4). The home of Uriah the prophet was in Kiriath-jearim (Je. 26:20).

Its precise location has not been determined, but the consensus of opinion favours Kuriet el-'Enab (commonly known as Abu Ghosh), a flourishing little village 14 km W of Jerusalem on the Jaffa road. It is a well-wooded district (or has been in the past) and it meets other geographical requirements. J.D.D.

KIRIATH-SEPHER (Heb. *qiryaṯ-sēp̄er*). The name used for *Debir in the story of Othniel and Achsah (Jos. 15:15ff., Jdg. 1:11ff.). J.P.U.L.

KIR OF MOAB, KIR-HARESETH. A fortified city of S Moab, attacked but not taken by the kings of Israel, Judah and Edom (2 Ki. 3:25). During the siege, Mesha, king of Moab, offered up his eldest son 'for a burnt offering upon the wall'.

The Hebrew name (*qîr ḥᵃrešeṯ*) means 'the wall of potsherds'. The LXX rendering of Is. 16:11 presupposes the Hebrew *qîr ḥᵃdešeṯ*, 'the new city'. Normally the town is called Kir of Moab (Is. 15:1). Some writers see in Je. 48:36–37 a play on words in which Kir Heres is parallel to 'bald' (Heb. *qorḥâ*). It is suggested that the original Moabite name was QRḤH, probably the town referred to in the *Moabite Stone (lines 22ff.), where Mesha established a sanctuary for Chemosh and carried out a building project. This would place it near Dibon.

Most writers, however, identify it with Kerak, following the Targum rendering, Kerak of Moab. If that is so, the place was built on a strategic rocky hill 1,027 m above sea-level, surrounded by steep valleys, some 18 km E of the Dead Sea and 24 km S of the Arnon River. Today a mediaeval castle crowns the hill.

BIBLIOGRAPHY. F. M. Abel, *Géographie de la Palestine*, 2, 1933, pp. 418–419; Nelson Glueck, *AASOR* 14, 1934, p. 65. J.A.T.

KISH (Heb. *qîš*, 'bow', 'power'). **1.** A Benjaminite, the son of Abiel and father of King Saul (1 Sa. 9:1; 14:51; *cf.* Acts 13:21). **2.** The son of Jehiel and Maacah (1 Ch. 8:30), perhaps the uncle of **1. 3.** A Levite, grandson of Merari (1 Ch. 23:21). **4.** Another Levite and Merarite who assisted in the cleansing of the Temple in Hezekiah's time (2 Ch. 29:12). **5.** A Benjaminite, great-grandfather of Mordecai (Est. 2:5). J.D.D.

6. Name of the capital of a city-state *c.* 20 km SE of Babylon (mod. Tell el-Ukheimer) where, according to Sumerian tradition (King List), the first dynasty after the *Flood ruled. It flourished *c.* 3200–3000 BC as a rival of *Erech when it was linked with the legendary Etana and with King Agga who opposed Gilgamesh. Documents from the earlier occupation and from the 2nd millennium are extant. It was excavated by the French (1914) and by a joint Oxford (Ashmolean Museum) and Chicago (Field Museum) expedition (1922–33). Finds include early palaces, tablets and a major flood-deposit level dated *c.* 3300 BC.

BIBLIOGRAPHY. L. C. Watelin, S. H. Langdon, *Excavations at Kish*, 1925–34; P. R. S. Moorey, *Oxford–Chicago Excavations at Kish*, 1976. D.J.W.

KISHON. The river, modern Nahr el-Muqaṭṭa', which, rising in the hills of N Samaria, drains the plain of Esdraelon and debouches in the bay of Acre, E of Mt Carmel. Though it winds about, in a general sense it flows in a NW direction parallel with, and to the NE of, the mountain range which runs from Samaria to Carmel and in the NE passes of which lay Taanach, Megiddo and Jokneam. The name Kishon is not often used, the river sometimes being indicated by reference to one of the towns overlooking it. Thus it is probably first mentioned in Jos. 19:11, where the 'brook which is east of Jokneam' is given as part of the boundary of Zebulun, though in this case it is only a small section of the river in the vicinity of Jokneam that is referred to.

The best-known reference to the river is that connected with the victory of the Israelites under Barak over the Syrians under Sisera (Jdg. 4–5; Ps. 83:9). The forces of Sisera, fully armed with chariots, were deployed in the plain, and the Israelites made their attack from the mountains SW of the river. The success of the Israelites was in large measure due to the river, which was running high, and must have made the surrounding plain too soft for Sisera's chariots, which became bogged down and useless.

The river is referred to in the Song of Deborah as 'the waters of Megiddo' (Jdg. 5:19), and the fact that Megiddo is not otherwise referred to in this account has been taken by Albright to indicate that it was at this time lying in ruins, while Taanach was flourishing. The excavations of *Megiddo have shown a gap in occupation about 1125 BC between Levels VII and VI, and it may be that the Israelite victory occurred during that period of abandonment, or about 1125 BC.

The river is next mentioned as the scene of the slaughter by Elijah of the prophets of Baal, after the contest on Mt Carmel (1 Ki. 18:40). It is referred to here as a brook (*naḥal*), suggesting that the long drought preceding these events had reduced the river to a low level. The rains which followed must have washed away the traces of the execution.

BIBLIOGRAPHY. G. A. Smith, *The Historical Geography of the Holy Land*[25], 1931, pp. 394–397; W. F. Albright, *The Archaeology of Palestine*, 1960, pp. 117–118; *LOB*, pp. 204f. T.C.M.

KISS. A common salutation in the E, this word occurs in the OT as a sign of affection between relatives (*e.g.* Gn. 29:11; 33:4), an expression of love (Ct. 1:2), or lust (Pr. 7:13), and perhaps as a token of homage (1 Sa. 10:1). The last, kissing 'God's anointed', possibly may be, as Ps. 2:10, a religious or cultic rite analogous to that found among idol cults: to kiss the hand (Jb. 31:27), or an image (1 Ki. 19:18; Ho. 13:2), is an act of religious worship. In the NT *phileō* is used as a sign of friendship or affection (*e.g.* Judas, Mt. 26:48), as is the stronger form *kataphileō* (*e.g.* Lk. 7:38; 15:20; Acts 20:37). The 'holy kiss' (Rom. 16:16; 1 Pet. 5:14), which later entered into the church's liturgy, was an expression of Christian love and presumably was restricted to one's own sex (*cf. Apostolic Constitutions* 2. 57, 12). See W. Günther, C. Brown, in *NIDNTT* 2, pp. 547–550. E.E.E.

KITTIM. One of the sons of Javan (Gn. 10:4 = 1 Ch. 1:7; Heb. *kittîm*) whose descendants settled on the island of Cyprus where their name was given to the town of Kition, modern Larnaka, which is referred to in the Phoenician inscriptions as *kt* or *kty*. They engaged in sea trade (Nu. 24:24), and the name seems to have come to apply to the whole island of Cyprus (Is. 23:1, 12), and then in a more general way to the coastlands and islands of the E Mediterranean (*'iyyê kittiyyîm*: Je. 2:10; Ezk. 27:6). The ostraca of *c.* 600 BC from Arad refer to *ktym*, probably mercenaries, principally perhaps Greeks, from the islands and coastlands. In Daniel's fourth vision, which probably deals with the period from Cyrus to Antiochus Epiphanes, the latter's failure to conquer Egypt, due to the intervention of Rome, is probably referred to in 11:30, where 'the ships of Kittim' must be Rome. The author probably saw in Rome's intervention the fulfilment of Nu. 24:24, where Vulg. translates Kittim by 'Italy' (so also in Dn. 11:30) and the Targum of Onkelos by 'Romans'. The name occurs in the Dead Sea Scrolls, also probably with reference to Rome, being used, for instance, in the commentary on Habakkuk as an interpretation of the 'Chaldeans' of that prophet (Hab. 1:6).

BIBLIOGRAPHY. A. Lemaire, *Inscriptions hébraïques*, 1, 1977, p. 156; Y. Yadin, *The Scroll of the War of the Sons of Light Against the Sons of Darkness*, 1962, pp. 22–26. T.C.M.

KNEADING-TROUGH. A large shallow bowl, made of pottery or wood, in which dough was prepared. Modern Arab nomads often use wooden bowls for this purpose. Heb. *miš'eret*, Ex. 12:34; *cf.* Dt. 28:5, 17 (AV 'store'). For a model, *c.* 700 BC, see *ANEP*, no. 152. (*BREAD.) A.R.M.

KNEE, KNEEL. The concrete imagery of the OT expresses weakness or fear as 'feeble knees' (Jb. 4:4; Is. 35:3) or as 'the knees tremble', 'knock together' (Na. 2:10; Dn. 5:6).

The fifteen references in the NT are, with the exception of Heb. 12:12, always used in connection with bowing. The action may indicate a sign of respect (Mk. 1:40; *cf.* 2 Ki. 1:13; Mk. 15:19), or subjection (Rom. 11:4; 14:11; *cf. 1 Clement* 57:1, 'bending the knees of your heart'), or of religious adoration or worship (Lk. 5:8). In the latter sense kneeling is sometimes the posture of prayer (Lk. 22:41; 1 Ki. 8:54, *cf.* 18:42). The universal recognition of Christ's Lordship is thus signified: 'every knee should bow' (Phil. 2:10; *cf.* Rom. 14:10f.; 1 Cor. 15:25). *Cf. TDNT* 1, pp. 738–740; 3, pp. 594–595; 6, pp. 758–766. E.E.E.

KNIFE. The primitive flint knife was current until recent times beside metal forms in the Near East. In the OT it is specified for the *circumcision of Moses' son and of Israel (Ex. 4:25; Jos. 5:2–3), perhaps for hygienic reasons, the once-used flint being discarded without cost. The Heb. *ḥereḇ* used in these passages, and for the self-mutilation of the frenzied priests of Baal (1 Ki. 18:28), usually denotes a short sword. In Pr. 30:14 this is parallel to Heb. *ma'ᵃḵeleṯ*, a knife used in eating. It was such a short sword that Abraham took to kill Isaac and the Levite used to dismember his concubine (Gn. 22:6, 10; Jdg. 19:29). Heb. *śakkîn* (Pr. 23:2) is to be connected with Aram. *sakkîn*, Arab. *sikkîn*, 'knife'.

AV and RV follow Vulg. *cultri* in rendering the unique Heb. *maḥᵃlāpîm*, 'knives' (Ezr. 1:9; *cf.* Syr. *ḥlāpâ*). RSV 'censers' is taken from 1 Esdras 2:9 (Gk. *thyiskai*). The LXX 'of a different sort' (Gk. *parēllagmena*) translates the Hebrew but does not throw light on the meaning. A.R.M.

KNOWLEDGE. The Gk. ideal of knowledge was a contemplation of reality in its static and abiding being; the Heb. was primarily concerned with life in its dynamic process, and therefore conceived knowledge as an entry into relationship with the experienced world which makes demands not only on man's understanding but also on man's will.

I. In the Old Testament

Thus it is that the OT speaks of knowing (*yāḏa'*) the loss of children (Is. 47:8), grief (Is. 53:3), sin (Je. 3:13), God's hand and his might (Je. 16:21), his vengeance (Ezk. 25:14). The intimate sexual relationship is spoken of as knowing a man or a woman (*e.g.* Gn. 4:1; Jdg. 11:39). Above all, to know God is not simply to be aware of his existence; for the most part this is taken for granted in

Heb. writings. To know him is to recognize him for what he is, the sovereign Lord who makes a demand on man's obedience and especially upon the obedience of his people Israel, with whom he has made a covenant. He is the God whose holiness and loving-kindness are 'known' in the experience of nation and individual. The criterion of this knowledge is obedience, and its opposite is not simply ignorance but rebellious, wilful turning away from God (*cf.* 1 Sa. 2:12; 3:7; 2 Ch. 33:13; Is. 1:3; Je. 8:7; 24:7; 31:34). Furthermore, the acknowledgment of the Lord's claims involves a rejection of the heathen gods, knowing that they are not gods (*cf.* Is. 41:23).

On God's side of the relationship between himself and man there is also knowledge. Here especially there can be no question of theoretical observation; for man and all things are God's creation. It is from this fact that God's omniscience springs: he knows the world and man within it because it is at his command that they come to be (Jb. 28:20ff.; Ps. 139). In particular, God knows those whom he has chosen to be his agents: his knowledge is spoken of in terms of election (Je. 1:5; Ho. 13:5; Am. 3:2).

II. In the New Testament

To speak of knowledge in these ways is natural in addressing a people who all formally believe that God exists but fail to acknowledge his claims. In Hellenistic Judaism and in the NT use of *ginōskein, eidenai*, and their derivatives we find Heb. thought modified by the fact that the Gentiles were ignorant even of God's existence (*IGNORANCE). In general, however, the Heb. conception is retained. All men ought to respond to the revelation in Christ which has made possible a full knowledge of God, no more intellectual apprehension but an obedience to his revealed purpose, an acceptance of his revealed love, and a fellowship with himself (*cf.* Jn. 17:3; Acts 2:36; 1 Cor. 2:8; Phil. 3:10). This knowledge of God is possible only because God in his love has called men to it (Gal. 4:9; 1 Cor. 13:12; 2 Tim. 2:19). The whole process of enlightenment and acceptance may be called coming to the knowledge of the truth (1 Tim. 2:4; 2 Tim. 2:25; 3:7; Tit. 1:1; *cf.* Jn. 8:32).

Both Paul and John write at times in conscious contrast with and opposition to the systems of alleged esoteric knowledge purveyed by the mystery cults and syncretistic 'philosophy' of their day (*cf.* 1 Tim. 6:20; Col. 2:8). To these knowledge was the result of an initiation or illumination which put the initiate in possession of spiritual discernment beyond mere reason or faith. Against them Paul (particularly in 1 Cor. and Col.) and all the Johannine writings stress that knowledge of God springs from committal to the historic Christ; it is not opposed to faith but forms its completion. We need no revelation other than that in Christ. (*GNOSTICISM.)

BIBLIOGRAPHY. E. Schütz, E. D. Schmitz, in *NIDNTT* 2, pp. 390–409; M. Williams, *The Psychology of Religious Knowing*, 1988. M.H.C.

KOA. Ezekiel (23:23) prophesies that this people, together with other dwellers in Mesopotamia, will attack Jerusalem. Koa has been identified by some with the people called in Assyr. texts *Qutu*, who lived E of the Tigris in the region of the upper 'Adhaim and Diyala rivers. Assyr. records often couple them with another tribe hostile to Assyria, the *Sutu*, perhaps to be equated with Shoa in Ezk. 23:23. Some (*e.g.* O. Procksch) find Koa in Is. 22:5, but only by a doubtful emendation of the word usually translated 'walls'. Vulg. misinterpreted Koa as *principes*, 'princes', an interpretation which was followed by Luther.

BIBLIOGRAPHY. F. Delitzsch, *Wo lag das Paradies?*, 1881, pp. 233–237; G. A. Cooke in *ICC*, 1936, on Ezk. 23:23. J.T.

KOHATH, KOHATHITES. Kohath, second son of Levi, was founder of one of the three great Levite families. His family was subdivided into the houses of Amram, Izhar, Hebron and Uzziel, and Moses and Aaron were Amramites (Ex. 6:20). In the wilderness the Kohathites carried the tabernacle furniture and vessels. They camped on the S side of the tabernacle. Their males over a month old numbered 8,600; those who actually served (age-group 30–50), 2,750 (Nu. 3:27–32; 4:36). In the land the Kohathites who, being sons of Aaron, were priests, were allotted thirteen cities, the rest ten cities (Jos. 21:4–5). Under David's reorganization the Kohathites held a wide variety of offices, including a share in the Temple singing (1 Ch. 6:31–38; *cf.* 9:31–32; 26:23–31). Kohathites are mentioned again under Jehoshaphat, Hezekiah and Josiah (2 Ch. 20:19; 29:12; 34:12), and at the return from the Exile (*cf.* Ezr. 2:42 with 1 Ch. 9:19; Korahites were Kohathites). See also *KORAH. D.W.G.

KORAH (Heb. *qōraḥ* = baldness?). **1.** Chief (AV 'Duke') of Edom, son of Esau (Gn. 36:5, 14, 18; 1 Ch. 1:35). **2.** Chief of Edom, son of Eliphaz (Gn. 36:16). As the name is omitted from Gn. 36:11 and 1 Ch. 1:36, some think this to be a gloss. **3.** A son of Hebron (1 Ch. 2:43). **4.** A grandson of Kohath and ancestor of a group of sacred musicians ('sons of Korah') who are mentioned in the titles of Ps. 42 and 11 other psalms (1 Ch. 6:22).

5. A Levite ('Core' in Jude 11, AV), a Kohathite of the house of Izhar, perhaps identical with **4.** With Dathan, his brother Abiram and another Reubenite, On, Korah rebelled against Moses and Aaron. Three grounds of revolt are stated, and although these have led some commentators to assume composite authorship according to the documentary hypothesis, the narrative reads naturally as a harmonious unity. Nu. 16 records discontent on the grounds: first, that Moses and Aaron have set themselves above the rest of Israel (vv. 3, 13); secondly, that Moses has failed to bring Israel to the promised land (v. 14); and thirdly, that he and Aaron have arrogated the priesthood to themselves (vv. 7–11). That different grievances should be used unitedly is not unfamiliar in both ancient history and modern. As the rebels prepare to offer incense, the wrath of God is kindled, and after Moses has interceded for the congregation of Israel the rebels and their followers are destroyed by the earth opening to swallow them, and by fire. *Cf.* Nu. 26:9; Dt. 11:6; Ps. 106:17. It has been argued that this narrative contains two differing versions which reflect variant traditions of the struggle for religious leadership among the Levites. T.H.J.

L

LABAN (Heb. *laḇan*, 'white'). **1.** A descendant of Abraham's brother Nahor (Gn. 22:20–23), son of Bethuel (Gn. 28:5), Rebekah's brother (Gn. 24:47ff.) and uncle and father-in-law of Jacob (Gn. 27:43; 28:2). Laban's branch of the family had remained in Harran, but the close ethnic affinity was maintained by both Isaac and Jacob, who found their wives there. Nevertheless, notable differences existed between the Harran and Palestinian groups. Laban is described as an Aramean (Gn. 28:5; 31:20), he spoke Aramaic (Gn. 31:47), practised marriage customs unknown to Jacob (Gn. 29:26) and worshipped other gods (Gn. 31:19ff., *cf.* v. 53), though he did acknowledge Yahweh's activity (Gn. 24:50–51). Though generous in his hospitality, Laban's chief characteristics were duplicity

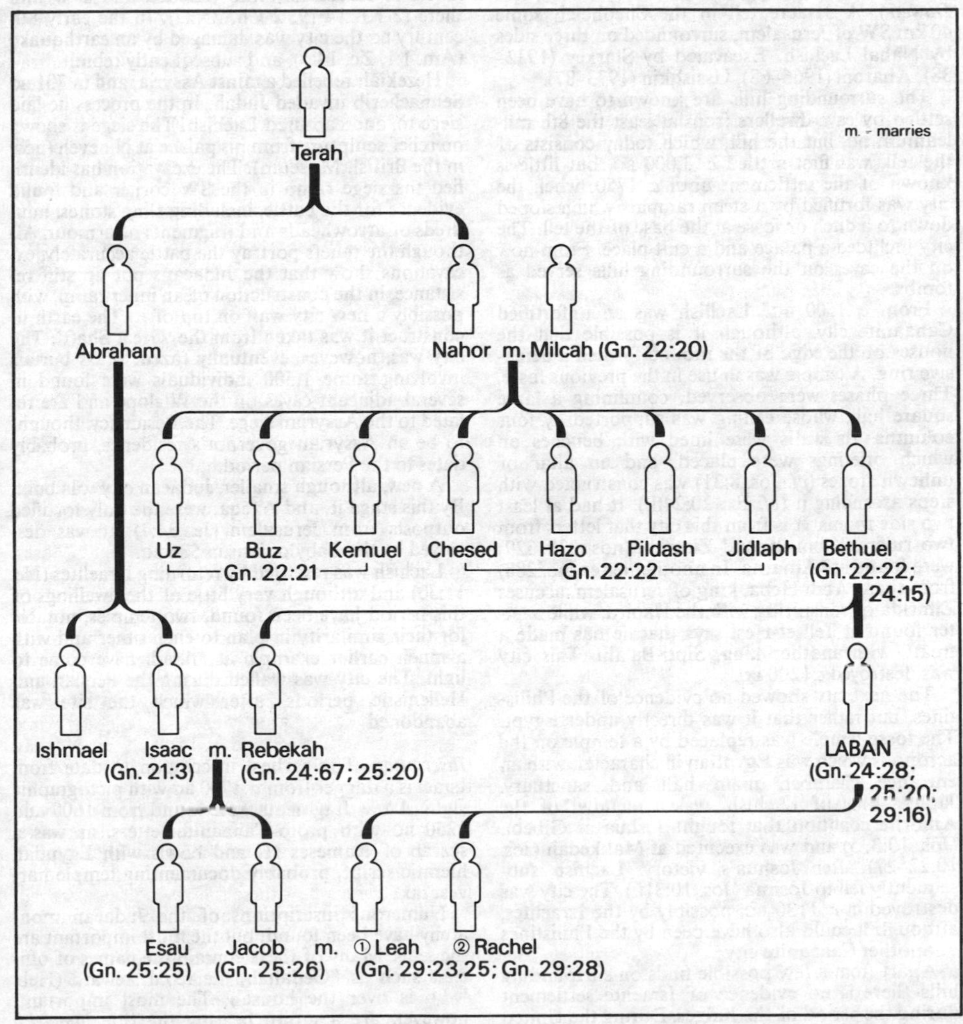

The family of Laban.

and self-interest, as demonstrated in his dealings with Jacob. Taking advantage of Jacob's love for Rachel, he made him work 14 years for his bride, though Jacob responded with his own brand of trickery (Gn. 29–30). When Jacob eventually left with his family for Palestine, Laban, being warned in a dream not to harm them, made a covenant or treaty with Jacob (Gn. 31:44–54). Laban was thwarted ultimately not by Jacob's cunning, but by God's overruling grace. Earlier, Laban rather than Bethuel had arranged Rebekah's marriage (Gn. 24:50ff.), though no usurping of the father's authority need be assumed here (*cf.* Gn. 31:18–28).

BIBLIOGRAPHY. D. Daube and R. Yaron, *JSS* 1, 1956, pp. 60–62; M. Greenberg, *JBL* 81, 1962, pp. 239–248.

2. An unknown place (Dt. 1:1), probably in the plains of Moab, or perhaps to be identified with *Libnah, a stopping-place in the wilderness (Nu. 33:20–21). M.J.S.

LACHISH (Heb. *lāḵîš*, LXX *Lachis*, Arab. *Tell ed-Duweir*). A 31-acre tell in the Shephelah some 40 km SW of Jerusalem, surrounded on three sides by Nahal Lachish. Excavated by Starkey (1932–38), Aharoni (1966–68), Ussishkin (1973–87).

The surrounding hills are known to have been settled by cave-dwellers from at least the 8th millennium BC, but the hill, which today consists of the tell, was first settled *c.* 3,000 BC, but little is known of the settlement until *c.* 1750, when the city was fortified by a steep rampart which sloped down to a ditch or fosse at the base of the tell. The city included a palace and a cult place. From now on the caves on the surrounding hills served as tombs.

From *c.* 1500 BC Lachish was an unfortified Canaanite city, although it is possible that the houses on the edge of the mound formed a defensive ring. A temple was in use in the previous fosse. Three phases were observed, containing a large square hall, whose ceiling was supported by four columns. Its walls were lined with benches on which offerings were placed, and an altar of unhewn stones (*cf.* Jos. 8:31) was constructed with steps ascending it (*cf.* Ex. 20:24ff.). It had at least two side rooms. It is from this city that letters from two rulers, Yabni-ilu and Zimrida (nos. 328–329) were found at *Amarna. In another letter (no. 288) from there, Abdi Heba, king of Jerusalem, accuses Zimrida of conspiring with the Hapiru, while a letter found at Tell el-Hesi says that he has made a treaty with another king, Šipti-Ba'alu. This city was destroyed *c.* 1200 BC.

The next city showed no evidence of the Philistines, but rather that it was directly under Egypt. The fosse temple was replaced by a temple on the acropolis which was Egyptian in character, with an entrance chamber, main hall and sanctuary. Japhia, king of Lachish, was a member of the Amorite coalition that fought Joshua at Gibeon (Jos. 10:3, 5) and was executed at Makkedah (Jos. 10:22–27) after Joshua's victory. Lachish subsequently fell to Joshua (Jos. 10:31f.). The city was destroyed in *c.* 1130 BC, possibly by the Israelites, although it could also have been by the Philistines or another Canaanite city.

Apart from a few possible finds on surrounding hills there is no evidence of Israelite settlement during the period of the Judges. During the United Monarchy there appears to have been a large fortified tower surrounded by farmhouses. A small shrine contained a large number of religious objects including an altar, a *maṣṣēbāh*, incense burners, and figurine fragments, indicating Canaanite religion in Israel. The prophet Micah (1:13) said that the city was 'the beginning of sin to the daughter of Zion'.

A new city was constructed during the 9th century BC, probably by Rehoboam (2 Ch. 11:5–10) on a new plan. The city was surrounded by two walls. An elaborate gate complex with an inner three-chambered gate led out to a fortified podium protruding from the tell which formed the outer gate. From here the road led down to the saddle connecting the tell with the surrounding hills. From the gate a road led to a large administrative building which now incorporated the earlier tower. This building had a large enclosed courtyard on its E side with storerooms and stables. The residential area of the city was in the S quadrant, and a water shaft is probably located in the NE corner. Amaziah took refuge at Lachish when fleeing from rebels in Jerusalem, who pursued and slew him there (2 Ki. 14:19; 2 Ch. 25:27). In the early 8th century BC the city was damaged by an earthquake (Am. 1:1, Zc. 14:5), and subsequently rebuilt.

Hezekiah rebelled against Assyria, and in 701 BC Sennacherib invaded Judah. In the process he laid siege to, and captured Lachish. The siege is shown on relief sculpture from his palace at Nineveh (now in the British Museum). The excavation has identified the siege ramp in the SW corner and found evidence for the battle, including sling stones, hundreds of arrowheads and fragments of armour. Although the reliefs portray the battle accurately, excavations show that the Judaeans put up stiff resistance, in the construction of an inner ramp, with possibly a new city wall on top of it. The earth to construct it was taken from the 'Great Shaft'. The city was, however, eventually razed. Mass burials involving some 1,500 individuals were found in several adjacent caves on the W slope and are related to the Assyrian siege. The Residency, thought to be an Assyrian governor's residence, probably dates to the Persian period.

A new, although smaller, Judaean city was built. By this stage it, and Azeqa, were the only fortified outposts from Jerusalem (Je. 34:7). It was destroyed by the Babylonians in 586 BC.

Lachish was resettled by returning Israelites (Ne. 11:30) and although very little of the dwellings of this period have been found, two temples, notable for their similarity in plan to each other and with a much earlier example at *Arad, have come to light. The city was walled during the Persian and Hellenistic periods, after which the site was abandoned.

Inscription. The earliest inscription to date from Israel is a dagger from *c.* 1700 BC with pictographic signs. A few fragments were found from 1600 and 1250 BC with proto-Canaanite letters, as was a scarab of Rameses III and bowls with Egyptian hieratic script, probably documenting temple harvest tax.

Numerous inscriptions of the Judaean monarchy have been found, but the most important are the seals. Many of these contain the names of officials such as *Gedaliah, the royal steward (Heb. 'who is over the house'). The most important, however, are a group bearing the title *lamelekh* (Heb. 'belonging to the king'). These contain an emblem of a disk with either two or four wings, and the name of one of four cities – Socoh, Ziph, Hebron, or *mmst.* The excavations at Lachish have shown that these belonged to an administrative organization instituted by Hezekiah in anticipation of Sennacherib's invasion.

A total of twenty-one ostraca (inscribed potsherds), which were written during the last few weeks before Nebuchadrezzar's conquest in 586 BC, were found in the gate house. Although the language is biblical Heb., the cursive script has been almost obliterated on many of the ostraca, making reading impossible. The legible examples reveal that the collection is the correspondence of a subordinate, Hoshayahu, who is in charge of an outpost, to his superior, Yaush, who is the commanding officer of the garrison at Lachish. Hoshayahu commences the letters with the greeting 'May YHWH cause my lord to hear tidings of peace this day' before proceeding with the business, which in most of the letters is answering the charge that he has read confidential letters from the king. In letter II, he replies (*cf.* 2 Sa. 9:8), 'Who is your servant (but) a dog . . . May YHWH afflict those who re[port] an (evil) rumour about which you are not informed.' It has been suggested that the ostraca were stored in the gate, pending a trial, but it is more likely that the military command to which the letters were sent was situated in the gate building.

Letter IV concludes, 'we are watching for the signals of Lachish, according to all the indications which my lord has given, for we cannot see Azeqah.' This recalls the situation mentioned by Jeremiah (34:7) when Azeqah, Lachish and Jerusalem were the only fortified Judaean cities left. Azeqah is 11 km NE of Lachish, and the fact that Hoshayahu could not see its signals may indicate it had already fallen.

Letters III and XVI refer to 'the prophet'. His identity has been much debated. Jeremiah is one possibility. Uriah who fled to Egypt (Je. 26:20–22) during Jehoiakim's reign is another suggestion which requires redating the letters. Others believe him to be an unnamed prophet. The letter testifies to the recognition of prophets in ancient Israel and their participation in affairs of state. Letter III also mentions an expedition to Egypt by the commander of the army, which may have been a last desperate attempt by Zedekiah to obtain Egyptian assistance to withstand the inevitable Babylonian attack.

BIBLIOGRAPHY. E. Stern, *NEAEHL*, pp. 897–911; D. Ussikishkin, *ABD* 4, pp. 114–126. J.W.
G.J.D.

LAHMI. A personal name found only in 1 Ch. 20:5 and applied to the brother of *Goliath the Gittite, who is there stated to have been slain by Elhanan. There is no valid reason why this should not be accepted, but it is possible that the reading may be a copyist's error for 'Bethlehemite' (*cf.* 2 Sa. 21:19), the last part of which is identical to 'Lahmi' in Hebrew. There is, however, no MS authority for this conjecture. G.W.G.

LAMB OF GOD. This expression occurs twice only in the NT (Jn. 1:29, 36). The word *amnos* is also found in Acts 8:32 and 1 Pet. 1:19, *arnos* occurs in Lk. 10:3, and *arnion* is found once in Jn. 21:15 and twenty-eight times in Revelation. The words 'Behold the Lamb of God, who takes away the sin of the world' (Jn. 1:29) are attributed to John the Baptist when acclaiming Jesus. Many possible interpretations of the word 'lamb' have been canvassed.

Some suggest that it refers to the lamb of the sin-offering, and the phrase 'who takes away the sin of the world' lends support to this. The fact that propitiatory ideas do not seem to be found elsewhere in the Fourth Gospel is not a sufficient reason for rejecting this.

Others believe there is a reference to the paschal lamb. The Jewish festivals have great significance in John, and Jn. 19:36 may well be alluding to the lamb of the Passover. But this would not explain the whole phrase, as the paschal lamb did not take away sins.

Some maintain that we have here a reference to the suffering servant of Is. 53. The word *amnos* occurs in the LXX of Is. 53:7. The Baptist quoted from Is. 40 the day before and he may have been meditating on those chapters. The sin-bearing function is clear in Is. 53. The suggestion that *amnos* is a mistranslation of the Aramaic *ṭalyā'* meaning 'servant' is ingenious, but it has not been proved.

Another possible reference is to the horned ram who led the flock. The 'lamb of God' would thus be the same as the 'king of Israel'. This view is acceptable only if it is claimed that *ho airōn tēn hamartian* has no propitiatory meaning.

It seems likely that, whatever the Baptist intended, the Evangelist intended his readers to think of the lamb offered in the Temple, the paschal lamb, and the suffering servant. The 'Lamb of God' also reminds us of God's provision of a lamb for Abraham to sacrifice (Gn. 22:8, 13–14).

BIBLIOGRAPHY. *BAGD*; J. Jeremias, *TDNT* 1, pp. 338–340; R. Tuente, *NIDNTT* 2, pp. 410–414; standard commentaries on John's Gospel; C. H. Dodd, *The Interpretation of the Fourth Gospel*, 1953, pp. 230–238; L. Morris, *The Apostolic Preaching of the Cross*[3], 1965, pp. 129ff. R.E.N.

LAMECH (Heb. *lemek̲*, possibly from an Arabic word meaning 'a strong young man'; so Dillmann, Holzinger). **1.** A descendant of Cain (Gn. 4:18f.), who introduced polygamy. One of his sons was Tubal-cain, the first worker in metals, and Lamech's song in Gn. 4:23f. is sometimes thought to be a 'sword-lay' glorifying the weapons of war invented by his son. He boasts to his wives, Adah and Zillah, that he has killed men, and because of his superior strength due to his weapons, he has no need of God's protection like Cain. Jesus may be referring to this in Mt. 18:22, substituting forgiveness for revenge.

2. A descendant of Seth and father of Noah (Gn. 5:25–31; 1 Ch. 1:3; Lk. 3:36). From the fact that 'Lamech' and 'Enoch' occur in both Cainite (Kenite) and Sethite genealogies, and from other likenesses, it is held by many that they are variants of one original list according to J and P (*e.g.* G. von Rad, *Genesis*, 1961). But there are differences, notably in the character of this Lamech, who voiced the pious hope that Noah would reverse the curse of Adam (Gn. 5:29; *cf.* 3:17ff.). J.G.G.N.

LAMENTATIONS, BOOK OF. In the Heb. Bible

Lamentations (called *'ēḵâ*, the characteristic lament 'how!'; *cf.* 1:1; 2:1; 4:1) is included among the five scrolls, since it is read on the ninth of Ab, the day of mourning over the destruction of the Temple. The EVV follow the LXX (*thrēnoi*, 'wailings' or 'dirges') and the Vulg. (whose sub-title *Lamentationes* supplied the English name) in placing Lamentations after the book of Jeremiah.

I. Outline of contents and literary structure

The first four chapters are acrostic poems, each containing sixty-six lines, except ch. 4, which has forty-four. Ch. 3 is noteworthy because each of the twenty-two Heb. letters is used for three successive one-line verses. One purpose of an acrostic is to aid memorization. But in a collection of acrostics the alphabetic pattern would not help one remember which verse beginning with a given letter belongs in which chapter. This carefully wrought, highly artificial style seems to have a further purpose: 'to encourage completeness in the expression of grief, the confession of sin and the instilling of hope' (N. K. Gottwald, *Studies in the Book of Lamentations*, 1954, p. 28). The acrostic speaks to the eye, not the ear, and conveys an idea not merely a feeling. Gottwald stresses the cathartic role of the acrostic: 'to bring about a complete cleansing of the conscience through a total confession of sin' (*op. cit.*, p. 30). Though curbing spontaneity, the acrostic lends a restraint, a gentle dignity, to what could have become an unfettered display of grief.

The dirge-like rhythm of chs. 1–4 helps to convey the feeling of grief. Characteristic of Heb. elegies (*e.g.* 2 Sa. 1:19ff.; Am. 5:2), this *qînâ* rhythm drives home its message with short, sobbing lines. An important device in *qînâ* poetry is *dramatic contrast* in which the former state of the deceased or bereaved is described in glowing terms to sharpen the sense of tragedy (*e.g.* 1:1; 4:1–2; *cf.* 2 Sa. 1:19, 23).

Ch. 3, though written in *qînâ* rhythm, is an *individual lament* rather than a funeral dirge (*cf.* Pss. 7; 22; *etc.*), containing elements typical of this category: a figurative description of suffering (3:1–18) and an affirmation that God will answer the suppliant's plea (3:19–66), the climax of the book. Though the form is *individual* the intent is *national*; the author speaks for the nation. Ch. 5, neither acrostic nor *qînâ*, resembles closely in form the psalms of *communal lament* (*e.g.* Pss. 44; 80).

II. Authorship and date

Though anonymous, Lamentations has been attributed to Jeremiah by the LXX, Vulg., and Jewish tradition (Targum at Je. 1:1; Talmud, *Baba Bathra* 15a), probably on the basis of 2 Ch. 35:25.

The evidences for and against a Jeremianic authorship approach a stalemate. S. R. Driver and E. J. Young cite similar lines of evidence and reach differing conclusions, Young voting *pro* and Driver *contra*. The chief arguments for the traditional view are the similarity in temperament between Lamentations and Jeremiah, their unanimity in attributing Jerusalem's destruction to God's judgment, and certain stylistic parallels. Against these one must consider the variation in alphabetic order of the acrostic poems (ch. 1, *s*, *'*, *p*; chs. 2–4, *s*, *p*, *'*), which may hint at multiple authorship, alleged conflicts in viewpoint, such as the author's apparent dependence on Egypt (*cf.* 4:17 with Je. 37:5–10) or his support of King Zedekiah (*cf.* 4:20 with Je. 24:8–10), and the contrast between Jeremiah's spontaneity and the stylized acrostics of Lamentations (see S. R. Driver, *LOT*, pp. 462–464, for details of the various arguments).

Attempts to attribute the first four poems to different times and authors have generally proved too subjective to gain wide acceptance. These chapters seem to be the work of an eye-witness of Jerusalem's calamity (*c.* 587 BC), who recorded his impressions while they were still fresh. Ch. 5 may date from a slightly later period when the intense anguish of the catastrophe had given way to the prolonged ache of captivity. No part of the book need be dated later than the return in 538 BC.

III. Message and significance

Lamentations is by no means barren theologically. Gottwald's analysis is convincing in its main thrusts if not in all details (*op. cit.*, pp. 47–110). Finding the central theme in the *tragic reversal*, the contrast between past glory and present degradation, he discusses the theology in terms of *doom* and *hope*.

The prophets had heralded Judah's doom, convinced that a righteous God would act in history to punish his people's sin. Lamentations continues this prophetic emphasis by seeing in the ashes of Jerusalem the vindication of God's righteousness (1:18). The city's destruction is no capricious coincidence; it is the logical and inevitable result of defying God's law. Even where God is chided (*e.g.* ch. 2) for his severity, the deep-seated sense of guilt which permeates the book is evident (2:14; *cf.* 1:5, 8–9, 18, 22; 3:40–42; 4:13, 22; 5:7). The sense of tragedy is heightened by the recognition that it was avoidable. The manifold picture of the wrath of God (*e.g.* 1:12ff.; 2:1–9, 20–22; 3:1–18; 4:6, 11) makes Lamentations a key source for any study of this aspect of God's nature.

Judah's plight is desperate but not hopeless. Though the aspects of her hope are not delineated, her reason for hope is cogently stated: the faithfulness of a covenant-keeping God (3:19–39). It was one thing for the prophets to forecast a better day before the disaster struck; it is another thing for our prophet to appropriate this hope in the midst of appalling circumstances. His recognition of the disciplinary role of suffering and its relationship to God's goodness (3:25–30) is cogent testimony to his prophetic insight.

Lamentations is a meeting-place of three great strands of Heb. thought: prophecy, ritual and wisdom. The priestly influence is evident in the liturgical forms of the poems. The wisdom emphasis is stressed in the willingness to contemplate the mysteries of God's ways with men, especially in regard to the timeless problem of suffering.

BIBLIOGRAPHY. B. Albrektson, *Studies in the Text and Theology of the Book of Lamentations*, 1963; N. Gottwald, *Studies in the Book of Lamentations*, rev. edn., 1962; D. Hillers, *Lamentations*, rev. edn., 1992; I. Provan, *Lamentations*, 1991; S. P. Re'emi, *God's People in Crisis*, pp. 73–134, 1984; W. Reyburn, *A Handbook on Lamentations*, 1992; C. Westermann, *Lamentations: Issues and Interpretation*, 1994.

D.H.

LAMP, LAMPSTAND, LANTERN.

I. Design and development

Small open pottery bowls with one or more slight lips, which can be identified as lamps (Heb. *nēr*,

Gk. *lychnos*, *lampas*), first appear in the Middle Bronze Age. This simple form continued in use throughout the Iron Age, the lip becoming more pronounced. The final development took place in the Hellenistic period when the Greek style of lamp with inward curving rim became completely enclosed, a small central hole alone remaining for feeding the oil (*cf.* Mt. 25:4). These lamps were mass-produced from moulds, one making the base, the other the lid. A very long spout for the wick characterizes Hellenistic lamps; this was shortened in the Roman period. Small handles were sometimes added. The moulds for the lids were frequently impressed with floral and other patterns, and, in the Roman period when the lid became broad and concave, with pictures that appear in relief on the lamps. From the 3rd century AD Christian symbols (cross, fishes, alpha and omega) form decorative motifs, while the seven-branched candlestick (*menorah*) marks Jewish lamps. The standard Palestinian lamp of the Gospel period was plain, round, with a fairly wide flanged filling hole, and a flared nozzle for the wick, sloping downwards.

Lamps could be held in the hand, set on a shelf or placed on a stand (Heb. *mᵉnôrâ*, 2 Ki. 4:10; Aram. *neḇraštâ*, Dn. 5:5; Gk. *lychnia*, Mt. 5:15; *cf.* *ANEP*, no. 657, left edge). A simple wooden stand would serve most households, but some Iron Age lamps were provided with thick bases or separate hollow pedestals. Where brighter light was needed lamps with several spouts were employed, seven-spouted examples having been found in Palestine from this and earlier times, and many with provision for multiple wicks are known from the Roman era.

Pottery forms were copied in metal, although few examples survive from the OT period. In the tabernacle stood the elaborate golden lampstand (Ex. 25:31ff.). Three branches ending in flower-shaped lamp-holders protruded from either side of the main stem, which also supported a lamp-holder. Representations on certain Maccabean coins, a Herodian period drawing on stone found in Jerusalem and a relief on the arch of Titus supplement Hebrew descriptions, and it may be assumed the pattern given in Exodus was followed closely throughout. Ten similar lampstands were made for Solomon's Temple (1 Ki. 7:49).

The single lamps described burnt coarse olive oil or fat, and could stay alight for 2 to 4 hours, it seems, with an occasional trimming of the wick which was made of flax or other fibre (Heb. *pištâ*, Is. 42:3; 43:17). It might be allowed to die away at night, or be kept alight (1 Sa. 3:3; Pr. 31:18).

Out-of-doors lamps could be carried in pottery vessels, although no examples are known earlier than the Roman era. These were dome-shaped with a flat base, a handle at the top and an opening at one side for the light. Such may have been the 'lantern' of Jn. 18:3 (Gk. *phanos*), or it may have been a more elaborate metal form. Gk. *phanos* can also mean 'torch', and that could be the sense here. Gideon's men had torches at an earlier date (Heb. *lappîḏ*, Jdg. 7:16).

II. Symbolic uses

Lamps were placed in tombs from the first, partly, no doubt, to illuminate the chamber, at the same time very likely serving as a symbol of life. The expression 'his lamp' is so used metaphorically in the OT (Jb. 21:17; Pr. 20:20; 24:20; *cf.* 2 Sa. 21:17; 1 Ki. 11:36, *etc.*). From its purpose the lamp became a symbol of joy and prosperity, and of guidance: see Ps. 119:105; 2 Sa. 22:29; Pr. 6:20, 23, and personal names such as Neriyah, 'The Lord is my light'.

BIBLIOGRAPHY. D. M. Bailey, *Greek and Roman Pottery Lamps*, 1963; R. H. Smith, *BA* 27, 1964, pp. 1–31, 101–124; 29, 1966, pp. 2–27. A.R.M.

III. Symbolic and other uses in the New Testament

In the NT 'lamp' occurs 7 times in AV, on each occasion rendering *lampas*. RV renders *lampas* as 'torch' in Jn. 18:3 (following AV) and in Rev. 8:10, as 'light' in Acts 20:8 (following AV), and as 'lamp' in Mt. 25:1, 3–4, 7–8; Rev. 4:5 (following AV). RV renders *lychnos* (AV 'light' 6 times, 'candle' 8 times) as 'lamp' on every occasion.

The RV rendering must be accepted apart from the translating of *lampas* by 'lamp' in Mt. 25 and Rev. 4:5. In the latter RSV has 'torch'. In the parable of the virgins (Mt. 25:1–13) RVmg. should be followed, where 'torch' is read. The conventional lamp was for indoor use, and what was needed (and what is still sometimes used) at a wedding was a * torch. The rags which formed its wick needed to be soaked in oil. It seems that the foolish virgins had no oil at all (v. 3), and therefore when they lit their torches they went out instantly (v. 8). The wise had taken oil in separate containers ready for use at the appropriate moment. The difference between them seems to have been not in the quantity of oil that they possessed but in the fact of their possessing or not possessing any at all. The foolish could have gone and bought some had they acted in time.

lychnos is used frequently in a symbolic sense. It is the lamp which must be put on a stand to give light to all in the house (Mt. 5:15). John the Baptist was 'a burning and shining lamp' (Jn. 5:35), who came 'to bear witness to the light' (Jn. 1:7). It is Christ who is the light (*phōs*). In Mt. 6:22 the eye is called 'the lamp of the body' because it receives the light from outside.

lychnia is rendered 'candlestick' by AV *passim* and 'stand' by RV in the Gospels. RV translates this 'candlestick' in Heb. 9:2 and also 7 times in Rev., but gives 'lampstand' in mg. RSV has 'lampstand' throughout. The seven churches (Rev. 1:12–13, 20; 2:1, 5) and the two witnesses (Rev. 11:4) are symbolized by lampstands, similar to those used in the tabernacle (Heb. 9:2). R.E.N.

LANDMARK. Canaan was divided among the Israelite tribes, and to each family was given a plot of land to provide its livelihood. This was passed from father to son, or at least kept within the tribe (Nu. 27:1–11; 36), from which it was, theoretically, inalienable (see the story of Naboth, 1 Ki. 21). Inevitably many lost their land through debt, so that the situation in which every man owned his own plot was looked upon as an ideal (Zc. 3:10). The boundaries were defined by stone pillars or cairns. (In Babylonia inscribed stones recorded the size of important estates, Bab. *kudurru*, *ANEP*, nos. 519–522, contemporary with the Israelite settlement of Canaan.) To remove these was tantamount to removing a man's claim, and was a lawless act (Dt. 19:14; 27:17; Pr. 22:28; 23:10). (For an Egyp. parallel, *cf.* *ANET*, p. 422, ch. 6.) It was a sign of evil times when men dared to do so (Jb. 24:2; Ho. 5:10). A.R.M.

LANGUAGE OF THE APOCRYPHA. The so-called *'Apocrypha' comprise a heterogeneous group of books, so that to talk of its language is in fact to talk of the individual books and the problems of language which they pose. They have been preserved for us in MSS of the LXX and so lie before us like that translation in Greek. Their Greek varies widely: *e.g.* an evident 'translation Greek' in Tobit, Judith, Ben-Sira, 1 Maccabees; a relatively idiomatic Greek in 1 Esdras and Wisdom of Solomon 1–9, in which nonetheless may be perceived traces of its original; the rest of Wisdom and 2 Maccabees in a Greek uninfluenced by any other tongue, although these two works differ widely in their literary merit. In this Greek dress, then, the Apocrypha present instances of a variety of popular Greek works current among Jewish people in the three centuries immediately before Christ. The writings pose textual problems which fall within the general pattern of the textual criticism of the LXX.

It has often been assumed that Hebrew is the original tongue of those works in this group which are evidently based on a Semitic original. C. C. Torrey, however, in this as in the NT field, opened the pertinent question whether Aramaic is not the original language, at least in certain cases. His knowledge of Aramaic was vast and his contributions to biblical learning always challenging and stimulating, sometimes providing solutions to problems old and new, but not always convincing or even necessary (see the review by G. R. Driver of his posthumously published work on the Apocalypse: *JTS* n.s. 11, 1960, pp. 383–389). This must be borne in mind in evaluating his views on the language of the Apocrypha.

The Hebrew origin of a number of books is not controverted even by Torrey. 1 Maccabees has been translated from Hebrew by one better acquainted with Greek than Hebrew: signs of its origin are to be seen in, for instance, 1:28; 9:24; 14:28. Judith is plainly from Hebrew, as phrases such as *apo prosōpou, eis prosōpon*, and instrumentally used *en* show. The prologue to the Wisdom of Ben-Sira, or Ecclesiasticus, as it is often called, expressly states Hebrew to be the original, and a large part of this was discovered in the Cairo Geniza in 1896. The additions to Daniel are shown to be Hebrew in origin by passages such as the Prayer of Azariah 17 (3:40 in continuous Greek text) and Susanna 15. The Greek of the Prayer of Manasses is fluent, but the obscurities of vv. 4 and 7, for example, appear to derive from imperfectly expressed Hebrew locutions. Baruch displays in 4:5 evidence of a scribal error in the Hebrew (*ziḵrôn* read instead of *ziḵrû*) translated into Greek. 1 Esdras is a rendering of a known original, part Hebrew, part Aramaic: it is idiomatically rendered. Finally, within this group, the first nine chapters of the Wisdom of Solomon are now widely acknowledged to be based on a Hebrew original; they are translated by the author of the rest of the book, to whose original additions we should perhaps also attribute 6:22–8:1.

Tobit is generally conceded to be translated from some Semitic language. Pfeiffer admits that both Hebrew and Aramaic can be proposed but that the case for Aramaic is the stronger. Torrey proposed to find evidence for this latter hypothesis in the meaningless Manasses of 14:10 (MSS B and A), an original participle with objective suffix *mᵉnassēh*, 'the one who exalted him', 'his benefactor'. (Fragments of Tobit in both Hebrew and Aramaic have been identified among the Qumran texts.) The Epistle of Jeremy admits of debate: some still maintain a Greek original. A crucial point is 'the harlots on the roof' (v. 11). Torrey sees here evidence of a misrendering of *'al 'agrā*, 'for their hire', as *'al 'iggārā*. However, both readings in the Greek (*stegous/tegous*) may be understood as 'brothel', so that mistranslation seems to be an unnecessary hypothesis in this case. In the case of 2 Esdras (not extant in Greek) variant hypotheses have been advanced for both Hebrew and Aramaic originals. The question of the additions to Esther is larger than merely discussion of language: if the argument of Torrey that this represents the original form of the book be correct, then Aramaic

Hebrew	Hebrew or Aramaic	Greek
1 Maccabees	Tobit	2 Maccabees
Judith	Epistle of Jeremy (or Greek?)	Wisdom of Solomon 9 to the end
Wisdom of Ben Sira (Ecclesiasticus)	(Part of) 1 Esdras	
Additions to Daniel; Susanna 15	2 Esdras	
Prayer of Azariah	Additions to Esther	
Prayer of Manasses		
Baruch	2 Maccabees (the letters in chs. 1 and 2)	
(Part of) 1 Esdras		
Wisdom of Solomon 1-9		

Table of languages used for the original texts in the books of the Apocrypha.

may well have been its original. But this argument has not been accepted by most scholars.

Lastly, 2 Maccabees is a composition in Greek, a highly artificial attempt at the attainment of rhetorical heights. The letters which are found in chs. 1 and 2 may be original, and appear to be from a Semitic source, perhaps in Aramaic.

In these linguistic debates it may be well to bear in mind the remarks of G. R. Driver (*op. cit.*) to the effect that in the case of one author at least both Hebrew and Aramaic must be considered. As the one was spoken increasingly during the time of the composition of the Apocrypha and the other was still a literary medium and sometimes spoken, it may be that both have left their imprint upon the eventual Greek form of these books: and that this fact has led to the possibility of such different arguments upon a single matter.

BIBLIOGRAPHY. R. H. Charles, *The Apocrypha and Pseudepigrapha of the Old Testament*, 2 vols., 1913; C. C. Torrey, *The Apocryphal Literature*, 1945; R. H. Pfeiffer, *History of New Testament Times with an Introduction to the Apocrypha*, 1949; E. A. Speiser, *JQR* n.s. 14, 1924, pp. 455–482; C. E. Purinton, 'Translation Greek in the Wisdom of Solomon', *JBL* 47, 1928, pp. 276–304; C. C. Torrey, 'The Older Book of Esther', *HTR* 37, 1944, pp. 1–40; *HJP*, 3.1 and 3.2, *passim*. J.N.B.

LANGUAGE OF THE OLD TESTAMENT.

I. Hebrew

Hebrew belongs to the W group of the Semitic languages (the word Semitic is formed from the name of Shem, Noah's eldest son). It is most closely related to the language of ancient Ugarit, and to Phoenician and Moabite. *Canaanite is known only from occasional words in the *Amarna letters. Probably it was the parent of Hebrew. In the OT it is called the 'language (lit. "lip") of Canaan' (Is. 19:18), or Judaic (2 Ki. 18:26f.; *cf.* Is. 36:11ff. and Ne. 13:24). The designation 'Hebrew' first occurs in the Prologue to Ecclesiasticus (Ben Sira, *c.* 180 BC).

Characteristic of the Semitic languages is the triconsonantal root acting as a kind of frame for a series of vowel-patterns. The insertion of the vowel-pattern into the frame gives it its specific meaning. In *kōhēn*, for instance, *k-h-n* would be the consonantal frame and *o-e* would be the vowel-pattern. The force of the *o-e* is roughly equivalent to that of the present participle in English, thus *kōhēn*, 'ministering (one)'.

Hebrew script is a descendant of the N Semitic or Phoenician script (*WRITING). It consists of 22 consonants (later *š* and *ś* were distinguished, making 23). It is written from right to left. It contains various sounds not found in Indo-European languages; *e.g.* emphatic consonants (*ṭ*, *ḳ* [*q*], and *ṣ*) and the laryngal *'ayin* ('). The latter was often transliterated into Greek by *gamma*, as for instance in 'Gomorrah'. When Hebrew was no longer widely current, systems of marks were inserted above, below and within the consonants to show the correct vowels (*TEXTS AND VERSIONS).

This vocalization represents an important synchronic stage in Hebrew, and it is the product of a highly enlightened and reliable tradition, as is shown, for instance, by the care with which it observes the distinction that originally obtained between certain vowels of 'substantival' and 'adjectival' verbs, where modifications of the consonantal frame reveal their primitive forms. There are also a number of extra-alphabetical and punctuation or intonation signs. For biblical Hebrew the pronunciation most commonly adopted is the Sephardic (Judaeo-Spanish).

The scribes scrupulously avoided making any change in the consonantal text. Where they presumed that there had been a transcriptional error, or where a word was no longer in polite use, they placed what they considered was the right or preferable word in the margin and the vowels of this word were added to the word in the text (over which a small circle was often placed). The consonants in the text are referred to as *Kᵉṯîḇ* ('the written'), those in the margin as the *Qᵉrē'* ('that which is to be read').

Hebrew possesses no indefinite article. The definite article (*ha-*) is prefixed to the noun. Its use differs in many details from that of the definite article in English. For example, demonstrative pronouns and adjectives take it when used attributively with a noun determinate in its reference (*e.g.* the book, the this; the man, the fat). It is also used with a member of a class or with something previously mentioned.

Nouns in Hebrew distinguish gender and number. Gender is grammatical: inanimate as well as animate things are assigned gender. The feminine has usually a specific termination (*-â*). A number of feminine nouns, however, have no termination, but their gender is indicated by the agreement of adjectives and verbs. Hebrew also possesses a specific termination for the dual, largely confined to members of the body occurring in pairs; case-endings were discarded early, but a few traces remain.

There are two main classes of verbs: those with *substantival* cognates and those with *adjectival* cognates. Broadly speaking, the 'substantival' verb is dynamic, whereas the 'adjectival' (often called 'stative') is static. The verb primarily indicates the kind of the action, and distinguishes two main aspects: completed action (perfective) and incompleted (imperfective). For the perfective, the pronominal element is suffixed: for the imperfective it is prefixed. In the perfective, gender is distinguished in the 3rd person singular and in the 2nd person singular and plural, and in the imperfective also in the 3rd person plural. Hebrew has a number of verb-forms for particular categories of action, such as iterative, causative, tolerative, *etc.*

Nouns are formed in many ways: by a variety of vowel-patterns, and with or without the addition of certain consonants. When consonants are used they are usually prefixed, *m* and *t* being the most common. Wide use is made of the singular as a collective, with the result that the feminine termination is sometimes used as a kind of singulative ending, *e.g.* *śē'ār*, 'hair', *śa'ᵃrâ* (fem.), 'single hair'. Zero forms, that is forms in which a morphological element common to a class is missing, are not uncommon; *ṣō'n* (fem.), 'flocks', *cf.* *ṣō'n 'ōḇᵉḏôṯ*, 'lost sheep', where *ôṯ* indicates the element missing. The noun preceding a genitive has its vowels reduced to the minimum and omits the definite article. The group is treated virtually as an inseparable compound. Possessive pronouns appear as suffixes to the noun.

Adjectives may be used either predicatively, when they do not take the definite article and usually precede the noun, or attributively, when they

SEMITIC LANGUAGE FAMILY (all dates are approximate)					
(N)–W SEMITIC		(N)–E SEMITIC		S SEMITIC	
'Eblaite' 2400 BC		Old Akkadian 2500–2000 BC			
Amorite 18th cent. BC		Old Assyrian = Akkadian = Old Babylonian 2000–1500 BC			
Ugaritic (Ras Shamra) 1450–1200 BC		Middle Assyrian	Middle Babylonian 1500–1000 BC		
Early Canaanite (Amarna Glosses) 14th cent. BC					
Canaanite	Aramaic				
Hebrew (Classical/Biblical) 1200–200 BC					
Phœnician/Punic 10th cent. BC– 2nd cent. AD	Old Aramaic dialects. 10th–7th cent. BC	Neo-Assyrian 1000–600 BC	Neo-Babylonian 1000 BC		
Moabite 9th cent. BC					Ancient (Epigraphic) S. Arabic 8th cent. BC– 6th cent. AD
	Classical/Imperial Aramaic. 7th–3rd cent. BC. Includes Biblical Aramaic		Late Babylonian 625 BC–1st cent. AD	N. Arabic 5th cent. BC– 4th cent. AD Dedanite Safaitic Lihyanic Thamudic	Sabaean Hadramautic Minaean Qatabanian
	W. Aramaic	E. Aramaic			
	Jewish Palestinian Aramaic, 150 BC– 4th cent. AD	Hatrene 1st cent. BC– 3rd cent. AD			
	Nabataean 100 BC–AD 200				
	Palmyrene 100 BC–AD 200				
Hebrew, Mishnaic 1st–4th cent. AD					Ancient Ethiopic (Ge'ez)
		Syriac 3rd–13th cent. AD			
	Samaritan 4th cent. AD	Mandaean 3rd cent. AD onwards			
		Babylonian Aramaic 4th–6th cent. AD		Classical Arabic 4th cent. AD	
	Christian Palestinian Aramaic 5th– 8th cent. AD	Neo-Syriac dialects			
					Harari Tigre Trigrina Amharic
Medieval Hebrew					
Modern Hebrew				Modern Arabic Dialects	Gurage

Chart showing the Semitic family of languages including biblical Hebrew and Aramaic.

follow the noun and take the definite article if the noun has it. The adjective may also take the definite article and be used independently, having the value of a substantive. Comparison is rendered by the use of the preposition *min*, 'from', equivalent to the English 'more . . . than'. The highest degree of a quantity is often left unexpressed, *e.g.* 'the good', namely 'the best', or the superlative is expressed by a phrase consisting of a singular form followed by a plural, *e.g.* 'song of the songs', *i.e.* the greatest or best song.

The use of the numerals shows several peculiarities. One and two agree in gender with their noun, but three to ten disagree. This may indicate a late introduction of grammatical gender.

The 'verbless' or nominal sentence in which the predicate consists of a noun, a pronoun, or adjective, is widely used. Usually we supply in translation some part of the verb 'to be', *e.g.* 'the servant of Abraham (am) I'. In sentences with a finite verb the word-order usually follows the pattern—verb, subject, object. Often with the accusative the particle *'eṯ* is used. If the object consists of a pronoun it can be appended to the accusative particle, or it can be added as an enclitic form to the verb. An indirect object consisting of a preposition and a pronominal suffix normally comes before the subject. If there is an adverbial extension it usually follows the object. Where English might use the impersonal 'one', *e.g.* in 'one says', Hebrew uses either the 2nd or 3rd singular masculine or the 3rd plural.

The most distinctive feature of Hebrew style is its syndetic or co-ordinative character, that is, the prevalence of the simple conjunction 'and', and the infrequent use of subordinating conjunctions. Compared with English, it might seem to be less abstract. Hebrew, for instance, makes extensive use of terms for physical attitudes to describe psychological states, or organs of the body are associated with mental attitudes. It is most difficult for anyone inured to Indo-European procedure to dissociate his mind from the original meanings; this is particularly so when a work is replete with them, as, for instance, in the Song of Songs.

The imagery of Hebrew is largely drawn from the things and activities of everyday life. It has, therefore, a universal quality and lends itself without difficulty to translation. Hebrew makes use of all the common figures of speech, parables (*e.g.* 2 Sa. 12), similes, metaphors, *e.g.* 'star' or 'lion' for hero, 'rock' for refuge, 'light' for life and for the divine revelation, 'darkness' for sorrow and ignorance.

Hebrew, in common with general linguistic usage, makes wide use of anthropomorphic expressions; that is, the transference or adaptation of terms for parts of the human body and for human activities to the inanimate world and other conditions to which they are not strictly attributable. These expressions have their origin in metaphor and come under the heading of 'extension of meaning', a device essential apparently to mechanism of languages in general. They occur as frequently in other Semitic languages as in Hebrew. Akkadian, for instance, refers to the keel of a ship as the 'backbone', to which the 'ribs' are attached. Hebrew speaks about the 'head' of a mountain, the 'face' of the earth, the 'lip' (shore) of the sea, the 'mouth' of a cave, the 'going' of water (a verb often used elsewhere with the meaning of 'walking'). These and many other expressions had obviously become 'fossilized' metaphors. When such expressions are applied to the activities or attributes of God it would be indefensible on linguistic grounds to interpret them in a literal sense, or to base theories of beliefs on what are intrinsic modes of expression dictated by the very nature of linguistic communication.

Elliptical expressions, by which the semantic content of a full phrase is vested in a single member of the group, are not uncommon, *e.g.* the omission of 'voice' after 'to lift up' (Is. 42:2). Although one of the earliest references to semantic change occurs in the OT (1 Sa. 9:9), there is little evidence of change in Hebrew in the course of the centuries. It is likely, however, that many parts have been revised to a standard Hebrew, perhaps that of late pre-exilic Jerusalem. Traces of dialects may be found in some books, *e.g.* Ruth, parts of 2 Kings. Later forms of the language can be traced in Esther, Chronicles and other passages. In the nature of the case, it would not be easy to detect loan-words from cognate languages. Examples are *hêḵāl*, 'temple', from Akkad. *ekallu*, 'palace', which in turn was borrowed from Sumerian *e-gal*, 'great house'; *'argāmān*, 'purple', comes from Hittite.

Recovery of numerous ancient texts in cognate languages has brought a more precise understanding of some points. There is a danger that the excitement of new discoveries may give rise to ill-founded proposals that contravene in-built safeguards of the language which prevent ambiguity. Frequent appeal to Arabic in this way mars NEB (see J. Barr, *Comparative Philology and the Text of the Old Testament*, 1968). The great divergences between Hebrew and the other cognate languages, largely due to the action of semantic change, make it extremely hazardous to attempt on etymological grounds to assign meanings to Hebrew words of infrequent occurrence.

The high literary style of much of the OT would seem to indicate the early existence of literary models or of a 'grand style'. The ancient Near East offers examples of high styles continuing in use for many centuries. Much that has been written about divergences in Hebrew style is, in the absence of proper criteria, valueless.

While it is now clear that the influence of Hebrew on NT Greek is not as extensive as was formerly held by many scholars, nevertheless it has left its mark both on vocabulary and syntax. There are a number of loan-words and many loan-translations, *e.g.* *hilastērion* for the covering of the ark which, on the Day of Atonement, was sprinkled with blood, and an expression like 'Blessed art thou among (lit. "in") women', where the Greek follows the Hebrew use of the preposition.

The influence of Hebrew on European literature is incalculable, even though much of it may have come indirectly through the Vulgate. Among the many Hebrew loan-words in English are: sabbath, sack, Satan, shekel, jubilee, hallelujah, aloes (fragrant resin) and myrrh. The use of 'heart' as the seat of the emotions and will and of 'soul' for person are probably loan-translations.

BIBLIOGRAPHY. A. B. Davidson, *An Introductory Hebrew Grammar*[25], 1962; G. Beer and R. Meyer, *Hebräische Gram.*, 1, 1952; 2, 1955; 3–4, 1972; J. Weingreen, *Practical Grammar for Classical Hebrew*, 1959: T. O. Lambdin, *Introduction to Biblical Hebrew*, 1971; H. Bauer and P. Leander, *Historische Gram. der Hebräischen Sprache*, 1918–19; P. Joüon, *Grammaire de l'Hébreu Biblique*, 1923;

F. I. Andersen, *The Hebrew Verbless Clause in the Pentateuch*, 1970; *idem*, *The Sentence in Biblical Hebrew*, 1974; Gesenius–Buhl, *Handwörterbuch*, 1921; L. Koehler, W. Baumgartner, *Hebräisches und aramaisches Lexicon zum Alten Testament*, 1967ff.; E. Y. Kutscher, *A History of the Hebrew Language*, 1982; B. Waltke and M. O'Connor, *An Introduction to Biblical Hebrew Syntax*, 1990; N. M. Waldman, *The Recent Study of Hebrew*, 1989; A. Sáenz-Badillos, *A History of the Hebrew Language*, 1993; L. McFall, *The Enigma of the Hebrew Verbal System*, 1982. B.D.B.

II. Aramaic

Aramaic, a close cognate, not a derivative, of Hebrew, is the language of Dn. 2:4–7:28; Ezr. 4:8–6:18; 7:12–26; Je. 10:11; two words in Gn. 31:47; and of the Targums (Aramaic translations of parts of the OT). In the 9th and following centuries BC, Aramaic and its script (taken from alphabetic Hebrew/Phoenician) rapidly became the international medium of commerce and diplomacy. Already in the 9th century BC, Israel and Damascus had merchants in each other's capitals (1 Ki. 20:34), and in 701 BC Hezekiah's officers sought to be addressed in Aramaic—understood by rulers or merchants, but not by (Hebrew) 'men in the street' (2 Ki. 18:26). In Assyria itself from *c.* 730 BC under Tiglath-pileser III, Aramaic steadily came into official use: Aramaic dockets on cuneiform tablets, Aramaic annotations by high Assyrian officials and Assyrian sculptures showing the recording of tribute by scribes who write (Aramaic) with pen on parchment as well as in cuneiform on clay tablets. (For full references, see R. A. Bowman, *JNES* 7, 1948, pp. 73–76, to which add the ostracon listing Hebrew exiles in Assyria found at Calah, J. B. Segal, *Iraq* 19, 1957, pp. 139–145, and Albright, *BASOR* 149, 1958, pp. 33–36.) Note here, too, the Aramaic letter of Adon of Ascalon to the pharaoh of Egypt in 604(?) BC (W. D. McHardy in *DOTT*, pp. 251–255 with bibliography). Unless it is a note to readers that Aramaic directly follows, the note in Dn. 2:4 'in Aramaic' when the Chaldeans address Nebuchadrezzar would fit in perfectly with Assyro-Babylonian court use of Aramaic. Besides examples above, Aramaic epigraphs occur on the very bricks used in constructing the great buildings of Nebuchadrezzar's Babylon and testify to the common use of that language there then (see R. Koldewey, *The Excavations at Babylon*, 1914, pp. 80–81, figs. 52–53). Aramaic ('Reichsaramäisch') became the official medium of communication throughout the polyglot Persian empire—Ezra is the classic biblical example. This is vividly illustrated by Aramaic papyri from Egypt (5th century BC); for these see A. Cowley, *Aramaic Papyri of the Fifth Century* BC, 1923; H. L. Ginsberg in *ANET*, pp. 222–223, 427–430, 491–492; E. G. Kraeling, *The Brooklyn Museum Aramaic Papyri*, 1953; G. R. Driver and others, *Aramaic Documents of the Fifth Century* BC, 1954 and abridged and revised, 1957.

The script is the same as Hebrew, and Aramaic has approximately the same phonological characteristics, including the position of the stress. The vowel-patterns are on the whole more attenuated and on occasions preserve more primitive forms. The consonantal shift between the two languages lacks the consistency of a law. Heb. *z* = Aram. *d* (*ḏ*), Heb. *š* = Aram. *t*, Heb. *ṣ* = Aram. *ṭ*, *etc.*, but the change of Heb. *ṣ* to Aram. ʿ and *q* is phonetically hard to explain.

The definite article is *-â* and is suffixed to its noun. The genitive relation can be expressed as in Hebrew, the noun preceding the genitive is shortened if possible and the group is treated as inseparable. The relationship is more often expressed by *dî*, originally a demonstrative pronoun, thus *ḥezwâ dî lēlyâ*, 'vision of the night'.

As in Hebrew, the noun has singular, dual and plural. There are two genders: masculine and feminine. The feminine termination is *-â*, but many feminine nouns are without any indication. Possessive pronouns are suffixed to the noun.

The verb possesses two tense-aspects: perfective (completed action) with pronominal elements suffixed, and imperfective (incompleted action) with the pronominal elements prefixed. The active participle is widely used to express present or future. There are some eight 'verb-forms' or conjugations: Primary Form, with modifications for active, passive and reflexive; Intensive; and the Causative, designated by either a prefixed *h*, ʾ or *š*. The verb 'to be', *hᵃwâ*, comes to be used very much like an auxiliary verb.

The verbless sentence is common. In verbal sentences either the verb or the subject may come first, but the latter order seems more common. Word-order is less rigid than in Hebrew.

The Aramaic of the OT is a subject of dispute. S. R. Driver (*LOT*, pp. 502ff.) affirmed that the Aramaic of Daniel was a *Western* Aramaic dialect and hence late. When he wrote, the only material available was too late to be relevant. Subsequently R. D. Wilson, making use of earlier material that had come to light, was able to show that the distinction between E and W Aramaic did not exist in pre-Christian times. This was amply confirmed by H. H. Schaeder. Schaeder also drew attention to the fact that the static nature of 'Imperial Aramaic', as it has come to be called, precludes the possibility of dating documents in it, including Daniel and Ezra. He showed that the criteria adduced to assign to Daniel and Ezra a late date are merely the result of a process of orthographical modernization going on in the 5th century BC (see F. Rosenthal, *Aramaistische Forschung*, pp. 67ff.). From what we know from contemporary documents of the extent of trade and diplomatic contacts, we are not surprised to find loan-words in the most unexpected places.

Advancing knowledge based upon old and new discoveries shows arguments for dating the Aramaic of the OT after the Persian period are often groundless. Recent evidence on one matter must suffice here. In early Aramaic there was a sound *ḏ* (*dh*) which by Persian times had become identical with ordinary 'd' in pronunciation. In the W (Syria) this consonant was written as 'z' (even in a non-Aramaic name, as Miliz for Milid(h), 'Melitene' in Zakir's stele), and this persisted as a 'historical' spelling in the Aramaic papyri of the Persian empire. But in the E, 'dh' was already represented by the Assyrians as 'd' from the 9th century BC (Adad-idri for (H)adad-ezer). The real pronunciation 'd' in Persian times is betrayed by various hints: a remarkable Aramaic text in Egyptian demotic script, 5th century BC, writes 't'/ 'd' (J. A. Bowman *JNES* 3, 1944, pp. 224–225 and n. 17), while in some of the normal Aramaic papyri there are cases of false archaism in writing 'z' for original 'd' (not 'dh'), *cf.* E. Y. Kutscher, *JAOS* 74, 1954, p. 235 (*zyn wzbb*).

OT Aramaic writes a phonetically true 'd', not a

W historic 'z'; this is no indicator of late date, but signifies one of two things. Either Daniel, Ezra, *etc.*, simply put Aramaic as spoken in 6th/ 5th-century Babylonia into a directly phonetic spelling, or else they used the historic spelling largely eliminated by a subsequent spelling-revision of rather later date.

BIBLIOGRAPHY. E. Y. Kutscher, in T. A. Seboek (ed.), *Current Trends in Linguistics* 6, 1970, pp. 347–412; R. D. Wilson, *Studies in the Book of Daniel*, 1917; F. Rosenthal, *Aramaistische Forschung*, 1939; H. H. Schaeder, *Iranische Beiträge*, 1, 1930; K. A. Kitchen, in D. J. Wiseman (ed.), *Notes on Some Problems in the Book of Daniel*, 1965, pp. 31–79; W. R. Garr, *Dialect-Geography of Syria–Palestine, 1000–586 BCE*, 1985. *Grammars*—by H. Bauer and P. Leander, 1927; H. Strack, 1921; W. B. Stevenson, 1924; F. Rosenthal, 1961; K. Beyer, *The Aramaic Language*, 1986; *Lexicons*—those listed under *Hebrew* contain Aramaic supplements.

W.J.M.
K.A.K.

LANGUAGE OF THE NEW TESTAMENT.

I. General characteristics

a. The nature of 'common Greek'

The language in which the NT documents have been preserved is the 'common Greek' (*koinē*), which was the *lingua franca* of the Near Eastern and Mediterranean lands in Roman times. It had been established over this wide territory by the conquests and express cultural purpose of Alexander the Great, whose colonies provided *foci* for the continued use of the language. It exercised influence in vocabulary upon Coptic, Jewish Aramaic, rabbinical Hebrew and Syriac, and was spoken as far W as the Rhone valley, colonized from the province of Asia. It represents, as its morphology and accidence show, a mingling of the Attic, Ionic and W Greek dialects, which in the course of Greek political history before and after Alexander's conquests became fused together into a fully unified language with little trace of dialectal differentiation, so far as our records go. It is the direct ancestor of Byzantine and modern Greek which have recently been much utilized to cast light on its development and normative forms.

A number of the writers of the Roman period strove to attain the Attic ideal, and thus the living dialect is largely obscured in their works (Dionysius of Halicarnassus, Dio Chrysostom, Lucian); and even those who wrote in the *koinē* were inevitably influenced at times by their literary background (Polybius, Diodorus Siculus, Plutarch, Josephus).

The language of the NT, however, belongs to a style which is not moulded by formal literary education, but stands in a tradition of the presentation of technical materials and practical philosophy. The antecedents of this are in the scientific writings of Aristotle and Theophrastus, and in the medical writings of the Hippocratic school. Contemporary parallels to NT Greek are to be found in popular philosophical writings such as the discourses of Epictetus, in business and legal documents known to us from papyrus discoveries, and in various Hellenistic writers on medical and other technical matters. This style provided a convenient medium for the presentation of the matters of general interest which the early church desired to convey, in a language which was likely to be that which the non-Greek speaker learnt when he entered Graeco-Roman society. It had an intellectual tradition but was not the property of a sophisticated lettered class: it was not the colloquial daily speech but had links with that, as the cultivated literary language did not. The language of the NT, from the solecisms of the Apocalypse to the highly-wrought style of Luke or Hebrews, stands within this common tradition. It is not a separate dialect but draws its peculiarities from its subject-matter, from the background of the LXX and from the imprint of the mother tongue of most of its writers.

The *koinē* is characterized by the loss or attenuation of many subtleties of the classical period, and by a general weakening in force of particles, conjunctions and the *Aktionsart* of verbal conjugations. The extent and particular instances of this tendency to simplification naturally vary even within the NT, and much more within the whole range of the linguistic monuments of the dialect. The dual number has totally disappeared. The optative mood is little used and scarcely ever strictly according to the canons of classical Attic. The distinction of perfect and aorist is sometimes not observed, a feature often reflected in variant readings. Certain particles, *e.g. te*, *hōs*, and even *ge*, are used as mere otiose supplements to others. Distinctions between different prepositions, *e.g. eis* and *en*, *hypo* and *apo*, are blurred; and similarly, the use of the same preposition (*e.g. epi*) with differing cases of the noun.

In vocabulary, compound verbs take the place of simple verbs, and thematic of non-thematic, while back-formations appear; in the noun there is a marked inclination to use diminutives without due implication of smallness. Similarly, the usage of such conjunctions as *hina* and *mē* has been greatly extended; and the pattern of conditional sentences (whether with *ei* or with a relative) has lost its clearly-defined nuances. This is not to imply that the language was in this form totally weakened and bereft of all its powers and subtleties—it remained a keen and precise instrument of expression—but without cognizance of the attenuating processes which were at work the expositor stands in danger of oversubtlety in exegesis.

During the period of our NT writings, under Roman domination, the *koinē* was exposed to the influence of Latin, and this has left its mark upon the language. However, this impression is mainly upon vocabulary and is to be seen in two forms, transliterated words (*e.g. kentyriōn*) and literally transposed phrases (*e.g. to hikanon poiein* = *satisfacere*). An attempt has been made to argue that the original tongue of Mark's Gospel was Latin, as some Syr. colophons say, and a plausible case erected; but the thesis has not met with acceptance, since much of its evidence may be paralleled either in the papyri or in modern Greek. It is in fact an unchallenged axiom of present-day scholarship in this field that that which is at home in modern Greek is the development of a natural Hellenistic locution, and in its appearance in the NT cannot be the result of a foreign influence upon NT Greek. As regards the language of Mark, it should also be noted that Latinisms of both kinds are to be found in Matthew and John and even in Luke, while the African Latin text, claimed as the original text, is in fact extant for all four Gospels, and not only for Mark.

b. Hebraisms in the New Testament

No local dialects are observable within the *koinē*, and in extant records there seems to be little local variation apart from pronunciation. A few 'Phrygianisms' and 'Egyptianisms' have been isolated. But in the NT writings we meet the particular problem of Semitisms, *i.e.* abnormal locutions which reveal an underlying or otherwise influencing Hebrew or Aramaic. We find that here we are dealing with an extremely subtle problem, in solving which a number of different types of influence and reflection may be discerned. Much that seemed curious to earlier scholars and was put down to Hebraism has, since the discoveries of the papyri, proved to be but the common Greek of the period. Yet certain features remain about which debate continues.

Hebraisms are mainly of Septuagintal origin. The Septuagint (LXX) was the Bible text chiefly known and used in the period of the formation of the NT. Its influence upon the NT writers varies. To trace this is again somewhat difficult, except in the case of explicit citation or phraseology, because of different strata in the LXX itself, some parts of which are written in idiomatic *koinē*, others in good literary *koinē*, while the Pentateuch and some other portions, largely for reverential reasons, closely adhere to the Heb. text, even when this entails a certain wrestling of the grammatical usage of Greek. Heb. phrases are rendered word for word into Greek, *e.g. pasa sarx*, 'all flesh'; *akrobystia*, 'uncircumcision', *enōpion tou kyriou*, 'before the Lord'; pronouns are much used, following Heb. usage; various verbal features of Hebrew, especially the infinitive absolute, are rendered as literally as possible into Greek, *e.g.* in this case by pleonastic participle or cognate noun in the dative case; various periphrastic prepositional forms are used in imitation of Hebrew, *e.g. en mesō, dia cheiros*. In some cases, for instance the last named, this represents simply an over-use of a development already observable in popular Greek of the period.

The Greek of the NT, however, is not translated from Hebrew; and where (citations, *etc*., apart) Hebraism is observable, it is in works otherwise high in the scale of stylistic and literary elegance in the NT. These are Luke, whose Septuagintalism is probably the result of deliberate pastiche, and Hebrews, whose author is steeped in the LXX while himself being capable of a highly complex and subtle Greek style. In Revelation the author's Greek, basically *koinē*, has been moulded by his Semitic mother-tongue. For instance, the verbal pattern of Hebrew and Aramaic has been imposed thoroughly upon his usage of the Greek verb, and Hebrew influence may be seen in the numerals. The resultant style is thoroughly Semitized but distinct from Septuagintal styles.

c. The so-called 'Aramaic approach'

This approach is a method even more difficult to pursue than the tracing of Hebraism. This is due to many factors. First, there has been considerable debate over the appropriate dialect of the widespread Aramaic language, in which the sayings of Jesus may be presumed to have been uttered and preserved. In the upshot it would appear that the Palestinian Targum, the Aramaic portions of the Talmud Yerushalmi, and Samaritan Aramaic sources are probably the safest guide, with biblical Aramaic and Christian Palestinian Syriac as useful auxiliary aids. Secondly, whereas for Hebraisms we have a known translation from Hebrew to guide us, in the case of Aramaic there is no translated literature apart from the versions of biblical books known to have been translated from Aramaic, and various pseudepigrapha presumably translated; and only in the first of these cases have we the originals by which to control our understanding. Josephus' *Jewish War*, originally composed in Aramaic, has been skilfully rendered into Greek in a version which shows little or no trace of its original language. Thirdly, a number of alleged signs of Aramaic origin (*e.g.* asyndeton, parataxis, an extended use of *hina* said to be based on the Aramaic *d*[e]) are also to be found in the *koinē*, where simplicity of construction is often found and finer shades of meaning are sometimes lost.

In view of these difficulties, one needs to proceed with care. The more ambitious hypotheses which find all the Gospels and parts of Acts to be translations from Aramaic have failed to meet with general acceptance. More sober positions need to be taken up. We have to assess the probabilities largely by an 'un-Greek' preponderance of, or predilection for, certain locutions, or by means of patent ambiguities directly attributable to errors of translation. We find, then, that, broadly speaking, sayings and discourse material prove to be that which displays the most unambiguous signs of translation out of Aramaic: *viz.* sayings, complexes of sayings, parables, in the Synoptics; peculiarly Johannine discourse material; speeches in Acts. In these sections a number of ambiguities have been resolved by recourse to the syntax and style of Aramaic: this is the most securely established conclusion of this method. The majority of attempts to find flagrant mistranslations, however, in the *cruces interpretum* of the Greek, have not met with general agreement; each scholar tends to put forward his own suggestions, to the detriment of others and in criticism of theirs. In the case of John not all would be willing to find Aramaic sources even behind the discourses: rather, the work of a bilingual author has been postulated, in which the more natural Aramaic has left its indelible imprint on the more mannered Greek. This is certainly so in the case of Paul, whose rugged and vigorous *koinē* is marked throughout by his close acquaintance with the LXX and sometimes, perhaps, by his native Aramaic.

II. Individual stylistic features

Having thus summarized the general characteristics of NT Greek, we may give a brief characterization of each individual author. Mark is written in the Greek of the common man; our increased knowledge of the papyri has done much to illuminate his usage, though Aramaisms still remain, notably his impersonal use of the third person plural of the active verb to express a general action or thought. Matthew and Luke each utilize the Marcan text, but each corrects his solecisms, and prunes his style, in accordance with principles which we may find illustrated in their extreme form in Phrynichus. Matthew's own style is less distinguished than that of Luke—he writes a grammatical Greek, sober but cultivated, yet with some marked Septuagintalisms; Luke is capable of achieving momentarily great heights of style in the Attic tradition, but lacks the power to sustain these; he lapses at length back to the style of his sources or to a very humble *koinē*. In both Evangelists, of course, the Aramaic background of the material reveals itself again and again, especially in sayings. The first two chapters of Luke have led to some debate: it is common to describe them as a pastiche of the LXX, but it may be plausibly argued that they are translated directly from a Heb. source. John's Greek can be closely paralleled from Epictetus, but in the opinion of most scholars appears to be a *koinē* written by one whose native thought and speech were Aramaic; there may even be passages translated from that language. Certain qualities of his style, notably the 'I AM' type of theophanic declaration, are most closely to be paralleled from the Mandaean writings which have their roots in W Syria; this too underlines the description of the Gospel as markedly Semitic. Acts is clearly the work of Luke, whose style fluctuates here as in the Gospel, and in spite of his spasmodic achievements remains at the mercy of his sources.

Paul writes a forceful Greek, with noticeable developments in style between his earliest and his latest Epistles. The development in Ephesians and in the Pastorals is so striking as to have led to hypotheses of pseudonymous composition; it is naturally patient of other explanations in the view of conservative scholars (*PSEUDONYMITY). Hebrews is written in very polished Greek of one acquainted with the philosophers, and with the type of thought and exegesis exemplified in Philo, yet the LXX has affected the language and style as it has not in Philo's case. James and 1 Peter both show close acquaintance with classical style, although in the former some very 'Jewish' Greek may also be seen. The Johannine Epistles are closely similar to the Gospel in language, but are more uniform and, even, duller in style, though the wide differences of literary type and subject may well be the operative factor in this. Jude and 2 Peter both display a highly tortuous and involved Greek; the latter has in fact with some justification been accused of Atticizing, and has been described as the one NT writing which gains by translation. The Apocalypse, as we have indicated, is *sui generis* in language and style; its vigour, power and success, though a *tour de force*, cannot be denied.

III. Conclusion

So NT Greek, while showing a markedly Semitic cast in places, remains in grammar, syntax and even style essentially Greek. Semantically, however, it has come to be increasingly acknowledged that its terminology is as strongly moulded by the usage of the LXX as by its origins, etymology and usage in Greek. This realization has led to the *TDNT* founded by Kittel, and has made a major contribution towards the current investigations of biblical theology; readily accessible to the English reader, there is also the work of C. H. Dodd in this field, especially in *The Bible and the Greeks* and *The Interpretation of the Fourth Gospel.* Behind 'righteousness' and 'justification', behind 'faith' and 'to believe', behind 'knowledge' and 'grace', stand Heb. concepts which quite transform the Gk. significance and which must be comprehended if the gospel is not to be misunderstood. The lack of this knowledge affects even the best of patristic and mediaeval exegesis, and later theologians too have suffered from lack of it. The realization of it is one of our greatest gains from modern biblical research: but note the criticism of J. Barr.

In summary, we may state that the Greek of the NT is known to us today as a language 'understanded of the people', and that it was used with varying degrees of stylistic attainment, but with one impetus and vigour, to express in these documents a message which at any rate for its preachers was continuous with that of the OT scriptures—a message of a living God, concerned for man's right relation with himself, providing of himself the means of reconciliation. This gospel has moulded the language and its meaning so that even the linguistic disciplines of its analysis become ultimately parts of theology.

BIBLIOGRAPHY. R. W. Funk, *A Greek Grammar of the New Testament*, 1961 (rev. of F. Blass and A. Debrunner, *Grammatik der neutestamentlichen Griechisch*) 9/10 ed.; latest Ger. ed. = ^{17}, 1990 (ed. F. Rehkopf); J. H. Moulton, *Grammar of New Testament Greek*, 1^3, 1908; 2 (ed. W. F. Howard), 1929; 3, 1963; 4, 1976; M. Black, *An Aramaic Approach to the Four Gospels and Acts*^{3}, 1967; L. Rydbeck, *Fachprosa, vermeintliche Volkssprache u. Neues Testament*, 1967; G. Mussies, *The Morphology of Koine Greek*, 1971; C. F. D. Moule, *TDNT*; Walter Bauer, *Griechisch-Deutsches Wörterbuch zu den Schriften des Neuen Testament und der früchristlichen Literatur* 6, völlig neu bearbeitete Auflage . . . von Kurt and Barbara Aland, 1988; *BAGD*; J. Barr, *The Semantics of Biblical Language*, 1961; *Biblical Words for Time*, 1962; J. A. Fitzmyer, *A Wandering Aramean*, 1979. J.N.B.

LAODICEA. A city of SW Phrygia, in the Roman province of Asia, in the W of what is now Asiatic Turkey. It was founded by the Seleucid Antiochus II in the 3rd century BC, and called after his wife Laodice. It lay in the fertile valley of the Lycus (a tributary of the Maeander), close to *Hierapolis and *Colossae, and was distinguished by the epithet 'on Lycus' from several other cities of the name. It was at a very important cross-road: the main road across Asia Minor ran W to the ports of *Miletus and *Ephesus about 160 km away and E by an easy incline on to the central plateau and thence towards Syria; and another road ran N to *Pergamum and S to the coast at *Attalia.

Laodicea, one of the 'seven churches of Asia' (*Rev.* *1–3*).

This strategic position made Laodicea an extremely prosperous commercial centre, especially under Roman rule. When destroyed by a disastrous earthquake in AD 60 (Tacitus, *Ann.* 14. 27) it could afford to dispense with aid from Nero. It was an important centre of banking and exchange (*cf.* Cicero, *ad Fam.* 3. 5. 4, *etc.*). Its distinctive products included garments of glossy black wool (Strabo, *Geog.* 12. 8. 16 [578], and it was a medical centre noted for ophthalmology. The site had one disadvantage: being determined by the road-system, it lacked a sufficient and permanent supply of good water. Water was piped to the city from hot springs some distance S, and probably arrived lukewarm. The deposits still encrusting the remains testify to its warmth. The site of Laodicea was eventually abandoned, and the modern town (Denizli) grew up near the springs.

The gospel must have reached Laodicea at an early date, probably while Paul was living at Ephesus (Acts 19:10), and perhaps through Epaphras (Col. 4:12–13). Although Paul mentions the church there (Col. 2:1; 4:13–16), there is no record that he visited it. It is evident that the church maintained close connections with the Christians in Hierapolis and Colossae. The 'letter from Laodicea' (Col. 4:16) is often thought to have been a copy of our Ephesians which had been received in Laodicea.

The last of the Letters to 'the seven churches of Asia' (Rev. 3:14–22) was addressed to Laodicea. Its imagery owes relatively little to the OT, but contains pointed allusions to the character and circumstances of the city. For all its wealth, it could produce neither the healing power of hot water, like its neighbour Hierapolis, nor the refreshing power of cold water to be found at Colossae, but merely lukewarm water, useful only as an emetic. The church was charged with a similar uselessness: it was self-sufficient, rather than half-hearted. Like the city, it thought it had 'need of nothing'. In fact it was spiritually poor, naked and blind, and needed 'gold', 'white garments' and 'eyesalve' more effective than its bankers, clothiers and doctors could supply. Like citizens inhospitable to a traveller who offers them priceless goods, the Laodiceans had closed their doors and left their real Provider outside. Christ turns in loving appeal to the individual (v. 20).

BIBLIOGRAPHY. C. J. Hemer, *NIDNTT* 1, pp. 317–319; *idem*, *Buried History* 11, 1975, pp. 175–190; E. M. Yamauchi, *New Testament Cities in Western Asia Minor*, 1980; C. J. Hemer, *The Letters to the Seven Churches of Asia in their Local Setting*, 1986.

M.J.S.R.
C.J.H.

LAPPIDOTH (Heb. *lappîḏôṯ*, 'torches'). The husband of Deborah (Jdg. 4:4). Some Jewish commentators, taking it as a description of Deborah, would render the Hebrew as 'a woman of lightning flashes', but there is little evidence to support this view; other Jewish commentators (with equal lack of evidence) identified him with Barak (Jdg. 4:6), whose name means 'lightning'. J.D.D.

LASEA, presumably the same town as the Lasos mentioned by Pliny (*NH* 4. 59), has been identified with ruins some 8 km E of *Fair Havens. If this identification is correct, one of the disadvantages of Fair Havens as a winter harbour would be the distance of the town from it. K.L.McK.

LASHA. Probably *leša'*, but written *lāša'* in the interests of prosody in its sole occurrence, which is at the end of a verse (Gn. 10:19). It figures in the designation of the limits of the territory of Canaan in a context which suggests that one travelling from the Mediterranean coast would encounter it as the farthest inland of a group consisting of Sodom, Gomorrah, Admah and Zeboim. This points to a locality somewhere near the SE shore of the Dead Sea, but no site of this name is known there. Ancient tradition equated it with the hot springs of *Kallirrhoē*, modern Zarqa Ma'in SW of Madaba near the E coast of the Dead Sea, and some modern scholars prefer to identify it with *layiš* of *Dan, but neither of these can be substantiated. T.C.M.

LASHARON (RV 'Lassharon', AVmg. 'Sharon'). A Canaanite royal city mentioned with Aphek as taken by Joshua (12:18). LXX (B) reads 'the king of Aphek in Sharon'. However, Eusebius (*Onomasticon, s.v.* 'Saron') mentions a district called Sarona, between Mt Tabor and the Sea of Tiberias, and this ancient site, 10 km SW of Tiberias, may be the biblical Lasharon. J.D.D.

LATIN. The word is mentioned only twice in the NT (Lk. 23:38, RSVmg.; Jn. 19:20). An Indo-European language, it was spoken first in Rome and the contiguous Latian plain by racial elements which entered Italy, probably from the N, before 900 BC. Latin was confined to the Latian enclave by the alien Etruscan language to the N, and to the E and S by the allied languages, Oscan and Umbrian, which came with a later wave of immigrants, possibly across the Adriatic. Latin expanded with Rome, became the second speech of the W Mediterranean, fathered the Romance languages, and contributed major elements to the vocabularies of the Teutonic and Slavonic languages. Latin words appearing in the NT are: *as, charta, census, centurio, colonia, custodia, denarius, forum, flagellum, grabbatus, legio, lenteum, libertini, lolium, praetorium, quadrans, macellum, membrana, modius, raeda, semi-cinctium, sicarius, speculator, sudarium, taberna, titulus, zizanium.* E.M.B.

LAW

I. In the Old Testament

Terminology

The OT has a variety of terms for law, the commonest of which are: *tôrāh*, 'law, instruction, teaching'; *ḥōq*, 'statute, decree'; *mišpāṭ*, 'judgment, legal decision'; *dābār*, 'word'; *miṣwāh*, 'command(ment)'. Their number reflects the importance of law within the Bible. Indeed the first five books are called *tôrāh*, 'law', by Jews and the NT, even though they appear to be as much about history as law. The specifically legal sections are embedded in narratives about Israel's early history, and this context is important for the understanding of biblical law. This article will therefore begin by describing the main groups of law within the Pentateuch; next it will review the relationship of OT law to other collections of laws from the ancient Near East; then it will look at the relationship of the law to the covenant, and finally at its relationship to the narratives.

a. The Ten Commandments

The Ten Commandments or Ten Words (Decalogue) (Ex. 20:1–17; Dt. 5:6–21) are rightly regarded as the quintessence of OT law. This is not merely the opinion of modern commentators, but is affirmed by Jesus and Paul and by the OT itself. They alone are said to have been written by 'the finger of God', a very emphatic statement of their inspiration.

The Ten Commandments are not case or statute law, or 'Israel's criminal law' (so Philips). No human penalties are specified for breaking them, but dire warnings of punishment by God or promises of his blessing are added to them. And the last commandment about coveting could never be enforced by a human court. This shows that the commandments should not be classed as civil or criminal law, but as a statement of basic religious and ethical principles.

These principles are illustrated and in the other legal collections of the Pentateuch are put into a form that judges could handle. Ex. 22:1–15 shows how theft should be punished, and Dt. 22:13–30, among other passages, gives directions about adultery and kindred offences. Indeed the order of topics in Dt. 12–25 seems to be dictated by the order of the commandments.

This order is not haphazard: it gives an insight into the religious and ethical priorities of the OT. Though every commandment expresses the will of God, and to breach them is to invite his punishment, the most important come first. Other collections of law are put in a similar order. Flagrant breaches of the first six commandments are punished by death. Death is made optional for the seventh, *i.e.* adultery. It is never invoked for ordinary cases of false witness or theft, and covetousness is not brought to court. Thus the Decalogue makes love for God, his name and his day, the Israelite's first duty, but almost as important is love for parents, human life and marriage. Then comes truth and property, and finally covetousness. Other societies tend to rank these matters differently.

b. The Book of the Covenant

Ex. 20:22–23:19 is often referred to as the Book or Code of the Covenant, a title suggested by Ex. 24:7. This was given at the same time as the Ten Commandments, and the context makes it plain that the writer of Exodus saw this collection of laws as an elaboration of the Decalogue. Yet about half of them find good parallels in non-biblical collections of laws, so that scholars assume that there has often been large-scale borrowing from Canaanite sources or a drawing on common Near-Eastern legal tradition which explains these parallels. But the differences between non-biblical collections and the Book of the Covenant are just as striking as the affinities. There has been no mechanical borrowing, for the laws within the Book have been added to or reordered to reflect biblical priorities. For example, oriental collections of law rarely contain rules about worship or other religious matters, but in the Book of the Covenant and the other collections these come first (20:22–26) and last (23:10–19). In the Mesopotamian collections, laws about slaves usually come towards the end, but Ex. 21:1–11 puts them near the beginning. This reflects the OT's insistence that slaves are human beings, not mere chattels, but it also recalls that as 20:2 puts it, 'I am the LORD . . . who brought you out . . . of slavery.' Israel must show kindness to slaves as God did to them (*cf.* Dt. 15:15). The primacy of human life over property is also reflected in these laws.

c. Leviticus and the Holiness Code

Source criticism splits the book of Leviticus into two parts: 1–16 is ascribed to the Priestly source and 17–27 to the Holiness Code, an earlier document subsequently incorporated into the Priestly source. The theme of holiness runs through the book of Leviticus. Its motto is: 'Be holy because I, the Lord your God, am holy.' The narrative which encases the laws in Leviticus sets their promulgation in Sinai, like the Book of the Covenant. Like the Book of the Covenant, Leviticus shows the same sense of priorities. It begins with seven chapters on sacrifice, showing the acceptable way to worship God. After a short narrative interlude (chs. 8–10), it proceeds with a long section on impediments to worship, *i.e.* unclean conditions (chs. 11–15), more laws on worship, before reaching its section on civil and criminal offences (chs. 18–25), with its acme 'Love your neighbour as yourself' (19:18). Once again, duties towards God precede duties to one's neighbour.

d. Deuteronomy

Deuteronomy is Gk. for 'second law'. This is not the aptest description of this book, for although chapters 12–25 contain much legal material, the genre of the book as a whole is different from the preceding collections. Deuteronomy is a series of sermons by Moses about the law, urging Israel to keep the law if they want to prosper in the land they are about to enter. Much critical debate focuses on whether Moses, the implied author of Deuteronomy, is the actual author, but that is not the issue here. The laws in Exodus and Leviticus profess to have been given by God to Moses, but Deuteronomy is an extended reflection by Moses on the law and an attempt by him to persuade the nation of Israel to keep the laws, especially when they enter Canaan.

The structure of the book owes much to the Near Eastern legal document form exemplified in treaties, law codes and *kudurru* stones. But as already mentioned the section of Deuteronomy that most closely corresponds to a law code, chapters 12–25, appears to follow the order of the Decalogue in its arrangement of laws. Some of the most obvious points are chs. 12–13//1st commandment 'no other gods', chs. 15–16//4th commandment 'sabbath' = 7th year and festivals, chs. 17–18//5th commandment 'parents' = authorities, chs. 19–21//6th commandment 'murder', chs. 22–23//7th commandment 'adultery', chs. 23–24//8th commandment 'theft, property' ch. 25//9th commandment 'false witness'. Once again the same sense of values emerges here as in the Decalogue itself.

e. OT law and ancient oriental parallels

In discussing the Book of the Covenant we noted that many parts parallel laws from other Near Eastern texts, such as the laws of Lipit-Ishtar *c.* 2100 BC, the laws of Eshnunna and Hammurapi *c.* 1750 BC, the Hittite laws and the Middle Assyrian laws. There are also thousands of legal documents dealing with marriage, wills, sale, and disputes spanning nearly three millennia, from Sumer to Egypt, which shed light on Israelite legal practice. Despite the multitude of documents now available, it is difficult to know how much legal practice differed from place to place and in different periods. Though scholars tend to presuppose much evolutionary development, Westbrook argues that the ancient world was a very static society, with relatively little change happening from place to place. Certainly legal texts from very different times and places have contributed to elucidating biblical law.

It is generally agreed that the extrabiblical collections of law are not comprehensive codes trying to cover every legal eventuality. Often the most obvious cases are not discussed, *e.g.* ordinary homicide or arson, but unusual cases are, *e.g.* looting at a fire. This suggests we are dealing with collections of traditional case law, perhaps introducing certain innovations or reforms. How far these collections were drawn up for the guidance of judges (they are hardly ever cited in legal cases), or how far they represent an academic exercise by learned scribes as propaganda on behalf of the king, is still a matter of debate. The biblical collections are similar in not being comprehensive and in presupposing at many points the normal legal practices of the Near East. For example, Lv. 18 does not prohibit incest with one's daughter, but presupposing it extends the incest boundaries considerably. The OT does not describe what constituted a legal marriage or divorce, but by using extrabiblical materials, and remarks in biblical law about unusual cases, it is possible to reconstruct more typical procedures. So with the aid of Near Eastern texts, biblical law may be interpreted much more exactly.

However, though legal practice in Israel may at many points have been similar to that of its neighbours, the framework of understanding was somewhat different. In Mesopotamia, the king was the author of the law, but Israel saw God as the lawgiver. This had profound consequences. First, it meant that all offences were sins. They did not merely affect human relationships, but also the relationship between God and people. Non-observance of the law was a breach of the covenant between God and Israel that was liable to provoke divine judgment. Second, if law comes from God, all life is related to God, therefore it is natural for collections of law to contain reference to religious duties as well as social ones. We have already noted this feature in all the biblical collections of law. Third, the duty of keeping the law fell on every Israelite, not just the king. So every Israelite was expected to know and teach the law, especially to members of his family (*cf.* Dt. 6:7).

The express purpose of the law was to create a 'kingdom of priests and a holy nation' (Ex. 19:6). But the prologue of Hammurapi's laws dwells on the political and economic benefits that law brings—justice, peace, prosperity and good government. But though the OT recognizes these benefits as flowing from national obedience to the law (*cf.* Dt. 28:1–14), it also sees a much greater benefit in the law. The law itself is the divine means of creating a holy people. Obedience to the law renews the divine image in man, enabling him to fulfil the command to 'Be holy, for I am holy' and to enjoy the presence of God in the midst of his people (*cf.* Lv. 11:44–45; 19:2; 20:7; 26).

f. Biblical law and the Covenant

All the biblical collections of law are set within a covenant framework. The Ten Commandments and the Book of the Covenant form the centrepiece of the first Sinai covenant, the laws in Leviticus form part of the renewal of that covenant after the golden calf incident, and Deuteronomy renews the covenant some 40 years later in the plains of Moab. It is widely recognized that the Israelite covenant roughly follows the pattern of Near Eastern vassal treaties made between great kings and their underlings. In the OT setting, the Lord is the great king and Israel is his vassal, pledged to total loyalty.

The covenant framework of the law has several implications for its understanding. First, it shows that the law forms part of a personal relationship between God and Israel: they are not anonymous rules imposed by an unknown authority. They are given by the creator God who has chosen one nation out of all the nations to be his treasured possession (Ex. 19:5) and his laws are a gift to them that no other people enjoy and proof of God's nearness to them (Dt. 4:7–8). Second, the law was given to Israel after she had experienced salvation, after they had been brought out of Egypt, not before. Israel was saved by divine mercy, not by their own good works or efforts. The giving of the law was part of God's ongoing grace towards Israel. Third, obedience to the law would lead to yet greater blessings for the nation: good harvests, numerous children, freedom from hunger and disease, victory over their enemies, and God's presence in their land. But, conversely, breaking the laws would lead to all sorts of disasters: drought, hunger, disease and, ultimately, expulsion from the land (Lv. 26; Dt. 28). So though obedience to the law did not earn Israel salvation, it was indispensable if they were to continue to enjoy its benefits.

g. The law in its narrative context

The law-giving at Sinai is not an isolated event. As explained above, it was part of the covenant made there, and this in turn is viewed as fulfilment of the promises made to Abraham, Isaac and Jacob (Ex. 3:7–17; 6:2–8). God promised to make Abraham a great nation, give his descendants the land of Canaan and make an everlasting covenant with them (*cf.* Gn. 12:1–3; 17). The Sinai covenant was a partial fulfilment of these patriarchal promises.

But the Sinai covenant does not simply hark back to these promises to Abraham. It reflects God's plan for mankind foreshadowed in Genesis 1–2. There God gave Adam the garden of Eden. He told him to 'be fruitful and multiply' and provided him with a wife, walked with them in the garden, and gave them a law 'not to eat of the tree'. It was transgression of this one law that led to Adam and Eve forfeiting the benefits of Eden. The story of the rest of Genesis is of God's planning and working to bring to pass his original plan for the human race. The call of Abraham was a first step, the covenant at Sinai was another. Not only did the Lord come down on Sinai but he guided them with the pillar of fire, and eventually 'walked' in the tabernacle as he once walked in Eden. Admittedly, it was only the high priest who could enter the divine presence, whereas in Eden the whole human race enjoyed such intimacy with God. But it was a step in the right direction.

Similarly, the laws given at Sinai, particularly the penal laws and those formulated negatively, *e.g.* most of the Ten Commandments, should not be regarded as God's ideals for human behaviour. Rather they represent the floor below which no one should fall—if they do, society or God must step in to punish. God's ideals are set out in the opening chapters of Genesis, where man is created in God's image and therefore expected to imitate him. In the exhortations and motive clauses scattered throughout the collections, similar lofty goals emerge: 'Be holy, for I am holy', 'Love the Lord your God with all your heart and with all your soul and with all your strength.' Therefore the OT law fixes no ceiling on human ethical endeavour: it too encourages man to 'be perfect, as your heavenly Father is perfect' (Mt. 5:48).

BIBLIOGRAPHY A. C. J. Phillips, *Ancient Israel's Criminal Law*, 1971; B. N. Kaye and G. J. Wenham (ed.), *Law, Morality and the Bible*, 1978; C. J. H. Wright, *Living as the People of God*, 1983; D. Patrick, *OT Law*, 1985; R. Westbrook, *Studies in Biblical and Cuneiform Law*, 1988; W. Janzen, *OT Ethics: A Paradigmatic Approach*, 1994; B. M. Levinson, *Theory and Method in Biblical and Cuneiform Law*, 1994; E. Otto, *Theologische Ethik des Alten Testaments*, 1994; J. M. Sprinkle, *'The Book of the Covenant': A Literary Approach*, 1994.

G.J.W.

II. In the New Testament

a. Jewish background

One of the most important features of OT religion was the law of Moses, which the Jews received when the Sinai covenant was ratified. Obedience to the law of Moses was not conceived as a way of earning God's favour but as a response to his grace in delivering Israel from Egypt (Ex. 20:1–17). Nonetheless, the basic storyline of the OT reveals that Israel failed to keep the law and forsook the God of Israel. Yahweh responded by sending his people into exile for their disobedience of the Torah (Lv. 26; Dt. 28; Jos. 23:14–16; 2 Ki 17:7–23; Dn. 9). In Paul's day the Jews believed that the promises of a glorious, national future were not yet fulfilled, since they were in subjection to Rome, and their servility continued to be ascribed to their failure to obey the Torah. The keeping of the law of Moses, therefore, was considered to be essential for the deliverance of the nation and the fulfilment of God's promises. Most Jews in Second Temple Judaism believed that by exercising their free will they had the ability to keep the law (Ecclus. 15:11–22; *Psalms of Solomon* 9:4–5; 2 *Apocalypse of Baruch* 54:15, 19; 85:7; *'Aboth* 3:16). What was required was commitment to carry out its prescriptions.

b. The meaning of the term 'law' and 'works of law' in the NT

Given the OT background, it is not surprising that the term 'law' (*nomos*) in the NT usually refers to the law of Moses. In most cases the focus is on Sinaitic legislation, *i.e.* the commands and prescriptions of the law (*e.g.* Lk. 2:22–24, 27, 39; Rom. 2:12–27; 1 Cor. 9:8–9). The phrase 'the law and the prophets' also occurs (*e.g.* Mt. 5:17; 7:12; 22:40; Lk. 16:16; Jn. 1:45; Acts 13:15; Rom. 3:21; *cf.* Lk. 24:44), denoting the OT scriptures as a whole. 'Law' in these cases refers to the Pentateuch, while 'prophets' designates the rest of the OT. The term 'law' also occasionally refers to the OT as Scripture and yet does not denote the Pentateuch, for Paul cites passages from Psalms, Proverbs and Isaiah and labels them as 'law' (*cf.* Rom. 3:10–19; 1 Cor. 14:21). There are a few other instances in which the term 'law' may not refer to the law of Moses. The 'law of Christ' (Gal. 6:2; *cf.* 1 Cor. 9:21) is understood by most scholars to be distinct from the law of Moses, although some see it as the fulfilment of the Mosaic law. It has often been said that the word 'law' means 'principle', 'order', or 'rule' in Rom. 3:27; 7:21, 23 and 8:2, although this has been vigorously contested in recent scholarship, with some insisting that the reference is to the law of Moses in every case.

The meaning of the term 'works of law' (*erga nomou*), which occurs eight times in Paul (Gal. 2:16 [three times]; 3:2, 5, 10; Rom. 3:20, 28), has also been the subject of considerable controversy. It has been suggested that the term is shorthand for legalism (Fuller), or that it focuses on the requirements which separate and distinguish Jews from Gentiles, *viz.*, circumcision, food laws, and observance of days (Dunn). More likely, the term refers broadly to all the works or deeds required by the law (Westerholm). This latter view is suggested by the Qumran literature (*Florilegium* 1:7; *Miqsat Ma'aseh Torah*) where the term 'works of the law' denotes all that is required by the law. Even more germane is the context in which the term is found in Romans. Paul asserts in Rom. 3:20 that no one is right before God by 'works of law'. This statement functions as a conclusion to the sustained argument of Rom. 1:18–3:18, where it is demonstrated that all people—both Jews and Gentiles—have sinned and fallen short of God's standard. Indeed, the Jews are indicted in Rom. 2:17–19 for failing to keep the law which they so avidly proclaim. The fundamental argument against the Jews in Rom. 2 is not that they are legalistic, nor that they exclude Gentiles. Rather, they are criticized for failing to observe the law which they treasure and teach. Thus, when Paul concludes his case in Rom. 3:20 by saying that no one is right before God by 'works of law', it follows from the preceding argument that the law, as a whole, is contemplated and that human beings failed to keep it perfectly. It is likely that a similar understanding should be applied in Gal. 2:16 and 3:10. A reference to the whole law is suggested particularly by Gal. 3:10, for Paul says that a curse rests upon those who do not 'abide by *all* that is written in the book of the law'. The emphasis on 'all' (Paul uses the LXX text which contains the word 'all', not the MT where the word is lacking) intimates that the whole law is in view and that perfect obedience is demanded. If 'works of law' do not justify, then what is the means by which the curse of the law can be removed? Gal. 3:13 proclaims that the curse is removed through the cross of Christ by which he becomes a curse-bearer for believers. Rom. 3:21–26 contains a similar argument: righteousness does not come via the law, but is available through faith by virtue of the atoning death of Christ which turned away the Father's wrath and wiped away our sins.

c. The law and human inability

We have seen that in both the OT and Second Temple Judaism, Israel's failure to realize the promises of national glory was ascribed to disobedience to the Torah. Paul (Rom. 1:18–3:20) also indicts both Gentiles and Jews for their failure to observe the law (*cf.* Gal. 2:17–18; 3:10; 5:3; 6:13). Other NT writers concur that disobedience was the fundamental problem with the Jews (*cf.*

Mt. 3:7–10 par.; Jn. 7:19; Acts 7:53; 15:10–11). Indeed, Jesus' most stinging criticism of the Pharisees is not that they are legalistic, but that they themselves do not keep the law (*cf.* Mt. 5:20; 23:3, 23, 25–26; Mk. 7:8, 13; Lk. 11:37–52).

NT writers do not depart from Second Temple Judaism in their conception that the promises have not yet been realized because of human sin. This would have been common ground between NT writers and their Jewish contemporaries. NT writers differed in their assertion that human beings are *unable* to keep the law (see Laato's work below). Paul is particularly emphatic on this point. He says that those who are in the flesh, *i.e.* unregenerate, 'cannot' keep God's law (Rom. 8:7). They are slaves to sin (Rom. 6:6, 17, 19, 20) and sold under the power of sin (Rom. 7:14) so that they are its captives (Rom. 7:23). Many Jews believed that the law could counter the 'evil impulse' (*yēṣer hāra'*) in human beings. Paul countered that to be 'under law' was to be under the power of sin (Rom. 6:14–15; 7:14; Gal. 3:22). Those who are of 'works of law' are 'under a curse' (Gal. 3:10). They are enslaved to the elements of the world (Gal. 4:3–5), and can be freed from the tyranny of being 'under law' only when they yield to the leading of the Spirit (Gal. 5:18). This is not to say that the law is evil *per se* (Rom. 7:12), for the 'under' phrases denote an era of salvation history in which the law was given and yet the Spirit was withheld from most of Israel. Thus, the law of Moses was given to increase sin (Rom. 5:20; 7:7–11; Gal. 3:19), and the law apart from the Spirit kills and condemns (2 Cor. 3:6, 9), for 'the power of sin is the law' (1 Cor. 15:56).

d. Is Jewish legalism criticized in the NT?

Ever since the Reformation, scholars have understood NT writers, and Paul in particular, to be opposing Jewish legalism which taught that one could merit right standing before God by doing the works of the law. A few dissenting voices have been raised along the way, but the consensus basically held until 1977. The year 1977 marks a watershed in NT studies, for E. P. Sanders published in that year his massive and influential work *Paul and Palestinian Judaism.* Sanders contends that scholarship has read Paul and Second Temple Judaism through the lenses of the Reformation struggle between Protestantism and Roman Catholicism instead of from a historical perspective. When the extant literary evidence of Judaism is examined, he claims, no evidence of legalism can be supported from the Jewish texts themselves – with the exception of 4 Ezra. Thus, the idea that Judaism was legalistic is a serious misreading of the evidence.

Sanders has convinced many scholars of the validity of his case, and he rightly strikes a balance against a caricature of Second Temple Judaism. Nonetheless, the claim that Judaism was as free of legalism as he suggests is questionable. The failure of Second Temple Judaism to emphasize the covenant and the stress on the minutiae of the law are at least a recipe for legalism which could easily creep into the practice, if not the theology, of some Jews. Neither can NT evidence that points to legalism among the Jews be explained away. The parable of the Pharisee and the tax collector (Lk. 18:9–14) demonstrates that the Pharisee believed he was righteous because of his morality and devotion to religious practices. His religion had become a mask for self-exaltation (v. 14). The Lukan inclusion of this parable can scarcely be accounted for if no one suffered from the problem of legalism.

Several texts in Paul also take aim at merit theology. For instance, Paul explicitly contrasts someone who works for a wage that is owed to him with someone who receives the gift of justification simply by believing (Rom. 4:4–5). This illustration occurs in a context in which all boasting is excluded, since righteousness is obtained by faith instead of works (Rom. 3:27–28; 4:2–3). One must strain the text unduly not to see a critique of legalism here. Those who are convinced that they have done the requisite works (an illusion, of course, since no one keeps the law perfectly—Rom. 1:18–3:20) do not need righteousness as a gift. They believe they have merited righteousness as a wage that is deserved, since they worked to attain it. And thus they believe (vainly!) they have grounds for boasting in their achievement. Rom. 9:30–10:8 should be understood similarly. The problem with the Jews is that they did not pursue the law with faith 'but as from works' (Rom. 9:32). Instead of submitting themselves to God's saving righteousness, they tried to establish their own righteousness by works (Rom. 10:3). The assertion by some (*e.g.* Dunn) that Paul's criticism of the Jews is limited to their nationalism and ethnocentrism can hardly be sustained here. Not a word is breathed in this context about circumcision, food laws, or observance of days. The text refers to 'works' in general—not even 'works of law'—and thus it would be illegitimate to conclude that the Jews are criticized for excluding Gentiles. The term 'works' should be interpreted in a broad sense, denoting their works-orientation rather than faith-orientation. Paul's critique of the Jews was not from an outsider's perspective, for he had suffered from the same tendency (Phil. 3:2–11). He attempted to obtain right-standing with God on the basis of 'his own righteousness from the law' instead of 'the righteousness of God on the basis of faith' (Phil. 3:9). The critique against legalism in the NT should not be understood as an attack against 'Jews' and an indication of anti-Semitism. Legalism is due to pride, and the desire for self-exaltation, which is a problem common to *all* humanity, not just the Jews.

e. Abrogation and fulfilment of the law

One of the perplexities in reading the NT is that it seems to say contradictory things about the law. In fact, Räisänen makes this his central plank in his book on Paul's view of the law, contending that Paul's theology of the law is inconsistent and contradictory. Räisänen's solution is unsatisfactory, and yet the difficulty is apparent to all careful readers of the NT, since the various statements made about the law are difficult to reconcile. This comes to the forefront in the matter of the abrogation and fulfilment of the law. Some statements imply that the law is still in force and fulfilled in Christ, while others teach that the law has come to an end. The solution to this vexing problem is paradoxical, for NT writers affirm that both are true, *i.e.* the law is abrogated and yet it is also fulfilled.

Matthew, for instance, emphasizes that Christ came to fulfil the law (5:17–20; *cf.* 5:21–48). What Matthew means by 'fulfil' is the subject of controversy, but it should be related to his christology, since he emphasizes that Christ fulfils OT prophecy (*cf.* 1:22; 2:15, 17, 23; 4:14; 8:17, *etc.*). Matthew hints (15:1–20) that the food laws of the OT are no longer binding. Mark, in the parallel text (Mk. 7:1–23), makes it explicit that all foods are now clean (Mk. 7:19). It is also possible that Matthew's words about the Sabbath suggest some change regarding Sabbath regulations (12:1–14). The fulfilment envisaged by Matthew, then, hints at some changes in the law. Food laws and perhaps the Sabbath laws are no longer binding in the same way (*cf.* also the texts on divorce in 5:31–32; 19:3–12). Nonetheless, the moral norms of the law are not jettisoned, but can now become a reality with the coming of the kingdom (4:17; 5:17–48).

Luke also emphasizes that Jesus fulfils prophecy (1:32–33, 54–55, 68–79; 4:18–19; 24:25–27, 44–49; Acts 2:16–36, *etc.*), and that the law is eternally valid (16:17). This does not mean that there is no shift in terms of the law, for Acts 10:1–11:18 communicates in unmistakable terms that food laws are no longer required. Moreover, at the Jerusalem council in Acts 15, circumcision is not imposed on the Gentiles. Luke's perspective seems to be a salvation historical one in which the law no longer functions in the same way now that Messiah has come, the Spirit has been poured out, and the gospel goes to the Gentiles (*cf.* Blomberg). The letter to the Hebrews depicts the covenantal shift in a beautiful argument which is unfolded in chapters 7–10. The law of the old covenant is no longer binding, since there has been a change of priesthood (Heb. 7:11–12). Indeed, the very fact that a Melchizedean priesthood was predicted in Ps. 110:4 signals that the Levitical priesthood was destined to become obsolete. If the Levitical priesthood has been superseded, the same is true of Levitical sacrifices. Ultimately, the blood of animals cannot atone for sin anyway, since they are brute beasts and unwilling victims. OT sacrifices actually anticipated and pointed forward to the sacrifice of Christ which is the fulfilment of what they adumbrated. Thus, the author of Hebrews does not criticize the OT law *per se.* He places it in salvation historical perspective, arguing that it must be interpreted in light of the fulfilment accomplished by Jesus Christ. The OT itself, in promising a new covenant, envisaged a day when the old would be dissolved.

Paul's theology follows the same basic paradigm. The gospel of Christ fulfils the OT scriptures (Rom. 1:2; 3:21). And now that Christ has come, circumcision, food laws and observance of days are not mandated for the people of God (Rom. 2:26–29; 4:9–12; 14:1–23; 1 Cor. 7:19; Gal. 4:10; 2:3–5; 5:2–6; 6:12–13; Col. 2:16–23). The Mosaic covenant has come to an end upon the arrival of Christ (Gal. 3:15 4:7; 2 Cor. 3:4–18), for the promises given to Abraham that all nations would be blessed have become a reality (Gal. 3:6–9, 14–18, 29; Rom. 4:9–17). Circumcision, food laws and Sabbath are not required, because the days of separation between Jews and Gentiles have ended. And yet the deeper reality to which these laws pointed has now been fulfilled. Curcumcision of the heart has become a reality through the work of the Holy Spirit (Rom. 2:28–29; Phil. 3:3) and the work of Christ on the cross (Col. 2:11–12). The purity laws of the OT are fulfilled in purity of life and in separation from all evil (*cf.* 2 Cor. 6:14; 7:1; *cf.* Peter's application of Lv. 11:44 in 1 Pet. 1:15–16). Paul himself does not enunciate how the Sabbath is fulfilled, but the author of Hebrews (Heb. 4:1–11) sees the Sabbath as coming to fruition in the Sabbath rest which believers now enjoy, and which will be consummated at the day of Christ's return. The fulfilment of the law for Paul (*cf.* also Jas. 2:8–12) also involves empowerment so that the moral norms of the law may be kept. Many scholars doubt that Paul operated with a distinction between the moral and ceremonial law, but texts such as Rom. 2:25–29; 8:4; 13:8–10; Gal. 5:2–6, 14; 1 Cor. 7:19, suggest that he operated with such a distinction. Of course, Paul never conceived that the law could be fulfilled in one's own strength. Fulfilling the law was due to the work of the Holy Spirit which enabled believers to obey God's commandments.

BIBLIOGRAPHY. E. P. Sanders, *Paul and Palestinian Judaism*, 1977; D. P. Fuller, *Gospel and Law: Contrast or Continuum?*, 1980; E. P. Sanders, *Paul, the Law, and the Jewish People*, 1983; H. Räisänen, *Paul and the Law*, 1983; C. L. Blomberg, 'The Law in Luke–Acts', *JSNT* 22, 1984, pp. 53–80; D. J. Moo, 'Jesus and the Authority of the Mosaic Law', *JSNT* 20, 1984, pp. 3–49; S. Westerholm, *Israel's Law and the Church's Faith*, 1988; J. D. G. Dunn, *Jesus, Paul, and the Law*, 1990; T. Laato, *Paulus und das Judentum*, 1991; N. T. Wright, *The Climax of the Covenant*, 1991; T. R. Schreiner, *The Law and Its Fulfilment*, 1993; F. Thielman, *Paul and the Law*, 1994; C. G. Kruse, *Paul, the Law and Justification*, 1996. T.R.S.

LAWGIVER (Heb. *mᵉḥōqēq*; Gk. *nomothetēs*). All six OT occurrences of the Heb. word are in poetry. In Gn. 49:10; Nu. 21:18; Ps. 60:7 (= Ps. 108:8) the rendering 'staff' or 'sceptre' makes better sense in context and with parallels. Dt. 33:21; Jdg. 5:14; Is. 33:22 ascribe judicial leadership to Gad, Manasseh and the Lord. James (4:12) rebukes censoriousness among his readers by reminding them that God alone is judge.

The idea of lawgiver in the NT, if not the word, is much more widespread. In particular, Christ is characterized as Lawgiver by his respect for the Mosaic Law (Mt. 5:17–18), and by comparison with Moses (Mt. 17:3; Jn. 1:17). The superiority of Christ is emphasized in his own pronouncements (Mt. 5:22ff.; 22:36–40) and elsewhere by stressing his status (Gal. 3:19; Heb. 7:11), the scope of his law (Rom. 10:4; 13:8ff.), and its spiritual nature (Rom. 7–8; Jas. 1:25, *etc.*). P.A.B.

LAWYER. The NT title *nomikos* was used of the scribes synonymously with *grammateus* (scribe) and *nomodidaskalos* (teacher of the law). All scribes were originally students of Scripture, but by the 2nd century BC lay scribes had begun to expound the minutiae of the law without direct reference to Scripture. Lawyers had seats in the Sanhedrin (Mt. 16:21; Lk. 22:66; Acts 4:5).

R.K.H.

LAYING ON OF HANDS. Actions with the *hands were an important part of ancient religious ritual, *e.g.* in prayer (1 Ki. 8:54; 1 Tim. 2:8) and invocation of divine blessing (Lv. 9:22; Ecclus. 50:20; Lk. 24:50). Jacob blessed the sons of Joseph by laying (*šîṯ*) his hands upon their heads (Gn. 48:8–20), and Jesus similarly blessed children brought to him (Mk. 10:16; Mt. 19:13–15; *cf. SB*, 1, pp. 807f.). Jesus also touched (*e.g.* Mk. 1:41; 7:33), or laid his hands on, the sick (Mk. 5:23; 6:5;

7:32; 8:23, 25; Mt. 9:18; Lk. 4:40; 5:13; 13:13), as did the apostles (Acts 9:12, 17; 28:8; Mk. 16:[18]; *cf.* 1 Qap Gen 20. 21, 28f. The action was symbolic of spiritual blessing flowing from one person to another (*cf.* Mk. 5:30).

I. In the Old Testament

On the Day of Atonement Aaron placed (*sāmaḵ*) his hands on the head of the goat which was to be sent into the wilderness and confessed the people's sins over it, thus putting them upon the goat (Lv. 16:21). A similar rite accompanied the burnt, peace, sin and ordination offerings (*e.g.* Lv. 1:4; 3:2; 4:4; Nu. 8:12), indicating the 'identification' of the people with their offering. (In Lv. 24:14 *(cf.* Susanna 34*)* the people who put their hands upon a blasphemer were probably 'thrusting' his guilt upon him.)

The Levites, who as priests represented the people before God, were ordained by the people placing their hands upon them (Nu. 8:10). Moses ordained his successor Joshua by placing his hands upon him and thus investing him with some of his authority (Nu. 27:18–23). This passage describes Joshua as 'a man in whom is the spirit' before his ordination, but Dt. 34:9 states that he was full of the spirit of wisdom because Moses had laid his hands upon him. The implication would appear to be that a worthy person, possessed of the divine Spirit, received additional spiritual gifts when commissioned for service by this rite. At the same time the rite indicated a transfer of authority.

II. In the New Testament

In the NT baptism and the reception of the Spirit were on occasion accompanied by the laying on of hands. In Acts 8:14–19 the gift of the Spirit was conferred only when baptism had been followed by apostolic laying on of hands. It is unlikely that the laying on of hands by Ananias in Acts 9:12, 17 (where it precedes baptism) is to be understood similarly. Acts 19:6 links laying on of hands with baptism and the gift of the Spirit expressed in tongues and prophecy, and Heb. 6:2 refers to teaching about baptisms and laying on of hands, probably as instruction given to new converts. Elsewhere, however, the gift of the Spirit was given without mention of laying on of hands, and once even before baptism (Acts 10:44–48), and it is unlikely that in the NT period baptism was always accompanied by laying on of hands.

Following the OT analogies and what may have been contemporary rabbinic practice, laying on of hands was also the rite of ordination for Christian service. After the congregation had chosen the seven helpers they (or possibly the apostles) prayed and laid hands on them (Acts 6:5f.; *cf. SB*, 2, pp. 647–661); similarly, the church at Antioch prayed and laid hands on Barnabas and Saul for mission work (Acts 13:3). In 1 Tim. 5:22 Timothy is urged not to be hasty in laying on of hands; this may refer to the ordination of elders or to the restoration of backsliders to fellowship with an act of blessing. 2 Tim. 1:6 refers to Timothy's own reception of the gift of God for the work of the ministry by the laying on of Paul's hands. *Cf.* 1 Tim. 4:14, where, however, it is the 'presbytery' which laid hands on him. The simplest and best solution is that Paul and the local elders were associated in the act, but D. Daube thinks that the phrase in question means 'ordination to the rank of presbyter'. Such ordination, carried out under divine guidance (Acts 13:3; *cf.* 1 Tim. 1:18), was an outward sign that God gave to the person his gifts for some task of ministry, and by it the church acknowledged the divine commission and enabling and associated itself with the Spirit in commissioning and authorizing the minister for his task.

Bibliography. G. W. H. Lampe, *The Seal of the Spirit*, 1951, ch. 5; E. Lohse, *Die Ordination im Spätjudentum und im Neuen Testament*, 1951; D. Daube, *The New Testament and Rabbinic Judaism*, 1956, pp. 224ff.; J. Newman, *Semikhah*, 1950; N. Adler, *Taufe und Handauflegung*, 1951; E. Ferguson, *HTR* 56, 1963, pp. 12–19; *JTS* n.s. 26, 1975, pp. 1–12; C. Maurer, *TDNT* 8, pp. 159–161; E. Lohse, *TDNT* 9, pp. 424–434; H.-G. Schütz, *NIDNTT* 2, pp. 148–153. I.H.M.

LAZARUS AND DIVES. In the story, which occurs in Lk. 16:19–31, Dives (Lat. 'rich man') is nowhere named. He failed to take notice of the plight of Lazarus, the beggar at his gate. After death Lazarus went to *Abraham's bosom and Dives to Hades. It was impossible for any contact to be made between them. Nor was there any point in Abraham's sending Lazarus to the brothers of Dives, as they had sufficient in Moses and the prophets to bring them to repentance.

The story teaches the dangers of wealth in blinding men to the need of their fellows and the irrevocable decision of our eternal destiny in our life on earth. It does not suggest that poverty is a virtue and wealth a vice, for Abraham was a rich man. Dives failed to learn the unjust steward's lesson (Lk. 16:9). The reference to resurrection in 16:31 applies more naturally to that of Christ than to that of Lazarus of Bethany. (*Gulf.)

Bibliography. I. H. Marshall, *The Gospel of Luke*, *NIGTC*, 1978, pp. 632–639. R.E.N.

LAZARUS. The name Lazarus is an abbreviation of the name Eleazar, which was the fourth most common male name among Palestinian Jews in the period 300 BC–AD 200. So it is not surprising that the name Lazarus is borne by two characters in the NT: one a character in a parable (Lk. 16:19–31), the other a close friend of Jesus and brother of Martha and Mary of Bethany (Jn. 11:1–44; 12:1–2, 9–11). Scholars have often postulated a connection between the two, supposing either that the parable in Luke was one of the sources out of which John created the story of the raising of Lazarus, or that the character in the parable was named after the man Jesus raised from the dead. But since the name was extremely common, such speculation is redundant. The fact that resurrection is mentioned in connection with both characters is an artificial similarity. In the parable, the rich man proposes that Lazarus be sent back to the world of the living to warn his brothers of the fate that awaits them after death. The proposal probably envisages only a temporary visit by Lazarus to this world, and it is rejected. This is quite unlike the raising of Lazarus of Bethany, where the purpose of the miracle is not that Lazarus should provide information from his experience of the world of the dead, but that Jesus should demonstrate his power to give life to the dead.

The Lazarus of the parable in Lk. 16 is the only character in a gospel parable who has a name. The reason may be simply that the demands of story-telling required him to be named. The point of the narrative is that the conditions of the destitute beggar and the wealthy aristocrat are reversed at death. Therefore they cannot be called 'the poor man' and 'the rich man' after their deaths. The telling of the story is greatly facilitated by naming the poor man. Since Eleazar means 'God has helped', the name may have been chosen for its appropriateness. But the naming of Lazarus may also help to associate the parable with the many stories, popular in the ancient world, about people who died, returned to life and were able to reveal the fate of people after death. Such stories usually named their characters. Jesus' parable plays on the notion familiar from such stories, but subverts it. In order to know that the rich should not live in luxury while the poor starve, a revelation from beyond the grave is not necessary because the scriptures are sufficient.

The raising of Lazarus in Jn. 11 plays a key role in both the theological and the historical sequence of John's narrative of Jesus. It is the greatest of the series of 'signs' which Jesus performs in the first half of the Gospel. John refers to the miracles of Jesus as 'signs', because they are acts of divine power whose purpose is to signify something even greater than the miracles themselves: Jesus' power to communicate eternal life. The raising of Lazarus is the most remarkable of the miracles. John emphasizes this by pointing out that Lazarus had been dead and buried for 4 days. According to popular Jewish belief, the spirit of a dead person did not finally desert the body until 3 days after death. So Lazarus is unambiguously dead. As a miracle of resurrection, this is the 'sign' which indicates most clearly that Jesus' mission is to give eternal life. Although Lazarus returns only to mortal life, Jesus' conversation with Martha (11:21–27) shows that the 'sign' points to the eternal life Jesus gives to believers.

By stressing both Jesus' love for Lazarus and his sisters (11:5, 36) and the fact that Jesus risks his own life by helping them (11:8, 16), the narrative foreshadows the way Jesus is soon to sacrifice his own life in order to give eternal life to those he loves. The remarkable stress on Jesus' emotions (11:33, 35, 38) may indicate not only his participation in the sorrow of the family he loves, but also his awareness that his act of helping them is going to lead to his own death. In the sequel to the raising of Lazarus (11:45–53), it becomes the event which determines the decision of the Jewish authorities to put Jesus to death. It also leads to a plot against the life of Lazarus himself (12:10–11). If Lazarus represents all those whom Jesus loves and for whom he gives his life, then there is perhaps the implication that followers of Jesus also risk their lives for him.

Thus history and theological meaning are closely intertwined in this story, as elsewhere in John. This need not mean that the events are not historical. Many have doubted the historicity of the miracle on the grounds that the other three gospels do not record it. However, this should be put in the context of the contrast between John's strong focus on events in and around Jerusalem and the Synoptic Gospels' focus on Galilee. Only one synoptic healing miracle (the healing of Bartimaeus in Jericho) occurs anywhere near Jerusalem. In this context, it is not surprising that the two synoptic resurrection miracles (Mk. 5:21–43; Lk. 7:11–17) occur in Galilee, while only John records one in the vicinity of Jerusalem. The synoptics are relatively vague about the historical causes of Jesus' execution, but John offers a detailed and plausible account of the political considerations that led to Jesus' death.

Since Lazarus is said to be one whom Jesus loved (11:3, 5, 36), it has sometimes been proposed that he is the anonymous 'disciple whom Jesus loved' (13:23–26; 19:25–27; 20:2–10; 21:7, 20–24). However, John also says that Jesus loved all his disciples (13:1). If Lazarus were *the* 'disciple Jesus loved', it would be odd that he is named in some passages and anonymous in others.

BIBLIOGRAPHY. R. Bauckham, 'The Rich Man and Lazarus: The Parable and the Parallels', *NTS* 37, 1991, pp. 225–246; B. Byrne, *Lazarus*, 1991; M. W. G. Stibbe, *John as Storyteller*, 1992. R.J.B.

LEAH (Heb. *lē'â*, 'wild cow' ?). The elder daughter of the Aramaean, Laban. Through his deception she became the wife of Jacob, because of the local custom prohibiting the younger daughter from marrying before the elder (Gn. 29:21–30). She was, not unnaturally, jealous of her more attractive sister Rachel.

As the mother of Reuben, Simeon, Levi, Judah, Issachar, Zebulun and Dinah she was acclaimed with Rachel as one of the builders of the house of Israel (Ru. 4:11). Together they allied with Jacob against Laban, and when they went to meet Esau she was given a place in the middle of the procession.

Her burial took place at Machpelah, in Hebron, presumably before Jacob's descent to Egypt (Gn. 49:31). M.B.

LEAVEN (Heb. *śᵉ'ōr*, 'leaven', 'leavened bread' in Dt. 16:4; *ḥāmēṣ*, 'anything leavened or fermented'; *cf. maṣṣâ*, 'without leaven', Lv. 10:12; Gk. *zymē*, 'leaven'; *cf.* Lat. *levare*, 'to raise').

In Heb. life leaven came to play an important part, not only in bread-making, but also in law, ritual and religious teaching. It was made originally from fine white bran kneaded with must; from the meal of certain plants such as fitch or vetch; or from barley mixed with water and then allowed to stand till it turned sour. As baking developed, leaven was produced from bread flour kneaded without salt and kept till it passed into a state of fermentation.

a. In bread-making

In bread-making the leaven was probably a piece of dough, retained from a former baking, which had fermented and turned acid. This was then either dissolved in water in the kneading-trough before the flour was added, or was 'hid' in the flour (Mt. 13:33) and kneaded along with it. The *bread thus made was known as 'leavened', as distinct from 'unleavened' bread (Ex. 12:15, *etc*.). There is no clear trace of the use of other sorts of leaven, although it has often been suggested that the Jews used also the lees of wine as yeast.

b. In law and ritual

The earliest Mosaic legislation (Ex. 23:18; 34:25) prohibited the use of leaven during the *Passover and the 'feast of unleavened bread' (Gk. *azymos*) (Ex. 23:15; Mt. 26:17, *etc*.). This was to remind the Israelites of their hurried departure from Egypt, when without waiting to bake leavened bread they carried dough and kneading-troughs with them, baking as they wandered (Ex. 12:34ff.; Dt. 16:3, *etc.*), much as the bedouin still do.

The prohibition on leaven, as that on honey (Lv. 2:11), was possibly made because fermentation implied disintegration and corruption, and to the Hebrew anything in a decayed state suggested uncleanness. Rabbinical writers often used leaven as a symbol of evil and of man's hereditary corruption (*cf.* also Ex. 12:8, 15–20). Plutarch echoes this ancient view when he describes leaven as 'itself the offspring of corruption, and corrupting the mass of dough with which it is mixed'. *fermentum* is used in Persius (*Sat.* 1. 24) for 'corruption'.

Doubtless for this reason it was excluded also from the offerings placed upon the altar of Yahweh, only cakes made from flour without leaven (*maṣṣôṯ*, Lv. 10:12) being allowed. (*SHOWBREAD.)

Two exceptions to this rule should, however, be noted (Lv. 7:13; *cf.* Am. 4:5). 'Leavened bread' was an accompaniment of the thank-offering, and leavened loaves were used also in the wave-offering—*i.e.* at the Feast of Pentecost.

c. In religious teaching

The figurative uses of leaven in the NT to a large extent reflect the former view of it as 'corrupt and corrupting'. Jesus utters warnings against the leaven of the Pharisees, Sadducees and Herodians (Mt. 16:6; Mk. 8:15): the Pharisees' hypocrisy and preoccupation with outward show (Mt. 23:14, 16; Lk. 12:1); the Sadducees' scepticism and culpable ignorance (Mt. 22:23, 29); the Herodians' malice and political guile (Mt. 22:16–21; Mk. 3:6).

The two Pauline passages in which the word occurs support this view (1 Cor. 5:6ff.; Gal. 5:9), with the former going on to contrast 'the leaven of malice and evil' with 'the unleavened bread of sincerity and truth', remembering the new significance of the old feast: that 'Christ, our paschal lamb, has been sacrificed'.

No such meaning attaches, however, to Jesus' brief but profoundly significant parable which (following that of the slow-growing mustard seed) compares the kingdom of God with 'leaven which a woman took and hid in three measures of flour, till it was all leavened' (Mt. 13:33; Lk. 13:21), clearly an allusion to 'the hidden, silent, mysterious, but all-pervading and transforming action of the leaven in the . . . flour' (*ISBE*, 3, p. 1862).

BIBLIOGRAPHY. *ISBE*; J. Lightfoot, *Horae Hebraicae*, 1659, 2, pp. 232–233; O. T. Allis, 'The Parable of the Leaven', *EQ* 19, 1947, pp. 254–273; R. S. Wallace, *Many Things in Parables*, 1955, pp. 22–25; H. Windisch, *TDNT* 2, pp. 902–906; G. T. D. Angel, *NIDNTT* 2, pp. 461–463. J.D.D.

LEBANON. A mountain range in Syria. The name is also more loosely applied to the adjoining regions (Jos. 13:5), and is also that of a modern republic.

I. Name

Heb. *lᵉḇānôn* is derived from the root *lbn*, 'white'. The range owes this name to two factors: the white limestone of the high ridge of Lebanon and especially the glittering snows that cap its peaks for 6 months of the year; *cf.* Je. 18:14. Lebanon is attested in ancient records from at least the 18th century BC onwards; see on history, below. The Assyrians called it *Lab'an*, then *Labnanu*; the Hittites, *Niblani*; the Egyptians, *rmnn* or *rbrn*; and the Canaanites themselves, *e.g.* at Ugarit, *Lbnn* just as in Hebrew.

II. Topography

The S end of the Lebanon range is a direct continuation of the hills of N Galilee, and is divided from them only by the deep E–W gorge of the lower reaches of the Litani river, which enters the sea a few km N of Tyre. The Lebanon range is a ridge almost 160 km long, following the SW to NE trend of the Phoenician coast from behind Sidon N to the E–W valley of the Nahr el-Kebir river (the river Eleutherus of antiquity), which divides Lebanon from the next N–S mountain range extending still farther N (Nuseiri or Ansariya Mts).

This ridge is marked by a series of peaks. From S to N, the principal ones are Gebel Rihan, Tomat and Gebel Niha (from over 1,630 m high to nearly 1,900 m) behind Sidon; Gebel Baruk, Gebel Kuneiyiseh and Gebel Sunnin (*c.* 2,200 m, 2,100 m and 2,600 m high respectively) behind Beirut; Qurnet es-Sauda, the highest at about 3,000 m, ESE of Tripoli; N is Qurnet Aruba, *c.* 2,230 m high. These high mountains and the coastal strip have a good rainfall, but in the 'rain-shadow' area Damascus and the N half of the Biqā' plain have less than 25 cm a year and must depend on stream water.

The W flanks of this range sweep right down to the Mediterranean, leaving only a narrow coastal plain for the Canaanite/Phoenician cities, and sometimes reach the sea, roads having had to be cut by man round such headlands. Typical of these is the headland of the Nahr el-Kelb just N of Beirut. The E flanks of Lebanon descend into the Biqā'. This plain, or broad vale, is highest in the vicinity of Baalbek, and it is the 'valley (*biq'aṯ*) of Lebanon' of Jos. 11:17. It descends N with the Orontes and S with the Litani and headwater streams of the Jordan. It is the classical *Coelesyria ('Hollow Syria') and is bounded along its E side by the corresponding mountain range of Anti-Lebanon. This latter range also runs from SW to NE and is broken in two by the plateau from which the Barada river descends E to water the incredibly rich oasis of Damascus. The highest peak is Mt Hermon (over 2,800 m) in the S half of the range. The structure of the whole region is clearly expressed in the diagram of D. Baly, *Geography of the Bible*, 1957, p. 11, fig. 3. For routes connecting the Biqā', AntiLebanon and Damascus, see *ibid.*, pp. 110–111.

Mt Hermon in Anti-Lebanon was called Sirion by the Sidonians (*i.e.* Phoenicians), and Senir by the Amorites (Dt. 3:9). Both names are independently attested in antiquity. Senir is mentioned as Saniru by Shalmaneser III of Assyria in 841 BC (*ANET*, p. 280b; *DOTT*, p. 48). Besides a Hittite mention of Sirion as Sariyana about 1320 BC (*ANET*, p. 205a), the use of the name Sirion for Hermon by the Canaanites/Phoenicians is confirmed by the Ugaritic texts of the 14th/13th centuries BC that picture Lebanon and Sirion as yielding timber for Baal's temple (*ANET*, p. 134a, § vi). Hermon is often thought to be the 'many-peaked mountain, mountain of Bashan' in Ps. 68:15; but Baly (*op. cit.*, pp. 194, 220, 222) suggests that it could equally well be the impressive peaks of the Gebel Druze. (*BASHAN, *HERMON, *SENIR, *SIRION.)

The biblical writers sometimes define the promised land in general terms as extending 'from the wilderness and Lebanon and from the River . . . Euphrates to the western sea' (Dt. 11:24; Jos. 1:4), *i.e.* within these S–N and E–W limits. For the Phoenician coastal cities, the Lebanon mountain ridge formed a natural barrier to invaders from inland. The Assyrian king Shamshi-Adad I reached Lab'an in the 18th century BC (*ANET*, p. 274b) and the Hittite emperor Suppiluliuma made it his SW boundary in the 14th century BC (Mt Niblani, *ANET*, p. 318b), without their disturbing the coastal cities to any extent.

III. Resources

Lebanon was above all famous for its former dense forest cover. The ample November and March rainfall and limestone ridges gave rise to many springs and streams flowing down to E and W (Ct. 4:15; Je. 18:14). The coastland, Biqā', and lower mountain-slopes support garden-cultivation, olive-groves, vineyards, fruit-orchards (mulberries, figs, apples, apricots, walnuts) and small cornfields (Rawlinson, *Phoenicia*, p. 17). Higher still rises the forest-cover of myrtles and conifers, culminating in the groves of mighty cedars, of which, alas, only one or two isolated groves survive (because of excessive deforestation), the main one being at Bsharreh SE of Tripoli (picture in L. H. Grollenberg, *Shorter Atlas of the Bible*, 1959, p. 13). The fertility and fruitfulness of the Lebanon region is reflected in scriptures such as Ps. 72:16; Ct. 4:11; Ho. 14:5–7, as well as in early inscriptions (Tuthmosis III, 5th and 7th campaigns, 15th century BC, *ANET*, p. 239a, b). Wild beasts also lurked there (*e.g.* 2 Ki. 14:9; Ct. 4:8).

The mighty cedars were apt symbols of majesty and strength in biblical imagery; *cf.* Jdg. 9:15; 1 Ki. 4:33; 2 Ki. 14:9 (= 2 Ch. 25:18); Pss. 92:12; 104:16; Ct. 5:15; Is. 35:2; 60:13. They were also symbols of earthly pride subject to divine wrath; *cf.* Ps. 29:5–6; Is. 2:13; 10:34; Je. 22:6; Ezk. 31:3–14; Zc. 11:1–2. These forests afforded a refuge (Je. 22:23). But above all, Lebanon's cedars and conifers (firs, cypresses, *etc.*) furnished the finest building timber in the ancient East, sought by the rulers of Egypt, Mesopotamia and Syria-Palestine alike. The most celebrated of such deliveries of timber were those sent to Solomon by Hiram I of Tyre for the Temple at Jerusalem (1 Ki. 5:6, 9, 14 (= 2 Ch. 2:8, 16); 7:2; 10:17, 21 (= 2 Ch. 9:20)). For the price in foodstuffs paid by Solomon for his timber, *etc.*, see *FOOD (Solomon's palace food-supplies). The firs of Lebanon and Anti-Lebanon (Sirion) provided ships for Tyre (Ezk. 27:5) and sacred barges for Egypt (*ANET*, pp. 25b, 27a; *c.* 1090 BC), as well as furniture (Ct. 3:9). Wood for the second Jerusalem Temple was also cut in Lebanon (Ezr. 3:7).

IV. History

The history of Lebanon is essentially that of the Phoenician cities on its littoral and the story of the exploitation of its splendid timber. From S to N, the Canaanite/Phoenician cities of Tyre, Ahlab, Zarephath, Sidon, Beirut, Byblos (Gebal, modern Jebail) and Simyra (N of Tripoli) all had the wealth of the Lebanon as their hinterland besides their maritime trade. For their detailed histories (except Beirut and Simyra), see separate articles; see also *CANAAN and *PHOENICIA.

The Lebanon timber-trade goes back to the earliest times. The 4th Dynasty pharaoh Snofru fetched forty shiploads of cedars as early as *c.* 2600 BC (*ANET*, p. 227a), and various of his successors followed suit in later centuries. Byblos in particular became virtually an Egyptian dependency and its princes thoroughly assimilated to Egyptian culture, even writing their Semitic names in hieroglyphs (*cf. ANET*, p. 229a). In exchange for timber, they received handsome gold jewellery from the 12th Dynasty pharaohs (*c.* 1900–1800 BC).

When the New Kingdom pharaohs conquered Syria they exacted a regular annual tribute of 'genuine cedar of Lebanon' (*ANET*, p. 240b: Tuthmosis III, *c.* 1460 BC), and a relief of Sethos I (*c.* 1300 BC) actually depicts the Syrian princes hewing down the timbers of Lebanon for the pharaoh (*ANEP*, p. 110, fig. 331, or Grollenberg, *Shorter Atlas of the Bible*, p. 14; *cf. ANET*, p. 254, § c, end). In later days (20th Dynasty) the pharaohs had to pay handsomely for such timber (*cf.* Solomon), as Wenamun, envoy of Rameses XI, found to his cost (*ANET*, p. 27a).

From Canaan itself in the 2nd millennium BC, the Ugaritic epics about Baal and Anath and Aqhat allude to 'Lebanon and its trees; Sirion, its choice cedars' providing timber for the house (*i.e.* temple) of Baal (*ANET*, p. 134a, § vi; C. H. Gordon, *Ugaritic Literature*, 1949, p. 34), and furnishing material for a bow (*ANET*, p. 151b, § vi; Gordon, *op. cit.*, p. 90).

The Assyrians, too, exacted a tribute of timber from Lebanon for temple-building—so Tiglath-pileser I, *c.* 1100 BC (*ANET*, p. 275a) and Esarhaddon about 675 BC (*ANET*, p. 291b)—but also often drew upon the Amanus forests farther N (*ANET*, pp. 276b, 278a); *cf.* here, 2 Ki. 19:23; Is. 37:24. Nebuchadrezzar followed their example (*ANET*, p. 307; *DOTT*, p. 87). Habakkuk (2:17) refers to Babylonian despoliation of Lebanon, which was also foreseen by Isaiah (14:8).

BIBLIOGRAPHY. P. K. Hitti, *History of Syria with Lebanon and Palestine*, 1951; *Lebanon in History*[2], 1962; J. P. Brown, *The Lebanon and Phoenicia*, 1, 1969 (on ancient sources); Kamal Salibi, *A House of Many Mansions*, 1989.

K.A.K.
A.K.C.

LEB-KAMAI. An artificial word (Je. 51:1, RV), formed by the device known as Athbash (explained under *SHESHACH). The Heb. consonants *l-b-q-m-y* really represent *k-ś-d-y-m*, *i.e. kaśdîm*, 'Chaldeans'; *cf.* RSVmg. The vowels added by the Massoretes give the word a quasi-meaning, 'the heart of those that rise up against me' (*cf.* RVmg.). The verse mentions Babylon openly, so the device is here word-play rather than cipher. NEB with some scholars prefers to emend the text.

D.F.P.

LEES (Heb. *šᵉmārîm*, 'preserves', Is. 25:6; Je. 48:11; Zp. 1:12). The dregs at the bottom of wine-jars. See *WINE AND STRONG DRINK, and an excellent comprehensive article under 'Shemarim' in Kitto, *A Cyclopaedia of Biblical Literature*. The expression is used only figuratively in the OT.

J.D.D.

LEG. 1. Heb. *kᵉrā'ayim* occurs chiefly in ritual passages, *e.g.* Ex. 12:9; 29:17; Lv. 1:9, 13; 4:11, *etc.* In

Lv. 11:21 it describes the bending hind-legs of locusts permitted for food, and provides an illustration of judgment in Am. 3:12.

2. *regel* normally means foot but is used of Goliath's legs in 1 Sa. 17:6.

3. *šôq* means the upper leg, and is synonymous with 'thigh'. It is used of men in Dt. 28:35; Ps. 147:10; Pr. 26:7; Ct. 5:15; Is. 47:2; Dn. 2:33. In Jdg. 15:8 it is translated 'hip'. It is also used with reference to animals. In several ritual passages, *e.g.* Ex. 29:22, 27; Lv. 7:32–34; 8:25–26; Nu. 6:20, *etc.*, it is translated 'thigh' in RSV, while in 1 Sa. 9:24 RSV translates as 'leg'. This was one of the choicest pieces of the animal, normally reserved for priests.

4. *šōḇel* is incorrectly translated 'leg' in AV of Is. 47:2 (RSV 'robe').

5. Gk. *skelos* occurs only in Jn. 19:31ff., when the legs of those crucified with Jesus were broken to hasten death. J.G.G.N.

LEGION. Gk. *legeōn* (from Lat. *legio*), used four times in the NT, was the main division of the Roman army and comprised between 4,000 and 6,000 men. It was divided into ten cohorts and these in turn into six centuries each. Sometimes a small cavalry division (*ala*) of about 120 was attached. In the 1st century AD three or four legions were normally on duty in Syria, but Palestine saw very few legionaries until the beginning of the first Jewish rebellion in AD 66; previously the policing had been done by auxiliary cohorts. The word is used in the NT to suggest a very great number, as in Mt. 26:53 (of angels) and in Mk. 5:9, 15; Lk. 8:30 (of the demons possessing the Gerasene demoniac). R.P.G.

LEHABIM. The third son of Mizraim (Gn. 10:13; 1 Ch. 1:11). The name (Heb. *lᵉhāḇîm*) is unknown apart from these references, but many scholars would equate it with *lûḇîm* of 2 Ch. 12:3, *etc.* (*LUBIM), which is generally identified as referring to the Libyans. In support of this is the LXX reading *Labieim* and the fact that these people, who figure in the ancient Egyp. inscriptions as *rbw*, are not elsewhere mentioned in Gn. 10, unless *lûdîm* (v. 13) is to be read for *lûḇîm*, as some scholars hold (*LUD, LUDIM). The matter therefore remains uncertain. T.C.M.

LEHI (Heb. *lᵉḥî*, *leḥî*, 'jawbone', Jdg. 15:9, 14, 19; 'Ramath-lehi' in Jdg. 15:17). The place in Judah where Samson slew 1,000 men with the jawbone of an ass. The site is unknown, but see F. F. Bruce, in *NBCR*, p. 271. J.D.D.

LEMUEL. King of *Massa, whose mother's instructions concerning good government and the dangers of sensuality and over-indulgence in wine are recorded in Pr. 31:1–9. Modern scholars have not generally accepted the rabbinic tradition, which says that Lemuel and the names in Pr. 30:1 are attributes of Solomon, an attempt to credit Proverbs entirely to Solomon (*cf.* L. Ginzberg, *The Legends of the Jews*, 6, 1946, p. 277). See W. McKane, *Proverbs*, 1970, pp. 407–412. D.A.H.

LEVI. The third son of Jacob and Leah (Gn. 29:34). The name (Heb. *lēwî*) is here linked with the root *lāwâ* (to join), and a play upon this meaning is found in Nu. 18:2, 4.

The only detail of his life known to us, apart from those events common to all Jacob's sons, is his treacherous attack on Shechem in company with Simeon (Gn. 34:25–26). It should in fairness be noted that the natural meaning of Gn. 34:13, 27 is that the two brothers were acting with the connivance of all. The two were specially concerned because Dinah was their full sister. The two lads could carry out the massacre with the help of their father's slaves.

It has almost universally been taken for granted that Gn. 49:5–7 refers to this incident, but this is most doubtful. There is no validity in the versional variation in the last clause of v. 6 represented by AV, 'they digged down a wall'; the Heb. 'they houghed an ox' (RV) is seemingly contradicted by Gn. 34:28. It is better to take the tenses in v. 6 as 'perfects of experience' and render, 'For in their anger they slay men, and in their wantonness they hamstring oxen' (RSV). They are cursed for a life of violence and cruelty in which Shechem was merely an early and outstanding example. Later history was to show that the loyalty of Levi's descendants to Yahweh could turn the curse to a blessing, and their division and scattering in Israel was as his representatives. None the less, the curse seems to have hit Levi very heavily. The total census figure in Nu. 3:22, 28, 34 of males from a month upward is strikingly below all the tribal figures in Nu. 1 of males from 20 years upwards. No indication is given how this happened. Levi seems to have had only three sons, Gershon, Kohath and Merari, all born before he went down with Jacob to Egypt.

Modern critical scholarship has questioned the biblical account of the origin of the tribe of Levi in various ways, but most of them have by now fallen into disfavour. We need mention only the conjecture of Lagarde that the Levites were those Egyptians that 'joined themselves' to the Israelites at the Exodus, and that of Baudissin that they were those 'joined to', *i.e.* escorting, the ark—in other words priestly servants. Much more important is Hommel's linking of *lēwî* with *lawi'a*, meaning 'priest', in Minaean N Arabian inscriptions. The facts and a valuable discussion will be found in G. B. Gray, *Sacrifice in the Old Testament*, pp. 242–245. He points out that the Minaeans *might* have borrowed the term from Israel. In fact, an overwhelming majority of scholars agree that Gn. 49:5–7 is proof positive that Levi must have originated as a secular tribe. The mention of Aaron as 'the Levite' in Ex. 4:14 is difficult, perhaps best explained as a later scribal addition.

For Levi the son of Alphaeus, one of the Twelve (Mk. 2:13), see *MATTHEW. The name also occurs twice in the genealogy of our Lord (Lk. 3:24, 29). H.L.E.

LEVIATHAN is a transliteration of a Heb. word which occurs in only five passages in the OT. It is generally thought to be from a root *lāwâ*, *cf.* Arab. *lawā*, 'bend', 'twist'. Its literal meaning would then be 'wreathed', *i.e.* 'gathering itself in folds'. Some scholars have suggested that it may be a foreign loan-word, possibly of Bab. origin. The context of its use in the OT indicates some form of aquatic monster. In Ps. 104:26 it is clearly of the sea and is generally thought to be the whale, although the dolphin has been suggested. It is used twice symbolically in Is. 27:1, referring to the empires of Assyria (the 'fleeing' serpent is the swift-flowing Tigris) and Babylonia (the 'twisting' serpent is the Euphrates). In Ps. 74:14 it occurs in reference to Pharaoh and the Exodus in parallel with the Heb. *tannîn*, 'sea or river monster'. This word occurs again in Ezk. 29:3–5 symbolically of Pharaoh and the Egyptians, where the description of its scales and jaws makes it clear that the crocodile is intended.

Leviathan is referred to twice in Job. In 3:8 it is generally held to be the dragon which, according to popular ancient mythology, was supposed to cause eclipses by wrapping its coils around the sun. The longest description of Leviathan occupies Jb. 41:1–34, and most scholars agree that here the creature is the crocodile (*ANIMALS). Some have objected that the crocodile would not have been described as unapproachable and that there is no reference in the OT to crocodiles in Palestine. However, the author probably had in mind the crocodile of the Nile, and the description of the creature's invincibility is rhetorical. The only alternative interpretation of any significance regards Leviathan as a mythical monster, perhaps to be identified with the Bab. mother goddess Tiamat (father Apsu) who, in the Creation Epic, even in battle against Marduk 'recites charms and casts spells'. The word is cognate with Ugaritic *ltn*, the seven-headed monster whose description as 'the fleeing serpent, . . . the tortuous serpent' smitten by Baal is so reminiscent of the language of Is. 27:1.

BIBLIOGRAPHY. C. F. Pfeiffer, 'Lotan and Leviathan', *EQ* 32, 1960, pp. 208ff.; J. N. Oswalt, 'The Myth of the Dragon and OT Faith', *EQ* 49, 1977, pp. 163ff.

D.G.S.

LEVITICUS, BOOK OF. The third book of the Pentateuch is referred to in Jewish usage as *way-yiqrā'* ('and he called'), this being the word with which it begins in Hebrew. In the Mishnah the book is variously named *tôraṯ kôhanîm*, 'priests' law', *sēper kôhanîm*, 'priests' book', *tôraṯ haqqorbānîm*, 'law of the offerings'; these names refer to the contents of the book. In the LXX it is called *Leueitikon* or *Leuitikon* (*sc. biblion*), 'the Levitical (book)'. The Latin Vulg. entitles it *Leviticus* (*sc. liber*), which similarly means 'the Levitical (book)'; in some Latin MSS the name appears as *Leviticum*. The Peshitta calls it 'the book of the priests'.

It can be objected to the name Leviticus that the book has much less to do with Levites than with priests. But the priests in question are levitical priests (*cf.* Heb. 7:11, 'the Levitical priesthood'). The name Leviticus indicates clearly enough that the book has to do with the cult; this name may indeed have been chosen because 'Levitical' was understood in the sense of 'cultic' or 'ritual'.

I. Outline of contents

Leviticus consists mainly of laws. The historical framework in which these laws are set is Israel's residence at Sinai. The book may be divided as follows:

a. Laws concerning offerings (1:1–7:38).

b. The tabernacle service put into operation (8:1–10:20).

c. Laws concerning purity and impurity (11:1–15:33).

d. The great Day of Atonement (16:1–34).

e. Various laws (17:1–25:55).

f. Promises and warnings (26:1–46).

g. Appendix: valuation and redemption (27:1–34).

As may be seen from this outline, the contents consist largely of ritual law. At the same time it must be noted that the intention is to continue the narrative of Israel's experiences at Sinai. This is evident from the first words of the book, and from the repeated formula 'And the Lord said to Moses' (1:1; 4:1; 5:14, *et passim*), with which we should compare 'And the Lord spoke to Aaron' (10:8) and 'And the Lord said to Moses and Aaron' (11:1; *cf.* 13:1, *etc.*). The historical setting must not be forgotten. As part of the complete Pentateuch, the book occupies its own place in the Pentateuchal narrative.

At Mt Sinai the nation of Israel is equipped for its task, a task stated in the words 'And you shall be to me a kingdom of priests and a holy nation' (Ex. 19:6). Israel had already had committed to it the Decalogue, the Book of the Covenant and the regulations with regard to the tabernacle. This dwelling-place for the Lord had already been set up in the midst of the camp (Ex. 40). It is possible that the laws concerning the offerings (Lv. 1–7) once existed as a separate unit (*cf.* 7:35–38). But they fit very well into the Pentateuchal context in which they now appear. The history of sacrificial offerings, about which the book of Leviticus provides such important information, and in which Christians ought to take a special interest because we know how perfectly their inmost significance was fulfilled by the obedience of Jesus Christ, begins as early in the Pentateuch as Gn. 4:3–5. There are also other passages in the Pentateuch before the book of Leviticus in which sacrifices and offerings are mentioned. But in Leviticus the Lord regulates the whole sacrificial service and institutes a special form of it as a means of atonement for Israel. Lv. 17:11 states the reason for the ban upon eating blood ('the life of the flesh is in the blood'); the ban has already been imposed in 3:17 and 7:26f., but in neither of these places is the reason for it explicitly stated. It is in the light of 17:11 that the shedding of blood and sprinkling with blood prescribed in chs.1–7 must be viewed. This is an indication of the unity of the book.

Another indication of its unity is the fact that 17:11 prepares us for the transition to the regulations regarding impurity, which come up for detailed treatment in chs. 11–15. Similarly, 10:10 looks forward to the transition to the detailed distinctions between clean and unclean which we have in ch. 11. Viewed in the light of the whole book of Leviticus, the laws concerning purity and impurity point to the necessity laid upon Israel to keep sin at a distance. It is sin which brings about separation between the Lord and his people, so that they have to approach him through the mediation of sacrifice (chs. 1–7) and priesthood (chs. 8–10). Lv. 16:1 follows close on 15:31 and refers back to 10:1f. In 20:25 we have a clear allusion to the law concerning clean and unclean animals in ch. 11; and this verse provides a closer link between the commandments of chs. 18–20 and those of chs. 11–15. This does not support the view of those who accept the existence at one time of a separate Holiness Code, preserved for us in chs. 17–26. In 21:1–22:16 expressions like those of 11:44f.; 19:2; 20:7 are repeated with reference to the priests (*e.g.* 21:8,

'I the Lord, who sanctify you, am holy'). Lv. 25:1 states that the words which follow were revealed to Moses on Mt Sinai, just as is stated of the laws summarized in 7:37f.

In the form in which we now possess Leviticus, it forms a well-knit and coherent whole. The historical portion is larger than one might think at first sight (*cf.* 10:1–7; 24:10–23; chs. 8–10 and the formula 'And the Lord said to Moses').

Attention is also paid to marriage and chastity, the sanctification of daily life, and Israel's attitude to the commandments of her God (*cf.* 18:3–5, 30; 19:1–3, 18, 37; 20:26; 22:31–33; 26, *etc.*).

In view of the character of its contents throughout, we can call Leviticus 'the book of the holiness of Yahweh', whose fundamental requirement is 'You shall be holy to me: for I the Lord am holy' (20:26).

II. Authorship and composition

The author of Leviticus is not named in the book. Yahweh does indeed speak repeatedly to Moses, to Moses and Aaron, or to Aaron; but no command is given to make a written record of what he says. We owe the contents of the book to divine revelation given at Sinai in the time of Moses (*cf.* 7:37f.; 26:46; 27:34); but that does not settle the question of the authorship of Leviticus. Moses is not named as the author of any single part of the book, as he is named with regard to certain sections of Exodus (*cf.* Ex. 17:14; 24:4; 34:27). It may be that a later writer set in order the Mosaic material of which Leviticus consists. It may equally well be that Moses himself set it in order in the form which has been handed down to us.

The question of authorship is bound up with the whole problem of the composition of the Pentateuch. Leviticus is commonly assigned to P (the Priestly Code). The objections to this documentary hypothesis in general are equally valid as regards their application to Leviticus. The name 'Holiness Code', given to Lv. 17–26, is due to August Klostermann, who in 1877 wrote for the *Zeitschrift für lutherische Theologie* an article entitled 'Ezechiel und das Heiligkeitsgesetz' ('Ezekiel and the Law of Holiness'), which was reprinted in his book *Der Pentateuch: Beiträge zu seinem Verständnis und seiner Entstehungsgeschichte* (*The Pentateuch: Contributions to its understanding and the history of its composition*), 1893, pp. 368–418. The name 'Holiness Code' came into wide vogue; many found it especially apt because of the explicit and repeated emphasis on holiness and sanctification in 19:2; 20:7–8, 26; 21:6–8, 15, 23; 22:9, 16, 32. It is not possible to debate the whole question here; reference should be made to the case for the separate existence of H, based upon distinctive features of style and language, as presented, *e.g.*, in S. R. Driver, *LOT*, pp. 47ff. A close relationship is pointed out between H and Ezekiel; indeed, some have seen in Ezekiel himself the author or redactor of H, while others take the view that Ezekiel was acquainted with H. But the majority opinion is that H is earlier than Ezekiel.

None of the arguments for the view that Lv. 17–26 should be regarded as a separate law-code seems to be conclusive. We must not forget that here as elsewhere the investigator of the OT is greatly influenced by the attitude which he adopts to Holy Scripture as the Word of God. For example, the argument that Lv. 26 must be dated in the time of the Exile, because this exile is foretold in that chapter, is far from doing justice to divine revelation. The absence of a special superscription at the head of Lv. 17 is best explained by the view that here the book of Leviticus continues quite ordinarily.

III. Significance

Leviticus is a book of great significance from many points of view.

First of all, it provides us with a background to all the other books of the Bible. If we wish to understand references to sacrificial offerings and ceremonies of purification, or institutions such as the sabbatical year or the year of jubilee, it is this book that we must consult.

In the second place, it is of interest from a general religious viewpoint. Thanks especially to archaeological excavation, we can compare the institutions dealt with in Leviticus with those of other people, *e.g.* the Phoenicians, Canaanites, Egyptians, Assyrians, Babylonians and Hittites.

In the third place, orthodox Jews have to this day found their binding regulations—*e.g.* with regard to food—in this book. Hoffmann, a Jewish exegete of Leviticus, points out that other confessions which draw upon the OT chiefly select Genesis as the subject of their study, while Jews pay special attention to Leviticus.

Fourthly, Leviticus proclaims to us who are Christians the way in which the God of Israel combats sin in Israel. He combats it by means of his institutions of sacrifice and purification—social sin by means of the sabbatical year and year of jubilee, sexual sins by means of the laws of chastity—and also by means of his promises and warnings. And in this combating of sin the book of Leviticus presents to us Christ as the means of atonement, the means of purification, the great Priest, Prophet and Teacher, the King who rules us through his ordinances. That is the abiding significance of Leviticus. It is the book of sanctification, of the consecration of life (the burnt-offering stands in the forefront of the book), the book of the avoidance and atonement of sin, the combating and removal of sin among the people of the Lord. The Day of Atonement occupies a central place in it (Lv. 16); the ceremony of the two goats prescribed for that day reminds us that 'as far as the east is from the west, so far does he remove our transgressions from us' (Ps. 103:12). (*Law.)

BIBLIOGRAPHY. A. A. Bonar, *Commentary on Leviticus*[4], 1861, reprinted 1959; S. R. Driver and H. A. White, *The Book of Leviticus*, 1898; A. T. Chapman and A. W. Streane, *The Book of Leviticus, CBSC*, 1914; W. H. Gispen, *Het Boek Leviticus*, 1950; N. Micklem, *Leviticus, IB*, 2, 1955; H. Cazelles, *Le Lévitique, Bible de Jérusalem*, 2, 1958; L. G. Vink, *Léviticus*, 1962; J. L. Mays, *LBC*, 1963; K. Elliger, *HAT*, 1966; N. H. Snaith, *NCB*, 1967; M. Noth, *Leviticus*, E.T. 1968; W. Kornfeld, *Das Buch Leviticus*, 1972; B. Maarsingh, *Leviticus*, 1974; A. Ibáñez Arana, *El Levitico*, 1975; G. J. Wenham, *Leviticus*, 1978; R. K. Harrison, *Leviticus, TOTC*, 1980; J. Milgram, *Leviticus 1–16*, 1991; J. E. Hartley, *Leviticus*, 1992.

W.H.G.

LIBERTY. The biblical idea of liberty (freedom) has as its background the thought of imprisonment or slavery. Rulers would imprison those whom they regarded as wrongdoers (Gn. 39:20); a conquered nation might be enslaved by its conqueror, or a prisoner of war by his captor, or an individual might, like Joseph, be sold into slavery. When the Bible speaks of liberty, a prior bondage or incarceration is always implied. Liberty means the happy state of having been released from servitude for a life of enjoyment and satisfaction that was not possible before. The idea of liberty appears in Scripture in its ordinary secular application (*e.g.* Ps. 105:20; Acts 26:32); but it also receives a significant theological development. This sprang from Israel's realization that such freedom from subjugation by foreigners as she enjoyed was God's gift to her. In the NT liberty becomes an important theological concept for describing salvation.

I. Israel's liberty

At the Exodus God set Israel free from bondage in Egypt, in order that henceforth the nation might serve him as his covenant people (Ex. 19:3ff.; 20:1ff.; Lv. 25:55; *cf.* Is. 43:21). He brought them into the 'land flowing with milk and honey' (Ex. 3:8; *cf.* Nu. 14:7ff.; Dt. 8:7ff.), settled them there, and undertook to maintain them in political independence and economic prosperity as long as they eschewed idolatry and kept his laws (Dt. 28:1–14). This meant that Israel's freedom would not depend upon her own efforts in either the military or the political realm, but on the quality of her obedience to God. Her freedom was a supernatural blessing, Yahweh's gracious gift to his own covenant people; unmerited and, apart from him, unattainable in the first instance, and now maintained only through his continued favour. Disobedience, whether in the form of religious impiety or social injustice, would result in the loss of freedom. God would judge his people by national disaster and enslavement (Dt. 28:25, 47ff.; *cf.* Jdg. 2:14ff.; 3:7ff., 12ff.; 4:1ff.; 6:1ff.); he would raise up hostile powers against them, and would ultimately cause them to be deported into a land where no tokens of his favour could be expected (Dt. 28:64ff.; Am. 5; 2 Ki. 17:6–23; *cf.* Ps. 137:1–4).

The structure of the theological idea of liberty is here fully evident. Liberty, as the OT conceives it, means, on the one hand, deliverance from created forces that would keep men from serving and enjoying their Creator, and, on the other hand, the positive happiness of living in fellowship with God under his covenant in the place where he is pleased to manifest himself and to bless. Liberty is *from* slavery to powers that oppose God *for* the fulfilment of his claims upon one's life. Liberty is not man's own achievement, but a free gift of grace, something which apart from God's action man does not possess at all. In its continuance, liberty is a covenant blessing, something which God has promised to maintain as long as his people are faithful. Liberty does not mean independence of God; it is precisely in God's service that man finds his perfect freedom. Man can enjoy release from bondage to the created only through bondage to his Creator. Thus, the way that God sets men free from their captors and enemies is to make them his own slaves. He frees them by bringing them to himself (Ex. 19:4).

The Isaianic prophecies of the release from captivity and the restoration of Jerusalem gave added religious content to the idea of liberty by stressing that these events would herald a new and unprecedented experience of joyful and satisfying fellowship with Israel's gracious God (Is. 35:3–10; 43:14–44:5; 45:14–17; 49:8–50:3; 51:17–52:12; 54; 61:1ff., *etc.*; *cf.* Ezk. 36:16–36; 37:15–28).

Since all members of the liberated nation were, as such, God's servants (Lv. 25:42, 55), Israelites who through pressure of poverty sold themselves into household service were not to be treated like foreign slaves, as mere property, in their master's hereditary possession (Lv. 25:44ff.). Every 7th year they were to be released (unless they had voluntarily chosen to make their service permanent) in memory of God's release of Israel from Egyptian bondage (Dt. 15:12ff.). Every 50th year, in addition to a release of Israelite servants, alienated land was also to revert to its hereditary owner (Lv. 25:10). Jeremiah denounced the people because, having thus 'proclaimed liberty' for Hebrew servants, they went back on it (Je. 34:8–17).

II. The Christian's liberty

The full development of the idea of liberty appears in the Gospels and Pauline Epistles, where the enemies from whom God through Christ liberates his people are revealed to be sin, Satan, the law and death.

Christ's public ministry was one of liberation. He opened it by announcing himself as the fulfilment of Is. 61:1: '... he has anointed me ... to proclaim release to the captives' (Lk. 4:16ff.). Ignoring Zealot hankerings after a national liberation from Rome, Christ declared that he had come to set Israelites free from the state of slavery to sin and Satan in which he found them (Jn. 8:34–36, 41–44). He had come, he said, to overthrow 'the prince of this world', the 'strong man', and to release his prisoners (Jn. 12:31f.; Mk. 3:27; Lk. 10:17f.). Exorcisms (Mk. 3:22ff.) and healings (Lk. 13:16) were part of this work of dispossession. Christ appealed to these (Lk. 11:20; *cf.* Mt. 12:28) as proof positive of the coming among men of the *kingdom of God (*i.e.* the promised eschatological state in which men effectively receive God's forgiveness and salvation and are effectively made subject to his will).

Paul makes much of the thought that Christ liberates believers, here and now, from destructive influences to which they were previously in bondage: from sin, the tyrannical overlord whose wages for services rendered is death (Rom. 6:18–23); from the law as a system of salvation, which stirred sin up and gave it its strength (Gal. 4:21ff.; 5:1; Rom. 6:14; 7:5–13; 8:2; 1 Cor. 15:56); from the demonic 'power of darkness' (Col. 1:13); from polytheistic superstition (1 Cor. 10:29; Gal. 4:8); and from the burden of Jewish ceremonialism (Gal. 2:4). To all this, Paul affirms, freedom from the remaining partial bondages to indwelling sin (Rom. 7:14, 23), and from physical corruption and death, will in due course be added (Rom. 8:18–21).

This freedom, in all its aspects, is the gift of Christ, who by death bought his people out of bondage (1 Cor. 6:20; 7:22f.). (There may be an allusion here to the legal fiction by which Greek deities 'bought' slaves for their manumission.) Present freedom from the law, sin and death is conveyed to believers by the Spirit, who unites them to Christ through faith (Rom. 8:2; 2 Cor. 3:17). Liberation brings with it adoption (Gal. 4:5); those set free from guilt become sons of God, and receive the Spirit of Christ as a Spirit of adoption, assuring them that they are in truth God's sons and heirs (Gal. 4:6f.; Rom. 8:15f.).

Man's response to the divine gift of liberty (*eleutheria*), and indeed the very means of his receiving it, is a free acceptance of bondservice (*douleia*) to

God (Rom. 6:17–22), to Christ (1 Cor. 7:22), to righteousness (Rom. 6:18), and to all men for the sake of the gospel (1 Cor. 9:19–23) and of the saviour (2 Cor. 4:5). Christian liberty is neither an abolishing of responsibility nor a sanctioning of licence. The Christian is no longer 'under law' (Rom. 6:14) for salvation, but he is not therefore 'without law toward God' (1 Cor. 9:21). The divine law, as interpreted and exemplified by Christ himself, remains a standard expressing Christ's will for his own freed bondservants (1 Cor. 7:22). Christians are thus 'under the law of Christ' (1 Cor. 9:21). The 'law of Christ' (Gal. 6:2)—James' 'law of liberty' (Jas. 1:25; 2:12)—is the law of love (Gal. 5:13f.; *cf.* Mk. 12:28ff.; Jn. 13:34), the principle of voluntary and unstinting self-sacrifice for the good of men (1 Cor. 9:1–23; 10:23–33) and the glory of God (1 Cor. 10:31). This life of love is the response of gratitude which the liberating gospel both requires and evokes. Christian liberty is precisely freedom for love and service to God and men, and it is therefore abused when it is made an excuse for unloving licence (Gal. 5:13; *cf.* 1 Pet. 2:16; 2 Pet. 2:19), or irresponsible inconsiderateness (1 Cor. 8:9–12).

Paul wrote the Epistle to the *Galatians to counter the threat to Christian liberty which Judaizing theology presented. The basic issue, as he saw it, was the sufficiency of Christ for salvation apart from works of law. The Judaizers held that Gentiles who had put faith in Christ still needed circumcision for salvation. Paul argued that if this were so, then by parity of reasoning they would need to keep the whole Mosaic law for salvation; but this would be seeking justification by the law, and such a quest would mean a falling away from grace and from Christ (Gal. 5:2–4). The Christian, Jew or Gentile, Paul maintained, is free from all need to perform works of law for acceptance, for as a believer in Christ he is fully accepted already (Gal. 3:28f.), as the gift of the Spirit to him proves (Gal. 3:2f., 14; 4:6; 5:18). There is no reason why a Gentile convert should burden himself with Mosaic ceremonies (circumcision, the festal calendar [Gal. 4:10], *etc.*), which in any case belonged to the pre-Christian era. The redeeming work of Christ has freed him completely from the need to seek salvation through law (Gal. 3:13; 4:5; 5:1). His task now is, first, to guard his God-given liberty against any who would tell him that faith in Christ alone is not enough to save him (Gal. 5:1) and, second, to put his liberty to the best use by letting the Spirit lead him into responsible fulfilment of the law of love (Gal. 5:13ff.).

Paul makes a similar point elsewhere. The Christian is free from the need to work for his salvation, and he is bound neither by Jewish ceremonialism nor by pagan superstition and taboos. There is a large realm of things indifferent in which 'all things are lawful for me' (1 Cor. 6:12; 10:23). In this realm the Christian must use his liberty responsibly, with an eye to what is expedient and edifying and with a tender regard for the weaker brother's conscience (*cf.* 1 Cor. 8–10; Rom. 14:1–15:7).

III. 'Free will'

The historic debate as to whether fallen men have 'free will' has only an indirect connection with the biblical concept of freedom. Distinctions must be made to indicate the issues involved.

1. If the phrase 'free will' be taken morally and psychologically, as meaning the power of unconstrained, spontaneous, voluntary, and therefore responsible, choice, the Bible everywhere assumes that all men, as such, possess it, unregenerate and regenerate alike.

2. If the phrase be taken metaphysically, as implying that men's future actions are indeterminate and therefore in principle unpredictable, the Bible seems neither to assert nor to deny an indeterminacy of future action relative to the agent's own moral or physical constitution, but it does seem to imply that no future event is indeterminate relative to God, for he foreknows and in some sense fore-ordains all things. (*PROVIDENCE, *PREDESTINATION.)

3. If the phrase be taken theologically, as denoting a natural ability on the part of unregenerate man to perform acts that are good without qualification in God's sight, or to respond to the gospel invitation, such passages as Rom. 8:5–8; Eph. 2:1–10; Jn. 6:44 seem to indicate that no man is free for obedience and faith till he is freed from sin's dominion by prevenient grace. All his voluntary choices are in one way or another acts of serving *sin till grace breaks sin's power and moves him to obey the gospel. (*Cf.* Rom. 6:17–22; *REGENERATION.)

BIBLIOGRAPHY. *BAGD*; *MM*; H. Schlier, *TDNT* 2, pp. 487–502; J. Blunck, *NIDNTT* 1, pp. 715–720; *LAE*, pp. 326ff.; Calvin, *Institutio*, 3. 19. J.I.P.

LIBNAH (Heb. *liḇnâh*). **1.** An important town in the Shephelah, taken by Joshua and assigned to the priests (Jos. 10:29f.; 15:42; 21:13); revolted from Jehoram (2 Ki. 8:22); besieged by Sennacherib (2 Ki. 19:8, 35); the birthplace of Josiah's wife Hamutal. The identification by Bliss and Macalister with Tell es-Safi (the Crusader Blanchegarde), on a limestone outlier 7 km W of Azekah, is now widely contested; Sennacherib would hardly have passed it to attack Lachish first, and Jos. 15:42 suggests a site further SE. Alternatives are scarce. Tell Bornat (W. F. Albright, *BASOR* 15, p. 19) is too small; Tell Judeideh (Tel Goded), N of the Beit Guvrin basin, is attractive but unproved. See G. E. Wright, *BA* 34, 1971, pp. 81–85; A. F. Rainey, *Tel Aviv* 7, 1980, pp. 195, 198.

2. An unidentified camping-place in the desert (Nu. 33:20; perhaps also Dt. 1:1). J.P.U.L.

LIBNI. A son of Gershon mentioned in Ex. 6:17; Nu. 3:18; 1 Ch. 6:17, 20. In 1 Ch. 6:29 Libni is listed as a son of Merari. The patronymic 'Libnites' is mentioned in Nu. 3:21; 26:58. Libni is 'Ladan' in 1 Ch. 23:7f.; 26:21. R.A.H.G.

LIBYA (LUBIM, AV). First occurs as *Rbw* (= Libu) in Egyp. texts of 13th–12th centuries BC, as a hostile Libyan tribe (Sir A. H. Gardiner, *Ancient Egyptian Onomastica*, 1, 1947, pp. 121*–122*). Libu as *lûḇîm* became a Heb. term for Libya, Libyans, and as *libys* became the general Gk. term 'Libyan' for the land and people W of Egypt. Thus the Heb. and Gk. terms cover other Libyans besides the tribe *Rbw*. During the 12th–8th centuries BC, Libyans entered Egypt as raiders, settlers or soldiers in Egypt's armies. Hence the prominence of Lubim in the forces of *Shishak (2 Ch. 12:3); of *Zerah (2 Ch. 14:9 with 16:8); and among the troops of the Ethiopian pharaohs that failed to protect No-Amon (Thebes) from Assyr. devastation (Na. 3:9). *Lubbîm*, Dn. 11:43, may be the same word. (*LEHABIM; *PUT.) K.A.K.

LIE, LYING (Heb. *šeqer*, 'falsehood', 'deception'; *kāzāḇ*, 'lie' or 'deceptive' thing'; Gk. *pseudos* and cognates). Essentially, a lie is a statement of what is known to be false with intent to deceive (Jdg. 16:10, 13). Biblical writers severely condemn aggravated forms of lying, *e.g.* those which perpetrate a fraud (Lv. 6:2–3) or secure wrongful condemnation (Dt. 19:15), and the testimony of false prophets (Je. 14:14). Lies may be expressed in words (Pr. 6:19), a way of life (Ps. 62:9), error (2 Thes. 2:11), or a false form of religion (Rom. 1:25). The prophets regarded lying as a specific expression of the principle of evil (Ho. 12:1). Lying is prohibited as repugnant to the moral conscience of Israel (Pr. 19:22), because of its anti-social effects (Pr. 26:28), and, above all, as incompatible with the divine nature (Nu. 23:19). Jesus declares that Satan is the father of lies (Jn. 8:44). All falsehood is forbidden in the Christian community (Col. 3:9).

Lying is characterized in various ways, *e.g.* Cain's evasive answer (Gn. 4:9), Jacob's deliberate falsehood (Gn. 27:19), Gehazi's misrepresentation of his master (2 Ki. 5:21–27), and the deception practised by Ananias and Sapphira (Acts 5:1–10). Lying is the sin of Antichrist (1 Jn. 2:22) and all habitual liars forfeit eternal salvation (Rev. 21:27).

1 Sa. 16:2 does not justify the expedient lie. God merely suggested an ostensible reason for Samuel's visit to Bethlehem, and the prophet was under no obligation to divulge his real purpose. Again, 1 Ki. 22:20–23 implies that God permitted a subterfuge that his righteous judgment should be enacted upon Ahab. In such passages as Gn. 12:10–20 it is clear that deception is not condoned nor recorded as an example to follow. (*TRUTH.)

BIBLIOGRAPHY. John Murray, *Principles of Conduct*, 1957, ch. 6; *HDB*, 3; H. Conzelmann, *TDNT* 9, pp. 594–603; U. Becker, H.-G. Link, *NIDNTT* 2, pp. 467–474. A.F.

LIFE.

I. In the Old Testament

a. Terms and concepts

1. Inherent in 'life' (Heb. *ḥayyîm*) is the idea of activity. Life is 'that which moves' (Gn. 7:21f.; Ps. 69:34; *cf.* Acts 17:28) in contrast to the relaxed, dormant or inert state of non-life (*cf.* Rom. 7:8; Jas. 2:17, 20). Running water is 'living' (Gn. 26:19), and rapid labour in childbirth indicates the mother's 'aliveness' (Ex. 1:19). The word's frequently plural form emphasizes the intensity of the concept. Life is associated with light, gladness, fullness, order and active being (Ps. 27:1; Jb. 33:25ff.; Pr. 3:16; Gn. 1) and contrasted with the darkness, sorrow, emptiness, chaos and silence which are characteristic of death and inanimate being (Ec. 11:8; Ps. 115:17).

2. Soul (Heb. *nep̄eš*), as 'being' or 'self', is common to man and beast, living and dead (Lv. 21:11; Jb. 12:10; Rev. 8:9; 16:3). But its meaningful state is 'living soul' (*nep̄eš ḥayyâ*, Gn. 2:7) and, therefore, may simply mean 'life'. To die is to breathe out one's soul, and to revive is to have it return (Je. 15:9; 1 Ki. 17:21; *cf.* Acts 20:10); or, seated in the blood, it is 'poured out' at death (Lv. 17:11; La. 2:12; Is. 53:12). While the soul may continue in spilt blood (Rev. 6:9; Gn. 4:10) or, corporately, in one's name or descendants, 'life' and 'self' are so closely parallel that to lose one's life means virtually to lose one's self (Pedersen, pp. 151ff.; Jb. 2:4; Ezk. 18).

3. Similarly, spirit (Heb. *rûaḥ*) or breath (*nešāmâ*), as the principle which distinguishes the living from the dead, often may be rendered life (1 Sa. 30:12; Jb. 27:3f.). To die is to lose one's breath or spirit (Jb. 27:3; Ps. 104:29f.; *cf.* Mt. 27:50); to revive is to 'have it come again' (*cf.* Lk. 8:55; Rev. 11:11; 13:15).

4. Life is given to man as a psychosomatic unity in which 'our own distinctions between physical, intellectual and spiritual life do not exist' (von Allmen, pp. 231f.); and the OT view of man may be described as 'animated body' (Robinson, p. 27). Thus soul may be paralleled with flesh (Ps. 63:1; *cf.* Mt. 6:25; Acts 2:31), life (Jb. 33:28) or spirit (Ps. 77:2f.; *cf.* Lk. 1:46f.), and all terms viewed as the self or 'I'. It is the 'I' which lives—and which dies (*cf.* Gn. 7:21; Ezk. 18:4).

b. Life unto death

1. What will man give for his life (Jb. 2:4; *cf.* Mk. 8:37)? Man is not only a unified being, he is a being threatened by death—mortal (Jb. 4:17), barred from the tree of life (Gn. 3:24), existing like cut grass or a morning's dew (Jb. 7:9; Pss. 39:4f.; 90:5f.; *cf.* 1 Pet. 1:24; Jas. 4:14). Death is at work in the midst of life, and life, therefore, is a battle against the dissolution of death, an ebb and flow, possessed in greater or less degree. The tired slave rests and is 'ensouled' (Ex. 23:12). Deliverance from sickness or an enemy or sorrow is deliverance from death, and to be sick or troubled is to be in Sheol (Nu. 21:8f.; Jos. 5:8; Ps. 30:2f.; *cf.* Pss. 71:20; 86:13). It is not that these are equated with death, but that anything threatening life is viewed as an invasion of death upon the soul. Thus, Adam and Eve 'died' when they disobeyed (Gn. 2:17); Abimelech, incurring God's displeasure, is a 'dead man' (Gn. 20:3); and Jonah (2:2) in the fish is in Sheol. Standing under threat of death, one may be viewed from that perspective (*cf.* Lk. 9:60).

2. Likewise long life as the gift of Wisdom or God (Pr. 3:16; Dt. 5:16) has implicit in it the idea of the good life. 'I have set before you . . . life and good, death and evil' (Dt. 30:15). 'Long live the king' (1 Sa. 10:24) does not mean merely length of life but a reign of peace, prosperity and victory. The death of the righteous at an old *age and full of years is a blessing in that life has been lived to the full and a progeny blessed by God carries on the name (Gn. 25:8; Nu. 23:10).

3. Nevertheless, the present life is life unto death. 'What man can live and never see death? Who can deliver his soul from the power of Sheol?' (Ps. 89:48). Man is a thing moulded of clay; his breath goes back to God, man dies and returns to dust (Gn. 3:19; Jb. 10:9; Ps. 144:4; Ec. 12:7). One may continue to 'live' in his name or progeny (Ps. 72:17; Is. 66:22), and in a very real way these are viewed as a corporate extension of one's own soul (Pedersen, pp. 254ff.). But personal life ends and personal being belongs no more to the 'land of the living' (*cf.* Ps. 52:5; Je. 11:19). To live is to speak of *my* life; in death a man's plans perish and he returns to the common earth, gathered to and sleeping with the fathers (Gn. 25:8; 37:35; Dt. 31:16). Man's end is 'like water spilt on the ground, which cannot be gathered up again' (2 Sa. 14:14).

4. Death is not merely the momentary event of dying; it is the death state, *i.e.* Sheol. Sheol is 'in the dust' (Jb. 17:13ff.) and is probably best understood generically as 'the grave'. As a synonym for death it is the common goal and final leveller of all life: man and beast, righteous and wicked, wise and foolish (Jb. 3:13ff.; Ps. 49; Ec. 2:14; 3:19). It is a state of sleep, rest, darkness, silence, without thought or memory (Jb. 3:16f.; 17:13ff.; Ps. 6:5; Ec. 9:5, 10) in which one does not praise God and from which one does not return (2 Sa. 12:23; Jb. 7:9; Ps. 30:9; Is. 38:18). It is like an insatiable monster and its prospect, except in the most desperate straits, is one of foreboding (Hab. 2:5; *cf.* 2 Sa. 22:5f.).

A few times Sheol is pictured as a massive grave in which, amid the maggots, an enfeebled ghost-life continues (Ezk. 31–32; Is. 14:4ff.) and from which one's 'shade' may be called up (1 Sa. 28:8ff., AV). While the first two passages are obviously poetic symbolism, the medium of Endor séance reflects a common—though forbidden—practice. It is not representative of the general OT view, which sees life and death in utter opposition (*contra* Johnson, p. 89).

Although not strictly non-being, Sheol is the end of meaningful existence and is 'virtual annihilation' (Johnson, p. 93). 'The paths of glory lead but to the grave', and this conclusion to human life gives rise to the Preacher's refrain: 'Vanity of vanities, all is vanity' (Ec. 12:8; Ps. 89:47). To this victory of death the OT does offer a hopeful answer; it lies not in the nature of man but in the power of the living God.

c. The living God

1. The common formula for an oath, 'as the Lord lives' (*cf.* Nu. 14:21, 28; 1 Sa. 14:39), stresses that God is the God who speaks and acts because he is 'the living God'. This quality distinguishes Yahweh from all idols and attests not only his own vitality but his creative power and providential activity (Jos. 3:10; Je. 10:10; Is. 46:5ff.). He is the source and upholder of all life, the spring of living water (Je. 17:13; Ps. 36:9f.), who gives man breath and who, delivering from Sheol, leads one in the path of life (Gn. 2:7; Ps. 16:11; Pr. 5:6). God is the God who makes alive and who kills (Gn. 6:17; Dt. 32:39; Jdg. 13:3, 23; 1 Sa. 2:6; 2 Ki. 5:7).

2. Such is man's dependence upon God for life that man's breath or spirit may be called God's breath and God's spirit (Jb. 27:3f.; 33:4; Gn. 6:3; Is. 42:5). God gave manna in the wilderness that Israel might learn that even physical life is maintained by 'everything that proceeds out of the mouth of the Lord' (Dt. 8:3; *cf.* Mt. 4:4; Lk. 12:15, 20). God imparts breath and man lives (Gn. 2:7; *cf.* Rev. 11:11); if God 'should take back his spirit to himself, and gather to himself his breath, all flesh would perish together, and man would turn to dust' (Jb. 34:14f.; *cf.* Ec. 12:7; Pss. 90:3; 104:29f.). Man's life then is loaned to him at God's good pleasure, and true life consists not in the transient, even though prosperous, life of the wicked, but in having God as 'my portion for ever' (Ps. 73:17, 26). One's life is assured if he is 'bound in the bundle of the living in the care of the Lord' (1 Sa. 25:29).

3. Because life is 'life in relatedness to God', life and death are moral alternatives. The fate of the individual and nation, whether blessing and life or misfortune and death, hangs upon one's righteousness or sinfulness, obedience or disobedience to Yahweh (Dt. 30:15ff.; Jdg. 2:18ff.; Ezk. 18). Universal death is viewed (when viewed at all) as a judgment upon sin; because of disobedience man is barred from the 'tree of life' (Gn. 3:17ff.; *cf.* Jb. 14:1ff., 16f.; contrast Ps. 89:47). Although not always apparent, righteousness tends to life and evil to death (*cf.* Ps. 73:17; Pr. 11:19); righteousness is a 'way of life', and by it one is delivered from the threats of Sheol (Am. 5:4, 14; Pr. 6:23; Hab. 2:4).

4. God has no relationship to Sheol or to those in it. But this must not be confused with the mistaken notion that God has no power in Sheol. It is basic to the OT faith—as expressed in all strata of the literature—that Yahweh, the living God, reigns over death and/or Sheol. To heal (2 Ki. 5:7, 14), to raise the dead (1 Ki. 17:20ff.; 2 Ki. 4:16, 33ff.), to deliver Israel from national death (Jdg. 7:2ff.; Ho. 13:14; Ezk. 37), to cause life to bud in a barren woman (Gn. 17:15ff.; Jdg. 13:2f.; 2 Sa. 1:19f.; 2:6)—all these reveal God's power over Sheol, for the maladies are themselves invasions of death into which God interjects resurrection power.

While God's power to deliver individuals from Sheol is implicit throughout the OT, his purpose to do so comes to explicit expression in comparatively few passages (*cf.* Is. 25:8; 26:19; Jb. 19:26; Pss. 16:8–11; 49:14f.; Dn. 12:2). When it does appear, however, the conviction is full-grown and seemingly is not an innovation (W. O. E. Oesterley, *The Jews and Judaism during the Greek Period*, 1941, p. 183). The concept is related to and perhaps an inference from: (i) God's expressed relationship to the righteous dead, and (ii) God's redemption of Israel understood within the framework of a 'corporate personality' in which the reality of the individual is preserved in the reality of the whole. In a later day Jesus Christ, as well as other rabbis, urged the former as a key to the proper understanding of the OT at this point (Mt. 22:31f.; Lk. 20:37f.; *cf.* *SB*, 1, pp. 893ff.): (i) God says to Moses, 'I am the God of Abraham.' (ii) Abraham is in Sheol. (iii) God is the God of the living and has no relationship with Sheol. (iv) Therefore, it is to be inferred that God will resurrect Abraham from Sheol.

5. Resurrection-life is pictured (as in intertestamental Judaism) in materialistic terms. It is restored life in which 'life', *i.e.* prosperity, peace and fullness, is multiplied and Sheol threats are removed (Is. 27; *cf.* Rev. 21–22). Its realization (in Is. 26:19; Dn. 12:2) belongs to the coming Messianic deliverance and, as creation life, it is solely the result of God's sovereign and gracious act. God, who by his creative word called man into being, again calls dust into life through resurrection.

II. In the New Testament

a. Terms and concepts

1. Life (Gk. *bios*), means 'course of life' or 'necessities of life maintenance' (Mk. 12:44; 1 Tim. 2:2; 1 Jn. 3:17). While *zōē* characteristically (and always in the Johannine literature) describes resurrection-life, it also denotes 'course of life' (Lk. 16:25; Phil. 1:20; *cf.* Lk. 15:13; Rom. 6:2), soul-life or natural vitality (Acts 8:33; 17:25; Phil. 1:20; 1 Tim. 4:8; *cf.* Jn. 4:50), and life duration (Jas. 4:14). Soul (*psychē*) and spirit (*pneuma*) continue their ambiguous role of 'self' and 'life'. As life, soul is simply 'being', 'natural-life' (Lk. 9:25; Mk. 8:36). It may be preserved to resurrection-life (Jn. 12:25), but at present it exists as natural vitality, lost at death (Mt. 2:20; Jn. 15:13; Acts 20:10; 1 Jn. 3:16) or, more importantly, as Adamic life, life of the old age, life under divine judgment (Lk. 12:20; *cf.* 1 Cor. 2:14; 15:44ff.; Jas. 3:15). While spirit can mean, as in ancient Israel, the vitalizing principle of Adamic life (Jn. 19:30; Acts 7:59), it tends to be associated with resurrection-life and, as such, to stand in contrast to soul-life, *i.e.* life under judgment (*cf.* Jude 19; Jn. 6:63; 1 Cor. 15:45).

2. As in the OT, man's life and being, although viewed from different aspects, is a psychosomatic unity (*cf.* Bultmann). The Gk. soul-body dualism is incidentally reflected in the parable of Lk. 16:19ff., but is not in accord with the general NT outlook or teaching.

b. Life under death

1. The OT view continues. (i) Life is borrowed, transitory, dependent upon and at the disposal of God (*cf.* Mt. 4:4). Man can neither prolong his soul-life nor destroy it (Mt. 6:25ff.; Lk. 12:25; Jas. 4:15); God can either forfeit it or redeem it to resurrection-life (Mt. 10:28; Lk. 12:20; 1 Cor. 15:44; 1 Jn. 5:16; *cf.* Jas. 5:20). (ii) Life is ebb and flow: to live is to live in health (Jn. 4:50).

2. In radical development of OT thought the moral quality of life as relationship to God comes into sharp focus. One related to God, although dead, may be viewed as 'living' (Lk. 20:38). On the other hand, soul-life alienated from the life of God (Eph. 4:18) is no life at all. Anyone in it—not only those under immediate threat of Sheol (Mk. 5:23; *cf.* Mt. 9:18)—may be regarded as 'dead' (Lk. 9:60; Rom. 8:10; 1 Jn. 3:14; Rev. 3:1; *cf.* Lk. 15:24). Even when called life, 'this life' is contrasted to real life (1 Cor. 15:19; 1 Tim. 6:19) and has meaning only in conjunction with the life of the coming age (Gal. 2:20; Phil. 1:22; 1 Tim. 4:8).

3. The cry of John the Baptist, 'Repent', sets the mood of the NT (Mt. 3:2; *cf.* Acts 11:18; 17:30f.). All life stands under imminent judgment, and decision is demanded of all who would share the life of the new age. Criminals suffering ignominious execution are not special sinners: 'unless you repent you will all likewise perish' (Lk. 13:3). Nor can prosperity be relied upon as a token of God's favour: in the midst of man's ease God speaks, 'Fool, this night your soul is required from you' (Lk. 12:20). While this (OT) view of the judgment of the soul-life by physical death is present, more often the *locus* of judgment shifts to the eschatological consummation—the parousia (Mt. 24:36ff.; 25:31ff.), the resurrection of judgment (Jn. 5:28f.), the second death (Rev. 21:8—in which God destroys 'soul and body' in hell (Mt. 10:28). Soul-life (*psychē*), in contrast to resurrection-life (*zōē*), is Adamic life, life under judgment, which without *zōē* must perish (Jn. 3:16). Indeed the 'soulish' man is one directing his life toward the perishing old age, the 'soulish' body one controlled by the Sheol-power dominating the old age (1 Cor. 2:14; 15:44; Jas. 3:15; Jude 19).

4. The judgment of death is executed corporately and representatively in Jesus Christ, the eschatological Adam (1 Cor. 15:45), who 'becomes sin' and voluntarily delivers his soul to Sheol as 'a ransom' (Mk. 10:45; Jn. 10:15; 2 Cor. 5:21; *cf.* Mk. 14:34; Is. 53:6, 10; Acts 8:32ff.; 1 Pet. 2:24) to give resurrection-life to the world (Jn. 6:51). However, Christ's soul is not left in Sheol; in resurrection victory he takes his soul again (Acts 2:31; Jn. 10:17). And by the power of an 'indestructible life' he becomes a 'life-giving spirit' who shares his victory and imparts resurrection-life to whom he will (Heb. 7:3; 1 Cor. 15:45; Eph. 4:8; Jn. 5:21; 17:2). Thereby, Christ removes for ever the Sheol threat to man's soul.

5. Man's soul-life, then, need not be forfeited. If he loves it or seeks to preserve it, he will lose it, but if he loses it or gives it up for Christ, the gospel, or the brethren, it will be preserved, caught up in resurrection-life (Mk. 8:35f.; Jn. 12:25; 1 Jn. 3:16; 2 Cor. 12:15; Phil. 2:30; Rev. 12:11). To believe or to convert a sinner is to save a soul from death (Heb. 10:39; Jas. 1:21; 5:20; 1 Pet. 1:9). One who believes shall never taste real death (Jn. 8:51f.; 11:26; *cf.* Jn. 10:28; Mk. 9:1), for in Christ death is transformed into a temporary 'sleep in Jesus' (1 Thes. 4:14; *cf.* Mk. 5:39; Jn. 11:11). Both soul-life and resurrection-life are the life of the self, the whole man. The latter does not displace the former, but preserves it and transforms it.

c. Resurrection-life

1. The OT ideal of the good life has in the NT an eschatological fulfilment as resurrection-life (*zōē*). Since it is the only true life, it may be called simply 'life' (Acts 5:20; 11:18; Rom. 5:17; 2 Pet. 1:3; 1 Jn. 5:16). It is associated with light (Jn. 8:12), glory (1 Pet. 5:1, 4; *cf.* Jas. 1:12), honour (Rom. 2:7), abundance (Jn. 10:10), immortality (2 Tim. 1:10), resurrection (Jn. 6:40; 11:25), eternal life, the kingdom of God (Col. 1:13; Mt. 25), holiness (Rom. 6:22f.), joy (1 Thes. 2:19), spirit (Jn. 6:63; *cf.* 1 Cor. 15:45), the imperishable (Heb. 7:16; 1 Pet. 1:23); and is contrasted with darkness (Col. 1:13), dishonour (Rom. 2:7), death (1 Jn. 3:14), mortality (2 Cor. 5:4), destruction (Mt. 7:13f.), judgment (Jn. 5:28f.), corruption (Gal. 6:8), wrath (Rom. 2:7f.; Jn. 3:36), eternal punishment (Mt. 25:46). To have life is to 'abide' (Jn. 6:27). To lack it is to wither and be burnt as a severed branch (Mt. 7:13, 19; Lk. 3:9; *cf.* Jn. 15:6) and to be destroyed in hell (Mt. 10:28; Mk. 9:43ff.; Rev. 20:14f.).

2. As in the OT, life is properly the life of God, the Ever-Living One (Rom. 5:21; Rev. 4:9), who has life in himself and alone has immortality (Jn. 5:26; 1 Tim. 6:16). He can make alive and he can kill (Rom. 4:17; 2 Cor. 1:9; 1 Tim. 6:13; Mt. 10:28f.; Jas. 4:14f.; Lk. 12:20).

3. This life of God is manifest in Jesus Christ. In the Synoptic Gospels Jesus simply assures his followers of resurrection-life (Mk. 8:34ff.; 9:41ff.; 10:29f.; Mt. 25:46) and evidences his power to bestow it: to heal is to 'save souls' (Lk. 6:9) and cause to 'live' (Mk. 5:23). Sheol itself is robbed by Christ's creative word (Mk. 5:39ff.; Lk. 7:14f.; *cf.* Jn. 11:43). The Fourth Gospel and the Epistles, written with Christ's resurrection in more deliberate perspective, are more explicit and elaborate: Christ is 'the true God, and eternal life' (1 Jn. 5:20; Jn. 1:4; 14:6), the 'Author of life' (Acts 3:15), to whom the Father has granted 'to have life in himself' (Jn. 5:26). He is 'the resurrection and the life' (Jn. 11:25), 'the bread of life' (Jn. 6:35), and his words are 'spirit and life' (Jn. 6:63). By his resurrection he manifests himself Lord and Judge over the living and the dead (Mt. 25:31ff.; Mk. 14:62; Jn. 5:27ff.; Acts 10:42; 17:31; Rom. 10:9f.; 14:9; 2 Tim. 4:1; *cf.* 1 Pet. 4:5; Rev. 11:18).

In Jesus Christ's resurrection immortal life has been actualized on the plane of history. His resurrection becomes the basis for all resurrection, and all resurrection is to be understood in terms of his (*cf.* 1 Cor. 15; Col. 3:4; 1 Jn. 3:2). No longer does the hope of resurrection rest, as in the OT, merely upon prophetic vision or upon inferences from God's covenant relationships. No longer is resurrection to be defined simply as renewed life out of Sheol. Resurrection-life now finds its meaning in the image of Jesus Christ (Rom. 8:29).

4. For man, then, true life is grounded in Jesus Christ who 'became a life-giving spirit' (1 Cor. 15:45; *cf.* Jn. 6:63; 2 Cor. 3:17). The core of the gospel proclamation is that he who was dead is 'alive for evermore' (Acts 2:31ff.; 1 Cor. 15:3ff.; Rev. 1:5, 18) and by the power of an indestructible life gives life to the world (Heb. 7:16; Jn. 6:33). If Christ has not been raised from death one must write over the Christian dead, *finis* (1 Cor. 15:18, 32). But Christ is risen and has the 'keys to Sheol'; because Sheol could not conquer him, neither can it prevail against his church (Mt. 16:18; Rev. 1:18). His Life is mediated to the believer through repentance, faith and baptism (Acts 11:18; Jn. 3:16; 11:25f.; Rom. 6:4); by it one is 'saved' (Rom. 5:10). In Christ's death and resurrection God pierces radically into the world of man to make him see the fatality of sin and the utter grace of the new life from God—an unfathomable, unexpected and freely-bestowed act of salvation.

5. Resurrection-life, like Adamic soul-life, is imparted and sustained by God's creative word. Man has no control over it. He may inherit, receive or enter it (Mk. 9:43ff.; 10:17, 30; Tit. 3:7; 1 Pet. 3:7). By evil deeds or rejection of the gospel he may judge himself unworthy of it (Acts 13:46; *cf.* Rom. 1:32) or, conversely, by the Spirit he may perform deeds yielding eternal life (Mk. 10:17ff.; Jn. 5:28f.; Rom. 2:7; 2 Cor. 5:10; Gal. 5:22; 6:8). Such deeds are possible only by a relationship to Christ through faith (Rom. 1:17; Jn. 20:31) which itself imparts life (Jn. 6:53f.; Rom. 6:23; Col. 3:3; 1 Jn. 3:14; 5:13). God gives life to those whom he wills (Jn. 1:13; 5:21), who are ordained for it, and who from the foundation of the world are written in the book of life (Acts 13:48; Rom. 9:11; Phil. 4:3; Rev. 17:8; 20:12ff.). The new life is a resurrection, a new birth, a sovereign and gracious act of the creator God (Jn. 5:24f.; Rom. 6:4; Col. 3:1ff.; Eph. 2:1ff.; Jn. 1:13).

6. In the Synoptic Gospels life is always viewed as future and associated with the coming kingdom of God (Mk. 10:17, 23; 9:43, 47; Mt. 25:46). The way to it is blocked by sin and found by few; yet to attain life is the highest possible goal and worthy of any sacrifice (Mk. 9:42ff.; Mt. 7:14; 13:44ff.), for only in this way can one's soul be preserved (Mk. 8:34ff.; *cf.* Jn. 12:25).

7. In the Johannine and Pauline literature this parousia perspective continues (Jn. 5:24, 28f.; 6:40; 11:24; 14:3, 6, 19; Rom. 5:10; 6:22; 2 Cor. 5:4; 13:4; Phil. 3:10f.; *cf.* 1 Cor. 15:52ff.), but resurrection-life is also viewed as a present possession of the believer. One passes 'from death to life' at conversion (1 Jn. 3:14; *cf.* Jn. 5:24; Eph. 2:1ff.), and one may even speak in the past tense of having been crucified, raised to life, brought into Christ's kingdom, glorified and made to sit in heaven (Gal. 2:20; Eph. 2:5f.; Col. 1:13; Rom. 8:30). However, in Paul (and probably in John) this is always viewed as a corporate participation in Christ's death and resurrection (Rom 6:4; 8:2; 2 Tim. 1:1; *cf.* Jn. 6:33, 51ff.) vouchsafed by the Spirit, the 'down-payment' of the new-age life (*cf.* 2 Cor. 4:12; 5:5). Our life is hid with Christ (Col. 3:3), and to have life means simply to have Christ (1 Jn. 5:11f.). Individually, resurrection-life is now being realized in ethical renewal and psychological transformation (Rom. 8:10; 12:1; Gal. 5:22f.; Col. 3:1ff., 9f.; Eph. 4:18ff.); but the self in its mortality remains under death. Only in the parousia is mortality 'swallowed by life' and Sheol's power vanquished (1 Cor. 15:26, 52ff.; 2 Cor. 5:4; *cf.* Rev. 20:13). At present the victory is actualized personally only in Jesus Christ, 'the first fruits of those who have fallen asleep', 'the first-born among many brethren' (1 Cor. 15:20; Rom. 8:29).

8. As in ancient Israel, the problem of death finds its answer neither in philosophical speculation about immortality nor in the sub-life of Sheol, but in deliverance from Sheol; to be a son of God is to be a son of the resurrection (Lk. 20:36). And it is the resurrected Son of God who imparts this victory to his church; in Adam all die, so in Christ all shall be made alive (1 Cor. 15:22). Not Bach's 'come, sweet death' but John's 'come, Lord Jesus' expresses the NT attitude towards death.

Resurrection-life is bodily life—the life of the whole man (Lk. 24:39ff.; Jn. 5:28f.; 1 Cor. 15; Phil. 3:21; Rev. 20:13). It is to be with Christ (Jn. 14:3; Col. 3:4; 1 Thes. 4:17), to have a full vision of God (1 Cor. 13:12; 2 Cor. 5:7; 1 Jn. 3:2; Rev. 22:4), to enter the kingdom (Mt. 25:34, 46), to enjoy the fulfilment of 'righteousness and peace and joy in the Holy Spirit' (Rom. 14:17; *cf.* Rev. 21–22) in which all Sheol-threats are removed.

Resurrection-life will be 'my life'. One's personal continuity does not rest, however, in the residual monad of Leibnitz nor in the escaping soul of Plato. It rests in God in whose mind 'all live' (Lk. 20:38) and 'who can bring the dead to life and can call to himself the things that do not exist as though they did' (Rom. 4:17, Williams).

Bibliography. R. Bultmann, *The Theology of the New Testament*, 1955, 1, pp. 191–227, 324–329; H. C. C. Cavallin, *Life after Death . . . in 1 Cor. 15*, 1, 1974; O. Cullmann, *Immortality of the Soul or Resurrection of the Dead?*, 1958; *idem*, *The Early Church*, 1956, pp. 165–173; C. H. Dodd, *The Interpretation of the Fourth Gospel*, 1954, pp. 144–150, 201ff.; E. E. Ellis, *Paul and his Recent Interpreters*[5], 1979, pp. 35–48; *idem*, *NTS* 10, 1963–64, pp. 274–279; *idem*, *Eschatology in Luke*, 1972; *idem*, in F. Neirynck (ed.), *L'Evangile de Luc*[2], 1989, pp. 296–303, *idem*, *Pauline Theology: Ministry and Society*, 1989, pp. 1–25; *idem*, *Int* 44, 1990, pp. 132–144; J. de Fraine, *Adam and the Family of Man*, 1965; R. H. Gundry, *Sōma in Biblical Theology*, 1976; K. Hanhart, *The Intermediate State in the New Testament*, 1966; H.-G. Link, *NIDNTT* 2, pp. 474–484; *TDNT* 2, pp. 832–872; 8, pp. 359–451; 9, pp. 617–656; A. R. Johnson, *The Vitality of the Individual in the Thought of Ancient Israel*, 1949; J. Pedersen, *Israel: Its Life and Culture*, 1, 1926, pp. 99–181, 453–496; H. W. Robinson, *Corporate Personality in Ancient Israel*, 1964; J. W. Rogerson, *Anthropology and the Old Testament*, 1979.

E.E.E.

LIGHT. The word is used in connection with joy, blessing and *life in contrast to sorrow, adversity and death (*cf.* Gn. 1:3f.; Jb. 10:22; 18:5f.). At an early time it came to signify God's presence and favour (*cf.* Ps. 27:1; Is. 9:2; 2 Cor. 4:6) in contrast to God's judgment (Am. 5:18). From this and other sources arises an ethical dualism between light and darkness, *i.e.* good and evil, which is quite marked in the NT (*cf.* Lk. 16:8; Jn. 3:19ff.; 12:36; 2 Cor. 6:14; Col. 1:12f.; 1 Thes. 5:5; 1 Pet. 2:9). Some, *e.g.* C. H. Dodd, have regarded Hellenistic parallels to be significant in this regard, but the presence of this usage in Judaism, *e.g. The War of the Sons of Light and the Sons of Darkness* in DSS, makes such an inference unnecessary and provides a more pertinent commentary on the NT concepts.

God's *holiness is expressed in terms of light, *e.g.* in 1 Tim. 6:16, where he is said to dwell 'in unapproachable light'; *cf.* 1 Jn. 1:5, where it is said that 'God is light', and other passages in that Epistle where the implications of this for the believer are worked out. The same thought is seen in the typically Heb. expression 'children of light' which is twice used by Paul (Eph. 5:8; *cf.* 1 Thes. 5:5; Jn. 12:36).

In John's Gospel the term light refers not so much to God's holiness as to the *revelation* of his love in Christ and the penetration of that love into lives darkened by sin. So Christ refers to himself as 'the light of the world' (Jn. 8:12; 9:5; *cf.* 12:46), and in the Sermon on the Mount applies this term to his disciples (Mt. 5:14–16). Similarly Paul can refer to 'the light of the gospel of the glory of Christ' and to God himself who 'has shone in our hearts' (2 Cor. 4:4–6).

BIBLIOGRAPHY. *BAGD; ISBE*; C. H. Dodd, *The Interpretation of the Fourth Gospel*, 1954, pp. 201–212; D. Flusser, 'The Dead Sea Sect and Pre-Pauline Christianity', *Aspects of the Dead Sea Scrolls*, ed. C. Rabin and Y. Yadin, 1958, pp. 215–266; H. Conzelmann, *TDNT* 9, pp. 310–358; H.-C. Hahn *et al.*, *NIDNTT* 2, pp. 484–496. E.E.E.

LIGHTNING. 1. Lightning which accompanies *thunder is a well-known phenomenon in Palestine, especially in the cool season, with a maximum in November or December. The word is sometimes rendered 'glitter' or 'glittering' (Dt. 32:41; Jb. 20:25; Ezk. 21:15; Na. 3:3; Hab. 3:11). Lightning is a figure used for brightness of countenance (Dn. 10:6; Mt. 28:3) and of raiment (Lk. 24:4). In some passages the usage of 'fire' refers to lightning (*e.g.* Ex. 9:23; 1 Ki. 18:38; 2 Ki. 1:10, 12, 14; 1 Ch. 21:26; Jb. 1:16; Ps. 148:8). Lightning is poetically described with thunderstorms (2 Sa. 22:15; Pss. 18:14; 97:4; 135:7; Je. 10:13; 51:16).

2. Lightning is associated with theophanies as at Sinai (Ex. 19:16; 20:18), in Ezekiel's vision (Ezk. 1:13–14) and several times in the Apocalypse (Rev. 4:5; 8:5; 11:19; 16:18). It is regarded as an instrument of God's judgment (Ps. 144:6; Zc. 9:14; Lk. 10:18). J.M.H.

LILITH (Heb. *lîlîṯ*, Is. 34:14, RVmg., JB; LXX *onokentauros*; Symm., Vulg. *lamia* (Jerome, 'avenging fury'); AV 'screech owl'; AVmg., RV 'night-monster'; RSV 'night hag'; NIV 'night creatures').

This name appears in a description of the terrible desolation of Edom, and presents great difficulties of interpretation. At a time when Bab. and Persian influence was developing, Lilith appears evidently as a loan-word derived from the Assyr. female demon of the night, *Lilitu*.

It may, however, be misleading to regard the creature as necessarily associated with the night: the darkness which some demons were said to love was that caused by desert storms (*cf.* Sumerian *LIL.LÁ*, 'storm-wind'; and also a possible conclusion from Jerome's translation cited above). Some scholars regard it as the equivalent of the English vampire.

Later Jewish literature speaks variously of Lilith as the first wife of Adam, but she flew away and became a demon; as a fabulous monster which stole and destroyed newly-born infants; and as a demon against which charms were used to keep it from the haunts of men, lest it enter and bring disease.

There is, however, no real evidence for insisting on a mythological interpretation of the word, and it is perhaps significant that most of the other creatures listed in Is. 34 are real animals or birds. If the LXX rendering is understood as something akin to a tail-less monkey (*cf.* G. R. Driver, *loc. cit.*, p. 55), it seems an unlikely habitué of a desolate place. A similar objection applies also to both the tawny and the night owl, neither of which is a desert bird. Driver suggests a goat-sucker or nightjar (NEB), several species of which are found in waste land.

BIBLIOGRAPHY. *JewE*; G. R. Driver, 'Lilith', *PEQ* 91, 1959, pp. 55–58. J.D.D.

LIME, LIMESTONE. Chemically, lime is calcium oxide, made by heating limestone in a kiln, of which there must have been many in ancient Palestine. The Heb. Bible uses three words, *śîḏ*, 'plaster', 'lime' or 'whitewash' (Dt. 27:2, 4; Is. 33:12; Am. 2:1), *gîr*, 'chalk' or 'lime' (Dn. 5:5) and *'aḇnê gîr*, 'stones of lime' (Is. 27:9, RSV 'chalkstones').

Limestone is abundant in Palestine. Geologically it was formed from the compacting together of shells, *etc.*, on the sea bed, which was then thrust up by earth movement. Palestine was under the sea more than once, at least in part. The bulk of the limestone visible today on both sides of the Jordan is from the Cretaceous period.

BIBLIOGRAPHY. D. Baly, *The Geography of Palestine*², 1974, pp. 17ff. J.A.T.

LINE. The commonest OT word is *qaw*, *qāw* or *qeweh*, denoting a measuring-line such as was used to measure the circumference of the Temple laver (1 Ki. 7:23) or to mark out a city, or land for building (Is. 34:17; Je. 31:39; Zc. 1:16). It is used for measuring distances of 1,000 cubits from Ezekiel's Temple to test the water depth (Ezk. 47:3), and by an extension of meaning it is the plumbline used to check the integrity of a city or land (2 Ki. 21:13; Is. 28:17; 34:11; La. 2:8), or the lines of instruction of a teacher (Is. 28:10, 13, where the picture is one of children reciting the alphabet, *qāw* being an alternative way of naming the letter *qōp̄*).

The word *ḥeḇel*, 'cord' or 'rope', also refers to an instrument for dividing up land or an inheritance (Pss. 16:6, AV; 78:55, AV; Am. 7:17; Zc. 2:1). In 2 Sa. 8:2 it is used of the lines of Moabites drawn up by David, some destined for life and some for death.

The words *ḥûṭ* (1 Ki. 7:15), *pāṯîl* (Ezk. 40:3) and *śereḏ* (Is. 44:13) have special uses. Rahab's red cord is *tiqwâ* (Jos. 2:18, 21, AV). (*WEIGHTS AND MEASURES, *ARTS AND CRAFTS.) J.A.T.

LINEN. The Heb. word *šēš* (Egyp. *šś*) is rendered 'fine linen'. The following Heb. words are rendered by 'linen': *baḏ*, *pištâ*, *bûṣ* and *'ēṭûn* (*cf.* Egyp. *'idmy*, 'yarn' in RV). The word *pištâ* means actually the flax of which linen was made. As early as the 14th century BC the word *pšt*, or plural *pštm*, was used in Ugarit for linen (*cf*. Virolleaud, *PRU*, Mission Ras Shamra 7, II). *bûṣ* is present only in later books (*cf*. Gk. *byssos*). RSV, AV translate the following Gk. words by linen: *sindōn*, *othonion* and *linon*.

Linen is made of flax (*Linum usitatissimum*). After treatment the thread of the rind gives linen and the seed linseed-oil. After the flax was treated it was spun by women and made into material (Pr. 31:13, 24). Flax was never extensively grown in Palestine in biblical times. According to Ex. 9:31; Ho. 2:5 and probably Jos. 2:6, it was, however, cultivated from early times. An extra-biblical witness is the Gezer calendar (*c*. 1000 BC), where we read in the fourth line: 'His month is hoeing up of flax' (Albright's translation in Pritchard, *ANET*²). The great cultivator and exporter of flax was Egypt. In Pr. 7:16 we read of Egyptian linen (*cf*. Heb. *ḥ*ᵃ*ṭuḇôṯ*, 'many coloured'). Red linen was especially precious in ancient Egypt and was called 'royal linen'. It is quite probable that linen (*cf*. Egyp. words *sś* and *'idmy* as possible loan-words in Hebrew and Canaanite) was imported from Egypt by the inhabitants of Palestine from the earliest times. We know from Egyp. documents that linen was exported from Egypt to Phoenicia (*cf*. also Ezk. 27:7) and especially Byblos through many centuries.

The use of linen in OT times was prescribed for priests (Ex. 28:39). The coat, turban and girdle must be of fine linen. This is, according to Ezk. 44:17, prescribed for the coolness of the material. The high priest used a woollen overcoat, but was draped in linen on the great Day of Atonement (Lv. 16:4, 23). Linen the Israelites brought along from Egypt was used for the ten curtains of the tabernacle (Ex. 26:1), the veil (26:31) and the screen of the door of the tent (26:36). Samuel wore an ephod (*'ēpôḏ*) of linen (1 Sa. 2:18); David danced in front of the ark draped in a linen ephod (2 Sa. 6:14). It seems as if the use of linen was associated with special, holy persons, *e.g*. the man with the writing-case in Ezk. 9:2 and the man Daniel saw in Dn. 10:5 and 12:6–7. Linen and fine linen were regarded as precious gifts to the woman a man loved. In Ezk. 16:10, 13 the Lord speaks to Jerusalem as a husband to his wife and reminds her how he has decked her with linen and fine linen. It is obvious from Pr. 31:22 that the use of linen by women was highly esteemed (as in *embroidery). It was a luxury (Is. 3:23). The word *bûṣ*, 'linen', is used in the later books as the material for the rich and important people, *e.g*. Mordecai went to the Persian king draped with a mantle of fine linen (Est. 8:15). Linen was commonly used for fine furnishings, sails and for protection of precious carpets.

The word linen is sparingly used in the NT. In the parable of the rich man and the beggar Lazarus the former is described as decked out in fine linen (Gk. *byssos*) and purple (Lk. 16:19). The young man who followed Jesus to Gethsemane lost his linen cloth (or sheet?) in his flight from the scene (Mk. 14:51). The body of Jesus was wrapped in linen according to Mt. 27:59 and parallel texts. According to Rev. 19:8, the Bride of the Lamb is clothed in fine linen, which is the righteous deeds of the saints. In Rev. 19:14 the eschatological armies are described as arrayed in fine white linen.

BIBLIOGRAPHY. L. M. Wilson, *Ancient Textiles from Egypt*, 1933; A. Bellinger, *BASOR* 118, 1950, pp. 9–11; G. M. Crowfoot, *PEQ* 83, 1951, pp. 5–31; *DEAD SEA SCROLLS. F.C.F.

LINUS. A Rom. Christian who greeted Timothy, 2 Tim. 4:21; for his relation to others *in loc*., see *CLAUDIA. The name (a son of Apollo) is not common. Succession lists show a Linus, identified by Irenaeus (*Adv. Haer*. 3. 3. 2) and subsequent writers with Timothy's friend, as first bishop of Rome after the apostles. On the problems of such lists, *cf*. Lightfoot, *Clement I*, pp. 201–345; A. Ehrhardt, *The Apostolic Succession*, 1953. Writers dominated by later practice (*e.g*. Rufinus, Preface to *Clem. Recog*.) labour to reconcile the apostolic appointment of both Linus and *Clement. Linus made little further mark on tradition or legend. (*Cf. Liber Pontificalis*, ed. Duchesne, 1, pp. 53, 121, for meagre notices; Tischendorf, *Acta Apocrypha*, pp. xixf., for martyrdoms of Peter and Paul.) A.F.W.

LION OF JUDAH. An abbreviated form of one of Christ's Messianic titles found in Rev. 5:5, 'the Lion of the tribe of Judah'. An obvious allusion to Gn. 49:9, 'Judah is a lion's whelp', this title depicts Christ as the culmination of the courage, might and ferocity of the tribe of Judah. Like a lion Satan stalks the saints (1 Pet. 5:8), but Christ is the conquering lion, worthy to open the seven seals of judgment. The use of the term 'lion' (*ANIMALS) in connection with judgment may reflect passages like Is. 38:13; La. 3:10; Ho. 5:14; 13:8, where God's judgment is likened to a lion's attack. Emperors of Ethiopia, convinced that they stemmed from Judah as descendants of Solomon and the Queen of Sheba, proudly appropriated this title ('Conquering Lion of Judah') until the overthrow of Haile Selassie's regime in 1974. D.A.H.

LIP. Both the Heb. word *śāpâ*, and (less frequently) the Gk. word *cheilos*, mean not only the human lip but also the brink or shore of the sea, or the bank of a river (Gn. 22:17; 41:3; Heb. 11:12) and, in the case of the Heb. word, edge of a garment (Ex. 28:26), though the primary application is to lips. Another Heb. word *śāpām* refers to the upper lip or moustache, usually in respect of covering it, with the hand or garment, as a sign of grief or shame (Lv. 13:45). *Cf*. the reference to covering the face in 2 Sa. 19:4.

In the case of the lips we find clear examples of the Hebrew way of speaking whereby the organs seem to feel and act themselves, which is partly synecdoche, and partly due to the lack of physiological understanding of the nervous system (*BODY). However, the connection of the lips with the mind or heart is brought out in Pr. 16:23. For an explanation of this connotation, see *HEART.

The lips not only speak (Jb. 27:4) but shout for joy (Ps. 71:23), quiver (with fear) (Hab. 3:16), guard knowledge (Pr. 5:2), offer praise (Ps. 63:3), plead (Jb. 13:6) and possess ethical qualities of truthfulness or righteousness, or, conversely, sinning or speaking lies (Jb. 2:10; Pr. 12:19; 16:13). The parallelism with *tongue or *mouth is natural, and these are used in much the same senses (Pss. 34:13; 51:15). Just as with these words, lip can be extended to mean speech, words (Jb. 12:20) or language (Gn. 11:1; Is. 19:18). B.O.B.

LIVER. Only in the OT does this word occur. The Heb. *kāḇēḏ* is from a root meaning 'to be heavy', or by extension of meaning 'to be honoured'. So, it is the heavy organ. Of the 14 occurrences, 11 are in Ex. and Lv., referring to the liver of a sacrificial beast.

The 'appendage (AV 'caul') of the liver' (Ex. 29:13, *etc.*), always associated with the kidneys, was burnt on the altar. Josephus lists the parts burnt on the altar (*Ant.* 3. 228) 'the kidneys, the caul, all the fat along with the lobe of the liver'.

It is, however, unlikely that the 'caul', *yōṯereṯ*, refers to a lobe of the liver, but probably to fat upon it, or possibly the pancreas. The word literally means 'remainder' or 'appendage' (RSV), so it is not stated specifically that the liver itself was burnt on the altar, but the internal fat and the kidneys.

From Ezekiel (21:21) it appears that the liver was the material for a form of divination, based on the internal markings of the liver. Many artificial livers of clay have been unearthed in the Middle East, and were made for this purpose. A similar practice was known among the Etruscans, from whom it passed to the Romans (Lat. *haruspices* = 'liver diviners'). B.O.B.

LO-DEBAR. Where Mephibosheth lived before David recalled him (2 Sa. 9:4); E of the Jordan (*cf.* 2 Sa. 2:29; 17:27); possibly *DEBIR, 3. J.D.D.

LOGOS. A common Gk. word used in a quasi-technical sense as a title of Christ in the Johannine writings. It carries a large number of different meanings: its basic translation is 'word', *i.e.* meaningful utterance, whence develop its many senses 'statement, declaration, discourse, subject-matter, doctrine, affair' and, by another development, 'reason, cause, sake, respect'. As a grammatical term it means a finite sentence, in logic a factual statement, definition or judgment, in rhetoric a correctly constructed piece of oratory. As a term of psychology and metaphysics it was used by the Stoa, following Herakleitos, to signify the divine power of function by which the universe is given unity, coherence and meaning (*logos spermatikos*, 'seminal Word', which, like seed, gives form to unformed matter): man is made in accordance with the same principle, and is himself said to possess Logos, both inwardly (*logos endiathetos*, reason) and expressed in speech (*logos prophorikos*). The term is also used as the pattern or norm of man whereby he lives 'according to Nature'.

In the LXX Logos is used to translate Heb. *dāḇār*. The root of this signifies 'that which lies behind', and so when translated as 'word' it, too, means meaningful sound; it may also mean 'thing'. In accordance with a common feature of Heb. psychology a man's *dāḇār* is regarded as in some sense an extension of his personality and further as possessing a substantive existence of its own. The Word of God, then, is his self-revelation through Moses and the prophets; it may be used to designate *both* single visions and oracles *and* the whole content of the total revelation, and thus especially the Pentateuch. The Word possesses a like power to the God who speaks it (*cf.* Is. 55:11) and effects his will without hindrance. Hence the term may refer to the creative word of God. In the Wisdom literature the creative power of God is referred to as his wisdom, and in a number of passages is spoken of as an *hypostasis* distinct from him (see especially Pr. 8:22–30: Wisdom of Solomon 7:21ff.).

Influenced both by the OT and by Hellenic thought, Philo made frequent use of the term Logos, to which he gave a highly-developed significance and a central place to his theological scheme. He derived the term from Stoic sources and, in accordance with his discovery of Gk. thought in the Heb. Scriptures, made use of it on the basis of such passages as Ps. 33:6 to express the means whereby the transcendent God may be the Creator of the universe and the Revealer of himself to Moses and the Patriarchs. On the Gk. side he equates the Logos with the Platonic concept of the World of Ideas so that it becomes both God's plan and God's power of creation. On the side of biblical exegesis the Logos is identified with the Angel of the Lord and the Name of God, and is described by a variety of terms as High Priest, Captain and Steersman, Advocate (Paraclete) and Son of God. It is termed a second God and, on the other hand, described as the Ideal Man, the Pattern of God's earthly creation of man. In spite of all this terminology of personification, however, the term remains—inevitably, in view of Philo's staunch Judaism (at least, in intention)—a philosophical and theological term and tool.

A further possible determining factor in the use of Logos in the passages which we need to review is the use of the term to signify the gospel message. The term is used absolutely (*e.g.* to preach the Word) and with a number of genitives (the Word of God, of Christ, of the cross, of reconciliation, of life, *etc.*). These show that the gospel story is seen in the NT as essentially a presentation of Jesus himself; he is the Word which is preached. But this is by no means always implicit in the phrase.

Three places are found at which the use of Logos in a technical sense has been concerned, *viz.* Jn. 1:1 and 14; 1 Jn. 1:1–3; Rev. 19:13.

Jn. 1:1 is the only unambiguous case. Here we have a highly metaphysical prologue to the Gospel in which the significance of the Christ is interpreted theologically. Divergence is found among scholars in the identification of the primary source of these verses and the chief meaning of Logos here. Attempts have been made to link the prologue primarily with the OT use of *dāḇār* alone, or with the rabbinical teaching concerning the Torah. These fail because these concepts are not sufficiently differentiated from the supreme Godhead to stand without alteration in v. 14. The figure of Wisdom provides more parallels but lacks identification in our sources with the Word: the teaching about the Primal or Heavenly Man which others have invoked is too conjectural to command much confidence. Only the Philonic Logos-teaching provides a clear theological scheme in which the Word possesses a like unity with God and a like distinction from him, and in which both creative and sustaining activity in the universe and revelatory activity towards man is ascribed to it. Further, the necessarily unique concept of incarnation is nevertheless a proper development of the identification of Philo's Logos with the Ideal Man. Either a direct use of Philo or a similar background in intellectual circles of Hellenistic Jewry may lie behind this.

In 1 Jn. 1:1 the phrase 'Word of life' is unlikely

to bear the meaning of Logos in its technical theological sense; both context and construction are against this. Even if this be from the same pen as the Gospel (which some scholars regard as doubtful), the letter may date from a time prior to the adoption of a full-grown Logos-doctrine. The sense of 'Christian gospel' fits this context best.

In Rev. 19:13 the sense of 'gospel' may lie behind the ascription of the title Logos of God to the triumphant figure; compare 6:2, where in the view of some exegetes the mounted figure is the triumphant advancing gospel.

We may compare also the imagery of Wisdom of Solomon 18:15–16. But since in Revelation the figure is explicitly declared to be King of kings and Lord of lords, some more metaphysical meaning must be latent here. The literary genre of the book amply explains why this meaning is not developed here in the same fashion as in the Fourth Gospel.

All three places illustrate how the fullness of Christ consistently exhausts all preparatory imagery and thought; and how many places need an exegesis which draws on many sources for full exposition. Jesus gives fresh meaning to terminology which prior to him was expressive of lesser mysteries.

BIBLIOGRAPHY. Pauly-Wissowa, art. 'Logos'; A. Debrunner *et al.*, *TDNT* 4, pp. 69–143; H. Haarbeck *et al.*, *NIDNTT* 3, pp. 1078–1123; R. Mortley, *From Word to Silence*, 2 vols., 1986. J.N.B.

LOIS. Timothy's grandmother, presumably the mother of *Eunice (2 Tim. 1:5). Paul doubtless alludes to her Christian faith: had she been simply a godly Jewess, her devotion is less likely to have been known to him. The name is hard to parallel in the period. A.F.W.

LORD'S DAY. The expression is found only once in Scripture. In Rev. 1:10 John discloses that the vision of the Apocalypse came to him while he was rapt 'in the Spirit on the Lord's day'. This is the first extant occurrence in Christian literature of *hē kyriakē hēmera*. The adjectival construction suggests that it was a formal designation of the church's worship day. As such it certainly appears early in the 2nd century (Ignatius, *Epistle to the Magnesians*, 1. 67).

Little support can be adduced for the theory that the term referred to Easter day, except, of course, in the sense that each Lord's day is a paschal recapitulation. But it must be noted that such reputable scholars as J. J. Wettstein, G. A. Deissmann and F. J. A. Hort, among others, prefer to interpret the verse as indicating that John was transported in his spiritual ecstasy to the great day of judgment itself (*cf.* Rev. 6:17; 16:14). J. B. Lightfoot believes that there are 'very good, if not conclusive reasons' for such a view (*The Apostolic Fathers*, 2, Section I, Part II, p. 129). The majority opinion, however, inclines to feel with H. B. Swete that such an interpretation is foreign to the immediate context and contrary to linguistic usage (LXX always has *hē hēmera tou kyriou* for the prophetic 'day of the Lord': *kyriakos* does not appear). It would seem reasonably safe, therefore, to conclude that as the actual location of John's vision is recorded in v. 9, so the actual occasion is recorded in v. 10.

Even if a late date for Revelation be accepted (*c.* AD 96), it is not necessary to assume with Harnack that *hē kyriakē hēmera* was not in use before the close of the 1st century. It may even have emerged as soon as AD 57 when Paul wrote 1 Corinthians. In 11:20 he speaks of *kyriakon deipnon* ('the Lord's supper'). It is interesting that Pesh. reads 'Lord's day' here. But it would hardly appear that the term was in current use, for later in the Epistle Paul has *kata mian sabbatou* (16:2).

Deissmann has thrown further light upon the title by showing that in Asia Minor and Egypt even before the Christian era the first day of each month was called Emperor's Day or *Sebastē*. This may eventually have been transferred to a day of the week, probably Thursday (*dies Iovis*). 'If these conclusions are valid,' comments R. H. Charles, 'we can understand how naturally the term "Lord's Day" arose; for just as the first day of each month, or a certain day of each week, was called "Emperor's Day", so it would be natural for Christians to name the *first day* of each week, associated as it was with the Lord's resurrection and the custom of Christians to meet together for worship, as "Lord's Day". It may have first arisen in apocalyptic circles when a hostile attitude to the Empire was adopted by Christianity' (R. H. Charles, *The Revelation of St. John*, 1, 1920, p. 23; *cf.* Deissmann, *Bible Studies*, pp. 218ff.).

'Lord' here clearly signifies Christ and not God the Father. It is Christ's own day. It belongs to him because of his resurrection, when he was 'designated Son of God in power' (Rom. 1:4). McArthur is surely right in claiming that the title ultimately derives from the Lordship of Jesus Christ which was made manifest in the resurrection on 'the first day of the week' (Mk. 16:2; see A. A. McArthur, *The Evolution of the Christian Year*, 1953, p. 21). Christian worship is essentially an *anamnēsis* (remembrance) of the Easter event which revealed the triumph of God's redemptive purpose. Hence the prevailing note of joy and praise. The first day was also appropriate, as it recalled the initial day of creation, when God made light, and the fact that the Christian Pentecost fell on Sunday. Furthermore, it may well have been the expectation of the primitive Christians that our Lord's return would take place on his own day.

The earliest piece of evidence relating to the Christian observance of the first day of the week lies in 1 Cor. 16:1–2, but there is no explicit reference to an actual assembly. Acts 20:7 is more specific and probably reflects the continued Christian use of the Jewish calendar under which the Lord's day would begin at sunset on Saturday. Alford sees in the readiness of Gentiles to accept this Jewish reckoning 'the greatest proof of all that this day was thus observed' (Henry Alford, *The New Testament for English Readers*[6], 1871, p. 788). On the other hand, there is no trace in the NT of any sabbatarian controversy. The Lord's day, while fulfilling all the beneficent purposes of God in the institution of the Sabbath for mankind, was kept 'not under the old written code but in the new life of the Spirit' (Rom. 7:6).

BIBLIOGRAPHY: H. P. Porter, *The Day of Light: the Biblical and Liturgical Meaning of Sunday*, 1960; W. Rordorf, *Sunday: the History of the Day of Rest and Worship in the Earliest Centuries of the Church*, E.T. 1968; R. T. Beckwith and W. Stott, *This is the Day*, 1978 (reply to Rordorf); D. A. Carson (ed.), *From Sabbath to Lord's Day: A Biblical, Historical and Theological Investigation*, 1984. A.S.W.

LORD'S PRAYER, THE. The prayer which our Lord taught his disciples as the model prayer for their regular use. In Mt. 6:9–13 it is given as an integral part of the Sermon on the Mount. But in Lk. 11:2–4 it is given by our Lord in different circumstances. It is probable that since he meant this prayer to serve as a pattern for all his disciples at all times, he would have repeated it on different occasions.

In Mt. 6:9–13 he gives it as an example which complies with all the requisites which he himself had laid down as essential for true prayer: 'Pray then like this,' he said (v. 9). He was thus continuing to teach his disciples *how* to pray. After having warned them not to pray as hypocrites (v. 5) nor to 'heap up empty phrases' as the heathen do (v. 7), he taught them what sort of prayer is acceptable before God. But in Lk. 11:1–4, in response to the request of a disciple, he gives the prayer this time, not only as an example of a prayer which complies with his teaching, but as a definite prayer which must be prayed by his followers: 'When you pray, say . . .' (v. 2).

In Lk. 11:2–4 the prayer is given in a shorter form than in Mt. 6:9–13, as follows: 'Father, hallowed be thy name. Thy kingdom come. Give us each day our daily bread; and forgive us our sins, for we ourselves forgive every one who is indebted to us; and lead us not into temptation.'

The short form probably represents the compass of the prayer as Jesus originally phrased it: the simple address 'Father' corresponds to the form 'Abba' which he used himself (*cf.* Mk. 14:36) and which the early Christians followed his example in using (*cf.* Rom. 8:15; Gal. 4:6). The amplified Matthaean text has been adapted for Christian liturgical use, the address 'Our Father who art in heaven' being taken over from synagogue usage. Here we shall consider the full Matthaean text.

It is obvious that our Lord gave the prayer originally in Aramaic. By the time Matthew and Luke wrote their Gospels, however, the prayer would naturally have been used by Christians in Greek also. This probably explains why Mt. 6 and Lk. 11 have general agreement in language and both use the unique term *epiousios* (rendered 'daily') in the prayer.

By the opening words of the prayer—'Our Father who art in heaven'—we are taught the correct attitude and spirit in which we should pray to God. Addressing him as 'Our Father', we look up to him in love and faith, as to the One who is near us in perfect love and grace. By the words 'who art in heaven' we give expression to our holy reverence for him who is the Almighty Ruler over all. The introductory words of the prayer also remind us of the fact that all Christian believers are one in him, for we are to pray to him as '*Our* Father'. The believer's heart being rightly attuned by the invocation, the first petitions are those concerning the glory and divine purpose of our heavenly Father. 'Hallowed be (*hagiasthētō*) thy name' is a prayer asking God to enable us and all men to recognize and honour him. His name, *i.e.* he himself in his self-revelation, is to be acknowledged as holy; and he is to receive all the honour and glory due to the One who perfectly loves us, our holy and omnipotent Creator. (*GOD, NAMES OF.) The petition 'Thy kingdom come' may, for general purposes, be used as a supplication that the divine dominion (*basileia*) of God will be extended 'here and now' (in this present age) in the heart of individuals as well as in the world as a whole. Primarily, however, this petition has an eschatological connotation; it is a supplication that the kingly rule of God may be established 'with power' (Mk. 9:1) at the glorious appearing of the Son of man. (*KINGDOM OF GOD.)

The third petition, 'Thy will be done on earth as it is in heaven', which is absent in the authentic text of Lk. 11:2, is practically an elaboration of the previous petition. In heaven, where the rule of God is gladly and unconditionally accepted by all, the will of God is continuously, spontaneously and joyfully obeyed by all. Believers should thus pray that God's will shall in the same way be obeyed by all on earth, and especially in their own lives. This petition has a partial reference to the present age, but it opens up vistas to the time when every knee shall bow before the King of kings and the powers of darkness will be finally destroyed. God will then be all in all and his will shall reign supreme (1 Cor. 15:25–28). The three imperatives *hagiasthētō* ('be hallowed'), *elthatō* ('come') and *genēthētō* ('be done') are all aorist and point to the final consummation.

The first three petitions having centred upon the glorification of God, the next three petitions are concerned with the physical and spiritual well-being of believers.

Believers should thus pray expressly for the aid and blessing of God regarding all aspects of life in this world. The petition 'Give us this day our daily bread' asks God as our heavenly Father to grant us the physical necessities of life. The word 'bread' here sums up all that we really need for our earthly existence. In view of the foregoing petitions, this is a supplication asking God continually to supply us with the material necessities of life so that we may most effectively sanctify his name, labour for the coming of his kingdom and do his will on earth. Our prayer for daily sustenance is thus not meant to be a selfish prayer, or a prayer for material luxury, but a prayer in which we confess our utter dependence on God and look to him in faith and love to supply us with all things which we really need to enable us to live according to his will.

The Gk. word *epiousios*, translated 'daily', occurs only in Mt. 6:11 and Lk. 11:3, and (reportedly) in one papyrus document (unfortunately no longer extant), where the neuter plural form *epiousia* appears to have meant 'daily rations'. Although finality has not yet been reached regarding its correct etymological derivation, and some prefer to translate it by 'for the coming day' or 'that is needful or sufficient', the translation 'daily' seems to be quite in order. The rendering 'supersubstantial bread' goes back to Jerome, as though the reference were to Jesus as the true bread of life. J. Jeremias relates this petition to the eschatological emphasis of its predecessors as though the reference were to 'eating bread in the kingdom of God' (*cf.* Lk. 14:15). But in the context, what is meant is the constant provision of what is really needed and adequate for us day by day in the realm of our physical, material existence.

The next petition, 'And forgive us our debts, as we also have forgiven our debtors', is both a prayer and a confession. For he who prays for forgiveness at the same time admits that he has sinned and is guilty. In Lk. 11:4 this petition reads: 'And forgive us our sins; for we ourselves forgive every one who is indebted to us.' The Gk. word *hamartias*, here rendered 'sins', has the primary meaning of 'missing the mark' and thus 'acting wrongly' and 'breaking the law of God'. In Mt. 6:12 *opheilēmata* ('debts') preserves the Aramaic idiom in which the word for 'debt' (*ḥôḇâ*) is also used in the sense of 'sin'. By sinning we have incurred a moral and spiritual debt to our Father and Creator, who has full authority over our lives. In this petition we therefore humbly ask him for a remission of our debts, seeing that we ourselves can never earn our forgiveness.

The words 'as we also [*hōs kai hēmeis*, 'in the same way also as we'] have forgiven [aorist] our debtors' (Mt. 6:12) and 'for we ourselves forgive [present indicative] every one who is indebted to us' (Lk. 11:4) do not mean that we are to ask forgiveness *on the ground* of our forgiving those who sin against us. We can receive forgiveness through grace alone. But in order to pray to God for forgiveness in sincerity and without hypocrisy, we must be free from all spirit of hatred and revenge. Only when God has given us the grace truly to forgive those who sin against us can we utter a true prayer for forgiveness. This was looked upon by our Lord as of such importance that he reiterated it in Mt. 6:14–15 (*cf.* Mt. 18:23–35; Mk. 11:25).

The final petition in Lk. 11:4 reads: 'And lead us not into temptation'. In Mt. 6:13, the words 'but deliver us from evil' (RSVmg. 'the evil one') follow. These additional words help to make the petition one of general application. Those who sincerely pray for forgiveness of sins long to be enabled not to sin again. Thus it is fitting that this petition follows the previous one. God never tempts anyone to do evil (Jas. 1:13), but he controls the circumstances of our lives. In this prayer we humbly confess that we are prone to sin and thus plead with him not to allow us to be brought into situations or conditions which involve grave temptation to sin. As a further elaboration of this there follows 'but deliver us from the evil one', *i.e.* shield, protect, guard (*rhyesthai*) us against the onslaughts of the devil (*tou ponērou*). This final petition, although applicable to every day in our lives, points very clearly to the consummation when our Lord will put an end to all that is evil, and establish his eternal kingdom of righteousness and holiness.

This brings us to the consideration that in the setting of Jesus' ministry this petition struck an eschatological note. The NEB rendering ('And do not bring us to the test') indicates this, albeit too cryptically. The test is that crucial test of the disciples' faith which, without divine strength, would prove too intense for them to resist. The form taken by that test was shown in the setting of Gethsemane (the final test also for Jesus himself). The exhortation to the disciples, 'Watch and pray that you may not enter into temptation' (Mk. 14:38) probably means 'Keep awake, and pray not to fail in the test'. This suggests that the petition in the Lord's Prayer means, 'Grant that we may not fail in the test' (*cf.* C. C. Torrey, *The Four Gospels*, 1933, p. 292). And today, over and above the general plea to be delivered from temptation, Christians may use the petition as a prayer for grace and power to keep them from failing when their faith is challenged by a supreme test.

In some ancient and many later MSS of Mt. 6:13 a doxology follows. In the AV it reads, 'For thine is the kingdom, and the power, and the glory, for ever. Amen.' Although the most authoritative MSS do not have the doxology, it has been used in the Christian church from the earliest times (*cf.* the *Didache* and the Western Text), and it is certainly a most suitable and worthy ending for the Lord's Prayer. That it does not, however, belong to the original text of Matthew is apparent from the fact that vv. 14 and 15 follow naturally after vv. 12 and 13a.

Someone has rightly said that the Lord's Prayer is Jesus' message of the kingdom of God summarized in prayer form. It is the prayer which all Christians should regularly offer to God in order to be enabled to live as his children ever more completely until the day when his sovereignty is perfectly established.

It should be noted that our Lord (when teaching his disciples this prayer) did not say, '*we* must pray' but '*you* pray'. The Lord's Prayer is the prayer which he taught, not one which he used. He does not appear ever to have used the expression 'Our Father' in such a way as to include his disciples with himself (*cf.* Jn. 20:17, 'my Father and your Father'), nor is there any hint that he ever felt the need to ask forgiveness for himself.

While the individual petitions in the Lord's Prayer are paralleled in various contexts in Jewish religious literature, nothing comparable to the prayer as a whole is found. The Lord's Prayer is unique, and unsurpassed even to this day—gathering in a few words all the essentials of true prayer.

BIBLIOGRAPHY. J. Jeremias, *The Lord's Prayer*, 1964 (reprinted in *The Prayers of Jesus*, 1967, pp. 82–107); E. Lohmeyer, *The Lord's Prayer*, 1965; T. W. Manson, *BJRL* 38, 1955–6, pp. 99–113, 436–448; B. M. Metzger, in *Historical and Literary Studies*, 1968, pp. 64ff.; W. O. Walker, *NTS* 28, 1982, pp. 237–256; commentaries on Matthew and Luke.

J.N.G.
F.F.B.

LORD'S SUPPER, THE. It will be most convenient to set out the NT evidence for the Christian ordinance under the headings of 'The Last Supper'; 'The breaking of bread'; 'The Pauline Eucharist'; and 'Other NT material'.

I. The Last Supper

a. Was it the Passover?

The precise nature of the meal which the Lord shared with his disciples on the night in which he was betrayed is one of the most warmly debated topics of NT history and interpretation. Various suggestions have been made.

1. The traditional explanation is that the meal was the customary Passover feast, and this can claim the support of the Gospel records, both Synoptic (*e.g.* Mk. 14:1–2, 12–16) and Johannine (*e.g.* 13:21–30). There are features of the meal which students of Judaism (notably P. Billerbeck and G. H. Dalman) have noted as distinguishing features of the Paschal feast, *e.g.* reclining at the table (*ABRAHAM'S BOSOM), the distribution of alms (*cf.* Jn. 13:29), and the use of the 'sop' which is dipped in the special *ḥarōseṯ* sauce as a memorial of the bitterness of the Egyp. bondage. See the full details in G. H. Dalman, *Jesus–Jeshua*, E.T. 1929, pp. 106ff., and J. Jeremias, *The Eucharistic Words of Jesus*, E.T. [2]1966, pp. 41ff. But the evidence is not so compelling as to exclude all other interpretations, although there is a tendency today, especially since the first publication of Jeremias' book in 1949, to give more respectful consideration to the Passover view than was formerly done. The earlier judgment was similar to that expressed by Hans Lietzmann, who dismissed the Paschal theory of the Supper as containing scarcely 'the least vestige of probability' (*Mass and Lord's Supper*, E.T. 1953, p. 173). There has been a reaction from this extreme negativism.

2. The data which caused some questioning of the traditional view are mainly derived from the Fourth Gospel, which apparently dates the events of the Supper evening and the passion a day earlier than the Synoptics. According to Jn. 13:1; 18:28; 19:14, 31, 42, the crucifixion happened a day before Nisan 15, which is the Synoptic reckoning, and the Last Supper was, of course, eaten on the evening before that. Thus it cannot have been the regular paschal meal, for the Lord died at the same time as the lambs for that meal were being immolated in the Temple ritual. Thus there is an apparent *impasse*, which is further complicated by the allegation that the Synoptic account is not consistent with itself; for instance, Lk. 22:15 may be read as an unfulfilled wish. For those scholars who prefer to support the Johannine dating (*e.g.* J. H. Bernard in the *ICC* on *John*) and believe that the last meal could therefore not have been the Passover, the question arises, what type of meal, then, was it? They answer this question by postulating a sabbath *Qiddūsh*, *i.e.*, according to this view, Jesus and his followers constituted a religious group which met on the eve of the sabbath and the Passover, and held a simple service in which a prayer of sanctification (*Qiddūsh*) over a cup of wine was said.

3. As a modification of this suggestion Hans Lietzmann put forward the idea that the meal was an ordinary one, and the Lord and his disciples, who shared it, formed a religious association called a *ḥaḇûrāh*, similar to the groups in which the Pharisees met. All these ideas have met with severe criticism, and there is apparent deadlock in the debate; though it is now being reopened through the investigation of the new evidence of the Qumran scrolls.

4. In the light of recent researches into the influence of separate calendars which were used for calculating feast-days, it is now possible to consider again the older submissions of P. Billerbeck and J. Pickl that the two strata of Gospel evidence may be harmonized on the assumption that both are understandable, with each reflecting a different tradition. Billerbeck and Pickl distinguished between the Pharisaic date of the Passover which Jesus used and the Sadducean dating a day earlier which lies behind the Fourth Gospel. This was dismissed by critics as lacking in supporting evidence, but the Dead Sea Scrolls show that there were divergent calendars in use in heterodox Jewry, and it is possible that separate traditions were, in fact, in vogue at the time of the passion. Mlle A. Jaubert has recently reconstructed the events on this basis so as to harmonize the data of the Gospels and early liturgical witnesses (in her book *The Date of the Last Supper*, E.T. 1965. See for an acceptance of her thesis, E. E. Ellis, *The Gospel of Luke*², *NCB*, 1974, pp. 249f. and Mlle Jaubert's later contribution in *NTS* 14, 1967–8, pp. 145–164.

Whether the date of the Supper will ever be conclusively determined is uncertain; but we may certainly believe that, whatever the exact nature of the meal, there were Passover ideas in the Lord's mind when he sat down with the disciples. The Jewish Passover, based on Ex. 12 and interpreted in the *Haggāḏāh* for Passover and the Mishnaic tractate *Pesaḥim*, provides the indispensable key to an understanding of the meal and also the meaning of the Lord's Supper in the early church. This conclusion is reinforced by recent studies in typology which have shown the importance of the OT events in their 'typological' significance for the NT writers; and no complex of saving events comes more decisively to the foreground in the thinking of early Christianity than the Exodus and redemption from Egypt (*cf.* H. Sahlin, 'The New Exodus of Salvation according to St Paul', in *The Root of the Vine*, ed. A. Fridrichsen, 1953, pp. 81–95; J. Daniélou, *Sacramentum Futuri*, 1950, Book IV, pp. 131ff.). Reference may also be made to the important contribution of T. Preiss, *Life in Christ*, E.T. 1954, p. 90, who shows the place of 'the totality of the events of the Exodus centring on the Passover' in both Jewish and Christian traditions.

b. The words of institution

We turn now to examine more closely the last meal in the upper room. Two questions immediately arise. What was the *form* of the words of institution, spoken over the bread and wine? And what was their *meaning*?

1. The original form of the words is not easily discoverable because there are several sets of variants, represented chiefly in the Marcan and the Pauline traditions respectively. Lk. 22:15–20 has peculiarities of its own, both textual and hermeneutical. There is a recent tendency to accept the longer recension of the Lucan text against the shorter readings of the Western MS D and certain Old Lat. and Syrian MSS which omit verses 19b and 20. The value of the Lucan *pericope* lies in its place as independent evidence of the same tradition as that used by Paul with the unusual order 'cup—bread' in Lk. 22:17–19 and 1 Cor. 10:16, 21 (*cf. Didache* 9); and the preservation in both accounts of the command to repeat the rite (Lk. 22:19b; 1 Cor. 11:25). The originality of the 'longer text' has been virtually established by H. Schürmann, *Bib* 32, 1951, pp. 364–392, 522–541. *Cf.* E. E. Ellis, *Luke*, pp. 254–256 (biblio.).

On the issue of Marcan versus Pauline form the arguments on both sides are inconclusive. Some scholars feel that Jesus could never have suggested that the disciples were to drink his blood, even symbolically, and the Pauline version, 'This cup is the new covenant in my blood' (1 Cor. 11:25), is more likely to be original, especially as the Marcan formula is liturgically symmetrical with that about the bread, and is aligned to Ex. 24:8 (LXX). Against this it has been contended by A. J. B. Higgins that the Marcan form is more primitive because of its harsh Semitisms in the Greek and the obvious dependence on the Servant passages in Isaiah, although Higgins would wish to excise some of the Marcan phrases. At all events, we may consider the following to be somewhere near the original: 'Jesus took a loaf, pronounced a blessing, broke it and said, This is my body. And he took a cup, blessed it and said, This cup is the new covenant in my blood (Paul), or, This is my blood of the covenant (Mark).' Then followed the eschatological pronouncement, *cf.* Mk. 14:25; 1 Cor. 11:26. On the 'vow of abstinence', see J. Jeremias, *New Testament Theology*, 1, E.T. 1971, pp. 298f.

2. If we begin with the eschatological utterance

this will be explained as the hope of the early believers, instructed by the Lord, that their fellowship with him will be fulfilled in the perfected kingdom of God; and this sets a *terminus ad quem* for the Pauline Eucharist, for when the Lord returns in glory to unite his people in fellowship the memorial table-fellowship will cease (*cf.* M. Dibelius, *From Tradition to Gospel*, E.T. 1934, p. 208).

The interpretative words over the elements have been variously estimated. There is no ground for a literal equivalence as in the doctrine of transubstantiation. The copula 'is' is the exegetical *significat* as in Gn. 41:26; Dn. 7:17; Lk. 8:11; Gal. 4:24; Rev. 1:20; and in the spoken Aramaic the copulative would be lacking, as in Gn. 40:12; Dn. 2:36; 4:22. The figurative, non-literal connotation 'ought never to have been disputed' (Lietzmann).

The words, 'body, blood', are sometimes taken in the sense that Jesus is referring to his impending death on the cross when his body was broken (but *cf.* Jn. 19:31–37) and his blood shed in violent death. The principal objection to this symbolic view is that the word over the bread was not spoken when it was broken but when it was distributed, and the wine had been poured out at an earlier part of the paschal meal. Also there is nothing unusual or unique in the fact that bread was broken. 'To break bread' was a common Jewish expression for the sharing of a meal.

Another view takes the Gk. term *sōma* (body) to denote the Aramaic *gûp̄*, which means not only 'body' but 'person', as though Jesus said, 'This is my person, my real self'; and points to his continuing fellowship as risen Lord with his people as they repeat the table-fellowship. Jeremias, however, has objected to this suggestion of Dalman (*op. cit.*, p. 143) by remarking that the true counterpart to 'blood' is not 'body', *sōma*, but 'flesh', *sarx*, for which the Aramaic is *bisrī*, 'my flesh'. But see E. Schweizer, *The Lord's Supper according to the New Testament*, E.T. 1967, pp. 14–17.

The most valuable clue to the meaning of the Lord's instituting words is to be found in the part which food and drink play in the Passover ritual. Following Higgins' interpretation, we may take the words of the institution to be the Lord's own addition to the order of the paschal liturgy at two vital points, before and after the main meal. He tells his disciples, by his words and prophetic symbolism, that the original meaning of the paschal rite has now been transcended, inasmuch as he is the paschal Lamb fulfilling the OT prefigurement (1 Cor. 5:7). His words and action in taking the bread and the cup are parables which announce a new significance. The bread becomes under his sovereign word the parable of his body yielded up in the service of God's redeeming purpose (*cf.* Heb. 10:5–10); and his blood outpoured in death, recalling the sacrificial rites of the OT, is represented in the cup of blessing on the table. That cup is invested henceforward with a fresh significance as the memorial of the new Exodus, accomplished at Jerusalem (Lk. 9:31).

The function of the elements is parallel, then, to that of the Passover dishes. At the annual feast the Israelite is linked, in a realistic and dynamic way, with his forebears whom the Lord redeemed from Egypt. The bread on the table is to be regarded as though it were 'the bread of affliction' which the Jews of old ate (Dt. 16:3 as interpreted in the Passover *Haggāḏāh*); he is to account himself as though he personally was set free from Egyp. tyranny in that first generation of his nation long ago (Mishnah, *Pesaḥim* 10. 5). At the Lord's Table which is genetically related to the upper room the church of the new Israel is gathered as the people of the new covenant (Je. 31:31ff.); is confronted afresh with the tokens of that once-offered sacrifice; and relives that experience by which it came out of the Egypt of sin and was ransomed to God by the precious death of God's paschal Victim. Further details of this 'dynamic' significance of the Lord's supper elements are given in R. P. Martin, *Worship in the Early Church*, 1974 ed., pp. 114ff.

II. The breaking of bread

In the early church of the Acts there are scattered references to table-fellowship, *e.g.* Acts 2:42, 46 where the phrase is 'breaking of bread'. In Acts 20:7 (but not 27:35, which describes an ordinary, non-cultic meal) there is a reference to a fellowship meal, using the identical phrase. The fact that no mention of the cup is ever made in Acts leads H. Lietzmann (see *ExpT* 65, 1953–54, pp. 333ff. for a clear, yet critical, statement of his theory) to the elaborate thesis that this Jerusalem communion in one kind is the earliest and most original form of the sacrament, though hardly deserving the name. It was, *ex hypothesi*, a fellowship meal beginning with the familiar Jewish custom of breaking of bread—a continuation, in fact, of the common meals of the Galilean ministry when the Lord fed the crowds and in which the Lord and his disciples formed a *ḥaḇûrāh*. The motif of the Jerusalem rite was not the death of Jesus, but the invisible presence of the exalted Lord in their midst. The Lord's Supper of 1 Cor. 11 with its emphasis on the atoning significance of the death of Christ was Paul's own new contribution, received by special revelation from the Lord in glory. So Lietzmann suggests.

But this elaboration is unnecessary. There is little suggestion that Paul was such an innovator. As A. M. Hunter remarks, 'It staggers belief that he could have successfully foisted his innovation . . . on the church at large' (*Paul and His Predecessors*[2], 1961, p. 75). The non-mention of the cup may not be significant; the name 'breaking of bread' may be a quasi-technical expression for the whole meal. What is significant about the early form of the Eucharist is the note of *joy* which stems directly, not so much from the Galilean meals as from the post-resurrection appearances, many of which are associated with a meal between the victorious Lord and his own (Lk. 24:30–35, 36–48; Jn. 21:9ff.; Acts 1:4 (RVmg.); 10:41; Rev. 3:20).

III. The Pauline Eucharist

The common meals of the Galilean ministry are more likely to find their fulfilment in the *agapē* or love feast of the Corinthian church (1 Cor. 11:20–34). At Corinth there were two parts of the cultic observance: a common meal, taken for the purpose of nourishment (*cf. Didache* 10. 1: 'after you are filled'), followed by a solemn rite of the Eucharist. (*LOVE FEAST.) There were serious excesses within the Corinthian assembly, such as greediness, selfishness, drunkenness and gluttony. Paul issued a grave warning, and the impression we gather is that it was his desire to have the two parts kept separate, as happened in the later church. Let the hungry eat at home, and come with reverence and self-examination to the Table, is his caution (11:22, 30–34).

Paul's distinctive eucharistic teaching serves to enhance the significance of the Supper by anchoring it firmly in God's redeeming purpose; so that it proclaims the Lord's death (1 Cor. 11:26) as the Passover ritual set forth (hence the title, *Haggāḏāh*, *i.e.* declaration, for which the Gk. equivalent would be the Pauline *katangellein* of 1 Cor. 11:26) the redeeming mercy of God under the old covenant. He also expounds the inner meaning of the Table as a communion (*koinōnia*) with the Lord in his death and risen life, signified in the bread and the wine (1 Cor. 10:16). Therein he discovers the unity of the church, for as the members share together the one loaf they sit down as the one body of Christ (*cf.* A. E. J. Rawlinson's essay in *Mysterium Christi*, ed. Bell and Deissmann, 1930, pp. 225ff.). There are eschatological overtones likewise, as in the evangelic tradition, with the forward look to the advent in glory. *Marānāthā* in 1 Cor. 16:22 may very well be placed in a eucharistic setting so that the conclusion of the letter ends with the invocation 'Our Lord, come!' and prepares the scene for the celebration of the meal after the letter has been read to the congregation (*cf.* Lietzmann, *op. cit.*, p. 229; J. A. T. Robinson, 'The Earliest Christian Liturgical sequence?', *JTS* n.s. 4, 1953, pp. 38–41; but see C. F. D. Moule, *NTS* 6, 1959–60, pp. 307ff.). See, too, G. Wainwright, *Eucharist and Eschatology*, 1971. Further exposition of Paul's teaching on the Supper is offered in R. P. Martin, *op. cit.*, ch. 11.

IV. Other New Testament material

It is surely significant that there is little other *direct* NT witness to the sacrament apart from the references we have already given. This fact is especially important when it comes to an assessment of Paul's so-called 'sacramentalism'. The writer of 1 Cor. 1:16–17 could never have been one who regarded the sacraments as the last word about the Christian faith and practice; yet we must equally admit that, in C. T. Craig's words, 'Paul would not have understood an expression of Christian faith apart from a community in which the Lord's Supper was celebrated' (quoted by A. M. Hunter, *Interpreting Paul's Gospel*, 1954, p. 105). Adolf Schlatter, we believe, gives the truest estimate in his observation on the apostle's sacramental theology: Paul 'can express the word of Jesus, not in half measure but completely, without mentioning the sacraments at all. But if they come into view he connects with them the entire riches of the grace of Christ, because he sees in them the will of Jesus, not partially but fully expressed and effective' (*Die Briefe an die Thessalonicher, Philipper, Timotheus und Titus*, 1950, p. 262).

What is true of Paul is true of the other NT writers. There may be allusions to the Lord's Supper in such places as Heb. 6:4; 13:10; and John's Gospel contains the notable synagogue discourse which many scholars relate to the eucharistic tradition of the later church (Jn. 6:22–59); but we should not overpress these references, as O. Cullmann seems to have done in finding numerous subtle references to sacramental worship in the Fourth Gospel (see his *Early Christian Worship*, 1953, pp. 37ff., especially p. 106).

There is the witness of 2 Pet. 2:13 and Jude 12 to the *agapē* meal. Apart from these somewhat exiguous data and meagre details, the NT is silent about the ordering and observance of eucharistic worship in the primitive communities, mainly owing to the fact that what is generally received and practised is not usually the subject of extended comment. For the development of the rite, and, it must be confessed, a fruitful source of heresy and confused doctrine, we must await the correspondence, epistles and liturgies of the 2nd and subsequent centuries, from *1 Clem.* 40. 2–4; Ignatius, *Smyrnaeans*. 8. 1; *Didache* 9–10, 14 onwards.

BIBLIOGRAPHY. This article has mentioned some of the main works of importance. Of special value is A. J. B. Higgins, *The Lord's Supper in the New Testament*, 1952; and for the later development, J. H. Srawley, *The Early History of the Liturgy*, 1947. Useful surveys of recent discussion of the NT evidence are books by E. Schweizer, *The Lord's Supper according to the New Testament*, E.T., 1967 (bibliography); H. Patsch, *Abendmahl und historisch Jesus*, 1972; I. H. Marshall, *Last Supper and Lord's Supper*, 1980. See, for a more popular treatment, R. P. Martin, *Worship in the Early Church*, 1974. R.P.M.

LOT (Heb. *lôṭ*, 'covering'?). The son of Haran, Abraham's youngest brother, and so Abraham's nephew. Apart from the account of his life in Genesis, his name is absent from the OT (except for references to his descendants in Dt. 2:9, 19; Ps. 83:8), but he is mentioned by our Lord in Lk. 17:28–32 and also by Peter in 2 Pet. 2:7f.

He accompanied Terah, Abram and Sarai as they journeyed from Ur to Harran, and went on with Abram and Sarai into Canaan, down into Egypt and then out again into Canaan (Gn. 11:31; 12:4–5; 13:1). Flaws in his character first appear when he selfishly chose the well-watered Jordan valley (Gn. 13:8–13). This brought him into the midst of the wicked men of Sodom, and he had to be rescued from the results of his folly, first by Abraham (Gn. 14:11–16), and then by the two angels (Gn. 19). In the latter incident he revealed both his weakness and his inclination to compromise. His salvation from Sodom is expressly linked with God's remembrance of Abraham in Gn. 19:29.

Through his drunkenness his two daughters obtained children by him, and these became the ancestors of the Moabites and the Ammonites (Gn. 19:30–38; *cf.* Dt. 2:9, 19; Ps. 83:8).

Our Lord illustrated his teaching on the subject of his return from the story of Lot and his wife (Lk. 17:28–32), thus setting his seal upon its historicity, and 2 Pet. 2:7f. emphatically asserts his righteousness. It is probable that Peter is here deliberately alluding to Abraham's prayer for the 'righteous' in Sodom. G.W.G.

LOVE, BELOVED.

I. In the Old Testament

a. Etymology

Love is the translation in the EVV primarily of the Heb. *'āhēḇ*, which is in every way as broad in its usage as the English word, and easily the most common word for every range of its meaning. Other Heb. words are *dôḏ* and *ra'yâ* (respectively of passionate love and its female object, especially in Ct.), *yāḏaḏ* (*e.g.* Ps. 127:2), *ḥāšaq* (*e.g.* Ps. 91:14), *ḥāḇaḇ* (only Dt. 33:3), *'āḡaḇ* (*e.g.* Je. 4:30, of paramours) and *rāḥam* (Ps. 18:1).

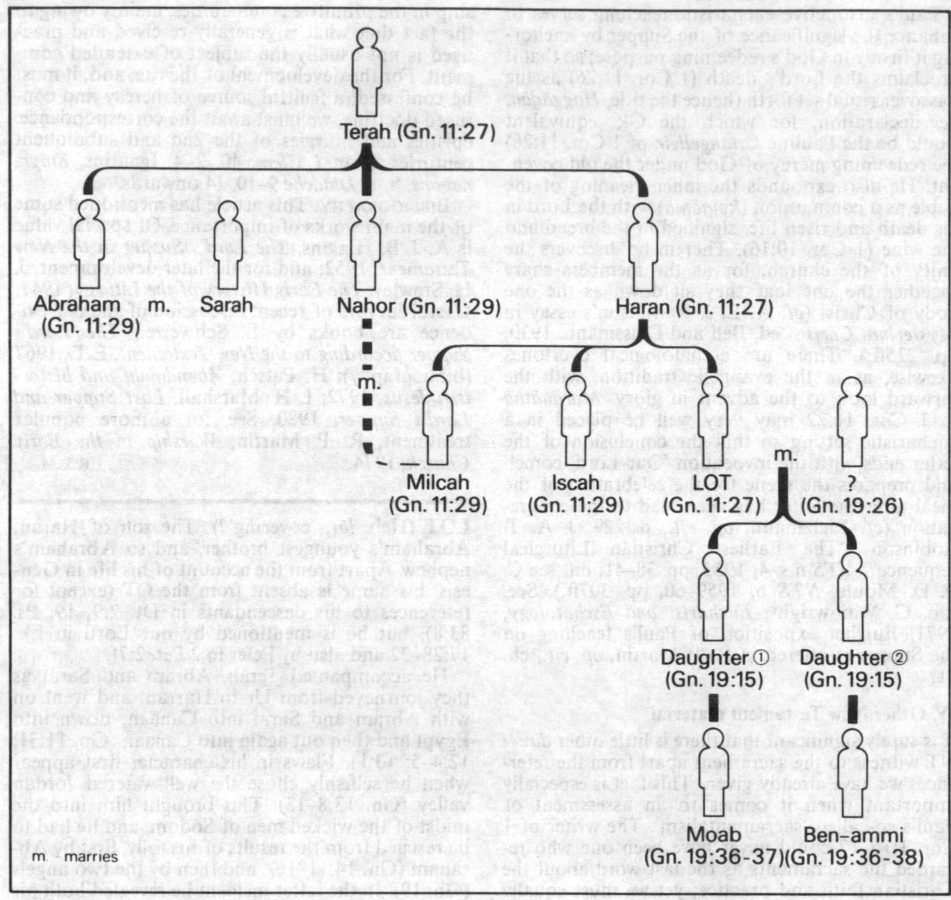

Lot's family (see p. 699).

In the OT love, whether human or divine, is the deepest possible expression of the personality and of the closeness of personal relations. In the non-religious sense *'āhēḇ* is most commonly employed of the mutual urge of the sexes, in which there is no restraint or sense of uncleanness (see Ct. for its most sublime expression). It is also used of a multitude of personal (Gn. 22:2; 37:3) and sub-personal (Pr. 18:21) relations which have no connection with the sexual impulse. Fundamentally it is an inner force (Dt. 6:5, 'might') which impels to performing the action which gives pleasure (Pr. 20:13), obtaining the object which awakens desire (Gn. 27:4), or in the case of persons to self-sacrifice for the good of the loved one (Lv. 19:18, 34), and unswerving loyalty (1 Sa. 20:17–42).

b. God's love for men

(i) *Its object*. This is primarily a collective group (Dt. 4:37, 'your fathers'; Pr. 8:17, 'those who love me'; Is. 43:4, 'Israel'), though the implication is clear that the individual shares in the divine regard for the group. Only in three places is God said in so many words to love an individual, and in each case it is a king (2 Sa. 12:24 and Ne. 13:26, Solomon; Is. 48:14, ?Cyrus). Here the special relationship may be because Israel's king is in some sense regarded as a son of God (*cf.* 2 Sa. 7:14; Pss. 2:7; 89:26f.), while Cyrus in the Isaianic passage may be a representative figure.

(ii) *Its personal nature*. Being rooted firmly in the personal character of God himself, it is deeper than that of a mother for her children (Is. 49:15; 66:13). This is most clear in Ho. 1–3, where (in whatever order the chapters are to be read) the relation between the prophet and his unfaithful wife Gomer is illustrative of the ultimate basis of the divine covenant in a deeper than legal relationship, in a love that is willing to suffer. God's love is part of his personality, and cannot be swayed by passion or diverted by disobedience (Ho. 11:1–4, 7–9; this passage is the nearest the OT approaches to a declaration that God is love). Israel's unfaithfulness can have no effect upon it, for 'I have loved you with an everlasting love' (Je. 31:3). The threat to 'love them no more' (Ho. 9:15) is best interpreted as one to be their God no more.

(iii) *Its selectiveness*. Dt. in particular bases the covenant relationship between Israel and God on God's prior love. Unlike the gods of other nations, who belong to them for natural and geographic reasons, Yahweh took the initiative and chose Israel because he loved her (Dt. 4:37; 7:6ff.; 10:15; Is. 43:4). This love is spontaneous, not evoked by any intrinsic worth in its object, but rather creating that worth (Dt. 7:7). The corollary is also true, that God hates those whom he does not love (Mal. 1:2f.). Although in various passages, notably Jon. and the Servant Songs of Is., a doctrine of universal love is foreshadowed, it nowhere finds concrete expression.

c. Love as a religious duty

(i) *Towards God.* Love for God with the whole personality (Dt. 6:5) is God's demand; though this is not to be understood as meaning merely a punctilious observance of an impersonal divine law but rather as summoning to a relationship of personal devotion created and sustained by the work of God in the human heart (Dt. 30:6).

It consists in the simple joyful experience of communion with God (Je. 2:2; Pss. 18:1; 116:1), worked out in daily obedience to his commandments (Dt. 10:12, 'to love him, to serve the Lord your God'; Jos. 22:5, 'to love the Lord your God and to walk in all his ways'). This obedience is more fundamental to the nature of love for God than any feeling. God alone will be the judge of its sincerity (Dt. 13:3).

(ii) *Towards fellow men.* Love is ordained by God to be the normal, ideal human relationship, and as such is given the sanction of the divine law (Lv. 19:18), though the parallel prohibition of hatred with its reference to the heart (Lv. 19:17) shows clearly that this too is deeper than a merely legal relationship. An enemy is never commanded to be loved, though he is to be helped (Ex. 23:4f.), even if for somewhat selfish motives (Pr. 25:21f.).

II. In the New Testament

a. Etymology

The commonest Gk. word in the NT for all forms of love is *agapē*, *agapaō*. This is one of the least frequent words in classical Greek, where it expresses, on the few occasions it occurs, that highest and noblest form of love which sees something infinitely precious in its object. Its use in the NT derives not directly from classical Greek so much as from the LXX, where it occurs in 95% of all cases where EVV translate the Hebrew by 'love', and in every case of love from God to man, man to God and man to his neighbour. The dignity which the word possesses in the NT has been contributed by its use as a vehicle of the OT revelation. It is pregnant with OT associations.

phileō is the alternative word to *agapaō*. It is more naturally used of intimate affection (Jn. 11:3, 36; Rev. 3:19), and of liking to do things which are pleasant (Mt. 6:5). though there is considerable overlapping of usage between the two words. Much exegesis of Jn. 21:15–17 has turned on Peter's willingness to say *philō se* ('I am your friend', J. B. Phillips), and apparent reluctance to say *agapō se*. It is difficult to see why a writer of such simple Greek as John should have used the two words in this context unless he intended a distinction to be drawn between their meanings. The existence of any clear distinction, here or elsewhere, is, however, seriously disputed by scholars, and is not noticed by ancient commentators, except perhaps by Ambrose (*On Luke* 10. 176) and in the Vulg., which in this passage employs *diligo* and *amo* to translate *agapaō* and *phileō* respectively. (B. B. Warfield, 'The Terminology of Love in the New Testament', *PTR* 16, 1918; J. H. Bernard, *St John*, *ICC*, 2, 1928, pp. 701ff.)

b. God's love

(i) *For Christ.* The relationship between the Father and the Son is one of love (Jn. 3:35; 15:9; Col. 1:13). The word 'beloved' (*agapētos*), carrying with it a strong sense of 'only-beloved', is employed in the Synoptics only of the Christ, either directly (Mt. 17:5; Mk. 1:11) or by inference (Mt. 12:18; Mk. 12:6) (B. W. Bacon, 'Jesus' Voice from Heaven', *AJT* 9, 1905, pp. 451ff.). This love is returned and mutual (Jn. 14:31; *cf.* Mt. 11:27). Since this love is historically prior to creation (Jn. 17:24), it follows that, though known by men only as revealed in Jesus Christ and in redemption (Rom. 5:8), it is of the very nature of the Godhead (1 Jn. 4:8, 16), and that Jesus Christ, who is love incarnate and personified (1 Jn. 3:16), is God's self-revelation.

(ii) *For men.* Jesus is not recorded in the Synoptic Gospels as using *agapaō* or *phileō* to express God's love for men. Rather he revealed it by his countless acts of compassionate healing (Mk. 1:41; Lk. 7:13), his teaching about God's acceptance of the sinner (Lk. 15:11ff.; 18:10ff.), his grief-stricken attitude to human disobedience (Mt. 23:37; Lk. 19:41f.), and by being himself a friend (*philos*) of tax-collectors and outcasts (Lk. 7:34). This saving activity is declared in Jn. to be a demonstration of the love of God, imparting an eternal reality of life to men (Jn. 3:16; 1 Jn. 4:9f.). The whole drama of redemption, centring as it does on the death of Christ, is divine love in action (Gal. 2:20; Rom. 5:8; 2 Cor. 5:14).

As in the OT, God's love is selective. Its object is no longer the old Israel, but the new, the church (Gal. 6:16; Eph. 5:25). God's love and his choosing are closely connected, not only in Paul but clearly too by inference in certain sayings of Jesus himself (Mt. 10:5f.; 15:24). Those whom God's life-giving love does not reach are 'children of wrath' (Jn. 3:35f.; Eph. 2:3ff.) and of 'the devil' (Jn. 8:44). God's intention, however, is clearly the salvation of the whole world (Mt. 8:5; 28:19; Rom. 11:25f.), which is ultimately the object of his love (Jn. 3:16; 6:51), through the preaching of the gospel (Acts 1:8; 2 Cor. 5:19). Individuals are loved by God under the new covenant (Gal. 2:20), though response to his love involves fellowship in the people of God (1 Pet. 2:9f., a passage generally regarded as having a baptismal context).

c. Love as a religious duty

(i) *Towards God.* Man's natural state is to be God's enemy (Rom. 5:10; Col. 1:21), and to hate him (Lk. 19:14; Jn. 15:18ff.), this enmity being seen for what it is in the crucifixion. This attitude is transformed into one of love by the prior action of God in loving man (1 Jn. 4:11, 19). So closely related is God's love for man and man's for God that it is often difficult to decide whether the phrase 'the love of God' denotes a subjective or objective genitive (*e.g.* Jn. 5:42).

Jesus himself, though he accepted and underlined the Shema with his own authority (Mk. 12:28ff.), and expected men to love God and himself when there was ample opportunity for them not to (Mt. 6:24; 10:37f.; Lk. 11:42; Jn. 3:19), preferred to speak of the ideal man–God relationship as one of faith (Mt. 9:22; Mk. 4:40). The word love appears not to have sufficiently emphasized for him the humble trust which he regarded as vital in man's relationship to God. Accordingly, though love to God, worked out in service to one's fellows, is enjoined in the rest of the NT (1 Cor. 2:9; Eph. 6:24; 1 Jn. 4:20; 5:2f.), the writers more commonly follow Jesus' example and enjoin faith.

(ii) *Towards fellow men.* As in the OT, mutual love is to be the ideal human relationship. Jesus corrected contemporary Jewish thought in two directions. (*a*) He insisted that the commandment to love one's neighbour is not a limiting ordinance (Lk. 10:29), as in much rabbinic exegesis of Lv. 19:18, but rather means that the neighbour is to be the first object, because the nearest, of the love which is the characteristic of the Christian heart (Lk. 10:25–37). (*b*) He extended this demand for love to include enemies and persecutors (Mt. 5:44; Lk. 6:27), though none but the new people of God can be expected to have this attitude, for the demand belongs to a new time (Mt. 5:38f.), involves supernatural grace ('reward', Mt. 5:46; 'credit', Lk. 6:32ff.; 'more', Mt. 5:47), and is addressed to a group of 'hearers' (Lk. 6:27), who are sharply differentiated from sinners (Lk. 6:32ff.) and tax-collectors (Mt. 5:46f.).

This new attitude is far from a sentimental utopianism, for it must issue in practical help to those who need it (Lk. 10:33ff.), nor is it a superficial virtue, for it involves a fundamental response of the heart (1 Cor. 13 *passim*) to the prior love of God (1 Jn. 4:19), and an acceptance of the Spirit's work in the depths of a man's being (Gal. 5:22).

The characteristic form of this love in the NT is love for the fellow Christian (Jn. 15:12, 17; Gal. 6:10; 1 Pet. 3:8; 4:8; 1 Jn. 2:10; 3:14), love for the outsider being expressed in the evangelistic outreach (Acts 1:8; 10:45; Rom. 1:15f.) and in the patient endurance of persecution (1 Pet. 2:20). The Christian loves his brother: (*a*) to imitate God's love (Mt. 5:43, 45; Eph. 5:2; 1 Jn. 4:11); (*b*) because he sees in him one for whom Christ died (Rom. 14:15; 1 Cor. 8:11); (*c*) because he sees in him Christ himself (Mt. 25:40). The very existence of this mutual love, issuing as it does in the unity of Christian people (Eph. 4:2f.; Phil. 2:1ff.), is the sign *par excellence* to the outside world of the reality of Christian discipleship (Jn. 13:35).

BIBLIOGRAPHY. J. Barr, in L. D. Hurst and N. T. Wright (eds.), *The Glory of Christ in the New Testament*, 1987; A Soble (ed.), *Eros, Agape and Philia*, 1990; W. Günther, C. Brown, *NIDNTT* 2, pp. 538–551. F.H.P.

LOVE FEAST. The Christian duty to love one another has always been expressed in gatherings for fellowship. Such fellowship was realized from early times by participation in a common meal, and love feasts, *agapai*, are mentioned by Jude (v. 12; *cf.* 2 Pet. 2:13, RV). Among the Jews meals for fellowship and brotherhood were common, and similar convivial gatherings took place among the Gentiles. It was natural, therefore, that both Jewish and Gentile Christians should adopt such practices. The name *agapē* was later given to the fellowship meal. It is an anachronism, however, to apply it in its later sense to the conditions described in Acts and 1 Corinthians. 'The breaking of bread' referred to in Acts 2:42, 46 may describe a common meal which included both Agapē and Eucharist (see F. F. Bruce, *Acts of the Apostles*, 1951). St Paul's account (in 1 Cor. 11:17–34) of the administration of the Eucharist shows it set in the context of a fellowship supper. His farewell discourse at Troas which continued till midnight was delivered at a fellowship meal on the first day of the week which included the Eucharist (Acts 20:7ff.).

Although the common custom of fellowship meals among the Jews may have been sufficient ground for the primitive Agapē, some would trace the practice to the actual circumstances of the Last Supper. The sacrament was instituted at a Passover meal. Some scholars contend for another type of fellowship meal customary in the *qiddûsh* and *ḥaḇûrāh* gatherings. The early disciples probably reproduced the setting of the first Eucharist, preceding it with such a fellowship meal. The separation of the meal or Agapē from the Eucharist lies outside the times of the NT. The theory of Lietzmann that Eucharist and Agapē can be traced to two different types of sacramental observance in the NT is generally rejected (*LORD'S SUPPER).

For later development of Agapē and Eucharist, see Pliny's letter to Trajan, *Didache*, Justin Martyr, *Apol.* 1. 67, Tertullian, *de Corona* 3.

BIBLIOGRAPHY. J. H. Srawley, *Early History of the Liturgy*, 1947; G. Dix, *Shape of the Liturgy*, 1944; P. F. Bradshaw, *The Search for the Origins of Christian Worship*, 1992. R.J.C.

LOVING-KINDNESS. One rendering of the Heb. word *ḥeseḏ* given prior to the 20th century in all EVV from the time of Coverdale. Most of its occurrences are in the Pss., but it comes seven times elsewhere in AV, which has ten other renderings, the most frequent being 'mercy', 'kindness' and 'goodness'. There have been many suggestions as to how it should best be translated, including 'leal-love' (G. Adam Smith), 'piety' (C. H. Dodd), 'solidarity' (*KB*) and 'covenant-love' (N. H. Snaith). RSV frequently, although not consistently, renders it 'steadfast love'. Its etymological origin is uncertain. An examination of the passages where it is found (*e.g.* Ps. 89, where it is rendered 'mercy' as well as 'loving kindness' in AV) reveals its close connection with the two ideas of covenant and faithfulness. Its meaning may be summed up as 'steadfast love on the basis of a covenant'. It is employed both of God's attitude towards his people and of theirs to him, the latter especially in Hosea.

BIBLIOGRAPHY. N. H. Snaith, *The Distinctive Ideas of the Old Testament*, 1944, pp. 94–130; K.-J. Dobel, *TDOT* 5, pp. 44–64. G.W.G.

LUCIFER (Lat. 'light-bearer'). This was the Lat. name for the planet Venus, the brightest object in the sky apart from the sun and moon, appearing sometimes as the evening, sometimes as the morning, star. In Is. 14:12 it is the translation of *hêlēl* ('shining one': LXX *heōsphoros*, 'light-bearer'; *cf.* the Arabic for Venus, *zuhratun*, 'the bright shining one'), and is applied tauntingly as a title for the king of Babylon, who in his glory and pomp had set himself among the gods. This name is appropriate, as the civilization of Babylon began in the grey dawn of history, and had strong astrological connections. Babylonians and Assyrians personified the morning star as Belit and Ištar. Some have considered that the phrase 'son of the morning' might refer to the crescent moon; *cf.* Gray in *ICC, ad loc.*; others (*e.g.* S. H. Langdon, *ExpT* 42, 1930–1, pp. 172ff.) argue for an identification with the planet Jupiter. The similarity of the description here with that of such passages as Lk.

10:18 and Rev. 9:1 (*cf.* 12:9) has led to the application of the title to Satan. The true claimant to this title is shown in Rev. 22:16 to be the Lord Jesus Christ in his ascended glory. D.H.W.

LUCIUS. Gk. *Loukios*, transcribing or imitating the Roman praenomen. *Loukas* (Luke) was a diminutive. (*Cf.* Ramsay, *BRD*, pp. 370–384, for inscriptions.)

1. A Cyrenian prophet and teacher of Antioch (Acts 13:1), probably one of its first missionaries (*cf.* Acts 11:19–21). A strange African quotation of Acts 13:1 noted by Zahn (*cf. INT*, 3, pp. 28f.) adds 'who remains to this day'. Probably this writer, like Ephraem Syrus *in loc.*, identifies Lucius with the traditionally Antiochene Luke.

2. A companion of Paul in Corinth, sending greetings in Rom. 16:21. He is Paul's 'kinsman', *i.e.* a Jew (*cf.* Rom. 9:3). Origen *in loc.* mentions an identification with Luke.

That either is Luke is improbable. They were undoubtedly Jews; Luke was almost certainly a Gentile (see Col. 4:11, 14).

BIBLIOGRAPHY. H. J. Cadbury, *BC*, 1. 5, pp. 489–495. A.F.W.

LUD, LUDIM. In Gn. 10:22 and 1 Ch. 1:17 Lud is one of the descendants of Shem, and Josephus (*Ant.* 1. 144) refers to the Lydians (*LYDIA) as his descendants. Herodotus' account of the Lydians (50. 7) does not preclude a Semitic origin. In Is. 66:19 Lud is a Gentile nation characterized by the use of the bow (probably not true of Lydia); in Ezk. 27:10 and 30:5 they are allies of Tyre and of Egypt respectively, and as such Lydia (*Lūdu*) is mentioned in Neo-Babylonian annals.

Ludim appears in Gn. 10:13 and 1 Ch. 1:11 as a descendant of Ham, and in Je. 46:9 as a bow-bearing auxiliary of Egypt. This may be an unknown African nation, but some scholars emend to *Lubim* (Libya), and even the singular *Lud* to *Lub* in some passages. K.L.McK.

LUHITH, ASCENT OF. A place in Moab where the people fled from the Babylonians (Is. 15:5; Je. 48:5). Eusebius places it between Areopolis and Zoar, but it has not yet been certainly identified. J.D.D.

LUKE. Among the companions of Paul who send their greetings in his letter to Colossae there appears 'Luke (Gk. *Loukas*) the beloved physician' (Col. 4:14); the way in which he is described suggests that he had given medical care to Paul, no doubt during the latter's imprisonment. In Phm. 24, probably written at the same time, he is described as a fellow worker of Paul, which suggests that his help in the work of the gospel was not confined to his medical skill. There is a third reference to him in what appears to have been one of Paul's last messages: 'Luke alone is with me' (2 Tim. 4:11), and this confirms the close link between the two men. He is generally thought to have been a Gentile, but E. E. Ellis (pp. 51–53) has argued that Col. 4:11 refers to a particular group within the wider circle of Jewish Christians, and that consequently Luke may have been a Jewish Christian of the Dispersion.

Irenaeus (*c.* AD 180) is the first person to refer clearly to Luke and to name him as the author of the third Gospel and Acts. The same tradition is found in the Muratorian Canon and the so-called anti-Marcionite Prologue to the Gospel of Luke. The last of these documents speaks of Luke as coming from Antioch in Syria, and as serving the Lord without the distractions of a wife or family until he died at the age of 84 in Boeotia; the earliness and reliability of this tradition are uncertain.

The tradition that Luke was the author of Lk. and Acts can probably be traced back to earlier in the 2nd century. The fact that Marcion, a fanatical follower of Paul's theology, chose Lk. as the one Gospel which he recognized, probably implies that he regarded it as the work of a companion of Paul. Acts contains a number of passages written in the 1st person plural which describe events from the point of view of a companion of Paul (Acts 16:10–17; 20:5–21:18; 27:1–28:16). The fact that the author of Acts made no attempt to rewrite these passages in the 3rd person is best explained by identifying him as their original author. Of the possible companions of Paul, known to us from his Epistles but not named in Acts, Luke stands out as the probable composer of Acts and hence of Lk. This identification is found in a variant reading of Acts 20:13 ('But I Luke, and those who were with me, went on board') which may go back to early in the 2nd century.

The argument from the internal evidence of Acts is strong. It is confirmed by the external evidence of 2nd-century tradition cited above, and especially by the fact that no other candidate for the authorship of Acts was ever suggested. The claim that the tradition rests on a deduction from the NT evidence and has no independent value is pure hypothesis. There is more force in the objection that the picture of the early church in Acts, and of Paul in particular, are not such as might be expected from a companion of Paul, but this objection can be answered (F. F. Bruce, *NBCR*, pp. 968–973).

The literary style of Lk. and Acts demonstrates that their author was a well-educated person with considerable gifts of expression. The traces of medical language and the interest in medical matters displayed in them are consistent with authorship by the 'beloved physician'. Luke's gifts as a historian have been recognized by many scholars who have viewed his work against its classical background and compared him favourably with the best of ancient historians.

Luke's admiration for Paul comes out clearly in the course of Acts. Through his close contact with him and with other Christian leaders, and as a consequence of his visits to Jerusalem and Caesarea (*cf.* Acts 21:17ff.), Luke had ample opportunities to gain first-hand knowledge about the life of Jesus and the history of the earliest Christian church. He could rightly claim in the prologue to his Gospel that he was well qualified for his task, having carefully and thoroughly investigated all the relevant facts, as they were handed down by responsible witnesses in the church (Lk. 1:1–4).

The picture which emerges is of a self-effacing man possessed of strong human sympathies who regarded himself as a servant of the Word. With his considerable literary, historical and theological gifts, he was well fitted to recount the story of the beginnings of Christianity in a new way, adapted to the needs of the second generation in the church.

BIBLIOGRAPHY. F. F. Bruce, *The Acts of the Apostles*[3], 1990, pp. 1–34; C. K. Barrett, *Luke the Historian in Recent Study*, 1961; E. E. Ellis, *The Gospel of Luke*[2], *NCB*, 1974, pp. 2–62; E. Haenchen, *The Acts of the Apostles*, 1971; C. J. Hemer, *BJRL* 60, 1977, pp. 28–51. I.H.M.

LUKE, GOSPEL OF.

I. Outline of contents

a. Preface (1:1–4).
b. The birth and childhood of Jesus (1:5–2:52).
c. John the Baptist and Jesus (3:1–4:13).
d. The ministry in Galilee (4:14–9:50).
e. Progress towards Jerusalem (9:51–19:10).
f. The ministry in Jerusalem (19:11–21:38).
g. The passion and resurrection of Jesus (22:1–24:53).

II. The sources of the Gospel

In its general pattern Lk. is similar to the other two *Synoptic Gospels. It shares with Mt. an interest in the birth of Jesus, although the two Gospels tell this story from different angles. It follows the general outline of the ministry of Jesus found in Mk. (and also in Mt.), but has a considerably longer section on the progress of Jesus from Galilee to Jerusalem. Whether or not Mk. originally included some account of the resurrection appearances of Jesus, Lk. and Mt. each contain their own individual accounts of these appearances.

To a considerable extent the contents of Lk. are also shared with the other Gospels. It is generally agreed that one of Luke's major sources was Mk., and that like Matthew he drew the most part of his account of the ministry and deeds of Jesus from the earlier Gospel. Nearly all of Mk. has been incorporated in Lk., but it has been rewritten in Luke's more developed literary style. Luke also includes a good deal of the teaching of Jesus which is found in Mt. (but not in Mk.), and it is generally assumed that the two Gospels were dependent on some common source (or a collection of sources), written or oral. It is much less likely that one Gospel was dependent on the other for this material. Although the relation between the sources of Jn. and the other Gospels continues to be uncertain, it is clear that Lk. and Jn. reflect some use of common traditions, especially in the story of the passion and resurrection. In addition, there is a good deal of information about Jesus peculiar to Lk., much of it to be found in the account of Jesus' journey to Jerusalem. In some places where Luke is at first sight dependent on Mk., such as the account of the Last Supper, it is highly probable that he had access to other traditions also.

All this means that Luke was dependent upon a variety of sources of information for his Gospel and illustrates his own statement (Lk. 1:1–4) that many other persons had made earlier attempts to draw up accounts of what had happened. The same statement suggests that Luke was acquainted not only with written accounts of the ministry of Jesus but also with persons who had been eyewitnesses of it, and that he wrote his Gospel after careful research into his various sources of information.

III. Authorship, date and place of composition

The question of the authorship of Lk. is closely bound up with that of Acts. The two books are parts of one work, and attempts to deny their common authorship have not been successful. The traditional ascription of both books to *Luke still remains the most probable view. The evidence is basically derived from *Acts. So far as the Gospel is concerned, it contains little concrete evidence for or against the traditional ascription of authorship. The claim that it breathes the atmosphere of the sub-apostolic period (*i.e.* the time after Luke's death) is too subjective to carry any conviction.

What the modern discussion of authorship has brought out is that Luke was not a slavish imitator of Paul in his theological outlook. He had his own distinctive slant on the Christian faith. His Gospel, therefore, is in no way a Pauline reinterpretation of the story of Jesus, but represents his own, independent assessment of the significance of Jesus, based on traditions handed down from the early church. We do not know how Paul regarded the earthly life of Jesus, since he makes so little mention of him in his letters, and we have, therefore, no way of comparing his views with those of Luke. If we cannot ascertain the measure of their agreement, we are equally unable to posit any disagreement between them.

In one sense, identification of the author of the Gospel sheds little light on it, since we know scarcely anything about the author additional to what can be gleaned from Lk. and Acts. In another sense, however, the knowledge of the author's identity is valuable because it confirms that he was a person well qualified (in accordance with his own explicit claim) to learn the contents of the Gospel tradition and to reformulate them. The historical credentials of the Gospel are greater than if it was the work of some unknown figure from a later date.

We do not know when or where the Gospel was written. There are two serious possibilities regarding the date, either in the early 60s or in the later decades of the 1st century. A decision depends on the date to be assigned to Mk. and on whether Luke was writing after the fall of Jerusalem prophesied by Jesus. A date before AD 70 is certainly not to be ruled out for Mk. In the case of Lk. the comparatively frequent and more precise references to the fall of Jerusalem, while based on genuine prophecy by Jesus, may be thought to reflect interest in the fulfilment of the prophecy. On the other hand, the lack of interest in the fall of Jerusalem in Acts, and the way in which that book ends its story before the death of Paul, are strong indications of a date before AD 70. It is possible that the composition of the books was largely complete before that date, although the date of completion may have been later.

Although there is a tradition of uncertain date connecting the composition of the Gospel with Achaia, there is nothing in the writing itself to substantiate this view. It is more likely that we should connect the Gospel with Rome (where Mk. was available and where Luke was present with Paul) or with Antioch in Syria (with which Luke is also connected by what is probably a more reliable tradition, and where the 'Q' source which he shared with Matthew was probably compiled). Behind the Gospel, however, there ultimately lie traditions current in Palestine. Luke's connection with the early church in Palestine and Syria is ultimately of more significance than where he adventitiously happened to produce his Gospel.

IV. Purpose and character

We are singularly fortunate in that Luke has given us his own statement of intention at the beginning of the Gospel. At the same time we can draw certain conclusions from the character of the work itself. His concern was to present the story of Jesus in such a way as to bring out its significance and its reliability for those who believed in him; and he did this in the context of a two-part work which went on to tell the story of the early church so as to demonstrate how the message of the gospel spread, in accordance with prophecy and God's command, to the ends of the earth and brought salvation to those who responded to it. Luke was writing for people at some remove from the ministry of Jesus, both in geography and in time. He addresses himself to a certain *Theophilus, whose identity remains quite unknown, but clearly this is no more than a literary dedication to a friend of the author and the book was intended for a wider audience. The dedication suggests that it was meant for members of the church, and its contents reinforce this view, but at the same time it could be used both as a handbook and as a tool for evangelism; its outward form, conforming to that of historical and literary works of the time, strongly suggests that a wider audience was in view.

Luke wrote as a man of culture and education, and his work has much more of a claim to being a deliberate literary production than the other Gospels have. It is clear that the author was a man of letters, well acquainted with the OT in Gk. and also with the style of contemporary literature, who was able to produce a work that would commend the gospel by its literary quality. Even if E. Renan intended to damn rather than to praise when he described Lk. as 'the most beautiful book that was ever written', his comment is not without some truth. Here literary art is employed as a servant of the gospel.

At the same time, Luke writes specifically as a historian. The evidence for his historical interests and abilities is more obvious in Acts, but the Gospel too is meant as a historical work whose aim is to demonstrate the reliability of the traditions about Jesus. Where we can compare his story with its sources, Luke has faithfully reproduced them, although of course he does not follow them with slavish literalness.

Literary art and historical skill are, however, servants of a conscious evangelistic and theological purpose. Two important groups of words take us to the centre of Luke's interest. The first is the verb 'to preach the gospel' (*euangelizomai*), a word which characterizes the Christmas message (Lk. 1:19; 2:10), the preaching of John (Lk. 3:18), the ministry of Jesus (Lk. 4:18, 43; 7:22; *et al.*) and the activity of the early church (Acts 5:42; 8:4; *et al.*). The fact that the verb, found frequently in Paul, is virtually absent from the other Gospels (Mt. 11:5; the corresponding noun, however, is used more often) is an indication of its significance for Luke in describing the nature of the work of Jesus and the early church. The other keyword is 'salvation' (with its cognates). Particularly in the birth stories the thought of God bringing a Saviour to his people is prominent (Lk. 1:47, 69, 71, 77; 2:11, 30); although the word-group is not so conspicuous elsewhere in Lk. and Acts, the opening emphasis on it gives the key to the nature of the gospel message, just as John's opening stress on the Word gives the key to his Gospel. By contrast with Mark, Luke brings out the nature of Jesus' message of the kingdom of God as salvation for the lost; and where Matthew tends to present Jesus as the Teacher of true righteousness, Luke lays more stress on his action as Saviour; these contrasts, however, can be misleading if taken too far.

Luke shows how the ministry of Jesus represents the fulfilment of OT prophecy (Lk. 4:18–21; 10:23f.; 24:26f., 44–47). The new era of salvation has dawned, characterized by the preaching of the good news of the kingdom (Lk. 16:16). Although the full realization of the reign of God belongs to the future (Lk. 19:11), nevertheless God has already begun to deliver men and women from the power of Satan and the demons (Lk. 11:20; 13:16), and sinners can enjoy forgiveness and fellowship with Jesus. In Jesus the saving power of God himself is manifested (Lk. 7:16; Acts 10:38).

The One through whom God acts in this way is clearly a prophet, anointed with the Spirit, but for Luke he is more than a prophet, more even than the unique prophet like Moses for whom the people were waiting (Lk. 24:19–21; Acts 3:22f.). He is the anointed King who will reign in the future kingdom (Lk. 22:29f.; 23:42), and already he can be described as the 'Lord', the title which indicates the role of Jesus confirmed by his resurrection and exaltation (Acts 2:36). Behind these roles fulfilled by Jesus there lies his unique nature as the Son of God (Lk. 1:32).

In his presentation of the ministry of Jesus Luke draws particular attention to the concern of Jesus for outcasts; all the Gospels bear witness to this undoubted historical fact, but it is Luke who takes most delight in drawing attention to it (Lk. 14:15–24; 15; 19:1–10). He demonstrates how Jesus was concerned for women (Lk. 7:36–50; 8:1–3), for the Samaritans (Lk. 9:51–56; 10:30–37; 17:11–19) and for the Gentiles (Lk. 7:1–9); yet Luke respects the historical fact that Jesus' ministry was almost exclusively to the Jews by confining himself to hints of the wider spread of the gospel in Acts (Lk. 2:32; 13:28f.; 24:47). Another concern of Jesus to which Luke draws attention is his care for the poor and his warnings that the rich who have lived for themselves thereby shut themselves out of the kingdom of God. In the kingdom human values are subjected to a radical reappraisal. There is no room for the self-sufficient who think that worldly wealth will shield them from judgment (Lk. 6:20–26; 12:13–21; 16:19–31) or for the self-righteous who see no need for repentance (Lk. 18:9–14). On the contrary, entry to the kingdom is reserved for the poor, *i.e.*, those who know their poverty and therefore trust in God, and the repentant who recognize their sin and cast themselves upon the mercy of God. Such repentance means whole-hearted turning from sin and readiness to follow Jesus, whatever the cost (Lk. 9:23); and that cost may involve renunciation of one's possessions (Lk. 14:33; 19:8).

The picture of Jesus in Lk. is no doubt meant as an example and a pattern for his disciples. This can be seen from a comparison of the life of Jesus in the Gospel with Luke's description of the church and its members in Acts. Thus, just as the life of Jesus was governed by the plan of God, partly revealed in OT prophecy, so the life of the church is at every point guided and directed by God. As Jesus did his work in the power of the Spirit (Lk. 4:14, 18), so the early church was filled with the Spirit for its task of witness (Lk. 24:49). Similarly, just as Jesus was a man of prayer, drawing guidance and inspiration from his communion with God (Lk. 3:21; 6:12; 9:18, 28f.; 22:32), so the church is to be continuously in prayer to God (Acts 1:14).

Such—in broadest outline—is the characteristic Lucan picture of Jesus and his teaching. It has a number of significant features. First, it presents the story of Jesus in terms of fulfilment of prophecy. For Luke the category of promise and fulfilment is of great significance and it provides the structure of his historical thinking. Second, Luke strongly emphasizes the actual presence of salvation in the ministry of Jesus. The accent falls on what Jesus accomplished rather than on the future, although the future dimension is by no means lacking. Third, Luke links the ministry of Jesus to the rise of the early church and shows how the latter follows on from the former. He is aware that the beginning of Christianity included both of the areas covered in the Gospel and Acts.

The effect of these considerations is to show that for Luke the story of Jesus was a part of history. The most important modern discussion of Luke, that of H. Conzelmann, argues that Luke saw the ministry of Jesus as the mid-point of history (preceded by the history of Israel and followed by the period of the church). Conzelmann claims that this was a new understanding of Jesus and stood in contrast with earlier views. The earlier understanding of Jesus was as the proclaimer of the imminent kingdom of God. Luke wrote at a time when the church was beginning to enjoy a settled existence and the future consummation of the kingdom had proved to be a disappointing hope. In effect he remoulded Christian theology to fit it for the second and subsequent generations by virtually abandoning hope of the imminent end of the world and regarding the ministry of Jesus as the midpoint in the history of God's dealings with men rather than as the immediate prelude to the end. The Christian summons to repent before the imminent end was turned into a historical account of the coming of Jesus, and the period of the church, during which the Holy Spirit would lead its members in mission, replaced the hope of the future kingdom of God.

Like so many first statements of a case, Conzelmann's understanding of Luke is one-sided and exaggerated, but it has had the merit of demonstrating that Luke was a careful theologian and of encouraging other scholars to offer a more balanced understanding of his theology. The truth is rather that the message of Jesus and the early church was not as one-sidedly futurist as Conzelmann suggests, and that Luke is simply drawing attention to the present features in that message. 'Salvation history' was by no means an invention of Luke. At the same time, Luke by no means gives up the hope of the coming of the end, and his work retains that element of tension between present realization and future hope which is typical of early Christianity. The effect of his work, however, is to lead the church away from looking for apocalyptic signs of the coming of the end to a concentration on the task of spreading the gospel.

We have to draw a distinction between the factors which moulded Luke's work and the conscious purposes which governed his writing. Among the former we must number the need to represent the story of Jesus in a way that brought it up-to-date for the church of his day. Among the latter the chief was the desire to present Jesus as the Saviour and to show how the Spirit of God had constituted the church as the witness to Jesus. In the combination of these factors and purposes we can find the key to the distinctive nature of this Gospel in which a historical record has become a means of equipping the church for evangelism.

BIBLIOGRAPHY. Commentaries on the English text: F. W. Danker, 1988; E. E. Ellis, *NCB*², 1974; L. Morris, *TNTC*², 1988; C. H. Talbert, 1982; D. Gooding, 1987; C. A. Evans, *NIBC*, 1990; C. F. Evans, *TPINTC*, 1990; on the Greek text: I. H. Marshall NIGTC, 1978; J. A. Fitzmyer, *AB*, 1981–5; J. Nolland, *WBC*, 1989–93. Studies: H. Conzelmann, *The Theology of St Luke*, 1960; S. G. Wilson, *The Gentiles and the Gentile Mission in Luke–Acts*, 1973; C. H. Talbert, *Literary Patterns, Theological Themes and the Genre of Luke–Acts*, 1974; E. Franklin, *Christ the Lord*, 1975; J. Drury, *Tradition and Design in Luke's Gospel*, 1976; R. J. Maddox, *The Purpose of Luke–Acts*, 1982; D. L. Bock, *Proclamation from Prophecy and Pattern*, 1987; F. Bovon, *Luke the Theologian*, 1987; I. H. Marshall, *Luke: Historian and Theologian*³, 1988; B. E. Beck, *Christian Character in the Gospel of Luke*, 1989; M. D. Goulder, *Luke a New Paradigm*, 1989.

I.H.M.

LUST. The Eng. word was originally a neutral term describing any strong desire; hence its use in early translations of Gn. 3:16; Jn. 1:13; Nu. 14:8; Heb. 10:6. In its modern restricted sense of sexual passion it cannot adequately render many familiar contexts in AV.

The Heb. *nep̄eš* expresses craving or desire in Ex. 15:9 and Ps. 78:18, and carries the promise of satisfaction in Pr. 10:24. Gk. *epithymia* expresses any strong desire, the context or a qualifying adjective determining its nature, whether good or evil. Hence it is used of the intensely pure desire of Christ, Lk. 22:15, and of Paul's desire to be with Christ, Phil. 1:23, and of his longing to see his converts, 1 Thes. 2:17. Yet in 1 Pet. 4:3 it stands among a list of Gentile vices, and the adjectives 'worldly', 'evil', 'youthful' and 'deceitful' are attached to it in Tit. 2:12; Col. 3:5; 2 Tim. 2:22; and Eph. 4:22 respectively. The restricted reference to sexual passion is found in Eph. 2:3; 1 Jn. 2:16; 1 Pet. 2:11 (*cf.* LXX and Jos., *Ant.*). The strong desire of the Spirit is set over against that of the flesh in Gal. 5:17. Other cognate words are *pathos*, 'passion' (1 Thes. 4:5); *orexis*, 'strong desire' (Rom. 1:27), and *hēdonē*, 'pleasure' (Jas. 4:3). The word 'lusty' when used in Jdg. 3:29 (AV); Is. 59:10 (RV); Ps. 73:4 (Prayer Book) carries no derogatory tone, and simply means able-bodied or vigorous.

BIBLIOGRAPHY. *BAGD*; *HDB*; B. S. Easton, *Pastoral Epistles*, 1947, pp. 186ff.; *MM*; H. Schönweiss *et al.*, *NIDNTT* 1, pp. 456–461. D.H.T.

LUZ. The ancient name of *Bethel, which was so named by Jacob after he had dreamed of the ladder from heaven to earth after spending the night near to the city (Gn. 28:19; 35:6; 48:3). It was the site of Jacob's sojourn near to the city, rather than the city itself, that received the name Bethel (Jos. 16:2), but this site later became so important that the name was applied to the city as well (Jos. 18:13; Jdg. 1:23). The city was, however, still known to the Canaanite inhabitants as Luz, because when the Israelites took the city at the time of the conquest a Canaanite whom they pressed to show them the entrance to it in return for his life escaped to the 'land of the Hittites' and founded another city of that name (Jdg. 1:24–26).

BIBLIOGRAPHY. F. M. Abel, *Géographie de la Palestine*, 2, 1938, p. 371. T.C.M.

LYCAONIA, a territory in S-central Asia Minor, so called from the *Lykaones* who inhabited it, mentioned by ancient writers from Xenophon (early 4th century BC) onwards. In Pompey's settlement of W Asia Minor (64 BC) the W part of Lycaonia was added to Cilicia, the E part to Cappadocia, and the N part to *Galatia, which became a Roman province in 25 BC. E Lycaonia later became independent of Cappadocia and from AD 37 onwards formed part of the client kingdom of Antiochus, king of Commagene, and was known as Lycaonia Antiochiana. In the NT 'Lycaonia' denotes that part of the territory which constituted a region of the province of Galatia, Lycaonia Galatica. Lystra and Derbe are designated 'cities of Lycaonia' in Acts 14:6, in a context which implies that Iconium lay on the Phrygian side of the frontier separating Lycaonia Galatica from Phrygia Galatica. W. M. Ramsay has put it on record that it was this geographical note that led to his 'first change of judgment' with regard to the historical value of Acts. Paul and Barnabas on their first 'missionary journey' (AD 47–8) doubtless recognized that they had crossed a linguistic frontier between Iconium and Lystra, for in the latter place (near modern Hatunsaray) they heard the indigenous population speak 'in Lycaonian' (Acts 14:11, Gk. *lykaonisti*). Lycaonian personal names have been identified in inscriptions hereabout, *e.g.* in one at Sedasa which records the dedication to Zeus of a statue of Hermes (*cf.* Acts 14:12). When, after leaving Lystra, Paul and Barnabas came to Derbe (modern Kerti Hüyük) and planted a church there, they turned back; had they gone farther they would have crossed into the kingdom of Antiochus, but it was no part of their plan to evangelize non-Roman territory.

BIBLIOGRAPHY. W. M. Ramsay, *Historical Commentary on Galatians*, 1899, pp. 185f., 215ff.; M. H. Ballance, *AS* 7, 1957, pp. 147ff.; 14, 1964, pp. 139f.; B. Van Elderen, 'Some Archaeological Observations on Paul's First Missionary Journey', in *Apostolic History and the Gospel*, ed. W. W. Gasque and R. P. Martin, 1970, pp. 156–161. F.F.B.

LYCIA. A small district on the S coast of Asia Minor containing the broad valley of the river Xanthus, mountains rising to over 3,000 m, and the seaports *Patara and *Myra (Acts 21:1; 27:5). Although some sculptures and inscriptions have been preserved, the origin of the Lycian people is obscure. They alone of the peoples of W Asia Minor successfully resisted the Lydian kings, but they succumbed in 546 BC to the Persians.

Freed by Greeks in the following century, they were greatly influenced by Gk. civilization and eventually submitted voluntarily to Alexander. They adopted the Gk. language and script, and were thoroughly Hellenized by the time they came under Roman protection in the 2nd century BC. Claudius in AD 43 annexed Lycia to the province of Pamphylia, but apparently Nero restored their freedom, for Vespasian again reduced them to provincial status (Suetonius, *Vespasian* 8). Through these changes the federation of Lycian cities maintained its general political framework. K.L.McK.

LYDDA. A town some 18 km SE of the coast at Jaffa, in the Shephelah plain. It is almost certainly to be identified with the OT Lod, which is mentioned in the Karnak list of Thothmes III. In Israelite times it was a Benjaminite town; reoccupied after the Bab. Exile, it later fell to the authority of the governor of Samaria, and was not reclaimed by the Jews till 145 BC (1 Macc. 11:34). It was burnt down in Nero's reign. After the fall of Jerusalem (AD 70) it became a rabbinical centre for a period. It had a bishop in the early Christian centuries. Since then it has borne the names Diospolis, Ludd and Lod again (today). D.F.P.

LYDIA. A woman of Thyatira in Lydia, who at Philippi became Paul's first European convert and gave him hospitality, with Silas and Luke (Acts 16:14–15, 40). Lydia may be an adjectival form, 'the Lydian woman' (such ethnic names were common), but it was also a personal name (*e.g.* Horace, *Od.* 1. 8; 3. 9). Evidently a woman of rank (*cf.* Acts 17:4, 12), she was head of a household, and thus either widowed or unmarried. Lydian purple dye, in which she traded, was renowned (*cf.* Homer, *Il.* 4. 141). She was a Jewish proselyte, engaging in prayers and ablutions at the riverside on the sabbath; her connection with the Jewish faith probably went back to the colony in Thyatira. For the Christian church established there, *cf.* Rev. 1:11; 2:18–29. Lydia may be included in Paul's reference in Phil. 4:3, but since she is unmentioned by name she may have died or left the city. Her hospitality became traditional in the church there (*cf.* Phil. 1:5; 4:10). B.F.H.

LYDIA, a district in the centre of the W slope of Asia Minor, included the Caÿster and Hermus valleys, the most fertile and highly cultivated areas of the peninsula, and between them the mountains of Tmolus, rising to 2,000 m. Besides its natural wealth its position on the main routes from the coast to the interior of Asia Minor gave its cities (including *Sardis, *Thyatira and *Philadelphia) great commercial importance. Lydia was bordered by Mysia, Phrygia and Caria. Some of the coastal cities (including Smyrna and Ephesus) were sometimes reckoned as Lydian, sometimes as Gk.

The origins of the Lydian race are obscure, but there may have been Semitic elements (*LUD). Croesus, the last king of Lydia, dominated the whole of Asia Minor before he was conquered by Cyrus the Persian in 546 BC. The region was subsequently ruled by Alexander and his successors, and became part of the Attalid kingdom of Pergamum before becoming part of the Roman province of Asia in 133 BC. Some Lydian inscriptions of the 4th century BC have been discovered, but by the beginning of the Christian era Gk. had become the common language and, according to Strabo, Lydian was little used.

Lydia was the first state to use coined money and was the home of some innovations in music.

K.L.McK.

LYSANIAS, listed in Lk. 3:1 as 'tetrarch of *Abilene', *c.* AD 27–8. So Josephus (*Ant.* 20. 138) speaks of 'Abila, which had been the tetrarchy of Lysanias'. His name appears on an inscription of Abila, dated between AD 14 and 29, recording a temple dedication by a freedman of 'Lysanias the tetrarch' (*CIG*, 4521). It is uncertain whether coins superscribed 'Lysanias tetrarch and high priest' refer to him or to an earlier Lysanias, 'king of the Ituraeans' (so Dio Cassius), executed by Antony *c.* 36 BC (Jos., *Ant.* 15. 92; *cf.* 14. 330). Two members of this family called Lysanias, of different generations, are named in *CIG*, 4523.

LYSTRA. An obscure town on the high plains of Lycaonia (near modern Hatunsaray), singled out by Augustus as the site of one of a number of Roman colonies that were intended to consolidate the new province of Galatia. Its advantages are not known. Its remote position and proximity to the unsettled S mountains suggest defensive motives, as also does the considerable Latin-speaking settlement implied by surviving inscriptions. If it was the security of such a place that attracted Paul and Barnabas in their hasty retreat from Iconium (Acts 14:6) they were badly let down. Superstitious veneration, disabused by the apostles themselves, was converted by agitators into drastic hostility, which apparently secured official support for the stoning that was inflicted upon Paul (v. 19). There is no suggestion of Roman order or justice. Nor does the NT even disclose that it was a colony. There was plainly a substantial non-hellenic population (v. 11), as well as the usual Greeks and Jews (Acts 16:1). Nevertheless, a church was established (Acts 14:20–23) which provided in Timothy (unless, as is just possible, he came from the nearby Derbe, Acts 16:1–2) Paul's most devoted 'son'.

BIBLIOGRAPHY. B. Levick, *Roman Colonies in Southern Asia Minor*, 1967. E.A.J.

M

MAACAH, MAACHAH. 1. Maacah is used as a man's name for the following: the father of Shephatiah, one of David's henchmen (1 Ch. 27:16); the father of Hanun, one of David's warriors (1 Ch. 11:43); the father of *Achish, king of Gath at the time of David and Solomon.

2. It is also used as a woman's name for the following: the concubine of Caleb, mother of Sheber and Tirhanah (1 Ch. 2:48); the wife of Machir, mother of Peresh (1 Ch. 7:16); the wife of Gibeon, or Jehiel, one of the ancestors of Saul (1 Ch. 8:29; 9:35); the daughter of Talmai, king of Geshur, who married David and was the mother of Absalom and Tamar (2 Sa. 3:3); the favourite wife of Rehoboam and the mother of Abijah and the daughter of Absalom (2 Ch. 11:20–22); the mother of Asa, the queenmother of Judah until she was removed because of her idolatry (2 Ch. 15:16). (*QUEEN.)

3. The child of Nahor, the brother of Abraham, and his concubine Reumah, was called Maacah, but there is no indication as to sex (Gn. 22:24).

4. It is also the name for a small state to the SW of Mt Hermon, on the edge of the territory of the half-tribe of Manasseh (Dt. 3:14; Jos. 13:8–13) and possibly extending across the Jordan to Abel-beth-Maacah. At the time of David, its Aramaean king provided 1,000 soldiers for the Ammonite and Aramaean attempt to crush Israel. Following the defeat at Helam, Maacah probably became tributary to David (2 Sa. 10). Maacah was later absorbed into the kingdom of Damascus, which had been reestablished during Solomon's reign (1 Ki. 11:23–25).

BIBLIOGRAPHY. B. Mazar, 'Geshur and Maacah', *JBL* 80, 1961, pp. 16ff.

M.B.
A.R.M.

MAAREH-GEBA (Jdg. 20:33, RV; AV 'meadows of Gibeah'). Heb. *ma'ᵃrēh* means 'open, bare place', but LXX(A) *dysmōn* and Vulg. *occidentali urbis parte* suggest Heb. *ma'ᵃrāḇ*, 'west', which yields a better sense here. (*GEBA. A.R.M.

MACCABEES. *Makkabaios* was the Gk. form of the surname of the Jewish hero Judas ben Mattathias (1 Macc. 2:4): its application has been extended to his family and his party. The derivation is quite obscure: 'the hammerer' or 'the eradicator' are perhaps the commonest modern interpretations. According to Josephus the family name seems to have been Ḥašmōn: hence the title 'Hasmonaeans' reflected in rabbinic literature.

I. The Maccabean revolt

Palestine was perennially a theatre for the power politics of the Seleucid and Ptolemaic heirs of Alexander the Great's empire. One result was the growth of a pro-Syrian and a pro-Egyptian party in Judaea, and tension between these groups was inextricably bound up with Jewish internal politics and family jealousies, and with a movement among 'liberal' Jews to adopt the customs and standards of the Gk. world. Resulting conflict brought about the decisive intervention of Syria. The Seleucid king, Antiochus IV (Epiphanes), who was mad, bad and dangerous, sold the high-priesthood to the highest bidder, one Menelaus, who was quite unentitled to it, and when, in 168 BC, his nominee was ejected, Antiochus sent his officer to sack Jerusalem and kill its inhabitants.

Soon afterwards, Antiochus instituted a religious persecution of unprecedented bitterness. Sabbath-keeping and the practice of circumcision were forbidden under pain of death: pagan sacrifices and prostitution were established in the Temple; and law-loving Jews were subjected to every degradation and brutality (*cf.* Dn. 11:31–33). Doubtless many succumbed, but many endured heroic suffering (1 Macc. 1:60ff.; 2:29ff.; 2 Macc. 6:18ff.), and Antiochus could not have estimated the sober resilience of the Ḥasidim (or men of the covenant), who 'offered (themselves) willingly for the law' (1 Macc. 2:42). More drastic action began in Modein, some 30 km from Jerusalem, where the aged Mattathias angrily killed a Jew who had come to sacrifice on the royal altar, and the Syrian officer who had come to supervise, and then called on everyone zealous for the Law to follow him and his five sons, John, Simon, Judas, Eleazar and Jonathan, to the mountains. The Maccabean revolt had begun.

II. Judas Maccabaeus

The Judaean hills were suited to guerrilla warfare. Mattathias and his sons were joined by many Ḥasidim, and at first were content with terrorizing apostates, destroying altars and enforcing the Law. Mattathias died, and his third son, Judas, proved a leader of Gideon's type and stature. Perhaps no army has ever had higher morale than the force with which he won his brilliant victories against numerically superior Syrian forces. Antiochus was occupied in larger wars with the Parthians, and his regent Lysias had no option but to conclude peace with Judas and withdraw the abominable decrees in 165 BC. Amid great rejoicing, Judas marched to Jerusalem, the Temple was solemnly cleansed, and the worship of God restored (1 Macc. 4)—an event commemorated by the Feast of Hanukkah, or the Dedication (Jn. 10:22).

Maccabean success had led to furious persecution of Jewish minorities in cities of mixed population. Judas raised the cry, 'Fight today for your brethren' (1 Macc. 5:32) and, with his brother Jonathan, carried out effective punitive expeditions

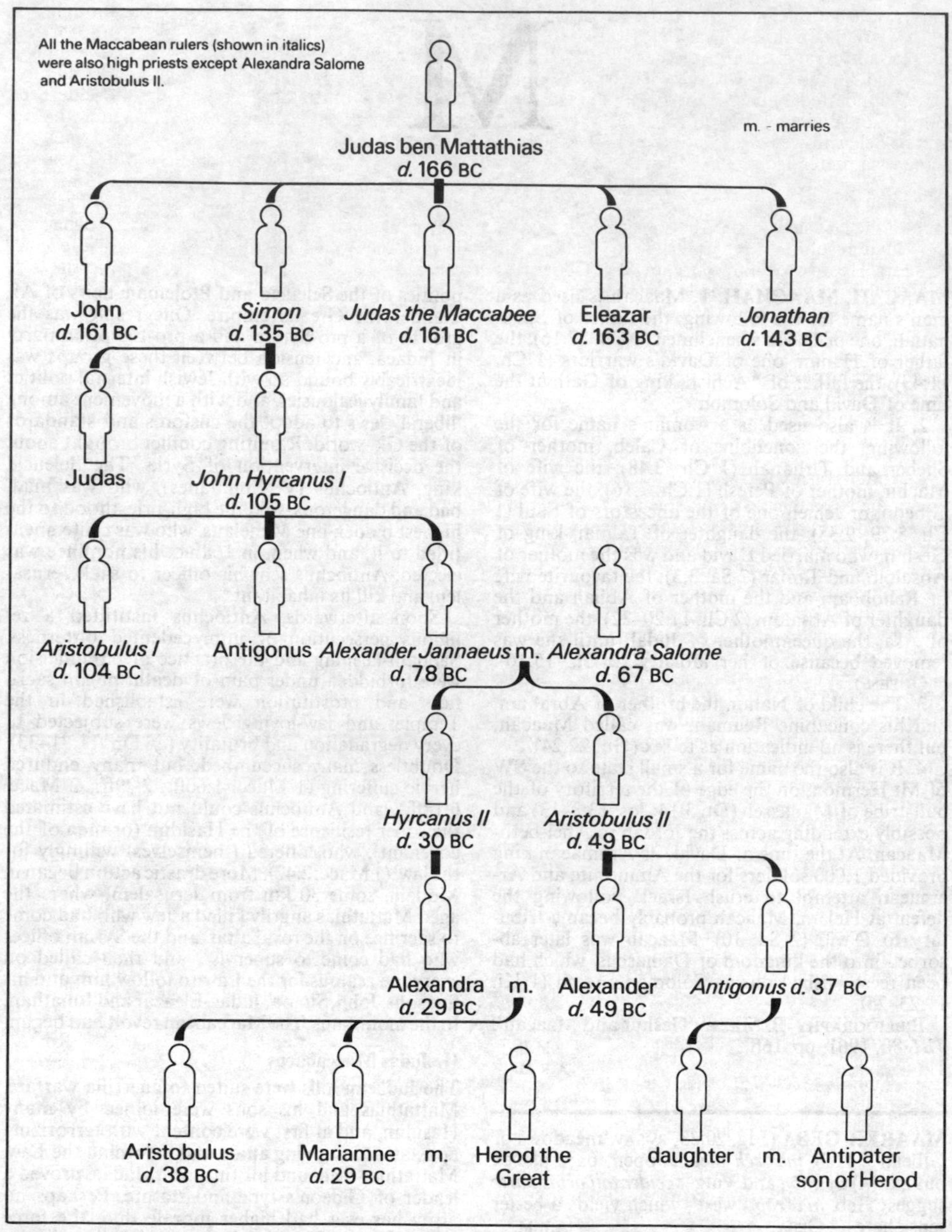

The family of the Maccabees.

in Transjordan, while Simon dealt similarly with Galilee. On the death of Antiochus Epiphanes in 164/3 BC Judas tried to seize the *Akra*, the Syrian fortress in Jerusalem, the symbol of Seleucid suzerainty: he was trapped, and was on the brink of disaster when political upheaval in Syria caused a diversion, and the Syrians had to be content with a treaty virtually securing the *status quo*.

Eventually Demetrius I (Soter) made good his claim to the throne, and he appointed a pro-Syrian high priest, Alcimus. Many Ḥasidim were prepared to support this man, since he was an Aaronite, but his outrageous actions played into Judas' hands. Judas took revenge on deserters, and a large Syrian force had to be called in. The Syrians were defeated at Adasa, but, after an interval, scattered the Jewish army at Elasa, where Judas was killed in battle in 161 BC.

III. Jonathan

Jonathan, youngest of the brothers, now headed the Maccabean party. For a long time he was reduced to guerrilla fighting in the hills, but internal faction had become endemic in the Seleucid empire, and he was more and more left to himself by the Syrians. In time he was the effective ruler of Judaea, and rival claimants to the Seleucid throne competed for his support. One such, Alexander Balas, appointed him high priest in 153 BC, and military and civil governor in 150. He continued to exploit Seleucid weakness until treacherously murdered by a pretended ally in 143 BC.

IV. Simon

Simon, the last survivor of the sons of Mattathias, showed a resolution not inferior to that of his brothers. He drove a hard bargain with Demetrius II whereby the latter virtually resigned the suzerainty of Judaea and 'the yoke of the Gentiles was removed from Israel' (1 Macc. 13:41). The Syrians were ejected from the *Akra*, Judaea was aggrandized at the expense of her neighbours at several points, and a period of relative peace and prosperity began, with Simon as high priest and unchallenged ruler.

V. The later Hasmonaeans

Simon died at the hand of his son-in-law in 135 BC. His son John Hyrcanus was forced into temporary submission to the disintegrating Seleucid empire, but at his death in 104 BC the Jewish realm was at its greatest extent since Solomon's time. His son Aristobulus (104–103 BC) formally claimed the title of king, and with him begins the sorry story of murder and intrigue and family jealousy which left the Jewish state a prey to the rising power of Rome. Antigonus, the last of the Hasmonaean high-priestly kings, was executed in 37 BC, and the pro-Roman *Herod the Great began a new era. Several later members of the house of Herod had Hasmonaean blood by the maternal side.

VI. The significance of the Maccabees

According to Dn. 11:34, the Maccabean revolt was to be only 'a little help' to God's people, for Daniel depicts events on the huge canvas of God's ultimate gracious purpose. Many Ḥasidim, looking for God to accomplish this, probably thought military action had gone far enough when the proscription of Judaism was abrogated and the Temple cleansed in 165 BC. At all events there are after that date increasing signs of Ḥasidim and Maccabees parting company. The assumption of the high-priesthood by Jonathan, and then Simon and his family, who were all of priestly but not Aaronic stock, must have been bitter to the Ḥasidim, and the latter's heirs, the Pharisees, were wholly alienated from the worldly and tyrannical Hasmonaean high-priest kings, who reached a grotesque climax in the drunken and unhinged Alexander Jannaeus (103–76 BC).

It would, nevertheless, be a mistake to divide Maccabean aims into the achievement first of religious liberty, and then of political liberty. Judas and his brethren were fighting for *Israel*, and desired, in the name of the God of Israel, to take away the 'yoke of the Gentiles'. The easy and natural process whereby the hereditary high-priesthood, which comprehended unquestioned civil leadership, assumed into itself the revived monarchy, is eloquent. John Hyrcanus and the Hasmonaean kings in their campaigns clearly have the ideal of the Davidic kingdom in mind, and there are records of some territories they conquered being forcibly Judaized.

In some respects, the Maccabees set the pattern of Jewish nationalism and Messianic thought for the NT period. Judas and his successors were invariably on good terms with the Romans, but in their day Rome was not yet ready to control Palestine. By NT times the Jews were firmly under 'the yoke of the Gentiles' once more, this time that of Rome. But the memory lingered of how Israel had once in the name of God defied another heathen empire, engaged her in single combat, and won; of how her borders had approached those of her Davidic glory. 'The ministry of Jesus falls . . . when the Jews of Palestine had still the memory of the Maccabean triumphs and no foreknowledge of the horrors of the siege under Titus' (T. W. Manson, *The Servant-Messiah*, 1953, p. 4).

W. R. Farmer has pointed to the preponderance of Maccabean names among anti-Roman agitators of NT times, and has associated the *Zealot party with Maccabean ideals, and the crowd's reaction to our Lord's triumphal entry with the deliberate recall of the triumphs of Judas and Simon.

The once fashionable habit of dating many Psalms in the Maccabean period has almost passed. For other literary questions, see *APOCRYPHA, *DANIEL, BOOK OF, *PSEUDEPIGRAPHA, *ZECHARIAH.

BIBLIOGRAPHY. 1 and 2 Maccabees (*APOCRYPHA); Josephus, *Ant.* 12–14; E. Schürer, *HJP*, 1, 1973, pp. 146–286; R. H. Pfeiffer, *History of New Testament Times*, 1949; E. Bickerman, *The Maccabees*, 1947; W. R. Farmer, *Maccabees, Zealots and Josephus*, 1956; B. Bar-Kochva, *Judas Maccabaeus*, 1988. A.F.W.

MACEDONIA. A splendid tract of land, centred on the plains of the gulf of Thessalonica, and running up the great river valleys into the Balkan mountains. It was famous for timber and precious metal. Anciently ruled by cavalry barons under a hellenized royal house, its kings dominated Greek affairs from the 4th century BC, and after Alexander Macedonian dynasties ruled throughout the E Mediterranean until superseded by the Romans. The home monarchy was the first to go when in 167 BC Macedonia was constituted a series of four federations of republics (to which structure Acts 16:12 may refer), thus completing its hellenization. They were subsequently grouped under Roman provincial control, and, until the consolidation of Moesia and Thrace as provinces in NT times, were heavily garrisoned against the intractable N frontier. The province embraced the N part of modern Greece from the Adriatic to the Hebrus river, and was crossed by the Via Egnatia, the main land route from Italy to the E. After 44 BC the proconsul sat at Thessalonica, while the assembly of the Greek states met at Beroea, the seat of the imperial cult. The province included six Roman colonies, of which Philippi was one. There were also tribally organized communities. In spite of this diversity, the area is normally treated in the NT as a unit, following Roman usage.

Paul's vision of 'a man of Macedonia' (Acts 16:9) marks a distinct development in his methods of evangelism. At Philippi (Acts 16:37) for the first time he took advantage of his high civil station. He now enjoyed support in the cultivated circles to which he naturally belonged (Acts 16:15; 17:4, 12) in contrast to their hostility at earlier points on his route (Acts 13:50; 14:5). He looked back upon Macedonia with profound affection (1 Thes. 1:3;

Phil. 4:1), and was always eager to return (Acts 20:1; 2 Cor. 1:16). The Macedonians were willing donors to his Jerusalem fund (2 Cor. 8:1–4), and several of their number were added to his regular retinue of assistants (Acts 19:29; 20:4). It was in Macedonia then, it seems, that Paul finally proved himself as an independent missionary leader.

BIBLIOGRAPHY. D. W. J. Gill, in *BA1CS* 2, pp. 397–418; J. Keil, *CAH*, 9, pp. 566–570; J. A. O. Larsen, in T. Frank, *An Economic Survey of Ancient Rome*, 5,1940, pp. 436–496. E.A.J.

MACHAERUS. A fortress E of the Dead Sea (modern el-Mekawar), near the S frontier of the region of Peraea, built by Alexander Jannaeus (103–76 BC), destroyed by the Roman commander Gabinius (57 BC), rebuilt by Herod (37–4 BC), who appreciated the hot springs at Calirrhoe not far away (Wadi Zerka Ma'in). Here, according to Josephus (*Ant.* 18. 112, 119), Herod Antipas imprisoned John the Baptist and later had him put to death; here too Antipas' first wife, the daughter of the Nabataean king Aretas IV, broke her journey on her way home to her father's capital at Petra when Antipas divorced her for Herodias. When Peraea was added to the province of Judaea (AD 44), Machaerus was occupied by a Roman garrison, which evacuated the place on the outbreak of war in AD 66. It was then occupied by a force of Jewish insurgents, but surrendered to the governor Lucilius Bassus in AD 71.

BIBLIOGRAPHY. Josephus, *BJ* 7. 163–209; S. Loffreda, *Annual of the Department of Antiquities of Jordan*, 25, 1981, pp. 85–94. F.F.B.

MACHIR (Heb. *māḵîr*). **1.** A grandson of Joseph and son of Manasseh was named Machir (Gn. 50:23). We later learn that he was the father of Gilead, ancestor of the Gileadites (Nu. 26:29). His children later took Gilead, dispossessing the Amorites (Nu. 32:39–40). Gilead is later attributed to Machir (Jos. 17:1–3). For other references, *cf.* Dt. 3:15; Jos. 13:31; Jdg. 5:14; 1 Ch. 2:21–23; 7:14–17.

2. The son of Ammiel who protected Mephibosheth in Lo-debar (2 Sa. 9:4–5). Later Machir was one of those who brought provisions to David (2 Sa. 17:27–29). E.J.Y.

MACHPELAH. The name applied to the field, cave and surrounding land purchased by Abraham as a burial-place for his wife Sarah (Gn. 23). It was purchased from Ephron, a Hittite, for 400 shekels of silver (vv. 8–16). It lay E of Mamre (v. 17) in the district of Hebron. Here were later buried Abraham (Gn. 25:9), Isaac and Rebekah (Gn. 49:31) and Jacob (Gn. 50:13).

The Heb. (*hammaḵpēlâ*) implies that the name is in some way descriptive and the Gk. (*to diploun*, 'the double') is taken to describe the form of the cave in Gn. 23:17 (LXX). The reading of Shechem for Hebron in Acts 7:16 may be due to the summary nature of the record of this speech, which originally referred also to Joseph's burial at Shechem.

The modern site of the burial-cave (60 m by 34 m), now incorporated in the S end of the Ḥaram al-Ḫalîl at Hebron, is much venerated by Jews, Christians and Muslims. It is jealously guarded by massive stone walls, probably of Herodian work, though the antiquity of the cave itself and its furnishings has not been verified by archaeological research. The 'cenotaph of Sarah' is still to be seen among others in the mosque above the cave (see Vincent, Mackay and Abel, *Hébron, le Haram al Khalîl*, 1923).

The antiquity of the details of Abraham's purchase of Machpelah (Gn. 23) had been thought to find support in Middle Assyr. and Hittite laws prior to 1200 BC (*BASOR* 129, 1953, pp. 15–23), but this claim has now been questioned (*JBL* 85, 1966, pp. 77–84). D.J.W.

MADMANNAH (*maḏmannâh*). A town in SW Judah. At one time Calibbite (1 Ch. 2:49), it may have passed to Simeon and become known as Beth-marcaboth (*cf.* Jos. 15:31 with 19:5; W. F. Albright, *JPOS* 4, 1924, pp. 159f.). Khirbet umm Deimneh, 6 km SW of Dhahiriyah, and Kh. Tatrit, 2½ km further S, have been suggested as possible locations. J.P.U.L.

MADMEN. A town of Moab against which Jeremiah prophesied (48:2).

Since this place is otherwise unknown, it has been suggested, either that the Heb. text read *gm-dmm tdmm*, 'also thou (Moab) shalt be utterly silenced' (LXX, Syr., Vulg.), or that it stands for Dimon, a possible (but unlikely) rendering of the name of the capital *Dîḇôn*. Modern Khirbet Dimneh may be the site. Madmen is unlikely to be the same as * Madmannah, which lay in the Negeb (Jos. 15:31; 1 Ch. 2:49), or * Madmenah, N of Jerusalem (Is. 10:31). D.J.W.

MADMENAH. A place mentioned only in Isaiah's description of the route whereby an invading army approached Jerusalem from the N (Is. 10:31). Shu'fat, 2 km N of Mt Scopus, is the supposed site. A.R.M.

MADON (Heb. *māḏôn*). A city of N Canaan (Jos. 11:1; 12:19; LXX *marrōn*, as in 11:7 for * Merom). If the names are identical (so *LOB*, pp. 117f., 226, 231f.), *d* is a transcription error for *r*. *Mḏn* of Tuthmosis III list (no. 20) is not equivalent. For Kh. Madjan/Qarn Hattin see *Adamah. J.P.U.L.

MAGBISH. Either a town in Judah (*GTT*, p. 380) or the name of a clan. Ezr. 2:30 records that 156 of its 'sons' (or 'inhabitants') returned after the exile. It is inexplicably omitted from the parallel list in Ne. 7. D.J.A.C.

MAGDALA, MAGDALENE. The name 'Magdala' occurs only once in the NT (Mt. 15:39, AV), where the best MSS (followed by RSV, NEB) read 'Magadan'. Some MSS, however, also read 'Magdala' or 'Magadan' for *'Dalmanutha' (otherwise unknown) in Mk. 8:10. The town of Magdala (or Tarichaea) stood on the W shore of the Sea of Galilee, N of Tiberias and Hammath, and S of Capernaum. The name derives from the Heb. *miḡdāl*, 'tower'. It is probable that the modern

Khirbet Mejdel stands on the site today. Magadan was the *locality* on the W shore of the lake to which Jesus crossed after feeding the crowds, and it probably included the town of Magdala. Evidently Mary called Magdalene came from this town or area. (For 'Mary Magdalene', see * MARY, **3**.) S.S.S.

MAGI. The term is used in Herodotus (1. 101, 132) of a tribe of the Medes who had a priestly function in the Persian empire; in other classical writers it is synonymous with priest. Complementing this, Daniel (1:20; 2:27; 5:15) applies the word to a class of 'wise men' or astrologers who interpret dreams and messages of the gods. In the NT the usage broadens to include all who practise magic arts (*cf.* Acts 8:9; 13:6, 8).

Both Daniel and Herodotus may contribute to the understanding of the Magi of Mt. 2:1–12. Apparently the Magi were non-Jewish religious astrologers who, from astronomical observations, inferred the birth of a great Jewish king. After inquiring of Jewish authorities, they came to Bethlehem to do homage. Whether 'the East' from which they came is Arabia, Babylon or elsewhere is uncertain.

The historicity of the visit of the Magi has been questioned on account of the silence of other sources concerning both the event and Herod's subsequent slaughter of the infants, and also because of what is regarded as the legendary character of parts of the narrative. While full weight must be given to the poetic descriptions in the story (*e.g.* the star standing over Bethlehem), descriptive symbolism neither affirms nor negates the historicity of the event involved. A literalist approach, either to dehistoricize the story or to exaggerate the miraculous, is out of keeping with the Evangelist's meaning. For Matthew the Magi's visit represents the Messiah's relationship to the Gentile world and is also a fitting introduction to other prophetically significant events of Christ's infancy. The story is in keeping with the 'royal' Messianic expectations of the Jews and with the character of Herod. Perhaps there is some astronomical confirmation of the * star in the conjunction of Jupiter and Saturn in 7 BC and in the report of a later (4 BC) evanescent star in Chinese records. But such parallels must be applied with caution.

Later Christian traditions regard the Magi as kings (because of Ps. 72:10; Is. 49:7; 60:3?) and number them at three (because of the gifts) or twelve. In the Christian calendar Epiphany, originally associated with Christ's baptism, reflects the importance of the Magi's visit for later Christendom. (* ANNUNCIATION; * MAGNIFICAT.) E.E.E.

MAGIC AND SORCERY.

I. The biblical view

Magic and sorcery attempt to influence people and events by supernatural or occult means. They may be associated with some form of * divination, though divination by itself is the attempt to use supernatural means to discover events without influencing them.

Magic is universal, and may be 'black' or 'white'. Black magic attempts to produce evil results through such methods as curses, spells, destruction of models of one's enemy and alliance with evil spirits. It often takes the form of witchcraft. White magic tries to undo curses and spells, and to use occult forces for the good of oneself and others. The magician tries to compel a god, demon or spirit to work for him; or he follows a pattern of occult practices to bend psychic forces to his will. There is no doubt that magic and sorcery are not always mere superstitions, but have a reality behind them. They must be resisted and overcome through the power of God in the name of Jesus Christ.

I. Biblical terms

The following root words are used in Scripture to denote magical practices and practitioners.

a. In the Old Testament

1. *kšp*. 'Sorcerer', 'sorcery', 'witch-(craft)'. The root probably means 'to cut', and could refer to herbs cut for charms and spells (Ex. 22:18; Dt. 18:10; Is. 47:9, 12; Je. 27:9, *etc.*).

2. *ḥrṭm*. 'Magician'. This term derives from Egyp. *ḥry-tp*, 'chief (lector-priest)', the title borne by Egypt's most renowned magicians (Gn. 41:8; Ex. 7:11, *etc.*).

3. *ḥbr*. 'Enchantment', 'charmer' (Dt. 18:11; Is. 47:9, 12, *etc.*). The root has the idea of binding, probably with amulets and charms.

4. *kaśdîm*. 'Chaldeans'. In Dn. the term is used racially (*e.g.* Dn. 5:30; 9:1) and of a special class linked with magicians (Dn. 2:2, 4, 10, *etc.*). The word is used in a similar sense by Herodotus (1. 181f.), and may have been current earlier with this special meaning. See A. R. Millard, *EQ* 49, 1977, pp. 69–71.

5. *qsm*. 'Divination', especially of future (Dt. 18:10; Ezk. 21:21). Of false prophets (Je. 14:14; Ezk. 13:6).

6. *lt*. 'Secret arts'. Pharaoh's magicians (Ex. 7:22).

7. *nḥš*. 'Enchantment' with spells (Nu. 23:23; 24:1).

8. *lḥš*. 'Expert in charms' (Is. 3:3). Snake charming (Ps. 58:5; Ec. 10:11; Je. 8:17).

b. In the New Testament

1. *magos* (and cognates). 'Magician', 'magic'; in Mt. 2, 'wise men'. Originally a Magian, a racial group in Media, it came, like 'Chaldean', to have a technical use (*e.g.* Acts 8:9, 11; 13:6, 8; found only in Mt. and Acts; * MAGI).

2. *pharmakos* (and cognates). 'Sorcerer', 'sorcery', 'witchcraft'. The root idea is that of drugs, potions (Rev. 9:21; 18:23; 21:8; 22:15; elsewhere only in Gal. 5:20).

3. *goēs*. 'Imposter' (AV 'seducer') (2 Tim. 3:13), it may also signify a spell-binding magician. It has the magical sense in classical and hellenistic Greek.

4. *perierga*. 'Magic arts', AV 'curious arts' (Acts 19:19). The adjective has the root idea of being exceedingly occupied, then of being occupied with other people's business, then of interfering with others by magical arts.

5. *baskainō*. In Gal. 3:1 metaphorically of Galatians bewitched into false beliefs.

II. The biblical judgment on magic

The references given in the first part of this article show that magic and sorcery are always condemned in Scripture. Magic is a rival to true religion, though it can be practised in conjunction with false religious ideas. True religion centres in the personal experience of the one God, with an attempt to live a life that is conformable to his will. The believer walks humbly with his God, prays to him, and is prepared to accept the circumstances of life as the sphere in which to glorify him. Magic, on the other hand, deals with lower supernatural beings, or attempts to force issues by using psychic forces, irrespective of whether the issues are for the glory of God. The following practices come under the specific condemnation of the Bible.

a. The wearing of charms

Among the list of women's ornaments in Is. 3:18–23 the word translated 'amulets' in v. 20 is the root *lḥš* (**I.** *a.* **8**, above); some consider that the word may originally have been *nḥš*, 'serpent', in which case the charm would have been a serpent figure. In this same passage there is a reference in v. 18 to 'crescents'. These are clearly moon-images, and the only other occurrence of the word (*śahᵃrōnîm*) is in Jdg. 8:21, 26, where they are worn both by camels and by the kings of Midian. The previous word in Is. 3:18 (*šᵉḇîsîm*), translated 'headbands' (AV 'cauls') occurs only here in Scripture, but a similar word in the Ras Shamra tablets apparently denotes sun-pendants.

It is probable that there is a reference to charms in Gn. 35:2–4, where Jacob's household put away their 'foreign gods' and their 'earrings'. This is the normal word for ear-ring, but the association with idols here suggests that they were charms of some kind.

b. Workers of magic; sorcerers; witches

Genesis and Exodus speak of the magicians of Egypt, and 2 Tim. 3:8 names two of them as Jannes and Jambres. The Exodus record says that the Egyp. magicians copied Moses in turning their rods into serpents (7:11), in turning water into blood (7:22), and in producing frogs (8:7), but failed to produce the lice (8:18–19), and were themselves incapacitated by the boils (9:11). The account leaves us free to decide whether they were clever conjurors or used occult methods.

There is little direct allusion to sorcerers and witches in Israel. It is incorrect to speak of the 'witch' of Endor (1 Sa. 28) since the Bible describes her as a medium, and not as a worker of magic. It is significant that Jezebel practised sorcery (2 Ki. 9:22), and Mi. 5:12 suggests that it was by no means rare in Israel. Manasseh personally encouraged it among other evils (2 Ki. 21:6).

There is an indication of magical practices in Is. 28:15, where people were initiated into some magical pact which they believed would give immunity from death.

The most striking reference to Heb. witchcraft is Ezk. 13:17–23. Here Heb. prophetesses were also practising magic arts for the preservation and destruction of individuals. In this they were going farther than the false prophets of Mi. 3:5, who gave messages of good or ill to individuals according to whether they were prepared to pay. The details of the magical practices here are not easy to follow. The armbands and veils are worn both by victims (18) and witches (20–21). Witchcraft practice suggests a psychic link between witch and client through interchange of material charged with good or evil spells. Alternatively, the veils are made to size (18), and maybe the witch made a veil of a size to represent one's enemy. The witch then wore it for a time and impregnated it with malevolent spells (*cf.* the use of doll figures). The wrist bands would bring luck to the wearers. J. G. Frazer, in his *Folk-Lore in the Old Testament*, suggests that the women professed to catch souls and bind them up in cloth bands. The imprisonment would cause the owner of the soul to waste away. The soul might be represented by some object from the victim, *e.g.* blood, hair or nails.

III. Does the Bible countenance magic?

We now deal with some of the passages where the Bible might seem to countenance magic and superstition.

a. The use of mandrakes

Down through the centuries E women have made use of mandrakes to ensure conception (*cf.* Gn. 30:14–18). Since modern investigations have shown that primitive medicines often contain some element that is really effective, it would be foolish to dismiss this example as magic.

b. Jacob and the peeled rods

In Gn. 30:37–41 Jacob was probably influenced by primitive ideas of the effect of seen objects upon the unborn young. But v. 40 indicates that the results really came about through selective breeding (see D. M. Blair, *A Doctor Looks at the Bible*, 1959).

c. Samuel and the water

This incident (1 Sa. 7:6) is often thought to denote sympathetic magic, the solemn pouring out of water to induce a storm. There is, however, not the slightest indication of this in the context. Water poured on the ground, according to 2 Sa. 14:14, is a symbol of human frailty and impermanence, and Samuel's action may best be interpreted as a sign of abasement and humiliation before God.

d. Samson's hair

Frazer and others have produced stories from all parts of the world in which the soul or the strength of someone resided in his hair, or even in some external object. The biblical story, however (Jdg. 16), shows that Samson's uncut hair denoted his faithfulness to the *Nazirite vow, and that the Spirit of God empowered him so long as he was faithful to this vow (*e.g.* Jdg. 13:25; 14:19). Those who wish to argue from a natural level may note that the loss of strength could be accounted for on psychological grounds when Samson realized his guilt. There are well-recognized cases of hysterical blindness, paralysis, *etc.*

e. Rousing up leviathan

Job asks that the day of his birth should be cursed by those who curse the day, who are ready to rouse up leviathan (Jb. 3:8). Some find here a reference to magicians who were thought to rouse up a dragon to swallow the sun at an eclipse. If this is correct, it is part of the extravagant language of Job, who calls upon everyone, bogus or true, who might claim to bring ill-luck on his birthday.

f. The power of blessing and cursing

The OT lays great stress on this. The Patriarchs bless their children, and Isaac cannot reverse what he has promised to Jacob (Gn. 27:33, 37). Balaam is called upon to curse Israel (Nu. 22f.). Throughout the rest of the OT there are other incidental references. It should be noted that the Bible does not visualize anyone's pronouncing an effective blessing or curse contrary to God's will. The Patriarchs believe that God is showing them the future of their descendants, and their blessing is declaratory of this. Balaam cannot effectively curse those whom God has blessed (Nu. 23:8, 20). The psalmist knows that God can turn the undeserved curse into a blessing (Ps. 109:28), while David's reluctance to interfere with Shimei is based on the fear that God may have inspired the curse for something that David had done (2 Sa. 16:10).

g. Miracles

The pagan world certainly regarded 'private' miracles as magic (Acts 8:9–11), but the Bible never treats divine miracles as superior magic, *i.e.* there is no use of incantations, invocation of spirits or spells. Moses did not silence Pharaoh's magicians by being a better magician, but acted solely as the agent of God, behaving when and how God instructed him. His rod was not a conjuror's magic wand, but the symbol of God's designation. It was 'the rod of God' (Ex. 4:20).

As regards exorcisms and healings, one need not be surprised to find linguistic resemblances between the Gospel records and pagan magic, since the vocabulary of demonology and illness is limited. But neither Christ nor the disciples are ever regarded as using the accompaniments of magical practice. For a full linguistic discussion see John M. Hull, *Hellenistic Magic and the Synoptic Tradition*, 1974. J.S.W.

2. Egyptian and Assyro-Babylonian

I. Ancient magic

Where the ordinary relationships and processes of life could readily be regulated through observation of obvious cause and effect, and by acting on an acquired modicum of knowledge and/or skill, this sufficed. But where mystery shrouded the causes of effects, and when ordinary means did not suffice to obtain desired results, then magic was appealed to. Magic was the exploitation of miraculous or occult powers by carefully specified methods to achieve ends otherwise unattainable.

Magic and religion were closely linked, in that whereas 'society' principally covers relationships between man and man, and 'religion' the relationship between deity and mankind, the powers of magic found application in both spheres. In general, *cf. Sources Orientales 7: Le monde du sorcier*, 1966.

II. Egyptian magic in the Bible

Learned in sacred writings, rituals and spells, trained in the 'House of Life' (temple 'schools' where this and other literature was composed, copied and taught), Egypt's greatest magicians were the chief lector-priests, in Egyp. *ḥry-ḥbt ḥry-tp*, later abbreviated by Moses' time (13th cent. BC) to *ḥry-tp*. This very title gave the Heb *ḥarṭōm*, 'magician'. This essentially Egyp. term recurs in an Assyr. document (7th century BC), as *ḫar-ṭibi*, and as *ḥrtb* in 1st-century AD tales of magicians. (See A. H. Gardiner, *JEA* 24, 1938, pp. 164–165; and, more fully, J. Vergote, *Joseph en Égypte*, 1959, pp. 66–94, 206, with full references.) Thus the association of 'magicians' with 'wise men' generally in Gn. 41:8 and Ex. 7:11 reflects authentic Egyp. tradition; see paragraphs *a* and *c*, below.

BIBLIOGRAPHY. For a good formal analysis of Egyptian magic, see A. H. Gardiner in *ERE*, 8, pp. 262–269. Much material is collected (texts and pictures) in F. Lexa, *La Magie dans l'Égypte Antique*, 3 vols., 1925.

a. Magicians and dreams of Joseph's pharaoh

In Gn. 41:8, Joseph's pharaoh calls upon his magicians and wise men to interpret his dreams. This reflects the importance of dreams in ancient Egypt and the E; dreams and their interpretations were gathered into manuals, veritable handbooks of dream-interpretation. The original of one such MS, Papyrus Chester Beatty 3 (19th Dynasty, 13th century BC) may date back to the Middle Kingdom age, while the Papyri Carlsberg 13 and 14 of the 2nd century AD contain further collections from early sources. The common pattern is, that if a man sees himself in a dream doing or experiencing such-and-such, it is good or bad, and means that so-and-so will befall him. For this whole topic, see A. L. Oppenheim, *The Interpretation of Dreams in the Ancient Near East*, 1956; *Sources Orientales 2: Les Songes et leurs Interprétations*, 1959.

b. Joseph and divination

In Gn. 44:4–5, 15, Joseph play-acts the learned Egyptian, master of the divinatory art, before his brothers. Two interpretations of this incident are possible.

(i) Joseph had it said by his steward, according to the usual translations of v. 5, that he divined by means of his silver cup; this would imply knowledge of cup-divination (lecanomancy) in Hyksos-period Egypt, *c.* 1700 BC. By this technique, omens for interpretation were obtained by observing the movement or configuration of drops of oil upon water in a cup. This technique is of Mesopotamian origin, apparently already used by the Sumerians (*cf.* B. Meissner, *Babylonien und Assyrien,* 2, 1925, p. 284). A handbook to this technique is preserved on two cuneiform tablets dating from the 19th–17th centuries BC, *i.e.* within Joseph's general period.

In Egypt, however, cup-divination is attested only twice, once doubtfully. Two small statuettes of apparently Middle Kingdom date (*c.* 1900–1700 BC) each show a figure kneeling with chin on a cup held in the hands, and it is just possible that these depict cup-divination (J. Capart, *Chronique d'Égypte* 19, 1944, p. 263). Egypt offers no further example until the technique recurs in papyri of the 2nd century AD. But Bab. influence, including divination, was already felt in Palestine in the 2nd millennium BC. Bab. divinatory practice is attested at Hazor: in Temple II of the 15th century BC was found a clay model liver inscribed in cuneiform (see Y. Yadin, *BA* 22, 1959, p. 7 with fig. 5). Hence on this evidence there is no difficulty whatever in presupposing some knowledge of other forms of Mesopotamian divination such as lecanomancy in the Palestine of Joseph's day or in the immediately adjacent Egyp. E Delta, then under Hyksos (Semitic) control.

(ii) One may, on the other hand, render Joseph's steward's speech as 'Is it not from this cup that my lord drinks, and *concerning* which he will assuredly divine?', *i.e.* to unmask the theft. On this rendering Joseph's cup is solely a drinking-vessel, cup-divination would not be alluded to, and the form of his pretended divination remains wholly unspecified. This fits well with v. 15 when Joseph says to his brothers, 'Do you not know that such a man as I can indeed divine?', *i.e.* he pretends to have apprehended them in their theft by divination, to recover his cup. For this view, see J. Vergote, *Joseph en Égypte*, 1959, pp. 172–173.

c. Moses and the magicians

In Ex. 7:8–13, when Aaron at Moses' command casts down his rod as a serpent before Pharaoh, his magicians and sorcerers 'did in like manner with their enchantments' (v. 11). For this kind of conjuring, it would appear that the Egyp. cobra (Arab. *naja ḥaye*) can be rendered immobile (catalepsy) if pressure be applied to the muscles at the nape of the neck; *cf.* L. Keimer, *Histoires de Serpents dans l'Égypte ancienne et moderne* (*Mémoires, Institut d'Égypte*, 50), 1947, pp. 16–17. The serpent must first be charmed, then seized at the neck as shown on several ancient Egyptian scarab-amulets (Keimer, *op. cit.*, figs. 14–21) and thus be temporarily immobilized (*cf.* H. S. Noerdlinger, *Moses and Egypt*, 1956, p. 26; *EBr*[11], 6, p. 613). Aaron's serpent restored to a rod manifested the wholly-other omnipotence of God, however. On the plagues, see *Plagues of Egypt.

III. Assyro-Babylonian magic

a. Its role

Defensive and curative magic was mainly resorted to to obtain deliverance from affliction—illness, demon possession, *etc.*—which may originate with the sufferer. The exorcist might then often employ rites and spells from the 'handbook' *Šurpu*, 'Burning' (*i.e.* in purificatory rite), listing every conceivable fault the sufferer might have committed. Or affliction may have entered from without—some sorcerer's evil spell. To counter such, there was the companion 'handbook' of tablets, *Maqlu*, also 'Burning' (of wax or wooden effigies of sorcerers). 'As this image quivers, dissolves and melts away, even so may the sorcerer and sorceress quiver, dissolve and melt away!' (E. A. W. Budge, *British Museum: A Guide to the Babylonian and Assyrian Antiquities*, 1922, p. 201). Collections of prayers for release or absolution also exist. There is a full modern translation of *Šurpu* in E. Reiner, *Šurpu, A Collection of Sumerian and Akkadian Incantations*, 1958; of *Maqlu* in G. Meier, *Die Assyrische Beschwörungssammlung Maqlû*, 1937.

Prognostic magic, i.e. divination, was based on the conviction that any event, good or ill, may be announced or accompanied by some portent observable by men. Learned priests systematically compiled long series of omens with interpretations in veritable reference-manuals. Omens were either observed from signs in nature or sought by specific techniques.

1. Natural portents were taken from the whole gamut of man's observation: haloes and eclipses of sun and moon, conjunctions of heavenly bodies, *etc.* (astrology); the flight of birds, actions and states of animals and insects; births of animals and humans, especially if abnormal—all in long series of omen-tablets. For a sick person, omens good or bad would determine their survival or decease (see R. Labat, *Traité Akkadien de Diagnostics et Prognostics Médicaux*, 2 vols., 1951). Is. 47:9–13 criticizes such proceedings.

2. Specific techniques of divination included observation of configurations of and on a sheep's liver (hepatoscopy, extispicy), and observation of patterns of oil on water (or vice versa) in a cup (lecanomancy). For translations of reports of the liver, see A. Goetze, *JCS* 11, 1957, pp. 89–105. This most famous form of Bab. divinatory magic penetrated among the Hittites of Asia Minor and the Canaanites in N Syria and Palestine alike (see Egyptian Magic, **II**.*b*, above). *Cf.* also Ezk. 21:21–22. Dream-interpretation was as important as in Egypt. *Cf.* also *La divination en Mésopotamie ancienne* (*Rencontre, Strasbourg*), 1966; A. Caquot, M. Leibovici, *La divination*, 1–2, 1968.

c. Its practitioners

As in Egypt, magic was practised by priestly scholars attached to the temples. Exorcisms were performed by the *āšipu*-priest (*cf.* Heb. *'aššāpîm*, 'enchanters', Dn. 1:20) by virtue of the gods Ea and Marduk, the master-magicians. The elaborate apparatus of divination was the province of the *bārû*-priest; he had to be physically perfect, undertake long studies and be initiated. Those attached to the royal court were called upon at any time to interpret all manner of things. See G. Contenau, *Everyday Life in Babylon and Assyria*, 1954, pp. 281–283, 286–295.

BIBLIOGRAPHY. On Mesopotamian magic, see also briefly L. W. King, *ERE*, 4, 1911, pp. 783–786; 8, 1915, pp. 253–255. Useful notes can be found in É. Dhorme and R. Dussaud, *Les Religions de Babylonie et d'Assyrie . . . des Hittites, etc.*, 1949, pp. 258–298. Fully detailed surveys of magic and divination respectively, with copious translations from texts, can be found in M. Jastrow, *Die Religion Babyloniens und Assyriens*, 1–2, 1912. Specific studies are by G. Contenau, *La Magie chez les Assyriens et les Babyloniens*, 1940; B. Meissner, *Babylonien und Assyrien*, 2, 1925, pp. 198–282.

IV. Assyro-Babylonian magic in the Bible

a. Balaam

Balaam of Nu. 22–24 is apparently a diviner turned prophet under divine constraint. Thus Balak sent emissaries to hire Balaam 'with the fees for divination in their hand' (Nu. 22:7; *cf.* v. 18), and at first Balaam went 'to meet with omens', their nature unspecified (Nu. 24:1). Balak evidently required of Balaam evil omens wherewith to curse Israel. An astrological text was found at Qatna (*Revue d'Assyriologie* 44, 1950, pp. 105–112) and *bārû*-diviners in 18th- and 14th-century BC texts from Alalaḫ (D. J. Wiseman, *The Alalakh Tablets*, 1953, p. 158 *sub* '*bârû*'), both in N Syria. Further, an early 2nd millennium seal of one 'Manum the *bârû*(-diviner)' turned up at Beth-shan in Jezreel in levels of the 13th century BC, Balaam's own period, to which his oracles can be dated linguistically (W. F. Albright, *JBL* 63, 1944, pp. 207–233). It is therefore wholly in keeping with known facts that a Moabite ruler should hire a diviner from N Syria (Pethor by the River [Euphrates]), in the land of the sons of Amaw (Nu. 22:5; *cf.* Albright, *BASOR* 118, 1950, pp. 15–16, n. 13).

b. The law and magic in Canaan

The prohibitions in the Mosaic law against the magic and sorcery practised by other nations (*e.g.* Lv. 19:26; 20:27; Dt. 18:10–14) were very relevant to conditions in contemporary Canaan. For Bab. influence there, see above. The N Canaanite epics from *Ugarit/Ras Shamra (tablets of the 14th/13th century BC) show Danil kissing the growing plants and grain, invoking an oracular blessing upon Aqhat (*ANET*, p. 153: 60ff.); Pugat's activities are much less certainly connected with sorcery. That Ex. 22:18 expressly condemns sorceresses is also noteworthy.

c. Daniel

In Dn. 1:4 the procedure for educating the well-favoured Heb. youths in Bab. learning as laid down by Nebuchadrezzar accurately reflects that which was usual for the *bārû* scholar-magicians.

To 'dissolve doubts' (Dn. 5:12, 16, AV), *i.e.* to dissipate anxiety caused by a (yet unexplained) dream or omen (*cf.* Dn. 4:5), was the purpose of interpreting or 'resolving' dreams. Then a good dream's benefits could be accepted and the threat from a bad one averted magically. On this, see A. L. Oppenheim, *The Interpretation of Dreams in the Ancient Near East*, pp. 218–220, 300–307. This emphasis on dreams is characteristic of the neo-Bab. kings, particularly Nabonidus, father of Belshazzar. For his dreams, see Oppenheim, *op. cit.*, pp. 202–206, 250, and, in part, T. Fish in *DOTT*, pp. 89f. New texts of, and new dreams by, Nabonidus and his venerable mother come from stelae of this king at Harran; see C. J. Gadd, *AS* 8, 1958, pp. 35–92 and pls. 1–16, especially pp. 49, 57, 63; *ANET*[3], pp. 560–563. Closely parallel to Dn. 4 is the 'Prayer of Nabonidus' in the Dead Sea Scrolls in which an exiled Jewish sage (name not preserved) is granted to the king to explain the cause of the latter's affliction. E.T. in M. Burrows, *More Light on the Dead Sea Scrolls*, 1958, p. 400; text published by J.-T. Milik, *RB* 63, 1956, pp. 407–415; brief comments, D. N. Freedman, *BASOR* 145, 1957, pp. 31–32.

BIBLIOGRAPHY. 'Magic (Jewish)' in *ERE*; E. Langton, *Good and Evil Spirits*, 1942; *idem*, 'The Reality of Evil Powers Further Considered', *HJ* 132, July 1935, pp. 605–615; M. F. Unger, *Biblical Demonology*, 1952, pp. 107–164; A. D. Duncan, *The Christian, Psychotherapy and Magic*, 1969; D. Basham, *Deliver us from Evil*, 1972. K.A.K.

MAGISTRATE. In Ezr. 7:25 'magistrate' translates the Heb. *šôpēṭ*, 'judge'. In Jdg. 18:7, AV 'there was no magistrate in the land' is a paraphrase of the Heb, idiom *yāraš 'eṣer*, 'to possess restraint' (RSV 'lacking nothing'). Dn. 3:2–3 lists magistrates (Aram. *tip̄tāye'*, AV 'sheriffs') among officials summoned by Nebuchadrezzar.

In the NT Luke uses in his Gospel (12:11, 58) the words *archē* and *archōn* ('rule' and 'ruler') to refer to civil authorities in general. Paul was beaten, imprisoned and subsequently released by the magistrates at Philippi (Acts 16:20, 22, 35–36, 38). Here the Gk. word is *stratēgoi*, which literally means generals, or leaders of the host, but came to be used in a political context as an equivalent for Lat. *praetores.* This latter was the title found in some inscriptions as a popular designation for the leading men of the colony, though their correct title was *duoviri*. Evidence for the titles of the Philippian magistrates is to be found in *CIL*, 3. 633, 654, 7339, 14206[15]. (*SANHEDRIN, *POLICE.) D.H.W.

MAGNIFICAT. Like other hymns in Lk. 1–2, the prophecy of Mary (Lk. 1:46–55) takes its name from the Lat. Vulg. Believing 'Mary' (Lk. 1:46) to be the secondary reading, some commentators accept the less well-attested reading 'Elizabeth' (*cf.* Creed). It may be that Luke originally wrote simply 'she said', and that both 'Mary' and 'Elizabeth' were attempts of copyists to assign the song to a particular person. The reading 'Mary' became universally accepted. Scholars are divided on the question of whether the contents of the hymn are more suitable to Mary or Elizabeth. The episode which forms the setting is, however, transitional from the annunciation to the birth stories; it stands in close conjunction with the former and continues its Messianic theme. Most probably, therefore, Luke viewed it as *Mary's* song regarding Christ.

This lyrical poem is modelled upon OT psalms and has also a special affinity to the Song of Hannah (1 Sa. 2:1–10). The sequence of the narrative is moulded by Luke's theme; and the hymn need not be regarded as Mary's spontaneous or exact reply. But neither should it be considered merely as an editorial reconstruction. Its significance for Luke lies in the fact that it is Mary's prophecy, *i.e.* that its contents sprang from her lips and express her mind and heart.

As this lyric forms a climax to the section, so also within the Magnificat itself the mood rises to a crescendo. It is divided into four strophes, describing (1) Mary's joyous exaltation, gratitude and praise for her personal blessing; (2) the character and gracious disposition of God to all who reverence him; (3) his sovereignty and his special love for the lowly in the world of men; and (4) his peculiar mercy to Israel. The cause of Mary's song is that God has deigned to choose her, a peasant maid of low estate, to fulfil the hope of every Jewish maiden. For it is probable that, in Judaism, that which gave deepest meaning and joy to motherhood was the possibility that this child might be the Deliverer.

The last part of the poem is a description of God's Messianic deliverance and is a virtual paraphrase of OT passages. This redemption is prophesied in terms of a national deliverance from human oppressors. This is a typical mode of expression of pre-Christian Messianism. The NT does not contradict it, but does transfer it to Messiah's parousia in the eschatological 'age to come' (*cf.* Acts 1:6ff.). As is often the case in OT oracles, these Messianic acts of God are viewed as though they were already accomplished: the promise of God has the efficacy of the act itself (*cf.* Gn. 1:3); his word is the word of power. The specific object of God's mercy is 'Israel his servant' (Lk. 1:54f.; *cf.* Acts 3:13, 26; 4:27, 30). Whether there is reflected here the OT distinction between the whole nation and the righteous remnant is uncertain; the concept is often left in an undifferentiated whole, and the contrast in vv. 51–53 may be only between the Jewish nation and the Gentile overlord. But in the mind of Luke—and in the mind of his first readers—certainly the distinctly Christian interpretation in such concepts as 'Israel' (*cf.* Lk. 24:21–26; Jn. 12:13; Acts 1:6; Rom. 9:6), 'servant', and 'the seed' (Jn. 8:39; Gal. 3:16, 29) is not absent, and it probably enters into his understanding and interpretation of Mary's prophecy. (*ANNUNCIATION; *BENEDICTUS.)

BIBLIOGRAPHY. R. Laurentin, 'Les Évangiles de l'enfance', *Lumière et Vie* 23, 1974, pp. 84–105; S. Farris, *The Hymns of Luke's Infancy Narratives*, 1985. E.E.E.

MAGOR-MISSABIB (Heb. *māḡôr missāḇîḇ*, 'terror on every side'). A symbolic name that

Jeremiah gave to Pashhur son of Immer (Je. 20:3, AV; see *PASHHUR, 1). J.D.D.

MAHANAIM (Heb. *maḥ^anayim*, 'two camps'). A place in Gilead where Jacob saw the angels of God before he reached Penuel and met Esau (Gn. 32:2). Appointed to be a levitical (Merarite) city from the territory of Gad (Jos. 21:38; 1 Ch. 6:80), Mahanaim was on the border of Gad with Gileadite Manasseh (Jos. 13:26, 30). It was briefly capital of Ishbosheth, Saul's son (2 Sa. 2:8, 12, 29), and later David's refuge from Absalom (2 Sa. 17:24, 27; 19:32; 1 Ki. 2:8), and then became the seat of a district-officer of Solomon's (1 Ki. 4:14). The location of Mahanaim is still uncertain; *cf.* J. R. Bartlett in *POTT*, p. 252, n. 47. It is usually placed in the middle of N Gilead at Khirbet Mahneh, 20 km N of the Jabbok river, but as the boundary of Gad is linked with the course of the Jabbok, Mahanaim is probably better located somewhere on (or overlooking) the N bank of the Jabbok. Mahanaim was at some distance from the Jordan, on the evidence of 2 Sa. 2:29, however 'Bithron' be interpreted. If (as is commonly taken) Bithron means 'cleft, ravine', Abner went from Jordan up the vale of the Jabbok E and through its narrow part before reaching Mahanaim. If the RSV reading be adopted, then 'the whole forenoon' was needed in any case for Abner's E flight. Hence perhaps Mahanaim was in the Jerash area, or up to 10–15 km SSW of Jerash, overlooking the N bank of the river Jabbok. See K.-D. Schunck, *ZDMG* 113, 1963, pp. 34–40. (*GAD, *GILEAD.) K.A.K.

MAHANEH-DAN (Heb. *maḥ^anēh-ḏān*, 'camp of Dan'). Where Samson experienced the stirring of God's Spirit (Jdg. 13:25), and the first staging-post of the Danites in their quest for an inheritance (Jdg. 18:12). The geographical references given, 'between Zorah and Eshtaol' and 'W of Kiriath-jearim', cannot be reconciled, and the name itself suggests a temporary settlement. As the Danites had no secure inheritance (Jdg. 18:1), probably due to Philistine pressure, there is no problem in two places bearing the same name. It is not surprising that no trace of such temporary encampments has survived. A.E.C.

MAHER-SHALAL-HASH-BAZ. A symbolical name ('speed the spoil, hasten the prey') given to one of the sons of *Isaiah to signify the speedy removal of Syria and Israel as enemies of Judah by the Assyrians. This removal was to take place before the child could lisp 'my father and my mother' (Is. 8:3–4). E.J.Y.

MAHLI (Heb. *maḥlî*, 'weak', 'sickly'). **1.** Eldest son of Merari and grandson of Levi (Ex. 6:19, AV 'Mahali'; Nu. 3:20; 1 Ch. 6:19, 29; 23:21; 24:26, 28; Ezr. 8:18). His descendants are mentioned in Nu. 3:33; 26:58. **2.** The son of Mushi, another son of Merari (1 Ch. 6:47; 23:23; 24:30); therefore nephew of **1**, above. J.D.D.

MAHOL (Heb. *māḥôl*, 'dance'). The father of certain sages whom Solomon excelled in wisdom (1 Ki. 4:31). But in 1 Ch. 2:6 they are said to be 'sons of Zerah'. 'Sons' may simply mean 'descendants' in either case. However, 'sons of Mahol' may be an appellative expression meaning 'sons of the dance' (*cf.* 'daughters of music' in Ec. 12:4). Such dancing would then be part of the ritual of worship, as in Pss. 149:3; 150:4 (*cf.* also the titles of Pss. 88–89). J.G.G.N.

MAKKEDAH (Heb. *maqqēḏâh*). A town in the Shephelah captured by Joshua (Jos. 10:28; 12:16); in the district of Lachish (15:41). Adonizedek and his allies hid in a cave nearby after their defeat (10:16ff.). Eusebius (*Onom.* p. 126) put Makkedah 8 Roman miles from Beit Guvrin; Khirbet el-Kheishum, NE of Azekah, seems to be too far, while Tell Bornat (Kallai-Kleinmann, *VT* 8, 1958, p. 155) is only 3 km from Beit Guvrin. El-Mughar, SE of Yibna, was once favoured but is unlikely.

BIBLIOGRAPHY. F. M. Abel, *Géographie de la Palestine*, 2, 1937, p. 378; D. Dorsey, *Tel Aviv* 7, 1980, pp. 185–193. J.P.U.L.

MAKTESH. A site in Jerusalem or near by (Zp. 1:11). The name means 'mortar' or 'trough'. The oldest suggestion is that it was the Kidron Valley; so says the Targum. But most scholars today believe it to have been some part of the Tyropoeon Valley, within the walls of the city, where foreign merchants gathered; *cf.* NEB 'Lower Town'. D.F.P.

MALACHI, BOOK OF.

I. Authorship, date and background

The LXX takes the word not as a proper name but as a common noun, and renders 'my messenger', which is the meaning of the Heb. word. Many scholars follow LXX, and believe that the name of the author is not given. But the analogy of the other prophetical books which give the author's name would support the view that the name is here intended to indicate the author. This is supported by the Targum, which adds the phrase 'whose name is called Ezra the scribe'.

From internal evidence the approximate date of the prophecy may be determined. Sacrifices were being offered in the Temple (1:7–10; 3:8). This implies that the Temple was standing; indeed, that it had been standing for some time, a fact which would point to the 5th century BC. This is substantiated by the reference in 1:8 to the *peḥâ* or Persian governor. Mixed marriages seem to have been practised (2:10–12). The phrase 'the daughter of a foreign god' means 'a woman of foreign religion'. Apparently this practice of marrying outside the covenant people was so widespread that the earlier prohibitions had long since been forgotten. Nor was great care exhibited in the offering of the sacrifices (1:7). The priests had despised the Lord in offering polluted bread. When blemished offerings are brought it is a sign of a lax attitude, and such an attitude would not well comport with the early zeal displayed by the returned exiles. This appears to have been accompanied by a neglect in paying the requisite tithes (3:8–10). The abuses which Malachi condemns are those which Nehemiah sought to correct.

It is impossible to date the book precisely, but it may be that it was composed during Nehemiah's visit to Susa. At least it would seem to come from approximately this time.

II. Outline of contents

The book falls into two main parts, and its purpose may best be ascertained through a study of its contents. The first part (chs. 1 and 2) deals with the sin of Israel, and the second part (chs. 3 and 4) with the judgment that will befall the guilty and the blessedness that will come upon those who repent.

We may analyse the book thus:

a. The superscription (1:1)

There is a connection between this heading and that found at the beginning of ch. 3. Whether or not Malachi is a proper name, it exemplifies the fact that he is a messenger of God.

b. The Lord's love for Israel (1:2–5)

God declares his love for the people in that he chose Jacob and rejected Esau. This fact is seen in that Edom is devastated and refugees from Edom will never be able to return and rebuild, whereas Israel is back in the promised land.

c. A delineation of Israel's sin (1:6–2:9)

In bold fashion the prophet now begins to delineate the chief and characteristic sins of the nation which were again bringing the wrath of God upon the nation's head. God is the Father of the people, for he has nourished and brought them up. A father deserves honour and love, but such have not been shown to God by Israel. This complaint is directed particularly to the priests who are the representatives of the people before God. These priests who should have set the example of godly fear in worship have, in fact, despised the name of the Lord. Unworthy worship had been characteristic of their predecessors in the 8th and 7th centuries until the Exile had been brought upon Judah. Now, however, the Exile is past, and its lessons have not yet been learnt. Restored to her land, able to worship in the Temple, Judah yet sins against the Lord in the same manner as before.

The accusation against Israel is carried on in the form of a dialogue. Against each charge of the Lord a question or challenge is raised. For example, God charges that the priests have offered polluted food. They reply, 'How have we polluted it?' (1:7). It is thus brought out in clear-cut fashion that the priests have been bringing blemished sacrifices. This was in direct contravention of the law, which required that the offerings should be perfect. Instead, they had brought what was blind and lame, and in so doing had exhibited contempt for the Lord.

When such sacrifices come from their hands, how can they expect to be accepted as individuals and to find favour with him? (1:9). It would be better that the gates of the Temple were closed entirely than for such offerings to be brought (1:10). Both the offerer and his offering are unacceptable to the Lord, and the priests are despised by the people.

Such sacrifices are not desired by God, for even among the Gentiles his name will prove itself to be great so that pure sacrifices are offered to him (1:11). This does not refer to the offerings which the heathen nations bring to their gods, but to the time when the true gospel will be spread throughout the world and the true God worshipped by all peoples. Israel, however, had profaned the Lord's table, and found his service boring, resulting in a people who practised deception and were selfish.

If there is no repentance, then a curse will come upon the priests. In 2:5–7 the Lord makes clear the true duty of the priests, and thus there appears a great contrast between what the priest should be and what he actually was. Indeed, through his own poor example, he, instead of instructing others, has led them astray. He has been partial in instructing others (2:9b).

d. Condemnation of mixed marriages and divorce (2:10–17)

Israel had a common Father: God had created the nation. Therefore, it should have manifested unity. Instead of that, however, it had dealt treacherously. It had profaned the holiness of the Lord in the practice of mixed marriages. Those who had thus acted, however, were to be cut off. Divorce was also common, and the Lord hates divorce. These sins had been glossed over and rationalized. The Lord declares that the people have wearied him with their words. They have ignored him and acted as though he did not exist.

e. The coming Day of the Lord (3:1–6)

Malachi now breaks into the exalted language of prophecy in declaring that the messenger of the Lord will truly come and prepare the day for the Lord whom the people seek. He will appear as a refiner, to purify and purge the nation, and who can face the day of his coming? As a result of his work, the offering of Judah and Jerusalem will be pleasing to the Lord (3:4). Yet the coming will bring judgment, and this will fall upon those in the nation who are oppressing others. Nevertheless, Jacob will not be entirely wiped out, for the Lord does not change; he remains faithful to his promises (3:6).

f. Repentance and tithing (3:7–12)

The nation's apostasy is not new, but has continued from of old. For one thing, it has shown itself in withholding from God the tithes which had been commanded. This amounted to robbing God. If the nation would bring the tithes as it should, God would respond to its worship and pour upon it an overflowing blessing which would call forth comment from other nations.

g. A promise of deliverance for the godly (3:13–4:3)

The nation had been saying resentful things against God. It would seem that the people considered it did not pay them to serve God. But among them there were also those who 'feared the Lord', and they encouraged one another. These the Lord takes note of, and he will not only spare them but make them his own possession. The day of judgment will surely come, and it will consume the arrogant, but to those who fear the Lord's name righteousness will rise like a sun, and in its wings there will be healing, joy and victory.

h. Conclusion (4:4–6)

The prophecy closes with an exhortation to remember the law of Moses, and with the announcement that Elijah will come before there appears the great and terrible Day of the Lord.

BIBLIOGRAPHY. J. G. Baldwin, *Haggai, Zechariah, Malachi, TOTC*, 1972; W. C. Kaiser, *Malachi: God's Unchanging Love*, 1984; R. L. Smith,

Micah-Malachi, WBC, 1984; P. A. Verhoef, *The Books of Haggai and Malachi, NIC*, 1987. E.J.Y. J.G.B.

MALCAM. 1. A Benjaminite, son of Shaharaim by Hodesh (1 Ch. 8:9).

2. God of the Ammonites, possibly their chief deity (Am. 1:15, AV, RSV 'their king'), almost certainly to be identified with *Milcom (1 Ki. 11:5, 33; 2 Ki. 23:13), and *Molech or Moloch (Lv. 18:21; 1 Ki. 11:7; Je. 32:35, *etc.*). All these terms have the basic root *mlk* which conveys the idea of king, kingship. Both AV and RV translate *malkām* as 'their king' in Je. 49:1, 3 (RSV 'Milcom'). *Cf.* Zp. 1:5 (RSV 'Milcom'). J.A.T.

MALACH IJAH('Yah is King'). This is a common OT name, sometimes translated as Malchiah. It was the name of the following: **1.** A descendant of Gershom and ancestor of Asaph (1 Ch. 6:40); **2.** a priest, the father of Pashhur (1 Ch. 9:12; Je. 21:1); **3.** the head of a priestly course (1 Ch. 24:9), perhaps the same as **2**; **4, 5, 6.** three Israelites who had taken foreign wives in post-exilic times (Ezr. 10:25, 31). In 1 Esdras 9:26, 32 they are called Melchias, Asibias and Melchias respectively; **7.** 'the son of Rechab', who repaired the dung gate (Ne. 3:14); **8.** 'the goldsmith's son', possibly the same as **4, 5, 6** or **7**, who helped to repair the wall (Ne. 3:31).

9. One who stood beside Ezra at the reading of the Law (Ne. 8:4); **10.** one who sealed the covenant, perhaps the same as **9** (Ne. 10:3); **11.** a priest who took part in the purification of the wall (Ne. 12:42), perhaps the same as **9** and/or **10**.

12. The owner of the pit in which Jeremiah was imprisoned and probably a member of the royal family (Je. 38:6). J.D.D.

MALCHUS (Gk. *Malchos* from Heb. *meleḵ*, 'king'). The high priest's servant whose ear Peter cut off when Jesus was arrested in the Garden of Gethsemane (Mt. 26:51; Mk. 14:47; Lk. 22:50; Jn. 18:10). Only John mentions the man's name, thus confirming his close acquaintance with the high priest Caiaphas and his household (*cf.* Jn. 18:15); and only Luke (22:51), with his interest in medical matters, mentions the healing of the ear. Malchus is a common Arab name in Nabatean and Palmyrene inscriptions. J.D.D.

MALICE. In the NT this translates Gk. *kakia*, which has the following meanings: **1.** 'Wickedness', 'evil' (1 Cor. 14:20; Jas. 1:21; 1 Pet. 2:1, 16; and also in Acts 8:22, of an individual sinful act). 'Malice' in 17th-century (AV) English had primarily this meaning. **2.** 'Ill-will', 'spitefulness'; *i.e.* 'malice' in the modern sense of the word. **3.** 'Trouble', 'harm' (Mt. 6:34). In lists of sins (*e.g.* Rom. 1:29; Col. 3:8; Tit. 3:3), sense **2** is probably to be preferred, except, perhaps, in 1 Pet. 2:1 and Eph. 4:31, where 'all *kakia*' implies 'all kinds of wickedness'.

Malice characterizes the life of men under the wrath of God (Rom. 1:29). It is not only a moral deficiency but destroys fellowship (W. Grundmann, *TDNT* 3, pp. 482–484). For believers it belongs to the old life (Tit. 3:3); but there is still need for exhortation to 'clean it out' (1 Cor. 5:7f.) or 'strip it off' (Jas. 1:21; Col. 3:8). Christians are to be 'babes in evil' (1 Cor. 14:20), for Christian liberty is not lawlessness (1 Pet. 2:16). P.E.

MALTA (Gk. *Melitē*; Acts 28:1, AV 'Melita'). An island in the centre of the Mediterranean, 100 km S of Sicily and in area about 246 sq km (not to be confused with the island Mljet or Melitene off the Dalmatian coast; *cf.* O. F. A. Meinardus, 'St Paul Shipwrecked in Dalmatia', *BA* 39, 1976, pp. 145–147.) Here Paul's ship was driven from Crete by the ENE wind Euraquilo (27:14, RSV 'the northeaster'; *WIND). After being shipwrecked he spent 3 months on the island before continuing his journey to Rome *via* Syracuse, Rhegium and Puteoli (28:11–13). Paul performed acts of healing, and the party was treated with great respect.

Malta had been occupied from the 7th century BC by Phoenicians. The name itself means 'refuge' in that language (J. R. Harris, *ExpT* 21, 1909–10, p. 18). Later, Sicilian Greeks also came; there are bilingual inscriptions of the 1st century AD on the island. In 218 BC the island passed from Carthaginian to Roman control (Livy, 21. 51), later gaining the 'civitas'. Its inhabitants were *barbaroi* (28:2, 4) only in the sense of not speaking Greek. Luke may refer to one of their gods in v. 4 as *Dikē* (Justice). Publius, 'the chief man' (v. 7), probably served under the propraetor of Sicily. His title (Gk. *prōtos*) is attested by inscriptions (*CIG*, 14. 601; *CIL*, 10. 7495).

The site of the shipwreck is thought to have been 'St Paul's Bay', 13 km NW of modern Valletta (*cf.* W. M. Ramsay, *SPT*, pp. 314ff.).

BIBLIOGRAPHY. J. Smith, *Voyage and Shipwreck of Paul*[4], 1880; W. Burridge, *Seeking the Site of St Paul's Shipwreck*, 1952; J. D. Evans, *Malta*, 1959; C. J. Hemer, 'Euraquilo and Melita', *JTS* n.s. 26, 1975, pp. 100–111. B.F.H.

MAMMON. This word occurs in the Bible only in Mt. 6:24 and Lk. 16:9, 11, 13, and is a transliteration of Aramaic *māmônâ*. It means simply wealth or profit, but Christ sees in it an egocentric covetousness which claims man's heart and thereby estranges him from God (Mt. 6:19ff.): when a man 'owns' anything, in reality it owns him. (*Cf.* the view that mammon derives from Bab. *mimma*, 'anything at all'.) 'Unrighteous mammon' (Lk. 16:9) is dishonest gain (F. Hauck, *TDNT* 4, pp. 388–390) or simply gain from self-centred motives (*cf.* Lk. 12:15ff.). The probable meaning is that such money, used for others, may be transformed thereby into true riches in the coming age (Lk. 16:12).

BIBLIOGRAPHY. C. Brown, *NIDNTT* 2, pp. 836–840; J. D. M. Derrett, *Law in the New Testament*, 1970. E.E.E.

MAMRE (Heb. *mamrē'*). **1.** A place in the Hebron district, W from Machpelah (Gn. 23:17, 19; 49:30; 50:13), associated with Abraham (Gn. 13:18; 14:13; 18:1) and Isaac (Gn. 35:27). Abraham resided for considerable periods under the terebinth of Mamre; there he built an altar, there he learnt of the capture of Lot, there he received Yahweh's promise of a son and pleaded for Sodom, and from there he saw the smoke of Sodom and its neighbour-cities ascend. The site has been identified at Râmet el-Khalîl, 4 km N of Hebron. Here Constantine built a basilica beside an ancient tere-

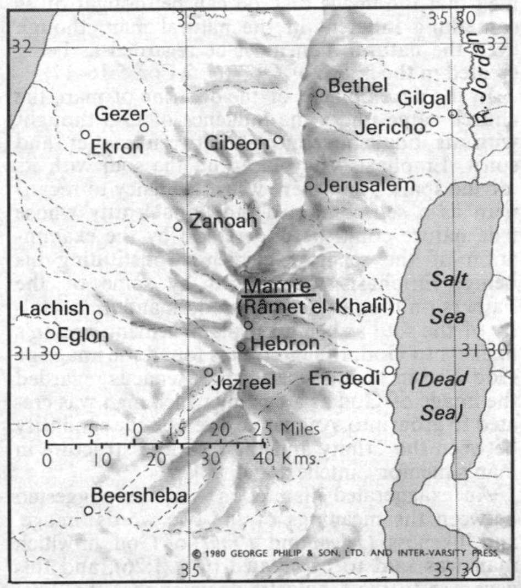

Mamre, identified with modern Râmet el-Khalîl.

binth which was pointed out in his day (as by Josephus 250 years earlier) as the tree beneath which Abraham 'entertained angels unawares' (Gn. 18:4, 8). There was a shrine there under the Monarchy, but it was a sacred place before Abraham's time in the Early Bronze Age.

2. An Amorite chief at Mamre who with his brothers Eshcol and Aner joined Abraham's expedition against Chedorlaomer (Gn. 14:13, 24).

BIBLIOGRAPHY. E. Mader, *Mambre*, 1957; *NEAEHL*, pp. 939–942. F.F.B.

MAN. The Genesis account of creation accords to man a supreme place in the cosmos. Not only is his creation the final work of God, but in it the work of the other 5 days finds its fulfilment and its meaning. Man is to possess the earth, make it serve him, and to rule the other creatures (Gn. 1:27–2:3). The same witness to man's dominion and centrality in creation is given elsewhere (Am. 4:13; Is. 42:5f.; Pss. 8:5f.; 104:14f.), and is supremely given in the incarnation (*cf.* Heb. 2).

a. Man in nature

It is emphasized throughout the Bible that man is part of nature. Being dust, and made from dust (Gn. 2:7), his biological and physical similarity to the animal creation is obvious in many aspects of his life (Gn. 18:27; Jb. 10:8–9; Ps. 103:14; Ec. 3:19–20; 12:5–7). Being 'flesh' he shares in the helpless dependence of the dumb creation on God's mercy (Is. 2:22; 40:6; Pss. 103:15; 104:27–30). Even in making nature serve him he has to serve nature, tend it, and bring it to fruition (Gn. 2:15). He is subject to the same laws as the natural world, and can find himself overwhelmed in the midst of the grandeur of the world in which he lives (Jb. 38–42).

Nature is not simply a neutral framework or background for man's life. Between nature and man there are deep and mysterious bonds. The natural world falls under the curse of corruption through the Fall of man (Gn. 3:17–18), and now suffers pain and death, waiting for the final redemption of mankind before it can expect its own (Rom. 8:19–23). Nature is regarded in the Bible as rejoicing in the events that lead to man's redemption (Ps. 96:10–13; Is. 35; 55:12–13) when it, too, shall enjoy deliverance (Is. 11:6–9; 65:25). Man, on his side, has an instinctive sympathy with nature (Gn. 2:19) and must respect its ordinances (Lv. 19:19; Dt. 22:9–10; Jb. 31:38–40), realize his dependence on it, and toil to gain from his natural environment sustenance for his life and enrichment for his culture (Gn. 3:17; 9:1–7).

b. Man's destiny

Yet man cannot find the true meaning of his life within this context. The animals can provide no 'helper fit for him' (Gn. 2:18). He has a history and a destiny to fulfil, unique among the rest of creation. He is made 'in the image of God' (Gn. 1:27). While some have suggested that this image is expressed in man's dominion over the earth, or in his power of reasoning, or even in his physical characteristics, it seems better to find it neither in man's relationship with the world nor in any static impress on man's being, but in his responsibility towards his Creator. In the Genesis account of creation God, when he creates man, is regarded as taking up an attitude of deeper personal concern for him (Gn. 1:26; *cf.* 1:3, 6, *etc.*), and an approach that involves himself in a closer relationship with man his creature (Gn. 2:7) than with the rest of creation. God approaches man and addresses him as a 'thou' (Gn. 3:9, AV), and man is made to respond to God's gracious word in personal love and trust. Only in this response can man be what he truly is. God's word by which he lives (*cf.* Mt. 4:4) offers him a relationship that lifts him above the rest of creation around him, and confers on him his dignity as a child of God, made in his image and reflecting his glory. This dignity, moreover, is not something he possesses as an isolated individual before God, but only as he also stands in responsible and loving relationship to his fellowmen. It is as man within his family and social relationships that he truly reflects the image of God (Gn. 1:27–28; 2:18).

c. Man's structure

Various words are used to describe man in his relationship to God and to his environment, and in the structure of his own being. These are: spirit (Heb. *rûah*, Gk. *pneuma*), soul (Heb. *nepeš*, Gk. *psychē*), body (only in NT Gk., *sōma*), flesh (Heb. *bāśār*, Gk. *sarx*). These words are used according to the different aspects of man's activity or being which it is intended to emphasize, but they must not be regarded as describing separate or separable parts which go to make up what man is. The use of the word 'soul' may emphasize his individuality and vitality with emphasis on his inner life and feeling and personal consciousness. The use of the word 'body' may emphasize the historical and outward associations that affect his life. But the soul is, and must be, the soul of his body, and vice versa. Man is also in such a relation to the Spirit of God that he has spirit, and yet not in such a way that he can be described as spirit, or that spirit can be regarded as a third aspect of his identity. Man as 'flesh' is man in his connection with the realm of nature and with humanity as a whole, not only in its weakness but also in its sinfulness and opposition to God.

Other words are used to define the seat of certain particular aspects or functions of man. In the

OT emotional impulses and feelings are attributed, really and metaphorically, to organs of the body such as the *heart (*lēḇ*), *liver (*kāḇēḏ*), *kidneys (*kᵉlāyôṯ*) and *bowels (*mēʿîm*). The *blood is also regarded as being closely identified with the life or *nep̄eš*. It is especially the heart (*lēḇ*) that is the seat of a wide range of volitional and intellectual as well as emotional activities, and tends to denote the soul, or man viewed from his inward and hidden side. In the NT the same use is made of the Gk. word *kardia* (= *lēḇ*, heart). Two more words, *nous*, 'mind', and *syneidēsis*, 'conscience', are brought into use, and a clearer distinction is made between the 'inward' and 'outward' man, but these two aspects of the one man cannot be separated, and the future holds not the mere 'immortality of the soul' but the 'resurrection of the body', which means the salvation and renewal of the whole man in the fullness of his being.

d. Man's sin

The Fall of man (Gn. 3) involves his refusal to respond to God's word, and to enter the relationship in which he can fulfil the purpose for which he was created. Man seeks to find within himself the justification for his existence (Rom. 10:3). Instead of seeking to enter a true relationship with God and his fellow-men in which he can reflect God's image and glory, he seeks to find the meaning of his destiny merely in his relationship with the created world in the context of his immediate environment (Rom. 1:25). The result is that his life has become characterized by bondage (Heb. 2:14–15), conflict with evil powers (Eph. 6:12), frailty and frustration (Is. 40:6; Jb. 14:1), and he is so perverted and evil in his mind and heart (Gn. 8:21; Jb. 14:4; Ps. 51:5; Mt. 12:39; 15:19–20) that he turns the truth of God into a lie (Rom. 1:25).

e. Man in God's image

Yet in spite of the Fall, man under the promise of Christ must still be regarded as in the image of God (Gn. 5:1ff.; 9:1ff.; Ps. 8; 1 Cor. 11:7; Jas. 3:9), not because of what he is in himself, but because of what Christ is for him, and because of what he is in Christ. In Christ is now to be seen the true meaning of the covenant which God sought to make with man in the Word, and the destiny which man was made to fulfil (*cf.* Gn. 1:27–30; 9:8–17; Ps. 8; Eph. 1:22; Heb. 2:6ff.), for the unfaithfulness of man does not nullify the faithfulness of God (Rom. 3:3). Therefore in the sight of God, man, seen both in the individual (Mt. 18:12) and corporate (Mt. 9:36; 23:37) aspects of his life, is of more value than the whole realm of nature (Mt. 10:31; 12:12; Mk. 8:36–37), and the finding of the lost man is worth the most painful search and complete sacrifice on God's part (Lk. 15).

Jesus Christ is the true image of God (Col. 1:15; 2 Cor. 4:4) and thus the true man (Jn. 19:5). He is both the unique individual and the inclusive representative of the whole race, and his achievement and victory mean freedom and life for all mankind (Rom. 5:12–21). He fulfils the covenant in which God bestows on man his true destiny. In Christ, by faith, man finds himself being changed into the likeness of God (2 Cor. 3:18) and can hope confidently for full conformity to his image (Rom. 8:29) at the final manifestation of his glory (1 Jn. 3:2). In 'putting on' this image by faith he must now 'put off the old nature' (Eph. 4:24; Col. 3:10), which seems to imply a further renunciation of the idea that the image of God can be thought of as something inherent in the natural man, though even the natural man must be regarded as being created in the image of God (*cf.* 2 Cor. 5:16–17).

In the development of the doctrine of man, the church came under the influence of Gk. thought with its dualistic contrast between matter and spirit. Emphasis was placed on the soul with its 'divine spark', and there was a tendency to regard man as a self-contained individual entity whose true nature could be understood by the examination of the separate elements constituting his being. Emphasis was placed by some of the Fathers on the rationality, freedom and immortality of the soul as being the main element in man's likeness to God, though others found the image of God also in his physical being. Irenaeus regarded the image of God as a destiny which man was created to grow into. Augustine dwelt on the similarity between the Trinity and the threefold structure in man's memory, intellect and will.

An exaggerated distinction was also suggested between the meanings of the two words 'image' and 'likeness' (*ṣelem* and *dᵉmûṯ*) of God, in which man was said to·be created (Gn. 1:26), and this gave rise to the scholastic doctrine that the 'likeness' (Lat. *similitudo*) of God was a supernatural gift given by God to man in his creation, *i.e.* an original righteousness (*justitia originalis*) and perfect self-determination before God, which could be, and indeed was, lost in the Fall. The 'image' (*imago*), on the other hand, consisted of what belonged to man by nature, *i.e.* his freewill, rational nature and dominion over the animal world, which could not be lost even in the Fall. This means that the Fall destroyed what was originally supernatural in man, but left his nature and the image of God in him wounded, and his will free.

At the Reformation Luther denied the distinction between *imago* and *similitudo*. The Fall radically affected the *imago*, destroyed man's freewill (in the sense of *arbitrium*, though not of *voluntas*), and corrupted man's being in its most important aspects, only a tiny relic of his original image and relationship to God being left. Calvin, however, also stressed the fact that the true meaning of man's creation is to be found in what is given to him in Christ, and that man comes to be in God's image as he reflects back to him his glory, in gratitude and faith.

In later Reformed dogmatics the concepts of *imago* and *similitudo* were again differentiated when theologians spoke of the essential image of God which could not be lost, and the accidental but natural endowments (including original righteousness) which might be lost without the loss of humanity itself. In more modern times Brunner has attempted to use the concept of the 'formal' *imago* consisting of the present structure of man's being, based on law. This has not been lost in the Fall, and is a point of contact for the gospel. It is one aspect of a unified theological nature of man which even in its perversion reveals traces of the image of God. 'Materially', however, for Brunner, the *imago* has been completely lost. R. Niebuhr has returned to the scholastic distinction between, on the one hand, the essential nature of man which cannot be destroyed, and, on the other hand, an original righteousness, the virtue and perfection of which would represent the normal expression of that nature.

Karl Barth, in formulating his doctrine of man,

has chosen a path different from that followed by church tradition. We cannot know real man till we know him in and through Christ, therefore we must discover what man is only through what we find Jesus Christ to be in the gospel. We must not take sin more seriously than grace, therefore we must refuse to regard man as being no longer the one God made him. Sin creates the conditions under which God acts, but does not so change the structure of man's being that when we look at Jesus Christ in relation to men and mankind, we cannot see within human life analogical relationships which show a basic form of humanity corresponding to and similar to the divine determination of man. Though man is not by nature God's 'covenant-partner', nevertheless in the strength of the hope we have in Christ human existence is an existence which corresponds to God himself, and in this sense is in the image of God. Barth finds special significance in the fact that man and woman together are created in the image of God, and stresses the mutual communication and helpfulness of man to man as being of the essence of human nature. But only in the incarnate Son, Jesus Christ, and through his election in Christ, can man know God and be related to God in this divine image.

BIBLIOGRAPHY. O. Weber, *Dogmatik*, 1, 1955, pp. 582–640; E. Brunner, *Man in Revolt*, E.T. 1939; K. Barth, *Church Dogmatics*, E.T. III/1, pp. 176–211, 235–249, and III/2, *Christ and Adam*, E.T. 1956; D. Cairns, *The Image of God in Man*, 1953; R. Niebuhr, *The Nature and Destiny of Man*, 1941; Gustaf Wingren, *Man and the Incarnation*, 1959; H. Heppe, *Reformed Dogmatics*, E.T. 1950, pp. 220–250; W. Eichrodt, *Man in the Old Testament*, E.T. 1951; C. H. Dodd, P. I. Bratsiotis, R. Bultmann and H. Clavier, *Man in God's Design*, 1952; R. P. Shedd, *Man in Community*, 1958; W. G. Kümmel, *Man in the New Testament*, 1963; K. Rahner, *Man in the Church* (= *Theological Investigations* 2), 1963; *idem*, *Theology, Anthropology, Christology* (= *Theological Investigations* 13), 1975; R. Scroggs, *The Last Adam: A Study in Pauline Anthropology*, 1966; W. Pannenberg, *What is Man?*, 1970; T. M. Kitwood, *What is Human?*, 1970; J. Moltmann, *Man*, 1971; R. Jewett, *Paul's Use of Anthropological Terms*, 1971; P. K. Jewett, *Man as Male and Female*, 1975; P. E. Hughes, *The True Image*, 1989; T. E. Pollard, *Fullness of Humanity*, 1982; R. S. Anderson, *On Being Human*, 1982; H. Vorländer, C. Brown, J. S. Wright in *NIDNTT* 2, pp. 562–572. R.S.W.

MANAEN. The Gk. form of the Heb. name Menahem ('comforter'). Brought up with ('foster-brother of') Herod Antipas, Manaen's life took a very different turn from that of the tetrarch, and he is found as one of the Christian leaders at Antioch along with Paul and Barnabas (Acts 13:1). He may have been related to an earlier Manaen or Menahem, an Essene who, according to Josephus (*Ant.* 15.373), was a friend of Herod the Great. J.D.D.

MANAHATH, MANAHATHITES. 1. Son of Shobal, son of Seir the Horite (Gn. 36:23; 1 Ch. 1:40), who was the eponymous ancestor of a clan of Mt Seir later absorbed by Edom.

2. The name of a city to which certain Benjaminites were carried captive (1 Ch. 8:6), and which seems to have been somewhere in the vicinity of Bethlehem (so *GTT*, p. 155). *ISBE* and Grollenberg suggest an identification with Manocho, a town in the hill-country of Judah listed in Jos. 15:59, LXX, and probably to be identified with the modern Malîha, SW of Jerusalem. Mahanath may also be the 'Nohah' of Jdg. 20:43, for both names mean 'resting-place'. Amarna Letter 292 (*ANET*, p. 489) mentions a Manhatu in the realm of Gezer which is probably the same place.

Manahathites, inhabitants of Manahath, are mentioned in 1 Ch. 2:52, 54. They were the descendants of Caleb. Half of them were the progeny of *Shobal, and the others of Salma (*SALMON). J.D.D.

MANASSEH ('making to forget'). **1.** Elder son of Joseph, born in Egypt of an Egyptian mother, *Asenath, daughter of *Potiphera, the priest of On (Gn. 41:51). Israel accepted Manasseh and Ephraim as co-equals with Reuben and Simeon, but Manasseh lost the right of *firstborn* (*bᵉḵôr*) in favour of his younger brother Ephraim (Gn. 48:5, 14). An interesting and early parallel is found in Ugaritic literature, *Keret Legend* (Tab. 128, 3. 15), 'The youngest of them I will make *firstborn* (*abrkn*).'

2. The tribe of Manasseh derived from seven families: one from Machir, and the remaining six from Gilead. They occupied land on both sides of Jordan; the E portion being granted by Moses, the W by Joshua (Jos. 22:7). After the crossing of Jordan and the settlement in the land, Joshua permitted the half-tribe of Manasseh, together with Reuben and Gad, to return to the conquered territory of Sihon, king of Heshbon, and Og, king of Bashan (Nu. 32:33). The E lot of the half-tribe of Manasseh covered part of Gilead and all of Bashan (Dt. 3:13). The W half of the tribe was granted good land N of Ephraim, and S of Zebulun and Issachar (Jos. 17:1 12). This W part was divided into ten portions: five to those families having male descendants, and five to Manasseh's sixth family, *i.e.* the posterity of Hepher, all females and daughters of Zelophehad (Jos. 17:3). W Manasseh included a chain of Canaanite fortresses and strong cities, among which were *Megiddo, *Taanach, *Ibleam and *Bethshan. These they failed to conquer but compelled their inhabitants eventually to pay tribute. Though the lot of Manasseh and Ephraim, the tribe of Joseph, was large, they lodged a complaint with Joshua for more land. In reply he advised them to show their worth by clearing the unclaimed forest areas (Jos. 17:14–18). Golan, a city of Bashan, in E Manasseh, was one of the six *'cities of refuge' (Jos. 20:8; 21:27; 1 Ch. 6:71).

The tribe was renowned for its valour; among its heroes was Gideon in the W (Jdg. 6:15), and Jephthah in the E (Jdg. 11:1). Some of the tribe of Manasseh deserted to David at Ziklag (1 Ch. 12:19–20), and also rallied to his support at Hebron (v. 31). Manassites were among those deported to Assyria by Tiglath-pileser (1 Ch. 5:18–26).

Difficulties have been found in the genealogies of the tribe of Manasseh, given in Nu. 26:28–34; Jos. 17:1–3; 1 Ch. 2:21–23; 7:14–19 (see *HDB* on 'Manasseh'). But if allowance is made for a corrupt text in 1 Ch. 7:14–15, then harmony can be restored. It is probable that the words 'Huppim

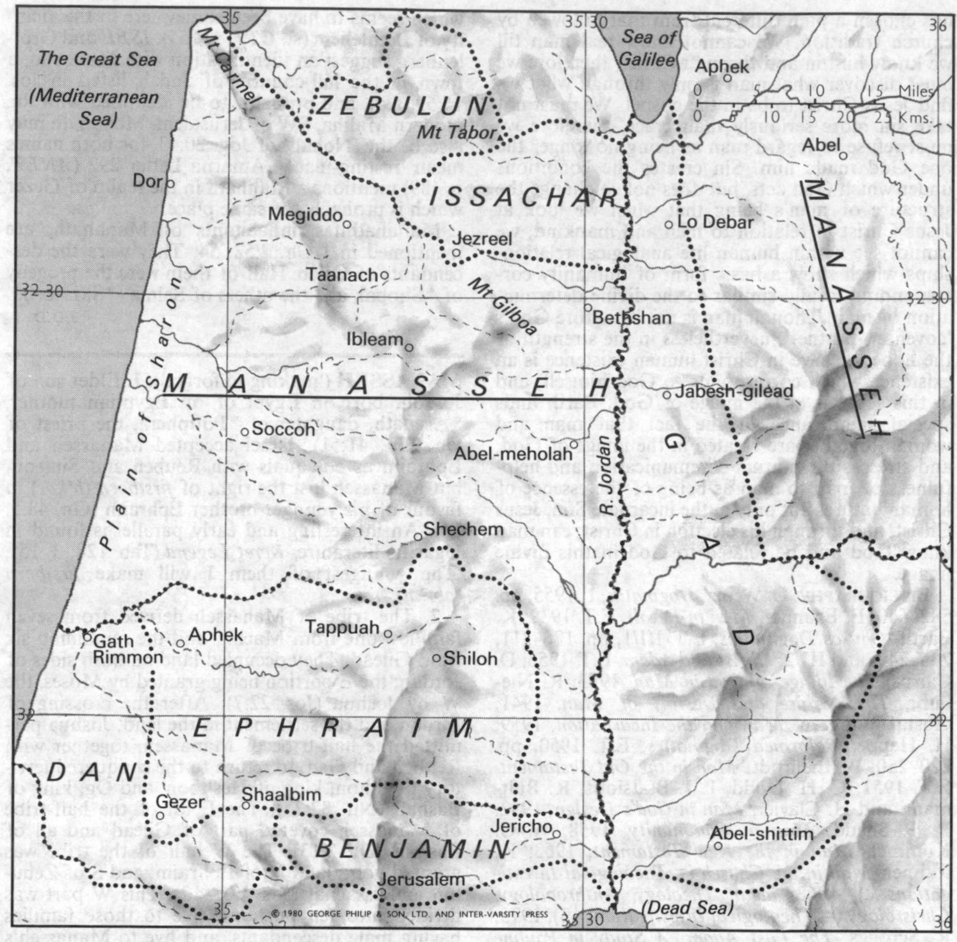

Map showing the land allotted to the tribe of Manasseh.

and Shuppim' are glossed into v. 15 from v. 12, and possible that the word 'Asriel' is a dittograph.

A comparison of the Heb. text of these verses with LXX, Syr. Peshitta and Vulg. indicates that the original text may have had the following words: 'The son of Manasseh (Asriel) . . . whom his Syrian concubine . . . bore Machir the father of Gilead and Machir took a wife . . . and his sister's name Maacha and the name of the . . Zelophehad and Zelophehad had daughters . . .' Apart from these verses, the genealogies are consistent.

3. Son of Hezekiah and Hephzibah, he began his reign in Jerusalem at the age of 12 and reigned 55 years (2 Ki. 21:1; 2 Ch. 33:1); probably as co-regent with his father 696–686 BC, and as sole ruler 686–642 BC (E. R. Thiele, *The Mysterious Numbers of the Hebrew Kings*, 1951, pp. 154ff.). His reign was a time of religious retrogression, caused by terror of Assyria and a fascination for her cults. This resulted in a syncretism of Baalism, a cult of Astarte at the 'high places', astral worship, with spiritism and divination. His long reign was bloody and reactionary, and notorious for the introduction of illegal altars into the Temple courts, and 'the passing of his sons through the fire' in the valley of the son of Hinnom.

The name 'Manasseh, king of Judah' appears on the Prism of Esarhaddon (*Me-na-si-i šar Ia-ú-di*), and on the Prism of Ashurbanipal (*Mi-in-si-e šar Ia-ú-di*), among twenty-two tributaries of Assyria (*ANET*, pp. 291, 294). The Chronicler narrates Manasseh's deportation to Babylon, his repentance and release (2 Ch. 33:10–13). A parallel to this is the capture and the subsequent release of Neco I, king of Egypt, by Ashurbanipal (*Rassam Cylinder*, *ANET*, p. 295). Since a revolt against Assyria occurred in Manasseh's reign, in support of Shamash-shum-ukin, viceroy of Babylon, he may well have been involved in it (*ANET*, p. 298). His reformation appears to have been superficial and was swept away in the reign of his son. R.J.A.S.

MANGER. The feeding-trough for animals in a stall or stable, translated 'crib' in Jb. 39:9 (AV, RSV); Pr. 14:4 (AV); Is. 1:3 (AV, RSV). Gk. *phatnē* has an extended meaning of 'stall' (Lk. 13:15), and is used in LXX to translate various Heb. words, *'urwâ*, 'stall' (2 Ch. 32:28), *repeṯ* (Hab. 3:17), *'ēḇûs* (Jb.

39:9; Pr. 14:4; Is. 1:3). In the NT it occurs in Lk. 2:7, 12, 16; 13:15.

Mangers are known in other lands besides Palestine. In Palestine the stable or stall was attached to the owner's house and was furnished with a manger. The stables at *Megiddo, now dated to the Omrid dynasty, had hollowed-out limestone blocks for feed boxes. Christian tradition holds that Jesus was born in a cave in the neighbourhood of Bethlehem. In that case the manger may have been cut out of the rock walls. J.A.T.

MANNA. A substance which was the Israelites' chief food during their 40 years' sojourn in the wilderness (Ex. 16:35). When Israel grumbled at the lack of food in the wilderness of Sin, God gave them 'bread from heaven' (Ex. 16:4; Ps. 78:23–24), and his provision did not cease until they crossed into Canaan and ate the food of that land (Jos. 5:12), despite their grumbling (Nu. 11:6; *cf.* Ne. 9:20). The Israelites were to collect an omer each for five days and double that amount on the sixth day to last them over the sabbath, as none would appear on that day. Usually it did not keep overnight but became maggoty and malodorous if left over, but the manna to be kept for sabbath use was preserved by being cooked or baked beforehand (Ex. 16:4–5, 16–30). Each morning after the dew had gone there was found on the ground a 'small, round thing' like hoar-frost, whitish, like coriander-seed and bdellium, with a honey taste; it could be ground and used in cooking and baking. The people said, 'What (Heb. *man*) is it?' and called it manna (*man*). Such are the data in Ex. 16:14–15, 31; Nu. 11:7–9. An omerful was preserved by Aaron at God's command as a witness for future generations (Ex. 16:33–34; Heb. 9:4).

Many have speculated on the precise nature of this manna, and several partial parallels are known. To the present time in Sinai, certain insects produce honeydew excretions on tamarisk-twigs seasonally every June for some weeks. At night these drops fall from the trees to the ground, where they remain until the heat of the sun brings forth the ants which remove them. These drops are small, sticky, light-coloured, and sugary-sweet, quite strikingly like the biblical descriptions in Ex. 16 and Nu. 11. Other honeydew-producing insects are known in Sinai and elsewhere, *e.g.* certain cicadas. However, these products do not fit the biblical description in all particulars. On them, see F. S. Bodenheimer, *BA* 10, 1947, pp. 1–6; for a photo of tamarisk-twigs with drops, see W. Keller, *The Bible as History*, 1956, plate between pp. 112–113. In S Algeria in 1932 and also about 70 years before, after unusual weather 'there were falls of a whitish, odourless, tasteless matter of a farinaceous kind which covered tents and vegetation each morning' (A. Rendle Short, *Modern Discovery and the Bible*[3], 1952, p. 152). Also in 1932, a white substance like manna one morning covered an area of ground 640 × 18 m on a farm in Natal and was eaten by the natives (H. S. Gehman in *WDB*, p. 375a). None of these phenomena satisfies the biblical data, and the provision of the manna remains ultimately in the realm of the miraculous, especially in its continuity, quantity and 6-day periodicity. The partial parallels cited above may indicate, however, the kind of physical bases used by God in this provision.

The manna was used by God to teach lessons for spiritual instruction as well as physical sustenance. Israel was told that with the failure of other food ('suffered thee to hunger'), his provision of manna was to 'make you know that man does not live by bread alone, but that man lives by everything that proceeds out of the mouth of the Lord' (Dt. 8:3, *cf.* v. 16). God used the provision of manna on 6 days and not the seventh to teach Israel obedience, and convicted them of disobedience (Ex. 16:19, *cf.* vv. 20, 25–30). Jesus Christ uses the manna, God-given 'bread from heaven', as a type of himself, the true bread of life, and contrasts the shadow with the substance: 'your fathers ate the manna in the wilderness, and they died' (Jn. 6:49), but he could say, 'I am the bread of life . . . which came down from heaven; if any one eats of this bread, he will live for ever' (Jn. 6:35, 51, and *cf.* vv. 26–59 *passim*). Eternal life was made available to man by the merits of Christ's death (v. 51). In Rev. 2:17 the 'hidden manna' represents spiritual sustenance imparted by the Spirit of Christ. K.A.K.

MANOAH. Samson's father. The name is identical in form with a word meaning 'resting-place, state or condition of rest' from the root *nwḥ*, 'to rest' (*BDB*), and with the Wâdi el-Munâḥ, which runs into Wâdi Ṣarâr from Tibneh (= Timnah). Manoah was a Danite from Zorah (*ṣorʿā*) (Jdg. 13:2), and one name may be derived from the other. A connection with the Manahathites of 1 Ch. 2:54 is more dubious. These were a Calebite clan of Judah (1 Ch. 2:50ff.), and may have been among those Judahites who lived in Zorah in post-exilic times (Ne. 11:29). For a discussion of these coincidences, see C. F. Burney, *Book of Judges*, 1920, p. 341. Manoah is best known for the angelic annunciation of Samson's birth. He appears as a man of prayer and godly fear, and he tried to dissuade his son from marrying outside the covenant people (Jdg. 14:3). He predeceased his son (Jdg. 16:31). A.G.

MANSIONS (AV) (Gk. *monai*, Vulg. *mansiones*, RVmg. 'abiding-places', RSV 'rooms'). Various speculations have been made about this figure of speech used by our Lord in Jn. 14:2 (*e.g.* B. F. Westcott, *The Gospel according to St John*, 2, 1908, p. 167). Most scholars agree that what is intended is that the Father will provide room and to spare in the eternal abode. The Gk. word elsewhere in NT occurs only in v. 23 of this chapter. See F. Hauck, *TDNT* 4, pp. 579–581. J.D.D.

MAON, MAONITES. 1. Descendants of the Calebite branch of the tribe of Judah. Maon was the son of Shammai and the father of the inhabitants of Beth-zur (1 Ch. 2:45). The town Maon features in Judah in the list in Jos. 15:55. In this area David and his men sheltered from Saul (1 Sa. 23:24–25), and the churlish Nabal lived there (1 Sa. 25:2). The Maonites are mentioned in the official list of those who returned from Exile (Ezr. 2:50, AV 'Mehunim', RSV 'Meunim'; Ne. 7:52, 'Meunim'). Khirbet-el-Maʿîn, 14 km S of Hebron and 65 km W of Gaza, marks the ancient site. Traces of Early Iron Age I pottery and a remarkable late 4th–6th century AD synagogue with mosaics were found there. It is surrounded by pasture-lands, probably the 'wilderness of Maon' where David sought refuge from Saul (1 Sa. 23:24–25) and was saved by a Philistine raid (1 Sa. 23:27f.).

2. A hostile people in Transjordan, linked with Amalek and the Zidonians as oppressors of Israel (Jdg. 10:12); a pastoral people attacked by Hezekiah (RSV 'Meunim', 1 Ch. 4:41), and Uzziah (2 Ch. 26:7). Their association with Arabs and Ammonites (2 Ch. 20:1) suggests *Ma'ān*, SE of Petra, as their home. J.A.T.

MARAH (Heb. *mārâ*, 'bitter'). This was the first named camp of the Israelites after the Red Sea crossing, called Marah because only bitter water was found there (Ex. 15:23; Nu. 33:8–9), and perhaps also by comparison with the sweet water of the Nile Valley to which they had been accustomed. On the likely assumption that the route from the crossing led to the mountains in the S of the Sinai peninsula, Marah is often identified with the modern Ain Hawarah, *c.* 75 km SSE of Suez. However, H. H. Rowley (*From Joseph to Joshua*, 1950, p. 104) and J. Gray (*VT* 4, 1954, pp. 149f.) identify Marah with *Kadesh, a view refuted by *GTT*, p. 252, n. 218; B. Rothenberg and Y. Aharoni, *God's Wilderness*, 1961, pp. 11, 93f., 142ff., present both views. (*WILDERNESS OF THE WANDERING.)

BIBLIOGRAPHY. B. S. Childs, *Exodus*, 1974, pp. 265–270. J.D.D. G.I.D.

MARANATHA. An Aramaic formula used in transliteration without explanation at 1 Cor. 16:22, AV. In the *Didache* (10. 6) it figures as part of the eucharistic liturgy. The phrase is probably to be resolved as *māranâ ṯâ*, 'our Lord, come!' (see G. H. Dalman, *Grammatik des jüdisch-palästinisch Aramäisch*, pp. 120, n. 2; 297, n. 2: also *Jesus–Jeshua*, 1929, p. 13, for the resolution *māran 'eṯâ* of identical meaning). The anticipation and longing expressed in this early Christian prayer may be seen reflected in 1 Cor. 11:26 (*cf.* the context in the *Didache*) and in Rev. 22:20. The occurrence of the phrase at 1 Cor. 16:22 derives from the idea of judgment implicit in v. 21, which is closely linked with the idea of the second coming (*cf.* the Old Latin MS g and the Ethiopic version, which render *maranatha* as 'at the coming of the Lord').

In Gk. MSS with accents and punctuation the phrase is often written as if it represented *māran 'aṯâ*, 'our Lord has come'. This seems less likely in view of the ideas of the Eucharist and the judgment with which it is linked in the context, unless it be a reference to the Lord's manifestation of himself through the Eucharist.

BIBLIOGRAPHY. T. Zahn, *INT*, 1909, 1, pp. 303–305; K. G. Kuhn, *TDNT* 4, pp. 466–472; W. Mundle, C. Brown, *NIDNTT* 2, pp. 895–898; C. F. D. Moule, 'A Reconsideration of the Context of *Maranatha*', *NTS* 6, 1959–60, pp. 307ff.; *BAGD*. J.N.B.

MARESHAH (Heb. *mārē'šâh*). A town in the Shephelah (Jos. 15:44), covering the road up the Wadi Zeita to Hebron; now Tell Sandahanna (Tel Maresha). The inhabitants claimed descent from Shelah (1 Ch. 4:21). Rehoboam fortified it, and in this area Zerah of Ethiopia was defeated by Asa; Eliezer the prophet was born here (2 Ch. 11:8; 14:9; 20:37). Later it was a Sidonian colony and an important stronghold of Idumaea (1 Macc. 5:66; 2 Macc. 12:35; Zeno, Cairo Museum pap. 59006; Josephus, *Ant.* 12. 353; 14. 75). The Parthians destroyed it in 40 BC (*Ant.* 14. 364); in its place rose Eleutheropolis, now Beit Guvrin or Jibrin, 1½ km to the N; a village to the W is now Khirbet Mar'ash. The name, probably derived from *rō'š* (head), was perhaps not unique (Rudolph on 1 Ch. 2:42). See *NEAEHL*, pp. 948–957. J.P.U.L.

MARI, mod. Tell Ḥariri, is a site located on the middle Euphrates river in mod. Syria. A. Parrot excavated the site from 1933. Since 1979 J. Margueron has continued the excavations. Situated midway up the valley, 2 km from the Euphrates, it forms a mid-point on the river between Babylon to the SE and Emar to the NW. The site was first built near the end of the fourth millennium BC. Its central importance grew throughout the third millennium BC. In the early second millennium BC it emerged as a centre of Amorite culture under the leadership of Yahdun-Lim and his successors. However, Hammurabi conquered the last of the dynasty, Zimri-Lim. The king of Babylon destroyed the city in the mid-18th century BC. The city never again flourished. Excavation of the site has revealed a palace preserving many rooms and organized around two large courtyards. The rooms contain frescoes. Although its foundations date earlier, Zimri-Lim made the structure a centre of international renown for its magnificence. It has been compared with other palaces of the mid-second millennium, especially that of the Minoan civilization found at Knossos on Crete.

Archaeologists have excavated more than 20,000 tablets and fragments. Although a few dozen date from the 23rd century and a handful from the following centuries, most originate in the final two decades of the Amorite dynasty (*c.* 1780–1760 BC). Many record the administration of the palace. From the palace there are numerous letters, and a few treaties, literary and religious texts. The gaps in the letters and treaties, as well as the mutilated state of the latter, led Durand in 1992 to suggest that Hammurabi removed these documents when he conquered the city. Many thousands of personal names of the citizens of Mari have come to light from census lists. These attest to the dominance of a W Semitic population, called Amorite. The OT dates the patriarchs to this period. As W Semitic ancestors of Israel, they too would have been Amorites. Sharing a common culture, Mari practices parallel those of Israel. Thus the *asakkum* at Mari resembled Israel's *ḥērem*, *i.e.* the 'ban' imposed on Canaanite property and lives, as in the conquest of Jericho (Jos. 6; Malamat). Both terms can refer to the property of a deity. As with Joshua, at Mari a military commander could impose a ban on the spoils of war by public proclamation. In both cases, violation of the ban incurred serious penalty. Study of the Mari texts has illuminated the OT in many areas, including patriarchal customs, prophecy and proper names.

Texts describe the making of peace treaties through the slaughter of various animals (Held, Malamat). This resembles the covenant God makes with Abram in Gn. 15 which also involves the slaughter of animals. Genesis portrays the lifestyle of the patriarchs as (enclosed) nomadic pastoralists, who move about with their herds while maintaining commercial relations with cities. This parallels Mari, where various nomadic tribal groups (Mari *gāyūm*, *cf.* Heb. *gôy* 'people, nation') sought water and pasture rights for their livestock (Mari *nawūm*, 'people, livestock, camp', *cf.* Heb. *nāweh*, 'pasture, abode'; Malamat). Both urban and tribal groups benefited. Nomads might settle in order to obtain a better life. The reverse also occurred. Jacob grew up in a nomadic family, settled at Haran, and then returned to a nomadic lifestyle. *Naḫālum*, 'to give or inherit property (especially land)' resembles Heb. *naḥ^{a}lāh*, 'inheritance' of land given to God's people.

The Heb. *m^{e}baśśēr*, 'bringer of good news' (Is. 40:9; 41:27; 52:7), underlies NT 'evangelize'. At Mari, the *mubassiru* was a military messenger who brought good news of victory (Fisher). Heb. *nābî'*, 'prophet', resembles the Mari (and Emar) *na-bi-i* who work with diviners (*bārûm*) and whose role is to invoke deities in prayer, blessing or inquiry. *Cf.* Baal's prophets (1 Ki. 18:26–29) and Naaman's expectation (2 Ki. 5:11) which contrast with the Heb. *nābî'* who responds to God's initiative (Nu. 11:25–27; 1 Sa. 10; 19; Fleming). Cruder, but reminiscent of Ezekiel's acts and Amos' wordplay, a *muḫḫûm* prophet devours a raw lamb and uses the same word to announce that the land will be devoured. Mari attests to a divine council (Ps. 82; Je. 23), to divine commissioning of a prophet (Is. 6:8), to prophets as messengers, and to critical and ethical messages towards the king (Gordon).

Mari gentilics (Benjaminites, Canaanites) and personal names or their elements (Adam [but feminine], Seth, Mahalalel, Reu, Shem, Ham, Milcah, Arioch, Ab[a]ram, Jacob, David) correspond to biblical names but refer to different namebearers. The relationship of the Ḫabiru, 'socially disenfranchised people', to Heb. is not established. Mari place names and divine names do refer to the same biblical sites (Haran, Nahor, Serug [but a personal name]) and deities (Hadad, Dagan, Baal, El). Hazor, a trading partner of Mari, is the only Israelite city mentioned.

BIBLIOGRAPHY. Texts are published in the continuing series, *Archives royales de Mari.* This series includes texts in photograph, hand copy, transliteration and translation into French. The major journal studying the archives is *MARI, Mari: Annales de recherches interdisciplinaires*; M. Held, 'Philological Notes on the Mari Covenant Rituals', in *Bulletin of the American Schools of Oriental Research* 200, 1970, pp. 32–40; V. H. Matthews, *Pastoral Nomadism in the Mari Kingdom (c. 1830–1760* BC*)*, 1978; A. Malamat, *Mari and the Early Israelite Experience* 1989; *IEJ 45, 1995, pp. 226–*229; J.-M. Durand, 'Mari (Texts)', *ABD* 4, 1992, pp. 529–536; R. W. Fisher, 'The *Mubassirū* Messengers at Mari', in Young, 1992, pp. 113–120; J.-C. Margueron, 'Mari (Archaeology)', in *ABD* 4, 1992, pp. 525–529; G. D. Young (ed.), *Mari in Retrospect. Fifty Years of Mari and Mari Studies*, 1992; D. E. Fleming, 'The Etymological Origins of the Hebrew *nābî'*: The One Who Invokes God', *CBQ* 55, 1993, pp. 217–224; R. P. Gordon, 'From Mari to Moses: Prophecy at Mari and in Ancient Israel', in *Of Prophets' Visions and the Wisdom of Sages. Essays in Honour of R. Norman Whybray on His Seventieth Birthday*, *JSOTSS* 162, 1993, pp. 63–73. R.S.H.

MARK, GOSPEL OF.

I. Outline of contents

a. Prologue (1:1–13)
The ministry of John (1:1–8); baptism and temptation of Jesus (1:9–13).

b. The earlier Galilean ministry (1:14–6:44)
The kingdom of God in Galilee (1:14–45); the beginning of conflict (2:1–3:6); conflict increases (3:7–35); division caused (parables of the Kingdom) (4:1–34); Jesus, by-passing the synagogue, communicates himself to Israel (4:35–6:44).

c. The later Galilean ministry (6:45–9:50)
Jesus, removing the barriers, communicates himself to Gentiles (6:45–8:10); the Pharisees are refused a sign and the disciples cannot see one when it is given (8:11–26); confession and transfiguration (8:27–9:10); the passion foretold (9:11–50).

d. The road to Jerusalem (10:1–52)
Debates in Peraea (10:1–34); the test of greatness (10:35–45); the healing of Bartimaeus (10:46–52).

e. The Jerusalem ministry (11:1–13:37)
Entry into Jerusalem (11:1–14); cleansing of the Temple (11:15–19); exhortation and debate (11:20–12:44); the *Olivet discourse (13:1–37).

f. Passion and resurrection (14:1–16:8)
The Last Supper (14:1–25); agony in Gethsemane (14:26–42); the arrest (14:43–52); Jesus before the Sanhedrin (14:53–72); Jesus before Pilate (15:1–15); the crucifixion (15:16–41); burial and resurrection (15:42–16:8).

(16:9–20 form a later addition to the Gospel.)

The scope of Mark's Gospel is thus identical with that of the primitive apostolic preaching, beginning with John the Baptist and ending with the resurrection (*cf.* Acts 10:36–43; 13:24–37). Those scholars who maintain that Mark originally ended at 13:37, at least in its 'first edition' (*e.g.* E. Trocmé), would say that verses like 9:9 assume the resurrection witness, so that the scope of the Gospel is still the same.

II. Authorship

This record of our Lord's ministry, the shortest and simplest of all the Gospels, was traditionally compiled by John Mark of Jerusalem, who at different times was a younger companion of Paul, Barnabas and Peter (*MARK (JOHN)). Other modern guesses have included Philip the evangelist.

a. Evidence of Papias

The earliest statement about the origin of this Gospel is that given by Papias (preserved in Eusebius, *EH* 3. 39): 'Mark, who was the interpreter of Peter, wrote down accurately all that he remembered, whether of sayings or doings of Christ, but not in order. For he was neither a hearer nor a companion of the Lord; but afterwards, as I have said, he accompanied Peter, who adapted his instruction as necessity required, not as though he were making a compilation of the Lord's oracles. So then Mark made no mistake when he wrote down thus some things as he remembered them; for he concentrated on this alone—not to omit anything that he had heard, nor to include any false statement among them.'

Papias' information (*c.* AD 140) is amplified a generation or so later in the anti-Marcionite prologue to Mark and in Irenaeus. The anti-Marcionite prologue, only part of which has survived, says that Mark 'was called "stumpy-fingered" (*kolobodaktylos*) because his fingers were short in relation to the rest of his body; he was Peter's interpreter, and after Peter's departure he committed his Gospel to writing in the parts of Italy'. Irenaeus (*Adv. Haer.* 3. 1. 1), after referring to Mark as having been written 'when Peter and Paul were preaching the gospel in Rome and founding the church there', adds that 'after their departure (*exodos*) Mark, Peter's disciple, has himself delivered to us in writing the substance of Peter's preaching'. Both of these authorities therefore suggest a date shortly after Peter's death, though later Fathers claim, perhaps tendentiously, that it was written in Peter's lifetime.

b. Influence of Peter

Mark's Gospel has sometimes been popularly called Peter's Gospel (to be distinguished from later heretical works with this or similar titles), not only because of the evidence of these 2nd-century writers but also since, even if the hand be Mark's, the voice is Peter's voice, to judge from the nature of the incidents, choice of matter, and manner of treatment. It is, however, only fair to say that alternative explanations can be found for all of these (see Nineham and Trocmé) taken individually: nevertheless, their cumulative evidence is strong. It may thus be no empty tradition that this is the written record of the preaching of Peter, originally delivered to Christian catechumens, whether at Rome, or in the Gk. East, and reduced to writing either on the death of its oral source or when the death became imminent. This would put the date of the Gospel somewhere in the second half of the 1st century, perhaps between the death of Peter in AD 65 and the fall of Jerusalem in AD 70, if ch. 13 was written before the fall, as seems most probable (unlike the parallel passages in Matthew and Luke). In any case, to allow use by Matthew and Luke, it could hardly be later than AD 75.

Others have chosen to describe it as the Gospel for the Romans (if it had the influence of the powerful Roman church behind it, then its rapid and apparently universal acceptance would be immediately explicable), or the Gospel for the Gentiles; but in the first of these identifications they may have been influenced more by the Lat. name borne by Mark, in addition to his Heb. name of John, and by the traditional place of origin of the Gospel, rather than by an examination of the contents of the book. Luke has more claim, in every way, to be regarded as the Gentile Gospel; and, while Peter was initially used by God for the conversion of the Gentile Cornelius (Acts 15:7), yet he was universally recognized in the early church as apostle to the circumcision (Gal. 2:8), not apostle to the Gentiles, as was Paul. Thus it is *a priori* unlikely that Peter's teaching forms would be initially aimed at, and adapted to, Gentile audiences. In any case, modern scholarship shows increasingly the thoroughly Jewish nature of *all* the Gospels, although it is true that Mark is at pains to explain Jewish words and customs, as though to a Hellenistic Gentile public.

III. Relationship to Matthew and Luke

For over a century, since Lachmann's day, the question of the literary relationship of Mark to the other Gospels has attracted the attention of W scholars. Apart from the Gospel of John, which in many ways stands by itself, it is obvious that some close link exists between the other three, usually called the Synoptic Gospels because, taken together, they present a very similar picture of the ministry and teaching of Christ. Source criticism is the science of investigation of the assumed direct literary dependence of one Gospel upon another, or of both alike upon some third document, either present or hypothetical.

a. Primacy of Mark's Gospel

Most subsequent Protestant scholars have held firmly, with Lachmann, to the primacy of Mark, considering it to be the earliest of the three Synoptic Gospels, if not in its present form, at least in what might be called an early edition, possibly containing only chs. 1–13. Indeed, most modern scholars consider that Mark was the originator of the form of the *gospel*, a form which became very popular later (Lk. 1:1–3), by his combination of various unconnected sayings and miracles of Jesus, setting them in a framework of his own making. How far this framework is chronological, and how far it is theological, is disputed: and nowadays, some scholars hold that even this framework was traditional within the church. If this were true, Mark would underlie both Matthew and Luke as a principal source. A second presumed early written source was a mass of non-Marcan matter common to Matthew and Luke; this, when isolated, was denoted by the symbol 'Q', for German *Quelle*, 'source'. Mark and Q were thus two of the earliest strands in the Gospel tradition, although Matthew and Luke were acknowledged each to have their own peculiar material as well, for which suitable alphabetical symbols were adopted. Mark, under this system, was considered as a product of the years immediately preceding the fall of Jerusalem in AD 70, and the first Gospel to be written; some of its peculiarities were thus explained, as arising from its 'primitive' nature. The danger was that, if Matthew and Luke seemed to deviate from Mark, they would be considered as less reliable, as having controlled their source for some end of their own. But it is more and more apparent that even Mark selected his material from a vastly larger store (*cf.* Jn. 21:25) and arranged it with a theological purpose (even if it was that of the whole church) so that these strictures are unjustified. All the Evangelists stand or fall together, as far as the historicity of their material is concerned.

b. Primacy of Matthew's Gospel

Roman Catholic scholars for a long time would have none of this, although the situation is very different nowadays; for them it was an article of faith to believe in the primacy of Matthew, and they argued their case with great ingenuity, although without producing much conviction outside their own ranks. They could at least argue that the early church believed in the primacy of Matthew—else why put Mark as the second Gospel? But the principle of arrangement of books within the various sections of the NT is still too little understood to make such a psychological argument valid. Their view, if true, would make

Mark only a secondary authority, and his words would tend to be treated as less weighty than those of Matthew. This is most unlikely: we can see reasons for Matthew's 'smoothing-out' or 'toning-down' of Mark, for instance, but no reasons at all for the reverse process taking place. The battle raged; mathematical symbols multiplied, and ultimately the multiplication of assumed literary sources led to fragmentation. Instead of Gospels, there were bundles of documents, and scholars were left in a morass of literary agnosticism. Was there a way out? As in contemporary OT scholarship, the literary hypothesis had broken down under its own weight.

c. Form criticism

Meanwhile, on the flank, a new force had arisen, which would in itself nullify and make meaningless the whole battle. This was form criticism, originated about 1920 by M. Dibelius, followed closely by R. Bultmann. This might be described as the abandonment of the study of the whole in favour of the study of the part, and, in origin, was purely a descriptive and classificatory science. The various incidents and sayings recorded in Mark (usually called 'pericopes', from the Gk. word for 'paragraph') were now examined, and classified by nature and content. So far, so good. This classification was made from a new angle, had the merit of freshness, and produced some positive and valuable results. But the next step was to examine the hypothetical circumstances and practical religious needs of the community that led to the preservation of each saying; and to make exegesis dependent upon hypothetical reconstruction is dangerous. In the case of extreme critics, this meant that the story was either created or moulded by the needs of the infant church; less extreme scholars would simply say that the story was selected and told with these needs in view. Thus, what had begun as a purely neutral movement ended by passing judgments on the historicity of the text of Scripture. In a sense, such a statement as the last phrase is meaningless to an adherent of this school, for documentary hypotheses have been abandoned in favour of oral tradition, exactly as in contemporary OT scholarship. It is doubtful, however, whether there is any ultimate difference between considering a particular mass of material as a written document or as a complex of oral tradition, especially in view of the fixity of oral tradition in the rabbinical world of the 1st century.

Nevertheless, this stress on form criticism and oral tradition has outdated rather than solved much of the old discussion. Further, it has made the question of the date of Mark's Gospel unanswerable, if not meaningless. The scholar may tentatively date the compilation of the tradition in its present literary form, but the origins of Mark lie much farther back, in the oral traditions of the generation of the crucifixion and resurrection. This, of course, has its good side, in that the reader is confronted directly with the recollections of those who had themselves been eyewitnesses of the events (Lk. 1:2). Much work along these lines has been constructive and cautious; and valuable results have emerged. In particular, it appears that many of the traditions used by Mark were 'church traditions' rather than 'individual traditions': the stories were already old when he used them, and represent the witness of a church (perhaps the Roman church?) to Christ.

d. History of tradition

A still more recent study is the attempt to discover by what means the oral tradition reached its present form, by delving further into the pre-literary history of the text. This, by its nature, is even more hypothetical. We can tell what a particular Marcan saying or incident became in Matthew or Luke, and we can suggest tentative reasons: but we have at present no way of getting behind the text of Mark except by guesswork. Ultimately, we must deal with the text that we have: the only Christ that we know is the Christ of the Gospels. To say that this is the Christ of faith is true: to deny that this is the Christ of history is unwarranted assumption.

e. Redaction criticism

Another recent movement concentrates on the contribution of the Evangelists themselves (redaction criticism). In the case of Mark's Gospel, this leads to an examination of Mark as a theologian. There is no doubt that the Evangelist has been selective in his use of material, but caution is needed to avoid the impression that he has imposed on it his own type of theology.

f. Liturgical approach

There has been an increasing tendency (probably representing the spirit of the times rather than any new discovery) to explain not only Matthew but also Mark as a 'church Gospel', and to see, for instance, his passion narrative as written around the 'holy week' observance of the primitive church. Sometimes this goes along with the belief that even the order of the Gospel may be linked with a primitive liturgic calendar. This, however, while not objectionable, seems too sophisticated for so early, especially outside Jerusalem: it sometimes goes along with the view that Mark was written by a 1st-century 'angry young man' to combat certain ecclesiological and un-missionary views in the early church. This again seems too modern a concept: young men did not act in that way in those days. In any case, Mark does not give the impression of being a brilliant individualist, but of a humdrum church member, faithfully reproducing the common tradition, whether in a liturgical context or not.

g. Recent discoveries

As against this swing towards oral tradition, a reaction in favour of early written documents as sources has been helped by the discovery in Egypt, during the last generation, of several early Gk. papyri containing portions of both canonical and uncanonical Gospels. By their early date, these have pushed back the emergence of written Gospels, in the modern sense of the word, to at least the end of the 1st Christian century. These finds, important as they are, have been overshadowed by the discovery in 1947 and the following years, in caves near Qumran, in the territory of Jordan, of caches of manuscripts in Heb., Aram. and Gk. These *Dead Sea Scrolls are largely of pre-Christian date, apparently the property of a semi-monastic community of Jewish sectaries. The very existence of these manuscripts proves that there is no *a priori* evidence against the existence of 1st-century Christian documents, Gk. or Aram., as sources of the Gospels, particularly collections of 'Messianic prophecies', or 'testimonies'.

h. Aramaic influences

Further, the discovery of such Sem. documents has raised again the issue, already live for half a century, as to whether Gk. or Aram. was the original language of the sources of the Gospels, and, in this instance, of Mark's Gospel. In the light of form criticism, this may well be a 'non-question': it all depends on what stage of the tradition we designate as 'sources' of the Gospel, since, the further back we go, the more likely they are to be in Aram., particularly in Galilee. This leads to the further question, as to how far the Gk. of Mark is not only *koinē* Gk., the *lingua franca* of the 1st-century Roman Mediterranean (*LANGUAGE OF THE NEW TESTAMENT), but actually 'translation Greek'. The many Semitisms in Mark would thus be due, not only to OT reminiscences, nor to influence by the 'translation Greek' of the Septuagint, the Gk. OT, nor even to Semitic speech-patterns persisting in the language of a Palestinian Jew (Mark's local knowledge can hardly be explained otherwise) even if he habitually spoke Gk. in later years at least, but directly to Aram. originals lying before the Evangelist. Indeed, to scholars pursuing this line, many difficult verses in Mark have appeared either as misunderstandings or mistranslations of a lost Aram. original, whether written or spoken. It appears certain that Aram. was the mother-tongue of the Lord and his apostles, to judge from the fossilized Aram. words and phrases that appear even in Gk. dress (*cf.* Mk. 5:41; 7:34; 15:34). While C. C. Torrey's theory of entirely translated Gospels has not generally commended itself to scholars, as being too extreme and involving too many forced arguments, yet few would deny the importance of the underlying Aram. substratum in every Gospel, and the value of considering Aram. vocabulary or idiom when the Gk. text presents difficulties. Recent and more cautious approaches in English have been made, especially by Matthew Black. There is traditional support for some such translation process in the evidence of Papias, preserved in Eusebius; but when he says that Mark was the 'interpreter' of Peter, he can hardly mean simply that Mark turned Peter's Aram. preaching into Gk. The Latinisms of Mark may support a Roman origin for the work: on the other hand, they may simply show the vulgar Gk. of the E part of the empire. In any case, they are not as significant as his Semitisms.

IV. Special characteristics

Basically, Mark is the most blunt and clipped of the Gospels; Matthew contains much of specifically Jewish interest nowhere to be found in Mark, and Luke has much of a 'medical' or of a 'human' interest not found in Mark, as for example the three famous parables of Luke 15. The abrupt ending of Mark is a problem in itself, although it is probably to be seen as a textual rather than a theological problem. The various alternatives put forward by the manuscripts suggest that the original ended abruptly at the same place, whether by accident or by design: this last is hard to believe. It will be objected that the above is a purely negative definition of Mark's nature and contents. Indeed, this was precisely why, in the heyday of source criticism, Mark was seen as the earliest and most primitive of the Gospels, and as a source for both the other Synoptists. But if all documentary sources alike disappear in a welter of oral tradition, what then? The basic observation as to the nature and style of Mark still holds good. Nor is this a purely subjective impression on the part of the 20th century; Papias of Hierapolis shows that the problem was felt equally keenly in the 2nd century. If Mark knew more facts about the Lord, why did he not recount them? Why does he omit so much that the other Evangelists record? Why, on the other hand, are his narratives commonly more detailed and more vivid than parallel accounts in the other Gospels? In addition, Mark appears on first sight to be constructed on a chronological framework of the Lord's life and thus to approach a 'biography' in the Hellenistic and modern sense of the word (although Mark himself warns us that it is a 'gospel', not a 'biography', Mk. 1:1). But is Mark so constructed? and, if not, is there any discernible principle of arrangement? In earlier days attempts were made to fit the other Gospels willy-nilly into Mark's assumed chronological framework. But this proved impossible, although Matthew and Luke do, broadly speaking, follow the same outline, and weave their own material into it—perhaps for the sake of convenience, or perhaps because the framework was already generally known and accepted.

Perhaps the answer is to be found in the cautious use of the new understanding of the nature and importance of oral tradition as underlying the present Gospel of Mark. For it is a plain fact that constant oral repetition leads not to diversity but to uniformity, especially when such repetition is by unimaginative and elderly teachers, whose aim is not to entertain but to instruct catechumens within the context of the church. Stories are not ramified but simplified, if told with a purely didactic end in view; events are boiled down to their bare bones. Variant stories do not grow from one original in such a tradition; if anything, the tendency is to assimilate original variants, all unconsciously. Scholars have not always recognized this, because they have too often considered the earliest custodians of Christian tradition in the light of professional story-tellers, Arabic, Celtic or Scandinavian, according to the culture-pattern the scholars already knew. The aged Sunday-school teacher in a country church might be a closer parallel, for with his continual practice of 'extempore prayer' he tends to become in such circumstances quasi-liturgical, and fixed in form. Seen in this light, Mark is not the most primitive and least developed of the Gospels. The second Gospel is not a bare recital of facts, to which other writers have added flowery details, as imagination prompted them. Rather, Mark is the most developed of the Gospels in the sense that it is threadbare with use, pared of all but significant fact, the record of teaching forms that have stood the test of time. After all, that is exactly what Papias said.

This does not say anything about the actual date of the writing of Mark in its present form; it is merely the empirical observation that it bears, more clearly than any other Gospel, the marks of being a virtual 1st-century Teachers' Handbook, a summary of facts, with all save what was deemed significant ruthlessly pruned. By contrast, Luke was specifically composed *de novo* as a written document, in the face of other existing written documents (Lk. 1:1–4), and in deliberate and pointed contrast to such disconnected instruction as Mark records. Luke, in fact, had claims to be regarded as a work of literature, as had Acts (Acts 1:1); Mark had none. He was not, in all probability, a well-educated man like Luke or Paul, and this may well account for some of the honest uncouthness of his Gospel. But his hearers were not well-educated men either, and his purpose was not to attain to literary excellence, but to communicate the truth. Even Matthew and John bear marks of careful arrangement, although on varying principles; but, for such matters as Mark contains, the principle of arrangement seems to be largely mnemonic. Stories and sayings are linked by keywords or similarity of subject rather than by strict chronological sequence. Where the order of incident varies, as against that given in Matthew and Luke, it is sometimes demonstrably because a different keyword or link is used.

All this would fit perfectly with the above sketch of the origin and nature of Mark, and when it is found to accord exactly with the earliest traditions about the Gospel the case becomes even stronger. For Papias, our oldest witness, in the extract quoted above, appears to be defending Mark against exactly the charges which a modern scholar might bring against him—omission of significant detail and lack of chronological arrangement. The defence is seen to lie in the very nature of the Gospel, which, says Papias, is but a permanent record of the teaching of Peter, thus preserved for posterity at a time when its primary source was passing away. Careful chronological order and full cataloguing of fact, says Papias, are not to be found in Peter because they were not his aim, which was purely practical and instructional; it is unfair to blame any man for failure to achieve something foreign to his purpose. If all this be so, Mark is absolved, along with Peter, and the reasons for many other aspects of his Gospel become apparent at once. (*GOSPELS.)

BIBLIOGRAPHY. Commentaries by V. Taylor, 1952; C. E. B. Cranfield, *CGT*, 1960; P. S. Minear, 1962; D. E. Nineham, *Pelican*, 1963; W. L. Lane, *NIC*, 1974; H. Anderson, *NCB*², 1981; S. E. Johnson, 1977; F. Belo, 1984; R. A. Cole, *TNTC*², 1990. Treatises by G. R. Beasley-Murray, *A Commentary on Mark Thirteen*, 1957; J. A. T. Robinson, *The Problem of History in Mark*, 1957; N. B. Stonehouse, *The Witness of Matthew and Mark to Christ*, 1958; W. Marxsen, *Mark the Evangelist, Studies on the Redaction History of the Gospel*, 1969; R. P. Martin, *Mark, Evangelist and Theologian*, 1972; É. Trocmé, *The Formation of the Gospel According to Mark*, E.T. 1975.

A.C.

MARK (JOHN). Traditional author of the second Gospel, apparently a Jew and a native of Jerusalem. His Heb. name was the OT *yôḥānān*, 'Yahweh has shown grace' (*cf.* 2 Ki. 25:23, *etc.*), shortened in English to the familiar 'John'. The reason for his adopted Lat. name of 'Marcus' is uncertain; sometimes Jewish families that had been captured as slaves in war, and later freed, took, as 'freedmen', the name of the Roman family to which they had been enslaved; but this is unlikely in his case, the more so as Marcus is a praenomen, not a family name. It was not uncommon for 1st-century Jews to bear a Gk. or Rom. name in addition to their Heb. name, 'in religion'; see Acts 1:23 for another such 'surname', again Lat. and not Gk. in origin. The same phenomenon is common among Jews today. If his early nickname of *kolobodaktylos*, 'stumpy-fingered', is a genuine tradition (see the anti-Marcionite prologue to Mark, dating from the later 2nd century, which is the earliest evidence for it), then it may refer either to a physical peculiarity on the part of the author or to some strange stylistic features of the Gospel which have puzzled critics of all ages. It may, however, be only a late conjecture, due to the confusion of 'Marcus' with the Lat. adjective *mancus*, 'maimed'.

Scripture gives some very clear evidence about his family, and there are also several conjectures of varying degrees of probability. His mother, named Mary, was related to Barnabas (Col. 4:10), the wealthy Levite from Cyprus, who was a landowner (Acts 4:36) and, whatever his country of origin, was a resident of Jerusalem in the days of the opening chapters of Acts. Mary herself appears to have been a woman of wealth and position, as well as a Christian; certainly her house was large enough to house a number of people, boasted at least one maidservant and was used as a meeting-place by the apostolic church even in time of persecution (Acts 12:12). It is significant that Peter, released from prison, has no doubt as to where he will find the Christians gathered. John Mark's father is nowhere mentioned in Scripture, and, from the fact that the house of Acts 12:12 is called Mary's, it has been inferred, probably correctly, that he was dead by that date, and Mary a widow. To John Mark himself there is no certain early reference, although the young man of Mk. 14:51, who saved himself by ignominious flight, is usually taken to be Mark. (Was he sleeping in a hut on the family property, guarding the fruit?) It would be neither safe nor customary for an author to mention his own name in such circumstances (*cf.* Jn. 21:24 for similar deliberate anonymity). Less likely, as partly dependent on the above tentative identification, is the theory that the Last Supper of Mk. 14 actually took place in John Mark's house; the shadowy 'goodman of the house' of v. 14 would thus be John Mark's father, still alive then, although dead before the date of Acts 12:12.

John Mark apparently remained at home until brought to Antioch by Barnabas and Paul, who were returning from a relief mission to Jerusalem (Acts 12:25). When the two departed to Cyprus on the first missionary journey some time later he accompanied them, as travelling companion and attendant on the two older men (Acts 13:5). When, however, the party reached Perga, on the mainland of Asia Minor, John Mark left them, and returned to Jerusalem (Acts 13:13), while Barnabas and Paul continued alone. Paul apparently regarded this as desertion, and thus, when Barnabas suggested Mark as a travelling companion for the second journey, he refused point-blank (Acts 15:38). With both men, the attitude towards John Mark was no whim, but a point of principle (*cf.* Acts 9:27 and 11:25 for the character of Barnabas), so a separation was inevitable, Barnabas taking Mark back to Cyprus with him, and Paul taking Silas instead.

After that, Mark is lost to view in Acts, but appears spasmodically in the Epistles. By the date of Col. 4:10 he is in the company of Paul the prisoner, presumably at Rome; Paul is apparently intending to send him on a mission to Colossae, so that he must have forgiven and forgotten the past. Phm. 24 also mentions him among the same apostolic group, which includes Luke. By the time of writing 2 Tim. 4:11 Mark is now away with Timothy, but there has been no rift; presumably this means that Paul had sent Mark on the mission to Asia Minor envisaged above, if Timothy was indeed in Ephesus.

In the Petrine correspondence there is one significant mention, in 1 Pet. 5:13, where the wording shows the 'paternal' relationship existing between the older and younger disciples. If, as is probable, 'Babylon' in this verse stands for 'Rome', then the tradition of the Roman origins of Mark's Gospel may well be true. The tradition that Mark later founded the church of Alexandria (Eusebius, *EH* 2. 16) lacks support. As 'Mark' was the commonest of all Roman names, some have argued that the biblical references concern more than one person. But, in such cases, the Bible differentiates (*e.g.* Jn. 14:22), so we may reject the objection. For Bibliography, see *MARK, GOSPEL OF. A.C.

MARKET, MARKET-PLACE. In the OT this translates Heb. *ma'ᵃrāḇ*, 'merchandise', in Ezk. 27:13, 17, 19, 25. In Is. 23:3 the word is *sāḥār*, 'emporium' (of Tyre). Both describe the trading centre of an E town.

In the NT the word used is *agora*, 'place of assembly', the chief place not only of trade but of public resort, often ornamented with statues and colonnades. Here the sick were brought (Mk. 6:56), children played games (Mt. 11:16; Lk. 7:32) and idlers waited to hire out their services (Mt. 20:3; *cf.* Acts 17:5, *agoraioi*, 'of the rabble'). In the market-places greetings were exchanged, according to social rank, and this the Pharisees particularly loved (Mt. 23:7; Mk. 12:38; Lk. 11:43; 20:46), but they were careful to remove any defilement (Mk. 7:4). Here also in Gentile towns preliminary trial hearings were held (Acts 16:19; *cf.* 19:38ff.) and philosophical or religious discussions took place, *e.g.* Paul in Athens (Acts 17:17–18). For an ancient description of this *agora*, *cf.* Pausanias 1. 2–17; for its modern excavation, Am. Sch. Class. Studs., *The Athenian Agora*, 1962. B.F.H.

MARKS. The variety of 'marks' mentioned in the Bible is reflected in the number of different Heb. and Gk. words which are used to describe them.

1. The various verbal forms which occur correspond to our Eng. verb 'to mark' in the sense of 'to consider' (Ps. 48:13), 'pay attention to' (Ps. 37:37), 'scrutinize with fixed gaze' (1 Sa. 1:12), 'observe closely' (Lk. 14:7), *etc.* With the meaning of 'to make a mark', Isaiah refers to the carpenter who draws a line with pencil and compasses (44:13), while Jeremiah speaks of Judah's sins being indelibly marked like a stain on cloth which neither lye nor soap can eradicate (2:22).

2. The first arresting use of 'mark' as a noun is found in Gn. 4:15. Here it is a translation of Heb. *'ôṯ*, which describes the mark on Cain's forehead. In the OT *'ôṯ* usually means 'sign', but it signifies also 'omens' (1 Sa. 10:7, 9), 'symbols' (Is. 8:18), 'miracles' (Ex. 7:3). However, underlying many of these different uses is the common idea of 'pledge', as, *e.g.*, of good (Ps. 86:17), of God's presence (Ex. 4:8f.), and of covenant (Gn. 9:12–13, 17). Hence *'ôṯ*, when used with reference to the mark on Cain's brow, should be understood in terms of a sign, a pledge or token, of the Lord's protection which would shield him from retribution. If this is correct, then *'ôṯ* might signify a token of some kind of covenant by which God promises to protect Cain (Gn. 4:15).

3. 'Mark' in the sense of 'target' is a rendering of the Heb. *maṭṭārā'* (1 Sa. 20:20). Job complains that God has made him a target at which he shoots his arrows (16:12; *cf.* La 3:12).

4. In Ezk. 9:4, 6, the Heb. word *tāw* is rendered 'mark' in the sense of 'sign'. This is the mark which is placed on the forehead of the righteous, and was an attestation that those who bore the sign were the Lord's people (*cf.* Jb. 31:35, RV, where *tāw* is rendered 'signature'), were distinguished from idolaters, and were therefore exempt from judgment because of the Lord's protection (*cf.* Ex. 12:22f.). Here 'mark' might have the meaning 'seal' (*cf.* Rev. 7:3; 14:1; 22:4).

5. Another word which is rendered 'mark' occurs only once in the Bible: *qa'ᵃqa'*. Its etymology is obscure, but in Lv. 19:28 it probably refers to tattoo marks which, along with 'cuttings in your flesh' (*i.e.* 'incisions' or 'lacerations'), the Israelites were forbidden to make. The prohibition probably points to their having pagan and magical associations.

6. In the well-known Pauline metaphor of 'pressing towards the mark' (*skopos*) in order to win the prize (Phil. 3:14, AV) 'mark' signifies the 'goal' (RSV). The apostle here uses the language of the chariot races to describe the intensity with which he concentrates on winning the crown—the honour of being called by God in Christ.

7. The next Gk. word rendered 'mark' is one that has entered the Eng. language without undergoing any alteration, *stigma.* Like *skopos*, it occurs only once (Gal. 6:17). The root means 'to prick', but probably Paul uses it in the sense of tattoo- or brand-marks with which slave-owners stamped their slaves for identification purposes. Paul was proud of being Christ's bondslave (*cf.* Rom. 1:1, RVmg.); for him no stigma attached to Christ's brand-marks with which he had been branded (Gal. 6:17) in the course of his Christian ministry (2 Cor. 11:23–27).

8. The last word, *charagma* (Rev. 13:16), is reminiscent of Heb. *tāw* in Ezk. 9:4, 6, but the circumstances are reversed. In Rev. 13:16 it is 'the mark of the beast', and is borne by the followers of Antichrist, who is the embodiment of apostasy. Whether a literal or a moral designation, this 'mark' may have stood for a travesty of God's 'seal' upon the Christians. J.G.S.S.T.

MARRIAGE. Marriage is the state in which men and women can live together in sexual relationship with the approval of their social group. Adultery and fornication are sexual relationships that society does not recognize as constituting marriage. This definition is necessary to show that in the OT polygamy is not sexually immoral, since it constitutes a recognized married state; though it is generally shown to be inexpedient.

I. The status of marriage

Marriage is regarded as normal, and there is no word for 'bachelor' in the OT. The record of the creation of Eve (Gn. 2:18–24) indicates the unique relationship of husband and wife, and serves as a picture of the relationship between God and his people (Je. 3; Ezk. 16; Ho. 1–3) and between Christ and his church (Eph. 5:22–33). Jeremiah's call to remain unmarried (Je. 16:2) is a unique prophetic sign, but in the NT it is recognized that for specific purposes celibacy can be God's call to Christians (Mt. 19:10–12; 1 Cor. 7:7–9), although marriage and family life are the normal calling (Jn. 2:1–11; Eph. 5:22–6:4; 1 Tim. 3:2; 4:3; 5:14).

Monogamy is implicit in the story of Adam and Eve, since God created only one wife for Adam. Yet polygamy is adopted from the time of Lamech (Gn. 4:19), and is not forbidden in Scripture. It would seem that God left it to man to discover by experience that his original institution of monogamy was the proper relationship. It is shown that polygamy brings trouble, and often results in sin, *e.g.* Abraham (Gn. 21); Gideon (Jdg. 8:29–9:57); David (2 Sa. 11; 13); Solomon (1 Ki. 11:1–8). In view of oriental customs Heb. kings are warned against it (Dt. 17:17). Family jealousies arise from it, as with Elkanah's two wives, one of whom is an adversary to the other (1 Sa. 1:6; *cf.* Lv. 18:18). It is difficult to know how far polygamy was practised, but on economic grounds it is probable that it was found more among the well-to-do than among the ordinary people. Herod the Great had nine wives at one time (Jos., *Ant.* 17. 19). Polygamy continues to the present day among Jews in Muslim countries.

When polygamy was practised the status and relationship of the wives can be gathered both from the narratives and the law. It was natural that the husband would be drawn to one rather than another. Thus Jacob, who was tricked into polygamy, loved Rachel more than Leah (Gn. 29). Elkanah preferred Hannah in spite of her childlessness (1 Sa. 1:1–8). In Dt. 21:15–17 it is admitted that the husband may love one wife and hate the other.

Since children were important to carry on the family name, a childless wife might allow her husband to have children by her slave. This was legal in civilized Mesopotamia (*e.g.* the Code of Hammurapi, §§ 144–147), and was practised by Sarah and Abraham (Gn. 16) and Rachel and Jacob (Gn. 30:1–8), though Jacob went farther and accepted Leah's maid also, even though Leah had already borne him children (Gn. 30:9). In these cases the rights of the wife are safe-guarded; it is she who gives her maid to her husband for a specific occasion. It is difficult to give a name to the status of the maid in such a relationship; she is a secondary, rather than a second, wife, though, if the husband continued to have relations with her, she would have the position of concubine. This is perhaps why Bilhah is called Jacob's concubine in Gn. 35:22, while Hagar is not classed with Abraham's concubines in Gn. 25:6.

Wives would normally be chosen from among the Hebrews (*e.g.* Ne. 13:23–28). Betrothal and marriage would then follow a normal pattern (see below). Sometimes they were bought as Heb. slaves (Ex. 21:7–11; Ne. 5:5). It is commonly asserted that the master of a household had sexual rights over all his female slaves. No doubt there were flagrant examples of such promiscuity, but the Bible says nothing about them. It is noteworthy that Ex. 21:7–11 and Dt. 15:12 distinguish between an ordinary female slave, who is to be released after 7 years, and one who has been deliberately taken as a wife, or concubine, and who cannot claim her release automatically. Since her rights are here established by law, the head of the house or his son must have gone through some ceremony, however simple, of which the law can take cognizance. In speaking of her rights this passage does not make them depend upon her word against the word of the head of the house, nor even upon her having borne him or his son a child. It is difficult to say what her status was. No doubt it varied according to whether she was the first, second, or only 'wife' of the householder. Where she was given to the son of the house, she might well have full status as his wife. The fact is that this law, as the context shows, deals with her rights as a slave and not primarily as a wife.

Wives might also be taken from among captives after a war, provided that they were not Palestinians (Dt. 20:14–18). Some writers regard these captives as concubines, but the regulations of Dt. 21:10–14 regard them as normal wives.

There is no law dealing with concubines, and we do not know what rights they had. Obviously they had an inferior position to the wives, but their children could inherit at their father's discretion (Gn. 25:6). Judges records the rise to power of Abimelech, the son of Gideon's concubine (Jdg. 8:31–9:57), and also tells the tragic story of the Levite and his concubine (Jdg. 19). The impression given by 19:2–4 is that this concubine was free to leave her 'husband', and that the man relied on persuasion to bring her home. David and Solomon copied oriental monarchs in taking many wives and concubines (2 Sa. 5:13; 1 Ki. 11:3; Ct. 6:8–9). In the last two passages it seems that the concubines were drawn from a lower class of the population.

In normal marriages the wife came to the husband's home. There is, however, another form of marriage in Jdg. 14–15. This is practised among the Philistines, and there is no record of it among the Israelites. Here Samson's wife remains at her father's home, and Samson visits her. It might be argued that Samson had intended to take her home after the wedding, but went off alone in a rage after the trick that she had played on him. Yet she is still at her father's house in 15:1, even though in the meantime she has been married to a Philistine.

II. Marriage customs

The marriage customs of the Bible centre in the two events of betrothal and wedding.

a. Betrothal

In the Near East betrothal (Talmudic *'ērûsîn* and *qiddûšîn*) is almost as binding as marriage itself. In the Bible the betrothed woman was sometimes called 'wife' and was under the same obligation of faithfulness (Gn. 29:21; Dt. 22:23–24; Mt. 1:18, 20), and the betrothed man was called 'husband' (Joel 1:8; Mt. 1:19). The Bible does not legislate for broken betrothals, but the Code of Hammurapi (§§ 159–160) stipulated that if the future husband broke the engagement the bride's father retained the bride-gift; while if the father changed his mind he repaid double the amount of the gift (see also the Law codes of Lipit-Ishtar, 29, and Eshnunna, 25). Presumably there was some formal declaration, but the amount of publicity would depend on the bridegroom. Thus Joseph wished to dissolve the betrothal to Mary as quietly as possible (Mt. 1:19).

God's love and faithfulness towards his people are pictured in terms of a betrothal in Ho. 2:19–20. The betrothal included the following steps:

(i) *Choice of a spouse.* Usually the parents of a young man chose his wife and arranged for the marriage, as Hagar did for Ishmael (Gn. 21:21) and Judah for Er (Gn. 38:6). Sometimes the young man did the choosing, and his parents the negotiating, as in the case of Shechem (Gn. 34:4, 8) and Samson (Jdg. 14:2). Rarely did a man marry against the wish of his parents, as did Esau (Gn. 26:34–35). The girl was sometimes asked whether she consented, as in the case of Rebekah (Gn. 24:58). Occasionally the girl's parents chose a likely man to be her husband, as did Naomi (Ru. 3:1–2) and Saul (1 Sa.18:21).

(ii) *Exchange of gifts.* Three types of gifts are associated with betrothal in the Bible: **1.** The *mōhar*, translated 'marriage present' in RSV and 'dowry' in AV (Gn. 34:12, for Dinah; Ex. 22:17, for a seduced maiden; 1 Sa. 18:25, for Michal). The *mōhar* is implied but not so named in such passages as Gn. 24:53, for Rebekah; 29:18, the 7 years' service performed by Jacob for Rachel. Moses' keeping of the sheep for his father-in-law may be interpreted in the same way (Ex. 3:1). This was a compensation gift from the bridegroom to the family of the bride, and it sealed the covenant and bound the two families together. Some scholars have considered the *mōhar* to be the price of the bride, but a wife was not bought like a slave. **2.** The dowry. This was a gift to the bride or the groom from her father, sometimes consisting of servants (Gn. 24:59, 61, to Rebekah; 29:24, to Leah) or land (Jdg. 1:15, to Achsah; 1 Ki. 9:16, to Pharaoh's daughter, the wife of Solomon), or other property (Tobit 8:21, to Tobias). **3.** The bridegroom's gift to the bride was sometimes jewellery and clothes, as those brought to Rebekah (Gn. 24:53). Biblical examples of oral contracts are Jacob's offer of 7 years' service to Laban (Gn. 29:18) and Shechem's promise of gifts to the family of Dinah (Gn. 34:12). In TB a contract of betrothal is called *šᵉṭar qiddûšîn* (*Moed Katan* 18b) or *šᵉṭar 'ērûsîn* (*Kiddushin* 9a). In the Near East today the contributions of each family are fixed in a written engagement contract.

b. Wedding ceremonies

An important feature of many of these ceremonies was the public acknowledgment of the marital relationship. It is to be understood that not all of the following steps were taken at all weddings.

(i) *Garments of bride and groom.* The bride sometimes wore embroidered garments (Ps. 45:13–14), jewels (Is. 61:10), a special girdle or 'attire' (Je. 2:32) and a veil (Gn. 24:65). Among the adornments of the groom might be a garland (Is. 61:10). Eph. 5:27; Rev. 19:8; 21:2 refer figuratively to the white garments of the church as the Bride of Christ.

(ii) *Bridesmaids and friends.* Ps. 45:14 speaks of bridesmaids for a royal bride, and we assume that lesser brides had their bridesmaids also. Certainly the bridegroom had his group of companions (Jdg. 14:11). One of these corresponded to the best man at our weddings, and is called 'companion' in Jdg. 14:20; 15:2, and 'the friend of the bridegroom' in Jn. 3:29. He may be the same as 'the steward (AV 'governor') of the feast' in Jn. 2:8–9.

(iii) *The procession.* In the evening of the day fixed for the marriage the bridegroom and his friends went in procession to the bride's house. The wedding supper could be held there: sometimes circumstances compelled this (Gn. 29:22; Jdg. 14), but it may have been fairly common, since the parable of the Ten Virgins in Mt. 25:1–13 is most easily interpreted of the bridegroom going to the bride's house for the supper. One would, however, expect that more usually the bridegroom escorted the bride back to his own or his parents' home for the supper, though the only references to this in Scripture are in Ps. 45:14f.; Mt. 22:1–14 (royal weddings), and probably in Jn. 2:9f.

The procession might be accompanied by singing, music and dancing (Je. 7:34; 1 Macc. 9:39), and by lamps if at night (Mt. 25:7).

(iv) *The marriage feast.* This was usually held at the house of the groom (Mt. 22:1–10; Jn. 2:9) and often at night (Mt. 22:13; 25:6). Many relatives and friends attended; so the wine might well run out (Jn. 2:3). A steward or friend supervised the feast (Jn. 2:9–10). To refuse an invitation to the wedding feast was an insult (Mt. 22:7). The guests were expected to wear festive clothes (Mt. 22:11–12). In special circumstances the feast could be held in the bride's home (Gn. 29:22; Tobit 8:19) The glorious gathering of Christ and his saints in heaven is figuratively called 'the marriage supper of the Lamb' (Rev. 19:9).

(v) *Covering the bride.* In two cases in the OT (Ru. 3:9; Ezk. 16:8) the man covers the woman with his skirt, perhaps a sign that he takes her under his protection. D. R. Mace follows J. L. Burckhardt (*Notes on the Bedouin*, 1830, p. 264) in saying that in Arab weddings this is done by one of the bridegroom's relations. J. Eisler, in *Weltenmantel und Himmelszelt*, 1910, says that among the bedouin the bridegroom covers the bride with a special cloak, using the words, 'From now on, nobody but myself shall cover thee.' The Bible references suggest that the second custom was followed.

(vi) *Blessing.* Parents and friends blessed the couple and wished them well (Gn. 24:60; Ru. 4:11; Tobit 7:13).

(vii) *Covenant.* Another religious element was the covenant of faithfulness which is implied in Pr. 2:17; Ezk. 16:8; Mal. 2:14. According to Tobit 7:14, the father of the bride drew up a written marriage contract, which in the Mishnah is called *kᵉṯûḇâ*.

(viii) *Bridechamber.* A nuptial chamber was specially prepared (Tobit 7:16). The Heb. name for this room is *ḥuppâ* (Ps. 19:5; Joel 2:16), originally a canopy or tent, and the Gk. word is *nymphōn* (Mk. 2:19). The word *ḥuppâ* is still used among Jews today of the canopy under which the bride and bridegroom sit or stand during the wedding ceremony.

(ix) *Consummation.* The bride and groom were escorted to this room, often by the parents (Gn. 29:23; Tobit 7:16–17; 8:1). Before coming together, for which the Heb. uses the idiom 'to know', prayer was offered by husband and wife (Tobit 8:4).

(x) *Proof of virginity.* A blood-stained cloth or chemise was exhibited as a proof of the bride's virginity (Dt. 22:13–21). This custom continues in some places in the Near East.

(xi) *Festivities.* The wedding festivities continued for a week (Gn. 29:27, Jacob and Leah) or sometimes 2 weeks (Tobit 8:20, Tobias and Sarah). These celebrations were marked by music (Pss. 45; 78:63) and by joking like Samson's riddles (Jdg. 14:12–18). Some interpret Canticles in the light of a custom among Syrian peasants of calling the groom and bride 'king' and 'queen' during the festivities after the wedding and of praising them with songs.

III. Forbidden degrees of marriage

These are listed in Lv. 18 in detail, and less fully in

Lv. 20:17–21; Dt. 27:20–23. They are analysed in detail by David Mace, *Hebrew Marriage*, pp. 152f. We presume that the ban held good both for a second wife during the first wife's lifetime and for any subsequent marriage after the wife's death, except for marriage with the wife's sister: for Lv. 18:18, in saying that the wife's sister may not be married during the wife's lifetime, implies that she may be married after the wife is dead.

Abraham (Gn. 20:12) and Jacob (Gn. 29:21–30) married within degrees of relationship that were later forbidden. The scandal in the church at Corinth (1 Cor. 5:1) may have been marriage of a stepmother after the father's death, but, since the woman is called 'his father's wife' (not *widow*), and the act is called *fornication*, it is more likely to be a case of immoral relationship with the man's young second wife.

IV. The levirate law

The name is derived from Lat. *levir*, meaning 'husband's brother'. When a married man died without a child his brother was expected to take his wife. Children of the marriage counted as children of the first husband. This custom is found among other peoples besides the Hebrews.

The custom is assumed in the story of Onan in Gn. 38:8–10. Onan took his brother's wife, but refused to have a child by her, because 'the seed should not be his' (v. 9), and his own children would not have the primary inheritance. This verse does not pass any judgment on birth control as such.

Dt. 25:5–10 states the law as applying to brethren who dwell together, but allows the brother the option of refusing.

The book of Ruth shows that the custom extended farther than the husband's brother. Here an unnamed kinsman has the primary duty, and only when he refuses does Boaz marry Ruth. A further extension of the custom here is that it is Ruth, and not Naomi, who marries Boaz, presumably because Naomi was too old to bear a child. The child is called 'a son to Naomi' (4:17).

The levirate law did not apply if daughters had been born, and regulations for the inheritance of daughters are given to the daughters of Zelophehad in Nu. 27:1–11. It might seem strange that vv. 9–11 seem to ignore, or even contradict, the levirate law. It could be argued that Dt. 25:5–10 had not yet been promulgated. On the other hand, when a law arises out of a specific occasion one must know the exact circumstances in order to judge what the law professes to cover. There would be no contradiction of the levirate law if Zelophehad's wife had died before he did, and the law here confines itself to similar cases. Nu. 27:8–11 would operate when there were daughters only, or when a childless wife had predeceased her husband, or when the late husband's brother refused to take the childless widow, or when the wife remained childless after the brother had married her.

In Lv. 18:16; 20:21 a man is forbidden to marry his brother's wife. In the light of the levirate law this clearly means that he may not take her as his own wife, whether she has been divorced during her husband's lifetime or has been left with or without children at her husband's death. John the Baptist rebuked Herod Antipas for marrying the wife of his brother Herod Philip (Mt. 14:3–4); Herod Philip was still alive.

In the NT the levirate law is used by the Sadducees to pose a problem about the resurrection (Mt. 22:23ff.).

V. Divorce

a. In the Old Testament

In Mt. 19:8 Jesus says that Moses 'allowed' divorce because of the hardness of the people's hearts. This means that Moses did not command divorce, but regulated an existing practice, and the form of the law in Dt. 24:1–4 is best understood in this sense. AV and RV imply a command in the second half of v. 1, but the RSV follows Keil, Delitzsch, S. R. Driver and LXX, in making the 'if' of the protasis extend to the end of v. 3, so that v. 4 contains the actual regulation. On any translation we gather from this section that divorce was practised, that a form of contract was given to the wife, and that she was then free to remarry.

The grounds of divorce here are referred to in such general terms that no precise interpretation can be given. The husband finds 'some uncleanness' in his wife. The Heb. words, *'erwaṯ dāḇār* (literally, 'nakedness of a thing'), occur elsewhere only as a phrase in Dt. 23:14. Shortly before the time of Christ the school of Shammai interpreted it of unfaithfulness only, while the school of Hillel extended it to anything unpleasing to the husband. We must remember that Moses is not here professing to state the grounds of divorce, but accepting it as an existing fact.

There are two situations in which divorce is forbidden: when a man has falsely accused his wife of pre-marital unfaithfulness (Dt. 22:13–19); and when a man has had relations with a girl, and her father has compelled him to marry her (Dt. 22:28–29; Ex. 22:16–17).

On two exceptional occasions divorce was insisted on. These were when the returned exiles had married pagan wives (Ezr. 9–10 and probably Ne. 13:23ff., although divorce is implied here, rather than stated). In Mal. 2:10–16 some had put away their Jewish wives so as to marry pagans.

b. In the New Testament

In comparing the words of Jesus in Mt. 5:32; 19:3–12; Mk. 10:2–12; Lk. 16:18, we find that he brands divorce and remarriage as adultery, but does not say that man *cannot* put asunder what God has joined together. In both passages in Matthew fornication (RSV 'unchastity') is given as the sole ground on which a man may put away his wife, whereas there is no such qualification in Mark and Luke. *Fornication* is commonly taken as here being equivalent to *adultery*; similarly, the conduct of the nation as Yahweh's wife is branded both as adultery (Je. 3:8; Ezk. 23:45) and as fornication (Je. 3:2–3; Ezk. 23:43); in Ecclus. 23:23 an unfaithful wife is said to have committed adultery in fornication (*cf.* also 1 Cor. 7:2 where 'immorality' is Gk. 'fornication').

The reason for the omission of the exceptive clause in Mark and Luke could be that no Jew, Roman or Greek ever doubted that adultery constituted grounds for divorce, and the Evangelists took it for granted. Similarly, Paul in Rom. 7:1–3, referring to Jewish and Rom. law, ignores the possibility of divorce for adultery which both these laws provided.

Other theories have been held about the meaning of Christ's words. Some refer *fornication* to pre-marital unfaithfulness, which the husband discovers after marriage. Others have suggested that the parties discover that they have married within the prohibited degrees of relationship, a thing which must have happened too rarely for it to be the subject of a special exception in Christ's words. Roman Catholics hold that the words sanction separation, but not remarriage. It is difficult to exclude permission to remarry from Mt. 19:9; and among the Jews there was no such custom as separation without permission to remarry.

Some have doubted the authenticity of Mk. 10:12, since a Jewish wife could not normally divorce her husband. But a wife could appeal to the court against her husband's treatment of her, and the court could compel the husband to divorce her. Moreover, Christ may have had Gk. and Rom. law in mind, and here the wife could divorce her husband, as Herodias had divorced her first husband.

There is a strong body of opinion both among Protestants and Roman Catholics that 1 Cor. 7:10–16 gives another ground for divorce. Here Paul repeats the teaching that the Lord had given when on earth, and then, under the guidance of the Spirit, gives teaching beyond what the Lord had given, since a new situation had arisen. When one party in a pagan marriage is converted to Christ he or she must not desert the other. But if the other insists on leaving the Christian 'a brother or sister is not under bondage in such cases'. This latter clause cannot simply mean that they are free to be deserted, but must mean that they are free to be remarried. This further ground, which on the face of it is of limited application, is known as the 'Pauline Privilege'.

In the present modern tangle of marriage, divorce and remarriage the Christian church, in dealing with converts and repentant members, is often compelled to accept the situation as it is. A convert who previously has been divorced, on sufficient or insufficient grounds, and who has remarried, cannot return to the original partner, and the present marriage cannot be branded as adulterous (1 Cor. 6:9, 11).

BIBLIOGRAPHY. W. R. Smith, *Kinship and Marriage in Early Arabia*, 1903; E. A. Westermarck, *The History of Human Marriage*, 3 vols., 1922; H. Granquist, *Marriage Conditions in a Palestinian Village*, 2 vols., 1931, 1935; M. Burrows, *The Basis of Israelite Marriage*, 1938; E. Neufeld, *Ancient Hebrew Marriage Laws*, 1944; D. R. Mace, *Hebrew Marriage*, 1953; J. Murray, *Divorce*, 1953; D. S. Bailey, *The Man–Woman Relation in Christian Thought*, 1959; R. de Vaux, *Ancient Israel*, 1961; E. Stauffer, *TDNT* 1, pp. 648–657; W. Günther *et al.*, *NIDNTT* 2, pp. 575–590; M. J. Harris, C. Brown, *NIDNTT* 3, pp. 534–543.

J.S.W.
J.T.

MARSHAL. There are two Heb. words rendered 'marshal'. **1.** *sōp̄ēr* (Jdg. 5:14. 'they who wield the marshal's staff'). The word *sōp̄ēr* usually means 'writer' (so AV and Syr., Targ.; *cf.* LXX *grammateus*, 'scribe'). **2.** *ṭip̄sār* (Je. 51:27) or *ṭap̄sēr* (Na. 3:17). Probably from Akkad. *ṭupšarru*, 'tablet writer'; hence 'official', 'marshal'. For both these instances, *cf.* 1 Macc. 5:42, where Gk. *grammateus* means 'marshal'.

The seeming proper name *Tartan (Is. 20:1; 2 Ki. 18:17) is from the Akkad. *turtanu*, a title of high military rank which may be rendered 'marshal'. R.J.W.

MARTHA. The name derives from an Aram. form not found in Heb., meaning 'lady' or 'mistress'. It occurs only in the NT, and is used of only one person (Lk. 10:38–41; Jn. 11:1, 5, 19–39; 12:2). Martha was the sister of the Mary who anointed our Lord shortly before his death (Mt. 26:6ff., and parallels); and Lazarus, whom Jesus raised from the dead (Jn. 11), was their brother. According to Jn. 11:1 the family came from Bethany, a village probably about 4 km from Jerusalem on the road to Jericho. Luke seems to suggest by his placing of events that Martha's house was in Galilee (Lk. 10:38). This difficulty is removed, however, if we either allow the possibility that the Lucan incident is chronologically misplaced (so *HDB*, 3, p. 277) or, more reasonably, assume that this was one of the several journeys undertaken by Jesus to Jerusalem during the last 6 months of his earthly life (*cf.* Jn. 10:22).

Matthew, Mark and John all agree that our Lord was anointed in Bethany, and Matthew and Mark specify (presuming the same occasion is referred to) that it took place in the house of Simon the leper. Since Jesus was received into Martha's house in the Lucan record, and Martha served at the supper in Simon's house at Bethany during which Mary anointed our Lord, it has been supposed that Martha was the wife (or even the widow) of Simon. The lead she takes on both occasions suggests that she was the elder sister.

In Luke's narrative (10:38ff.) Martha is gently rebuked by Christ for her impatience with her sister, and her excessive concern for the practical details of the meal (v. 40). She was no less devoted to Jesus than Mary (*cf.* her faithful response to the Lord recorded at Jn. 11:27), but she failed to see the way of receiving him which would please him most—'one thing is needful'. Some of the oldest MSS read at this point, 'few things are needful, or only one' (so RSVmg.). 'Few' refers presumably to material provision, 'one' to spiritual apprehension.

See J. N. Sanders, 'Those whom Jesus loved', *NTS* 1, 1954–5, pp. 29ff.; and the comment on Lk. 10:38–42 in E. E. Ellis, *The Gospel of Luke*, *NCB*², 1974, pp. 161f. (*MARY, 2.) S.S.S.

MARY. The name appears as *Maria* or *Mariam* in the NT. Both are Graecized forms of the Heb. name Miriam, which appears in LXX as Mariam (used of the sister of Moses), and may just possibly be derived from the Egyp. *Maryē*, 'beloved' (but see A. H. Gardiner, *JAOS* 56, 1936, pp. 194–197). In the NT the name is used to refer to the following:

1. Mary the mother of the Lord. Our information about the mother of Jesus is largely confined to the infancy narratives of Mt. and Lk. There we learn that when the angelic announcement of the birth of Jesus occurred, Mary was living at Nazareth, in Galilee, and was engaged to a carpenter named Joseph (Lk. 1:26f.). Luke tells us that Joseph was of Davidic descent (*ibid.*), and although no mention of Mary's lineage is made it is possible that she came from the same line, particularly if, as seems likely, the *genealogy of Christ in Lk. 3 is to be traced through his mother. The conception of Jesus is described as 'of the Holy Spirit' (Mt. 1:18; *cf.* Lk. 1:35), and his birth as taking place at Bethlehem towards the end of Herod the Great's reign (Mt. 2:1; Lk. 1:5; 2:4). (*VIRGIN BIRTH.)

It is recorded in both Mt. 2:23 and Lk. 2:39 that after the birth the holy family lived at Nazareth. Matthew alone mentions the flight into Egypt, where Joseph and Mary and the child Jesus took refuge from the jealous anger of Herod. Luke records Mary's visit to her cousin Elizabeth, who greeted her as 'the mother of my Lord' with the words 'Blessed are you among women' (1:42f.). Luke also has Mary's song of praise (1:46–55, where a few ancient witnesses read 'Elizabeth' for 'Mary' as the name of the speaker; *MAGNIFICAT). A single appealing glimpse of Christ's childhood is given to us by Luke (2:41–51), who records the typically anxious words of his mother at the discovery of the lost boy (v. 48), and the well-known reply, 'Did you not know that I must be in my Father's house?' (v. 49).

The remaining references to Mary in the Gospels are few and relatively uninformative. Apparently she did not accompany our Lord on his missionary journeys, although she was present with him at the marriage in Cana (Jn. 2:1ff.). The rebuke uttered by Jesus on this occasion, 'O woman, what have you to do with me?' (v. 4), reveals amazement rather than harshness (*cf.* Lk. 2:49, and the tender use of the same word *gynai*, 'woman', in Jn. 19:26; see also Mk. 3:31ff., where the Lord places spiritual fidelity above family relationship; with v. 35 *cf.* Lk. 11:27f.). Finally, we meet Mary at the foot of the cross (Jn. 19:25), when she and the beloved disciple are entrusted by him to each other's care (vv. 26–27). The only other explicit NT reference to Mary is in Acts 1:14, where she and the disciples are described as 'devoting themselves to prayer'.

The brief NT sketch of Mary and her relationship to our Lord leaves many gaps in the record which pious legend has not been slow to fill. But we are not able to press the Gospel records beyond their historical limit, and this means that we must be content at least to notice Mary's humility, obedience and obvious devotion to Jesus. And as she was the mother of the Son of God, we cannot say less about her than did her cousin Elizabeth, that she is 'blessed *among* women'.

BIBLIOGRAPHY. J. de Satgé, *Mary and the Christian Gospel*, 1976; R. E. Brown (ed.), *Mary*, 1977; J. McHugh, *The Mother of Jesus in the New Testament*, 1975.

2. Mary the sister of Martha. She appears by name only in Lk. and Jn. In Lk. 10:38–42 it is recorded that after the return of the Seventy Jesus came into 'a village' (identified subsequently in Jn. 11:1 as Bethany, about 2 km E of the summit of the Mount of Olives), where *Martha, who had a sister called Mary, received him into her house. In the account which follows Martha is rebuked by the Lord for complaining about her sister Mary, who listened to his 'word' rather than helping with the work.

Jn. 11 gives us the description of the meeting at Bethany between Jesus and the sisters Martha and Mary, on the occasion of the death of Lazarus their brother. Mary is now described (v. 2) as the one who 'anointed the Lord with ointment, and wiped his feet with her hair'; and after the raising of Lazarus by Jesus (11:43f.) we are told almost immediately of this anointing (12:1ff.).

All four Gospels contain an account of the anointing of Jesus by a woman (Mt. 26: 6–13; Mk. 14:3–9; Lk. 7:37–50; Jn. 12:1–8). The difficulty is to decide whether these four accounts report an identical occasion, and if not whether more than one woman is involved. Matthew and Mark more or less agree in their versions; the Lucan account differs widely (particularly in placing the event in Galilee while John the Baptist was in prison, rather than in Bethany shortly before the death of Christ); while the Johannine account is independent of all three. Only in John is the woman named, and there, as we have seen, she is clearly identified as Mary the sister of Martha. Luke alone adds that the woman was 'a sinner' (7:37); Matthew and Mark set the scene specifically 'in the house of Simon the leper'; and Matthew and Mark agree against Luke and John that it was the head and not the feet of Jesus that the woman anointed.

There have been various attempts to resolve these differences. One is to suggest that Luke describes a different occasion, but that it is the same woman who performs the anointing. The difficulty in this view (mostly held in the Latin church) is the earlier description 'sinner' for the saintly Mary of Bethany. It was this ascription indeed, together with the absence of further information, which led mediaeval scholars to identify the sinful woman of Luke's account with Mary Magdalene (for a discussion of which see below under 'Mary Magdalene'), and the Magdalene herself, by the further confusion just noted, with Mary of Bethany. Yet John could not have been unaware of the real identity of the two Marys, or been content to confuse his readers. There is really no justification for identifying Mary of Bethany with Mary Magdalene, and certainly none for associating either with the sinful woman of Lk. 7.

The second main view is that two anointings of our Lord occurred during his earthly ministry, one administered by a penitent sinner of Galilee, and the other by Mary of Bethany. In this case the description of Mary in Jn. 11:2, as the one who 'anointed the Lord', has a prospective reference. The only difficulty in this view is the repetition of what is evidently regarded by Jesus as an otherwise unique action, the singular character of which he clearly intends to underline by his commendation (Mt. 26:13; Mk. 14:9). This interpretation seems the most satisfactory one, however, and it solves more problems than it raises. Origen suggested that at least three anointings took place, involving either two or three different people.

The action of Mary is recognized as a spontaneous expression of devotion to Jesus, which in its character as well as its timing anticipates his death and is therefore associated with it.

3. Mary Magdalene. The name probably derives from the Galilean town of *Magdala. Her appearance prior to the passion narratives is confined to Lk. 8:2, where we read that among the women cured of possession by evil spirits who accompanied the Lord and his disciples during their evangelistic ministry was 'Mary called Magdalene, from whom seven demons had gone out' (*cf.* Mk. 16:9, in the longer ending).

It is not possible, at least from the biblical evidence, to limit the illness from which Mary was healed to one sphere alone, the physical, the mental or the moral. This is a further reason for resisting any identification between Mary Magdalene and the 'sinful woman' of Lk. 7 (see above, under **2**). If Luke had known that the Mary of ch. 8 was the same person as the sinner of ch. 7, would he not probably have made the connection explicit?

Mary reappears at the crucifixion, in company with the other women who had journeyed with our

Lord from Galilee (see below, under **4**). In the Johannine account of the resurrection we have the description of the Lord's appearance to Mary alone. Mark's version, in the longer ending, is brief and not placed chronologically. Slight differences occur in the reports of the arrival of the women at the tomb. Mary sets out with the others (Mt. 28:1; Mk. 16:1), but apparently runs ahead of them and arrives first at the tomb (Jn. 20:1). She then tells Peter and the beloved disciple what has happened (Jn. 20:2), and is joined there by the other women (Lk. 24:10). She returns with Peter and the beloved disciple to the tomb, and lingers behind weeping after they have gone (Jn. 20:11). It is then that she sees two angels (v. 12), and finally the risen Christ himself (v. 14), who addresses to her the famous *noli tangere* injunction (v. 17). Clearly Mary's relationship to her Lord, following his resurrection, is to be of a different kind and to continue in another dimension.

4. Mary the mother of James; 'the other Mary'; Mary 'of *Clopas'. It is very probable that these three names all refer to the same person. Mary the mother of James and Joses is listed with Mary Magdalene among the women who accompanied our Lord to Jerusalem and were present at the crucifixion (Mt. 27:55f.). When Mary Magdalene and 'the other Mary' are described immediately afterwards (v. 61) as 'sitting opposite the sepulchre' after the burial it seems likely that the same Mary, the mother of James, is intended. 'The other Mary' again appears with Mary Magdalene on the resurrection morning (Mt. 28:1).

From the other Synoptists we learn further details. Mark refers to her (15:40) as 'Mary the mother of James the younger and of Joses', who was present at the crucifixion in the company of Mary Magdalene and Salome. In Mk. 15:47 she is called *Maria hē Iōsētos*, and in 16:1 she reappears (as 'Mary the mother of James') with Salome and Mary Magdalene as one who brought spices to the tomb on the morning of the resurrection to anoint the dead body of Jesus. Luke adds (24:10) that Joanna, as well as Mary Magdalene and Mary the mother of James, was among the women who had been onlookers at the passion of Christ, and who reported the events of the resurrection to the apostles.

John uses the descriptive term *Klōpa* ('of Clopas') for this Mary, when he records (19:25) that standing by the cross of Jesus were his mother and his mother's sister, Mary 'the wife of Clopas' and Mary Magdalene. It appears correct to translate the genitive *Klōpa* as '(wife) of Clopas', rather than as '(daughter) of Clopas'. Judging, then, by the list given in Mk. 15:40, and noted above, it seems fairly clear that Mary of Clopas (*pace* Jerome) is the same person as Mary of James. Hegesippus tells us (see Eus., *EH* 3. 11) that *Clopas (AV Cleophas) was the brother of Joseph, the husband of the Virgin Mary. (The 'Cleopas' of Lk. 24:18 is a different name.)

5. Mary the mother of Mark. The sole NT reference to this Mary occurs in Acts 12:12. After Peter's escape from prison (12:6ff.) it is to her house in Jerusalem, evidently a meeting-place for Christians, that he goes first. Since *Mark is described as the cousin of Barnabas (Col. 4:10), Barnabas was evidently Mary's nephew.

6. Mary greeted by St Paul. Her name appears among the 24 people listed in Rom. 16 to whom Paul sent greetings (v. 6). There she is described as one who 'worked hard' in (or for) the church. Otherwise nothing is known of her. S.S.S.

MASSA. The seventh of the twelve princes of Ishmael according to Gn. 25:14 and 1 Ch. 1:30, who apparently settled in N Arabia. Probably this tribe is to be identified with the Mas'a who paid tribute with Tema to Tiglath-pileser III (*ANET*, p. 283) and with the *Masanoi*, located by Ptolemy (5. 19, 2) NE of Duma. Perhaps Meshech in Ps. 120:5 should be emended to Massa, which more closely parallels Kedar. In Pr. 30:1 and 31:1 *hammaśśā'* ('the prophecy' in AV) should possibly be read as a proper name. If Agur and *Lemuel are Massaites, their collections of proverbs are examples of the international character of Heb. *wisdom literature, which on occasion was adopted and shaped by the Israelites to conform to their historic faith.

D.A.H.

MASSAH. According to Dt. 6:16 and 9:22, a place in the wilderness where Israel put God to the test: Massah (from *nissâ*, 'to test') means 'testing'. In Ex. 17:7 the name is coupled with Meribah (= 'quarrel, complaint', from *rîḇ* = 'strive, complain') in a story from the older Pentateuchal sources which shows the Israelites protesting because of lack of water at *Rephidim, close to Mt Horeb (v. 6). The two names again appear together in Ps. 95:8, a warning to later generations which could refer to this episode.

The name Meribah also occurs (without Massah) in conjunction with *Kadesh, both in a boundary-list (Ezk. 47:19) and as the location of a similar episode (mainly drawn from P), which results in both Moses and Aaron being denied the privilege of entering the promised land (Nu. 20:1–13 (*cf.* v. 24); 27:14; Dt. 32:51; Ps. 106:32).

Both narratives are aetiological, *i.e.* imply that the names were given as a result of these events of the Mosaic period. But because of the legal connotations of the verb *rîḇ* it has often been suggested that Meribah was first of all a place where legal disputes were settled (*cf.* En-mishpat, 'well of judgment', another name for Kadesh [Gn. 14:7]). This can only be a hypothesis, but there are other reasons for wondering whether the straightforward explanation of the names is historically correct.

The attempt has frequently been made to separate out a Massah-story and a Meribah-story in Ex. 17:1–7, but, although there is a little unexpected repetition (vv. 2–3), it is not sufficient to justify analysis into two separate stories, deriving from different sources. The same must be said for Nu. 20:1–13. What is more likely is that, in both cases, there has been some amplification of the original account by a later author. In Ex. 17:1–7 this amplification may be responsible for the introduction of the allusion to Meribah (and perhaps Massah also) in vv. 2 and 7.

Dt. 33:8 and Ps. 81:7, where these names also occur, can scarcely refer to the same episodes, since here there is no hint of criticism and it is God, not the people of Israel, who is doing the 'testing'. The theme of God testing Israel is one that is encountered several times in Exodus (15:25; 16:4; 20:20). It seems likely that other events, perhaps mentioned elsewhere in the Bible (Ex. 32?), perhaps not, were at one time connected with these places. To date, no fully satisfactory correlation of the various passages has been made, and it may be that the literary and historical problems are insoluble. For some ingenious, if speculative, suggestions see H. Seebass, *Mose und Aaron*, 1962, pp. 61ff.

BIBLIOGRAPHY. B. S. Childs, *Exodus*, 1974, pp. 305–309. G.I.D.

MASTER. The translation of five Heb. and seven Gk. words. In the OT the most common term is *'āḏôn*, 'lord', 'sir', found 96 times, particularly when the reference is to persons other than God—*e.g.* a master of servants (Gn. 24:14, *etc.*; *TDOT* 1, pp. 59–72). *ba'al*, 'owner', 'master', appears five times, generally denoting the master of a house (Jdg. 19:22; *cf.* Mt. 10:25, Gk. *oikodespotēs*; *TDNT* 2, p. 49; *TDOT* 2, pp. 181–200). (For the Phoenician god, see *BAAL.) *raḇ*, 'great', 'elder', occurs four times, notably in combination with another word—*e.g.* 'chief of the magicians' (Dn. 4:9; 5:11), 'chief eunuch' (Dn. 1:3). On two occasions the Heb. word is *śar*, 'prince', 'chief', 'commander' (Ex. 1:11; 1 Ch. 15:27), and once it is *'ēr*, 'to awake', 'to stir up' (Mal. 2:12), where RV and AVmg. render 'him that waketh' and RSV has 'any to witness' (reading *'ēḏ* for *'ēr*).

In the NT the most frequent term is *didaskalos* (*TDNT* 2, pp. 148–159), 'teacher', 'instructor', found 47 times, all in the Gospels except for Jas. 3:1. *despotēs* (*TDNT* 2, pp. 44–49) generally denotes a master over slaves, and is used five times (*e.g.* 1 Tim. 6:1–2). A word peculiar in this connection to Luke's Gospel and found there six times, always when the disciples are addressing Jesus, is *epistatēs* (*TDNT* 2, pp. 622–623), 'superintendent', 'overseer' (*e.g.* Lk. 5:5). *kyrios* (*TDNT* 3, pp. 1039–1095), 'lord', 'sir', is translated 'master' 14 times, often signifying God or Christ (*e.g.* Mk. 13:35; Eph. 6:9). Another word translated as master is *kathēgētēs*, 'a leader', 'a guide' (in the scholastic sense) (Mt. 23:8, 10). Gk. *rhabbi* (*TDNT* 6, pp. 961–965), *'Rabbi', from Heb. *rabbî*, 'my master', is used of Jesus (*e.g.* Jn. 4:31) in 12 of its 15 NT occurrences. Finally, *kybernētēs* (*TDNT* 3, pp. 1035–1037), 'ship-master', 'pilot', is found twice (Acts 27:11; Rev. 18:17). J.D.D.

MATTHEW. Matthew appears in all the lists of the twelve apostles (Mt. 10:3; Mk. 3:18; Lk. 6:15; Acts 1:13). In Mt. 10:3 he is further described as 'the tax-collector'. In Mt. 9:9 Jesus finds him 'sitting at the tax-office' and bids him follow him. In the parallel passages in Mark and Luke the tax-collector called from the tax-office is designated Levi, Mark adding that he was 'the son of Alphaeus'. The *Gospel of Peter* also speaks of Levi the son of Alphaeus as a disciple of Jesus. Subsequently, Jesus is a fellow-guest with many tax-collectors and sinners. Neither Mt. 9:10 nor Mk 2:15 makes it clear at whose house the meal was held, but Lk. 5:29 states that 'Levi made him a great feast in his house'. From the evidence it is usually supposed that Matthew and Levi were the same person.

The statement of Papias that Matthew 'compiled the oracles' (*synegrapsato ta logia*) in Hebrew was taken by the early church as evidence that Matthew was the author of the Gospel which had been handed down as 'according to Matthew'. Most modern scholars believe that Papias was referring to a compilation by Matthew either of the sayings of Jesus or of Messianic proof-texts from the OT. It may be that the subsequent embodiment of some of these sayings or proof-texts in the Gospel was the reason why that document came to be styled 'according to Matthew' from the middle of the 2nd century. For Bibliography, *MATTHEW, GOSPEL OF. R.V.G.T.

MATTHEW, GOSPEL OF.

I. Outline of contents

a. Events associated with the birth of Jesus the Messiah (1:1–2:23).

b. Jesus is baptized and tempted and begins his Galilean ministry (3:1–4:25).

c. The ethics of the kingdom of God are taught by Jesus by injunctions and illustrations (5:1–7:29).

d. Jesus demonstrates his power over disease, the devil and nature (8:1–9:34).

e. Jesus commissions the Twelve and sends them out as preachers (9:35–10:42).

f. Jesus commends John the Baptist, issues a gracious invitation to the heavy laden, claims to be Lord of the sabbath day, argues that he cannot be Beelzebub and explains the qualifications for membership in his new family (11:1–12:50).

g. Jesus gives seven parables about the kingdom of heaven (13:1–52).

h. Jesus is rejected by his fellow-townsmen of Nazareth, and John the Baptist is martyred (13:53–14:12).

i. Further miracles are performed by Jesus, who is acknowledged to be the Christ by Peter. Later Jesus is transfigured before three disciples and predicts his coming death and resurrection (14:13–17:27).

j. Jesus teaches his disciples to be humble, careful in conduct, and very forgiving in practice (18:1–35).

k. Jesus travels to Jerusalem. On the way he gives teaching on divorce, the position of children, the snare of riches and the wickedness of God's people the Jews; he heals two blind men at Jericho (19:1–20:34).

l. After making a triumphal but humble entry into Jerusalem, Jesus shows his authority by cleansing the Temple, by cursing a fruitless fig-tree, and by attacking and counter-attacking the chief priests and Pharisees (21:1–23:35).

m. Jesus predicts the fall of Jerusalem and his own glorious second coming (24:1–51).

n. Jesus gives three parables on judgment (25:1–46).

o. Jesus is betrayed, tried, denied, mocked, crucified and buried (26:1–27:66).

p. Jesus is raised from the dead and is seen by his friends (28:1–10).

q. Jesus gives his final orders before returning to God in heaven (28:11–20).

II. Characteristics and authorship

In this Gospel the incidents in the life of Jesus which constituted 'the gospel' preached by the apostles are combined to a greater extent with the ethical teaching of Jesus than elsewhere in the NT; and it is this feature of the book, together with the orderly manner in which the material is presented, which made it from the earliest days the most widely read and in some respects the most influential of the four Gospels. Modern scholars hesitate to accept the tradition that its author was the apostle *Matthew, for he seems to have been dependent upon a document composed by a non-apostolic writer, the Gospel of Mark, to a degree improbable in an original apostle. For a full discussion of the question of authorship see the writer's Introduction to the *TNTC*.

III. The influence of Mark

It is clear that Matthew has included almost the whole of Mark, though he has greatly abbreviated the Marcan stories of the miracles to make space for the large amount of non-Marcan material he desires to insert (*Gospels; *Mark, Gospel of). Along with the stories from Mark, the Evangelist inserts numerous sayings of Jesus, taken, it would seem, from a source common to himself and Luke; and he conflates these sayings with others found only in his Gospel, the resultant groupings constituting five blocks of teaching, chs. 5–7, 10, 13, 18 and 24–25, each block ending with the formula: 'When Jesus had finished these sayings.' The subject-matter of the Gospel is rendered complete by the addition of several narratives found nowhere else. These would appear for the most part to be elaborations of traditions used by Christians for apologetic purposes in defence against Jewish slanders. Evidence of style suggests that these particular narratives were first put in writing by the Evangelist himself (see G. D. Kilpatrick, *The Origins of the Gospel according to St. Matthew*, 1946).

IV. Differences from Mark's Gospel

The fact that this Gospel originated in a Gk.-speaking Jewish–Christian community accounts largely for the particular emphasis which it places upon the different elements that composed the primitive Christian preaching, and also for the manner in which the teaching of Jesus is presented. The note of *fulfilment* finds stronger emphasis here than in the Gospel of Mark. The author is most concerned to establish the truth that the earthly history of Jesus, in its origin and its purpose, and in the actual manner of its unfolding, was the activity of God himself, who was therein fulfilling his own words spoken by the prophets. No Gospel so closely links together OT and NT; and no document in the NT sets forth the person of Jesus, and his life and teaching, so clearly as the fulfilment of 'the law and the prophets'. Not only does the Evangelist add OT references to passages taken over from Mark, as, *e.g.*, at 27:34 and 43; but at various points in the narrative he introduces with the impressive formula 'this was to fulfil what was spoken by the prophet' some eleven special quotations from the OT, the cumulative effect of which is remarkable (see 1:23; 2:18; 2:23; 4:15f.; 8:17; 12:18ff.; 13:35; 21:5, and 27:9f.). Events are recorded as happening in the way they did because God had willed that it should be so. They were not freak events isolated and unexplained. They happened 'according to the scriptures', in which God's will had been expressed.

V. The story of Jesus

The record of the events in the life and death of Jesus which were of special importance and significance for the Christian gospel that we find presented in Matthew is for the most part Mark's story. Our Evangelist collects in chs. 8 and 9, in three groups of three, many of the Marcan narratives of the miracles; and in chs. 11 and 12 he combines from Mark and other sources stories about the relations of Jesus with prominent people of his day such as John the Baptist and the Pharisees. He makes no attempt to relate these incidents in chronological sequence. Such sequence is to be found only in the story of the passion, which, because it lay at the centre of the Christian gospel, was probably told in chronological form from very early days. Matthew, however, renders Mark's story of the life of Jesus more complete by prefacing it with a *genealogy and traditions about the infancy of Jesus and by following it with accounts of two of the appearances of the risen Jesus. The infancy narratives of Matthew do not contain an account of the birth of Jesus, which is mentioned only in passing in 2:1. The purpose of the Evangelist seems to be, by the genealogy, to show that Jesus, though born of a virgin-mother, was nevertheless legally of Abraham's seed and a son of the royal house of David; and, by the material contained in 1:18–25, to answer the calumny that Jesus was an illegitimate child of Mary, and to defend the action of Joseph. The subsequent story of the flight into Egypt is partly an answer to the Jewish cavil why, if Jesus, known as Jesus of Nazareth, was really born in Bethlehem, so much of his life was spent at Nazareth.

The two resurrection appearances peculiar to Matthew (28:9–10, 16–20) may be an attempt to round off the Marcan story. Certainly, the abruptness of Mark's ending is avoided by the statement that the women, instead of saying nothing to anybody of what they had heard and seen, at once obeyed the angel's command to report to the Lord's brethren that they were to go to Galilee where they would see him, and that, as the women were setting out on their errand, they met the risen Jesus. The momentous disclosure by the risen Jesus in Galilee that by his victory over death universal sovereignty had been given him, and his commission to the eleven disciples to embark upon a world-wide evangelistic mission with the assurance that he would be with them to the end of time, provide the climax of the Gospel of Matthew.

In these infancy and post-resurrection narratives Matthew is making definite additions to the story of Jesus as it had been set forth in Mark. Where he expands such Marcan stories as he embodies, it is usually by adding material which reflects interests that were of concern to the Christian church at the time he was writing. For example, the story of Peter walking over the waves to Jesus (14:28–31) and the famous Petrine passage in 16:18–19 were important at a time when that apostle was playing a leading part in the church; and the problem presented by taxation, especially after AD 70, when, on the destruction of the Temple, the tax for its upkeep was transferred to the temple of Jupiter Capitolinus, would receive some elucidation from the narrative recorded in 17:24–27. Moreover, as time went on, and biographical curiosity tended to increase, greater attention seems to have been paid to the secondary characters in the story of Jesus. Thus the Matthean account of the fate of Judas Iscariot (27:3–10) and the incident of Pilate's wife (27:19) would help to answer the puzzling questions, 'Why did Judas betray his Master?' and, 'Why did Pilate condemn Jesus?'

In his account of the crucifixion and resurrection Matthew makes four main additions to the Marcan narrative which at this point he is following closely. He relates that at the moment of Jesus' death an earthquake occurred accompanied by a resurrection of the saints, who had foretold the coming of the Messiah and who now rose to salute his death on Calvary (27:51–53). The three further additions of Matthew to Mark's resurrection narrative, *viz.* the special guarding and sealing of the tomb (27:62–66); the failure of these precautions due partly to the semi-mortification of the guards after another earthquake and partly to the presence of an angelic visitor who rolled the stone from the tomb (28:2–4); and the bribing of the guards to circulate the story, still current in the Evangelist's day, that the disciples of Jesus had come during the night and stolen the body (28:11–15)—are all of an apologetic nature. Their purpose is to dismiss the possibility that the body of Jesus could have been removed from the grave except in a supernatural manner. In many respects the Gospel of Matthew might be called an early Christian apology.

VI. The new Israel

The chief consequence of the life and death of Jesus emphasized in the Gospel of Matthew is the coming into being of the universal church of God, the new Israel, in which Gentiles as well as Jews find a place. The Gospel opens with the prophecy that Jesus is Emmanuel, God with us (1:23); and it closes with the promise that this same Jesus, now the risen Christ, will be with his disciples, drawn from all the nations, till the end of time. The note of universality, sounded at the beginning in the story of the manifestation of Jesus to the Magi, is re-echoed in the command with which the Gospel closes to go into all the world and make disciples of all nations. The Evangelist finds significance in the fact that the ministry of Jesus was exercised partly in 'Galilee of the Gentiles' (4:15); and describes him as God's servant who would 'proclaim justice to the Gentiles . . . and in his name will the Gentiles hope' (12:18, 21). The Christian church, universal in its membership, is, however, no new church. It is the old Israel transformed and widened because of Jesus' rejection by the majority of the Jews. It was to 'the lost sheep of the house of Israel' that Jesus confessed himself primarily to have been sent (15:24); and it was to the same lost sheep that he despatched his apostles to proclaim the arrival of the kingdom (10:6). But greater faith was found in a Roman centurion than in any in Israel (8:10); and in consequence the places at the Messianic banquet, unfilled by the Jew, would be thrown open to believers from E and W, while 'the sons of the kingdom' would remain outside (8:11–12). Because the Messiahship of Jesus had become to the Jews 'a stone of stumbling', the kingdom would be taken away from them and given to a nation 'producing the fruits of it' (21:42–43). The patriarchs of the new Israel, the apostles, would share in the Messiah's final victory, acting as his co-assessors in judgment, as Jesus makes clear in the words recorded by Matthew in 19:28, and as the Evangelist emphasizes by inserting the words 'with you' in the Marcan saying inserted at 26:29.

VII. Jesus as Judge

The fourth element in the primitive preaching was the call to repentance in view of the return of Jesus as Judge of living and dead. This call is sounded loudly in Matthew. John the Baptist in this Gospel calls Israel to repent in the same words as Jesus because they stand on the threshold of the Messiah's ministry (3:2); and at the close of the teaching of Jesus we read the parable of the great assize, found only in this Gospel (25:31–46). This parable concludes a group of sayings and parables concerned exclusively with the coming of the Messiah in judgment. By the time the Gospel was written, perhaps in the early 80s of the 1st century, part of the divine judgment had already descended upon Israel in the fall of Jerusalem; and the words of 21:41 and 22:7 had indeed been fulfilled.

Many of the parables peculiar to Mt., such as the tares of the field, the unforgiving debtor, the guest without a wedding garment and the ten virgins, stress the inevitability and the serious nature of the divine judgment; and it is in them that we find constantly repeated the solemn phrases peculiar to this Gospel, 'the outer darkness', 'the close of the age' and 'the weeping and gnashing of teeth'. In the perspective of this Gospel this final coming of the Christ, though absolutely certain, is not pictured as immediate, because, as we have seen, the closing pronouncement of the risen Christ implies a period of indefinite duration, during which he is present and exercises his reign in his church, before his final appearance as Judge. It is probable, therefore, that in the light of the teaching of the Gospel as a whole we ought to interpret the two very difficult sayings in 10:23 and 16:28 as referring to the exaltation of Jesus to the right hand of God after the triumph of his resurrection, when he entered upon a more extended reign in the hearts of his followers. Otherwise we are forced to the unsatisfactory conclusion that either they remained unfulfilled, and were therefore false prophecies, or that they are not genuine sayings of Jesus.

VIII. Ethical teaching

The Gospel of Matthew is also remarkable for the extent to which and the manner in which the ethical teaching of Jesus is presented. To this Evangelist, as to Jewish Christians generally, and also to Paul (for the very phrase is his), there is such a thing as 'the law of Christ'. Some scholars have thought that the five groups of teaching in this Gospel were regarded by the author as comparable to the five books of the law. Be this as it may, it would seem clear that he presents Jesus as the great Teacher who proclaims a revised law for the new Israel from the mountain (5:1), even as Moses had spoken the divine law given to him on Mt Sinai. The Messiah calls Israel not only to repentance but to good works; and the desire to do them, and the willingness to suffer for doing them, render the doers blessed (5:6, 10). The righteousness of Christ's disciples must exceed that of the Pharisees (5:20). It is true that by their traditions, by their slavery to isolated texts and their failure to grasp the wider implications of the law, the Pharisees had rendered much of it void; but the law remained an integral part of divine revelation. It is this law which finds its fulfilment in Christ, who came not to destroy it but to supply what it lacked and to correct scribal misinterpretations of it (5:17). Accordingly, a large part of the Sermon on the Mount is taken up with an explanation of the Decalogue in which Jesus lays down the moral standards by which the conduct of his disciples is to be judged.

One of the major difficulties of this Gospel is that it presents Jesus as upholding the validity of the Mosaic law and also claiming authority so to 'fulfil' it that sometimes he has been thought to be contradicting it. That he regarded the OT as possessing permanent validity as the Word of God is explicit in the uncompromising saying of 5:17–19. At the same time, so strongly is the binding authority of Christ's own utterances stressed, that in certain instances the abiding nature of the old law *seems* to be denied. In view, however, of the categorical statement about the law's validity, the Evangelist cannot have meant his readers to infer that there was any real antithesis between the statements contained in it and Jesus' comments upon them. Six times in the Sermon on the Mount he appears to be setting his own pronouncements against what had been previously spoken, and in each instance what had been previously spoken consists of, or at least includes, a quotation from the Mosaic law.

It has, however, been well pointed out that the expressions in ch. 5, 'You have heard that it was said' or 'It was said', do not correspond exactly to 'It is written', which Jesus so often uses when he is appealing to the authority of Scripture. By them he is, in fact, drawing attention not only to what the law said but to what the people had been told by their teachers was its meaning. In Judaism the law occupied the supreme position. In Christianity that place is occupied by Christ himself. In the Jewish–Christian Gospel of Matthew Christ remains the dominant authority. It is significant that it is in this Gospel alone that we read his gracious but imperious invitation, 'Come to me, all who labour and are heavy laden, and I will give you rest. Take my yoke upon you, and learn from me; for I am gentle and lowly in heart, and you will find rest for your souls. For my yoke is easy, and my burden is light' (11:28–30).

BIBLIOGRAPHY. Commentaries by D. Hill, *NCB*, 1972; E. Schweizer, 1976; D. A. Carson, *EBC*, 1984; R. T. France, *TNTC*, 1986; W. D. Davies and D. C. Allison, *ICC*, 1988, 1991. See also J. D. Kingsbury, *Matthew: Structure, Christology, Kingdom*, 1975; R. T. France, *Matthew: Evangelist and Teacher*, 1989; G. N. Stanton, *A Gospel for a New People: Studies in Matthew*, 1991. R.V.G.T.

MATTHIAS. The successor of Judas Iscariot, following the latter's defection from the Twelve (Acts 1:15–26). The fact and manner of his election have sometimes been called in question as hasty and unspiritual, and supervening on the place intended for Paul (*cf.*, *e.g.*, G. Campbell Morgan, *Acts,* 1924, *ad loc.*), but Luke gives no hint of such a view: the basis of the lot-casting, with its OT precedent (*cf.* 1 Sa. 14:41; * URIM AND THUMMIM), was that God had *already chosen* his apostle (v. 24), and it was fitting that the foundational apostolate should be complete at the outpouring of the Spirit on the church and its first preaching (*APOSTLE). That Matthias fulfilled the qualifications of vv. 21–22 makes the statement of Eusebius (*EH* 1. 12) that he was one of the Seventy not unlikely.

Of his later career nothing is known. His name was often confounded with that of Matthew, a process doubtless encouraged by the Gnostic groups who claimed secret traditions from him (Hippolytus, *Philos.* 7. 8). A book of so-called traditions was known to Clement of Alexandria (*Strom.* 2. 9; 3. 4; *cf.* 7. 17). Other apocryphal literature was fathered upon him.

The early identification of Matthias with Zacchaeus (Clement, *Strom.* 4. 6) may also arise from confusion with Matthew the tax-collector. The substitution of 'Tholomaeus' in the Old Syriac of Acts 1 is harder to understand.

The name is probably a contraction of Mattathias. A.F.W.

MATTOCK. Heb. *maḥ^{a}rēšā* in 1 Sa. 13:20 (end), 21, and the similar form *maḥ^{a}rešeṯ* (earlier in v. 20) represent cutting instruments (root *ḥrš*, 'to plough, engrave'), *i.e.* probably mattocks and hoes. Among other terms in these verses, the second one, Heb. *'ēṯ*, is a metal head: of an axe in 2 Ki. 6:5 and so perhaps of a ploughshare or more strictly a metal cap for a wooden plough (rather than AV's 'coulter'); *cf.* Is. 2:4 = Mi. 4:3; Joel 3:10, feasible adaptations as well as evocative. The third term in v. 20 (*qardōm*) is a pickaxe (AV 'axe').

In AV 'mattock' also translates Heb. *ma'dēr* in Is. 7:25, hoe, used in the vineyard terraces (*cf.* also Is. 5:6) and *b^{e}ḥarbōṯêhem* in 2 Ch. 34:6, which should probably be rendered 'in their ruins' with RV, RSV (from *ḥorbâ*).

For an iron mattock of about 10th century BC found at Tell Jemmeh in SW Palestine, see G. E. Wright, *Biblical Archaeology*, 1957, p. 92, fig. 57:3. (* ARTS AND CRAFTS.) K.A.K.

MEADOW. 1. Heb. *'āḥū*: AV 'meadow'; RV, RSV 'reed grass'. This Heb. word is a loan-word from Egyp. *'ḫ(y)* and, like it, means 'papyrus thicket(s)'. The picture of cattle pasturing in the papyrus thickets and marshes (Gn. 41:2, 18) is typically Egyptian: cattle are shown thus in tomb-scenes, while texts mention bringing 'best grass from the papyrus marshes' for livestock. In Jb. 8:11 *gōme'* and *'āḥū* are parallel: 'papyrus' or 'reeds' and 'papyrus thicket', which must have mud and water. In Ho. 13:15 it is possible to render *'aḥîm* as 'reed thickets' rather than 'brothers' (*cf.* RSV). See J. Vergote, *Joseph en Égypte*, 1959, pp. 59–66 (especially 62ff.) for full references; also *cf.* T. O. Lambdin, *JAOS* 73, 1953, p. 146, for other related Egyp. and Ugaritic terms.

2. In Jdg. 20:33 AV renders *ma'^{a}rēh-geḇa'* as 'meadows of Geba'. This may be the 'bare place' by Geba, or perhaps a Maareh-geba close by, or even (with LXX) to be read as *ma'^{a}raḇ-geḇa'*, '(on) west of Geba' (RSV). K.A.K.

MEALS.

I. Non-biblical sources

What is probably the oldest banquet scene in the world has been preserved on a lapis-lazuli cylinder seal recovered from the mound at Ur in Mesopotamia. Now in the University of Philadelphia Museum, the artefact dates from the time of Queen Shub-ad (*c.* 2600 BC). It depicts a meal at which the royal guests are seated on low stools and are being served with beakers of wine by attendants who wear skirts of fleece. Musical entertainment is provided by a harpist, while other servants employ fans in an attempt to cool the guests in the hot Mesopotamian air.

Similar scenes have been preserved by Bab. artists from subsequent periods, one of the more interesting of which is a large bas-relief from Assyria. King Ashurbanipal is seen eating with his wife in the garden of the royal palace at Nineveh. As the king reclines on a pillowed dining-couch he raises a bowl of wine to his lips. His wife is also shown drinking from an elegant bowl, but she is seated upon a small chair which has a low shelf in the form of a foot-rest. As in the case of the Ur artefact, attendants stand ready with fans to cool the diners and dispel annoying insects. The relief shows a few musical instruments placed on the ground beside some vines and palm trees in readiness for the court musicians.

The earliest detailed menu of which we have any record relates to a feast given by Ashurnasirpal II at the dedication of his new palace at Nimrud. It was attended by 69,574 persons and lasted for 10 days. The details are given on a monument set up in 879 BC (see *IBA*, fig. 43).

II. Biblical references

a. Palace meals

The type of elegance mentioned above, which was characteristic of Mesopotamian antiquity, was far surpassed by the delicacy and expertise which surrounded the royal meals of ancient Egypt. Paintings on the walls of tombs and other buildings have furnished remarkable evidence of the splendour such a celebration as the palace birthday banquet of pharaoh in the time of Joseph (Gn. 40:20). On such occasions the guests, elegantly bewigged and perfumed, were seated on couches near to low tables. Their food would include a variety of roast fowl, vegetables, roast beef, a wide range of pastries and numerous sweetmeats. Popular beverages included beer brewed from barley, and wine. Representations on tomb walls show servants bringing in large containers of wine and handing the guests bent glass tubes which were then dipped into the jar. The guests drank until they were inebriated and fell to the floor near their dining-couches.

Banqueting customs in Persia in the 5th century BC have been preserved by the book of Esther, which describes no fewer than five such festive occasions at Susa. The first was a marathon feast lasting 180 days, given by the king in honour of the Persian and Median princes (Est. 1:3ff.). This was followed by a 7-day banquet in the royal gardens, to which all the palace staff were invited. The guests were shielded from the sunlight by awnings of blue, green and white, the royal Persian colours, while the dining-couches were inlaid with gold and silver. The other feasts mentioned included one for the palace women (Est. 1:9), the wedding feast of Queen Esther (2:16–18), the wine-banquet given to Ahasuerus and Haman (5:4; 7:1–8) and the festival period known as Purim (9:1–32).

By contrast the Heb. palace meals were austere until the days of Solomon. Guests and retainers were numerous even in the time of Saul, and the royal displeasure could be incurred by refusing an invitation to dine with the king (1 Sa. 20:6). The generosity of David was shown in the provision made at the royal board for Mephibosheth, the crippled son of Jonathan (2 Sa. 9:7). Solomon imitated the monarchs of surrounding nations in the elaborateness and splendour of his feasts. It has been suggested that Solomon would probably have his summer meals served in some such garden as that mentioned in Canticles. In the royal court at Samaria Queen Jezebel supported a retinue of 400 prophets of the Asherah and 450 Baal prophets (1 Ki. 18:19). The poverty of post-exilic Judaea contrasted sharply with the fare provided by Nehemiah the governor. He supported 150 Jews in addition to other guests, and the day's food included six sheep, an ox, numerous fowls, fruit and wine (Ne. 5:17–19).

b. Working-class meals

For the labouring classes in biblical times, however, the situation was very different. The day began early, and instead of eating a formal breakfast, the workers carried in their girdles or in other containers small loaves, goat's-milk cheese, figs, olives and the like, which they ate as they journeyed to work. The Egyptians apparently had their main meal of the day at noon (Gn. 43:16), but Heb. workers generally contented themselves with a light repast and a rest period (Ru. 2:14). Abstinence from this meal constituted fasting (Jdg. 20:26; 1 Sa. 14:24). Supper, the most important meal of the day, took place after the work had been done (Ru. 3:7). Once the food had been prepared, the entire family dined together along with any guests who might be present. On festive occasions it was customary for entertainment to be provided, and this included riddles (Jdg. 14:12), music (Is. 5:12) and dancing (Mt. 14:6; Lk. 15:25). In the patriarchal period the diners sat in a group on the ground (Gn. 18:8; 37:25), but at a later time it became customary for them to sit at a table (1 Ki. 13:20; Ps. 23:5; Ezk. 23:41) after the Egyp. fashion, but perhaps in a semi-recumbent position (Est. 7:8).

c. Seating arrangements

In NT times meals were often eaten on a floor above that normally occupied by animals and domestic pets (*cf.* Mk. 7:28). Guests invariably reclined on couches, which were arranged on three sides of a square around a low table. Normally not more than three persons reclined on each couch, though occasionally this number was increased to four or five. Each couch was provided with cushions on which the left elbow rested and the right arm remained free, following the contemporary Graeco-Roman fashion. The guests so arranged themselves on the couches that each person could rest his head near the breast of the one who was reclining immediately behind him. He was thus reclining 'in the bosom' of his neighbour (Jn. 13:23; *cf.* Lk. 16:22), the close proximity of whom furnished adequate opportunity for an exchange of confidential communications. The place of greatest honour or 'highest couch' was the one immediately on the right of the servants as they entered the room to serve the meal. Conversely, the 'lowest room' was on the left of the servants, directly opposite to the 'highest couch'. The three guests on each couch were spoken of as highest, middle and lowest, a designation which was suggested by the fact that a guest who reclined on another's bosom always appeared to be below him. The most coveted seat (Mt. 23:6) was therefore the 'highest' place on the 'highest' couch. No questions of physical elevation were involved in such a usage of 'high' and 'low'.

d. The meal itself

The main meal of the day was generally a relaxed, happy occasion. Guests always washed their hands before partaking of food, since it was customary for all of them to eat from a communal dish. This was a large pottery container filled with meat and vegetables, and placed on a table in the centre of the couches. Only one instance is recorded in the OT of a blessing being pronounced before food was eaten (1 Sa. 9:13), but the NT mentions several occasions on which Christ pronounced grace before a meal commenced (Mt. 15:36; Lk. 9:16; Jn. 6:11).

While the general practice was for each guest to dip his hand into the common bowl (Mt. 26:23), there were occasions when separate portions were served to each guest (Gn. 43:34; Ru. 2:14; 1 Sa. 1:4–5). In the absence of knives and forks, small pieces of bread were held between the thumb and two fingers of the right hand to absorb the gravy from the dish (Jn. 13:26). They were also used after the fashion of spoons to scoop up a piece of meat, which was then conveyed to the mouth in the form of a sandwich. If a guest acquired a particularly delectable morsel by such means it was deemed an act of great politeness for him to hand it over to a companion (Jn. 13:26). When the meal was at an end it was customary for grace to be pronounced once again in compliance with the injunction of Dt. 8:10, after which the guests washed their hands a second time.

It would appear from instances such as those of Ruth among the reapers (Ru. 2:14), Elkanah and his two wives (1 Sa. 1:4–5), and the sons and daughters of Job (Jb. 1:4) that the womenfolk commonly partook of their meals in company with the men. But since it is probable that the task of preparing the food and waiting upon the guests normally devolved upon the women of the household (Lk. 10:40), they would doubtless be forced to take a somewhat more irregular and brief repast.

An ordinary family meal would not involve the preparation of more than one dish of food, so that when it had been served the member of the household who had cooked the meal would have no further work to do. This thought probably underlies the rebuke to *Martha (Lk. 10:42), when Christ suggested that only one dish was really necessary. In OT times, when the meal had been brought in by the person who had prepared it (1 Sa. 9:23), the head of the household allotted the various servings (1 Sa. 1:4), the size of which might well vary with the preference which he exercised towards individuals in the assembled group (Gn. 43:34; 1 Sa. 1:5).

e. Special meals

Special feasts celebrating birthdays, marriages or the presence of honoured guests were normally marked by an increased degree of ceremony. Visitors were received by the host with a kiss (Lk. 7:45) and provided with a refreshing footbath (Lk. 7:44). On certain occasions special clothing was furnished (Mt. 22:11) and the guests were decked out with floral wreaths (Is. 28:1). The head, beard, face and sometimes even the clothes were anointed with perfumes and ointments (Ps. 23:5; Am. 6:6; Lk. 7:38; Jn. 12:3) in celebration of an important festal occasion. The conduct of the banquet itself was under the direction of a special person known in NT times as the 'steward' of the feast (Jn. 2:8), to whom fell the task of sampling the various items of food and drink before they were placed on the table.

Guests were seated according to their respective rank (Gn. 43:33; 1 Sa. 9:22; Mk. 12:39; Lk. 14:8; Jn. 13:23), and were often served with individual portions of food (1 Sa. 1:4–5; 2 Sa. 6:19; 1 Ch. 16:3). Honoured guests were usually singled out by being offered either larger (Gn. 43:34) or more delectable (1 Sa. 9:24) portions than the others who were present at the banquet.

In the days of Paul the banquet was an elaborate meal which was generally followed by a symposium or intellectual discussion. On such occasions the discourse would often last far into the night, and would treat of such subjects as politics and philosophy.

f. Jesus' presence at meals

The NT records a number of occasions on which Jesus was a guest at an evening meal. The wedding feast at Cana (Jn. 2:1–11) was a festal occasion for which formal invitations had been issued, as was also the case in the parable of the king who gave a feast when his son was married (Mt. 22:2–14). The occasion on which Matthew was host at a banquet (Mt. 9:10) followed the more formal pattern of 1st-century AD Graeco-Roman meals. Jesus reclined at the table in company with his disciples, the tax-collectors and other invited guests. It is probable that the dining-room opened on to the street, with curtains placed near the entrance so that the guests would be shielded to some extent from the curious gaze of passers-by. The customs of the day, however, permitted people to look in through the curtains and gossip about those present at the feast. It was this practice which prompted the Pharisees to question the propriety of Christ's dining with publicans and sinners (Mt. 9:11).

On another occasion in a similar dining-room (Lk. 7:36–50) Jesus was noticed by a passing woman who returned with an alabaster flask from which she poured ointment on the feet of Christ. Her action was interpreted as supplying the traditional unguent of hospitality which the host had neglected to furnish in honour of his guest. It would also appear that he had failed to provide a container of water in which the guest could wash his feet, an omission which constituted a grave breach of courtesy in those days. The meal served to Jesus in Jericho by Zacchaeus (Lk. 19:6) was probably of lavish proportions. More modest were the family gatherings in Bethany (Lk. 10:40; Jn. 12:2), and the interrupted meal at Emmaus (Lk. 24:30–33) on the first Easter day. Occasionally Christ omitted the traditional hand-washing as a preliminary to a meal in order to teach an important spiritual principle (Lk. 11:37–42).

g. Meals on journeys

Persons undertaking journeys to parts of the country where hospitality was uncertain usually carried an earthen bottle of water (Gn. 21:14) and items of food, such as cakes of figs or raisins, bread and parched corn. The plight of those who 'forgot to take bread' (Mk. 8:1–9, 14) could be very serious under certain circumstances.

III. Religious significance of meals

a. Among the Semites

The communal aspect of a meal was carried over into the religious sphere by all Semitic peoples. Archaeological discoveries at Ras Shamra (Ugarit) have shown the prevalence of such meals in Canaanite religious life. Baal temples were frequently dedicated amidst prolonged feasting and revelry. At Shechem the remains of a Hyksos temple indicated the presence of rooms for banquets consequent upon the performance of sacrificial rites. The Hebrews sought both divine fellowship and pardon by means of meals (*PASSOVER, *SACRIFICE, *FEASTS) at which the blood and fat were the divine perquisite, while the priests and people received their appointed portions (Lv. 2:10; 7:6). Such sacrifices were common in the kingdom period (1 Sa. 9:11–14, 25; 1 Ch. 29:21–22; 2 Ch. 7:8–10), but were devoid of the licentiousness and debauchery which characterized Canaanite religious meals.

b. In Christianity
The principal sacred meal of Christianity was the *Lord's Supper, instituted by Christ just prior to his crucifixion (Mk. 14:22–25; Mt. 26:26–29; Lk. 22:14–20). In the early church the Agape, a communal meal denoting brotherly love among believers, frequently preceded celebrations of the Lord's Supper. (*LOVE FEAST; *FOOD.)

BIBLIOGRAPHY. *ISBE* 2, pp. 327–331; E. W. Heaton, *Everyday Life in Old Testament Times*, 1956, pp. 81ff.; A. C. Bouquet, *Everyday Life in New Testament Times*, 1954, pp. 69ff. R.K.H.

MEAT MARKET (Gk. *makellon*; Lat. *macellum*). Jewish law forbade dealing in such pagan markets, which sold the flesh of ritually unclean animals. In 1 Cor. 10:25 Paul counsels his readers to avoid what in a later age was known as scrupulosity. On the meat market in Corinth see *JBL* 80, 1934, pp. 134–141. J.D.D.

MECONAH (AV, **MEKONAH**). A town near Ziklag occupied by the Jews under Nehemiah (Ne. 11:28). Simons (*GTT*, p. 155) equates it with Madmannah, but Grollenberg with Machbena, named separately from Madmannah as a Calebite settlement (1 Ch. 2:49). The site is unknown. J.P.U.L.

MEDAN. A son of Abraham by *Keturah (Gn. 25:2; 1 Ch. 1:32). The names of some of the other sons and descendants of Keturah, such as Midian and Dedan, were later known as those of N Arabian tribes (*ARABIA), so it may be assumed that Medan likewise settled in this area, though the name is unknown outside the Bible. Medanites were associated with Midianites in the sale of Joseph, according to Gn. 37:36, *MT*. T.C.M.

MEDEBA (Heb. *mêḏᵉḇā'*, possibly 'water of quiet'). A plain and city of Reuben (Jos. 13:9, 16) N of the Arnon. An old Moabite town taken from Moab by Sihon (Nu. 21:21–30), it was used by the Syrian allies of Ammon as a camping-site after their defeat at the hand of Joab (1 Ch. 19:6–15). Thereafter it seems to have changed hands several times. It is mentioned in the *Moabite Stone as having been taken by Omri, perhaps from Moab, and as recovered by Mesha and fortified. Recaptured from Moab by Jeroboam II, it is again Moabite in Is. 15:2.

It figured also in the history of the intertestamental era (1 Macc. 9:36ff. as 'Medaba'; Jos., *BJ* 1. 63), before being captured by Hyrcanus after a long siege (Jos., *Ant.* 13. 11, 19).

The site, today called Mādabā, is 10 km S of Heshbon. There in 1896, during excavation of the site of a church, was discovered a 6th-century AD mosaic map showing part of Palestine from Beth-shan to the Nile. See M. Avi-Yonah, *The Madaba Mosaic Map*, 1954. In addition, there are considerable ruins, dating mainly from the Christian era, including a large temple and extensive cisterns. Tombs of Iron Age date have also been found. *NEAEHL*, pp. 992–1001. J.D.D.

MEDES, MEDIA (Heb. *madai*; Assyr. *(A)mada*; Old Pers. *Mada*; Gk. *Medai*).

Media was the name for NW Iran, SW of the Caspian Sea and N of the Zagros Mountains, covering the modern province of Azerbaijan and part of Persian Kurdistan. The inhabitants were called Medes or Medians and were Japhethites (Gn. 10:2), whose Aryan lineage is confirmed by Herodotus (7. 62), Strabo (15. 2. 8) and by the surviving traces of their language. The Medes were steppe-dwellers whose name is first mentioned by Shalmaneser III who raided their plains in 836 BC to obtain their famous, finely bred horses. Later Assyr. kings followed him and sought to keep the E passes open to the traders. Adad-nirari III (810–781 BC) claims to have conquered 'the land of the Medes and Parsua (Persia)', as did Tiglath-pileser III (743 BC) and Sargon II (716 BC). The latter transported Israelites to Media (2 Ki. 17:6; 18:11) after he had overrun the part of the land ruled by Dayaukku (Deioces), whom he exiled for a time to Hamath.

Esarhaddon bound his Median vassals by treaty (*Iraq* 20, 1958, pp. 1–91), but they soon rebelled and joined the Scythians (Ashguza) and Cimmerians against the declining power of Assyria after 631 BC. Under Phraortes there began the open attacks which culminated in the fall of Nineveh (612 BC) and Harran (610 BC) to Kyaxares of Media and his Bab. allies. The Medes controlled all lands to the N of Assyria and clashed with Lydia until peace was ratified in 585 BC.

In 550 BC *Cyrus of Anshan (*ELAM) defeated Astyages and brought Media under control, capturing the capital Ecbatana and adding 'King of the Medes' to his titles. Many Medes were given positions of responsibility and their customs and laws were combined with those of the Persians (Dn. 6:8, 15). Media was sometimes used to denote Persia but more usually combined with it as a major part of the new confederation (Dn. 8:20; Est. 1:19). The Medes, as seen by the prophets Isaiah (13:17) and Jeremiah (51:11, 28), took part in the capture of Babylon (Dn. 5:28). The new ruler of Babylon, *Darius, was called 'the Mede' (Dn. 11:1), being the son of Ahasuerus of Median origin (Dn. 9:1).

The Medes later rebelled under Darius I and II (409 BC). The history of the Jews in Media is recounted in Esther (1:3, 14, 18–19) and the Medians under Syrians (Seleucids) and Parthians are referred to in 1 Macc. 14:1–3; Josephus, *Ant.* 10. 232. Media was organized as the 11th and 18th Satrapies. The Medes are mentioned, with the Parthians and Elamites, in Acts 2:9. After the Sassanids Media was used only as a geographical term.

BIBLIOGRAPHY. E. Yamauchi, *Persia and the Bible*, 1990. D.J.W.

MEDIATOR. The term occurs infrequently in the Scriptures (Gal. 3:19–20; 1 Tim. 2:5; Heb. 8:6; 9:15; 12:24; Jb. 9:33, LXX). But the idea of mediation and therefore of persons acting in the capacity of mediator permeates the Bible. The function of a mediator is to intervene between two parties in order to promote relations between them which the parties themselves are not able to effect. The situation requiring the offices of a mediator is often one of estrangement and alienation, and the mediator effects reconciliation. In the sphere of human relations Joab acted the part of mediator between David and Absalom (2 Sa. 14:1–23). Job expresses the need in regard to his relations to God when he said, 'There is no umpire (AV 'daysman') between us, who might lay his hand upon us both' (Jb. 9:33).

I. In the Old Testament

In the OT the prophet and the priest fulfilled, most characteristically, the office of mediator in the institution which God established in terms of covenant relations with his people. The prophet was God's spokesman; he acted for God in the presence of men (*cf.* Dt. 18:18–22). The priest acted on behalf of men in the presence of God (Ex. 28:1; Lv. 9:7; 16:6; Nu. 16:40; 2 Ch. 26:18; Heb. 5:1–4; *cf.* Jb. 42:8). In the OT, however, Moses, of all human instruments, was the mediator *par excellence* (*cf.* Ex. 32:30–32; Nu. 12:6–8; Gal. 3:19; Heb. 3:2–5). He was the mediator of the old covenant, because it was through his instrumentality that the covenant at Sinai was dispensed and ratified (*cf.* Ex. 19:3–8, 24:3–8; Acts 7:37–39). It is with Moses that Jesus as Mediator of the new covenant is compared and contrasted.

II. Christ as mediator

The designation 'Mediator' belongs pre-eminently to Christ, and even those men who executed mediatory offices in the OT institution were thus appointed only because the institution in which they performed these functions was the shadow of the archetypal realities fulfilled in Christ (*cf.* Jn. 1:17; Heb. 7:27–28; 9:23–24; 10:1). Jesus is the Mediator of the new covenant (Heb. 9:15; 12:24). And it is a better covenant (Heb. 8:6) because it brings to consummate fruition the grace which *covenant administration embodies. Christ is the 'one mediator between God and men' (1 Tim. 2:5). To invest any other with this prerogative is to assail the unique honour that belongs to him as well as to deny the express assertion of the text.

Though the title 'Mediator' is not often used, the Scripture abounds in references to the mediatory work of Christ.

a. Pre-incarnate mediation

As the eternal and pre-existent Son he was Mediator in the creation of the heavens and the earth (Jn. 1:3, 10; Col. 1:16; Heb. 1:2). This activity in the economy of creation is correlative with his mediatorship in the economy of redemption. The omnipotence evidenced in the former and the prerogatives that belong to him as Creator are indispensable to the execution of redemption. It is in redemption, however, that the extensiveness of his mediation appears. All along the line of the redemptive process from its inception to the consummation his mediacy enters.

Election as the ultimate fount of salvation did not take place apart from Christ. The elect were chosen in him before the foundation of the world (Eph. 1:4) and they were predestinated to be conformed to his image (Rom. 8:29).

b. Mediation in salvation and redemption

It is particularly in the once-for-all accomplishment of salvation and redemption that his mediatory action is patent (*cf.* Jn. 3:17; Acts 15:11; 20:28; Rom. 3:24–25; 5:10–11; 7:4; 2 Cor. 5:18; Eph. 1:7; Col. 1:20; 1 Jn. 4:9). The accent falls upon the death, blood and cross of Christ as the action through which redemption has been wrought. In the Scriptures the death of Christ is always conceived of as an event in which Jesus is intensely active in obedience to the Father's commandment and in fulfilment of his commission (*cf.* Jn. 10:17–18; Phil. 2:8). It is Jesus' activity as Mediator in the shedding of his blood that accords to his death its saving efficacy. When salvation wrought is viewed as reconciliation and propitiation, it is here that the mediatory function is most clearly illustrated. Reconciliation presupposes alienation between God and men and consists in the removal of that alienation. The result is peace with God (*cf.* Rom. 5:1; Eph. 2:12–17). Propitiation is directed to the wrath of God and Jesus, as the propitiation, makes God propitious to us (*cf.* 1 Jn. 2:2).

c. Continued mediation

Christ's mediation is not confined to his finished work of redemption. His mediatory activity is never suspended. In our participation of the fruits of redemption we are dependent upon his continued intervention as Mediator. Our access to God and our introduction into the grace of God are through him; he conveys us into the Father's presence (Jn. 14:6; Rom. 5:2; Eph. 2:18). It is through him that grace reigns through righteousness to eternal life, and grace and peace are multiplied to the enjoyment of the fullness of Christ (*cf.* Rom. 1:5; 5:21; 2 Cor. 1:5; Phil. 1:11). The most characteristic exercises of devotion on the part of the believer are offered through Christ. Thanksgiving and prayer are not only exercised in the grace which Christ imparts but are also presented to God through Christ (*cf.* Jn. 14:14; Rom. 1:8; 7:25; Col. 3:17; Heb. 13:15). The acceptableness of the believer's worship and service springs from the virtue and efficacy of Christ's mediation, and nothing is a spiritual sacrifice except as rendered through him (1 Pet. 2:5). Even the pleas presented to others for the discharge of their obligations derive their most solemn sanction from the fact that they are urged through Christ and in his name (Rom. 15:30; 2 Cor. 10:1; *cf.* Rom. 12:1).

The continued mediation of Christ is specially exemplified in his heavenly ministry at the right hand of God. This ministry concerns particularly his priestly and kingly offices. He is a Priest for ever (Heb. 7:21, 24). An important aspect of this priestly ministry in the heavens is intercession directed to the Father and drawing within its scope every need of the people of God. Jesus is exalted in his human nature, and it is out of the reservoir of fellow feeling forged in the trials and temptations of his humiliation (Heb. 2:17–18; 4:15) that he meets every exigency of the believer's warfare. Every grace bestowed flows through the channel of Christ's intercession (Rom. 8:34; Heb. 7:25; *cf.* 1 Jn. 2:1) until the salvation which he has secured will reach its fruition in conformity to his image. The priestly ministry of Christ, however, must not be restricted to intercession. He is High Priest over the house of God (Heb. 3:1–6), and this administration involves many other functions. In his kingly office he is exalted above all principality and power (Eph. 1:20–23), and he will reign to the end of bringing all enemies into subjection (1 Cor. 15:25). This is Christ's mediatorial dominion, and it embraces all authority in heaven and in earth (Mt. 28:18; Jn. 3:35; 5:26–27; Acts 2:36; Phil. 2:9–11).

It is eschatology that will finally manifest and vindicate Christ's mediatorship; the resurrection and judgment will be wrought by him. All the dead, just and unjust, will be raised by his summons (Jn. 5:28–29). It is in him that the just will be raised to immortality and incorruption (1 Cor. 15:22, 52–54; 1 Thes. 4:16), and with him they will be glorified (Rom. 8:17; *cf.* Jn. 11:25; Rom. 14:9). The final judgment will be executed by him (Mt. 25:31–46; Jn. 5:27; Acts 17:31).

d. Conclusion

Christ's mediatorship is thus exercised in all the phases of redemption from election in God's eternal counsel to the consummation of salvation. He is Mediator in humiliation and exaltation. There is, therefore, multiformity attaching to his mediatorial activity, and it cannot be defined in terms of one idea or function. His mediatorship has as many facets as his person, office and work. And as there is diversity in the offices and tasks discharged and in the relations he sustains to men as Mediator, so there is also diversity in the relations he sustains to the Father and the Holy Spirit in the economy of redemption. The faith and worship of him require that we recognize this diversity. And the unique glory that is his as Mediator demands that we accord to no other even the semblance of that prerogative that belongs to him as the one Mediator between God and man.

BIBLIOGRAPHY. J. Calvin, *Institutes of the Christian Religion*, 2. 12; G. Stevenson, *Treatise on the Offices of Christ*, 1845; R. I. Wilberforce, *The Doctrine of the Incarnation of Our Lord Jesus Christ*, 1875, pp. 166–211; P. G. Medd, *The One Mediator*, 1884; T. F. Torrance, *The Mediation of Christ*, 1983; W. L. Alexander, *A System of Biblical Theology*, 1888, 1, p. 425, 2, p. 212; J. S. Candlish, *The Christian Salvation*, 1899, pp. 1–12; E. Brunner, *The Mediator*, 1934; H. B. Swete, *The Ascended Christ*, 1916, pp. 87–100; V. Taylor, *The Names of Jesus*, 1954, pp. 110–113; A. Oepke, *TDNT* 4, pp. 598–624; J. Guhrt, O. Becker, *NIDNTT* 1, pp. 365–376.

J.M.

MEEKNESS. The high place accorded to meekness in the list of human virtues is due to the example and teaching of Jesus Christ. Pagan writers paid greater respect to the self-confident man. However, its roots lie in the OT. The adjective *'ānāw* is usually translated 'meek' in AV but by a variety of words in RSV related to its basic meaning, 'poor and afflicted', from which the spiritual quality of patient submission, humility, is derived, *e.g.* Pss. 22:26; 25:9; Is. 29:19. Meekness is a quality of the Messianic King (Zc. 9:9) and the theme of Ps. 37:11, 'the meek shall inherit the earth' (AV), is repeated by our Lord in the Beatitudes (Mt. 5:5). In meekness Moses, while maintaining strength of leadership, was ready to accept personal injury without resentment or recrimination (Nu. 12:1–3).

In the NT meekness (*prautēs* and adjective *praus*) refers to an inward attitude, whereas *gentleness is expressed rather in outward action. It is part of the fruit of Christlike character produced only by the Spirit (Gal. 5:23, AV). The meek do not resent adversity because they accept everything as being the effect of God's wise and loving purpose for them, so that they accept injuries from men also (as Moses above), knowing that these are permitted by God for their ultimate good (*cf.* 2 Sa. 16:11). The meekness and gentleness of Christ was the source of Paul's own plea to the disloyal Corinthians (2 Cor. 10:1). He enjoined meekness as the spirit in which to rebuke an erring brother (2 Tim. 2:25, AV), and when bearing with one another (Eph. 4:2). Similarly, Peter exhorted that the inquiring or arguing heathen should be answered in meekness (1 Pet. 3:15, AV). Supremely meekness is revealed in the character of Jesus (Mt. 11:29, AV; 21:5, AV), demonstrated in superlative degree when he stood before his unjust accusers without a word of retort or self-justification.

BIBLIOGRAPHY. F. Hauck, S. Schulz, *TDNT* 6, pp. 645–651.

J.C.C.

MEGIDDO. An important OT city which lay in the Carmel range some 30 km SSE of the modern port of Haifa.

I. Biblical evidence

The city of Megiddo (Heb. *m^eḡiddô*) is first mentioned among the cities which Joshua captured during his conquest of Palestine (Jos. 12:21) and was subsequently allotted to Manasseh in the territory of Issachar (Jos. 17:11; 1 Ch. 7:29). Manasseh, however, did not destroy the Canaanites in the city, but put them to menial labour (Jdg. 1:28). A curiously indirect reference is made to Megiddo in the Song of Deborah, where *Taanach is described as 'by the waters of Megiddo' (*'al-mê m^eḡiddô*, Jdg. 5:19), but no mention of Megiddo as a city as opposed to the name of a watercourse is made (*KISHON). The next reference to the city comes from the time of Solomon, when it was included in his fifth administrative district under Baana (the son of Ahilud) (1 Ki. 4:12) and was selected, with Hazor and Gezer, to be one of his main fortified cities outside Jerusalem, in which he had accommodation for chariots and horses (1 Ki. 9:15–19). Megiddo is briefly mentioned as the place where Ahaziah of Judah died after being wounded in his flight from Jehu (2 Ki. 9:27), and it was later the scene of the death of Josiah when he tried to prevent *Neco of Egypt from going to the aid of Assyria (2 Ki. 23:29–30; 2 Ch. 35:22, 24). The name occurs in the form *m^eḡiddôn* in Zechariah (12:11), and it is this form which is used in the NT *Armageddon (Rev. 16:16), from *harm^eḡiddôn*, 'hill of Megiddo'.

II. Extra-biblical sources

The site of ancient Megiddo has been identified with the modern deserted mound of Tell el-Mutesellim, which lies on the N side of the Carmel ridge and commands the most important pass from the coastal plain to the valley of Esdraelon. The tell stands nearly 21 m high, with an area on the summit of over 10 acres, and the earlier cities lower down in the mound were still larger than this.

MEGIDDO

The first excavations were carried out by a German expedition under G. Schumacher from 1903 to 1905. A trench was cut across the top of the mound, and a number of buildings were found, but owing to the limited knowledge of pottery at the time little was learnt. The site was not excavated again until 1925, when the Oriental Institute of the University of Chicago under the direction of J. H. Breasted selected it as the first major project in an ambitious scheme of excavations all over the Near East. The work was directed successively by C. S. Fisher (1925–7), P. L. O. Guy (1927–35), and G. Loud (1935–9). The original intention was to clear the entire mound, level by level, to the base, and to this end an area at the foot of the slope was excavated at an early stage to release it for the subsequent dumping of earth from the tell. War brought the work to an end, and though the lay-out of the entire city in Iron Age times had been revealed, the earlier levels were known only in a relatively small area. Further excavations were carried out in 1960, 1966–7 and 1971 by Y. Yadin to elucidate some problems, notably those by Yadin in the 60s. Recently Finkelstein and Ussishkin have renewed large-scale excavations.

Twenty main occupation levels were identified, dating back to Chalcolithic settlements in the early 4th millennium (levels XX, XIX). An interesting feature of level XIX is a small shrine with an altar in it. During the Early Bronze Age (3rd millennium) there was a considerable city at Megiddo (levels XVIII–XVI), one interesting feature of which was a circular platform of boulders approached by a flight of steps, which was covered with animal bones and broken pottery. It may be that this was a *bāmâ* or *'high place'. This platform continued in use in the Middle Bronze Age (levels XV–X; first half of the 2nd millennium), a period of Egyp. influence the start of which was marked by widespread rebuilding, in which the circular platform became the nucleus of three megaron-shaped temples with *altars. A fine triple-piered gateway, of a type which originated in Mesopotamia, was also found in these levels, and the necessity of such strong gates was shown by the evidence of a number of major destructions in the latter part of the period, culminating in a great devastation probably to be connected with the Egyp. reconquest of Palestine following the expulsion of the Hyksos from Egypt.

The evidences of periodical violence are less frequent in the Late Bronze Age (levels VIII, VII), and though this was a period of Egyp. domination the culture of Palestine reflected the Canaanite civilization of the N to a considerable extent. It was in this period that perhaps the most fully reported battle of antiquity was fought when Tuthmosis III routed an Asiatic coalition at Megiddo *c.* 1468 BC. Architectural remains of this period include a temple, a palace and a gate, and the N cultural influence is clearly seen in a great hoard of over 200 objects of carved ivory which was found in a subterranean treasury under the level VII palace. This is one of the earliest collections of a type of art which was well known in Iron Age times from *Samaria and from as far afield as Assyria, and though practically no examples have yet been discovered in Phoenicia it is probable that many of them were made either in Phoenician workshops or by expatriate Phoenician craftsmen. That there were contacts with Mesopotamia at this period is shown by the recent discovery on the edge of the mound of a fragment of the Bab. Epic of Gilgamesh which can be dated by its cuneiform script to the 14th century BC.

The final Canaanite city (VIIA) was destroyed in *c.* 1150 BC and was replaced by a small short-lived village (VIB). It has been suggested that the Israelites destroyed VIIA and established the village of VIB. This was a period of great instability and both could be the result of a number of other forces, which is likely since Jdg. 1:27–28 indicates that the Canaanite inhabitants of Megiddo were not driven out in the Israelite conquest. Following the renewed strength of Egypt under Merenptah the flourishing city of VIA was established. As well as showing clear Egyptian influence it also contained pottery of the Philistines or one of the other Sea Peoples. Following the destruction of this city, a new town was established (VB) which was composed of houses along the perimeter of the site forming a defensive ring. This town has been dated to the reign of David. This was replaced by VA-IVB which has been attributed to Solomon. It is in this town that first major public buildings appear, including palaces and a six-chambered gate.

A fragment of a stela of Pharaoh Sheshonq (*SHISHAK) comes from the destruction of the Solomonic city (probably VA-IVB). The next city (IV) was built by Omri or Ahab and was a very substantial city with palaces, a four-chambered gate and a solid wall. In this city a large number of stables were found which clearly illustrate the large chariot force that the annals of Shalmaneser claim that Ahab had.

Another discovery, probably of this period, was the city water-supply systems. An unbuilt zone of the mound was excavated by a pit 37 m deep, the bottom section of which consisted of a shaft with a staircase round its side, cut into the rock at the base. From the foot of the shaft, the staircase entered a tunnel which, finally levelling off, led, some 50 m father on, into a cave with a spring of water at the far end. It appeared that this spring had originally given on to a slope outside the city, but at a later period the tunnel had been cut from inside the city and the cave was blocked and masked from the outside for strategic reasons.

Tiglath Pileaser III conquered N Israel, destroying the city built by Ahab. This city was replaced by a new one (III) which became the capital of the Assyrian province of Megiddo. The excavations uncovered a number of Assyrian palaces near the gate, and show that the city was built on an entirely new plan which was very different from any known in Israel. When the Egyptians took over the city from the Assyrians, they appear to have constructed a very substantial fortress (II). There is little evidence to show that Megiddo continued to serve as a provincial capital in the Babylonian and Persian periods.

BIBLIOGRAPHY. G. Schumacher and C. Steuernagel, *Tell el-Mutesellim*, 1, *Fundbericht*, 1908; C. Watzinger, 2, *Die Funde*, 1929; R. S. Lamon and G. S. Shipton, *Megiddo I: Seasons of 1925–34*, 1939; G. Loud, *Megiddo II: Seasons of 1935–1939*, 1948; H. G. May, *Material Remains of the Megiddo Cult*, 1935; P. L. O. Guy and R. M. Engberg, *Megiddo Tombs*, 1938; G. Loud, *The Megiddo Ivories*, 1939; W. F. Albright, *AJA* 53, 1949, pp. 213–215; G. E. Wright, *JAOS* 70, 1950, pp. 56–60; *idem*, *BA* 13, 1950, pp. 28–46; Y. Yadin, *BA* 33, 1970, pp. 66–96; *idem*, *Hazor* (Schweich Lectures, 1970), 1972, pp. 150–164; A. Goetze and S. Levy, 'Fragment of the

Gilgamesh Epic from Megiddo', *'Atiqot*, 2, 1959, pp. 121–128; *IDBS*, 1976, pp. 583–585; G. I. Davies, *Megiddo*, 1986, *NEAEHL*, pp. 1003–1024.

T.C.M.

MELCHIZEDEK (Heb. *malkîṣeḏeq*, 'Ṣedeq is (my) king' or, as in Heb. 7:2, 'king of righteousness'). He was the king of Salem (probably Jerusalem) and priest of 'God Most High' (*'ēl 'elyôn*) who greeted Abram on his return from the rout of *Chedorlaomer and his allies, presented him with bread and wine, blessed him in the name of God Most High and received from him a tenth part of the booty which had been taken from the enemy (Gn. 14:18ff.). Abram thereupon declined the king of Sodom's offer to let him keep all the booty apart from the recovered prisoners, swearing by God Most High that he would allow no man to have the honour of making him rich (v. 22, where *MT*, but not Samaritan, LXX, or Pesh., adds *Yahweh* before *'ēl 'elyôn*, thus emphasizing that the two names denote one and the same God). The incident is probably to be dated in the Middle Bronze Age (*ABRAHAM). Melchizedek's name may be compared with that of a later king of Jerusalem, Adoni-zedek (Jos. 10:1ff.).

In Ps. 110:4 a Davidic king is acclaimed by divine oath as 'a priest for ever after the order of Melchizedek'. The background of this acclamation is provided by David's conquest of Jerusalem *c.* 1000 BC, by virtue of which David and his house became heirs to Melchizedek's dynasty of priest-kings. The king so acclaimed was identified by Jesus and his contemporaries as the Davidic Messiah (Mk. 12:35ff.). If Jesus is the Davidic Messiah, he must be the 'priest for ever after the order of Melchizedek'. This inevitable conclusion is drawn by the writer to the Hebrews, who develops his theme of our Lord's heavenly priesthood on the basis of Ps. 110:4, expounded in the light of Gn. 14:18ff., where Melchizedek appears and disappears suddenly, with nothing said about his birth or death, ancestry or descent, in a manner which declares his superiority to Abram and, by implication, to the Aaronic priesthood descended from Abram. The superiority of Christ and his new order to the levitical order of OT times is thus established (Heb. 5:6–11; 6:20–7:28).

A fragmentary text from Cave 11 at Qumran (11QMelch.) envisages Melchizedek as divinely appointed judge in the heavenly court, expounding Pss. 7:7ff.; 82:1ff. in this sense (*cf.* A. S. van der Woude, 'Melchisedech als himmlische Erlösergestalt', *OTS* 14, 1965, pp. 354ff.).

BIBLIOGRAPHY. Commentaries on Genesis, Psalms, Hebrews; F. F. Bruce, *The Epistle to the Hebrews, NIC*², 1990, pp. 94ff., 133ff.; H. H. Rowley, 'Melchizedek and Zadok', *Festschrift für A. Bertholet* (ed. W. Baumgartner *et al.*), 1950, pp. 461ff.; A. R. Johnson, *Sacral Kingship in Ancient Israel*, 1955; O. Cullmann, *The Christology of the New Testament*, 1959, pp. 83ff.; J. A. Fitzmyer, *Essays on the Semitic Background of the NT*, 1971, pp. 221–269; F. L. Horton, *The Melchizedek Tradition*, 1976; B. A. Demarest, *A History of Interpretation of Hebrews 7:1–10 from the Reformation to the Present*, 1976.

F.F.B.

MELZAR. The subordinate official in charge of Daniel and his companions, to whom Daniel appealed for a change of diet (Dn. 1:11–16). In AV it is translated as a proper name, as in Theodotion, Lucian, and in Syr., Vulg. and Arab. vss. LXX gives 'Abiesdri', and identifies him with the chief of the eunuchs in v. 3. Most scholars now regard it as a title, probably a loan-word from the Assyr. *maṣṣāru*, 'guardian' (see *BDB*). Probably we should read 'steward' (RSV), 'overseer' (Nowack), or 'warden' (J. A. Montgomery, *Daniel*, *ICC*, 1926).

J.G.G.N.

MEMPHIS (Egyp. *Mn-nfr*; Heb. *Mōp̄* and *Nōp̄*). Situated on the Nile, at about 24 km from the apex of the Delta. It was a foundation of Menes (the White Walls), the pharaoh who united Upper and Lower Egypt. The name *Mn-nfr* is short for that of the temenos of the pyramid of Pepi (*c.* 2400 BC). It was the capital of Egypt during the Old Kingdom. It remained an important city up to the conquest by Alexander the Great (332 BC). Principal gods were Ptah, the demiurge, Sekhmet, Nefertem and Sokaris. The name *Hwt-k'-Ptḥ*, 'mansion of the Ka of Ptah', is the origin of the name Egypt. Very little remains of the city of the living (Mît-Rahîna); the necropolis is better known with the important ruins of Djeser at Saqqara, the pyramid of Djedefrê at Abu Rawash, the pyramids of Kheops, Khephren and Mykerinos at Gîza, and those of the 5th Dynasty at Abusîr. Rameses II, Merenptah and Psammetichus pursued extensive building in the region. The temple is described by Herodotus (2. 153), and writers of old describe the place where the living Apis bull was kept. During the New Kingdom, as a consequence of Asiatic immigration, we find that foreign gods, such as Qadesh, Astarte and Baal, were worshipped at Memphis.

The city was taken by the Ethiopians (Piankhy 730 BC), the Assyrians (Esarhaddon 671, Ashurbanipal 666) and the Persians (Cambyses 525).

From the 7th century BC, colonies of foreigners established themselves in the place, and, after the destruction of Jerusalem, also Jews (Je. 44:1). The city is mentioned several times by the prophets (Ho. 9:6; Is. 19:13; Je. 2:16; 46:14, 19; Ezk. 30:13, 16).

BIBLIOGRAPHY. F. Petrie, *Memphis*, 1, 2, 3, 1909–10; Kees, in *RE, s.v.*; Porter and Moss, *Topographical Bibliography*, 3, 1931.

C.D.W.

MENAHEM. The son of Gadi, and military governor of Tirzah, became king of Israel (752–742, or 747–737 BC, 2 Ki. 15:17–22) after taking the throne as a usurper, having captured Samaria and ousted Shallum. He had to suppress opponents who were aware, as were the Assyrians, that he was not related to the ruling House of Omri. Menahem is named *menihimme* of Samaria in a list of states which paid tribute to the Assyrian king Tiglath-pileser III about 743 BC. The Assyrians were incorporating neighbouring states as vassals, and made Samaria the centre of an Assyrian province. The cost to Israel was her independence since she had to pay a tribute of 1,000 talents of silver, recouped by a tax of 50 shekels a head per wealthy male (*i.e.* total of 36,000 men); that was the equivalent of the current redemption price for each male slave. Menahem, the last Israelite king to be succeeded by his son (Pekahiah), was a primary cause for anti-Assyrian opposition which resulted in the capture of Samaria in 722 BC and the exile of its inhabitants.

BIBLIOGRAHY. D. J. Wiseman, *DOTT*, pp. 53–58; *idem. 1 & 2 Kings*, *TOTC*, 1993, pp. 254–255; L. D. Levine, *Iran*, 1972, pp. 11–24. D.J.W.

MENE, MENE, TEKEL, UPHARSIN. The writing on the wall at Belshazzar's feast (Dn. 5:25, RSV 'MENE, MENE, TEKEL, and PARSIN', since the *u* of *upharsin* is the conjunction 'and', after which *p* becomes the spirant *ph* [*(p̄)*]). In Daniel's interpretation (vv. 26–28) *m*^{e}*nē'* is derived from Aram. *m*^{e}*nā'*, 'to number', indicating that the days of the Chaldean empire have been *numbered* and brought to an end; *t*^{e}*qēl* is derived from Aram. *t*^{e}*qal*, 'to weigh' (*cf.* Heb. *šāqal*, whence 'shekel'), indicating that Belshazzar has been *weighed* in the divine scales and found wanting; and the plural *parsîn* is replaced by the singular *p*^{e}*rēs*, which is derived from Aram. *p*^{e}*ras*, 'to divide', indicating that his empire is to be *divided* between the Medes and the Persians (*pārās*, with a further play on the root *prs* (RSV, AV, NIV, 'PERES').

The mystery lay not in the decipherment of the Aram. words, but in their significance. On the surface they denoted a series of weights or monetary units, 'a mina, a mina, a shekel, and half-shekel' (Bab. *parisu*)—or, if the first word were regarded as imperative of the verb *m*^{e}*nā'*, 'number a mina, a shekel, and half-shekel'. But there was no context which could make these words seem relevant to the king or his wise men.

Various attempts have been made by several scholars to relate the specified units to successive rulers of Babylon, *e.g.* Nebuchadrezzar (a mina), Belshazzar (a shekel), Medes and Persians (divisions) (C. S. Clermont-Ganneau, A. H. Sayce); Evil-merodach and Neriglissar (two minas), Labashi-marduk (a shekel), Nabonidus and Belshazzar (two half-minas) (E. G. Kraeling); Nebuchadrezzar (a mina), Evil-merodach (a shekel), Belshazzar (one half-mina) (H. L. Ginsberg); Nebuchadrezzar (a mina), Nabonidus (a shekel), Belshazzar (one half-mina) (D. N. Freedman, who concludes from the Qumran *Prayer of Nabonidus* that the Daniel story originally knew these three Chaldean kings). These attempts are fascinating but inconclusive.

BIBLIOGRAPHY. Commentaries on Daniel by J. A. Montgomery, 1927, E. W. Heaton, 1956, A. Jeffery, *IB*, 6, 1956; J. G. Baldwin, *TOTC*, 1978; J. E. Goldingay, 1989; J. J. Collins, 1993, *ad. loc.*; A. H. Sayce, *The Higher Criticism and the Verdict of the Monuments*, 1895, pp. 530f.; E. G. Kraeling, *JBL* 63, 1944, pp. 11ff.; H. L. Ginsberg, *Studies in Daniel*, 1948, pp. 24ff.; O. Eissfeldt, 'Die Menetekel-Inschrift', *ZAW* 62, 1951, pp. 105ff.; D. N. Freedman, *BASOR* 145, February 1957, pp. 31f. F.F.B.

MEONENIM, OAK OF. The RV rendering of the phrase *'ēlôn m*^{e}*'ôn*^{e}*nîm* in Jdg. 9:37, which is translated 'plain of Meonenim' in AV and 'Diviners' Oak' in RSV. The word *m*^{e}*'ôn*^{e}*nîm* is the intensive participle of the verb *'ānan*, 'to practise soothsaying', used, for instance, in 2 Ki. 21:6 = 2 Ch. 33:6 (RV 'observed times') and Lv. 19:26, where the practice is forbidden. The participial form, meaning 'soothsayer' or 'diviner' (*DIVINATION), occurs also in Dt. 18:10, 14 and in Mi. 5:12 (13, Heb.) but is treated only as a proper name by AV and RV in the passage in Judges. The reference is probably to a tree where Canaanite or apostate Israelite soothsayers carried out their business. The site is unknown. T.C.M.

MEPHIBOSHETH. The original form of the name may have been Meribba'al, perhaps *'Baal is advocate' (1 Ch. 8:34; 9:40a), or Meribba'al, 'hero of Baal' (1 Ch. 9:40b). In the Lucianic recension of the LXX (except at 2 Sa. 21:8) the form is Memphibaal, perhaps 'one who cleaves Baal in pieces' (*cf.* Dt. 32:26). This transitional form was perhaps further modified by the replacement of *ba'al* with *bōšeṯ*, 'shame' (*cf.* Ishbosheth, Jerubbesheth in 2 Sa. 11:21, and the LXX 'prophets of shame' for 'prophets of Baal' in 1 Ki. 18:19, 25). See *BDB*; Smith, *ICC*, *Samuel*, 1899, pp. 284–285; S. R. Driver, *Notes on the Hebrew Text of the Books of Samuel*[2], 1913, pp. 253–255 with references. On the other hand, Mephibosheth and Meribba'al may have been alternative names (*ISHBOSHETH).

There were two men of this name. **1.** The son of Jonathan, Saul's son. When they were killed he was 5 years old and became lame owing to an injury sustained in flight with his nurse (2 Sa. 4:4). David spared his life, gave him an honourable place at court for Jonathan's sake, and appointed Ziba, one of Saul's slaves, to serve him (2 Sa. 9; 21:7). Ziba's treachery and Mephibosheth's reconciliation with David at the time of Absalom's revolt are related in 2 Sa. 16:1–6; 19:24–30. **2.** Saul's son by his concubine Rizpah. He was among those executed by the Gibeonites to expiate Saul's massacre (2 Sa. 21:8). A.G.

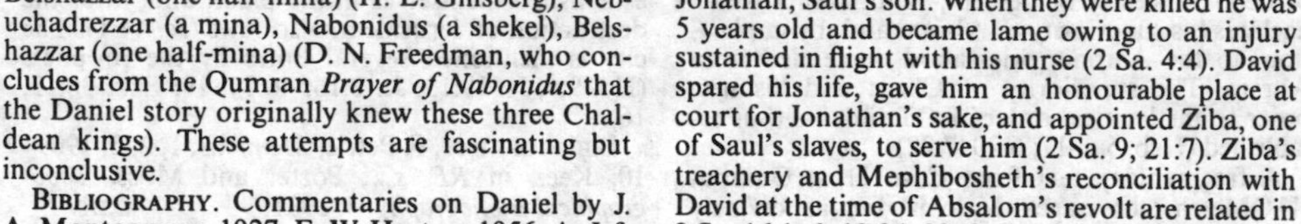

'MENE, MENE, TEKEL, and PARSIN' (mn' mn' tql prs), *written in the Aramaic script of the 6th–5th cent.* BC, *was interpreted by Daniel at Belshazzar's feast.*

MERAB. Saul's elder daughter (1 Sa. 14:49). She was promised to David but given instead to Adriel, the Meholathite (1 Sa. 18:17–20), an incident the LXX omits. Many scholars substitute Merab for Michal in 2 Sa. 21:8, regarding it as an ancient scribal error, saying that after her death her sons were hanged to atone for Saul's slaughter of the Gibeonites, a breaking of Israel's covenant (Jos. 9). M.B.

MERARI, MERARITES. Merari, third son of Levi, was founder of one of three great Levite families. His family was subdivided into the houses of Mahli and Mushi. In the wilderness the Merarites carried the tabernacle frames (boards), bars and sockets, and the court pillars, sockets, pins and cords. Four wagons and eight oxen were given them to help in the task. They encamped on the N side of the tabernacle. Their males over a month old numbered 6,200; those who actually served (age-group 30–50), 3,200 (Nu. 3:33–39; 4:42–45; 7:8). In the land they were assigned twelve cities (Jos. 21:7).

Under David's reorganization the Merarite family of Ethan (Jeduthun) shared in the Temple singing duties, while others were porters (1 Ch. 6:31–48; 25:3; 26:10–19). Merarites are mentioned as being present at the bringing up of the ark (1 Ch. 15:6), and again at the successive cleansings of the Temple under Hezekiah and Josiah (2 Ch. 29:12; 34:12). Some also are recorded as serving under Ezra (Ezr. 8:18–19) and Nehemiah (*cf.* Ne. 11:15 with 1 Ch. 9:14). D.W.G.

MERATHAIM (Heb. *m^erāṯayim*). A term found in Je. 50:21, having the dual meaning of 'double bitterness' or 'double rebellion'. Some hold that the dual expresses merely intensity of rebellion against the Lord (*cf.* v. 24); other scholars now suggest an identification of the word with Bab. *nār marrātu* (Persian Gulf) = S Babylonia (so *BDB*; *GTT*), but this is questionable. J.D.D.

MERCY, MERCIFUL. The tracing of the concept of mercy in the Eng. Bible is complicated by the fact that 'mercy', 'merciful' and 'have mercy upon' are translations of several different Heb. and Gk. roots, which are also variously rendered in other occurrences by other synonyms, such as 'kindness', 'grace', 'favour' (and cognate verbs). To picture this concept we would require a group of overlapping linguistic circles.

I. In the Old Testament

1. *ḥesed*: the etymological origin of this root is possibly 'keenness, eagerness' (Snaith). Its semantic core is best expressed by 'devotion'. Used nearly 250 times, it is translated in AV predominantly by 'mercy', but also by 'kindness', *'lovingkindness', 'goodness' (LXX, *eleos*; Luther, *Gnade*). Its range of meaning is: 'solidarity, kindness, grace' (G. Lisowsky, *Konkordanz*, 1958). It denotes devotion to a covenant, and so, of God, his covenant-love (Ps. 89:28). But God's faithfulness to a graciously established relationship with Israel or an individual, despite human unworthiness and defection, readily passes over into his mercy. 'This steady, persistent refusal of God to wash his hands of wayward Israel is the essential meaning of the Heb. word which is translated loving-kindness' (Snaith). RSV renders it often by 'loyalty', 'deal loyally', chiefly by 'steadfast love'.

2. *ḥānan* is translated in AV chiefly as 'have mercy upon', be 'gracious', 'merciful'; and *ḥēn* by 'grace' and 'favour' (LXX mostly *charis*). 'It is the gracious favour of the superior to the inferior, all undeserved' (Snaith).

3. *rāḥam* may share common origin with *reḥem*, meaning 'womb', and hence denote 'brotherly' or 'motherly feeling' (*BDB—cf.* Is. 13:18; 49:15). AV 'have mercy' or 'compassion', and once (Ps. 18:1) 'love'. The plural *raḥ^amîm* is rendered 'tender mercies' (LXX *splanchna*, *oiktirmoi*, *eleos*). It expresses the affective aspect of love: its compassion and pity. 'The personal God has a heart' (Barth).

II. In the New Testament

In NT the meanings of *ḥeseḏ* and *ḥēn* are largely combined in *charis*, *'grace'. The specific notion of mercy—compassion to one in need or helpless distress, or in debt and without claim to favourable treatment—is rendered by *eleos*, *oiktirmos* and *splanchnon* (and cognate verbs). Grace is concerned for man, as guilty; mercy, as he is miserable (R. C. Trench, *Synonyms of the New Testament*, pp. 166ff.).

God is 'the Father of mercies' (2 Cor. 1:3; Ex. 34:6; Ne. 9:17; Pss. 86:15; 103:8–14; Joel 2:13; Jon. 4:2). 'His compassion is over all that he has made' (Ps. 145:9), and it is because of his mercy that we are saved (Eph. 2:4; Tit. 3:5). Jesus was often 'moved with compassion' and he bids us to be 'merciful, as your Father also is merciful' (Lk. 6:36; Mt. 18:21ff.). Christians are to put on 'heartfelt compassion' (Col. 3:12). The merciful are blessed, and will receive mercy (Mt. 5:7; also Jas. 2:13, on which see R. V. G. Tasker, *TNTC*, *ad loc.*).

BIBLIOGRAPHY. N. H. Snaith, *The Distinctive Ideas of the Old Testament*, 1944; *TWBR*, ('Lovingkindness', 'Mercy'); Karl Barth, *Church Dogmatics*, 2, 1, 1957, section 30, pp. 368ff.; H.-H. Esser, *NIDNTT* 2, pp. 593–601. J.H.

MERODACH. The Heb. form of the Babylonian divine name Marduk. By the time of *Hammurapi (*c.* 1750 BC), on whose stela this god may be represented (*IBA*, fig. 24), the god Marduk (Sumerian *amar. utu*) had taken over many of the attributes of the god Enlil. Marduk was the primary deity of *Babylon and was later called by his epithet Bēl (Ba'al), so that his defeat was synonymous with that of his people (Je. 50:2) as was that of the earlier Canaanite *Ba'al'. The Babylonian epic of creation (*enuma eliš*) commemorates the god's victory over forces of evil and his honour as 'king of the gods'. Merodach occurs as the divine element in the Heb. rendering of Babylonian names, *Evil-merodach, *Merodach baladan and *Mordecai. D.J.W.

MERODACH-BALADAN. Known from cuneiform texts as the name of Marduk-apla-iddina II, the king of Babylon who sent an embassy to Hezekiah (Is. 39:1). The Heb. writing reflects the consonants of the name according to the methods of transcription used in the 8th and 7th centuries BC (*mrdkbldn*; 2 Ki. 20:12, Berodach-baladan, has a phonetic variant), the vowels being added by later

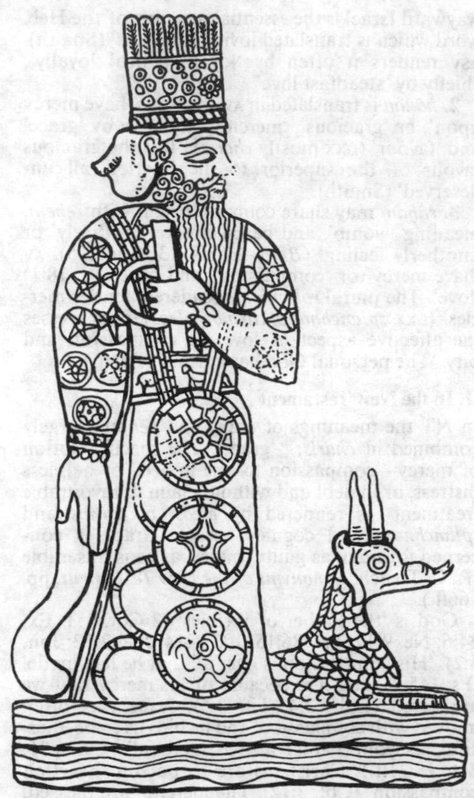

The Babylonian god Marduk (Heb. Merodach) wears a royal crown and holds the rod and ring, symbols of authority. He is here depicted on his symbol, a composite creature (mušruššu) *whose body was a serpent. Drawn from a curved cylinder found at Babylon (see p. 751).*

tradition. His father, not named in cuneiform sources, could have been called B l-iddin, giving the same consonants as Baladan (*bldn*) when transcribed into Hebrew (Is. 39:1). See *TynB* 22, 1971, pp. 125–126.

He was a ruler of the Chaldean district of Bit-Yakin, N of the Persian Gulf, who claimed descent from Eriba-Marduk king of Babylon 782–762 BC. When Tiglath-pileser III entered Babylonia in 731 BC, Merodach-baladan brought presents to him at Sapia and supported the Assyrians against a rebellious sheikh Ukīn-z r (*Iraq* 17, 1953, pp. 44–50). On the succession of Sargon in 721 BC Merodach-baladan entered babylon and claimed the throne. The assyrians reacted and attacked the elamite allies of babylon the following year.

The outcome of the battle is obscure except in that Merodach-baladan remained on the throne until 710 BC, when Sargon, having previously neutralized the Elamites, entered Babylon unopposed. When the Assyrians moved S into Bit-Yakin, Merodach-baladan was retained as local ruler and did not openly oppose his overlord during the rest of his reign.

On Sargon's death in 705 BC, however, Merodach-baladan began to work for his independence from Assyria. It was probably at this time that he sent an embassy to Hezekiah, which was shown the resources of Judah (2 Ki. 20:12–19; Is. 39), with the aim of encouraging action against Assyria by the W. Not only did Isaiah's opposition to this scheme thwart Merodach-baladan's plan, but the Babylonians themselves forestalled him by setting up their own nominee, Marduk-zakir-šum, in 704 BC. He deposed the newly appointed king in Babylon and ruled from nearby friendly Borsippa. Despite the aid of Elamite troops under Imbappa sent by Šutur-Naḫundu, Sennacherib defeated the rebels in battles at Kutha and Kish and entered Babylon, where he set Bel-ibni on the throne. Bit-Yakin alone was despoiled, and Merodach-baladan fled to SW Elam, where he subsequently died.

BIBLIOGRAPHY. J. A. Brinkman, in *Studies presented to A. L. Oppenheim*, 1964, pp. 6–53; *CAH* 3/2, 1991, pp. 26–36. D.J.W.

MEROM, WATERS OF (Heb. *mērôm*). Rendezvous of the Hazor confederacy against Joshua, who surprised and routed them there (Jos. 11:5, 7). It is not clear whether Merom is (*a*) modern Meiron, a village 5 km WNW of Safed (Safat), near springs which feed the Wadi Leimun or W Meiron (M. Noth, *Josua*², p. 67); or (*b*) Maroun er-Ras, 15 km to the N, above a valley leading to the Huleh basin N of Hazor (*LOB*, pp. 225f., proposing Tell el-Khirbeh, 3 km to the SSW). Whether or not it is the same as *Madon, Merom appears to have been an important site (Tuthmosis III list no. 85; *ANET*, p. 283); no such remains have been found at Meiron (E. Meyers, *BASOR* 214, 1974, pp. 2f.). J.P.U.L.

MERONOTHITE. Jehdeiah (1 Ch. 27:30) and Jadon (Ne. 3:7) were Meronothites. Ne. 3:7 seems to suggest that Meronoth was close to Gibeon and Mizpah, but Mizpah is a doubtful reading (*GTT*, p. 387). Grollenberg, *Atlas*, identifies it as Beitûniyeh, NW of Gibeon, following earlier studies. A.R.M.

MEROZ (Heb. *mērôz*), in Jdg. 5:23 a community (doubtfully identified with Khirbet Maruṣ, 12 km S of Barak's home at Kedesh-naphtali) on which Deborah pronounces a curse for its failure to take part in the campaign against Sisera. The bitterness of the curse suggests that Meroz was under a sacred obligation to obey Barak's summons. F.F.B.

MESHA. 1. King of Moab, succeeding his father who had reigned for 30 years and worshipped *Chemosh (Moabite Stone, 2–3). He rebelled after Ahab's death (2 Ki. 1:1; 3:5). Since an invasion of his territory by Judah, Israel and Edom failed, his breakaway may have occurred *c*. 853 BC while Ahab and Israel were engaging the Assyrians. The details of his reign on the *Moabite Stone record his building of towns and regulating the water-supply. His rebellion may have been an attempt to gain direct control of his considerable wool trade with Tyre (2 Ki. 3:4–5; *POTT*, pp. 235, 275).

2. Caleb's first-born son (1 Ch. 2:42, RSVmg.).

3. A Benjaminite born in Moab, son of Shaharaim by Hodesh (1 Ch. 8:9). D.J.W.

MESHA. A place mentioned as the limit of the territory of the descendants of Joktan (Gn. 10:30), the other limit being *Sephar. Some scholars would identify it with *maśśā'* in N Arabia (*MASSA), but the probable location of Sephar in S Arabia suggests a similar locality for Mesha, though no place of that name has been suggested in that region. T.C.M.

MESHACH (Heb. *mēšaḵ*). The name given to Mishael ('who is what God is'?), one of Daniel's companions in captivity at Babylon, by Nebuchadrezzar's chief eunuch (Dn. 1:7; 2:49, *etc.*). The most plausible meaning of the name suggested is the Bab. *mēšāku* ('I have become weak') perhaps given as similar to the Heb. name. D.J.W.

MESHECH (*MT mešeḵ*; LXX *Mosoch*). One of the sons of Japheth (Gn. 10:2 = 1 Ch. 1:5) here and elsewhere associated with Tubal. 1 Ch. 1:17 names him as a descendant of Shem by Aram, while the parallel passage (Gn. 10:23) gives the name as Mash. One of these is, presumably, an error, and LXX *Mosoch* in Gn. 10:23 suggests *k* has been lost there. The intermarriage implied by the presence of the same name among the children of Japheth and Shem, which such a view would involve, would not be impossible (*NATIONS, TABLE OF).

The descendants of Meshech are later mentioned as exporting slaves and copper (Ezk. 27:13), as a warlike people threatening from the N (Ezk. 32:26; 38:2–3; 39:1), and as typical of a barbarous society (Ps. 120:5). The close association of the name with Tubal renders likely their identification with the people often named together as *Tabâl* and *Musku* or *Mušku* in the Assyr. inscriptions and *Tibarēnoi* and *Moschoi* in Herodotus. The *muš-ka-a-ia* are first mentioned in the annals of Tiglath-pileser I (*c.* 1100 BC) as mounting an army of 20,000 men in the N, and it may be that they were already in the region SE of the Black Sea a century earlier when the Hittite texts mention one Mitas in that area, for this name is similar to that of the king of the Muški in the 8th century. They are mentioned in the annals of Tukulti-Ninurta II and Ashurnasirpal II in the 9th century and of Sargon in the 8th. This king gives their ruler's name as *mita-a*, which some scholars suggest is to be equated with Midas of Phrygia, the kingdom which succeeded the Hittites in Asia Minor, and that the Muški are therefore to be equated with the Phrygians. The name Mušku is not mentioned in the Achaemenian inscriptions, but Herodotus names the Moschoi as falling within the 19th Satrapy of Darius (3. 94) and as forming a contingent in the army of Xerxes (7. 78). This information leads to the conclusion that Meshech refers to a people perhaps speaking an Indo European language who entered the Near East from the N steppe, and imposed themselves as rulers upon the indigenous population of an area in E Anatolia.

BIBLIOGRAPHY. S. Parpola, *Neo-Assyrian Toponyms*, 1970, pp. 252–253; R. D. Barnett, *CAH*[3], 1975, pp. 417–442; J. N. Postgate, *Iraq* 35, 1973, pp. 21–34. T.C.M.

MESOPOTAMIA. The Gk. *Mesopotamia*, 'between the two rivers', is AV borrowing from LXX to render the Heb. *'ᵃram nahᵃrayim* (except in the title of Ps. 60). This was the fertile land E of the river Orontes covering the upper and middle Euphrates and the lands watered by the rivers Habur and Tigris, *i.e.* modern E Syria–N Iraq. It includes Harran (to which Abraham moved after leaving Ur in Babylonia) and its surrounding townships, to which Eliezer was sent to find a wife for Isaac (Gn. 24:10). Mesopotamia was the original home of Balaam (Dt. 23:4; *PEOR) and was the country ruled by Cushan-rishathaim when he oppressed Israel (Jdg. 3:8–10). In David's time Mesopotamia provided charioteers and horsemen to support his Ammonite opponents (1 Ch. 19:6). This accords with the evidence for the occupation of this whole area by horse-rearing Indo-Aryan Mitanni and Hurrians (*HORITES) in the 2nd millennium.

Greek and Roman writers after the 4th century BC extended the use of 'Mesopotamia' to describe the whole Tigris–Euphrates valley, that is, the modern state of Iraq. Thus Stephen referred to Abraham's original home of Ur in Babylonia as in 'Mesopotamia, before he lived in Haran' (Acts 7:2). The inclusion of Mesopotamians with Parthians, Medes and Elamites may indicate that the Jews of the Diaspora in Babylonia were present in Jerusalem to hear Peter (Acts 2:9). Thus the NT follows the wider use of the geographical name which is still adopted by some modern scholars.

See also *ARAM, *SYRIA, and for the history of the region, *ASSYRIA and *BABYLONIA.

BIBLIOGRAPHY. *JNES* 21, 1962, pp. 73–92, *Aram* 1, 1989, pp. 24–30. D.J.W.

MESSIAH.

I. In the Old Testament

This word, used as the official title of the central figure of expectation, is in the main a product of later Judaism. Its use is, of course, validated by the NT, but the term is found only twice in the OT (Dn. 9:25–26).

The idea of *anointing and of the anointed person is a well-established OT usage. One particular example, which has sometimes caused difficulty to OT students, is in fact specially helpful in defining the term. In Is. 45:1 the Persian, Cyrus, is addressed as 'his (*i.e.* Yahweh's) anointed (*mᵉšîḥô*)'. There are here five features which, in the light of the rest of Scripture, are clearly definitive of certain main lines of OT Messianism. Cyrus is a man of God's choice (Is. 41:25), appointed to accomplish a redemptive purpose towards God's people (45:11–13), and a judgment on his foes (47). He is given dominion over the nations (45:1–3); and in all his activities the real agent is Yahweh himself (45:1–7). The anointed status of Cyrus, as such, simply shows that there is a 'secular' (so to speak) usage of the terminology of Messiahship (*cf.* the 'anointing' of Hazael, 1 Ki. 19:15; and the description of Nebuchadrezzar as 'my servant', Is. 25:9). There could be no better summary of the OT view of the 'anointed' person; furthermore it is quite clear that these five points are pre-eminently true of the Lord Jesus Christ, who saw himself as the fulfilment of the OT Messianic expectations. In the light of this, the best and simplest plan for our study is to apply the word 'Messianic' to all those prophecies that place a person in the limelight as the figure of salvation (so Vriezen).

How old is the Messianic expectation? One major line of argument on this question (suggested by Mowinckel) is that the Messiah is an eschatological figure in the strict sense of the term: that is to say, not merely a figure of future hope, but emphatically belonging to the 'last days'. Consequently, since all properly defined eschatological passages look back upon the fall of the Davidic monarchy as a fact of past history, the Messiah must belong to post-exilic times, and is not found as a matter of prediction in pre-exilic documents. Seemingly Messianic passages belonging to monarchic times must be interpreted as simple addresses to the reigning king, and of no Messianic, that is, eschatological, significance. Later editing, it is urged, may have adapted them Messianically, and later Messianic writers may have drawn from them some of their imagery, but in themselves, and properly considered, they are not Messianic.

Against this it is urged (*e.g.* by Knight), with great weight, that it is hardly credible that the monarchs known to us in the books of Kings could have been seriously addressed or thought of in the terms used, for example, in the royal Psalms. We shall demonstrate this contention presently, and for the moment must be content to say that such passages point to a conception of Israelite kingship as such, and to an expectation resident in the kingly office itself. Even if Mowinckel has correctly insisted that Messiah must be an eschatological figure, by no means all OT specialists would agree that eschatology must be post-exilic (*cf.*, *e.g.*, Vriezen), but it may certainly be asked if he has not defined the concept of eschatology too rigidly. If, for example, he denies the description 'eschatological' to any passage which depicts the survival and life of a remnant after the divine intervention, the logical consequence of this is to deny that the Lord Jesus Christ is an eschatological figure, and thereby contradict the biblical view of the 'last days' (*e.g.* Heb. 1:2; 1 Jn. 2:18). It is much more satisfactory to define the Messiah as a 'teleological figure'. Unique in Israel was their apprehension of purpose in life. They possessed this awareness from the beginning (*cf.* Gn. 12:1–3), and this made them alone the true historians of the ancient world.

The specific attachment of this hope to a royal figure of the future is in no way dependent on the historical fall of the Monarchy, for the Davidic line was a failure from the start, and the expectation, even longing, for the royal Messiah need not be later than the time of Solomon. Our plan therefore will be to seek in the OT for a 'figure of salvation', and, by associating our search with Israelite teleology, rather than with a narrowly defined eschatology, we will find good reasons to hold that such a hope was early embraced by the chosen people, taking its rise from the famous 'protevangelium' of Gn. 3:15.

a. Messiah as the antitype of great historical figures

Israel's teleological view of life on earth, already mentioned, was rooted in the knowledge of the unique God who revealed himself to them. The faithfulness and self-consistency of their God provided them with a key to the future, in so far as it was necessary for faith to discern things to come. God had acted 'typically' and characteristically in certain great persons and events of the past, and, because God does not change, he will so act again. Three such persons of the past were specially woven into the Messianic pattern: Adam, Moses and David.

1. *The Messiah and Adam.* There are certain features of the Messianic future which are very clearly reminiscent of the Edenic state: for convenience we group them under the two headings of prosperity (Am. 9:13; Is. 4:2; 32:15, 20; 55:13; Ps. 72:16) and peace (the harmony of the world of living creatures: Is. 11:6–9; and of the world of human relations: Is. 32:1–8). Viewing the Fall in its effects purely upon this world, these were the things lost as God's curse took effect. When the curse is reversed and God's Man restores all things the Edenic scene reappears. This is not merely wishful thinking, but a logical and proper extension of the doctrine of creation by a holy God. All the passages cited above concern the Messianic King and the nature of his rule and kingdom. Here is the real recapitulation of the first man, who had 'dominion' over the rest of created things (Gn. 1:28; 2:19–20), but fell when he allowed his dominion to be usurped (*cf.* Gn. 3:13). Dominion will be restored in the Messiah. It may frankly be admitted that the notion of the Messiah as a new *Adam is neither lengthily nor specifically developed, 'but it is not unlikely that we have evidence that the royal ideology was sometimes influenced by the conception of the king of paradise' (Mowinckel). The NT doctrine of the 'Second Adam' has a clear OT root in the passages quoted.

2. *The Messiah and Moses.* It is not surprising that the Exodus and its leader should have so impressed the mind of Israel that the future was seen in this mould. As it was recorded and presented to succeeding generations of the nation, the pattern of the first Exodus constituted an eternal revelation of God (Ex. 3:15). The conception of the second Exodus is not always in a specifically Messianic setting. Sometimes the fact is stressed that God will do again what he did at the Exodus, only in a surpassing way, but without mentioning any man by whom God will so work as formerly he wrought by Moses (*e.g.* Ho. 2:14–23; Je. 31:31–34; Ezk. 20:33–44—note 'king' (RV, RSV) in v. 33: it may be that Moses is called 'king' in Dt. 33:5). Sometimes, however, the forecast of the second Exodus is Messianic, *e.g.* Is. 51:9–11; 52:12; Je. 23:5–8. Once again, it is only fair to notice that the matter is, at best, inferentially expressed. However, in the case of Moses we can take the study a stage farther, for we have his own prophecy recorded in Dt. 18:15–19 that the Lord will raise up a prophet 'like me'.

In general, the exegesis of this passage has tended to the exclusive advocacy of one or other point of view: either that the Messiah is here foretold or that the reference is simply to the providential provision of a continuing line of prophets. In recent work the latter has the support of the majority, although sometimes it has been allowed that the Messianic meaning may also, though secondarily, be admitted. However, the passage itself seems to require both interpretations, for some features in it can be satisfied only by the line of prophets, and others only by the Messiah.

Thus the context is very weighty for the former view. Moses insistently warning his hearers against Canaanite abomination stresses especially divinatory practices for ascertaining the future. The warning is buttressed by this prophecy of the Mosaic Prophet. Here, says Moses, is the Israelite alternative to divination; the living are not to consult the dead, for the God of Israel will speak to his people through a man raised up for that purpose. This seems to be a promise of continuous revelation; a prediction of a far-off Messiah would not meet the need for guidance of which Moses is speaking.

Again, vv. 21–22, supplying a test for prophets, may be seen as anticipating the situation which often arose in the days of the canonical prophets, and which caused such bitterness of soul to Jeremiah (23:9ff.). However, this consideration is not of equal weight with the foregoing, for it would not be at all improper that some test for the Messiah should be provided. A false Messiah is as likely as a false prophet and, indeed, to take the matter no farther, Jesus himself rested his claims on the coincidence of his words and works, and his Jewish opponents were continually pressing for an unequivocal Messianic sign.

If we take Moses' words as prophetic of a line of prophets, they were, of course, amply fulfilled. Every true prophet was 'like Moses', for he existed to teach Moses' doctrine. Both Jeremiah (23:9ff.) and Ezekiel (13:1–14:11) distinguish the true prophet from the false by the content of his message: the true prophet has a word to speak against sin, the false prophet has not. This is simply to say that the theology of true *prophecy derives from Sinai. This truth is taught also in Deuteronomy, for the question of false prophecy is raised in ch. 13, and it is precisely required that every prophet must be brought into comparison with the Exodus revelation (vv. 5, 10) and with the teaching of Moses (v. 18). Moses is the normative prophet; every true prophet, as such, is a prophet 'like Moses'.

But there is another side to the exegesis of this passage. According to Dt. 34:10, Moses is unique, and his like has not yet appeared. On any view of the date of Deuteronomy, this verse points to an understanding of Dt. 18:15ff. as Messianic: for if Deuteronomy is as late as some hold, or if 34:10 represents later editorial comment, then we are here being informed that no single prophet, nor yet the prophets collectively, fulfilled the prediction of 18:15ff.

Furthermore, when we come to the passage itself, special regard ought to be paid to the very precise terms of the comparison with Moses. The passage does not say, in a large and undefined way, that there will arise a prophet 'like Moses', but specifically a prophet who, in his person and work, may be compared with Moses at Horeb (v. 16). Now this comparison was not fulfilled by any of the OT prophets. Moses at Horeb was the mediator of the covenant; the prophets were preachers of the covenant and foretellers of its successor. Moses was an originator; the prophets were propagators. With Moses, Israel's religion entered a new phase; the prophets fought for the establishment and maintenance of that phase, and prepared the way for the next, to which they looked forward. The strict requirement of vv. 15–16, therefore, can be met only by Messiah.

How, then, are these two interpretations to be reconciled? We remarked above, relative to Israel's continuing need of the voice of God, that a far-off Messiah would not meet that need. In so saying, we spoke as if 20th-century information was at the disposal of the ancient Israelite. This passage certainly foretells the prophet-Messiah, but it says nothing about his being 'far off'. Only the actual passage of time could show that. Here, then, is the reconciliation: in respect of prophets, Israel was in exactly the same situation as in respect of kings (see further, below). The line of kings proceeded under the shadow of the promise of the coming great King, and each successive king was hailed in deliberately Messianic terms, both to remind him of his vocation to a certain type of kingship and to express the national longing that at last Messiah might have come. So too with the prophets. They likewise live under the shadow of the promise; they too have a pattern to fulfil. Each king must be, as best he can, like the king of the past (David) until the coming of the One who is able to reformulate the Davidic type and be the king of the future; so, too, each prophet must be, as best he can, like the prophet of the past (Moses) until the coming of the One who is able to reformulate the Mosaic type and be the prophet, lawgiver and mediator of the future, new covenant.

3. *The Messiah and David.* The dying Jacob is recorded (and there is no good reason for doubting the ascription) as prophesying about the future of his sons. The prophecy about Judah has deservedly attracted great attention (Gn. 49:9–10). Dispute has necessarily centred on the meaning of *'aḏ kî yāḇô' šîlôh*. Ezk. 21:27 seems to suggest the interpretation 'until he come, whose right it is', and this certainly is the most venerable approach to the problem. More recently the view has been taken that we have here an Akkadian loan-word meaning 'his (*i.e.* Judah's) ruler'. At all events, tribal rule is vested in Judah, and some pre-eminent Judahite ruler is foreseen as the consummation of the sovereignty. In an initial, and at the same time normative, sense, this came to pass in David of Judah, with whom all succeeding kings, for good or ill, were compared (*e.g.* 1 Ki. 11:4, 6; 14:8; 15:3, 11–14; 2 Ki. 18:3; 22:2). However, it is one thing to see that David, as a matter of fact, was the normative king; it is another matter altogether to say just why he should be the type of the king to come. The prophecy of Nathan (2 Sa. 7:12–16) does not precisely require a single king as its fulfilment, but rather predicts a stable house, kingdom and throne for David. We must presume that, as from Solomon's later years failure and declension set in, the days of David glowed brighter and brighter in Israel's memory, and hope crystallized into the 'David' of the future (*e.g.* Ezk. 34:23). This expectation is shown particularly by two groups of passages.

(i) The Psalms. There are certain psalms which centre on the king, and they depict a very precise character and career. Summarizing, this king meets world-opposition (2:1–3; 110:1), but, as a victor (45:3–5; 89:22–23), and by the activity of Yahweh (2:6, 8; 18:46–50; 21:1–13; 110:1–2), he establishes world-rule (2:8–12; 18:43–45; 45:17; 72:8–11; 89:25; 110:5–6), based on Zion (2:6) and marked by a primary concern for morality (45:4, 6–7; 72:2–3, 7, 101.1–8). His rule is everlasting (21.4, 45.6, 72:5); his kingdom is peaceful (72:7), prosperous (72:16) and undeviating in reverence for Yahweh (72:5). Pre-eminent among men (45:2, 7), he is the friend of the poor and the enemy of the oppressor (72:2–4, 12–14). Under him the righteous flourish (72:7). He is remembered for ever (45:17), possesses an everlasting name (72:17) and is the object of unending thanks (72:15). In relation to Yahweh, he is the recipient of his everlasting blessing (45:2). He is the heir of David's covenant (89:28–37; 132:11–12) and of Melchizedek's priesthood

(110:4). He belongs to Yahweh (89:18) and is devoted to him (21:1, 7; 63:1–8, 11). He is his son (2:7; 89:27), seated at his right hand (110:1), and is himself divine (45:6).

The Messianic pattern as deduced from Cyrus above is clearly here. It is inconceivable that such notions were entertained in any directly personal way concerning the line of monarchs who followed David in Judah. We have here, therefore, either the most blatant flattery the world has ever heard, or else the expression of a great ideal. Some comment is necessary on the ascription of divinity in Ps. 45:6. Unquestionably there are ways in which the address to the king as 'God' may legitimately be avoided (see Johnson), but such interpretations are not necessary in the light of the fact so clearly taught elsewhere in the OT that a divine Messiah was expected. It is no argument against this that v. 7 of the psalm, still addressing the king, speaks of 'God, your God'. Certainly we are intended to gather that there is some distinction between God and the king, even if the king can be spoken of as 'God', but this need occasion no surprise, because exactly the same thing occurs throughout Messianic expectation, as we shall see, and also in the case, for example, of the * Angel of the Lord, who is both himself divine and also distinct from God.

(ii) Isaiah 7–12, *etc*. The most sustained treatment of the Davidic–Messianic theme occurs in Isaiah 1–37 and in particular in the self-contained unit, chs. 7–12. From 745 BC onwards, pressure towards the W from the awakening imperialism of Assyria forced all the Palestinian states to look to their security. Aram and Israel (Ephraim) allied themselves for mutual defence and sought the additional strength of a united Palestinian front. When, as it seems, Judah stood aloof from this Syro-Ephraimite alliance, pressure was exerted to bring the S kingdom to a better mind. It is unnecessary to review the course of the events (*cf*. 2 Ki. 15:37–16:20; 2 Ch. 28); rather we must concentrate on sharing Isaiah's view of the matter. It is clear that he saw the threat as transitory (7:7, 16) but the moment as decisive for the future of the people of God. If in the face of this threat there should be a refusal to find security in Yahweh alone and a seeking of security in any sort of worldly pact, then in the prophet's view not just the current king (Ahaz) but the Davidic dynasty itself would be exposed as faithless; it would have rejected the promises and pleadings of its God in a decisive and final way and doom would follow. For this reason he identifies Ahaz with the dynasty (7:2, 13, 17), calls for a policy of total reliance on Yahweh (7:4, 'Take care that you do nothing'), warns that the issue of faith will settle the fortunes of the dynasty and nation (7:9), offers in Yahweh's name the provision of a sign of such magnitude as would virtually compel faith (7:10–11) and when this is rejected speaks of another sign, Immanuel, wherein the hope of the nation is seen as overwhelmed in the triumph of Assyria (7:14ff.).

There is a logic, therefore, about 7:1–25. There comes a moment when faith is decisively offered and beyond that offer lies only the doom which comes on unbelief. But for Isaiah this creates as many problems as it solves. It is one thing to say that the unbelieving Ahaz is doomed by his faithlessness, and dooms the dynasty and nation with him. But what of the promises themselves? Does God go back on his word? Does the promise of a Davidic king itself fail simply because Ahaz faithlessly refuses to enter into it? Is God's Messianic plan to that extent dependent on the choice of man? It is to this problem that Isaiah addresses himself in this section of his book and his treatment of it centres on the figure of Immanuel.

Immanuel must be approached first in relation to what is said of his birth: it is described as a 'sign' and as birth of an *'almâ*. On neither count is Isaiah's meaning uncontroverted. 'Sign' is used in the OT of a present persuader (as in 7:11; *cf*. Dt. 13:1) and of a future confirmation (*e.g*. Ex. 3:12). In which sense is Immanuel a 'sign'? Regarding Immanuel's mother, the majority opinion of specialists insists that the word *'almâ* means a young woman of marriageable age who, in this case, in the light of her pregnant state, must be assumed to be married and that if Isaiah had meant *virgo intacta* he must needs use another word, *bᵉṯûlâ*. The issue, however, is not as settled as some commentators would suggest. 'From a survey of non-biblical evidence we may safely conclude that the word *'almâ*, in so far as may be ascertained, was never used of a married woman,' says E. J. Young (*Studies in Isaiah*, 1954, p.170); and of the eight other occasions on which the word is used in the Bible, there is no reason in any case to assume married state. The sequence of Gn. 24:14, 16, 43 is specially notable: Abraham's servant prays for a 'girl' (v. 14, *naᵃrâ*); when Rebekah comes he notes that she is marriageable but unmarried (v. 16, a *bᵉṯûlâ* whom man had not known); with this knowledge at his disposal he summarizes the whole story for Rebekah's family using *'almâ* (v. 43). In passing, it is important to ask why, if *bᵉṯûlâ* is virtually a technical term for 'virgin', it needs to be qualified on a number of significant occasions, as in Gn. 24:16 (*cf*. Lv. 21:3; Jdg. 11:39; 21:12). There is, in fact, strong ground for urging that Isaiah used *'almâ* because it is the nearest word in Hebrew which expresses *virgo intacta* and that Matthew practised no sleight of hand in accepting the rendering *parthenos* (1:23).

Secondly, Isaiah sets Immanuel in the context of the hope of Israel. Chs. 7–11 form an integrated unit of prophetic teaching in which 7:1–9:7 focuses on the S kingdom (Judah) and 9:8–11:16 on the N (Jacob, 9:8). Each section passes through the same four sub-sections: the moment of decision (7:1–17; 9:8–10:4), the judgment (7:18–8:8; 10:5–15), the remnant (8:9–22; 10:16–34) and the glorious hope (9:1–7; 11:1–16). As this sequence is followed through, the wonder-child, Immanuel (the possessor, 8:8, and security, 8:10, of his people) becomes, as the focus clarifies, the royal deliverer of 9:1–7 and the righteous king of 11:1–16. In each place he is a world-ruler (9:7; 11:10) and in each place the element of mystery regarding his person remains. In 9:6 he who sits on David's throne (v. 7) is also 'mighty God'—and in the light of the identical wording referring without equivocation to Yahweh in 10:21 it is exegetically unworthy to refuse either the translation or its clear implication here—and in 11:1, 10 he who springs out of the stock of Jesse is also the root of Jesse.

Thirdly, we must attempt to relate Immanuel and Maher-shalal-hash-baz (8:1–4). We noted above a problem whether, considered as a sign, Immanuel must be understood as a present persuader or a future confirmation. The implication of 7:15–17 that he would be born heir to the Assyrian devastations of Judah might appear to settle the point. Yet Isaiah seems, with a certain amount of emphasis and deliberation, to transfer the task of being an immediate sign to his own son (8:1–4) and in the rest of chs. 8–9 there is a plain contrast between this immediate child with a fourfold name of doom (8:1–4) and one whose birth comes 'in the latter time' (9:1) and who has a fourfold name of glory (9:6). Did Isaiah then change his mind about Immanuel and the date of his birth? Or how are we to understand this odd tension in the evidence? We come nearest to a solution if we assume that from the start Isaiah saw Immanuel's birth as a coming confirmation of the divine rejection of Ahaz and the Davidic dynasty as represented by him: the great, expected king would be born in the line of Ahaz to inherit an empty title, a meaningless crown, and a subjugated people. Were Immanuel to have been born there and then, that would have been the case; when, as we know, Immanuel was born, it was still the case. Isaiah gently eases the birth of Immanuel out of the present and into the undated future by the substitution of the birth of his own son and the open dating of 'the latter time' (9:1).

b. Other Messianic figures

1. *The Servant*. Isaiah 40–55 is dominated by the Messianic portrayal of the Servant (42:1–4; 49:1–6; 50:4–9; 52:13–53:12). The Servant is Yahweh's anointed (42:1), exercises the royal functions of 'judgment' (*mišpāṭ*, 42:1, 3–4) and dominion (53:12), displays prominently the marks of a prophet (49:1–2; 50:4), extends a ministry to Gentiles (42:1, 4; 49:6b) and to Israel (49:5–6a), is the agent in a world-wide revelation (42:1, 3–4) and salvation (49:6), and, not as priest but as victim, voluntarily submits to a death interpreted in the substitutionary terms of the levitical sacrifices (53:4–6, 8, 10–12).

The link between the first Servant Song and its context may be seen in the double 'behold' of 41:29; 42:1. The former verse is the climax of Isaiah's awareness of Gentile need; the latter is the introduction of one who will bring *mišpāṭ* to the Gentiles ('The religion of Jehovah regarded as a system of practical ordinances', Skinner, *Isaiah*, 1905, *ad loc.*). Both in relation to creation (40:12–31) and history (41:1–29) the God of Israel is the only God. This constitutes the ground for a word of comfort to Israel (40:1–11; 41:8–20) but it also exposes the plight of the larger part of the created and historical world (40:18–20, 25; 41:5–7, 21–24, 28–29). The Servant is divinely endowed (42:1) precisely to meet this need (42:1b, 3b–4).

Between the first and second Servant Songs a significant movement of thought develops. The first Song does not raise the question of the identity of the Servant but concentrates on his task. No sooner, however, has Yahweh confirmed this task as his will for his Servant (42:5–9) and committed himself to its accomplishment (42:10–17) than the prophet turns to an exposure of the plight of Israel (42:18–25). This significant passage must be deeply pondered by all who would understand this central section of the Isaianic literature: the nation of Israel is blind, deaf (vv. 18–19), enslaved (v. 22), under judgment for sin (vv. 23–25a) and spiritually unperceptive (v. 25b). In the sequence of the chapters, we have thus been informed that the Servant cannot be the nation. But Isaiah has not our preoccupation with the Servant's identity and proceeds (43:1–44:23) to indicate in promissory fashion that both the political (43:1–21) and spiritual (43:22–44:23) needs of Israel will be met by Yahweh. His provision in the former category is Cyrus (44:24–48:22), before whom Babylon falls (46:1–47:15) and by whom Israel leaves captivity (48:20–22).

A major preoccupation in Is. 48 is the sinfulness of Israel (vv. 1, 4–5, 7–8, 18, 22). Two things thus lie side by side: release from Babylon and continuance in sin. V. 22 is an apt climax and an equally apt introduction to the second Song. A change of address (from Babylon to home) is not a change of heart; the people may have come back to the land but they have yet to come back to Yahweh. That which has been promised of spiritual redemption (43:22–44:23) is to be fulfilled by the Servant who inherits the name they have forfeited (49:3; *cf.* 48:1) and, without loss of the task of bringing salvation to the Gentiles, adds the task of bringing Jacob to Yahweh (49:5–6).

The third Song in its content displays the Servant as the totally obedient one, suffering for obedience' sake, and in its context sets the Servant apart from even the faithful among the people of God. In contrast to Zion, despondent (49:14–26), and unresponsive (50:1–3), the Servant responds to Yahweh (50:4–5) with buoyant, optimistic faith (50:6–9) and becomes the Exemplar of all who would fear Yahweh (50:10): indeed, apart from the Servant, man is left to his own powers of self-illumination and under divine disapproval (50:11).

The command to watch ('Behold', 52:13) is in effect the climax of a number of addresses to the faithful (51:1, 4, 7) seen in their own persons or typified as Jerusalem/Zion (51:17; 52:1). Thus Isaiah continues to distinguish the Servant from the remnant until he stands out in terms 'unmistakably individual' (H. H. Rowley, *The Servant of the Lord*, 1965, p.52), internationally triumphant (52:13–15), rejected (53:1–3), sin-bearing (53:4–6), voluntarily the innocent sufferer of lawlessness, consigned to have 'his grave with wicked men, but with a rich man in his death' (53:7–9), yet living to dispense the fruits of his dying, the worthy recipient of the divine accolade, 'I will give him the many as his portion and he will take the strong as spoil' (53:10–12). And in all this, the universality of the Servant's redemptive work is not forgotten. The call goes first to the barren Zion (54:1–17) to enter peace (54:10) and to inherit righteousness (54:14, 17), and then to the whole world to enter a free salvation (55:1–2) and to enjoy the mercies promised to David (55:3).

The delineation of the Servant is thus straightforward and unified, but the person of the Servant retains its proper element of mystery: a man among men (53:2–3) who is also 'the arm of the Lord' (53:1). Aptly, Mowinckel brings out the proper emphasis: 'Who could have believed what we have heard? Who could have seen here the arm of Yahweh?' (53:1). For the 'arm of Yahweh' is none other than Yahweh himself (52:10) acting again as he acted at the Exodus and the Red Sea to redeem and ransom (51:9–11).

2. *The anointed Conqueror*. The third section of the Isaianic literature completes the Messianic forecast. Isaiah has shown in chs. 1–37 a world-wide king but yet without indicating how the Gentiles will be gathered in. In his delineation of the Servant he has foretold a world-wide salvation, bringing all the redeemed under David's rule. Both these sections have included but without emphasis the exacting of vengeance on Yahweh's foes (*e.g.*

9:3–5; 42:13, 17; 45:16, 24; 49:24–26). This topic now predominates as one who, like the King (11:2, 4) and the Servant (42:1; 49:2), is anointed with the Spirit and the Word (59:21), steps on to the scene.

The vision of the world-wide house of prayer (56:1–8) is in danger of perishing under the weight of self-seeking princes (56:9ff.), religious corruption (57:3ff.), inability to rise to the heights of truly spiritual religion (58:1ff.) and to find the way of peace (59:1ff.). Under these circumstances, and in default of there being any other Saviour, Yahweh himself dons the garments of salvation (59:16–20) bringing a Redeemer to Zion. Mysteriously, however, the covenant which ensues is addressed to one endowed with Yahweh's Spirit and speaking Yahweh's words (59:21), but plainly this Zion-orientated work is world-wide for at once the universal call is issued (60:1ff.). In a manner reminiscent of the literary method of chs. 40–55, the affirmation that Yahweh will hasten the great vision to its fulfilment (60:22) merges into the testimony of one endowed with Yahweh's Spirit and Word to comfort (61:1–2a) and avenge (v. 2b). The work of comfort occupies the prophet until the end of ch. 62 and it is now the endowed One who dons the garments of Salvation (61:10–11) as formerly (59:16f.) did Yahweh himself. The mighty 63:1–6 relates the work of redemption to its counterpart in vengeance wherein one working alone (as Yahweh was alone, 59:16) treads the winepress and exacts a full penalty.

In his person, this Messianic Conqueror hardly differs from the king and the Servant. He has the same spiritual endowment; he is a man among men. But two other sidelights are given. First, he is described as the conqueror of Edom, a task accomplished by no other Israelite king but David (*cf.* Nu. 24:17–19). May we not see here the identity of the anointed Conqueror with the Davidic Messiah? Secondly, in the development of the theme it is he who at the last wears the garments of salvation and vengeance which Yahweh himself was seen to don (59:16ff.). Once more the prophet introduces the Messianic motif: the identity and the distinction of Yahweh and his Anointed.

3. *The Branch*. Under this Messianic label there is a beautifully unified series of predictions. Je. 23:5ff. and 33:14ff. are virtually identical. Yahweh will raise a Branch 'for David'. He is a king in whose days Israel will be saved. His rule is marked by judgment and righteousness. His name is 'Yahweh our Righteousness'.

The second of these passages associates the Branch prophecy with the assertion that the priests shall never want a man to offer sacrifice. This might seem somewhat extraneous were it not for the subsequent use made by Zechariah of the same Messianic figure. In Zc. 3:8 Joshua and his fellow-priests are declared to be a sign of Yahweh's purpose to bring forth 'my servant the Branch', who will accomplish the priestly work of removing the iniquity of the land in one day. Again, in 6:12ff., Zechariah returns to the Branch, who shall grow up in his place, build the Temple of Yahweh, be a priest upon his throne, and enjoy perfect, covenanted peace with Yahweh. The Branch is clearly, therefore, the Messiah in his kingly and priestly offices. He is the fulfilment of Ps. 110, with its designation of the king as an eternal Melchizedek-priest.

Having reached this point, it is now fair to refer to Is. 4:2–6. The Messianic reference of v. 2 is a matter of dispute, and is often denied, but, seeing that the following verses agree exactly with the use of the Branch in the passages already cited, the inference need not be resisted that the Messiah is found here too. He is the Branch of Yahweh, and he is associated with the priestly work of washing away the filth of the daughters of Zion (v. 4) and with the kingly reign of Yahweh in Jerusalem (vv. 5–6). The picture of the Branch summarizes in one figure what Isaiah elsewhere extended and analysed into the work of King, Servant and Conqueror. The Messianic motifs of humanity and divinity, and of identity and distinction in Deity, are present, for the Branch 'belongs to David' and yet is 'Yahweh's'—the very imagery speaking of origin and nature; he is 'my servant', and yet his name is 'Yahweh our righteousness'.

4. *The seed of the woman*. We have noticed throughout this study that the humanity of the Messiah is stressed. In particular, it is often through the mother that the human origin is described. It is easy to over-emphasize small details, but nevertheless it should be noted that both Immanuel (Is. 7:14) and the Servant (Is. 49:1) are cases in point. Likewise, Mi. 5:3 speaks of 'she who is in travail', and very likely the difficult Je. 31:22 refers to the conception and birth of a remarkable child. The most notable prophecy of the seed of the woman, and the one from which the whole notion may well have arisen, is given in Gn. 3:15. It has become almost an accepted thing to refuse any Messianic reference here, and to regard the verse as 'a quite general statement about mankind and serpents, and the struggle between them' (Mowinckel). But as a direct matter of the exegesis of these chs. in Genesis, it is unfair to isolate this verse from its context and to treat it aetiologically. In order to see the force of the promise made in 3:15, we must pay heed to the part played by the serpent in the tragedy of the Fall. Gn. 2:19 shows man's superiority over the animal creation. The Creator graciously instructs the man as to his difference from the mere animals: he can impose his order upon them, but among them is not found any 'help meet for him'. His like is not there.

But now, in Gn. 3, another phenomenon meets us: a talking animal, an animal which somehow has risen above its station, and presents itself as man's equal, able to engage him in intelligent conversation, and even as his superior, able to instruct him in matters wherein he was formerly misguided, to give him what purports to be a correct understanding of God's law and God's person. The serpent speaks as one well able to weigh God in the balances and find him wanting, to discern the inner thoughts of the Almighty and to expose his underhand motives! Even more, he displays open hostility to God; a hatred of God's character, a readiness to destroy his creation-plan, a sneering mockery of the Most High. It is simply not good enough to see in the serpent the spirit of man's irrepressible curiosity (Williams) or any such thing. The Bible knows only one who displays this ungodly arrogance, this hatred of God, and it is no wonder that the serpent in Eden becomes 'that ancient serpent, who is the Devil and Satan' (Rev. 20:2). But where sin abounds, grace superabounds, and so it is that at the very moment when Satan seems to have scored a signal triumph it is declared that the seed of the woman will crush and destroy Satan. He will be himself bruised in the process, but will be victorious. The seed of the woman will reverse the whole calamity of the Fall.

5. *The Son of man.* On Dn. 7, a passage which has aroused so much discussion and difference of opinion, it is only possible here, as throughout this article, to state one point of view. The essence of the vision is the judgment scene, wherein the Ancient of Days disposes of the worldly and hostile powers—we note in passing the reappearance of the kingly motif of Ps. 2—and there is brought to him 'with the clouds of heaven . . . one like a son of man' who receives a universal and everlasting dominion. It is clear that the general reference here must be associated in some way with the universal dominion already generally observed in the Messianic passages, but the question whether the 'one like a son of man' is the Messianic individual or is intended to be a personification of the people of God must not be thus summarily settled. It is urged that vv. 18 and 22 speak of judgment and the kingdom being given to the 'saints of the Most High', and that therefore reason demands that the same recipients must be intended by the single figure of vv. 13–14.

However, we may also notice that there is a double description of the beasts who are the enemies of the saints. V. 17 says 'these four great beasts . . . are four kings' and v. 23 says the fourth beast 'shall be a fourth kingdom'. The figures are both individual (kings) and corporate (kingdoms). We must adopt the same preliminary reference for the 'one like a son of man'. Next, we must view the king–kingdom relationship in its OT context. The king is prior, and the kingdom is derivative. It is not the kingdom which fashions the king, but the reverse. As for the beast-kings, they are the personal enemies of the kingdom of the saints, and they involve their kingdoms with them; equally the 'one like a son of man' receives universal dominion, and in this is implicated the dominion of his people (*cf.* the dominion of Israel in the dominion of the conqueror, Is. 60, *etc.*). On this ground it is urged that the 'one like a son of man' is the Messianic individual. As such, he fits into the general pattern found throughout the whole series of expectations: he is a king, opposed by the world, but achieving universal dominion by the zeal of the Lord, *i.e.* from the Ancient of Days, in Daniel's imagery; he is man, by the terms of his title, and yet he does not originate among men but comes 'with the clouds of heaven', a position characteristic of God (see, *e.g.*, Ps. 104:3; Na. 1:3; Is. 19:1). Here is the same polarity of human and divine which is found almost without exception in OT Messianism, and which ought by now to occasion us no surprise.

6. *The anointed Prince.* It is something to say of any passage of the OT that it has attracted more interpretative enquiry and suggestion than any other, yet this is probably the case with Dn. 9:24–27. There is, however, a measure of appropriateness in attempting to urge one or two generalities in connection with it for, having begun our review with a secular 'anointed prince', Cyrus, it has at least the virtue of neatness to end it with the anointed Messiah himself.

The verses themselves fall into two unequal parts: clearly vv. 25–27 indicate a programme to be worked out in history. It starts with a command to rebuild Jerusalem (v. 25), from which a period of 62 weeks stretches until the coming of 'an anointed one, a prince'. V. 26 looks to what happens 'after the sixty-two weeks', and v. 27 brings matters to a 'decreed end'. V. 24, however, stands apart as offering a total statement of the purposes which are thus to be accomplished: three are negative, to finish transgression, put an end to sin and to atone for (*kipper*, to pay the atonement price) iniquity; three are positive, to introduce everlasting righteousness, to attest the veracity of vision and prophet and to anoint a most holy place (lit., a 'holiness of holinesses', elsewhere referring to the innermost shrine of the tabernacle, Ex. 26:33, the altar of burnt offering, Ex. 29:37, the tabernacle and all its furnishings, Ex. 30:29, the incense, Ex. 30:36, the priestly portions of the cereal-offerings, sin-offering, guilt-offering, Lv. 2:3, 10; 6:17, 25; 7:1, 6, the bread of the Presence, Lv. 24:9 (Nu. 4:7), and every 'devoted thing' including persons, Lv. 27:28). While there are in this statement of purpose a few difficulties with individual words and some unique expressions, the meaning of the whole cannot be in doubt: 'that the messianic age is to be marked by the abolition and forgiveness of sin, and by perpetual righteousness' (S. R. Driver, *Daniel*, 1900, p. 136).

It is very difficult to see how any such exalted purpose is explicable in terms of those interpretations which focus the prophecy on Antiochus Epiphanes: 7 'weeks' elapse between Jeremiah's prophecy (*cf.* Dn. 9:2) and the anointed prince, Cyrus; 62 weeks cover the history of Jerusalem to the high-priesthood of Onias III in 175 BC who was 'cut off', anointed one though he was, being assassinated and replaced by his brother. The 'prince' of v. 26 is Antiochus himself. But where, one might reasonably ask, is the finishing of transgression, the paying of the atoning price, the bringing in of everlasting righteousness?

To base the passage on the Lord Jesus Christ involves no greater exercise of hindsight than does the Antiochus-theory and, on the contrary, provides a more persuasive use of individual expressions and a complete satisfaction of the purposes stated in v. 24. The period between the decree and the anointed prince is in total 69 weeks (v. 25, lit. as NASB, 'From the issuing of a decree . . . [there will be] seven weeks and sixty-two weeks.') The division into two may well mark the period between Cyrus and Ezra–Nehemiah (a noteworthy point in the city's history) and between then and the coming of 'an anointed one, a prince'. During his 'week' the anointed one 'empowers a covenant with many' (v. 27) and causes sacrifice to cease—though, as we know, the meaningless, post-Calvary ritual slaughter of animals continued till the desolator brought the old Temple itself to an end.

It is one thing to wrest words into unnatural shapes to make them fit later knowledge. It is another altogether to refuse the aid of later light in trying to elucidate obscurities. That Daniel was instructed to expect one who would mean the end of sin's long reign, the eternal establishment of righteousness, and the inauguration of true religion, cannot be controverted, nor can it be controverted even remotely, that not until Jesus, nor with any necessity after him, has such been accomplished, nor in any other has the whole range of OT Messianism found its goal, the attestation of both vision and prophet.

BIBLIOGRAPHY. H. Ringgren, *The Messiah in the OT*, 1956; A. Bentzen, *King and Messiah*, 1956; S. Mowinckel, *He that Cometh*, 1956; J. Klausner, *The Messianic Idea in Israel*, 1956; H. L. Ellison, *The Centrality of the Messianic Idea for the Old Testament*, 1953; B. B. Warfield, 'The Divine

Messiah in the Old Testament', in *Biblical and Theological Studies*, 1952; H. H. Rowley, *The Servant of the Lord*, 1952; A. R. Johnson, *Sacral Kingship in Ancient Israel*, 1955; *IDB*, *s.v.* 'Messiah'; Y. Kaufmann, *The Religion of Israel*, 1961; G. A. F. Knight, *A Christian Theology of the Old Testament*, 1959; J. A. Motyer, 'Context and Content in the Interpretation of Is. 7:14', *TynB* 21, 1970; G. J. Wenham, '*Bᵉ TULAH*, "A Girl of Marriageable Age"' *VT* 22, 1972, pp. 326–347; E. J. Young, *Daniel's Vision of the Son of Man*, 1958; P. and E. Achtemeier, *The Old Testament Roots of our Faith*, 1962. J.A.M.

II. In the New Testament

Christos, 'anointed', is the Gk. equivalent of Heb. *māšîaḥ*, Aram. *mᵉšîḥā'* (transliterated as *messias* in Jn. 1:41; 4:25, in both cases glossed by *christos*). In the vast majority of NT uses, either alone or in the combination *Iēsous Christos*, it is apparently used as a name for Jesus without necessary reference to its original sense, as 'Christ' is in modern usage. Such uses (largely found in the NT letters, though some also in Acts and Rev., and a few in the Gospels) are not discussed in this article.

a. The Gospels

Particularly in the Gospel of John (1:20, 25, 41; 4:25, 29; 7:26f., 31, 41f.; 9:22; 10:24; 11:27) but also in the Synoptic Gospels (Mk. 8:29; 14:61; Lk. 2:11, 26; 3:15; 4:41) *christos* usually denotes the expected deliverer in a quite general sense. Such uses convey the impression of a widespread and eager expectation, without implying any specific figure or theme of OT hope. Sometimes, however, a nationalistic note is present when *christos* is used in connection with Jesus in the Gospels, particularly, when it is linked with the title 'king of the Jews' (Mt. 2:4; 26:68; 27:17, 22: Mk. 12:35; 15:32; Lk. 23:2). While there were many strands to Messianic expectation in 1st-century Palestine, some of which find an echo in the NT (especially the prophet like Moses (above, **I.** *a.* 2) expected by Jews and Samaritans: see Jn. 6:14; *cf.* Mt. 21:11; Lk. 7:16; this expectation is the background also to Jn. 4:25), the dominant popular hope was of a king like David, with a role of political liberation and conquest, and it seems clear that this would be the popular understanding of *christos*.

It is against this background that we must understand Jesus' remarkable reluctance to apply the title *christos* to himself. The only time when he is recorded as doing so (apart from two passages where it seems to mean no more than 'I', and is probably an editorial addition, Mk. 9:41; Mt. 23:10) is with the Samaritan woman, to whom it would convey the idea of a prophet like Moses, not of a Jewish king (Jn. 4:25f.). His discussion of the status of the Messiah in Mark 12:35–37 does not explicitly claim the title for himself, and is aimed at dissociating it from the political connotations of 'son of David'.

Not that he denied that he was the Messiah. His constant stress on the fulfilment of OT hopes in his ministry (*Jesus Christ, **VII.** *b*, *c*) must carry this implication. John the Baptist, hearing of the works of the *christos*, asked if he was the 'coming one', and Jesus replied by pointing to his literal fulfilment of Isaiah 35:5f. and 61:1, the latter an unambiguously Messianic passage (Mt. 11:2–5). He declared at Nazareth that the same passage was fulfilled 'today' (Lk. 4:18ff.).

Yet when Peter acclaimed him as the *christos*, Jesus swore his disciples to secrecy, and went on to teach that his role was to suffer and be rejected, a role which Peter found quite incompatible with his idea of Messiahship; and the title he used to teach this was not *christos* but 'Son of man' (Mk. 8:29–33). When the high priest challenged Jesus to say whether he was the *christos*, he replied affirmatively (though the wording in Matthew and Luke suggests hesitation over the term used), but went on to speak of his role (as 'Son of man' not *christos*) as one of future vindication and authority, not present political power (Mk. 14:61f. and parallels).

All this indicates that Jesus' conception of his Messianic role was so much at variance with the popular connotations of *christos* that he preferred to avoid the title. His mission had been launched by God's declaration at his baptism (Mk. 1:11; *Jesus Christ, **IV.** *b*) whose words alluded to two key OT passages, the one (Ps. 2:7) marking out his role as Messianic king of the line of David, but the other (Is. 42:1) indicating that this role was to be accomplished through the obedience, suffering and death of the *Servant of the Lord. This declaration clearly moulded Jesus' understanding of his Messianic vocation, as may be seen from his careful selection of OT passages in explaining his mission, among which Is. 53, with its explicit portrayal of a Servant who would suffer and die to redeem his people, took pride of place (*Jesus Christ, **VII.** *g*). But he did not apply to himself the many predictions of a Davidic king (except by implication in Mk. 12:35–37, and there his intention was to play down this aspect of Messiahship), and avoided such titles as 'son of David' and 'king of Israel' which others used of him (*e.g.* Mk. 10:47f.; 15:2; Mt. 12:23; 21:9, 15; Jn. 12:13; 18:33ff.) as consistently as he did *christos*. The openly Messianic demonstration of the entry to Jerusalem (Mk. 11:1–10) was deliberately staged to call to mind Zechariah's prophecy of a humble king, bringer of peace not war (Zc. 9:9f.). But when the excited crowd wanted to make him a king of the more traditional nationalistic type he ran away (Jn. 6:15). It was only after his death and resurrection, when a misunderstanding of his mission as one of political liberation was no longer possible, that he referred to his mission of suffering explicitly as that of the *christos* (Lk. 24:26, 46).

On two significant occasions, as we have seen, while Jesus did not reject the suggestion that he was the *christos*, he quickly dropped the title in favour of 'Son of man'. That this was his chosen title for himself is indisputable in the light of its use in the NT (41 times, not counting parallels, in the Synoptic Gospels and 12 in John, *all* on the lips of Jesus; with no clear use as a title in the rest of the NT except in Acts 7:56), and is denied by radical scholarship only on the basis of large-scale excision of the relevant sayings as unauthentic. It is also clear that he applied this title to himself not only in his future glory (as its origin in Dn. 7:13f. would suggest), but in his earthly humiliation and particularly in his suffering and death. It was thus apparently his chosen term to convey the whole scope of his Messianic vocation as he conceived it, as distinct from the popular notion of the *christos*. This was because, apart from the special use of 'Son of man' in the *Similitudes of Enoch* (probably an isolated work, and possibly later than the time of Jesus; *Pseudepigrapha, I), it was not in current use as a Messianic title. (For this point see R.

T. France, *Jesus and the Old Testament*, 1971, pp. 187f.; Dn. 7:13f. was understood as a Messianic prophecy, but without turning the common Aram. phrase 'son of man' into a title.) Jesus could thus use it to carry his own unique conception of Messiahship without importing alien ideas already inherent in the title, as would have been the case with *christos* or 'son of David'. See further *JESUS CHRIST, TITLES OF.

b. Acts and Epistles

At the centre of the earliest Christian preaching as recorded in Acts is the declaration that Jesus, rejected and crucified by the Jewish leaders, is in fact the Messiah. This certainty is based on the resurrection, which has finally vindicated his claim: 'Let all the house of Israel therefore know assuredly that God has made him both Lord and Christ, this Jesus whom you crucified' (Acts 2:36).

This assertion was so improbable in the light of the popular conception of Messiahship that much attention was given to the scriptural ground for the rejection, death and resurrection of the Messiah (*e.g.* Acts 2:25–36; 3:20–26; 13:27–37; 18:28). In this apologetic and preaching activity among Jews the early Christians apparently had no inhibitions about using the actual term *christos*, and frequently in Acts it occurs in this context, not as a name of Jesus but as a title in its original sense of the expected deliverer (*e.g.* Acts 2:31, 36; 3:18, 20; 5:42; 9:22; 17:3; 18:5, 28). What had been during Jesus' ministry a misleading term was now, since his death and resurrection, no longer open to a political construction, and was taken up enthusiastically by his followers in presenting his claims to the Jews.

Their message was not only, or even mainly, that Jesus had been the Messiah while on earth, but that now, exalted to the right hand of God, he was enthroned as the Messianic King. Ps. 110:1, which Jesus had alluded to in this connection (Mk. 14:62), is taken up by Peter at Pentecost (Acts 2:34–36), and becomes perhaps the most quoted OT verse in the NT. Jesus is not a king on David's throne in Jerusalem, but, as David's lord, the ruler of an eternal and heavenly kingdom, waiting at God's right hand until all his enemies will be placed under his feet. The Messiah whose earthly humiliation was in such striking contrast with the political power of popular Messianic expectation now far transcends that popular hope of a merely national kingdom.

The triumphant proclamation of the first Christians that despite all appearances Jesus was indeed the *christos* seems quickly to have given way to such an unchallenged assumption of this truth within Christian circles that *Christos*, either alone or in combination with *Iēsous*, came to be used as a name of Jesus, and Jesus' followers could be known as *Christianoi* (Acts 11:26). Already by the time of the earliest letters of Paul *Christos* has ceased to be a technical term and has become a name. No doubt it was a name which continued to be full of deep meaning for a Jewish Christian, but it is remarkable that in the nearly 400 uses of *christos* in the letters of Paul (most of them written, of course, to predominantly Gentile churches) there is only one clear case of its use in its original technical sense (Rom. 9:5, significantly in a passage discussing the question of the Jews). The same is true, if less strikingly, of the other NT letters, though 1 Pet. 1:11 uses *christos* of the Messiah of OT prophecy, and 1 Jn. 2:22; 5:1 shows that the issue of whether Jesus was the *christos* was still a live one (though now in a different sense, probably, confronting Gnostic rather than Jewish opposition).

But if the technical sense of *christos* was quickly eclipsed by its use as a personal name, this does not mean that the church lost interest in the question of Jesus' fulfilment of OT hopes. Paul stressed that the basic elements of Jesus' work were 'according to the scriptures' (1 Cor. 15:3f.). This emphasis was not only necessary for effective preaching to Jews, but was clearly of absorbing interest to the Christians themselves; building on Jesus' expounding to them 'in all the scriptures the things concerning himself' (Lk. 24:27), they searched further in the OT for passages to throw light on his Messianic role. Beginning with the sermons in Acts 2, 7 and 13, they continued to draw together collections of relevant texts (*e.g.* Rom. 10:5–21; 15:9–12; Heb. 1:5–13; 2:6–13, *etc.*), and to explore OT themes which pointed forward to the ministry of Jesus (*e.g.* the recurring theme of the *'stone', or the *Melchizedek priesthood of Ps. 110:4 which provides such rich material for the author of Hebrews, 5:5–10; 7:1–28). See further *QUOTATIONS.

Hebrews in particular, while it makes very sparing use of the title *christos*, consists largely of extended exposition of OT themes and their fulfilment in Jesus, who has come to bring in the new covenant and to provide the true reality of which the features of the OT dispensation were only shadows.

So if the term *christos* tended increasingly to be used simply as a name of Jesus, the fact that Jesus was the one through whom God was now working out his long-promised purpose of salvation remained of central importance in early Christian thought, as the NT writers went beyond the simple assertion of the fact of Jesus' Messiahship to explore more and more deeply the content and the meaning of that saving work.

BIBLIOGRAPHY. O. Cullmann, *The Christology of the New Testament*, 1959 (esp. ch. 5); R. H. Fuller, *The Foundations of New Testament Christology*, 1965; F. F. Bruce, *This is That*, 1968; F. Hahn, *The Titles of Jesus in Christology*, 1969; R. N. Longenecker, *The Christology of Early Jewish Christianity*, 1970; M. Hengel, *The Charismatic Leader and His Followers*, 1981; A. E. Harvey, *Jesus and the Constraints of History*, 1982, ch. 6; R. Leivestad, *Jesus in His Own Perspective*, 1987; L. Grollenberg, *Unexpected Messiah*, 1988; D. Juel, *Messianic Exegesis*, 1988. R.T.F.

METHEG-AMMAH. Apparent textual corruption in 2 Sa. 8:1 makes this name difficult to understand. No certainty seems possible, and at least three alternative interpretations present themselves. **1.** That it is a place-name, evidently near Gath in the Philistine plain (*cf.* 'hill of Ammah', 2 Sa. 2:24). **2.** That the RV translation, 'the bridle of the mother city', be preferred—*i.e.* regarding it as a figurative name for Gath, a chief city of the Philistines (*cf.* 1 Ch. 18:1). **3.** That LXX be followed and the verse rendered as 'and David took the tribute out of the hand of the Philistines'. J.D.D.

METHUSELAH (Heb. *m^etûšelaḥ*, meaning apparently 'man of [the deity] Lach'). The eighth Patriarch listed in the genealogy of Gn. 5. He was the son of Enoch and grandfather of Noah. He lived to the great age of 969 years according to the Heb. and the LXX (the Samaritan gives 720 years). Though they are both rendered in the LXX by *Mathousala*, there is no reason to assume that *mᵉtûšelaḥ* and *mᵉtûšā'ēl* (Methushael, Gn. 4:18) were the same person. T.C.M.

MEZAHAB. The grandfather of Mehetabel who was the wife of Hadar, king of Edom (Gn. 36:39 = 1 Ch. 1:50). The form is that of a place- rather than personal-name (*mê zāhāḇ*, 'waters of gold'), but a man may sometimes be named after a place with which he is associated. T.C.M.

MICAH, MICAIAH ('who is like Yah?'). A common Hebrew name, variously spelt in both EVV and *MT*. Of the many men named with one of these forms, three are better known than the rest. **1.** Micah of Moresheth the prophet. (See next article.) **2.** Micah of Mt Ephraim, whose strange story is told in Jdg. 17–18, presumably to explain the origin of the sanctuary at Dan and incidentally relating the migration of the Danites to their new territory. **3.** Micaiah the son of Imlah, a prophet in Israel in the days of Ahab (1 Ki. 22:8–28; 2 Ch. 18:3–27). Nothing is known of him except for this single interview he had with Ahab, but we may infer that he had prophesied before and that Ahab was aware of his unfavourable messages. Probably he was brought out of prison to appear before Ahab, and there may be some truth in Josephus' tradition that he was the unknown prophet of 1 Ki. 20:35–43. J.B.Tr.

MICAH, BOOK OF (Heb. *mîḵâ*, abbreviated form of *mîḵāyᵉhû*, 'who is like Yahweh?').

I. Outline of contents

a. The coming judgment upon Israel (1:1–16).

b. Israel to be punished, then restored (2:1–13).

c. Condemnation of the princes and prophets (3:1–12).

d. The coming glory and peace of Jerusalem (4:1–13).

e. The suffering and restoration of Zion (5:1–15).

f. Prophetic and popular religion contrasted (6:1–16).

g. Corruption of society; concluding statement of trust in God (7:1–20).

II. Authorship and date

Authorship is usually attributed to Micah of Moresheth (1:1), whose home, identified with *Moresheth-gath in the Shephelah or lowlands of Judah, was the general locale of his prophetic activity (1:14). A younger contemporary of Isaiah, he uttered his sayings during the reigns of Jotham (*c.* 742–735 BC), Ahaz (*c.* 735–715 BC) and Hezekiah of Judah (*c.* 715–687 BC).

Some modern scholars have maintained that only Mi. 1:2–2:10 and parts of chs. 4 and 5 are the work of the prophet himself. While the last two chapters of the book have much in them that is akin to the work of Micah, critics have urged that the difference in background and style from earlier portions of the prophecy, and the comparatively subordinate position which they occupy in the book, require them to be assigned to a time later than the 8th century BC. In particular, 7:7–20 is held to be definitely post-exilic.

Other scholars have claimed that the forceful, descriptive style which is evident in each chapter of the prophecy, and the consistent revelation of divine judgment, compassion and hope, are powerful arguments for the unity of authorship of the prophecy. Arguments from style are never particularly strong at the best, since style can be altered so easily with a change of subject-matter. Furthermore, it is not easy to see why 7:7–20 should be assigned to a post-exilic period, since there is nothing in the content which is in the slightest degree at variance with the language or theology of the 8th-century BC prophets. The closing verses of the book are read each year by Jewish worshippers in the afternoon service on the Day of Atonement.

III. Background and message

Although he lived in rural surroundings, Micah was familiar with the corruptions of city life in Israel and Judah. His denunciations were directed particularly at Jerusalem (4:10), and like Amos and Isaiah he noted how the wealthy landowners took every advantage of the poor (2:1f.). He condemned the corruption rampant among the religious leaders of his day (2:11) and the gross miscarriages of justice perpetrated by those dedicated to the upholding of the law (3:10). The fact that all this was carried on in an atmosphere of false religiosity (3:11) proved for Micah to be the crowning insult.

Like his 8th-century BC contemporaries Amos, Hosea and Isaiah, Micah stressed the essential righteousness and morality of the divine nature. He was concerned also to point out that these qualities had pressing ethical implications for the life of the individual and the community alike. If the people of Israel and Judah were to take their covenant obligations at all seriously the justice which characterized the nature of God must be reflected in a similar state of affairs among the people of God.

Whereas Amos and Hosea had a good deal to say about the idolatry and immorality which were rampant in Israel and Judah as a result of the influence of pagan Canaanite religion, Micah confined his utterances to the problems arising from the social injustices perpetrated upon the small landowners, farmers and peasants. He warned those who wrongfully deprived others of their possessions that God was devising a drastic punishment for them. His denunciation of the rulers of Israel (3:1–4) and the false prophets (3:5–8) envisaged the ultimate destruction of Jerusalem because the corruption which they represented had permeated to the very core of national life.

Micah was in general accord with Amos, Hosea and Isaiah in his belief that God would use a pagan nation to punish his own guilty people. As a result he foretold the depredations of Shalmaneser V in the N kingdom, and the ultimate destruction of Samaria, capital of Israel (1:6–9). He did not view the collapse of the N kingdom in quite the same broad terms as did Isaiah, however. To Micah it brought the threat of invasion to the very doors of 'this family' (2:3), making the Assyr. invader Sennacherib the herald of a larger doom (5:5ff.).

There is a striking resemblance between the prophecies of devastation proclaimed for Samaria

(1:6) and Jerusalem (3:12). A century after his death the words of Micah concerning the downfall of Zion were still remembered (Je. 26:18f.). On that occasion the prophet Jeremiah might well have been put to death for prophesying destruction for the Temple and the Holy City had not certain elders of the land recalled that Micah of Moresheth had said precisely the same thing a hundred years earlier. For Micah there could be no question as to the ultimate fate of the house of Judah. So pervasive and influential was the depraved religion of Canaan, and so widespread was the resultant corruption of society that nothing short of the exercise of divine judgment upon the S kingdom could avail for the ultimate salvation of the people of God. But before the remnant of Jacob could experience this saving grace it would be necessary for all idolatry and social corruption to be rooted out (5:10–15).

This experience would be one of tribulation and sorrow, during which the voice of prophecy would cease (3:6–7), and the sin of the nation would become evident (3:8). Consequent upon this would come the destruction of Jerusalem and the shame of captivity in the midst of other peoples (5:7–8). Restoration would be marked by a new universalistic religion in a restored Jerusalem. Under divine judgment swords would be beaten into ploughshares and spears into pruning-hooks (4:3), and the people of God would honour his name only (4:5). Prominent in the thought of Micah was the expectation of a Messiah to be born in Bethlehem (5:2). This personage would come forth from the common people, delivering them from oppression and injustice and restoring the remainder of the Israelite family to fellowship with the remnant in Zion.

Micah was at pains to point out that the saving grace of God could not be earned (6:6–8), either by pretentious sacrificial offerings or by indulgence in elaborate ritual forms of worship. Humility, mercy and justice must be an everyday experience in the life of the person who was to be well-pleasing to God.

BIBLIOGRAPHY. J. M. P. Smith, *ICC*, 1911, pp. 5–156; G. A. Smith, *The Book of the Twelve Prophets*, 1, 1928, pp. 381ff.; R. K. Harrison, *IOT*, 1969, pp. 919–925; L. C. Allen, *The Books of Joel, Obadiah, Jonah and Micah*, *NIC*, 1976; T. E. McComiskey, *ISBE* 3, pp. 343–346. R.K.H.

MICHAEL (Heb. *mîḵā'ēl*, 'who is like God?'—synonymous with Micaiah and Micah). The name of eleven biblical characters, only one of whom gets more than a passing reference. The exception is the *angel Michael, who in pseudepigraphic literature is regarded as the patron of, and intercessor for, Israel (*1 Enoch* 20:5; 89:76). In the book of Daniel he is more particularly the guardian of the Jews from the menace of the godless power of Greece and Persia (12:1), and is styled as 'one of the chief princes' and as 'your prince' (10:13, 21). In this capacity it is peculiarly fitting that he should be the archangel represented (Jude 9) as 'contending with the devil . . . about the body of Moses', that great leader of God's people to whom an angel (perhaps Michael) spoke in Mt Sinai (Acts 7:38). Michael further appears in Rev. 12:7 as waging war in heaven against the dragon. See R. H. Charles, *Studies in the Apocalypse*, 1913, pp. 158–161. J.D.D.

MICHAL (Heb. *mîḵal*) was Saul's younger daughter (1 Sa. 14:49). Instead of her sister *Merab she was married to David, for a dowry of a hundred Philistine foreskins (1 Sa. 18:20ff.). Her prompt action and resourcefulness saved him from Saul (1 Sa. 19:11–17). During his exile she was given in marriage to Palti(el), son of Laish, of Gallim (1 Sa. 25:44). After Saul's death, when Abner wanted to treat with him, David demanded her restitution—a political move to strengthen his claim to the throne (2 Sa. 3:14–16). Having brought the ark to Jerusalem, he danced before it with such abandon that Michal despised him (2 Sa. 6:12ff.). For this reason she remained childless for ever (2 Sa. 6:23). Five sons are mentioned (2 Sa. 21:8), but tradition holds that they were Merab's (so LXX and two Heb. MSS), and that Michal 'reared them'.

On one view David married Michal at Hebron 'to unite the tribes of Israel and the clans of Judah' (*EBi*); but the idea that she had one son, Ithream, her name being corrupted to Eglah (2 Sa.3:5), is without foundation. M.B.

MICHMASH, MICHMAS. A city of Benjamin E of Bethel and 12 km N of Jerusalem, 600 m above sea-level, on the pass from Bethel to Jericho. In Geba, just S of this pass, Jonathan made a successful foray against the Philistine garrison (1 Sa. 13:3), whereupon the Philistines gathered a large well-equipped army and occupied Michmash, causing the scattered flight of the Hebrews (13:5ff.). Thereafter Saul's army camped at Geba (or Gibeah) with the Philistines on the other side of the pass (13:23).

Unknown to Saul, Jonathan and his armour-bearer descended from Geba and, ascending the S slope, surprised the Philistines and caused confusion in the enemy camp (for a description of this feat, see S. R. Driver, *Notes on the Hebrew Text of the Books of Samuel*[2], 1913, p. 106). Aided by Hebrew prisoners who had been in Philistine hands, by refugees from the previous defeat and by Saul's army, they put the Philistines to rout (1 Sa. 14:1ff.).

In his prophetic description of the coming attack on Jerusalem Isaiah (10:24, 28) represents the taking of Michmash by the Assyrians. After

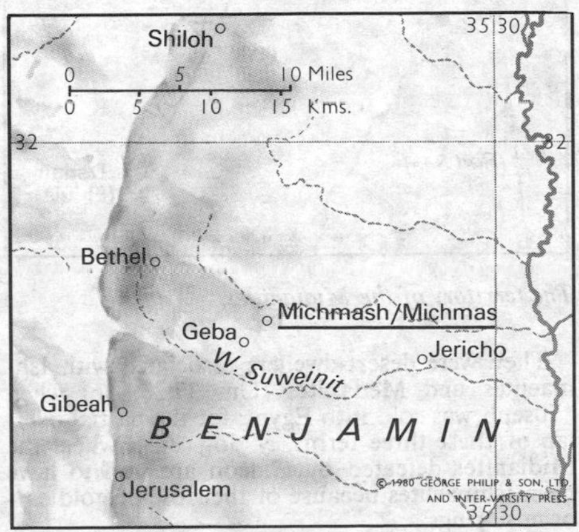

The location of Michmash.

the Exile members of the Jewish community lived in Michmash (Ezr. 2:27; Ne. 7:31; 11:31), and it was later the residence of Jonathan Maccabeus (1 Macc. 9:73).

It is the present Mukhmâs, a ruined village on the N ridge of the Wadi Suweinit. J.D.D.

MIDIANITES. They consisted of five families, linked to Abraham through Midian, son of the concubine Keturah. Abraham sent them away, with all his other sons by concubines, into the E (Gn. 25:1–6). Thus the Midianites are found inhabiting desert borders in Transjordan from Moab down past Edom.

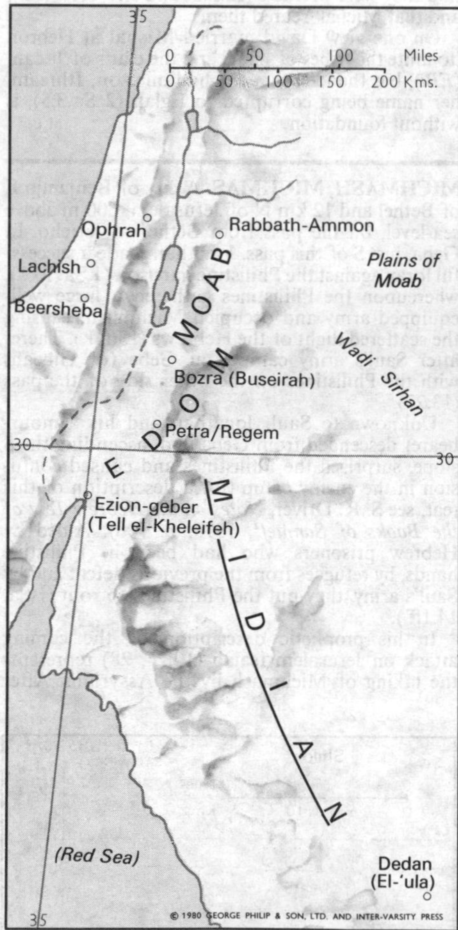

The territory of the Midianities.

They were desert-dwellers associated with Ishmaelites and Medanites (Gn. 37:28, 36) when *Joseph was sold into Egypt; for the partial overlap of these three terms, *cf.* Jdg. 8:24, where the Midianites defeated by Gideon are said to have been Ishmaelites because of their use of gold ear- or nose-rings.

Moses had a Midianite wife, Zipporah, father-in-law, Jethro/Reuel (Ex. 2:21; 3:1, *etc.*), and brother-in-law, Hobab (Nu. 10:29; Jdg. 4:11). As a man of the desert, Hobab was asked by Moses to guide Israel in travelling through the steppe (or 'wilderness') (Nu. 10:29–32).

Later, in the plains of Moab, the chiefs of Midian and Moab combined in hiring Balaam to curse Israel (Nu. 22ff.) and their people led Israel into idolatry and immorality (Nu. 25), and so had to be vanquished (Nu. 25:16–18; 31). The five princes of Midian were confederates of the Amorite king Sihon (Jos. 13:21). In the time of the judges, through Gideon and his puny band (Jdg. 6–8; 9:17), God delivered Israel from the scourge of camel-riding Midianites, Amalekites and other 'children of the east', an event remembered by psalmist and prophet (Ps. 83:9; Is. 9:4; 10:26). This is at present the earliest-known reference to full-scale use of camels in warfare (W. F. Albright, *Archaeology and the Religion of Israel*, 1953, pp. 132–133), but by no means the first occurrence of domesticated camels (*ANIMALS, Camel; and W. G. Lambert, *BASOR* 160, 1960, pp. 42–43, for indirect Old Babylonian evidence). The dromedaries of Midian recur in Is. 60:6. In Hab. 3:7 Midian is put in parallel with Cushan, an ancient term that probably goes back to *Kushu* mentioned in Egyp. texts of *c.* 1800 BC (see W. F. Albright, *BASOR* 83, 1941, p. 34, n. 8; *cf.* G. Posener, *Princes et Pays d'Asie et de Nubie*, 1940, p. 88, and B. Maisler, *Revue d'Histoire Juive en Égypte* 1, 1947, pp. 37–38; *ETHIOPIAN WOMAN. K.A.K.

MIDWIFE (Heb. *mᵉyalleḏeṯ*, 'one who helps to bear'). The midwife helped at childbirth by taking the new-born child, cutting its umbilical cord, washing the babe with water, salting and wrapping it (Ezk. 16:4); news of the birth was then brought to the father (Je. 20:15).

In Hebrew tradition, midwives are first mentioned in the time of Jacob, attending on Rachel (Gn. 35:17) and Tamar (Gn. 38:28); in the latter case the midwife tied a red thread to mark the first twin born, technically the eldest.

In Mesopotamia and Egypt and among the Hebrews women very often crouched in childbirth upon a pair of bricks or stones—the *'oḇnayim* of Ex. 1:16—or on a birthstool of similar pattern. All this can be well illustrated from ancient sources. The Egyptian Papyrus Westcar, written in the Hyksos period (*c.* 1700/1600 BC), records how three goddesses delivered a priest's wife of three sons: each took one child in her arms; they cut the umbilical cord, washed the children and put them on a cloth on a little brick bench, then went to announce the births to the waiting husband (M. Lichtheim, *Ancient Egyptian Literature*, 1, 1973, pp. 220–221). This text also illustrates the giving of punning names to children at birth as in Genesis and elsewhere. In Egyptian the two bricks or stones (and also birthstools) were called *ḏb't*, 'the brick(s)', or *msḫnt*, the latter word being followed in writing by the hieroglyph of a brick or of a pair of bricks, or of a birthstool (plan-view), *etc*. The Egyptian word *msi*, 'to give birth', was often followed by the hieroglyph of a crouching woman in the act of birth, and in one late text the figure is actually shown crouching on two bricks or stones. See W. Spiegelberg, *Aegyptologische Randglossen zum Alten Testament*, 1904, pp. 19–25; H. Rand, *IEJ* 20, 1970, pp. 209–212, pl. 47. K.A.K.

MIGDOL. The name is used of a Canaanite fort. Mentioned as a place-name in Ex. 14:2; Nu. 33:7; Je. 44:1; 46:14; Ezk. 29:10; 30:6. Several Migdols were built in the neighbourhood of the Egyptian border, but none of them can be accurately located. The Migdol of the Prophets, in the N of Egypt (possibly at Tell el-Her), is different from that in the S (P. Anastasi V), which is probably the Migdol of Succoth (Old Egyp. *ṯkw*). The Migdol in the N may be the Magdolum of *Itinerarium Antonini*, 12 Roman miles from Pelusium. See *NEAEHL*, pp. 1392–1393. (* ENCAMPMENT BY THE SEA.) C.D.W.

MIGRON. 1. A place mentioned in 1 Sa. 14:2 situated on the outskirts of Saul's home at Gibeah, where he remained during the first stage of the Philistine invasion after his election as king. It is possibly identical with **2**, a locality mentioned in the march of the Assyr. army in Is. 10:28, the modern Tell Miryam, N of Michmash. J.D.D.

MILCAH (Heb. *milkâ*, 'counsel'). **1.** The daughter of Haran (Abraham's brother) and wife of Nahor (Gn. 11:29). Her children are named in Gn. 22:20ff. Rebekah was her granddaughter (Gn. 24:15, 24, 47). **2.** One of the five daughters of * Zelophehad of the tribe of Manasseh. Because they had no brothers, they were given an inheritance when the land was divided (Nu. 26:33; 27:1; 36:11; Jos. 17:3). J.D.D.

MILCOM. In this form of spelling we have a distortion (or alternative form) of the name of the national deity of the * Ammonites. The basic root *mlk* enables an identification of the three biblical forms of the name (*milkōm*, *malkām*, *mōleḵ*). Solomon is described in 1 Ki. 11:5 as marrying an Ammonite princess and going 'after Milcom the abomination of the Ammonites'. Josiah broke down the high place which Solomon had erected for this god (2 Ki. 23:13).

In some passages in the OT, however, the term *mōleḵ* may refer to a sacrifice as in some Phoenician (Punic) inscriptions from N Africa. Certain OT passages may be read as saying that men caused children to go through fire for (or, as) a *mōleḵ* sacrifice. However in other passages the reference is to a deity. (* MALCAM, * MOLECH.)

BIBLIOGRAPHY. W. F. Albright, *Archaeology and the Religion of Israel*, 1953, pp. 162–164; D. R. Ap-Thomas in *POTT*, p. 271; R. de Vaux, *Studies in Old Testament Sacrifice*, 1964, pp. 52–90; A. R. W. Green, *The Role of Human Sacrifice in the Ancient Near East*, 1976. J.A.T.

MILETUS. The most S of the great Ionian (Gk.) cities on the W coast of Asia Minor. It flourished as a commercial centre, and in the 8th, 7th and 6th centuries BC established many colonies in the Black Sea area and also had contact with Egypt. Pharaoh Neco dedicated an offering in a Milesian temple after his victory at Megiddo in 608 BC (2 Ki. 23:29; 2 Ch. 35:20ff.). The Milesians resisted the expansion of Lydia, and in 499 BC initiated the Ionian revolt against Persia, but their city was destroyed in 494 BC. In its period of great prosperity Miletus was the home of the first Gk. philosophers Thales, Anaximander and Anaximenes, and of Hecataeus the chronicler. Its woollen goods were world famous.

After its Persian destruction the city had many vicissitudes, and when Paul called there (Acts 20:15; 2 Tim. 4:20) it was largely living on its past glories. At this time it was part of the Roman province of Asia, and due to the silting up of its harbour (nowadays an inland lake) by deposits from the river Maeander it was declining commercially. An inscription in the ruins shows the place reserved in the stone theatre for Jews and 'god-fearing' people. K.L.MCK.

MILK (Heb. *ḥālāḇ*; Gk. *gala*). Milk was part of the staple diet of the Hebrews from patriarchal times, and where there was abundance of milk (Is. 7:22) it was possible to enjoy the added delicacy of cream or curdled milk (Heb. *ḥem'â*, 'butter'). Hence the attraction of the land of Canaan as a land flowing with milk and honey (Ex. 3:8), for the rich supply of milk was an indication of the pasturage available. *ḥālāḇ* might be the milk of cows or sheep (Dt. 32:14; Is. 7:22), goats (Pr. 27:27), or possibly in patriarchal times of camels also (Gn. 32:15). It was contained in buckets, if RVmg. is the correct rendering of the *hapax legomenon* in Jb. 21:24, and in skin-bottles (Jdg. 4:19), from which it could conveniently be poured out for the refreshment of strangers (Gn. 18:8) or as a drink with meals (Ezk. 25:4). It is frequently coupled with honey, and with wine (Gn. 49:12; Is. 55:1; Joel 3:18), with which it may sometimes have been mingled as a rich delicacy (Ct. 5:1). The phrase 'honey and milk are under thy tongue' (Ct. 4:11) refers to the sweet conversation of the loved one.

Its metaphorical use to describe the land of Canaan has been mentioned; Egypt was also so described by the embittered Israelites during the years of wandering (Nu. 16:13). Elsewhere it stands alone as a symbol of prosperity and abundance (Is. 60:16; Joel 3:18), and it is therefore not surprising that later Judaism compared it with the Torah. Kimchi says of Is. 55:1, 'As milk feeds and nourishes a child, so the law feeds and nourishes the soul.' This is a similar figure to that used in the NT of young converts imbibing the 'pure spiritual milk' (1 Pet. 2:2), though Paul carries the metaphor further and considers milk unworthy of mature disciples (1 Cor. 3:2; *cf.* Heb. 5:12f.).

The strange Mosaic prohibition of seething a kid in its mother's milk (Ex. 23:19; 34:26; Dt. 14:21) probably referred originally to a Canaanite ritual. On this verse, however, has been built the entire Jewish dietary law forbidding milk to be consumed at any meal at which meat is eaten, the cleavage between the two foods being so great that among orthodox Jews separate kitchen equipment has to be provided for the preparation and cooking of milk and meat dishes. J.B.TR.

MILL, MILLSTONE. The oldest and most common method of grinding corn was to spread it on a flat stone slab and rub it with a round stone muller. Such stone querns have been found in the early Neolithic town at Jericho, together with stone * mortars (*PEQ* 85, 1953, pl. 38. 2; for an Egyptian model, see *ANEP*, no. 149). The rotary quern came into general use in the Iron Age. This consisted of two circular stone slabs, each about 50 cm across, the upper one (Heb. *reḵeḇ*, 'rider') pierced through to revolve on a pivot fixed to the lower (*cf.* the illustration of a potter's wheel). A wooden stick projecting from a hole near the outer edge of the upper stone was the handle. The grain was poured through the pivot-hole in the upper stone and crushed as this turned, so that the flour spilled from between the two stones (Heb. *rēḥayîm*) on to the ground. It was the woman's task to grind the corn (Ex. 11:5; Mt. 24:41), but it was also imposed upon prisoners as a menial service (Is. 47:2; La. 5:13). Larger types of rotary quern were turned by animals, or by prisoners (Samson, Jdg. 16:21) and were kept in a mill-house (Mt. 24:41, Gk. *mylōn*).

Since the Israelite depended on the hand-mill for his daily bread, he was forbidden to give it in pledge (Dt. 24:6). Cessation of the steady, constant sound of grinding was a sign of desolation and death (Je. 25:10; Rev. 18:22, a simile for the old man's teeth; Ec. 12:4). The upper stone was used on occasion as a missile in war (Jdg. 9:53; 2 Sa. 11:21) and as a weight (Mt. 18:6, Gk. *mylos onikos*, the largest sort of millstone, turned by an ass; Rev. 18:21). A.R.M.

MILLO. A place-name derived from the verb *mālē'*, 'to be full', 'to fill'. It is used in Jdg. 9:6, 20 of a place near Shechem, the 'house of Millo', perhaps a fortress; but its principal use is in connection with *Jerusalem, where it evidently formed part of the Jebusite city, for it was already in existence in the time of David (2 Sa. 5:9 = 1 Ch. 11:8). It was rebuilt by Solomon (1 Ki. 9:15, 24; 11:27; the 'breach' here referred to was probably a different thing) as part of his programme of strengthening the kingdom, and was again strengthened some 2½ centuries later when Hezekiah was preparing for the Assyrian invasion (2 Ch. 32:5). This verse is taken by some to indicate that Millo was another name for the whole city of David, but it can very plausibly be connected with a system of terraces, consisting of retaining walls with levelled filling, which have been discovered by Kathleen Kenyon on the E slope of Ophel Hill at Jerusalem. These terraces provided space for the construction of buildings on the slope.

Millo is otherwise mentioned as the place where Joash was murdered (2 Ki. 12:20). The LXX usually translates Millo by the name Akra, but this was a Maccabean structure. For a suggestion as to the type of construction indicated by the term *millô'*, see *ARCHITECTURE.

BIBLIOGRAPHY. J. Simons, *Jerusalem in the Old Testament*, 1952, pp. 131–144; K. M. Kenyon, *Digging up Jerusalem*, 1974, pp. 100–103. T.C.M.

MINAEANS. The people of the kingdom of Ma'īn which flourished in SW Arabia (in the N of modern Yemen) in the 1st millennium BC. The name is that of a tribe which became dominant in a state known from inscriptions to have been established with Qarnāwu as its capital by about 400 BC. It was active in establishing trade links with the N, having colonies along the Red Sea coastal route to Palestine, the best known being *Dedan. Late in the 1st century BC Ma'īn was absorbed by the expansion of its S neighbour Saba (*SHEBA, 7) and its N colonies lost their Minaean identity. The name does not occur with certainty anywhere in the Bible, though some scholars would see it in Jdg. 10:12 (Maonites); 1 Ch. 4:41 (AV 'habitation'); 2 Ch. 20:1 (altering Ammonites); 2 Ch. 26:7 (Mehunims); or Ezr. 2:50 = Ne. 7:52 (Mehunim). (*MAON; *ARABIA.)

BIBLIOGRAPHY. J. A. Montgomery, *Arabia and the Bible*, 1934, pp. 60–61, 133–138, 182–184; S. Moscati, *Ancient Semitic Civilizations*, 1957, pp. 184–194. T.C.M.

MINING AND METALS. The theatre of OT history is the so-called 'Fertile Crescent' (*i.e.* Mesopotamia, Syria, Palestine and the Nile Delta). The alluvial plains of the Tigris–Euphrates and Nile valleys provide but little stone. Much of Assyria's gypsum, indeed, comes from stone quarries near Mosul; and there is a worked vein of stone near Ur. But for the most part in those valleys clay bricks were used for building purposes in ancient times (Gn. 11:3; Ex. 1:11–14; 5:7–19).

The 'Crescent' is bounded on the N and E by high folded mountain chains consisting of rocks of many types and ages. The ranges are well mineralized and provide ores of gold, silver, copper, tin, lead and iron. On the S a complex of ancient rocks appears in which such types as granite, diorite and porphyry occur. This group extends along the E desert between the river Nile and the Red Sea, across the S half of the Sinai peninsula and E into the Arabian plateau. In some of these rocks occur gold, silver, iron, turquoise and other semi-precious stones, together with building stones of many kinds.

N of Sinai and the Arabian plateau lie the desert, Transjordan and Palestine. These are composed mainly of Cretaceous rocks (limestone, chalk and sandstone), but N and E of the upper Jordan are areas of newer volcanic basalts.

I. Non-metallic materials

a. Flint

Flint occurs abundantly in the chalk of the area and in gravels derived from the chalk. Flint is a close-grained hard rock which a steel blade will not scratch. It may be worked by percussion or pressure to produce a sharp cutting-edge. The earliest cutting tools available to man were made from flint. Stone-Age man made arrow-heads, chisels, scrapers and knives of it, and it continued to be used well into the Bronze period. Zipporah, wife of Moses, circumcised her son with a flint knife (Ex. 4:25). Flint is referred to in Scripture to denote hardness, inflexibility, steadfastness (Dt. 8:15; Ps. 114:8; Is. 50:7; Ezk. 3:9).

b. Stone

Away from the alluvial plains of Mesopotamia and Lower Egypt supplies were plentiful. In Egypt limestone and sandstone were at hand in the river cliffs, and granite, diorite and other igneous rocks are found in outcrops. In Palestine limestone and sandstone occur throughout the hill country, and basalt is found E of the upper Jordan valley. The quarrying and erection of huge standing stones in Neolithic times gave experience for future quarrying and mining. Limestone is easily worked, being fairly soft, and was used for the excavation of cisterns and tombs, and the making of such things as water-pots (Je. 2:13; Mt.

27:60; Jn. 2:6). The term 'alabaster' as used in Mt. 26:7 properly refers to calcite (calcium carbonate), a much harder stone than English alabaster (calcium sulphate).

c. Marble

This is a close-grained crystalline limestone, usually white or cream in colour. It may be pink or veined in red or green. The best statuary marble in the Near East came from Paros (Minoa), but it also occurs on the W coast of the Gulf of Suez, in S Greece and in Assyria E of the river Tigris. 'Great quantities of marble' are mentioned in 1 Ch. 29:2, and may have been polished local limestone, but, considering that trade was vigorous and far-flung in David and Solomon's time, it may have been brought by sea or from the NE.

II. Metals and mining

The order in which the principal metals came into use was gold, copper (bronze) and iron. Gold is the first metal mentioned in Scripture (Gn. 2:11), and is thereafter closely associated with silver, the other *noble* metal of antiquity. All the above can occur in the native state, and as such they were first used. Silver is often found alloyed with gold. After the period when native metals were used, mainly for ornament (*ARTS AND CRAFTS), copper ores were won from outcrops at the surface, but mining began at a very early date and an advanced stage of the working of the metal (not mining) had been reached at Ur more than 1,000 years before Abraham's time. According to R. J. Forbes (*Metallurgy in Antiquity*, 1950, p. 297), 'it is certain that every form of mining from open-cut mining to the driving of galleries into the mountainside to follow up the copper-bearing strata was practised in Antiquity. But the details given on ancient mines are few.'

Mining for turquoise and for copper probably began in the time of the 1st Dynasty of Egypt *c.* 3000 BC at Magharah and Serabit el-Khadim in W Sinai, and evidence for large-scale copper working by Egyptians in the Ramesside period (13th century BC) has been found in the Arabah at Timna. Shafts more than 35 m in depth have been found in mines in Egypt. Tunnels, ventilated by shafts, were driven into hillsides, pillars being left in broad excavations to support the roof.

At first stone tools were used, but later bronze and stone continued to be used together. Wedges and fire were used to split the rock, and the ore was separated by crushing, washing and hand-picking. Smelting was usually done by feeding a charge of finely-ground copper ores and fluxes (iron oxides, limestone or sea shells) mixed with charcoal through the open top of the furnace on to the charcoal fire. As the ore was reduced the copper globules sank to the bowl-shaped bottom of the furnace. The slag which formed above the copper was drawn off into a slag-pit while still liquid and the copper ingot removed as soon as it had solidified. The ingot would need remelting in a crucible before it could be used for casting in a mould. Crucibles and slag-heaps are found at many old sites. Baskets were used for carrying the ore, and drainage tunnels constructed to get rid of surplus water. Moffatt's translation of Jb. 28:1–11 gives a vivid picture of mining in ancient times.

a. Gold

This occurs native, usually alloyed with silver in varying amounts. It is extremely malleable and ductile and does not tarnish. This property made it a very acceptable material for ornaments, such as beads and rings, even to Stone-Age man. Gold was prescribed for use in the most important furnishings in the Mosaic tabernacle (Ex. 25) and in

Reconstruction of a copper-smelting furnace found at Timnah. Air is supplied by bellows: the removal of a plug allows the slag to run off, leaving the copper ore in the bottom of the furnace. This was retrieved by breaking open the furnace. Ramesside. c. 1250 BC.

Solomon's Temple (1 Ki. 6). The metal was especially abundant in the alluvium of the E desert of Egypt, and the Israelites must have removed large quantities of it at the Exodus. Other sources known to the ancient world were the W coast of Arabia, the mountains of Armenia and Persia, W Asia Minor, and the Aegean islands. Gold early became a valuable article of currency.

b. Silver

This is ranked next to gold as a noble metal, with which it is often linked in Scripture. It does not tarnish in a pure atmosphere and will take a mirror-like polish. It is usually extracted from the sulphide ore of lead (galena), but may occur native. Silver was so plentiful in biblical times that the extraction and refining processes must have been known from an early date. Jeremiah (6:29–30) uses the failure of the refining process of lead and silver as an illustration of the refusal of the people to become obedient to God. Sources of the metal are the same as those for lead, namely, Asia Minor, the islands of the Aegean, Laurion in S Greece, Armenia and Persia, and 3 or 4 localities occur in the E desert of Egypt.

c. Lead

This occurs in Scripture in a few lists of metals. It was used occasionally as tablets for inscriptions (Jb. 19:24).

d. Copper (*Bronze, Brass*)

Heb. *nᵉḥōšeṯ* is translated 'copper' in Ezr. 8:27, AV, but elsewhere in AV is called 'brass'. Bronze is not mentioned in Scripture, but it was in common use from before patriarchal times (Abraham lived in the Middle Bronze Age). The 'brass' of Scripture may therefore be any of the three, except that true brass, an alloy of copper and zinc, came into use only at a late stage. Heb. *ḥašmal* in Ezk. 1:4 (AV, RV 'amber'; RSV 'gleaming bronze') may denote true brass. The first metal in general use was more or less pure copper, although the methods of production meant that some impurities were usually present, and eventually the alloy of copper and tin (bronze) was developed and produced deliberately. Some examples of brass (copper and zinc) are also known, but they were probably produced accidentally until the Romans began the production of brass for coinage and other uses about 20 BC. The ores of copper which appear at the surface are brightly coloured green and blue carbonates, and were used as eye paint or to produce a blue colour in glaze. Accidental heating of these ores could have led to the production of copper. There is no evidence in Egypt of the common use of native copper, although it was used at an early stage in the Palestinian copper industry. The ores were widespread around the 'Fertile Crescent' in Sinai, Midian, E Egypt, Armenia, Syria and Persia, and of course in Cyprus, which takes its name from the metal. The metal was used for a host of purposes. In addition to its use in the tabernacle and Temple, household articles, such as basins, ewers, idols, musical instruments, as well as armour, mirrors, *etc*., were all made of it.

e. Tin

Tin is mentioned in Scripture only in lists of metals. It was often confused with lead in ancient times. A small percentage mixed with copper produces bronze. As tin often occurs in association with copper, the first bronze was probably made by accident. The dark heavy oxide ore, cassiterite, was taken mainly from stream-sands and was not mined, as were the other metals, until about Roman times.

f. Iron

Rare and occasional uses of iron are known in very ancient times, but only in the native form, which has its origin in fragments of 'shooting stars' or meteors. This is probably the explanation of its early mention in Gn. 4:22, which belongs to a time long before the true Iron Age begins. Experiments with iron went on for a long time before tools could be made of it, since this depends for success on producing a metal with the properties of steel. The Hittites were the first people known to have used iron consistently, although on a limited scale, and when their kingdom came to an end the knowledge spread farther. The Philistines brought the art to Palestine, and the Israelites found themselves at a disadvantage in this respect (Jdg. 1:19; 1 Sa. 13:19–22). The balance was restored in the reigns of David and Solomon (1 Ch. 29:7). Iron was abundant along with copper in the Wadi Arabah between the Dead Sea and the Gulf of Aqabah. Iron ores were plentiful around Palestine and were to be found near Mt Carmel, Mt Hermon, SW Midian and the E Egyptian desert, in Syria, Cyprus, the Pontus coast of Asia Minor and in the Aegean Islands. The fact that both copper and iron could be mined within Solomon's realm near Ezion-geber was a literal fulfilment of Dt. 8:9.

Steel is mentioned in the AV of 2 Sa. 22:35 (= Ps. 18:34); Jb. 20:24; Je. 15:12, but the Heb. word is that for copper or bronze (*nᵉḥōšeṯ*); accordingly, RV renders 'brass' and RSV, more accurately, 'bronze'.

BIBLIOGRAPHY. R. J. Forbes, *Metallurgy in Antiquity*, 1950; L. Woolley, *Ur of the Chaldees*, 1938; W. A. Ruysch (ed.), *The Holy Land, Antiquity and Survival*, II, 2–3, 1957; T. Löw, *Die Mineralia der Juden*, 1935; A. Lucas (ed. J. R. Harris), *Ancient Egyptian Materials and Industries*, 4, 1962; A. Guillaume, 'Metallurgy in the Old Testament', *PEQ*, 1962, pp. 129–132; H. Hodges, *Technology in the Ancient World*, 1970; B. Rothenberg, *Timna*, 1972; R. F. Tylecote, *A History of Metallurgy*, 1976; Jane Waldbaum, *From Bronze to Iron*, 1978.

A.S.
J.Ru.

MINISTER. The Heb. term *mᵉšārēṯ* (LXX *leitourgos*) and its correlates normally refer to temple service, or else to the ministration of angels (Ps. 104:4); but in a more general sense Joshua is the *mᵉšārēṯ* or 'minister' of Moses (Ex. 24:13; Jos. 1:1), and Solomon's ministers (1 Ki. 10:5) are his domestic servants. In the NT the characteristic word is *diakonos*, at first in a non-technical sense, and then in Phil. 1:1 and in the Pastorals as the title of a subordinate church-officer. It refers to service in general, temporary or permanent, either by bond or free; but it has the special connotation of waiting at table (the corresponding verb is used in this sense, Lk. 12:37; 17:8, and Martha's trouble was excess of *diakonia*, Lk. 10:40). Christ appears among the disciples as *ho diakonōn*, 'one who serves' (Lk. 22:27), and he can be described as a *diakonos* of the circumcision (Rom. 15:8); following the example of this lowly service, the greatest of Christians should be a minister to the rest (Mt. 20:26; Mk. 10:43).

Thus we find the apostles and their helpers designated as ministers of God (2 Cor. 6:4; 1 Thes. 3:2), of Christ (2 Cor. 11:23; Col. 1:7; 1 Tim. 4:6), of the gospel (Eph. 3:7; Col. 1:23), of the new covenant (2 Cor. 3:6), of the church (Col. 1:25), or absolutely (1 Cor. 3:5; Eph. 6:21; Col. 4:7). But it is to be noted that Satan can also have his ministers (2 Cor. 11:15), and that there might be a minister of sin (Gal. 2:17); further, the secular power can be regarded as a minister of God (Rom. 13:4). The Seven were appointed to serve tables (*diakonein trapezais*, Acts 6:2); it is unlikely that the word is here used to denote a technical office, since it is immediately afterwards (v. 4) contrasted with the apostles' *diakonia* of the word, and in fact Stephen and Philip did the work of evangelists rather than of deacons; moreover, poor-relief at Jerusalem seems to have been managed by elders, not deacons (Acts 11:30). However, the Seven may in some sense have provided a prototype for the later assistants to the bishops, mentioned in Phil. 1:1, and characterized in 1 Tim. 3:8ff. as men of serious, honest, sober and faithful disposition. Their primary work seems to have been, not that of teaching, but visiting from house to house and relieving the poor and sick; deacons were thus the chief agents through which the church expressed its mutual fellowship of service. They seem also to have assisted at corporate worship.

It is uncertain whether 1 Tim. 3:11 refers to deacons' wives or to deaconesses; Phoebe is described (Rom. 16:1) as a *diakonos* (common gender) of the church at Cenchrea, but this perhaps means that she was a helper rather than that she held an official position; the two *ministrae* mentioned by Pliny in his letter to Trajan may have been deaconesses, but this office was not really developed until the 3rd century.

The lowliness of Christian service is emphasized even more strongly by the use of the word *doulos* or slave; it was the form of such a bond-servant that Christ assumed (Phil. 2:7), and, following his example, the apostles and their fellow-labourers are designated as the slaves of God or Christ (Rom. 1:1; Gal. 1:10; Col. 4:12; Tit. 1:1; Jas. 1:1; 2 Pet. 1:1).

Another term is *hypēretēs*, properly meaning an under-rower in a galley, and then anyone in a subordinate position. This word is used for the *ḥazzān*, a sort of verger in the Jewish synagogue, who had custody of the sacred books (Lk. 4:20); it also describes John Mark (Acts 13:5) when he acted in the capacity of batman to Paul and Barnabas. But Paul himself was proud to claim a similar position in relationship to Christ (Acts 26:16; 1 Cor. 4:1), and Luke (1:2) employs it as a generic term for the servants of the word.

Finally, the term *leitourgos* is taken over by the NT in a Christian sense. Originally it referred to public service, such as might be offered by wealthy citizens to the State; then it acquired a distinctively religious connotation, as in the LXX usage. Thus Christ appears as a *leitourgos* of the heavenly temple (Heb. 8:2), and the angels are 'liturgical', *i.e.* ministering spirits (Heb. 1:14). The corresponding verb is used when prophets and teachers minister to the Lord at Antioch (Acts 13:2); similarly, Paul describes himself as the *leitourgos* of Christ Jesus, ministering (*hierourgōn*) in the priestly service of the gospel of God (Rom. 15:16). But the NT terminology remains sufficiently fluid for the same word to be used of Epaphroditus as a minister to Paul's wants (Phil. 2:25), of Gentile assistance to Jews in material things (Rom. 15:27), and of the civil power as the servant of God (Rom. 13:6). In the Christian understanding of *ministry, whether official or otherwise, the minister renders a lowly but loving service to God or man.

BIBLIOGRAPHY. See under *MINISTRY.

G.S.M.W.
R.T.B.

MINISTRY. To express the idea of professional or priestly ministration, the OT normally employs the verb *šārat̲* and its correlates (LXX *leitourgein*), while *'āb̲ad̲* (*latreuein*) refers rather to the religious service of the whole congregation or of an individual. In the NT the characteristic term is *diakonia*, which appears only in Esther among OT books, but is not there used of any priestly function; and the change in language implies a change also in doctrine, since ministry in the NT sense is not the exclusive privilege of a priestly caste. *leitourgia* is retained to describe the work of the Jewish priesthood (Lk. 1:23, RSV 'service'; Heb. 9:21, RSV 'used in worship'), and it is applied also to the more excellent ministry of Christ (Heb. 8:6); further, it can be applied, in a metaphorical sense, to the spiritual service rendered by prophets and preachers of the gospel (Acts 13:2; Rom. 15:16). But it remains true in general that the NT uses priestly language only in reference to the body of believers as a whole (Phil. 2:17; 1 Pet. 2:9).

I. Christ the pattern

The pattern of Christian ministry is provided by the life of Christ, who came not to receive service but to give it (Mt. 20:28; Mk. 10:45); the verb used in these texts is *diakonein*, which suggests something like waiting at table, and recalls the occasion when he washed the disciples' feet (Jn. 13:4ff.). It is significant that in the first recorded instance of ordination to the Christian ministry, the purpose of the office is stated to be that of 'serving tables' (Acts 6:2); and the same word is used in the same chapter (v. 4) to describe the service of the word exercised prior to this by the twelve apostles. The *minister of Christ, following the example of his Master, renders a humble but loving service to the needs of humanity at large, in the same spirit as that in which angels (Mt. 4:11; Mk. 1:13) and women (Mt. 27:55; Lk. 8:3) had ministered to the Lord on earth. Such service is reckoned as being done to Christ in the persons of the needy (Mt. 25:44); it is most frequently rendered to the saints (Rom. 15:25; 1 Cor. 16:15; 2 Cor. 8:4; 9:1; Heb. 6:10); but it is a mutual service within the fellowship of Christ's body (1 Pet. 4:10); and, as the ministry of the gospel (1 Pet. 1:12), it is in fact a ministry of reconciliation (2 Cor. 5:18) for the world.

The ability to perform such work is a gift of God (Acts 20:24; Col. 4:17; 1 Tim. 1:12; 1 Pet. 4:11); already in Rom. 12:7 it is being classified in a list of other spiritual gifts; and in 1 Tim. 3:8ff. the diaconate has become a recognized church office, probably open to women as well as men (*cf.* Rom. 16:1). But even so, the term is still being used in a wider sense; Timothy is to fulfil his ministry by doing the work of an evangelist (2 Tim. 4:5); and this work of service has as its great object the edification of the body of Christ (Eph. 4:12). In the words of Hort, Christ lifted 'every grade and pattern of service into a higher sphere . . . ministration thus became one of the primary aims of all Christian actions'; and the generic term is applied to all forms of ministry within the church.

II. Pastoral ministry

Christ is not only the pattern of the diaconate, but also, as the good Shepherd (Jn. 10:11), he is the great *Bishop of men's souls (1 Pet. 2:25, AV). In a sense, both of these offices originate from the example of Christ himself, while that of the *presbyter is a reflection of the ministry instituted by him in the apostolate (*cf.* 1 Pet. 5:1). But it would be wrong to stress these distinctions, since the terms bishop and presbyter are virtually synonymous, and the diaconate embraces many forms of assistant ministry. Pastoral care of the flock is an outstanding part of ministerial duty (Jn. 21:15–17; Acts 20:28; 1 Pet. 5:2), and is closely associated with the preaching of the word (1 Cor. 3:1–2) as the bread of life (Jn. 6:35), or pure nourishing milk (1 Pet. 2:2). The parable in Lk. 12:41–48 implies that some ministry of this character is to continue in the church until Christ's return.

III. Sacramental duties

The NT has comparatively little to say on the subject of sacramental duties; Paul regarded the administration of baptism as a subordinate activity, which he was accustomed to delegate to his assistants (1 Cor. 1:17; *cf.* Jn. 4:1f.; Acts 10:48); and although it is natural for an apostle, if present, to preside at the breaking of bread (Acts 20:7), the celebration of the Lord's Supper is nevertheless regarded as an activity of the entire congregation (1 Cor. 10:16f.; 11:25). However, a president must have been needed from the first; and in the absence of an apostle, prophet or evangelist, this duty would naturally fall to one of the local presbyters or bishops.

IV. Spiritual gifts

In its earliest form the Christian ministry is charismatic, *i.e.* it is a spiritual gift or supernatural endowment, whose exercise witnesses to the presence of the Holy Spirit in the church. Thus prophecy and glossolalia occur when Paul lays his hands on some ordinary believers after baptism (Acts 19:6); and the words there used imply that the occurrence was to some extent a repetition of the Pentecostal experience (Acts 2).

Three lists are provided in the Pauline Epistles of the various forms which such ministry may take, and it is notable that in each list administrative functions are included along with others more obviously spiritual (*CHURCH GOVERNMENT). In Rom. 12:6–8 we have prophecy, *service (*diakonia*), teaching, exhortation, contributing (almsgiving), aiding and doing acts of mercy (?visitation of the sick and poor). 1 Cor. 12:28 lists apostles, prophets, teachers, together with those endowed with power to work miracles, heal the sick, help, administer, or speak with tongues. The more official catalogue in Eph. 4:11 mentions apostles, prophets, evangelists, pastors-cum-teachers, who all labour to perfect the saints in their Christian service, so that the whole church grows up in organic connection with her divine Head. Here, emphasis is laid on the ministration of the word, but the fruit of such ministry is mutual service in love. The various gifts listed in these passages are functions or ways of serving, rather than regular and stereotyped offices; one man might act in several capacities, but his ability to fulfil any depended on the prompting of the Spirit. All Christians are in fact called to minister, in their various capacities (Rom. 15:27; Phil. 2:17; Phm. 13; 1 Pet. 2:16), and it is for this ministry that the ministers of the word equip them (Eph. 4:11f.).

Not only the Twelve were included in the apostolate, but also Paul, James the Lord's brother (Gal. 1:19), who had also seen the risen Lord, Barnabas (Acts 14:14; 1 Cor. 9:5f.), who was Paul's fellow-evangelist, and Andronicus and Junias (Rom. 16:7). The primary qualification of an *'apostle' was that he had been an eye-witness of Christ's earthly ministry, particularly of the resurrection (Acts 1:21–22), and his authority depended on the fact that he had been in some way commissioned by Christ either in the days of his flesh (Mt. 10:5; 28:19) or after he was risen from the dead (Acts 1:24; 9:15). Apostles and elders might meet in council to decide a common policy for the church (Acts 15:6ff.), and apostles could be sent as delegates from the original congregation to superintend some new development in another locality (Acts 8:14ff.). But the picture of an apostolic college in permanent session at Jerusalem is quite unhistorical, and the great work of an apostle was to act as a missionary for the propagation of the gospel, in which capacity his labours should be confirmed by signs of divine approval (2 Cor. 12:12). Thus the apostolic ministry was not confined by local ties, though a division of labour might be made, as for example between Peter and Paul (Gal. 2:7–8).

The 'evangelist' exercised a similar ministry of unrestricted mission, and his work seems to have been identical with that of the apostle, except in so far as he lacked the special qualifications for the higher function; Philip, one of the original Seven, became an evangelist (Acts 21:8), and Timothy is called by the same title (2 Tim. 4:5), though he is by implication excluded (2 Cor. 1:1) from the rank of apostle.

Prophecy was by its very nature a gift of intermittent occurrence, but some individuals were so regularly endowed with it that they formed a special class of 'prophets'. Such men were found at Jerusalem (Acts 11:27), Antioch (Acts 13:1), and Corinth (1 Cor. 14:29); those mentioned by name include Judas and Silas (Acts 15:32), and Agabus (Acts 21:10), together with Anna (Lk. 2:36) and the pretended prophetess Jezebel (Rev. 2:20). Prophecy provided edification, exhortation and comfort (1 Cor. 14:3; *cf.* Acts 15:32), and might therefore be described as inspired preaching. The prophet could issue a specific direction (Acts 13:1–2) or on occasion foretell the future (Acts 11:28). Being delivered in a known tongue, his messages were more profitable than mere glossolalia (1 Cor. 14:23–25). But the gift was particularly liable to the danger of imposture, and although it should be controlled only by those possessing it (1 Cor. 14:32; 1 Thes. 5:19f.), its content must agree with the fundamental teaching of the gospel (1 Cor. 12:1–3; 1 Thes. 5:20; 1 Jn. 4:1–3), or else the prophet must be dismissed as one of the false pretenders whose coming had been foretold by Christ (Mt. 7:15).

'Pastors and teachers' (Eph. 4:11) are presumably to be identified with the local ministers instituted by the apostles (Acts 14:23) or their assistants (Tit. 1:5) to serve the needs of a particular congregation, and described indifferently as presbyters or bishops. 'Administrators' (AV 'governors') seems to be a generic name for those who administered the affairs of local congregations, while 'helpers' were engaged in works of charity, especially in attending to the sick and poor. Miraculous powers of healing and speaking with tongues were a marked feature of the apostolic age, and their renewal has been claimed at various periods from the Montanist revival onwards.

V. The origin of the ministry

There has been much debate over the precise relationship between the original and unrestricted mission of apostles and evangelists, on the one hand, and the permanent and local ministry of pastors, teachers, administrators and helpers, on the other. The latter class appears usually to have been appointed by the former; but if Acts 6 may be taken as describing a typical ordination, popular election played a part in the choice of candidates. Rom. 12 and 1 Cor. 12 might seem to imply that the church, as the Spirit-filled community, produces its own organs of ministration; on the other hand, Eph. 4:11 asserts that the ministry is given to the church by Christ. It may be suggested that, while Christ is the source of all authority and the pattern of every type of service, the church as a whole is the recipient of his divine commission. At all events, the NT is not concerned to indicate possible channels of transmission; its main preoccupation in this regard is to provide a doctrinal test for the orthodoxy of ministerial teaching.

BIBLIOGRAPHY. J. B. Lightfoot, 'Dissertation on the Christian Ministry', in *Philippians*, 1868, pp. 181–269; A. von Harnack, *The Constitution and Law of the Church in the First Two Centuries*, E.T., 1910; H. B. Swete, *Early History of the Church and Ministry*, 1918; K. E. Kirk (ed.), *The Apostolic Ministry*, 1946; D. T. Jenkins, *The Gift of Ministry*, 1947; T. W. Manson, *The Church's Ministry*, 1948; J. K. S. Reid, *The Biblical Doctrine of the Ministry*, 1955; E. Schweizer, *Church Order in the NT*, E.T., 1961; L. Morris, *Ministers of God*, 1964; J. R. W. Stott, *One People*, 1969; J. N. Collins, *Diakonia*, 1990; E. M. B. Green, *Freed to Serve*[2], 1996.

G.S.M.W.
R.T.B.

MINNI. A people summoned by Jeremiah, with Ararat (Armenia) and Ashkenaz, to make war on Babylonia (Je. 51:27). The Mannai, whose territory lay SE of Lake Urmia, are frequently named in texts of the 9th–7th centuries BC. The Assyrians dominated them until 673 BC, when they were controlled by the Medes (v. 28). In the light of Jeremiah, it is interesting to note that the Mannai were allied with the Assyrians, their former enemies, against the Babylonians in 616 BC (Bab. Chronicle). They were probably present with the Guti and other hill-folk at the capture of Babylon in 539 BC. D.J.W.

MINNITH (Heb. *minnîṯ*). Mentioned in Jdg. 11:33 as the limit of Jephthah's invasion of Ammon. Eusebius (*Onom*. p. 132) indicates that it lay at the head of a natural route from the Jordan to the uplands between Rabbath-Ammon (Amman) and Heshbon. The exact site is unknown.

Ezk. 27:17 may refer to the same; but see W. Zimmevli, *Ezekiel*, 1983, *ad loc*. J.P.U.L.

MIRACLES. A number of Heb., Aram. and Gk. words are used in the Bible to refer to the activity in nature and history of the living God. They are variously translated in the EVV by 'miracles', 'wonders', 'signs', 'mighty acts', 'powers'. Thus, for example, the Heb. word *môp̄ēṯ*, which is of uncertain etymology, is translated in RSV by 'miracle' (Ex. 7:9; Ps. 78:43), 'wonder' (*e.g.* Ex. 7:3; Dt. 4:34) and 'sign' (*e.g.* 1 Ki. 13:3, 5).

The words used by the English translators preserve in general, though not always in particular instances, the three distinctive emphases of the originals. These characterize God's activity as being:

1. Distinctive, wonderful; expressed by Heb. derivatives of the root *pl'*, 'be different', particularly the participle *nip̄lā'ôṯ* (*e.g.* Ex. 15:11; Jos. 3:5), by Aramaic *ṯ*ᵉ*māh* (Dn. 4:2–3; 6:27), and by Gk. *teras* (*e.g.* Acts 4:30; Rom. 15:19).

2. Mighty, powerful; expressed by Heb. *g*ᵉ*ḇûrâ* (Pss. 106:2; 145:4) and Gk. *dynamis* (*e.g.* Mt. 11:20; 1 Cor. 12:10; Gal. 3:5).

3. Meaningful, significant; expressed by Heb. *'ôṯ* (*e.g.* Nu. 14:11; Ne. 9:10), by Aramaic *'āṯ* (Dn. 4:2–3; 6:27), and by Gk. *sēmeion* (*e.g.* Jn. 2:11; 3:2; Acts 8:6).

I. Miracles and the natural order

A great deal of confusion on the subject of miracles has been caused by a failure to observe that Scripture does not sharply distinguish between God's constant sovereign providence and his particular acts. Belief in miracles is set in the context of a world-view which regards the whole of creation as continually dependent upon the sustaining activity of God and subject to his sovereign will (*cf.* Col. 1:16–17). All three aspects of divine activity—wonder, power, significance—are present not only in special acts but also in the whole created order (Rom. 1:20). When the psalmist celebrates the mighty acts of God he moves readily from the creation to the deliverance from Egypt (Ps. 135:6–12). In Jb. 5:9–10; 9:9–10 the word *nip̄lā'ôṯ* refers to what we would call 'natural events' (*cf.* Is. 8:18; Ezk. 12:6).

Thus when the biblical writers refer to the mighty acts of God they cannot be supposed to distinguish them from 'the course of nature' by their peculiar causation, since they think of all events as caused by God's sovereign power. The particular acts of God highlight the distinctive character of God's activity, different from and superior to that of men and more particularly that of false gods, almighty in power, revealing him in nature and history.

The discovery of, say, causal connections between the different plagues of Egypt, a repetition of the blocking of the Jordan, or increased knowledge of psychosomatic medicine could not of themselves contradict the biblical assertion that the deliverance from Egypt, the entry to Canaan and the healing works of Christ were mighty acts of God. 'Natural laws' are descriptions of that universe in which God is ever at work. It is only by an unwarranted philosophical twist that they are construed as the self-sustaining working of a closed system or the rigid decrees of a God who set the universe to work like some piece of machinery.

It has been argued by some philosophers and theologians that the working of miracles is inconsistent with God's nature and purpose. He is the

Alpha and Omega, he knows the end from the beginning; he is the Creator who fashioned all things unhampered by any limitation imposed by pre-existent matter; he is the unchanging One. Why, then, should he need to 'interfere' with the working of the natural order?

This objection based on the character of God arises from a failure to grasp the biblical understanding of God as living and personal. His changelessness is not that of an impersonal force but the faithfulness of a person: his creative act brought into being responsible creatures with whom he deals, not as puppets but as other persons over against himself. Miracles are events which dramatically reveal this living, personal nature of God, active in history not as mere Destiny but as a Redeemer who saves and guides his people.

A fuller knowledge of the ways of God's working may show that some supposedly unique events were part of a regular pattern. It can, however, never logically exclude the exceptional and extraordinary. While there is no such radical discontinuity between miracles and the 'natural order' as has been assumed by those who have most keenly felt the modern doubts on the subject, it is clear that Scripture speaks of many events which are extraordinary or even unique so far as our general experience of nature goes.

II. Miracles and revelation

If it be granted that *a priori* objections to miracle stories are invalid, it still remains to ask what precise function these extraordinary events perform in the total self-revelation of God in history. Orthodox theologians have been accustomed to regard them primarily as the authenticating marks of God's prophets and apostles and supremely of his Son. More recently it has been argued by liberal critics that the miracle stories of OT and NT are of the same character as the wonder-stories told of pagan deities and their prophets. Both these views fail to do justice to the integral relationship between the miracle stories and the whole self-revelation of God. Miracles are not simply an external authentication of the revelation but an essential part of it, of which the true purpose was and is to nourish faith in the saving intervention of God towards those who believe.

a. False miracles

Jesus consistently refused to give a *sign from heaven, to work useless and spectacular wonders, simply to guarantee his teaching. In any case the simple ability to work miracles would have been no such guarantee. There is frequent reference both in Scripture and elsewhere to wonder-working by those who were opposed to the purposes of God (*cf.* Dt. 13:2–3; Mt. 7:22; 24:24; 2 Thes. 2:9; Rev. 13:13ff.; 16:14; 19:20). The refusal to do wonders for their own sake sharply marks off the biblical miracle stories from the general run of *Wundergeschichten.*

It is noteworthy that the word *teras*, which of all the biblical terms has most nearly the overtones of the English 'portent', is always used in the NT in conjunction with *sēmeion* to stress that only significant portents are meant. The only exception is the OT quotation in Acts 2:19 (but *cf.* Acts 2:22).

The mere portent or the false miracle is distinguished from the true by the fact that the true miracle is congruous with the rest of the revelation. It harmonizes with the knowledge which believers already possess concerning God, even where it also carries that knowledge farther and deeper. Thus Israel is to reject any miracle-worker who denies the Lord (Dt. 13:2–3) and thus also we may rightly discern between the miracle stories of the canonical Gospels and the romantic tales or ludicrous stupidities of the apocryphal writings and mediaeval hagiography.

b. Miracles and faith

The working of miracles is directed to a deepening of men's understanding of God. It is God's way of speaking dramatically to those who have ears to hear. The miracle stories are intimately concerned with the faith of observers or participants (*cf.* Ex. 14:31; 1 Ki. 18:39) and with the faith of those who will hear or read them later (Jn. 20:30–31). Jesus looked for faith as the right response to his saving presence and deeds; it was faith which 'made whole', which made the difference between the mere creation of an impression and a saving communication of his revelation of God.

It is important to observe that faith on the part of human participants is not a necessary condition of a miracle in the sense that God is of himself unable to act without human faith. Mk. 6:5 is often quoted to support such a view, but Jesus could do no mighty work in Nazareth, not because the people's unbelief limited his power—Mark tells us that he healed a few sick people there—but rather because he could not proceed with his preaching or with the deeds which proclaimed his gospel in action where men were unready to accept his good news and his own person. Wonder-working for the crowds or the sceptics was inconsistent with his mission: it is in this sense that he could not do it in Nazareth.

c. Miracles and the Word

It is a notable feature—in some cases the chief feature—of miracles that even where the matter of the event is such that it can be assimilated to the ordinary pattern of natural events (*e.g.* some of the plagues of Egypt), its occurrence is predicted by God to or through his agent (*cf.* Jos. 3:7–13; 1 Ki. 13:1–5) or takes place at an agent's command or prayer (*cf.* Ex. 4:17; Nu. 20:8; 1 Ki. 18:37–38); sometimes both prediction and command are recorded (*cf.* Ex. 14). This feature emphasizes yet again the connection between miracles and revelation, and between miracles and the divine creative Word.

d. The crises of the sacred history

Another connection between miracles and revelation is that they cluster about the crises of sacred history. The pre-eminently mighty acts of God are the deliverance at the Red Sea and the resurrection of Christ, the first the climax of the conflict with Pharaoh and the gods of Egypt (Ex. 12:12; Nu. 33:4), the second the climax of God's redeeming work in Christ and the conflict with all the power of evil. Miracles are also frequently noted in the time of Elijah and Elisha, when Israel seemed most likely to sink into complete apostasy (*cf.* 1 Ki. 19:14); in the time of the siege of Jerusalem under Hezekiah (2 Ki. 20:11); during the Exile (Dn. *passim*); and in the early days of the Christian mission.

III. Miracles in the New Testament

Some liberal treatments of the question of miracles draw a marked distinction between the miracles of the NT, particularly those of our Lord himself, and those of the OT. Both more radical and more conservative critics have pointed out that in principle the narratives stand or fall together.

The contention that the NT miracles are more credible in the light of modern psychology or psychosomatic medicine leaves out of account the nature miracles, such as that at the wedding-feast in Cana and the calming of the storm, the instantaneous cures of organic disease and malformation, and the raising of the dead. There is no *a priori* reason to suppose that Jesus did not make use of those resources of the human mind and spirit which today are employed by the psychotherapist; but other narratives take us into realms where psychotherapy makes no assertions and where the claims of spiritual healers find least support from qualified medical observers.

There is, however, evidence for regarding the miracles of Christ and those done in his name as different from those of the OT. Where before God had done mighty works in his transcendent power and revealed them to his servants or used his servants as the occasional agents of such deeds, in Jesus there confronts us God himself incarnate, freely active in sovereign authority in that world which is 'his own'. When the apostles did similar works in his name they acted in the power of the risen Lord with whom they were in intimate contact, so that Acts continues the story of the same things which Jesus began to do and teach in his earthly ministry (*cf.* Acts 1:1).

In stressing and direct presence and action of God in Christ we do not deny the continuity of his work with the previous course of God's dealing with the world. Of the list of works given by our Lord in answering the Baptist's inquiry (Mt. 11:5) it is the most wonderful, the healing of lepers and the raising of the dead, which have OT parallels, notably in the ministry of Elisha. What is remarkable is the intergral relationship between the works and words of Jesus. The blind receive their sight, the lame walk, the deaf hear, and at the same time that the gospel is preached to the poor by which spiritual sight and hearing and a power to walk in God's way are given to the spiritually needy.

Again, the frequency of healing miracles is far greater in the time of the NT than at any period of the OT. The OT records its miracles one by one and gives no indication that there were others unrecorded. The Gospels and the NT in general repeatedly claim that the miracles described in detail were but a fraction of those wrought.

Jesus' works are clearly marked off from others by their manner or mode. There is in Jesus' dealing with the sick and demon-possessed a note of inherent authority. Where prophets did their works in the name of God or after prayer to God, Jesus casts out demons and heals with that same air of rightful power as informs his pronouncement of forgiveness to the sinner; indeed, he deliberately linked the two authorities (Mk. 2:9–11). At the same time Jesus stressed that his works were done in constant dependence on the Father (*e.g.* Jn. 5:19). The balance between inherent authority and humble dependence is the very mark of the perfect unity of deity and humanity.

NT teaching on the virgin birth, the resurrection and the ascension emphasizes the newness of what God did in Christ. He was born of a woman in the genealogy of Abraham and David, but of a virgin; others had been raised from death, only to die again; he 'always lives' and has ascended to the right hand of power. It is, moreover, true of the resurrection as of no other individual miracle that on it the NT rests the whole structure of faith (*cf.* 1 Cor. 15:17). This event was unique as the decisive triumph over sin and death.

The miracles of the apostles and other leaders of the NT church spring from the solidarity of Christ with his people. They are works done in his name, in continuation of all that Jesus began to do and teach, in the power of the Spirit he sent from the Father. There is a close link between these miracles and the work of the apostles in testifying to the person and work of their Lord; they are part of the proclamation of the kingdom of God, not an end in themselves.

The debate continues over the contention that this function of miracle was of necessity confined to the apostolic age. But we may at least say that the NT miracles were distinct from any subsequent ones by virtue of their immediate connection with the full manifestation of the incarnate Son of God, with a revelation then given in its fullness. They do not, therefore, afford grounds in themselves for expecting miracles to accompany the subsequent dissemination of the revelation of which they formed an integral part.

BIBLIOGRAPHY. D. S. Cairns, *The Faith that Rebels*, 1927; A. Richardson, *The Miracle Stories of the Gospels*, 1941; C. S. Lewis, *Miracles, A Preliminary Study*, 1947; E. and M.-L. Keller, *Miracles in Dispute*, 1969; C. F. D. Moule (ed.), *Miracles: Cambridge Studies in their Philosophy and History*, 1965; C. Brown, *Miracles and the Critical Mind*, 1984; *That You May Believe*, 1985. M.H.C.

MIRIAM. (For derivation, see *MARY.) **1.** The daughter of Amram and Jochebed, and the sister of Aaron and Moses (Nu. 26:59). It is generally agreed that it was she who watched the baby Moses in the bulrushes and suggested her mother as his nurse. The term 'the prophetess' was used to describe her as she led the women in music, dancing and singing a paean of praise to celebrate the crossing of the Red Sea (Ex. 15:20f.).

Miriam and Aaron rebelled against Moses, supposedly because of his marriage to the Cushite woman, but in reality because they were jealous of his position. Divine judgment descended upon Miriam and she became leprous, whereupon Moses interceded for her and she was cleansed, but she was excluded from the camp for 7 days (Nu. 12). She died at Kadesh and was buried there (Nu. 20:1). There is no record of her marriage in the Bible, but rabbinical tradition makes her the wife of Caleb and mother of Hur.

2. In his genealogy the Chronicler lists a Miriam as one of the children of Ezrah, of the tribe of Judah (1 Ch. 4:17). M.B.

MIRROR. During the OT period mirrors were made of metal, cast and highly polished (Jb. 37:18). Several bronze examples dating from the Middle Bronze Age onwards have been found in Palestine. These are of a form common throughout the Near East; *cf.* those used by the Israelite women in Ex. 38:8 (see *ANEP*, No. 71). The meaning of Heb. *gillāyôn* in Isaiah's list of finery (3:23, rendered 'tablet' in Is. 8:1) is uncertain; it may mean mirrors (Targ., AV, RV); others suggest garments of gauze (LXX, RSV). Glass mirrors were probably introduced in the 1st century AD. Whether of metal or glass, these mirrors never gave a perfect reflection (1 Cor. 13:12). It is probable that in 2 Cor. 3:18 (Gk. *hēmeis . . . katoptrizomenoi*) Paul's idea is that we see merely a reflection (AV); but it may be that we reflect (RV; see Arndt, pp. 425–426; R. V. G. Tasker, *2 Corinthians*, *TNTC*, 1958, pp. 67–68). James gives a simple illustration from the use of a mirror (1:23). A.R.M.

MISHAEL (Heb. *mîšā'ēl*, 'who is what God is'?). **1.** A son of *Uzziel, a Levite (Ex. 6:22) who, with his brother *Elzaphan, carried the bodies of Nadab and Abihu outside the camp after they had been killed for desecrating the altar (Lv. 10:1–5). **2.** A colleague of Daniel (Dn. 1:6, 11, *etc*.; 1 Macc. 2:59) whose name was changed to Meshach by the Babylonians (Dn. 1:7). D.W.B.

MISREPHOTH-MAIM (Heb. *miśrᵉpôṯ-mayim*). A limit of pursuit from *Merom (Jos. 11:8); the S border of Sidon (Jos. 13:6). If it was the rocky headland of Rosh Haniqra, Khirbet el-Mushreifeh (at the N end of the Acre plain) preserved the name; the gap in Late Bronze and Early Iron occupation would not be relevant. However, there were Israelite settlements to the N, and the river Litani is a possible identification (*LOB*, p. 238). See *NEAEHL*, p. 1288. J.P.U.L.

MITHREDATH ('given by Mithra', the Persian god of light. *Cf.* Gk.–Lat. 'Mithridates'). **1.** The treasurer of Cyrus king of Persia, who in 536 BC restored to Sheshbazzar the sacred vessels confiscated by Nebuchadrezzar from Jerusalem (Ezr. 1:8). **2.** A Persian officer in Samaria, one of those who wrote in Aram. to Artaxerxes ('Longimanus') protesting against the rebuilding of the walls of Jerusalem (Ezr. 4:7). B.F.H.

MITRE (AV; Heb. *miṣnepeṯ*). One of the high priest's holy garments. From the use of the Heb. verb in Is. 22:18 it is thought to have been a kind of turban (RSV) wound round the head. It is described in Ex. 28:4, 36–39. On it was worn 'the plate of the holy crown' engraved 'Holy to the Lord' (Ex. 39:28, 30f.). Aaron wore it for his anointing (Lv. 8:9) and on the Day of Atonement (Lv. 16:4). To be uncovered was a sign of mourning (Ezk. 24:17) and uncleanness (Lv. 13:45; *cf.* 10:6) and was specifically forbidden to the high priest (Lv. 21:10–12)—*cf.* the 'bonnets' (AV) or 'caps' (Ex. 28:40; 29:9) (*miḡbā'ôṯ*) of inferior priests—so that Ezekiel (21:26) prophesies of the removal of the mitre because of the profanity of Israel, and Zechariah (3:5) sees Joshua invested with it (*ṣānîp̄*) as a sign of his cleansing and acceptance by God. Israel's ultimate renewal is symbolized by calling her a royal mitre (diadem) in the hand of God (Is. 62:3). P.A.B.

MITYLENE. An ancient republic of the Aeolian Greeks and the principal state of the island of Lesbos. Its situation at the cross-roads of Europe and Asia frequently placed its political fortunes in jeopardy, until under the pax Romana it settled down as an honoured subordinate, highly favoured by the Romans as a holiday resort. A capacious harbour facing the mainland of Asia Minor across the straits made it a natural overnight stop for Paul's vessel on the S run to Palestine (Acts 20:14).

BIBLIOGRAPHY. R. Herbst, *RE*, 16. 2. 1411. E.A.J.

MIZAR. A hill mentioned in Ps. 42:6, in connection with Mt Hermon. It may be presumed that Hermon was visible from it; in which case it would have been in the Galilee region—note the reference to the Jordan. The word in Heb. (*miṣ'ār*) means 'smallness'. Some scholars emend the text of Ps. 42:6 slightly, making *miṣ'ār* an adjective, 'small', referring to Mt Zion. In this case the psalmist would be stating his preference for Zion rather than Hermon's great bulk. D.F.P.

MIZPAH, MIZPEH. The basic meaning of the word is 'watchtower', 'place for watching'. It is vocalized as *miṣpâ* and *miṣpeh*, and is found usually with the article. It is natural to look for places so named on high vantage-points. The following may be distinguished:

1. The place where *Jacob and Laban made a covenant and set up a cairn of stones as a witness (Galeed, *gal'ēḏ* in Hebrew, or *yᵉḡar śāhᵃḏûṯā'* in Aramaic). God was the watcher between them (Gn. 31:44–49).

2. Either the same place as **1** or a town in Gilead, E of the Jordan. The article is used both in Gn. 31:49 (*hammiṣpâ*), and in Jdg. 10:17; 11:11, 34. The place features in the story of Jephthah. When Ammon encroached on Gilead the Israelites assembled at Mizpah (Jdg. 10:17), the home of Jephthah, from which he commenced his attack and to which he returned to carry out his rash vow (Jdg. 11:11, 29, 34). Its identification with Ramoth-gilead is urged by some writers (J. D. Davis, *WDB*, p. 401), but is rejected by F. M. Abel and du Buit, who identify it with Jal'ûd. It is possibly the same as Ramath-mizpeh or height of Mizpeh (Jos. 13:26).

3. A place in Moab to which David took his parents for safety (1 Sa. 22:3), possibly the modern Rujm el-Meshrefeh, WSW of Madaba. **4.** A place at the foot of Mt Hermon (Jos. 11:3), referred to as 'the land of Mizpeh' or 'the valley of Mizpeh' (v. 8), the home of the Hivites. Opinions differ as to its identification, but Qal'at eṣ-Ṣubeibeh on a hill 3 km NE of Banias has much support. **5.** A town in the Shephelah (lowlands) of Judah named along with Joktheel, Lachish and Eglon (Jos. 15:38–39). The sites of Khirbet Ṣāfiyeh, 4 km NE of Beit Jibrin, and Ṣufiyeh, 10 km N, are possible choices for this Mizpeh.

6. A town of Benjamin (Jos. 18:26), in the neighbourhood of Gibeon and Ramah (1 Ki. 15:22). In the days of the Judges, when the Benjaminites of Gibeah outraged the Levite's concubine, the men of Israel assembled here (Jdg. 20:1, 3; 21:1, 5, 8). Here Samuel assembled Israel for prayer after the ark had been restored to Kiriath-jearim (1 Sa. 7:5–6). The Philistines attacked them, but were driven back (vv. 7, 11), and Samuel erected a stone of remembrance near by at Ebenezer (v. 12). Here also Saul was presented to the people as their king (1 Sa. 10:17). Mizpeh was one of the places visited by Samuel annually to judge Israel (1 Sa. 7:16).

King Asa fortified Mizpeh against Baasha of Israel, using materials his men took from Baasha's fort at Ramah, after Asa had asked the Syrian Ben-hadad to attack Israel (1 Ki. 15:22; 2 Ch. 16:6). After the destruction of Jerusalem by Nebuchad-rezzar in 587 BC, Gedaliah was appointed governor of the remainder of the people, the governor's residence being fixed at Mizpeh (2 Ki. 25:23, 25). The prophet Jeremiah, released by Nebuzaradan, the captain of the guard, joined Gedaliah at Mizpeh (Je. 40:6), and refugee Jews soon returned (Je. 40:8, 10, 12–13, 15), Soon after, Ishmael of the royal seed slew Gedaliah and the garrison at the instigation of Baalis, king of Ammon. Two days later he murdered a company of pilgrims and threw their bodies into the great cistern Asa had built. He imprisoned others and sought to carry them to Ammon, but was frustrated by Johanan (Je. 41:1, 3, 6, 10, 14, 16).

Two references to a Mizpah in post-exilic times occur in Ne. 3:15, 19. It is possible that one or both of these refer to Mizpah of Benjamin, though they may represent different places.

Mizpah was the scene of an important assembly in the days when Judas Maccabaeus called the men of Judah together for counsel and prayer (1 Macc. 3:46), 'because Israel formerly had a place of prayer in Mizpah'.

Two identifications are offered today—Nebi Samwil 7 km NW of Jerusalem, 895 m above sea-level and 150 m above the surrounding country, and Tell en-Nasbeh on the top of an isolated hill about 13 km N of Jerusalem. The evidence in favour of Tell en-Nasbeh is stronger than for Nebi Samwil, because it can be seen how the consonants *mzph* could become *nzbh* phonetically and the archaeological evidence supports the identification.

The site itself is ancient and was occupied in the Early Bronze Age, to judge from tombs in the area. It seems to have been deserted in the Middle and Late Bronze periods but was re-occupied in the Iron I period and continued during the years *c.* 1100–400 BC, so that it belongs to the period of Israelite settlement. In the days of the kings and during the Persian period the town was prosperous, as the relatively rich tombs suggest. Prosperity is also suggested by architectural remains, the massive gate, a large number of cisterns and silos, some dye-plants, numerous spinning-whorls, loom-weights, wine and oil presses, pottery, beads of semi-precious stones, pins, bangles and metal jewellery. The city expanded beyond its walls during the Iron II period, but began to decline in the 5th century BC. Fragments of Gk. pottery in the later city suggest trade with the Aegean areas. Numerous epigraphic discoveries, scarabs, stamped jar handles bearing the letters *MṢH* and *MṢP* (*i.e.* Miṣpah), a cuneiform inscription bearing the words *šar kiššati*, 'king of the universe', dating to the period *c.* 800–650 BC, and a beautiful seal bearing the inscription *ly'znyhw 'bd hmlk*, 'belonging to Jaazaniah, slave of the king', all attest the importance of the town.

BIBLIOGRAPHY. *LOB*, *passim*; D. Diringer, 'Mizpah', in *AOTS*, pp. 329–342; C. C. McCowan, *Excavations at Tell En-Nasbeh*, 2 vols., 1947; J. F. Muilenburg, *IDB* 3, pp. 407–409; M. Broshi, *NEAEHL*, pp. 1098–1102. J.A.T.

MIZRAIM. 1. Second son of Ham and progenitor of Ludim, Anamim, Lehabim, Naphtuhim, Casluhim and Caphtorim (Gn. 10:6, 13; 1 Ch. 1:8, 11). See *NATIONS, TABLE OF, and individual articles.

2. *miṣrayim* is also the regular Heb. (and common Semitic) term for Egypt. For details on this name, see *EGYPT (Name).

3. In 1 Ki. 10:28–29, it is possible to argue that the first *miṣrayim* is not Egypt but a land Muṣur in SE Asia Minor, and to render (modifying RSV) 'Solomon's import of horses was from Muṣur and from Que' (Cilicia), but this would require the *miṣrayim* of 2 Ch. 9:28 to be taken also as Muṣur and not Egypt. It is perhaps better to render *miṣrayim* as Egypt in these two passages as in all other OT references. See also P. Garelli, *Muṣur*, in *DBS*, 5, fasc. 29, 1957, cols. 1468–1474; H. Tadmor, 'Que and Muṣri', *IEJ* 11, 1961, pp. 143–150. K.A.K.

MNASON. 'An early (original) disciple'—*i.e.* at least from Pentecost—and Paul's host (Acts 21:16). Like Barnabas, he was a Jewish Cypriot. The name is Greek, and common.

Vulg., AV, RV, NEB understand the passage 'Caesarean disciples brought Mnason' (but why should they bring the prospective host?); RSV, TEV translate 'bringing *us* to the house of Mnason'. Neither is easy; probably *Mnasōni* has been attracted into the case of its relative (*cf.* A. T. Robertson, *Gram.*, p. 719). One would infer Mnason's residence in Jerusalem: a Hellenist host might not embarrass Paul's Gentile friends. The Western reading, valueless in itself, has 'reaching a village, we were with Mnason': perhaps a guess—the journey would require a night-stop—but perhaps correctly interpreting Luke. Mnason's house would then lie between Caesarea and Jerusalem: hence the escort, and the reference to Jerusalem in v. 17.

Luke's allusion may indicate Mnason provided source-material (*cf.* Ramsay, *BRD*, p. 309n.).

BIBLIOGRAPHY. F. F. Bruce, *The Acts of the Apostles*, 1951, *ad loc*; *The Pauline Circle*, 1985. A.F.W.

MOAB, MOABITES. Moab (Heb. *mô'āḇ*) was the son of Lot by incestuous union with his eldest daughter (Gn. 19:37). Both the descendants and the land were known as Moab, and the people also as Moabites (*mô'āḇî*). The core of Moab was the plateau E of the Dead Sea between the wadis Arnon and Zered, though for considerable periods Moab extended well to the N of the Arnon. The average height of the plateau is 100 m, but it is cut by deep gorges. The Arnon itself divides about 21 km from the Dead Sea and several times more farther E into valleys of diminishing depth, the 'valleys of the Arnon' (Nu. 21:14). The Bible has preserved the names of many Moabite towns (Nu. 21:15, 20; 32:3; Jos. 13:17–20; Is. 15–16; Je. 48:20ff.).

In pre-Exodus times Moab was occupied and had settled villages until about 1850 BC. Lot's descendants found a population already there, and must have intermarried with them to emerge at length as the dominant group who gave their name to the whole population. The four kings from the E invaded Moab and overthrew the people of Shaveh-kiriathaim (Gn. 14:5). Either as a result of this campaign, or due to some cause unknown,

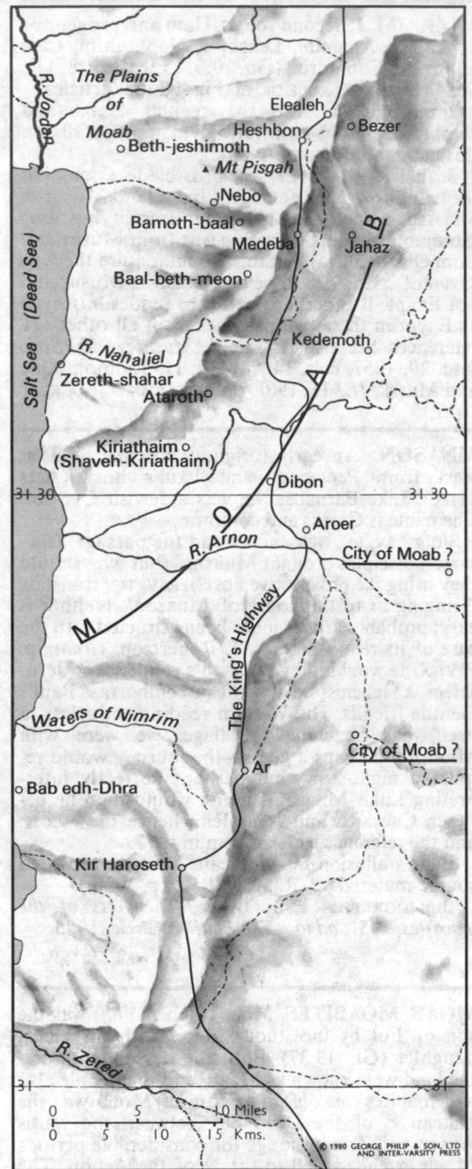

Moab and possible sites of the 'city of Moab'.

Transjordan entered on a period of non-sedentary occupation till just before 1300 BC, when several of the Iron Age kingdoms appeared simultaneously. Moab, like the others, was a highly organized kingdom with good agricultural and pastoral pursuits, splendid buildings, distinctive pottery, and strong fortifications in the shape of small fortresses strategically placed around her boundaries. The Moabites overflowed their main plateau and occupied areas N of the Arnon, destroying the former inhabitants (Dt. 2:10–11, 19–21; *cf.* Gn. 14:5). These lands were shared with the closely related Ammonites.

Just prior to the Exodus, these lands N of the Arnon were wrested from Moab by Sihon, king of the Amorites. When Israel sought permission to travel along 'the King's Highway' which crossed the plateau, Moab refused (Jdg. 11:17). They may have had commercial contact (Dt. 2:28–29). Moses was forbidden to attack Moab despite their unfriendliness (Dt. 2:9), although Moabites were henceforth to be excluded from Israel (Dt. 23:3–6; Ne. 13:1).

Balak, king of Moab, distressed by the Israelite successes, called for the prophet Balaam to curse Israel now settled across the Arnon (Nu. 22–24; Jos. 24:9).

As Israel prepared to cross the Jordan, they camped in the 'plains of Moab' (Nu. 22:1; Jos. 3:1) and were seduced by Moabite and Midianite women to participate in idolatrous practices (Nu. 25; Ho. 9:10).

In the days of the Judges, Eglon, king of Moab, invaded Israelite lands as far as Jericho and oppressed Israel for 18 years. Ehud the Benjaminite assassinated him (Jdg. 3:12–30). Elimelech of Bethlehem migrated to Moab and his sons married Moabite women, Orpah and Ruth. Ruth later married Boaz and became the ancestress of David (Ru. 4:18–22; Mt. 1:5–16). Saul warred with the Moabites (1 Sa. 14:47) and David lodged his parents there while he was a fugitive (1 Sa. 22:3–4). Later David subdued Moab and set apart many Moabites for death (2 Sa. 8:2, 12; 1 Ch. 18:2, 11). After Solomon's death, Moab broke free, but was subdued by Omri of Israel. (*MESHA, *MOABITE STONE.) Towards the close of Ahab's life Moab began to break free again. Jehoram of Israel sought the help of Jehoshaphat, king of Judah, and the king of Edom to regain Moab, but the campaign was abortive (2 Ki. 1:1; 3:4–27). Later, Jehoshaphat's own land was invaded by a confederacy of Moabites, Ammonites and Edomites, but confusion broke out and the allies attacked one another so that Judah was delivered (2 Ch. 20:1–30).

In the year of Elisha's death, bands of Moabites raided Israel (2 Ki. 13:20). During the latter part of the 8th century BC Moab was subdued by Assyria and compelled to pay tribute (Is. 15–16), but after Assyria fell Moab was free again. Moabites entered Judah in the days of Jehoiakim (2 Ki. 24:2). At the fall of Jerusalem in 587 BC some Jews found refuge in Moab, but returned when Gedaliah became governor (Je. 40:11ff.). Moab was finally subdued by Nebuchadrezzar (Jos., *Ant.* 10. 181) and fell successively under the control of the Persians and various Arab groups. The Moabites ceased to have independent existence as a nation, though in post-exilic times they were known as a race (Ezr. 9:1; Ne. 13:1, 23). Alexander Jannaeus subdued them in the 2nd century BC (Jos., *Ant.* 13. 374).

In the prophets they are often mentioned and divine judgment pronounced on them (see Is. 15–16; 25:10; Je. 9:26; 25:21; 27:3; Ezk. 25:8–11; Am. 2:1–3; Zp. 2:8–11).

The archaeological story of Moab is slowly being unravelled. Excavation in Jordan has not proceeded as rapidly as it has in areas to the W of the Jordan, although in recent decades the programme has been increased. Important sites which have yielded significant results are Dibon, Aroer, Bab edh-Dhra and several sites in the area of the Lisan.

Our knowledge of Moab in early archaeological periods has been greatly expanded with new information about the transition between the Chalcolitic and the Early Bronze Age and the later transition between the Early and Middle Bronze Ages. At Bab edh-Dhra a vast cemetery of the Early Bronze Age has provided material from EB I to EB IV. The excavations at Aroer have given support to the theory that much of Moab was unoccupied during the greater part of the 2nd millennium. This site and the site of Dibon were typical of important Iron Age walled settlements contemporary with the period of the kings of Israel. At Dibon the important *Moabite (or Mesha) Stone was discovered. Sedentary life in these sites declined from the end of the 6th century BC down to the end of the 4th century.

BIBLIOGRAPHY. F. M. Abel, *Géographie de la Palestine*, 1, 1933, pp. 278–281; N. Glueck, *The Other Side of Jordan*, 1940, pp. 150ff.; *idem*, *AASOR* 14–15, 18–19; A. D. Tushingham, *The Excavations at Dibon (Dhiban) in Moab*, *AASOR* 40, 1972; A. H. van Zyl, *The Moabites*, 1960; J. R. Bartlett, in *POTT*, pp. 229–258; E. D. Grohman, *IDB* 3, pp. 409–419; J. A. F. Sawyer and D. J. A. Clines, *Midian, Moab and Edom*, *JSOT Suppl.* 24, 1983; P. Bienkowski (ed.), *Early Edom and Moab*, 1992.

J.A.T.

MOABITE STONE. A black basalt inscription left by *Mesha, king of *Moab, at Dhiban (biblical *Dibon) to commemorate his revolt against Israel and his subsequent rebuilding of many important towns (2 Ki. 3:4–5).

The stone was found on 19 August 1868, by the Rev. F. Klein, a German missionary working with the Church Missionary Society. An Arab sheikh named Zattam showed him an inscribed slab some 120 cm high, 60 cm broad and 6 cm thick, rounded at the top and containing thirty-four lines of writing. Klein copied a few words and reported his find to Dr Petermann the German consul, who began negotiations to obtain the inscription for the Berlin Museum. Unfortunately, C. S. Clermont-Ganneau of the French Consulate sought to obtain it for the Paris Museum. He sent independent messengers to obtain a squeeze of the inscription, but a dispute arose and the messengers fled with the squeeze in several pieces. The Arabs, sensing the value of the stone, had forced the price up. When Turkish officials interfered the local Arabs kindled a fire under the stone and poured water over it to break it into fragments, which were carried away as charms to bless their grain. Clermont-Ganneau subsequently recovered several fragments, made fresh squeezes, and finally reconstructed the stone in the Louvre in Paris (see *IBA*, p. 54). Out of an estimated 1,100 letters, 669 were recovered, rather less than two-thirds, but the original squeeze, though somewhat marred, preserved the greater part of the story.

The inscription refers to the triumph of 'Mesha, ben *Chemosh, king of Moab', whose father reigned over Moab 30 years. He tells how he threw off the yoke of Israel and honoured his god Chemosh by building a high place at Qarḥoh (QRḤH) in gratitude. The account continues as follows—'As for Omri king of Israel, he humbled Moab many years [lit. days] for Chemosh was angry at his land. And his son followed him and he also said "I will humble Moab". In my time he spoke (thus) but I have triumphed over him and over his house, while Israel hath perished for ever! (Now) Omri had occupied the land of Medeba and (Israel) had dwelt there in his time and half the time of his son (Ahab), forty years; but Chemosh dwelt there in my time.'

This account seems to imply that Mesha broke free from Israel before Ahab's death and thus appears to clash with 2 Ki. 1:1. There need not be any contradiction, however, for during the last years of Ahab's life he was sore pressed by the Syrian wars and probably lost his control over Moab. From Mesha's angle, his freedom dated from then, but from Israel's viewpoint Moab could not be regarded as free till after the abortive campaign conducted by Ahab's son Joram (2 Ki. 3).

The stone continues with an account of the building of Baal-meon, Qaryaten, Qarḥoh, Aroer, Beth-bamoth, Bezer, Medeba, Beth-diblathen, Beth-baal-meon. Ataroth, built by the king of Israel for the men of Gad, was captured, its people slain and its chieftain Arel (or Oriel) dragged before Chemosh in Kerioth. Nebo was taken and 7,000 devoted to Ashtar-Chemosh. Yahaz, built by the king of Israel, and his centre during the fighting, was taken and attached to Dibon.

Mesha referred to the reservoirs and cisterns, the walls, gates, towers and the king's palace he constructed in Qarḥoh with Israelite slave labour. He also made a highway in the Arnon valley.

The great importance of this inscription linguistically, religiously and historically lies in its close relation to the OT. The language is closely akin to Hebrew. Both Chemosh the god of Moab and Yahweh the God of Israel are mentioned, and we have an interesting insight into Moabite beliefs, akin in some ways to those of Israel. Chemosh may be angry with his people, forsake them, deliver them to their enemies and finally save them. He might command Mesha in words like those that Yahweh used for his servants. The rite of *ḥerem* and the existence of sanctuaries in high places occur here as well as in the OT. Although the authenticity of the stone has been disputed, there are no adequate grounds for this. It must be dated towards the end of Mesha's reign, *c.* 830 BC.

BIBLIOGRAPHY. W. F. Albright, *ANET*, pp. 320f.; *BASOR* 89, 1943, p. 16; F. I. Andersen, 'Moabite Syntax', *Orientalia* 35, 1966, pp. 81–120; A. Dearman (ed.), *Studies in the Mesha Inscription and Moab*, 1989; H. Donner and W. Röllig, *Kanaanäische and aramäische Inschriften*, I, 1962; R. Dussaud, *Les monuments palestiniens et judaïque*, 1912, pp. 4–22; E. Ullendorff in *DOTT*; A. H. van Zyl, *The Moabites*, 1960; J. R. Bartlett in *POTT*, pp. 229–258; J. C. L. Gibson, *Textbook of Syrian Semetic Inscriptions*, I, 1971, pp. 71–83.

J.A.T.

MOLADAH. A town of Simeon in the Negeb near Beersheba (Jos. 15:26; 19:2; 1 Ch. 4:28). Occupied by returning Judahite exiles (Ne. 11:26), it was later turned into an Idumean fortress. The site is not clearly identified. Tell el-Milḥ, SE of Beersheba, has regularly been identified with Moladah, but this mound is now thought to be Canaanite Arad. The more likely location is Khereibet el-Waṭen, E of Beersheba, which is possibly the Arabic equivalent of the Hebrew name.

BIBLIOGRAPHY. *LOB*, pp. 110, 298; *GTT*, p. 144.

W.O.

MOLECH. The name of a deity, usually written

MOLECH

Molech (Heb. *mōleḵ*, 2 Ki. 23:10; Je. 32:35), Melech ('king', *meleḵ*, Is. 57:9), Malcham ('their king', Je. 49:1, 3) or once Moloch (Am. 5:26 quoted Acts 7:43, Gk. *moloch*, AV).

Molech was worshipped in the ancient Near East in the second millennium BC (Mari and Ugarit) and associated with death and the underworld. He may be attested in the element *malik* found in personal names. His cult was practised by the Ammonites (1 Ki. 11:7, 33) and probably by the Canaanites (Dt. 12:31). It was considered the equivalent of Baal worship, hence the definite article before the name in Lv. 18:21; 20:2–5; 2 Ki. 23:10; Je. 22:35. Weinfeld links it especially with death and the worship of the god Baal-Hadad as 'king'. Solomon built a high place for Molech on

The Moabite Stone commemorates the revolt of Mesha, king of Moab, against Israel (see 2 Ki. 3:5ff.) and his rebuilding of several towns, e.g. Aroer, Medeba, Qarhoh, using Israelite slave labour. Black basalt. Height 1·0 m, breadth 0·60 m. c. 830 BC (see p. 777).

the Mount of Olives, probably to please his foreign wives (1 Ki. 11:7).

The type and extent of the ritual associated with this deity is the subject of debate. The phrase 'to pass (*h'br*) the son/daughter through the fire to Molech' (2 Ki. 16:3; 17:17; 23:10) could refer to a dedication or votive ceremony, possibly fire-walking. King Ahaz was condemned for this (2 Ch. 28:3) as were Manasseh (2 Ki. 21:6) and Samaria (2 Ki. 17:17). Eissfeldt compared this with *molk*, a dedicatory offering found from the 6th century onwards. However, no extant Phoenician inscription has *mlk* in connection with child-sacrifice (except later Sanchuniathon). Nor is child sacrifice common in OT or surrounding cultures. It was a rare and detested practice to the true Israelite, as shown in 2 Ki. 3:27; Ps. 106:37–38. This is also shown by the use of 'sacrifice' (*zbḥ*) or immolation (*śrp*) on occasions (Lv. 21:9; Dt. 12:31; 18:10). The majority of scholars, however, interpret all references to Molech as child sacrifice and compare it with later Phoenician-Carthaginian (Punic) practice in N Africa where *mlk* denotes the sacrifice. Whether death by child sacrifice or dedication through fire, both are abhorrent to God. They are associated with Topheth (2 Ki. 23:10; Je. 7:31–32; 19:11–12) and the smouldering rubbish dumps in the Hinnom valley outside Jerusalem. The reforms of Josiah in Judah were marked by the destruction of the high places dedicated to Molech (2 Ki. 23:10, 13) yet the ritual did not die out until after Ezekiel (16:20ff.; 20:26, 31; 23:27).

BIBLIOGRAPHY. M. Weinfeld, 'The Worship of Molech and the Queen of Heaven', *UF* 4, 1972, pp. 133–154; G. C. Heider, *The Cult of Molek: A Reassessment*, 1985; D. Edelman, 'Biblical Molek Reassessed', *JAOS* 107, 1987, pp. 727–731; J. Day, *Molech, a God of Human Sacrifice in the Old Testament*, 1989; S. Brown, *Late Carthaginian Child Sacrifice and Sacrificial Monuments in their Mediterranean Context*, 1991.

D.J.W.

MOLID. A name found in the genealogy of Jerahmeel (1 Ch. 2:29). Moladah may be connected, but evidence is lacking (*GTT*, pp. 48, 144).

J.D.D.

MONEY.

I. In the Old Testament

Before the introduction of coinage in the late 8th century BC (see *c*, below) the medium of exchange in commercial transactions was a modified form of barter. Throughout the ancient Near East staple commodities, both those which were perishable, such as wool, barley, wheat and dates, and those which were non-perishable, including metals, timber, wine, honey and livestock, served as 'exchangeable goods'. The texts show that from the earliest times periodic attempts were made to stabilize the values of these commodities with respect to each other. Thus wealth was measured by possession of cattle (Jb. 1:3) and precious metals. Abraham was 'very rich in cattle, in silver, and in gold' (Gn. 13:2).

a. Metal as an exchange commodity

Since silver (Heb. *kesep̄*) was the commonest precious metal available in Palestine (as in Assyria and Babylonia), it appears as the most frequently used (AV, RSV often translate *kesep̄* as 'money', *e.g.* Gn. 17:13). Thus in ordinary transactions the term silver is often omitted, as understood; Solomon purchased chariots at 600 (shekels weight of silver) and horses at 150 (1 Ki. 10:29; *cf.* Lv. 5:15). His revenue was reckoned in silver by talents (1 Ki. 10:14; *WEIGHTS AND MEASURES), for silver was as common in Jerusalem as stones (1 Ki. 10:27). Until post-exilic times the 'shekel' bears its literal meaning of a certain *weight rather than denoting a coin.

Silver was used for the purchase of real estate, such as the field purchased by Jeremiah at Anathoth for 17 shekels of silver (Je. 32:9), the cave at Machpelah bought by Abraham for 400 shekels of silver (Gn. 23:15–16), the village and hill of Samaria by Omri for 2 talents of silver (1 Ki. 16:24), or the threshing-floor of Araunah by David for 50 shekels (2 Sa. 24:24). Silver was also the basis of a dowry (Ex. 22:17) or a bride purchase-price (Ho. 3:2).

Gold, being more rarely obtained, often figures after silver in the payment of tribute. Thus Hezekiah paid Sennacherib in 701 BC 300 talents of silver and 30 talents of gold (2 Ki. 18:14), while Menahem had bought off the Assyrians for 1,000 talents of silver (2 Ki. 15:19). Gold played a prominent part in inter-state border transactions, and Hiram paid 120 talents of gold to Solomon for the villages ceded to him (1 Ki. 9:10–14).

In many transactions payment in goods might be agreed as a supplement or substitute for precious metal. Mesha of Moab offered sheep and wool (2 Ki. 3:4); Sennacherib was given precious stones, in addition to gold and silver, by Hezekiah according to the Assyr. annals, and the tribute of *Jehu to Shalmaneser III included blocks of antimony, lead, golden vessels and rare fruits. Barley (Ho. 3:2), spices (2 Ki. 20:13) or clothing might be part of the agreed price or gift (2 Ki. 5:23). Copper (AV 'brass') was another metal in use as currency (Ex. 35:5; 2 Sa. 21:16) of less value than gold (Is. 60:17).

To control the use of metals as currency they had to be weighed out (Heb. *šql*, hence 'shekel') by the purchaser and checked by the vendor in the presence of witnesses (Gn. 23:16; Je. 32:9–10). The standard of weight agreed was that in force by local standards called the 'silver of city X' or 'the silver (current with) the merchant' (Gn. 23:16; Bab. *kaspum ša tamqarim*). This agreed standard is also implied by payment 'in full weight' (Gn. 43:21). Thus merchants were 'weighers of silver'. Another check was made on the quality of the metal by marking it with its place of origin. Gold of Ophir (1 Ki. 10:11) or Parvaim (2 Ch. 3:6) was highly prized, while gold and silver were sometimes classified as 'refined' (AV 'pure, purified').

b. Forms of currency

To enable metal used as currency to be transportable it was kept either in the form of jewellery (often as arm-rings), of objects in daily use or in characteristic shapes. Thus Abraham gave Rebekah a gold ring (weighing) half a shekel and bracelets of 10 shekels (Gn. 24:22). Gold was often carried as thin bars or wedges (Heb. 'tongue'), like that weighing 50 shekels found by Achan at Jericho (Jos. 7:21) or the 'golden wedge of Ophir' (Is. 13:12). Gold and silver were also held as ingots, vessels, dust (Jb. 28:6) or small fragments, and could be melted and used immediately for many purposes. In these forms Joseph increased the revenue of Egypt (Gn. 47:14).

On a journey the small pieces of metal were carried in a pouch or bag of leather or cloth ('bundles of money', Gn. 42:35; Pr. 7:20) which, if holed, would easily lead to loss (Hg. 1:6). A talent of silver seemed to require two bags (2 Ki. 5:23). To guard against loss the money bags were often placed inside other sacks or receptacles (Gn. 42:35). Silver was also moulded into small drops or beads (1 Sa. 2:36, *ᵃgōrâ*) or lumps. It is probable that the half-shekel used for payment into the sanctuary was an unminted lump of silver (Ex. 30:13; 2 Ki. 12:9–16), though normally such temple dues as taxes could be paid either in silver or in kind (Dt. 26; Ne. 5:10).

Copper, being of less value than gold and silver, was transported as flat circular discs, hence the term *kikkār* ('a round', 'flat round of bread', Assyr. *kakkāru*) was used for the 'talent', the heaviest weight.

c. The introduction of coinage

Coinage, a piece of metal struck with a seal authenticating its title and weight so that it would be accepted on sight, first appears in Asia Minor in the mid-7th century BC. Though Sennacherib (*c.* 701 BC) refers to the 'minting of half-shekel pieces', there is no evidence that this refers to anything more than a bronze-casting technique, for no coins of this early period have been found as yet in Assyria, Syria or Palestine. The first known coins were struck in electrum (a natural alloy of gold and silver) in Lydia. Herodotus (1. 94) attributes the introduction of coinage to Croesus of Lydia (561–546 BC), his gold coins being called 'Croesides'. It would seem that coinage was introduced into Persia by Darius I (521–486 BC), whose name was used to denote the thick gold coin, or *daric*, which portrays the king, half-length or kneeling, with bow and arrow; with the die-punch mark in reverse (see Herodotus 4. 166). This daric weighed 130 gr., the silver *siglos* or shekel 86½ gr. It has been suggested (*PEQ* 87, 1955, p. 141) that Hg. 1:6 (520 BC) is the earliest biblical allusion to coined money.

The daric (AV 'dram') was known to the Jews in exile (Ezr. 2:69; 8:27; Ne. 7:70–71) and the reference to a daric in the time of David (1 Ch. 29:7) shows that the text at this point was giving the equivalent term at the time of compilation of this history. The change to payment of workmen in coin instead of in kind is attested by the Persepolis Treasury texts (*c.* 450 BC), confirming a ratio of 13:1 gold to silver. The spread of coinage to Judah seems to have been slow, perhaps because of the images they bore. It is therefore uncertain whether the silver shekels of Ne. 5:15; 10:32 were weights, as in the earlier period, or money in coin.

Phoenician traders quickly took up the use of coins, and mints were active by the 5th–4th centuries BC at Aradus, Byblos, Tyre and Sidon. The coinage of cities in Asia Minor and Greece, and of the kings of Ptolemaic Egypt and Seleucid Syria entered Judah and circulated there alongside coins of Persian kings. The Persian-approved Jewish governors were evidently allowed to issue small silver coins from about 400 BC. The designs of the half-dozen or so found follow Athenian patterns, but include the word *yhd*, 'Judah'. One also bears the name Hezekiah, perhaps the High Priest at the time of Alexander the Great.

After the independent Jewish state was established, Simon Maccabaeus was given the right to strike coins (1 Macc. 15:6), but does not seem to have used it (coins once attributed to him have been shown to belong to the First and Second Revolts, AD 67–70, 132–5). Alexander Jannaeus (103–76 BC) was probably the first Jewish ruler to strike coins. They are small bronze pieces bearing various designs, his name in Greek and Hebrew, and sometimes the words 'Yehonathan the high priest and the community of the Jews'. Following kings continued to strike small bronze coins, the Roman overlords retaining the prerogative to strike silver ones. Only in the Jewish Revolts were local silver coins issued.

BIBLIOGRAPHY. E. S. G. Robinson, 'The Beginnings of Achaemenid Coinage' in *Numismatic Chronicle* (6th Series) 18, 1958, pp. 187–193; Y. Meshorer, *Ancient Jewish Coinage*, 1983; *ABD* 1, pp. 1076–1089. D.J.W.

II. In the New Testament

During NT times money from three different sources was in circulation in Palestine. There was the official imperial money coined on the Roman standard; provincial coins minted at Antioch and Tyre, which held mainly to the old Gk. standard, and circulated chiefly among the inhabitants of Asia Minor; and the local Jewish money, coined perhaps at Caesarea. Certain cities and client-kings were also granted the right to strike their own bronze coins. With coins of so many different scales in circulation it is obvious that there was need of money-changers at Jerusalem, especially at feasts when Jews came from all parts to pay their poll-tax to the Temple treasury. On these occasions the money-changers moved their stalls into the Court of the Gentiles, whence Jesus expelled them (Jn. 2:15; Mt. 21:12; Mk. 11:15; Lk. 19:45f.) because of their avaricious practices.

Mt. 10:9 serves as a useful reminder that in those days, as now, money was coined in three principal metals, gold, silver and copper, bronze or brass. Bronze (Gk. *chalkos*) is used as a general word for money in Mk. 6:8 and 12:41, but as only the coins of smaller value, the Roman *as* (Gk. *assarion*) and Jewish *lepton* were minted in bronze, the more common general term for money in the NT is silver (Gk. *argyrion*; see Lk. 9:3; Acts 8:20; *etc.*). The most common silver coins mentioned in the NT are the Attic tetradrachm and the Roman *denarius*. Gk. *chrysos*, gold, is most frequently used to refer to the metal itself, except in Mt. 10:9; Acts 3:6, possibly also Acts 20:33; 1 Pet. 1:18; Jas. 5:3; Mt. 23:16f., though these instances might equally well refer to gold vessels and ornaments.

Other general terms used for money in the NT are the common Gk. word *chrēma*, meaning property or wealth, as well as money (Acts 4:37; 8:18, 20; 24:26); *kerma*, or small change (from Gk. *keirō*, 'I cut up'), used in Jn. 2:15, and nearly always denoting copper coins; and *nomisma*, or money introduced into common use by law (*nomos*). This last is found only in Mt. 22:19, where the phrase *nomisma tou kēnsou* means the legal coin for paying the tax.

a. Jewish coins

In 141–140 BC Antiochus VII granted permission to Simon Maccabaeus 'priest and ethnarch of the Jews . . . to mint your own coinage as money for your country' (1 Macc. 15:6), and from that time

Jewish coins were minted, mainly in bronze, as neighbouring cities produced an abundance of silver coins. Early Jewish coins heeded the second commandment, and so their devices adhered strictly to horticultural designs and inanimate objects. Coins minted under the Herods show one or two breaches of this rule, as they displayed sometimes the reigning emperor's head, sometimes their own, on the obverse (see Wiseman, *IBA*, p. 86). During the time of the First Revolt (AD 66–70) the Jews proudly coined their own silver for the first time, issuing silver shekels and quarter- and half-shekel pieces as well as their own bronzes. Following this revolt, the Temple treasures were seized, and so the Jews had no further supplies of metal to coin their own silver during the Second Revolt (AD 132–135). They therefore celebrated their independence by overstriking old foreign coins with Jewish dies containing the inscription 'deliverance of Jerusalem'.

The only Jewish coin mentioned in the NT is the bronze *lepton* (from Gk. *leptos*—'small, fine'). This is the widow's 'mite' (AV) of Mk. 12:42; Lk. 21:2, also called a 'farthing' in Lk. 12:59 (AV), where it stands for the smallest coin imaginable. It was equivalent to half the Roman *quadrans*, and so one-eighth of the *assarion* (see below). Such coins were minted locally by the procurator or tetrarch, and * Pilate appears to have introduced designs on his coins calculated to affront the Jews.

b. Greek coins

The basic Greek coin was the silver *drachmē*, of which there were 100 to the *mna*, or mina, and 6,000 to the talent. About 300 BC the drachm was the price of a sheep: an ox cost 5 *drachmai* (Demetrius Phalereus).

The *drachmē* is mentioned only in Lk. 15:8f., RSV 'silver coins', AV 'pieces of silver', which the woman in the parable may have worn as an ornament. It was regarded as approximately equivalent to the Roman *denarius* (see below).

The *didrachmon* or 2-drachm piece was used among the Jews for the half-shekel required for the annual Temple tax (Mt. 17:24). This regulation derived from the atonement-money prescribed in Ex. 30:11–16, which, according to Maimonides, later developed into a regular annual poll-tax (see Jos., *Ant*. 16. 160). After the fall of Jerusalem and the destruction of the Temple this tax had to be paid into the Roman treasury (Jos., *BJ* 7. 217). It seems most likely that the coins used for this tax would be those of Tyre, for the Talmudic law forbade the use of Antiochene money for the Temple treasury, not for any religious reasons, but because it did not contain enough silver.

The *statēr*, *tetradrachmon*, or 4-drachm piece, is found only in Mt. 17:27, where it is the coin which would pay the Temple tax for Jesus and Peter. As it was a more common coin than the didrachm, it would appear that Jews frequently united to pay the Temple tax in pairs by means of the tetradrachm. It was minted at Antioch, Caesarea in Cappadocia and in Tyre. Pompey fixed the rate of exchange of tetradrachms from Antioch and Tyre at 4 *denarii* (*c*. 65 BC), and Josephus refers to the same rate for the Tyrian tetradrachm in his day (*BJ* 2. 592). Antiochene tetradrachms were, however, tariffed by the imperial government at 3 *denarii* only. Most numismatists agree that this was the coin in which Judas received his thirty pieces of silver (Mt. 26:15). The use of the term *argyria hikana*, 'large silver-money', in Mt. 28:12–13 has been thought by some to suggest that the coins with which the Sanhedrin bribed the guards of the tomb were the large silver staters and not the smaller *drachmai* or *denarii*, though it is possible that the adjective here refers to quantity rather than size.

The *mna*, translated 'pound', occurs in the parable of Lk. 19:11–27.

The 'talent' was not a coin, but a unit of monetary reckoning. Its value was always high, though it varied with the different metals involved and the different monetary standards. The Roman–Attic was equivalent to 240 *aurei* (see below). It was mentioned by Jesus in two parables: in Mt. 18:24 'ten thousand talents' is figurative for a very large sum of money, and in the parable of the talents in Mt. 25:15–28 it is referred to in v. 18 as *argyrion*, which may suggest that our Lord had the silver talent in mind.

c. Roman coins

The basic Roman coin, mentioned above, was the silver *denarius*. There were 25 *denarii* to the golden *aureus*, the weight of which was fixed by Julius Caesar in 49 BC at 126·3 grs., though subsequent debasing of the coinage under Augustus and his successors brought the weight down to 115 grs. by Nero's time.

The *quadrans* (Gk. *kodrantēs*) was one-quarter of the copper *as* (see below). It is referred to by both Horace (*Satires* 2. 3. 93) and Juvenal (7. 8) as the smallest Roman coin: Mk. 12:42 states that the widow's 2 *lepta* (see *a*, above) were equivalent to a *quadrans*. Mt. 5:26 uses *quadrans* for the smallest coin, which must be paid to clear a debt in full, while the Lucan parallel (12:59) has *lepton*, except in the Western Text, which agrees with Matthew.

The copper *as* (Gk. *assarion*) was a quarter of the bronze *sestertius* and one-sixteenth of the silver *denarius*. It occurs in Mt. 10:29 and Lk. 12:6, where it is translated by the AV as 'farthing' and RV, RSV as 'penny', the price at which two sparrows are sold (Lk. has five sparrows for 2 farthings).

The *denarius* (Gk. *dēnarion*) gained its name (*deni* = ten at a time) from the fact that at first it was the equivalent in silver of 10 copper *asses*. From 217 BC it was worth 16 *asses*, when the weight of the latter coin was fixed at 28 gr. It was rendered consistently as 'penny' by the translators of the AV and RV (but see the note on Mt. 18:28 in the RVmg.), owing to the fact that British currency, modelled on that of Rome, used *d*. for *denarius* as the abbreviation for penny.

It would appear from the parable of Mt. 20:1–16 to have been the daily wage of a labourer, and 2 *denarii* was the sum paid by the good Samaritan to the innkeeper (Lk. 10:35): that should give some idea of its purchasing power. In Rev. 6:6 'a quart of wheat for a *denarius*, and three quarts of barley for a *denarius*' is an indication of famine prices (* WEIGHTS AND MEASURES).

From Mt. 22:19; Mk. 12:15; Lk. 20:24 we learn that it was the coin used to trick Jesus in the question concerning the payment of tribute-money. Silver *denarii* of the time have been discovered which carry the laureate head of the emperor Tiberius on the obverse, with his mother, Livia, in the role of Pax, holding a branch and sceptre, on the reverse (see *IBA*, p. 87, fig. 90).

The *aureus*, or *denarius aureus* (golden denarius), was a gold coin introduced by Julius Caesar in his financial reforms of 49 BC. It finds no mention in the Bible, but is referred to in Jos., *Ant.* 14. 147: it may be the 'gold' of Mt. 10:9.

BIBLIOGRAPHY. K. A. Jacob, *Coins and Christianity*, 1959; R. G. Bratcher, 'Weights, Money, Measures and Time', *The Bible Translator* 10, No. 4, Oct. 1959, pp. 165ff.; Garnet R. Halliday, *Money Talks about the Bible*, 1948; E. Rodgers, *A Handy Guide to Jewish Coins*, 1914; Paul Romanoff, *Jewish Symbols on Ancient Jewish Coins*, 1944; F. A. Banks, *Coins of Bible Days*, 1955; A. Reifenberg, *Israel's History in Coins from the Maccabees to the Roman Conquest*, 1953; D. Kanael, *BA* 26, 1965, pp. 38–62; E. W. Klenowsky, *On Ancient Palestinian and Other Coins*, 1974; Y. Meshorer, *Jewish Coins of the Second Temple Period*, 1967; R. Gower, *The New Manners and Customs of Bible Times*, 1987. D.H.W.

MONEY-CHANGERS. The 'exchangers' of Mt. 25:27 (AV) were regular bankers (*trapezitai*); *cf.* the saying commonly ascribed to our Lord, 'Be expert bankers'—*i.e.* trustworthy and skilled in detecting counterfeits. A specialized class of money-changers officiated in the Temple precincts, probably in the Court of the Gentiles—*kollybistai* (Mt. 21:12; Mk. 11:15; Jn. 2:15) or *kermatistai* (Jn. 2:14). The former title derived from a word of Semitic origin denoting exchange-rate or commission; the latter would, strictly speaking, relate to a dealer in small change. The trade arose from the fact that money for the Temple, including the obligatory half-shekel (Ex. 30:13; *cf.* Mt. 17:24, and see E. Schürer, *HJP*, 2, 1978) had to be in Tyrian standard coin, with its high level of silver purity, and not in the current Roman standard. A surcharge was made (Mishnah tractate *Sheqalim*, *passim*) and the way opened for various malpractices (add passages in *HHT* on Mt. 21:12 to those in *SB*). The Lord's cleansing of the Temple included the overthrow of the counters of these dealers at the Passover season. A.F.W.

MOON. The creation of the moon is recorded in Gn. 1:16, where it is referred to as 'the lesser light' in contrast to the sun. It was placed in the heavens to rule the night, and with the other luminaries to be 'for signs and for seasons and for days and years' (1:14). Its appearance in regular phases in the night sky afforded a basis for early *calendars, and the word most commonly used for it (*yārēaḥ*) is closely related to *yeraḥ*, 'month'. The same word occurs in Akkad. ([w]*arḫu*), Ugaritic (*yrḫ*), Phoen. (*yrḥ*) and other Semitic languages. Another word, used less often for it, is *l^{e}ḇānâ*, 'white one' (Ct. 6:10; Is. 24:23; 30:26).

The first day of each new month was considered holy. Hence the association in the OT of the monthly 'new moon' with the weekly sabbath (*e.g.* Is. 1:13). This fresh beginning was marked by special sacrifices (Nu. 28:11–15) over which the trumpets were blown (Nu. 10:10; Ps. 81:3). Amos depicts the merchants of his day anxiously awaiting the end of the new moon and of the sabbath so that they could resume their fraudulent trading. It seems therefore to have been regarded, like the sabbath, as a day on which normal work was not done. The reference may be, however, to the new moon of the 7th month, regarding which the law stated specifically that no servile work was to be done on it (Lv. 23:24–25; Nu. 29:1–6). 2 Ki. 4:23 suggests that both new moon and sabbath were regarded as providing opportunity for consulting the prophets, and Ezekiel marks out the new moon as a special day for worship (Ezk. 46:1, 3).

The moon is mentioned with the sun as a symbol of permanence (Ps. 72:5). It is quoted as a wonder of creation (Ps. 8:3), and as marking by its behaviour the coming of the Messiah (Mk. 13:24; Lk. 21:25). Ps. 121:6 suggests that it was recognized as capable of affecting the mind, and in the NT Gk. words meaning literally 'moon-struck' are used in Mt. 4:24 and 17:15.

The moon is named as an object of idolatrous worship in Jb. 31:26, and archaeology has shown that it was deified in ancient W Asia from early Sumerian to Islamic times. In Mesopotamia the Sumerian god Nanna, named *Sin by the Akkadians, was worshipped in particular at Ur, where he was the chief god of the city, and also in the city of Harran in Syria, which had close religious links with Ur. The Ugaritic texts have shown that there a moon deity was worshipped under the name *yrḫ*. On the monuments the god is represented by the symbol of a crescent moon (*AMULETS). At Hazor in Palestine a small Canaanite shrine of the late Bronze Age was discovered which contained a basalt stela depicting two hands lifted as if in prayer to a crescent moon, perhaps indicating that the shrine was dedicated to the moon god (see *IBA*, fig. 112). T.C.M.

MORDECAI (Heb. *mord^{e}ḵay*; *mord^{o}ḵay*; Ezr. 2:2).

1. A leader of the exiles who returned with Zerubbabel (Ezr. 2:2; Ne. 7:7; 1 Esdras 5:8).

2. A Jewish exile who had moved to the Persian capital *Susa, where he was employed in the palace. He was a Benjaminite son of Jair and descendant of Kish, taken prisoner to Babylon by Nebuchadrezzar (Est. 2:5–6). He brought up his orphaned cousin Hadassah (*ESTHER) and was rewarded, by being mentioned in the royal chronicles, for revealing a plot against King Xerxes (Est. 2:7, 21–23). (Mordecai has been identified by some with a finance officer at Susa under Xerxes.)

He opposed the vizier Haman who plotted to kill all Jews (Est. 3). When this evil deed was turned against Haman, Mordecai succeeded him in office, being then next in rank to the king (chs. 5–6; 10). He used this position to encourage the Jews to defend themselves against the massacre inspired by Haman. In respect for Mordecai the Persian provincial officials to whom he wrote assisted in protecting the Jews. The celebration of this event by the annual feast of *Purim was later connected with the 'day of Mordecai' (2 Macc. 15:36).

Mordecai is probably the Heb. rendering of a common Bab. personal name Mardukaya. This is found in texts, including one *c.* 485 BC (*AfO* 19, 1959–60, pp. 79–81) and another concerning an official of Ushtannu, satrap of Babylon.

BIBLIOGRAPHY. E. Yamauchi, *Persia and the Bible*, 1990, pp. 234–236. D.J.W.

MOREH (Heb. *mōreh*, 'teacher', 'diviner'). **1.** The name of a place near Shechem mentioned in Gn. 12:6, where *'ēlôn mōreh* may be translated 'the teacher's oak' (or 'terebinth'). Dt. 11:30 makes reference to the 'oak of Moreh' in the district of Gilgal (*i.e.* the Shechemite Gilgal). It is recorded that Abraham pitched his camp there on arriving in Canaan from Harran, and it was there that God revealed himself to Abraham, promising to give the land of Canaan to his descendants (*MAMRE). This tree may also be the one mentioned in Gn. 35:4 where Jacob hid foreign gods, and a reference to the place also occurs in the story of Abimelech (Jdg. 9:37).

2. The hill of Moreh at the head of the N side of the valley of Jezreel, S of Mt Tabor, 2 km S of Nain, and *c.* 13 km NW of Mt Gilboa, is the modern Jebel Dahi; it features in Jdg. 7:1, where, in the encounter between Gideon and the Midianites, the Midianites encamped in the valley, by the hill of Moreh, to the N of Gideon's camp by the spring of Harod.

3. Moreh has a quasi-technical sense in the Qumran phrase *mōrēh ṣeḏeq*, commonly translated 'teacher of righteousness' and used as a designation of the first organizer of the Qumran community and possibly of each succeeding leader. There may be an allusion to Joel 2:23, where *mōreh liṣᵉḏāqāh* is rendered '(he hath given you) a teacher of righteousness' in AVmg., or to Ho. 10:12, where *yōreh ṣeḏeq* is rendered '(he will) teach (you) righteousness' in RVmg., as though the coming of the Qumran teacher were greeted as a fulfilment of these promises. *Cf.* F. F. Bruce, *The Teacher of Righteousness in the Qumran Texts*, 1957; J. Weingreen, *From Bible to Mishna*, 1976, pp. 100ff.

R.A.H.G.
F.F.B.

MORESHETH-GATH. Home-town of the prophet Micah (Mi. 1:1; Je. 26:18) near the Philistine territory of Gath (Mi. 1:14); probably the modern Tell ej-Judeieh, 32 km SW of Jerusalem and 10 km NE of Lachish. Moresheth-gath (Mi. 1:14) is one of twelve cities listed by the prophet Micah, whose names are by word-play associated with the form of their imminent judgment through invasion. Lachish, so to speak, will have to give a parting bridal-gift or dowry (*cf.* 1 Ki. 9:16) to Moresheth (*môrešeṯ*, which sounds like *mᵉ'ôrešeṯ*, betrothed), as that city is lost to the enemy. See *NEAEHL*, pp. 837–838. N.H.

MORIAH. In Gn. 22:2 God commanded Abraham to take Isaac to 'the land of Moriah' (*'ereṣ hammōriyyâ*) and there to offer him as a burnt offering upon one of the mountains (*har*). The mountain chosen was 3 days' journey (22:4) from the land of the Philistines (21:34; the region of *Gerar), and was visible from a distance (22:4).

The only other mention of the name occurs in 2 Ch. 3:1, where the site of Solomon's Temple is said to be 'on mount Moriah (*bᵉhar hammôriyyâ*), on the threshing-floor of Ornan the Jebusite where God appeared to David (3:2). It should be noted that no reference is made here to Abraham in connection with this site. It has been objected that Jerusalem is not sufficiently distant from S Philistia to have required a 3 days' journey to get there, and that one of the characteristics of Jerusalem is that the Temple hill is not visible until the traveller is quite close, so that the correctness of the biblical identification is called in question. The Samaritan tradition identifies the site with Mt Gerizim (as though Moriah = Moreh; *cf.* Gn. 12:6), and this is claimed to fulfil the conditions of Gn. 22:4 adequately. However, the distance from S Philistia to Jerusalem is *c.* 80 km, which might well have required 3 days to traverse, and in Genesis the place in question is not a 'mount Moriah' but one of several mountains in a land of that name, and the hills on which Jerusalem stands are visible at a distance. There is no need to doubt therefore that Abraham's sacrifice took place on the site of later Jerusalem, if not on the Temple hill.

BIBLIOGRAPHY. F. M. Abel, *Géographie de la Palestine*, 1, 1933, pp. 374–375. T.C.M.

MORTAR AND PESTLE. This formed an alternative to the stone *mill. While in the wilderness the Israelites ground the *manna either in mills or in a mortar (Nu. 11:8; Heb. *mᵉḏōḵâ*), and olive oil was produced in the same way ('beaten oil', Ex. 27:20). Pr. 27:22 shows that evil cannot be removed from a wicked man even if he were to be crushed small (Heb. *maḵtēš*, 'mortar'; *'ᵉlî*, 'pestle'). For Egyptians using mortar and pestle, see *ANEP*, no. 153, upper right, and 154, lower part. The mortar was either a hollowed stone or a deep wooden bowl, the pestle a stout wooden pole. A small hollow in the land could also be called 'mortar' from its form, so Jdg. 15:19; Zp. 1:11. (*MAKTESH.) A.R.M.

MOSERAH, MOSEROTH. A camp-site of the Israelites in the wilderness (Nu. 33:30f.), where Aaron died (Dt. 10:6). The name could mean 'chastisement(s)', with reference to the trespass at Meribah (*cf.* Nu. 20:24; Dt. 32:51). The site is unidentified, but may have been close to Mt *Hor, which also figures as the place of Aaron's death and burial. See J. A. Thompson, *Deuteronomy*, *TOTC*, 1974, p. 145. D.F.P.

MOSES. The great leader and lawgiver through whom God brought the Hebrews out of Egypt, constituted them a nation for his service, and brought them within reach of the land promised to their forefathers.

I. Name

In Ex. 2:10 it is said that 'she called his name *Mōšeh*: and she said, Because I drew him (*mᵉšîṯihû*) out of the water'. Most interpreters identify the 'she' as Pharaoh's daughter, and this has led many to assume an Egyp. origin for the name *Mōšeh*, Egyp. *ms*, 'child' or '(one) born' being the best possibility. However, the antecedent of 'she' could as easily be 'the woman', *i.e.* Moses' own mother and nurse, who '*had* called his name . . .' (so W. J. Martin). Ex. 2:10 clearly links the name of *Mōšeh* with his being taken from the waterside (*māšâ*, 'to draw forth'). This pun would come naturally to a Hebrew speaker but not to an Egyptian: which fact would favour the view just mentioned that it was Moses' own mother who first named him, rather than Pharaoh's daughter.

Mōšeh as it stands is an active participle meaning 'one who draws forth', and may be an ellipsis for some longer phrase. In the 14th/13th centuries BC Egyp. *ms*, 'child' (and the related grammatical form in such names as Ramose, 'Rē, is born') was pronounced approximately *măsĕ*, and there is no philological or other reason why Moses' Egyp. adoptive mother should not have assimilated a

Semitic *māši* or *Mōšeh* to the common name-word *Māšĕ*, *Mōšeh* in her own tongue. Compare assimilations such as German Löwe to English Lowe in our own day. Hence Moses' name may simply be Semitic assimilated to Egyp. while in Egypt. The majority view, however, is that the daughter of Pharaoh called him *Mōse*, 'child' (or—less suitably—a theophoric name in *-mose*), which passed into Heb. speech as *Mōšeh*. This view, however, fails to account adequately for the Semitic pun, which there is no objective reason to reject as unhistorical, as it is a common practice in Egypt and elsewhere (including the OT) long before Moses; such a view, moreover, runs into real phonetic difficulties over Egyp. *s* appearing as *š* in *Mōšeh* but as *s* in Ra'amses and Phinehas in Hebrew, as was pointed out long ago by A. H. Gardiner, *JAOS* 56, 1936, pp. 192–194—a problem in no way solved by J. G. Griffiths, *JNES* 12, 1953, pp. 225–231, the best statement of this view.

II. Life and background

a. Ancestry

Moses belonged to the tribe of Levi, to the clan of Kohath, and to the house or family of Amram (Ex. 6:16ff.). That he was the distant descendant, not the son, of Amram by Jochebed is hinted at inasmuch as his parents are not named in the detailed account of his infancy (Ex. 2), and is made almost certain by the fact that Amram and his three brothers had numerous descendants within a year of the Exodus (Nu. 3:27f.). (*CHRONOLOGY OF THE OT, **III.** *b.*)

b. Egyptian upbringing

To save her baby son from the pharaonic edict ordering the destruction of Hebrew male infants, Moses' mother put him into a little basket of pitch-caulked reeds or papyrus among the rushes by the stream bank and bade his sister Miriam keep watch. Soon a daughter of Pharaoh came with her maidservants to bathe in the river, found the child, and took pity on him. Miriam discreetly offered to find a nurse for the child (in fact, his mother), and so Moses' life was saved. When weaned, he was handed over to his adoptive 'mother', the Egyptian princess (Ex. 2:1–10). Of Moses' growth to adult maturity in Egyptian court society no detail is given, but a boy in his position in New Kingdom period court circles could not avoid undergoing a substantial basic training in that 'wisdom of the Egyptians' with which Stephen credits him (Acts 7:22).

Modern knowledge of ancient Egypt yields a rich background for the early life of Moses in Egypt. The pharaohs of the New Kingdom period (*c.* 1550–1070 BC) maintained residences and *harîms* not only in the great capitals of Thebes, Memphis and Pi-Ramessē (Ra'amses) but also in other parts of Egypt. Typical is the long-established *harîm* in the Fayum, where the royal ladies supervised a hive of domestic industry (A. H. Gardiner, *JNES* 12, 1953, pp. 145–149, especially p. 149). One such *harîm* must have been Moses' first Egyptian home.

Anciently, children of *harîm*-women could be educated by the Overseer of the *harîm* ('a teacher of the children of the king', F. Ll. Griffith and P. E.

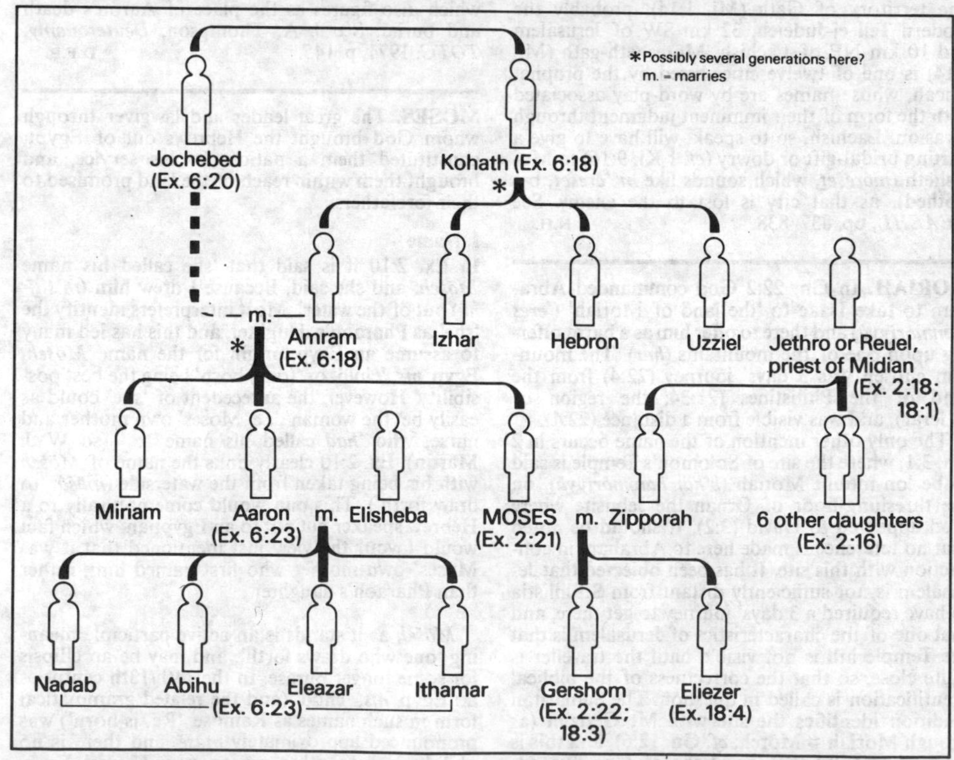

The family of Moses

Newberry, *El Bersheh*, 2, 1894, p. 40). In due course princes were given a tutor, usually a high official at court or a retired military officer close to the king (H. Brunner, *Altägyptische Erziehung*, 1957, pp. 32–33); Moses doubtless fared similarly.

Moreover, as a Semite in Egypt, Moses would have had no difficulty whatever in learning and using the twenty or so letters of the proto-Canaanite linear alphabet, especially if he had been submitted to the much more exacting discipline of a training in the scores of characters and sign-groups of the Egyptian scripts (though even these require only application, not genius, to learn them). The fact that Egypt, not Palestine, was his home would be no barrier to familiarity with this simple linear script. The 'proto-Sinaitic' inscriptions of the early 15th century BC are certainly just informal dedications, work-notes and brief epitaphs (for offerings) by Semitic captives from the Egyp. E Delta (or Memphis settlements) employed in the turquoise-mines (*cf.* W. F. Albright, *BASOR* 110, 1948, pp. 12–13, 22), and illustrate free use of that script by Semites under Egyptian rule nearly two centuries before Moses. Still more eloquent of the ready use of the linear script by Semites in Egypt is an ostracon from the Valley of the Queens at Thebes, some 560 km S of Palestine, Sinai, or the Delta (J. Leibovitch, *Annales du Service des Antiquités de l'Égypte* 40, 1940, p. 119, fig. 26, and pl. 16, 19:50); the one word fully preserved can be reasonably read *'mht*, 'maid-servants' (Albright, *op. cit.*, p. 12, n. 33).

c. Foreigners at the Egyptian court

Semites and other Asiatics could be found at every level of Egyptian society in the New Kingdom. Besides thousands of prisoners brought from Canaan to be slaves (*cf. ANET*, pp. 246b, 247b), foreign artisans, Syrian warriors in Egyptian service (*e.g. ANEP*, fig. 157), Asian youths as attendants, fan-bearers, *etc.*, at court (R. A. Caminos, *Late-Egyptian Miscellanies*, 1954, pp. 117, 200–201), Semites in Egypt could rise to the highest levels of the social pyramid. They were couriers between Egypt and Syria (*ANET*, p. 258b), charioteers who themselves owned servants (J. Černý, *JEA* 23, 1937, p. 186), and merchants (Caminos, *op. cit.*, p. 26: 'Aper-Ba'al); the daughter of a Syrian sea-captain Ben-'Anath could marry a royal prince (W. Spiegelberg, *Recueil de Travaux*, 16, 1894, p. 64).

Under the Ramesside kings Asiatics were still more prominent. Thus, one of King Merenptah's trusted cupbearers was the Syrian Ben-'Ozen of Ṣûr-Bashan ('Rock-of-Bashan'), who accompanied the vizier in overseeing work on that pharaoh's tomb in the Valley of the Kings (*JEA* 34, 1948, p. 74). Further, at the very end of the 19th Dynasty, a Syrian very briefly took over control of Egypt itself: he was very possibly the immensely powerful Chancellor Bay (Černý in Gardiner, *JEA* 44, 1958, pp. 21–22).

In New Kingdom Egypt, Canaanite and other Asiatic deities were accepted (Baal, Resheph, 'Ashtaroth, 'Anath, *etc.*; *cf. ANET*, pp. 249–250); and as well as innumerable loan-words, Canaanite literary themes were current, either borrowed or assimilated to Egyp. ones (W. F. Albright, *Archaeology and the Religion of Israel*, 1953, pp. 197–198 (rape of 'Anath); T. H. Gaster, *BO* 9, 1952, pp. 82–85, 232; and G. Posener, *Mélanges Isidore Lévy*, 1955, pp. 461–478 (the greed of the Sea); and reference to a story of Qazardi, *ANET*, p. 477b). Some Egyp. officials prided themselves on being able to speak the lip of Canaan as well as know its geography (*ANET*, p. 477b), not to mention those who had to learn Babylonian cuneiform for diplomatic purposes (*cf.* Albright, *Vocalization of the Egyptian Syllabic Orthography*, 1934, p. 13, n. 50, and *JEA* 23, 1937, pp. 191, 196–202).

d. In Midian and Sinai

Moses felt for his labouring brethren (*cf.* Acts 7:24) and slew an Egyp. overseer whom he found beating a Hebrew (Ex. 2:11f.); but the deed reached Pharaoh's ears, so Moses fled E over the border to Midian for safety (Ex. 2:15ff.). Flight over the E border was the escape chosen also by Sinuhe 600 years earlier (*ANET*, p. 19) and by runaway slaves later in the 13th century BC (*ANET*, p. 259b). Moses helped the daughters of a Midianite shepherd-priest Reuel/Jethro to water their flocks, and married one of them, Zipporah, who bore him a son, Gershom (Ex. 2:16–22).

Through the wonder of the burning bush that was not consumed came Moses' call from God, the God of ancestral Abraham, Isaac and Jacob (Ex. 3:6) and not just of his Midianite/Kenite in-laws, except in so far as they too were descendants of Abraham (*cf.* Gn. 25:1–6) and may have retained the worship of Abraham's God. After some procrastination, Moses obeyed the call (Ex. 3–4). Apparently Moses had omitted to circumcise one of his sons, perhaps under Zipporah's influence. At any rate, under threat of Moses' death by God's agency, she circumcised the boy, calling her husband 'a bridegroom of blood' (Ex. 4:24–26) because circumcision was binding on him and his people (but perhaps not on her people?). Moses may have gone on alone from this point, as later on Zipporah returns to Moses from Jethro's care (Ex. 18:1–6).

e. On the eve of the Exodus

After meeting his brother and the elders of Israel (Ex. 4:27–31), Moses with Aaron went before the pharaoh to request that he release the people to hold a feast to the Lord in the wilderness. But Pharaoh contemptuously dismissed them—there were already enough religious holidays and festivals on which no work was done, and this was just an excuse to be idle (Ex. 5:8, 17).

That Moses should be able to gain ready access to the pharaoh is not very surprising, especially if the pharaoh of the Exodus was Rameses II. P. Montet (*L'Égypte et la Bible*, 1959, p. 71) appositely refers to Papyrus Anastasi III, which describes how the 'young people of (Pi-Ramessē) Great of Victories . . . stand by their doors . . . on the day of the entry of Wosermaetrē'-Setepenrē' (*i.e.* Rameses II) . . ., every man being like his fellow in voicing his petitions' (*i.e.* to the king), *cf. ANET*, p. 471b. For the brickmaking of the Israelites and use of straw, see *Brick. The organization of labour into gangs of workmen under foremen responsible to taskmasters is at once authentic and natural.

As for absence from work, Egyp. ostraca (*Papyri) include journals of work that give a day-to-day record of absenteeism, names of absentees and reasons. One ostracon shows that the workmen of the royal tomb were idle at one period for 30 days out of 48. One journal of absences takes note of several workmen, 'offering to his god' (A. Erman, *Life in Ancient Egypt*, 1894, pp. 124–125), and the laconic entry *wsf*, 'idle', is not infrequent in such journals. That the Hebrews should go 3 days' journey into the wilderness to celebrate their feast and not arouse Egyp. religious antagonism (Ex. 8:26f.; 10:9, 25f.) is, again, thoroughly realistic, as is pointed out by Montet (*op. cit.*, pp. 99–101 with references), in connection with sacred animals, especially the bull-cults in the Egyp. Delta provinces (*CALF, GOLDEN).

After the rebuff from Pharaoh, Moses was reassured by God that he would fulfil his covenant to their descendants, bringing them from Egypt to Palestine (Ex. 6:2–9). It should be noted that Ex. 6:3 does *not* deny knowledge of the name of YHWH to the Patriarchs, though it may possibly deny real knowledge of the significance of the name: see on this, W. J. Martin, *Stylistic Criteria and the Analysis of the Pentateuch*, 1955, pp. 16–19, and J. A. Motyer, *The Revelation of the Divine Name*, 1959, pp. 11–17. Successive *plagues demonstrated the God of Israel's power to Pharaoh in judgment (Ex. 7:14–12:36). On the eve of the last plague, the smiting of the first-born, the families of Israel had to kill a spotless lamb and mark the jambs and lintels of their house-doors with the blood, so that God should not destroy their first-born: 'the sacrifice of the Lord's passover' (Ex. 12:27). It has been suggested by B. Couroyer (*RB* 62, 1955, pp. 481–496) that the Hebrew *psḥ* is derived from the Egyptian *p(')-sḫ*, 'the stroke, blow' (*i.e.* of God), but this meaning does not fit all the Hebrew evidence, and so remains doubtful.

f. From Succoth to Sinai

On the date of the Exodus, see *Chronology of the OT; also J. J. Bimson, *Redating the Exodus and Conquest*, 1978; for its route from Ra'amses and Succoth out of Egypt, see *Encampment by the Sea, *Pithom; for travels in Sinai, see *Wilderness of Wandering. When Israel encamped by the *yam sûp̄*, 'sea of reeds', the pharaoh and his people imagined that the Hebrews were trapped (Ex. 14:1–9). For the figure of over 600 chariots (Ex. 14:7), compare the figures of 730 and 1,092 (*i.e.* 60 [+] 1032) Syr. chariots captured in Canaan on two campaigns by Amenophis II (*ANET*, pp. 246–247); on the role of chariots in the Egyptian army, *cf.* R. O. Faulkner, *JEA* 39, 1953, p. 43. But God divided the waters, led his people to safety and turned the waters upon the Egyp. forces. Then Moses and the Hebrews raised their song of God's triumph (Ex. 15).

Israel encamped at the foot of Mt Sinai and Moses went up to commune with God and receive the terms of the covenant (the 'ten commandments' of Ex. 20), which were the foundation of Israel's subsequent role as the people of God (he being their great King), and also the series of statutes carrying the commandments into effect (Ex. 21–23).

After the idolatrous lapse over the golden *calf and the restoration of the covenant so quickly violated (Ex. 32:1–35:3), the tabernacle, ark and furnishings were duly made and inaugurated for the worship of God (Ex. 35:4–40:33). The techniques used for the portable tabernacle reflect Moses' Egyp. training in so far as such techniques had been used in Egypt for portable structures (religious and otherwise) for over 1,000 years before his time (*cf.* K. A. Kitchen, *THB* 5/6, 1960, pp. 7–13). However, the representational and didactic nature of the tabernacle sacrifices stands out in marked contrast to Egyp. ritual. The Heb. sacrifices speak in picture-language of the offensiveness of sin in God's sight, and of the need of atonement for its cancellation, and were not merely a magically efficacious re-enactment of daily life needed to keep the god fed and flourishing as in Egyp. ritual.

At Sinai a census was taken, the manner of Israel's camp and marching order laid down. Levitical care for the tabernacle and its contents was arranged (Nu. 1–4) among other things on the eve of leaving Sinai (Nu. 5:1–10:10). The arrangement of the tribes by their standards in a 'hollow rectangle' round the tabernacle is also probably a mark of God's use of Moses' Egyp. training (*cf.* Kitchen, *op. cit.*, p. 11). The long, silver trumpets and their use for civil assembly and military and religious purposes (Nu. 10:1–10) is illustrated by contemporary Egyp. use of such trumpets (*cf.* H. Hickmann, *La Trompette dans l'Égypte Ancienne*, 1946, especially pp. 46–50). Ox-wagons were regularly used on campaigns in Syria by the pharaohs from Tuthmosis III (*c.* 1470 BC) onwards (*ANET*, p. 204a, 'chariot'), *e.g.* by Rameses II, *c.* 1270 BC, at Qadesh (C. Kuentz, *La Bataille de Qadech*, 1928/34, pl. 39, left centre). With Moses' wagons each drawn by a span of (two) oxen in Sinai, compare the ten wagons (Egyp. *'grt* from Heb. *'glt*, same word, in Nu. 7:3, 6–7) each drawn by six spans of oxen that carried supplies for 8,000 quarrymen of Rameses IV (*c.* 1160 BC) from the Nile valley into the deserts of Wadi Hammamat between the Nile and the Red Sea, in very similar conditions to Sinai (*ARE*, 4, § 467).

g. From Sinai to Jordan

In their 2nd year out from Egypt (Nu. 10:11), Israel left Sinai and reached Kadesh-barnea. Moses thence sent spies into Canaan. The land was a goodly one, but its inhabitants were powerful (Nu. 13:17–33). At this report, faithless Israel rebelled, but Moses pleaded with God to spare Israel (Nu. 14:5–19). Therefore the Lord decreed instead that Israel's travels in the wilderness should last 40 years until the rebellious generation had died and given place to a new one (Nu. 14:20–35).

It is very easy to forget that, prior to this tragic episode, Israel was intended to have crossed from Egypt—*via* Sinai—directly to the Promised Land within a few years; the 40 years in the wilderness was purely a commuted sentence (Nu. 14:12, 20–30, 33) and *not* part of God's 'first and best' plan for Israel. This should be remembered when reading the laws in Ex. 22–23, relating to agriculture, vineyards, *etc.*; Israel at Sinai had had 4 centuries living in Egypt amid a pastoral and agricultural environment (*cf.* Dt. 11:10), neither they nor their patriarchal forefathers were ever true desert nomads (*cf.* Gn. 26:12 and 37:6–8), and at Sinai they might well count themselves within striking distance of the land where these laws would find a speedy application. Israel had no need to settle in Canaan before such laws could be given, as is so often asserted (*cf.* Kitchen, *op. cit.*, pp. 13–14).

On the twin rebellion of Korah against the ecclesiastical role (Nu. 16:3), and Dathan and Abiram against the civil authority (Nu. 16:13), of Moses and Aaron, see *Wilderness of Wandering. This double revolt was followed by the threat of general revolt (Nu. 16:41–50). Back at Kadesh-barnea, where Miriam died, Moses himself and Aaron sinned blasphemously casting themselves in God's role: 'Hear now, you rebels; shall *we* [not

God] bring forth water for you out of this rock?' (Nu. 20:10); their punishment was that neither should enter the Promised Land, and was one which Moses later felt very keenly (Dt. 3:24–27). The Edomites (Nu. 20:14–21; also Moab, *cf.* Jdg. 11:17) refused Israel passage through their territories so that Israel must go round their borders. At this time Aaron died and was buried in Mt Hor (Nu. 20:22–29). Yet again Israel rebelled. God punished them by sending serpents among them, and again Moses interceded for them. God commanded him to set up a bronze *serpent on a pole (Nu. 21:4–9), to which those bitten might look and live, through faith in the Healer. Thereafter Israel reached the Amorite kingdom of Sihon. Sihon marched—unprovoked—to attack Israel, into whose hand God then delivered him and his land; Og of Bashan, likewise hostile, met a similar fate (Nu. 21:21–35).

At last, Israel encamped in the plains of Moab (Nu. 22:1; 25:1). A second census was carried out, and preparations for apportioning the Promised Land were begun. A punitive war was conducted against Midian, and the tribes of Reuben, Gad and half-Manasseh were allowed to take Transjordan as their portion on condition that they would help their brethren beyond Jordan after Moses' death.

*Deuteronomy gives Moses' farewell addresses to his people; the covenant between God and Israel was renewed and placed under sanctions of blessing and cursing in a manner calculated to be widely understood in the 14th/13th centuries BC (as shown by *covenants or treaties from the contemporary Hittite state archives, *cf.* G. E. Mendenhall, *BA* 17, 1954, pp. 53–60 and *passim*). Finally, Moses saw to it that Israel had her covenant-law in written form, appropriately placed alongside the ark of the covenant (Dt. 31:24), left them a song to enjoin on them obedience to that law (Dt. 32, especially vv. 44–47), and laid upon them his dying blessing (Dt. 33) before ascending Mt Nebo to view the land he was not destined to enter, and being laid to rest in the land of Moab (Dt. 32:48–52; 34:1–8).

III. The work of Moses

a. Leader

As a leader of his people, Moses was not only equipped technically through his Egyp. upbringing and training (Acts 7:22), but was also, on a much more fundamental level, a supreme leader by being a close follower of his God by faith (Heb. 11:23–29; *cf.* Acts 7:23–37). Israel repeatedly failed to have faith in their God in all circumstances, broke the commandments, and rejected God's leadership in rebelling against Moses (sometimes Moses and Aaron) through whom that leadership was manifested (*e.g.* Nu. 14:4, 10; 16:41f.). Moses' own family let him down (Ex. 32:1ff., 21; Nu. 12:1f.). Great indeed was Moses' forbearance (Nu. 12:3); he was constantly interceding with God for sinning Israel (*e.g.* Nu. 14:13ff.; 16:46, *etc.*) and pleading with Israel to be faithful to their delivering God (*e.g.* Nu. 14:5–9). That he was a man of enduring faith in the invisible God (Heb. 11:27b) and so jealous for God's name (*cf.* Nu. 14:13ff.) can alone explain his achievement (*cf.* Phil. 4:13).

b. Prophet and lawgiver

As one especially prominent in declaring and teaching the will, commandments and nature of God, Moses was characteristically the model of all later true prophets until the coming of that One of whom he was forerunner (Dt. 18:18; Acts 3:22f.), to whom all the prophets bear witness (Acts 10:43). He was called by God (Ex. 3:1–4:17) not only to lead the people out of bondage but to make known God's will. Typical is Ex. 19:3, 7: God speaks to Moses, and he to the people.

Moses communed with God long (Ex. 24:18) and often (*e.g.* Ex. 33:7–11), as did later prophets (*cf.* Samuel's life of prayer, 1 Sa. 7:5; 8:6; 12:23; 15:11). Just as the covenant was declared and renewed (Dt. 29:1) through Moses, so the later prophets in turn repeatedly reproved Israel for breaking the covenant and its conditions (*e.g.* 1 Ki. 18:18; 2 Ki. 17:15, 35–40; 2 Ch. 15:1f., 12; Je. 6:16, 19; 8:7f., 11:1–5, 6–10; Ho. 6:7; Am. 2:4; Hg. 2:5; Mal. 2:4ff.), though Jeremiah (31:31–34) could also look forward to a new covenant.

The term 'code' often given to various parts of the Pentateuch is misleading: Moses was not simply the promulgator of some kind of ideal, civil '*code Napoléon*' for Israel. Contemporary Near Eastern treaty-documents of the 13th century BC show that Moses was moved by God to express Israel's relationship to God in the form of a 'suzerainty' treaty or *covenant, by which a great king (in this case, God, the King of kings) bound to himself a vassal-people (here, Israel), the form in question being uniquely transmuted to the religious and spiritual plane. This was a kind of formulation that would be universally understood at the time. For Israel, the basic stipulations of their covenant were the Ten Commandments, in effect moral law as the expression of God's will; and the detailed covenant-obligations took the form of 'civil' statute rooted in the moral law of the Ten Commandments (*e.g.* Ex. 21–23; Dt. 12–26, *etc.*), and even of prescriptions governing the forms of permissible and authorized religious practice (*e.g.* Ex. 25:1ff.; 35:10ff.; Lv.); Israel's life in every way was to be marked by righteousness and holiness as issuing from obedience to the covenant, or, in other words, fulfilling the law. Attainment, however, waited upon further divine provision; *cf.* Gal. 3:23ff. (also 15–22, especially 21f.).

Because Israel's covenant was not merely a treaty of political obligations but regulated their daily life before God, its ordinances served also as a minimum basis of 'civil' law for the people. The existence of long series of laws promoted by individual heads of state from the end of the 3rd millennium BC onwards makes it superfluous to date the giving of the pentateuchal laws any later than Moses (13th century BC).

The number or quantity of 'civil' laws in the Pentateuch is in no way excessive or exceptional when compared with other collections. In Ex. 21–23 may be discerned about 40 'paragraphs', in Lv. 18–20 more than 20 'paragraphs', and in Dt. 12–26 nearly 90 'paragraphs', of very variable length from a chapter or half-chapter of the present-day text-divisions down to one short sentence; say, about 150 'paragraphs' in these sections altogether, leaving aside the more obviously religious prescriptions. This figure compares very reasonably with the 282 paragraphs of Hammurapi's laws, the 115 surviving paragraphs of the Middle Assyrian laws (many more being lost) or the 200 paragraphs of the Hittite laws.

c. Author

In modern times estimates of Moses' role as an author have varied over the whole range of conceivable opinion between the two extremes of either attributing to him every syllable of the present Pentateuch, or denying his very existence.

That Moses' name was attached to parts of the Pentateuch right from the start is clearly shown by the biblical text itself. Thus, at an utter minimum, Moses as a writer is undeniably credited with the following: a brief document on God's judgment against Amalek (Ex. 17:14); the 'book of the covenant' (Ex. 24:4–8; on the external parallels, this must include Ex. 20 and 21–23, the commandments and attendant laws); the restoration of the covenant (Ex. 34:27, referring to 34:10–26); an itinerary (Nu. 33:1f., referring to the document that furnished 33:3–40); the major part of Dt. to 31 (Dt. 31:9–13, 24ff., referring to renewal of the covenant and re-enforcement of its laws that precede ch. 31); and two poems (Dt. 32; *cf.* 31:22; and Ps. 90 by title, which there is no objective evidence to doubt). Later OT and NT references to Moses in this connection are collected by various scholars, *e.g.* by E. J. Young, *IOT*, 1949, pp. 50f.

The ability to write historical narrative, record laws and compose poetry in one man is not unique. An Egyp. example of this kind of ability 7 centuries before Moses is probably furnished by Khety (or Akhtoy), son of Duauf, a writer under the pharaoh Amenemhat I (*c.* 1991–1962 BC), who was apparently educator, political propagandist and poet. He wrote the *Satire of the Trades* for use in scribal schools, was probably commissioned to give literary form to the 'Teaching of Amenemhat I', a political pamphlet, and may have been author of a well-known Hymn to the Nile often copied out by scribes along with the other two works (*cf.* Gardiner, *Hieratic Papyri in the British Museum, Third Series*, 1935, 1, pp. 40, 43–44, and Posener, *Littérature et Politique dans l'Égypte de la XIIe Dynastie*, 1956, pp. 4–7, 19, n. 7, 72–73). However, beyond the 'utter minimum' already mentioned above, there is no objective reason why Moses should not have written, or have caused to be written (at dictation—hence third person pronouns), considerably more of the contents of the present Pentateuch, though just how much more must remain a matter of opinion.

d. Later fame

From Joshua (8:31; *cf.* 1 Ki. 2:3; 2 Ki. 14:6; Ezr. 6:18, *etc.*) to NT times (Mk. 12:26; Lk. 2:22; Jn. 7:23), the name of Moses was associated with the OT, especially the Pentateuch; note 2 Cor. 3:15, where 'Moses' stands *pars pro toto* for the OT. And it was Moses and Elijah, the representatives of OT law and prophecy, who stood with Christ on the Mount of Transfiguration (Mt. 17:3f.).

BIBLIOGRAPHY. O. T. Allis, *God Spake by Moses*, 1951; G. von Rad, *Moses*, 1960; H. H. Rowley, *Men of God*, 1963, pp. 1–36; *idem*, *From Moses to Qumran*, 1963, pp. 35–63; R. Smend, *Das Mosebild von Heinrich Ewald bis Martin Noth*, 1959; H. Schmid, *Mose, Überlieferung und Geschichte*, 1968.

K.A.K.

MOUNT, MOUNTAIN. The topographical terms *giḇ'â* and *hār* in Heb., and *bounos* and *oros* in Gk., are best translated by the Eng. 'hill' and 'mountain' respectively. The term *giḇ'â*, 'hill', is specific, referring to an elevated site, slope or ascent. Its root meaning, 'bowl' or 'hump-backed', refers accurately to the rounded hills which form the backbone of central Palestine, carved out of the hard and folded arches of Cenomanian limestone. Their eroded form is distinct from the deep dissection of the soft Senonian limestones which flank the Judaean highlands, which are graphically described in AV as 'slippery places' (Dt. 32:35; Pr. 3:23; Je. 23:12; 31:9). Specific sites of the hills and mountains are personified in Scripture with descriptive titles. Such are: head (Gn. 8:5; Ex. 19:20; Dt. 34:1; 1 Ki. 18:42), ears (Jos. 19:34), shoulder (Jos. 15:8; 18:16), side (1 Sa. 23: 26; 2 Sa. 13:34), loins (Jos. 19:12), rib (2 Sa. 16:13), back—possible derivation of Shechem, backed by Mt Gerizim—and thigh (Jdg. 19:1, 18; 2 Ki. 19:23; Is. 37:24).

The term *hār*, generally translated 'mountain' in modern VSS, is more general, used indiscriminately of a single mount, a mountain range, or a tract of mountainous terrain. In Eng. mountain and hill are relative terms associated with altitudinal differences, but AV regards the Heb. OT terms *giḇ'â* and *hār* as almost interchangeable. Similarly, in NT, Jesus, *e.g.*, is described as coming down the 'hill' (Lk. 9:37) which he ascended the previous day as the 'Mount' of Transfiguration. In the following passages AV would be better rendered 'mountain', as RSV: Gn. 7:19; Ex. 24:4; Nu. 14:44–45; Dt. 1:41, 43; 8:7; 11:11; Jos. 15:9; 18:13–14; Jdg. 2:9; 16:3; 1 Sa. 25:20; 26:13; 2 Sa. 13:34; 16:13; 21:9; 1 Ki. 11:7; 16:24; 20:23; 22:17; 2 Ki. 1:9; 4:27; Pss. 18:7; 68:15–16; 80:10; 95:4; 97:5; 98:8; 104:10, 13, 18, 32; 121:1; Lk. 9:37. On the other hand, Heb. *hār* is correctly termed 'hill country' (Jos. 13:6; 21:11; *cf.* Gk. *oreinē*, Lk. 1:39, 65, when applied to a regional tract of land such as Ephraim and Judah . It is also used of the land of the Amorites (Dt. 1:7, 19–20), of Naphtali (Jos. 20:7), of the Ammonites (Dt. 2:37) and Gilead (Dt. 3:12).

The identification of specific sites is therefore not always possible, as in the cases of the high mountain of temptation (Lk. 4:5), the mount of the Beatitudes (Mt. 5:1), and the Mount of Transfiguration (Mt. 17:1; Mk. 9:2; Lk. 9:28). Mt *Sinai cannot be identified if, as some have suggested, it was a previously active volcano (Ex. 19:16; Pss. 104:32; 144:5). The traditional location in the Sinai Peninsula (Jebel Mūsa) would in that case be impossible geologically, as the ancient rocks of the district show no evidence of recent volcanicity. Two pleistocene volcanic cones, perhaps active in historic times, occur on the E side of the Gulf of Aqabah, but some authorities cannot see how this fits with the route of the *Exodus described.

The mount of assembly mentioned in Is. 14:13 occurs in the boast of the king of Babylon, and may be an allusion to a probable Bab. legend relating to the dwelling of the gods (*cf.* Jb. 37:22; Ezk. 28:13f.).

Armageddon, Hebraicized Har-magedon in AV (Rev. 16:16), may refer to the mountain district of *Megiddo, *i.e.* Mt Gerizim, which overlooks the plain of Megiddo, the location of other apocalyptic scenes (*cf.* Zc. 12:11).

Mountains have great significance in the geography and history of *Palestine. Consequently they are frequently referred to in the Scriptures. They provide vistas—'go up to the top of Pisgah and lift up your eyes' (Dt. 3:27; *cf.* Lk. 4:5). Their influence on higher rainfall makes them a symbol of fertility (Dt. 33:15; Je. 50:19; Mi. 7:14), grazing-places (Ps. 50:10) and hunting-grounds (1 Sa. 26:20). They are associated with pagan sanctuaries (1 Ki. 18:17–46; Is. 14:13; 65:7; Ezk. 6:13). Their inaccessibility makes them places of refuge (Jdg. 6:2; 1 Sa. 14:21–22; Ps. 68:15, 22; Mt. 24:16).

Mountains are a symbol of eternal continuance (Dt. 33:15; Hab. 3:6) and stability (Is. 54:10). They are considered as the earliest created things (Jb. 15:7; Pr. 8:25), of ancient origin (Ps. 90:2) and objects of the Creator's might (Ps. 65:6) and majesty (Ps. 68:16). They are the scenes of theophanies, melting at Yahweh's presence (Jdg. 5:5; Ps. 97:5; Is. 64:1; Mi. 1:4) and shuddering at his judgments (Ps. 18:7; Mi. 6:1f.). They are called to cover the guilty from his face (Ho. 10:8; Lk. 23:30). When God touches them they bring forth smoke (Pss. 104:32; 144:5). They also rejoice at the advent of Israel's redemption (Ps. 98:8; Is. 44:23; 49:13; 55:12), leap at the praise of the Lord (Ps. 114:4, 6) and are called to witness his dealings with his people (Mi. 6:2).

Mountains are also symbols of difficult paths in life (Je. 13:16), obstacles (Mt. 21:21), and other difficulties (Zc. 4:7), the removal of which is possible to those of strong faith (Mt. 17:20).

J.M.H.

MOUTH. Heb. *peh* with several other words occasionally translated mouth, and Gk. *stoma.* Both are used not only of the mouth of man or beast, or anthropomorphically of God, but are often translated 'edge', in the phrase 'edge of the sword'. *peh* is used also of the mouth of a well (Gn. 29:2), a sack (Gn. 42:27), or a cave (Jos. 10:22).

The general usage is very close to and almost interchangeable with *lip or *tongue. The hand laid upon the mouth, like the lip, was a sign of shame (Mi. 7:16). The mouth can sin (Ps. 59:12) or utter good. The tendency to speak of the mouth as acting independently, by synecdoche or ignorance of physiology, is not as marked as in the case of lip. This may be because the Heb. did not distinguish clearly between the supposed functions of the internal organs, and the mouth, being partly internal, was obviously connected with them (see *HEART and *cf.* Pr. 16:23 where *peh* is translated in RSV as 'speech').

Frequently the mouth is said to be filled with words of one kind or another, or a spirit which causes certain words to be spoken (1 Ki. 22:22; Ps. 40:3). By extension the word *peh* came to mean words or commandments (Ex. 17:1). B.O.B.

MUSIC AND MUSICAL INSTRUMENTS.

I. Music

It is evident from the frequent references in the OT that music played an important part in Heb. culture. According to tradition Jubal, the son of Lamech, who 'was the father of all those who play the lyre and pipe' (Gn. 4:21), was the inventor of music. The close relation between the pastoral and the musical arts is shown in that Jubal had an elder brother Jabal who was 'father of those who dwell in tents, and have cattle' (Gn. 4:20).

At a later stage music was consecrated to the service of the Temple worship, but found secular use also, from early times. Thus Laban reproached Jacob for stealing away without allowing him to cheer his departure 'with mirth and songs, with tambourine (AV tabret) and lyre' (Gn. 31:27). It was frequently used on occasions of rejoicing, when it was regularly linked with the *dance. There were songs of triumph after victory in battle (Ex. 15:1ff.; Jdg. 5:1ff.). Miriam and the women celebrated the downfall of Pharaoh and his horsemen 'with timbrels and dancing' (Ex. 15:20ff.), and Jehoshaphat returned victorious to Jerusalem 'with harps (AV psalteries) and lyres and trumpets' (2 Ch. 20:28). Music, singing and dancing were common at feasts (Is. 5:12; Am. 6:5). In particular, they were features of the vintage festivals (Is. 16:10) and of marriage celebrations (1 Macc. 9:37, 39). Kings had their singers and instrumentalists (2 Sa. 19:35; Ec. 2:8). The shepherd boy also had his lyre (1 Sa. 16:18). The young men at the gates enjoyed their music (La. 5:14). Even the harlot increased her seductive powers with song (Is. 23:16).

Music was used at times of mourning as well as at times of gladness. The dirge (*qînâ*) which constitutes the book of Lamentations and David's lament over Saul and Jonathan (2 Sa. 1:18–27) are notable examples. It became the custom to hire professional mourners to assist at funerals. These regularly included flautists (Mt. 9:23). According to Maimonides, the poorest husband was expected to provide at least two flautists and one mourning woman for the funeral of his wife (*Mišnāyôṯ* 4).

As music formed an integral part of Heb. social life, so it had its place in their religious life. 1 Ch. 15:16–24 contains a detailed account of the organization by David of the levitical choir and orchestra. Apart from this passage there are only scattered and indirect references to the use of music in religious worship, and there is little evidence on which to form any clear impression of the character of the musical service of the Temple.

Of the nature of the music performed by the Heb. musicians we have no knowledge whatever. It is uncertain whether they had any system of notation. No identifiable system has survived. Attempts have been made to interpret the accents of the Heb. text as a form of notation, but without success. These accents were a guide to recitation rather than music and were, in any case, of late origin. Although we have no evidence regarding the instrumental music of the Temple, we can discover from the form of the psalms that they were intended to be sung antiphonally either by two choirs (Pss. 13; 20; 38), or by a choir and the congregation (Pss. 136; 118:1–4). It appears that after the captivity the choirs were formed of an equal number of male and female voices (Ezr. 2:65). But it is not clear whether each choir was of mixed voices or whether one was of male and the other of female voices. They probably chanted rather than sang, although the manner of their chanting is obscure and was certainly very different from modern ecclesiastical chanting.

From Mesopotamia comes written evidence (early 2nd millennium BC) on the stringing and tuning of harps, and musical instruments with a litany (6th century BC); *cf.* D. Wulstan, O. R. Gurney, *Iraq* 30, 1968, pp. 215–233; W. G. Lambert, in H. Goedicke (ed.), *Near Eastern Studies . . . W. F. Albright*, 1971, pp. 335–353. At Ugarit (from *c.* 1400 BC) was found a group of cuneiform tablets bearing hymns in the Hurrian language, accompanied by a form of musical notation; *cf.* A. D. Kilmer, *RA* 68, 1974, pp. 69–82; *ibid.* (with D. Wulstan), pp. 125–128, with earlier references.

ISRAELITE					
	Selected Bible references	Hebrew	AV	RSV	NIV
Stringed instruments					
Harp	1 Sa. 10:5	*nēḇel*	psaltery	harp	lyres
	Is. 5:12		viol	harp	lyres
	Is. 14:11; Am. 5:23; 6:5		viol(s)	harp(s)	harp(s)
(Zither?)	Pss. 33:2; 144:9	*nebel ʿāśôr*	psaltery and an instrument of ten strings	harp of ten strings; ten-stringed harp	ten-stringed lyre
Lyre	Gn. 4:21	*kinnôr*	harp	lyre	harp
Wind instruments					
Horn	Jos. 6:4	*qeren hayyôḇēl*	trumpets of rams' horns	trumpets of rams' horns	trumpets of rams' horns
	1 Ch. 15:28; 2 Ch. 15:14; Ps. 98:6	*šôpār*	cornet, trumpet	the horn, trumpets	rams' horns, trumpets
	Ex. 19:13	*yôḇēl*	trumpet	trumpet	ram's horn
Trumpet	Nu. 10:2	*ḥᵃṣōṣᵉrâ*	trumpet	trumpet	trumpet
	Ezk. 7:14	*?tāqôaʿ*	trumpet	trumpet	trumpet
Vertical flute?	Gn. 4:21; Jb. 21:12; 30:31; Ps. 150:4	*ʿûgaḇ*	organ	pipe	flute
Double pipe (?)	1 Sa. 10:5; Is. 5:12; 1 Cor. 14:7	*ḥālîl*	pipe	flute	flutes
	1 Ki. 1:40		pipe	pipe	flutes
Percussion instruments					
Tambour or hand drum	Ex. 15:20; Ps. 81:2	*tōp̄*	timbrel	timbrel	tambourine

	Selected Bible references	Aramaic	AV	RSV	NIV
	Jb.21:12		timbrel	tambourine	tambourine
	Gn. 31:27; 1 Sa. 10:5		tabret	tambourine	tambourine
	Is. 5:12		tabret	timbrel	tambourine
Cymbals	1 Ch. 15:19	*ṣelṣ^elîm*	cymbals of brass	bronze cymbals	bronze cymbals
	2 Sa. 6:5; 2 Ch. 5:13; Ezr. 3:10; Ps. 150:5	*m^eṣiltayim*	cymbals	cymbals	cymbals
Sistrum (?)	2 Sa. 6:5	*m^ena'an'îm*	cornets	castanets	sistrums
Bells	Ex. 28:33–34 39:25–26	*pa'^amôn*	bells	bells	bells
	Zc. 14:20	*m^eṣillâ*	bells of horses	bells of horses	bells of horses
BABYLONIAN					
Stringed instruments					
Horizontal harp?	Dn. 3:5, 7, etc.	*sabb^eḵâ*	sackbut	trigon	lyre
Vertical harp?	Dn. 3:5, 7, etc.	*p^esanṭērîn*	psaltery	harp	harp
Lyre	Dn. 3:5, 7, etc.	*qîṯrôs/qaṯrōs*	harp	lyre	zither
Wind instruments					
Horn	Dn. 3:5, 7, etc.	*qeren*	cornet	horn	horn
Double pipe	Dn. 3:5, 7, etc.	*mašrôqîṯâ*	flute	pipe	flute
Percussion?					
Drum?	Dn. 3:5, 7, etc.	*sûmpônyâ*	dulcimer	bagpipe	pipes

Table showing musical instruments mentioned in the Bible, with names used in three current translations.

An attempt has been made to reproduce the harp-tuning and hymnology in musical form on a gramophone record; *cf.* A.D. Kilmer, R. L. Crocker, R. R. Brown, *Sounds of Silence*, 1977.

II. Musical instruments

We have a little more knowledge of the musical instruments of the Bible, although there is no definite information regarding their form or construction. Instruments have, however, been found belonging to other ancient nations of the Middle East, notably the Egyptians. The etymology of the Heb. words helps a little, and also the ancient vss, but still our knowledge is very slight. The instruments mentioned in the Bible can be divided into the three main groups: strings, wind and percussion.

a. Strings

(i) *Lyre.* The *kinnôr*, which is regularly rendered 'harp' by AV, is the first musical instrument mentioned in the Bible (Gn. 4:21) and is the only stringed instrument referred to in the Pentateuch. It is one of the instruments with which Laban the Syrian would have wished to send Jacob on his way, had he not departed so suddenly (Gn. 31:27). This allusion suggests that the instrument may have been of Syrian origin. There has been difference of opinion whether it was truly a harp or a lyre. The balance of opinion is in favour of the lyre, which word is used in RSV. That it was portable and therefore small is evidenced by the fact that it was one of the four musical instruments borne before the young prophets (1 Sa. 10:5). Ancient Egyp. tomb-paintings represent foreigners, Semites from Shutu (Transjordan), bearing lyres played with a plectrum in their hands. Nor is it clear whether the *kinnôr* was played with a plectrum or by hand. In 1 Sa. 16:23 'David took the lyre and played it with his hand'; but the absence of mention of a plectrum is no proof that the strings were plucked by the fingers alone. There is no certainty about the number of strings on the *kinnôr*. Josephus thought it had ten. Another suggestion, based on the association of the instrument with Heb. *šᵉmînîṯ* ('eighth', LXX *hyper tēs ogdoēs*) in 1 Ch. 15:21, is that it had eight strings; but the allusion in the passage is far from certain.

The *kinnôr* was a wooden instrument, David's being made probably of cypress (2 Sa. 6:5). Those which Solomon had made for the Temple were constructed of almug (1 Ki. 10:12), and were evidently very valuable. Josephus (*Ant.* 8. 94) records that their framework was fitted with electrum, *i.e.* either a mixed metal or amber.

The word 'harp' is used also by AV in translating Aram. *qîṯrôs* (RSV 'lyre'), which occurs only among the instruments of Nebuchadrezzar's orchestra in Dn. 3. It is the same root from which the European word 'guitar' has sprung.

(ii) *Psaltery.* This word is derived from Gk. *psaltērion*, which denotes an instrument plucked with the fingers instead of with a plectrum. The Gk. verb *psallō* means to touch sharply or pluck. It is the word most often used to translate Heb. *nēḇel*, although occasionally the rendering 'viol' is found, and in the Prayer Book version of the Psalms the word 'lute' is used. In LXX *nēḇel* is variously rendered (*psaltērion, psalmos, kithara, nablion, nabla, nablē, naula* and *nablas*). It is generally accepted that it was a kind of harp, as it is rendered in RSV, although its exact description is uncertain. It is first mentioned in 1 Sa. 10:5, and this seems to confirm the opinion that it was of Phoenician origin, since there was little close contact between Israel and Phoenicia before this date. Attempts have been made to reconstruct the shape of the *nēḇel* by identifying it with a root meaning a skin-bottle, jar or pitcher. It has been suggested that it had a bulging resonant body at its lower end. This identification of the root has even led to the supposition that the instrument was a form of bagpipe. But these suggestions are mere conjecture.

Like the *kinnôr*, the *nēḇel* was made of cypress wood, and later of almug. It is clear that David was able to play the *nēḇel* as well as the *kinnôr*. As it is commonly linked in the Bible with other musical instruments, it is generally thought to have supplied the bass.

Heb. *'āśôr* is frequently linked with *nēḇel*. This word is from the root meaning 'ten', and is generally thought to indicate that the instrument had ten strings. This interpretation is found also in LXX and Vulg. (*psaltērion decachordon* and *psalterium decem chordarum*). In all probability the *nēḇel 'āśôr* was simply a variety of *nēḇel*.

The word 'psaltery' appears also in AV as a translation of Aram. *psantērîn* (Dn. 3:5ff.), another of the instruments in Nebuchadrezzar's orchestra. The Aram. word appears to be a rendering of Gk. *psaltērion*, and is translated in RSV 'harp'. J. Stainer (*The Music of the Bible*, pp. 40–55) argues at some length that the instrument referred to is in fact the dulcimer. It is, however, impossible to say more with confidence than that it was a stringed instrument.

(iii) *Sackbut*. This word occurs in AV only in Dn. 3 as a translation of Aram. *sabbᵉḵâ*. It was one of the instruments of Nebuchadrezzar's orchestra, and was therefore not a Heb. instrument. The AV translation is clearly wrong, as the sackbut was a wind instrument, being in fact a kind of bass trumpet with a slide rather like a modern trombone. The *sabbᵉḵâ* is usually identified with Gk. *sambykē*, by which it is translated in Dn. 3, LXX. This has been described as either a small triangular harp of four or more strings and high pitch, or a large, many-stringed harp. Whichever description is correct, it was a stringed and not a wind instrument. According to Strabo (10. 471) it was of barbaric origin. RSV more correctly renders 'trigon'.

(iv) *Dulcimer*. This is the AV translation of Aram. *sûmpônyâ*, which is generally regarded as a Gk. loan-word. It occurs in the Bible only in the orchestra of Dn. 3. The AV rendering is incorrect, as it is not a stringed instrument. It is now generally supposed to have been a form of bagpipe (as rendered in RV, RSV). The modern Italian rendering of the word is *sampogna*, a kind of bagpipe in current use in that country. Alternatively, it may derive from Gk. *ty(m)panon*, a kind of drum.

b. Wind instruments

(i) *Pipe*. This is Heb. *ḥālîl*, rendered 'pipe' in AV, 'flute' in RSV. The word occurs only six times in the OT. In the NT the pipe is Gk. *aulos*, used in LXX for the *ḥālîl*. Vulg. uses *tibia*. Both *aulos* and *tibia* are general terms covering both reed instruments, such as the oboe and the clarinet, and instruments played by blowing across or through a hole, such as with the flute.

The word *ḥālîl* derives from a root meaning to bore or pierce. The word *aulos* is from a root meaning to blow. But neither the derivation of *ḥālîl*, nor its rendering in LXX, gives any indication of the nature of the instrument. The balance of opinion seems to be in favour of the oboe rather than the flute, but there is no certainty on the matter. Just as today, it was apparently customary in ancient times for the player of a reed instrument to carry with him a supply of reeds in a box (Gk. *glōssokomon*). It was in fact a reed-box and not a 'bag', as AV renders it, which Judas used as a money-box (Jn. 12:6; 13:29).

The pipe was used in festival processions (Is. 30:29), at times of national rejoicing (1 Ki. 1:40), and also in mourning at funerals (Mt. 9:23). That it could produce a plaintive note is evidenced by the allusion to it in Je. 48:36.

(ii) *Flute*. This is the AV translation of Aram. *mašrôqîṯâ*. It occurs only in Dn. 3, and is derived from the root *šāraq*, an onomatopoeic word meaning 'to whistle' or 'hiss'. The playing of most types of pipe or flute is usually accompanied by a hissing sound. It is therefore a reasonable supposition that the instrument referred to is of that class.

(iii) *Organ*. This word (Heb. *'ûgāḇ*) occurs only four times in the OT. In Gn. 4:21 it is evidently a generic term covering all wind instruments, just as the parallel word in the verse, *kinnôr*, is the general term for all stringed instruments. In Jb. 30:31 it again occurs in association with the *kinnôr*, and in Jb. 21:12 it represents the wind section in parallel with members of the stringed and percussion families. We find it again in Ps. 150:4 among numerous other instruments. LXX gives no guide as to the nature of the instrument, for it uses three different words. (In Gn. 4:21 *kithara*, 'guitar'; in the two passages in Job *psalmos*, 'psaltery'; and in Ps. 150:4 *organon*, 'organ'.) The derivation of the Heb. word is uncertain. Some have linked it with a root meaning 'to lust', 'have inordinate affection', thus alluding to its sensuous or appealing tones; but this is no more than conjecture. The instrument must be some form of pipe or possibly a group of pipes.

(iv) *Horn*. This word (Heb. *qeren*) occurs frequently in the OT. Cognate with it are Gk. *keras* and Lat. *cornu*. It appears to have been used in biblical times for two purposes: as a flask for carrying oil and as a kind of trumpet. In this latter sense it occurs in only three passages. In Jos. 6 it is used synonymously with *šôp̄ār* ('trumpet', see (v) below) in the account of the capture of Jericho. In 1 Ch. 25:5 are listed those who were appointed by David to play it, and in Dn. 3 it is one of the instruments of Nebuchadrezzar's orchestra. The earliest trumpets were evidently made out of the horns of animals and later imitated in metal.

(v) *Trumpet*. There is frequent mention of the trumpet in the Bible. In AV it is used chiefly as a translation of two different Heb. words, *šôp̄ār* and *ḥᵃṣōṣᵉrâ*. It is used once also for Heb. *yôḇēl*, which means literally a ram's horn. LXX renders uniformly *salpinx*, which is used also in the NT.

The *šôp̄ār*, a long horn with a turned-up end, was the national trumpet of the Israelites. It was used on military and religious occasions to summon the people. The *šôp̄ār* is still used in Jewish synagogues today.

The *ḥᵃṣōṣᵉrâ* was a trumpet made of beaten silver. Moses was commanded by God to make two of them for summoning the congregation and for breaking camp. Nu. 10:1–10 contains God's instructions to Moses regarding the occasions for the blowing of the trumpet. It was principally a sacred and not a martial instrument.

(vi) *Cornet*. The word appears in AV as the translation of three different words. In Dn. 3 it is used for *qeren*, elsewhere translated 'horn' (see (iv) above). In four passages the Heb. word is *šôp̄ār*, which occurs frequently in the OT and is in all other instances translated 'trumpet' (see (v) above).

In 2 Sa. 6:5 the Heb. word is *mᵉna'an'îm*, which occurs only in this passage. It is used in conjunction with the cymbals (see *c* (ii) below) among other instruments on which David and the children of Israel played before the Lord. The root from which it is derived means 'to quiver', 'vibrate', and it is probable that the instrument was a kind of rattle. LXX renders *kymbala*, 'cymbals', and is therefore less accurate than Vulg. *sistra*, 'rattles' (Gk. *seistron* from *seiō*, 'shake', 'move to and fro'). RSV renders 'castanets'. Illustrations have been preserved of ancient Egyp. rattles consisting of an oval hoop on a handle, to which were affixed rods carrying loose rings which jangled together when shaken.

c. Percussion

(i) *Bells*. Two Heb. words are rendered 'bells' in AV: *pa'ᵃmôn*, from a root meaning 'strike', occurs four times in Exodus, referring to the bells of gold on Aaron's high-priestly robes; the other word, *mᵉṣillâ*, is found only in Zc. 14:20. AVmg. follows LXX (*chalinoi*), reading 'bridles'. The Heb. word is from the same root as that rendered 'cymbals' in AV, and probably refers to the metal discs or cups fixed to the bridles of horses either as an ornament or in order to produce a jingling sound of bells.

(ii) *Cymbals*. This word comes from Gk. *kymbalon*, which occurs once in the NT (1 Cor. 13:1) and also in LXX as a translation of Heb. *mᵉṣiltayim* and *ṣelṣᵉlîm*. *kymbalon* is derived from *kymbē*, which means a bowl or hollowed plate. The two Heb. words are derived from the same root, an onomatopoeic word meaning to whirr or quiver. *mᵉṣiltayim* seems to be a later form of the word occurring about twelve times in the books of Chronicles and once each in Ezra and Nehemiah. The earlier form *ṣelṣᵉlîm* is found in the Psalms and once in 2 Samuel. In Ps. 150 the word is used twice in one verse with different adjectives. Two kinds of cymbals are known to have existed in ancient times. One kind consisted of two shallow metal plates held one in each hand and struck together. The others were cup-like in shape, one being held stationary while the other was brought down sharply against it. It has been suggested that in Ps. 150 these two kinds of cymbals are alluded to, but this is merely conjecture.

In all the passages where cymbals are mentioned they are used in religious ceremonies. Gk. *kymbalon* is used in 1 Sa. 18:6 LXX to translate Heb. *šālîš*, which is from the root meaning 'three'. The Vulg. renders *sistrum*, 'rattle'. Suggestions have been made that it was a triangle or a three-stringed instrument, but there is no certainty as to what is denoted.

(iii) *Timbrel* and *tabret*. These are each used eight times in AV, translating Heb. *tōp̄* (LXX *tympanon*). The instrument was a kind of tambourine held and struck with the hand. It was used as an accompaniment to singing and dancing (Ex. 15:20). It is always associated in the OT with joy and gladness, and is found accompanying the merriment of feasts (Is. 5:12) and the rejoicing of triumphal processions (1 Sa. 18:6).

BIBLIOGRAPHY. I. H. Jones, *Bible Translator* 37,

1986, pp. 101–116; 38, 1987, pp. 129–145; *BA* 54, 1991, pp. 16–27; T. C. Mitchell, *PEQ* 124, 1992, pp. 124–143; H. Hartmann, *Die Musik der sumerischen Kultur*, 1960; T. C. Mitchell and R. Joyce in D. J. Wiseman (ed.), *Notes on some Problems in the Book of Daniel*, 1965, pp. 19–27; J. Rimmer, *Ancient Musical Instruments of Western Asia* (*British Museum*), 1969; L. Manniche, *Music and Musicians in Ancient Egypt*, 1991. D.G.S.
K.A.K.

MYRA. With its port, about 4 km away, Myra was one of the chief cities of Lycia, a province on the SW tip of Asia Minor. There Paul and his centurion escort boarded an Alexandrian corn ship bound for Italy (Acts 27:5–6). Called Dembre by the Turks, Myra displays some impressive ruins, including a well-preserved theatre. J.D.D.

MYSIA. The homeland of one of the pre-hellenic peoples of Asia Minor, never a political unit in classical times, and therefore never precisely defined. It centred on the heavily forested hill country on either side of the main N road from Pergamum to Cyzicus on the Sea of Marmora, a tract which stretched from the border of Phrygia W to the promontory of the Troad. Troas itself, together with Assos and a number of other Gk. coastal states, and even Pergamum may be regarded as part of Mysia. It was the N portion of the Rom. province of Asia. Paul had reached its E limits on his way through Phrygia to Bithynia (Acts 16:7) when he was diverted through Mysia (v. 8) to Troas, probably following a route through the S of the region. E.A.J.

MYSTERY.

I. In the Old Testament

The only OT appearance of the word is in the Aram. section of Dn. (2:18–19, 27–30, 47; 4:9), where LXX renders Aram. *rāz* by *mystērion* (AV, NEB 'secret'; RSV 'mystery'). In this context the word carries a specialized reference, and, as in the phrase 'there is a God in heaven who reveals mysteries' (2:28), it means primarily that which is hidden and still needs to be made known. Yet even here the meaning of the term is not unrelated to its NT use and significance, since the mysteries of which Daniel speaks in this chapter are contained within the eternal plan of God, and also made known by him in advance to his servants ('thoughts of what would be hereafter', 2:29).

Daniel's use of *rāz*, 'mystery', with the correlative *pᵉšar*, 'solution', 'interpretation', was taken over by the Qumran sect, whose use of this terminology has provided an illuminating background for understanding the NT occurrences of the term *mystērion*.

II. In the New Testament

a. Meaning

The meaning of the term *mystērion* in classical Gk. is 'anything hidden or secret' (*HDB*, 3, p. 465), and it was used in the plural particularly (*ta mystēria*) to refer to the sacred rites of the Gk. mystery religions in which only the initiated shared. The root verb is *myō*, which means primarily 'to close the lips (or eyes)' (Lat. *mutus*). But whereas 'mystery' may mean, and in contemporary usage often does mean, a secret for which no answer can be found, this is not the connotation of the term *mystērion* in classical and biblical Gk. In the NT *mystērion* signifies a secret which is being, or even has been, revealed, which is also divine in scope, and needs to be made known by God to men through his Spirit. In this way the term comes very close to the NT word *apokalypsis*, 'revelation'. *mystērion* is a temporary secret, which once revealed is known and understood—a secret no longer; *apokalypsis* is a temporarily hidden eventuality, which simply awaits its revelation to make it actual and apprehended (*cf.* 1 Cor. 1:7, for example, where *apokalypsis* is used, as so often, in reference to Christ himself; and Rom. 8:19, where Paul describes the creation as waiting with eager longing for its *apokatastasis* in the coming age of glory, which is to be revealed (*apokalyphthēnai*) at the *apokalypsis* of the sons of God themselves).

b. Usage

(i) *In the Gospels.* The single occurrence of the word *mystērion* in the Gospels is in Mk. 4:11 = Mt. 13:11 (plural) = Lk. 8:10 (AV 'mystery', RSV, NEB 'secret'). Here the term is used to refer to the kingdom of God, the knowledge of which, just because it is *God's* kingdom, is reserved for those to whom it is 'given'. As a result the unrevealed mystery is, for those 'outside' (*exō*), hidden in *'parables'.

(ii) *In the Pauline Letters.* Paul uses the word frequently, and indeed, apart from four occurrences of the word in Rev. and the three just noted in the Synoptic Gospels, the appearance of *mystērion* in the NT is confined to the Pauline Letters (21 times). The character of *to mystērion* in Paul's theology is fourfold.

1. It is eternal in its scope, in so far as it relates to the divine plan of salvation, the *Heilsgeschichte* itself. The 'mystery' is the good news which forms the content of God's revelation (*cf.* Eph. 6:19); it is the mystery of God himself, the focus of which is in Christ (Col. 2:2, reading *tou mystēriou tou theou, Christou*, with P[46], B, *et al.*; *cf.* 1 Cor. 2:1, where B, D, and other MSS read *martyrion* for *mystērion*). As such it is contained within God's everlasting counsels and hidden in him (Eph. 3:9), decreed 'before the ages' (1 Cor. 2:7) and declared as God's *sophia*, and veiled to human understanding, but awaiting its disclosure, throughout the ages (1 Cor. 2:8; Rom. 16:25, where the adjectival participle is *sesigēmenon*).

2. It is historical in its announcement. This mystery is also the 'mystery of Christ', announced historically and definitively by God in Christ himself (Eph. 1:9; 3:3f., where the *mystērion* is described as revealed to Paul *kata apokalypsin*; *cf.* Col. 4:3) when 'the time had fully come' (Gal. 4:4). It is precisely this mystery, centred and declared in the person of the Lord Jesus Christ, through whose death God reconciles us to himself (2 Cor. 5:18f.; *cf.* 1 Cor. 2:2), that Paul was commissioned to proclaim (Eph. 3:8f.; *cf.* 1 Cor. 4:1). In his letter to the Ephesians Paul considers particularly, against the background of a general and gradual movement towards a Christ-centred inclusiveness (see J. A. Robinson, *Ephesians*, 1903, pp. 238f.), the dominant and related notions of 'hope' and 'mystery'. Christ is the hope of men (1:12) and of the universe (1:10), and we possess as a result a hope which is both glorious (1:18) and real; already the

Christian is saved, and raised with him (2:4–6, where the verbs are in the aorist). Not only so, but also—and this is the particular character of the *mystērion* which Paul has been sent to preach, and which in Eph. he is chiefly concerned to outline—the new hope, and thus also the new *life* in Christ, are available for Jew and Gentile alike (3:8; *cf.* Col. 1:27, where the content of the mystery is qualified as 'Christ in you, the hope of glory').

3. It is spiritual in its perception. We have seen already from the Synoptic Gospels that the mystery of the kingdom is spiritually perceived. Paul retains this idea when he regards the mystery of Christ (the focus of which is particularly 'the Gentiles as fellow-heirs') as revealed to apostles and prophets by the Spirit (*en pneumati*, Eph. 3:5; *cf.* also 1 Cor. 13:2; 14:2). In line with this must be understood the term as it is used derivatively by Paul in connection with Christian marriage (Eph. 5:32), and the 'man of lawlessness (or sin)' (2 Thes. 2:7). The divine significance of these 'mysteries' is apprehended by a conjunction of revelation and spiritual understanding (*cf.* also Rev. 17:3–7).

4. It is eschatological in its outcome. The mystery which has been revealed in time still awaits its divine consummation and fulfilment in eternity. This is the sense in which the term must be understood in Rev. 10:7: the 'mystery of God' already announced will be corporately fulfilled without delay, 'in the days of the trumpet call to be sounded by the seventh angel'. And this is equally true in terms of personal salvation—the 'mystery' of 'being changed' when the trumpet sounds, of mortality's being finally replaced by immortality (1 Cor. 15:51ff.). Such a mystery, even when it is made known, overwhelms us still with the depth of nothing less than the wisdom and the knowledge of God himself (Col. 2:2).

The use of the word 'mystery' with reference to the sacraments (Vulg. translates *mystērion* as *sacramentum*) is entirely post-biblical.

BIBLIOGRAPHY. E. Hatch, *Essays in Biblical Greek*, 1889, pp. 57–62; G. Bornkamm, *TDNT* 4, pp. 802–828; G. Finkenrath, *NIDNTT* 3, pp. 501–506.

S.S.S.

MYTH, MYTHOLOGY. Gk. *mythos*, 'story'; *mythologia*, 'story-telling'. In LXX the word-group appears rarely, and never in books translated from the Hebrew Bible. In Ecclus. 20:19 an ungracious man is compared to 'a story told at the wrong time (*mythos akairos*)'; in Baruch 3:23 the 'story-tellers (*mythologoi*) . . . have not learned the way to wisdom'. In NT *mythos* occurs only in the Pastoral Epistles and 2 Peter, and always in a disparaging sense. Timothy is told to discourage interest in 'myths and endless genealogies which promote speculations' (1 Tim. 1:4). There are similar references to 'godless and silly myths' (1 Tim. 4:7), 'myths' into which false teachers beguile hearers who have 'itching ears' (2 Tim. 4:4), and 'Jewish myths' to which Christians must lend no credence (Tit. 1:14). A mixture of judaizing and gnosticizing speculation is perhaps implied. Such 'myths' are set in contrast to gospel truth: 'we did not follow cleverly devised myths when we made known to you the power and coming of our Lord Jesus Christ, but we were eyewitnesses' (2 Pet. 1:16).

In modern usage the word-group has a wide variety of meaning.

1. *The 'myth and ritual' school.* The 'myth' is the story of which the ritual is the dramatic enactment. T. H. Gaster (*Thespis*, 1950) interprets the Ugaritic religious texts as 'myths' of seasonal rites of emptying and filling which he tries to reconstruct. The *Akitu* or New Year festival of Babylon has been thought to be an instance of a Near Eastern ritual pattern in which the king played the part of the dying and rising god, being regarded as his embodiment or as his mediatorial representative with the people. In this sense a historical event, or series of historical events, could serve as the 'myth', as when the narrative of Ex. 1–15 is regarded as the *mythos* of the annually re-enacted Passover meal, or the passion narrative as the *mythos* of the even more frequently repeated Lord's Supper (*cf.* 1 Cor. 11:26).

2. *The 'demythologizing' programme.* This programme was launched in an essay by R. Bultmann (*New Testament and Mythology*, 1941) which maintained that, if the genuine 'offence' of the cross is to be presented effectively today, the gospel must be relieved ('de-mythologized') of features belonging to the world-view of those to whom it was first preached—not only the 'three-decker' universe but the concept of this world as being open to invasion by transcendent powers. Part of this mythological apparatus detected in the NT has been thought (on inadequate grounds) to belong to a redeemer-myth of Iranian origin developed in various gnostic schools, especially in Mandaism.

3. *'Myth' in Theology*. This is the title of an essay by M. F. Wiles (*BJRL* 59, 1976–7, pp. 226ff.) which refers to another modern usage—that implied, *e.g.*, in the title of the symposium *The Myth of God Incarnate*, 1977 (to which Wiles is a contributor), in which a myth seems to be the pictorial and imaginative presentation of an ontological reality (such as the union of the divine and human at the heart of the human personality). The theological use of the word-group goes back to D. F. Strauss (*Life of Jesus*, 1835) but in wider parlance remains unacceptable because the dominant popular understanding of myth is something that is not simply factually untrue but positively misleading, like a mirage.

Quite different and much more adequate is the approach of C. S. Lewis and others, according to whom 'Myth became Fact' when God became man, so that the aspirations and insights of the human soul which formerly found mythological expression have been given a satisfying response in the historical events of the gospel, not least in the incarnation and redemption which it announces.

BIBLIOGRAPHY. H. W. Bartsch (ed.), *Kerygma and Myth*, 1, 1953; 2, 1962; F. F. Bruce, in C. Brown (ed.), *History, Criticism and Faith*, 1976, pp. 79ff.; *NIDNTT* 2, pp. 643–647, with bibliography; D. Cairns, *A Gospel without Myth*, 1960; A. Dundes, *Sacred Narrative, Readings in the Theory of Myth*, 1984; S. H. Hooke (ed.), *Myth, Ritual and Kingship*, 1958; G. V. Jones, *Christology and Myth in the New Testament*, 1956; C. S. Lewis, *Till we have Faces*, 1956; W. Pannenberg, *Basic Questions in Theology*, 3, 1972, pp. 1ff.; J. W. Rogerson, *Myth in Old Testament Interpretation*, 1974.

F.F.B.

N

NAAMAH ('pleasant'). **1.** A daughter of Zillah and sister of Tubal-cain (GN. 4:22). **2.** 'The Ammonitess', the mother of Rehoboam (1 Ki. 14:21). **3.** A city in lowland Judah (Jos. 15:41), probably identical to modern Nā‘neh, 10 km S of Lydda. Zophar, one of Job's 'comforters', was a Naamathite, but it is unlikely that he originated from the same Naamah. G.W.G.

NAAMAN (Heb. *na‘*^{a}*mān*, 'pleasant'). A common N Syrian name during the mid-2nd millennium as shown by texts from *Ugarit.

1. A dependant of Benjamin; forefather of the Naamite clan (Gn. 46:21; Nu. 26:40; 1 Ch. 8:4, 7).

2. A military commander of the Syrian army during the reign of *Ben-hadad I (2 Ki. 5). Although afflicted with leprosy, he still held his high position (v. 1). At the suggestion of an Israelite prisoner of war, he took a letter from his king, along with gifts, to the king of Israel, probably *Jehoram. He was referred to *Elisha who offered him a cure by bathing in the River Jordan, which Naaman indignantly refused until prevailed upon by his servants (vv. 8–14). Upon being cleansed, he took two mule-loads of earth, which he saw as a necessity for worshipping Yahweh, the one true god (vv. 15–17). Although a Yahwist, Naaman still needed to worship at the temple of *Rimmon, probably because of social obligation.

Jewish legend, recorded in Josephus (*Ant.* 8. 414) but unsubstantiated, identifies Naaman as the one who killed *Ahab by drawing 'his bow at a venture' (1 Ki. 22:34). He is also briefly mentioned in Lk. 4:27. D.W.B.

NABAL ('fool'). A wealthy inhabitant of Maon, SE of Hebron, of the tribe of Caleb, who pastured sheep and goats on adjacent *Carmel (2). During his exile in the reign of Saul, David heard that Nabal was shearing his sheep, a traditional time of hospitality, and sent ten of his men with the request that Nabal should provide David's force with hospitality on a feast-day in return for the protection from brigands David had given his flocks.

Nabal, whose aggressive *folly matched his name (1 Sa. 25:25), replied with insults, whereupon David with 400 men marched up. When Abigail, the beautiful and intelligent wife of Nabal, heard of the messengers' visit she arranged for food and wine to be sent on ahead and went to meet David. This prevented David from committing the crime of blood guilt upon Nabal.

On her return Abigail found her husband drunk. The following day Nabal suffered a paralytic stroke on hearing of his wife's action, and he died about 10 days later (1 Sa. 25). R.A.H.G.

NABATAEANS. Nebaioth, son of Ishmael and brother-in-law of Edom (Gn. 25:13; 28:9), is possibly to be considered the ancestor of the Nabataeans, who may also be the Nabaiate of inscriptions of Ashurbanipal of Assyria (*c.* 650 BC, *ANET*, pp. 298–299). A difference in spelling between these two names (with *tāw*) and the native *nbṭw* (with *ṭêth*) precludes certain identification. Diodorus Siculus (*c.* 50 BC) brings the Nabataeans into recorded history in his account of the end of the Persian empire and the career of Alexander. Quoting from an earlier source, he describes them as a nomadic Arab tribe who neither built houses nor tilled the soil. Their territory, the area S and E of the river Jordan, straddled the trade routes from the Orient to the Mediterranean, and their capital, Petra, 80 km S of the Dead Sea, formed a base from which caravans could be attacked. Antigonus, who gained power in Syria after Alexander's death, sent two expeditions to Petra to subdue the Nabataeans and gain control of the trade (312 BC). Both were unsuccessful. It is clear that at this time Petra was at least a stronghold, and Gk. potsherds of *c.* 300 BC found there suggest a permanent settlement.

Contact with the settled communities of Palestine during the 2nd and 3rd centuries BC resulted in the development of Nabataean villages and towns and in intensive cultivation of formerly barren desert areas. This was aided by well-organized lines of frontier posts to guard against Arab marauders and by the skill of Nabataean engineers in constructing irrigation systems to conserve the scanty rainfall. Many of their dams and reservoirs are still usable. Petra is surrounded by high cliffs, pierced by narrow ravines, which form an almost impregnable defence.

When a Nabataean ruler arose (the earliest known king is Aretas I, *c.* 170 BC, 2 Macc. 5:8) who was able to safeguard the caravans, Nabataean merchants led trade from S Arabia and from the Persian Gulf to Petra, whence it was forwarded to the coast, particularly Gaza. Increased demands by the Rom. world for spices, silks and other luxuries from India and China swelled enormously the revenues of a power which could levy tolls on all goods passing through its territory. The redirection of the trade routes across the Red Sea to Egypt after Augustus' failure to conquer Arabia (25 BC) was an important factor in the decline of Nabataean prosperity.

Native records (coins and dedicatory inscriptions) are written in Aram. in a curiously heightened form of the 'square' script (*WRITING). Papyri from the Judaean desert and ostraca from Petra exhibit a cursive form of this writing from which the Arab. scripts are derived. Use of Aram. indicates a wide assimilation to the culture of

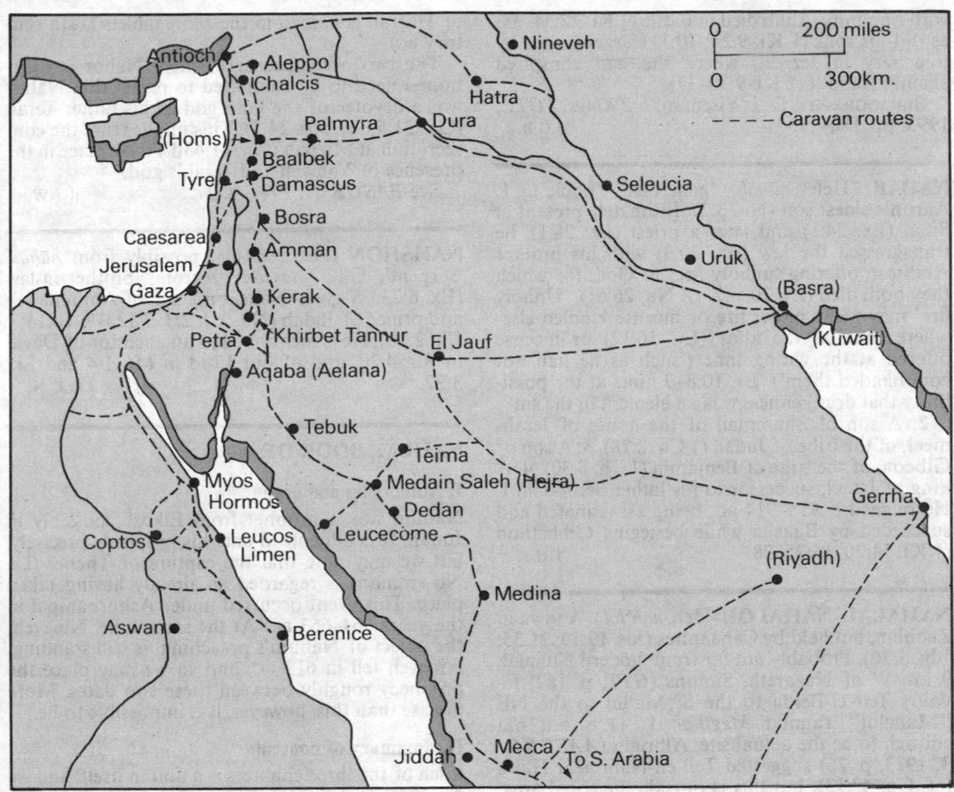

Caravan routes of Nabataean times.

neighbouring settled peoples. This is evidenced by Nabataean sculptures which contain features found in Syrian work and traceable in early Islamic ornamentation. It may be seen also in the acceptance of Syrian deities, Hadad and Atargatis (Astarte-Anat) into the Nabataean pantheon. These two may have been identified with Dushara and his consort Allat, the national deities. Many open-air shrines (*e.g.* the high place at Petra) and temples (*e.g.* Khirbet et-Tannur) have been discovered on isolated hill-tops. The gods worshipped were especially associated with weather and fertility. Nabataean *potters developed a distinctive ware of their own unsurpassed in Palestine.

Nabataean history, as reconstructed from incidental references by Jewish and Gk. authors, consists mainly of struggles to gain control of the Negeb in the S and of Damascus in the N. Aretas III (*c.* 70 BC) and Aretas IV (*c.* 9 BC–AD 40) succeeded in holding both these areas for a few years, so obtaining complete control of E–W trade. It was an officer (Gk. *ethnarchēs*) of Aretas IV who attempted to detain Paul in Damascus (2 Cor. 11:32). Malichus III and Rabbel II, the last Nabataean kings, moved the capital from Petra to Bostra, 112 km E of Galilee. This became the capital of the Rom. province of Arabia following Trajan's conquests in AD 106. Petra enjoyed considerable prosperity during the 2nd century AD when many of the rock-cut façades were made. The rise of Palmyra diverted the trade which formerly went to Petra from the E, and that city gradually declined. The Nabataean people, subject to Arab raids, became absorbed in the surrounding population, although the script continued in use into the 4th century.

Bibliography. J. Starcky, 'The Nabataeans: A Historical Sketch', *BA* 18, 1955, pp. 84–106; G. L. Harding, *The Antiquities of Jordan*, 1959; N. Glueck, *Deities and Dolphins*, 1966; Y. Meshorer, *Nabataean Coins*, 1975; S. Moscati, *The Semites in Ancient History*, 1959, pp. 117–119. A.R.M.

NABOTH. This Israelite commoner had the misfortune of owning a vineyard close to the palace of King Ahab in Jezreel, who wanted to extend his gardens (1 Ki. 21). Though the king offered fair terms for the land, Naboth exercised his right to keep intact his ancestral inheritance. Ahab felt aggrieved and sulked, but Queen Jezebel, who owed no allegiance to Israel's ideals of kingship (Dt. 17:14–20), plotted Naboth's murder. In the king's name she ordered the proclamation of a fast, implying some calamity. This would be seen as God's punishment for some crime. Naboth was accused by fellow members of the judiciary of cursing both God and the king (Ex. 22:28); for this the sentence was death by stoning (*cf.* Dt. 13:10). Elijah pronounced the Lord's judgment on Ahab and his dynasty for the crime of murder. Jezebel's punishment would be a gory death and no burial.

This incident demonstrates that, in Israel at least, the king was subject to God's laws, and could not ride roughshod over the rights of his citizens with impunity. Ahab died in battle (1 Ki. 22:34–38) as did his sons (1 Ki. 9:24; 10:11). Jezebel died by treachery in Jezreel, where she had conspired against Naboth (2 Ki. 9:30–37).

BIBLIOGRAPHY. D. J. Wiseman, *1–2 Kings*, *TOTC*, 1993, pp. 180–183. J.G.B.

NADAB (Heb. *nāḏāḇ*, 'generous', 'noble'). **1.** Aaron's eldest son (Nu. 3:2). Intimately present at Sinai (Ex. 24:1) and later a priest (Ex. 28:1), he transgressed the law (Ex. 30:9) with his brother Abihu in offering 'unholy fire' to God, for which they both died (Lv. 10:1–7; *cf.* Nu. 26:61). 'Unholy fire' may mean either fire or incense kindled elsewhere than at the altar (Lv. 16:12) or incense offered at the wrong time ('such as he had not commanded them'). Lv. 10:8–9 hints at the possibility that drunkenness was an element in the sin.

2. A son of Shammai, of the house of Jerahmeel, of the tribe of Judah (1 Ch. 2:28). **3.** A son of Gibeon, of the tribe of Benjamin (1 Ch. 8:30). **4.** A king of Israel, successor to his father, Jeroboam I. He reigned *c.* 915–914 BC, being assassinated and succeeded by Baasha while besieging Gibbethon (1 Ki. 14:20; 15:25–28). T.H.J.

NAHALAL, NAHALOL (Heb. *nah^a^lol*). A town in Zebulun, but held by Canaanites (Jos. 19:15; 21:35; Jdg. 1:30). Probably not far from modern Nahalal, 9 km W of Nazareth. Simons (*GTT*, p. 182) favours Tell el-Beida to the S; Ma'lul to the NE ('Mahalul', Talmud *Megillah* 1. 1) is not old enough to be the actual site. Albright (*AASOR* 2–3, 1923, p. 26) suggested Tell en-Nahl near Haifa (*cf.* Gn. 49:13), but this is outside the tribal area. J.P.U.L.

NAHALIEL (Heb. *naḥ^a^lî'ēl*, 'valley of God'). N of the Arnon (Nu. 21:19); now Wadi Zerka Ma'in; famous in Rom. times for its warm springs, which flow into the Dead Sea 16 km from the Jordan (Josephus, *BJ* 1. 657; 7. 185). J.P.U.L.

NAHASH (Heb. *nāḥāš*). **1.** An Ammonite king who attacked Jabesh-gilead in Saul's reign (1 Sa. 11–12). His relations with David were friendly (2 Sa. 10:2; 1 Ch. 19:1). **2.** Father of Abigail and Zeruiah, David's sisters (2 Sa. 17:25). LXX(B) and Origen support this reading against other Gk. MSS which give 'Jesse' (Driver, *Samuel*), perhaps assimilating to 1 Ch. 2:13–16. The Chronicler may mean that Abigail and Zeruiah were Jesse's step-daughters; their sons appear to have been of about David's age. J.P.U.L.

NAHOR. 1. Son of Serug, and grandfather of Abraham (Gn. 11:22–25; 1 Ch. 1:26).

2. Son of Terah, and brother of Abraham and Haran. He married his niece Milcah, Haran's daughter (Gn. 11:26–27, 29). Nahor probably journeyed to Harran with Terah, Abram and Lot despite the silence of Gn. 11:31 to this effect, for Harran became known as 'the city of Nahor' (Gn. 24:10; *cf.* 27:43). He was the progenitor of twelve Aramaean tribes which are listed in Gn. 22:20–24. This reflects the close relationship of the Hebrews and the Aramaeans. A place Nahur in the vicinity of Harran is named in the Mari tablets (18th century BC).

The two other passages where Nahor is mentioned need to be compared to reveal that Nahor was a devotee of the false god of his father Terah (Gn. 31:53; *cf.* Jos. 24:2). This implies that the consecration at Mizpah (Gn. 31:43ff.) took place in the presence of Yahweh and Terah's god.

See *BASOR* 67, 1937, p. 27. R.J.W.

NAHSHON (Heb. *naḥšôn*, possibly from *nāḥāš*, 'serpent'; Gk. *Naassōn*). Aaron's brother-in-law (Ex. 6:23; AV gives 'Naashon'), son of Amminadab and prince of Judah (Nu. 1:7; 2:3; 7:12, 17; 10:14; 1 Ch. 2:10). He is mentioned as an ancestor of David in Ru. 4:20, and of our Lord in Mt. 1:4 and Lk. 3:32. J.G.G.N.

NAHUM, BOOK OF.

I. Authorship and date

Nahum was a prophet from Elkosh, possibly in Judah. It is difficult to date his prophecy precisely, but we may note that the capture of Thebes (*i.e.* No-ammon) is regarded as already having taken place. This event occurred under Ashurbanipal in the years 664–663 BC. At the same time, Nineveh, the object of Nahum's preaching, is still standing. Nineveh fell in 612 BC, and so we may place the prophecy roughly between these two dates. More precise than this, however, it is impossible to be.

II. Summary of contents

Each of the three chapters is a unit in itself, and we may best understand the prophecy by considering these chapters one after another.

a. An acrostic poem and declaration of judgment, 1:1–15

Chapter 1 falls into three principal sections: the superscription (v. 1), the description of God's majesty (vv. 2–8), and the declaration of judgment to come (vv. 9–15). The superscription describes the message as a *maśśā'*, *i.e.* 'burden', a word which often denotes a message involving threatening. It also declares that the work is a 'book of the vision of Nahum', *i.e.* a book in which the vision received by Nahum is written down. The supernatural character of the message is thus early acknowledged.

The prophet immediately plunges into a statement of the jealousy of God. The zeal of the Lord is his determination to carry out his purposes both in the bringing in of his own kingdom and in the punishment of his adversaries. It is this latter aspect of God's jealousy which is here prominent. God is slow to anger, says the prophet (v. 3); nevertheless, he will take vengeance on his enemies. When these terms are applied to God we must understand that they are used anthropomorphically; they do not contain the sinister connotations that adhere to them when they are used of men. That God is able so to carry out his purposes is a matter that admits of no doubt. He can control the forces of nature, the storm, the rivers, the sea, Bashan, *etc.* For those who trust in him he is a stronghold, but for the wicked he is darkness.

The enemies of the Lord refuse to believe that he will smite them. Hence, God announces that in a time when they expect it not the enemy will be devoured as stubble that is wholly dry. Yet there is also to be an announcement of salvation, and Judah is commanded to keep her solemn feasts and to perform her vows.

b. The siege and sack of Nineveh, 2:1–13

In 2:1–6 Nahum describes the enemy who lay siege to Nineveh. These are the Medes who came from the plain of Persia and were turning their attention against the Assyrians of the Mesopotamian plain. They are described as those that dash in pieces (v. 1). In attacking the city they open the sluices so that the waters of the river may overflow and then they enter the city to destroy her palace.

Huzzab, a word which possibly designates the queen (*cf.* RSV 'its mistress'), is taken away into captivity, and her female attendants follow her. (NEB renders the word 'train of captives'; J. D. W. Watts suggests the pedestal of a temple image.) Nineveh, the object of attack, has become like a pool of water. Into her much trade has poured and many goods have been brought, so that she is now filled. Nevertheless, men will flee from her, and those who cry 'Stand!' will not be able to stay those who would take refuge in flight. Plunder then begins in earnest, and the few survivors who remain behind look on in grief and terror as the city is despoiled.

Nineveh had once been a lion, a veritable den of lions. She had engaged in search for prey. Now, however, she is herself the object of such search and herself becomes a prey. What has become of Nineveh? The answer is that the Lord of hosts is against her, and he has determined to act in such a way as to remove her strength and power from her.

c. A description of the city and a comparison with Thebes, 3:1–19

Chapter 3 consists of a description of the wicked character of the city of Nineveh. She was a bloody city and full of cruelty. She was a warring city, and there were many that were slain. Through her whoredoms she sold nations and dealt in witchcrafts. Hence, the Lord had set himself against her and would expose her so that she would become a laughing-stock to all who looked upon her.

Nahum then makes a brief comparison with Thebes (3:8–15). Thebes, as the capital of Upper Egypt, had become strong, had revelled in her strength and acted as had Nineveh, yet her ruin had surely come. So also would it be with Nineveh. There could be no escape. Thus the prophet works up to a mighty climax, and announces that there is no healing for the bruise of Assyria, 'Your wound is grievous' (3:19a).

In this small prophecy of doom we learn that the God of Israel, the nation whom Assyria had despised, is truly the God who controls the destinies and the actions of all nations.

BIBLIOGRAPHY. J. H. Eaton, *Obadiah, Nahum, Habakkuk, Zephaniah, TBC*, 1961; J. D. W. Watts, *Joel, Obadiah, Jonah, Nahum, etc., CBC*, 1975; R. L. Smith, *Micah–Malachi*, 1984; D. W. Baker, *Nahum, Habakkuk and Zephaniah, TOTC*, 1988.

E.J.Y.

NAIL. 1. Finger-nail (Heb. *ṣippōren*; Aram. *ṭᵉpar*). Captive women were commanded to shave the head and pare the nails (Dt. 21:12). Nebuchadrezzar had 'nails like birds' claws' (Dn. 4:33; *cf.* 7:19).

2. A wooden tent peg (Jdg. 4:21, Heb. *yāṯēḏ*), used by Jael to slay Sisera. It was sometimes used for suspending objects as in Ezk. 15:3. Isaiah (22:25 AV; RSV 'peg') likened Eliakim to 'a nail in a sure place' on which the 'whole weight of his father's house' might hang. Such a nail was driven into a wall.

3. A metal nail or pin (*yāṯēḏ*) for driving into wood or other material to hold objects together, or left projecting to suspend objects. In the tabernacle the nails were of bronze (Ex. 27:19; 35:18; 38:20, 31; 39:40; Nu. 3:37; 4:32). Delilah used such a nail (pin) to bind Samson (Jdg. 16:14). The word *masmēr* refers to nails of iron (1 Ch. 22:3) or of gold (2 Ch. 3:9), driven into a wall (Ec. 12:11), or used to secure idols in their place (Is. 41:7; Je. 10:4). Nails have been found at many Palestinian sites including Tell Abu Hawam, an ancient harbour city near Mt Carmel.

4. In NT times victims were affixed to a *cross by nails driven through hands and feet (Gk. *hēlos*, Jn. 20:25). J.A.T.

NAIN. Mentioned only in Lk. 7:11. There is a small village still bearing this name in the Plain of Jezreel, a few miles S of Nazareth, at the edge of Little Hermon, and it is generally accepted as the scene of the Gospel narrative. It is certainly to be distinguished from the Nain of Jos., *BJ* 4. 511, which was E of the Jordan. The name is perhaps a corruption of the Heb. word *nā'îm*, 'pleasant', which adjective well describes the area and the views, if not the village itself. A problem is raised, however, by the reference to the city gate (Lk. 7:12); for the village today called Nain was never fortified, and so would never have had a gate in the proper sense of the word. But the word 'gate' may be used loosely, to indicate the place where the road entered between the houses of Nain. An ingenious suggestion solves the difficulty by proposing that the site was Shunem (as in the similar story of 2 Ki. 4), an original *synēm* becoming accidentally reduced to *nēm*, and then confused with Nain. Shunem, in any case, is in the same general area. D.F.P.

NAIOTH. A place or quarter in Ramah where Samuel supervised a community of prophets and to which David fled from Saul (1 Sa. 19:18–19, 22–23). When Saul sent messengers there to seek David, each in turn 'prophesied'. Later, when Saul came in person he too 'prophesied' (v. 24), giving rise to a proverb: 'Is Saul also among the prophets?' The Heb. word *nāyôṯ* is related to *nāweh*, 'pasture ground' or 'abode', and is commonly translated 'habitation'. J.A.T.

NAME. The Bible is no stranger to the custom, now virtually normative, of giving a name simply because it appeals to the parents. What else is likely to lie behind calling a little girl Deborah (meaning 'bee', Jdg. 4:4) or Esther (Heb. *hᵃḏassâ*, 'myrtle')? Even in cases where it offers some high-sounding, moralistic or religious sentiment, it would run beyond the evidence to assume without question that the name was conferred with that thought in mind rather than that the parents were indulging a preference for that rather than any other label. One can, for example, weave sad fancies round a name like Ahikam ('my brother has risen') as indicating a tragic earlier bereavement in the family which the subsequent birth of another son was seen to rectify, but Ahikam is a pleasant-sounding name and in default of evidence to the contrary may well have been chosen for no better reason.

Nevertheless, while we can be too high-minded in our approach to names and naming in the Bible, there is no question but that there is, throughout, a conceptual background which was often given full play in the conferring of a name and which, even if it seemed to have no part (or none that we know) in the original naming yet in later life asserted its claim on the person concerned. Thus, for example, whereas Isaiah named his two sons with deliberation so that they would embody certain aspects of the word of God to his people (Is. 7:4; 8:1–4) his own name ('Yahweh saves'), as we should have to say, 'by coincidence', could not have been bettered as the name for this prophet above all. The Bible's view of names and naming would be offended by the idea of a mere coincidence or accident of parental choice: the link it sees between name and person is both too close and also too dynamic for that.

I. Significant naming

The general evidence dispersed throughout the Bible would insist that it is no coincidence that the great prophet of salvation is called by a theophoric name on the salvation theme. It would see the directive providence of God determining beforehand the whole course of the life; it would probably more typically see the name as embodying a word of God which would henceforth mould its recipient into the man whose life would express what the word declared. This, at any rate, is the dynamic view of names and naming which runs throughout Scripture and which differs so dramatically from our static view of a name as a differentiating label.

The following seven categories cover most of the dynamic name-giving situations:

a. The status-name. Of his new-found wife, the man said that she would be called 'Woman', thus according to her a co-equal (or, better, counterpart) status with her husband: he is *'îš*; she is *'iššâ*. In general in the Bible name-giving is an authority function: the imposition of the name 'Man' on the couple by their Creator (Gn. 5:2), the giving of animal names by the man, in his capacity as creation's lord (Gn. 2:19f.), the naming of children by parents (by the mother on 28 and by the father on 18 occasions), the naming of a conquered king (2 Ki. 23:34), *etc.* But in Gn. 2:23 the 'man' acknowledges his complementary equal, the one who, with him, shares the God-given dominion of the world (Gn. 1: 28ff.).

b. The occasion-name. The birth of her first-born is to Eve the significant moment of the fulfilling of the promise of a victorious seed; therefore 'along with Yahweh' as she said (Gn. 4:1)—he, fulfilling his promise, she bringing forth a child—she 'gained possession' (verb *qānâ*) of a child whom she therefore called 'Cain' (*qayin*).

c. The event-name. Sometimes names encapsulate a whole situation: *e.g.* Babel (Gn. 11:9) or Peleg (Gn. 10:25). Both these namings have the same quality, but we can see what was afoot more clearly in the fully-documented case of Babel: the name was in effect a word of God. Men had already discerned in themselves a tendency to separate or scatter (11:4) and they purposed by their technological advance (v. 3) to be their own saviours in this regard. The divine edict goes forth against man's confidence that his own cleverness can save him, and the word which imposes judicially on the human race the disability which it feared (v. 8) is succinctly built into the fabric of earthly things by the place-name 'Babel' ('confusion') which is to be henceforth the evil genius of the Bible story until the end (*cf.*, *e.g.*, Is. 13:1; 21:1–10; 24:10; Rev. 18:2; *etc.*; *BABYLON).

d. The circumstance-name. Isaac was named because of the attendant laughter of his parents (Gn. 17:17; 18:12; 21:3–7); Samuel, because of the prayer of his mother (1 Sa. 1:20); Moses, because his princess-mother drew him from the water (Ex. 2:10); Ichabod, because of the loss of the ark, seen as significant of the withdrawal of divine favour (1 Sa. 4:21); Jacob, because of the position of the twins at birth (Gn. 25:26). In many of such cases the Bible provides the evidence to show that such 'accidents' were truly symbolic: the victory at the Red Sea makes Moses pre-eminently the man who came up out of the water; the story of Samuel is precisely the story of the man who knew that prayer is answered, and so on. In other words, there is a continuing link between the idea of giving a name and the dynamism of the ever-potent word of God effecting that which it declares.

e. The transformation- or alteration-name. Names were bestowed in order to show that something new had entered the life of the person concerned, one chapter was complete and a new chapter was opening. Though this giving of a new name is usually hopeful and promissory, the category opens with the sad re-naming of *'iššâ* (Gn. 2:23) as Eve (Gn. 3:20), the name expressive of co-equality of status and complementariness of relationship becoming the name of function; the former name expressed what her husband saw in her (and was glad), the latter expressed what he would use her for, giving her domination in return for her longing (Gn. 3:16). But to the same category belongs the re-naming of Abram as Abraham, signifying the beginning of the new man with new powers: the childless Abram (whose name 'high father' was only a sour joke) becoming Abraham, which, though it does not grammatically mean 'father of many nations', has sufficient assonance with the words which would (at greater length) express that thought. Many significant names operate on just such a basis of assonance. Thus also on one and the same day Benoni became Benjamin (Gn. 35:18), the circumstance-name of pain and loss becoming the status-name of 'right-hand man'. The dominical bestowal of the name Peter (Jn. 1:42) has the same significance, *cf.* Mt. 16:18; as indeed does the (presumably) self-chosen change from Saul to Paul (Acts 13:9).

f. The predictive/admonitory-name. Isaiah's two sons are pre-eminent in this class. It is significant of the prophet's certainty of the word of God through him that he was willing to embody it in his sons who thus were, within their own time, 'the word become flesh', the greatest of the acted oracles (*PROPHECY) of the OT. *Cf.* Is. 7:3; 8:1–4, 18. See also 2 Ki. 24:17, where the name Zedekiah embodies the righteousness element (*ṣedeq*, 'righteousness') which Pharaoh thus warns the new king to practise. The Lord's naming of James and John as 'Boanerges' was equally a warning against the unacceptable element of fire in their zeal (Mk. 3:17; *cf.* Lk. 9:54) and once again the name proved itself to be an effective word of God.

g. Precative- and theophoric-names. A name like Nabal (*nāḇāl*, 'fool') (1 Sa. 25:25) can only have been given on the basis of a mother's prayer—'Let him not grow up to be a fool'—a prayer for which a cogent background could be provided without too much stretch of the imagination. It is likely that many theophoric names had this same element of prayer in them—or at the very least, most of those which are based on an imperfect tense of the verb: thus Ezekiel ('May God strengthen!'); Isaiah ('May Yah[weh] save!'). Even those which in direct translation make an affirmation (*e.g.* Jehoahaz, 'Yahweh has grasped') are most likely the product of pious parental aspirations—not always realized, as the sad case of Nabal (1 Sa. 25) may show, or the case of King Ahaz whose name is probably an abbreviation of 'Jehoahaz': it is fully in accord with the story of that politically astute, spiritually inept king to think that he deliberately dropped the theophoric element in his name.

The naming of the Lord Jesus Christ does not fit any single one of the foregoing categories. In its relation to OT prophecies (Mt. 1:23 with Is. 7:14; Lk. 1:31–33 with Is. 9:6f.) the name Jesus is a status-name, declaring the recipient to be God, born of a virgin and the promised king of David's line. It is a significant thing that the first person named in the NT receives (not a prediction-name but) a fulfilment-name: the purposes of God are being rounded out to completion. The name Jesus itself is a prediction-name looking forward to what he will himself do, and this is itself significant, for the prediction-names of the OT looked forward to what Yahweh would do and stood in relation to that act as external heralds or pointers. But Jesus is himself the fulfilment of what his name declares.

II. The name of God

Any and all evidence which helps to show that on the human level a name is a significant and indeed potent thing, not only labelling but moulding its recipient, finds its focus in the concept of the 'name of God' (*GOD, NAMES OF) which lies at the centre of the Bible. A 'divine name' is not, of course, a distinctively biblical notion. Amongst the ancient Greeks, for instance, Hesiod tried to enter more deeply into an understanding of the gods by a study of their names, an exercise which, *mutatis mutandis*, might well be seen as central to biblical theology.

There is a real sense in which the Bible is poised upon the revelation of the divine name. In the OT, the Patriarchs knew their God by titles (*e.g.* Gn. 14:22; 16:13; 17:1), among which was the so far unexplained 'Yahweh'. The significance of Moses and the Exodus is that at that point what had hitherto been no more than a label was revealed to be not a title, however exalted, but a personal name. The revelation enshrined in the name was opened up and confirmed in the Exodus events, the redemption of the people of God, the Passover and the Red Sea. In the NT the balancing event was the ministry and redemptive work of Jesus: the definitive 'name' of God as the Holy Trinity, Father, Son and Holy Spirit, coinciding with the public commencement of Jesus' ministry when at his baptism he began deliberately to be numbered with the transgressors (*cf.* Mk. 1:9–11). John sees the significance of this in his deliberate association of Jesus at his baptism with the Lamb of God (Jn. 1:29ff.). This comparison should warn against identifying the God of the OT ('Yahweh') with the NT revelation of God the Father. Yahweh is rather the Holy Trinity *incognito*.

In form the divine name *Yahweh* is either a simple indicative or a causative indicative of the verb 'to be', meaning 'he is (alive, present, active)' or 'he brings into being', and the formula in which the name is disclosed (Ex. 3:14, *I am who I am*) means either 'I reveal my active presence as and when I will' or 'I bring to pass what I choose to bring to pass'. In the setting of Ex. 3–20 this refers both to the events of the Exodus as those in which Yahweh is actively present (and which indeed he has deliberately brought to pass) and also to the preceding theological interpretation (Ex. 3:1–4:17; 5:22–6:8) of those events vouchsafed to Moses. Yahweh is thus the God of revelation and history and in particular reveals himself as the God who saves his people (according to covenant promise) and overthrows those who oppose his word.

Abundant though this revealed knowledge of God is, yet in the divine name there is a clear element of secrecy. The formula *I am who I am* in itself expresses no more than that God knows his own nature: it is a formula of the sovereignty of God in the revelation of himself. If anything is to be told, he must tell it; he will tell only what he pleases. *Cf.* Gn. 32:29; Jdg. 13:17. This is not in any way to be related to the concepts of magic. In the surrounding pagan world to know a god's name was supposed to confer some power over that god—a logical extension (as so much false religion is a logical embroidering upon a truth) of the idea that 'naming' is the act of a superior. Yahweh did not withhold any revelation of himself in fear lest man should gain power over him. Rather the revelation of himself belongs in a programme of privilege which he has designed for his people, whereby the somewhat 'external' relationship expressed in titles becomes the highly personal relationship to a God who has given his people the liberty to call him by name, and what is at that point held back is concealed only because the moment of supreme revelation is yet to come. Nevertheless what is already known is not a falsehood later to be set aside nor a partial truth (for *this is my name for ever*, Ex. 3:15) awaiting completion, but one way of expressing the whole truth which will yet achieve greater and fuller expression. The 'name' of God lies at the heart of progressive revelation.

But though the name does not confer 'power' in any magical sense (*cf.* Acts 19:13ff.), the knowledge of the name brings people into a wholly new relationship with God. They are his intimates, for this is the significance of 'knowing by name' (*cf.* Ex. 33:12, 18–19; Jn. 17:6). The initiation of the relationship thus described lies on the divine side: collectively and individually the people of God are 'called by his name' (*cf.* 2 Ch. 7:14; Is. 43:7; Je. 14:9; 15:16; Am. 9:12). Furthermore the motive which lies behind this divine outreach is often described as the Lord acting 'for the sake of his name' (*cf.* especially Ezk. 20:9, 14, 22, 44) by means of works through which he 'made for himself a name' (*e.g.* 2 Sa. 7:23; Ne. 9:10). The name is thus a summary way of stating what God is in himself (his name is all that is known to be true about him and his motives of action) and also what God is to others, allowing them to know his name (letting them into his truth) and sharing his name with them (letting them into his fellowship).

There are five aspects of this basic situation strongly enough attested in Scripture to warrant a brief statement of each, even though not all are evenly spread through the Bible.

a. It is a particularly Johannine emphasis to express the human side of the experience of God as 'believing in the name' (*e.g.* Jn. 3:18; 1 Jn. 3:23), *i.e.* personal commitment to the Lord Jesus as thus revealed in the essence of his Person and work.

b. Those who are of the people of God are 'kept' in his name (*e.g.* Jn. 17:11), taking up the distinctive OT picture of the name as a strong tower (*e.g.* Pr. 18:10) to which they may run for safety, and also the name given as a husband's name to a wife whereby provision and protection are guaranteed (*cf.* 'called by the name' above). When Christians are said to be 'justified in the name' (1 Cor. 6:11) the implication is the same: the name, as the unchangeable nature of Jesus and as the summary of all that he is and has done, is the ground of secure possession of all the implied blessings.

c. God's presence among his people is secured by 'making his name dwell' among them. *Cf.* Dt. 12:5, 11, 21; 14:23f.; 16:2, 6; 2 Sa. 7:13; *etc.* It has sometimes been foolishly pressed that there is a distinction if not a rift between a 'name-theology' and a 'glory-theology' in the OT, but these are two ways of expressing the same thing: *e.g.* when Moses sought to see Yahweh's glory, he found that the glory had to be verbalized by means of the name (Ex. 33:18–34:8). There is no sense in which the Deuteronomist is replacing a crude notion of indwelling glory by a refined notion of the indwelling name: it is rather that the 'glory' tends to express the 'sense' of God's real presence, including much that is rightly unapproachable and ineffable; 'name' explains why this is so, verbalizes the numinous, for nowhere does the God of the Bible deal in dumb sacraments but always with intelligible declarations.

d. The name of God is described as his 'holy name' more often than all other adjectival qualifications taken together. It was this sense of the sacredness of the name that finally led to the obtuse refusal to use 'Yahweh', leading as it has done to a deep loss of the sense of the divine name in EVV (with the notable exception of JB). The 'holiness' of the name, however, does not remove it from use but from abuse: this is the reason why the revelation of the divine name must never be confused with any thought of magical 'power with the divine'. Far from man being able to use the name to control God, it is the name which controls man, both in worship Godward (*e.g.* Lv. 18:21) and in service manward (*e.g.* Rom. 1:5). The 'name' is thus the motive of service; it is also the message (*e.g.* Acts 9:15) and the means of power (*e.g.* Acts 3:16; 4:12).

e. Throughout the Bible the name of God is the ground of prayer: *e.g.* Ps. 25:11; Jn. 16:23–24.

Distinctively the NT associates baptism with the name, either of the Holy Trinity (Mt. 28:19) or of the Lord Jesus (*e.g.* Acts 2:38): the distinction is that the former stresses the total reality of the divine nature and purpose and the totality of blessedness designed for the recipient, whereas the latter stresses the effective means of entry into these things through the sole mediation of Jesus.

BIBLIOGRAPHY. *s.v.* 'Name' in J.-J. von Allmen, *The Vocabulary of the Bible*, 1958; *IDB*, 1962, and Supp. Vol., 1976; *see also*, J. Pedersen, *Israel* 1 and 2, 1926, pp. 245–259; J. Barr, 'The Symbolism of Names in the OT', *BJRL* 52, 1969–70, pp. 11–29; L. Hartman, 'Into the Name of Jesus', *NTS* 20, 1973–4, pp. 432–440; J. A. Motyer, *The Revelation of the Divine Name*, 1959; R. de Vaux, 'The Revelation of the Divine Name YHWH', in J. I. Durham and J. R. Porter, *Proclamation and Presence*, 1970, pp. 44, 48–75; G. von Rad, *Studies in Deuteronomy*, 1953, pp. 37–44; G. T. Manley, *The Book of the Law*, 1957, pp. 33, 122ff.; H. Bietenhard, F. F. Bruce, *NIDNTT* 2, pp. 648–656. J.A.M.

NAOMI (Heb. *no'ᵒmî*, 'my delight'). During the period of the Judges there was a famine in Bethlehem of Judah, which caused Elimelech, a citizen of that place, to take his wife Naomi, and their two sons, Mahlon and Chilion, to Moab. There she was widowed, and her sons married Moabite girls, Orpah and *Ruth, who were widowed in their turn.

Naomi decided to return to her own people alone, while her daughters-in-law remarried, but Ruth insisted on accompanying her. She told them that her name was now Mara (Heb. *mārā'*, 'bitter') (Ru. 1:20f.). At Bethlehem she planned a levirate marriage for Ruth with her near kinsman, Boaz. Their first child, Obed, was reckoned as hers, and he was the grandfather of David (Ru. 4:16f.). M.B.

NAPHISH. The eleventh son of Ishmael (Gn. 25:15; 1 Ch. 1:31). His descendants have not been definitely identified, but may be the 'Naphish' of 1 Ch. 5:19; 'the sons of Nephisim' of Ezr. 2:50; and the 'Nephushesim' of Ne. 7:52. J.D.D.

NAPHTALI (Heb. *naptālî*, 'wrestler'). The sixth son of Jacob, and the second son of Bilhah, Rachel's maidservant; the younger brother of Dan, with whom he is usually associated (Gn. 30:5–8). In the Blessing of Jacob he is described as 'a hind let loose' which may allude to either his agility or his impetuosity.

In most of the administrative lists the tribe of Naphtali comes last (*e.g.* Nu. 1:15, 42f.; 2:29ff.; 7:78; 10:27). The Blessing of Moses commands Naphtali to 'possess the lake and the south' (Dt. 33:23) and following the settlement its tribal portion comprised a broad strip W of the Sea of Galilee and the upper Jordan, including the greater portion of E and central Galilee. This territory is roughly delineated in Jos. 19:32–39, including nineteen fortified cities. But the N boundary is undefined and since two of the cities mentioned, Beth-anath and Beth-shemesh, parts of a chain of Canaanite fortresses extending from the coast across upper Galilee, are noted in Jdg. 1:33 as not completely subjugated, it is probable that it varied considerably in the earlier period. Naphtali included also the largest Canaanite city, Hazor, covering about 80 hectares and dominating a vital trade route. Hazor, although destroyed by the Israelites under Joshua (Jos. 11:10f.), reasserted itself and, whilst never regaining its former prestige, it was not finally vanquished until well into the Judges' period (Jdg. 4:2, 23f.). Another important city was Kedesh, a levitical city and one of the cities of refuge (Jos. 20:7; 21:32).

The strong Canaanite element is reflected in Jdg. 1:33, 'Naphtali . . . dwelt among the Canaanites'. This would encourage syncretism and partly accounts for the relative insignificance, historically, of this tribe. But there were moments of glory. Barak, Deborah's partner in delivering Israel from Canaanite domination, was a Naphtalite (Jdg. 4:6) and his tribe was conspicuous in the same campaign (Jdg. 5:18). A later generation served valiantly under Gideon (Jdg. 6:35; 7:23), and the Chronicler records their support for David (1 Ch. 12:34, 40). Thereafter, Naphtali, vulnerable because of its frontier situation, suffered from attacks from the N. During the reign of Baasha its territory was ravaged by Ben-hadad I of Syria (1 Ki. 15:20). Approximately 150 years later (734 BC) the tribe of Naphtali was the first W of the Jordan to be deported (2 Ki. 15:29). A probable reconstruction of Tiglath-pileser III's account of this campaign notes his annexation of the region, '. . . the wide land of Naphtali, in its entire extent, I united with Assyria'. Is. 9:1 alludes to the same event.

The territory of Naphtali included some of the most fertile areas of the entire land. During David's reign its 'chief officer' was Jeremoth (1 Ch. 27:19). It was one of the districts from which Solomon provisioned his court; at this time its governor was one of Solomon's sons-in-law, Ahimaaz (1 Ki. 4:15). Hiram, the principal architect of Solomon's Temple, was the son of 'a widow of the tribe of Naphtali' (1 Ki. 7:14). In Ezekiel's redistribution of the tribal allotments, Dan, Asher and Naphtali are assigned portions in the N, but the other N tribes, Issachar and Zebulun, are included further S (Ezk. 48:1–7, 23–29).

Jesus spent the greatest part of his public life in this area which, because of its chequered history of deportations and infusion of new settlers, was greatly despised by the Jews of Jerusalem, an attitude which partly explains why Galilee became the headquarters of the reactionary Zealots, bitterly opposed to Roman rule.

BIBLIOGRAPHY. Y. Aharoni, *The Settlement of the Israelite Tribes in Upper Galilee*, 1947; *idem*, *LOB*, pp. 201f., 238f. A.E.C.

NAPHTUHIM. Classed with Mizraim (Egypt), Gn. 10:13; 1 Ch. 1:11. Its identity is uncertain, but Lower Egypt, specifically the Nile Delta, would be appropriate alongside Pathrusim (*PATHROS) for Upper Egypt. Hence Brugsch and Erman emended the Heb. to fit Egyp. *p' t'-mḥw*, 'Lower Egypt'. Another Egyp. equivalent, without emendation, might be a *n'(-n-)/n'(yw-) p' idḥw*, 'they of the Delta (lit. marshland)', Lower Egypt(ians). Alternatively, *nap̄tuḥîm* may be an Egyp. *n'(-n-)/n'(yw-) p' t' wḥ'(t)*, 'they of the Oasis-land', *i.e.* the oases (and inhabitants) W of the Nile valley. K.A.K.

NARCISSUS. Paul salutes those 'who belong to the family of Narcissus' (Rom. 16:11). The phrase suggests the slaves of a prominent household. The rich freedman Narcissus, who brought about the fall of Messalina (Tacitus, *Annals* 11, *passim*), had committed suicide some little time before Rom. was written (*ibid.*, 13. 1); but his slaves ('Narcissiani' are mentioned in *CIL*, 3, 3973; 6, 15640) would pass to Nero and still be a recognizable entity. Though the name is also common outside Rome, it is tempting to see in Rom. 16:11 a Christian group within this body. A.F.W.

NATHAN (Heb. *nāṯān*, 'he [*i.e.* God] has given'). Of some eleven men of this name in the OT the following at least can be identified as separate individuals:

1. A prophet (Heb. *nāḇî'*) involved in the story of King David. He appears without introduction when David expresses his wish to build a temple (2 Sa. 7 = 1 Ch. 17). Nathan approves at first, but after speaking with God informs David that this task is for David's descendant, though David apparently arranges, at Nathan's instigation, the music for Temple worship (2 Ch. 29:25). When Adonijah plans to seize his father's throne, Nathan advises Bathsheba to remind David of his promise to name Solomon his successor. Supporting this reminder, Nathan is instructed to proclaim Solomon (1 Ki. 1:11–45). Nathan is best known for his fearless denunciation of David's double sin against Uriah the Hittite, and the parable in which it was couched (2 Sa. 12).

2. Relative of two of David's warriors (2 Sa. 23:36; 1 Ch. 11:38). **3.** Son of David, born in Jerusalem (2 Sa. 5:14). This line of descent is cited in Zc. 12:12 and in our Lord's genealogy in Lk. 3:31. Either this Nathan or the prophet is referred to in 1 Ki. 4:5. **4.** A man of Judah (1 Ch. 2:36). **5.** One of Ezra's companions to Jerusalem (Ezr. 8:16). **6.** Son of Bani, who put away his foreign wife at Ezra's instigation (Ezr. 10:39). T.H.J.

NATHANAEL. The name means 'gift of God', and it occurs only in Jn. 1:45–51; 21:2. He seems to be one of the Twelve and he has been variously identified, especially with Bartholomew. The name Bartholomew is a patronymic, and its bearer would have another name too. Bartholomew is next to Philip in the lists of the Twelve in the Synoptics (Mt. 10:3; Mk. 3:18; Lk. 6:14). Some, with but little justification, have identified Nathanael with Matthew, Matthias, John, Simon the Cananaean or Stephen. Others, with even less justification, have denied his real existence.

He was from Cana in Galilee and he was brought by Philip to Jesus, sceptical about the possibility of a Messiah from Nazareth. He was astonished that Jesus knew him already, having seen him under the fig tree. (This means a display of supernatural power, though the 'fig tree' may be symbolic of the study of the Law or of prosperity.) He confessed that Jesus was Son of God and King of Israel. This was the confession of an 'Israelite indeed, in whom is no guile', but it seems to limit the Messiahship to Israel. Christ promised him a greater vision, that of the Son of man as the link between heaven and all mankind (Jn. 1:45–51). He was one of those who saw Christ on his resurrection appearance by the Sea of Tiberias (Jn. 21:2).

BIBLIOGRAPHY. C. F. D. Moule, *JTS* N.S. 5, 1954, pp. 210f. R.E.N.

NATIONS, TABLE OF. An account, recorded in Gn. 10, and with a few minor variations in 1 Ch.

1:5–23, of the descendants of Noah by his three sons, *Shem, *Ham and *Japheth.

I. The Table

The table on p. 816 represents the relationships by placing the names of the descendants of an individual below and to the right of the ancestor's name.

II. Position in Genesis

If Genesis is divided into sections by means of the recurring formula 'these are the *generations (Heb. *tôl^eḏôṯ*) of . . .', the Table of Nations falls within the section Gn. 10:2–11:9, the formula occurring in Gn. 10:1 and 11:10. Different views are held as to whether these formulae constitute headings or colophons, but it does not affect the issue in the present case whether the Table of the Nations, together with the account of the tower of Babel, be regarded as part of the *tôl^eḏôṯ* of the sons of Noah (if 10:1 is the heading) or of Shem (if 11:10 is the colophon).

III. Arrangement

V. 32 summarizes the Table, stating that it gives the families (*mišp^eḥōṯ*; *FAMILY, OT) of the sons or descendants (*b^enê*) of Noah, according to their genealogies (*l^eṯôl^eḏôṯ*; *GENERATION) in their nations (*b^egôyīm*), and from these (*mē'ēlleh*, *i.e.* either the 'families' or the 'nations' making these up) the nations (*gôyim*) spread abroad on the earth (*'ereṣ*) after the Flood. While this verse forms a colophon to the Table as a whole, vv. 5, 20 and 31 form colophons to the subsections vv. 2–4, 6–19 and 21–30 which give the descendants of Japheth, Ham and Shem respectively. Their general tendency is the same as v. 32, but they further state that their lists give the names 'with reference to' their families (*mišp^eḥōṯ*) and their languages (AV 'tongues', *l^ešōnôṯ*; Japheth's colophon varies with 'each with his own language'), and in their lands and their nations (*gôyim*). In Japheth's colophon these are presented in a different order, and it is further stated that 'from these the coastland peoples spread'. Many commentators consider that this phrase applies to the descendants of Javan alone, since the designation 'coastland peoples' (AV 'isles') is not appropriate to the other members of the group. It is further suggested on the basis of the analogous statements in vv. 20 and 31 that the phrase 'these are the sons of Japheth' originally stood before 'in their lands . . .' in v. 5, and inadvertently dropped out in transmission. This view is adopted in the RSV and may be correct.

Japheth	Ham	Shem
Gomer	Cush	Elam
Ashkenaz	Seba	Asshur
Riphath	Havilah	Arpachshad
Togarmah	Sabtah	Shelah
Magog	Raamah	Eber
Madai	Sheba	Peleg
Javan	Dedan	Joktan
Elishah	Sabteca	Almodad
Tarshish	Nimrod	Sheleph
Kittim	Mizraim	Hazarmaveth
Dodanim	Ludim	Jerah
Tubal	Anamin	Hadoram
Meshech	Lehabim	Uzal
Tiras	Naphtuhim	Diklah
	Pathrusim	Obal
	Casluhim	Abimael
	Philistines	Sheba
	Caphtorim	Ophir
	Put (Phut)	Havilah
	Canaan	Jobab
	Zidon	Lud
	Heth	Aram
	Jebusite	Uz
	Amorite	Hul
	Girgashite	Gether
	Hivite	Mash
	Archite	
	Sinite	
Descendants of an individual are placed below and to the right of the ancestor's name	Arvadite	
	Zemorite	
	Hamathite	

The Table of Nations, according to Gn. 10, showing the descendants of Noah's sons, Shem, Ham and Japheth.

Within the three lineages the names are related to each other, either by the formula 'these are the sons of (*bᵉnê*) . . .' or '. . became the father of (AV 'begat') (*yālad*) . . .' (*GENEALOGY). The latter is not found in the list of Japheth's descendants, but under Ham is used of Nimrod, and the descendants of Mizraim and of Canaan, and under Shem is used of the section from Shelah to Jobab, that is, all the descendants of Arpachshad. One exception to these two formulae is found in the Philistines who 'came' or 'were begotten' (*yāṣā'*) from Casluhim (v. 14). The regular arrangement into three lists of names is modified by the insertion of other verses which give additional information, either in relating the names to each other, or in giving further information about individuals. The arrangement of the chapter may be summarized as follows:

- Heading (or colophon to previous section) (1)
  - Japheth's descendants (2–4)
    - Details concerning Javan (5a)
    - Colophon (5b)
  - Ham's descendants (6–7, 13–18a)
    - Details concerning Nimrod (8–12) and Canaan (18b–19)
    - Colophon (20)
  - Shem's descendants (22–29a)
    - Details concerning Shem (21), and Joktan (29b–30)
  - Colophon (31)
- Colophon to whole (32)

The order, in which Shem is given last, follows the usage of Genesis whereby the chosen line is treated after the collateral lines have been discussed. The genealogy in Gn. 11 carries on the line through Peleg to Abraham.

IV. Contents

Many of the names in the Table have been connected with names of peoples or regions known in the ancient inscriptions, and there is sufficient agreement on a number of these to make possible a general idea of the scope of the three lists.

a. Preliminary consideration

The names in the Table were probably the names of individuals, which came to be applied to the people descended from them, and in some cases to the territory inhabited by these people. It is important to note that such names could have different meanings at different points in history, so that the morphological identification of a name in Gn. 10 with one in the extra-biblical sources can be completely valid only if the two occurrences are exactly contemporary. The changes in significance of names of this kind are due largely to movements of peoples, in drift, infiltration, conquest or migration.

There are three principal characteristics of a people which are sufficiently distinctive to form some nuance of their name. These are race or physical type; language, which is one constituent of culture; and the geographical area in which they live or the political unit in which they are organized. Racial features cannot change, but they can become so mixed or dominated through intermarriage as to be indistinguishable. Language can change completely, that of a subordinate group being replaced by that of its rulers, in many cases permanently. Geographical habitat can be completely changed by migration. Since at times one, and at other times another, of these characteristics is uppermost in the significance of a name, lists in Gn. 10 are unlikely to have been drawn up on one system alone. Thus, for instance, the descendants of Shem cannot be expected all to have spoken one language, or even to have lived all in one area, or even to have belonged to one racial type, since intermarriage may have obscured this. That this could have taken place may be indicated by the presence of apparently duplicate names in more than one list, Asshur (*ASSYRIA), Sheba, Havilah and Lud(im) under both Shem and Ham, and probably Meshek (Mash in Shem's list; *MESHECH) under Shem and Japheth. Though these may indicate names that are entirely distinct, it is possible that they represent points where a strong people has absorbed a weaker.

It is necessary to observe that names have been adopted from this chapter for certain specific uses in modern times. Thus in language study the terms 'Semitic' and 'Hamitic' are applied, the former to the group of languages including Heb., Aram., Akkad., Arab., *etc*., and the latter to the group of which (ancient) Egyp. is the chief. This is a usage of convenience, however, and does not mean that all the descendants of Shem spoke Semitic languages or all those of Ham Hamitic. Thus the entry of Elam under Shem, and Canaan under Ham, is not necessarily erroneous, even though Elamite was a non-Semitic and Canaanite was a Semitic tongue. In short, the names in Gn. 10 probably indicate now geographical, now linguistic, and now political entities, but not consistently any one alone.

b. Japheth

In this list the following identifications receive general, though not universal, agreement: Gomer = Cimmerians; Ashkenaz = Scythians; Madai = Medes; Meshek = Muški, peoples who entered the ancient Near East from the N steppe. Javan = Ionians, and his descendants, including Elishah = Alašia (in Cyprus) and Dodanim [probably a corruption for Rodanim; *cf*. 1. Ch. 1:7, RSV] = Rhodes, were probably a W group of the N peoples who passed through Ionia to the islands and coastlands (*'iyyê*, v. 5) of the Aegean and Mediterranean. Thus it appears that the descendants of Japheth were people who in the 2nd millennium were found in the regions to the N and NW of the Near East.

c. Ham

Here the following identifications are accepted in general: Cush = Ethiopia; Sheba = Saba (in S Arabia); Dedan = Dedan (in N Arabia); Mizraim = Egypt; Ludim = Lydia (?); Philistines = Philistines; Caphtorim = Cretans; Put = Libya; Canaan = Canaan; Zidon = Sidon; Heth = Hittites; Amorite = Amorites; *Hivites = Hurrians; Hamathites = Hamathites.

Under *Nimrod an additional note is provided to the effect that the beginning of his kingdom was in *Shinar = Babylonia where he ruled in Babel = Babylon, Erech = Uruk, Accad = Agade, and *Calneh (possibly to be vocalized *kullānâ*, 'all of them'), the first three being important cities in S Mesopotamia, though the site of Agade is as yet unknown. From there he went to Asshur = Assyria (or 'Asshur went forth'; *cf*. AV) and built Nineveh, Rebohoth-ir, Calah = Kalḫu, and Resen. Nineveh and Kalḫu were Assyrian royal cities, but the other two names are unknown.

According to the situation revealed in the extra-biblical inscriptions, the statements that the inhabitants of Mesopotamia (Nimrod) came from Ethiopia, and that the Philistines and Cretans came from Egypt might appear to be erroneous, but the nature and origins of all the elements in the early population of Mesopotamia are still obscure, and Egypt's early connections with Crete and the Aegean area show the possibility of earlier unrecorded contacts. In general, the peoples to the S of the Near East are indicated in this list.

d. Shem

In Shem's list a few identifications are generally accepted: Elam = Elam (the SE part of the Mesopotamian plain); Asshur = Aššur (or Assyria); Hazarmaveth = Ḥaḍramaut (in S Arabia); Sheba = Saba; Lud = Lydia (?); Aram = Aramaeans. These names suggest that the general area settled by the group stretched from Syria in the N, through Mesopotamia to Arabia.

V. Sources

The study of the ancient Near East gives some idea of the horizons of geographical knowledge of the 2nd millennium BC and earlier.

a. Mesopotamia

In the 4th millennium BC the evidence of prehistoric archaeology shows that at times a common culture flourished over an area stretching from the Persian Gulf to the Mediterranean. By about 3000 BC contacts through trade are attested with the Arabian peninsula, Anatolia, Iran and India. The cuneiform records take up the tale in the late 3rd and the 2nd millennia. Early rulers had business relations and other contacts with Iran, the Lebanon ('Cedar Forest'), the Mediterranean ('Upper Sea'), the Taurus ('Silver Mountain') and Anatolia (Burušḫatum) in the N, and in the S with Bahrain (Dilmun), where excavations have revealed a centre trading with Arabia and India. In the 18th century BC a colony of Assyr. merchants maintained themselves in Cappadocia (Kültepe), and from about this period a merchant's itinerary from S Mesopotamia to this station is known (*JCS* 7, 1953, pp. 51–72).

Movements in the 3rd millennium on the N steppe resulted in the arrival in the Near East during the early 2nd millennium of such peoples as the Kassites and later the rulers of Mitanni, who probably brought with them a knowledge of the N lands.

b. Egypt

In pre-historic times the inhabitants of the lower Nile had trading contacts with the Red Sea, Nubia, Libya and perhaps other places in the Sahara, and during the early Dynasties in the 3rd millennium regular expeditions were made to Sinai, and to Byblos on the Syrian coast. In the early 2nd millennium trade contacts with Cyprus, Cilicia and particularly Crete are attested by finds of objects at both ends. The Egyptians were given to listing names, and the Execration Texts of the 18th century and the lists of 'subject' cities and peoples of the pharaohs of the 15th show a geographical knowledge of Palestine and Syria. In the 14th century the archive of cuneiform tablets found at el-Amarna shows that one language (Akkadian) was used for diplomacy over the whole Near East and that a good knowledge of other areas was possible.

c. Literary criticism

It is believed by many scholars that the distinction between the *bᵉnê* and *yālaḏ* formulae in the arrangement of the Table betrays composite authorship. According to this, the main framework, making use of the *bᵉnê* formula, is to be ascribed to the Priestly Code (P), and the parts introduced by *yālaḏ*, together with other matter which gives additional information on some names in the lists, is derived from the earlier less scientific Yahwistic document (J) which was woven into their framework by the more methodical Priestly writers. The resulting division is: P = 1a, 2–7, 20, 22–23, 31–32; J = 1b, 8–19, 21, 24–30. This variation can be just as well understood, however, as the licence of style, and in the light of the geographical knowledge of the 2nd millennium BC it is no longer necessary to assume a date of composition as late as the early monarchy (J) and the post-exilic period (P). Indeed, the absence of Persia from the list would be difficult to explain if the Table was largely compiled and put into its final form by priests who owed their very return from exile to the tolerant policy of the Persians.

VI. Scope

Apart from those theories which would set the Table down as late and unreliable, there are two main views as to its scope. Some maintain that this Table names the peoples of the whole world, others that it mentions only those peoples of the Near East with whom the Israelites were likely to come in contact. This depends largely upon the word *'ereṣ* in v. 32. This is taken in EVV in the sense of '*earth', but it is a term whose significance could vary from 'the whole earth' through 'the known world' to a limited 'country' according to the context. The general view which can be obtained from the commonly accepted identifications of names in the Table supports the opinion that *'ereṣ* here means 'the known world'; but the fact that many of the names in the Table are as yet unidentified shows that the other view cannot be completely ruled out. To accept the former view does not imply that others besides Noah survived the flood, for, while the implication of Gn. 9:19 is that the earth was peopled by the descendants of Noah's three sons (*NOAH, *d*), the Table does not claim to name all of them.

VII. Authorship and date

The facts mentioned above show that the contents of the Table would not necessarily have been beyond the knowledge of a person educated in the Egyp. schools of the 15th or 14th century. Those who argue for a post-Mosaic date do so largely on the basis of the fact that such peoples as the Cimmerians, Scythians, Medes and perhaps Muški do not appear in the written documents until the 1st millennium and on the basis of this a date in the early 1st millennium is postulated. These peoples must, however, have existed as tribes or larger groups before they are mentioned in the extant records, and it is possible that such earlier invaders as the Kassites and the rulers of Mitanni, who had had contacts with the more N tribes, might have preserved a knowledge of them. It is also commonly held that the *Philistines (v. 14) did not appear in the biblical world until the 12th century, but various considerations point to the possibility of earlier contacts with these people. Likewise the

S Arabian peoples mentioned in the Table, who do not appear in the written records until the 1st millennium, must have existed as tribes before then.

In brief, therefore, though there are some difficulties in the view, it is not impossible that the Table of Nations could have been compiled in the 13th century BC, perhaps by Moses.

BIBLIOGRAPHY. W. F. Albright, *Recent Discoveries in Bible Lands*, 1955, pp. 70–72; W. Brandenstein, 'Bemerkungen zur Völkertafel der Genesis', *Festschrift . . . Debrunner*, 1954, pp. 57–83; G. Hölscher, *Drei Erdkarten . . . .*, 1949, ch. 5; J. Simons, 'The Table of Nations (Gen. 10): Its General Structure and Meaning', *OTS* 10, 1954, pp. 155–184; D. J. Wiseman, 'Genesis 10: Some Archaeological Considerations', *JTVI* 87, 1955, pp. 14–24, 113–118 and *POTT*, pp. xv–xxi; E. A. Speiser, *Genesis*, 1964, pp. 64–73; most of the earlier views are discussed in S. R. Driver, *The Book of Genesis*[12], 1926, pp. xxvi-xxvii, 112–132; G. R. Driver, *ibid.*, pp. 444–447; J. Skinner, *Genesis*[2], 1930, pp. 196–207.

T.C.M.

NATURE. There are few words more dangerously ambiguous than 'nature'. It is impossible here to distinguish carefully all its various uses; the following analysis deals only with the words translated 'nature', 'natural', 'naturally' in AV and RSV. It is significant that even these spring from four distinct roots, one Heb. and three Gk.

1. The Heb. word *lēaḥ*, rendered 'natural force' at Dt. 34:7, has the root idea of 'freshness', 'moistness', and so of the vigour usually associated with the suppleness of youth.

2. The Gk. adverb *gnēsiōs* and the noun *genesis* stem from a root indicating 'birth', 'coming into being'. The former, although rendered 'naturally' in AV, Phil. 2:20, had lost its etymological sense in Hellenistic Greek and is better translated 'genuinely' (as RSV), 'sincerely' (*cf. MM s.v.* for the history of this change in meaning). The noun *genesis* occurs in the genitive case in Jas. 1:23; 3:6. In the first case RSV renders the genitive by 'natural', in the second 'of nature'. The idea is that of the successive birth, decay and new birth characteristic of the world around us. A man sees in a mirror the face which has come to be what it is through this process (1:23): 3:6 further brings out the sense of continuous process with the phrase 'the wheel' or 'course' of the changing world. There is abundant evidence in Philo for the contrast between *genesis*, the changing scene around us, and the eternity of God.

3. The word translated 'natural' in 1 Cor. 2:14; 15:44, 46 (AV) is the Greek *psychikos*. This adjective is used in the NT to refer to that which belongs to *psychē*, not in the most general sense of 'life', 'soul', but as it is distinguished from *pneuma*. *psychē* in this sense is the life of sensation, emotion, intellect apart from all conscious contact with God. The natural body of 1 Cor. 15 is a body which answers to the needs of this lower *psychē*; similarly, the spiritual body, otherwise undefined, will be a body not necessarily 'composed of spirit' but a fit 'vehicle', as it were, for the functioning of the spirit.

4. The words most frequently translated 'nature', 'natural', are *physis* and *physikos*. The basic meaning of *physis* is 'the process of growth' and hence that which comes into being by such a process; *cf.* Rom. 11:21, 24 for the distinction between *physis*, the normal growth of a plant, and the results of grafting. Every order of beings has its own *physis*, Jas. 3:7 (*cf.* RV mg.); it is even possible to speak of the distinctive *physis* of God (2 Pet. 1:4), though no process of growth is conceivable within the divine Being itself.

The precise meaning of *physis*, *physikos*, is often determined by that with which *physis* is contrasted. Thus it may be regarded as characteristic of brute beasts as opposed to humanity (2 Pet. 2:12; Jude 10) or to be contrasted with that which is commonly but falsely believed (Gal. 4:8, Moffatt—'gods who are really', *physei*, 'no gods at all'; *cf.* 1 Cor. 8:5).

Of special importance are the Pauline uses of *physis* in contrast with (i) the perversions of Gentile society, (ii) the free grace of God in Christ and its consequences in man's life.

The former use is found in Rom. 1:26–27; sexual perversion is there viewed as a departure from the norm recognized by 'natural' man. The same idea is probably present in 1 Cor. 11:14, though here *physis* could have a reference to its primary sense 'the process of growth' and physiological facts about the length of uncut hair.

physis as distinguished from grace gives the Jew a place of comparative privilege (Gal. 2:15); it marks him off from the Gentile outside the covenant (Rom. 11:21, 24), though it does not of itself save. On the other hand, the Gentile, despite his not having the sign of the covenant and being, *ek physeōs*, uncircumcised, is sometimes able *physei* to do the works demanded by the law (Rom. 2:14, 27). Over against all privilege or good works, however, stands the fact that all men are *physei* children of wrath (Eph. 2:3). Thus *physis, physikos*, in these passages refer to all that belongs to the state of the world, Jewish and Gentile, apart from God's gracious act in Christ.

M.H.C.

NAZARENE. According to Mk., the designation *Nazarēnos* was applied to our Lord by demons (1:24), the crowd (10:47), a domestic (14:67), and the messenger of the resurrection (16:6). It is used also in Lk. 4:34 (= Mk. 1:24) and Lk. 24:19 (the Emmaus disciples). But Mt., Lk. and Jn. normally employ *Nazōraios* (Mt. 26:71; Lk. 18:37; Jn. 18:5ff.; 19:19; Acts 2:22; 3:6; 4:10; 6:14; 22:8; 26:9). Both terms are translated in AV and RSV as 'of Nazareth'. *Nazōraios*, 'Nazarene', is applied also to Jesus in Mt. 2:23, and occurs as a popular designation of the Christian 'sect' in Acts 24:5. This is maintained in Jewish use (*cf.* the oldest Palestinian form of the *Shemoneh 'Esreh*, where at about AD 100 execration is pronounced on the *noṣrîm*) and in Arabic, apparently as a general designation for Christians (*cf.* R. Bell, *The Origin of Islam in its Christian Environment*, 1926, pp. 147ff.). The Christian Fathers knew of Jewish-Christian groups who called themselves 'Nazarenes' (Jerome, *De vir. ill.* 2–3, *Epist.* 20. 2) or 'Nazorenes' (Epiphanius, *Haer.* 29. 7, 9), and Epiphanius—never too reliable on such matters—mentions an aberrant Jewish sect, the Nasarenes (*Haer.* 1. 18).

In the NT the title is never applied to our Lord without the name 'Jesus', and to identify a man by his place of origin (*e.g.* John of Gischala) was a common Jewish practice. Linguistic objections have been raised, however, against deriving *Nazarēnos*, still more *Nazōraios*, from 'Nazareth', even issuing in a suggestion that Nazareth was created out of a misunderstanding of the title Nazorean (*cf.* E. Nestle, *ExpT* 19, 1907–8, pp. 523f.). These objections have been faithfully dealt with by G. F. Moore, but are still sometimes raised.

The allusion to *Nazōraios* as a title given to the Messiah in prophecy (Mt. 2:23) has been frequently taken as a reference to the 'Branch' (*nēṣer*) of Is. 11:1 and similar passages, or to the Nazirite (*nāzîr*, *cf.* Jdg. 13:7) in his character as God's holy one (*nāzîr* is used non-technically, and was perhaps interpreted Messianically, in Gn. 49:26; Dt. 33:16; see H. Smith, *JTS* 28, 1926, p. 60). Another ancient suggestion (Jerome, *in loc.*) is that Mt. alludes to the passages which speak of the Messiah as despised (*cf.* Jn. 1:46). At all events the different quotation formula in Mt. 2:23 from that in, *e.g.*, Mt. 1:22; 2:15, 17, suggests that a prophetic *theme*, not a specific prediction, is in mind.

The fact that the Mandaean Manichaean–Gnostic sect call themselves *Naṣorayya* has attracted attention. Moore has sufficiently disposed of the 'evidence' for a pre-Christian 'Nazarene' cult adapted to a Jewish *milieu*, but M. Black accepts Lidzbarski's derivation of *Naṣorayya* from *nāṣar*, 'to guard' (*sc.* the tradition), and points to the Mandaean claim to preserve the rites of John the Baptist. Rejecting on linguistic grounds any connection of *Nazōraios* with either *nēṣer* or *nāzîr*, he suggests the suitability of 'Nazarenes' as a title for the followers of John, that it is preserved by the Mandaeans and perhaps Epiphanius, and became applied to the 'Jesus-movement' which arose in the wake of John's. Ingenious as this is, it is perhaps over-subtle. It may be that word-play between *nēṣer* or *nāzîr* or both and the name 'Nazareth' is all that is involved; and it is noteworthy that the Syriac versions, doubtless reflecting Aram. speech, spell Nazareth with *ṣ* not *z*. A different paronomasia is used in the Qur'an (*Sura* 3. 45; 11. 14), and yet another derivation has appeared in the Chenoboskion *Gospel of Philip*, Log. 47.

Bibliography. W. F. Albright, *JBL* 65, 1946, pp. 397ff.; M. Black, *Aramaic Approach to the Gospels and Acts*[3], 1967, pp. 197ff.; R. A. Pritz, *Nazarene Jewish Christianity from the end of the New Testament period until its disappearance in the fourth century*, 1988. For the modern Mandaeans, see the works of Lady E. S. Drower, and especially *The Secret Adam*, 1960.

A.F.W.

NAZARETH. A town of Galilee where Joseph and Mary lived, and the home of Jesus for about 30 years until he was rejected (Lk. 2:39; 4:16, 28–31). He was therefore called Jesus of Nazareth. It is not mentioned in the OT, the Apocrypha, by Josephus, or in the Talmud. (The earliest Jewish reference to it is in a Hebrew inscription excavated at Caesarea in 1962, which mentions it as one of the places in Galilee to which members of the twenty-four priestly courses emigrated after the foundation of Aelia Capitolina in AD 135.) The reason for this was first geographical and later theological. Lower Galilee remained outside the main stream of Israelite life until NT times, when Rom. rule first brought security. Even then Sepphoris was the chief town of the area, a little to the N of Nazareth. But Nazareth lay close enough to several main trade-routes for easy contact with the outside world, while at the same time her position as a frontier-town on the S border of Zebulun overlooking the Esdraelon plain produced a certain aloofness. It was this independence of outlook in Lower Galilee which led to the scorn in which Nazareth was held by strict Jews (Jn. 1:46).

Nazareth is situated in a high valley among the most S limestone hills of the Lebanon range; it runs approximately from SSW to NNE. To the S there is a sharp drop down to the plain of Esdraelon. The base of the valley is 370 m above sea-level. Steep hills rise up on the N and E sides, while on the W side they reach up to 500 m and command an impressive view. Major roads from Jerusalem and Egypt debouched into the Esdraelon plain in the S; caravans from Gilead crossed the Jordan fords and passed below; the main road from Ptolemais to the Decapolis and the N, along which the Rom. legions travelled, passed a few kms above Nazareth. Such a location may have given rise to the name, which is possibly derived from the Aramaic *nāṣ*ᶜ*raṯ*, 'watch-tower'. Another suggested derivation is from the Heb. *nēṣer*, 'shoot', advocated in Eusebius' *Onomasticon* and by Jerome (*Epist.* 46, *Ad Marcellam*). The mild climate in the valley causes wild flowers and fruit to flourish.

To judge by the rock-tombs, the early town was higher up the W hill than the present Nazareth. There are two possible water-supplies. The first, which is the larger, lies in the valley and has been called 'Mary's Well' since AD 1100, but there is no trace of early dwellings near by. The second is a very small fountain, called 'the New Well', in an angle formed by a projection of the W hill; the Byzantine church and town lay closer to this. The steep scarp of Jebel Qafsa, overlooking the plain, is traditionally but erroneously called 'the Mount of Precipitation', since this was not the hill 'on which their city was built' (Lk. 4:29).

Bibliography. *NEAEHL*, pp. 1103–1106.

J.W.C.

NAZIRITE (Heb. *nāzîr*, from *nāzar*, 'to separate, consecrate, abstain'; *cf.* *nēzer*, 'a diadem', the 'crown of God', sometimes identified with the Nazirite's uncut hair). In Israel the Nazirite was one who separated himself from others by consecration to Yahweh with a special vow.

The origin of the practice is pre-Mosaic and obscure. Semites and other primitive peoples often left the hair uncut during some undertaking calling for divine help, and thereafter consecrated the hair (*cf.* modern echoes of this among Arab tribes in A. Lods, *Israel*, 1932, p. 305; see also Jdg. 5:2).

I. Legislation in Numbers 6

Although chronologically not the first biblical reference to the subject, the rules for the Nazirite outlined in Nu. 6 provide the fullest and most convenient basis for discussion. The legislation has three sections.

a. Prohibitions

(i) The Nazirite had to abstain from wine and intoxicating drinks, vinegar and raisins. This may have been aimed at safeguarding the integrity and holiness of the Nazirite from possession by a spirit other than that of Yahweh (*cf.* Pr. 20:1). Like an officiating priest, the Nazirite renounced wine so as the more worthily to approach God. R. Kittel, however, sees in the abstention a protest against Canaanite culture, and a desire to return to nomadic customs (*Geschichte des Volkes Israel*[6], 2, 1925, p. 250).

(ii) He must not cut his hair during the time of consecration (*cf. nāzîr* = 'unpruned vine', Lv. 25:5, 11). The hair was regarded as the seat of life, 'the favourite abode of spirits and magical influences', to be kept in its natural state until its burning ensured its disappearance without fear of profanation.

(iii) He must not go near a dead body, even that of his nearest relation, a prohibition which applied also in the case of the high priest.

b. Violation

If the last-named rule were inadvertently broken, the Nazirite had to undergo closely-detailed purificatory rites, and to begin all over again. It is notable, however, that the terms of the Nazirite vow did not preclude the carrying out of other domestic and social duties.

c. Completion

At the end of his vow the Nazirite had to offer various prescribed sacrifices, and thereafter cut his hair and burn it on the altar. After certain ritual acts by the priest, the Nazirite was freed from his vow.

The distinctive features of the original Nazirate were a complete consecration to Yahweh, in which the body, not regarded merely as something to be restrained, was enlisted into holy service; an extension to the layman of a holiness usually associated only with the priest; and an individualistic character in contrast to groups such as *Rechabites.

II. Problems concerning the Nazirate

It is clear from the provisions in *c.* above that the Nazirate was for a fixed term only. But against that, and pre-dating the above legislation (for the dating of which, *NUMBERS, BOOK OF), there are instances during the pre-exilic era of parents dedicating children to be Nazirites all their lives. There is, for example, the consecration of Samuel (1 Sa. 1:11), who is not called a Nazirite in *MT* (but in a Qumran text, 4Q Sam[a], 1 Sa. 1:22 ends with the words, 'a Nazirite for ever all the days of his life'). There is also the express Nazirate of Samson (Jdg. 13), elements of whose story may date from the 10th century BC. That Samuel and Samson were Nazirites has been questioned (see G. B. Gray, *Numbers*, *ICC*, 1903, pp. 59–60). The Samson narrative conspicuously does not give the impression that he abstained from wine! It may be that the term 'Nazirite' was loosely applied to one devoted to Yahweh.

Absalom, moreover, has often been regarded as a type of perpetual Nazirite (for the cutting of the hair of such, see G. B. Gray, 'The Nazirite', *JTS* 1, 1900, p. 206). Amos, in whose day Nazirites appear to have been numerous, clearly speaks of Nazirites whom the people seek to deflect from their abstinence (2:11–12). During the whole pre-exilic period it is difficult to find direct evidence of temporary Nazirites.

III. Later developments

From the time of the Exile the Nazirate seems to have been for a fixed term only. Extraneous elements crept in, and no longer was the motive for taking the vow exclusively one of penitence and devotion. On occasion it was practised in order to gain certain favours from Yahweh (*cf.* Jos., *BJ* 2. 313, where Bernice undertakes a 30 days' vow), as a meritorious ritual activity, or even for a bet (Mishnah, *Nazir* 5. 5ff.). Wealthy Jews often financed the final sacrifice; Herod Agrippa I is said to have done so (Jos., *Ant.* 19. 293), and Paul was persuaded to perform this service for four members of the church of Jerusalem (Acts 21:23ff.; *cf.* 18:18 for Paul's personal undertaking of a Nazirite vow). Casuistry was inevitably introduced, and a special tractate of the Mishnah (*Nazir*) fixed the minimum duration of the Nazirate at 30 days.

From the references in Josephus it appears that Nazirites were a common feature of the contemporary scene. For the suggestion that John the Baptist and James the Lord's brother were Nazirites, and for the whole subject, see G. B. Gray, *JTS, art. cit.* J.D.D.

NEAPOLIS (the 'new city'). A town, mod. Kavalla, in Macedonia which served as the port of Philippi, 16 km inland. Originally thought to have been called Daton, it occupied a position on a neck of land between two bays, which gave it a useful harbour on both. Paul arrived here from Troas on his second missionary journey (Acts 16:11), after receiving his call to Macedonia. He may have visited it on his third journey also. J.H.P.

NEBAIOTH. The eldest son of Ishmael (Gn. 25:13; 28:9; 36:3; 1 Ch. 1:29). His descendants, an Arabian tribe mentioned in conjunction with Kedar in Is. 60:7 (the two are also named together in Assyr. records), are possibly to be identified with the later *Nabataeans (see *JSS* 18, 1973, pp. 1–16). J.D.D.

NEBAT. A name which occurs only in the phrase 'Jeroboam the son of Nebat' (1 Ki. 11:26, *etc.*), apparently to distinguish Jeroboam I from the later son of Joash. J.D.D.

NEBO (Heb. $n^e\underline{b}\hat{o}$). **1.** The Bab. deity Nabû, son of Bēl (Marduk), and thus descriptive of the power of Babylon itself (Is. 46:1). The name occurs as part of such appellatives as Nebuchadrezzar and perhaps *Abednego. Nabû was considered the god of learning and thus of writing, astronomy and all science. His symbol was a wedge upon a pole, signifying either the cuneiform script or a sighting instrument used in astronomy. He was the principal deity of Borsippa (12 km SSW of Babylon), but a temple Ezida ('the House of Knowledge') was dedicated to him in each of the larger cities of Babylonia and Assyria.

2. The (abbreviated?) name of the ancestor of Jews who married foreign women and thus incurred Ezra's displeasure (Ezr. 10:43). D.J.W.

NEBO. 1. Mt Nebo, from which Moses viewed the Promised Land, a prominent headland of the Transjordan plateau range, *Abarim, with which it is sometimes equated (Dt. 32:49; 34:1). Usually identified with Jebel en Neba, some 16 km E of the N end of the Dead Sea. It commands extensive views from Mt Hermon to the Dead Sea. Jebel Osha, about 45 km further N, is preferred by local Muslim tradition and some scholars (see G. T. Manley, *The Book of the Law*, 1957, pp. 163f.), but is outside the land of Moab. The original border was near Wadi Hesban (Nu. 21:26ff.; the *Moabite Stone also implies Jebel en Neba). (*ABARIM, *PISGAH.)

2. A town in Moab (Nu. 32:3, 38; Is. 15:2), possibly Khirbet Ayn Musa or Khirbet el Mukkayet near Jebel en Musa. Taken by Mesha of Moab *c.* 830 BC.

3. A town in Judah (Ezr. 2:29; Ne. 7:33).

G.G.G.

NEBUCHADREZZAR, NEBUCHADNEZZAR. The king of Babylon (605–562 BC) frequently named by the prophets Jeremiah, Ezekiel and Daniel, and in the history of the last days of Judah. His name in Heb. (*nᵉḇūḵaḏreʾṣṣar*) transliterates the Bab. *Nabū-kudurri-uṣur*, meaning perhaps 'Nabû has protected the succession-rights'. The alternative Heb. rendering (*nᵉḇūḵaḏneʾṣṣar*; *cf.* Gk. *Nabochodonosor*) is a not improper form of the name (*ZA* 65, 1975, pp. 227–230).

According to the Bab. Chronicle this son of the founder of the Chaldean dynasty, Nabopolassar, first commanded the Bab. army as 'crown-prince' in the fighting in N Assyria in 606 BC. In the following year he defeated Neco II and the Egyptians at Carchemish and Hamath (2 Ki. 23:29f.; 2 Ch. 35:20ff.; Je. 46:2). 'At this time he conquered the whole of Hatti' (*i.e.* Syria and Palestine, so Bab. Chronicle; 2 Ki. 24:7; Jos., *Ant.* 10. 86). Daniel was among hostages taken from Judah (Dn. 1:1), where Jehoiakim was in his 4th regnal year (Je. 36:1). While in the field Nebuchadrezzar heard of his father's death and rode across the desert to claim the Bab. throne, which he ascended on 6 September 605 BC.

In the following year, the first of his reign, Nebuchadrezzar received tribute in Syria from the kings of Damascus, Tyre and Sidon and others, including Jehoiakim, who was to remain his faithful vassal for only 3 years (2 Ki. 24:1; Je. 25:1). Ashkelon refused and was sacked. In the campaign of 601 BC the Babylonians were defeated by Egypt, whereupon Jehoiakim transferred his loyalty, despite the warnings of Jeremiah (27:9–11), to the victors. When his army had been re-equipped Nebuchadrezzar raided the Arab tribes of Qedar and E Jordan in 599/8 BC, as predicted by the same prophet (Je. 49:28–33), in preparation for subsequent reprisals on Jehoiakim and Judah (2 Ch. 36:6). Thus in his 7th year Nebuchadrezzar 'marched to Palestine and besieged the city of Judah which he captured on the second day of the month Adar' (= 16 March 597 BC). He then 'seized its king and appointed a king of his own choice, having received heavy tribute which he sent back to Babylon' (Bab. Chronicle B.M. 21946). This capture of Jerusalem and its king Jehoiachin (Jehoiakim's son and successor), the choice of Mattaniah-Zedekiah as his successor, and the taking of booty and prisoners, form the subject of the history recorded in 2 Ki. 24:10–17. Nebuchadrezzar removed the temple vessels to the temple of Bel-Marduk in Babylon (2 Ch. 36:7; 2 Ki. 24:13; Ezr. 6:5). The Judaean captives were marched off about April 597, 'in the spring of the year' (2 Ch. 36:10), which marked the beginning of his 8th regnal year (2 Ki. 24:12). Jehoiachin and other Jewish captives are named in inscriptions from Babylon dated in the years of this Bab. king (*ANET*, p. 308; *DOTT*, pp. 83–86).

In 596 BC Nebuchadrezzar fought with Elam (so also Je. 49:34), and in the next year mastered a rebellion in his own country. Thereafter Bab. historical texts are wanting, but in his 17th–19th years he campaigned again in the W. From his headquarters at Riblah he directed the operations which led to the sack of Jerusalem in 587 BC and the capture of the rebel Zedekiah (Je. 39:5–6; ch. 52). For a time the siege was raised when Apries, the successor of Neco II of Egypt, invaded Phoenicia and Gaza (Je. 47:1). In Nebuchadrezzar's 23rd year (582) a further deportation of Judaeans to Babylon was ordered (Je. 52:30). About this time also the 13-year siege of *Tyre was undertaken (Ezk. 26:7).

A fragmentary Bab. text tells of Nebuchadrezzar's invasion of Egypt in 568/7 BC (*cf.* Je. 43:8–13). Since little is yet known of the last 30 years of his reign, there is no corroboration of his madness which occurred for 7 months (or 'times') as recorded in Dn. 4:23–33. With the aid of his wife Amytis, he undertook the rebuilding and embellishment of his capital Babylon. A religious man, he rebuilt the temples of Marduk and Nabû with many shrines in *Babylon and provided regular offerings and garments for the divine statues (*cf.* the golden image of Dn. 3:1). He also restored temples in Sippar, Marad and Borsippa and boasted of his achievements, especially in the two defence walls, the gateway of Ishtar, the ziggurat and the sacred processional way through his own city, which he provided with new canals (Dn. 4:30). Some of his architectural works were classed among the seven wonders of the world. Herodotus calls both Nebuchadrezzar and Nabonidus (556–539) by the name of Labynetus. Nebuchadrezzar died in August–September 562 BC and was succeeded by his son Amēl-Marduk (*EVIL-MERODACH).

BIBLIOGRAPHY. D. J. Wiseman, *Chronicles of Chaldaean Kings*, 1956; *Nebuchadrezzar and Babylon*, 1985.

D.J.W.

NECK. 1. Heb. *ʿōrep̄* is used of the neck, or back of the neck; it is also translated 'back', when used of enemies turning their back in flight (*e.g.* Ex. 23:27). It is used of similar ideas in respect of conflict (Gn. 49:8; Jb. 16:12), and also in the descriptive metaphor of the hardened or stiffnecked, meaning obstinate or rebellious (Dt. 31:27; 2 Ki. 17:14; Is. 48:4).

2. Heb. *gārôn* is also used, meaning the front of the neck (Is. 3:16; Ezk. 16:11), or throat (Ps. 5:9; Je. 2:25), and so voice (Is. 58:1, 'cry aloud', lit. 'with your throat').

3. The commonest Heb. word is *ṣawwāʾr*, used of the neck generally; bearing a yoke, symbolizing servitude (Gn. 27:40; Je. 30:8); wearing a necklace (Gn. 41:42); of falling on a person's neck in embrace (Gn. 33:4), or of the neck placed under the *foot of a conqueror (Jos. 10:24).

4. Gk. *trachēlos* is used of embrace (Lk. 15:20), of being under a yoke (Acts 15:10), or of wearing a millstone, a large flat stone with a hole in the centre, to weigh the body down (Mt. 18:6). Paul also speaks of risking the neck in respect of the custom of beheading (Rom. 16:4). From *trachēlos* comes the verb *trachēlizō*, 'to expose the neck or throat', used in the perfect participle passive in Heb. 4:13 in the sense of 'laid bare'.

B.O.B.

NECO, NECHO. Egyp. *Ni-k'w*, Gk. *Nechao.* Pharaoh of Egypt *c.* 610–595 BC, and son and successor of Psammetichus I, the founder of the 26th Dynasty. In 609 BC, following his father's policy of maintaining a balance of power in W Asia (*EGYPT. History), Neco II marched into Syria to assist Aššur-uballiṭ II, last king of Assyria, against Babylon. But Josiah of Judah forced a battle with Neco at Megiddo; this delay of Egyp. help for the Assyrians sealed their fate at the cost of Josiah's own life (2 Ki. 23:29; 2 Ch. 35:20–24). On his return S, Neco deposed and deported Josiah's son Jehoahaz and appointed instead another son, Jehoiakim, as vassal-king in Jerusalem, which was obliged to pay tribute to Egypt (2 Ki. 23:31–35; 2 Ch. 36:1–4). Egypt claimed Palestine as her share of the former Assyr. empire, but in the battle of Carchemish, in May/June 605 BC, Nebuchadrezzar stormed that Egyp. outpost and pursued the remnants of the Egyp. forces through Syria as they scurried home to Egypt; Judah thus exchanged an Egyp. for a Bab. master (2 Ki. 24:1, 7).

Neco wisely desisted from any further Palestinian adventures. But the Bab. Chronicle shows that in 601 BC Nebuchadrezzar marched against Egypt; Neco met him in open battle, and both sides suffered heavy losses. Nebuchadrezzar therefore had to spend the next year at home in Babylon to refit his army. This Egyp. rebuff for the Babylonians perhaps tempted Jehoiakim to revolt against Babylon as recorded in 2 Ki. 24:1, but no help came from neutral Egypt.

At home, Neco II followed his father's policy of fostering Egypt's internal unity and prosperity, granting trading-concessions to Gk. merchants to this end. He undertook the cutting of a canal from the Nile to the Red Sea, completed by Darius the Persian, and sent out a Phoenician fleet that circumnavigated Africa as recorded by Herodotus (4. 42), whose scepticism of this achievement is refuted by its cause, namely, that the voyagers reported that the sun eventually rose on their right hand.

BIBLIOGRAPHY. For Neco, see Drioton and Vandier, *L'Égypte*, Coll. Clio, 1952; H. De Meulenaere, *Herodotos over de 26ste Dynastie*, 1951. For his conflicts with Babylon, see D. J. Wiseman, *Chronicles of Chaldaean Kings (626–556 BC)*, 1956.

C.D.W.

NEGEB. Heb. *negeḇ*, 'the dry', refers to the S lands of Palestine. Misconceptions arise from its translation as 'the South' in both AV and RV, where some forty passages have described it inaccurately in this way. An indefinite region, it covers *c.* 1,200,000 hectares (4,520 sq. mls) or nearly half the area of modern Israel. The N boundary may be drawn conveniently S of the Gaza–Beersheba road, roughly the 20 cm-mean annual isohyet, then due E of Beersheba to the Dead Sea through Ras ez-Zuweira. The S boundary which merged traditionally into the highlands of the Sinai Peninsula is now drawn politically S of the Wadi el-Arish to the head of the Gulf of Aqabah at Eilat. The Wadi Arabah, now the political frontier with Jordan, is overlooked to the E by the Arabah escarpment, the traditional boundary. For the description of the geographical features to the Negeb, see *PALESTINE.

Mention of the Negeb is almost entirely confined to pre-exilic times, apart from allusions in Zc. 7:7 and Ob. 20. Five districts in the N Negeb are referred to: the Negeb of Judah, of the Jerahmeelites, of the Kenites (1 Sa. 27:10), of the Cherethites and of Caleb (1 Sa. 30:14). These occupied the grazing and agricultural lands between Beersheba and Bir Rikhmeh and the W slopes of the central highlands of Khurashe-Kurnub. This district was settled by the Amalekites (Nu. 13:29), the ruins of whose fortified sites are still seen between Tell Arad (Nu. 21:1; 33:40), 32 km E of Beersheba and Tell Jemmeh or Gerar (Gn. 20:1; 26:1). At the Exodus the spies had been awed by their defences (Nu. 13:17–20, 27–29), which lasted until the early 6th century BC, when they were probably destroyed finally by the Babylonians (Je. 13:19; 33:13). The sites of the twenty-nine cities and their villages in the Negeb (Jos. 15:21–32) are unknown, only Beersheba ('well of seven', or 'well of oath', Gn. 21:30), Arad, Khirbet Ar'areh or Aroer (1 Sa. 30:28). Fein or Penon (Nu. 33:42), and Tell el-Kheleifeh or Ezion-geber, having been identified.

The strategic and economic importance of the Negeb has been significant. The 'Way of Shur' crossed it from central Sinai NE to Judaea (Gn. 16:7; 20:1; 25:18; Ex. 15:22; Nu. 33:8), a route followed by the Patriarchs (Gn. 24:62; 26:22), by Hadad the Edomite (1 Ki. 11:14, 17, 21–22), and probably the escape route used by Jeremiah (43:6–12) and later by Joseph and Mary (Mt. 2:13–15). The route was dictated by the zone of settled land where well-water is significant, hence the frequent references to its wells (*e.g.* Gn. 24:15–20; Jos. 15:18–19; Jdg. 1:14–15). Uzziah reinforced the defence of Jerusalem by establishing cultivation and defensive settlements in his exposed S flank of the N Negeb (2 Ch. 26:10). It seems clear from the history of the Near East that the Negeb was a convenient vacuum for resettlement whenever population pressure forced out migrants from the Fertile Crescent. Also significant was the location of copper ores in the E Negeb and its trade in the Arabah. Control of this industry explains the Amalekite and Edomite wars of Saul (1 Sa. 14:47f.) and the subsequent victories of David over the Edomites (1 Ki. 11:15f.). It also explains the creation by Solomon of the port of Ezion-geber, and, when it was silted up, the creation of a new port at Elath by Uzziah (1 Ki. 9:26; 22:48; 2 Ki. 14:22). The abiding hatred of the Edomites is explained by the struggles to control this trade (*cf.* Ezk. 25:12 and the book of Obadiah).

Between the 4th century BC and the beginning of the 2nd century AD, when the Nabataeans finally disappeared, these Semitic people of S Arabian origin created a brilliant civilization of small hydraulic works in the Negeb. Deployed across the strategic trade routes between Arabia and the Fertile Crescent, they waxed rich on the spice and incense trade of Arabia, and other exotic goods from Somaliland and India. Later, in the Christian era, the Negeb became a stronghold of Christianity. Glueck has identified some 300 early Christian Byzantine sites in the Negeb, dating from the 5th and 6th centuries AD.

BIBLIOGRAPHY. For the occupation of the Negeb at various archaeological periods, see *ARCHAEOLOGY; Y. Aharoni, *IEJ* 8, 1958, pp. 26ff.; 10, 1960, pp. 23ff., 97ff.; N. Glueck, *Rivers in the Desert*,

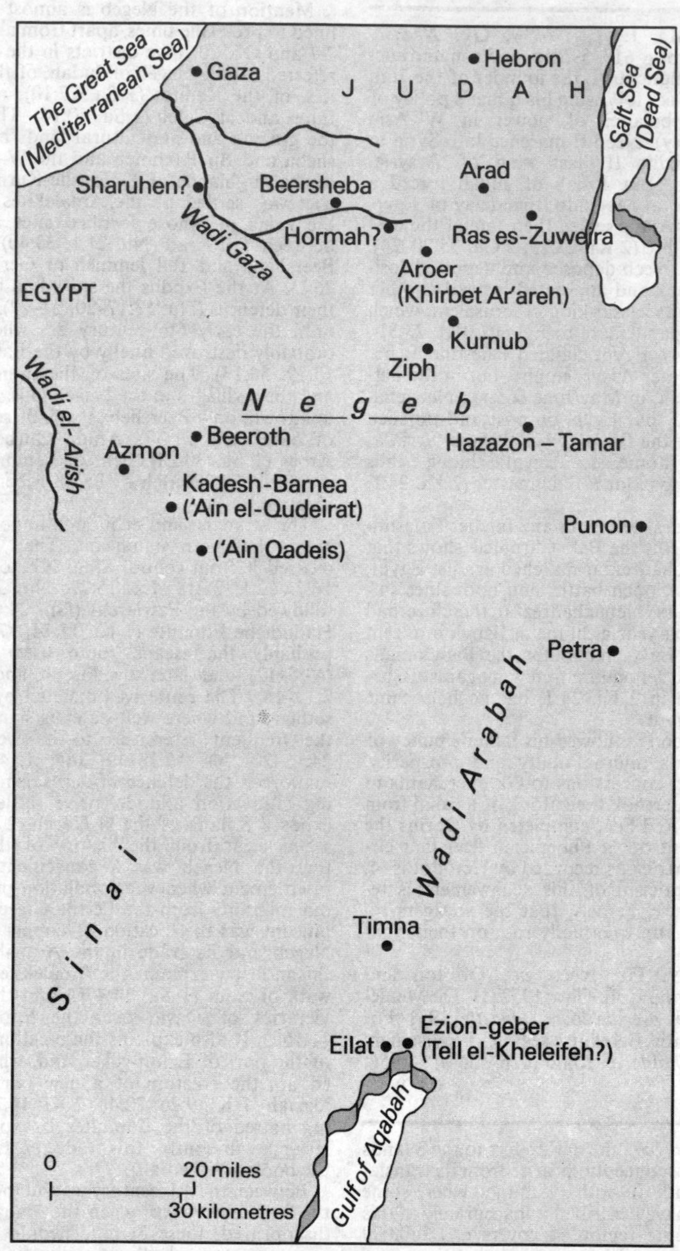

The Negeb.

1959; *idem, Deities and Dolphins* (*The story of the Nabataeans*), 1966; C. L. Woolley and T. E. Lawrence, *The Wilderness of Zin*, 1936. J.M.H.

NEHELAM. Family name or place of origin of Shemaiah, a false prophet who withstood Jeremiah (Je. 29:24, 31f.). The name is otherwise unknown. V. 24 AVmg. renders the word as 'dreamer', thus implying some connection with Heb. *ḥālam*, 'to dream'. M. F. Unger suggests a punning allusion to the dreams of the false prophets. J.D.D.

NEHEMIAH. Our only knowledge of Nehemiah comes from the book that bears his name. He was cupbearer to the Persian king, Artaxerxes I (465–424 BC). This was a privileged position. Since there is no mention of his wife, it is likely that he was a eunuch. On receiving news of the desolate state of Jerusalem (probably the result of the events of Ezr. 4:7–23), he obtained permission to go to his own country, and was appointed governor. In spite of intense opposition (*SANBALLAT, *TOBIAH), he and the Jews rebuilt the walls of Jerusalem in 52 days. He and the other Jews then called on Ezra to read the Law, and pledged themselves to observe its commands. During his absence in Persia, some of the abuses that he had put down reappeared, and on his return he had to carry out fresh reforms. His personal memoirs occupy a large part of the book of Nehemiah, and they reveal him as a man of prayer, action and devotion to duty.

For dating his movements we have the following references:

2:1. His appointment as governor in 445 BC.
5:14; 13:6. His return to Persia in 433 BC.
13:7. His return to Jerusalem 'after certain days' (AV).

The suggestion in 2:6 is that his first appointment was short, and he may have returned to Persia for a brief time between 445 and 433 BC. Since his absence from Jerusalem in 13:6 was long enough for considerable abuses to arise, and for the Levites to be driven out to work in the fields, we must conclude that the 'certain days' were at least 18 months, and possibly more. J.S.W.

NEHEMIAH, BOOK OF.

I. Outline of contents

a. Nehemiah's mission (1:1–7:73a)

i. Nehemiah hears news from Jerusalem (1:1–11).
ii. He receives permission to visit Jerusalem (2:1–8).
iii. He arrives in Jerusalem, and makes plans to rebuild the walls (2:9–20).
iv. The list of wall-builders, with their allotted sections of wall (3:1–22).
v. Opposition from the Samaritans (4:1–23).
vi. Economic difficulties and Nehemiah's solution (5:1–13).
vii. Nehemiah's behaviour as governor (5:14–19).
viii. The wall is completed, in spite of plots against Nehemiah (6:1–19).
ix. Preparations for the re-peopling of Jerusalem (7:1–73a).

b. Ezra's work (continued from Ezr. 7–10) (7:73b–9:37)

i. Ezra's reading of the law (7:73b–8:12).
ii. Celebration of the festival of booths (8:13–18).
iii. A day of repentance and its penitential psalm (9:1–37).

c. Nehemiah's community (9:38–13:31)

i. The pledge of reform (9:38–10:39)
ii. The population of Jerusalem and Judaea (11:1–36).
iii. The clergy of the post-exilic community (12:1–26).
iv. The dedication of the wall (12:27–43).
v. An ideal community (12:44–13:3).
vi. Reforms during Nehemiah's second governorship (13:4–31).

II. Composition

It is commonly thought that the book of Nehemiah originally formed part of the Chronicler's work, which included also the books of 1 and 2 *Chronicles and *Ezra. Very little, however, of the book of Nehemiah was especially composed by the Chronicler (12:44–47 is probably one such passage), since he had ample source materials at his disposal.

Chief among these were the 'memoirs' of Nehemiah (Ne. 1:1–7:73a; 11:1–2; 12:31–43; 13:4–31), which may more properly be regarded as Nehemiah's formal record of his activities presented to God for his approval (note the places where Nehemiah appeals to God to 'remember' him: 5:19; 13:14, 22, 31). This first-person narrative is unique in the OT as a record made by a leading Jewish statesman about affairs he was personally involved in; though Nehemiah obviously looks at matters from his own point of view, there can be little serious doubt about the authenticity of this record. It has been subject to practically no editorial revision, and its simple and direct style marks it off quite clearly from the work of the Chronicler.

The other main source of the book is a section of the Ezra narrative (Ne. 8–9) which is inserted within the story of Nehemiah either because the activity of Ezra and Nehemiah overlapped or because the Chronicler has arranged his material thematically. The first explanation, though the most natural, creates the difficulty that though Ezra had been sent by the Persian emperor in 458 BC to proclaim the Pentateuchal law to the Jews, it was not until Nehemiah's arrival in 444 BC that he read it publicly to the people. The second explanation would imply that the Chronicler regarded the work of Ezra and Nehemiah as an integral whole; he then showed in his account that the community that came to live within the walls of rebuilt Jerusalem (Ne. 11:1–2) was united in its allegiance to the law of Moses (Ne. 8), penitent for its disobedience to that law (Ne. 9), and resolved to maintain its fidelity to the smallest detail of the law (Ne. 10).

Other sources used by the compiler of the book were lists of various kinds:

a. Wall-builders (Ne. 3). This may have been included in Nehemiah's 'memoirs'.

b. Returned exiles (7:6–73a). The same list, with minor variations, is found in Ezr. 2. It was apparently used by Nehemiah to prove the pure Jewish ancestry of the intended inhabitants of Jerusalem.

c. Signatories of the pledge to observe the Mosaic law (9:38–10:27), together with various particular interpretations of the law which the community bound itself to obey (10:28–39). This pledge seems to reflect reforms undertaken by Nehemiah during his second governorship (Ne. 13).

d. Family heads resident in Jerusalem (11:3–19).

e. Country towns with Jewish population (11:25–36).

f. Priests, Levites and high priests (12:1–26).

III. Message of the book

If, as most believe, Nehemiah formed part of the Chronicler's history (*CHRONICLES, BOOKS OF), its significance must be assessed within the context of the whole work. The Chronicler's purpose, broadly speaking, was to show that the Judaean community of his own time, probably the 4th century BC, was the legitimate heir of the promises made by God to Israel and to the Davidic dynasty. Although there was no longer a Davidic king, in the Chronicler's view the chief function of the Davidic kingship had been the establishment of the Temple and its worship; now that the Temple is restored, the worship of God can be carried on effectively by the community itself without the presence of a king. Characteristically, the Chronicler concludes his history proper with an almost idyllic picture of pure and joyful worship in the restored Temple, its clergy being willingly maintained by the tithes of the people (12:44–47). After his long story of Israel's disappointments, failures and grim periods of judgment, the finale to his history must have brought reassurance to his own community. Though they were only a tiny enclave in a vast Gentile empire, they could at least have the satisfaction of knowing that they were under the immediate leadership of men of God's choice and that they were fulfilling the purpose for which Israel had been created: the worship of God. Such a message can of course lead to self-congratulation and laxity. We have no way of knowing how the Chronicler's readers reacted to his encouragement, but it is worth while knowing that the people of God does not have to be always castigating itself, but is sometimes entitled to rejoice in what it has achieved.

As for the 'memoirs' of Nehemiah, which, apart from the lists, form the bulk of the book, their original purpose may well have been a kind of report such as a civil servant might make to his superior, in this case God. When Nehemiah's 'report' was read by others, they would have seen in it a revealing picture of a man of spirit, haughty and quick-tempered, and over-suspicious, no doubt, but passionately concerned for the well-being of his people (chs. 1–2), quick to respond to the appeals of brotherhood (ch. 5) and zealous for the purity of Jewish worship (13:4–9); above all, a leader who was the opposite of a self-made man, one who was always conscious of the 'good hand' and the 'fear' of his God upon him (2:8; 5:15; *cf.* 2:12, 18; 4:9, 14–15, 20; 6:9).

BIBLIOGRAPHY. L. H. Brockington, *Ezra, Nehemiah and Esther*, *NCB*, 1969; P. R. Ackroyd, *I and II Chronicles, Ezra, Nehemiah, TBC*, 1973; D. Kidner, *Ezra and Nehemiah*, *TOTC*, 1979; H. G. M. Williamson, *Ezra and Nehemiah*, 1987; *Ezra, Nehemiah*, 1985; M. Roberts, *Ezra–Nehemiah*, 1992. D.J.A.C.

NEHUSHTA (Heb. *neḥuštā'*). The wife of Jehoiakim and mother of Jehoiachin, a native of Jerusalem (2 Ki. 24:8) who was taken prisoner with her son when the Babylonians captured the city in 597 BC (v. 12; also Jos., *Ant.* 10. 84ff.). Her name may allude to her complexion (*cf.* Jb. 6:12) or to bronze (Heb. *neḥūšâ*) or even to the *serpent. Heb. personal names relating to colours, metals (*BARZILLAI) or to animals are typical of this period.

D.J.W.

NEIGHBOUR. In the OT 'neighbour' translates the Heb. *šāḵēn*, *'āmîṯ*, *qārôḇ* and *rēa'*. In Lv. 19:18 LXX has *ho plēsion*. In the NT (in which this commandment is quoted eight times) Luke and John alone use the words *geitōn* and *perioikos*; elsewhere (and also Lk. 10:27–36; Acts 7:27) the LXX expression appears.

The Heb. *rēa'* is of more general application than English 'neighbour'. It is used, even of inanimate objects (Gn. 15:10), in the expression 'one *another*'; but it is also used in the sense of 'bosom friend' (Pr. 27:10), 'lover' (Ct. 5:16), even 'husband' (Je. 3:20). Like *'āmîṯ*, *rēa'* is almost exclusively used in contexts where moral principles are in question (*qārôḇ* and *šāḵēn* expressing mere geographical or physical proximity). Of passages where *rēa'* is defined in the context (*i.e.* refers to particular people) there are only three (1 Sa. 15:28; 28:17; 2 Sa. 12:11) which do not admit the translation 'friend', and these are all susceptible of ironical interpretation. Thus it is either used definitely, in which case it means one who has acted—or *surprisingly* has not acted (Ps. 38:11)—in the appropriate manner, hence a 'friend'; or indefinitely of those towards whom appropriate behaviour is due. *rēa'* is often found in parallel with *'āḥ*, 'brother', and the Bible uses this dichotomy of other people in a developing series of senses. Thus a relative is contrasted with another within the clan, a fellow Hebrew with a Gentile, and finally a fellow Christian with an unbeliever.

It is important to love those to whom one has a natural or covenanted obligation, but it is as important to love those with whom one's only contact is through circumstances: the distinct ideas *ḥeseḏ* and *'ahᵃḇâ* ('covenant' and 'elective' love—*cf.* N. H. Snaith, *Distinctive Ideas of the Old Testament*, 1944, pp. 94–95) merge in the NT into the one *agapē* required of a Christian both to those within and without the church. The Bible teaches this in the following ways:

1. It praises those who were exemplary neighbours to those whom they might have been expected to hate: particularly *cf.* Rahab's treatment of the spies (Jos. 2:1); Ruth's refusal to desert her mother-in-law, though in a sense free from obligation after the death of her husband (the whole story is most instructive in this connection, and it is perhaps no accident that 'Ruth' is the abstract noun from the same root as *rēa'*); the widow's entertainment of Elijah (implicity compared with the unclean birds [1 Ki. 17:6] who fed him: Zarephath was in the territory of Sidon from which Jezebel came).

2. It rebukes the proud independence of the Jew (*cf.* Am. 2:6ff.; Is. 1:17; Jonah *passim*; Jb. 12:2).

3. In the parable of the Good Samaritan an explicit epitome of biblical teaching is given which combines **1** and **2**. To the question, 'Who is my neighbour?' Jesus replies, 'Who proved neighbour to the man who fell among the robbers?' (Lk. 10:36).

BIBLIOGRAPHY. U. Falkenroth, *NIDNTT* 1, pp. 258f. J.B.J.

NEPHTOAH. Mentioned only in the expression 'the spring of the Waters of Nephtoah' (Jos. 15:9; 18:15). The context shows that it was on the borders of Judah and Benjamin. It is usually identified with Lifta, a village 4 km NW of Jerusalem. The linguistic equation Nephtoah = Lifta is very doubtful, but no other site seems to have strong claims. L.M.

NEREUS. A Christian greeted with his sister (not named, but conceivably Nereis) in Rom. 16:15. He is grouped with three others and 'the saints which are with them', perhaps because they belonged to the same house-church. The name (a Greek sea-god) is found in many areas, usually of freedmen and the lower orders (including slaves of 'Caesar's household'). Strangely, Paul's friend seems not to have been assimilated to the early Roman martyr commemorated in the Acts of SS. Nereus and Achilleus (*Acta Sanctorum*, 3, Maii, pp. 4f.; *cf.* Lightfoot, *Clement*, 1, pp. 42ff., especially p. 51n.).

A.F.W.

NERGAL (Heb. *nērᵉgal*; Sumerian U.GUR; Bab. *ner(i)gal*, 'Lord of the great city', *i.e.* the underworld). This Bab. deity had his cult-centre at Cuthah (modern Tell Ibrahim, NE of Babylon), where he was worshipped with his consort Ereshkigal, as lord of the underworld. Men from Cuthah continued to worship him as exiles in Samaria (2 Ki. 17:30), but, though he was the god of hunting, they feared the lion (his cult animal) sent by Yahweh (v. 26). Nergal was worshipped throughout Assyria and Babylonia as a deity having the sinister aspects of the sun, bringing plague, war, flood and havoc. He has been identified with Mekal, the god of *Bethshan and later with Mars. Temples at Larsa, Isin and Assur were dedicated to him. His name is commonly found as the divine element in personal names, as *Nergal-sharezer (Je. 39:3, 13).

BIBLIOGRAPHY. E. von Weiher, *Der babylonische Gott Nergal*, 1971. D.J.W.

NERGAL-SHAREZER. Heb. equivalent of Bab. *Nergal-šar-uṣur* (Gk. Neriglissar) meaning 'O Nergal, protect the king'. The name of a senior official with Nebuchadrezzar's army at Jerusalem in 587 BC (Je. 39:3, 13). It is possible that two persons of the same name are listed in v. 3; if so, the first may be the Neriglissar who was one of the Bab. army commanders, son of Bel-šum-iškun and married to Nebuchadrezzar's daughter. He succeeded to the throne at Babylon in 560 BC. The Nergal-sharezer qualified as *Rabmag seems to have held a position of lower rank. D.J.W.

NERO. Son of a distinguished family of the old Roman aristocracy, the Domitii, and on his mother's side the great-great-grandson of Augustus, he was adopted by Claudius as his heir and duly took his place in the Caesarian succession in AD 54. His atrocities and feebleness finally

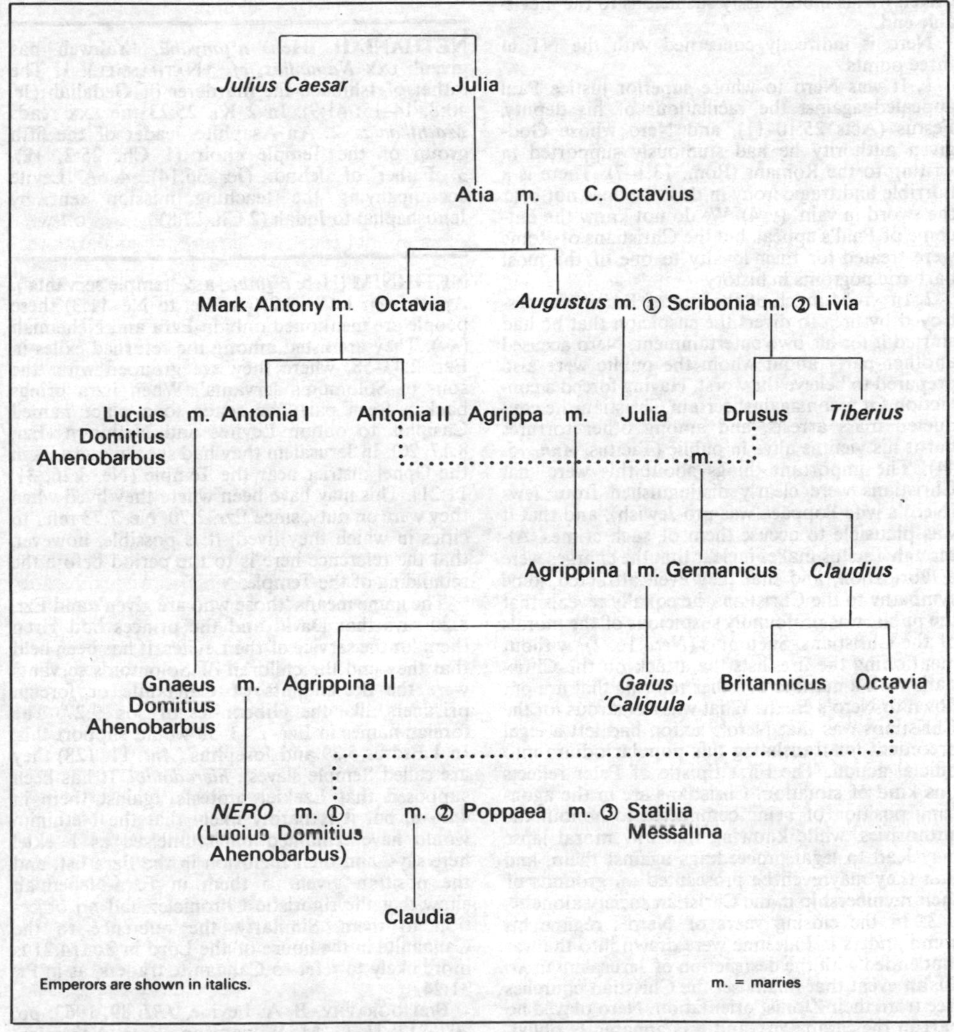

Simplified family tree of the Roman imperial house, showing the position of Nero in it.

destroyed the credit of his house, whose long ascendancy he finally brought to an end with his suicide in the face of the revolts of AD 68. A youth of exquisite taste, he fascinated and scandalized his contemporaries with his artistic pursuits. To the Greeks in particular he endeared himself; they never tired of flattering his longing for prizes in literary festivals; and he reciprocated this whimsy by abolishing Rom. control over the states of Achaia. After his premature death his legend flourished in the E, and his reincarnation was fervently expected, and even announced. On the other hand, within his domestic circle and among his aristocratic peers, his behaviour was monstrously sinister. The belief that his mother had murdered Claudius after marrying him to ensure her son's succession scarcely mitigated the horror when Nero himself had her done to death. Although there seems to have been a period of stable government while he remained under the influence of the senators Burrus and Seneca, he eventually freed himself from their restraints as well and was driven by his bloodthirsty suspicions to the inevitable end.

Nero is indirectly concerned with the NT at three points.

1. It was Nero to whose superior justice Paul appealed against the vacillations of his deputy, Festus (Acts 25:10–11), and Nero whose God-given authority he had studiously supported in writing to the Romans (Rom. 13:1–7). There is a horrible and tragic irony in this: 'he does not bear the sword in vain' (v. 4). We do not know the outcome of Paul's appeal, but the Christians of Rome were treated for their loyalty to one of the most barbaric pogroms in history.

2. In AD 64 much of the city of Rome was destroyed by fire. To divert the suspicion that he had started it for his own entertainment, Nero accused another party about whom the public were also prepared to believe the worst. Having forced a conviction for arson against certain Christians he conducted mass arrests, and among other tortures burnt his victims alive in public (Tacitus, *Ann.* 15. 44). The important things about this were that Christians were clearly distinguished from Jews (Nero's wife Poppaea was pro-Jewish), and that it was plausible to accuse them of such crimes. Although Tacitus makes it clear that the charges were a fabrication, and that they even attracted some sympathy to the Christians, he equally reveals that the public was profoundly suspicious of the morals of the Christians. Suetonius (*Nero* 16. 2), without mentioning the fire, lists the attack on the Christians with a number of other reforms that are put down to Nero's credit. What was disastrous for the Christians was that Nero's action had left a legal precedent for translating this popular odium into official action. The First Epistle of Peter reflects this kind of situation. Christians are in the agonizing position of being committed to honour the authorities, while knowing that any moral lapse may lead to legal proceedings against them, and that they may even be prosecuted on grounds of their membership in the Christian society alone.

3. In the closing years of Nero's régime his commanders in Palestine were drawn into the war that ended with the destruction of Jerusalem in AD 70, an event that finally set the Christian churches free from their Zionist orientation. Nero played no part in the campaigns, and was apparently oblivious of the issues involved: the critical year AD 67 found him engrossed in literary triumphs on the stages of Greece.

BIBLIOGRAPHY. J. H. Bishop, *Nero*, 1964; B. H. Warmington, *Nero*, 1969; M. Grant, *Nero*, 1970; M. T. Griffin, *Nero, the End of a Dynasty*, 1984.

E.A.J.

NEST (Heb. *qēn* from *qinnēn*, 'make a nest'; Gk. *kataskēnōsis*, 'place for roosting in'). The word is employed in its customary sense in Dt. 22:6; 32:11 (speaking of 'nestlings'); Jb. 39:27; Ps. 104:17; Pr. 27:8; Is. 16:2. It is found metaphorically (notably of a lofty fortress) in Nu. 24:21; Je. 49:16; Ob. 4; with reference to the secure home of Israel in Ps. 84:3–4; and of the Chaldeans' strong abode in Hab. 2:9. Job (29:18) speaks of his lost home as a 'nest'. In Gn. 6:14 'nests' (*qinnîm*, 'rooms') is used to describe the subdivisions within the ark. In Mt. 8:20; Lk. 9:58 Jesus contrasts his homeless situation with that of the *birds who have their nests (RVmg. 'lodging-places'). J.D.D.

NETHANIAH (Heb. *nᵉtanyāhū*, 'Yahweh has given'; LXX *Nathanias*; *cf.* *NATHANAEL). **1.** The father of Ishmael, the murderer of Gedaliah (Je. 40:8, 14–15; 41:9). In 2 Ki. 25:23 the LXX reads *Maththanias.* **2.** An Asaphite, leader of the fifth group of the Temple choir (1 Ch. 25:2, 12). **3.** Father of Jehudi (Je. 36:14). **4.** A Levite accompanying the teaching mission sent by Jehoshaphat to Judah (2 Ch. 17:8). D.J.W.

NETHINIM (Heb. *nᵉṯînîm*, RSV 'temple servants'). Apart from 1 Ch. 9:2 (parallel to Ne. 11:3) these people are mentioned only in Ezra and Nehemiah (AV). They are listed among the returned exiles in Ezr. 2:43–58, where they are grouped with 'the sons of Solomon's servants'. When Ezra brings back a fresh party he sends to a place named Casiphia to obtain Levites and Nethinim (Ezr. 8:17, 20). In Jerusalem they had special quarters in the Ophel district near the Temple (Ne. 3:26, 31; 11:21). This may have been where they lived when they were on duty, since Ezr. 2:70; Ne. 7:73 refer to cities in which they lived; it is possible, however, that the reference here is to the period before the rebuilding of the Temple.

The name means 'those who are given', and Ezr. 8:20 says that David and the princes had given them for the service of the Levites. It has been held that they and the children of Solomon's servants were the descendants of Canaanite or foreign prisoners, like the Gibeonites of Jos. 9:27. The foreign names in Ezr. 2:43–58 would support this. In 1 Esdras 5:29 and Josephus (*Ant.* 11. 128) they are called 'temple slaves', *hierodouloi.* It has been supposed that Ezekiel protests against them in 44:6–8, but it is hardly likely that the Nethinim would have remained uncircumcised as Ezekiel here says, and their inclusion in the Ezra list, and the position given to them in Ezra-Nehemiah show that the rigoristic Chronicler had no objection to them. Similarly, the reference to the Canaanite in the house of the Lord in Zc. 14:21 is more likely to refer to Canaanite traders, as in Pr. 31:24.

BIBLIOGRAPHY. B. A. Levine, *JBL* 89, 1963, pp. 207–212; H. G. M. Williamson, *Ezra, Nehemiah*, 1985, pp. 35–36.

J.S.W.

NETOPHAH ('a dropping'). A city, or group of villages (1 Ch. 9:16; Ne. 12:28), near Bethlehem (Ne. 7:26). The inhabitants are called Netophathites in EVV. 'Netophathi' in Ne. 12:28, AV, should be 'the Netophathites' as RSV. It was the home of some of David's mighty men (2 Sa. 23:28–29). It is mentioned as a place to which returning exiles came (Ezr. 2:22). That it was near Bethlehem is clear, but it cannot be identified conclusively with any modern site. G.W.G.

NETS. Nets in the Bible are instruments of meshed strings for fishing or hunting, or reticulate designs or gratings.

a. Nets for fishing and hunting

Words from four Heb. roots are translated 'net' in the OT. **1.** From *yrš*, 'take', *rešeṯ* is a net to catch birds (Pr. 1:17) or water creatures (Ezk. 32:3), and is often used figuratively of the plots of evil men (*e.g.* Ps. 9:15, laid to catch the feet), or of God's judgments (*e.g.* Ezk. 12:13, cast over the prey). **2.** *ḥerem*, 'something perforated', is a large net which may be spread out on the shore to dry (Ezk. 26:5) and is used figuratively of an evil woman's heart (Ec. 7:26), of God's judgment of Pharaoh (Ezk. 32:3), of predatory individuals (Mi. 7:2), and of the Chaldeans' military power (Hab. 1:15). **3.** From the root *ṣûḏ*, 'hunt', *mᵉṣôḏâ* is a fish-net (Ec. 9:12), *māṣûḏ* and *mᵉṣûḏâ* are used of God's judgments (Jb. 19:6, surrounding the prey; Ps. 66:11), and *māṣôḏ* in Pr. 12:12 is perhaps a snare for evil men. **4.** From the root *kmr*, which in Arabic means 'overcome' or 'cover', Heb. *mikmōreṯ* is the net which Egyptian fishermen spread over the water (Is. 19:8), *mikmereṯ*, AV 'drag', RSV 'seine', is a symbol of the Chaldeans' army (Hab. 1:15), *mikmôr* is used to catch an antelope (Is. 51:20), and *mikmār* is figurative of the plots of the wicked (Ps. 141:10).

In the NT three Gk. words are translated 'net'. **5.** From *diktyō*, 'to net', *diktyon*, the most common and general word for net. This type of net was used by Jesus' disciples (Mt. 4:20–21); it was let down (Lk. 5:4) or cast (Jn. 21:6) in the water, and emptied into a boat (Lk. 5:7) or dragged to shore (Jn. 21:8). **6.** From *amphiballō*, 'cast around', *amphiblēstron*, 'a casting net', also used by the disciples of Jesus (Mt. 4:18). **7.** From *sassō*, 'fill', *sagēnē* (related to English 'seine'), a drag-net to which our Lord compared the kingdom of heaven (Mt. 13:47). It required several men to draw this large net to shore (Mt. 13:48).

The care of nets included washing (Lk. 5:2), drying (Ezk. 47:10) and mending (Mt. 4:21).

BIBLIOGRAPHY. G. Dalman, *Arbeit und Sitte*, 6, 1939, pp. 335–337, 343–363.

b. Nets as designs or gratings

Around the base of the brazen altar of burnt offering of the tabernacle was grating of net design (*rešeṯ*, Ex. 27:4–5) or net work (*ma'aśēh rešeṯ*, Ex. 38:4). This grating may have had both artistic and practical purposes, since it would be lighter to carry than solid metal and allow draught for burning.

The capitals of the two pillars before Solomon's Temple were decorated with a net design (Heb. *śᵉḇāḵâ* from a root meaning 'interweave', 1 Ki. 7:17; Je. 52:22). Those who think these pillars were cressets point out that open net work would give air for burning inside the capital, but this feature is not mentioned in the Bible.

BIBLIOGRAPHY. H. G. May, *The Two Pillars before the Temple of Solomon, BASOR* 88, December 1942, pp. 19–27. J.T.

NEW TESTAMENT APOCRYPHA. The extent of the NT apocrypha is more difficult to determine than that of the OT. The term will here be confined to non-canonical works attributed to, or purporting to give extra-canonical information about, Christ or the apostles. Works written without such pretensions are thus excluded, even where they enjoyed quasi-canonical status in some churches for a time (*PATRISTIC LITERATURE); so are Christian attributions to (or Christianized versions of works attributed to) OT characters (*PSEUDEPIGRAPHA), and the interpolation or rehandling of NT texts with alien material (*TEXTS AND VERSIONS, NT section).

A huge literature remains, preserved partly in Gk. and Lat., but still more in Coptic, Ethiopic, Syriac, Arabic, Slavonic, and even in Anglo-Saxon and contemporary W European languages. Some works that we know to have been very influential have been almost lost, and many of the most important exist only in fragmentary state. New discoveries, however, often of much importance for early Christian history, are constantly being made. Complex literary problems are frequently met, for many of the apocryphal works lent themselves to re-telling, interpolation and plagiarization.

I. Forms

A large proportion of the apocryphal literature falls into one of the NT literary forms: Gospel, Acts, Epistle, Apocalypse. But this formal similarity is often accompanied by a huge difference in conception. This is particularly noticeable with the Gospels: we have Infancy Gospels, Passion Gospels, sayings documents and theological meditations; but (if we exclude the early fragmentary Gospels on which we are in any case ill-informed), it is hard to find works which, like the canonical Gospels, have any interest in the words and works of the incarnate Lord. Acts form a numerous and probably the most popular class, doubtless through the wide and non-sectarian appeal of many of the stories. Epistles are not common: despite the fact that nearly all the works in the NT sometimes said to be pseudepigraphic are Epistles. For apocalypses, there was Jewish precedent for attributing them to a celebrity of the past.

Another class of literature developed which took over some features of apocryphal literature: the Church Orders of Syria and Egypt. These collections of canons on church discipline and liturgy, of which the *Apostolic Constitutions* is the most popular, claiming to represent apostolic practice, came by convention to claim apostolic origin: and the most daring, the *Testament of our Lord*, purports to be a post-resurrection discourse of Christ. The custom was perhaps stimulated by its success in the 3rd-century *Didascalia*, and misunderstanding of the claim to apostolicity of the *Apostolic Tradition* of Hippolytus—two works which they plundered heavily—together with, in some cases, the popularity of the Clementine romance. (*Cf. Studia Patristica*, eds. K. Aland and F. L. Cross, 2, 1957, pp. 83ff.)

II. Motives

The creation of apocryphal literature had begun in apostolic times: Paul has apparently to authenticate his signature because of forgeries circulating (*cf.* 2 Thes. 3:17). In the 2nd century the literature comes into its own, and gathers momentum thenceforth, particularly in Egypt and Syria. It continues into the Middle Ages (where the older legends were still loved), and, occasionally, through sentiment, *parti pris* or sheer eccentricity, in our own day. The various motives behind it are thus related to the whole trend of Christian and sub-Christian history; but some of the motives operative at the beginning are particularly important.

a. Romance and the literary impulse

This shows itself in various forms. There is the desire to satisfy curiosity on matters of which the NT says nothing. A flood of worthless Infancy Gospels covers the silent years from Bethlehem to the baptism. As the Virgin Mary becomes more prominent in theology and devotion, pseudo-apostolic works describe her birth, life and, eventually, her assumption into heaven. A reader of Col. 4:16 felt it incumbent upon him to supply the apparently missing letter to the Laodiceans. It appears above all in the novelistic Acts and romances and some of the Gospels—bizarre, fetid, but packed with wonders and anecdotes, and many of them, with all their faults, having a certain animation. We best understand this movement as a branch of popular Christian literature, and, studied in this light, the earliest books reveal some of the issues which occupied congregations in the 2nd and 3rd centuries: relationships with the state, controversies with the Jews, debates on marriage and celibacy: and, by their belligerent insistence on miracles, reveal that the real age of miracles had passed. The productions are crude, even vulgar; but their authors knew their public. For many they must have replaced erotic pagan popular literature, and in many cases, with a real desire to edify. The authors would doubtless be hard put to it to differentiate their motives from those of the 20th-century author of *The Robe* or *The Big Fisherman*. There is no need to question the sincerity of the Asian presbyter who was unfrocked for publishing the *Acts of Paul* when he said that he did so 'for love of Paul', who had died 100 years before the presbyter wrote. This helps to explain how stories and whole books originating in heretical circles retained and increased their currency in orthodox quarters. It was heretical teachers who made the earliest effective use of this form of literature; and so successful was it that others transmitted, expurgated and imitated the forms designed as vehicles for their propaganda.

b. The inculcation of principles not, to the author's mind, sufficiently clearly enunciated in the New Testament books

Naturally, even in a work 'for love of Paul' any doctrinal disproportion or aberration of the author passed into his work; indeed part of his edificatory aim might well be to inculate the aberration: the Asian presbyter, for instance, had an obsession with virginity which makes his work, otherwise more or less orthodox, remote from evangelic spirit. But there are many works the aim of which is deliberately sectarian: to promulgate a body of doctrine to supplement or supersede that of the undisputed books. These were mainly the fruit of the two great reactionary movements of the 2nd century, *Gnosticism and Montanism. The Montanist 'Scriptures' arose almost by accident, and were not in our sense strictly apocryphal, for, though they claimed to preserve the living testimony of the Holy Spirit, they were not pseudonymous; they have virtually disappeared (but *cf.* those collected in R. M. Grant, *Second Century Christianity*, pp. 95ff.). Writings from the multiform expressions of Gnosticism, however, have survived in quantity. Such works as the *Gospel of Truth*, a meditation in Gnostic terms reflecting the language of the undisputed Scriptures, are less common than works which select, modify and interpret those Scriptures in a sectarian direction (*cf.* the Nag Hammadi *Gospel of Thomas*), those which blatantly profess to contain secret doctrine not available elsewhere (*cf.* the *Apocryphon of John*), and those which simply attribute to the Lord or the apostles the commonplaces of Gnostic teaching. And for all these purposes the apocryphal form became conventional.

The reason is not far to seek. In the sub-apostolic age and after, with the immense expansion of the church, the intensifying of the danger of persecution and the proliferation of false teaching, apostolicity became the norm of faith and practice: and, as the living memory of the apostles receded, apostolicity was increasingly centred in the Scriptures of our NT, over the majority of which there was unanimity in the church. If, therefore, a new form of teaching was to spread, it had to establish its apostolicity. This was commonly done by claiming a secret tradition from an apostle, or from the Lord through an apostle, either as a supplement to the open tradition of the Gospels or as a corrective. The favoured apostle varies: many sects had Judaic leanings, and James the Just and, curiously, Salome, are frequent sources of tradition; Thomas, Philip, Bartholomew and Matthias also appear constantly. In the *Gospel of Thomas*, for instance, it is Thomas who shows fullest understanding of the Lord's person (Matthew and Peter—perhaps as the apostles behind the church's first two Gospels—appear to their disadvantage). The still more weird *Pistis Sophia* envisages a sort of congress of the apostles and the women with the Lord, but indicates that Philip, Thomas and Matthias are to write the mysteries (*Pistis Sophia*, ch. 42, Schmidt). Local factors probably contribute something to the choice of apostle—all those named were associated with Syria and the East, some of the most fertile soil for literature of this type; and speculations about Thomas as the Lord's twin exercised an additional fascination. The process brought about a new emphasis on the post-resurrection period, in which discourses of the Lord were usually set; significantly, for little is said of this period in the undisputed Gospels, and it was a constant Gnostic feature to undervalue the humanity of the incarnate Lord. It is worth noticing that, while those syncretistic sects who adopted some Christian elements could get their revelations whence they would, Christian Gnosticism had to show that its knowledge was derived from an apostolic source.

c. The preservation of tradition

Inevitably in early days words of the Lord were handed down outside the canonical Gospels. Some were probably transformed out of recognition in the process, others tendentiously twisted. The celebrated preface of Papias (Eusebius, *EH* 3. 39), showing him collecting oracles of the Lord for his Expositions, reveals how conscious orthodox Christians in the early 2nd century were of this floating material and the problems of collecting it. Papias, whatever his shortcomings, was conscientious in scrutinizing his material: yet the results were not always happy, and perhaps not all his contemporaries had his compunction. Genuine material may thus sometimes have been preserved amid undisputed rubbish.

Similarly, memories of the lives and deaths of apostles would be likely to linger, and the apocryphal Acts, even when dubious theologically, may sometimes preserve genuine traditions, or reflect appropriate situations.

The desire to transmit such memories undoubtedly played its part in the production of the apocryphal literature; but it could not defeat the tendency to invent, elaborate, improve, or redirect. Any winnowing process is thus hazardous: and, as scholars like Origen knew, was already hazardous in patristic times. In consequence, the necessity of building squarely upon what was undisputed was universally recognized.

III. The apocryphal literature in the early church

The presence of such various writings under apostolic names when apostolicity was the norm made it urgent to be assured which the truly apostolic writings were, and the early Christian scholars were not deficient in insight and critical acumen (*CANON OF THE NEW TESTAMENT). But it is striking how little the generally received list of canonical books is affected by discussions over apocryphal literature. Some churches were slow in receiving books now regarded as canonical. Some gave high place to such works as *1 Clement* and the *Shepherd* of Hermas. But hardly any books in, say, M. R. James' *Apocryphal New Testament* were ever in any sense 'Excluded books of the NT'. They were beyond consideration. The Petrine literature caused more heart-searching than any other (*cf.* R. M. Grant and G. Quispel, *VC* 6, 1952, pp. 31ff.). By Eusebius' time the discussion, save on 2 Peter, is closed (*EH* 3. 3), but there is positive evidence that at least the *Apocalypse of Peter* was for a time employed in some areas (see below).

In this connection the letter of Serapion, bishop of Antioch, to the congregation at Rhossus about AD 190, is of interest (*cf.* Eusebius, *EH* 6. 12). The church had begun to use the *Gospel of Peter.* There had evidently been opposition to it, but Serapion, satisfied of the stability of the congregation, had, after a cursory glance, sanctioned its public reading. Trouble followed. Serapion read the Gospel more carefully and found not only that it was accepted by churches whose tendencies were suspect, but that it reflected at some points the Docetic heresy (denying the reality of Christ's manhood). He sums it up 'most is of the Saviour's true teaching', but some things (of which he appended a list) were added. He says, 'We accept Peter and the other apostles as Christ, but as men of experience we test writings falsely ascribed to them, knowing that such things were not handed down to us.'

In other words, the list of apostolic books was already traditional. Other books might be read, provided they were orthodox. The *Gospel of Peter* was *not* traditional: its use at Rhossus was the result of a specific request, and was not unopposed. At first Serapion had seen nothing to require prolonged controversy: if spurious, it was at least harmless. When closer examination revealed its tendencies its use in any form in church was forbidden.

The course of events seems best understood if, following the hint of Serapion's action, we recognize that the acknowledgment of a book as spurious did not necessarily involve complete refusal to allow its public reading, providing it had some devotional value and no heretical tendency: a sort of intermediate status analogous to that of the Apocrypha in the sixth Anglican Article. But even a heretical book, if it had other appeal, might still be read privately and laid under tribute. By these means the apocryphal literature came to have a lasting effect on mediaeval devotion and Christian art and story.

There is, however, nothing to suggest that it was an accepted part of catholic practice in the 1st or 2nd century to compile works in the name of an apostle, a process implied in some theories of the authorship of certain NT books (*cf.* D. Guthrie, *ExpT* 67, 1955–6, pp. 341f.), and the case of the author of the *Acts of Paul* is one example of drastic action against such publication.

Passing from any NT writings to the best NT apocrypha—the true creation of the early Christian community—one moves into a different world. If 2 Peter—to take the NT writing most commonly assigned to the 2nd century—be an apocryphon, it is unique among the apocrypha.

IV. Some representative works

A few representatives of different apocryphal forms may be given. They are, generally speaking, some of the more important older works. Few have a complete text: for some we are dependent on quotations from early writers.

a. Early apocryphal Gospels

A number of fragments from early Gospels are quoted by 3rd- and 4th-century writers. Debate continues on the nature and inter-relationships of these Gospels. The *Gospel according to the Hebrews* was known to Clement of Alexandria, Origen, Hegesippus, Eusebius, and Jerome, who says (though he is not always believed) that he translated it into Gk. and Lat. (*De Viris Illustribus* 2) from Aramaic in Heb. characters, and that it was used by the Nazarenes, a Jewish–Christian group. Most people, he says, mistakenly thought it was the Heb. original of the Gospel of *Matthew mentioned by Papias, which recalls that Irenaeus knew of sects which used only Matthew (*Adv. Haer*. 1. 26. 2; 3. 11. 7). Some of the extracts we possess have certainly points of contact with Matthew; others reappear in other works, most recently the *Gospel of Thomas.* There is a strong Jewish–Christian tone, and a resurrection appearance to James the Just is recorded. Eusebius refers to a story, found both in Papias and in the *Gospel of the Hebrews*, of a woman accused before Jesus of many sins. This has been often identified with the story of the adulteress found in many MSS of Jn. 8.

The Gospel probably reflects the activity of Syrian Jewish Christians using Matthaean (the 'local' Gospel) and other local tradition, some of it doubtless valid. The Nazarenes called it 'The Gospel according to the Apostles' (Jerome, *Contra Pelag.* 3. 2)—a suspiciously belligerent title. (See V. Burch, *JTS* 21, 920, pp. 310ff.; M. J. Lagrange, *RB*

31, 1922, pp. 161ff., 321ff.; and for its defence as a primary source, H. J. Schonfield, *According to the Hebrews*, 1937.)

Epiphanius, ever a confused writer, mentions a mutilated version of Matthew used by the Jewish-Christian sect he calls 'Ebionites'. This has been identified with the Hebrews Gospel, but the extracts given show a different view of the nativity and baptism, and the work is clearly sectarian and tendentious. It may be the same as the *Gospel of the Twelve Apostles* mentioned by Origen (*Lk. Hom.* 1; *cf.* J. R. Harris, *The Gospel of the Twelve Apostles*, 1900, pp. 11f.).

The *Gospel of the Egyptians* is known mainly through a series of quotations in the *Stromateis* of Clement of Alexandria. Some Gnostics used it (Hippolytus, *Philosophoumena* 5. 7), and it doubtless arose in an Egyptian sect. Extant portions relate to a dialogue of Christ and Salome on the repudiation of sexual relations. A document with the same title is included in the Nag Hammadi library, but is not related to the work known to Clement. It is an esoteric Gnostic tractate.

The papyri have yielded a number of fragments of uncanonical Gospels. The most celebrated, P. Oxy. 1. 654–655, will be considered later under the *Gospel of Thomas*. Next in interest comes the so-called *Unknown Gospel* (P. Egerton 2) published by H. I. Bell and T. C. Skeat in 1935, describing incidents after the Synoptic manner but with a Johannine dialogue and vocabulary. The MS, dated *c.* AD 100, is one of the oldest known Christian Gk. MSS. It has been held by some to draw on the Fourth Gospel and perhaps one of the Synoptics also, and by others to be an early example of Christian popular literature independent of these (*cf.* Lk. 1:1). (See H. I. Bell and T. C. Skeat, *The New Gospel Fragments*, 1935; C. H. Dodd, *BJRL* 20, 1936, pp. 56ff. = *New Testament Studies*, 1953, pp. 12ff.; G. Mayeda, *Das Leben-Jesu-Fragment Egerton 2*, 1946; H. I. Bell, *HTR* 42, 1949, pp. 53ff.)

b. Passion Gospels

The most important Gospel of which we have any substantial part is the (mid?) 2nd-century *Gospel of Peter*, of which a large Coptic fragment, covering from the judgment to the resurrection, exists (The Akhmim Fragment). It has been identified with the 'memoirs of Peter', perhaps mentioned by Justin (*Trypho* 106), but this is inappropriate. (*Cf.* V. H. Stanton, *JTS* 2, 1900, pp. 1ff.)

The miraculous element is heightened. The watch see three men come out from the tomb, two whose heads reach the sky and one who overpasses it. A cross follows them. A voice from heaven cries, 'Hast thou preached to them that sleep?' and a voice from the cross says, 'Yes' (*cf.* 1 Pet. 3:19). Pilate's share of blame is reduced, and that of Herod and the Jews emphasized: perhaps reflecting both an apologetic towards the state and controversy with the Jews.

Serapion's judgment (see above) did not err; most of it is lurid, but not dangerous. But there are tell-tale phrases: 'He kept silence as one feeling no pain', and the rendering of the cry of dereliction, 'My power, thou hast forsaken me', followed by the pregnant 'he was taken up', show that the author did not properly value the Lord's humanity. (See L. Vaganay, *L'Évangile de Pierre*, 1930.)

The *Gospel of Nicodemus* is the name given to a composite work existing in various recensions in Gk., Lat. and Coptic, of which the principal elements are 'The Acts of Pilate', supposedly an official report of the trial, crucifixion and burial, an abstract of the subsequent debates and investigations of the Sanhedrin, and a highly-coloured account of the 'Descent into Hell'. There are various appendices in the different versions; one, a letter of Pilate to the emperor Claudius, may give the earliest example of 'Acts of Pilate'. Apologists like Justin (*Apol.* 35. 48) appeal confidently to the trial records, assuming they exist. Tertullian knew stories of Pilate's favourable reports to Tiberius about Jesus (*Apol.* 5. 21). Such 'records' would be constructed in time: especially when a persecuting government, *c.* AD 312, used forged and blasphemous reports of the trial for propaganda purposes (Eusebius, *EH* 9. 5). Our present 'Acts' may be a counter to these. The 'Descent into Hell' may be from rather later in the century, but both parts of the work probably draw on older material. The striking feature is the virtual vindication of Pilate, doubtless for reasons of policy. As the stories passed into Byzantine legend, Pilate became a saint, and his martyrdom is still celebrated in the Coptic Church.

There is no proper critical text. See J. Quasten, *Patrology*, 1, pp. 115ff. for versions.

c. Infancy Gospels

The *Protevangelium of James* had a huge popularity; many MSS exist in many languages (though none in Lat.), and it has deeply influenced much subsequent Mariology. It was known to Origen, so must be 2nd century. It gives the birth and presentation of Mary, her espousal to Joseph (an old man with children) and the Lord's miraculous birth (a midwife attesting the virginity *in partu*). It is clearly written in the interests of certain theories about the perpetual virginity. The supposed author is James the Just, though at one point Joseph becomes the narrator. (See M. Testuz, *Papyrus Bodmer 5*, 1958; E. de Strycker, *La forme plus ancienne du Protévangile de Jacques*, 1961.)

The other influential infancy Gospel of antiquity was the *Gospel of Thomas*, which tells some rather repulsive stories of the silent years. Our version seems to have been shorn of its Gnostic speeches. It is distinct from the Nag Hammadi work of the same name (see below); it is sometimes difficult to know to which work patristic writers refer.

d. The Nag Hammadi Gospels

In the Nag Hammadi library there are several Gospels in Coptic which were not previously known, besides new versions of others (*CHENOBOSKION).

One text opens 'The Gospel of Truth is a joy' (an *incipit*, not a title), and proceeds to a verbose and often obscure meditation on the scheme of redemption. Gnostic terminology of the type of the Valentinian school is evident, but not in the developed form we meet in Irenaeus. It alludes to most of the NT books in a way which suggests recognition of their authority. It has been commonly identified with the 'Gospel of Truth' ascribed to Valentinus by Irenaeus, though this has been denied (*cf.* H. M. Schenke, *ThL* 83, 1958, pp. 497ff.). Van Unnik has attractively proposed that it was written before Valentinus' break with the Roman church (where he was once a candidate for an episcopal chair), when he was seeking to establish his orthodoxy. It would thus be an important witness to the list of authoritative books (and substantially similar to our own) in Rome *c.* AD 140. (See G. Quispel and W. C. van Unnik in *The Jung Codex*, ed. by F. L. Cross, 1955; text by M. Malinine *et al.*, *Evangelium Veritatis*, 1956 and 1961; commentary by K. Grobel, *The Gospel of Truth*, 1960.) The most recent English translation is by G. W. MacRae in *The Nag Hammadi Library*, 1977.

The now famous *Gospel of Thomas* is a collection of sayings of Jesus, numbered at about 114, with little obvious arrangement. A high proportion resemble sayings in the Synoptic Gospels (with a bias towards Luke) but almost always with significant differences. These often take a Gnostic direction, and among other Gnostic themes the OT is minimized and the necessity for obliterating consciousness of sex is stressed. It has been identified with the Gospel used by the Naassene Gnostics (*cf.* R. M. Grant with D. N. Freedman, *The Secret Sayings of Jesus*, 1959; W. R. Schoedel, *VC* 14, 1960, pp. 225ff.), but its originally Gnostic character has been doubted (R. McL. Wilson, *Studies in the Gospel of Thomas*, 1961), and some are prepared to see independent traditions of some value in it. G. Quispel has found the variants similar in type to those in the Bezan ('Western') Text (*VC* 14, 1960, pp. 204ff.) as well as in Tatian's *Diatessaron* and the Pseudo-Clementines (see below). In a more recent article Quispel connects the *Gospel of Thomas* with the Encratites rather than the Gnostics (*VC* 28, 1974, pp. 29f.) The Oxyrhynchus Logia P. Oxy. 1. 654–655, including the celebrated 'Raise the stone and thou shalt find me', recur in a form which suggests that they were part of an earlier Gk. version of the book. Thomas (probably thought of as the twin of Jesus) plays the central role in the tradition (see above), but James the Just is said to become chief of the disciples—one of several indications that a Jewish–Christian source is under tribute.

Many problems beset this curious and inconsistent book, but so far it seems safe to place its origin in Syria (which may explain the Semitisms of the language), where there was always a freer attitude to the Gospel text and more contamination than elsewhere. (See text and translation by A. Guillaumont *et al.*, 1959; H. Koester and T. O. Lambdin in *The Nag Hammadi Library in English*, pp. 117–130; B. Gärtner, *The Theology of the Gospel of Thomas*, 1961; bibliography to 1960 in J. Leipoldt and H. M. Schenke, *Koptisch-Gnostische Schriften aus den Papyrus-Codices von Nag-Hamadi*, 1960, pp. 79f.)

The chief interest of the *Gospel of Philip* (Gnostic, though the sect is hard to identify) lies in its unusually developed sacramental doctrine, in which there are greater mysteries in chrism and the 'bridechamber' than in baptism (see E. Segelberg, *Numen* 7, 1960, pp. 189ff.; R. McL. Wilson, *The Gospel of Philip*, 1962, provides a translation and commentary. *Cf.* also *The Nag Hammadi Library in English*, pp. 131–151 [tr. by W. W. Isenberg]. The language is repulsive: interest in sexual repudiation amounts to an obsession.

e. The 'Leucian' Acts

The five major apocryphal Acts must serve as representatives of a large number. They were gathered into a corpus by Manicheans, who would inherit them from Gnostic sources. The 9th-century bibliophile Photius found the whole attributed to one 'Leucius Charinus' (*Bibliotheca*, 114), but it is probable that Leucius was simply the fictitious name of the author of the *Acts of John*, the earliest (and most unorthodox) of the corpus.

It belongs to about AD 150–160 and describes miracles and sermons (definitely Gnostic) by John in Asia Minor. It reflects ascetic ideals, but has some pleasant anecdotes amid more disreputable matter. It affects also to relate John's own accounts of some incidents with the Lord, and his farewell and death. Liturgically it is of some interest, and includes the first known eucharist for the dead.

The *Acts of Paul* is also early, for Tertullian knew people who justified female preaching and baptizing therefrom (*De Baptismos* 17). He says it was written ostensibly 'for love of Paul' by an Asian presbyter, who was deposed for the action. This must have happened before AD 190, probably nearer AD 160. The Acts reflect a time of persecution. There are three main sections:

(i) The Acts of Paul and Thecla, an Iconian girl who breaks off her engagement at Paul's preaching, is miraculously protected from martyrdom (winning the interest of 'Queen Tryphaena'—*TRYPHAENA AND TRYPHOSA), and assists Paul's missionary travels. There may have been some historical nucleus even if not a written Thecla source (so Ramsay, *CRE*, pp. 375ff.).

(ii) Further correspondence with the Corinthian church.

(iii) The martyrdom of Paul (legendary).

The tone is intensely ascetic (*cf.* Paul's Beatitudes for the celibate, ch. 5), but otherwise orthodox. There are many incomplete MSS, including a sizeable section of the original Gk. See L. Vouaux, *Les Actes de Paul*, 1913; E. Peterson, *VC* 3, 1949, pp. 142ff.

The *Acts of Peter* is somewhat later, but still well within the 2nd century. The main MS, in Latin (often called the Vercelli Acts), opens with Paul's farewell to the Roman Christians (perhaps from another source). Through the machinations of *Simon Magus the Roman church falls into heresy, but, in response to prayer, Peter arrives, and defeats Simon in a series of public encounters. There follows a plot against Peter initiated by pagans whose wives have left them as a result of his preaching, Peter's flight including the *Quo Vadis?* story, and his return to crucifixion, which was head downwards. A Coptic fragment and allusions to a lost portion suggest that other stories dealt with questions raised in the community about suffering and death. Like other Acts, it sees Peter's work and Paul's as supplementing each other: and the Roman church is a *Pauline* foundation. The ascetic tone is as intense as ever, but otherwise the Gnostic element is not often obtruded; we may, however, have expurgated editions. The place of origin is disputed, but it was almost certainly Eastern. See L. Vouaux, *Les Actes de Pierre*, 1922. It is worth noting that in the Nag Hammadi library the only two documents described as Acts are related to Peter. The Coptic *Acts of Peter* has some affinity with the Lat. *Acts of Peter*, but the latter is more extreme in its ascetic emphasis.

The *Acts of* (*Judas*) *Thomas* stand apart from the other Acts. They are a product of Syriac Christianity, and were almost certainly written in Syriac in Edessa in the early 3rd century. They describe how the apostles divided the world by lot, and Judas Thomas the Twin was appointed to India. He went as a slave, but became the means of the conversion of King 'Gundaphar' and many other notable Indians. Everywhere he preaches virginity and is frequently imprisoned in consequence of his success. Finally, he is martyred.

The Acts have certain Gnostic features: the famous 'Hymn of the Soul' which appears in them has the familiar Gnostic theme of the redemption of the soul from the corruption of matter—the king's son is sent to slay the dragon and bring back the pearl from the far country. There is clearly some relation, as yet unascertained, to the *Gospel of Thomas*: and the title of Thomas, 'Twin of the Messiah', is eloquent. The appeal for virginity is louder, shriller, than in any of the other Acts, but this was a characteristic of Syriac Christianity. Of Gnosticism in the sense of the possession of hidden mysteries there is little trace: the author is too much in earnest in preaching and recommending his Gospel.

There are complete versions in Syriac and Gk. The Acts seem to show some real knowledge of the history and topography of *India. (See A. A. Bevan, *The Hymn of the Soul*, 1897; F. C. Burkitt, *Early Christianity outside the Roman Empire*, 1899; A. F. J. Klijn, *VC* 14, 1960, pp. 154ff.; *idem, The Acts of Thomas*, 1962.)

The *Acts of Andrew* is the latest (*c.* AD 260?) and, in our MSS, the most fragmentary of the 'Leucian' Acts. It is closely related to the *Acts of John*, and its Gnostic character is mentioned by Eusebius (*EH* 3. 25). It describes preachings among the cannibals, miracles, exhortations to virginity, and, perhaps added from another source, martyrdom in Greece. An abstract is given by Gregory of Tours. (See P. M. Peterson, *Andrew, Brother of Simon Peter*, 1958; F. Dvornik, *The Idea of Apostolicity in Byzantium and the Legend of the Apostle Andrew*, 1958, pp. 181ff.; G. Quispel, *VC* 10, 1956, pp. 129ff.; *cf.* D. Guthrie, 'Acts and Epistles in Apocryphal Writings', in W. W. Gasque and R. P. Martin (eds.), *Apostolic History and the Gospel*, 1970.

f. Apocryphal Epistles

The most important are the *Third Epistle to the Corinthians* (see *Acts of Paul*, above); the *Epistle of the Apostles*, really a series of early 2nd-century apocalyptic visions cast in the form of an address in the name of all the apostles, to convey post-resurrection teaching of Christ (important as one of the earliest examples of this form); the *Correspondence of Christ and Abgar*, in which the king of Edessa invites the Lord to his state, and of which Eusebius affords an early translation from the Syriac (*EH* 1. 13); the Latin *Correspondence of Paul and Seneca* (see Jerome, *De Viris Illustribus* 12), a 3rd-century apology for Paul's diction, evidently intended to gain a reading of the genuine Epistles in polite circles; and the *Epistle to the Laodiceans*, in Latin, a cento of Pauline language evoked by Col. 4:16. The Muratorian Fragment mentions Epistles to the Laodiceans, and to the Alexandrians, of Marcionite origin: of these there is no trace. The commonly quoted *Letter of Lentulus* describing Jesus and allegedly addressed to the Senate is mediaeval. (See H. Duensing, *Epistula Apostolorum*, 1925; J. de Zwaan in *Amicitiae Corolla* edited by H. G. Wood, 1933, pp. 344ff.; for all the pseudo-Pauline letters, L. Vouaux, *Les Actes de Paul*, 1913, pp. 315ff.)

g. Apocalypses

The *Apocalypse of Peter* is the only strictly apocryphal work of which there is positive evidence that it held quasi-canonical status for any length of time. It occurs in the Muratorian Fragment, but with the accompanying note that some will not have it read in church. Clement of Alexandria seems to have commented on it as if it were canonical in a lost work (Eusebius, *EH* 6. 14), and in the 5th century it was read on Good Friday in some Palestinian churches (Sozomen, *Eccles. Hist.* 7. 19). But it was never universally accepted, and its canonicity was not a live issue in Eusebius' day (*EH* 3. 3). Its substantial orthodoxy seems certain. An old stichometry gives it 300 lines: about half of this appears in the main copy of the *Gospel of Peter* (see above). It contains visions of the transfigured Lord, and lurid accounts of the torments of the damned: with perhaps a confused reference to future probation. (See M. R. James, *JTS* 12, 1911, pp. 36ff., 362ff., 573ff.; 32, 1931, pp. 270ff.)

There were several Gnostic *Apocalypses of Paul*, one known to Origen, inspired by 2 Cor. 12:2ff. A version of one (which influenced Dante) has survived (see R. P. Casey, *JTS* 24, 1933, pp. 1ff.).

In the Nag Hammadi library Book V consists of four apocalypses, one of *Paul*, two of *James* and one of *Adam*. The *Apocalypse of Paul* in this collection is distinct from those previously known. All these works are Gnostic in their teaching. *Cf.* A. Böhlig and P. Labib, *Koptisch-gnostische Apocalypsen aus Codex V von Nag Hammadi*, 1963.

h. Other apocryphal works

The *Kerygmata Petrou*, or *Preachings of Peter*, is known to us only in fragments, mostly preserved by Clement of Alexandria. Origen had to deal with Gnostic scholars who employed it, and challenged them to prove its genuineness (in Jn. 13:17, *De Principiis* Pref. 8). It has been postulated as a source of the original Clementine romance (see below). The fragments we have claim to preserve words of the Lord and of Peter, and at least one accords with the *Gospel of the Hebrews*.

The *Clementine Homilies* and the *Clementine Recognitions* are the two chief forms of a romance in which Clement of Rome, seeking for ultimate truth, travels in the apostle Peter's footsteps and is eventually converted. It is probable that both derive from an immensely popular 2nd-century Christian novel, which may have used the *Preachings of Peter*. The literary and theological problems involved are very complex. The Homilies in particular command a Judaized sectarian form of Christianity. (See O. Cullmann, *Le Problème Littéraire et Historique du Roman Pseudo-Clémentin*, 1930; H. J. Schoeps, *Theologie und Geschichte des Judenchristentums*, 1949; E.T. of Homilies and Recognitions in Ante-Nicene Christian Library.)

The *Apocryphon of John* was popular in Gnostic circles, and has reappeared at Nag Hammadi. The Saviour appears to John on the Mount of Olives, bids him write secret doctrine, deposit it safely and impart it only to those whose spirit can understand it and whose way of life is worthy. There is a curse on anyone imparting the doctrine for reward to an unworthy person. It is to be dated before AD 180, probably in Egypt. (See W. C. Till, *Die Gnostischen Schriften des koptischen Papyrus Berol. 8502*, 1955; *cf. JEH* 3, 1952, pp. 14ff.) In the Nag Hammadi documents, an account is given of the creation, the Fall and the redemption of humanity.

The *Apocryphon of James* has also been discovered at Nag Hammadi. It is an exhortation to seek the kingdom, cast in the form of a post-resurrection discourse to Peter and James, who ascend with the Lord but are unable to penetrate the third heaven. Its interest lies in its early date (AD 125–150?), the prominence of James (the Just?), who sends the apostles to their work after the ascension, and, in van Unnik's opinion, its freedom from Gnostic influence. (See W. C. van Unnik, *VC* 10, 1956, pp. 149ff.) F. E. Williams in his introductory remarks to his translation of the Nag Hammadi text in *The Nag Hammadi Library in English*, p. 29, finds some evidence of Gnostic themes and suggests Christian Gnosticism as its source.

The *Pistis Sophia* and the *Books of Jeû* are obscure and bizarre Gnostic works of the 2nd or 3rd century. (See C. Schmidt, *Koptisch-gnostische Schriften*[3], edited by W. Till, 1959; G. R. S. Mead, *Pistis Sophia*[3], 1947, E.T.—*cf.* F. C. Burkitt, *JTS* 23, 1922, pp. 271ff.; C. A. Baynes, *A Coptic Gnostic Treatise*, 1933.)

GENERAL BIBLIOGRAPHY. Critical editions of many of these works are still needed. Gk. and Lat. texts of the earlier Gospel discoveries are provided by C. Tischendorf, *Evangelia Apocrypha*, 1886, to be supplemented by A. de Santos, *Los Evangelios Apocrifos*, 1956 (with Spanish translations). The best collection of texts of the Acts is R. A. Lipsius and M. Bonnet, *Acta Apostolorum Apocrypha*, 1891–1903. Some newer texts and studies are provided in M. R. James, *Apocrypha Anecdota*, 1, 1893; 2, 1897. M. R. James, *ANT* (a splendid collection of English translations up to 1924); E. Hennecke–W. Schneemelcher (E.T. by R. M. Wilson), *New Testament Apocrypha*, 1, 1963; 2, 1965 (indispensable for serious study). Non-canonical sayings: J. Jeremias, *Unknown Sayings of Jesus*, 1957; J. Finegan, *Hidden Records of the Life of Jesus*, 1969; F. F. Bruce, *Jesus and Christian Origins outside the New Testament*, 1974; C. Hendrick (ed.), *The Historical Jesus and the Rejected Gospels*, 1988. Church orders: J. Cooper and A. J. Maclean, *The Testament of our Lord*, 1902; R. H. Connolly, *The So-Called Egyptian Church Order and its Derivatives*, 1917. A.F.W.

NICODEMUS. The name is Gk. and means 'conqueror of the people'. He is mentioned only in the Fourth Gospel, where he is described as a Pharisee and ruler of the Jews (*i.e.* a member of the Sanhedrin) who visited Jesus by night (Jn. 3:1–21). He seems to have been an earnest man attracted by the character and teaching of Jesus but afraid to allow this interest to be known by his fellow Pharisees. He could not understand the spiritual metaphors used by Christ. Nicodemus fades from the scene and we are left with Christ's word to a Judaism wrapped in darkness.

Nicodemus is mentioned again in Jn. 7:50–52, where he showed more courage in protesting against the condemnation of Christ without giving him a hearing. The final reference is in Jn. 19:40, where he is said to have brought a lavish gift of spices to anoint the body of Christ. Nothing more is known of him despite a large number of legends (*e.g.* in the apocryphal *Gospel of Nicodemus*). His identification with the wealthy and generous Naqdimon ben-Gorion of the Talmud is uncertain.

BIBLIOGRAPHY. M. Pamment, *ExpT* 97, 1985, pp. 71–75; J. S. King, *ExpT* 98, 1986, p. 45; D. D. Sylva, *NTS* 34, 1988, pp.148–151. R.E.N.

NICOLAUS, NICOLAITANS. Nicolaus of Antioch (Acts 6:5) is supposed to have given his name to a group in the early church who sought to work out a compromise with paganism, to enable Christians to take part without embarrassment in some of the social and religious activities of the close-knit society in which they found themselves. It is possible that the term Nicolaitan is a Graecized form of Heb. Balaam, and therefore allegorical, the policy of the sect being likened to that of the OT corrupter of Israel (Nu. 22). In that case the Nicolaitans are to be identified with groups attacked by Peter (2 Pet. 2:15), Jude (11) and John (Rev. 2:6, 15 and possibly 2:20–23), for their advocacy within the church of pagan sexual laxity. References in Irenaeus, Clement and Tertullian suggest that the group hardened into a Gnostic sect. E.M.B.

NICOPOLIS ('city of victory'). A town built as the capital of Epirus by Augustus on a peninsula of the Ambraciot Gulf, where he had camped before his victory at Actium in 31 BC. It was a Rom. colony, and derived some of its importance from the Actian games, also established by Augustus.

Although there were other towns named Nicopolis, this was the only one of sufficient standing to warrant Paul's spending a whole winter in it (Tit. 3:12), and its geographical position would suit its selection as a rendezvous with Titus. Paul may have planned to use it as a base for evangelizing Epirus. There is no ancient authority for the AV subscription to the Epistle to Titus. K.L.McK.

NILE.

I. Terminology

The origin of Gk. *Neilos* and Lat. *Nilus*, our 'Nile', is uncertain. In the OT, with a few rare exceptions, the word *y*[e]*'ôr*, 'river, stream, channel', is used whenever the Egyp. Nile is meant. This Heb. word is itself directly derived from Egyp. *itrw* in the form *i'r(w)* current from the 18th Dynasty onwards, meaning 'Nile-river, stream, canal', *i.e.* the Nile and its various subsidiary branches and channels. (A. Erman and H. Grapow, *Wörterbuch der Aegyptischen Sprache*, 1, 1926, p. 146; T. O. Lambdin, *JAOS* 73, 1953, p. 151). In AV the word *y*[e]*'ôr* is hidden under various common nouns, 'river, flood', *etc*. Just once the word *nāhār*, 'river', is used of the Nile as the river of Egypt in parallel with the Euphrates, the *nāhār*, 'river' *par excellence*, the promised land lying between these two broad limits (Gn. 15:18). *nahal*, 'wadi', is apparently never used of the Nile, but of the Wadi el-'Arish or 'river of Egypt', while the Shihor is the seaward end of the E Delta branch of the Nile (*EGYPT, RIVER OF).

II. Course of the river

The ultimate origin of the Nile is the streams such as the Kagera that flow into Lake Victoria in Tanzania; from the latter, a river emerges N, *via* Lake Albert Nyanza and the vast Sudd swamps of the S Sudan, to become the White Nile. At Khartoum this is joined by the Blue Nile flowing down from Lake Tana in the Ethiopian (Abyssinian) highlands, and their united stream is the Nile proper. After being joined by the Atbara river some 320 km NE of Khartoum, the Nile flows for 2,700 km through the Sudan and Egypt N to the Mediterranean without receiving any other tributary; the total length of the river from Lake Victoria to the Mediterranean is roughly 5,600 km. Between Khartoum and Aswan, six 'sills' of hard granite rocks across the river's course give rise to the six cataracts that impede navigation on that part of its course.

Within Nubia and Upper Egypt, the Nile stream flows in a narrow valley which in Egypt is never much more than 20 km wide and often much less, bounded by hills or cliffs, beyond which stretch rocky deserts to E and W (*Egypt, II). Some 20 km N of Cairo, the river divides into two main branches that reach the sea at Rosetta in the W and Damietta in the E respectively; between and beyond these two great channels extend the flat, swampy lands of the Egyptian Delta. In Pharaonic Egypt three main branches of the Delta Nile seem to have been recognized ('Western river', Canopic branch?; 'the Great river', very roughly the present Damietta branch; 'the Waters of Rē'', or Eastern, Pelusiac branch, Heb. Shihor), besides various smaller branches, streams and canals. Gk. travellers and geographers reckoned from five to seven branches and mouths of the Nile. See A. H. Gardiner, *Ancient Egyptian Onomastica*, 2, 1947, pp. 153*–170*, with map between pp. 131* and 134*, on this tricky question; also J. Ball, *Egypt in the Classical Geographers*, 1942; M. Bietak, *Tell El-Dab'a*, 2, 1975.

III. The inundation and agriculture

The most remarkable feature of the Nile is its annual rise and flooding over its banks, or inundation. In spring and early summer in Ethiopia and S Sudan the heavy rains and melting highland snows turn the Upper Nile—specifically the Blue Nile—into a vast torrent bringing down in its waters masses of fine, reddish earth in suspension which it used to deposit on the lands flooded on either side of its banks in Egypt and Nubia. Thus, until the perennial irrigation-system of dams at Aswan and elsewhere was instituted last century, those areas of the Egyptian valley and Delta within reach of the floods received every year a thin, new deposit of fresh, fertile mud. The muddy flood-waters used to be held within basins bounded by earthen banks, to be released when the level of the Nile waters sank again. In Egypt the Nile is lowest in May; its rise there begins in June, the main flood-waters reach Egypt in July/August, reach their peak there in September and slowly decline again thereafter. But for the Nile and its inundation, Egypt would be as desolate as the deserts on either hand; wherever the Nile waters reach, vegetation can grow, life can exist. So sharp is the change from watered land to desert that one can stand with a foot in each. Egypt's agriculture depended wholly on the inundation, whose level was checked off against river-level gauges or Nilometers. A high flood produced the splendid crops that made Egypt's agricultural wealth proverbial. A low Nile, like drought in other lands, spelt famine; too high a Nile that swept away irrigation-works and brought destruction in its wake was no better. The regular rhythm of Egypt's Nile was familiar to the He-

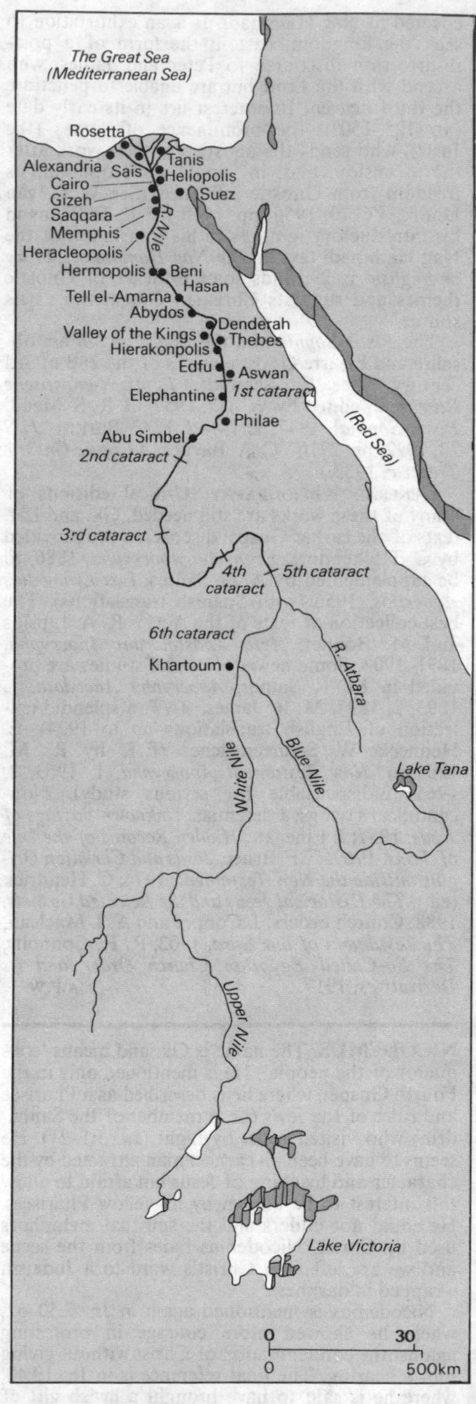

The course of the river Nile.

brews (*cf.* Is. 23:10; Am. 8:8; 9:5), and likewise the dependence of Egypt's cultivators, fisherfolk and marshes on those waters (Is. 19:5–8; 23:3). More than one prophet proclaimed judgment on Egypt in terms of drying up the Nile (Ezk. 30:12; *cf.*

29:10; Zc. 10:11), as other lands might be chastised by lack of rain (*cf.* *FAMINE). Jeremiah (46:7–9) compares the advance of Egypt's army with the surge of the rising Nile. On the inundation of the Nile, see G. Hort, *ZAW* 69, 1957, pp. 88–95; J. Ball, *Contributions to the Geography of Egypt*, 1939, *passim*; D. Bonneau, *La crue du Nil*, 1964.

IV. Other aspects

The Nile in dominating Egypt's agriculture also affected the form of her calendar, divided into three seasons (each of four 30-day months and excluding 5 additional days) called *'Akhet*, 'Inundation'; *Peret*, 'Coming Forth' (*i.e.* of the land from the receding waters); and *Shomu*, 'Dry(?)' or Summer season. The waters of the Nile not only supported crops but formed also the marshes for pasture (*cf.* Gn. 41:1–3, 17–18) and papyrus (*PAPYRI AND OSTRACA), and contained a wealth of fish caught by both line and net (Is. 19:8), *cf.* R. A. Caminos, *Late-Egyptian Miscellanies*, 1954, pp. 74, 200 (many sorts), and G. Posener *et al.*, *Dictionnaire de la Civilisation Égyptienne*, 1959, figures on pp. 214–215. On the plagues of a blood-red Nile, dead fish and frogs, *etc.*, *PLAGUES OF EGYPT. For Na. 3:8, *THEBES. The Assyrian's boast of drying up Egypt's streams (2 Ki. 19:24 = Is. 37:25) may refer to moats and similar river-defence works. For Moses in the rushes by the Nile, *MOSES. The Nile was also Egypt's main arterial highway; boats could sail N by merely going with the stream, and could as readily sail S with the aid of the cool N wind from the Mediterranean. In the religious beliefs of the Egyptians the spirit of the Nile-flood was the god Ha'pi, bringer of fertility and abundance. K.A.K.

NIMRIM, WATERS OF. The waters of Nimrim are mentioned twice (Is. 15:6; Je. 48:34). In substantially identical terms the prophets tell of the overthrow of Moab; cries of anguish go up from the cities of Moab, and 'the waters of Nimrim are a desolation'. Both in Isaiah and (especially) in Jeremiah the sequence of place-names suggests a site in S Moab, the now-customary identification with Wadi en-Numeirah, 16 km S of the Dead Sea. This is to be distinguished from Nimrah (Nu. 32:3) or Beth-nimrah (Nu. 32:36) about 16 km N of the Dead Sea. J.A.M.

NIMROD. The name of the son of Cush, an early warrior, or hero (*gibbōr*), who lived in Babylonia, where his kingdom included Babylon, Erech and Akkad (Gn. 10:8–10; 1 Ch. 1:10). He was father or founder of Nineveh and Calah in Assyria (Gn. 10:11) and was famous as a hunter (v. 9). The land adjacent to Assyria was later referred to as the 'land of Nimrod' (Mi. 5:6).

His name is perpetuated in several place-names, including Birs Nimrud, SW of Babylon, and Nimrud in Assyria (*CALAH). This, with the legends concerning him preserved in Sumerian, Assyr. and later literature, implies a wider basis in the tradition than is provided in Genesis. Many scholars therefore compare him with Sargon of Agade, *c.* 2300 BC, who was a great warrior and huntsman and ruler of Assyria. He led expeditions to the Mediterranean coast and into S Anatolia and Persia, and the splendour of his age and achievements led to its being recalled as a 'golden age'. Since only the throne-name of Sargon is known, it is possible that he bore other names. Others see in Nimrod exploits attributed to such early rulers as Naram-Sin of Agade, Tukulti-Ninurta I of Assyria (*Eretz Israel* 5, 1958, pp. 32*–36*); or deities as Ninurta (Nimurda), the Bab. and Assyr. god of war, and the hunter, or Amarutu, the Sumerian name of the god Marduk. No certain identification is yet possible. D.J.W.

NINEVEH. A principal city, and last capital, of Assyria. The ruins are marked by the mounds called Kuyunjik and Nabi Yunus ('Prophet Jonah') on the river Tigris opposite Mosul, N Iraq.

I. Name

The Heb. *nînʿwēh* (Gk. *Nineuē*; classical *Ninos*) represents the Assyr. *Ninuā* (Old Bab. *Ninuwa*), a rendering of the earlier Sumerian name *Nina*, a name of the goddess Ishtar written with a sign depicting a fish inside an enclosure. Despite the comparison with the history of Jonah, there is probably no connection with the Heb. *nūn*, 'fish'.

According to Gn. 10:11 Nineveh was one of the N cities founded by *Nimrod or Ashur after leaving Babylonia. Excavation 25 m down to virgin soil shows that the site was occupied from prehistoric times (*c.* 4500 BC). 'Ubaid (and Samarra) type pottery and pisée-buildings may indicate a S influence. Although first mentioned in the inscriptions of Gudea of Lagash who campaigned in the area *c.* 2200 BC, the texts of Tukulti-Ninurta I (*c.* 1230 BC) tell how he restored the temple of the goddess Ishtar of Nineveh founded by Manishtusu, son of Sargon, *c.* 2300 BC.

By the early 2nd millennium the city was in contact with the Assyr. colony of Kanish in Cappadocia, and when Assyria became independent under Shamshi-Adad I (*c.* 1800 BC) the same temple of Ishtar (called E-mash-mash) was again restored. Hammurapi of Babylon (*c.* 1750 BC) adorned the temple, but the expansion of the town followed the revival of Assyr. fortunes under Shalmaneser I (*c.* 1260 BC), and by the reign of Tiglath-pileser I (1114–1076 BC) it was established as an alternative royal residence to Assur and Calah. Both Ashurnasirpal II (883–859 BC) and Sargon II (722–705 BC) had palaces there. It was, therefore, likely that it was to Nineveh itself that the tribute of Menahem in 744 BC (2 Ki. 15:20) and of Samaria in 722 BC (Is. 8:4) was brought.

Sennacherib, with the aid of his W Semitic queen Naqi'a-Zakutu, extensively rebuilt the city, its defensive walls, gates and water-supply. He built a canal leading 48 km from a dam on the river Gomel to the N, and controlled the flow of the river Khasr, which flowed through the city, by the erection of another dam at Ajeila to the E. He also provided new administrative buildings and parks. The walls of his new palace were decorated with reliefs depicting his victories, including the successful siege of *Lachish. The tribute received from Hezekiah of Judah (2 Ki. 18:14) was sent to Nineveh, to which *Sennacherib himself had returned after the campaign (2 Ki. 19:36; Is. 37:37). It is possible that the temple of *Nisroch, where he was murdered, was in Nineveh. His account of his attack on Hezekiah in Jerusalem is recorded on clay prisms used as foundation inscriptions in Nineveh.

Ashurbanipal (669–*c.* 627 BC) again made

Nineveh his main residence, having lived there as crown prince. The bas-reliefs depicting a lion hunt (British Museum), which were made for his palace, are the best examples of this form of Assyr. art. The fall of the great city of Nineveh, as predicted by the prophets Nahum and Zephaniah, occurred in August 612 BC. The Bab. Chronicle tells how a combined force of Medes, Babylonians and Scythians laid siege to the city, which fell as a result of the breaches made in the defences by the flooding rivers (Na. 2:6–8). The city was plundered by the Medes, and the king Sin-shar-ishkun perished in the flames, though his family escaped. The city was left to fall into the heap of desolate ruin which it is today (Na. 2:10; 3:7), a pasturing-place for the flocks (Zp. 2:13–15), which gives the citadel mound its modern name of Tell Kuyunjik ('mound of many sheep'). When Xenophon and the retreating Gk. army passed in 401 BC it was already an unrecognizable mass of debris.

At the height of its prosperity Nineveh was enclosed by an inner wall of *c.* 12 km circuit within which, according to Felix Jones' survey of 1834, more than 175,000 persons could have lived. The population of 'this great city' of Jonah's history (1:2; 3:2) is given as 120,000, who did not know right from wrong. This has been compared with the 69,574 persons in *Calah (Nimrud) in 865 BC, then a city of about half the size of Nineveh. The 'three days' journey' may not necessarily designate the size of Nineveh (Jon. 3:3) whether by its circumference or total administrative district. It could refer to a day's journey in from the suburbs (*cf.* 3:4), a day for business and then return. The Heb. translation by using *nînᵉwēh* in each case could not differentiate between the district (Assyr. *ninua*[*ki*]) and metropolis ([*al*]ninuā). There is no external evidence for the repentance of the people of Nineveh (Jon. 3:4–5), unless this is reflected in a text from Guzanu (*GOZAN) of the reign of Ashur-dān III when a total solar eclipse in 763 BC was followed by flooding and famine. Such signs would be interpreted by the Assyrians as affecting the king who would temporarily step down from the throne (Jon. 3:6). Such portents, including an earthquake about the time of Jonah ben Amittai (2 Ki. 14:25), could well have made the Ninevites take the step commended by Jesus (Lk. 11:30; Mt. 12:41).

II. Exploration

Following reports made by such early travellers as John Cartwright (17th century) and plans drawn by C. J. Rich in 1820, interest was reawakened in the discovery of the OT city. Excavation was at first undertaken by P. E. Botta (1842–3), but with little success, and he abandoned the site, believing Khorsabad (16 km to the N) to be the biblical Nineveh. However, the diggings of Layard and Rassam (1845–54), which resulted in the discovery of the reliefs from the palaces of Sennacherib and Ashurbanipal together with many inscriptions, placed the identification beyond question. Following the discovery, among the 25,000 inscribed tablets from the libraries of Ashurbanipal and of the temple of Nabu (*ASSYRIA), of a Bab. account of the Flood (Epic of Gilgamesh) in 1872, the British Museum reopened the excavations under G. Smith (1873–6); E. A. W. Budge (1882–91); L. W. King (1903–5) and R. Campbell Thompson (1927–32). The Iraqi Government has continued work at the site (1963, 1966–74). The mound of Nabi Yunus covering a palace of Esarhaddon has been as yet little explored because it is still inhabited.

Nineveh, with its many reliefs and inscriptions, has done more than any other Assyrian site to elucidate the ancient history of *Assyria and *Babylonia, while the epics, histories, grammatical and scientific texts and letters have made Assyr. literature better known than that of any ancient Semitic peoples except the Hebrews (*ARCHAEOLOGY, *WRITING).

BIBLIOGRAPHY. R. Campbell Thompson and R. W. Hutchinson, *A Century of Exploration at Nineveh*, 1929; A. Parrot, *Nineveh and the Old Testament*, 1955. The exploration of Nineveh is described in full by A. H. Layard, *Nineveh and its Remains*, 1849; G. Smith, *Assyrian Discoveries*, 1875; R. Campbell Thompson (and others), *Liverpool Annals of Archaeology and Anthropology* 18–20, 1931–3; *Iraq* 1–52, 1934–90; *BA* 55, 1992, pp. 227–233. D.J.W.

NISROCH (Heb. *nisrōḵ*). The deity in whose temple Sennacherib was murdered by his sons as he worshipped (2 Ki. 19:37; Is. 37:38). The place of this assassination, which is mentioned also in Assyr. records (*DOTT*, pp. 70–73), is variously identified with one of the major cities, Nineveh, Assur or Calah. Nisroch may then be a rendering of the name of the Assyr. national god, Ashur (*cf.* LXX *Esdrach*, *Asorach*; *JRAS*, 1899, p. 459). A form of the god Nusku (assuming an original *nswk*) of Marduk, or a connection with the eagle-shaped army standards has also been suggested. D.J.W.

NITRE (Heb. *neṯer*). The modern name denotes saltpetre (sodium or potassium nitrate), but the biblical name refers to natron (carbonate of soda), which came chiefly from the 'soda lakes' of Lower Egypt. In Pr. 25:20 the effect of songs on a heavy heart is compared to the action of vinegar on nitre (RVmg. 'soda')—*i.e.* producing strong effervescence. RSV follows LXX: 'it is like pouring vinegar on a wound'. In Je. 2:22 nitre ('lye') is used in a purificatory sense: mixed with oil it formed a kind of *soap. (*ARTS AND CRAFTS, **III**. *h.*)

BIBLIOGRAPHY. R. J. Forbes, *Studies in Ancient Technology*, 3, 1955. J.D.D.

NOAH. The last of the ten antediluvian Patriarchs and hero of the *Flood. He was the son of Lamech, who was 182 (Samaritan Pentateuch, 53; LXX, 188) years old when Noah was born (Gn. 5:28–29; Lk. 3:36).

a. Name

The etymology of the name, *nōaḥ*, is uncertain, though many commentators connect it with the root *nwḥ*, 'to rest'. In Genesis (5:29) it is associated with the verb *nḥm* (translated 'comfort' in AV and RV; 'bring relief' in RSV), with which it is perhaps etymologically connected; though this is not necessarily required by the text. The element *nḥm* occurs in Amorite personal names and in the name Naḫmizuli which figures in a Hurrian fragment of the Gilgamesh epic found at Boğazköy, the Hittite capital in Asia Minor. The LXX gives the name as *Nōe*, in which form it appears in the NT (AV).

b. Life and character

Noah was a righteous man (Gn. 6:9, *ṣaddîq*), having the righteousness that comes of faith (Heb. 11:7, *hē kata pistin dikaiosynē*, lit. 'the according to faith righteousness'), and had close communion with God, as is indicated by the expression he 'walked with God' (Gn. 6:9). He is also described as without fault among his contemporaries (Gn. 6:9; AV 'perfect in his generations') who had all sunk to a very low moral level (Gn. 6:1–5, 11–13; Mt. 24:37–38; Lk. 17:26–27), and to them he preached righteousness (2 Pet. 2:5), though without success, as subsequent events showed. Like the other early Patriarchs, Noah was blessed with great length of years. He was 500 years old when his first son was born (Gn. 5:32), 600 when the *Flood came (Gn. 7:11) and died at the age of 950 (Gn. 9:28–29). According to the most likely interpretation of Gn. 6:3, together with 1 Pet. 3:20, when Noah was 480 years old God informed him that he was going to destroy man from the earth but would allow a period of grace for 120 years, during which time Noah was to build an *ark, in which he would save his immediate family and a representative selection of animals (Gn. 6:13–22). It was probably during this period that Noah preached, but there was no repentance, and the *Flood came and destroyed all but Noah, his three sons and their four wives (Gn. 7:7; 1 Pet. 3:20).

After the Flood Noah, who had probably been a farmer before it, planted a vineyard (Gn. 9:20; 'And Noah, the husbandman, began and planted a vineyard . . .', which is to be preferred to the EVV) and, becoming drunk, behaved in an unseemly way in his tent. *Ham, seeing his father naked, informed his two brothers, who covered him, but it is probable that Canaan, Ham's son, did something disrespectful to his grandfather, for Noah placed a curse on him when he awoke (Gn. 9:20–27).

c. God's covenant with Noah

The covenant implied in Gn. 6:18 might be interpreted as salvation for Noah conditional upon his building and entering the ark, which obligations he fulfilled (v. 22). On the other hand, it may be that this passage simply makes reference to the covenant which God made with Noah after the Flood, and which he sealed by conferring a new significance on the rainbow (Gn. 9:9–17; *cf.* Is. 54:9). The main features of this covenant were that it was entirely instituted by God, that it was universal in scope, applying not only to Noah and his seed after him but to every living creature, that it was unconditional, and that it was everlasting. In it God undertook from his own free lovingkindness never again to destroy all flesh with a flood.

d. Descendants

Noah had three sons, *Shem, *Ham and *Japheth (Gn. 5:32, 9:18–19; 10:1), who were born before the Flood, and accompanied him in the ark. We are told that after the Flood, from them 'was the whole earth (*'ereṣ*) overspread', or 'the whole (population of) the earth dispersed' (Gn. 9:19). Their descendants later spread out over a wide area, and an account is given of some of them in the Table of the *Nations in Gn. 10.

e. Cuneiform parallels

In the *flood accounts which have been preserved in Akkadian the name of the hero is Utanapishtim, which corresponds to the name Ziusuddu in a Sumerian account of the early 2nd millennium BC, which probably lies behind the Akkadian versions. Though in the principal version of the Sumerian king list only eight rulers are named before the Flood, of whom Ziusuddu is not one, other texts list ten rulers, the tenth being Ziusuddu, who is credited with a reign of 36,000 years. The same is found in a late account in Gk. by the Babylonian priest Berossos, whose flood hero Xisouthros is the tenth of his pre-flood rulers.

BIBLIOGRAPHY. J. Murray, *The Covenant of Grace*, 1954, pp. 12–16; E. A. Speiser, *Mesopotamian Origins*, 1930, pp. 160–161; H. B. Huffmon, *Amorite Personal Names in the Mari Texts*, 1965, pp. 237–239; E. Laroche, *Les noms des Hittites*, 1966, p. 125; T. Jacobsen, *The Sumerian King List*, 1939, pp. 76–77 and n. 34; F. F. Bruce, *NIDNTT* 2, pp. 681–683. T.C.M.

NOB. A locality mentioned in three passages of the OT, all of which may refer to the same place.

In 1 Sa. 22:19 it is referred to as a city of priests; presumably Yahweh's priests had fled there with the ephod after the capture of the ark and the destruction of Shiloh (1 Sa. 4:11). David visited Nob after he had escaped from Saul when Ahimelech was priest there and ate holy bread (1 Sa. 21:6). When Saul heard that the priest of Nob had assisted the fugitive David he raided the shrine and had Ahimelech, along with eighty-five other priests, put to death (1 Sa. 22:9, 11, 18–19).

Isaiah prophesied that the Assyrian invaders would reach Nob, between Anathoth, 4 km NE of Jerusalem, and the capital (Is. 10:32), and the city is also mentioned in Ne. 11:32 as a village which was reinhabited after the return from exile.

The latter two references indicate a locality near Jerusalem, probably the modern Râs Umm et-Tala on the E slopes of Mt Scopus, NE of Jerusalem (Grollenberg, *Atlas of the Bible*, 1956). S. R. Driver (*Notes on the Hebrew Text of the Books of Samuel*[2], 1913, p. 172) suggests perhaps a spot on the Rās el-Meshārif, under 2 km N of Jerusalem, a ridge from the brow of which (818 m) the pilgrim along the N road still catches his first view of the holy city (790 m). R.A.H.G.

NOBAH (Heb. *nōḇaḥ*). **1.** An Amorite locality settled and renamed by Nobah (see **2**) and his clan (Nu. 32:42). If the Amorite name Kenath indicates modern Kanawat (Eusebius' *Kanatha*), 96 km E of lake Tiberias, this can hardly be the Nobah of Jdg. 8:11, which must be in Mt Gilead.

2. A Manassite leader (Nu. 32:42). J.P.U.L.

NOD. A land E of, or in front of, Eden (*qiḏmaṯ-'ēḏen*, Gn. 4:16), to which Cain was banished by God after he had murdered Abel. The name (*nôḏ*) is the same in form as the infinitive of the verb *nûḏ* (*nwd*), 'to move to and fro, wander', the participle of which is used in Gn. 4:14 when Cain bemoans the fact that he will become a 'vagabond' (RSV 'wanderer'). The name is unknown outside the Bible, but its form and the context suggest that it was a region where a nomadic existence was necessary, such as is today found in several parts of the Middle East. T.C.M.

NODAB. A tribe which, among others, is mentioned in 1 Ch. 5:19 as having been conquered by Reuben, Gad and half-Manasseh, and about whom nothing more is definitely known. (*HAGARITES.) J.D.D.

NOMADS. A human group which changes its area of residence seasonally within a larger domain which is its home territory.

I. In the Bible

The word 'nomad' does not occur in EVV of the Bible, the nomadic groups being called by other names.

The first was *Cain, who was banished from his kindred to be a wanderer (Gn. 4). A number of nomadic groups are mentioned in the Table of the Nations in Gn. 10 (*NATIONS, TABLE OF). Among the descendants of *Japheth are *Gomer (Cimmerians), Madai (*MEDES), Meshek (perhaps Phrygians) and *Ashkenaz (Scythians), all peoples who probably came originally from the N steppe. Heth, among the children of Ham, may be the *Hittites of Asia Minor, though it is perhaps more probable that the reference is to the later Neo-Hittite states of N Syria. Among the descendants of Shem are listed *Aram (Aramaeans), and a number of Arabian tribes, some of them still nomadic in historical times, who stemmed from the Arabian peninsula.

The patriarchal period was largely a time of nomadism for God's chosen remnant. It is uncertain whether Abraham was actually living a sedentary life within the city of Ur when he was called by God. He is later called 'the Hebrew' (Gn. 14:13), and this may indicate that he was one of the Habiru (*HEBREWS) living outside the city in perhaps a client status. In such a situation he could still be a man of substance, as he undoubtedly was. How long he and his fathers had been at Ur is not stated, but when he left he began a nomadic life which was continued by Isaac and Jacob for two long generations, before the children of Israel settled to the sedentary life of Egypt (*cf.* Heb. 11:9). This was not the regular seasonal movement of nomads within a set territory, but a wandering from place to place; and, though Abraham had camels (*e.g.* Gn. 24; for the view of some scholars that patriarchal camels are anachronistic, see *CAMEL), his herds were largely of sheep and goats, and included asses (Gn. 22:3), so that some would class him as a semi-nomad or an 'ass-nomad'. Such a life would fit in well with the times as illuminated by the *Mari archives. Terah and his sons Nahor and Haran by remaining at Harran established affiliations with another nomadic group, the Aramaeans, as is shown by the reference to a 'wandering Aramaean' as the ancestor of the Israelites (Dt. 26:5).

After experiencing the luxuries of a sedentary life in Egypt, even though oppressed, the Israelites at the Exodus were reluctant to return to the rigours of wandering. The 40 years in the wilderness was a unique episode, for without the miraculous supply of food provided by God the numbers of the people would have been far too great to be supported by the natural resources of the area.

After the settlement in the Promised Land the true nomadic life ceased for the Israelites, but various reminiscences of it survive in the OT. For instance, in many cases a man's house is referred to as his 'tent' (*e.g.* Jdg. 20:8; 1 Sa. 13:2; 2 Sa. 20:1; 1 Ki. 12:16). To express the idea of rising early the verb *šāḵam* (in the Hiph'îl stem), which properly means 'to load the backs (of beasts)', is used (*e.g.* Jdg. 19:9; 1 Sa. 17:20). Certain metaphors used in poetry suggest a nomadic background: in Jb. 4:21 (RSV) the plucking up of a tent-cord signifies death; in Je. 10:20 the breaking of tent-cords indicates desolation, and conversely, a sound tent speaks of security (Is. 33:20); in Is. 54:2 a prosperous people is signified by an enlarged tent space.

The Israelites came in contact with various nomadic groups after they had settled in the land. The Aramaeans had by the 1st millennium largely settled in the city states of Syria, so that the nomadic threat came mostly from the E and S, where the *bᵉnê qeḏem*, 'the Children of the East' (*cf.* Ezk. 25:4) and such associated peoples as the *Midianites, *Amalekites, *Moabites, *Edomites, *Ammonites and *Kedarites would always take advantage of weakness in the settled territories. Solomon's commercial expansion in the 10th century brought contacts with *Arabia and the caravan traders of that area. In the 9th century Jehoshaphat was able to exact tribute from the Arabs (2 Ch. 17:11), but the family of Jehoram were carried off by this people in a raid (2 Ch. 21:16–17). Throughout the Monarchy, the Arabs are mentioned in various capacities (*e.g.* Is. 13:20; 21:13; Je. 3:2; 25:23–24; Ezk. 27:21).

After the return from the Exile the nomadic traders who were settling on the E fringes of Syria–Palestine are exemplified by *Geshem the Arab, who tried to hinder the rebuilding of Jerusalem (Ne. 2:19; 6:6). These people were followed in NT times by the *Nabataeans.

With the moral corruption which accompanied the settlement in the land, the prophets used the ideal of the nomadic life as a figure of spiritual health. They condemned the luxuries of city life (Am. 3:15; 6:8) and spoke of a return to the simplicity of the early days of Israel in the wilderness (Ho. 2:14–15; 12:9). It is probable that this call to the desert was put into practice from time to time, as is evidenced by the Qumran Community (*DEAD SEA SCROLLS) in the intertestamental period, and by John the Baptist, and Jesus Christ and his disciples in NT times. Though this was not nomadism in the strict sense, it was a manifestation of that value of nomadism which has always been held forth as an aim for God's people; to be pilgrims in this world, and to avoid the laying up of treasure upon earth. (*RECHABITES; *KENITES.)

II. Way of life

A nomadic group depends for its livelihood upon herds of animals such as the horse, camel, sheep, goat or ox, and the pasturing needs of the herds determine the movements of the community. This way of life is required by the terrain inhabited, which usually consists mainly of an area of steppe or plain which provides temporary pasture in the wet or cool season, and either oases or uplands to which a retreat is made in the dry season. Under normal conditions a nomadic tribe will have a recognized home territory, visiting different parts regularly in a seasonal cycle. Thus each tribe or, in more barren areas, smaller group visits annually its recognized tract of pasture, and returns annually to the same oasis or upland territory. Mobile dwellings are provided by tents of skins, felt or wool, and all equipment is strictly limited. There are variations from area to area. Some groups, mainly camel herders, abandon the plain for an oasis or upland only when compelled by drought; others, particularly shepherds, have semi-permanent dwellings at the oasis, even planting and raising crops, and go out on the plain only when the animals' needs for pasture compel it. Peoples of this latter type are sometimes called semi-nomads.

Such an economy is finely adjusted, and the natural increase of population disturbs the balance. In consequence, a growing group may encroach on a neighbour's traditional territory, and the weaker group be displaced, perhaps setting up a chain effect which may cause the fringe groups to look abroad. Sedentary farming communities fall an easy prey to the overspilling nomads who may set themselves as a military aristocracy over the less-vigorous population. A few generations, however, usually suffice for the interlopers to be absorbed by the dominant though less-aggressive culture of the settled peoples.

The most advantageous situation for a nomadic group is in a mixed country where city-states and their surrounding tilled territory are interspersed by less-intensively settled areas where the nomad can make his encampments and exploit the vulnerable settlements. This may be done either by mobile raids or by taking service either as mercenary troops or as labourers.

Certain values arise from the demands of the nomadic life. The mutual dependence of the members of a tribe, together with the consciousness of common descent, lead to great solidarity (*FAMILY) and to such concomitant practices as blood revenge (*AVENGER OF BLOOD) for murder or manslaughter. The need for mobility results in the reduction of property to that which is movable, wealth being accumulated in livestock. The rigours of life lead also to hospitality to the traveller and to chivalry, sometimes of a kind strange to the sedentary farmer.

III. The ancient Near East

There were two main areas supporting nomadic populations in ancient times, from which the more settled regions of the Near East suffered the influx of marauders. These were the peninsula of Arabia and the steppe of S Russia. Access from Arabia was easier than from the N, since the latter area lay across a mountain barrier, and for the nomads of N Arabia some of the oases visited seasonally lay on the very margins of the settled areas of Palestine and Syria.

a. The southern nomads

It is probable that Arabia was the immediate homeland of the Semites (Semitic speakers), and since from the earliest historical times in Mesopotamia the Semitic Akkadians formed part of the population, a continual influx of nomads from the Arabian peninsula may be inferred. Knowledge of the arrival of nomads from Arabia is very much conditioned by the surviving evidence. Written records are meagre from Palestine, intermittent from Syria, but more extensive from Mesopotamia. In Mesopotamia, however, the fullest records come from periods of political strength, when encroaching nomads could be most effectively resisted, and indeed, according to the records, the best-attested route of overt entry to Mesopotamia was from the N, though a peaceful infiltration into Babylonia from the W may be assumed. The early part of the 2nd millennium BC, following the fall of the 3rd Dynasty of Ur, was a period of weakness in Babylonia, and of consequent nomadic invasions from the N, the invaders, particularly the *'Amorites', finally establishing themselves as ruling dynasties in the cities of Babylonia. During the time of the greatest of these dynasties, the 1st of Babylon, the diplomatic archives discovered at the city of *Mari on the Middle Euphrates give a glimpse of the situation in N Mesopotamia–Syria, where the city-states were interspersed by territory occupied by nomadic groups. One group known as the Hanaeans (*Ḫanû*) provided the king of Mari with mercenary troops, and, though they lived in encampments, some of them were beginning to settle in permanent dwellings. A more troublesome group were the Yaminites (sometimes read Bini-Yamin; the writing is more likely to have been read *mārū yamīn*; *BENJAMIN, TUR [pl]-*ya-mi-in*), who spread through the steppe area between the Ḫabur river and the Euphrates and farther W, particularly in the vicinity of Harran, being frequently mentioned as raiding settlements and even attacking towns. The Sutaeans (*Sutû*) likewise raided farther S, particularly on the trade routes connecting the Euphrates with Syria. Another group of people, the Habiru (*HEBREWS), who are mentioned in the second half of the 2nd millennium in documents from Nuzi, Alalaḫ, Hattusas, Ugarit, el-Amarna and in native Egyp. documents, are already mentioned earlier (18th century BC) in the Mari letters and in documents of the same general period from Alalaḫ, Cappadocia and S Mesopotamia. These people seem to have been nomads or semi-nomads who are found now as raiders, now as settlers in the towns, serving sometimes as mercenary troops, and sometimes as labourers or even slaves.

These are the principal nomadic groups mentioned in the Mari archives from this period, but they were no doubt typical of peoples at other periods who menaced the isolated city-states, particularly of N Mesopotamia and Syria–Palestine. Some were probably more in the nature of travelling craftsmen than raiders, and such a group is depicted on a 19th-century BC wall painting at Beni Hasan in Egypt (see *IBA*, fig. 25).

In the succeeding centuries another nomadic group which spread through Syria–Palestine and into *Egypt was the Hyksos, and again mainly during the 2nd millennium yet another body of nomads, the *Aramaeans, and a related group, the Aḫlamu, began to come into prominence. During the centuries around the turn of the 2nd to the 1st millennium, these people and their congeners flooded W Asia, putting a halt to the growing dominion of Assyria, and founding many city-states in the area of Syria and N Mesopotamia.

These groups of nomads are the principal ones known from the written documents, who probably came ultimately from the Arabian peninsula. More directly from the peninsula were groups of Arabs (*ARABIA), who are mentioned in the Assyr. inscriptions and depicted in the bas-reliefs as riding camels and living in tents. Later in the 1st millennium such posts as Petra and Palmyra were settled by Arab tribes who were able to profit from the caravan traffic.

b. The northern nomads

Access to the Near East was more difficult for the N nomads who inhabited the S Russian steppe; the principal route of entry was between the Caspian and the Black Seas and into Asia Minor and Iran. Signs of the influx of the N nomads are found already in the middle of the 3rd millennium at the 'Royal Tombs' of Alaca Hüyük in central Asia Minor, where a warrior aristocracy had imposed itself on the peasant population. These were predecessors of the Indo-European-speaking Hittites who established an empire in Asia Minor in the 2nd millennium. It is clear that, like the Hittites, many of the invaders from the N were Indo-European-speaking. In the 2nd millennium the Kassites in Babylonia and the rulers of Mitanni in N Mesopotamia betray, in their names and certain elements of vocabulary, their Indo-European origins. These people were among the first to introduce the *horse and *chariot to W Asia, and it is probable that this was a combination developed on the steppe. In the late 2nd millennium the Phrygians in Asia Minor repeated the pattern of a dominating warrior aristocracy, and later the Cimmerians are encountered as warlike raiders. In the 1st millennium the Medes and Persians came to prominence in Iran, the latter finally founding an empire which dominated the entire Near East. In the Assyr. inscriptions the earlier groups of the raiding warriors are known as Ummanmanda (*ASSYRIA).

BIBLIOGRAPHY. *General:* C. D. Forde, *Habitat, Economy and Society*[4], 1942, pp. 308–351. *Bible:* R. de Vaux, *Ancient Israel*, 1961, pp. 3–15, 519–520; D. J. Wiseman, *The Word of God for Abraham and Today*, 1959, pp. 10–12; *DBS* 6, coll. 541–550. *Ancient Near East:* F. Gabrieli (ed.), *L'Antica Società Beduina*, 1959; J. R. Kupper, *Les nomades en Mésopotamie au temps des rois de Mari*, 1957; S. Moscati, *The Semites in Ancient History*, 1959; T. T. Rice, *The Scythians*, 1958, esp. pp. 33–55; M. B. Rowton, 'Autonomy and Nomadism in Western Asia', *Or* 42, 1973, pp. 247–258; 'Dimorphic Structure and the Problem of the 'Apirû-'Ibrîm', *JNES* 35, 1976, pp. 13–20. T.C.M.

NOSE, NOSTRILS (Heb. *'ap̄*, 'nose' or 'nostril'). The organ of breathing, used also of the face, perhaps by synecdoche, especially in the expression 'face to the ground' in worship or homage. The Hebrews apparently thought no further into the respiratory process, and no word for lung occurs in the Bible. The presence of breath in the nostrils was connected with *life (Gn. 2:7; Jb. 27:3), and the temporary nature thereof (Is. 2:22). The word also denotes the nose as the organ of smelling (Ps. 115:6; Am. 4:10). When breath was emitted visibly (called 'smoke', Ps. 18:8) it was connected with the expression of inner emotion, principally anger. By metonymy the word *'ap̄* often comes to mean 'anger' (Gn. 27:45; Jb. 4:9), and is used figuratively thus in the OT far more frequently than in the literal sense. It is apparent from cognate languages (*e.g.* Akkad. *appu*, 'face') that the physical designation is the original. The word is not found in the NT. B.O.B.

NUMBER.

I. General usage

Israel shared with most of her Mediterranean and Near Eastern neighbours, *e.g.* Assyria, Egypt, Greece, Rome and Phoenicia, the decimal system of counting. The numbers recorded in the Heb. text of the OT are written in words, as in the main are the figures in the Gk. text of the NT. Numbers are also written in word form on the Moabite Stone and the Siloam Inscription.

In Heb. the number one is an adjective. A series of nouns denote the numbers 2 to 10. Combinations of these numbers with 10 give 11 to 19. After 20 the tens are formed in a pattern similar to that used in Eng., *i.e.* 3, 30. A separate word denotes 100; 200 is the dual form of this, and from 300 to 900 there is again a pattern similar to that found in the Eng. numeral system. The highest number expressed by one word is 20,000, the dual form of 10,000.

Aram. papyri from Egypt from the 6th to the 4th centuries BC, Aramaic endorsements on cuneiform tablets from Mesopotamia and Heb. ostraca and weights provide evidence of an early system of numerical notation within the OT period. Vertical strokes were used for digits and horizontal strokes for tens, written one above the other for multiples of ten, often with a downward stroke on the right. A stylized *mem* represented 100 with vertical strokes for additional hundreds. An abbreviation of the word 'a thousand' was used to indicate this figure. It is considered that the Heb. material shows that a sign resembling a Gk. *lambda* represented 5 and a sign similar to an early *gimel* stood for 4. See Y. Yadin, *Scripta Hierosolymitana*, 8, 1961, pp. 9–25. (*WEIGHTS AND MEASURES.)

H. L. Allrick (*BASOR* 136, 1954, pp. 21–27) proposes that originally the lists in Ne. 7 and Ezr. 2 were written in the early Heb.–Aram. numeral notation, and he suggests that an explanation of certain differences between the lists may be found in this fact. See A. R. Millard, *TynB* 11, 1962, pp. 6–7, for evidence of Heb. numerical signs.

The idea of using letters of the alphabet for numerals originated from Gk. influence or at least during the period of Gk. influence, and, as far as is known, first appeared on Maccabean coins. See however G. R. Driver, *Textus* 1, 1960, pp. 126f.; 4, 1964, p. 83, for indication of earlier origin. The first nine letters were used for the figures 1 to 9, the tens from 10 to 90 were represented by the next nine and the hundreds from 100 to 400 by the remaining four letters. The number 15, however, was denoted by a combination of *teṭh* (9) and *waw* (6), as the two letters *yod* (10) and *he* (5) were the consonants of Yah, a form of the sacred name Yahweh. Further numbers were denoted by a combination of letters. There are ordinal numbers in biblical Heb. from 1 to 10, after which the cardinal numbers are used. There are also words for fractions from a half to a fifth. Numbers in biblical Gk. follow the pattern used in Hellenistic Gk.

An indication of the mathematical concept of infinity may be found in the statement in Rev. 7:9 where the redeemed are 'a great multitude, which no man could number'. In a concrete image this concept is expressed in the OT as, *e.g.*, Gn. 13:16. *Cf.* also Gn. 15:5.

The elementary processes of arithmetic are recorded in the OT, *e.g.* addition, Nu. 1:17ff. and Nu. 1:45; subtraction, Lv. 27:18; multiplication, Lv. 25:8.

In certain passages it is evident that numbers are being used in an approximate sense. The numbers '2', '2 or 3', '3 or 4', '4 or 5' are sometimes used with the meaning of 'a few', *e.g.* 1 Ki. 17:12, where the widow of Zarephath says, 'I am gathering a couple of sticks', and also Lv. 26:8 'five of you shall chase a hundred'. Similar usages are found in 2 Ki. 6:10; Is. 17:6; for 'three or four', see Am. 1:3ff. and Pr. 30:15ff. From the NT we may quote the use of round numbers by Paul in 1 Cor. 14:19. 'Nevertheless in the church I would rather speak five words with my mind, in order to instruct others, than ten thousand words in a tongue.' *Cf.* also Mt. 18:22.

It would seem that '10' was used as the equivalent of 'quite a number of times', and we may instance Jacob's words in Gn. 31:7, where it is recorded that Laban changed his wages '10 times'; *cf.* also Nu. 14:22. That Saul, David and Solomon are recorded as having reigned for 40 years, and the recurring statement in the book of Judges that the land had rest 40 years (Jdg. 3:11; 5:31; 8:28) seem to indicate that 40 was used to stand for a generation, or quite a considerable number, or length of time. 100, *e.g.* Ec. 6:3, would equal a large number, and 1,000, 10,000 (Dt. 32:30; Lv. 26:8), and 40,000 (Jdg. 5:8) provide instances of round numbers which indicate an indefinitely large number. In the case of large numbers for the strength of armies, *e.g.* 2 Ch. 14:9, these are in all probability approximate estimates, as also seems to be the case with the number of David's census (2 Sa. 24:9; *cf.* 1 Ch. 21:5), and perhaps the 7,000 sheep sacrificed in Jerusalem (2 Ch. 15:11).

II. Large numbers in the Old Testament

The large numbers recorded in certain parts of the OT have occasioned considerable difficulties. These are concerned chiefly with the chronology of the early periods of OT history, where the problem is further complicated by the presence of differing figures in the various texts and versions, with the numbers of the Israelites at the time of the Exodus, and the numbers of warriors in various armies, and especially of the numbers of the slain of enemy forces. With regard to the first problem one may instance that the Heb. text gives 1,656 years as the time between the creation and the Flood, the LXX 2,262 years and the Samaritan 1,307. Or for the age of Methuselah the Heb. text gives 969 years and the Samaritan 720. (*GENEALOGY; *CHRONOLOGY OF THE OLD TESTAMENT.) A similar problem exists in the NT regarding the number of persons on board the ship on which Paul travelled to Rome. Some MSS give 276 and others 76 (Acts 27:37). Again the number of the beast (Rev. 13:18) is given variously as 666 and 616.

An indication that numbers might suffer textual corruption in transmission is provided by differing numbers in parallel texts, *e.g.* the age of Jehoiachin at the beginning of his reign is given as 18 in 2 Ki. 24:8 and 8 in 2 Ch. 36:9.

Archaeological discoveries have contributed considerable background information to the age of the Exodus and the conquest of Palestine, and the contemporary population. Given that the Israelites were less in number than the Canaanites, as may be inferred from Ex. 23:29 and Dt. 7:7, 17, 22, the census numbers of Nu. 1 and 26 which imply a population of 2–3 million require investigation.

Divergent interpretations of the figures have been proposed, from acceptance at face value, *e.g.* *NBC*, 1953, p. 165, to J. Bright, *A History of Israel*[2], 1972, p. 130: 'these lists . . . represent a later period of Israel's history'. Attempts have been made to retranslate the figures and so reduce them. The Heb. word *'elep̄*, 'a thousand', can be translated 'family', 'tent group', or 'clan': *e.g.* Jdg. 6:15, 'my clan (*'alpî*) is the weakest in Manasseh'. The following may also be consulted: F. Petrie, *Egypt and Israel*, 1911, pp. 42ff.; G. E. Mendenhall, 'The Census Lists of Numbers 1 and 26', *JBL* 77, 1958, pp. 52ff.; C. S. Jarvis, *Yesterday and Today in Sinai*, 1936; R. E. D. Clark, 'The Large Numbers of the OT', *JTVI* 87, 1955, pp. 82ff.

J. W. Wenham (*TynB* 18, 1967, pp. 19–53), following R. E. D. Clark's repointing of *'elep̄* 'thousand' to *'allûp̄*, translated 'officer' or 'trained warrior', and interpreting *mē'ôṯ* 'hundreds' as 'contingents', suggests that the individual large numbers consist of a coalescence of these two terms in a specific ratio. The number of fighting men would then be reduced to 18,000 and, allowing for Levites and those too old to fight, an estimated male population would total 36,000, consistent with the figure for first-born males (22,273) in Nu. 3:43. This figure, doubled to include women, gives a calculated Israelite population of 72,000.

Revocalization of *'elep̄* to *'allûp̄* 'officer', 'captain', provides a possible solution to the enormous numbers of fallen in battle, recorded in thousands, and is consistent with practice in ancient battles where mighty men did most of the fighting, *e.g.* David and Goliath.

III. Significant numbers

Numbers are also used with a symbolical or theological significance.

One is used to convey the concept of the unity and uniqueness of God, *e.g.* Dt. 6:4, 'The Lord our God is one Lord'. The human race stems from one (Acts 17:26). The entry of sin into the world is through one man (Rom. 5:12). The gift of grace is by one man, Jesus Christ (Rom. 5:15). His sacrifice in death is a once-for-all offering (Heb. 7:27), and he is the first-born from the dead (Col. 1:18), the firstfruits of the dead (1 Cor. 15:20). 'One' also expresses the unity between Christ and the Father (Jn. 10:30), the union between believers and the Godhead, and the unity which exists among Christians (Jn. 17:21; Gal. 3:28). 'One' further expresses singleness of purpose (Lk. 10:42). The concept of union is also found in the saying of Jesus concerning marriage, 'and the two shall become one' (Mt. 19:6).

Two can be a figure both of unity and of division. Man and woman form the basic family unit (Gn. 1:27; 2:20, 24). Animals associate in pairs and enter the ark in twos (Gn. 7:9). Two people often work together in companionship, *e.g.* Joshua's spies (Jos. 2:1), and the Twelve and Seventy disciples were sent out in pairs (Mk. 6:7; Lk. 10:1). In addition, at Sinai there were two stone tablets, and animals were often offered for sacrifice in pairs. By contrast two is used with separating force in 1 Ki. 18:21, as it is also implied in the two 'ways' of Mt. 7:13–14.

Three. It is natural to associate the number 3 with the Trinity of Persons in the Godhead, and the following references among others may be instanced: Mt. 28:19; Jn. 14:26; 15:26; 2 Cor. 13:14; 1 Pet. 1:2, where this teaching is implied. The number 3 is also associated with certain of God's mighty acts. At Mt Sinai the Lord was to come down to give his Law on 'the third day' (Ex. 19:11). In Hosea's prophecy the Lord would raise up his people 'on the third day', probably meaning a short time (Ho. 6:2). There is a similar usage of

	AKKADIAN	EGYPTIAN		EARLY HEBREW	PHOENICIAN	POST-EXILIC HEBREW	GREEK	
		Hieroglyphic	Hieratic				Before 200BC	After 200BC
1	𒁹	|	ǀ	|	|	𐡀 א	|	A
2	𒈫	||	ıı	||	||	𐡁 ב	||	B
3	𒐈	|||	ııı	|||	|||	𐡂 ג	|||	Γ
4	𒐉	||||	ıııı	||||	||||	𐡃 ד	||||	Δ
5	𒐊	|||||	[illegible]	ᒣ	|||||	𐡄 ה	Γ	E
6	𒐋	||||||	[illegible]		||||||	ו	ΓΙ	F
7	𒐌	|||||||	[illegible]		|||||||	ז	ΓΙΙ	Z
8	𒐍	||||||||	=		||||||||	ח	ΓΙΙΙ	H
9	𒐎, [illegible]	|||||||||	[illegible]		|||||||||	ט	ΓΙΙΙΙ	Θ
10	𒌋	∩	[illegible]	Λ	𐤗	י	Δ	I
20	𒎙	∩∩	[illegible]	χ	𐤘, [illegible]	כ	ΔΔ	K
30	𒌍			ϯ	𐤗𐤘, [illegible]	ל	ΔΔΔ	Λ
40	𒐏					מ	ΔΔΔΔ	M
50	𒐐			ʔ		נ	𐅄	N
60	𒁹					ס	𐅄Δ	Ξ
70	𒁹𒌋					ע		O
80						פ		Π
90						צ		Ϙ

100	[illegible]	[illegible]	[illegible]		צ׳, א׳	ק	Η	Ρ
200			[illegible]			ר	ΗΗ	Σ
300						ש		Τ
400						ת		Υ
500						תק	𐅅	Φ
600	[illegible]							Χ
700								Ψ
800								Ω
900								Ͳ
1,000	[illegible]	[illegible]	[illegible]		ח	תתר	Χ	/Α
2,000			[illegible]					
3,600	[illegible]							
10,000		[illegible]	[illegible]				Μ	
20,000			[illegible]					
100,000		[illegible]	[illegible]					
200,000			[illegible]					
1,000,000			[illegible]					
2,000,000			[illegible]					
5,000,000		[illegible]						

Table of numerals in use during the biblical period.

'three' in Lk. 13:32, where 'third day' is 'poetical for the moment when something is finished, completed, and perfected' (N. Geldenhuys, *Commentary on the Gospel of Luke*, 1950, p. 384, n. 4). Jonah was delivered (Jon. 1:17; Mt. 12:40), and God raised Christ from the dead, on the third day (1 Cor. 15:4). There were three disciples admitted to special terms of intimacy with Christ (Mk. 9:2; Mt. 26:37), and at Calvary there were three crosses. Paul emphasizes three Christian virtues (1 Cor. 13:13). A further instance of three being used in connection with periods of time is the choice offered to David of 3 days' pestilence, 3 months' defeat or 3 years' famine (1 Ch. 21:12). The deployment of Gideon's army furnishes an example of division into three (Jdg. 7:16), and the fraction, a third, is employed in Rev. 8:7–12.

Four, the number of the sides of a square, is one of symbols of completion in the Bible. The divine name Yahweh has 4 letters in Heb. (*YHWH*). There were 4 rivers flowing out of the garden of Eden (Gn. 2:10) and there are 4 corners of the earth (Rev. 7:1; 20:8), from whence blow the 4 winds (Je. 49:36; Ezk. 37:9; Dn. 7:2). In his vision of the glory of God, Ezekiel saw 4 living creatures (ch. 1), and with these we may compare the 4 living creatures of Rev. 4:6.

The history of the world from the time of the Babylonian empire is spanned by 4 kingdoms (Dn. 2; 7). Four is a prominent number in prophetic symbolism and apocalyptic literature, as the following additional references show: 4 smiths and 4 horns (Zc. 1:18–21), 4 chariots (Zc. 6:1–8), 4 horns of the altar (Rev. 9:13), 4 angels of destruction (Rev. 9:14). In addition, there are 4 Gospels, and at the time when the gospel was extended to the Gentiles Peter saw in a vision a sheet let down by its 4 corners.

Five and *ten*, and their multiples, occur frequently on account of the decimal system used in Palestine. In the OT 10 Patriarchs are mentioned before the Flood. The Egyptians were visited with 10 plagues and there were Ten Commandments. The fraction one-tenth formed the tithe (Gn. 14:20; 28:22; Lv. 27:30; 2 Ch. 31:5; Mal. 3:10). In the parable of Lk. 15:8 the woman possessed 10 coins, and in the parable of the pounds mention is made of 10 pounds, 10 servants and 10 cities (Lk. 19:11–27). Of the 10 virgins, 5 were wise and 5 foolish (Mt. 25:2). 5 sparrows were sold for 2 farthings (Lk. 12:6); Dives had 5 brothers (Lk. 16:28); the woman by the well had had 5 husbands (Jn. 4:18), and at the feeding of the 5,000 the lad had 5 loaves. There are 10 powers which cannot separate the believer from the love of God (Rom. 8:38f.) and 10 sins which exclude from the kingdom of God (1 Cor. 6:10). The number 10, therefore, also signifies completeness; 10 elders form a company (Ru. 4:2).

Six. In the creation narrative God created man and woman on the 6th day (Gn. 1:27). 6 days were allotted to man for labour (Ex. 20:9; 23:12; 31:15; *cf*. Lk. 13:14). A Heb. servant had to serve for 6 years before he was freed. The number 6 is therefore closely associated with man.

Seven has an eminent place among sacred numbers in the Scriptures, and is associated with completion, fulfilment and perfection. In the creation narrative God rested from his work on the 7th day, and sanctified it. This gave a pattern to the Jewish sabbath on which man was to refrain from work (Ex. 20:10), to the sabbatic year (Lv. 25:2–6), and also to the year of jubilee, which followed 7 times 7 years (Lv. 25:8). The Feast of Unleavened Bread and the Feast of Tabernacles lasted 7 days (Ex. 12:15, 19; Nu. 29:12). The Day of Atonement was in the 7th month (Lv. 16:29), and 7 occurs frequently in connection with OT ritual, *e.g.* the sprinkling of bullock's blood 7 times (Lv. 4:6) and the burnt-offering of 7 lambs (Nu. 28:11); the cleansed leper was sprinkled 7 times (Lv. 14:7), and Naaman had to dip 7 times in Jordan (2 Ki. 5:10). In the tabernacle the candlestick had 7 branches (Ex. 25:32).

Other references to be noted are: the mother of 7 sons (Je. 15:9; 2 Macc. 7:1ff.); 7 women for one man (Is. 4:1); a loving daughter-in-law preferable to 7 sons (Ru. 4:15). The Sadducees proposed a case of levirate marriage with 7 brothers (Mt. 22:25). The priests encompassed Jericho 7 times (Jos. 6:4). Elijah's servant looked for rain 7 times (1 Ki. 18:43). The psalmist praised God 7 times a day (Ps. 119:164), and Gn. 29:18; 41:29, 54 and Dn. 4:23 mention 7 years (times). The early church had 7 deacons (Acts 6:3) and John addresses 7 churches in the book of Revelation, where there is mention of 7 golden candlesticks (1:12) and 7 stars (1:16). At the miraculous feeding of 4,000 from 7 loaves and a few fishes (Mk. 8:1–9), the 7 basketsful collected afterwards may indicate that Jesus can satisfy completely. The complete possession of Mary Magdalene is effected by 7 demons (Lk. 8:2), while the dragon of Rev. 12:3 and the beast of Rev. 13:1; 17:7 have 7 heads.

Eight. 1 Pet. 3:20 records that 8 people were saved in the ark of Noah. Circumcision of a Jewish boy took place on the 8th day (Gn. 17:12; Phil. 3:5). In Ezekiel's vision of the new Temple the priests make their offering on the 8th day (43:27).

Ten. See *Five*.

Twelve. The Heb. year was divided into 12 months, the day into 12 hours (Jn. 11:9). Israel had 12 sons (Gn. 35:22–27; 42:13, 32) and there were 12 tribes of Israel, the people of God (Gn. 49:28). Christ chose 12 apostles (Mt. 10:1ff.). Twelve is therefore linked with the elective purposes of God.

Forty is associated with almost each new development in the history of God's mighty acts, especially of salvation, *e.g.* the Flood, redemption from Egypt, Elijah and the prophetic era, the advent of Christ and the birth of the church. The following periods of 40 days may be listed: the downpour of rain during the Flood (Gn. 7:17); the despatch of the raven (Gn. 8:6); Moses' fasts on the mount (Ex. 24:18; 34:28; Dt. 9:9); the spies' exploration of the land of Canaan (Nu. 13:25); Moses' prayer for Israel (Dt. 9:25); Goliath's defiance (1 Sa. 17:16); Elijah's journey to Horeb (1 Ki. 19:8); Ezekiel's lying on his right side (Ezk. 4:6); Jonah's warning to Nineveh (Jon. 3:4); Christ's stay in the wilderness prior to his temptation (Mt. 4:2), his appearances after his resurrection (Acts 1:3).

For 40 years, the general designation of a generation, the following may be quoted: the main divisions of Moses' life (Acts 7:23, 30, 36; Dt. 31:2); Israel's wandering in the wilderness (Ex. 16:35; Nu. 14:33; Jos. 5:6; Ps. 95:10); the recurring pattern of servitude and deliverance in the era of the judges (*e.g.* Jdg. 3:11; 13:1); the reigns of Saul, David and Solomon (Acts 13:21; 2 Sa. 5:4; 1 Ki. 11:42); the desolation of Egypt (Ezk. 29:11).

Seventy is often connected with God's administration of the world. After the Flood the world was repopulated through 70 descendants of Noah (Gn. 10); 70 persons went down to Egypt (Gn. 46:27); 70 elders were appointed to help Moses administer Israel in the wilderness (Nu. 11:16); the people of Judah spent 70 years of exile in Babylon (Je. 25:11; 29:10); 70 weeks, 'sevens', were decreed by God as the period in which Messianic redemption was to be accomplished (Dn. 9:24); Jesus sent forth the Seventy (Lk. 10:1); he enjoined forgiveness 'until seventy times seven' (Mt. 18:22).

666 (or *616*) is the number of the beast in Rev. 13:18. Many interpretations of this number have been proposed, and by *gematria*, in which figures are given the value of corresponding letters, the number 666 has been identified with the numerical values of the names of a variety of personalities from Caligula and Nero Caesar onwards, and with such concepts as the chaos monster.

For a full discussion, and of 'thousand', see commentaries on the book of Revelation, especially *NBCR*; H. B. Swete, *The Apocalypse of St. John*, 1906, pp. 175–176; J.-J von Allmen, art. 'Number' in *Vocabulary of the Bible*, 1958; D. R. Hillers, *BASOR* 170, 1963, p. 65.

Rev. 7:4; 14:1 records the number *144,000* 'which were sealed'. It is the number 12, the number of election, squared, and multiplied by 1,000, an indefinitely large number, and symbolizes the full number of saints of both covenants who are preserved by God.

BIBLIOGRAPHY. E. D. Schmitz, *et al.*, *NIDNTT* 2, pp. 683–704; W. Roth, *Numerical Sayings in the OT*, 1965. R.A.H.G.

NUMBERS, BOOK OF. The synagogue named this book after its first word or after one of the first words (*wayᵉḏabbēr*, 'and he spoke'; or *bᵉmiḏbar*, 'in the desert'). The Gk. translators called it *arithmoi*, 'numbers'. Where the four other parts of the Pentateuch are concerned, the Gk. names are commonly used; in this fifth part, in some countries the Gk. has been translated into the native language: 'Numbers', *etc.*; in other countries the Lat. translation of the Gk. name is used: *Numeri*. The title is given because the book's first few chapters (and ch. 26) contain many numbers, especially census-numbers.

I. Outline of contents

a. The numbering of the Israelites. The marshalling of the tribes (1:1–4:49).

b. The law regarding jealousy, legislation for the Nazirites and other laws (5:1–6:27).

c. The offerings for the consecration of the tabernacle (7:1–89).

d. The candlestick. The consecration of the Levites; their time of service (8:1–26).

e. The second Passover; the cloud; the two silver trumpets (9:1–10:10).

f. The departure from Sinai (10:11–36)

g. Taberah. The quails. The 70 elders (11:1–35).

h. Miriam and Aaron against Moses (12:1–16).

i. The twelve spies (13:1–14:45).

j. Miscellaneous commandments regarding, *inter alia*, meat and drink offerings, offerings where a person has sinned through ignorance, and commandments about sabbath-breaking (15:1–41).

k. Korah, Dathan and Abiram. The blossoming rod of Aaron (16:1–17:13).

l. The position of the priests and Levites (18:1–32).

m. The water of separation for purification of sins (19:1–22).

n. The death of Miriam. Meribah (20:1–13).

o. Edom refuses to give Israel passage. Death of Aaron (20:14–29).

p. The struggle at Hormah. The serpent of bronze. To the plains of Moab. The fight against Sihon and Og (21:1–35).

q. Balaam (22:1–24:25).

r. Baal-peor (25:1–18).

s. The second numbering of the Israelites (26:1–65).

t. The right of inheritance of daughters. The successor of Moses (27:1–23).

u. Commandments regarding offerings. Vows of the women (28:1–30:16).

v. Vengeance taken against the Midianites (31:1–54).

w. The allotment of the land on the E side of Jordan (32:1–42).

x. The places where Israel camped during their journeys through the desert (33:1–49).

y. Directions concerning the conquest of Canaan. The borders of Canaan. Regulations concerning the division of the land. The cities of the Levites. Cities of refuge (33:50–35:34).

z. The marriage of daughters having an inheritance (36:1–13).

II. Authorship and date

Many scholars today consider that the tradition according to which Moses is the author of the entire book must be seriously questioned. They draw attention to the following considerations. Only for ch. 33 is a literary activity of Moses mentioned (v. 2, *cf.* 5:23; 11:26); this is not mentioned for any other part of Nu.; for the contrary case, see *e.g.* Dt. 31:9. Various data point to a later time than that of Moses, or at least to another author than Moses; *cf.* 12:3; 15:22f. (Moses in the third person); 15:32; 21:14 (perhaps the 'book of the wars of the Lord' originates from the post-Mosaic time); 32:34ff. Nevertheless, the book repeatedly states that the regulations and the laws have been given through the agency of Moses (and Aaron), 1:1, *etc.*; it is also clear that the laws and regulations give the impression that they were enacted during the wanderings through the desert (5:17; 15:32ff., *etc.*). For that matter it is possible that the laws have gone through a process of growth: afterwards there may have been alterations made in them, *e.g.* for the purpose of adapting them to altered circumstances. Sometimes there are definite marks of these processes; thus there are differences between Nu. 15:22–31 and Lv. 4:1f.; in addition, we note the fact that Nu. 15:22f. speaks about Moses in the third person, and it is not unlikely that Nu. 15:22–31 is a later version of Lv. 4.

We shall have to assume that the laws substantially originate from the Mosaic time. We can also assume that the noting down of both the laws and the stories was already begun during the Mosaic time. The time when the book received its final form is unknown to us. In the opinion of the present writer, it is a plausible view that the major points were already recorded in writing, *e.g.* in the early days of the Monarchy. It is significant that there are no *post-Mosaica* pointing unmistakably to a time much later than that of Moses.

Since the critical activity of Wellhausen and others, many scholars have adopted the view that

Nu. belongs for the greater part to the so-called Priestly Code, which is said to have its origin in the post-exilic age. At present, however, scholars are inclined, more than Wellhausen was, to accept the view that Nu. contains material dating from old, even very remote, times, admitting that in Nu. 5:11ff. and ch. 19, ancient rites are described, and that other material points to a similar conclusion. Many scholars are willing to accept that the cult, as it is described in Nu., was in use, so far as concerns the main points, in pre-exilic Jerusalem. See also the articles on *PENTATEUCH, *MOSES, *WILDERNESS OF THE WANDERING, *etc.*, and articles under particular subjects such as *BALAAM, *CITIES OF REFUGE, *etc.*

III. Further summary of contents

1. The division of the Pentateuch into five books is not original. Thus, even though it is not without meaning that with Nu. 1:1 a new book begins (in which the first four chapters form the preparation for the departure from Sinai), this book nevertheless forms a unity with the preceding books. In the same way it may be said that Dt. is the continuation of Nu., but the separation between Nu. and Dt. is more fundamental than the separation of Lv. and Nu.

2. The history narrated in Nu. covers 38 years—the period between the 2nd year and the 40th year after the Exodus (see the definitions of the time in 1:1; 7:1; 9:1, 15; 10:11; 33:38; *cf.* Ex. 40:2; Dt. 1:3).

In the first part Israel is still staying near Mt Sinai (Ex. 19:1 tells of their arrival at Sinai). Nu. 10:11–12:16 deals with the departure from Sinai and the journey to Kadesh (*cf.* 13:26); in the 2nd year after the Exodus Israel had already arrived at Kadesh (*cf.* Dt. 2:14). Because Israel put faith in the defeatist words of the spies, there ensued a prolonged wandering in the desert (chs. 13–14). Little is known to us of the fortunes of Israel during the 38 years of their wanderings (15:1–20:13). We should reckon with the possibility that Kadesh was for a long time a sort of centre for Israel, while various groups of Israelites were wandering about the Sinai Peninsula. After these 38 years Israel leaves Kadesh for Canaan, marches round Edom, comes into the plains of Moab, and defeats Sihon and Og (20:14–21:35). The last part of the book describes the actions of Balaam, Israel's idol-worship of Baal-peor and the punishment of the Midianites.

3. Besides dealing with history, this book contains all kinds of regulations and laws. The relation between laws and history and between one law and another is often not very clear to us. Nevertheless, the author will, at least in many cases, have intended a connection. The simplest solution is to suppose that there is a chronological connection. Sometimes there is also a material connection; see, *e.g.*, how well 5:1–4 and ch. 18 correspond with what precedes, and 10:1–10 with what follows; after a survey of the journey through the desert has been given (33:1–49), the narrative continues (33:50–35:34) with regulations concerning the conquest of Canaan and laws for when they are dwelling in it. Finally, we should bear in mind that the construction of many OT books raises similar questions to those we have referred to here (*PSALMS, *PROVERBS, *ISAIAH, *etc.*).

Many laws (but not all of them) concern ritual matters. The Israelites did not distinguish between cultic, moral, juridical and social laws in the same way as we usually do. All the laws and regulations have as their object that Israel should be prepared to live in Canaan in the sight of the Lord, as an independent and well-conducted nation.

4. In Nu. Moses is again the dominant figure, depicted in all his greatness and weakness, and guiding the people in every respect. Through his mediation the Lord gives Israel a variety of laws and regulations, speaking to his servant 'mouth to mouth' (12:6–8). Over and over again Moses acts as intercessor for the people (11:2; 12:13; 14:13ff.; 16:22; 21:7). He was 'very meek, more than all men that were on the face of the earth' (12:3; *cf.* 14:5; 16:4ff.), yet he had his share of human failings. Contrary to the Lord's order he strikes the rock (20:10f.), and on occasion he makes temperamental complaints (11:10ff.; *cf.* 16:15). Next to Moses in prominence is Aaron (1:3, 17, 44; 2:1, *etc.*, especially chs. 12; 16–17).

IV. The message of the book

In Nu., as in the case of the whole Bible, the almighty and faithful God of the covenant reveals himself; it is this revelation that joins the different parts of Nu. into a unity. In the regulations and laws he imposes, God shows his care of his people. Israel frequently revolts against him. As a result the anger of the Lord is kindled: he does not allow the sin to go unpunished (11:1–3, 33f.; 12:10ff.; 14, *etc.*); Moses and Aaron are not allowed to enter Canaan (20:12f.). But the Lord does not repudiate his people; he remains faithful to his covenant. He guides Israel through the desert, so that the land promised to their fathers is reached. This is prevented neither by Israel's unfaithfulness nor by the power of the nations that turn against Israel.

Special attention should be paid to certain aspects of the revelation of God in Numbers.

1. The Lord is, indeed, unchangeable in his faithfulness (*cf.* 23:19), but this does not imply that he is an unmovable being (see especially the touching story in 14:11ff.). In this connection we should note the strong anthropomorphisms (see, *e.g.*, 10:35f.; 15:3, 'a pleasing odour to the Lord'; 28:2, 'my food', *etc.*); expressions which, while we must not take them in a strictly literal sense, show at the same time how deeply the Lord is involved in the doings of Israel.

2. God's holiness is specially emphasized. The stories do this (see, *e.g.*, 20:12f.), and so also, in a different way, do the laws and regulations: when a man approaches God he has to fulfil all kinds of prescribed rules, he has to be free from every uncleanness (*cf.* also 1:50ff., *etc.*).

3. Very detailed prescriptions are given in this book: God exercises his sovereign dominion over everything, even over the smallest details.

4. As soon as the children of Israel have arrived at the borders of the promised country they yield to the temptation to serve the gods of the new land. But the Lord is not only the Lord of the desert: he engages a heathen fortune-teller (22–24), and punishes Israel for their idol-worship (25), together with those who had seduced his people (31).

In what is said above, the Christological character of this book has already been mainly indicated. In Nu., as elsewhere, God reveals himself as the faithful God of the covenant. In other words, he reveals himself in the face of Christ. In addition, there is much in this book which has a typological meaning: in persons (especially Moses and Aaron), in occurrences, and in laws, the coming

Christ casts his shadow before him (*cf.* Jn. 3:14; 1 Cor. 10:1ff.; Heb. 3:7ff.; 9:13; *etc.*).

BIBLIOGRAPHY. See various *IOT*s and the commentaries—*e.g.* G. B. Gray, *Numbers, ICC*, 1903 (1955); L. E. Binns, *The Book of Numbers, WC*, 1927; S. Fish, *The Book of Numbers*², 1950, in *The Soncino Books of the Bible*; J. Marsh, *Numbers, IB*, 2, 1953; W. H. Gispen, *Het boek Numeri*, 1, 1959; 2, 1964, in *Commentaar op het Oude Testament*; N. H. Snaith, *Leviticus and Numbers, NCB*, 1967; M. Noth, *Numbers, OTL*, 1968; P. J. Budd, *Numbers, WBC*, 1984. N.H.R.

NUNC DIMITTIS. The prophecies accompanying Christ's advent occur not (as with John the Baptist) at circumcision but at the rites of purification a month later. According to an ancient custom babies were brought to an old doctor or rabbi in the Temple for a blessing. Perhaps in this setting Simeon, taking the Lord Jesus, uttered his *nunc dimittis* (Lk. 2:29–35). Simeon is characterized as receiving a 'spirit which was holy', which in Jewish tradition is equated with the 'spirit of prophecy'. According to the rabbis the Spirit departed from Israel after the prophet Malachi, and his return was indicative of the Messianic age (*cf. SB, in loc.*). In the case of Simeon three specific 'acts of the Spirit' occur: (1) he receives by divine revelation assurance that he shall see the Lord's Messiah; (2) under the influence of the Spirit (*cf.* Rev. 1:10) he is led to encounter and recognize Jesus as Messiah (*cf.* 1 Sa. 16:6ff.); (3) he utters a prayer and prediction which, in Luke's context, is clearly to be regarded as prophetic.

Nunc Dimittis is divided into two parts, the first a prayer to God (liturgically, this alone came to be designated the 'Nunc Dimittis') and the second a prophecy spoken to Mary. Their mood and theme stand in stark contrast to each other. The prayer is joyful, expressing the Messianic hope of Judaism in its most exalted tone: in Messiah the Gentiles will receive the truth of God and thus, in him, Israel's glory as God's instrument of revelation and redemption will be fully manifest (*cf.* Is. 49:6; Acts 1:8; Rom. 15:8ff.). But, in the second section, as if to counterbalance the impression of the prayer, praise gives way to warning. The Messiah shall cause division and shall be rejected by many (*cf.* Rom. 9:33).

In Simeon's prophecy to Mary the concept of a suffering Messiah appears. Israel's destiny is glorious, but it is one of conflict. As a sign or pointer to the redemption of Israel Jesus shall be attacked and rejected (*cf.* Lk. 11:30), for the kind of redemption he represents will not be welcomed by all. Although this will bring anguish to Mary, through it men will be brought to decision and thus their real selves, their hidden selves, be uncovered. (*BENEDICTUS.) E.E.E.

NURSE. 'Nurse' in the EVV may mean a wet-nurse, translating Heb. *mêneqeṯ*, used of Deborah (Gn. 24:59), of Moses' mother (Ex. 2:7), and of the nurse of the infant Joash (2 Ki. 11:2; 2 Ch. 22:11). Suckling is usually continued in the Near East for 2 years, and the nurse often remains with the family as a trusted servant, as in the case of Deborah (Gn. 35:8). The same word is used in a figurative sense of queens who will care for God's people in the glorious future (Is. 49:23). Paul compares his care for believers to that of a nurse (Gk. *trophos*) for her own children (1 Thes. 2:7).

In the more general sense of one who cares for children, 'nurse' translates Heb. *'ōmeneṯ*; for example, Naomi (Ru. 4:16) and the governess of 5-year-old Mephibosheth (2 Sa. 4:4) are so described. The masculine form of this Heb. word, *'ōmēn*, translated 'nursing father' AV, 'nurse' RSV, is used figuratively of Moses' care for the Israelites (Nu 11:12) and of kings who will serve the people of God (Is. 49:23). *Cf.* Acts 13:18, RVmg.

BIBLIOGRAPHY. H. Granquist, *Birth and Childhood among the Arabs*, 1947, pp. 107–117, 246–252; *RAC*, 1, pp. 383–385. J.T.

NUZI. The excavations at Nuzi (Yorghan Tepe) and adjacent mounds near Kirkuk, Iraq, were carried out by E. Chiera and others between 1925 and 1931 through the co-operation of the American Schools of Oriental Research, the Iraq Museum and the Semitic Museum, Harvard. The earliest level of occupation was dated to the Ubaid period, while the latest traces came from Roman times. The two main periods of occupation were in the 3rd millennium BC when the site was known as Gasur, and in the 15th–14th centuries BC when the town was under Hurrian influence and known as Nuzi. In the palace and private homes more than 4,000 clay tablets were found, written in a local Hurrian dialect of Akkadian. These included several archives, among which those of Tehiptilla (*c.* 1,000 tablets), prince Shilwateshub and a successful business woman, Tulpunnaya, are the best known. The texts cover approximately five generations, thus providing a detailed picture of life in an ancient Mesopotamian community in a comparatively short period.

The tablets from Nuzi contain mainly private contracts and public records. Apart from lists of various kinds of goods and equipment, a wide range of topics is covered, including land, prices, family law, women, law and order, and slaves. Of particular importance are documents relating to various kinds of adoption, wills, marriage, lawsuits, antichretic security and exchange of persons, goods and land. Until comparatively recently several of the Nuzi text types were scarcely represented elsewhere, but excavation at Tell al-Fikhar (Kurruhanni), *c.* 30 km SW of Nuzi, has revealed similar material of comparable date, though it remains largely unpublished.

By contrast, the political history and religious life is poorly understood. Nuzi appears to have been situated within the Hurrian kingdom of Mitanni, though the extant texts make little reference to this or to the rising power of Assyria. Literature, including myths, epics, wisdom texts and scholarly documents, is also sparsely represented.

The Nuzi texts contain a significant number of points of contact with the OT, notably with the patriarchal narratives. These links between the customs and social conditions of the people of Nuzi and the biblical Patriarchs have led some scholars to argue for a similar 15th-century date for Abraham and his descendants, though there is evidence that many of these customs had already been observed for centuries. More recently attempts have been made to reduce considerably any connection between Nuzi and the Patriarchs (Thompson, van Seters). The examples listed below, however, indicate the existence of several significant parallels, and some of the customs concerned are also found elsewhere in Mesopotamia. Nuzi practice, in fact, followed mainly a Mesopotamian rather than a Hurrian pattern.

A large group of documents deals with *inheritance.* Throughout the ancient Near East an eldest son received a larger inheritance share than his brothers, though the exact proportion varied. The double share, which is most prominent at Nuzi and which also appears in other 2nd-millennium cuneiform texts, is closely paralleled in Dt. 21:17, though the Patriarchs seem to have followed a different practice (Gn. 25:5–6). The most frequent description of the eldest son at Nuzi (*rabû*, 'eldest'), also found at Ugarit, Alalaḫ and in Middle Assyrian texts, occurs in Hebrew (*raḇ*) in Gn. 25:23 instead of the usual *bᵉḵôr*.

It remains uncertain whether or not one's birthright could be exchanged at Nuzi, as in the case of Jacob and Esau (Gn. 25:29–34). Although several examples are known where at least part of an inheritance changed hands between brothers, in no instance can an eldest son be definitely identified in such transactions. In any case similar examples of the transfer of an inheritance occur in Assyria and Babylonia and are not confined to Nuzi.

However, any heir could be disinherited. Such drastic action was permitted only for offences against the family and the references to 'disrespect' and 'disobedience' towards parents provides a useful background to Reuben's demotion (Gn. 35:22; 49:3–4), though again similar examples can be found elsewhere.

The suggestion has been made that possession of the household gods in Nuzi formed an effective entitlement to an inheritance and that Rachel's theft of Laban's images, perhaps on Jacob's behalf, could be similarly explained (Gn. 31:19ff.). It is more probable, however, that the family deities could only be bequeathed by the father, normally to the first-born son, and that their theft did not improve an heir's claim.

Adoption also occupies an important place in the Nuzi texts. A man without an heir could adopt an outsider who would carry out certain responsibilities towards his adoptive parents, though of course similar customs are known from other Mesopotamian texts. The duties included the provision of food and clothing, particularly in old age, and ensuring proper burial and mourning rites, while in return the adoptee received an inheritance. It is quite possible that Abram adopted Eliezer in this manner prior to Isaac's birth (Gn. 15:2–4), especially since at Nuzi a son born subsequently usually gained a larger inheritance share than any adoptee and that the adoption of slaves is occasionally mentioned. The process of adoption at Nuzi was also extended to become a fiction whereby property, apparently legally inalienable, could be sold. Tehiptilla, for example, was 'adopted' in this way some 150 times!

Apart from adoption, the Nuzi texts mention three further solutions for a childless marriage. The husband could remarry or take a concubine or the wife could present her own slave-girl to her husband. The latter custom, which afforded the barren wife some protection, parallels that of Sarah, Rachel and Leah (Gn. 16:1–4; 30:1–13), and though only one example occurs at Nuzi (*HSS* 5. 67), others are known from Babylonia and Assyria. A son born to a slave-girl in this way would normally have to be adopted or legitimated by the father according to Mesopotamian custom, though the Nuzi text is not specific on this point. *HSS* 5. 67 does indicate, however, that the wife maintained authority over her slave-girl's children and there are indications that Sarah, Rachel and Leah took responsibility for their slave-girls' offspring right from the naming of the children.

Although the Nuzi texts do not refer to a paternal blessing such as in Gn. 27:29, 33; 48:1ff., they do occasionally contain oral statements which were clearly regarded as having legal validity. One of these was made by a father to his son while the former lay ill in bed (*cf.* Isaac). In both Nuzi and Genesis such oral statements were supported by legal or customary safeguards, and symbolic actions involving the hands were frequently used.

Women are often mentioned in the Nuzi documents. The right of daughters to inherit property is attested, usually in the absence of sons, as in Babylonian contracts (*cf.* Nu. 27:8). Sometimes a marriage contract included a clause prohibiting the husband from marrying a second wife, a safeguard sought for Rachel by Laban (Gn. 31:50). Not every bride was so fortunate, however. A girl could be acquired by a man for optional marriage to himself or to his son (*cf.* Ex. 21:7–11), while the complaint of Laban's daughters that their father had held back their dowry (Gn. 31:15) is paralleled by an identical phrase (*kaspa akālu*) in five Nuzi texts.

Several Nuzi references to business transactions have some relevance to the OT. Land was sometimes apportioned by lot (Nu. 26:55f.; Jos. 18:2–10) and there was a periodic 'release' from debt (Dt. 15). Sale of land was sometimes confirmed by the seller lifting his foot and placing the buyer's on the soil, while shoes functioned as legal symbols in some transactions (*cf.* Ru. 4:7–8; 1 Sa. 12:3, LXX; Am. 2:6; 8:6). 1 Sa. 1:24 has been reinterpreted in the light of Nuzi evidence to read 'a bullock, three years old'.

Finally, the Nuzi references to *'apiru* (*habiru*), indicating various persons, many apparently foreigners who had accepted voluntary servitude, recalls the phrase 'Hebrew slave' and the derogatory use of 'Hebrews' by Egyptians and Philistines when referring to Israelites (Gn. 39:14; Ex. 1:15; 21:1–6; 1 Sa. 14:21).

BIBLIOGRAPHY. *Archaeology*: R. F. S. Starr, *Nuzi, Report on the Excavations at Yorghan Tepe*, 2 vols., 1939. *Texts:* E. Chiera *et al.*, *Joint Expedition at Nuzi*, 7 vols., 1927–39, 1989; E. R. Lacheman *et al.*, *Excavations at Nuzi*, 9 vols., 1929–62, 1987–93. *General:* C. H. Gordon, *BA* 3, 1940, pp. 1–12; C. J. Mullo Weir, *AOTS*, pp. 73–86; M. Dietrich *et al.*, *Nuzi-Bibliographie*, 1972; T. L. Thompson, *The Historicity of the Patriarchal Narratives*, 1974, pp. 196–297; M. J. Selman, *TynB* 27, 1976, pp. 114–136; D. I. Owen, *et al.* (ed.), *Studies on the Civilization and Culture of Nuzi and the Hurrians*, 5 vols., 1981–93.

M.J.S.

NYMPHA, NYMPHAS. Owner of a house in Laodicea (or possibly somewhere else near Colossae) in which a church met (Col. 4:15). Though many MSS read 'his house', as AV, most of the best read either 'her house' (*cf.* RSV, NEB) or 'their house' (*cf.* RV). The name is in the accusative and, unaccented, could represent a masculine Nymphas (pet-form for Nymphodorus?) or a feminine Nympha (*cf.* J. H. Moulton, *Grammar*, 1, p. 48, for alleviation of the cause of Lightfoot's reserve). On either rendering the reading 'their house' is so hard to explain that it may well be correct. Perhaps it refers back to 'the brethren which are in Laodicea' (Lightfoot proposes a Colossian family there, or, alternatively, that *autōn* stands for 'Nymphas and his friends').

Nympha(s), like *Philemon and *Archippus, displays Paul's friendships (made in Ephesus?) in an area he had not visited (*cf.* Col. 2:1). A.F.W.

OATHS. In ancient Israel: **1.** Oaths were attributed to God (Num. 14:21) in relation to his covenant with Israel (Dt. 31:7f.), his promises (Gn. 22:16–18; 26:3), his judgments (Am. 4:2) and his word (Ezk. 20:3; 33:11). **2.** It followed that oaths ensured a norm of morality (Gn. 34:1–7; Je. 29:20–23). Oaths in God's name were sacrosanct (Dt. 10:20), maintaining family honour and tribal loyalty. To ratify one's oath by invoking Yahweh's name, while knowingly perjuring oneself, was to profane the name (Lv. 19:12; Ex. 20:7). **3.** In ancient Israel the absence of jurisprudence made the oath obligatory in administering justice at the town gate.

Of the two Heb. words translated oath, *šᵉbū'â* and *'ālâ*, the second is stronger, meaning a curse (Is. 14:24). The first more commonly conveys the weaker sense of solemn promise. When one reinforced his oath by invoking Yahweh to witness it, the swearer placed himself under a curse if proved to 'have sworn deceitfully'. Prof. de Vaux reconstructs the various contexts in which this judicial oath applied (*e.g.* Ex. 22:1–11; Dt. 2:1–8). Nu. 5:21 describes how the judicial oath became an imprecatory or adjuratory oath.

Oaths applied when making covenants (Gn. 26:28), promises (Gn. 24:2–4), decisions (1 Sa. 25:22), when emphasizing the veracity of statements (Jdg. 8:19; 1 Sa. 20:3), the certainty of prophetic predictions (1 Ki. 17:1), guaranteeing against perjury (Jdg. 11:10; Je. 42:5), reinforcing a command (Gn. 24:41), in legal proceedings (1 Ki. 8:31; 2 Ch. 6:22f.) and concerning property (Lv. 5:1ff.; 6:1ff.). Perjury outraged the prophets (Ezk. 17:13–19; Je. 5:2; 6:2; Ho. 4:2; Zc. 5:23f.; Mal. 3:5).

God swore by himself: to confirm his covenant with Abraham (Gn. 22:16–18; Ps. 105:9f.; Lk. 1:73), his promise to David relative to Christ's resurrection (Ps. 89:3f.; 132:11f.; Acts 2:29–32) and Christ's unchangeable high priesthood (Ps. 110:4; Heb. 7:17–28).

Christ prohibited oaths absolutely (Mt. 5:34). The reasoning behind this was: the old covenant was ending (Mk. 1:14f.; Mt. 5:33); Jesus is 'the truth' (Jn. 14:6); the Christian is in 'him that is true' (1 Jn. 5:20); therefore an unambiguous 'yes' or 'no' suffices (Mt. 5:37; Jas. 5:12). Jesus condemned scribal casuistry (Mt. 23:16–22) but implied the value of oaths (Mt. 26:63f.). Christians follow his example (Lk. 22:70; 23:3), remembering Peter's bitter experience (Mk. 14:72; Mt. 26:70, 72, 74).

The Apostle Paul condemns 'perjured persons' (1 Tim. 1:10), but calls God to witness to his blameless life (1 Thes. 2:5; 2 Cor. 1:23), his sincerity (Gal. 1:20) and his affection for fellow-believers (2 Cor. 11:11; Phil. 1:8; Rom. 1:9).

BIBLIOGRAPHY. W. Eichrodt, *The Theology of the OT* (trans. by J. A. Baker), 1, 1961, pp. 206, 219; 2, 1967, p. 318; R. de Vaux, *Ancient Israel* (trans. by John McHugh), 1961, pp. 106, 157f., 169, 255, 420; G. von Rad, *OT Theology* (trans. by D. M. G. Stalker), 1, 1962, pp. 129, 223, 311, 378, 414f.; 2, 1963; *TDNT*, pp. 683, 729.

J.G.S.S.T.

OBADIAH (*'ōḇaḏyāhû*, *'ōḇaḏyâ*). A Heb. name meaning 'servant of Yahweh' or 'worshipper of Yahweh'. At least twelve men in the OT bear this name.

1. The steward, or major-domo, in charge of the palace of King Ahab of Israel (1 Ki. 18:3–16). From his youth he was a devout worshipper of Yahweh. When Jezebel was persecuting the prophets of Yahweh, Obadiah hid 100 of them in two caves. During a drought while Obadiah was seeking grass for the royal horses and mules, Elijah met him and persuaded him to arrange a meeting with Ahab, which led to the contest between Elijah and the prophets of Baal. The TB (*Sanhedrin* 39b) mistakenly identifies him with the prophet Obadiah. An ancient Hebrew seal reading 'To Obadiah servant of the King' may have belonged to this man.

2. A descendant of David (1 Ch. 3:21). **3.** A chief of Issachar (1 Ch. 7:3). **4.** A descendant of Saul (1 Ch. 8:38; 9:44). **5.** A Levite (1 Ch. 9:16), identical with Abda (Ne. 11:17) and probably with Obadiah, a gate-keeper of the Temple (Ne. 12:25). **6.** A Gadite captain who joined David at Ziklag (1 Ch. 12:9).

7. A Zebulonite in the time of David (1 Ch. 27:19). **8.** One of the princes sent out by King Jehoshaphat to teach the law in the cities of Judah (2 Ch. 17:7). **9.** A Levite overseer of the repair of the Temple in the time of Josiah (2 Ch. 34:12). **10.** An Israelite leader who returned from Babylonia to Jerusalem with Ezra (Ezr. 8:9). **11.** A priest who sealed the covenant with Nehemiah (Ne. 10:5).

12. A prophet, presumably of Judah (Ob. 1). The Bible gives nothing directly about his life. Though some locate him before the Exile, it is more likely that he lived in the 5th century BC (see below, *OBADIAH, BOOK OF). If the latter view is correct it is chronologically impossible to identify him with Ahab's steward, as does the TB (*Sanhedrin* 39b), or with Ahaziah's captain (2 Ki. 1:13–15) as Pseudo-Epiphanius does in *The Lives of the Prophets.* The talmudic tradition that he was a proselyte of Edomite origin is improbable in view of his strong denunciation of Edom.

J.T.

OBADIAH, BOOK OF. The fourth of the Minor Prophets in the Heb. Bible and the fifth in the order of the LXX. For a note on the author, see the previous article (**12**).

I. Outline of contents

a. The judgment of Edom (vv. 1–14).

(i) Title (v. 1a).
(ii) Warning of Edom's doom (vv. 1b–4).
(iii) Completeness of Edom's destruction (vv. 5–9).
(iv) Reasons for Edom's judgment (vv. 10–14).

b. Universal judgment (vv. 15–16).

c. Restoration of Israel (vv. 17–21).

II. Historical background

a. Before the Exile

Jewish tradition in the Talmud (*Sanhedrin* 39b) placed Obadiah in the reign of Ahab in the 9th century BC, and the order of the Minor Prophets in the Heb. Bible includes Obadiah among the pre-exilic prophets. Some scholars have suggested that the background for the whole of Obadiah is the attack of the Arabians and Philistines on Judah in the reign of Jehoram mentioned in 2 Ch. 21:16–17 (so Keil), or the Edomite attack on Judah in the reign of Ahaz described in 2 Ch. 28:17 (so J. D. Davis). Many think that only the older oracle against Edom, which Obadiah embodies in vv. 1–6, 8–9, has a pre-exilic background. Arab raids on Palestine, and presumably on Edom, are recorded in the 9th century BC (2 Ch. 21:16–17) and in the 7th century BC (Assyr. Annals).

b. After 587 BC

Most scholars consider that the calamity to Jerusalem described in Ob. 11–14 is its capture by the Chaldeans in 587 BC. This is the only capture of Jerusalem in which it is recorded that Edomites participated (Ps. 137:7; 1 Esdras 4:45). The references to the sufferings caused by the fall of Jerusalem are so vivid that G. A. Smith would place Obadiah soon afterwards during the exilic period. Many, however, feel that the latter part of Obadiah reflects a post-exilic background. V. 7 states that the Edomites have been driven out of their old land (*cf.* Mal. 1:3–4). After the fall of Jerusalem Edomites under Arab pressure began moving into the Negeb (1 Esdras 4:50), which came to be called Idumaea, and by the late 6th century BC Arabs had largely pushed them out of the area of Petra, once the Edomite capital. Vv. 8–10 announce the future wiping out of the Edomites as a nation, and this prophecy must have been made before the fulfilment which took place in the Maccabean period (Jos., *Ant.* 13. 257). The territory occupied by the Jews according to vv. 19–20 is the area around Jerusalem, as in the days of Nehemiah (Ne. 11:25–36). Thus the latest clear indication of date in the prophecy is in the mid-5th century BC, about the time of Malachi.

III. Parallels in other prophecies

Other prophetic denunciations of Edom include: Is. 34:5–17; 63:1–6; Je. 49:7–22; La. 4:21–22; Ezk. 26:12–14; Joel 3:19; Am. 1:11–12.

The many identical phrases in Ob. 1–9 and Je. 49:7–22 suggest some literary relationship between the two passages. The different order of the phrases in the two prophecies makes it probable that they are both quoting some earlier divine oracle against Edom. Since some of the additional material in Jeremiah is characteristic of that prophet, and since the order is more natural in Obadiah, it is likely that the latter is closer in form to the original prophecy. Some scholars, however, hold that either Jeremiah (so Keil) or Obadiah (so Hitzig) made use of the other.

Several phrases are found in both Obadiah and Joel: Ob. 10 = Joel 3:19; Ob. 11 = Joel 3:3; Ob. 15 = Joel 1:15; 2:1; 3:4, 7, 14; Ob. 18 = Joel 3:8. In 2:32 Joel indicates by the words 'as the Lord has said' that he is quoting, probably from Ob. 17. Therefore Obadiah preceded Joel and doubtless influenced him in some of the other phrases common to the two prophets.

IV. Style

Obadiah, the shortest book of the OT, is marked by vigorous poetic language. The prevailing poetic metre is the pentameter (3 + 2), but other metres are used for variety (*e.g.* 3 + 3 and 3 + 3 + 3). Much of the prophecy consists of God's own words to personified Edom (vv. 2–15), and this feature gives a direct and personal quality to the book. Vividness is enhanced by the use of the prophetic perfect tense (v. 2) to describe a judgment yet to be fulfilled, and by the use of prohibitions (vv. 12–14) forbidding atrocities which had actually been perpetrated. Various striking comparisons and metaphors are used: the mountain fastness of Edom is like an eagle's eyrie (v. 4); the plunderers of Edom are compared to night thieves and gleaners of grapes (v. 5); the judgment of the nations is a bitter drink which they must swallow (v. 16); the avenging Israelites are called a fire, and the Edomites are called stubble (v. 18). Edom's crimes are listed in climactic order (vv. 10–14). The completeness of Israel's restoration is expressed by the specification of its expansion in the four cardinal directions (vv. 19–20). Sin and doom in vv. 1–16 are sharply contrasted with hope and victory in vv. 17–21. Obadiah proceeds from the particular to the general, from the judgment of Edom to the universal judgment, from the restoration of Israel to the establishment of the kingdom of God.

V. Literary analyses

Some hold that Obadiah was the original author of the whole prophecy (so Keil). Most scholars believe that he adapted an older oracle in vv. 1–6, 8–9. Some have found various other fragments, but the uniform historical background supports the literary unity of the remainder of the prophecy.

VI. Leading messages

1. *Divine inspiration.* Four times (vv. 1, 4, 8, 18) the prophet claims a divine origin for his words.

2. *Divine judgment.* The main message of this prophecy is God's moral judgment of nations. Edom is judged because of inhumanity to Israel, who also has been punished. Ultimately all nations will be judged in the Day of the Lord.

3. *The divine kingdom.* The final goal, according to Obadiah, is that 'the kingdom shall be the Lord's' (*cf.* Rev. 11:15). His hope for the restoration of his own people rises above mere nationalism, for in their victory he sees the establishment of the kingdom of God (v. 21). That kingdom will be characterized by 'deliverance' and 'holiness' (v. 17), ideas which are amplified in the NT.

BIBLIOGRAPHY. *Commentaries* by E. B. Pusey, 1860; C. F. Keil in *Biblischer Commentar über das Alte Testament*, 1888; J. A. Bewer in *ICC*, 1911; H. C. O. Lanchester in *CBSC*, 1918; G. W. Wade in *WC*, 1925; G. A. Smith in *EB*, 1928; E. Sellin in

KAT, 1929; T. H. Robinson in *HAT*, 1954; J. H. Eaton, *Obadiah, Nahum, Habakkuk, Zephaniah, TBC*, 1961; D. W. B. Robinson in *NBCR*, 1970; J. A. Thompson in *IB*, 1956; G. F. Wood in *The Jerome Biblical Commentary*, 1968; L. C. Allen, *The Books of Joel, Obadiah, Jonah and Micah, NIC*, 1976; D. W. Baker, T. D. Alexander, B. K. Waltke, *Obadiah, Jonah and Micah, TOTC*, 1988.

Special studies: G. L. Robinson, *The Sarcophagus of an Ancient Civilization*, 1930; W. Rudolph, 'Obadja', *ZAW* 8, 1931, pp. 222–231. J.T.

OBED (Heb. *'ôḇēḏ*, 'servant'). **1.** The son of Ruth and Boaz (Ru. 4:17), and grandfather of David (Ru. 4:21f.; 1 Ch. 2:12; Mt. 1:5; Lk. 3:32). Obed's birth brought comfort to Naomi's old age. **2.** A Jerahmeelite (1 Ch. 2:37f.). **3.** One of David's mighty men (1 Ch. 11:47). **4.** A son of Shemaiah and grandson of Obed-edom, of the Korahite family (1 Ch. 26:7). **5.** The father of Azariah, a captain who served under Jehoiada (2 Ch. 23:1). J.D.D.

OBED-EDOM (Heb. *'ōḇēḏ 'eḏôm*, 'servant of [god?] Edom'). **1.** A Philistine of Gath living in the neighbourhood of Jerusalem. Before taking it to Jerusalem David left the ark in his house for 3 months after the death of Uzzah, during which time its presence brought blessing to the household (2 Sa. 6:10ff. = 1 Ch. 13:13f.; 15:25).

2. The ancestor of a family of doorkeepers (1 Ch. 15:18ff.; 16:38; 26:4ff.; 2 Ch. 25:24). **3.** A family of singers in pre-exilic times (1 Ch. 15:21; 16:5). J.D.D.

OBEDIENCE. The Heb. verb translated 'obey' in EVV is *šāma' bᵉ*, lit. 'hearken to'. The verb used in LXX and the NT is *hypakouō* (noun, *hypakoē*; adjective, *hypēkoos*), a compound of *akouō*, which also means 'hear'. *hypakouō* means literally 'hear *under*'. The NT also uses *eisakouō* (1 Cor. 14:21), lit. 'hear *into*', *peithomai*, and *peitharcheō* (Tit. 3:1). The two latter words express respectively the ideas of yielding to persuasion and submitting to authority. The idea of obedience which this vocabulary suggests is of a hearing that takes place *under* the authority or influence of the speaker, and that leads *into* compliance with his requests.

For obedience to be due to a person, he must: (*a*) have a right to command, and (*b*) be able to make known his requirements. Man's duty to obey his Maker thus presupposes: (*a*) God's Lordship, and (*b*) his revelation. The OT habitually describes obedience to God as obeying (hearing) either his *voice* (accentuating (*b*)) or his *commandments* (assuming (*b*), and accentuating (*a*)). Disobedience it describes as not hearing God's voice when he speaks (Ps. 81:11; Je. 7:24–28).

According to Scripture, God demands that his revelation be taken as a rule for man's whole life. Thus obedience to God is a concept broad enough to include the whole of biblical religion and morality. The Bible is insistent that isolated external acts of homage to God cannot make up for a lack of consistent obedience in heart and conduct (1 Sa. 15:22; *cf.* Je. 7:22f.).

The disobedience of Adam, the first representative man, and the perfect obedience of the second, Jesus Christ, are decisive factors in the destiny of everyone. Adam's lapse from obedience plunged mankind into guilt, condemnation and death (Rom. 5:19; 1 Cor. 15:22). Christ's unfailing obedience 'unto death' (Phil. 2:8; *cf.* Heb. 5:8; 10:5–10) won righteousness (acceptance with God) and life (fellowship with God) for all who believe on him (Rom. 5:15–19).

In God's promulgation of the old covenant the emphasis was on obedience as his requirement if his people were to enjoy his favour (Ex. 19:5, *etc.*). In his promise of the new covenant, however, the emphasis was on obedience as his gift to them, in order that they might enjoy his favour (Je. 31:33; 32:40; *cf.* Ezk. 36:26f.; 37:23–26).

Faith in the gospel, and in Jesus Christ, is obedience (Acts 6:7; Rom. 6:17; Heb. 5:9; 1 Pet. 1:22), for God commands it (*cf.* Jn. 6:29; 1 Jn. 3:23). Unbelief is disobedience (Rom. 10:16; 2 Thes. 1:8; 1 Pet. 2:8; 3:1; 4:17). A life of obedience to God is the fruit of faith (*cf.* what is said of Abraham, Gn. 22:18; Heb. 11:8, 17ff.; Jas. 2:21ff.).

Christian obedience means imitating God in holiness (1 Pet. 1:15f.) and Christ in humility and love (Jn. 13:14f., 34f.; Phil. 2:5ff.; Eph. 4:32–5:2). It springs from gratitude for grace received (Rom. 12:1f.), not from the desire to gain merit and to justify oneself in God's sight. Indeed, law-keeping from the latter motive is not obedience to God, but its opposite (Rom. 9:31–10:3).

Obedience to divinely-established authority in the family (Eph. 5:22; 6:1ff.; *cf.* 2 Tim. 3:2), in the church (Phil. 2:12; Heb. 13:17), and in the state (Mt. 22:21; Rom. 13:1ff.; 1 Pet. 2:13ff.; Tit. 3:1), is part of the Christian's obedience to God. When claims clash, however, he must be ready to disobey men in order not to disobey God (*cf.* Acts 5:29).

BIBLIOGRAPHY. W. Mundle, *NIDNTT* 2, pp. 172–180. J.I.P.

ODED. 1. Father of Azariah the prophet (2 Ch. 15:1) in the reign of Asa. V. 8 has either included a marginal gloss or omitted 'Azariah the son of'. **2.** A prophet of Samaria (2 Ch. 28:9–15) who met the victorious army of the N kingdom returning with a number of enslaved captives from Judah, and remonstrated with them to return the slaves. His pleadings, joined by those of some Samaritan leaders, were successful. M.A.M.

OFFICERS. A term used of various subordinate officials whether civil, judicial or military. The status of these officers as assisting and recording on behalf of their superiors originally may imply the ability to write (Heb. *šōṭēr*; *cf.* Akkad. *šaṭāru* 'to write'). The Egyptians used 'officers' to record the work of Hebrew slaves there (Ex. 5:6, 14), a practice attested in Egyp. records. Moses developed this in his employment of such officers as clerks to assist him and *judges by recording legal decisions (Nu. 11:16) and this became the later custom (Dt. 16:18; 1 Ch. 23:4; 2 Ch. 19:8; *cf.* Josephus, *Ant.* 4. 214; *EQ* 28, 1951, pp. 149–157). These men had responsibilities also relating to call-up for war-service (Dt. 20:5; Jos. 1:10) and as military aides (Jos. 3:2). Their duties related them to the local governors and elders (Jos. 8:33; 23:2; 24:1). By the time of the Monarchy these were numerous (1,700) both in the Temple and civilian administration as well as in royal service (1 Ch. 26:29; 27:1) and as such were clearly distinguished in the time of Jehoshaphat (2 Ch. 19:11; 26:11; 34:13).

Officers were sometimes 'princes' (*sarîm*; Ezr. 7:28) with military duties (2 Ch. 32:3; Ne. 2:9) or were designated 'third man' or officer-in-charge of a *chariot crew (Ex. 14:7; 15:4, *šlš*; *cf.* Assyr. *šalšu*; J. V. Kinnier Wilson, *The Nimrud Wine Lists*, 1972). 'Officer' is also sometimes used to translate 'chief' (*rôš*, *rāḇ*) as in Est. 1:8; Je. 41:1; Ezk. 23:15 or even 'eunuch' (*sarîs*; 2 Ki. 24:12).

An officer was an appointee (*pqd*) set to oversee all work on behalf of the king, whether in one region (Jdg. 9:28; Is. 60:17) or in a specific sphere (Ezk. 2:3). The term is also used of subordinates within the Temple organization (2 Ch. 21:11; Je. 20:1) including those on guard duties (2 Ki. 11:18). Sometimes the use of the Heb. term *nṣb* stresses that the official owed his appointment to the king (1 Ki. 4:5; 22:47; 2 Ch. 8:10).

In the NT an officer may denote the 'prison guard' (Lk. 12:58; *cf.* Mt. 5:25), the deputies (*hypēretēs*, lit. 'under oarsmen') who acted for the chief priests and Sanhedrin as bailiffs (Jn. 7:32, 45–46; *cf.* v. 36; *cf.* Acts 5:22, 26). Such officials served in Herod's court (Mk. 6:21) and Paul considered himself in similar relationship to God (1 Cor. 4:1). D.J.W.

OG (Heb. *'ôḡ*). An Amorite king of Bashan, of the giant race of Rephaim at the time of the Conquest of Palestine (Nu. 21:33; Jos. 13:12). His kingdom was a powerful one, having sixty cities 'fortified with high walls, gates and bars' (Dt. 3:4–5), extending from Mt Hermon to the Jabbok. These included two royal cities, Ashtaroth and Edrei, at the latter of which the Israelites defeated and slew him. His territory was given to the half tribe of Manasseh (Dt. 3:13), which remained E of the Jordan. His defeat was one of the signal victories of Israel (*cf.* Jos. 9:10; Ne. 9:22; Pss. 135:11; 136:20).

His bed (*'ereś*) was renowned as made of black basalt. Some have conjectured that it was in reality a sarcophagus, although the word nowhere else bears this meaning; but many such sarcophagi have been found in the region. It appears to have fallen into the hands of the Ammonites and was kept in Rabbah (Dt. 3:11). M.A.M.

OHOLIAB (AV **AHOLIAB**), a Danite, son of Ahisamach, specially gifted by God and appointed to assist *Bezalel in the design and construction of the tabernacle, its furniture and furnishings, and in teaching other craftsmen (Ex. 31:6; 35:34–35). D.W.G.

OHOLIBAMAH, OHOLAH, OHOLIBAH. Oholibamah was an Edomite name used for both men and women. It was the name of *Esau's second wife, a Canaanite woman, daughter of Anah and mother of Jeush, Jalam and Korah (Gn. 36:1–28). There was also an Edomite chief of this name (Gn. 36:41; 1 Ch. 1:52) which means 'tent of the high place'. In Gn. 36:34 and 1 Ch. 1:52 the name appears alongside Timnah and it is interesting to note that a tent shrine has been discovered at Timnah in the Negeb, the region of ancient Edom. The shrine is dated to the Midianite period and is a parallel to the desert *tabernacle. The name suggests that some early *'high places' may have been tents (*cf.* Ezk. 16:16).

Oholah and Oholibah (AV Aholah and Aholibah) are allegorical names given to the N and S kingdoms in Ezk. 23. Both names mean 'tent worshipper' and were inspired by the term Oholibamah. They imply criticism of Israel's unfaithfulness to God. The two kingdoms are portrayed as sisters married to Yahweh but who have persisted in adultery by their entanglements with other nations. Oholibah is warned against following her sister's example and judgment is predicted. The sexuality of the imagery (*cf.* Ezk. 16; Ho. 1–3; Am. 5:1–2) is particularly appropriate as many of the neighbouring nations' religions involved fertility rites. J.T.W.

OIL. Unless cosmetic ointments (Ru. 3:3; 2 Sa. 14:2; Ps. 104:15) or oil of myrrh (Est. 2:12) are indicated, all other biblical references to oil are to the expressed product of the *olive fruit. The abundance of olive-trees (*Olea europaea*) in ancient Palestine enabled a flourishing trade in oil to be carried on with Tyre and Egypt. Solomon supplied large quantities of oil to Hiram as part-payment for the construction of the Temple (1 Ki. 5:11; Ezk. 27:17), while Egypt imported substantial quantities of Palestinian oil (*cf.* Ho.

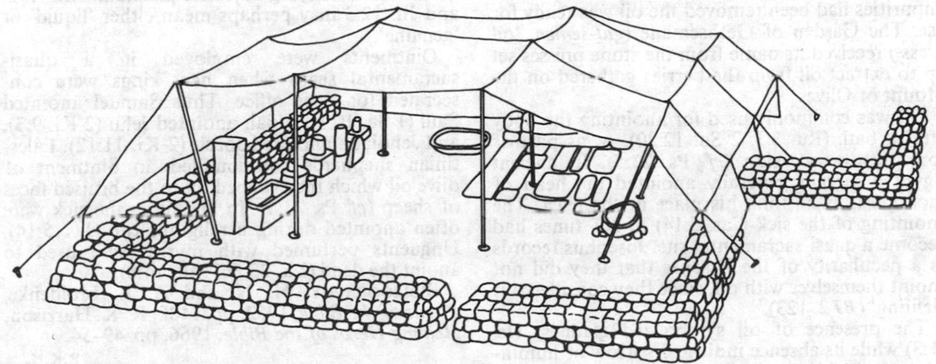

Reconstruction of the Midianite tent-shrine discovered at Timnah. This was probably similar in concept to the Hebrew tabernacle and furnishes archaeological evidence for Oholibamah, 'tent of the high place'. Mid-12th cent. BC.

12:1), because the Egyp. climate is not conducive to successful cultivation.

As an important element of religious observances, oil was prominent among the firstfruit offerings (Ex. 22:29) and was also an object of tithing (Dt. 12:17). The meal-offerings were frequently mixed with oil (Lv. 8:26; Nu. 7:19), while the sanctuary lamp (Ex. 25:6) was replenished from a supply of freshly processed oil (Lv. 24:2). Oil was employed ceremonially at the consecration of priests (Ex. 29:2), at the purification of lepers (Lv. 14:10–18), during the daily sacrifice (Ex. 29:40), and at the completion of the Nazirite's vow (Nu. 6:15). But certain ceremonies were devoid of oil, such as the jealousy-offering (Nu. 5:15) and the sin-offering (Lv. 5:11).

Olive oil was widely employed in the preparation of food, replacing butter in cooking (1 Ki.17:12–16). An equally popular usage in the domestic sphere was that of a fuel for the small lamps found in abundance from an early period in Palestine. Both portable and other types of lamps generally had an indentation in the brim into which the wick of flax (Is. 42:3) or hemp was put. When the lamp was filled with olive oil the wick maintained a steady flame until the supply of fuel was depleted. When such lamps were being carried about it was customary in NT times for the bearer to attach a small container of olive oil to one finger by means of a string. Then if the lamp needed to be replenished at any time an adequate supply of oil was readily available (*cf.* Mt. 25:1–13).

Apart from the use of oil at the consecration of the priests (Ex. 29:2), it was an important ritual element in the ceremonial recognition of the kingly office (1 Sa. 10:1; 1 Ki. 1:39).

As a medicine olive oil was used both internally and externally. Its soothing protective qualities made it a valuable remedy for gastric disorders, while its properties as a mild laxative were also recognized in antiquity. Externally it formed a popular unguent application for bruises and wounds (Is. 1:6; Mk. 6:13; Lk. 10:34).

In OT times olive oil was produced either by means of a pestle and mortar (Ex. 27:20) or by grinding the olives in a stone press. Excavations at Taanach, Megiddo and Jerusalem have uncovered presses hewn out of the solid rock. A large stone roller manipulated by two people crushed the olives to a pulp, which was then either trodden out (Dt. 33:24) or subjected to further pressing. After impurities had been removed the oil was ready for use. The Garden of Gethsemane (*gaṯ-šemen*, 'oil press') received its name from the stone presses set up to extract oil from the berries gathered on the Mount of Olives.

Oil was commonly used for anointing the body after a bath (Ru. 3:3; 2 Sa. 12:20), or as part of some festive occasion (*cf.* Ps. 23:5). In ancient Egypt a servant generally anointed the head of each guest as he took his place at the feast. The anointing of the sick (Jas. 5:14) in NT times had become a quasi-sacramental rite. Josephus records as a peculiarity of the Essenes that they did not anoint themselves with oil, since they considered it 'defiling' (*BJ* 2. 123).

The presence of oil symbolized gladness (Is. 61:3) while its absence indicated sorrow or humiliation (Joel 1:10). Similarly oil was used as an image of comfort, spiritual nourishment, or prosperity (Dt. 33:24; Jb. 29:6; Ps. 45:7).

BIBLIOGRAPHY. H. N. and A. L. Moldenke, *Plants of the Bible*, 1952, pp. 97f., 158ff.; J. F. Ross, *IDB* 3, pp. 592–593; J. A. Balchin, *ISBE* 3, pp. 585–586.

R.K.H.

OINTMENT (Heb. *mirqaḥaṯ*, *šemen*; Gk. *myron*). Unguent preparations of various kinds were widely used throughout the whole of the ancient Near East. Their primary use was cosmetic in nature, and they probably originated in Egypt. Toilet boxes, of which alabaster ointment containers formed a part, have been recovered in considerable numbers from Palestinian sites.

The Egyptians apparently found that the application of unguents was soothing and refreshing. It was their custom at feasts to place small cones of perfumed ointment upon the foreheads of guests. Bodily heat gradually melted the ointment, which trickled down the face on to the clothing, producing a pleasant perfume. This practice was adopted by the Semites (Ps. 133:2), and continued into NT times (Mt. 6:17; Lk. 7:46).

Other ancient peoples followed the Egyptians in using ointments to reduce chafing and irritation caused by the heat. In localities where water was frequently at a premium, aromatic unguents were employed to mask the odour of perspiration. At other times they were used along with cosmetics in personal toilet procedures. Ointments were compounded either by apothecaries (2 Ch. 16:14), perfumers (Ex. 30:35), priests or by private individuals, using a wide variety of aromatic substances.

The holy anointing oil (Ex. 30:23–25) prescribed for use in tabernacle rituals was required to be compounded according to the art of the perfumer. It consisted of olive oil, myrrh, cinnamon, calamus and cassia, the solid ingredients probably being pulverized and boiled in the olive oil (*cf.* Jb. 41:31). The manufacture of this preparation by unauthorized persons was strictly prohibited (Ex. 30:37–38).

According to Pliny, unguents were preserved most successfully in alabaster containers. Under such conditions they improved with age, and became very valuable after a number of years. Thus the alabaster flask of ointment mentioned in the Gospels (Mt. 26:7; Mk. 14:3; Lk. 7:37) was a very costly one containing spikenard (*Nardostachys jatamansi*). This herb, related to valerian, was imported from N India and used widely by Hebrews and Romans alike in the anointing of the dead. The qualifying adjective *pistikē* in Mk. 14:3 and Jn. 12:3 may perhaps mean either 'liquid' or 'genuine'.

Ointments were employed in a quasi-sacramental sense when new kings were consecrated for their office. Thus Samuel anointed Saul (1 Sa. 10:1), Elijah anointed Jehu (2 Ki. 9:3), and Jehoiada anointed Joash (2 Ki. 11:12). Palestinian shepherds compounded an ointment of olive oil which they rubbed on to the bruised faces of sheep (*cf.* Ps. 23:5). In NT times the sick were often anointed during a religious rite (Jas. 5:14). Unguents perfumed with myrrh were used to anoint the dead (Lk. 23:56; Mk. 14:8).

BIBLIOGRAPHY. H. N. and A. L. Moldenke, *Plants of the Bible*, 1952, pp. 148f.; R. K. Harrison, *Healing Herbs of the Bible*, 1966, pp. 49–54.

R.K.H.

OLIVE (Heb. *zayiṯ*; Gk. *elaia*). One of the most valuable *trees of the ancient Hebrews, the olive is first mentioned in Gn. 8:11, when the dove returned to the ark with an olive branch. When the Israelites took possession of Canaan it was a conspicuous feature of the flora (*cf.* Dt. 6:11). At a later time the olive was esteemed with the vine as a profitable source of revenue (1 Sa. 8:14; 2 Ki. 5:26).

Although the botanical name of the olive is *Olea europaea*, the tree is thought to be a native of W Asia, being introduced subsequently into the Mediterranean region. Oriental peoples regarded the olive as a symbol of beauty, strength, divine blessing and prosperity. In harmony with the Noahic tradition, the olive and the dove have been venerated ever since as symbols of friendship and of peace (*cf.* Ps. 52:8).

In many parts of Palestine the olive, of which there are many varieties in the Near East, is still very often the only tree of any size in the immediate locality. The cultivated olive grows to about 6 m in height, with a contorted trunk and numerous branches. The tree develops slowly, but often attains an age of several centuries if left undisturbed. If cut down, new shoots spring up from the root, so that as many as five new trunks could thus come into being. Moribund olives usually sprout in this manner also (*cf.* Ps. 128:3). Olive groves were chiefly valued for their potential *oil resources, although they were also highly esteemed as a shelter from the burning sun and as a place where one could meditate (Lk. 22:39).

In antiquity olive-trees were distributed profusely across Palestine. The groves on the edge of the Phoenician plain were particularly impressive, as were those in the plain of Esdraelon and the valley of Shechem. Bethlehem, Hebron, Gilead, Lachish and Bashan were all renowned in Bible times for their wealth of olive groves.

The berries borne by the olive ripened in the early autumn, and were harvested towards the end of November. The primitive and rather injurious method of gathering the olive berries described in Dt. 24:20, whereby the trees were either shaken or beaten with poles, is still widely employed. In antiquity a few berries were left on the tree or on the ground beneath it for the benefit of the poor. The olive harvest was normally transported to the presses in baskets on the backs of donkeys. The oil was usually extracted from the berries by placing them in a shallow rock cistern and crushing them with a large upright millstone. Occasionally the berries were pounded by the feet of the harvesters (Dt. 33:24; Mi. 6:15), but this was a rather inefficient procedure. After being allowed to stand for a time the oil separated itself from foreign matter, and was then stored in jars or rock cisterns.

The cherubim of the Solomonic Temple were fashioned from olive wood (1 Ki. 6:23), and since they were some 4·5 m high with the same wingspread, it has been conjectured that they were composed of several pieces of wood joined together. While olive-wood is still used in Palestine for fine cabinet-work, the short gnarled trunks do not provide very lengthy pieces of timber. After it has been seasoned for a number of years the rich amber-grained wood can be polished to a high gloss.

So prolific a tree as the olive was naturally turned to a wide variety of usages. It was deemed worthy of being called the king of the trees (Jdg. 9:8), and at coronations its oil was employed as an emblem of sovereignty. Olive boughs were used to construct booths during the Feast of Tabernacles (Ne. 8:15). Fresh or pickled olives eaten with bread formed an important part of ancient Palestinian diet. The oil constituted the base of many unguent preparations, and was also used as a dressing for the hair. In addition it did duty as a fuel (Mt. 25:3), a medicine (Lk. 10:34; Jas. 5:14) and a food (2 Ch. 2:10).

The olive-tree enjoyed wide symbolic usage among the Hebrews. The virility and fruitfulness of the tree suggested the ideal righteous man (Ps. 52:8; Ho. 14:6), whose offspring was described as 'olive branches' (Ps. 128:3). An allusion to the facility with which the olive sometimes sheds its blossoms is found in Jb. 15:33, where Eliphaz states that the wicked will 'cast off his blossom, like the olive-tree.' In Zc. 4:3 the two olive-trees were emblems of fruitfulness, indicating the abundance with which God had provided for human needs.

The olive mentioned in Is. 41:19 (Heb. *'ēṣ šāmen*; AV 'oil-tree') has been equated with the botanically unrelated *Elaeagnus angustifolia*, which yields an inferior oil; but the context favours the true olive.

The fruit of the olive in its wild state is small and worthless. To become prolific the olive must be grafted, a process by which good stock is made to grow upon the wild shrub. Paul uses this fact as a powerful allegory (Rom. 11:17) in showing how the Gentiles are under obligation to the true Israel, indicating that it is contrary to nature for the wild olive slip to be grafted on to good stock.

BIBLIOGRAPHY. W. M. Ramsay, *Pauline and Other Studies*, 1906, pp. 219ff.; H. N. and A. L. Moldenke, *Plants of the Bible*, 1952, pp. 157–160; F. N. Hepper, *IEBP*, pp. 103–109; A. Goor and M. Nurock, *The Fruits of the Holy Land*, 1968, pp. 89–120.

R.K.H.
F.N.H.

OLIVES, MOUNT OF. Olivet, or the Mount of Olives, is a small range of four summits, the highest being 830 m, which overlooks Jerusalem and the Temple Mount from the E across the Kidron Valley and the Pool of Siloam. Thickly wooded in Jesus' day, rich in the olives which occasioned its name, the mount was denuded of trees in the time of Titus. All the ground is holy, for Christ unquestionably walked there, though particularized sites, with their commemorative churches, may be questioned. From the traditional place of Jesus' baptism, on Jordan's bank, far below sea level, Olivet's distant summit 1,200 m higher, a traditional site of the ascension, is clearly visible, for Palestine is a small land of long perspectives.

The OT references to Olivet at 2 Sa. 15:30; Ne. 8:15; Ezk. 11:23 are slight. 1 Ki. 11:7 and 2 Ki. 23:13 refer to Solomon's idolatry, the erection of high places to Chemosh and Molech, which probably caused one summit to be dubbed the Mount of Offence. In the eschatological future the Lord will part the Mount in two as he stands on it (Zc. 14:4).

Jews resident in Jerusalem used to announce the new moon to their compatriots in Babylonia by a chain of beacons starting on Olivet, each signalling the lighting of the next. But since Samaritans lit false flares, eventually human messengers had to replace the old beacons. G. H. Dalman considers the Mishnaic claim that this beacon service stretched as far afield as Mesopotamia perfectly feasible (*Sacred Sites and Ways*, 1935, p. 263, n. 7). The Mount has close connections with the red heifer (*CLEAN AND UNCLEAN) and its ashes of purification (Nu. 19; *Parah* 3. 6–7, 11), as with other ceremonies of levitical Judaism. According to one legend, the dove sent forth from the ark by Noah plucked her leaf from Olivet (Gn. 8:11; Midrash *Genesis Rabba* 33. 6). Some believed that the faithful Jewish dead must be resurrected in Israel, that those who died abroad would eventually be rolled back through underground cavities (*Ketuboth* 111a), emerging at the sundered Mount of Olives (H. Loewe and C. G. Montefiore, *A Rabbinic Anthology*, 1938, pp. 660ff.). When the Shekinah, or radiance of God's presence, departed from the Temple through sin, it was said to linger for 3½ years on Olivet, vainly awaiting repentance (*Lamentations Rabba*, Proem 25; *cf.* Ezk. 10:18). The name 'Mountain of Three Lights' comes from the glow of the flaming Temple altar reflected on the hillside by night, the first beams of sunrise gilding the summit, and the oil from the olives which fed the Temple lamps.

Near the Church of All Nations, at the base of Olivet, are some venerable olive-trees, not demonstrably 2,000 years old. This is the area of Gethsemane, and the precise spot of the Agony, though undetermined, is close by. Half-way up the hill is the Church of Dominus Flevit. But why should our Lord weep there, half-way down? *HDB* cogently argues that he really approached Jerusalem by Bethany, round the S shoulder of Olivet, weeping when the city suddenly burst into view. A succession of churches of the ascension have long crowned the reputed summit of our Lord's assumption, and his supposed footprints are carefully preserved there as a tangible fulfilment of Zc. 14:4. Yet Luke's Gospel favours the Bethany area as the real scene of the Ascension. The visitor to Palestine learns the futility of pondering insolubles. R.A.S.

OLIVET DISCOURSE. Sometimes known as the Synoptic Apocalypse, this is the last major discourse of Jesus recorded by Matthew, Mark and Luke (Mt. 24:3–25:46; Mk. 13:3–37; Lk. 21:5–36), and is the longest and most important section of teaching about the future in the Synoptics. The core is similar in each Gospel, but Matthew has the fullest form, adding at the end some parables and other teaching about the coming judgment. (References in this article will be to Mark's version, unless otherwise stated.)

I. Structure

The discourse is introduced by the disciples asking about (a) when Jesus' prediction of the destruction of the Temple will be fulfilled; (b) 'when these things are all to be accomplished' (v. 4). The wording in Matthew and the subsequent context in Mark suggest that 'all these things' include the end of the age and Jesus' second coming.

Jesus replies: **1.** Do not be misled by the appearance of false Christs, wars, earthquakes and famines: these are the beginning of sufferings, not an indication of the end (vv. 5–8). **2.** Be ready to endure bitter persecution as you witness to me (vv. 9–13). **3.** There will be a period of great distress when the 'desolating sacrilege' is set up (vv. 14–20). **4.** Do not be misled by the activities of false Christs (vv. 21–23). **5.** In those days after the distress the heavenly bodies will be shaken, and you will see the Son of man coming in power and gathering his elect (vv. 24–27). **6.** 'These things' are signs of the Lord's nearness and will happen in this generation (vv. 28–31). **7.** 'That day and hour' are unknown; so keep awake (vv. 32–37).

II. Problems of interpretation

The following are some of the most important points of interpretation on which there is dispute.

a. Particular exegetical problems

1. The phrase 'desolating sacrilege' (v. 14), one of the many OT allusions in the discourse, echoes Dn. 11:31; 12:11. In Daniel the primary reference is to the setting up of a pagan altar in the Jerusalem Temple in 168 BC by *Antiochus Epiphanes; but the intended meaning in the Synoptic Apocalypse is difficult to determine. The injunction 'let the reader understand' (probably to be taken as addressed to the reader of the Gospel, or possibly to the reader of Daniel) suggests that the phrase is deliberately cryptic. Some modern scholars associate it with the abortive attempt of the Roman emperor Gaius to have his statue set up in the Temple in AD 40. They argue that the prophecy derives from that time (so not from Jesus), and that it was unfulfilled. Others take the phrase to refer to the still future appearance of the *Antichrist in the last day, pointing to the similar description of the 'lawless one' in 2 Thes. 2. Others again see the fulfilment of the prophecy in the events leading up to the fall of Jerusalem in AD 70, a view apparently supported by Luke's slightly different version in 21:20. This last view seems the simplest, though it is possible to maintain that the prophecy has a double reference, both to the period of the Roman attack on Jerusalem in AD 66–70 and to the last days.

2. The reference in vv. 24–27 to the disturbances in the heavens and to the coming of the Son of man has been taken in at least two different ways. Some scholars argue that it is figurative language taken from the OT with a historical reference to the fall of Jerusalem: the coming of the Son of man is a coming in victory, not his return to earth, and the gathering of the elect by God's 'messengers' is the missionary outreach of the church. The more usual view is that the verses refer to the second coming, and this is supported by other similarly worded passages in the NT which undoubtedly refer to the parousia (*e.g.* Mt. 13:41ff.; 1 Thes. 4:14ff.).

3. The assertion 'this generation will not pass away before all these things take place' (v. 30) raises particularly difficult questions. Does it mean that the coming of the Son of man and everything else described in the discourse will take place within the lifetime of Jesus' contemporaries? If so—and if the coming referred to is the seond coming (see point **2** above)—then this is evidently a mistaken prediction. Some scholars accept it as such and maintain that the error was a reflection of Jesus' humanity. Many others have been unhappy about this view and have looked for alternative explanations. Some argue that the saying was not Jesus' at all but the teaching of the early church; this explanation probably creates as many difficulties as it solves. Others suggest that the word *genea* does not here mean 'generation' (so RSV and other versions) but 'race' or 'kind of people'. These proposed alternatives do not fit well into the context. A more satisfactory explanation based on the text is that 'these things' in v. 29 are the *signs* of the end, not the end itself; so 'all these things' in v. 30 may also be taken as a reference to the signs of the end. This view can claim support from v. 32; although this verse may simply be saying that Jesus is ignorant of the precise moment in 'this generation' when the Son of man will return, it may also be taken as a general disavowal of knowledge of the timing of 'that day' (= the last day in biblical terminology). Thus Jesus does know that the signs will take place within a generation, but he does not know when the end itself will come.

Even on this view the strong impression is still that the coming is near. Perhaps the best explanation of this strong sense of imminence, which pervades the whole NT, is to say that it is a theological awareness of the fact that, once Jesus has come, the parousia is near in God's plan, rather than a particular chronological conviction. The end began in Jesus, and ever afterwards we live in eager anticipation of the consummation.

b. More general questions

1. Many scholars have doubts about ascribing some or all of the discourse to Jesus. Many have felt, *e.g.*, that the apocalyptic teaching in the discourse is unlike Jesus' teaching elsewhere in the Gospels. T. Colani's famous *Little Apocalypse Theory*, propounded in 1864 and taken up with modification by many since, was that vv. 5–31 were a Jewish–Christian apocalyptic tract incorporated into the Gospel by the Evangelist. This theory was founded on a mistaken view of Jesus as one who taught eternal ethical truths and not an eschatological gospel. But although scholars today reject Colani's view of Jesus, some still argue that the teaching on signs contradicts Jesus' teaching elsewhere on the unexpectedness of the parousia (*e.g.* Lk. 17:20ff.). This view fails to take seriously the fact that in biblical apocalyptic teaching about suddenness and signs is regularly found together. Other objections to regarding the teaching as deriving from Jesus, *e.g.* that the OT quotations are based on the LXX and not on the Hebrew text, are equally indecisive.

2. There are important literary critical questions about the discourse. The differences between the Gospels force the critic to try to explain the relationship between the accounts; many scholars argue that two or more of the Evangelists had independent accounts of this discourse, and not simply that Matthew and Luke used Mark. Many also believe that one or more of the Evangelists has included in his version material that originally belonged in a different context; thus Matthew is thought to have imported 'Q' material into his account.

3. More important than the simply literary questions are questions about the theological teaching of the discourse in the three Gospels. One debated question is whether the prime intention is to give apocalyptic teaching about the signs of the end, or to exhort hearers and readers. The probability is that both purposes are present: Jesus taught his disciples that the rule (or *kingdom) of God had come with his ministry, but that it would be fully established in the future. Here he does give information about what will occur before the end, but his purpose is not so that anyone may draw up a timetable of future events but to prepare people practically for the future; thus the note of exhortation is very strong. Jesus' disciples are (a) not to get excited by false teachers and rumours before the end; (b) to endure hardship until the end; (c) to be awake for the return of Christ.

BIBLIOGRAPHY. G. R. Beasley-Murray, *Jesus and the Future*, 1954; commentaries on Mark by C. E. B. Cranfield, 1959, and W. Lane, *NIC*, 1974; D. Ford, *The Abomination of Desolation in Biblical Eschatology*, 1979; D. Wenham, *The Rediscovery of Jesus' Eschatological Discourse*, 1984; T. J. Geddert, *Watchwords: Mark 13 in Biblical Eschatology*, 1989.

D.W.

OLYMPAS. An otherwise unknown but influential Christian greeted by Paul in Rom. 16:15. As the name, probably an abbreviation of Olympiodorus, was common throughout the empire, its presence in this verse throws no light on the problem of the destination of Rom. 16. R.V.G.T.

OMRI (Heb. *'omrî*). **1.** An officer from Issachar during David's reign (1 Ch. 27:18). **2.** Sixth king of the N kingdom of Israel and founder of a new dynasty after the death of *Elah. During the period of anarchy following the death of *Baashah, the army, besieging Gibbethon, proclaimed their leader Omri as king upon hearing of the coup by Zimri (*c.* 885 BC; 1 Ki. 16:15–17). He thereupon marched to the capital, *Tirzah, and besieged the town until Zimri committed suicide (v. 18). Tibni, another claimant to the throne, resisted Omri for 4 years but was finally defeated. Omri then reigned for 7 years, from the 31st to the 38th year of *Asa (vv. 23, 29), a total of 12 years (v. 23).

Aram, which under *Ben-hadad I had been strong enough to annex part of Israel during Baasha's reign, still threatened Omri (*cf.* 1 Ki. 20:34). He allied himself with Ethbaal, king of Sidon, by taking his daughter *Jezebel for *Ahab, his son (16:31), thus averting some of the danger. He was strong enough to make Moab his vassal, as recorded by Mesha in the *Moabite stone (11:4–5) (*ANET*, p. 320; *DOTT*, p. 196; *cf.* 2 Ki. 3:4).

Omri is also remembered for his building activities. The most important of these was the new Israelite capital at *Samaria on a site purchased from Shemer, its previous owner (1 Ki. 16:24). The city had an excellent strategic position, and served as capital until the fall of Israel in 722 BC. Archaeological excavations at Megiddo and Hazor have also revealed buildings attributed to him.

Details of Omri's reign are sparse, but Assyrian sources show that until the reign of *Sargon II, Israel was also known as *mātbīt Ḫumri*, 'the land/house of Omri' (*ANET*, pp. 281–285). Because he condoned pagan worship he was remembered as a bad king (1 Ki. 16:25–26). D.W.B.

ON. 1. A venerable city, Egyp. *'Iwnw* ('city of the pillar'), Gk. Heliopolis, now represented by scattered or buried remains at Tell Ḥiṣn and Maṭariyeh, 16 km NE of Cairo. From antiquity it was the great centre of Egyp. sun-worship, where the solar deities Rē' and Atum were especially honoured, and the home of one of Egypt's several theological 'systems'. The pharaohs embellished the temple of Rē' with many obelisks—tall, tapering, monolithic shafts of square or rectangular section, each

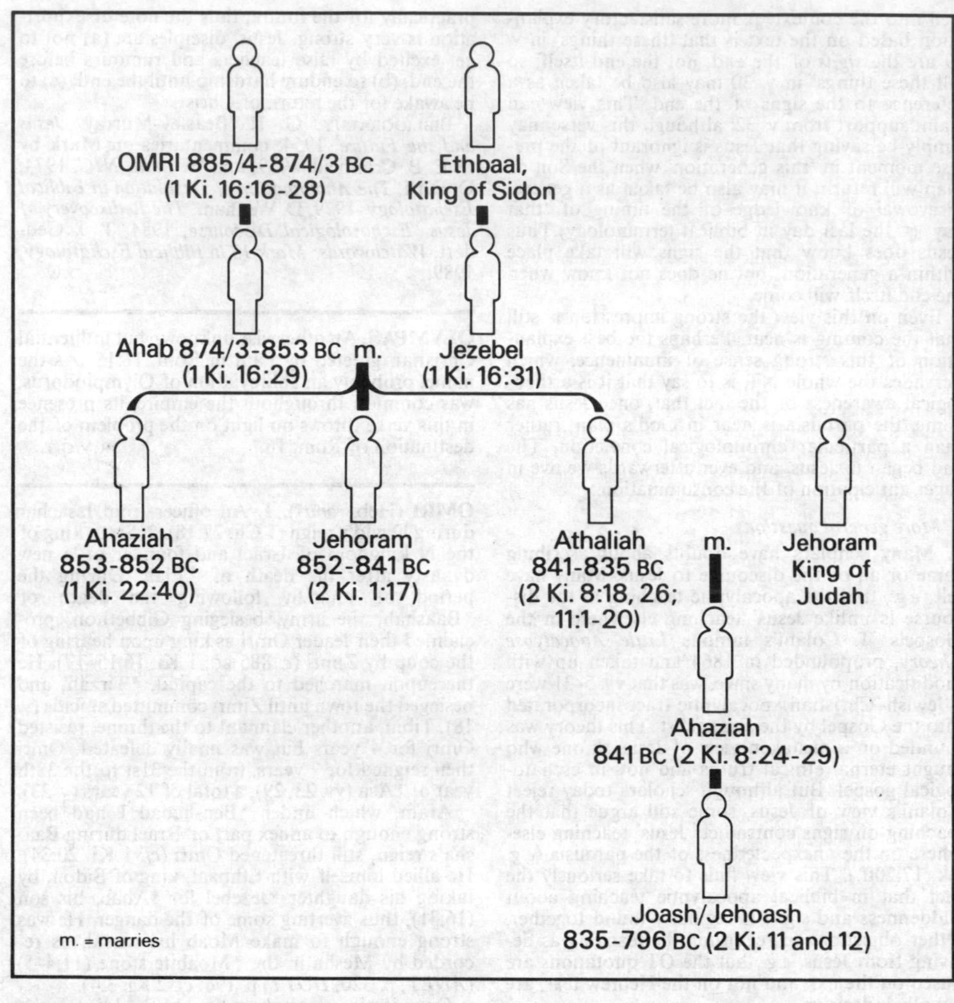

The dynasty of Omri, king of Israel (c. 885–874 BC) (see p. 847).

ending at the top in a pyramidally shaped point; such a 'pyramidion' represented the *benben* or sacred stone of Rēʿ, as first to catch the rays of the rising sun. Each pharaoh from the 5th Dynasty onward (25th century BC) was styled 'son of Rēʿ', and the priestly corporations of On/Heliopolis were equalled in wealth only by that of the god Ptah of Memphis and exceeded only by that of the god Amūn of Thebes, during *c.* 1600–1100 BC.

The prominence of On is reflected in Gn. 41:45, 50; 46:20, where Joseph as Pharaoh's new chief minister is married to Asenath, daughter of *Potiphera, 'priest of On'. This title might mean that Potiphera was high priest there. His name, very fittingly, is compounded with that of the sun-god Rēʿ. *Cf.* A. Rowe, *PEQ* 94, 1962, pp. 133–142.

On next recurs in Heb. history under the appropriate pseudonym Beth-shemesh, 'House of the Sun', when Jeremiah (43:13) threatens that Nebuchadrezzar will smash 'the pillars of Beth-shemesh', *i.e.* the obelisks of On/Heliopolis. Whether Isaiah's 'city of the sun' (19:18) is On is less clear. Aven (Heb. *'awen*) of Ezk. 30:17 is a variant pointing of *'ôn*, 'On', perhaps as a pun on *'awen*, 'trouble, wickedness', in Ezekiel's judgment on Egypt's cities.

2. On, son of Peleth, a Reubenite chief, rebelled with Korah against Moses in the wilderness (Nu. 16:1). K.A.K.

ONAN (Heb *'ōnān,* 'vigorous'). The second son of Judah (Gn. 38:4; 46:12; Nu. 26:19; 1 Ch 2:3). On the death of his elder brother Er, Onan was commanded by Judah to contract a levirate marriage with Tamar, Er's widow. Onan, unwilling to follow this traditional practice, took steps to avoid a full consummation of the union, thus displeasing the Lord, who slew him (Gn. 38:8–10). Judah evidently attached some blame for his sons' deaths to Tamar herself (v. 11). For levirate marriage see *MARRIAGE, IV. J.D.D.

ONESIMUS. A runaway slave belonging to Philemon, an influential Christian at Colossae. He made the acquaintance of Paul, while the latter was a prisoner, either at Rome or Ephesus (according to the view which is taken of the provenance of Colossians). He was converted by the apostle (Phm. 10), and became a trustworthy and dear brother (Col. 4:9). His name, which means 'useful', was a common name for slaves, though not confined to them; and he lived up to it by making himself so helpful to Paul that the latter would have liked to have kept him to look after him as, Pauls feels, Philemon would have wished (Phm. 13). But the apostle felt constrained to do nothing without Philemon's willing consent; so he returned the slave to his former owner, with a covering note—the canonical *Philemon. In this the apostle plays on the slave's name by describing him as 'once so little use to you, but now useful indeed, both to you and me'; and hints, tactfully but clearly, that he expects Philemon to take Onesimus 'back for good, no longer as a slave, but as more than a slave—as a dear brother, very dear indeed to me and how much dearer to you, both as man and as Christian' (Phm. 15–16, NEB). Nevertheless, Paul admits that sending him back is like being deprived of a part of himself (Phm. 12).

The mention of Onesimus is one of the links which bind together Colossians and Philemon, and shows that they were sent from the same place at the same time. Some scholars believe that the Onesimus known to Ignatius and described by him in his Epistle to the Ephesians as 'a man of inexpressible love and your bishop' was none other than the runaway slave. This hypothesis, though not impossible, would seem improbable on chronological considerations. It is urged in its support that it supplies a reason why Philemon was preserved as a canonical book. On the other hand, its close connection with Colossians, and its importance for the light it throws on the Christian treatment of slaves, would seem to provide adequate reasons for its canonicity.

Bibliography. Onesimus' later career has been made the subject of an elaborate theory by E. J. Goodspeed, *INT*, 1937, pp. 109–124, and J. Knox, *Philemon among the Letters of Paul*[2], 1959. For a criticism (with bibliography), see R. P. Martin, *Colossians and Philemon, NCB*[2], 1982, introduction. See also R. P. Martin, *Ephesians, Colossians and Philemon, Interpretation*, 1992; S. S. Bartchy, *ABD* 5, pp. 305–310.

R.V.G.T.
R.P.M.

ONESIPHORUS. In the Second Epistle to Timothy, written by Paul to Timothy at Ephesus, the apostle sends greetings to the household of Onesiphorus (4:19), and prays that the Lord's mercy may rest upon it, and that Onesiphorus himself may find mercy from the Lord on the great day of judgment. This true Christian friend had often brought relief to the apostle in his troubles, and had taken pains to search out and find him in Rome, where Paul was now in prison. His conduct in this respect, Paul notices, stood out in marked contrast to other Asian Christians who had deserted Paul in his hour of need. Like Onesimus, Onesiphorus had lived up to his name, which means 'profit-bringer'. The apostle reminds Timothy that he knew better than Paul himself about the many services rendered by Onesiphorus to the Christians who lived at Ephesus (1:16–18).

Bibliography. E. E. Ellis, *NTS* 17, 1970–71, pp. 437–452, 'Paul and his Co-Workers'; and for the view that Onesiphorus played a significant role regarding the collection in Galatia, and that the setting of 2 Tim. 1:16–18 is Pisidian Antioch, not Rome, see F. J. Badcock, *The Pauline Epistles*, 1937, especially pp. 150–158.

Problems to do with Paul's remembrance of Onesiphorus, who may or may not have been deceased when 2 Tim. 1:18 was written, are considered by D. Guthrie (*TNTC*, 1957) and J. N. D. Kelly (Harper-Black, 1963) *ad loc.*

R.V.G.T.
R.P.M.

ONO. A town first mentioned in the lists of Thothmes III (1490–1436 BC). The Benjaminites rebuilt it after the conquest of Canaan (1 Ch. 8:12) and reoccupied it after the Exile (Ne. 11:31–35). Identified with Kafr 'Anâ, it lay near Lydda. The area was called the Plain of Ono (Ne. 6:2).

D.F.P.

ONYCHA. Pungent component of holy incense made by Moses at God's command, by burning claw-shaped valves closing shell apertures of certain molluscs—Heb. *šᵉḥēleṯ*, Ex. 30:34 only. This is the Gk. accusative of *onyx*, meaning talon, claw, anything so shaped, the precious stone. The accusative form, misunderstood as nominative in Vulg., passed into EVV usage, thus conveniently distinguishing the specialized meaning in Ex. 30:34.

R.A.S.

OPHIR (Heb. *'ôp̄ir*, Gn. 10:29; *'ôp̄îr*, 1 Ki. 10:11). **1.** The name of the son of Yoqtān in the genealogy of Shem (Gn. 10:29 = 1 Ch. 1:23). This tribe is known from pre-islamic inscriptions (G. Ryckmans, *Les noms propres sud-sémitiques*, 1934, pp. 298, 339f.). Their area lies between Saba in the Yemen and Ḥawilah (Ḥawlān) as described in Gn. 10:29. Islamic tradition equates Yoqtān with Qaḥtān, a son of Ishmael and 'father of all Arabs'.

2. The country from which fine gold was imported to Judah (2 Ch. 8:18; Jb. 22:24; 28:16; Ps. 45:9; Is. 13:12), sometimes in large quantities (1 Ch. 29:4), and with valuable almug(sandal?)-wood (1 Ki. 10:11), silver, ivories, apes and peacocks (1 Ki. 10:22), and precious stones (2 Ch. 9:10). It was reached by Solomon's fleet from Ezion-geber on the Gulf of Aqabah (1 Ki. 9:28) employing 'ships of Tarshish', which might be *ships normally used for carrying ore (1 Ki. 22:48). These voyages took 'three years', that is perhaps one entire year and parts of two others. The trade was sufficiently well known for Ophir to be synonymous with the fine gold which was its principal product (Jb. 22:24). In Is. 13:12 Ophir is paralleled with *'ôqir*, 'I will make precious' (*HUCA* 12–13, 1937–8, p. 61). A confirmation of this trade is found in an ostracon, found at Tell Qasileh NE of Tel Aviv in 1946, inscribed *zhb 'p̄r lbyt ḥrn š=*, 'gold from Ophir for Beth Horon 30 shekels' (*JNES* 10, 1951, pp. 265–267).

Various theories have been put forward for the site of Ophir.

a. S Arabia (as in **1** above). R. North links (Š)ōpha(i)r(a) (= Ophir) with Parvaim (= Farwa) in Yemen as the source of Sheba gold (*cf.* Ps. 72:15; Is. 60:6).

b. SE Arabia: Oman. These are not far from Ezion-geber, and it is necessary to assume both that the 3-year voyage included laying up during the hot summer and that some commodities (*e.g.* apes) not commonly found in S Arabia were brought to Ophir as an entrepôt from more distant places.

c. E African coast: Somalia, *i.e.* the Egyp. *Punt*, a source of the frankincense and myrrh and those items described as from Ophir (W. F. Albright, *Archaeology and the Religion of Israel*, 1953, pp. 133–135, 212; van Beek, *JAOS* 78, 1958, p. 146).

d. (S)upāra, 75 km N of Bombay, India. Josephus (*Ant.* 8. 164), LXX and Vulg. (Jb. 28:16) interpreted Ophir as India. In favour of this interpretation are the facts that all the commodities named are familiar in ancient India, and it is known that from the 2nd millennium BC there was a lively sea-trade between the Persian Gulf and India.

e. Other, more doubtful, suggestions include Apir, Baluchistan (possibly ancient Meluhha, *cf.* *BSOAS* 36, 1973, pp. 554–587) and Zimbabwe, S Rhodesia.

BIBLIOGRAPHY. V. Christides, *RB* 77, 1970, pp. 240–247; R. North, *Fourth World Congress of Jewish Studies*, Papers, 1, 1967, pp. 197–202.

D.J.W.

OPHRAH. (Heb. *'oprâh*). **1.** A town in Benjamin (Jos. 18:23; 1 Sa. 13:17, called Ephron (*Q^e^rē' 'eprāim*); 2 Ch. 13:19); modern et-Tayibeh, on a commanding height 9 km N of Michmash. Arabs often substituted *tayibeh* ('fortunate') where a place-name *'ofra* persisted in the Middle Ages, as it suggested black magic (Abel, *JPOS* 17, 1937, p. 38). It is doubtful whether *'oprâh* developed into *Ephraim* (= Heb. *'eprāim*) of Jn. 11:54; see K.-D. Schunck, *VT* 11, 1961, pp. 188–200, and J. Heller, *VT* 12, 1962, pp. 339ff.

2. Ophrah of Abiezer in Manasseh, Gideon's home, where his altar of Jehovah-shalom (Jdg. 6:24, AV) was shown in later times. Possible sites are: (*a*) Fer'ata, W of Mt Gerizim (Conder), near Shechem but rather remote from the area of conflict, and probably *Pirathon of Jdg. 12:15; (*b*) et-Tayibeh, half-way between Beth-shan and Tabor (Abel), but well inside Issachar, and perhaps the Hapharaim of Jos. 19:19; (*c*) Afula in the Jezreel plain (*LOB*, p. 263). Tell el-Far'a, 10 km NE of Shechem, is now known to be *Tirzah.

3. A town or family in Judah (1 Ch. 4:14).

J.P.U.L.

ORACLE. The translation 'oracle' occurs 17 times in the AV of the OT. Sixteen times it is the consistent mistranslation of the Heb. *d^e^bîr*, used exclusively of the inner shrine of Solomon's *Temple. The faulty derivation from *dibber*, 'speak', rather than from *dābar* in the sense of 'to be behind' stems from the translations of Aquila and Symmachus (who used *chrēmatistērion*, 'oracle') and the Vulgate (*oraculum*). That in heathen temples the chambers where the gods delivered their utterances (the oracular shrine of Apollo at Delphi was the most famous of these) were designated 'oracles' undoubtedly influenced the change as well.

In 2 Sa. 16:23 'oracle' translates the Heb. *dābār* and refers simply to the *word* or *utterance* of God without any specific indication of how this would be elicited; although some have here inferred a reference to the *Urim and Thummim (1 Sa. 28:6). In the RVmg. 'oracle' is sometimes used in place of 'burden' in the title of certain prophecies as a translation of the Heb. *maśśā'*.

In the NT 'oracles' translates the Gk. *logia*, meaning divine utterances and generally referring to the entire OT or some specific part of it. In Acts 7:38 the reference is either to the Decalogue or to the entire content of the Mosaic law. These oracles are said to be 'living', *zōnta*, that is, 'enduring' or 'abiding'. In Rom. 3:2 the reference is to all the written utterances of God through the OT writers, but with special regard to the divine promises made to Israel. The 'oracles of God' in Heb. 5:12, AV ('word', RSV) represent the body of Christian doctrine as it relates both to its OT foundation and to God's final utterance through his Son (Heb. 1:1). 1 Pet. 4:11 teaches that the NT preacher must speak as one who speaks the oracles of God, treating his words as carefully as if they were inspired Scripture.

The theological significance of the oracle is emphasized by B. B. Warfield who concludes that *ta logia*, as employed in the NT, are 'divinely authoritative communications before which men stand in awe and to which they bow in humility' (*The Inspiration and Authority of the Bible*, 1948, p. 403).

R.H.M.

ORCHARD. Well known in various Bible lands throughout antiquity, these were plantations of fruit trees, specifically including pomegranates (Ec. 2:5, AV and Ct. 4:13 where 'orchard' renders Heb. *pardēs*). The *pardēs* of Ne. 2:8 furnished timber, and so is there rendered *'forest'. K.A.K.

ORDINATION. Considering the role played by the ministry throughout the history of the church, references to ordination are surprisingly few in the NT. Indeed, the word 'ordination' does not occur, and the verb 'to ordain' in the technical sense does not occur either. A number of verbs are translated 'ordain' in AV, but these all have meanings like 'appoint'. For example, *cheirotoneō* is used of the institution of elders in certain Galatian churches (Acts 14:23), but before we think of this as denoting 'ordination' in our sense of the term we must note its use in passages such as 2 Cor. 8:19, where it refers to the brother who was 'appointed by the churches to travel with us . . .'

The Twelve were chosen by Christ to be very near to himself and to be sent forth to minister (Mk. 3:14). But there is no word of any ceremony of ordination. Mark says that Jesus 'made (*poieō*)' twelve, and Luke that he 'chose (*eklegō*)' them (Mk. 3:14; Lk. 6:13). This was a very solemn occasion (Luke tells us that Jesus prayed all night before making his selection). But there is no 'ordination' mentioned. John speaks of the risen Lord as breathing on the ten, saying, 'Receive the Holy Spirit' (Jn. 20:22); but it is difficult to see an ordination in this. It is probably significant that when Matthias took the place of Judas there is again no mention of any ordination. Lots were cast, and when the choice of Matthias was known he was simply 'enrolled' or 'numbered' with the others (Acts 1:26). Similarly, prophets and others are called directly by God, though some at least are said to be 'for the work of ministry' (Eph. 4:12; the word 'ministry' here is, of course, used of service in a wide sense).

Luke tells us of the appointment of the Seven (Acts 6), and this is often understood as the institution of the diaconate. This may indeed be the case, but it is far from certain. Some think that the presbyterate is meant, and others deny that there is ordination to any ecclesiastical office. They think that Luke is describing nothing more than a temporary measure to meet a difficult situation. If the traditional view is accepted, then the essential thing about ordination is the laying on of hands with prayer. But in view of the uncertainties, and the wide use in antiquity of the laying on of hands, it is not possible to build much on this passage. Nor are we any better off when we read of elders as being appointed in the Galatian churches (Acts 14:23), for, while we may be tolerably sure that they were ordained in some way, nothing at all is told us of how this was done or what was expected of it.

Our most important information comes from the Pastoral Epistles. Paul counsels Timothy, 'Do not neglect the gift you have, which was given you by prophetic utterance when the council of elders laid their hands upon you' (1 Tim. 4:14). This passage yields us three items of information about Timothy's ordination. First, it meant the giving to him of a *charisma*, the spiritual *gift needed for the work of ministering. Secondly, this came to him 'by (*dia*) prophecy'. Thirdly, it came with (*meta*) the laying on of hands by the elders. The essential thing about ordination is the divine gift. Nothing can compensate for its lack. But there is also an outward act, the laying on of hands. It is possible that Paul refers to the same rite when he speaks of his own laying on of hands on Timothy (2 Tim. 1:6), though it should not be overlooked that some other rite may be in mind, perhaps something more akin to Anglican confirmation than to ordination. We might be able to make a better judgment if we knew when this took place, whether at the beginning of Paul's association with Timothy, or not long before the writing of the letter. If with most commentators we take this to refer to ordination, the meaning will be that Paul joined with the elders in the *laying on of hands, which in any case would be antecedently likely. It is probable that we have another reference to the same ordination in the words about 'the prophetic utterances which pointed to you' (1 Tim. 1:18).

Ordination is always a solemn affair, and it may be that the words 'Do not be hasty in the laying on of hands' (1 Tim. 5:22) emphasize this. But in view of the context it is perhaps more likely that they refer to the reception of penitents back into fellowship.

All this makes for a somewhat meagre harvest, which is all the more disappointing, since the Pastorals show us how important the *ministry was, especially the offices of presbyter and deacon. Titus, for example, is bidden 'appoint (*kathistēmi*) elders in every town' (Tit. 1:5), and much attention is paid to the qualifications for ministers. It is possible to suggest that the Christians took over the ordination of elders from the similar Jewish institution, but this does not get us far. All that we can say for certain is that the important thing for ministering is the divine gift, and that the essential rite in the earliest time appears to have been that of the laying on of hands with prayer. (*SPIRITUAL GIFTS.) L.M.

OREB (Heb. *'ōrēḇ*, 'raven'). **1.** A Midianite prince in the army routed by Gideon. **2.** The rock of Oreb, named after this prince, and remembered for the great defeat of Midian (Jdg. 7:25; Is. 10:26). The Ephraimites cut off the enemy's retreat at the Jordan fords, presumably opposite Jezreel; Beth-barah might be a ford (*'āḇar*, 'cross') some 20 km S of the Sea of Galilee. J.P.U.L.

ORNAMENTS. From Palaeolithic times ornament has been used by man to adorn the objects which surround him in his daily life. When the intention is right, the skill of the craftsman is a thing pleasing to God, and indeed for the building of the tabernacle Bezalel was filled with the spirit (*rûaḥ*) of God (Ex. 31:1–5), as were those who were to make the garments for the high priest (Ex. 28:3).

Archaeological discoveries have shown that in biblical times the carving of wood and ivory was done with great skill; weaving and embroidery reached a high standard; and the techniques involved in fine metalwork were well understood (*ARTS AND CRAFTS). Three main divisions of ornamented objects may be distinguished.

I. Personal

There is no evidence for the practice of ornamental tattooing in the ancient Near East, but clothing was often elaborately decorated, and jewellery was widely used. Though few examples of textiles have been recovered outside Egypt, the Assyrian and Persian sculptured reliefs and mural paintings at Mari on the Euphrates give, sometimes in great detail, representations of garments with fine embroidery. The Egyp. tomb-paintings likewise depict clothing in detail, and in one tomb at Beni-hasan a group of Asiatic nomads with brightly-coloured costumes (see *IBA*, fig. 25) gives an idea of the sort of ornamental clothing perhaps worn by the Patriarchs (*DRESS).

Many examples of jewellery (*JEWELS AND PRECIOUS STONES) have been found in excavations, perhaps the most outstanding being those from the 'Royal Tombs' at *Ur.

Various terms referring to objects of personal adornment are translated 'ornament', but their precise significance is in many cases uncertain. Among these are the following: **1.** *ḥ^{a}lî* (Pr. 25:12), perhaps from a Semitic root *ḥlh*, 'to adorn'; all EVV translate 'ornament'. The word also occurs in Ct. 7:1 where EVV translate it 'jewel'. **2.** *liwyâ* (Pr. 1:9; 4:9; lit. 'twisted thing'); RV renders 'chaplet' and RSV 'garland'. **3.** *'^{a}ḏî* (Ex. 33:4–6; 2 Sa. 1:24; Is. 49:18; Je. 2:32; 4:30; Ezk. 7:20; 16:7, 11; 23:40), derived from *'āḏâ*, 'to ornament', 'to deck oneself'; all EVV translate 'ornament'. **4.** *p^{e}'ēr* (Is. 61:10), from *pā'ar* in the Pi'el, meaning 'to beautify'; RV and RSV translate 'garland'. **5.** *ṣ^{e}'āḏâ* (Is. 3:20), of unknown etymology. It probably signifies an 'armlet' (so RSV); RV gives 'ankle chain'. **6.** *'eḵes* (Is. 3:18), perhaps connected with Arab. *'ikāsu*, 'to hobble (a camel)', from *'akasa*, 'to reverse, tie backwards', whence RV, RSV 'anklet'. The root occurs as a verb in Is. 3:16, where it is translated 'making a tinkling'.

Though on an occasion such as a wedding the putting on of ornaments and jewels by the participants is treated as right and proper (Is. 61:10), the immoderate use of personal ornament is roundly condemned (Is. 3:18–23; 1 Tim. 2:9). Is. 3 provides a catalogue of different kinds of ornaments which are translated variously in EVV. Some of these are *hapax legomena*, and little can be added to the RSV interpretation. The 'bracelet' (*šērâ*) of v. 19 is supported by the probable Akkad. cognate *šemêru* (*šewêru*) with this meaning. Likewise in v. 21, 'ring' (*ṭabba'aṯ*, RSV 'signet ring') is supported by Akkad. *ṭimbu'u*, *ṭimbûtu*, 'seal ring' (*SEAL). AV renderings which have been radically altered in the later versions are v. 20 'earring' (*laḥaš*; RV, RSV *'amulet'), v. 22 'wimple' (*miṭpaḥaṯ*; RV 'shawl', RSV 'cloak') and 'crisping pin' (*ḥārîṭ*; RV 'satchel', RSV 'handbag').

Among other articles of personal adornment were: **1.** *ḥāḥ*, usually a hook or ring for holding a man (2 Ki. 19:28) or animal (Ezk. 29:4) captive, but in Ex. 35:22 an ornament (AV 'bracelet', RV, RSV 'brooch'); **2.** *śah^arôn*, probably a crescent-shaped object which was used on camels (Jdg. 8:21; AV 'ornament', RV 'crescent') and humans (Jdg. 8:26; Is. 3:18, AV 'round tire like the moon', RV 'crescent'); and many different kinds of chain ornaments, including **3.** *rāḇîḏ*, probably a twisted circlet for the neck (Gn. 41:42; Ezk. 16:11); **4.** *ᵃnāq*, a more elaborate form made of plaited wire which might have pendants attached (Jdg. 8:26; Pr. 1:9; Ct. 4:9); **5.** *šarš^erâ*, probably a more flexible chain of the link type (Ex. 28:14, 22; 39:15; 1 Ki. 7:17; 2 Ch. 3:5, 16); **6.** *ḥārûz*, a necklace of beads strung on a thread (Ct. 1:10; RV 'string of jewels'). Another type of ornament, mentioned in 1 Macc. 10:89; 11:58; 14:44, is the 'buckle' (Gk. *porpē*, 'buckle pin', 'buckle brooch').

A special case of personal ornament is found in the garments of the high priest (*DRESS). The linen coat was of an ornamental weave (Ex. 28:39, RV, RSV), the ephod and the girdle were decorative (Ex. 28:6, 8) and round the hem of the robe of the ephod were alternate bells and pomegranates (Ex. 28:31–35). In addition to these the breastplate (see *BREASTPIECE OF THE HIGH PRIEST) contained ornamental elements.

The ancient Hebrews, like their neighbours, probably wore *amulets and personal *seals for ornamentation.

In Ex. 13:16 and Dt. 6:8; 11:18 the word 'frontlets' (*ṭôṭāpôṯ*) may refer to some ornament of the head. A connection with Akkad. *ṭaṭāpu*, 'to encircle', has been suggested, but this remains uncertain.

II. Movable objects

From very early times painted or incised decoration was used on *pottery, and though in historical times the abundance of other possessions resulted in absence of decoration, certain wares such as Mycenaean and that called 'Philistine' are easily distinguishable and provide useful criteria for dating to the archaeologist. *Archaeology has shown that tools and weapons had, on occasion, appropriate decorations, but the class of small object which often called forth the most elaborate and delicate ornamentation was that of cosmetic equipment. Boxes, jars for unguents, palettes for mixing pigments and mirror handles of elaborately carved bone and ivory have been excavated in Syria, Palestine, Mesopotamia and Egypt. Furniture, especially in royal palaces, was sometimes richly ornamented with carved ivory panels (*cf.* 1 Ki. 10:18; 2 Ch. 9:17; Am. 6:4 and *IVORY). That ornamental carpets were used is shown by stone paving slabs carved in replica of carpets from the Assyrian royal palaces. Elaborately ornamented horse harnesses are portrayed on the Assyrian palace reliefs and camel harness was also evidently decorated (Jdg. 8:21, 26).

The *tabernacle and its contents were ornamented, under the skill of *Bezalel, with cunning workmanship. This was also a pagan practice, as is shown by discoveries of temple furniture from Megiddo, Beth-shan and other sites, where incense and offering stands are decorated with birds, animals, serpents (symbol of fertility) and human figures. These were the common trappings of the pagan cults of the Israelites' neighbours, and often the most elaborate ornament was reserved for the casket of the deceased. Elaborately carved stone sarcophagi are known from Phoenicia and Egypt, and the discoveries in the 'Royal Tombs' at *Ur and in the tomb of Tutankhamūn show the wealth of ornamental riches that accompanied the dead to the grave.

III. Architectural

Buildings in antiquity, particularly palaces, were decorated both inside and out. The inside walls of important rooms in the palaces of the Assyrian kings at Nineveh and Khorsabad were adorned by carved bas-reliefs and the doorways guarded by great composite beasts (*IBA*, fig. 44). These reliefs were probably partially coloured in antiquity, being in fact glorified murals, examples of which from the Assyrian period were discovered at Til Barsip. In the early 2nd-millennium palace at Mari remains of several mural paintings were recovered suggesting that such decoration has not been discovered more often only on account of its perishable nature.

In Egypt, while the best-known mural paintings are found in rock-cut tombs, palaces with murals have been excavated at Malkata (Amenophis III) and el-Amarna (Amenophis IV). The great temples at Karnak and Luxor were decorated with carved and painted murals and hieroglyphic inscriptions, the hieroglyphs forming ornamental elements. *Ivory was probably used not only for the decoration of furniture but also for application to suitable parts of important rooms, as is suggested by caches of carved ivories found at Nimrud, Arslan Tash, Megiddo and Samaria (*cf.* 1 Ki. 22:39; Ps. 45:8; Am. 3:15).

Outside decoration, while in earlier periods it might consist of revetted walls, or in Assyria guardian beasts at gateways, reached a sumptuous level in Nebuchadrezzar's Babylon, where excavation has revealed great façades of coloured glazed bricks with animals and rosettes at intervals.

The Persians in the latter part of the 1st millennium BC recruited craftsmen from all over the Middle East to build and decorate the great ceremonial city of Persepolis, even employing men from as far afield as the Aegean. Aegean influences had already been felt in the 2nd millennium (Alalaḫ, Ugarit), and it is probable that the term *kap̄tôr* in Ex. 25:31–36; 37:17–22 (AV 'knop') and Am. 9:1; Zp. 2:14 (AV 'lintel') refers to some decorative architectural feature, perhaps a column capital, derived from Crete or the Aegean (*CAPHTOR).

There is reason to believe that under the Monarchy the kings and the wealthy would have followed the customs of the surrounding peoples, particularly the Phoenicians, in the decoration of their palaces and houses.

BIBLIOGRAPHY. No one work covers the whole subject. Relevant material is to be found incidentally in C. Singer, E. Holmyard and A. Hall, *A*

History of Technology, 1, 1954, especially pp. 413–447, 623–703, and *passim* in H. Frankfort, *The Art and Architecture of the Ancient Orient*, 1954; W. S. Smith, *The Art and Architecture of Ancient Egypt*, 1958; and for Palestine, A. G. Barrois, *Manuel d'Archéologie Biblique*, 1–2, 1939–53; Y. Shiloh, *PEQ* 109, 1977, pp. 39–42 ('Proto-Aeolic' capital); K. R. Maxwell-Hyslop, *Western Asiatic Jewellery*, 1971.

T.C.M.

ORPAH. A Moabitess, the daughter-in-law of Naomi, and Ruth's sister-in-law (Ru. 1:4). After their husbands died they came from Moab to Judah, but Orpah, following Naomi's advice, remained, to return to her former home and the worship of Chemosh (Ru. 1:15; 1 Ki. 11:33). Even so, Naomi commended her to Yahweh's protection.

M.B.

ORPHAN, FATHERLESS (Heb. *yāṯôm*; Gk. *orphanos*). The care of the fatherless was from earliest times a concern of the Israelites, as of the surrounding nations. The Covenant Code (Ex. 22:22), and the Deuteronomic Code particularly, were most solicitous for the welfare of such (Dt. 16:11, 14; 24:17), protecting their rights of inheritance and enabling them to share in the great annual feasts and to have a portion of the tithe crops (Dt. 26:12). It is specifically stated, moreover, that God works on their behalf (Dt. 10:18), and that condemnation awaits those who oppress them (Dt. 27:19; *cf.* Mal. 3:5).

Though many orphans would be aided by kindred and friends (Jb. 29:12; 31:17), there was a general failure to fulfil the provisions of the Codes, testified by the accusations and laments found in the prophets, in the Psalms, and in the book of Job. 'In you,' says Ezekiel (22:7), speaking of Jerusalem, 'the fatherless and the widow are wronged'. Justice, it is averred, is withheld from orphans; their plight is pitiable, for they are robbed and killed (Jb. 24:3, 9; Ps. 94:6; Is. 1:23; 10:2; Je. 5:28), making even more vivid the Psalmist's words against the wicked: 'May his children be fatherless . . .!' (109:9).

God, however, is specially concerned for the fatherless (Pss. 10:18; 68:5; 146:9; Ho. 14:3; *cf.* Jn. 14:18), especially when they look in vain to men for help (*cf.* Ps. 27:10).

The only NT occurrence of the word makes an integral part of true religion the visiting of 'orphans and widows in their affliction . . .' (Jas. 1:27).

BIBLIOGRAPHY. J. Pridmore, *NIDNTT* 2, pp. 737f.; H. Seesemann, *TDNT* 5, pp. 487f.

J.D.D.

OTHNIEL (Heb. *'oṯnî'ēl*). **1.** A *Kenizzite, brother (or perhaps nephew) of Caleb ben Jephunneh (Jdg. 1:13; *cf.* Jos. 15:17); if 'son of Kenaz' is a patronymic, he and Caleb may have been brothers or half-brothers. Distinguishing himself in the sack of *Kiriath-sepher, he married Achsah, Caleb's daughter. Later he saw the beginnings of apostasy and the domination by *Cushan-rishathaim, against whom he led a successful revolt, becoming the first of the *judges. Jdg. 3:10 indicates that he was a charismatic leader, who restored order and authority ('judged' means this as well as deliverance; *cf.* 1 Sa. 7:15; 8:20).

2. A *Netophathite, whose descendant Heldai was one of David's officers (1 Ch. 27:15).

J.P.U.L.

P

PADDAN, PADDAN-ARAM. The 'field' or 'plain' of Aram (RSV *'Mesopotamia') is the name given in the area around Harran in Upper Mesopotamia, N of the junction of the rivers Ḫabur and Euphrates in Gn. 25:20; 28:2; 31:18, *etc.*, and is identical with Aram-naharaim, 'Aram of the rivers', of Gn. 24:10; Dt. 23:4; Jdg. 3:8. Abraham dwelt in this area before emigrating to Canaan. He sent his servant there to obtain a bride for Isaac, and thither Jacob fled from Esau. For a suggested identification of Paddan-aram, near Harran, see *AS* 2, 1952, p. 40; *POTT*, pp. 134f., 140. R.A.H.G.

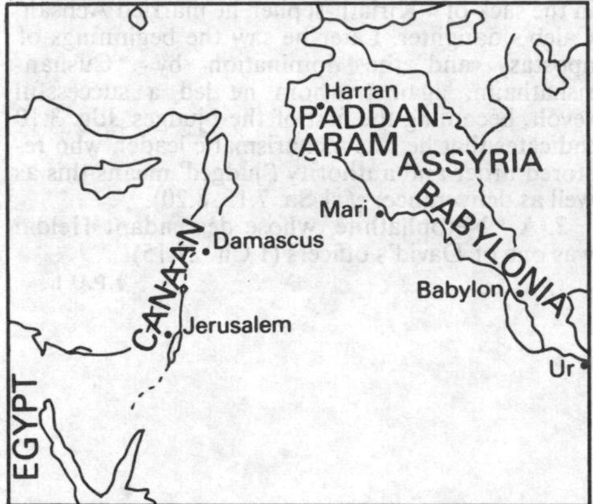

The location of Paddan-aram.

PAHATH-MOAB (lit. 'Governor of Moab'). Perhaps an ancestor had been a governor of Moab when Moab was subject to Israel. The name of a Jewish clan consisting of two families, Jeshua and Joab, 2,812 of whom returned to Judah with Zerubbabel (Ezr. 2:6. Ne. 7:11 gives the figure 2,818) and 201 with Ezra (Ezr. 8:4). Of this clan certain members are listed in Ezr. 10:30 as having married foreign women. Ne. 10:14 records that Pahath-moab among princes, priests and Levites set his seal to the covenant made on the return of the exiles to Jerusalem. R.A.H.G.

PALACE. The word designates a large residential building or group of buildings which accommodate a ruler and his administration. During the Israelite Monarchy, the administrative centre was called *'armôn*, AV 'palace', RSV 'citadel, palace, stronghold or castle'. A large portion of the nation's wealth was safeguarded in the citadel. Its capture was therefore the aim of a conquest and so substantial fortifications were constructed around the citadel so that the king and the loyal remnants of his army would be able to resist capture even when the remainder of the capital city had fallen. When predicting the overthrow of nations, the prophets specifically refer to the citadels of *Babylon (Is. 25:2), *Jerusalem (Is. 32:14; Je. 6:5; 9:21; 17:27; Am. 2:5), Damascus (Je. 49:27; Am. 1:4) and Edom (Is. 34:14; Am. 1:12). Amos also speaks about the destruction of the citadels of Gaza (1:7), Tyre (1:10), Rabbah (1:14), Moab (2:2) and *Samaria (3:11).

One of the most complete citadels in Syria/Palestine was excavated at Zinjirli (ancient Sam'al) used between *c.* 900 and 600 BC. Here three palaces and many storehouses were surrounded by walls and towers and the complex could be entered only after passing through two gates. In Palestine, only meagre remains of the citadel at *Samaria have been found. A similar but smaller citadel was built by King *Jehoiakim at Ramat Raḥel and is most probably referred to by Jeremiah (22:13–14). As at Samaria, the citadel was fortified with a casemate wall constructed with rectangular masonry and within the wall was a large courtyard, a storehouse and a palace.

Excavation has revealed that at the time of Solomon both *Hazor and *Megiddo had administrative buildings enclosed within citadel areas. Solomon chose a similar system at Jerusalem where the citadel embraced the *Temple, the king's palace (1 Ki. 3:1), the 'House of the Forest of Lebanon' (1 Ki. 7:2–5), halls and porches (7:6–7), a palace for Pharaoh's daughter (7:8; 9:24) and courts (7:12). One of the large buildings at Megiddo for which Solomon was probably responsible has been reconstructed as a *bīt-ḫilāni* (*PORCH), a style of palace which seems to have been adopted in the Hall of Pillars and the Hall of the Throne at Jerusalem (1 Ki. 7:6–7). The 'House of the Forest of Lebanon' was a hypostyle hall of 100 × 50 cubits. Its purpose was, at least in part, to display the kingdom's wealth (1 Ki. 10:17), but whether it was a banqueting-hall, as would be suggested by some of its contents (10:21), a magazine (Is. 22:8) or an entrance-hall is not clear. The royal residence (*bêṯ hammeleḵ*) would have been a number of storeys high, providing sufficient accommodation for the king, his wives and family and their advisers and servants.

Although the term 'great house' (Heb. *hêḵāl*) normally refers to a temple, it is also used of a palace (so Akkad. *ekallu*) when it is the principal building in a city. The palace of *Ahab at Jezreel (1 Ki. 21:1), the Assyrian king's palace at Nineveh (Na. 2:6) and the palaces at *Babylon (2 Ki. 20:18; Dn. 4:4, 29, *etc.*) and Susa (Ezr. 4:14) are described in this way. The palaces of Assyria, Babylon and Persia accommodated the administration for large empires and also considerable quantities of tribute.

In addition to offices and magazines, temples were included in the palace complex, thus enabling the king to fulfil his religious duties to ensure the favour of the gods. Senior officials each possessed their own residences and other parts of the palace housed schools (Dn. 1:4) for the princes, future civil servants and priests. The wealth of the king was suitably displayed to visitors and so public courtyards and the state rooms were richly decorated and lavishly furnished. Sometimes gardens of exotic plants were grown within the palace area (Est. 7:7–8).

After the Exile palaces are sometimes referred to as fortresses (Aram. *bîrâ*); palaces at Jerusalem (1 Ch. 29:1, 19; Ne. 2:8; 7:2), Susa (Dn. 8:2; Ne. 1:1, Est. 1:2, 5, *etc.*) and Ecbatana (Ezr. 6:2) are so described. Daniel (11:45) mentions the residence of the king of the N as *'appeḏen* (AV 'palace', RSV 'palatial tents') which is similar to the Old Persian word (*apadāna*) meaning columned hall and may in this case indicate large tents with many supports.

The palace (*aulē*) of the high priest (Mt. 26:3; Jn. 18:15) was probably a large hellenistic residence built around colonnaded courtyards. Jesus speaks about the need to guard such a palace which contains wealth (Lk. 11:21). *Herod the Great built palaces at Jerusalem, *Machaerus, *Jericho, the Herodium near Bethlehem, and Masada. In Jerusalem he built a strongly fortified palace with three towers, named Hippicus, Phasael and Mariamne, by the corner gate. This building forms the foundations of the present-day Citadel. There were two palaces at Masada and both have been excavated and partially restored. The N palace is amazingly positioned on the cliff face of the flat-topped mountain which was fortified by Herod.

Palaces or citadels often represent the fortunes of a nation in the OT. The palace of the faithful nation possesses peace (Ps. 122:7), while that of a sinful nation is destroyed (Je. 17:27; Am. 2:5) and becomes deserted (Is. 34:13–14).

BIBLIOGRAPHY. D. Ussishkin, *BA* 36, 1973, pp. 78–105; G. Turner, *Iraq* 32, 1970, pp. 177–213; W. G. Dever, *IEJ* 35, 1985, pp. 217–230. C.J.D.

PALESTINE. The term 'Palestine', originally applied to the territory of Israel's foes, the Philistines, was first used by Herodotus as a designation of S Syria. In the form of *Palaestina*, it was also used by the Romans. The older term 'Canaan' has a similar history. In the el-*Amarna letters (14th century BC) Canaan was limited to the coastal plains, then with the Canaanite conquests of the interior it was applied to all the lands W of the Jordan valley. The terms 'land of Israel' (1 Sa. 13:19) and 'the land of promise' (Heb. 11:9) are associated with the Israelites in the same area, the latter usually connected with the area from Dan to Beersheba, N of the Negeb. The Israelite settlement of two-and-a-half tribes E of the Jordan seems to have resulted from unforeseen circumstances and the hold on that side of the valley appears to have been generally precarious. After the division of the kingdom, the name Israel was usually given to the N realm. In the Middle Ages, the term 'the Holy Land' was often adopted (*cf.* Zc. 2:12).

I. The position and highways of Palestine

The mediaeval perspective of Jerusalem as the centre of the earth is not so absurd as might be thought, for on the tiny Syrian corridor that unites the world island of Europe, Asia and Africa, the five seas of the Mediterranean, Black Sea, Caspian, Red Sea and the Persian Gulf narrow the greatest land mass of our planet into a single isthmus. All the important continental routes must go across this corridor, and the great sea-routes of antiquity between the Indies and the Mediterranean must in turn be linked by land communications across the Sinai Peninsula. The high mountain chains which run E from Asia Minor to Kurdistan and the deserts to the S and E further help to concentrate the routeways of 'the Fertile Crescent', which, sickle-shaped, runs from Palestine and S Syria to the alluvial valley basins of the Tigris and Euphrates. It is, of course, 'fertile' only in comparison with the surrounding desert and mountainous terrain, since most of it is either Mediterranean scrub or steppe. At either end of the Fertile Crescent a great locus of civilization developed in the lower basin of Mesopotamia and the lower Nile valley respectively, whose fortunes dominated the history of the Near East for almost two millennia.

Three great trade routes have always traversed Palestine. The great Trunk Road, perhaps described in Is. 9:1 as 'the way of the sea', runs along the low coast from Egypt to the Vale of Esdraelon. Then it is diverted inland by the Syrian mountains to skirt the W side of the Lake of Galilee, then through the Syrian Gate and central depression to Damascus, where it joins the desert caravan trails across to Mesopotamia. Two other routes are of great antiquity although of lesser importance. The *King's Highway follows the edge of the Transjordan plateau from the Gulf of Aqabah towards Damascus. It marks a zone of increased rainfall and was followed in part by the Israelites during the Exodus (Nu. 21–22), and all the towns enumerated in Nu. 21; 27–30 lie along it. The watershed of central Palestine is followed by another route, the shortest between Sinai and Canaan. In the N *Negeb it links an important series of wells, keeping W of the forbidding, barren depressions of the E Negeb that are still difficult to traverse. It links all the important historic centres from Kadesh-barnea and Beersheba to Hebron, Jerusalem, Shechem and Megiddo. Heavily travelled from the Abramic (Middle Bronze I) period onwards, it was also made famous by the journey of Joshua and his fellow-spies. All these routes emphasized the N–S alignment of Palestine, which benefited from their fertilizing contacts of trade and culture. But Israel was rarely able to control these highways without upsetting the strategic interests of the great powers that dominated their terminals. Even in Solomon's day the coastal highway was too tightly controlled by the sea-powers to warrant interference there (1 Ki. 9:11; 10:22; Ezk. 27:17), while Edom was for long Israel's deadly enemy because it dominated the routes from the Gulf of Aqabah where Israel obtained its copper (Ob. 3).

A number of minor transverse routes have joined these parallel highways. Of these the most important have been: (1) Gaza–Beersheba–Petra; (2) Ashkelon–Gath–Helvan; (3) Joppa–Bethel–Jericho (*cf.* Jos. 10:6–14) and Joppa–Shechem–Adam–Gilead (Jos. 3:16); (4) Vale of Esdraelon–Megiddo–Gilead. Exposed to coastal sedimentation from the Nile, the coast of Palestine as far as Carmel has been unfavourable for port development, so the chief towns have been route centres at important road junctions, either in the strategic plain of Esdraelon or along the hilly dorsal of Judaea and Samaria. The sea was an unfamiliar medium of communication to the Hebrews (*cf.* Ps. 107), while the desert was also feared as 'a land of trouble and anguish' (Is. 30:6; *cf.* Dt. 8:15). Perched precariously between them, the Hebrew highlanders sought a protracted aloofness from both environments and their peoples. Thus autonomy of spirit became a major characteristic of the Israelites, despite their nodal position at the hub of the ancient world's trade routes.

II. The geological structure and relief

For some 675 km from the borders of Egypt to Asia Minor, the Levant consists of five major zones: (1) the littoral; (2) the W mountain chain (the Judaean–Galilean highlands, Lebanon and Ansariya mountains); (3) the rift valleys (Arabah, Jordan valley, Biqa' and Ghôr); (4) the E mountains (highlands of Transjordan, Hermon and Anti-lebanon); and (5) the deserts of Negeb, Arabia and Syria. But the contrasts between the N and S sections of these zones explain the individuality of Palestine. N of Acre, the mountains rise abruptly from the sea, limiting the narrow coastal plains to discontinuous stretches but providing the famous harbours of Sidon, Tyre, Beirut, Tripoli and Ras Shamra. The limited hinterlands of each unit have encouraged independent maritime city-states where 'the families of the Canaanites spread abroad' (Gn. 10:18). S of Mt Carmel, however, the coast opens into a broad continuous plain, harbourless except for artificial ports erected by the Philistines and later sea-peoples.

A second contrast is to be found in the Rift Valley sectors. In Syria the Biqa' depression is a broad, fertile plain between the lofty ranges of Lebanon and Anti-Lebanon, with wide access to other rolling plains, and studded with historic centres such as Kadesh, Homs and Hamath. To the S, the depression blocked by recent basaltic lavas narrows into deep gorges before opening into the swamp of Lake Huleh, making N–S communication difficult. These features have tended to isolate Palestine from the N territory.

The rocks of Palestine are notably limestone, volcanics and recent deposits such as marls, gravels and sands. The Rift Valley represents an ancient planetary lineament that is traceable as far as the E African Lakes. Broadly speaking, it has operated like a hinge, so that the areas to the W of it have been mostly under the sea, whereas the Arabian block has been generally continental. Thus, W of the Rift the rocks are predominantly limestone laid down specially during the Cretaceous and Eocene eras. Some of these are hard and dolomitic (Cenomanian and Eocene), explaining the steep headland of Mt Carmel, the twin mountains of Ebal and Gerizim above Shechem, and generally all the rugged, higher relief of the Judaean–Galilean dorsal. But the Senonian is a soft chalk, easily eroded into gaps and valleys that breach the highlands, notably at Megiddo, the valley of Aijalon and the moat of Beth-shemesh which separates the Eocene foothills of the Shephelah from the Judaean plateau. These limestones have been upworked along the central dorsal and gently folded in a series of arches which become more complicated farther N in Samaria and Galilee. They occur, however, horizontal in Transjordan, resting upon the continental block beneath them. The ancient block is exposed in the SE in the high cliffs of the Wadi Arabah and in the Sinai Peninsula. Overlapping them are the so-called Nubian sandstones, whose desert origin prolonged over vast geological periods explains the red colour from which Edom probably derives its name ('the red'). In the NE, recent basaltic lavas cap the limestones in the broad, undulating plateaux in the land of Bashan, and extending into the Jordan trough around the Lake of Galilee. These weather into the rich soils which attracted to the Galilean shores a high density of population from early times.

Palestine suffers from crustal instability. Volcanic eruptions have continued into historic times, notably in the cases of Harrat en-Nar, SE of the Gulf of Aqabah, which were active as late as the 8th and 13th centuries AD. It is tempting to equate the descriptions of Ex. 19:18 and Ps. 68:8 with volcanic manifestations, but the traditional site of Sinai is in an area of ancient, crystalline rocks where no recent volcanic action has occurred. The fate of Sodom and Gomorrah (Gn. 14:10; 19:23–28) is a memory of some kind of volcanic phenomena, associated probably with the intrusion of sulphurous gas and liquid asphalt. There are also the biblical records of earthquakes (Gn. 19:25; 1 Sa. 14:15; Am. 1:1) and geological faulting (Nu. 16:31–35). All these are associated with the Great Rift Valley of the Jordan and Dead Sea, or with the series of transverse faults that form the Vale of Esdraelon and divide Samaria and Galilee into a complicated series of highland blocks and depressions floored with sediments.

Under the semi-arid conditions, badland relief is typical, especially around the E and S rims of the Judaean highlands and the W edge of the Transjordan plateau. Within the deep Jordan valley, soft marls deposited by a lake more extensive than the present Dead Sea have been dissected to form the Ghôr in the middle of the trough, lying at more than 365 m below sea-level. The seasonal wadis that drain into the Arabah trough have also deeply dissected their slopes. Thus the AV references to the 'slippery places' are a characteristic feature of many parts of the Negeb and the Jordan (Dt. 32:35; Pr. 3:23; Je. 23:12; 31:9). Much of the Negeb is a rock waste of hammadas, and direct reference to the wind-borne loessial deposits is made (Ex. 10:20–23; Dt. 28:24; Na. 1:3).

III. The climate and vegetation

In the Levant three climatic zones may be distinguished: a Mediterranean, a steppe and a desert zone, each with its distinct type of vegetation. Along the coast as far S as Gaza, the Mediterranean zone has mild winters (53·6°F, 12°C, mean monthly average for January at Gaza) compared with the severer conditions of the interior hills (Jerusalem 44·6°F, 7°C, in January). But summers are everywhere hot (Gaza 78·8°F, 26°C, in July, Jerusalem 73·4°F, 23°C). The prolonged snow cover of the high Lebanon mountains (Je. 18:14) is exceptional, though snow is not infrequent in the Hauran. Elsewhere it is a rare phenomenon (2 Sa. 23:20). Less than one-fifteenth part of the annual rainfall occurs in the summer months from June to October; nearly all of it is concentrated in winter to reach a maximum in mid-winter. The total amount varies from about 35–40 cm on the coast to about 75 cm on Mt Carmel and the Judaean, Galilean and Transjordan mountains. In the Beersheba area to the S, and in parts of the Jordan valley and of the Transjordan plateau the climate is steppe, with

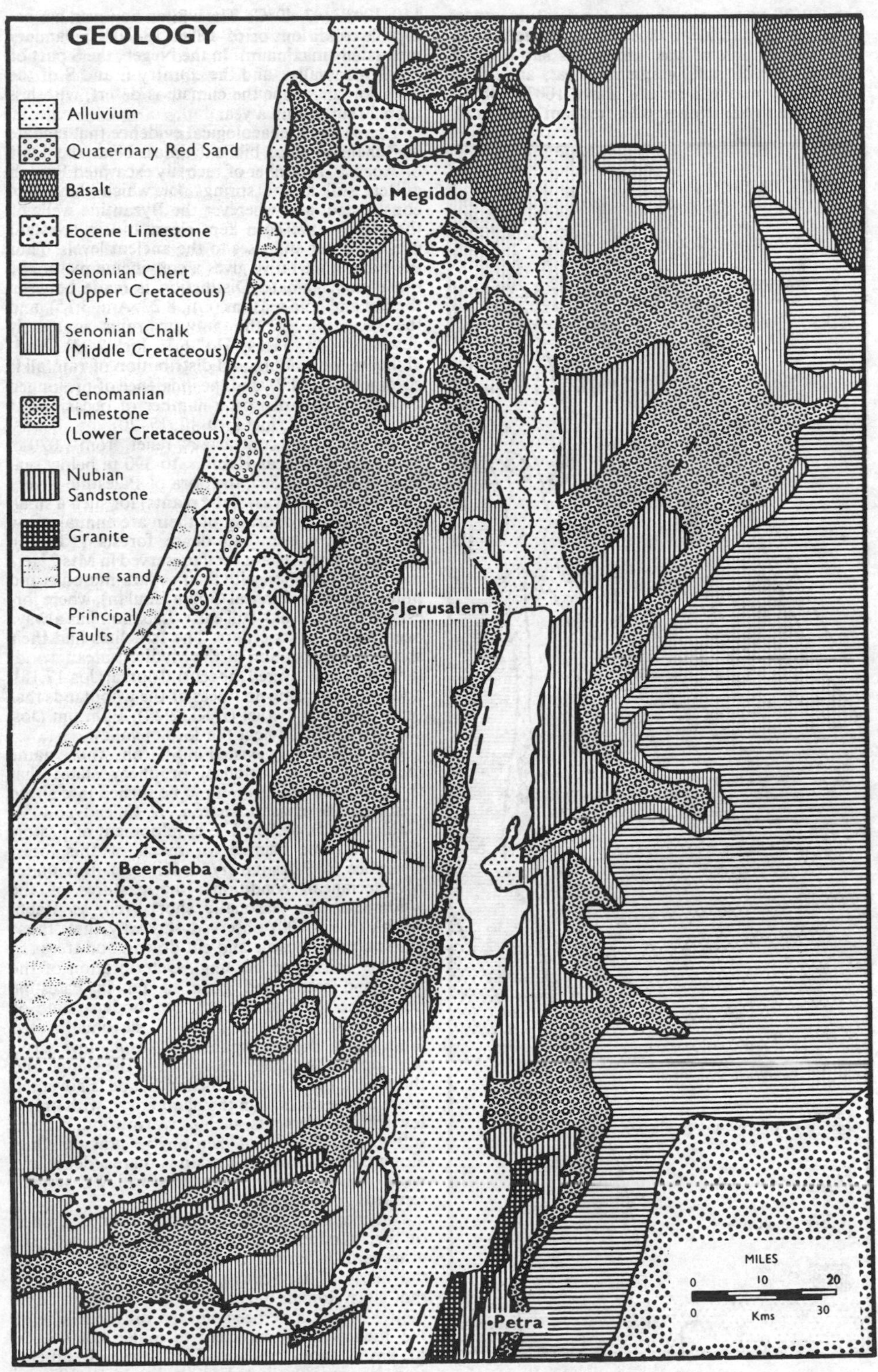

Palestine: geological structure.

only 20–30 cm of rain, though temperature conditions are comparable to those of the Judaean hills. The deep trough of the Jordan has sub-tropical conditions with stifling summer heat; at Jericho mean daily maxima remain above 100°F (38°C) from June to September, with frequent records of 110–120°F (43–49°C). The winter, however, has enjoyable conditions of 65–68°F (18–20°C) (January mean daily maximum). In the Negeb, the S part of the Jordan valley, and the country E and S of the Transjordan steppe the climate is desert, with less than 20 cm of rain a year.

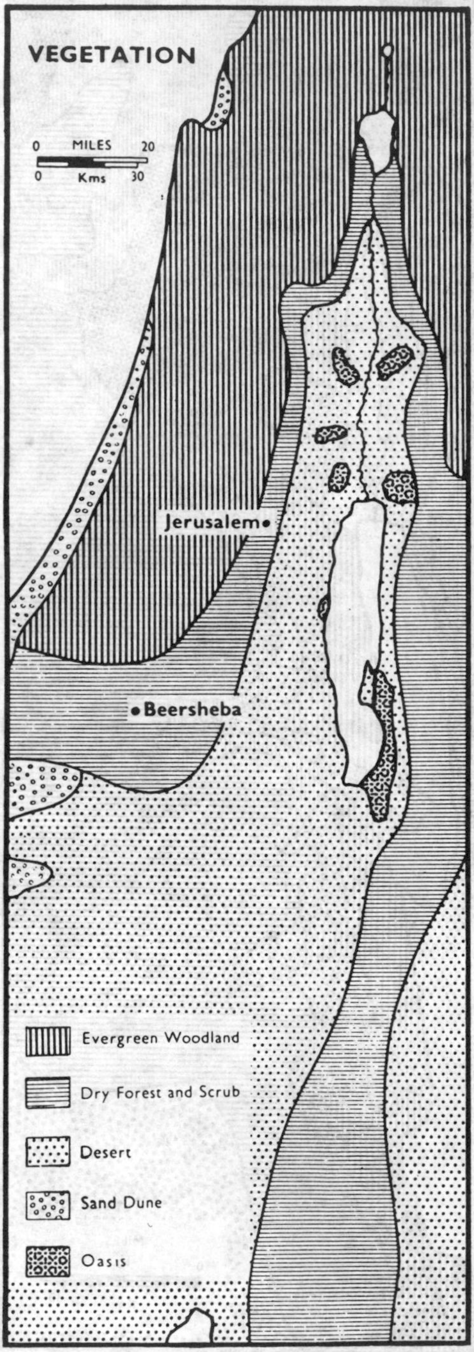

There is no archaeological evidence that climate has changed since biblical times. Near the Gulf of Aqabah, a number of recently excavated Roman gutters still fit the springs for which they were constructed, and wherever the Byzantine wells of the Negeb have been kept clean and in constant use, the water still rises to the ancient levels. Thus the biblical narrative gives a convincing picture of the present climate. Distinction is made between the hot and cold seasons (Gn. 8:22; Am. 3:15), and the inception of the autumn rains is clearly described (Dt. 11:14; Ho. 6:3; Joel 2:23). Variability in the amount and distribution of rainfall is common (Am. 4:7), and the incidence of prolonged drought is recorded on a number of occasions (1 Ki. 17:7; Je. 17:8; Joel 1:10–12, 17–20).

Because of the contrasts of relief, from 1,020 m above sea-level near Hebron, to 390 m below sea-level at the Dead Sea, the flora of Palestine is very rich (about 3,000 vascular *plants) for such a small area. A large proportion of them are annuals. Few districts have ever had dense forests (*Trees), though remnants have been preserved in Mts *Hermon and *Lebanon with their cedars, firs, oaks and pines, and in the biblical Golan (Jaulan), where forests of pine and oak still exist. Lebanon has always been noted for its cedars. The Israelites had their share in deforestation of the Mediterranean woodland that once covered the central dorsal (Jos. 17:18), and today there are no traces of the woodlands that once existed at Bethel (2 Ki. 2:24), Ephraim (Jos. 17:15) and Gilead near the Jordan valley.

Oak forests long existed in Sharon, whose name means forest, but biblical prophecy states that three forested regions were to be turned into sheep pastures, the coastal Sharon, N Gilead and SE Galilee (see Is. 65:10). The development of pastoralism must be blamed for much of this forest clearance in Palestine (*cf.* 2 Ki. 3:4). But under Mediterranean conditions 'the pastures of the wilderness' are seasonally short-lived, so Rabbi Akiba (*c.* AD 100) observed shrewdly that 'those who rear small cattle and cut down good trees . . . will see no sign of blessing'. Deterioration of the woodland scrub had gone so far in Palestine before the establishment of the modern state of Israel in AD 1948 that most of the uncultivated land was a dreary expanse of *batha*, low scrub with open, rock outcrops. Towards the steppe and the desert, the colour of the landscape is governed more by the rocks than the plant cover, with only a few shrubby elements, such as wormwood, broom, saltwort and tufts of xerophytic grasses. Only along the banks of the Jordan is there a dense and wide gallery forest of various willows, poplar, tamarisk, oleander, *etc.*

But many of the Palestinian hill lands, eroded of their productive *terra vessa* soils, have been the graveyard of former civilizations, especially with the decay of terrace-cultivation. One estimate is that since Roman times 2,000–4,000 million cubic metres of soil have been worked off the E side of the Judaean hills, sufficient to make 4,000–8,000 sq. km of good farmland. This threat of soil erosion is possibly alluded to in Jb. 14:18–19, and the easy spread of fire during the summer

Palestine: vegetation.

drought is described (Ps. 83:13–14). These features of Mediterranean instability are recognized in the need for balance and restraint, in a land which lies so precariously between the desert and the sown (Ex. 23:29–30; Pr. 24:30–34). (*DEW, *RAIN, *WIND.)

MEAN ANNUAL RAINFALL IN MMS. 1901–1930

Haifa
Gaza
Jericho
Jerusalem
Hebron
Beersheba
Sdom
Petra
Aqabah

MILES 0 10 20 30
0 30 50
Kms

Left and top right: Palestine: rainfall.

IV. Water-supply and agriculture

It is not by chance that the names of over seventy ancient sites in Palestine contain the word *'ain*, 'spring', and another sixty such sites the word *bîr*, 'well'. Apart from the Jordan, a few of its tributaries and four or five small coastal streams that

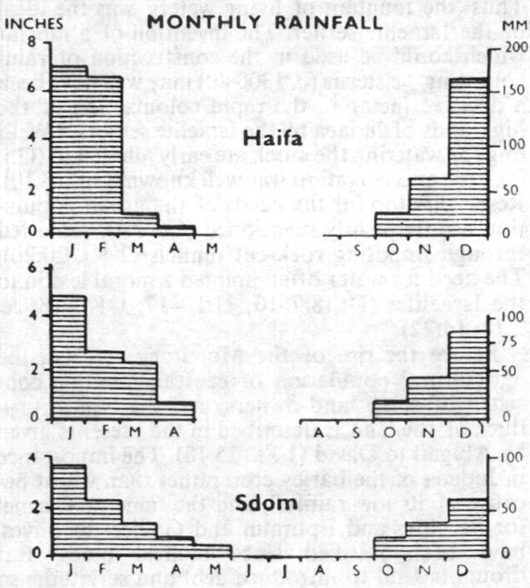

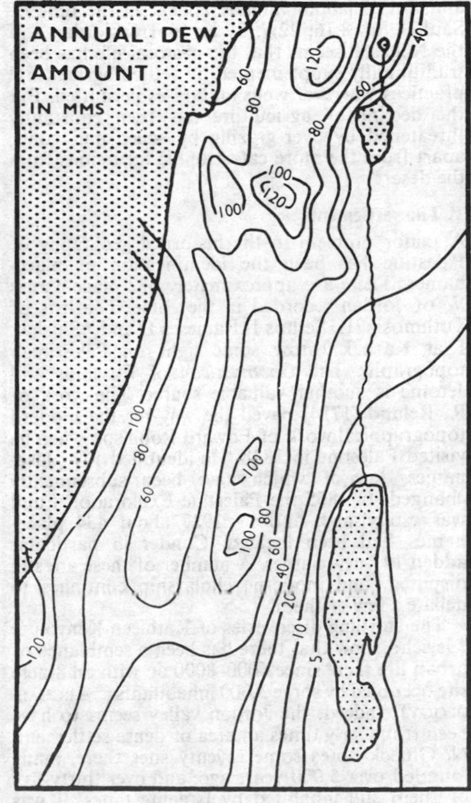

Palestine: dewfall.

are fed from springs, all the remaining rivers of Palestine are seasonal. Snow-fed streams account for their maximum volume in May–June (Jos. 3:15), but the majority dry up in the hot summer (1 Ki. 17:7; Jb. 24:19; Joel 1:20), notably in the Negeb (Ps. 126:4). With the autumn rains the sudden spate is graphically described (Jdg. 5:21; Mt. 7:27). Thus 'the fountain of living waters' was the ideal of the Israelite settler. The invention of a mortar which could be used in the construction of rain-collecting *cisterns (*c.* 1300 BC) may well have been a decisive factor in the rapid colonization of the highlands of Judaea by the Israelite settlers. *Wells dug for watering the stock are early alluded to (Gn. 26, *etc.*) and irrigation was well known (Gn. 13:10). Reservoirs too for the needs of the urban population are frequently mentioned (Ct. 7:4), some fed through imposing rock-cut tunnels (2 Ki. 20:20). The need for water often pointed a moral lesson to the Israelites (Dt. 8:7–10; 11:10–17; 1 Ki. 18; Je. 2:13; 14:22).

Before the rise of the Monarchy at least, the agricultural population of central Palestine consisted of small land-owners, and the typical produce of the land is described in the presents given by Abigail to David (1 Sa. 25:18). The importance in Judaea of the barley crop rather than wheat because of its low rainfall, and the fame of Carmel for its vines and Ephraim and Galilee for olives, have been justified since biblical times. But droughts tend to introduce debt and servitude, so that despite the ideological democracy envisaged in the jubilee year (Lv. 25), crownlands, large estates and forced labour already appear in the time of Saul (1 Sa. 8:16; 22:7; 25:2). In Transjordan and the Negeb it seems that the pastoral life has been traditionally supplemented by settled agricultural practices wherever wells and oases permitted. But the decline of agriculture has been constantly threatened by over-grazing by sheep and goats, apart from the more catastrophic incursions from the desert.

V. The settlements

A major problem in the historical geography of Palestine has been the identification of place-names. There are approximately 622 place-names W of Jordan recorded in the Bible. The lists of Tuthmosis III, Sethos I, Rameses II and *Shishak I at Karnak throw some light on Palestinian topography. The *Onomasticon* of Eusebius and Jerome is another valuable source. The work of R. Reland (1714) paved the way for the modern topographical work of Edward Robinson when he visited Palestine in 1838. He identified 177 place-names, few of which have been subsequently changed. In 1865 the Palestine Exploration Fund was established, and by 1927 about 434 place-names had been located; Conder in particular added 147 new names. A number of these are still disputed, and modern scholarship continues to debate a few of them.

The startling discoveries of Kathleen Kenyon at *Jericho show that there has been a semblance of urban life there since 6000–8000 BC with an 8-acre site occupied by some 3,000 inhabitants (*ARCHAEOLOGY). Indeed, the Jordan valley seems to have been from early times an area of dense settlement. N. Glueck notes some seventy sites there, many founded over 5,000 years ago, and over thirty-five of them still inhabited by Israelite times. It was only later that this valley which Lot found so attractive (Gn. 13:10) became more desolate, probably with the advent of malaria. It has been suggested that some of the Tells were artificial mounds built deliberately above the swampy ground, though added to by subsequent settlement. But everywhere water-supply has been the decisive factor of settlement. Fortified towns and castles were built at important perennial springs such as Jericho, Beth-shan and Aphek (famous from the wars of the Israelites with the Philistines). Indeed, it is a corollary that sites with abundant springs have usually had the most continuous settlement from remote times.

Along the coastal plain S of Carmel settlement has been relatively dense since antiquity, favoured by the ease with which wells could be dug through the sandy soils to the lenticular beds of clay that hold suspended water-tables. But farther N in the Vale of Sharon and Upper Galilee, where the water-supply is abundant, relatively dense woodland made human occupancy difficult until more recent centuries. In the basins of lower Galilee and Samaria population has for long been dense, scattered in numerous villages, but S of Jerusalem village sites become fewer and more nucleated, until around Beersheba settlement has been limited to strategic fortified well-sites. In Transjordan the edge of the plateau is marked by a number of fortresses such as Petra, Bozrah (Buseira) and Tophel (Tafileh). Beyond them to the E is the narrow stretch of agricultural land with its scattered villages along which ran the King's Highway. Within these patterns of settlement dictated largely by water conditions, the strategic and most important towns have grown up at cross-roads where the proximity of some defile enabled the transverse roads to link with the main N–S highways. Such were in biblical times Beersheba, Hebron, Jerusalem, Bethel, Shechem, Samaria, Megiddo, Beth-shan and Hazor. Hence the psalmist could exclaim: 'He led them by a straight way, till they reached a city to dwell in' (Ps. 107:7).

VI. The regions of Palestine

The geographer can create as many regions as there are problems worth studying, so it is absurd to suggest that the delimitation of areas within Palestine has a permanent validity. But certain regional units have appeared again and again in the history of Palestine, and should be recognized. The broad divisions already noted are distinct: the coastal plains, the central hill lands, the Rift Valley, the plateaux of Transjordan and the desert.

The coastal plains stretch for a distance of about 200 km from the borders of Lebanon to Gaza, interrupted by Mt Carmel in the N. To the N of it, the plain of Asher runs for 40 km to the ancient Ladder of Tyre, where the Galilean hills crowd close to the coast. It played no part in the life of Israel, but to the SE of it the valley of Jezreel and plain of Esdraelon have been of major significance. Stretching for 50 km into the interior and some 20 km at its widest, this formed the main road from Egypt to Damascus and the N. Along it were situated the strategic centres of Megiddo, Jezreel and Beth-shan, famous in many of Israel's wars (Jdg. 5; 7:1; 1 Sa. 29:1; 31:12) and the apocalyptic site of the future (Rev. 16:16). S of Carmel, which shelters the small plain of Dor, is the plain of Sharon with its five great Philistine strongholds of Ekron, Ashdod, Ashkelon, Gath and Gaza,

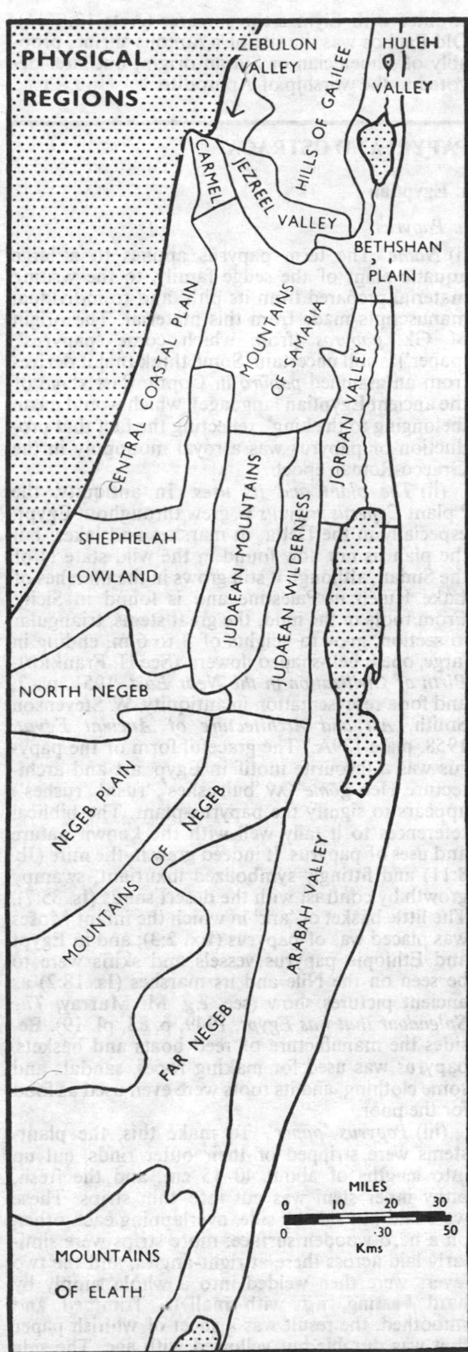

Palestine: physical regions.

merging E into the hill lands of the Shephelah, a buffer between Israel and Philistia. These hills were once heavily wooded with sycamores (1 Ki. 10:27; 2 Ch. 1:15; 9:27) and crossed transversely by narrow valleys which witnessed the early struggles of Israel from the times of the Judges to David, notably Aijalon (Jos. 10:10–15; 1 Sa. 14:31); Sorek (Jdg. 16), and Elah (1 Sa. 17:1–2).

The Central Hills run some 300 km from N Galilee to Sinai, made up of interlocking hills and plateaux. In the S, Judah has gently undulating folds except in the E, where the deeply dissected chalky relief of the Wilderness of Judah, or Jeshimon, descends steeply to the Rift Valley. This Judaean plateau runs N into the hill country of Ephraim with its easy transverse passages, but to the N the hills of Samaria decrease gently from the Judaean heights of over 1,000 m to an average of just over 300 m in the central basin, in which are situated the biblical sites of Gibeah, Shalem, Shechem and Sychar. Above it tower the heights of Ebal (945 m) and Gerizim (890 m). Together with other fertile basins, Samaria was exposed to outside influences, and its faith early corrupted. N of the plain of Esdraelon lies Galilee, divided into S or lower Galilee, which has a similar landscape to the lands of Samaria, and N or upper Galilee, where the mountains reach over 900 m. A number of basins, notably Nazareth, provide easy passage and rich cultivation between the coast and the Lake area, densely settled in our Lord's day.

Slicing across Palestine for over 100 km, the Jordan follows the great Rift Valley. Its N sector is occupied also by the lakes Huleh and Galilee, surrounded by high mountains, notably Hermon, the source of the Jordan (Dt. 3:9; 4:48). Below the basin of Huleh, the Jordan has cut through the basaltic dam that once blocked the depression in a gorge to enter the lake Tiberias or Sea of Galilee 200 m below sea-level. Beyond it the river Yarmuk adds its waters to the Jordan and the valley gradually widens S towards the Dead Sea trough. S of the cliffs of 'Ain Khaneizer commences the Arabah, stretching 160 km to the Gulf of Aqabah, a desert dominated by the great wall of the Transjordan tableland. W stretches the desolate hilly relief of the central Negeb and its steppe plains, towards Beersheba. E over the edge of the Transjordan plateaux extend a series of regions well known in Bible times: the tableland of Bashan dominated E by the great volcanic caves of Jebel Druze; Gilead situated in a huge oval dome 55 km by 40 km wide and famed for its forests (Je. 22:6; Zc. 10:10); the level steppes of Ammon and Moab; and S of the Zered valley (Dt. 2:13; Is. 15:7) the faulted and tilted block of Edom with its impregnable strongholds. Beyond to the E and the S are the deserts, tablelands of rock and sand, blasted by the hot winds. See also *JORDAN, *NEGEB, *SHARON, *ZIN. For archaeology of Palestine, see *ARCHAEOLOGY and individual sites, for history, see *CANAAN, *ISRAEL, *JUDAH, *PHILISTINES, *etc.*

BIBLIOGRAPHY. F.-M. Abel, *Géographie de la Palestine*, 1937 (2 vols.); D. Baly, *The Geography of the Bible*[2], 1974; G. Dalman, *Sacred Sites and Ways*, 1935; M. du Buit, *Géographie de la Terre Sainte*, 1958; N. Glueck, *The River Jordan*, 1946; W. J. Phythian-Adams, 'The Land and the People' in *A Companion to the Bible* (ed. T. W. Manson), 1944, pp. 133–156; A. Reifenberg, *The Struggle between the Desert and the Sown in the Levant*, 1956; G. A. Smith, *The Historical Geography of the Holy Land*[25], 1931; *National Atlas of Israel* (in Hebrew), in course of publication since 1958.

J.M.H.

PALTITE, THE. The name given to the inhabitants of Beth-pelet, situated in the Judaean Negeb (Jos. 15:27; Ne. 11:26). Helez, one of David's 30 heroes, was a native of this town (2 Sa. 23:26). In 1 Ch. 11:27 and 27:10 he is called 'the *Pelonite'.

R.A.H.G.

PAMPHYLIA. A coastal region of S Asia Minor on the great bay of the Mare Lycium, lying between *Lycia and *Cilicia. It is mentioned in Acts 13:13; 14:24 and 15:38 in connection with Paul's first journey, a visit which Ramsay believed was cut short through illness and the enervating climate (*SPT*, pp. 89ff.). According to tradition, the area was colonized by Amphilochus and Calchas (or Mopsus, his rival and successor) after the Trojan War. Linguistic evidence confirms a mixed settlement. The chief towns were Attaleia, Paul's probable landing-place, founded by Attalus II of Pergamum after 189 BC with Athenian colonists; Aspendus, a Persian naval base which claimed Argive foundation; Side, founded by Aeolian colonists; and *Perga. The region was under Persian rule until Alexander, after which, apart from brief occupations by Ptolemy I and Ptolemy III, it passed to the possession of the Seleucids of Syria. After the defeat of Antiochus III, C. Manlius took the region over for Rome and the main cities were associated in alliance. The Attalids at this time (189 BC) received the coastal strip, where they founded Attaleia. Many readjustments followed. From 102 BC Pamphylia was a part of the province of Cilicia, but about 44 BC was included in Asia. In 36 BC Antony made the territory over to his ally Amyntas, king of Galatia. Thanks to his timely desertion to Octavian before Actium, Amyntas retained possession until his death in battle against a highland tribe in 25 BC. From this date until AD 43 Pamphylia was part of the province of Galatia. In that year Claudius formed the province of Lycia-Pamphylia. There were later reorganizations under Galba and Vespasian. The church founded at Perga is the only one mentioned in the 1st century, but there were at least twelve foundations at the time of Diocletian's persecution in AD 304.

BIBLIOGRAPHY. A. H. M. Jones, *Cities of the Eastern Roman Provinces*², 1971, pp. 123ff.

E.M.B.

PANNAG. A Heb. word, found only in Ezk. 27:17, denoting some type of merchandise, presumably edible. AV and RV transliterated, since the meaning was unknown. Scholars and EVV have often emended the Heb., either to *dônaḡ*, 'wax' (JB) or to *paggaḡ*, 'early figs' (RSV); but recent evidence from Hittite and Akkad. texts supports MT. 'Meal' (NEB), or some baked product, seems to be meant.

D.F.P.

PAPHOS. The name of two settlements in SW Cyprus in NT times, distinguished by scholars as Old and New Paphos. The former was a Phoenician foundation of great antiquity lying slightly inland from the coast. New Paphos grew up, after the Romans annexed the island in 58 BC, as the centre of Rom. rule, and it was here that Paul met the proconsul Sergius (Acts 13:6–7, 12) on his first missionary journey. Here, too, he had his encounter with Elymas the sorcerer (Acts 13:6–11). Old Paphos was the site of a famous shrine, probably of Phoenician or Syrian origin, but later devoted to the worship of Aphrodite.

J.H.P.

PAPYRI AND OSTRACA.

I. Egyptian

a. Papyrus

(i) *Name.* The term papyrus applies to a large aquatic plant of the sedge family, to the writing material prepared from its pith, and to individual manuscripts made from this material. The origin of Gk. *papyros* (from which come 'papyrus', 'paper') is still uncertain. Some think that it derives from an assumed *papūro* in Coptic (last stage of the ancient Egyptian language), which would mean 'belonging to the king', reflecting the fact that production of papyrus was a royal monopoly in the Graeco-Roman epoch.

(ii) *The plant and its uses.* In antiquity, the *plant *Cyperus papyrus* L. grew throughout Egypt, especially in the Delta, in marshes and lakes; but the plant is not now found in the wild state N of the Sudan, although it still grows in the marshes of Lake Huleh in Palestine and is found in Sicily. From roots in the mud, the great stems, triangular in section, grew to heights of 3 to 6 m, ending in large, open, bell-shaped flowers. (See H. Frankfort, *Birth of Civilization in the Near East*, 1951, pl. 2, and for a representation in antiquity, W. Stevenson Smith, *Art and Architecture of Ancient Egypt*, 1958, plate 129A.) The graceful form of the papyrus was a favourite motif in Egyp. art and architecture. Heb. *gōme'* (AV 'bulrushes', 'rush', 'rushes') appears to signify the papyrus-plant. The biblical references to it tally well with the known nature and uses of papyrus. It indeed grew in the mire (Jb. 8:11) and fittingly symbolized luxuriant, swampy growth by contrast with the desert sands (Is. 35:7). The little basket or 'ark' in which the infant Moses was placed was of papyrus (Ex. 2:3); and in Egypt and Ethiopia papyrus vessels and skiffs were to be seen on the Nile and its marshes (Is. 18:2) as ancient pictures show (see, *e.g.* M. Murray, *The Splendour that was Egypt*, 1949, p. 83, pl. 19). Besides the manufacture of reed boats and baskets, papyrus was used for making ropes, sandals and some clothing, and its roots were even used as food for the poor.

(iii) *Papyrus 'paper'.* To make this, the plant-stems were stripped of their outer rinds, cut up into lengths of about 40–45 cm, and the fresh, pithy inner stem was cut into thin strips. These were laid out side by side, overlapping each other, on a hard wooden surface; more strips were similarly laid across these at right-angles; and the two layers were then welded into a whole simply by hard beating, *e.g.* with mallets. Trimmed and smoothed, the result was a sheet of whitish paper that was durable but yellowed with age. The side showing horizontal fibres was usually written on first (except for letters) and is called the recto; the 'back' with the vertical fibres is termed the verso. These sheets were pasted end to end, with slight overlaps, to form a papyrus roll. The standard length was twenty sheets, but this could be shortened by cutting or lengthened by pasting on more, as need arose. The longest known papyrus is the great *Papyrus Harris I*, *c.* 1160 BC, in the British

Museum; it is some 40 m long. The height of a papyrus varied according to the use to which it was to be put: the larger sizes (maximum, 47 cm; usually 35·5 cm and 42 cm in Dynasties 18 and 19–20) for official and business papers and accounts (with long columns of figures); and the smaller ones (about 18 cm and 21 cm, but often less) for literary compositions.

(iv) *The use of papyrus*. This was governed by definite conventions. As Egyp. script usually runs from right to left, the scribes always began at the right-hand end of a papyrus and wrote to the left—at first in vertical lines (usual until *c.* 1800 BC), thereafter in horizontal lines of modest length, grouped in successive 'columns' or 'pages'. For scripts used, punctuation, writing equipment, manuscripts, *etc.*, see *WRITING; *TEXTS AND VERSIONS.

Papyrus was used from the beginning of Egyp. history (*c.* 3000 BC) down into the early Islamic period (7th century AD and later). The oldest (blank) rolls are of Dynasty 1, the first written ones are of Dynasty 5, *c.* 2500 BC. Large quantities were made and used in Egypt in the 2nd and 1st millennia BC for every kind of written record; but papyrus was not cheap, and the backs and blank spaces of old rolls were often used up, or an old text washed off to make room for a new one.

Before the end of the 2nd millennium BC, papyrus was being exported extensively to Syria–Palestine and doubtless beyond. About 1075 BC Zakarbaal, the prince of Phoen. Byblos, quoted timber-prices to the Egyp. envoy Wenamun from the rolls of accounts kept by his predecessors, and in Wenamun's part-payment for timber were included '500 (rolls of) finished papyrus' (*ANET*, pp. 27a, 28a). For the use of papyrus for Heb. and Aram., and in NT times, see separate sections below. On all aspects of papyrus as a writing-medium in Egypt, see J. Černý, *Paper and Books in Ancient Egypt*, 1952. For pictures of funerary and administrative papyri respectively, see *IBA*, pp. 36–37, figs. 30–31.

b. Ostraca

The plural of *ostrakon*, a Gk. word originally meaning 'oyster-shell', but applied by the Greeks to the potsherds on which they recorded their votes (hence English 'ostracize'). In Egypt this term is applied to slips of limestone or potsherds bearing ink-written inscriptions and drawings. Although such ostraca are known from most periods in Egyp. history and from various sites, the vast majority are of New Kingdom date (*c.* 1550–1070 BC) and come from Thebes in Upper Egypt, specifically from the Valleys of the Tombs of the Kings and the Queens and the village for the workers at these tombs (modern Deir el-Medineh). Most Egyp. ostraca are written in the cursive hieratic script; those in the more formal, pictorial hieroglyphic script are much rarer. The ostraca with drawings are often delightful, sketched by artists in their spare time. The inscribed ostraca fall into two classes: literary and non-literary. The former contain portions of Egyp. literary works (stories, poems, wisdom, hymns, *etc.*), written out as school exercises, test of memory, or for pleasure; these ostraca often preserve literary works (or parts of them) still unknown from any other source. Much more varied are the non-literary ostraca. These were the Egyptians' equivalent of memo-pads, jotters and scrap paper, and reflect every conceivable aspect of daily life: rosters of workmen with note of absentees, reports on work done (*cf.* Ex. 5:18–19), distribution of food-allowances and oil, innumerable accounts of bricks, straw, vegetables, vessels, *etc.*, lawsuits, marriage-contracts, bills of sale and demand-notes for debts, many letters and memoranda, and much else besides. The total of this material gives a vivid insight into Egyp. daily life during and after the time of Israel's sojourn and exodus and can provide useful background for the Exodus narratives. (*LACHISH, *SAMARIA.)

BIBLIOGRAPHY. On scope and importance of ostraca, see J. Černý, *Chronique d'Égypte*, 6/No. 12, 1931, pp. 212–224, and S. Sauneron, *Catalogue des Ostraca Hiératiques Non Littéraires de Deir el Medineh*, 1959, Introduction, pp. vi–xviii, who gives ample reference to other publications. In English, see W. C. Hayes, *The Scepter of Egypt*, 2, 1959, pp. 176–178, 390–394, 432. For pictures of typical ostraca, see Hayes, *op. cit.*, p. 177, fig. 98.

K.A.K.

II. Hebrew, Aramaic and Greek

a. Hebrew papyri

The oldest known Heb. papyrus (Mur 17) was discovered at Wadi Murabba'at by the Dead Sea in 1952. Mur 17 is a palimpsest written in palaeo-Hebrew script and dates from the late 8th or early 7th century BC. The original letter, of which a few words may still be read, was erased and a list of personal names superimposed. Most of the scrolls found at Qumran are of parchment but there are a few papyri worthy of mention. Cave 4 yielded papyrus fragments of *The Rule of the Community* and *The Thanksgiving Hymns*. Hundreds of papyrus pieces were found in Cave 6, among them fragments of the biblical books of Kings and Daniel written in a semi-cursive script. Before the Qumran discoveries the Nash Papyrus, containing parts of Dt. 5 and 6, had occupied a unique position as the oldest biblical Heb. MS extant; it is possibly to be dated as early as the 2nd century BC. Wadi Murabba'at has also produced assorted Heb. papyri from the time of the Bar Kokhba rebellion (AD 132–135). The most noteworthy finds were a couple of letters written by Bar Kokhba himself and containing his real name—Simeon Ben Kosebah.

b. Hebrew ostraca

Ostraca, being cheap and of limited use, tended to have only information of secondary importance inscribed on them. Nevertheless, ostraca bearing Heb. inscriptions have shed valuable light on the language and literature of the OT. The Samaria ostraca, discovered in the main during the Harvard excavations of 1908–10, are among the most important. They date from the time of the Jehu dynasty, possibly from the reign of Jehoahaz at the end of the 9th century. Discovered in a royal storehouse, they record information concerning the payment of oil and wine; it is possible that they refer to the produce from crown property in the vicinity of Samaria. In each case the regnal year is given and, though not uniformly, they contain many personal and place-names, the former including compounds of Yahweh, El and Baal. See *LOB*, pp. 315–327. Many ostraca inscribed in Aramaic, and some in Hebrew, have been discovered at

Arad. The Hebrew-inscribed date from the late 7th century BC and concern supplies of wine, flour and bread which an official had to provide for travellers (troops?). Some smaller ostraca found in the temple ruins record names of priestly families, among them the Korahites (*bny qrḥ*). The Yavneh-Yam ostraca are dated to the same era. Special interest attaches to one of this collection which preserves an agricultural worker's plea for the return of his cloak which had been removed by an overseer who wrongly accused him of laziness (*cf.* Ex. 22:26–27). Of roughly similar date is the Ophel ostracon found in Jerusalem in the 1923–5 excavations. It contains a list of names and provenances in palaeo-Hebrew script. Probably best known of all are the Lachish ostraca, twenty-one of which were discovered on the site of the ancient city (mod. Tell ed-Duweir) in 1935 and 1938. These have a particular merit in that many of them can be dated with certainty to the year 587 BC. They are mostly letters and the name of Yaosh, military governor of Lachish, occurs as that of the addressee in some of them. The letters reflect the desperate situation in Judah as the Babylonians took city after city; there are some points of contact with the book of Jeremiah. Features of interest include the free use of the tetragrammaton and a reference to a prophet acting as postman. Some Heb.-inscribed sherds have also been discovered at Qumran, Wadi Murabba'at and Masada (where one with the name Ben Yair inscribed on it has aroused particular interest because of its probable connection with the Zealot leader Eleazar Ben Yair).

c. Aramaic papyri

Possibly the earliest extant papyrus written in Aramaic is that which was found in 1942 at Saqqarah in Egypt. It represents part of a letter from a king Adon to the pharaoh and would seem to have been written from somewhere on the Philistine or Phoenician coast. Thus the use of Aramaic in international diplomacy before the Persian era is illustrated, for the letter cannot have been written after the time of Nebuchadrezzar (d. 562 BC). But by far the most significant corpus of Aram. papyri is that which comes from the island of Elephantine in Egypt. Here and at Memphis and Hermopolis a large number of papyri written by Jews in the late 6th and 5th centuries BC have been preserved. Legal documents and private letters are well represented, and there is also a fragment of the oldest known version of the *Sayings of Ahikar*. The type of Aramaic is, as we should expect, rather like that in the biblical Ezra. These Jewish colonists had their own temple (despite Dt. 12:5–7) and went so far as to compound the name of the God of Israel with Canaanite divine names (*e.g.* Anath-Yahu, Anath-Bethel). Representing the 4th century are the papyri from Wadi Daliyeh, 19 km NW of Jericho. These were discovered in a cave and it is surmised that they were hidden there by refugees from Samaria where they were actually written. They are legal and administrative documents which were drawn up *c.* 375–365 BC; they may have been abandoned by people who had fled before Alexander the Great. Some Aram. papyri are included in the finds at Qumran (*e.g.* one containing OT genealogies, from Cave 4) and at Wadi Murabba'at (*e.g.* deeds of sale). Some Nabataean fragments have also been recovered in the vicinity of Wadi Murabba'at.

d. Aramaic ostraca

An early example is the letter on a potsherd found at Asshur and probably written in the 7th century BC. Aram. ostraca at Elephantine (*vid. sup.*) are mainly tax receipts. Fragments from the Persian period found at Tell al-Khalayfa evidently served as receipts for wine. Scores of Aram. sherds are among the finds at Arad. A few have turned up at Qumran and Wadi Murabba'at but they are of little significance. A fragment of a letter(?) at Wadi Murabba'at is dated to the early 1st century BC.

e. Greek Old Testament papyri

A considerable number are extant, though invariably they are in fragmentary condition. Perhaps the oldest is the John Rylands Pap. Gk. 458 containing parts of Dt. 23–28 and dating from the 2nd century BC. Pap. Fouad 266 is almost as old and preserves fragments of Gn. 7 and 38 and Dt. 17–33. The Chester Beatty Gk. OT papyri include parts of various OT books and range in date from the 2nd to the 4th centuries AD. From the 3rd century AD comes the Freer Gk. MS V, a papyrus codex of the Minor Prophets. Qumran Cave 4 has yielded fragments of Lv. 2–5, while in Cave 7 fragments containing Ex. 28:4–7 and the *Epistle of Jeremiah* 43–44 have been found. The Qumran finds may be given approx. dates in the 1st century BC.

BIBLIOGRAPHY (for Heb., Aram. and Gk. OT material): A. Cowley, *Aramaic Papyri of the Fifth Century BC*, 1923; E. G. Kraeling, *The Brooklyn Museum Aramaic Papyri*, 1953; *DOTT*, pp. 204–208, 212–217, 251–269; P. Benoit *et al.*, *Discoveries in the Judaean Desert*, 2, 1961; F. F. Bruce, *The Books and the Parchments*[3], 1963; S. Jellicoe, *The Septuagint and Modern Study*, 1968; B. Porten, *Archives from Elephantine*, 1968; K. Aland, *Repertorium der Griechischen Christlichen Papyri: I. Biblische Papyri*, 1976; A. Lemaire, *Inscriptions hébratiques 1. Les ostraca*, 1977. R.P.G.

III. New Testament

a. Introduction

The discovery of the Gk. papyri in Egypt during the last century has had important results for NT studies. In the initial finds biblical papyri were rare, but with the commencement of systematic excavations by Grenfell and Hunt in 1896 large quantities of papyri came to light, including either portions of the NT books themselves or documents of the early centuries which helped our understanding of them. The most fruitful sites were in the Fayyûm and to the S, particularly at Oxyrhynchus, Hermopolis, Tebtynis, Aphroditopolis and Panopolis.

It had long been assumed by many scholars that NT Greek was *sui generis*, 'a language of the Holy Ghost', but there were some, such as Masson, Lightfoot and Farrar, who anticipated the fact soon to be proved, that the NT writers used the common tongue of the Gk. world in the 1st century AD, approximating more often to the spoken than to the literary form of *koinē* Greek. Thanks to the papyri, we now have illustrations of the contemporary 'secular' use of the vast majority of NT words. It is still true, in a restricted sense, that the language is *sui generis*, because of the frequent substratum of Hebrew and Aramaic. 'The tension between the Jewish heritage and the Greek world vitally affects the language of the New Testament' (Hoskyns and Davey, *The Riddle of the New Tes-*

tament, 1931, p. 20). Another tendency corrected by the study of the papyri was the inclination of scholars to judge the NT by Attic standards of grammar and syntax, and also of literary taste. It was now made doubly clear that the *koinē* of the first Christian centuries was in a comparatively rapid state of evolution, which culminated in Byzantine and finally in modern Greek, and must therefore be evaluated in the light of this. It would be wrong to claim too much for these advances, but they have provided an indispensable aid to the study of the NT text, language and literature, and thus for its theological interpretation. In his Schweich Lecture of 1946 (published in 1953 as *The Text of the Epistles*) G. Zuntz makes a plea for the active conjunction of these two fields of study. 'The theologian who studies the New Testament must assume the quality also of the philologist' (p. 3). Perhaps the finest work exemplifying this is *TDNT*.

The original documents of the NT were all written on papyrus rolls (apart from one or two of the shortest Epistles, which may have been written on individual sheets of papyrus), and it may here be mentioned that the transmission of the text played an important part in the development of new techniques. In the rest of the Roman world papyrus codices did not begin to replace rolls until the 3rd century AD, but from Egypt we have evidence that the Christian communities developed the codex form considerably earlier. Ten Bible fragments have been found dated to the 2nd and early 3rd centuries, and of 111 fragments of the 3rd and 4th only twelve were in the form of papyrus rolls. The text of Romans would have required a roll of 4 m, Mark 6 m, Acts about 10 m (*cf.* 2 Tim. 4:13 referring to rolls and the parchment wrappings which protected them). But as the need arose for copies of the Gospels and Epistles in larger bulk, the use of codices naturally developed, *i.e.* leaves of papyrus folded and arranged in quires, much as in modern books. A single codex could now contain the four Gospels and Acts, or the whole of Paul's Epistles.

b. List of the most notable papyri

The latest tabulation, edited by K. Aland (1976), contains more than 241 entries, of which 68 are listed in the critical editions of the NT text. Many are comparatively small, but the importance of the more substantial texts is great.

P^1 (3rd or 4th cent.) contains Mt. 1:1–9, 12–20; P^4 (4th cent.) Lk. 1:74–80; 6:1–4; P^5 (3rd cent.) Jn. 1:23–31, 33–41 and 20:11–17, 19–25; it comprises the two leaves of a single quire, and illustrates the family from which the Codices Sinaiticus and Vaticanus later derived. P^8 (4th cent.) contains Acts 4:31–37; 5:2–9; 6:1–6, 8–15; P^{13} (3rd cent., written on the back of an Epitome of Livy) Heb. 2:14–5:5; 10:8–22; 10:29–11:13; 11:28–12:17; P^{20} (3rd cent.) Jas. 2:19–3:9; P^{22} (3rd cent.) Jn. 15:25–16:2, 21–32; P^{27} (3rd cent.) Rom. 8:12–22, 24–27, 33–9:3; 9:5–9; P^{37} (3rd cent.) contains Mt. 26:19–52; P^{38} (4th cent.) Acts 18:27–19:6; 19:12–16.

Of the Chester Beatty Papyri ($P^{45, 46, 47}$), Nos. 1 and 2 are of particular interest. P^{45} (early 3rd cent.) contains portions of 30 leaves out of a codex of 220 including the Gospels and Acts; it has parts of Matthew, Mark, Luke, John (17 leaves) and Acts (13 leaves). P^{46} (also early 3rd cent.) contains 86 leaves, found over a period in three groups, and has Romans, Hebrews, 1, 2 Corinthians, Galatians, Ephesians, Philippians, Colossians, 1, 2 Thessalonians, except for small gaps. It is notable that the concluding doxology of Romans here occurs at the end of ch. 15. P^{47} (3rd cent., 10 leaves) has Rev. 9:10–17:2; P^{48} (3rd cent., similar to P^{38}) has Acts 23:11–16, 24–29. P^{52} (the famous 'John Rylands' fragment, 9 cm by 6 cm) was identified by C. H. Roberts in 1935 as Jn. 18:31–33, 37–38 and belonging to the early 2nd cent. P^{64} (2nd cent.) contains portions of Mt. 26; P^{66} (*c.* AD 200), the 'Bodmer papyrus II', has 108 leaves in 5 quires, each 16 cm by 14 cm, and contains Jn. 1:1–14:26.

The textual relation of these and many lesser papyri to the most important vellum codices and early versions of the NT has been the subject of close study.

c. Effect on the textual study of the New Testament

To describe this, a brief sketch of the history of the Gk. text up to the papyrus discoveries is necessary. The AV of 1611 was based on the Gk. NT edition prepared by Stephanus (Robert Etienne) in 1550, the 'Textus Receptus', which itself drew largely on the edition of Erasmus published in 1516. Stephanus had made use of only fifteen MSS, all of them of late date, and representing the Byzantine or Eastern tradition of the text. The event which stimulated a serious search for all available MSS was the appearance in England in 1627 of the Codex Alexandrinus, a vellum codex of the 5th century AD. But it was not until the discovery of Codex Sinaiticus and the appearance of Tischendorf's edition of Vaticanus, in 1859 and 1867 respectively, that any great advance in textual study was possible. This came just as scholars began to realize the potential wealth of Egypt in papyri. Westcott and Hort published a revised Gk. text in 1881, which was used extensively in the Eng. RV of that year. These scholars postulated four main families of texts, Syrian, Neutral, Alexandrian and Western, and themselves gave most weight to the Neutral family, consisting of the Codices Vaticanus and Sinaiticus, the Coptic Versions and kindred MSS.

NT papyri have played a prominent part in the extension and modification of their results. Further study convinced scholars that Westcott and Hort's groups had been distinguished too sharply from each other; and B. H. Streeter, using the minuscule groups of MSS isolated by Ferrar and Abbott, and by K. Lake, together with the Koridethi MS (9th cent.) demonstrated the close relation these all bore to Origen's text of the NT, and postulated at any rate for the Gospel of Mark the 'Caesarean' family (Origen having spent his latter years at Caesarea). The text of the Gospels in the Freer MSS (the 'Washington Gospels') and the Chester Beatty papyri further showed that the 'Caesarean' family of texts probably originated in Egypt, and went from Alexandria to Caesarea with Origen. The Chester Beatty group, especially P^{46}, have been of immense value. They prove that the codex was early in use for collections of the Gospels and Pauline Epistles, the circulation of which greatly assisted towards the formation of the canon of the NT. Their firm dating to the 3rd century AD means that we now possess a line of textual evidence going beyond the great vellum codices of the 4th and 5th centuries, upon which scholars had depended so heavily, and earlier than the NT collections which Eusebius was ordered to produce for use in the churches, following the Edict of Milan in AD 313. Further valuable help has been provided by the Bodmer papyri, especially P^{66}, a late 2nd-century codex of John. Still earlier fragments, in particular the 'John Rylands' fragment of John's Gospel, take us into the first half of the 2nd century, *i.e.* to within a single generation of the last writings of the NT, the Johannine Corpus.

The general picture of the transmission of the text which emerges is that of many groups or families arising, as copies were made for public and private use, sometimes by trained scribes, but more often by untrained Christians. The need for a standard text had not yet arisen, and local attempts at the collation of different texts were never very widely used. We must also assume that in the persecutions, *e.g.* that of Decius in AD 250, many copies of the NT perished. The papyri have helped to reveal the complexity of this early stage of transmission; if we are still far from fulfilling Bentley's aim to make the text so undoubtedly true 'ut e manibus apostolorum vix purior et sincerior evaserit' ('that it could scarcely have come from the hands of the apostles themselves in a form purer or more free from corruption'), at least the story is one of continuous advance. (*TEXTS AND VERSIONS (NT).)

d. Effect on the study of New Testament language and literature

As noted above, the Gk. of the NT has affinities with both the literary and the non-literary forms of the *koinē*, principally the latter, which is now known so fully from papyrus documents of every type from Graeco-Roman Egypt—Imperial rescripts, judicial proceedings, tax and census papers, marriage contracts, birth, death and divorce notices, private letters, business accounts, and a host of others. There are without doubt many Semitisms in the NT, all the writers except one being Jewish, but their estimated number has been greatly reduced by the discovery of parallel expressions in the papyri. 'Even Mark's Semitisms are hardly ever barbarous Greek, though his extremely vernacular language makes us think so, until we read the less educated papyri' (Howard). An example is the expression *blepein apo* at Mk. 8:15. Many new word formations of NT Greek have been paralleled, *e.g.* substantives ending in*-mos*, *-ma*, *-sis*, *-ia*; adjectives ending in *-ios*, new compound adjectives and adverbs, new words with the privative *a-* prefix; foreign words, technical words used of the Roman army and administration. Problems of orthography have been settled, *e.g.* *genēma* (Mt. 26:29), *tameion* (Lk. 12:3), *sphyris* (Mt. 15:37); and of morphology, *e.g.* *gegonan* (Rom. 16:7), *elthatō* (Mt. 10:13), *ēlthan* (Mk. 3:8); and of syntax, *e.g.* the consecutive use of *hina* clauses (as in Jn. 17:3), the interchangeability of *eis* and *en* (as in Jn. 1:18; Mt. 18:19).

NT vocabulary was abundantly illustrated. Instead of the numerous *voces biblicae* of the older scholars, it became possible to show, as did Deissmann and Bauer, that only about 1 per cent of the vocabulary, about fifty words, was in fact peculiar to it. A better sense could be given to words like *hēlikia* (*e.g.* Lk. 2:52 = 'age'), *meris* (Acts 16:12 = 'district'), *anastatoō* (lit. 'drive out of hearth and home', used metaphorically in Acts 17:6 and Gal. 5:12), *hypostasis* (Heb. 11:1 = 'title-deeds', RSV 'assurance'), *parousia* (*passim*; = visit of royalty or other notable person), *arrhabōn* (*e.g.* Eph. 1:14 = 'deposit paid', RSV 'guarantee'), *leitourgia* (2 Cor. 9:12; of both private and public service). The common terms *adelphoi* and *presbyteroi* were frequently illustrated, from social and religious fraternities and from village and temple officials.

At the time the NT was written a revised Atticism was popular, an essentially artificial movement which affected to recognize only 5th-century Attic Greek as the norm. But there were notable secular writers, such as Plutarch, Strabo, Diodorus Siculus and Epictetus, who shunned Atticism, and the NT itself represents a revolt against it by its use of the vernacular tongue. '*Koinē* is not, as it were, pure gold accidentally contaminated, but something more like a new and serviceable alloy' (Moule). The LXX had already set a precedent for such a use of popular Greek, and the writers, all of whom might have written in Aramaic, wrote in Greek from deliberate choice. The literary standard of their work of course varies enormously. 2 Peter most nearly approaches a fully literary level, and Luke and the author of Hebrews are also conscious stylists. But Luke and Paul, though obviously capable of speaking and writing Greek in its classical form (*cf.* the prefaces to Luke and Acts, and Acts 17:22ff.) did not hesitate to use highly colloquial forms. The extreme case is the Revelation, written in laboured and sometimes barbarous Greek, which clearly reflects the influence of Semitic terms and modes of thought. But it still remains true that 'the Greek in which the author expresses himself was more like the Greek of the Egyptian papyri' (A. Robinson). (*LANGUAGE OF THE NEW TESTAMENT.)

e. Ostraca

We have noted already that ostraca or 'potsherds' were used extensively in antiquity as the cheapest possible writing material. Their seeming insignificance (*cf.* Is. 45:9) caused them to be neglected as being of any value for the study of *koinē* Greek. As we might expect, among the large numbers found in Egypt, covering a period of nearly 1,000 years, the vast majority are documents, or fragments of them, belonging to the life of the lower classes. A few have been found bearing short literary texts, no doubt for use in schools, and we have ostraca with short passages of the NT inscribed on them (verses from Mk. 9 and Lk. 22) and one of the 6th century AD with a hymn to Mary influenced by Lk. 1. But more comprise brief letters, contracts, and, above all, tax receipts. Many languages are used, including Greek, Latin, Aramaic, Coptic and Old Egyptian.

Occasionally a NT expression is illuminated. Several ostraca give details of receipts dated to the day called *Sebastē*, meaning 'Emperor's Day', and perhaps parallel to the use by Christians of *kyriakē* as 'the *Lord's day'. The title *Kyrios*, 'Lord', appears on ostraca referring to the emperors Nero and Vespasian (*cf.* Jude 4). Receipts from Thebes dated to the 1st century have thrown light on the NT use of *logeia* (*e.g.* 1 Cor. 16:1–2 = 'collections') and also on the verb *apechō* signifying the receipt of a payment (*cf.* Mt. 6:2 = 'they have received their reward in full'). The common phrase *eis to onoma* ('in the name') is shown by ostraca to have been a regular legal formula, of the authority under which something is done. Ostraca thus supplement, on a comparatively minor scale, the evidence of the papyri as to NT language and idiom.

f. Apocryphal and non-canonical papyri

These deserve mention because of the assistance they have given to the understanding of the form and content of NT writings. Most notable are the *Logia* or Sayings of Jesus. The first of these (found at Oxyrhynchus in 1896 and 1897) was the leaf of a codex dated to the 3rd century, containing sayings some of which were familiar, others of a more mystical type; the second, of the late 2nd century, had the sayings written on the back of a roll about land surveys. A third contained fragments of a non-canonical Gospel, and another of this type was discovered in 1934; it comprises fragments of three leaves of a codex, assigned to *c.* AD 150, and narrates four incidents from Christ's life, similar to those in the Gospels. Then, among thirteen papyrus rolls found near Nag Hammadi in 1946 was the *Gospel of Thomas*, an important collection of Sayings in which Gnostic influence mingles with the Synoptic, Johannine and other traditions, evidently a Coptic version of the work of which the Oxyrhynchus Logia are fragments.

Several apocryphal works have been recovered in whole or in part. The Chester Beatty collection includes fourteen leaves of the *Book of Enoch*, from a 4th-century codex, and part of a homily by Melito of Sardis on the passion. One papyrus leaf of Gnostic origin has come to light (early 3rd century), out of the *Gospel of Mary*. At Akhmim fragments were found of the *Gospel* and *Apocalypse of Peter* (probably written in the 2nd century). The former has Docetic tendencies, and the latter is much inferior to the Revelation of John. In the Amherst collection is the major portion of the *Ascension of Isaiah*, and in the Hamburg State Library are eleven leaves of the *Acts of Paul*, a late 2nd-century 'religious romance'. Finally, the Oxyrhynchus papyri have provided some of the Gk. text of the well-known *Shepherd* of Hermas. This work later appears in full in the Codex Sinaiticus. (*CANON OF THE NEW TESTAMENT.)

BIBLIOGRAPHY (*listed according to above sections*).

a. E. G. Turner, *Greek Papyri*², 1980; F. F. Bruce, *The New Testament Documents: Are They Reliable?*⁵, 1960; C. H. Roberts, *Manuscript, Society and Belief in Early Christian Egypt*, 1979; C. H. Roberts and T. C. Skeat, *The Birth of the Codex*, 1983.

b. K. Aland, *Repertorium der griechischen christlichen Papyri*, 1, 1976; K. Treu, *Archiv für Papyrus-forschung* 19, 1969, pp. 169–206 and subsequent vols.; M. Grunewald and K. Junack, *Das Neue Testament auf Papyrus* 1-2, 1986 and 1989.

c. B. M. Metzger, *The Manuscripts of the Greek Bible*, 1981; *A Textual Commentary on the Greek New Testament*, 1971; B. and K. Aland, *The Text of the New Testament*², 1989.

d. Blass-Debrunner–Funk, *A Greek Grammar of the New Testament*¹⁰, 1961; C. F. D. Moule, *An Idiom Book of New Testament Greek*², 1959; G. H. R. Horsley, *et al.*, *New Documents Illustrating Early Christianity*, 1-6, 1981–92.

e. Portions of NT found on *ostraca* are included in the papyri lists of *b.* above.

f. B. P. Grenfell, A. S. Hunt *et al.*, *The Oxyrhynchus Papyri* I–LVIII, 1898–1991; R. M. Grant and D. N. Freedman, *The Secret Sayings of Jesus*, 1960; R. McL. Wilson, *Studies in the Gospel of Thomas*, 1960; E. Hennecke, *New Testament Apocrypha* 1, 1963; J. Jeremias, *The Unknown Sayings of Jesus*, 1964.

B.F.H.

PARABLE.

I. Parables and allegories

'Parable' is ultimately derived from Gk. *parabolē*, literally 'putting things side by side'. Etymologically it is thus close to 'allegory', which by derivation means 'saying things in a different way'. Both parables and allegories have usually been regarded as forms of teaching which present the listener with interesting illustrations from which can be drawn moral and religious truths; 'parable' is the somewhat protracted simile or short descriptive story, usually designed to inculcate a single truth or answer a single question, while 'allegory' denotes the more elaborate tale in which all or most of the details have their counterparts in the application. Since 'truth embodied in a tale shall enter in at lowly doors', the value of this method of instruction is obvious.

The line between parables and allegories is obviously a fluid one, and both forms are found in the Gospels. There is, however, a more basic difference than that of amount of detail present. While the developed allegory is essentially illustrative, so that one might almost say that the details of the story have been derived from the application, many of the parables of Jesus are not merely illustrations of general principles; rather they embody messages which cannot be conveyed in any other way. The parables are the appropriate form of communication for bringing to men the message of the kingdom, since their function is to jolt them into seeing things in a new way. They are means of enlightenment and persuasion, intended to bring the hearers to the point of decision. Jesus, as it were, stands where his hearers stand, and uses imagery familiar to them to bring new and unfamiliar insights to them. Just as a lover finds himself restricted by the language of prose and must resort to poetry to express his feelings, so Jesus expresses the message of the kingdom in the appropriate forms of language.

II. The interpretation of the parables

In the NT the actual word 'parable' is used with the same broad variety of meaning as Heb. *māšāl* to refer to almost any kind of non-literal utterance. What we should normally call a *proverb can be termed a parable (Lk. 4:23, Gk.; RSV has 'proverb'). The 'parable' in Mt. 15:15 has almost the nature of a conundrum. The simple illustration, that leaves on a tree are signs of the approach of summer, is a 'parable' (Mk. 13:28). The more elaborate comparison between children at play and the reaction of Jesus' contemporaries to John the Baptist and himself is usually spoken of as 'the *parable* of the children's game' (Lk. 7:31f.). On the other hand, the parables of the sower and the tares are both given detailed allegorical interpretations (Mt. 13:18–23, 36–43), and the parables of the drag-net (Mt. 13:47–50), the wicked husbandmen (Mk. 12:1–12), the marriage feast (Mt. 22:1–14) and the great supper (Lk. 14:16–24) obviously contain details with allegorical significance.

Christian preachers in all ages have striven, for homiletic purposes, to express their message afresh for their own audiences. This is obviously an entirely legitimate procedure; it is justified by the nature of the parables themselves as art-forms and it is already to be seen in the NT itself (*cf.* perhaps Paul's use of the 'sower' motif in Col. 1:6). Unfortunately a tendency developed to allegorize small details in the parables so as to teach truths not in the least obvious in the stories themselves, and irrelevant to the context in which they are found. As a result, the inevitable critical reaction set in. Scholars, such as A. Jüicher, asserted that the parables were intended to illustrate one truth only; and they regarded the allegorical interpretations of the parables of the sower and the tares as early examples of the dangerous process of allegorization which had done so much harm in the Christian church. But it is in reality impossible to draw a clear-cut distinction between parable and allegory in the stories told by Jesus; some of his stories were clearly intended to illustrate *several* lessons, as in the parable of the prodigal son, where stress is laid on the joy which God as Father has in forgiving his children, the nature of repentance, and the sin of jealousy and self-righteousness (Lk. 15:11–32).

It was the mistake of Jülicher to reduce the messages of the parables to moral platitudes. More recent scholars have rightly recognized that they formed part of Jesus' proclamation of the kingdom of God. In an effort to define more precisely their meaning, J. Jeremias and other scholars have insisted that the parables must be understood in their original historical settings within the ministry and teaching of Jesus. In some cases, according to Jeremias, the parables have been re-worded by those who transmitted them in the early church in order to bring out their abiding significance for fresh generations of hearers; in order to hear them again in their pristine freshness as they fell from the lips of Jesus we must attempt to remove any secondary elements which they have acquired and free the original, comparatively simple lessons taught by Jesus from the more elaborate meanings added by early Christian teachers. While some valuable light can be shed on the parables in this way, such analysis of primary and secondary elements tends to be subjective. It is certainly the case that the Evangelists did not always know the occasion on which particular parable was first spoken or the persons to whom it was originally addressed. In the case of the parables of the good Samaritan (Lk. 10:25), the two debtors (Lk. 7:41), the children's game (Lk. 7:31f.) and the pounds (Lk. 19:11), the context is given and provides a clue to the interpretation. Often, however, it would seem that the stories of Jesus were remembered long after the circumstances that gave rise to them were forgotten; and the Evangelists have fitted them into their narratives in suitable places, sometimes suggesting the original motive for their utterance (Lk. 18:9). On occasion collections of parables, detached from their original contexts, were made (Mt. 13).

Recent scholars have claimed that the parables constitute an art-form whose interpretation is not entirely dependent on a reconstruction of their original content and form; as parables, the stories told by Jesus are capable of showing fresh facets of meaning. It is clear, however, that exposition of the parables for today must be based on as careful an understanding of what Jesus meant by the parables as is possible; otherwise we fall back into the error of regarding them as illustrations of general truths.

The study of the parables with the aid of insights from modern linguistics and semantics has shown that they are not simply ways of conveying information in an attractive form. They have a variety of logical forms and functions. Very often their aim is to jolt the audience into seeing things from a new point of view and to be the actual means of bringing them into a new situation. The parables were meant to force people to *decide* about their attitude to Jesus and his message and thus to bring them into a new relationship with him. They have been described (by E. Fuchs) as 'language-events': *i.e.* they are the form which the kingdom of God takes in the sphere of language. Through the parables the kingly rule of God comes to men with its promises, judgments, demands and gifts.

It is on these points that interpretation of the parables must concentrate. We should not expect to find the whole of the gospel in any given parable: 'It is, for example, misleading to say that the parable of the prodigal son contains "the gospel within the Gospels" and to deduce from it that no doctrine of atonement is vital to Christianity; or to suppose from the story of the good Samaritan that practical service to our fellow men is the be-all and end-all of Christianity' (R. V. G. Tasker, *The Nature and Purpose of the Gospels*, 1957, pp. 57f.). Nor should we attempt to bring ethical and economic considerations to bear upon the interpretation of the parables when these are in fact irrelevant. The parable of the unjust steward (Lk. 16:1–9) teaches that men must prepare themselves for the future; but the morality of the steward (if he was in fact acting immorally—see J. D. M. Derrett, cited below) has no bearing on this lesson. It is futile to suggest that the parable of the labourers in the vineyard (Mt. 20:1–16) is meant to throw light on the problem of wages; it illustrates the goodness of God, who deals with men generously and not strictly in accordance with their merits.

III. Characteristics of the parables

Jesus took the illustrations for his parables sometimes from nature, as in the various parables about seeds and their growth (Mt. 13:24–30; Mk. 4:1–9, 26–29, 30–32); sometimes from familiar customs and incidents of everyday life, as in the parables of the leaven (Mt. 13:33), the lost sheep and the lost coin (Lk. 15:3–10), the importunate man (Lk. 11:5–8) and the ten virgins (Mt. 25:1–13); sometimes from recent events (Lk. 19:14); and sometimes from what might be regarded as occasional happenings or not improbable contingencies, as in the parables of the unjust judge (Lk. 18:2–8), the unjust steward (Lk. 16:1–9) and the prodigal son (Lk. 15:11–32). The style varies from the brief simile or metaphor (Mk. 2:21f.; 3:23) to the description of a typical event or a full-scale short story of a particular happening.

Sometimes the lesson of a parable is quite obvious from the story itself, as in the story of the rich fool, where the rich man dies at the very moment when he has completed his preparations to retire in security and comfort (Lk. 12:16–21), but even here the story is 'capped' with the dictum: 'So is he who lays up treasure for himself, and is not rich toward God'. On other occasions the point is elicited by means of a question, *e.g.* 'Now which of them will love him more?' (Lk. 7:42). A parable itself may be told in the form of a question which invites the hearer to think how he would act, and then to make the application (Lk. 11:5–8; 14:28–32). Jesus may draw out the point himself, either at the conclusion of a story (*e.g.* Mt. 18:23) or in response to a subsequent request for elucidation (*e.g.* Mt. 15:15). But more often the story is told without additions, and the hearers are left to draw their own deductions from it. Thus in Mk. 12:12 it is clear that the religious leaders knew that Jesus had spoken the parable of the wicked husbandmen against them.

IV. The kingdom of God

Many of the parables of Jesus are specifically related to the *kingdom of God (*e.g.* Mk. 4:26, 30), and in general the parables are related to its nature, its coming, its value, its growth, the sacrifices it calls for, and so on. Very naturally the interpretation of the parables is dependent on the view of the kingdom held by individual interpreters, and vice versa. Theologians of the 'thoroughgoing' school of eschatology, such as A. Schweitzer, who believed that Jesus envisaged the coming of the kingdom of God as a supernatural event which would take place suddenly and catastrophically in the near future, found here the clue to the meaning of the parables of the kingdom. They referred to the imminent crisis prophesied by Jesus. Even parables which implied growth or progress were regarded in this way. It was, for example, in the suddenness of the rising of leaven, not in its slow working, that the meaning of the parable was to be found (Mt. 13:33). Theologians of the school of 'realised' eschatology, such as C. H. Dodd, who argued that the kingdom had fully arrived in the ministry of Jesus, interpreted the parables in terms of fulfilment. The harvest prepared for in past ages had already come; the mustard seed planted long ago had now become a tree (Mk. 4:26–32).

Both of these interpretations are one-sided and fail to do justice to the undoubted elements of future hope (Mk. 13:28–37) and present fulfilment (Mt. 9:37f.; Jn. 4:35) in the teaching of Jesus. While Jesus regarded the kingdom or kingship of God as present indeed in his own words and actions, he also anticipated a period, the length of which he did not know (Mk. 13:32), during which that kingship would be a reality in the society of his followers who would constitute his world-wide church, and he predicted that the kingdom would not come in its fullness until he himself came as the Son of man in glory. The contrast between the apparent lack of response with which his teaching was at first received and the final outcome of it is suggested in the parables recorded in Mk. 4. Many of the parables are concerned with the grace shown by God through Jesus in the present time and indicate that the new age has dawned. Others are concerned with how men are to live in the light of the kingdom until its final consummation: they are to be persistent in prayer, to forgive others, to serve their neighbours, to use the gifts God has given them, to be free from covetousness, to remain alert, to be faithful stewards, and to remember that their final judgment is being determined by their present conduct.

V. The purpose of the parables

Some have found Mk. 4:10–12 very difficult to understand, for it seems to suggest that Jesus' purpose in the parables was not to enlighten the unenlightened, but that the unbeliever might become hardened in his unbelief. It is possible, however, that what seems to be a clause of purpose in Mk. 4:12 is in fact a clause of consequence (so Mt. 13:13). The parables of Jesus may have the effect of hardening the unbeliever, just as Isaiah prophesied with regard to the effects of preaching the Word of God. The truth is that Jesus' parables are unique. The parables of other teachers can to some extent be separated from the teachers themselves, but Jesus and his parables are inseparable. To fail to understand *him* is to fail to understand his parables. 'For those outside everything is in parables' (Mk. 4:11); the *whole* of Jesus' ministry, not merely the parables, remains on the level of earthly stories and portents devoid of any deeper significance. Here 'parables' has virtually come to mean 'riddles'. It is, therefore, possible for men to decline the invitation to understanding and commitment found in the parables, and in them Isaiah's prophecy (Is. 6:9f.) is fulfilled (*cf.* Jn. 12:40 where the same prophecy is cited with reference to the disbelief of the Jews in the face of Jesus' mighty works).

VI. Parables in John's Gospel

In Jn. 10:6 the word *paroimia* (a variant translation of *māšāl*, usually rendered 'proverb', *e.g.* Pr. 1:1) is used to describe the allegory of the true and false shepherds. In Jn. 16:25 the same word is closer to its OT sense of a difficult saying which needs further explanation. The Gospel of John is apparently lacking in parables of the kind found in the other Gospels, but C. H. Dodd and A. M. Hunter have drawn attention to a number of brief parables which lie almost hidden in this Gospel (Jn. 3:8, 29; 4:35–38; 5:19f.; 8:35; 10:1–5; 11:9f.; 12:24, 35f.; 16:21). Nor should we overlook the many 'figurative' descriptions which Jesus uses of himself in this Gospel, *e.g.* 'the good shepherd', 'the true vine', 'the door', 'the light of the world', and 'the way, and the truth, and the life'.

Bibliography. F. Hauck, *TDNT* 5, pp. 744–761; C. H. Dodd, *The Parables of the Kingdom*², 1961; J. Jeremias, *The Parables of Jesus*², 1963; G. V. Jones, *The Art and Truth of the Parables*, 1964; J. D. M. Derrett, *Law in the New Testament*, 1970; D. O. Via, Jr., *The Parables: Their Literary and Existential Dimension*, 1967; J. D. Crossan, *In Parables: The Challenge of the Historical Jesus*, 1973; J. R. Michaels, *Servant and Son*, 1981; R. H. Stein, *An Introduction to the Parables of Jesus*, 1981; H. Hendrickx, *The Parables of Jesus*, 1986; D. Wenham, *The Parables of Jesus*, 1989; C. L. Blomberg, *Interpreting the Parables*, 1990. On parables in Jn. see C. H. Dodd, *Historical Tradition in the Fourth Gospel*, 1963; A. M. Hunter, *According to John*, 1968. On hermeneutics and the parables, see A. C. Thiselton, *SJT* 23, 1970, pp. 437–468.

R.V.G.T.
I.H.M.

PARADISE. Paradise is a loan-word from ancient Iranian (*pairidaēza-*) and means a garden with a wall. The Gk. word *paradeisos* is used for the first time by Xenophon for the gardens of the Persian kings. LXX translates *gan 'ēḏen* of Gn. 2:8 by *paradeisos*.

a. In the Old Testament

The word paradise (Heb. *pardēs*) appears in Ne. 2:8; Ec. 2:5; Ct. 4:13. RSV renders it by 'king's forest' in Ne., 'park' in Ec. and 'orchard' in Ct. The actual word is thus nowhere used in the OT in an eschatological sense, which meaning developed in the later Jewish world. The following trends can be discerned. The word paradise (Aram. *pardēsā'*) was used to give expression to the meaning of primeval times (German *Urzeit*) and then expanded to include fantastic speculations on the glory and bliss of those times. This was connected with the expectations of a wonderful Messianic time in the future. This coming age of glory would be identical with the garden of Eden of ancient times. The Jews believed also that paradise was present in their own time, but concealed. This concealed paradise was the place to which the souls of the Patriarchs, the chosen and the righteous people, were taken. The ancient, future and present paradise were regarded as being identical.

b. In the New Testament

The word paradise (Gk. *paradeisos*) occurs in only three instances in the NT (Lk. 23:43; 2 Cor. 12:3; Rev. 2:7). The context shows that the predominating sense is that of the later development of the word. In Lk. 23:43 the word 'paradise' is used by Jesus for the place where souls go immediately after death, *cf.* the concealed paradise in later Jewish thought. The same idea is also present in the parable of the rich man and Lazarus (Lk. 16:19–31).

In 2 Cor. 12:2–4 Paul wrote in the third person of his experience of being caught up into paradise where he heard unspeakable words (Gk. *arrhēta rhēmata*). In this case paradise is the 'third *heaven' with its glory, perhaps the same as in Lk. 23. The only place where paradise is used in an eschatological sense is in Rev. 2:7. The promise is made by Christ that he will give paradise as a gift to the one who overcomes. The present paradise will come in its full glory with the final consummation. The idea of a garden of God in the world to come is strongly emphasized in the last chapters of Revelation. The symbols of the tree of life, of life-giving water, and of the twelve kinds of fruit are all witnesses to the glory of the coming paradise (Rev. 22). F.C.F.

PARAN. A wilderness situated in the E central region of the Sinai peninsula, NE from the traditional Sinai and SSE of Kadesh, with the Arabah and the Gulf of Aqabah as its E border. It was to this wilderness that Hagar and Ishmael went after their expulsion from Abraham's household (Gn. 21:21) It was crossed by the Israelites following their Exodus from Egypt (Nu. 10:12; 12:16), and from here Moses despatched men to spy out the land of Canaan (Nu. 13:3, 26). The wilderness was also traversed by Hadad the Edomite on his flight to Egypt (1 Ki. 11:18).

1 Sa. 25:1 records that David went to the wilderness of Paran on the death of the prophet Samuel, but in this instance we may read with the Greek 'wilderness of Maon'.

El-paran, mentioned in Gn. 14:6 as on the border of the wilderness, may have been an ancient name for Elath. Mt Paran of the Song of Moses (Dt. 33:2) and of Hab. 3:3 was possibly a prominent peak in the mountain range on the W shore of the Gulf of Aqabah. (*ZIN.) R.A.H.G.

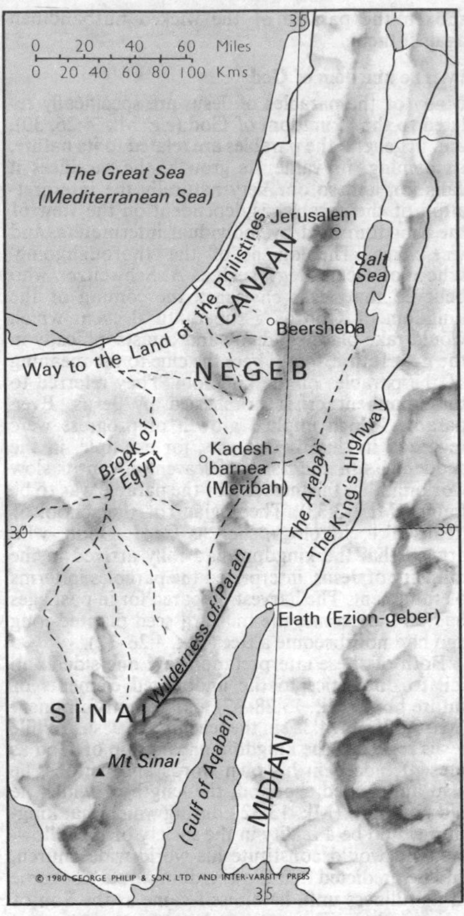

The location of the wilderness of Paran.

PARBAR. A room or partly-roofed gateway or courtyard building to W of the Temple where gatekeepers were stationed (1 Ch. 26:18), perhaps used for disposal of sacrificial waste. It may correspond with the 'building' seen by Ezekiel (41:12) and with the word in 2 Ki. 23:11 which has been associated with Pers. *parwār* ('having light'; LXX *pharoureim*). The location of Nathan-melek's house is given as 'in *parwārim*'. RV 'precincts', AV 'suburbs', follow Targ. and Mishnah, for the city suburbs contained 'summer' or veranda-houses.

The precise meaning of the non-Heb. word is uncertain. It has been associated with an Aram.-Lydian *parbar* which describes an open anteroom of a tomb at Sardis. The suggested emendation to *pᵉrādīm* ('who was over the mules') and any link with Iranian *frabada* remain unsupported. D.J.W.

PARTHIANS. Parthia, a district SE of the Caspian Sea, was part of the Persian empire conquered by Alexander the Great. In the middle of the 3rd century BC Arsaces led the Parthians in revolt against their Seleucid (Macedonian) rulers, and his successors eventually extended their empire from the Euphrates to the Indus. Their exclusive use of cavalry-bowmen made them a formidable enemy, as the Romans discovered to their cost. In the 1st century AD the Parthians changed their capital from Ecbatana to Ctesiphon and sought to revive the Iranian elements of their civilization at the expense of the Greek.

The Parthians were governed by a land-owning aristocracy, and controlled the lucrative trade with the Far East. Their own religion was Iranian Mazdaism, but they were generally tolerant of other peoples' religions.

Parthia was one of the districts in which the deported Israelites had been settled, and according to Josephus their descendants continued to speak an Aram. dialect and to worship the true God, sending tribute to the Temple at Jerusalem. Consequently the Parthians in Jerusalem on the Day of Pentecost (Acts 2:9) may have been only Israelites from that district ('language' in v. 8 could equally well be 'dialect'), but there may have been Parthian proselytes with them.

BIBLIOGRAPHY. N. C. Debevoise, *Parthia*, 1938; M. A. R. Colledge, *The Parthians*, 1967.

K.L.McK.

PARVAIM. The place which produced the gold used for ornamenting Solomon's Temple (2 Ch. 3:6). The location is obscure. Some suggest Farwa in Yemen. Gesenius, identifying it with Sanskrit *parvam*, understands it to be a general term for the E regions. (*OPHIR.) J.D.D.

PASHHUR. This name is probably of Egyptian origin: Heb. *paš-ḥûr* from Egyp. *p(') š(ri n) Ḥr*, 'the son (of) (the god) Horus'; *cf.* Š. Ahituv, *IEJ* 20, 1970, pp. 95–96.

1. Pashhur son of Immer. A priest, the chief officer of the house of the Lord, in the reign of Zedekiah or earlier, who put Jeremiah in the stocks and whose fate Jeremiah prophesied as exile in Babylon (Je. 20:1–6).

2. Pashhur son of Malchijah. Sent by King Zedekiah to inquire of Jeremiah (Je. 21:1), he was among those who incarcerated the prophet in the slimy pit-dungeon of the king's son Malchijah (the father of this Pashhur?) (Je. 38:1–13). He is possibly identical with the head of a priestly family of which some members were exiled to Babylonia. Some later members of this family returned to Jerusalem with Zerubbabel (Ezr. 2:38 = Ne. 7:41), six of them having to put away foreign wives there (Ezr. 10:22). Others volunteered for the fuller reoccupation of Jerusalem under Nehemiah (Ne. 11:12; probably the same Adaiah as in 1 Ch. 9:12).

3. Pashhur father of Gedaliah. His son Gedaliah was among those who imprisoned Jeremiah in Malchijah's dungeon (Je. 38:1–13); see **2** above. This Pashhur may possibly be identical with **1** or **2** above.

4. Pashhur, a priest, was among those who set their seal to the covenant under Nehemiah which followed Ezra's reading of the law (Ne. 10:3).

K.A.K.

PASSION. 1. In Acts 1:3 'passion' translates *pathein* and refers to Christ's suffering and death. This use of the term is still current. Elsewhere the same word is translated 'suffer' (*e.g.* Lk. 17:25; 24:26; Acts 17:3; Heb. 13:12, *etc.*).

2. In Acts 14:15 and Jas. 5:17 AV uses 'passion' to translate *homoiopathēs*. RSV 'of like nature' gives the sense of the Greek.

3. In its bad sense 'passion' translates *pathos* in Rom. 1:26; Col. 3:5; 1 Thes. 4:5 (in the NT this word always has the meaning 'evil desire'), and *pathēmata* in Rom. 7:5 and Gal. 5:24 (a word which usually has the sense of 'sufferings'). RSV also uses it 15 times to translate *epithymia*, 'desire' (usually in the plural) in the bad sense of that word. (*LUST.) P.E.

PASSOVER. The Passover of Ex. 12 concerns (1) the original historic event of Israel's deliverance from Egyp. bondage; (2) the later recurrent institutional commemoration of that event (*Mishnah Pesaḥim* 9:5). Closely conjoined, though separate, are (3) the prohibition of *leaven, symbolizing the haste of that unforgettable night of exodus, and (4) the later dedication of the *first-born, with statutory offerings, commemorating those first-born divinely spared in the blood-sprinkled houses. Moses quite possibly adapted more ancient ceremonials, Unleavened Bread being an agricultural festival, Passover nomadic and pastoral (*EBr*, 1974, Makropaedia, vol. 10, pp. 219f.). Passover may have had original links with circumcision, demonism, fertility cult or the first-born oblation (*cf.* H. H. Rowley, *Worship in Ancient Israel*, 1967, pp. 47ff.). Until AD 70, Passover was celebrated in Jerusalem, in any house within the city bounds, and in small companies; the lamb was ritually slaughtered in the Temple precincts. When Temple and Palestinian nation were both destroyed by war, Passover inevitably became a domestic ceremony.

The *Samaritans still meticulously observe their ancient N Israelite Passover ritual annually on Mt *Gerizim, in close conformity to the Pentateuch, keeping Passover and Unleavened Bread entirely separate entities. Unlike the Jews, they still employ a lamb. The slopes of Gerizim are now used, as the summit is ritually defiled by a Muslim cemetery (*EBr*, Mikropaedia, vol. 4, p. 494). They buttress their claims by the variant reading 'Gerizim' in place of 'Ebal' in Dt. 27:4, also by referring Dt. 12:5, 14; 16:16 to Gerizim, not Zion. There was for some time a rival Samaritan temple on Gerizim (*cf.* R. de Vaux, *Ancient Israel*, E.T. 1961, pp. 342f.), though its precise dates of functioning are disputed (*cf.* also John Macdonald, *The Theology of the Samaritans*, 1964, *passim*).

I. In the Old Testament

Ex. 12, the natural starting-point of study, suggests the following principal considerations.

1. Passover (Heb. *pesaḥ*) comes from a verb meaning 'to pass over', in the sense of 'to spare' (Ex. 12:13, 27, *etc.*). This affords excellent sense; there is no need to jettison the time-honoured view that God literally passed over the blood-sprinkled Israelite houses, whilst smiting the Egyptian ones. The term is used both for the ordinance and for the sacrificial victim. *BDB* note another verb with the same radicals, meaning 'to limp', which has suggested alternative theories (*cf.* T. H. Gaster, *Passover: Its History and Traditions*, 1949, pp. 23–25); but *KB* modify this conclusion.

2. Abib, later called Nisan, the month of the ripening ears and of the first Passover, was made in honour the first month of the Jewish year (Ex. 12:2; Dt. 16:1; *cf.* Lv. 23:5; Nu. 9:1–5; 28:16).

3. Was the Paschal victim customarily a lamb, as popularly conceived? In Dt. 16:2 the choice of animal is unquestionably wider; in Ex. 12 it depends on exegesis. The Heb. word *śeh* (v. 3) is restricted by *BDB* to the sheep and goat categories, irrespective of age; *KB* restrict it further to lamb or kid. There is some controversy as to the meaning of the phrase *ben-šānâ* (v. 5), lit. 'son of a year'. Some take this to signify a yearling, 12–24 months

in age, *i.e.* a full-grown animal (*cf.* Gesenius-Kautzsch-Cowley, *Hebrew Grammar*, section 128 v; G. B. Gray, *Sacrifice in the OT*, 1925, pp. 345–351). But the traditional exegesis, which takes 12 months as the upper, not the lower, age-limit, is by no means disproved. Talmudic evidence seems to limit the legitimacy of the Passover victim to the sheep and goat families, following Exodus rather than Deuteronomy (*cf. Menaḥoth* 7:6, with Gemara). The choice of lamb or kid, lamb or goat, is several times asserted (*Pesaḥim* 8:2; 55b; 66a), yet the over-all evidence does suggest a certain preference for the lamb (*Shabbath* 23:1; *Kelim* 19:2; *Pesaḥim* 69b; *etc.*). One ruling excludes a female animal, or a male which has passed the age of 2 years—which would lend tacit support to the yearling interpretation (*Pesaḥim* 9:7). Yet a contradictory passage declares categorically that a Passover offering is valid from the eighth day of its life (*Parah* 1:4). If the universal use of a lamb cannot be certainly demonstrated from Scripture or Talmud, it is at least clear that this acquired strong consuetudinary sanction. It is of interest and significance that the Samaritans, following age-old precedents, sacrifice a lamb on the slopes of Mt Gerizim to this very day.

4. On the Passover night in Egypt, the lintels and side-posts of all Israelite doors were smeared (apotropaically, some suggest) with the victim's blood. This was carried in a basin, Heb. *sap̄*, v. 22 (which could also, with slight change of exegesis, mean 'threshold'), applied therefrom with hyssop, the foliage of the marjoram plant, a common emblem of purity. See further N. H. Snaith, *The Jewish New Year Festival*, 1947, pp. 21ff.

5. The phrase 'between the two evenings' in Ex. 12:6 (also Ex. 16:12; Lv. 23:5; Nu. 9:3, 5, 11) has been accorded two variant interpretations, according to variant community practice—either between 3 p.m. and sunset, as the Pharisees maintained and practised (*cf. Pesaḥim* 61a; Josephus, *BJ* 6. 423); or, as the Samaritans and others argued, between sunset and dark. The earlier time, as Edersheim points out, allows more leeway for the slaughtering of the innumerable lambs, and is probably to be preferred.

6. Ex. 12:43–49 excludes Gentiles from participating in the Passover, but not of course proselytes, who were expected, even obliged, to conform fully.

The whole drama and inner meaning of Ex. 12 is concentrated into seventeen pregnant Gk. words in Heb. 11:28.

The Passover of Dt. 16 differs in important minor respects from that of Ex. 12. The blood emphasis has disappeared; an essentially domestic ceremony has become a more formal sacrifice at a central sanctuary with a wider choice of victim; v. 7 stipulates boiling, not roasting, the animal; Passover and Unleavened Bread, here termed the bread of affliction, are integrated more thoroughly than in Exodus. This is development, event changing to institution, not contradiction; moreover it approximates better to the NT evidence concerning Passover. It is not necessary to assume a great time-gap between the passages; the changed circumstances could have been prophetically foreseen in the wilderness period. It is further recorded that a second Passover, celebrated a month later, was instituted for the benefit of those who had been levitically unclean at the time of the first (Nu. 9:1–14).

Passover was celebrated in the plains of Jericho during the Conquest (Jos. 5:10f.). In the observances of Hezekiah (2 Ch. 30:1–27) and Josiah (2 Ch. 35:1–19), the proper place is considered to be the Jerusalem Temple. Hezekiah's ceremony takes advantage of the legitimate second Passover mentioned above, because the people are not gathered in Jerusalem, and the priests are not in a state of levitical purity, at the earlier date. The brief reference of Ezekiel (45:21–24) deals with Passover in the ideal Temple of his conceiving. The three points of interest are the fuller participation of the secular leader, the fact of a sin-offering, and the complete change-over from family celebration to public ceremony. The victims specified include bullocks, rams and kids. The prescriptions of Deuteronomy are considerably extended, though not in any new thought-pattern.

Jewish usage in the last days of the Herodian Temple is reflected in the Mishnah tractate *Pesaḥim*. The people gathered in the outer Temple court in companies to slaughter the Passover victims. The priests stood in two rows; in one row each man had a golden, in the other each man a silver, basin. The basin which caught the blood of the expiring victim was passed from hand to hand in continuous exchange to the end of the line, where the last priest tossed the blood in ritual manner on the altar. All this was done to the singing of the *Hallel* (Pss. 113–118). The celebrating companies were generally family units, but other common ties were possible, such as that which bound our Lord to his disciples.

II. In the New Testament

In NT times, all Israelite males were expected to appear in Jerusalem thrice annually, for the Feasts of Passover, of Weeks or Pentecost and of Tabernacles. Even Dispersion Jews sometimes conformed; the temporary population of the Holy City (*cf.* the Pentecost gathering of Acts 2) could swell to almost 3,000,000 according to Josephus (*BJ* 6. 425)—a figure reduced to the more realistic 180,000 by J. Jeremias (*Jerusalem in the Time of Jesus*, 1969, pp. 83f.). After candlelight search for the forbidden leaven, and other careful preparations (*cf.* Mk. 14:12–16 and parallels), the Paschal supper proper was taken reclining. It included the symbolic elements of roasted lamb, unleavened bread, bitter herbs, some minor condiments and four cups of wine at specified points. The stipulated ritual hand-washings were carefully observed. The table (more probably the floor) was cleared before the second cup of wine, the story of the Egyp. Passover and Exodus recounted in a dialogue between father and son (or some suitable substitutes). The dishes of food were then brought back, part of the Hallel was sung, the second cup of wine followed. Then came the breaking of bread. In the Last Supper, it was probably at this point that Judas received the sop, and departed into the night to betray his Master (Jn. 13:30). On that fateful night, it may be assumed that the institution of the Lord's Supper or Eucharist was associated with the third cup of wine. The singing of the Hallel was completed with the fourth cup—doubtless the hymn of Mt. 26:30. It is assumed here that the Last Supper did coincide with the statutory Passover, despite the denials of certain expositors. A. Plummer, *e.g.* (*Luke, ICC*, 1896, pp. 491f.), postulates an ante-dated Passover, 20 hours before the lambs were slaughtered, maintaining that at the proper time Jesus was dying or dead. Others suggest a Passover Qiddush, or ritual purification meal in anticipation. J. N. Geldenhuys argues at length that the Last Supper was itself the Passover, that it was held on the 14th of Nisan, the day before the crucifixion, that there is no contradiction whatever between Synoptics and Fourth Gospel, when the relevant passages are correctly expounded. The Passion, he says, is to be dated on or about 6 April, AD 30. Variant views will be found in other standard commentaries.

The symbolism, 'Christ our Passover', 'Lamb of God', is familiar from NT usage. We have seen that the traditional lamb, if not provable in all instances, has widespread precedent. It is laid down in Ex. 12:46 and Nu. 9:12 that no bone of the Passover victim is to be broken. This small detail is typologically fulfilled when it is reverently applied to the crucified One (Jn. 19:36).

After the destruction of the Jerusalem Temple in AD 70, any possibility of slaughtering a victim in ritual manner utterly ceased, and the Jewish Passover reverted to the family festival it had been in the earliest days—the wheel had turned full circle. Whilst church and synagogue eventually went their separate ways, the habit of celebrating Passover would continue for some time among certain Christians, particularly those of Jewish or proselyte background. But the Lord's Supper came to replace the Jewish ordinance, just as baptism came to replace circumcision.

BIBLIOGRAPHY. See lit. cited in article; also J. Jeremias, *TDNT* 5, pp. 896–904; *SB*, 4.1, pp. 41–76; B. Schaller, *NIDNTT* 1, pp. 632–635; R. A. Stewart, 'The Jewish Festivals', *EQ* 43, 1971, pp. 149–161; G. B. Gray, *Sacrifice in the OT*, 1925, pp. 337–397; A. Edersheim, *The Temple: Its Ministry and Services as they were in the Time of Jesus Christ*; J. B. Segal, *The Hebrew Passover from Earliest Times to A.D. 70*, 1963; B. Bokser, *BRev*, 1987, pp. 24–33; A. Guilding, *The Fourth Gospel and Jewish Worship*, 1960; J. Jeremias, *Jerusalem in the Time of Jesus*, 1969.

R.A.S.

PASTORAL EPISTLES. The three Epistles, 1 and 2 Timothy and Titus, were first called the Pastoral Epistles in the 18th century, and the name has become generally used to denote them as a group. The title is only partially an accurate description of their contents, for they are not strictly pastoral in the sense of giving instruction on the care of souls.

D.G.

PATARA. A seaport of SW *Lycia, in the Xanthus valley. Besides local trade it was important as being a suitable starting-point for a sea passage direct to Phoenicia (*SHIPS AND BOATS). According to the commonly accepted Alexandrian text of Acts 21:1, Paul trans-shipped at Patara on his way to Jerusalem. The Western Text, possibly influenced by Acts 27:5–6, adds 'and *Myra', which would imply that he coasted farther E before trans-shipment. There is reason to believe that the prevailing winds made Patara the most suitable starting-point for the crossing, and Myra the regular terminal for the return journey.

Patara was also celebrated for its oracle of Apollo.

K.L.McK.

PATHROS, PATHRUSIM. Classed under Mizraim (Egypt), Gn. 10:14; 1 Ch. 1:12. Pathros is Egyp. *p' t'-rs(y)*, 'the Southland', *i.e.* Upper Egypt, the long Nile valley extending N–S between Cairo and Aswan; the name is attested in Assyr. inscriptions as Paturisi. Thus, the terms Mizraim for Egypt, especially Lower Egypt, Pathros for Upper Egypt and *Cush for 'Ethiopia' (N Sudan) occur in this significantly geographical order both in a prophecy of Isaiah (11:11) and in a subsequent inscription of Esarhaddon, king of Assyria, who also boasts himself 'king of Muṣur, Paturisi and Cush'. Jeremiah similarly identifies Pathros with Egypt (Je. 44:15) and specifically Upper Egypt as distinct from the cities (and land) of Lower Egypt (Je. 44:1). Pathros also appears as Upper Egypt and as the homeland of the Egyp. people in Ezk. 29:14; 30:14.

K.A.K.

PATIENCE. Biblical patience is a God-exercised, or God-given, restraint in face of opposition or oppression. It is not passivity. The initiative lies with God's love, or the Christian's, in meeting wrong in this way. In the OT, the concept is denoted by Heb. *'ārēḵ*, meaning 'long'. God is said to be 'long' or 'slow' to anger, *'ereḵ 'appayim* (see Ex. 34:6; Nu. 14:18; Ne. 9:17; Pss. 86:15; 103:8; 145:8; Joel 2:13; Jon. 4:2). This idea is exactly represented in the Gk. *makrothymia*, often translated in AV as 'longsuffering', and defined by Trench as 'a long holding out of the mind' before it gives room to anger.

Such patience is characteristic of God's dealings with sinful men, who are fully deserving of his wrath (Is. 48:9; Ho. 11:8). His protecting mark on the murderer Cain (Gn. 4:15), his providential rainbow sign to a world that had forfeited its existence (Gn. 9:11–17; *cf.* 1 Pet. 3:20), his many restorations of disobedient Israel (Ho. 11:8–9), his sparing of Nineveh (Jonah), his repeated pleadings with Jerusalem (Mk. 12:1–11; Lk. 13:1–9, 34; Rom. 9:22), his deferment of Christ's second coming (2 Pet. 3:9)—these are all expressions of his patience. Christians are to show a like character (Mt. 18:26, 29; 1 Cor. 13:4; Gal. 5:22; Eph. 4:2; 1 Thes. 5:14). In Proverbs the practical value of patience is stressed; it avoids strife, and promotes the wise ordering of human affairs especially where provocation is involved.

The patience of God is a 'purposeful concession of space and time' (Barth). It is opportunity given for repentance (Rom. 2:4; 9:22; 2 Pet. 3:9). God's forbearance has been a 'truce with the sinner' (Trench, on *anochē*, Rom. 2:4; 3:25), awaiting the final revelation and redemption in Christ (Acts 17:30). Prayer may prolong the opportunity for repentance (Gn. 18:22ff.; Ex. 32:30; 1 Jn. 5:16).

The Christian's patience in respect of persons (*makrothymia*) must be matched by an equal patience in respect of things (*hypomonē*), that is, in face of the afflictions and trials of the present age (Rom. 5:3; 1 Cor. 13:7; Jas. 1:3; 5:7–11; Rev. 13:10). God is the God who gives such Christlike patience (Rom. 15:5; 2 Thes. 3:5), and Jesus is the great Exemplar of it (Heb. 12:1–3). He who thus endures to the end, by his patience will gain his soul (Mk. 13:13; Lk. 21:19; Rev. 3:10).

BIBLIOGRAPHY. R. C. Trench, *Synonyms of the New Testament*[9], 1880, pp. 195ff.; Karl Barth, *Church Dogmatics,* 2. 1, 1957, sect. 30, pp. 406ff.: 'The Patience and Wisdom of God'; U. Falkenroth, C. Brown, W. Mundle, in *NIDNTT* 2, pp. 764–776.

J.H.

PATMOS. An island of the Dodecanese, lying some 55 km off the SW coast of Asia Minor, at 37° 20′ N, 26° 34′ E. To this island the apostle John was banished from Ephesus, evidently for some months about the year AD 95, and here he wrote his Revelation (Rev. 1:9). The island is about 12 km long, with a breadth of up to 7 km, and it has been suggested that the scenery of its rugged volcanic hills and surrounding seas find their reflection in the imagery of the Apocalypse. See Pliny, *Nat. Hist.* 4. 69. The island now belongs to Greece.

J.H.P.

PATRIARCHAL AGE.

I. The biblical picture

The patriarchal age covering the life-spans of Abraham, Isaac and Jacob is described in Gn. 12–50, although chs. 39–50 are concerned more with Joseph. It is extremely difficult to give a date for the patriarchal period and scholars hold widely differing views within a range of about 1900 BC to 1500 BC. Biblical data is insufficient to settle the matter and we are forced to propose tentative dates by comparing data within the patriarchal stories in Gn. with extra-biblical data from the first part of the 2nd millennium BC. There is a further difficulty in drawing a general picture of the patriarchal age because Gn. concentrates on only a few individuals. The total group which made up the kinspeople of this narrowly defined family was probably quite extensive, all of them having originated in lands to the NE of Palestine. Further, the biblical writers must have selected their own material from a wide range of traditions which were available to them in order to stress important religious and theological points. Hence, if we restrict ourselves to the biblical narratives alone there are severe limitations for the historian.

The Patriarchs are depicted in Gn. as moving across a wide canvas from Mesopotamia to Egypt. Among the towns referred to in the biblical narratives which modern archaeology has shown to have been occupied from early in the 2nd millennium are Ur (Gn. 11:28, 31; 15:7), Harran (Gn. 11:31–32; 12:4–5; 27:43; 28:10; 29:4), Shechem (Gn. 12:6; 33:18), Salem (Jerusalem, Gn. 14:18), Gerar (Gn. 20:1; 26:1, 6, *etc.*), Dothan (Gn. 37:17), and probably Hebron (Gn. 13:18; 23:2, 19; 35:27) and Bethel (Gn. 12:8). The * Ebla documents (*c.* 2300 BC) attest the existence of Sodom, Gomorrah, Admah, Zeboiim, Bela (Gn. 14:2) at an early date. Significant towns not referred to in the Bible which were flourishing in the patriarchal era were Megiddo, Hazor, Lachish, Gezer and Jericho. The Mesopotamian town of Ur at this period was not the city of great political importance that it had been at the end of the 3rd millennium BC, although

'Asiatic' soldiers of the 'patriarchal age' depicted on an Egyptian tomb-painting at Beni Hasan. Sesostris I. c. 1950 BC

it retained a considerable influence in religion and literature. The town of *Mari on the Euphrates also flourished in this period and, although not mentioned in the Bible, has produced some 20,000 tablets which throw considerable light on the age.

In some passages in Gn. lists of towns are given, *e.g.* Ashteroth-karnaim, Ham and Shaveh-kiriathaim, towns along the road traversed by the invading kings of the E (Gn. 14:5); the 'cities of the valley' (Gn. 13:12; 19:25, 29); the towns which Jacob passed through on his way back to Bethel (Gn. 35:5), and towns in Egypt (Gn. 41:35, 48; 47:21 mg.). It is clear that from Mesopotamia to Egypt there were centres of settlement, either open villages or walled towns, both small and large. In Palestine proper most of the towns were to be found in the lowlands or along the highways.

Outside the settled areas the semi-nomads moved about with their flocks forming one part of a dimorphic society in which urban dwellers and semi-nomadic pastoralists lived side by side. The latter group frequently camped in the vicinity of the towns (Gn. 12:6–9; 13:12–18; 33:18–20; 35:16–21; 37:12–17), occasionally practised agriculture (Gn. 26:12f.), were able to engage in social and economic exchange with townspeople (Gn. 21:25–34; 23:1–20; 26:17–33; 33:18–20) and even dwelt in towns as 'resident aliens' for various periods of time (Gn. 12:10; 15:13; 17:8; 20:1; 21:23, 34; 26:3; 28:4; 32:4; 35:27; 36:7; 37:1; 47:4–5). Thus when Lot and Abraham separated, Lot took up residence in the town of Sodom and pitched his tent 'toward Sodom' and 'was sitting in the gate'. The two figures of Jacob and Esau present contrasting yet complementary ways of life (Gn. 25:27–34) and Jacob and his sons at Shechem settled for a time and entered into the society of the town-dwellers (Gn. 33:18–34:31).

We gain glimpses of the semi-nomadic life of shepherds living in tents, moving with their flocks, sometimes over considerable distances, seeking pasture-lands and wells and sometimes clashing with other people (Gn. 13:5–11; 18:1–8; 21:25–31; 24:62–67; 26:1–33; 29–31; 33:12–17; 36:6–8). The valued possessions of the Patriarchs were sheep, asses, oxen, flocks and herds, and even *camels (Gn. 12:16; 13:5, 7; 20:14; 21:27–30; 30:29; 31:1–10, 38; 32:13–16; 34:28; 46:32; 47:16–18). The term *'cattle' (*bᵉhēmâ*) in some passages is a comprehensive one for small beasts, although the Patriarchs did have cattle in one sense of the word, 'oxen', *bāqār* (Gn. 12:16; 20:14; 21:27; 34:28).

*Travel seems to have been common. Abraham moved from Ur in Mesopotamia to Egypt in the course of his life; Jacob travelled from Palestine to Harran and back (Gn. 28; 35) and later to Egypt. Probably there were well-trodden trade-routes used by merchants, a group of whom took Joseph to Egypt (Gn. 37:28–36).

The patriarchal narratives make references to contemporary rulers, the pharaoh of Egypt (12:15, 17, 20), certain 'kings' (Heb. *meleḵ*) from the E, Amraphel of Shinar, Arioch of Ellasar, Chedorlaomer of Elam and Tidal king of the Goiim (14:1), petty rulers of the Sodom and Gomorrah region (14:2), *Melchizedek king of Salem (14:18), Abimelech king of Gerar (20:2; 26:1, *etc.*), certain 'chiefs' of Edom (Heb. *'allûp̄*) and later kings of Edom (Gn. 36:19, 31), 'chiefs' of the Horites (Gn. 36:29) and the chiefs of Esau (Gn. 36:40–43). None of these personalities can be identified in any historical records to date. Some of them must have been very insignificant rulers indeed and the semi-nomadic patriarchal families paid attention to them only as they were required for reasons of pasture or watering places. In some cases they entered into a covenant with them (Gn. 14:13; 21:27; 26:28f.), but for the most part they moved about freely in the dimorphic society of the day.

The daily life of the Patriarchs was governed by a variety of customs of long standing and widespread usage. The Patriarchs and their kinspeople were tribally organized into inter-related social units comprising extended families or clans (Gn. 12:1–5; 24:1–9; 28:1–5). The system was patriarchal. We read of the 'paternal house' (*bêṯ 'āḇ*) in Gn. 12:1; 24:38–40, or simply the 'house of the patriarch' (Gn. 24:2; 31:14, 43; 36:6; 46:26–27, 31; 47:12; 50:8). In such a society the father, as head of the family, had wide powers. Normally the eldest son succeeded him as heir to his position and his property. In the absence of a natural heir a slave might become heir (Gn. 15:2f.) or the son of a slave-girl who had become a subsidiary wife (Gn. 16:1ff.). In the latter case if a son was born he was regarded as the son of the true wife who had presented the slave-girl to her husband. The arrangement arose out of the wife's consent and not when the husband took a secondary wife of his own accord. The marriages of Abraham with Hagar (Gn. 16:1–4) and Keturah (Gn. 25:1–6) provide examples of these two types of union (*cf.* Gn. 30:3, 9). Problems arose if the true wife gave birth to a son after the birth of a son to the secondary wife. In patriarchal society the true son seems to have become heir (Gn. 15:4; 17:19), although Gn. 21:10 suggests that this may not have been automatic. Sarah had to insist that Ishmael should not be heir along with her own son Isaac.

Marriage was a complex affair. In the society of the times the rich and the powerful could take more than one wife but mostly marriage was monogamous. In practice, however, a husband could take a concubine or secondary wife relatively easily either through his own initiative or, if the couple could not produce the desired heir, the wife might provide a slave-girl. In patriarchal society Jacob and Esau had more than one wife of equal status (Gn. 26:34f.; 29). Abraham remarried after Sarah's death (Gn. 25:1f.) and Nahor had children by a concubine (Gn. 22:20ff.).

It would seem that there was a preference for endogamous marriage, that is, within the family, *e.g.* Abraham and Sarah, Nahor and Milcah (Gn. 11:27–30), Jacob and Rachel, Jacob and Leah, Isaac and Rebekah, Esau and Ishmael's daughter.

It is clear also that some of the patriarchal customs were forbidden in later Mosaic law, *e.g.* marriage to two sisters (*cf.* Lv. 18:18), and marriage to one's half-sister (Gn. 20:12; *cf.* Lv. 18:9, 11, Dt. 27:22).

In the case of Jacob we learn that he was required to render service to his prospective father-in-law in return for his wife (Gn. 29:18f., 27f.). We have no means of knowing whether this practice was common or not. It may have been an Aramaean custom or have been confined to an area in N Mesopotamia. Probably the practice was more widespread than our evidence allows us to say.

In at least one case further marriage was forbidden to a man (Gn. 31:50).

The patriarchal blessing was important and once given could not be revoked (Gn. 27; 48–49). In Gn. 27 the eldest son surrendered the birthright and the younger son received the blessing (vv. 22–29). It would have been normal, however, for the eldest son to receive the blessing, though not automatic.

We shall discuss below possible comparisons with other ancient Near Eastern documents. There are certain parallels between the patriarchal customs and contemporary practices, but there are also a number of features not paralleled elsewhere which seem to be specific to the patriarchal customs portrayed in the Gn. records.

In matters of religion few details are given. It is clear that the Patriarchs knew the need for a personal faith in God who guided them through life and who encouraged them with his promises (Gn. 12:1–3; 15:4f.; 17; 28:11–22, *etc.*). In the matter of guidance God was not restricted to a particular place but was active in Ur, Harran, Canaan or Egypt (*cf.* Gn. 35:3). Once God's will became known to the Patriarchs the only course was to believe and obey (Gn. 22). Prayer and the offering of sacrifices were part of the regular worship of the Patriarchs (Gn. 12:8; 13:4, 18; 26:25; 35:1, 3, 7). Circumcision was a religious rite to mark those who were in the covenant family. An intense awareness of God's activity among them caused the Patriarchs to name places and children according to some evidence of God's dealings with them (Gn. 16:11, 14, all the names of Jacob's children in Gn. 29:31ff.; *cf.* Gn. 32:30; 35:15, *etc.*). Each Patriarch seems to have had his own special name for God, which suggests a sense of special personal relationship, the 'Fear', or as W. F. Albright suggested, the 'Kinsman' (*paḥaḏ*) of Isaac (Gn. 31:42, 53) the 'Mighty One' (*'ᵃḇîr*) of Jacob (Gn. 49:24). This sense of personal relationship, the knowledge of God's promises and the awareness that obedience to the will of God is of the essence of true faith, may be said to form the heart of patriarchal religion.

Two features of patriarchal society should be stressed, namely the concepts of covenant and election. Either directly (Gn. 15:18; 27:7, 10–11, 13, 19) or indirectly, God's covenant with Abraham, Isaac and Jacob is deeply significant in patriarchal religion. In the covenant God bound himself to Abraham and his descendants and bound them to himself in a most solemn engagement which involved the divine promise to, and the divine election of, Abraham and his descendants (Gn. 12:1–3; 13:14–17; 15:18–21; 17:5–8, *etc.*). Through Abraham and his descendants God would reach out to all mankind (Gn. 12:3; 18:18; 22:17–18; 26:4; 28:14). And it was specifically through this elect family that God would act in this way (Gn. 17:18–19; 21:12). The twin concepts of covenant and election are powerful motifs in the Gn. picture of patriarchal religion.

II. Modern discovery and the patriarchal age

The precise date of the patriarchal age is difficult to determine, but there are strong reasons for placing it in the Middle Bronze Age, *c.* 1850–1570 BC (*ABRAHAM). This is based on the assumption that archaeological and epigraphic knowledge can give us contemporary information. This view is widely held today, although some writers like T. L. Thompson and J. van Seters assign the patriarchal traditions in their entirety to the Iron Age on the assumption that they are late literary inventions. For such writers archaeology cannot reconstruct a 'historical' background for the contents of the patriarchal age, since by their definition there is none. We shall return to the point below. The following outline will give an idea of the more important of the discoveries of recent years. It should be recognized that the great collections of ancient documents recovered represent only a tiny proportion of all that was written in ancient times, and are largely accidental survivors.

a. Peoples

There is a variety of peoples mentioned in the patriarchal narratives—Egyptians, Amorites, Elamites, Canaanites, Horites, Edomites, Hittites. Gn. 14 appears to refer to four specific groups. It is not possible to identify all the groups mentioned. Thus the Horites may not be the same as the Hurrians. Indeed they are connected with Edom and S Palestine in Gn. 36:20f. Nor need the Hittites of Gn. 23 be the Hittites of Anatolia. They are rather a group of indigenous people related to Canaanites (Gn. 10:15). It is true that in the early part of the 2nd millennium there were considerable movements of peoples in the ancient Near East and one might expect to find all kinds of people in Canaan. To that extent the patriarchal narratives reflect the circumstances of the period in a general way.

Two groups of people may be of particular interest, the Hapiru and the Binyaminites of Mari. The Hapiru were widely known both geographically and over a long period of time. Abraham is called a Hebrew in Gn. 14:13. This may mean that he was recognizable as being like one of the ubiquitous Hapiru people. The Binyaminites were seminomadic elements in the dimorphic society in the region of Mari and there is much to be gained by studying what may be known about this group from the Mari documents. There are numerous parallels on the sociological level with patriarchal society.

b. Cities

Excavation has shown that in the first part of the 2nd millennium BC the ancient Near East was heir to an ancient civilization and that several of the towns in the patriarchal records were already in existence (see I, above). Details of the life lived in these towns may be learnt from the ruins of the houses, the pottery and art work, the tools and weapons, and in some cases from the written records left behind in the ruins. The town of Harran (Gn. 11:31–32), for example, is known on clay tablets found in *Mari. The *Ebla tablets refer to a number of towns in Canaan which were within the ambit of its trading interest. The important Egyp. records known as the Execration Texts, dating to the 19th century BC, refer to several which were in existence in Canaan at the time, including Jerusalem (Gn. 14:18). Certainly it could be claimed that a number of the towns of the patriarchal narratives were in existence in the early part of the 2nd millennium. In Canaan itself the great Middle Bronze Age cities like Megiddo, Hazor, Lachish, Gezer, Jericho and Shechem, among others, had already been established. Outside Canaan were great towns like Mari on the Euphrates, whose written records are of considerable significance in depicting the society of the region. Despite this wealth of material we are no nearer to determining the exact date of the Patriarchs, since these cities were in existence over many centuries. Probably all we can claim with certainty is that the patriarchal stories could not refer to a period earlier than when the cities referred to came into existence.

c. Personal names

The numerous names in the patriarchal records enable a comparison with name systems which are known from the tablet records. Numerous comparisons can be made. Thus the name Abram is known in a number of variant forms, such as *A-ba-am-ra-am*, *A-ba-am-ra-ma*, *A-ba-ra-ma*, on a variety of texts in W Semitic areas over a long period of time, so that the name is of little use for specific dating. Names like *Ya'qub-ilu* (Jacob-el) occur both early and late in the 2nd millennium. Some of the names of the twelve tribes such as Simeon, Ashur, Benjamin, may also be attested. The names Ishmael and Israel consist of a verbal element plus the name for deity, El. Other names like Isaac are probably hypocoristic (a special or pet name) formed from verbal elements only, *e.g.* Isaac (*yiṣḥāq*), 'he laughs', 'mocks', 'plays' or 'fondles' (Gn. 17:17; 18:12; 21:6). Extensive studies of W Semitic names, Amorite names, Mari names, *etc.*, have been undertaken and it may be claimed that the patriarchal name system has many parallels, certainly in the early part of the 2nd millennium, but also over a longer period, so that while we gain valuable insight into the patriarchal name system as such, we are not assisted in dating the Patriarchs.

d. Travel, trade and commerce

There was a good deal of *trade and *travel all over the Near East at this time. Clay tablets from Cappadocia indicate that as early as 2000 BC there was trade in copper and wool between Asia Minor and Assyria. Other records tell of movements of armies and the transport of booty, *etc.*, all over the Near East. Great routes crossed from Mesopotamia to Asia Minor and Palestine, and others down into Egypt. That a great road traversed Transjordan (the *King's Highway, Nu. 20:17) is clear from the line of ancient towns strung out along the route not far from the modern highway. Pictures from Beni-hasan in Egypt dating to about 1900 BC depict travelling nomads, possibly metal-workers, from the general area of Palestine. From these we gain a good idea of the dress and the possessions of these people in Abraham's time. Their main beasts of burden seem to have been asses and donkeys. Finally, the *Ebla tablets of *c.* 2300 BC introduce us to the vast trading area over which the Ebla merchants ranged and point to wide activities in travel, trade and commerce well before the period we are proposing for the patriarchal age.

e. The customs of the age

These have come to light from the tens of thousands of clay tablets which represent the documents of everyday life, legal, commercial, religious and private. There are in addition some important lists of laws, such as the Laws of Hammurapi (about 1750 BC), the Code of the town of Eshnunna (19th or 18th century BC), and the fragmentary Sumerian Codes of the kings of Lipit-Ishtar and Ur-nammu (21st–19th centuries BC). Of the private and personal documents, those of *Nuzi (15th and 14th centuries BC), *Mari (18th century BC), Ras Shamra (*Ugarit, 14th century BC) and *Alalaḫ (17th and 15th centuries BC) should be mentioned. These combine to give a picture of the life in N Mesopotamia in the period 2000–1500 BC and form a body of information against which we can study the patriarchal customs. Clearly documents from the 15th and 14th centuries take us beyond what we are proposing as the patriarchal age, so that they have to be used with some caution. Customs change in the course of time, but they often reflect earlier practices and it would not be impossible to find helpful clues to life in the 18th century BC by reading documents from the 15th century BC. In general, however, documents from the same age are the most reliable source of data.

Shortly after the discovery of the Nuzi documents in the years 1925 to 1931 scholars proposed many parallels between the customs at Nuzi and the patriarchal customs. With the discovery of an increasing number of documents from other sites and from earlier centuries the Nuzi texts can now be seen to be not quite so relevant to the patriarchal narratives as was once thought. Parallels in the areas of adoption, marriage, inheritance, wife–sister marriages, sistership adoption, the 'dying words' of a patriarch, the performance of a period of service before a man could claim a wife, the giving of a slave-girl as a marriage gift and several other customs, were all sought for and found in Nuzi. Writers like C. H. Gordon and E. A. Speiser were strong proponents of the view that the Nuzi documents provided a kind of quarry for patriarchal parallels. It has now become clear that of the 4,000 cuneiform tablets from Nuzi no more than a dozen have been quoted. A concomitant of this view is that the patriarchal age was sought in the 14th century BC on the basis of links with the customs portrayed in the Ugarit, the el-Amarna and the Nuzi documents.

In fact, with a growing volume of tablet evidence parallels are more easily discovered in earlier material. Thus the most suitable example of adoption is found on an old Babylonian letter from Larsa where it is stated that a childless man could adopt his own slave, an aspect of adoption not found at Nuzi. The adoption of the son of the wife's slave-girl is found in only one Nuzi text. It was more common for the husband to marry a second wife or take his own slave-girl as a concubine. But most of the practices concerning secondary wives are known in texts from other ancient Near Eastern sites. The dying words of a patriarch are not paralleled in Nuzi and the wife–sister marriage proposed by E. A. Speiser lacks any real foundation either in Nuzi or in Gn. 12–50. It would seem that no special relationship exists between the Nuzi tablets and the patriarchal narratives. Yet such a search for parallels is not without value. One senses in a general way that the customs of the patriarchal narratives belong to a society not unlike the one we know from the tablet records of the early part of the 2nd millennium BC. However, many of the customs were current for several centuries and are not sufficiently precise for chronological purposes, though they may be useful for sociological purposes. One of the most fruitful lines of investigation is a study of nomadism and sedentarization in the ancient Near Eastern dimorphic societies such as that at Mari. If such a study is combined with a continued search for parallels in customs we may be able to gain a better idea both of patriarchal society and of the period of the patriarchal age. It is also important to realize that there may not be a specific parallel in extra-biblical material to a particular patriarchal custom, since it was peculiar to the patriarchal group.

III. The historical value of the patriarchal records

It may be claimed that in general a notable change has come over scholarship since the days of J. Wellhausen at the end of the 19th century. His view was that we can attain to no historical knowledge of the Patriarchs from the biblical records, but that these are rather a reflection of the times of those men who wrote the stories in a much later day. The view is not quite forgotten and has been brought forward again by Thomas L. Thompson (1974) and J. van Seters (1975). Van Seters has raised questions about the degree to which oral tradition lies behind the stories in Gn. and is inclined to minimize its influence. He argues that it is impossible to identify specifically the personal names, places, peoples and customs of the patriarchal narratives. He can find no specific place for the Patriarchs in world events and holds that archaeology contributes very little, if anything, in elucidating their background. He also makes much of the so-called anachronisms like camels and Philistines. Hence he calls into question the whole scholarly search for parallels with the 2nd millennium and suggests instead that the traditions were largely moulded by and for the social and religious community of a later date, including the period of the Exile. This later literary activity must take priority in discussing the Gn. records. The themes of the divine promise to Abraham and the covenant were used by writers to support the dynastic ideology of the Monarchy, but they were late inventions. Thompson follows a somewhat similar line, although there are differences in detail between his approach and that of van Seters. There have been severe criticisms of these two writers. Other modern writers who have questioned the historical value of the patriarchal records are A. Alt and M. Noth, although both appear to admit that there may well be important elements of tradition which are of historical value, carried over from earlier times.

It may be agreed that a generation of scholars in recent years has made some excessive claims about several aspects of the patriarchal narratives. But it is an over-reaction to deny to these narratives any historical value. Even if we recognize them as literary-theological documents woven together from the traditions which were handed down from past centuries, there is no good reason to deny that they contain a good deal of archaic and historical material. The very strength of the theological ideas of promise and covenant required that the Patriarchs were more than mere literary inventions.

Many historical issues remain unsolved. Exact dating is impossible and precise definition of the patriarchal society and its customs in terms of a related contemporary society is not possible at present. But most present-day scholars show a disposition to treat the patriarchal records with far more respect from the point of view of their historical value than did some earlier scholars. The wisest course to follow at present is to await further evidence from all the sources. More research should enable the scholars to synthesize more accurately the biblical and the non-biblical material. In the meantime great theological doctrines like covenant, election, faith, obedience, promise, remain unobscured. Such doctrines have been the foundation of Israel's faith over the centuries and have also played a significant role in the faith of Christians. Few writers would disagree with this latter statement, whatever their view about the historicity of the Gn. narratives.

BIBLIOGRAPHY. J. Bright, *A History of Israel*[2], 1972, ch. 2; H. Cazelles, *DBS*, fasc. 36, cols. 81–156; W. G. Dever, 'Palestine in the Second Millennium BCE: the Archaeological Picture', in J. H. Hayes and J. M. Miller, *Israelite and Judaean History*, 1977, pp. 70–120; N. Glueck, 'The Age of Abraham in the Negeb', *BA* 18, 1955, pp. 2ff.; *BASOR* 149, Feb. 1958, pp. 8ff.; 152, Dec. 1958, pp. 18ff.; C. H. Gordon, 'Biblical Customs and the Nuzu Tablets', *BA* 3, 1940, pp. 1ff.; K. M. Kenyon, 'Palestine in the Middle Bronze Age', *CAH*, 2/1, pp. 77–116; J. R. Kupper, *Les Nomads en Mésopotamie au temps des rois de Mari*, 1957; J. T. Luke, 'Abraham and the Iron Age, Reflections on the New Patriarchal Studies', *JSOT* 4, 1977, pp. 35–47; A. R. Millard and D. J. Wiseman (eds.), *Essays on the Patriarchal Narratives*, 1980; H. H. Rowley, 'Recent Discovery and the Patriarchal Age', *BJRL* 32, 1949–50, pp. 44ff.; M. J. Selman, 'The Social Environment of the Patriarchs', *TynB* 27, 1976, pp. 114–136; E. A. Speiser, *JBL* 74, 1955, pp. 252ff.; *idem*, *Genesis, AB*, 1964; T. L. Thompson, *The Historicity of the Patriarchal Narratives*, 1974; R. de Vaux, *Histoire ancienne d'Israel*, 1971, pp. 157–273; J. van Seters, *Abraham in History and Tradition*, 1975; C. J. Mullo Weir, 'Nuzi', in D. W. Thomas (ed.), *Archaeology and Old Testament Study*, 1967, pp. 73–86; D. J. Wiseman, *BS* 134, 1977, pp. 123–130; 137, 1977, pp. 228–237.

J.A.T.

PATRISTIC LITERATURE. The importance for many branches of NT study of the extra-canonical early Christian literature, both the fragments from unorthodox writings and *NT Apocrypha, on the one hand, and the patristic writings (*i.e.* the non-apocryphal and non-sectarian ancient Christian writings), on the other, is widely recognized. For the history of the *Canon of the NT and the establishment of its text (*TEXTS AND VERSIONS, IV) the patristic allusions and quotations from biblical books are obviously indispensable. In exegesis, also, the Gk. Fathers in particular have to be taken into account and what writers such as Irenaeus, Clement of Alexandria and, above all, Origen say about unwritten traditions demands attention. But, in a wider aspect, the 2nd-century Gk. and Lat.-speaking church, with all its differences in ethos from the apostolic age, is the outcome of the Jerusalem Pentecost assembly, and any illumination of the path between them is likely to cast its light backwards as well as forwards.

Unfortunately, at present a very ill-lit tunnel extends from the later apostolic age to the great apologists of the middle and later 2nd century. It is a period of intensified persecution and pernicious propaganda (as predicted in 2 Tim. 3 and elsewhere); the church is widely spread through and (in the E) beyond the Roman empire; Israel has been repudiated in AD 70, and with it any effective primacy of the Jerusalem church has ended. The name 'Apostolic Fathers', originally meant to designate men in contact with, or appointed by, the apostles, has long been given to writings associated with this period; but lists of the Apostolic Fathers vary considerably. To three—Clement of Rome,

Ignatius, Polycarp—this title is regularly applied, though only for Polycarp is there unmistakable evidence of direct contact with the apostles. All these early writings are practical, not scholarly or speculative. If one senses the immediate drop from the NT, the contrast of their directness with the tortuous intellectualism of, say, the *Gospel of Truth*, their contemporary, or with the fetid atmosphere of the apocrypha is also marked.

The works listed below represent some earlier patristic writings.

I. Clement of Rome

A long Gk. letter addressed from the church of God sojourning in Rome to that in Corinth has come down under the name of Clement (*1 Clement*). There is no ground for identifying him with the Clement of Phil. 4:3, or with Flavius Clemens, Domitian's cousin. He is doubtless the person who appears third in Roman episcopal succession lists, but the term 'bishop of Rome' in the usual sense would be an anachronism, for in the letter 'bishop' is equivalent to 'presbyter'.

The occasion is a disturbance in the church at Corinth in which legitimately appointed presbyters have been ejected. Clement, on behalf of his church, appeals for peace and order, and asks them to remember the analogy of the ordered worship of old Israel and the apostolic principle of appointing a continuance of reputable men.

The date is almost certainly about the time of Domitian's persecution, AD 95–96, *i.e.* within the NT period.

The so-called second Epistle of Clement (*2 Clement*) is a homily of unknown (though 2nd-century) date and authorship. *Cf.* K. P. Donfried, *The Setting of Second Clement in Early Christianity*, 1974.

II. Ignatius

Ignatius, bishop of Antioch, was on his way to martyrdom in Rome in Trajan's reign (AD 98–117, probably late in that period) when he wrote seven letters which were gathered into a corpus: to the Asian churches at Ephesus, Magnesia, Tralles, Philadelphia and Smyrna, to his friend Polycarp, bishop of Smyrna, and to the Roman church, asking them not to intervene to prevent his martyrdom.

Ignatius approaches nearer than any other 2nd-century writer to sublimity as he speaks of the mysteries of incarnation and salvation. But he writes hurriedly and often obscurely: and he is consumed with the desire for martyrdom and obsessed with the necessity for close adhesion to the bishop. Some have taken this to imply that government by a single bishop, as distinct from presbyters, was still fairly new in Asia. Ignatius mentions no bishop when writing to Rome.

The letters were heavily interpolated and others added by forgers, usually dated in the 4th-century (but see J. W. Hannah, *JBL* 79, 1960, pp. 221ff.). On the setting see V. Corwin, *St. Ignatius and Christianity in Antioch*, 1960.

III. Polycarp

Polycarp was one of the most revered figures of Christian antiquity. He was bishop of Smyrna when Ignatius wrote: at a great age he was martyred. The date of his martyrdom, of which a moving early account survives, is disputed: AD 155/6 and AD 168 are canvassed (see W. Telfer, *JTS* n.s. 3, 1952, pp. 79ff.). He had known the apostles, and John in particular, and he taught Irenaeus (Irenaeus, *Adv. Haer*. 3. 3. 4; Eusebius, *EH* 5. 20). He thus links the apostolic age and the late 2nd-century church. A letter to the Philippians survives, earnest and gracious. Ch. 13 is written without news of Ignatius' fate. P. N. Harrison (*Polycarp's Two Epistles to the Philippians*, 1936) argues that it is a separate early letter, and that chs. 1–12 were written *c.* AD 135–7 and conflated with it.

IV. The Didache

The *Didache* is a problematical work, consisting of teaching (which appears in other works) on the ways of life and of death, a brief church order, dealing with baptism, fasting, prayer, eucharist, ministers and prophets, and closing with an apocalypse. It has many peculiar features, according exactly neither with church order in the NT nor with what we know of the 2nd-century church. It has been argued that it is a genuine early work (*e.g.* J. P. Audet, *La Didachè*, 1958, dates it AD 60), that it is a late-2nd-century reconstruction, or that it represents a church out of the main stream. It seems to be Syrian.

V. Papias

Papias was bishop of Hierapolis in the early 2nd century and devoted much care to a five volume 'Exposition of the Oracles of the Lord', which survives only in tantalizing fragments in Irenaeus and Eusebius. Its date is uncertain: nothing later than AD 130 is likely. At all events he was in contact with hearers of the apostles (*MARK, GOSPEL OF; *MATTHEW).

VI. Barnabas

The *Epistle of Barnabas* is probably Alexandrine, from the early 2nd century. It is strongly anti-Jewish in tone, and marked by forced allegorical exegesis. It includes a form of the 'Two Ways'. The work is anonymous; its attribution to Barnabas (if the apostle is meant) is doubtless an early guess. It may, however, have led to its being read for a time in some churches (*cf.* Eusebius, *EH* 3. 25). See further P. Prigent, *L'Epître de Barnabé 1–16*, 1962.

VII. Hermas

The *Shepherd* of Hermas is a symbolic work intended to rouse a lax church and call to repentance Christians who had sinned: making clear—obviously a disputed point—that post-baptismal sin was not necessarily unforgivable. It is divided, rather artificially, into Visions, Tractates and Mandates.

Critical and historical problems abound. The Muratorian Fragment says it was written recently, by the brother of bishop Pius of Rome (*c.* AD 140), but there are some marks of earlier date, and, inferior work as it seems now, it had a period of reception as Scripture in some churches. It appears in Codex Sinaiticus of the NT. See H. Chadwick, *JTS* n.s. 8, 1957, pp. 274ff. *Cf.* also J. Reiling, *Hermas and Christian Prophecy*, 1973, for a study of the eleventh Mandate.

BIBLIOGRAPHY. J. B. Lightfoot, *The Apostolic Fathers*, 5 vols. (a mine of information and judicious comment, with texts of Clement, Ignatius and Polycarp); J. B. Lightfoot–J. R. Harmer, *The Apostolic Fathers*, 1891 (handy texts and translations); K. Lake, *The Apostolic Fathers* (texts and translations), 1917–19; J. A. Kleist, *Ancient*

Christian Writers 1, 4, 1946–8; C. C. Richardson, *Early Christian Fathers*, 1953; R. M. Grant (ed.), *The Apostolic Fathers*, 1–6, 1964–8; T. F. Torrance, *The Doctrine of Grace in the Apostolic Fathers*, 1948; J. Quasten (ed.), *Patrology*, 1950; B. Altaner, *Patrology*, 1960; J. Lawson, *A Theological and Historical Introduction to the Apostolic Fathers*, 1961; L. W. Barnard, *Studies in the Apostolic Fathers and their Background*, 1966. A.F.W.

PAUL.

I. Life

a. Background

From Paul's birth until his appearance in Jerusalem as a persecutor of Christians there is little information concerning his life. Although of the tribe of Benjamin and a zealous member of the Pharisee party (Rom. 11:1; Phil. 3:5; Acts 23:6), he was born in Tarsus a Roman citizen (Acts 16:37; 21:39; 22:25ff.). Jerome cites a tradition that Paul's forbears were from Galilee. It is not certain whether they migrated to Tarsus for commercial reasons or were settled there as colonists by a Syrian ruler. That they were citizens suggests that they had resided there for some time.

Sir William Ramsay and others have shown that Tarsus truly was 'no mean city'. It was a centre of learning, and scholars generally have assumed that Paul became acquainted with various Gk. philosophies and religious cults during his youth there. Van Unnik has challenged this assumption. He argues that the relevant texts (Acts 22:3; 26:4f.) place Paul in Jerusalem as a very small child; Acts 22:3 is to be read in sequence: (i) born in Tarsus; (ii) brought up at my mother's knee (*anatethrammenos*) in this city; (iii) educated at the feet of Rabban *Gamaliel the elder. As a 'young man' (Acts 7:58; Gal. 1:13f.; 1 Cor. 15:9) Paul was given official authority to direct the persecution of Christians and as a member of a synagogue or Sanhedrin council 'cast my vote against them' (Acts 26:10). In the light of Paul's education and early prominence we may presume that his family was of some means and of prominent status; his nephew's access to the Jerusalem leaders accords with this impression (Acts 23:16, 20).

Of Paul's personal appearance the canonical account suggests only that it was not impressive (1 Cor. 2:3f.; 2 Cor. 10:10). A more vivid picture, which Deissmann (p. 58) and Ramsay (*CRE*, pp. 31f.) incline to credit, occurs in the apocryphal *Acts of Paul and Thecla*: 'And he saw Paul coming, a man little of stature, thin-haired upon the head, crooked in the legs, of good state of body, with eyebrows joining, and nose somewhat hooked, full of grace: for sometimes he appeared like a man, and sometimes he had the face of an angel.'

b. Conversion and early ministry

While there is no evidence that Paul was acquainted with Jesus during his earthly ministry (2 Cor. 5:16 means only to 'regard from a human point of view'), his Christian kinsmen (*cf.* Rom. 16:7) and his experience of the martyrdom of Stephen (Acts 8:1) must have made an impact upon him. The glorified Jesus' question in Acts 26:14 implies as much. The result of Paul's encounter with the risen Christ gives ample assurance that it was an experience of a healthy mind; and it can be adequately interpreted, as indeed Luke does interpret it, only as a miraculous act, which transformed Christ's enemy into his apostle. The three accounts in Acts (chs. 9, 22, 26) attest not only the significance of Paul's conversion for Luke's theme (*cf. CBQ* 15, 1953, pp. 315–338), but also, as J. Dupont and M. E. Thrall have suggested in the Bruce *Festschrift*, its essential importance for Paul's Christology and his interpretation of his ministry to the Gentiles. *Cf.* Kim, *Origin*, pp. 135–138, 170ff., 338.

Apart from an interval in the Transjordan desert, Paul spent the 3 years following his baptism preaching in Damascus (Gal. 1:17; Acts 9:19ff.). Under pressure from the Jews he fled to Jerusalem, where Barnabas ventured to introduce him to leaders of the understandably suspicious Christians. His ministry in Jerusalem lasted scarcely 2 weeks, for again certain Hellenistic Jews sought to kill him. To avoid them, Paul returned to the city of his birth, spending there a 'silent period' of some 10 years. No doubt it is silent only to us. Barnabas, hearing of his work and remembering their first meeting, requested Paul to come to Antioch to help in a flourishing Gentile mission (Gal. 1:17ff.; Acts 9:26ff.; 11:20ff.). These newly named 'Christians' soon began their own missionary work. After a year of notable blessing Paul and Barnabas were sent on a 'famine visit' to help stricken colleagues in Judaea.

c. Mission to Galatia—the Council of Jerusalem—mission to Greece

Upon their return from Jerusalem—about AD 46—Paul and Barnabas, commissioned by the church in Antioch, embarked on an evangelistic tour. It took them across the island of Cyprus and through 'S Galatia' (Acts 13–14). Their strategy, which became a pattern for the Pauline missions, was to preach first in the synagogue. Some Jews and Gentile 'Godfearers' accepted the message and became the nucleus for a local assembly. When the mass of Jews rejected the gospel, sometimes with violence, the focus of the preaching shifted to the Gentiles (*cf.* Acts 13:46f.). Despite these perils and the defection at Perga of their helper, John Mark, the mission succeeded in establishing a Christian witness in Pisidian Antioch, Iconium, Lystra, Derbe and possibly Perga.

Meanwhile the influx of Gentiles into the church raised serious questions concerning their relations to Jewish laws and customs. A number of Jewish Christians were insisting that Gentiles must be circumcised and observe the Mosaic law if they were to be received 'at par' in the Christian community. Upon his return to Antioch (*c.* AD 49), Paul, seeing in this Judaizing movement a threat to the very nature of the gospel, expressed his opposition in no uncertain terms. First, he rebuked Peter publicly (Gal. 2:14), after the latter, to avoid a breach with certain Judaizers, had separated himself from Gentile Christians. Secondly, hearing that the Judaizing heresy was infecting his recently established churches, Paul wrote a stinging letter of warning to the Galatians in which the Pauline *credo*, 'Salvation by grace through faith', was forcefully presented.

These events in Antioch gave rise to the first great theological crisis in the church. To resolve the problems which it raised, the church in Antioch sent Paul and Barnabas to confer with the 'apostles and elders' in Jerusalem (*c.* AD 50, Acts 15). The ensuing council gave the judgment that Gentiles should have 'no greater burden' than to abstain from food offered to idols, blood-meat, meat from strangled animals and unchastity (or incest marriage). The effect of this decision was to sustain Paul's contention that Gentiles were under no obligation to keep the Mosaic law. The restrictions mentioned seem to have been principally for local application (*cf.* 1 Cor. 8) and as an aid to Jewish–Gentile relations.

Because of differences with Barnabas (over taking John Mark with them again) Paul took a new companion, Silas, on his 2nd missionary tour (Acts 15:40–18:22). From Antioch they travelled overland to the churches of 'S Galatia' and at Lystra added young Timothy to the party. Forbidden by the Holy Spirit to evangelize W, they journeyed N through 'N Galatia', where some converts may have been made (*cf.* Acts 16:6; 18:23). At Troas Paul in a vision saw a 'man of Macedonia' beckoning to him. Thus his evangelization of Greece began. In Macedonia missions were established in Philippi, Thessalonica and Beroea; in Achaia, or S Greece, Athens and Corinth were visited. In the latter city Paul remained almost 2 years founding a Christian fellowship that was to be the source of both joy and trial in the future. Through his co-workers (Luke the physician joined the party in Troas) and by correspondence (the Epistles to the Thessalonians) he kept in touch also with the struggling young churches in Macedonia. The Holy Spirit now moved Paul to turn his eyes once more upon the earlier forbidden province of Asia. Departing from Corinth, he stopped briefly at Ephesus, the commercial metropolis of Asia, and left as an advance party his Corinthian colleagues Priscilla and Aquila. In a quick trip back to Antioch—*via* Jerusalem—Paul completed his 'second missionary journey' and, after a final sojourn in Antioch, prepared to move his base of operation W to Ephesus.

d. The Aegean ministry

In many ways the Aegean period (*c.* AD 53–58; Acts 18:23–20:38) was the most important of Paul's life. The province of Asia, so important for the later church, was evangelized; and the Christian outposts in Greece secured. During these years he wrote the Corinthian letters, Rom. and perhaps one or more of the Prison Epistles (Eph., Phil., Col., Phm.), which in the providence of God were to constitute a holy and authoritative Scripture for all generations. For the apostle this was a time of triumph and defeat, of gospel proclamation and threatening heresies, of joy and frustration, of activity and prison meditation. The risen Christ used all these things to mould Paul into his image and to speak through Paul his word to the church.

From Antioch Paul travelled overland through the familiar Galatian region to Ephesus. There he met certain 'disciples', including Apollos, who had known John the Baptist and, presumably, Jesus (Acts 18:24ff.). On this foundation the church grew, and God performed such extraordinary miracles that certain Jewish exorcists began, without success, to use the name of 'Jesus whom Paul preaches'. Opposition from devotees of the city's patron goddess, Artemis (Diana), was soon aroused; and Demetrius, a prosperous idol-maker, succeeded (from motives other than piety) in inciting the people to riot. Paul doubtless had made a number of short trips from Ephesus; he took this occasion, some 3 years after his arrival, to make a final visit to the churches in the Aegean area. Through Troas he came to Macedonia, where he wrote 2 Cor. and, after a time, travelled S to Corinth. There he spent the winter and wrote a letter to the 'Romans' before retracing his steps to Miletus, a port near Ephesus. After a touching farewell Paul, 'bound in the Spirit' and under threatening clouds, sailed towards Jerusalem and almost certain arrest. This did not deter him, for Asia had been conquered and he had visions of Rome.

e. The Caesarean and Roman imprisonment—Paul's death

Paul disembarked at Caesarea and, with a collection for the poor, arrived at Jerusalem at Pentecost (Acts 21:23f.; *cf.* 1 Cor. 16:3f.; 2 Cor. 9; Rom. 15:25ff.). Although he was careful to observe the Temple rituals, Jewish pilgrims from Ephesus, remembering 'the apostle to the Gentiles', accused him of violating the Temple and incited the crowds to riot. He was placed under arrest but was permitted to address the crowd and later the Sanhedrin.

To prevent his being lynched, Paul was removed to Caesarea, where *Felix, the Roman governor, imprisoned him for 2 years (*c.* AD 58–60, Acts 23–26). At that time Festus, Felix's successor, indicated that he might give Paul to the Jews for trial. Knowing the outcome of such a 'trial', Paul, as a Roman citizen, appealed to Caesar. After a moving interview before the governor and his guests, King Agrippa and Bernice, he was sent under guard to Rome. Thus, under circumstances hardly anticipated, the risen Christ fulfilled the apostle's dream and his own word to Paul: 'You must bear witness also at Rome' (Acts 23:11). Paul had a stormy sea-voyage and, after being wrecked, spent the winter on Malta (*c.* AD 61). He reached Rome in the spring and spent the next 2 years under house-arrest 'teaching about the Lord Jesus Christ quite openly' (Acts 28:31). Here the story of Acts ends, and the rest of Paul's life must be pieced together from other sources. (A helpful survey of the apostolic age, and Paul's place in it, is F. F. Bruce, *New Testament History*, 1969.)

Most probably Paul was released in AD 63 and visited Spain and the Aegean area before his re-arrest and death at the hands of Nero (*c.* AD 67). *1 Clement* (5. 5–7; ?AD 95), the Muratorian Canon (*c.* AD 170), and the apocryphal (Vercelli) *Acts of Peter* (1. 3; *c.* AD 200) witness to a journey to Spain; and the Pastoral Epistles appear to involve a post-Acts ministry in the East. To the end Paul fought the good fight, finished the course and kept the faith. His crown awaits him (*cf.* 2 Tim. 4:7f.).

II. Chronology

a. General reconstruction

The book of Acts, augmented with data from the Epistles and from Jewish and secular sources, continues to serve as the chronological framework of most scholars. Its essential compatibility with the sequence of Paul's mission, detectable (in part) in his letters, is evident (*cf.* T. H. Campbell, *JBL* 74, 1955, pp. 80–87). However, its sketchiness and chronological vagueness, even in those periods treated, is increasingly conceded; and there is a growing willingness to interpolate (*e.g.* an Ephesian imprisonment) into the framework from other data or reconstructions. Fixed dates with secular history are not numerous. The most certain is the proconsulship of Gallio (*cf.* Acts 18:12), which may be fixed in AD 51–2 (Deissmann) or AD 52–3 (Jackson and Lake; *cf.* K. Haacker, *BZ* 16, 1972, pp. 252–255). If in Acts 18:12 Gallio had only recently assumed office (Deissmann), Paul's sojourn in Corinth may be dated between the end of AD 50 and the autumn AD 52. This accords with the 'recent' expulsion of Priscilla and Aquila from Rome (Acts 18:2), which may be dated *c.* AD 50 (Ramsay, *SPT*, p. 254). The accession of Festus (Acts 24:27) is often placed in AD 59 or 60. But the lack of any clear evidence leaves the matter uncertain (*cf.* C. E. B. Cranfield, *Romans*, *ICC*, 1975, pp. 14f.; Robinson, pp. 43–46).

Besides the three dates above, the mention of King Aretas of Nabatea (2 Cor. 11:32), the famine in Judaea (Acts 11:28) and Paul's trip to Spain and martyrdom in Rome under Nero (Rom. 15:28; *1 Clement* 5; Eus., *EH* 2. 25–3. 1) provide some less specific chronological data as follows. First, Damascus coins showing Roman occupation are present until AD 33, but from AD 34 to 62 they are lacking; this places a *terminus a quo* for Paul's conversion at AD 31 (*i.e.* AD 34 minus 3; *cf.* Gal. 1:18; *ICC* on 2 Cor. 11:32). (But the Nabateans apparently took control at the accession of Caligula in AD 37; *cf.* A. H. M. Jones, *The Cities of the Eastern Roman Provinces*², 1971.) Secondly, Josephus (*Ant.* 20. 101) notes a severe famine *c.* AD 44–48, probably to be located in AD 46. Thirdly, from tradition Paul's death may be dated with some probability in the latter years of Nero, *c.* AD 67.

b. The relation of Acts and Galatians

The only fully satisfying chronology is one in which there is a consensus of Acts, the Epistles and extra-biblical sources. One continuing problem for such a synthesis has been the relation between Acts and Galatians. The identification of Paul's visit to Jerusalem in Gal. 1:18 with Acts 9:26ff. is seldom questioned: the second visit in Gal. 2:1ff. poses the basic problem. Three views are current: Gal. 2 equals Acts 15, or Acts 11: 27–30, or Acts 11 and 15. In the past the first view has commanded the largest advocacy (*cf.* E. de W. Burton, *The Epistle to the Galatians*, 1921, pp. 115ff.), and it continues to attract some commentators (*cf.* H. Schlier, *An die Galater*, 1951, pp. 66ff.; H. Ridderbos, *Galatians*, 1953, pp. 34f.). The following objections, among others, have combined to undermine it: Gal. 2 pictures a second visit and a private meeting without reference to any document; Acts 15 is a third visit involving a public council and culminating in an official decree. Many scholars regard it as incredible that Gal. would, in a highly relevant context, omit mention of the Apostolic Council and decree.

The second view, often associated with the S Galatian theory, revives an interpretation of Calvin and removes a number of these objections. Acts 11 is a second visit, by revelation, and concerned with the poor (*cf.* Gal. 2:1–2, 10); the Apostolic Council in Acts 15 occurs after the writing of Gal. and, therefore, is not germane to the problem. Advanced in modern times by Ramsay (*SPT*, pp. 54ff.) and recently advocated by Bruce (*BJRL* 51, 1968–9, pp. 305ff.; 54, 1971–2, pp. 266f.), it is probably the prevailing view among British scholars (*cf.* C. S. C. Williams, *The Acts of the Apostles*, 1957, pp. 22ff.).

Dissatisfied with both alternatives, most Continental writers (*e.g.* Goguel, Jeremias), followed by a number in Britain and America (*e.g.* K. Lake, A. D. Nock), regard Acts 11 and Acts 15 as duplicate accounts of Gal. 2, which Luke, using both sources, failed to merge (*cf.* Haenchen, pp. 64f., 377). Against Ramsay, Lake urges that if the Judaizing problem is settled in Acts 11 (= Gal. 2), Acts 15 is superfluous. Gal. 2:9, however, pictures not a settlement but only a private, tacit approval of Paul's gospel and is incidental to the purpose of the visit which, as Lake admits, is the 'care of the poor' (*BC*, 5, pp. 201f.). Haenchen (p. 377) rejects Ramsay's 'crucial' application of Gal. 2:10 to the famine visit. He may be correct in identifying the 'poor' with the Gentile mission (Gal. 2:9), but it scarcely has the vital significance which he attributes to it. Ramsay's reconstruction, even with some exegetical gnats, remains the more probable alternative. Basically the view identifying Acts 11 and Acts 15 arises from the traditional equation of Gal. 2 and Acts 15, and also from an excessively negative estimate of Luke's acquaintance with and interpretation of the primary sources. Since Gal. 2 = Acts 11 provides 'a perfectly clear historical development' (W. L. Knox, *The Acts of the Apostles*, 1948, p. 49), the other is unnecessarily complex. Other views of the problem are expressed by T. W. Manson (*BJRL* 24, 1940, pp. 58–80), who identifies Gal. 2 with a visit prior to Acts 11, and M. Dibelius (*Studies in Acts*, 1956, p. 100), whose excessive *tendenz* criticism denies to both Acts 11 and Acts 15 any claim to historicity.

c. A new reconstruction

Convinced that the Acts framework is unreliable, John Knox (*Chapters in a Life of Paul*, 1950, pp. 74–88) offers an imaginative chronological reconstruction from the evidence of the letters. A 14-year 'silent period' (AD 33–47) is impossible; therefore, the apostle's missionary activities and some letters are largely to be placed between his first (AD 38; Gal. 1:18) and second (AD 51; Gal. 2 = Acts 15) visits to Jerusalem. The final tour ends with his 'collection visit' and arrest (AD 51–3; Rom. 15:25; 1 Cor. 16:3f.). Why a silent period (which means simply that it yields no extant letters and did not fit Luke's theme) is so impossible is not readily apparent; and the traditional equation of Acts 15 and Gal. 2 also is open to question. Knox's fertile mind has found here more admirers than followers, for 'it is difficult to exchange tradition with imagination (as we find it in Acts) for imagination (however reasonable) without tradition' (Davies, *TCERK*, p. 854). Nevertheless, further attempts have been made to reconstruct the Pauline mission solely from the letters. *Cf.* Kümmel, *INT*, pp. 253f.; G. Lüdemann, *Paulus der Heidenapostel*, 1979.

III. History of criticism

a. Early developments

In a brilliant historical survey Albert Schweitzer (*Paul and his Interpreters*; *cf.* also Feine, *Paulus*, pp. 11–206; Ridderbos, *Paul*, 1976, pp. 13–43) traces the development of critical studies in Germany following the Reformation. For the orthodox, Scripture sometimes was little more than a mine of credal proof texts; exegesis became the servant of dogma. The 18th century witnessed a reaction by pietists and rationalists, who, each for his own purpose, sought to distinguish exegesis from credal conclusions. Philological exegesis and the interpretation of Scripture by Scripture became normative for scientific interpretation.

This development perhaps finds its most important expression in J. S. Semler, who, with J. D. Michaelis, pioneered the development of literary–historical criticism. His 'Prolegomena' to theological hermeneutics, 'Paraphrases' of Rom. and Cor., and other writings emphasize that the NT is a temporally conditioned document in which the purely cultural references are to be distinguished and/or eliminated. Philology exists to serve historical criticism. Our copies of Paul's letters have a 'church liturgy' format and we must, then, face the possibility that they originally had a different form. Specifically, Semler suggests that Rom. 15 and 16; 2 Cor. 9; 12:14–13:14 were separate documents, later incorporated into the larger Epistles. Foreshadowing the conclusions of F. C. Baur, Semler contrasts Paul's non-Jewish ideas with the Jewish-Christian party whom the apostle opposed; the General Epistles reflect an effort to mediate in this conflict. On questions of authorship a trend appeared in J. E. C. Schmidt (1805), who, on literary grounds, doubted the authenticity of 1 Tim. and 2 Thes. Schleiermacher (1807), Eichhorn (1812), and De Wette (1826) brought 2 Tim., Tit. and Eph. under question.

b. The Tübingen School

In 19th-century Germany exegesis was fully transformed from the 'servant of dogma' to the 'servant of scientific philosophy' (*cf.* Kümmel, *Problems*, pp. 130–143; S. Neill, *The Interpretation of the New Testament, 1861–1961*, 1964, pp. 10–28). Most significant in this regard for Pauline studies was F. C. Baur of Tübingen. He was not content merely to test the authenticity of ancient documents, a popular practice since the Renaissance. His was a 'positive criticism' which sought to find the documents' true historical setting and meaning. In *Symbolik und Mythologie*, the book which brought about his faculty appointment, he revealed the set of his mind and of his future work with the declaration that 'without philosophy history seems to me for ever dead and mute' (1. xi). In this matter Baur found in Hegelian dialectic—which viewed all historical movement as a series of theses (advance), antitheses (reaction) and syntheses (= a new thesis)—an appropriate key to interpret the history of the apostolic age (*cf.* Ellis, *Prophecy*[1], pp. 86–89; Haenchen, pp. 15–24). He had argued earlier (1831) that 1 Cor. 1:12 depicted a conflict between Pauline–Gentile and Petrine–Jewish Christianity. He later saw in Acts and the smaller Pauline Epistles and in the 'Gnostic' opponents of 'the so-called Pastoral letters' (1835) a more developed stage of the conflict in which, in the fight against Gnosticism, the original Pauline 'thesis' and Petrine 'antithesis' were finally resolved by the late 2nd century into an early Catholic 'synthesis'. In this 'tendency criticism' all NT writings which 'tended' towards compromise between Paul and the original apostles were viewed as later attempts to read back a subsequent unity into the apostolic period. After Baur's thoroughgoing scything only five NT documents remained uncontested witnesses from the apostolic period. Apart from Rev. all were Paul's: Rom., Cor. and Gal. The then current literary analysis of Paul's letters favoured Baur's reconstruction and, in turn, the latter accentuated and confirmed the suspicions of the more extreme literary critics. The Tübingen school rapidly became the dominant factor in NT criticism.

Using Baur's logic and sparked by Bruno Bauer's commentary on Acts (1850), an ultra-radical school questioned the genuineness of all Pauline literature. First, Acts knows no Pauline letters, and its simple picture of the apostle may be more primitive than the letters; disagreements even within Rom. and Gal. suggest several hands and a later time. Secondly, if Pauline thought (Paulinism) is the Hellenization of Christianity, as Baur thought, is it possible that this was accomplished so quickly and by one man? Could anti-Jewish feeling or Paul's high Christology have developed in a Palestinian-based church so soon after Jesus' death? No; the conflict itself is the climax of a long development, and Paulinism is to be identified with a 2nd-century Gnostic party who used the apostle's 'letters' as an authoritative vehicle for their own ideas. Why letters? Because apostolic letters already had a position of authority. Why Paul? This is impossible to say.

For all their logic the radicals succeeded only in convincing themselves. The citation of Paul in *1 Clement* (?AD 95) and Ignatius (AD 110), and the neglect of Paulinism and lack of any anti-Jewish conflict in the post-apostolic literature were fatal to their argument. The omission in Acts of Pauline literary activity was a (not very strong) argument from silence. The net result of the 'ultra-Tübingen school' was to undermine Tübingen itself. For, within their common assumption that Paul was the Hellenizer of Christianity and that Hegel supplied the key to history, the radicals had the better argument.

Baur's views came under attack from the conservatives (*e.g.* J. C. K. von Hofmann) and the followers of Schleiermacher (*e.g.* Ewald); perhaps the cruellest and most telling blow was from A. Ritschl, a former disciple. Both Ritschl and von Hofmann rejected the alleged hostility between Paul and the original disciples. The latter's emphasis upon the unity of apostolic teaching was in the next century to find renewed expression in the writings of P. Feine and A. Schlatter and in the kerygmatic theology of C. H. Dodd. A moderating literary criticism, even among Baur's disciples (*e.g.* Pfleiderer), revised the estimate of genuine Pauline Epistles sharply upward. Apart from the Pastorals, the majority excluded only 2 Thes. and Eph., and their acceptance (*e.g.* by Harnack, Jülicher) was no longer a mark of conservatism.

With its literary and philosophical presuppositions undermined, the influence of Tübingen waned. Nevertheless, by tying literary analysis to an imaginative philosophical synthesis Baur, whom Godet called Semler *redivivus*, dominated NT criticism (as Semler never did) for half a century. Again, although his own exegesis proved to have a philosophical bias unacceptable to later historians (and to all committed to a theistic interpretation of history), Baur brought into prominence an inductive historical approach to earliest Christianity and freed research from a tradition which came to much of the data with its conclusions already assumed. For this, all students can appreciate his labours. Finally, because Baur's reconstruction placed in bold relief the problems facing historians of the apostolic age, he largely set the course of future studies. What was the relationship between Paul and Jesus? What was the influence of Jewish and Hellenistic thought in the apostolic church? What are the proper philosophical presuppositions for a study of Christian origins? The Tübingen school died, and there is no apparent sign of an early resurrection. (Its airing in S. G. F. Brandon's *The Fall of Jerusalem and the Christian Church*, 1951, does not appear to have imparted life.) But the forces which gave it birth continued fecund and, for a corpse, Tübingen retained a remarkable familiarity with the following generations.

c. British contributions in the 19th century

British (and American) scholars interacted with the Tübingen reconstruction; but, with one or two exceptions (*e.g.* S. Davidson), they did not find it persuasive. Likewise, the Pauline Corpus (minus Heb.) continued to find acceptance. In America some rejected the Pastorals (*e.g.* B. W. Bacon, A. C. McGiffert); Britain, following J. B. Lightfoot (*Biblical Essays*, 1904, pp. 397–410), generally accepted them in a post-Acts setting. Nevertheless, with characteristic caution, British scholars influenced future criticism more than is generally realized by solid historical exegesis (*e.g.* Lightfoot, Ramsay) and by relating Paul to contemporary Jewish thought (*e.g.* F. W. Farrar, H. St J. Thackeray). W. M. Ramsay's espousal of the Lucan authorship of Acts after thoroughgoing archaeological and historical research was particularly influential for the critical reconstruction of Paul's life (*cf. SPT*, pp. 20ff.; W. K. Hobart's conclusions regarding *The Medical Language of St Luke*, 1882, also remain, with qualifications, a valid contribution in this area). With the advocacy of the German scholars Harnack and Deissmann this conclusion has been strengthened, although some recent students, as Haenchen, have argued anew against the tradition.

d. Trends in the 20th century

Literary criticism in the present century has focused upon: (i) a continuing effort towards a general historical reconsruction (*cf.* **IV**, below); (ii) the publication of the Pauline corpus; (iii) the provenance and date of the Prison Epistles; (iv) authorship; and (v) other questions concerning individual Epistles.

(i) *Historical reconstructions.* In spite of the demise of the Tübingen school its historical reconstruction, and some of its literary foibles, have continued to be assumed in much contemporary critical study. Johannes Munck (pp. 70–77) has rightly objected that when the literary conjectures failed, the dependent historical conjectures ought to have been revised ('It was not enough merely to transfer the problem from the two centuries to the three decades'; p. 70). Munck himself proposes such a revision. (1) The Jerusalem church, *i.e.* the original disciples, even as Paul, had no interest in excluding or 'Judaizing' Gentiles. (2) It was Paul's conviction, and his sole difference with the Jerusalem church, that Gentiles must *first* be won. Thus, as *the* apostle to the Gentiles (Gal. 2:7) he restrains antichrist (2 Thes. 2:7), by evangelism brings in (representatively) the 'fullness of the Gentiles' (Rom. 11:25; 15:19) and, as a decisive eschatological act, initiates Israel's redemption by making her jealous (Rom. 11:11) in taking the 'Gentile' collection to Jerusalem (Acts 20:4; 1 Cor. 16:3). Israel's 'No' issues in Paul's arrest and death, but Paul dies, as did Jesus, knowing God will yet save 'all Israel' in the fullness of time. In interpreting Paul's ministry within the framework of his initial call and of his eschatology, Munck gives due heed to critical emphases; on balance, his work marks a constructive advance.

Like F. C. Baur and W. Schmithals, E. E. Ellis (*Prophecy*[1], pp. 69ff., 78f., 104–128) also interprets Paul's mission in terms of his conflict with opponents: (1) Because the Hebraists (= 'the circumcision party', Acts 11:2f.; Gal. 2:12) and the Hellenists of Acts 6:1 had respectively a strict and a loose attitude towards the ritual law, they pursued somewhat separate missions in the Diaspora. (2) There a faction of the Hebraists, the Judaizers, sought to impose circumcision on Gentile believers. After the Council of Jerusalem they apparently subordinated their judaizing interests to a boastful triumphalism, licentious tendencies and a claim to mediate divine *gnōsis* through visions of angels. (3) Seeking to maintain the unity of the church, Paul counselled with Hebraist leaders (Gal. 2), worked with Hebraist colleagues (Col. 4:11) and took offerings to the Hebraist church of Jerusalem. (4) Against the opponents and their sympathizers he emphasized justification apart from works together with judgment according to one's works (Gal., Rom., Pastorals), the cruciform model of Christian ministry (Cor., Phil.), the Christocentric character of divine *gnōsis* and of all the charisms (Cor., Col.) and, at length, a church order that would protect the congregations from the false teachers (Pastorals).

(ii) *The Pauline corpus.* E. J. Goodspeed, departing from Harnack and earlier authorities, drew fresh attention to the formation of the Pauline corpus. He conjectured that about AD 90 an admirer of Paul in Ephesus published the apostle's letters (excepting the Pastorals) and wrote Eph. himself as an 'Introduction'. J. Knox (*Philemon among the Letters of Paul*, 1959, pp. 98ff.) took the hypothesis a step further and identified that admirer with Onesimus the slave, and later bishop of Ephesus. While receiving considerable acceptance (*cf.* C. L. Mitton, *The Formation of the Pauline Corpus of Letters*, 1955), the theory has been unpersuasive to many. (1) The text demands some addressee, and the primitive omission of such points to a circular letter, hardly suitable for a corpus introduction. (2) Eph. never introduces or ends the Pauline corpus in any ancient MS. (3) It is very doubtful that the content of Eph. can be properly described as a non-Pauline summation of Pauline thought. (4) G. Zuntz (pp. 14ff., 276–279), while recognizing the possibility of an earlier pre-corpus collection in Ephesus, finds that the textual and other evidence points to *c.* AD 100 and to 'the scholarly Alexandrian methods of editorship'. C. F. D. Moule suggests that Luke may be the collector of Paul's letters (*BJRL* 47, 1964–5, pp. 451f.).

(iii) *The provenance and date of the Prison Epistles.* The provenance of Paul's prison letters (Eph., Phil., Col., Phm.), traditionally assigned to Rome, has been a matter of increasing interest since G. S. Duncan, following Lisco and Deissmann, located them in *St Paul's Ephesian Ministry* (1929). Although Acts mentions no Ephesian imprisonment, Paul's letters imply it (*e.g.* 1 Cor. 15:32; 2 Cor. 1:8; 6:5; 11:23); also the setting, journeys and personages of the prison letters fit Ephesus better than distant Rome (*cf.* Phm. 22; Phil. 2:24 with Rom. 15:24ff.; *NTS* 3, 1956–7, pp. 211–218). J. Knox (*Philemon*, p. 33), Michaelis (pp. 205ff., 220), and as to Phil., Bruce (*Acts*[1], English text, p. 341) and T. W. Manson (*BJRL* 22, 1939, pp. 182ff.) are sympathetic to Duncan. C. H. Dodd (*Studies*, pp. 85–108) and Percy (pp. 473f.) object. (1) The tradition apart from Marcion's Prologue is unanimous for Rome, and such probably (though not certainly) is the meaning of Phil. 4:22. (2) Such references as 1 Cor. 15:32 are to be taken metaphorically. (3) The 'developed theology' of the captivity Epistles suggests the later Roman date. On balance, the Ephesian provenance is inviting and, at least in the case of Phil., may prove to be a permanent advance. However, a Caesarean provenance is advocated by Reicke (in the Bruce *Festschrift*) and by J. A. T. Robinson (*Redating the New Testament*, 1976, pp. 60f.).

(iv) The *authorship* of Paul's letters has been regarded traditionally as the individual enterprise of the apostle. On this assumption it is thought that the 'authentic' letters can be identified in terms of vocabulary, style, idiom and subject-matter and, on the same basis, that they can be divided into Pauline and 'interpolated' sections (*cf.* Schweitzer, *Interpreters*, pp. 141–150; Schmithals, *Gnosticism*, pp. 302–325; J. C. O'Neill, *Galatians*, 1972; *Romans*, 1975).

However, the effort to determine authorship on the basis of literary criteria has now been brought into question by several factors. (1) As Otto Roller showed, *the role of the amanuensis* in ancient letter-writing included an influence on the vocabulary and style of the letter. The hand of such secretaries is clearly present in the Pauline letters—even in the brief note to Philemon (Rom. 16:22; Gal. 6:11; 2 Thes. 3:17; Phm. 19). (2) The *role of the co-senders* of some letters is not entirely clear but, as H. Conzelmann (*NTS* 12, 1965–6, p. 234n.; *cf.* Roller, pp. 153–187) has observed, it probably involved some influence on their composition. (3) Paul worked within a circle of prophets and teachers (*cf.* Acts 13:1; Rom. 16:21f.; Col. 4:10–14), and the work of these colleagues is sometimes incorporated into his letters (*cf.* Ellis, *Prophecy*[1], pp. 25f., 213). It is reflected in the *many pre-formed pieces* that are used by the apostle — hymns (*e.g.* Phil. 2:5–11; 1 Tim. 3:16), expositions (*e.g.* 1 Cor. 2:6–16; 2 Cor. 6:14–7:1) and creeds (*e.g.* Rom. 1:3f.; 1 Cor. 15:3–7)—a phenomenon widely recognized today, and shows that even the undisputed Pauline letters are not a literary unity.

Paul is the author of the letters under his name in the sense that they were written under his supervision and in part by his hand or dictation, and they were sent out under his authority. But they are not, as a whole, solely his *de novo* compositions. Consequently, the literary criteria traditionally used to determine Pauline authorship can be given little weight in their present form, for they were devised under mistaken assumptions about the Pauline mission praxis and about the process by which the letters were composed.

(v) *Individual Epistles*. Critical emphases within the individual letters have shifted, except in the case of Eph. and the Pastorals, from authorship to other matters. (See separate articles on the various Epistles.) Many British and American scholars favour an early date for *Galatians* (*c.* AD 49 from Antioch) and a S Galatia destination, *i.e.* to the churches founded on Paul's first mission tour. On the Continent, N Galatia, *i.e.* the ethnic region (Acts 16:6; 18:23), and a post-Acts 15 chronology remain popular. The order of *1* and *2 Thessalonians* is reversed by T. W. Manson. Differences of style and subject-matter caused Harnack to suppose that 2 Thes. was written to the Jewish Christians but, more likely, it was directed to Paul's Thessalonian co-workers (Ellis, *Prophecy*[1], pp. 19ff.). Munck (pp. 36ff.; contrast *NIC*), following Cullmann, identifies the restraining power in 2 Thes. 2:6f. with Paul himself.

The *Corinthians correspondence* includes, in addition to the canonical Epistles, a letter prior to 1 Cor. (5:9) and a 'painful letter' (*cf.* 2 Cor. 2:4; 7:8) which are identified by some scholars with 2 Cor. 6:14–7:1 and 2 Cor. 10–13 respectively. C. K. Barrett (*Second . . . Corinthians*, 1973) and R. V. G. Tasker (*TNTC*) argue for the unity of our second Epistle. A more plausible case for the combination of two letters occurs in *Romans*, where the concluding doxology occurs after 14:23 and 15:33 in a number of MSS, and the addressees in Rom. 1:7, 15 are missing in a few. Of several explanations the one given by T. W. Manson (pp. 225–241), among others, is quite attractive: Rom. 1–15 was a circular letter to which ch. 16, an introduction of Phoebe to the Ephesians, was attached in the Ephesus copy. Nevertheless, the traditional view continues to find wide support (*e.g.* C. E. B. Cranfield, *ICC*, 1975; K. P. Donfried, *The Romans Debate*, 1977).

A 'circular letter' appears to be indicated in the case of *Ephesians* by: (1) the currency of the practice in the 1st century (*cf.* Zuntz, p. 228), and (2) the necessity for, and yet manuscript omission of, an addressee. Such a view would militate against Goodspeed's corpus introduction theory, but it would leave open Sanders' view (*cf.* F. L. Cross, below) that Ephesians is not an Epistle but Paul's 'spiritual testament'. It might also explain the title 'to the Laodiceans', which, according to Tertullian, Marcion gave the letter (*cf.* Col. 4:16). E. Percy, M. Barth and A. van Roon have given the most recent arguments for Pauline authorship; C. L. Mitton in *Epistle to the Ephesians* (1951) argues against it. A more popular 'pro and con' is found in F. L. Cross's symposium, *Studies in Ephesians* (1956). 'Which is more likely,' asks H. J. Cadbury (*NTS* 5, 1958–9, p. 101), 'that an imitator of Paul in the 1st century composed a writing 90 or 95% in accordance with Paul's style or that Paul himself wrote a letter diverging 5 or 10% from his usual style?' With the increased tendency to allow for variation in Pauline literary and theological expression and a different perception of the nature of authorship (above) the arguments against genuineness become less convincing; they are weakened even further by the Dead Sea Scrolls parallels (*cf.* Murphy-O'Connor, pp. 115–131, 159–178).

Outside Germany most students consider the 19th-century 'non-Pauline' verdicts valid only for the Pastorals. (In recent years Pauline authorship of the Epistle to the Hebrews has been seriously argued only by the Roman Catholic scholar William Leonard.) Anglo-American opinion (and also Schmithals, *Gnostics*) has tended to agree with P. N. Harrison's 'fragment hypothesis' *i.e.* Pauline fragments supplemented and edited; most Continentals who reject the Pastorals favour, with Kümmel (*INT*, a later Paulinist author. The case for genuineness has found suppport in Roller's 'secretary hypothesis', *i.e.* that stylistic variations stem from Paul's amanuensis, whom some suggest to be Luke (*e.g.* C. F. D. Moule, *BJRL* 47, 1965, pp. 430–452); the traditional view has been argued anew by Spicq and Michaelis. The growing dissatisfaction with Harrison's hypothesis expressed, *e.g.*, in Guthrie (*TNTC*), Kelly and Metzger (*ExpT* 70, 1958–9, pp. 91ff.) may represent a general reappraisal of the prevailing view (*cf. EQ* 32, pp. 151–161). But see M. Dibelius and H. Conzelmann, *The Pastoral Epistles*, 1972. See also * Timothy and Titus, Epistles to (**IV**).

IV. Pauline thought

a. Background

The Reformation emphasis upon righteousness or justification by faith (Rom. 1:17) continued in the following centuries to be the controlling factor in the interpretation of Paul's doctrine. With the rise of literary criticism the absence of this motif became sufficient reason to suspect or even reject a 'Pauline' letter; and in the incipient development of Paulinism, *i.e.* the system of Pauline thought, 'righteousness' was regarded as the key to the apostle's mind. (In the following sketch compare especially Schweitzer, *Interpreters*.)

(i) *Paul's doctrine of redemption.* L. Usteri (1824) and A. F. Daehne (1835) sought to explain the whole of Pauline thought in terms of the imputed righteousness of Romans (*e.g.* 3:21ff.). In contrast, the rationalist H. E. G. Paulus, starting from texts stressing the 'new creation' and sanctification (*e.g.* 2 Cor. 5:17; Rom. 8:29), insisted that Pauline righteousness was an ethical, moral concept; faith in Jesus meant ultimately the faith of Jesus. These two ideas and their relationship had a continuing significance through the 19th century.

F. C. Baur, within the framework of Hegelian idealism, sought at first (1845) to explain Paul in terms of the Spirit given through union with Christ by faith. Later, however, Baur reverted to the Reformation pattern, a compartmentalized presentation of the various Pauline doctrines without any attempt to view them from a unified concept. This *loci* approach was followed by succeeding writers who gave minute descriptions of Pauline doctrine, innocently supposing 'that in the description they possessed at the same time an explanation' (Schweitzer, *Interpreters*, p. 36).

Nevertheless, some writers pressed towards the discovery of a unifying concept for Pauline thought. R. A. Lipsius (1853) had recognized two views of redemption in Paul, the juridical (justification) and the ethical ('new creation'). Hermann Luedemann, in his book *The Anthropology of the Apostle Paul* (1872), concluded that the two views of redemption actually rested on two views of the nature of man. In Paul's earlier 'Jewish' view (Gal.; Rom. 1–4) redemption was a juridical verdict of acquittal; for the mature Paul (Rom. 5–8) it was an ethical–physical transformation from 'flesh' to 'spirit' through communion with the Holy Spirit. The source of the first idea was Christ's death; the second, his resurrection. On the other hand, Richard Kabisch concluded that Pauline redemption essentially meant deliverance from coming judgment, and its significance, therefore, was to be found in the eschatology of the apostle. The Christian must walk in newness of life to show that he actually shared Christ's resurrection. 'Spiritual' life and death in the modern religious sense are unknown to Paul; both concepts are, *e.g.* in Rom. 6, always physical; and the new life is a mystical union with Christ. Thus, future deliverance from satanic powers is anticipated by the possession of the Holy Spirit, who manifests the new age in the present and inseminates our corporal being with a super-earthly substance.

For both Luedemann and Kabisch: (1) Paul's doctrine of redemption emanates from one fundamental concept. (2) It is a physical redemption to be understood in terms of Pauline anthropology. (3) To be redeemed means to share Christ's death and resurrection, which involves union with Christ and the abolition of the 'flesh'. (4) Although future, this redemption is mediated in the present by the Holy Spirit.

But questions remained. In what sense can Christ's death and resurrection be repeated in the believer? In what sense can the Christian be 'a new creation' and yet outwardly appear unchanged? Albert Schweitzer, building upon the interpretations of Luedemann and Kabisch, sought an answer in the following synthesis. (1) Paul, as did Jesus, interpreted Jesus' death and resurrection to be eschatological, *i.e.* an end of the world event, bringing the kingdom of God and the resurrection life to all the elect. (2) But the world did not end, and believers did not in fact enter into resurrection life; in time the temporal separation between Christ's resurrection and the (anticipated) resurrection of believers became the chief problem for Paul's teaching. (3) To answer it Paul posits a 'physical mysticism': through the sacraments the Holy Spirit mediates in the present time Christ's resurrection to the 'last generation' believers. (4) This present union with Christ in the Spirit ensures to the believer a share in the 'Messianic resurrection' at the parousia.

(ii) *Pauline eschatology*. Thus, Schweitzer set the stage for 20th-century discussions of Pauline eschatology. It was his great merit that he sought to understand Paul's thought in terms of one fundamental concept, that he recognized the central importance of eschatology and (Jewish) anthropology in the apostle's doctrine of redemption, and that he recognized the Holy Spirit and the *en Christō* union as the realization of the new age in the present. But Schweitzer's interpretation of Paul's eschatology as a makeshift expedient (and as a sacramental mysticism) is questionable, to say the least. For, as N. Q. Hamilton's critique has pointed out (*The Holy Spirit and Eschatology in Paul*, 1957, pp. 50ff.), the exalted Christ, not the 'delay' in the parousia, determines Paul's eschatology. Also, if Paul's thought patterns are Jewish (as Schweitzer rightly recognized), sacramental mysticism is a rather awkward explanation of the realism of the 'new creation' in Christ.

(iii) *Paul's thought patterns.* In addition to eschatology as the key to Paulinism, a closely related question important for the future also had its rise in the 19th century. Are Paul's thought patterns Jewish or Hellenistic? Kabisch and Schweitzer insisted that Pauline thought was Jewish to the core. Others, following F. C. Baur's reconstruction of Paul as the 'Hellenizer of Christianity', interpreted Pauline anthropology and eschatology from the standpoint of a modified Platonic dualism. The antithesis between 'flesh' and 'spirit' in Rom. 6–8 was an ethical dualism, and 'dying' and 'rising' a spiritual transformation. This has its roots in an anthropological dualism; thus, in the future, redemption involves the deliverance of the 'soul' from its house of clay. But Paul also speaks of the resurrection of the whole man from death (1 Thes. 4; 1 Cor. 15). Otto Pfleiderer (*Paulinism*, 1877, I, p. 264) concluded that Paul held Jewish and Gk. views simultaneously, 'side by side, without any thought of their essential inconsistency'. In interpreting Pauline eschatology elsewhere (*cf.* Schweitzer, *Interpreters*, p. 70) he posits a development from 1 Thes. 4 through 1 Cor. 15 to 2 Cor. 5. The first is simply Jewish resurrection eschatology; in 2 Cor. 5 the believer goes to the heavenly realms at death.

b. The origin of Paul's religion: Hellenism

20th-century studies of Pauline thought have devoted themselves primarily to three questions. What is the relation between Paul and Jesus? What are the sources for Pauline thought? What is the role of eschatology in the mind of Paul?

(i) *Paul's relation to Jesus.* The distinction raised a half century earlier between 'juridical' (Rom. 1–4) and 'ethical' (Rom. 5–8) righteousness had borne much fruit, and the latter came to be regarded as the more central and decisive Pauline concept. A. Deissmann (pp. 148ff.) viewed 'in Christ' as an intimate spiritual communion with Christ, a Christ mysticism; more often the 'mysticism' was interpreted as a sacramental reality based upon Jewish eschatology (Schweitzer) or the pagan mysteries (J. Weiss, *Earliest Christianity*, 1959 (1937), 2, pp. 463f.). Somewhat later J. S. Stewart (*A Man in Christ*, 1935, pp. 150ff.) reflected this trend in British scholarship, regarding union with Christ as the central element in Paul's thought. This emphasis had important consequences for the course of Pauline studies in the 20th century.

The contrast between the 'liberal Jesus' and Paul's indwelling and yet transcendent Christ called forth at the turn of the century a spate of books on the relationship of Jesus and Paul (*cf.* P. Feine, *Paulus*, pp. 158ff.). W. Wrede's influential *Paulus* (1905) put the matter in the starkest terms: Paul was not truly a disciple of Jesus; he was actually the second founder of Christianity. The individual piety and future salvation of the Rabbi Jesus had been transformed by the theologian Paul into a present redemption through the death and resurrection of a christ-god. Paul's ideas could not, of course, be accepted at face value. To do so would, as Weinel (*St Paul*, 1906, p. 11) remarked, 'stifle the claims of reason for the sake of Christianity, for reason is ever-repeating . . . that the modern conception of the world is the right one'. Nevertheless, the historian's task remained. If Paul's doctrines did not arise from and build upon Jesus' mind, what was their origin?

(ii) *Sources of Pauline thought.* F. C. Baur sought to explain the mind of Paul in the context of church controversy: Paul was the champion of Gentile freedom. For Schweitzer the origin of Paul's thought was his peculiar eschatological problem forged in the mental cauldron of late Judaism. However, the rising 'History of Religion' (*Religionsgeschichte*) school found no evidence to ground Paul's sacramental mysticism in Judaism. While recognizing the eschatological problem, it built upon Baur's 'Gentile' Paul and developed still another elaborate reconstruction of the apostolic age. Represented most notably by R. Reitzenstein and W. Bousset, it interpreted Paulinism in the framework of Oriental–Hellenistic mystery religions. The Mysteries spoke, as did Paul, of a dying-rising god, of 'Lord', of sacramental redemption, of 'mysteries', *gnōsis* and 'spirit'. As a boy in Tarsus and later as a missionary the apostle came under the influence of these ideas, and they exerted a profound influence on his theology. Schweitzer (*Interpreters*, pp. 179–236), H. A. A. Kennedy, G. Wagner and J. G. Machen (pp. 255–290) subjected this reconstruction to a thorough critique, pointing out that, in ignoring the OT–Judaism background of the parallels (which Kennedy showed to be quite plausible) and the late date of its sources, the theory reflected a weakness in method. (*Cf.* also R. E. Brown, *The Semitic Background of the Term 'Mystery'* . . ., 1968). The principal contribution of the History of Religion school was to raise the important question of Paul's theological relation to the Gentile religious world. The 'mystery religion' reconstruction did not win general approval, but in a more recent gnostic dress its general outlines continue to be strongly advocated.

The mystery religion parallels paled; nevertheless, the conviction remained strong that Paul's thought was substantially influenced by the Greek world of ideas. R. Bultmann (1910) had shown the affinity of Paul's literary style with the Stoic diatribe. Others regarded Paul's doctrine of the 'corporate body' (*cf.* W. L. Knox, *Gentiles*, pp. 160ff.), his natural theology in Rom. 1 (*cf.* Acts 17) and his concept of conscience (E. Norden, *Agnostos Theos*, 1913) as rooted in Stoicism. The inadequacy of these conclusions was pointed out, respectively, by E. Best (pp. 83ff.), B. Gaertner (pp. 133–169) and C. A. Pierce (pp. 16ff.). Gaertner argues that Paul's 'natural theology' is thoroughly OT–Jewish; however, Pierce (pp. 22ff., 57ff.) concludes that the NT adopts in the case of 'conscience' a general usage of popular Gk. thought.

To determine the relationship of Paul to pagan religious thought, the area currently receiving most attention is Gnosticism. This religious–philosophical movement stressed a metaphysical dualism, deliverance from 'matter' through a divine gift and power of *gnōsis*, *i.e.* a special knowledge of God, and mediating angels to assist one to salvation. Long ago J. B. Lightfoot (*Colossians and Philemon*, 1886, pp. 71–111) detected elements of Gnosticism in the Colossian heresy. Early in the 20th century Bousset and J. Weiss (*op. cit.*, 2, pp. 650f.) urged that aspects of Paul's own thought lay in this direction. R. Bultmann and his pupil W. Schmithals became the chief representatives and developers of Bousset's reconstruction today. From existentialist considerations Bultmann again made 'justification' a central Pauline motif, although it was far from a return to Baur or to the Reformers; for the same reasons Paul's anthropology was given a thorough exposition (*Theology* 1, pp. 190–227). But the real clue to Bultmann's understanding of Paulinism is his grounding of Pauline thought in a syncretistic Judaism and Christianity. From this background Paul obtained a number of concepts, *e.g.* sacramental redemption and ethical dualism, which were Gnostic or gnosticized in some degree (*Theology* 1, pp. 63ff., 124ff., 151–188). While Paul opposed the Gnostics, *e.g.* at Colossae, in the process he modified not only his terminology but also his concepts, particularly his Christology (Messiah Jesus becomes a heavenly Lord; *cf.* Bousset) and cosmogony (the demon-controlled world is redeemed by a heavenly man; *cf.* W. L. Knox, *Gentiles*, pp. 220ff.; but see G. B. Caird, *Principalities and Powers*, 1956; W. Foerster, *TDNT* 2, pp. 566–574).

Schweitzer (*Interpreters*, p. 231) predicted that a

'Hellenized' Paulinism was a half-way house which must carry its conclusions even to the genesis of Christianity. His prediction was more than fulfilled by the discovery in 1947 of the Dead Sea Scrolls with their ethical dualism and emphasis on 'knowledge'. The Scrolls were an embarrassment for Bultmann's reconstruction, for 'pre-Gnostic' was about the closest identification most scholars cared to make for them. Also, there is little reason to believe that Paul reflects, *e.g.*, 'an earlier Gnostic doctrine about the descent of a redeemer, especially since there is no evidence that such a doctrine existed' (R. M. Grant, *Gnosticism*, p. 69; *cf.* pp. 39–69; R. McL. Wilson, pp. 27f., 57f.). Almost all else Bultmann chose to refer to Gnostic influences likewise suffered from the same chronological strictures. Grant, looking back to Schweitzer, interprets Gnosticism as arising from a failure of the apocalyptic hope; unlike Schweitzer, Grant views Paul as a man whose spiritual world lies somewhere between Jewish apocalyptic and the fully developed Gnosticism of the 2nd century (p. 158). Grant sees the latter tendency in Paul's interpretation of Christ's resurrection as a realized (eschatological) victory over the cosmic powers. More cautiously R. McL. Wilson, in a valuable assessment (*The Gnostic Problem*, 1958, pp. 75–80, 108, 261), concludes that Paul adopts a contemporary cosmogony and terminology only to oppose Gnosticism and to interpret Jesus' authority over the (Gnostic) 'powers'; the apostle rejects the gnosticizing interpretation. However, J. Dupont (*Gnosis: La Connaissance Religieuse dans les Épîtres de Saint Paul*[2], 1960) and Ellis (*Prophecy*[1], pp. 45–62) argue that Pauline *gnōsis* is strictly OT–Jewish.

All the 'Greek' reconstructions of Paul have their root in Baur's interpretation of Paul as the exponent of Gentile Christianity. When W. Wrede and others recognized the redemptive–eschatological character of Pauline thought, the apostle was set in opposition not only to Jewish Christianity but to the 'liberal' Jesus himself. But, as Schweitzer had shown, the 'liberal' Jesus was not the Jesus of the Gospels. Bultmann (*Theology* 1, pp. 23, 30ff.) accepted Schweitzer's 'apocalyptic' Jesus but insisted that God's demand for man's decision, not the apocalyptic window-dressing, was the essence of Jesus' eschatology. The suffering, resurrected and returning Son of man was a 'mythologized' picture of the later 'Hellenized' Christology. The mind of Paul remained far distant from the mind of the earthly Jesus or of his earliest disciples. One's estimate of Paulinism is closely tied, therefore, to one's estimate of the Gospels' picture of Jesus.

A number of mediating scholars, taking their cue from B. Weiss, see 'development' as the key to Paul's thought. In view of fading parousia hopes Paul's anthropology and eschatology move towards a Platonic dualism (Dodd) and his cosmogony towards Gnosticism (R. M. Grant).

In its present *religionsgeschichtliche* format the interpretation of Paul in terms of pagan religious ideas is subject to a number of criticisms. There is a tendency to convert parallels into influences and influences into sources. Some of its 'sources' for Pauline thought come from a period considerably later than the apostle's lifetime. (Bultmann's Paul may have more than a casual relation to the Gnostic 'Paul' of the ultra-Tübingen school.) Also, its historical inquiry has sometimes been compromised by an inadequate world-view. For example, Bultmann, like Weinel, views the natural world as a 'self-subsistent unity immune from the interference of supernatural powers' (*Kerygma and Myth*, ed. H. W. Bartsch, 1953, p. 7; *cf.* pp. 5–8, 216, 222).

Perhaps the most basic questions are these: Is Paulinism best understood as an amalgam, gathered here and there, or as the expansion and application of a central tradition rooted in the mind of Jesus Christ and the earliest church? Is Paul's mind most adequately explained within a religious syncretism or within the context of apocalyptic Judaism and the primitive church? Does the 'gnosticizing' of Christian thought begin in Paul and pre-Pauline Christianity (Bultmann) or in Paul's opponents and wayward converts; and does it arise from a failure of the primitive eschatology in Paul (Grant) or from a misunderstanding of it (and of Paul) in his churches? *Cf.* Ellis, *Prophecy*[1], pp. 45–62, 101–115.

c. The origin of Paul's religion: Judaism

(i) *Paul's link with the earliest church.* Both Ritschl and von Hofmann had argued, *contra* Baur, for the unity of Paul's teaching with that of the earliest church. A. Resch, in the 'Jesus or Paul' debate, upheld this view. His thorough investigation of *Der Paulinismus und die Logia Jesu* (1904) concluded that the words of Jesus were a primary source of Pauline thought. But could not rather Paul be the source of the Synoptic Jesus? The research of several writers (*e.g.* Dungan; F. F. Bruce, *BJRL* 56, 1973–4, pp. 317–335) has substantiated the priority argued by Resch.

C. H. Dodd (*Preaching*, p. 56) established that a *kerygma*, *i.e.* a gospel-core proclamation, underlay both the Gospels and Paul, 'a tradition coeval with the Church itself'. The same writer (*According to the Scriptures*, 1952, pp. 108ff.), building upon Rendel Harris' *Testimonies* (1916, 1920), found a 'substructure of NT theology' to which Paul was indebted and whose origin pointed to Christ himself. E. E. Ellis, examining the hermeneutical principles of *Paul's Use of the Old Testament*[1] (pp. 97f., 107–112; *idem*, *Prophecy*[1], *passim*), suggested that some common (pre-Pauline) exegetical tradition originated with 'prophets' of the earliest church. E. Lohmeyer (*Kyrios Jesus*, 1928) interprets Phil. 2:5ff. as a primitive Christian hymn probably arising in Aram. circles (*cf.* L. Cerfaux, pp. 283ff.; R. P. Martin, *Carmen Christi*[2], 1983; E. G. Selwyn, *First Epistle of St Peter*, 1946, pp. 365–369, 458–466). Similarly, the pre-Pauline character of the *Primitive Christian Catechism* (1940) was demonstrated by P. Carrington.

O. Cullmann ('Tradition', pp. 69–99), K. H. Rengstorf (*TDNT* 1, pp. 413–443), H. Riesenfeld (*The Gospel Tradition*, 1969, pp. 1–29) and B. Gerhardsson point to a rationale for this understanding of Christian origins. The NT concept of apostle has a similar origin to that of the rabbinic *šālîaḥ*, an authorized agent equivalent to the sender himself. The apostles witnessed to a tradition or *paradosis*, given to them by Christ. 'But since everything has not been revealed to each individual apostle, each one must first pass on his testimony to another (Gal. 1:18; 1 Cor. 15:11), and only the entire *paradosis*, to which all the apostles contribute, constitutes the *paradosis* of Christ' (Cullmann, 'Tradition', p. 73). Thus, as an 'apostle' Paul's message is defined in terms of what he has received: his catechesis, kerygma, and the wider 'tradition' should be, and critical study finds them to be, rooted in the earliest church and ultimately in the teaching of Jesus. This teaching of Jesus seems to have included not merely moral instruction or apocalyptic warning, but also biblical exposition (Ellis, *Prophecy*[1], pp. 240–253) and a creative, theological synthesis which envisaged a post-resurrection ministry by his disciples (*cf.* J. Jeremias, *Jesus' Promise to the Nations*, 1958). If these writers are correct, the dichotomy between Paul and the primitive Jewish church, which has been urged from Baur to Bultmann, is an assumption which must be abandoned.

(ii) *Paul's background.* To understand a writer it would seem to be proper to give priority to that milieu to which he appeals and to which he presumably belongs. In interpreting Pauline concepts it is not the categories of a 2nd-century Gnosticism (however easily they may be 'read back') but the categories of 1st-century rabbinic/apocalyptic Judaism which demand first claim upon the critical historian's mind.

The nature of 1st-century Judaism is complex, and it is easy to overdraw or wrongly define the contrast between the 'syncretistic' and 'orthodox', terms not to be equated with 'Hellenist' and 'Hebraist' or with '*diaspora*' and 'Palestinian' (*cf.* Acts 6:1; Ellis, *Prophecy*, pp. 106f., 125f., 245ff.; Davies, pp. 1–8). Nevertheless, considerable research relates the thought of Paul, the Pharisee and 'Hebrew of the Hebrews' (Phil. 3:5), with Palestinian rabbinism and apocalypticism rather than with a syncretistic Judaism. Van Unnik has raised at least the probability that Paul's early youth was passed not in Tarsus but in Jerusalem. Certainly Paul used the Septuagint, but this translation has now been found among the DSS. He preached among the *diaspora*, and he may have been acquainted with the syncretistic Judaism exemplified by Philo. But with the doubtful exception of the Wisdom of Solomon, his relationship to the *diaspora* literature is not direct and probably reflects only traditions which both had in common. His more significant relationships lie in another direction. W. D. Davies and others have shown that Qumran and Rabbinic Judaism form the background of many Pauline concepts formerly labelled 'Hellenistic'. Likewise, the literary form of Paul's biblical exposition agrees with rabbinic models. The Dead Sea Scrolls have confirmed in remarkable fashion the Jewishness of Pauline and NT backgrounds. (*Cf.* Bruce, *Qumran Texts*, pp. 66–77; Flusser; M. Black, *The Scrolls and Christian Origins*, 1961; Ellis, *Prophecy*[1], pp. 35, 57ff., 213–220; Murphy-O'Connor.)

(iii) *Specific Pauline concepts.* Passing to specific Pauline concepts, anthropology and the nature of the 'in Christ' relationship have had a central importance since the days of F. C. Baur. It is widely recognized today that Paul views man in an OT–Jewish framework and not in the Platonic dualism of the Hellenistic world (*cf.* *LIFE; Bultmann, *Theology* 1, pp. 209f.; Cullmann, *Immortality*, pp. 28–39; J. A. T. Robinson, *The Body*, 1952). The corporate 'body of Christ' also is best understood not in terms of a Gnostic mythology (Käsemann) nor a Stoic metaphor (W. L. Knox) but as the OT–Jewish concept of corporate solidarity. Davies (*Judaism*, pp. 53ff.) has related Paul's thought here to the rabbinic speculations on the body of Adam. R. P. Shedd's *Man in Community* (1958) correctly finds Paul's ultimate rationale in the realism of Semitic thought patterns, as they are applied to Messiah and his people (*cf.* J. A. T. Robinson, *The Body*, 1953, pp. 56ff.; Kümmel, *Man*; J. deFraine, *Adam and the Family of Man*, 1965, pp. 245–270; Ellis, *Prophecy*[1], pp. 170ff.). R. Gundry (pp. 228–241) falls short of this realism in viewing the concept metaphorically. D. R. G. Owen, in *Body and Soul* (1956), offers an illuminating comparison of biblical anthropology with the modern scientific view of man. The study of D. Cox (*Jung and St Paul*, 1959) seeks to define in other areas the relevance of Paul for current faith and practice.

Whether Paul's eschatology is rooted in Jewish or Greek concepts is a matter of continuing debate. The importance of this question for Paulinism requires that some detailed attention now be given to it.

d. The eschatological essence of Pauline thought

C. A. A. Scott's well-written *Christianity according to Saint Paul* (1927), over against Albert Schweitzer's eschatological interpretation, identifies salvation as the fundamental concept of Paulinism. But what is the factor determining the character of Paul's 'already but not yet' redemption theology? Not grasping Schweitzer's real question, Scott did not really pose an alternative: he found a motif to describe Paul, not a key to explain him. (*Cf.* also Christological approaches, *e.g.* L. Cerfaux, *Christ in the Theology of St Paul*, 1959.) Schweitzer may not have stated the problem, or the solution, satisfactorily; but his identification of the key concept remains valid.

(i) *The views of Schweitzer and Dodd.* Until recently discussion of NT eschatology has revolved about the views of Schweitzer and C. H. Dodd. (For Bultmann, eschatology has nothing to do with the future or with history; it is the realm of existential living. Like F. C. Baur, Bultmann uses NT language to clothe an imposing philosophy of religion; exegesis becomes the servant of existentialism. *Cf.* Hamilton, pp. 41–90, for a lucid summation and critique of the eschatology of Schweitzer, Dodd and Bultmann.) Schweitzer argued that Paul's '*en Christō*' concept arose from the failure of the kingdom of God, *i.e.* the end of the world, to arrive at Christ's death and resurrection. Against Schweitzer, Dodd contended that in Christ's death the 'age to come' did arrive; eschatology was 'realized' as much as it ever would be in history. The believer already participates in the kingdom (*e.g.* Col. 1:13), and at death he fully enters the eternal, *i.e.* eschatological, realm. Eschatology, therefore, does not refer to an endof-the-world event; in Platonic fashion it is to be understood 'spatially' rather than temporally, eternity over against time. How, then, is Paul's anticipation of a future parousia to be accounted for? Believing it to be a hangover from apocalyptic Judaism (and quite alien to the central message of Jesus), Dodd goes back to Pfleiderer for an answer: in 1 Thes. 4 Paul has a strictly Jewish eschatology but in 1 Cor. 15 modifies it with the concept of a 'spiritual' body; 2 Cor. 5, which then places the believer in heaven at death, expresses the view of the mature (and 'Greek') Paul. J. A. T. Robinson's *Jesus and His Coming* (1958, pp. 160ff.) is essentially an elaboration of Dodd's thesis.

It is Dodd's great merit that he saw, as Schweitzer did not, the essential meaning for NT thought (and for the relevance of the gospel in the present world) of the 'realized' aspect of the kingdom of God. But in adopting an unbiblical

Platonic view of time Dodd failed to do justice to the futurist and temporal character of eschatological redemption. Also, his development of Pauline eschatology involved an un-Pauline anthropological dualism and, in part, reflected a misunderstanding of the texts. Both Schweitzer and Dodd made admirable attempts to achieve a comprehensive interpretation of NT eschatology. Although 'futurist or realized' has now been recognized as an improper either/or, the contributions of Schweitzer and Dodd remain fundamental landmarks in the progress of the research.

The important monographs of W. G. Kümmel (*Promise and Fulfilment*, 1957, pp. 141–155; and *NTS* 5, 1958–9, pp. 113–126) argued convincingly that both 'present' and 'future' eschatology are equally and permanently rooted in the teaching of Jesus and of Paul. Oscar Cullmann's most significant publications, *Christ and Time* (1951) and *Salvation in History* (1967), contrasted the Platonic idea of redemption, *i.e.* to escape the time 'circle' at death, with the biblical concept that redemption is tied to resurrection in future 'linear' time, *i.e.* at the parousia. These works, plus a proper appreciation of Paul's OT–Jewish anthropology and of the Semitic concept of corporate solidarity, form a proper foundation for understanding Paul's eschatology—and thus his total doctrine of redemption.

(ii) *The pre-eminence of a theology of redemption.* Historical research since the Reformation has recognized that Pauline theology is above all a theology of redemption. The 19th century witnessed a growing emphasis upon the present 'union with Christ' (rather than imputed righteousness) as the central aspect of this redemption. Since Albert Schweitzer two eschatological *foci*, Christ's death and resurrection and the parousia, have been recognized as the key to the meaning of 'union with Christ'.

Jesus Christ in his death and resurrection defeated for all time the 'powers' of the old aeon—sin, death and the demonic 'rulers of this darkness' (Eph. 6:12; Col. 2:15). Now Christians were crucified, resurrected, glorified and placed at God's right hand with Christ (Gal. 2:20; Eph. 2:5f.). 'In Christ' Christians have entered the resurrection age; the solidarity with the first Adam in sin and death has been replaced by the solidarity with the eschatological Adam in righteousness and immortal life. (*LIFE.)

This corporate redemption in and with Jesus Christ, this 'new age' reality, which the believer enters at conversion (*cf.* Rom. 6), finds an individual actualization in the present and the future (*cf.* Ellis, *NTS* 6, 1959–60, pp. 211–216). In the present life it means a transformation through the indwelling Spirit, the firstfruits of the new resurrection life (Rom. 8:23; 2 Cor. 5:5), of one's ethic (Col. 2:20; 3:1, 9f., 12) and of one's total world view (Rom. 12:1ff.). However, in the midst of moral–psychological renewal the Christian remains, in his mortality, under the death claims of the old age. But this too is to be understood no longer in terms of 'in Adam', but as a part of the 'in Christ' reality; for 'the sufferings of Christ abound to us' (2 Cor. 1:5; *cf.* Phil. 3:10; Col. 1:24), and the Christian dead have fallen asleep 'in Jesus' (1 Thes. 4:14; *cf.* Phil. 2:17; 2 Tim. 4:6). The individual actualization of Christ's sufferings is, of course, in no way a self-redemption process; rather, it means to be identified with Christ 'in the likeness of his death' (Rom. 6:5). The 'likeness of his resurrection' awaits its actualization at the parousia, when the individual Christian, raised to immortal life, shall be 'conformed to the image of his Son, that he might be the firstborn among many brethren' (Rom. 8:29; *cf.* 1 Cor. 15:53ff.).

Thus, Pauline redemption is not a 'spiritual' deliverance culminating in the escape of the 'soul' at death (Dodd); it is a physical redemption culminating in the deliverance of the whole man at the parousia (Cullmann). It is to be understood not in terms of a Platonic dualism but in the framework of an OT–Jewish view of man as a unified being and as one who lives not only as an individual but in 'corporate solidarities'. The future that has become present in the resurrection of Jesus Christ is a future which the Christian realizes now only corporately, as the 'body of Christ'. However, at the parousia faith shall become sight, 'away' shall become 'at home', and the solidarities of the new age shall become individually actualized in all their glory, both in man and in the whole created order (Rom. 8:19–21). This is the living hope of Paul's heart; it is also the meaning of his theology.

BIBLIOGRAPHY. M. Barth, *Ephesians*, 2 vols., 1974; E. Best, *One Body in Christ*, 1955; G. Bornkamm, *Paul*, 1971; W. Bousset, *Kurios Christos*, 1913, E.T. 1970; F. F. Bruce, *The Acts of the Apostles*[3], 1990 (*NIC*[2], 1988); *idem*, *Biblical Exegesis in the Qumran Texts*, 1959; *idem*, *Paul and Jesus*, 1974; *idem*, *Paul*, 1978; R. Bultmann, *Theology of the New Testament*, 2 vols., 1952; H. C. C. Cavallin, *Life after Death . . . in 1 Cor. 15*, 1974; O. Cullmann, *Immortality of the Soul or Resurrection of the Dead?*, 1958; *idem*, 'The Tradition', *The Early Church*, 1956, pp. 57–99; W. D. Davies, *Paul and Rabbinic Judaism*, 1955; A. Deissmann, *Paul*, 1927; C. H. Dodd, *New Testament Studies*, 1953; *idem*, *The Apostolic Preaching and its Development*, 1936; J. W. Drane, *Paul, Libertine or Legalist?*, 1976; D. L. Dungan, *The Sayings of Jesus in the Churches of Paul*, 1971; E. E. Ellis, *Paul's Use of the Old Testament*[5], 1991; *idem*, *Prophecy and Hermeneutic*[4], 1993; F. J. Foakes-Jackson and K. Lake, *BC*, 5 vols., 1933; B. Gaertner, *The Areopagus Speech and Natural Revelation*, 1955; W. W. Gasque and R. P. Martin, *Apostolic History and the Gospel*, 1970; B. Gerhardsson, *The Gospel Tradition*, 1986; E. J. Goodspeed, *The Meaning of Ephesians*, 1933; R. M. Grant, *Gnosticism and Early Christianity*, 1959; R. H. Gundry, *Soma*, 1974; E. Haenchen, *Acts*, 1971; A. T. Hanson, *Studies in Paul's . . . Theology*, 1974; P. N. Harrison, *The Problem of the Pastoral Epistles*, 1921; H. Hübner, *Law in Paul's Thought*, 1984; J. N. D. Kelly, *The Pastoral Epistles*, 1963; H. A. A. Kennedy, *Saint Paul and the Mystery Religions*, 1913; S. Kim, *The Origin of Paul's Gospel*[2], 1984; W. L. Knox, *Saint Paul and the Church of the Gentiles*, 1939; W. G. Kümmel, *Man in the New Testament*, 1963; *idem*, *The New Testament . . . Problems*, 1972; J. G. Machen, *The Origin of Paul's Religion*, 1947 (1925); T. W. Manson, *Studies in the Gospels and Epistles*, 1962; I. H. Marshall, *The Origins of New Testament Christology*, 1976; W. Michaelis, *Einleitung in das Neue Testament*, 1954; C. F. D. Moule, *The Origin of Christology*, 1977; J. Munck, *Paul and the Salvation of Mankind*, 1960; J. M. Murphy-O'Connor, *Paul and Qumran*, 1968; E. Pagels, *The Gnostic Paul*, 1975; E. Percy, *Probleme der Kolosser- und Epheserbriefe*, 1946; C. A. Pierce, *Conscience in the New Testament*, 1955; R.

Reitzenstein, *Die hellenistischen Mysterienreligionen*, 1927 (E.T. 1977); K. H. Rengstorf (ed.), *Das Paulusbild in der neueren deutschen Forschung*, 1969; H. Ridderbos, *Paul and Jesus*, 1958; O. Roller, *Das Formular der Paulinischen Briefe*, 1933; E. P. Sanders, *Paul, the Law, and the Jewish People*, 1983; W. Schmithals, *Gnosticism in Corinth*, 1971; *idem, Paul and the Gnostics*, 1972; *idem, Paul and James*, 1965; H. J. Schoeps, *Paul*, 1961; A. Schweitzer, *The Mysticism of Paul the Apostle*, 1931; *idem, Paul and his Interpreters*, 1912; K. Stendahl (ed.), *The Scrolls and the New Testament*, 1957; W. C. van Unnik, *Tarsus or Jerusalem?*, 1962; G. Wagner, *Pauline Baptism and the Pagan Mysteries*, 1967; D. E. H. Whiteley, *The Theology of St Paul*², 1985; R. McL. Wilson, *Gnosis and the New Testament*, 1968; G. Zuntz, *The Text of the Epistles*, 1953.

Recent studies include: E. E. Ellis, *Pauline Theology: Ministry and Society*, 1989; *idem* '*Soma* in I Corinthians', *Int* 44, 1990, pp. 132–144; *idem* 'The Pastoral Epistles'; 'Co-workers, Paul and his', in R. P. Martin and G. F. Hawthorne (eds.) *Dictionary of Paul and his Letters*, 1993; *idem, The Making of the New Testament Documents*, 1994; C. J. Hemer, *The Book of Acts in the Setting of Hellenistic History*, 1989; M. Hengel, *The Son of God*, 1976; *idem, The Pre-Christian Paul*, 1991; O. Hofius, *Paulusstudien*, 1989; R. P. Martin, *The Spirit and the Congregation*, 1984; E. R. Richards, *The Secretary in the Letters of Paul*, 1991; W. Schrage, *The Ethics of the New Testament*, 1988, pp. 163–278; P. Stuhlmacher, *Reconciliation, Law, and Righteousness*, 1986; P. J. Tomson, *Paul and the Jewish Law*, 1990; N. T. Wright, *The Climax of the Covenant*, 1991. E.E.E.

PAULUS, SERGIUS, more correctly **PAULLUS,** was the proconsul (Gk. *anthypatos*) of *Cyprus in AD 47/8 when the apostle Paul visited that island (Acts 13:7). His name suggests that he was a member of an old Roman senatorial family: if he was the L. Sergius Paullus mentioned in *CIL*, 6. 31545, he was one of the Curators of the Banks of the Tiber under Claudius. Another inscription (*IGRR*, 3. 930; *cf. EGT*, 2, 1900, p. 286) found in Cyprus refers to the proconsul *Paulos*, while an inscription discovered at Pisidian Antioch in honour of a L. Sergius Paullus, propraetor of Galatia in AD 72–4, is possibly a commemoration of his son.

B. van Elderen (in W. W. Gasque and R. P. Martin (eds.), *Apostolic History and the Gospel*, 1970, pp. 151–156) considers that the inscription *IGRR*, 3. 935 is more likely to refer to this proconsul. Commentators disagree over the reality of Paullus' profession of Christian faith. D.H.W.

PAVILION (Heb. *sōḵ*, *sukkâ*). A covered place, tent, booth or shelter, where a person or beast may hide or be sheltered. The same word is translated in AV as den (Ps. 10:9), tabernacle (Ps. 76:2), covert (Je. 25:38), booth (Jon. 4:5) and lodge (Is. 1:8), and thus represents something used by beasts, worshippers, travellers and soldiers. It is translated only six times in the AV as pavilion. In 1 Ki. 20:12, 16 it refers to the army tents in which Ben-hadad and his soldiers were resting and drinking when they were campaigning against Ahab. Such tents are illustrated on the sculptured reliefs of the Assyr. kings Shalmaneser III and Sennacherib (BM). The other uses of the word are metaphorical. It represents the place of divine protection in the day of trouble (Pss. 27:5; 31:20), or the place where God is hidden with dark waters and thick clouds for his pavilion (Ps. 18:11; 2 Sa. 22:12).

RSV translates a difficult phrase in Jb. 36:29 as 'the thunderings of his pavilion' (*sukkâ*, AV 'tabernacle'). NEB takes it differently: as the sky is sometimes described as God's tent, clouds, viewed from the earth, might appear as carpeting on the tent floor.

The term is also used for the bough shelters erected at the Feast of Booths (Tabernacles) commemorating the shelters in which Israel dwelt in the wilderness. In Ps. 19:5 the reference is to the canopy (RSV 'tent') under which a bridegroom stands with his bride on their wedding day.

For Egyp. data, *cf.* K. A. Kitchen, *THB* 5–6, 1960, pp. 7–11. J.A.T.

PEACE. Basically the OT word for peace, *šālôm*, means 'completeness', 'soundness', 'well-being'. (See *BDB*.) It is used when one asks of or prays for the welfare of another (Gn. 43:27; Ex. 4:18; Jdg. 19:20), when one is in harmony or concord with another (Jos. 9:15; 1 Ki. 5:12), when one seeks the good of a city or country (Ps. 122:6; Je. 29:7). It may mean material prosperity (Ps. 73:3) or physical safety (Ps. 4:8). But also it may mean spiritual well-being. Such peace is the associate of righteousness and truth, but not of wickedness (Ps. 85:10; Is. 48:18, 22; 57:19–21).

Because of the world's chaos through man's sin, and because peace comes only as God's gift, the Messianic hope was of an age of peace (Is. 2:2–4; 11:1–9; Hg. 2:7–9), or of the advent of the Prince of peace (Is. 9:6f.; *cf.* Je. 33:15f.; Ezk. 34:23ff.; Mi. 5:5; Zc. 9:9f.). The NT shows the fulfilment of this hope. In Christ peace has come (Lk. 1:79; 2:14, 29f.). By him it is bestowed (Mk. 5:34; Lk. 7:50; Jn. 20:19, 21, 26), and his disciples are its messengers (Lk. 10:5f.; Acts 10:36).

In classical Greek *eirēnē* had a primarily negative force; but by way of the LXX, the word in the NT has the full content of the OT *šālôm*, and nearly always carries a spiritual connotation. The breadth of its meaning is especially apparent from its linking with such keywords as grace (Rom. 1:7, *etc.*), life (Rom. 8:6), righteousness (Rom. 14:17), and from its use in benedictions such as 1 Thes. 5:23 and Heb. 13:20f. (*cf.* 2 Pet. 3:14).

For sinful man there must first be peace with God, the removal of sin's enmity through the sacrifice of Christ (Rom. 5:1; Col. 1:20). Then inward peace can follow (Phil. 4:7), unhindered by the world's strife (Jn. 14:27; 16:33). Peace between man and man is part of the purpose for which Christ died (Eph. 2) and of the Spirit's work (Gal. 5:22); but man must also be active to promote it (Eph. 4:3; Heb. 12:14), not merely as the elimination of discord, but as the harmony and true functioning of the body of Christ (Rom. 14:19; 1 Cor. 14:33).

BIBLIOGRAPHY. W. Foerster, G. von Rad, *TDNT* 2, pp. 400–420; D. Gillett, *Them* 1, 1976, pp. 80ff.; H. Beck, C. Brown, *NIDNTT* 2, pp. 776–783.

F.F.

PEDAIAH ('Yahweh has redeemed'). **1.** Father of Joel, ruler (under David) of Manasseh, W of the

Jordan (1 Ch. 27:20). **2.** Grandfather of King Jehoiakim (2 Ki. 23:36). **3.** Third son of King Jehoiachin (1 Ch. 3:18). According to 1 Ch. 3:19, he was called the father of Zerubbabel, who elsewhere is named as the son of Shealtiel, brother of Pedaiah. **4.** A son of Parosh, who helped to repair the wall of Jerusalem (Ne. 3:25). **5.** One who stood on Ezra's left when he read the law to the people (Ne. 8:4); perhaps identical with **4** above. **6.** A Levite appointed by Nehemiah to assist in distributing the tithes (Ne. 13:13). **7.** A Benjaminite (Ne. 11:7). J.D.D.

PEKAH (Heb. *peqaḥ*, 'opening'). Pekah, the son of Remaliah, was the 'third man' (Heb. *šālîšâ*) in Pekahiah's war chariot. With the help of Gileadites he murdered Pekahiah, successor of Menahem, at Samaria (2 Ki. 15:21ff.). He then seized the throne and reigned as king of Israel from *c.* 737 to 732 BC. His accession was in the 52nd year of Uzziah of Judah (v. 27), and in his 2nd year Jotham succeeded Uzziah (v. 32).

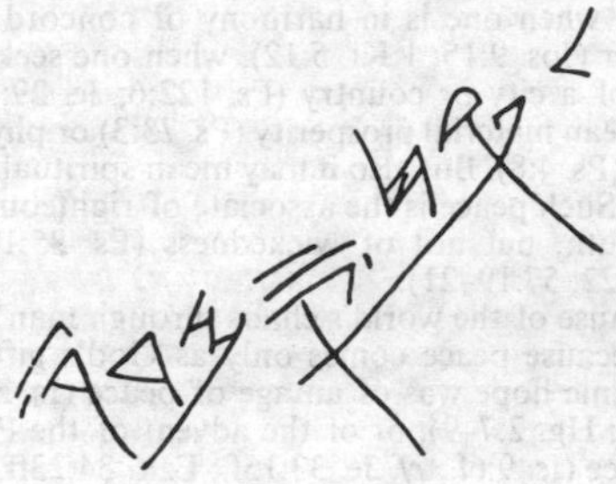

This Hebrew inscription from a fragment of a store-jar from Hazor reads 'For Peqah, Semader', probably a reference to Pekah, king of Israel, and to a type of oil. Stratum V A. 740–732 BC.

Pekah adopted an anti-Assyrian policy and allied himself to *Rezin of Syria. Together they brought pressure on Jotham of Judah, probably to join them (v. 37). Isaiah, however, advised him and his successor Ahaz to be neutral. Pekah moved in force against Jerusalem, which was unsuccessfully besieged (2 Ki. 16:5; Is. 7:1). His Syrian allies took Elath, while Pekah fought the Judaeans, slaying many and taking many prisoners from the Jericho district back to Samaria (2 Ch. 28:7–8). These were later released on the intercession of the prophet Oded (vv. 8–15).

Faced with this invasion Ahaz appealed for help to Tiglath-pileser III of Assyria, who was campaigning in Syria. In 732 BC the Assyrians captured Damascus and invaded N Israel. A list of the places invaded, as far S as Galilee, is given in 2 Ki. 15:25–29 and is partly paralleled by Tiglath-pileser's own Annals. Excavation at Hazor confirms the Assyrian destruction there at this time. A wine-jar inscribed *lpqḥ*, 'belonging to Pekah', was found among the objects from the period of Pekah's occupation.

Following the swift Assyrian invasion of more than half of Israel, Hoshea, son of Elah, conspired against Pekah, whom he slew. Since Tiglath-pileser claims in his Annals to have replaced Pekah (*Paqaḫa*) by Hoshea (*'Ausi*), it is clear that this act was approved, if not instigated, by the Assyrians. Pekah's reign was considered to have followed the evil tradition of Jeroboam (2 Ki. 15:28). D.J.W.

PEKAHIAH (Heb. *peqaḥyâ*, 'Yahweh has opened [his eyes]'). Son of *Menahem, king of Israel, whom he succeeded *c.* 742/1 BC (2 Ki. 15:23–26; *CHRONOLOGY OF THE OT). His assassination in the 2nd year of his reign suggests that he continued his father's policy of submission to Assyria. The revolutionaries, led by *Pekah son of Remaliah, may have been in league with *Rezin, king of Damascus, for they came from Gilead, adjacent to his territory. The king was killed while in the keep (Heb. *'armôn*) of the palace at *Samaria. The words 'with *Argob and Arieh' (2 Ki. 15:25) seem to have been transposed from v. 29. A.R.M.

PEKOD. A small *Aramaean tribe E of the lower Tigris. Akkadian sources record the temporary subjugation of *Puqūdu* under *Tiglath-pileser III (747–727 BC), *Sargon II (722–705 BC) and *Sennacherib (705–681 BC). Mentioned in Jeremiah's oracle against Babylon (50:21), Pekod is also among other Mesopotamian peoples who, though formerly lovers of Israel, will rise against Jerusalem (Ezk. 23:23). Eponymous for a city and irrigation system mentioned in TB (*Beṣah* 29a, *Kethuboth* 27b, *Ḥullin* 127a).

BIBLIOGRAPHY. S. Parpola, *Neo-Assyrian Toponyms*, 1970, pp. 280–281; M. Dietrich, *Die Aramäer Südbabyloniens*, 1970. D.W.B.

PELATIAH (Heb. *pelaṭyāh(û)*, 'Yahweh delivers'; Gk. *Phaltias*, *Phalettia*). **1.** A witness to the covenant in Ne. 10:22. This may well be the same man as the grandson of Zerubbabel, a descendant of Solomon (1 Ch. 3:21). **2.** A Simeonite captain who occupied ex-Amalekite territory (1 Ch. 4:42). **3.** A leader whom Ezekiel pictured as devising mischief and giving wicked counsel in Jerusalem. He fell dead while Ezekiel prophesied (Ezk. 11:1–13).

Names composed with element *plṭ* are attested from the Amorite period and were common at Ugarit (*RAS SHAMRA) in the 13th century BC as well as in later Aramaic (*e.g.* F. Gröndahl, *Personnamen der Texte aus Ugarit*, 1967, p. 173). D.J.W.

PELEG (Heb. *peleḡ*, 'water-course, division'). The son of Eber, brother of Yoqtan (*JOKTAN), and grandson of Shem (Gn. 10:25). In his time the earth was 'divided', the word used (*nip̄leḡâ*) being a play on, or explanation of, his name. This is commonly held to refer to the splitting up of the world's population into various geographical and linguistic groups (Gn. 11:1–9). It may equally well mark the development by the semi-nomad sons of *Ebel of cultivation, using artificial irrigation canals (Assyr. *plagu*); *peleḡ* is used in this sense in Is. 30:25, 32:2; Jb. 29:6; 38:25. Alternatively it may be a reference to division of territory by borders (Akk. *pulukku*; *JCS* 18, 1964, p. 69; *palāku*, 'to divide at borders'). Peleg was father of Reu (Gn. 11:19). D.J.W.

PELONITE. The name given to two of David's mighty men, Helez and Ahijah (1 Ch. 11:27, 36; 27:10). The former is described as the *Paltite in the parallel text, 2 Sa. 23:26, and the Syriac has this reading in 1 Ch. 11:27. In view of 2 Sa. 23:34 some commentators prefer to emend 1 Ch. 11:36b to 'Eliam the son of Ahithophel the Gilonite'.

R.A.H.G.

PENTATEUCH. The first five books of the OT (Gn., Ex., Lv., Nu., Dt.) constitute the first and most important section of the threefold Jewish *Canon. Usually called by the Jews *sēp̄er hattôrâ*, 'the book of the law', or *hattôrâ*, 'the law' (see *KB*, p. 403, for suggested derivations of the word, which seems to mean basically 'teaching' or 'instruction'), the Pentateuch (Gk. *pentateuchos*, 'five-volumed [*sc.* book]') is also known as the 'five-fifths of the law'. For the past century or so, many higher critics, following the lead of Alexander Geddes (*c.* 1800), have tended to disregard the traditional five-book division in favour of a Hexateuch comprising the Pentateuch and Joshua (*cf.* J. Wellhausen, *Die Composition des Hexateuchs*, 1876–7). On the other hand, I. Engnell has suggested the word 'Tetrateuch' to separate Deuteronomy from the first four books (*Gamla Testamentet*, 1, 1945). The critical presuppositions which underlie these suggestions are evaluated below.

The antiquity of the fivefold division is attested by the Samaritan Pentateuch and the LXX, which gave the books their traditional names; the Jews identify them by the first word or phrase. The divisions between the books were determined both by topical and practical considerations: papyrus scrolls could contain only about one-fifth of the *tôrâ*. Jewish tradition prescribes that a section of the Law be read weekly in the synagogue. Three years were required for the completion of the Pentateuch in Palestine; the modern lectionary, in which the Pentateuch is read through in one year, is derived from that used in Babylonia. It may well be that a psalm was read along with the traditional reading from the prophetic writings (*hap̣ṭārâ*). The five books of the Psalter are probably patterned after the Pentateuch (*cf.* N. H. Snaith, *Hymns of the Temple*, 1951, pp. 18–20).

References to the Pentateuch in the OT are largely restricted to the writings of the Chronicler, who uses several designations: the law (Ezr. 10:3; Ne. 8:2, 7, 14; 10:34, 36; 12:44; 13:3; 2 Ch. 14:4; 31:21; 33:8); the book of the law (Ne. 8:3); the book of the law of Moses (Ne. 8:1); the book of Moses (Ne. 13:1; 2 Ch. 25:4; 35:12); the law of the Lord (Ezr. 7:10; 1 Ch. 16:40; 2 Ch. 31:3; 35:26); the law of God (Ne. 10:28–29); the book of the law of God (Ne. 8:18); the book of the law of the Lord (2 Ch. 17:9; 34:14); the book of the law of the Lord their God (Ne. 9:3); the law of Moses the servant of God (Dn. 9:11; *cf.* Mal. 4:4). One cannot say for certain whether references to the law in the historical writings refer to the Pentateuch as a whole or to parts of the Mosaic legislation, *e.g.* the law (Jos. 8:34); the book of the law (Jos. 1:8; 8:34; 2 Ki. 22:8); the book of the law of Moses (Jos. 8:31; 23:6; 2 Ki. 14:6); the book of the law of God (Jos. 24:26).

The NT uses similar designations: the book of the law (Gal. 3:10); the book of Moses (Mk. 12:26); the law (Mt. 12:5; Lk. 16:16; Jn. 7:19); the law of Moses (Lk. 2:22; Jn. 7:23); the law of the Lord (Lk. 2:23–24). The descriptions of the Pentateuch in both Testaments serve to emphasize its divine and human authorship, its binding authority as *the law*, and its inscripturated form in *the book*.

I. Contents

The Pentateuch narrates God's dealings with the world, and especially the family of Abraham, from creation to the death of Moses. There are six main divisions. First, the origin of the world and of the nations (Gn. 1–11). This section describes the *creation, the Fall of man, the beginnings of civilization, the Flood, the Table of the Nations and the tower of Babel. Secondly, the patriarchal period (Gn. 12–50) depicts the call of Abraham, the initiation of the Abrahamic covenant, the lives of Isaac, Jacob and Joseph, and the settling of the covenant-clan in Egypt. Thirdly, Moses and the Exodus from Egypt (Ex. 1–18). Fourthly, legislation at Sinai (Ex. 19:1–Nu. 10:10), which includes the giving of the law, the building of the tabernacle, the establishment of the levitical system and the final preparations for the journey from Sinai to Canaan. Fifthly, the wilderness wanderings (Nu. 10:11–36:13). This section describes the departure from Sinai, the acceptance of the majority report of the spies, God's consequent judgment, the encounter with Balaam, the appointment of Joshua as Moses' successor and the apportionment of the land to the twelve tribes. Sixthly, the final speeches of Moses (Dt. 1–34) recapitulate the Exodus events, repeat and expand the Sinaitic commandments, clarify the issues involved in obedience and disobedience, and bless the tribes, who are poised to enter Canaan. This section ends with the cryptic description of Moses' death and burial.

II. Authorship and unity

For centuries both Judaism and Christianity accepted without question the biblical tradition that Moses wrote the Pentateuch. Ben-Sira (Ecclus. 24:23), Philo (*Life of Moses* 3. 39), Josephus (*Ant.* 4. 326), the Mishnah (*Pirqê Abôth* 1. 1), and the Talmud (*Baba Bathra* 14b) are unanimous in their acceptance of the Mosaic authorship. The only debate centred in the account of Moses' death in Dt. 34:5ff. Philo and Josephus affirm that Moses described his own death, while the Talmud (*loc. cit.*) credits Joshua with eight verses of the *tôrâ*, presumably the last eight.

a. Pentateuchal criticism before AD *1700*

The tradition expressed in 2 Esdras 14:21–22, that the scrolls of the Pentateuch, burned in Nebuchadrezzar's siege of Jerusalem, were rewritten by Ezra, was apparently accepted by a number of the early church Fathers, *e.g.* Irenaeus, Tertullian, Clement of Alexandria, Jerome. They did not, however, reject the Mosaic authorship of the original law. The first recorded instance of such a rejection is the statement of John of Damascus concerning the Nasaraeans, a sect of Jewish Christians (*cf. PG* 94. 688–689). The *Clementine Homilies* teach that diabolical interpolations were made in the Pentateuch to try to put Adam, Noah and the Patriarchs in a bad light. Any passage out of harmony with the Ebionite assumptions of the author was suspected in this early attempt at higher criticism. Among the stumbling-blocks to the faith which Anastasius the Sinaite, patriarch of Antioch (7th century AD), attempted to remove were questions dealing with the Mosaic authorship of, and alleged discrepancies in, Genesis (*cf. PG* 89. 284–285).

During the mediaeval era, Jewish and Muslim scholars began to point out supposed contradictions and anachronisms in the Pentateuch. For instance, Ibn Ezra (d. 1167), following a suggestion of Rabbi Isaac ben Jasos (d. 1057) that Gn. 36 was written not earlier than Jehoshaphat's reign because of the mention of Hadad (*cf.* Gn. 36:35; 1 Ki. 11:14), maintained that such passages as Gn. 12:6; 22:14; Dt. 1:1; 3:11 were interpolations.

The Reformer A. B. Carlstadt (1480–1541), observing no change in the literary style of Deuteronomy before and after Moses' death, denied that Moses wrote the Pentateuch. A Belgian Roman Catholic, Andreas Masius, produced a commentary on Joshua (1574) in which he credited Ezra with certain pentateuchal interpolations. Similar positions were maintained by two Jesuit scholars, Jacques Bonfrère and Benedict Pereira. Two famous philosophers helped to pave the way for modern higher critics by voicing in their widely circulated writings some of the contemporary criticisms of the unity of the law: Thomas Hobbes (*Leviathan*, 1651) credited Moses with everything attributed to him in the Pentateuch, but suggested that other parts were written more about Moses than by him; Benedict Spinoza (*Tractatus Theologico-politicus*, 1670) carried the observations of Ibn Ezra farther by noting doublets and alleged contradictions, and concluding that Ezra, who himself wrote Deuteronomy, compiled the Pentateuch from a number of documents (some Mosaic). 17th-century criticism of the Pentateuch was climaxed in the works of the Roman Catholic Richard Simon and the Arminian Jean LeClerc in 1685. LeClerc replied to Simon's view that the Pentateuch was a compilation based on many documents, both of divine and human origin, by asserting that the author must have lived in Babylonia between 722 BC and Ezra's time.

b. Pentateuchal criticism from AD 1700 to 1900

(i) *The question of Mosaic authorship.* Despite the questions raised by Catholics, Protestants and Jews in the period discussed above, the vast multitude of scholars and laymen clung firmly to belief in the Mosaic authorship. A milestone in pentateuchal criticism was reached in 1753, when the French physician Jean Astruc published his theory that Moses had composed Genesis from two main ancient *mémoires* and a number of shorter documents. The clue to the identification of the two *mémoires* was the use of the divine names: one employed *Elohim*; the other, *Yahweh.* Astruc maintained the Mosaic authorship of Genesis, but posited his theory of multiple sources to account for some of the repetitions and alleged discrepancies which critics had noted. J. G. Eichhorn (*Einleitung*, 1780–83) expanded Astruc's views into what is called 'the early documentary theory'. Abandoning the Mosaic authorship, he credited the final editing of the Elohistic and Yahwistic documents of Genesis and Ex. 1–2 to an unknown redactor. K. D. Ilgen (*Die Urkunden des Jerusalemischen Tempelarchivs in ihrer Urgestalt*, 1798) carried the documentary theory a step farther when he discovered in Gn. 17 independent sources traceable to three authors, two of whom use *Elohim* and the other *Yahweh.*

A Scottish Roman Catholic priest, Alexander Geddes, pursued Astruc's identification of several *mémoires* and developed (between 1792 and 1800) the *fragmentary theory* which holds that the Pentateuch was composed by an unknown redactor from a number of fragments which had originated in two different circles—one Elohistic, the other Yahwistic. Two German scholars embraced and expanded the fragmentary theory: J. S. Vater (*Commentar über den Pentateuch*, 3 vols., 1802–5) tried to trace the growth of the Pentateuch from over thirty fragments; W. M. L. De Wette (*Beiträge zur Einleitung in das Alte Testament*, 1807) stressed the comparatively late nature of much of the legal material and, significantly for later research, identified Josiah's book of the law as Deuteronomy (in this identification he had been anticipated by Jerome 1,400 years earlier).

De Wette's emphasis on one basic document augmented by numerous fragments was developed by H. Ewald, who in 1831 suggested that the chief document was the Elohistic source which carried the narrative from the creation into the book of Joshua and was supplemented by the account of the Yahwist, who was also the final redactor. Though Ewald later retreated from this 'supplementary theory', it survived in the writings of F. Bleek (*de libri Geneseos origine*, 1836) and F. Tuch (*Genesis*, 1838).

The 'new documentary theory' was fathered by H. Hupfeld (*Die Quellen der Genesis und die Art ihrer Zusammensetzung*, 1853), who, like Ilgen, found three separate sources in Genesis—the original Elohist (E^1), the later Elohist (E^2), and the Yahwist (J). A year later, when E. Riehm published his *Die Gesetzgebung Mosis im Lande Moab* in 1854, which purported to demonstrate the independent character of Deuteronomy, the four major documents had been isolated and dated in the order E^1, E^2, J, D.

K. H. Graf (in 1866) developed the suggestion of E. G. Reuss, J. F. L. George and W. Vatke and affirmed that E^1 (called P for Priestly Code by modern scholars), rather than being the earliest of the documents, was the latest. The debate then centred in the question as to whether E^2(E)JDP(E^1) or JEDP was the proper chronological order. A. Kuenen's work, *The Religion of Israel* (1869–70), assured the triumph of the latter order and set the stage for the appearance of the star actor in the drama of pentateuchal criticism, Julius Wellhausen.

(ii) *Wellhausen's views.* Wellhausen's important publications from 1876 to 1884 gave the documentary theory its most cogent and popular setting. Stated simply, this theory holds that J (*c.* 850 BC) and E (*c.* 750 BC) were combined by a redactor (R^{JE}) about 650 BC. When D (the Deuteronomic laws, *c.* 621) was added by R^D (*c.* 550) and P (*c.* 500–450) by R^P *c.* 400 BC, the Pentateuch was basically complete. In Wellhausen's presentation more was involved than mere documentary analysis. He linked his critical studies to an evolutionary approach to Israel's history which minimized the historicity of the patriarchal period and tended to detract from Moses' prominence. The religion of Israel advanced from the simple sacrifices on family altars in the days of the settlement to the intricately legalistic structure of Leviticus (P), which stemmed from Ezra's era (*PRIESTS AND LEVITES). Similarly, Israel's concept of God evolved from the animism and polytheism of the patriarchal days, through the henotheism of

Moses' time and the ethical monotheism of the 8th-century prophets to the sovereign Lord of Is. 40ff.

So fundamental for later scholarship were Wellhausen's ideas that his influence in biblical studies has frequently been likened to Darwin's in the natural sciences. Largely through the writings of W. Robertson Smith and S. R. Driver, Wellhausen's documentary analysis gained a widespread acceptance throughout the English-speaking world. The following summary (somewhat oversimplified) outlines the basic characteristics of the pentateuchal documents according to the Wellhausenian school.

The *Yahwist's narrative* (J) is said to date from early in the Monarchy (*c.* 950–850 BC). Allusions to territorial expansion (Gn. 15:18; 27:40) and the ascendancy of Judah (Gn. 49:8–12) allegedly point to a Solomonic date. The J document tells the story of God's dealings with man from the creation of the universe to Israel's entry of Canaan. The combination of majesty and simplicity found in J marks it as an outstanding example of epic literature worthy of comparison with Homer's *Iliad.* Originating in Judah, the Yahwist document has some distinctive literary traits in addition to the preference for the name Yahweh: *šip̄ḥâ*, 'maidservant', is preferred to *'āmâ* (E); Sinai is used instead of Horeb (E); popular etymologies occur frequently, *e.g.* Gn. 3:20; 11:9; 25:30; 32:27.

Intensely nationalistic, the J narrative records in detail the exploits of the patriarchal families, even those that are not particularly praiseworthy. Theologically J is noted for its anthropopathisms and anthropomorphisms. God in quasi-human form walks and talks with men, although his transcendence is never doubted. The transparent biographies of the Patriarchs, deftly and simply narrated, are an outstanding feature of J.

The *Elohist's narrative* (E) is usually dated about a century after J, *i.e.* 850–750 BC. A N (Ephraimitic) origin for E has been suggested on the basis of the omission of the stories of Abraham and Lot, which centre in Hebron and the Cities of the Plain, and the special emphasis given to Bethel and Shechem (Gn. 28:17; 31:13; 33:19–20). Joseph, the ancestor of the N tribes Ephraim and Manasseh, plays a prominent role. More fragmentary than J, E nevertheless has its own stylistic peculiarities: 'the River' is the Euphrates; repetition is used in direct address (*cf.* Gn. 22:11: Ex. 3:4); 'Here am I' (*hinnēnî*) is used in replies to the Deity.

Though less noteworthy as a literary composition than J, the E document is noted for its moralistic and religious emphases. Sensitive to the sins of the Patriarchs, E attempts to rationalize them, while the anthropomorphisms of J are replaced by divine revelations through dreams and angelic mediation. An outstanding contribution of E is the story of God's testing of Abraham in the command to sacrifice Isaac (Gn. 22:1–14). With powerful simplicity the picture of conflict between love of family and obedience to God is painted, and with prophetic force the lesson concerning the inwardness of true sacrifice is conveyed.

The *Deuteronomist document* (D), in Pentateuchal studies, corresponds roughly with the book of *Deuteronomy. Essential to the documentary hypothesis is the view that Josiah's book of the law (2 Ki. 22:3–23:25) was part, at least, of Dt. The correspondences between D and the terms of Josiah's reformation are noteworthy: the worship is centralized at Jerusalem (2 Ki. 23:4ff.; Dt. 12:1–7); acts of false worship are specifically forbidden (2 Ki. 23:4–11, 24; Dt. 16:21, 22; 17:3; 18:10, 11). D lays great stress on God's love for Israel and her obligation to respond, a philosophy of history which spells out the terms of God's blessing and judgment, and the necessity for a vigorous sense of social justice under the terms of the covenant. A collection of sermons rather than narratives, D is a collection of legal and hortatory materials compiled during the exigencies of Manasseh's reign and combined with JE after the time of Josiah.

The *Priestly document* (P) draws together laws and customs from various periods of Israel's history and codifies them in such a way as to organize the legal structure of post-exilic Judaism. P contains some narratives, but is more concerned with genealogies and the patriarchal origins of ritual or legal practices. Formal divisions such as the ten 'generations' of *Genesis and the covenants with Adam, Noah, Abraham and Moses are generally credited to P. The complexity of the legal and ritual structure of P is usually interpreted as a sign of a post-exilic date, especially when P (*e.g.* Ex. 25–31; 35–40; Lv.; the laws in Nu.) is compared with the simple ritualism of Jdg. and 1 Sa. As a literary document P cannot be compared with the earlier sources, because the penchant for laborious details (*e.g.* the genealogies and detailed descriptions of the tabernacle) tends to discourage literary creativity. The concern of the priestly movement for the holiness and transcendence of God reveals itself in P, where the entire legislation is viewed as a means of grace whereby God bridges the gap between himself and Israel.

c. Pentateuchal criticism after AD 1900

Documentary analysis did not stop with Wellhausen's researches. Rudolf Smend, expanding a suggestion made in 1883 by Karl Budde, attempted to divide the Yahwistic document into J^1 and J^2 throughout the Hexateuch (*Die Erzählung des Hexateuch auf ihre Quellen untersucht*, 1912). What Smend had called J^1, Otto Eissfeldt identified as a Lay-source (L), because it contrasts directly with the Priestly document and emphasizes the nomadic ideal in opposition to the Canaanite mode of life. Julian Morgenstern's *Kenite document (K), purportedly dealing with Moses' biography and the relations between Israel and the Kenites (*HUCA* 4, 1927, pp. 1–138), R. H. Pfeiffer's S (South or Seir) document in Genesis, corresponding somewhat to Eissfeldt's L (*ZAW* 48, 1930, pp. 66–73), and Gerhard von Rad's division of the priestly document into P^A and P^B (*Die Priesterschrift im Hexateuch*, 1934) are further refinements of a documentary criticism which had reached its extreme in the detailed dissections of P in B. Baentsch's work on Leviticus (1900), where seven main sources of P are further modified by the discovery of one or more redactors. This atomizing tendency is represented in the works of C. A. Simpson (notably *The Early Traditions of Israel: a Critical Analysis of the Pre-Deuteronomic Narrative of the Hexateuch*, 1948).

d. Reactions to the Graf–Wellhausen theory

Conservatives, convinced that their view of inspiration and the whole structure of theology built on it were at stake, joined battle almost immediately with pentateuchal critics. In the van of this reaction were E. W. Hengstenberg (*Dissertations on the Genuineness of the Pentateuch*, 1847) and C. F. Keil. After the appearance of Wellhausen's monumental synthesis the battle was continued by W. H. Green (*The Higher Criticism of the Pentateuch*, 1895) and James Orr (*The Problem of the Old Testament*, 1906), whose careful scrutiny of the documentary analyses found them wanting in terms of both literary evidence and theological presuppositions. The pattern set by these scholars was continued in the researches of R. D. Wilson (*A Scientific Investigation of the Old Testament*, 1926, reprinted 1959), G. Ch. Aalders (*A Short Introduction to the Pentateuch*, 1949), O. T. Allis (*The Five Books of Moses*, 1943) and E. J. Young (*IOT*, 1949).

(i) *The use of the divine names.* Conservative attacks on the Wellhausenian theory have generally taken shape along the following lines. The use of the divine names as a criterion for separating documents has been questioned at four points: (1) The evidence of textual criticism, especially from the Pentateuch of the LXX, suggests that there was less uniformity and more variety in early manuscripts of the Pentateuch than in the *MT*, which has traditionally been used as the basis of documentary analysis (although J. Skinner's *The Divine Names in Genesis*, 1914, has weakened the force of this argument).

(2) R. D. Wilson's study of the divine names in the Qur'an (*PTR* 17, 1919, pp. 644–650) brought to light the fact that certain suras of the Qur'an prefer *Allah* (4; 9; 24; 33; 48, *etc.*), while others prefer *Rab* (18; 23; 25–26; 34, *etc.*), just as certain sections of Genesis use *Elohim* (*e.g.* Gn. 1:1–2:3; 6:9–22; 17:2ff., 20, *etc.*) and others *Yahweh* (*e.g.* Gn. 4; 7:1–5; 11:1–9; 15; 18:1–19:28, *etc.*), although there is no support among scholars for a documentary approach to Qur'anic studies based on the divine names.

(3) The use of *Yahweh Elohim* (Gn. 2:4–3:24; *cf.* also Ex. 9:30) presents a special problem for the Wellhausen theory, since it involves a combining of the names which are supposed to be clues to separate documents; the LXX contains many more instances of this combination (*e.g.* Gn. 4:6, 9; 5:29; 6:3, 5), while there is ample evidence of compound names for deities in Ugaritic, Egyp. and Gk. literature (*cf.* C. H. Gordon in *Christianity Today*, 23 Nov. 1959).

(4) It is likely that the interchange of Yahweh and Elohim in the Pentateuch reflects an attempt on the part of the author to stress the ideas associated with each name (*cf.* I. Engnell, *Gamla Testamentet*, 1, 1945, pp. 194ff.). These and similar problems pertaining to the divine names have long since caused documentary critics to minimize what was once the starting-point of the whole process of documentary analysis.

(ii) *Diction and style.* Differences in diction and style, an important link in the chain of evidence for the Wellhausen theory, have been called into question by a number of conservatives. Stress has been laid on the fact that the pentateuchal stories are too fragmentary to give an adequate sampling of an author's vocabulary and that insufficient attention has sometimes been given to the fact that different types of literature call for differing vocabularies. Words supposedly peculiar to one document are sometimes credited to a redactor when they occur in another source. This use of a redactor when the facts call in question critical theories seems a somewhat too convenient method of dealing with difficulties. As for matters of style, conservatives and others have frequently pointed out the subjectivity in such judgments and the very great difficulty involved in subjecting such opinions to scientific examination. What seems to be a graphic, vibrant narrative to one critic may seem dull or turgid to another. W. J. Martin has highlighted some of the difficulties encountered by literary critics in his *Stylistic Criteria and the Analysis of the Pentateuch*, 1955, although caution is imperative in the use of analogies from western literary criticism for the study of oriental literature.

(iii) *Double narratives.* The occurrence of double narratives (sometimes called doublets) has been considered key evidence for a diversity of sources. Aalders (*op. cit.*, pp. 43–53) and Allis (*op. cit.*, pp. 94–110, 118–123) have examined a number of these repetitions (*e.g.* Gn. 1:1–2:4a; 2:4b–25; 6:1–8, 9–13; 12:10–20; 20; 26:6–11) and have sought to show that their presence in the text need not be interpreted as evidence for multiplicity of sources. On the contrary, repetition within Heb. prose may be connected with the characteristically Heb. (and indeed Semitic) use of repetition for emphasis. Ideas are underscored in Heb. literature not by the logical connection with other ideas but by a creative kind of repetition which seeks to influence the reader's will. (*Cf.* J. Muilenburg, 'A Study in Hebrew Rhetoric: Repetition and Style' in *VT Supp* 1, 1953, pp. 97–111; J. Pedersen, *Israel*, 1–2, 1926, p. 123.) Liturgical use may also help to account for repetition in both narrative and legislative portions of the Pentateuch.

So far as Gn. is concerned, a conservative contribution was made by P. J. Wiseman in *New Discoveries in Babylonia about Genesis*, 1936; rev. ed., *Clues to Creation in Genesis*, 1977. He suggested that the *tôlēḏôt* passages (those beginning or ending with some such phrase as 'These are the generations . . .') mark the various sources available to Moses for compiling earlier narratives. This approach was popularized by J. Stafford Wright in *How Moses Compiled Genesis: A Suggestion*, 1946. For replies to the Wellhausenian theory of the development of the levitical system, see *Priests and Levites.

Conservatives have been quick to draw upon the conclusions of non-conservatives when these conclusions tended to question the validity of the documentary hypothesis. The sustained attack on the theories of Wellhausenians by B. D. Eerdmans is a case in point. Though denying the Mosaic authorship of the Pentateuch, Eerdmans staunchly defended the basic authenticity of the patriarchal narratives and affirmed his confidence in the antiquity of the ritual institutions of P. Further, T. Oestreicher and A. C. Welch endeavoured to tumble the documentary theory by removing the keystone —the identification of D with Josiah's book of the law. E. Robertson (*The Old Testament Problem*, 1950) regards Dt. as having been compiled under Samuel's influence as a law-book for 'all Israel', as having fallen into disuse when the disruption of the nation made its application impossible, and as having been opportunely rediscovered in Josiah's reign at a time when it was possible to treat 'all Israel' as a religious unit once more. The Decalogue and the Book of the Covenant, with which the Hebrews entered Canaan, were preserved in the early days of the settlement at various local sanctuaries, where they gathered around themselves bodies of divergent though related laws and traditions; the beginnings of national reunion in Samuel's day necessitated the compilation, on the basis of this material, of a law-book for the central administration. R. Brinker, a pupil of E. Robertson, elaborated certain aspects of this theory in *The Influence of Sanctuaries in Early Israel*, 1946. Using linguistic and stylistic criteria, U. Cassuto (*La Questione della Genesi*, 1934) argued for the unity of Gn., while F. Dornseiff (*ZAW* 52–53, 1934–5) defended the literary unity of the whole Pentateuch; *cf.* his *Antike und Alter Orient*, 1956.

From another angle A. R. Johnson warns us against what 'seems to be a real danger in OT study as a whole of misinterpreting what may be different but contemporary *strata* in terms of corresponding *stages* of thought, which can be arranged chronologically so as to fit into an over-simplified evolutionary scheme or similar theory of progressive revelation' (*The Vitality of the Individual in the Thought of Ancient Israel*, 1949, p. 3).

(iv) *Form criticism.* While not abandoning the documentary hypothesis, the pioneer form critics, H. Gunkel and H. Gressmann, laid stress both on the literary qualities and on the lengthy process of oral tradition which had shaped the various narratives into aesthetic masterpieces. This welcome relief from the coldly analytical approach of the documentary critics, who in their detailed dissection of the Pentateuch tended to neglect the power and beauty of the stories, paved the way for the researches of a group of Scandinavian scholars who have discarded the documentary approach in favour of an emphasis on oral tradition. Following the lead of J. Pedersen who in 1931 formally rejected the documentary theory (*ZAW* 49, 1931, pp. 161–181), I. Engnell (*Gamla Testamentet*, 1, 1945) affirmed that, far from being the result of the compilation of written documents, the Pentateuch is a combination of reliable oral traditions collected and shaped in two main traditionist circles: a 'P-circle' responsible for the Tetrateuch and a 'D-circle' which formulated Dt., Jos., Jdg., Sa. and Ki. The actual writing of the books is relegated to exilic or post-exilic times. Key factors in the development of this traditio-historical school are the advanced knowledge of Heb. psychology and the growing understanding of ancient oriental literature. According to Engnell, the devotees of the Wellhausenian approach tend to interpret the OT in terms of European literary methods and western logic. See Eduard Nielsen, *Oral Tradition*, 1954, for a concise presentation of the views of the Scandinavian School.

As H. Gunkel's preoccupation with the various literary units (identifiable by literary *form* within the Pentateuch) represented a kind of return to the *fragmentary* approach of Geddes, Vater and De Wette, so P. Volz (and to some extent W. Rudolph) called for a revival of a *supplementary* hypothesis by minimizing the importance of the Elohist, who is at the most, in Volz's view, a later editor of the great author of Gn., the Yahwist. In somewhat similar fashion G. von Rad (*The Problem of the Hexateuch and Other Essays*, E.T. 1966) has stressed the dominant role played by the Yahwist as both collector and author of the pentateuchal materials which took shape over a lengthy period of time and have a rich history of tradition behind them. The generally accepted dates for the documents are highly tentative, according to von Rad, and represent the final stages in compiling the materials.

The theological application of von Rad's theories of the Pentateuch is to be found in his *Old Testament Theology*, 1, E.T. 1962. His theory that the Pentateuch developed around Israelite creeds like Dt. 26:5ff. has recently been turned around with the suggestion that the creeds are not the source of the pentateuchal narrative but its summary (J. A. Soggin, *IOT*, E.T. 1976, p. 93).

M. Noth (*The Laws in the Pentateuch, and Other Essays*, E.T. 1966) has approximated some of the results of the Uppsala school of Engnell *et al.* without abandoning a documentary approach. Rather, he has paid close attention to the history of the oral traditions which lie behind the documents, while maintaining an approach to J, E and P which is quite conventional. Perhaps his divergence from the Wellhausenian tradition is best seen in his refusal to recognize a 'Hexateuch' and his removal of most of Dt. from the province of pentateuchal criticism.

In general, contemporary scholars are paying more attention to the forms of narrative, liturgical, contractual or legislative material than they are to the alleged sources of the documentary hypothesis, as recent introductions to the OT indicate. *Cf.* O. Kaiser, *IOT*, E.T. 1975, who lists the following chapter titles: Literary Types of Israelite Narrative, Literary Types of Israelite Law, The Growth of the Pentateuchal Narrative at the Pre-Literary Stage; also J. A. Soggin, *op. cit.* The precise relationship of form criticism to the more traditional source criticism is still under debate. What is clear is that much more attention must be paid to redaction criticism, the study of the import and thrust of the five individual books and the Pentateuch as a whole, whatever their process of composition may have been.

(v) *The evidence of archaeology.* The march of modern archaeology has contributed to the re-evaluation of the documentary hypothesis. The basic reliability of the historical narratives has been confirmed time and again, especially in the patriarchal period. (See H. H. Rowley, 'Recent Discovery and the Patriarchal Age' in *The Servant of the Lord*[2], 1965.) The evolutionary reconstruction of Israel's history and religion has been questioned more than once by outstanding archaeologists such as W. F. Albright (*e.g. From the Stone Age to Christianity*, 1957, pp. 88ff., 282) and C. H. Gordon (*e.g. Ugaritic Literature*, 1949, pp. 5–7; 'Higher Critics and Forbidden Fruit', *Christianity Today*, 23 Nov. 1959). A drastic re-appraisal of the documentary hypothesis from the standpoint of Israel's religion is found in the researches of Yehezkel Kaufmann, who affirms the antiquity of P and its priority to D. Furthermore, he separates Gn. from the rest of the Pentateuch, maintaining that it is 'a stratum in itself whose material is on the whole most ancient' (*The Religion of Israel*, 1960, p. 208).

e. The position today

The insights gained from these criticisms of the Graf–Wellhausen hypothesis, together with the continuing researches of its exponents, have resulted in considerable modification of the old theory. The simple evolutionary views of Israel's history and religion have been cast aside. The basic authenticity of the patriarchal stories is recognized by many scholars, since the light of archaeology has illuminated the setting of these stories. The Egyp. *milieu* of the Joseph cycle and the Exodus account has been established by archaeological, literary and linguistic considerations (*cf.* A. S. Yahuda, *The Language of the Pentateuch in its Re-*

lation to Egyptian, 1931; C. H. Gordon, *The World of the Old Testament*, 1958, p. 139). The role of *Moses as the great lawgiver and the dominant figure in Israel's religion has been reaffirmed.

Though not discarded, the documentary theory has been modified by contemporary scholars. The development of each document is exceedingly complex and is generally considered to represent a whole 'school' rather than a single author. The growth of the various documents is not consecutive but parallel, since there are ancient elements found in each, as the use of pentateuchal elements by the prophets indicates (*cf.* Aalders, *op. cit.*, pp. 111–138). Minute dissections of verses and positive assignment of their parts to diverse sources have generally been abandoned. These modifications in the documentary hypothesis should be viewed by conservatives as a medical chart, not as an obituary. The Wellhausenian theory is still very much alive and remains a constant challenge to conservative scholarship, which has sometimes been content to take comfort in the reactions against the documentary hypothesis without producing a thorough introduction to the Pentateuch, which states positively the evidence for the basic unity of the law while taking into full consideration the indications of diversity on which the documentary theory is based. Our increased knowledge of Middle Eastern literature—thanks to discoveries in *Mari, *Nuzi, *Ugarit, Hatti, *Sumer and *Egypt—should be of measurable help in this task. Since the texts from *Ebla (Tell Mardikh) seem to be contemporary with the earlier chapters of biblical history, they are likely to illuminate both the literature of the Pentateuch and its cultural background.

Aalders' studies have broken fresh ground and point the way for further advance. Of particular interest are his recognition of post-Mosaic and non-Mosaic elements in the Pentateuch (*e.g.* Gn. 14:14; 36:31; Ex. 11:3; 16:35; Nu. 12:3; 21:14–15; 32:34ff.; Dt. 2:12; 34:1–12) and his awareness of the fact that neither Testament ascribes the entire work to Moses, although both attribute substantial parts of it to him. The great legal codes, for instance, are credited specifically to Moses (*e.g.* Ex. 20:2–23:33; 34:11–26; Dt. 5–26; *cf.* Dt. 31:9, 24), as is the Israelites' itinerary mentioned in Nu. 33:2. As far as the Gn. stories are concerned, Moses may or may not have been the one who compiled them from their written and oral forms. The evidences of post-Mosaic editing of the Pentateuch are found in the references cited above, and especially in the mention of such ancient documents as 'the Book of the Wars of the Lord' (Nu. 21:14). It is difficult to date the final redaction of the Pentateuch. Aalders' suggestion that it took place some time within the reigns of Saul and David is credible, although some further allowance should probably be made for the modernizing of vocabulary and style.

III. The religious message of the Pentateuch

'*The Pentateuch must be defined as a document which gives Israel its understanding, its aetiology of life.* Here, through narrative, poetry, prophecy, law, God's will concerning Israel's task in the world is revealed' (A. Bentzen, *IOT*[2], 1952, 2, p. 77). A record of revelation and response, the Pentateuch testifies to the saving acts of God who is sovereign Lord of history and nature. The central act of God in the Pentateuch (and indeed the OT) is the *Exodus from Egypt. Here God broke in upon the consciousness of the Israelites and revealed himself as the redeeming God. Insights gained from this revelation enabled them under Moses' leadership to re-evaluate the traditions of their ancestors and see in them the budding of God's dealings which had bloomed so brilliantly in the liberation from Egypt.

Having powerfully and openly proved himself as Lord in the Exodus, God led the Israelites into the realization that he was the Creator and Sustainer of the universe as well as the Ruler of history. The order is important: a knowledge of the *Redeemer* led to a knowledge of the *Creator*; an understanding of the God of *grace* prompted an understanding of the God of *nature*. The display of control over nature apparent in the plagues, the crossing of the sea, and the sustenance in the wilderness may well have influenced the Israelites to view God as Lord of nature as well as of history.

God's grace is revealed not only in his deliverance and guidance, but in the giving of the law and the initiation of the covenant. Israel's pledge of obedience, her oath of loyalty to God and his will is her response; but even her response is a gift of God's grace, for it is he who, though free from obligation, has fixed the terms of the covenant and provided the sacrificial system as a means of spanning the gap between himself and his people. God's grace demands a total recognition of his Lordship, a complete obedience to his will in every sphere of life. This demand is gracious because it involves what is good for Israel, what will help her to realize her true potential, and what she could not discover without divine revelation.

Whatever the origin of the Pentateuch, it stands now as a document possessing a rich inner unity. It is the record of God's revelation in history and his Lordship over history. It testifies both to Israel's response and to her failure to respond. It witnesses to God's holiness, which separates him from men, and his gracious love, which binds him to them on his terms. (*GENESIS, *EXODUS, *LEVITICUS, *NUMBERS, *DEUTERONOMY.)

BIBLIOGRAPHY. J. Blenkinsopp, *The Pentateuch*, 1992; E. Carpenter, 'Pentateuch', *ISBE*[3], 1986, pp. 740–753; U. Cassuto, *The Documentary Hypothesis and the Composition of the Pentateuch*, E.T. 1961; D. Clines, *The Theme of the Pentateuch*, 1978; I. Engnell, *Critical Essays on the Old Testament*, 1970; K. Koch, *The Growth of the Biblical Tradition*, 1969; McCarthy, *Treaty and Covenant*, 1963; R. W. L. Moberly, *The Old Testament of the Old Testament*, 1992; J. A. Motyer, *The Revelation of the Divine Name*, 1959; C. R. North, 'Pentateuchal Criticism', *OTMS*, pp. 48–83; M. North, *The Laws in the Pentateuch and Other Essays*, 1966; M. Noth, *A History of Pentateuchal Traditions*, 1972; G. von Rad, *The Problem of the Hexateuch and Other Essays*, 1966; N. H. Ridderbos, 'Reversals of Old Testament Criticism', in C. F. H. Henry (ed.), *Revelation and the Bible*, 1958; H. H. Rowley, 'Moses and the Decalogue', *BJRL* 34, 1951, pp. 81–118; *idem, The Biblical Doctrine of Election*, 1950; R. de Vaux, *The Bible and the Ancient Near East*, 1971; R. N. Whybray, *The Making of the Pentateuch: A Methodological Study*, 1987.

D.A.H.

PENTECOST, FEAST OF. In Lv. 23:16 LXX reads *pentēkonta hēmeras* for the Heb. *ḥ[a]miššîm yôm*, 'fifty days', referring to the number of days from the offering of the barley sheaf at the beginning of the Passover. On the 50th day was the Feast of Pentecost. Since the time elapsed was 7 weeks, it was called *ḥag̱ šāḇuʿôṯ*, 'feast of weeks' (Ex. 34:22; Dt. 16:10). It marks the completion of the barley harvest, which began when the sickle was first put to the grain (Dt. 16:9), and when the sheaf was waved 'the morrow after the sabbath' (Lv. 23:11). It is also called *ḥag̱ haqqāṣîr*, 'feast of harvest', and *yôm habbikkûrîm*, 'day of the first fruits' (Ex. 23:16; Nu. 28:26). The feast is not limited to the times of the Pentateuch, but its observance is indicated in the days of Solomon (2 Ch. 8:13), as the second of the three annual festivals (*cf.* Dt. 16:16).

The feast was proclaimed as a 'holy convocation' on which no servile work was to be done, and at which every male Israelite was required to appear at the sanctuary (Lv. 23:21). Two baked loaves of new, fine, leavened flour were brought out of the dwellings and waved by the priest before the Lord, together with the offerings of animal sacrifice for sin-and peace-offerings (Lv. 23:17–20). As a day of joy (Dt. 16:16) it is evident that on it the devout Israelite expressed gratitude for the blessings of the grain harvest and experienced heartfelt fear of the Lord (Je. 5:24). But it was the thanksgiving and fear of a redeemed people, for the service was not without sin-and peace-offerings, and was, moreover, a reminder of their deliverance from Egypt (Dt. 16:12) as God's covenant people (Lv. 23:22). The ground of acceptance of the offering presupposes the removal of sin and reconciliation with God.

In the intertestamental period and later, Pentecost was regarded as the anniversary of the law-giving at Sinai (Jubilees 1:1 with 6:17; TB, *Pesaḥim* 68b; Midrash, *Tanḥuma* 26c). The Sadducees celebrated it on the 50th day (inclusive reckoning) from the first Sunday after Passover (taking the 'sabbath' of Lv. 23:15 to be the weekly sabbath); their reckoning regulated the public observance so long as the Temple stood, and the church is therefore justified in commemorating the first Christian Pentecost on a Sunday (Whit Sunday). The Pharisees, however, interpreted the 'sabbath' of Lv. 23:15 as the Festival of Unleavened Bread (*cf.* Lv. 23:7), and their reckoning became normative in Judaism after AD 70, so that in the Jewish calendar Pentecost now falls on various days of the week.

In the NT there are three references to Pentecost: (1) Acts 2:1 (Gk. *tēn hēmeran tēs pentēkostēs*). On this day, after the resurrection and ascension of Christ (*c.* AD 30), the disciples were gathered in a house in Jerusalem, and were visited with signs from heaven. The Holy Spirit descended upon them, and new life, power and blessing was evident, which Peter explained was in fulfilment of the prophecy of Joel. (2) Acts 20:16. Paul was determined not to spend time in Asia and made speed to be in Jerusalem by the day of Pentecost (AD 57). (3) 1 Cor. 16:8. Paul purposed to stay at Ephesus until Pentecost (AD 54 or 55), because an effectual door was opened to him for his ministry.

BIBLIOGRAPHY. Mishnah, *Menaḥoṯ* 10. 3; Tosefta, *Menaḥoṯ* 10. 23, 528; TB, *Menaḥoṯ* 65a; L. Finkelstein, *The Pharisees*, 1946, pp. 115ff. D.F.

PENUEL. 'The face of God' was the name that Jacob gave to the place where he crossed the Jabbok on his way back to meet Esau. It is possible that it had been called Penuel before, perhaps after a peculiarly shaped rock, and that Jacob endorsed the name as a result of his experience with the angel. The blessing which he sought (Gn. 32:26) materialized in Esau's conciliatory attitude (*cf.* 33:10: 'Truly to see your face is like seeing the face of God').

That Penuel was the site of an important pass is shown by the fact that a tower was built there, which Gideon destroyed after defeating the Midianites (Jdg. 8:8ff.), and Jeroboam rebuilt the city there, presumably to defend the invader's route from the E to his new capital at Shechem. The exact site is unknown, but S. Merrill, *East of Jordan*, 1881, pp. 390–392, makes a good case for the ancient ruins 6 km E of Succoth on two hills called Tulul ed-Dahab. J.B.J.

PEOPLE. 1. Heb. *lᵉʾôm*, occasionally sing., more frequently plur. *lᵉʾummîm*, may mean: (*i*) a race or ethnic aggregate (Gn. 25:23, sing. and plur.); (*ii*) the sum total of the populace subject to a ruler, the same concept from a different viewpoint (Pr. 14:28, sing.); (*iii*) the totality or a large section of an ethnic community considered as the vehicle of judgment and feeling (Pr. 11:26, sing.); (*iv*) exceptionally, the Jewish people (Is. 51:4, sing.); (*v*) frequently, in the plur., the non-Jewish nations (*e.g.* Is. 55:4).

2. Heb. *gôy*, 'nation', 'people', came by association rather than etymology to mean specifically the Gentiles; or, when applied to Israelites, to imply backsliding and religious unfaithfulness (Jdg. 2:20; Is. 1:4; *etc.*) The term is used in a vivid metaphor for a swarm of locusts in Joel 1:6. LXX regularly uses *ethnos* for *gôy*, yet NT sometimes uses *ethnos* for Israel, showing that these acquired associations cannot be pressed too rigidly.

3. With trifling exceptions (*cf.* Gn. 26:11, 'Philistines'; Ex. 9:15, 'Egyptians') Heb. *ʿam*, 'people', came to be applied fairly exclusively to Israel as the chosen race, but this meaning is acquired, not intrinsic. The LXX equivalent is *laos*. Further exceptions to Israelite reference are the metaphorical descriptions of ants and conies in community (Pr. 30:25f.). The unusual negative of Dt. 32:21, directly attached to the noun, denies to a flesh-and-blood people those spiritual characteristics which would justify their title (*cf.* 'Loammi', Ho. 1:9, AV). The biblical phrase *ʿam hāʾāreṣ* means in the earlier books the common people of the land, as distinct from the rulers and aristocracy. In the Ezra-Nehemiah period, the phrase sharpened to focus those Palestinians whose Judaism was mixed or suspect, with whom scrupulous Jews could not intermarry; *cf.* Ezr. 9:1–2, *etc.* In the rabbinic literature the term—now used in the sing. of an individual, in the plur. (*ʿammê hāʾāreṣ*) of a class—came to mean specifically all those who failed to observe the whole traditional law in all its details. A clear premonition of the rabbinic contempt for such persons is seen in Jn. 7:49.

4. The common NT equivalent to *ʿam* is *laos* or *dēmos*, as opposed to *ochlos*, which means merely a crowd. R.A.S.

PEOR. 1. A mountain somewhere to the N of the Dead Sea and opposite Jericho, described as looking towards the desert, but its location is not certainly identified. It was the last place from which Balaam blessed Israel (Nu. 23:28). See J. A. Jaussen-R. Savignac, *Mission en Arabie*, 1909, pp. 2, 650f.

2. The name of a deity, more fully Baal-peor, to which the Israelites were attracted (Nu. 25:3) and for the worship of which they were severely punished. Their punishment left a vivid impression and was recalled as a warning and example (Nu. 31:16; Dt. 4:3; Jos. 22:17). M.A.M.

PERAEA. A district in Transjordan, corresponding roughly to the *Gilead of the OT. It is never mentioned by name in the NT—that is left to Josephus—but is the district referred to several times (*e.g.* Mt. 19:1) as the land 'beyond Jordan'. The name Peraea came into use after the Exile, to denote an area E of the Jordan *c.* 16 km wide, stretching from the river Arnon in the S to some point between the Jabbok and the Yarmuk in the N. It comprised essentially the edge of the 1,000 m scarp overlooking the Jordan, with its towns, and was thus a highland region, with adequate (750 mm [30 in.]) per annum) rainfall and tree cover in its higher parts. At intermediate elevations there were olives and vines, and cultivation tailed off E through the wheatfields and then the steppe pastures of lower lands. It was evidently an attractive region in OT times, for after seeing it and adjacent areas the tribes of Gad and Reuben (Nu. 32:1–5) lost interest in crossing Jordan with their cattle.

In the time of Christ Peraea was occupied by Jews and ruled by Herod Antipas, and by Jews it was regarded as possessing equality of status with Judaea and Galilee. As it adjoined both of these across the Jordan, it was possible by traversing its length to follow an all-Jewish route from Galilee to Judaea, thus by-passing the territory of the Samaritans. J.H.P.

PERDITION (Gk. *apōleia*, 'loss', 'destruction'). A word employed in the NT, in the sense of 'destruction' and with special reference to the fate of the wicked and their loss of eternal life (Rev. 17:8, 11). (*HELL, *ESCHATOLOGY.)

In addition, the phrase 'son of perdition' occurs, a form of speech in which the Jews often expressed a man's destiny (*e.g.* 'sons of light', 'children of disobedience'; *cf.* Mt. 23:15; Lk. 10:6). It is applied to Judas Iscariot (Jn. 17:12) in a vivid sense which the Eng. does not fully convey as meaning literally 'not one perished but the son of perishing'. The term is used also by Paul to describe the 'man of lawlessness' (2 Thes. 2:3), for which see *Antichrist. The phrase 'sons of perdition' is found in *Jubilees* 10:3, with reference to those who perished in the Flood.

The Gk. word stands in direct antithesis to full and complete blessedness (*sōtēria*). J.D.D.

PEREZ, PEREZITES. Perez (Heb. *pereṣ*), one of the sons of Judah by Tamar his daughter-in-law (1 Ch. 2:4; 4:1), was so named because though his twin Zarah put out his hand first, Perez was the first delivered, and it was said that he had 'made a breach' (RSV) or 'broken forth' (AV) (*pāraṣ*; Gn. 38:29). He was the father of Hezron and Hamul (Gn. 46:12; Nu. 26:21; 1 Ch. 2:5), whose descendants were called Perezites (*parṣî*; Nu. 26:20; AV 'Pharzites'; see also Ne. 11:4, 6). Through him and Hezron passed the genealogy of the Messiah (1 Ch. 9:4; Ru. 4:18; Mt. 1:3; Lk. 3:33; *cf.* Ru. 4:12). The name occurs in LXX and NT as *Phares*, and this name is taken over unchanged into the AV NT. In the OT the AV gives 'Pharez' in all occurrences except 1 Ch. 27:3, and Ne. 11:4–6. In the later EVV the form Perez is used throughout. It may be compared with the Assyr. personal name *Parṣi* found in documents of the 8th century BC. See K. Tallqvist, *Assyrian Personal Names*, 1914, p. 180. T.C.M.

PERFECTION. The biblical idea of perfection is of a state of ideal wholeness or completion, in which any disabilities, shortcomings or defects that may have existed before have been eliminated or left behind.

In the OT, two Heb. roots express this idea: *šlm* and *tmm*. (For the literal sense of the adjective *šālēm*, see Dt. 25:15, RSV 'full', AV 'perfect'; 27:6, 'whole'; for that of *tāmîm*, see Lv. 3:9; 23:15.) In the NT the usual adjective (19 times) is *teleios* (noun *teleiotēs*, Col. 3:14; Heb. 6:1), which expresses the thought of having reached the appropriate or appointed *telos* ('end' in the sense of 'goal', 'purpose'). The corresponding verb, *teleioō* (16 times in this sense), means to bring into such a condition. In secular Greek *teleios* means also: (i) adult, full-grown, as opposed to immature and infantile, and (ii), in connection with mystery-cults, fully initiated. The former sense shines through in 1 Cor. 14:20; Eph. 4:13; Heb. 5:14; *cf.* 6:1; the latter in 1 Cor. 2:6 and perhaps Phil. 3:15; Col. 1:28. Two adjectives of similar meaning are: (i) *artios* (2 Tim. 3:17; AV 'perfect', RSV 'complete'), denoting ability and readiness to meet all demands made upon one, and (ii) *holoklēros* (Jas. 1:4, with *teleios*; 1 Thes. 5:23, RV 'entire', RSV 'sound'), for which Arndt gives 'whole, complete, undamaged, intact, blameless'. The NT also uses (7 times) the verb *katartizō*, translated 'perfect' in AV, meaning 'put in order', or 'bring to a fit state', by training, or supplying some lack, or correcting some fault.

Perfection is a relative term, meaning simply the attainment of a due end, or the enjoyment of an ideal state. What that end and state is varies in different cases. The Bible speaks of perfection in three distinct connections.

I. The perfection of God

Scripture speaks of God (Mt. 5:48), his 'work' (Dt. 32:4), his 'way' (2 Sa. 22:31 = Ps. 18:30), and his 'law' (Ps. 19:7; Jas. 1:25) as perfect. In each context some feature of his manifested moral glory is in view, and the thought is that what God says and does is wholly free from faults and worthy of all praise. In Mt. 5:48, Christ holds up the ideal conduct of the heavenly Father (particularly, in the context, his kindness to those who oppose him) as a pattern which his children must imitate.

II. The perfection of Christ

The writer to the Hebrews speaks of the incarnate Son of God as having been made 'perfect through sufferings' (Heb. 2:10). The reference here is not to any personal probation of Jesus as man, but to his being fitted by his experience of the power of temptation and the costliness of obedience for the high-priestly ministry to which God had called him (Heb. 5:7–10; *cf.* 7:28, RV). As high priest, having 'offered for all time a single sacrifice for sins' (Heb. 10:12), he became 'the source of eternal salvation to all who obey him' (Heb. 5:9), securing for them by his intercession constant access to God (Heb.

7:25; 10:19ff.) and giving them the constant sympathy and help that they need in their constant temptations (Heb. 4:14ff.). It was his own firsthand experience of temptation that fitted him to fulfil this latter ministry (Heb. 2:17f.; 5:2, 7ff.).

III. The perfection of man

This is spoken of with reference (*a*) to God's covenant relationship with man and (*b*) to his work of grace in man.

a. God's covenant relationship with man

The Bible speaks of *man's perfection in the covenant with God.* This is the perfection which the OT demands of God's people (Gn. 17:1; Dt. 18:13) and ascribes to individual saints (Noah, Gn. 6:9; Asa, 1 Ki. 15:14; Job, Jb. 1:1): loyal, sincere, wholehearted obedience to the known will of their gracious God. It is faith at work, maintaining a right relationship with God by reverent worship and service. This perfection is essentially a matter of the heart (1 Ki. 8:61; 2 Ki. 20:3; 1 Ch. 29:9); outward conformity to God's commands is not enough if the heart is not perfect (2 Ch. 25:2). Perfection is regularly linked with uprightness, as its natural outward expression (Jb. 1:1, 8; 2:3; Ps. 37:37; Pr. 2:21). In Mt. 19:21 *teleios,* as well as expressing the negative thought, 'lacking nothing', would seem to carry the positive meaning, 'sincerely and truly in covenant with God'.

The Bible also speaks of *God's perfecting of his covenant relation with man.* This is the perfecting of men through Christ with which the writer to the Hebrews deals. 'The perfecting of men refers to their covenant condition. . . . To perfect . . . is to put the People into the true covenant relation of worshippers of the Lord, to bring them into His full fellowship' (A. B. Davidson, *Hebrews*, p. 208). God did this by replacing the old covenant, priesthood, tabernacle and sacrifices by something better. The 'old covenant' in Hebrews means the Mosaic system for establishing living fellowship between God and his people; but, says the writer, it could never 'perfect' them in this relationship, for it could not give full assurance of the remission of all sins (Heb. 7:11, 18; 9:9; 10:1–4). Under the new covenant, however, on the ground of Christ's single sacrifice of himself, believers receive God's assurance that he will remember their sins no more (10:11–18). Thus they are 'perfected for ever' (v. 14). This perfection of fellowship with God is something that OT saints did not know on earth (11:40)—though, through Christ, they enjoy it now, in the heavenly Jerusalem (12:23f.).

b. God's work of grace in man

The Bible speaks of *God's perfecting of his people in the image of Christ.* God means those who through faith enjoy fellowship with him to grow from spiritual infancy to a maturity (perfection) in which they will lack nothing of the full stature of Christ, in whose likeness they are being renewed (Col. 3:10). They are to grow till they are, in this sense, complete (*cf.* 1 Pet. 2:2; Heb. 5:14; 6:1; Gal. 3:14; Eph. 4:13; Col. 4:12). This thought has both a corporate and an individual aspect: the church corporately is to become 'a perfect man' (Eph. 4:13; *cf.* 2:15; Gal. 3:28), and the individual Christian will 'be perfect' (Phil. 3:12). In either case the conception is Christological and eschatological. The realm of perfection is 'in Christ' (Col. 1:28), and perfection of fellowship with Christ, and likeness to Christ, is a divine gift that will not be enjoyed till the day of his coming, the church's completing, and the Christian's resurrection (*cf.* Eph. 4:12–16; Phil. 3:10–14; Col. 3:4; 1 Jn. 3:2). Meanwhile, however, mature and vigorous Christians may be said to have attained a relative perfection in the realms of spiritual insight (Phil. 3:15, *cf.* v. 12), tempered Christian character (Jas. 1:4) and confident love towards God and men (1 Jn. 4:12, 17f.).

The Bible nowhere relates the idea of perfection directly to law, nor equates it directly with sinlessness. Absolute sinlessness is a goal which Christians must seek (*cf.* Mt. 5:48; 2 Cor. 7:1; Rom. 6:19) but which they do not as yet find (Jas. 3:2; 1 Jn. 1:8–2:2). No doubt when the Christian is perfected in glory he will be sinless, but to equate the biblical idea of perfection with sinlessness and then to argue that, because the Bible calls some men perfect, therefore sinlessness on earth must be a practical possibility, would be to darken counsel. The present perfection which, according to Scripture, some Christians attain is a matter, not of sinlessness, but of strong faith, joyful patience, and overflowing love. (*SANCTIFICATION.)

BIBLIOGRAPHY. *BAGD; R. C. Trench, New Testament Synonyms*[10], 1880, pp. 74–77; B. B. Warfield, *Perfectionism*, 1, 1931, pp. 113–301; R. N. Flew, *The Idea of Perfection in Christian Theology*, 1934, pp. 1–117; V. Taylor, *Forgiveness and Reconciliation*, 1941, ch. v; commentaries on Hebrews by A. B. Davidson, 1882, pp. 207–209, and B. F. Westcott[3], 1903, pp. 64–68; J. Wesley, *A Plain Account of Christian Perfection*, 1777. J.I.P.

PERGA. An ancient city of unknown foundation in *Pamphylia; well sited in an extensive valley, watered by the Cestrus. It was the religious capital of Pamphylia, like Ephesus, a 'cathedral city' of Artemis, whose temple stood on a nearby hill. Like most cities on that pirate-ridden coast, Perga stands a little inland, and was served by a river-harbour. Attaleia, founded in the 2nd century BC, later served as Perga's port, but also absorbed her prosperity. Some ruins remain giving a pleasant impression of the ancient Perga, but Attaleia survives as an active port, the modern Adalia, one of the beauty-spots of Anatolia, so completely did Attalus' foundation overwhelm the more ancient towns. E.M.B.

PERGAMUM. A city of the Roman province of Asia, in the W of what is now Asiatic Turkey. It occupied a commanding position near the seaward end of the broad valley of the Caicus, and was probably the site of a settlement from a very early date. It became important only after 282 BC, when Philetaerus revolted against Lysimachus of Thrace and made it the capital of what became the Attalid kingdom, which in 133 BC was bequeathed by Attalus III to the Romans, who formed the province of *Asia from it. The first temple of the imperial cult was built in Pergamum (*c.* 29 BC) in honour of Rome and Augustus. The city thus boasted a religious primacy in the province, though *Ephesus became its main commercial centre.

Pergamum is listed third of the 'seven churches of Asia' (Rev. 1:11): the order suits its position in geographical sequence. This was the place 'where Satan's throne is' (Rev. 2:13). The phrase has been referred to the complex of pagan cults, of Zeus,

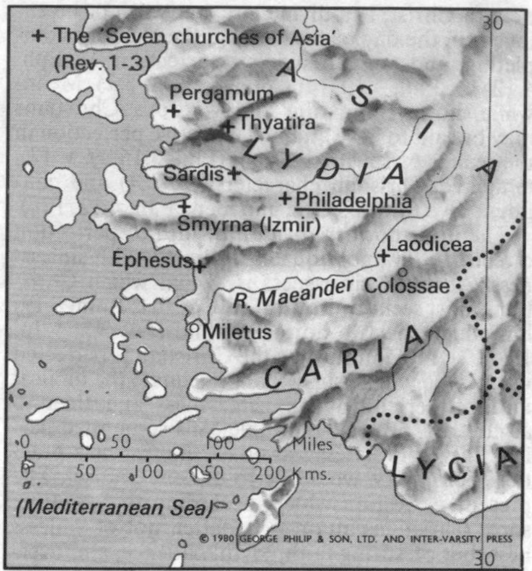

Pergamum, one of the 'seven churches of Asia' (Rev. 1–3).

Athena, Dionysus and Asclepius, established by the Attalid kings, that of Asclepius Soter (the 'saviour', 'healer') being of special importance. These cults are illustrative of the religious history of Pergamum, but the main allusion is probably to emperor worship. This was where the worship of the divine emperor had been made the touchstone of civic loyalty under Domitian. It marked a crisis for the church in Asia. Antipas (v. 13) is probably cited as a representative (perhaps the first) of those who were brought to judgment and execution here for their faith.

This letter is the primary source for the *Nicolaitans, who are emphatically equated with Balaam, and seem to be a party which advocated compromise under pagan pressures.

Here Christ possesses the real and ultimate authority, symbolized by the 'sharp two-edged sword' (v. 12), in the place where the Roman proconsul exercised the 'power of the sword' in judgment. The church is blamed for tolerating a party whose teaching would subvert it into idolatry and immorality like that of Balaam. But the 'conqueror' receives a pledge of Christ's inward relationship with him. The meaning of the 'white stone' (v. 17) is uncertain: it is properly a 'pebble' or *tessera* (tablet; Gk. *psēphos*). These had many uses, more than one of which may be apposite here. They represented acquittal, or served as a token or ticket of many kinds. The written name here is of the individual, and marks Christ's individual acceptance of the believer.

A small town (Bergama) still stands on the plain below the acropolis of the ancient city.

BIBLIOGRAPHY. C. J. Hemer, *The Letters to the Seven Churches of Asia in Their Local Setting*, 1986; E. M. Yamauchi, *New Testament Cities in Western Asia Minor*, 1980. M.J.S.R.
C.J.H.

PERIZZITES. These are mentioned: (1) among the occupants of Canaan generally (Gn. 15:20; Ex. 3:8; Dt. 7:1; 20:17; Jos. 3:10; 9:1; Jdg. 3:5; 1 Ki. 9:20; 2 Ch. 8:7; Ezr. 9:1; Ne. 9:8); (2) with the Jebusites, *etc.*, in the hills (Jos. 11:3); (3) with the Canaanites near Bethel (Gn. 13:7), near Shechem (Gn. 34:30), and in the Judaean hills (Jdg. 1:4f.); (4) with the Rephaim (Jos. 17:15). They were apparently hill-dwellers; this suits the interpretation of 'Perizzites', favoured by most commentators, as 'villagers' (from Heb. *pᵉrāzâ*, 'hamlet'). The fact that Gn. 10:15ff. does not name Perizzites among Canaan's 'sons' supports this possibility. See *POTT*, p. 101. J.P.U.L.

PERSECUTION. As encountered by Christians, this was nothing new. It was part of their Jewish heritage. The association of witness and suffering, begun as early as the second part of Isaiah, was crystallized in the Seleucid struggle. A theory of martyrdom rewarded by personal immortality grew up till it dominated the outlook of the Jews towards the Roman government (4 Macc. 17:8ff.). The possibility of death for Torah became accepted as a demand of Judaism. Thus the Jews were not averse to martyrdom; despite official Roman toleration of their religion, their cohesiveness, non-co-operation and uncanny financial success won them widespread hatred and spasmodic persecution, especially outside Palestine: pogroms were common in Alexandria. This legacy was taken over by the Christians. Their willingness to face suffering was intensified by the example of Jesus and by the association of persecution with the longed-for end of the age (Mk. 13:7–13). Even so, we must ask what aroused such animosity towards them among both the Jews and the Romans.

a. Opposition from the Jews

This gradually grew in intensity. The preaching of a crucified Messiah whose death was publicly blamed on the Jewish leaders was highly provocative. Even so, the people were favourable (Acts 2:46f.; 5:14) and the Pharisees moderate (Acts 5:34ff.; 23:6ff.), while opposition arose, naturally enough, among the Sadducees (Acts 4:1, 6; 5:17). Stephen's preaching of the transitoriness of the law (Acts 6:14) turned public opinion and brought about the first persecution in Jerusalem and elsewhere, *e.g.* Damascus. In AD 44 James was executed by Herod Agrippa, and throughout the Acts the Jews appear as Paul's most vehement enemies. This attitude could only have been made worse by the Apostolic Council which repudiated the need for circumcision, and it culminated in the excommunication of Christians at Jamnia, *c.* AD 80.

b. Opposition from the Romans

Rome's attitude underwent a marked change. At first, as we see in Acts, she gave Christians toleration and even encouragement. This soon gave way to fierce opposition. In Rome (Tacitus, *Ann.* 15. 44) such was their unpopularity by AD 64 that Nero could make them scapegoats for the fire. In Bithynia (Pliny, *Ep.* 10. 96–97) by *c.* AD 112 persistence in Christianity was a capital offence, though Trajan would not allow anonymous delation and he deprecated 'witch hunting'. Three explanations of this changed attitude are suggested:

(i) That Christians were prosecuted only for specific offences, such as cannibalism, incendiarism, incest, magic, illicit assembly and *majestas* (in their case, refusal to sacrifice to the *numen* of the emperor). There is, indeed, evidence that they were accused on all these counts, but 1 Pet. 2:12; 4:14–17; Pliny, *Ep.* 10. 97; and Suetonius, *Nero* 16, all make clear that at an early date the *nomen ipsum* of Christian, irrespective of the *cohaerentia flagitia* associated with it in the popular mind, was punishable.

(ii) That there was a general law throughout the empire, the *institutum Neronianum*, which proscribed Christianity. Tertullian makes this claim, and says that this was the only one of Nero's *acta* not rescinded later (*Ad. Nat.* 50. 7, see also *Apol.* 5), and the evidence of Suetonius, 1 Pet. and Rev. is patient of this interpretation. However, Christianity was probably not important enough to evoke such a general law, and if there was one it is hard to explain Pliny's ignorance of it, Trajan's failure to mention it, the property rights enjoyed by the church prior to the Decian persecution, and the remarkable lack of uniformity in its execution.

(iii) That persecution was at the discretion of the governor, who acted only in response to private accusation: there was no public prosecutor in Roman society. Whatever the formal charge, it is clear that by Pliny's time active membership of an organization believed to be criminal, and therefore, like the Bacchanals and the Druids, banned because in all three cult and *scelera* appeared indistinguishable, constituted an actionable offence, and *contumacia*, persistent refusal to recant, met with death. The competence of proconsuls and city prefects in *crimina extra ordinem* has been shown in recent years to have been very great. If a governor wished to take action against Christians he had the Neronian precedent to guide him and his coercive *imperium* to support him. Alternatively, it lay within his discretion, like Gallio (Acts 18:14–16), to refuse jurisdiction. If in doubt he could refer to the emperor, whose rescript would be binding on him as long as he remained in the province, though not necessarily upon his successors.

It is because the governors enjoyed such discretion that Tertullian addressed his Apology not to the emperor but to the governor: for it was in his hands that the remedy lay. This accounts for the spasmodic nature of persecution until the days of Decius. It depended so much on the policy of the governor and whether the extent of the unpopularity of Christians in the province was such as to drive private individuals to prosecute them. There is no satisfactory evidence (despite Orosius, 7. 7) for believing that there was any general action against Christians throughout the empire under Nero, though the sect seems to have become *illicita* in Rome itself (Suetonius, *Nero* 16). The actual evidence for a Domitianic persecution of the church is precarious despite the invective heaped on that emperor by the Fathers. A broad generalization in Dio (67. 14), concerning the death of Flavius Clemens, who was possibly, and Acilius Glabrio, who was probably, a Christian, and the banishment of Domitilla, is about all that can be summoned. But it is quite possible that Domitian, who minutely inspected and vigorously exacted the Jewish revenue (Suetonius, *Domit.* 12), discovered uncircumcised Christians sheltering under the religious privileges of the Jews and instituted against them a general persecution of which we have vivid traces in the Apocalypse, if this is to be dated under Domitian rather than Nero.

Persecution was therefore restricted by three factors: (i) that the Roman governors were reluctant to admit charges concerning private religious opinions (*superstitiones*) and tried to confine their attention to real offences; (ii) that accusations had to be made personally and publicly—and to bring a capital charge was both dangerous and difficult; (iii) that in each province only one man, the governor, could pass the death sentence.

These three factors combined to protect the majority of Christians long enough for the church to become firmly established throughout the empire.

BIBLIOGRAPHY. W. H. C. Frend, *Martyrdom and Persecution in the Early Church*, 1965; T. W. Manson, *BJRL* 39, 1956–7, pp. 463ff.; H. B. Mattingley, *JTS* n.s. 9, 1958, pp. 26ff.; F. W. Clayton, *CQ* 41, 1947, pp. 83ff.; A. N. Sherwin-White, *JTS* n.s. 3, 1952, pp. 199ff.; E. M. Smallwood, *Classical Philology* 51, 1956, pp. 5–11; G. Ebel, R. Schippers, *NIDNTT* 2, pp. 805–809; A. Oepke, *TDNT* 2, pp. 229f.; H. Schlier, *TDNT* 3, pp. 139–148; R. J. Lane Fox, *Pagans and Christians*, 1986. E.M.B.G.

PERSEVERANCE. The strictly biblical, as distinct from the later theological, significance of this term is indicated by the context of its sole occurrence in AV as a rendering of *proskarterēsis* in Eph. 6:18. The implication of steadfastness, patience, persistence is confirmed by the use of the verb *proskartereō*, to attend constantly, continue unswervingly, adhere firmly, hold fast to (*MM*, p. 548). It is used in Mk. 3:9 to describe a skiff quietly waiting to carry Jesus from the surging crowd, and in Acts 10:7 of the soldiers in Cornelius' bodyguard who were in uninterrupted attendance upon him. In its spiritual application it always has to do with continuance in the Christian way, particularly in relation to prayer (*cf.* Acts 1:14; 2:42, 46; 6:4; 8:13; Rom. 12:12; 13:6; Col. 4:2). RSV translates *hypomonē* as 'perseverance' in Heb. 12:1.

No doctrinal undertones attach to the term in the NT. It relates simply to the continual and patient dependence of the Christian upon Christ. Our Lord's parable of the importunate widow is the most relevant commentary (*cf.* Lk. 18:1–8). Christian perseverance is only a quality in the believer because initially it is a gift of God. It is by his power that those who trust in him are 'guarded through faith for a salvation ready to be revealed in the last time' (1 Pet. 1:5).

BIBLIOGRAPHY. I. H. Marshall, *Kept by the Power of God*, 1969; W. Mundle, *NIDNTT* 2, pp. 767f. A.S.W.

PERSIA, PERSIANS. The Indo-European Persians, nomadic pastoralists from S Russia, probably entered the Iranian plateau late in the 2nd millennium BC. In 836 BC Shalmaneser III of Assyria received tribute from rulers of a Parsua near Lake Urmia. His successor found the land of Parsuash in the S where several tribes finally settled. This area, E of the Persian Gulf, is still called Farsistan. Persepolis and Parsagarda were the chief towns. Heb. *pāras*, 'Persia', refers to this land.

I. Persian and Jewish history

The early traditions of the Persian people are recorded in the sacred book, the Zend-Avesta. The earliest recorded kings ruled from Anshan, NW of Susa. The Achaemenes who was claimed as founder of the dynasty by later kings probably reigned

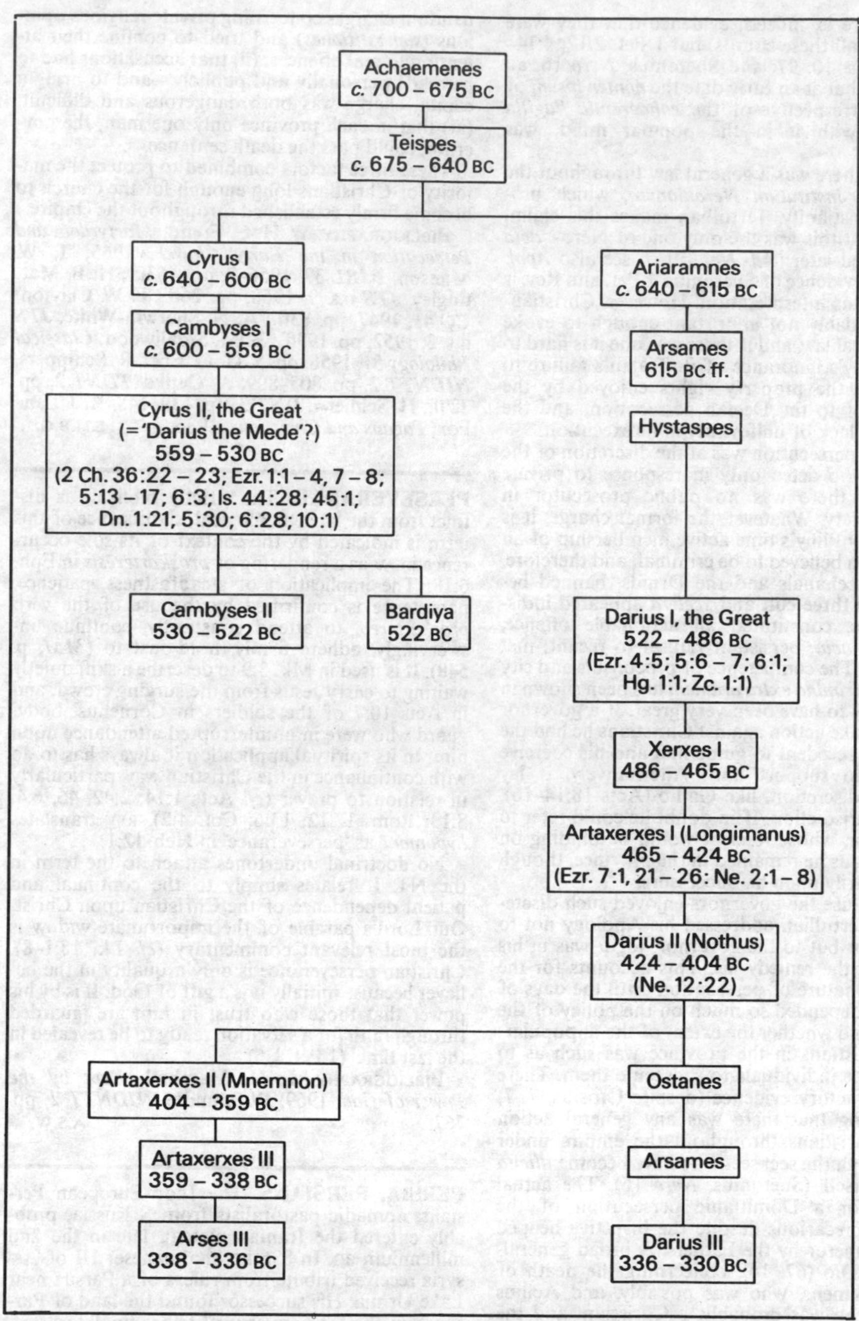

Persian rulers of the Archaemenid dynasty, with selected biblical references.

c. 680 BC. His grandson, Cyrus I, opposed Ashurbanipal of Assyria, but later submitted. Cyrus II, grandson of Cyrus I, rebelled against his Median suzerain, Astyages, killing him and taking over his capital, *Ecbatana, in 550 BC. Thereafter Median language and customs had strong influence on the Persians. This success was followed by the subjugation of Anatolia and the conquest of Croesus of Lydia (547 BC). Cyrus then turned E to extend his realm into NW India. By 540 BC he was sufficiently strong to attack Babylonia. After several battles he entered Babylon in triumph on 29 October 539 BC, 17 days after the city had fallen to his army (Dn. 5:30f.; *CYRUS). The king soon returned to Susa, but his son Cambyses remained in Babylon to represent him in religious ceremonies. The whole

empire was divided into large regions ruled by *satraps, chosen from Persian or Median nobles but with native officers under them (*cf.* Dn. 6). Various statues of gods which had been collected into Babylon by the last native king, Nabonidus (perhaps reflected in Is. 46:1f.), were returned to their own shrines. As there was no image of Yahweh to return to Jerusalem, Cyrus gave to back the Jews the precious vessels looted from the Temple by Nebuchadrezzar (Ezr. 1:7ff.; *cf. DOTT*, pp. 92–94). More important, he gave royal authorization for the rebuilding of the Temple to any Jew who wished to return to Judah (Ezr. 1:1–4). One Sheshbazzar was appointed governor (Ezr. 5:14). He was evidently a special officer responsible to the king. The governor of the province of 'Across the River' (the country W of the Euphrates) was clearly unaware of Cyrus' edict when in 520 BC he attempted to delay the work. His letter went to his superior, the satrap who had charge of Babylon and the W. No record was found among the archives kept at Babylon, but a memorandum was found at Ecbatana, where Cyrus had resided during his first regnal year. Darius I (522–486 BC) confirmed the decree and ordered his officials to help the Jews.

Darius and his successor Xerxes I (486–465 BC) expended considerable energy in an attempt to conquer the Greeks of the Peloponnese, almost the only area remaining outside the Persian empire in the known world, for Cambyses II (530–522 BC) had annexed Egypt in 525 BC. The defeat at Marathon (490 BC) by a small Gk. army was the only rebuff suffered by Darius. His reorganization of the satrapies, his system of military commanders, and his introduction of coinage, legal and postal systems lasted as long as the empire. These facilities coupled with the considerable degree of autonomy allowed to subject peoples contributed greatly to the stability of the empire and allowed such a small community as Judah to survive, Jewish officers acting as governors (*pḥh*) there.

Under Artaxerxes I (465–424 BC) Jewish affairs had official representation at court. *Ezra, it seems, was 'Secretary of State for Jewish Affairs' (Ezr. 7:12). He was accredited as special envoy to reorganize the Temple services at Jerusalem (458 BC). The eager Jews were led on by the encouragement they received to exceed the terms of Ezra's commission and rebuild the city wall. This was reported to the king by the governor of Samaria, who evidently had some responsibility for Judah. The royal reply (Ezr. 4:17–23) ordered the cessation of the work, for search of the records had shown that the city had revolted against earlier kings. Artaxerxes was faced with rebellion in Egypt (*c.* 460–454 BC), so he could not allow the construction of a fortress so near to that country. However, the royal cupbearer was a Jew, *Nehemiah, who was able to reverse the effects of this decree by having himself appointed *governor of Judah (Heb. *tiršāṯā'*, a Persian word, Ne. 8:9) with permission to rebuild the walls (445 BC). No record remains of relations between the Persian rulers and the Jews after this period. When the Persian empire was in the power of Alexander (331 BC) the Jews simply transferred their allegiance from one monarch to another.

II. Persian culture

The Indo-European Persian language was written in a cuneiform script composed of 51 simple syllabic signs (*WRITING) but this was restricted to imperial monuments almost exclusively. The imperial chancery used *Aramaic language and characters for official communications (*e.g.* the letters in Ezra, *cf. DOTT*, pp. 256–269). Translations were made into local tongues (*cf.* Est. 3:12; 8:9).

The luxury of the Persian court as described in the book of *Esther is attested by objects found at several sites. A number of stone bas-reliefs depict the king and his courtiers and the tribute of the vanquished. Portraits of the different racial groups are especially fine examples of Persian stone carving. The Oxus treasure (now mostly in the British Museum) and other chance finds show the skill of goldsmiths and jewellers. Solid gold and silver bowls and vases illustrate the wealth of the kings. Gk. influences may be seen in some Persian works and Gk. craftsmen appear among lists of palace dependants.

III. Persian religion

The early Persians revered gods of nature, fertility and the heavens. The tribe of the Magi were nearly exclusively the priests. Some time after 1000 BC Zoroaster proclaimed a religion of lofty moral ideals based on the principle 'Do good, hate evil'. For him there was one god, Ahura-mazda, the Good, represented by purifying fire and water. Opposed to the good was a dark power of Evil. This creed was adopted by Darius I, but soon became lost among the more ancient cults. Zoroaster's doctrines survived and were spread abroad. Their influence has been traced in the writings of early Judaism (*DEAD SEA SCROLLS) and, by some scholars, in the NT.

BIBLIOGRAPHY. A. T. Olmstead, *History of the Persian Empire*, 1948; R. N. Frye, *The Heritage of Persia*^{2}, 1975; E. Porada, *Ancient Iran*, 1965; M. Boyce, *A History of Zoroastrianism*, 1, 1975; E. M. Yamauchi, *Persia and the Bible*, 1990. A.R.M.

PETER.

I. Early background

Peter's original name was apparently the Heb. Simeon (Acts 15:14; 2 Pet. 1:1): perhaps, like many Jews, he adopted also 'Simon', usual in the NT, as a Gk. name of similar sound. His father's name was Jonah (Mt. 16:17); he himself was married (Mk. 1:30), and in his missionary days his wife accompanied him (1 Cor. 9:5). The Fourth Gospel gives *Beth-saida, just inside Gaulanitis, and a largely Gk. city, as his place of origin (Jn. 1:44), but he had also a home in Capernaum in Galilee (Mk. 1:21ff.). Both places were at the lakeside, where he worked as a fisherman, and in both there would be abundant contact with Gentiles. (His brother's name is Gk.) Simon spoke Aramaic with a strong N-country accent (Mk. 14:70), and maintained the piety and outlook of his people (*cf.* Acts 10:14), though not trained in the law (Acts 4:13; literacy is not in question). It is likely that he was affected by John the Baptist's movement (*cf.* Acts 1:22): his brother Andrew was a disciple of John (Jn. 1:39f.).

II. Call

The Fourth Gospel describes a period of Christ's activity before the commencement of the Galilean ministry, and to this may be referred Peter's first introduction to him, by Andrew's agency (Jn.

1:41). This makes the response to the subsequent call by the lakeside (Mk. 1:16f.) more intelligible. The call to the intimate band of the Twelve followed (Mk. 3:16ff.).

It was as a disciple that Simon received his new title, the Aramaic *Kepha* ('Cephas'), 'rock' or 'stone' (1 Cor. 1:12; 15:5; Gal. 2:9), usually appearing in NT in the Gk. form *Petros*. According to Jn. 1:42, Jesus conferred this title (not known as a personal name previously) at their first encounter. John's usual designation is 'Simon Peter'. Mark calls him Simon up to 3:16, and Peter almost invariably thereafter. There is nothing in any case to suggest that the solemn words of Mt. 16:18 represented the first bestowal of the name.

III. Peter in the ministry of Jesus

Peter was one of the first disciples called; he always stands first in the lists of disciples; he was also one of the three who formed an inner circle round the Master (Mk. 5:37; 9:2; 14:33; *cf.* 13:3). His impulsive devotion is frequently portrayed (*cf.* Mt. 14:28; Mk. 14:29; Lk. 5:8; Jn. 21:7), and he acts as spokesman of the Twelve (Mt. 15:15; 18:21; Mk. 1:36f.; 8:29; 9:5; 10:28; 11:21; 14:29ff.; Lk. 5:5; 12:41). At the crisis near Caesarea Philippi he is the representative of the whole band: for the question is directed to them all (Mk. 8:27, 29), and all are included in the look that accompanies the subsequent reprimand (8:33).

On any satisfactory interpretation of Mk. 9:1 the transfiguration is intimately related to the apostolic confession which precedes it. The experience made a lasting impression on Peter: 1 Pet. 5:1; 2 Pet. 1:16ff. are most naturally interpreted of the transfiguration, and, for what they are worth, the *Apocalypse* and *Acts of Peter* (*NEW TESTAMENT APOCRYPHA) show that their authors associated the preaching of this subject with Peter.

In a measure, the disastrous boast of Mk. 14:29ff. is also representative of the disciples; and, as Peter's protestations of loyalty are the loudest, so his rejection of the Lord is the most explicit (Mk. 14:66ff.). He is, however, specially marked out by the message of the resurrection (Mk. 16:7), and personally receives a visitation of the risen Lord (Lk. 24:34; 1 Cor. 15:5).

IV. The commission of Peter

Mt. 16:18ff. is one of the most discussed passages of the NT. Rejection of the genuineness of the saying is arbitrary, and generally based on dogmatic assumptions (sometimes the assumption that Jesus never meant to found the church). Others have argued that the saying is genuine but displaced. Stauffer would see it as a resurrection commission, like Jn. 21:15; Cullmann would set it in a passion context, like Lk. 22:31f. Such reconstructions hardly do justice to the distinctiveness of Mt. 16:18ff. It is a benediction and a promise: the other passages are commands. We need not undervalue Mark's vivid account of the Caesarea Philippi incident, which concentrates attention on the disciples' failure to understand the nature of the Messiahship they have just confessed, to acknowledge that the 'rock' saying belongs to the occasion of the confession.

There is still no unanimity in interpreting the passage. The suggestion that 'rock' is simply a misunderstanding of a vocative 'Peter' in the underlying Aramaic (*SB*, 1, p. 732) is too facile: the passage has obviously something to do with the significance of Peter's name, which various Gospel sources show as having been solemnly bestowed by Jesus. From early times two main interpretations have been held, with many variants.

1. That the rock is substantially what Peter has said: either Peter's faith or the confession of the Messiahship of Jesus. This is a very early interpretation (*cf.* Origen, *in loc.*, 'Rock means every disciple of Christ'). It has the great merit of taking seriously the Matthean context, and emphasizing, as Mk. 8 does in a different way, the immense significance of the Caesarea Philippi confession. In historical perspective we should probably see the rock as, not simply faith in Christ, but the apostolic confession of Christ, spoken of elsewhere as the foundation of the church (*cf.* Eph. 2:20). The 'rock' saying touches the core of the apostolic function, and Peter, first among the *apostles, has a name which proclaims it. That his own faith and understanding are as yet anything but exemplary is irrelevant: the church is to be built on the confession of the apostles.

2. That the rock is Peter himself. This is found almost as early as the other, for Tertullian and the bishop, whether Roman or Carthaginian, against whom he thundered in *De Pudicitia*, assume this, though with different inferences. Its strength lies in the fact that Mt. 16:19 is in the singular, and must be addressed directly to Peter even if, like Origen, we go on to say that to have Peter's faith and virtues is to have Peter's keys. Comparison might also be made with the Midrash on Is. 51:1. When God looked on Abraham who was to appear, he said, 'Behold, I have found a rock on which I can build and base the world. Therefore he called Abraham a rock' (*SB*, 1, p. 733).

Many Protestant interpreters, including notably Cullmann, take the latter view; but it is perhaps significant that he cuts the saying from the Matthean setting. To read it where Matthew places it is surer than to treat it as an isolated logion.

It must be stressed, however, that the exegesis of this point has nothing to do with the claims for the primacy of the Roman Church or its bishop with which it has through historical circumstances become involved. Even if it could be shown that Roman bishops are in any meaningful sense the successors of Peter (which it cannot), the passage does not allow for the transfer of its provisions to any successors whatever. It refers to the foundation of the church, which cannot be repeated.

The words that follow about the keys of the kingdom should be contrasted with Mt. 23:13. The Pharisees, for all their missionary propaganda, shut up the kingdom: Peter, recognizing the Son who is over the house and who holds the keys (*cf.* Rev. 1:18; 3:7; 21:25), finds them delivered to him (*cf.* Is. 22:22) to open the kingdom. (*POWER OF THE KEYS.) The 'binding and loosing', a phrase for which there are illuminating rabbinic parallels, is here addressed to Peter, but elsewhere is assigned to all the apostles (*cf.* Mt. 18:18). 'The apostle would, in the coming Kingdom, be like a great scribe or Rabbi, who would deliver decisions on the basis, not of the Jewish law, but of the teaching of Jesus which "fulfilled" it' (A. H. McNeile, *in loc.*).

But that here and elsewhere a primacy among the apostles is ascribed to Peter is not in doubt. Lk. 22:31ff. shows the strategic position of Peter as seen by both the Lord and the devil and, in full knowledge of the approaching desertion, marks out his future pastoral function. The risen Lord reinforces this commission (Jn. 21:15ff.), and it is the Fourth Gospel, which demonstrates the peculiar relationship of the apostle John to Christ, that records it.

V. Peter in the apostolic church

The Acts shows the commission in exercise. Before Pentecost it is Peter who takes the lead in the community (Acts 1:15ff.); afterwards, he is the principal preacher (2:14ff.; 3:12ff.) the spokesman before the Jewish authorities (4:8ff.), the president in the administration of discipline (5:3ff.). Though the church as a whole made a deep impression on the community, it was to Peter in particular that supernatural powers were attributed (5:15). In Samaria, the church's first mission field, the same leadership is exercised (8:14ff.).

Significantly also, he is the first apostle to be associated with the Gentile mission, and that by unmistakably providential means (10:1ff.; *cf.* 15:7ff.). This immediately brings criticism upon him (11:2ff.); and not for the last time. Gal. 2:11ff. gives us a glimpse of Peter at Antioch, the first church with a significant ex-pagan element, sharing table-fellowship with the Gentile converts, and then meeting a barrage of Jewish-Christian opposition, in the face of which he withdraws. This defection was roundly denounced by Paul; but there is no hint of any theological difference between them, and Paul's complaint is rather the incompatibility of Peter's practice with his theory. The old theory (revived by S. G. F. Brandon, *The Fall of Jerusalem and the Christian Church*, 1951), of persistent rivalry between Paul and Peter, has little basis in the documents.

Despite this lapse, the Gentile mission had no truer friend than Peter. Paul's gospel and his had the same content, though a somewhat different expression: the Petrine speeches in Acts, Mark's Gospel and 1 Peter have the same theology of the cross, rooted in the concept of Christ as the suffering Servant. He was ready with the right hand of fellowship, recognizing his mission to Jews and Paul's to Gentiles as part of the same ministry (Gal. 2:7ff.); and at the Jerusalem Council is recorded as the first to urge the full acceptance of the Gentiles on faith alone (Acts 15:7ff.).

Peter's career after the death of Stephen is hard to trace. The references to him in Joppa, Caesarea and elsewhere suggest that he undertook missionary work in Palestine (James no doubt now assuming leadership in Jerusalem). He was imprisoned in Jerusalem, and on his miraculous escape he left for 'another place' (Acts 12:17). Attempts to identify this place are fruitless. We know that he went to Antioch (Gal. 2:11ff.); he may have gone to Corinth, though probably not for long (1 Cor. 1:12). He is closely associated with Christians in N Asia Minor (1 Pet. 1:1), and possibly the prohibition on Paul's entry into Bithynia (Acts 16:7) was due to the fact that Peter was at work there.

Peter's residence in Rome has been disputed, but on insufficient grounds. 1 Peter was almost certainly written from there (1 Pet. 5:13; *PETER, FIRST EPISTLE OF). That book shows signs of being written just before or during the Neronian persecution, and *1 Clement* 5 implies that, like Paul, he died in this outburst. Doubts cast on the interpretation of *1 Clement* (*cf.* M. Smith, *NTS* 9, 1960, pp. 86ff.) have little foundation. On the other hand, Cullmann's suggestion, based on the context in *1 Clement* and Paul's hints in Philippians of tensions in the church in Rome, that Peter, perhaps at Paul's request, came specifically to heal the breach, and that bitterness among Christians led to the death of both, is worth serious consideration. The story in the *Acts of Peter* of his martyrdom by crucifixion (*cf.* Jn. 21:18ff.) head downwards cannot be accepted as reliable, but this work (*NEW TESTAMENT APOCRYPHA) may preserve some valid traditions. Certainly these Acts, like other 2nd-century witnesses, emphasize the co-operation of the apostles in Rome.

Excavations in Rome have revealed an early cultus of Peter under St Peter's (*cf.* Eusebius, *EH* 2. 25): it is not safe to claim more for them. (*PETER, FIRST and SECOND EPISTLES OF.)

BIBLIOGRAPHY. O. Cullmann, *Peter: Disciple—Apostle—Martyr*[2], 1962; *JEH* 7, 1956, pp. 238f. (on excavations); J. Toynbee and J. Ward Perkins, *The Shrine of St. Peter and the Vatican Excavations*, 1956; H. Chadwick, *JTS* n.s. 8, 1957, pp. 31ff.; O. Karrer, *Peter and the Church*, 1963; R. E. Brown, K. P. Donfried, J. Reumann (eds.), *Peter in the New Testament*, 1973; C. P. Thiede, *Simon Peter*, 1986; K. B. Quast, *Peter and the Beloved Disciple*, 1989; P. Perkins, *Peter*, 1994; *BAICS* 6, f.c.

A.F.W.

PETER, FIRST EPISTLE OF. The letter is sent in the name of the apostle, to whose status and experience there is a modest allusion in 5:1. A certain function is ascribed to Silvanus (5:12)—almost certainly the *Silas of Acts. The address is the widest in the NT (1:1); to the Christians of five provinces (of which Bithynia and Pontus were for administrative purposes merged).

I. Outline of contents

a. Address and greeting (1:1–2)

Trinitarian in form and concerned with the work of salvation.

b. Thanksgiving (1:3–12)

In form a *berakhah*, or blessing of God, for the privileges of salvation (contrast Paul's thanksgivings), making reference to present suffering.

c. The implications of salvation (1:13–2:10)

God's purpose for his people: the nature of redemption and the call of the redeemed to fear God and love one another: the privileges of belonging to the people of God. The section includes the call to 'put off' the characteristics of the old life.

d. Christian relationships (2:11–3:12)

The appeal to good behaviour among the Gentiles: careful subjection to lawfully constituted authority; the duties of slaves, under good and bad masters, with the example of Christ; the duties for wives and husbands; the call to unity; love, gentleness and humility, swelling into Ps. 34.

e. Suffering and the will of God (3:13–22)

Preparedness to suffer injustice: Christ's suffering and its triumphant consequences.

f. Holy living (4:1–11)

Includes a call to watch: culminates in a benediction.

g. The fiery trial (4:12–19)

A sudden resumption of the theme of imminent suffering: its inherent blessing: the glory of suffering for the Name: the coming judgment.

h. Address to elders (5:1–4)

i. General address and benediction (5:5–11)

Including a renewal of the call to vigilance and to resistance to the evil one.

j. Personalia and greetings (5:12–14)

II. External attestation

The use of 1 Peter in the primitive church is at least as well attested as most other Epistles. Eusebius says that 'the ancient elders' made free use of it (*EH* 3. 3); some have found echoes of it in Clement of Rome (*c.* AD 96), and rather more in Ignatius, Hermas and Barnabas, belonging to different parts of the world, but all to the early 2nd century. Beyond question is its use by Polycarp (who may have been baptized as early as AD 69) and Papias, also of the sub-apostolic generation (Eusebius, *EH* 3. 39). It is reflected in the *Gospel of Truth*, which seems to use the books regarded as authoritative in Rome *c.* AD 140 (*NEW TESTAMENT APOCRYPHA). From the second half of the century onwards it seems universally known and read, at least in the Gk.-speaking church. There are fewer signs of it in Lat. writers. It is not mentioned—possibly by accident (*cf.* T. Zahn, *Geschichte des Neutestamentlichen Kanons*, 2. 1, 1890, pp. 105ff., 142)—in the Muratorian Fragment. By Eusebius' time, no question was raised about its authenticity, though other writings bearing Peter's name had long caused discussion (*EH* 3. 3).

Obviously the Epistle had considerable influence on the thought and expression of early Christians, and nothing suggests that it was ever attributed to anyone but Peter. Some who have on other grounds questioned its authenticity have been driven by its evident early attestation to the desperate conclusion that it must have circulated anonymously.

A date about AD 100–111 has often been urged for the passages about persecution. But this is tenable only if the traditional authorship is denied, and in any case is a dubious understanding of these passages (see section V, below). It is also worth remembering that Polycarp and Papias, both Asians, were, the one certainly, the other almost certainly, mature men at that time.

III. Place of writing

The letter conveys greetings from the church in 'Babylon' (5:13). Mesopotamian Babylon is unlikely: it is too much of a coincidence that Mark and Silvanus, old colleagues of Paul, should be there too. Still less can be said for Babylon on the Nile, a military depot. It is far more likely that, as in Rev. 14:8; 17:5, *etc.*, Babylon stands for Rome. The OT had compared it as a symbol of godless prosperity (*cf.* Is. 14); theories that it is a general allegory for 'the world' or a cryptogram for security purposes are needless. There are grounds for believing Peter worked in Rome, and the presence of Mark and Silvanus would be explained.

IV. Style and language

The Gk. of the Epistle is good and rhythmic, the style not pretentious but with a certain delicacy. Simple rhetorical devices are effectively used, but there are also some grammatical features best explained by Semitic influence. The quotations from and allusions to the OT almost invariably follow the LXX in a way which suggests thorough familiarity with it.

Some of these facts, reinforced by an exaggeration of the classical character of the Gk., have seemed at once to overthrow any claim to authorship by an Aramaic-speaking Galilean. A number of assumptions here, however, require testing. Gk. was widely understood and spoken, and was a vital cultural force, throughout 1st-century Palestine, and especially Galilee. Peter's own brother has a Gk. name, and Peter would doubtless be quite at home in the language. Further, the LXX was the 'Authorized Version' of most early Christians, and everyone connected with the Gentile mission would be familiar with it, and especially with the key passages most frequently in use.

These factors, however, would not themselves justify an easy assumption that Peter could write Gk. prose of the type of 1 Peter. But we must here ask, in what sense is the letter 'by' Silvanus (5:12)? Were he simply the messenger, one would expect the expression 'sent by' (*cf.* Acts 15:27). Contemporary literature attests that in the ancient world secretaries were often entrusted with considerable powers (*cf.* J. A. Eschlimann, *RB* 53, 1946, pp. 185ff.). Probably, therefore, 1 Pet. 5:12 indicates, and the diction and style evidence, the assistance of Silvanus in drafting the letter.

Silvanus, we learn from Acts, was a Jew, a Roman citizen, acceptable for the delicate task of explaining the resolutions of the Jerusalem Council (Acts 15:22ff.) and a devoted worker in the Gentile mission. He had been associated with Paul in the sending of 1 and 2 Thes. (1 Thes. 1:1; 2 Thes. 1:1). Selwyn has pointed to verbal parallels and connections of thought between those Epistles and 1 Peter (pp. 369ff., 439ff.) which, after due weight has been given to the criticisms of B. Rigaux (*Les Épîtres aux Thessaloniciens*, 1956, pp. 105ff.) and others, will repay careful study. An interesting light may be cast, for instance, on 1 Pet. 3:7 and 1 Thes. 4:3–5 if the one is read in the light of the other.

Those who deny the Petrine authorship usually write off the reference to Silvanus as part of the pseudepigraphic machinery. If, however, the hypothesis of a secretary introduces factors beyond proof it is also true that this method was used in antiquity, and must be allowed for.

V. The historical background

The principal data come from the references to persecution (1:6f.; 3:13–17; 4:12–19; 5:9). In the first two passages trials exist, unjust suffering is a possibility; in the second two a fierce ordeal is imminent: so much so that some have even urged that 4:12ff. comes from a later period. The vocabulary, however, is very similar: in each case *peirasmos*, 'trial', is used (1:6 and 4:12); persecution is a ground of rejoicing (1:6; 4:13); the same beatitude is applied (3:14; 4:14); the glory of suffering for doing good, or as a Christian, is proclaimed (3:17; 4:16); the undeserved suffering of Christians is linked with the will of God (3:17; 4:19); obedience to the civil power in things lawful and honest is enjoined (2:13ff.; 4:15), and the example of Christ's sufferings is set forth (1:11; 3:18; 4:13). The readers are also told that their fiery trial should be no surprise (4:12): and suffering they already know (*cf.* 1:6ff.). All this suggests that if the peril in 4:12ff. is new, it is in degree, not kind.

The antithesis in 4:12ff. between suffering for wrong committed and suffering for the name of Christ has attracted comparison with a letter from Pliny, appointed governor of Bithynia–Pontus in AD 110/111 to the usually liberal-minded emperor Trajan (Pliny, *Ep.* 10. 96).

Pliny, faced with vast numbers of Christians in his province, asks whether age, sex or recantation is to be allowed for in prescribing punishment: and, further, if the name of Christian (*nomen ipsum*) is sufficient reason for punishment, or only the crimes (putatively) congruent therewith (*flagitia cohaerentia*).

His own line of conduct had been to inquire whether people were Christians and to give them free pardon if they sacrificed to the emperor's genius; and, if they refused, to execute them for contumacy (*contumacia*). Some of those who sacrificed said they had ceased to be Christians 20 years back; but neither from them nor from two Christian girls (*DEACONESS), whom he tortured, could he find anything very reprehensible save a rather disgusting superstition. His vigorous action was having effect, and disused heathen rites were recommencing.

Trajan's reply (*Ep.* 10. 97) generally approves these actions but lays down that Christians are not to be sought out: if they are regularly accused and fail to recant they must suffer.

Pliny also says that Christians took an oath of abstention from crime (*cf.* 1 Pet. 4:15). And this all takes place in part of the area to which 1 Peter is addressed.

There is no evidence of widespread state-sponsored persecution in the provinces before this date: the savage pogroms of Nero and Domitian were directed at Roman Christians. Accordingly, many have seen in 1 Peter a tract designed for Pliny's time (*cf., e.g.,* J. Knox, *JBL* 72, 1953, pp. 187ff.).

To this thesis there are four strong objections.

1. 'The name' is used in 1 Peter in a primitive Christian, not a juristic Roman, sense. The 'name' of Jesus was immensely significant for Christians of the apostolic age, and in particular the accounts which we have of Peter's Jerusalem preaching (*cf.* Mk. 9:37, 41; 13:13; Lk. 21:12; Acts 2:21, 38; 3:6, 16; 4:12, 17f., 30; 5:28). Even in Jerusalem days persecution was for 'the name' (Acts 5:41; 9:16; *cf.* 9:4f.). The background of 'the name' in 1 Pet. 4 surely lies in these passages.

2. When Pliny talks of *flagitia cohaerentia* he is doubtless thinking of the common slander that Christians were guilty of cannibalism, incest and other horrors in their rites—he is looking for evidence. But the warnings in 1 Pet. 4:15f. have no such undertones: and 'a mischief-maker' does not denote a criminal offence at all.

3. The language of 1 Peter does not necessarily indicate legislative action. It is implied in 2:14; 3:15ff. that, in the ordinary administration of justice, Christians would have nothing to fear: though the same passages make clear that they might on occasions be subjected to flagrant injustice. In 3:15ff. the danger seems to be primarily from ill-disposed neighbours; in 4:14 reproach is specifically mentioned; and the readers' sufferings are the same as other Christians know elsewhere (5:9). Jewish jealousy, private spite, enraged commercial interests, mob violence and ill-judged actions by local magistrates could have dire effects (Acts *passim*; 2 Cor. 11:22ff.; 1 Thes. 2:14f.; 2 Tim. 3:11f.; Heb. 12:4ff.).

4. Pliny's jurisdiction extended over Bithynia–Pontus only: nothing suggests an enforcement of his policy in the other areas to which 1 Peter is addressed.

Pliny's action must have had its roots well in the past (*cf.* Ramsay, *CRE*, pp. 245ff.). Though not sure of the technicalities, he takes for granted that Christians must be punished for *something*: and even he does not execute for the *nomen ipsum* but for *contumacia*. Nor does Trajan give him a straight answer: it is still not clear whether Christianity is a crime or not. The law, kept deliberately vague, puts Christians at the mercy of gossips.

There is no need, however, to look to Vespasian's or Domitian's time: nothing in the *language* of 1 Peter requires a date later than the 60s. If a note of particular urgency appears at 4:12ff. the outbreak of the Neronian persecution would afford ample justification for this.

It seems certain that *Peter suffered in Rome under Nero, and 'Babylon' (5:13) almost certainly indicates that city. The E provinces tended to copy imperial actions on their own initiative. Rev. 2–3 suggests that this happened in Domitian's persecution in the 90s. From Rome, in the first rumblings of Nero's anti-Christian movement that became literally a fiery trial, Peter would have reason to predict an intensification of the suffering of his brethren in the East.

A suitable date for 1 Peter would thus be just before the outbreak of Nero's persecution: AD 63 or early 64; perhaps after Paul had died and left his colleagues Silvanus and Mark.

VI. The author's background

A rewarding study can be made of the connection between 1 Peter and the other parts of the NT with which Peter is associated: Mark's Gospel and the early speeches in Acts. It is not simply a matter of verbal links between 1 Pet. 2:20ff. and Mark's passion narrative (*cf.* Selwyn, p. 30). Mark, the Petrine speeches and 1 Peter all set forth Christ in terms of the suffering Servant of Isaiah 53; 1 Peter and Mk. both expound the Lord's death as a ransom (*cf.* Mk. 10:45 with 1 Pet. 1:18). Other NT writings, of course, are indebted to Is. 53, but it is remarkable that these three have this prophetic passage so deeply impressed that it may be regarded as their central thought about Christ. 1 Pet. 2, like Is. 53, describes both the Servant's conduct and sufferings and the significance of them. Much has been said of the call to the imitation of Christ in 1 Peter; but there is far more than a description of the passion and an appeal to imitation: the thought moves on to what is for ever inimitable, the redemption which only his suffering could effect.

The Petrine speeches in Acts share with 1 Peter the same sense of prophetic fulfilment (Acts 2:16ff.; 3:18; 1 Pet. 1:10ff., 20), the insistence on the cross as the foreordained action of God (Acts 2:23; 1 Pet. 1:20), the same connection of the resurrection and exaltation (Acts 2:32ff.; 1 Pet. 1:21); the call to repentance and faith-baptism (Acts 2:38, 40; 1 Pet. 3:20ff.); the certainty of Christ's judgment of the living and dead (Acts 10:42; 1 Pet. 4:5); joyous recognition of the Gentile mission and its blessings (Acts 10:9ff.; 11:17; 15:7ff.; 1 Pet. 1:1, 4–12; 2:3–10), expressed from a Jewish standpoint. It would take a Jew of Peter's views to speak of Gentile Christians as 'elect . . . sojourners of the Dispersion' (1:1, RV), and to describe them as entering Israel (2:9f.—note the modification of Hosea: the readers had *never been* God's people before). A Jew, too, could describe their background as 'what the Gentiles like to do' (4:3).

Again, in both 1 Peter and the Petrine speeches we are, as we have seen, in an atmosphere where the 'name' of Jesus means much (see **V**, above). Even details may be significant: the use of the oracle about the stone (Acts 4:10ff.; 1 Pet. 2:7) and the use of *xylon*, properly 'wood', for the cross (Acts 5:30; 10:39; 1 Pet. 2:24).

1 Peter contains an unusual number of apparent reminiscences of the Lord's words: generally not as formal quotations, but woven into the framework of the discourse (*e.g.* 1 Pet. 1:16 = Mt. 5:48; 1:17 = Mt. 22:16; 1:18 = Mk. 10:45; 1:22 = Jn. 15:12; 2:19 = Lk. 6:32 and Mt. 5:39; 3:9 = Mt. 5:39; 3:14 = Mt. 5:10; 4:11 = Mt. 5:16; 4:13 = Mt. 5:10ff.; 4:18 = Mt. 24:22; 5:3 = Mt. 20:25f.; 5:7 = Mt. 6:25ff.), and other passages take on a richer meaning if Peter were in fact the author. These connections are not exclusively from the Marcan tradition: but 1 Peter and Mk. alike display the theme of the suffering and the glory.

Some have sought the author's background in the Asian mystery cults (see R. Perdelwitz, *Die Mysterienreligionen und das Problem des 1 Petrusbriefes*, 1911, and *cf.* Beare) and found the letter too colourless in its treatment of the Lord's life for the work of one of the Twelve. The proponents of the mystery religion theory have, however, not made their case in a matter where dating is notoriously uncertain; and the parallels with the Galilean Gospel tradition are far more impressive. Eloquent is the judgment of Cullmann, who, while not discussing the authorship of 1 Peter, can be assured that it was written with knowledge of Peter's dominant theological themes (*Peter*, p. 68).

VII. 1 Peter and the rest of the New Testament

The theology of 1 Peter is essentially Pauline. This is not, as some think, an argument against authenticity: there is reason to hold that *Peter stood close to Paul in theology and none to think that he was an original theologian. Silvanus, too, had long worked with Paul. Moreover, though the agreement is close, the setting and expression of the theology in terms of the Servant is quite independent of Paul. It is worth remarking that K. Lake, drawn to a late date by the persecution passages, could say, 'The simplicity of the theology is marked, and affords an argument for an early date' (*EBr*[11], 21, p. 296) and that F. L. Cross can point to 'that remarkable co-presence of the end as future and yet as already here from which second century writings depart' (pp. 42f.).

More remarkable are the literary resemblances between 1 Peter and other NT writings, especially Rom., Eph., Heb. and Jas. Not all can be fortuitous: for instance, the unusual divergence from the LXX in the quotation in 1 Pet. 2:4–8 appears also in Rom. 9:32f. Problems of priority in literary relationships are always difficult and can rarely command certainty. C. L. Mitton claims to have proved the dependence of 1 Pet. on Eph. (*JTS* n.s. 1, 1950, pp. 67ff.)—the significance of this, if ascertained, will depend on the date given to Eph. Beare claims, with less demonstration, that the author of 1 Peter must have had access to the published Pauline Corpus (*The First Epistle of Peter*[3], p. 219).

A fruitful development in recent literary criticism has been the attention given to the common patterns of Christian teaching which appear in diverse NT writings (see P. Carrington, *The Primitive Christian Catechism*, 1946). A pattern of instruction for converts has been recovered, associated by many scholars, perhaps too categorically, with baptism. Jas. and 1 Peter, as well as Eph. and Col., reflect this pattern, which had among its components:

1. The call to put away sins and desires of the old pagan life (1 Pet. 2:1, 11).
2. The call to Christian humility, subjection and the subordination of self-interest—addressed to particular classes of society (1 Pet. 2:11–3:9—these are parentheses).
3. The call to watch and pray: twice in 1 Peter (1 Pet. 4:7; 5:8).
4. The call to resist the devil (1 Pet. 5:8f.).

Many of the strongest resemblances between 1 Peter and other Epistles occur in just these sections, and it seems probable that the explanation lies in the common forms of catechetical training, not in direct literary dependence.

Selwyn has gone further and seen other common patterns reflected in 1 Peter, more especially a body of teaching on persecution which declared it to be a ground of rejoicing, a test of character, a necessary visitation and a sign of the imminence of divine judgment and vindication: and which was anchored in the words of the Lord. Selwyn finds this same pattern in 1 and 2 Thes., also associated with Silvanus. In common with other writers, he sees various hymns and liturgical fragments (*e.g.* 1 Pet. 2:6–10; 3:18–22; and use of Ps. 34 in 3:10f.).

VIII. The nature and purpose of 1 Peter

1 Peter has long been treated as a sermon cast into epistolary form, dealing with baptism. This was given a new form by H. Preisker in 1951, who saw in the section 1:3–4:11 indications of a rite in progress and references to baptismal practice, and declared the work to be a baptismal liturgy with the rubrics omitted. Preisker's hypothesis was marred by stylistic hypercriticism, but this feature has been removed by F. L. Cross, who urges, with a wealth of illustration from patristic sources and especially from the *Apostolic Tradition* of Hippolytus, that 1 Peter is the president's part for an Easter baptismal eucharist: 1:3–12 is the president's opening solemn prayer; 1:13–21 his formal charge to the candidates. The baptism takes place at this point, and 1:22–25 gives the welcome to the newly baptized: passing to a discourse on the fundamentals of sacramental life (2:1–10), an address on Christian duties (2:11–4:6), and closing with admonitions and a doxology (4:7–11). It is a weakness of the theory that no explanation is given of 4:12ff.

This thesis rests on a vast amount of detailed study which cannot be discussed here. Many of the details have been called in question. (See the examination by T. C. G. Thornton, *JTS* n.s. 12, 1961, pp. 14ff.). A few general points, however, suggest the need for reserve.

First, baptism is far less prominent in the Epistle than the discussions of recent years suggest. There is only one explicit reference to it, and that is a parenthesis (3:21). Other allusions to baptism which some find are highly dubious: the 'born anew' (1:3; *cf.* 1:23) is already realized, and its result enjoyed: it cannot refer to an event to take place after 1:21. Its corresponding member in the catechetical form in Jas. 1:18 makes it clear that the begetting relates to the gospel, not baptism, and this is confirmed by 1:23, where the 'word of God' is defined as the enduring gospel preached to the readers. The repeated 'now' need not relate to a rite in progress; it is due rather to an exultant sense of the last times: and the 'now' in 3:21 in the context of baptism surely only points to a contrast with the ancient Flood.

Second, many of the allusions can be readily understood without the theory. The emphasis on Exodus typology is valuable, but this typology is not restricted to baptism. Van Unnik, for example, points to a rabbinic saying that proselytes entered Israel in the same way as Israel entered the covenant and infers that 1 Peter stresses the transition that the readers have made. They know God's election and covenant sprinkling (1:2ff.); they are now Israel (1:18f.); those who had never been God's people have become that people (2:10); the work of Christ is to bring us (*prosagein*) to God: and *prosagein* represents a technical term for becoming a proselyte.

On a reading like this, while conversion and the radical break with the old life are much to the fore, baptism in itself is not. The question of authorship is not, of course, directly affected by the formal nature of the work. Peter might preach a sermon and send it as a letter (though it is very hard to see a motive for converting a liturgical text into a letter). But 1 Peter as we have it *is* a letter, and on the sound critical principle of making sense of what we have, we must so read it. (*DESCENT INTO HADES; *PERSECUTION.)

BIBLIOGRAPHY. Commentaries by R. Leighton (d. 1684), *Practical Commentary upon 1 Peter*; F. J. A. Hort (posthumous, unfinished, Gk. text); E. G. Selwyn, 1946 (indispensable for Gk. text); H. Windisch–H. Preisker, 1951; F. L. Cross, *1 Peter: a Paschal Liturgy*[2], 1957; C. E. B. Cranfield, *TBC*[2], 1961; C. Spicq, *Les Épitres de Saint Pierre*, 1966; J. N. D. Kelly, *The Epistles of Peter and Jude*, *BNTC*, 1969; F. W. Beare[3], 1970 (denies Petrine authorship); E. Best, *1 Peter*, *NCB*, 1971; K. H. Schelkle, *Die Petrusbriefe und der Judasbrief*[3], 1976; L. Goppelt, *Der Erste Petrusbrief*, 1978; W. Grudem, *The First Epistle of Peter*, *TNTC*, 1988; J. Michaels, *1 Peter*, *WBC*, 1988. See also W. C. van Unnik, *ExpT* 68, 1956–7, pp. 79ff.; C. F. D. Moule, *NTS* 3, 1957, pp. 1ff.; R. H. Gundry, *NTS* 13, 1967, pp. 336–350; N. Hillyer, 'Rock-stone Imagery in 1 Peter', *TynB* 22, 1971, pp. 58–81. A.F.W.

PETER, SECOND EPISTLE OF.

I. Outline of contents

After the salutation (1:1–2) the author speaks of the reliability of the Christian faith, attested as it is by growing personal experience (1:3–11), the testimony of eyewitnesses (1:12–18) and inspired ancient prophecy (1:19–21). Mention of true prophecy leads him on to condemn false prophecy (2:1–3:10). Current false teachers are the successors of the OT false prophets, and will incur the same judgment (2:1–9). Their depravity is shown by throwing off God's restraints in unbridled licence (2:10–18), which brings not liberty but bondage (2:19–22). Therefore judgment awaits them, despite their scepticism about the parousia. They should recall that a catastrophic end of the world had been foretold (3:1–4), and the certainty of this prophecy is substantiated by the Flood (3:5–7). The second coming is delayed because of the long-suffering of a God who is outside time (3:8–9), but, though delayed, it is none the less certain (3:10). It is the duty of the faithful not to be led away by the libertinism and scepticism of the false teachers, but to live an upright life in anticipation of Christ's return (3:11–end).

II. Occasion

The recipients are not defined, though their having 'a faith of equal standing *with ours*' (1:1) and their having escaped 'the corruption that is in the world' (1:4) suggests a predominantly Gentile audience. The writer has had a long and intimate acquaintance with them (1:12–13; 3:1) and writes to warn them against a false teaching both antinomian in practice and radical in belief. The immorality (2:12ff.), insubordination to church leaders (2:10), scepticism (3:3), twisting of Scripture (they exploited in particular, no doubt, the Pauline doctrine of justification, 3:16), and greed of these false teachers (2:3, 15) evoke his most stringent denunciation. He writes to warn the church members of their moral and intellectual danger, to assure them of the basis for their belief, to explain their main problem—the parousia—and to encourage holy living and growth in grace. If the author was Peter the date would be around the mid-60s (he is anticipating death, 1:14). If not, the letter may have been written in the late 1st or early 2nd century. No mention is made of its provenance or destination: it may well have been written, like 1 Peter, from Rome to Asia Minor.

III. Authorship and date

The authorship of this Epistle is hotly contested on both external and internal grounds.

a. The external evidence

This is inconclusive. While no book in the Canon is so poorly attested in the Fathers, no book excluded from the Canon can claim comparable support. Origen, early in the 3rd century, is the first to cite it by name; he records the doubts which surrounded it, but himself accepts it. So does Jerome, while Eusebius is uncertain. After its inclusion in the Festal Letter of Athanasius in AD 367 and its ratification by the Council of Carthage in AD 397, its position in the Canon was unquestioned until the Reformation, when Luther accepted it, Erasmus rejected it and Calvin was dubious. Though not quoted by name until Origen, it was used much earlier; Clement of Alexandria had it in his Bible; Valentinus in the *Gospel of Truth*, Aristides in his *Apology* (AD 129) and Clement of Rome (*c.* AD 95) appear to allude to it. More probable still is its use by the author of the *Apocalypse of Peter*, whose existence is attested by the end of the 2nd century AD. For this reason many of the scholars who on other grounds reject the Epistle nevertheless regard its external attestation as sufficient.

b. The internal evidence

Many scholars are inclined to adjudge it a pseudepigraph, on the following grounds:

(i) *Its relationship with Jude.* There is an undeniable literary relationship between the two letters; which way it lies has not been fully established, although the majority today think 2 Peter borrowed from Jude. This, it is argued, would in itself rule out the possibility of apostolic authorship. No such conclusion is warranted. If, as is certain, Paul borrowed from a variety of sources, and if, as is possible, 1 Peter borrowed from James, it would not be surprising to find the same thing in 2 Peter. On the other hand, both 2 Peter and Jude may have incorporated a common document denouncing false teaching, just as Matthew and Luke appear to have drawn from 'Q' their common sayings-material. In neither case need the priority of Jude affect the authenticity of 2 Peter, whereas if Jude drew from 2 Peter (as Bigg and Zahn maintain), the apostolic authorship of the Epistle could hardly be denied.

(ii) *Its relationship with 1 Peter.* The marked difference of diction and style between the two letters led to the doubts of the early church about 2 Peter. Jerome thought that Peter used two different amanuenses (a possibility enhanced by the researches of E. G. Selwyn into the probable influence of Silvanus on 1 Peter), and this suggestion must be taken seriously, for despite the wide differences no book in the NT is so like 2 Peter as 1 Peter. They have been shown (by A. E. Simms, *The Expositor*, 5th series, 8, 1898, pp. 460ff.) to have as close an affinity on a purely linguistic basis as 1 Timothy and Titus, where unity of authorship is universally admitted.

Modern writers concentrate less on the linguistic than on the doctrinal differences between the Epistles, and they are very different in this respect. The subject-matter of 1 Peter is hope, of 2 Peter knowledge. 1 Peter is written to Christians facing persecution, and therefore stresses the great events of the life of Christ for emulation and comfort; 2 Peter is written to Christians facing false doctrine and practice and therefore stresses the great hope of the return of Christ for warning and challenge. The best safeguard against the false teaching is full knowledge (*gnōsis*, *epignōsis*) of Christ, and it is this, accordingly, which is stressed in 2 Peter. The teaching of both letters is conditioned by the pastoral needs which evoked them. The differences can, in fact, easily be exaggerated; both letters draw attention to the warnings of the Flood, the small number saved, the longsuffering of God. Both emphasize prophecy, the inspiration of the OT, the solidarity of the old and the new Israel, and the value of eyewitness testimony. Both emphasize the primitive eschatological tension derived from the Christian's dual membership of this age and the age to come, with its consequences in holy living, in sharp contrast with the 2nd-century neglect of this doctrine. In short, the divergence of doctrinal emphasis in the two letters is great, but not impossible.

(iii) *Its anachronisms.* **1.** Such concepts as 'partakers of the divine nature' (1:4), escaping 'the corruption that is in the world' (1:4), and the repeated emphasis on knowledge and eyewitness (*epoptai*, 1:16, is a favourite word of the mystery-religions) suggest to some scholars a 2nd-century origin for the letter. There is no need to postulate so late a date, since the discovery of the Carian Inscription of AD 22 and parallel passages in Philo and Josephus show that this was the common cultural language of the day in the 1st century.

2. The destruction of the world by fire (3:7) was a common topic in the 2nd century, and may thus be an indication of a late date for 2 Peter. On the other hand, there is some reason to believe that the distinctly Christian belief in the destruction of the world by fire (as seen in Barnabas and Justin) may ultimately derive from this Epistle (see J. Chaine, *RB* 46, 1937, pp. 207ff.).

3. The phrase 'since the fathers fell asleep' (3:4) is held to favour a late date when the first Christian generation had almost disappeared. Even if these words did apply to the Christian 'fathers', it would not necessitate a late date. As early as 1 Thes. 4:15–17 or 1 Cor. 15:6, the state of those who had died before the parousia was a burning topic that had to be faced. However, here the context suggests that 'the fathers' refers to the OT fathers ('from the beginning of *creation*') as elsewhere in the NT (*e.g.* Heb. 1:1; Rom. 9:5).

4. The inclusion of Paul's letters among the 'other scriptures' favours the hypothesis of a late date, and suggests the formation of the Pauline Corpus of letters. If this is the case, to make Peter call Paul a 'beloved brother' was a stroke of genius in the *falsarius* unparalleled in the 2nd century, when divergencies between Peter and Paul were constantly exacerbated. No mention is made here of a corpus of letters, and the only real difficulty lies in one apostle's regarding the letters of another as Scripture. In view, however, of the apostolic assertion that the same Holy Spirit who inspired the OT writings was active in their own (1 Cor. 2:13), and the claims of Paul to have the mind of Christ (1 Cor. 2:16) and to lay down rules for all the churches (1 Cor. 7:17) which are equated with the commandment of Christ (1 Cor. 14:37) and rejection of which will bring rejection by God (1 Cor. 14:38), this possibility cannot be excluded.

IV. Conclusion

The evidence does not suffice to justify a dogmatic answer one way or the other to the question of authorship. There is nothing that forbids us to entertain the possibility of Petrine authorship, though many regard it as unlikely in view of the cumulative effect of the difficulties outlined above. However, no alternative solution is free from difficulty. The doctrine of the letter and the character of the false teaching do not readily fit into the 2nd-century scene. 2 Peter as a pseudepigraph has no satisfactory *raison d'être*; it adds nothing to our knowledge of Peter, has no unorthodox tendency, is no romance, makes no reference to burning 2nd-century problems, such as chiliasm, gnosticism or church leadership; in fact, it bears no resemblances to the undoubted pseudepigrapha of the Petrine circle. At all events, it is certain that the early church which deposed the author of the *Acts of Paul* for forgery (Tertullian, *de Baptismo* 17) and forbade the use of the *Gospel of Peter* because it was Petrine neither in authorship nor doctrine (Eus., *EH* 6. 12) thoroughly investigated 2 Peter's claims to authenticity. It passed the test before that same Council of Carthage which excluded from the Canon *Barnabas* and *Clement of Rome*, which had long been read in the churches. It cannot be shown that they were right; but it has still to be shown that they were wrong.

BIBLIOGRAPHY. Among those who reject the Petrine authorship are E. A. Abbott, *The Expositor* 2, 3, 1882, pp. 49ff., 139ff., 204ff.; F. H. Chase, *HDB*, 3, 1900, pp. 796ff.; J. B. Mayor, *The Epistle of Jude and the Second Epistle of Peter*, 1907; J. Moffatt, *INT*[3], 1918, pp. 358ff.; E. Käsemann, *ZTK* 49, 1952, pp. 272ff.; C. E. B. Cranfield, *I and II Peter and Jude*, *TBC*, 1960; C. Spicq, *Les Épitres de Saint Pierre*, 1966; J. N. D. Kelly, *The Epistles of Peter and of Jude*, *BNTC*, 1969; K. H. Schelkle, *Die Petrusbriefe und der Judasbrief*[3], 1976; R. J. Bauckham, *Jude, II Peter*, 1983. Those who accept the Epistle as Peter's include C. Bigg, *St. Peter and St. Jude*, *ICC*, 1902; T. Zahn, *INT*, 2, 1909, pp. 194ff.; E. I. Robson, *Studies in 2 Peter*, 1915; J. Chaine, *Les Épîtres Catholiques*, 1939; E. M. B. Green, *2 Peter Reconsidered*, 1961; *idem*, *The Second Epistle General of Peter and the General Epistle of Jude*[2], *TNTC*, 1987. See also R. V. G. Tasker, *The Old Testament in the New Testament*[2], 1954, p. 129. E.M.B.G.

PETHOR. A city of N Mesopotamia, S of Carchemish, mentioned in Nu. 22:5 as by the river (*i.e.* the Euphrates) and in Dt. 23:4 as in Mesopotamia, it was the home of Balaam. Thither Balak sent messengers to call him to curse Israel. Pethor in 'Amaw is the Pitru of Assyr. texts (*cf. ANET*, p. 278), described as on the river Sāgūr (modern Sājūr), near its junction with the Euphrates. On 'Amaw, see Albright, *BASOR* 118, 1950, pp. 15–16, n. 13, and for 'the eastern mountains (or hills)' note that in a 15th-century BC Egyp. text, chariot-wood from 'Amaw is said to come from 'god's land (= the E) in the hill-country of Naharen'—*i.e.* hills overlooking 'Amaw on the Sājūr river flowing into the Euphrates on its W bank; this W extension of (Aram-) Naharaim is attested by both Heb. and Egyp. references. R.A.H.G.

PHARAOH.

I. The term

The common title in Scripture for the kings of Egypt. It derives from Egyp. *pr-''*, 'great house'. This term was by origin simply a name for the royal palace and the Egyp. court, and is so used in the Old and Middle Kingdoms in the 3rd and first half of the 2nd millennium BC. But in the mid-18th Dynasty (*c.* 1450 BC) the term came to be applied to the person of the king himself, as a synonym for 'His Majesty'. The first examples of this usage apparently date from the reigns of Tuthmosis III(?) and IV, then under Amenophis IV/Akhenaten. From the 19th Dynasty onward, the simple term 'pharaoh' is constantly used in documents, just as it is particularly in Gn. and Ex. From the 22nd Dynasty onward (945 BC), the term 'pharaoh' could also be coupled with the king's name: thus, 'Pharaoh Sheshonq' occurs on a stele then, just like the slightly later OT references to Pharaoh Neco and Pharaoh Hophra. See Sir A. H. Gardiner, *Egyptian Grammar*[3], 1957, p. 75; J. Vergote, *Joseph en Égypte*, 1959, pp. 45–48, and the references cited.

II. Specific pharaohs

1. A contemporary of Abraham (Gn. 12:15–20). As Abraham lived *c.* 1900 BC, his pharaoh was most likely one of the several kings Amenemhat and Sesostris of the 12th Dynasty (*c.* 1991 1778 BC).

2. A contemporary of *Joseph (Gn. 37–50). Joseph lived *c.* 1700 BC; his pharaoh therefore would most likely be one of the Hyksos kings of the 15th Dynasty.

3. The pharaoh(s) of the oppression. The number of individual rulers covered by the terms 'king of Egypt' and 'pharaoh' in Ex. 1–2 is a matter of interpretation—one, or two. In any case, he/they would directly precede the pharaoh of the Exodus.

4. The pharaoh of the Exodus (Ex. 5–12). If the Exodus occurred in the first half of the 13th century BC, as seems likeliest on the evidence available, the pharaoh of the Exodus and last oppressor would be Rameses II.

5. The father of Bithiah, wife of Mered of the tribe of Judah (1 Ch. 4:18). The date of Bithiah and so of her royal father is uncertain, and therefore he has not yet been identified.

6. The pharaoh who received the young prince Hadad of Edom as a refugee from David and Joab's devastation of the Edomites (1 Ki. 11:18–22), and married him off to his sister-in-law. The pharaoh in question would be late in the 21st Dynasty, *i.e.* Amenemope or Siamūn. The obscurities of 21st Dynasty chronology forbid any closer dating.

7. The pharaoh who reduced Gezer and bestowed it as dowry on that daughter of his whom he gave in marriage to Solomon (1 Ki. 9:16; *cf.* also 3:1; 7:8; 9:24; 11:1). Shishak's raid into Palestine in 925 BC, the 5th year of Rehoboam, was not later than his own 21st year, and he acceded *c.* 945 BC. Solomon died in 931/30 BC after a 40-year reign which began *c.* 970 BC; hence Shishak acceded in Solomon's 25th year. Therefore Solomon's Egyp. contemporaries for his first 25 years of reign would be the last two kings of the 21st Dynasty, Siamūn and Psusennes II. Of these two, Siamūn is perhaps the pharaoh who took Gezer and bestowed it with his daughter upon Solomon; a triumphal scene of his from Tanis (Zoan) may provide evidence for warlike activity of Siamūn in Philistia. On this period of Egypto-Israelite relations, *cf.* K. A. Kitchen, *Third Intermediate Period in Egypt*, 1972, pp. 273ff., 280ff.

8. *Shishak, who is Sheshonq I, founder of the 22nd (Libyan) Dynasty. **9.** *So, contemporary of Hoshea. **10.** *Tirhakah, of the 25th (Ethiopian) Dynasty. **11.** *Neco, second king of the 26th Dynasty, is the pharaoh of Je. 25:19. **12.** *Hophra, fourth king of the 26th Dynasty, is apparently the pharaoh of Je. 37:5, 7, 11; Ezk. 17:17; 29:2–3; and possibly of Je. 47:1. *Zerah was almost certainly *not* a pharaoh.

III. Other references

These are found mainly in the prophets. Is. 19:11 is part of a passage reflecting disruption in Egypt. Such internal fragmentation first became chronic early in Isaiah's time, in the late 22nd–24th

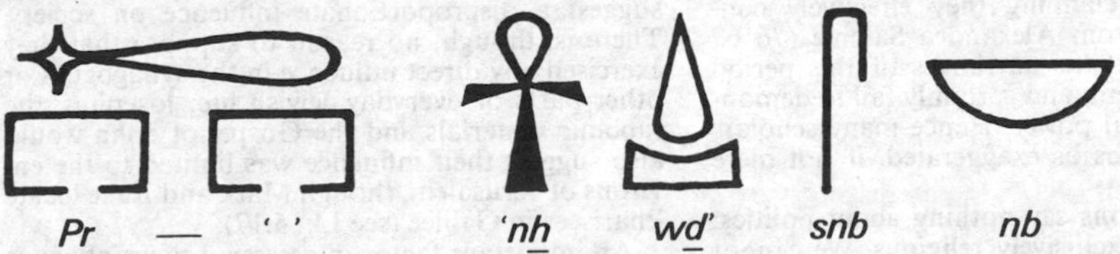

This address on a 14th-century BC letter reads: 'Pharaoh, life, prosperity, health, the Master.'

Dynasties (*c.* 750–715 BC), and continued under the overlordship of the Ethiopian kings of the 25th Dynasty (*c.* 715–664 BC). Pride in the long and exalted continuity of pharaonic tradition in accordance with v. 11 was reflected in the deliberate archaisms fostered by the 25th and 26th Dynasty kings, who sought thus to recall the glories of earlier epochs. The deceptive outward repute of the Ethiopian kings and their actual inability to help Israel against Assyria's armies are epitomized in Is. 30:2–3. Shebitku ('Shabataka') was on the throne in 701 BC when the Assyrian Rabshakeh dismissed pharaoh as a 'broken reed' (Is. 36:6 = 2 Ki. 18:21). For 'Pharaoh's house in Tahpanhes' (Je. 43:9), *TAHPANHES.

Both Jeremiah (46:25–26) and Ezekiel (30:21–25; 31:2, 18; 32:31–32) from 587 BC onward prophesied that Egypt would be worsted by *Nebuchadrezzar II of Babylon. In 568 BC Nebuchadrezzar did actually war against Egypt, as indicated by a fragmentary Babylonian text, though the extent of his success against Ahmose II (Amasis) is still unknown because of the lack of relevant documents. Lastly, Ct. 1:9 merely reflects the great fame of the chariot-horses of the pharaohs of the New Kingdom (*c.* 1550–1070 BC) and later. (*EGYPT, History; *CHRONOLOGY OF THE OLD TESTAMENT.)

K.A.K.

PHARISEES.

I. History

Reconstructing any Jewish sects (including *Sadducees, *Essenes, *Zealots, *Samaritans, and probably many others) is very difficult. Apart from the Jewish historian, Josephus, all the sources we have are 'travellers' tales' (*e.g.* Pliny, *NH* 5.73) and passing references, with the later rabbinic traditions which are of questionable value and strongly influenced by the destruction of the *Temple. All authors are biased, and most modern reconstructions use these sources far too uncritically.

While not presuming his readers to be familiar with the Pharisees, Josephus says nothing about aspects we would find most significant: their origins, doctrines, self-understanding and social structures.

His discussion of Jewish sects is part of his overall purpose to explain the downfall of God's chosen people. He therefore focuses on divine providence, predestination and free will. Josephus' Pharisees appear to occupy a mediating position between the rigid predestinarianism of the *Essenes and the human freedom asserted by the *Sadducees. He regards them as an attractive, popular and powerful faction, ascetic in lifestyle, concerned to present themselves as rigorists for the Torah. They have a body of additional interpretations and traditions, and religious practises are performed according to their interpretation (see especially *Ant.* 18:12–17). But he sees their major role as political, claiming they effectively controlled the state from Alexandra Salome (76–67 BCE) to Herod. Yet his narratives of this period hardly mention them, and certainly fail to demonstrate their political power. Hence many scholars see Josephus' claims as exaggerated, if not mere propaganda.

Rabbinic traditions say nothing about politics: the concerns are exclusively religious. We cannot assume the terms 'Pharisees', 'sages' or 'rabbis' refer to the group we know as Pharisees. The majority of the earliest traditions focus on purity laws; particularly washing, eating, tithing and festival Sabbath observance. Neusner therefore suggested that the Pharisees saw themselves, though laymen, as the 'kingdom of priests' of Ex. 19:6, observing the legislation relevant to a priest on Temple duty. (Similar motivation and concerns, interestingly, appear in the *Dead Sea Scrolls.) In the NT, too, cultic purity seems to be a major Pharisaic concern.

II. Relationship to other groups

All four gospels link *scribes and Pharisees (Mt. 5:20; 12:38; 15:1; 23; Mk. 2:16; 7:1; Lk. 5:21, 30; 6:7; 7:30; 11:53; 15:2; Jn. 8:3; *cf.* Acts 23.9). This only indicates that some scribes were Pharisees, and likely from their learning to take leading roles within the movement.

Matthew alone links Pharisees with *Sadducees (3:7; 16:1, 6, 11, 12). They might thus represent the leaders of the people, but generally the evangelists see various combinations of chief priests, elders and scribes in that role. Perhaps these two were seen as most doctrinally distinctive from other strands of Judaism. The opposition between them is important to Josephus and the rabbis; *cf.* also Acts 23:6–10.

Matthew once links Pharisees with the chief priests (21:45), and in John this combination is the moving force behind the formal opposition to Jesus (7:32, 45; 11:47, 57; 18:3). This might support Josephus' claims that they wielded political power. Although Matthew appears to intend two separate groups, Josephus notes that some priests were themselves Pharisees.

III. Teaching

The problems discussed above make it hard to be certain what was distinctively Pharisaic. Josephus' statements about the Pharisees being 'accurate interpreters of the Law' (*e.g.* *BJ* 2.162) must be tempered by his other comments attributing such accuracy to *all* Jewish sects, especially the priesthood. That they were conservative on some parts of the Law and liberal on others, adding also their own traditions, is neither surprising nor unique to their group. Any claim to be the definitive exponents of the Law would, however, give a cutting edge to Jesus' fierce denunciations.

The only point on which all sources agree is the Pharisees' belief in an afterlife. Josephus appears to contrast their position with Essene dualism: unrighteous souls are punished while the righteous pass into 'other bodies' (*BJ* 2.163), perhaps at a general resurrection.

IV. Influence

The traditional image of the all-powerful legalistic Pharisee is manifestly incorrect. Claims that they controlled cultic practice are incredible and contradicted by the evidence. However, our sources do suggest a disproportionate influence on society. There is, though, no reason to suppose that they exercised any direct influence in the synagogues or other parts of everyday Jewish life. Josephus, the rabbinic materials and the Gospel of John would also suggest their influence was limited to the environs of Jerusalem, though Mark and Luke locate Pharisees in Galilee (see Lk. 5:17).

An important factor in assessing their influence is the impression given by the synoptic writers that it was the Pharisees who took it upon themselves to vet Jesus' credentials and to seek to destroy his subversive new teaching. Hence they are portrayed as natural authorities in the community of faith, or at least in that part of most interest to the early Christian community. This coheres with both Josephus' report of their claims to 'accuracy' in interpretation, and with what we know of the early life of the erstwhile Pharisee, Paul (Gal. 1:13–14; Phil. 3.5f.). In Luke, in particular, they appear to regard Jesus as an equal, even while suffering his biting criticisms. In Acts they appear as a voice of moderation in the *Sanhedrin. But in general 'the Pharisees' quickly became a stereotype for the opponents of Jesus.

BIBLIOGRAPHY. See the items listed under SADDUCEES; J. Neusner, *The Rabbinic Traditions about the Pharisees before 70*, 3 vols., 1971; *idem*. 'Josephus' Pharisees: A Complete Repertoire', in L. H. Feldman & G. Hata (eds), *Josephus, Judaism, and Christianity*, 1987, pp. 274–292; S. Van Tilborg, *The Jewish Leaders in Matthew*, 1972; J. Lightstone, 'Sadducees *versus* Pharisees: The Tannaitic Sources', in Neusner (ed.), *Christianity, Judaism and other Greco-Roman Cults: Studies for Morton Smith at 60*, 3, 1975, pp. 206–217.; M. J. Cook, *Mark's Treatment of the Jewish leaders*, 1978; E. Rivkin, *The Hidden Revolution: An Historical Reconstruction of the Pharisees*, 1978; R. L. Brawley, *Luke–Acts and the Jews*, 1987; J. T. Sanders, *The Jews in Luke–Acts*, 1987; J. T. Carroll, 'Luke's Portrayal of the Pharisees', *CBQ* 50, 1988, pp. 604–621; D. B. Gowler, *Host, Guest, Enemy and Friend: Portraits of the Pharisees in Luke and Acts*, 1991; S. Mason, *Flavius Josephus on the Pharisees: A Composition-Critical Study*, 1991; *idem*, 'Chief Priests, Sadducees, Pharisees and Sanhedrin in Acts' in R. J. Bauckham (ed.), *The Book of Acts in its Palestinian Setting*, 1995. D.R. de L.

PHARPAR ('swift'). One of the two 'rivers of Damascus' of which Naaman boasted (2 Ki. 5:12). 64 km long, it is one of the tributaries of the *Abana or Barada, flows E from Hermon a little S of Damascus, and is now called the 'Awaj'. J.D.D.

PHILADELPHIA. A city in the Rom. province of Asia, in the W of what is now Asiatic Turkey. It was perhaps founded by Eumenes, king of Pergamum, in the 2nd century BC, and certainly named after his brother Attalus, whose loyalty had earned him the name Philadelphus. It was situated near the upper end of a broad valley leading down through Sardis to the sea near Smyrna; and it lay at the threshold of a very fertile tract of plateau country, from which much of its commercial prosperity derived. The area was subject to frequent earthquakes. A severe one in AD 17 destroyed the city; and as the shocks continued intermittently the people took to living outside the city (Strabo, *Geography* 12.8.18 *(579)*; 13.4.10 *(628)*). After an imperial bounty had helped it to recover, the city voluntarily assumed the new name of Neocaesarea. Later, under Vespasian, it took another imperial name, Flavia. The city was remarkable for the number of its temples and religious festivals. The site is now occupied by the town of Alaşehir.

The letter to 'the angel of the church in Philadelphia' (Rev. 3:7–13) probably alludes to some of

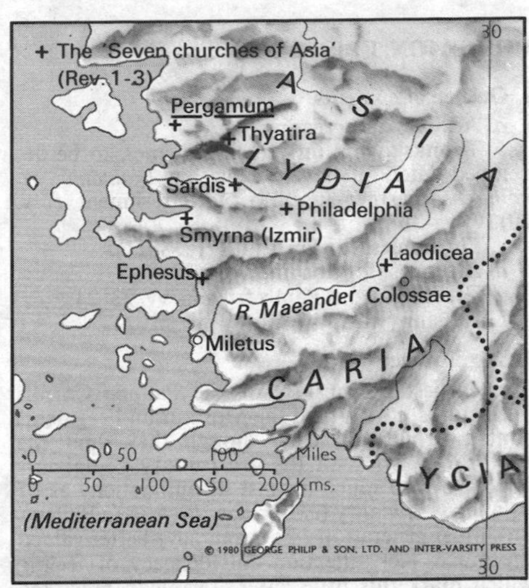

Philadelphia, one of the 'seven churches of Asia' (Rev. 1–3).

the circumstances of the city. As Philadelphus was renowned for his loyalty to his brother, so the church, the true Philadelphia, inherits and fulfils his character by its steadfast loyalty to Christ (vv. 8, 10). As the city stands by the 'open door' of a region from which its wealth derives, so the church is given an 'open door' of opportunity to exploit (v. 8; *cf.* 2 Cor. 2:12). The symbols of the 'crown' and the 'temple' (vv. 11–12) point to a contrast with the games and religious festivals of the city. In contrast with the impermanence of life in a city prone to earthquakes, those who 'overcome' are promised the ultimate stability of being built into the temple of God. As at Smyrna, this church had met rejection from the Jews in the city (v. 9), but the conqueror shall enjoy final acceptance by the Lord whose name he had confessed (v. 8), signified again by the conferring on him of the divine names (v. 12), which recall the new names taken by the city from the divine emperors. Ignatius later visited the city on his way from Antioch to martyrdom in Rome, and sent a letter to the church there.

BIBLIOGRAPHY. C. J. Hemer, *The Letters to the Seven Churches of Asia in their Local Setting*, 1986; E. M. Yamauchi, *New Testament Cities in Western Asia Minor*, 1980. M.J.S.R. C.J.H.

PHILEMON. The owner of the slave *Onesimus and almost certainly a resident of Colossae (*PHILEMON, EPISTLE TO, for other views). Though Paul had not himself visited Colossae (Col. 2:1), Philemon was apparently converted through him (Phm. 19) and had been a colleague (the normal meaning of 'fellow-worker', Phm. 1, RSV)—both, perhaps, in Ephesus, the provincial capital (*cf.* Acts 19:31). The argument of J. Knox (who applies Phm. 19 to Archippus), that Paul would regard the work of any of his associates as his own, is hardly borne out by Col. 1:7f., which he cites, nor is Phm. 5 ('*hear* of your love') incompatible with past acquaintance. A.F.W.

PHILEMON, EPISTLE TO.

I. Outline of contents

a. Address and greeting (vv. 1–3).

b. Thanksgiving: introducing themes, to be developed later, of love, fellowship (*koinōnia*; *cf.* *koinōnos*, 'partner' in v. 17) and refreshment (*cf.* v. 20) (vv. 4–7).

c. The request for Onesimus (vv. 8–21).

d. A request for hospitality (v. 22).

e. Greetings from Paul's friends (vv. 23–24).

f. Blessing (v. 25).

II. Significance

The earliest extant lists of the Pauline Corpus (Marcion's 'canon' and the Muratorian Fragment) contain Philemon, even though they omit the Pastoral Epistles. In the 4th century complaints appear not so much against its authenticity as of its alleged triviality (*cf.* Jerome, *Preface to* Philemon): most generations, however, have better valued the grace, tact, affection and delicacy of feeling which mark this little letter. Tertullian remarked that it was the only Epistle which Marcion left uncontaminated by 'editing' (*Adv. Marc.* 5, 21), and its authenticity has never been responsibly questioned. In recent years it has become a bastion of the theory of the Pauline Corpus associated with E. J. Goodspeed and John Knox (*PAUL, **III.** *d.* ii); gratitude for the fresh interest they have stimulated in Philemon, and the adoption of some of their suggestions, does not, however, demand acceptance of this highly dubious reconstruction.

III. Form

The personal and informal nature of Philemon (*cf.* Deissmann, *LAE*, pp. 234f., and *EPISTLE) may distract attention from its extremely careful composition and observance of literary forms (*cf.* Knox, pp. 18f.). It should also be noted that a house-church is in mind as well as the people named in the address (v. 2). Goodspeed and Knox over-emphasize the part the church is expected to play in swaying the slave-owner to 'do the Christian thing' (Goodspeed, p. 118): the second person singular is used throughout, even for the greetings: the only exceptions are in vv. 22 (the hoped-for visit) and 25 (the benediction). This affords a contrast with Ignatius' letter to Polycarp, which is addressed to an individual but with frequent passages in the second person plural which show that the church is being harangued. Philemon is addressed to the slave-owner, with his family and church presumably linked with him after the manner of Rom. 16:5; Col. 4:15. Comparison has often been invited with Pliny's letter (*Ep.* 9. 21) on behalf of an errant but repentant freedman.

IV. Purpose and occasion

The core of the Epistle is an appeal by Paul on behalf of one Onesimus, a slave from Colossae (Col. 4:9) whose conduct had contrasted with his name ('useful'—a pun is involved in Phm. 10–11). It seems that Onesimus had robbed his master (18) and run away (15—not quite explicit). By some means unstated—perhaps his fellow-townsman Epaphras (Col. 4:12) was instrumental—he was brought into contact with the imprisoned Paul and radically converted. Not only so, but strong affection developed between Paul and his new 'son', in whom the veteran saw rich potential.

Under contemporary law, almost limitless vengeance could be wreaked on Onesimus by his owner: Graeco-Roman society was never free from the phobia of a servile war, and even an otherwise good master might think it his duty to society to make an example of the runaway. Frightful penalties also awaited those who harboured runaways (*cf.* P. Oxy. 1422). It is at this point that Paul interposes with his brother (7, 20), not commanding, but begging (8–9) that his owner will receive Onesimus as he would Paul himself (17), and solemnly undertaking all the slave's debts (18–19).

But probably Paul is asking more than mercy. Knox points out that *parakaleō* followed by *peri* (as in v. 10) usually means in late Gk. 'to ask *for*' rather than 'on behalf of'. Paul highly valued Onesimus; his departure caused him great sorrow; and but for the necessity of obtaining his owner's permission would have liked to keep him with him (11–14). The fullness of Paul's request would be that Onesimus might be released to Paul for Christian service. He would thenceforth stand in an unspeakably closer and more permanent relationship than the old domestic one (15–16). In any case, to Paul's ministry this correspondent owes his own conversion (19).

Paul is in prison (9–10): the occasion is the same as that indicated in Colossians, for Onesimus is to accompany Tychicus, the bearer of that letter (Col. 4:9). Paul's party in Phm. 23f. is the same as that in Col. 4:10–14, with the exception of Jesus Justus (unless this is a scribal omission; *cf.* E. Amling, *ZNW* 10, 1909–10, p. 261). The place of imprisonment will be decided mainly on grounds external to the letter: the real alternatives are Rome, in the first imprisonment (*c.* AD 62) or Ephesus about AD 55 (*PAUL; *CHRONOLOGY OF THE NEW TESTAMENT). Either city might have attracted Onesimus. Ephesus was near home, but large enough to be lost in; Rome was a haven for displaced persons of every kind. In either case there is some expectation of release and a journey to Philemon's area in the foreseeable future.

There are other links with Colossians. Col. 3:22ff. (*cf.* Eph. 6:5–9) could hardly have been written without Onesimus, and the possible effect on his career, in mind. Knox and Goodspeed have, however, little reason to associate the charge to Archippus and the 'Epistle from Laodicea' (Col. 4:16–17) with the Onesimus case. Knox himself has disposed of Goodspeed's suggestion that Onesimus' owner lived at Laodicea (pp. 40ff.), but his own suggestion that Philemon received the letter first as the (Laodicean) superintendent of the Lycus churches and that Archippus in Colossae was the slave-owner and principal addressee, fares no better. It requires an unnatural reading of the address, and a heavy burden on a few words (*e.g.* 'fellow worker' and 'fellow soldier' in vv. 1 and 2). Whether the epistle of Col. 4:16 was *Ephesians or some unknown letter is uncertain, but nothing suggests that it was Philemon. (*APPHIA; *ARCHIPPUS; *ONESIMUS; *PHILEMON.)

BIBLIOGRAPHY. Commentaries (with Colossians) on the Gk. text by C. F. D. Moule, 1957; P. T. O'Brien, *WBC*, 1982; commentaries on the Eng. text by J. Knox, *IB*, 1955; R. P. Martin, *NCB*, 1974; N. T. Wright, *TNTC*, 1986. See also J. Knox, *Philemon among the Epistles of Paul*[2], 1959; F. F. Bruce, *BJRL* 48, 1965, pp. 81–97; S. C. Winter, *NTS* 33, 1987, pp. 1–15.

A.F.W.

PHILETUS. A teacher representative of those undermining the Christian doctrine of the resurrection (2 Tim. 2:17). (*HYMENAEUS.) J.D.D.

PHILIP (Gk. *philippos*, 'horse-lover'). There are 4 characters of this name known to the NT writers.

1. A son of Herod the Great and Mariamne, the daughter of Simon the high priest. For a time he was next in succession to Antipater (Jos., *Ant.* 17. 53), but this arrangement was revoked by later wills, and he lived as a private citizen. A. H. M. Jones (*The Herods of Judaea*, 1938, p. 176n.) claims that his name was Herod, not Philip. (Jos., *Ant.* 18. 137, calls him Herod, but so many members of the *Herod family bore this name that an additional name was almost obligatory.) His wife *Herodias, the mother of Salome, left him in order to live with Herod Antipas, his half-brother (Mt. 14:3; Mk. 6:17; Lk. 3:19).

2. A son of Herod the Great by his fifth wife, Cleopatra of Jerusalem; Jos., *Ant.* 17. 21 states that he was brought up at Rome. By Augustus' settlement of Herod's will Philip was granted the tetrarchy of Gaulanitis, Trachonitis, Auranitis, Batanaea (Jos.), and Ituraea (Lk. 3:1). He ruled for 37 years until his death in the winter of AD 33/ 34, and differed from his kinsfolk in the moderation and justice of his rule (Jos., *Ant.* 18. 106). At his death the territory was incorporated into the province of Syria until AD 37, when the emperor Gaius Caligula granted it to Agrippa (the Herod of Acts 12:1, 19–23), son of Aristobulus and grandson of Herod and Mariamne. Philip rebuilt Panias (modern Banyas) as Caesarea Philippi (Mt. 16:13; Mk. 8:27) and Beth-saida Julias (Jos., *Ant.* 18. 28; *BJ* 2. 168), both names reflecting his pro-Roman sympathies. He was the first Jewish prince to impress the heads of Roman emperors on his coins. He married Salome, the daughter of *Herodias, and had no children (Jos., *Ant.* 18. 137).

3. Philip the apostle was called to follow Jesus on the day following the call of Andrew and Simon, and was instrumental in bringing Nathanael to follow him (Jn. 1:43–46). His home was *Beth-saida (Jn. 1:44): this was the Beth-saida of Galilee (Jn. 12:21), the home town of Andrew and Simon, and is thought to have been a fishing-village on the W shore of the lake. In the lists of the apostles in Mt. 10:3; Mk. 3:14; Lk. 6:14 he is placed fifth in order, with Bartholomew sixth: Acts 1:13 places him fifth, but puts Thomas in the sixth place. The only other references to him in the NT tell of his inability to suggest to Jesus how to supply the food for the 5,000 (Jn. 6:5), his bringing the Greeks to Jesus (Jn. 12:21f.), and his request of Jesus to see the Father (Jn. 14:8). Papias 2. 4 refers to him as one of the *presbyteroi* (see further below).

4. Philip was one of the 'Seven' who were chosen as officials (the first *'deacons') of the church at Jerusalem (Acts 6:5). On the persecution of the church following the martyrdom of Stephen he took the gospel to Samaria, where his ministry was much blessed (Acts 8:5–13), and subsequently he was sent S to the Jerusalem–Gaza road to lead the Ethiopian eunuch to Christ (Acts 8:26–38). After this incident he was 'Spirited' away to Azotus, the Philistine Ashdod, and from there conducted an itinerant ministry until he reached the port of Caesarea (Acts 8:39–40), where he appears to have settled (Acts 21:8). He was known as 'the evangelist',

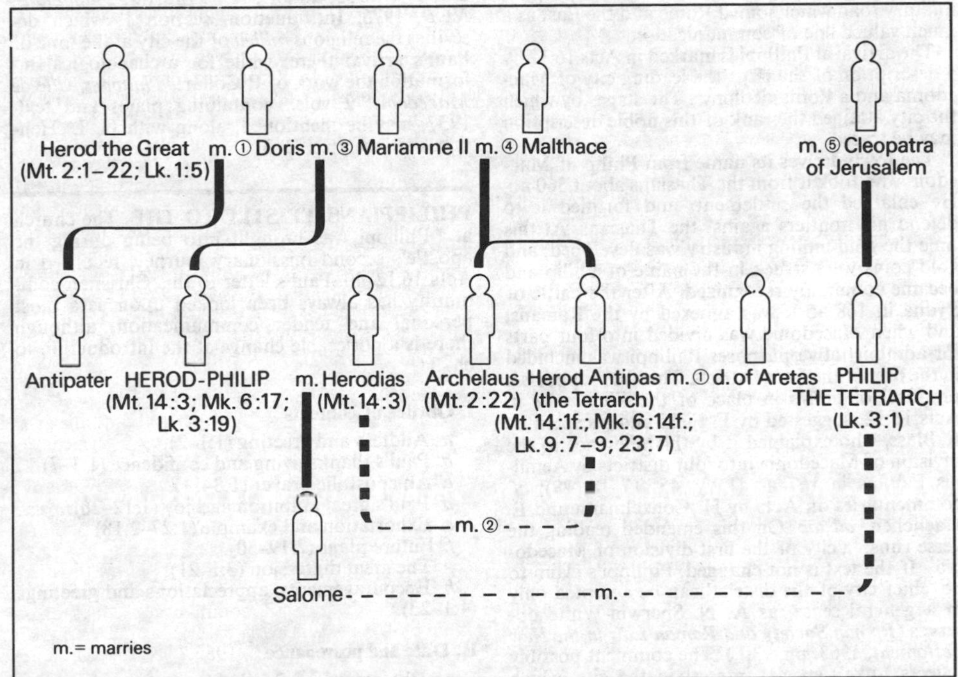

Two of the members of Herod's family, according to the NT, were named Philip. Simplified family tree.

presumably to distinguish him from the apostle (3, above), and had four daughters who were prophetesses (Acts 21:9). Luke is here at great pains to distinguish the evangelist from the apostle. Eusebius twice (*EH* 3. 31; 5. 24) quotes Polycrates as referring to Philip, 'one of the twelve apostles', and his two aged virgin daughters as being buried at Hierapolis, while another daughter was buried at Ephesus. Perhaps this last was the one mentioned in 3. 30 (quoting Clement of Alexandria, who may use the plural here loosely) as having been given in marriage. Papias is also cited (*EH* 3. 39) as stating that 'the apostle Philip' and his daughters lived at Hierapolis and the daughters supplied him with information. A quotation from the *Dialogue of Gaius and Proclus* in Eus., *EH* 3. 31 that the tomb of Philip and his four prophesying daughters may be seen at Hierapolis, followed by a reference to Acts 21:8–9, shows that the historian had confused the apostle and the evangelist. It would seem most likely that both the apostle and the evangelist had daughters, which would lead to their confusion. Lightfoot (*Colossians*, pp. 45ff.) is probably right in maintaining that it was the apostle who died in Hierapolis.

The papyrus finds at Nag Hammadi (*CHENOBOSKION) have revealed an apocryphal *Gospel according to Philip*: see R. McL. Wilson, *The Gospel of Philip*, 1962. D.H.W.

PHILIPPI. In the course of his apostolic travels Paul received in a vision an invitation from a man of Macedonia who implored, 'Come over to Macedonia, and help us' (Acts 16:9). Interpreting this plea as a summons from God, Paul and his party sailed for Neapolis, the port of Philippi, 13 km S of the city and the terminus of the Egnatian Way, a military road which joined Rome and the East as a much valued line of communication.

The arrival at Philippi is marked in Acts 16:12 by a description of the city: 'the leading city of Macedonia and a Roman colony'. The stages by which the city attained the rank of this noble description may be traced.

The town derives its name from Philip of Macedon, who took it from the Thasians about 360 BC. He enlarged the settlement, and fortified it to defend his frontiers against the Thasians. At this time the gold-mining industry was developed, and gold coins were struck in the name of Philip and became commonly recognized. After the battle of Pydna in 168 BC it was annexed by the Romans; and when Macedonia was divided into four parts for administrative purposes Philippi was included in the first of the four districts. This fact supports a proposal of *prōtēs* in place of the TR's *prōtē* in Acts 16:12, suggested by F. Field and accepted by F. Blass, who explained it by this reference to the division of Macedonia into four districts by Aemilius Paullus in 167 BC (Livy, 45. 17–18, 29); *cf.* commentaries on Acts by H. Conzelmann and E. Haenchen, *ad loc.* On this emended reading the verse runs: 'a city of the first division of Macedonia'. If the text is not changed, Philippi's claim to be 'chief city of the district' can be accepted only in a general sense, as A. N. Sherwin-White observes (*Roman Society and Roman Law in the New Testament*, 1963, pp. 93ff.). The comment possibly reflects Luke's special interest in the city, which may have been his birth-place.

In 42 BC the famous battle of Philippi was fought with Antony and Octavian ranged against Brutus and Cassius. After this date the town was enlarged, probably by the coming of colonists; the title *Colonia Iulia* is attested at this time. This prominence was enhanced further when, after the battle of Actium in 31 BC, in which Octavian defeated the forces of Antony and Cleopatra, the town 'received a settlement of Italian colonists who had favoured Antony and had been obliged to surrender their land to the veterans of Octavian' (Lake and Cadbury, p. 187). Octavian gave the town its notable title, *Col*(*onia*) *Iul*(*ia*) *Aug*(*usta*) *Philip*(*pensis*), which has appeared on coins. Of all the privileges which this title conferred, the possession of the 'Italic right' (*ius Italicum*) was the most valuable. It meant that the colonists enjoyed the same rights and privileges as if their land were part of Italian soil.

The civic pride of the Philippians (who are given the equivalent of their Latin name *Philippenses* in Paul's letter, 4:15) is a feature of the Acts narrative, and reappears in allusions the apostle makes in the Epistle. See Acts 16:21; *cf.* 16:37. Official names are used (*duoviri* in 16:20, 22, and 'lictors' in 16:35). The Gk. word translated 'uncondemned' in 16:37 probably reflects the Latin *re incognita* or *indicta causa*, *i.e.* 'without examination'. In the letter to the Philippian church two passages, 1:27 and 3:20, speak of 'citizenship', a term which would have special appeal to the readers; and the virtues listed in 4:8 are those which the Roman mind would particularly appreciate.

After the apostle's first visit with his preaching, imprisonment and release, his further contact with the city is inferred from references in Acts 20:1, 6; 1 Tim. 1:3.

BIBLIOGRAPHY. Historical details are supplied in *BC*, 1, 4, 1933, *ad loc.*; R. P. Martin, *Philippians*, *NCB*, 1976, Introduction, section 1, which describes the religious *milieu* of the city at the time of Paul's arrival there; while for archaeological information the work of P. Collart, *Philippes, ville de Macédoine*, 2 vols., containing plates and text, 1937, may be mentioned, along with H. L. Hendrix, *ABD* 5, pp. 313–317. R.P.M.

PHILIPPIANS, EPISTLE TO THE. The church at *Philippi was brought into being during the apostle's second missionary journey, recorded in Acts 16:12–40. Paul's letter to this Christian community has always been looked upon as a most personal and tender communication, although there is a noticeable change at the introduction to ch. 3.

I. Outline of contents

a. Address and greeting (1:1–2).
b. Paul's thanksgiving and confidence (1:3–7).
c. An apostolic prayer (1:8–11).
d. Paul's great ambition and joy (1:12–26).
e. Exhortation and example (1:27–2:18).
f. Future plans (2:19–30).
g. The great digression (3:1–21).
h. Encouragements, appreciations and greetings (4:1–23).

II. Date and provenance

From the record of Paul's life in the Acts of the Apostles we know of only three imprisonments (16:23–40; 21:32–23:30; 28:30), during one of which this letter was written (Phil. 1:7, 13–14, 16). It obviously cannot have been written during the first; and it seems at first sight that the choice is a simple one between his captivity at Caesarea and the 2 years' detention at Rome.

a. The Caesarean hypothesis

This view goes back to 1799, when it was propounded by H. E. G. Paulus. Rather surprising support came later from E. Lohmeyer in the Meyer commentary, and there have been several suggestive studies (see Martin, *Philippians*, *NCB*, 1976, pp. 45–48) in support of this setting of the letter. The suggestion of the letter's composition during the imprisonment at Caesarea contains some difficulties, which may be enumerated as follows:

1. The custody of Acts 23:35 does not suggest the imminent martyrdom which Lohmeyer takes as the controlling theme of the entire letter (*cf.* his analysis of the letter in these terms, pp. 5f.).

2. The size and type of the Christian community at the place of his captivity do not tally with what we know of the church at Caesarea (1:14ff.), as Moffatt indicates (*An Introduction to the Literature of the New Testament*, 1918, p. 169).

3. The apostle's outlook at the time of Acts 23–24 was bound up with a visit to Rome, but of this desire there is no hint in Philippians; rather he looks forward to a return visit to Philippi (2:24ff.).

b. The Roman hypothesis

The alternative proposal is that the letter was written and despatched during the apostle's Roman captivity; and this remains the traditional view, with many adherents. It has considerable evidence in its favour:

1. The allusions to the *praetorium* (1:13) and to 'Caesar's household' (4:22) correspond to the historical detail of the Roman detention, whatever the precise meaning of the terms may be.

2. The gravity of the charge and of the impending verdict (1:20ff.; 2:17; 3:11) suggests that Paul is on trial for his life in the highest judicial court, from which there can be no appeal. It is submitted that this piece of evidence shows that it cannot have been a provincial court whose judgment Paul awaits, for even if the verdict there were unfavourable, he would still have a 'trump card' (in C. H. Dodd's phrase) to play which would quash this local sentence and transfer his case to Rome. That he does not appear to have recourse to this is presumptive evidence that he has in fact so appealed, and that the appeal has brought him to the imperial city.

3. The church at Rome would correspond, in size and influence, to the references in 1:12ff., which point to a Christian fellowship of considerable importance.

4. The length of the imprisonment is sufficient, according to the proponents of this view, to allow for the journeys mentioned or implied by the letter. But this is a matter of debate.

5. There is indirect witness to the Roman provenance of the Epistle in the Marcionite prologue to the letter, which says, 'The apostle praises them from Rome in prison by Epaphroditus.'

There are, however, certain difficulties about this time-honoured view which have made scholars hesitate before accepting it. A. Deissmann was apparently the first to formulate these doubts, which we may state thus:

1. Deissmann drew attention to the fact that journeys to and from the place of captivity imply that the place cannot have been far from Philippi. It was argued that on the Roman hypothesis it is difficult to fit 'those enormous journeys', as he called them, into the 2 years mentioned as the duration of the Roman imprisonment.

2. Moreover, the situation reflected in the letter, with its foreboding of imminent martyrdom, hardly corresponds with the comparative freedom and relaxed atmosphere of Acts 28:30–31. If the letter came out of that detention it is clearly necessary to postulate an unfavourable development in the apostle's relations with the authorities which led to a change for the worse in his conditions and prospects.

3. A telling criticism of the traditional theory is the witness of 2:24, which expresses the hope that, if the apostle is set free, he intends to revisit the Philippians, and also to take up his missionary and pastoral work in their midst once again. This is an important *datum* from the internal evidence of the letter itself, for we know from Rom. 15:23–24, 28 that at that time he considered his missionary work in the E as completed, and was setting his face to the W, notably to Spain. If the letter emanates from Rome (*i.e.* if it is later than the writing of Rom. 15) it is necessary to believe that a new situation had arisen which led him to revise his plans. This possibility, indeed, is not unthinkable, as we know from his movements at Corinth; but it does show that the Roman view is not entirely free from weaknesses.

c. The Ephesian hypothesis

In place of the Roman dating it is proposed to place the letter in a putative Ephesian captivity. The evidence for this imprisonment is inferential and therefore lacking in complete cogency; but the scholars who support it find that the locating of the letter in this period of Paul's life eases the difficulties which the Roman theory encounters. For example, the intended re-visit to Philippi is then fulfilled in Acts 20:1–6, with Timothy's movements also tallying with the record of Acts. W. Michaelis, who has consistently championed the Ephesian origin, shows persuasively how, on this view, the movements mentioned both in Acts and in Philippians dovetail like the pieces of a jig-saw puzzle. The shorter distance between Philippi and Ephesus makes the journeys more within the bounds of likelihood, while there is inscriptional evidence that satisfies the requirement of 1:13 and 4:22. Ephesus was the centre of the imperial administration in Asia, and there would be a *praetorium* there.

The main difficulties which stand in the way of accepting this novel theory are:

1. Its speculative character. The Ephesian imprisonment cannot be proved from a direct source, although there is much indirect attestation of it, especially in 1 and 2 Cor.

2. The absence of any mention of a matter which (so it is argued) must have filled the apostle's mind at the time of this suggested dating, *viz.* the collection for the churches in Judaea.

3. Perhaps the strongest counter-objection is the failure to explain why it was that, if Paul were in jeopardy at Ephesus, he did not use his right as a Roman citizen and extricate himself by an appeal to the emperor to be tried in Rome. Of this possibility there is no mention in the letter.

Our conclusion, then, must be a disappointing

one to those who expect a firm answer. The evidence, we feel, is finely balanced, and a final decision is not possible. The Roman dating may still be accepted with caution and one or two lingering doubts. The Ephesian hypothesis would have to be sufficiently strong to reverse the judgment of centuries, and this it fails to do, although it has many points in its favour; and were it more securely anchored in direct evidence it would command wider support. The tide of critical opinion is, however, running in favour of a dating in the Ephesian period (see Martin, *op. cit.*, pp. 36–57). (*PAUL.)

III. The unity of the letter

In the textual history the letter is known only as a complete whole; but there are many suggestions which contest its unity, mainly on the ground of an abrupt change in tone, style and content at the beginning of ch. 3. Explanations of this sudden change are given under the headings of 'Interpolation' and 'Interruption'.

a. Interpolation

On this view the reason for the abrupt change at 3:1b is that this verse introduces an interpolated fragment from another Pauline letter which has somehow become interwoven into the canonical Epistle. There is little agreement as to where the interpolation ends, whether 4:3 (so K. Lake), 4:1 (A. H. McNeile–C. S. C. Williams, F. W. Beare), or 3:19 (J. H. Michael). Beare envisages the letter as a composite document made up of three elements: a letter of thanks, acknowledging the Philippians' gift by Epaphroditus (4:10–20); an interpolated fragment which denounces the false teaching of the Jewish missionaries and the antinomianism of Gentile Christians (3:2–4:1), and may be directed to some church other than Philippi, as J. H. Michael earlier proposed; and the framework of the Epistle (1:1–3:1; 4:2–9, 21–23), regarded as being the last of Paul's extant letters and, in a sense, his farewell message to the church militant on earth. This analysis has several variations (see Martin, *op. cit.*, pp. 14–21 for details), but in the main the partition into three fragments is widely held. For a convincing defence of the letter's unity, see R. Jewett, *NovT* 12, 1970, pp. 40–53.

b. Interruption

The sudden change in style and outlook may more plausibly be accounted for by the interruption of the apostle as he dictated his letter, as Lightfoot suggested. See also E. Stange, 'Diktierpausen in den Paulusbriefen', in *ZNW* 18, 1917–18, pp. 115f.

On this interpretation, 3:1a is the intended conclusion of the letter. Paul is disturbed by stirring news which has just reached him, and quickly turns aside to dictate a vehement warning. 'The same things' is a prospective term, looking forward to the serious admonitions to watchfulness against the Judaizers which are to follow. See V. P. Furnish, *NTS* 10, 1963–4, pp. 80–88.

The integrity of the letter is, therefore, to be accepted, with a possible reservation only in the case of 2:5–11, which some regard as a pre-Pauline or post-Pauline composition, while F. W. Beare breaks new ground with the submission that this section owes its origin to an unknown Gentile writer who came under Pauline influence during the apostle's lifetime. Paul accepts his writing with his *imprimatur* by including it in his Epistle. There is a full discussion of the authorship and provenance of the Christological hymn in 2:5–11 in the writer's monograph; see below.

IV. The occasion and purpose of the letter

The most obvious reason why the letter came to be written is to be found in Paul's situation as a prisoner, and his desire to commend his colleagues Timothy and Epaphroditus to the church. Paul writes as though he wanted to prepare the way for the coming of these men, and particularly to disarm any criticism which might be raised against Epaphroditus (*cf.* 2:23ff.).

There is also the note of appreciation for the Philippians' gift, to which he alludes in several places (1:5; 4:10, 14ff.). This gift had evidently come through Epaphroditus, and Paul gratefully acknowledges both the gift and the presence of their messenger (2:25).

Epaphroditus had, it is clear, also brought news of the outbreak of various troubles at Philippi, especially the disturbing news of disunity within the ranks of the church members. This is clear from 2:2–4, 14; 4:2, where the disputants are named, and perhaps 1:27. Paul gently reproaches them for this, and recalls them to agreement in the Lord.

Another source of confusion in the fellowship seems to have been the existence and influence of a 'perfectionist' group within the church. There are grounds—known by inference from Paul's counter-arguments—for believing that the Philippians' confidence in being 'perfect' was based on a gnosticized eschatology that eliminated the future hope of the Christians and transferred it to a present experience. Paul's response in ch. 3 is directed to a rebuttal of this. (For details, see Martin, *op. cit.*, pp. 22–34.)

The Christian cause at Philippi seems to have been the object of persecution and attack from the outside world. There is definite allusion to the church's 'enemies' (1:28), and a description of the type of society in which the church was called upon to live and bear witness to Christ is given (2:15). Hence the oft-repeated call to stand fast (1:27; 4:1). We may detect in a ministry of encouragement a further reason for the letter, although Lohmeyer's interpretation of the entire Epistle as a 'tract for martyrs' is somewhat extreme.

V. The value of the letter

Two outstanding features of the letter may be mentioned. First, the Philippian letter will always remain as a tribute to the apostle's attitude to his sufferings. By the grace of God he is able to rejoice under the most trying circumstances of his captivity and impending fate. His constant call to rejoicing (the word 'joy' and its cognate forms is found 16 times) is a distinguishing characteristic, as Bengel noted in his famous phrase: '*summa epistolae; gaudeo, gaudete*'. And the secret of that joy is fellowship with the Lord who is the centre of his life, whatever the future may hold (1:20–21).

Secondly, no introduction to the letter would be complete without a reference to the great passage in 2:5–11. Here we find the *locus classicus* of Paul's doctrine of the person of Christ and the nature and scope of Christian salvation, and for that reason the Philippian Epistle will ever remain in the forefront of Pauline studies so long as the great apostle's writings continue to engage the attention of Christian students.

BIBLIOGRAPHY. Commentaries by F. W. Beare, 1959; K. Barth, E.T. 1962; K. Grayston, *CBC*,

1967; R. P. Martin, *NCB*, 1976 and *TNTC*², 1987; G. F. Hawthorne, *WBC*, 1983; J. A. Motyer, *BST*, 1984; P. T. O'Brien, *NIGTC*, 1991. See also J. L. Houlden, *Paul's Letters from Prison*, 1970; G. B. Caird, *Paul's Letters from Prison*, 1976; R. P. Martin, *Carmen Christi: Philippians 2:5–11*², 1983; J. T. Fitzgerald, *ABD* 5, pp. 318–326. R.P.M.

PHILISTINES, PHILISTIA.

I. Name

In the OT the name Philistine is written *pᵉlištî*, usually with the article, and more commonly in its plural form *pᵉlištîm* (rarely *pᵉlištiyyîm*) generally without the article. The territory which they inhabited was known as 'the land of the Philistines' (*'ereṣ pᵉlištîm*) or Philistia (*pᵉlešeṯ*). The modern name 'Palestine' is derived from this through Assyr. *Palastu*, Gk. *Palaestine* and Lat. *Palaestina*. In the Septuagint the word is variously rendered *Phylistieim* (mainly in the Pentateuch, Joshua and Judges). *Hellenas* (Is. 9:12 [11, Heb.]), and *allophylos, -oi*, 'stranger, foreigner' (but not in the Pentateuch or Joshua). It is probable that the name is to be identified with *prst* in the Egyp. texts (the sounds *l* and *r* are not separately represented in the hieroglyphic script) and *palaštu* in the Assyr. cuneiform inscriptions.

II. In the Bible

a. Origin of the Philistines

According to the *Table of Nations (Gn. 10:14; 1 Ch. 1:12), the Philistines derived from Casluhim, the son of Mizraim (Egypt) the son of Ham (Gn. 10:14; 1 Ch. 1:12). When they later appeared and confronted the Israelites they came from *Caphtor (Am. 9:7).

b. In the time of the Patriarchs

Abraham and Isaac had dealings with a Philistine, Abimelech, the king of Gerar, and his general Phichol (Gn. 20–21; 26). In the time of the Monarchy the Philistines were almost proverbially aggressive, but Abimelech was a reasonable man. He had adopted many of the customs of the country, had a Semitic name, and engaged with Isaac in a covenant.

c. At the time of the Exodus and the Judges

When the Israelites left Egypt the Philistines were extensively settled along the coastal strip between Egypt and Gaza, and they were obliged to detour inland to avoid 'the way of the land of the Philistines' (Ex. 13:17). The adjacent section of the Mediterranean was in fact referred to as the sea of the Philistines (Ex. 23:31). The Philistines probably did not settle in the area until after the time of the exodus, so in these references the name is presumably used retrospectively. It is presumably the Philistines in this area who are referred to as Caphtorim in Dt. 2:23.

The Israelites did not encounter the Philistines in Canaan during the Conquest, but by the time Joshua was an old man they were established in the five cities of Gaza, Ashkelon, Ashdod, Ekron and Gath (Jos. 13:2–3). From this time for many generations these people were used by God to chastise the Israelites (Jdg. 3:2–3). Shamgar ben Anath repulsed them temporarily (Jdg. 3:31), but they constantly pressed inland from the coast plain, and the Israelites even adopted their gods (Jdg. 10:6–7). The great Israelite hero of the period of the Judges was Samson (Jdg. 13–16). In his time there were social links between Philistines and Israelites, for he married a Philistine wife, and later had relations with Delilah, who, if not a Philistine herself, was in close contact with them. The hill-country was not under Philistine control, and Samson took refuge there after his raids. When he was finally taken by them he was bound with bronze fetters (16:21) and forced to make sport for them while they watched from inside and on the roof of a pillared building (16:25–27).

d. In the reigns of Saul and David

Continuing Philistine pressure was probably one reason Israel felt the need for a strong military leader. The Philistines captured the Ark and destroyed Shiloh (1 Sa. 4), and had control of Esdraelon, the coastal plain, the Negeb and much of the hill-country. By restricting the distribution of iron, they prevented the Israelites from having new-style weapons (1 Sa. 13:19–22). It was probably largely due to the continuing pressure of the Philistines that the need for a strong military leader was felt in Israel. The ark was captured by the Philistines in a disastrous battle at Aphek and the shrine at Shiloh was destroyed (1 Sa. 4), and at this time they probably controlled Esdraelon, the coast plain, the Negeb, and much of the hill-country. They also controlled the distribution of iron, and thus prevented the Israelites from having useful weapons (1 Sa. 13:19–22). Saul was anointed king by Samuel, and after a victory over the Philistines at Michmash, drove them from the hill-country (1 Sa. 14). His erratic rule, however, allowed the Philistines to continue to assert themselves, as when they challenged Israel at Ephes-dammim, and David killed Goliath (1 Sa. 17–18). Saul turned against David, who became an outlaw and finally a feudatory vassal of Achish king of Gath (1 Sa. 27). He was not called upon to fight against Israel at the battle of Mt Gilboa when Saul and his sons were killed, and when he took over the kingship of Israel he must have remained on peaceful terms with Gath at least, and in fact maintained a personal Philistine bodyguard throughout his reign (*CHERETHITES). A final conflict had to come, however. David drove the Philistines out of the hill-country and struck a heavy blow in Philistia itself (2 Sa. 5:25), putting an end to the power of the Philistines as a serious menace.

e. During the divided Monarchy

The Philistines continued to cause trouble throughout the Monarchy. With the weakening of the kingdom at the death of David the Philistine cities (except for Gath, 2 Ch. 11:8) were independent and there was fighting on the frontier (1 Ki. 15:27; 16:15). Jehoshaphat received tribute from some of the Philistines (2 Ch. 17:11), but under Jehoram the border town of Libnah was lost to Israel (2 Ki. 8:22). They were still aggressive in the time of Ahaz (Is. 9:8–12), and the last time they are mentioned in the Bible is in the prophecy of Zechariah, after the return from the Exile.

III. Philistia

The area which took its name from the Philistines was that of the nucleus of their settlement. This centred on the five main Philistine cities of Gaza, Ashkelon, Ashdod, Ekron and Gath, and largely comprised the coastal strip S of Carmel, extending inland to the foot of the Judaean hills. There is still uncertainty concerning the identification of the sites of some of the five principal cities of the Philistines (see under separate city names). Other cities particularly associated with the Philistines in the Bible are *Bethshean and *Gerar.

IV. In the inscriptions

The Philistines are first mentioned by name (*prst*) in the annals of Rameses III for his 5th (1185 BC) and subsequent years, inscribed in his temple to Ammon at Medinet Habu near Thebes. This describes his campaign against an invasion of Libyans and various other peoples generally known as the 'Sea Peoples', of whom the *prst* were one. Other members of the 'Sea Peoples' had already been mentioned in the inscriptions of Merenptah, Rameses II and in the 14th-century Amarna Letters (Lukku, Sˇzerdanu, Danuna). The carved reliefs in the temple at Medinet Habu show the Sea Peoples arriving with their families and chattels by wagon and ship, and the *prst* and another group closely associated with them, the *ṯkr* (Tjekker), are depicted wearing head-dresses of feathers rising vertically from a horizontal band. However, not all *prst* are depicted in this way; one at Medinet Habu is shown wearing a beard and tight-fitting cap. A head wearing a similar head-dress is one of the pictographic signs on a clay disk found at Phaistos in Crete, and usually dated to the 17th century BC.

The Assyr. inscriptions mention Philistia as an area often in revolt. The first occurrence is in an inscription of Adad-nirari III (810–782 BC), where Philistia is mentioned among other tribute-paying states, including Israel. Philistia is subsequently named by Tiglath-pileser III, Sargon and Sennacherib, usually as a defeated rebel area. Philistines are later listed in an archive of cuneiform documents of the time of the exile found at Babylon as expatriates receiving rations.

In a group of cuneiform documents of the time of the Exile found at Babylon, the issue of rations to expatriates is recorded. Among these are mentioned men from Philistia.

V. Archaeology

a. Pottery

A type of pottery has been found in a number of sites centring on Philistia and from levels of the late 2nd millennium BC. Since this was the area and period of the Philistines, this pottery is usually attributed to them. This type of pottery is found at Ekron and Ashdod after what seems to have been a sequence from about 1200 BC, of locally made pottery decorated in a style derived from the Aegean and known in Cyprus (classified as Mycenaean III.c. 1.b) first with simple, then with elaborate decoration, the latter perhaps being the prototype in the early 12th century of distinctively Philistine pottery, Excavations at other sites (*e.g.* Tell Batash, Tell Mor and Tell Qasile) suggest a gradual expansion during the 12th and 11th centuries BC.

It is clear also that there were Philistine enclaves at a number of other sites, notably Tell Beit Mirsim, Gezer, Beth-shemesh and Deir el-Balah.

b. Clay coffins

Clay coffins, each with a face moulded in relief at the head end, have been discovered at *Bethshean, Tell el-Far'a, Lachish and in Transjordan, which are probably to be connected with similar coffins found in Egypt, notably at Tell el-Yehudiyeh in the Delta. The date and distribution of these suggest that they may be attributed to the Philistines, a view supported by the fact that some of the faces are surmounted by a row of vertical strokes, perhaps indicating the feathered head-dress.

c. Weapons

The Egyp. reliefs show the *prst*, with the Tjekker and Serdanu, armed with lances, round shields, long broadswords and triangular daggers. They arrived in Palestine at the period of transition from the Bronze to Iron Age, so that the biblical statements that they bound Samson with fetters of bronze but, by the time of Saul, controlled the iron industry of the area are quite consistent.

VI. Culture

The Philistines, while retaining a few cultural features bespeaking their foreign origin, were largely assimilated to the Canaanite culture that surrounded them.

a. Government

The five Philistine cities were each ruled by a *seren* (Jos. 13:3; Jdg. 3:3; 16:5, 8, 18, 27, 30; 1 Sa. 5:8, 11; 6:4, 12, 16, 18; 7:7; 29:2, 6–7; 1 Ch. 12:19). The term is probably cognate with Luwian (Hieroglyphic Hittite) *tarwana*, 'judge' or the like, and pre-Hellenic (probably Indo-European) Gk. *turannos*, 'absolute ruler'. The precise meaning of *seren* is uncertain, but 'ruler' (RSV) is a reasonable rendering.

b. Language

No Philistine inscriptions have been recovered, and the language is largely unknown. Claims that semi-pictographic inscriptions on clay tablets from Deir 'Alla are Philistine are unsubstantiated. The Mycenaean associations of the Philistines, together with the probable Indo-European affiliations of *seren* (above), as well as the word *kôba'l qôbaʿ*, 'helmet' (first of Goliath), probably cognate with Hittite *kupahi*, 'helmet, hat', and probably *'argāz*, 'box', perhaps cognate with Hittite *ark-*, 'to put, shut in' and Gk. *arkeō*, 'to keep off, defend', together with personal names (below), suggest the possibility that the Philistine language was Indo-European. This can be no more than a hypothesis, however. The name, Achish (*'āḵîš*) is probably the same as *'kš*, which is listed as a *kftyw* (*CAPHTOR) name in an Egyp. inscription of about the 18th Dynasty and Goliath (*golyat*) is perhaps linked by its *-yat* termination with Luwian (Hieroglyphic Hittite) and Lydian names ending respectively in *-wattaš* and *-uattes*. Aside from these few words, it is clear that once they had settled in Palestine, the Philistines adopted the Semitic tongue of the peoples they dispossessed.

c. Religion

Knowledge of the Philistine religion depends greatly upon the Bible. The three gods mentioned, *Dagon, *Ashtoreth and *Baalzebub, were all Near Eastern, and it is perhaps to be assumed that they identified their own gods with those they found in Palestine, and accommodated their own religion to that already there. Three successive temples were found at Tell Qasile (strata XII–X), which have similarities with temples found in the Aegean and Cyprus. A circular hearth, uncovered in a public building near the temple, belongs to a type known in cult contexts at Mycenae, Pylos and other sites in the Aegean, while a similar 'hearth sanctuary' was found at Ekron. At the latter site also, wheels from a bronze laver stand (Heb. *m*ᵉ*kônāh*; AV 'base') were part of the cult equipment.

VII. Origin and role

The cumulative evidence leaves little doubt that the Philistines came immediately, though probably not ultimately, from the Aegean. Some scholars would equate the name with that of the *Pelasgoi*, the pre-Greek inhabitants of the Aegean, a view which is weighted by the occurrence of the name twice in Gk. literature, spelt with a *t* rather than a *g*. This view is still debated, and even granting it, the classical references to the *Pelasgoi* are too inconsistent to be helpful.

It seems that the Philistines were one of the Sea Peoples who, in the later 2nd millennium, moved out of the Aegean, probably as a result of other folk movements, and migrated by land and sea, some *via* Crete and Cyprus, to the Near East, where they forced a foothold, first as mercenary troops of the pharaohs, the Hittite kings and the Canaanite rulers, and finally as settlers who were absorbed in the basic population. Though they retained their name for many centuries, the biblical Philistines, the Tjekker who occupied an adjacent coastal region, and doubtless others of the Sea Peoples, became for all practical purposes Canaanites.

VIII. Philistines in the patriarchal narratives

Since the Philistines are not named in extra-biblical inscriptions until the 12th century BC, and the archaeological remains associated with them do not appear before this time, many commentators reject references to them in the patriarchal period as anachronistic. Two considerations must be entertained, however. There is evidence of a major expansion of Aegean trade in the Middle Minoan II period (*c.* 1900–1700 BC; *CRETE) and objects of Aegean manufacture or influence have been found from this period at Ras Shamra in Syria, Hazor and perhaps Megiddo in Palestine, and Tôd, Harageh, Lahun and Abydos in Egypt. It is likely that a large part of this trade consisted in perishable goods such as textiles. A new type of spiral design which appears in Egypt and Asia (Mari) at this time may support this. Further evidence of contacts is afforded by a tablet from Mari (18th century) recording the sending of gifts by the king of Hazor to Kaptara (*CAPHTOR). Secondly, ethnic names in antiquity were not used with particular precision. The members of a mixed group such as the Sea Peoples were unlikely to be carefully distinguished by name, so that the absence of one name from the inscriptions may simply mean that the particular group was not sufficiently prominent to find special mention. The Sea Peoples, and their predecessors who traded with the Near East, arrived in waves, the Luka being known already in the 14th century (Amarna Letters), and dominant in a 12th-century wave were the Philistines, who consequently figured in the records. In this context the term 'Philistine' could have been applied retrospectively to early Aegean migrants, rather as today reference is made to 'American Indians'. There is no reason why small groups of Philistines could not have been among the early Aegean traders, not prominent enough to be noticed by the larger states.

BIBLIOGRAPHY. R. A. S. Macalister, *The Philistines, Their History and Civilization*, 1914; A. H. Gardiner, *Ancient Egyptian Onomastica*, Text, 1, pp. 200*–205*; *AASOR* 49, 1989, pp. 1–15; G. E. Wright, *BA* 22, 1959, pp. 54–66; T. C. Mitchell in *AOTS*, pp. 404–427; K. A. Kitchen in *POTT*, pp. 53–78. T. Dothan and M. Dothan, *People of the Sea: The Search for the Philistines*, 1992.

T.C.M.

PHILO. Among the many bearers of the name Philo in antiquity, the most important for the student of the Bible is Philo of Alexandria, a member of a rich and influential Jewish family in that city in the 1st century. His brother Alexander was one of the richest men of his day, while his nephew Tiberius Alexander became in due time Procurator of Judaea and Prefect of Egypt, having apostatized from the Jewish faith.

Little is known of the life of Philo himself; neither his birth nor his death may be dated, the one sure date in his career being his membership in the embassy to Gaius (Caligula) in AD 39. From this it is evident that he was quite old at that time, and conjecturally we may place his dates as approximately 20 BC to AD 45. From his writings it may be deduced that, as a leader of the Jewish community, he spent much of his life in the duties of public service. His natural bent, however, was to the life of contemplation and the pursuit of philosophy, in which, as he asserts, he spent his youth (*Concerning the Special Laws*, 3. 1), perhaps in such a community as the Therapeutae, described by him in *Concerning the Contemplative Life*. Although he was obliged to leave this to take up his duties, he found opportunity to produce a body of writings on philosophical and theological topics.

His early work was on philosophical themes, in which he shows little originality, but provides valuable source material for the study of a little-known period of Hellenistic philosophy. His main work, however, was the production of expositions of the Pentateuch; he was motivated by the desire to demonstrate that the philosophical and religious quests of the Gentile world of the day found their true goal in the God of Abraham. Three large works remain, none of them complete nor in exact order, their several sections having been transmitted often as separate treatises in the MS tradition: *The Allegory of the Laws* (a commentary on Genesis); *Questions and Answers on Genesis and Exodus* (a shorter work of the same kind); and *The Exposition of the Laws* (a review of the history in the Pentateuch). By means of allegorical exegesis he is able to extract moral and mystical teaching from all parts of these books. His method of allegory is derived from that already applied to the Homeric books by philosophers. It may be analysed as: (i) 'cosmological' ('physiological' in his own terminology) in which allegory concerning the nature (*physis*) of things is perceived (*e.g.* the high priest and his vestments seen as the Logos and the universe, *Life of Moses*, 2. 117ff.), and (ii) 'ethical', in which reference to human psychology and moral struggle is seen (*e.g.* etymological interpretations of such figures as Isaac (= joy)). The basis of both the cosmology and psychology is the Stoic system, although it is evident that Pythagorean and Platonist are also laid under contribution in some details, a feature which probably reflects the eclecticism of the period.

Philo's greatest contribution to thought, according to recent students, is his use of philosophy in this way to provide a rationale of religion; he is in fact the 'first theologian', and philosophy is significant to him primarily as the handmaid of theology. The motivation of his work may be seen not simply in his missionary zeal, common to many Jews of that era, but also in the mystical experiences of the reality of his God of which he writes movingly in several places (*e.g. Special Laws, loc. cit.*). Central to his understanding both of the universe and of religious experience is the concept of the Logos, a term of Stoic origin which, in Philo, linked with such a concept as the Platonic World of Ideas, signifies the mode whereby the transcendent God creates and sustains the world, and further, reveals himself to his creatures. Moses is expounded as a type of the Logos by whom men are led to knowledge of God; the Patriarchs as instances of those who have freed themselves from the bondage of material things and are united with the divine Wisdom.

The definitive edition of the Gk. text of Philo is the six volumes by L. Cohn and P. Wendland, published 1896–1914, with a seventh volume of Indexes (1926–30) by H. Leisegang. A number of works, extant only in Armenian, were edited by the Mechitarist J. B. Aucherian in 1822 and 1826; the version dates from the 5th century. There is also an Old Lat. version of Philo, of some value for the construction of his text. The most recent translation of Philo's extant works, both Gk. and Armenian, is that in the Loeb Classical Library by F. H. Colson, G. H. Whittaker and R. Marcus (10 vols. plus 2 supplementary vols., 1929–62).

As the best preserved and most extensive of Hellenistic Jewish writings, Philo's works are of value in illuminating the thought world of the NT. Certain of his OT citations bear upon the problem of the origin of the LXX (see P. Katz, *Philo's Bible*, 1950). Two writings at least of the NT may not be adequately understood without reference to his thought and method. The Epistle to the Hebrews in its treatment of the tabernacle and the figure of Melchizedek shows close affinity to his allegory, while its doctrine of the Son is related in several particulars to his Logos-teaching. The Gospel of John bears no resemblance to Philonic allegory (as has sometimes been asserted), but in the cosmology explicit in the Prologue and elsewhere implicit there is evidently close kinship to the Philonic allegory. This need not imply that these writers were directly dependent on Philo. A plausible explanation might be that they come from a like background of thought. Both possibilities have been pursued and demand still further investigation.

BIBLIOGRAPHY. H. Leisegang, 'Philo' in *RE*; E. R. Goodenough, *An Introduction to Philo Judaeus*, 1939; *By Light, Light*, 1935; S. Sandmel, *Philo of Alexandria*, 1979; R. Williamson, *Philo and the Epistle to the Hebrews*, 1970; J. Cazeaux, *La trame et la chaîne . . . dans . . . des traités de Philon* (1983, 1989); R. Radice and D. T. Runia, *Philo of Alexandria: an Annotated Bibliography 1937–1986*, 1988. J.N.B.

PHINEHAS. A name of Egyp. origin, *P'-nḥsy*, 'the Nubian'; popular in Egypt during the New Kingdom (16th to 12th centuries BC). It is borne in the OT by three individuals.

1. Son of Eleazar, and grandson of Aaron (Ex. 6:25; 1 Ch. 6:4, 50; Ezr. 7:5), with priestly descendants (Ezr. 8:2). He slew an Israelite and the (pagan) Midianite woman he had taken, after Israel became involved in paganism at Shittim (Nu. 25; Ps. 106:30), and shared in the subsequent war against Midian (Nu. 31:6). Under Joshua, Phinehas helped settle the dispute with the Transjordanian tribes over their memorial altar (Jos. 22:9ff.). After burying his father in his own hill (Jos. 24:33) Phinehas was officiating priest early in the Judges' period (Jdg. 20:28; perhaps 1 Ch. 9:20).

2. Younger of the high priest Eli's two disreputable sons, late in the Judges' period (1 Sa. 1:3; *cf.* 2:12–17, 34). He was slain in the battle of Aphek when the Philistines captured the ark (1 Sa. 4). A grandson of this Phinehas was a priest in Saul's reign (1 Sa. 14:3).

3. The father of a priest Eleazar in Ezra's time (Ezr. 8:33). K.A.K.

PHOEBE (AV 'Phebe'). Lady Bountiful of Cenchreae (E port of Corinth, where hospitality would be important); *'deaconess' (AV 'servant') of the church and 'patroness' (AV 'succourer') of many, including Paul (Rom. 16:1–2; the terms are probably semi-technical). She apparently carried Paul's letter, and he asks worthy hospitality for her. E. J. Goodspeed (*HTR* 44, 1951, pp. 55ff.) holds that Rom. 16 is a separate letter to Ephesus to secure her a reception with those named. But would such oblique personal references be necessary?

The name (meaning 'radiant') is a surname of Artemis. A striking epitaph to 'The second Phoebe', a later deaconess, is cited in *MM* (*s.v. koimaomai*). See further M. D. Gibson, *ExpT* 23, 1911–12, p. 281. A.F.W.

PHOENICIA, PHOENICIANS. The territory on the E Mediterranean coast covering *c.* 240 km between the rivers Litani and Arvad (mod. Lebanon–S Latakia) and its inhabitants.

Phoenicia (AV Phenice) as such is named only in the NT as the place of refuge for Christians fleeing from persecution following the death of Stephen (Acts 11:19); through this land Paul and Silas journeyed on their way from Samaria to Antioch (Acts 15:3). Later Paul landed on the Phoenician coast near Tyre on his way to Jerusalem (Acts 21:2–3). In the time of Christ Phoenicia was referred to as 'the sea-coast and district of Tyre and Sidon' (Mt. 15:21; Lk. 6:17), and the inhabitants, including Greeks, were considered 'Syro-Phoenicians' (Mk. 7:26).

In OT times the territory occupied by the Phoenicians was called by the Hebrews 'Canaan' (Is. 23:11), 'Canaanite' (*i.e.* 'merchant') being probably the name applied by the inhabitants to themselves (Gn. 10:15). It was, however, the common practice in all periods to refer to Phoenicia by the name of its principal cities (*TYRE, *SIDON), since there was little political cohesion between them except for periods such as the reign of Hiram I. Other major settlements were Arvad, Simyra, Gebal/Byblos, Be(i)rut and Zarephath (*ZAREPTA).

I. History

The origin of the sea-faring Phoenicians is obscure, though according to Herodotus (1. 1; 7. 89) they arrived overland from the Persian Gulf area, via the Red Sea, and first founded Sidon. The earliest archaeological evidence of their presence may come from the 'proto-Phoenician' finds at Byblos (ancient Gubla or Gebal, Ezk. 27:9, modern Gebail) dated *c.* 3000 BC. This important site has been excavated since 1924 by the French under Montet and Dunand. Byblian ships are depicted on Egyp. reliefs of the time of Sahure in the 5th Dynasty (*c.* 2500 BC) and there can be no doubt that by the 18th century there was an extensive trade in timber and artistic commodities between Phoenicia and Egypt (*SHIPS). The Phoenicians by this time had settled in their first colonies along the coast at Joppa, Dor (Jdg. 1:27–31), Acre and Ugarit (Ras Shamra). They chose easily defensible natural harbours and gradually dominated the local population as at Ras Shamra (level IV).

For some centuries Phoenicia was under the economic and quasi-military control of the Egyptian 18th and 19th Dynasties, and Arvad was among the places claimed to have been captured by Tuthmosis III (*c.* 1485 BC). Nevertheless, the letters written by Rib-Addi of Byblos and Abi-milki of Tyre to Amenophis III at Amarna in Egypt show that, by *c.* 1400 BC, Ṣumur and Berut had disaffected and with Sidon, which appears to have maintained its independence, were blockading

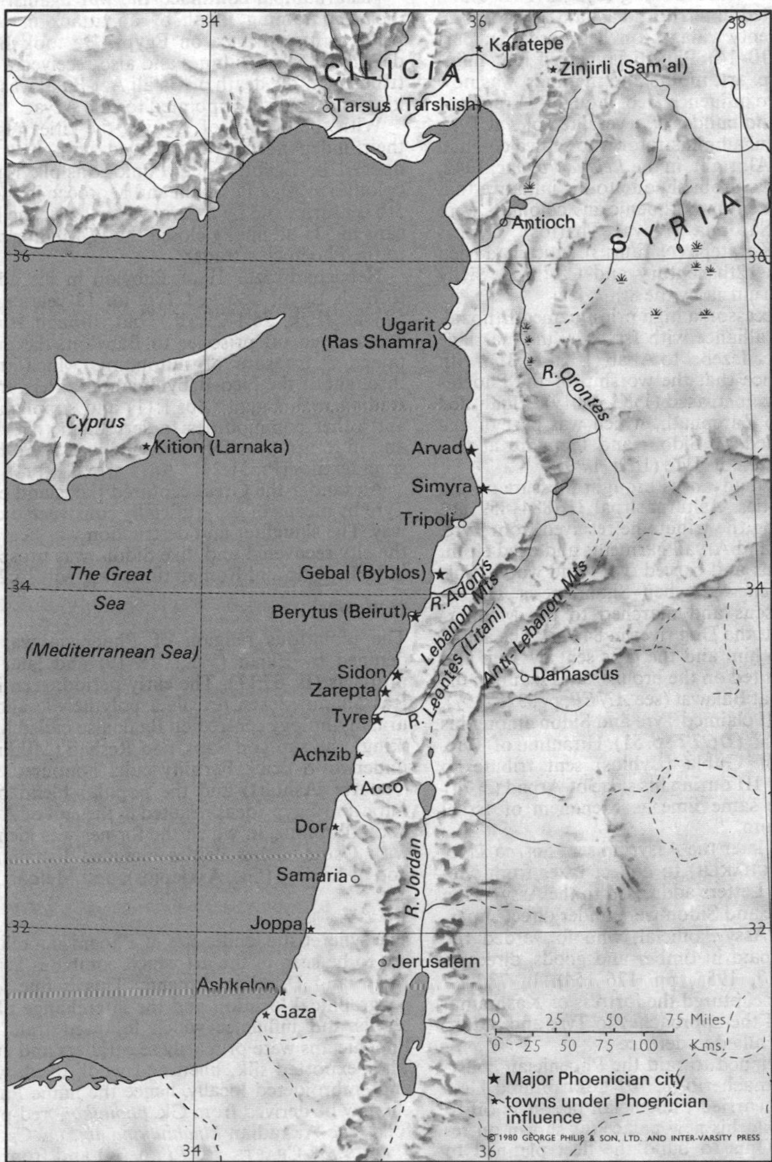

The major cities of Phoenicia.

Phoenician cities (*AMARNA). When the 'sea-peoples' invaded the coast *c.* 1200 BC, Byblos, Arvad and Ugarit were destroyed and the Sidonians fled to Tyre, which now became the principal port, or, as Isaiah claims, the 'daughter of Sidon' (23:12).

By the time of David, Tyre was ruled by Hiram I son of Abi-Baal and his reign began a golden age. Phoenicia was allied commercially with David (2 Sa. 5:11; 1 Ki. 5:1) and Hiram by treaty supplied Solomon with wood, stone and craftsmen for the construction of the Temple and palace (1 Ki. 5:1–12; 2 Ch. 2:3–16), and ships and navigators to assist the Judaean fleet and to develop the port of Ezion-geber as a base for long voyages (1 Ki. 9:27). This aid resulted in territorial advantages, for Tyre was given twenty villages on her border in part payment (vv. 10–14). Phoenicia, herself long influenced by Egyp. art, motifs and methods, was now in a position to influence Heb. thought. Hiram was a conqueror and builder of several temples at Tyre, and a successful administrator who settled colonial revolts (W. F. Albright, in the *Leland Volume*, 1942, pp. 43f.). It was probably due to his initiative that by the 9th century Phoenician colonies were founded in Sardinia (Nova, Tharros), Cyprus (Kition) and Karatepe (N Taurus). Utica had been settled in the 12th century and Carthage, Sicily (Motya) and Tunisia by the 8th.

Hiram's successor, a high priest named Ethbaal, furthered the alliance with Israel by the marriage of his daughter Jezebel to Ahab (1 Ki. 16:31), with the consequence that the worship of the Phoenician Baals was increased (1 Ki. 18:19). Elijah fled for a while to Zarephath, which was part of the coast controlled by Sidon, and therefore at this time independent of Tyre (1 Ki. 17:9).

The Assyrian advances brought pressure on the Phoenician cities. Ashurnasirpal II (884–859 BC) counted among the tribute he received from Tyre, Sidon, Gebal and Arvad garments and dyed cloth, precious metals and carved ivory and wood. This tribute was renewed when Shalmaneser III besieged Damascus and marched to the Mediterranean coast at the Dog river in 841 BC. The act of submission to him and the gifts sent by Tyre and Sidon are pictured on the bronze gates set up in the Assyr. temple at Balawat (see *ANEP*, pp. 356–357). Adad-nirari III claimed Tyre and Sidon among his vassals in 803 BC (*DOTT*, p. 51). Hirammu of Tyre, Sibitti-Bi'ili of Gubla (Byblos) sent tribute to Tiglath-pileser III during his siege of Arpad (*c.* 741 BC) about the same time as Menahem of Israel submitted to him.

A few years later the Assyrian sent his *rab šaqe*-official (*RABCHAKEH) to collect taxes from Metenna of Tyre. Letters addressed to the Assyr. king show that Tyre and Sidon were under direct supervision of an Assyr. official, who forwarded the taxes, mostly paid in timber and goods, direct to Calah (*Iraq* 17, 1955, pp. 126–154). In 734 BC Tiglath-pileser captured the fortress of Kashpuna, which guarded the approaches to Tyre and Sidon, who were now allied in defence.

Sargon continued to raid the Phoenician coastlands, and Sennacherib (*c.* 701 BC) captured Ušše near Tyre and carried Phoenician prisoners off to Nineveh to build his new palace (as shown on reliefs) and to Opis to build the fleet planned to pursue the rebel *Merodach-baladan across the Persian Gulf. Nevertheless, the larger cities clung to their independence until Esarhaddon sacked Sidon and settled the survivors from it in a new town called 'Walled City of Esarhaddon' and in 15 adjacent villages. Other towns were placed under Ba'ali of Tyre, who was bound by treaty to Esarhaddon. This named Arvad, Acre, Dor, Gebal and Mt Lebanon and regulated trade and shipping. However, Ba'ali, incited by Tirhakah of Egypt, revolted. Tyre was besieged and Phoenicia subordinated to a province. The rulers of the cities, including Milki-asapa of Gebal, and Matan-Ba'al of Arvad, were made to 'bear the corvée basket', that is, to act as labourers at the foundation of Esarhaddon's new palace at Calah, as Manasseh did in Babylon (2 Ch. 33:11).

Ashurbanipal continued the war against Phoenicia, containing Ba'ali by an attack in 665 BC prior to his advance on Egypt. He took Ba'ali's daughters as concubines and also received a heavy tribute. On the death of Ba'ali Azi-Ba'al was made king and Yakinlu appointed to rule Arvad.

With the decline of Assyria the cities regained their independence and traded with new ports opened in Egypt. Their Punic kinsfolk founded colonies in Algeria, Spain and Morocco in the 7th–5th centuries and by a naval victory over the Etruscans in 535 BC finally closed the W Mediterranean to the Phoenician traders.

Nebuchadrezzar II of Babylon in his advance towards Egypt besieged Tyre for 13 years *c.* 585–573 BC (Ezk. 26:1–29:1ff.), but, though Ithobaal was carried off prisoner to Babylon, the city retained a measure of autonomy, which it held throughout the Neo-Babylonian and Persian rule, trading with Egypt (Zp. 1:11) and supplying fish and other commodities to Jerusalem (Ne. 13:16) and in return probably receiving wood and homespun textiles (Pr. 31:24; *ARTS AND CRAFTS).

Alexander the Great captured the island city of Tyre by means of an artificially constructed causeway. The slaughter and destruction was heavy, but the city recovered and, like Sidon, was prosperous in Hellenistic and Roman times (*e.g.* Mt. 15:21).

II. Religion

The idolatrous religion of Phoenicia was condemned by Elijah (1 Ki. 18–19) and later Heb. prophets (Is. 65:11). The early period, seen in the Ras Shamra texts, reveals a polytheistic and natural mythology centred on Baal, also called Melek, 'king', the sun-god Saps, and Reshep (Mikkal) an underworld deity. Fertility cults honoured 'Anat (Astarte, Ashtart) and the popular blend of Semitic and Egyp. ideas resulted in the cult of Adonis and *Tammuz, in which the former was identified with Osiris. Other deities included Eshmun, the god of healing (Gk. Asklepios), and Melqart.

III. Art

The syncretistic tendencies of Phoenician religions are to be seen in the art which combines Semitic, Egyp. and Hurrian elements. This is due to the geographical location and the interchange of materials and influence which followed trade. The Phoenicians were primarily sea-traders and artists. They exported silk, linen and wool, dyed, woven and embroidered locally, hence the name Phoenicia may be derived from Gk. *phoinikoi*, 'red-purple folk' (the Akkadian *kinahhi/kina'ain, i.e.* Canaan) (*ARTS A^nd^ CRAFTS; *POTT*, p. 34) and from their unbounded supplies in the hinterland of the Lebanon shipped wood and its products. The craftsmen worked stone (*e.g.* Ahiram sarcophagus *c.* 900 BC;

BASOR 134, 1954, p. 9; *Syria* 11, 1930, pp. 180ff.), *ivory, and *glass, and though the Hebrews did not themselves allow images or the portrayal of the human figure (*ART), Phoenician silver and bronze coins are found inland in numbers from the 4th century BC onwards. The requirements of their trade led to the development of *writing (the so-called Phoenician, Byblian and Ugaritic alphabets), the *abacus* for counting, and *papyrus books. It is much to be regretted that the Phoenician literature, including the mythology of Sanchuniathon of Byblos and the history of Menander of Tyre, has survived only in a few quotations in later authors, for it was probably through their literature that much of the learning of the East reached Greece.

BIBLIOGRAPHY. D. B. Harden, *The Phoenicians*, 1962; S. Moscati, *The World of the Phoenicians*, 1968; D. R. Ap-Thomas in *POTT*, pp. 259–286; *Studia Phoenicia*. D.J.W.

PHOENIX. 1. A mythical bird, anciently thought to be born directly from its parent's corpse. Some early Christians (Tertullian, *De Resurr.* 13.6; *cf. 1 Clement* 25), seeing an analogy of resurrection, warranted it by Ps. 92:12 (LXX 91:13), but *phoinix* there clearly means 'palm-tree'. Phoenix-and-palm was frequent in Christian art.

2. The harbour (AV 'Phenice') the nautical experts, despite Paul's entreaties, made for in winter (Acts 27:12). Data given by Strabo, Ptolemy and other writers seem to indicate the Cape Mouros area, where modern Loutro is the only safe harbour in S Crete (James Smith, *Voyage and Shipwreck of St. Paul*[4], 1880, p. 90n.). But Luke (AV) says Phoenix 'lieth toward the south-west and north-west (*sc.* 'winds')', *i.e.* faces W, while Loutro faces E. A narrow peninsula separates it from a W-facing bay, but one offering little shelter. Smith, urging the danger of W winter gales, suggested that Luke meant the direction *towards which* the winds blew, *i.e.* looking NE and SE (*cf.* RV, RSV); but this is unsubstantiated unless we assume some lost nautical idiom. Ramsay thought that Luke might have excusably misunderstood Paul's account of the discussion, but left open the possibility of a change in coastline (*cf. HDB*). Ogilvie's recent examination strongly suggests this occurred. The W bay was once better protected, and earthquake disturbance has apparently covered an inlet facing NW in classical times. A SW-facing inlet remains, and the disused W bay is still called Phinika. Ogilvie also found that locally the winter winds are N and E: in Acts 27 it was an ENE wind (*EURAQUILO) which caused the disaster.

BIBLIOGRAPHY. J. B. Lightfoot on *1 Clement* 25; J. Smith, *op. cit.*, pp. 87ff., 251ff.; R. M. Ogilvie, *JTS* n.s. 9, 1958, pp. 308ff. A.F.W.

PHRYGIA. A tract of land centred on the W watershed of the great Anatolian plateau, and reaching N into the valley of the upper Sangarius, SW down the valley of the Maeander, and SE across the plateau, perhaps as far as Iconium. The Phrygians formed the (legendary?) kingdom of Midas. They fell under direct Hellenic influence during the era of the Attalid kings of Pergamum, and in 116 BC most of Phrygia was incorporated by the Romans into their province of Asia. The E extremity (Phrygia Galatica) was included in the new province of Galatia in 25 BC. The Romans were deeply impressed by the ecstatic Phrygian cult of Cybele, and the national fanaticism apparently lies behind the defiant tombstones, presumably Montanist, of the 2nd century AD, which represent the earliest extant public manifesto of Christianity. There is no evidence of any indigenous Christian church in NT times, however. Such churches as fall technically within Phrygia (Laodicea, Hierapolis, Colossae, Pisidian Antioch and probably Iconium) were established in Gk. communities. It was most probably Jewish members of these Gk. states who visited Jerusalem (Acts 2:10). If Col. 2:1, as is just possible, is not taken to exclude a visit by Paul, it would be natural to assume that it is the first three of these cities, on the upper Maeander, that are referred to in Acts 16:6; 18:23. Failing that, we may resort to the view that 'the region of Phrygia and *Galatia' is a composite technical term for Phrygia Galatica and refers in particular to the churches at Iconium and Pisidian Antioch. Otherwise we cannot identify the disciples Paul left in 'Phrygia'.

BIBLIOGRAPHY. Strabo, 12; J. Friedrich, *RE*, 20, 1, pp. 781–891; W. M. Ramsay, *Cities and Bishoprics of Phrygia*, 1895–7; A. H. M. Jones, *Cities of the Eastern Roman Provinces*, 1937; D. Magie, *Roman Rule in Asia Minor*, 2 vols., 1950; W. M. Calder, *AS* 5, 1955, pp. 25–38. E.A.J.

PHYLACTERIES. The name is a transliteration of Gk. *phylaktērion*, meaning 'a means of protection' or *'amulet'. Though some Jews have regarded them superstitiously, this attitude has always been marginal, so the Gk. name probably derives from heathen misinterpretation. The Jew speaks of *tᵉp̄illâ* (lit. 'prayer'), pl. *tᵉp̄illîn*. They represent the interpretation by the pious of Ex. 13:9, 16; Dt. 6:8; 11:18. Their present form became standardized by the early years of the 2nd century AD and consists of two hollow cubes made of the skin of clean animals. They vary between 1·25 cm and 4 cm a side. That for the head is divided into four equal compartments; that for the hand has no divisions. In them are placed the four passages Ex. 13:1–10; 13:11–16; Dt. 6:4–9; 11:13–21 written by hand on parchment (on four pieces for the head, on one for the hand). The phylacteries are attached to leather straps by which they are fastened to the left hand and the centre of the forehead by the men before morning prayers, whether in the home or the synagogue, except on the sabbath and high festivals. They are put on after the praying shawl (*ṭallîṯ*), that for the hand coming first. Both they and the straps are always coloured black. The phylactery for the head can be recognized by a three-and four-armed *šin* on its right and left sides.

In the *Qumran discoveries portions of phylacteries have been found, which show they were not absolutely standardized before the destruction of the Temple. The main difference, however, was the inclusion of the Ten Commandments on the parchment in them. Their exclusion later, just like their exclusion from the daily services, was a reaction against the Jewish Christians.

Though Christian exegesis has always understood the above-mentioned passages as metaphorical, our increasing knowledge of the ancient Near East would not rule out their possible literal intent (or for that matter of Dt. 6:9; 11:20, which the Jew fulfils by enclosing a parchment containing

Dt. 6:4–9; 11:13–21 in a box called a *mᵉzûzâ* and affixing it to his door-post). All available evidence suggests, however, that they were a late innovation brought in by the *ḥᵃsîḏîm* (*HASIDAEANS), being intended as a counterblast to increasing Hellenistic influence. There is no mention of them in the OT, and they seem always to have been unknown to the Samaritans. LXX clearly takes the passages on which the custom is based as metaphorical. The *Letter of Aristeas* mentions apparently only that for the arm and Philo that for the head.

Both the somewhat later Talmudic acknowledgment that they were not worn by the common people (*'am hā-'āreṣ*) and the failure of pagan writers to mention them indicate that in the time of Christ they were still worn only by a minority of the people. We may be sure that all Pharisees wore them, not merely during morning prayer but throughout the hours of daylight. Their later restriction to the time of prayer was due to their providing an all too easy mark of recognition of the Jew in times of persecution. We have no reason for thinking that they were worn either by Christ or his disciples. Even the condemnation in Mt. 23:5 suggests the temptation to the ultra-pious of stressing their adherence to a custom that was only slowly winning its way. Their use became universal before the end of the 2nd century AD.

The orthodox Jew interprets their use in a highly spiritual way. This is shown by the meditation to be used while putting them on, which is given early in the morning service in any standard Jewish Prayer Book.

BIBLIOGRAPHY. Articles in *JewE*, *EJ*, 1971; Y. Yadin, *Tefillin from Qumran*, 1969. H.L.E.

PI-BESETH. Bubastis (Egyp. *Pr-B'stt*, 'mansion of the goddess Ubastet'), today Tell Basta, is situated on the Nile (Tanitic branch) SE of Zagazig. It is mentioned in Ezk. 30:17 with the more important city of Heliopolis (On or Aven). Of the main temple described by Herodotus (2. 138), little remains. Ubastet was a lioness or cat-goddess. Bubastis existed already in the time of Kheops and Khephren (4th Dynasty, *c.* 2600 BC) and Pepi I (6th Dynasty, *c.* 2400 BC). There are a few remains of the 18th Dynasty (14th century BC). The town was important under the Ramesside kings (19th Dynasty, 13th century BC) and gave its name to the 22nd Dynasty—that of Shishak, *c.* 945 BC—for whom it served as a residence like Tanis or Qantir.

BIBLIOGRAPHY. E. Naville, *Bubastis*, 1891, and *The Festival Hall of Osorkon II*, 1892; Labib Habachi, *Tell Basta*, 1957. C.D.W.

PIETY. AV used this word in 1 Tim. 5:4, of dutiful care for a widowed mother or grandmother (*cf.* the Lat. *pietas*, and the Eng. 'filial piety'). The verb is *eusebeō*, the regular Hellenistic word for performing acts of religious worship (so in Acts 17:23), which indicates that, to Paul, care for these widowed relatives was part of a Christian's religious duty. This is understandable in the light both of the fifth commandment and of the fact that hereby the Christian relieves the church of responsibility for supporting the widows concerned.

The corresponding noun, *eusebeia*, usually translated *'godliness' in EVV, appears 14 times in the Pastorals and 2 Peter (elsewhere only in Acts 3:12, where RSV renders 'piety') as a comprehensive term for the practice of Christian personal religion, the worship and service of God and the rendering of reverent obedience to his laws. In the plural the word denotes specific acts of piety (2 Pet. 3:11). Christian *eusebeia* springs from the divine gift of an inner principle of life and power (2 Pet. 1:3; 2 Tim. 3:5), which in its turn is bestowed with and through the sinner's believing response to the prior gift of saving truth (1 Tim. 3:16: the 'mystery'—revealed secret—from which 'godliness' springs is the gospel message of the incarnate and reigning Christ). It is characteristic of gospel truth that it is 'according to godliness' (1 Tim. 6:3; Tit. 1:1), *i.e.* godliness is the natural and necessary outcome of receiving it, so that ungodliness in those who profess it is presumptive evidence that they have not truly and heartily received it at all (*cf.* 2 Tim. 3:2–8; Tit. 1:16; 2 Pet. 2:19–22). All allegedly evangelical teaching should be tested by asking whether it makes for godliness—*i.e.* whether it enforces God's demands adequately, and whether it exhibits correctly the gift of renewal in Christ from which alone godliness can spring (2 Tim. 3:5–8).

The Bible views the piety that it inculcates from several complementary standpoints. The OT calls it 'the *fear of God', or 'the Lord' (over 30 times), thus showing that true piety is rooted in an attitude of reverence, submission and obedience towards God. The NT calls it 'obeying the gospel' or 'the truth' (Rom. 10:16; Gal. 5:7; 2 Thes. 1:8; 1 Pet. 1:22; *cf.* Rom. 6:16), thus characterizing piety as a response to revelation. From another standpoint, as the maintaining of a state of separation from the world and consecratedness to God, the NT calls it simply *'holiness' (*hagiasmos*, *hagiōsynē*: see 1 Thes. 4:3; Heb. 12:14; 2 Cor. 7:1; 1 Thes. 3:13; *etc.*). Christ taught that the 'work of God', the single comprehensive divine requirement in which all the individual 'works of God' are embraced, is faith in himself (Jn. 6:28f.); and Christian piety means simply living by this faith, and living it out. Accordingly, John characterizes the piety that God commands and accepts by singling out the two features that are most essential to it, and most distinctive of it—faith in Christ, and love to Christians (1 Jn. 3:22–24).

A full analysis of NT piety would include the practical expression of faith in a life of repentance, resisting temptation and mortifying sin; in habits of prayer, thanksgiving and reverent observance of the Lord's Supper; in the cultivation of hope, love, generosity, joy, self-control, patient endurance and contentment; in the quest for honesty, uprightness and the good of others in all human relations; in respect for divinely constituted authority in church, State, family and household. All these attitudes and practices are commanded by God, and glorify him.

BIBLIOGRAPHY. *BAGD*; *MM*; Richard Baxter, *A Christian Directory* (*Practical Works*), 1830, 1–5; 1838, 1); W. Mundle, W. Günther, *NIDNTT* 2, pp. 90–95; W. Foerster, *TDNT* 7, pp. 175–185.

J.I.P.

PIHAHIROTH. An unidentified place on the border of Egypt (Ex. 14:2, 9; Nu. 33:7–8). Of Egyptian equivalents proposed, the likeliest is either *Pi-Ḥrt*, 'House of the goddess *Ḥrt*' (*BASOR* 109, 1948, p. 16) or *P'-ḥr*, a canal near Ra'amses

(*cf.* Caminos, *Late-Egyptian Miscellanies*, 1954, p. 74, two mentions). C.D.W.
K.A.K.

PILATE. Pontius Pilatus was a Roman of the equestrian, or upper middle-class, order: his *praenomen* is not known, but his *nomen*, Pontius, suggests that he was of Samnite extraction and his *cognomen*, Pilatus, may have been handed down by military forbears. Little is known of his career before AD 26, but in that year (see P. L. Hedley in *JTS* 35, 1934, pp. 56–58) the emperor Tiberius appointed him to be the fifth *praefectus* (*hēgemōn*, Mt. 27:2, *etc.*; the same title is used of Felix in Acts 23 and Festus in Acts 26) of Judaea. Evidence of this title was discovered in 1961 on an inscription at Caesarea, and E. J. Vardaman (*JBL* 88, 1962, p. 70) suggests that this title was used in Pilate's earlier years, being replaced by *procurator* (the title used by Tacitus and Josephus) later. In accordance with a recent reversal in the policy of the Senate (in AD 21—Tacitus, *Annals* 3. 33–34) Pilate took his wife with him (Mt. 27:19). As procurator he had full control in the province, being in charge of the army of occupation (1 ala—*c.* 120 men—of cavalry, and 4 or 5 cohorts—*c.* 2,500–5,000 men—of infantry), which was stationed at Caesarea, with a detachment on garrison duty at Jerusalem in the fortress of Antonia. The procurator had full powers of life and death, and could reverse capital sentences passed by the Sanhedrin, which had to be submitted to him for ratification. He also appointed the high priests and controlled the Temple and its funds: the very vestments of the high priest were in his custody and were released only for festivals, when the procurator took up residence in Jerusalem and brought additional troops to patrol the city.

Even pagan historians mention Pilate only in connection with his authorization of the death of Jesus (Tacitus, *Annals* 15. 44): his only appearance on the stage of history is as procurator of Judaea.

Josephus relates (*Ant.* 18. 55; *BJ* 2. 169) that Pilate's first action on taking up his appointment was to antagonize the Jews by setting up the Roman standards, bearing images of the emperor, at Jerusalem: previous procurators had avoided using such standards in the holy city. Because of the determined resistance of their leaders in spite of threats of death, he yielded to their wishes after 6 days and removed the images back to Caesarea. Philo (*De Legatione ad Gaium* 299ff.) tells how Pilate dedicated a set of golden shields in his own residence at Jerusalem. These bore no image, only an inscription with the names of the procurator and the emperor, but representations were made to Tiberius, who sensibly ordered them to be set up in the temple of *Roma et Augustus* at Caesarea (*cf.* P. L. Maier, 'The Episode of the Golden Roman Shields at Jerusalem', *HTR* 62, 1969, pp. 109ff.).

Josephus (*Ant.* 18. 60; *BJ* 2. 175) and Eusebius (*EH* 2. 7) allege a further grievance of the Jews against Pilate, in that he used money from the Temple treasury to build an aqueduct to convey water to the city from a spring some 40 km away. Tens of thousands of Jews demonstrated against this project when Pilate came up to Jerusalem, presumably at the time of a festival, and he in return sent his troops in disguise against them, so that a large number were slain. It is generally considered that this riot was caused by the Galileans mentioned in Lk. 13:1–2 (whose blood Pilate had mingled with their sacrifices), and C. Noldius (*De Vita et Gestis Herodum*, 1660, 249) claimed that Herod's enmity against Pilate (Lk. 23:12) arose from the fact that Pilate had slain some of Herod's subjects. This explains Pilate's subsequent care (Lk. 23:6–7) to send Jesus to be tried before Herod. It is not known whether the tower at Siloam which collapsed (Lk. 13:4) was part of this aqueduct.

Pilate finally over-reached himself by the slaughter of a number of Samaritans who had assembled at Mt Gerizim in response to the call of a deceiver who had promised to show them that Moses had hidden the sacred vessels there. In spite of the obvious falsehood of this claim (Moses had never crossed Jordan: some consider that there is a textual error, *Mōÿseōs* for *Ōseōs*, and Josephus is referring to the Samaritan tradition that Uzzi the high priest (1 Ch. 6:6) had hidden the ark and other sacred vessels in Mt Gerizim), a great multitude came armed to the mountain, and Pilate surrounded and routed them, capturing many and executing their ringleaders. A Samaritan delegation went with a protest to Vitellius, who was then governor of Syria, and he ordered Pilate to answer this accusation of the Jews before the emperor, ordering Marcellus to Judaea in Pilate's place (Jos., *Ant.* 18. 85–89). Pilate was on his journey to Rome when Tiberius died (AD 37). (*Cf.* E. M. Smallwood, 'The Date of the Dismissal of Pontius Pilate from Judaea', *JJS* 5, 1954, p. 12ff.) We know nothing of the outcome of the trial, but Eusebius (*EH* 2. 7) preserves a report of otherwise unknown Gk. annalists that Pilate was forced to commit suicide during the reign of Gaius (AD 37–41).

The above incidents are all related by Josephus or Philo. E. Stauffer (*Christ and the Caesars*, E.T. 1955, pp. 119f.) draws attention to a further instance of provocation of the Jews by Pilate. According to G. F. Hill (*Catalogue of the Greek Coins of Palestine*, 1914), the procurators minted small copper coins to meet local needs in Palestine. Normally these bore symbolic designs of natural features, such as trees and ears of corn, in deference to the second commandment. In AD 29–31 Pilate issued coins bearing imperial religious insignia, the *lituus*, or augur's staff, and the *patera*, or pagan libation bowl. Such issues ceased after AD 31, and the British Museum has a coin of Pilate on which his successor Felix appears to have overstamped the staff with a palmbranch, though Y. Meshorer (*Jewish Coins of the Second Temple Period*, 1967) states that Felix also produced coins with symbols of a provocative nature, such as Roman weapons, which underlined the Roman subjugation of Judaea.

Philo can find no good thing to say of Pilate: in *De Legatione ad Gaium* 301 he describes him as 'by nature rigid and stubbornly harsh' and 'of spiteful disposition and an exceeding wrathful man', and speaks of 'the bribes, the acts of pride, the acts of violence, the outrages, the cases of spiteful treatment, the constant murders without trial, the ceaseless and most grievous brutality' of which the Jews might accuse him. The verdict of the NT is that he was a weak man, ready to serve expediency rather than principle, whose authorization of the judicial murder of the Saviour was due less to a desire to please the Jewish authorities than to fear of imperial displeasure if Tiberius heard of further unrest in Judaea. This is made abundantly evident by his mockery of the Jews in the wording of the superscription (Jn. 19:19–22). It is most unfortunate that we do not know anything of his record apart from his government of the Jews, towards whom he would appear to have shown little understanding and even less liking.

For an interesting discussion of the significance of the inclusion of 'suffered under Pontius Pilate' in Christian creeds see S. Liberty, *JTS* 45, 1944, pp. 38–56.

There are a number of *Acta Pilati* in existence: none of which is considered to be genuine.

BIBLIOGRAPHY. P. L. Maier, *Pontius Pilate*, 1968; B. Reicke, *The New Testament Era*, 1969.

D.H.W.

PILGRIMAGE. Sojourners in foreign lands may return home; sojourners in the flesh, with a foreshortened view of heavenly things, may enter the eternal realm by the portal of death. By established metaphor, the mortal life-span is called a pilgrimage, which simply means a sojourning. Biblical terminology is a little flexible.

The common Heb. phrase *'ereṣ m^e^gûrîm* means literally 'land of sojournings' (the latter term is grammatically rather than numerically plural, and should be singular in idomatic English). In the typical passages Gn. 17:8; 28:4; 36:7; 37:1; Ex. 6:4, LXX generally uses the verb *paroikeō* or a cognate; AV has 'land wherein thou art a stranger', or some variant; RV and RSV have, correctly if rather woodenly, 'land of sojournings', but the singular would be preferable. *Cf.* Ezk. 20:38; also Ps. 55:15; Jb. 18:19, where a cognate Heb. term means 'dwellings' or 'habitations', the singular being again preferable in English. The AV and RV text perceptively render the same word twice as 'pilgrimage' in Gn. 47:9—this may be upheld against RVmg. and RSV, because the meaning here is life's total span and experience. The LXX underlines this by using *zōē*, 'life'. There is a close parallel in Ps. 119:54, where 'the house of my pilgrimage' means simply 'my mortal body throughout its earthly existence'.

There are two technical terms for a resident alien—usually a Gentile dweller in Palestine—*gēr*, from the same Heb. root as *m^e^gûrîm*, and *tôšāḇ*. The first word usually implies a longer, the second a shorter, association, so that the difference is chiefly one of intensity. The coupling of the two lays a heavy emphasis on transitoriness. The second then follows climactically. The LXX translates the first term by *paroikos*, the second in its happier moments by *parepidēmos*. The four words may be found literally used in Gn. 22:4, *MT* and LXX. The metaphorical usages, stressing the brevity of life, are Ps. 39:12; 1 Ch. 29:15. The LXX spoils the sense in the second passage by substituting *katoikountes* for *parepidēmoi*, for the change of word would suggest settled dwelling, whereas the entire emphasis is the reverse. In both contexts 'pilgrim(s)' would afford a good translation.

The 'weary pilgrimage' of the oft-sung paraphrase has a similar ring about it, though strictly speaking it is a mistranslation. Jacob in his vow (Gn. 28:20) actually uses the word *dereḵ*, 'road' or 'way'. Metaphorically, this signifies manner of life, human or animal—even the behaviour of inanimate but propelled objects. (Pr. 30:19 aptly illustrates all three pictorial usages.) Jacob's reference is personal, practical, specific and contemporary. The 'weary pilgrimage', generalized in reference, is not strict translation, but good poetic licence, true to the spirit of the original prayer.

paroikos and *parepidēmos* or their cognates are used in the NT independently (1 Pet. 1:1, 17) and in OT quotation (Heb. 11:13; 1 Pet. 2:11). By NT times it is probably true to say that the *paroikos* not only resided longer in a place than the *parepidēmos*, but also that he was more fully incorporated into the civic life and fiscal obligations of his adopted community. The *eklektoi parepidēmoi* of 1 Pet. 1:1 are more than 'elect sojourners'. Their political status is strong metaphor for the fact that they are God's pilgrims, persons now in time and flesh, yet chosen for eternal life through Christ Jesus, therefore fundamentally different from the worldling. The *paroikia* of 1 Pet. 1:17 reverts by stylistic variation to the *gēr* emphasis, but still means essentially 'pilgrimage'. The *'strangers and pilgrims' of Heb. 11:13 AV, 'strangers and exiles' RSV, translates the Greek beautifully. There is a verbal echo of Ps. 39:12 and 1 Ch. 29:15, with perhaps a sidelong glance at Gn. 47:9. The phrase is more telling in view of the writer's 'idealist epistemology'—the Temple and all earthly things are but copies and shadows of heavenly things; the real world is the unseen one. *Cf.* 1 Pet. 2:11.

The concept of pilgrimage as a journey of religious volition or obligation to a sacred spot, such as Abraham's visit to Mt Moriah, is known from remote antiquity, though the Bible lacks a technical term for it. Any place held in veneration was liable to attract pilgrims, as even the earliest OT records show. Journeys to the statutory feasts at Jerusalem, where the Temple enjoyed exclusive prestige, were well established by NT times (*cf.* notably Lk. 2:41ff.). Each of them was a 'pilgrimage-festival' (Heb. *ḥaḡ*; *cf.* Arabic *ḥajj*). Before the Arab–Israeli partition of Jerusalem in 1948, and since the Six Days' War of 1967, Jews have regularly prayed at the Western Wall (formerly the Wailing Wall), which is all that remains of the Herodian Temple.

BIBLIOGRAPHY. D. J. Wiseman, *The Word of God for Abraham and To-day*, 1959; D. J. Estes, *From Patriarch to Pilgrim*, diss. Cambridge, 1988; W. Grundmann, *TDNT* 2, pp. 64f.; O. Michel, *TDNT* 5, pp. 153–155; R. Meyer, K. L. and M. A. Schmidt, *TDNT* 5, pp. 841–853.

R.A.S.

PILLAR.

a. Structural

Pillars of wood, stone or mud-brick were used from the earliest times to support the roofs of large rooms or to provide monumental decoration (as at Erech in S Mesopotamia; H. Frankfort, *Art and Architecture of the Ancient Orient*, 1954, pl. 2). From the latter part of the 2nd millennium onwards rectangular stone pillars or wooden posts on stone bases were used in larger Palestinian houses for carrying upper storeys or balconies on one or all sides of the central courtyard (*HOUSE). The evidence of Philistine sites suggests that the pillars held by Samson were of wood, set on stone bases (Jdg. 16:23–30; *cf.* R. A. S. Macalister, *Bible Sidelights from the Mound of Gezer*, 1906, pp. 135–138).

From the early Monarchy have survived several examples of official storehouses with rows of pillars (*cf.* the seven pillars of Wisdom's house, Pr. 9:1). At Megiddo these pillars also served as hitching-posts (see *ANEP*, nos. 741–742, and for official buildings, Z. Herzog in Y. Aharoni, *Beer-Sheba*, 1, 1973, pp. 23–30). Of finer quality are the carved capitals, imitating the top of a palm-tree (called proto-Aeolic or Ionic), found at several sites. While the majority were made for rectangular attached pillars (*e.g.* those from the palace at Samaria, *cf.* W. F. Albright, *Archaeology of Palestine*, 1960, p. 127, fig. 35), a few belonged to free-standing columns. Solomon's Temple may have been enhanced with similar capitals, Heb. *timorâ*, 1 Ki. 6:29ff.; 7:36; *cf.* Ezk. 40:22ff.; 41:18ff.; 2 Ch. 3:5; see Y. Shiloh, *PEQ* 109, 1977, pp. 39–52. This simple design was elaborated, producing finally the complicated capitals at the Persian palaces of Persepolis and Susa (Est. 1:6, see R. Ghirshman, *Iran*, 1954, pl. 17b). Simple cylindrical pillars of this period have been found at Lachish (*PEQ* 69, 1937, p. 239) and possibly Bethel (*BASOR* 137, 1955, fig. 3).

During the Hellenistic and Roman periods pillars were widely employed as decorative features, *e.g.* lining the main streets of towns, as at Jerash (G. L. Harding, *Antiquities of Jordan*, 1959, pl. 10). The entrance to Solomon's Temple was flanked by two gigantic bronze pillars of uncertain significance (1 Ki. 7:15–22; see *JACHIN AND BOAZ). It was apparently by one of these that the king stood on ceremonial occasions (2 Ki. 11:14; 23:3; 2 Ch. 23:13; *cf.* the coronation of Abimelech, Jdg. 9:6, RV).

'Pillar' is also used to describe: Lot's wife smothered by salt (Gn. 19:26); the smoke and fire which protected the camp of Israel (Ex. 13:21); a palm-like column of smoke spreading at the top (Ct. 3:6; Joel 2:30, Heb. *tîmārâ*; *cf. timorâ*, above). The supporting function is used figuratively of: (i) the pillars of heaven and earth over which God alone has power (1 Sa. 2:8; Jb. 9:6; 26:11; Ps. 75:3); (ii) the legs of the beloved and the feet of an angel (Ct. 5:15; Rev. 10:1); (iii) the church as upholding the truth (1 Tim. 3:15); (iv) the position of James, Cephas and John in the church of Jerusalem (Gal. 2:9).

b. Monumental

Stones set up on end are found throughout the ancient world, often associated with a shrine or temple (*e.g.* an early Neolithic shrine at Jericho contained a niche in which was a stone cylinder, see *PEQ* 84, 1952, p. 72, pl. XIX. 1) or standing alone (the Celtic *menhir*). A consideration of all the OT passages in which such a pillar (Heb. *maṣṣēḇâ*, something erected) is mentioned shows that the basic significance was that of a memorial. Rachel's grave was thus marked (Gn. 35:20), and Absalom, being childless, set up a pillar, to which he gave his own name, as his own memorial (2 Sa. 18:18). The name conferred on the stone identified it with the bearer of that *name (*WORD). Important events were likewise commemorated. Jacob set up the stone he had used as a pillow, clearly a small slab, after the first theophany at Bethel and another stone after the second theophany. Libations were poured on both of these, marking them out from other stones. By naming the stones 'House of God' (Heb. *bêṯ'ēl*), Jacob recorded their significance to him (Gn. 28:18–22; 35:13–15). The covenants between Jacob and Laban and between Yahweh and Israel were also visibly indicated in this way (Gn. 31:45–54; Ex. 24:4; Jos. 24:26–27). So too were the crossing of the Jordan (Jos. 4:1–9) and the victory over the Philistines at Mizpah (1 Sa. 7:12, named 'stone of help', Heb. *'eḇen hā'ēzer*). This is the import of the victorious Christian who will be a pillar in the temple of God, bearing the names of God, the new Jerusalem and the Son of man's new name (Rev. 3:12).

In Canaanite religion the pillar had so far become identified with deity (particularly male deity) as to be an object of veneration. It was therefore forbidden to the Israelites, who were to destroy all they found (Ex. 23:24; Dt. 16:22; *cf.* /ASHERAH). Of the many standing stones found in and around Palestine (*e.g.* at Gezer, Lejjun, Byblos, Ras Shamra) the best examples are those at Hazor. An upright stone, with the top broken off, was found standing by the entrance to an important building in the Canaanite citadel, an offering before it (*BA* 22, 1959, p. 14, fig. 12). In the lower city lay a small shrine containing a row of several slabs about 45 cm high and many more stacked in a side room (*BA* 19, 1956, p. 10, fig. 7). These may well be ancestral monuments destroyed by the Israelites (*cf. ANEP*, nos. 630, 635). The practice continued in neighbouring countries and Isaiah foretold that the Egyptians would set up a pillar to Yahweh on their border when they turned to him (Is. 19:19). See C. F. Graesser, 'Standing Stones in Ancient Palestine', *BA* 35, 1972, pp. 34–63. A.R.M.

PINNACLE (Gk. *pterygion*, 'a little wing'; Vulg. *pinnaculum*; NEB 'highest ledge'). A part of the buildings of the Temple (Mt. 4:5; Lk. 4:9) mentioned in connection with the temptation of Jesus. Its precise location is uncertain, but two relevant factors should be noted. (i) Despite the AV's use of the indefinite article, we should follow other EVV in reading '*the* pinnacle of the temple' (*i.e.* suggesting that there was only one). (ii) The context calls for a position from which there was both a fearful drop and an impressive view of the surrounding countryside. These latter conditions are met if we locate the pinnacle in the SE corner of the Temple area, overlooking the Kidron Valley (*cf.* Jos., *Ant.* 15. 410f.). Different opinions have, however, been expressed. See, *e.g.*, *HHT*, 4, pp. 85–86. J.D.D.

PIRATHON. Fer'ata, 9 km WSW of Shechem, home of the Ephraimite judge Abdon ben Hillel (Jdg. 12:13, 15) and of David's captain Benaiah (2 Sa. 23:30; 1 Ch. 11:31; 27:14); probably not the Pharathon in Benjamin (1 Macc. 9:50) as Moore suggested (*ICC*, Jdg. 12:13); *Sellem* in LXX (A) is a corruption of 'Hillel' rather than a pointer to Shaalim or *Shalisha; *cf.* J. Soggin, *Judges*, 1987, p. 224. The district was known as the Amalekite hills (*MT* and LXX B; LXX A, 'hill of Anak'); *cf.* Jdg. 5:14, though here also LXX A ('in the valley') disagrees. J.P.U.L.

PISGAH, ASHDOTH-PISGAH. Always accompanied by the definite article, Pisgah is associated with the ascent and either 'top' (head) or 'slope' (Ashdoth). From these facts it may be deduced that Pisgah is a common noun denoting a ridge crowning a mountain or hill. 'The Pisgah' would then be one or more of the ridges common on the Transjordan plateau. 'The slopes of Pisgah' (Ashdoth-pisgah) may refer to the entire edge of the Moabite plateau E of the Dead Sea (Dt. 3:17,

AV; 4:49; Jos. 12:3; 13:20). These references relate to the territorial borders of the Amorites and later of the Reubenites.

Apart from the general plateau, Pisgah refers to a specific ridge or peak associated with Mt *Nebo. Nu. 21:20, a location on the route of the Israelites, and Nu. 23:14, one peak from which Balaam tried to curse God's people, are both close to the wilderness N and E of the Dead Sea (*JESHIMON), so also probably refer to the same ridge.

It was from 'the top of Pisgah, Mt Nebo' that Moses viewed the promised land before his death (Dt. 3:27; 34:1). This plateau headland is probably to be identified with Ras es Siyaghah, the second and slightly lower N ridge of Mt Nebo. As this ridge protrudes further W, it provides a wider and less obstructed view over the land, and so is more likely to be the place of Moses' vision.

BIBLIOGRAPHY. G. T. Manley, *EQ* 21, 1943, pp. 81–92. G.G.G.

PISIDIA. A highland area in Asia Minor bounded by Lycaonia to the E and N, Pamphylia to the S, and the province of Asia to the N and W. The district lay at the W end of the Taurus range, and was the home of lawless mountain tribes who defied the efforts of the Persians and their Hellenistic successors to subdue them. The Seleucids founded Antioch (called 'the Pisidian' to distinguish it rather from the Phrygian Antioch on the Maeander than from the Seleucid capital of Syria) in order to control the Pisidian highlanders, and Amyntas with like aim founded a colony there about 25 BC, and linked the city with similar strong-points by a system of military roads. Paul's 'perils of robbers . . . perils in the wilderness' (2 Cor. 11:26) may have reference to this area, and it is a fair guess that, even in his day, the tradition of predatory independence was not yet dead among the mountaineers. Pisidia was part of the kingdom of Galatia assigned by Antony to Amyntas in 36 BC, and it was in warfare against the Pisidian hill tribes that Amyntas perished in 25 BC. Sulpicius Quirinius finally imposed some sort of order, and incorporated the region in the province of Galatia. The Roman Peace brought prosperity to the district and in the 2nd century several prosperous towns sprang up together with at least six strong churches. E.M.B.

PIT. Basically a deep hole, either natural or artificial, in the ground.

1. Heb. *bôr*, 'a deep hole', used to describe the place where Joseph was cast by his brethren (Gn. 37:20, 22, 24, *etc.*), a place to hide (1 Sa. 13:6), a place where lions lurked (2 Sa. 23:20; 1 Ch. 11:22), a place where prisoners were shut up (Is. 24:22; Zc. 9:11; *cf.* Je. 38:6), and where the rebel Ishmael cast the bodies of the men of Shechem, Shiloh and Samaria (Je. 41:7, 9).

The laws of Ex. 21:33–34 were directed to Israelites who opened up holes and left them uncovered (*cf.* Ec. 10:8, where the word is *gûmmāṣ*).

Metaphorically the word is used to describe the underworld, the place of departed spirits (Pss. 28:1; 30:3; 88:4, 6; 143:7; Pr. 1:12; Is. 14:15, 19; 38:18; Ezk. 26:20; 31:14, 16; 32:18, 24, *etc.*). A second metaphorical use describes the place from which God brings up his saints (Ps. 40:2; Is. 51:1).

2. Heb. *bᵉ'ēr*, a well. The vale of Siddim was full of slime (bitumen) pits (Gn. 14:10). Used metaphorically, it is the pit of destruction (Pss. 55:23; 69:15). A harlot is described in Pr. 23:27 as a narrow pit.

3. Heb. *gēḇ* or *geḇe'*, a place where water is collected (Is. 30:14; Je. 14:3). **4.** Heb. *paḥaṯ*, 'a hole for trapping animals' (2 Sa. 17:9; 18:17; Is. 24:17–18; Je. 48:43–44). **5.** Heb. *šᵉ'ôl*, Sheol, the underworld (Nu. 16:30, 33; Jb. 17:16). The same Heb. word is translated elsewhere in other ways. (*HELL.)

6. Three words from the Heb. root *šwḥ*: (i) *šûḥâ*, 'a pit in the desert' (Je. 2:6), a place where Jeremiah was trapped by wicked men (Je. 18:20, 22), and the mouth of a strange woman (Pr. 22:14). (ii) *šaḥaṯ*, a trap in the ground for wild animals (Ps. 35:7; Ezk. 19:4, 8), or, more usually, the underworld (Jb. 33:18, 24, 28, 30; Pss. 9:15; 30:9; 94:13; Is. 38:17; 51:14; Ezk. 28:8). (iii) *šîḥâ*, a trap (Pss. 57:6; 119:85; Je. 18:22).

7. Two words from the Heb. root *šḥh*. *šᵉḥuṯ*, the pit which the wicked prepare for the righteous, into which they fall themselves (Pr. 28:10), and *šᵉḥiṯ*, the lot of Zedekiah in 587 BC when he was taken in the pits of the enemy (La. 4:20).

8. In the NT the pit into which an ass falls is *bothynos* in Mt. 12:11 and *phrear* in Lk. 14:5. The bottomless pit of Rev. 9:1–2 is also *phrear*. (*ABYSS.)

Some idea of pits is to be obtained from archaeological discoveries. Quite regularly the cistern which served as a pit had a neck about the width of a man about 1 m in depth, and then opened out into a large bulbous cavity of varying size. Broken pottery and other remains in these pits are useful aids to dating the period when they were in use. (*POOL, *ARCHAEOLOGY.) The use of pits for trapping animals and men is also attested in extrabiblical texts. J.A.T

PITHOM (Old Egyp. *Pr-fitm*, 'mansion of the god Atum'). A city of Egypt where the Israelites were afflicted with heavy building burdens (Ex. 1:11). Most accept that it was situated in Wadi Tumilat, at Tell el-Maskhuta or Tell er-Retaba. Not far away from this place was the migdol of Tjeku, which may be the biblical Succoth (Ex. 12:37; 13:20; Nu. 33:5–6). In Papyrus Anastasi, V, 19. 5–20. 6 we read that the chief of the archers went to Tjeku to prevent slaves from running away, but he came too late. Somebody had seen them crossing the N wall of the migdol of Seti-Merenptah. A second report, in Papyr. Anas., V, 18. 6–19. 1, refers to Libyan mercenaries who tried to flee and were taken back to Tjeku. A third mention, in Papyr. Anas., VI, 5. 1, emanates from a civil servant who had finished passing Shasu-nomads from Edom, S of the Dead Sea, into Egypt, at the fort of Tjeku, towards the marshes of Pithom of Merenptah of Tjeku. (*ENCAMPMENT BY THE SEA.)

BIBLIOGRAPHY. E. Naville, *The Store-City of Pithom*, 1903; Montet, *Géographie de l'Égypte ancienne*, 1, 1957, pp. 214–219. C.D.W.

PLAGUES OF EGYPT. In commissioning Moses to lead Israel out of Egypt, God had warned him that this would come about only through God's supreme power overcoming all the might of Pharaoh, whereby Egypt would be smitten with wonders or signs from God (*cf.* Ex. 3:19–20). After the sign of the rod that became a serpent and swallowed up those of the Egyptian magicians, which left Pharaoh unmoved, God's power was demonstrated to him and his people in a series of ten judgments. They were so applied as to portray clearly the reality and power of Israel's God, and thus by contrast the impotence of Egypt's gods. The first nine of these plagues bear a direct relation to natural phenomena in the Nile valley, but the tenth, the death of the first-born, belongs wholly to the realm of the supernatural.

These first nine plagues demonstrate the divine vine use of the created order to achieve his ends, and recent studies tend to confirm both the reality of what is described in Ex. 7–12 and the powers of accurate, first-hand observation of the narrator of this part of Exodus. The element of miracle in these plagues is usually bound up with their intensity, timing and duration. By far the most painstaking study of the plague phenomena is that by G. Hort in *ZAW* 69, 1957, pp. 84–103, and *ZAW* 70, 1958, pp. 48–59. While her treatment of the first nine seems excellent, her attempt to explain the tenth as 'firstfruits' instead of first-born is decidedly artificial and unlikely.

Hort has pointed out that the first nine plagues form a logical and connected sequence, beginning with an abnormally *high* Nile-inundation occurring in the usual months of July and August and the series of plagues ending about March (Heb. *Abib*). In Egypt too high an inundation of the Nile was just as disastrous as too low a flood.

The first plague (Ex. 7:14–25)

Moses was commanded to stretch his rod over the Nile waters, that they should be 'turned to blood'; the fish in the river would die, the river stink, and its water be unpalatable; no immediate ending of these conditions is recorded. This would correspond with the conditions brought about by an unusually high Nile. The higher the Nile-flood, the more earth it carries in suspension, especially of the finely-divided 'red earth' from the basins of the Blue Nile and Atbara. And the more earth carried, the redder became the Nile waters. Such an excessive inundation could further bring down with it microcosms known as *flagellates* and associated bacteria: besides heightening the blood-red colour of the water, these would create conditions so unfavourable for the fish that they would die in large numbers as recorded. Their decomposition would foul the water and cause a stench. The rise of the Nile begins in July/August, reaches its maximum about September, and then falls again; this plague would therefore affect Egypt from July/August to October/November.

The second plague (Ex. 8:1–15)

Seven days later (7:25) Egypt was afflicted by swarms of frogs which, in accordance with God's promise, died *en masse* the following day and quickly decayed. That the frogs should swarm out of the river in August was most unusual. The numerous decomposing fish washed along the banks and backwaters of the Nile would pollute and infect the river-shore haunts of the frogs and the frogs themselves, which then came ashore in numbers, heading for the shelter of houses and fields. The sudden death and malodorous and rapid putrefaction of the frogs would indicate internal anthrax (from *Bacillus anthracis*) as the infection and cause.

The third plague (Ex. 8:16–19)

Hort suggests that this was an abnormal plague of mosquitoes (AV 'lice', RSV 'gnats'), whose already high rate of reproduction would be further encouraged by the specially-favourable breeding-conditions provided by an unusually high Nile.

The fourth plague (Ex. 8:20–32)

The particular 'fly' in question here was probably *Stomoxys calcitrans*. See below on the sixth plague, for which this insect is the likeliest agent.

The fifth plague (Ex. 9:1–7)

A 'very severe plague' upon all the Egyptians' cattle actually in the fields (not all livestock). A cattle pest that affected only the animals out in the fields might indicate that they had contracted anthrax from the infection carried into their fields by the frogs. If the Israelites' cattle were in their stalls they would not have been affected.

The sixth plague (Ex. 9:8–12)

The *boils 'breaking out in sores' were probably skin anthrax passed on by the bites of the carrier-fly *Stomoxys calcitrans*, which breeds in decaying vegetation and would have become a carrier of the disease from the infected haunts of the frogs and cattle. The boils may have affected particularly the hands and feet (Ex. 9:11: the magicians could not stand before Moses; *cf.* Dt. 28:27, 35), which would be a further clue in favour of the proposed identifications of the disease and its carrier, which would strike by about December/January.

The seventh plague (Ex. 9:13–35)

Heavy hail with thunder, lightning and rain. This ruined the barley and flax, but not the wheat and spelt, which were not yet grown up. This would fit early February. The concentration at this season of this sudden plague in Upper Egypt, but not in Goshen nearer the Mediterranean seaboard, fits the climatic phenomena of these areas.

The eighth plague (Ex. 10:1–20)

The heavy precipitation in Ethiopia and the Sudan which led to the extraordinarily high Nile would also provide favourable conditions for a dense plague of locusts by about March. These, following the usual route, would in due course be blown into N Egypt by the E wind; the 'west wind', *rûaḥ-yām*, is literally 'sea-wind'; *i.e.* really a N (or NW) wind, and this would blow the locusts right up the Nile valley. Hort would then emend 'Red Sea' (*yām sûp̄*) to 'South' (*yāmîn*), but this is not strictly necessary.

The ninth plague (Ex. 10:21–29)

The 'thick darkness' which could be felt. This was a *khamsin* dust-storm, but no ordinary one. The heavy inundation had brought down and deposited masses of 'red earth', now dried out as a fine dust over the land. The effect of this when whirled up by a *khamsin* wind would be to make the air extraordinarily thick and dark, blotting out the light of the sun. The 'three days' of Ex. 10:23 is the known length of a *khamsin*. The intensity of the *khamsin* may suggest that it was early in the season, and would thus come in March. If the Israelites were dwelling in the region of Wadi Tumilat, they would miss the worst effects of this plague.

The tenth plague (Ex. 11:1–12:36)

So far God had demonstrated his full control over the natural creation. He had caused his servant Moses to announce the successive plagues and brought them to pass in invincible sequence and growing severity when the pharaoh ever more persistently refused to acknowledge Israel's God in face of the clearest credentials of his authority and power. In this final plague came the most explicit sign of God's precise and full control: the death of the first-born only. Nor did it come without adequate warning (Ex. 4:23); the pharaoh had had every opportunity to acknowledge God and obey his behest, and so had to take the consequences of refusal.

Other aspects

In later days Joshua reminded Israel in Canaan of their mighty deliverance from Egypt through the plagues (Jos. 24:5). The Philistines also knew of them and feared their Author (1 Sa. 4:8). Later still, the psalmist sang of these awe-inspiring events (Ps. 78:43–51).

In Ex. 12:12 God speaks of executing judgments against all the gods of Egypt. In some measure he had already done so in the plagues, as Egypt's gods were much bound up with the forces of nature. Ha'pi, the Nile-god of inundation, had brought not prosperity but ruin; the frogs, symbol of Heqit, a goddess of fruitfulness, had brought only disease and wasting; the hail, rain and storm were the heralds of awesome events (as in the Pyramid Texts); and the light of the sun-god Rē' was blotted out, to mention but a few of the deities affected.

The account of the plagues is emphatically a literary unity: it is only the *total* details of the whole and unitary narrative that correspond so strikingly with observable physical phenomena. The mere fragments of plagues that would feature in supposed documentary sources (J, E, P, *etc.*) and the schematic uniformity of features postulated for these correspond to no known phenomena. Arbitrary adaptation of such partial and stylized accounts into a new and conflated narrative that somehow then happens to correspond exactly to observable phenomena long past and in a distant land is surely beyond serious belief (so Hort). The plainer explanation and the unity of the narrative is to be preferred to a theory which involves unattested phenomena. K.A.K.

PLAIN, CITIES OF THE. The cities of the plain were, chiefly, Sodom, Gomorrah, Admah, Zeboiim and Bela or Zoar (Gn. 14:2). It has been held that these were located N of the Dead Sea, where the Jordan Valley broadens into the 'Circle' or 'Plain' of the Jordan (*cf.* Dt. 34:3), the evidence being 'that Abraham and Lot looked upon the cities from near Bethel (Gn. 13:10), that *Circle of Jordan* is not applicable to the S of the Dead Sea, that the presence of five cities there is impossible and that the expedition of the Four Kings (Gn. 14:7), as it swept N from Kadesh-barnea, attacked Hazazon-tamar, probably Engedi, *before* it reached the Vale of Siddim and encountered the king of Sodom and his allies' (G. A. Smith, *Historical Geography of the Holy Land*[25], 1931, pp. 505f.).

On the other hand the view that the cities lie buried beneath the shallow waters of the S tip of the Dead Sea (G. E. Wright, *Westminster Historical Atlas*, 1945, pp. 26, 65–66; *idem*, *Biblical Archaeology*, 1957, p. 50) can be maintained. First, Gn. 13:10 says that Lot saw, not the cities of the plain, but the 'Circle' of Jordan. He was attracted not by urban facilities but by good pasturage. Secondly, refusal to give the name 'Circle of Jordan' to, and denial of the possibility of five cities at, the S of the Dead Sea depends on present-day configuration, and disregards any alterations made by the overthrow. Thirdly, there is the identification of Hazazon-tamar with En-gedi. This depends on 2 Ch. 20:2, where the advancing Moabites and Ammonites are said to be 'in Hazazon-tamar (that is, En-gedi)'. The qualifying phrase ought not to be taken in this case as identifying the two places (as, *e.g.*, in Gn. 14:3), unless we make the absurd assumption that after the time of Jehoshaphat the name En-gedi replaced Hazazon-tamar, thus necessitating an explanation of the archaism. The qualification 'that is, En-gedi' must, therefore, state more precisely where the enemy was in the general district designated by the first place-name. This suits the usage in Gn. 14:7 where, in a chapter full of parenthetic explanations of archaic place-names, Hazazon-tamar is left unexplained. We may therefore picture the cities of the plain as sited in the now-flooded area which once formed the S extension of the Circle of the Jordan.

As Lot saw it, the Circle was supremely attractive from every material viewpoint (Gn. 13:10), but it was to become desolate. The efficient cause of this destruction of the cities was probably an earthquake, with an accompanying release and explosion of gaseous deposits. Biblically and fundamentally it was God's judgment, remembered again and again throughout the Bible (Dt. 29:23; Is. 1:9; Je. 49:18; La. 4:6; Am. 4:11; Lk. 17:29; 2 Pet. 2:6); and Sodom became synonymous with brazen sin (Is. 3:9; La. 4:6; Jude 7). Whereas Ezk. 16:49–51 lists the sins of Sodom as pride, prosperous complacency and 'abominations', Gn. 19:4–5 concentrates on sexual perversion, particularly homosexuality. Lot's vicious offer of his daughters (v. 8) indicates the life and demoralizing influence of Sodom. The report that a cuneiform tablet from *Ebla lists the five cities rests on a misidentification.

The story of Sodom does not merely warn, but provides a theologically documented account of divine judgment implemented by 'natural' disaster. The history is faith's guarantee that the Judge of all the earth does right (Gn. 18:25). Being personally persuaded of its justice and necessity (Gn. 18:20–21), God acts; but in wrath he remembers mercy, and in judgment discrimination (Gn. 19: 16, 29). (*Cf.* *ARCHAEOLOGY for bibliography.)

J.A.M.

PLANTS. Any attempt to pronounce upon the nature and identity of the various biblical plants must avoid a number of pitfalls. One of these is the tacit assumption that they are identical with those designated by the same names in different parts of the world today. Another is the assumption that plants found in Palestine today were also native to that area in biblical times. In addition, different versions of Scripture frequently reflect wrong identifications and there is confusion of botanical nomenclature and the like by the translators. This is partly due to the fact that for the original writers present-day standards of accuracy in botanical matters were not pressing considerations, and, in addition, their terminology was by no means as comprehensive as that of the modern botanist. The AV, made at a time when little was known of the natural history of the Holy Land and before scientific classification had begun, contributed materially to the degree of confusion already existing regarding the identification of plants. The RSV and other modern versions correct obvious errors, but there remain differences of opinion as to the identity of some plant names, including that of *trees.

The following represent some wild biblical plants and those not included in single or composite entries.

Broom (Heb. *rōṯem* and variants; AV 'juniper'). A common Palestinian shrub (*Retama raetam*) of sandy places, 2–4 m high, with numerous white pea flowers in the spring. Elijah in despair sat under one (1 Ki. 19:4–5). Its roots produce excellent charcoal which was used for incendiary arrows (Ps. 120:4) and for warmth (Jb. 30:4), although some authors consider the latter verse refers to the parasitic plant *Cynomorium coccineum*, which grows upon broom roots and may be edible (*cf.* AV).

Castor-oil. The correct rendering of the Heb. *qîqāyôn* (Jon. 4:6) has been disputed by many scholars. Pliny and Herodotus assumed it to be the castor-oil plant (*Ricinus communis*, the *kroton* of the Greeks) and they are followed by many versions (RSVmg.). It is a rapidly-growing shrub which could have afforded shade to Jonah and is said to wither even after only slight handling, as Jonah's did. Others, starting from LXX (Gk. *kolokyntha*, but not the ground-trailing colocynth) suggest the bottle-gourd (*Cucurbita lagenaria*, Arab. *qar'ah*, AV 'gourd') which is more adequate botanically, since the biblical context requires a vine rather than a small tree like the castor-oil. The reference may therefore be to such a 'lodge' as sheltered watchers over cucumbers (see Is. 1:8), and which would also be subject to rapid withering, although there may not be a satisfactory natural explanation to an event that was clearly under the control of the Lord.

Crocus. In Is. 35:1 the Heb. *ḥᵃḇaṣṣeleṯ* means bulb, hence the RSV rendering 'crocus' (although strictly a corm). There are many species of *crocus* in Palestine flowering during the winter. The LXX rendered it as *krinon* ('lily'), AV 'rose', and NEB 'asphodel', which has root tubers. The polyanthus narcissus (*Narcissus tazetta*) would be an even better suggestion since it is a truly bulbous plant. Crocus may also be intended in the reference to the 'rose of Sharon', Ct. 2:1. See **Rose**, below.

Hyssop (Heb. *'ēzôḇ*; Gk. *hyssōpos*). Several distinct species of plant are evidently referred to by this name in the Bible, but there is considerable discussion as to their identity. It is certain, however, that the present-day herb known as hyssop (*Hyssopus officinalis*) was not one of them, since it is native to S Europe.

In the OT 'hyssop' was used in the Passover rites (Ex. 12:22) for the purification of lepers (Lv. 14:4, 6), for plague (Lv. 14:49–52) and at the red heifer sacrifice (Nu. 19:2–6; *cf.* Heb. 9:19). The purifying qualities of 'hyssop' are referred to in Ps. 51:7. This plant is generally considered to be the Syrian marjoram (*Origanum syriacum*) which is a fragrant grey-leaved wiry-stemmed perennial herb, 20–30 cm high, with white flowers in small heads, growing in dry rocky places. A different plant is considered to be mentioned in 1 Ki. 4:33, probably the caper (*Capparis spinosa*) which is commonly seen in walls of old buildings: it has very prickly woody stems and large whitish flowers.

In the NT the 'hyssop' employed at the crucifixion (Jn. 19:29, where NEB reads *hyssō*, 'on a javelin') was probably a reed or stick, but the reed-like cereal durra (*Sorghum vulgare*) has been considered the most likely suggestion.

Lily (Heb. *šôšân*, and variants; Gk. *krinon*). As with the 'rose' of the Bible there has been considerable speculation as to the botanical identity of the 'lily'. In common usage the word may be applied to several decorative plants. Most of the references in Ct. are thought to be to the hyacinth (*Hyacinthus orientalis*), a bulbous plant with blue flowers, although the lily-like lips of Ct. 5:13 may allude to the scarlet tulip (*Tulipa sharonensis*) or red poppy anemone (*Anemone coronaria*), myrrh resin also mentioned, being red. Although the white madonna lily (*Lilium candidum*) is wild in Palestine, it inhabits rocky places and it is unlikely to be the plant referred to in Ct. 6:2–3, as has been suggested. The 'lily' of Ho. 14:5 is by implication of a moist habitat likely to be the yellow flag (*Iris pseudacorus*), the 'fleur de lis' of the French.

The references to 'lily-work' on the columns of Solomon's Temple in 1 Ki. 7:19, 22, 26 and 2 Ch. 4:5 are probably to carved representations of the water-lily. The Egyptian lotus (the blue flowered *Nymphaea caerulea* and white *N. lotus*) exercised a wide influence over ancient Near Eastern art, as evidenced by the presence of the lotus motif in many Egyptian and Palestinian archaeological *objets d'art.*

The 'lilies of the field' (Mt. 6:28; Lk. 12:27) could refer to any of the spectacular and beautiful flowers of the Palestinian countryside. Many have been suggested, including the poppy anemone *Anemone coronaria* and the white daisy *Anthemis palaestina* or the crown marguerite *Chrysanthemum coronarium.*

Mallow (Heb. *mallûaḥ*, AV 'mallows', Jb. 30:4). The term implies 'saltiness', whether referring to the taste of the plant or to its habitat. The most likely species is the shrubby orache (*Atriplex halimus*), of salty places by the Dead Sea or Mediterranean. The mallow (*Malva rotundifolia*) may be used like spinach, but it is not salty to the taste and it is a common weed of waste but not saline places.

Mandrake (Heb. *dûḏā'îm*; *Mandragora officinarum*). A perennial herb of the nightshade family with a rosette of large leaves, mauve flowers during the winter and fragrant round yellow fruits in the spring (Ct. 7:13). It is reputed to have emetic, purgative and narcotic qualities. The forked, torso-like shape of the tap-root gave rise to many superstitions. Aphrodisiac properties have been ascribed to it since an early period, which explains the argument between Rachel and Leah (Gn. 30:14). It grows in fields and rough ground in Palestine and the Mediterranean region.

Mildew (Heb. *yērāqôn*, 'paleness', 'greenness'; *cf.* LXX *ikteros*, 'jaundice'). A common species of fungus (*Puccinia graminis*) which, in moist conditions, attacks the crops in Palestine. In biblical times it was regarded as God's punishment on the disobedient (Dt. 28:22; Am. 4:9; Hg. 2:17), and Solomon prayed for deliverance from it (1 Ki. 8:37; 2 Ch. 6:28). The Bible always mentions mildew in conjunction with the opposite conditions, 'blight' or 'blasting' (Heb. *šiddāpôn*, lit. 'scorching'), a drying up of plants by the hot sirocco or *ḥamsîn* wind from the S.

Mustard. Much controversy surrounds the identification of the plant (Gk. *sinapi*) whose seed was used by Christ as an illustration of something which develops rapidly from small beginnings, such as the kingdom of heaven (Mt. 13:31; Mk. 4:31; Lk. 13:19), or the faith of an individual (Mt. 17:20; Lk. 17:6). Some scholars consider that the black mustard (*Brassica nigra*) is indicated, since in NT times its seeds were cultivated for their oil as well as for culinary purposes. It can grow to a height of 5 m, although it is usually much smaller. One interpretation sees the 'mustard' as a monstrous plant foretelling the worldly expression of Christendom, with evil, as exemplified by the birds, in its branches.

Myrtle (Heb. *hᵃḏas*; *Myrtus communis*). A shrub of Palestinian hillsides, usually 2–3 m high, with fragrant evergreen leaves and scented white flowers used as perfumes. Scriptural references envisage the myrtle as symbolizing divine generosity. Isaiah foresaw the myrtle as replacing the brier in the wilderness (Is. 41:19; 55:13). Zechariah in a vision symbolizing peace saw a grove of myrtle trees (Zc. 1:8–11), while in Ne. 8:15 the Jews brought myrtle branches from Olivet to construct shelters at the Feast of Booths (Tabernacles) of Lv. 23:40; Dt. 16:16. The name Hadassah (Esther) was derived from the Heb. term.

Nettles. There is some uncertainty about the precise plants referred to in the above translation of the two Heb. words. **1.** *ḥārûl*, perhaps from the obsolete root *ḥāral*, 'to be sharp', 'to sting'. Found in Jb. 30:7 (LXX 'wild brushwood'); Pr. 24:31; Zp. 2:9; RVmg. in each case renders 'wild vetches' and NEB as 'scrub' or 'weeds'. **2.** *qimmôś* (Is. 34:13; Ho. 9:6). Probably the true nettle, of which the most common Palestine species is *Urtica pilulifera*, which occurs in waste places. (See also **Thistles**, below.)

Nuts. Two Heb. words are thus translated. **1.** *'ᵉgôz* (Arab. *gawz*), in Ct. 6:11 only, probably referring to the walnut (*Juglans regia*), an introduction from Persia. **2.** *boṭnîm* (Gn. 43:11 only) is usually considered to be the pistachio nut (*Pistachia vera*), the fruits of which must have been imported from further E where it grew before it was cultivated in the E Mediterranean area. However, the native terebinths (*P. atlantica* and *P. terebinthus* var. *palaestina*) also yield edible nuts of a small size. Some Jewish authors identify this Heb. word with the carob. (See **Pods**.)

Pods (Gk. *keratia*). A sweet dry fruit eaten by animals and by the poor. The prodigal son in his hunger would gladly have done so (Lk. 15:16, AV 'husks'). It is the seed-pod of the carob tree (*Ceratonia siliqua*), common in the Mediterranean region, where it is also called the locust bean and St John's bread from a tradition that they were the 'locusts' which John the Baptist ate, although these are more likely to have been the actual locust insect (*ANIMALS).

Reed. 1. Heb. *'āḥû* (Jb. 8:11, AV 'flag'; Gn. 41:2, 18, AV 'meadow'). This is a general word for water-loving plants found in swamps and by river-banks—hence Bildad's rhetorical question ('Can the reed grow without water?').

2. Heb. *sûp̄*, 'reed' (Ex. 2:3, 5; Is. 19:6). Evidently specifically applied to the moisture-loving cat-tail or reed-mace (*Typha angustata*) still common around the Nile and its canals. The Red Sea (*yam sûp̄*) is literally the 'sea of Reeds' (*cf.* Egyp. *p'-ṯwf*).

3. Heb. *qāneh*; Gk. *kalamos*. Tall grasses growing in wet places (marshes, river-banks, *etc.*), often the haunts of large aquatic animals (*cf.* Jb. 40:21; Is. 19:6–7; 35:7). The Heb. and Gk. words are both quite general terms, although some think that the *Arundo donax* of Palestine and Egypt, growing to 3 m high or more, and the smaller common reed (*Phragmites communis*) are the plant usually intended. Israel under God's judgment is like a reed shaken in the water (1 Ki. 14:15); and in Christ's words, wind-blown reeds and richly dressed courtiers will not be found in a dry wilderness (Mt. 11:7–8; Lk. 7:24). If undue weight be rested on a reed-stalk it will break irregularly, and the snags will pierce the hand. Just so did Egypt fail Israel in the days of Isaiah (Is. 36:6; 2 Ki. 18:21), Jeremiah and Ezekiel (Ezk. 29:6–7). The 'bruised reed' could be symbolic of the weak whom the Messiah would not break off (Is. 42:3; Mt. 12:20).

Before the crucifixion, the soldiers gave Christ a reed as a mock sceptre, and then struck him with it (Mt. 27:29–30; Mk. 15:19). On the cross he was offered a spongeful of vinegar on the end of a reed (Mt. 27:48; Mk. 15:36; or 'hyssop', Jn. 19:29). A reed could serve as a measuring-rod, and gave its name to a measure of 6 cubits (Ezk. 40:3–8; 41:8 *(*the 6 cubits*)*; 42:16–19; Rev. 11:1; 21:15–16), as did the same term *qanu* in Mesopotamia. (*WEIGHTS AND MEASURES.)

Rose. The true rose, *e.g. Rosa phoenicia*, is uncommon in Palestine and the 'rose of Sharon' (Ct. 2:1) is unlikely to be this plant. *Anemone*, *Cistus*, *Narcissus*, *Tulipa* and *Crocus* have been mentioned as possibilities.

In the Apocrypha the 'rose' of Ecclus 1:8 bloomed in spring and may be either a tulip, narcissus or crocus. In Ecclus 24:14 and 39:13 the references are probably to oleander (*Nerium oleander*) which is a tall, pink-flowered shrub with poisonous leaves that inhabits rocky streams. The 'roses' of 2 Esdras 2:19 and 'rosebuds' of Wisdom 2:8 have been variously regarded as species of rock-rose (*Cistus*), rose (*Rosa*) or oleander.

Rush. The word rush should apply to species of *Juncus*, but the term is loosely applied to other water-loving plants (except marsh grasses, which are reeds), such as reed-mace also called cat-tail (*Typha*), and sedges such as papyrus (*Cyperus papyrus*) and corresponds to the Heb. *'ağmōn* and *gōme'*. The former is a general word, 'rushes', 'reed'. For her unfaithfulness to God, Israel is stripped even of such ordinary basic raw materials as 'palm branch and reed' (Is. 9:14), while these, for all their utility, will not avail Egypt in her troubles (Is. 19:15). Rushes could be woven into rope, or used as fuel (Jb. 41:2, 20). The head bowed in outward penitence is like the bent-over tip of the rush (Is. 58:5); here the papyrus plant is probably intended since it does not snap off but is easily bent by the wind and hangs down.

The term *gōme'* may signify the papyrus-plant (for which see *PAPYRI AND OSTRACA, I), or else reeds generally; either meaning suits the biblical references to *gōme'*, which is depicted growing in the marsh (Jb. 8:11), symbolizing swampy growth (Is. 35:7), used for papyrus skiffs in Egypt and Ethiopia (Is. 18:2) and Moses' basket of bulrushes (Ex. 2:3). Heb. *gōme'* is probably the same as Egyp. *gmy* and *ḳmy*, 'reeds', 'rushes', attested from the 13th century BC onwards, and *kam* in Coptic. (See R. A. Caminos, *Late-Egyptian Miscellanies*, 1954, pp. 167–168, 412; *cf.* W. Spiegelberg, *Koptische Etymologien*, 1920, pp. 4–6; T. O. Lambdin, *JAOS* 73, 1953, p. 149.)

Shrub (Heb. *'ar'ār*, Je. 17:6). The Heb. word, rendered 'shrub' in RSV (AV 'heath'), is considered by Jewish scholars to be the Phoenician juniper (*Juniperus phoenicea*). The tamarisk (*Tamarix* sp.) has also been suggested. A similar word *'ᵃrô'ēr* in Je. 48:6 appears as 'wild ass' in RSV and 'heath' in AV.

Thistles, Thorns. Botanists have difficulty identifying the thistles, thorns, briers, bramble and other prickly plants mentioned in Scripture, owing to the fact that over twenty different words are employed to describe such plants, of which there are many in the dry Palestinian countryside. These prickly *weeds fall into genera such as *Centaurea*, *Ononis*, *Silybum*, *Notobasis* and *Poterium*. In many instances the Heb. and Gk. words for them are as imprecise as Eng. ones.

In general, thorns expressed the concept of fruitlessness or vexatious endeavour (Gn. 3:18; Nu. 33:55; Jos. 23:13). They were evidence of divine judgment on the ungodly (Na. 1:10), or of sheer misfortune (Ezk. 2:6). If allowed to grow unchecked in orchards or vineyards they made serious inroads on the productivity of the trees and vines (Pr. 24:31; Is. 5:6; Je. 12:13), but when kept in control and arranged in the form of hedges they served as effective barriers to wild animals (Ho. 2:6; Mt. 21:33). Thorns were popular quick-burning fuel in OT times, as among the modern bedouin Arabs (Ps. 58:9; Is. 9:18; 10:17). The destructive nature of thistles and thorns was expressed graphically in the Gospel parables (Mt. 13:7; Mk. 4:7; Lk. 8:7), as was their essential fruitlessness (Mt. 7:16). Thistles are herbaceous plants, whereas thorns are woody. In the parable of the sower (Mt. 13:7, *etc.*) the 'thorns' among which the grain fell were likely to have been the milk thistle (*Silybum marianum*) which infests field margins and grows rapidly.

Some of the biblical references to 'thorns' are to the holy bramble (*Rubus sanguineus*). Those of Pr. 15:19 and Ho. 2:6 may be the latter, while 'thorns of the wilderness' (Jdg. 8:7) may be an acacia, or *Ziziphus lotus*, and the 'briers' boxthorn (*Lycium* sp.), which is the 'bramble' of Jotham's parable (Jdg. 9:14). The crown of *thorns (Mt. 27:29; Mk. 15:17; Jn. 19:5) plaited for Jesus before his crucifixion would have been made of some locally available material. Although the 'Christ thorn' shrub (*Paliurus spina-christi*), which has long thorny branches, is not now found around Jerusalem, it is known to have grown near there in ancient times. However, some authors consider that the small spiny burnet (*Poterium spinosum*) or tree *Ziziphus spina-christi* was used; others have suggested the thorns of the *Phoenix dactylifera*, in mock imitation of the radiate crown (*cf.* H. St J. Hart, *JTS* n.s. 3, 1952, pp. 66ff.). (See also **Nettles**, above.)

Tumbleweed. Heb. *galgal* is rendered in EVV 'wheel', 'rolling thing', 'thistle down' and 'whirling dust' (Is. 17:13; Ps. 83:13, RSV 'tumble weed'). It implies one of the wind-distributed fruiting bodies of certain plants growing in open dry habitats. Such Palestinian plants are *Grundelia tournefortii* and *Cachrys goniocarpa*, as well as the hairy grains of some grasses that collect as rolling balls. *Anastatica hierochuntica* is not one of these, as has often been suggested, since it remains firmly anchored by its root even when dead.

Vine of Sodom. A variety of opinion exists regarding the nature of the allusions in the Song of Moses (Dt. 32:32). There is a distinct possibility that the expression may be figurative, describing the bitterness of Israel's enemies. If a real plant, one which conceals a powdery substance underneath an attractive rind is indicated. *Solanum sodomeum*, or *Calotropic procera*, with feathery seeds in an inflated fruit, has been suggested. More probably the phrase arose from association with the colocynth, a wild *gourd, *Citrullus colocynthis*, which trails on sandy ground near the Dead Sea and has bitter, light-weight fruits.

Weeds. Usually applied to wild plants of cultivated and waste ground. In the Bible represented as a scourge of useless, troublesome plants as indeed they were to the farmer. RSV renders several words as 'weeds', especially Gk. *zizania*, Arab. *zuwān*, which AV calls 'tares', and is probably more correctly considered (as in NEB) to be the darnel grass (*Lolium temulentum*). In the leafy stage this grass resembles wheat, but if the biblical counsel be followed and both are allowed to grow together till harvest (Mt. 13:30) the small ear is clearly distinguished, and usually to women and children falls the tedious manual task of separation. If the wheat grain is contaminated with the bitter darnel grains subsequent poisoning causes illness and vomiting. Sowing darnel in a field for purposes of revenge (*cf.* Mt. 13:25f.) was a crime under Roman legislation. The necessity for a law on the subject suggests that the action was not infrequent.

NEB renders other words as 'weeds' which appear in RSV as *nettles or *thorns.

The cockle (*Agrostemma githago*) was a curse of English wheat fields at the time the AV was being translated, but there is no evidence that it occurred in Palestine. Later translations are probably correct in rendering the Heb. *bo'šâ*, referred to by Job while defending his integrity (31:38–40), by some general term such as 'stinking weeds', AVmg.; 'noisome weeds', RVmg.; 'foul weeds', RSV; 'weeds', NEB. Evidently this weed was prickly and it has been identified with the oyster thistle (*Scolymus maculatus*) and the rest-harrow (*Ononis antiquorum*).

Wild vine, wild gourds (Heb. *paqqu'ōt*, 'bursters'). Mentioned in 2 Ki. 4:39 these gourds were the colocynth (*Citrullus colocynthis*). Like small melons in appearance, the fruits are a violent purge which may be dangerous. The colocynth trails along the ground in sandy places by the Dead Sea.

Wormwood (Heb. *la'ᵃnâ*, Gk. *apsinthos*). Many species of wormwood grow in Palestine, but the biblical references are either to *Artemisia herba-alba* or *A. judaica*. All species have a strong, bitter taste, leading to the use of the plant as a symbol of bitterness, sorrow and calamity (Pr. 5:4; La. 3:15, 19; Am. 5:7; 6:12 (AV 'hemlock')). Moses used it to show the perils of secret idolatry (Dt. 29:18, RSV 'bitter root'), as did Jeremiah in warning of the punishment awaiting disobedient Israel (Je. 9:15; 23:15).

BIBLIOGRAPHY. N. Feinbrun-Dothan and A. Danin, *Analytical Flora of Eretz-Israel*, 1991 (Heb.); A. Goor and M. Nurock, *Fruits of the Holy Land*, 1968; F. N. Hepper, *IEBP*; I Löw, *Die Flora der Juden*, 1–4, 1924–34; H. N. and A. L. Moldencke, *Plants of the Bible*, 1952; U. Pitman *et al.*, *Pictorial Flora of Israel*, 1983 (Heb.); D. Zohary and M. Hopf, *Domestication of Plants in the Old World*, 1988; M. Zohary, *Plant-life of Palestine*, 1962; *idem*, *Plants of the Bible*, 1982; *idem* and N. Feinbrun-Dothan, *Flora Palaestina*, 1–4, 1966–86.

F.N.H. *et al.*

PLASTER. 1. The inner, and sometimes outer, walls of buildings were covered with a plaster commonly made of clay (Lv. 14:42–43; Heb. *ṭûaḥ*, 'to coat, overlay'; Arab. *ṭāḫa*). Such plaster is attested from prehistoric times (*JERICHO). A better plaster was made by heating crushed limestone or gypsum (Heb. *śîḏ*, 'to boil'). This enabled rough stones or brickwork to be covered with a fine surface which could be painted or inscribed, as was done on the altar at Ebal (Dt. 27:2, 4). (An example has been found at Deir 'Alla in the Jordan Valley.) It was used for basins, cisterns and walls. A glazed surface on brickwork was obtained by firing in a kiln (Is. 27:9; Heb. *gîr*). Such a 'plaister' (AV) was broken by the handwriting on the palace wall in Babylon (Dn. 5:5; Aram. *gîrâ*). (*GLASS.)

2. The 'plaister' used to cure Hezekiah (Is. 38:21, AV; Heb. *māraḥ*) was a poultice made of crushed figs. A similar medical term is used in the Ras Shamra texts and Egyp. Ebers Papyrus. D.J.W.

PLOUGHMAN. In the OT there are three Heb. expressions which are rendered 'ploughman'.

1. *'ikkār*. The cognate Akkadian ideogram describes the *'ikkār* as 'man of the plough'. The exact social position and function of the *'ikkār* is uncertain, but the code of Hammurapi suggests that he was a hired agricultural foreman. The OT contrasts the shepherd with the *'ikkār* (Is. 61:5).

2. *yōḡēḇ* (2 Ki. 25:12; Je. 52:16). Consideration of the related Heb. *gûḇ* and Arab. *ǧāba*, 'to bore', 'hollow out', may suggest that the *yōḡēḇ* was a spade labourer.

3. *'îš 'ᵃḏāmâ* means literally 'man of soil', but a comparison of Gn. 9:20 and Zc. 13:5 shows that it refers indifferently to an arable or cattle farmer.

LXX and NT employ *geōrgos*, 'farmer, tenant farmer', throughout. God is pictured as the husbandman of the true vine (Jn. 15:1) and of the church (1 Cor. 3:9). R.J.W.

POETRY.

I. In the Old Testament

Although poetry occurs very frequently in the OT, the division between prose and poetry in ancient Heb. is not precise. No single literary trait occurs only in what we call poetry to the exclusion of prose. Nonetheless, certain literary devices in poetry allow us to identify poems with a high level of confidence. These traits may be discussed under four headings: terseness, parallelism, imagery, and secondary literary devices.

Ancient Heb. poetry is terse. The lines are short, usually containing only three or four Heb. words. Economy of expression is further achieved by a relative lack of conjunctions. The result is something noticed by even casual readers of English Bibles: wider margins.

The poems of the Bible are comprised of cola, which are grouped into lines, which in turn are grouped into stanzas. Prose narrative, on the other hand, is built with sentences which are grouped into paragraphs. The typical poetic line is a bicolon: *i.e.*, two cola which are united by parallelism into a single line. An example is Psalm 78:1:

Oh my people, hear my teaching:
 listen to the words of my mouth.

Parallelism is a major element in biblical poetry and was named by Bishop Robert Lowth (*Lectures on the Sacred Poetry of the Hebrews*) in 1753. Lowth borrowed the term from mathematics and thus implied symmetry, *i.e.* the first colon (A) and the second (B) are equal. Hence the popular understanding that a parallel line 'says the same thing twice'.

The above example best illustrates what Lowth called 'synonymous parallelism'. He also described 'antithetical parallelism' in which the same truth is seen from two different perspectives:

The tongue of the wise commends knowledge,
 but the mouth of the fool gushes folly.
 (Pr. 15:2)

A third category, into which all anomalous cases fell, he called 'synthetic parallelism':

'I have installed my King
 on Zion, my holy hill.' (Ps. 2:6)

More recently James Kugel, Robert Alter and Adele Berlin have redefined parallelism in a subtle but far-reaching manner. Rather than continuing Lowth's approach, which saw the A and B cola as essentially restatements of the same proposition, they observe that the second colon always specifies, and carries forward the thought expressed in the first colon. In Kugel's formulation 'A, what's more B'. Berlin applied this formula to grammatical parallelism. An illustration of parallelism is Psalm 131:1:

My heart is not proud, O Lord,
 my eyes are not haughty;
I do not concern myself with great matters . . .

As we read these three cola, we take them as a unit because of their similarity of content and intent. In all three the psalmist distances himself from pride. But there is also progress as we move from A to B to C. In A, the psalmist denies pride in his heart, the very core of his personality. In B, he denies pride in his demeanor. In C, he denies pride in his actions.

Besides terseness and parallelism, biblical poetry contains intense imagery. Imagery stimulates the imagination by embodying multiple meanings in a concise form. An image not only triggers a train of thinking about a subject but also evokes an emotional response.

Imagery is often the result of comparison, the two most common types being metaphor and simile. Simile, on one level, is not even figurative language; it is capable of being understood on a literal level. A simile is a comparison between two things and is marked by the use of 'like' or 'as'. Song of Songs 4:1b is a clear example:

Your hair is like a flock of goats
descending from Mount Gilead.

Metaphor presents a stronger connection between the two objects of comparison and is truly figurative language, as in Song. 4:1a:

Your eyes behind your veil are doves.

A well-known example comes from the first line of Psalm 23:

The Lord is my shepherd.
I shall not be in want.

What does it mean to compare the Lord to a shepherd? To read the image in context, we would immediately suggest that the poem speaks of God's protection, his guidance, and his care. We would stop short, however, if we did not remember that the shepherd image was a well-used royal image in the ancient Near East. Reading the text sympathetically, we would experience assurance and feel comfort even in the midst of danger.

Terseness, parallelism and imagery are the three main primary traits of biblical poetry. The acrostic form is a striking example of a secondary poetic device. These devices are secondary because they occur only occasionally.

An acrostic is a poem in which the first letters of successive lines form a recognizable pattern. The examples found in the OT all follow the order of the Heb. alphabet. The two most famous are perhaps the so-called Giant Psalm (119), which is broken up into eight-verse stanzas by the acrostic, and the book of Lamentations. One of the more interesting acrostic patterns is found in the first chapter of Nahum. The acrostic covers only half the alphabet and even skips an occasional letter. Other acrostics in Heb. occur as Pss. 9, 10, 25, 34, 37, 111, 112, 145; Pr. 31:10–31; La. 1–4.

The purpose of acrostic form may only be guessed. It may help in the process of memorization. It may also communicate a sense of wholeness. As Watson points out, 'By using every letter of the alphabet the poet was trying to ensure that his treatment of a particular topic was complete' (Watson 198).

A neglected secondary convention of Heb. poetry is the use of stanzas and strophes. Most studies of biblical poetry have concentrated on the level of the parallel line. Little has been done to describe rhetorical patterns that encompass the whole poem.

There is no doubt that most poems are unified wholes, but the relationship between the parts is almost always described in terms of content. For instance, grief psalms share a similar structure, *e.g.* Psalm 69: invocation and initial plea to God for help (v. 1a); complaints (vv. 1b–4, 7–12, 19–21); confession of sin (vv. 5–6); further pleas for help (vv. 13–18); imprecation (vv. 22–28); hymn of praise (vv. 30–36).

Each of these sections is composed of at least one and usually more than one parallel line. Are these broader groupings stanzas and/or strophes? Watson (160–200) argues that they are, as long as these terms are understood in the broad sense as 'units within the poem'.

Biblical poems then, may have a structure (in content and in style) that goes beyond the individual line and encompasses the whole poem.

The question of the existence of meter in biblical poetry has been widely discussed since the church fathers. In recent years a consensus has grown that either the meter of biblical poetry is undetectable or else, as seems more likely, it is non-existent.

Old Testament poetic types

Four principal types of poems can be discerned in the OT: lyric, epic, prophetic and dramatic. These four types often overlap.

The psalms are clear examples of biblical lyric, as is the Song of Songs, as both are personal expressions of deeply-held emotions. Indeed, the psalms explore the whole emotional spectrum, from the brightest joy to the darkest anger and grief, just as the love poems in the Song of Songs portray the full range of romantic sentiments.

Historical poems differ from lyric in that they recall past events, in particular the great acts of God. They are usually expressions of thanks to God for these events. Exodus 15 is a prime example, as it recalls in loving detail the miraculous deliverance of Israel from the Egyptians at the Red Sea.

The poetry of the prophets has a lyrical and a historical dimension. But the prophets use poetry with a more intense appeal to the wills of their hearers. They seek to persuade and to convict, and to achieve this they use the heightened language of poetry.

Conclusion

The extensive occurrence of poetry throughout the OT and its continued use in the NT remind us that the Bible is not simply an informative book. The biblical authors stimulate our imaginations as they fill our minds with images that give us an adequate, but partial, glimpse of the nature of God and of his relationship with his creatures.

BIBLIOGRAPHY. M. H. Abrams, *A Glossary of Terms*, 4, 1981; R. Alter, *The Art of Biblical Poetry*, 1985; A. Berlin, *The Dynamics of Biblical Parallelism*, 1985; E. W. Bullinger, *Figures of Speech Used in the Bible, Explained and Illustrated*, 1898, 1968; A. S. Cooper, 'Biblical Poetics: A Linguistic Approach', 1976; J. L. Kugel, *The Idea of Biblical Poetry*, 1981; T. Longman III, *How to Read the Psalms*, 1988; *idem*. 'Poetry', in *A Complete Literary Guide to the Bible*, 1993; L. Ryken, *How to Read the Bible as Literature*, 1984; *idem. Words of Delight: A Literary Introduction to the Bible*, 1987; W. G. E. Watson, *Classical Hebrew Poetry*, 1984.

T.L.

II. In the New Testament

a. Psalms

Three, perhaps four, typical Heb. hymns are preserved in Luke's Gospel: the *Magnificat* (Lk. 1:46–55), the *Benedictus* (Lk. 1:68–79), the *Nunc Dimittis* (Lk. 2:29–32) and the *Gloria* (Lk. 2:14). All of these passages are in the style and spirit of OT psalms, majestic in language, and constructed on the pattern of verbal parallelism proper to Heb. poetry.

b. Hymns

Early Christian hymns may have been poems of mixed tradition (Eph. 5:19), reflecting both the form of the Heb. psalm and that of the Gk. lyric. It has been suggested that numerous passages in the NT are direct and indirect quotations from this corpus of sacred poetry: *e.g.* Eph. 5:14 and 1 Tim. 3:16, where the Hebraic structure is especially striking. Perhaps Col. 1:13–20 and 2 Cor. 5:14–18 are of the same order.

c. Poetic language

This may be discussed under three heads:

(i) It is impossible decisively to distinguish between what may have been direct quotation of rhythmical and poetic utterance, and exalted prose couched in poetic language. In the warm, emotive style of Heb. writing it is always difficult to distinguish sharply poetry from prose, and in passages of deep emotion the NT often adopts such a style. Consider brief ascriptions of praise such as Jude 24–25, and Rev. 5:12–14; rhythmic constructions such as Jn. 14:27; Rom. 11:2, 33 and 1 Cor. 15:54–57; or parallelisms strong in their antitheses such as Jn. 3:20–21, or Rom. 2:6–10; and parallelism of chiastic form and pattern such as Phil. 3:3–10, and Jn. 10:14–15. All these passages, and many others, reveal the influence of the poetry of the OT on the language of the NT, both in form and colouring. Less in debt to Heb. speech, but still of the nature of poetry, are such lofty passages as Rom. 12; 1 Cor. 13 and Phil. 2.

(ii) Tropes and figures are part of the language and tradition of poetry, and have found some mention under *c* (i), above. Paronomasia and alliteration may, however, be separately considered. In several passages the Greek of the NT reveals an artificial assonance, accompanied sometimes by alliteration: *e.g.* Lk. 21:11 (*loimoi, limoi*); Rom. 1:29 (*phthonou, phonou*); Acts 17:25 (*zōēn, pnoēn*); Heb. 5:8 (*emathen, epathen*); Rom. 12:3 (*hyperphronein, phronein, sōphronein*). Mt. 16:18 (*Petros, petra*) and Phm. 10 and 20 (*Onēsimus, onaimēn*) involve puns. Acts 8:30 (*ginōskeis, anaginōskeis*) is probably accidental.

(iii) Mt. 24 and the parallel Synoptic passages, together with the whole of the Apocalypse, are couched in the traditional language of Heb. apocalyptic poetry or prophecy, a type of literature found in Daniel, Ezekiel and Zechariah. It is based on imagery of an allusive nature, and is sometimes designed for private interpretation. It is not unlike certain forms of modern poetry, first brought into fashion by G. M. Hopkins, and practised with some skill by T. S. Eliot. It follows that the 'poetic' interpretation is one legitimate approach to the Apocalypse, and certainly a rewarding one. It may also be remarked that some of the imagery of the book may lack interpretation because of the loss of the key to the allusion, once doubtless possessed.

d. Quotation

The NT is uncommonly full of quotation from the poetic literature of the OT. Parts of the Epistle to the Hebrews are composed almost entirely of such references. So are parts of the Epistle to the Romans. More elusive and less frequent are some direct quotations from Gk. literature. Acts 17:28, 'for we are indeed his offspring', is the former half of an hexameter by Aratus of Soli in Cilicia (315–240 BC). The same phrase occurs in a surviving fragment of Cleanthes, who was the head of the Stoic school from 263 to 232 BC. There is some evidence that the passage contains a more remote quotation from Epimenides, the half-legendary Cretan poet from whom Paul quotes a complete hexameter at Tit. 1:12. Then, in 1 Cor. 15:33 an iambic trimeter of Menander (342–291 BC), the Athenian comic poet, is quoted ('evil communications corrupt good manners'). Again, the Greek of Jas. 1:17 contains a pure hexameter. So do Acts 27:34b (omitting the conjunction *gar*, 'for'), Heb. 12:13 (reading the aorist imperative) and there is an iambic measure at Acts 23:5. It is impossible to say whether quotation is involved in these cases. Metrical writing can be accidental, *e.g.* 'Husbands love your wives and be not bitter against them.'

BIBLIOGRAPHY. C. F. Burney, *The Poetry of our Lord*, 1925; J. T. Sanders, *The New Testament Christological Hymns*, 1971. E.M.B.

POISON. In Israelite thinking poison came either from plants, water or food, or from adders, vipers, serpents, *etc.* The commonest Heb. word for poison, *ḥēmâ*, basically means heat, and may derive from the burning sensation which followed the taking of poison or from the sting of a reptile.

There were poisonous *plants in Palestine like hemlock (Ho. 10:4), and the poisonous gourd (2 Ki. 4:39), and, although the word is not used, the waters of Marah (Ex. 15:23) and Jericho (2 Ki. 2:19) were clearly regarded as poisonous (2 Ki. 2:21). (*GALL, *WORMWOOD.)

Several passages refer to the poison of reptiles, serpents (Dt. 32:24; Ps. 58:4), dragons (Dt. 32:33) and adders (Ps. 140:3). Zophar, in the story of Job, told how the wicked would suck the poison (*rō'š*) of asps (Jb. 20:16).

Metaphorically, the Almighty is said to send forth his arrows which give forth poison to distress one's spirit (Jb. 6:4). Again, the poison of the wicked is as the poison of serpents (Ps. 58:4), and the poison of adders is under their lips (Ps. 140:3). With this latter verse compare Rom. 3:13 (Gk. *ios*). Jas. 3:8 describes the tongue as full of poison (*ios*). J.A.T.

POLICE. A Roman magistrate was attended by a staff of lictors (the number depending on his rank) who carried bundles of rods (hence Gk. *rhabdouchoi*, 'rod-bearers', Acts 16:35) and axes symbolizing his capital powers. There being no regular police force, these lictors (AV 'serjeants') carried out police duties as well as escorting the magistrate. They occur at Philippi because it was a Roman colony. E.A.J.

PONTUS. The coastal strip of N Asia Minor, reaching from Bithynia in the W into the highlands of Armenia to the E. The region was politically a complex of Greek republics, temple estates and Iranian baronies in the interior. One of these houses established a kingdom whose greatest ruler, Mithridates, temporarily ejected the Romans from Asia Minor early in the 1st century BC. After his defeat the western part of Pontus was administered with Bithynia as a Roman province, the E part being left under a Greek dynasty. The Jews from Pontus (Acts 2:9; 18:2) presumably came from the Greek coastal states. We know nothing of the origin of Christianity there, but it was represented by the time of 1 Pet. 1:1.

BIBLIOGRAPHY. J. Keil, *CAH*, 11, pp. 575ff.; D. Magie, *Roman Rule in Asia Minor*, 2 vols., 1950.

E.A.J.

POOL. During the summer, water which had collected in pools during the winter and spring formed an important source of supply. The ability to collect and keep water in artificial pools enabled the Israelites to settle uninhabited parts of Palestine (*CISTERN). Artificial pools were dug inside walled cities (the *MOABITE STONE records one) often fed through a tunnel leading from a spring outside, ensuring a supply in time of siege. Examples have been found at Gezer, *Hazor, Megiddo, Gibeon (*cf.* 2 Sa. 2:13) and elsewhere (see J. B. Pritchard, 'The Water System at Gibeon', *BA* 19, 1956, pp. 65–75). 'Hezekiah's tunnel' and the pool of *Siloam in Jerusalem are perhaps the best-known examples (Jn. 9:7, 11; Ne. 3:15). Lack of evidence precludes the certain location of the other pools named in Jerusalem (the lower and old pools, Is. 22:9, 11; the king's pool and the artificial pool, Ne. 2:14; 3:16; see also *SAMARIA, *BETHESDA.)

A.R.M.

PORCH. Heb. *'ûlām, 'êlām* (*cf.* Assyr. *ellamu*, 'front') is used of the vestibule of Solomon's Temple (1 Ki. 6:3) and of the gateways of Ezekiel's Temple (Ezk. 40). Solomon's palace included a porch of pillars with a porch in front and another porch for the judgment throne (1 Ki. 7:6–7). These buildings may well be derived from the Syrian *bit hilāni*, a suite of rooms, consisting of a portico entered by a flight of steps and leading to an audience chamber, various other rooms and a stairway to an upper floor or roof. The unique Heb. *misdᵉrôn* (Jdg. 3:23, from root *sdr*, 'to set in order, arrange') is perhaps a portico of this nature in an upper storey, the word describing the row of pillars (see H. Frankfort, *Art and the Architecture of the Ancient Orient*, 1954, pp. 167–175, and the reconstruction in Sir Leonard Woolley's *A Forgotten Kingdom*, 1953, p. 113). Five porches (Gk. *stoa*) surrounded the pool of Bethesda to give shelter (Jn. 5:2). Peter denied his Lord in the entrance to the courtyard of the high priest's house (Mt. 26:71, *pylōn*; Mk. 14:68, *proaulion*). Solomon's Porch was a covered walk 30 cubits wide with two rows of pillars 25 cubits high along the E side of the Court of the Gentiles in Herod's Temple (Jn. 10:23; Acts 3:11; 5:12; Jos., *Ant.* 15. 380–425). (*TEMPLE.)

A.R.M.

POTIPHAR. A high officer of Pharaoh, to whom the Midianites sold Joseph (Gn. 37:36; 39:1), and in whose household Joseph became chief steward (Gn. 39). His name is Egyptian, of the type *P'-dfi-X*, X being a deity. The simplest, but not wholly satisfactory, explanation of Potiphar is that it is an abbreviated variant of *Potiphera with loss of final *'ayin*. Two high officials at court with the same or similar names is not without parallel in Egyp. history.

K.A.K.

POTIPHERA (Potipherah, AV). The 'priest of On', whose daughter, Asenath, Joseph received in marriage from Pharaoh (Gn. 41:45, 50; 46:20). He was possibly high priest of the sun-god Rēʿ in *On (Gk. Heliopolis). Potiphera (Heb. *pôṭîp̄era'*) is universally admitted to be Egyp. *P'-di-P'R'*, 'he whom P'Rēʿ (= sun-god) has given', on pattern *P'-di-X*, X being a deity. The exact form *P'-di-P'R'* is inscriptionally attested only late (*c.* 1000–300 BC), but is merely a full Late-Egyptian form of this name-type which is known from the Empire period, especially the 19th Dynasty (13th century BC), the age of Moses. Potiphera/*P'-di-P'R'* may be simply a modernization in Moses' time of the older form *Didi-R'*, with the same meaning, of a name-pattern (*Didi-X*) which is particularly common in the Middle Kingdom and Hyksos periods, *i.e.* the patriarchal and Joseph's age (*c.* 2100–1600 BC).

K.A.K.

POTTER, POTTERY. A reasonable explanation of the introduction of pottery is that a clay-lined basket was accidentally burnt, baking the lining and rendering it usable (see S. Cole, *The Neolithic Revolution*, 1959, p. 41). Pottery first appears in Neolithic times in the Near East. Until the invention of the potter's *wheel late in the 4th millennium BC, all pots were built up by hand, by the same methods which continue to be used for making large vessels in Palestine (G. M. Crowfoot, 'Pots Ancient and Modern', *PEQ* 64, 1932, pp. 179–187). Examples of the professional potter's workshop discovered in Palestine (*e.g.* at Lachish (*PEQ* 70, 1938, p. 249, pl. XXV) and Khirbet Qumran (*RB* 63, 1956, p. 543, pl. XI)) show that the potter sat on the edge of a small pit in which stood the wheels (Heb. *'oḇnayim*), usually two stones, one pivoted upon the other, which he turned with his feet. Pebbles, shells, bone implements and broken shards were used to smooth and burnish the surface, to shape and to decorate. The power of the potter (Heb. *yôṣēr*; Gk. *kerameus*) over the clay (Heb. *ḥōmer*; Gk. *pēlos*) is used as a simile in Je. 18:1–12 and by Paul (Rom. 9:21). See R. H. Johnston, *BA* 37, 1974, pp. 86–106.

I. Ancient pottery

Simply because it is common, but fragile, pottery in large quantities lies strewn on every ancient tell (*cf.* Jb. 2:8). Careful observation of the stratigraphical relationship of fragments found on one site enables a distinction to be made between the earliest pieces and the latest (usually those found at the bottom and the top of the mound respectively). Comparison with similar shards from other sites shows the contemporaneity or otherwise of the various levels (*ARCHAEOLOGY). Records of pottery finds from several sites in Palestine have enabled a sequence of forms to be drawn up which can be dated by other evidence. As a result, it is now possible to date pottery found on one site—and thus the site—by comparison with recognized dated forms. It is dangerous, however, to give a date more precisely than approximately 50 years either way solely on the evidence of pottery. Plotting the distribution of pottery types over a wide area can reveal trade routes and cultural boundaries.

The following brief description of some features of pottery found in Palestine should be read in conjunction with the chart. The superior figures refer to the numbers of the various objects included in it.

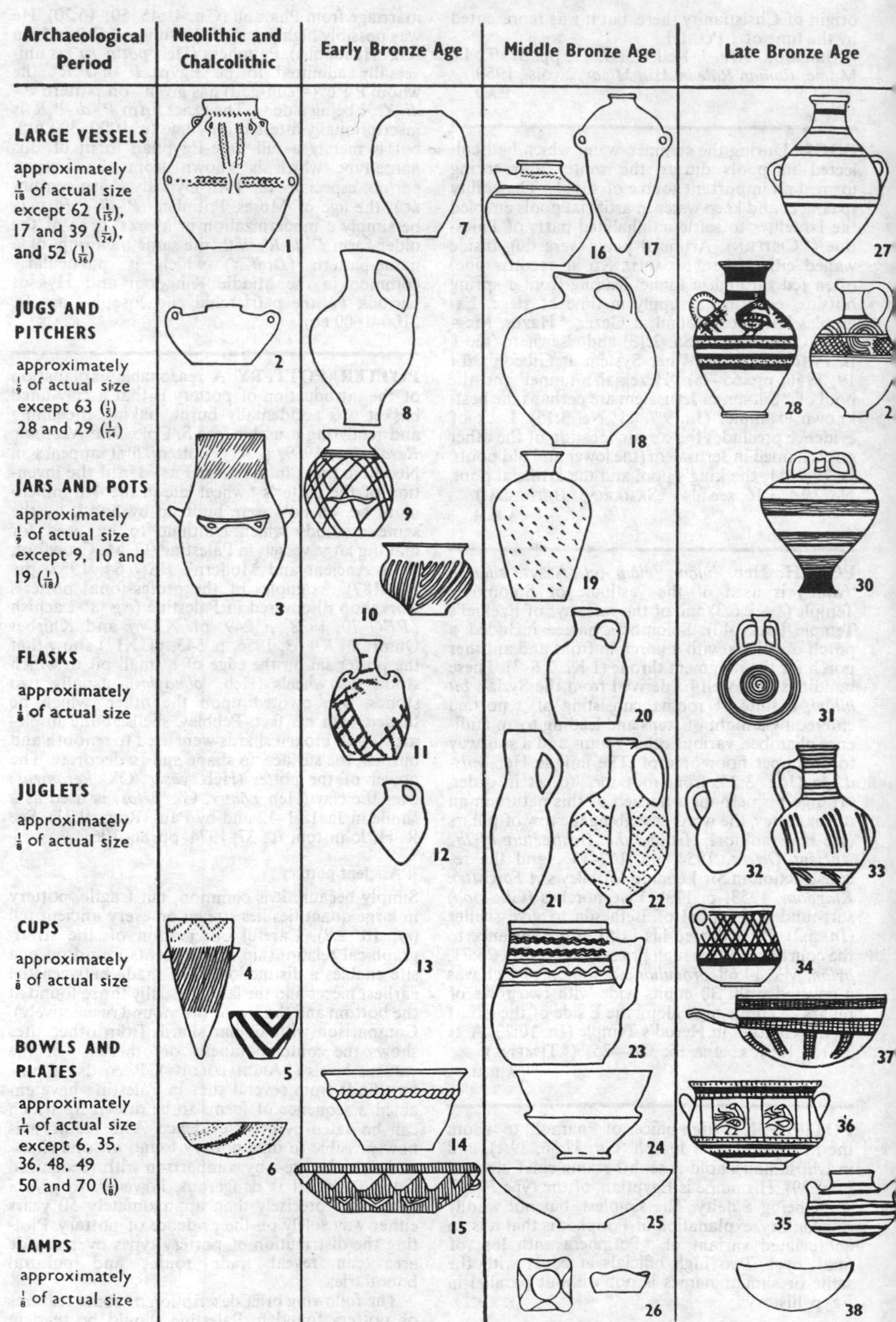

Chart showing the development of pottery in Palestine from Neolithic to Roman times. For a discussion of the objects in this chart.

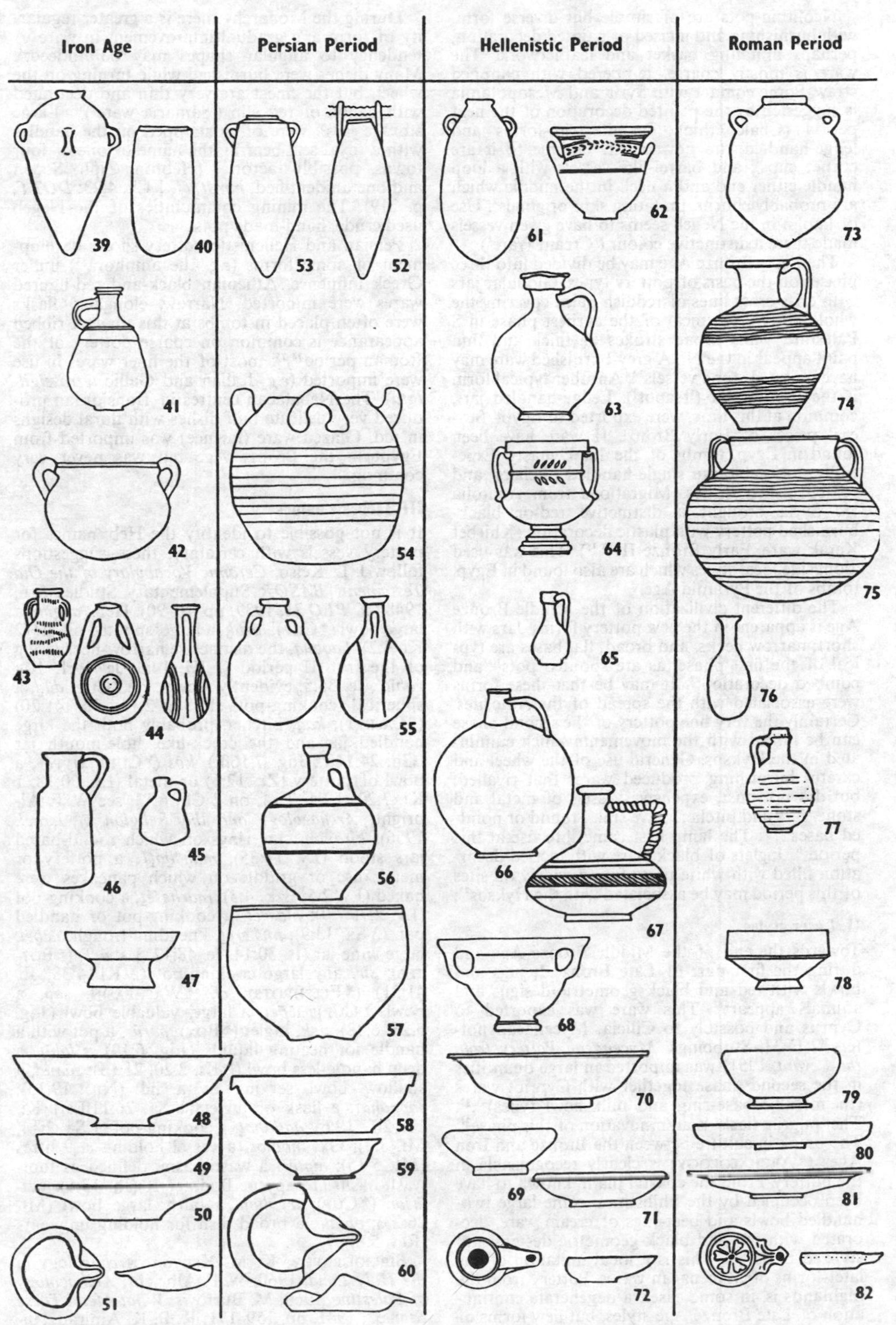

special features see article POTTER, POTTERY, *where reference is made by means of superior figures of some of*

Neolithic pots are of simple but diverse form, with burnishing and incised or painted decoration, perhaps imitating basket and leatherwork. The ware is mostly coarse, tempered with chopped straw. Some contact with Syria and Mesopotamia is suggested by the painted decoration of the next period (Chalcolithic). Definite rim-forms and ledge-handled jars now occur. Unique to it are cornet cups[4], and barrel-like vessels with a loop handle either end and a neck in the middle which are probably churns, imitating skin originals[2]. Use of kaolin in the Negeb seems to have given vessels made there a distinctive colour ('Cream Ware').

The Early Bronze Age may be divided into three phases on the basis of pottery types. Globular jars with criss-cross lines of reddish paint covering the whole body are typical of the earliest phase in S Palestine, while broad strokes of thick and thin paint appear in the N[9]. A grey-burnished ware may have imitated stone vessels[14]. Another typical form is the spouted jar ('teapot'). Ledge-handled jars, common at this time, were exported to Egypt. Several pieces of Early Bronze II ware have been found in Egyp. tombs of the 1st Dynasty. Especially noticeable are single-handled pitchers[8] and red-burnished dishes. Migrations from Anatolia *via* Syria brought a distinctive red-or black-burnished pottery with plastic decoration (Khirbet Kerak ware, Early Bronze III[10],[15]). This was used alongside local styles which are also found in Egyp. tombs of the Pyramid Age.

The different civilization of the Middle Bronze Age is apparent in the new pottery forms. Jars with short, narrow necks, and broad, flat bases are typical of the first phase, as are spouted pots[16] and combed decoration[23]. It may be that these forms were associated with the spread of the Amorites. Certainly the very fine pottery of the second phase can be linked with the movements which culminated in the Hyksos. General use of the wheel and careful burnishing produced wares that rivalled, but did not oust, expensive vessels of metal and stone. Jars and pitchers have small round or pointed bases[17],[21]. The lamp first came into use at this period[26]. Juglets of black ware with incised decoration filled with white paste found widely on sites of this period may be associated with the Hyksos[22].

II. Later styles

Towards the end of the Middle Bronze Age and during the first part of Late Bronze I, jugs and bowls with red and black geometric designs and animals appear[28]. This ware was exported to Cyprus and possibly to Cilicia. Mycenaean pottery[30] (F. H. Stubbings, *Mycenaean Pottery from the Levant*, 1951) was imported in large quantities in the second phase together with Cypriot wares (the metallic 'base-ring' and 'milk-bowl' types)[33],[37]. The 'pilgrim flask' is an innovation of this phase[31]. The break in culture between the Bronze and Iron Ages (*ARCHAEOLOGY) is clearly recognizable in the pottery. From the coastal plain, known to have been occupied by the Philistines, come large two-handled bowls and beer-jugs of cream ware, decorated with red and black geometric designs and stylized birds[36],[29]. This is a local imitation of the later forms of Mycenaean wares. Pottery from the highlands is, in some cases, a degenerate continuation of Late Bronze Age styles, but new forms of coarse ware and crude shape also appear. Heavy storage jars with short 'collar rims' and handles are reckoned typical of the Settlement period.

During the Monarchy there is a greater regularity of form and gradual improvement in ware. A tendency to angular shapes may be noticed[41]. Many dishes were burnished while turning on the wheel, but the finest are very thin and decorated with bands of red slip ('Samaria ware')[48]. Large storage jars[39] were often stamped on the handles with a royal seal bearing the name of one of four towns, possibly factories (Hebron, Ziph, Socoh and one unidentified, *mmšt*, *cf.* 1 Ch. 4:23; *DOTT*, p. 219). The mining communities of the Negeb used crude, hand-made pots.

Persian and Hellenistic pottery shows development of some forms (*e.g.* the amphora[52]) under Greek influence. Athenian black-and red-figured wares were imported. Narrow, elongated flasks were often placed in tombs at this time. A ribbed appearance is common on coarse pottery of the Roman period[74],[75]; most of the finer wares in use were imported (*e.g.* Italian and Gallic *terra sigillata*). The Nabataean centres in Transjordan produced very delicate buff dishes with floral designs in red. Glazed ware (faience) was imported from Egypt in the Bronze Age but was never very common.

III. Hebrew names

It is not possible to identify the Heb. names for pottery vessels with certainty; these suggestions follow J. L. Kelso, *Ceramic Vocabulary of the Old Testament*, *BASOR* Supplementary Studies 5–6, 1948 (*cf. PEQ* 71, 1939, pp. 76–90). Heb. *'aggān*, a large bowl (*CUP); *'āsûḵ*, a large, spouted oil-jar (2 Ki. 4:2); *baqbûq*, the distinctive narrow-necked jug of the Iron II period (1 Ki. 14:3; Je. 19:1, 10); *gaḇîa'*, Je. 35:5, evidently a ewer, *cf.* *CUP; *dûḏ*, a spherical cooking-pot (1 Sa. 2:14; Jb. 41:20) (*BASKET); *kaḏ*, pitcher, probably both the large handled jar and the crock-like, hole-mouth jar (Gn. 24:14ff.; Jdg. 7:16ff.); *kôs* (*CUP); *kiyyôr*, a bowl of pottery (Zc. 12:6) or metal (Ex. 30:18; 1 Ki. 7:20; 1 Sa. 2:14; on 2 Ch. 6:13, see W. F. Albright, *Archaeology and the Religion of Israel*, 1956); *kîrayîm*, clay rings on which round-based jars stood (Lv. 11:35); *maḥ^{a}ḇaṯ[*, a pottery or metal disc or griddle on which pancakes were baked (Lv. 2:5; Ezk. 4:3); *marḥešeṯ*, a cooking-pot (Lv. 2:7; 7:9); *maśrēṯ*, a cooking-pot or handled pan (2 Sa. 13:9); *miš'ereṯ*, kneading-trough; *nēḇel*, large wine jar (Is. 30:14; Je. 48:12; La. 4:2) (*BOTTLE); *sîr*, any large cooking-pot (2 Ki. 4:38; Jb. 41:31) (*FLESHPOTS); *cf.* *WASHBASIN; *sap̄*, a bowl (*CUP); *sēp̄el*, a large, valuable bowl (Jdg. 5:25; 6:38); *paḵ*, juglet (*BOX); *pārûr*, a pot with a handle for heating liquids (Jdg. 6:19); *ṣ^{e}lōḥîṯ*, a deep handle-less bowl (2 Ki. 2:20; 21:13); *ṣāmîḏ*, a shallow bowl serving as a lid (Nu. 19:15); *ṣappaḥaṯ*, a flask or juglet (1 Sa. 26:11ff.; 1 Ki. 17:12ff.; 19:6); *qallaḥaṯ*, a cooking-pot (1 Sa. 2:14; Mi. 3:3); Gk. *modios*, a vessel holding *c.* 9 litres (Mt. 5:15); *niptēr*, a wash-basin, defined as foot-wash-basin in papyrus Bodmer II (Jn. 13:5); *potērion* (*CUP); *tryblion*, a fairly large bowl (Mt. 26:23); *phialē*, a broad dish for holding unguents (Rev. 5:8).

BIBLIOGRAPHY. K. M. Kenyon, *Archaeology in the Holy Land*, 1960; W. F. Albright, *Archaeology of Palestine*, 1960; M. Burrows, *What Mean These Stones?*, 1941, pp. 159–171; R. B. K. Amiran, *Ancient Pottery of the Holy Land*, 1969; P. W. and N. Lapp, *Palestinian Ceramic Chronology, 200 B.C.–A.D. 70*, 1961.

A.R.M.

POVERTY.

I. In the Old Testament

The impression is sometimes given that God prospered the righteous with material possessions (Ps. 112:1–3). While it is true that the benefits of industry and thrift to individuals and to the nation are clearly seen, and that God promises to bless those who keep his commandments (Dt. 28:1–14), there were numbers of poor people in Israel at every stage of the nation's history. Their poverty might have been caused through natural disasters leading to bad harvests, through enemy invasion, through oppression by powerful neighbours or through extortionate usury. There was an obligation on the wealthier members of the community to support their poorer brethren (Dt. 15:1–11). Those who were most likely to suffer poverty were the fatherless and the widows and the landless aliens (*gērîm*). They were often the victims of oppression (Je. 7:6; Am. 2:6–7a), but Yahweh was their vindicator (Dt. 10:17–19; Ps. 68:5–6). The law commanded that provision should be made for them (Dt. 24:19–22), and with them were numbered the Levites (Dt. 14:28–29) because they had no holding of land. A man could sell himself into slavery, but if he were a Hebrew he had to be treated differently from a foreigner (Lv. 25:39–46).

It was a problem to some of the psalmists to understand how in so many cases wealth had come into the wrong hands. On purely material grounds it might seem vain to serve Yahweh (Ps. 73:12–14), but in the end the wicked would come to destruction while the righteous enjoyed the richest possession—the knowledge of Yahweh himself (Ps. 73:16–28). But so often were the rich oppressors that 'the poor' became almost a synonym for 'the pious' (Ps. 14:5–6).

II. In the New Testament

There were heavy taxes of various kinds imposed on the Jews in NT times. Probably many were in severe economic straits, while others made considerable profits from collaborating with the Romans. The worldly-minded Sadducees were generally wealthy, as were the tax-collectors.

Jesus was the son of poor parents (Lk. 2:24), but there is no reason to suppose he lived in abject poverty. As the eldest son, he would probably have inherited something from Joseph, and it appears that he used to pay the Temple tax (Mt. 17:24). Some of his disciples were reasonably well-to-do (Mk. 1:20) and he had some fairly wealthy friends (Jn. 12:3). He and the Twelve, however, shared a common purse (Jn. 12:6). They were content to go without the comforts of home life (Lk. 9:58), and yet found occasion for giving to the poor (Jn. 13:29).

In the teaching of Jesus material possessions are not regarded as evil, but as dangerous. The poor are often shown to be happier than the rich, because it is easier for them to have an attitude of dependence upon God. It was to them that he came to preach the gospel (Lk. 4:18; 7:22). It is they who are the first to be blessed and to be assured of the possession of the kingdom of God (Lk. 6:20), if their poverty is the acknowledgment of spiritual bankruptcy (Mt. 5:3). A poor person's offering may be of much greater value than a rich man's (Mk. 12:41–44). The poor must be shown hospitality (Lk. 14:12–14), and given alms (Lk. 18:22), though charity was to be secondary to worship (Jn. 12:1–8).

The early church made an experiment in the communal holding of wealth (Acts 2:41–42; 4:32). This led at first to the elimination of poverty (Acts 4:34–35), but it has often been held that it was responsible for the later economic collapse of the church at Jerusalem. Much of the ministry of Paul was concerned with raising money in the Gentile churches to assist the poor Christians in Jerusalem (Rom. 15:25–29; Gal. 2:10). These churches were also taught to provide for their own poor members (Rom. 12:13, *etc.*). James is especially vehement against those who allowed distinctions of wealth in the Christian community (Jas. 2:1–7). The poor were called by God and their salvation brought glory to him (1 Cor. 1:26–31). The material wealth of the church of Laodicea was in sad contrast with her spiritual poverty (Rev. 3:17).

The most systematic exposition about poverty and wealth in the Epistles is found in 2 Cor. 8–9, where Paul sets the idea of Christian charity in the context of the gifts of God and especially that of his Son who, 'though he was rich, yet for your sake he became poor, so that by his poverty you might become rich'. In the light of that, running the risk of material poverty will lead to spiritual blessing, just as the apostles were poor but made many rich (2 Cor. 6:10). (*ALMS; *ORPHAN.)

BIBLIOGRAPHY. L. Schottroff and W. Stegemann, *Jesus and the Hope of the Poor*, 1986.

R.E.N.

POWER.

I. In the Old Testament

Various Heb. words are rendered 'power', the principal ones being *ḥayil*, *kōaḥ* and *ʿōz*. True power, the ability to exercise authority effectively, belongs to God alone (Ps. 62:11). The power of God is shown in the creation (Ps. 148:5) and the sustaining of the world (Ps. 65:5–8). Some of his authority is delegated to mankind (Gn. 1:26–28; Pss. 8:5–8; 115:16), but God actively intervenes on many occasions, showing his power in miraculous deeds of deliverance. It was 'with mighty hand and outstretched arm' that he brought his people out of Egypt (Ex. 15:6; Dt. 5:15, *etc.*), and he demonstrated his power in giving them the promised land (Ps. 111:6).

II. In the New Testament

'Power' in EVV represents chiefly Gk. *dynamis* and *exousia*. *exousia* means derived or conferred 'authority', the warrant or right to do something (Mt. 21:23–27); from this it comes to denote concretely the bearer of authority on earth (Rom. 13:1–3), or in the spirit world (Col. 1:16). *dynamis* is ability (2 Cor. 8:3) or strength (Eph. 3:16), or it may mean a powerful act (Acts 2:22) or a powerful spirit (Rom. 8:38). Christ had all authority given him by his Father (Mt. 28:18) and he used it to forgive sins (Mt. 9:6) and to cast out evil spirits (Mt. 10:1). He gave authority to his disciples to become sons of God (Jn. 1:12) and to share in his work (Mk. 3:15).

Jesus came to his ministry in the power (*dynamis*) of the Spirit (Lk. 4:14), and his power was operative in healing miracles (Lk. 5:17) and he did many mighty works (Mt. 11:20). This was evidence of the power of the kingdom of God as a prelude to the new Exodus (Lk. 11:20; *cf.* Ex. 8:19). But the kingdom had not yet come in its full power. That would happen at Pentecost (Lk. 24:49; Acts 1:8; ?Mk. 9:1) and there would be the consummation at the parousia (Mt. 24:30, *etc.*).

In the Acts we see the power of the Spirit operative in the life of the church (4:7, 33; 6:8; *cf.* 10:38). Paul looks back to the resurrection as the chief evidence of God's power (Rom. 1:4; Eph. 1:19–20; Phil. 3:10) and sees the gospel as the means by which that power comes to work in men's lives (Rom. 1:16; 1 Cor. 1:18). (*AUTHORITY.)

BIBLIOGRAPHY. G. B. Caird, *Principalities and Powers*, 1956; A. Richardson, *An Introduction to the Theology of the New Testament*, 1958, pp. 62ff.; Cyril H. Powell, *The Biblical Concept of Power*, 1963; O. Betz in *NIDNTT* 2, pp. 601–611; J. P. M. Walsh, *The Mighty from their Thrones*, 1987; W. Wink, *The Powers*, vol. 1, 1984; D. Prior, *Jesus and Power*, 1987. R.E.N.

POWER OF THE KEYS. This is the phrase used to describe the authority given by our Lord to his disciples as described in Mt. 16:19; 18:18; Jn. 20:22–23. It is a power which may be said to operate in two ways. First, by preaching the gospel the kingdom of God is opened to believers and shut to the impenitent, and secondly, by discipline, serious offenders are excluded from the church until they repent, whereupon they are readmitted. In either case, forgiveness is mediated through the church, acting in the Spirit and through the Word.

'Since it is the doctrine of the gospel that opens heaven to us, it is beautifully expressed by the metaphorical appellation of "keys".' 'Binding and loosing are simply nothing other than the preaching and application of the gospel' (Luther). That keys and doctrine are so connected is seen from the fact that the delivery of a key was part of a scribe's ordination (Mt. 13:52; Lk. 11:52). Through the preaching of the gospel some men are reconciled to God by faith, others are more firmly bound by unbelief. The church, acting as Christ's representative (Lk. 10:16), pronounces absolution to the penitent. This is a real transaction only in so far as the church is filled with the Spirit of God, so that then it gives the actual judgment of God himself. *Binding and loosing mean not merely the authoritative announcement of the conditions of entrance into the kingdom; a stronger sense is necessary—determining which individuals have accepted the conditions.

This power was given in a special sense to Peter, for he, at Pentecost, opened the door of faith to the Jews, and later to the Gentiles and Samaritans. But it was given to all the apostles (Jn. 20:23) and to men of like faith and spirit ever since.

In the further exercise of the power of the keys, in ecclesiastical discipline, the thought is of administrative authority (Is. 22:22) with regard to the requirements of the household of faith. The use of censures, excommunication and absolution is committed to the church in every age, to be used under the guidance of the Spirit. 'Whoever, after committing a crime, humbly confesses his fault and entreats the church to forgive him, is absolved not only by men, but by God himself; and, on the other hand, whoever treats with ridicule the reproofs and threatenings of the church, if he is condemned by her, the decision which men have given will be ratified in heaven' (Calvin on 1 Cor. 5).

Since the Reformers it has been accepted that 'the power of the keys' represented this *duplex ministerium*, a real power of spiritual binding and loosing. But this judicial sense has been sharply challenged in favour of a legislative sense whereby 'loose' means 'permitted', and 'bind' means 'forbidden'. This is in agreement with rabbinic usage: the school of Shammai was said to *bind* when it declared that there was only one ground for divorce; the school of Hillel *loosed* when it allowed more laxity in this and other questions. For this use, see also Mt. 23:4; Rom. 7:2; 1 Cor. 7:27, 39. So Peter, in T. W. Manson's words, is to be 'God's vicegerent . . . The authority of Peter is an authority to declare what is right and wrong for the Christian community. His decisions will be confirmed by God' (*The Sayings of Jesus*, 1954, p. 205). But note that this special rabbinical application of the words was based on the juristic character of the rabbinic literature, and that it was originally used of the full power of the judge (*cf. TDNT* 3, p. 751). Even granting a late origin for Mt. 18:18, we are left with the question as to why a context of church discipline should early seem suitable for the words 'bind' and 'loose'. A. H. McNeile questions the authenticity of this passage altogether, but J. Jeremias has argued ingeniously for its trustworthiness (*TDNT* 3, pp. 752f.).

In any case, it is hardly right to make Peter, as this view does, a scribe in the kingdom of God. 'The apostle would, in the coming kingdom, be like a great scribe or Rabbi, who would deliver decisions on the basis . . . of the teaching of Jesus' (A. H. McNeile). But there is a great difference between the pronouncements of the apostles on ethical matters and the encyclopaedic casuistry of the scribes. Mt. 23:8 made it impossible for Peter to aspire to such a function. The principle of Christian ethics is to look after the big things (mercy, love, truth) and the little things will then look after themselves; not detailed prescribed legislation, but the guidance of the Spirit.

BIBLIOGRAPHY. Calvin's Commentaries on the Matthaean passages and on 1 Cor. 5 present a fair representation of the views of all the Reformers. In addition to the modern writers cited, R. N. Flew discusses these questions in *Jesus and His Church*, 1938, pp. 131f. See also *DCG* (*s.v.* 'Absolution'); *ERE* (*s.v.* 'Discipline'); Calvin, *Institutes*, 4. 12; J. Jeremias, *TDNT* 3, pp. 744–753; D. Müller, C. Brown, *NIDNTT* 2, pp. 731–733. R.N.C.

PRAETORIUM. Originally the tent of the commander, or praetor, and, in consequence, the army headquarters (Livy, 7. 12; Caesar, *Bellum Civile* 1. 76). By extension the word came to mean the residence of a provincial governor (Mt. 27:27; Mk. 15:16; Jn. 18:28, 33; 19:9; Acts 23:35). If Paul was writing from Rome, Phil. 1:13 may refer to the emperor's residence on the Palatine. The word seems not to have been used for the permanent camp of the praetorian guards by the Porta Viminalis. It does, however, sometimes mean the forces of the praetorian guards (*CIL*, 5. 2837; 8. 9391), and, whether the letter was written at Ephesus or Rome, this gives good sense to Paul's phrase. Detachments of *praetoriani* were sent to the provinces, and in Rome they would have charge of prisoners in imperial custody. E.M.B.

PRAISE. In the OT the words for praise mainly used are *hālal*, the root meaning of which is connected with making a noise; *yāḏâ*, which was originally associated with the bodily actions and gestures which accompany praising; and *zāmar*, which is associated with the playing or singing of music. In the NT *eucharistein* (lit. 'to give thanks') is the favourite word, implying on the part of the person who praises the attitude of one more intimate with the person praised than in the more formal *eulogein*, 'to bless'.

The whole of the Bible is punctuated with outbursts of praise. They rise spontaneously from the 'basic mood' of joy which marks the life of the people of God. God takes pleasure and delight in his works of creation (Gn. 1; Ps. 104:31; Pr. 8:30–31), and all creation, including the angels, expresses its joy in praise (Jb. 38:4–7; Rev. 4:6–11). Man also was created to rejoice in God's works (Ps. 90:14–16) and fulfils this purpose by accepting God's gifts (Ec. 8:15; 9:7; 11:9; Phil. 4:4, 8; *cf.* also W. Eichrodt, *Man in the Old Testament*, 1951, p. 35).

The coming of the kingdom of God into the midst of this world is marked by the restoration of joy and praise to the people of God and the whole creation (Is. 9:2; Ps. 96:11–13; Rev. 5:9–14; Lk. 2:13–14), a foretaste of which is already given in the ritual and worship of the Temple where praise arises from sheer joy in the redeeming presence of God (Dt. 27:7; Nu. 10:10; Lv. 23:40). The praise of God is rendered on earth for the works both of creation and redemption (Pss. 24; 136), this being an echo on earth of the praise of heaven (Rev. 4:11; 5:9–10). Praise, therefore, is a mark of the people of God (1 Pet. 2:9; Eph. 1:3–14; Phil. 1:11). It is the mark of the heathen that they refuse to render it (Rom. 1:21; Rev. 16:9). The act of praising implies the closest fellowship with the One who is being praised. 'Therefore praise not merely expresses but completes the enjoyment; it is its appointed consummation. . . . In commanding us to glorify Him, God is inviting us to enjoy Him' (C. S. Lewis, *Reflections on the Psalms*, 1958, p. 95).

Yet praise to God is frequently commanded from men as a duty and is obviously not meant to depend on mood or feeling or circumstances (*cf.* Jb. 1:21). To 'rejoice before the Lord' is part of the ordered ritual of the common life of his people (Dt. 12:7; 16:11–12), in which men encourage and exhort one another to praise. Though there are psalms which express the praise of the individual, it was always felt that praise could best be rendered within the congregation (Pss. 22:25; 34:3; 35:18), where praise not only gives honour and pleasure to God (Ps. 50:23) but also bears testimony to God's people (Ps. 51:12–15).

Elaborate arrangements were made for the conduct of praise in the Temple by the Levites. The Psalms were used in the liturgy and in sacred processions with 'glad shouts and songs' (Ps. 42:4). The singing was probably antiphonal, involving two choirs, or soloist and choir. Dancing, from earliest times a means of expressing praise (Ex. 15:20; 2 Sa. 6:14), was also used in the Temple to this end (Pss. 149:3; 150:4). Ps. 150 gives a list of musical instruments used in the praise. (*MUSIC AND MUSICAL INSTRUMENTS.)

The early Christians continued to express their gladness by attending worship in the Temple (Lk. 24:53; Acts 3:1). But their experience of new life in Christ was bound to express itself in new forms of praise (Mk. 2:22). Joy was the dominant mood of the Christian life, and though the formal worship and praise which it inspired is not explicitly described or prescribed, this was because it was so much taken for granted. As those who experienced and witnessed the healing and cleansing power of Jesus broke out spontaneously into praise (Lk. 18:43; Mk. 2:12), so also in the apostolic church there are frequent examples of such spontaneous outbursts, as men began to see and understand the power and goodness of God in Christ (Acts 2:46; 3:8; 11:18; 16:25; Eph. 1:1–14).

The Psalms were undoubtedly used to express the praise of the early church (Col. 3:16; *cf.* Mt. 26:30). There were also new Christian hymns (*cf.* Rev. 5:8–14), referred to in Col. 3:16; 1 Cor. 14:26. We have examples of such inspiration to new forms of praise in the *Magnificat, *Benedictus and *Nunc Dimittis (Lk. 1:46–55, 68–79; 2:29–32). Elsewhere in the text of the NT there are examples of the formal praise of the early church. It seems likely from its literary form and content that Phil. 2:6–11 was composed and used as a hymn of praise to Christ. Probably there are echoes of, or quotations from, early hymns in such passages as Eph. 5:14 and 1 Tim. 3:16. The doxologies in the book of Revelation (*cf.* Rev. 1:4–7; 5:9–14; 15:3–4) must have been used in public worship to express the praise of the congregation (*cf.* A. B. Macdonald, *Christian Worship in the Primitive Church*, 1934).

The close connection between praise and sacrifice should be noted. In the sacrificial ritual of the OT a place was found for the sacrifice of thanksgiving as well as of expiation (*cf.* Lv. 7:11–21). Gratitude was to be the fundamental motive behind the bringing of the first-fruits to the altar (Dt. 26:1–11). In the sincere offering of praise itself there is a sacrifice which pleases God (Heb. 13:15; Ho. 14:2; Ps. 119:108). In the priestly self-offering of Jesus this aspect of thanksgiving finds its place (Mk. 14:22–23, 26; Jn. 17:1–2; Mt. 11:25–26). The life of the Christian should, correspondingly, be a self-offering of gratitude (Rom. 12:1) in fulfilment of his royal priesthood (Rev. 1:5–6; 1 Pet. 2:9), and the fact that such a sacrificial self-offering can be made in a real way in the midst of suffering, links suffering and praise together in the Christian life (Phil. 2:17). Thanksgiving sanctifies not only suffering but all aspects of the life of the Christian (1 Tim. 4:4–5; 1 Cor. 10:30–31; 1 Thes. 5:16–18). Whatever else be the burden of prayer, it must include praise (Phil. 4:6).

BIBLIOGRAPHY. H. Ringgren, *The Faith of the Psalmists*, 1963; C. Westermann, *The Praise of God in the Psalms*, 1965; J. R. Taylor, *The Hallelujah Factor*, 1985; H.-G. Link, *NIDNTT* 1, pp. 206–215; H. Schultz, H.-H. Esser, *NIDNTT* 3, pp. 816–820. R.S.W.

PRAYER.

I. Introduction

In the Bible prayer is worship that includes all the attitudes of the human spirit in its approach to God. The Christian worships God when he adores, confesses, praises and supplicates him in prayer. This highest activity of which the human spirit is capable may also be thought of as communion with God, so long as due emphasis is laid upon divine initiative. A man prays because God has already touched his spirit. Prayer in the Bible is not a 'natural response' (see Jn. 4:24). 'That which is born of the flesh is flesh.' Consequently, the Lord does not 'hear' every prayer (Is. 1:15; 29:13). The biblical doctrine of prayer emphasizes the character of God, the necessity of a man's being in saving or covenant relation with him, and his entering fully into all the privileges and obligations of that relation with God.

II. In the Old Testament

Köhler (*Old Testament Theology*, 1957, p. 251, n. 153) finds 'about eighty-five original prayers in the OT. In addition there are about sixty whole psalms and fourteen parts of psalms which may be called prayers.'

a. The patriarchal period

In the patriarchal period prayer is calling upon the name of the Lord (Gn. 4:26; 12:8; 21:33); *i.e.* the sacred name is used in invocation or appeal. There is, consequently, an unmistakable directness and familiarity in prayer (Gn. 15:2ff.; 18:23ff.; 24:12–14, 26f.). Prayer is also closely connected with sacrifice (Gn. 13:4; 26:25; 28:20–22), although this association appears in later periods too. This offering of prayer in a context of sacrifice suggests a union of man's will with God's will, an abandonment and submission of the self to God. This is especially so in Jacob's conjoining prayer with a vow to the Lord. The vow, itself a prayer, promises service and faithfulness if the blessing sought is granted (Gn. 28:20ff.).

b. The pre-exilic period

1. In this period one of the main emphases in prayer is intercession; although this was also a factor in patriarchal times (Gn. 18:22ff.). Intercession was especially prominent in the prayers of Moses (Ex. 32:11–13, 31f.; 33:12–16; 34:9; Nu. 11:11–15; 14:13–19; 21:7; Dt. 9:18–21; 10:10). Dt. 30 is also largely a prayer of intercession, as are also the prayers of Aaron (Nu. 6:22–27), Samuel (1 Sa. 7:5–13; 12:19, 23), Solomon (1 Ki. 8:22–53), and Hezekiah (2 Ki. 19:14–19). The inference seems to be that intercession was confined to outstanding personalities who, by virtue of their position assigned to them by God as prophets, priests and kings, had peculiar power in prayer as mediators between God and men. But the Lord always remained free to execute his will; hence we hear of unsuccessful intercession (Gn. 18:17ff.; Ex. 32:30–35). In Am. 7:1–6 'the Lord repented' concerning a certain course of action in answer to the prophet's intercession, and in the next verses (7:7–8:2) Israel is to be led away captive after all. Jeremiah is even forbidden to intercede with God (Je. 7:16; 11:14; 14:11). On the other hand, success attended the intercession of Lot (Gn. 19:17–23), Abraham (Gn. 20:17), Moses (Ex. 9:27–33; Nu. 12:9ff.), and Job (Jb. 42:8, 10). It is the strongly personal relation with God in which those mediators stood that underlies these intercessory prayers.

2. It is surprising that among all the legal enactments of the Pentateuch there is nothing about prayer apart from Dt. 26:1–15. Even here it is formulae for worship rather than prayer that are being emphasized. In vv. 5–11 there is thanksgiving, and in vv. 13–14 there is a profession of past obedience, but only in v. 15 is there supplication. However, we are probably right in assuming that sacrifice would often be offered with prayer (Ps. 55:14), and where it was not it might be reproved (Ps. 50:7–15). On the other hand, the almost total absence of prayer in those parts of the Pentateuch where sacrifice is regulated suggests that sacrifice without prayer was fairly common.

3. Prayer must have been indispensable in the ministry of the prophets. The very reception of the revelatory Word from God involved the prophet in a prayerful relation with Yahweh. Indeed, it might well have been that prayer was essential to the prophet's receiving the Word (Is. 6:5ff.; 37:1–4; Je. 11:20–23; 12:1–6; 42:1ff.). The prophetic vision came to Daniel while he was at prayer (Dn. 9:20ff.). On occasion the Lord kept the prophet waiting for a considerable time in prayer (Hab. 2:1–3). We know from Jeremiah's writings that while prayer was the essential condition of, and reality in, the prophet's experience and ministry, it was often a tempestuous exercise of the spirit (18:19–23; 20:7–18), as well as a sweet fellowship with God (1:4ff.; 4:10; 10:23–25; 12:1–4; 14:7–9, 19–22; 15:15–18; 16:19; 17:12ff.).

4. In the Psalms there is a blending of pattern and spontaneity in prayer. Alongside the more formal 'sanctuary' prayers (*e.g.* 24:7–10; 100; 150) there are personal prayers for pardon (51), communion (63), protection (57), healing (6), vindication (109) and prayers that are full of praise (103). Sacrifice and prayer also blend in the psalms (54:6; 66:13ff.).

c. The exilic period

During the Exile the important factor in religion for the Jews was the emergence of the synagogue. The Jerusalem Temple was in ruins, and altar rites and sacrifices could not be performed in unclean Babylon. A Jew was now no longer one who had been born into the community, and was residing in it, but rather one who *chose* to be a Jew. The centre of the religious community was the synagogue, and among the accepted religious obligations such as circumcision, fasting and sabbath observance, prayer was important. This was inevitable because each little community in exile now depended upon the synagogue service where the Word was read and expounded, and prayers were offered. And after the return to Jerusalem, just as the Temple was not allowed to displace the synagogue, nor the priest the scribe, nor sacrifice the living Word, so ritual did not displace prayer. Both in Temple and synagogue, in priestly ritual and scribal exposition, the devout worshipper now sought the face of Yahweh, his personal presence (Pss. 100:2; 63:1ff.), and received his blessing in terms of the light of his countenance shining upon him (Ps. 80:3, 7, 19).

d. The post-exilic period

After the Exile there was undoubtedly a framework of devotion, but within it freedom was secured for the individual. This is exemplified in Ezra and Nehemiah, who, while insisting upon cult and law, and upon ritual and sacrifice and, therefore, upon the social aspects of worship, yet emphasized also the spiritual factor in devotion (Ezr. 7:27; 8:22f.; Ne. 2:4; 4:4, 9). Their prayers are also instructive (Ezr. 9:6–15; Ne. 1:5–11; 9:5–38; *cf.* also Dn. 9:4–19). We may also note here that concerning posture in prayer there were no fixed rules (Ps. 28:2; 1 Sa. 1:26; 1 Ki. 8:54; Ezr. 9:5; 1 Ki. 18:42; La. 3:41; Dn. 9:3 and v . 20 where we should read 'towards' instead of 'for'). So also in the matter of hours for prayer: prayer was effective at any time, as well as at the stated hours (Ps. 55:17; Dn. 6:10). In the post-exilic period, then, we find a blending of orderliness of Temple ritual, the simplicity of the synagogue meeting, and the spontaneity of personal devotion.

Prayer being what it is, it would be manifestly impossible to systematize it completely. Within the OT there are certainly patterns for prayer but no binding regulations governing either its contents or its ritual. Mechanical prayer, prayer hemmed in by coercive prescriptions, did not come until towards the close of the intertestamental period, as the Gospels make clear. Then, alas, both through Temple sacrifice in Jerusalem, and in the *diaspora* through the praise, prayer and exposition of the synagogue service, and through circumcision, sabbath observance, tithes, fasting and supererogatory deeds, worshippers in both Temple and synagogue sought to merit acceptance with God.

III. In the New Testament

There are certain clearly-defined areas where the NT teaching on prayer is set forth, but the fountain-head from which all its instruction in prayer flows is Christ's own doctrine and practice.

a. The Gospels

1. As to Jesus' doctrine of prayer, this is set out principally in certain of his parables. In the parable of the friend who borrowed three loaves at midnight (Lk. 11:5–8) the Lord inculcates importunity in prayer; and the ground on which the confidence in importunate prayer is built is the Father's generosity (Mt. 7:7–11). The parable of the unjust judge (Lk. 18:1–8) calls for tenacity in prayer, which includes persistence as well as continuity. God's delays in answering prayer are due not to indifference but to love that desires to develop and deepen faith which is finally vindicated. In the parable of the tax collector and the Pharisee (Lk. 18:10–14) Christ insists on humility and penitence in prayer, and warns against a sense of self-superiority. Self-humiliation in prayer means acceptance with God, self-exaltation in prayer hides God's face. Christ calls for charity in prayer in the parable of the unjust servant (Mt. 18:21–35). It is prayer offered by a forgiving spirit that God answers. Simplicity in prayer is taught in Mt. 6:5f.; 23:14; Mk. 12:38–40; Lk. 20:47. Prayer must be purged of all pretence. It should spring from simplicity of heart and motive, and express itself in simplicity of speech and petition. The Lord also urged intensity in prayer (*cf.* Mk. 13:33; 14:38; Mt. 26:41). Here watchfulness and faith combine in sleepless vigilance. Again, in Mt. 18:19f. unity in prayer is emphasized. If a group of Christians who have the mind of Christ pray in the Holy Spirit their prayers will be effectual. But prayer must also be expectant (Mk. 11:24). Prayer that is an experiment achieves little; prayer which is the sphere where faith operates in surrender to God's will achieves much (Mk. 9:23).

2. On objectives in prayer Jesus had singularly little to say. Doubtless he was content to let the Holy Spirit prompt his disciples in prayer. What aims he referred to in prayer are to be found in Mk. 9:28f.; Mt. 5:44; 6:11, 13; 9:36ff.; Lk. 11:13.

3. As to method in prayer, the Lord had two important things to teach. First, prayer is now to be offered to him, as it was offered to him when he was on earth (*e.g.* Mt. 8:2; 9:18). As he insisted on faith then (Mk. 9:23), and tested sincerity (Mt. 9:27–31), and uncovered ignorance (Mt. 20:20–22) and sinful presumption (Mt. 14:27–31), in those who petitioned him, so he does today in the experience of those who offer prayer to him. Secondly, prayer is now also to be offered in the name of Christ (Jn. 14:13; 15:16; 16:23f.), through whom we have access to the Father. To pray in the name of Christ is to pray as Christ himself prayed, and to pray to the Father as the Son has made him known to us: and for Jesus the true focus in prayer was the Father's will. Here is the basic characteristic of Christian prayer: a new access to the Father which Christ secures for the Christian, and prayer in harmony with the Father's will because offered in Christ's name.

4. As to the Lord's practice of prayer, it is well known that he prayed in secret (Lk. 5:15f.; 6:12); in times of spiritual conflict (Jn. 12:20–28; Lk. 22:39–46); and on the cross (Mt. 27:46; Lk. 23:46). In his prayers he offered thanksgiving (Lk. 10:21; Jn. 6:11; 11:41; Mt. 26:27), sought guidance (Lk. 6:12ff.), interceded (Jn. 17:6–19, 20–26; Lk. 22:31–34; Mk. 10:16; Lk. 23:34) and communed with the Father (Lk. 9:28ff.). The burden of his high-priestly prayer in Jn. 17 is the unity of the church.

5. Since the *Lord's Prayer is treated more fully elsewhere, it will suffice to point out that after the invocation (Mt. 6:9b) there follow six petitions (9c–13b), of which the first three have reference to God's name, kingdom and will, and the last three to man's need of bread, forgiveness and victory: the Prayer then closes with a doxology (13c) which contains a threefold declaration concerning God's kingdom, power and glory. It is 'like this' that Christians are bidden to pray.

b. The Acts of the Apostles

The Acts is an excellent link between the Gospels and the Epistles, because in Acts the apostolic church puts into effect our Lord's teaching on prayer. The church was born in the atmosphere of prayer (1:4). In answer to prayer the Spirit was poured out upon her (1:4; 2:4). Prayer continued to be the church's native air (2:42; 6:4, 6). There remained in the church's thinking a close connection between prayer and the Spirit's presence and power (4:31). In times of crisis the church had recourse to prayer (4:23ff.; 12:5, 12). Throughout the Acts the church leaders emerge as men of prayer (9:40; 10:9; 16:25; 28:8) who urge the Christians to pray with them (20:28, 36; 21:5).

c. The Pauline Epistles

It is significant that immediately after Christ revealed himself to Paul on the Damascus road it is said of Paul, 'Behold, he is praying' (Acts 9:11). Probably for the first time Paul discovered what prayer really was, so profound was the change in his heart which conversion had effected. From that moment he was a man of prayer. In prayer the Lord spoke to him (Acts 22:17f.). Prayer was thanksgiving, intercession, the realization of God's presence (*cf.* 1 Thes. 1:2f.; Eph. 1:16ff.). He found that the Holy Spirit assisted him in prayer as he sought to know and do God's will (Rom. 8:14, 26). In his experience there was a close connection between prayer and the Christian's intelligence (1 Cor. 14:14–19). Prayer was absolutely essential for the Christian (Rom. 12:12). The Christian's armour (Eph. 6:13–17) included prayer which Paul describes as 'all prayer', to be offered at 'all seasons', with 'all perseverance', for 'all saints' (v. 18). And Paul practised what he preached (Rom. 1:9; Eph. 1:16; 1 Thes. 1:2); hence his insistence upon prayer when writing to his fellow-believers (Phil. 4:6; Col. 4:2).

In his Epistles Paul is constantly breaking out into prayer, and it is instructive to glance at some of his prayers because of their content.

1. In Rom. 1:8–12 he pours out his heart to God in thanksgiving (v. 8), insists upon serving Christ with his spirit (v. 9a), intercedes for his friends in Rome (v. 9b), expresses his desire to impart to them a spiritual gift (vv. 10f.), and declares that he too is depending upon them for spiritual uplift (v. 12).

2. In Eph. 1:15–19 Paul again thanks God for his converts (vv. 15f.), and prays that they may receive the Spirit through whom comes knowledge of God and illumination of heart (vv. 17–18a), in order that they may know the hope of God's calling, the wealth of God's inheritance, and the greatness of God's power which had been demonstrated in Christ's resurrection (vv. 18b–19).

3. Again, in Eph. 3:14–18 the apostle pleads with the Father (vv. 14f.) for his fellow-Christians that they might be increasingly conscious of God's power (v. 16), to the end that Christ might indwell them, and that they might be rooted in love (v. 17), that each together, being perfected, might be filled with the fullness of God (vv. 18f.). Both of these 'Ephesian' prayers are well summed up in Paul's threefold desire that Christians should receive knowledge and power issuing in the love of Christ, through which as individuals and a group they should achieve perfection.

4. In Col. 1:9ff. Paul again prays that the believers should know God's will through spiritual wisdom and understanding (v. 9), that practice might agree with profession (v. 10), that they might have power for their practice (v. 11), and be thankful for their immense privilege and position in the Lord Jesus (vv. 12f.).

But perhaps Paul's greatest contribution to our understanding of Christian prayer is in establishing its connection with the Holy Spirit. Prayer is in fact a gift of the Spirit (1 Cor. 14:14–16). The believer prays 'in the Spirit' (Eph. 6:18; Jude 20); hence prayer is a co-operation between God and the believer in that it is presented to the Father, in the name of the Son, through the inspiration of the indwelling Holy Spirit.

d. Hebrews, James and 1 John

The Epistle to the Hebrews makes a significant contribution to an understanding of Christian prayer. 4:14–16 shows why prayer is possible: it is possible because we have a great High Priest who is both human and divine, because he is now in the heavenly place and because of what he is now doing there. When we pray it is to receive mercy and find grace. The reference to the Lord's prayer life in 5:7–10 really teaches what prayer is: Christ's 'prayers' and 'supplications' were 'offered up' to God, and in this spiritual service he 'learned obedience' and therefore 'was heard'. In 10:19–25 the emphasis is upon corporate prayer, and the demands and motives which it involves. The place of prayer is described in 6:19.

The Epistle of James has three significant passages on prayer. Prayer in perplexity is dealt with in 1:5–8; correct motives in prayer are underlined in 4:1–3; and the significance of prayer in time of sickness is made clear in 5:13–18.

In his first Epistle, John points the way to boldness and efficacy in prayer (3:21f.), while in 5:14–16 he establishes the relation between prayer and the will of God, and shows that efficacy in prayer is especially relevant to intercession, but that situations do arise where prayer is powerless.

IV. Conclusion

The heart of the biblical doctrine of prayer is well expressed by B. F. Westcott: 'True prayer—the prayer that must be answered—is the personal recognition and acceptance of the divine will (Jn. 14:7; *cf.* Mk. 11:24). It follows that the hearing of prayer which teaches obedience is not so much the granting of a specific petition, which is assumed by the petitioner to be the way to the end desired, but the assurance that what is granted does most effectively lead to the end. Thus we are taught that Christ learned that every detail of His life and passion contributed to the accomplishment of the work which He came to fulfil, and so He was most perfectly "heard". In this sense He was "heard for his godly fear".'

BIBLIOGRAPHY. F. Heiler, *Prayer*, 1932; J. G. S. S. Thomson, *The Praying Christ*, 1959; Ludwig Köhler, *Old Testament Theology*, 1957; Th. C. Vriezen, *An Outline of Old Testament Theology*, 1958; H. Schönweiss, C. Brown, G. T. D. Angel, *NIDNTT* 2, pp. 855–886; H. Greeven *et al.*, *TDNT* 2, pp. 40–41, 685–687, 775–808; 3, pp. 296–297; 5, pp. 773–799; 6, pp. 758–766; 8, pp. 244–245; *DBT*, pp. 445–449.

J.G.S.S.T.

PREACHING. In the NT, preaching is 'the public proclamation of Christianity to the non-Christian world' (C. H. Dodd, *The Apostolic Preaching and its Development*, 1944, p. 7). It is not religious discourse to a closed group of initiates, but open and public proclamation of God's redemptive activity in and through Jesus Christ. The current popular understanding of preaching as biblical exposition and exhortation has tended to obscure its basic meaning.

I. The biblical terms

The choice of verbs in the Gk. NT for the activity of preaching points us back to its original meaning. The most characteristic (occurring over 60 times) is *kēryssō*, 'to proclaim as a herald'. In the ancient world the herald was a figure of considerable importance (*cf.* G. Friedrich, *TDNT* 3, pp. 697–714). A man of integrity and character, he was employed by the king or State to make all public proclamations. Preaching is heralding; the message proclaimed is the glad tidings of salvation. While *kēryssō* tells us something about the activity of preaching, *euangelizomai*, 'to bring good news' (from the primitive *eus*, 'good', and the verb *angellō*, 'to announce'), a common verb, used over 50 times in the NT, emphasizes the quality of the message itself. It is worthy of note that the RSV has not followed the AV in those places where it translates the verbs *diangellō*, *laleō*, *katangellō* and *dialegomai* by 'to preach'. This helps to bring into sharper focus the basic meaning of preaching.

It is not unusual to distinguish between preaching and teaching—between *kērygma* (public proclamation) and *didachē* (ethical instruction). An appeal is made to such verses as Matthew's summary of Jesus' Galilean ministry, 'He went about all Galilee, *teaching* . . . *preaching* . . . and *healing*'

(Mt. 4:23), and Paul's words in Rom. 12:6–8 and 1 Cor. 12:28 on the gifts of the Spirit. While the two activities ideally conceived are distinct, both are based upon the same foundation. The *kērygma* proclaims what God has done: the *didachē* teaches the implications of this for Christian conduct.

While we have defined preaching within narrow limits in order to emphasize its essential NT meaning, this is not to suggest that it is without precedent in the OT. Certainly the Heb. prophets as they proclaimed the message of God under divine impulse were forerunners of the apostolic herald. Jonah was told to 'preach' (LXX *kēryssō*; Heb. *qârâ'*, 'to call out'), and even Noah is designated a 'preacher (*kēryx*) of righteousness' (2 Pet. 2:5). The LXX uses *kēryssō* more than 30 times, both in the secular sense of official proclamation for the king and the more religious sense of prophetic utterance (*cf.* Joel 1:14; Zc. 9:9; Is. 61:1).

II. New Testament features

Perhaps the most prominent feature in NT preaching is the sense of divine compulsion. In Mk. 1:38 it is reported that Jesus did not return to those who sought his healing power but pressed on to other towns *in order that he might preach there also*—'for that is why I came out'. Peter and John reply to the restrictions of the Sanhedrin with the declaration, 'We cannot but speak the things which we have seen and heard' (Acts 4:20). 'Woe to me if I do not preach the gospel', cries the apostle Paul (1 Cor. 9:16). This sense of compulsion is the *sine qua non* of true preaching. Preaching is not the relaxed recital of morally neutral truths: it is God himself breaking in and confronting man with a demand for decision. This sort of preaching meets with opposition. In 2 Cor. 11:23–28 Paul lists his sufferings for the sake of the gospel.

Another feature of apostolic preaching was its transparency of message and motive. Since preaching calls for faith, it is vitally important that its issues not be obscured with eloquent wisdom and lofty words (1 Cor. 1:17; 2:1–4). Paul refused to practise cunning or to tamper with God's Word, but sought to commend himself to every man's conscience by the open statement of the truth (2 Cor. 4:2). The radical upheaval within the heart and consciousness of man which is the new birth does not come about by the persuasive influence of rhetoric but by the straightforward presentation of the gospel in all its simplicity and power.

III. The essential nature of preaching

In the Gospels Jesus is characteristically portrayed as One who came 'heralding the kingdom of God'. In Lk. 4:16–21 Jesus interprets his ministry as the fulfilment of Isaiah's prophecy of a coming Servant-Messiah through whom the kingdom of God would at last be realized. This kingdom is best understood as God's 'kingly rule' or 'sovereign action'. Only secondarily does it refer to a realm or people within that realm. That God's eternal sovereignty was now invading the realm of evil powers and winning the decisive victory was the basic content of Jesus' *kērygma*.

When we move from the Synoptics into the rest of the NT we note a significant change in terminology. Instead of the 'kingdom of God' we find 'Christ' as the content of the preached message. This is variously expressed as 'Christ crucified' (1 Cor. 1:23), 'Christ . . . raised' (1 Cor. 15:12), 'the Son of God, Jesus Christ' (2 Cor. 1:19), or 'Christ Jesus as Lord' (2 Cor. 4:5). This change of emphasis is accounted for by the fact that Christ *is* the kingdom. The Jews anticipated the universal establishment of the sovereign reign of God, viz. his *kingdom*: the death and resurrection of Jesus Christ was the decisive act of God whereby his eternal sovereignty was realized in human history. With the advance of redemptive history the apostolic church could proclaim the kingdom in the more clear-cut terms of decision concerning the King. To preach Christ *is* to preach the kingdom.

One of the most important advances of NT scholarship in recent years has been C. H. Dodd's crystallization of the primitive *kērygma*. Following his approach (comparing the early speeches in Acts with the pre-Pauline credal fragments in Paul's Epistles) but interpreting the data with a slightly different emphasis, we find that the apostolic message was 'a proclamation of the death, resurrection and exaltation of Jesus that led to an evaluation of His person as both Lord and Christ, confronted man with the necessity of repentance, and promised the forgiveness of sins' (R. H. Mounce, *The Essential Nature of New Testament Preaching*, 1960, p. 84).

True preaching is best understood in terms of its relation to the wider theme of revelation. Revelation is essentially God's self-disclosure apprehended by the response of faith. Since Calvary is God's supreme self-revelation, the problem is, How can God reveal himself in the present through an act of the past? The answer is, through preaching—for preaching is the timeless link between God's redemptive act and man's apprehension of it. It is the medium through which God contemporizes his historic self-disclosure in Christ and offers man the opportunity to respond in faith.

BIBLIOGRAPHY. In addition to the books mentioned above, *cf.* C. K. Barrett, *Biblical Problems and Biblical Preaching*, 1964; E. P. Clowney, *Preaching and Biblical Theology*, 1961; H. H. Farmer, *The Servant of the Word*, 1950; P. T. Forsyth, *Positive Preaching and the Modern Mind*, 1949; J. Knox, *The Integrity of Preaching*, 1957; J. S. Stewart, *Heralds of God*, 1946; J. R. W. Stott, *The Preacher's Portrait*, 1961. R.H.M.

PREDESTINATION.

I. Biblical vocabulary

The English 'predestinate' comes from Lat. *praedestino*, which the Vulgate uses to translate the Gk. *prohorizō*. RSV renders *prohorizō* as 'predestine' in Acts 4:28; Rom. 8:29–30; and 'destine' in Eph. 1:5, 12; though as 'decree' in 1 Cor. 2:7. RV has 'foreordain' in all six places.

prohorizō, which the NT uses only with God as subject, expresses the thought of appointing a situation for a person, or a person for a situation, in advance (*pro-*). The NT uses other *pro-* compounds in a similar sense: (1) *protassō*, 'arrange beforehand' (Acts 17:26); (2) *protithemai*, 'propose' (Eph. 1:9; of a human proposal, Rom. 1:13; *cf.* use of the cognate noun *prothesis*, 'purpose', 'plan', Rom. 8:28; 9:11; Eph. 1:11; 3:11; 2 Tim. 1:9); (3) *prohetoimazō*, 'prepare beforehand' (Rom. 9:23; Eph. 2:10); (4) *procheirizō*, 'appoint beforehand' (Acts 3:20; 22:14); (5) *procheirotoneō*, 'choose beforehand' (Acts 10:41). *problepō*, 'foresee', carries the thought of God's effective pre-ordaining in Gal. 3:8; Heb. 11:40; as the context shows. So does *proginōskō*, 'foreknow' (Rom. 8:29; 11:2; 1 Pet. 1:20), and its cognate noun *prognōsis* (1 Pet. 1:2; Acts 2:23). The same sense is sometimes conveyed by the uncompounded verbs *tassō* (Acts 13:48; 22:10) and *horizō* (Lk. 22:22; Acts 2:23), the former implying a precise setting in order, the latter an exact marking out. This varied vocabulary well suggests the different facets of the idea expressed.

The NT formulates the thought of divine foreordination in another way, by telling us that what motivates and determines God's actions in his world, and among them the fortunes and destiny which he brings upon men, is his own will (nouns, *boulē*, Acts 2:23; 4:28; Eph. 1:11; Heb. 6:17; *boulēma*, Rom. 9:19; *thelēma*, Eph. 1:5, 9, 11; *thelēsis*, Heb. 2:4; verbs, *boulomai*, Heb. 6:17; Jas. 1:18; 2 Pet. 3:9; *thelō*, Rom. 9:18, 22; Col. 1:27), or his 'good pleasure' (noun, *eudokia*, Eph. 1:5, 9; Mt. 11:26; verb, *eudokeō*, Lk. 12:32; 1 Cor. 1:21; Gal. 1:15; Col. 1:19), *i.e.* his own deliberate, prior resolve. This is not, indeed, the only sense in which the NT speaks of the will of God. The Bible conceives of God's purpose for men as expressed both by his revealed commands to them and by his ordering of their circumstances. His 'will' in Scripture thus covers both his law and his plan; hence some of the above terms are also used with reference to particular divine demands (*e.g. boulē*, Lk. 7:30; *thelēma*, 1 Thes. 4:3; 5:18). But in the texts referred to above it is God's plan of events that is in view, and it is this that predestination concerns.

The OT lacks words for expressing the idea of predestination in an abstract and generalized form, but it often speaks of God purposing, ordaining or determining particular things, in contexts which call attention to the absolute priority and independence of his purposing in relation to the existence or occurrence of the thing purposed (*cf.* Ps. 139:16; Is. 14:24–27; 19:17; 46:10f.; Je. 49:20; Dn. 4:24f.).

The usage of the NT word-group is in favour of the traditional practice of defining predestination in terms of God's purpose regarding the circumstances and destinies of men. The wider aspects of his cosmic plan and government are most conveniently subsumed under the general head of *providence. To grasp the meaning of predestination as Scripture presents it, however, it must be set in its place in God's plan as a whole.

II. Biblical presentation

a. In the Old Testament

The OT presents God the Creator as personal, powerful and purposeful, and assures us that as his power is unlimited, so his purposes are certain of fulfilment (Ps. 33:10f.; Is. 14:27; 43:13; Jb. 9:12; 23:13; Dn. 4:35). He is Lord of every situation, ordering and directing everything towards the end for which he made it (Pr. 16:4), and determining every event, great or small, from the thoughts of kings (Pr. 21:1) and the premeditated words and deeds of all men (Pr. 16:1, 9) to the seemingly random fall of a lot (Pr. 16:33). Nothing that God sets before himself is too hard for him (Gn. 18:14; Je. 32:17); the idea that the organized opposition of man could in any way thwart him is simply absurd (Ps. 2:1–4). Isaiah's prophecy expands the thought of God's plan as the decisive factor in history more fully than does any other OT book. Isaiah stresses that God's purposes are everlasting, that Yahweh planned present and future happenings 'long ago', 'from the beginning' (*cf.* Is. 22:11; 37:26; 44:6–8; 46:10f.), and that, just because it is he, and no-one else, who orders all events (Is. 44:7), nothing can prevent the occurrence of the events that he has predicted (Is. 14:24–27; 44:24–45:25; *cf.* 1 Ki. 22:17–38; Ps. 33:10f.; Pr. 19:21; 21:30). Yahweh's ability to predict the seemingly incredible things that are going to happen proves his control of history, whereas the inability of the idols to foretell these things shows that they do not control it (Is. 44:6–8; 45:21; 48:12–14).

Sometimes Yahweh is pictured as reacting to developing situations in a way that might seem to imply that he had not anticipated them (*e.g.* when he repents, and reverses his prior action, Gn. 6:5; Je. 18:8, 10; 26:3, 13; Joel 2:13; Jon. 4:2). But in their biblical context it is clear that the purpose and point of these anthropomorphisms is simply to emphasize that Israel's God is really personal, and not to throw doubt on whether he really foreordains and controls human affairs.

That Yahweh governs human history teleologically, to bring about his own predestined purpose for human welfare, is made clear in the Bible story as early as the protevangelium (Gn. 3:15) and the promise to Abraham (Gn. 12:3). The theme develops through the wilderness promises of prosperity and protection in Canaan (*cf.* Dt. 28:1–14), and the prophetic pictures of the Messianic glory which would succeed God's work of judgment (Is. 9:1ff.; 11:1ff.; Je. 23:5ff.; Ezk. 34:20ff.; 37:21ff.; Ho. 3:4f., *etc.*); and it reaches its climax in Daniel's vision of God overruling the rise and fall of pagan world-empires in order to set up the rule of the Son of man (Dn. 7; *cf.* 2:31–45). A global eschatology of this order could not be seriously put forward save on the presupposition that God is the absolute Lord of history, foreseeing and foreordaining its whole course.

It is in terms of this view of God's relation to human history that the OT describes God's choice of Israel to be his covenant people, the object and instrument of his saving work. This choice was *unmerited* (Dt. 7:6f.; Ezk. 16:1ff.) and wholly gracious. It was *purposeful*; Israel was appointed a destiny, to be blessed and so to become a blessing to other nations (*cf.* Ps. 67; Is. 2:2–4; 11:9f.; 60; Zc. 8:20ff.; 14:16ff.). It was, however, for the time being *exclusive*; the selection of Israel meant the deliberate passing-by of the rest of the nations (Dt. 7:6; Ps. 147:19f.; Am. 3:2; *cf.* Rom. 9:4; Eph. 2:11f.). For more than a millennium God left them outside the covenant, objects only of his judgment for their national crimes (Am. 1:3–2:3) and for their malice against the chosen people (*cf.* Is. 13–19, *etc.*).

b. In the New Testament

The NT writers take for granted the OT faith that God is the sovereign Lord of events, and rules history for the fulfilling of his purposes. Their uniform insistence that Christ's ministry and the Christian dispensation represented the fulfilment of biblical prophecies, given centuries before (Mt. 1:22; 2:15, 23; 4:14; 8:17; 12:17ff.; Jn. 12:38ff.; 19:24, 28, 36; Acts 2:17ff.; 3:22ff.; 4:25ff.; 8:30ff.; 10:43; 13:27ff.; 15:15ff.; Gal. 3:8; Heb. 5:6; 8:8ff.; 1 Pet. 1:10ff., *etc.*), and that God's ultimate aim in inspiring the Heb. Scriptures was to instruct Christian believers (Rom. 15:4; 1 Cor. 10:11; 2 Tim. 3:15ff.), is proof enough of this. (Both convictions, be it noted, derive from our Lord himself: *cf.* Lk. 18:31ff.; 24:25ff., 44ff.; Jn. 5:39.) A new development, however, is that the idea of election, now applied, not to national Israel, but to Christian believers, is consistently individualized (*cf.* Ps. 65:4) and given a pre-temporal reference. The OT assimilates election to God's historical 'calling' (*cf.* Ne. 9:7), but the NT distinguishes the two things sharply, by representing election as God's act of predestinating sinners to salvation in Christ 'before the foundation of the world' (Eph. 1:4; *cf.* Mt. 25:34; 2 Tim. 1:9); an act correlative to his foreknowing Christ 'before the foundation of the world' (1 Pet. 1:20). The uniform NT conception is that all saving grace given to men in time (knowledge of the gospel, understanding of it and power to respond to it, preservation and final glory) flows from divine election in eternity.

Luke's language in the narrative of Acts bears striking witness to his belief, not merely that Christ was foreordained to die, rise and reign (Acts 2:23, 30f.; 3:20; 4:27f.), but that salvation is the fruit of prevenient grace (2:47; 11:18, 21–23; 14:27; 15:7ff.; 16:14; 18:27) given in accordance with divine foreordination (13:48; 18:10).

In John's Gospel Christ says that he has been sent to save a number of particular individuals whom his Father has 'given' him (Jn. 6:37ff.; 17:2, 6, 9, 24; 18:9). These are his 'sheep', his 'own' (10:14ff., 26ff.; 13:1). It was for them specifically that he prayed (17:20). He undertakes to 'draw' them to himself by his Spirit (12:32; *cf.* 6:44; 10:16, 27; 16:8ff.); to give them eternal life, in fellowship with himself and the Father (10:28; *cf.* 5:21; 6:40; 17:2; Mt. 11:27); to keep them, losing none (6:39; 10:28f.; *cf.* 17:11, 15; 18:9); to bring them to his glory (14:2f.; *cf.* 17:24), and to raise their bodies at the last day (6:39f.; *cf.* 5:28f.). The principle that those who enjoy salvation do so by reason of divine predestination is here made explicit.

The fullest elucidation of this principle is found in the writings of Paul. From all eternity, Paul declares, God has had a plan (*prothesis*) to save a church, though in earlier times it was not fully made known (Eph. 3:3–11). The aim of the plan is that men should be made God's adopted sons and be renewed in the image of Christ (Rom. 8:29), and that the church, the company of those so renewed, should grow to the fullness of Christ (Eph. 4:13). Believers may rejoice in the certainty that as part of his plan God predestinated them personally to share in this destiny (Rom. 8:28ff.; Eph. 1:3ff.; 2 Thes. 2:13; 2 Tim. 1:9; *cf.* 1 Pet. 1:1f.). The choice was wholly of grace (2 Tim. 1:9), having no regard to desert—being made, indeed, in defiance of foreseen ill-desert (*cf.* Jn. 15:19; Eph. 2:1ff.). Because God is sovereign, his predestinating choice guarantees salvation. From it flows an effectual 'calling', which elicits the response of faith which it commands (Rom. 8:28ff.; *cf.* 9:23f.; 1 Cor. 1:26ff.; Eph. 1:13; 2 Thes. 2:14); justification (Rom. 8:30); sanctification (1 Thes. 2:13); and glorification (Rom. 8:30, where the past tense implies certainty of accomplishment; 2 Thes. 2:14). Paul gives this teaching to Christians, persons who were themselves 'called', in order to assure them of their present security and final salvation, and to make them realize the extent of their debt to God's mercy. The 'elect' to whom, and of whom, he speaks in each Epistle are himself and/or the believers to whom he addresses it ('you', 'us').

It has been argued that God's foreknowledge is not foreordination, and that personal *election in the NT is grounded upon God's foresight that the persons chosen will respond to the gospel of themselves. The difficulties in this view seem to be: (1) this asserts in effect election according to works and desert, whereas Scripture asserts election to be of grace (Rom. 9:11; 2 Tim. 1:9), and grace excludes all regard to what a man does for himself (Rom. 4:4; 11:6; Eph. 2:8f.; Tit. 3:5); (2) if election is *unto* faith (2 Thes. 2:13) and good works (Eph. 2:10, AV) it cannot rest upon foresight of these things; (3) on this view, Paul ought to be pointing, not to God's election, but to the Christian's own faith, as the ground of his assurance of final salvation; (4) Scripture does appear to equate foreknowledge with foreordination (*cf.* Acts 2:23).

III. Election and reprobation

*'Reprobate' appears first in Je. 6:30 (*cf.* Is. 1:22), in a metaphor taken from metal refining. The thought is of something that, by reason of its corrupt condition, does not pass God's test, and which he therefore rejects. The metaphor reappears in the NT. It is used of the Gentile world (Rom. 1:28) and of professing Christians (1 Cor. 9:27; 2 Cor. 13:5f.; *cf.* 2 Tim. 3:8; Tit. 1:16). Christian theology since Augustine has, however, spoken of reprobation, not as God's rejection of particular sinners in history, but as that which (it is held) lies behind it—God's resolve, from all eternity, to pass them by, and not to give them his saving grace (*cf.* 1 Pet. 2:8; Jude 4). It has thus become common to define predestination as consisting of election and reprobation together.

It is disputed whether reprobation ought to be thus included in God's eternal *prothesis*. Some justify the inclusion by appeal to Rom. 9:17f., 21f.; 11:7f. It seems hard to deny, in face of 9:22, that the hardening and non-salvation of some, which in vv. 19–21 Paul proved to be within God's right, is actually part of his predestinating purpose; though it should be noticed that Paul is concerned to stress, not God's implacability towards the reprobate, but his long restraint of his wrath against persons who have become ripe for destruction (*cf.* 2:4). But to determine the exact scope of these verses in their context is not easy; see the commentaries.

BIBLIOGRAPHY. *BAGD*; B. B. Warfield, 'Predestination', and J. Denney, 'Reprobation', in *HDB*; Calvin, *Institutes*, 3. 21–24; *idem*, *Concerning the Eternal Predestination of God*, E.T. by J. K. S. Reid, 1960; E. Jacob, *Theology of the Old Testament*, E.T. 1958, pp. 183–207; G. C. Berkouwer, *Divine Election*, 1960; commentaries on Rom. 9–11, esp. W. Sanday and A. C. Headlam, *ICC*, 1902; P. Jacobs, H. Krienke, *NIDNTT* 1, pp. 692–697.

J.I.P.

PREPARATION. The Gk. word *paraskeuē* is found in the NT with a twofold connotation. In its meaning of a definite day of preparation, it is used of the day preceding the weekly sabbath and the day which prepares for the annual Jewish Passover festival (*cf.* Jos., *Ant.* 16. 163), see Mt. 27:62; Mk. 15:42; Lk. 23:54; and especially Jn. 19, which mentions both types of preparation day. The reference in Jn. 19:14 is to *'ereḇ ha-pesaḥ*, *i.e.* the eve of the Passover (*cf.* *Pesaḥim* 10. 1 in the Mishnah). In Jn. 19:31, 42 there is no accompanying genitive, so the word must mean *'ereḇ šabbāṯ*, *i.e.* the day before the sabbath (as clearly in Mk. 15:42). This would be the 24 hours from 6 p.m. Thursday to 6 p.m. Friday. The second meaning is extended, in later Christian literature, to designate the sixth day of the week, *i.e.* Friday (*cf. Martyrdom of Polycarp* 7. 1; *Didache*, 8. 1); and this is the sense of *paraskeuē* in modern Greek.

For the controverted meaning of the phrase in Jn. 19:14, see J. Jeremias, *The Eucharistic Words of Jesus*, E.T.[2] 1966, pp. 80–82 (biblio.). R.P.M.

PRESBYTER, PRESBYTERY. These terms, in EVV usually rendered 'elder', 'eldership', *etc.*, are derived from the Gk. words *presbyteros*, *presbyterion* (as is also the contracted Eng. term 'priest'). The Heb. equivalent of *presbyteros* is *zāqēn*, and the Aram. equivalent is *śîb*, and all three words have the basic meaning 'old(er) man', in which sense *zāqēn* is used in Gn. 25:8; 1 Ki. 12:8; Ps. 148:12; Pr. 17:6; Je. 31:13, *etc.*, and *presbyteros* in Acts 2:17; 1 Tim. 5:1. This suggests that originally elders were men of advancing years; and that such still tended to be the case in NT times is indicated by 1 Pet. 5:1, 5; *Mishnah Aboth* 5. 21. *presbyteroi* can also mean 'men of old time', as in Mk. 7:3, 5; Heb. 11:2, and perhaps Rev. 4:4, 10, *etc.*, where the twenty-four elders may symbolize the authors of the books of the OT, which the Jews reckon as twenty-four in number (*CANON OF THE OT).

Throughout the Bible, seniority entitles people to respect (Lv. 19:32; 1 Tim. 5:1) and *age is thought of as bringing experience and therefore wisdom (1 Ki. 12:6–15; Pr. 4:1; 5:1). Consequently, the leading men of Israel, right through its OT history, are the elders of the nation (Ex. 3:16, 18; Lv. 4:15; Jdg. 21:16; 1 Sa. 4:3; 2 Sa. 3:17; 1 Ki. 8:1, 3; 2 Ki. 23:1; 1 Ch. 11:3; Ezr. 5:5, 9; Je. 26:17; Ezk. 8:1, *etc.*). Seventy of them are chosen to share the burden of ruling with Moses (Nu. 11:16–30), and the elders later do something similar for the king. Along with the priests, they are entrusted with the written Law, and charged to read it to the people (Dt. 31:9–13). When the people settle in the promised land, and are dispersed throughout its cities, the elders of the cities act as judges there (Dt. 19:12; 21:19f.; 22:15–18; Jos. 20:4; Ru. 4:2, 4, 9, 11; 1 Ki. 21:8, 11; 2 Ki. 10:1, 5), thus continuing the practice of having lay judges for lesser questions, which began in the wilderness (Ex. 18:13–26; Dt. 1:9–18). The appeal judges at Jerusalem, however, are partly lay, partly priestly (Dt. 17:8–13; 2 Ch. 19:8–11).

The lay judges of Ex. 18 and Dt. 1 are selected for their wisdom, piety and integrity. Similarly, the choice made among the elders in Nu. 11 probably reflects a recognition that age does not bring wisdom invariably. Indeed, a wise youth is better than a foolish old king (Ec. 4:13). This recognition continues in the intertestamental literature. Wisdom befits the aged, and elders ought to be wise (Ecclus. 6:34; 8:8f.; 25:3f.), but even the young are honoured if wise (Wisdom 8:10) and are treated as elders (Susanna 45, 50). Judges are men specially selected from among the elders (Susanna 5f., 41). The elders said to have been chosen from each tribe to translate the Pentateuch into Greek are marked not so much by age (*Letter of Aristeas* 122, 318) as by virtuous life and by knowledge and understanding of the Mosaic Law (32, 121f., 321). In conformity with Dt. 31, they include both laymen and priests (184, 310), but now with a large lay majority.

At Jerusalem also, the ancient link between elders and priests continues (La. 1:19; 4:16; 1 Macc. 7:33; 11:23) and is prominent in the NT (Mt. 21:23; 26:3, 47; 27:1, 3, 12, 20; 28:11f.; Acts 4:23; 23:14; 25:15). Out of it has now grown the Sanhedrin, which is the ruling council of the nation and its supreme court of justice, presided over by the high priest. The elders and chief priests are included among its seventy-one members (Mt. 27:1; Mk. 8:31; 14:53; 15:1; Lk. 22:66; Acts 4:5, 8, 23; 22:5), along with 'scribes' and 'rulers', terms which probably have very similar meanings to the other two. The elders also appear as rulers in the intertestamental literature, at Jerusalem and elsewhere (Judith 8:10f.; 1 Macc. 12:35).

For their duty of judging the people according to God's law, the priests and elders need a knowledge of God's law, and this is why the priests are given the further duty of teaching it (Lv. 10:10f.; Dt. 33:10; Mal. 2:6f.). In 1st-century Alexandria we still find the priests as well as the elders performing this duty, by expounding the Scriptures to the people in the synagogue on the sabbath (Philo, *Hypothetica* 7. 13), but in Palestine the task of teaching seems to have passed over almost entirely to the elders, who are called by this name in Lk. 7:3, in a Jerusalem synagogue inscription from before AD 70, and in the rabbinical literature, but in the NT are usually called 'scribes' (Scripture-experts), 'teachers of the law', 'lawyers' or 'rabbis'. They teach on occasion in the Temple (Lk. 2:46) but have their great centre of influence in the synagogue (Mt. 23:6; Mk. 1:21f.; Lk. 5:17; 6:6f.; 7:3–5). In the rabbinical literature, their primary duty is still to be judges, and this is why we read in the NT of excommunications from the synagogue (Jn. 9:22; 12:42; 16:2), and of punishments being inflicted in the synagogue (Mt. 23:34; Mk. 13:9; Acts 22:19; 26:11). The synagogue also has one or more 'synagogue-rulers', responsible for keeping order there (Lk. 13:14) and for choosing who should preach (Acts 13:15), read the lessons or lead the prayers; and an 'attendant' (Lk. 4:20). The non-biblical evidence suggests that these are local appointments attached to the synagogue building. The elder, on the other hand, is ordained by his teacher and thus has a wider scope for his ministry, though he usually settles and earns his living by a trade. He in turn ordains his own pupils, often with the co-operation of two other elders, and usually by the laying on of hands and thus a succession of teachers and judges, and a tradition of teaching and legal interpretation, is established and continued. Then, in the 2nd century AD, the right to ordain or authorize ordinations is concentrated in the national patriarch. *Cf.* esp. *Tosefta Sanhedrin* 1. 1; *Jerusalem Sanhedrin* 1. 2–4.

It is against this background that the Christian eldership is established, and the Jewish-Christian institution of eldership helps to unify the diversities of NT ministry, more than is often realized. Christ is the one great teacher or rabbi (Mt. 23:8). His disciples call themselves elders (1 Pet. 5:1; 2 Jn. 1; 3 Jn. 1). They pass on the teaching they have received and commit it to others, who are to commit it to others again (1 Cor. 11:23; 15:1, 3; 2 Thes. 2:15; 3:6; 2 Tim. 2:2). Those to whom it is committed are likewise called elders (Acts 14:23; Tit. 1:5). They are apparently appointed by the laying on of hands (Acts 6:6; *cf.* 11:30; 1 Tim. 4:14; 5:22; 2 Tim. 1:6). They must be ready to earn their own living if necessary (Acts 20:17, 33–35). They have the tasks of teaching (1 Tim. 5:17; Tit. 1:5, 9) and of acting as judges (Acts 15:2, 6, 22–29; 16:4). It is an open question whether a parallel is to be seen between the Jerusalem council or appeal court, consisting of apostles and elders, presided over by James the Lord's brother, and the Sanhedrin, consisting of chief priests and elders, presided over by the high priest. In addition to the tasks of teaching and judging, the task of ruling is re-emphasized in the Christian eldership, and given a pastoral rather than a political character (Acts 20:17, 28; 1 Tim. 5:17; Jas. 5:14; 1 Pet. 5:1–4; *cf.* Mt. 9:36–38; Eph. 4:11); hence the elder's other title of *bishop, and hence the disappearance of the separate office of 'synagogue-ruler' in Christianity, his task being partly absorbed by the elder, and partly, no doubt, by the owner of the house-church. The 'attendant', on the other hand, survives as the Christian deacon, though his office is still local to the extent that deacons appear in the NT only occasionally.

The Christian eldership is thus primarily an office of teaching, of adjudicating questions of right and wrong, and of providing pastoral oversight. Though elders are specially ordained, their office is not a priestly or a ceremonial one. The sacraments are under the supervision of the ordained ministry, but are not their personal prerogative. When the office of bishop becomes separated from that of elder in the 2nd century, the tasks of teaching, pastoral oversight and supervision of the sacraments are shared between the two offices; the task of acting as judge, in matters of excommunication and reconciliation, adheres primarily to the bishop; so too, for a time, does the assistance of the deacon; and so does the duty of ordination, the practice of having two others to co-operate in the bishop's own ordination, and the concept of a succession of teachers, each committing to his successor, through instruction and ordination, the message with which he has himself been entrusted. Elders, however, continue to have certain judicial duties, in the repelling of impenitent offenders from the Lord's table, and certain ordaining duties, in assisting with the ordination of other elders. (*Church Government, *Ministry.)

Bibliography. J. Newman, *Semikhah* (*Ordination*), 1950; E. Ferguson, *JTS* n.s. 26, 1975, pp. 1–12. R.T.B.

PRESS, WINEFAT. A rectangular cavity hollowed out of rock or constructed artificially within which grapes were trampled underfoot, and from which the resultant juice drained into a lower receptacle. The term is applied to the whole apparatus. Its fullness was a sign of prosperity, while its emptiness represented famine.

It is used metaphorically in Is. 63:3 and in Joel 3:13, where the full press and overflowing vats indicate the greatness of the threatened carnage. It serves as a striking simile in La. 1:15, and in Rev. 14:18–20 forms part of the apocalyptic language following on the predicted fall of Babylon.

Bibliography. M. Noth, *The Old Testament World*, 1966. F.S.F.

PRIDE. The emphasis placed on pride, and its converse humility, is a distinctive feature of biblical religion, unparalleled in other religious or ethical systems. Rebellious pride, which refuses to depend on God and be subject to him, but attributes to self the honour due to him, figures as the very root and essence of sin.

We may say with Aquinas that pride was first revealed when Lucifer attempted to set his throne on high in proud independence of God (Is. 14:12–14). The fallen devil (Lk. 10:18) instilled the craving to be as gods into Adam and Eve (Gn. 3:5), with the result that man's entire nature was infected with pride through the Fall (*cf.* Rom. 1:21–23). The 'condemnation of the devil' is associated with pride in 1 Tim. 3:6 (*cf.* 'the snare of the devil' in 1 Tim. 3:7; 2 Tim. 2:26); pride was his undoing and remains the prime means by which he brings about the undoing of men and women. Hence we find a sustained condemnation of human arrogance throughout the OT, especially in the Psalms and Wisdom Literature. In Pr. 8:13 both *gē'â*, 'arrogance', and *ga'ᵃwâ*, 'insolence', are hateful to the divine wisdom: their manifestation in the form of national pride in Moab (Is. 16:6), Judah (Je. 13:9) and Israel (Ho. 5:5) are especially denounced by the prophets. The notorious 'pride which goes before a fall' is called *gā'ôn*, 'swelling excellence', in Pr. 16:18, and is rejected in favour of the lowly spirit. 'Haughtiness', *gōḇah*, appears as a root cause of atheism in Ps. 10:4. It is the downfall of Nebuchadrezzar in Dn. 4:30, 37. A milder word, *zāḏôn*, 'presumption', is applied to David's youthful enthusiasm in 1 Sa. 17:28, but in Ob. 3 even this is regarded as a deceitful evil. Further warnings against pride occur in the later Wisdom Literature, *e.g.* Ecclus. 10:6–26.

Greek teaching during the four last centuries BC was at variance with Judaism in regarding pride as a virtue and humility as despicable. Aristotle's 'great-souled man' had a profound regard for his own excellence; to underestimate it would have stamped him as mean-spirited. Similarly, the Stoic sage asserted his own moral independence and equality with Zeus. Insolence (*hybris*), however, is a deep source of moral evil in the Greek tragedy (*cf.*, *e.g.*, the *Antigone* of Sophocles).

The Christian ethic consciously rejected Greek thought in favour of the OT outlook. Humility was accorded supreme excellence when Christ pronounced himself 'gentle and lowly in heart' (Mt. 11:29). Conversely, pride (*hyperēphania*) was placed on a list of defiling vices proceeding from the evil heart of man (Mk. 7:22). In the Magnificat (Lk. 1:51f.) God is said to scatter the proud and exalt the meek. In both Jas. 4:6 and 1 Pet. 5:5, Pr. 3:34 is quoted to emphasize the contrast between the meek (*tapeinois*), whom God favours, and the proud (*hyperēphanois*), whom God resists. Paul couples the insolent (*hybristas*) and the boastful (*alazonas*) with the proud sinners in his sketch of depraved pagan society in Rom. 1:30; *cf.* 2 Tim. 3:2. Arrogant display or ostentation (*alazoneia*) are disparaged in Jas. 4:16 and 1 Jn. 2:16. Love, in 1 Cor. 13:4, is stated to be free from both the arrogance and the self-conceit which mar the heretical teachers of 1 Tim. 6:4.

Paul saw pride ('boasting' in knowledge of the law and in works/righteousness) as the characteristic spirit of Judaism and a direct cause of Jewish unbelief. He insisted that the gospel is designed to exclude boasting (Rom. 3:27) by teaching men that they are sinners, that self-righteousness is therefore out of the question, and that they must look to Christ for their righteousness and take it as a free gift by faith in him. Salvation is 'not because of works, lest any man should boast'; it is all of grace. No man, therefore, not even Abraham, may glory in the achievement of his own salvation (see Eph. 2:9; 1 Cor. 1:26–31; Rom. 4:1–2). The gospel message of righteousness through Christ sounds the death-knell of self-righteousness in religion; that is why it was a stumbling-block to the proud Jews (Rom. 9:30–10:4).

This NT emphasis made a deep impact on early and mediaeval ethics. Augustine, Aquinas and Dante all characterized pride as the ultimate sin, while Milton and Goethe dramatized it.

BIBLIOGRAPHY. *ERE*; *BAGD*; *MM*; R. Niebuhr, *The Nature and Destiny of Man*, 1944–5, ch. 7; E. Güting, C. Brown, *NIDNTT* 3, pp. 27–32; G. Bertram, *TDNT* 8, pp. 295–307, 525–529. D.H.T.

PRIESTS AND LEVITES. The relationship between the priests, who are the descendants of Aaron, and the Levites, the other members of Levi's tribe, is one of the thorny problems of OT religion. Any treatment of the Levites must deal with the biblical evidence, Julius Wellhausen's reconstruction of it and the numerous ways in which contemporary scholars have reacted to his evolutionary approach.

I. The biblical data

a. The Pentateuch

The Levites come into prominence in the Pentateuch in connection with Moses and Aaron (Ex. 2:1–10; 4:14; 6:16–27). After Aaron led the people into apostasy with the golden calf (Ex. 32:25ff.), the sons of Levi avenged the Lord's honour by punishing many of the miscreants. This display of fidelity to God may partially account for the signal responsibilities given the tribe in the pentateuchal legislation.

The role of the Levites as ministers in the tabernacle, clearly detailed in Numbers, is anticipated in Ex. 38:21, where they co-operate in the construction of the tabernacle under the supervision of Aaron's son, Ithamar. In the laws preparatory to the wilderness march, Levi was separated by God from the other tribes and placed in charge of the dismantling, carrying and erecting of the tabernacle (Nu. 1:47–54). The sons of Levi camped around the tabernacle and apparently served as buffers to protect their fellow-tribes from God's wrath, which threatened them if they unwittingly came in contact with the holy tent or its furnishings (Nu. 1:51, 53; 2:17).

Forbidden to serve as priests, a privilege reserved, on penalty of death, for Aaron's sons (Nu. 3:10), the Levites were dedicated to an auxiliary ministry for the priests, especially in regard to the manual labour of caring for the tabernacle (Nu. 3:5ff.). In addition, they performed an important service for the other tribes by substituting for each family's first-born, to whom God was entitled in view of the fact that he spared Israel's first-born at the Passover in Egypt (*cf.* Ex. 13:2ff., 13). As representatives of the tribes' first-born (Nu. 3:40ff.) the Levites were part of 'the far-reaching principle of *representation*' by which the concept of a people utterly dependent upon and totally surrendered to God was put across (*cf.* H. W. Robinson, *Inspiration and Revelation in the Old Testament*, 1953, pp. 219–221).

Each of the three families of Levi had specific duties. The sons of *Kohath* (numbering 2,750 in the age-group from 30 to 50 according to Nu. 4:36) were in charge of carrying the furniture after it had been carefully covered by the priests, who alone could touch it (Nu. 3:29–32; 4:1ff.). The Kohathites were supervised by Aaron's son, Eleazar. The sons of *Gershon* (2,630; Nu. 4:40) cared for the coverings, screens and hangings under the supervision of Aaron's son Ithamar (Nu. 3:21–26; 4:21ff.). *Merari's* sons (3,200; Nu. 4:44) had the task of carrying and erecting the frame of the tabernacle and its court (Nu. 3:35–37; 4:29ff.).

The representative function of the Levites is symbolized in the rituals of cleansing and dedication (Nu. 8:5ff.). For instance, both the fact that the Israelites (probably through their tribal leaders) laid hands on the Levites (8:10), acknowledging them as substitutes (*cf.* Lv. 4:24, *etc.*), and the fact that the priests offered the Levites as a wave-offering (probably by leading them to and then from the altar) from the people (8:11), suggest that the Levites were given by the Israelites to serve Aaron's sons in their stead. This is made explicit in 8:16ff., where Levi's sons are called *n*ᵉ*ṯûnîm*, 'gifts'.

Their service began at 25 years of age and continued until the 50th year, when the Levite went into a kind of semi-retirement with limited duties (Nu. 8:24–26). There may have been a 5-year apprenticeship, because apparently the full responsibility of carrying the tabernacle and its furnishings fell on the shoulders of the men from 30 years to 50 (Nu. 4:3ff.). When David established a permanent site for the ark, the age was lowered to 20 years because there was no longer a need for mature Levites as porters (1 Ch. 23:24ff.).

The levitical responsibility of representing the people carried with it certain privileges. Although they had no inheritance in the land (*i.e.* no portion of it was appointed for their exclusive use: Nu. 18:23–24; Dt. 12:12ff.), the Levites were supported by the tithes of the people, while the priests received the parts of the offerings not consumed by sacrifice, the firstlings of flock and herd, and a tithe of the levitical tithes (Nu. 18:8ff., 21ff.; *cf.* Dt. 18:1–4). Occasionally both priests and Levites shared in the spoils of battle (*e.g.* Nu. 31:25ff.). In addition, the Levites had permission to reside in forty-eight cities set aside for their use (Nu. 35:1ff.; Jos. 21:1ff.). Surrounding each city an area of pasture-land was marked off for them. Six of the cities, three on each side of the Jordan, served as *cities of refuge.

The transition from the wilderness marches to settled life in Canaan (anticipated in Nu. 35 in the establishing of levitical cities) brought with it both an increased concern for the welfare of the Levites and an expansion of their duties in order to cope with the needs of the decentralized pattern of life. In Deuteronomy great stress is laid on the Israelites' responsibilities towards the sons of Levi, who were to share in the rejoicing of the tribes (12:12), in their tithes and certain offerings (12:18–19; 14:28–29), and in their chief festivals, especially Weeks and Tabernacles (16:11–14). The Levites dispersed throughout the land were to share equally both the ministry and the offerings with their brethren who resided at the central shrine (18:6–8).

Whereas Numbers characteristically calls the priests the *sons of Aaron* (*e.g.* 10:8), Deuteronomy frequently uses the expression 'the *Levitical priests*' (*e.g.* 18:1). Though some scholars (see below) have held that no distinction is made between priest and Levite in Deuteronomy, the fact that different portions are ascribed to priests in Dt. 18:3ff. and to Levites in 18:6ff. suggests that the distinction is maintained. The phrase 'the Levitical priests' (*e.g.* Dt. 17:9, 18; 18:1; 24:8; 27:9; *cf.* Jos. 3:3; 8:33) seems to mean 'the priests of the tribe of Levi'. To them the Deuteronomic code assigns numerous duties in addition to the care of the sanctuary: they serve as judges in cases involving difficult decisions (17:8–9), regulate the control of lepers (24:8), guard the book of the law (17:18) and assist Moses in the ceremony of covenant renewal (27:9).

Within the family of Kohath the office of high priest (Heb. *hakkōhēn*, 'the priest' (Ex. 31:10, *etc.*); *hakkōhēn hammāšîaḥ*, 'the anointed priest' (Lv. 4:3, *etc.*); *hakkōhēn haggāḏōl*, 'the high priest' (Lv. 21:10, *etc.*)) was exercised by the eldest representative of Eleazar's family, unless the sanctions of Lv. 21:16–23 were applicable. He was consecrated in the same manner as the other priests and shared in their routine duties. He alone wore the special vestments (Ex. 28; *BREASTPIECE OF THE HIGH PRIEST, *MITRE, *DRESS) and interpreted the oracles (*URIM AND THUMMIM). On the Day of *Atonement he represented the chosen people before Yahweh, sprinkling the blood of the sacrificial goat on the mercy-seat (*SACRIFICE AND OFFERING).

b. The Former Prophets

The priests play a more prominent role than the Levites in the book of Joshua, especially in the story of the crossing of Jordan and the conquest of Jericho. Sometimes called 'the priests the Levites' (*e.g.* Jos. 3:3; 8:33) and more often simply 'the priests' (*e.g.* Jos. 3:6ff.; 4:9ff.), they had the crucial task of bearing the ark of the Lord. The tabernacle, however, carried by the Levites is not mentioned (with the possible exception of 6:24) until it was pitched at Shiloh (18:1; 19:51) after the conquest of Canaan. Apparently the carrying of the ark was entrusted to the priests rather than the Kohathites (*cf.* Nu. 4:15) because of the supreme importance of these journeys: God, whose presence the ark symbolized, was marching forth conquering and to conquer. The Levites came into the forefront only when the time for dividing the land was at hand (*cf.* Jos. 14:3ff.). The distinction between priests and Levites is clearly maintained: the Levites remind Eleazar, the priest, and Joshua of Moses' command concerning levitical cities (Jos. 21:1–3); the Kohathites are divided into two groups—those who have descended from Aaron (*i.e.* the priests) and the rest (Jos. 21:4–5).

The general laxness of worship during the days between the conquest of Canaan and the establishment of the Monarchy is illustrated in the two levitical stories in Judges. Micah's Levite (Jdg. 17–18) is said to hail from Bethlehem and to be a member of the family of Judah (17:7). How was he both Levite and Judahite? The answer hangs on whether the Levite is to be identified with *Jonathan, the son of Gershom (18:30). If they are identical (as seems likely), then the Levite's relationship to Judah must be geographical, not genealogical, in spite of the phrase 'family of Judah' (17:7). If the two men are not identical, then the Levite may be an example of the possibility that men of other tribes could, in this period, join themselves to the priestly tribe. This may have been the case with *Samuel, an Ephraimite (*cf.* 1 Sa. 1:1; 1 Ch. 6:28). There is some evidence that the term *Levite* may have been a functional title meaning 'one pledged by vow' as well as a tribal designation (*cf.* W. F. Albright, *Archaeology and the Religion of Israel*[3], 1953, pp. 109, 204ff.); however, T. J. Meek (*Hebrew Origins*[3], 1960, pp. 121ff.) maintains that the Levites were originally a secular tribe who assumed a priestly function not only in Israel but perhaps in Arabia as well. The macabre story of the Levite and his concubine (Jdg. 19) is further testimony to the itinerations of the Levites and to the general laxness of the era. Lack of central authority curtailed the control which the central sanctuary at Shiloh should have enjoyed (Jdg. 18:31) and allowed numerous shrines to exist which paid little heed to the Mosaic regulations.

Levites appear only rarely in the rest of the Former Prophets, usually in connection with their role in carrying the ark (1 Sa. 6:15; 2 Sa. 15:24; 1 Ki. 8:4). When *Jeroboam I set up rival shrines at Dan and Bethel, he staffed them with non-levitical priests, probably in order to sever relationships with the Jerusalem Temple as completely as possible (1 Ki. 12:31; *cf.* 2 Ch. 11:13–14; 13:9–10). Royal control of the centre of worship in both kingdoms was an important feature of the Monarchy.

c. The Chronicles

The priestly perspective of the writer of the books of *Chronicles tends to accentuate the role of the Levites and fills in numerous details of their ministry which the authors of Kings have omitted. In the genealogies of 1 Ch. 6, which also describe the role of Aaron's sons (6:49–53) and the distribution of levitical cities (6:54–81), special attention is focused on the levitical singers, Heman, Asaph, Ethan and their sons, who were put in charge of the Temple music by David (6:31ff.; *cf.* 1 Ch. 15:16ff.). The list of Levites in 1 Ch. 9 bristles with problems. The similarities between it and Ne. 11 have led some (*e.g.* ASV, RSV) to treat it as the roll of Levites who returned to Jerusalem from the captivity (*cf.* 1 Ch. 9:1). Others (*e.g.* C. F. Keil) view it as a list of early inhabitants of Jerusalem. Both the carefully organized assignments of duty and the numbers of Levites involved (*cf.* the 212 gatekeepers of 1 Ch. 9:22 with the 93 of 1 Ch. 26:8–11) suggest a period subsequent to that of David. The close co-operation between Levites and sons of priests (*cf.* 1 Ch. 9:28ff.) and the fact that Levites cared for some of the holy vessels and helped to prepare the showbread may indicate that the rigid division of duties suggested in Nu. 4 and 18 broke down during the Monarchy, perhaps because the sons of Aaron were not numerous enough (the 1,760 in 1 Ch. 9:13 probably refers to the number of kinsmen, not to the number of heads of houses) to cope with the demands of their office. Therefore, in addition to their regular tasks as singers and musicians, gatekeepers, porters, *etc.*, the Levites had to help in the actual preparation of the sacrifices, as well as in the care of the courts and chambers, the cleansing of the holy things and the preparation of the showbread, the cereal offering, the unleavened bread, the baked offering, *etc.* (23:14).

David's orders in 1 Ch. 23 illustrate the two dominant factors which produced substantial changes in the levitical offices: the permanent location of the ark in Jerusalem, which automatically made obsolete all the regulations concerning the Levites' function as porters; and the centralization of responsibility for the official religion (as for all other affairs of life) in the king. The Heb. view of corporate personality saw the king as the great father of the nation whose essential character was derived from him. As David brought the central shrine to Jerusalem (1 Ch. 13:2ff.) and established the patterns of its function (1 Ch. 15:1ff.; 23:1ff.) in accordance with the principles of the Mosaic legislation, so Solomon built, dedicated and supervised the Temple and its cult according to his father's plan (1 Ch. 28:11–13, 21; 2 Ch. 5–8, note especially 8:15: 'And they did not turn aside from what the king had commanded the priests and Levites . . .').

Similarly, Jehoshaphat commissioned princes, Levites and priests to teach the law throughout Judah (2 Ch. 17:7ff.) and appointed certain Levites, priests and family heads as judges in Jerusalem (2 Ch. 19:8ff.) under the supervision of the chief priest. Joash (2 Ch. 24:5ff.), Hezekiah (2 Ch. 29:3ff.) and Josiah (2 Ch. 35:2ff.) supervised the priests and Levites and re-established them in their functions according to the Davidic pattern.

The relationship between the levitical office and the prophetic is a moot question. Were some Levites cult-prophets? No firm answer is possible, but there is some evidence that Levites sometimes exercised prophetic activity: Jahaziel, a Levite of the sons of Asaph, prophesied Jehoshaphat's victory over the Moabite–Ammonite coalition (2 Ch. 20:14ff.) and Jeduthun, the Levite, is called the king's *seer* (2 Ch. 35:15).

d. The Latter Prophets

Isaiah, Jeremiah and Ezekiel touch briefly upon the role of the Levites after the Exile. Is. 66:21 speaks of God's gathering of dispersed Israelites (or perhaps converted heathen) to serve him as priests and Levites. Jeremiah (33:17ff.) envisages a covenant with the levitical priests (or perhaps priests and Levites; *cf.* Syr. and Vulg.) which is as binding as God's covenant with David's family (*cf.* 2 Sa. 7). Ezekiel forces a sharp cleavage between the levitical priests, whom he calls the sons of Zadok (*e.g.* 40:46; 43:19), and the Levites. The former are deemed to have remained faithful to God (44:15; 48:11), while the latter went astray after idols and therefore could not approach the altar or handle the most sacred things (44:10–14). Actually Ezekiel's suggestion seems to be a return to the careful distinction between priest and Levite found in Numbers from the somewhat more lax view which prevailed during the Monarchy.

e. The post-exilic writings

Under Joshua and Zerubbabel 341 Levites returned (Ezr. 2:36ff.) with the 4,289 members of priestly families, and the 392 Temple servants (*nᵉṯînîm, i.e.* 'given', 'appointed', who were apparently descendants of prisoners of war pressed into Temple service; *cf.* Jos. 9:23, 27; Ezr. 8:20). The difference between the large number of priests and the comparatively small number of Levites may be due to the fact that many Levites took on priestly status during the Exile. The other Levites responsible for menial tasks in the Temple seem to have been reluctant to return (Ezr. 8:15–20). The Levites played a prominent part at the laying of the foundation (Ezr. 3:8ff.) and at the dedication of the Temple (Ezr. 6:16ff.). Ezra, after recruiting Levites for his party (Ezr. 8:15ff.), instituted a reform to ban foreign marriages in which even priests and Levites had become involved (Ezr. 9:1ff.; 10:5ff.).

Similarly in Nehemiah, the Levites and priests engaged in their full range of duties. After repairing a section of the wall (Ne. 3:17), the Levites were busily occupied with instruction in the law (Ne. 8:7–9) and participation in the religious life of the nation (Ne. 11:3ff.; 12:27ff.). They were to receive tithes from the people and in turn to give a tithe of the tithes to Aaron's sons (Ne. 10:37ff.; 12:47). The need for a central authority to enforce the levitical regulations was shown by the deterioration of the cult during Nehemiah's absence from Jerusalem: Tobiah, the Ammonite, was allowed to occupy the room in the Temple which should have served as a storeroom for the levitical tithes (Ne. 13:4ff.); deprived of their support, the Levites had forsaken the Temple and fled to their fields in order to sustain themselves (Ne. 13:10ff.).

It may have been during this period that the priests put personal gain above their covenanted responsibility to teach the law and accepted corrupt sacrifices (Mal. 1:6ff.; 2:4ff.). For Malachi, the purification of the sons of Levi was one of God's central eschatological missions (3:1–4).

The high priesthood remained in the family of Eleazar until the time of *Eli, a descendant of Ithamar. The conspiracy of *Abiathar led Solomon to depose him (1 Ki. 2:26f.). The office thus returned to the house of Eleazar in *Zadok and remained in that family until political intrigues resulted in the deposition of Onias III by the Seleucid king Antiochus Epiphanes (*c.* 174 BC). Thereafter it became the patronage of the ruling power.

II. Wellhausen's reconstruction

The development of the documentary hypothesis with its emphasis on the post-exilic date for the completion of the priestly code (*PENTATEUCH) brought with it a drastic re-evaluation of the development of Israel's religion. The classical form of this re-evaluation was stated by Julius Wellhausen (1844–1918) in his *Prolegomena to the History of Israel* (1878; E.T. 1885).

The crux of the relationship between priest and Levite for Wellhausen was Ezekiel's banning of Levites from priestly duties (44:6–16). From Ezekiel's statement Wellhausen drew two inferences: the separation of the holy from the profane was not part of the temple procedure, as the use of heathen temple servants (see above) indicates; Ezekiel reduced the Levites, who had hitherto performed priestly functions, to the status of temple-slaves. The sons of Zadok were exempt from Ezekiel's indictment because they served at the central sanctuary in Jerusalem and, unlike the Levites, had not defiled themselves by service at the high places throughout the land. When the sons of Zadok objected to relinquishing their exclusive control, Ezekiel devised 'moral' grounds for maintaining their exclusiveness, although actually the distinction between priests and Levites was accidental not moral (the priests *happened* to be at Jerusalem, the Levites at the high places). Wellhausen concluded that the priestly law of Numbers did not exist in Ezekiel's time.

Since the Aaronic priesthood is stressed only in the priestly code, it was viewed by Wellhausen as a fiction in order to give the priesthood an anchor in the Mosaic period. The genealogies in Chronicles are artificial attempts to link the sons of Zadok with Aaron and Eleazar.

Central in Wellhausen's reconstruction was the

striking contrast between the 'elaborate machinery' of the wilderness cult and the decentralization of the period of the Judges, when worship played apparently only a minor role according to Jdg. 3–16. The latter period he took to be the authentic time of origin of Israelite worship, which began simply as various family heads offered their own sacrifices, and developed as certain families (*e.g.* Eli's at Shiloh) gained prominence at special sanctuaries. A startling example of the contrast between the complexity of the wilderness religion and the simplicity during the settlement was the fact that Samuel, an Ephraimite, slept nightly beside the ark (1 Sa. 3:3) in the place where, according to Lv. 16, only the high priest could enter annually.

When Solomon built the permanent shrine for the ark, the prominence of the Jerusalem priests (under Zadok, whom David had appointed) was assured. Like Judah, like Israel: Jeroboam's shrines were royal shrines and the priests were directly responsible to him (Am. 7:10ff.). In Judah the process of centralization reached its acme when Josiah's reform abolished the high places, reduced their priests to subsidiary status in the central sanctuary and set the stage for Ezekiel's crucial declaration.

Against this evolutionary schematization, Wellhausen set the various strata of the Pentateuch and found a remarkable degree of correspondence. In the laws of J (Ex. 20–23; 34) the priesthood is not mentioned, while the other parts of J mark Aaron (Ex. 4:14; 32:1ff.) and Moses (Ex. 33:7–11) as founders of the clergy. The mention of other priests (*e.g.* Ex. 19:22; 32:29) was disregarded by Wellhausen, who considered these passages as interpolations. It was in D (Dt. 16:18–18:22) that he saw the beginning of the use of the name *Levites* for the priests. The hereditary character of the priesthood began not with Aaron (who, according to Wellhausen, 'was not originally present in J, but owed his introduction to the redactor who combined J and E') but during the Monarchy with the sons of Zadok. Recognizing the basic authenticity of the inclusion of Levi in the tribal blessings of Gn. 49, Wellhausen believed that this tribe 'succumbed at an early date' and that the supposed tie between the official use of the term *Levite* and the tribe of Levi was artificial.

The priestly code (P) not only strengthened the hand of the clergy but introduced the basic division into the ranks of the clergy—the separation of priests (Aaron's sons) from Levites (the rest of the tribe). Therefore, while the Deuteronomist spoke of levitical priests (*i.e.* the priests the Levites) the priestly writers, especially the Chronicler, spoke of priests and Levites.

Another priestly innovation was the figure of the high priest, who loomed larger in Exodus, Leviticus and Numbers than anywhere else in the pre-exilic writings. Whereas in the historical books the king dominated the cult, in the priestly code it was the high priest, whose regal status, according to Wellhausen, could only reflect a period when the civil government of Judah was in the hands of foreigners and Israel was not so much a people as a church—the post-exilic period.

One need only consult such representative works as Max Loehr's *A History of Religion in the Old Testament*, 1936, *e.g.* pp. 136–137; W. O. E. Oesterley and T. H. Robinson's *Hebrew Religion*, 1930, *e.g.* p. 255; and R. H. Pfeiffer's *IOT*, 1948, *e.g.* pp. 556–557, to see the stubbornness with which Wellhausen's reconstruction has persisted.

III. Some reactions to Wellhausen's reconstruction

Among the conservatives who have set out to tumble Wellhausen's structure, three names are noteworthy: James Orr (*The Problem of the Old Testament*, 1906), O. T. Allis (*The Five Books of Moses*², 1949, pp. 185–196), G. Ch. Aalders (*A Short Introduction to the Pentateuch*, 1949, pp. 66–71).

Basic to Wellhausen's reconstruction is the assumption that the Levites who were invited in Dt. 18:6–7 to serve at the central shrine were the priests who had been disfranchised by the abolition of their high places during Josiah's reform. But solid evidence for this assumption is lacking. In fact, 2 Ki. 23:9 affirms the opposite: the priests of the high places did not come up to the altar of the Lord in Jerusalem. The critical view that priests and Levites are not clearly distinguished in Deuteronomy has been discussed above, where it was seen that a clear distinction was made between them in regard to the people's responsibility towards them (Dt. 18:3–5, 6–8). Nor can the view that the phrase 'the priests the Levites' (Dt. 17:9, 18; 18:1; 24:8; 27:9), not found elsewhere in the Pentateuch, argues for the identity of the two offices in Deuteronomy be maintained. The phrase serves merely to link the priests with their tribe. Confirmation for this seems to be found in 2 Ch. 23:18 and 30:27, where the 'Levitical priests' are distinguished from other Levites (30:25), gatekeepers, *etc.* (23:19).

Attention has frequently been directed by Wellhausen and others to the apparent discrepancy between the law of *tithes in Nu. 18:21ff. (*cf.* Lv. 27:30ff.), which earmarks the tithes for the Levites, and the counterpart in Dt. 14:22ff., which allows Israelites to eat of the tithes in a sacrificial meal while enjoining them to share it with the Levites. Judaism has traditionally reconciled these passages by calling the tithe of Deuteronomy 'a second tithe', *e.g.* in the Talmudic tractate *Ma'aśer Sheni*. This explanation may not be so acceptable as James Orr's (*op. cit.*, pp. 188–189): the laws of Deuteronomy, he held, apply to a time when the tithe-laws (and those relating to levitical cities) could not be fully enforced, since the conquest was not complete and there was no central agency to enforce them. In other words, Nu. 18:21ff. deals with Israel's ideal while Dt. 14:22ff. is an interim programme for the conquest and settlement.

Pivotal in Wellhausen's reconstruction is his interpretation of Ezekiel's denunciation of the Levites (44:4ff.), in which he finds the origin of the cleavage between priests (the sons of Zadok) and Levites (priests who had previously engaged in idolatry at the high places). But James Orr (*op. cit.*, pp. 315–319, 520) calls attention to the deplorable condition of the priesthood just prior to Ezekiel's time and points out that Ezekiel did not establish the law but rather re-established it by depriving Levites of privileges not rightly theirs, which they had usurped during the Monarchy and by demoting idolatrous priests to the already well-established lower rank of Levite. Furthermore, the ideal context of Ezekiel's pronouncement suggests that the degradation in view may never have been carried out, at least not literally. The tone of Ezekiel stands in contradiction to that of the priestly code in that the latter knows nothing of priestly degradation but stresses divine appointment. In addition, the priests in P are not Zadok's sons but Aaron's sons.

The office of high priest has been largely relegated to the post-exilic period by the Wellhausenian school. Though the title itself occurs only in 2 Ki. 12:10; 22:4, 8; 23:4 in pre-exilic writings (usually considered by documentary critics to be post-exilic interpolations), the existence of the office seems to be indicated by the title '*the* priest' (*e.g.* Ahimelech, 1 Sa. 21:2; Jehoiada, 2 Ki. 11:9–10, 15; Urijah, 2 Ki. 16:10ff.) and by the fact that a priesthood of any size at all involves an administrative chief, even if the king is the head of the cult. (*Cf.* J. Pedersen, *Israel*, 3–4, p. 189.)

In *The Religion of Israel*, 1960, Yehezkel Kaufmann examines a number of Wellhausen's key conclusions and finds them wanting. The high priest, for instance, far from being a royal figure reflecting the post-exilic religious leaders, faithfully mirrors the conditions of the military camp which is subject to the authority of Moses, not Aaron (*op. cit.*, pp. 184–187).

Kaufmann turns his attention to 'the one pillar of Wellhausen's structure that has not been shaken by later criticism'—the reconstruction of the relationship between priests and Levites. Noting the absence of evidence for the demotion of the rural priests, he then calls attention to a basic weakness in the documentary view: 'Nothing can make plausible a theory that the very priests who demoted their colleagues saw fit to endow them with the amplest clerical due, a theory the more improbable when the great number of priests and paucity of Levites at the Restoration (4,289 priests, Ezr. 2:36ff.; 341 Levites plus 392 temple servants, Ezr. 2:43ff.) is borne in mind' (p. 194).

Why did the priests preserve the story of the Levites' faithfulness during Aaron's defection (Ex. 32:26–29), while glossing over the idolatry, which, for Wellhausen, was responsible for their degradation, and according the Levites the honour of divine appointment rather than punishment? After affirming that the Levites are clearly a distinct class in the Exile, Kaufmann points out that they could not have developed as a distinct class in the brief period between Josiah's reform (to say nothing of Ezekiel's denunciation) and the return, and that on foreign soil.

Kaufmann's own reconstruction may not prove entirely satisfactory. He denies a hereditary connection between the sons of Aaron and the Levites, since he deems the Aaronids to be 'the ancient, pagan priesthood of Israel' (p. 197), and thus rejects the firm biblical tradition connecting Moses, Aaron and the Levites (*cf.* Ex. 4:14). In the golden calf incident the old secular tribe of Levi rallied with Moses against Aaron, but was forced to yield the privilege of altar service to the Aaronids (p. 198), while they themselves had to be content as *hierodules*. This raises the question as to how, apart from a connection with Moses, the Aaronids survived the catastrophe of the golden calf and continued as priests. Kaufmann's opinion that the Deuteronomic legislation was compiled during the latter part of the Monarchy and thus is considerably later than the priestly writings may be more of a return to an old critical position (*i.e.* that of Th. Noeldeke and others) than a fresh thrust at Wellhausen.

Rejecting the linear view of institutional evolution which was a main plank in Wellhausen's platform, W. F. Albright notes that Israel would be unique among her neighbours had she not enjoyed during the period of the Judges and afterwards a high priest, usually called (in accordance with Semitic practice) *the priest* (*Archaeology and the Religion of Israel*[3], 1953, pp. 107–108). The lack of emphasis on the high-priestly office during the Monarchy represents a decline, while, after the Monarchy's collapse, the priesthood again rose to a position of prestige. Albright accepts the historicity of Aaron and finds no reason for not considering Zadok an Aaronid. Concluding that the Levite had first a functional (see above) and then a tribal significance, Albright points out that Levites may sometimes have been promoted to priests and that 'we are not justified either in throwing overboard the standard Israelite tradition regarding priests and Levites, or in considering these classes as hard and fast genealogical groups' (*op. cit.*, p. 110).

The assumption that the tabernacle in the wilderness was the idealization of the Temple and had no historical existence, so basic to Wellhausen's reconstruction, has now largely been abandoned (although *cf.* R. H. Pfeiffer's *Religion in the Old Testament*, 1961, pp. 77–78). Both arks and portable tent-shrines are attested among Israel's neighbours, as archaeology has revealed. Far from being figments of a later period, these, as John Bright notes, are 'heritages of Israel's primitive desert faith' (*A History of Israel*, 1960, pp. 146–147).

Obviously the last word has not been said on this puzzling problem of the relationship between priests and Levites. The data from the period of the conquest and settlement are meagre. It is hazardous to assume that the pentateuchal legislation, representing the ideal as it often does, was ever carried out literally. Even such stalwart kings as David, Jehoshaphat, Hezekiah and Josiah were not able to ensure complete conformity to the Mosaic pattern. But it is even more tenuous to hold that because laws were not enforced they did not exist. The combination of argumentation from silence, straight-line evolutionary reconstruction, and a resort to textual emendations and literary excisions when passages prove troublesome, has resulted more than once in interpretations of biblical history which have proved to be too facile to stand permanently in the face of the complexities of biblical data and Semitic culture. Wellhausen's ingenious reconstruction of the history of the Levites may prove to be a case in point.

BIBLIOGRAPHY. In addition to works cited above, R. Brinker, *The Influence of Sanctuaries in Early Israel*, 1946, pp. 65ff.; R. de Vaux, *Ancient Israel: Its Life and Institutions*, E.T. 1961; A. Cody, *A History of the Old Testament Priesthood*, 1969; M. Haran *et al.*, 'Priests and Priesthood', *EJ*, 13, 1970; H.-J. Kraus, *Worship in Israel*, E.T. 1966.

IV. Priesthood in the New Testament

a. Continuity with the Old Testament

With the single exception of the priest of Zeus, who wrongly seeks to venerate Paul and Barnabas in Lystra (Acts 14:13), references to priest and high priest in the Gospels and Acts assume an historical and religious continuity with the OT: no explanation is needed of the priest's function in the story of the good Samaritan (Lk. 10:31) or of the duties of the 'priest named Zechariah', father of John the Baptist (Lk. 1:5); Jesus recognized the lawful function of the priests in declaring lepers clean (Mt.

8:4; Mk. 1:44; Lk. 5:14; 17:14; see Lv. 14:3). Jesus also pitted the freer practice of some OT priests against the legalism of his opponents (Mt. 12:4–5). He had no basic quarrel with the prescribed functions of the Temple and priesthood.

b. Conflict with Judaism

The lion's share of references to priests, especially high priests (or chief priests as RSV usually has them) are found, however, in contexts of conflict. Matthew depicts the high priests as actively involved in the gospel events from beginning (Mt. 2:4) to end (Mt. 28:11). Their opposition mounts as the claims and mission of Jesus become clear, *e.g.* in his challenge to the Sabbath legislation (Mt. 12:1–7; Mk. 2:23–27; Lk. 6:1–5) and in his parables that censured the religious leaders (Mt. 21:45–46). This conflict to the death was anticipated immediately after Peter's confession at Caesarea Philippi (Mt. 16:21; Mk. 8:31; Lk. 9:22), was intensified at the Palm Sunday reception and the subsequent Temple cleansing (Mt. 21:15, 23, 45–46; Mk. 11:27; Lk. 19:47–48; 20:1), and reached its bitter climax in the arrest and trial (Mt. 26–27). The Fourth Gospel also bears witness to the conflict (Jn. 7:32, 45; 11:47, where Pharisees are the partners in crime; 12:10, where the hostility focuses on Lazarus; 18:19, 22, 24, 35, where Caiaphas' role in Jesus' trial is stressed; *cf.* 19:15).

The chief priests (*archiereus*) rarely acted alone in their desire to crush Jesus' influence. Depending on the issue and circumstances, they were joined by other officials of the Sanhedrin (*archontes*, Lk. 23:13; 24:20), by scribes (*grammateis*, Mt. 2:4; 20:18; 21:15), by scribes and elders (*grammateis, presbyteroi*, Mt. 16:21; 27:41; Mk. 8:31; 11:27; 14:43, 53; Lk. 9:22), by elders (Mt. 21:23; 26:3). The singular 'high priest' usually refers to the president of the Sanhedrin (*e.g.* Caiaphas, Mt. 26:57; Jn. 18:13; Annas, Lk. 3:2; Jn. 18:24; Acts 4:6; Ananias, Acts 23:2; 24:1). The plural 'chief priests' describes members of the high-priestly families who serve in the Sanhedrin; ruling and former high priests together with members of the prominent priestly families (Acts 4:6). J. Jeremias has argued that 'chief priests' include Temple officers like treasurer and captain of police (*Jerusalem in the Time of Jesus*, E.T. 1969, pp. 160ff.).

The death and resurrection of Jesus did not quell the conflict, as Acts amply documents. The apostolic witness to the resurrection drew the Sadducees into the struggle alongside the chief priests and other Temple officials (Acts 4:1; 5:17). Priestly involvement in the story of Saul of Tarsus is noteworthy. The proposed persecution of Christians in Damascus apparently had the official sanction of the high priest (Acts 9:1–2, 14); the 'itinerant Jewish exorcists' who sought to duplicate Paul's miracles in Ephesus were described as 'seven sons of a Jewish high priest named Sceva' (Acts 19:13–14); like his Master, Paul stood trial before a high priest, Ananias, who also pressed charges against him before the Roman governors Felix and Festus (Acts 24:1ff.; 25:1–3). Almost nothing in the apostle's life illustrates so clearly the radical change wrought by his conversion than the dramatic reversal in his relationships to the priestly establishment: the beginning of his story found him riding with the hounds; the end, running with the foxes.

c. Consummation in Christ

At root this conflict sprang from the Christian conviction and the Jewish suspicion that Jesus' life, death, resurrection and ascension spelt the eclipse if not the destruction of the old priestly structures. Jesus' own teaching had placed him at the heart of a new sacerdotal structure: 'something greater than the temple is here' (Mt. 12:6); 'destroy this temple, and in three days I will raise it up' (Jn. 2:19); 'for the Son of man also came not to be served but to serve, and to give his life as a ransom for many' (Mk. 10:45).

Of the NT writers, it is the author of Hebrews who picks up these threads and weaves them into a many-coloured fabric. In its passion to prove that the Christian faith is superior to, indeed has replaced, the OT patterns of worship, Hebrews presses persistently its claim that Jesus has been appointed by God (5:5–10) to be the new, the true high priest who can finally deal with human sin. His priesthood, surpassing Aaron's (7:11) and reaching back to Melchizedek's (7:15–17), contains the perfection missing in the older sacrificial system (7:18): 1. It is based on God's own oath (7:20–22); 2. It is permanent because it is centred in the eternal Christ (7:23–25); 3. It partakes of the perfection of Christ who had no need to be purged of sin, as did the sons of Aaron (7:26–28); 4. It continues in the heavens where God himself has erected the true sanctuary of which Moses' tent was but 'a copy and shadow' (8:1–7); 5. It is the fulfilment of God's promise of a new covenant (8:8–13); 6. Its sacrifice needs no repeating but was rendered 'once for all' (7:27; 9:12); 7. Its offering was not 'the blood of bulls and goats', unable to take away sins, but 'the body of Jesus Christ', through which believers are sanctified (10:4, 10); 8. Its result is full and regular access to God for all Christians not just a priestly order (10:11–22); 9. Its promises and hopes are assured by the faithfulness of God and the assurance of Christ's second coming (9:28; 10:23); 10. Its full forgiveness provides the highest motivation for our works of love and righteousness (10:19–25); 11. Its effectiveness in the lives of God's people is guaranteed by Christ's constant intercession (7:25). Though Paul did not choose to make Christ's priesthood a dominant theme in his writings (probably because his ministry was largely to Gentiles, for whom a knowledge of their freedom from law and their new place in God's purpose was the pre-eminent need), we can be grateful that the rich insights of Hebrews are among God's gifts in the canon of Scripture. See G. E. Ladd, *A Theology of the New Testament*, 1974, pp. 578–584.

d. Commission of the church

As Christ's body and as his new Israel (*cf.* Ex. 19:6), the church is anointed to a priesthood in the world—a mediatorial service that declares the will of God to humankind and bears human needs before God's throne in prayer. Two related duties of this priesthood are mentioned by Peter: 1. 'to offer spiritual sacrifices acceptable to God through Jesus Christ' (1 Pet. 2:5), *i.e.* to worship God and do his loving will; 2. to 'declare the wonderful deeds of him who called you out of darkness into his marvellous light', *i.e.* to bear witness to his saving work in the world (1 Pet. 2:9).

Peter's 'royal priesthood' is echoed and amplified in Rev. where the beloved and forgiven church is called 'a kingdom, priests to his God and Father' (Rev. 1:6; *cf.* 5:10; 20:6). This royal role not only entails obedience to Christ 'the ruler of kings on earth' (Rev. 1:5) but also participation in his rule over others: 'and they shall reign on earth' (Rev. 5:10; *cf.* 20:6). Here the circle of conflict has taken a full turn: the people of Christ, afflicted by a priesthood that opposed their Master, will share in his victory as triumphant high priest and demonstrate his loving sovereignty in a hostile world.

The church's priesthood in the NT is corporate: no individual minister or leader is called 'priest'. The post-apostolic writings, however, move quickly in that direction: Clement (AD 95–96) describes Christian ministry in terms of high priest, priests and Levites (*1 Clem.* 40–44); the *Didache* (13:3) likens prophets to high priests. Tertullian (*On Baptism* 17) and Hippolytus (*Refutation of All Heresies*, preface) seemed to have pioneered the use of the titles 'priest' and 'high priest' for Christian ministers (*c.* AD 200).

BIBLIOGRAPHY. T. W. Manson, *Ministry and Priesthood: Christ's and Ours*, 1958; R. de Vaux, *Ancient Israel*, 1961, pp. 271–517; bibliography, pp. 537–552; H. Seebas, *NIDNTT* 2, pp. 232–236; J. Baehr, *NIDNTT* 3, pp. 32–44. D.A.H.

PRINCE. A variety of Heb. words are translated 'prince', but are not always so rendered. 'Ruler', 'leader', 'captain', *etc.*, are also used. The frequency of the use of the word is an effect (still discernible in RSV) of the AV translators' so rendering, though not with entire consistency, the LXX *archōn*, which itself represents no less than 20 Heb. words, the most important being the word for 'head', *rō'š*.

The Heb. words fall into two categories. First, loan-words from other languages, usually referring to foreign dignitaries. For example, *xšaQ- rapavan*, 'satrap', and *fratama*, 'foremost', are Persian words transliterated in Dn. 3:2, *etc.* (Aram. *'ăḥašdarpan*), 1:3 (Heb. plur. *parṯ'mîm*). The *satrapies of the Persian empire were originally coextensive with the conquered kingdoms. But Darius reduced the number to twenty (Herodotus 3. 89–94). The power of the satrap was checked by certain officials responsible directly to the Great King, but otherwise approximated to that of a vassal king.

Secondly, words of indigenous origin representing the following salient ideas: (1) *śar*, 'exercising dominion', whether as supreme or subordinate to an overlord; (2) *nāgîḏ*, 'being in front', especially of military leader; (3) *nāśî'*, 'being exalted'; (4) *nāḏîḇ*, 'a volunteer', perhaps signifying a contrast with those whom a king might compel to fight on his behalf; (5) *qāṣîn*, 'a judge'.

Ezekiel often uses *nāśî'* of the Messiah: it corresponds with his conception of the true David (Ezk. 37:24–25). In Daniel, *śar* and *nāgîḏ* are used of him, corresponding to the military imagery with which the cosmic struggle is depicted. *śar* is also used of the guardian angels of countries, and particularly of Michael (Dn. 10:13, 21).

In the NT *archōn* is used of Satan, 'ruler of this world', and in the plural, of the Roman and Jewish authorities ('rulers'). It is once used of Christ (Rev. 1:5), 'ruler of the kings of the earth', but elsewhere where 'prince' is used in AV. The LXX *archēgos* (for Heb. *nāśî'* and *qāṣîn*) is used of Christ (*cf.* Acts 5:31), gathering from its Greek connections the additional idea of 'author' (Acts 3:15) and 'pioneer' (Heb. 2:10; 12:2).

J.B.J.

PRISON.

I. In the Old Testament

The first mention of a prison in Scripture is that of *Joseph in Egypt (Gn. 39:20–23). For this the Hebrew text uses a special term *bêṯ-sōhar*; *sōhar* is usually compared with other Semitic words for 'round' or 'enclosure', and Joseph's prison is therefore commonly considered to be, or be in, a fortress. The comparison of Heb. *sōhar* with Egyp. *Ṯ'rw*, 'Silē' (mod. Qantara), is false, as this word is really *Ṯl* (J. Vergote, *Joseph en Égypte*, 1959, pp. 25–28). However, there is an Egyp. word *ṯ'rt*, occurring as early as *c.* 1900 BC as well as later, which means 'enclosed building', 'store', '(ship's) cabin', and this might just conceivably be connected with *sōhar*. Egyp. prisons served as forced-labour compounds, as 'lock-ups' and as places of remand for people like Joseph awaiting trial. The butler and baker were put in *mišmār*, detention, virtually house-arrest, in Joseph's prison (Gn. 40:2–3) until their case was decided. Joseph's brothers were likewise detained for 3 days (Gn. 42:17, 19). After capture by the Philistines, Samson was kept in prison, the 'house of the prisoners' (Jdg. 16:21, 25; lit. 'those bound'); a very similar term is used in Ec. 4:14.

In Judah the guardrooms of the palace guards served as a temporary prison for Jeremiah (32:2, 8, 12; 33:1; 37:21; 38:28; *cf.* also Ne. 3:25; 12:39). Both there and in a private residence, a cistern could be used as a dungeon, which would often be very unpleasant (Je. 37:16, 20; 38:6, 13) and dark (Is. 42:7), a symbol of bondage from which the Lord's servant should deliver his people (Acts 26:15–18; Lk. 1:79). Nor was Jeremiah the only prophet imprisoned for his faithfulness in declaring God's message: Asa of Judah put Hanani the seer into the stocks (2 Ch. 16:10), and Ahab had Micaiah put in prison on rations of bread and water (1 Ki. 22:27; 2 Ch. 18:26). Defeated kings were sometimes imprisoned by their conquerors: so Hoshea of Israel by the Assyrians (2 Ki. 17:4), Jehoiachin of Judah by Nebuchadrezzar (*cf.* Je. 24:1, 5; D. J. Wiseman, *Chronicles of Chaldaean Kings*, pp. 33–35, 73), and Zedekiah of Judah likewise (Je. 52:11). At Babylon Jehoiachin was but one of many noble captives and artisans detained under 'house-arrest' at the royal palace and environs. Ration-tablets for him, his five sons and many other foreigners were found at Babylon (*ANET*, 308b; *DOTT*, pp. 84–86; E. F. Weidner, *Mélanges R. Dussaud*, 2, 1939, pp. 923–935; Albright, *BA* 5, 1942, pp. 49–55). Eventually Evil-merodach granted him a greater measure of freedom (2 Ki. 25:27, 29; Je. 52:31, 33). Ezekiel (19:9) pictures Jehoiachin being brought to Babylon in a cage; for a much earlier Egyp. picture of a Semitic prince as a prisoner in a cage, see P. Montet, *L'Égypte et la Bible*, 1959, p. 73, fig. 12.

K.A.K.

II. In the New Testament

Four Greek words are translated by 'prison' in the EVV. John the Baptist was imprisoned in a *desmōtērion*, a 'place of bonds'. This was at Herod's fortress at Machaerus in Peraea, E of the Dead Sea (Jos., *Ant.* 18. 119), where two dungeons have been discovered, one still showing traces of fetters. *phylakē*, a 'place of guarding', is the most general and frequently used term. It suggests a place where the prisoners were closely watched. The chief priests imprisoned the apostles (Acts 5:19) in what is also called a *tērēsis dēmosia*, a 'public place of watching' (*cf.* Acts 4:3).

When Herod put Peter in prison, probably in the fortress of Antonia, where Paul was later lodged (Acts 21:34; 23:30) and referred to here as an *oikēma*, 'house', the apostle was guarded continually by four soldiers, two chained to him and two outside the door (Acts 12:3–6). Beyond this there would appear to have been another guard and then the iron outer gate (Acts 12:10). At Philippi Paul was in custody in the town jail, under the charge of a keeper, where there was an inner, perhaps underground, chamber containing stocks (Acts 16:24). These would have several holes, allowing the legs to be forced wide apart to ensure greater security and greater pain. In Caesarea Paul was imprisoned (Acts 23:35) in Herod's castle, but when a prisoner at Rome he was allowed to stay in his own lodging, with a soldier always chained to him (Acts 28:16, 30). D.H.W.

PROCONSUL (Gk. *anthypatos*, AV 'deputy'). In the Roman empire as organized by Augustus this was the title of governors of provinces which were administered by the Senate because they did not require a standing army. Proconsuls mentioned in the NT are L. Sergius *Paullus, proconsul of Cyprus when Paul and Barnabas visited that island *c.* AD 47 (Acts 13:7), and L. Junius *Gallio, whose proconsulship of Achaia (AD 51–2) overlapped Paul's 18-month stay in Corinth (Acts 18:12). In Acts 19:38 'proconsuls' may be a generalizing plural; the proconsul of Asia had recently been assassinated (October AD 54) and his successor had not yet arrived. F.F.B.

PROCURATOR. In Roman imperial administration the word indicated the financial officer of a province, but was also used as the title of the governor of a Roman province of the third class, such as Judaea (Gk. *epitropos*; but in the NT the procurator of Judaea is regularly described as the 'governor', Gk. *hēgemōn*). *Judaea was governed by imperial procurators or prefects from AD 6 to 41 and from 44 to 66. Three are mentioned in the NT: Pontius *Pilate, AD 26–36 (Mt. 27:2, *etc.*), Antonius *Felix, 52–59 (Acts 23:24ff.) and Porcius *Festus, 59–62 (Acts 24:27ff.). The procurators were generally drawn from the equestrian order (Felix, a freedman, was an exception). They had auxiliary troops at their disposal and were generally responsible for military and financial administration, but were subject to the superior authority of the imperial legate (propraetor) of Syria. Their seat of government was Caesarea. From the Pilate inscription found at Caesarea in 1961, where he is called 'prefect' of Judaea, it has been inferred that before AD 41 the governors of Judaea were officially called 'prefects', but Tacitus gives Pilate the title 'procurator' (*Ann.* 15. 44). F.F.B.

PROMISE. There is in the Heb. OT no special term for the concept or act of promising. Where our English translations say that someone promised something, the Hebrew simply states that someone said or spoke (*'āmar*, *dāḇar*) some word with future reference. In the NT the technical term, *epangelia*, appears—chiefly in Acts, Galatians, Romans and Hebrews.

A promise is a word that goes forth into unfilled time. It reaches ahead of its speaker and its recipient, to mark an appointment between them in the future. A promise may be an assurance of continuing or future action on behalf of someone: 'I will be with you', 'They that mourn shall be comforted', 'If we confess our sins, God will forgive us our sins.' It may be a solemn agreement of lasting, mutual (if unequal) relationship: as in the covenants. It may be the announcement of a future event: 'When you have brought the people from Egypt, you will serve God on this mountain.' The study of biblical promises must therefore take in far more than the actual occurrences of the word in the EVV. (See also *WORD, *PROPHECY, *COVENANT and *OATHS.) An oath often accompanied the word of promise (Ex. 6:8; Dt. 9:5; Heb. 6:13ff.).

That what he has spoken with his mouth he can and will perform with his hand is the biblical sign manual of God, for his word does not return void. Unlike men and heathen gods, he knows and commands the future (1 Ki. 8:15, 24; Is. 41:4, 26; 43:12, 19, *etc.*; Rom. 4:21; *cf.* Pascal, *Pensées*, 693). Through the historical books, a pattern of divine promise and historical fulfilment is traced (G. von Rad, *Studies in Deuteronomy*, 1953, pp. 74ff.), expressive of this truth.

The point of convergence of the OT promises (to Abraham, Moses, David and the Fathers through the prophets) is Jesus Christ. All the promises of God are confirmed in him, and through him affirmed by the church in the 'Amen' of its worship (2 Cor. 1:20). The OT quotations and allusions in the Gospel narratives indicate this fulfilment. The Magnificat and the Benedictus rejoice that God has kept his word. The promised Word has become flesh. The new covenant has been inaugurated—upon the 'better promises' prophesied by Jeremiah (Je. 31; Heb. 8:6–13). Jesus is its guarantee (Heb. 7:22), and the Holy Spirit of promise its first instalment (Eph. 1:13–14).

Awaiting the promise of Christ's coming again and of the new heavens and a new earth (2 Pet. 3:4, 9, 13), the church sets forth on her missionary task with the assurance of his presence (Mt. 28:20) and with the news that 'the promise of the Father'—the Holy Spirit (after Joel 2:28)—is given to Jew and pagan in Jesus Christ, fulfilling the promise to Abraham of universal blessing through his posterity. The promise is correlated to faith and open to all who, by imitating Abraham's faith, become 'children of the promise' (Gal. 3; Rom. 4; 9). (*ESCHATOLOGY, *SCRIPTURE.)

BIBLIOGRAPHY. J. Jeremias, *Jesus' Promise to the Nations*, E.T. 1958; W. G. Kümmel, *Promise and Fulfilment*, E.T.[2] 1961; F. F. Bruce (ed.), *Promise and Fulfilment: Essays presented to S. H. Hooke*, 1963; J. Moltmann, *Theology of Hope*, E.T. 1967; J. Bright, *Covenant and Promise*, 1977; T. E. Mc Comiskey, *The Covenants of Promise*, 1985; J. Schniewind and G. Friedrich, *epangellō, etc.*, *TDNT* 2, pp. 576–586; E. Hoffmann, *NIDNTT* 3, pp. 68–74. J.H.

PROMISED LAND. 'The land of promise' (Heb. 11:9) refers to Canaan before the Israelites entered it under Joshua. By his covenant with Abraham, God promised to make him 'into a great nation', to be a 'blessing to all the peoples on earth' and have an inheritance of land (Gn. 12:1–2; *cf.* 12:7; 13:15; 24:7). The patriarchs lived in the land as 'sojourners' (Gn. 17:8; 24:4, *etc.*) but the promise was often repeated (Gn. 26:3–4; 13; 35:12; 48:4; 50:24) and provided sustaining hope for the Israelites after the Exodus (Ex. 3:8, 17; Nu. 10:29, *etc.*). The promise became reality under Joshua and reached greatest fulfilment under David and Solomon (2 Sa. 3:10; 1 Ki. 4:21; 8:65; *cf.* Ezk. 47:15–20). The Assyrian and Babylonian invasions led to exile in a 'strange land' (Ps. 137:4), yet prophets predicted a 'restoration' (Is. 27:12–13; 43:19–21; 60:18; Je. 16:15; 23:8; 30–33; Ezk. 36–37; 47–48; Zp. 3:10) which partially occurred under Zerubbabel, Ezra and Nehemiah.

The land 'flowing with milk and honey' (Nu. 13:27; Dt. 6:3) was Yahweh's gracious gift, yet it still had to be conquered (Dt. 1:25; 5:31; 9:6; 11:17). Yahweh remained its owner (Lv. 25:23) and received the first fruits of the land (Dt. 26:9–15) so ownership was not transferred (see Lv. 25:8–10, 13–16). Israel would possess the land 'forever' but the gift was conditional (Dt. 28:63–64; Jos. 23:13, 15; 1 Ki. 9:7; 2 Ki. 17:23; Je. 12:10–12).

The NT says little about the land, despite many references to the divine promises being fulfilled in Jesus (*e.g.* 2 Cor. 1:20; *cf.* Rom. 15:8). Some argue that the land is not a NT concern (it is mentioned but passed over in Acts 7:3–7; 13:17–19), but it is more likely that 'the land' is now reinterpreted in the light of Christ. The promise of 'the land' is now seen as an advanced metaphor for the world (Rom. 4:13). It is also understood eschatalogically as a symbol of the heavenly 'rest' (Heb. 4:9). Abraham was looking towards a 'better country – a heavenly one' (11:16). Gentile believers who previously had been 'far away' were now 'brought near as fellow-citizens' (Eph. 2:12–13, 19). So the NT discourages interest in the literal land, as it does in the Temple and the city of Jerusalem (*e.g.* Gal. 4:25–26; Heb. 8:13; 12:22; Rev. 3:12; 11:9; 21:2 – 22:5). This has implications regarding modern Zionism which denies that the promises of the land were fulfilled in Christ (*c.f.* also Lk. 21:24; Rom. 11:26).

Yet we must be wary of over-spiritualizing. In a society with keen ecological concern and often marked by a sense of alienation, the promise of a 'land' for God's people is a continual reminder of the divine concern, both for the earth and for those who feel rootless. Still more, the socio-political background of the 'land' (such that 'land' should be understood as a Hebraic 'concretization' standing for political, social and economic relationships) alerts us to the OT's concern that God's holiness be exemplified and practised in society ('in the land'). Some of the NT references to the 'earth' (a normal translation of *gē*: see *e.g.* Matt. 5:5) need to be seen against this specific Hebraic concern with 'the land'. Thus Wright argues that, whilst emphasizing the typological and 'universalizing' understanding of the 'land' in the NT, we must also understand the 'land' as a paradigm which gives us important principles for society.

BIBLIOGRAPHY. W. Brueggemann, *The Land*, 1977; C. Chapman, *Whose Promised Land?*', 1989; W. D. Davies, *The Gospel and the Land*, 1974; T. Donaldson, *Jesus on the Mountain*, 1985; R. T. France, 'Old Testament Prophecy and the Future of Israel', *TB* 26, 1975, pp. 53–78; J Jeremias, *Jesus' Promise to the Nations*, E.T. 1956; L. Lambert, *The Uniqueness of Israel*, 1979; G. von Rad, 'Promised Land and Yahweh's Land in the Hexateuch', in *Problems of the Hexateuch and Other Essays*, E.T. 1966, pp. 79–93; P. W. L. Walker (ed.), *Jerusalem Past & Present in the Purposes of God*, 1994; C. J. H. Wright, *Living as the People of God*, 1983; *God's People in God's Land*, 1990.

P.W.L.W.

PROPHECY, PROPHETS.

I. The prophetic office

a. The normative prophet

The first person whom the Bible calls a prophet (Heb. *nāḇî'*) was Abraham (Gn. 20:7; *cf.* Ps. 105:15), but OT prophecy received its normative form in the life and person of Moses, who constituted a standard of comparison for all future prophets (Dt. 18:15–19; 34:10; *MESSIAH). Every feature which characterized the true prophet of Yahweh in the classical tradition of OT prophecy was first found in Moses.

He received a specific and personal call from God. The initiative in making a prophet rests with God (Ex. 3:1–4:17; *cf.* Is. 6; Je. 1:4–19; Ezk. 1–3; Ho. 1:2; Am. 7:14–15; Jon. 1:1), and it is only the false prophet who dares to take the office upon himself (Je. 14:14; 23:21). The primary object and effect of the call was an introduction into God's presence, as the passages noted above show. This was the 'secret' or 'counsel' of the Lord (1 Ki. 22:19; Je. 23:22; Am. 3:7). The prophet stood before men, as a man who had been made to stand before God (1 Ki. 17:1; 18:15).

Again, the prophetic awareness of history stemmed from Moses. When Isaiah makes his tremendous polemic against idolatry, one of his most potent contentions, that Yahweh alone is the Author of prophecy and that the idols are at best wise after the event (*e.g.* 45:20–22), stems directly from Moses and the Exodus. Yahweh sent Moses into Egypt possessed of the clues necessary to interpret the great events which were to follow. History became revelation because there was added to the historical situation a man prepared beforehand to say what it meant. Moses was not left to struggle for the meaning of events as or after they happened; he was forewarned of events and of their significance by the verbal communications of God. So it was with all the prophets. Alone of the nations of antiquity, Israel had a true awareness of history. They owed it to the prophets, and, under the Lord of history, the prophets owed it to Moses.

Likewise they owed to him their ethical and social concern. Even before his call Moses concerned himself with the social welfare of his people (Ex. 2:11ff.; *cf.* v. 17), and afterwards, as the prophetic lawgiver, he outlined the most humane and philanthropic code of the ancient world, concerned for the helpless (Dt. 24:19–22, *etc.*) and the enemy of the oppressor (*e.g.* Lv. 19:9ff.).

Many of the prophets were found confronting their kings and playing an active, statesman's part in national affairs. This was a function of the prophet which found its prototype in Moses, who legislated for the nation, and was even called 'king' (Dt. 33:5). It is interesting that the first two kings of Israel were also prophets, but this union of offices did not continue, and the Mosaic–theocratic rule was prolonged by the association of the anointed king and the anointed prophet.

We also see in Moses that combination of proclamation and prediction which is found in all the prophets. This will concern us in greater detail presently, as a feature of prophecy at large. We will pause only to show that Moses established the norm here also, namely, that in the interests of speaking to the present situation the prophet often undertakes to enlarge upon events yet to come. It is this interlocking of proclamation and prediction which distinguishes the true prophet from the mere prognosticator. Even when Moses uttered his great prophecy of the coming Prophet (Dt. 18:15ff.) he was dealing with the very pressing problems of the relation of the people of God to the practices and allurements of pagan cults.

Two other features characteristic of the prophets who were to succeed him are found in Moses. Many of the prophets used symbols in the delivery of their message (*e.g.* Je. 19:1ff.; Ezk. 4:1ff.). Moses used the uplifted hand (Ex. 17:8ff.) and the uplifted serpent (Nu. 21:8), not to mention the highly symbolic cultus which he mediated to the nation. And finally, the intercessory aspect of the prophetic task was also displayed in him. He was 'for the people to Godward' (Ex. 18:19, AV; Nu. 27:5) and on at least one notable occasion literally stood in the breach as a man of prayer (Ex. 32:30ff.; Dt. 9:18ff.; *cf.* 1 Ki. 13:6; 2 Ki. 19:4; Je. 7:16; 11:14).

b. The titles of the prophets

Two general descriptions appear to have been used for prophets: the first, 'man of God', describes how they appeared to their fellow-men. This title was first used of Moses (Dt. 33:1) and continued in use till the end of the Monarchy (*e.g.* 1 Sa. 2:27; 9:6; 1 Ki. 13:1, *etc.*). That it was intended to express the difference of character between the prophet and other men is made perfectly clear by the Shunammite: 'I perceive that this is a holy man of God . . .' (2 Ki. 4:9). The other general title was 'his, your or my servant'. It does not appear that any ever addressed the prophet as 'servant of God', but God often described the prophets as 'my servants' and consequently the other pronouns, 'his' and 'your', were also used (*e.g.* 2 Ki. 17:13, 23; 21:10; 24:2; Ezr. 9:11; Je. 7:25). Here the other relationship of the prophet, that towards God, is expressed, and this also was first a title of Moses (*e.g.* Jos. 1:1–2).

There are three Hebrew words used of the prophet: *nāḇî'*, *rō'eh* and *ḥōzeh*. The first of these is always translated 'prophet'; the second, which is, in form, an active participle of the verb 'to see', is translated 'seer'; the third, also an active participle of another verb 'to see', is unfortunately without distinctive English equivalent and is translated either 'prophet' (*e.g.* Is. 30:10) or 'seer' (*e.g.* 1 Ch. 29:29).

The derivation of *nāḇî'* has been the subject of long debate. The word can be traced to an Akkadian root, and the choice is between the prophet as one who is called, or one who calls, *i.e.* to men in the name of God. Either of these will admirably suit the nature of the prophet as found in the OT. The possibility that the prophet is one who calls to God, in prayer, has not been canvassed, but that too, and apparently from the start (Gn. 20:7), was a mark of a prophetic man.

Equally extensive discussion has centred on the relation of the three words *nāḇî'*, *rō'eh* and *ḥōzeh* to each other. Verses such as 1 Ch. 29:29, which appear to use the words with great discrimination (Gad is described in the Heb. as *ḥōzeh*), suggest that we ought to find a precise shade of meaning in each word. This, however, is not borne out by an examination of OT usage as a whole. The use of the words falls into two periods, marked out by 1 Sa. 9:9: first, there was the period when *nāḇî'* and *rō'eh* meant something different, the early period; then came the period, in which the author of 1 Sa. 9:9 lived, when *nāḇî'* had taken on the force of a synonym of *rō'eh*, with or without losing its own earlier meaning. The source document for the early period is 1 Sa. 9–10, and it certainly seems that we can decide the force of the two words as far as those chapters are concerned: the *nāḇî'* is a member of a group, given to corporate and infectious ecstasy (1 Sa. 10:5–6, 10–13; 19:20–24), whereas the *rō'eh* is solitary, and altogether a more important and impressive person. Out of a total of ten occurrences of the title, it is used six times of Samuel (1 Sa. 9:11, 18–19; 1 Ch. 9:22; 26:28; 29:29). He, therefore, demonstrates the *rō'eh par excellence*.

However, when we move to the later period indicated in 1 Sa. 9:9 it is impossible to be so precise. While it is noticeable that throughout Chronicles the *ḥōzeh* is always (except in 2 Ch. 29:30) mentioned in association with the king, the attractive suggestion that he was employed as a resident clairvoyant is not in accordance with the evidence. Even in Chronicles he often acts precisely as a *nāḇî'* would have done (*e.g.* 2 Ch. 19:2; 33:18), and the task most frequently attributed to him was that of court historian —a task equally found in the *nāḇî'* and the *rō'eh* (2 Ch. 9:29; 12:15; *cf.* 1 Ch. 29:29).

In general OT usage every shade of meaning in the verb *ḥāzâ* can be paralleled in the verb *rā'â*: both are used in connection with divination (Zc. 10:2; Ezk. 21:21), a connection which they share also with the *nāḇî'* (Mi. 3:11); both are used for the perception of the meaning of events (Ps. 46:8; Is. 5:12), and of the assessment of character (Ps. 11:4, 7; 1 Sa. 16:1); both are used of the vision of God (Ps. 27:4; Is. 6:5), and of prophetic activity (Is. 1:1; Ezk. 13:3); both are used of seeing vengeance carried out (Pss. 58:10; 54:7). In Is. 29:10 *nāḇî'* and *ḥōzeh* are parallel; in Is. 30:10, *rō'eh* and *ḥōzeh* are parallel; in Am. 7:12ff. Amaziah addresses Amos as *ḥōzeh*, urging him to prophesy (*nibbā'*) in Judah, and Amos replies that he is not a *nāḇî'*; in Ezk. 13:9 the reverse procedure is found: the noun *nāḇî'* is the subject of the verb *ḥāzâ*. These references could be prolonged extensively, and we conclude that the words are synonymous.

c. Foretelling and forthtelling

Too often in studies of the phenomenon of prophecy lip-service has been paid to the uniqueness of this movement in Israel, and at the same time it has been brought under judgment and criticism as though it were not unique, and as though the evidence could be explained on purely rationalistic grounds. We have only one mine of information about the OT prophet, however, and that is the OT itself, which must therefore be treated as a primary source document.

The prophet was first a man of the word of God. Even when he seemed to undertake other functions, such as the elaborate 'miming' of Ezekiel, it was subordinated to the interests of bringing the word of God to his fellow men. This word was not, so to speak, a mere passive opinion, as though

God were anxious simply that men should be aware how he saw matters before they decided for themselves. It was rather the prophets' conviction that the proclamation of God's word radically changed the whole situation. For example, Is. 28–29 shows us a picture of a people struggling for a satisfactory solution to a pressing problem of political expediency, and, in the process, rejecting God's word; chs. 30 onwards reveal the situation which then transpires: the problem is no longer one of political balance of power as between Judah, Assyria and Egypt, but one of spiritual relationship between Judah, Assyria and Egypt, on the one hand, and the word of God, on the other. The word is an active ingredient added to the situation, which is henceforth impelled forward in terms of the word spoken (Is. 40:8; 55:11; see, *e.g.*, *CURSE).

Clearly, however, the prophets spoke to their situation primarily by means of warnings and encouragements concerning the future. Almost every prophet first appears as a foreteller, *e.g.* Am. 1:2. There are three grounds of this practice of foretelling: in the first place, it is clearly necessary, if people are to exercise due moral responsibility in the present, that they should be aware of the future. This at once lifts OT prediction out of the realm of mere prognostication and carnal curiosity. Calls to repentance (*e.g.* Is. 30:6–9) and calls to practical holiness (*e.g.* Is. 2:5) are equally based on a word concerning the future; the vision of wrath to come is made the basis of a present seeking of the mercy of God; the vision of bliss to come calls to a walking in the light now.

Secondly, prediction arises from the fact that the prophets speak in the name of the holy Ruler of history. We have already mentioned that the prophets' call was primarily to a knowledge of God. Out of this knowledge sprang the awareness of what he would do, as he guided history according to the unchangeable principles of his holy nature. This is to say, that, as prophets, they possessed all the basic information, for by Moses and the Exodus God had declared his name for ever (Ex. 3:15). They were 'in the know' (Am. 3:7).

Thirdly, prediction seems to belong to the very idea of the prophetic office. We may see this in Dt. 18:9ff.: Israel, entering the land of Canaan, is not only warned about the abominations of the Canaanite cults, such as infant sacrifice, but also about Canaanite religious practitioners, such as diviners. Certainly these men were concerned with what we call 'fortune-telling'; they offered to probe the future by one means or another. For Israel, instead of all these, there will be a prophet whom the Lord will raise up from among their brethren. This prophet, speaking in the name of the Lord, is to be judged by the accuracy of his forecasts (v. 22)—a clear proof that Israel expected prophetic prediction, and that it belonged to the notion of prophecy.

We may note here the extraordinarily detailed telepathic and clairvoyant gifts of the prophets. Elisha had the reputation of knowing what was said in secret afar off (2 Ki. 6:12) and gave evidence that it was not an inaccurate assessment of his powers. Ezekiel is justly famed for his detailed knowledge of Jerusalem at the time of his residence in Babylon (Ezk. 8–11). While it would be unrealistic to rule out direct communication between Ezekiel and Jerusalem, it is equally needless to try to evade this part of the biblical testimony. The prophets were men of remarkable psychic powers. It is, for example, unnecessary to question foreknowledge of personal names, such as is exemplified in 1 Ki. 13:2; Is. 44:28 (*cf.* Acts 9:12). Since there is no textual uncertainty at these points, the question is simply one of whether we accept the OT evidence as to what constitutes OT prophecy or not. The occurrence of such detailed prediction is perfectly 'at home' in the general picture of prophecy as the Bible reveals it. We should remember that it is illegitimate to pose the problem in terms of our knowledge of the lapse of time between prediction and fulfilment: 'How could the prophet know the name of someone not born till hundreds of years after his time?' There is nothing about 'hundreds of years' in the passages mentioned. This is our contribution to the question, because we know of the time-lapse. The real question is much simpler in statement: 'From what we know of the OT prophet, is there anything against his foreknowledge of personal names?' In the light of the OT, the negative reply may justly be made.

II. Prophetic inspiration and methods

a. Modes of inspiration

How did the prophet receive the message which he was commissioned to convey to his fellows? The answer given in the vast majority of cases is perfectly clear and yet tantalizingly vague: 'The word of the Lord came . . .', literally, the verb being the verb 'to be', 'the word of the Lord became actively present to . . .'. It is a statement of a direct, personal awareness. This is the basic experience of the prophet. It is stated for the first time in Ex. 7:1–2 (*cf.* 4:15–16). God is the author of the words which he conveys to the prophet, and through him to the people. It is this same experience which Jeremiah had when the Lord's hand touched his mouth (Je. 1:9), and this passage tells us as much as we are permitted to know: that in the context of personal fellowship which God has brought about the prophet receives a donation of words. Jeremiah later expressed this experience as 'standing in the counsel of the Lord' (23:22), whereby he was then able to make the people hear God's words. This, however, adds nothing in the way of psychological explanation.

Dreams and visions also had their place in the inspiration of the prophet. It is sometimes urged that Je. 23:28 teaches the invalidity of dreams as a method of ascertaining the word of the Lord. However, in the light of Nu. 12:6–7 and 1 Sa. 28:6, 15, which teach the validity of the dream, we see that Je. 23:28 is to be understood as 'a mere dream' or 'a dream of his own fancy'. Indeed, Jeremiah himself appears to have enjoyed the word of God through a dream (31:26). The experience of visions is best exemplified in the prophet Zechariah, but, like dreams, it adds nothing to our knowledge—or rather our ignorance—of the mechanics of inspiration. Exactly the same may be said of the cases where the word is perceived through a symbol (Je. 18; Am. 7:7ff.; 8:1–3). Inspiration is a miracle; we do not know in what way God makes the mind of a man aware of his word.

This raises the question of the activity of the Spirit of God in prophetic inspiration. There are 18 passages which associate prophetic inspiration with the activity of the Spirit: in Nu. 24:2 the reference is to Balaam; Nu. 11:29; 1 Sa. 10:6, 10; 19:20, 23 deal with the prophetic ecstasy; the plain assumption that prophecy arises from the Spirit of

God is found in 1 Ki. 22:24; Joel 2:28–29; Ho. 9:7; Ne. 9:30; Zc. 7:12; a direct claim to the inspiration of the Spirit is made in Mi. 3:8; the Spirit's inspiration of the prophetic word is claimed by 1 Ch. 12:18; 2 Ch. 15:1; 20:14; 24:20; Ne. 9:20; and Ezk. 11:5. It is clear that this evidence is not evenly spread through the OT, and in particular that the pre-exilic prophets are sparsely represented. Indeed, Jeremiah does not mention the Spirit of God in any context whatever. This has been taken as showing a distinction between the 'man of the word' and the 'man of the Spirit' (see L. Koehler, *Old Testament Theology*, 1957; E. Jacob, *Theology of the Old Testament*, 1958; T. C. Vriezen, *An Outline of Old Testament Theology*, 1958), suggesting that the early prophets were anxious to dissociate themselves from the group inspiration of the so-called spirit-possessed men. This is not a necessary, nor even a probable, conclusion. For one thing, a straightforward identification of the earlier group-ecstatics with the later false prophets is not possible; and, for another, as E. Jacob points out, 'the word presupposes the spirit, the creative breath of life, and for the prophets there was such evidence of this that they thought it unnecessary to state it explicitly'.

b. Modes of communication

The prophets came before their contemporaries as men with a word to say. The spoken oracle is the form in which the word of God is expressed. Each prophet stamped the marks of his own personality and experience on this word: the oracles of Amos and Jeremiah are as unlike as are the personalities of the two prophets. There is, therefore, a double awareness in the books of the prophets: on the one hand, these words are the words which God gave to the prophet. God took this man to be his mouthpiece; they are the words of God. On the other hand, these words are the words of a certain man, spoken at a certain time, under certain circumstances. It is customary among modern writers (*e.g.* H. H. Rowley, *The Servant of the Lord*, 1952, p. 126) to draw the conclusion that the word thus became to an extent imperfect and fallible, because it was the word of imperfect and fallible men. We ought to be clear that such a conclusion must rest on grounds other than the testimony of the prophets themselves in so far as we have it in the books. This is not the place to discuss the relation between the words of inspired men and the words of the God who inspired them (*INSPIRATION), but it is the place to say that the books of the prophets may be searched without discovering any trace of suggestion that the prophets thought the word through them was in any way less than the word of God. We shall note presently that most of the prophets seemed totally unaware of the existence of voices other than, or contradictory to, their own. They possessed an overwhelming certainty concerning their words, such as is proper either to lunatics or to men who have stood in the counsel of God and received there what they are to say on earth.

Sometimes the prophets couched their oracles in the form of parable or allegory (*e.g.* Is. 5:1–7; 2 Sa. 12:1–7; and especially Ezk. 16 and 23), but the most dramatic presentation of their message was by means of the 'acted oracle'. If we start by thinking of the acted oracle as a 'visual aid' we will undoubtedly end with the wrong conception of its nature and function. Of course, it was a visual aid, but, in association with the Heb. notion of the efficacy of the word, it served to make the discharge of the word into the contemporary situation rather more powerful. This is best seen in the interview between King Joash and the dying Elisha (2 Ki. 13:14ff.). In v. 17 the arrow of the Lord's victory is shot against Syria. The prophet has introduced the king into a sphere of symbolic action. He now inquires how far the king has faith to embrace that word of promise: the king smites three times, and that is the extent to which the effective word of God will achieve accomplishment and not return void. Here we see very vividly the exact relation in which the symbol stood to the word, and in which both stood to the course of events. The word embodied in the symbol is exceedingly effective; it cannot fail to come to pass; it will accomplish exactly what the symbol declared. Thus, Isaiah walked naked and barefoot (Is. 20), Jeremiah smashed a potter's vessel in the place of potsherds (Je. 19), Ahijah tore his new coat into twelve pieces and gave Jeroboam ten (1 Ki. 11:29ff.), Ezekiel besieged a model city (Ezk. 4:1–3), dug through the house wall (12:1ff.), did not mourn for his dead wife (24:15ff.). We need to distinguish sharply between the acted oracle of the Israelite prophet and the sympathetic magic of the Canaanite cults. Essentially the latter is a movement from man to God: the performance of a certain action by man is an attempt to coerce Baal, or whatever god was in mind, to function correspondingly. The acted oracle was a movement from God to man: the word of God, the activity on which God had already decided, was thus declared and promoted on earth. In this, as in every other aspect of biblical religion, the initiative rests solely with God.

c. The books of the prophets

The question of the formation of the *Canon does not concern us here, but we cannot evade the question of the compilation of the writings of each prophet. It ought to be taken for granted that each of the prophetic books contains only a selection of the utterances of that prophet, but who did the selecting, editing and arranging? For example, the Judaean references in the book of Hosea are probably correctly seen as editorial work after the fall of Samaria, when the prophet's oracles were carried S. But who was the editor? Or, again, the series of questions and answers in Malachi are clearly a deliberate arrangement to convey a total message. Who arranged them? Or, on a larger scale, the book of Isaiah is manifestly a well-edited book; we have only to think of the way in which the series of six 'woes' (chs. 28–37) fall into two groups of three within which the first three respectively are exactly matched by the second three, or of the way chs. 38–39 have been taken out of chronological order so that they may become a historical preface to chs. 40–55. But who was the careful editor?

If we consult the books themselves we find three hints as to their written composition. First, that the prophets themselves wrote at least some of their oracles (*e.g.* Is. 30:8; Je. 29:1ff.; *cf.* 2 Ch. 21:12; Je. 29:25; *cf.* the use of the first person in Ho. 3:1–5); secondly, that in the case of Jeremiah, at least, a lengthy statement of his prophecies so far was made out with the help of a secretary (Je. 36), and that the command is both given and received without any sign that it was at all out of the way; and thirdly, that the prophets are sometimes associated with a group which was, presumably, the recipient

Name of prophet	Approximate dates of ministry	Contemporary rulers of			Historical setting
		Judah	Israel	Babylon/Persia	
Joel	c. ?810–750 BC	Joash (=Jehoash), Amaziah, Uzziah (=Azariah)			2 Ki. 11:1–15:7
Amos	c. 760 BC	Uzziah (=Azariah)	Jeroboam II		2 Ki. 14:23; 15:7
Jonah	c. 760 BC		Jeroboam II		2 Ki. 14:23–29
Hosea	760–722 BC		Jeroboam II, Zechariah, Shallum, Menahem, Pekahiah, Pekah, Hoshea		2 Ki. 14:23–18:37
Micah	742–687 BC	Jotham, Ahaz, Hezekiah			2 Ki. 15:32–20:21; 2 Ch. 27:1–32:33; Is. 7:1–8:22; Je. 26:17–19
Isaiah	740–700 BC	Uzziah (=Azariah), Jotham, Ahaz, Hezekiah			2 Ki. 15:1–20:21; 2 Ch. 26:1–32:33
Nahum	somewhere between 664 and 612 BC	Josiah			2 Ki. 22:1–23:30; 2 Ch. 34:1–36:1; Zp. 2:13–15
Zephaniah	c. 640 BC onwards	Josiah			2 Ki. 22:1–23:34; 2 Ch. 34:1–36:4
Jeremiah	626–587 BC	Josiah, Jehoahaz, Jehoiakim, Jehoiachin, Zedekiah			2 Ki. 22:1–25:30; 2 Ch. 34:1–36:21
Habakkuk	c. 605 BC	Jehoiakim			2 Ki. 23:31–24:7
Daniel	605–535 BC	Jehoiakim, Jehoiachin, Zedekiah		Nebuchadrezzar, Belshazzar, Darius, Cyrus	2 Ki. 24:1–25:30; 2 Ch. 36:5–23
Ezekiel	593–570 BC			Nebuchadrezzar	2 Ki. 24:8–25:26; 2 Ch. 36:9–21
Obadiah	c. ?587 BC onwards			Nebuchadrezzar	2 Ki. 25; 2 Ch. 36:11–21
Haggai	520 BC			Darius	Ezr. 5:1–6:22
Zechariah	c. 520 BC onwards			Darius onwards	Ezr. 5:1–6:22
Malachi	c. 433 BC			Artaxerxes I	Ne. 13

The approximate dates of the ministries of the OT prophets (see also CHRONOLOGY OF THE OT*).*

of the teaching of the master-prophet, and may have been the repository of his oracles. Such a group is mentioned as 'my disciples' in Is. 8:16. These slender pieces of evidence suggest that the prophet himself was behind the recording of his words, whether by personal act, or by dictation, or by teaching. It could easily have been that the oracles of Isaiah took their present form as a manual of instruction for the prophet's disciples.

The name 'sons of the prophets' is used of these groups of disciples. It is actually found in the times of Elijah and Elisha, though Am. 7:14 shows that it survived as a technical term long after. We would gather from 2 Ki. 2:3, 5 that there were known groups of men settled here and there in the land under the general superintendence of the 'authorized' prophet. Elijah, in his effort to spare Elisha the strain of parting, appears to make a customary journey. Elisha in his turn had the management of the prophetic groups (2 Ki. 4:38; 6:1ff.), and availed himself of their services (2 Ki. 9:1). Clearly the members of these groups were men of prophetic gift (2 Ki. 2:3, 5), but whether they joined the group by divine call or attached themselves to the prophet, attracted by his teaching, or were called by him, we are not in a position to say.

There is no need to see in Am. 7:14 a slur on the prophetic groups, as though Amos were indignantly distinguishing himself from them. Amos could hardly be denying prophetic status to himself, seeing he is about to assert that the Lord commanded him to 'prophesy' (Heb. *hinnāḇē'*, to perform the part of a *nāḇî'*, 7:15). We may therefore take the words either as an indignant rhetorical question: 'Am I not a prophet, and a prophet's son? Indeed, I was a herdsman . . . and the Lord took me', or, preferably, 'I am no prophet . . . I am a herdsman, . . . and the Lord took me.' Amos is making no sinister accusation against the sons of the prophets as necessarily professional time-servers, but is alleging the authority of a spiritual call as against the accusation of lack of official status and authorization.

Very likely, at any rate, it is to such men, grouped round the great prophets, that we owe the safeguarding and transmission of their oracles, while at the same time it is going far beyond any information we possess regarding the groups of the 'sons of the prophets', their continuance and their work, to ascribe to them wholesale modifications, adaptations and additions to the inherited work of the 'master' prophet, as is becoming increasingly fashionable in specialist study.

III. True and false prophets

When Micaiah the son of Imlah and Zedekiah the son of Chenaanah confronted each other before King Ahab, the one warning of defeat and the other promising victory, and both appealing to the authority of the Lord (1 Ki. 22), how could they have been distinguished, the true from the false? When Jeremiah faced Hananiah, the former bowing under a yoke symbolizing servitude and the latter breaking the yoke symbolizing liberation (Je. 28), how could they have been distinguished? Or, a more extreme case, when the 'old prophet in Bethel' brought back the 'man of God' out of Judah with a lying message, and then rounded upon him with the true word of God (1 Ki. 13:18–22), was it possible to tell when he spoke with truth and when he spoke with deceit? The question of the discrimination of prophets is by no means academic but thoroughly practical and of the highest spiritual importance.

Certain external characteristics of a general kind have been alleged as distinguishing the true from the false. It has been urged that the prophetic ecstasy was the mark of the false prophet. We have already noted that group-ecstasy was the common mark of the *nāḇî'* in the time of Samuel (1 Sa. 9–10; *etc.*). This ecstasy was apparently spontaneous, or it could be induced, notably by music (1 Sa. 10:5; 2 Ki. 3:15) and by the ritual dance (1 Ki. 18:28). The ecstatic person apparently became very forgetful and quite insensible to pain (1 Sa. 19:24; 1 Ki. 18:28). It is easy, and indeed almost inevitable, that we should look with suspicion on a phenomenon such as this: it is so alien to our taste, and it is known as a feature of Baalism, and of Canaan in general. But these are not sufficient grounds for a plain identification between ecstatic and false. For one thing, there is no indication that the ecstasy was in any way frowned upon either by the people at large or by the best of their religious leaders. Samuel foretold with apparent approbation that Saul would join the ecstatic prophets and that this would signify his becoming a new man (1 Sa. 10:6). Also, the emissary of Elisha is called by Jehu's fellow captains 'this mad fellow' (2 Ki. 9:11), probably indicating that the ecstasy was still a feature of the prophetic group. Furthermore, Isaiah's Temple experience was certainly an ecstasy, and Ezekiel was without doubt an ecstatic.

Another suggested identification of false prophecy is professionalism: they were the paid servants of some king or other and it was to their interest to say what would please the king. But, again, this will hardly serve as a criterion. Samuel was clearly a professional prophet but was not a false prophet; Nathan was very likely a court official of David, but yet professionalism was by no means equivalent to sycophancy. Even Amos may have been professional, but Amaziah urges upon him that the living is better in Judah for a prophet like him (Am. 7:10ff.). Like the ecstatics, the court prophets are found in groups (1 Ki. 22), and no doubt their professional status could have been a corrupting influence, but to say that it was so is to run beyond the evidence. Jeremiah made no such accusation against Pashhur (Je. 20), though it would have been greatly to his advantage to have had a ready-made proof of his adversary's error.

There are three notable discussions of the whole question of false prophecy in the OT. The first is in Dt. 13 and 18. Dealing with the latter chapter first, it states a negative test: what does not come to pass was not spoken by the Lord. The wording here ought to be strictly observed; it is not a simple statement that fulfilment is the hall-mark of genuineness, for, as 13:1ff. indicates, a sign may be given and come to pass and yet the prophet be false. Inevitably, fulfilment was looked for as proof of genuine, godly utterance: Moses complained when what was spoken 'in the name' failed to have the desired effect (Ex. 5:23); Jeremiah saw in the visit of Hanamel a proof that the word was from the Lord (Je. 32:8). But Deuteronomy states only the negative, because that alone is safe and correct. What the Lord says will always find fulfilment, but sometimes the word of the false is fulfilled also, as a test for God's people.

Thus, we turn to Dt. 13, and the answer to the problem of discerning the false prophet: the test is a theological one, the revelation of God at the

Exodus. The essence of the false prophet is that he calls the people 'after other gods, which you have not known' (v. 2), thus teaching 'rebellion against the Lord your God, who brought you out of the land of Egypt' (vv. 5, 10). Here we see the final feature of Moses, the normative prophet: he also fixed the theological norm by which all subsequent teaching could be judged. A prophet might allege that he spoke in the name of Yahweh, but if he did not acknowledge the authority of Moses and subscribe to the doctrines of the Exodus he was a false prophet.

This is substantially the answer, also, of Jeremiah. This sensitive prophet could not carry off the contest with the robust assurance which seemed so natural to Isaiah and Amos. The question of personal certainty was one which he could not evade, and yet he could not answer it except by the tautologous 'certainty is certainty'. We find him in the heat of the struggle in 23:9ff. It is clear from a reading of these verses that Jeremiah can find no external tests of the prophet: there is here no allegation of ecstasy or professionalism. Nor does he find the essence of the false prophet to consist in the acquisition of his oracles by dreams: that is, there is no test based upon prophetic technique. This, rather, is what Jeremiah alleges: the false prophet is a man of immoral life (vv. 10–14) and he places no barrier to immorality in others (v. 17); whereas the true prophet seeks to stem the tide of sin and to call people to holiness (v. 22). Again, the message of the false prophet is one of peace, without regard to the moral and spiritual conditions which are basic to peace (v. 17); whereas the true prophet has a message of judgment upon sin (v. 29).

We might interject here that Jeremiah ought not to be understood to say that the true prophet cannot have a message of peace. This is one of the most damaging notions that has ever entered the study of the prophets. There is a time when peace is the message of God; but it will always be in Exodus terms, that peace can come only when holiness is satisfied concerning sin. And this is exactly what Jeremiah is urging: the voice of the true prophet is always the voice of the law of God, once for all declared through Moses. Thus Jeremiah is bold to say that the false prophets are men of borrowed testimony, feigned authority and self-appointed ministry (vv. 30–32), whereas the true prophet has stood in the counsel of Yahweh and heard his voice, and has been sent by him (vv. 18, 21–22, 28, 32). Jeremiah's final position is in fact that 'certainty is certainty', but he is rescued from tautology by the positive revelation of God. He knows he is right because his experience is the Mosaic experience of standing before God (*cf.* Nu. 12:6–8; Dt. 34:10), and his message accords, as that of the false prophets does not, with the 'Exodus Quadrilateral' of Holiness (obedience), Peace, Sin, Judgment.

The answer of Ezekiel is substantially that of Jeremiah, and is found in Ezk. 12:21–14:11. Ezekiel tells us that there are prophets who are guided by their own wisdom and have no word from Yahweh (13:2–3). Thus they make people trust in lies and leave them without resource in the day of trial (13:4–7). The mark of these prophets is their message: it is one of peace and shallow optimism (13:10–16), and it is devoid of moral content, grieving the righteous and encouraging the wicked (v. 22). By contrast, there is a prophet who insists on piercing to the core of the matter, answering folk not according to their ostensible queries but according to their sinful hearts (14:4–5), for the word of Yahweh is always a word against sin (14:7–8). We see again that the true prophet is the Mosaic prophet. It is not just that in a vague sense he has a direct experience of God, but that he has been commissioned by the God of the Exodus to reiterate once again to Israel the moral requirements of the covenant.

IV. The prophets in the religion of Israel

a. Cultic prophets

Prophecy in a cultic setting is found in 2 Ch. 20:14. In a time of national anxiety King Jehoshaphat has led his people in public prayer in the court of the Lord's house. Immediately upon the conclusion of the prayer, a Levite, inspired by the Spirit of God, brings a word from the Lord promising victory. Here, then, is a Levite, that is, a cultic official, with a prophetic capacity. A further indication of the same happening may occur in some psalms (*e.g.* 60; 75; 82; *etc.*). In all these psalms there is a section in which a first person singular voice speaks: this is the oracular response, the prophet associated with the cult, bringing the contemporary utterance of God to his people. The suggestion made is that the guilds of levitical singers in the post-exilic period are the survival of groups of cultic prophets attached to the various sanctuaries in pre-exilic times. At every sanctuary, working alongside the priests, who had charge of the sacrificial aspect of the worship, there were prophets who declared the word of God publicly for the nation or privately for individual guidance.

The evidence for this practice, known, of course, in Canaanite circles, is largely inferential: we first meet a prophetic guild at the high place at Gibeah (1 Sa. 10:5); Samuel the prophet was an official at Shiloh (1 Sa. 3:19), and presided at a cultic meal at Ramah (1 Sa. 9:12ff.); the prophet Gad commanded David to erect the altar in Araunah's threshing-floor (2 Sa. 24:11, 18), and revealed God's will concerning the guilds of temple singers (2 Ch. 29:25); the prophet Nathan was consulted about the building of the Temple (2 Sa. 7:1ff.); Elijah staged a cultic scene at an ancient shrine (1 Ki. 18:30ff.); it was customary to visit the prophet on cultic occasions (2 Ki. 4:23); there are numerous references in which prophet and priest are coupled together in a way suggesting professional association (2 Ki. 23:2; Is. 28:7; Je. 2:26; 8:10; 13:13, *etc.*); there were prophetic quarters within the Temple (Je. 35:4).

It is difficult to see how any theory could be stable when it rests on such slight foundation. For example, the apparently strong connection established between prophet and Temple by the allocation of quarters, in Je. 35:4, is utterly negatived by the fact that the same verse speaks of chambers allocated to the princes. Again, the fact that prophets and guilds are found at cultic centres need mean nothing more than that they too were religious people! Amos was found at the sanctuary of Bethel (7:13), but this does not prove that he was paid to be there. David's consultation of his prophets tells us more about David's good sense than about his prophets' cultic associations. The theory of the cultic prophet remains a theory.

b. The prophets and the cultus

Even if the theory of the cultic prophet could be proved, it would still leave unsettled the relation of the canonical, or writing, prophet to the cultus. Their view of the cultus is somewhat of a crux of interpretation, and centres round six brief passages which are supposed by some to contain an outright condemnation of all cultic worship and a denial that it was ever the will of God (Am. 5:21–25; Ho. 6:6; Is. 1:11–15; 43:22–24; Mi. 6:6–8; Je. 7:21–23).

We may remark at once on the small number of verses involved. If the prophets were so opposed to the cultus, as some commentators have urged, it is extraordinary that their opposition was so rarely voiced, and then in such a manner as to leave it open to doubt whether they intended to condemn the cultus as such or the cultus as then abused. Furthermore, in other parts of their writings some of these prophets do not seem to take such a strong line about ceremonial and sacrifice. Isaiah, in his inaugural vision, certainly met with God and with peace of heart in a cultic setting. Are we to believe that he thought the cultus was worth nothing? Or again, Jeremiah, in ch. 7, the chapter from which the proof-text is drawn, does not condemn people for offering cultic worship (vv. 9–10) because Yahweh has forbidden it but because they couple it with moral indifference and iniquity; in v. 11 the Temple is 'this house, which is called by my name' and in v. 12, Shiloh is 'my place', which was destroyed, not to manifest divine rejection of the cultus but because of the iniquity of the worshippers. This all suggests, what detailed study of the verses will also indicate, that the anger of the prophets is directed against the cultus abused.

The heart of the exegetical problem in Am. 5:21–25 is in the last verse: 'Did you bring to me sacrifices and offerings the forty years in the wilderness . . . ?' In order to support the theory that Amos is a root-and-branch opponent of sacrifice, we must see him confidently expecting the answer 'No' to this question. But this is exactly what he could not have done. On any view of the origin of the Pentateuch, the traditions current in Amos' day would have spoken of sacrifice in the time of Moses, and of the Patriarchs before him. Vv. 21–23 tell of God's spurning of their current cultic practice. V. 24 tells us what is missing: a moral concern, a holy life. V. 25 is intended to enforce the truth that these things are not an 'either/or' but are the inseparable sides of religion according to the will of God. It should be stressed that the form of the question in the Hebrew does not suggest, let alone require, a negative answer, and if we translate v. 25 so as to bring out the emphasis of the prophet, we read: 'Was it sacrifices and offerings you brought to me in the wilderness forty years . . . ?' If they trace their religion back to its root in revelation, what do they find but a divine requirement of sacrifice in the context of a life obedient to the law of God? Because of their failure to follow this pattern (vv. 26f.) they will go into captivity. Mere *opus operatum* ritual is not worship of the God of the Bible.

According to Pr. 8:10, we are to 'Take my instruction instead of silver, and knowledge rather than choice gold.' Clearly this is a statement of priorities, not an exclusion of one thing in favour of the other. The importance of this verse is that its Hebrew is exactly parallel in construction to that of Ho. 6:6. In the light therefore of Hosea's failure to maintain an attitude of rejection towards the cultus throughout the rest of his prophecy, we may hold that he intends here a statement of priorities such as was given classical expression by Samuel: 'To obey is better than sacrifice' (1 Sa. 15:22).

The difficulty with the passage in Is. 1 is that it proves a great deal too much if it is taken simply as outright condemnation. Certainly vv. 11–12 appear to be a very strong attack on sacrifice, but no stronger than the attack upon the sabbath in v. 13, and upon prayer in v. 15. It cannot be that the prophet is utterly repudiating the sabbath and prayer. It must be that the final clause of v. 15, while referring directly to the earlier part of the verse, refers also to all the preceding condemnations. The prophet is simply urging that no religious activity avails in the context of a blatantly sinful life. This interpretation is proved to be correct by the initial verbs of v. 16, the first of which is constantly used throughout the levitical code for ceremonial purification, a very unlikely verb for the prophet to use if he considered all such things contrary to God's will; the second verb applies to moral purgation. The prophet's message is thus the Bible's message: the message of the joint requirement of the moral and ceremonial law.

We notice next Mi. 6:6–8. We have a somewhat analogous situation in the words of our Lord to the rich young ruler (Mk. 10:17ff.). By his exclusive reply in terms of the moral law does he intend to deny the divine authority of the ceremonial law of atoning sacrifice? In view of his constant regard for the Mosaic legislation (*e.g.* Mt. 8:4), not to mention his authentication of the terms of OT sacrifice by his teaching concerning his own death (Mk. 14:24), this is an unlikely interpretation of the words. Or again, we might ask if Lv. 18:5, presenting the moral law as a way of life, intends to invalidate the ceremonial law. Likewise, in the case of Micah, we must not understand him to reject whatever he does not specifically approve.

We have already noted certain background facts relative to the study of Je. 7:21–23. If Jeremiah, in the immediate context, seems, at the least, not to condemn sacrifice as *per se* unacceptable, may we so interpret 7:22? The difficulty is that, on the face of it, the words seem to require us to do so. However, closer examination of the Hebrew suggests that the difficulty belongs more to the English translation than to the original. The preposition which the English gives as 'concerning'—the vital word in the whole verse—is the Hebrew *'al-diḇrê*, which can only mean 'concerning' by a weakening of its real significance 'because of' or 'for the sake of' (*cf.* Gn. 20:11; 43:18; Ps. 7, title; Je. 14:1; *etc.*). According to this, the verse says that Yahweh did not address Israel either 'because of' sacrifices: that is to say, the performance of sacrifice is not a means whereby pressure may be applied to God; nor did he address them 'for the sake of' sacrifices, for the living God stands in no need of anything man can supply. The nation has missed the divine priority by its concentration on the mere operation of a cult, for the cult is not a thing which exists on its own but rather for the sake of the spiritual needs of a people committed to obedience to the moral law of God.

We may allude finally to Is. 43:22ff., which is, in many ways, the most difficult verse of all. The emphasis in v. 22 requires the translation, 'Not me have you called . . .' On the supposition that this sets the tone of address throughout the verses, we are clearly within the same circle of possibilities: either, there is an indignant repudiation of the whole idea of divine authorization of sacrifice: 'whoever you may think you appeal to in your cultus, it is not to me, for I did not burden you with offerings'; or the accusation is that they abused the divine intention: 'in all your cultic labour you have not really called upon me, for it was never my plan that the cultus should turn you into slave-labour of ritual'. These alternatives of interpretation are so clear in the text that we may simply ask whether there are any other evidences whereby we might decide between them. The general consent of Scripture points to the second suggestion. Since there is no need to interpret the other crucial verses as an outright denial of sacrifice, we ought to reject that meaning here also. Moreover, within Isaiah, we have to reckon with 44:28, clearly approving the rebuilding of the Temple: for Isaiah to repudiate sacrifice and yet rejoice in the Temple would involve a complete contradiction in terms. There is also the inescapably sacrificial language of Is. 53.

c. The unity of Israel's religion

The religion of Israel began, as to its normative form, with the prophet-priest Moses, and it continued as a religion jointly of prophet and priest. This is declared in the covenant ceremony in Ex. 24:4–8. Yahweh has redeemed his people according to promise and they have acquiesced in the law he has imposed upon them as his redeemed people. Moses expressed the relationship symbolically: twelve pillars grouped round an altar (24:4). Here is the visual expression of the fulfilment of the covenant promise: 'I will take you for my people, and I will be your God' (Ex. 6:7). Notably, God is represented as an altar, for the holy God—the primary revelation of God to Moses (Ex. 3:5)—can dwell among sinners only by virtue of the atoning blood. Hence, the first thing Moses does with the blood is to sprinkle it upon the altar. As at the Passover, the initial movement of the blood is towards God in propitiation (Ex. 12:13).

The ceremony proceeds with the people's self-dedication to obedience to the law, and then the blood is sprinkled upon them. It is thus declared that while the people are brought to God by means of the blood of propitiation, the people themselves need the blood also in the context of their obligation to keep God's holy law. This, then, is the unity of prophet and priest: the former calls continually to obedience; the latter reminds constantly of the efficacy of the blood. If we drive them asunder the former becomes a moralist and the latter a ritualist; if we keep them together, as the religion of Israel does, and as the Bible does, we see the whole wonder of the God whom prophet and priest—and apostle too—proclaimed: a just God, and a Saviour, who will never relax his demand that his people walk in the light and be holy as he is holy, and who sets alongside that inflexible demand the blood which cleanses from all sin.

BIBLIOGRAPHY. H. W. Robinson, *Inspiration and Revelation in the Old Testament*, 1946, Parts 3 and 4; A. R. Johnson, *The Cultic Prophet in Ancient Israel*, 1944; A. B. Davidson, *Old Testament Prophecy*, 1904; C. Kuhl, *The Prophets of Israel*, 1960; E. J. Young, *My Servants the Prophets*, 1955; A. Lods, *The Prophets and the Rise of Judaism*, 1937; T. H. Robinson, *Prophecy and the Prophets in Ancient Israel*, 1923; J. Skinner, *Prophecy and Religion*, 1926; A. Guillaume, *Prophecy and Divination*, 1938; M. Noth, *BJRL* 32, 1949–50, pp. 194ff.; O. T. Allis, *The Unity of Isaiah*, 1950, chs. 1–2; J. Lindblom, *Prophecy in Ancient Israel*, 1962; Y. Kaufmann, *The Religion of Israel*, 1961, Part 3; C. Westermann, *Basic Forms of Prophetic Speech*, 1967; R. E. Clements, *Prophecy and Covenant*, 1965; W. McKane, *Prophets and Wise Men*, 1965; C. H. Peisker, C. Brown, in *NIDNTT* 3, pp. 74–92; J. Bright, 'Jeremiah's Complaints—Liturgy or Expressions of Personal Distress?' in J. I. Durham and J. R. Porter (eds.), *Proclamation and Presence*, 1970, pp. 189ff.; H. H. Rowley, *From Moses to Qumran*, 1963, ch. 4; J. Blenkinsopp, *A History of Prophecy in Israel*, 1983,; R. Coggins, A. Phillips and M. Knibb (eds.), *Israel's Prophetic Tradition*, 1982; J. Barton, *Oracles of God*, 1986; K. Koch, *The Prophets*, 2 vols., 1982–3; R. P. Gordon (ed.), *The Place is too small for us*, f.c. J.A.M.

V. Prophecy in the New Testament

a. Continuity with the Old Testament

Prophecy and the prophets form the greatest line of continuity between the OT and NT. This is evident from the attitude of Christ and the apostles to OT prophecy, from the continuance of the phenomenon of prophecy both up to and after the ministry of Jesus, from the prophetic character of his own ministry, from the placing of the inspiration of NT apostles and prophets alongside that of OT prophets, and from the general outpouring of the Holy Spirit—the spirit of prophecy—upon the church, leading to a continuing acceptance of prophets and prophesying in NT churches.

The OT prophetic line did not end with Malachi, but with John the Baptist, as our Lord expressly declares (Mt. 11:13). Prophetic utterances of John's father Zechariah, and of Anna, Simeon and Mary at the beginning of Luke's Gospel all bear witness to the continuance of prophetic inspiration (Lk. 1:46–55, 67–79; 2:26–38). The customary division into two 'Testaments' unfortunately obscures this marvellous unity of God's programme of revelation, but the line is continuous from Moses to John—and indeed beyond him, as we shall see.

Furthermore the NT stands in a relation of fulfilment to the actual message of the OT prophets. Time and again this is the burden of the NT: what God said of old he has now brought to pass (*e.g.* Mt. 1:22; 13:17; 26:56; Lk. 1:70; 18:31; Acts 3:21; 10:43, *etc.*). They all bore witness ultimately to Christ and his saving work (Lk. 24:25, 27, 44; Jn. 1:45; 5:39; 11:51). He came not to abolish the law and the prophets but to fulfil them (Mt. 5:17), and indeed based his understanding of his own mission and destiny principally upon their predictions.

The importance of this feature of the NT in authentication of the OT can scarcely be overemphasized. Though a persecuted minority (Mt. 5:12; 23:29–37; Lk. 6:23, *etc.*), the OT prophets are no mere idle speculative dreamers, but the most important voice coming to us from the ancient past, confirmed as proclaimers of eternal truth by the fulfilment of their greatest words in the greatest event of all time, the person and work of Jesus Christ. He himself points us back to them and their message as a permanent revelation of God, sufficient to lead to repentance and therefore to render culpable those who fail to listen to them (Lk. 16:29–31). They are authorized teachers of the Christian church, men whose words are still to be heeded as the word of God (*cf.* 2 Pet. 1:19–21).

b. The greatest prophet and more

One of his commonest assessments of the person of Jesus of Nazareth by his contemporaries in Palestine was that he was a prophet from God, or a teacher from God, or both (Mt. 14:5; 21:11, 46; Lk. 7:16; Jn. 3:2; 4:19; 6:14; 7:40; 9:17, *etc.*). Their basic concept of a prophet was clearly based upon the OT prophetic ministry, and included declaring God's word, having supernormal knowledge, and evidencing the power of God (*cf.* Jn. 3:2; 4:19 *in loc.*; Mt. 26:68; Lk. 7:39).

Jesus accepted this title among others, and used it of himself (Mt. 13:57; Lk. 13:33), as well as accepting the title of teacher (Jn. 13:13), and even of scribe by implication (Mt. 13:51–52). The apostles came to realize that the ultimate fulfilment of Moses' prophecy (Dt. 18:15ff.) of the prophet like him whom God would raise up was found in Christ himself (Acts 3:22–26; 7:37; *MESSIAH). Only, in the case of Jesus we do not merely have a prophet, but the Son to whom the Spirit is not given by measure, in whose teaching ministry therefore the ministry of prophet and teacher are perfectly combined, and with whom the acme of prophetic revelation is reached (Mt. 21:33–43; Lk. 4:14–15; Jn. 3:34). However, more than the greatest prophet, we see in Jesus the one who sent the prophets (Mt. 23:34, 37), and one who not merely speaks the words of God, but is himself the Word made flesh (Jn. 1:1–14; Rev. 19:13; *LOGOS).

c. The Spirit of prophecy and the Christian church

Christ promised his disciples that after his ascension he would send them his Holy Spirit who would empower them to bear witness to him in the world, and would bear witness with them (Lk. 24:48–49; Jn. 14:26; 15:26–27; Acts 1:8). That this includes prophetic inspiration is clear from Mt. 10:19–20; Jn. 16:12–15, *etc.* The apostles and those who preached the gospel at the first did so in the power of the same 'Holy Spirit sent from heaven' who inspired the predictions of the OT prophets as they looked forward to the coming sufferings and glory of Christ (1 Pet. 1:10–12). Hence it is no surprise that when the Holy Spirit is poured out at Pentecost, the immediate result includes manifestations in speech (Acts 2:1–12), and Peter's explanation cites Joel 2:28–32, where a major result of the effusion of the Spirit on all flesh is that 'they shall prophesy', including not only prophetic words but also visions and dreams (Acts 2:18). Every Christian is potentially a prophet (thus realizing Moses' wish expressed in Nu. 11:29), for the Spirit given generally to the church for its testimony to Jesus is the Spirit of prophecy (1 Cor. 14:31; Rev. 19:10). Therefore Paul tells the Corinthian Christians, 'Earnestly desire the spiritual gifts, especially that you may prophesy' (1 Cor. 14:1).

When Christians initially received the power of the Holy Spirit, the commonest manifestations resulting at the time seem to have been speaking in another language (of praise and prayer) and prophesying (Acts 2:4, 17–18; 10:44–46; 19:6; 1 Cor. 1:5–7). It is not clear whether those who so spoke under the inspiration of the Spirit retained this faculty in all cases, or whether it was simply an initial confirmatory evidence of their reception of the Spirit, as in the case of the seventy elders, the nearest OT parallel in Nu. 11:25, where they prophesied only when the Spirit came upon them initially, 'but they did so no more'.

Jesus predicted that people would prophesy in his name (Mt. 7:22; though attention should be paid to his warning against reliance on this or any other work for one's spiritual standing), so prophecy is repeatedly mentioned as one of the gifts of the Holy Spirit with which Christ equips his members to function as his body in each place (Rom. 12:4–7; 1 Cor. 12:10–13; 1 Thes. 5:19–20; 1 Pet. 4:10–11; Rev. *passim*). This gift is differentiated both from tongues and interpretation and also from teaching. It differs from the former in being Spirit-inspired speech from God to man, whereas tongues and interpretations are addressed from man to God (Acts 2:11; 10:46; 1 Cor. 14:2–3); it differs from the latter (as in the OT) in being an utterance (frequently in the Lord's name) immediately inspired by direct revelation from the Holy Spirit, whereas teaching is mediated through patient study and exposition of truth already revealed. (Prophecy under the Spirit's inspiration will also often partly take the form, as in the OT, of a reiteration of truths already revealed in Scripture.)

The fullest guidance on the use of this gift in a church is given by Paul in 1 Cor. 14, along with instruction on the use of 'tongues'. From this and other references the following picture emerges. The exercise of this gift is in principle open to any Christian, under the sovereign distribution of the Spirit of Christ, including to women on occasion (vv. 5, 31; 11:5; 12:11; *cf.* Acts 21:9), although whether such feminine ministry was generally welcomed in the churches of the time is doubtful in view of 1 Cor. 14:33–36. Prophetic utterances are an intelligible word of revelation from God to the hearts and minds of those present, 'for their upbuilding and encouragement and consolation' (vv. 3–5, 26, 30–31). The reaction of the unbeliever to this prophetic ministry (vv. 24–25) shows that it could proclaim the whole message, of sin and judgment, as well as of grace and salvation.

'The spirits of prophets are subject to prophets' (v. 32), so that prophecy is neither to be abused by people succumbing to any supposedly uncontrollable ecstatic frenzy, nor to be exercised without the check of other members of the body, notably the elders and prophets weighing or discerning the accuracy and reliability of utterances purporting to issue from the Holy Spirit (vv. 29–33). It was doubtless just such abuses which led the apostle to write to another young church, 'Do not quench the Spirit, do not despise prophesying, but test everything; hold fast what is good' (1 Thes. 5:19–21)—a similar balance to that shown by him towards tongues in 1 Cor. 14:39–40.

Testing or weighing prophetic utterances is all the more necessary in view of the warnings of the NT (following the OT) against false prophets and false prophecy, by which Satan seeks to lead the unwary astray (Mt. 7:15; 24:11, 24; 2 Pet. 2:1; 1 Jn. 4:1ff.), and an example of which appears in Bar-Jesus at Paphos (Acts 13:5ff.). In the latter case occult sources are specified, although in other cases selfish human desires are blamed; but in either case the devil's anti-Christian cause is being served, as the symbolic figure of the false prophet serving the dragon in Rev. 13:11 and 19:20 makes plain. False prophets will on occasion work miracles (Mk. 13:22), but as in the OT (Dt. 13:1–5) are not to be given undiscerning credence merely on that account. The testing of any prophetic utterance will be in accordance with our Lord's warning, 'You will know them by their fruits' (Mt. 7:20 *in loc.*), and will include these criteria: *i.* their conformity to the teachings of Scripture, of Christ and of his apostles in both content and character (similar to OT, Dt. 18; but notice that a test of any man claiming spirituality or prophetic gifts is that 'he should acknowledge that what I am writing to you is a command of the Lord', 1 Cor. 14:37–38; 1 Jn. 4:6); *ii*. their over-all tendency and result or fruits (*e.g.*, do they glorify Christ and edify the church, as *per* Jn. 16:14 and 1 Cor. 14:3ff.?); *iii*. the consensus of the recognized prophets, and presumably elders and teachers, in that place weighing or discerning what is said (1 Cor. 14:29, 32); *iv*. the consistency of this utterance with other prophetic utterances in the body of Christ in that place (vv. 30–31); and *v*. the reverent confession of Jesus as the incarnate Lord by the Spirit speaking through the prophet (1 Cor. 12:2–3; 1 Jn. 4:1–3). In common with other spiritual gifts, Paul stresses that this gift is unprofitable and jarring in its exercise unless it proceeds from a loving heart and is ministered in a loving way in the church (1 Cor. 12:31–13:3).

Besides the possibility of any believer exercising this gift on occasions, there were also in the NT church those particularly recognized and set apart as 'prophets' for a more regular ministry of this nature. They are mentioned next after apostles in 1 Cor. 12:28–29 and Eph. 4:11, and they appear alongside teachers there and in the church at Syrian Antioch (Acts 13:1). Probably the best known in Acts is Agabus (11:28; 21:10–11), but others are also named (15:32), and the whole of the book of Revelation is an extended prophecy revealed to John (1:3; 10:11; 22:7, 10, 18–19). The ministry of prophets appears to have operated along with that of elders when Timothy was set apart for his ministry as an evangelist (1 Tim. 1:18; 4:14).

d. The character and form of New Testament prophecy

All the evidence from the examples of prophetic ministry in the NT shows that it was entirely of a piece with OT prophecy in its character and form. The ministries of John the Baptist, Agabus and the John who wrote the Apocalypse alike comprise the classic unity of prediction and proclamation, of foretelling and forth-telling, and the same is true of Zechariah, Simeon and others. Similarly they combined prediction of wrath to come or trouble in store and of coming grace (Lk. 3:7, 16ff.; Jn. 1:29ff.; Acts 11:28; Rev. 19–21). Equally we find prophecy and revelation by vision and occasionally by dream, as well as by the word of the Lord (Lk. 3:2; Rev. 1:10, 12, *etc.*; Acts 10:9–16; Mt. 1:20). The use of parable and symbol are well attested, including the acted oracle (Acts 21:11). It should be noted that in the last-named instance, Agabus' word was accepted by Paul as descriptively accurate, but not personally directive (vv. 12–14), although it agreed with the words he had received in other cities (Acts 20:23). However, both here and in 1 Tim. 4:14 and Acts 13:9ff. we see the power of the prophetic word still fully able to effect and convey that of which it speaks (*cf.* also Rev. 11:6).

e. Prophecy in the apostolic and later ages

It has often been assumed or argued that there can be no prophecy or prophets in the NT sense of the word in the church today, or in any other post-apostolic age, and many of those who use the term 'prophecy' to describe any current ministry have often diluted its meaning as equivalent to relevant preaching. But while evangelistic proclamation or a teaching ministry may on occasion approximate to prophecy, they are not the same. The biblical arguments for denying the possibility of prophets today (as summarized by J. R. W. Stott, in *Baptism and Fullness*, 1975, pp. 100–102) are twofold: first, besides being mentioned immediately after apostles in Eph. 4:11 and 1 Cor. 12:28, the two are bracketed together as constituting the foundation of the NT church in Eph. 2:20 and 3:5; and secondly, the formation of a completed or closed canon of the NT precludes the possibility of any fresh revelation of divine truth (Heb. 1:1–2). Others have sometimes sought to identify this completion of the NT canon with the time when prophecy will pass away according to 1 Cor. 13:8ff.; but this does violence to the context, which clearly shows that these gifts will pass away 'when the perfect comes', which is defined as when we 'see face to face' (*i.e.* beyond this life and age altogether). Nor will the Ephesian texts bear the weight thus placed on them, since the association of prophets with the founding of the church does not automatically rule out their ministry in its continuance. (There are other reasons for asserting the uniqueness of the original apostolate, which do not apply equally to prophets.) Some would maintain that the prophets referred to are OT prophets, but this is very doubtful. The argument appears to rest in fact upon an equation of prophecy with 'fresh revelation', that is, some material addition to God's saving revelation of himself to mankind as a whole in Christ. But there does not seem to be any solid ground for making such an inevitable equation in either the OT or NT. All may agree that there is no new revelation to be expected concerning God in Christ, the way of salvation, the principles of the Christian life, *etc.* But there appears to be no good reason why the living God, who both speaks and acts (in contrast to the dead idols), cannot use the gift of prophecy to give particular local guidance to a church, nation or individual, or to warn or encourage by way of prediction as well as by reminders, in full accord with the written word of Scripture, by which all such utterances must be tested. Certainly the NT does not see it as the job of the prophet to be a doctrinal innovator, but to deliver the word the Spirit gives him in line with the truth once for all delivered to the saints (Jude 3), to challenge and encourage our faith.

Always in the NT the prophets of both Testaments are regarded as the pioneers of faith, who stand in the front line in every age and reap the full blast of the wind of persecution stirred up in the world by the devil against the people of God, whether through Jewish or Gentile opposition (Mt. 23:37; Lk. 11:47–50; Acts 7:52; 1 Thes. 2:15; Rev. 11:3–8; 16:6; 18:20, 24). Sometimes they are bracketed with our Lord, sometimes with the apostles and sometimes with the saints, but the treatment they receive as God's spokesmen is typical of what all his servants and children who are faithful in their testimony may expect in a fallen world, together with their victory, resurrection and inheritance beyond it by God's grace (Mt. 5:10–12; Heb. 11:39–12:2). For 'the testimony of Jesus is the spirit of prophecy', and all his people are called to bear that testimony faithfully in various ways by the power of the same Spirit.

BIBLIOGRAPHY. H. A. Guy, *New Testament Prophecy, its origin and significance*, 1947; M. C.

Harper, *Prophecy*, 1964; A. Bittlinger, *Gifts and Graces*, 1967; *idem*, *Gifts and Ministries*, 1974; G. Friedrich, *TDNT* 6, pp. 828–861; J. Lindblom, *Gesichte und Offenbarungen*, 1968; E. E. Ellis, in W. W. Gasque and R. P. Martin (eds.), *Apostolic History and the Gospel*, 1970; D. Hill, *NTS* 20, 1973–4, pp. 262–274; *idem*, *New Testament Prophecy*, 1979; J. D. G. Dunn, *Jesus and the Spirit*, 1975, pp. 170ff., 225ff.; U. B. Müller, *Prophetie und Predigt im Neuen Testament*, 1975; J. Panagopoulos (ed.), *Prophetic Vocation in the New Testament and Today* (*NovT Supp.* 45), 1977; C. H. Peisker, C. Brown, *NIDNTT* 3, pp. 74–92; F. F. Bruce, *The Time is Fulfilled*, 1978, pp. 97–114; D. E. Aune, *Prophecy in Early Christianity and the Ancient Mediterranean World*, 1983; W. Grudem, *The Gift of Prophecy in the New Testament and Today*, 1988. J.P.B.

PROPHETESS (Heb. *nᵉḇî'â*; Gk. *prophētis*). Throughout both Testaments 'prophetess' is used in as wide a sense of women as 'prophet' is of men.

Prophetesses specifically named are Miriam, sister of Moses, who led a choral dance in celebration of Israel's deliverance from Egypt (Ex. 15:20); Deborah, wife of Lappidoth, 'a mother in Israel' (Jdg. 5:7), who was consulted as an inter-tribal judge (Jdg. 4:4); Huldah, wife of the keeper of the royal wardrobe, who declared the divine will to Josiah after the discovery of the law-book (2 Ki. 22:14); Noadiah, who joined other prophets in attempting to intimidate Nehemiah (Ne. 6:14); and Anna, who praised God in the Temple at the appearance of the infant Jesus (Lk. 2:36ff.).

Isaiah's wife is called 'the prophetess' (Is. 8:3), perhaps because she was a prophet's wife. Philip's 4 unnamed daughters prophesied in Caesarea (Acts 21:9). In the early church, as Paul's Corinthian correspondence indicates, the gift of *prophecy was exercised by various Christians irrespective of sex (*cf.* 1 Cor. 11:4f.). This was in accordance with the prediction of Joel 2:28 ('your sons and your daughters shall prophesy'), fulfilled on the day of Pentecost (Acts 2:16ff.).

There were false prophetesses as well as false prophets in Israel (*cf.* Ezk. 13:17). In the NT unenviable notoriety is attained by 'the woman Jezebel, who calls herself a prophetess' (Rev. 2:20). M.B.

PROPITIATION. Propitiation properly signifies the removal of wrath by the offering of a gift. In the OT it is expressed by the verb *kipper* (*ATONEMENT). In the NT the *hilaskomai* word group is the important one. In modern times the whole idea of propitiation has been strongly criticized as savouring of unworthy ideas of God. Many suggest that the term 'propitiation' should be abandoned in favour of *expiation, and this is done, for example, in RSV.

The objection to propitiation arises largely from an objection to the whole idea of the wrath of God, which many exponents of this view relegate to the status of an archaism. They feel that modern men cannot hold such an idea. But the men of the OT had no such inhibitions. For them 'God is angry with the wicked every day' (Ps. 7:11, AV). They had no doubt that sin inevitably arouses the strongest reaction from God. God is not to be accused of moral flabbiness. He is vigorously opposed to evil in every shape and form. While he may be 'slow to anger' (Ne. 9:17, *etc.*), his anger is yet certain in the face of sin. We may even read 'The Lord is slow to anger, and abounding in steadfast love, forgiving iniquity and transgression, but he will by no means clear the guilty' (Nu. 14:18). Even in a passage dealing with the longsuffering of God his refusal to condone guilt finds mention. The thought that God is slow to anger is to men of the OT far from being a truism. It is something wonderful and surprising. It is awe-inspiring and totally unexpected.

But if they were sure of the wrath of God against all sin, they were equally sure that this wrath might be put away, usually by the offering of the appropriate sacrifice. This was ultimately due, not to any efficacy in the sacrifice, but to God himself. God says, 'I have given it for you upon the altar to make atonement for your souls' (Lv. 17:11). Pardon is not something wrung from an unwilling deity. It is the gracious gift of a God who is eager to forgive. So the psalmist can say, 'He, being compassionate, forgave their iniquity, and did not destroy them; he restrained his anger often, and did not stir up all his wrath' (Ps. 78:38). The averting of the wrath of God is not something which men bring about. It is due to none less than God himself, who 'turned his anger away' (AV).

In the NT there are several passages where the expression 'the wrath of God' occurs, but the relevant evidence is not limited to these alone. Everywhere in the NT there is the thought that God is vigorously opposed to evil. The sinner is in no good case. He has put himself in the wrong with God. He can look for nothing other than the severity of the divine judgment. Whether we choose to call this 'the wrath of God' or not, it is there. And, while wrath is a term to which some objections may legitimately be raised, it is the biblical term and no satisfactory substitute has been suggested.

We see the force of the NT idea of propitiation from the occurrence of the term in Rom. 3:24f. We are 'justified freely by his grace through the redemption that is in Christ Jesus: whom God hath set forth to be a propitiation through faith in his blood' (AV). The force of Paul's argument up to this point is that all, Jew and Gentile alike, are under the condemnation of God. 'The wrath of God is revealed from heaven against all ungodliness and wickedness of men' (Rom. 1:18). Paul shows first that the Gentile world stands under God's condemnation and then that the Jewish world is in the same plight. It is against this background that he sees the work of Christ. Christ did not save men from nothing at all. He delivered them from a very real peril. The sentence of judgment had been passed against them. The wrath of God hung over them. Paul has strongly emphasized the wrath of God throughout these opening chapters, and therefore Christ's saving work must include deliverance from this wrath. This deliverance is described by the word 'propitiation'. There is nothing else to express this thought in the critical passage Rom. 3:21ff., which sets out the way in which God has dealt with this aspect of man's plight. *hilastērion* must be held here to signify something very like 'propitiation'. (See further *NTS* 2, 1955–6, pp. 33–43.)

In 1 Jn. 2:2 Jesus is described as 'the propitiation for our sins'. In the previous verse he is our 'advocate with the Father'. If we need an advocate with God, then our position is indeed a dangerous one.

We are in dire peril. All this helps us to see that 'propitiation' is to be taken here in its usual sense. Jesus' activity for men is described as turning away the divine wrath.

But the Bible view of propitiation does not depend on this or that specific passage. It is a reflection of the general import of its teaching. 'Propitiation' is a reminder that God is implacably opposed to everything that is evil, that his opposition may properly be described as 'wrath', and that this wrath is put away only by the atoning work of Christ.

BIBLIOGRAPHY. C. H. Dodd, *The Bible and the Greeks*, 1935; R. Nicole, *WTJ* 17, 1954–5, pp. 117–157; L. Morris, *NTS* 2, 1955–6, pp. 33–43; *idem*, *The Apostolic Preaching of the Cross*[2], 1965; *idem*, *The Atonement*, 1983; H.-G. Link, C. Brown, H. Vorländer, *NIDNTT* 3, pp. 145–176. L.M.

PROSELYTE. A proselyte was a Gentile who, through conversion, committed himself/herself to the practice of the Jewish law, exclusive devotion to Yahweh and integration into the Jewish community.

The Heb. term *gēr* first meant a resident alien, not necessarily with religious affiliations – indeed the same word is used for Jews on foreign soil (Gn. 15:13; Ex. 23:9). Within the OT canon, or possibly later, it came to designate full proselytes. The LXX renders *gēr* by *proselytos* seventy-seven times, with other terms being used occasionally. There is both in Heb. and in Gk. an advance in significance of meaning with these terms, although we cannot always define precisely where one phase shades into another.

Several OT passages show a warmth of welcome to proselytes. Note the willingness in Ex. 12:48 to receive foreigners into religious fellowship on condition of circumcision. The prayer of 1 Ki. 8:41–43, and the glowing potential universalism of Is. 2:2–4; 19:18–25; 49:6; 56:3–8; Je. 3:17; Zp. 2:11; 3:9 are striking. The short book of Ruth is the story of a particular woman proselyte whose memory later Judaism greatly honoured. Political and geographical circumstances doubtless kept the number of proselytes relatively small in OT times. Such persons would normally be aliens, resident in Palestine, voluntarily accepting circumcision, and with it the whole of the law.

We have evidence for a number of proselytes in the Graeco-Roman period which shows that Jewish morality and monotheism appealed to a number of Gentiles who accordingly became converts. Their existence is clear in literary works of the period and in a number of inscriptions. Notable examples are the members of the royal family from Adiabene (see Josephus, AJ 20.17–95) and Nicolaus the proselyte from Antioch (Acts 6:5; see also Acts 2:10; 13:43; Tobit 1:8; Judith 14:10). Josephus also writes of forced conversion to Judaism in the Hasmonaean period (see AJ 13.257–258, 319).

Another group of Gentiles, who have been called 'Godfearers', were attracted to Judaism and worshipped in the synagogue without becoming converts. A recently discovered inscription from Aphrodisias in Asia Minor, probably from the early 3rd century AD, gives the names of seventy-one Jews but also lists fifty-four people, none of whom have distinctly Jewish names, who are described as 'Godfearers' (*theosebis*). This is clear evidence that the Jews in Aphrodisias at this time used the term 'Godfearers' as a semi-technical term for a group of Gentiles who revered the Jewish God, adopted some Jewish customs and were connected with the Jewish community in some definite way, but had not become proselytes. We have further evidence for Godfearers in other areas in Asia Minor and elsewhere. Although only one of these inscriptions (from Panticapaeum) is to be dated in the 1st century AD, texts in Josephus, Juvenal and Acts also suggest that there were Godfearers in some synagogues in this earlier period, although at this stage no one term seems to have been used to describe them, and Godfearers probably varied in their degree of adherence to Judaism. According to Acts, a number of these Godfearers (called *phoboumenoi* or *sebomenoi tōn theōn*) became Christians (Acts 10:1–2; 17:4).

In the rabbinic literature, the term *gēr* unquestionably means a full proselyte. According to the rabbis, proselytes were instructed and then underwent circumcision and baptism, followed by offering a sacrifice in the temple while this was possible. The elements of conversion in the 1st century are debated. Although the duties and rights of proselytes were in some respects more limited than those of born Jews, in essentials proselytes were probably regarded by the rabbis as of equal status with born Jews and many rabbinic texts evince a positive attitude towards proselytes. However, some rabbis viewed proselytes unfavourably. In deprecating the admission of proselytes to Judaism, the Babylonian Talmud likens them to a sore on the skin of Israel (*b. Yebamoth* 109b) and one rabbi argued that proselytes delayed the coming of the Messiah, and so were presumably, therefore, not to be actively sought (*b. Niddah* 13b).

Many scholars have held the view that Jews had an active proselytizing mission in the 1st century AD. However, it has recently been argued that Jews in this period did not engage in an active mission to convert outsiders. Although Jews welcomed non-Jews, who elected to join them and their religion, Jews in this period did not undertake a mission to win converts whenever the opportunity offered itself. The initiative for conversion seems to have generally come from the would-be Gentile convert. The proselytizing impulse within the early church was therefore something which arose within Christianity itself, and was not something taken over from the Judaism of the 1st century. However, by the 3rd century AD, some Jews do seem to have regarded winning proselytes as a religious duty.

There has been much controversy about the meaning of the words of Jesus given in Mt. 23:15. It seem likely that here Jesus attacked Pharisees for their eagerness to try and persuade other Jews to become Pharisees. 'To make a proselyte' in this verse therefore probably involves persuading someone to become a Pharisee, and shows that the term 'proselyte' was still in the process of becoming a technical term for converted Gentile at this time. Alternatively, the verse may refer to Pharisees seeking to convert Godfearers into full proselytes, who then came under the law as the Pharisees understood it.

BIBLIOGRAPHY. M. Goodman, *Mission and Conversion. Proselytizing in the Religious History of the Roman Empire*, 1994; K. G. Kuhn, in *TDNT* 6, pp. 727–744; S. McKnight, *A Light Among the Gentiles. Jewish Missionary Activity in the Second Temple Period*, 1991; E. Schürer *et al.*, *The History of the Jewish People in the Age of Jesus Christ (175 BC–AD 135)*, rev. edn., 3, 1986, pp. 150–176; P. Trebilco, *Jewish Communities in Asia Minor*, 1991, pp. 145–166. P.T.

R.A.S.

PROSTITUTION. The OT speaks of both common prostitutes, *zōnôṯ*, and sacred prostitutes of both sexes, *qᵉḏēšôṯ* and *qᵉḏēšîm*, who were votaries of fertility cults. The NT term for a prostitute is *pornē* (*cf.* the word 'pornography').

Tamar is described as both a harlot (Gn. 38:15) and a cult prostitute (Gn. 38:21, RSVmg.). The two Heb. words are used as parallels in Ho. 4:14. Rahab the harlot (Jos. 2) hid the two spies in her home at Jericho. She was acclaimed for her faith (Heb. 11:31; Jas. 2:25) and became an ancestress of Christ (Mt. 1:5). The two mothers who claimed the same baby before Solomon were prostitutes (1 Ki. 3:16).

In the NT period prostitutes were among those who repented at the preaching of John the Baptist (Mt. 21:31–32).

In Dt. 23:17–18 the contemptuous phrase 'dog' evidently refers to a male cult prostitute. In Rehoboam's time the presence of such male prostitutes became widespread (1 Ki. 14:24). Asa, Jehoshaphat and Josiah attempted to root out this abomination (1 Ki. 15:12; 22:46; 2 Ki. 23:7).

Other passages which may contain possible allusions to sacred prostitution include Nu. 25:1–3; 1 Sa. 2:22; Je. 13:27; Ezk. 16; 23:37–41; Am. 2:7–8; 2 Macc. 6:4.

Numerous nude female figurines found throughout the Near East depict the goddesses who were venerated in sacred prostitution. Their votaries believed that they could stimulate the fertility of their crops by sympathetic magic when they engaged in intercourse.

We may assume that the worship of the major Canaanite goddesses —Ashera, Astarte, Anath—involved sacred prostitution, though there are no explicit texts which can prove this. In the Ugaritic texts of temple personnel we find the *qdšm*, who were probably male cult prostitutes. Explicit references to sacred prostitution in Syria and Phoenicia are found in the late texts of Lucian's *De Dea Syria* (2nd century AD). The prostitution of women in the service of Venus at Heliopolis (Baalbek) is attested as late as the 4th century AD.

There is good reason to believe that Phoenician influence was responsible for the importation of cultic prostitution as part of the Greek worship of Aphrodite by way of Cyprus and Cythera (*cf.* Homer's *Odyssey* 8. 288, 362).

Aphrodite was the goddess of Corinth and the patroness of prostitutes. Strabo 8. 6. 20 asserted that her temple on the Acrocorinthus had more than 1,000 hierodoules. When Paul warned the congregation at Corinth against immorality (1 Cor. 6:15–16), he was no doubt warning them in part against these cult prostitutes.

Prostitution is condemned as defiling our bodies which are the temples of the Holy Spirit (1 Cor. 6:18–20). Those who do not repent of such practices will be excluded from heaven (Rev. 21:8; 22:15).

The Scriptures often use the imagery of harlotry to depict the evil of idolatry and apostasy (Is. 57:3–5; Je. 2:23–25; Rev. 17:1ff.). Hosea was commanded to marry Gomer the harlot to illustrate Israel's infidelity (Ho. 1:2).

BIBLIOGRAPHY. E. Yamauchi, in H. Hoffner (ed.), *Orient and Occident*, 1973, pp. 213–222; J. Oswalt, *ZPEB*, 4, pp. 910–912; E. Fisher, *Biblical Theology Bulletin* 6, 1976, pp. 225–236; P. E. Dion, *CBQ* 43, 1981, pp. 41–48; K. van der Toorn, *JBL* 108, 1989, pp. 193–205. E.M.Y.

PROVERB. In RSV the word 'proverb' has a wider range of meanings than in normal English usage, due especially to the many meanings of *māšāl* (probably related to *mšl*, 'to be like', 'to be compared with', although some relate it to *mšl*, 'to rule'; hence a word spoken by a ruler). In addition to denoting 'a pithy saying, especially one condensing the wisdom of experience' (*cf.* 1 Sa. 10:12; 24:13; 1 Ki. 4:32; Pr. 1:1, 6; 10:1; 25:1; Ec. 12:9; Ezk. 12:22–23; 16:44; 18:2–3), 'proverb' may also serve as a synonym for 'byword' (*e.g.* Dt. 28:37; 1 Ki. 9:7; 2 Ch. 7:20; Ps. 69:11; Je. 24:9; Ezk. 14:8). The point seems to be that the sufferer becomes an object-lesson from which others may learn appropriate lessons. Similarly, 'proverb' may mean 'taunt-song' as in Is. 14:4ff., where the disastrous effects of the king of Babylon's presumptuous pride are paraded. In Hab. 2:6 (AV) 'proverb' translates *ḥîḏâ*, 'riddle', 'perplexing question'.

Two words are rendered 'proverb' in the NT: *parabolē* (Lk. 4:23) and *paroimia* (Jn. 16:25, 29, AV; 2 Pet. 2:22). In the Johannine passages *paroimia* apparently denotes a 'dark saying' or 'figure of speech in which . . . lofty ideas are concealed' (Arndt). The didactic role of proverbs in both Testaments should not be underestimated. Along with *parables, proverbs played a major part in the teaching ministry of Christ (*e.g.* Mt. 6:21; Lk. 4:23; Jn. 12:24). (*WISDOM LITERATURE.)

BIBLIOGRAPHY. D. A. Hubbard, *ISBE*[3], 1986, pp. 1012–1015; W. McKane, *Proverbs*, 1970, pp. 10–33; R. B. Y. Scott, *Proverbs, Ecclesiastes*, *AB*, 1965, pp. 3–9; G. von Rad, *Wisdom in Israel*, 1972, pp. 24–34. D.A.H.

PROVERBS, BOOK OF. The Heb. title *mišlê*, 'proverbs of', is an abbreviation of *mišlê šᵉlōmōh*, 'the proverbs of Solomon' (1:1). The English name is derived from the Vulg. *Liber Proverbiorum*. A collection of collections, Proverbs is a guidebook for successful living. Without overtly stressing the great prophetic themes (*e.g.* the covenant), the proverbs show how Israel's distinctive faith affected her common life.

I. Outline of contents

a. The importance of wisdom (1:1–9:18)

Following an introductory statement of purpose (1:1–6), the writer instructs his son or pupil concerning the worth and nature of wisdom. In contrast to the proverbs of 10:1ff., each idea is discussed at some length in a didactic poem. These poetic essays are a highly polished development of the *māšāl* (*PROVERB, *WISDOM LITERATURE).

The author's aim is to paint the strongest possible contrast between the results of seeking wisdom and living a life of folly. He sets the stage for the several hundred specific proverbs which follow. Certain temptations loom large in the sage's mind: crimes of violence (1:10–19; 4:14–19); the binding of oneself by a rash pledge (6:1–5); sloth

(6:6–11); duplicity (6:12–15); and especially sexual impurity (2:16–19; 5:3–20; 6:23–35; 7:4–27; 9:13–18). To the one who avoids these snares, *Wisdom offers happiness, long life, wealth and honour (3:13–18). The deeply religious nature of this section (*e.g.* 1:7; 3:5–12), its sensitive moral tone and its hortatory, didactic style are reminiscent of Deuteronomy.

Apparently the writer of these chapters is anonymous, since 1:1–6 probably refers to the entire book and 10:1 introduces a collection of proverbs which purport to be Solomonic. This section is customarily dated among the latest in the collection. Though its final editing may be relatively late (*c.* 600 BC), much of the material may be considerably earlier. W. F. Albright has drawn attention to the number of parallels in thought and structure between this section, especially chs. 8–9, and Ugaritic or Phoenician literature (*Wisdom in Israel*, pp. 7–9). He also suggests that 'it is entirely possible that aphorisms and even longer sections go back into the Bronze Age in substantially their present form' (p. 5). For the personification of Wisdom in 8:22ff., see *WISDOM.

b. The proverbs of Solomon (10:1–22:16)

This section is probably the oldest in the book, and there is a growing tendency among scholars to accept the accuracy of the tradition reflected in 1 Ki. 4:29ff.; Pr. 1:1; 10:1; 25:1 honouring *Solomon as the sage *par excellence.* His contacts with the court of Egypt, the far-reaching network of his empire and the combination of wealth and respite from war enabled him to devote himself to cultural pursuits on a scale denied his successors.

About 375 proverbs occur in this collection. Their structure is largely *antithetic* in chs. 10–15 and *synthetic* or *synonymous* in chs. 16–22. Most of the proverbs are unrelated; no system of grouping is discernible.

Though a religious note is by no means absent (*cf.* 15:3, 8–9, 11; 16:1–9, *etc.*), the bulk of the proverbs contain no specific reference to Israel's faith but are based on practical observations of everyday life. The extremely practical nature of the instruction which stresses the *profits* of wisdom has drawn the criticism of those who hold that pure religion should be disinterested. But how would a practical sage to whom God had not yet revealed the mystery of life after death make the issues clear without pointing out the blessings of the wise and the pitfalls of the fool?

c. The words of the wise (22:17–24:22)

The title is obscured in *MT* and EVV, being incorporated in 22:17. However, the obvious title 'These also are sayings of the wise' (24:23) suggests that 22:17–24:22 should be considered a separate collection. These maxims are more closely related and sustained in theme than those of the previous section. The topics are manifold: regard for the poor (22:22, 27), respect for the king (23:1–3; 24:21–22), discipline of children (23:13–14), temperance (23:19–21, 29–35), honour of parents (23:22–25), chastity (23:26–28), *etc.* Religious emphasis, though not dominant, is not lacking (*e.g.* 22:19, 23; 24:18, 21).

A formal relationship between the Egyp. proverbs of Amenemope and 22:17–23:11 is widely recognized. The debate centres in the question, Which influenced which? W. Baumgartner (*The Old Testament and Modern Study*, ed. by H. H. Rowley, 1951, p. 212) notes that 'the . . . theory that Amenemope is the original . . . has now been generally accepted'. This view, however, has now been challenged from within Egyptology itself, by E[ua]. Drioton, who has put up weighty reasons for a view that the Egyp. Amenemope is, in fact, merely a translation (sometimes too literal) from a Heb. original into Egyp.; this Heb. original would then be the 'words of the wise' from which Proverbs independently drew. See E[ua]. Drioton, *Mélanges André Robert*, 1957, pp. 254–280, and *Sacra Pagina*, 1, 1959, pp. 229–241. Against this, however, see R. J. Williams, *JEA* 47, 1961, pp. 100–106. The passage has been so refined by Israel's faith that, whatever its origin, it belongs to the OT revelation.

d. Additional sayings of the wise (24:23–34)

This brief collection exhibits the same irregularity of form as the one above. There are brief proverbs (*e.g.* v. 26) and extended maxims (*e.g.* vv. 30–34; *cf.* 6:6–11). The religious element is not prominent, but there is a keen sense of social responsibility (*e.g.* vv. 28–29). These two collections are apparently not Solomonic but are part of the legacy of Israel's sages, who created or collected and polished a vast body of wisdom sayings (*cf.* Ec. 12:9–11).

e. Additional proverbs of Solomon (25:1–29:27)

In content this section is not unlike 10:1–22:16 (*e.g.* 25:24 = 21:9; 26:13 = 22:13; 26:15 = 19:24, *etc.*). However, the proverbs here are less uniform in length; antithetic parallelism, the backbone of the earlier section, is less common, although chs. 28–29 contain numerous examples; comparison, rare in 10:1ff., occurs frequently (*e.g.* 25:3, 11–14, 18–20, *etc.*).

The statement in 25:1 has influenced the Talmudic opinion (*Baba Bathra* 15a) that Hezekiah and his company wrote the Proverbs. The role of Hezekiah's men in the editing of the book is not clear, but there is no reason to question the accuracy of 25:1, which relates to the sayings in chs. 25–29. Hezekiah's interest in Israel's literature is attested in 2 Ch. 29:25–30, where he restores the Davidic order of worship, including the singing of the psalms of David and Asaph. A. Bentzen suggests that these proverbs were preserved *orally* until Hezekiah's time, when they were transcribed (*IOT*, 2, p. 173). S. R. Driver (*An Introduction to the Literature of the Old Testament*, p. 401) lists those proverbs which reflect a restiveness concerning the Monarchy (28:2, 12, 15f., 28; 29:2, 4, 16). In the selection of these proverbs, is there a reflection of the turbulence of the 8th century BC?

f. The words of Agur (30:1–33)

Agur, his father Jakeh, Ithiel and Ucal (30:1) defy identification. See *ITHIEL for an adjustment in the word divisions which eliminates the last two names completely. *Oracle* (30:1, RSVmg.) should probably be read as a proper name *Massa.

The first few verses are difficult to interpret, but seem to be agnostic in tone. This agnosticism is answered (5–6) with a statement about the unchangeable word of God. Following a brief but moving prayer (7–9), the chapter concludes with a series of extended proverbs describing some commendable or culpable quality. In many of these the number *four* is prominent. Several exhibit the x, x + 1 pattern well attested in the OT (*e.g.* Am. 1–

2; Mi. 5:5) and common in Ugaritic (*cf.* C. H. Gordon, *Ugaritic Handbook*, 1947, pp. 34, 201).

*g. The words of *Lemuel* (31:1–9)

This king of *Massa is unknown. His mother's advice includes warnings against sexual excess and drunkenness and encouragement to judge even the poor with rectitude. The influence of Aramaic on this section is noteworthy (*e.g. bar*, 'son'; *mᵉlāḵîn*, 'kings').

h. In praise of a virtuous wife (31:10–31)

This well-wrought acrostic poem has no title, but is so different from the preceding section that it must be considered separately. Its stylized form suggests that it should be viewed among the latest sections of the book. The description of an industrious, conscientious and pious woman is a fitting conclusion to a book which discusses the practical outworkings of a God-directed life.

II. Date

Proverbs could not have been completed before Hezekiah's time (*c.* 715–686 BC). However, the acrostic poem (31:10–31) and the sayings of the Massaites (30:1–33; 31:1–9) may well have been added in the exilic or post-exilic period. A reasonable date for the final editing is the 5th century BC. The individual proverbs date in most cases from well before the Exile. W. F. Albright notes (*op. cit.*, p. 6) that the contents of Proverbs must, on literary grounds, be dated before the Aramaic sayings of Ahiqar (7th century BC).

III. Proverbs and the New Testament

Proverbs has left its stamp on the NT by several quotations (*e.g.* 3:7a = Rom. 12:16; 3:11–12 = Heb. 12:5–6; 3:34 = Jas. 4:6 and 1 Pet. 5:5b; 4:26 = Heb. 12:13a; 10:12 = Jas. 5:20 and 1 Pet. 4:8; 25:21–22 = Rom. 12:20; 26:11 = 2 Pet. 2:22) and allusions (*e.g.* 2:4 and Col. 2:3; 3:1–4 and Lk. 2:52; 12:7 and Mt. 7:24–27). As Christ fulfilled the Law and the Prophets (Mt. 5:17), so he fulfilled the wisdom writings by revealing the fullness of God's wisdom (Mt. 12:42; 1 Cor. 1:24, 30; Col. 2:3). If Proverbs is an extended commentary on the law of love, then it helps to pave the way for the One in whom true love became incarnate. See C. T. Fritsch, 'The Gospel in the Book of Proverbs', *Theology Today* 7, 1950, pp. 169–183.

BIBLIOGRAPHY. R. Alden, *Proverbs*, 1983; D. A. Hubbard, *Proverbs*, 1989; D. Kidner, *Proverbs*, *TOTC*, 1964; W. McKane, *Proverbs: A New Approach*, 1970; R. Murphy, *Wisdom Literature*, *FOTL* 13, 1981; R. B. Y. Scott, *Proverbs, Ecclesiastes*, 1965; R. C. Van Leeuwen, *Context and Meaning in Proverbs 25–27*, 1988; R. N. Whybray, *The Book of Proverbs*, 1972. D.A.H.

PROVIDENCE. No single word in biblical Hebrew or Greek expresses the idea of God's providence. *pronoia* is used for God's purposive foresight by Plato, Stoic writers, Philo, who wrote a book *On Providence* (*Peri pronoias*), Josephus, and the authors of Wisdom (*cf.* 14:3; 17:2) and 3, 4 Macc.; but in the NT *pronoia* occurs only twice (Acts 24:2; Rom. 13:14), both times denoting, not God's care and forethought, but man's. The cognate verb *pronoeō*, too, is used only of man (Rom. 12:17; 2 Cor. 8:21; 1 Tim. 5:8).

Providence is normally defined in Christian theology as the unceasing activity of the Creator whereby, in overflowing bounty and goodwill (Ps. 145:9 *cf.* Mt. 5:45–48), he upholds his creatures in ordered existence (Acts 17:28; Col. 1:17; Heb. 1:3), guides and governs all events, circumstances and free acts of angels and men (*cf.* Ps. 107; Jb. 1:12; 2:6; Gn. 45:5–8), and directs everything to its appointed goal, for his own glory (*cf.* Eph. 1:9–12). This view of God's relation to the world must be distinguished from: (*a*) *pantheism*, which absorbs the world into God; (*b*) *deism*, which cuts it off from him; (*c*) *dualism*, which divides control of it between God and another power; (*d*) *indeterminism*, which holds that it is under no control at all; (*e*) *determinism*, which posits a control of a kind that destroys man's moral responsibility; (*f*) the doctrine of *chance*, which denies the controlling power to be rational; and (*g*) the doctrine of *fate*, which denies it to be benevolent.

Providence is presented in Scripture as a function of divine sovereignty. God is King over all, doing just what he wills (Pss. 103:19; 135:6; Dn. 4:35; *cf.* Eph. 1:11). This conviction, robustly held, pervades the whole Bible. The main strands in it may be analysed as follows.

a. Providence and the natural order

God rules all natural forces (Ps. 147:8f.), all wild animals (Jb. 38–41), and all happenings in the world, great and small, from thunderstorms (Jb. 37; Ps. 29) and plagues (Ex. 7:3–11:10; 12:29ff.; Joel 2:25) to the death of a sparrow (Mt. 10:29) or the fall of a lot (Pr. 16:33). Physical life, in men and animals, is his to give and to take away (Gn. 2:17; 1 Sa. 1:27; 2 Sa. 12:19; Jb. 1:21; Pss. 102:23; 104:29–30; 127:3; Ezk. 24:16ff.; Dn. 5:23, *etc.*); so are health and sickness (Dt. 7:15; 28:27, 60), prosperity and adversity ('evil', Am. 3:6; *cf.* Is. 45:7), *etc.*

Since the regularity of the natural order is thought of as depending directly upon the divine will (*cf.* Gn. 8:22), the Bible finds no difficulty in the idea of an occasional miraculous irregularity; God does what he wills in his world, and nothing is too hard for him (*cf.* Gn. 18:14).

God's providential government of the created order proclaims his wisdom, power, glory and goodness (Pss. 8:1, RV; 19:1–6; Acts 14:17; Rom. 1:19f.). The man who in face of this revelation does not acknowledge God is without excuse (Rom. 1:20).

The Bible presents God's constant fulfilling of his kindly purposes in nature both as matter for praise in itself (*cf.* Pss. 104; 147) and as a guarantee that he is lord of human history, and will fulfil his gracious promises in that realm also (*cf.* Je. 31:35ff.; 33:19–26).

b. Providence and world history

Since the Fall, God has been executing a plan of redemption. This plan pivots upon Christ's first coming and culminates in his return. Its goal is the creation of a world-wide church in which Jew and non-Jew share God's grace on equal terms (Eph. 3:3–11), and through this the reintegration of the disordered cosmos (Rom. 8:19ff.), under the rule of Christ at his second coming (Eph. 1:9–12; Phil. 2:9ff.; Col. 1:20; 1 Cor. 15:24ff.). Through Christ's present reign and future triumph, the OT prophecies of God's Messianic kingdom (*cf.* Is. 11:1–9; Dn. 2:44; 7:13–27) are fulfilled. The unifying theme of the Bible is God's exercise of his kingship in setting up this kingdom. No foe can thwart him; he laughs at opposition to his plan (Ps. 2:4), and uses it to his own ends (*cf.* Acts 4:25–28, quoting Ps. 2:1f.). The climax of history will be the overthrow of those who fight against God and his kingdom, as the book of Revelation shows (Rev. 19, *etc.*).

Paul analyses the steps in God's plan in terms of the Jew–Gentile and law–grace relationships in Gal. 3; Rom. 9–11; *cf.* Eph. 2:12–3:11.

c. Providence and personal circumstances

God told Israel as a nation that he would prosper them while they were faithful but bring disaster on them if they sinned (Lv. 26:14ff.; Dt. 28:15ff.). The attempt to understand the fortunes of individual Israelites in the light of this principle raised problems. Why does God allow the wicked to prosper, even when they are victimizing the just? And why is disaster so often the lot of the godly?

The first question is always answered by affirming that the wicked prosper only for a moment; God will soon visit them and take vengeance (Pss. 37 *passim*; 50:16–21; 73:17ff.), though for the present he may forbear, in order to give them further opportunity for repentance (Rom. 2:4f.; 2 Pet. 3:9; Rev. 2:21). The NT identifies the day of God's visitation with the final judgment (*cf.* Rom. 2:3ff.; 12:19; Jas. 5:1–8).

The second question is tackled in several ways. It is asserted: (i) that the righteous will be vindicated when the day of visitation for the wicked comes (Ps. 37; Mal. 3:13–4:3); (ii) that meanwhile suffering is valuable as a God-given discipline (Pr. 3:11f.; Ps. 119:67, 71); (iii) that suffering, faithfully borne, even if not understood, glorifies God and leads to blessing in the end (Jb. 1–2; 42); (iv) that communion with God is the supreme good, and to those who enjoy it outward impoverishments are of no ultimate importance (Ps. 73:14, 23ff.; Hab. 3:17f.).

In the NT the fact that believers suffer ill-treatment and adverse circumstances is no longer a problem, since it is recognized that fellowship in Christ's sufferings is fundamental to the Christian vocation (*cf.* Mt. 10:24f.; Jn. 15:18ff.; 16:33; Acts 9:16; 14:22; Phil. 3:10ff.; 1 Pet. 4:12–19). This recognition, in conjunction with the OT principles mentioned above, completely disposed of the 'problem of suffering' for the first Christians. Knowing something of their glorious hope (1 Pet. 1:3ff.), and of the strengthening and sustaining power of Christ (2 Cor. 1:3ff.; 12:9f.), they could contentedly face all situations (Phil. 4:11) and rejoice in all troubles (Rom. 8:35ff.), confident that through adversity their loving Father was disciplining them in sanctity (Heb. 12:5–11), developing their Christian character (Jas. 1:2ff.; 1 Pet. 5:10; *cf.* Rom. 5:2ff.), proving the reality of their faith (1 Pet. 1:7), and so ripening them for glory (1 Pet. 4:13). In all things God works for the spiritual welfare of his people (Rom. 8:28); and he supplies them with whatever material things they need throughout their earthly pilgrimage (Mt. 6:25–33; Phil. 4:19).

Belief in providence determines many of the basic attitudes of biblical piety. The knowledge that God determines their circumstances teaches the faithful to wait on him in humility and patience for vindication and deliverance (Pss. 37; 40:13ff.; Jas. 5:7ff.; 1 Pet. 5:6f.). It forbids them to grow despondent or despairing (Pss. 42–43), and brings them courage and hope when harassed (Pss. 60; 62). It inspires all prayers for help, and praise for every good thing that is enjoyed.

d. Providence and human freedom

God rules the hearts and actions of all men (*cf.* Pr. 21:1; Ezr. 6:22), often for purposes of his own which they do not suspect (*cf.* Gn. 45:5–8; 50:20; Is. 10:5ff.; 44:28–45:4; Jn. 11:49ff.; Acts 13:27ff.). God's control is absolute in the sense that men do only that which he has ordained that they should do; yet they are truly free agents, in the sense that their decisions are their own, and they are morally responsible for them (*cf.* Dt. 30:15ff.). A distinction, however, must be drawn between God's allowing (or 'giving up') sinners to practise the evil that they have preferred (Ps. 81:12f.; Acts 14:16; Rom. 1:24–28), and his gracious work of prompting his people to will and do what he commands (Phil. 2:13); for in the former case, according to the biblical rule of judgment, the blame for the evil done belongs entirely to the sinner (*cf.* Lk. 22:22; Acts 2:23; 3:13–19), whereas in the latter case the praise for the good done must be given to God (*cf.* 1 Cor. 15:10).

BIBLIOGRAPHY. *BAGD*; A. E. Garvie, in *HDB*; A. H. Strong, *Systematic Theology*[12], 1949, pp. 419–443; L. Berkhof, *Systematic Theology*[4], 1949, pp. 165–178; Calvin, *Institutes*, 1. 16–18; K. Barth, *Church Dogmatics*, 3. iii, E.T. 1960, pp. 3–288; A. S. Peake, *The Problem of Suffering in the Old Testament*, 1904; O. Cullmann, *Christ and Time*, E.T. 1951; G. C. Berkouwer, *The Providence of God*, 1952; P. Jacobs, H. Krienke, *NIDNTT* 1, pp. 692–697; J. Behm, *TDNT* 4, pp. 1009–1017. J.I.P.

PROVINCE. Originally the word denoted a sphere of duty or administration. The *praetor urbanus*, *e.g.*, held an *urbana provincia*, and this was defined as the administration of justice within the city (Livy, 6. 42; 31. 6). Tacitus speaks of the suppression of a slave revolt at Brundisium in AD 24 by a quaestor 'whose province was the hill-country pastures', *calles* (*Annals* 4. 27). The reading is confirmed by Suetonius (*Iul.* 19), who speaks of 'provinces' covering the supervision of 'woods and pasture-lands'. The reference shows that, long after the term developed territorial and geographical significance, it retained its ancient meaning. The intermediate use is seen in the employment of the term of a military command. 'To Sicinius,' says Livy, 'the Volsci were assigned as his province, to Aquilius the Hernici' (2. 40). That is, the task of pacification in these two Italian tribal areas was allotted respectively to these two consuls. It was an easy step from, *e.g.*, Spain as a military command to Spain as a conquered territory and defined area of administration. In this later, commoner and wider sense of the word, there were no provinces until Rome extended her conquests beyond the Italian peninsula. Sicily was the first country to be made thus into 'a Roman province' (Cicero, *In Verr.* 2. 2). This was in 241 BC. Sardinia followed in 235 BC. In 121 BC Rome annexed a piece of territory in S Gaul between the Alps and the Cévennes to secure communications with Spain, and this area, Gallia Narbonensis, became known as 'the Province' above all others, and its inhabitants *provinciales.* (Hence Provence today.) Similarly the rest of the provinces were acquired piecemeal, the list being closed by the annexation of Britain by Claudius and Dacia by Trajan.

The earliest provinces were administered by magistrates elected for the purpose. *E.g.*, two additional praetors were elected from 227 BC for Sicily and Sardinia, and two more 20 years later, to govern the two Spanish provinces. The scheme was then discontinued for over a century, Macedonia (148 BC), Achaea and Africa (146 BC) and Asia (133 BC), *e.g.*, being ruled by *magistrates already in office, their *imperium* being extended for the purpose. The term *proconsul signified a consul whose *imperium* was thus 'prorogued' after his year of office, for the purpose of a provincial governorship. A proconsulship could, however, be held without preceding tenure of the consulship. This was the case with Pompey in 77, 66 and 65 BC.

Under the principate the provinces were divided into senatorial and imperial. The former were governed by ex-consuls and ex-praetors with the title of **proconsul*, normally in yearly tenure; the latter were administered by legates of the emperor (*legati Augusti pro praetore*), men of senatorial rank or selected equestrian officials. Tenure of office was at the emperor's pleasure. Imperial provinces were usually those involving legionary garrisons. Transference from one list to another was not uncommon. Tacitus mentions the transfer of Achaea and Macedonia from the senate to the emperor in AD 15 (*leuari proconsulari imperio tradique Caesari* . . .) (*Ann.* 1. 76). Cyprus is a similar example. Annexed in 57 BC, it was incorporated in Cilicia in 55 BC and made an imperial province in 27 BC. In 22 BC Augustus transferred it and Gallia Narbonensis to the senate in exchange for Dalmatia. Hence there was a proconsul in command, as Luke, with his usual accuracy, indicates (Acts 13:7). (*ROMAN EMPIRE.)

BIBLIOGRAPHY. T. Mommsen, *The Provinces of the Roman Empire from Caesar to Diocletian*, 1909; G. H. Stevenson, *Roman Provincial Administration*, 1939; *BA1CS* 2. E.M.B.

PSALMS, BOOK OF.

I. The importance of the Psalter

It would be difficult to overestimate the significance, for Jew and Gentile, of the book of Psalms. Here are mirrored the ideals of religious piety and communion with God, of sorrow for sin and the search for perfection, of walking in darkness, unafraid, by the lamp of faith; of obedience to the law of God, delight in the worship of God, fellowship with the friends of God, reverence for the Word of God; of humility under the chastening rod, trust when evil triumphs and wickedness prospers, serenity in the midst of storm.

The Hebrew poets were inspired to take these spiritual insights and experiences and make them the themes of their songs. But it should be remembered that 'the Psalms are poems, and poems intended to be sung, not doctrinal treatises, nor even sermons' (C. S. Lewis, *Reflections on the Psalms*, 1958, p. 2)—hence the Hebrew title of the Psalms, *tᵉhillîm*, 'songs of praise'—also that they were giving expression to the religion of Israel to which the psalmists were heirs, not merely to their personal religious experiences. So the Psalms belong to all believers, Jew and Gentile.

II. The formation of the Psalter

It has been customary to describe the book of Psalms as 'the hymn-book of the second Temple', and such it undoubtedly was. The title is misleading, however, if it is interpreted to mean that all the psalms were written in the exilic or post-exilic periods. It is important to notice that this type of literature is not only confined to the Psalter in the OT but is found in many different periods in Hebrew history. It is found among the Hebrews as early as the Exodus period (Ex. 15), and another example comes from a time subsequent to, but relatively close to, the invasion of Canaan under Joshua (Jdg. 5). Hannah's psalm (1 Sa. 2:1–10) comes at the close of the Judges period.

The pre-exilic prophetic literature also contains examples of psalm composition (*cf.*, *e.g.*, Ho. 6:1–3; Is. 2:2–4; 38:10–20; Je. 14:7–9; Hab. 3:1ff., *etc.*). And from the post-exilic period come such passages as Ezr. 9:5–15 and Ne. 9:6–39, which are strongly reminiscent of many of the psalms. Clearly, then, the Psalter is not an isolated literary phenomenon. Indeed, the same type of *poetry is found among the Babylonians and the citizens of Ugarit as the Ras Shamra tablets testify. The OT Psalter is a collection of poems which are typical of a literary form which the Hebrews, in common with other cultures, used from at least the Exodus right up until the post-exilic or second Temple period. And, of course, if one reckons with the non-canonical psalms it is clear that this literary form persisted among the Jews until quite a long way into the Christian era.

a. Authorship

No fewer than 73 psalms are attributed to David. Other authors named in the titles are Asaph (50; 73–83), the sons of Korah (42–49, 84–85, 87–88), Solomon (72; 127), and Heman (88), Ethan (89), both Ezrahites, and Moses (90), who have one psalm each attributed to them. Davidic authorship of many of the psalms has often been denied, principally on the ground that David the psalmist of popular belief bears no resemblance to David the warrior of the books of Samuel and Kings. It can also be argued that the ascription *lᵉḏāwiḏ* ('of David') need not be a note of authorship, but only a rubic appointing certain psalms to be used in a royal ritual for the 'David' (the Davidic king) of the time. We do know, however, that David was a musician (1 Sa. 16:14ff.) and a poet (2 Sa. 1:17ff.; 3:33f.). The attempts of some scholars to disprove the Davidic authorship assigned to 2 Sa. 22:1ff.; 23:1–7, and to excise the words 'like David' from Am. 6:5 (where the tradition of David and his music and songs is referred to 300 years after his death) have the air of special pleading. Moreover the NT not only accepts but bases arguments upon Davidic authorship of this material. On this, see also section **IV**, below.

This hymn-book of the second Temple contains very ancient material. This is not at all surprising when it is recalled that the Ras Shamra tablets show that, when Israel invaded Canaan, the type of poetry represented in the Psalms was already a long-established tradition among the inhabitants of Ugarit. The Song of Moses, then, in Ex. 15, and the Song of Deborah (Jdg. 5), were neither isolated nor unprecedented examples of Semitic poetry. The Mosaic and Solomonic authorships referred to in the titles of three psalms suggest that the ancient religion of the tabernacle and the first Temple would require its sacred music. Religion in the days of Amos (5:21–23) and Isaiah (30:29), during the Exile (Ps. 137:1ff.) and the period following the return, and also the building of the second Temple, would also require its solemn chants. But it is the prominence of the king in the Psalter (see section IV) which has done most to convince recent scholars that the classical period of psalm composition was the Monarchy, *i.e.* from David to the beginning of the Exile.

b. Organization

The OT Psalter as we now have it consists of five books. This division goes back to the LXX version, which was begun as early as the 3rd century BC. Every section is easily recognizable because a doxology closes each book. These doxologies are short except the one that ends Book V; there an entire psalm is given over to the closing doxology. The five divisions of the Psalter are as follows: Book I, Pss. 1–41; Book II, Pss. 42–72; Book III, Pss. 73–89; Book IV, Pss. 90–106; Book V, Pss. 107–150. Many have seen in this fivefold division an attempt to imitate the division of the Torah into five books, the Pentateuch. (See N. H. Snaith, *Hymns of the Temple*, 1951, pp. 18–20, where the significance of this is discussed.)

Various features suggest that there were separate collections of psalms in use before the final compilation. *E.g.* certain psalms, in whole or in part (notably Pss. 14 and 53; Ps. 40:13–17 and Ps. 70; Pss. 57:7–11 plus 60:6–13 to make Ps. 108), occur in more than one part of the Psalter. Further, a large group (42–83) speaks predominantly of 'God' rather than 'the LORD', whereas other blocks (1–41; 84–89; 90–150) have the opposite preference, even in psalms attributed to some of the authors of the former group (42–83). Again, Ps. 72:20 evidently marks the close of a particular set of Davidic psalms, but not of David's whole output, as the rest of the Psalter demonstrates.

It seems likely, as various scholars have suggested, that the penultimate stage in compiling the Psalter was the gathering of groups of psalms into three main psalters, perhaps used at different centres or periods, as follows: *a.* the Davidic Pss. 3–41 or 2–41, which prefer the divine name Yahweh (the LORD); *b.* the Korahite, Asaphite and Davidic Pss. 42–83 (the 'Elohistic psalter'), where the term *'ᵉlōhîm* (God) predominates (to which group was added an appendix, 84–89, in which 'Yahweh' prevails); *c.* a collection of mostly anonymous psalms, 90–150 (with 'Yahweh' again), containing certain clusters marked by particular themes or uses (*e.g.* God's kingship, 93–100; the 'Egyptian Hallel', 113–118, traditionally associated with the Passover; the Songs of Ascents, 120–134; the closing Hallelujah psalms, 146–150). Finally, on this view, to match the books of Moses the three collections were further divided to make five, and Ps. 1 (or 1 and 2) placed at the beginning to introduce the whole.

III. Technical terms in the Psalter

The title of the book in Hebrew is *tᵉhillîm*, 'Songs of Praise', or 'Praises'. In English the title *Psalter* comes from LXX A *Psaltērion*, while *The Psalms* comes from LXX B *Psalmoi* or the Vulg. *Liber Psalmorum*. In addition to the title given to the book, the majority of individual psalms have separate headings. Since, however, many of the technical terms in the titles and elsewhere were already obscure to the Jewish translators of the LXX (3rd to 2nd centuries BC), any comments must be tentative.

1. *Technical designations of psalms.* The most frequent term is *mizmôr*, 'a psalm', a word which suggests the use of an instrumental accompaniment. 'A song' (*šîr*) is a more general term, not confined to worship. In the Psalter it is often coupled with *mizmôr* (*e.g.* 48, title), and there are 15 consecutive 'Songs of Ascents' (120–134), probably pilgrim songs or else processional songs for the festivals. Thirteen psalms have the heading *maśkîl*, which would seem to mean 'making wise or skilful'. The psalms in question (32; 42; 44–45; 52–55; 74; 78; 88–89; 142) reflect extremely chastening experiences—with one striking exception (45). The title may, however, refer not to the content or context of the psalm but to its literary style. We have to confess ignorance. Six psalms are called *miḵtām*, which LXX interprets as 'an inscription', and AV mg. (hardly less improbably) as 'a golden psalm' (from *keṯem*, 'gold'). Mowinckel, however, draws attention to Akkad. *katamu*, to cover, and infers a psalm for atonement, since he classifies all these psalms (16; 56–60) as laments. But the 'cover' which they seek is not atonement but defence, and the most likely meaning is 'a plea for protection'; almost, in our terms, 'an SOS'. Other titles are 'a prayer' (17; 86; 90; 102; 142), 'a praise' or 'doxology' (145) and 'a shiggaion' (*šiggāyôn*, Ps. 7; *cf.* Hab. 3:1, plur.). This last term is not clear to us; it has been linked with *šgh*, to wander or reel, and (Mowinckel) with Akkad. *šegu*, to howl or lament. But both Ps. 7 and Hab. 3, while they face desperate situations, react to them with notable faith and hope.

2. *Musical directions.* Many directions which appear to be of this kind occur in conjunction with the heading *lamᵉnaṣṣēahḏ*, 'to (or 'of') the choirmaster' (*cf.* RSV of Pss. 4ff., *etc.*), which may indicate a special collection of psalms (there are 55, scattered through all five books) more elaborately performed than the rest. But that is a guess, and various other meanings have been suggested for this Heb. term derived from a root meaning to excel, endure or shine: *e.g.* LXX has 'to the end'; Mowinckel, 'to dispose Yahweh to mercy' (making his face shine)—to mention only two.

*Musical instruments prescribed in the titles include *nᵉgînôṯ* (strings) and *nᵉḥîlôṯ* ('flutes', RSV), and the pitch of instruments or voices may perhaps be indicated by *'ᵃlāmôṯ* (Ps. 46), 'trebles'(?)—lit. 'girls'—and *sᵉmînîṯ* (Pss. 6 and 12), 'an octave below'(?)—lit. 'eighth'—on the admittedly enigmatic basis of 1 Ch. 15:20f.

Some terms, usually coupled with the preposition *'al* (RSV 'according to'), have been interpreted as either liturgical directions (see 3, below) or tune-names. The chief examples are *a.* Gittith (*gittîṯ*, 8; 81; 84), a word derived from Gath or from the wine or olive press; *b.* Muth-labben (*'al-mûṯ labbēn*, 9), 'death of the son' (but revocalized as *'ᵃlāmôṯ lāḇîn*, as L. Delekat suggests, it could perhaps be construed as 'trebles for clarity'); *c.* 'The Hind of the Dawn' (*'ayyeleṯ ha-šaḥar*, 22); but LXX has 'the help at dawn' (*cf.* *'ᵉyālûṯî*, 'my help', in v. 19 (20, Heb.), as B. D. Eerdmans points out). See, however, 3, below. *d.* 'Lilies' (*šōšannîm*, 45; 69; 80), 'Lily of testimony or covenant' (*šûšan 'ēḏûṯ*, 60); but instead of 'lilies', LXX has 'those who make changes' (*šeššōnîm*?). *e.* 'The Dove on Far-off Terebinths', or, 'The Silent Dove of Far-off Places' (*yônaṯ 'ēlem rᵉḥōqîm*, 56): is this, however, a concluding note to Ps. 55, in view of 55:6f. (7f., Heb.)? On a cultic interpretation, see 3, below. *f.* 'Do Not Destroy' (*'al-tašḥēṯ*, 57 – 59; 75) is a phrase from the vineyards in Is. 65:8, and conceivably the name of a vintage-song and its tune. But the same words occur more significantly in Dt. 9:26, which may underlie both Is. 65:8b and this title. *g.* 'Mahalath' (*mahᵃlaṯ*, 53; 88) appears to be derived from *ḥlh*, either 'be ill' or 'propitiate'. It could be 'a catch-word in a song, giving the name to a tune' (*BDB*), and the additional word *lᵉʿannôṯ* in the title of Ps. 88 could mean either 'to sing antiphonally' (*cf.* Vulg.) or 'to afflict or humble'. But see the next paragraph, against the notion of tune-names.

3. *Liturgical directions.* The preposition *ʿal* (RSV 'according to'), which introduces most of the terms in the above paragraph, means basically 'on'. Mowinckel therefore relates the above titles, *a.* to *g.*, to cultic acts, 'over' which the psalms would be sung. So, *e.g.*, *e.* would refer to a ritual such as that of Lv. 14:5–7, where one bird was sacrificed and one released to fly away, and *g.* would indicate a ritual for the sick. Likewise *ʿal-yᵉḏûṯûn* (62; 77; *cf.* 39) would refer not to the singer Jeduthun (2 Ch. 5:12) but to an act of confession over which the psalms were to be sung. Mowinckel's suggestions are speculative; but so, admittedly, are most others. Perhaps his most dubious example is the title of Ps. 22, taken to refer to the sacrifice of a hart, a non-sacrificial animal (Dt. 12:15, *etc.*).

Selah (*selâ*) occurs 71 times, and is still obscure to us. Since it often seems to mark a division in a psalm, it may be an instruction to the worshippers to 'lift up' (*sll*) their voices or instruments in a refrain or interlude.

Higgaion (*higgāyôn*, 9:16 [17, Heb.]). like Selah, evidently calls for music. It is a term in Ps. 92:3 (4, Heb.) for the sound of a stringed instrument.

IV. The liturgical approach to the Psalter

A landmark in the modern study of the Psalter was the work of H. Gunkel in the early decades of this century. To him it was all-important to start by distinguishing the different classes (*Gattungen*) of psalms by attending to *a.* the worship-situations from which they had sprung ('some definite divine service', rather than some event in the history of the nation or the writer); *b.* the thoughts and moods which different psalms were found to have in common; and *c.* the recurrent features of style, form and imagery which served these various ends. He found the following main types: Hymns of Praise, Personal Thanksgivings, Communal Laments and Personal Laments. In addition there were smaller categories such as Entrance Liturgies, Blessings and Cursings, Wisdom Psalms, Royal Psalms; and there were also mixed types. His classification has been widely adopted, and his insistence on the importance of such an approach seldom questioned.

While Gunkel regarded most of the canonical psalms as literary descendants of Israel's original psalmody, S. Mowinckel saw them as products of the living cultus. He set himself to reconstruct the rites and festivals of Israel from the clues which he confidently detected there, independently of any confirmation from the Pentateuch. His early psalm studies, in the 1920s, made much of a postulated festival of Yahweh's accession as King, supposedly celebrated at the New Year somewhat after the fashion of the Babylonian *akitu* festival, leaving its traces in about 40 of the psalms and in the development of OT eschatology. This lead was quickly followed, sometimes to excess, by other scholars, notably the so-called Myth and Ritual School of British and Scandinavian scholars in the 1930s, who drew heavily upon comparative religion to construct in detail a cultic drama of divine combat and nuptials and the fixing of destinies, which accounted for many of the cries of anguish or triumph in the Psalter and most of its allusions to seas and springs, enemies and monsters, defeat and victory, and the attributes and activities of the king.

Not all scholars, however, who acknowledge a debt to Mowinckel have agreed in detail with him or (still less) with those who carried his methods to extremes. Mowinckel himself makes less of the Accession motif in his later writings than in his early studies, and other scholars who emphasize the influence of the new year festival on the Psalter would see its main aspect as covenant-renewal (A. Weiser) or the reaffirming of God's choice of Zion and the house of David (H. J. Kraus). But the legacy of Gunkel and Mowinckel remains, in the preoccupation of most commentators with the task of assigning each psalm to its proper class, and in the viewing of almost all the material as ecclesiastical.

This is distinct from the view, with which there can be no quarrel, that the psalms were collected and used for worship, and in many cases written expressly for such use. Instead, it assumes that even those psalms which profess to have sprung from episodes in the life of David (*e.g.* the bulk of Pss. 51–60), or which are attested as his writings by the NT (*e.g.* Pss. 16; 69; 109–110), arose on the contrary out of the cult-drama or were anonymously composed as set pieces for worship situations that might arise for the individual, the Davidic king or the congregation. Thus Ps. 51, despite the introductory statement which is part of the Hebrew text, is allegedly not David's prayer after his sin with Bathsheba, and Ps. 110, despite our Lord's account of it, is not allowed to be the work of (as he himself put it in Mk. 12:36) 'David himself, inspired by the Holy Spirit'. Within this dominant school of thought, however, there are varicties of opinion as to the right classification of individual psalms, and there is more confidence in saying who did not write the psalms than in deciding who did.

The attempt to place the psalms within their setting, we suggest, should be governed by the evidence in each separate case. This will include the internal characteristics to which Gunkel and his successors have drawn attention, but it will be controlled by the statements, where there are such, in the titles and other scriptures. It will also bear in mind the fact that a psalmist could speak (as Peter pointed out in Acts 2:30f.) as 'a prophet', aware of God's promises and foreseeing what was far beyond his own horizon.

V. The theology of the Psalter

1. The marrow of the religious life of the psalmists was undoubtedly their *knowledge of God.* They never tire of singing his majesty in creation. In all his works in the heavens, the earth and the sea he has made himself known as the all-powerful, the all-knowing, the everywhere-present God. He is also the God of all history who guides everything towards the final goal which he has purposed to fulfil. But this Ruler of the world, this King of kings, is also Lawgiver and Judge, the Vindicator of all who are oppressed and their Saviour. He is therefore merciful and faithful, just and righteous, the Holy One whom men and angels adore. But the God of the psalmists is also, and uniquely, the God

of Israel. The God who revealed himself to Abraham, Isaac and Jacob, who through Moses delivered Israel from Egypt, entered into covenant with them and gave them the promised land, is the God of Israel still, the Lord and Defender of the chosen people.

With such a high conception of God it is not surprising that the psalmists found their chief delight and privilege in prayer to God. There is a directness, a spontaneity and an immediacy in the prayers of the psalmists that convince us of the reality of prayer for them. They believe in his providence, trust in his presence, rejoice in his righteousness, rest in his faithfulness, confide in his nearness. In their prayers they praise, petition and commune with their God, and find refuge from sickness, want, pestilence and slander, and humble themselves under his mighty hand. In the progressive life of the community their behaviour is marked by fidelity to God, reverent obedience to the law, kindness to the oppressed and joy in the worship of God's people.

2. Set against such a background of faith and obedience *the imprecatory psalms* (see especially 35:1–8; 59; 69; 109) may be felt to constitute a moral difficulty. Similar prayers for vengeance are found in Jeremiah 11:18ff.; 15:15ff.; 18:19ff.; 20:11ff. The underlying idea in these passages in the Psalter, where curses and revengeful punishments are invoked upon the enemy, is expressed in 139:21f., 'Do I not hate them that hate thee, O Lord? . . . I count them my enemies.' That is to say, the psalmists are motivated by zeal for the Holy One of Israel who must exercise retribution in the present moral order in the world. Behind the imprecations is a recognition of a divine moral governance in the world, a belief that right and wrong are meaningful for God, and that therefore judgment must operate in the moral world order as well as grace. It was natural, then, for men living under the dispensation of the law to pray for the destruction of *God's* enemies through judgment, although Christians now living in the dispensation of grace pray for all men that they may be saved, while still believing in the reality of a here-and-now judgment as well as judgment that is a future event.

It should be remembered too that while the psalmists were aware of the tensions between righteousness and unrighteousness, between the people of God and the enemies of God, they had as yet no conception of judgment in an eschatological sense, nor had they any doctrine of a future state in which the ungodly would be punished and the godly rewarded. Therefore if righteousness is to be vindicated it has to be vindicated now, if wickedness is to be punished it has to be punished now. For when the righteous man prayed for the destruction of wickedness he did not distinguish in his mind between the ungodly and his ungodliness. The destruction of the one without the other was unthinkable to the pious Hebrew. It was even difficult if not impossible for some psalmists to distinguish between the ungodly man and his family. All that belonged to the wicked man was involved with him in his wickedness. The Christian therefore must have these things in mind when he reads these imprecatory psalms. He must not empty them of all significance. They are at least a powerful reminder of the reality of judgment in this moral world, and they testify to a burning zeal for the cause of righteousness which flamed in the hearts of some of the psalmists, and to their refusal to condone sin.

3. Has the Psalter a theology of a *future life*? The answer here is, No. There is a hope but no assured belief concerning the future. There is no *certain* reference to resurrection in the Psalter. Flashes of revelation or insight concerning the future life there may be, but there is no doctrine, no such article of religious faith. The germ of such a hope may be found in Pss. 16–17; 49; 73, but simply a hope it remains. Nowhere does a psalmist attain to an assured belief in resurrection.

4. The *Messianic psalms.* One of the most important factors in the national survival of Israel has been the Messianic hope. This hope centres on the return of the age of David whose reign in the past marked the golden age in Israel's history; and it is against this background that the Messianic hope in the Psalter should be viewed. The picture of the Messiah that emerges from the Psalter is a twofold one.

First, since Messiah is to be a scion of the Davidic dynasty, he is to be the *King* of the Messianic age. The Psalter envisages a divine Messianic King against whom nations will rebel in vain (Ps. 2). The Messianic age is depicted in Ps. 72, while in Ps. 2 the kingdom is described as a universal kingdom which belongs to God but over which Messiah rules in association with the Lord. In Ps. 110 Messiah is King, Priest and Victor who sits in glory at God's right hand. Ps. 45 speaks of eternal dominion, while Ps. 72 emphasizes the universality of Messiah's rule.

But secondly, the Psalter also prepares men's minds for a suffering Messiah. Is. 53 has its counterpart in the Psalter. The anointed Son of Yahweh, the Priest-King whose throne will stand for ever and whose reign of peace and righteousness will cause all nations to be blessed in him, is to submit himself to dreadful suffering (Pss. 22; 69, *etc.*). However, not until Christ interpreted the Psalter to the apostles were these and similar psalms considered to be Messianic (Lk. 24:27–46). Only as the Lord enlightened the disciples' minds did the church understand the meaning of these passages in the Psalter and make it the hymn-book and the prayer-book of the church.

VI. The Christian and the Psalter

Apart from the inherent religious and devotional qualities of the psalms two factors have compelled the Christian church to make the Psalter her prayer-book.

1. There is the fact that the Psalter occupied such a large place in the life and teaching of our Lord. It was the prayer-book which he would use in the synagogue service, and his hymn-book in the Temple festival. He used it in his teaching, met temptation with it, sang the Hallel from it after the Last Supper, quoted it from the cross and died with it on his lips.

2. Moreover, from earliest times the Psalter has been both the hymn-book and the prayer-book of the Christian church. Some of her great hymns of praise are modelled on the psalms (Lk. 1:46ff., 68ff.; 2:29ff.). The Psalter was the inspiration of the apostles in persecution (Acts 4:25f.), it was embedded in their message (Acts 2:25ff.; 13:33), it was used to set forth their profoundest beliefs concerning the Lord (Heb. 1:6, 10–13; 2:6–8; 5:6; 10:5–7). In all ages the church has found in the Psalter 'a Bible in miniature' (Luther), or 'the Bible within

the Bible'. And while this 'Bible in miniature' originated in the Jewish church, and is intimately related to the OT, yet, because it is illuminated by the light that breaks from the Gospels, the Christian church claims it and uses it too in all her access to God whom she evermore worships and adores.

BIBLIOGRAPHY. *Commentaries*: A. F. Kirkpatrick, 1901; H. C. Leupold, 1959; A. Weiser, 1962; J. H. Eaton, 1967; M. J. Dahood, 1966–70; A. A. Anderson, 1972; D. Kidner, *TOTC*, 1975 H.-J. Kraus, E.T. 1988–89; Word Commentary, 1983–90. *Other Studies*: H. Gunkel, *The Psalms* (E.T. 1967, Facet Books); S. Mowinckel, *The Psalms in Israel's Worship*, 1962; H. Ringgren, *The Faith of the Psalmists*, 1963; B. S. Childs, 'Psalm Titles and Midrashic Exegesis', *JSS* 16, 1971, pp. 137–150; C. C. Broyles, *The Conflict of Faith and Experience in the Psalms*, 1989; C. Westermann, *The Living Psalms*, 1989; A. Weiser, *The Psalms*, 1965.

J.G.S.S.T.
F.D.K.

PSEUDEPIGRAPHA. The term is used to describe those Jewish writings which were excluded from the OT Canon and which find no place in the Apocrypha. For the purpose of this article the term will also exclude the sectarian documents of the Qumran library (*DEAD SEA SCROLLS). Unlike the Apocrypha, which were included in the Greek Scriptures, these pseudepigrapha never approached canonical status. They nevertheless played an important role during the intertestamental period and are valuable for the light they shed on the Jewish background of the NT. While not all the writings included in this group are pseudepigraphic in the strict sense of writings published under assumed names (*PSEUDONMITY), the majority of them are and the name is therefore generally appropriate. It will be convenient to divide them roughly between Palestinian and Jewish–Hellenistic groups, as their place of origin strongly affected their form and purpose. Because of a dominant thread which runs through the majority of these writings they have aptly been described as the literature of the apocalyptic movement.

I. The Palestinian group

The Palestinian group contains three different literary types, poetry, legend and apocalypse, the *Psalms of Solomon* almost certainly belongs to the second half of the 1st century BC and is an example of the anti-Sadducean polemic of the Pharisees at that period. In the majority of these 18 psalms, which are modelled on the Davidic Psalms, there is no reference to the Messiah (*Ps. Sol.* 17 is the main exception), but much about the Messianic kingdom. The overthrow of the Hasmonaean dynasty by the Roman Pompey is regarded as a divine act, although Pompey himself is condemned for his profanation of the Temple. There were other psalm collections during the intertestamental period, an example of which is the *Psalms of Joshua* found in the Qumran library.

There were many books which were legendary expansions of biblical history, based mainly on the law, although including some legends about the prophets. Among the earliest of these is the *Testaments of the Twelve Patriarchs*, based on Gn. 49. Each of Jacob's sons gives his instructions to his descendants and much of this teaching is of a high moral order. They are represented as reviewing their own failings to serve as a warning to others, but two of the Patriarchs, Joseph and Issachar, are able to commend their own virtues. The original work was a Pharisaic production written towards the end of the 2nd century BC, but this was later expanded by additions. The library at Qumran contained certain parts of an earlier recension of the *Testaments* of Levi and Naphtali, in Aramaic and Hebrew, but does not appear to have possessed the whole. This new evidence has confirmed Charles' opinion that the *Testaments* contained some late Jewish and Christian additions. Some have supposed that the final editing was completed by a Christian, *c.* AD 200. There are in these writings some similarities to the teachings of Jesus, as, for example, exhortations to humility, brotherly love and almsgiving. These parts represent some of the best moral injunctions of pre-Christian Judaism.

Another book based on Genesis is the *Book of Jubilees*, so styled from its system of dating. The author advocated a 364-day year in order to assist the Jews to keep the feasts on the proper day. This is typical of his legalistic approach. The whole book, in fact, purports to be a revelation to Moses on Mt Sinai and is clearly intended to uphold the eternal validity of the law. The Pharisaic author was intent on combating the encroachments of Hellenism during the latter part of the 2nd century BC. In the course of the revelations there are many legendary accretions to the biblical history, as for example the attribution to Satan and not to God of the suggestion that Abraham should sacrifice Isaac (17:16; 18:9, 12). The author insisted on the strict observance of Jewish rites, particularly circumcision and sabbath observance (15:33f.; 2:25–31; 50:6–13). The book was well known at Qumran and possesses many points of contact with the Damascus Document.

In a similar vein to the *Testaments of the Twelve Patriarchs* is the *Testament of Job*, in which Job delivers to the children of his second wife a parting address. He is represented as reviewing his past life, and the book concludes with an account of the special ability granted to his three daughters to sing heavenly songs while his soul is transported by chariot to heaven. The book appears to have been the work of an author belonging to one of the stricter Jewish sects (possibly the *ḥasidim*) and may be dated possibly about 100 BC.

Several legendary works of a similar character, but which at least in their extant texts appear to have been subjected to Christian influence, must be included among this group of writings. The *Life of Adam and Eve*, which exists only in a Latin text, although it runs parallel in parts to the *Apocalypse of Moses* (in Greek), is an imaginative reconstruction of the history subsequent to the Fall, and in the course of it Adam has a vision in which he sees a picture of the developments of Jewish history to post-exilic times. It can confidently be dated before AD 70, since it supposes that Herod's Temple is still standing (29:6f.).

The *Martyrdom of Isaiah* is a partly Jewish and partly Christian book, extant only in Ethiopic. It tells how Isaiah came to be 'sawn asunder' (*cf.* Heb. 11:37) with a wood saw (1–5). A *Vision of Isaiah*, which has been interpolated into the original work, is clearly a Christian addition because it records the devil's indignation over Isaiah's foretelling of redemption through Christ and mentions Christian history up to the time of the Neronian persecutions (3:13–4:18). The part of the book known as the *Ascension of Isaiah* is also Jewish-Christian, for Isaiah is not only told by God of the coming of Jesus but witnesses the birth, death and resurrection of the Coming One. It is thought that the Jewish part may date from the 2nd century BC, but no trace of it has so far been found at Qumran.

In addition to these there was some pre-Christian pseudo-Jeremianic and pseudo-Danielic literature which has only recently come to light from the Qumran library and which has not been sufficiently investigated at the time of writing for an account of it to be included in this survey. But a previously extant work known as the *Paralipomena of Jeremiah the Prophet*, which shows marked Christian influences, may well look back to some earlier Jeremianic cycle. It is aimed particularly against mixed marriages.

By far the most important group of Jewish pseudepigrapha is the apocalypses, among which the *Book of Enoch* takes pride of place. It is a composite work, of which the various parts were composed at different times during the last two centuries BC. The oldest sections belong to the Maccabean period, according to Rowley and Torrey, although Charles had earlier maintained a pre-Maccabean date. There are five main divisions in the book as it now exists. The first describes a vision given to Enoch of future judgment, especially of the fallen angels. The second, known as *The Similitudes of Enoch*, consists of three parables dealing mainly with the theme of judgment upon the world, but with assurances to the righteous through the Messianic hope. The third is an astronomical book. The fourth consists of two visions, one about the flood and the other recounting the history of the world down to the Messianic age. The fifth is a miscellaneous collection of exhortations and other material, of which the most notable is an *Apocalypse of Weeks* which divides world-history into 10 weeks, the last 3 being apocalyptic. This book is of great importance for studies in the intertestamental period and furnishes valuable data for pre-Christian Jewish theology. It is also of interest in being cited in the NT Epistle of Jude. The *Apocalypse of Weeks* has been thought to be connected with the Qumran sect, but because there is no trace of the *Similitudes* at Qumran it is possible that this part should be dated in the Christian era (*cf.* J. C. Hindley).

There was another book which circulated under the name of Enoch, commonly known as the *Book of the Secrets of Enoch* or *2 Enoch.* It is also sometimes described as the *Slavonic Enoch* because it is extant only in some Slavonic MSS. Unlike *1 Enoch* it comes from a Hellenistic background and parts of the work are believed to belong to the Christian period. Since it was cited in the later parts of the *Testaments of the Twelve Patriarchs*, at least a section of *2 Enoch* must have preceded those parts. The whole is generally dated during the 1st century AD. It consists of an account of Enoch's journey through the seven heavens, together with certain revelations given to Enoch about creation and the history of mankind and includes Enoch's admonitions to his children. Much of the ethical instruction is noble in character and is reminiscent of the type of teaching in Ecclesiasticus.

The *Assumption of Moses* may have consisted of two distinct works known as the *Testament*, and *Assumption, of Moses* respectively (according to Charles, but Pfeiffer is reserved about this). In any case no MS is extant which gives the dispute over the body of Moses, which formed the basis of the *Assumption* (it is alluded to in the Epistle of Jude), but in the *Testament* Moses gives to Joshua an apocalyptic review of Israel's history from the occupation of Canaan until the end of time. There is a marked absence of any Messianic hope in the book. Because of close parallels with the Qumran War Scroll and the Damascus Document, it has recently been concluded that the author was probably an Essene.

Another work belonging to the Christian period is the *Apocalypse of Ezra* (or *2* [or *4*] *Esdras*). In this book various visions are ascribed to Ezra in Babylon which deal with the problem of Israel's sufferings and bring the issue down to the author's own day (*i.e.* to the period after AD 70 when the problem became acute). The sense of hopelessness pervading the account is finally relieved only by the vague belief in a coming golden age. The book is a sincere but unsuccessful attempt to solve a pressing problem. It is generally dated towards the end of the 1st century AD.

About the same time appeared the *Apocalypse of Baruch* (or *Syriac Baruch*), which has many similarities of thought with the last-mentioned book. It is in fact regarded by some scholars as an imitation of the more brilliant *2 Esdras*. Through the pessimism resulting from the overthrow of the city of Jerusalem there is faint hope until the Messianic reign of peace begins. The present is unrelieved despair, typified by very dark waters, but the coming of Messiah, represented by lightning, brings consolation.

II. The Jewish–Hellenistic group

Among the more notable Jewish–Hellenistic pseudepigrapha are propaganda works (the *Letter of Aristeas* and parts of the *Sibylline Oracles*), legendary history (*3 Maccabees*), philosophy (*4 Maccabees*) and apocalyptic (part of the *Slavonic Enoch* already mentioned and part of the *Greek Baruch*; *APOCRYPHA).

The *Letter of Aristeas* purports to come from the time of the production of the LXX said to have been proposed by Ptolemy II, Philadelphus, of Egypt (285–245 BC). The narrative itself is legendary and was written in fact by a Jew (*c.* 100 BC) who wished to commend the Jewish law and religion to his Hellenistic contemporaries. It is an apology for Judaism against its Gentile detractors.

About 140 BC an Alexandrian Jew produced some *Sibylline Oracles* in imitation of the ancient Greek oracles attributed to the Sibyl, a pagan prophetess held in high regard not only by contemporary Greeks but also among many Jews and even Christians at a later period. Numerous additions were subsequently made to these oracles. Of the twelve extant books the majority appear to be Christian in origin, but books 3–5 are generally regarded as Jewish. These are specifically devoted to propaganda and consist particularly of judgments on Gentile nations. In book 3 occurs a review of Israelitish history from Solomon's time down to Antiochus Epiphanes and his successors, but the Jews are to benefit by the coming Messiah. There is a special appeal to Greece to cease its pagan worship, and this strong apologetic purpose is further seen in the claim that the Sibyl is in reality a descendant of Noah.

3 Maccabees, like *2 Maccabees*, is a legendary embellishment designed for the glorification of the Jews in Egypt under Ptolemy Physcon. *4 Maccabees* is a philosophical homily in which a Hellenistic Jewish author, of a definitely legalistic persuasion, discourses on the main theme of the control of the passions by reason, and in this he betrays his Stoic leanings. But his real admiration is nevertheless for the Mosaic law, and he seeks unsuccessfully to achieve a synthesis between the two.

As a whole this pseudepigraphic literature throws interesting light on the preparation period for the gospel. It belongs to times when prophetic declarations had ceased and when there was an increasing reverence for the law. They were times of perplexity, and apocalyptic emerged to attempt to reconcile the prophetic promises with the disastrous course of current history and to project the fulfilment of these promises into an age yet to come. These books had wide circulation among the Jews, and many of the NT writers may have known them.

The literary device used seems strange to modern ideas, but the great preponderance of pseudonymous ascriptions in these books is evidence of its contemporary effectiveness. It may have been adopted by reason both of security and of the need to ensure the maximum authority for the writings (*PSEUDONYMITY).

There are many theological differences and developments in this literature as compared with the earlier prophetical period. The future age differs essentially from the present. It has a supernatural origin and will displace the present age, which is conceived of as under the domination of evil influences. This doctrine of the two ages is characteristic of the intertestamental period and finds some echoes in NT thought. It is significant that owing to this apocalyptic approach to future history the Messianic hope was not as dominant during this period as it had been earlier. The clearest picture is in the *Book of Enoch*, where the Messianic conception has become more transcendental, parallel with the increasing transcendentalism of the conception of God. The Son of man as a heavenly pre-existent Being is conceived as sharing with God in judgment. Another striking feature of this literature is the receding interest in pure nationalism and in the development of individualism, on the one hand, and universalism, on the other. But perhaps the greatest service rendered by the literature was its antidote to the increasing legalism of Judaism, particularly among the Pharisees, in spite of the fact that this legalism is not entirely lacking from many of these books. (*APOCALYPTIC; *APOCRYPHA.)

BIBLIOGRAPHY. J. H. Charlesworth (ed.), *The OT Pseudepigrapha*, 1983–85; *The OT Pseudepigrapha and the NT*, 1987; A.-M. Denis, *Introduction aux Pseudepigraphes Grecs d'Ancien Testament*, 1970; R. H. Pfeiffer, *History of New Testament Times with an Introduction to the Apocrypha*, 1949; L. Rost, *Judaism outside the Hebrew Canon*, E.T. 1976; H. H. Rowley, *The Relevance of Apocalyptic*, 1944; D. S. Russell, *The Method and Message of Jewish Apocalyptic*, 1964; D. S. Russell, *The OT Pseudepigrapha*, 1987; E. P. Sanders, *Paul and Palestinian Judaism*, 1977, pp. 346–418; E. Schürer, *HJP*², 1, 1973; M. E. Stone, *Jewish Writings of the Second Temple Period*, 1984.

D.G.

PSEUDONYMITY. Pseudonymity is the practice of attributing literary works to assumed names, a device widely used in the ancient world. Numerous examples are known from the Graeco-Roman world, but in studying the Christian attitude towards such a device the Jewish pseudepigrapha are very much more significant (*PSEUDEPIGRAPHA, I). The former were not, as the latter were, expressions of a religious approach, and because of the wide differences in content between secular and religious writings the Jewish writings naturally form a closer parallel with the numerous Christian pseudepigrapha circulating during the first 3 centuries AD.

There is no doubt that these writings enjoyed considerable popularity, and for this reason demand some explanation of their character and method. It is difficult for modern minds accustomed to the literary condemnation of plagiarism (the use of another's material) to appreciate this ancient practice of using another's name. But it is often assumed that the ancient approach was essentially different from the modern and implied nothing reprehensible. Undoubtedly many of the authors who resorted to this practice were men of sincerity, and herein lies the problem. Are there any ascertainable principles which throw any light on the apparent contradiction?

I. The Greek approach

There are many causes which are thought to account for the abundance of pseudonymous writings among the Greeks. There was a tendency to ascribe anonymous works to some well-known author of works of the same kind, for instance, epics to Homer or Virgil. Many writings by scholars were attributed to their masters, from whom they had learnt their wisdom, as, for example, among the followers of Plato. Moreover, rhetorical exercises were frequently attributed to famous persons (*cf.* the forgery known as the *Epistle of Phalaris*). A more deliberate type of forgery prevalent in the Greek world was the practice of publishing MSS under the names of popular authors as a method of selling them. A later motive was the desire to produce documents in support of certain doctrines by attributing them to some ancient and honoured teacher (*e.g.* among the Neopythagoreans, and in a Christian context the Clementine literature and the works attributed to Dionysius the Areopagite).

II. The Jewish approach

This seems to have inherited little directly from Greek practices, since the majority of the pseudonymous writings were the products of Palestinian Judaism. The widespread Greek secular usage may have had some small impact, although the *Letter of Aristeas* and the *Slavonic Enoch* are almost the only clear instances of the practice even among the Hellenistic Jews (*PSEUDEPIGRAPHA, **II**). The main causes for pseudonymity must clearly be sought elsewhere. Undoubtedly the most significant factor was the rigidity of the law and the cessation of prophecy. An authoritative message for the contemporary Jews of the 2 centuries before Christ could be established, it was thought, only by attributing such a message to some hero of the past whose authority was unquestioned. This accounts for the prominence of the patriarchal names among the pseudepigrapha. Indeed, all the assumed authors except Aristeas are mentioned either in the Law or the Prophets. This illustrates clearly the fundamental difference between Greek and Jewish pseudonymous practice. The latter possessed what the former lacked, an authoritative body of writings which formed the basis of their religious beliefs, and their pseudonymous productions were therefore extensions of canonical material (the nearest Greek parallel is the *Sibylline Oracles*). It is this phenomenon which raises problems for Jewish pseudonymity which were almost entirely absent from the Greek world. The Jewish authors were religious men, and it is not easy to see how they could resort to a literary method which to us seems morally questionable. There are a number of possible explanations.

The false ascription may have been occasioned by the use of materials traditionally handed down in association with some famous name. Some scholars, for instance, have virtually maintained this viewpoint when suggesting that Jude cites not the *Book of Enoch* but an earlier oral ascription believed to have been a true saying of Enoch which was later incorporated into the pseudonymous book (*cf.* Jude 14). But unfortunately data for verifying this procedure are practically non-existent. Another suggestion arises from the nature of apocalyptic. This mode of thought frequently made use of symbolic figures of speech, which the readers were clearly not expected to take literally, and the same tacit assumption may have been made over the pseudonym. Sometimes the device may have been used in self-defence when the author was not anxious to parade his identity for fear of arousing the suspicions of the tyrannical occupying power. In this case the readers would readily appreciate the reason for the pseudonym and would absolve the writer from any moral censure. Yet in few cases is this explanation clearly applicable. It is possible that the Jews paid little attention to literary property and were far more concerned with contents than authorship, and if this were generally so it might explain the readiness with which the writings circulated.

III. The Christian approach

There is no doubt that the prevalence of pseudonymous early Christian writings owed more to Jewish than to Greek influences. By the 2nd century AD a canon of Christian writings had come into existence which, although lacking formal codification (except in the case of Marcion), was nevertheless real and authoritative. There were pseudonymous counterparts to all 4 types of NT literature—Gospels, Acts, Epistles and Apocalypses. The majority of these sprang from heretical sources, and in these cases the use of the pseudonymous device is transparent. Esoteric doctrines outside the theology of orthodoxy sought support by the theory that secret teachings had been handed down to the initiates of a particular sect but had been hidden from others. The production of pseudonymous apostolic writings was thus made easy. Since the interval separating the assumed author from the real author was not as great as in the majority of Jewish writings of this character, it did not stretch the credulity of the readers too much to be told that some new writing was in fact an apostolic production, assuming that they were ignorant of its true source.

In spite of the fact that pseudonymity was a widespread practice, it must not be assumed that it would have been regarded as a harmless literary device among the orthodox Christians. What external evidence there is suggests rather that the church took a firm stand against the practice (*e.g.* the Muratorian Canon, Serapion, Tertullian). Tertullian in fact records the unfrocking of the Asian presbyter who confessed to writing the *Acts of Paul* out of his love for Paul, which does not suggest it was an acknowledged practice to produce such literature. For this reason the assumption by some scholars that certain NT books are really pseudonymous raises an acute psychological and moral problem, which few of the supporters of these hypotheses are willing to admit. There is a presumption against NT canonical pseudepigrapha which can be nullified only by overwhelming and conclusive evidence to the contrary, and even here each case must be judged entirely on its own merits.

On the question of pseudonymity in OT literature, see *DANIEL, BOOK OF; *DEUTERONOMY; *ECCLESIASTES; *PENTATEUCH.

BIBLIOGRAPHY. R. H. Charles, *Religious Development between the Old and New Testaments*, 1914; D. Guthrie, 'Epistolary Pseudepigraphy', *New Testament Introduction*, 1970, pp. 671–684; J. Moffatt, *An Introduction to the Literature of the New Testament*[2], 1912, pp. 40ff.; H. J. Rose, 'Pseudepigraphic Literature', *Oxford Classical Dictionary*, 1949; R. D. Shaw, *The Pauline Epistles*[4], 1913, pp. 477ff.; A. Sint, *Pseudonymität im Altertum: ihre Formen und Gründe*, 1960; and especially F. Torm, *Die Psychologie der Pseudonymität im Hinblick auf die Literatur des Urchristentums*, 1932. D.G.

PTOLEMAIS.

I. In the Old Testament

The name given in the late 3rd or early 2nd century BC by Ptolemy I or II of Egypt to the seaport of Accho, on the N point of the Bay of Acre (named from Accho), about 13 km N of Carmel headland which faces it across the bay. Accho was the only natural harbour on the coast S of Phoenicia in OT times, and various routes connected it with Galilee and its lake, the Jordan valley and beyond. The only reference to Accho in the OT is in Jdg. 1:31, where it is assigned to Asher, but the tribe failed to capture it, and it probably remained Phoenician throughout the OT period. Some would emend Ummah in Jos. 19:30 to read Accho (*e.g. GTT*, p. 139), though this is but a conjecture.

Accho is more frequently mentioned in non-biblical texts. A prince of Accho (Egyp. *'ky*) is apparently already mentioned in the Egyp. Execration Texts of the 18th century BC (G. Posener, *Princes et Pays d'Asie et de Nubie*, 1940, p. 87, E49; *ANET*, p. 329, n. 9). Accho later appears in topographical lists of the 15th and 13th centuries BC, in the Amarna tablets of the 14th century BC (*e.g. ANET*, pp. 484–485, 487), and in an Egyp. satirical letter of *c.* 1240 BC (*ANET*, p. 477b). In later days Sennacherib of Assyria mentions Accho as part of the realm of Tyre and Sidon on his Palestinian campaign of 701 BC (*ANET*, p. 287b), and Ashurbanipal attacked it in the 7th century BC (*ANET*, p. 300b). On the relation of Accho to Asher and Galilee inland, see D. Baly, *Geography of the Bible*[2], 1974, pp. 121–124. K.A.K.

II. In the New Testament

During the intertestamental period the name Accho was changed to Ptolemais, presumably in honour of Ptolemy Philadelphus (285–246 BC). Under this name it played an important role in the Jews' struggle for freedom under the Maccabees (*cf.* 1 Macc. 5:15; 12:45–48), but is only once noticed in the NT (Acts 21:7). Paul, sailing from Tyre to Caesarea towards the end of his missionary journey, put in at Ptolemais, and while his ship lay at anchor in the harbour he spent a day with the Christians of the place. This was probably not the only time he passed through the city, since he came along the Phoenician coast several times.

In Paul's day Ptolemais was a *colonia*, the emperor Claudius having settled a group of veterans there. After the Roman period it assumed its original name 'Akka and has maintained it to the present day. During the Crusades Ptolemais rose to importance under the Gallicized name Acre or St Jean d'Acre. Today it is overshadowed by the prominence of the city of Haifa, which lies directly across the bay. (See *NEAEHL*, pp. 16–31.)

W.W.W.

PTOLEMY. The name borne by the 14 kings of the purely Macedonian Greek dynasty that ruled Egypt *c.* 323 to 30 BC.

I. The early Ptolemies

After the death of Alexander the Great at Babylon in 323 BC one of his marshals, Ptolemy son of Lagus, had himself appointed as satrap of Egypt, recognizing the nominal reigns of Alexander's half-brother Philip Arrhidaeus and infant son Alexander the younger, as did the great conqueror's other marshals in Babylon, Syria, Asia Minor and Greece. But in 310 BC the boy Alexander had been murdered, and each marshal tried unsuccessfully to take the whole empire from his rivals, so that it was carved up between them. Ptolemy therefore took the title king of Egypt in 304 BC, reigning till 285. Under him, his son Ptolemy II Philadelphus (285–246 BC), and his grandson Ptolemy III Euergetes I (246–222 BC), Egypt became once more a power in the Near East, no longer as a pharaonic but as a Hellenistic monarchy. Ptolemy IV Philopator (222–204 BC) was a dissolute ruler, echoes of whose Syrian wars occur in 3 Macc. 1:1–5.

Like the Ptolemaic kings themselves, all their chief ministers, all the upper ranks of the vast, centralized bureaucracy now instituted to govern Egypt, the main armed forces, the official language of administration—all were Greek. Egypt was the king's personal estate and run on strictly business lines to extract the maximum profit for the crown. *Alexandria was the capital, famous for its buildings, institutions ('Museum', Library, Serapeum, *etc.*), and its exports of grain, papyrus, perfumes, glass, *etc.* There was early a large community of Greek-speaking Jews in Alexandria; in the 3rd century BC the law was rendered into Greek for their use, and the rest of the OT followed, and thus was born the Septuagint version (*TEXTS AND VERSIONS).

The Ptolemies endeavoured to retain the loyalty of the native population of Egypt by gifts of money, lands and new temple buildings to the great, traditional Egyptian priesthoods. Large new temples arose (*e.g.* at Edfu, Dendera, Kom Ombo) in the old pharaonic style, but the 'pharaohs' sculptured on their walls bear in hieroglyphs the names of the Ptolemies.

The long hieroglyphic texts in these temples were written in a specially intricate way by the nationalistic priests so that no foreigners should penetrate their secret traditions; they contain a vast deposit of information on Egyptian religion and mythology, much of it handed down from, and valuable for the study of, pharaonic Egypt.

At first, Palestine—including the Jewish community—and *Coele-Syria formed part of the Ptolemaic kingdom along with Cyprus and Cyrenaica. But after a series of battles in 202–198 BC Antiochus III of Syria finally drove the forces of young Ptolemy V Epiphanes (204–180 BC) out of Syria–Palestine; this area, with its Jewish inhabitants, thus passed under Syrian (Seleucid) rule.

The Rosetta Stone is a decree of Ptolemy V, *c.* 196 BC, inscribed in both Egyptian (hieroglyphs and demotic) and Greek; its discovery in 1799 provided the key for the decipherment of the Egyptian hieroglyphs and the founding of modern Egyptology (*WRITING).

II. The later Ptolemies

The change from an Egyptian to a Syrian overlord was to have drastic consequences for the Jews some 30 years later, under *Antiochus IV. Down to this period, some of the clashes between the kingdoms of Egypt and Syria (of the 'South' and 'North') are foreshadowed in Dn. 11:4ff. (*DANIEL, BOOK OF). Under Ptolemy VI Philometor (180–145 BC) dynastic strife first divided the royal family; his ruthless brother Ptolemy VII Euergetes II was for a time joint king and eventually succeeded him. Ptolemy VI favoured the Jews in Egypt and permitted the son of the dispossessed high priest, Onias III of Jerusalem, to establish a rival temple in Egypt at Leontopolis, about 16½ km N of Heliopolis. Ptolemy VI's activities in Syria are mentioned in 1 Macc. 10:51–57; 11:1–18; those of Ptolemy VII (145–116 BC) in 1 Macc. 1:18 and 15:16 (links with Rome). Other, non-royal, Ptolemies who are named in the Apocrypha are a general of Antiochus IV Epiphanes (1 Macc. 3:38; 2 Macc. 4:45; 6:8; 8:8; and perhaps 10:12) and a son-in-law of Simon Maccabaeus who murdered Simon and two brothers-in-law at Dok near Jericho in 135 BC (1 Macc. 16:11ff.).

Under the later Ptolemies the Egyptian state steadily declined. Native revolts were more frequent; the kings and their ruthless queens (Cleopatras and Berenices) were dissolute (family murders being common), while the power of Rome grew apace. Last of the line were the brilliant but unscrupulous Cleopatra VII and her son by Julius Caesar, Ptolemy XIV Caesarion. She captivated both Caesar and Antony, but made no impression on Octavian (Augustus), and so committed suicide to avoid the humiliation of appearing in a Roman triumphal procession. So Egypt passed under the heel of Rome in 30 BC.

BIBLIOGRAPHY. E. Bevan, *A History of Egypt under the Ptolemaic Dynasty*, 1927; see also *CAH*, 7, 1928; and for the religious background, Sir H. I. Bell, *Cults and Creeds in Graeco-Roman Egypt*, 1953. For the numbering and reigns of the Ptolemies, *cf.* T. C. Skeat, *The Reigns of the Ptolemies*, 1954; also A. E. Samuel, *Ptolemaic Chronology*, 1962.

K.A.K.

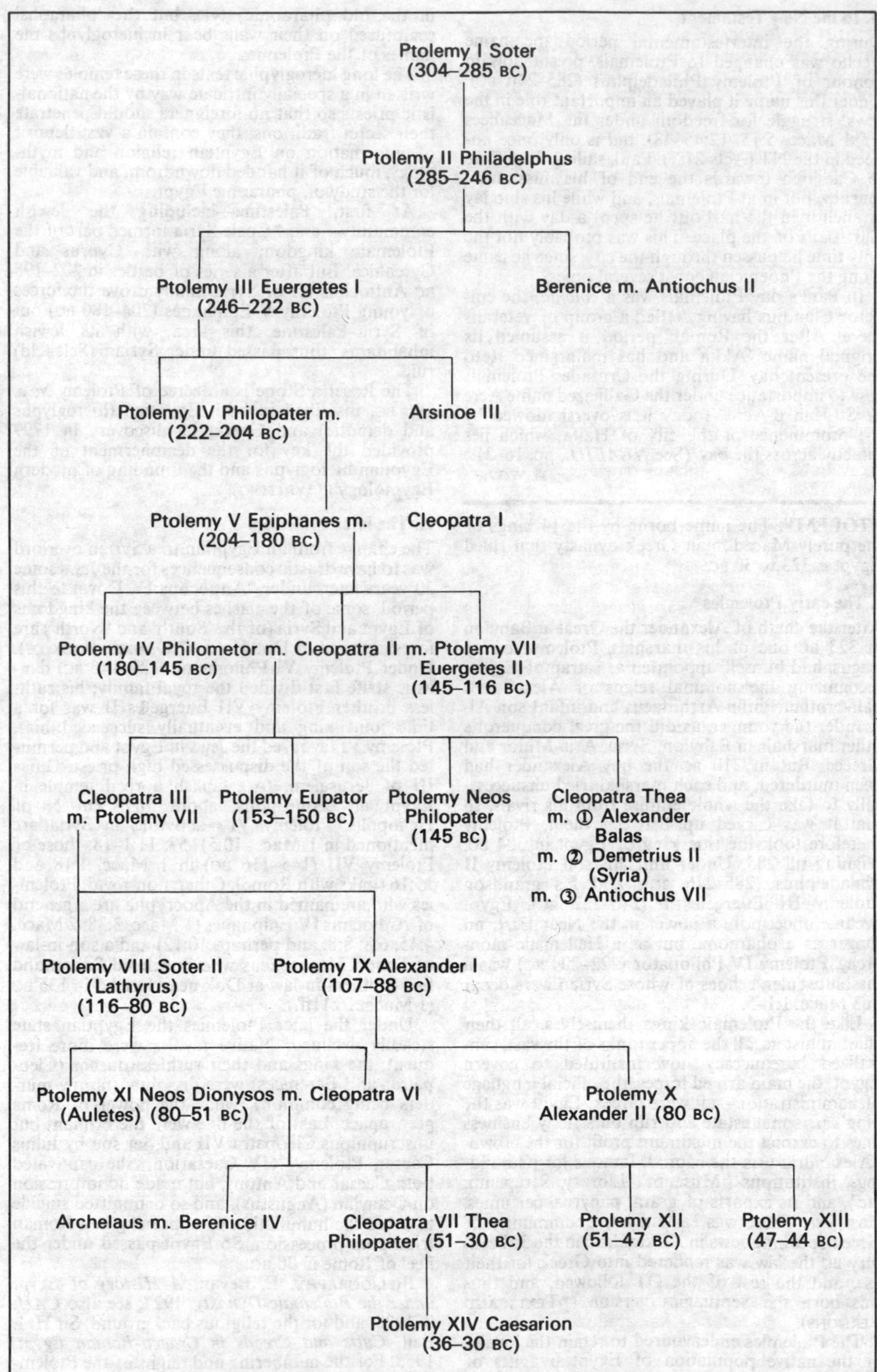

Simplified family tree of the Ptolemies, the Hellenistic rulers of Egypt.

PUBLIUS. *Poplios* is the Greek version of the Latin name, probably *praenomen*, of the 'chief man of the island' of Malta in Acts 28:7. The title 'chief man' appears to be correct local usage (*IG*, 14. 601; *CIL*, 10. 7495), and may refer either to a native officer or to the chief Roman official. In the latter case the use of *praenomen* alone may perhaps be explained as the familiar usage of the local inhabitants.

BIBLIOGRAPHY. W. M. Ramsay, *SPT*, p. 343; *BC*, 4, *in loc.*; *BAGD*. J.H.H.

PUDENS. A Roman Christian who joined *Claudia and others in greeting Timothy (2 Tim. 4:21). Martial (4. 13) salutes Aulus Pudens and his bride Claudia, and another Pudens ('modest') and Claudia are linked in an inscription (*CIL*, 6. 15066): but identification with Timothy's friends is improbable. Tradition called Pudens a senator, locating his house-church at the church of S Pudentiana (*cf.* *Liber Pontificalis*, ed. Duchesne, 1, pp. 132f.); for excavations, *cf.* R. Lanciani, *Pagan and Christian Rome*, 1895, pp. 110ff. A.F.W.

PURIM. A Jewish festival celebrated during the 13–15th days of the month Adar. On this occasion the book of Esther is read, and traditionally the congregation in the synagogue shouts and boos whenever the name of Haman is mentioned. The book of Esther gives the origin of the festival. In the reign of Ahasuerus, probably Xerxes (486–465 BC) but possibly Artaxerxes II (404–359 BC), *Haman, the vizier, determined to massacre all the Jews. Since he was a superstitious man, he cast lots to find an auspicious day. The word *pûr*, which in Est. 3:7; 9:24, 26, is said to mean 'lot', is not a Hebrew word, but is almost certainly the Assyrian *puru*, which means a pebble, or small stone, which would be used for casting lots.

The earliest reference to the festival outside the OT is 2 Macc. 15:36, where a decree is made in 161 BC to celebrate annually the defeat of Nicanor by Judas Maccabaeus on 'the thirteenth day of the twelfth month, which is called Adar in the Syrian language—the day before Mordecai's day'. If 2 Maccabees is dated somewhere in the middle of the 1st century BC, this shows that by 50 BC Purim was celebrated on the 14th of Adar. The parallel passage in 1 Macc. 7:49 speaks of the institution of what was later called Nicanor's Day on the 13th of Adar, but makes no reference to Purim on the 14th. No conclusions can be drawn from this silence.

Josephus, at the end of the 1st century AD, says that Nicanor's Day was kept on Adar 13 (*Ant.* 12. 412) and Purim on Adar 14 and 15 (*Ant.* 11. 295). Curiously enough, Josephus does not use the term *Purim*, but says that the Jews call the 2 days *phroureas* (other readings are *phrouraias*, *phroureous*, *phrouraios*). This Gk. word seems to be based on the verb *phroureō*, meaning 'guard', 'protect'.

Nicanor's Day was not observed after the 7th century AD, but Adar 13 was gradually made part of Purim. As opposed to Adar 14 and 15, which were days of celebration, Adar 13 was a day of fasting.

Suggestions (*e.g.* J. C. Rylaarsdam, *IB*, 3, pp. 968f.) that the festival is a Jewish adaptation of a myth of a struggle between Babylonian or Persian deities have little to commend them. It is unlikely that for a supremely national celebration the Jews would have adapted a drama of pagan polytheism.

BIBLIOGRAPHY. J. H. Greenstone, *Jewish Feasts and Fasts*, 1946; W. Hallo, *BA* 46, 1983, pp. 19–29. J.S.W.

PURITY. The original biblical significance was ceremonial. It was to be obtained by certain ablutions and purifications which were enjoined upon the worshipper in the performance of his religious duties. Purifications were common to many other religions, but there they were merely ceremonial and had no ethical significance. In the case of Israel most of the ceremonial purifications had both sanitary and ethical significance. Though Gn. 35:2 and Ex. 19:14 indicated that the general idea did not originate with the Mosaic law, it is clear that only with the giving of the ceremonial law under Moses were these regulations codified and detailed. In the teaching of the prophets the significance largely passed from the merely ceremonial to the ethical. In the NT the teaching of Christ and the descent of the Spirit lifted the meaning of purity into the moral and spiritual sphere.

In the general sense common to the NT, and to the devotional literature of the OT, purity indicates a state of heart where there is complete devotion to God. As unadulterated water is said to be pure, and gold without alloy is pure gold, so the pure heart is the undivided heart where there is no conflict of loyalties, no cleavage of interests, no mixture of motives, no hypocrisy and no insecurity. It is whole-heartedness God-wards. This is probably the sense in which our Lord used it in the Beatitudes (Mt. 5:8). The reward of the undivided heart is the vision of God. No vision of God can come to the heart that is unclean because it is out of harmony with the nature and character of God. In the further teaching of Christ (see Mk. 7:14–28) he transfers the state of defilement, and so of purity, entirely from the outer to the inner man. Purity in this sense may be said to be a state of heart reserved completely for God and freed from all worldly distractions.

In the specialized sense purity came to mean freedom from sensual pollution, particularly in the sexual life, though the NT does not teach that sexual activity is polluting in itself and, indeed, makes it clear that rightly ordered sexual behaviour is not (*cf.* Heb. 13:4). Nevertheless, the NT teaches the sanctity of the body as the temple of the Holy Spirit (*cf.* 1 Cor. 6:19f.) and inculcates the duty of self-restraint and self-denial even to the extent of personal loss. Purity is thus the spirit of renunciation and of the obedience which brings every thought and feeling and action into subjection to Christ. It begins within and extends outwards to the entire life, cleansing all the centres of living and controlling all the movements of body and spirit.

BIBLIOGRAPHY. H. Baltensweiler *et al.*, *NIDNTT* 3, pp. 100–108; F. Hauck, *TDNT* 1, pp. 122f.; R. Meyer, F. Hauck, *TDNT* 3, pp. 413–431.

R.A.F.

PUT, PHUT. 1. Third son of Ham (Gn. 10:6; 1 Ch. 1:8). **2.** Warriors alongside *Lubim, Egyptians and Ethiopians unable to save No-Amon (Thebes) from Assyria (Na. 3:9). Elsewhere the word is found only in Je. 46:9; Ezk. 30:5 (as Egyp. allies), in Ezk. 38:5 (in Gog's armies; AV 'Libya[ns]') and in Ezk. 27:10 (warriors of Tyre). Put is certainly African, but its location is disputed. Claiming that Lubim (Libyans) and Put are distinct in Na. 3:9, some wish to equate Put with *Pw(n)t* (E Sudan?) of Egyp. texts. But Old Persian *putiya* and Bab. *puṭa* (= Heb. *pûṭ*) become *T' Ṯmḥw*, 'Libya', in Egyp. thus making Put Libya (G. Posener, *La Première Domination Perse en E[ua]gypte*, 1936, pp. 186–187). Lubim and Put in Na. 3:9 are like Lubim and *Sukkiim in 2 Ch. 12:3. Also, Tyre would employ Libyan rather than Somali auxiliaries. *pûṭ* may derive from Egyp. *pḏty*, 'foreign bowman', or similar; T. C. Mitchell, *Proceedings, Seminar for Arabian Studies* 22, 1992, pp. 69–80. K.A.K.

PUTEOLI. Mod. Pozzuoli, near Naples, a Samian colony from Cumae founded in the 6th century BC. Puteoli probably fell into Roman hands with Capua in 338 BC, and rapidly became an important arsenal and trading port. Livy mentions a garrison of 6,000 during the Hannibalian invasion (24. 13), and the embarkation of large reinforcements for Spain (26. 17). Rome's E traffic, notably the Egyp. grain, passed through Puteoli. Seneca describes the arrival of the Alexandrian corn-fleet (Ep. 77), and Paul arrived on an Alexandrian freighter (Acts 28:13). The recently discovered chapel in Herculaneum probably marks the home of some who met Paul at nearby Puteoli. The Via Domitiana linked Puteoli with the Via Appia. E.M.B.

PYTHON. This is the Greek name given to the mythological serpent or dragon which lived at Pytho beneath Mt Parnassus, and guarded the Delphic oracle. Apollo slew it, but the name was then applied to anyone who prophesied under the inspiration of Apollo. Such persons generally spoke with the mouth closed, uttering words quite beyond their own control, and so were also known as *engastrimythoi* or ventriloquists (Plutarch, *De Defectu Oraculorum*, 9, p. 414E).

Acts 16:16 records how Paul met and subsequently exorcized a young woman with such a spirit of *divination at Philippi: it is significant that Luke uses a word with pagan connections, *manteuomenē*, not elsewhere employed in the NT, to describe her oracular speech, obviously inspired by a demonic power. D.H.W.

Q

QUARRY. 1. Heb. *šᵉḇārîm*, a place from which stone is dug. In Jos. 7:5 'Shebarim' is better understood as 'quarries' (so RVmg.) in describing the place to which the Israelites fled after their abortive attack on Ai. Stone was quarried through the centuries in Palestine. Good limestone lies close to the surface in most places and is broken out of its bed by cracking the stone along lines of cleavage. The so-called stables of Solomon in Jerusalem near to the Temple area are almost certainly ancient quarries. (*MINING.)

2. The word *pᵉsîlîm* refers to a carved stone, and should be so translated in Jdg. 3:19, 26 (as in Dt. 7:5; Ps. 78:58; Is. 10:10; Mi. 5:13), rather than AV 'quarries'. J.A.T.

QUARTUS. The Latin name, meaning 'fourth', of a Christian at Corinth whose greetings Paul conveys (Rom. 16:23). He is called 'the brother'. This may mean either 'brother of Erastus', mentioned with him (several Corinthian Christians have Latin names); or 'our brother', *i.e.* our 'fellow-Christian', the title balancing the appellations of the others in vv. 21–23; or 'your brother', *i.e.* 'fellow-Roman Christian' (*cf.* 1 Cor. 1:1; *SOSTHENES). If Tertius and he were not separated by two other names, one might conjecture that they were third and fourth sons in the same family. Later, menologies allocated him to the Seventy (*Acta Sanctorum*, Nov. 1, p. 585). A.F.W.

QUEEN (Heb. *malkâ*, Gk. *basilissa*). The word 'queen' is not widely used in the Bible. It is used to describe women from countries outside Palestine who were reigning monarchs in their own right. Examples of this are the queen of *Sheba (1 Ki. 10:1; *cf.* Mt. 12:42; Lk. 11:31), and *Candace, queen of *Ethiopia (Acts 8:27).

In this same sense the word is used once in Israelite history with reference to Athaliah, who usurped the throne of Judah and reigned for 6 years (2 Ki. 11:3). In post-biblical Jewish history Salome Alexandra, widow of Alexander Jannaeus, succeeded her husband as queen regnant for 9 years (76–67 BC).

As consort the wife of the reigning monarch did not as a rule concern herself with affairs of state. Among the most noteworthy exceptions to this are Bathsheba (1 Ki. 1:15–31) and Jezebel (1 Ki. 21). The most important woman in the royal household, in Israel and Judah as in neighbouring lands, was the queen-mother. She was pre-eminent among the ladies of the court, and sat at the monarch's right hand (Bathsheba, 1 Ki. 2:19), crowned (Nehushta, Je. 13:18). In the history of Judah the queen-mothers were always named. A king might have many wives, but he had only one mother, and he was under obligation to honour her (Ex. 20:12). That her position was more than an honorary one is evident from the record of Maacah, who was queen-mother not only during the reign of her son Abijam but also during the reign of her grandson Asa, until the latter deposed her for idolatry (1 Ki. 15:2, 10, 13; 2 Ch. 15:16). The Chaldean queen of Dn. 5:10 was probably the queen-mother; the same may be true of the Persian queen of Ne. 2:6. M.B.

QUEEN OF HEAVEN. Cakes, possibly in the shape of figurines or crescent moons, were made for the *mᵉleḵeṯ* of the heavens by the inhabitants of Jerusalem (Je. 7:18) and incense burnt as to a deity (Je. 44:17–19, 25). The unusual word is rendered as 'queen' (*malkaṯ*), and may be Phoen., a title of Astarte, Assyr. Ishtar. It may refer to *Ashtaroth or to the Canaanite Anat (so Egyp. 19th century *BETHSHEAN); *cf.* the female personal name (*Ham*)*mōleḵeṯ* (1 Ch. 7:18). Alternatively, this may be a rare writing of *mᵉle'ḵeṯ*, 'heavenly handiwork' (*i.e.* stars), also denoting an idolatrous practice. D.J.W.

QUICKSANDS. (Gk. *syrtis*, 'a sandbank', RSV 'Syrtis', Acts 27:17). The ship in which Paul was travelling found it necessary to take precautions against being driven on to the Greater Syrtis, quicksands W of Cyrene on the N African coast. Now called the Gulf of Sidra, its treacherous sands and waters were greatly feared by sailors. J.D.D.

QUIRINIUS (Lk. 2:2, RV, RSV, NEB; AV 'Cyrenius' corresponds closely to Gk. *Kyrēnios*). Publius Sulpicius Quirinius was consul at Rome in 12 BC, and not long afterwards conducted a campaign against the unruly Homanadensians of central Asia Minor. In 3 BC he became proconsul of Asia; in AD 3–4 he was adviser to the imperial heir-apparent, Gaius Caesar, during the latter's Armenian expedition; from AD 6 to 9 he was imperial legate (*legatus pro praetore*) of Syria-Cilicia. This appears to have concluded his public career; thereafter he lived at Rome, where he died in AD 21. At the beginning of his governorship of Syria–Cilicia he organized the census in Judaea when that territory became a Roman province on the deposition of Archelaus (*HEROD, 2). This census, recorded by Josephus (*Ant.* 18. 1–3, 26), is that referred to in Acts 5:37. From the *Lapis Venetus* (*CIL*, 3. 6687) we gather that it was not only in Judaea that a census was held under Quirinius' auspices; this inscription records the career of an officer who served under Quirinius during his legateship of

Syria–Cilicia and held a census on his behalf in the Syrian city of Apamea. The *census of Lk. 2:1ff., however, must be at least 9 years earlier.

The statement in Lk. 2:2 about this earlier census has for the most part been understood in two alternative ways: 'This was the first registration of its kind; it took place when Quirinius was governor of Syria' (NEB), or 'This was the first registration carried out while Quirinius was governor of Syria' (NEBmg.). The possibility that Quirinius may have been governor of Syria on an earlier occasion (*CHRONOLOGY OF THE NT) has found confirmation in the eyes of a number of scholars (especially W. M. Ramsay) from the testimony of the *Lapis Tiburtinus* (*CIL*, 14. 3613). This inscription, recording the career of a distinguished Roman officer, is unfortunately mutilated, so that the officer's name is missing, but from the details that survive he could very well be Quirinius. It contains a statement that when he became imperial legate of Syria he entered upon that office 'for the second time' (Lat. *iterum*). The question is: did he become imperial legate of Syria for the second time, or did he simply receive an imperial legateship for the second time, having governed another province in that capacity on the earlier occasion?

The wording is ambiguous. Ramsay held that he was appointed an additional legate of Syria between 10 and 7 BC, for the purpose of conducting the Homanadensian war, while the civil administration of the province was in the hands of other governors, including Sentius Saturninus (8–6 BC), under whom, according to Tertullian (*Adv. Marc.* 4. 19), the census of Lk. 2:1ff. was held. A strong case, however, has been made out (especially by R. Syme) for the view that Quirinius's earlier legateship was not over Syria but over Galatia, where the Homanadensians would have been on his doorstep. It has been suggested that 'Saturninus', which Tertullian appears to have read in his copy of Lk. 2:2, was the original reading rather than 'Quirinius' (so B. S. Easton, *The Gospel according to St Luke*, 1926, p. 20; J. W. Jack, 'The Census of Quirinius', *ExpT* 40, 1928–9, pp. 496ff.); another possibility is that the verse should be rendered: 'This enrolment was earlier than that held when Quirinius was governor of Syria' (so M. J. Lagrange, *RB* n.s. 8, 1911, pp. 60ff.; F. M. Heichelheim in T. Frank (ed.), *An Economic History of Ancient Rome*, 4, 1938, pp. 160ff.; N. Turner, *Grammatical Insights into the NT*, 1965, pp. 23f.).

BIBLIOGRAPHY. W. M. Ramsay, *Was Christ Born in Bethlehem?*, 1905; L. R. Taylor, 'Quirinius and the Census of Judaea', *American Journal of Philology* 54, 1933, pp. 120ff.; R. Syme, 'Galatia and Pamphylia under Augustus', *Klio* 27, 1934, pp. 122ff.; and other literature listed in *TCERK*, 1, 1955, p. 222 (*s.v.* 'Census'). F.F.B.

QUMRAN, the name of a wadi near the NW shore of the Dead Sea, but also applied to ruins on its N bank and, more generally, to caves in the surrounding cliffs.

R. de Vaux excavated the ruins in 1951 and 1953–6 in the hope of throwing light on the origin of some scrolls which had recently been discovered in a nearby cave. During the period of excavation ten further scroll-bearing caves were found. Ceramic remains, and the proximity of the caves to the settlement, indicate that the *Dead Sea Scrolls belonged to the group (probably *ESSENES) which inhabited the site from the latter half of the 2nd century BC to AD 68.

De Vaux proposed that sometime in the latter half of the 2nd century BC (period 1a), a small community of Essenes resettled a modest Israelite stronghold from the 8th century BC. Extensive building in the following period (1b), beginning in the reign of Alexander Jannaeus (103–76 BC) or perhaps John Hyrcanus I (135–104 BC), attests a greatly enlarged population. A layer of ash betrays a destruction no earlier than the reign of Antigonus Mattathias (40–37 BC; see *MACCABEES, V). De Vaux interpreted several cracks in cisterns and walls as testimony to the earthquake of 31 BC which he believed caused the fire. Accumulated sediment in the decantation basin and beyond betrays a period of abandonment, which de Vaux believed lasted until near the turn of the era because of the scarcity of Herodian coins in the ruins. Apparently the same group resettled the site (period 2), as suggested by the similarity in pottery types and burials of animal bones under pottery sherds in both periods 1b and 2. The end of period 2 is again marked by a black powdery destruction layer. Roman arrowheads and Jewish coins from the second and third years of the Jewish Revolt (but none from the fourth) suggest that Jewish (Essene) occupation of Khirbet Qumran came to a violent end in AD 68/69.

De Vaux suggested that Essenes lived in nearby caves and/or temporary shelters and that the buildings at Qumran were for public functions. They farmed and worked on the Buqeia plain above the cliffs and at Ain Feshka, an agricultural and industrial installation 3 km to the S. On the evidence of 1,200 graves in a cemetery to the E, he estimated a population of approximately 200. He believed most of them were celibate men, because skeletons of women and children seemed to be confined to two small 'secondary' cemeteries, with only one exception in the 'main cemetery' set apart by orientation and type.

Other theories, interpreting the remains at Qumran as a Hasmonean fortress, a villa or a trading post, have not proved to be more plausible. Nevertheless, a number of serious questions have been raised about various details in de Vaux's reconstruction. All the dates which he assigned can be questioned, in particular his early date for the beginning of period 1, his association of the destruction layer with the earthquake of 31 BC, the long abandonment and the Roman destruction in AD 68. Newer data indicates substantial commercial trade at Qumran and reveals his interpretation of numismatic and ceramic evidence to be problematic. There is no justification for distinguishing a 'main cemetery' from 'secondary cemeteries', and the remains of women and children need to be more adequately explained. Despite these problems, the main lines of the proposed history of the site have enjoyed the acceptance of most scholars.

BIBLIOGRAPHY. M. Broshi, 'The Archaeology of Qumran–a Reconsideration', in D. Dimant and U. Rappaport (eds.), *The Dead Sea Scrolls: Forty Years of Research*, 1992, pp. 103–115; A. D. Crown and L. Cansdale, 'Qumran: Was It an Essene Settlement?', *BAR* 20, 1994, pp. 24–35, 73–78; P. R. Davies, *Qumran*, 1982; R. de Vaux, *Archaeology and the Dead Sea Scrolls*, 1973 (rev. ed.); J.-B. Humbert, 'L'espace sacré à Qumrân. Propositions pour l'archéologie', *RB* 101, 1994, pp. 161–214;

J.-B. Humbert and A. Chambon (eds.), *Fouilles de Khirbet Qumrân et de Aïn Feschkha I*, 1994; J. Murphy-O'Connor, 'Qumran, Khirbet', in *ABD* 5, 1992, pp. 590–594; M. O. Wise, *et al* (eds.), *Methods of Investigation of the Dead Sea Scrolls and the Khirbet Qumran Site*, 1994; *NEAEHL*, pp. 1235–1241. D.K.F.

QUOTATIONS (IN THE NEW TESTAMENT). There are some 250 express citations of OT in NT. If indirect or partial quotations and allusions are added, the total exceeds 1,000. The book of Rev., *e.g.*, has no quotations, but is virtually interlaced with allusions to OT texts. The importance of the OT, which is indicated by this usage, is further defined by the introductory formulas: to say 'the Scripture says' is equivalent to saying 'God says' (*e.g.* Mt. 19:4); 'that it might be fulfilled' (*e.g.* Mt. 2:15) points to the essential connection between the message of God in the old covenant and in the new (*cf.* Ellis, *Prophecy*, pp. 148ff., 165–169; *idem*, *Paul*[1], pp. 22–25).

Some citations are taken from an OT Targum (Rom. 12:19) or from the Heb. text itself (Rom. 11:35; 1 Cor. 3:19). However, as one would expect in a Gk. document written for Gk. readers, the large majority of quotations are derived from the LXX, but with varying degrees of exactness. (Although textually dated, Turpie's manual is still helpful for classification and comparison of the Gk. and Heb. texts.) The inaccuracies which occur show the lack of concern (more than memory lapse) of the biblical writers for verbal exactness: it is the meaning rather than the words in themselves that are important.

In a considerable number of cases variant renderings are deliberately chosen, *ad hoc* or from other known versions, in order to bring out the 'fulfilment' as seen by the NT writer (*e.g.* 1 Cor. 15:54f.). In this process, known from its use at Qumran as *midrash pesher*, the commentary is merged into the quotation to give it a present-time, eschatological application. K. Stendahl has shown the affinity of this hermeneutical method in Mt. with the practices of the Qumran community; it is also present elsewhere in the NT (see Ellis, *Prophecy*[1]). Interpretative renderings may not have originated with the NT writer himself. Rendel Harris suggested that behind some NT quotations lay a pre-canonical 'testimony book', a collection of selected, combined (*e.g.* Mk. 1:2f.), and interpreted OT passages, worked out in the early Christian community for apologetic purposes. While C. H. Dodd has suggested some modifications to this theory, the presence of *testimonia* in the Dead Sea Scrolls shows that the practice was not unknown and substantiates, in some measure, Harris's conjecture. It also appears probable that some of these paraphrases originated in the teachings of primitive Christian prophets (Ellis, *Paul*[1], pp. 107–112; *idem, Prophecy*[1], pp. 130–138, 182–187, 224–229). Thus the problem of textual variation points beyond itself to the larger question of interpretation and application of OT by NT.

Often OT passages are applied quite at variance with the original historical meaning. Hosea's reference to the Exodus of Israel is 'fulfilled' in the baby Jesus' return from Egypt (Mt. 2:15). A number of passages having historical reference to Israel are referred by the NT to the church (*e.g.* Rom. 8:36; Eph. 4:8). A passage referring to Solomon, king of Israel, is applied both to Jesus Christ (Heb. 1:5) and to the church (2 Cor. 6:18). The rationale for this usage seems to lie (1) in a typological correspondence between OT *Heilsgeschichte* and the 'new age' fulfilment in Jesus Christ; (2) in the Semitic idea of corporate solidarity in which the king of Israel and Israel, Christ (Israel's true king) and the 'body of Christ', stand in realistic relationship to one another; and (3) in the conviction that the church is the true Israel and, therefore, the heir to the promises and the object of the prophecies. While the subject-matter of NT quotations covers virtually all doctrinal issues, the emphasis throughout is on the Messiah and Messianic-age fulfilments. Sometimes the application of the quotations is dependent upon the wider context of the OT (*e.g.* Acts 8:29f.); such 'pointer' quotations also may have been designed to call the reader's attention to a wider theme or topic (Dodd, p. 126).

A number of quotations occur in expository patterns similar, in varying degree, to those found in Philo (*cf.* Borgen), Qumran and the rabbinic literature (*cf.* Ellis, *Prophecy*[1], pp. 147–236). One such pattern opens with an OT quotation (or summary) followed by commentary, sometimes including a parable and/or supporting citations, and ends with a final quotation (Mt. 21:33–46; 1 Cor. 1:18–31; Gal. 4:21–5:1; Heb. 10:5–39; 2 Pet. 3:5–13; *cf.* Acts 13:17–41). It may be that some *testimonia* represent excerpts from such expositions. Quotations other than from the OT also appear. Eph. 5:14 (*cf.* 1 Cor. 15:45b; 1 Tim. 5:18b) may be an excerpt from an early Christian hymn or oracle; Jude 14 is taken from the pseudepigraphical book of *Enoch*; and Acts 17:28 is a quotation from a pagan writer.

BIBLIOGRAPHY. G. L. Archer, *Old Testament Quotations in the New Testament*, 1983; P. Borgen, *Bread from Heaven*, 1965; C. H. Dodd, *According to the Scriptures*, 1953; E. E. Ellis, *Paul's Use of the Old Testament*[1], 1957([5], 1991); *Prophecy and Hermeneutic*[1], 1978 ([4], 1993); *The Old Testament in Early Christianity*, 1991; R. T. France, *Jesus and the Old Testament*, 1971; L. Goppelt, *TYPOS*[2], 1969 (E.T. 1982); J. R. Harris, *Testimonies*, 1916, 1920; W. C. Kaiser, Jr., *The Uses of the Old Testament in the New*, 1985; C. A. Kimball, *Jesus' Exposition of the Old Testament in Luke's Gospel*, 1994; R. L. Longenecker, *Biblical Exegesis in the Apostolic Period*, 1975; D. J. Moo, *The Old Testament in the Gospel Passion Narratives*, 1983; K. Stendahl, *The School of St Matthew*[1], 1969; D. M. Turpie, *The Old Testament in the New*, 1868.

E.E.E.

R

RAAMAH (Heb. *ra'mâ, ra'mā*, 'trembling'). A 'son' of Cush (Gn. 10:7; 1 Ch. 1:9). The tribe of Raamah has not been identified, but inscriptions found in Sheba suggest a location N of Marib in Yemen. With Sheba, Raamah sold spices, precious stones and gold to Tyre (Ezk. 27:22). A.R.M.

RA'AMSES, RAMESES (Egyp. *Pr-R'mssw*, Pi-Ramessē, 'Domain of Ramesses'). A city of Egypt mentioned with Pithom, where the Hebrews were afflicted with heavy burdens (Ex. 1:11; 12:37; Nu. 33:3). This was the famous E-Delta residence of Rameses II (*c*. 1290–1224 BC). The kings of the 18th Dynasty did no building here. Scholars once located Pi-Ramessē at Pelusium, then at Tanis (*ZOAN), following Montet's excavations there. But all the Ramesside stonework at Tanis is re-used material from elsewhere. Remains of a palace, a glaze-factory and of houses of princes and high officials (with trace of a temple) at and near Qantir, 30 km S of Tanis, almost certainly mark the real site of Ra'amses/ Pi-Ramessē. The Exodus began from Ra'amses (Ex. 12:37) (*ENCAMPMENT BY THE SEA). Centuries before, Jacob had settled in the district (Gn.47:11).

BIBLIOGRAPHY. A. H. Gardiner, *JEA* 5, 1918, pp. 127–138, 179–200, 242–271; P. Montet, *RB* 39, 1930, pp. 5–28; L. Habachi, *ASAE* 52, 1954, pp. 443–562; J. van Seters, *The Hyksos*, 1966, pp. 127–151; M. Bietak, *Tel el-Dab'a*, 2, 1975, especially pp. 179–221, pl. 44f. C.D.W. K.A.K.

RABBAH. 1. A town with associated villages in the hill country of Judah (Jos. 15:60), possibly Rubute of the Amarna letters and Tuthmosis III, which lay in the region of Gezer.

2. The capital of Ammon, now Amman, capital of Jordan, 35 km E of the river Jordan. Its full name occurs in Dt. 3:11; 2 Sa. 12:26; 17:27; Je. 49:2; Ezk. 21:20 as 'Rabbah of the Ammonites' (*rabbat bᵉnê ammôn*), and is shortened to Rabbah (*rabbâ*) in 2 Sa. 11:11; 12:27; Je. 49:3, *etc*. The name evidently means 'Main-town' (LXX has *akra*, 'citadel', at Dt. 3:11). The iron coffin of Og, king of Bashan, rested there (Dt. 3:11; AV 'iron bedstead').

Ammonite power grew simultaneously with Israelite, so that David faced a rival in Hanun, son of Nahash. After defeating Hanun's Aramaean allies and the Ammonite army, David and Joab were able to overrun Ammon, Joab besieging Rabbah, but leaving David the honour of taking the citadel. The inhabitants were put to forced labour (2 Sa. 10; 12:26–31; 1 Ch. 20:3). After Solomon's death, Ammon reasserted her independence and troubled Israel. The prophets spoke against Rabbah as representing the people of Ammon (Je. 49:2–3; Ezk. 21:20; 25:5; Am. 1:14).

Rabbah, rebuilt and renamed Philadelphia by Ptolemy Philadelphus (285–246 BC), became one of the cities of the Decapolis and an important trading centre.

Considerable archaeological remains exist in the vicinity of Amman today. At the airport a building of the 13th century BC (Late Bronze Age) has been unearthed. It was used as a depository for cremated human remains, many of them of young children, perhaps sacrificed to *Molech. On the citadel itself are extensive ruins of the mediaeval, Byzantine, Roman and Hellenistic cities, and among them sculptures and inscriptions of the 8th and 7th centuries BC have been found. Traces of Middle Bronze and Iron Age fortifications have been discovered.

BIBLIOGRAPHY. G. L. Harding, *Antiquities of Jordan*, 1967, pp. 61–70; J. B. Hennessy, *PEQ* 98, 1966, pp. 155–162; C. M. Bennett, *Levant* 10, 1978, pp. 1–9; *NEAEHL*, pp.1243–1252. J.A.T. A.R.M.

RABBI, RABBONI. Heb. *raḇ* meant 'great', and came to be used for a person in a respected position; *rabbi*, 'my great one', was used as a reverential form of address. By the end of the 2nd century BC the word *raḇ* was used for a teacher, and *rabbi* as the respectful address, 'my teacher'. Later the suffix lost its possessive significance, and the word 'rabbi' came to be used as the title of the authorized teachers of the Law; in modern Judaism it is used for those who are ordained to this work. By NT times the word had not come to be restricted to the official usage. It was certainly a title of honour, applied once to John the Baptist and twelve times to our Lord. In Mt. 23:7f., in contrast to the scribes' delight in being called 'rabbi', the disciples are told not to be so called—'for you have one teacher', Jesus said to them, 'and you are all brethren'. The Heb. word is transliterated into Gk. as *rhabbi* or *rhabbei* and in this passage quoted, and also in Jn. 1:38 and 20:16, it is made clear that the Heb. word was equivalent in meaning to the Gk. *didaskalos*.

'Rabboni' (*rhabbouni*) is a heightened form of 'rabbi' used to address our Lord in Mk. 10:51 and Jn. 20:16.

BIBLIOGRAPHY. G. H. Dalman, *The Words of Jesus*, 1902, pp. 331–340; E. Lohse, on *rhabbi*, *rhabbouni*, *TDNT* 6, pp. 961–965; H. L. Ellison, *NIDNTT* 3, pp. 115f. F.F.

RABMAG. The official position of the Bab. *Nergal-sharezer at the sack of Jerusalem in 587 BC (Je. 39:3, 13). It is the heb. form of *rabu emga*, 'noble

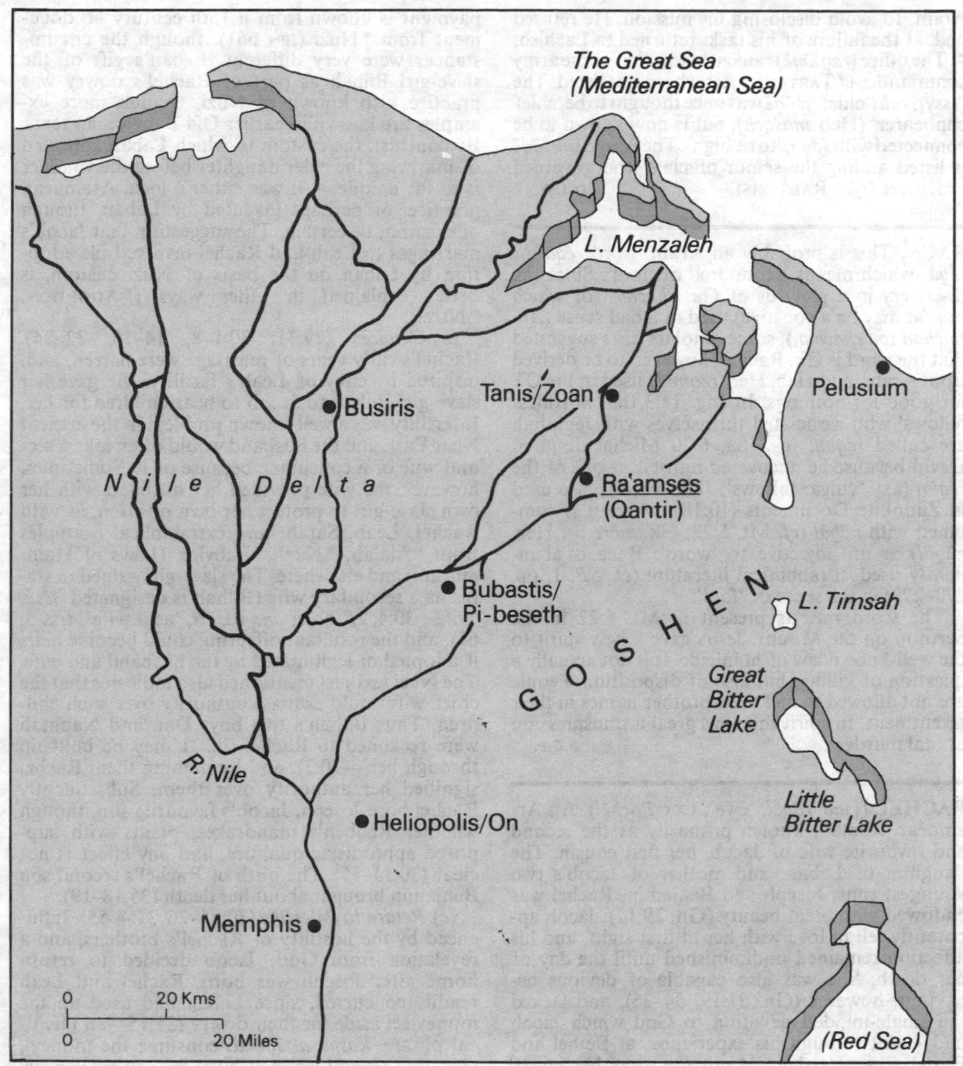

Ra'amses (Qantir) in Goshen.

and wise', a royal title claimed by Neriglissar, and of *rab maḫḫu*, 'chief of the *maḫḫu* (administrative, not religious) officials'. It is probably, however, the Heb. form of *rab mu(n)gi*, the title of an Assyr. and Bab. military official, sometimes sent as envoy to foreign kings. The precise meaning is unknown.

D.J.W.

RABSARIS. The title, 'chief official', of the following: **1.** One of the three Assyrians sent by Sennacherib to parley with Hezekiah at Jerusalem (2 Ki. 18:17; *cf.* Is. 36:3, where it is omitted). **2.** The Bab. Nabushazban who removed Jeremiah from prison and handed him over to Gedaliah (Je. 39:13). **3.** *Sarsechim, one of three Babylonians who sat as judges in the gate of Jerusalem after its capture in 587 BC (Je. 39:3).

The office of 'chief of the court eunuchs' (Bab. *rab ša rēši*) was held by a high-ranking palace dignitary (*cf.* Dn. 1:7). It is common in Assyr. texts and is attested in an Aram. docket from Nineveh (*rbsrs*, B.M. 81–2–4, 147). On this official see J. V. Kinnier Wilson, *The Nimrud Wine Lists*, 1972, pp. 47f. An Assyr. eponym, whose usual title of *šaknu* of the land of Marqasu, is glossed in an Aram. contract as *rbsrs*, *i.e. rab ša rēši* (*JAOS* 87, 1967, p. 523).

D.J.W.

RABSHAKEH. The title of the Assyr. official who, with the *Tartan and *Rabsaris, was sent by Sennacherib, king of Assyria, from Lachish to demand the surrender of Jerusalem by Hezekiah (2 Ki. 18:17, 19, 26–28, 37; 19:4–8; Is. 36:2, 4, 11–13, 22; 37:4, 8). He acted as spokesman for the delegation, addressing the citizens in the Judaean dialect. Hezekiah's representatives asked him to speak in

Aram. to avoid disclosing his mission. He refused and, at the failure of his task, returned to Lachish.

The office (*raḇšāqē*) ranked below that of the army commander (*TARTAN), after whom it is listed. The Assyr. *rab* ('chief') *šāqē* was once thought to be 'chief cupbearer' (Heb. *mašqeh*), but is now known to be connected with *šaqû*, 'to be high'. The Assyr. *rab šāqē* is listed among the senior officials who governed provinces (*cf.* *RABSARIS). D.J.W.

RACA. This is probably an Aram. word *rêqā'* or *rêqâ*, which means 'scoundrel' or 'fool'. Since the discovery in a papyrus of Gk. *rhachas* (of which *rhacha* may be a vocative) used in a bad sense (*Antiochon ton rhachan*), some scholars have suggested that the word is Gk. Raca is, however, to be derived from Aram. and Heb. Heb. *rêqîm* is used in the OT for good-for-nothings. In Jdg. 11:3 the 'worthless fellows' who associated themselves with Jephthah are called *rêqîm*; in 2 Sa. 6:20 Michal despised David because he uncovered himself as one of the *rêqîm* (RSV 'vulgar fellows'). The word is also used in Zadokite Documents (10:18), where it is combined with *nāḇāl* (*cf.* Mt. 5:22, Gk. *mōre* for Heb. *nāḇāl*) as an adjective to 'word'. Raca is abundantly used in rabbinical literature (*cf. SB*, 1, pp. 278–279) in the sense of 'fool'.

The word *raca* is present in Mt. 5:22 in the Sermon on the Mount. Jesus gave a new spirit to the well-known law of homicide. It is not actually a question of killing, but also of disposition. People are not allowed to call their brother names in their resentment. In spirit this is as great a transgression as real murder. F.C.F.

RACHEL (Heb. *rāḥēl*, 'ewe'; LXX *Rachēl*). An Aramaean woman, known primarily as the second and favourite wife of Jacob, her first cousin. The daughter of Laban, and mother of Jacob's two youngest sons, Joseph and Benjamin, Rachel was endowed with great beauty (Gn. 29:17). Jacob apparently fell in love with her at first sight, and his affection remained undiminished until the day of her death. She was also capable of devious behaviour, however (Gn. 31:19, 34–35), and lacked the single-minded devotion to God which Jacob had learnt through his experiences at Bethel and Peniel. She probably did not put away her pagan gods until shortly before she died. Rachel was the ancestress of three tribes, Benjamin, Ephraim and Manasseh, and she and her sister Leah were honoured by later generations as those 'who together built up the house of Israel' (Ru. 4:11).

(*a*) *Marriage* (Gn. 29:6–30). Jacob had been sent by Isaac and Rebekah to find a wife among his mother's relatives in Paddan-aram (28:1–2; *FAMILY). He met Rachel in the region of Harran as she was shepherding her father's flocks, and he at once helped her to water the animals by rolling the stone from the well's mouth. Laban welcomed him into his household where he lived for 20 years. Jacob's love for Rachel is one of the Bible's outstanding examples of human love—7 years 'seemed to him but a few days because of the love he had for her' (29:20). As a result of Laban's trickery in making Leah Jacob's first wife, presumably accomplished by the veiling of the bride, Jacob served another 7 years for Rachel, but his love did not waver.

Some details of Rachel's marriage can be paralleled outside the OT. Serving for a wife in lieu of payment is known from a 15th century BC document from *Nuzi (JEN 661), though the circumstances were very different. Laban's gift of the slave-girl Bilhah as part of Rachel's dowry was practice also known at Nuzi, though more examples are known in earlier Old Babylonian texts. By contrast, the custom to which Laban appealed of marrying the elder daughter before the younger is so far unique — it was either a local Aramaean practice, or perhaps invented by Laban, though one cannot be certain. The suggestion that Jacob's marriages to Leah and Rachel involved his adoption by Laban on the basis of Nuzi custom, is better explained in other ways (*ADOPTION, *NUZI).

(*b*) *Children* (29:31; 30:1–8, 14–15, 22–24). Rachel's early years of marriage were barren, and, inspired by envy of Leah's fertility, she gave her slave-girl Bilhah to Jacob to bear children for her. Infertility was a well-known problem in the ancient Near East, and the husband would often take a second wife or a concubine because of it. Sometimes, however, the wife provided her husband with her own slave-girl to protect her own position, as with Rachel, Leah, Sarah, and extrabiblical examples from *Alalaḫ, *Nuzi, *Babylon (Laws of Hammurapi) and elsewhere. The slave-girl gained in status as a secondary wife (Bilhah is designated *'iššâ*, 'wife', 30:4; *cf.* Nuzi *ana aššūti*, 'as a wife', HSS 5. 67), and the resultant offspring could become heirs if adopted or legitimated by the husband and wife. The Nuzi text just mentioned also indicates that the chief wife could exercise authority over such children. Thus Bilhah's two boys Dan and Naphtali were reckoned to Rachel (lit. 'I may be built up through her'—30:3), and by naming them Rachel signified her authority over them. Subsequently Rachel bore Joseph, Jacob's favourite son, though whether Reuben's mandrakes, plants with supposed aphrodisiac qualities, had any effect is not clear (30:14–15). The birth of Rachel's second son Benjamin brought about her death (35:18–19).

(*c*) *Return to Palestine* (30:25–26; 31:4–55). Influenced by the hostility of Rachel's brothers, and a revelation from God, Jacob decided to return home after Joseph was born. Rachel and Leah readily concurred, since Laban had used up the money set aside for their dowry (31:15—an identical phrase, *kaspa akālu* 'to consume the money', was used several times at Nuzi in very similar circumstances). Without any inheritance from their father, the girls were regarded by him as 'foreigners'. It is frequently suggested that Rachel's theft of her father's household gods or *teraphim (*tᵉrāp̄îm*) was an attempt to regain an inheritance for herself and Jacob, but the fact that they were stolen rules out this interpretation. Perhaps Rachel sought for protection on the long journey, or simply wanted to deprive her father of his valued possessions. Jacob, however, who was unaware of his wife's action, regarded the offence as worthy of death, though the threat was never carried out. Rachel continued as Jacob's favourite wife after the incident (33:2, 7), and the *tᵉrāp̄îm* were probably among the images later disposed of because their existence was a hindrance to the worship of God (35:2–4). On the same journey, Laban and Jacob agreed a covenant by which Jacob undertook not to maltreat his wives nor to marry any other. Both these conditions are found in marriage contracts from various periods in the ancient Near East.

(*d*) *Death* (35:16–20). Rachel died between

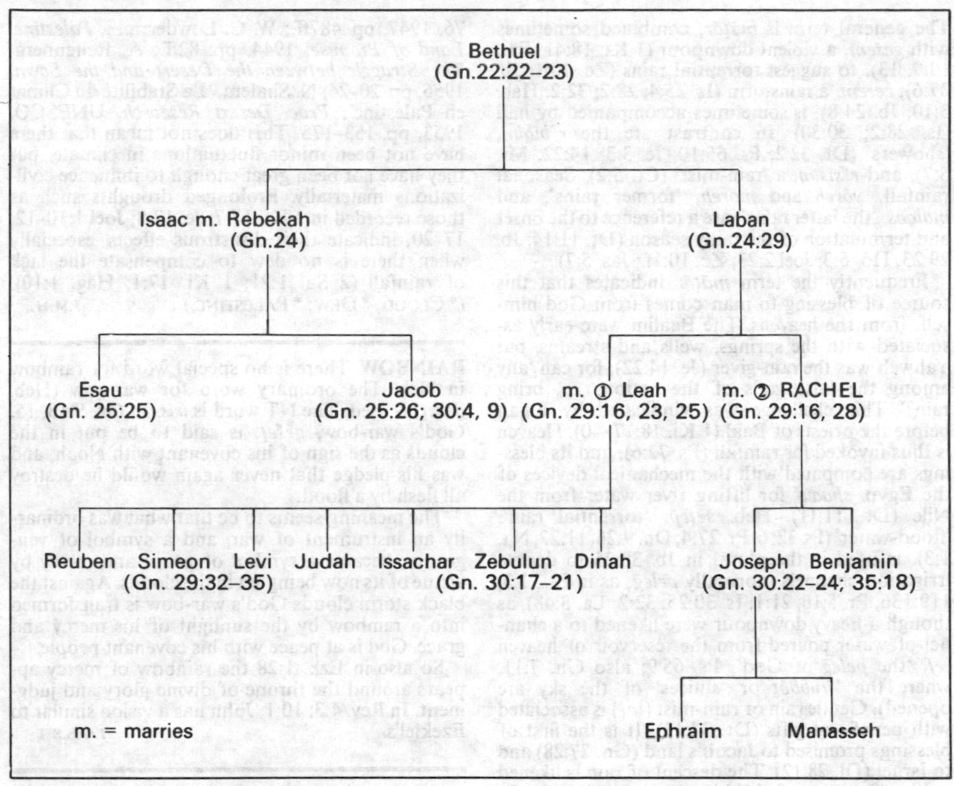

Rachel's lineage.

Bethel and Bethlehem when her second son Benjamin was born. Jacob's continuing love for her is evidenced by the memorial pillar (*maṣṣēḇâ*) he set up over her grave, and its location was still known in Saul's day, when it was described as being on the border of Benjamin at Ṣelṣaḥ (*ZELZAH, 1 Sa. 10:2). The site is unknown today, though Je. 31:15 (*cf.* Mt. 2:18) suggests it may have been near Ramah, *c.* 8 km N of Jerusalem. However, Rachel's memory was also preserved at Bethlehem in the time of Ruth (Ru. 4:11), probably because it was near her burial-place.

BIBLIOGRAPHY. M. J. Selman, *TynB* 27, 1976, pp. 114–136; J. Z. Abrams, *JBQ* 18, 1989–90, pp. 213–221.

M.J.S.

RAHAB (Heb. *rāḥāḇ*, possibly connected with root *rḥb*, 'broad'). A harlot who lived in a house which formed part of the town wall of Late Bronze Age Jericho. Joshua's two spies lodged with her. When they were pursued she hid them under drying stalks of flax on the roof. The pursuers were sent off on a false trail and then Rahab made terms with her lodgers. She knew that Jericho must fall to the servants of Yahweh and so she asked for protection for herself and her family. The spies escaped from a window, with her help. When Jericho was destroyed the family was saved and Rahab joined up with the Israelites (Jos. 2:6–17, 22–25).

In the NT the writer to the Hebrews includes her among ancient examples of faith in God (Heb. 11:31), and she is quoted as one who was justified by her works in Jas. 2:25. She is almost certainly to be identified with Rahab (AV 'Rachab'), the wife of Salmon and mother of Boaz, ancestor of David, who is included in our Lord's genealogy in Mt. 1:5.

BIBLIOGRAPHY. M. Newman in J. T. Butler (ed.), *Understanding the Word*, 1985, pp. 167–181.

M.B.

RAHAB (Heb. *rahaḇ*, lit. 'pride', 'arrogance'), the female monster of chaos (*cf.* Bab. Tiamat), closely associated with *Leviathan. The curbing of the forces of chaos (pre-eminently the unruly sea) at the creation is poetically described in terms of God's smiting Rahab (*cf.* Jb. 26:12, and more generally Jb. 9:13; 38:8–11). But this imagery in the OT is usually transferred from the creation story to the narrative of the redemption of Israel from Egypt, when God again showed his mastery over the sea and other forces opposed to his will; it is the Exodus that is indicated by references to the smiting of Rahab in Ps. 89:10; Is. 51:9 (*cf.* Ps. 74:12ff., where the sense is the same, although Rahab is not expressly mentioned). From this usage Rahab comes to be employed quite generally as a poetic synonym for Egypt, as in Ps. 87:4 ('Among those who know me I mention Rahab and Babylon') and Is. 30:7 ('Rahab who sits still'); and her dragon-associate becomes a figure of Pharaoh (*cf.* Ezk. 29:3).

F.F.B.

RAIN. The importance and character of rainfall is emphasized in the OT by the use of several words.

The general term is *māṭār*, combined sometimes with *gešem*, a violent downpour (1 Ki. 18:41; Ezr. 10:9, 13), to suggest torrential rains (Zc. 10:1; Jb. 37:6); *zerem*, a rainstorm (Is. 25:4; 28:2; 32:2; Hab. 3:10; Jb. 24:8), is sometimes accompanied by hail (Is. 28:2; 30:30). In contrast are the *rᵉbîḇîm*, 'showers' (Dt. 32:2; Ps. 65:10; Je. 3:3; 14:22; Mi. 5:7), and *rᵉsîsîm*, a 'rain-mist' (Ct. 5:2). Seasonal rainfall, *yôreh* and *môreh*, 'former rains', and *malqôš*, 'the latter rains', are a reference to the onset and termination of the rainy season (Dt. 11:14; Jb. 29:23; Ho. 6:3; Joel 2:23; Zc. 10:1f.; Jas. 5:7).

Frequently the term *māṭār* indicates that this source of blessing to man comes from God himself, from the heavens. The Baalim were early associated with the springs, wells and streams, but Yahweh was the rain-giver (Je. 14:22), for can 'any among the false gods of the nations ... bring rain?' This challenge was vindicated by Elijah before the priests of Baal (1 Ki. 18:17–40). Heaven is thus invoked for rainfall (Ps. 72:6), and its blessings are compared with the mechanical devices of the Egyp. *shaduf* for lifting river water from the Nile (Dt. 11:11). Heb. *šeṭep̄*, 'torrential rain', 'flood-water' (Ps. 32:6; Pr. 27:4; Dn. 9:26; 11:22; Na. 1:3), is used in the plural in Jb. 38:25 to denote irrigation channels (normally *peleḡ*, as in Pss. 1:3; 119:136; Pr. 5:16; 21:1; Is. 30:25; 32:2; La. 3:48), as though a heavy downpour were likened to a channel of water poured from the reservoir of heaven (*cf.* 'the *peleḡ* of God', Ps. 65:9; also Gn. 7:11, where the *'ᵃrubbôṯ* or 'sluices' of the sky are opened). Gentle rain or rain-mist (*ṭal*) is associated with beneficent gifts (Dt. 33:13). It is the first of blessings promised to Jacob's land (Gn. 27:28) and to Israel (Dt. 28:12). The descent of rain is likened to the blessings of the kingdom (Ps. 72:6–7). In contrast, the presence of clouds and wind without rain is likened to a man who 'boasts of a gift he does not give' (Pr. 25:14). (*DEW.)

The rainfall of Palestine is so closely identified with the cool season that the Arab. *šitā'* refers to both winter and rain. There is the same significance in Ct. 2:11, 'For, lo, the winter is past, the rain is over and gone.' Equally the summer season is suggestive of the hot, dry period, *e.g.* 'My strength was dried up as by the heat of summer' (Ps. 32:4). During the preliminary period of mid-Sept. to mid-Oct. the moist sea air encountering the very hot dry air from the land surface causes thunderstorms and the irregular distribution of rainfall. This is vividly described in Am. 4:7, 'I would send rain upon one city, and send no rain upon another city: one field would be rained upon, and the field on which it did not rain withered.' The onset of the effective rains usually begins in mid- or late Oct., but may be delayed until even Jan. These 'former rains', so earnestly longed for, cause a fall in temperature so that convectional currents are eliminated and the damp atmosphere produces a brilliance in the sky, described by Elihu: 'And now men cannot look on the light when it is bright in the skies, when the wind has passed and cleared them' (Jb. 37:21). The cool, rainy season is the pastoral setting to the joys described by the psalmist (Ps. 65:12–13). Between April and early May, the 'latter rains' describe the last showers at the close of the rainy season (Am. 4:7).

Modern scholars agree that no climatic change has occurred within historic times. See J. W. Gregory, 'The Habitable Globe: Palestine and the Stability of Climate in Modern Times', *Geog. Journ.* 76, 1947, pp. 487ff.; W. C. Lowdermilk, *Palestine, Land of Promise*, 1944, pp. 82ff.; A. Reifenberg, *The Struggle between the Desert and the Sown*, 1956, pp. 20–24; N. Shalem, 'La Stabilité du Climat en Palestine', *Proc. Desert Research*, UNESCO, 1953, pp. 153–175. This does not mean that there have not been minor fluctuations in climate, but they have not been great enough to influence civilizations materially. Prolonged droughts such as those recorded in 1 Ki. 17:7; Je. 17:8; Joel 1:10–12, 17–20, indicate their disastrous effects, especially when there is no dew to compensate the lack of rainfall (2 Sa. 1:21; 1 Ki. 17:1; Hag. 1:10). (*CLOUD; *DEW; *PALESTINE.) J.M.H.

RAINBOW. There is no special word for rainbow in Heb. The ordinary word for war-bow (Heb. *qešeṯ*) is used. The NT word is *iris*. In Gn. 9:13, 15, God's war-bow, *qešeṯ*, is said to be put in the clouds as the sign of his covenant with Noah, and was his pledge that never again would he destroy all flesh by a flood.

The meaning seems to be that what was ordinarily an instrument of war, and a symbol of vengeance, became a symbol of peace and mercy by virtue of its now being set in the clouds. Against the black storm clouds God's war-bow is transformed into a rainbow by the sunlight of his mercy and grace. God is at peace with his covenant people.

So also in Ezk. 1:28 the rainbow of mercy appears around the throne of divine glory and judgment. In Rev. 4:3; 10:1, John has a vision similar to Ezekiel's. J.G.S.S.T.

RAMAH. The Heb. name *rāmâ*, from the root *rûm*, 'to be high', was used of several places, all of them on elevated sites.

1. Ramah of Benjamin, near Bethel, in the area of Gibeon and Beeroth (Jos. 18:25), was a resting-place on the road N. Here the Levite and his concubine planned to stay (Jdg. 19:13). Deborah the prophetess lived close by (Jdg. 4:5). When Asa of Judah and Baasha of Israel were at war, Baasha built a fort here, but when the Syrians attacked Israel Asa destroyed it and built Geba and Mizpah with the materials (1 Ki. 15:17, 21–22; 2 Ch. 16:1, 5–6).

Here Nebuzaradan gathered the exiles after the fall of Jerusalem and released Jeremiah (Je. 40:1). The town was reoccupied after the return from Babylon (Ezr. 2:26; Ne. 11:33).

Ramah features in the messages of some of the prophets (Ho. 5:8; Is. 10:29; Je. 31:15). It is probably to be identified with Er-Ram 8 km N of Jerusalem, or Ramat Rahel (Beth Haccherem), near the traditional tomb of Rachel (Je. 31:15; 1 Sa. Mt. 2:18; Jos., *Ant.* 8. 303).

2. The birthplace and subsequent home of Samuel, also called Ramathaim-zophim (1 Sa. 1:19; 2:11), from which he went on circuit annually (1 Sa. 7:17). Here Saul first met him (1 Sa. 9:6, 10), and here the elders of Israel came to demand a king (1 Sa. 8:4ff.). After his dispute with Saul Samuel came here (1 Sa. 15:34ff.). David found refuge in Ramah and later fled to Nob (1 Sa. 19:18; 20:1).

There are four sites proposed for Ramah today: Ramallah, 13 km N of Jerusalem; Beit Rama, 19 km NW of Bethel; Er-Ram, the Ramah of Benjamin; and Nebi Samwil. There still remains some uncertainty.

The word is also used as the name for **3.** a town on

the boundary of Asher (Jos. 19:29); **4.** a walled town of Naphtali (Jos. 19:36); **5.** a town of Simeon (Jos. 19:8; 1 Sa. 30:27); and **6.** an abbreviation for Ramoth-gilead (*cf.* 2 Ki. 8:28–29 and 2 Ch. 22:5–6).

See F. M. Abel, *Géographie de la Palestine*, 2, 1933, p. 427; D. Baly, *Geography of the Bible*[2], 1974. J.A.T.

RAMOTH-GILEAD. A walled city in the territory of Gad, E of the Jordan, which featured frequently in Israel's wars with Syria. It was one of the * cities of refuge (Dt. 4:43; Jos. 20:8) and was assigned to the Merarite Levites (Jos. 21:38; 1 Ch. 6:80). It has been identified with Mizpeh, Mizpeh of Gilead (Jdg. 11:29) and Ramath-mizpeh ('height of Mizpeh', Jos. 13:26). Modern equivalents suggested are Huṣn-'Ajlûn and Remtheh, but the suggestion of Nelson Glueck (*BASOR* 92, 1943) that it is Tell-Rāmîth has strong claims.

It was probably the home of Jephthah (Jdg. 11:34). Ben-geber, one of Solomon's twelve administrators, lived here (1 Ki. 4:13). According to Josephus (*Ant.* 8. 399), the city was taken by Omri from Ben-hadad I. The town changed hands between Israel and the Syrians several times. Even after Ahab had defeated the Syrians (1 Ki. 20), it remained in their hands and Ahab enlisted the help of Jehoshaphat of Judah to retake it (1 Ki. 22:3–4). He was wounded and died (1 Ki. 22:1–40; 2 Ch. 18). His son Joram took up the attack but was likewise wounded (2 Ki. 8:28ff.). During his absence from the camp at Ramoth-gilead, Jehu the army captain was anointed at Elisha's instigation (2 Ki. 9:1f.; 2 Ch. 22:7). Jehu later murdered all the seed royal, but Josephus says that the city was taken before Jehu departed (*Ant.* 9. 105).

BIBLIOGRAPHY. N. Glueck, 'Ramoth Gilead', *BASOR* 92, 1943, pp. 10ff.; F. M. Abel, *Géographie de la Palestine*, 2, 1933, pp. 430–431; H. Tadmor, *IEJ* 12, 1962, pp. 114–122; W. A. Lasor, *ISBE* 4, pp. 40–41; *NEAEHL*, pp. 1291–1293. J.A.T.

REBEKAH, REBECCA (Heb. *riḇqâ*, *cf.* Arab. 'a looped cord for tying young animals' from *rabaqa*, 'to tie fast'; Gk. *rhebekka*). The wife of Isaac, daughter of Bethuel, Abraham's nephew (Gn.

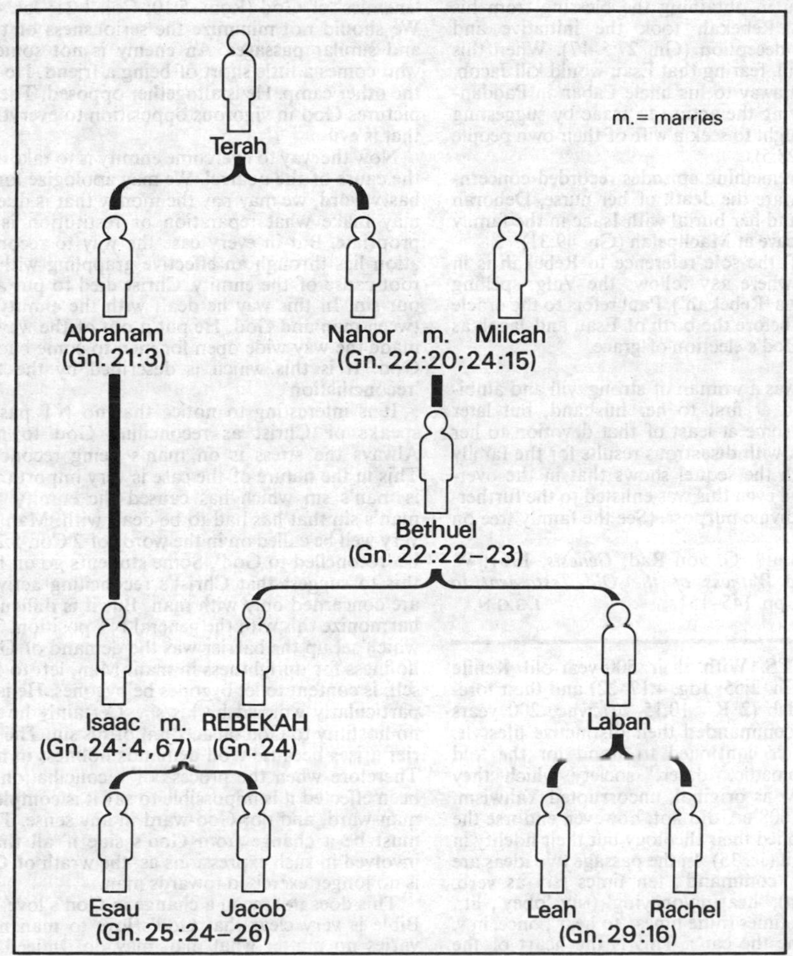

The family of Rebekah.

22:23). The account of the choice of Rebekah as Isaac's wife (Gn. 24) strongly emphasizes the guidance and overruling providence of God. Abraham sent his chief steward, not named but probably Eliezer, to his home-country to seek a wife for his son. After prayer, the steward was led directly to Rebekah. Bethuel and her brother, Laban, having heard all the circumstances, agreed to the marriage.

She was barren for the first 20 years of her marriage. Isaac entreated God, and she bore twin sons, Esau and Jacob, receiving from Yahweh before the birth an oracle in which their divergent destinies were foretold (Gn. 25:20–26). The beginning of tragedy is foreshadowed in Gn. 25:28, where we read of the favouritism of Isaac and Rebekah for different sons, which made inevitable the destruction of family unity.

Reminiscent of Abraham and Sarah was the incident during Isaac's sojourn in Gerar, when he deceived Abimelech and the Philistines by pretending that Rebekah was his sister (Gn. 26:1–11; *cf.* Gn. 20). Both Isaac and Rebekah were grieved at Esau's marriages to women of an alien race, the Hittites (Gn. 26:34f.).

In the deed of treachery whereby Jacob supplanted Esau in obtaining the blessing from his aged father, Rebekah took the initiative and planned the deception (Gn. 27:5–17). When this was successful, fearing that Esau would kill Jacob, she sent him away to his uncle Laban in Paddan-aram, justifying the action to Isaac by suggesting that Jacob ought to seek a wife of their own people (Gn. 27:42–28:5).

The only remaining episodes recorded concerning Rebekah are the death of her nurse, Deborah (Gn. 35:8), and her burial with Isaac in the family grave in the cave at Machpelah (Gn. 49:31).

In the NT, the sole reference to Rebekah is in Rom. 9:10, where RSV follows the Vulg. spelling 'Rebecca' (NEB 'Rebekah'). Paul refers to the oracle she received before the birth of Esau and Jacob as illustrating God's election of grace.

Rebekah was a woman of strong will and ambition, devoted at first to her husband, but later transferring some at least of that devotion to her younger son, with disastrous results for the family unity, though the sequel shows that in the overruling of God even this was enlisted to the furtherance of the divine purpose. (See the family tree on p. 1001.)

BIBLIOGRAPHY. G. von Rad, *Genesis*, 1961; W. Vischer, *The Witness of the Old Testament to Christ*, 1949, pp. 145–151. J.G.G.N.

RECHABITES. With their 500-year-old Kenite ancestry (1 Ch. 2:55; Jdg. 4:17–22) and their forefather Jonadab (2 Ki. 10:15–27) who, 200 years earlier, had commanded their distinctive lifestyle, the Rechabites continued to stand for the 'old ways': a nomadic, 'desert' society which they doubtless saw as original, uncorrupted Yahwism. Jeremiah, in 608 BC, did not, however, endorse the way they applied their theology but their fidelity in maintaining it (Je. 35). In the passage two ideas are pre-eminent: 'command', ten times (six as verb, four as noun); 'hearing/obeying' (NIV 'obey', lit., 'to hear') ten times (nine times, 'to hear', once, in v. 15, 'to incline the ear'). This is the heart of the matter: the Rechabites obeyed the human word of their forefather. Why do the people of God disobey the divine word of their God? Jeremiah placed the incident between the promise-breakers of 34:18 and the imperishable divine word of ch. 36 to enforce the message. The distinctive reality of the people of God is to obey the Word of God. The Rechabites wanted to change society by a separatist stance; Jeremiah called for change in society by a return to obedience.

BIBLIOGRAPHY. J. Pedersen, *Israel 3–4*, 1953, *s.v.* 'Rechabites'; F. D. Kidner, *The Message of Jeremiah*, *BST*, 1987; J. Guest, *Jeremiah*, 1988; M. H. Pope, *Interpreter's Bible*. J.A.M.

RECONCILIATION. There are four important NT passages which treat of the work of Christ under the figure of reconciliation, namely, Rom. 5:10f.; 2 Cor. 5:18ff.; Eph. 2:11ff.; Col. 1:19ff. The important Gk. words are the noun *katallagē* and the verbs *katallassō* and *apokatallassō*. Reconciliation properly applies not to good relations in general but to the doing away of an enmity, the bridging over of a quarrel. It implies that the parties being reconciled were formerly hostile to one another. The Bible tells us bluntly that sinners are 'enemies' of God (Rom. 5:10; Col. 1:21; Jas. 4:4). We should not minimize the seriousness of these and similar passages. An enemy is not someone who comes a little short of being a friend. He is in the other camp. He is altogether opposed. The NT pictures God in vigorous opposition to everything that is evil.

Now the way to overcome enmity is to take away the cause of the quarrel. We may apologize for the hasty word, we may pay the money that is due, we may make what reparation or restitution is appropriate. But in every case the way to reconciliation lies through an effective grappling with the root cause of the enmity. Christ died to put away our sin. In this way he dealt with the enmity between man and God. He put it out of the way. He made the way wide open for men to come back to God. It is this which is described by the term 'reconciliation'.

It is interesting to notice that no NT passage speaks of Christ as reconciling God to man. Always the stress is on man's being reconciled. This in the nature of the case is very important. It is man's sin which has caused the enmity. It is man's sin that has had to be dealt with. Man may very well be called on in the words of 2 Cor. 5:20 to be 'reconciled to God'. Some students go on from this to suggest that Christ's reconciling activities are concerned only with man. But it is difficult to harmonize this with the general NT position. That which set up the barrier was the demand of God's holiness for uprightness in man. Man, left to himself, is content to let bygones be bygones. He is not particularly worried by his sin. Certainly he feels no hostility to God on account of his sin. The barrier arises because God demands holiness in man. Therefore when the process of reconciliation has been effected it is impossible to say it is completely man-ward, and not God-ward in any sense. There must be a change from God's side if all that is involved in such expressions as 'the wrath of God' is no longer exercised towards man.

This does not mean a change in God's love. The Bible is very clear that God's love to man never varies no matter what man may do. Indeed, the whole atoning work of Christ stems from God's great love. It was 'while we were yet sinners' that

'Christ died for us' (Rom. 5:8). This truth must be zealously guarded. But at the same time we must not allow ourselves to slip into the position of maintaining that reconciliation is a purely subjective process. Reconciliation in some sense was effected outside man before anything happened within man. Paul can speak of Christ 'through whom we have now received our reconciliation' (Rom. 5:11). A reconciliation that can be 'received' must be proffered (and thus in some sense accomplished) before men received it. In other words, we must think of reconciliation as having effects both God-ward and man-ward.

BIBLIOGRAPHY. L. Morris, *The Apostolic Preaching of the Cross*[3], 1965; R. P. Martin, *Reconciliation*, 1980; P. Stuhlmacher, *Reconciliation, Law and Righteousness*, 1986; H.-G. Link, *et al.*, *NIDNTT* 3, pp. 145–176; F. Büchsel, *TDNT* 1, pp. 254–258. L.M.

REDEEMER, REDEMPTION. Redemption means deliverance from some evil by payment of a price. It is more than simple deliverance. Thus prisoners of war might be released on payment of a price which was called a 'ransom' (Gk. *lytron*). The word-group based on *lytron* was formed specifically to convey this idea of release on payment of ransom. In this circle of ideas Christ's death may be regarded as 'a ransom for many' (Mk. 10:45).

Again, slaves might be released by a process of ransom. In the fictitious purchase by a god the slave would pay the price of his freedom into the temple treasury. Then he would go through the solemn formality of being sold to the god 'for freedom'. Technically he was still the slave of the god, and some pious obligations might accordingly be laid upon him. But as far as men were concerned he was thenceforth free. Alternatively, the slave might simply pay his master the price. The characteristic thing about either form of release is the payment of the ransom price (*lytron*). 'Redemption' is the name given to the process.

Among the Hebrews we may discern a different situation, well illustrated in Ex. 21:28–30. If a man had a dangerous ox he must keep it under restraint. If it got out and gored someone so that he died the law was plain, 'the ox shall be stoned, and its owner also shall be put to death'. But this is not a case of wilful murder. There is no malice aforethought. Thus, it is provided that a ransom (Heb. *kōper*) might be 'laid on him'. He could pay a sum of money and thus redeem his forfeited life.

Other usages of redemption in antiquity provide for the redemption of property, *etc.*, but the three we have noticed are the most important. Common to them all is the idea of freedom secured by payment of a price. Outside the Bible the usage is practically unvarying. A few metaphorical passages occur, but these serve only to make clear the basic meaning of the word. The payment of a price for deliverance is the basic and characteristic thing.

It is this which makes the concept so useful for the early Christians. Jesus had taught them that 'everyone who commits sin is a slave to sin' (Jn. 8:34). In line with this, Paul can think of himself as 'carnal, sold under sin' (Rom. 7:14), sold as under a cruel slave-master. He reminds the Romans that in earlier days they had been 'slaves of sin' (Rom. 6:17). From another point of view men were under sentence of death on account of their sin. 'For the wages of sin is death' (Rom. 6:23). Sinners are slaves. Sinners are doomed to death. Either way the ancient world would have regarded the situation as crying out for redemption. Failing redemption, the slavery would continue, the sentence of death be carried out. The cross of Christ is seen against this background. It is the price paid to release the slaves, to let the condemned go free.

What gives the metaphor force is the constant presence of the price-paying idea. But it is precisely this that is disputed by some who think that redemption is no more than another way of saying 'deliverance'. The big reason for thinking this is that there are some OT passages where Yahweh is said to have redeemed his people (Ex. 6:6; Ps. 77:14f., *etc.*), and it is unthinkable that he should pay a price to anyone. But too much is being deduced. The metaphor has not been robbed of its point (*cf.* the saying 'he sold his life dearly'). Sometimes in the OT Yahweh is thought of as being so powerful that all the might of the nations is but a puny thing before him. But redemption is not used in such passages. Where redemption occurs there is the thought of effort. Yahweh redeems 'with a stretched out arm'. He makes known his strength. Because he loves his people he redeems them at cost to himself. His effort is regarded as the 'price'. This is the whole point of using the redemption terminology.

The characteristic NT word for redemption is *apolytrōsis*, a comparatively rare word elsewhere. It is found ten times in the NT but apparently there are only eight occurrences in all the rest of Gk. literature. This may express the conviction of the early Christians that the redemption wrought in Christ was unique. It does not mean, as some have thought, that they understand redemption simply as 'deliverance'. For that they use such a word as *rhyomai*, 'rescue'. *apolytrōsis* means deliverance on payment of a price, and that price is the atoning death of the Saviour. When we read of 'redemption through his blood' (Eph. 1:7), the blood of Christ is clearly being regarded as the price of redemption. It is not otherwise with Rom. 3:24f., 'Being justified freely by his grace through the redemption that is in Christ Jesus: whom God hath set forth to be a propitiation through faith in his blood' (AV). Here Paul is using three metaphors, those of the law court, and of the sacrifices, and of manumission. Our concern is with the last. Paul envisages a process of freeing, but by the payment of a price, the blood of Christ. Redemption is linked with Christ's death also in Heb. 9:15. Sometimes, again, we have the mention of price, but not redemption, as in references to being 'bought with a price' (1 Cor. 6:19f.; 7:22f.). The basic idea is the same. Christ bought men at the price of his blood. In Gal. 3:13 the price of redemption is given thus: 'having become a curse for us'. Christ redeemed us by taking our place, by bearing our curse. This points us to the definitely substitutionary idea in redemption, an idea which sometimes receives stress, as in Mk. 10:45 ('a ransom for many').

Redemption not only looks back to Calvary, but forward to the freedom in which the redeemed stand. 'You were bought with a price,' Paul can say, 'so glorify God in your body' (1 Cor. 6:20). Precisely because they have been redeemed at such a cost believers must be God's men. They must show in their lives that they are no longer caught up in the bondage from which they have been released and are exhorted to 'stand fast therefore in the liberty wherewith Christ hath made us free' (Gal. 5:1, AV).

BIBLIOGRAPHY. *LAE*, pp. 318ff.; L. Morris, *The Apostolic Preaching of the Cross*[3], 1965, ch. 1; A. J. Hultgren, *Christ and His Benefits*, 1987; O. Procksch, F. Büchsel, in *TDNT* 4, pp. 328–356; C. Brown *et al.*, in *NIDNTT* 3, pp. 177–223. L.M.

RED SEA. In modern geography, the sea that divides NE Africa from Arabia and extends some 1,900 km from the straits of Bab el-Mandeb near Aden N to the S tip of the Sinai peninsula. For nearly another 300 km, the Gulfs of Suez and Aqabah continue the sea N on the W and E sides of the Sinai peninsula respectively. In classical antiquity the name Red Sea (*erythra thalassa*) included also the Arabian and Indian Seas to the NW coast of India. In the OT the term *yam sûp̄*, 'sea of reeds' (and/or 'weed'), is used to cover: (*a*) the Bitter Lakes region in the Egyptian Delta N of Suez along the line of the present Suez Canal; and (*b*) the Gulfs of Suez and Aqabah and possibly the Red Sea proper beyond these.

I. The Bitter Lakes region

In general terms, the Israelites were led from Egypt on the way of the wilderness and the *yam sûp̄* (Ex. 13:18). Ex. 14 and 15 are more specific: on leaving Succoth (Tell el-Maskhuta) and Etham, Israel were to turn back and camp before Pihahiroth, between Migdol and the 'sea', before Baal-zephon (Ex. 14:1–2, 9; *cf.* *ENCAMPMENT BY THE SEA). It was this 'sea', near all these places, that God drove back and divided by a 'strong east wind' for Israel to cross dryshod, and then brought back upon the pursuing Egyptians (Ex. 14:16, 21–31; 15:1, 4, 19, 21). From the 'sea of reeds', *yam sûp̄*, Israel went into the wilderness of Shur (Ex. 15:22; Nu. 33:8) and then on towards Sinai. Various points suggest that this famous crossing, the Exodus in the narrow sense, took place in the Bitter Lakes region, roughly between Qantara (48 km S of Port Said) and just N of Suez. First, geographically, the wilderness of Shur, which Israel entered directly from crossing the *yam sûp̄* (Ex. 15:22), is opposite this very area (*SHUR). Secondly, geophysically, the reedy waters of the Bitter Lakes and Lake Menzaleh can be affected by strong E winds precisely in the way described in Ex. 14:21 and experienced on a small scale by Aly Shafei Bey in 1945–6 (*Bulletin de la Société Royale de Géographie d'Égypte* 21, August 1946, pp. 231ff.; *cf.* also *JTVI* 28, 1894–5, pp. 267–280). Thirdly, philologically, the Heb. word *sûp̄* is generally admitted to be a loanword from Egyp. *ṯwf(y)*, 'papyrus', and *p'-ṯwf*, a location, 'the papyrus-marshes' *par excellence* in the NE part of the Delta between Tanis (Zoan), Qantir and the present line of the Suez Canal N of Ismailia, on the former Pelusiac arm of the Nile. For details and references, see A. H. Gardiner, *Ancient Egyptian Onomastica*, 2, 1947, pp. 201*–202*; R. A. Caminos, *Late-Egyptian Miscellanies*, 1954, p. 79; Erman and Grapow, *Wörterbuch d. Aegypt. Sprache*, 5, 1931, p. 359: 6–10. Ps. 78:12, 43, puts the great events preceding the Exodus in the 'field of Zoan', *i.e.* in the NE Delta. There is no sufficient factual basis for taking *sûp̄* to mean 'end'; more likely it is derived from the Egyptian *ṯwf*, despite F. Batto, *JBL* 102, 1983, pp. 27–35, and *BAR* 10/4, 1984, pp. 57–62; *cf.* survey, J. R. Huddlestun, *ABD* 5, 1992, pp. 633–642.

II. The Gulfs of Suez and Aqabah

Turning S from Shur *via* Etham, Marah and Elim, the Israelites pitched by the *yam sûp̄* and then went on to Sin and Dophkah (Nu. 33:10–11). This would appear to refer to the Gulf of Suez. Whether Ex. 10:19 during the plagues refers to the Lakes region, the Gulf of Suez or the Red Sea proper is not certain; see *Plagues of Egypt (eighth plague) and G. Hort, *ZAW* 70, 1958, pp. 51–52. The *yam sûp̄* of Ex. 23:31 is ambiguous, but perhaps it is the Gulf of Aqabah.

Various references clearly show that the term *yam sûp̄* applied to the Gulf of Aqabah. After their first halt at Kadesh-barnea (*KADESH), the Israelites were ordered into the wilderness by the way to the *yam sûp̄* (Nu. 14:25; Dt. 1:40; 2:1), *i.e.* by the Arabah towards the Gulf of Aqabah as suggested by the physical circumstances in which the earth swallowed Korah and his company (*WILDERNESS OF WANDERING; G. Hort, *Australian Biblical Review* 7, 1959, pp. 19–26). After a second sojourn at Kadesh, Israel went by the way of the *yam sûp̄* to go round Edom (Nu. 21:4; Jdg. 11:16), again with reference to the Gulf of Aqabah. Solomon's seaport of Ezion-geber or *Elath on this gulf is placed on the *yam sûp̄* by 1 Ki. 9:26; Teman in Edom is associated with it (Je. 49:21).

The use of the term *yam sûp̄* to refer to a wider area than the reedy lakes or the N arms of the Red Sea is not unparalleled. About 1470 BC, for example, Egyp. texts of a single epoch can use the name *Wadj-wer*, 'Great Green (Sea)', of both the Mediterranean and Red Seas (Erman-Grapow, *op. cit.*, 1, p. 269: 13–14, references), and *Ta-neter*, 'God's Land', of both Punt (E Sudan?) in particular and E lands generally (*ibid.*, 5, p. 225: 1–4, references). K.A.K.

REFINER, REFINING. The Heb. root *ṣrp* expresses the melting, testing, and refining of metals, especially precious metals such as gold and silver. This same terminology was also used of God testing men and of God's tried and tested word. A less-common term for refining or purifying was *zqq*. In the ancient world crude metal was customarily remelted to remove impurities and to make metal castings (tools, weapons, images, *etc.*). The metal was heated in pottery crucibles (Pr. 17:3; 27:21) in ovens or hearths, bellows often being used to provide a draught to create greater heat.

The Heb. term *ṣōrēp̄* for refiner, metal-worker, is often rendered as goldsmith in EVV. In the days of the Judges Micah's mother had a silver image cast (Jdg. 17:4), while much later Isaiah (40:19; 41:7; 46:6) and Jeremiah (10:8–9; 51:17) graphically describe the futile manufacture of metal and metal-plated idols. David provided refined gold and silver for the future Temple at Jerusalem (1 Ch. 28:18; 29:4); various metal-smiths shared in the repair of Jerusalem's walls under Nehemiah (Ne. 3:8, 31–32).

God, like a master-refiner seeking the pure metal, is often said to try or test (*ṣrp*) men's hearts. *Cf.* Jdg. 7:4 (Gideon's men); Pss. 17:3b; 26:2b; 66:10; 105:19; Is. 48:10; Je. 9:7; Zc. 13:9; Mal. 3:2–3. See also the graphic pictures in Ps. 12:6 and Pr.

30:5 of God's Word. For the latter concept, *cf.* also 2 Sa. 22:31 (= Ps. 18:30); Ps. 119:140. Pure metal was used for casting (*cf.* Pr. 25:4). God sought to purify his people from sin as the removal of dross and alloy (Is. 1:25), but in simile even a fire heated with the bellows was sometimes not enough to do this (Je. 6:29–30). Trials are sometimes used to refine men, and the wise refine (purify) themselves (Dn. 11:35; 12:10). Wine is once so referred to (Is. 25:6). (*ARTS AND CRAFTS.)

BIBLIOGRAPHY. For Egyp. scenes of such metal-working, actual moulds and crucibles, see *ANEP*, p. 40, figs. 133–136; Singer, Holmyard and Hall, *A History of Technology*, 1, 1954, p. 578, fig. 383 (use of bellows). In general, see *ibid.*, pp. 577–584; R. J. Forbes, *Studies in Ancient Technology*, 6, 1958, pp. 70–73, 81–85; 8, 1964, pp. 133ff., 170ff., 239ff.; 9, 1964, pp. 67ff.; A. Lucas, *Ancient Egyptian Materials and Industries*, 1962, ch. 11. K.A.K.

REGENERATION. The Gk. noun *palingenesia* occurs only twice in the NT (Mt. 19:28, RSV 'new world', AV 'regeneration'; Tit. 3:5, 'regeneration'). In the Mt. passage it is used eschatologically to refer to the restoration of all things, reminding us that the renewal of the individual is part of a wider and cosmic renewal. In Tit. the word is used with an individual reference.

Elsewhere various words are used to express the change which the Holy Spirit effects. *gennaō* (with *anōthen*, Jn. 3:3, 7), meaning 'to beget' or 'give birth to', is used in Jn. 1:13; 3:3–8; 1 Jn. 2:29; 3:9; 4:7; 5:1, 4, 18. In 1 Pet. 1:3, 23 the word *anagennaō*—'to beget again' or 'to bring again to birth'—is found. These words are used to describe the initial act of renewal. The words *anakainōsis* (Rom. 12:2; Tit. 3:5) with the verb *anakainoō* (2 Cor. 4:16; Col. 3:10) denote a making anew or renewing. The references will indicate that the use of these two words is not limited to the initial renewal but extends to the resultant process. We may note with reference to the result of the new birth such terms as *kainē ktisis*, 'a new creation' (2 Cor. 5:17; Gal. 6:15), and *kainos anthrōpos*, 'a new man' (Eph. 2:15; 4:24). Twice we have the term *synzōopoieō*, 'to make alive with' (Eph. 2:5; Col. 2:13), which hints at a change, not only as dramatic as birth, but as dramatic as resurrection. *apokyeō* (Jas. 1:18) denotes to bear or bring forth.

Surveying these terms, we notice that they all indicate a drastic and dramatic change which may be likened to birth, rebirth, re-creation or even resurrection. Several of the terms in their context indicate that this change has permanent and far-reaching effects in its subject.

I. Old Testament presentation

The idea of regeneration is more prominent in the NT than in the OT. Many OT passages have the concept of national renewal. This thought is present in the statements concerning the new covenant and the law being written in the heart or the giving of a new heart (Je. 24:7; 31:31f.; 32:38f.; Ezk. 11:19; 36:25–27, and the 'valley of dry bones' passage, 37:1–14).

Although it is the nation that is in view in these scriptures, a nation can be renewed only when the individuals within it are changed. Thus, in the very idea of national renewal we find the concept of 'new hearts' being given to individuals. Other passages deal more directly with the individual (*cf.* Is. 57:15). We notice especially Ps. 51, where David's prayer is expressed in v. 10. Considering the serious view of sin and its effects expressed in this Psalm, it is hardly surprising to find more than a hint of the need for individual renewal.

II. New Testament presentation

This doctrine must be considered in the context of man in sin (Jn. 3:6; Eph. 2:1–3, 5). The effects of sin on human nature are considered to be so serious that, without the new birth, the sinner cannot see, let alone enter into, the kingdom of God (Jn. 3:3, 5; *cf.* 1 Cor. 2:6–16).

The initiative in regeneration is ascribed to God (Jn. 1:13); it is from above (Jn. 3:3, 7) and of the Spirit (Jn. 3:5, 8). The same idea occurs in Eph. 2:4–5; 1 Jn. 2:29; 4:7; *etc.* This divine act is decisive and once for all. Aorists are used in Jn. 1:13; 3:3, 5, 7. The use of perfects indicates that this single, initial act carries with it far-reaching effects, as in 1 Jn. 2:29; 3:9; 4:7; 5:1, 4, 18. The abiding results given in these passages are doing righteousness, not committing sin, loving one another, believing that Jesus is the Christ, and overcoming the world. These results indicate that in spiritual matters man is not altogether passive. He is passive in the new birth; God acts on him. But the result of such an act is far-reaching activity; he actively repents, believes in Christ, and henceforth walks in newness of life.

Jn. 3:8 serves to warn us that there is much in this subject that is inscrutable. Yet we must inquire what actually happens to the individual in the new birth. It would be safe to say that there is no change in the personality itself; the person is the same. But now he is differently controlled. Before the new birth sin controlled the man and made him a rebel against God; now the Spirit controls him and directs him towards God. The regenerate man walks after the Spirit, lives in the Spirit, is led by the Spirit, and is commanded to be filled with the Spirit (Rom. 8:4, 9, 14; Eph. 5:18). He is not perfect; he has to grow and progress (1 Pet. 2:2), but in every department of his personality he is directed towards God.

We may define regeneration as a drastic act on fallen human nature by the Holy Spirit, leading to a change in the person's whole outlook. He can now be described as a new man who seeks, finds and follows God in Christ.

III. The means of regeneration

In 1 Pet. 3:21 baptism is closely connected with entry into a state of salvation, and in Tit. 3:5 we have the reference to the washing of regeneration. 1 Pet. 1:23 and Jas. 1:18 mention the Word of God as a means of new birth. Many, from such scriptures, contend that these are the necessary channels by which regeneration comes to us. With 1 Cor. 2:7–16 in mind, we must question whether the Word of God is a means of regeneration in this way. Here we are clearly taught that the natural man is in such a state that he cannot receive the things of the Spirit of God. A divine intervention which makes the natural man receptive to God's Word must be antecedent to hearing the Word in a saving manner. When this has occurred the Word of God brings the new life into expression. It is clear that the new birth of 1 Pet. 1:23; Jas. 1:18 is conceived more comprehensively than in John. John distinguishes between regeneration and the faith which results from it (*e.g.* Jn. 1:12–13; 1 Jn. 5:1); Peter and James, by including the reference to the Word as the means, show that they have in mind the whole process whereby God brings men to conscious faith in Christ.

We can also think of the issue in terms of conception and birth. The Holy Spirit plants or begets new life by a direct action on the soul. It is subsequently brought to the birth (*apokyeō*, Jas. 1:18) by the word. *gennaō* (1 Pet. 1:23) can have the meaning of birth as well as begetting.

There are further biblical objections to the idea that baptism itself conveys regenerating grace. To look at baptism in this *ex opere operato* manner is contrary to other scriptures, especially the prophetic protest against the abuse of priestly rites, and Paul's strictures on Jewish views concerning circumcision (*cf.* Rom. 2:28f.; 4:9–12). We actually have incidents of conversion without baptism (Acts 10:44–48; 16:14–15). The latter case is especially interesting, for the opening of Lydia's heart is specifically mentioned before baptism. If it be argued that things are different concerning Christians of subsequent generations, Paul's attitude to similar views with regard to circumcision ought to settle the issue. Regenerating grace comes direct by the Spirit to lost sinners. The Word of God brings it into expression in faith and repentance. *Baptism bears witness to the spiritual union with Christ in death and resurrection through which new *life is conveyed, but does not convey it automatically where *faith is not present.

Bibliography. Arts. 'Regeneration' by J. V. Bartlet (*HDB*), J. Denney (*DCG*), A. Ringwald *et al.*, *NIDNTT* 1, pp. 176–188; R. D. Knudsen (*ZPEB*); H. Burkhardt (*NDT*), 'New Birth' by W. L. Kynes (*DJG*). Appropriate sections of most systematic theologies; B. Citron, *The New Birth*, 1951; J. Murray, *Redemption Accomplished and Applied*, 1955, pp. 119–129. M.R.G.

REHOB (Heb. *rʰōḇ*, 'open place, market-place [of town or village]', a name occuring in the Bible as a personal and as a place-name).

1. The most N city observed by Joshua's spies in Canaan (Nu. 13:21). It was an Aramaean centre which supplied the Ammonites with troops in the time of David (2 Sa. 10:6–8). The name is written 'Beth-rehob' in 2 Sa. 10:6 and in Jdg. 18:28, which latter passage suggests that it was situated near the source of the Jordan, though the precise location is unknown.

2. A city in Canaan which fell to the lot of Asher (Jos. 19:28, 30) and was declared a levitical city (Jos. 21:31; 1 Ch. 6:75), though it was among the cities not taken at the time of the Conquest (Jdg. 1:31). Identification with Tell Bir el-Gharbi (Tel Bira), SE of Acco, is proposed; see *NEAEHL*, pp. 262–263.

3. The father of Hadadezer, the king of Zobah in the time of David (2 Sa. 8:3, 12). Compare Ruḫubi, the name of the father of Ba'sa, the Ammonite ally of Ahab at the battle of Qarqar in 854 BC (Shalmaneser III, Kurḫ Stele 2. 95).

4. One of the Levites who sealed the covenant in the time of Nehemiah (Ne. 10:11).

(*Rehoboth; *Rehoboth-ir.)

Bibliography. W. F. Albright, *BASOR* 83, 1941, p. 33; H. Tadmor, *Scripta Hierosolymitana* 8, 1961, p. 245. T.C.M.

REHOBOAM (Heb. *rᵉḥaḇʿām*,' expansion of the people'). The son of *Solomon and Naamah who, upon his father's death, became the last king of a united Israel and the first of the S kingdom of Judah.

The chronology of Rehoboam's reign is disputed. Assuming a 17-year reign (1 Ki. 14:21; 2 Ch. 12:13) the dating would be *c.* 931–913 BC (*Chronology of the OT), but some have truncated the reign to *c.* 922–915 BC (W. F. Albright, *BASOR* 100, 1945, pp. 16–22).

The oppressive measures needed by Solomon to ensure the funds for his public and royal expenditures led to a confrontation between Rehoboam and the N kingdom. His arrogance led him to accept ill-considered advice to increase this burden, which Israel would not accept. When Rehoboam sent his *corvée*-officer to the N, he was stoned, and *Jeroboam was made king over the ten tribes of Israel (1 Ki. 12:1–20; 2 Ch. 10). When Rehoboam mustered troops to quell the revolt, Shemaiah, a prophet, forestalled him (1 Ki. 12:21–24).

Judah built fortified towns (2 Ch. 11:5–12), probably against incursions by the Philistines (*cf.* 1 Ki. 15:27; 16:15) and Egypt. Rehoboam was also in conflict with Israel (14:30), from which the priests and Levites had fled, in reaction to the pagan practices there (2 Ch. 11:13–17). The Egyp. king, *Shishak (Shoshenq), came against Palestine *c.* 926 BC and plundered it from end to end (*LOB*, pp. 283–290; fully studied by K. A. Kitchen, *The Third Intermediate Period in Egypt*, 1972, pp. 432–447), pillaging Jerusalem (1 Ki. 14:25–27).

Pagan cultic practices appeared in Judah (1 Ki. 14:22–24), possibly influenced by the presence of foreign women in important positions, such as the king's mother, Naamah (1 Ki. 14:21, 31), and his favourite wife, Maacah (15:13; *cf.* W. F. Albright, *Archaeology and the Religion of Israel*, 1968, pp. 152f.). When Shemaiah the prophet pointed out that the invasion by Egypt was divine punishment for this apostasy, Rehoboam repented (2 Ch. 12:5–8, 12).

When he died, Rehoboam was buried in Jerusalem, 'with his fathers' (1 Ki. 14:31; 2 Ch. 12:16). His name is mentioned in the genealogy of Jesus (Mt. 1:7). D.W.B.

REHOBOTH (Heb. *rᵉḥōḇôt*, 'broad places, room'; LXX *eurychōria*). **1.** A well dug by Isaac near Gerar (Gn. 26:22), so named because no quarrel ensued with the herdsmen of Gerar. **2.** A city 'by the river' (Gn. 36:37), probably beside the Wadi el-Hesā, which divides Moab from Edom. 'The River' is normally the Euphrates (see RSV), but the context here forbids it. J.W.C.

REHOBOTH-IR (Heb. *rᵉḥōḇōṯ ʿîr*). One of four cities built by As(s)hur (RSV *Nimrod) in Assyria (Gn. 10:11–12). Of these Nineveh and Calah are well known, but no Assyr. equivalent is known for this place. Since the large and ancient city of Aššur (80 km S of Nineveh) would be expected in the context, some consider this name an interpretation from the Sum. *AŠ.UR* (*AŠ* = Assyr. *rebâtu*; *UR* = Assyr. *ālu*; Heb. *ʿîr*). A suburb of Nineveh (*rebit Ninua*) is mentioned in Assyr.

texts (Esarhaddon), and this may have been founded at the same time. The phrase 'open-places of the city' may here be a description of Nineveh itself. The LXX read as a proper name(*Rhoōbōth*).

BIBLIOGRAPHY. G. Dossin, *Le Muséon* 47, 1934, pp. 108ff.; J. M. Sasson, *RB* 90, 1983, pp. 94–96.

D.J.W.

REHUM. A name borne by several men in post-exilic times, including Rehum the 'commander' (RSV), or 'high commissioner' (NEB), who joined in writing the letter of complaint in Ezr. 4:8. His title *be'ēl ṭe'ēm* means 'lord of judgment' (or 'report'), and may refer either to administration or to communication (A. H. Sayce suggested 'postmaster').

J.S.W.

REI. Occurs in 1 Ki. 1:8 only. EVV render it as a personal name, thus linking Rei with the group of Solomon's supporters. J. Taylor (*HDB*, *ad loc.*) suggests that he was an officer of the royal guard. Josephus (*Ant.* 7. 346) translates 'the friend of David' instead of 'and Rei, and the mighty men which belonged to David', but this indicates that he was probably following a shorter Heb. text, and the longer form is difficult to account for if it is not original. Suggested conjectural emendations and identification with other persons of the Davidic period are unconvincing.

G.W.G.

RELIGION. The word 'religion' came into Eng. from the Vulg., where *religio* is in a 13th-century paraphrase of Jas. 1:26f. In Acts 26:5 it denotes Judaism (*cf.* Gal. 1:13f.). Here and in the Apocrypha, *thrēskeia* refers to the outward expression of belief, not the content, as when we contrast the Christian religion with Buddhism. RSV uses the word, however, in something approaching this sense in 1 Tim. 3:16, to translate Gk. *eusebeia* (AV 'godliness'), and in 2 Tim. 3:5, where again our instinct would be to use the word 'Christianity'. Because of the association of *thrēskeia* with Judaism, James's use is probably ironical. The things which he calls the elements of '*thrēskeia* that is pure and undefiled' would not in the view of his opponents, who restricted it to ritual, have counted as *thrēskeia* at all.

Hesitance today in using the word 'religion' either of the content of the Christian faith or of its expression in worship and service, is due to the conviction that Christianity is not simply one among many religions, but differs from all others in that its content is divinely revealed and its outward expression by believers is not an attempt to secure salvation but a thank-offering for it.

J.B.J.

REPENTANCE. In the OT two words are regularly translated 'repent' or some near equivalent—*nāḥam* ('be sorry, change one's mind') and *šûḇ* (in the sense, 'turn back, return').

nāḥam is used infrequently of man (Ex. 13:17; Jb. 42:6; Je. 8:6; 31:19), but regularly of God, where it is often said that God 'repents of evil' proposed or initiated. This vigorous speech arises out of Israel's understanding of God's attitude to men in terms of personal relationship. The language of course did not imply anything fickle or arbitrary on God's side, but simply that the *relation* was a changing one. In particular, when man removes himself by his self-will from God's direction and care he finds that the God-willed consequence of his evil is more evil (Gn. 6:6f.; 1 Sa. 15:11, 35; 2 Sa. 24:16; Je. 18:10). But whoever repents, even at the eleventh hour, whoever turns (again) to God, finds a God of mercy and love, not of judgment (Je. 18:8; 26:3, 13, 19; Jon. 3:9f.; the importance of the intercessor who is willing to stand before God on behalf of his people is emphasized in Ex. 32:12–14 and Am. 7:3, 6). So even though God's firmness of judgment against *sin is in no doubt (Nu. 23:19; 1 Sa. 15:29; Ps. 110:4; Je. 4:28; Ezk. 24:14; Zc. 8:14), he has shown himself more often as a gracious God, faithful to his people even when they are faithless—a God, in other words, 'who repents of evil' (Ex. 32:14; Dt. 32:36; Jdg. 2:18; 1 Ch. 21:15; Pss. 106:45; 135:14; Je. 42:10; Joel 2:13f.; Jon. 4:2).

The call for repentance on the part of man is a call for him to return (*šûḇ*) to his creaturely (and covenant) dependence on God. Such calls are particularly frequent in the pre-exilic prophets. Am. 4:6–11 makes it clear that the evil that God intends as a consequence of Israel's sin is not malicious or vindictive, but rather is intended to bring Israel to repentance. He who commits evil finds further evil willed by God. But he who repents of his evil finds a God who repents of *his* evil. One of the most eloquent pleas for repentance comes in Ho. 6:1–3 and 14:1–2—a plea alternating with hope and despair (3:5; 5:4; 7:10), with 11:1–11 particularly poignant. Equally moving are the hopes of Isaiah expressed in the name of his son, Shearjashub ('a remnant shall return', 7:3; see also 10:21f.; 30:15; *cf.* 19:22) and the pleadings of Jeremiah (3:1–4:4; 8:4–7; 14:1–22; 15:15–21), both mingled with foreboding and despair (Is. 6:10; 9:13; Je. 13:23).

Other powerful expressions are Dt. 30:1–10; 1 Ki. 8:33–40, 46–53; 2 Ch. 7:14; Is. 55:6–7; Ezk. 18:21–24, 30–32; 33:11–16; Joel 2:12–14. See also particularly 1 Sa. 7:3; 2 Ki. 17:13; 2 Ch. 15:4; 30:6–9; Ne. 1:9; Ps. 78:34; Ezk. 14:6; Dn. 9:3; Zc. 1:3f.; Mal. 3:7. The classic example of national repentance was that led by Josiah (2 Ki. 22–23; 2 Ch. 34–35).

In the NT the words translated 'repent' are *metanoeō* and *metamelomai*. In Gk. they usually mean 'to change one's mind', and so also 'to regret, feel remorse' (*i.e.* over the view previously held). This note of remorse is present in the parable of the tax collector (Lk. 18:13), probably in Mt. 21:29, 32; 27:3 and Lk. 17:4 ('I am sorry'), and most explicitly in 2 Cor. 7:8–10. But the NT usage is much more influenced by the OT *šûḇ*; that is, repentance not just as a feeling sorry, or changing one's mind, but as a turning round, a complete alteration of the basic motivation and direction of one's life. This is why the best translation for *metanoeō* is often 'to convert', that is, 'to turn round' (*CONVERSION). It also helps to explain why John the Baptist demanded *baptism as an expression of this repentance, not just for obvious 'sinners', but for 'righteous' Jews as well—baptism as a decisive act of turning from the old way of life and a throwing oneself on the mercy of the Coming One (Mt. 3:2, 11; Mk. 1:4; Lk. 3:3, 8; Acts 13:24; 19:4).

Jesus' call for repentance receives little explicit

mention in Mk. (1:15; *cf.* 6:12) and Mt. (4:17; 11:20f.; 12:41), but is emphasized by Lk. (5:32; 10:13; 11:32; 13:3, 5; 15:7, 10; 16:30; 17:3f.; *cf.* 24:47). Other sayings and incidents in all three Gospels, however, express very clearly the character of the repentance which Jesus' whole ministry demanded. Its radical nature, as a complete turning round and return, is emphasized by the parable of the Prodigal Son (Lk. 15:11–24). Its unconditional character appears from the parable of the Pharisee and tax collector—repentance means acknowledging that one has no possible claim upon God, and submitting oneself without excuse or attempted justification to God's mercy (Lk. 18:13). The 'turn round' in previous values and life-style is highlighted by the encounter with the rich young man (Mk. 10:17–22) and Zacchaeus (Lk. 19:8). Above all, Mt. 18:3 makes it clear that to convert is to become like a child, that is, to acknowledge one's immaturity before God, one's inability to live life apart from God, to accept one's total dependence on God.

The call for repentance (and promise of forgiveness) features regularly in Luke's record of the preaching of the first Christians (Acts 2:38; 3:19; 8:22; 17:30; 20:21; 26:20). Here *metanoeō* is complemented by *epistrephō* ('to turn round, return'—Acts 3:19; 9:35; 11:21; 14:15; 15:19; 26:18, 20; 28:27), where *metanoeō* means more a turning away (from sin) and *epistrephō* a turning to (God) (see particularly Acts 3:19; 26:20), though each by itself can embrace both senses (as in Acts 11:18; 1 Thes. 1:9).

It is clear from Acts 5:31 and 11:18 that no difficulty was felt in describing repentance both as God's gift and as man's responsibility. At the same time Is. 6:9–10 is cited several times as an explanation of men's failure to convert (Mt. 13:14f.; Mk. 4:12; Jn. 12:40; Acts 28:26f.).

The writer to the Hebrews also indicates the importance of initial repentance (6:1), but whereas he questions the possibility of a second repentance (6:4–6; 12:17), others are even more emphatic in their belief that *Christians* can and need to repent (2 Cor. 7:9f.; 12:21; Jas. 5:19f.; 1 Jn. 1:5–2:2; Rev. 2:5, 16, 21f.; 3:3, 19).

There are only a few other references to repentance in the NT (Rom. 2:4; 2 Tim. 2:25; 2 Pet. 3:9; Rev. 9:20f.; 16:9, 11). We should not assume that talk of repentance and *forgiveness invariably featured in the earliest preaching. In particular Paul rarely uses either concept, and they do not occur at all in the Gospel and Epistles of John, whereas both strongly emphasize that the Christian life starts from the positive commitment of *faith.

BIBLIOGRAPHY. G. Bertram, *epistrephō*, *TDNT* 7, pp. 722–729; G. Bornkamm, *Jesus of Nazareth*, 1960, pp. 82–84; J. P. Healey and A. B. Luter, *ABD* 5, pp. 671–674; J. Jeremias, *New Testament Theology*, 1: *The Proclamation of Jesus*, 1971, pp. 152–158; O. Michel, *metamelomai*, *TDNT* 4, pp. 626–629; E. Würthein and J. Behm, *metanoeō*, *TDNT* 4, pp. 975–1008; F. Laubach, J. Goetzmann, *NIDNTT* 1, pp. 353–359; D. Guthrie, *New Testament Theology*, 1981, pp. 574–601 *passim*.

J.D.G.D.

REPHAIM (Heb. *rᵉpā'îm*). One of the pre-Israelite peoples of Palestine mentioned, together with the Zuzim and Emim, in the time of Abraham as having been defeated by Chedorlaomer (Gn. 14:5). They are also listed among the inhabitants of the land God promised to Abraham's seed (Gn. 15:20). At the time of the conquest the Rephaim seem to have inhabited a wide area, but were known by different local names. In Moab the Moabites, who succeeded them there, called them *Emim (Dt. 2:11), and likewise in Ammon, where they preceded the Ammonites, they were known as *Zamzummim (Dt. 2:20–21).

They were a formidable people, being compared in stature with the Anakim (*ANAK) (Dt. 2:21), and LXX renders the name by *gigas*, 'giant' in Gn. 14:5; Jos. 12:4; 13:12, and 1 Ch. 11:15; 14:9; 20:4, a rendering adopted by AV in Dt. 2:11, 20; 3:11, 13; Jos. 12:4; 13:12; 15:8; 17:15; 18:16; 1 Ch. 20:4. (LXX translates it *Titanes* in 2 Sa. 5:18, 22.)

It may be that the forms *rāpā'* and *rāpâ* (2 Sa. 21:16, 18, 20, 22; 1 Ch. 20:6, 8), which are rendered 'giant' in EVV (LXX *gigas* in 2 Sa. 21:22; 1 Ch. 20:6), are variant forms of the name *rᵉpā'îm*, but the context of these occurrences, in connection with a Philistine, is perhaps better suited by the meaning *'giant'. The name is unknown in an ethnic sense outside the Bible.

In Ps. 88:11 (v. 10, RSV); Pr. 2:18; 9:18; 21:16; Jb. 26:5; Is. 14:9; 26:14, 19, the word *rᵉpā'îm* occurs in the sense of 'ghosts of the dead', and it is suggested by some that the name Rephaim was applied by the Israelites to the early inhabitants of the land as persons long since dead. The word occurs in Ugaritic (*rpu'm*), perhaps referring to a class of minor gods or a sacred guild, though the meaning is uncertain, and in Phoenician tomb inscriptions (*rp'm*) in the sense of 'ghost'.

BIBLIOGRAPHY. J. Gray, 'The Rephaim', *PEQ* 81, 1949, pp. 127–139, and 84, 1952, pp. 39–41; H. W. F. Saggs, *FT* 90, 1958, pp. 170–172.

T.C.M.

REPHAN (AV **REMPHAN**). The name of a god identified or connected with the planet Saturn, quoted in Acts 7:43 from the LXX of Am. 5:26. The LXX reading, *Rhaiphan* (cod. B, A; *Rhemphan* 239), is thought by some to be a mistaken transliteration of the *MT* reading, *kiyyûn* (RSV *KAIWAN, AV Chiun), by others to be a deliberate substitution of *Repa*, a name of Seb, the Egyp. god of the planet Saturn.

D.W.G.

REPHIDIM. The last stopping-place of the Israelites on the Exodus from Egypt, before they reached Mt Sinai (Ex. 17:1; 19:2; Nu. 33:14–15). Here the Israelites under Joshua fought against Amalek, and the successful outcome of the battle depended on Moses' holding up his hands, which he did with the support of Aaron and Hur (Ex. 17:8–16). After the battle, Jethro, Moses' father-in-law, persuaded Moses to give up judging the people entirely by himself, and to appoint deputies for this purpose (Ex. 18). The site of Rephidim is uncertain, the usual suggestion being the Wadi Refayid in SW Sinai.

BIBLIOGRAPHY. B. Rothenberg, *God's Wilderness*, 1961, pp. 143, 168.

T.C. M.

REPROBATE. It is convenient to retain the AV term as a heading under which to include words used in RSV (unfit, refuse, dross, disqualified) to translate Heb. and Gk. equivalents which present the idea of divine investigation leading to rejection because of an ineradicable sin. OT prophets compare the sin of Israel to impurity in metal (Is. 1:22; Je. 6:30; Ezk. 22:19–20). In Je. 6:30, 'Refuse silver they are called, for the Lord has rejected them', the Heb. verb *mā'as* is rendered 'reprobate' in AV (AVmg., RSV, RV 'refuse'), *i.e.* 'tested and rejected by Yahweh because of ineradicable sin'. In Is. 1:22 LXX renders Heb. *sîgîm* by the adjective *adokimos*, which occurs eight times in the NT with the meaning 'rejected after a searching test'.

In Rom. 1:28, the Gk. puns *dokimazein* with *adokimos*, and may be rendered 'since they did not see fit to retain God in their mind he handed them over to an unfit mind', where 'unfit' (AV 'reprobate', AVmg. 'a mind void of judgment') means 'unfit to pass judgment', in the active or passive sense, because of wickedness, *etc*. (vv. 29–30).

In 1 Cor. 9:27 Paul concludes 'an exhortation to self-denial and exertion' (Hodge), given in athletic metaphors, by attributing his personal bodily discipline to fear of disqualification, 'lest I . . . be disqualified (*adokimos*)'. But from what? Salvation or ministerial reward? The context favours reward (*cf.* 3:10–15) and stresses the need of ceaseless vigilance against sin (*cf.* 10:12). The remaining occurrences of *adokimos* are in 2 Cor. 13:5–7, where the test proposed is 'whether you are holding to your faith', and the context implies that faith has empirical proofs, lacking which the Corinthians are failures, and even Paul himself would be a failure, since he would be unable to demonstrate his apostolic authority; in 2 Tim. 3:8 and in Tit. 1:16, where *adokimos* means 'proved to be morally worthless'; and in Heb. 6:8, where 'barren' (*adokimos*) soil illustrates the situation of hardened backsliders. None of these occurrences necessarily implies judicial abandonment to *perdition, yet all are consonant with such a doctrine: in each case the rejection follows demonstrable faults; in some God, in others man, makes the test. The human verdict anticipates the divine.

BIBLIOGRAPHY. J. Denney in *HDB*; E. K. Simpson, *Words Worth Weighing in the Greek New Testament*, 1946, p. 17; H. Haarbeck, *NIDNTT* 3, pp. 808–810; R. E. Davies, *ZPEB* 5, p. 66. M.R.W.F.

RESEN (Gk. *Dasen*). The city located between Nineveh and Calah founded by *Nimrod or Ashur (so AV) and with them part of a great populated area (Gn. 10:12). *rēš-êni* ('fountain-head') designated a number of places in Assyria. The sites of this name on the Ḫabur and Khosr Rivers (NE of Nineveh) do not, however, easily fit the geographical situation given in Gn. 10. The proposed equation with Selamiyeh (3 km N of Calah) is based on the false identification of this place with Larissa (Xenophon, *Anabasis* 3. 4), now known to be the Gk. name for Calah itself. A possible site for Resen is the early ruins of Hamam Ali with its adjacent sulphur springs on the right bank of the river Tigris about 13 km S of Nineveh.

D.J.W.

REST. The non-theological sense of 'rest' is prominent in the Bible. *E.g.* the Lord rests from activity (Gn. 2:2f.); the sabbath is to be a day of rest (Ex. 31:15); the land of promise was to have rest every 7th year (Lv. 25:4f.); and the Temple was the Lord's resting-place among his people (Ps. 132:8, 14).

In its theological sense 'rest' is even more prominent in the Bible. Israel was promised rest by the Lord in the land of Canaan (Dt. 3:20), and to this rest the exiles would return from Babylon (Je. 46:27). Rest and felicity were to be David's great gifts to Israel (1 Ch. 22:7–10). Alas, this great ideal of rest remained unfulfilled in Israel's experience (Heb. 3:7–4:10) because of unbelief and disobedience (Ps. 95:8–11).

However, although rest in the OT remains in the sphere of promise, in the NT there is fulfilment. Christians, by faith in Christ, have entered into rest (Heb. 12:22–24). He is their peace. To all who come to him he gives rest, rest that is relief, release and satisfaction to the soul (Mt. 11:28–30).

But 'rest' in Scripture has also an eschatological content. 'There remains a sabbath rest' for the Christian as for Israel (Heb. 4:9). The celestial city and the heavenly country (Heb. 11:10, 16) are still in the future. Today there is the task (1 Cor. 3:9), the good fight of faith (Eph. 6:10–20), the pilgrimage (Heb. 11:13–16). And even the rest to which death is the prelude (Rev. 14:13) is not fullness of rest (Rev. 6:9–11). But those who have entered into the rest of faith, by casting anchor within the veil where Christ has gone, know that the final state of rest is secure. J.G.S.S.T.

RESTORATION. The Gk. noun *apokatastasis* is found only in Acts 3:21, while the corresponding verb is used three times in the sense of a final restoration.

The idea goes back to the great prophets of the OT. They foresaw the Exile, but they also prophesied that God would restore his people to their own land (Je. 27:22; Dn. 9:25, *etc*.). When this took place conditions in Judah were far from ideal, and thus men looked and longed for a further restoration, a restoration of prosperity and bliss.

In time this came to be associated with the Messiah. The Jews as a whole understood this restoration in terms of material prosperity, but Jesus saw it in the work of John the Baptist, who fulfilled the prophecy of Mal. 4:5 (Mt. 17:11; Mk. 9:12). Here, as elsewhere, he reinterpreted the Messianic category which had become distorted among the Jews.

In the full sense the restoration is yet future. Though they had Jesus' interpretation of the prophecy of Malachi, the disciples could ask on the eve of the ascension, 'Lord, will you at this time restore the kingdom to Israel?' (Acts 1:6). Jesus' answer discourages them from speculation about matters which do not concern them, but it does not deny that there will be a restoration. The fullest reference comes in Acts 3:19ff. Here Peter looks for 'times of refreshing' which he associates with the return of the Lord Jesus Christ (v. 20), who is in heaven 'until the time for establishing (*i.e.* restoration) all that God spoke . . .'. From one point of view the restoration awaits the return of the Lord, and Peter sees this as a subject of prophecy from the very first. It is legitimate to infer that the restoration points to some such state as that of pre-fallen man, though there is no biblical passage which says this in so many words. Some have reasoned from the expression 'time for establishing all that God spoke' to the thought of universal salvation. This is more than the expression will bear. That question must be determined by the teaching of Scripture as a whole.

BIBLIOGRAPHY. H.-G. Link, *NIDNTT* 3, pp. 146–148. L.M.

RESURRECTION. The most startling characteristic of the first Christian preaching is its emphasis on the resurrection. The first preachers were sure that Christ had risen, and sure, in consequence, that believers would in due course rise also. This set them off from all the other teachers of the ancient world. There are resurrections elsewhere, but none of them is like that of Christ. They are mostly mythological tales connected with the change of the season and the annual miracle of spring. The Gospels tell of an individual who truly died but overcame death by rising again. And if it is true that Christ's resurrection bears no resemblance to anything in paganism it is also true that the attitude of believers to their own resurrection, the corollary of their Lord's, is radically different from anything in the heathen world. Nothing is more characteristic of even the best thought of the day than its hopelessness in the face of death. Clearly the resurrection is of the very first importance for the Christian faith.

The Christian idea of resurrection is to be distinguished from both Greek and Jewish ideas. The Greeks thought of the body as a hindrance to true life and they looked for the time when the soul would be free from its shackles. They conceived of life after death in terms of the immortality of the soul, but they firmly rejected all ideas of resurrection (*cf.* the mockery of Paul's preaching in Acts 17:32). The Jews were firmly persuaded of the values of the body, and thought these would not be lost. They thus looked for the body to be raised. But they thought it would be exactly the same body (*Apocalypse of Baruch* 1:2). The Christians thought of the body as being raised, but also transformed so as to be a suitable vehicle for the very different life of the age to come (1 Cor. 15:42ff.). The Christian idea is thus distinctive.

I. Resurrection in the Old Testament

There is little about resurrection in the OT. That is not to say that it is not there. It is. But it is not prominent. The men of the OT were very practical men, concentrating on the task of living out the present life in the service of God, and they had little time to spare for speculation about the next. Moreover, it must not be forgotten that they lived on the other side of Christ's resurrection, and it is this which gives the doctrine its basis. Sometimes they used the idea of resurrection to express the national hope of the re-birth of the nation (*e.g.* Ezk. 37). The plainest statement on the resurrection of the individual is undoubtedly that in Dn. 12:2, 'many of those who sleep in the dust of the earth shall awake, some to everlasting life, and some to shame and everlasting contempt'. This clearly envisages a resurrection both of the righteous and of the wicked, and it sees also eternal consequences of men's actions. There are other passages which look for resurrection, chiefly some in the Psalms (*e.g.* Pss. 16:10f.; 49:14f.). The precise meaning of Job's great affirmation (Jb. 19:25–27) is disputed, but it is difficult to think that there is no thought of resurrection here. Sometimes the prophets also give utterance to this thought (*e.g.* Is. 26:19). But on the whole the OT says little about it. This may, perhaps, be due to the fact that some doctrine of resurrection was found among such peoples as the Egyptians and Babylonians. At a time when syncretism was a grave danger this would have discouraged the Hebrews from taking too great an interest in it.

During the period between the two Testaments, when that danger was not so pressing, the idea is more prominent. No uniformity was reached, and even in NT times the Sadducees still denied that there was a resurrection. But by then most Jews accepted some idea of resurrection. Usually they thought that these same bodies would be brought back to life just as they were.

II. The resurrection of Christ

On three occasions Christ brought back people from the dead (the daughter of Jairus, the son of the widow of Nain, and Lazarus). These, however, are not to be thought of as resurrection so much as resuscitation. There is no indication that any of these people did other than come back to the life that they had left. And Paul tells us explicitly that Christ is 'the first fruits of those who have fallen asleep' (1 Cor. 15:20). But these miracles show us Christ as the master of death. This comes out again in the fact that he prophesied that he would rise 3 days after he was crucified (Mk. 8:31; 9:31; 10:34, *etc.*). This point is important. It shows Christ as supremely the master of the situation. And it also means that the resurrection is of the very first importance, for the veracity of our Lord is involved.

The Gospels tell us that Jesus was crucified, that he died and that on the third day the tomb in which he had been placed was found to be empty. Angels told certain women that he had risen from the dead. Over a period of some weeks Jesus appeared to his followers from time to time. Paul lists some of these appearances but he does not explicitly mention the empty tomb and some scholars accordingly suggest that it was absent from the earliest tradition. But it may be fairly countered that Paul implies that the tomb was empty. What else does he mean by saying that Jesus 'was buried, that he was raised on the third day . . .' (1 Cor. 15:4)? The express mention of burial is pointless if he does not have the empty tomb in mind. And it is referred to in all four Gospels. It must be accepted as part of the authentic Christian tradition. Some have suggested that the disciples went to the wrong tomb, where a young man in white said, 'He is not here', meaning 'He is in another tomb'. But in the first place this is pure speculation, and in the second it raises all sorts of questions. It is impossible to hold that the right tomb was completely forgotten by all, friend and foe alike. When the first preaching laid such stress on the resurrection we can be sure that the authorities would have spared no effort in the attempt to find the body.

But if the tomb was empty it would seem that there are only three possibilities: that friends took the body away, that foes took the body away, or that Jesus rose. The first hypothesis is more than difficult to maintain. All our evidence goes to show that there was no thought of resurrection in the minds of the disciples, and that they were men without hope on the evening of the first Good Friday. They were dispirited, beaten men, hiding away for fear of the Jews. Moreover, Matthew tells us that a guard was set over the tomb, so that they could not have stolen the body even had they wanted to do so. But the crowning improbability is that they would have suffered for preaching the resurrection as Acts tells us they did. Some were imprisoned, and James was executed. Men do not suffer such penalties for upholding what they know to be a lie. It must also be borne in mind that when the Christian sect was troublesome enough for the authorities to persecute it, the chief priests would have been very ready to have paid for information as to the stealing of the body, and the case of Judas is sufficient to show that a traitor could be found in the ranks. All in all, it is impossible to hold that Christians stole away the body of Christ.

It is just as difficult to maintain that his foes removed the body. Why should they? There seems no conceivable motive. To have done so would have been to start the very rumours of a resurrection that the evidence shows they were so anxious to prevent. Moreover, the guard over the tomb would have been just as big an obstacle to them as to the friends of the Lord. But the absolutely decisive objection is their failure to produce the body when the first preaching began. Peter and his allies put great emphasis on the resurrection of their Lord. Clearly it had gripped their imagination. In this situation, had their enemies produced the body of Jesus, the Christian church must have dissolved in a gale of laughter. The silence of the Jews is just as significant as the speech of the Christians. The failure of the enemies of Jesus to produce the body is conclusive evidence that they could not do so.

Since it seems impossible to hold either that friends or foes removed the body, and since the tomb was empty, it seems that we are shut up to the hypothesis of the resurrection. This is confirmed also by the resurrection appearances. Altogether there are ten different appearances recorded in our five accounts (the four Gospels and 1 Cor. 15). These accounts are not easy to harmonize (though this is not impossible, as is often asserted; the attempt made in the *Scofield Reference Bible*, for example, may or may not be the right one, but it certainly shows that harmonization is possible). The difficulties show only that the accounts are independent. There is no stereotyped repetition of an official story. And there is impressive agreement on the main facts. There is great variety in the witnesses. Sometimes one or two saw the Lord, sometimes a larger number, as the eleven apostles, once as many as 500 disciples. Men as well as women are included in the number. Mostly the appearances were to believers, but possibly that to James was to one who had not believed up till that point. Specially important is Paul. He was not credulous, but an educated man who was bitterly hostile to the Christians. And he is emphatic that he saw Jesus after he had risen from the dead. Indeed, so sure was he of this that he based the whole of the rest of his life on the certainty. Canon Kennett puts this point trenchantly. He speaks of Paul as having been converted within 5 years of the crucifixion and says, 'within a very few years of the time of the crucifixion of Jesus, the evidence for the resurrection of Jesus was in the mind of at least one man of education absolutely irrefutable' (*Interpreter* 5, 1908–9, p. 267).

We should not overlook the transformation of the disciples in all this. As noted before, they were beaten and dispirited men at the crucifixion, but they were ready to go to prison and even to die for the sake of Jesus shortly afterwards. Why the change? Men do not run such risks unless they are very sure of themselves. The disciples were completely convinced. We should perhaps add that their certainty is reflected in their worship. They were Jews, and Jews have a tenacity in clinging to their religious customs. Yet these men observed the Lord's day, a weekly memorial of the resurrection, instead of the sabbath. On that Lord's day they celebrated the holy communion, which was not a commemoration of a dead Christ, but a thankful remembrance of the blessings conveyed by a living and triumphant Lord. Their other sacrament, baptism, was a reminder that believers were buried with Christ and raised with him (Col. 2:12). The resurrection gave significance to all that they did.

Sometimes it is said that Christ did not really die, but swooned. Then in the coolness of the tomb he revived. This raises all sorts of questions. How did he get out of the tomb? What happened to him? Why do we hear no more? When did he die? Questions multiply and the answers do not appear. Some have thought the disciples to have been the victims of hallucination. But the resurrection appearances cannot be so explained. Hallucinations come to those who are in some sense looking for them, and there is no evidence of this among the disciples. Once started they tend to continue, whereas these stop abruptly. Hallucinations are individual affairs, whereas in this case we have as many as 500 people at once seeing the Lord. There seems no point in exchanging a miracle on the physical level for one on the psychological level, which is what this view demands.

But many scholars today deny outright the possibility of a physical resurrection. They may lay it down that 'the bones of Jesus rest in the soil of Palestine'. They may say that Jesus rose into the *kerygma*; the disciples came to see that he had survived through death and that they could thus preach that he was alive. Or they may locate the change in the disciples. These men had known Jesus to live in true freedom and now they entered that experience for themselves. This meant that they came to see that Jesus was not dead but a living influence. There are two big difficulties in the way of all such views. The first is that this is not what the sources say. As plain as words can do it they say that Jesus died, was buried, and rose to life again. The second is the moral difficulty. There is no question but that the disciples believed that Jesus had risen. It was this that gave them their drive and it was this that formed the theme of their preaching. If Jesus was in fact dead then God has built the church on a delusion, an unthinkable conclusion. Moreover, such views ignore the empty tomb. This is a stubborn fact. Perhaps it is worth adding that these views are quite modern (though occasionally there have been forerunners, *cf.* 2 Tim. 2:17f.). They form no part of historic Christianity, and if they are correct nearly all Christians have at all times been in serious error concerning a cardinal doctrine of the faith.

III. The resurrection of believers

Not only did Jesus rise, but one day all men too will rise. Jesus refuted the scepticism of the Sadducees on this point with an interesting argument from Scripture (Mt. 22:31–32). The general NT position is that the resurrection of Christ carries with it the resurrection of believers. Jesus said, 'I am the resurrection and the life; he who believes in me, though he die, yet shall he live' (Jn. 11:25). Several times he spoke of raising believers up at the last day (Jn. 6:39–40, 44, 54). The Sadducees were grieved because the apostles were 'proclaiming in Jesus the resurrection from the dead' (Acts 4:2). Paul tells us that 'as by a man came death, by a man came also the resurrection of the dead. For as in Adam all die, so also in Christ shall all be made alive' (1 Cor. 15:21f.; *cf.* 1 Thes. 4:14). Likewise Peter says, 'we have been born anew to a living hope through the resurrection of Jesus Christ from the dead' (1 Pet. 1:3). It is plain enough that the NT writers did not think of Christ's resurrection as an isolated phenomenon. It was a great divine act, and one fraught with consequences for men. Because God raised Christ he set his seal on the atoning work wrought out on the cross. He demonstrated his divine power in the face of sin and death, and at the same time his will to save men. Thus, the resurrection of believers follows immediately from that of their Saviour. So characteristic of them is resurrection that Jesus could speak of them as 'sons of God, being sons of the resurrection' (Lk. 20:36).

This does not mean that all who rise rise to blessing. Jesus speaks of 'the resurrection of life' but also of 'the resurrection of judgment' (Jn. 5:29). The plain NT teaching is that *all* will rise, but that those who have rejected Christ will find the resurrection a serious matter indeed. For believers the fact that their resurrection is connected with that of the Lord transforms the situation. In the light of his atoning work for them they face resurrection with calmness and joy.

Of the nature of the resurrection body Scripture says little. Paul can speak of it as 'a spiritual body' (1 Cor. 15:44), which appears to mean a body which meets the needs of the spirit. He expressly differentiates it from the 'physical body' which we now have, and we infer that a 'body' answering to the needs of the spirit is in some respect different from that which we now know. The spiritual body has the qualities of incorruptibility, glory, and power (1 Cor. 15:42f.). Our Lord has taught us that there will be no marriage after the resurrection, and thus no sexual function (Mk. 12:25).

Perhaps we can gain some help by thinking of the resurrection body of Christ, for John tells us that 'we shall be like him' (1 Jn. 3:2), and Paul that 'our lowly body' is to be 'like his glorious body' (Phil. 3:21). Our Lord's risen body appears to have been in some sense like the natural body and in some sense different. Thus on some occasions he was recognized immediately (Mt. 28:9; Jn. 20:19f.), but on others he was not (notably the walk to Emmaus, Lk. 24:16; *cf.* Jn. 21). He appeared suddenly in the midst of the disciples, who were gathered with the doors shut (Jn. 20:19), while contrariwise he disappeared from the sight of the two at Emmaus (Lk. 24:31). He spoke of having 'flesh and bones' (Lk. 24:39). On occasion he ate food (Lk. 24:41–43), though we cannot hold that physical food is a necessity for life beyond death (*cf.* 1 Cor. 6:13). It would seem that the risen Lord could conform to the limitations of this physical life or not as he chose, and this may indicate that when we rise we shall have a similar power.

IV. Doctrinal implications of the resurrection

The Christological significance of the resurrection is considerable. The fact that Jesus prophesied that he would rise from the dead on the third day has important implications for his Person. One who could do this is greater than the sons of men. Paul clearly regards the resurrection of Christ as of cardinal importance. 'If Christ has not been raised,' he says, 'then our preaching is in vain, and your faith is in vain. . . . If Christ has not been raised, your faith is futile and you are still in your sins' (1 Cor. 15:14, 17). The point is that Christianity is a gospel, it is good news about how God sent his Son to be our Saviour. But if Christ did not really rise, then we have no assurance that our salvation has been accomplished. The reality of the resurrection of Christ is thus of deep significance. The resurrection of believers is also important. Paul's view is that if the dead do not rise we may as well adopt the motto 'Let us eat and drink, for tomorrow we die' (1 Cor. 15:32). Believers are not men for whom this life is all. Their hope lies elsewhere (1 Cor. 15:19). This gives them perspective and makes for depth in living.

The resurrection of Christ is connected with our salvation, as when Paul says that 'Jesus our Lord was put to death for our trespasses and raised for our justification' (Rom. 4:25; *cf.* 8:33f.). There is no need here to go into the precise significance of the two uses of 'for'. That is a task for the commentaries. We content ourselves with noting that the resurrection of Christ is connected with the central act whereby we are saved. Salvation is not something that takes place apart from the resurrection.

Nor does it stop there. Paul speaks of his desire to know Christ 'and the power of his resurrection' (Phil. 3:10), and he exhorts the Colossians, 'If then you have been raised with Christ, seek the things that are above . . .' (Col. 3:1). He has already reminded them that they were buried with Christ in baptism, and in the same sacrament were raised with him (Col. 2:12). In other words, the apostle sees the same power that brought Christ back from the dead as operative within those who are Christ's. The resurrection is ongoing.

BIBLIOGRAPHY. G. Vos in *PTR* 27, 1929, pp. 1–35, 193–226; K. Barth, *The Resurrection of the Dead*, E.T. 1933; A. M. Ramsey, *The Resurrection of Christ*, 1946; N. Clark, *Interpreting the Resurrection*, 1967; W. Marxsen, *The Resurrection of Jesus of Nazareth*, 1970; L. Coenen, C. Brown in *NIDNTT* 3, pp. 257–309; M. J. Harris, *Raised Immortal*, 1983; P. Perkins, *Resurrection*, 1984; P. Carnley, *The Structure of Resurrection Belief*, 1987; *From Grave to Glory*, 1990; G. Lüdemann, *The Resurrection of Jesus*, 1994. L.M.

REUBEN (*MT r*^{e}*'ûḇēn*; LXX *Roubēn*; Pesh. *Roubîl*; Jos. *Roubēlos*; Arab. *Ra'ûbîn*; Lat. *Rubin*). **1.** The first-born of Jacob by Leah (Gn. 29:32), whose choice of name is connected with the phrase, 'the Lord *has looked upon my affliction*' (Heb. *rā'â . . . b*^{e}*'onyî*). That this meaning was attached to the name is clear from the other names in this section: 'Simeon (Heard) . . . the Lord has *heard*', 'Levi (Attached) . . . my husband . . . will be *attached*', 'Judah (Praise) . . . I will *praise* the Lord', 'Dan (Judge) . . . God has *judged* me', *etc.* Attempts have been made to give the desired meaning, 'He has looked upon my affliction', to the Heb. consonants for 'Reuben', which in our present text appears to mean, 'Behold a son'. Possibly the vocalization of the name is at fault.

Reuben had some admirable qualities in his character; unfortunately, they were offset by his incestuous act with Bilhah, his father's concubine

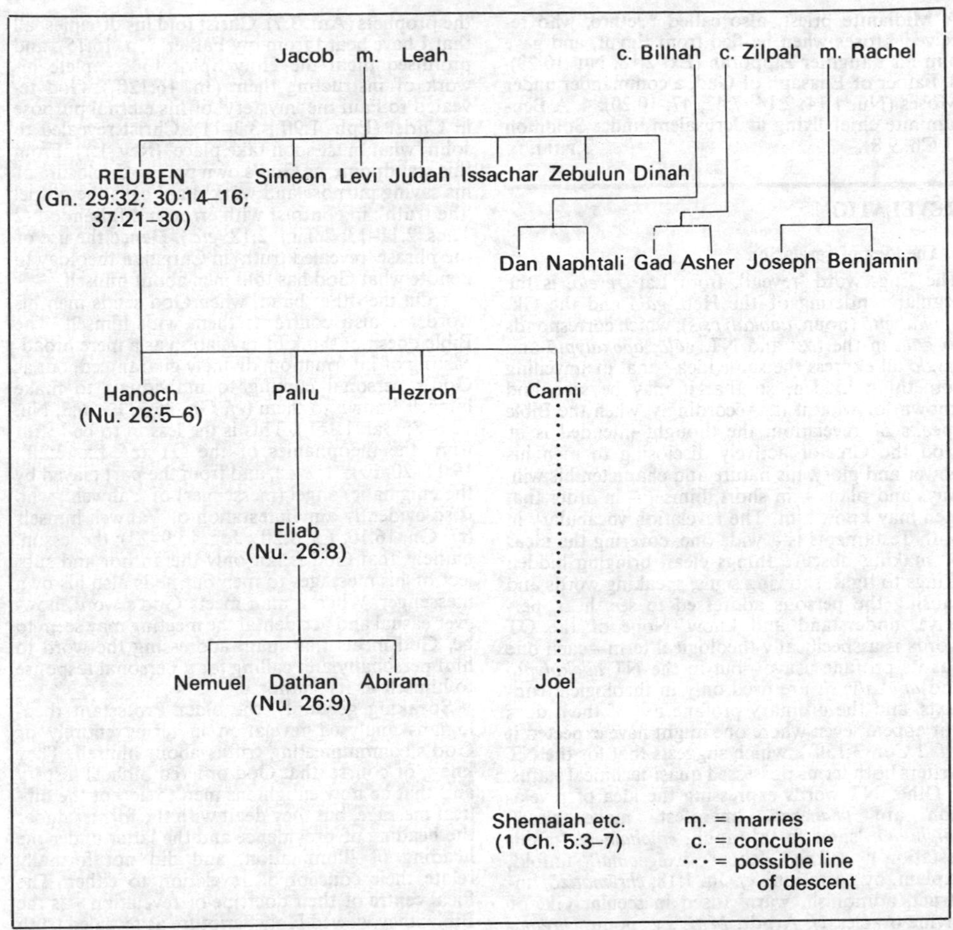

The family and descendants of Reuben

(Gn. 35:22). It was Reuben who advised his brothers not to kill Joseph, and returned to the pit to release him (Gn. 37:21, 29). Later he accused them of bringing calamity upon themselves, when they were held in the Egyp. court as suspected spies (Gn. 42:22). Again, it was Reuben who offered his own two sons as sufficient guarantee for the safety of Benjamin (Gn. 42:37).

In the blessing of the sons of Jacob, Reuben is recognized legally as the first-born, although in actual fact the double-portion which went with the birthright (Dt. 21:17) was symbolically bequeathed to Joseph, through his two sons, Ephraim and Manasseh. However, after a eulogy of Reuben, no doubt sincerely meant, there is added a significant and prophetic utterance by the Patriarch: 'Unstable as water, you shall not have pre-eminence . . .' (Gn. 49:4). This legal recognition as first-born is upheld in 1 Ch. 5:1, where we are told that the birthright belonged to Joseph *de facto* but not *de jure*, for 'he [Joseph] is not to be enrolled in the genealogy according to the birthright' (*cf.* Gesenius, *Heb. Gram.*[28], p. 349, § 114k). So it is that in Gn. 46:8; Ex. 6:14; Nu. 26:5, Reuben retains his status as first-born. Reuben had four sons before the descent into Egypt.

2. The tribe of Reuben was involved in the rebellion in the wilderness (Nu. 16:1). The tribe was linked with Gad and occupied territory E of Jordan. In the N it was contiguous with Gad, in the S it was bounded by the Arnon. The tribe's pursuits would be mainly pastoral, but those to the W of Jordan were mainly agricultural. This may have led to a separation of interests, for Reuben took no part in repelling the attack of Sisera (Jdg. 5:15f.). In the time of Saul they united with Gad and Manasseh in an attack on the Hagarites, apparently a nomad people (1 Ch. 5:10, 19f.).

Though there is mention of Gad on the Moabite Stone, there is none of Reuben, and thus it appears that at that time, *c.* 830 BC, they had lost their importance as warriors. However, they were never forgotten by their brethren; a place is reserved for the tribe of Reuben in Ezekiel's reconstructed Israel (Ezk. 48:7, 31), and they are numbered among the 144,000, sealed out of every tribe of the children of Israel, in the Apocalypse of John (Rev. 7:5). R.J.A.S.

REUEL (Heb. *rᵉʿûʾēl*, Gk. *raguel*; the name appears to mean 'friend of God').

1. A son of Esau (Gn. 36:4, 10, 17; 1 Ch. 1:35). **2.**

REUEL

A Midianite priest, also called *Jethro, who received Moses when he fled from Egypt, and gave him his daughter Zipporah (Ex. 2:18; Nu. 10:29). **3.** Father of Eliasaph of Gad, a commander under Moses (Nu. 1:14; 2:14; 7:42, 47; 10:20). **4.** A Benjaminite chief living at Jerusalem under Solomon (1 Ch. 9:8). J.P.U.L.

REVELATION.

I. The idea of revelation

The Eng. word 'reveal', from Lat. *revelo*, is the regular rendering of the Heb. *gālâ* and the Gk. *apokalyptō* (noun, *apokalypsis*), which corresponds to *gālâ* in the LXX and NT. *gālâ*, *apokalyptō* and *revelo* all express the same idea—that of unveiling something hidden, so that it may be seen and known for what it is. Accordingly, when the Bible speaks of revelation, the thought intended is of God the Creator actively disclosing to men his power and glory, his nature and character, his will, ways and plans —in short, himself—in order that men may know him. The revelation vocabulary in both Testaments is a wide one, covering the ideas of making obscure things clear, bringing hidden things to light, showing signs, speaking words and causing the persons addressed to see, hear, perceive, understand and know. None of the OT words is a specifically theological term—each one has its profane usage—but in the NT *apokalyptō* and *apokalypsis* are used only in theological contexts, and the ordinary profane use of them does not appear, even where one might have expected it (*cf.* 2 Cor. 3:13ff.); which suggests that for the NT writers both terms possessed quasi-technical status.

Other NT words expressing the idea of revelation are *phaneroō*, 'manifest, make clear'; *epiphainō*, 'show forth' (noun, *epiphaneia*, 'manifestation'); *deiknuō*, 'show'; *exēgeomai*, 'unfold, explain, by narration', *cf.* Jn. 1:18; *chrēmatizō*, 'instruct, admonish, warn' (used in secular Gk. of divine oracles, *cf.* Arndt, *MM*, *s.v.*; noun, *chrēmatismos*, 'answer of God', Rom. 11:4).

From the standpoint of its contents, divine revelation is both indicative and imperative, and in each respect normative. God's disclosures are always made in the context of a demand for trust in, and obedience to, what is revealed—a response, that is, which is wholly determined and controlled by the contents of the revelation itself. In other words, God's revelation comes to man, not as information without obligation, but as a mandatory rule of faith and conduct. Man's life must be governed, not by private whims and fancies, nor by guesses as to divine things unrevealed, but by reverent belief of as much as God has told him, leading to conscientious compliance with as many imperatives as the revelation proves to contain (Dt. 29:29).

Revelation has two focal points: (1) God's purposes; (2) God's person.

1. On the one hand, God tells men about himself—who he is, what he has done, is doing and will do, and what he requires them to do. Thus he took Noah, Abraham and Moses into his confidence, telling them what he had planned and what their part in his plan was to be (Gn. 6:13–21; 12:1ff.; 15:13–21; 17:15–21; 18:17ff.; Ex. 3:7–22). Again, he declared to Israel the laws and promises of his covenant (Ex. 20–23, *etc.*; Dt. 4:13f.; 28, *etc.*; Pss. 78:5ff.; 147:19). He disclosed his purposes to the prophets (Am. 3:7). Christ told his disciples 'all that I have heard from my Father' (Jn. 15:15), and promised them the Holy Spirit to complete his work of instructing them (Jn. 16:12ff.). God revealed to Paul the 'mystery' of his eternal purpose in Christ (Eph. 1:9ff.; 3:3–11). Christ revealed to John 'what must soon take place' (Rev. 1:1). From this standpoint, as God's own precise disclosure of his saving purpose and work, Paul calls the gospel 'the truth', in contrast with error and falsehood (2 Thes. 2:11–13; 2 Tim. 2:18; *etc.*). Hence the use of the phrase 'revealed truth' in Christian theology to denote what God has told men about himself.

2. On the other hand, when God sends men his word, he also confronts them with himself. The Bible does not think of revelation as a mere broadcasting of information, divinely guaranteed, but as God's personal coming to individuals to make himself known to them (*cf.* Gn. 35:7; Ex. 6:3; Nu. 12:6–8; Gal. 1:15f.). This is the lesson to be learnt from the theophanies of the OT (*cf.* Ex. 3:2ff.; 19:11–20; Ezk. 1; *etc.*), and from the part played by the enigmatic 'angel (messenger) of Yahweh', who is so evidently a manifestation of Yahweh himself (*cf.* Gn. 16:10; Ex. 3:2ff.; Jdg. 13:9–23): the lesson, namely, that God is not only the author and subject of his messages to men but he is also his own messenger. When a man meets God's word, however casual and accidental the meeting may seem to be, God meets that man, addressing the word to him personally and calling for a personal response to himself as its Author.

Speaking generally, the older Protestant theologians analysed revelation in terms entirely of God's communicating truths about himself. They knew, of course, that God ordered biblical history and that he now enlightens men to accept the biblical message, but they dealt with the former under the heading of providence and the latter under the heading of illumination, and did not formally relate their concept of revelation to either. The focal centre of their doctrine of revelation was the Bible; they viewed Holy Scripture as revealed truth in writing, and revelation as the divine activity that led to its production. They correlated revelation with inspiration, defining the former as God's communication to the biblical writers of otherwise inaccessible truth about himself, and the latter as his enabling them to write it all down truly, according to his will. (This formulation evidently has its roots in the book of Daniel: *cf.* Dn. 2:19, 22, 28ff., 47; 7:1; 10:1; 12:4.)

Many modern theologians, reacting against this view under pressure of a supposed need to abandon the notion of Scripture as revealed truth, speak of revelation wholly in terms of God's directing biblical history and making individuals aware of his presence, activity and claims. The focal centre of the doctrine of revelation is thus shifted to the redemptive history which the Bible records. With this commonly goes the assertion that there is, properly speaking, no such thing as communicated truth ('propositional revelation') from God; revelation is essentially non-verbal in character. But this is to say in effect that the biblical idea of God *speaking* (the commonest and most fundamental revelatory act which Scripture ascribes to him) is only a misleading metaphor; which seems implausible. On these grounds, it is further held that the Bible is not, properly speaking, revelation, but a human response to revelation. This, however, seems unbiblical, since the NT uniformly quotes OT statements—prophetic, poetic, legal, historical, factual and admonitory—as authoritative utterances of God (*cf.* Mt. 19:4f.; Acts 4:25f.; Heb. 1:5ff.; 3:7ff.; *etc.*). The biblical view is that God reveals himself by both deeds and words: first by ordering redemptive history, then by inspiring a written explanatory record of that history to make later generations 'wise unto salvation' (*cf.* 2 Tim. 3:15ff.; 1 Cor. 10:11; Rom. 15:4), and finally by enlightening men in every age to discern the significance and acknowledge the authority of the revelation thus given and recorded (*cf.* Mt. 16:17; 2 Cor. 4:6). Thus, the positive emphases in the two sets of ideas contrasted above are complementary rather than contradictory; both must be combined in order to cover the full range of the biblical concept of revelation.

II. The necessity of revelation

The Bible assumes throughout that God must first disclose himself before men can know him. The Aristotelian idea of an inactive God whom man can discover by following out an argument is quite unbiblical. A revelatory initiative is needed, first, because *God is transcendent.* He is so far from man in his mode of being that man cannot see him (Jn. 1:18; 1 Tim. 6:16; *cf.* Ex. 33:20), nor find him out by searching (*cf.* Jb. 11:7; 23:3–9), nor read his thoughts by shrewd guesswork (Is. 55:8f.). Even if man had not sinned, therefore, he could not have known God without revelation. In fact, we read of God speaking to unfallen Adam in Eden (Gn. 2:16). Now, however, there is a second reason why man's knowledge of God must depend on God's revelatory initiative. *Man is sinful.* His powers of perception in the realm of divine things have been so dulled by Satan (2 Cor. 4:4) and sin (*cf.* 1 Cor. 2:14), and his mind is so prepossessed by his own fancied 'wisdom', which runs contrary to the true knowledge of God (Rom. 1:21ff.; 1 Cor. 1:21), that it is beyond his natural powers to apprehend God, however presented to him. In fact, according to Paul, God presents himself constantly to every man through his works of creation and providence (Rom. 1:19ff.; Acts 14:17; *cf.* Ps. 19:1ff.), and the spontaneous operations of natural conscience (Rom. 2:12–15; *cf.* 1:32); yet he is not recognized or known. The pressure of this continual self-disclosure on God's part produces idolatry, as the fallen mind in its perversity seeks to quench the light by turning it into darkness (Rom. 1:23ff.; *cf.* Jn. 1:5), but it does not lead to knowledge of God, or to godliness of life. God's 'general revelation' (as it is usually called) of his eternity, power and glory (Rom. 1:20; *cf.* Ps. 19:1), his kindness to men (Acts 14:17), his moral law (Rom. 2:12ff.), his demand for worship and obedience (Rom. 1:21) and his wrath against sin (Rom. 1:18, 32), thus serve only to render men 'without excuse' for their 'ungodliness and wickedness' (Rom. 1:18–20).

This shows that fallen man's need of revelation goes beyond Adam's in two respects. First, he needs a revelation of God as a redeemer and restorer, one who shows mercy to sinners. God's revelation through creation and conscience speaks of law and judgment (Rom. 2:14f.; 1:32), but not of forgiveness. Second, supposing that God grants such a revelation (the Bible is one long proclamation that he does), fallen man still needs spiritual enlightenment before he can grasp it; otherwise he will pervert it, as he has perverted natural revelation. The Jews had a revelation of mercy in the OT, which pointed them to Christ, but on most of their hearts there was a veil which kept them from understanding it (2 Cor. 3:14ff.), and so they fell victim to a legalistic misconception of it (Rom. 9:31–10:4). Even Paul, who calls attention to these facts, had himself known the Christian gospel before his conversion—and tried to stamp it out; not till 'it pleased God . . . to reveal his Son in me'—*in*, by inward enlightenment — did Paul recognize it as the word of God. The need of divine enlightening to reveal to individuals the reality, authority and meaning of revelation objectively given, and to conform their lives to it, is occasionally indicated in the OT (Ps. 119:12, 27, *etc.*; Je. 31:33f.); in the NT it is stressed most by Paul and in the recorded teaching of Christ (Mt. 11:25; 13:11–17; Jn. 3:3ff.; 6:44f., 63ff.; 8:43–47; 10:26ff.; *cf.* 12:37ff.).

III. The content of revelation

a. Old Testament

The foundation and framework of Israel's religious outlook was the covenant which God announced between himself and Abraham's seed (Gn. 17:1ff.). A *covenant is a defined relationship of promise and obligation binding two parties together. This covenant was a royal imposition whereby God pledged himself to Abraham's clan as *their* God, thus authorizing them to invoke him as *our* God and *my* God.

The fact that God made known his name (Yahweh) to Israel (Ex. 3:11–15; 6:2ff.; on the exegesis, *cf.* J. A. Motyer, *The Revelation of the Divine Name*, 1960) was a witness to this relationship. The 'name' stands for all that a person is, and for God to tell the Israelites his name was a sign that, such as he was, in all his power and glory, he was pledging himself to them for their welfare. The goal of his relationship with Israel was the perfecting of the relationship itself: that is, that God should bless Abraham's seed with the fullness of his gifts, and that Abraham's seed should perfectly bless God by a perfect worship and obedience. Hence God continued to reveal himself to the covenant community by his words of law and promise, and by his redemptive deeds as Lord of history for the realizing of this covenant eschatology.

God made the royal character of his covenant more explicit at Sinai, where, having dramatically shown his saving power in the Exodus from Egypt, he was formally acknowledged as Israel's Sovereign (Ex. 19:3–8; Dt. 33:4f.), and through the mouth of Moses, the archetypal prophet (*cf.* Dt. 18:15), promulgated the laws of the covenant, making it clear that enjoyment of covenant blessing was conditional upon obedience to them (Ex. 19:5; *cf.* Lv. 26:3ff.; Dt. 28). These laws were committed to writing, the Decalogue in the first instance by God himself (Ex. 24:12; 31:18; 32:15f.), the whole code eventually by Moses, as, in effect, God's amanuensis (Ex. 34:27f.; Dt. 31:9ff., 24ff.; *cf.* Ex. 24:7). It is noteworthy that God through Hosea later spoke of the entire work of writing the law as his own work, though tradition was unanimous that Moses did it (Ho. 8:12); here are some of the roots of the idea of biblical *inspiration. The law, once written, was regarded as a definitive and permanently valid disclosure of God's will for his people's life, and the priests were made permanently responsible for teaching it (Dt. 31:9ff.; *cf.* Ne. 8:1ff.; Hg. 2:11f.; Mal. 2:7f.).

God forbade Israelites to practise sorcery and divination for day-to-day guidance, as the Canaanites did (Dt. 18:9ff.); they were to seek guidance from him only (Is. 8:19). He promised them a succession of prophets, men in whose mouths he would put his own words (Dt. 18:18; *cf.* Je. 1:9; 5:14; Ezk. 2:7–3:11; Nu. 22:35, 38; 23:5), to give his people such periodic direction as they needed (Dt. 18:15ff.). Prophets in Israel fulfilled a vital ministry. The great prophets, at Yahweh's bidding, spoke God's words and interpreted his mind to kings and to the nation; they expounded and applied his law, pleading for repentance and threatening judgment in his name, and they declared what he would do, both in judgment and also in fulfilling the covenant eschatology by bringing in his kingdom after the judgment was over. And prophets may also have had a place in the cult as seers, men who could give answers from God to individuals who asked particular questions about guidance and the future (*cf.* 1 Sa. 9:6ff.; 28:6–20; 1 Ki. 22:5ff.; see A. R. Johnson, *The Cultic Prophet in Ancient Israel*, 1944). A further means of guidance in pre-exilic Israel was the sacred lot, *Urim and Thummim, manipulated by the priests (Dt. 33:8ff.; *cf.* 1 Sa. 14:36–42; 28:6). Divine guidance for life of a more general sort was supplied also by the maxims of the 'wise men', whose wisdom was held to be from God (*cf.* Pr. 1:20; 8).

In addition to these arrangements for verbal or quasi-verbal communication from God, Israel knew certain theophanic and experimental manifestations which betokened the nearness of God: the *'glory' (*cf.* Ex. 16:10; 40:34; Nu. 16:19; 1 Ki. 8:10f.; Ezk. 1, *etc.*); the thunderstorm (Pss. 18:6–15; 29); the sight of his 'face' and the joyful awareness of his 'presence' to which faithful worshippers aspired (Pss. 11:7; 16:11; 17:15; 51:11f.).

The chief emphases in the OT revelation of God are upon: (*a*) God's uniqueness, as the Maker and Ruler of all things; (*b*) his *holiness, *i.e.* the conjunction of awesome characteristics which set him apart from men—majesty and greatness and strength, on the one hand, and purity and love of righteousness and hatred of wrongdoing, on the other; (*c*) his covenant faithfulness and patience and mercy, and his loyalty to his own gracious purposes towards the covenant people.

b. New Testament

In the NT Christ and the apostles are organs of new revelation, corresponding to Moses and the prophets in the OT. The fulfilment of OT covenant eschatology is found in the kingdom of Christ and the Christian hope of glory. The one God of the OT is revealed as Triune, by the coming first of Christ and then of the Spirit, and the disclosing of the divine redemptive purpose as one in which all three Persons of the Godhead work together (*cf.* Eph. 1:3–14; Rom. 8). Two events which will bring God's plan of human history to its climax are spoken of as acts of revelation still to come (the appearing of antichrist, 2 Thes. 2:3, 6, 8, and of Christ, 1 Cor. 1:7; 2 Thes. 1:7–10; 1 Pet. 1:7, 13). The NT claims that the revelation of the OT has been augmented along two chief lines.

(i) *The revelation of God in Christ.* The NT proclaims that 'God . . . in these last days . . . has spoken to us by a Son' (Heb. 1:1f.). This is God's crowning and final revelation, his last word to man. By his words and works, and by the over-all character of his life and ministry, Jesus Christ perfectly revealed God (Jn. 1:18; 14:7–11). His personal life was a perfect revelation of the character of God; for the Son is the image of God (2 Cor. 4:4; Col. 1:15; Heb. 1:3), his *logos* ('word', regarded as expressing his mind, Jn. 1:1ff.), in whom, as incarnate, all the divine fullness dwelt (Col. 1:19; 2:9). Equally, his Messianic work revealed perfectly the saving purposes of God; for Christ is the wisdom of God (1 Cor. 1:24), through whom, as Mediator (1 Tim. 2:5), all God's saving purposes are worked out and all the wisdom that man needs for his salvation may be found (Col. 2:3; 1 Cor. 1:30; 2:6f.). The revelation of the Father by the Son, whom the Jews condemned as an impostor and blasphemer for declaring his Sonship, is a major theme of John's Gospel.

(ii) *The revelation of God's plan through Christ.* Paul declares that the 'mystery' (secret) of God's 'good pleasure' for the saving of the church and the restoring of the cosmos through Christ is now revealed, after having been kept hidden up to the time of the incarnation (Rom. 16:25f.; 1 Cor. 2:7–10; Eph. 1:9ff.; 3:3–11; Col. 1:19ff.). He shows how this revelation abolishes the old wall of partition between Jew and Gentile (Rom. 3:29ff.; 9–11; Gal. 2:15–3:29; Eph. 2:11–3:6); similarly, the writer to the Hebrews shows how it abolishes the old priestly and sacrificial Jewish cultus (Heb. 7–10).

IV. The nature of revelation

It is clear from the foregoing that the Bible conceives of revelation as primarily and fundamentally verbal communication—God's *tôrâ* ('teaching, instruction, law'), or *d*^{e}*ḇārîm* ('words'), in the OT, and his *logos* or *rhēma*, 'word, utterance', in the NT. The thought of God as revealed in his actions is secondary, and depends for its validity on the presupposition of verbal revelation. For men can 'know that he is Yahweh' from seeing his works in history only if he speaks to make it clear that they are his works, and to explain what they mean. Equally, men could never have guessed or deduced who and what Jesus of Nazareth was, apart from God's statements about him in the OT, and Jesus' own self-testimony (*cf.* Jn. 5:37–39; 8:13–18). (*Inspiration, *Prophecy.)

Bibliography. Arndt; A. Oepke, *TDNT* 3, pp. 563–592; C. F. D. Moule, *IDB*, 4, pp. 54–58; B. B. Warfield, *The Inspiration and Authority of the Bible*, 1951; H. H. Rowley, *The Faith of Israel*, 1956; L. Köhler, *Old Testament Theology*, E.T. 1953; H. W. Robinson, *Inspiration and Revelation in the Old Testament*, 1946; E. F. Scott, *Revelation in the New Testament*, 1935; J. Orr, *Revelation and Inspiration*, 1910; B. Ramm, *Special Revelation and the Word of God*, 1961; G. C. Berkouwer, *General Revelation*, 1955. J.I.P.

REVELATION, BOOK OF. The last book of the Bible is, for most Christians, one of the least read and most difficult. A few passages from it are well known and well loved (*e.g.* 7:9–17); but for the most part modern readers find the book unintelligible. This is largely because it abounds in symbolism of a type that we do not use and to which we no longer possess the key. Yet this kind of imagery was readily comprehensible to the men of the day. Indeed, this partly accounts for our difficulties. The author could assume that his readers would detect his allusions, and therefore he felt no need to make explanations.

The 'seven churches of Asia' of Rev. 1–3 and the island of Patmos where John received the revelation.

Revelation is classed with the literature known as *apocalyptic. It is the only book of this type in the NT, though there are apocalyptic passages in other books (*e.g.* Mt. 24), and the OT visions of Daniel belong to the same class. Characteristic of apocalyptic is the thought that God is sovereign, and that ultimately he will intervene in catastrophic fashion to bring to pass his good and perfect will. He is opposed by powerful and varied forces of evil, and these are usually referred to symbolically as beasts, horns, *etc.* There are visions; angels speak; there is the clash of mighty forces; and ultimately the persecuted saints are vindicated. Much of this is conventional (which is why the first readers of Revelation would have understood it quite easily), but in the hands of many enthusiasts it led to turgid and grotesque phantasies. Biblical apocalyptic is much more restrained.

Another difference between Revelation and the usual run of apocalyptic is that the author's name is given, whereas apocalypses were usually pseudonymous. The writers took names from the great ones of the past and ascribed their works to them. For our present purpose it is important to notice that in this book the Holy Spirit has made use of a recognized literary form, but that the book is not simply a conventional apocalypse. It has features of its own, and is a genuine prophecy, as the first three verses indicate.

I. Outline of contents

The book begins with a vision of the risen Lord, who gives messages to seven churches, those in Ephesus, Smyrna, Pergamum, Thyatira, Sardis, Philadelphia and Laodicea, a group of cities in the Roman province of Asia (1:1–3:22). The messages rebuke these churches where they have failed and encourage them on the path of Christian service. Then come visions of God and of the Lamb (4:1–5:14), after which we read of the 7 seals. As each seal is opened there is a vision recorded (6:1–17; 8:1). This leads on to the 7 trumpets, with a vision recorded after each trumpet is sounded (8:2–9:21; 11:15–19). Between the 6th and 7th seals there is an interlude (7:1–17), and another between the 6th and 7th trumpets (10:1–11:14). John then records various wonders in heaven, a woman bringing forth a man child, and opposed by Satan (12:1–17), beasts opposing themselves to God (13:1–18), the Lamb on Mount Zion and his followers (14:1–20). Next the 7 last plagues are recounted. John sees 7 angels with bowls, and as each pours out his bowl upon the earth one of the plagues follows (15:1–16:21). Further judgments are then denounced on the scarlet woman and on Babylon (17:1–19:21), and the book concludes with visions of the millennium, of the new heavens and the new earth (20:1–22:21).

It is uncertain how much of the book duplicates other sections. The recurrence of the number 7 makes it fairly clear that some, at least, of the series are described in more than one way. What is certain is that the book envisages terrific opposition to God and the people of God, but that in the end God will triumph over every evil thing.

II. Authorship and date

The author tells us that his name was John, and he describes himself as God's 'servant' (Rev. 1:1), as one of the 'prophets' (Rev. 22:9) and as 'your brother' (Rev. 1:9). Tradition has affirmed this John to be identical with John the apostle, and further, that he was the author of the Fourth Gospel and of the three Johannine Epistles. The view that the author was John the apostle goes back to Justin

Martyr (*c.* AD 140), and is supported by Irenaeus and many others. The principal objection is the style of Revelation. The Greek is in many respects unlike that of the other Johannine writings. It is so unusual and sometimes shows such scant respect for the rules of Gk. grammar that it is felt that it cannot come from the same pen as do the Gospel and the Epistles. (Charles speaks of it as 'unlike any Greek that was ever penned by mortal man'.) The question is too intricate to be discussed fully here. Suffice to say that, whereas most scholars today deny the apostolic authorship, there are some who find it best to think of all five Johannine writings as from one author, and that author the apostle John (*e.g.* E. Stauffer).

The book was obviously written at a time when the church was undergoing persecution and difficulty. During the possible time for the composition of the book the two most important periods when this was so were during the reigns of Nero and of Domitian. The principal argument for the former date is Rev. 17:9f., 'This calls for a mind with wisdom: the seven heads are seven mountains on which the woman is seated; they are also seven kings, five of whom have fallen, one is, the other has not yet come.' If this refers to the emperors of Rome, then Nero was the fifth, and the writing would date from shortly after his reign. This is strengthened by the prophecy that 'the beast that was and is not, it is an eighth but it belongs to the seven' (Rev. 17:11). This appears to refer to the 'Nero *redivivus*' myth, the idea that Nero, though dead, would appear once more on this earth. Support is adduced from Rev. 13:18, which gives 'the number of the beast' as 666. Numbers were written in the 1st century, not with our convenient notation, but with letters of the alphabet. Each letter had a numerical value. By taking the numerical values of the letters making up 'Nero Caesar' in Hebrew we get 666. But it is difficult to see why it should be in Hebrew (when the book is in Greek), and anyway to get the desired result a variant spelling has to be adopted.

The later date is attested by a number of ancient authors, such as Irenaeus and Eusebius, who state categorically that the book was written in the time of Domitian. This is supported by certain indications of a general type within the book, though not by specific allusions to identifiable events. Thus the book speaks of certain groups of Christians as complacent and declining in spirituality. In Nero's reign the church was still very young and vigorous. By the time of Domitian there is much more possibility of development and of degeneration. Most scholars today are agreed that the later date is to be preferred.

III. Interpretation

How are we to understand all this? Four chief ways of looking at the book have emerged in the Christian church.

a. The preterist view

This takes the book to describe past events. It sees all the visions as arising out of conditions in the Roman empire of the 1st century AD. The seer was appalled at the possibilities for evil inherent in the Roman empire and he used symbolic imagery to protest against it, and to record his conviction that God would intervene to bring about what pleased him. In general, liberal scholars endorse this point of view. It enables them to understand the book without finding much place for predictive prophecy, and at the same time to see in Revelation a much-needed assertion of the truth of God's moral government of the world. Such a view roots the book in the circumstances of the writer's own day, which is surely right. But it overlooks the fact that the book calls itself a 'prophecy' (Rev. 1:3), and that some at any rate of its predictions refer to what is still future (*e.g.* chs. 21–22).

b. The historicist view

This regards the book as setting forth in one grand sweep a panoramic view of history from the 1st century to the second coming of Christ. The writer's own day is mentioned, and so is the final time, but there is no indication of a break anywhere. Therefore, upholders of such views reason, the book must be held to give a continuous story of the whole period. Such views were held by most of the Reformers, who identified papal Rome with the beast. But the difficulties seem insuperable, and it is significant that, while stoutly maintaining that all history is here set forth, historicists have not been able to agree among themselves as to the precise episodes in history which the various visions symbolize. In 1,900 years at least the main outlines should have emerged with clarity. It is also difficult to see why the outline of history should confine itself to W Europe, especially since in earlier days at least much of the expansion of Christianity was in E lands.

c. The futurist view

This maintains that from ch. 4 onwards Revelation deals with events at the end-time. The book is not concerned with the prophet's own day, nor with later historical events, but with those happenings that will take place in connection with the second coming of the Lord. This view takes seriously the predictive element in the book (Rev. 1:19; 4:1). And it has in its favour the fact that Revelation undeniably leads up to the final establishment of the rule of God, so that some of the book must refer to the last days. The principal objection is that this view tends to remove the book entirely from its historical setting. It is not easy to see what meaning it would have had for its first readers if this is the way it is to be understood.

d. The idealist or the poetic view

This insists that the main thrust of the book is concerned with inspiring persecuted and suffering Christians to endure to the end. To bring about this aim the writer has employed symbolic language, not meaning it to be taken for anything other than a series of imaginative descriptions of the triumph of God. Such views can be linked with other views, and are often found, for example, in combination with preterist ideas. The difficulty is that the seer does claim to be prophesying of later days.

None of the views has proved completely satisfying, and it is probable that a true view would combine elements from more than one of them. The outstanding merit of preterist views is that they give the book meaning for the men of the day in which it was written, and, whatever else we may say of the book, this insight must be retained. Historicist views similarly see the book as giving light on the church throughout its history, and this cannot be surrendered. Futurist views take with the greatest seriousness the language of the book about the end-time. The book does emphasize the ultimate triumph of God and the events associated with it. Nor can the idealist view be abandoned, for the book does bring before us a stirring challenge to live for God in days when the opposition is fierce. Moreover, the Christian must always welcome the assurance that God's triumph is sure.

BIBLIOGRAPHY. Commentaries by R. H. Charles, *ICC*, A. Farrer, 1964; G. E. Ladd, 1972; G. R. Beasley-Murray, 1974; J. M. Ford, *NCB*², 1981; R. H. Mounce, *NIC*, 1977; L. Morris, *TNTC*², 1987; M. Wilcock, *BST*, 1991; C. Rowland, 1993. See also N. B. Stonehouse, *The Apocalypse in the Ancient Church*, 1929; M. C. Tenney, *Interpreting Revelation*, 1957; D. T. Niles, *As Seeing the Invisible*, 1962; A. Y. Collins, *Crisis and Catharsis* 1984; C. J. Hemer, *The Letters to the Seven Churches of Asia*, 1986; L. I. Thompson, *The Book of Revelation*, 1990. L.M.

REWARD. Thirteen Heb. roots, of which *śāḵār* and *šōḥaḏ* are the chief, lie behind OT expressions of 'reward'. In Gk. the verb *apodidōmi* and noun *misthos* are used. All convey the meaning of payment, hire or wages, and there are instances of 'reward' as pay for honest work done (1 Tim. 5:18) and dishonest gain, *i.e.* bribe (Mi. 3:11).

1. Any reward depends for its significance upon the character of its bestower, and God's rewards, with which the biblical writers are chiefly concerned, both as blessings and as punishments, are manifestations of his justice, *i.e.* of himself (*e.g.* Ps. 58:11) and inseparable from the covenant (Dt. 7:10) to which his commands are annexed. Thus the second commandment relates the penalty of disobedience to the jealousy of God, and the reward of obedience to his mercy (Ex. 20:5). Dt. 28 explains Israel's well-being in terms of submission to the covenant, a theme developed by the later prophets (*e.g.* Is. 65:6–7; 66:6). That obedience to God will bring visible temporal rewards is rightly expected throughout the Bible, but two false conclusions were also drawn from such teaching as Dt. 28, namely (i) that righteousness is automatically rewarded materially, and (ii) that suffering is a certain sign of sin (Job; Pss. 37; 73, all reflect the tension created by these false deductions, and Ec. 8:14 marks an extreme cynicism). Yet it must be noted that in the OT God himself and his salvation are already known to be the supreme reward (Is. 62:10–12; Ps. 63:3), rather than his gifts.

2. Jesus promised rewards to his disciples (Mk. 9:41; 10:29; Mt. 5:3–12), so coupled with self-denial and suffering for the gospel's sake as to prevent a mercenary attitude. He slew the Pharisaic notion of meritorious service (Lk. 17:10) and discouraged desire for human reward (Mt. 6:1), since the Father is the disciple's best reward. Jesus shows that reward is inseparable from himself and from God, and the apostles laboured to establish the complete dependence of man's obedience and faith upon mercy and grace (Rom. 4:4; 6:23). Work, and therefore reward, is certainly looked for, but simply as an index of living faith (Jas. 2:14–16; Jn. 6:28), not as a basis of claim upon God. The reward of salvation in Christ begins in time (2 Cor. 5:5) and its fulfilment is looked for after *judgment (final rewards and punishments) when the covenant people enter into full enjoyment of the vision of God which is their enduring reward (Rev. 21:3).

BIBLIOGRAPHY. *BAGD*; K. E. Kirk, *The Vision of God* (abridged ed.), 1934, pp. 69–76; P. C. Böttger *et al.*, *NIDNTT* 3, pp. 134–145; W. White Jr, *ZPEB* 5, p. 99; T. B. Dozeman, *ISBE* 4, pp. 179–180. M.R.W.F.

REZEPH. A town destroyed by the Assyrians and named in a letter to Hezekiah sent by Sennacherib as a warning to Jerusalem of the fate of those cities who resisted their demands for surrender (2 Ki. 19:12 = Is. 37:12). The details of any revolt or sack of Assyr. Raṣappa are not known, though Assyr. texts mention the town and name several governors in the years 839–673 BC. This important caravan-centre on the route from the Euphrates to Hamath was identified by Ptolemy (5. 16; Gk. *Rhēsapha*) and is the modern *Reṣāfa*, about 200 km ENE of Hama, Syria. D.J.W.

REZIN. The king of *Damascus who, in alliance with *Pekah of Samaria, threatened *Ahaz of Judah (2 Ki. 15:37; 16:5). Their aim was probably to form an anti-Assyrian front, but in fact they drove Ahaz into alliance with Assyria, despite Isaiah's advice that Rezin was not to be feared (Is. 7:1, 8; 8:6). *Tiglath-pileser III listed Rezin as tributary about 738 BC, but captured Damascus and killed him in 732 BC (2 Ki. 16:9). See W. Pitard, *Ancient Damascus*, 1987, pp. 179–187. A.R.M.

REZON. The son of Eliadah, who fled with a band of followers when David attacked Hadadezer of Zobah (1 Ki. 11:23–24). He occupied Damascus and became its ruler, opposing Israel during the reign of Solomon in alliance with Hadad of Edom (v. 25). He later 'reigned over Syria', and is thus thought to have outlived the united Hebrew monarchy and to be identified with Hezion, father of Tab-Rimmon and grandfather of *Benhadad I, the king of *Damascus, with whom Asa of Judah made an alliance (1 Ki. 15:18). If this is correct, Rezon was the founder of the dynasty of *Aram who opposed Israel. Rezon (and Rezin) may be a title meaning 'prince' (*cf.* Pr. 14:28). *Cf.* M. F. Unger, *Israel and the Aramaeans of Damascus*, 1980; W. T. Pitard, *Ancient Damascus*, 1987. D.J.W.

RHEGIUM. The modern Reggio di Calabria, a port-city on the Italian shore of the Strait of Messina, in S Italy. An old Gk. colony, Rhegium owed its importance under the Roman empire to its position in relation to the navigation of the Strait and the Italian W coast. With the whirlpool of Charybdis and the rock of Scylla endangering navigation through the Strait, it was important to attempt the passage only with the most favourable sailing wind, and shipping moving N would wait at Rhegium for a S wind. This was done by the master of the ship which was taking Paul to Rome (Acts 28:13). J.H.P.

RHODA (Gk. *rhodē*, 'rose'). A slave-girl in the house of John Mark's mother who announced Peter's arrival (Acts 12:13ff.) after the angel had released him from prison. See *BRD*, pp. 209ff. J.D.D.

RHODES. The large island extending towards Crete from the SW extremity of Asia Minor, and thus lying across the main sea route between the Aegean and the Phoenician ports. It was partitioned among three Gk. states, of Dorian stock, early federated and sharing a common capital at the NE point of the island. It was this city, also called Rhodes, that Paul touched at on his last journey to Palestine (Acts 21:1). After Alexander's conquests, and the establishment of the Macedonian kingdoms and many Hellenized states throughout the E periphery of the Mediterranean, Rhodes grew to be the leading Gk. republic, outstripping those of the old homeland. This was not only because she was now the natural clearing-house for the greatly increased E–W traffic, but because her position gave her an effective diplomatic leverage against the pressures of the rival kingdoms who disputed the hegemony of the strategic Aegean islands. As the champion of the old autonomy principle, she took the lead in calling for Roman intervention to protect it. Rhodes fell from favour with the Romans, however, who deliberately advanced Delos to destroy her ascendancy. By Paul's time her importance was gone, except as a resort of mellow distinction in learning and leisure.

BIBLIOGRAPHY. M. Rostovtzeff, *CAH*, 8, pp. 619–642. E.A.J.

RIBLAH, RIBLATH. 1. A place in the district of Hamath, on the river Orontes in Syria, on the right bank of which are ruins near a modern village, Ribleh, 56 km NE of Baalbek and S of Hama. The site is easily defended and commands the main route from Egypt to the Euphrates as well as the neighbouring forests and valleys, from which ample supplies of food or fuel are obtained. For such reasons Riblah was chosen by Neco II as the Egyp. headquarters, following his defeat of Josiah at Megiddo and the sack of Qadesh in 609 BC. Here he deposed Jehoahaz, imposed tribute on Judah and appointed Jehoiakim its king (2 Ki. 23:31–35). When Nebuchadrezzar II defeated the Egyptians at Carchemish and Hamath in 605 BC he likewise chose Riblah as his military base for the subjugation of Palestine. From it he directed operations against Jerusalem in 589–587 BC, and here was brought the rebel Zedekiah to be blinded after watching the death of his sons (2 Ki. 25:6, 20–21; Je. 39:5–7; 52:9–27). The AV Diblath (RV 'Diblah') of Ezk. 6:14 may be the same place (see RSV), since an otherwise unknown situation is unlikely in the context.

2. Riblath at the NE corner of the ideal boundary of Israel (Nu. 34:11) might be the same place as **1**, though the border is generally considered to lie farther S (*cf.* Ezk. 47:15–18). The suggestion commonly adopted, that this is to be read 'to Harbel' (LXX), modern Harmel in the Beqa', helps little in evaluating the border, since this place lies only 13 km SW of Riblah **1** itself. D.J.W.

RIGHTEOUSNESS (Heb. *ṣeḏeq, ṣᵉḏāqâ*; Gk. LXX and NT, *dikaiosynē*). The Heb. *ṣeḏeq* probably derives from an Arab. root meaning 'straightness', leading to the notion of an action which conforms to a norm. There is, however, a considerable richness in the biblical understanding of this term and it is difficult to render either the Heb. or Gk. words concerned by a simple Eng. equivalent. One basic ingredient in the OT idea of righteousness is relationship, both between God and man (Ps. 50:6; Je. 9:24) and between man and man (Dt. 24:13; Je. 22:3).

Referred to relations between men, righteous action is action which conforms to the requirements of the relationship and in a more general sense promotes the well-being and peace of the community (1 Sa. 24:17; Pr. 14:34). It is therefore linked in a forensic sense with *justice though even then the idea is less that of conformity to some formal legal norm as the strongly ethical notion of action which is to be legally upheld because it is productive of communal well-being (Dt. 1:16; Am. 5:7). In the prophetic period righteousness comes to include the idea of helping the poor and needy (Dn. 4:27; Am. 5:12, 24), and hence almsgiving (Mt. 6:1f.).

When we move from relations between men to those between God and men (though this distinction is arguably somewhat formal since the thought of God was probably never completely absent whenever the Hebrew used the word *ṣeḏeq*) righteousness implies a correct relationship to the will of God which was particularly expressed and interpreted by Israel's covenant with God. Righteous action is hence action which flows out of God's gracious election of Israel and accords with the law of the covenant (Dt. 6:25; Ezk. 18:5–9). God himself is righteous (2 Ch. 12:6; Ps. 7:9), and hence may be relied upon to act in accordance with the terms of his relationship with Israel. God is therefore a righteous judge who acts for his people (Ps. 9:4; Je. 11:20), and upon whose righteousness his people depend for deliverance and vindication (Ps. 31:1; Je. 11:20).

Thus emerges the conflation of the notions of righteousness and salvation. God is 'a righteous God and (therefore) a Saviour' (Is. 45:21; *cf.* Ps. 36:6; Is. 61:10). For the OT God is Creator and therefore he is the ground and guarantor of the moral order. His righteousness is hence intimately related to other more general moral attributes such as his holiness. The Creator, however, is also the Redeemer, and his righteousness is interpreted by his redemptive activity. Further, Israel's experience of God's righteous deliverance in the past led her to an expectation of a future act of salvation. The coming Messianic ruler is seen as the special recipient and instrument of the divine righteousness (Ps. 72:1f.; Is. 11:3–5; 32:1–20; Je. 23:5). The 'Righteous One' was a Messianic title (Is. 53:11; *cf.* Acts 3:14; 7:52; 22:14).

The NT uses righteousness in the sense of conformity to the demands and obligations of the will of God, the so-called 'righteousness of the law' (Gal. 3:21; Phil. 3:6, 9; *cf.* Tit. 3:5). Human attainment of righteousness is at points relatively positively viewed (Lk. 1:6; 2:25; Mt. 5:20), but in the end this attainment in all men falls far short of a true conformity to the divine will (Rom. 3:9–20; Lk. 18:9–14; Jn. 8:7). In contrast to this human unrighteousness stands the righteousness of God (Rom. 1:17) which in consistency with OT understanding conveys the thought of God's active succour of man in the miracle of his grace.

This righteousness is proclaimed by Jesus as a gift to those who are granted the kingdom of God (Mt. 5:6). By faith in Jesus Christ and his work of atonement man, unrighteous sinner though he is, receives God's righteousness, *i.e.* he is given a true relationship with God which involves the forgiveness of all sin and a new moral standing with God in union with Christ 'the Righteous One' (Rom. 3:21–31; 4:1–25; 10:3; 1 Cor. 1:30; 2 Cor. 5:21; Phil. 3:9). By dealing with all the consequences of man's sin and unrighteousness (both Godward and manward) in the cross, God at once maintains the moral order in which alone he can have fellowship with man *and* in grace delivers the needy (Rom. 3:26).

The gift of God's righteousness involves entry into the new realm of divine salvation, the gift of eternal life under the reign of God (Rom. 6:12–23; 2 Cor. 6:7, 14; Phil. 1:11; Eph. 4:24). Hence the extrinsic righteousness imputed through the cross finds inevitable expression in the intrinsic righteousness of a life which in a new way conforms to the will of God, even though the ultimate realization of this conformity must await the consummation of the kingdom (1 Jn. 3:2; Phil. 3:12–14; 1 Cor. 13:12f.; 2 Pet. 3:11–13). (*Justification.)

Bibliography. G. Schrenk, in *TDNT* 2, pp. 192–210; N. Snaith, *Distinctive Ideas of the Old Testament*, 1944; J. Denney, *The Death of Christ*, reprinted 1951; A. Nygren, *Commentary on Romans*, E.T. 1952; H. Seebass, C. Brown, in *NIDNTT* 3, pp. 352–377; A. H. Leitch, *ZPEB* 5, pp. 104–118; C. E. B. Cranfield, *Romans*, *ICC*, 2 vols., 1979.

B.A.M.

RIMMON. 1. 'Thunderer', a title of the storm-god Hadad (*cf.* *Hadad-rimmon) worshipped in Damascus. Grateful for his cure from leprosy by Elisha, the Syrian army commander Naaman requested two mule-loads of earth from Israel. He proposed to erect an altar on this soil in Rimmon's temple so that he might worship Israel's God on his own ground (2 Ki. 5:17–18). The temple was probably on the site in Damascus occupied by the Roman temple of Zeus, whose emblem, like Rimmon's, was a thunderbolt. The famous Umayyad mosque now stands there. See J. C. Greenfield, *IEJ* 26, 1976, pp. 195–198.

2. A Benjaminite from Beeroth, father of Baanah and Rechab, who assassinated Ishbosheth (2 Sa. 4:2, 9). This personal name, like the similar place-names, if not an abbreviation of a form including the divine element Rimmon, is probably to be derived from the Heb. *rimmôn*, 'pomegranate'. See following article. D.J.W.

RIMMON (Heb. *rimmôn*, 'pomegranate'). **1.** En (Ain)-Rimmon was a place in the Negeb near Edom assigned to Simeon (Jos. 19:7; 1 Ch. 4:32) but incorporated into the Beersheba district (Jos. 15:32). Zechariah envisaged it as the S part of the high plateau seen from Jerusalem (14:10). It was settled by returning exiles (Ne. 11:29), and usually identified with Khirbet er-Ramamim *c.* 16 km NNE of Beersheba. Some identify this with the Rimmon-perez between Hazeroth and Moseroth where the Israelites encamped (Nu. 33:19–20).

2. A village in Zebulun (Jos. 19:13), possibly mod. Rummaneh 10 km NNE of Nazareth (the Crusader Romaneh). AV 'Remmon-methoar' is to be translated 'Rimmon as it bends towards . . .', as in RSV. A Levitical city (1 Ch. 6:77), Dimnah (Jos. 21:35), read by some vss as Remmon, may be the site; it was captured by the Assyrians *en route* to Jerusalem (so Is. 10:27, RSV).

3. A rocky cliff with caves near Gibeah, to which the Benjaminites escaped (Jdg. 20:45–47); perhaps modern Rammon, 8 km E of Bethel. D.J.W.

RIVER. Hebrew has a good many different words often rendered 'river', although this is not always an accurate translation of the original term.

The Heb. word *naḥal* is common, meaning a wadi or torrent-valley; in summer a dry river-bed or ravine, but a raging torrent in the rainy season. The Jabbok was such a wadi (Dt. 2:37), as were all the streams mentioned in the Elijah stories. Because these river-beds could suddenly become raging torrents, they often symbolize the pride of nations (Is. 66:12), the strength of the invader (Je. 47:2), and the power of the foe (Ps. 124:4). In his vision it was a *naḥal* that Ezekiel saw issuing from the Temple (47:5–12).

The second term, *nāhār*, is the regular word for 'river' in Heb. It is used of particular rivers: *e.g.* the rivers of Eden (Gn. 2:10, 13–14), the Euphrates (Dt. 1:7), and the rivers of Ethiopia (Is. 18:1), Damascus (2 Ki. 5:12), *etc.* In Ex. 7:19; Ps. 137:1, the word should almost certainly be rendered 'canals'. The waters from the rock struck by Moses formed a *nāhār* (Ps. 105:41).

The word used most frequently of the Nile is *y*e*'ôr*. The term is also found in Coptic, and was probably an Egyp. loan-word (*BDB*): see, *e.g.*, Gn. 41:1; Ex. 1:22. It is used by Jeremiah (46:7f.) as a similitude of Egyp. invasion.

Other Heb. terms for 'river' are *peleḡ*, irrigating canals (Pss. 1:3; 65:9); *'āp̄îq*, channel or river-bed (Ps. 42:1; Is. 8:7; and *yûḇāl* or *'ûḇāl*, a stream or watercourse (Is. 30:25; Dn. 8:2–3, 6). In the NT the word for 'river' is *potamos*. It is used of the Euphrates (Rev. 16:12) and the Jordan (Mk. 1:5); of the river issuing from God's throne (Rev. 22:1f.); and of the Holy Spirit under the figure of living water (Jn. 7:38f.). J.G.S.S.T.

RIZPAH (Heb. *riṣpâ*, 'a hot stone', 'a live coal'). **1.** Feminine form of *reṣep*, 'a live coal (from the altar)' (Is. 6:6); 'a cake baked on heated stones' (1 Ki. 19:6).

2. A town in N Mesopotamia (2 Ki. 19:12). Sennacherib, king of Assyria, spoke of its gods, as well as the gods of other nations, as being powerless to resist him (2 Ki. 19:12; Is. 37:12). Israel too was unable to resist the Assyrians.

3. A daughter of a certain Aiah, a concubine (*pîleḡeš*) of Saul (2 Sa. 3:7; 21:8, 10, 11). On Saul's death, Abner took Rizpah himself (2 Sa. 3:7–11).

Rizpah gave two sons to Saul, Mephibosheth and Armoni (2 Sa. 21:8). When, in later years, King David learnt that the Gibeonites required the death of seven of Saul's sons as an atonement for the bloody deeds of Saul among them, he surrendered the two sons of Rizpah along with the sons of Michal (2 Sa. 21:1ff.). All were hanged and left unburied, and the grief-stricken Rizpah watched over the bodies for several months. This devotion led David to undertake the proper burial of the bones of Jonathan and Saul along with those of the men who had been hanged. J.A.T.

ROCK. In the OT rock (Heb. *sela'*; *ṣûr*) symbolizes the security and defence of a steep and inaccessible refuge (*cf.* Is. 32:2; 33:16). Similarly, it is used of an immovable foundation (*cf.* Ps. 40:2): to remove 'the rock' is equivalent to shaking the world (*cf.* Jb. 18:4). In an interplay of these symbols it is not surprising to find God spoken of as a rock who gives security and safety to his people (*cf.* 2 Sa. 22:32). In Is. 8:14 *ṣûr* is used of the Messianic stone rejected by the Jewish 'temple builders'. Together with Ps. 118:22 and Is. 28:16 it becomes important for NT typology: Jesus Christ, the rejected 'rock of offence', becomes the *cornerstone of God's true Temple, the Christian *ekklēsia* (Rom. 9:33; 1 Pet. 2:6ff.; *cf.* Ellis, *Paul*, pp. 88ff.). In Paul the typology is extended to the identification of Christ with the rock whose nourishing water followed the Israelites in the wilderness (1 Cor. 10:1ff.; *cf.* Ellis, *Prophecy*, pp. 209–212). The relation (and probable identification) of *Peter with the rock in Mt. 16:18 is the subject of continuing discussion (*cf.* Cullmann, pp. 155–212).

BIBLIOGRAPHY. 'Cornerstone', *Baker's Dictionary of Theology*, 1959; O. Cullmann, *Peter: Disciple, Apostle, Martyr*, 1953; E. E. Ellis, *Paul's Use of the Old Testament*[5], 1991; *idem.*, *Prophecy and Hermeneutic*[4], 1993; O. Cullmann, in *TDNT* 6, pp. 95–112; W. Mundle *et al.*, in *NIDNTT* 3, pp. 381–394. E.E.E.

ROD (STAFF). A word with a variety of meanings. **1.** A stem, branch (Gn. 30:37; Je. 1:11). **2.** A support carried by travellers (Gn. 32:10; Mk. 6:8), shepherds (Ex. 4:2; Ps. 23:4, 'staff'), old men (Zc. 8:4; Heb. 11:21) and men of rank (Gn. 38:18); figurative in 2 Ki. 18:21; Is. 3:1; Ezk. 29:6. Passing under a rod or staff was a shepherd's way of counting his sheep (Lv. 27:32; *cf.* Ezk. 20:37). **3.** An instrument of punishment (Pr. *passim*; 1 Cor. 4:21). **4.** A club carried by soldiers (1 Sa. 14:27; 2 Sa. 23:21) and shepherds (1 Sa. 17:40; *cf.* Ps. 23:4, where rod and staff respectively are used figuratively of divine protection and guidance; *cf.* Mi. 7:14). **5.** A symbol of authority, both human (Jdg. 5:14), *e.g.* a sceptre (Gn. 49:10; Je. 48:17), and divine, like Moses' rod (Ex. 4:20) and Aaron's which confirmed the levitical priesthood (Nu. 17; Heb. 9:4). **6.** A pole upon which ring-shaped loaves were hung. Breaking it is figurative of famine (Lv. 26:26; Ps. 105:16; Ezk. 4:16; 5:16; 14:13). Alternatively it may be simply a symbol for bread as a staple means of supporting life. **7.** A magician's or diviner's wand (Ex. 7:12; Ho. 4:12). **8.** A threshing-stick (Is. 28:27). **9.** A measuring stick (Rev. 11:1; 21:15f.; *cf.* Ezk. 40:3).

In Ezk. 7:10 probably *MT hammaṭṭeh*, 'rod' (RSVmg.), has been rightly revocalized as *hammuṭṭeh*, 'injustice'.

BIBLIOGRAPHY. *BAGD*; *BDB*. L.C.A.

ROMAN EMPIRE. The term in its modern usage is neither biblical nor even classical, and does not do justice to the delicacy and complexity of Roman methods of controlling the peoples of the Mediterranean. The word *imperium* signified primarily the sovereign authority entrusted by the Roman people to its elected magistrates by special act (the *lex curiata*). The *imperium* was always complete, embracing every form of executive power, religious, military, judicial, legislative and electoral. Its exercise was confined by the collegiality of the magistracies, and also by the customary or legal restriction of its operation to a particular *provincia*, or sphere of duty. With the extension of Rom. interests abroad, the province became more and more often a geographical one, until the systematic use of the magisterial *imperium* for controlling an 'empire' made possible the use of the term to describe a geographical and administrative entity. In NT times, however, the system was still far from being as complete or rigid as this implies.

I. The nature of Roman imperialism

The creation of a Rom. *province, generally speaking, neither suspended existing governments nor added to the Rom. state. The 'governor' (there was no such generic term, the appropriate magisterial title being used) worked in association with friendly powers in the area to preserve Rome's military security, and if there was no actual warfare his work was mainly diplomatic. He was more like the regional commander of one of the modern treaty organizations which serve the interests of a major power than the colonial governor with his monarchical authority. The solidarity of the 'empire' was a product of the sheer preponderance of Roman might rather than of direct centralized administration. It embraced many hundreds of satellite states, each linked bilaterally with Rome, and each enjoying its individually negotiated rights and privileges. While the Romans obviously had it in their power to cut their way clean through the web of pacts and traditions, this suited neither their inclination nor their interest, and we find them even struggling to persuade dispirited allies to enjoy their subordinate liberties. At the same time there was going on a process of piecemeal assimilation through individual and community grants of Rom. citizenship which bought out the loyalty of local notabilities in favour of the patronal power.

II. Growth of the provincial system

The art of diplomatic imperialism as explained above was developed during Rome's early dealings with her neighbours in Italy. Its genius has been variously located in the principles of the fetial priesthood, which enforced a strict respect for boundaries and allowed no other grounds for war, in the generous reciprocity of early Rom. treaties, and in the Rom. ideals of patronage, which required strict loyalty from friends and clients in return for protection. For whatever reason, Rome soon acquired the leadership of the league of Latin cities, and then over several centuries, under the impact of the sporadic Gallic and German invasions, and the struggles with overseas powers such as the Carthaginians and certain of the Hellenistic monarchs, built up treaty relations with all of the Italian states S of the Po valley. Yet it was not until 89 BC that these peoples were offered Rom. citizenship and thus became municipalities of the republic. Meanwhile a similar process was taking place throughout the Mediterranean. At the end of the first Punic War Sicily was made a province (241 BC), and the Carthaginian threat led to further such steps in Sardinia and Corsica (231 BC), Hither and Further Spain (197 BC), and finally to the creation of a province of Africa itself after the destruction of Carthage in 146 BC. By contrast the Romans at first hesitated to impose themselves on the Hellenistic states of the E, until after the repeated failure of free negotiation provinces were created for Macedonia (148 BC) and Achaia (146

BC). In spite of a certain amount of violence, such as the destruction of both Carthage and Corinth in 146 BC, the advantages of the Rom. provincial system soon became recognized abroad, as is made clear by the passing of three states to Rome by their rulers' bequest, leading to the provinces of Asia (133 BC), Bithynia and Cyrene (74 BC). The Romans had been busy tidying up on their own account, and the threat to communications caused by piracy had by this time led to the creation of provinces for Narbonese Gaul, Illyricum and Cilicia.

The careerism of Rom. generals now began to play a prominent part. Pompey added Pontus to Bithynia and created the major new province of Syria as a result of his Mithridatic command of 66 BC, and in the next decade Caesar opened up the whole of Gaul, leaving the Romans established on the Rhine from the Alps to the North Sea. The last of the great Hellenistic states, Egypt, became a province after Augustus' defeat of Antony and Cleopatra in 31 BC. From this time onwards the policy was one of consolidation rather than expansion. Augustus pushed the frontier up to the Danube, creating the provinces of Raetia, Noricum, Pannonia and Moesia. In the next generation local dynasties were succeeded by Rom. governors in a number of areas. Galatia (25 BC) was followed by Cappadocia, Judaea, Britain, Mauretania and Thrace (AD 46).

The NT thus stands at the point where the series of provinces has been completed and the whole Mediterranean has for the first time been provided with a uniform supervisory authority. At the same time the pre-existing governments still flourished in many cases, though with little prospect of future progress. The process of direct incorporation into the Rom. republic went ahead until Caracalla in AD 212 extended citizenship to all free residents of the Mediterranean. From this time onwards the provinces are imperial territories in the modern sense.

III. The administration of the provinces

Until the 1st century BC the provinces had fallen to the Rom. magistrates either for their year of office itself or for the immediately subsequent year, when they continued to exercise the *imperium* as promagistrate. For all the high sense of responsibility of the Rom. aristocrat, and his life-long training in politics and law, it was inevitable that his province was governed with a single eye to his next step in the capital. The first standing court at Rome was established for the trial of provincial governors for extortion. So long as the competition for office remained unrestrained, the creation of 3-, 5- and 10-year commands only worsened the position. They became the basis for outright attempts at military usurpation. The satellite states were left in a hopeless plight. They had been accustomed to protect their interests against capricious governors by seeking the patronage of powerful houses in the senate, and justice was done in the long run. Now during the 20 years of civil war that followed the crossing of the Rubicon (49 BC) they were compelled to take sides and risk their wealth and liberty in an unpredictable conflict. Three times the great resources of the East were mustered for an invasion of Italy itself, but in each case the invasion was abortive. It then fell to the victor, Augustus, during 45 years of unchallenged power to restore the damage. He first accepted a province for himself embracing most of the regions where a major garrison was still needed, notably Gaul, Spain, Syria and Egypt. This grant was renewed periodically until the end of his life, and the custom was maintained in favour of his successors. Regional commanders were appointed by his delegation, and thus a professional class of administrators was established, and consistent long-term planning was possible for the first time.

The remaining provinces were still allotted to those engaged in the regular magisterial career, but the possibilities of using the position improperly were ruled out by the overwhelming strength of the Caesars, and inexperience tended to defer to them in any case, so that the Caesarian standard of administration was widely maintained.

If it came to the worst a maladministered province could be transferred to the Caesarian allotment, as happened in the case of Bithynia in Pliny's day.

Three of the main responsibilities of the governors are well illustrated in the NT. The first was military security and public order. Fear of Rom. intervention on this ground led to the betrayal of Jesus (Jn. 11:48–50), and Paul was arrested by the Romans on the assumption that he was an agitator (Acts 21:31–38). The governments at Thessalonica (Acts 17:6–9) and at Ephesus (Acts 19:40) demonstrate the paralysis that had crept in through fear of intervention. On the other hand, among the Phoenician states (Acts 12:20) and at Lystra (Acts 14:19) there are violent proceedings with no sign of Rom. control. The second major concern was with the revenues. The Caesars straightened out the taxation system and placed it on an equitable census basis (Lk. 2:1). Jesus (Lk. 20:22–25) and Paul (Rom. 13:6–7) both defended Rom. rights in this matter. The third and most onerous of their duties was jurisdiction. Both by reference from the local authorities (Acts 19:38) and by appeal against them (Acts 25:9–10) litigation was concentrated around the Rom. tribunals. Long delays ensued as the cost and complexity of procedure mounted up. Hard-pressed governors struggled to force the onus back on to local shoulders (Lk. 23:7; Acts 18:15). Christians, however, freely joined in the chorus of praise for Rom. justice (Acts 24:10; Rom. 13:4).

IV. The Roman empire in New Testament thought

While the intricate relations of governors, dynasts and republics are everywhere apparent in the NT and familiar to its writers, the truly imperial atmosphere of the Caesarian ascendancy pervades it all. Caesar's decree summons Joseph to Bethlehem (Lk. 2:4). He is the antithesis of God in Jesus' dictum (Lk. 20:25). His distant envy seals Jesus' death warrant (Jn. 19:12). Caesar commands the perjured loyalty of the Jews (Jn. 19:15), the spurious allegiance of the Greeks (Acts 17:7), the fond confidence of the apostle (Acts 25:11). He is the 'emperor' to whom Christian obedience is due (1 Pet. 2:13). Yet his very exaltation was fatal to Christian loyalty. There was more than a grain of truth in the repeated insinuation (Jn. 19:12; Acts 17:7; 25:8). In the last resort the Christians will defy him. It was the hands of 'lawless' men that crucified Jesus (Acts 2:23). The vaunted justice is to be spurned by the saints (1 Cor. 6:1). When Caesar retaliated (Rev. 17:6) the blasphemy of his claims revealed his doom at the hand of the Lord of lords and King of kings (Rev. 17:14).

Thus, while Rom. imperial peace opened the way for the gospel, Rom. imperial arrogance flung down a mortal challenge.

BIBLIOGRAPHY. *CAH*, 9–11; A. N. Sherwin-White, *Roman Society and Roman Law in the New Testament*, 1963; F. Millar, *The Roman Empire and its Neighbours*, 1967; J. P. V. D. Balsdon, *Rome: the Story of an Empire*, 1970; E. A. Judge, *The Social Pattern of the Christian Groups in the First Century*, 1960; C.Wells, *The Roman Empire*, 1984; *BA1CS* 2; P. Garnsey and R. Saller, *The Roman Empire: Economy, Society and Culture*, 1987. E.A.J.

ROMANS, EPISTLE TO THE.

I. Outline of contents

a. Introduction (1:1–15)

The apostle gives a long greeting followed by his reasons for his desire to visit the Roman church.

b. Doctrinal exposition (1:16–8:39)

The major theme is the righteousness of God.

(i) Both Gentiles and Jews are equally guilty in face of God's righteousness (1:18–3:20). This is in spite of the many privileges of the Jews.

(ii) God has nevertheless dealt with this situation. He has provided a propitiatory sacrifice in Christ (3:21–26). Since the benefits of this are appropriated by faith, the way is open for both Jews and Gentiles (3:27–31). The example of Abraham shows justification to be by faith and not works (4:1–25). Many blessings attend the believer's justification (5:1–11). As sin is universal through Adam, so life comes through Christ (5:12–21).

(iii) Righteousness must have an application to life. This is achieved through union with Christ, for as the believer has died with him so he now lives in him (6:1–14). This new life involves a new type of service, for the believer, although freed from the law, has become a slave of God (6:15–7:6). Law is no help towards sanctification, since it produces inner conflict (7:7–25). But life in the Spirit brings victory to the believer, for sin is robbed of its power and a new status of sonship replaces the bondage of sin (8:1–17). The believer has great hope for the future, which is shared even by the material creation (8:18–25). The present life is strengthened by the Spirit's intercession and by the security provided by God's love (8:26–39).

c. The problem of Israel (9:1–11:36)

The theme of God's righteousness is now treated historically in answer to its apparent conflict with the rejection of Israel.

(i) God's actions are sovereign and just. No creature has the right to question the Creator's decisions (9:1–29).

(ii) Israel's rejection is not arbitrary but due to their own fault, for they have had ample opportunity to repent (9:30–10:21).

(iii) Nevertheless Israel may hope for restoration. God has always preserved a remnant (11:1–6). Israel's own failing has led to the inclusion of the Gentiles (11:7–12). The Gentiles will be the means of Israel's restoration (the olive-tree analogy) (11:13–24). The final state of Israel is in the hands of God in whom is inscrutable wisdom (11:25–36).

d. Practical exhortations (12:1–15:13)

(i) Duties resulting from dedicated lives of a personal and general character (12:1–21).

(ii) Duties affecting society as a whole, such as the duty of civic obedience, neighbourliness and sober conduct (13:1–14).

(iii) The need for toleration among Christians. This is worked out in relation to the special problem of foods (14:1–15:13).

e. Conclusion (15:14–16:27)

(i) The writer states his motive in writing (15:14–21).

(ii) His future plans are then mentioned (15:22–29).

(iii) He asks for prayer support for his Jerusalem visit (15:30–33).

(iv) Many Christians are greeted by name (16:1–16).

(v) Warnings are given about false teachers (16:17–19).

(vi) Further personal greetings, a benediction and doxology close the Epistle (16:20–27).

II. The Christian church at Rome

In the world of Paul's day the name of Rome meant much and was not without its strong fascination for the apostle himself, since he expresses a strong desire to preach the gospel there. As a missionary strategist he recognized the immense importance of the Christian church at the centre of the empire, and this may well have influenced the form of the Epistle which he addressed to it. Of the origin of this important church we know little, and it is perhaps useless to conjecture. It may have been founded by converts from the day of Pentecost who returned to their Roman homes rejoicing in their new-found faith, but, although some Romans are mentioned in Acts 2, there is no indication whether any of these were converted to Christianity on that day. But travel between Rome and her provinces was relatively easy in those days, and many Christians must have been among the travellers along the imperial highways. All that is certainly known is that by the time Paul writes to them the church was not only established but of considerable proportions. If the expulsion of Jews from Rome under the emperor Claudius had anything to do with the Christian church, as seems most probable from the reference to 'Chrestus' in the report of Suetonius, it is evident that it was of sufficient dimensions for such drastic action to be taken. And certainly under the Neronian persecutions not many years after this Epistle was written the Christians numbered a considerable multitude.

The question of Peter's connection with Rome cannot be answered with any conciseness, although any claims that Peter was founder of the church there may at once be dismissed. The apostle was still in Jerusalem at the time of the edict of Claudius, and the church must have been started many years before this. Moreover, Paul makes no mention of Peter in this Epistle, which would be hard to explain if Peter were in fact the head of the church at Rome at this time, as well as being directly opposed to his statement in 15:20. Nevertheless, tradition strongly supports the view that Peter and Paul both suffered martyrdom in Rome, since so early a witness as Clement of Rome attests to this.

There has been some discussion regarding the composition of the Roman church, but it would seem most probable that it consisted of both Gentiles and Jews, with the former in the majority. Such a composition is to be expected in a cosmopolitan city with a strong Jewish colony, and is supported by an analysis of the Epistle itself. In some parts of his argument Paul seems to be addressing Jews, as, for instance, when he appeals to Abraham as 'our father' (4:1) and his direct address to a Jewish questioner in ch. 2; in other parts he turns his thought exclusively towards Gentiles (*cf.* 1:5ff.; 11:13, 28–31). It is an interesting question from what source the Christian tradition within this church had been mainly derived, but there is little indication that it had been derived from the narrower Jewish–Christian stream and it is most natural to suppose that these Christians maintained an outlook similar to that of Paul himself. There is no evidence of the tension of the Jewish–Gentile controversy so apparent in the Galatian Epistle.

III. Date and place of writing

Such indications as are given in this Epistle about Paul's present location all point to the period of his stay in Greece at the close of his third missionary journey (Acts 20:2). His face is now definitely turned towards the W, for he plans not only soon to visit Rome but to proceed with further missionary work in Spain (Rom. 15:24, 28). His E travels are therefore at an end, and this would well fit his situation in Acts 20. Moreover, he is there on his way to Jerusalem, and in Rom. 15:25 he says that his present plans are to go to Jerusalem with the contributions which many churches have made for the support of poverty-stricken Christians there. No doubt can exist, therefore, that the apostle writes this letter just before the final part of his third journey.

In confirmation of this conclusion there are certain indications in ch. 16 which point to Corinth as the place of despatch, although not all scholars are prepared to appeal to this chapter in support, since some believe it was sent to Ephesus and not Rome (see below). But leaving this aside, it is significant that *Phoebe is commended, and she was a deaconess of the church at Cenchrea, one of the two ports of Corinth. There is also a passing reference to a certain *Gaius who was Paul's host at the time of writing, and it is possible that he is the Christian mentioned in 1 Cor. 1:14. Possibly the *Erastus referred to in Rom. 16:23 is the Erastus mentioned in 2 Tim. 4:20 as being left at Corinth, but this is by no means certain. More significant is the mention of Timothy and Sopater (Sosipater) (Rom. 16:21), both of whom accompanied Paul on his visit to Jerusalem (Acts 20:4).

The Epistle may therefore be dated with relative accuracy, although the problems of NT *chronology in general and Paul-ine chronology in particular forbid any absolute dating. Some time between AD 57 and 59 would fit all the known data.

IV. The purpose of the Epistle

Certain immediate circumstances suggest themselves as the occasion which prompted the production of this Epistle. Paul's intention to do further missionary work in Spain caused him to appeal to the Christians at Rome to support him in this venture (*cf.* Rom. 15:24). As he contemplates his visit to the Roman church he realizes that he may have a spiritual gift to impart to them and that he as well as they may be mutually encouraged (1:11–12).

The apostle may have heard of some practical difficulties which the Christians were experiencing, and he intends to correct in the ethical part of his letter (especially in ch. 14) any wrong emphases. There is an allusion to false teachers in 16:17–19, where the Christians are told to avoid them, but this cannot be considered as part of the primary purpose of the letter, since it is appended almost as an afterthought. Clearly an anti-heretical purpose does not dominate the Epistle.

But the incidental purposes so far considered do not account for the theological form of the main part of the letter. What prompted the apostle to give such a prolonged theological exposition? He scarcely needed to have done this in order (on his approaching visit) to encourage interest in his western missionary plans. He must obviously have had some other dominating purpose. The first eleven chapters after the introductory portion (1:1–15) read more like a treatise than a letter, and it is important to consider the reason for this.

The view that Paul wished to deposit with the Roman church a full statement of his doctrinal position has much to commend it. Here are enshrined for posterity some of the noblest concepts of Christianity which have rightly been accorded an honoured place in Christian theology. But a clear distinction must be made between the basic use that Christians have made of this Epistle and the purpose for which Paul originally intended it. It cannot be maintained that he envisaged laying the foundations of Pauline theology in this way. Moreover, there are some aspects of this theology which find no part in the argument of this Epistle, such as eschatology and the doctrine of the church. It is not possible, therefore, to regard this Epistle as a full statement of Paul's doctrine. Nevertheless, it provides a well-reasoned presentation of some of his most dominant concepts, and it may well be that it was Paul's intention to inform the Roman church of these so that when he visited them the Christians would be intelligently acquainted with his teaching.

It is most probable that the apostle is deeply conscious that he has now reached the turning-point of his missionary career and his mind dwells upon some of the major concepts which have formed part of his continuing teaching work. In this case the inclusion of his matured reflections in a letter addressed to Rome may have been no more than an accident of circumstances in that at the time his face was turned Romeward. But it seems better to attach some importance to Paul's own esteem for the strategic importance of this church and to suppose that consciousness of this played some part in the character of his letter.

A more precise problem relating to the dogmatic purpose of the letter is the relative importance of the section dealing with the Jews' position (chs. 9–11). Some of the earlier critical scholars (*i.e.* of the Tübingen school) regarded this portion as the kernel of the letter, in which case the purpose was supposed to be an endeavour to reconcile opposing Jewish and Gentile elements. But this theory is now wholly discounted. It is more in harmony with the facts to maintain that this section naturally follows on the earlier, more theological, debate. The problem in these chapters is the difficulty of reconciling the righteousness of God, the theme of the earlier chapters, with the apparent non-fulfilment of the ancient promises in the rejection of Israel. This theme must have been a burning one for all Jewish

Christians, and would have been relevant in an address to any church with a group of such Christians.

V. The integrity of the Epistle

Few scholars have had the temerity to question the authenticity of this Epistle, and the arguments of those who have done so are now recognized as wholly unfounded and subjective. But there are many scholars who question the concluding chapter, not on grounds disputing Pauline authorship but on the grounds that it does not belong to this Epistle. This opinion is based on several considerations: the large number of personal greetings which are supposed to be improbable to a church which Paul had never visited; the fact that three people, Aquila, Priscilla and Epaenetus, had connections with Asia rather than Rome (although the first two originally came from Rome); the commendation of Phoebe, which is considered less appropriate when addressed to a church where Paul was unknown; the unexpectedness of the allusions to the false teachings in vv. 17–19; and the suitability of 15:33 as an ending to the Epistle. But these considerations are not conclusive and can be otherwise explained. It was not Paul's practice to single out individuals in churches where he was known, and in view of travel facilities it is not surprising that he knew many at Rome or that some last heard of in Asia were then at Rome. Since Paul was well enough known at Rome to write them an Epistle, the commendation of Phoebe presents no difficulty, while the warnings regarding false teachers may have been abruptly introduced either because Paul's notice had just been drawn to them or else because he purposely left the matter to the end so as not to emphasize it disproportionately. The ending 15:33 may be possible as an ending, but is unparalleled in Paul's other Epistles. On the internal evidence from the Epistle there would seem to be insufficient grounds for regarding the chapter as originally detached and as sent to a quite different destination, either Ephesus or anywhere else.

Something must be said about the textual evidence for the ending of this Epistle, although this is not the place for a full discussion. It is sufficient to mention that there are different streams of textual evidence for the position of the benediction and the doxology, and some variations in the reference to Rome in 1:7, 15. There are even some indications that in some quarters the Epistle circulated without its two concluding chapters. This seems to have been particularly associated with Marcion. It is by no means easy to find a theory which accounts for all the variations in the textual evidence, and many different hypotheses have been proposed, some regarding chs. 1–14 as original, some 1–15, and others 1–16. It is probable that the Epistle is original as it now stands, but that Marcion shortened it. In that case his text would have been responsible for the various textual traditions.

VI. The leading themes of the Epistle

a. The righteousness of God

At the commencement of the doctrinal part of the Epistle Paul introduces the theme of God's righteousness, which he claims is now revealed to the believer (1:17). To understand the development of Paul's argument as a whole it is necessary to consider in what ways he uses the concept of *righteousness (*dikaiosynē*). Sanday and Headlam, in their excellent article on the righteousness of God (*A Critical and Exegetical Commentary on the Epistle to the Romans*, 1895, pp. 34–39), point out four different aspects of the manifestation of divine righteousness in this Epistle. The first is fidelity; for the promises of God must be fulfilled to accord with the divine nature (3:3–4). The second is wrath, a particular aspect of righteousness in its abhorrence of all sin, and not as is sometimes supposed a quality opposed to righteousness (*cf.* 1:17f.; 2:5). Righteousness and wrath are, in fact, indivisible, and it is a false exegesis which can treat of God's righteousness without allowing for the operation of God's wrath. The third is the manifestation of righteousness in the death of Christ, of which the classic statement is found in 3:25f. More will be said of this later, but for the present purpose it is necessary to note that in some way God's gift of Christ as a propitiatory sacrifice manifests his righteousness. It is not considered arbitrary or capricious, but is pre-eminently right and just. Only so could it reveal righteousness. The fourth aspect is the linking of righteousness with faith. It may be said to be characteristic of Pauline theology that the righteousness of God which has been manifested can also be appropriated by faith. God's righteousness is therefore considered as being active as well as passive, and in its active role it declares as righteous those who by nature are at enmity with God (see 5:10). This is the meaning of justification; not that men are actually made righteous but that they are accounted as righteous. The whole Epistle is in reality an exposition of this theme, and it has become basic not only to Pauline theology but to the subsequent Reformed theology which draws so much from it.

b. The goodness of God

In case anyone should think that Paul's conception of God was mainly influenced by God's righteousness irrespective of his other attributes, it is well to be reminded that in this Epistle Paul has much to say about the loving character of God. The mere fact that God's righteousness is conceived of as active in man's salvation points to a motive of love linked with holiness. But Paul specifically draws attention to God's kindness and forbearance and patience (2:4). He points out that the supreme manifestation of God's love is in the amazing fact that Christ died for us while we were still sinners (5:8). And the classic statement of the enduring quality of that love is found in 8:35ff., where Paul can think of nothing, either circumstantial or spiritual, which could possibly separate us from God's love.

When dealing with the problem of the rejection of Israel, Paul makes much of God's mercy and flatly refuses to acknowledge the possibility of his injustice (9:15). He quotes approvingly the statement of Isaiah that all day long God had stretched out his hands to the disobedient people of Israel (10:21). Even when the apostle is obliged to speak of the severity of God, he at once reminds his readers of God's kindness to those who continue to abide in him (11:22). It is the great prerogative of God to have mercy (11:32). Even in the practical part of the Epistle, Paul frequently thinks of the gracious character of God. His will is good, acceptable and perfect (12:2). He receives both the weak and the strong, and this is cited as a reason why the one should not judge the other. He is called the God of steadfastness and encouragement (*tēs hypomonēs kai tēs paraklēseōs*, 15:5), and this forms the basis of an exhortation to develop similar qualities in ourselves. Similarly, because God is a God of hope (15:13), Christians by the power of the Spirit are to abound in hope. Throughout the Epistle, in fact, Paul's thought is dominated by his conception of God. But one other aspect demands a brief comment on its own.

c. The sovereignty of God

It is mainly in chs. 9–11 that God's sovereignty comes into focus. Here Paul is discussing the destiny of Israel and its relationship to the destiny of the Gentiles. The theme at once raises the problem of the justice of God, and Paul sets out his view of God's choice. He illustrates his point by reference to both patriarchal and Mosaic times. To any who still dispute the sovereign choice of God through Israel's past history, he uses the illustration of the potter and the clay (9:19ff.) and shows that the power of God is always mixed with mercy. His sovereign purposes are seen not only in the inclusion of the Gentiles, but also in the promise of Israel's restoration. Throughout this discussion Paul is at pains to affirm the sovereignty of God even if it leads to problems. It is the conviction that God's ways must be right which leads the apostle to the majestic doxology in 11:33–36.

d. The grace of God

No account can be given of God's grace until full appreciation has been made of man's sin, and this is well illustrated in this Epistle. The first three chapters are designed to show man's failure to attain to God's righteousness. Not only does Paul give a startling inventory of Gentile sins (ch. 1) but he points out Israel's culpability in spite of their privileges. As his argument develops, Paul lays stress on the sinful nature of man under the terminology of flesh (*sarx*), by which he means moral rather than physical sinfulness. When speaking of Christ Paul is careful to differentiate his flesh, which was only in the likeness of sinful flesh, and man's flesh. It is clear that Christ had to become man to redeem man, for that is basic to Paul's doctrine of the two *Adams (5:12ff.). In his description of his own struggles with sin (ch. 7) Paul has an acute sense of the power of sin. It is almost a personal enemy which does its utmost to destroy the soul. It takes advantage of the flesh. It brings all the members into bondage to its principles, which Paul calls the law of sin (7:23). It reduces man to the utmost wretchedness, from which only God through Christ can deliver.

This leads to a consideration of the saving activity of God in Christ. There has been much discussion over the significance of the word *hilastērion* (propitiatory) in 3:25, and this is not the place to discuss its meaning. But it is important to remember that the most significant aspect of Paul's statement is that God took the initiative. This is in line with Paul's whole approach to the processes of redemption in this Epistle. The work of Christ on the cross is seen as an objective sacrifice provided by God on the basis of which sins may be remitted.

Paul deals in ch. 6 with the operation of God's grace and shows that the superabundance of that grace must never be regarded as an occasion to commit greater sin. This is impossible because of the believer's close union with Christ, a doctrine which has an important place in Paul's thought. The illustration of baptism is used to show the character of the transformation which has been effected. Sin no longer has dominion because we are now under grace (6:14). Nevertheless, grace has made us slaves of God, so that a new obligation has replaced the old (6:20f.).

e. The law of God

That the apostle had a high regard for the Jewish law is made clear by his statement that the commandment is holy, just and good (7:12). He also recognizes the useful function of the law in manifesting the character of sin (7:7). Yet he is convinced by bitter experience that the law is completely ineffective as a means of salvation, not because of any inherent deficiencies in the law, for man's better self delights in the law (7:22), but because of man's own deficiencies.

Yet as he considers the law of God, the apostle at once perceives that for the Christian this comprises more than the mere letter of the Mosaic law. It involves what he calls the law of the Spirit (8:2), and his doctrine of the Holy Spirit, especially in his work of sanctification (in ch. 8), ought not to be divorced from its close connection with the law of God. Under the new covenant the commandments were to be written on the heart, and this is effected only through the indwelling Spirit. He introduces a new way of looking at God's requirements, for these become the laws of a Father under an entirely new relationship.

The Spirit of God is set over against the flesh (8:4f.), gives life in place of death (8:11), bears witness to the Christian's sonship (8:14f.) and intercedes for them in accordance with God's will (8:26f.). Christian life is, therefore, not a matter of submission to a legal code, but a life controlled by the Spirit on the basis of a new law which involves such qualities as righteousness, peace, joy, hope and love (*cf.* 5:3f.; 12:11; 14:17; 15:13, 30).

BIBLIOGRAPHY. Commentaries by H. C. G. Moule, *EB*, 1893; J. Denney, *EGT*, 1900; W. Sanday and A. C. Headlam, *ICC*, 1902; C. H. Dodd, *MNT*, 1932; K. Barth, E.T. 1933; C. K. Barrett, *BNTC*, 1957; F. J. Leenhardt, 1957; J. Murray, *NIC*, 1960, 1965; O. Michel, *KEK*[12], 1963; D. Guthrie, *New Testament Introduction*, 1970, pp. 393ff.; M. Black, *NCB*, 1973; C. E. B. Cranfield, *ICC*, 2 vols., 1975; 1979; J. G. D. Dunn, *WBC*, 2 vols., 1988; F. F. Bruce, *TNTC*², 1985; J. A. Fitzmyer, *AB*, 1993; J. Stott, *BST*, 1994. See also T. W. Manson, *BJRL* 31, 1947–8, pp. 224ff. D.G.

ROME. Founded traditionally in 753 BC on its seven hills (the bluffs formed where the Latin plain falls away into the Tiber bed at the first easy crossing up from the mouth), Rome, as the excavations have shown, was in origin a meeting-place and a melting-pot, rather than the home of a pre-existing people. The process of accretion, stimulated at an early stage by the strategic requirements of the Etruscan states to the N and S, acquired its own momentum, and by a liberal policy of enfranchisement unique in antiquity Rome attracted to herself men and ideas from all over the Mediterranean, until nearly 1,000 years from her beginning she had incorporated every other civilized community from Britain to Arabia. Rome was cosmopolitan and all the world was Roman. Yet this very comprehensiveness destroyed the uniqueness of the city, and the strategic centrality that had dictated her growth was lost with the opening up of the Danube and the Rhine, leaving Rome in the Middle Ages little more than a provincial city of Italy.

In NT times Rome was in the full flush of her growth. Multi-storey tenement blocks housed a proletariat of over a million, drawn from every quarter. The aristocracy, becoming just as international through the domestic favours of the Caesars, lavished the profits of three continents on suburban villas and country estates. The Caesars themselves had furnished the heart of the city with an array of public buildings perhaps never equalled in any capital. The same concentration of wealth provided the overcrowded masses with generous economic subsidies and entertainment. It also attracted literary and artistic talent from foreign parts. As the seat of the senate and of the Caesarian administration Rome maintained diplomatic contact with every other state in the Mediterranean, and the traffic in foodstuffs and luxury goods fortified the links.

I. Rome in New Testament thought

The Acts of the Apostles has often been supposed to be an apostolic odyssey set between Jerusalem and Rome as the symbols of Jew and Gentile. The opposite pole to Jerusalem is, however, given as the 'end of the earth' (Acts 1:8), and, while the narrative certainly concludes at Rome, no great emphasis is laid on that. Attention is concentrated on the legal struggle between Paul and his Jewish opponents, and the journey to Rome serves as the resolution of this, culminating in Paul's denunciation of the Jews there and the unhindered preaching to the Gentiles. The theme of the book seems to be the release of the gospel from its Jewish matrix, and Rome provides a clear-cut terminal point in this process.

In Revelation, however, Rome acquires a positively sinister significance. 'The great city, which has dominion over the kings of the earth' (Rev. 17:18), seated upon seven mountains (v. 9), and upon 'the waters' which are 'peoples and multitudes and nations and tongues' (v. 15), is unmistakably the imperial capital. The seer, writing in Asia Minor, the greatest centre of luxury trade in antiquity, discloses the feelings of those who suffered through the consortium with Rome. He scorns the famous compromise with 'the kings of the earth' who 'were wanton with her' (Rev. 18:9), and catalogues the sumptuous traffic (vv. 12–13) of the 'merchants of the earth' who have 'grown rich with the wealth of her wantonness' (v. 3). He stigmatizes the artistic brilliance of the city (v. 22). How widespread such hatred was we do not know. In this case the reason is plain. Rome has already drunk the 'blood of the martyrs of Jesus' (Rev. 17:6).

II. The origin of Christianity at Rome

So far as the NT goes, it is not clear how the circle of Christians was established in Rome, nor even whether they constituted a church in the regular way. There is no unequivocal reference to any meeting or activity of the church as such, let alone to bishops or sacraments. The church of Rome simply fails to appear in our documents. Let it be said at once that this need not mean that it was not yet formed. It may merely be the case that it was not intimately connected with Paul, with whom most of our information is concerned.

Paul's first known link with Rome was when he met *Aquila and Priscilla at Corinth (Acts 18:2). They had left the city as a result of Claudius' expulsion of the Jews. Since it is not stated that they were already Christians, the question must be left open. Suetonius says (*Claudius*, 25) that the trouble in Rome was caused by a certain Chrestus. Since this could be a variant of Christus, it has often been argued that Christianity had already reached Rome. Suetonius, however, knew about Christianity, and, even if he did make a mistake, agitation over Christus could be caused by any Jewish Messianic movement, and not necessarily by Christianity alone. There is no hint in the Epistle to the Romans that there had been any conflict between Jews and Christians at Rome, and when Paul himself reached Rome the Jewish leaders professed personal ignorance of the sect (Acts 28:22). This not only makes it unlikely that there had been a clash, but sharpens the question of the nature of the Christian organization at Rome, since we know that by this stage there was a considerable community there.

Some few years after meeting Aquila and Priscilla, Paul decided that he 'must also see Rome' (Acts 19:21). When he wrote the Epistle shortly afterwards his plan was to visit his friends in the city on the way to Spain (Rom. 15:24). A considerable circle of these is named (ch. 16), they had been there 'many years' (Rom. 15:23), and were well known in Christian circles abroad (Rom. 1:8). Paul's reference to his not building 'on another man's foundation' (Rom. 15:20) does not necessarily refer to the situation in Rome; it need only mean that this was the reason why his work abroad had been so lengthy (Rom. 15:22–23); indeed, the authority he assumes in the Epistle leaves little room for an alternative leader. The most natural assumption, on the internal evidence, is that Paul is writing to a group of persons who have collected in Rome over the years after having had some contact with him in the various churches of his foundation. A number of them are described as his 'kinsmen', others have worked with him in the past. He introduces a new arrival to them (Rom. 16:1). Although some bear Roman names, we must assume that they are recently enfranchised foreigners, or at least that the majority of them are not Romans, since Paul's references to the government allude to its capital and taxation powers over non-Romans in particular (Rom. 13:4, 7). Although some are Jews, the group seems to have a life of its own apart from the Jewish community (ch. 12). The reference in at least five cases to household units (Rom. 16:5, 10–11, 14–15) suggests that this may have been the basis of their association.

When Paul finally reached Rome several years later, he had been met on the way by 'the brethren' (Acts 28:15). They do not appear again, however, either in connection with Paul's dealings with the Jewish authorities or, so far as the brief notice goes, during his 2 years' imprisonment. The seven letters that are supposed to belong to this period do sometimes contain greetings from 'the brethren', though they are mainly concerned with personal messages. The reference to rival preachers (Phil. 1:15) is the nearest we come to any positive NT evidence for a non-Pauline contribution to Roman Christianity. On the other hand, the assumption of a church organized independently of Paul might explain the amorphous character of Roman Christianity in his writings.

III. Was Peter ever in Rome?

In the late 2nd century AD the tradition appears

that Peter had worked in Rome and died there as a martyr, and in the 4th century the claim that he was first bishop of the Roman church appears. These traditions were never disputed in antiquity and are not inconsistent with NT evidence. On the other hand, nothing in the NT positively supports them. Most students assume that 'Babylon' (1 Pet. 5:13) is a cryptic designation for Rome, but, although there are parallels for this in apocalyptic literature, it is difficult to see what the need for secrecy was in a letter, nor who was likely to be deceived in this case when the meaning was supposed to be plain to so wide a circle of readers. The so-called *First Epistle of Clement*, written when the memory of the apostles was still preserved by living members of the church at Rome, refers to both Peter and Paul in terms which imply that they both died martyrs' deaths there. The tantalizing fact that this is not positively asserted may, of course, simply mean that it was taken for granted. From about a century later comes the information that there were 'trophies' of Peter on the Vatican hill and of Paul on the road to Ostia. On the assumption that these were tombs, the two churches bearing the apostolic names were erected over them at later times. The Vatican excavations have revealed a monument which could well be the 2nd-century 'trophy' of Peter. It is associated with a burial-ground that was used in the late 1st century.

We still lack any positive trace of Peter in Rome, however. The excavations strengthen the literary tradition, of course, and in default of further evidence we must allow the distinct possibility that Peter died in Rome. That he founded the church there and ruled it for any length of time has much feebler support in tradition, and faces the almost insuperable obstacle of the silence of Paul's Epistles.

The tradition of the martyrdom of the apostles is supplied with a lurid occasion by the massacre of AD 64 (*NERO). The account by Tacitus (*Annals* 15. 44) and the shorter notice by Suetonius (*Nero* 16) supply us with several surprising points about the Christian community at Rome. Its numbers are described as very large. Its connection with Jesus is clearly understood, and yet it is distinguished from Judaism. It is an object of popular fear and disgust for reasons which are not explained, apart from a reference to 'hatred of the human race'. Thus Nero's mad atrocities merely highlight the revulsion with which the Christians were received in the metropolis of the world.

BIBLIOGRAPHY. See under *ROMAN EMPIRE. G. Alfoldy, *The Social History of Rome*, 1988; J. P. V. D. Balsdon, *Life and Leisure in Ancient Rome*, 1974. E.A.J.

ROSH. 1. In the RV this word occurs in the title of Gog who is described as 'prince of Rosh' (Ezk. 38:2–3; 39:1). AV, RVmg. and RSV interpret as a title itself, 'chief', 'prince'. However, the name of a N people or country such as Meshech and Tubal is more probable. Gesenius suggested Russia, but this name is not attested in the area, and a very distant people named thus early is unlikely in the context. Most follow Delitzsch in identifying Rosh with Assyr. *Rašu* on the NW border of Elam (*i.e.* in Media).

2. The name of the seventh son of Benjamin (Gn. 46:21). LXX makes him son of Bela, grandson of Benjamin; but *cf.* lists in Nu. 26:38f.; 1 Ch. 8:1–5. D.J.W.

RUFUS ('red'). A name of Italic rather than Latin origin, found twice in the NT (Mk. 15:21; Rom. 16:13), probably referring to the same man. In Mk. 15:21 Simon of Cyrene is identified for the benefit of a later generation as the father of Alexander and Rufus, brothers who were presumably known in Rome when Mark's Gospel was published there. The Roman Rufus who is greeted by Paul (on the assumption that Rom. 16 was sent to Rome) can hardly have been a different man. Paul describes him as a choice Christian. His mother had shown herself a mother to Paul (perhaps in Antioch, if we may further identify Simon of Cyrene with Simeon of Acts 13:1). F.F.B.

RUHAMAH (Heb. *ruḥāmâ*, 'pitied'). A symbolic name of Israel (Ho. 2:1, AV; *cf.* Rom. 9:25–26; 1 Pet. 2:10) used to indicate the return of God's mercy. A play on words is involved, for the second child of Gomer, wife of *Hosea, was called Lo-ruhamah ('unpitied'), denoting a time when God had turned his back on Israel because of her apostasy. J.D.D.

RUMAH. Mentioned in 2 Ki. 23:36 only. Josephus, in a parallel account, calls it 'Abouma', and probably means 'Arumah', a place mentioned in Jdg. 9:41, in the vicinity of Shechem. But the name Rumah is quite possible; the name and site are probably preserved in Khirbet al-Rumah, some 35 km inland from Mt Carmel. D.F.P.

RUNNER. Urgent messages were sent in antiquity by a swift runner (Heb. *rāṣ*), often a member of the royal bodyguard or 'out-runners' (2 Sa. 15:1). So the late term 'runner' or royal messenger (Je. 51:31) was used for those who carried letters between cities (2 Ch. 30:6, 10), usually on fast horses (Est. 8:10, 14). Thus the term 'post' (AV) was synonymous with speed (Jb. 9:25). Throughout the Persian empire, as in earlier Babylonian times, regular posts were established between provincial capitals (G. R. Driver, *Aramaic Documents of the Fifth Century BC*, 1956, pp. 10–12). D.J.W.

RUTH (Heb. *rûṯ*, perhaps contracted from *r*e*'ûṯ*, 'female companion'). Ruth is the heroine of the book which bears her name (see next article). She was a Moabitess who lived in the time of the Judges.

In her own land Ruth had married Mahlon (Ru. 4:10), the elder son of Elimelech and Naomi, Israelites from Bethlehem judah who came to Moab during a famine. Naomi was widowed and then her two sons died without heirs. She determined to return to her native country, whereupon Ruth announced that she intended to accompany her, adopting both her nation and her God. Only by death would they be separated (Ru. 1:17).

During the barley harvest in Bethlehem Ruth went to glean in the fields of Boaz, a wealthy relative of Elimelech. Boaz noticed her and gave her his protection in acknowledgment of her loyalty to Naomi. She was invited to eat with the reapers, and was favoured throughout the barley harvest and the wheat harvest.

When all was harvested and the threshing had begun, acting on Naomi's instructions Ruth went to the threshing-floor at night and claimed Boaz's protection by appealing to his chivalry. He sent her back home as soon as it was light, with a present of six measures of barley, and the undertaking that, if her near kinsman was not prepared to marry her under the levirate marriage law, he would act as her kinsman-redeemer (*cf.* Lv. 25:25, 47–49).

With ten elders of the city as witnesses, he appealed to Naomi's kinsman to redeem a plot of land which had belonged to Elimelech, and which was a sacred trust that must not pass out of the family (*cf.* Lv. 25:23). To this he added the obligation of levirate marriage to Ruth (Ru. 4:5). The kinsman could not afford this and renounced his right in favour of Boaz.

Ruth was married to Boaz, and their first child Obed was given to Naomi to continue the names of Elimelech, Mahlon and Chilion. He was the grandfather of David (1 Ch. 2:12; Mt. 1:5).

M.B.

RUTH, BOOK OF. In the Heb. Bible Ruth is one of the five *Megilloth* or 'rolls', included in the 'Writings', the third division of the Canon. It is read annually by the Jews at the Feast of Weeks. In the LXX, Vulg., and most modern versions it comes immediately after Judges; Josephus (*Contra Apionem* 1. 8) apparently reckons it to be an appendix to Judges and does not count it separately in enumerating the total number of books in the Canon.

For the plot of the book, see *RUTH.

I. Outline of contents

a. Naomi, widowed and bereft of her sons, returns from Moab to her native Bethlehem with her Moabite daughter-in-law Ruth (1:1–22).

b. Ruth gleans in the field of Naomi's wealthy kinsman Boaz (2:1–23).

c. Ruth appeals to Boaz to perform the part of a kinsman-redeemer (3:1–18).

d. Ruth is married to Boaz and gives birth to Obed (4:1–17).

e. Genealogy from Perez to David (4:18–22).

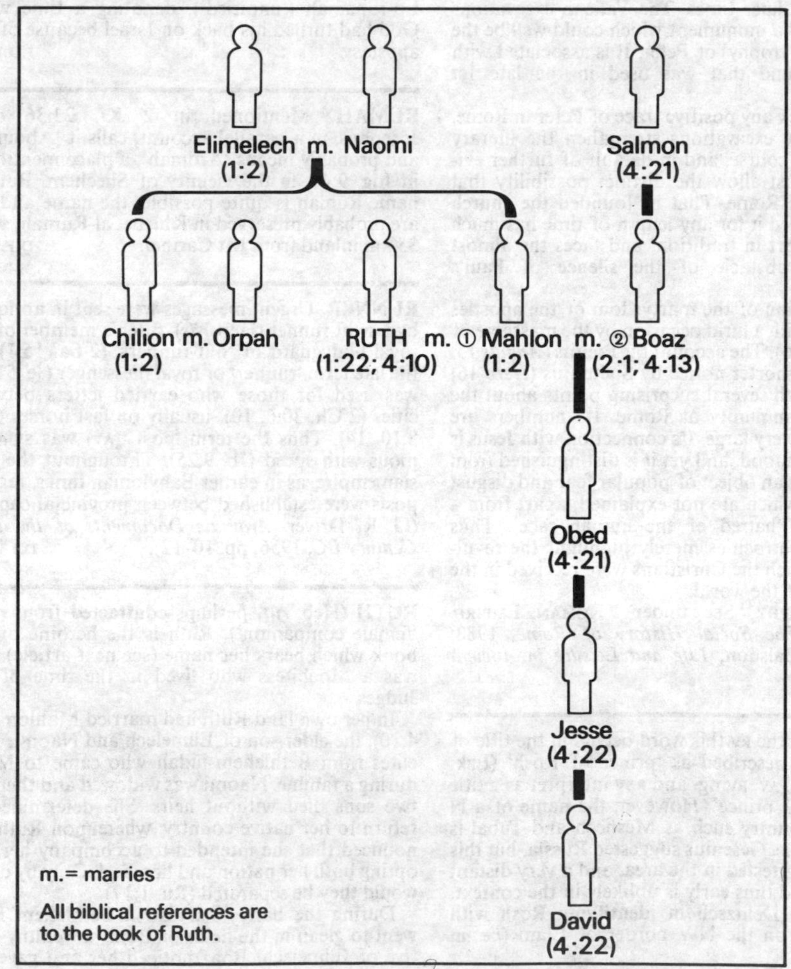

The family of Ruth.

II. Authorship, date and purpose

The book of Ruth is fraught with difficulties for the critic, because, like Job, it contains no clue to its authorship. Tradition alone ascribes this idyllic pastoral to the last of the Judges, the prophet-priest Samuel.

The setting is that of the period of the Judges (Ru. 1:1), but its writing belongs to a later date. This is indicated when the author explains former customs (Ru. 4:1–12). A very wide range of dating is offered for its actual composition, ranging from early pre-exilic times to a late post-exilic date.

The classical style and language do point to an early date, as does the attitude to foreign marriages, for under the Deuteronomic law a Moabite could not enter the congregation (Dt. 23:3). The late dating is based on the antiquarian interest displayed in the book, and on its supposed connection with the reforms of Ezra and Nehemiah. One school of thought sees evidence of both early and late work in the book, supposing that the genealogy of David (Ru. 4:18–22) and the explanations of early customs belong to a much later date than the book itself.

Many suggestions as to the purpose of the book have been put forward, among them the following. It was intended to supply a family tree for the greatest of the kings of Hebrew history, David, because this was omitted from the books of Samuel. It was a political pamphlet, an anti-separatist tract, written to counteract the stringency of Ezra and Nehemiah on the subject of mixed marriages. It was a humanitarian plea on behalf of the childless widow so that the next of kin would assume responsibility for her. It was designed to depict an overruling providence. It was to present a case for racial tolerance. Perhaps there was no ulterior motive at all, but it was a tale that had to be told. It certainly presents a most pleasing contrast with the narratives at the end of Judges, which belong to the same general period (Jdg. 17–21).

BIBLIOGRAPHY. H. H. Rowley, 'The Marriage of Ruth', *HTR* 40, 1947, pp. 77ff.; E. Robertson, 'The Plot of the Book of Ruth', *BJRL* 32, 1949–50, pp. 207ff.; A. E. Cundall and L. Morris, *Judges and Ruth*, *TOTC*, 1968; R. E. Murphy, *FOTL* 13, 1981; M. D. Gow, *The Book of Ruth*, 1992.

M.B.

S

SABBATH (Heb. *šabbāṯ*, from the root *šāḇaṯ*, 'to cease', 'to desist'). In the Bible the principle is laid down that one day in 7 is to be observed as a day holy to God. From the reason given for keeping the sabbath day in the Ten Commandments we learn that the example for the sabbath rest had been set by God himself in the creation. The sabbath therefore is a creation ordinance (Ex. 20:8–11).

In the account of creation the actual word 'sabbath' is not found, but the root from which the word is derived does occur (Gn. 2:2). The work of creation had occupied 6 days; on the 7th God rested (lit. 'ceased') from his labour. Thus there appears the distinction between the 6 days of labour and the one day of rest. This is true, even if the 6 days of labour be construed as periods of time longer than 24 hours. The language is anthropomorphic, for God is not a weary workman in need of rest. Nevertheless, the pattern is here set for man to follow. Ex. 20:11 states that God 'rested' (Heb. *wayyānaḥ*) on the 7th day, and Ex. 31:17 says that he ceased from his work and 'was refreshed' (*wayyinnāp̄aš*). The language is purposely strong so that man may learn the necessity of regarding the sabbath as a day on which he himself is to rest from his daily labours.

It has been held in contradistinction to what has been stated above that the institution of the sabbath derived from Babylonia. It is true that the Babylonian word *šabbatum* is related to the corresponding Hebrew word, but the force of the words is quite different. For one thing the Babylonians had a 5-day week. Examination of contract tablets reveals that the days designated *šabbatum* were not days of cessation from labour. Contracts from Mari (Tel el-Harîrî) show that work was performed, sometimes over a period of several days, without any interruption every 7th day. The Bible clearly attributes the origin of the sabbath to the divine example.

The fourth commandment enjoins observance of the sabbath. In Genesis there is no mention of the sabbath apart from the creation account. There is, however, mention of periods of 7 days (*cf.* Gn. 7:4, 10; 8:10, 12; 29:27ff.). We may also note in the narrative in Job that the seven sons celebrated a feast each on his day, and this was followed by the prayers and sacrifices of Job for the benefit of his children (Jb. 1:4–5). This was not a single round, but was regularly practised. It may be that here is an intimation of worship on the 1st day of the cycle. At least the principle that one day in 7 is holy to the Lord appears to be recognized here.

In Ex. 16:21–30 explicit mention is made of the sabbath in connection with the giving of manna. The sabbath is here represented as a gift of God (v. 29), to be for the rest and benefit of the people (v. 30). It was not necessary to work on the sabbath (*i.e.* to gather manna), for a double portion had been provided on the 6th day.

The sabbath was therefore known to Israel, and the injunction to remember it was one that would be understood. In the Decalogue it is made clear that the sabbath belongs to the Lord. It is therefore primarily his day, and the basic reason for observing it is that it is a day which belongs to him. It is a day that he has blessed and that he has set apart for observance. This is not contradicted by the Decalogue given in Dt. 5:12ff. In this latter passage the people are commanded to keep the sabbath in the manner in which the Lord has already commanded them (the reference is to Ex. 20:8–11), and the fact that the sabbath belongs to the Lord is again stated (v. 14). An additional reason, however, is given for the observance of the command. This reason is merely additional; it does not conflict with those already given. Israel is commanded to observe the sabbath day, in order 'that your manservant and your maidservant may rest as well as you'. Here is a humanitarian emphasis; but here also is emphasis upon the fact that the sabbath was made for man. Israel had been a slave in Egypt and had been delivered; so Israel must show the mercy of the sabbath towards those in her own midst who were slaves.

Throughout the remainder of the Pentateuch the sabbath legislation is found. It is interesting to note that there is a reference to the sabbath in each of the four last books of the Pentateuch. Genesis presents the divine rest; the remaining books emphasize the sabbatical legislation. This shows the importance of the institution. Sabbath legislation, it may be said, is integral and essential to the basic law of the OT and the Pentateuch (*cf.* Ex. 31:13–16; 34:21; 35:2ff.; Lv. 19:3, 30; 23:3, 38).

In this connection the significance of the sabbatical legislation appears in the severe punishment that is meted out upon a sabbath-breaker. A man had been gathering sticks upon the sabbath day. For this act a special revelation from God decreed that he should be put to death (*cf. J. Weingreen, From Bible to Mishna*, 1976, pp. 83ff.) This man had denied the basic principle of the sabbath, namely, that the day belonged to the Lord, and therefore was to be observed only as the Lord had commanded (*cf.* Nu. 15:32–36).

Upon the Pentateuchal legislation the prophets build; their utterances are in accordance with what had been revealed in the Pentateuch. The 'sabbaths' are often linked together with the 'new moons' (2 Ki. 4:23; Am. 8:5; Ho. 2:11; Is. 1:13; Ezk. 46:3). When prophets like Hosea (2:11) pronounced divine judgment on new moons, sabbaths and other appointed feasts, they were not condemning the sabbath as such; they were condemning a misuse of the sabbath and of the other Mosaic institutions.

On the other hand, the prophets do point out the blessings that will follow from a proper observance of the sabbath. There were those who polluted the sabbath and did evil on that day (Is. 56:2–4), and it was necessary to turn from such things. In a classic passage (Is. 58:13) Isaiah sets forth the blessings that will come from a true observance of the day. It is not a day in which man is to do what pleases him, but rather one on which he is to do the will of God. God, not man, must determine how the sabbath is to be observed. Recognizing that the day is holy to the Lord will bring the true enjoyment of the promises.

During the Persian period emphasis was again laid upon observance of the sabbath day. The preexilic ban on engaging in commercial transactions on the sabbath (Am. 8:5) or carrying burdens on that day (Je. 17:21f.) was reinforced by Nehemiah (Ne. 10:31; 13:15–22). During the period between the Testaments, however, a change gradually crept in with respect to the understanding of the purpose of the sabbath. In the synagogues the law was studied on the sabbath. Gradually oral tradition made its growth among the Jews, and attention was paid to the minutiae of observance. Two tractates of the Mishnah, *Shabbath* and *'Erubin*, are devoted to a consideration of how the sabbath was to be observed in detail. It was against this burdening of the commands of God with human tradition that our Lord inveighed. His remarks were not directed against the institution of the sabbath as such and not against the OT teaching. But he did oppose the Pharisees who had made the Word of God of none effect with their tradition. Christ identified himself as the Lord of the sabbath (Mk. 2:28). In so speaking, he was not depreciating the importance and significance of the sabbath nor in any way contravening the OT legislation. He was simply pointing out the true significance of the sabbath with respect to man and indicating his right to speak, inasmuch as he himself was the Lord of the sabbath.

As Lord of the sabbath, Jesus went to the synagogue on the sabbath day, as was his custom (Lk. 4:16). His observance of the sabbath was in accord with the OT prescription to regard the day as holy to the Lord.

In his disagreement with the Pharisees (Mt. 12:1–14; Mk. 2:23–28; Lk. 6:1–11) our Lord pointed out to the Jews their complete misunderstanding of the OT commands. They had sought to make the observance of the sabbath more rigorous than God had commanded. It was not wrong to eat on the sabbath, even if the food must be obtained by plucking corn from the ears. Nor was it wrong to do good on the sabbath day. To heal was a work of mercy, and the Lord of the sabbath is merciful (*cf.* also Jn. 5:1–18; Lk. 13:10–17; 14:1–6).

On the first day of the week the Lord rose from the dead, and therefore it early and increasingly became the day above all others—'the *Lord's day' (Rev. 1:10)—on which Christians met for worship (*cf.* Acts 20:7; also *Didache* 14. 1; Justin, *First Apology* 67. 3).

Bibliography. W. Rordorff, *Sunday*, 1968; F. N. Lee, *The Covenantal Sabbath*, 1972; A. Lamaire, *RB* 80, 1973, pp. 161–185; R. T. Beckwith and W. Stott, *This is the Day*, 1978; W. Stott, *NIDNTT* 3, pp. 405–415; D. A. Carson (ed.), *From Sabbath to Lord's Day*, 1982; S. Bacchiocchi, *The Sabbath in the New Testament*, 1985; G. Robinson, *The Origin and Development of the Old Testament Sabbath*, 1988; E. Fisher (ed.), *The Jewish Roots of Christian Liturgy*, Part 3, 1990, pp. 119–157.

E.J.Y.
F.F.B.

SABBATICAL YEAR. This term refers to the provision made concerning the land. Lv. 25:2 has *w^ešāḇ^eṯâh ā'āreṣ šabbāṯ*, 'the land shall keep a sabbath'. It is also called 'sabbath of solemn rest' and 'year of solemn rest' (Lv. 25:4–5). After 6 years of sowing, pruning and gathering, the land lay fallow for one year. The unattended growth of the field was for the poor to glean and what remained was for the beasts (Ex. 23:11; Dt. 15:2–18). To quiet fears of privation the Israelites were assured by the Lord that the 6th year would provide enough for 3 years (Lv. 25:20f.). From the time of its institution this year of rest was observed in Israel (Ne. 10:31; 1 Macc. 6:49, 53; *cf.* Jos., *Ant.* 12. 378; 14. 206). Lv. 26:34–43; 2 Ch. 36:21; Je. 34:14–22 refer to God's anger concerning the violation of this ordinance.

The culmination of the sabbatical years was reached each 50th year. This was a jubilee (Heb. *yôḇēl*, 'ram', thence 'trumpet' (ram's horn) by which the year was heralded). The sanctions of the sabbatical year were enforced. In addition, property reverted to its original owners, debts were remitted, and Hebrews who had been enslaved for debt were released. It was a time of thanksgiving and an occasion for the exercise of faith that God would provide food (Lv. 25:8, *etc.*).

The significance of rest for the land every 7th year does not lie merely in principles of soil chemistry. Neither does it follow the Canaanite pattern of a 7-year cycle without a harvest followed by 7 years of plenty. In the text the land lies fallow for one year. (See C. H. Gordon, *Ugaritic Literature*, 1949, pp. 5f.) The underlying reason for this arrangement lies in the disclosure that the 7th year of rest is a sabbath of rest both for the land and for the Lord (Lv. 25:2, 4). There is evident here a relation to the *sabbath institution which is grounded in God's creative activity. In accord with this disclosure other elements may be observed, namely, that man is not the sole owner of the soil and he does not hold property in perpetuity but possesses it in trust under God (Lv. 25:23). The Israelite was also to remember he possessed nothing by inherent right, for he was a slave in Egypt (Dt. 15:15). Generosity is motivated by gratitude. D.F.

SABTA, SABTAH. The third son of Cush (Gn. 10:7, *saḇtâ*; 1 Ch. 1:9, *saḇtā'*) whose name also applied to his descendants. From the fact that among the other descendants of *Cush there are names later associated with S Arabia, it is probable that Sabta refers to a tribe in this area.

Bibliography. J. A. Montgomery, *Arabia and the Bible*, 1934, p. 42. T.C.M.

SABTECA. The fifth son of Cush (Gn. 10:7 = 1 Ch. 1:9) whose name also referred to his descendants. The other descendants of Cush include names later associated with S Arabian tribes, indicating that the descendants of Sabteca probably later lived in this area. The name is otherwise unknown. T.C.M.

SACKCLOTH. A coarse cloth (Heb. *śaq*, Gk. *sakkos*, from which the Eng. word is derived), usually made of goats' hair (*Siphra* 53b) and black in colour (Rev. 6:12). The same Heb. word sometimes means 'sack' (*e.g.* Gn. 42:27), which was evidently made of this material.

Sackcloth was worn as a sign of mourning for the dead (Gn. 37:34; 2 Sa. 3:31; Joel 1:8; Judith 8:5), or of mourning for personal or national disaster (Jb. 16:15; La. 2:10; Est. 4:1; 1 Macc. 2:14), or of penitence for sins (1 Ki. 21:27; Ne. 9:1; Jon. 3:5; Mt. 11:21), or of special prayer for deliverance (2 Ki. 19:1–2; Dn. 9:3; Judith 4:10; Baruch 4:20; 1 Macc. 3:47).

The form of the symbolic sackcloth was often a band or kilt tied around the waist (1 Ki. 20:31–32; Is. 3:24; 20:2; 2 Macc. 10:25). It was usually worn next to the skin (2 Ki. 6:30; Jb. 16:15; 2 Macc. 3:19), and was sometimes kept on all night (1 Ki. 21:27; Joel 1:13). In one case it replaces a robe, presumably over other clothes (Jon. 3:6). Sometimes the sackcloth was spread out to lie on (2 Sa. 21:10; Is. 58:5), or spread out before the altar or on the altar (Judith 4:11).

Palestinian shepherds wore sackcloth because it was cheap and durable (TB, *Shabbath* 64a). Prophets sometimes wore it as a symbol of the repentance which they preached (Is. 20:2; Rev. 11:3). According to Jon. 3:8 and Judith 4:10 even animals were clothed in sackcloth as a sign of national supplication. Wearing sackcloth for mourning and penitence was practised not only in Israel but also in Damascus (1 Ki. 20:31), Moab (Is. 15:3), Ammon (Je. 49:3), Tyre (Ezk. 27:31) and Nineveh (Jon. 3:5).

Clothing with sackcloth is used figuratively of the darkening of the heavenly bodies in Is. 50:3.

BIBLIOGRAPHY. G. Dalman, *Arbeit und Sitte*, 5, 1939, pp. 18, 165, 176, 202; H. F. Lutz, *Textiles and Costumes among the Peoples of the Ancient Near East*, 1923, pp. 25–26, 176–177; P. Heinisch, 'Die Trauergebräuche bei den Israeliten', *Biblische Zeitfragen* 13, 1931, 7–8, pp. 16–17. J.T.

SACRAMENTS. The word 'sacrament' (Lat. *sacramentum*) in its technical theological sense, when used to describe certain rites of the Christian faith, belongs to the period of the elaboration of doctrine much later than the NT. The Vulgate in some places thus renders Gk. *mystērion* (Eph. 5:32; Col. 1:27; 1 Tim. 3:16; Rev. 1:20; 17:7), which was, however, more commonly rendered *mysterium* (*MYSTERY). In early ecclesiastical usage *sacramentum* was used in a wide sense of any ritual observance or sacred thing.

In everyday usage the word had been applied in two ways: (1) as a pledge or security deposited in public keeping by the parties in a lawsuit and forfeited to a sacred purpose; (2) as the oath taken by a Roman soldier to the emperor, and thence to any oath. These ideas later combined to produce the concept of a sacred rite which was a pledge or token, the receipt of which involved an oath of loyalty, and this led in time to the limitation of the word 'sacrament' to the two major rites of divine institution, Baptism and the Lord's Supper. The wider use continued for many centuries. Hugo of St Victor (12th century) can speak of as many as thirty sacraments, but Peter Lombard in the same period estimated seven as the number. The latter estimation is officially accepted by the Roman Church.

The common definition of a sacrament accepted by the Reformed and Roman Churches is that of an outward and visible sign, ordained by Christ, setting forth and pledging an inward and spiritual blessing. The definition owes much to the teaching and language of Augustine, who wrote of the visible form which bore some likeness to the thing invisible. When to this 'element', or visible form, the word of Christ's institution was added, a sacrament was made, so that the sacrament could be spoken of as 'the visible word' (see Augustine, *Tracts on the Gospel of John* 80; *Epistles* 98; *Contra Faustum* 19. 16; *Sermons* 272).

Does the NT teach the obligation of sacramental rites on all Christians? What spiritual benefit is there in their reception, and how is it conveyed?

The obligation to continue sacramental rites depends on: (1) their institution by Christ; (2) his express command for their continuance; (3) their essential use as symbols of divine acts integral to the gospel revelation. There are only two rites obligatory in these ways on all Christians. There is no scriptural warrant for giving the other so-called sacramental rites (*i.e.* Confirmation, Orders, Matrimony, Penance, Extreme Unction) the same status as *Baptism and the *Lord's Supper, which from the beginning are together associated with the proclamation of the gospel and the life of the church (Acts 2:41–42; *cf.* 1 Cor. 10:1–4). They are linked with circumcision and the Passover, the obligatory rites of the OT (Col. 2:11; 1 Cor. 5:7; 11:26). The Christian life is associated in its beginning and in its continuance with sacramental observance (Acts 2:38; 1 Cor. 11:26). Some of the deepest lessons of holiness and perfection are implicit in what Scripture says regarding the Christian's sacramental obligations (Rom. 6:1–3; 1 Cor. 12:13; Eph. 4:5). References to the sacraments may underlie many passages where there is no explicit mention of them (*e.g.* Jn. 3; 6; 19:34; Heb. 10:22). The risen Lord's great commission to the disciples to go to all nations with the gospel specifically commands the administration of Baptism and clearly implies observance of the Lord's Supper (Mt. 28:19–20). Christ promises to be with his servants until the end of time. The work to which he has called them, including the observance of the sacraments, will not be completed before then. Paul also has no doubt that the Lord's Supper is to be continued, as a showing forth of the death of Christ, till he comes again (1 Cor. 11:26). It is true that Matthew and Mark do not record the command 'this do in remembrance of me', but the evidence of the practice of the early church (Acts 2:42; 20:7; 1 Cor. 10:16; 11:26) more than compensates for this.

The efficacy of the sacraments depends on the institution and command of Christ. The elements in themselves have no power; it is their faithful use that matters. For through them men are brought into communion with Christ in his death and resurrection (Rom. 6:3; 1 Cor. 10:16). Forgiveness (Acts 2:38), cleansing (Acts 22:16; *cf.* Eph. 5:26) and spiritual quickening (Col. 2:12) are associated with baptism. Participation in the body and blood of Christ is realized through Holy Communion (1 Cor. 10:16; 11:27). Baptism and the cup are linked together in the teaching of our Lord when he speaks of his death, and in the mind of the church when it remembers its solemn obligations (Mk. 10:38–39; 1 Cor. 10:1–5).

The sacraments are covenant rites: 'This cup is the new covenant' (Lk. 22:20; 1 Cor. 11:25). We are baptized 'into the name' (Mt. 28:19, RV). The new covenant was initiated by the sacrifice of the death of Christ (*cf.* Ex. 24:8; Je. 31:31–32). Its blessings are conveyed by God through his word and promise in the gospel and its sacraments. There is clear evidence that many in apostolic days received blessing through the administration of the sacraments accompanied by the preaching of the word (Acts 2:38ff.). It was the gospel word or promise accompanying administration which gave meaning and efficacy to the rite. Those who had received only John's baptism were baptized again 'in the name of the Lord Jesus' (Acts 19:1–7). It is apparent also that some received the sacraments without spiritual benefit (Acts 8:12, 21; 1 Cor. 11:27; 10:5–12). In the case of Cornelius and his household (Acts 10:44–48) we have an example of some who received the gifts which baptism seals, before they received the sacrament. Nevertheless, they still received the sacrament as bestowing benefit and as an obligation.

In the NT there is no conflict suggested between the use of sacraments and spirituality. When they are rightly received the sacraments do convey blessings to the believer. But these blessings are not confined to the use of the sacraments, nor when they are conveyed through the sacraments does their bestowal conflict in any way with the strong, scriptural emphasis on faith and godliness. The sacraments, when administered in accordance with the principles laid down in Scripture, recall us continually to the great ground of our salvation, Christ in his death and resurrection, and remind us of the obligations we have to walk worthily of the calling wherewith we are called.

BIBLIOGRAPHY. J. Jeremias, *The Eucharistic Words of Jesus*, 1955; W. F. Flemington, *The New Testament Doctrine of Baptism*, 1957; A. M. Stibbs, *Sacrament, Sacrifice and Eucharist*, 1961; G. R. Beasley-Murray, *Baptism in the New Testament*, 1962; J. I. Packer (ed.), *Eucharistic Sacrifice*, 1962; D. Cairns, *In Remembrance of Me*, 1967; C. K. Barrett, *Church, Ministry and Sacraments in the New Testament*, 1985. R.J.C.

SACRIFICE AND OFFERING.

I. In the Old Testament

a. Terms

The OT has no general word for 'sacrifice', except the rather sparsely used *qorbān*, 'that which is brought near' (*qrb*), which is practically confined to the levitical literature. (AV renders this term 'Corban' in the single NT reference of Mk. 7:11.) *'iššêh* may also serve this purpose in the laws, but it is debated whether it should not be limited to 'fire-offerings' (*'ēš*) (but *cf.* Lv. 24:9). The other frequently used words describe particular kinds of sacrifice, and are derived either from the mode of sacrifice, as *zebah* (sacrifice), 'that which is slain' (*zāḇaḥ*), and *'ôlâ* (burnt-offering), 'that which goes up', or from its purpose, as *'āšām* (guilt-offering), 'for guilt' (*'āšām*), and *ḥaṭṭā'ṯ* (sin-offering), 'for sin' (*ḥaṭṭā'ṯ*). These may be distinguished in part by the disposal of the victim, whether wholly burnt (*'ôlâ*, Lv. 1), or eaten by priests and worshippers together (*zeḇaḥ*, Lv. 3), or eaten by the priests alone (*ḥaṭṭā'ṯ* and *'āšām*, Lv. 4–5). For the distinction of *'ôlâ* and *zeḇaḥ*, see Dt. 12:27 (*cf.* Je. 7:21, where the prophet ironically suggests an obliteration of the distinction).

Also included under *qorbān* were the non-blood offerings 'offering, oblation', the cereal-offering (*minḥâ*, Lv. 2), the firstfruits (*rē'šîṯ*, *bikkûrîm*), the sheaf of 16 Nisan, the dough of the Feast of Weeks, and the tithes.

b. Theories of the beginnings

Sacrifice was not confined to Israel among the nations of antiquity (*cf.* Jdg. 16:23; 1 Sa. 6:4; 2 Ki. 3:27; 5:17), and many parallels from surrounding nations have been adduced in explanation of Israelite sacrifice. W. R. Smith ('Sacrifice', *EBr*[9], 21, 1886, pp. 132–138; *The Religion of the Semites*, 1889) constructed, from the pre-Islamic nomadic Arabs, a hypothetical 'Semite', to whom the sacrificial meal was the earliest form, and the communion of the worshippers and the deity the controlling idea. The Pan-Babylonian movement (H. Winckler, A. Jeremias, from *c.* 1900 onwards) looked to the higher civilization of Mesopotamia, and to the developed ritual of propitiatory sacrifice practised there.

R. Dussaud preferred a Canaanite background, and found parallels first in the Carthaginian sacrificial tariffs (*Le sacrifice en Israel et chez les Phéniciens*, 1914; *Les origines cananéennes du sacrifice israélite*, 1921), and later in the Ras Shamra texts (*Les découvertes de Ras Shamra et l'Ancien Testament*, 1937). Here the materials of ancient Ugarit (*c.* 1400 BC) indicated a developed ritual of sacrifices bearing names similar to those of the OT. The *šrp* was a burnt-offering, the *dbḥ*, a slain-offering for a meal, the *šlm*, possibly a propitiatory sacrifice, and the *'aṯm*, the equivalent of the Heb. *'āšām*. (These were not Dussaud's identifications.) The myth and ritual school (S. H. Hooke, *The Origins of Early Semitic Ritual*, 1938; I. Engnell, *Studies in Divine Kingship in the Ancient Near East*, 1943) stressed this sedentary background and laid weight on the substitutionary role of the suffering king in the cult.

This was not convincing to A. Alt, who had earlier claimed (*Der Gott der Väter*, 1929, now in *Essays on OT History and Religion*, 1966, pp. 1–77) that the real antecedents of Israelite faith were to be sought rather among the nomad Patriarchs, who had practised a form of religion centring in the god of the head of the clan (the 'God of Abraham', the 'God of Isaac', the 'God of Jacob'). V. Maag ('Der Hirte Israels', *Schweizerische Theologische Umschau* 28, 1958, pp. 2–28) took this further by noticing the dominance of the shepherd metaphor in the descriptions of this God, and from a background of the migrant shepherd cultures of the Asiatic steppes, suggested that their sacrifice was the fellowship meal in which the god took over the responsibility of the shed blood, which would otherwise have exacted vengeance (*cf.* A. E. Jensen, 'Über das Töten als kulturgeschichtliche Erscheinung', *Paideuma* 4, 1950, pp. 23–38; H. Baumann, 'Nyama, die Rachemacht', *ibid.*, pp. 191–230). Israelite religion, as it appears in the OT, is a syncretism in which the nomadic *zeḇaḥ* sacrifice exists alongside of gift sacrifices of the *'ôlâ* type, which come in from the sedentary Canaanite side (V. Maag, *VT* 6, 1956, pp. 10–18).

Such a view finds place for both the sedentary and nomadic aspects, but becomes subjective when applied to particular OT narratives. The OT depicts early Israel less as nomadic than as a people in process of sedentarization. The Patriarchs already have the larger bovines and engage in some

Animals to be offered	Bullocks	Rams	Lambs	Goats
OCCASIONS FOR OFFERINGS				
Daily (morning & evening)			2	
Additional offerings on the Sabbath			2	
New Moons	2	1	7	1
ANNUAL FESTIVALS				
Unleavened Bread (daily offering)	2	1	7	1
Total for 7 days	14	7	49	7
Weeks (Firstfruits)	2	1	7	1
1st day of 7th month	1	1	7	1
Day of Atonement	1	1	7	1
Tabernacles Day 1	13	2	14	1
Day 2	12	2	14	1
Day 3	11	2	14	1
Day 4	10	2	14	1
Day 5	9	2	14	1
Day 6	8	2	14	1
Day 7	7	2	14	1
Day 8	1	1	7	1
Total for 8 days	71	15	105	8

Numbers of animals to be offered at the public sacrifices, daily, weekly and at festivals.
The two lambs on the Sabbath are additional to the usual daily 2.
The total for seven days refers to the seven days of the Festival of Unleavened Bread (*i.e.* 2 bullocks per day for 7 days = 14).
Similarly, the total for eight days refers to the eight days of the Feast of Tabernacles (*i.e.* 1 goat per day for 8 days = 8 goats).

Chart of the occasions laid down for public sacrifice and offerings (Nu. 28–29).

agriculture, and it may well be that a closer parallel to Hebrew sacrifice may be found among a tribe such as the African Nuer, whose sacrifice, as described by E. Evans-Pritchard (*Nuer Religion*, 1956) involved the offering of an ox in substitution for sin. The Wellhausen school, which traced an evolution from a joyous sacrificial meal in the earlier time to sin-offerings and guilt-offerings only in the post-exilic period (J. Wellhausen, *Prolegomena to the History of Israel*, 1885; W. R. Smith, *op. cit.*), regarded the connection of sacrifice with sin as the latest element. But this is no longer probable (*cf.* the writer's *Penitence and Sacrifice in Early Israel*, 1963), as the following historical sketch will show.

c. The development in the history

1. *Patriarchal.* It is significant that the first sacrifices mentioned in Gn. were not *zᵉḇāḥîm* meals, but the gift-offerings of Cain and Abel (*minḥâ*, Gn. 4:3–4), and the burnt-offering of Noah (*'ôlâ*, Gn. 8:20; we have here the first reference to an altar). Patriarchal altars are often described (*e.g.* Gn. 12:6–8), but unfortunately details as to the type of sacrifice are lacking. Maag thinks of the *zeḇaḥ* communion meal, but T. C. Vriezen (*An Outline of Old Testament Theology*, 1958, p. 26) thinks the *'ôlâ* more typical. Gn. 22 gives some support to the latter position. Isaac knows that Abraham is in the

habit of offering *'ôlâ* and that a lamb is the likely victim (v. 7). Sacrificial meals do, however, seal covenants (Gn. 31:54, first use of *zeḇaḥ*), but not all covenants are of this type. Gn. 15:9–11 is best understood as a purificatory ritual like that of the Hittite text translated by O. Masson (*RHR* 137, 1950, pp. 5–25; *cf.* O. R. Gurney, *The Hittites*, 1952, p. 151).

As to the motives of sacrifice in this period, honouring of God and thanksgiving for his goodness were prominent, but more solemn thoughts cannot be ruled out. Noah's offering is to be seen, not simply as a thank-offering for deliverance, but as an expiation or atonement. When Jacob goes to Egypt (Gn. 46:1), he pauses to seek God's will, and offers sacrifices (*zeḇaḥ*), which were possibly expiatory (*cf.* I. Rost, *VTSupp* 7, 1960, p. 354; *ZDPV* 66, 1943, pp. 205–216). In Egypt Israel is called to a solemn sacrifice in the wilderness (Ex. 5:3, *zeḇaḥ*), which required animal victims (Ex. 10:25–26) and was distinguished from any offered by the Egyptians (Ex. 8:26).

2. *Tribal.* The establishment of Israel as a tribal organization, which Noth thinks of as coming into being only on the soil of Palestine in the time of the Judges (*cf. The History of Israel*, 1958), is taken back by strong biblical tradition to the time of Moses. Chief among tribal occasions were the three festivals, at which sacrifice was to be offered: 'none shall appear before me empty-handed' (Ex. 23:15). The sacrifices we know best were those of the *Passover and the *covenant. The Passover combined the elements of sacrifice as an apotropaic and sacrifice as a communion meal. Secure in the knowledge that the blood had been shed to ward off evil, the members of each family could sit down to joyful fellowship (Ex. 12; Jos. 5:5–12). Similar elements probably entered into the covenant sacrifice and its renewals (Ex. 24:1–8; Dt. 27:1ff.; Jos. 8:30ff.; 24; *cf.* Ps. 50:5). The blood-sprinkling purified the covenant and the eating of the meal marked its consummation.

In addition, many other sacrifices both national and local were offered. Typical of national sacrifices were those in times of disaster or war (Jdg. 20:26; 21:4; 1 Sa. 7:9), when penitence seems to have been the main note (*cf.* Jdg. 2:1–5). Dedications and new beginnings were marked by sacrifice (Jdg. 6:28; Ex. 32:6; 1 Sa. 6:14; 11:15; 2 Sa. 6:17), as were individual occasions of celebration (1 Sa. 1:3), intercession (Nu. 23:1ff.), and perhaps hospitality (Ex. 18:12).

3. *Monarchic.* The building of the Temple by Solomon provided opportunity for initiatory (1 Ki. 8:62ff.) and regular sacrifices (1 Ki. 9:25), but as the sources are books of 'kings' they speak rather of royal participation (*cf.* 2 Ki. 16:10ff.) than of that of the people. That the everyday cult was in progress, however, is attested by such a verse as 2 Ki. 12:16, and by the frequent mention of sacrifice in the prophets and psalms. The many favourable references in the latter show that the condemnations of the former are not to be taken in an absolute sense, as if prophet and priest were opposed. The prophets object less to the cult itself than to the magic-working ideas borrowed from the fertility cults (Am. 4:4–5; Is. 1:11–16), and to such innovations as idolatry and child sacrifice introduced by apostatizing rulers (Je. 19:4; Ezk. 16:21).

An Isaiah can receive his call in the Temple (Is. 6), and a Jeremiah or an Ezekiel can find a place for a purified cult in the future (Je. 17:26; Ezk. 40–48). This is also the predominant feeling of the psalmists, who constantly speak of their sacrifices of thanksgiving in payment of their vows (*e.g.* Ps. 66:13–15). Expressions of penitence and the joy of forgiveness are also present (Pss. 32; 51) and, although sacrifice is not often mentioned in these contexts, it is probably to be assumed from the fact that forgiveness is experienced in the Temple (Ps. 65:1–5). While there is no need to make all such references post-exilic, the prophets' complaint that penitence did not often enough accompany sacrifice in the late kingdom period should also be borne in mind.

4. *Post-exilic.* The disaster of the Exile is usually seen as resulting in a deeper sense of sin, and no doubt this is true (*cf.* 2 Ki. 17:7ff.; Ne. 9), but not in the sense of Wellhausen that only then could the expiatory note of Lv. 1–7 and Lv. 16 have entered Israelite religion. References to sacrifice in the non-levitical writings before and after the Exile, although usually too fragmentary to decide the issue, give little support to such an evolution. Joy, as well as penitence, continues to characterize sacrifice (Ezr. 6:16–18; Ne. 8:9ff.). Temple and cult are valued (Hg. 1–2; Joel 2:14, and especially Chronicles), but only as they are the vehicles of sincere worship (Mal. 1:6ff.; 3:3ff.). Apocalyptic and Wisdom literature take the cult for granted (Dn. 9:21, 27; Ec. 5:4; 9:2) and also continue the prophetic moral emphasis (Ec. 5:1; Pr. 15:8).

d. The regulations of the laws

Laws for sacrifice are scattered through all the codes (Ex. 20:24ff.; 34:25ff.; Lv. 17; 19:5ff.; Nu. 15; Dt. 12, *etc.*), but the sacrificial 'torah' *par excellence* is Lv. 1–7. Chs. 1–5 deal in turn with the burnt-offering (*'ôlâ*), cereal-offering (*minḥâ*), peace-offering (*zeḇaḥ*), sin-offering (*ḥaṭṭā'ṯ*) and guilt-offering (*'āšām*), while chs. 6–7 give additional regulations for all five—6:8–13 (burnt); 6:14–18 (cereal); 6:24–30 (sin); 7:1–10 (guilt); 7:11ff. (peace). From these and other references the following synthetic account is compiled.

1. *The materials.* The sacrificial victim had to be taken from the clean animals and birds (Gn. 8:20), and could be bullock, goat, sheep, dove or pigeon (*cf.* Gn. 15:9), but not camel or ass (Ex. 13:13) (*Clean and Unclean). These provisions are not to be traced to the idea of sacrifice as 'food for the gods' (*viz.* that the gods ate what man ate)—as might be suggested by Lv. 3:11; 21:6; Ezk. 44:7—for fish (Lv. 11:9) and wild animals (Dt. 12:22) could be eaten but not sacrificed. The principle seems rather to have been that of property (*cf.* 2 Sa. 24:24), the wild animals being regarded as in some sense already God's (Ps. 50:9ff.; *cf.* Is. 40:16), while the domestic animals had become man's by his labours (Gn. 22:13 is only apparently an exception), and were in a kind of 'biotic rapport' with him. This was even more clearly the case with the non-blood offerings, which had been produced by 'the sweat of his brow' (cereals, flour, oil, wine, *etc.*), and were also staple articles of the kitchen. Property unlawfully acquired was not acceptable (Dt. 23:18).

The principle of 'the best for God' was observed throughout—as to sex, males being preferred to females (Lv. 1:3; but *cf.* Lv. 3:1; Gn. 15:9; 1 Sa. 6:14; 16:2); as to age, maturity being especially valuable (1 Sa. 1:24); as to physical perfection, 'without blemish' being constantly emphasized

(Lv. 1:3; 3:1; Dt. 15:21; 17:1; 22:17–25; *cf.* Mal. 1:6ff., but note the exception for free-will offerings Lv. 22:23); and in some cases as to colour, red being chosen (Nu. 19:2), perhaps as representing blood (*cf.* prehistoric cave paintings of animals). The difference between Israel and her neighbours is clearly seen in the rejection of the extension of this principle to what might be thought its logical climax in the human first-born. The child sacrifice, which was present in the late kingdom (2 Ki. 21:6), and the human sacrifices occasionally reported of earlier times (Jdg. 11:29ff.), were from outside influences, and were condemned by prophet (Je. 7:31ff.), precept (Lv. 20:4) and example (Gn. 22). Ex. 22:29b is clearly to be interpreted by Ex. 34:19–20 and Ex. 13:12–16. The principle of substitution is present, not only in this replacing of the human first-born by an animal victim but in the provision given to the poor to offer the cheaper doves for a sin-offering (Lv. 5:7) and, if even this was too much, a cereal-offering (Lv. 5:11). The words 'such as he can afford' (Lv. 14:22, *etc.*) are very significant here.

Libations of oil (Gn. 28:18), wine (Gn. 35:14) and water (?1 Sa. 7:6) seem to have had a place in the cult, but only the wine-offerings are referred to in the basic laws (Nu. 28:7, *etc.*). The prohibition of leaven and honey (with some exceptions), and possibly also of milk, is probably to be put down to their liability to putrefaction. For the opposite reason salt was probably added to the sacrifices, because of its well-known preservative qualities (mentioned only in Lv. 2:13 and Ezk. 43:24, but *cf.* Mk. 9:49). *Incense (*l^e^bônâ, q^e^ṭōreṯ*) played a considerable role, both as an independent offering (Ex. 30:7, *cf.* the instructions for its making in vv. 34–38) and as an accompaniment of the cereal-offering (Lv. 2). Many scholars, doubting its early use on the ground that it was neither edible nor home-grown property (Je. 6:20), think *q^e^ṭōreṯ* in the historical books describes the burning of the fat (*qṭr*) rather than incense, but this is not certain. (See N. H. Snaith, *IB*, 3, 1954, p. 40, and J. A. Montgomery, *ICC*, *Kings*, 1952, p. 104, also *VT* 10, 1960, pp. 113–129.)

2. *The occasions.* The regulations cover both national and individual offerings, and daily and festival occasions. The first public sacrifices with good attestation are the seasonal ones, the Feast of Unleavened Bread, Firstfruits or Weeks and Ingathering or *Tabernacles (Ex. 23:14–17; 34:18–23; Dt. 16). With the first the *Passover was early connected (Jos. 5:10–12), and with the last, in all probability, covenant renewal ceremonies (*cf.* Ex. 24; Dt. 31:10ff.; Jos. 24) and possibly new year and atoning rites (*cf.* Lv. 23:27ff.) (*PENTECOST.) A full tariff of sacrifices for these, and for additional observances, monthly (new moon), weekly (sabbath) and daily (morning and evening), is found in Nu. 28–29, and may be set out in tabular form (see the chart on p. 1046).

The date of the beginning of the twice-daily burnt-offering is controverted, and certainty is difficult to arrive at, because of the ambiguous nature of *minḥâ* for both cereal- and burnt-offerings. (See the chart on p. 1050.) *'ôlâ* and *minḥâ* are also referred to without time notes in 1 Sa. 3:14; Je. 14:12; and Ps. 20:3, and continual *'ōlôṯ* and *minḥôṯ* in Ezr. 3:3ff. and Ne. 10:33.

Sacrifices of a more private nature were the Passover, for which the unit was the family (Ex. 12; *cf.* 1 Sa. 20:6, but this was a new moon, not a full moon), and individual sacrifices, such as those in fulfilment of a vow (1 Sa. 1:3, *cf.* v. 21; 2 Sa. 15:7ff.), or in confirmation of a treaty (Gn. 31:54), veneration of God (Jdg. 13:19), personal dedication (1 Ki. 3:4), consecration (1 Sa. 16:3) or expiation (2 Sa. 24:17ff.). Whether the extending of hospitality to a guest was always regarded as a sacrificial occasion is not clear (Gn. 18; Nu. 22:40; 1 Sa. 28:24 may not have involved altar rites, but *cf.* 1 Sa. 9). Additional occasions mentioned in the laws are the cleansing of the leper (Lv. 14), purification after child-birth (Lv. 12), the consecration of a priest (Lv. 8–9) or a Levite (Nu. 8), and the release of a Nazirite from his vows (Nu. 6). Less frequent sacrifices were those of sanctuary dedication (2 Sa. 6:13; 1 Ki. 8:5ff.; Ezk. 43:18ff.; Ezr. 3:2ff.), royal coronations (1 Sa. 11:15; 1 Ki. 1:9), and days of national penitence (Jdg. 20:26; 1 Sa. 7) or preparation for battle (1 Sa. 13:8ff.; Ps. 20).

Among seasonal offerings brought annually in recognition of God's share in productivity were firstlings and firstfruits (Ex. 13; 23:19; Dt. 15:19ff.; 18:4; 26; Nu. 18; *cf.* Gn. 4:3–4; 1 Sa. 10:3; 2 Ki. 4:42), *tithes, and the offerings of the first sheaf (Lv. 23:9ff.) and the first dough (Nu. 15:18–21; Ezk. 44:30; *cf.* Lv. 23:15ff.). Their purpose was probably not to consecrate the rest of the crop, but to deconsecrate it. All was God's until the first portion had been offered and accepted in lieu of the whole. Only then was the restriction on the human use of the remainder removed (Lv. 23:14, *cf.* 19:23–25). Even the portion brought was usually presented only in token at the altar, and afterwards taken away for the use of the priests or for a sacrificial meal. This was also the final fate of the weekly *showbread.

3. *The ritual.* The major altar sacrifices of Lv. 1–5 are described in a framework of a stereotyped ritual comprising six acts, of which three belong to the worshipper and three to the priest. They may be illustrated from the *'ôlâ* and the *zeḇaḥ* (*cf.* R. Rendtorff, *Die Gesetze in der Priesterschrift*, 1954). (See the chart on p. 1051.) The provisions for the sin-offering, several times repeated for various classes (Lv. 4:1–12, 13–21, 22–26, 27–31), follow the same scheme, except in minor details. The burnt-offering of a bird (Lv. 1:14–17) and the cereal-offering (Lv. 2) of necessity present greater variations, but are not entirely dissimilar. A similar formula for the guilt-offering is not given (*cf.*, however, 7:1–7), but it may be understood as coming under the law of the sin-offering (Lv. 7:7).

(i) The worshipper brings near (*hiqrîḇ*) his offering (also *hēḇî'*, *'āśâh*). The place of the sacrifice is the tabernacle forecourt on the N side of the altar (for burnt-, sin- and guilt-offerings, but not for the more numerous peace-offerings), although in earlier times it may have been the door of the tabernacle (Lv. 17:4), or local sanctuary (1 Sa. 2:12ff.), or a rough altar of stone or earth (Ex. 20:24ff.) or a rock (1 Sa. 6:14) or pillar (Gn. 28:18). Killing *on* the altar, although implied by Gn. 22:9 and Ex. 20:24 (Ps. 118:27 is corrupt), is not normal in the cult.

(ii) He lays (*sāmaḵ*) his hands, or in the biblical period more probably one hand (*cf.* Nu. 27:18), upon the victim, and possibly confesses his sin. This latter is mentioned, however, only in connection with the scapegoat, where the blood was not shed (Lv. 16:21) and with some sin-offerings (Lv. 5:5) and guilt-offerings (Nu. 5:7) (*cf.*, however, Dt. 26:3; Jos. 7:19–20), so that the *s^e^mîḵâ* cannot certainly be claimed as a transferring of sin. On the other hand, it seems inadequate to regard it simply as an identification by the owner of his property, for such an identification is not made with the non-blood sacrifices, where it would have been equally appropriate. Representation, if not transference, seems to be clearly involved (*cf.* the use of the same word for the commissioning of Joshua (Nu. 27:18) and the Levites (Nu. 8:10) and the stoning of a blasphemer (Lv. 24:13f.)). See P. Volz, *ZAW* 21, 1901, pp. 93–100, and for an opposite view J. C. Matthes, *ibid.* 23, 1903, pp. 97–119.

(iii) The slaughtering (*šāḥaṭ*) is performed by the worshipper, except for the national offerings (Lv. 16:11; 2 Ch. 29:24). In the non-levitical literature the verb *zābaḥ* is used, but this may have referred to the subsequent cutting up of the sacrifice, and the laying of the parts on the altar (*mizbēaḥ*, not *mišḥaṭ*) (so K. Galling, *Der Altar*, 1925, pp. 56ff.). For this, however, *ntḥ* is normally used (1 Ki. 18:23; Lv. 1:6), and *zābaḥ* describes rather the *zᵉbāḥîm* sacrifices, except for a few passages (Ex. 20:24; 1 Ki. 3:4; *cf.* 2 Ki. 10:18ff.) where it occurs with *'ōlôṯ*. These are perhaps to be put down to a loose use of the verb, which in the cognate languages can even be used of vegetable offerings, and in the *Piēl* in Heb. seems to be used quite generally for the whole round of the (usually apostate) cult. It is not certain, then, that every use of *zebaḥ* was sacrificial, or that meat could be eaten only on occasions of sacrifice, although this was often the case in antiquity (*cf.* the problem of the idol-meat at Corinth) (see N. H. Snaith, *VT* 25, 1975, pp. 242–246).

(iv) The manipulation (*zāraq*) of the blood is in the hands of the priest, who collects it in a basin and dashes it against the NE and SW corners of the altar in such a way that all four sides are spattered. This takes place with the animal burnt-offerings (Lv. 1), peace-offerings (Lv. 3) and guilt-offerings (Lv. 7:2), but not with the burnt-offering of birds (Lv. 1:15), where the quantity of blood was insufficient, and so was drained out on the side of the altar. The sin-offering (Lv. 4) uses a different set of verbs, *hizzâ* ('sprinkle') or *nāṯan* ('put') according to whether the offering is of primary or secondary rank (see below). The remainder of the blood is then poured out (*šāp̄aḵ*) at the base of the altar. The blood rite is referred to in the historical books only in 2 Ki: 16:15 (but *cf.* 1 Sa. 14:31–35; Ex. 24:6–8). (See Th. C. Vriezen, *OTS* 7, 1950, pp. 201–235; D. J. McCarthy, *JBL* 88, 1969, pp. 166–176; 92, 1973, pp. 205–210; N. H. Snaith, *ExpT* 82, 1970–71, pp. 23f.)

(v) Some burning (*hiqṭîr*) took place with all the sacrifices. Not only the blood but also the fat belonged to God, and this was first burnt (Gn. 4:4; 1 Sa. 2:16). This was not the fat in general, but specifically the fat of the kidneys, liver and intestines. From the peace-, sin- and guilt-offerings only this was burnt, from the cereal-offerings a portion called the *'azkārâ* was separated off and burnt, but the burnt-offering was wholly burnt except for the skin, which became the perquisite of the priests (Lv. 7:8). A different kind of burning (*śārap̄*) away from the altar was the fate of the primary rank sin-offerings. In this burning the skin was also included.

(vi) The remaining portions of the sacrifice were eaten (*'āḵal*) in a sacrificial meal, either by the priests and worshippers together (peace-offering), or by the priests and their families, or by the priests alone. Priestly food was classified as either holy or most holy. The former included the peace-offerings (Lv. 10:14; 22:10ff.) and firstfruits and tithes (Nu. 18:13), and could be eaten by the priest's family in any clean place, but the latter included the sin-offerings (Lv. 6:26), guilt-offerings (Lv. 7:6), cereal-offerings (Lv. 6:16), and showbread (Lv. 24:9), and could be eaten only by the priests themselves, and within the Temple precincts. The people's sacrificial meal from the peace-offering was the popular accompaniment of local worship in early times (1 Sa. 1; 9), but with the centralization of the cult in Jerusalem (*cf.* Dt. 12) tended to recede before the formal aspects of worship. As late as Ezk. 46:21–24, however, provision continued to be made for it.

4. *The kinds.* (i) *'ôlâ.* The burnt-offering seems to have a better claim to be regarded as the typical Hebrew sacrifice than the *zebaḥ* favoured by the Wellhausen school. It is present from the beginning (?Gn. 4; 8:20; 22:2; Ex. 10:25; 18:12; Jdg. 6:26; 13:16), early became a regular rite (1 Ki. 9:25; *cf.* 1 Ki. 10:5), was never omitted on great occasions (1 Ki. 3:4; Jos. 8:31), and retained its dominant role to the latest times (Ezk. 43:18; Ezr. 3:2–4) (see R. Rendtorff, *Studien zur Geschichte des Opfers im alten Israel*, 1967). Whatever may be said for Robertson Smith's view of a primary peace-offering, from which the burnt-offering later developed, as far as the OT is concerned it is from the *'ôlâ* that the *minḥâ*, *'āšām*, *ḥaṭṭā'ṯ* and even *šᵉlāmîm* seem to have arisen. The *kālîl* referred to five times (1 Sa. 7:9; Ps. 51:19; Dt. 33:10; *cf.* Dt. 13:16 and Lv. 6:22–23) is also another name for the *'ôlâ*, although apparently differing somewhat in the Carthage and Marseilles tariffs.

While there is truth in Rost's view that the incidence of the *'ôlâ* is confined to Greece and the region 'bordered by the Taurus in the N, the Mediterranean in the W and the desert in the E and S' ('Erwägungen zum israelitischen Brandopfer', *Von Ugarit nach Qumran* (Eissfeldt Festschrift), 1958, pp. 177–183), it does not follow that its origins in Israel are in human sacrifice (2 Ki. 3:27) or rites of aversion of the Greek kind. Its undoubted gift character is apparent from the sublimation of the elements into a form in which they can be transported to God (Jdg. 6:21; 13:20; *cf.* Dt. 33:10), but this does not say anything about the purpose of the gift, which may have been of homage and thanksgiving, or to expiate sin. The latter note is present in Jb. 1:5; 42:8 and many early passages, and is given as the reason for the sacrifice in Lv. 1:4 (*cf.* the Ugaritic Text 9:7, where the burnt-offering (*šrp*) is connected to forgiveness of soul (*slḥ npš*)). When the sin-offering came to take precedence as the first of the series of sacrifices (Mishnah, *Zebahim* 10. 2) it tended to take over this function, but this was not originally the case (*cf.* Nu. 28–29, and *cf.* Nu. 6:14 with 6:11).

(ii) *minḥâ* ('meal-offering', AV 'meat-offering', RSV 'cereal-offering'). It is somewhat confusing that this term is used in three different ways in the OT: 34 times it simply means 'present' or 'tribute' (*cf.* Jdg. 3:15; 1 Ki. 4:21—the root is probably *mānaḥ*, 'to give', *cf.* the peculiar form of the plural in the *MT* of Ps. 20:3), 97 times in the levitical literature it is the cereal-offering (*e.g.* in Lv. 2), and an indeterminate number of the remaining instances also have this meaning (*e.g.* Is. 43:23; 66:20), but in the others it refers to sacrifice generally (1 Sa. 2:29; 26:19, and probably in Malachi), and to animal sacrifice in particular (1 Sa. 2:12–17; Gn. 4:3–4; but see N. H. Snaith, *VT* 7, 1957, pp.

314–316). S. R. Driver rightly defines *minḥâ* as not merely expressing the neutral idea of gift, but as denoting 'a present made to secure or retain goodwill' (*HDB*, 3, 1900, p. 587; *cf.* Gn. 33:10), and this propitiatory sense is to the fore also in such sacrificial references as 1 Sa. 3:10–14; 26:19.

In these references the *minḥâ* is an independent sacrifice, whereas in the laws it is the accompaniment of burnt-offerings and peace-offerings (Nu. 15:1–16), except in Nu. 5:15, 25; Lv. 5:11–13; 6:19–23. According to Lv. 2, it is to consist of either flour (2:1–3), baked cakes (2:4–10) or raw grain (2:14–16), together with oil and frankincense (*lᵉḇônâ*). With this '*minḥâ* of the forecourt' may be compared what J. H. Kurtz called the '*minḥâ* of the holy place'—the altar of incense, the showbread on the table and the oil in the lamp (*The Sacrificial Worship of the Old Testament*, 1865). Other ingredients might be salt (Lv. 2:13) and wine (Lv. 23:13). None of these offerings was eaten by the worshippers (but ? Lv. 7:11–18). They went to the priests, but only after a 'memorial portion' (Lv. 2:2) had been burnt on the altar. This RSV translation implies a derivation of *'azkārâ* from *zāḵar*, but G. R. Driver has suggested the meaning 'token', a part for the whole (*JSS* 1, 1956, pp. 97–105), and this would be yet another instance of the principle of substitution in the sacrifices.

(iii) *zeḇaḥ* and *šᵉlāmîm*. Again there is a variety of usage, in which *zeḇaḥ* and *šᵉlāmîm* are sometimes interchangeable (Lv. 7:11–21; 2 Ki. 16:13, 15), sometimes distinguished (Jos. 22:27; *f.* Ex. 24:5; 1 Sa. 11:15), sometimes independent (2 Sa. 6:17–18; Ex. 32:6), and sometimes combined into a compound expression *zeḇaḥ šᵉlāmîm* or *ziḇᵉḥê šᵉlāmîm* (so usually in the levitical law). It is doubtful if all these uses are to be understood as referring simply to the *zeḇaḥ* sacrificial meal. *šᵉlāmîm*, when used alone, was possibly not a meal at all (*cf.*, however, 2 Sa. 6:19), but a solemn expiatory offering akin to the *'ôlâ* (so R. Rendtorff, *Studien zur Geschichte des Opfers*), and in conjunction with other sacrifices may still have retained this meaning. A *šlm* of a propitiatory kind seems to have been known at Ugarit (D. M. L. Urie, 'Sacrifice among the West Semites', *PEQ* 81, 1949, pp. 75–77) and is reflected in such passages as Jdg. 20:26; 1 Sa. 13:9; 2 Sa. 24:25. It is in no way inconsistent that a joyous meal followed, if the joy was the joy of forgiveness, for the *zeḇaḥ* covenant meal also usually marked a reconciliation after estrangement (Gn. 31:54; *cf.* S. I. Curtiss, 'The Semitic Sacrifice of Reconciliation', *The Expositor*, 6th series, 6, 1902, pp. 454–462).

Either of the proposed derivations of *šelem*—from *šālôm*, 'peace', so 'to make peace' (*cf.* G. Fohrer, 'to make complete' so 'concluding offering'; *TDNT* 7, pp. 1022–1023) or from *šillēm*, 'compensate', so 'to pay off, expiate' (*cf.* B. A. Levine, 'a tribute, a present, a gift of greeting', *In the Presence of the Lord*, 1974)—would be in keeping and preferable to the reduction of the peace-offering to what were in fact only segments 'vow-offering' or 'thank-offering'. These two, together with the freewill-offering, made up three classes within the peace-offering proper, and the regulations governing them (Lv. 7:11ff.) are a supplement to those of Lv. 3. All three were thank-offerings, but the vow-offering, which discharged an earlier promise at the time of its accomplishment, was no longer optional, while the others were. Possibly it was for this reason that the vow reverted to the stricter regulation of a victim without blemish (Lv. 22:19; *cf.* Mal. 1:14, where it is added that it should be a male), while this requirement was relaxed for the freewill-offering (Lv. 22:23). Lv. 7 also adds the rules for the sacrificial meal, which had been missing in Lv. 3—*viz.* that the thank-offering was to be eaten the same day, and the vow and freewill-offering not later than the next. The priests' portions are defined (Lv. 7:32ff.) as the 'wave' breast and the 'heave' shoulder (thigh). G. R. Driver (*op.*

Offerings	**Morning**		**Evening**	
Bible references	*'ôlâ* (burnt-offering)	*minḥâ* (cereal-offering)	*'ôlâ* (burnt-offering)	*minḥâ* (cereal-offering)
Ex. 29: 38-42	☐	☐	☐	☐
Nu. 28: 3-8	☐	☐	☐	☐
1 Ki. 18: 29				☐
2 Ki. 3: 20		☐		
2 Ki. 16: 15	☐			☐
Ezk. 46:13-14	☐	☐		

The main references to the twice-daily offerings. the 'ôlâ *and the* minḥâ.

Order of acts	1	2	3	4	5	6
Hebrew terms	*hiqrîḇ*	*sāmaḵ*	*šāḥaṭ*	*zāraq*	*hiqṭîr*	*'āḵal*
'ôlâ (burnt-offering) Leviticus 1:1-17						
Bull	Lv. 1:3	Lv. 1:4	Lv. 1:5a	Lv. 1:5b	Lv. 1:9b	–
Sheep or goat	Lv. 1:10b	–	Lv. 1:11a	Lv. 1:11b	Lv. 1:13b	–
zeḇaḥ (peace-offering) Leviticus 3:1-17						
Bull	Lv. 3:1b	Lv. 3:2a	Lv. 3:2a	Lv. 3:2b	Lv. 3:5	–
Lamb	Lv. 3:6b	Lv. 3:8a	Lv. 3:8a	Lv. 3:8b	Lv. 3:11	–
Goat	Lv. 3:12b	Lv. 3:13a	Lv. 3:13a	Lv. 3:13b	Lv. 3:16	–

The ritual procedures laid down for sacrifices or burnt- and peace-offerings (Lv. 1 and 3).

cit.) suggests some such meaning as 'contribution' for the terms 'wave' (*tᵉnûp̄â*) and 'heave' (*tᵉrûmâ*), and this seems better than the older suggestion of horizontal and vertical motions at the altar, which are scarcely appropriate when rams, he-goats and Levites are the objects of the actions (Nu. 8:11). (See W. B. Stevenson, 'Hebrew *'Olah* and *Zebach* Sacrifices', *Festschrift Alfred Bertholet*, 1950, pp. 488–497; *cf.* J. Milgrom, 'The Alleged Wave-Offering in Israel and in the Ancient Near East', *IEJ* 22, 1972, pp. 33–38.)

(iv) *'āšām and ḥaṭṭā'ṯ*. The names of these offerings, guilt-offering (trespass-offering) and sin-offering, are the names of the offences for which they are to atone, *'āšām* ('guilt') and *ḥaṭṭā'ṯ* ('sin'). In a cultic context these terms refer, not so much to moral offences, as to those which are ceremonially defiling, although the moral aspect is by no means ruled out. Of the former kind are the sin-offerings of the leper (Lv. 14; *cf.* Mk. 1:44) and the mother after childbirth (Lv. 12; *cf.* Lk. 2:24), and of the latter, those of deception and misappropriation in Lv. 6:1–7, and passion in Lv. 19:20–22. These examples can have been but little more than random specimens to illustrate the laws, and should not be regarded as giving a full account of sacrifice for sin in these laws, much less in the cult as a whole. In the history, for example, these sacrifices scarcely figure at all. They are not mentioned in Deuteronomy (*cf.* Dt. 12), and are probably not to be understood in Ho. 4:8. But this is to be put down less to their post-exilic origin as Wellhausen argued—for they are well known to Ezekiel (*cf.* 40:39; 42:13) and may be hinted at in Ps. 40:6; 2 Ki. 12:16; 1 Sa. 6:3 (unless these are only monetary)—than to their individual nature (this might explain the silence concerning the *'āšām*, which was not a festival sacrifice), and the fragmentary character of the records. They are equally silent for the post-exilic period (*'āšām* is mentioned, doubtfully, only in Ezr. 10:19 and *ḥaṭṭā'ṯ* in Ne. 10:33 and what appears a formula of the Chronicler in Ezr. 6:17; 8:35; 2 Ch. 29:21ff.).

Equally obscure is the relation between the two offerings (*e.g.* they are used synonymously in Lv. 5:6). All that can certainly be said is that sins against the neighbour are more prominent in the *'āšām* and those against God in the *ḥaṭṭā'ṯ*. The *'āšām* therefore requires a monetary compensation in addition to the sacrifice. The value of the misappropriation plus a fifth is to be repaid to the wronged neighbour (Lv. 6:5) or, if he or his representative is not available, to the priest (Nu. 5:8). The sacrificial victim in the guilt-offering, usually a ram, also became the priest's, and after the regular blood and fat ritual could be eaten by the priests as 'most holy' (Lv. 7:1–7). The same provision applies (Lv. 6:24–29) to the sin-offerings of the ruler (Lv. 4:22–26) and the common man (Lv. 4:27–31), but in these cases the blood is put on the horns of the altar.

The sin-offerings of the high priest (Lv. 4:1–12) and the whole community (Lv. 4:13–21) follow a still more solemn ritual, in which the blood is sprinkled (*hizzâ*, not *zāraq*) before the veil of the sanctuary, and the bodies of the victims are not eaten but burnt (*śārap̄*, not *hiqṭîr*) outside the camp (Lv. 6:30; *cf.* Heb. 13:11). In addition to these four classes provisions are made for substitute offerings from the poor (Lv. 5:7–13). Chs. 4 and 5 thus contain a graduated scale of victims: bull (high priest and congregation, but *cf.* Nu. 15:24; Lv. 9:15; 16:5), he goat (ruler), she goat or lamb (common man), turtle-doves or pigeons (poor), flour (very poor). The following principles may be remarked: everyone must bring some sin-offering, no-one may eat of his own sin-offering, and the more propitiatory the rite the nearer the blood must come to God. On the Day of Atonement the veil itself was penetrated and the blood sprinkled on the ark. (See D. Schötz, *Schuld- und Sündopfer im Alten Testament*, 1930; L. Morris, '*'Asham*', *EQ* 30, 1958, pp. 196–210; J. Milgrom, *VT* 21, 1971, pp. 237–239; D. Kellerman, *TDOT* 1, pp. 429–437.)

5. *The meaning.* The oft-stated purpose of the sacrifices in Lv. is 'to atone' (*kipper*, Lv. 1:4, *etc.*). This verb may be explained in one of three ways: 'to cover', from the Arab. *kafara*; 'to wipe away', from the Akkad. *kuppuru*; 'to ransom by a substitute', from the Heb. noun *kōper.* Although the second is favoured by most modern writers, it is the third which seems most in keeping with the theory of sacrifice given in Lv. 17:11, AV, 'the life of the flesh is in the blood . . . it is the blood that maketh an atonement for the soul' (but *cf.* RSV and J. Milgrom, *JBL* 90, 1971, pp. 149–156), and with the principle at work in many of the practices encountered above: the choice of offering material in 'biotic rapport'; their designation by the laying on of the hand; the burning of a token such as the fat or the *'azkārâ*; the offering of a first portion and the redemption of the first-born (*cf.* S. H. Hooke, 'The Theory and Practice of Substitution', *VT* 2, 1952, pp. 1–17, and for an opposite view A. Metzinger's articles, *Bib* 21, 1940). To these might be added the ritual of the heifer in Dt. 21 and the scapegoat in Lv. 16, which, although not blood sacrifices, reflect ideas which must *a fortiori* have been true of blood sacrifices. It was in this light that Lv. 16 was understood in the Jewish tradition (*e.g.* Mishnah, *Yoma* 6. 4, 'bear our sins and be gone').

Such passages are a warning against confining the atonement to a single act, as if it were the death alone, or the presentation of the blood, or the disposal of the victim, which atoned. The death was important—the live goat is only half of the ritual in Lv. 16 (*cf.* v. 15 with 14:4–7; 5:7–11). The blood manipulation was also important—in 2 Ch. 29:24 it seems to make atonement subsequent to the killing. The final disposal of the victim by fire or eating or to Azazel also had its place—in Lv. 10:16–20 the priestly eating of the sin-offering is more than just declaratory. The view that the death of the victim was only to release the life that was in the blood, and that the atonement consisted only of the latter, is as one-sided as that which sees the death as a quantitative penal satisfaction. To the latter view it has been objected that the sins for which sacrifice was offered were not those meriting death, that sin-offerings did not always require death (*cf.* Lv. 5:11–13), and that the killing could not have been central or it would have been in the hands of the priest, not the layman. These objections tell only against extreme forms of the substitution theory, not against the principle of substitution itself.

The real advantage of the substitution theory is that it retains the categories of personal relationships, where other views tend to descend to sub-personal dynamistic categories, in which the blood itself is thought of as effecting mystic union or revitalizing in a semi-magical way (*cf.* the theories of H. Hubert and M. Mauss, *Sacrifice: Its Nature and Function*, 1964; A. Loisy, *RHLR* n.s. 1, 1910, pp. 1–30, and *Essai historique sur le sacrifice*, 1920; S. G. Gayford, *Sacrifice and Priesthood*, 1924; A. Bertholet, *JBL* 49, 1930, pp. 218–233, and *Der Sinn des kultischen Opfers*, 1942; E. O. James, *The Origins of Sacrifice*, 1933).

A weightier objection to the substitution theory is that which finds difficulty in the description of the sin-offering after the sacrifice as 'most holy', and as fit for priestly food. If a transfer of sin had taken place, would it not be unclean and fit only for destructive burning (*śārap̄*)? This was in fact the case with the primary rank sin-offerings. In the other cases the priestly eating is perhaps to be similarly interpreted, as if the power of superior 'holiness' in the priests through their anointing absorbed the uncleanness of the offering (*cf.* Lv. 10:16–20 and the article 'Sin-Eating', *ERE*, 11, 1920, pp. 572–576 (Hartland)). That we are dealing here with categories of 'holiness', which are not ours, is evident from the instruction to break the earthen vessels in which the sin-offering has been boiled (Lv. 6:28; *cf.* *CLEAN AND UNCLEAN). Alternatively, the death of the victim could be understood as neutralizing the infection of sin, so that the fat and blood could come unimpeded to the altar as an offering to God.

Whether other views of sacrifice such as 'homage' and 'communion' are possible alongside that outlined here, as favoured by most scholars (A. Wendel, *Das Opfer in der altisraelitischen Religion*, 1927; W. O. E. Oesterley, *Sacrifices in Ancient Israel*, 1937; H. H. Rowley, *The Meaning of Sacrifice*, 1950), or whether certain types of sacrifice express one of these aspects more than another (*e.g.* burnt-offering, homage, and peace-offering, communion) is best left an open question. But in the laws at least the burnt-offering, the cereal-offering and even the peace-offering (but only rarely; *cf.* Ex. 29:33; Ezk. 45:15), as well as the sin- and guilt-offerings, are said to atone. And what is true of the laws seems to be true also of the history.

The question as to whether the offering was both an expiation (*i.e.* of sins) and a propitiation (*i.e.* of wrath) or only an expiation is also difficult to answer. *kipper* undoubtedly means propitiation in some instances (Nu. 16:41–50; Ex. 32:30), and this is supported by the use of the expression *rēaḥ nîḥōaḥ*, 'sweet-smelling savour', throughout the laws (*cf.* also Gn. 8:21, and LXX of Dt. 33:10). *rēaḥ nîḥōaḥ* may, however, have a weakened sense (G. B. Gray, *Sacrifice in the Old Testament*, 1925, pp. 77–81, points out that it is used where we should hardly expect it, with cereal and *zeḇaḥ* offerings, but not where we do expect it with sin- and guilt-offerings), and this is even more evidently the case with *kipper* when it is used in connection with such material things as the tabernacle furniture (Ex. 29:37; Ezk. 43:20; 45:19), and must be rendered simply 'cleanse'.

Of importance to the discussion here is the recognition that God himself gave the ritual to sinful man (Lv. 17:11, 'the blood . . . I have given it for you upon the altar to make atonement for your souls'). The sacrifices are to be seen as operating within the sphere of the covenant and covenanting grace. They were not 'man's expedient for his own redemption' as L. Köhler (*Old Testament Theology*, 1957) suggests, but were 'the fruit of grace, not its root' (A. C. Knudson, *The Religious Teaching of the Old Testament*, 1918, p. 295). The question as to whether within this context propitiation has a place is similar to the NT one, and will depend on the view taken of sin, and law and the nature of God (*ATONEMENT; also L. Morris, *The Apostolic Preaching of the Cross*, 1955).

It remains to be said that within the OT itself there is much to suggest that its system was not a final one. No sacrifices availed, for example, for breach of covenant (*cf.* Ex. 32:30ff.)—it is in this light that the prophetic rejection of sacrifice is to be understood—or for sins of a 'high hand' that put man outside the covenant (Nu. 15:30), though perhaps idolatry and apostasy would be illustrations here. While not accepting the view, on the one hand, that the efficacy of sacrifice was limited to inadvertent sins, which were no real sins at all, or, on the other, that prophets and pious psalmists saw no value in sacrifice whatsoever, it remains true that the cult was liable to abuse, when the inward tie between worshipper and means of worship was loosed, and prophetic religion became necessary to emphasize the priority of a personal relation to God. It is no accident, however, that when priestly and prophetic religion meet in the figure of the Servant of the Lord in Is. 53 the highest point of OT religion is reached, as all that is valuable in cult is taken up into a person, who both makes a sacrificial atonement (*hizzâ*, 'lamb', 'guilt-offering') and calls for the love and personal allegiance of the human heart.

BIBLIOGRAPHY. Articles. in *ABD, EB, EJ, ERE, HDB, IDB, ISBE, ZPEB*; *JSOT* 56 (Kiuchi), 91 (Gorman), 106 (Jenson); F. D. Kidner, *Sacrifice in the OT*, 1952; H. Ringgren, *Sacrifice in the Bible*, 1962; R. H. Elliott, *R&E* 59, 1962, pp. 9–26; R. J. Thompson, *Penitence and Sacrifice in Early Israel*, 1963; N. Snaith, *VT* 7, 1957, pp. 308–317; 15, 1965, pp. 75–80; R. de Vaux, *Studies in OT Sacrifice*, 1965; B. A. Levine, *In the Presence of the Lord*, 1974; F. M. Young, *Sacrifice and the Death of Christ*, 1975; J. W. Rogerson, in M. F. C. Bourdillon and M. Fortes (eds.), *Sacrifice*, 1980, pp. 45–60; R. D. Hecht, *RSR*, 1982, pp. 253–259. R.J.T.

II. In the New Testament

The Greek words used are *thysia*, *dōron*, *prosphora* and their cognates, and *anapherō*, translated 'sacrifice, gift, offering, offer' (*thysia* in Mk. 12:33 probably means 'meal-offering'); *holokautōma*, 'whole burnt offering'; *thymiama*, 'incense'; *spendō*, 'pour out as a drink-offering'. All were adopted, with the other terms given below, from LXX.

a. Old Testament sacrifices in the New

The OT sacrifices (see **I**, above) were still being offered during practically the whole period of the composition of the NT, and it is not surprising, therefore, that even their literal significance comes in for some illuminating comment. Important maxims are to be found in Mt. 5:23–24; 12:3–5 and parallels, 17:24–27; 23:16–20; 1 Cor. 9:13–14. It is noteworthy that our Lord has sacrifice offered for him or offers it himself at his presentation in the Temple, at his last Passover, and presumably on those other occasions when he went up to Jerusalem for the feasts. The practice of the apostles in Acts removes all ground from the opinion that after the sacrifice of Christ the worship of the Jewish Temple is to be regarded as an abomination to God. We find them frequenting the Temple, and Paul himself goes up to Jerusalem for Pentecost, and on that occasion offers the sacrifices (which included sin-offerings) for the interruption of vows (Acts 21; *cf.* Nu. 6:10–12). However, in principle these sacrifices were now unnecessary, for the old covenant was now indeed 'old' and 'ready to vanish away' (Heb. 8:13), so that when the Romans destroyed the Temple even the non-Christian Jews ceased to offer the sacrifices.

The Epistle to the Hebrews contains the fullest treatment of the OT sacrifices. The teaching of this writer has its positive side (11:4), but his great concern is to point out their inadequacy except as types. The fact that they cannot gain for men entrance into the Holy of holies proves that they cannot free the conscience from guilt, but are simply carnal ordinances, imposed until a time of reformation (9:6–10). Their inadequacy to atone is shown also by the fact that mere animals are offered (10:4), and by the very fact of their repetition (10:1–2). They are not so much remedies for sin as reminders of it (10:3).

b. 'Spiritual sacrifices'

'Spiritual sacrifices' (1 Pet. 2:5; *cf.* Jn. 4:23–24; Rom. 12:1; Phil. 3:3) are the NT substitute for carnal ordinances, and appear frequently (Rom. 12:1; 15:16–17; Phil. 2:17; 4:18; 2 Tim. 4:6; Heb. 13:15–16; Rev. 5:8; 6:9; 8:3–4). Even in the OT, however, the psalmists and prophets sometimes use the language of sacrifice metaphorically (*e.g.* Pss. 50:13–14; 51:16–17; Is. 66:20), and the usage is continued in the intertestamental literature (Ecclus. 35:1–3; *Testament of Levi* 3. 6; *Manual of Discipline* 8–9; Philo, *De Somniis* 2. 183). The attempt of F. C. N. Hicks (*The Fulness of Sacrifice*[3], 1946) to refer such passages to literal sacrifices must be reckoned on the whole a failure. The sacrifices mentioned in these passages are not always immaterial, and sometimes involve death: the sense in which they are 'spiritual' is that they belong properly to the age of the Holy Spirit (Jn. 4:23–24; Rom. 15:16). But sometimes they are immaterial, and they never have a prescribed ritual. It appears, in fact, that every act of the Spirit-filled man can be reckoned as a spiritual sacrifice, and the sense in which it is a sacrifice is that it is devoted to God and is acceptable to God. It does not, of course, atone. The antitype of atoning sacrifice is to be sought not here but in the sacrifice of Christ, without which spiritual sacrifices would not be acceptable (Heb. 13:15; 1 Pet. 2:5).

c. The sacrifice of Christ

The sacrifice of Christ is one of the chief themes of the NT. His saving work is sometimes spoken of in ethical, sometimes in penal, but often also in sacrificial terms. He is spoken of as the slain lamb of God, whose precious blood takes away the sin of the world (Jn. 1:29, 36; 1 Pet. 1:18–19; Rev. 5:6–10; 13:8)—a lamb being an animal used in various sacrifices. More specifically, he is spoken of as the true Passover lamb (*pascha*, 1 Cor. 5:6–8), as a sin-offering (*peri hamartias*, Rom. 8:3, *cf.* LXX Lv. 5:6–7, 11; 9:2–3; Ps. 40:6, *etc.*), and in Heb. 9–10 as the fulfilment of the covenant sacrifices of Ex. 24, the red heifer of Nu, 19, and the Day of Atonement offerings. The NT constantly identifies our Lord with the suffering Servant of Is. 52–53, who is a guilt-offering (Is. 53–10), and with the Messiah (Christ) of Dn. 9, who is to atone for iniquity (v. 24). The NT uses the terms 'propitiate' and 'ransom' (*PROPITIATION, *REDEEMER) of Christ in a sacrificial sense, and the idea of being cleansed by his blood (1 Jn. 1:7; Heb. *passim*) is sacrificial (*ATONEMENT, **III.** *b*; *SANCTIFICATION).

The doctrine is most fully worked out in the Epistle to the Hebrews. The writer stresses the importance, in Christ's sacrifice, of his death (2:9, 14; 9:15–17, 22, 25–28; 13:12, 20), and the fact that his sacrifice is over (1:3; 7:27; 9:12, 25–28; 10:10, 12–14, 18), but his other statements have led some Anglo-Catholics (*e.g.* S. C. Gayford, *Sacrifice and Priesthood*, 1924) and the Presbyterian W. Milligan (*The Ascension and Heavenly Priesthood of our Lord*, 1892) to suppose, on the contrary, that the death is not the important element in Christ's sacrifice, and that his sacrifice goes on for ever. It is quite true that the Epistle confines Christ's priesthood and sanctuary to heaven (8:1–5; 9:11, 24), but it emphatically does not confine his sacrifice there. It states indeed that he offered there (8:3), but 'offer' is a word used equally of the donor who brings and kills a sacrifice outside the sanctuary and of the priest who presents it, either there on the altar or within. The reference here is doubtless to the sprinkling or 'offering' of blood in the Holy of holies on the Day of Atonement by the high priest (9:7, 21–26), a typical action fulfilled by Christ. All that was costly in the sacrifice—the part of the donor and the victim—took place at the cross: there remained only the priestly part—the presentation to God by an acceptable mediator—and this Christ performed by entering into his Father's presence at the ascension, since when his sprinkled blood has remained there (12:24). There is no call to think of any *literal* presentation of himself or of his blood at the ascension: it is enough that he entered as the Priest of the sacrifice slain once for all at the cross, was immediately welcomed, and sat down in glory. His everlasting priestly intercession in heaven (7:24f.; *cf.* Ps. 99:6; Joel 2:17) is not some further activity, but is all part of his 'now appearing in the presence of God on our behalf' (9:24). On the basis of his finished work on the cross, and with his sufferings now all past, his simple appearance in God's presence on our behalf is both continual intercession for us and continual *'expiation' or *'propitiation' for our sins (2:10, 17f.; note present tense in the Gk.). See also *PRIESTS AND LEVITES.

It is a mistake to view Christ's sacrifice as being any more a literal sacrifice than the spiritual sacrifices are. Both transcend their OT types, and neither is ritual. The contention of Owen and others that Christ's sacrifice was a real sacrifice was directed against the Socinian view that Christ's death does not fulfil what the OT sacrifices set out to do, and failed to do—the view which denied that Christ's death makes propitiation. But apart from the slaying (and this is not performed, as in OT ritual, by the donor), everything in his sacrifice is spiritualized. For the body of an animal we have the body of God's Son (Heb. 10:5, 10). For spotlessness, we have sinlessness (Heb. 9:14; 1 Pet. 1:19). For a sweet smell, we have true acceptableness (Eph. 5:2). For the sprinkling of our bodies with blood, we have forgiveness (Heb. 9:13–14, 19–22). For symbolical atonement, we have real atonement (Heb. 10:1–10).

d. Sacrifice and the Lord's Supper

Sacrifice and the *Lord's Supper are indissolubly connected—not indeed in the way that Romanists, Non-jurors and Tractarians have wished to connect them, by making the eucharist an act of oblation, but as complementary to each other. To give 'do' and 'remembrance' (Lk. 22:19; 1 Cor. 11:24–25) a technical sacrificial sense is merely an afterthought of those who have already accepted the eucharistic sacrifice on non-scriptural grounds. The same is true of the attempt to exclude a future meaning from the participles 'given' and 'shed' (Mt. 26:28; Mk. 14:24; Lk. 22:19–20). And to correlate the eucharist with the eternal sacrifice of Christ in heaven is impossible if the eternal sacrifice is disproved. But to regard the eucharist as a *feast* upon Christ's sacrifice is demanded by the argument of 1 Cor. 10:14–22, in which it is made to correspond with Jewish and Gentile sacrificial meals; by the allusion to Ex. 24:8 in Mt. 26:28 and Mk. 14:24; and by the traditional interpretation of Heb. 13:10. Since the sacrifice of Christ is in so many points to be spiritualized, the language about the feast on his sacrifice is doubtless to be spiritualized also, but it is not to be bereft of its meaning. The meaning of the sacrificial meal was not so much the appropriation of atonement as the fellowship with God which it effected, and this was betokened by a feast with God upon the victim. Whether in enjoying this fellowship with God we also truly partake of Christ or of his body and blood is the central point of controversy about the sacrament. But since Jn. 6 teaches that those who believe on Christ when they see him or hear his words do feed on him, on his body and blood, through the Spirit, there does not seem to be any reason for doubting that what happens through his words also happens through the tokens of bread and wine which he instituted, though in an equally spiritual manner.

BIBLIOGRAPHY. Commentaries on the Epistle to the Hebrews; B. B. Warfield, *The Person and Work of Christ*, 1950, pp. 391–426; N. Dimock, *The Doctrine of the Death of Christ*, 1903; A. Cave, *The Scriptural Doctrine of Sacrifice and Atonement*, 1890; G. Vos, *The Teaching of the Epistle to the Hebrews* (ed. J. G. Vos), 1956; T. S. L. Vogan, *The True Doctrine of the Eucharist*, 1871; H.-G. Link *et al.*, *NIDNTT* 3, pp. 415–438; F. M. Young, *The Use of Sacrificial Ideas in Greek Christian Writers*, 1979. R.T.B.

SADDUCEES. On the various problems in reconstructing the nature of Jewish groups in the 1st century see *PHARISEES.

No materials survive from the Sadducees themselves. Our only sources are the NT itself, Josephus (*BJ* 2. 119, 164–166; *Ant.* 13. 171–173, 293–298; 18. 11, 16–17; 20. 199; *Vit.* 10–11) and scattered rabbinic texts of varying value. These are all to a greater or lesser extent hostile. It is therefore impossible to derive a balanced view of this group. Their name has been derived from *ṣaddîq* ('righteous') and from the name Zadok (either the high priest or another). They have been seen as a primarily religious group (of priestly conservatives); as the Judaean aristocracy (again through a supposed link with the priesthood), and as a political party. They have been identified by some scholars (and by some of the later rabbinic traditions) with the Boethusians, an equally obscure group whose major difference with the Pharisees appears to have been over the *calendar.

None of our sources actually link the Sadducees with the priesthood, stating only that certain priests were also Sadducees. 1 Macc. 2:1 derives the Hasmonean priesthood not from Zadok (as one might expect on the conventional understanding of Sadducee origins) but from one Joarib. When the polemic is stripped from the rabbinic materials, all that remains is that the Pharisees and Sadducees had differing understandings of certain laws, particularly purity laws, and the afterlife. They first appear as an entity in Josephus' narrative of John Hyrcanus (*Ant.* 13. 293–299), as a political group subordinate to the Pharisees, until the Sadducee, Jonathan, persuades the ruler to support their cause – a move which Josephus regards as extremely unpopular. Apart from Ananus the high priest, who is incidentally identified as a Sadducee (*Ant.* 20. 199), they otherwise feature very little in

Josephus' narrative of political events. We are therefore left quite uncertain about their origins, social status and *raison d'être.*

In his descriptions of the three philosophies, Josephus contrasts the Sadducees with the Pharisees and *Essenes as denying divine action in the world, affirming human freedom, and believing that the soul perishes along with the body. He also notes that they have the support of the rich and accept only the written laws in contrast to the Pharisaic traditions.

The only issue on which all our sources agree is that the Sadducees rejected beliefs in the afterlife, resurrection and a post-mortem judgment. However, even here one must be cautious. Josephus sees no incongruity in people switching allegiance between Pharisees and Sadducees (John Hyrcanus, *Ant.* 293–299, and himself, *Vita* 2), which suggests that he did not see such beliefs as central or burning issues.

In the gospels, they appear only once in Mark and Luke (Mk. 12:18; Lk. 20:27; Mt. 22:23), with their question about the resurrection. Matthew, however, adds them to two other narratives (assuming Marcan priority), at 3:7 and 16:1–12, simply as part of the Jewish religious scene.

In Acts their concerns are again primarily over the question of resurrection (4:2; 23:6–8). They are said to be the party of the high priest (5:17), and we are also informed that they were represented in the *Sanhedrin (23:6).

BIBLIOGRAPHY. G. W. E. Nickelsburg, *Resurrection, Immortality and Eternal Life in Intertestamental Judaism*, 1972; J. LeMoyne, *Les Sadducéens*, 1972; G. G. Porton, 'Diversity in Postbiblical Judaism', in R. A. Kraft and G. W. E. Nickelsburg (ed.), *Early Judaism and its Modern Interpreters*, 1986, pp. 57–80; S. J. D. Cohen, 'The Political and Social History of the Jews in Greco-Roman Antiquity: The State of the Question', in R. A. Kraft and G. W. E. Nickelsburg (ed.), *Early Judaism and its Modern Interpreters*, 1986, pp. 33–56; A. J. Saldarini, *Pharisees, Scribes and Sadducees in Palestinian Society*, 1988; G. Baumbach, 'The Sadducees in Josephus', in L. H. Feldman and G. Hata (ed.), *Josephus, the Bible, and History*, 1989, pp. 173–195; J. C. VanderKam, 'The People of the Dead Sea Scrolls: Essenes or Sadducees?' *Bible Review* 7, 1991, pp. 42–47; L. L. Grabbe, *Judaism from Cyrus to Hadrian*, 2, 1992, pp. 463ff.; S. Mason, *Josephus and the New Testament*, 1992.

D.R. de L.

SAKKUTH, SIKKUTH, SICCUTH. *MT sikkûṯ* is translated 'tabernacle' (as though it were equivalent to *sukkaṯ*) in Am. 5:26, AV—a verse which refers to Israel's adoption of Assyrian gods. In this verse the unvocalized consonants are *skkt mlkkm*, which are better translated, 'Sakkuth your king', than by AV and LXX. 'the tabernacle of your Moloch'. The consonants *skkt* were vocalized to read *sikkûṯ*, 'tabernacle', probably by using the vowels of *šiqqûṣ*, 'an abominable thing'. However, the verse makes good sense if we read Sakkuth instead of 'tabernacle'. Sakkuth was the name of the god of war, and of sun and light, Adar-malek or Saturn (*cf.* 2 Ki. 17:31, Adrammelech), otherwise known as Ninurta (SAG.KUT). Kaimanu or Kaiwanu are alternative names for the planet. Hence Am. 5:26 should be translated, as in RSV, 'You shall take up Sakkuth your king, and Kaiwan your star-god, your images, which you made for yourselves . . .' (Others, however, like NEB, regard this astral interpretation as improbable, and follow LXX in seeing in *Sikkuth* a reference to tent-shrines, while translating *Kaiwan* as 'pedestal(s)'—an interpretation attested as early as the *Zadokite Work* of the 1st century BC.) (*REMPHAN.) J.A.T.

SALAMIS. A town on the E coast of the central plain of *Cyprus, not to be confused with the famous island off the coast of Attica. It rivalled in importance Paphos, the Roman capital of the whole island, and eventually superseded it. The harbour which made Salamis a great commercial centre is now completely silted up. In the 1st century AD the Jewish community there was large enough to have more than one synagogue (Acts 13:5). Destroyed by earthquakes, the town was rebuilt in the 4th century AD as Constantia. Its ruins are 5 km from Famagusta. K.L.McK.

SALECAH, SALCAH. A place in the extreme E of *Bashan (Dt. 3:10; Jos. 12:5; 13:11). Though Bashan fell to the lot of Manasseh, the area occupied by Gad included Salecah (1 Ch. 5:11). It probably was within the area conquered by David, but after Solomon's time it lay outside Israelite territory. The site is possibly the modern Ṣalḫad (Nabataean *ṣlḥd*) on a S spur of the Hauran, though this identification is not universally accepted. See *LOB*, p. 383. T.C.M.

SALEM. The place where Melchizedek ruled (Gn. 14:18; Heb. 7:1, 8) near the valley of Shaveh (Gn. 14:17; explained as 'the King's Valley'). It is mentioned in parallel with Zion (Ps. 76:2). Following Jos. (*Ant.* 1. 180), it is usually identified with the ancient site of *Jerusalem, the city of Salem, *Uru-salem, uru-salimmu* of the cuneiform and Egyptian inscriptions. This would suit the route probably taken by Abraham on his return from Damascus to Hebron when he encountered Melchizedek. Those who assume his return down the Jordan valley look for a more E location such as *Salim. The Samaritans link Salem with *Shalem, a city of Shechem (Gn. 33:18, AV), E of Nablus, but this may be due to their ancient rivalry with Judah, where a 'Valley of Salem' is known as late as Maccabean times (Judith 4:4). In Je. 41:5 the LXX (B) reads Salem for Shiloh.

The name *šālēm* (Gk. *Salem*) means 'safe, at peace', though Jerusalem has been interpreted as 'Salem founded' implying a divine name Salem. For the early occurrence of this name form, *cf.* *šillēm* (Gn. 46:24; Nu. 26:49). D.J.W.

SALIM. An apparently well-known place (Gk. *Saleim*) near Aenon on the river Jordan where John baptized (Jn. 3:23). Of the many identifications proposed, the Salim (Salumias) or Tell Abu Sus about 12 km S of Beisan (*Bethshan-Scythopolis) is the most likely. The ruins of Tell Ridgha or Tell Sheikh Selim, as it is also called after the local shrine, lie near several springs which might have been called Aenon (Arab. *'ain*, 'spring'). This site would be under the control of Scythopolis. Salim is mentioned by Eusebius, and marked on the 6th century AD Medaba map. The

Salim E of Nablus with which the Samaritans identify the *Salem of Gn. 14:18 lies in the heart of Samaria. The land of Salim (RSV 'Shaalim') is a region in hilly Ephraim, possibly between Aijalon and Ramah (1 Sa. 9:4). *Cf.* W. F. Albright, *The Archaeology of Palestine*, 1960, p. 247; *idem*, in *The Background of the New Testament and its Eschatology* (ed. W. D. Davies and D. Daube), 1956, p. 159. (*SHAALBIM.) D.J.W.

SALMON, SALMA. 1. Of Judah's line (Mt. 1:4–5; Lk. 3:32). The son of Nahshon, and father of Boaz the husband of Ruth and the great-grandfather of David the son of Jesse (Ru. 4:20; 1 Ch. 2:11). According to Mt. 1:5 he married Rahab (of Jericho). **2.** Also of Judah's line. A son of Caleb (not to be confused with Caleb, son of Jephunneh), and father of the Bethlehemites, Netophathites and other groups associated with the Kenites (1 Ch. 2:51–54). C.H.D.

SALMONE. A promontory at the extreme E end of Crete, now known as Cape Sidero. On his way to Rome Paul's ship was prevented by a NW wind from proceeding from off Cnidus along the N coast of Crete, and, tacking past Salmone, sheltered in the lee of the island (Acts 27:7). K.L.McK.

SALOME (Heb. *šālôm*, 'peace', with Gk. suffix). **1.** According to Mk. 15:40 and 16:1, of three women who saw the crucifixion and went to the tomb on Easter morning two were called Mary and one Salome. Mt. 27:56 names two women called Mary, and the mother of the sons of Zebedee, who is probably to be identified with Salome. Jn. 19:25 refers to two women called Mary, plus the mother of Jesus and his mother's sister, who stood near the cross. If his mother's sister is identified with Salome, then James and John, the sons of Zebedee, would be cousins of Jesus. It is equally possible, however, that John has made a different selection of names out of the 'many other women' who, according to Mk. 15:41, were present at the crucifixion.

2. The daughter of Herodias, by her first husband Herod Philip (Josephus, *Ant.* 18. 136f.). Though not named in the Gospel accounts, she is usually identified with the girl who danced before Herod (Mk. 6:22; Mt. 14:6). She married her father's half-brother Philip the tetrarch. D.R.H.

SALT. Whereas the Phoenicians obtained quantities of salt from the Mediterranean by evaporation in salt-pans, the Hebrews had access to an unlimited supply on the shores of the Dead Sea (Zp. 2:9) and in the hill of Salt (Jebel Usdum), a 15-square-mile (4,000 hectares) elevation at the SW corner of the Dead Sea. This area was traditionally associated with the fate of Lot's wife (Gn. 19:26).

Such salt was of the rock or fossil variety, and, because of impurities and the occurrence of chemical changes, the outer layer was generally lacking in flavour. The reference in Mt. 5:13 is to this latter, much of which was discarded as worthless. Salt was valued as a preservative and for seasoning food (Mt. 5:13; Mk. 9:50; Col. 4:6). It was often used among Oriental peoples for ratifying agreements, so that salt became the symbol of fidelity and constancy. In the levitical cereal-offerings (Lv. 2:13) salt was used as a preservative to typify the eternal nature of the 'covenant of salt' existing between God and Israel (Nu. 18:19; 2 Ch. 13:5).

The effect of salt on vegetation was to render the land infertile (Dt. 29:23). Thus the 'parched places of the wilderness' (Je. 17:6) were synonymous with a barren salt land (Jb. 39:6). Abimelech followed an ancient custom in sowing ruined Shechem with salt (Jdg. 9:45) as a token of perpetual desolation. Elisha used salt to sweeten the brackish waters of the Jericho spring (2 Ki. 2:19–22). New-born infants were normally rubbed with salt prior to swaddling (Ezk. 16:4). Under Antiochus Epiphanes Syria imposed a tax upon salt, which was paid to Rome.

BIBLIOGRAPHY. E. P. Deatrick and F. C. Fensham, *BA* 25, 1962, pp. 41–49; L. G. Hevv, *ISBE* 4, pp. 286–287. R.K.H.

SALT, CITY OF (Heb. *'îr hammelaḥ*). In Jos. 15:62 one of the frontier posts of the tribal territory of Judah 'in the wilderness', S of Middin, Secacah and Nibshan (now identifiable, on the basis of excavations, with the Buqei'a Iron Age II settlements at Khirbet Abū Ṭabaq, Khirbet es-Samrah and Khirbet el-Maqāri), and N of Engedi. Its identification with Khirbet Qumran, first suggested by M. Noth (*Josua*, 1938, p. 72; *ZDPV* 71, 1955, pp. 111ff.), has been confirmed by the discovery of an Iron Age II fortress beneath the *Qumran community settlement (*cf.* F. M. Cross Jr., J. T. Milik, *BASOR* 142, 1956, pp. 5ff.; R. de Vaux, *Archaeology and the Dead Sea Scrolls*, 1973, pp. 91ff. F.F.B.

SALT, VALLEY OF. Saline encrustations in steppe and desert lands are common. Some are of climatic origin; in other cases the climate has preserved geological salinity in the rocks. It is not possible to identify one topographic location from the biblical references. David and his lieutenant Abishai had memorable victories over the Edomites in the Valley of Salt (2 Sa. 8:13; 1 Ch. 18:12). Later Amaziah had a similar victory (2 Ki. 14:7; 2 Ch. 25:11). Traditionally the site has been accepted as the plain SSW of the Dead Sea, opposite the oasis of the Zered delta, where a plain 10–13 km long is overlooked by the salt range of Jebel Usdum, 8 km long and 200 m high. This plain passes imperceptibly into the glistening lowland of the Sebkha to the SE, a soft, impassable waste of salt marsh, where an army could well be routed in confusion. But, equally well, the site could be Wadi el-Milh (salt), E of Beersheba, also overlooked by a rocky hill, Tel el-Milh. All that the more precise reference of 2 Ch. 25:11 suggests is that the plain was overlooked by a rocky hill, somewhere between Judah and Edom, presumably in the Arabah. J.M.H.

SALVATION (Heb. *yēša'*; Gk. *sōtēria*).

I. In the Old Testament

The principal Heb. term translated 'salvation' is *yēša'* and its cognates. Its basic meaning is 'bring into a spacious environment' (*cf.* Pss. 18:36; 66:12), but it carries from the beginning the metaphorical sense of 'freedom from limitation' and the means to that; *i.e.* deliverance from factors which constrain and confine. It can be referred to deliverance from disease (Is. 38:20; *cf.* v. 9), from trouble (Je. 30:7) or enemies (2 Sa. 3:18; Ps. 44:7). In the vast majority of references God is the author of salvation. Thus God saves his flock (Ezk. 34:22); he rescues his people (Ho. 1:7) and he alone can save them (Ho. 13:10–14); there is no other saviour besides him (Is. 43:11). He saved the fathers from Egypt (Ps. 106:7–10) and their sons from Babylon (Je. 30:10). He is the refuge and saviour of his people (2 Sa. 22:3). He saves the poor and needy when they have no other helper (Ps. 34:6; Jb. 5:15). The word of Moses, 'stand firm, and see the salvation of the Lord' (Ex. 14:13), is of the essence of the OT idea. Thus to know God at all is to know him as a saving God (Ho. 13:4) so that the words 'God' and 'Saviour' are virtually identical terms in the OT. The great normative instance of God's saving deliverance was the exodus (Ex. 12:40–14:31). The redemption from Egyptian bondage through the intervention of God at the Red Sea was determinative of all Israel's subsequent reflection on God's nature and activity. The exodus was the mould into which all the subsequent interpretation of the drama of Israel's history was poured. It was sung in worship (Ps. 66:1–7), retold in story (Dt. 6:20–24), re-enacted in ritual (Ex. 13:3–16). Thus the notion of salvation emerged from the exodus indelibly stamped with the dimension of God's mighty acts of deliverance in history.

This profoundly significant element laid the basis in turn for a further major OT contribution to the idea of salvation, *viz.* eschatology. Israel's experience of God as saviour in the past projected her faith forward in anticipation of his full and final salvation in the future. Precisely because Yahweh has shown himself to be the Lord of all, creator and ruler of the whole earth, and because he is a righteous and faithful God, he will one day effect his total victory over his foes and save his people from all their ills (Is. 43:11–21; Dt. 9:4–6; Ezk. 36:22–23). In the earlier period this hope of salvation centres more upon immediate historic intervention for the vindication of Israel (*cf.* Gn. 49; Dt. 33; Nu. 23f.). In the prophetic period it finds expression in terms of a 'Day of Yahweh' in which judgment would combine with deliverance (Is. 24:19f.; 25:6–8; Joel 2:1f., 28–32; Am. 5:18f.; 9:11f.). The experience of the Exile gave concrete imagery and a concrete setting for the expression of this hope as a new exodus (Is. 43:14–16; 48:20f.; 51:9f.; *cf.* Je. 31:31–34; Ezk. 37:21–28; Zc. 8:7–13); but the disappointing and limited results of the restoration projected the hope forward again and transmuted it into what has been termed the *transcendental-eschatological* (Is 64:1f.; 65:17f.; 66:22), the hope of the *'olām habba'*, the new world at the end of the present age in which God's sovereign rule and righteous character would be manifested among all the nations.

Reference should also be made to other related terms which the LXX renders by *sotēria*; in particular the root *g'l*, 'to redeem', to recover property which had fallen into alien hands, to 'purchase back', often by payment. The person effecting this redemption, or salvation, is the *gō'ēl*, the 'kinsman-redeemer' (*cf.* Lv. 25:26, 32; Ru. 4:4, 6). God is the great *gō'ēl* of Israel (Ex. 6:6; Ps. 77:14f.). This usage is synonymous with *yēša'* in the latter part of Isaiah (Is. 41:14; 44:6; 47:4). They appear as parallel terms in Is. 43:1–2; 60:16; 63:9 (*cf.* *TDNT* 7, pp. 977–978).

Finally we note that the saving activity of God in the OT is expanded and deepened in terms of a particular instrument of this salvation, the Messiah-Servant. Salvation implies an agent, or saviour, though not necessarily one other than Yahweh himself. In general while Yahweh may employ particular human agents, or saviours, at particular historical junctures (Gn. 45:7; Jdg. 3:9,15; 2 Ki. 13:5; Ne. 9:27), he alone is the saviour of his people (Is. 43:11; 45:21; Ho. 13:4). This general assertion however requires qualification in the context of the development of the hope of salvation in the OT where in the Servant Songs we encounter a personal embodiment of Yahweh's moral salvation, even though the Servant is never directly referred to as saviour. Corporate imagery is clearly present here but the personification of the Servant's ministry is clear in the text, and in the light of NT fulfilment needs no further defence. In the song, Is. 49:1–6, he is to be the instrument of God's universal salvation (v. 6; *cf.* too v. 8). The final song, 52:13–53:12, does not contain the term but the idea of salvation is everywhere present in terms of a deliverance from sin and its consequences. Thus the OT leads us finally to the understanding that God delivers his people through his saviour-Messiah.

II. In the New Testament

In the NT we begin with the general observation that the 'religious' usage of a moral/spiritual deliverance becomes almost wholly dominant as far as the idea of salvation is concerned. Non-religious usage is virtually confined to saving from acute danger to life (Acts 27:20, 31; Mk. 15:30; Heb. 5:7).

a. The Synoptic Gospels

The word salvation is mentioned by Jesus only once (Lk. 19:9), where it may refer either to himself as the embodiment of salvation imparting pardon to Zacchaeus, or to that which is evidenced by the transformed conduct of the publican. Our Lord, however, used 'save' and kindred terms to indicate first what he came to do (by implication, Mk. 3:4; and by direct statement, Lk. 4:18; Mt. 18:11; Lk. 9:56; Mt. 20:28), and secondly, what is demanded of man (Mk. 8:35; Lk. 7:50; 8:12; 13:24; Mt. 10:22). Lk. 18:26, and context, shows that salvation calls for a contrite heart, childlike, receptive helplessness, and the renunciation of all for Christ—conditions it is impossible for man unaided to fulfil.

The testimony of others to our Lord's saving activity is both indirect (Mk. 15:31) and direct (Mt. 8:17). There is also the witness of his own name (Mt. 1:21, 23). All these varied usages suggest that salvation was present in the person and ministry of Christ and especially in his death.

b. The Fourth Gospel

This double truth is underlined in the Fourth Gospel, in which each chapter suggests different aspects of salvation. Thus in 1:12f. men are born as sons of God by trusting in Christ; in 2:5 the situation is remedied by doing 'whatever he tells you'; in 3:5 new birth from the Spirit is essential for entering the kingdom, but 3:14, 17 make it clear that this new life is not possible apart from trust in the death of Christ, without which men are already under condemnation (3:18); in 4:22 salvation is of the Jews—by revelation historically channelled through God's people—and is a gift inwardly transforming and equipping men for worship.

In 5:14 the one made whole must sin no more lest a worse thing come; in 5:39 the Scriptures testify of life (=salvation) in the Son, to whom life and judgment are committed; in 5:24 believers have already passed from death to life; in 6:35 Jesus declares himself the bread of life, to whom alone men should go (6:68) for the quickening words of eternal life; in 7:39 water is the symbol of the saving life of the Spirit who was to come after Jesus had been glorified.

In 8:12 the Evangelist shows the safety of the guidance of light and in vv. 32, 36 the liberty through truth in the Son; in 9:25, 37, 39 salvation is spiritual sight; in 10:10 entrance into the safety and abundant life of the fold and of the Father is through Christ; in 11:25f. resurrection-life belongs to the believer; in 11:50 (*cf.* 18:14) the saving purpose of his death is unwittingly described; in 12:32 Christ, lifted up in death, draws men to him; in 13:10 his initial washing signifies salvation ('clean all over'); in 14:6 he is the true and living way to the Father's abode; in 15:5 abiding in him, the Vine, is the secret of life's resources; in 16:7–15 for his sake the Spirit will deal with the obstacles to salvation and prepare for its realization; in 17:2–3, 12 he keeps safely those who have knowledge of the true God and of himself; in 19:30 salvation is accomplished; in 20:21–23 the words of peace and pardon accompany his gift of the Spirit; in 21:15–18 his healing love reinstils love in his follower and reinstates him for service.

c. The Acts

Acts traces the proclamation (*cf.* 16:17) of salvation in its impact first upon the crowds which are exhorted to be saved 'from this crooked generation' (2:40) by repentance (itself a gift and part of salvation, 11:18), remission of sins, and receiving the Holy Spirit; then upon a sick individual, ignorant of his true need, who is healed by the name of Jesus, the only name whereby we must be saved; and thirdly, upon the household of him who asked 'What must I do to be saved?' (16:30ff.).

d. The Pauline Epistles

Paul claims that the Scriptures 'are able to instruct you for salvation through faith in Christ Jesus' (2 Tim. 3:15ff.) and provide the ingredients essential for the enjoyment of a full-orbed salvation. Enlarging and applying the OT concept of the righteousness of God, which itself had adumbrations of the saving righteousness of the NT, Paul shows how there is no salvation by means of the law, since it could only indicate the presence and excite the reactionary activity of sin and stop men's mouths in their guilt before God (Rom. 3:19; Gal. 2:16). Salvation is provided as the free gift of the righteous God acting in grace towards the undeserving sinner who, by the gift of faith, trusts in the righteousness of Christ who has redeemed him by his death and justified him by his resurrection. God, for Christ's sake, justifies the unmeriting sinner (*i.e.* reckons to him the perfect righteousness of Christ and regards him as if he had not sinned), forgives his sin, reconciles him to himself in and through Christ 'making peace by the blood of his cross' (2 Cor. 5:18; Rom. 5:11; Col. 1:20), adopts him into his family (Gal. 4:5f.; Eph. 1:13; 2 Cor. 1:22), giving him the seal, earnest, and firstfruits of his Spirit in his heart, and so making him a new creation. By the same Spirit the subsequent resources of salvation enable him to walk in newness of life, mortifying the deeds of the body increasingly (Rom. 8:13) until ultimately he is conformed to Christ (Rom. 8:29) and his salvation is consummated in glory (Phil. 3:21).

e. The Epistle to the Hebrews

The 'great' salvation of the Epistle to the Hebrews transcends the OT foreshadowings of salvation. The NT salvation is described in the language of sacrifice; the oft-repeated offerings of the OT ritual that dealt mainly with unwitting sins and provided only a superficial salvation are replaced by the one sacrifice of Christ, himself both saving Priest and Offering (Heb. 9:26; 10:12). The outpouring of his life-blood in death effects atonement, so that henceforth man with a cleansed conscience can enter the presence of God in terms of the new covenant ratified by God through his Mediator (Heb. 9:15; 12:24). Hebrews, which lays such stress on Christ's dealing with sin by his suffering and death to provide eternal salvation, anticipates his second appearing, not then to deal with sin, but to consummate his people's salvation and, presumably, their attendant glory (9:28).

f. The Epistle of James

James teaches that salvation is not by 'faith' only but also by 'works' (2:24). His concern is to disillusion anyone who relies for his salvation on a mere intellectual acknowledgment of the existence of God without a change in heart resulting in works of righteousness. He does not discount true faith, but urges that its presence be shown by a conduct that in turn indicates the saving energies of true religion at work through the ingrafted Word of God. He is as concerned as any to bring back the sinner from the error of his way and save his soul from death (5:20).

g. 1 and 2 Peter

1 Peter strikes a similar note to Hebrews about the costly salvation (1:19) which was searched for and foretold by the prophets but is now a present reality to those who, like straying sheep, have returned to the Shepherd of their souls (2:24f.). Its future aspect is known by those who 'are guarded . . . for a salvation ready to be revealed' (1 Pet. 1:5).

In 2 Peter salvation involves escaping the corruption that is in the world through lust by being partakers of the divine nature (1:4). In the context of sin the believer yearns for the new heavens and the new earth wherein dwells righteousness, but recognizes that the postponement of the parousia is due to the longsuffering of his Lord, which is itself an aspect of salvation (3:13, 15).

h. 1, 2 and 3 John

For 1 John the sacrificial language of Hebrews is congenial. Christ is our salvation by being the propitiation for our sins, as the outcome of God's love. It is God in his love in Christ's outpoured life-blood who covers our sins and cleanses us. As in the Fourth Gospel, salvation is conceived in terms of being born of God, knowing God, possessing eternal life in Christ, living in the light and truth of God, dwelling in God and knowing his dwelling in us through love by his Spirit (3:9; 4:6, 13; 5:11). 3 John has a significant prayer for general prosperity and bodily health (natural well-being) to accompany prosperity of soul (v. 2).

i. The Epistle of Jude

Jude 3, in referring to the 'common salvation', has in mind something akin to the 'common faith' of Tit. 1:4, and allies it to the 'faith' (*cf.* Eph. 4:5) for which believers are to contend. This salvation comprises the saving truths, privileges, demands and experiences common to the variety of his readers. In vv. 22f. he would urgently present this salvation to various groups in doubt, danger and degradation.

j. The Revelation

Revelation reiterates the theme (of 1 Jn.) of salvation as liberation or cleansing from sin by virtue of the blood of Christ and its constitution of believers as royal priests (1:5f.). In a manner reminiscent of the psalmist, the seer, in adoration, ascribes salvation in its comprehensiveness to God (7:10). The closing chapters of the book depict salvation in terms of the leaves of the tree of life which are for the healing of the nations, to which tree, as to the city of salvation, admission is given only to those whose names are written in the book of life.

III. Relation to other views of salvation

a. The Essenes

Considerable attention has been given in the years since the discovery of the *Dead Sea Scrolls (1947 onwards) to this monastic movement within Judaism, and various attempts made to evaluate its contribution to NT origins. As far as the doctrine of salvation is concerned the Qumran Essenes shared the biblical sense of man's inherent sinfulness apart from God, and one notable passage (1QS 11. 9f.; *cf.* also the *Hymn of Thanksgiving*) approaches very near to the NT doctrine of salvation as acquittal by the action of God's righteousness, salvation through utter reliance upon the grace and mercy of God. This however is not altogether surprising bearing in mind the debt of the Qumran covenanters to the psalter and the great OT prophets. It would be wrong to overstress the points of correspondence; at other points the parallel with NT teaching is much more tenuous. The universalism of the Christian gospel is totally lacking; salvation is certainly *not* for the common mass of sinners. The Qumran understanding of the Suffering Servant of Is. 53 is disputed, but the prophecy appears to have been seen as fulfilled in the inner council (*sôḏ*) of the community. Nor can one entirely evade the simple fact that there is not one unambiguous reference to the Essenes in the entire NT.

b. Gnosticism

The precise dating of gnostic teaching is disputed, and the attempt to demonstrate a Christian dependence upon gnostic ideas is today a distinctly uncertain enterprise. There is however evidence in the NT (*cf.* 1 and 2 Cor.; Col.; 1 and 2 Tim; Tit.; 1 Jn.; Rev.) that the early church had to distinguish its salvation teaching from views which were embodied in later gnostic doctrines. In essence the gnostic claimed salvation by an immediate knowledge of God. This knowledge was intellectual as against moral, and esoteric in its being confined to the élite circle of initiates. Gnosticism also taught a dualism of soul and body, only the former being significant for salvation; and a hierarchy of spiritual and angelic intermediaries between God and man. Salvation was the escape from the domination of alien astrological forces and human passions by coming to 'know' in response to a 'call' from the divine world expressed in the so-called 'gnostic-redeemer myth', the story of the heavenly man who came down from the world of celestial light to 'save' 'fallen' men by the impartation of this secret knowledge.

As has already been implied, the attempt to locate such a view in the pre-Christian period and hence to see it as lying behind NT notions of salvation falls a long way short of demonstration. The evidence is far more compatible with the view that in the syncretistic religious atmosphere of the time certain latent gnostic tendencies were in the 2nd and 3rd centuries wedded to Christian salvation motifs to produce the doctrines of the gnostic sects which we have outlined above and of which we hear from writers such as Irenaeus in the post NT period. Against incipient forms of such notions of salvation the biblical writers stress the universal scope of God's offer of salvation, its essentially moral nature, the true humanity and the true deity of the mediator, and the focus of salvation in the historic acts of God in the birth, life, death and resurrection of Jesus Christ (*cf.* NT sections cited above).

c. The mystery religions

Another point at which the NT writers had to distinguish their doctrine of salvation from current ideas was in relation to the mystery cults. This 1st-century phenomenon was a combination of Hellenistic and oriental elements which had their origin in ancient fertility rites. They claimed to offer 'salvation' from fate, and a life beyond the grave free from the unsatisfactory and oppressive conditions of the present. Salvation was attained by the meticulous performance of certain cultic rituals. Language similar to the NT occurs at points. The initiates could be referred to as 'born again to eternal life'. Cult deities such as Dionysius attained the title 'Lord and Saviour'. Links with Christian theology have been alleged, particularly at the sacramental level, since sacred lustrations and the idea of uniting with the gods in a solemn meal were known. At even a cursory examination, however, the differences from the early Christian message and the life of the early Christian communities are stark and obvious. Salvation in the mysteries was essentially non-moral. The 'saved' worshipper was not expected to be a better man than his pagan neighbour, nor in most cases was he. The rational element was minimal; there were no great saving acts, and so no great common theological affirmations.

The alleged parallels to the Christian (Pauline) baptismal and eucharistic teaching have also been shown to be almost certainly without foundation; the evidence rather pointing to the apostle's debt to biblical salvation-history centred in God's mighty deed of redemption in Jesus Christ.

d. The imperial cult

The age-long mirage of salvation through political power and organization was reflected in the 1st century in the imperial cult. The myth of a God-King who was the saviour and benefactor of his people appears widely in various forms in the ancient world particularly in the orient. In Rome the impetus for the official cult stems from the career of Augustus who after Actium in 31 BC established the *Pax Romana*, the golden age of peace after decades of bloodshed. He was commonly addressed as *sōtēr*, 'Saviour of the world', and through his relationship to Julius Caesar, 'the Son of God'. Even in Augustus' case however some caution needs to be exercised since it has been shown that the title *sōtēr* was certainly not confined to the emperor, nor was the title always invested with the full oriental implications. The successive emperors of the 1st century showed varying degree of enthusiasm for the claims made on their behalf in the official cult. Caligula, Nero and Domitian certainly took their divine status seriously and this may account to some extent for some of the appearances of the title referred to Jesus Christ and the Father in the NT (*cf.* 1 Tim. 1:1; 4:10; Tit. 1:3; 3:4; 1 Jn. 4:14; Jude 25; Rev. 7:10; 12:10; 19:1).

e. Summary

In general, while there are clear parallels in language, the case for the dependence of Christian salvation teaching upon any or all of these contemporary movements has certainly not been made. In attempting to communicate the gospel to their contemporaries the NT preachers and writers certainly were not unprepared to translate the message, including its salvation language, into 1st-century thought-patterns, but the true origin and justification of their salvation language lies outside that world, in the salvation-history tradition of the OT as focused and fulfilled in the person and mission of Jesus Christ.

IV. Biblical salvation: Summary

1. Salvation is historical. The OT view of salvation as effected through historic, divine intervention is fully honoured in the NT. As against Gnosticism, man is not saved by wisdom; as against Judaism, man is not saved by moral and religious merit; as against the Hellenistic mystery cults, man is not saved by a technique of religious practice; as against Rome, salvation is not to be equated with political order or liberty. Man is saved by God's action in history in the person of Jesus Christ (Rom. 4:25; 5:10; 2 Cor. 4:10f.; Phil. 2:6f.; 1 Tim. 1:15; 1 Jn. 4:9–10, 14). While the birth, life and ministry of Jesus are not unimportant, the stress falls upon his death and resurrection (1 Cor. 15:5f.); we are saved by the blood of his cross (Acts 20:28; Rom. 3:25; 5:9; Eph. 1:7; Col. 1:20; Heb. 9:12; 12:24; 13:12; 1 Jn. 1:7; Rev. 1:5; 5:9). As this message is proclaimed and men hear and come to respond in faith God's salvation is brought to them (Rom. 10:8, 14f.; 1 Cor. 1:18–25; 15:11; 1 Thes. 1:4f.).

2. Salvation is moral and spiritual. Salvation relates to a deliverance from sin and its consequences and hence from guilt (Rom. 5:1; Heb. 10:22), from the law and its curse (Gal. 3:13; Col. 2:14), from death (1 Pet. 1:3–5; 1 Cor. 15:51–56), from judgment (Rom. 5:9; Heb. 9:28), also from fear (Heb. 2:15; 2 Tim. 1:7, 9f.) and bondage (Tit. 2:11–3: 6; Gal. 5:1f.). It is important to indicate the negative implications of this, *i.e.* what Christian salvation does *not* include. Salvation does not imply material prosperity or worldly success (Acts 3:6; 2 Cor. 6:10), nor does it promise physical health and well-being. One must be careful not to overstate this particular negative, as clearly remarkable healings did and do take place and 'healing' is a gift of the Spirit to the church (Acts 3:9; 9:34; 20:9f.; 1 Cor. 12:28). But healing is not invariable, and hence is in no sense a 'right' of the saved man (1 Tim. 5:23; 2 Tim. 4:20; Phil. 2:25f.; 2 Cor. 12:7–9). Further, salvation does not include deliverance from physical hardship and danger (1 Cor. 4:9–13; 2 Cor. 11:23–28), nor even, perhaps, seemingly tragic events (Mt. 5:45?). It does not mean being absolved from social injustice and ill-treatment (1 Cor. 7:20–24; 1 Pet. 2:18–25).

3. Salvation is eschatological. There is a danger of stating the meaning of salvation too negatively. Here we recall the recognition above of the paucity of references to salvation from the lips of Jesus. His central category was the kingdom of God, the manifestation of God's sovereign rule. In Rev. 12:10 however salvation and the kingdom are virtually equated. For the author of the Apocalypse as for Jesus salvation is equivalent to life under the reign of God, or, as in the witness of the Fourth Gospel, eternal life. Salvation therefore gathers up all the contents of the gospel. It includes deliverance from sin and all its consequences, and positively, the bestowal of all spiritual blessings in Christ (Eph. 1:3), the gift of the Holy Spirit and the life of blessedness in the future age. This future perspective is crucial (Rom. 8:24; 13:11; 1 Cor. 5:5; Phil. 3:20; Heb. 1:14; 9:28; 1 Pet. 1:5, 9). All that is known of salvation now is but a preliminary and foretaste of the fullness of salvation which awaits the fullness of the kingdom at the parousia of the Lord.

(*ATONEMENT; *ELECTION; *FORGIVENESS; *JUSTIFICATION; *SANCTIFICATION; *SIN; *GRACE; *RECONCILIATION.)

BIBLIOGRAPHY. W. Foerster, G. Fohrer, in *TDNT* 7, pp. 965–1003; M. Green, *The Meaning of Salvation*, 1965; G. Wagner, *Pauline Baptism and the Pagan Mysteries*, E.T. 1967; M. Black (ed.), *The Scrolls and Christianity*, 1969; E. Yamauchi, *Pre-Christian Gnosticism*, 1973; J. R. W. Stott, *Christian Mission in the Modern World*, 1975, ch. 5; *Let the Earth Hear His Voice*, 1975; *NIDNTT* 3, *s.v.* 'Reconciliation', 'Redemption'; D. F. Wells, *The Search for Salvation*, 1978; H. D. McDonald, *Salvation*, 1982.

G.W.
B.A.M.

SAMARIA. The name of the N Israelite capital and of the territory surrounding it.

I. History

After reigning 6 years at Tirzah, Omri built a new capital for the N kingdom on a hill 11 km NW of Shechem commanding the main trade routes through the Esdraelon plain. He purchased the site for two talents of silver and named it after its owner Shemer (1 Ki. 16:24). The place is otherwise unknown unless it is to be identified with Shamir, the home of Tola (Jdg. 10:1; F. M. Abel, *Géographie de la Palestine*, 2, p. 444). The hill, which is *c.* 100 m high and commands a view over the plain, was impregnable except by siege (2 Ki. 6:24), and the name (*šōmᶜrôn*) may be connected with the Heb. 'watch-post'.

Omri allowed the Syrians of Damascus to set up bazaars (AV 'streets') in his new city (1 Ki. 20:34). For 6 years he worked on the construction of Samaria, and this was continued by Ahab, who built a house decorated or panelled with ivory (1 Ki. 22:39). In a temple for Baal of Sidon (Melqart), the deity whose worship Jezebel encouraged (1 Ki. 18:22), Ahab set up a pillar (*'ăšērâ*) near the altar which Jehoram later removed (2 Ki. 3:2). Other shrines and buildings used by the idolatrous priests must have been in use from this time until the reform undertaken by Jehu (2 Ki. 10:19). Samaria itself was long considered by the prophets a centre of idolatry (Is. 8:4; 9:9; Je. 23:13; Ezk. 23:4; Ho. 7:1; Mi. 1:6).

Ben-hadad II of Syria besieged Samaria, at first unsuccessfully (1 Ki. 20:1–21), but later the Syrians reduced it to dire famine (2 Ki. 6:25). It was relieved only by the panic and sudden withdrawal of the besiegers, which was discovered and reported by the lepers (2 Ki. 7). Ahab was buried in the city, as were a number of Israelite kings who made it their residence (1 Ki. 22: 37; 2 Ki. 13:9, 13; 14:16). His descendants were slain there (2 Ki. 10:1), including Ahaziah, who hid in vain in the crowded city (2 Ch. 22:9). Samaria was again besieged in the time of Elisha and miraculously delivered (2 Ki. 6:8ff.).

*Menahem preserved the city from attack by paying tribute to *Tiglath-pileser III (2 Ki. 15:17–20). His son *Pekah, however, drew the Assyrian army back again by his attack on Judah, then a vassal-ally of Assyria. The city, called *Samerina* or *Bit-Ḫumri* ('House of Omri') in the Assyrian Annals, was besieged by Shalmaneser V of Assyria in 725–722 BC. 2 Ki. records that he captured the city, agreeing with the Babylonian Chronicle, but evidently his death intervened before it was finally secured for Assyria. The citizens, incited by Iaubi'di of Hamath, refused to pay the tax imposed on them, and in the following year (721 BC) Sargon II, the new king of Assyria, initiated a scheme of mass deportation for the whole area. According to his annals, Sargon carried off 27,270 or 27,290 captives, and the effect was to terminate the existence of the N kingdom of Israel as a homogeneous and independent state. The exiles were despatched to places in Syria, Assyria and Babylonia and replaced by colonists from other disturbed parts of the Assyrian empire (2 Ki. 17:24). The resultant failure to cultivate the outlying districts led to an increase in the incursions of lions (v. 25). Some Israelites, called *Samaritans (v. 29), still inhabited part of the city and continued to worship at Jerusalem (Je. 41:5). The town, according to a cuneiform inscription (*HES*, 247) and to other records, was under an Assyrian governor and both Esarhaddon (Ezr. 4:2) and Ashurbanipal (Ezr. 4:9–10) brought in additional peoples from Babylonia and Elam. The contention between Samaria and Judah, of earlier origin, gradually increased in intensity, though Samaria itself declined in importance.

The discovery of papyri from Samaria in a cave of the Wadi ed-Dâliyeh 14 km N of Jericho seems to confirm the reports of ancient historians that Samaria was initially favourable to Alexander who captured the city in 331 BC. However, while Alexander was in Egypt they murdered his prefect over Syria. On his return, Alexander destroyed Samaria, massacred the city's leaders in the cave to which they had fled and resettled the area with Macedonians. Information contained in the papyri enables a list of Samaritan governors to be constructed, beginning with Sanballat I *c.* 445 BC.

Samaria was besieged by John Hyrcanus, and the surrounding countryside was devastated *c.* 111–107 BC. Pompey and Gabinius began to rebuild (Jos., *Ant.* 14. 75), but it was left to Herod to embellish the city, which he renamed Sebaste (Augusta) in honour of his emperor. In it he housed 6,000 veterans, including Greeks. On his death, Samaria became part of the territory of Archelaus and later a Roman colony under Septimus Severus. Despite the mutual antagonism between Judah and Samaria, Jesus Christ took the shorter route through Samaria to Galilee (Lk. 17:11), resting at Sychar near Shechem, a Samaritan city (Jn. 4:4). Philip preached in Samaria, but perhaps the district rather than the city is intended, since the definite article is absent in Acts 8:5.

II. Archaeology

The site was occupied in the Early Bronze Age, then deserted until the Iron Age. Sixteen levels of occupation were recognized by the Harvard (1908–10) and, later, joint Harvard–Hebrew University–British School of Archaeology in Jerusalem expeditions (1931–5). Further excavations were made by the Department of Antiquities of Jordan in 1965 and the British School of Archaeology in Jerusalem in 1968. The site is difficult to work because of the dense and continuous habitation, with constant rebuilding. Of the periods of occupation unearthed, seven have been assigned to the Israelites: Levels I–II = Omri–Ahab (28 years). The inner (1·5 m thick) and outer (6 m thick) fortification wall, completed by the latter king, enclosed the summit. A main gateway seems to have had a columned entrance court. The palace, which was later adapted by Jeroboam II, had a wide court in which lay a reservoir or pool (10 by 5m), probably the one in which Ahab's bloodstained chariot was washed down (1 Ki. 22:38). In an adjacent storeroom more than 200 plaques or fragments of ivories were discovered. These show Phoenician and pseudo-Egyptian styles and influences and may well have been inlays for furniture in Ahab's ivory house (1 Ki. 22:39) (*IVORY). Sixty-five ostraca, inscribed in Old Hebrew, noted the capacity and original owners of the wine-jars, with the date of their contents (*DOTT*, pp. 204–208; *WRITING). These are probably to be assigned to the reign of Jeroboam II.

Level III marks the period of Jehu with adaptations of earlier buildings. Then, after an interval, come levels IV–VI, the Israelite period covering Jeroboam and the 8th century BC. The city was repaired in the last decades before its fall to the Assyrians in 722 BC, which is marked by the destruction level VII.

The remains of the Hellenistic buildings are well preserved, with a round tower standing nineteen courses of stone high, a fortress, the city wall (near the West Gate), coins, stamped jar-handles and Greek pottery remaining.

The Roman city of Herod is notable for the great temple dedicated to Augustus, built over the Israelite palaces. Other remains include the enclosure wall, and West Gate, with three round towers, a 820-m long colonnaded street bordered by porticos and shops, the temple of Isis rededicated to Kore, a basilica (68 by 32 m), divided into three naves by

Corinthian columns, a forum, a stadium and an aqueduct. Many of the visible ruins are probably to be dated to later restorers, especially Septimus Severus (AD 193–211).

BIBLIOGRAPHY. A. Parrot, *Samaria*, 1958; J. W. Crowfoot, K. Kenyon, *etc.*, *Samaria*, 1, *The Buildings at Samaria*, 1943; 2, *Early Ivories at Samaria*, 1938; 3, *The Objects from Samaria*, 1957; *NEAEHL*, pp. 1300–1310; A. Mazar, *Archaeology and the Land of the Bible*, 1990, pp. 406–410; R. E. Tappy, *The Archaeology of Israelite Samaria*, 1992.

D.J.W.

SAMARITANS. In EVV of the OT, Samaritans are mentioned only in 2 Ki. 17:29, a passage which describes the syncretistic religion of those peoples whom the king of Assyria transported to the N kingdom of Israel to replace the exiled native population after the fall of Samaria (722/721 BC).

Several reasons argue strongly against the identification, favoured by Josephus and many others since, of this group with the Samaritans as they are more widely known from the NT (Mt. 10:5; Lk. 9:52; 10:33; 17:16; Jn. 4:9, 39–40; 8:48; Acts 8:25), some of whose descendants survive to the present day in two small communities at Nablus and Holon: (*i*) the word used (*haššōmrōnîm*) seems merely to mean 'inhabitants of (the city or province of) Samaria (*šōmrôn*)', and this fits the context of 2 Ki. 17 best; (*ii*) there is no evidence that the later Samaritans inhabited Samaria. The earliest certain references to them, by contrast, all point clearly to their residence at Shechem (Ecclus. 50:26; 2 Macc. 5:22f.; 6:2; *cf.* Jn. 4:5f., 20), whilst one of Josephus' sources refers to them as 'Shechemites' (*cf. Ant.* 11. 340–347; 12. 10); (*iii*) nothing whatever that is known of later Samaritan religion and practice suggests the pagan influence of 2 Ki. 17 or Ezr. 4.

The origins of the Samaritans of the NT as a distinctive group should probably not be sought before the start of the Hellenistic period (end of the 4th century BC), when Shechem was rebuilt after a long period of desolation. The enemies of the Jewish community in the earlier Persian period mentioned in Ezr. and Ne. would then be some of the inhabitants of the N province whose opposition to the rebuilding of Jerusalem was mainly stirred by political motives. That some adhered to the Israelite faith (Ezr. 4:2) is not surprising, since the OT itself acknowledges that not all the inhabitants of the old N kingdom were exiled in 721 BC (2 Ch. 30) and some of the newcomers could well have assimilated to those who remained.

It is not known precisely what factors led to the resettlement of Shechem and the consequent crystallization of the Samaritan community. An attractive suggestion is that following the complete Hellenization of Samaria after the conquests of Alexander the Great, a group of religious purists (possibly joined by some priests whose marriage to women of the N made their continued residence in Jerusalem impracticable) decided to make a fresh start where they could practise their religion unmolested. The find of over 200 skeletons (together with papyri which originated in Samaria) in a remote cave in Wadi ed-Dâliyeh, about 14 km N of Jericho, suggests that other refugees may not have been so fortunate.

Be that as it may, once the community had taken on a distinctive identity, and a temple had been built on Mt Gerizim (both Josephus, *Ant.* 11. 321ff., for all the other difficulties of his narrative at this point, and archaeological remains, if correctly identified, agree on a date in the Hellenistic period), it was inevitable that attitudes between the Jews of Jerusalem and the Samaritans should have begun to harden. Whilst it may be misleading to speak of a particular schism, it is clear that Ben-Sira (*c.* 180 BC) regarded the Samaritans as a quite separate group (Ecclus. 50:26), and this would have been accentuated by their capitulation in the period of the Maccabean revolt, when their temple was dedicated to Zeus Xenios. Perhaps, however, the breach was made final when, *c.* 128 BC, John Hyrcanus extended the Hasmonaean dominance of the area by capturing Shechem and destroying the Gerizim temple.

This by no means marked the end of the friction, however. From the scanty sources available, we learn that between AD 6 and 9 some Samaritans scattered bones in the Jerusalem Temple during a certain Passover. In AD 52 Samaritans massacred a group of Galilean pilgrims at En-gannim, though in the consequent dispute before Claudius, which followed a Jewish reprisal raid, the decision was given in favour of the Jews. Furthermore, the Samaritans suffered at the hands of the Roman rulers: in AD 36 a Samaritan fanatic assembled a crowd on Mt Gerizim, promising to reveal the sacred vessels thought to have been hidden there by Moses, and many of them were massacred by Pilate. A year after the start of the Jewish War (AD 66–70), a group of Samaritans switched allegiance to join the revolt, only to be slaughtered on Mt Gerizim by Vettulenus Cerealis.

Since the main theological writings of the Samaritans (*e.g. Memar Marqah*, the Samaritan liturgy known as the *Defter*, and a number of Chronicles) come from only the 4th century AD, and often much later, it is almost impossible to reconstruct in detail their beliefs in the NT period. For this reason, attempts to find a *distinctively* Samaritan background to (*e.g.*) Jn., Acts 7 or Heb. should be treated with the greatest caution.

Only the five books of the Pentateuch in their Samaritan recension (2nd century BC) were regarded as canonical, and this is reflected in their creed, whose elements must date back to early times: belief in one God, in Moses the prophet, in the law, in Mt Gerizim as the place appointed by God for sacrifice (which is made the tenth commandment in the SP), in the day of judgment and recompense, and in the return of Moses as *Taheb* (the 'restorer' or 'returning one').

The attitude of the Jewish Mishnah and Talmud towards the Samaritans, as of Josephus, is ambiguous. This may reflect a favourable attitude which recognized an essential affinity of both race and religion with the Samaritans, but which was subsequently heavily overlaid with later polemic, encouraged by the developing antagonism and based on 2 Ki. 17 and Ezr. 4.

It is thus noteworthy that the NT is almost consistently favourable towards them (see refs. above), and that the Samaritans are portrayed as responding enthusiastically both to Jesus himself and to the preaching of the early Christian church.

BIBLIOGRAPHY. Still of value is: J. A. Montgomery, *The Samaritans*, 1907, repr. 1968. More recent studies include: J. Macdonald, *The Theology of the Samaritans*, 1964; J. D. Purvis, *The Samaritan Pentateuch and the Origin of the Samaritan Sect*, 1968;

H. G. Kippenberg, *Garizim und Synagoge*, 1971; R. J. Coggins, *Samaritans and Jews*, 1975; K. Haacker, *NIDNTT* 3, pp. 449–467; J. Isser, *The Dositheans*, 1976; R. Pummer, *JSS* 21, 1976, pp. 39–61, and 22, 1977, pp. 27–47; A. D. Crown, *A Bibliography of the Samaritans*, 1984; J. D. Purvis, 'The Samaritans and Judaism', in R. A. Kraft and G. W. E. Nickelsburg (eds.), *Early Judaism and its Modern Interpreters*, 1986, pp. 81–98; A. D. Crown (ed.), *The Samaritans*, 1989. H.G.M.W.

SAMGAR-NEBO (Heb. *samgar-n^e^bô*; Gk. many variants, *e.g. Samagoth, Eissamagath*). Je. 39:3 lists officers of Nebuchadrezzar who sat in the middle gate of Jerusalem after its capture in 587 BC: 'Nergal-sharezer, Samgar-nebo, Sarsechim the Rabsaris, Nergal-sharezer the Rabmag'. Since a list of Nebuchadrezzar's courtiers includes a Nergal-shar-uṣur with the title Sinmagir (*ANET*, p. 308), it is thought that the text is confused and should read 'Nergal-sharezer the Simmagir'. The following Nebo would then belong with *Sarsechim as the name of the *Rabsaris, perhaps corrupted from Nebushazban as in v. 13. All this remains conjecture. A.R.M.

SAMOS. One of the larger islands in the Aegean Sea, off the coast of Asia Minor SW of Ephesus. An Ionian settlement, it had been an important maritime state. Under the Romans it was part of the province of Asia until Augustus made it a free state in 17 BC. On his way back to Judaea from his third missionary journey Paul sailed between Samos and the mainland (Acts 20:15). K.L.McK.

SAMOTHRACE (modern Samothraki). A small mountainous island in the N of the Aegean off the coast of Thrace, with a town of the same name on the N side. One of its peaks rises above 1,700 m, forming a conspicuous landmark. Sailing NW from Troas on his way to Neapolis, Paul must have had a favourable wind to reach Samothrace in one day and Neapolis in one more (Acts 16:11; *cf.* 20:6).

Samothrace was renowned as a centre of the mystery cult of the Kabeiroi, ancient fertility deities who were supposed to protect those in danger, especially at sea. K.L.McK.

SAMSON. Greater attention is given to Samson than to any other of Israel's judges before Samuel (Jdg. 13–16). His name, *šimšôn* (Jdg. 13:24), derives from Heb. *šemeš*, 'sun', which has led some scholars to suggest a connection with a sun-mythology, Samson's exploits being equated with the 'twelve labours' of Gilgamesh or Hercules. The proximity of Beth-shemesh to Samson's birthplace, Zorah, the fact that one of his feats of strength took place 'at the time of wheat harvest' (Jdg. 15:1), *i.e.* approaching mid-summer, and his death between the pillars of a Philistine temple, possibly symbolic of sunset, are used in support of this view. But the essential historicity of the biblical record can hardly be doubted. Samson's birth and death are carefully documented and there is a close connection with an actual historical situation. Names like Samson are found in Ugaritic texts of the 14th and 15th centuries BC and most likely a common Canaanite name like this was widely used by Israel also.

I. Historical background

The Samson narratives provide an invaluable background to the earlier part of the Philistine oppression. The Philistines settled on the coastal plain *c.* 1200 BC, a generation after the Conquest, and once established they attempted to expand into the Israelite hill-country. Shamgar's exploit probably gave temporary relief (Jdg. 3:31), but a combination of Philistine and Amorite pressure (Jdg. 1:34) forced part of Samson's tribe, the Danites, to migrate N (Jdg. 18). The Danite remnant which remained, with Judah, bore increasingly the brunt of Philistine pressure. At this stage Philistine rule was not onerous, Judah accepting it without demur (Jdg. 15:11). It was established by infiltration rather than by force, and promised obvious economic advantages to the subject peoples. The insidious nature of this domination was a major threat to Israel's continued independence. Samson's activities were significant in this light. Nowhere had he armed support from his compatriots but his one-man campaign highlighted the danger and brought the conflict into the open. Even so, Israel eventually overcame the Philistines only with the greatest difficulty. Samson may be dated in the period of open Philistine aggression, *c.* 1070 BC, contemporary with Jephthah, who dealt with the Ammonite menace (*cf.* Jdg. 10:7) and *c.* 20 years before Israel's double defeat at Aphek (1 Sa. 4:1–11).

II. Personal history

a. Samson was the son of Manoah, whose wife, like Sarah, Hannah and Elizabeth, was barren. His birth, like those of Isaac and John the Baptist, was announced by an angel (Jdg. 13:3). He was to be a *Nazirite (Heb. *nāzîr*, 'separated' or 'consecrated') from birth. Usually the Nazirite vow was voluntarily taken for a limited period (Nu. 6:1–21). Of the stipulations required by the Nazirite vow, Samson took only one seriously, that concerning his hair. He was often in contact with corpses (*e.g.* 14:8f.) and it is unlikely that he abstained from strong drink.

Samson's parents lived at Zorah, on the border between Dan and Judah, in the Shephelah *c.* 22 km W of Jerusalem.

b. Samson's first love (14:1–15:8). Seeing a Philistine woman in Timnah, 6 km SW of Zorah, he demanded that his unwilling parents arrange a marriage. Understandably they were aggrieved that he should seek a wife outside the covenant-community. At the wedding feast he used a riddle to test the thirty young men, who appear more as protection against Samson than as guests (14:11). They put pressure upon Samson's bride to extract the answer, whereupon an enraged Samson slew thirty Philistines at Ashkelon to pay his debt and then departed (14:13–19). To escape disgrace his bride was given to his 'best man' (14:20). The type of marriage indicated did not involve permanent cohabitation, but when Samson arrived back in the early summer with the present customary in such a relationship (15:1) he was refused entrance. He took his revenge by catching 300 'foxes', probably jackals, which unlike foxes are not solitary and are more easily caught, tying fire-brands to their tails and releasing them (15:2–5). At harvest-time the loss would be considerable. The Philistines, in their turn, took an equally vicious revenge upon the Timnite and his family (15:6). In a further escalation of violence Samson retaliated by slaughtering the offending Philistines (15:7f.).

c. The attempt to capture Samson at Lehi (15:9–20). Seeking refuge at the rock of Etam, Samson was taken into custody by 3,000 men of Judah, resentful that he had disturbed their peaceful situation under the Philistines (15:9–13). His abnormal strength enabled him to break free and attack the surprised Philistines with a jawbone of an ass, a formidable weapon in the hands of a determined man (15:14–17). Samson was weakened with thirst after this spectacular success and God provided miraculously for his need (15:18f.). V. 20, with its formal statement of Samson's judgeship, probably marked the end of one account of his life.

d. His downfall and death (16:1–31). Samson's uncontrolled sexual urge, involving foreign prostitutes, eventually proved his undoing. A warning of his vulnerability in such circumstances was given at Gaza, but his unique strength enabled him to escape (16:1–3). Gaza, the southernmost of the five Philistine cities, was 60 km from Hebron, but the narrative may indicate that Samson lifted the city-gates to a hill in the general direction of Hebron.

After this Samson became infatuated with Delilah, whose home in the valley of Sorek lay just below Zorah (16:4). She collaborated with the Philistines and with heartless tenacity extracted from Samson the secret of his strength (16:5–20). Blinded and humiliated, 'eyeless in Gaza', he was paraded as the butt at a festival (16:21–27). For the first time a religious act on Samson's part is noted, and in answer to his prayer, coupled with the fact that the Philistines had carelessly allowed his hair to grow again, Samson was able to demolish a probably over-stressed temple, killing both himself and more Philistines than he had slain during his life (16:28–31). As the Philistines formed a ruling class superimposed upon native population, the effect of this decimation would be considerable.

e. Moral problems raised by the Samson narratives. Most of the judges had moral and religious shortcomings, but these are greatly accentuated in the case of Samson, whose sensuality, irresponsibility and lack of true religious concern are apparent. Yet he is included in the catalogue of heroes of faith (Heb. 11:32). Especially perplexing is the relationship of his enduement with the Spirit of God to his character. A clue to the significance of chs. 13–16 is the absence of the religiously motivated comment which abounds elsewhere in the book of Judges, as though the editor deems further comment unnecessary, the narratives themselves testifying openly to the prevailing low standards. We should distinguish between the level of appreciation of the average contemporary Israelite, who would thoroughly approve of the hated Philistines' discomfiture, and that of the godly men who finally collected Israel's traditions; they would be well aware of Samson's blemishes. Nor must we read back the clear NT connection between Spirit-endowment and holiness—a charismatic anointing in the OT period did not necessarily produce purity of life. God could still make use of a person apart from the quality of his life. Amongst his unlikely instruments were Balaam (Nu. 22–24), Nebuchadrezzar (Je. 25:9; 27:6; 43:10) and Cyrus (Is. 44:28; 45:1–4). We may question his use of an agent like Samson, and be embarrassed by the details, but God is sovereign, and he used Samson, in the 'Dark Ages' of the Judges' period, to fulfil a lone but vital role.

BIBLIOGRAPHY. J. Gray, *Joshua, Judges and Ruth, CB*, 1967, pp. 342–362; A. E. Cundall and L. Morris, *Judges and Ruth, TOTC*, 1968, pp. 153–181; F. F. Bruce, 'Judges', *NBCR*, 1970, pp. 269–272; R. G. Boling, *Judges, AB*, 1975, pp. 217–253; J. C. Moyer, 'Samson', *ZPEB*, 5, pp. 249–252; J. A. Soggin, *Judges, OTL*, 1981, pp. 225–259.

A.E.C.

SAMUEL (Heb. *šᵉmû'ēl*, '(?)name of God'). **1.** A Simeonite leader (Nu. 34:20), in NEB; most EVV have *Shemuel. **2.** Grandson of Issachar (1 Ch. 7:2), in NEB; most EVV have *Shemuel. **3.** The prophet, contemporary with Saul and David, whose career is related in 1 Sa., and who has given his name to the two books of Samuel. Acts 3:24 views him as the first of the prophets, Acts 13:20 as the last of the judges.

I. Career

Samuel was born into an Ephraimite family of Ramah (though of levitical stock, according to 1 Ch. 6:33f.). His parents were Elkanah and Hannah; the latter had previously been barren, and she dedicated Samuel before his birth as a *Nazirite. After his weaning, therefore, he was brought up in the Shiloh temple by Eli (1 Sa. 1). While still a boy, he experienced the prophetic call, and in due course 'was established as a prophet of the Lord' (1 Sa. 3).

A major Philistine victory was accompanied by the capture of the ark of the covenant, the death of Eli and the transfer of the priesthood from *Shiloh (1 Sa. 4); Samuel's movements are not recorded. He subsequently mustered the Israelite troops at Mizpah and won a victory over the Philistines (*EBENEZER). He now fulfilled the role of judge in Israel, with a circuit in Bethel, Gilgal, Mizpah and Ramah (1 Sa. 7).

In his old age, his leadership was challenged by the tribal elders who clamoured for a king. Samuel at first resisted this pressure but received divine guidance to agree to it (1 Sa. 8). He then met *Saul and was told by God to anoint him; and in a complex of events Samuel presided over the institution of the Israelite monarchy, though not without issuing stern warnings to king and people alike (1 Sa.9–12)

Before long, a breach occurred between Samuel and Saul, when the latter took it upon himself to offer sacrifice before battle (1 Sa. 13). This breach became absolute when Saul later broke a solemn oath in sparing the life of the Amalekite king Agag. Samuel himself killed Agag, and then retired to Ramah. He explicitly rejected Saul, and never had any further dealings with him (1 Sa. 15). His final act was to anoint David, privately, to be next king of Israel (1 Sa. 16). He died in Ramah and was buried there (1 Sa. 25:1). Even afterwards a desperate Saul tried to ascertain God's will through him (1 Sa. 28).

II. Critical evaluation

Recent critical assessments of Samuel tend to be negative. The minimal view would see him as a mere local seer, quite unknown to Saul, on the

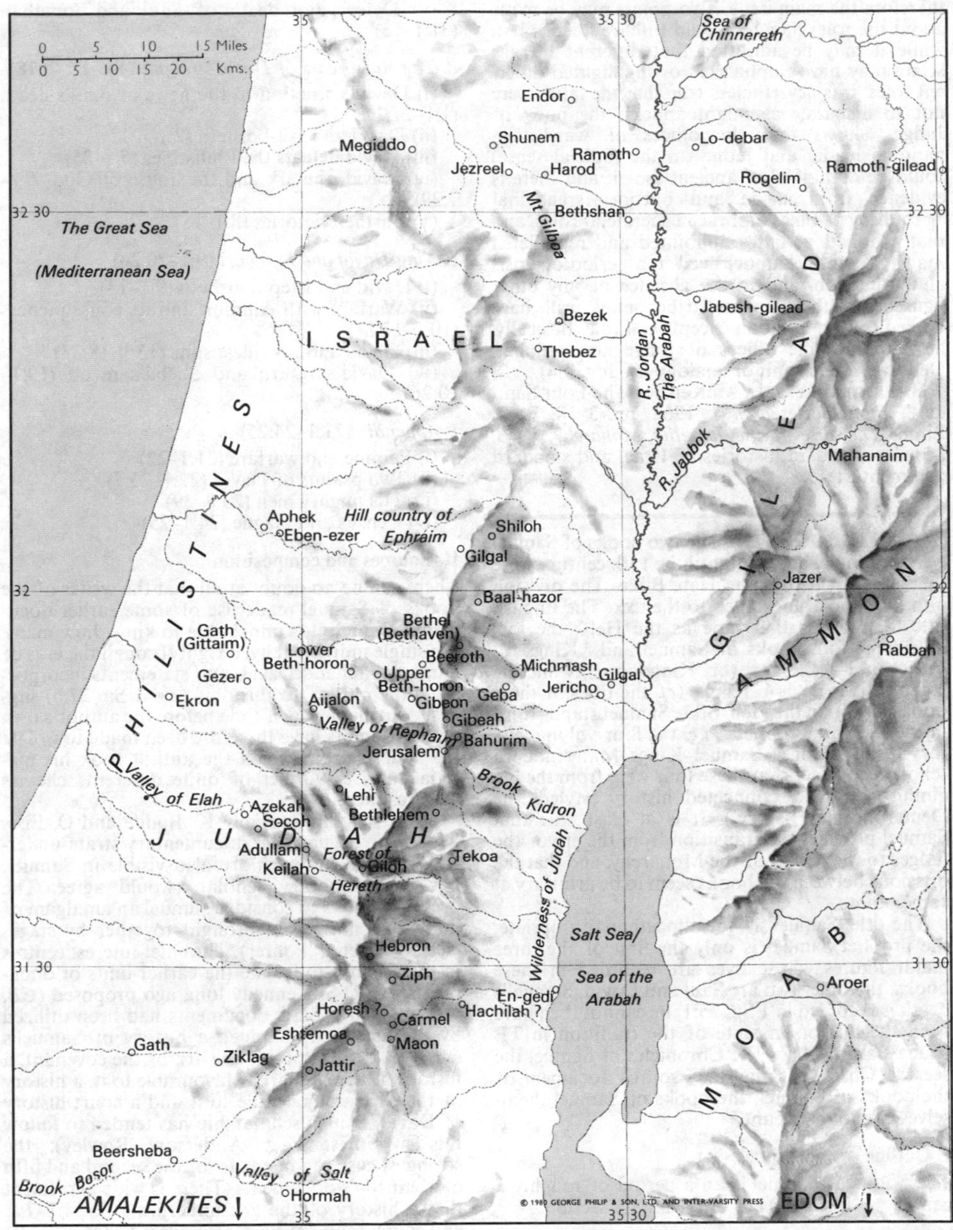

Israel and Judah at the time of Samuel.

basis of 1 Sa. 9:6, 18. Few scholars, however, would deny that he not only superintended the institution of the Monarchy but also later broke with Saul and repudiated him. Saul's subsequent insecurity strongly supports the biblical picture of Samuel as a man of power and influence.

The chief arguments against historicity are (i) the 'legendary' character of some of the stories (*e.g.* the infancy narrative), (ii) the fact that Samuel is depicted in such a diversity of roles (prophet, judge, war-leader, national leader and perhaps priest), and (iii) the problem of aligning these various roles with the supposed literary sources or unwritten traditions underlying 1 Sa. In the absence of extra-biblical data about Samuel, the first of these arguments admits of no objective criteria. The third problem, moreover, offers no secure basis for judgment in view of the fact that there is so little certainty about the sources utilized in the *books of Samuel. The second problem is therefore the main issue. Two points may be made about the roles Samuel is said to have filled. First, while it may be admitted that different literary strata may have emphasized or highlighted different roles, it is nevertheless true that the latter were not so disparate as might appear: the book of Judges shows that the offices of war-leader, national leader and judge (in the judicial sense) could be combined in ancient Israel; and there is evidence from inside and outside Israel that *prophecy at times embraced sacrificial roles, and that prophets at times appointed and repudiated kings. Secondly, Samuel lived in a period of crisis and transition, and in the absence of any other figurehead, the Israelite tribes may well have looked to him to fill an exceptional role. Basically, he combines the offices of judge and prophet; Deborah offers a minor analogy (*cf.* Jdg. 4:4).

BIBLIOGRAPHY. J. L. McKenzie, 'The Four Samuels', *Biblical Research* 7, 1962, pp. 3–18; B. C. Birch, *The Rise of the Israelite Monarchy*, 1976. See also standard histories of Israel and standard commentaries. D.F.P.

SAMUEL, BOOKS OF. The two books of Samuel were originally one; not until the 15th century were they ever divided in the Heb. Bible. The division into two books goes back to the LXX. The English title 'Samuel' is the same as the Heb.; the LXX linked the four books of Samuel and *Kings together as 1–4 'Reigns' (or 'Kingdoms'), while the Vulg. calls them 1–4 'Kings' (*cf.* the titles of these books in AV). In the Heb. Bible Samuel stands third in the 'Former Prophets', *i.e.* the four-volume history Joshua–Judges–Samuel–Kings. Many modern scholars consider that these four were from the beginning a single, connected history (styled 'the Deuteronomic History'). It is at least true that Samuel provides the transition from the era of the judges to the period of the Monarchy, and that the divisions between the books seem to be arbitrary at some points.

The title 'Samuel' is not altogether appropriate; the prophet Samuel is only the first of the three major figures whose lives are recorded in these books; the other two are Saul and David. Samuel's death is recorded in 1 Sa. 25:1; he cannot then have been the author, in spite of the tradition in TB (Baba Bathra 14*b*). 'The Chronicles of Samuel the seer' (1 Ch. 29:29) may be a source document of the books of Samuel; the books of Samuel themselves cannot be meant.

I. Outline of contents

The books of Samuel span a period of roughly a century, *c.* 1050–950 BC. There are six sections:

a. Samuel's early years (1 Sa. 1:1–7:14)

(i) Samuel and Eli (1:1–3:21)
(ii) War with the Philistines (4:1–7:14)

b. Samuel and Saul (7:15–15:35)

(i) Saul becomes king (7:15–12:25)
(ii) War with the Philistines (13:1–14:52)
(iii) The defeat of Amalek (15:1–35)

c. Saul and David (16:1–31:13)

(i) David reaches the royal court (16:1–17:58)
(ii) David and Jonathan (18:1–20:42)
(iii) David as a fugitive (21:1–26:25)
(iv) David in Philistine territory (27:1–30:31)
(v) Defeat and death of Saul and Jonathan (31:1–13)

d. The early years of David's reign (2 Sa. 1:1–8:18)

(i) David's reaction to the news of Saul's death (1:1–27)
(ii) David and Ish-bosheth (2:1–4:12)
(iii) David defeats the Philistines (5:1–25)
(iv) David, the ark and the house of God (6:1–7:29)
(v) Further victories (8:1–18)

e. King David and his court (9:1–20:26)

(i) David and Mephibosheth (9:1–13)
(ii) Warfare with Ammon and its consequences (10:1–12:21)
(iii) David and his eldest sons (13:1–18:33)
(iv) David's return and Sheba's revolt (19:1–20:26)

f. Appendix (21:1–24:25)

(i) Famine and warfare (21:1–22)
(ii) Two psalms of David (22:1–23:7)
(iii) His mighty men (23:8–39)
(iv) Census and plague (24:1–25)

II. Sources and composition

There can be no doubt at all that the writer of the books of Samuel made use of some earlier documents, though it is impossible to know how many. No single individual lived right through the eras of Samuel, Saul and David; and statements incorporating the phrase 'to this day' (*e.g.* 1 Sa. 27:6) suggest a further lapse of time before the author's own date. Attempts have therefore been made to isolate the sources from which the author took his material; and a number of quite different schemes have resulted.

Some scholars (notably K. Budde and O. Eissfeldt) have argued that documentary strata underlying the *Pentateuch are also visible in Samuel. Few contemporary scholars would agree. The present trend is to consider Samuel an amalgam of individual narratives, brought together by stages (see, *e.g.*, Weiser, Fohrer). The chief interest centres in the attempt to isolate the earlier units or documents. A. R. S. Kennedy long ago proposed (*CB*, 1904) that five basic documents had been utilized by the author of Samuel: a history of Samuel's early years, a history of the ark of the covenant, a history of the Monarchy favourable to it, a history of the Monarchy hostile to it and a court history of David. British scholarship has tended to follow this hypothesis (*e.g.* Anderson, Rowley); the strongest case can be made for the second and fifth of Kennedy's documents. There is wide agreement that a history of the ark underlies 1 Sa. 4:1–7:1, and many scholars have also agreed that 2 Sa. 9–20, with 1 Ki. 1f., constitute a distinct unit (usually known as 'The Succession Narrative'), though some recent studies have challenged this view (Delekat, Würthwein). The Succession Narrative is usually considered to have been composed by, or at least to derive from, an eyewitness. Absent from this section are 'doublets', a feature characteristic of the rest of Samuel; many scholars have stressed the significance of such 'duplicate narratives' in arguing for a variety of (conflicting) sources. This argument has been over-pressed (see D. F. Payne, 'Duplicate Accounts', in *NBCR*, pp. 284f.), but on the other hand it may be admitted that such doublets tend to suggest separate sources: historicity is, or should be, a different issue from source criticism. Thus 1 Sa. 16:14–23 tells how Saul first met David as a musician; 1 Sa. 17:55–58 may well derive from a separate source, in which the challenge from Goliath provided the circumstances for David's first coming to the attention of the king. If so, the compiler of the book has drawn on both earlier sources, and made his own clear decision as to which was the earlier event; the 'duplication' denies the historicity of neither story.

Both the number and the nature of the sources of Samuel remain unclear and disputed, then. The author himself undoubtedly made his own contribution, as references to his own day (1 Sa. 27:6) and explanatory remarks (1 Sa. 9:9) make clear. By general consent, however, his activity was very discreet; apart from such minor touches, it is only in 1 Sa. 7, 12 and 2 Sa. 7 that his hand is generally thought to be clearly visible. It is noteworthy that the clear editorial structures and formulae of *Judges and *Kings are absent from Samuel; this fact, among others, argues for a distinct origin for Samuel and militates against the hypothesis of a unified Deuteronomic history, Joshua–Kings. It may be, nevertheless, that a final redaction, of limited extent, took place when Samuel and Kings were brought together, in the exilic period or soon afterwards.

III. Purpose

In covering the era of the transition from a loose tribal constitution under the judges to a monarchy, the books of Samuel necessarily offer a view on the value of the monarchy; but different passages give rather differing impressions. 1 Sa. 8 offers a biting critique of kingship, and in 1 Sa. 12:19 the people acknowledge that they had done evil in seeking a king; but in 1 Sa. 10:24–27; 11:14f. a positive view is taken. Recent studies have found a similar tension within the Succession Narrative, some passages being favourable to David and Solomon, while others are distinctly critical of them. These differing viewpoints have often been used as a criterion, as regards sources and historicity; but as Bright and others have argued, the tension is certainly an original one, on any credible historical reconstruction, and the value of the criteria is dubious. In any case, since he incorporated material tending in both directions, it is unlikely that the final author was either pro-monarchic or anti-monarchic. Rather his attitude was typically prophetic, seeing the monarchy as a constitution which had been ordained by God, but taking a detached and objective view of each individual monarch. J. A. Soggin is right to emphasize that the primary interests of the author are election and rejection.

It is important not to overlook the biographical motive. There was a genuine interest in the careers and achievements of leading Israelites. It was the biblical writers' conviction that God had involved himself in history, and that he governed its whole course, which gave the historical books of the OT their theological quality and content. Theologically-coloured history is none the less history.

IV. Text

There are numerous problems in the Heb. text (*MT*) of Samuel, and commentaries and translations often turn to the LXX (especially LXX[B] and LXX[L]) for help. The LXX MSS not only elucidate many verses where the Heb. is obscure or problematic but also offer variant readings where the Heb. makes good sense. The most notable variation is in 1 Sa. 17f., where LXX[B] is much shorter than *MT* (17:12–31 and 17:55–18:5 are entirely absent). (See D. F. Payne, *NBCR*, p. 318.) Two other sources of evidence are parallel passages in Chronicles, and fragmentary copies of Samuel found at Qumran. The Qumranic material tends to support LXX where it differs from *MT*, and recent EVV, especially NEB, have made considerable use of its evidence. It is widely held that the evidence suggests not so much that the Heb. text of Samuel was poorly preserved as that there existed different recensions of the book.

BIBLIOGRAPHY. R. A. Carlson, *David, the Chosen King*, 1964; R. N. Whybray, *The Succession Narrative*, 1968; G. Wallis, *Geschichte und Überlieferung*, 1968, pp. 45–66. Commentaries by H. W. Hertzberg, *OTL*, E.T. 1960; J. Mauchline, *NCB*, 1971; H. J. Stoebe, *KAT*, 1973; P. K. McCarter, *AB*, 1980–84; R. P. Gordon, 1986; R. W. Klein (on 1 Sa.), *WBC*, 1986; J. Baldwin, *TOTC*, 1988; A. A. Anderson (on 2 Sa.), *WBC*, 1989. See also standard introductions to the OT. D.F.P.

SANBALLAT. The name is Babylonian, *Sinuballiṭ*, *i.e.* 'Sin (the moon-god) has given life'. In Ne. 2:10, 19; 13:28 he is called the Horonite, probably denoting that he came from Beth-horon, about 30 km NW of Jerusalem (*cf.* Jos. 10:10, *etc.*). He was one of the chief opponents of Nehemiah. The Elephantine Papyri show that in 407 BC he was governor of Samaria. If when Nehemiah came in 445 BC he was either governor or hoping to be governor, he doubtless wanted to have control of Judaea also. The Elephantine Papyri speak of his two sons, Delaiah and Shelemiah, and these names may show that Sanballat was a worshipper of Yahweh. This means that he was descended either from an Israelite family which had not gone into captivity in 721 BC or from one of the peoples whom the Assyrian kings had imported into Palestine. In either case his religion was probably syncretistic (2 Ki. 17:33), though he put Yahweh first, and so won sympathy even from the high priest's family, into which his daughter married (Ne. 13:28). Josephus (*Ant.* 11. 302) makes Sanballaṭ responsible for the building of the Samaritan temple, which he dates under Darius III (336–331 BC). If the story is true, Josephus has confused the date; unless he is referring to a second governor with the same name. (There was at least one further Sanballat, if not two, among the governors of Samaria under the Persian empire.)

BIBLIOGRAPHY. H. H. Rowley, 'Sanballat and the Samaritan Temple', *BJRL* 38, 1955–6, pp. 166ff. F. M. Cross, 'Discovery of Samaria Papyri', *BA* 26, 1963, pp. 110ff.; H. G. M. Williamson, *TynB* 39, 1988, pp. 59–82. J.S.W.

SANCTIFICATION, SANCTIFY

a. Meaning

Sanctification is one of several possible English translations of *qdš*, *hagios* and their cognates. See *HOLINESS for usage. Context alone determines whether the translation should be holy, holiness, holy one, saints, consecrate, consecration, sanctify or sanctification. Even in individual passages translators do not always agree. Its broad meaning is the process by which an entity is brought into relationship with or attains the likeness of the holy.

b. Old Testament

In the OT, the primary use of the *qdš* word group, in the sense of consecration or sanctification, has to do with the way in which the holiness necessary for earthly people or things to relate to the holy God could be received. The primary means of sanctification in the OT was through the cultic system.

The whole cultic system centred on the way the earthly realm relates to the divine. Crucial to this relationship was the consecration of the pure but profane person or thing to God through the means provided by God. Recent studies have shown that the priestly theology of holiness structured all Israelite society in terms of earthly relations to the divine. This is seen in the holiness word group: holy – profane and clean – unclean (Lv. 10:10). Both pairs have gradations between them, with varying levels of sanctity and cleanness. 'The sense of the distinction, however, is less a gradation of the holiness which derives from God than a gradation of human dealings with the Holy One' (Seebass, 227).

Consecration does not rest upon intrinsic holiness: 'it requires a special act of God to make a thing or person holy' (Jenson, 48). The sacrificial system was God's gracious means to enable his people to move from uncleanness or defilement to cleanness as the basis upon which to approach the holy God. Holiness and purity are not synonymous, however; purity is a presupposition for approaching the holy 'because antipathy between holiness and impurity was absolute' (Jenson, 53). Hence, in the priestly tradition, there is a great deal of emphasis on purity and separation. Sanctification occurs as a consequence of movement towards the Holy One, not as the basis for holiness.

Earlier studies sought to contrast priestly ritualistic notions of holiness and sanctification with the ethical standards of the prophets. But that dichotomy does justice to neither. The highest ethical standards, centred in wholehearted love of God and neighbour (Dt. 6:4; Lv. 19:18b), are embedded in the priestly cultus: 'Consecrate yourselves therefore, and be holy; for I am the Lord your God. Keep my statutes, and do them; I am the Lord who sanctify you' (Lv. 20:7). The prophets demanded worship which issued in concrete expression of covenantal standards in societal and personal ethics. They saw clearly that the experience of God's holiness would necessarily result in the transformation of the person (Is. 6:5–7) and society (Am. 4:4f.; 5:21–24; Mi. 6:6–8). In short, 'for Israel to be and remain the people of God, it must be holy, not merely in the ritual sense but also in the ethical sense' (Muller, 322).

c. New Testament

Fundamental to all NT theology is the shift in eschatological perspective brought about by the coming of Jesus Messiah, and the coming of the Holy Spirit. God has come amongst his people to reconcile them to himself and the *future* has already been set in motion, although the *end* has only just begun. Sanctification cannot be understood outside this framework.

The terminology of sanctification is rare in the gospels. In John, sanctification concerns relationship with the triune God on the one hand and mission on the other. Jesus is the one sanctified by the Father and sent into the world (10:36). If the disciples are to continue that mission, they too must be sanctified, *i.e.* brought into that intimate fellowship enjoyed by Father and Son (20:20–23). Jesus prays that the Father would sanctify the disciples in the truth (17:17). In order that they may be filled with God's being and power, Jesus sanctifies himself (17:19) through his death, then sends the disciples into the world just as the Father had sent him (20:21–22), imparting to them the Holy Spirit.

The presence of the Holy Spirit is the key to Paul's view of sanctification. Paul holds that sanctification is based on the historical reality of the atoning death of Christ which is brought to experiential reality by the Spirit (Gal. 3:2–5; 1 Cor. 6:11; Eph. 1:13–14; Tit. 3:4–7). It partakes fully of the eschatological tension of salvation: 'already'/'not yet'.

Paul's main emphasis is ethical rather than cultic. He echoes Jesus' own summation of God's ethical requirements for the new people as given in the great commandments (Gal. 5:14; Rom. 13:8–10) and models them before his converts (1 Thes. 2:10; 3:12). He urges them to continue to work out these principles of wholehearted devotion to God and love of neighbour in the context of everyday existence (1 Thes. 4:9–10). In 1 Thes. 3:10–13 and 5:23, Paul prays that his readers will be established in holiness and that God will sanctify them wholly. They are ever to be what they are now, *i.e.* a people called to be holy.

But these are also wish-prayers which means that the 'not yet' is equally important here. Paul has the Parousia, which perhaps he expected before his death (1 Thes. 4:17; 5:6), firmly in his view. He prays that these Christians will be found blameless (note, not faultless) in holiness on that soon-to-arrive day, with lives that reflect their anticipation of it.

The ethical thrust of sanctification continues in Rom. 6, where Paul uses the term *hagiasmos* twice. In 6:19, he urges his readers to yield their members to righteousness for sanctification, clearly focusing on the ethical living expected of those who have been freed from the dominion of sin. Since in and with Christ they have died to the lordship of sin (6:6), they are now to live lives which reflect their new relationship to God as sharers in Christ's risen life (6:13–14). In no sense, however, is Paul stating that holiness is achieved by personal striving (see Wynkoop, 326).

Paul uses the terms 'righteousness' and 'sanctification' here in a way which shows their inseparability. Paul could not conceive of a person brought into a right relationship with God whose life would not issue in sanctification (6:22), *i.e.* in a life of holiness. Debate about whether Paul has in mind a state or a process of sanctification is beside the point. Paul intends both.

That Paul can speak of both aspects of sanctification is confirmed in 2 Cor. 7:1. Here, in language reminiscent of the OT cultic context of purity and holiness, he urges his alienated readers to 'cleanse [y]ourselves from every defilement of body and spirit, and make holiness perfect.' His Christian readers are to purge themselves in every part, inwardly and outwardly (see Ps. 24:2–3, 'clean hands and pure heart'), and live out the implications of their grace-given relationship to the holy God.

Were it not for the indwelling presence of the

Spirit, all of this might seem to be mere wishful thinking. But Paul considers the sanctified life to be possible because of the indwelling presence of God's empowering Spirit (2 Thes. 2:13). Indeed, he says, anyone who rejects this way of living, rejects God who gives his Holy Spirit to you (1 Thes. 4:8). It is the presence of the Spirit which enables the believer to live a life which is not *according* to the flesh (Gal. 5:16, 24; Rom. 8:5) although life is still lived *in* the flesh (Gal. 2:20; Rom. 8:11, 23). To be sure, the Spirit has not brought the fulness of the end but only its beginning, so the Spirit's presence does not confer final perfection in the present age but rather leads to growing maturity in Christ, whereby Christians are ripened for their final transformation. 'We are both already and not yet' (Fee, p. 826).

The writer of the Epistle to the Hebrews is in conscious dialogue with Judaism. For this writer, sanctification is the work of Christ, the eternal high priest (5:8–10; 7:23–25) and the sanctifier (2:11; 13:12) who, as the enthroned Lord, now exercises all the prerogatives of God (ch. 1). The means of sanctification is through the death of Christ, who through the shedding of his blood, established the new and better covenant relationship between God and humans (10:10, 14). This new sacrifice is efficacious because, in contrast to sacrifices under the old covenant which could purify the flesh and restore a defiled Israelite to the community (Nu. 19:9), the blood of Christ is able to deal with the inner condition of sinful people (9:13f.; 10:22).

The heart of the matter in Hebrews, therefore, is the new covenant relationship promised in the OT (Je. 31:31–34; Ezk. 36:25–27). The verb *hagiadzein* is used 'with reference to the establishment of New Covenant relations between God and man' (D. F.Peterson, *Hebrews and Perfection*, *SNTSMS* 47, 1982, p. 72). The notion of the perfecting of believers (7:11, 19; 10:14), relates primarily to their covenantal acceptance by God (Peterson, p. 136).

Hebrews is the most explicit of the epistles on the present reality and enjoyment of the sanctified life. A crucial verse in this regard is Heb. 10:14 which emphasizes the single offering for sanctification made by Christ on the one hand and the experiential realization of the new relationship between God and humanity on the other. The new covenant relationship has already been established in Christ's death and exaltation; Christians are consciously to embrace in their ongoing experience what has already been accomplished for them. 'The terminology of perfection is used by our writer here to stress the realized aspect of Christian salvation' (Peterson, p. 153).

But Hebrews also applies the 'already'/'not yet' tension to sanctification. For while it is the present experience of believers, it is neither static nor final (12:10, 14, 22–24). This relationship is the earnest of that ultimate goal of sanctification which 'is to share Christ's glory (2:10), to enter God's rest (4:11ff.), to see the Lord (12:14), and to inhabit the heavenly Jerusalem (12:22; 13:14)' (Peterson, p. 129).

In some ways, 1 Pet. provides a summary of the NT view of sanctification: it has to do with God's choice (1:2; 2:9), the work of the Spirit in applying the benefits of Christ's sacrificial death and resurrection (1:2–3), and lives lived in obedience to God's call to holiness (1:14–15; 2:5) and love (1:22; 4:8). Sanctification, in sum, is essentially a relational reality, completed in Christ's death on the cross, experienced through the indwelling Holy Spirit and brought to its final goal when we see God (Heb. 12:14; 1 Jn. 3:2–3).

BIBLIOGRAPHY. E. C. Blackman, 'Sanctification', *IDB* 4, pp. 211–213; M. E. Dieter, *et al.*, *Five Views on Sanctification*, 1987; G. Fee, *God's Empowering Presence*, 1994; P. P. Jenson, *Graded Holiness*, *JSOTSS* 104, 1992; R. A. Muller, 'Sanctification', *ISBE* 4, pp. 321–331; D. F. Peterson, *Hebrews and Perfection*, *SNTSMS* 47, 1982; H. Seebass and C. Brown, 'Holy, Consecrate, Sanctify, Saints, Devout', *DNTT* 2, pp. 223–238; D. F. Peterson, *Possessed by God*, 1995; M. B. Wynkoop, *A Theology of Love*, 1972. K.B.

SANCTUARY. The Heb. words *miqdāš*, and its correlative *qōḏeš*, define a place set apart for the worship of God or gods. Whereas the Bible uses these words almost entirely of the place where Yahweh was worshipped, a study of cognate languages such as Canaanite shows that the same terms were used for the worship of the earlier inhabitants of Palestine. Excavation has revealed a wide variety of sanctuaries extending back to the 4th millennium BC. The most complete range of these at present known was excavated at Megiddo. A considerable variety of cult images and tools is now available for study.

Israel's earliest sanctuary was the movable tent known as the *tabernacle where the ark containing the tables of the covenant was housed (Ex. 25:8, *etc.*). Detailed descriptions of the various parts of this structure occur in Ex. 25–31 and 36–40, and the elaborate ritual associated with it is detailed in Leviticus.

With the settlement of Israel in the land, David planned, and Solomon completed, a permanent place of worship (1 Ch. 22:19; 28:10, *etc.*).

Apostasy during the days of the kings brought foreign cult-practices into the Temple. Ezekiel and Zephaniah reproached God's people for defiling his sanctuary (Ezk. 5:11; 23:39; 28:18, *etc.*; Zp. 3:4).

Israel's early sanctuaries were set up in the places where God appeared to his people or 'caused his name to dwell'. Finally Jerusalem became the official centre of worship. (*HIGH PLACE; *TEMPLE.)

In NT the 'sanctuary' (Gk. *naos*) is the holy house, the dwelling-place of God, whether literal (*e.g.* Mk. 14:58; 15:38; Jn. 2:19) or figurative (*e.g.* 1 Cor. 3:16f.; 6:19), as distinct from 'temple' (*hieron*), the whole sacred enclosure (*e.g.* Mk. 11:11, 15; Lk. 2:27, 46; Jn. 2:14). J.A.T.

SAND (Heb. *ḥôl*; Gk. *ammos*). The Heb. word derives from the verb *ḥûl* ('to whirl, dance'), doubtless a reference to the ease with which the light particles of silex, mica, felspar, *etc.*, are lifted and whirled by the wind. Sand is found extensively along the Mediterranean shores of S Palestine and Egypt, and in desert regions, thus providing a striking symbol of countless multitude (*e.g.* Gn. 22:17; Is. 10:22; Rev. 20:8). It is used also to convey an idea of weight (Jb. 6:3), longevity (Jb. 29:18) and instability (Mt. 7:26). A somewhat obscure allusion (Dt. 33:19) speaks of 'the hidden treasures of the sand'; perhaps a source of prosperity would be found in the seas (fishing, maritime commerce) and on the shores (shellfish; dye, from shellfish; glass, from sand; *cf.* Jos., *BJ* 2. 190; Pliny, *NH* 5. 17; 36. 65). The promise probably applies only to Zebulun, the tribe associated with the sea in the last words of Jacob (Gn. 49:13–15). J.D.D.

SANHEDRIN, the transcription used in the Talmud for Gk. *synedrion* (from which Heb. *sanhedrîn* is a loan-word). Both before and at the time of Christ, it was the name of the highest tribunal of the Jews which met in Jerusalem and also for various lesser tribunals. In EVV the term is often translated 'council'. There are parallels in classical writings to similar courts in Greece and Rome. Josephus used the word for the council that governed the five districts into which the Roman Gabinius, proconsul of Syria 57–55 BC, divided Judaea (*Ant.* 14. 90; *BJ* 1.170). Josephus first uses it of the Jews when referring to the summoning of the young Herod before it for alleged misdemeanours (*Ant.* 14. 163–184). In the NT the term refers either to the supreme Jewish court (Mt. 26:59; Mk. 14:55; Lk. 22:66; Jn. 11:47; Acts 4:15; 5:21ff.; 6:12ff.; 22:30; 23:1ff.; 24:20) or simply to any court of justice (Mt. 5:22). In a few cases other words are substituted for *synedrion*, *e.g.* *presbyterion*, 'body of elders' (Lk. 22:66; Acts 22:5), and *gerousia*, 'senate' (Acts 5:21).

I. History

The history of the Sanhedrin is not clear at all points. Traditionally it originated with the seventy elders who assisted Moses (Nu. 11:16–24). Ezra is supposed to have reorganized this body after the Exile. The Persians gave authority to the Jews in local affairs (Ezr. 7:25–26; 10:14), and it is possible that the elders of Ezr. 5:5, 9; 6:7, 14; 10:8, and the rulers of Ne. 2:16; 4:14, 19; 5:7; 7:5, made up a body which resembled the later Sanhedrin. Later, the Greeks permitted a body known as the *gerousia* ('senate') which was made up of elders and represented the nation (Jos., *Ant.* 12. 142; 1 Macc. 12:3, 6; 14:20). In the days of the Seleucids this *gerousia* had dealings with such rulers as Antiochus the Great in 208 BC and with Antiochus V (Jos., *Ant.* 12. 128), and was then apparently composed of elders drawn from the aristocracy (1 Macc. 12:6; 2 Macc. 1:10; 4:44; 11:27). In the days of the Maccabean revolt it was this council that united with Jonathan, the high priest and leader of the people, to make an alliance with Sparta (1 Macc. 12:5ff.), and it was they who advised him about building fortresses in Judaea (1 Macc. 12:35; *cf.* 13:36; 14:20, 28, 47). It would appear that the high priest presided over this body.

Under the Romans, except for a short period under Gabinius, this body had wide powers. The term used for the district councils was subsequently adopted for the more powerful *gerousia* at Jerusalem, and by the close of the 1st century BC this council was known as the *synedrion*, though other terms such as *gerousia* and *boulē* ('council') were also used at times. It was Julius Caesar who reversed the plan of Gabinius and extended the power of the Sanhedrin once again over all Judaea, although during the reign of *Herod (37–4 BC) its powers were severely curtailed. Under the procurators (AD 6–66) the powers of the Sanhedrin were extensive, the internal government of the country being in its hands (Jos., *Ant.* 20. 200), and it was recognized even among the *diaspora* (Acts 9:2; 22:5; 26:12) in some ways. From the days of Archelaus, son of *Herod the Great, its direct powers were, however, limited to Judaea, since it had no power over Jesus while he was in Galilee. In Judaea there were, of course, the local authorities who tried cases locally but reported certain cases to the central authority. The councils (*synedria*) of Mt. 5:22; 10:17; Mk. 13:9, and the *boulai* of Jos., *Ant.* 4. 214, *etc.* were local courts of at least seven elders, and in large towns up to twenty-three elders.

After AD 70 the Sanhedrin was abolished and replaced by the Beth Din (Court of Judgment) which is said to have met at Jabneh (AD 68–80), Usah (80–116), Shafran (140–163), Sepphoris (163–193) and Tiberias (193–220). Though regarded in the Talmud as continuous with the Sanhedrin, it was essentially different, being composed of scribes whose decisions had only moral and religious authority.

II. Constitution and composition

The constitution of the Sanhedrin was modified during the years. Originally composed basically of the predominantly Sadducean priestly aristocracy, its membership changed from the days of Queen Alexandra (76–67 BC) when *Pharisees were included, as well as *scribes. The method of appointment is not clear, but the aristocratic origin of the body suggests direct appointment of members of ancient families, to which were added secular rulers. Under Herod, who favoured the Pharisees and desired to restrict the *Sadducees and the influence of the old nobility, the Sadducean element became less prominent, and the Pharisaic element, which had been growing in strength since the days of Queen Alexandra, became more influential. In NT times the Great Sanhedrin in Jerusalem comprised the high priests (*i.e.* the acting high priest and those who had been high priest), members of the privileged families from which the high priests were taken, the elders (tribal and family heads of the people and the priesthood), and the scribes, *i.e.* the legal experts. The whole comprised both Sadducees and Pharisees (Mt. 26:3, 57, 59; Mk. 14:53; 15:1; Lk. 22:66; Acts 4:1, 5ff.; 5:17, 21, 34; 22:30; 23:6). The members were councillors (*bouleutēs*, Mk. 15:43; Lk. 23:50), as, for example, Joseph of Arimathaea.

According to Josephus and the NT, the high priest at the time was president (Jos., *Ant.* 4. 224; 20. 224ff.; Mt. 26:57; Acts 5:17ff.; 7:1; 9:1ff.; 22:5; 24:1). Thus, Caiaphas was president at the trial of Jesus, and Ananias at the trial of Paul (Acts 23:2). It would seem that in earlier times the high priest had supreme authority, but this was curbed somewhat later. The appointment was no longer hereditary, but political, and ex-high priests with their close associates (such as the captain of the Temple) were the 'rulers' (Jn. 7:26; Acts 4:5–8, *etc.*).

III. Extent of jurisdiction

The jurisdiction was wide at the time of Christ. It exercised not only civil jurisdiction according to Jewish law but also criminal jurisdiction in some degree. It had administrative authority and could order arrests by its own officers of justice (Mt. 26:47; Mk. 14:43; Acts 4:1ff.; 5:17ff.; 9:2). It was empowered to judge cases which did not involve capital punishment (Acts 4–5). Capital cases required the confirmation of the Roman procurator (Jn. 18:31), though the procurator's judgment was normally in accordance with the demands of the Sanhedrin, which in Jewish law had the power of life and death (Jos., *Ant.* 14. 168; Mt. 26:66). In the special case where a Gentile passed the barrier which divided the inner court of the Temple from that of the Gentiles the Sanhedrin was granted the power of death by Roman administrators (Acts 21:28ff.); and this concession may have extended to other offences against the Temple by deed or, as with Stephen (Acts 6:13f.), by word. The only case of capital sentence in connection with the Sanhedrin in the NT is that of our Lord, but the execution was carried out by the judgment of the Roman governor. The case of Stephen has some features of an illegal mob act.

A study of the NT will give a cross-section of the kinds of matters that came before the Sanhedrin. Thus, Jesus was charged with blasphemy (Mt. 26:57ff.; Jn. 19:7), Peter and John were charged with teaching the people false doctrine (Acts 4), Paul with transgressing the Mosaic law (Acts 22–24). These, of course, were religious matters. But at times the collection of revenue was the responsibility of the Sanhedrin, as in the time of Florus (Jos., *BJ* 2. 406). There was, however, always a theoretical check on the powers of the Sanhedrin, for the Romans reserved the right to interfere in any area whatever, if necessary independently of the Jewish court. Paul's arrest in Acts 23 is a case in point. It is probably best to regard the Sanhedrin as having two main areas of responsibility, political (administrative and judicial) and religious. It is not always clear how these two were carried out, and some writers have even suggested two different bodies, each known as the Sanhedrin. This is probably not necessary, but is suggested because of our lack of clear knowledge of procedures.

IV. Procedure

There were correct times and places for meeting, according to the tradition preserved in the Mishnaic tractate *Sanhedrin*. Local courts met on the 2nd and 5th days of the week, and the Sanhedrin in Jerusalem at definite (though unknown to us) times. They did not meet on festival days and on sabbaths.

There were proper procedures. The Sanhedrin sat in a semicircle and had two clerks of court, one to record votes of acquittal and the other votes of condemnation. Disciples attended the courts and sat in front. Prisoners attended dressed in humble fashion. In capital cases the arguments for acquittal were presented, then those for conviction. If one spoke for acquittal he could not reverse his opinion, but if he spoke for condemnation he could later change his vote. Students could speak in favour of acquittal but not for condemnation. Acquittal might be declared on the day of the trial, but condemnation must wait till the day following. In voting, members stood, beginning with the youngest. For acquittal a simple majority sufficed, for condemnation a two-thirds majority was required. If 12 of the 23 judges necessary for a quorum voted for acquittal, and 11 for conviction, the prisoner was discharged. If 12 voted for conviction, and 11 against, the number of judges had to be increased by 2, and this was repeated up to a total of 71, or until an acquittal was achieved. The benefit of the doubt was allowed to persons where the case was as doubtful as this. Indeed, always, the benefit lay with the accused (Mishnah, *Sanhedrin* 5. 5).

In this regard, the legality of the trial of Jesus has been discussed by many writers, and it is fairly clear that there are elements about it which point in the direction of a miscarriage of justice.

BIBLIOGRAPHY. E. Schürer, *HJP*, 1901, 2, i, pp. 163–195; J. Z. Lauterbach, *JewE*, 11, 1905, pp. 41–44; I. Abrahams, *ERE*, 2, 1920, pp. 184–185; H. Danby, *The Mishnah*, E.T. 1933, tractate *Sanhedrin*, pp. 382–400; *idem*, 'The Trial of Jesus', *JTS* 21, 1919–20, pp. 51–76; P. Winter, *On the Trial of Jesus*, 1961; W. J. Moulder, *ISBE*, 4, pp. 331–334.

J.A.T.

SAPPHIRA (Gk. *sappheira*, transliteration of Aram. *šappîrâ*, fem. sing., 'beautiful'). In Acts 5:1ff. wife of *Ananias, a member of the primitive Jerusalem church. The name, in Greek and Aramaic, was found on an ossuary in Jerusalem in 1923, but J. Klausner's theory (*From Jesus to Paul*, 1944, pp. 289f.) that the Sapphira of Acts is intended requires confirmation. F.F.B.

SARAH, SARAI (Heb. *śārâ*, 'princess'). The principal wife of Abram, and also his half-sister on his father Terah's side (Gn. 20:12). She went with him from Ur of the Chaldees, through Harran, to the land of Canaan. Famine caused them to turn aside to Egypt, and, as Abram feared that her outstanding beauty might endanger his life, Sarai posed as his sister. Pharaoh was attracted by her and took her into his harem. Then he suspected the truth, and husband and wife were sent away (Gn.12).

She posed as Abraham's sister on a second occasion, at the court of Abimelech, king of Gerar, in accordance with her husband's instructions: 'This is the kindness you must do me; at every place to which we come, say of me, He is my brother' (Gn. 20:13)—words which suggest a settled policy. This incident further increased Abraham's wealth, for gifts were given him as compensation to an injured husband (Gn. 20:14).

Her barrenness was a continual reproach to Sarai, and she gave her handmaiden, the Egyptian *Hagar, to her husband as his concubine. Hagar's pregnancy aroused her jealousy, and she ill-treated her to such an extent that Hagar ran away for a time. On her return Ishmael was born (Gn.16).

At the age of 90, Sarai's name was changed to Sarah, and her husband's from Abram to Abraham. Yahweh blessed her and said she would bear a son, and become the 'mother of nations' (Gn.17).

When Abraham was granted a theophany, Sarah was asked to make cakes for the divine visitors. She overheard the prophecy about her son, and laughed; then, afraid, she denied her derision in face of the words, 'Is anything too hard for the Lord?' (Gn. 18:14). On the birth of Isaac, Sarah's reproach was removed. She was so incensed by Ishmael's scorn at the feast to celebrate Isaac's weaning that she asked for Hagar and her son to be cast out (Gn. 21).

Aged 127, she died in *Kiriath-arba and was buried in the cave of the field of Machpelah (Gn. 23:1ff.) (*HEBRON).

Sarah is named in Is. 51:2 as an example of trust in Yahweh. In the NT Paul mentions both Abra-

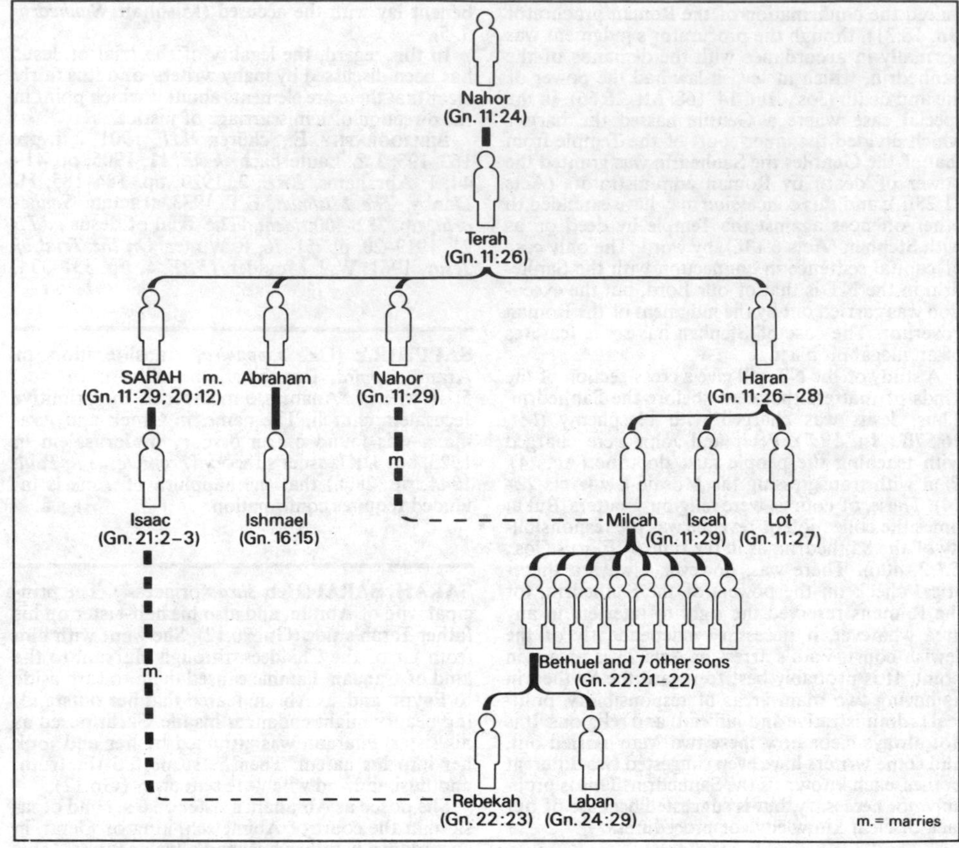

The family of Sarah.

ham and Sarah among those whose faith was counted for righteousness (Rom. 4:19), and he writes of Sarah as the mother of the children of promise (Rom. 9:9). The writer of the Epistle to the Hebrews includes Sarah in the list of the faithful (11:11). She is named also as an example of a wife's proper regard for her husband (1 Pet. 3:6).

M.B.

SARDIS. A city in the Roman province of Asia, in the W of what is now Asiatic Turkey. It was the capital of the ancient kingdom of Lydia, the greatest of the foreign powers encountered by the Greeks during their early colonization of Asia Minor. Its early prosperity, especially under Croesus, became a byword for wealth; its riches are said to have derived in part from the gold won from the Pactolus, a stream which flowed through the city. The original city was an almost impregnable fortress-citadel, towering above the broad valley of the Hermus, and nearly surrounded by precipitous cliffs of treacherously loose rock. Its position as the centre of Lydian supremacy under Croesus was ended abruptly when the Persian king Cyrus besieged the city and took the citadel (546 BC), apparently by scaling the cliffs and entering by a weakly defended point under cover of darkness. The same tactics again led to the fall of the city in 214 BC, when it was captured by Antiochus the Great. Though it lay on an important trade route down the Hermus valley, it never regained under Roman rule the spectacular prominence it had had in earlier centuries. In AD 26 its claim for the honour of building an imperial temple was rejected in favour of its rival Smyrna. There is now only a small village (Sart) near the site of the ancient city.

The letter to 'the angel of the church in Sardis' (Rev. 3:1–6) suggests that the early Christian community there was imbued with the same spirit as the city, resting on its past reputation and without any present achievement, and failing, as the city had twice failed, to learn from its past and be vigilant. The symbol of 'white garments' was rich in meaning in a city noted for its luxury clothing trade: the faithful few who are vigilant shall be arrayed to share in the triumphal coming of their Lord.

Important current excavations have brought much to light, including a superb late synagogue. Sardis had evidently been for centuries a principal centre of the Jewish Diaspora, and was probably the Sepharad of Ob. 20.

BIBLIOGRAPHY. G. M. A. Hanfmann, regular reports in *BASOR*; C. J. Hemer, *Buried History* 11, 1975, pp. 119–135; E. M. Yamauchi, *New Testament Cities in Western Asia Minor*, 1980; C. J. Hemer, *The Letters to the Seven Churches of Asia in Their Local Setting*, 1986.

E.M.B.G.
C.J.H.

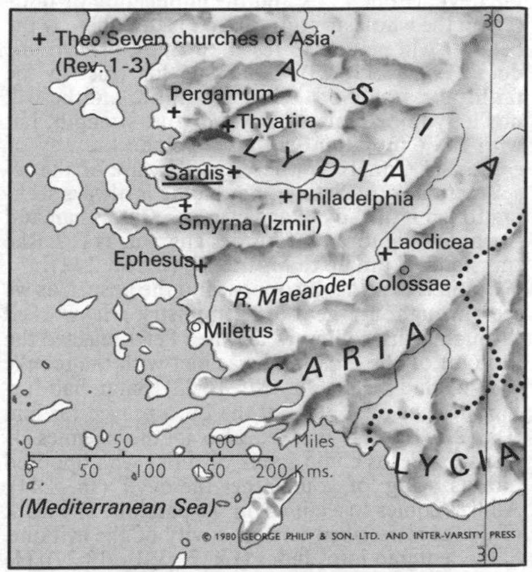

Sardis, one of the 'seven churches of Asia' (Rev. 1–3).

SARGON. Sargon (Heb. *sargōn*; LXX *Arna*; Assyr. *sargen*, ([the god] has established the king[ship]') ruled Assyria 722–705 BC. His reign is known in much detail from inscriptions at his palace at Khorsabad built in 717–707 BC, and from historical texts and letters found at Nineveh and Nimrud. Although he is named only once in the OT (Is. 20:1), his campaigns in Syro-Palestine are of importance in understanding the historical background of the prophecies of Isaiah.

Sargon claimed the capture of Samaria, which had been besieged by his predecessor Shalmaneser V for 3 years (2 Ki. 17:5–6) until his death on 20 December 722 BC or 18 January 721 BC. It is probable that Sargon completed this operation and hurried back to Assyria to claim the throne. Although he bore the same royal name as the heroic Sargon I of Agade (*c.* 2350 BC; *ACCAD; *NIMROD), there is evidence that he was the legal successor to the throne and not a usurper.

During the first months of his reign he faced a major domestic crisis which was settled only by the grant of privileges to the citizens of Assur. In the spring of 720 BC he moved S against the Chaldean Marduk-apla-iddina II (*MERODACH-BALADAN), who had seized the Babylonian throne. An indecisive battle at Der arrested the advance of the supporting Elamites and Arabian tribes, but disturbances in the W rendered it expedient for Sargon to leave Marduk-apla-iddina as king in Babylon (721–710 BC).

In the W, Yaubi'di of Hamath led Damascus, Arpad, Simirra, Samaria, and possibly Hatarikka, in an anti-Assyrian coalition. Late in 720 BC Sargon marched to defeat these allies in a battle near Qarqar, N Syria, and, reducing the participating cities once more to vassalage, he moved to destroy Raphia and thus cut off the rebel Hanun of Gaza from an Egyptian force, under its commander, which was defeated. This interpretation follows the identification of *So or Sib'e (2 Ki. 17:4) as a Hebrew rendering of the term for leader (*re'e*) and not as the proper name of an unidentified Egyptian king (*JNES* 19, 1960, pp. 49–53) or of a king of Sais (*s'w* = So; *BASOR* 171, 1963, pp. 64–67).

During these operations Isaiah warned Judah of the inadvisability of participating, or of trusting, in Egyptian help, illustrating his message by the fate of Carchemish, Hamath, Arpad, Samaria and Damascus (Is. 10:9). On his return from the Egyptian border Sargon deported a large part of the population of Samaria, which he began to rebuild as the capital of a new Assyrian province of Samaria. The process of repopulating the city with foreigners took several years and appears to have continued in the reign of Esarhaddon (Ezr. 4:2).

In 716 BC Sargon sent his army commander (*turtan*; the *'tartan') to war against the Arabs in Sinai. This led to the reception of tribute from the pharaoh Shilkanni (Osorkon IV) of Egypt and from Samsi, queen of the Arabs. Despite these Assyrian successes, the people of Ashdod displaced their Assyrian-nominated ruler, Ahimetu, by a usurper Iadna (or Iamani) who initiated yet another Syro-Palestinian league against Assyria, doubtless relying on Egyptian help. In 712 BC the same *turtan* was sent to conquer Ashdod (Is. 20:1), which was reduced to the status of an Assyrian province. Since Azaqa ('Azeqah or Tell es-Zakariye) on the Judaean border near Lachish surrendered in this campaign, it will be seen how narrowly independent Judah escaped a further invasion. Iamani fled to Nubia for refuge, only to be extradited to Nineveh by the ruler Shabaka.

On other fronts Sargon fought many battles, defeating the Mannaeans and Rusas of Urarṭu in 719–714 BC, and incorporating the defeated Carchemish as a provincial centre. In 710 and 707 BC, following raids into Media to neutralize the hill tribes, Sargon once more advanced against Merodach-baladan, who fled to Elam. Sargon's latter years were spent in suppressing rebellions in Kummukh and Tabal (where he was killed in action). He was succeeded by his son Sennacherib on 12 Ab, 705 BC. That he was 'not buried in his house' was later attributed to his sin in adopting a pro-Babylonian policy following his 'taking the hands of the god Bel (Marduk)' as king there in 709 BC.

BIBLIOGRAPHY. S. Parpola, *The Correspondence of Sargon II*, 1987; H. W. F. Saggs, in *Iraq* 17, 1955, pp. 146–149; 37, 1975, pp. 11–20; D. J. Wiseman, *DOTT*, pp. 58–63; *ANET*, pp. 284–287; *CAH* 3/2, 1991, pp. 86–96. D.J.W.

SARID. A town on the S boundary of Zebulun (Jos. 19:10, 12). Some ancient MSS of LXX read *Sedoud*, and this has given rise to the common identification with Tell Shadud, 8 km SE of Nazareth (*LOB*, p. 106). The weight of textual evidence, however, favours the *MT* Sarid of unknown location. W.O.

SARSECHIM. The name of a Babylonian official present in Jerusalem after the capture of the city in 587 BC (Je. 39:3). The name is as yet unidentified. It has been proposed to identify him with Nebushazban the *Rabsaris (Je. 39:13). This would require taking Nebo from the preceding *Samgar-nebo to read Nebo-sar-sechim as a corruption of Nabū-šezibanni (*nᵉḇô-šazibôn*?). Or *śar-sᵉkîm* could be a title, 'chief of the ...' D.J.W.

SATAN. The name of the prince of evil, Heb. *śāṭān*, Gk. *Satanas*, means basically 'adversary' (the word is so rendered, *e.g.*, in Nu. 22:22). In the first two chapters of Job we read of 'the Satan' as presenting himself before God among 'the sons of God'. It is sometimes said that in such passages Satan is not thought of as especially evil, but as simply one among the heavenly hosts. Admittedly we have not yet the fully developed doctrine, but the activities of 'the Satan' are certainly inimical to Job. The OT references to Satan are few, but he is consistently engaged in activities against the best interests of men. He moves David to number the people (1 Ch. 21:1). He stands at the right hand of Joshua the high priest 'to accuse him', thus drawing down the Lord's rebuke (Zc. 3:1f.). The psalmist thinks it a calamity to have Satan stand at one's right hand (Ps. 109:6, AV, but *cf.* RV 'an adversary', RSV 'an accuser'). John tells us that 'the devil sinned from the beginning' (1 Jn. 3:8), and the OT references to him bear this out.

Most of our information, however, comes from the NT, where the supremely evil being is referred to as Satan or as 'the devil' (*ho diabolos*) indifferently, with Beelzebub (or Beelzeboul, or Beezeboul) also employed on occasion (Mt. 10:25; 12:24, 27). Other expressions, such as 'the ruler of this world' (Jn. 14:30) or 'the prince of the power of the air' (Eph. 2:2), also occur. He is always depicted as hostile to God, and as working to overthrow the purposes of God. Matthew and Luke tell us that at the beginning of his ministry Jesus had a severe time of testing when Satan tempted him to go about his work in the wrong spirit (Mt. 4; Lk. 4; see also Mk. 1:13). When this period was completed the devil left him 'until an opportune time', which implies that the contest was later resumed. This is clear also from the statement that he 'in every respect has been tempted as we are' (Heb. 4:15). This conflict is not incidental. The express purpose of the coming of Jesus into the world was 'to destroy the works of the devil' (1 Jn. 3:8; *cf.* Heb. 2:14). Everywhere the NT sees a great conflict between the forces of God and of good, on the one hand, and those of evil led by Satan, on the other. This is not the conception of one writer or another, but is common ground.

There is no doubting the severity of the conflict. Peter stresses the ferocious opposition by saying that the devil 'prowls around like a roaring lion, seeking some one to devour' (1 Pet. 5:8). Paul thinks rather of the cunning employed by the evil one. 'Satan disguises himself as an angel of light' (2 Cor. 11:14), so that it is small wonder if his minions appear in an attractive guise. The Ephesians are exhorted to put on 'the whole armour of God, that you may be able to stand against the wiles of the devil' (Eph. 6:11), and there are references to 'the snare of the devil' (1 Tim. 3:7; 2 Tim. 2:26). The effect of such passages is to emphasize that Christians (and even archangels, Jude 9) are engaged in a conflict that is both relentlessly and cunningly waged. They are not in a position to retire from the conflict. Nor can they simply assume that evil will always be obviously evil. There is need for the exercise of discrimination as well as stout-heartedness. But determined opposition will always succeed. Peter urges his readers to resist the devil 'firm in your faith' (1 Pet. 5:9), and James says, 'Resist the devil and he will flee from you' (Jas. 4:7). Paul exhorts 'give no opportunity to the devil' (Eph. 4:27), and the implication of putting on the whole armour of God is that thereby the believer will be able to resist anything the evil one does (Eph. 6:11, 13). Paul puts his trust in the faithfulness of God. 'God is faithful, and he will not let you be tempted beyond your strength, but with the temptation will also provide the way of escape' (1 Cor. 10:13). He is well aware of the resourcefulness of Satan, and that he is always seeking to 'gain the advantage over us'. But he can add 'we are not ignorant of his designs' (or, as F. J. Rae translates, 'I am up to his tricks') (2 Cor. 2:11).

Satan is continually opposed to the gospel, as we see throughout the Lord's ministry. He worked through Jesus' followers, as when Peter rejected the thought of the cross and was met with the rebuke 'Get behind me, Satan' (Mt. 16:23). Satan had further designs on Peter, but the Lord prayed for him (Lk. 22:31f.). He worked also in the enemies of Jesus, for Jesus could speak of those who opposed him as being 'of your father the devil' (Jn. 8:44). All this comes to a climax in the passion. The work of Judas is ascribed to the activity of the evil one. Satan 'entered into' Judas (Lk. 22:3; Jn. 13:27). He 'put it into the heart of Judas Iscariot, Simon's son, to betray him' (Jn. 13:2). With the cross in prospect Jesus can say 'the ruler of this world is coming' (Jn. 14:30).

Satan continues to tempt men (1 Cor. 7:5). We read of him at work in a professed believer, Ananias ('why has Satan filled your heart . . .?', Acts 5:3), and in an avowed opponent of the Christian way, Elymas ('You son of the devil', Acts 13:10). The general principle is given in 1 Jn. 3:8, 'He who commits sin is of the devil'. Men may so give themselves over to Satan that they in effect belong to him. They become his 'children' (1 Jn. 3:10). Thus we read of 'a synagogue of Satan' (Rev. 2:9; 3:9), and of men who dwell 'where Satan's throne is' (Rev. 2:13). Satan hinders the work of missionaries (1 Thes. 2:18). He takes away the good seed sown in the hearts of men (Mk. 4:15). He sows 'the sons of the evil one' in the field that is the world (Mt. 13:38f.). His activity may produce physical effects (Lk. 13:16). Always he is pictured as resourceful and active.

But the NT is sure of his limitations and defeat. His power is derivative (Lk. 4:6). He can exercise his activity only within the limits that God lays down (Jb. 1:12; 2:6; 1 Cor. 10:13; Rev. 20:2, 7). He may even be used to set forward the cause of right (1 Cor. 5:5; *cf.* 2 Cor. 12:7). Jesus saw a preliminary victory in the mission of the Seventy (Lk. 10:18). Our Lord thought of 'eternal fire' as 'prepared for the devil and his angels' (Mt. 25:41), and John sees this come to pass (Rev. 20:10). We have already noticed that the conflict with Satan comes to a head in the passion. There Jesus speaks of him as 'cast out' (Jn. 12:31), and as 'judged' (Jn. 16:11). The victory is explicitly alluded to in Heb. 2:14; 1 Jn. 3:8. The work of preachers is to turn men 'from the power of Satan unto God' (Acts 26:18). Paul can say confidently, 'the God of peace will soon crush Satan under your feet' (Rom. 16:20).

The witness of the NT then is clear. Satan is a malignant reality, always hostile to God and to God's people. But he has already been defeated in Christ's life and death and resurrection, and this defeat will become obvious and complete in the end of the age. (*ANTICHRIST; *EVIL SPIRITS.)

BIBLIOGRAPHY. W. O. E. Oesterley in *DCG*; E. Langton, *Essentials of Demonology*, 1949; W. Robinson, *The Devil and God*, 1945; H. Bietenhard, C.

Brown, in *NIDNTT* 3, pp. 468–473; E. Ferguson, *Demonology of the Early Christian World*, 1985; P. L. Day, *An Adversary in Heaven*, 1988. L.M.

SATRAP (Heb. *'ᵃḥašdarpān*; Aram. *'ᵃḥašadrpān*; Akkad. *aḫšad(a)rapannu*; from Old Persian *ḫšaṯapāvan*, 'protector of the kingdom', originally *Median *khshathrapā*). Provincial governor under the Persians (Ezr. 8:36; Est. 3:12; Dn. 3:2; 6:1, *etc.*). The provincial system in the ancient Near East had been in use since the 3rd millennium BC (*e.g.* at *Ur and under *Assyria and *Babylonia). The system was adopted by the Persians. Possibly under *Darius I the empire was divided into twenty satrapies, each comprising smaller units (Herodotus 3. 89–95). Syro-Palestine was part of the satrapy 'Beyond the River' (Ne. 3:7).

BIBLIOGRAPHY. J. M. Cook, *The Persian Empire*, 1983. D.W.B.

SATYR (*śā'îr*, 'hairy one', 'he-goat'). The Heb. plural (*śᵉ'îrîm*) is rendered 'satyrs' in Lv. 17:7 and 2 Ch. 11:15 (AV 'devils', RV 'he-goats'). A similar meaning may be intended in 2 Ki. 23:8 if Heb. *šᵉ'ārîm* ('gates'), which seems meaningless in the context, be regarded as a slip for *śᵉ'îrîm*. The precise nature of these 'hairy ones' is obscure. They may have been he-goats in the ordinary sense, or gods having the appearance of goats. Sacrifices were made to them in high places, with special priests performing the ritual.

From goat to demon in Semitic belief was an easy transition (*cf.* *SCAPEGOAT). Satyrs, apparently demonic creatures, danced on the ruins of Babylon (Is. 13:21), and figured also in the picture of the desolation of Edom (Is. 34:14).

BIBLIOGRAPHY. Oesterley and Robinson, *Hebrew Religion*, 1930, pp. 13, 64ff.; *EBi* (*s.v.* 'satyr'). J.D.D.

SAUL (Heb. *šā'ûl*, 'asked', *i.e.* of God). **1.** King of ancient Edom, from Rehoboth (Gn. 36:37). **2.** A son of Simeon (Gn. 46:10; Ex. 6:15; Nu. 26:13).

3. First king of Israel, son of Kish, of the tribe of Benjamin. The story of Saul occupies most of 1 Sa. (chs. 9–31) and depicts one of the most pathetic of all God's chosen servants.

Head and shoulders above his brethren, a man whose personal courage matched his physique, kingly to his friends and generous to his foes, Saul was the man chosen by God to institute the monarchy, to represent within himself the royal rule of Yahweh over his people. Yet three times over he was declared to have disqualified himself from the task to which he had been appointed, and even in that appointment there was a hint of the character of the man whom God, in his sovereignty, chose to be king.

Under the pressure of the Philistine suzerainty, the Israelites came to think that only a visible warrior-leader could bring about their deliverance. Rejecting the spiritual leadership of Yahweh, mediated through the prophetic ministry of Samuel, they demanded a king (1 Sa. 8). After warning them of the evils of such government—a warning which they did not heed—Samuel was instructed by God to grant the people's wish, and was guided to choose Saul, whom he anointed secretly in the land of Zuph (1 Sa. 10:1), confirming the appointment later by a public ceremony at Mizpeh (10:17–25). Almost immediately Saul had the opportunity of showing his mettle. Nahash the Ammonite besieged Jabesh-gilead and offered cruel terms of surrender to its inhabitants, who sent for help to Saul, who was on the other side of the Jordan. Saul summoned the people by means of an object-lesson typical of his race and age, and with the army thus raised won a great victory (11:1–11). It is an evidence of his finer instincts that he refused at this time to acquiesce in the desire of his followers to punish those who had been unwilling to pay him homage (10:27; 11:12–13).

Following this, a religious ceremony at Gilgal confirmed the appointment of Saul as king, which had obviously received divine approval in the defeat of the Ammonites. With a parting exhortation to the people to be assiduous in their obedience to God, which was accompanied by a miraculous sign, Samuel left the new king to the government of his nation. On three occasions only, one of them posthumously, was the old prophet to emerge from the background. Each time it was to remonstrate with Saul for disobeying the terms of his appointment, terms involving utter obedience to the slightest command of God. The first occasion was when Saul, through impatience, arrogated to himself the priestly office, offering sacrifice at Gilgal (13:7–10). For this sacrilege his rejection from kingship was prophesied by Samuel, and Saul received the first hint that there was already, in the mind of God, the 'man after his heart' whom the Lord had selected to replace him.

The second occasion was when Saul's disobedience brought forth the prophet's well-known dictum that 'to obey is better than sacrifice, and to hearken than the fat of rams' (15:22). Again Saul's rejection from rule over Israel is declared and symbolically shown, and Samuel severs all contact with the fallen monarch. It is from the grave that Samuel emerges to rebuke Saul for the third and last time, and, whatever problems are raised by the story of the medium of Endor (ch. 28), it is clear that God permitted this supernatural interview with the unhappy king in order to fill Saul's cup of iniquity and to foretell his imminent doom.

For the long conflict between Saul and David, see *DAVID, which deals with other aspects of Saul's character. It is significant that when the public anointing of David was made in Bethlehem, Samuel rejected Eliab, David's most manly brother, and was warned against assuming that natural and spiritual power necessarily went together (16:7).

Saul is an object-lesson in the essential difference between the carnal and the spiritual man, as his NT namesake was to distinguish the two (1 Cor. 3, *etc.*). Living in a day when the Holy Spirit came upon men for a special time and purpose, rather than indwelling the children of God permanently, Saul was peculiarly susceptible to moodiness and uncertainty within himself (*HEALTH). Yet his disobedience is presented by the authors of 1 Sa. and 1 Ch. as inexcusable, for he had access to the Word of God, as it was then ministered to him through Samuel.

His downfall was the more tragic because he was a public and representative figure among the people of God.

4. The Jewish name of the apostle *Paul (Acts 13:9).

BIBLIOGRAPHY. J. C. Gregory, 'The Life and Character of Saul', *ExpT* 19, 1907–8, pp. 510–513;

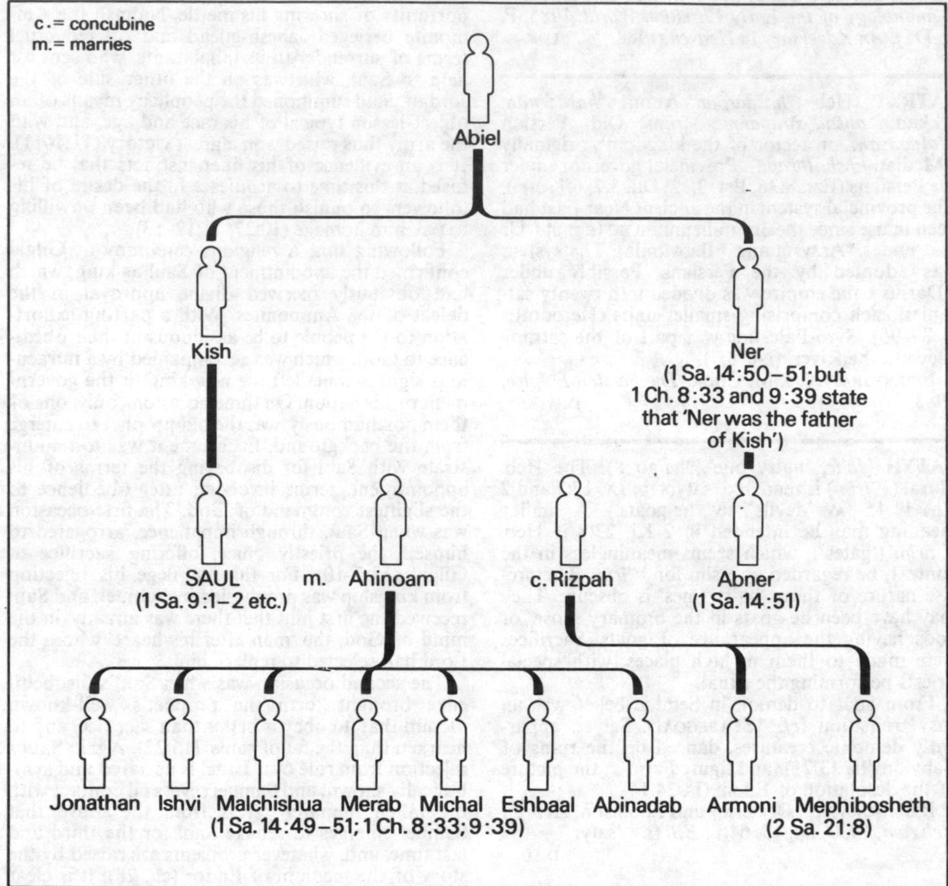

Saul's family.

A. C. Welch, *Kings and Prophets of Israel*, 1952, pp. 63–79; E. Robertson, *The Old Testament Problem*, 1946, pp. 105–136; J. Bright, *A History of Israel*[3], 1981.

T.H.J.

SAVOUR. With one exception (Joel 2:20) the word is used in AV of a sweet or acceptable smell. It is characteristic of sacrifice; and in this connection it is used pointedly of the effect of the Christian's life on his fellows (2 Cor. 2:15–16; RSV 'aroma', 'fragrance'). In Eph. 5:2 it is used of the sacrifice of Christ (RSV 'fragrant offering').

Two other references, referring to a loss of savour (Mt. 5:13; Lk. 14:34), connect this with insipidity or foolishness.

Common to all is the implicit association of cost, or distinctiveness, or strength with savour. Something is missing from God's people or the worship of God when there is no 'savour'.

In Mt. 16:23; Mk. 8:33, AV 'savour' renders Gk. *phronein*, 'to set the mind on' (RSV 'be on the side of').

C.H.D.

SCAPEGOAT. The word Azazel (Heb. *'ᵃzā'zēl*) occurs only in the description of the Day of Atonement (Lv. 16:8, 10 (twice), 26). There are four possible interpretations. **1.** The word denotes the 'scapegoat' and is to be explained as 'the goat (*'ēz*) that goes away (from *'āzal*)'. **2.** It is used as an infinitive, 'in order to remove'; *cf.* Arab. *'azala*, 'to remove' **3.** It means a desolate region (*cf.* Lv. 16:22) or 'precipice' (G. R. Driver; *cf.* NEB). **4.** It is the name of a demon haunting that region, derived from *'āzaz* 'to be strong' and *'ēl* 'God'.

Most scholars prefer the last possibility, as in v. 8 the name appears in parallelism to the name of the Lord. As a fallen angel Azazel is often mentioned in *Enoch* (6:6 onwards), but probably the author got his conception from Lv. 16. The meaning of the ritual must be that sin in a symbolical way was removed from human society and brought to the region of death (*cf.* Mi. 7:19). It is not implied that a sacrifice was presented to the demon (*cf.* Lv. 17:7).

BIBLIOGRAPHY. G. R. Driver, *JSS* 1, 1956, pp. 97f.; D. P. Wright, *The Disposal of Impurity*, 1987.

A. van S.

SCEPTRE. A staff or rod (Heb. *šēḇeṭ*) carried by kings and high officials. It was also used as a weapon (Is. 30:31), as a symbol of the exercise of justice and law (Ps. 45:6) or to indicate political and military oppression (Is. 14:5; Am. 1:5; Zc. 10:11). Judah was God's sceptre (Nu. 24:17; Pss. 60:7; 108:8; Ezk. 21:13). Rulers of Egypt (Zc. 10:11), Syria (Am. 1:5), Ashkelon (Am. 1:8), Babylon (Is. 14:5), Persia (Est. 4:11) and Israel (Ezk. 19:14) held a sceptre. The handle was of wood (Ezk. 19:11–14), metal (Ps. 2:9; Rev. 2:29) or gold (Est. 4:1).

Decorated sceptres are found in excavations (Royal Graves, Ur, Tel Dan) or depicted on palace reliefs and paintings (*e.g.* Darius I relief from Persepolis; *cf.* Gn. 49:10). A tiny ivory pomegranate, perhaps found in Jerusalem, seems to have decorated a ceremonial staff. It is inscribed in old Heb. script 'Belonging to the te[mple of the Lor]d? holy for the priests' (*lby[t yhw]h qdš lkhnm*) and was made about 700 BC. (A. Lemaire, *RB* 88, 1981, pp. 236–239; *BAR* 10, 1984, pp. 24–29; *cf.* *BAR* 18, 1992, pp. 42–45). D.J.W.

SCEVA. Actual or putative father of a group of seven magical practioners who, endeavouring to imitate Paul in Ephesus, used a spell with the name of Jesus for exorcism, were repudiated by the demon and set upon by the demoniac: an incident which deeply impressed Jew and Gentile alike (Acts 19:13ff.). The story was doubtless valued as a demonstration that the 'name' was no magical formula with automatic effect.

Sceva is described as a 'Jewish high priest'. Though this could denote a member of the senior priestly families, it is probably here a self-adopted title for advertisement—rather as a modern conjuror styles himself 'Professor'. 'The Sons of the High Priest Sceva' may have been the collective designation for this 'firm' of itinerant mountebanks (*cf.* v. 13); a Jewish high priest would, in the eyes of superstitious pagans, be an impressive source of esoteric knowledge. B. A. Mastin, however, argues that, as befitted priests, they were genuine, if unsuccessful, exorcists.

The MSS show many variants in detail.

BIBLIOGRAPHY. K. Lake and H. J. Cadbury, *BC*, 1. 4, pp. 241–243; B. A. Mastin, *JTS* n.s. 27, 1976, pp. 405–412. A.F.W.

SCHOOL.

I. In the Old Testament

From the earliest times in the ancient Near East schools were used for regular instruction in reading and writing. Among the Hebrews Moses, trained in Egypt (Acts 7:22), was commanded to teach the people the law (Dt. 4:10) and statutes (Lv. 10:11). This was done by repetition and example (Dt. 11:19), public reading (Dt. 31:10–13), and the use of specially composed songs (v. 19). Parents were responsible for their children's education (Gn. 18:19; Dt. 6:7).

With the establishment of local sanctuaries and the Temple, young men were doubtless taught by the prophets (1 Sa. 10:11–13; 2 Ki. 4:1), and among other instruction reading and writing was given (Jdg. 8:14; Is. 10:19). The alphabet was learned by repetition (Is. 28:10, 'precept upon precept . . .' being literally '*ṣ* after *ṣ*, *q* after *q* . . .'), but most subjects were imparted orally by question and answer (Mal. 2:12, AV 'master and scholar', lit. 'he who rouses and he who answers', may, however, refer to watchmen).

The pupils (*limmûḏîm*, AV 'disciples') were taught by the prophets (Is. 8:16; 50:4; 54:13), as were kings (*e.g.* 2 Sa. 12:1–7). There are no direct references in the OT to special school buildings, but the introduction *c.* 75 BC in Judah by Simon ben-Sheṭaḥ of compulsory elementary education for boys aged 6–16 indicates the prior existence of such schools from the time of the second Temple. 1 Ch. 25:8 refers to scholars (*talmîḏ*) at the time of the first Temple.

*Education played a significant part in the cultural influence of Mesopotamia from the 3rd millennium, and its school texts and curriculum appear to have been copied in Anatolia, Syria (*UGARIT, *MARI) and Palestine itself (*MEGIDDO). For Mesopotamian education and the part played by the scribe, see S. N. Kramer, *The Sumerians*, 1963, pp. 229–248; and for the Egyptian, R. J. Williams, *JAOS* 92, 1972, pp. 214–222. D.J.W.

II. In the New Testament

There is no trace in the NT of schools for Hebrew children. It seems that the home was the place of elementary instruction. The synagogue was the centre of religious instruction with teaching in the hands of the scribes (Mt. 7:29; Lk. 4:16–32; Acts 19:9). The word 'school' occurs in only one NT context (Acts 19:9, AV; RSV, 'hall'). There is nothing to indicate whether 'the school of Tyrannus' was devoted to elementary teaching (6–14 years) or to the advanced subjects of the Greek curriculum, philosophy, literature and rhetoric (14–18 years). A 'Western' addition to Acts 19:9 runs: 'from the fifth to the tenth hour'. Tyrannus' accommodation was available for hire from 11 a.m. onwards. Instruction began at dawn simultaneously with the obligations of Paul's own calling (Acts 18:3). He used the afternoon for teaching in the hired school-house. (*EDUCATION.) E.M.B.

SCHOOLMASTER. AV thus renders the Greek *paidagōgos* in Gal. 3:24–25 (RSV 'custodian'; RV reads 'tutor', as also in 1 Cor. 4:15). There is no satisfactory rendering, for the word has passed into a derivative of quite dissimilar meaning, and the office it signified passed with the social conditions which devised it. The Greek and Roman pedagogue was a trusted male attendant, commonly a slave, who had the general supervision of the boy and saw him safely to and from school. This is the point of Paul's metaphor. E.M.B.

SCOURGING, SCOURGE. The Eng. translation of several Heb. and Gk. words. **1.** Heb. *biqqōreṯ*, translated in Lv. 19:20, AV as 'she shall be scourged'; or (AVmg.), 'there shall be a scourging'. The Heb. term, however, expresses the idea of investigation, conveyed by RSV, 'an inquiry shall be held'.

2. Heb. *šôṭ* (Jb. 5:21; Is. 10:26, *etc.*), *šōṭēṭ* (Jos. 23:13), 'a scourge', but generally used in a metaphorical sense.

3. Gk. *mastigoō* (Mt. 10:17; Jn. 19:1, *etc.*), *mastizō* (Acts 22:25), 'to whip', 'to scourge'; *phragelloō*, derived from Lat. *flagello* (Mt. 27:26; Mk. 15:15). The scourging in Mt. 27:26; Mk. 15:15, was a preliminary stage in the execution of the sentence

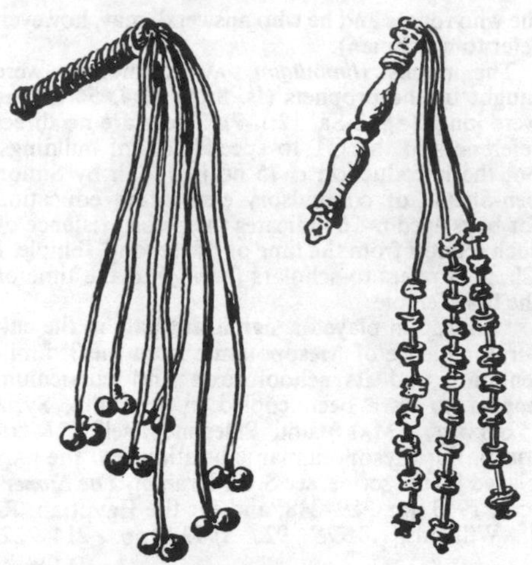

Roman scourges, barbed with lumps of lead and pieces of bone.

to *crucifixion; that proposed in Lk. 23:16, 22 (*paideuō*) and carried out in Jn. 19:1 preceded the death-sentence and may have been intended as a milder penalty.

J.D.D.
F.F.B.

SCRIBE. In ancient Israel, following the spread of the alphabet, the scribes' monopoly of writing was broken, but theirs remained an important profession. The words for 'scribe' in Heb. (*sôpēr*, from *sāpar*, 'to count, tell'; Pi'el, 'to recount'), Canaanite (*spr*) and Akkad. (*šapāru*, 'to send', 'write') cover the main duties of this highly skilled trade. Many scribes were employed by the public as secretaries to transcribe necessary legal contracts (Je. 32:12), write letters, or keep accounts or records, usually from dictation (Je. 36:26). Others, known as 'the king's scribes' (2 Ch. 24:11), were employed in public administration and were attached to the royal household, where the Chief Scribe acted as 'Secretary of State' and ranked before the Chronicler (*mazkîr*), who kept the state records (2 Sa. 8:16; 1 Ki. 4:3). As a high official the Chief Scribe was one of the royal advisers (1 Ch. 27:32). Thus Shebna the scribe, who later rose to be 'over the household' (*i.e.* Prime Minister), was sent by Hezekiah with the Prime Minister and elders to parley with the Assyrians besieging Jerusalem (2 Ki. 18:18; 19:2; Is. 36:3). Some scribes were especially employed for military duties, which included the compilation of a list of those called out for war (Jdg. 5:14) or of the booty won, their senior official being designated 'principal scribe of the host' (2 Ki. 25:19; Je. 52:25). Although other scribes were allotted to tasks in the Temple involving the collection of revenues (2 Ki. 12:10), the scribal profession was, until the Exile, separate from the priesthood, who had their own literate officials. Senior scribes had their own rooms in the palace (Je. 36:12–21) or Temple (Je. 36:10).

Shaphan the scribe was given the newly discovered scroll of the law to read before the king (2 Ki. 22:8), but it was only in the post-exilic period that the scribes assumed the role of copyists, preservers and interpreters of the law (Ezr. 7:6). *Ezra was both priest and scribe (7:11) and may well have acted as adviser on Jewish affairs to the Babylonian court, in the same way as did the specialist scribes of Assyria and Babylonia. By the 2nd century BC the majority of scribes were priests (1 Macc. 7:12) and were the prototypes of the religious *scribes of the NT day.

The scribe, as a person of education and means, was able to wear fine garments with a pen-case or 'inkhorn' hanging from his girdle (Ezk. 9:2). His equipment included reed-pens (Je. 8:8); a small knife for erasures and cutting papyrus (Je. 36:23), and, in some cases, styli for *writing in the cuneiform script. The profession was often followed by whole families (1 Ch. 2:55), and several sons are named as following their fathers in office. (*EDUCATION; *WRITING.)

D.J.W.

SCRIBES (Heb. *sōp̄ᵉrîm*; Gk. *grammateis*, *nomikoi* (lawyers) and *nomodidaskaloi* (teachers of the law)). Scribes were experts in the study of the law of Moses (*Torah*). At first this occupation belonged to the priests. Ezra was priest and scribe (Ne. 8:9); the offices were not necessarily separate. The chief activity of the scribe was undistracted study (Ecclus. 38:24). The rise of the scribes may be dated after the Babylonian Exile. 1 Ch. 2:55 would suggest that the scribes were banded together into families and guilds. They were probably not a distinct political party in the time of Ben-Sira (beginning of the 2nd century BC), but became one by the repressive measures of Antiochus Epiphanes. Scribes were found in Rome in the later imperial period, and in Babylonia in the 5th and 6th centuries AD. Not until about AD 70 are there detailed facts concerning individual scribes. They were mainly influential in Judaea up to AD 70, but they were to be found in Galilee (Lk. 5:17) and among the Dispersion.

The scribes were the originators of the synagogue service. Some of them sat as members of the Sanhedrin (Mt. 16:21; 26:3). After AD 70 the importance of the scribes was enhanced. They preserved in written form the oral law and faithfully handed down the Heb. Scriptures. They expected of their pupils a reverence beyond that given to parents (*Aboth* 4. 12).

The function of the scribes was threefold.

1. They preserved the law. They were the professional students of the law and its defenders, especially in the Hellenistic period, when the priesthood had become corrupt. They transmitted unwritten legal decisions which had come into existence in their efforts to apply the Mosaic law to daily life. They claimed this oral law was more important than the written law (Mk. 7:5ff.). By their efforts religion was liable to be reduced to heartless formalism.

2. They gathered around them many pupils to instruct them in the law. The pupils were expected to retain the material taught and to transmit it without variation. They lectured in the Temple (Lk. 2:46; Jn. 18:20). Their teaching was supposed to be free of charge (so Rabbi Zadok, Hillel and others), but they were probably paid (Mt. 10:10; 1 Cor. 9:3–18, for Paul's statement of his right), and even took advantage of their honoured status (Mk. 12:40; Lk. 20:47).

3. They were referred to as 'lawyers' and 'teachers of the law', because they were entrusted with the administration of the law as judges in the Sanhedrin (*cf.* Mt. 22:35; Mk. 14:43, 53; Lk. 22:66; Acts 4:5; Jos., *Ant.* 18. 16f.). 'Lawyer' and 'scribe' are synonymous, and thus the two words are never joined in the NT. For their services in the Sanhedrin they were not paid. They were therefore obliged to earn their living by other means if they had no private wealth.

The OT Apocrypha and Pseudepigrapha are sources for the origin of the scribal party. The books of Ezra, Nehemiah, Daniel, Chronicles and Esther also indicate something of the beginnings of the movement, whereas Josephus and the NT speak of this group in a more advanced stage of development. There is no mention of the scribes in the Fourth Gospel. They belonged mainly to the party of the Pharisees, but as a body were distinct from them. On the matter of the resurrection they sided with Paul against the Sadducees (Acts 23:9). They clashed with Christ, for he taught with authority (Mt. 7:28–29), and he condemned external formalism which they fostered. They persecuted Peter and John (Acts 4:5), and had a part in Stephen's martyrdom (Acts 6:12). However, although the majority opposed Christ (Mt. 21:15), some believed (Mt. 8:19).

BIBLIOGRAPHY. G. F. Moore, *Judaism*, 1, 1927, pp. 37–47; G. H. Box in *EBr*, 1948 edn.; J. D. Prince in *EBi*; D. Eaton in *HDB*; E. Schürer, *HJP*, 2, 1978; W. Robertson Smith, *The Old Testament in the Jewish Church*, 1892, pp. 42–72 (with bibliography on p. 42); A. Finkel, *The Pharisees and the Teacher of Nazareth*[2], 1974; J. W. Bowker, *Jesus and the Pharisees*, 1973; N. Hillyer, *NIDNTT* 3, pp. 477–482; J. Jeremias, *TDNT* 1, pp. 740–742; *idem*, *Jerusalem in the Time of Jesus*, 1969, ch. 10; *EJ* (*s.v.* 'Scribes').

C.L.F.

SCRIPTURE, SCRIPTURES.

I. Vocabulary

Two Gk. words are translated 'Scripture(s)' in EVV. *gramma*, originally 'an alphabetical character', is used in NT for 'document' (Lk. 16:6; Acts 28:21), in a special sense by Paul for the law (Rom. 2:27, 29; 7:6; 2 Cor. 3:6) and in the plural for the 'writings' of Moses (Jn. 5:47); for 'learning', sacred or profane (Jn. 7:15; Acts 26:24), and only once in the phrase *ta hiera grammata*, 'the holy scriptures' (2 Tim. 3:15). *graphē*, on the other hand, which in secular Gk. meant simply 'a writing' (though sometimes an authoritative writing in particular), is in the NT appropriated to 'the Scriptures' in a technical sense some 50 times, in most cases unmistakably the OT. Associated with *graphē* is the formula *gegraptai*, 'it is written', occurring some 60 times in the NT, and found in Greek usage for legal pronouncements (*cf.* A. Deissmann, *Bible Studies*[2], 1909, pp. 112ff.). Analogous forms occur in the Mishnah, but the rabbis more often used formulae like 'It is said . . .'. The term 'the Scripture' (*hakāṯûḇ*) is also employed. (See B. M. Metzger, *JBL* 70, 1951, pp. 297ff., for quotation formulae in rabbinic and NT documents.)

II. Significance

gegraptai meant 'It stands written in the Scriptures', and all Christians or Hellenistic Jews recognized that these comprised (Lk. 24:44) 'the law, . . . the prophets, and . . . the psalms' (*i.e.* the *Keṯuḇim*, or Writings; *CANON OF THE OLD TESTAMENT). Though the AV, RSV translation of 2 Tim. 3:16 ('every [all] scripture is inspired . . .') is probably preferable to that of RV, NEB, no contemporary would doubt the extent of 'every inspired scripture'. It was what Christians called the OT, in which the gospel was rooted, of which Christ was the fulfilment, which was through faith in Christ able to lead a man to salvation, and was used in the primitive church for all the purposes outlined in 2 Tim. 3:15–17.

The question arises, however, at what date and in what sense Christians began to use the term 'Scriptures' for *Christian* writings. It has sometimes been suggested that 'according to the scriptures' in 1 Cor. 15:3f. refers to Christian testimony books or early Gospels, since no OT passage specifies the resurrection on the third day. This is unacceptable: Paul means the OT, as the groundwork of Christian preaching (*GOSPEL), and probably relates simply the fact of resurrection, not its occurrence on the third day, to prophecy (*cf.* B. M. Metzger, *JTS* n.s. 8, 1957, pp. 118ff.). Still less acceptable is Selwyn's suggestion that the anarthrous *en graphēi* in 1 Pet. 2:6 means 'in writing' (*e.g.* in a hymn), for the passage quoted is from the OT. Nevertheless, there were undoubtedly collections of authoritative sayings of the Lord in the apostolic church (*cf.* O. Cullmann, *SJT* 3, 1950, pp. 180ff.; *TRADITION), and 1 Tim. 5:18 seems to represent a quotation from such a collection, linked with an OT citation, the two together being described as 'scripture'. Again, Paul in 1 Cor. 2:9 cites by *gegraptai* a passage which, unless it is an extremely free rendering of Is. 64:4; is unidentifiable. It occurs in various forms elsewhere in early literature, however, and now as Logion 17 of the *Gospel of Thomas* (*NEW TESTAMENT APOCRYPHA). It is perhaps worth considering whether Paul is quoting a saying of the Lord not recorded in our Gospels (as in Acts 20:35) and citing it as he would 'scripture'.

If indeed the tradition of the Lord's words was so early called 'Scripture' it would be an easy step so to describe apostolic letters read in church; and, despite many dogmatic statements to the contrary, there would be no reason why this should not have occurred in apostolic times, as 2 Pet. 3:16, as usually translated, represents: though perhaps we should translate 'they wrest the Scriptures *as well*' (*cf.* C. Bigg, *St. Peter and St. Jude*[2], *ICC*, 1901, *in loc.*).

We have, however, reached a dark place in NT history, though one where we may hope for future light. (*BIBLE; *CANON; *INSPIRATION.)

BIBLIOGRAPHY. C. H. Dodd, *According to the Scriptures*, 1952; E. E. Ellis, *Paul's Use of the Old Testament*, 1957; J. Barton, *Reading the Old Testament*, 1984; H. G. Reventlow, *The Authority of the Bible and the Rise of the Modern World*, 1985.

A.F.W.

SCYTHIANS. Though sometimes used of highly skilled semi-nomadic horsemen migrating from the Russian steppes, Scythian denotes a group of tribes who lived N and E of the Black Sea. They had invaded E Anatolia (Urarṭu) and NW Iran (Media) by the 8th century BC, driving the Cimmerians (*GOMER) before them. Their progress was checked by the Assyrians under Sargon II (722–705 BC) and they were defeated in 676 by Esarhaddon. According to Herodotus (1.116, 4.1) they dominated the Near East for 28 years (653–625 BC). At one time they were allied with the Assyrians to relieve Nineveh in 630 but later sided with the Babylonians, perhaps as part of the Ummanmanda hordes, to conquer that same city in 612 BC. A raid against Egypt was bought off in the reign of Psammetichus I (664–610). Later they were involved with Cyrus in the capture of Babylon. Some descendants or mercenaries settled at Beth Shean, called Scythopolis (Jdg. 1:27, LXX). By the 1st century BC they still controlled trade N of the Black Sea and were known to the Greeks as ruthless warriors with a reputation for savagery, reflected in 2 Macc. 4:47, 3 Macc. 7:5, 4 Macc, 10:7 and known to Paul in Col. 3:11.

The Scythians, known as Ashkenaz (Gn. 10:2; 1 Ch. 1:6; Je. 51:27) and by the Assyrians as *Ishkuza* have left no writings of their own. However, archaeological finds indicate a highly cultured people (Karmir Blur, the Ziwiye Treasure and widespread distinctive three-bladed barbed arrows).

BIBLIOGRAPHY. E. Yamauchi, *Foes from the Northern Frontier*, 1982, pp. 63–85; *BA* 46, 1983, pp. 90–99. D.J.W.

SEA (Heb. *yām*; Gk. *thalassa* and *pelagos*: this latter term, meaning 'open sea', occurs only once, Acts 27:5).

The predominating sea in the OT is, of course, the Mediterranean. Indeed, the word *yām* also means 'west', 'westward', *i.e.* 'seaward', from the geographical position of the Mediterranean with reference to Palestine. The Mediterranean is termed 'the Great Sea' (Jos. 1:4), 'the western sea' (Dt. 11:24), and 'the sea of the Philistines' (Ex. 23:31).

Other seas mentioned in the OT are the Red Sea, lit. 'sea of reeds' (Ex. 13:18); the Dead Sea, lit. 'sea of salt' (Gn. 14:3); the Sea of Galilee, lit. 'sea of *kinneret*' (Nu. 34:11). The word *yām* was also used of a particularly broad river, such as the Euphrates (Je. 51:35f.) and the Nile (Na. 3:8). It is used with reference to the great basin in the Temple court (1 Ki. 7:23).

As one would expect, the NT *thalassa* is used with reference to the same seas as are mentioned in the OT.

The Hebrews betrayed little interest in, or enthusiasm for, the sea. Probably their fear of the ocean stemmed from the ancient Semitic belief that the deep personified the power that fought against the deity. But for Israel the Lord was its Creator (Gn. 1:9f.), and therefore its Controller (Ps. 104:7–9; Acts 4:24). He compels it to contribute to man's good (Gn. 49:25; Dt. 33:13) and to utter his praise (Ps. 148:7). In the figurative language of Isaiah (17:12) and Jeremiah (6:23) the sea is completely under God's command. Many of the manifestations of the Lord's miraculous power were against the sea (Ex. 14–15; Ps. 77:16; Jon. 1–2). So also Christ's walking on the sea and stilling the storm (Mt. 14:25–33; *cf.* G. Bornkamm, 'The Stilling of the Storm in Matthew', in G. Bornkamm, G. Barth and H. J. Held, *Tradition and Interpretation in Matthew*, 1963, pp. 52ff.). God's final triumph will witness the disappearance of the sea in the world to come (Rev. 21:1). J.G.S.S.T.

SEA OF GLASS. Twice John saw in heaven 'as it were a sea of glass' (*hōs thalassa hyalinē*), 'before the throne' of God 'like crystal' (Rev. 4:6) and later 'mingled with fire' (Rev. 15:2). The picture of a sea in heaven may be traced through the apocalyptic literature (*e.g. Testament of Levi* 2:7; *2 Enoch* 3:3) back to 'the waters which were above the firmament' of Gn. 1:7; Pss. 104:3; 148:4. The likeness to crystal stands in contrast with the semi-opacity of most ancient *glass and speaks of the holy purity of heaven; the mingling with fire suggests the wrath of God (*cf.* Gn. 7:11; *1 Enoch* 54:7–8). Beside or on the sea stand the victors over the beast: their song (Rev. 15:3) recalls that of the Israelites beside the Red Sea (Ex. 15:1ff.). M.H.C.

SEAL, SEALING.

I. In the Old Testament

In the Near East, from which many thousands of individual seals have been recovered, engraved seals were common in ancient times, the Hebrews using a general term which did not specify the form of the seal itself (*ḥōtām*; Egyp. *htm*). The varied uses of such seals were much the same as in modern times.

a. Uses

(i) As a mark of authenticity and authority. Thus pharaoh handed a seal to Joseph his deputy (Gn. 41:42) and Ahasuerus sealed royal edicts (Est. 3:10; 8:8–10). The action describes the passing of the master's word to his disciples (Is. 8:16) and Yahweh granting authority to Zerubbabel (Hg. 2:23; *cf.* Je. 22:24). For a non-biblical example of delegated seals on a covenant, see *Iraq* 21, 1958.

(ii) To witness a document. The seal was impressed on the clay or wax (*WRITING). Thus, his friends witnessed Jeremiah's deed of purchase (Je. 32:11–14) and Nehemiah and his contemporaries attested the covenant (Ne. 9:38; 10:1) and Daniel a prophecy (Dn. 9:24).

(iii) To secure by affixing a seal. Thus, a clay document within its envelope or other receptacle, or a scroll tied by a cord to which was attached a lump of clay bearing a seal impression, could be examined and read only when the seal had been broken by an authorized person (*cf.* Rev. 5:1f.). A sealed prophecy (Dn. 12:9) or book (Is. 29:11) was thus a symbol for something as yet unrevealed.

To prevent unauthorized entry doors would be sealed by a cord or clay, with the sealing stretched across the gap between the door and its lock. This was done to the lions' den at Babylon (Dn. 6:17; Bel and the Dragon 14) and to tombs (Herodotus, 2. 121; *cf.* Mt. 27:66). A crocodile's close-knit scales were likened to a sealed item (Jb. 41:15).

Metaphorically the seal stood for what is securely held, as are the sins of man before God (Dt. 32:34; Jb. 14:17), who alone has the authority to open and to seal (Jb. 33:16). He sets his seal as a token of completion (Ezk. 28:12). The metaphor in Ct. 4:12 is probably of chastity.

b. Form

With the invention of writing in the 4th millennium BC seals were used in large numbers. The cylinder-seal was the most common and was rolled on clay, though stamp seals are also found in contemporary use. In Palestine, under both Mesopotamian (often through Syrian and Phoenician) and Egyptian influences, cylinder-seals and scarabs were in use in the Canaanite period. The latter predominated for use on wax or clay lumps appended to papyrus. With the Monarchy, stamp seals, 'button', conoid or scaraboid prevail.

The seal was pierced so that it could be worn on a cord round the neck (Gn. 38:18; Je. 22:24; Ct. 8:6) or on a pin, traces of which sometimes remain, for attachment to the dress. The scaraboid seals or seal stones were set in a ring to be worn on the hand or arm (Est. 3:12).

c. Materials

Poor persons could purchase roughly engraved seals made of local terracotta, bitumen, limestone, frit or wood. The majority of seals, however, were specially engraved by a skilled seal-cutter who used copper gravers, a cutting wheel, and sometimes a small bow-drill, perhaps the 'pen of iron; with a point of diamond' (Je. 17:1; *ARTS AND CRAFTS), to work the hard semi-precious stones (*ART). In Palestine, as elsewhere, carnelian, chalcedony, agate, jasper, rock crystal and haematite were imported and frequently used. Imported Egyptian scarabs were of glazed steatite and, later, glazed composition.

Engraved stones (Ex. 28:11-23; 39:8) were used as insets in the high priest's breast ornament. The fine stones and workmanship led to these seal stones or signet-rings (Heb. *ṭabba'aṯ*; Akkad. *ṭimbu'u*) being used as ornaments (Is. 3:21), votive offerings, or for sacred purposes (Ex. 35:22; Nu. 31:50), like the group of seals in the Canaanite shrine at Hazor, or as *amulets. The Heb. *ṭabba'aṯ* is used also of rings in general (Ex. 25:12).

d. Designs

Before the Monarchy cylinder-seals followed the Phoenician or Syrian style, showing patterns, well-filled designs, rows of men or designs characteristic of the different fashions prevailing at various periods in Mesopotamia. The later Palestinian seals, usually oval, bear representations of lions (see *IBA*, fig. 52), winged human-headed lions or sphinxes (cherubim), griffins or the winged uraeus-snake. Egyptian motifs, with the lotus flower, the *ankh*-symbol of life or the Horus-child, frequently occur. Scenes of worship, seated deities and animals and birds seem to show that this art did not offend Hebrew religious feeling. After the 7th century BC, however, the majority of seals bear only a two-line inscription.

e. Inscriptions

More than 200 Hebrew seals have been recovered, inscribed with their owners' names. The name may stand alone, or be followed by the father's name or by a title. Several belonged to royal retainers, described as 'servant of the king'. The finest of them is the jasper seal 'Of Shema, servant of Jeroboam' (*i.e.* Jeroboam II), found in excavations at Megiddo. Another shows a cock, with an inscription reading 'Of Jaazaniah, servant of the king', and may indicate as owner the Jaazaniah of 2 Ki. 25:23, or a contemporary of the same name (Je. 35:3; 40:8; *cf.* Ezk. 11:1). The seals were impressed into lumps of clay, and some of these have been recovered, carrying on the back the marks of the papyrus documents they once secured. One such sealing, termed *bulla*, had been stamped by the seal 'Of Gedaliah who is over the household'. It was found at Lachish, and may have belonged to the governor of Judah (2 Ki. 25:22–25; for the title *cf.* 2 Ki. 18:18, and *SHEBNA). One impression is particularly important because its date is certain. The seal was inscribed 'Of Jehozerah, son of Hilkiah, servant of Hezekiah' (*IEJ* 24, 1974, pp. 27–29), Hezekiah being the king of Judah, and Hilkiah his steward's father (2 Ki. 18:18, *etc.*). Several men are entitled 'son of the king', although it is not clear whether these were members of the royal family or of the larger palace community. Also uncertain is the identity of the master on the seal inscribed 'Of Eliakim, retainer (*na'ar*) of Yawkin'. Yawkin may have been *Jehoiachin, king of Judah, but the masters on other seals so inscribed were not all kings. Some seals certainly belonged to women, *e.g.* the seal of one Hannah (*ḥnh*; *PEQ* 108, 1976, pp. 59–61), or 'Of Abigail, wife of Asaiah'.

The value of these seals lies in the range of Hebrew personal names they reveal, not all known from the OT (*e.g.* Gamariah, Halasiah). The titles they reveal widen our knowledge of the administration. The large number of seals, many bearing no design apart from the names, implies a widespread ability to read in the relatively small state of Judah, whence most of the seals come.

Important historical information is supplied by a collection of clay sealings and some stamps on jar-handles, apparently carrying the names of three post-exilic governors of Judah (Elnathan, Yehoezer, Ahzai) each styled *peḥa*, to be placed after Zerubbabel, and before Ezra. These names are otherwise unknown. (See N. Avigad, *Bullae and Seals from a Post-Exilic Judaean Archive*, 1976.)

f. Stamped jar-handles

Excavations in Palestine have produced about 1,000 jar-handles bearing seal impressions. Some appear to be royal pottery marks (*cf.* 1 Ch. 4:23) giving the place of manufacture. The impressions are usually of four-winged scarabeus or a flying scroll with 'Of the king' (*lammeleḵ*) above, and (below) a place, *e.g.* Hebron, Ziph, Socoh and *mmšt*. Others bear personal names (perhaps of the potter), *e.g.* Shebnaiah, Azariah, Yopiah. Such stamped jar-handles have been found in quantity at Megiddo, Lachish and Gibeon. A group of fiscal stamp impressions inscribed in Aramaic *yhd* (Judah) dated 400–200 BC are of special interest (*MONEY; *BASOR* 147, Oct. 1957, pp. 37–39; 148, Dec. 1957, pp. 28–30; *IEJ* 7, 1957, pp. 146–153).

BIBLIOGRAPHY. (1) Palestinian seals: A. Rowe, *Catalogue of Egyptian Scarabs in the Palestine Archaeological Museum*, 1936; B. Parker, 'Cylinder Seals of Palestine', *Iraq* 11, 1949; J. Nougayrol, *Cylindres sceaux et empreintes . . . trouvés en Palestine au cours des fouilles régulières*, 1939; A. Reifenberg, *Ancient Hebrew Seals*, 1950; D. Diringer, in *DOTT*, pp. 218–226. (2) For other Near Eastern seals: H. Frankfort, *Cylinder Seals*, 1939; D. J. Wiseman, *Cylinder Seals of Western Asia*, 1958.

D.J.W.
A.R.M.

II. In the New Testament

a. Literal use

The verb *sphragizō* (noun *sphragis*) is occasionally used in the NT in a literal sense, *e.g.* of the sealing of the tomb of Christ after his burial (Mt. 27:66 *cf.* *Ev. Petr.* 8:33), the sealing of Satan in the abyss (Rev. 20:3) and the sealing of the apocalyptic roll against unauthorized scrutiny (Rev. 5:1–8:1, *passim*). The practice of 'sealing' mentioned in this latter context would have been as familiar to Jews as to Romans (*cf.* Rev. 22:10, where the *logoi* are not 'sealed' because 'the time is at hand', and they are to be imminently used; contrast Dn. 12:4, 9).

b. Figurative use

(i) In Rom. 15:28 Paul refers to his intention of delivering a contribution (*koinōnia*) of the Gentiles to the saints in Jerusalem, and so of having 'sealed' (*sphragisamenos*) their offering. This may possibly imply a guarantee of his honesty ('under my own seal', NEB), but it will in any case denote Paul's *approval* of the Gentile action (so Theodore of Mopsuestia; *cf.* Jn. 3:33, where *esphragisen* is used of man's 'approval' of the truth of God, and Jn. 6:27, where precisely the same form of the verb is used with reference to God's attestation of the Christ).

(ii) An unusual use of the word *sphragis*, which carries still the sense of 'authentication', occurs in 1 Cor. 9:2, when Paul describes his converts in the church at Corinth as the 'seal' affixed by Christ to his work; the vindication, indeed, of his apostolate.

(iii) In the discussion of Abraham's exemplary faith in Rom. 4, Paul mentions the *sēmeion* of circumcision as the confirming 'seal' (v. 11; NEB 'hallmark') of a righteousness which existed, by faith, before the rite itself was instituted. This use of the term 'seal' compares with that in the Apocalypse (Rev. 7:2–8; 9:4), where the servants of God are described as being 'sealed' with 'the seal of the living God' (7:2f.; *cf.* Ezk. 9:4; Rev. 14:1), as a safeguard as well as a mark of possession, A. G. Hebert suggests (*TWBR*, p. 222) that these passages 'readily fall into a baptismal context'.

III. Sealing by the Spirit

One important NT image associates *sphragis* with *pneuma.* The Pauline characterization of the Christian inheritance in Eph. 1, for example, proceeds against a background filled with Christian hope. In v. 13, accordingly, the Ephesian Christians are described as 'sealed with the promised Holy Spirit'; they have received in time, that is to say, an earnest of what they will become in eternity. Once more this use of 'sealing' includes the concept of 'possession' (*cf.* 2 Tim. 2:19; Gal. 6:17). Similarly, mention of the Holy Spirit in Eph. 4:30, during a piece of practical exhortation to Christ-like behaviour, is followed by the qualifying phrase, 'in whom (*en hō*) you were sealed for the day of redemption'; while in 2 Cor. 1:21f. believers are described as 'anointed' by God, who has 'put his seal' upon them, and given them the Holy Spirit as an eternal guarantee. We have to consider the nature of this 'seal', as well as the moment and results of the 'sealing'.

a. The nature of the seal. Considerable discussion has taken place on this point. R. E. O. White, for example (*The Biblical Doctrine of Initiation*, 1960, p. 203 and n.), takes the aorists of *sphragizō* in Eph. 1:13; 4:30; 2 Cor. 1:22 to refer to the gift of the Spirit, acting as a 'divine seal upon baptism'. He discovers in support of this suggestion a 'regular' NT use of the aorist tense in connection with the reception of the Spirit by the believer in baptism. W. F. Flemington, on the other hand (*The New Testament Doctrine of Baptism*, 1953, pp. 66f.), proposes baptism itself as the seal, and relates this to the word *sphragis* used in connection with the Jewish rite of circumcision. (So also O. Cullmann, *Baptism in the New Testament*, 1950, p. 46.)

Clearly the Heb. background to the theology of baptism, and to the notion of 'seal' itself, cannot be discounted; and Gregory Dix has indicated the extent to which the early Fathers were indebted to their Jewish antecedents in this respect (*Th* 51, 1948, pp. 7–12). At the same time, as Dix points out, it is not necessarily the NT which justifies any later connection made between 'baptism' and 'seal'; even the *Didachē* does not call water baptism a 'sealing', or connect the sacrament in any way with the gift of the Holy Spirit.

b. The moment of sealing. These considerations will suggest the doubt that also exists about the precise moment of the believer's 'sealing'. If we are right to associate the gift of the Holy Spirit with baptism (which is a frequent but not altogether regular pattern in the NT, *cf.* Acts 8:36ff.; 10:44), we may consider that this 'sealing' by the Spirit takes place at baptism, or more precisely, perhaps, at the moment of commitment that finds its focus and expression in the sacrament of baptism. So, *e.g.*. G. W. H. Lampe (*The Seal of the Spirit*, 1951) has carefully examined the origin and meaning of the cognate NT terms *sphragis* and *chrisma*, associated with the 'chrism' of Christ himself in whom the Spirit of God was actively present, and shown that (in Pauline language) incorporation into the body of Christ is effected by baptism (rather than by any equivalent of 'confirmation', incidentally), and 'sealed' by the gift of the Holy Spirit (pp. 6, 61f.; for a summary of the arguments involved, and their proponents, see further White, *op. cit.*, pp. 352ff.).

c. The results of sealing. It has become clear from 1st-century papyri that the language of 'sealing' came to acquire in the E the extended and important meaning, particularly in legal circles, of giving validity to documents, guaranteeing the genuineness of articles and so on. (The possible parallels that exist between *sphragizō* and initiation into Gk. mystery cults are less likely to be significant.) It is easy as a result to see how the word *sphragis* and its cognates fit naturally into NT contexts which presuppose the theology of the covenant, and denote, in terms of the gift of the Holy Spirit, authentication as well as ownership. We have already discovered these to be aspects of the meaning of the term in other NT passages.

The occurrence of similar ideas in other contexts may be noticed in this connection. The 'mark' of initiation administered by John the Baptist, *e.g.*, was an entirely eschatological rite (Lk. 3:3ff.; note the reaction of the people to John's identity in v. 15); and in line with normative Jewish apocalyptic his baptism signified an 'earmarking' for salvation in view of coming judgment comparable to certain parts of the *Psalms of Solomon* (*e.g.* 15:6f., 8; *cf.* 2 Esdras 6:5), and of the NT itself (2 Tim. 2:19; and *cf.* the thought of 'sealing for security' already noticed in Rev. 7:2ff., *etc.*; see White, *op. cit.*, p. 88).

In the NT uses of the term 'seal' we have considered, the ideas of ownership, authentication and security predominate. The three Pauline passages reviewed (Eph. 1:13; 4:30; 2 Cor. 1:22) together indicate that the *arrabōn* of the Holy Spirit given to the believer, incorporated *en Christō* by baptism through faith, is a 'token and pledge of final redemption' (Lampe, *op. cit.*, p. 61). In this way the gift of the Spirit is equivalent to 'putting on' Christ, sharing his *chrisma*, and becoming members of his body, the true Israel of God (*ibid.*; *cf.* 1 Cor. 12:13). The gift of the Holy Spirit, in fact, confirms the covenant in which believers are 'sealed' as God's own.

BIBLIOGRAPHY. The standard English work on this subject (NT) is G. W. H. Lampe, *The Seal of the Spirit*, 1951 (esp. Part 1). For the history of the idea see also G. Dix, *Th* 51, 1948, pp. 7–12. For a fuller discussion of the relevant texts see the major works on baptism in the NT, notably O. Cullmann, *Baptism in the New Testament*, 1950; W. F. Flemington, *The New Testament Doctrine of Baptism*, 1953; P.-Ch. Marcel, *The Biblical Doctrine of Infant Baptism*, 1953; R. E. O. White, *The Biblical Doctrine of Initiation*, 1960; R. Schnackenburg, *Baptism in the Thought of St. Paul*, 1964; J. D. G. Dunn, *Baptism in the Holy Spirit*, 1970; R. Schippers, *NIDNTT* 3, pp. 497–501. S.S.S.

SEBA. 1. Son of Cush, classed under Ham (Gn. 10:7; 1 Ch. 1:9). **2.** Land and people in S Arabia, apparently closely related to the land and people of *Sheba; in fact *sᵉḇā'* (Seba) and *šᵉḇā'* (Sheba) are commonly held to be simply the Old Arab. and Heb. forms of the one name of a people, *i.e.* the well-known kingdom of Sheba. In a psalm (72:10) dedicated to Solomon, he is promised gifts from 'the kings of Sheba and (or: "yea") Seba'. In Isaiah's prophecies, Israel's ransom would take the wealth of Egypt, Ethiopia (Cush) and Seba (Is. 43:3), and the tall Sabaeans were to acknowledge Israel's God (Is. 45:14), first fulfilled in the wide spread of Judaism and first impact of Christianity there during the first 5 centuries AD. The close association of Seba/Sheba with Africa (Egypt and Cush) may just possibly reflect connections across the Red Sea between S Arabia and Africa from the 10th century BC onwards; for slender indications of this, see W. F. Albright, *BASOR* 128, 1952, p. 45 with nn. 26–27. Strabo (16. 4. 8–10) names a town Sabai and harbour Saba on the W or Red Sea coast of Arabia. K.A.K.

SECACAH (Heb. *sᵉḵāḵâh*). A settlement in NE Judah (Jos. 15:61); probably Khirbet es-Samrah, the largest (68 m by 40 m) of three fortified sites in el-Buqei 'a, controlling irrigation works which made it possible to settle in this area; first occupied in the 9th century BC, doubtless to secure the frontier. See L. E. Stager, *BASOR* 221, 1976, pp. 145–158; *NEAEHL*, pp. 267–269. J.P.U.L.

SECU (RSV), **SECHU** (AV). The Heb. name, perhaps meaning 'outlook', of a place near Ramah, which Saul visited when seeking David and Samuel (1 Sa. 19:22). A possible but uncertain identification is Khirbet Shuweikeh, 5 km N of el-Râm (biblical Ramah). Some MSS of LXX read the unknown town Sephi, which represents, according to some scholars, Heb. *šᵉpî*, 'bare hill'; and the Pesh. similarly renders *sûpâ*, 'the end', but other Gk. MSS and the Vulg. support the Massoretic Hebrew.

BIBLIOGRAPHY. F. M. Abel, *Géographie de la Palestine*, 2, 1938, p. 453; C. R. Conder and H. H. Kitchener, *The Survey of Western Palestine*, 3, 1883, p. 52. J.T.

SECUNDUS. A Thessalonian Christian accompanying Paul (Acts 20:4), probably as a delegate, with Aristarchus, of his church, to bring the collection for Jerusalem (*cf.* 1 Cor. 16:1ff.). Agreement on the precise significance of Acts 20:4 is incomplete, but Secundus seems included among those who awaited Paul at Troas. Zahn (*INT*, 1, 1909, p. 213) conjectured that Secundus was another name of the Macedonian Gaius (mentioned with Aristarchus in Acts 19:29), distinguished here from his companion *Gaius of Derbe.

The name is Latin, and attested in Thessalonian inscriptions. A.F.W.

SEED. The fertilized and mature ovule of a flowering plant which enables the species to perpetuate itself. Seed-bearing plants are of great antiquity (Gn. 1:11).

The progeny of the species *Homo sapiens* was also regarded as 'seed' (Gn. 3:15; 13:15). Thus the seed of Abraham constituted Isaac and his descendants (Gn. 21:12; 28:14). The relationship between God and his people provided a perpetual establishment for the seed of Israel (Ps. 89:4), who would be ruled over by a descendant of the house of David (Acts 2:30), interpreted by the early Christians in terms of Christ the Messiah (2 Tim. 2:8).

The idea of the seed as the unit of reproduction of plant life found expression in several of Christ's parables. The spiritual significance of the seed varied with the differing circumstances under which the parables were narrated. In that of the seeds and the sower (Mt. 13:3–23; Lk. 8:5–15), the seed was interpreted in Matthew as the 'word of the kingdom', while in Mark (4:3–20) and Luke it was the 'word of God'. In the parable of the seed and the tares (Mt. 13:24–30), the 'good seed' represented the children of the kingdom, while in the parable of the mustard seed (Mt. 13:31–32; Mk. 4:30–32) the seed represented the kingdom of heaven. In Mk. 4:26–29 the mystery surrounding the development of the divine kingdom was likened to that connected with the germination and growth of a seed.

The Pauline doctrine of the resurrection body (1 Cor. 15:35ff.) reflected the thought of Christ concerning the necessity of wheat-grains dying before they could produce abundantly (Jn. 12:24). The resurrection body of the believer will be significantly different in kind and degree from that laid to rest in the grave, bearing a relationship to it similar to that existing between an acorn and the mature oak. R.K.H.

SEIR. 1. The word *śē'îr* defines a mountain (Gn. 14:6; Ezk. 35:15), a land (Gn. 32:3; 36:21; Nu. 24:18) and a people (Ezk. 25:8) in the general area of old Edom. Esau went to live there (Gn. 32:3), and his descendants overcame the original inhabitants, the Horites (Gn. 14:6; 36:20; Dt. 2:12; Jos. 24:4). The Simeonites later destroyed some Amalekites who took refuge there (1 Ch. 4:42–43).

2. A landmark on the boundary of Judah (Jos. 15:10). J.A.T.

SELA. Etymologically the Heb. word (*has-*)*sela'* means '(the) rock' or 'cliff' and may be used of any rocky place. The name occurs several times in the Bible.

1. A fortress city of Moab, conquered by Amaziah king of Judah and renamed Joktheel (2

Ki. 14:7; 2 Ch. 25:12). Obadiah, in condemning Edom, refers to those who dwelt in the clefts of the rock (Sela, Ob. 3). Is. 42:11 may refer to the same place. For centuries the site has been identified with a rocky outcrop behind Petra, an identification which goes back to the LXX, Josephus and Eusebius. The massive rocky plateau Umm el-Biyara towers 300 m above the level of Petra (the Gk. translation of Sela), and 1,130 m above sea level. It was investigated by Nelson Glueck in 1933 and W. H. Morton in 1955. C. M. Bennett uncovered parts of Iron Age stone houses there in 1960–65, built in the 7th century BC. The site was taken by the *Nabataeans *c.* 300 BC and they converted the great valley to the N, some 1,370 m long and 225–450 m across, quite enclosed by mountain walls, into the amazing rock-cut city of Petra—the 'rose-red city half as old as time'.

More recently it has been claimed that another Iron Age site, *es-Sela'*, 4 km NW of Bozra (Buseira) suits the biblical and post-biblical evidence better. This site was overlooked because of the impressive and continuous support for Petra. (See A. F. Rainey, *IDBS*, p. 100.)

2. An unidentified site, on the border of the Amorites in the time of the Judges (Jdg. 1:36), apparently within Judah. **3.** Isaiah, referring to the coming judgment of Moab, spoke of fugitive Moabites sending tribute to Judah from distant Sela (Is. 16:1). The site is unidentified.

BIBLIOGRAPHY. On Umm el-Biyara, see P. C. Hammond, *ISBE* 4, pp. 383–384; W. H. Morton, *BA* 19, 1956, pp. 26f.; *RB* 71, 1964, pp. 250–253; C. M. Bennett, *RB* 73, 1966, pp. 372–403. On the identity of Sela, see J. Starcky, *DBS*, 1966, cols. 886–900; *NEAEHL*, pp. 1488–1490. J.A.T.

SELAH. An isolated word occurring 71 times in the Psalms and three times in Habakkuk (3:3, 9, 13; 'the minor Psalter'). Since all of these, except Pss. 41 and 81, name the kind of melody or psalmody in the title, it is generally agreed that Selah must be a musical or liturgical sign, though its precise import is not known. The following are the main suggestions:

1. A term in *music or a musical direction to the singers and/or orchestra to 'lift up', *i.e.* to sing or play *forte* or *crescendo*. Thus LXX has *diapsalma* in each instance, perhaps a musical rather than a doxological interlude.

2. A liturgical mark (*sālal*, 'to lift up'; *cf.* Akkad. *sullu*, 'prayer'), perhaps to lift up the voice or the hands in prayer. It may have come into use, possibly in the exilic period, in connection with psalms used in public worship to denote those places at which the priest should pronounce a benediction. Some take it to mean 'to lift up' the eyes, for the purpose of repeating the verse, thus the equivalent of '*da capo*'. Others would derive it from an Aramaic root *sl*, 'to bow', and so interpret it as directing the worshipper at this point to prostrate himself.

3. The Targ. Aquila and Vulg. render Selah by phrases implying an ejaculation 'for ever', and make it a cry of worship like 'Amen' and 'Hallelujah' (Ps. 46:3) at the close of the liturgy or at specified points within it (Ps. 3:2, 4, *etc.*). D.J.W.

SELEUCIA. 1. The former port of Antioch in Syria (1 Macc. 11:8) which lay 8 km N of the

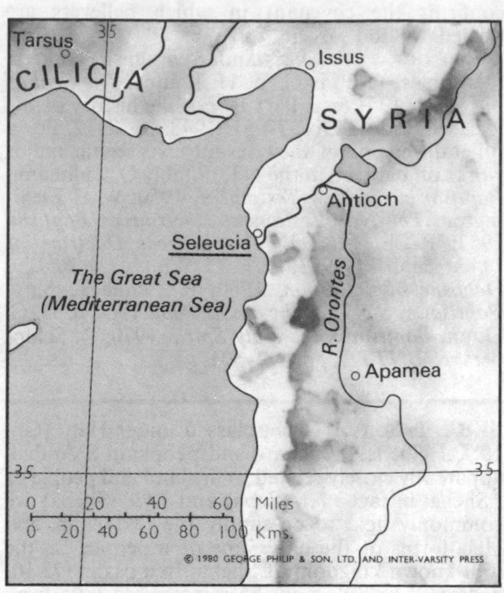

Seleucia was a seaport near the mouth of the R. Orontes in Syria.

mouth of the Orontes river and 25 km away from Antioch. Seleucia (*Seleukeia*) was founded by Seleucus Nicator in 301 BC, 11 years after he had established the Seleucid kingdom. The city lay at the foot of Mt Rhosus, to the N, and was itself in the NE corner of a beautiful fertile plain still noted for its beauty. It was fortified on the S and W and surrounded by walls, but, although regarded as impregnable, it was taken by the Ptolemy Euergetes (1 Macc. 11:8) in the Ptolemaic–Seleucid wars and remained in the hands of the Ptolemies till 219 BC, when Antiochus the Great recaptured it. He greatly beautified it, and, although it was lost again for a short time to Ptolemy Philometor in 146 BC, Seleucia was soon retaken. The Romans under Pompey made it a free city in 64 BC, and from then on it flourished until it began to decay fairly early in the Christian era. It is known in the Bible only in Acts 13:4, as the port of embarkation of Paul and Barnabas after they had been commissioned by the church in Antioch. From Seleucia they set sail for Cyprus on their first missionary journey. It is probably the port inferred in Acts 14:26; 15:30, 39, though it is not named.

Seleucia today is an extensive ruin, subject to archaeological investigation by a number of expeditions since 1937. The city area can be traced, and evidence of buildings, gates, walls, the amphitheatre, the inner harbour and the great water conduit built by Constantius in AD 338 in solid rock to carry off the mountain torrent from the city are all to be seen. The channel which connected the inner harbour to the sea has long been silted up.

2. A city in Gaulanitis SE of Lake Huleh captured by Alexander Yannai during his campaign in Transjordan in the 1st century AD. Josephus records that Agrippa II persuaded the people of the strongly fortified town to surrender to the Romans.

3. A city on the Tigris S of Baghdad founded by Seleucus I (312–280 BC) and occupied by Greeks and Syrians. It became a home for Jews in the 1st century of the Christian era. Animosity against them led to the slaughter of 50,000; the survivors fled to Nisibis and other towns. This site has been partially excavated by the Italians. J.A.T.

SELEUCUS. One of Alexander's lesser generals, who took control of the far E satrapies after his death and became a leading advocate of partition. After the battle of Ipsus in 301 BC he founded the port of *Seleucia (in Pieria) (Acts 13:4) to serve his new W capital of Antioch, and the Seleucid domains were later extended over most of Asia Minor. The dynasty, many of whose kings bore the names of Seleucus or Antiochus, ruled from Syria for *c.* 250 years, until suspended by the Romans. The vast and heterogeneous population called for a policy of active hellenization if their power was to be established. This and the fact that Palestine was the disputed frontier with the Ptolemies of Egypt caused trouble for the Jews. The Maccabaean revolt, with its legacy of petty kingdoms and principalities, and the religious sects of Jesus' time, was the result of the Seleucid attempt to secure Palestine.

BIBLIOGRAPHY. E. R. Bevan, *The House of Seleucus*, 1902; V. Tcherikover, *Hellenistic Civilization and the Jews*, 1959. E.A.J.

SELF-CONTROL (AV 'temperance') translates the Gk. *enkrateia*, which occurs in three NT verses. The corresponding adjective *enkratēs* and verb *enkrateuomai* are used both positively and negatively. Another word translated 'temperate', *nēphalios*, sometimes carries a restricted reference to drinking, such as is often read into the modern word 'temperance'.

The verb *enkrateuomai* is first used in the LXX in Gn. 43:31 to describe Joseph's control of his affectionate impulses towards his brothers. It refers also to the false self-restraint of Saul in 1 Sa. 13:12, and of Haman in Est. 5:10. According to Josephus, the Essenes exercised 'invariable sobriety' (*BJ* 2. 133), and some of them rejected marriage as incompatible with continence. The Greeks held temperance to be a cardinal virtue.

A very significant use of *enkrateia* is found in Acts 24:25. Since an adulteress sat beside Felix while Paul discussed self-control, its bearing on unchastity is easily apparent, and the verse compares naturally with 1 Cor. 7:9. This restricted reference to chastity often features in later literature. The Encratites enjoined complete abstinence from marriage; and some Christian clergy today may not marry. This distorted interpretation is called demonic in 1 Tim. 4:2–3, and the qualification 'self-controlled' (*enkratēs*) is applied to the married bishop in Tit. 1:8 (*cf.* 1 Pet. 3:2).

The association of *enkrateia* with righteousness in Acts 24:25 is parallel to other contexts where it is listed in catalogues of graces. In Gal. 5:22–23 it is the last of nine virtues, and seems to be opposed to drunkenness and carousing in the corresponding list of vices. In 2 Pet. 1:6 it forms a midway stage in a distinct moral progress of the believer, which commences in faith and culminates in love. (The form of the passage recalls expositions of Stoic moral *prokopē*.) The related words *nēphalios* and *sōphrōn* (sober-minded) appear in a list of virtues demanded of older Christian men in Tit. 2:2, 12.

The precise reference of *nēphalios*, 'temperate', is to drunkenness, and the word is actually opposed to 'drunkard' in 1 Tim. 3:2–3. It can broaden out, however, to include other forms of self-control, as in Tit. 2:2 and 1 Tim. 3:11. This extended application should be recollected when rendering the verb *nēphō*, which in RSV is translated 'to be sober', but which usually means 'to be vigilant' in contexts like 1 Thes. 5:6 and 1 Pet. 1:13; 4:7; 5:8. In 1 Cor. 9:25 the widest possible reference is given to *enkrateuomai* when the Christian athlete is said to exercise self-control in all things.

In the NT self-control is essentially a 'fruit of the Spirit' (Gal. 5:22–23). A deliberate antithesis between spiritual life and carnal drunkenness is introduced into several passages describing prophetic inspiration (*e.g.* Acts 2:15–17 and Eph. 5:18). Believers who 'drink of the Spirit' (1 Cor. 12:13) are thought by the world to be 'drunk'; and indeed so they are, not with wine, but with zeal for the Christian warfare. This passion to be good soldiers of Christ expresses itself not in excess but in sober discipline; it is the true imitation of a Master, whose life, as Bernard says, was the 'mirror of temperance'.

BIBLIOGRAPHY. R. L. Ottley in *ERE* (*s.v.* 'Temperance'); *BAGD*; H. Rashdall, *Theory of Good and Evil*, 1907; H. Baltensweiler, *NIDNTT* 1, pp. 494–497. D.H.T.

SENAAH. In the list of exiles who returned with Zerubbabel there are 3,630 (Ezr. 2:35) or 3,930 (Ne. 7:38) belonging to the town of Senaah. In Ne. 3:3 the name of the town occurs again with the definite article. Since in both passages Jericho is mentioned in close proximity, Senaah may have been near Jericho. J.S.W.

SENATE, SENATOR. 1. The AV translation in Ps. 105:22 (Heb. *zᵉqēnîm*; LXX *presbyteroi*), where RSV has *'elders'. **2.** Gk. *gerousia*, 'assembly of elders', Acts 5:21 (*SANHEDRIN). J.D.D.

SENEH ('pointed rock') and **BOZEZ** ('slippery'?) were two rocks between which Jonathan and his armour-bearer entered the garrison of the Philistines (1 Sa. 14:4ff.). (*MICHMASH.) No precise identification of the location of these two rocky crags has been made, but see *GTT*, p. 317. J.D.D.

SENIR. According to Dt. 3:9, the Amorite name for Mt Hermon (*śᵉnîr*; AV Shenir); but in Ct. 4:8 and 1 Ch. 5:23, apparently one of the peaks in the ridge, the name being loosely applied to the whole. Manasseh expanded N to Senir (1 Ch. 5:23), and the slopes supplied fir (*TREES) for Tyrian ships, Lebanon yielding cedars (Ezk. 27:5). Shalmaneser III names Senir (*sa-ni-ru*) as a stronghold of Hazael (*ANET*, p. 280). A.R.M.

SENNACHERIB. Sennacherib (Heb. *sanḥērîb* [but possibly pronounced *śnhrîb* as in Aram. papyri; *JSS* 21, 1976, p. 9]; Assyr. *Sin-aḫḫē-eriba*, 'Sin [moon-god] has increased the brothers') ruled Assyria 705–681 BC. When his father, whom he had served as governor of the N frontier, was assassinated, Sennacherib first marched to Babylonia, where Marduk-apla-iddina II (*MERODACH-BALADAN) was in revolt. He had ousted a local nominee Marduk-zakir-šum in 703 BC and was rallying support against Assyria. It was probably about this time that Merodach-baladan sent envoys to Hezekiah of Judah (2 Ki. 20:12–19; Is. 39). Late in 702 BC Sennacherib defeated the Chaldean and his Elamite and Arab allies in battles at Cutha and Kish. He was then welcomed in Babylon, where he set Bel-ibni on the throne. The Assyrians ravaged Bît-Yakin and returned to Nineveh with many prisoners, Merodach-baladan himself having escaped to Elam.

Sennacherib had little difficulty in controlling his N frontier, an area well known to him while crown prince. After a series of raids against the hill peoples in the E he moved against the W, where an anti-Assyrian coalition, backed by Egypt, was gaining power. The leader, Hezekiah of Judah, had seized Padi, the pro-Assyrian ruler of Ekron (2 Ki. 18:8), strengthened the fortifications and improved the water supplies at Jerusalem by building the *Siloam tunnel (2 Ki. 20:20), and called for help from Egypt (Is. 30:1–4).

Sennacherib's third campaign in Hezekiah's 14th year (701 BC) was directed against this coalition. He first marched down the Phoenician coast, capturing Great and Little Sidon, Zarephath, Mahalliba (*AHLAB), Ushu, Akzib and Acco, but not attempting to lay siege to Tyre. He replaced Luli (Elulaeus), king of Sidon, who fled and died in exile, by Ethba'al (Tuba'al). The kings of Sidon, Arvad, Byblos, Beth-ammon, Moab and Edom submitted, but Ashkelon refused and, with its neighbouring towns, including Beth-Dagon and Joppa, was despoiled. Sennacherib claims to have marched to Eltekeh, where he defeated an Egyptian army. He then slew the nobles of Ekron for handing over Padi to Hezekiah, and sent detachments to destroy forty-six walled towns and many villages in Judah, from which he took 200,150 people and much spoil. He himself took part in the siege and capture of *Lachish, and is depicted on his palace reliefs reviewing the spoil. From here he sent officers to demand the surrender of Jerusalem (2 Ch. 32:9).

Sennacherib's own account of this campaign claims tribute from Hezekiah (Annals) and describes how he besieged 'Hezekiah the Jew . . . I shut him up like a caged bird within his royal capital, Jerusalem. I put watch-posts closely round the city and turned back to his fate anyone who came out of the city gate' (Taylor Prism, BM). Hezekiah paid the Assyrians tribute (2 Ki. 18:13–16; Is. 36:1f.) which was later sent to Nineveh (Taylor Prism, dated 691 BC) and freed Padi, to whom some of the former Judaean territories were now given.

Sennacherib's account makes no mention of any conclusion of the siege (*cf.* 2 Ki. 19:32–34) or of the defeat of the Assyrian army by the hand of the Lord, perhaps by a plague (v. 35) described by Herodotus (2. 141) as 'a multitude of field mice which by night devoured all the quivers and bows of the enemy, and all the straps by which they held their shields . . . next morning they commenced their fight and great numbers fell as they had no arms with which to defend themselves'.

The majority of scholars hold that the mention of the approach of the Egyptian forces under *Tirhakah (2 Ki. 19:9; Is. 37:9) is an anachronism (but see K. A. Kitchen, *Third Intermediate Period in Egypt*, 1972). Moreover, they consider 2 Ki. 19:37 implies that the death of Sennacherib occurred soon after his return to Nineveh. They therefore postulate a second, and unsuccessful, Assyrian campaign against Jerusalem, perhaps following the attack on the Arabs 689–686 BC. Neither the extant Assyrian annals nor Babylonian chronicles mention such a campaign, and vv. 36f. do not necessarily state the length of time between Sennacherib's return from Palestine and his death in 681 BC, and this must have been some years on any interpretation. Thus the theory of a single campaign in 701 BC can still reasonably be held.

In 700 BC the Assyrians once more marched to Babylonia, where Bel-ibni had rebelled. Sennacherib placed his own son, Aššur-nadin-šum, on the throne, and he held sway until captured by the Elamites. In the series of campaigns which followed, Sennacherib fought the Elamites, and in 694 mounted a naval expedition across the Persian Gulf directed against those who had harboured Merodach-baladan. Erech was captured and, finally, Babylon sacked in 689 BC. On other frontiers Sennacherib invaded Cilicia and captured Tarsus, as well as raiding the Arabs S and E of Damascus.

At home Sennacherib was aided by his energetic W Semitic wife, Naqi'a-Zakutu, in the reconstruction of Nineveh, where he built a 'palace without a rival', an armoury, new city walls and gates. By providing a new source of water-supply from the river Gomel (Bavian), led by an aqueduct (Jerwan) down to a dam (Ajeila) E of the metropolis, he was able to irrigate parks and large tracts of land as well as to improve the natural defences of Nineveh formed by the rivers Tigris and Khosr.

He also built extensively at Assur and Kakzi and introduced many technological advances.

Sennacherib was assassinated by his sons while worshipping in the temple of Nisroch (2 Ki. 19:37). The flight of the sons, possibly *Adrammelech and *Sharezer, may be reflected in an account of the disturbances following his death in December 681 BC given by his younger son Esarhaddon, who had been elected crown prince in 687 BC, and now succeeded to the throne (v. 37). There is little support for the theory that Esarhaddon was the unnamed 'son' mentioned as assassin by the Babylonian Chronicle, or that the death took place in Babylon.

BIBLIOGRAPHY. D. D. Luckenbill, *The Annals of Sennacherib*, 1924; D. J. Wiseman in *DOTT*, pp. 64–73. D.J.W.

SEPHAR. The name of a 'mountain of the east' (*har haq-qeḏem*), mentioned in the Table of *Nations in defining the boundary of the territory of the sons of Joktan (Gn. 10:30). Judging from the names of other sons of Joktan, a mountain or promontory in S Arabia seems likely, and the coastal town of Ẓafār in the E Hadramaut has been suggested. In view, however, of the lack of precision in the Bible statement, and the discrepancy in the sibilants, there can be no certainty.

See J. A. Montgomery, *Arabia and the Bible*, 1934, p. 41. T.C.M.

SEPHARAD. The place in which captives from Jerusalem were exiled (Ob. 20). The location is as yet unidentified. Of many conjectures, the most plausible identifies the place as Sardis, capital of Lydia in Asia Minor. Known in Persian times as Sfard, it is written in Aramaic with the same consonants as in Obadiah. It may be the Saparda named in the Assyrian Annals of Sargon and Esarhaddon as a country allied to the Medes. The Targum of Jonathan interpreted it as Spain, hence the term Sephardim for Spanish Jews. A location in Anatolia is favoured by the Vulgate (*in Bosphoro*). See *JNES* 22, 1963, pp. 128–132. D.J.W.

SEPHARVAIM. A city captured by the Assyrians (2 Ki. 17:24, 31; 18:34; 19:13; Is. 36:19; 37:13). The context implies that it lies in Syria or adjacent territory and this is supported by the name of its deities (*ADRAMMELECH; *ANAMMELECH). The place is unidentified, though Halévy's suggestion that it is the same as the later Sibraim near Damascus (Ezk. 47:16) is possible. It cannot be the same as the Šab/mara'in of the Babylonian Chronicle, as this is Samaria. The usual interpretation of Sepharvaim as the twin cities of Sippar (of Šamaš and Anunitum) in Babylonia is unsupportable (though Sippar-amnanim is mentioned in texts), as Sippar had no independent king (*cf.* 2 Ki. 19:13). D.J.W.

SEPULCHRE OF THE KINGS, SEPULCHRE OF DAVID. The Bible indicates that the kings of Israel were buried in a special area near Jerusalem. Expressions like 'tombs of the kings of Israel' (2 Ch. 28:27), 'sepulchres of David' (Ne. 3:16), 'tombs of the sons of David' (2 Ch. 32:33), refer specifically to the royal tombs of the Judaean kings of David's line in the city of David. These tombs were close to the King's Garden and the pool of Shelah (1 Ki. 2:10; 2 Ch. 21:20; Ne. 3:15–16). Thus when Nehemiah was building the wall of Jerusalem one of his parties worked 'over against the sepulchres of David', not far from the 'pool of Shelah (Shiloah)' (Ne. 3:15–16).

Most of the kings from David to Hezekiah were buried in the city of David, though some kings had their own private sepulchres, *e.g.* Asa (2 Ch. 16:14), and possibly Hezekiah (2 Ch. 32:33), Manasseh (2 Ki. 21:18), Amon (2 Ki. 21:26) and Josiah (2 Ki. 23:30; 2 Ch. 35:24). Several kings died outside the bounds of Palestine: Jehoahaz in Egypt, Jehoiachin and Zedekiah in Babylon. Possibly Jehoiakim was not buried at all (Je. 22:19), and Jehoram, Joash, Uzziah and Ahaz were not admitted to the royal sepulchre (2 Ch. 21:20; 24:25; 26:23; 28:27).

The location of the tombs in the city of David was still referred to after the Exile. Josephus reported that they were plundered by the Hasmonean king John Hyrcanus and also by Herod (*Ant.* 13. 249; 16. 179).

In the NT the sepulchre of David was still remembered (Acts 2:29) and Josephus (*BJ*, 5. 147) spoke of the third wall passing by the sepulchred caverns of the kings. An inscribed tablet found by E. Sukenik states that the bones of King Uzziah had been removed to the top of the Mount of Olives.

The exact site of the tombs of the kings is not known today. Monuments in the Kedron Valley are late, both architecture and epigraphy pointing to the time of Herod the Great.

The term 'City of David' in the vicinity of which these tombs lay does not denote the entire city of Jerusalem but merely the citadel of the stronghold of Zion. Evidence points to the spur which juts S between the Tyropoean and Kedron valleys, later known as Ophel, as the location of the City of David. It overlooks the gardens and pools of Siloam. In this general area long horizontal tunnels have been found in the rock and these may have been the burial-place of the kings of David's line. But the site was desecrated and destroyed, possibly at the time of the Bar-Kokhba revolt (AD 135), and thereafter the exact location forgotten.

Various other sites have been proposed over the centuries. A popular tradition reaching back for 1,000 years places the tomb of David on the W hill at the place now called Mt Zion. The tradition was accepted by Jewish, Muslim and Christian traditions, and Benjamin of Tudela (*c.* AD 1173) reported the miraculous discovery of David's Tomb on Mt Zion during the repair of a church on the site. Pilgrimages are still made to the site, but there is little to commend its authenticity.

The so-called Tombs of the Kings of Judah some distance to the N of the modern wall mark the tomb of Helen, queen of Adiabene, a district in Upper Mesopotamia referred to by Josephus (*Ant.* 20. 17, 35).

BIBLIOGRAPHY. S. Krauss, 'The Sepulchres of the Davidic Dynasty', *PEQ* 1947, pp. 102–112; S. Yeivin, 'The Sepulchres of the Kings of the House of David', *JNES* 7, 1948, pp. 30–45. J.A.T.

SERAIAH (Heb. *śᵉrāyâ*, *śᵉrāyāhû*, 'Yahweh has prevailed'). **1.** David's scribe (2 Sa. 8:17, RSV 'secretary'), called also 'Sheva' (2 Sa. 20:25), 'Shisha' (1 Ki. 4:3), and *'Shavsha' (1 Ch. 18:16).

2. Son of Azariah and a chief priest in the time of Zedekiah. He was put to death by the king of Babylon at Riblah (2 Ki. 25:18= Je. 52:24). **3.** A son of Tanhumeth the Netophathite, and a captain who was among those whom Gedaliah, governor of Judaea, advised to submit to the Chaldeans (2 Ki. 25:23 = Je. 40:8). **4.** A son of Kenaz (1 Ch. 4:13–14). **5.** A Simeonite, son of Asiel (1 Ch. 4:35). **6.** A priest who returned with Zerubbabel to Jerusalem (Ezr. 2:2; Ne. 12:1, 12). **7.** One who sealed the covenant (Ne. 10:2), perhaps the same as **6** above. **8.** A priest, son of Hilkiah (Ne. 11:11) and 'ruler of the house of God' in post-exilic Jerusalem. **9.** One of the officers of King Jehoiakim, ordered by him to arrest Baruch and Jeremiah (Je. 36:26). **10.** A prince of Judah who accompanied King Zedekiah to Babylon in the 4th year of his reign. Seraiah carried Jeremiah's prophecy against Babylon (Je. 51:59, 61). Some would associate him with **3** above. J.D.D.

SERAPHIM. The only mention of these celestial beings in Scripture is in the early vision of Isaiah (Is. 6). The seraphim (incorrectly rendered in AV as 'seraphims') were associated with *cherubim and ophanim in the task of guarding the divine throne. The heavenly beings seen by Isaiah were human in form, but had six wings, a pair to shield their faces, another to conceal their feet and a third for flight. These seraphim were stationed above the throne of God, and appear to have led in divine worship. One chanted a refrain which Isaiah recorded: 'Holy, holy, holy is the Lord of hosts; the whole earth is full of his glory.'

So vigorous was this act of worship that the thresholds of the divine Temple shook, and the holy place was filled with smoke. The prophet lay in self-abasement before God and confessed his iniquity. Then one of the seraphim flew to him with a burning coal taken from the altar, and in an act of purification announced to Isaiah that his sin had been forgiven and his guilt removed.

It would appear that for Isaiah the seraphim were angelic beings responsible for certain functions of guardianship and worship. However, they appear to have been distinct moral creatures, not just projections of the imagination or personifications of animals. Their moral qualities were employed exclusively in the service of God, and their position was such that they were privileged to exercise an atoning ministry while at the same time extolling the ethical and moral character of God.

The origin and meaning of the Heb. term are uncertain. The *śārāp̄* of Nu. 21:6; Dt. 8:15 was a venomous serpent which bit the Israelites in the desert, while Is. 14:29; 30:6 referred to a reptile popular in folklore (see D. J. Wiseman, *TynB* 23, 1972, pp. 108–110). If the noun be derived from Heb. *śārap̄* 'to burn up', the seraphim may be agents of purification by fire, as Is. 6. indicates. A meaning 'bright, shining ones' cannot be taken from *śārap̄*.

A sculpture found at Tell Halaf (*GOZAN) depicts a creature with a human body, two wings at the shoulders and four below the waist (*ANEP*, no. 655). It is dated about 800 BC. For other ancient representations, see *CHERUBIM.

BIBLIOGRAPHY. H. S. Nash in *SHERK* (*s.v.* 'angel'); J. de Savignac, *VT* 22, 1972, pp. 320–325; S. Steck, *BZ* 16, 1972, pp. 188–206; G. V. Smith, *ISBE* 4, p. 410.

R.K.H.
A.R.M.

SERMON ON THE MOUNT. The Sermon on the Mount is the title commonly given to the teachings of Jesus recorded in Mt. 5–7. Whether the name can be properly used for the somewhat parallel portion in Luke (6:20–49) depends upon one's interpretation of the literary relationship between the two. The latter is often called the Sermon on the Plain because it is said to have been delivered on 'a level place' (Lk. 6:17) rather than 'on the mountain' (Mt. 5:1). But both expressions probably denote the same place approached from two different directions (see W. M. Christie, *Palestine Calling*, 1939, pp. 35f.).

Canon Liddon, in his Bampton Lectures, refers to the Sermon as 'that original draught of essential Christianity'. If this be interpreted to mean that the Sermon on the Mount is Christianity's message to the pagan world, we must counter with the reminder that it is manifestly *didachē* (teaching), not *kerygma* (proclamation). By no stretch of the imagination can it be considered 'good news' to one depending upon fulfilment of its demands for entrance into the kingdom. (Imagine a man outside of Christ, without the empowering aid of the Holy Spirit, trying to exceed the righteousness of the scribes and Pharisees.) It is rather a character sketch of those who have already entered the kingdom and a description of the quality of ethical life which is now expected of them. In this sense, it is true, it is 'essential Christianity'.

I. Composition

In times past it was taken for granted that the Sermon on the Mount was a single discourse delivered by Jesus on a specific occasion. Certainly this is what appears to be the case as it is reported in Matthew. The disciples sat down (v. 1), Jesus opened his mouth and taught them (v. 2), and when it was over the crowds were astonished at his teaching (7:28). However, most scholars are of the opinion that the Sermon is really a compilation of sayings of the Lord—'a kind of epitome of all the sermons that Jesus ever preached' (W. Barclay, *The Gospel of Matthew*, 1, p. 79). It is argued that: (1) There is far too much concentrated material here for one sermon. The disciples, not noted for acute spiritual perception, could never have assimilated such a wealth of ethical teaching. (2) The wide range of topics (description of kingdom blessedness, counsel on divorce, admonition concerning anxiety) is inconsistent with the unity of a single discourse. (3) The abruptness with which certain sections emerge in the Sermon (*e.g.* the teaching on prayer in Mt. 6:1–11) is very noticeable. (4) Thirty-four verses occur in other, and often more suitable, contexts throughout Luke (*e.g.* the Lord's Prayer in Luke is introduced by a request from his disciples that he teach them to pray, Lk. 11:1; the saying about the narrow gate comes in response to the question, 'Will those who are saved be few?' Lk. 13:23), and it is more likely that Matthew transposed sayings of Jesus into the Sermon than that Luke found them there and then scattered them throughout his Gospel. (5) It is characteristic of Matthew to gather together teaching material under certain headings and insert them into the narrative of Jesus' life (*cf.* B. W. Bacon, *Studies in Matthew*, 1930, pp. 269–325), and that the Sermon on the Mount is therefore simply the first of these didactic sections. (Others deal with the themes of discipleship (9:35–10:42), the kingdom of heaven (13), true greatness (18) and the end of the age (24–25).)

These considerations, however, do not force one to view the entire Sermon as an arbitrary composition. The historical setting in Mt. 4:23–5:1 leads us to expect an important discourse delivered on a specific occasion. Within the Sermon itself are various sequences which appear to be 'sermonettes' of Jesus and not topical collections of separate *logia*. A comparison with Luke's Sermon shows enough points of similarity (both begin with Beatitudes, close with the parable of the builders, and the intervening Lucan material—on loving one's enemies (6:27–36) and judging (6:37–42)—follows in the same sequence in Matthew) to suggest that behind both accounts there was a common source. Before either Evangelist wrote there was in all probability a primitive framework which corresponded to an actual discourse delivered on a definite occasion. Such questions as whether the Sermon as it occurs in Matthew is closer to the original than the Lucan version, or whether Matthew followed a framework supplied by an earlier source, are still matters of scholarly debate. For our purpose it is enough to conclude that Matthew took a primitive sermon source and expanded it for his particular purpose by the introduction of relevant material.

II. Language of the Sermon

In the last generation Aramaic scholarship has taught us much about 'The Poetry of Our Lord'—to borrow the title of C. F. Burney's book (1925). Even in translation we can recognize the various types of parallelism, which are the distinguishing feature of Semitic poetry. Mt. 7:6, for example, is a fine illustration of 'synonymous' parallelism:

'Do not give dogs what is holy;
and do not throw your pearls before swine.'

It appears that the Lord's Prayer is a poem of two stanzas, each of which has three lines of four beats apiece (*cf.* Burney, pp. 112f.). The practical value of recognizing poetry where it occurs is that we are not so likely to interpret the text with such an inflexible literalism as we might employ in interpreting prose. How tragic if someone should (and history records that some have done so) literally 'pluck out his eye' or 'cut off his hand' in an attempt to do away with the passion of lust. A. M. Hunter notes that 'proverbs indeed are principles stated in extremes'. We must always avoid interpreting paradox with a crude literalism, but rather seek the principle that underlies the proverb (*Design for Life*, pp. 19–20).

In this connection let us consider the quality of absoluteness in Jesus' moral imperatives. Verses like Mt. 5:48, 'You, therefore, must be perfect, as your heavenly Father is perfect', have long troubled men. Part of the answer lies in the fact that these are not 'new laws' but broad principles set forth in terms of action. They fall into the category of prophetic injunction, which was always deeper and demanded more than the mere letter of the law. And they were ethics of the new age, designed for those who partook of a new power (*cf.* A. N. Wilder, 'The Sermon on the Mount', *IB*, 7, 1951, p. 163).

III. Circumstances

Both Matthew and Luke place the Sermon in the first year of Jesus' public ministry; Matthew a little earlier than Luke, who locates it immediately after the choosing of the Twelve and implies that it should be understood as somewhat of an 'ordination sermon'. In either case, it came in that period before the religious teachers could muster their opposition, and yet late enough for Jesus' fame to have spread through the land. The first months of his Galilean ministry were spent in synagogue preaching, but soon the enthusiasm of his crowds necessitated some sort of outdoor preaching. A corresponding change can be seen in the character of his message. The early proclamation, 'Repent: for the kingdom of heaven is at hand' (Mt. 4:17), has given way to exposition on the nature of the kingdom for those who seriously desired to learn.

Since the Sermon falls within the Galilean ministry of Jesus, it is natural to assume that the scene of the Sermon would be one of the foothills which surrounded the N plain. As Jesus entered Capernaum soon after (Mt. 8:5), it was perhaps located in that general area. A Latin tradition, dating from the 13th century, names a two-peaked hill, Karn Hattin, which lies a bit farther to the S, but only guides and tourists seem to take this identification with any degree of seriousness.

The Sermon is addressed primarily to disciples. This is the apparent meaning of both Mt. 5:1–2 and Lk. 6:20. Luke's use of the second person in the Beatitudes, in sayings like 'You are the salt of the earth' (Mt. 5:13), and the exalted ethic of the Sermon as a whole, can only mean that it was designed for those who had deserted paganism for life in the kingdom. Yet at the close of each account (Mt. 7:28–29; Lk. 7:1) we learn of the presence of others. The solution seems to be that the crowd was there and heard Jesus as he taught, but that the discourse itself was directed primarily to the circle of disciples. Occasional utterances, such as the 'woes' of Lk. 6:24–26, unless rhetorical devices, seem to be 'asides' to some who might be listening in and who needed such admonition.

IV. Analysis

Regardless of whether one sees the Sermon as the summary of an actual discourse or as a mosaic of ethical sayings arranged by Matthew, there is little doubt that Mt. 5–7 has a real unity marked by the logical development of a basic theme. This theme is presented in the Beatitudes and can be expressed as 'the quality and conduct of life in the kingdom'. The following is a descriptive analysis of the content of the Sermon.

a. The blessedness of those in the kingdom, 5:3–16

(i) The Beatitudes (5:3–10).

(ii) An expansion of the final Beatitude and a digression to show the role of the disciple in an unbelieving world (5:11–16).

b. The relationship of the message of Jesus to the old order, 5:17–48

(i) The thesis stated (5:17). Jesus' message 'fulfils' the law by penetrating behind the letter and clarifying its underlying principle, thus bringing it to its ideal completion.

(ii) The thesis enlarged (5:18–20).

(iii) The thesis illustrated (5:21–48).

1. In the command not to kill, anger is the culpable element (5:21–26).

2. Adultery is the fruit of an evil heart nourished on impure desire (5:27–32).

3. Kingdom righteousness demands an honesty so transparent that oaths are unnecessary (5:33–37).

4. *Lex talionis* must give way to a spirit of non-retaliation (5:38–42).

5. Love is universal in application (5:43–48).

c. Practical instructions for kingdom conduct, 6:1–7:12

(i) Guard against false piety (6:1–18).

1. In almsgiving (6:1–4).
2. In prayer (6:5–15).
3. In fasting (6:16–18).

(ii) Dispel anxiety with simple trust (6:19–34).

(iii) Live in love (7:1–12).

d. Challenge to dedicated living, 7:13–29

(i) The way is narrow (7:13–14).

(ii) A good tree bears good fruit (7:15–20).

(iii) The kingdom is for those who hear and *do* (7:21–27).

V. Interpretation

The Sermon on the Mount has had a long and varied history of interpretation. For Augustine, who wrote a treatise on the Sermon while still a bishop at Hippo (AD 393–396), it was the 'perfect rule or pattern of Christian life'—a new law in contrast with the old. Monastic orders interpreted it as a 'counsel of perfection' designed not for the populace but for the chosen few. The Reformers held it to be the 'uncompromising expression of divine righteousness directed towards all'. Tolstoy, the Russian novelist and (in later life) social reformer, resolved it into five commandments (suppression of all anger, chastity, no oaths, non-resistance, unreserved love of enemies), which if literally obeyed would do away with the existing evils and usher in a Utopian kingdom. Weiss and Schweitzer held that the demands were too radical for all times, and thus declared them 'interim ethics' for the early Christians, who believed that the end of all things was at hand. Still others, making great allowance for figurative language, understood the Sermon as the expression of a noble way of thinking—teaching which dealt with what man should *be* rather than with what he should *do*.

Thus the 20th-century interpreter is presented with a bewildering number of 'keys' with which to unlock the essential meaning of the Sermon on the Mount. With Kittel he can take the demands as purposely exaggerated so as to drive man to a sense of failure (and hence to repent and believe), or with Windisch he can differentiate between historical and theological exegesis and defend the practicability of the demands. With Dibelius he can interpret the great moral imperatives as the absolute ethic of the inbreaking kingdom, or with the Dispensationalists he can relegate the entire sermon to a future millennial reign of Christ.

How, then, shall we interpret the Sermon? The following will at least give us our guide-lines: *a.* Although couched in poetry and symbol, the Sermon still demands a quality of ethical conduct which is breath-taking in its dimensions. *b.* Jesus is not laying down a new code of legal regulations but stating great ethical principles and how they affect the lives of those within the kingdom. 'It would be a great point gained if people would only consider that it was a Sermon, and was *preached*, not an *act* which was passed' (J. Denney). *c.* The Sermon is not a programme for the direct improvement of the world, but is directed to those who have denied the world in order to enter the kingdom. *d.* It is neither an impractical ideal nor a fully attainable possibility. In the words of S. M. Gilmour, it is 'the ethic of that transcendental order which broke into history in Jesus Christ, has built itself into history in the church, but whose full realization lies beyond history when God will be "all in all"' (*Journal of Religion* 21, 1941, p. 263).

Bibliography. In addition to the extensive literature cited in other Bible dictionaries (see, *e.g.*, Votaw's article in *HDB*, extra vol., pp. 1–45), see H. K. McArthur, *Understanding the Sermon on the Mount*, 1960; J. W. Bowman and R. W. Tapp, *The Gospel from the Mount*, 1957; W. D. Davies, *The Setting of the Sermon on the Mount*, 1964; M. Dibelius, *The Sermon on the Mount*, 1940; A. M. Hunter, *Design for Life*,1953; D. M. Lloyd-Jones, *Studies in the Sermon on the Mount*[2], 1976; A. N. Wilder's article in *IB*, 7, 1951, pp. 155–164; H. Windisch, *The Meaning of the Sermon on the Mount*, 1951 (translation of revised edition of *Der Sinn der Bergpredigt*, 1929); D. Bonhoeffer, *The Cost of Discipleship*, 1948; C. F. H. Henry, *Christian Personal Ethics*, 1957, pp. 278–326; J. Jeremias, *Die Bergpredigt*[7], 1970; J. R. W. Stott, *The Message of the Sermon on the Mount*, 1978. R.H.M.

SERPENT.

I. General.

Serpents or snakes (*Animals) are reptiles that have head, body and tail but no limbs, and move over the ground on their belly, so that with their flickering tongue they are often described as licking or eating the dust (Gn. 3:14; *cf.* Is. 65:25; Mi. 7:17; and implicitly, Pr. 30:19). In simile, compare the nations creeping like snakes, to acknowledge Israel's God (Mi. 7:17) and Egypt's flight from battle like a hissing snake down its bolt-hole (Je. 46:22, in contrast to the Egyptian concept of the sacred uraeus-snake on a pharaoh's brow leading him to victory). The ability of various snakes to inject deadly poison into a wound when they bite or strike (Gn. 49:17; Ec. 10:8, 11; implicitly, Mt. 7:10; Lk. 11:11) enters into many biblical similes. Subjects of such similes include the harmfulness of the wicked (Dt. 32:33 (rebellious Hebrews); Pss. 58:4; 140:3) or of overmuch wine (Pr. 23:32), the Day of the Lord (Am. 5:19), and in metaphor foreign oppressors (Is. 14:29). Like war, famine, *etc.*, snake-bite could feature among divine judgments and punishments (Nu. 21:4–6; Je. 8:17; Am. 9:3), and deliverance from this harm could be granted to God's servants (Mk. 16:18; Lk. 10:19; *cf.* Acts 28:3–6). Some snakes could be charmed (Ec. 10:11), others were considered 'deaf' to the charmer's techniques (Ps. 58:4–5; Je. 8:17). Snake-charmers may possibly be represented on Egyptian scarab-amulets (P. Montet, *L'Égypte et la Bible*, 1959, pp. 90–94, fig. 17). On snake-charming in Egypt, ancient and modern, *cf.* L. Keimer, *Histoires de Serpents dans l'Égypte Ancienne et Moderne*, 1947, and for Mesopotamia, see N. L. Corkill, 'Snake Specialists in Iraq', *Iraq* 6, 1939, pp. 45–52.

Besides the general word *nāḥāš*, 'snake, serpent' and *śārāp̱*, 'burning' (see **II**, below), Heb. possesses several other words for serpents. The old word *peṯen* (Dt. 32:33; Jb. 20:14, 16; Pss. 58:4; 91:13; Is. 11:8; AV 'adder, asp') occurs as *bṯn* in the Ugaritic texts of the 14th century BC. This is often considered to be the Egyptian cobra (Arab. *naja haje*; and the related *naja nigricollis*, M. A. Murray, *JEA* 34, 1948, pp. 117–118), and is the 'asp' of classical writers. The cobra gave rise to two Egyptian hieroglyphs. This venomous beast gave point to passages like Dt. 32:33 and Jb. 20:14, 16. The word *'ep̄'eh* (Jb. 20:16; Is. 30:6; 59:5; AV 'viper') is identical with Arab. *afa'â*, and like that word appears to be a further general term for serpents and sometimes more specifically for vipers (*cf.* L. Keimer, *Études d'Égyptologie*, 7, 1945, pp. 38–39, 48–49). In Gn. 49:17 (AV 'adder'), Heb. *š^{e}p̄îp̄ôn* is often thought to represent the *cerastes* vipers: either or both the 'horned viper', *Cerastes cornutus*, and the hornless *Vipera cerastes*. In Egypt and Palestine these have been familiar from ancient times, and in Egypt became the hieroglyph for 'f', from the onomatopoeic words *fy*, *fyt*, 'cerastes-viper' (Keimer, *Études d'Égyptologie* 7, 1945; P. E. Newberry, *JEA* 34, 1948, p. 118). The identification of *'aḵšûḇ* in Ps. 140:3 is uncertain; in Rom. 3:13 it is rendered by Gk. *aspis*, 'asp'. The word *ṣip̄'ônî* is rendered by AV as 'adder' in Pr. 23:32, and, like *ṣep̄a'* in Is. 14:29, as 'cockatrice' in Is. 11:8; 59:5; Je. 8:17; these words certainly denote snakes of some kind. The animal that fastened on Paul's hand in Acts 28:3 is often considered to be the common viper of the Mediterranean region; the same Greek word (*echidna*) is used in the powerful metaphors of Mt. 3:7; 12:34; 23:33; Lk. 3:7.

II. Specific

a. The first serpent in Scripture is the subtle creature of Gn. 3, used by Satan to alienate man from God (Rom. 16:20; 2 Cor. 11:3), controlled by the devil like the demons in men and swine in NT days. For its part, the serpent was put under a curse that it would never rise above its (already customary) creeping posture (Gn. 3:14). The serpent thus remained a biblical symbol of deceit (Mt. 23:33), and the arch-deceiver himself is 'that old serpent' (Rev. 12:9, 14–15; 20:2); Christians should match the serpent in his fabled wisdom if in no other respect (Mt. 10:16).

b. A sign performed by Moses before Israel (Ex. 4:2–5, 28–30) and by Moses and Aaron before pharaoh (Ex. 7:8–12) was to cast down his rod so that it became a serpent and take it up again as a rod, having on the latter occasion swallowed up the serpent-rods of the Egyptian magicians (*MAGIC AND SORCERY, **2. II.** *c*).

c. In the wilderness rebellious Israel was once punished by the onset of 'fiery serpents' (*nāḥāš śārāp̄*), whose venom was fatal (Nu. 21:4–9; *cf.* Dt. 8:15). When Israel sought deliverance God commanded Moses to set up a bronze figure of a serpent on a pole, that those bitten might look to it, trusting in God's healing power, and live (*SERPENT, BRONZE). The term *śārāp̄*, 'burning', or 'fiery', may refer to the effect of the venom or poison of the snakes concerned; it recurs in Is. 14:29 and 30:6 (where 'flying' might refer to the speed with which such reptiles may strike, as though 'winged'—so, modern Arab usage; for this and other explanations, see Keimer, *Histoires de Serpents*, p. 10, n. 2; D. J. Wiseman, *TynB* 23, 1972, pp. 108–110).

d. Some Hebrew references to 'serpents' apply rather to other fearful creatures, or are metaphorical of certain great military powers in the biblical world. Thus, the 'serpent' of Am. 9:3 is probably some large denizen of the deep rather than a snake. In Is. 27:1 the sword to be raised against 'Leviathan the fleeing (or, swift) serpent, Leviathan the twisting (or, winding) serpent, and . . . the dragon that is in the sea' (*cf.* RSV) most probably expressed coming judgment upon Assyria (land of the swift Tigris), Babylonia (of the winding Euphrates) and Egypt (*tannîn*, 'dragon, monster', as in Ezk. 29:3; 32:2) respectively. Isaiah may here be announcing God's judgment on these pagan lands in terms of the ancient Canaanite myth of Baal's destruction of Lôtan or Leviathan and the many Mesopotamian tales of slaying dragons and serpents (Labbu, Zu, *etc.*), not to mention the Egyptian overthrowing of 'Apep, condemning them under their own popular imagery. In Jb. 26:13 the identity of the 'fleeing serpent' as associated with the sky is uncertain. Since the serpent can stand for Satan (*cf. a*, above, and Rev. 12:7–10, 14–15; 20:2) one may possibly compare here his alternative (?) designation of fallen Day Star (AV 'Lucifer'), to whom the king of Babylon is likened in Is. 14:12, 15; *cf.* Jude 6 and 2 Pet. 2:4.

In no case does any of these passages, biblical or non-biblical, refer to a creation-struggle of deity and monster, as all the serpent-slaying in them is done within an already created world. Furthermore, the Babylonian Ti'amat, whose death at Marduk's hands *is* associated with creation, was *not* a serpent or dragon, and therefore gives no support for assuming a struggle of deity and serpent/dragon at creation either (*cf.* A. Heidel, *The Babylonian Genesis*, 1951, pp. 83–88, 102–114). (*DRAGON; *LEVIATHAN; *RAHAB.)

In Canaanite, Mesopotamian, Anatolian and Egyptian mythology and cults, serpent deities are known, and serpents in various contexts are symbols of protection (Egyptian uraeus), of evil (*e.g.* Egyptian 'Apep or Apopis), of fecundity (Egypto-Canaanite goddesses of sex; *ANEP*, figs. 471–474), or of continuing life (symbolized by repeated shedding of its skin, *cf.* A. Heidel, *The Gilgamesh Epic and Old Testament Parallels*, 1949, p. 92, n. 212). For Canaanite altar-stands with serpents modelled on them, see *ANEP*, figs. 585, 590. In the texts from Ugarit note the prescribed sacrifice of 'a head of small cattle (for) 'Anat-Lôtan' (C. H. Gordon, *Ugaritic Literature*, 1949, pp. 114, 107, n. 1) and an incantation against snakes (C. Virolleaud, in *Ugaritica* 5, 1968, pp. 564ff., No. 7; M. Astour, *JNES* 27, 1968, pp. 13–36; A. F. Rainey, *JAOS* 94, 1974, pp. 189f., 194; M. Dietrich *et al.*, *UF* 7, 1975, pp. 121–125.
K.A.K.

SERPENT, BRONZE. On the borders of Edom, rebelious Israel suffered deadly snakebite as a punishment and begged Moses to intercede with God for them, to save them from the serpents. God then commanded Moses to make a bronze figure of a serpent and set it up on a pole, so that anyone bitten by a serpent need only look at the bronze serpent-figure and he would live (Nu. 21:4–9; 1 Cor. 10:9, 11). By this means God granted the people deliverance and enforced the lesson of dependence upon himself both for that deliverance and as a general principle. Centuries later, during his purge of idolatrous objects and customs, King Hezekiah of Judah destroyed the bronze serpent because the people had turned it into an idol, burning incense to it (2 Ki. 18:4). The following phrase *wayyiqrā' lô nᵉḥuštān* may mean either 'he (= Hezekiah) called it Nehushtan' *i.e.* 'only a bit of bronze'), or 'it was called Nehushtan' (*i.e.* by the people from of old). In either case it is a pun on the phrase *nᵉḥaš-nᵉḥōšeṯ*, 'serpent of bronze', two very similar-sounding words in Heb. The significance of serpents in surrounding paganism made Hezekiah's action especially imperative (*cf.* *SERPENT, end of section **II.** *d*; see also H. H. Rowley, 'Zadok and Nehushtan', *JBL* 58, 1939, pp. 113ff.). A bronze serpent was found at Gezer (see R. A. S. Macalister, *The Excavation of Gezer*, 2, 1912, pp. 398–399 and fig.; or I. Benzinger, *Hebräische Archäologie*³, 1927, p. 327, fig. 418), a serpent standard at Hazor, and a gilded copper snake from a shrine at Timna (B. Rothenberg, *Timna, Valley of the Biblical Copper Mines*, 1972, pp. 152, 183–184, pls. XIX–XX).

When speaking of his coming crucifixion, Jesus Christ used the incident of the serpent, which was lifted up that man might look in faith and live, in order to illustrate the significance of that impending event. Those who put faith in him, uplifted on the cross for their sins, would have life eternal (Jn. 3:14).
K.A.K.

SERPENT'S STONE ('Stone of Zoheleth', AV) (*'eḇen hazzōḥeleṯ*). A stone near En-rogel, to the SE of Jerusalem, the scene of the slaughtering of animals by Adonijah (1 Ki. 1:9). The meaning of *zōḥeleṯ* is uncertain, but it is usually connected with *zāḥal*, 'to withdraw, crawl away'. From this, some would interpret the phrase as 'the stone of slipping' and connect it with a steep and slippery rock slope, called by the Arabs *zaḥweileh*, or some neighbouring surface, near Siloam. The translation 'serpent's stone' may be linked with a possible identification of *En-rogel with the Jackal's Well (Ne. 2:13).

BIBLIOGRAPHY. J. Simons, *Jerusalem in the Old Testament*, 1952, pp. 160–162. T.C.M.

SERVANT OF THE LORD.

I. In the Old Testament

a. The 'Servant Songs'

B. Duhm's commentary on Isaiah (1892) distinguished four passages which have since been regarded as the 'Servant Songs': Is. 42:1–4; 49:1–6; 50:4–9; 52:13–53:12. Some scholars (*e.g.* S. Mowinckel) have gone so far as to assign these passages to a separate author and period from the surrounding text. Modern scholarship is generally agreed, however, that they are an integral part of Isaiah 40ff., with many echoes in neighbouring passages. The term 'servant' (*'eḇeḏ*) occurs as frequently outside Duhm's selected passages as within them (*e.g.* Is. 41:8f.; 43:10; 44:1f., 21; 45:4; 48:20), with reference to the nation of Israel. It is also used in the OT for individuals in a close relationship with God, such as the Patriarchs, prophets and kings, and particularly Moses and David (*e.g.* Gn. 26:24; Ex. 14:31; Dt. 34:5; 2 Sa. 7:5; Is. 20:3; Am. 3:7). But in the 'Servant Songs' a distinctive conception of 'servanthood' comes into sharper focus, so that without divorcing these passages from their context most scholars continue to speak of a 'Servant figure' as a distinct element in the prophet's message; and the most distinctive element in this figure is that of obedient, undeserved suffering, leading to death, as the means of taking away the sin of his people and 'making many to be accounted righteous'.

For a fuller treatment of the character and mission of the Servant in the context of the message of Is. 40ff., see *Messiah, I. *b.* 1.

b. The identity of the Servant

The following are the main lines of interpretation suggested.

1. *Collective.* The explicit description of Israel as God's 'servant' both in the 'Servant Songs' (Is. 49:3) and in the surrounding text leads many to regard the Songs as a description of the prophet's ideal for Israel, identifying the Servant either as the nation as a whole or, more probably, a pious remnant within the nation, with a mission to Israel (49:5f.), involving suffering to redeem the whole nation (53:4–6, 8, 11f.).

2. *Individual.* The language about the Servant is often strongly individual, describing the birth, suffering, death and eventual triumph of what is apparently a person rather than a group. Various historical identifications have been proposed, such as Moses, Jeremiah, Cyrus, Zerubbabel or the prophet himself. But the traditional interpretation, Jewish and Christian, is that the Servant is an ideal individual figure of the future, God's agent in redeeming his people, *i.e.* the *Messiah. In later Palestinian Judaism this was the dominant interpretation (Hellenistic Judaism was apparently more favourable to a collective interpretation), so that the *Targum of Jonathan on Is. 53, while clearly embarrassed by the idea of Messianic suffering to the extent of drastically reconstructing the text to eliminate this implication, still explicitly identifies the Servant as the Messiah (see text in Zimmerli and Jeremias, *The Servant of God*², pp. 69–71; and for other early Jewish interpretations, *ibid.*, pp. 37–79).

3. *Cultic.* Some Scandinavian scholars find the background to the Servant in the Babylonian myth of the dying and rising god *Tammuz and its associated liturgy. The Servant would then be a mythological concept rather than a historically identifiable figure or group. The existence of such myth and ritual in Israel is, however, highly debatable.

4. *'Corporate personality'.* Interpretations **1** and **2** above reflect important characteristics of the texts: both collective and individual aspects are clearly present in the Servant figure. Most scholars today tend, therefore, to look for an exegesis similar to H. W. Robinson's concept of 'corporate personality', *i.e.* the recognition that in the OT an individual (*e.g.* king or father) may represent and embody the group of which he is the head, so that he both *is* that group and yet can also be placed over against it as its leader. So the Servant *is* Israel (49:3), he sums up in himself all that Israel represents, and yet he is an individual with a mission *to* Israel (49:5f.) and his experiences on their behalf are the object of the nation's interest (53:1–6). The close juxtaposition of 49:3 and 49:5f. shows that these two aspects of the Servant are inseparable. The individual character of the Servant is most clearly expressed in 52:13–53:12, so that in this passage 'what began as a personification (has) become a person' (Rowley), and here all the emphasis is on the vicarious nature of his suffering as a substitute for his people. But this role is only possible because he *is* Israel, as its representative head.

II. In the New Testament

Some recent scholarship (esp. M. D. Hooker; also C. K. Barrett, C. F. D. Moule) has argued that the Servant figure was a minor element in the NT understanding of Jesus' redemptive work, and that the OT ground for his role of suffering and rejection was found rather in the 'son of man' of Dn. 7. It is pointed out that relatively few formal quotations from Servant passages occur in the NT, and that several of these quotations are of parts of the Songs which do not speak explicitly of suffering, or at least of redemptive suffering.

It is not legitimate, however, to restrict consideration to formal quotations, as allusive references are if anything even more impressive evidence of the influence of the Servant figure, and even where the words alluded to are not directly concerned with redemptive suffering, it is hard to believe that these passages could be referred to with no thought of their most distinctive theme and of its relevance to the mission of Jesus. Above all, it is indisputable that Is. 53 is by far the clearest indication of Messianic suffering in the OT, so that even if no explicit allusions to the Servant occurred, it would be very likely that this was the main source (together with certain psalms and parts of Zc. 9–13) of the repeated conviction that the Messiah *must* suffer, because 'it is written' of him. No such role of Messianic suffering is explicit in Dn. 7, nor did contemporary Jewish exegesis find it there.

In fact the explicit evidence of the influence of the Servant figure (esp. Is. 53, where the redemptive element is emphatic) is far from negligible.

a. In the teaching of Jesus

Is. 53:12 is explicitly quoted in Lk. 22:37. There are further clear allusions to Is. 53:10–12 in Mk. 10:45 and 14:24. Mk. 9:12 probably echoes Is. 53:3, and other possible allusions have been found in Mt. 3:15 (*cf.* Is. 53:11), Lk. 11:22 (*cf.* Is. 53:12; not a very likely allusion) and in the use of *paradidosthai* ('be delivered') in Mk. 9:31; 10:33; 14:21 (*cf.* Is. 53:12). In addition the voice at Jesus' baptism (Mk. 1:11), outlining his mission in terms of Is. 42:1, must have influenced Jesus' thinking.

Note the concentration in these allusions on Is. 53, and particularly on vv. 10–12 where the redemptive role of the Servant is most explicit. In Mk. 10:45 and 14:24 in particular the vicarious and redemptive character of Jesus' death is stressed, in terms drawn from Is. 53.

b. In the rest of the New Testament

The actual title 'servant' (*pais*) is confined to Peter's speech in Acts 3:13, 26 and the prayer of the church in Acts 4:27, 30, but the influence of the Servant figure is clear also in 1 Pet. 2:21–25; 3:18, suggesting that it featured prominently in Peter's understanding of Jesus' mission. Paul's explanations of Christ's redemptive work often contain ideas, and sometimes verbal allusions, which suggest that he too saw Jesus' work foreshadowed in Is. 53. (See *e.g.* Phil. 2:6–11; Rom. 4:25; 5:19; 8:3f., 32–34; 1 Cor. 15:3; 2 Cor. 5:21.) The use of 'lamb of God' by John (1:29, 36) also probably shows the influence of Is. 53:7. Heb. 9:28, 'to bear the sins of many', echoes Is. 53:12.

There are also a number of formal quotations from Servant passages, with reference to Jesus and the gospel, *viz.* Mt. 8:17; 12:18–21; Jn. 12:38; Acts 8:32f.; Rom. 10:16; 15:21. None of these is with specific reference to Jesus' redemptive work, and some focus on other aspects of his mission, but all testify further to the early church's conviction that the Servant figure, and particularly Is. 53, was a divinely ordained pattern for the Messianic mission of Jesus.

BIBLIOGRAPHY. For the whole article: W. Zimmerli and J. Jeremias, *The Servant of God*[2], 1965 (=*TDNT* 5, pp. 654–717).

For section I: C. R. North, *The Suffering Servant in Deutero-Isaiah*, 1948; H. H. Rowley, *The Servant of the Lord*, 1952, pp. 1–88; H. Blocher, *Songs of the Servant*, 1975; D. J. A. Clines, *I, He, We and They. A Literary Approach to Isaiah 53*, 1976; J. E. Goldingay, *God's Prophet, God's Servant*, 1984, pp. 77–159; R. N. Whybray, *Thanksgiving for a Liberated Prophet: an Interpretation of Isaiah Chapter 53*, 1978; J. D. W. Watts, *Isaiah* (Word Biblical Themes), 1989, pp. 47–109.

For section II: C. K. Barrett, in A. J. B. Higgins (ed.), *New Testament Essays*, 1959, pp. 1–18; O. Cullmann, *The Christology of the New Testament*, 1959, pp. 51–82; M. D. Hooker, *Jesus and the Servant*, 1959; C. F. D. Moule, *The Phenomenon of the New Testament*, 1967, pp. 82–99; R. T. France, *TynB* 19, 1968, pp. 26–52; *idem, Jesus and the Old Testament*, 1971, pp. 110–132; J. Jeremias, *New Testament Theology* 1, 1971, pp. 286–299; D. J. Moo, *The Old Testament in the Gospel Passion Narratives*, 1983, pp. 79–172; D. Juel, *Messianic Exegesis*, 1988, pp. 119–133.

R.T.F.

SETH. 1. The third son of Adam and Eve, born after the murder of Abel, and called Seth (*šēṯ*) because, Eve said, 'God has appointed (*šāṯ*) me another seed instead of Abel' (Gn. 4:25). It was through Seth that the genealogy of Noah passed (Gn. 5:3–4; 1 Ch. 1:1; Lk. 3:38). His son Enosh was born when he was 105 years old (*MT* and SP; LXX reads 205) and he lived to the great age of 912 years (*MT*, SP and LXX agree; Gn. 4:26; 5:6–8). The individual in the Sumerian King List, Alalgar, who corresponds to Seth is credited with a reign of 36,000 years.

2. An unknown individual whose name is rendered Sheth (Nu. 24:17, AV and RSV; RV gives 'tumult'), the ancestor of a people mentioned by Balaam as enemies of Israel.

T.C.M.

SEVEN WORDS, THE. The 'seven words' are so reckoned by bringing the data of all four Gospels together and identifying the 'loud cry' of Mk. 15:37 with one of the articulate utterances quoted by another Evangelist.

The first of the words spoken by our Lord from the cross (Lk. 23:34) reveals a love that is utterly unexpected and utterly undeserved. He prayed for the Roman soldiers and even, as Peter suggests (Acts 3:17), for the religious guides of the nation. (This saying is omitted by some ancient witnesses to the text, but the omission is probably due to an editor who considered that the events of AD 70 showed that God had not forgiven the Jewish authorities who accused Jesus before Pilate, as though the prayer had them in view.)

The second word was spoken to the penitent brigand (Lk. 23:43), who, beyond the cross, saw the crown and the coming glory, and who said, 'Jesus, remember me when you come in your kingly power' (v. 42). To him Jesus said in effect, 'Not far down the ages, but before the sun sets, you will be with me in the bliss of Paradise'.

The third word (Jn. 19:25–27), comprising sayings addressed both to the mother of Jesus and to the beloved disciple, proves that we have in Jesus the supreme example of a 'heart at leisure from itself, to soothe and sympathize'. Though suffering severe physical pain and enduring far more awful agony of soul, he thought of his mother and made provision for her future. The sword was piercing her heart (Lk. 2:35), but the tender words of her Son must have brought to her deep comfort and healing.

The first three words were spoken during the bright morning hours before noon. The fourth awe-inspiring word (Mt. 27:46; Mk. 15:34) was probably spoken by Jesus as the mysterious, supernatural 3 hours' darkness was lifting (*ELOI, ELOI, LAMA SABACHTHANI).

The fifth word (Jn. 19:28) followed close upon the fourth. It is the only word that speaks of physical suffering. Jesus had refused a drugged drink (Mk. 15:23), but he accepted another kind of drink, in order to moisten his parched throat and lips, so that, with a loud voice, he might make the declaration contained in the sixth word. The Evangelist notes the fulfilment of Ps. 69:21b.

That word (Jn. 19:30) consists of one comprehensive Gk. verb, *tetelestai*, 'It is finished'. It is the cry, not of a vanquished victim but of a Victor, who has finished the work he had to do, has fulfilled all the OT prophecies and types, and has once for all offered the one final sacrifice for sin (Heb. 10:12).

In the final word (Lk. 23:46) Jesus quoted Ps. 31:5, traditionally the pious Jew's evening prayer.

The redeemed are so really brothers of the Redeemer (Heb. 2:11–13) that, in the moment of dying, they can use the same language, as they commend their souls into the hands of the Father—his Father, and their Father in him.

BIBLIOGRAPHY. V. Taylor, *Jesus and His Sacrifice*, 1937, pp. 157ff., 197ff.; R. G. Turnbull, *The Seven Words from the Cross*, 1956. A.R.

F.F.B.

SEVENEH. The RV, ASV rendering of the *MT* *sᵉwēnēh* (Egyp. *Swn*, 'place of barter', 'market', Coptic *Suan*, Arab. *'Aswân*) in Ezk. 29:10; 30:6, where AV, RSV retain the classical form, *Syene. Located on the first cataract of the Nile, Syene (modern 'Aswân) marked the boundary between Egypt and Ethiopia. 'From Migdol ('tower' in AV, RV) to Syene' means 'the length of Egypt from N to S'. *MT sᵉwēnēh* should be read *sᵉwēnâ* or *sᵉwānâ*, the *â* signifying direction: 'to Syene'. A border fortress and a base for expeditions up the Nile, a terminus for river traffic and a source of red granite for Egyp. monuments (syenite), Syene was of special importance to the Jews because of its proximity to the island of Elephantine, which housed a colony of Jews who sought refuge in Egypt after Jerusalem fell (587 BC). The Qumran MS of Is. suggests that 'Syenites' should replace *sînîm* (Is. 49:12); LXX reads *Syene* for *Sin* in Ezk. 30:16.

BIBLIOGRAPHY. *BA* 15, 1952, pp. 50–68; B. Porten, *Archives from Elephantine*, 1968.

D.A.H.

SHAALBIM. A village inhabited by Amorites near Mt Heres and Aijalon when they withstood the Danites. Later the Amorites were subjugated by the house of Joseph (Jdg. 1:35). With Makaz, Beth-shemesh and Elon-beth-Hanan, Shaalbim formed part of Solomon's second administrative district (1 Ki. 4:9). It is almost certainly the same as Shaalabbin, included with Aijalon in the list of Dan's territory (Jos. 19:42), and Shaalbon, the house of Eliahba, one of David's warriors (2 Sa. 23:32; 1 Ch. 11:33). Because of the similar area covered it has been suggested that Shaalbim of Jdg. 1:35; 1 Ki. 4:9 may also be the same place. The position of modern Selbīṭ, 5 km NW of Aijalon and 13 km N of Beth-shemesh, suits all these contexts well, though the name is philologically different. Shaalbim, *etc.*, may mean 'haunt of foxes'.

D.J.W.

SHAARAIM (Heb. *šaʿᵃraim*). **1.** On the line of the Philistine flight from Azekah, before the parting of the ways to Gath and Ekron (1 Sa. 17:52). This is compatible with Jos. 15:36. See *GTT*, p. 318. **2.** In 1 Ch. 4:31, for *Sharuhen. J.P.U.L.

SHADOW (Heb. *ṣēl*, 'shadow', 'shade', 'defence'; Gk. *skia*, 'a shade', 'a shadow'; both words with derivative forms). The representation made by any solid body interposing between the sun or light and another body. As a shadow is constantly varying till at last, perhaps suddenly, it ceases to be, so are our days unsubstantial and fleeting, our death sudden (1 Ch. 29:15; Jb. 14:2; 17:7). Darkness and gloominess are associated with shadows, and thus with 'the shadow of death' (Jb. 3:5; 16:16; 24:17; Ps. 23:4), though this common interpretation of Heb. *ṣalmûṯ* is strictly inaccurate and should be rendered 'deep darkness', as usually in RSV.

As a man can find welcome relief in the shade from the scorching heat (*cf.* Jon. 4:5–6), so the rule and shelter of the Almighty are called a shadow (La. 4:20; Ezk. 31:6; Ps. 91:1; Is. 25:4; *cf.* Ct. 2:3). The servant's eagerly anticipated time for stopping work is called the 'shadow' (Jb. 7:2). In contrast to the signs of approaching desolation and ruin, the 'shadows of evening' (Je. 6:4), the day of everlasting glory is when 'the shadows flee' (Ct. 2:17).

The ancient ceremonies are called a 'shadow of the good things to come' (Heb. 10:1; *cf.* Col. 2:17). The unchangeableness of God is contrasted with the 'play of passing shadows' (Jas. 1:17, NEB). In Heb. 9:5 AV 'shadowing' (RSV 'overshadowing') comes from *kataskiazō*, 'to (cause a) shadow' or 'to shade fully' (*cf.* Heb. *ṣālal*). J.D.D.

SHALEM. A word treated by AV as the name of a place near Shechem, which was visited by Jacob (Gn. 33:18). RV ('in peace') and RSV ('safely'), however, prefer to take it in an adverbial sense, from the verb *šālēm*, 'to be complete, sound', and this appears to make better sense. The word *šālēm*, identical in form, does occur as a place-name in connection with Melchizedek, but is given as *Salem in EVV. T.C.M.

SHALISHAH. The district reached by Saul after passing through the hills of Ephraim and before reaching the land of Shaalim, or *Salim, in pursuit of his father's lost asses (1 Sa. 9:4). The place seems to have had its own deity or shrine, Baal-shalishah (2 Ki. 4:42). Since the places in conjunction with which Shalishah is cited are of uncertain location, its own situation is not known. Conder proposed the ruins of Khirbet Kefr Thilth, 30 km NE of Jaffa. D.J.W.

SHALLUM (Heb. *šallûm, šallum*). **1.** A Jerahmeelite through the line of an ancestress who married an Egyp. slave (1 Ch. 2:40–41; *cf.* vv. 34–35). **2.** A descendant of Korah who served under David as chief gatekeeper at the King's Gate in the sanctuary (1 Ch. 9:17–19; Ezr. 2:42). Apparently this was an inherited position of some importance (*cf.* Ezr. 2:42; Ne. 7:45). Possibly a short form of Meshelemiah (1 Ch. 26:1; 9:21) and of Selemiah (26:14). **3.** Son of Jabesh and 16th king of the N kingdom of Israel (*c.* 745 BC). By assassinating *Zechariah, son of *Jeroboam II, he brought an end to the dynasty of *Jehu (2 Ki. 15:10), thus fulfilling prophecy (10:30; *cf.* 15:12). He was killed in turn in Samaria by *Menahem after a reign of only 1 month (15:13–15). **4.** The husband of *Huldah, the prophetess who was 'keeper of the wardrobe' (2 Ki. 22:14; 2 Ch. 34:22). **5.** Son of *Josiah (1 Ch. 3:15; Je. 22:11) and 18th king of Judah (*c.* 609 BC) whose throne-name was *Jehoahaz. He was deposed after a 3-month reign (2 Ki. 23:31). **6.** An Aaronide predecessor of *Ezra (Ezr. 7:2; *cf.* 1 Ch. 6:12–13). Possibly an abbreviated form of Meshullam (1 Ch. 9:11; Ne. 11:11; 12:13).

The various forms of this name are based on the same root in different nominal patterns.

D.W.B.

SHALMAN. The person who sacked Beth-arbel (Ho. 10:14). This action was sufficiently well known to serve as a warning to Israel. It is generally assumed that this could be a reference to *Shalmaneser V, the Assyr. king who besieged Samaria in 725–723 BC. In this event Arbel might be Arbela, W of Galilee (1 Macc. 9:2). But against this, Shalmaneser's name is elsewhere written fully and the Galilee area fell to Tiglath-pileser III in 734–732 BC. Thus Shalman may refer to Salamanu, king of Moab, mentioned in the annals of *Tiglath-pileser. Identification remains uncertain.

D.J.W.

SHALMANESER (Heb. *šalman'eser*; Gk. *Salmennasar*; Assyr. *Šulmanu-ašaridu*, 'the god Šulman is chief'). The Heb. may have been read *šlmn'sr* (*JSS* 21, 1976, p. 8).

Shalmaneser was the name borne by several rulers of *Assyria. The king of Assyria to whom Hoshea of Israel became subject (2 Ki. 17:3) was Shalmaneser V (727–722 BC), son of Tiglath-pileser III. When Hoshea failed to pay tribute in his 7th regnal year Shalmaneser began a 3-year siege of the Israelite capital *Samaria. There are no annals of this king extant, but the Assyr. Eponym List records the siege and the Bab. Chronicle says that Shalmaneser 'broke (the resistance of) the city of Shamara'in'. It is likely that the 'king of Assyria' to whom the city fell (2 Ki. 17:6) was this same Shalmaneser, though the final capture of the city is claimed by his successor Sargon II in 722/1 BC. It is possible that Sargon usurped the throne during the siege and continued the campaign (*DOTT*, pp. 58–63).

Shalmaneser III, king of Assyria 859–824 BC, frequently raided the W, and the first recorded Assyr. contact with the Israelites is found in his Annals. In 853 BC he fought a coalition of Syrian kings under Irhuleni of Hamath and Hadadezer of Damascus at Qarqar. Among their allies was 'Ahab the Israelite', who, according to the Assyrians, provided 2,000 chariots and 10,000 men as his contribution. The Assyr. advance was temporary and Shalmaneser did not return for 3 years (1 Ki. 16:29; 20:20; 22:1).

In his account of operations against Syria in 841 BC, Shalmaneser III claims to have defeated Hazael of Damascus (see 1 Ki. 19:15). He did not, however, capture the city and moved *via* the Hauran to the Lebanon, where he received tribute from 'Jehu, son of Omri', an event not mentioned in the OT portrayed on the Black Obelisk from Nimrud (*CALAH).

BIBLIOGRAPHY. *CAH*³, 3, 1978.

D.J.W.

SHAME. The Eng. word and its cognates appear about 190 times in OT and 46 times in NT. These occurrences are translations of original forms representing at least 10 different Heb. and 7 different Gk. roots and a considerably larger number of Heb. and Gk. words.

Two main meanings can be distinguished: descriptions of states of mind, and descriptions of physical states. The states of mind may be classified into three broad categories: first, those where an individual is or might be the object of contempt, derision or humiliation; second, those where he feels bashfulness or shyness; third, those where he feels respect or awe. The physical states involve a degree of exposure or nudity, or the words are used as euphemisms for the sexual organs.

The most frequent usage by far involves the ideas connected with contempt, derision and humiliation. Shame follows when the law of God is disregarded or forgotten (Ho. 4:6–7). God sends it upon the enemies of his people (Ps. 132:18). It is the result of sin and is removed in the day of liberty and restoration (Is. 61:7). It appears at times to be a punishment (Ps. 44:7, 9, 15). In contrast, it is also sometimes a positive preventive manifestation of the grace of God (Ezk. 43:10). It may induce positive action (Jdg. 3:25). False shame at that which is not shameful, *viz.* allegiance to Christ, is to be avoided (Mk. 8:38). There is also a figurative use of the term, as in Is. 24:23 and in Jude 13.

The usage representing shyness or bashfulness is not as important, since it occurs infrequently. A clear example is the statement concerning the man and his wife before the fall in Gn. 2:25. The usage which represents awe or respect is also rare. An OT instance is Ezr. 9:6; and there is the apostolic injunction of 1 Tim. 2:9. In the former instance the common Heb. root *bôš*, which appears on over 90 other occasions in the OT text in the Qal stem alone, is used; whereas 1 Tim. 2:9 is the only passage where *aidōs* occurs in the NT.

The uses of the words with a physical reference are concerned with nakedness. These occurrences are not frequent.

The biblical concept of shame is basically that of the mental state of humiliation due to sin, and to departure from the law of God, which brings obloquy and rejection by both God and man. The development of the concept is most extensive in the prophets and in the Pauline Epistles. The references to matters connected with sex are illustrative or figurative, and do not indicate that there is any more basic connection between shame and sexual functions than between shame and other functions which may occasion embarrassment by sinful use.

BIBLIOGRAPHY. R. Bultmann, *TDNT* 1, pp. 189–191; H.-G. Link, E. Tiedtke, *NIDNTT* 3, pp. 561–564.

P.W.

SHAMGAR (Heb. *šamgar*, probably from Hurrian *šimiqari*). A personal name repeatedly attested in Nuzian texts (*cf.* R. H. Pfeiffer and E. A. Speiser, *AASOR* 16, 1936, p. 161), called 'the son of Anath' (Jdg. 3:31; 5:6), *i.e.* a native of Beth-anath (presumably a S Beth-anath; *cf.* Jos. 15:59). His killing of 600 Philistines must belong to the earliest period of Philistine settlement in Canaan, since the reference to him in the Song of Deborah (Jdg. 5:6) indicates that he flourished before the battle of Kishon (*c.* 1125 BC). The ox-goad (Heb. *malmāḏ*) with which he wrought such havoc would have a metal tip which was sharpened as required (*GOAD). He is not described as a judge of Israel—indeed, he may well have been a Canaanite—but his exploit afforded the neighbouring Israelites some relief. Some LXX and other recensions repeat Jdg. 3:31 at the end of ch. 16, in a more 'Philistine' context. J. Garstang's surmise that Shamgar is identical with Ben-anath, a Syrian sea-captain and son-in-law of Rameses II (*c.* 1260 BC) is not convincing (*Joshua–Judges*, 1931, pp. 63f., 284ff.); still less so is Sir C. Marston's suggestion that 'The Ox-goad' was the name of his ship (*The Bible is True*, 1934, pp. 247ff.).

BIBLIOGRAPHY. G. F. Moore, 'Shamgar and Sisera', *JAOS* 9, 1898, pp. 159f.; F. C. Fensham, *JNES* 20, 1961, pp. 197–198; B. Maisler, 'Shamgar ben Anath', *PEQ* 66, 1934, pp. 192ff.; E. Danelius, *JNES* 22, 1963, pp. 191–193. F.F.B.

SHAMMAH. 1. A tribal chieftain (Heb. *'allûp̄*) of Edom, descended from Esau (Gn. 36:17). **2.** A brother of King David, and son of Jesse (1 Sa. 16:9). Variant forms of the name are Shammua, Shimea, Shimeah, Shimeam and Shimei. **3.** One of the outstanding three of David's warriors (2 Sa. 23:11), described as a Hararite. The Shammah of 2 Sa. 23:30 is almost certainly the same man, but there are textual problems; *cf.* NEB. **4.** Another of David's warriors, a Harodite (2 Sa. 23:25). 1 Ch. 11:27 renders his name as Shammoth (a plural form of the name), and the Shamhuth of 1 Ch. 27:8 may well be the same man. D.F.P.

SHAPHAN. 1. The son of Azaliah who was state secretary (AV 'scribe') to Josiah. Hilkiah reported to him the discovery of the book of the law in the Temple (2 Ki. 22:3; 2 Ch. 34:8–24). He read from this book before Josiah who sent him to the prophetess Huldah. Shaphan was father of at least three sons. (i) Ahikam who assisted the prophet Jeremiah (2 Ki. 22:12; 2 Ch. 34:20; Je. 26:24); (ii) Elasah who, with another man, was entrusted by Jeremiah with a letter to the exiles in Babylonia (Je. 29:3); (iii) Gemariah who tried to prevent Jehoiakim from burning the scroll containing Jeremiah's prophecies (Je. 36:10–12, 25). Shaphan had as grandsons Micaiah (Je. 36:11, 13) and Gedaliah, the governor of Judah after the Babylonian invasions of 589–587 BC, who helped Jeremiah (Je. 39:14).

2. The father of Jaazaniah, seen sacrificing to idols in Ezekiel's vision (Ezk. 8:11).

Even if the name is to be connected with Heb. *šāp̄ān*, 'rock-badger', there is no evidence that it betokens totem worship (as G. B. Gray, *Hebrew Proper Names*, 1896, p. 103). D.J.W.

SHAPHIR (AV Saphir). A town in the Philistine plain against which Micah prophesied (Mi. 1:11). The exact site is uncertain, but may be one of the three hut settlements es-Sūāfir near Ashdod. The identification of Shaphir with Shamir (Jos. 15:48; Jdg. 10:1–2) is tenuous. R.J.W.

SHAREZER. 1. A brother of Adrammelech who with him murdered their father Sennacherib in 681 BC (2 Ki. 19:37; Is. 37:38). His name is known only from this reference and is probably an abbreviation from the Assyr.–Bab. *šar-uṣur*, 'He has protected the king', normally prefixed by the name of a deity. By reference to *Nergilus* in the account by Abydenus of the same event Nergal-sharezer has been proposed. Johns considered the name a corruption of Šzar-eṭir-Aššur, the known name of a son of Sennacherib. Alternatively, a Nabū-šar-uṣur, governor of Marqasi and eponym for the year 682 BC, may be in mind.

2. A contemporary of Zechariah who inquired concerning the propriety of continuing the fast celebrating the anniversary of the destruction of the Temple (Zc. 7:2). Because the text is difficult (see RVmg.) it has been suggested that 'the people of Bethel' may imply that the full name was the common Belshazzar (Bab. Bel-šar-uṣur) or Bethel-sharezer. D.J.W.

SHARON (Heb. *šārôn*; 'Saron', Acts 9:35, AV) means a level place or plain. It comprises the largest of the coastal plains in N Palestine. Lying between the extensive marshes of the lower Crocodile river (Nahr ez-Zerka) and the valley of Aijalon and Joppa in the S, it runs some 80 km N–S and is 15 km wide. Its features have been largely determined by the Pleistocene shorelines and deposits. Inland from the belt of recent sand-dunes which divert and choke some of the coastal rivers, rises a zone of Mousterian red sands to *c.* 60 m, forming in the N a continuous belt of some 30 km. Formerly, this zone was thickly forested with oaks, probably *Quercus infectoria*, and today this is one of the richest agricultural districts of Israel, planted with citrus groves. Inland from the belt of Mousterian sands, the streams have partially excavated a longitudinal trough along the foothills of an earlier Pleistocene shoreline. The river valleys, especially in the N of this trough, tended to be marshy until modern drainage developments. In the past, only in the S border of Sharon was the land more favourable for settlement, and it is clear that most of Sharon was never colonized by the Israelites (but Tell Qasile, N of Joppa, was founded *c.* 1200 BC). In the N, Socoh, a district centre under Solomon (1 Ki. 4:10), and Gilgal, seat of the petty kings defeated by Joshua (Jos. 12:23), lay in the Samaritan foothills E of the plain.

References to Lod and Ono in the S, which were both fortified outposts (1 Ch. 8:12; Ezr. 2:33; Ne. 7:37), and 'the valley of the craftsmen' separating them (Ne. 11:35; *cf.* 1 Sa. 13:19–20) appear to indicate they were settled by the returning exiles.

The 'majesty' of Sharon (Is. 35:2), like the 'jungle' of Jordan (Je. 12:5; 49:19), would suggest the dense vegetation cover rather than the fertility which Sharon has subsequently proved to possess in its Pleistocene sands, now under orange groves. For settlement it has long remained a 'desert' (Is. 33:9), and was used only for pasturage (1 Ch. 5:16; Is. 65:10). It was here that Shitrai supervised King David's flocks (1 Ch. 27:29). The 'rose of Sharon' (Ct. 2:1–3) suggests the flowers (*PLANTS) of the dense undergrowth. Four red flowers still follow each other in quick succession, an anemone (*Anemone coronaria*), a buttercup (*Ranunculus asiaticus*), a tulip (*Tulipa montana*) and a poppy (*Papaver sp.*).

BIBLIOGRAPHY. D. Baly, *The Geography of the Bible*, 1957, pp. 133–137. J.M.H.

SHARUHEN. A Simeonite settlement (Jos. 19:6). Egyp. sources mention *Srḥn*, a Hyksos fortress which resisted Ahmose for 3 years *c.* 1550 BC, barring his way to further conquests; usually identified with Tell el-Far'a, 24 km S of Gaza (*NEAEHL*, pp. 441–444). Petrie's brief excavation revealed a strong Philistine occupation. The Joshua context also suits Tell el-Huweilfeh, ½ km N of Khirbet Rammamein (Ain Rimmon?), proposed earlier by Albright, *JPOS* 4, 1924, p. 135. See also A. Kempinski, *IEJ* 24, 1974, pp. 145–152; W. Shea, *IEJ* 29, 1979, pp. 1–5; J. M. Weinstein, *BASOR* 241, 1981, pp. 7f. J.P.U.L.

SHAUL (Heb. *šā'ûl*, 'asked for'). In Heb., the same as *'Saul'. **1.** A king of Edom (1 Ch. 1:48–49; *cf.* Gn. 36:37–38), belonging to Rehoboth. **2.** A son of Simeon by a Canaanitess (Gn. 46:10), from whom the Shaulites took their name (Nu. 26:13). **3.** A son of Kohath (1 Ch. 6:24), called 'Joel' in 1 Ch. 6:36.
G.W.G.

SHAVEH, VALLEY OF. A valley near Salem (Gn. 14:17f.), also known as 'the King's Valley', where Absalom raised his memorial pillar (2 Sa. 18:18). If Salem is Jerusalem, the site may be at the top of the Valley of Hinnom. But an ancient Jewish tradition reads *ś-r-h*, another word meaning 'king', for *š-w-h* ('Shaveh'). (This involves only one slight consonantal change.) D.F.P.

SHAVSHA. The name of a secretary of state under David (2 Sa. 8:17, where he is called Seraiah). He is called Shisha in 1 Ki. 4:3, Shavsha in 1 Ch. 18:16, and Sheva in 2 Sa. 20:25. Following de Vaux, Grollenberg (*Atlas of the Bible*) suggests that the form which must underlie these names indicates that the official was an Egyptian. His eldest son's name, Elihoreph, could mean 'my god is the Nile (god)', or in its LXX form Elihaph, 'my god is Apis'. If so, then the Egyp. father gave his son a hybrid name, the first element being Heb. but the second expressing his allegiance to the religion of his Egyp. ancestors. This would further suggest that David brought in Egyptians to fill offices in his kingdom, organizing it at least in part on Egyp. models. But both of these names (and their bearers) may in fact be Semitic; if so, the evidence for Egyp. influence in the organization of David's kingdom is then much less.

T. N. D. Mettinger (*Solomonic State Officials*, 1971, pp. 25–30), largely following A. Cody (*RB* 72, 1965, pp. 381–393), explains Shavsha as a misunderstood corruption of the Egyp. title *sẖ-š'*, 'secretary' ('scribe of letters'); while possible, the assumed phonetic changes are highly dubious.

BIBLIOGRAPHY. *KB*, p. 958 (*s.v.* 'Shavsha'); K. A. Kitchen, *VT Suppl.* 40, 1988, pp. 112–113; G. H. Jones, *1 and 2 Kings*, *NCBC*, 1984, p. 135; P. K. McCarter, Jr., *II Samuel*, *AB*, 1984, pp. 254, 433.
R.A.H.G.
K.A.K.

SHEAR-JASHUB. A symbolical name ('a remnant will return') given to one of Isaiah's sons to express the truth that out of the judgment God would save a remnant (*e.g.* Is. 1:9). When Isaiah went to Ahaz, Shear-jashub accompanied him as a reminder that the nation, even at that dark time, would not completely perish (Is. 7:3). E.J.Y.

SHEBA. 1. A city (Heb. *šeḇa'*) in the territory allotted to Simeon in S Palestine near Beersheba and Moladah (Jos. 19:2; *MT* at 1 Ch. 4:28 omits it in the parallel list, but LXX has 'Sama'). LXX reads 'Samaa' in MS B (*cf.* Jos. 15:26) and 'Sabee' in MS A. S. Cohen (*IDB*, 4, p. 311) suggests that Sheba ('seven') was named for the seven lambs with which Abraham made covenant with Abimelech (Gn. 21:28–29) and may have been the older part of Beersheba.

2. A Benjaminite (*šeḇa'*) who revolted unsuccessfully against David after Absalom's death (2 Sa. 20:1–2, 6–7, 10, 21–22). **3.** A leader (*šeḇa'*) of the tribe of Gad (1 Ch. 5:13). **4.** A descendant (*šᵉḇā'*) of Cush through Raamah (Gn. 10:7; 1 Ch. 1:9); brother of *Dedan. **5.** A descendant (*šᵉḇâ'*) of Shem through Joktan (Gn. 10:28; 1 Ch. 1:22). **6.** Son of Jokshan (*šᵉḇā'*) and grandson of Abraham and Keturah (Gn. 25:3; 1 Ch. 1:32); brother of Dedan.

7. The land (*šᵉḇā'*) whose queen (*SHEBA, QUEEN OF) visited Solomon (1 Ki. 10:1ff.; 2 Ch. 9:1ff.) was in all probability the home of the Sabaeans in SW Arabia. J. A. Montgomery (*ICC*, *Kings*, 1951, pp. 215f.) contends that the Sabaeans were still in N Arabia in the 10th century BC although they controlled the trade routes from S Arabia. On the other hand, J. Bright (*History of Israel*², 1972, p. 211), while recognizing that the Sabaeans were originally camel nomads, affirms, with greater probability, that by Solomon's time they had settled in the E area of what is modern Yemen. So also G. W. Van Beek, *IDB*, 4, p. 145.

The relationship between the Sabaeans and the three Shebas mentioned in Gn. is by no means clear. They may be distinct tribes, but the similarities among the groupings are striking: Raamah's sons (Gn. 10:7, Hamites, bear the same names as Abraham's grandsons—Sheba and Dedan (25:3); both Cush, the Hamite (10:7), and Joktan, the Semite, have descendants named Sheba and Havilah (10:28–29). The Table of *Nations in Gn. 10 may reflect both the Semitic origin of the Sabaeans and also the fact that they settled in close proximity to Hamitic groups, *i.e.* Egyptians and Ethiopians. Indeed, classical Abyssinian culture testifies to a blending of Hamitic and Semitic elements, and the role that S Arabians who crossed the Bab al-Mandab as traders and colonists played in shaping this culture is impressive.

It is as traders or raiders (Jb. 1:15, although E. Dhorme, *Job*, E.T. 1967, p. xxv, identifies Sheba here with an area near Tema and Dedan, oases substantially N of the Sabaean homeland) that the OT most frequently speaks of the people of Sheba. Gold (1 Ki. 10:2; Ps. 72:15; Is. 60:6), frankincense (Is. 60:6; Je. 6:20), spices and jewels (1 Ki. 10:2; Ezk. 27:22) were brought to N markets in their caravans (Jb. 6:19). Commercial opportunists, they were not above engaging in slave trade according to Joel 3:8 (where less preferably LXX reads 'into captivity' for 'to the Sabaeans'). This extensive trading activity apparently led the Sabaeans to found colonies at various oases in N Arabia. These served as caravan bases and probably gave the colonists a degree of control over the N area. Testimony to intercourse between Sheba and Canaan is found in a S Arabian clay stamp (*c.* 9th century BC) unearthed at Bethel (*BASOR* 151, 1958, pp. 9–16).

The most prominent of the Arab states (which included Hadramaut, Ma'īn and Qatabān) during the first half of the 1st millennium BC, Sheba was ruled by *mukarribs*, priest-kings, who supervised both the political affairs and the polytheistic worship of the sun, moon and star gods. Explorations by the University of Louvain with H. St J. Philby (1951–2) and the American Foundation for the Study of Man (1950–3) found some outstanding examples of Sabaean art and architecture, especially the temple of the moon-god at Mārib, the capital, which dates from the 7th century BC, and the sluices, hewn through solid rock at the dam in Mārib (*c.* 6th century BC).

BIBLIOGRAPHY. R. L. Bowen, Jr., and F. P. Albright, *Archaeological Discoveries in South Arabia*, 1958; *GTT*; S. Moscati, *Ancient Semitic Civilizations*, 1957, pp. 181–194; G. Ryckmans, *Les religions arabes préislamiques*², 1951; J. Ryckmans, *L'institution monarchique en Arabie méridionale avant l'Islam*, 1951; G. W. Van Beek in *BA* 15, 1952, pp. 2–18; *ibid.*, 'South Arabian History and Archaeology', in G. E. Wright (ed.), *The Bible and the Near East*, 1961; A. K. Irvine in *POTT*, pp. 299ff. D.A.H.

SHEBA, QUEEN OF. An unnamed Sabaean (*SHEBA) monarch who journeyed to Jerusalem to test Solomon's wisdom (1 Ki. 10:1–10, 13; 2 Ch. 9:1–9, 12). A major purpose of her costly (1 Ki. 10:10) yet successful (1 Ki. 10:13) visit may have been to negotiate a trade-agreement with Solomon, whose control of the trade routes jeopardized the income which the Sabaeans were accustomed to receive from the caravans which crossed their territory—an income on which Sheba (or better Saba) was dependent despite considerable achievement in agriculture due to favourable rainfall and an effective irrigation system. The spices, gold and precious stones with which she sought Solomon's favour (1 Ki. 10:3, 10) would have been typical of the luxurious cargoes of these caravans, which linked the resources of E Africa, India and S Arabia to the markets of Damascus and Gaza by way of oases like Mecca, Medina and Tema.

Both Assyr. and S Arab. inscriptions testify to the presence of queens in Arabia as early as the 8th century BC. (See N. Abbott, 'Pre-Islamic Arab Queens', *AJSL* 58, 1941, pp. 1–22.) The widespread domestication of the camel 2 centuries or so before Solomon's time made the Queen of Sheba's trip of about 2,000 km feasible (1 Ki. 10:2).

Her willingness to make this arduous journey is contrasted by Christ with the Jews' complacency in Mt. 12:42, where she is called 'Queen of the South', a title which reflects a Semitic construction like *malkaṯ sᵉḇā'* or *malkaṯ yāmîn*, Queen of Sheba or Yemen.

This queen is enshrined in Ethiopian legends, particularly the *Kebra Nagast* ('Glory of the Kings'), as the queen of Ethiopia who bore by Solomon the first king of Ethiopia. This legend reflects the close tie which existed in antiquity between S Arabia and E Africa, which Josephus also notes when he calls this ruler 'Queen of Egypt and Ethiopia' (*Ant.* 8. 165–175; *cf.* also Gregory of Nyssa, *Homilies on the Song of Songs* 7). Arabian legends remember her as Bilqis.

BIBLIOGRAPHY. Samuel Abramsky, *EJ*, 15, pp. 96–111; J. Gray, *I and II Kings*², 1970, pp. 258–262; James B. Pritchard (ed.), *Solomon and Sheba*, 1974.

D.A.H.

SHEBNA. A high official under Hezekiah, variously designated minister ('which is over the house', Is. 22:15), secretary (*sōp̄ēr*, 'scribe', 2 Ki. 18:18; 19:2; Is. 36:3), and state official (*sōḵēn*, 'treasurer', Is. 22:15). A man of wealth, he was rebuked by Isaiah for preparing a conspicuously monumental rock-hewn tomb and his downfall predicted (Is. 22:15–19). Part of the inscribed lintel from such a tomb has been recovered (N. Avigad, *IEJ* 3, 1953, pp. 137–152; D. J. Wiseman, *IBA*, 1958, p. 59). The full name of Shebna may be Shebanyah(u), a name which occurs in contemporary inscriptions and on Heb. seals (*IEJ* 18, 1968, pp. 166–167), and which may be compared with that later borne by levitical priests (Ne. 9:4–5; 10:10; 1 Ch. 15:24). D.J.W.

SHECHEM. 1. The son of Hamor, the Hivite, prince of Shechem (Gn. 34; Jos. 24:32; Jdg. 9:28) who defiled Jacob's daughter Dinah. **2.** A descendant of Joseph's son Manasseh (Nu. 26:31), founder of a family (Jos. 17:2). **3.** Son of Shemidah, of the tribe of Manasseh (1 Ch. 7:19).

4. An important town in central Palestine with a long history and many historical associations. Normally it appears in the Bible as Shechem (*šᵉḵem*), but also once as Sichem (Gn. 12:6, AV) and twice as Sychem (Acts 7:16, AV). It was situated in the hill country of Ephraim (Jos. 20:7), in the neighbourhood of Mt Gerizim (Jdg. 9:7). The original site is today represented by Tell Balaṭa, which lies at the E end of the valley running between Mt Ebal on the N and Mt Gerizim on the S, about 50 km N of Jerusalem and 9 km SE of Samaria.

Shechem (Sichem) is the first Palestinian site mentioned in Gn. Abram encamped there at the 'oak of Moreh' (Gn. 12:6). The 'Canaanite was then in the land', but the Lord revealed himself to Abram and renewed his covenant promise. Abram thereupon built an altar to the Lord (Gn. 12:7).

Abram's grandson, Jacob, on his return from Harran, came to Shalem, a city of Shechem, and

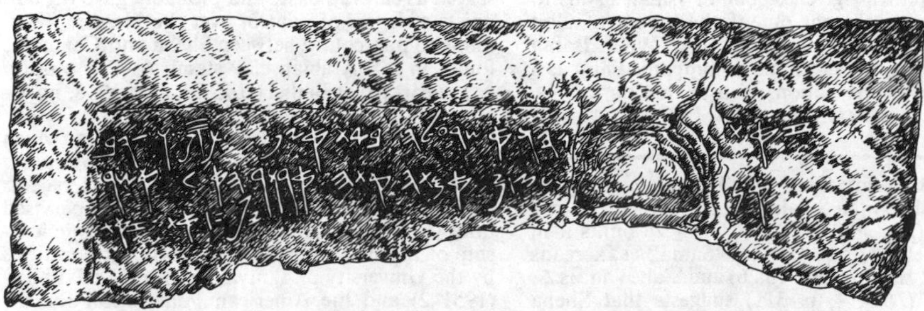

The early Hebrew inscription formed the lintel of the tomb of one []-yahu, *a royal steward ('he who is over the house'), at Siloam, Jerusalem. This may well be the tomb of Shebna, accused by Isaiah of carving a sumptuous grave for himself in the rock (Is. 22:15–16). Length 2·2 m. 7th cent.* BC

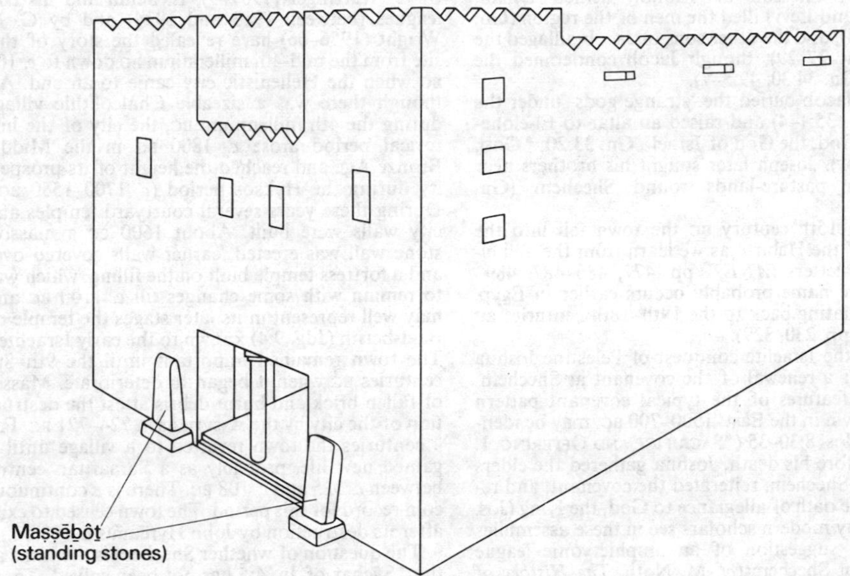

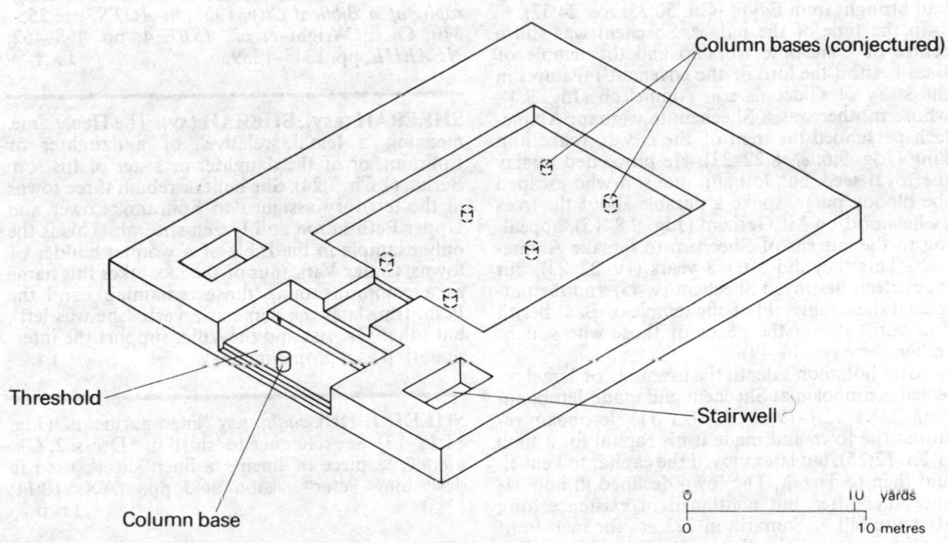

Plan and suggested reconstruction of the early phase of the fortress-temple (migdol) *excavated at Shechem. The standing stones may not have been erected until the later phase of the building. 17th cent.* BC.

pitched his tent (Gn. 33:18–19) on a parcel of ground which he bought from Hamor, the Hivite prince of the region (Gn. 33:18–19; 34:2). When Shechem, the son of Hamor, defiled Dinah, Simeon and Levi killed the men of the region (Gn. 34:25–26), and the other sons of Jacob pillaged the town (vv. 27–29), though Jacob condemned the action (Gn. 34:30; 49:5–7).

Here Jacob buried the 'strange gods' under the oak (Gn. 35:1–4) and raised an altar to El-elohe-Israel ('God, the God of Israel', Gn. 33:20; *God, Names of). Joseph later sought his brothers near the rich pasture-lands round Shechem (Gn. 37:12ff.).

In the 15th century BC the town fell into the hands of the Habiru, as we learn from the Tell el-Amarna letters (*ANET*, pp. 477, 485–487, 489–490). The name probably occurs earlier in Egyp. records dating back to the 19th–18th centuries BC (*ANET*, pp. 230, 329).

After the Israelite conquest of Pelestine Joshua called for a renewal of the covenant at Shechem. Various features of the typical covenant pattern well known in the East, 1500–700 BC, may be identified in Jos. 8:30–35 (*Sacrifice and Offering, **I**. *c*. 2). Before his death, Joshua gathered the elders again to Shechem, reiterated the covenant, and received the oath of allegiance to God, the King (Jos. 24). Many modern scholars see in these assemblies a strong suggestion of an amphictyonic league centred at Shechem (*cf.* M. Noth, *The History of Israel*, 1958).

The boundary between Ephraim and Manasseh passed near the town (Jos. 17:7), which was one of the cities of refuge, and a levitical city assigned to the Kohathite Levites (Jos. 20:7; 21:21; 1 Ch. 6:67). The town lay in Ephraim (1 Ch. 7:28). Here the Israelites buried the bones of Joseph which they had brought from Egypt (Gn. 50:25; Jos. 24:32).

In the time of the judges, Shechem was still a centre of Canaanite worship and the temple of Baal-berith ('the lord of the covenant') features in the story of Gideon's son Abimelech (Jdg. 9:4), whose mother was a Shechemite woman. Abimelech persuaded the men of the city to make him king (Jdg. 9:6; *cf.* 8:22–23). He proceeded to slay the royal seed, but Jotham, one son who escaped the bloody purge, spoke a parable about the trees as he stood on Mt Gerizim (Jdg. 9:8–15), appealing to the citizens of Shechem to forsake Abimelech. This they did after 3 years (vv. 22–23), but Abimelech destroyed Shechem (v. 45) and then attacked the stronghold of the temple of Baal-berith and burnt it over the heads of those who sought refuge there (vv. 46–49).

After Solomon's death the assembly of Israel rejected Rehoboam at Shechem and made Jeroboam king (1 Ki. 12:1–19; 2 Ch. 10:1–11). Jeroboam restored the town and made it his capital for a time (1 Ki. 12:25), but later moved the capital to Penuel, and then to Tirzah. The town declined in importance thereafter, but continued in existence long after the fall of Samaria in 722 BC, for men from Shechem came with offerings to Jerusalem as late as 586 BC (Je. 41:5).

In post-exilic times Shechem became the chief city of the Samaritans (Ecclus. 50:26; Jos., *Ant.* 11. 340), who built a temple here. In 128 BC John Hyrcanus captured the town (Jos., *Ant.* 13. 255). In the time of the first Jewish revolt Vespasian camped near Shechem, and after the war the town was rebuilt and named Flavia Neapolis in honour of the emperor Flavius Vespasianus (hence the modern Nablus).

Important excavations conducted at Tell Balaṭa by C. Watzinger (1907–9), E. Sellin and his colleagues (between 1913 and 1934) and by G. E. Wright (1956–66) have revealed the story of this site from the mid-4th millennium BC down to *c.* 100 BC when the Hellenistic city came to an end. Although there was a sizeable Chalcolithic village during the 4th millennium BC, the city of the historical period arose *c.* 1800 BC in the Middle Bronze Age and reached the height of its prosperity during the Hyksos period (*c.* 1700–1550 BC). During these years several courtyard temples and city walls were built. About 1600 BC a massive stone wall was erected, earlier walls covered over and a fortress temple built on the filling, which was to remain with some changes till *c.* 1100 BC and may well represent in its later stages the temple of Baal-berith (Jdg. 9:4) known to the early Israelites. The town remained important until the 9th–8th centuries BC when it began to deteriorate. Masses of fallen brick and burnt debris attest the destruction of the city by the Assyrians in 724–721 BC. For 4 centuries the town reverted to a village until it gained new life, probably as a Samaritan centre, between *c.* 325 and *c.* 108 BC. There is a continuous coin record for this period. The town ceased to exist after its destruction by John Hyrcanus *c.* 108 BC.

The question of whether Shechem is the same as the *Sychar of Jn. 4:5 has not been solved. There are only a few traces of Roman occupation at Tell Balaṭa. Sychar may have lain in the same general vicinity.

Bibliography. E. F. Campbell, Jr., and J. F. Ross, *BA* 26, 1963, pp. 2–26; E. Sellin, *ZDPV*, 1926, 1927, 1928; E. Sellin and H. Steckeweh, *ZDPV*, 1941; G. E. Wright, *Shechem, The Biography of a Biblical City*, 1965; in *AOTS*, pp. 355–370; G. E. Wright *et al.*, *ISBE* 4, pp. 458–462; *NEAEHL*, pp. 1345–1359.

J.A.T.

SHEERAH (RSV), **SHERAH** (AV). The Heb. name, meaning 'a female relative', of a daughter of Ephraim, or of the daughter or sister of his son, Beriah (1 Ch. 7:24). She built or rebuilt three towns in the territory assigned to Ephraim, Lower and Upper Beth-horon and Uzzen-sheerah. This is the only example in the Bible of a woman builder of towns. Codex Vaticanus of the LXX takes this name as a common noun, 'those remaining', and the Pesh. translates the name as a verb, 'she was left', but other Gk. MSS and the Vulg. support the interpretation as a proper name.

J.T.

SHEET. 1. Heb. *sāḏîn*, RSV 'linen garments' (Jdg. 14:12–13). See reference to 'shirt' in *Dress. **2.** Gk. *othonē*, 'a piece of linen', 'a linen sheet', used in describing Peter's vision at Joppa (Acts 10:11; 11:5).

J.D.D.

SHEKINAH. The Shekinah (Heb. *šᵉḵînâ*), the radiance, glory or presence of God dwelling in the midst of his people, is used by Targumist and Rabbi to signify God himself, for legal Judaism dislikes ascribing form or emotion to deity. Nevertheless the God conceived in purified human terms inspired the noblest prophetic utterances, whereas the legalist God became cold, abstract, aloof. The

Shekinah, nearest Jewish equivalent to the Holy Spirit, became, with other OT ideas or derivatives (Word, Wisdom, Spirit, *etc.*) a bridge between man's corporeality and God's transcendence. The term is post-biblical, but the concept saturates both Testaments. It underlies the teaching that God dwells in his sanctuary (Ex. 25:8, *etc.*), or among his people (Ex. 29:45f., *etc.*). These and cognate passages use the root verb *šāḵan*, 'to dwell', from which Shekinah is derived.

The glory of God (*kāḇôḏ* in the Heb. Bible, *doxa* in LXX and NT) is another name for the Shekinah. The Heb. and Gk. words may be applied to the glory of mere human beings, such as Jacob (Gn. 31:1, AV) or Solomon (Mt. 6:29), but it is clear enough when they refer to God. Thunder, lightning and cloud may be the outward concomitants of God's glory (Ex. 19:16; 24:15ff.; Pss. 29; 97; Ezk. 1:4); or it may be specially associated with the tent of meeting (Ex. 40:34–38) or with the Temple (Ezk. 43:2, 4); but it is manifest also in creation (Ps. 19), and possesses elements more numinous and mysterious than any of these (Ex. 33:18–23). In fact, the glory of God regularly becomes more glorious when it is deliberately divorced from Temple or mercy-seat.

In the NT as in the OT, glory may be predicated of God (Lk. 2:9; Acts 7:55; 2 Cor. 3:18) or ascribed to him (Lk. 2:14; Rom. 11:36; Phil. 4:20; Rev. 7:12, *etc.*). The attribution of this glory is mentioned as a human duty, whether fulfilled (Rom. 4:20) or unfulfilled (Acts 12:23; Rev. 16:9). The glory is present in a special way in the heavenly temple (Rev. 15:8) and in the heavenly city (Rev. 21:23).

The NT freely ascribes comparable glory to Christ as divine, before as well as after the dividing-point of Easter. The Synoptics are slightly reticent about associating this glory with the earthly Jesus, except in reference to the parousia (Mk. 8:38; 10:37; 13:26; also parallels), or in reference to Christ transfigured (Lk. 9:32). John ascribes this glory much more freely (*cf.* 1:14; 2:11; 11:4); nevertheless he distinguishes a fuller or final revelation as subsequent to the earthly ministry (7:39; 12:16, *etc.*). This seeming fluctuation is not unnatural—the view of the earthly Jesus and the heavenly Christ would sometimes become foreshortened after the Passion. The cognate verb *doxazō* frequently replaces the noun (Jn. 12; 17, *etc.*). The resemblance between the Heb. word and Gk. *skēnē*, *etc.*, may suggest the *shekinah* motif in Jn. 1:14 (*eskēnōsen*, 'dwelt') and Rev. 21:3 (*skēnē*, 'dwelling').

Other passages are worthy of special attention—*cf.* 1 Tim. 3:16; Tit. 2:13; Heb. 1:3; 13:21; Jas. 2:1; 1 Pet. 1:11, 21; 4:13; 5:1; Rev 5:12f.

BIBLIOGRAPHY. See *HDB* (*s.v.* 'Shekinah'); *JewE* (*s.v.* 'Anthropomorphism', 'Shekinah'); *EJ*, 14, 1971 (*s.v.* 'Shekhinah'); G. Kittel, G. von Rad, in *TDNT* 2, pp. 237–251; R. A. Stewart, *Rabbinic Theology*, 1961, pp. 40–42. R.A.S.

SHELAH. 1. Son of Arpachshad of the family of Shem, and father of Eber (Gn. 10:24; 11:12–15; 1 Ch. 1:18, 24; Lk. 3:35). **2.** Youngest son of Judah by Shua (Gn. 38:5; 46:12; 1 Ch. 2:3; 4:21), promised by Judah to his daughter-in-law Tamar after Er and Onan had died (Gn. 38:11, 14, 26). Father of the Shelanites (Nu. 26:20). The Syr. gives 'Shelanite' for 'Shilonite' in Ne. 11:5 (*cf.* 1 Ch. 9:5). **3.** In Ne. 3:15 (RSV) the name of the pool better known as Siloam. AV gives 'Siloah'. J.G.G.N.

SHEM. The eldest son of Noah (Gn. 5:32; 6:10; 1 Ch. 1:4), and the ancestor of many descendants (Gn.10). He was one of the eight people to escape the Flood in the ark (Gn. 7:13), and after it, when Noah was drunk, he and Japheth covered their father's nakedness (Gn. 9:18, 23, 26–27). Two years after the Flood, when Shem was 100 years old, he became father of Arpachshad (Gn. 11:10), through whom passed the line of descent to the Messiah (Lk. 3:36), and it may be in reference to this fact that Noah made his prophetic statement (Gn. 9:26). Since among the descendants of Shem listed in Gn. 10:21–31 a number are identified with peoples who are known to have spoken related languages in antiquity, the term 'Semitic' has been applied for convenience to this group by modern philologists. This is a modern use of the term, however, and does not imply that all the descendants of Shem spoke Semitic languages. It is stated that Shem lived for 500 years after the birth of Arpachshad (Gn. 11:11), giving him a life of 600 years. All the major versions agree on these figures. An early theory (Poebel) has been recently revived (Kramer), to the effect that the name *šem* is derived, through various phonetic changes, from *šumer*, written *ki.en.gi* by the Sumerians, the Akkadian name of this people who formed an important element in the early population of Mesopotamia. This theory has not been widely accepted.

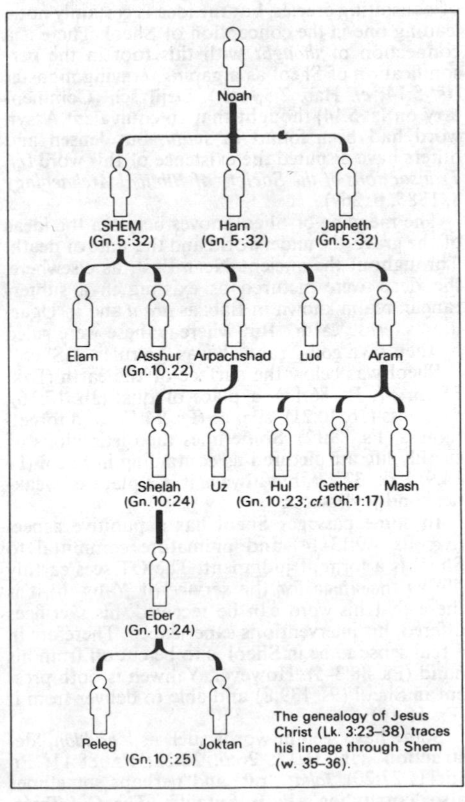

The genealogy of Shem.

Bibliography. S. N. Kramer, *Analecta Biblica* 12, 1959, pp. 203–204; *The Sumerians*, 1963, pp. 297–299. T.C.M.

SHEMUEL (Heb. *šᵉmûʼēl*, '(?) name of God'; *cf.* Samuel).

1. The son of Ammihud, leader of the tribe of Simeon, appointed to assist in the division of Canaan (Nu. 34:20). In Nu. 1:6; 2:12; 7:36, 41; 10:19 the leader of the tribe is called Shelumiel, the son of Zurishaddai, and the LXX gives the name Salamiēl in all these instances.

2. A grandson of Issachar (1 Ch. 7:2). R.A.H.G.

SHEOL. This word is used in the OT for the place of the dead. The derivation of the Heb. word *šᵉʼôl* is uncertain. Two main theories have been proposed.

a. Some have suggested that it comes from a weakened form of the root *šʻl*, from which derive the words for a hollow hand (Is. 40:12) and a hollow way (between vineyards, Nu. 22:24). In post-biblical Heb. *šaʻal* means the 'deep' of the sea. If this derivation is correct, the original sense will be the hollow, or more probably deep, place.

b. More scholars now hold the view that it is derived from the root *šʼl* meaning 'ask' or 'enquire'. In this case it may have been originally the place of enquiry, where oracles could be obtained. The root *šʼl* is frequently used in the OT of consulting oracles, but the idea is certainly not a leading one in the conception of Sheol. There is a connection of *thought* with this root in the personification of Sheol as a gaping, craving monster (Is. 5:14; *cf.* Hab. 2:5, *etc.*). Delitzsch (Commentary on Is. 5:14) thought that an equivalent Assyr. word had been found in *šualu*, but Jensen and others have disputed the existence of this word (*cf. Transactions of the Society of Biblical Archaeology* 8, 1885, p. 269).

The meaning of Sheol moves between the ideas of the grave, the underworld and the state of death. Throughout the ancient Near East, as elsewhere, the dead were pictured as existing in a subterranean realm known in Bab. as *aralu* and in Ugaritic as *'ereṣ*, 'earth'. But whereas these were ruled by their own gods, Yahweh was the ruler of Sheol.

Sheol was below the surface of the earth (Ezk. 31:15, 17; Ps. 86:13), a place of dust (Jb. 17:16), darkness (Jb. 10:21), silence (Ps. 94:17) and forgetfulness (Ps. 88:12). Sometimes the distinctions of earthly life are pictured as continuing in Sheol (Is. 14:9; Ezk. 32:27), but always it is a place of weakness and joylessness.

In some passages Sheol has a punitive aspect (*e.g.* Ps. 49:13–14) and premature committal to Sheol is a form of judgment. The OT sees earthly life as the arena for the service of Yahweh; it is there that his word can be received, his sacrifices offered, his interventions experienced. Therefore in a real sense to be in Sheol is to be cut off from his hand (Ps. 88:3–5). However, Yahweh is both present in Sheol (Ps. 139:8) and able to deliver from it (Ps. 16:10).

Some have seen in words such as *'ᵃḇaddôn*, 'destruction' (Jb. 31:12; 26:6; 28:22; Ps. 88:11; Pr. 15:11; 27:20), *šaḥaṯ*, 'pit' and perhaps sometimes also 'corruption' (E. F. Sutcliffe, *The Old Testament and the Future Life*, 1946, pp. 39f.; Jb. 33:24; Ps. 16:10; Ezk. 28:8, *etc.*) and *bôr*, 'pit' (Ps. 30:3; Ezk. 31:14), a place of punishment within Sheol. But no passage where they occur necessitates this interpretation, and the idea is not explicitly formulated in the OT. These words are better regarded as synonyms of Sheol, with which they all sometimes occur in parallelism.

In the later Jewish literature we meet with divisions within Sheol for the wicked and the righteous, in which each experiences a foretaste of his final destiny (*Enoch* 22:1–14). This idea appears to underlie the imagery of the parable of the rich man and Lazarus in Lk. 16:19–31. The Gk. *hadēs* used in this passage represents the underworld, or realm of the dead, in the classics. In the LXX it almost always translates *šᵉʼôl*, and in the NT the Pesh. renders it by *šᵉyûl*. It is therefore the NT equivalent of Sheol. It is used in connection with the death of Christ in Acts 2:27, 31, which quotes Ps. 16:10. In Mt. 16:18 Christ says that the gates of Hades (*cf.* Is. 38:10; Pss. 9:13; 107:18) shall not prevail against his church. As the gates of a city are essential to its power, the meaning here is probably the power of death. The phrase 'brought down to Hades' in Mt. 11:23 is best understood metaphorically of the depths of shame. In Rev., Christ holds the keys of Death and Hades (1:18). Their power (6:8) is broken and they are banished to the lake of fire (20:13–14).

Bibliography. R. H. Charles, *A Critical History of the Doctrine of a Future Life*, 1913; A. Heidel, *The Gilgamesh Epic and OT Parallels*, 1946, pp. 137–223; N. J. Tromp, *Primitive Conceptions of Death and the Nether World in the OT*, 1969; H. Bietenhard, in *NIDNTT* 2, pp. 205–210. D.K.I.

SHEPHELAH (Heb. *šᵉp̄ēlâ*), a geographical term for the low hill tract between the coastal plain of *Palestine and the high central ranges. The term is used only in the AV of 1 Macc. 12:38, which elsewhere translates as 'vale', 'valley' or (low) 'plain(s)', although the district is frequently referred to in the OT. The RV rendering 'lowland' (sometimes also in RSV) would give a truer picture if used in the plural form, to indicate its rolling relief of both hills and valleys. But its root-meaning ('to humble' or 'make low') suggests more accurately a district of relatively low relief at the foot of the central mountains. In RSV 'Shephelah' occurs in 1 Ki. 10:27; 1 Ch. 27:28; 2 Ch. 1:15; 9:27; 26:10; 28:18; Je. 17:26; 32:44; 33:13; Ob. 1:19. Passages such as 2 Ch. 26:10 and 28:18 clearly distinguish it from the coastal plain. The location of the 'Shephelah' of Jos. 11:2, 16 is distinct. There it refers to the hills around the town of Carmel (v. 2). 'Israelite Shephelah' in v. 16, according to G. A. Smith, may mean the land between Carmel and Samaria, a structural continuation of the true Shephelah farther S.

Bibliography. D. Baly, *The Geography of the Bible*, 1957, pp. 142–147; *LOB*. J.M.H.

SHEPHERD. Biblical shepherds may be literal or metaphorical: those in charge of sheep; those also, divine or mortal, in charge of men. Similar praise or censure may be applied to both types. The Heb. term for shepherd is the participial *rōʻeh*, the Gk. *poimēn*. Care exercised over fellow-mortals may be political or spiritual. Homer and other secular writers frequently called kings and governors shepherds (*Iliad* 1. 263; 2. 243, *etc.*), a usage reflected, in deeper metaphors, in Ezk. 34.

The literal shepherd pursued, and still pursues, an exacting calling, one as old as Abel (Gn. 4:2). He must find grass and water in a dry and stony land (Ps. 23:2), protect his charges from weather and from fiercer creatures (*cf.* Am. 3:12), and retrieve any strayed animal (Ezk. 34:8; Mt. 18:12, *etc.*). When his duties carried him far from human haunts, a bag held his immediate necessities (1 Sa. 17:40, 49), and a tent might be his dwelling (Ct. 1:8). He might use dogs to assist him, like his modern counterpart (Jb. 30:1). When shepherds and flocks take up their more permanent abode in any city, this is a mark of depopulation and disaster through divine judgment (Je. 6:3; 33:12; Zp. 2:13–15). The shepherd on duty was liable to make restitution for any sheep lost (Gn. 31:39), unless he could effectively plead circumstances beyond his foresight or control (Ex. 22:10–13). Ideally the shepherd should be strong, devoted and selfless, as many of them were. But ruffians were sometimes found in an honourable profession (Ex. 2:17, 19), and some shepherds inevitably failed in their duty (Zc. 11, *passim*; Na. 3:18; Is. 56:11, *etc.*).

Such is the honour of the calling that the OT frequently delineates God as the Shepherd of Israel (Gn. 49:24; Pss. 23:1; 80:1), tender in his solicitude (Is. 40:11), yet able to scatter the flock in wrath, or gather it again in forgiveness (Je. 31:10). Sometimes the note is predominantly one of judgment, when human shepherd and sheep alike stand condemned and punished (Je. 50:6; 51:23; Zc. 13:7; and Gospel applications). These unfaithful shepherds may well tremble to stand before the Lord (Je. 49:19; 50:44). Sometimes there is a note of compassion when the sheep are deserted by those responsible for them (Nu. 27:17; 1 Ki. 22:17; Mk. 6:34, *etc.*). Two shepherds mentioned with special approval are Moses (Is. 63:11) and, surprisingly enough, that heathen executor of God's purposes, Cyrus (Is. 44:28). Scripture earnestly stresses the serious responsibility of human leaders to those who follow them. One of the most solemn chapters in the OT is the denunciation of the faithless shepherds in Ezk. 34 (*cf.* Je. 23:1–4, and even more sternly Je. 25:32–38). These, for their belly's sake, have fed themselves and not their sheep; they have killed and scattered their charges for their own profit; they have grievously neglected their proper pastoral care; therefore God will re-gather the sheep and judge the shepherds. He will in fact appoint one shepherd (Ezk. 34:23). This is critically interpreted as signifying the union of the N and S kingdoms, but it portrays much better the expected Christ.

In the NT it is Christ's mission to be Shepherd, even Chief Shepherd (Heb. 13:20 and 1 Pet. 2:25; also 1 Pet. 5:4). This is worked out in detail in Jn. 10, which merits detailed comparison with Ezk. 34. John's main points are: the iniquity of those who 'creep, and intrude and climb into the fold'; the using of the door as a mark of the true shepherd; the familiarity of the sheep with the voice of their appointed leader (modern shepherds in the E use precisely the same methods); the teachings regarding the Person of Christ, who is likened to the door (E shepherds frequently slept right across the 'door' or opening in the fold wall); likened to the good shepherd, but contrasted with the worthless hireling. John stresses also the relationship of Christ, his followers and God; the bringing into the 'one flock' of the 'other sheep' (v. 16); and the rejection of those who are not the true sheep of Christ. (*Cf.* Milton, *Lycidas*, esp. lines 113–131.)

BIBLIOGRAPHY. E. Beyreuther, in *NIDNTT* 3, pp. 564–569; J. Jeremias, in *TDNT* 6, pp. 485–502; J. Beutler and R. T. Fortna, *The Shepherd Discourse of John 10 and Its Context*, 1991. R.A.S.

SHESHACH. Probably an artificial word (Je. 25:26; 51:41, AV, RSV mg.), formed by the device known as Athbash. The Eng. equivalent would be to replace *a* by *z*, *b* by *y*, *c* by *x*, *etc.* The Heb. consonants *š-š-k*, then, really represent *b-b-l*, *i.e.* *bāḇel*, 'Babylon'. The vowels have no value. The device is here word-play, not cipher, since Je. 51:41 later mentions Babylon explicitly. Possibly, however, Sheshach was a genuine name for Babylon. D.F.P.

SHESHBAZZAR. The person made governor (Heb. *nāśî*, 'prince') of Judah by Cyrus (Ezr. 1:8), to whom the temple vessels captured by Nebuchadrezzar II were entrusted for return to Jerusalem (Ezr. 5:14–15). His name may represent the Bab. *Šaššu-aba-uṣur* ('May Šaššu/Shamash protect the father'). His role and identity have been much discussed, some taking this as another, perhaps court, name for *Zerubbabel, others that he was the Bab. official leader of the returning party of Jewish exiles. He may well be the person entitled *Tirshatha in Ezr. 2:63; Ne. 7:65, 70. An identity with Shenazzar (Gk. *Sanesar*; *cf.* 1 Esdr. 2:11), an uncle of Zerubbabel (1 Ch. 3:8) is unlikely (P.-R. Berger, *ZAW* 83, 1971, pp. 98–100). D.J.W.

SHIBAH. The name of a well dug by Isaac's servants and named Shibah (Heb. *šiḇ'â*), or Shebah (Gn. 26:33, AV), because of a covenant with Abimelech. The word itself means 'seven' or 'oath'. Already, before Isaac's time, Abraham had encountered trouble with Abimelech king of Gerar and had finally entered into a covenant (Gn. 21:22–34). Seven ewe lambs were presented to Abimelech as a witness to the fact, and Abraham preserved the memory of this covenant by calling the place Beersheba ('well of seven', 'well of an oath'). Isaac revived the old name, using the feminine form *šiḇ'â* of the word *šeḇā'*. J.A.T.

SHIBBOLETH. A test-word by which the Gileadites under Jephthah detected the defeated Ephraimites who tried to escape across the Jordan after the battle (Jdg. 12:5–6). Since in the Ephraim local Semitic dialect initial *sh* became *s*, their true identity was disclosed when they pronounced *šibbōleṯ* as *sibbōleṯ*. Both words mean 'a stream in flood' (*cf.* Ps. 69:2; Is. 27:12), though the former is also apt to be confused with *šibbōleṯ*, 'an ear of corn'. Those Ephraimites who were thus discovered were slain immediately (v. 6). In modern usage the word stands for the catchword or mark of a sect or party, often used disparagingly. D.J.W.

SHIHOR-LIBNATH. A small river forming part of the S boundary of the tribe of Asher (Jos. 19:26). Probably the modern Nahr ez-Zerqa, which runs S of Mt Carmel (*EGYPT, RIVER OF). See

GTT, p. 190, n. 78; L. H. Grollenberg, *Atlas of the Bible*, 1957, pp. 58–59. Aharoni (*LOB*, pp. 237–238) argued for the *Kishon. T.C.M.

SHILOH. According to Jdg. 21:19, Shiloh is situated 'north of Bethel, on the east of the highway that goes up from Bethel to Shechem, and south of Lebonah'. This identifies it as the modern Seilun about 14 km N of Bethel (Beitin) and 5 km SE of el-Lubban. The site was excavated by Danes between 1926 and 1932, and by Finkelstein, 1981–84. A fortified town with a glacis existed in the Middle Bronze Age (2100–1600 BC); following its destruction, occupation existed on a reduced scale until about 1200 BC when an Israelite settlement was constructed which included complexes of storehouses on the slopes of the MBA glacis. The site was destroyed about 1050 BC, probably by the Philistines. No sign was found of a temple from this period.

According to the biblical record, it was at Shiloh that the tent of meeting was set up in the early days of the Conquest (Jos. 18:1), and it was the principal sanctuary of the Israelites during the time of the Judges (Jdg. 18:31). It was the site of a local annual festival of dancing in the vineyards, perhaps at the Feast of Ingathering (Ex. 23:16), which once provided the men of Benjamin with an opportunity to seize the maidens for wives (Jdg. 21:19ff.), and this festival probably developed into the annual pilgrimage in which Samuel's parents were later to take part (1 Sa. 1:3). By the time of Eli and his sons the sanctuary had become a well-established structure for centralized worship, and the tent of Joshua had been replaced by a temple (*hêḵāl*) with door and door-posts (1 Sa. 1:9). Although Scripture does not refer directly to its destruction, it is possible from archaeological evidence that this did take place and this would fit in well with the references to Shiloh as an example of God's judgment upon his people's wickedness (Ps. 78:60; Je. 7:12, 14; 26:6, 9). On the other hand, Ahijah the Shilonite is mentioned in 1 Ki. 11:29; 14:2, and other inhabitants of Shiloh in Je. 41:5. Some limited habitation must have continued after 1050 BC, but the priesthood transferred to Nob (1 Sa. 22:11; *cf.* 14:3) and Shiloh ceased to be a religious centre.

A reference of peculiar difficulty comes in Gn. 49:10, 'the sceptre shall not depart from Judah, nor the ruler's staff from between his feet, until Shiloh come' (RV). The Heb. *'aḏ kî-yāḇō' šîlōh* can be rendered in several ways. (i) As RV, taking Shiloh as a Messianic title. (ii) As RVmg. 'till he come to Shiloh', with the subject as Judah and the fulfilment in the assembling of Israel to Shiloh in Jos. 18:1, when the tribe of Judah nobly relinquished the pre-eminence it had formerly enjoyed. (iii) By emending *šîlōh* to *šellōh* and translating with the LXX 'until that which is his shall come', *i.e.* 'the things reserved for him', a vaguely Messianic hope. (iv) By emending *šîlōh* to *šay lô*, as in NEB, 'so long as tribute is paid to him'. (v) Following a variant reading in LXX, 'until he comes to whom it belongs' (RSV), whatever 'it' may be (Onkelos says it is the kingdom).

The last of these was generally favoured by the Fathers, while the first does not seem to have been put forward seriously until the 16th century except in one doubtful passage in the Talmud. Against (i) is its uniqueness: nowhere else is Shiloh used as a title for the Messiah and the NT does not recognize it as a prophecy. If it were taken as a title it would have to mean something like 'the peace-giver', but this is not very natural linguistically. (ii) is plausible, but it scarcely fits in with what we know of the subsequent history of Judah; nor is it usual for a patriarchal blessing to have such a time-limit. A variant to get round that objection is the translation 'as long as people come to Shiloh', *i.e.* 'for ever', but it strains the Heb. (iii), (iv) and (v) involve a minor emendation, and the renderings leave much to the imagination, but Ezk. 21:27 (v. 32 in Heb.) shows that a similar construction can stand; indeed, Ezk. 21:27 is probably a deliberate echo and interpretation of Gn. 49:10. The use of *še-* for the relative particle is, however, normally regarded as late (but *cf.* Jdg. 5:7).

For reviews of the possible interpretations, see especially the commentaries of J. Skinner and E. A. Speiser; an interesting theory by J. Lindblom is found in *VT Supp*. 1 (= Congress Volume, 1953), pp. 78–87. For archaeological information, see H. Kjaer, 'Shiloh 1981', *IEJ* 32, 1982; I. Finkelstein, *Tel Aviv* 12, 1985, pp. 123–180; *idem. BAR* 12, 1986; A. S. Kaufman, 'The Site of the Tabernacle at Shiloh', *BAR* 14, 1988, pp. 46f.; *NEAEHL*, pp. 1364–1370. J.B.Tr.
J.W.

SHIMEATH. In 2 Ki. 12:21 an Ammonitess, the mother of Jozacar (called Zabad in 2 Ch. 24:26), one of the murderers of Joash. J.D.D.

SHIMEI (Heb. *šim'î*, perhaps abridged from *š^ema'yāhû*, 'Yahweh has heard'). The OT records 19 men named Shimei. The first of note was a grandson of Levi (Nu. 3:21), and his family (the Shimeites) had part of the responsibility for maintaining the tent of meeting as their sacred charge (Nu. 3:25–26).

The best-known is Shimei the son of Gera, a Benjaminite and a kinsman of Saul, who cursed David for being a man of blood (2 Sa. 16:5ff.). The reference appears to be twofold: *a.* to David's conciliation of the Gibeonites (2 Sa. 21:1–10) by delivering to them seven of Saul's sons and grandsons to be hanged for Saul's slaughter of the Gibeonites (v. 1); *b.* to Absalom's rebellion, which would bring an end to David's reign, a just recompense for the blood of Saul's house which had been shed before the union of Judah and Israel; in fact David had not been responsible for the killings (2 Sa. 3:6–27; 4:8–11). David seems to have accepted this meekly, believing that Shimei spoke an admonition from the Lord (2 Sa. 16:11–12), as if acknowledging that at all events he was the occasion of the deaths. Later in life, however, David concluded that Shimei had sown dissension, and was not therefore a guiltless man (1 Ki. 2:8–9). Solomon showed clemency to Shimei, giving him a place in Jerusalem; but, to take revenge on Shimei for his bitterness towards David, had him slain, after 3 years, on the (wrong) grounds of his suspected complicity with the Philistines of Gath (1 Ki. 2:36–46). C.H.D.

SHIMRON-MERON. A Canaanite city whose king was allied with Hazor (Jos. 11:1, simply 'Shimron') and so defeated by Joshua in his Galilean war

(Jos. 12:20); probably identical with Shimron in the territory assigned to Zebulun, in the Bethlehem district (Jos. 19:15). If so, it is possibly the present Tell es-Semuniyeh, about 5 km SSE of Bethlehem, but this is disputed (see A. F. Rainey, *Tel Aviv*, 3.2, 1976, pp. 57–69). *Merom in 'Waters of Merom' is quite distinct from Shimron-meron. Whether Shimron should be identified with the *Šmw'nw/Šm'n* of the Egyp. lists of the 18th and 15th centuries BC (the Šamḫuna of the El-Amarna letters) through the LXX form *Symoōn* is highly doubtful. K.A.K.

SHINAR. The land in which were situated the great cities of Babylon, Erech and Akkad (Gn. 10:10). It lay in a plain to which early migrants came to found the city and tower of Babel (Gn. 11:2) and was a place of exile for the Jews (Is. 11:11; Dn. 1:2). The LXX interprets it as 'Babylonia' (Is. 11:11) or the 'land of Babylon' (Zc. 5:11), and this accords with the location implied in Gn. 10:10. (*ACCAD or Agade, which gave its name to N Babylonia.) Heb. *šin'ār* represents *šanhar* of cuneiform texts from the Hittite and Syrian scribal schools of the 2nd millennium BC, and was certainly a name for Babylonia. This equation is proved by several texts (see H. G. Güterbock, *JCS* 18, 1964, p. 3; R. Zadok, *ZA* 74, 1984, pp. 240–244), ruling out older ideas. D.J.W.

SHIPS AND BOATS. Rafts constructed from bundles of reeds were in use from a very early period in both Egypt and Mesopotamia and appear as an early pictographic sign on a clay tablet from *c.* 3500 BC. The raft has remained a popular craft in the marshes of S Mesopotamia. A clay model of a boat found at Eridu from *c.* 3500 BC is very similar to the round coracle (*quffa*) made from wood and hide depicted in Assyr. relief sculpture of *c.* 870 BC and which remain in use on the river Euphrates. Rafts of skins, inflated or stuffed with straw, are another ancient craft with a long and continuous history. Official transport in Sumer, however, was undertaken in vessels with high swinging stems and sterns which were propelled by paddles or poles or maybe on occasions towed from the bank. A model of this type of craft was found in a tomb at Fara from *c.* 3000 BC, enabling a reliable reconstruction of the hull shape which also appears on Sumerian cylinder seals and in Egyp. carvings of the same period. During the 3rd millennium, overseas trade developed from Mesopotamia through the Persian Gulf and into the N Indian Ocean. One text from *c.* 2000 BC mentions a craft weighing 300 *gur* (28,400 kg or 28 tonnes).

In Egypt the earliest wooden boats were replicas of reed craft, and although hull shape developed to suit timber, decorative motifs such as lotus bud ends common on reed vessels continue. The oldest actual Egyp. boat was found adjacent to the pyramid of Cheops at Giza (*c.* 2600 BC) and is 43.4 m long; two others, about 10 m in length, were found at Dahshur and belong to the 12th Dynasty (1991–1786 BC). The absence of good timber in Egypt necessitated its importation from Lebanon and so seagoing ships were developed. The presence of Egyp. vessels along the coast of Palestine gives force to Moses' warning that Israel may return to Egypt by ship (Dt. 28:68) especially as Asiatic slaves are depicted being transported to Egypt in ships as early as in the reign of Sahuré, *c.* 2500 BC. Expeditions were also made on the Red Sea in ships of about 30 m length and powered by sail and oars. Early Egyp. seagoing ships were kept rigid by a rope truss which passed around each end of the vessel and over forked sticks above the deck where it was tensioned like a tourniquet.

I. In the Old Testament

The tribes of Zebulun, Issachar, Dan and Asher had at some time seaside territories (Gn. 49:13; Dt. 33:19; Jdg. 5:17) and Israel's neighbours, the *Phoenicians and *Philistines, were leading maritime powers. The ship, however, remained a source of wonder for the Hebrews (Pr. 30:19) and a safe passage was considered a demonstration of God's goodness and power (Ps. 107:23–30). A ship's motion was reminiscent of the drunkard (Pr. 23:34) and its swift transit like the passing of life (Jb. 9:26).

The general Heb. word for ship, *'ᵒniyyâ*, refers most commonly to seagoing merchant vessels (*e.g.* Pr. 31:14) which are often described as 'ships of Tarshish' (1 Ki. 22:48f.). Whether or not *Tarshish is to be identified with a geographical location such as Tartessus in S Spain or Tarsus in Cilicia or is thought to mean something like 'ore-carrier', the ship so described is a Phoenician long-range merchantman. Barnett (*Antiquity* 32, 1958, p. 226) believes that the Phoenician transport vessels with round bows depicted on relief sculptures of Sennacherib (*c.* 700 BC) are 'ships of Tarshish', but the absence of sail makes this identification questionable. Phoenician shipping developed during the 2nd millennium BC and is known to us from Egyp. tomb paintings and from texts. The paintings reveal that, unlike contemporary Egyp. ships, Canaanite (early Phoenician) vessels were built with a keel and had a fence-like structure along the deck, which some believe acted as a lee cloth, while others believe that it barricaded the cargo. A document from Ras Shamra, *c.* 1200 BC, refers to one of these merchantmen as having a cargo of 457,000 kg (450 tonnes) with no indication that it was at all unusual. Such a large vessel had to rely on sail power and could be rowed only for brief periods in an emergency.

The ship that Jonah embarked on at Joppa is called a *sᵉpînâ* (Jon. 1:5), which may indicate that it was a large vessel with a deck, possibly similar to a Gk. merchantman painted on a cup of *c.* 550 BC. It was manned by sailors, Heb. *mallāḥîm* (Jon. 1:5) and captained by one called *raḇ hahōḇēl* (Jon. 1:6), the 'chief pilot'.

Smaller vessels were used by the Phoenicians for short-range cargo assignments. These vessels were paddled and were distinctive because of their high stem and stern posts, one of which bore the carved head of a horse and so they were naturally called *hippos* by the Greeks. An Assyr. relief sculpture, *c.* 710 BC, depicts these vessels in a logging operation which was no doubt similar to that undertaken by King Hiram of Tyre for Solomon (1 Ki. 5:9).

Another Heb. word for ship, *ṣî*, would appear to apply specifically to warships. This vessel is mentioned with a 'galley with oars', *'ᵒnî šayiṭ* (Is. 33:21), where it is stated that no such ship will approach Jerusalem when the city is at peace. These warships had streamlined hulls being built for speed and with a ram at the front. In order to shorten the vessel and increase its manoeuvrability without losing speed, the oarsmen, *šāṭîm* (Ezk. 27:8), were double-banked on each side. The Greeks were particularly skilful at fighting in these vessels, which may be referred to as the feared 'ships of Kittim' (Dn. 11:30; *cf.* Nu. 24:24). Because of their speed warships were particularly suited for delivering urgent messages over water (Ezk. 30:9; Thucydides 3. 49. 3).

BIBLIOGRAPHY. G. Bass, *A History of Seafaring*, 1972; B. Landström, *The Ship*, 1971; L. Casson, *Ships and Seamanship in the Ancient World*, 1971; N. Avigad, 'A Hebrew Seal Depicting a Sailing Ship', *BASOR* 246, 1982, pp. 59–62 (8–7 cent. BC); R. R. Stieglitz, 'Long Distance Seafaring in the Ancient Near East', *BA* 47, 1984, pp. 134–142; *BA* 53, 1990, pp. 13–18; *BAR* 18, 1992, pp. 25–33.

C.J.D.

II. In the New Testament

a. On the Sea of Galilee

The Galilean boats were used mainly for *fishing (*e.g.* Mt. 4:21f.; Mk. 1:19f.; Jn. 21:3ff.), but also generally for communications across the lake (*e.g.* Mt. 8:23ff.; 9:1; 14:13ff.; Mk. 8:10ff.). Our Lord sometimes preached from a boat so that his voice might not be restricted by the crowd's pressing too close (Mk. 4:1; Lk. 5:2f.).

These vessels were not large: one could accommodate Jesus and his disciples (*e.g.* Mk. 8:10), but an unusually large catch of fish enclosed by a single net was enough to overload two of them (Lk. 5:7). While they were no doubt fitted with sails, they were regularly equipped with oars to enable them to progress in calm weather and in the heavy storms which occasionally sweep across the lake (Mk. 6:48; Jn. 6:19).

b. On the Mediterranean

The main characteristics of Mediterranean ships had changed little over several centuries. Warships ('long ships', their length being eight or ten times their width) were regularly propelled by oars and rarely went far from the coast. Merchant ships ('round ships', their length being three or four times their width) relied on sails, but might carry some oars for emergencies. Under favourable conditions they would cross the open sea (*PATARA). Most seagoing ships were of between 70 and 300 tonnes, but Pliny mentions one of apparently 1,300 tonnes.

Most of Paul's missionary voyages were probably undertaken in small coastal vessels, but on his journey to Rome he sailed in two of the great grain ships plying between Egypt and Italy, which might easily carry a complement of 276 crew and passengers (Acts 27:37). About the same period Josephus travelled in a ship carrying 600 (*Vita* 15). Lucian (*Navigium* 1ff.) gives a description of a large grain ship of AD 150; and in recent years underwater archaeologists have examined a number of ancient wrecks. Thus we can get some idea of Paul's 'Twin Brothers' (*CASTOR AND POLLUX). Such a ship would have a central mast with long yard-arms carrying a large square mainsail and possibly a small topsail, and a small foremast sloping forward almost like a bowsprit, with a foresail (Gk. *artemōn*) which might be used to give the ship steerage way when it was not desired to take full advantage of the wind (Acts 27:40), and to head the ship round and check drifting in a storm (in Acts 27:17 'lowered the gear' may mean 'set the foresail' or 'let out a sea-anchor' or 'let down the mast-top gear'). By bracing the sails these ships could sail within about 7 points of the wind.

The bows were swept up to a carved or painted figure to represent the name of the ship (Acts 28:11), and on the stern, which was also raised, generally into a goose-neck shape, was a statue of the patron deity of the vessel's home port. Two large oars in the stern served as rudders, either operated separately or rotated together by means of tiller bars or ropes attached to a central piece of gear. These could be lashed in position in bad weather (*cf.* Acts 27:40).

Some anchors were wholly of iron, but most had a wooden stock with lead or stone arms. They might weigh more than 600 kg, and had small marker-buoys attached. There would be three or more on board, and when anchoring off a beach one or two of them would be let down from the bows, mooring cables from the stern being attached to the shore. For manoeuvring or riding out a gale, however, anchors might be let out from the stern (Acts 27:29). A sounding-lead was used to check the depth when near shallows (Acts 27:28), and might be greased to bring up samples of the bottom.

A dinghy was towed astern in good weather, but hoisted on board in a storm (Acts 27:16f.) to prevent its being swamped or smashed. This was for use in harbour rather than as a lifeboat: if the ship was wrecked, survivors had to rely on spars. Paul had been shipwrecked three times before his journey to Rome (2 Cor. 11:25).

The risks of any voyage were great, but so were the profits if it was successful (*cf.* Rev. 18:19). The owner often commanded his ship, perhaps with the assistance of a professional steersman or navigator; but in doubtful situations the passengers might share in making decisions (Acts 27:9–12: the centurion was responsible for his party, not for the ship). There might be as many as three decks on a large merchantman, and some luxuriously fitted cabins, but most passengers camped on deck or in the hold.

Ships were normally dismasted and laid up to avoid the winter storms from mid-November to mid-February (Acts 20:3, 6; 28:11; 1 Cor. 16:6ff.; 2 Tim. 4:21; Tit. 3:12), and periods of about a month before and after this season were considered dangerous (Acts 27:9). The main difficulty seems to have been the obscuring of the sky by storm clouds, thus making navigation by the sun and stars impossible. Delays due to weather were common. According to Josephus (*BJ* 2. 203) one letter from the emperor Gaius in Rome to Petronius in Judaea took 3 months to get there (*SAMOTHRACE).

There is some doubt about the meaning of 'undergirding the ship' in Acts 27:17. The traditional, and most likely, view is frapping, that is, passing ropes under the ship, from side to side, to hold its timbers firm; but some explain it as the use of a hogging truss (unlikely in a large ship with decks to strengthen it), or horizontal cables round the hull.

Our knowledge of Greeco-Roman boats is extended by finds from underwater archaeology and boats raised. Construction techniques and equipment such as anchors are now well known. A 26-foot fishing boat with angular bow and high stern dating from the time of Jesus (*c.* 120 BC–AD 40) has been found near Ginosar, Galilee. It had a mast, could be rowed by four people (*cf.* Mk. 1:20) and is similar to that shown on a 2nd-century mosaic from nearby Migdal.

c. Figurative use

Nautical metaphors are rare in the NT. In Heb. 6:19 hope is called 'an anchor of the soul'; and Jas. 3:4–5 compares the tongue with a ship's rudder.

BIBLIOGRAPHY. L. Casson, *Ships and Seamanship in the Ancient World*, 1971; J. Smith, *The Voyage and Shipwreck of St. Paul*[4], 1880; C. Torr, *Ancient Ships*[2], 1964; K. L. McKay, *Proceedings of the Classical Association* 61, 1964, pp. 25f.; H. J. Cadbury in *BC*, 5, pp. 345ff.; S. Wachsmann, 'Excavations of an Ancient Boat in the Sea of Galilee', *'Atiqot* 19, 1990, 'The Galilee Boat', *BAR* 19, 1988, pp. 19–33; *BA* 53, pp. 46–53; E. Linder, 'Excavating an Ancient Merchantman', *BAR* 18, 1992, pp. 204–235.

D.J.W.
K.L.McK.

SHISHAK. Libyan prince who founded Egypt's 22nd Dynasty as the Pharaoh Sheshonq I. He reigned for 21 years, *c.* 945–924 BC. He harboured Jeroboam as a fugitive from Solomon, after Ahijah's prophecy of Jeroboam's future kingship (1 Ki. 11:29–40). Late in his reign, Shishak invaded Palestine in the 5th year of Rehoboam, 925 BC. He subdued Judah, taking the treasures of Jerusalem as tribute (1 Ki. 14:25–26; 2 Ch. 12:2–12), and also asserted his dominion over Israel, as is evidenced by a broken stele of his from Megiddo. At the temple of Amūn in Thebes, Shishak left a triumphal relief-scene, naming many Palestinian towns; see *ANEP*, p. 118, fig. 349, p. 290. See also *LIBYA, *SUKKIIM. For Shishak's invasion, see K. A. Kitchen, *The Third Intermediate Period in Egypt*[2], 1986.

K.A.K.

SHITTIM. 1. One of the names given to the final Israelite encampment before they crossed the Jordan, opposite Jericho (Nu. 25:1; Jos. 2:1; 3:1; *cf.* Mi. 6:5). Nu. 33:49 uses a longer form of the name, Abel-shittim ('the brook(?) of the acacias', since *šiṭṭîm* means 'acacias'), for one extremity of the camp. Josephus mentions a city of his time called Abila, which was 60 stades from the Jordan in this general area (*Ant.* 5. 4), which appears to represent the element 'Abel' of this name. Abila was probably located at Tell el-Hammam (Glueck, Aharoni),

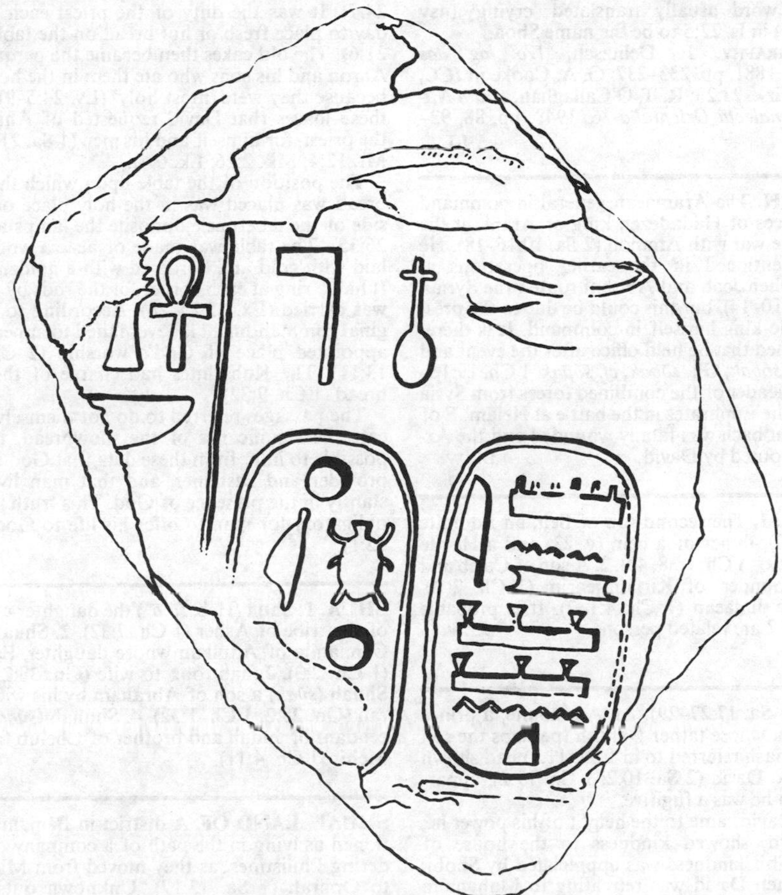

The name of Pharaoh Shishak is shown in Egyptian hieroglyphs on this fragment of a triumphal inscription found at Megiddo. c. 926 BC.

though other scholars have preferred Tell el-Kefrein, which lies a little to the NW. See *IDB*, 4, p. 339.

2. The 'valley of Shittim/acacias' in Joel 3:18, which is to be watered by a stream flowing from the Temple (*cf.* Ezk. 47:1–12), cannot be the same place, because a location for it W of the Jordan is required. It is most likely to be either a general term for the wadis of the Judaean wilderness or a name for the lower part of the Kidron valley, which leads into the Dead Sea from the W (rather than referring to the Wadi es-Sanṭ).

BIBLIOGRAPHY. H. W. Wolff, *Joel and Amos* (*Hermeneia*), on Joel 4:18 (3:18). For Shittim wood see *TREES (Acacia). G.I.D.

SHOA. Ezekiel (23:23) prophesies that this people, together with other dwellers in Mesopotamia, will attack Jerusalem. Shoa has been identified with the people called *Sutu* or *Su* in Akkadian sources, though some now question this identification. According to the Amarna letters, they were Semitic nomads living in the Syrian desert in the 14th century BC. Later they migrated to the area E of Baghdad, and Assyr. records often mention them with the *Qutu*, called Koa in Ezk. 23:23, as warring against Assyria. Some scholars (*e.g.* O. Procksch) take the word usually translated 'crying' (RSV 'shouting') in Is. 22:5 to be the name Shoa.

BIBLIOGRAPHY. F. Delitzsch, *Wo lag das Paradies?*, 1881, pp. 233–237; G. A. Cooke in *ICC*, 1936, on Ezk. 23:23; R. T. O'Callaghan, *Aram Naharaim, Analecta Orientalia* 26, 1948, pp. 88, 92–98, 101. J.T.

SHOBACH. The Aramaean general in command of the forces of Hadadezer, king of Aram, at the time of the war with Ammon (2 Sa. 10:16–18). He is not mentioned in the earlier operations at Rabbah when Joab and Abishai routed the Syrian army (vv. 10–14), but this could be due to the presence of the king himself in command. It is therefore assumed that he held office after the event and is named (*šôḇaḵ*; Gk. *sōbak*; *cf.* *šôp̄aḵ*, 1 Ch. 19:16–18) as the leader of the combined forces from Syria and E of the Euphrates in the battle at Helam, E of Jordan. Shobach was fatally wounded and the Aramaeans routed by David. D.J.W.

SHOBAL. 1. The second son of Seir, an Edomite (Gn. 36:20), father of a clan (v. 23) and a Horite leader (v. 29 = 1 Ch. 1:38, 40). **2.** A son of Caleb and 'father' (founder' of Kiriath-jearim (1 Ch. 2:50, 52), also a Judaean (1 Ch. 4:1–2). It is probable that **1** and **2** are related persons. D.J.W.

SHOBI (2 Sa. 17:27–29). An Ammonite, a prince of Rabbah, whose father Nahash (perhaps the son of the Nahash referred to in 1 Sa. 11:1) had shown kindness to David (2 Sa. 10:2; 1 Ch. 19:2), apparently when he was a fugitive.

When David came to the height of his power he, in his turn, showed kindness to the house of Nahash. This kindness was appreciated by Shobi, so that when David was retreating to Mahanaim before Absalom, Shobi was one of those who provided rest and refreshment for David's company. C.H.D.

SHOVEL (Heb. *yā'*). Bronze shovels were made for clearing ashes from off the altar of burnt-offering (Ex. 27:3) and later by Hiram for Solomon's Temple (1 Ki. 7:40, 45). Some Canaanite shovels have been discovered, *e.g.* at Megiddo (*BA* 4, 1941, p. 29 and fig. 9).

Heb. *raḥaṯ* is mentioned in Is. 30:24; it was probably wooden. (*FAN, *AGRICULTURE.) A.R.M.

SHOWBREAD. Heb. *leḥem happānîm*, lit. 'bread of the face', *i.e.* bread set before the face or presence of God (Ex. 25:30; 35:13; 39:36, *etc.*) or *leḥem hamma 'areḵeṯ*, lit. 'bread of ordering' (1 Ch. 9:32, *etc.*). After Moses had received divine instructions concerning the making of a table, dishes, spoons, covers and bowls for the holy place of the tabernacle, he was directed to place 'showbread' on the table. This arrangement was never to cease (Ex. 25:30). The showbread consisted of twelve baked cakes, made of fine flour, each containing two-tenths of an ephah (*WEIGHTS AND MEASURES). These were set in two rows, six to a row (*ma'areḵeṯ*, Lv. 24:6). Upon each row (lit. 'the row', Lv. 24:7) of cakes frankincense was placed 'as a memorial' (*le'azkārâ*) and was offered by fire to the Lord (Lv. 24:7). It was the duty of the priest each sabbath day to place fresh or hot bread on the table (1 Sa. 21:6). The old cakes then became the perquisite of Aaron and his sons who ate them in the holy place because they were 'most holy' (Lv. 24:5–9). It was these loaves that David requested of Ahimelech, the priest, for himself and his men (1 Sa. 21:1–6; *cf.* Mt. 12:4; Mk. 2:26; Lk. 6:4).

The position of the table upon which the showbread was placed was in the holy place on the N side of the tabernacle opposite the lampstand (Ex. 26:35). The table was made of acacia wood overlaid with gold and bordered with a golden crown. It had a ring at each corner for the rods by which it was carried (Ex. 25:23–28). According to the original commandment it never failed to appear in the appointed place of God's worship (2 Ch. 4:19; 13:11). The Kohathites had charge of the showbread (1 Ch. 9:32).

The passages referred to do not themselves indicate the significance of the showbread, but it is possible to infer from these data that God is man's provider and sustainer, and that man lives constantly in the presence of God. This truth makes it obligatory for man to offer his life to God (Rom. 12:1). D.F.

SHUA. 1. Shua (Heb. *šû'ā'*) the daughter of Heber of the tribe of Asher (1 Ch. 7:32). **2.** Shua (*šûa'*) a Canaanite of Adullam whose daughter, Bathshua (1 Ch. 2:3), Judah took to wife (Gn. 38:2, 12). **3.** Shuah (*šûaḥ*) a son of Abraham by his wife Keturah (Gn. 25:2; 1 Ch. 1:32). **4.** Shuhah (*šûḥâ*) a descendant of Judah and brother of Chelub father of Mehir (1 Ch. 4:11). T.C.M.

SHUAL, LAND OF. A district in Benjamin mentioned as lying in the path of a company of plundering Philistines, as they moved from Michmash to Ophrah (1 Sa. 13:17). Unknown outside the Bible, but probably near Michmash. Shual ('fox') is identified by some with Shaalim where Saul searched for lost donkeys (1 Sa. 9:4). T.C.M.

SHULAMMITE. A feminine noun (*šûlammîṯ*) applied to the heroine in Ct. 6:13, 'Shulammite' has been a formidable problem to scholars. Some (*e.g.* Koehler's *Lexicon*) have connected it with an unknown town, Shulam; some (*e.g. ISBE*) classify it as a variant of Shunammite (below); others (*e.g.* L. Waterman and H. Torczyner) identify the Shulammite with *Abishag, the Shunammite. E. J. Goodspeed (*AJSL* 50, 1934, pp. 102ff.) and H. H. Rowley (*AJSL* 56, 1939, pp. 84–91) deny any connection with Shunem but view the word as a feminine counterpart of Solomon, 'the Solomoness'. Attempts have been made to derive the names Solomon and Shulammite from the god Shelem. See H. H. Rowley, *The Servant of the Lord*, 1952, p. 223. D.A.H.

SHUNEM, SHUNAMMITE. A town (probably modern Solem) in the territory of Issachar near Jezreel (Jos. 19:18), Shunem (*šûnēm*) was the site of the Philistine camp before the battle of Gilboa (1 Sa. 28:4).

Elisha sojourned in Shunem frequently in the home of a generous woman (called the Shunammite, a feminine adjective derived from Shunem) whose son, born according to Elisha's prediction, was miraculously raised up by the prophet after being smitten with sun-stroke (2 Ki. 4:8ff.). It is this woman whose property was restored at Gehazi's behest after she had temporarily abandoned it to seek relief from famine in Philistia (2 Ki. 8:1–6). From Shunem also David's men brought the beautiful *Abishag to comfort their aged king (1 Ki. 1:3, 15). Adonijah's request for her hand in marriage cost him his life (1 Ki. 2:17, 21–22). (*SHULAMMITE.) D.A.H.

SHUR. A wilderness-region in the NW part of the Sinai isthmus, S of the Mediterranean coastline and the 'way of the land of the Philistines', between the present line of the Suez Canal on its W and the 'River of *Egypt' (Wadi el-'Arish) on its E. Abraham and Sarah's handmaid Hagar fled to a well past Kadesh on the way to Shur (Gn. 16:7).

For a time Abraham 'dwelt between Kadesh and Shur' and then sojourned at Gerar (Gn. 20:1); Ishmael's descendants ranged over an area that reached as far as 'Shur, which is opposite [*i.e.* E of] Egypt' (Gn. 25:18). After passing through the sea (*RED SEA), Israel entered the wilderness of Shur before going S into Sinai (Ex. 15:22). Shur lay on the direct route to Egypt from S Palestine (1 Sa. 15:7 and, most explicitly, 27:8). K.A.K.

SIBMAH. A town wrested from Sihon king of the Amorites and allotted by Moses to the tribe of Reuben (*śibmâ*, Jos. 13:19, 21). It is identical with Sebam ('Shebam', AV); possibly its name was changed when it was rebuilt (Nu. 32:3, 38). By the time of Isaiah and Jeremiah, who bewailed its devastation, it had reverted to the Moabites (Is. 16:8–9; Je. 48:32). Originally a land for cattle (Nu. 32:4), it became famous for its vines and summer fruit. Jerome (*Comm. in Is.* 5) placed it about 500 paces from Heshbon: Khirbet Qurn el-Qibsh, 5 km WSW, is a feasible site. J.W.C.

SIDDIM, VALLEY OF (Heb. *siddîm*, perhaps derived from Hittite *siyantas*, 'salt'). In Gn. 14:3, 10 a valley identified with the 'Salt Sea' and described as 'full of bitumen pits'. Here the kings of the Jordan pentapolis were defeated by Chedorlaomer and his allies from the E. It was probably a fertile, well-watered region S of the Lisan peninsula, later submerged by the S extension of the Dead Sea through earthquake action and consequent faulting of the rock-formation. From the bituminous products of the Dead Sea (still in evidence) the Greeks called it *Asphaltitis.*

BIBLIOGRAPHY. J. P. Harland, 'Sodom and Gomorrah', *BA* 5, 1942, pp. 17ff.; 6, 1943, pp. 41ff. F.F.B.

SIDON (Heb. *ṣîḏôn, ṣîḏōn*). A major walled city and port in ancient *Phoenicia (now located on the coast of Lebanon). Sidon (AV also 'Zidon'; modern Saida) had twin harbours and was divided into Greater Sidon (Jos. 11:8) and Lesser Sidon.

According to tradition, Sidon was the first Phoenician city to be founded and became a principal Canaanite stronghold (Gn. 10:19; 1 Ch. 1:13). For some centuries the harbour was subordinate to the Egyptian 18th–19th Dynasties. With declining Egyptian military control the city ruler Zimri-ada committed defection *c.* 1390 BC (so *Amarna tablets). It is possible that the attempt to include Dor in Sidonian territory led to war with the Philistines, who *c.* 1150 BC plundered Sidon, whose inhabitants fled to Tyre. The city was, however, strong enough to oppose Israel (Jdg. 10:12), and during a period of active colonization apparently made an unsuccessful attempt to settle at Laish in the Upper Jordan (Jdg. 18:7, 27). Opposition to Phoenician expansion came also from the Assyrians, who under *Tiglath-pileser I, *c.* 1110 BC, began to exact tribute from the ports, including Sidon. Ashurnasirpal II (*c.* 880 BC) claimed the city as a vassal, and in 841 BC *Shalmaneser III marched to the Dog river to receive the tribute of Tyre, Sidon and Israel (*JEHU), and depicted this on the temple gates at Balawat (now in BM). The Assyrian demands increased and the Sidonians rebelled. Tiglath-pileser III captured Tyre and perhaps Sidon in 739–738 (H. Tadmor, *Scripta Hierosolymitana* 8, 1961, p. 269, makes Zc. 9:2 refer to this time). When Sennacherib marched, in an attack foretold by Isaiah (23:2–12), Luli fled and died in exile and was replaced by Ethba'al (Tuba'lu) when Great and Little Sidon had been captured.

On Sennacherib's death Sidon once more revolted and Esarhaddon invaded Sidon, killed the ruler Abdi-milkutti, sacked the port and moved its inhabitants to Kar-Esarhaddon, and brought prisoners from Elam and Babylonia to replace the depleted population.

Sidon recovered its independence with the decline of the Assyrians, only to be besieged again and captured by Nebuchadrezzar *c.* 587 BC as foretold by Jeremiah (25:22; 27:3; 47:4). Under the Persians it provided the majority of the Persian fleet (*cf.* Zc. 9:2). About 350 BC, under Tabnit II (Tannes), Sidon led the rebellion of Phoenicia and Cyprus against Artaxerxes III (Ochus). The city was betrayed and 40,000 perished, the survivors burning the city and fleet. The fortifications were never rebuilt. The city under Strato II yielded to

Alexander the Great without opposition and helped his siege of Tyre.

Under Antiochus III Sidon was a prosperous part of the kingdom of Ptolemy and later passed to the Seleucids and then to the Romans, who granted it local autonomy. Through all its history the principal temple was that of Eshmun, the god of healing. It is thus significant that it was in the region of Sidon that Christ healed the Syro-Phoenician woman's daughter (Mk. 7:24–31; *cf.* Mt. 11:21). Many Sidonians listened to his teaching (Mk. 3:8; Lk. 6:17; 10:13–14). Herod Agrippa I received a delegation from Sidon at Caesarea (Acts 12:20) and Paul visited friends in the city on his way to Rome (Acts 27:3). The inhabitants of Sidon, which was renowned as a centre of philosophical learning, were mainly Greek (*cf.* Mk. 7:26). Many coins bear inscriptions of Sidonian rulers, and among the discoveries in the area are remains from the Middle Bronze Age onwards, the inscribed sarcophagus of Eshmunazar (*c.* 300 BC) and buildings in the port area of NT times (A. Poidebard and J. Lauffray, *Sidon*, 1951). For Phoenician inscriptions from Sidon, see G. A. Cooke, *North Semitic Inscriptions*, 1903, pp. 26–43, 401–403. D.J.W.

SIGN. In the OT the Heb. word *'ōṯ* is used with several shades of meaning.

1. A visible mark or object intended to convey a clear message, *e.g.* the sun and moon (Gn. 1:14), the mark of Cain (Gn. 4:15), tribal standards (Nu. 2:2).

2. An assurance or reminder, *e.g.* rainbow (Gn. 9:12), to Rahab (Jos. 2:12), stones from the Jordan (Jos. 4:6).

3. Omens named by prophets as pledges of their predictions, *e.g.* the death of Eli's sons (1 Sa. 2:34); Saul's prophetic ecstasy (1 Sa. 10:6f.); the young woman with child (Is. 7:10–14); various symbolic acts (as in Is. 20:3; Ezk. 4:1–3).

4. Works of God. When the word 'sign' is used in the plural together with 'wonders' (*mōp̄ēṯ*) the events are understood to be the works of God, or attestations of his active presence among his people. This is seen in the account of the Exodus, where the plagues are described as signs (Ex. 4:28; 7:3; 8:23). The Exodus itself, with the deaths of the Egyptian first-born, the crossing of the Red Sea and the destruction of the Egyptian army, provides the supreme example of such signs and wonders (Dt. 4:34; 6:22; 7:19). This conviction is found throughout the OT (*e.g.* Nu. 14:11; Jos. 24:17; Ps. 78:43; Je. 32:21; Ne. 9:10), and Israel was assured that when God revealed himself again it would be with 'signs and wonders' to herald his coming (Joel 2:30).

Similarly in the NT Gk. *sēmeion* can mean simply some act or object conveying a recognizable meaning (Mt. 26:48; Lk. 2:12; Rom. 4:11; 2 Thes. 3:17). In 1 Cor. 14:22 tongues are 'a sign for unbelievers', since Is. 28:11f. shows that utterance in an unknown language is a sign of God's judgment on unbelief. Signs in heaven are quite frequently mentioned as indications of the last days (Mt. 24:30; Lk. 21:11, 25; Acts 2:19; Rev. 12:1, 3; 15:1). In Mk. 13 the tribulations accompanying the fall of Jerusalem and the end of the age are not a sign (Mk. 13:4; Mt. 24:3; Lk. 21:7) which enables a calculation of the end (Mk. 13:32), but an assurance to those caught up in the tribulation that the end cannot be long delayed.

So too 'signs and wonders' (miraculous healings, exorcisms, *etc.*) are regarded as proofs of God's powerful activity in the missionary work of the churches (Rom. 15:19; Heb. 2:4). Acts in particular gives a special prominence to such miracles ('wonders and signs', Acts 2:22, 43; 4:30; 5:12; 6:8; 7:36; 14:3; 15:12; see also 4:16, 22; 8:6, 13). Elsewhere however the NT writers (and Jesus) are a good deal more cautious in their talk of signs. Jesus responds critically to the Pharisees' request for signs (Mk. 8:11f.; Mt. 12:38f.; 16:1–4; Lk. 11:16, 29; so with Herod, 23:8f.), and warns against 'false Christs and false prophets' who 'show signs and wonders' (Mk. 13:22; Mt. 24:24). In similar vein Paul warns against the 'pretended signs and wonders' of 'the lawless one' (2 Thes. 2:9) and the seer of Rev. against the signs of the beast, the false prophet and the demonic spirits (Rev. 13:13f.; 16:14; 19:20). Paul is equally critical of the Jews' demand for signs (1 Cor. 1:22); and although he can point to 'signs and wonders' in his own ministry (2 Cor. 12:12), the context of his 'boasting' shows that he values such acts much less highly than the 'false apostles' at Corinth (2 Cor. 10–13).

The Fourth Gospel uses *sēmeion* more often (17 times) than any other NT writing, almost always in reference to Jesus' miracles. John is particularly concerned to demonstrate the true relation between 'sign' (significant action) and faith. Thus he is critical of a faith based on miracles as such—faith in Jesus (merely) as a miracle worker is defective faith, the shallow applause of the fickle crowd (Jn. 2:23–3:2; 4:48; 6:2, 14, 30; 7:31; 9:16; 12:18). The real significance of the miracles of Jesus is that they point forward to Jesus' death, resurrection and ascension, to the transformation brought by the new age of the Spirit, and thus lead to a faith in Jesus the (crucified) Christ, the (risen) Son of God (2:11; 6:26; 12:37; 20:30f.).

The problem with any sign is that it is ambiguous. It can be interpreted in different ways. The message it holds for faith can be seen only by faith. So, *e.g.*, 'the sign of the prophet Jonah' (Mt. 12:39f.) means nothing to those who do not believe in the resurrection (*cf.* Jn. 2:18f.; Lk. 2:34; 16:31). Consequently a faith based or nurtured exclusively on signs, rather than on the reality to which they point, is immature and at grave risk. Mature faith rejoices in what signs it perceives, but does not depend on them. (*MIRACLE; *POWER; *SYMBOL; *WONDER.)

BIBLIOGRAPHY. K. H. Rengstorf, *TDNT* 7, pp. 200–261; A. Richardson, *IDB*, 4, pp. 346–347; O. Hofius, C. Brown, *NIDNTT* 2, pp. 626–635.

J.D.G.D.

SIHON. An Amorite king (13th century BC), whose capital was *Heshbon. According to Nu. 21:26–30 and Je. 48:45, Sihon conquered the Moabites and took their territory as far S as the river Arnon. His vassals included five Midianite princes (Jos. 13:21). His domain included the area from the Arnon on the S to the Jabbok on the N, and from the Jordan on the W to the desert on the E (Nu. 21:24; Jdg. 11:22), and Jos. 12:3 and 13:27 seem to extend his control N of the Jabbok to the Sea of Chinnereth. Moses sent an embassy to Sihon asking permission for the Israelites to pass through his kingdom (Nu. 21:21–22; Dt. 2:26–28). When Sihon refused, the Israelites defeated and killed him at Jahaz and occupied his territory (Nu.

21:21–32). This area was assigned to the tribes of Reuben and Gad (Nu. 32:33–38; Jos. 13:10). The victory over Sihon is often recalled in the subsequent history of Israel (Dt. 31:4, by Moses; Jos. 2:10, by Rahab; Jos. 9:10, by the Gibeonites; Jdg. 11:19–21, by Jephthah; Ne. 9:22, by Levites in a prayer of confession; and Pss. 135:11; 136:19). The name Jebel Šîḥân for the mountain S of Ḍîbân (biblical Dibon) preserves in Arabic form the name of this king in the area which he once ruled. TB *Niddah* 61a records a tradition not found in the Bible that Sihon was the brother of King Og (also an Amorite), and a son of Ahijah, son of the legendary fallen angel Shamhazai.

BIBLIOGRAPHY. G. A. Smith, *The Historical Geography of the Holy Land*[25], 1931, pp. 588–591, 691–693; A. Musil, *Arabia Petraea*, 1. *Moab*, 1907, pp. 375–376; M. Noth, *ZAW* 58, 1940, pp. 161–189.

J.T.

SILAS. A leading member of the church at Jerusalem who also had prophetic gifts (Acts 15:22, 32). Silas may be a Semitic name, possibly *šᵉʾîlā'*, the Aram. form of Saul. There is little doubt that he is to be identified with 'Silvanus' (2 Cor. 1:19; 1 Thes. 1:1; 2 Thes. 1:1; 1 Pet. 5:12), which is probably the Latinized form of 'Silas', though it may be a separate *cognomen* chosen for its similarity.

In Acts Silas was sent by the church at Jerusalem to welcome into fellowship the Gentiles converted through the church of Antioch (Acts 15:22–35). When Paul and Barnabas quarrelled about John Mark, Barnabas went off with Mark and Paul took Silas as his companion on his second missionary journey (15:36–41). The fact of his Roman citizenship (16:37–39) may have been one of the reasons for the choice, and his membership of the Jerusalem church would have been helpful to Paul. His role seems to have been to replace Mark rather than Barnabas. Nowhere is he referred to in a general way as an 'apostle' (contrast Barnabas in Acts 14:14) and his position seems to be subordinate. Mark was the 'minister' (*hypēretēs*) of the apostles before (13:5), and that may indicate that he had some function similar to the synagogue attendants (Lk. 4:20) in looking after the Scriptures and possibly catechetical scrolls later developed into his Gospel. If the function of Silas was similar we can more readily see how he could have the literary role assigned to Silvanus in the Epistles. He accompanied Paul through Syria, Asia Minor, Macedonia and Thessalonica. When Paul left for Athens Silas stayed at Beroea and then joined Paul at Corinth (Acts 16–18). Paul mentions his work there in 2 Cor. 1:19. He was associated with Paul in the letters written from Corinth (1 Thes. 1:1; 2 Thes. 1:1) and is not named again until the reference to him in 1 Peter.

Peter says that he is writing *dia Silouanou* (1 Pet. 5:12). This implies a literary function with probably a good amount of freedom. This could account for some of the resemblances in wording between 1 Peter, 1 and 2 Thessalonians, and the apostolic decree of Acts 15. See E. G. Selwyn, *The First Epistle of St. Peter*, 1946, pp. 9–17. R.E.N.

SILK. The RSV rendering of two biblical words. **1.** Heb. *mešî* (Ezk. 16:10, 13), perhaps 'silken thread', but the sense is obscure. Since the Heb. word seems to be an Egyp. loan-word (usually meaning linen in Egyp.) and silk was not introduced into Egypt until the Roman period, some doubt is cast on the identification. LXX has *trichaptos*, 'woven hair'; variants occur in other versions. **2.** Gk. *sērikon* (Rev. 18:12) 'silk', 'silken', listed among the precious wares sold in the markets of Babylon.

AV also renders as silk the Heb. *šēš* (Pr. 31:22 and mg. of Gn. 41:42 and Ex. 25:4) which other versions consider to be fine *linen.

True silk is obtained from the cocoon of a Chinese moth fed on the leaves of white mulberry (*Morus alba*). Silk thread was a precious article of trade obtained direct from China, since the rearing of these moths did not take place in the W until the Middle Ages. There is, however, another species of silk moth indigenous to the E Mediterranean that feeds on cypress and oak. It has been generally overlooked that from it in ancient times an industry arose in Cos and Sidon producing transparent silk that may have been intended in the biblical references.

J.D.D.
F.N.H.

SILOAM. One of the principal sources of water supply to Jerusalem was the intermittent pool of Gihon ('Virgin's Fountain') below the Fountain Gate (Ne. 3:15) and ESE of the city. This fed water along an open canal, which flowed slowly along the SE slopes, called *šilôaḥ* ('Sender'; LXX *Silōam*, Is. 8:6). It followed the line of the later 'second aqueduct' (Wilson) which fell only 5 cm in 300 m, discharging into the Lower or Old Pool (mod. *Birket el-Ḥamra*) at the end of the central valley between the walls of the SE and SW hills. It thus ran below 'the wall of the Pool of Shelah' (Ne. 3:15) and watered the 'king's garden' on the adjacent slopes.

This Old Pool was probably the 'Pool of Siloam' in use in NT times for sick persons and others to wash (Jn. 9:7–11). The 'Tower of Siloam' which fell and killed 18 persons—a disaster well known in our Lord's day (Lk. 13:4)—was probably sited on the Ophel ridge above the pool which, according to Josephus (*BJ* 5. 145), was near the bend of the old wall below Ophlas (Ophel). According to the Talmud (*Sukkoth* 4. 9), water was drawn from Siloam's pool in a golden vessel to be carried in procession to the Temple on the Feast of Tabernacles. Though there are traces of a Herodian bath and open reservoir (about 18 m by 5 m, originally 22 m square with steps on the W side), there can be no certainty that this was the actual pool in question. It has been suggested that the part of the city round the Upper Pool (*'Ain Silwān*) 100 m above was called 'Siloam', the Lower being the King's Pool (Ne. 2:14) or Lower Gihon.

When Hezekiah was faced with the threat of invasion by the Assyrian army under Sennacherib he 'stopped all the springs', that is, all the rivulets and subsidiary canals leading down into the Kedron 'brook that flowed through the land' (2 Ch. 32:4). Traces of canals blocked at about this time were found by the Parker Mission. The king then diverted the upper Gihon waters through a 'conduit' or tunnel into an upper cistern or pool (the normal method of storing water) on the W side of the city of David (2 Ki. 20:20). Ben Sira tells how 'Hezekiah fortified his city and brought water into the midst of it; he tunnelled the sheer rock with iron and built pools for water' (Ecclus. 48:17–19). Hezekiah clearly defended the new source of supply with a rampart (2 Ch. 32:30). The digging

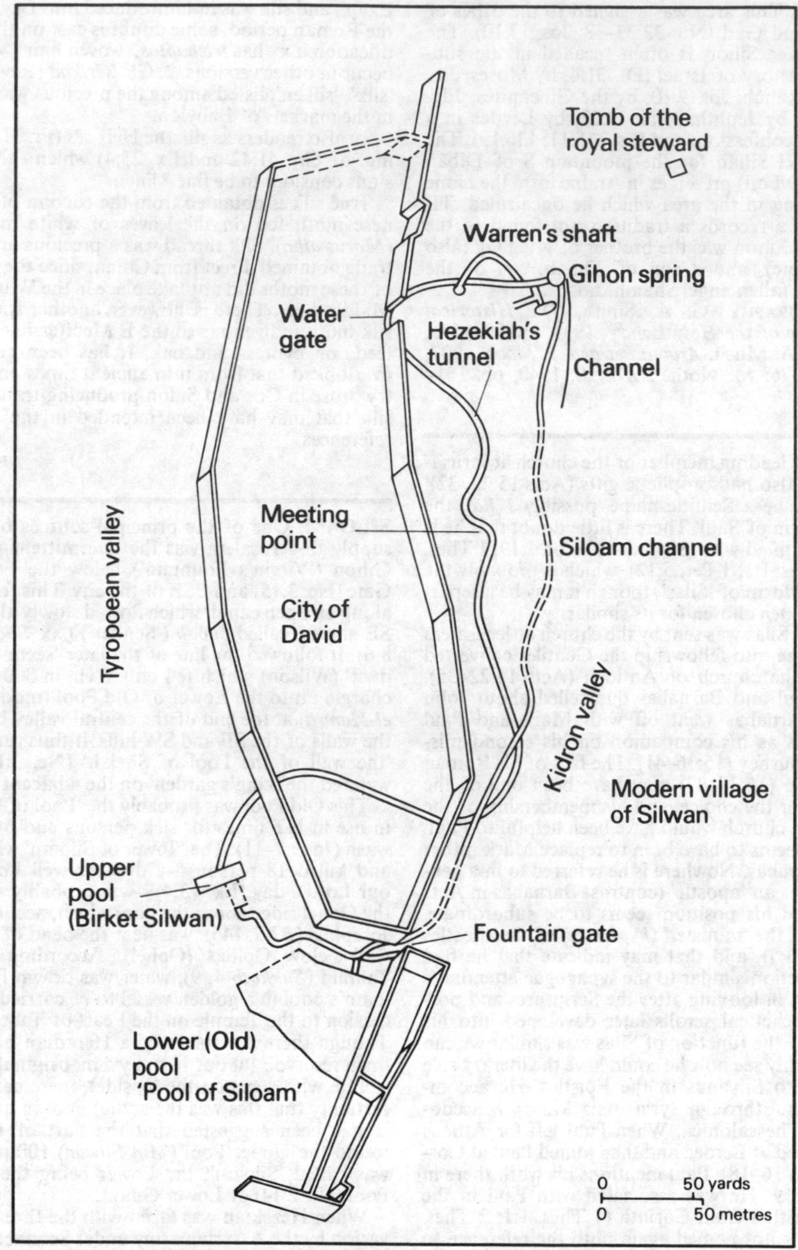

Plan of the Siloam area, including the pools and the channels which carried the water into the city of Jerusalem.

of the reservoir may be referred to by Isaiah (22:11).

In 1880 bathers in the upper pool (also called *birket silwān*) found about 5 m inside the tunnel a cursive Heb. inscription, now in Istanbul (*WRITING), which reads: '. . . was being dug out. It was cut in the following manner . . . axes, each man towards his fellow, and while there were still 3 cubits to be cut through, the voice of one man calling to the other was heard, showing that he was deviating to the right. When the tunnel was driven through, the excavators met man to man, axe to axe, and the water flowed for 1,200 cubits from the spring to the reservoir. The height of the rock above the heads of the excavators was 100 cubits' (D. J. Wiseman, *IBA*, pp. 61–64).

When this remarkable Judaean engineering feat was excavated the marks of the picks and deviations to effect a junction midway were traced. The tunnel traverses 540 m (or 643 m, Ussishkin),

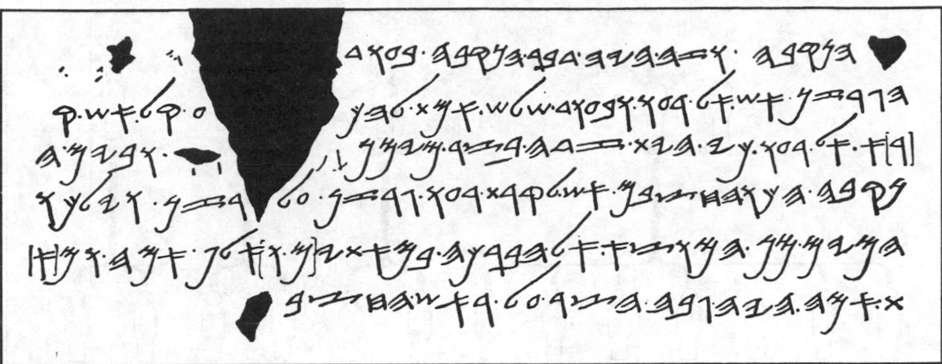

Facsimile of the inscription found in the Siloam tunnel describing how the miners excavating the water conduit from each end finally met. The archaic Hebrew script supports a date in Hezekiah's reign. Jerusalem. Length 75 cm. c. 710 BC.

twisting to avoid constructions or rock faults or to follow a fissure, to cover a direct line of 332 m. It is about 2 m high and in parts only 50 cm wide. Modern buildings prevent any archaeological check that the upper pool is the 'reservoir' (b^e*rēkâ*) of Hezekiah or that from this the waters overflowed direct to the lower pool. The pool was probably underground at first, the rock roof collapsing or being quarried away later.

Hezekiah's tunnel begins from an earlier tunnel which channelled water from the spring of Gihon to the bottom of a shaft which rises to join an inclined tunnel which led to a point inside the Jebusite city. This shaft and tunnel system was built by the Jebusites to provide a secure water-supply and is possibly the 'gutter' or 'water shaft' (*ṣinnôr*) that David's men climbed to capture the city (2 Sa. 5:8).

Below the modern village of Siloam (Silwān, first mentioned in 1697) on the E escarpment opposite the hill of Ophel are a number of rock-cut tombs. These were prepared for the burial of 'Pharaoh's Daughter' and for ministers and nobles of the kingdom of Judah. One of these bore a Heb. inscription, the epitaph of a royal steward, probably the *Shebna who was rebuked by Isaiah (22:15–16). See *IBA*, p. 59; *IEJ* 3, 1953, pp. 137–152; D. Ussishkin, *The Village of Siloam*, 1986.

BIBLIOGRAPHY. J. Simons, *Jerusalem in the Old Testament*, 1952; D. Ussishkin, 'The Original Length of the Siloam Tunnel', *Levant* 8, 1976, pp. 82–95; J. Wilkinson, 'The Pool of Siloam', *Levant* 10, 1978, pp.116–125. D.J.W.

SIMEON. 1. The second son of Jacob by Leah (Gn. 29:33). Heb. *šim'ôn* was derived from *šāma'* ('to hear'), and its significance is given in Gn. 29:33. Simeon took part with Levi in the massacre of the men of Shechem for dishonouring their sister Dinah (Gn. 34). He also played a prominent part in the affair of Joseph and his brothers, being given as a hostage so that they should return with Benjamin. Simeon may have been chosen by Joseph because he played a leading part in selling him to Egypt, or it may be because he was second to Reuben, who had acted more responsibly than the others (Gn. 37:21–22; 42:22). In the blessing of Jacob, Simeon and Levi were rebuked for their violent nature, and they were to be divided and scattered (Gn. 49:5–7). The sons of Simeon were Jemuel, Jamin, Ohad, Jachin, Zohar and Shaul, the son of a Canaanite woman (Gn. 46:10; Ex. 6:15).

2. The tribe of Simeon. The number of the tribe is given as 59,300 in Nu. 1:22–23 and 22,200 'families' in Nu. 26:14. They were to camp next to Reuben (Nu. 2:12–13). The tribe of Simeon was among those to be set on Mt Gerizim and blessed (Dt. 27:12), but it was not named (along with Issachar) in the blessing of Moses in Dt. 33. In the Promised Land it was given a portion at the S extremity and it came almost to be absorbed into the territory of Judah (Jos. 19:1–9). The towns of the area were reckoned to belong to Judah in Jos. 15:26–32, 42 and elsewhere. Judah and Simeon joined forces at the beginning of the conquest of Canaan (Jdg. 1:3, 17), but Judah was clearly the more powerful tribe. The sons of Simeon, despite keeping a genealogical record, did not multiply as fast as Judah (1 Ch. 4:24–33). They did, however, win a victory over the Amalekites under Hezekiah (1 Ch. 4:41–43), and they provided more men for David than did Judah (1 Ch. 12:24–25). The Chronicler seems to imply that Simeon belonged to the N kingdom, but numbers of Simeonites joined Asa in restoring the worship of Yahweh (2 Ch. 15:9). The tribe is not mentioned after the Exile, and the only other reference to it is among those sealed in Rev. 7:7, where it comes seventh in the list.

3. An ancestor of Jesus (Lk. 3:30).

4. A man in Jerusalem who was righteous and devout and who was looking for 'the consolation of Israel' (Lk. 2:25–35). He is not to be identified with Rabbi Simon ben Hillel. He was one of the remnant who were longing for the coming of the Messiah, and had received a direct revelation that he would not die before seeing the Messiah with his own eyes. When the presentation of Jesus was about to take place he was guided by the Spirit to come into the Temple. On seeing Jesus he uttered the hymn of praise now known as the *Nunc Dimittis. He saw that the Messiah would vindicate Israel in the eyes of the Gentiles. Simeon went on to speak to the astonished Mary of the role of Christ within Israel. He was to be like a stone causing some to fall and some to rise. He was to be a sign which would not be heeded but spoken against (34). Her own suffering as she watched his life and death was to be acute and he was to reveal the

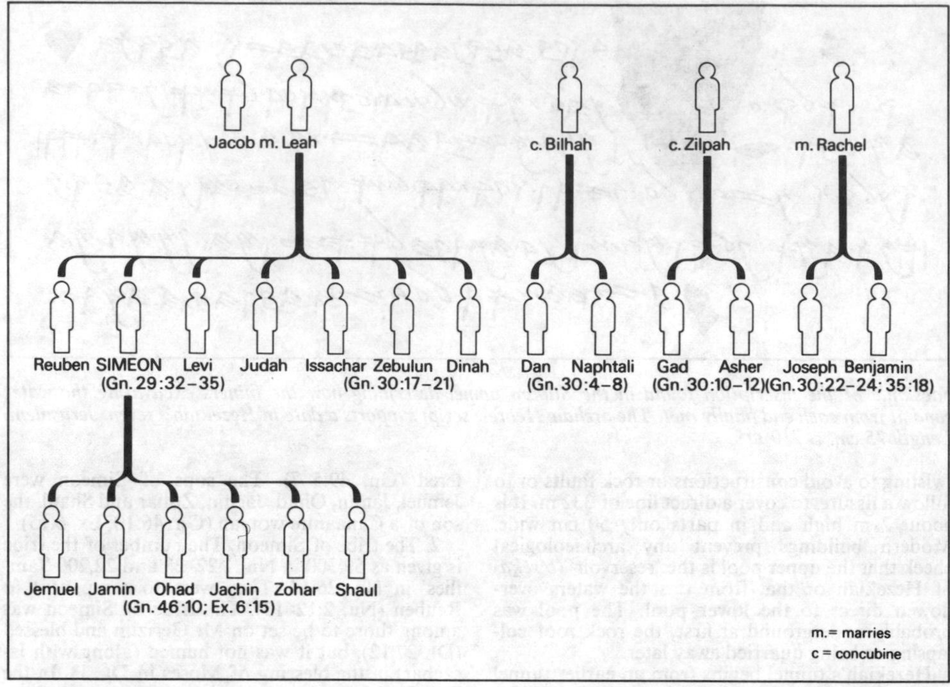

The family of Simeon.

inmost thoughts of men (35). Having given his testimony to the Christ, Simeon fades silently from the picture.

5. A disciple at Antioch, with prophetic and teaching gifts, who was one of those who ordained Barnabas and Saul for their first missionary journey (Acts 13:1–2). He was surnamed Niger, which suggests that he was an African, but he has not been proved to be the same person as Simon of Cyrene (Lk. 23:26, *etc.*). Here RV and RSV read 'Symeon', which is the more normal rendering of the Gk. but not of the Heb.

6. The archaic version of the name of Simon Peter used by James in his speech to the Council of Jerusalem (Acts 15:14). RV and RSV render 'Symeon'. Some good MSS read *Symeon* also in 2 Pet. 1:1 (*cf.* RVmg., NEB). R.E.N.

SIMON. A later form of the OT name of Simeon (see Acts 15:14, where James uses the older form; also 2 Pet. 1:1, RVmg., NEB).

1. The chief disciple and apostle of Jesus, who was the son of Jonas (or John) and the brother of Andrew. Jesus gave him the name of *Peter.

2. The 'Canaanite' (Mt. 10:4; Mk. 3:18, AV). 'Canaanite' here cannot mean an inhabitant of Canaan, nor can it represent one who dwells at Cana. Rather it should be rendered *Cananaean (RV, RSV), an adherent of the party later known as the *Zealots and rendered so by Luke (Lk. 6:15; Acts 1:13). Whether Simon was a zealot in the political sense or the religious sense is a matter of some debate.

3. One of the brothers of our Lord (Mt. 13:55; Mk. 6:3). **4.** A leper in Bethany in whose house the head of Jesus was anointed with oil (Mt. 26:6; Mk. 14:3), probably related to *Martha, *Mary and *Lazarus (see J. N. Sanders, 'Those whom Jesus loved', *NTS* 1, 1954–5, pp. 29–41). **5.** A man of Cyrene who was compelled to carry the cross of Jesus (Mk. 15:21), possibly the Simeon of Acts 13:1 (*RUFUS). **6.** A Pharisee in whose house the feet of Jesus were washed with tears and anointed (Lk. 7:40). Some scholars equate this Simon with **4** above and regard the stories as doublets; but they are strikingly different in their details (*MARY). **7.** Simon Iscariot, the father of *Judas Iscariot (Jn. 6:71; 12:4; 13:2). **8.** *Simon Magus. **9.** A tanner at Joppa in whose house Peter lodged (Acts 9:43). F.S.F.

SIMON MAGUS. In the NT we meet Simon in 'the city of Samaria' (Sebaste?—Acts 8:9–24), where he has 'swept the Samaritans off their feet with his magical arts' (NEB, v. 9). Luke does not suggest that Simon was himself a Samaritan. In essence a Levantine mountebank, Simon cultivated the legend that he was a divine emanation—'that Power of God which is called the Great Power'. The concept and the title were pagan enough (*cf.* for analogies, Ramsay, *BRD*, p. 117; Deissmann, *Bible Studies*[2], 1909, p. 336 n.), but the Samaritans would by 'God' intend 'Yahweh', and Simon must have acclimatized himself to his religious surroundings. He already represents, then, a significant syncretism of magical, Hellenistic and erratic Jewish elements.

In the mass movement attending Philip's preaching Simon professed conversion and was baptized. Luke uses his regular expression 'believed', and there is no reason to doubt Simon's sincerity thus far. The sequel, however, shows that his basic attitudes were still those of the magician. So impressed was he with the visible manifestations of the Holy Spirit following the apostles' laying on of hands, that he applied to them, as to higher proficients in the same trade, for the formula at an appropriate price. Peter's crushing rebuke evidently terrified him, for he begged the apostles' intercession to avert the threatened peril. Simon was obsessed with the idea of *power*: throughout he conceived of it as residing in the apostles as super-magicians.

Here, rather abruptly, Luke leaves Simon; but a tangle of traditions about his later career survive in primitive Christian literature. If they include incongruities and legends there is no need, with E. de Faye, to discount the patristic descriptions, or to deny a connection between the Simon of Acts and the Simonian sect. Even Lucian's rascally oraclemonger Alexander discoursed on the errors of Epicurus: and there is nothing incredible in Simon, with striking ability and personality, and real psychic powers, and perhaps some education, combining the charlatan and the heresiarch.

Justin (*Apology* 26, *cf.* 56, and *Trypho* 120), himself from Samaria, says that Simon was born in the village of Gitta; that his companion Helen, a former prostitute, was widely regarded as his first divine 'idea', while he himself was acclaimed by multitudes in Samaria and Rome as a divinity. Indeed, Roman adulation had erected a statue inscribed *Simoni Deo Sancto*, 'to Simon the Holy God'. (This statue may actually have been erected to the Sabine deity Semo Sancus, but the Simonians, who worshipped at statues, perhaps saw opportunities in this one.)

Irenaeus (*Adv. Haer.* 1. 16, Harvey), Hippolytus (*Philos.* 6. 7ff.) and Epiphanius (*Panarion.* 21. 2ff.) describe Simonian doctrine, the two latter employing publications which they allege, perhaps erroneously in Hippolytus' case, to emanate from the sect of Simon. He seems to have developed his old theme of 'the Great Power of God' into a Trinitarian scheme: Simon appeared to the Samaritans as the Father, to the Jews as the Son (he only *seemed* to suffer) and to the world at large as the Holy Spirit. He had a Redemption myth in which he rescued Helen ('the lost sheep') from the bondage of successive transmigrations in various female bodies; and he preached salvation by grace, requiring faith in Helen and himself, but allowing unrestrained liberty in morals afterwards. But Simon also borrowed heavily from Gk. paganism and Gk. philosophy, and some concepts appear which recur in more sophisticated Christian *Gnosticism. Irenaeus and the others regard him as the first major heretic, the initiator of a long chain of interrelated errors. The modern association of Gnostic origins with heretical forms of Judaism may suggest that their instinct was not far wrong.

Literature such as the Clementine romance and the *Acts of Peter* has many imaginative stories of encounters between Simon and Peter in Rome. The once-popular idea that in the Clementines Simon is a cipher for Paul need no longer be taken seriously.) According to Hippolytus, his final exhibition misfired. He was buried alive, promising to reappear in 3 days; but he did not, for, in Hippolytus' laconic phrase, 'he was not the Christ'.

BIBLIOGRAPHY. R. P. Casey in *BC*, 5, 1933, pp. 151ff.; J. W. Drane, 'Simon the Samaritan and the Lucan Concept of Salvation History', *EQ* 47, 1975, pp. 131–137; E. de Faye, *Gnostiques et Gnosticisme*², 1925, pp. 413ff.; J. Fossum, in A. Crown (ed.), *The Samaritans*, pp. 357–389; R. M. Grant, *Gnosticism and Early Christianity*, 1960, pp. 70–96; G. Ludemann, *NTS* 33, pp. 420–426. A.F.W.

SIN. The Egyp. *sỉnw*, *swn*, 'fortress', is connected later with Egyp. *sỉn*, 'clay, mud', hence its Gk. name Pelusium, 'mud-city'. A fortress-city, it is now Tell Farama, on the seashore about 32 km SE of Port Said; an Egyp. key defence-post against invasion from the E through Palestine. Emendation in Ezk. 30:15–16 to Seven(eh) (=Aswan) is unnecessary. On the name Sin, see Gardiner, *JEA* 5, 1918, pp. 253–254. K.A.K.

SIN.

I. Terminology

As might be expected of a book whose dominant theme is human sin and God's gracious salvation from it, the Bible uses a wide variety of terms in both OT and NT to express the idea of sin.

There are four main Heb. roots. *ḥṭ'* is the most common and with its derivatives conveys the underlying idea of missing the mark, or deviating from the goal (*cf.* Jdg. 20:16 for non-moral usage). The vast proportion of its occurrences refer to moral and religious deviation, whether in respect of man (Gn. 20:9), or God (La. 5:7). The noun *ḥaṭṭā'ṯ* is frequently used as a technical term for a sin-offering (Lv. 4, *passim*). This root does not address the inner motivation of wrong action but concentrates more on its formal aspect as deviation from the moral norm, usually the law or will of God (Ex. 20:20; Ho. 13:2; *etc.*). *pš'* refers to action in breach of relationship, 'rebellion', 'revolution'. It occurs in a non-theological sense, *e.g.*, with reference to Israel's secession from the house of David (1 Ki. 12:19). Used of sin it is perhaps the profoundest OT term reflecting as it does the insight that sin is rebellion against God, the defiance of his holy lordship and rule (Is. 1:28; 1 Ki. 8:50; *etc.*). *'wh* conveys a literal meaning of deliberate perversion or 'twisting' (Is. 24:1; La. 3:9). Used in relation to sin it reflects the thought of sin as deliberate wrongdoing, 'committing iniquity' (Dn. 9:5; 2 Sa. 24:17). It occurs in religious contexts particularly in a noun form *'āwôn* which stresses the idea of the guilt which arises from deliberate wrongdoing (Gn. 44:16; Je. 2:22). It can also refer to the punishment which is consequent upon the sin (Gn. 4:13; Is. 53:11). *šāḡâh* has as its basic idea straying away from the correct path (Ezk. 34:6). It is indicative of sin as arising from ignorance, 'erring', 'creaturely going astray' (1 Sa. 26:21; Jb. 6:24). It often appears in the cultic context as sin against unrecognized ritual regulations (Lv. 4:2). Reference should also be made to *rāša'*, to be wicked, to act wickedly (2 Sa. 22:22; Ne. 9:33); and *'āmal*, mischief done to others (Pr. 24:2; Hab. 1:13).

The principal NT term is *hamartia* (and cognates), which is equivalent to *ḥṭ'*. In classical Gk. it is used for missing a target or taking a wrong road. It is the general NT term for sin as concrete wrongdoing, the violation of God's law (Jn. 8:46; Jas. 1:15; 1 Jn. 1:8). In Rom. 5–8 Paul personifies the term as a ruling principle in human life (*cf.* 5:12; 6:12, 14; 7:17, 20; 8:2). *paraptōma* occurs in classical contexts for an error in measurement or a blunder. The NT gives it a stronger moral connotation as misdeed or trespass (*cf.* 'dead through . . .',

Eph. 2:1; Mt. 6:14f.). *parabasis* is a similarly derived term with similar meaning, 'transgression', 'going beyond the norm' (Rom. 4:15; Heb. 2:2). *asebeia* is perhaps the profoundest NT term and commonly translates *pš'* in the LXX. It implies active ungodliness or impiety (Rom. 1:18; 2 Tim. 2:16). Another term is *anomia*, lawlessness, a contempt for law (Mt. 7:23; 2 Cor. 6:14). *kakia* and *ponēria* are general terms expressing moral and spiritual depravity (Acts 8:22; Rom. 1:29; Lk. 11:39; Eph. 6:12). The last of these references indicates the association of the latter term with Satan, the evil one, *ho ponēros* (Mt. 13:19; 1 Jn. 3:12). *adikia* is the main classical term for wrong done to one's neighbour. It is translated variously as 'injustice' (Rom. 9:14), 'unrighteousness' (Lk. 18:6), 'falsehood' (Jn. 7:18), 'wickedness' (Rom. 2:8), 'iniquity' (2 Tim. 2:19). 1 Jn. equates it with *hamartia* (1 Jn. 3:4; 5:17). Also occurring are *enochos*, a legal term meaning 'guilty' (Mk. 3:29; 1 Cor. 11:27), and *opheilēma*, 'debt' (Mt. 6:12).

The definition of sin, however, is not to be derived simply from the terms used in Scripture to denote it. The most characteristic feature of sin in all its aspects is that it is directed against God (*cf.* Ps. 51:4; Rom. 8:7). Any conception of sin which does not have in the forefront the contradiction which it offers to God is a deviation from the biblical representation. The common notion that sin is selfishness betrays a false assessment of its nature and gravity. Essentially, sin is directed against God, and this perspective alone accounts for the diversity of its form and activities. It is a violation of that which God's glory demands and is, therefore, in its essence the contradiction of God.

II. Origin

Sin was present in the universe before the Fall of Adam and Eve (Gn. 3:1f.; *cf.* Jn. 8:44; 2 Pet. 2:4; 1 Jn. 3:8; Jude 6). The Bible however does not deal directly with the origin of evil in the universe, being concerned rather with sin and its origin in human life (1 Tim. 2:14; Jas. 1:13f.). The real thrust of the demonic temptation in the account of the Fall in Gn. 3 lies in its subtle suggestion of man's aspiring to equality with his maker ('you will be like God . . .', 3:5). Satan's attack was directed against the integrity, veracity and loving provision of God, and consisted in an enticement to wicked and blasphemous rebellion against man's proper Lord. In this act man snatched at equality with God (*cf.* Phil. 2:6), attempted to assert his independence of God, and hence to call in question the very nature and ordering of existence whereby he lived as creature in utter dependence upon the grace and provision of his creator. 'Man's sin lies in his pretension to be God' (Niebuhr). In this act, further, man blasphemously withheld the worship and adoring love which is ever his proper response to God's majesty and grace, and instead paid homage to the enemy of God and to his own foul ambitions.

Thus the origin of sin according to Gn. 3 ought not to be sought so much in an overt action (2:17 with 3:6) but in an inward, God-denying aspiration of which the act of disobedience was the immediate expression. As to the problem of how Adam and Eve could have been subject to temptation had they not previously known sin, Scripture does not enter into extended discussion. However, in the person of Jesus Christ it witnesses to a Man who, though without sin, was subject to temptation 'in every respect as we are' (Heb. 4:15; *cf.* Mt. 4:3f.; Heb. 2:17f.; 5:7f.; 1 Pet. 1:19; 2:22f.). The ultimate origin of *evil is part of the 'mystery of lawlessness' (2 Thes. 2:7), but an arguable reason for Scripture's relative silence is that a 'rational explanation' of the origin of sin would have the inevitable result of directing attention away from the Scripture's primary concern, the confession of *my personal guilt* (*cf.* G. C. Berkouwer, *Sin*, 1971, ch. 1). In the end, sin, by the nature of the case, cannot be 'known' objectively; 'sin posits itself' (S. Kierkegaard).

III. Consequences

The sin of Adam and Eve was not an isolated event. The consequences for them, for posterity and for the world are immediately apparent.

a. Man's attitude to God

The changed attitude to God on the part of Adam indicates the revolution that took place in their minds. They 'hid themselves from the presence of the Lord God' (Gn. 3:8; *cf.* v. 7). Made for the presence and fellowship of God, they now dreaded encounter with him (*cf.* Jn. 3:20). *Shame and fear were now the dominant emotions (*cf.* Gn. 2:25; 3:7, 10), indicating the disruption that had taken place.

b. God's attitude to man

Not only was there a change in man's attitude to God, but also in God's attitude to man. Reproof, condemnation, curse, expulsion from the garden are all indicative of this. Sin is one-sided, but its consequences are not. Sin elicits God's wrath and displeasure, and necessarily so, because it is the contradiction of what he is. For God to be complacent towards sin is an impossibility, since it would be for God to cease to take himself seriously. He cannot deny himself.

c. Consequences for the human race

The unfolding history of man furnishes a catalogue of vices (Gn. 4:8, 19, 23f.; 6:2–3, 5). The sequel of abounding iniquity results in the virtual destruction of mankind (Gn. 6:7, 13; 7:21–24). The Fall had abiding effect not only upon Adam and Eve but upon all who descended from them; there is racial solidarity in sin and evil.

d. Consequences for creation

The effects of the Fall extend to the physical cosmos. 'Cursed is the ground because of you' (Gn. 3:17; *cf.* Rom. 8:20). Man is the crown of creation, made in God's image and, therefore, God's vicegerent (Gn. 1:26). The catastrophe of man's Fall brought the catastrophe of curse upon that over which he was given dominion. Sin was an event in the realm of the human spirit, but it has its repercussions in the whole of creation.

e. The appearance of death

*Death is the epitome of sin's penalty. This was the warning attached to the prohibition of Eden (Gn. 2:17), and it is the direct expression of God's curse upon man the sinner (Gn. 3:19). Death in the phenomenal realm consists in the separation of the integral elements of man's being. This dissolution exemplifies the principle of death, namely, separation, and it comes to its most extreme expression in separation from God (Gn. 3:23f.). Because of sin death is invested with a fear and terror for man (Lk. 12:5; Heb. 2:15).

IV. Imputation

The first sin of Adam had unique significance for the whole human race (Rom. 5:12, 14–19; 1 Cor. 15:22). Here there is sustained emphasis upon the one trespass of the one man as that by which sin, condemnation and death came upon all mankind. The sin is identified as 'the transgression of Adam', 'the trespass of the one', 'one trespass', 'the disobedience of the one', and there can be no doubt that the first trespass of Adam is intended. Hence the clause 'because all men sinned' in Rom. 5:12 refers to the sin of all in the sin of Adam. It cannot refer to the actual sins of all men, far less to the hereditary depravity with which all are afflicted, for in v. 12 the clause in question clearly says why 'death spread to all men', and in the succeeding verses the 'one man's trespass' (v. 17) is stated to be the reason for the universal reign of death. If the same sin were not intended, Paul would be affirming two different things with reference to the same subject in the same context. The only explanation of the two forms of statement is that all sinned in the sin of Adam. The same inference is to be drawn from 1 Cor. 15:22, 'in Adam all die'. If all die in Adam, it is because all sinned in Adam.

According to Scripture the kind of solidarity with Adam which explains the participation of all in Adam's sin is the kind of solidarity which Christ sustains to those united to him. The parallel in Rom. 5:12–19; 1 Cor. 15:22, 45–49 between Adam and Christ indicates the same type of relationship in both cases, and we have no need to posit anything more ultimate in the case of Adam and the race than we find in the case of Christ and his people. In the latter it is representative headship, and this is all that is necessary to ground the solidarity of all in the sin of Adam. To say that the sin of Adam is imputed to all is but to say that all were involved in his sin by reason of his representative headship.

While the imputation of Adam's sin was immediate according to the evidence of the relevant passages, the judgment of condemnation passed upon Adam, and hence upon all men in him, is in Scripture seen as confirmed in its justice and propriety by every man's subsequent moral experience. Thus Rom. 3:23 'all have sinned' is amply proved by reference to the specific, overt sins of Jews and Gentiles (Rom. 1:18–3:8) before Paul makes any reference whatever to imputation in Adam. In similar vein Scripture universally relates man's ultimate judgment before God to his 'works' which fall short of God's standards (*cf.* Mt. 7:21–27; 13:41; 25:31–46; Lk. 3:9; Rom. 2:5–10; Rev. 20:11–14).

Rejection of this doctrine betrays not only failure to accept the witness of the relevant passages but also failure to appreciate the close relation which exists between the principle which governs our relation to Adam and the governing principle of God's operation in salvation. The parallel between Adam as the first man and Christ as the last Adam shows that the accomplishment of salvation in Christ is based on the same operating principle as that by which we have become sinners and the heirs of death. The history of mankind is finally subsumed under two complexes, sin–condemnation–death and righteousness–justification–life. The former arises from our union with Adam, the latter from union with Christ. These are the two orbits within which we live and move. God's government of men is directed in terms of these relationships. If we do not reckon with Adam we are thereby excluded from a proper understanding of Christ. All who die die in Adam; all who are made alive are made alive in Christ.

V. Depravity

Sin never consists merely in a voluntary act of transgression. Every volition proceeds from something that is more deep-seated than the volition itself. A sinful act is the expression of a sinful heart (*cf.* Mk. 7:20–23; Pr. 4:23; 23:7). Sin must always include, therefore, the perversity of heart, mind, disposition and will. This was true, as we saw above, in the case of the first sin, and it applies to all sin. The imputation to posterity of the sin of Adam must, therefore, carry with it involvement in the perversity apart from which Adam's sin would be meaningless and its imputation an impossible abstraction. Paul states that 'by one man's disobedience many were made sinners' (Rom. 5:19). The depravity which sin entails and with which all men come into the world is for this reason a direct implicate of our solidarity with Adam in his sin. We come to be as individuals by natural generation, and as individuals we never exist apart from the sin of Adam reckoned as ours. Therefore the psalmist wrote, 'Behold, I was brought forth in iniquity, and in sin did my mother conceive me' (Ps. 51:5) and our Lord said, 'That which is born of the flesh is flesh' (Jn. 3:6).

The witness of Scripture to the pervasiveness of this depravity is explicit. Gn. 6:5; 8:21 provides a closed case. The latter reference makes it clear that this indictment was not restricted to the period before the judgment of the Flood. There is no evading the force of this testimony from the early pages of divine revelation, and later assessments are to the same effect (*cf.* Je. 17:9–10; Rom. 3:10–18). From whatever angle man is viewed, there is the absence of that which is well-pleasing to God. Considered more positively, all have turned aside from God's way and become corrupted. In Rom. 8:5–7 Paul refers to the mind of the flesh, and flesh, when used ethically as here, means human nature directed and governed by sin (*cf.* Jn. 3:6). Further, according to Rom. 8:7, 'The mind that is set on the flesh is hostile to God'. No stronger condemnatory judgment could be arrived at, for it means that the thinking of the natural man is conditioned and governed by enmity directed against God. Nothing less than a judgment of total depravity is the clear implication of these passages, *i.e.* there is no area or aspect of human life which is absolved from the sombre effects of man's fallenness, and hence no area which might serve as a possible ground for man's justification of himself in the face of God and his law.

Depravity however is not registered in actual transgression to an equal extent in all. There are multiple restraining factors. God does not give over all men to uncleanness, to a base mind, and to improper conduct (Rom. 1:24, 28). Total depravity (total, that is, in the sense that it touches everything) is not incompatible with the exercise of the natural virtues and the promotion of civil righteousness. Unregenerate men are still endowed with conscience, and the work of the law is written upon their hearts so that in measure and at points they fulfil its requirement (Rom. 2:14f.). The doctrine of depravity, however, means that these works, though formally in accord with what God commands, are not good and well-pleasing to God in terms of the full and ultimate criteria by which his judgment is determined, the criteria of love to God as the animating motive, the law of God as the directing principle, and the glory of God as the controlling purpose (Rom. 8:7; 1 Cor. 2:14; *cf.* Mt. 6:2, 5, 16; Mk. 7:6–7; Rom. 13:4; 1 Cor. 10:31; 13:3; Tit. 1:15; 3:5; Heb. 11:4, 6).

VI. Inability

Inability is concerned with the incapacity arising from the nature of depravity. If depravity is total, *i.e.* affecting every aspect and area of man's being, then inability for what is good and well-pleasing to God is likewise comprehensive in its reference.

We are not able to change our character or act differently from it. In the matter of understanding, the natural man cannot know the things of the Spirit of God because they are spiritually discerned (1 Cor. 2:14). In respect of obedience to the law of God he is not only not subject to the law of God but he cannot be (Rom. 8:7). They who are in the flesh cannot please God (Rom. 8:8). A corrupt tree cannot bring forth good fruit (Mt. 7:18). The impossibility in each case is undeniable. It is our Lord who affirms that even faith in him is impossible apart from the gift and drawing of the Father (Jn. 6:44f., 65). This witness on his part is to the same effect as his insistence that apart from the supernatural birth of water and the Spirit no-one can have intelligent appreciation of, or entrance into, the kingdom of God (Jn. 3:3, 5f., 8; *cf.* Jn. 1:13; 1 Jn. 2:29; 3:9; 4:7; 5:1, 4, 18).

The necessity of so radical and momentous a transformation and re-creation as regeneration is proof of the whole witness of Scripture to the bondage of sin and the hopelessness of our sinful condition. This bondage implies that it is a psychological, moral and spiritual impossibility for the natural man to receive the things of the Spirit, to love God and do what is well-pleasing to him, or to believe in Christ to the salvation of his soul. It is this enslavement which is the premise of the gospel, and the glory of the gospel lies precisely in the fact that it provides release from the bondage and slavery of sin. It is the gospel of grace and power for the helpless.

VII. Liability

Since sin is against God, he cannot be complacent towards it or indifferent with respect to it. He reacts inevitably against it. This reaction is specifically his wrath. The frequency with which Scripture mentions the wrath of God compels us to take account of its reality and meaning.

Various terms are used in the OT. In Heb., *'ap̄* in the sense of 'anger', and intensified in the form *ḥarôn 'ap̄* to express the 'fierceness of God's anger' is very common (*cf.* Ex. 4:14; 32:12; Nu. 11:10; 22:22; Jos. 7:1; Jb. 42:7; Ps. 21:9; Is. 10:5; Na. 1:6; Zp. 2:2); *ḥēmâ* is likewise frequent (*cf.* Dt. 29:23; Pss. 6:1; 79:6; 90:7; Je. 7:20; Na. 1:2); *'eḇrâ* (*cf.* Ps. 78:49; Is. 9:19; 10:6; Ezk. 7:19; Ho. 5:10) and *qeṣep̄* (*cf.* Dt. 29:28; Ps. 38:1; Je. 32:37; 50:13; Zc. 1:2) are used with sufficient frequency to be worthy of mention; *za'am* is also characteristic and expresses the thought of indignation (*cf.* Pss. 38:3; 69:24; 78:49; Is. 10:5; Ezk. 22:31; Na. 1:6). It is apparent that the OT is permeated with references to the wrath of God. Often more than one of these terms appear together in order to strengthen and confirm the thought expressed. There is intensity in the terms themselves and in the constructions in which they occur to convey the notions of displeasure, fiery indignation and holy vengeance.

The Gk. terms are *orgē* and *thymos*, the former frequently predicated of God in the NT (*cf.* Jn. 3:36; Rom. 1:18; 2:5, 8; 3:5; 5:9; 9:22; Eph. 2:3; 5:6; 1 Thes. 1:10; Heb. 3:11; Rev. 6:17), and the latter less frequently (*cf.* Rom. 2:8; Rev. 14:10, 19; 16:1, 19; 19:15; see *zēlos* in Heb. 10:27).

The *wrath of God is therefore a reality, and the language and teaching of Scripture are calculated to impress upon us the severity by which it is characterized. There are three observations which particularly require mention. First, the wrath of God must not be interpreted in terms of the fitful passion so commonly associated with anger in us. It is the deliberate, resolute displeasure which the contradiction of his holiness demands. Secondly, it is not to be construed as vindictiveness but as holy indignation; nothing of the nature of malice attaches to it. It is not malignant hatred but righteous detestation. Thirdly, we may not reduce the wrath of God to his will to punish. Wrath is a positive outgoing of dissatisfaction as sure as that which is pleasing to God involves complacency. We must not eliminate from God what we term emotion. The wrath of God finds its parallel in the human heart, exemplified in a perfect manner in Jesus (*cf.* Mk. 3:5; 10:14).

The epitome of sin's liability is, therefore, the holy wrath of God. Since sin is never impersonal, but exists in, and is committed by, persons, the wrath of God consists in the displeasure to which we are subjected; we are the objects. The penal inflictions which we suffer are the expressions of God's wrath. The sense of guilt and torment of conscience are the reflections in our consciousness of the displeasure of God. The essence of final perdition will consist in the infliction of God's indignation (*cf.* Is. 30:33; 66:24; Dn. 12:2; Mk. 9:43, 45, 48).

VIII. The conquest of sin

Despite the sombreness of the theme, the Bible never completely loses a note of hope and optimism when dealing with sin; for the heart of the Bible is its witness to God's mighty offensive against sin in his historical purpose of redemption centred in Jesus Christ, the last Adam, his eternal Son, the Saviour of sinners. Through the whole work of Christ, his miraculous birth, his life of perfect obedience, supremely his death on the cross and resurrection from the dead, his ascension to the right hand of the Father, his reign in history and his glorious return, sin has been overcome. Its rebellious, usurping authority has been vanquished, its absurd claims exposed, its foul machinations unmasked and overthrown, the baleful effects of the Fall in Adam counteracted and undone, and God's honour vindicated, his holiness satisfied and his glory extended.

In Christ, God has conquered sin; such are the great glad tidings of the Bible. Already this conquest is demonstrated in the people of God, who by faith in Christ and his finished work are already delivered from the guilt and judgment of sin, and are already experiencing, to a degree, the conquest of sin's power through their union with Christ. This process will be culminated at the end of the age when Christ will return in glory, the saints will be fully sanctified, sin banished from God's good creation and a new heaven and earth brought into being in which righteousness will dwell. (*Cf.* Gn. 3:15; Is. 52:13–53:12; Je. 31:31–34; Mt. 1:21; Mk. 2:5; 10:45; Lk. 2:11; 11:14–22; Jn. 1:29; 3:16f.; Acts 2:38; 13:38f.; Rom. *passim*; 1 Cor. 15:3f., 22f.; Eph. 1:3–14; 2:1–10; Col. 2:11–15; Heb. 8:1–10:25; 1 Pet. 1:18–21; 2 Pet. 3:11–13; 1 Jn. 1:6–2:2; Rev. 20:7–14; 21:22–22:5.)

BIBLIOGRAPHY. J. Orr, *Sin as a Problem of Today*, 1910; C. Ryder Smith, *The Bible Doctrine of Sin*, 1953; E. Brunner, *Man in Revolt*, 1939; R. Niebuhr, *The Nature and Destiny of Man*, 1941 and 1943; M. Luther, *Bondage of the Will*, E. T. 1957; J. Murray, *The Imputation of Adam's Sin*, 1959; G. C. Berkouwer, *Sin*, 1971; B. Ramm, *Offence to Reason*, 1985; W. Günther, W. Bauder, *NIDNTT* 3, pp. 573–587; *TDNT* 1, pp. 149–163, 267–339; 3, pp. 167–172; 5, pp. 161–166, 447–448, 736–744; 6, pp. 170–172, 883–884; 7, pp. 339–358. J.M.

B.A.M.

SINAI, MOUNT.

I. Situation

The location of this mountain is uncertain. The following mountains are regarded by various scholars as Mt Sinai: Jebel Mûsa, Ras eṣ-ṣafṣafeh, Jebel Serbāl and a mountain near al-Hrob. The tradition in favour of Jebel Serbāl can be traced back as far as Eusebius; the tradition in favour of Jebel Mûsa only as far as Justinian. The situation of Jebel Serbāl, *e.g.* the fact that there is no wilderness at its foot, makes it improbable as the mountain of the covenant. The once widely accepted view of A. Musil that the volcanic mountain near al-Hrob is to be identified with Mt Sinai is no longer popular with scholars, because it makes the reconstruction of the route of the Exodus impossible and it reads too much into Ex. 19. Modern attempts to identify Sinai with volcanic mountains E of the Gulf of Aqabah are so uncertain that not much can be derived from them. This leaves two possibilities: Jebel Mûsa and Ras eṣ-ṣafṣafeh. These two mountains are situated on a short ridge of granite of about 4 km stretching from NW to SE. Ras eṣ-ṣafṣafeh (1,993 m) is situated at the N edge and Jebel Msa (2,244 m) at the S one. Tradition and most of the modern scholars accept Jebel Mûsa as Mt Sinai. There is, none the less, a strong preference among certain scholars for Ras eṣ-ṣafṣafeh as the mountain of the covenant because of the considerable plain at its foot which would have been spacious enough for the large body of Israelites (*cf.* Ex. 20:18: 'they stood afar off'). However, tradition in favour of Jebel Mûsa is so ancient (about 1,500 years) and the granite formations so imposing that it is quite probably Mt Sinai. Furthermore, a few stations *en route* to the mountain point to the same conclusion.

II. In the Old Testament

Mt Sinai is also called Horeb in the OT. Travelling past Marah and Elim, the Israelites reached Sinai in the 3rd month after their departure from Egypt (Ex. 19:1), and camped at its foot on a plain from which the top was visible (Ex. 19:16, 18, 20). The Lord revealed himself to Moses on this mountain and gave the Ten Commandments and other laws. The covenant made here between God and the people played a major role in binding the tribes together and moulding them into one nation serving one God. Although the authenticity of this account is rejected by certain modern schools, it is clear from Jdg. 5:5 that the Sinai tradition is an ancient part of Israelite belief. The prominent role of Mt Sinai in the OT and the strong tradition attached to it provide ample evidence in support of the historicity of the account (*EXODUS).

At the foot of Jebel Mûsa is the monastery of St Catherine. It was here that Tischendorf discovered the famous 4th-century uncial MS of the Greek Bible called Codex Sinaiticus. The library of St Catherine has ancient MSS in Gk., Arabic, Ethiopic and Syriac (many of which have recently been made generally available on microfilm).

BIBLIOGRAPHY. B. Rothenberg, *God's Wilderness*, 1961; W. Beyerlin, *Origins and History of the Oldest Sinaitic Traditions*, 1965; G. I. Davies, in J. A. Emerton (ed.), *Studies in the Pentateuch*, 1990.

F.C.F.

III. In the New Testament

1. During his last speech before martyrdom, Stephen twice mentions Mt Sinai in a reference to the theophany to Moses at the burning bush (Acts 7:30, 38; in Ex. 3:1ff. the synonym Horeb is used). Stephen reminds his accusers that even a Gentile place like Sinai in NW Arabia became holy ground because God was pleased to reveal himself there; he was not limited by Jewish geography.

2. In Gal. 4:21–31 Paul uses an allegory to identify Israel first with the slave-wife Hagar (Gn. 16:15; 21:2, 9) and then with Mt Sinai 'in Arabia' (*i.e.* appropriately in a barren wilderness area). Hagar and Sinai are symbolic respectively of being outside the covenant of promise and of bondage to the law of Moses. Together they are taken as representing 'the present Jerusalem', *i.e.* Judaism, which is slavery (to the Law and its intolerable burden of Pharisaic additions as well as to the Romans). By contrast 'the Jerusalem above' is 'free' (freeborn) and 'our mother', the mother of all who are Christians, *i.e.* 'children of promise, as Isaac was'.

3. In Heb. 12:19–29, although not named directly, Mt Sinai, symbolizing the old covenant, is contrasted with Mt Zion, symbolizing the offer of the gospel under the new covenant. The awesome terrors of Sinai at the giving of the Law are described in terms of Ex. 19:16–19; 20:18–21; Dt. 4:11f.; and the reader is warned that rejecting the gospel and its privileges incurs a far more dreadful judgment even than that which followed disobedience to the Law.

BIBLIOGRAPHY. C. Brown, *NIDNTT* 3, pp. 1013–1015; E. Löhse, *TDNT* 7, pp. 282–287. N.H.

SINEW. Heb. *gîḏ*, the sinew viewed as that which bound the bones together (Ezk. 37:6; Jb. 10:11).

The custom mentioned in Gn. 32:32 is obscure. C. A. Simpson in *IB* quotes Robertson Smith as explaining it from the idea that the thigh was sacred as the seat of life, and Wellhausen as calling attention to a trace of it in ancient Arabia. The application of the custom involves the removing of the sinew in the thigh-joint before the flesh is cooked.

The term is not found in the NT. B.O.B.

SIN, WILDERNESS OF. A wilderness through which the Israelites passed between Elim and Mt Sinai (Ex. 16:1; 17:1; Nu. 33:11–12). It is usually identified with Debbet er-Ramleh, a sandy tract below Jebel et-Tih in the SW of the Sinai peninsula; but another suggested location is on the coastal plain of el-Markhah. As its position depends on the fixing of Mt *Sinai, which is uncertain, it is impossible to determine the exact site.

J.M.H.

SION. A synonym for, or part of, Mt Hermon (Dt. 4:48, AV; *cf.* RSV mg.). It is probably another form of 'Sirion' (Dt. 3:9); indeed, Pesh. reads 'Sirion' here, as also do RSV, NEB. A different word from 'Zion'.

J.D.D.

SIRAH, CISTERN OF (AV 'well of Sirah'). The place from which Joab secretly recalled Abner, former captain of Saul's armies, following his visit to David to discuss the surrender of Israel. Unknown to David, Joab slew Abner (2 Sa. 3:26). Probably modern Ain Sarah, 2½ km NW of Hebron.

J.A.T.

SIRION (Heb. *śiryōn*). The Canaanite name for Mt *Hermon as used in the Bible by the Sidonians (Dt. 3:9; *cf.* Ps. 29:6) and found in the form *šryn* in the Ugaritic texts. See C. H. Gordon, *Ugaritic Textbook*, 1965, p. 495. (*SION.)

T.C.M.

SISERA (*sîs*ʿ*rā'*, a non-Semitic, possibly Illyrian name).

1. The commander of *Jabin's army (Jdg. 4:2f.) and possibly the petty king of Harosheth-ha-goiim (Haroseth of the nations), tentatively identified with Tell el-'Amr, 19 km NW of Megiddo, a strategic location for the deployment of Jabin's 900 chariots. His dominant military role in the battle against Deborah and Barak explains his prominence in the biblical record when compared with his overlord, Jabin (who is not mentioned at all in Jdg. 5). After his crushing defeat at Mt Tabor and subsequent flight, he was treacherously slain by *Jael (Jdg. 4:15–21; 5:24–27). See A. E. Cundall, *Judges and Ruth*, *TOTC*, 1968, pp. 81–100.

2. The family-name of a class of Temple servants of foreign origin who returned with Zerubbabel from Exile in 537 BC (Ezr. 2:53; Ne. 7:55).

A.E.C.

SITNAH (Heb. *śiṭnâ*, 'hatred', 'contention'). A name given to a well which Isaac's servants dug in Gerar (Gn. 26:21) and which was seized by the servants of Abimelech. For general location, see *GERAR.

J.D.D.

SKIRT. The translation of three Heb. words. **1.** *kānāp̄*, 'wing', 'extremity', is the usual term (Ru. 3:9; 1 Sa. 24:4; *etc.*). **2.** *šûl* (Je. 13:22, 26; La. 1:9; Na. 3:5) means 'hem', and is so rendered elsewhere in AV. **3.** *peh* (Ps. 133:2, AV) is the common word for 'mouth', and the context is clearer if we follow RSV, which in the verse concerned renders the Heb. as 'collar'.

J.D.D.

SLAVE, SLAVERY.

I. In the Old Testament

a. Introduction

Under the influence of Roman law, a slave is usually considered to be a person (male or female) owned by another, without rights, and—like any other form of personal property—to be used and disposed of in whatever way the owner may wish. In the ancient biblical East, however, slaves could and did acquire various rights before the law or by custom, and these included ownership (even of other slaves) and the power to conduct business while they were yet under their masters' control. Slavery is attested from the earliest times throughout the ancient Near East, and owed its existence and perpetuation primarily to economic factors.

b. Sources of slaves

(i) *By capture.* Captives, especially prisoners of war, were commonly reduced to slavery (Gn. 14:21, claimed by the king of Sodom; Nu. 31:9; Dt. 20:14; 21:10ff.; Jdg. 5:30; 1 Sa. 4:9 (*cf.* RSV); 2 Ki. 5:2; 2 Ch. 28:8, 10ff.), a custom that goes back as far as written documents themselves, to roughly 3000 BC and probably further (references in I. Mendelsohn, *Slavery in the Ancient Near East*, 1949, pp. 1–3).

(ii) *By purchase.* Slaves could readily be bought from other owners or general merchants (*cf.* Gn. 17:12–13, 27; Ec. 2:7). The law allowed Hebrews to buy foreign slaves from foreigners at home or abroad (Lv. 25:44f.). In antiquity, slaves were sold among all kinds of other merchandise and from country to country. Thus, the Midianites and Ishmaelites sold *Joseph to an Egyptian high official (Gn. 37:36; 39:1), and Phoenician Tyre imported slaves and bronzeware from Asia Minor (Ezk. 27:13) and sold Jews to the Ionians, thereby incurring a threat of like treatment of her own nationals (Joel 3:4–8). For evidence of the large numbers of Semitic slaves that reached Egypt in Joseph's general period, probably mainly by trade, see references in *Joseph or in Bibliography below. For Babylonian merchant-enterprise in slave-trading abroad in places such as Tyre, see Mendelsohn, *op. cit.*, pp. 3–5.

(iii) *By birth.* Children 'born in the house' of slave-parents became 'house-born slaves'; such are mentioned in Scripture from patriarchal times onward (Gn. 15:3; 17:12–13, 27; Ec. 2:7; Je. 2:14), and equally early in Mesopotamian documents (Mendelsohn, pp. 57–58).

(iv) *As restitution.* If a convicted thief could not make restitution and pay his fines and damages, funds towards this could be raised by selling him as a slave (Ex. 22:3; *cf.* a similar provision in Hammurapi's Code, §§ 53–54: *ANET*, p. 168).

(v) *By default on debts.* Debtors who went bankrupt were often forced to sell their children as slaves, or their children would be confiscated as slaves by the creditor (2 Ki. 4:1; Ne. 5:5, 8). The insolvent debtor himself, as well as his wife and family, commonly became the slave of his creditor and gave him his labour for 3 years to work off the debt and then go free, in Hammurapi's Code (§ 117: *DOTT*, p. 30, or *ANET*, pp. 170–171). This seems to be the background to the Mosaic law in Ex. 21:2–6 (and 7–11), and in Dt. 15:12–18, where a Hebrew slave must work 6 years, explicitly a 'double' period of time (Dt. 15:18) compared with

Hammurapi's 3 years (*cf.* Mendelsohn, pp. 32–33), but on release he was to be granted stock to start up on his own again (see also *d.* (i) 1, below). Insolvency was a major cause of reduction to slave status in the biblical East (Mendelsohn, pp. 23, 26–29).

(vi) *Self-sale.* Selling oneself voluntarily into slavery, *i.e.* dependence on another, to escape poverty, was widely known (Mendelsohn, pp. 14–19, for data). Lv. 25:39–43, 47ff., recognized this, but provided for redemption at (or with foreign owners, even before) Jubilee year.

(vii) *Abduction.* To steal a person, and to reduce a kidnapped person to slavery, was an offence punishable by death in the laws of both Hammurapi (§ 14: *DOTT*, p. 30; *ANET*, p. 166) and Moses (Ex. 21:16; Dt. 24:7). The brothers of *Joseph were guilty of essentially such an offence (Gn. 37:27–28 with 45:4), and might well be 'dismayed' and need reassurance not to be 'distressed' (Gn. 45:3, 5, and *cf.* Gn. 50:15).

c. Price of slaves

The price of slaves naturally varied somewhat according to circumstances and the sex, age and condition of slaves, but the average price of slaves gradually rose like that of other commodities during the course of history; the female of child-bearing age being always more valuable than the male slave. In the late 3rd millennium BC in Mesopotamia (Akkad and 3rd Ur Dynasties) the average price of a slave was 10–15 shekels of silver (references in Mendelsohn, pp. 117–155). About 1700 BC Joseph was sold to the Ishmaelites for 20 shekels of silver (Gn. 37:28), precisely the current price for the patriarchal period, where 1/3 of a mina is 20 shekels (§§ 116, 214, 252: *DOTT*, p. 35; *ANET*, pp. 170, 175–176, in (*e.g.*) Hammurapi's Code, *c.* 1750 BC), in contemporary Old Babylonian tablets (*cf.* Mendelsohn, *loc. cit.*), and at Mari (G. Boyer, *Archives Royales de Mari*, 8, 1958, p. 23, No. 10, lines 1–4). By about the 15th century BC the average price was 30 shekels at Nuzi (B. L. Eichler, *Indenture at Nuzi*, 1973, pp. 16–18, 87), and could be 20, 30 or 40 shekels at Ugarit in N Syria (Mendelsohn, pp. 118–155; J. Nougayrol, *Palais Royal d'Ugarit*, 3, 1955, p. 228: 2 with refs., p. 23 n. 1) in the 14th/13th centuries BC, comparing well with the contemporary price of 30 shekels reflected in Ex. 21:32. In later days the average price for a male slave rose steadily under the Assyrian, Babylonian and Persian empires, to about 50–60 shekels, 50 shekels and 90–120 shekels respectively (Mendelsohn, pp. 117–118, 155). For 50 shekels in Assyrian times, *cf.* 2 Ki. 15:20, where the Israelite notables under Menahem had to pay their value as slaves, presumably as ransom to avoid deportation to Assyria (D. J. Wiseman, *Iraq* 15, 1953, p. 135, and *JTVI* 87, 1955, p. 28). The successive and identical rises in average price for slaves in both the biblical and external records strongly suggest that the former are based directly on accurate traditions from the specific periods in question, *i.e.* the early and late 2nd millennium and early 1st millennium BC, and are not at these points the elaboration of later traditionists or of over-statistical priestly redactors.

d. Privately owned slaves in Israel

(i) *Hebrew slaves.* 1. The law sought (like Hammurapi's Code 5 centuries earlier) to avoid the risk of wholesale population-drift into slavery and serfdom under economic pressure on small farmers, by limiting the length of service that insolvent debtors (see *b.* (v), above) had to give to 6 years, their release to be accompanied by the provision of sufficient assets to make a new start (Ex. 21:2–6; Dt. 15:12–18). A man already married when thus enslaved took his wife with him at release, but if he was formerly single and was given a wife by his master, that wife and any children remained the master's. Hence, those who wished to stay in service and keep their family could do so permanently (Ex. 21:6; Dt. 15:16f.); at Jubilee he would be released in any case (Lv. 25:40) in connection with the restoration of inheritance then (Lv. 25:28), even if he chose to stay on with his master permanently. Insolvent debtors in temporary enslavement similar to that of Ex. 21:2ff. are probably the subject of Ex. 21:26–27, the permanent loss of a member cancelling the debt and so bringing immediate release from the creditor/ master (Mendelsohn, *op. cit.*, pp. 87–88). In Jeremiah's day the king and the wealthy flagrantly abused the law of 7th-year release by freeing their slaves only to seize them again, and were duly condemned for this very sharp practice (Je. 34:8–17).

2. A Hebrew who voluntarily sold himself into slavery to escape from poverty was to serve his master until Jubilee year, when he would go free (Lv. 25:39–43) and receive back his inheritance (Lv. 25:28). But if his master was a foreigner he had the option of purchasing his freedom or being redeemed by a relative at any time before Jubilee (Lv. 25:47–55).

3. Female slaves were the subject of further specific law and custom. That a chief wife's servant-maids might bear children to their master for the childless wife is attested both in the patriarchal narrative (Gn. 16) and in cuneiform documents, *e.g.* from Ur (Wiseman, *JTVI* 88, 1956, p. 124). Under the law, if a Hebrew girl was sold as a slave (Ex. 21:7–11) her marital status was carefully safeguarded: she might marry her master (and be redeemed if rejected), or his son, or become a properly maintained concubine, but would go free if the master failed to implement whichever of the three possibilities he had agreed to. In Mesopotamia such contracts were usually harsher, often having no safeguards whatever (*cf.* Mendelsohn, pp. 10ff., 87).

(ii) *Foreign slaves.* 1. Unlike Hebrew slaves, these could be enslaved permanently and handed on with other family property (Lv. 25:44–46). However, they were included in the commonwealth of Israel on patriarchal precedent (circumcision, Gn. 17:10–14, 27) and shared in festivals (Ex. 12:44, Passover; Dt. 16:11, 14) and sabbath-rest (Ex. 20:10; 23:12).

2. A woman captured in war could be taken as full wife by a Hebrew, and would thereby cease to have slave status; thus, if she was subsequently divorced she went free and did not become a slave (Dt. 21:10–14).

(iii) *General conditions.* 1. The treatment accorded to slaves depended directly on the personality of their masters. It could be a relationship of trust (*cf.* Gn. 24: 39:1–6) and affection (Dt. 15:16), but discipline might be harsh, even fatal (*cf.* Ex. 21:21), though to kill a slave outright carried a penalty (Ex. 21:20), doubtless death (Lv. 24:17, 22). It is just possible that Hebrew slaves, like some Babylonians, sometimes carried an outward token of their servitude (Mendelsohn, p. 49), though this remains uncertain. In some circumstances slaves could claim justice (Jb. 31:13) or go to law (Mendelsohn, pp. 65, 70, 72), but—like the Egyptian spared by David—could be abandoned by callous masters when ill (1 Sa. 30:13). In patriarchal times a childless master could adopt a house-slave and make him his heir, as is recorded of Abraham and Eliezer before the births of Ishmael and Isaac (Gn. 15:3), and of various people in cuneiform documents (Ur, *cf.* Wiseman, *JTVI* 88, 1956, p. 124).

2. Throughout ancient history, the available documents bear witness to the large numbers of people who tried to escape from slavery by running away, and those who in any way aided and abetted them could expect punishment, especially in early times (Mendelsohn, pp. 58ff.). However, slaves that fled from one country to another came under a different category. States sometimes had mutual extradition clauses in their treaties; this may explain how Shimei so easily recovered two runaway slaves of his from King Achish of Gath in Philistia (1 Ki. 2:39–40; *cf.* Wiseman, *op. cit.*, p. 123). However, some states also at times decreed that if any nationals of theirs enslaved abroad returned to their homeland they would be set free and not be extradited. This was stipulated by Hammurapi of Babylon (Code, § 280: *DOTT*, p. 35; *ANET*, p. 177; *cf.* Mendelsohn, pp. 63–64, 75, 77–78), and is probably the meaning of Dt. 23:15f. (Mendelsohn, pp. 63–64).

(iv) *Manumission.* In the Heb. laws an enslaved debtor was to be released after 6 years (Ex. 21:2; Dt. 15:12, 18), or as compensation for injury (Ex. 21:26–27), and a girl could be redeemed or set free if repudiated, or if conditions of service were not honoured (Ex. 21:8, 11; see *d.* (i) 3 above). A Hebrew who sold himself into slavery was to be freed at Jubilee, or could be redeemed by purchase at any time from a foreign master (Lv. 25:39–43, 47–55; *d.* (i) 2 above). On Dt. 23:15f., see preceding section. A female captive could become a freedwoman by marriage (Dt. 21:10–14).

In 1 Ch. 2:34f., a Hebrew Sheshan had no sons, and so married his daughter to his Egyptian slave Jarha in order to continue his family line; it is most probable that Jarha would be made free in these circumstances (Mendelsohn, p. 57), and likewise Eliezer of Damascus (Gn. 15:3), if he had not been replaced as heir to Abraham by Ishmael and then Isaac.

In Heb. the term which denotes that a person is 'free', not (or no longer) a slave (*e.g.* Ex. 21:2, 5, 26–27; Dt. 15:12–13, 18; Jb. 3:19; Je. 34:9–11, 14, 16; *etc.*), is *ḥop̄šî*, which has a long history in the ancient East, occurring as *ḫupšu* in cuneiform texts from the 18th to the 7th centuries BC, and usually referring to freedmen who are small landholders, tenant farmers or hired labourers. When a Hebrew was freed this is the class he would be in. He would become a small landholder if he regained his inheritance (as at Jubilee) or a tenant or labourer on land held by others. On manumission in the ancient East, see Mendelsohn, pp. 74–91; on *ḥop̄šî*, see Bibliography below.

e. State and Temple slavery

(i) *State slavery in Israel.* This was practised on a restricted scale. David caused the conquered Ammonites to do forced labour (2 Sa. 12:31), and Solomon conscripted the surviving descendants of the peoples of Canaan into his *mas-'ōḇēḏ*, permanent state labour-levy, but not true Israelites (see 1 Ki. 9:15, 21–22; burden-bearers and quarriers, v. 15 and 2 Ch. 2:18). The Israelites served on temporary corvée (*mas*) in Lebanon only, by rota (1 Ki. 5:13f.). There is no contradiction between 1 Ki. 5 and 9 on the corvées; *cf.* M. Haran, *VT* 11, 1961, pp. 162–164, following and partly correcting Mendelsohn, pp. 96–98. *Cf.* A. F. Rainey, *IEJ* 20, 1970, pp. 191–202. The famous coppermines near Ezion-geber (*ELATH) were most likely worked with Canaanite and Ammonite/Edomite slave-labour (N. Glueck, *BASOR* 79, 1940, pp. 4–5; Mendelsohn, p. 95; Haran, *op. cit.*, p. 162). Such use of war-captives was common throughout the Near East, and in other countries outside Israel their less fortunate nationals and ordinary slaves could sometimes be taken over by the state (Mendelsohn, pp. 92–99).

(ii) *Temple slaves in Israel.* After the war with Midian, Moses levied from the warriors and Israel at large 1 in 500 and 1 in 50 respectively of their spoils in persons and goods, for service with the high priest and Levites at the tabernacle, obviously as menials (Nu. 31:28, 30, 47). Then there were added to these the Gibeonites spared by Joshua, who became 'hewers of wood and drawers of water' for the house and altar of the Lord (Jos. 9:3–27), *i.e.* menials for the tabernacle and its personnel. Also, David and his officers had dedicated foreigners (Nethinim) for similar service with the Levites who served the Temple, some of their descendants returning from captivity with Ezra (8:20); to these were added 'Solomon's servants' (Ezr. 2:58). Ezekiel (44:6–9) possibly warned against allowing these uncircumcised menials to usurp a place in the worship of a Temple that was not theirs. Under Nehemiah (3:26, 31) some of these lived in Jerusalem and helped repair its walls.

f. Conclusion: general trends

Generally, a more humane spirit breathes through the OT laws and customs on slavery, as illustrated by the repeated injunctions in God's name not to rule over a brother Israelite harshly (*e.g.* Lv. 25:43, 46, 53, 55; Dt. 15:14f.). Even when Heb. law and custom on slaves shares in the common heritage of the ancient Semitic world, there is this unique care in God's name for these people who by status were not people, something absent from the law codes of Babylon or Assyria. It should, moreover, be remembered that, by and large, the economy of the ancient Near East was never one substantially or mainly based on slave-labour as in 'classical' and later Greece or above all in imperial Rome (*cf.* Mendelsohn, pp. 111–112, 116:117, 121; I. J. Gelb, *Festschrift for S. N. Kramer*, 1976, pp. 195–207, on statistics and comparisons; limited numbers and economic opportunities of Neo-Babylonian slaves, *cf.* F. I. Andersen (summary of Dandamayer), *Buried History* 11, 1975, pp. 191–194). And Job (31:13–15) heralds the concept of the equality of all men, of whatever station, before their creator God.

BIBLIOGRAPHY. A fundamental work which makes frequent reference to the OT data is I. Mendelsohn, *Slavery in the Ancient Near East*, 1949, following up earlier studies, and supplemented by *IEJ* 5, 1955, pp. 65–72. The biblical data are summarized and evaluated by A. G. Barrois, *Manuel d'Archéologie Biblique*, 2, 1953, pp. 38, 114, 211–215, and by R. de Vaux, *Ancient Israel: its Life and Institutions*, 1961, pp. 80–90, 525). On Temple slaves in Israel, see M. Haran, *VT* 11, 1961, pp. 159–169. On *ḥop̄šî*, 'free(dman)', see Mendelsohn, *BASOR* 83, 1941, pp. 36–39, and *ibid.*, 139, 1955, pp. 9–11; E. R. Lacheman, *ibid.*, 86, 1942, pp. 36–37; D. J. Wiseman, *The Alalakh Tablets*, 1953, p. 10. For the Egyp. data on slavery, see the monograph by A. M. Bakir, *Slavery in Pharaonic Egypt*, 1952, supplemented for Joseph's period by W. C. Hayes, *A Papyrus of the Late Middle Kingdom in the Brooklyn Museum*, 1955, pp. 92–94, 98–99, 133–134, and especially G. Posener, *Syria* 34, 1957, pp. 147, 150–161. K.A.K.

II. In the New Testament

a. Systems of slavery in NT times

Jewish slavery, to judge by the Talmud, remained governed as always by the tight national unity of the people. There was a sharp distinction between Jewish and Gentile slaves. The former were subject to the sabbath-year manumission, and the onus fell upon Jewish communities everywhere to ransom their nationals held in slavery to Gentiles. Thus no fundamental division into bond and free was recognized. At the same time the whole people might be thought of as the servants of Yahweh.

By contrast, Greek slavery was justified in classical theory by the assumption of a natural order of slaves. Since only the citizen class were, strictly speaking, human, slaves were merely chattels. While this idea was carried into practice only in the rare cases where common sense and humanity broke down, the fact remains that throughout classical antiquity the institution of slavery was simply taken for granted, even by those who worked for its amelioration.

There was a very great diversity at different times and places in the extent and uses of slavery. Modern sentiment is dominated by the horrors of the mass agricultural slavery in Italy and Sicily during the 2 centuries between the Punic wars and Augustus, which were dramatized by a series of heroic slave-revolts. This was a by-product of the rapid Roman conquest of the Mediterranean, the main source of the glut of slaves being war prisoners. In NT times, however, there was very little warfare, and in any case the slave ranches were a peculiarly Roman method of farming. In Egypt, for instance, there was practically no agricultural slavery, the land being worked by a free peasantry under bureaucratic supervision. In Asia Minor and Syria there were great temple estates whose tenant farmers were in a kind of serfdom. In Palestine, to judge by the parables of Jesus, slaves were employed on country estates more in administrative positions, the labour being recruited on a casual basis.

Domestic and public slavery were the most widespread forms. In the former case the slaves were purchased and employed as an index of wealth. Where only one or two were owned, they worked beside their master at the same occupations. At Athens they were indistinguishable in the streets from free men, and the familiarity of slaves towards their owners was a stock theme of comedy. At Rome the great houses employed scores of slaves for sheer luxury. Their work was highly specialized and often largely effortless. In the case of public slaves, their status conferred a good deal of independence and respect. They performed all sorts of duties in the absence of a civil service, including even police services in some cases. Professions such as medicine or education were commonly filled by slaves.

The main sources of slavery were: (1) birth, depending on the law of the particular state concerning the various degrees of servile parentage; (2) the widespread practice of exposing unwanted children, who were then available for the use of anyone who cared to rear them; (3) the sale of one's own children into slavery; (4) voluntary slavery as a solution to problems such as debt; (5) penal slavery; (6) kidnapping and piracy; (7) the traffic across the Roman frontiers. Not all these sources were open in one place at any one time: there was a great deal of variation in local law and sentiment. The degree of slavery also varied greatly, and is impossible to calculate. It may have reached one-third of the population in Rome and the great metropolitan cities of the east. In areas where there was a peasant economy, however, it was reduced to a small fraction of that.

Manumission could be readily arranged at any time if owners wished. In Rome it was most commonly performed by testament, and limits had to be placed on the generosity of owners to prevent the too rapid dilution of the citizen body with persons of foreign extraction. In Gk. states 2 common forms were a type of self-purchase, in which the legal incompetence of the slave was overcome by the ownership technically passing to a god, and manumission in return for a contract of services which simply meant that the slave continued in the same employment though legally free.

The condition of slavery was everywhere being steadily mitigated in NT times. Although slaves had no legal personality, owners recognized that they worked better the more their condition approximated to freedom, and the owning of property and contracting of marriages were normally allowed. Cruelty was condemned by the growing sentiment of common humanity, and in some cases legally controlled; in Egypt, for instance, the death of a slave was subject to a coroner's inquest. While in Gk. states emancipated slaves became resident aliens of their former master's city, at Rome they automatically became citizens on manumission. Thus the vast flow of slaves into Italy, especially during the last 2 centuries before Christ, had the effect of internationalizing the Roman republic, anticipating the government's own policy of steadily broadening membership.

b. The NT attitude to slavery

The twelve disciples of Jesus apparently had no part in the system of slavery. They included neither slaves nor owners. The institution figures frequently in the parables, however (*e.g.* Mt. 21:34; 22:3), because the regal and baronial households to which it belonged afforded a nice analogy for the kingdom of God. Jesus repeatedly spoke of the relation of the disciples to himself as that of servants to their lord (*e.g.* Mt. 10:24; Jn. 13:16). At the same time he stressed the inadequacy of this figure. The disciples were emancipated, as it were, and admitted to higher privileges of intimacy (Jn. 15:15). Or again, to their acute embarrassment, Jesus himself adopted the servile role (Jn. 13:4–17), with the object of encouraging them to mutual service.

Outside Palestine, however, where the churches were often established on a household basis, the membership included both masters and servants. Slavery was one of the human divisions that became meaningless in the new community in Christ (1 Cor. 7:22; Gal. 3:28). This apparently led to a desire for emancipation (1 Cor. 7:20) and perhaps even to the active encouragement of it by some (1 Tim. 6:3–5). Paul was not opposed to manumission if the opportunity was offered (1 Cor. 7:21), but studiously refrained from putting pressure on owners, even where personal sentiment might have led him to do so (Phm. 8, 14). Not only was there the practical reason of not laying the churches open to criticism (1 Tim. 6:1f.), but the point of principle that all human stations are allotted by God (1 Cor. 7:20). Slaves should therefore aim to please God by their service (Eph. 6:5–8; Col. 3:22). The fraternal bond with a believing master should be an added reason for serving him well (1 Tim. 6:2). A master, on the other hand, might well let the fraternal sentiment prevail (Phm. 16), and certainly must treat his slaves with restraint (Eph. 6:9) and strict equity (Col. 4:1).

The fact that household slavery, which is the only kind referred to in the NT, was generally governed by feelings of goodwill and affection, is implied by its figurative use in the 'household of God' (Eph. 2:19). The apostles are regularly God's stewards (1 Cor. 4:1; Tit. 1:7; 1 Pet. 4:10) and even plain servants (Rom. 1:1; Phil. 1:1). The legal character of 'the yoke of slavery' (Gal. 5:1) was not forgotten, however, and the idea of manumission and adoption into the family itself was a proud conclusion to this train of thought (Rom. 8:15–17; Gal. 4:5–7). Thus, whether in practice or by analogy, the apostles clearly branded the institution as part of the order that was passing away. In the last resort the fraternity of the sons of God would see all its members free of their bonds.

BIBLIOGRAPHY. W. L. Westermann, *The Slave Systems of Greek and Roman Antiquity*, 1955 (with full bibliography); M. I. Finley (ed.), *Slavery in Classical Antiquity: Views and Controversies*, 1960; S. S. Bartchy, *Mallon Chresai: First-Century Slavery and the Interpretation of 1 Cor. 7:21*, 1973; J. Vogt, *Ancient Slavery and the Ideal of Man*, 1974; F. Lyall, *Slaves, Citizens, Sons*, 1984; K. R. Bradley, *Slaves and Masters in the Roman Empire*, 1987; A. Kirschenbaum, *Sons, Slaves and Freedmen in Roman Commerce*, 1987; A. Watson, *Roman Slave Law*, 1987. E.A.J.

SLEEP. The OT uses several words for 'sleep', the NT has fewer; but no particular significance attaches to them. They signify sleep in the sense of physical rest and recuperation.

As might be expected, 'sleep' is used in a figurative sense in both Testaments. In Pr. 19:15, *etc.*, it describes mental torpor, and in Pr. 24:33 it refers to physical sloth and laziness. Paul uses the figure to describe the state of spiritual torpor of the non-Christians (Eph. 5:14), which unmans them and renders them unprepared for Christ's second advent (Mt. 25:22). By contrast, the Christian has awakened from this spiritual torpor, but he is challenged to remain awake (1 Thes. 5:4–8; Rom. 13:11f.; Mt. 25:13; 26:41).

Sleep is also a synonym for physical death (Jb. 14:12; Jn. 11:11–14; 1 Cor. 15:18). This signifies that death, like sleep, is neither a permanent state, nor does it 'destroy the identity of the sleeper' (Lk. 24:39f.), in spite of the change to be effected at the resurrection (1 Cor. 15:13ff.).

'Deep sleep', *tardēmâ*, was supernaturally induced (Gn. 2:21; 1 Sa. 26:12), and was equivalent almost to a *'trance' (Gn. 15:12), in which visions were granted (Jb. 4:13; Dn. 8:18). Its NT equivalent is *hypnos* (Acts 20:9). But visions also came in the course of 'ordinary' sleep (Gn. 28:10ff.; 1 Sa. 3:2ff.). See also *DREAM; L. Coenen, *NIDNTT* 1, pp. 441–443. J.G.S.S.T.

SLEIGHT. AV rendering (RSV 'cunning') of Gk. *kybeia*, 'dice-playing', Eph. 4:14 (*cf. kybeuō*, 'to deceive', in Epictetus 2. 19; 3. 21). NEB approaches the Greek differently from AV and RSV, and renders the last part of the verse 'dupes of crafty rogues and their deceitful schemes'. Paul is warning against instability and against those whose slick dealings present a plausible mixture of truth and error. J.D.D.

SMYRNA. A city in the Roman province of Asia, on the Aegean shore of what is now Asiatic Turkey. There was a Gk. colony near by from very early times, but it was captured and destroyed by the Lydians about the end of the 7th century BC and virtually ceased to exist until it was refounded on its present site by Lysimachus in the early 3rd century BC. It grew to be one of the most prosperous cities in Asia Minor. It was the natural port for the ancient trade route through the Hermus valley, and its immediate hinterland was very fertile. Smyrna was a faithful ally of Rome long before the Roman power became supreme in the E Mediterranean. Under the empire it was famous for its beauty and for the magnificence of its public buildings. It is now Izmir, the second largest city in Asiatic Turkey.

The gospel probably reached Smyrna at an early date, presumably from Ephesus (Acts 19:10). The 'angel of the church in Smyrna' is the recipient of the second (Rev. 2:8–11) of the letters to the 'seven churches . . . in Asia'. As in other commercial cities, the church encountered opposition from the Jews (Rev. 2:9; *cf.* 3:9). The description of the Christ as the one who was dead and lived again (v. 8) may allude to the resurgence of the city to new prosperity after a long period in obscurity. The 'crown' (v. 10) was rich in associations at Smyrna. It may suggest the victor's wreath at the games, or current forms of eulogy which used the image of

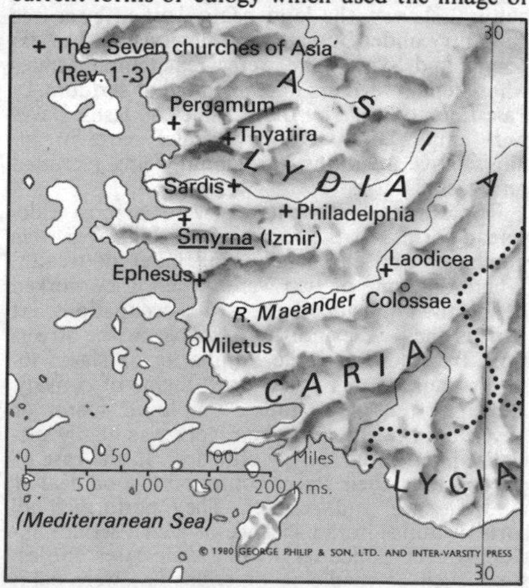

Smyrna, one of the 'seven churches of Asia' (Rev. 1–3).

the beauty and glory of the city and its buildings. *Cf.* also Jas. 1:12. The call to faithfulness (v. 10) is a call to the church to fulfil in the deepest way the historic reputation of the city. It was exemplified in the courage with which the aged bishop Polycarp refused to recant; he was martyred there *c.* AD 155 or later. (See C. J. Hemer, *Buried History* 11, 1975; *The Letters to the Seven Churches of Asia in Their Local Setting*, 1986; E. M. Yamauchi, *New Testament Cities in Western Asia Minor*, 1980.)

E.M.B.G.
C.J.H.

SNARE. Mechanical device, often with a bait, for catching birds or animals. AV uses 'snare' for 7 Heb. and 2 Gk. words, but RSV translates more accurately by other terms in Jb. 18:8, 10; La. 3:47; 1 Cor. 7:35. Heb. *paḥ* (*cf.* Egyp. *pḫ'*) is translated 'snare' 22 times in RSV; literally it is used of bird traps only (see Ps. 124:7; Pr. 7:23; Ec. 9:12; Am. 3:5). The last passage mentions two kinds of traps used by fowlers, one which pins the bird to the ground and one with a noose which catches the bird around the neck and springs up. In the majority of cases *paḥ* is used figuratively, for example in Jos. 23:13; Jb. 22:10; Ps. 119:110. AV translates *paḥ* by 'gin' in Jb. 18:9; Is. 8:14. Heb. *môqēš*, perhaps meaning 'striker', is translated 'snare' in RSV 22 times, literally only in Jb. 40:24, which implies that a snare cannot take the behemoth or hippopotamus. Examples of the figurative use of *môqēš* are: Ex. 10:7; 23:33; 2 Sa. 22:6; Ps. 64:5; Pr. 20:25; 22:25; Is. 8:14. AV translates *môqēš* by 'gin' in Pss. 140:5; 141:9; Am. 3:5. Other Heb. words translated 'snare' in a figurative sense are: *māṣôḏ*, 'means of hunting' (Ec. 7:26) and the related *mᵉṣûḏâ* (Ezk. 12:13; 17:20).

In the Apocrypha 'snare' (Gk. *pagis*) is used in reference to a gazelle (Ecclus. 27:20) and also figuratively (Ecclus. 9:3, 13; 27:26, 29).

In the NT Gk. *pagis* is translated 'snare' in a literal sense only in Lk. 21:34, which compares the suddenness of the Lord's coming to the springing of a trap. The figurative uses of *pagis* are Rom. 11:9; 1 Tim. 3:7; 6:9; 2 Tim. 2:26.

In Egypt today the following kinds of snares, some with ancient counterparts, are used: a clap-net, a clap-board over a hole, a clap-box, a springing noose, a trap with two jaws which close on the neck of the victim, and a cage with a sliding or springing door.

BIBLIOGRAPHY. G. Dalman, *Arbeit und Sitte* 6, 1939, pp. 321–340; G. Gerleman, *Contributions to the Old Testament Terminology of the Chase*, 1946; G. R. Driver, 'Reflections on Recent Articles, 2. Heb. *môqēš*, "striker" ', *JBL* 73, 1954, pp. 131–136.

J.T.

SNOW (Heb. *šeleḡ*). The few references to it indicate its rarity in Palestine, where it is scarcely ever found S of Hebron and is unknown along the sea coast and Jordan valley. Only twice is a snowfall recorded (in 2 Sa. 23:20 [= 1 Ch. 11:22] and in 1 Macc. 13:22). But the snow cover of Lebanon, 'the white mountain', is proverbial (Je. 18:14), and lower down in the Hauran it is not infrequent (Ps. 68:14). Elsewhere it is a rare feature, as the biblical incident of Benaiah would suggest (2 Sa. 23:20).

Snow as a symbol is variously employed. It is God-given and controlled (Jb. 38:22), one of the wonders of God's power (Jb. 37:6; Ps. 147:16), and given for fertility (Is. 55:10f.) and to accomplish moral ends (Jb. 38:22–23). It expresses whiteness (Ex. 4:6; Nu. 12:10; 2 Ki. 5:27; La. 4:7; Dn. 7:9), and therefore moral purity (Dn. 7:9; Mk. 9:3; Mt. 28:3; Rev. 1:14). It describes the complete acceptance of the penitent sinner (Ps. 51:7; Is. 1:18).

J.M.H.

SNUFFERS. For trimming and adjusting the wicks of the lamps in the tabernacle and Temple two, clearly distinct (see 1 Ki. 7:49–50; 2 Ch. 4:21–22), instruments were used: **1.** *mᵉzammᵉrôṯ*, translated 'snuffers' (1 Ki. 7:50; 2 Ki. 12:13 *(14)*; 25:14; 2 Ch. 4:22; Je. 52:18), probably a kind of scissors. **2.** *melqāḥayim*. These latter were 'tongs' (*cf.* Is. 6:6), but they are variously translated: 1 Ki. 7:49; 2 Ch. 4:21, 'tongs'; Ex. 37:23 'snuffers'; Ex. 25:38; Nu. 4:9, RSV 'snuffers', AV 'tongs'. See G. E. Wright, *Biblical Archaeology*, 1957, pp. 141f.

D.W.G.

SO. By conspiring with 'So king of Egypt' *c.* 726/5 BC (2 Ki. 17:4), Hoshea brought Assyrian retribution upon Israel. If So is the proper name of an Egyp. king, he must be either the last shadowy Libyan pharaoh, Osorkon IV (Aa-kheper-rēʿ) *c.* 727–716 BC, or the *de facto* W-Delta ruler Tefnakht, *c.* 727–720 BC, or some lesser and unidentified E-Delta kinglet. No mere kinglet could have helped Hoshea, nor can *Sô'* derive from Tefnakht's name; it is possible that *Sô'* could be an abbreviation for Osorkon (IV), as Egyp. *Sese* for Rameses (II).

Some identify So, vocalized *Siwe'* or *Sewe'*, with the Ethiopian Pharaoh Shabako (omitting formative *-ko*) who acted as army commander in Egypt before his accession. This is impossible in 726/5 BC, because the Ethiopians' W-Delta rivals, Tefnakht and Bekenranef (Bocchoris), held Lower Egypt until 716 BC. Others identify So/Siwe with 'Sib'e the *turtan* (army commander) of Egypt' whom Sargon II of Assyria defeated at Raphia in 720 BC. But So cannot be a king in 726/5 BC and then simply army commander in 720 BC, unless he were throughout a petty Delta kinglet acting as commander for Osorkon IV (or Tefnakht and Bekenranef). Therefore, if So is an Egyp. ruler's name, he would be either Osorkon IV abbreviated (but *not* Sib'e the *turtan*) or else a lesser kinglet and army commander under Osorkon IV, Tefnakht or Bekenranef.

S. Yeivin's suggestion in *VT* 2, 1952, pp. 164–168, that *Sô'* is not a proper name but merely a transcription of Egyp. *ṯ'*, 'vizier', then *sô' meleḵ miṣrayim* = 'the vizier of the king of Egypt' is phonetically unsuitable. The cuneiform name of the Egyp. commander of 720 BC, hitherto read as Sib'e, must now almost certainly be read as Re'e (R. Borger, *JNES* 19, 1960, pp. 49–53); this name cannot be identified with So as a proper name. It is possible that Re'e could be the name of the Egyp. vizier. H. Goedicke (*BASOR* 171, 1963, pp. 64–66) improbably read 'to (city) Sa(is), [to] the king of Egypt', with Tefnakht in mind. See K. A. Kitchen, *The Third Intermediate Period in Egypt*, 1972, pp. 182, 372–376.

K.A.K.

SOAP. 'Soap' is the rendering in the EVV of Heb. *bōriṯ* (Mal. 3:2; Je. 2:22), a word derived from *bārar*, 'to purify'. It probably means 'lye', a solution of potash (potassium carbonate) and soda (sodium carbonate) in water, which acts as a simple detergent. This is obtained by filtering water through vegetable ash, various alkaline salts being produced, of which potash is the principal. The Heb. term *bōr* is also best rendered 'lye' in Is. 1:25 and Jb. 9:30 (RVmg., RSV), though this is not observed by AV. (*ARTS AND CRAFTS, **III**. *h*.)

BIBLIOGRAPHY. R. Campbell Thompson, *A Dictionary of Assyrian Chemistry and Geology*, 1936, p. 14; M. Levey, *Chemistry and Chemical Technology in Ancient Mesopotamia*, 1959, p. 122.

T.C.M.

SOCOH, SOCO. 1. A town SE of Azekah in the Shephelah, the scene of the Philistine defeat (1 Sa. 17; see G. A. Smith, *The Historical Geography of the Holy Land*[25], 1966, pp. 161–162, for tactical description). The name is preserved in Khirbet Suweike (Roman and Byzantine); slightly farther W, the Early Iron fortification Khirbet Abbad commands the Wadi es-Sunt (Vale of Elah) from the S. Here the Wadi es-Sur from the S is joined by wadis coming down from the hills W of Bethlehem. Either this or **2** below was fortified by Rehoboam and later taken by the Philistines (2 Ch. 11:7; 28:18). Socoh is one of the cities named on royal jar-handle stamps found at *Lachish and other sites, which probably points to its importance as a major Judaean administrative centre in the reign of Hezekiah (*WRITING). *Cf. LOB*, pp. 353, 394–398.

2. A place in the highlands near Debir (Jos. 15:48; v. 35 refers to **1**); Khirbet Suweike, 3 km E of Dhahiriya (1 Ch. 4:18 probably refers to this place). **3.** A town in Solomon's tribute-area of Hepher (1 Ki. 4:10); probably the Bronze Age–Byzantine site Tell er-Ras by Suweike, N of Tulkarm in the plain of Sharon, and 24 km NW of Shechem (Tuthmosis III list no. 67). *Cf. ANET*, pp. 246f., *LOB* pp. 60, 310. J.P.U.L.

G.I.D.

SOLOMON. The third king of Israel (*c*. 971–931 BC), son of David and Bathsheba (2 Sa. 12:24); also named Jedidiah ('beloved of the Lord') by Nathan the prophet (2 Sa. 12:25). Solomon (*šᵉlōmōh*, probably 'peaceful') does not figure in the biblical narrative until the last days of David (1 Ki. 1:10ff.) despite the fact that he was born (in Jerusalem; 2 Sa. 5:14) early in his father's reign.

I. The rise to power

Solomon's path to the throne was far from smooth. Absalom's opposition was carried on by David's oldest surviving son, Adonijah (2 Sa. 3:4), who made a strong bid for the throne during his father's last days (1 Ki. 1:5ff.). Supported by David's deposed general, Joab, who had slain Absalom (2 Sa. 18:14–15), and the influential priest, Abiathar, Adonijah rallied support and actually held a coronation feast at En-rogel. But Solomon was not without allies. Benaiah, the son of Jehoiada, had his eye on the generalship; Zadok coveted a prominent priestly position. Their spokesman was Nathan the prophet, a confidant of David and Bathsheba (1 Ki. 1:11ff.). After Nathan and Bathsheba reminded David of his unexecuted promise concerning Solomon, the king gave instructions for Solomon's accession and sealed them with an oath (1 Ki. 1:28ff.).

The news of Solomon's coronation, for which David's storied bodyguard of Cherethites and Pelethites offered protection, broke up Adonijah's festivities (1 Ki. 1:41ff.) but not his stratagems to control the kingdom. He implored Bathsheba to influence Solomon to give him Abishag, David's handmaiden (1 Ki. 1:3–4), as wife (1 Ki. 2:13ff.). Solomon, apparently fearing that such a marriage would give Adonijah leverage with which to prise him from the throne, refused. Adonijah paid with his life for his rash proposal (1 Ki. 2:25); when Abiathar the priest was banished from office (1 Ki. 2:26–27) and Joab vengefully slain before the altar (1 Ki. 2:28ff.), Solomon reigned without a rival. The prominent role of the queen-mother in this whole intrigue is noteworthy. Bathsheba seems to have blazed the trail for other queen-mothers in Judah, for the author of Kings faithfully records the name of each king's mother (*e.g.* 1 Ki. 15:2, 10). The arbitrary manner in which Solomon was chosen boded ill for the future. The elders of Judah and Israel, on whose goodwill true national harmony depended, were bypassed in the decision.

II. The master sage

Solomon was Israel's first *dynastic* ruler. Saul and David, like the judges, were chosen because God had given them a special measure of power: they were *charismatic* rulers. Although Solomon took office without God's *charisma*, he received it during his vision at Gibeon, when the Lord offered him his choice of gifts (1 Ki. 3:5ff.). Realizing the enormity of his task, Solomon chose an 'understanding heart' (v. 9). The story of the harlots' dispute over the baby (1 Ki. 3:16ff.) has become a classic display of Solomon's royal wisdom.

Surpassing his contemporaries in Egypt, Arabia, Canaan, and Edom in wisdom (1 Ki. 4:29ff.), Solomon became the great patron of Israel's *Wisdom literature. No other period of the Monarchy provided the combination of international contacts, wealth and relief from war necessary for literary productivity. Solomon took the lead in this movement, collecting and composing thousands of proverbs and songs (1 Ki. 4:32). The statement that he spoke of trees, beasts, *etc.* (1 Ki. 4:33) probably refers to his use of plants and animals in his proverbs rather than to accomplishments in botany and zoology, although close observation of these creatures would be necessary before he could use them in his sayings (*cf.* Pr. 30:24–31).

Two extensive collections in Proverbs (10:1–22:16; 25:1–29:27) are credited to him, and the entire collection bears his name as the chief contributor (1:1). Canticles and Ecclesiastes have traditionally been ascribed to him, although the latter does not mention his name. Though the final composition of these books seems to be much later than the 10th century BC, both may contain accurate descriptions of Solomon's glory and wisdom. Two psalms (72, a royal psalm; 127, a wisdom psalm) complete the list of canonical writings attributed to him. The relationship of *corporate personality* (the view that members of a clan are so inter-related that when one member acts, the others may be viewed as taking part in the act) to problems of authorship is not clear: it is possible that some of the Solomonic writings are products of sages who felt their kinship with their intellectual father so strongly that they credited him with their work. Solomon's literary sponsorship may also have included substantial endeavours in

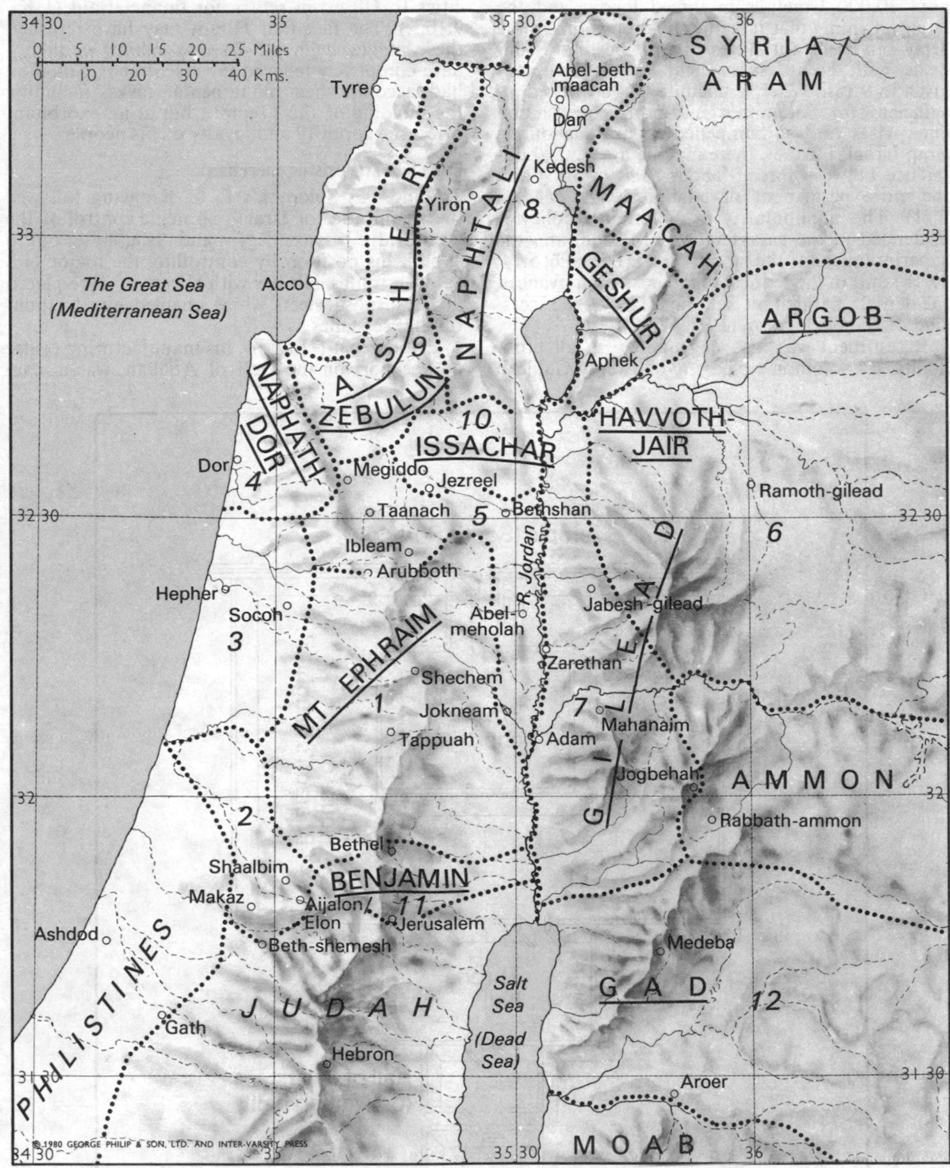

Solomon's administrative districts as described in 1 Ki. 4:7–19.

collecting and recording Israel's early traditions and the accounts of the beginning of the monarchy.

III. The iron ruler

Solomon's task was to maintain and control the expanse of territory bequeathed him by David. Further, he had to effect as smooth a transition as possible from the tribal confederacy which had characterized pre-Davidic political life to the strong central government which alone could maintain Israel's empire.

The traditional tribal boundaries were replaced by administrative districts: twelve in Israel (1 Ki. 4:7ff.) and perhaps one in Judah; *cf.* the problematic 4:19 in RSV. (See J. Bright, *A History of Israel*, 3, 1981, p. 206 n. 51, for the view that Jos. 15:20–62 contains the list of the twelve districts of Judah.) Each of these tax districts was obligated to provide support for the court for a month during the year (1 Ki. 4:7), which would appear an onerous task according to the list in 1 Ki. 4:22–23. (*FOOD, **I.** *d* (iii).)

In addition to this, Solomon began recruiting labourers from among the Israelites, a measure unpalatable to a people who relished freedom. There is an apparent contradiction between 1 Ki. 5:13ff. and 9:22, the former stating that Solomon used 30,000 Israelites in forced labour and the latter affirming that Israelites held positions in the army but were not slaves. It may be that 5:13ff. deals with events subsequent to the summary given in 9:15ff. When Canaanite labour proved insufficient for Solomon's enormous construction enterprises he was compelled to draft labourers from Israel. Further, there may be a technical difference between forced labour (*mas* in 5:13) and the more permanent slave-labour (*mas 'ôbēd* in 9:21). The unpopularity of Solomon's policy is evidenced in the assassination of Adoniram, the superintendent of the labour crews (1 Ki. 4:6; 5:14; 12:18) and in the request for redress of grievances, the denial of which by Rehoboam led to the secession of the N kingdom (1 Ki. 12:4ff.).

Resentment was also engendered, in all probability, by Solomon's pledging of twenty Galilean cities to Hiram in return for financial aid (1 Ki. 9:10ff.). The fact that Hiram may have returned these later (as 2 Ch. 8:1–2 seems to hint) would not have completely relieved the resentment. Solomon had accomplished monumental tasks, including the building of the *Temple, but at an exorbitant price: the goodwill and loyalty of his people.

IV. The enterprising merchant

Trading was Solomon's forte. Knowing full well the significance of Israel's strategic control of the land-bridge between Egypt and Asia, he set out to exploit his position by controlling the major N-S caravan routes. His ties with Hiram of Tyre placed at his disposal fleets which enabled him to monopolize sea lanes as well.

Ezion-geber (*ELATH), his manufacturing centre and seaport on the Gulf of Aqabah, was a main

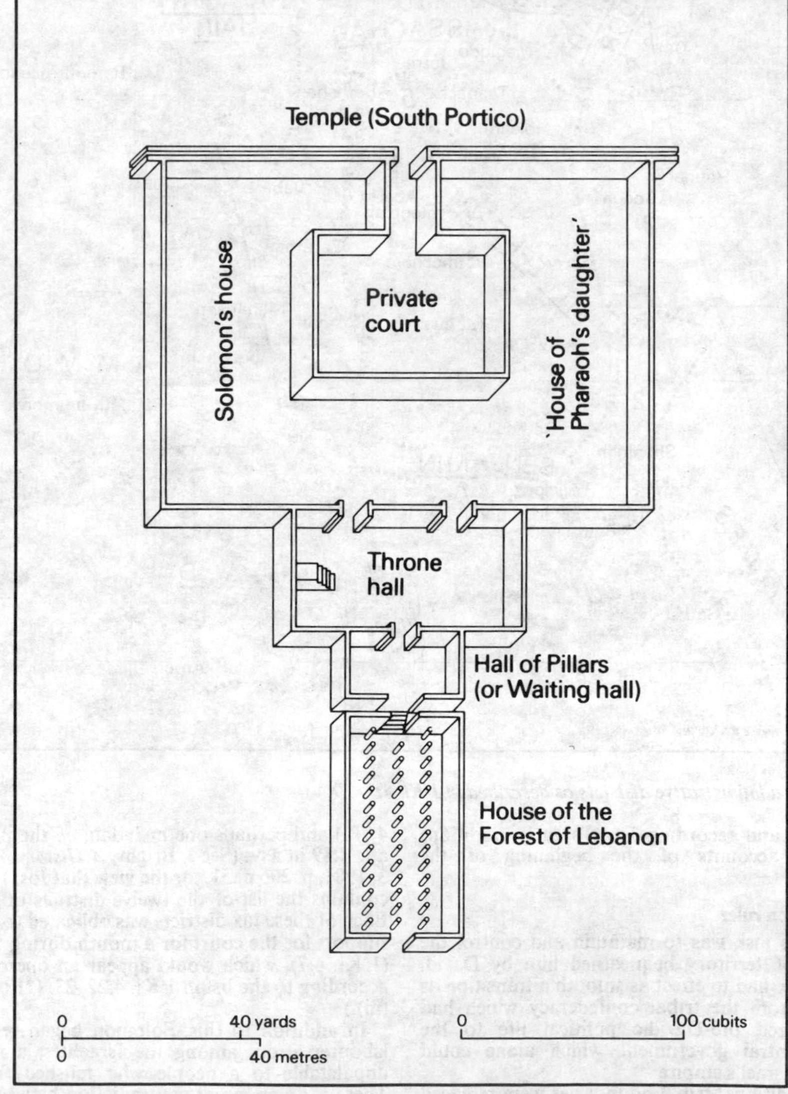

Suggested arrangement of the buildings of Solomon's palace at Jerusalem.

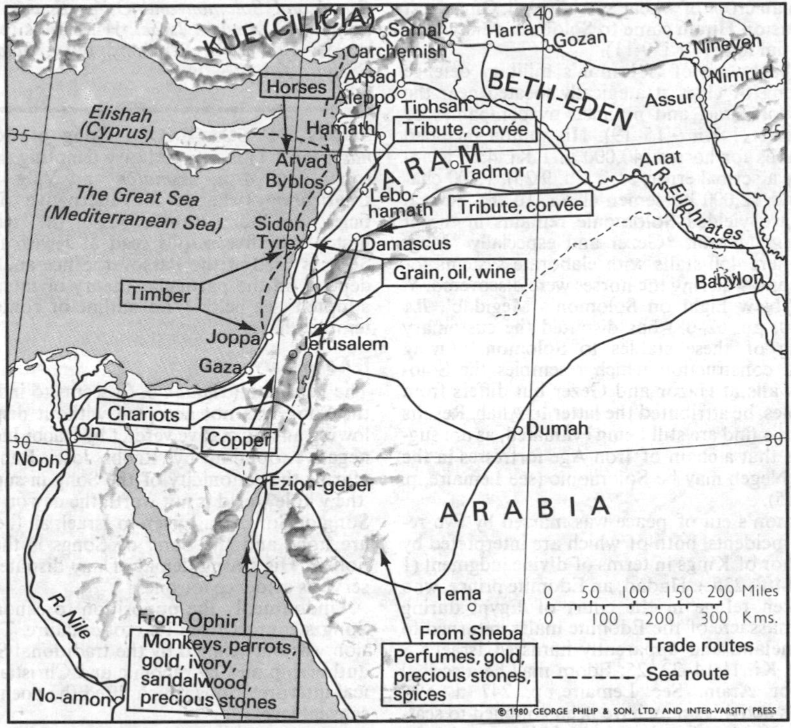

Trade routes in Solomon's time, showing principal imports and their sources.

base of his trading activities. From here his fleet, manned by Phoenicians (the Israelites apparently had neither love for nor knowledge of the sea), sailed to *Ophir carrying smelted copper, whose source is yet undiscovered. The phrase 'ships of *Tarshish' is probably to be translated 'refinery ships', *i.e.* ships equipped to carry smelted ore. In return, these ships brought back splendid cargo: gold, silver, hardwood, jewels, ivory, and varieties of apes (1 Ki. 9:26–28; 10:11–12, 22; 'peacocks' in v. 22 should probably be translated 'baboons', NIV).

The visit of the Queen of *Sheba (1 Ki. 10:1–13) may have had a commercial purpose. Solomon's control of the trade routes and his sea ventures in the S made him a serious financial threat to the Sabaeans, whose strategic position in SW Arabia enabled them to control trade in incense and spice. The queen's journey was successful, but she probably had to share her profits with Solomon, as did other Arabian monarchs (10:13–15).

Solomon's business acumen took advantage of Israel's location when he became the exclusive agent through whom the Hittites and Aramaeans had to negotiate in order to buy horses from Kue (Cilicia) or chariots from Egypt (1 Ki. 10:28–29). These and other enterprises made silver as common as stone and cedar as sycamore in Jerusalem, where the king lived in oriental splendour, in marked contrast to Saul's rustic simplicity in Gibeah. Although Israel's standard of living was undoubtedly raised, Israelites did not profit uniformly. The tendency towards centralization of wealth which brought the censure of the 8th-century prophets began during Solomon's golden reign.

V. The peaceful emperor

Solomon, who had inherited a large empire from his father, apparently conducted no major military campaigns. His task was to maintain Israel's extensive boundaries and to exploit his position of strength during the power-vacuum created by the temporary eclipse of Egypt and Assyria. The two main pillars of Solomon's foreign policy were friendly alliances, sometimes sealed by marriage, and the maintenance of a formidable army. Among his wives Solomon numbered pharaoh's daughter, an accomplishment almost unprecedented among ancient oriental monarchs. Because of her high station, Solomon built a special wing on his palace for her (1 Ki. 3:1; 7:8). This alliance was profitable for Solomon, for pharaoh (probably one of the last members of the impotent Dynasty 21) gave him the frontier city of Gezer as a dowry (1 Ki. 9:16; see J Bright, *op. cit.*, p. 191, n. 63, for the view that 'Gerar' is a preferable reading to 'Gezer'). In view of Solomon's numerous foreign marriages (1 Ki. 11:1–3), it is not surprising that Arabian, Jewish, and especially Ethiopian traditions describe his amorous relations with the Queen of *Sheba, who according to the Ethiopians bore him a son, Menelik I, the traditional founder of their royal house.

Solomon made the most of his alliance with Hiram (*c.* 969–936 BC) of Tyre (1 Ki. 5:1–12). The Phoenicians, just entering their colonial heyday, supplied the architectural skill and many of the materials, especially the fine Lebanese woods, for Solomon's Temple and palaces; they designed and manned his ships; they provided a market for the

Palestinian crops of wheat and olive oil. On at least one occasion Hiram came to Solomon's aid with a substantial loan (1 Ki. 9:11).

The backbone of Solomon's military defence was a ring of cities strategically located near the borders of Israel and manned by companies of charioteers (1 Ki. 9:15–19). His militia included 4,000 stalls for horses (40,000 in 1 Ki. 4:26 is apparently a scribal error; *cf.* 2 Ch. 9:25), 1,400 chariots, and 12,000 horsemen (1 Ki. 10:26). Several cities have yielded Solomonic remains in recent years, *e.g.* *Hazor, *Gezer and especially *Megiddo, where 450 stalls with elaborate systems for feeding and watering the horses were discovered. Y. Yadin ('New Light on Solomon's Megiddo', *BA* 23, 1960, pp. 62–68) has disputed the customary crediting of these stables to Solomon. Having found a construction which resembles the Solomonic walls at Hazor and Gezer but differs from the stables, he attributed the latter to Ahab. Results of Yadin's find are still being evaluated, as are suggestions that a chain of Iron Age fortresses in the central Negeb may be Solomonic (see Lemaire, p. 248 n. 85).

Solomon's era of peace was marred by two recorded incidents, both of which are interpreted by the author of Kings in terms of divine judgment (1 Ki. 11:14ff., 23ff.). Hadad, an Edomite prince, who had taken refuge in the court of Egypt during Joab's massacre of the Edomite males, returned to his homeland and apparently harassed Israel's S flank (1 Ki. 11:14–22, 25; Edom may be a scribal error for Aram. See Lemaire, p. 247 n. 59). Hadad's activities may have been confined to scattered skirmishes, for there is no indication that he posed a major threat to Solomon's S port, Eziongeber. The zest with which the pharaoh courted Hadad's favour is further indication of the Egyptian's *penchant* for forming beneficial alliances during this period.

Solomon's second antagonist was Rezon, who wrested Damascus from Israel and set up an independent kingdom in the city which had been David's N headquarters (2 Sa. 8:6). Solomon's loss of this strategically located, commercially important Aramaean city greatly weakened his control of N and central Syria. The monolithic empire, which at the outset of Solomon's reign had stretched from the Gulf of Aqabah to the Orontes and Euphrates and from the Mediterranean coast to the Transjordan (*cf.* 1 Ki. 4:24), was in danger of crumbling. (See M. F. Unger, *Israel and the Aramaeans of Damascus*, 1957, pp. 47–57.)

VI. The fatal flaw

Marrying foreign wives was expedient politically, but not spiritually,. The historian does not chide Solomon for sensuality but for disobedience to Israel's monotheistic ideal. Foreign marriages brought foreign religions, and the king compromised the convictions expressed in the dedicatory prayer for the Temple (1 Ki. 8:23, 27) by engaging in syncretistic worship to placate his wives. This violent breach of Israel's covenant could not go unpunished. Though judgment was stayed during Solomon's lifetime for David's sake, the seeds of dissatisfaction sown among the people by Solomon's harsh policies of taxation and *corvée* were to bear bitter fruit during the reign of his son and successor, Rehoboam (1 Ki. 11:1–13).

BIBLIOGRAPHY. E. H. Heaton, *Solomon's New Men*, 1974; T. Ishida (ed.), *Studies in the Period of David and Solomon and Other Essays*, 1982; A. Lemaire in *Ancient Israel*, H. Shanks (ed.), 1988, pp. 98–108; J. B. Pritchard (ed.), *Solomon and Sheba*, 1974. D.A.H.

SONG OF SOLOMON.

SONG OF SOLOMON. 'Song of Songs' (*šîr haššîrîm*, 1:1) is a superlative denoting the best of songs. LXX *Asma Asmatōn* and Vulg. *Canticum Canticorum* (whence the alternative title 'Canticles') are literal translations of the Hebrew. The first of the five scrolls read at Jewish feasts, the Song is used at the Passover. Since analysis must depend on the particular theory of interpretation adopted (see below), no outline of contents is attempted here.

I. Canonicity

The Mishnah (*Yadaim* 3. 5) seems to indicate that the Song was not accepted without dispute. Following an affirmative verdict by Rabbi Judah and a negative opinion by Rabbi Jose, Rabbi Akiba affirms the canonicity of the Song in superlatives: 'the whole world is not worth the day on which the Song of Songs was given to Israel; all the Writings are holy, and the Song of Songs is the holy of holies'. His strong denial of any dispute may well serve as evidence for one.

Undoubtedly the opposition to canonizing the Song stemmed from its erotic nature. This objection was outweighed by the traditional Solomonic authorship and by rabbinic and Christian allegorical interpretations which lifted the poems above a sensual level.

II. Authorship and date

The traditional attribution to Solomon is based on the references to him (1:5; 3:7, 9, 11; 8:11), especially the title verse (1:1). The phrase *lišlômôh* probably intimates authorship but can mean 'for Solomon'. Solomon's prowess as a song-writer is attested in 1 Ki. 4:32 (*cf.* Pss. 72; 127). The opinion expressed in *Baba Bathra* 15a that Hezekiah and his scribes wrote the Song of Songs is probably based on Pr. 25:1.

The presence of what seem to be Persian (*pardēs*, 'orchard', 4:13) or Greek (*'appiryôn* from *phoreion*, AV 'chariot', better RSV 'palanquin', 3:9) loanwords, a consistent (except for 1:1) use of *š* as the relative pronoun, and numerous words and phrases akin to Aramaic (see S. R. Driver, *Literature of the Old Testament*, p. 448) suggest to some that the final redaction of the book, if not its actual composition, took place after Solomon's time. It seems unnecessary, however, to date the composition as late as the Greek period (*c.* 300 BC) in view of the evidences for intercourse between Canaan and Ionia from the Solomonic period onwards. Likewise the presence of Aramaisms is no proof of a late date. S. R. Driver (*op. cit.*, p. 449) notes that the linguistic evidence, together with a number of geographical allusions (*e.g.* Sharon, 2:1; Lebanon, 3:9; 4:8, 11, 15, *etc.*; Amana, Senir, Hermon, 4:8; Tirzah, 6:4; Damascus, 7:4; Carmel, 7:5), points to a *northern* origin. But there is no provincialism here. The author is acquainted with the geography of Palestine and Syria from En-gedi, by the Dead Sea (1:14), to the mountains of Lebanon.

III. Literary qualities

The intensely personal speeches of Canticles take two main forms: dialogue (*e.g.* 1:9ff.) and soliloquy (*e.g.* 2:8–3:5). It is not easy to identify the participants in the conversation apart from the two lovers. Daughters of Jerusalem are mentioned (1:5; 2:7; 3:5, *etc.*), and brief responses have been credited to them (1:8; 5:9; 6:1, *etc.*). Statements have been attributed to citizens of Jerusalem (3:6–11) and Shulem (8:5). In highly figurative lyrical poetry it is possible that the central figures are reconstructing the responses of others (*e.g.* the Shulammite seems to quote her brothers in 8:8–9).

The power of the poetry lies in the intensity of love and devotion expressed and especially in the rich imagery which permeates the descriptions of the lovers and their love. If these descriptions are too intimately detailed to suit Western tastes we must remember that they are the product of a distant time and place. If some of the similes sound less than complimentary (*e.g.* teeth like ewes, neck like the tower of David, 4:2ff.), A. Bentzen's reminder is apposite: 'Orientals fix the eye on one single striking point, which according to our conceptions is perhaps not characteristic' (*IOT*, 1, p. 130). L. Waterman's opinion that the compliments are back-handed (*JBL* 44, 1925, pp. 179ff.) has not gained scholarly support. The pastoral qualities of the imagery have been noted frequently. The poems abound in references to animals and especially plants. This fact has not gone unnoticed by those who find the source of the Song in pagan fertility rites (see below).

IV. Theories of interpretation

Interpretations of the Song have been legion, and there is little agreement among scholars as to its origin, meaning and purpose. The vividly detailed, erotic lyrics, the virtual absence of overt religious themes, and the vagueness of its plot make it a challenge to scholarship and a temptation to imaginative ingenuity. Indispensable to the study of the varieties of interpretation is H. H. Rowley's essay 'The Interpretation of the Song of Songs' in *The Servant of the Lord*, 1952.

The problem of accepting a group of love poems into the Canon was solved for rabbis and church Fathers by an *allegorical* method of interpretation. Traces of this method are found in the Mishnah and Talmud, while the Targum of the Song sees in the love-story a clear picture of God's gracious dealings with Israel throughout her history. Once the allegorical trail had been blazed, the rabbis vied with one another in attempts to expand and redirect it. Allusions to Israel's history were squeezed from the most unlikely parts of the Song. The church Fathers and many subsequent Christian interpreters baptized the Song into Christ, finding within it an allegory of Christ's love for the church or the believer. Various mediaeval writers followed the example of Ambrose in finding the Virgin Mary foreshadowed in the *Shulammite. Christian interpreters have yielded nothing to the rabbis in imaginative interpretation of details. The allegorical approach has been predominant in Protestant thought until recently, and includes as its advocates such stalwarts as Hengstenberg and Keil.

Closely related is the *typical* method which preserves the literal sense of the poem but also discerns a higher, more spiritual meaning. Avoiding the excesses in detailed interpretation of the allegorical method, typology stresses the major themes of love and devotion and finds in the story a picture of the love relationship between Christ and his believers. This approach has been justified by analogies from Arabic love-poems which may have esoteric meanings, by Christ's use of the story of Jonah (Mt. 12:40) or the serpent in the wilderness (Jn. 3:14), and by biblical analogies of spiritual marriage, *e.g.* Ho. 1–3; Je. 2:2; 3:1ff.; Ezk. 16:6ff.; 23; Eph. 5:22ff. Not a few modern conservatives have espoused the *typical* view, *e.g.* J. H. Raven (*Old Testament Introduction*, 1910), M. F. Unger (*Introductory Guide to the Old Testament*^{2}, 1956).

Though Jews and Christians have found devotional benefits in allegorical or typical approaches to the Song, the exegetical basis of these approaches is questionable. Both the abundance of details and the absence of clues as to deeper spiritual significance within the book itself speak against the finding of allegory or type in the Song.

The *dramatic* interpretation of Canticles, suggested by both Origen and Milton, was developed in the 19th century in two major forms. F. Delitzsch found two main characters, Solomon and the Shulammite girl. Taking her from her village home to Jerusalem, Solomon learnt to love her as his wife with an affection that rose above physical attraction. H. Ewald formulated an interpretation based on three main characters: Solomon, the Shulammite and her shepherd lover to whom she remains true despite the king's desperate efforts to win her. While Ewald's approach (called the *shepherd hypothesis*), which was accepted by S. R. Driver and refined by other scholars, avoids some of the difficulties of Delitzsch's view by explaining why the lover is pictured as a shepherd (1:7–8) and why the poem ends in a N pastoral setting, it has its own difficulties, *e.g.* the absence of dramatic instructions, the complexities involved in the dialogues when Solomon describes the Shulammite's beauty while she responds in terms of her shepherd lover. Dramatic interpretations face another difficulty: the scarcity of evidence for dramatic literature among the Semites, especially the Hebrews.

J. G. Wetzstein's study of Syrian marriage customs prompted K. Budde to interpret the Song as a collection of *nuptial songs* akin to those used in the week-long marriage feast in which the bride and groom are crowned as king and queen. Critics of this view have pointed out the danger of using modern Syrian customs to illustrate ancient Palestinian practices. Also, the Shulammite is not called by the name of 'queen' anywhere in the Song.

The view of T. J. Meek that the Song is derived from the *liturgical rites* of the *Tammuz cult (*cf.* Ezk. 8:14) has gained widespread attention. But it is unlikely that a pagan liturgy with overtones of immorality would be incorporated in the Canon without a thorough revision in terms of Israel's faith, and the Song bears the marks of no such redaction.

Leroy Waterman, who had originally supported Meek's theory (*JBL* 44, 1925), has recently returned to a historical basis for the Song. This he finds in the story of Abishag, David's *Shunammite maiden (1 Ki. 1:3), who allegedly refused Solomon's overtures in favour of her shepherd lover. This interpretation hangs on the conjectural connection between Shunammite and *Shulammite.

An increasing number of scholars have viewed Canticles as a collection of *love-poems* not necessarily connected with wedding festivities or any other specific occasion. Attempts to assign the various sections to different authors (*e.g.* W. O. E. Oesterley divided the Song into 28 distinct poems and emphatically denied the unity of the book; *Song of Songs*, 1936, p. 6b) have been resisted by a number of scholars, especially H. H. Rowley: 'The repetitions that occur leave the impression of a single hand . . .' (*op. cit.*, p. 212).

V. Purpose

If the Song is not an allegory or type conveying a spiritual message, what place does it have in the Canon? It serves as an object-lesson, an extended *māšāl* (*PROVERB), illustrating the rich wonders of human love. As biblical teaching concerning physical love has been emancipated from sub-Christian asceticism, the beauty and purity of marital love have been more fully appreciated. The Song, though expressed in language too bold for Western taste, provides a wholesome balance between the extremes of sexual excess or perversion and an ascetic denial of the essential goodness of physical love. E. J. Young carries the purpose one step further: 'Not only does it speak of the purity of human love, but by its very inclusion in the Canon it reminds us of a love that is purer than our own' (*IOT*, 1949, p. 327).

BIBLIOGRAPHY. J. C. Rylaarsdam, *Proverbs to Song of Solomon*, 1964; W. J. Fuerst, *Ruth, Esther, Ecclesiastes, The Song of Songs, Lamentations*, 1975; S. C. Glickman, *A Song for Lovers*, 1976; J. C. Exum, *ZAW* 85, 1973, pp. 47–79; G. L. Carr, *The Song of Solomon*, *TOTC*, 1984; M. V. Fox, *The Song of Songs and the Ancient Egyptian Love Songs*, 1985; D. A. Hubbard, *Ecclesiastes, Song of Solomon*, 1991; R. Murphy, *The Song of Songs*, 1990; M. Pope, *Song of Songs*, 1977. D.A.H.

SONS (CHILDREN) OF GOD.

I. In the Old Testament

a. Individuals of the class 'god'

'Son' (Heb. *bēn*, Aram. *bar*) is commonly used in Semitic languages to denote membership of a class, as 'son of Israel' for 'Israelite', 'son of might' for 'valorous'. 'Son of God' in Heb. means 'god' or 'god-like' rather than 'son of (the) God (Yahweh)'. In Jb. 1:6; 2:1; 38:7; Ps. 29:1; 89:6, the 'sons of God' form Yahweh's heavenly train or subordinates, though LXX Job calls them *angeloi* of God (*cf.* Dt. 32:8 LXX, whence RSV 'according to the number of the sons of God' supported by a Heb. Dead Sea Scroll text, 4Q Dt[q], against *MT* 'sons of Israel'). Similarly the 'son of the gods' in Dn. 3:25 is called the 'angel of the Jews' God' in 3:28.

In Gn. 6:1–2 the 'sons of God' are contrasted with human women in a way which seems to preclude their identification with the line of Cain. Many commentators treat these verses as pagan myth, hardly altered from a polytheistic background. Others argue that the phrase denotes demon-possessed men or fallen angels (*cf.* 1 Pet. 3:19–20; Jude 6). A more attractive interpretation falls into the next category.

b. Men who by divine appointment exercise God's prerogative of judgment

In Ex. 21:6; 22:8–9, 28, 'God' (Heb. *'ĕlōhîm*) may stand for 'judges' (so AV, RVmg.), his deputies, exercising power of life and death (*cf.* 2 Ch. 19:6), as may be the case in Ps. 82:6.

Kings were titled 'son of god X' in the OT world, and in Israel in sense *c*, below. M. G. Kline has proposed that this usage be seen in Gn. 6:1–2, referring to rulers of the remote antediluvian era (*WTJ* 24, 1962, pp. 187–204).

c. Those who are related to Yahweh by covenant

Sonship of God chiefly denotes relationship by *covenant and is used (i) of Israel as a whole ('Israel is my first-born son', Ex. 4:22; *cf.* Ho. 11:1); (ii) of the Israelites generally ('You are the sons of the Lord your God', Dt. 14:1; *cf.* Ho.1:10—of an individual Israelite in later Judaism, *e.g.* Wisdom 2:18); (iii) of the Davidic king, Yahweh's anointed, who will rule his people for ever ('You are my Son; today I have begotten you', Ps. 2:7). This relationship is not biological, though metaphors of birth, infancy and growth are sometimes used (Ho. 11:1; Dt. 32:6; Is. 1:2; 63:8) and conformity to the Father's character expected. But basically sonship is established by God through his covenant. Dt. 14:1–2 well illustrates the covenantal context of Israel's sonship. The Messiah-King, though called (like Israel with whom he is so closely identified) 'my first-born' (Ps. 89:27) and 'begotten' of Yahweh (Ps. 2:7), no less owes his status to God's covenant with him (Ps. 89:28; 2 Sa. 23:5). The terms of this covenant ('I will be his father, and he shall be my son', 2 Sa. 7:14) are parallel to the terms of the covenant with Israel ('I . . . will be their God, and they shall be my people', Je. 31:33).

D.W.B.R.
A.R.M.

II. In the New Testament

Both expressions, 'sons (Gk. *hyioi*) of God' and 'children (Gk. *tekna*) of God', occur in the NT, but without obvious distinction in meaning. The NT usage is based on one or other of the OT uses of 'sons of God'.

a. Lk. 20:36

This reference, 'they are equal to angels and are sons of God, being sons of the resurrection', reflects the use of 'sons of God' as in Pss. 29:1; 89:6; Dt. 32:8 (LXX), where it means non-terrestrial beings in the presence of God, in contrast to 'the sons of this age'. That the elect should have this destiny before them was already the belief of many Jews, but it was to acquire a more distinctive meaning in the light of Christ's resurrection.

b. Those who act like God

Lk. 6:35, 'you will be sons of the Most High', means little more than 'you will be like God'. 'Son of . . .' is an idiom for 'having the characteristics of' or 'doing the work of' (*cf.* the parabolic description of the apprentice son in Jn. 5:19), and the 'sons of God' in Mt. 5:9 and 5:45 belong to this category. Ps. 82:6, discussed by Jesus in Jn. 10:34–36, may be an OT example of this sense, judges being men who exercise God's power of life and death. Paul's simple metaphor in Eph. 5:1, 'be imitators of God, as beloved children', reflects this idiom, though it also presupposes a deeper relation between the 'children' and their Father.

c. The sonship of Israel

The collective sonship of Israel ('Israel is my first-born son', Ex. 4:22) is prominent in the thought of

Paul (*e.g.* Rom. 9:4, 'they are Israelites, and to them belong the sonship . . .') and elsewhere in the NT. Sometimes this sonship is seen as represented and fulfilled in Jesus Christ, as in Mt. 2:15 and in the narratives of his baptism and temptation. However, even without a direct connection with Christ's sonship, 'sons (or children) of God' recalls the OT application of the term to God's covenant people who are to reflect his holiness. If Eph. 5:1 is little more than metaphorical, Phil. 2:15, 'children of God without blemish in the midst of a crooked and perverse generation', is based on the Song of Moses (Dt. 32:5–6, 18–20), and 2 Cor. 6:18 combines a number of covenantal passages (*e.g.* Is. 43:6; 2 Sa. 7:14). 'The children of God who are scattered abroad' in Jn. 11:52 are the lost sheep of the house of Israel (*cf.* 10:16). The idea is derived from Ezk. 34 and 37, though whether the reference in John is to Jewish believers only or all believers is a matter of debate.

The sonship of God's people is, however, linked with the special sonship of Jesus in Heb. 2:10–17. (A different word, *paidia*, is used for 'children' in the quotation in vv. 13–14.) Here, Jesus' sonship is that conferred on the Messiah-King, David's son (Ps. 2:7; 2 Sa. 7:14, quoted in Heb. 1:5), which itself is parallel to, and perhaps epitomizes, Israel's covenantal sonship. The 'many sons' are the 'descendants of Abraham' and 'children' by election even before Christ's incarnation. But they are brought 'to glory' through the Son sharing in their 'flesh and blood' in which he secured their salvation by his death.

d. Paul in Romans and Galatians

Though Paul acknowledges that 'the sonship' belongs to Israelites (Rom. 9:4), he insists that not all the offspring of Israel are 'Israel' in the true sense, and that therefore it is not 'the children of the flesh' but 'the children of the promise' who are 'children of God' and true partakers of the privilege (Rom. 9:6ff.).

By this test, Gentiles as well as Jews are included, 'for in Christ Jesus you are all sons of God, through faith' (Gal. 3:26). This doctrine of sonship is expounded in Rom. 8, where Paul invokes the idea of *hyiothesia*, usually rendered *'adoption'. But, though the term was used in contemporary Gk. to denote legal adoption of children (see *MM*), it is not clear how far this enters Paul's thought. Despite the contrast with a former status of slavery, both in Rom. 8:15 (where RSV renders *hyiothesia* as 'sonship') and Gal. 4:5, at least in the latter passage *hyiothesia* seems to correspond to the entering of a child on his inheritance at 'the date set by the father'. The primary model is the sovereign act of God's grace when he declared Israel, and then the Davidic king, to be his son. Neither Israel's sonship (Ex. 4:22) nor that of Messiah (Pss. 2:7; 89:27) was inconsistent with the recipient's being called God's 'first-born', and the *hyiothesia* of the believer is practically identical with the notion of spiritual generation. In Rom. 8:23 the *hyiothesia* is yet to come. Though again associated with the notion of 'redemption' (from slavery?), the positive act is really 'the revealing of the sons of God', showing them to be what they already are. This sonship is indissolubly linked with the sonship of Christ (Rom. 8:17), is attested and controlled by the Spirit (8:14, 16), and its ultimate nature disclosed when Christ's sonship is disclosed and when God's elect are seen as 'conformed to the image of his Son, in order that he might be the first-born among many brethren' (8:19, 29).

e. John

John's concept of 'children of God' differs only in emphasis from that of Paul, although he employs simply *tekna*, and reserves *hyios* exclusively for Christ. Westcott held that John deliberately avoided *hyios*, 'the name of definite dignity and privilege', to describe the relation of Christians to God, since 'he regards their position not as the result of an "adoption" (*hyiothesia*), but as the result of a new life which advances from the vital germ to full maturity'. However, Westcott overstated the case. While John undoubtedly exploits the imagery of natural birth and consequent relationship (*e.g.* 1 Jn. 3:9), he is also aware of the OT background where Israel became God's son by election and calling. We have already referred to Jn. 11:52. In Jn. 1:12 the 'children of God' may be interpreted as believing Israelites before the Word became flesh. In any case, they are described not only as being 'born of God' but also as becoming 'children of God' by having that status conferred on them: 'to them gave he the right to become children of God' (RV). Again in 1 Jn. 3 and 4 believers are described as 'born of God', with special reference to their reproducing God's character of love and righteousness; nevertheless the title 'children of God' is also a privilege bestowed through God's 'calling' (3:1). Though it 'may be seen' now who are children of God by their behaviour (3:10), their final form 'does not yet appear', but will be manifested in the day when the Son of God is manifested and they fully reflect the image of their Father (3:2); which image is in the Son.

BIBLIOGRAPHY. *BAGD*, *s.v.* *hyios*, *teknon*; E. Schweizer, *TDNT* 8, pp. 334ff.; F. Lyall, *JBL* 88, 1969, pp. 458ff.; J. D. G. Dunn, *Jesus and the Spirit*, 1975, pp. 21ff.; B. Byrne, '*Sons of God*' – '*Seed of Abraham*', 1979; J. M. Scott, *Adoption as Sons of God*, 1992.

D.W.B.R.

SOPATER, SOSIPATER, a believer from Beroea in Macedonia (Acts 20:4), was one of the missionary party which waited for Paul at Troas, and then accompanied him to Asia on his way to Syria. Sosipater is called, in Rom. 16:21, a kinsman (*syngenēs*) of Paul. His greeting was sent to the church at Rome.

Some consider that the references are to the same man. Perhaps Sopater was a fruit of Paul's preaching in Macedonia, and was therefore Paul's kinsman in Christ. He probably represented the Beroean church in the delegation which was about to set sail with Paul to carry the Gentile churches' contributions to Jerusalem. C.H.D.

SOREK, VALLEY OF. The home of Delilah (Jdg. 16:4). There is little doubt that this may be equated with the Wadi al-Sarar, a large valley lying between Jerusalem—starting some 20 km from it—and the Mediterranean. It must always have offered a convenient route inland (it is today followed by the railway line). There is a ruin near the valley called Khirbet Surik, preserving the biblical name. Eusebius and Jerome made the same identification.

D.F.P.

SOSTHENES. The chief ruler of the synagogue at Corinth, and successor (or possibly colleague) of the converted *Crispus. He was assaulted in court after Gallio disallowed a Jewish prosecution of Paul (Acts 18:17), either in an anti-Semitic demonstration by Greeks (as Western Text) or in Jewish spite against an unsuccessful or lukewarm spokesman.

The latter might indicate pro-Christian sympathy: did 'Paul sow, Apollos water' (*cf.* 1 Cor. 3:6)? 'Sosthenes the brother' is co-sender of 1 Corinthians (1:1), and Sosthenes is not the commonest of Gk. names. Paul's tact and modesty, in approaching a sensitive church in association with the ex-archisynagogue, then at Ephesus, best explain the allusion. Joint-authorship is not implied.

Sosthenes' inclusion in the Seventy (Clem. Alex., *Hyp.* 5, in Eus., *EH* 1. 12. 1–2) doubtless reflects his assumed participation in a canonical letter.

A.F.W.

SOUL. 1. The usual Heb. word *nepeš* (*nᵉšāmâ*, Is. 57:16, is an exception) occurs 755 times in the OT. As is clear from Gn. 2:7, the primary meaning is 'possessing life'. Thus it is frequently used of animals (Gn. 1:20, 24, 30; 9:12, 15–16; Ezk. 47:9). Sometimes it is identified with the blood, as something which is essential to physical existence (Gn. 9:4; Lv. 17:10–14; Dt. 12:22–24). In many cases it stands for the life-principle. This sense is common in the book of Psalms, though not confined to it.

The numerous occurrences with a psychical reference cover various states of consciousness: (a) where *nep̄eš* is the seat of physical appetite (Nu. 21:5; Dt. 12:15, 20–21, 23–24; Jb. 33:20; Pss. 78:18; 107:18; Ec. 2:24; Mi. 7:1); (b) where it is the source of emotion (Jb. 30:25; Pss. 86:4; 107:26; Ct. 1:7; Is. 1:14); (c) where it is associated with the will and moral action (Gn. 49:6; Dt. 4:29; Jb. 7:15; Pss. 24:4; 25:1; 119:129, 167). In addition there are passages where *nep̄eš* designates an individual or person (*e.g.* Lv. 7:21; 17:12; Ezk. 18:4) or is employed with a pronominal suffix to denote self (*e.g.* Jdg. 16:16; Ps. 120:6; Ezk. 4:14). A remarkable extension of the latter is the application of *nep̄eš* to a dead body (*e.g.* Lv. 19:28; Nu. 6:6; Hg. 2:13). Usually the *nep̄eš* is regarded as departing at death (*e.g.* Gn. 35:18), but the word is never used for the spirit of the dead. Since Hebrew psychology lacked precise terminology, there is some overlapping in the use of *nep̄eš*, *lēḇ* (*lēḇāḇ*) and *rûaḥ* (*HEART, *SPIRIT).

2. Gk. *psychē*, the corresponding term to *nēpeš* in the NT, occurs in the Gospels with similar meanings, but in certain instances, indicating life, more is implied than physical life, ceasing at death (Mt. 10:39; Mk. 8:35; Lk. 17:33; 21:19; Jn. 12:25). In all four Gospels *pneuma*, the equivalent of *rûaḥ*, sometimes denotes the principle of life, although in other cases it means the higher level of psychical life.

Of 12 occurrences in Paul, 6 represent life (Rom. 11:3; 16:4; 1 Cor. 15:45; 2 Cor. 1:23; Phil. 2:30; 1 Thes. 2:8), 2 are personal (Rom. 11:3; 13:1) and 4 are psychical, 3 of these representing desire (Eph. 6:6; Phil. 1:27; Col. 3:23), while the remaining one indicates emotion (1 Thes. 5:23). For the higher aspects of ordinary life and especially the higher life of a Christian he uses *pneuma*. In line with this is his use of the adjectives *psychikos* and *pneumatikos* (1 Cor. 2:14–15). When he employs *psychē* along with *pneuma* (1 Thes. 5:23) he is merely describing the same immaterial part of man in its lower and higher aspects.

Other NT writers provide examples of a somewhat heightened use of *psychē*. The Word of God can save it and recovery from error rescues it from death (Jas. 1:21; 5:20). The outcome of faith is the salvation of the *psychē* (Heb. 10:29; 1 Pet. 1:10), while fleshly desires are inimical to it (1 Pet. 2:11). Hope of what shall be firmly anchors it (Heb. 6:19). In the description of what follows the opening of the fifth seal, *psychē* is used with reference to the martyrs seen below the altar (Rev. 6:9). (*SPIRIT.)

BIBLIOGRAPHY. A. R. Johnson, *The Vitality of the Individual in the Thought of Ancient Israel*, 1949; E. White, 'A Preface to Biblical Psychology', *JTVI* 83, 1951, pp. 51ff.; *idem*, 'The Psychology of St Paul's Epistles', *JTVI* 87, 1955, pp. 1ff.; J. Laidlaw, *The Bible Doctrine of Man*, 1879, pp. 49–96, 179–220; H. W. Robinson, *The Christian Doctrine of Man*³, 1926, pp. 11–27, 104–111; G. Bertram *et al.*, *TDNT* 9, pp. 608–656; G. Harder, C. Brown, *NIDNTT* 3, pp. 676–689.

W.J.C.

SPAIN. For the discussion of possible OT references to Spain, see *TARSHISH. A series of Gk. commercial colonies founded from Massilia (Marseilles) introduced Spain into world history, and in the 3rd century BC it became a theatre for the long struggle between Carthage and Rome. By 197 BC, the Carthaginians being dispossessed, two Roman provinces, Hispania Citerior and Hispania Ulterior, were set up; but the forcible reconciliation of the Spanish tribes to Roman rule took almost 2 centuries more. Later, however, Spain developed, economically and culturally, perhaps faster than any other part of the empire. Augustus reorganized the peninsula into three provinces, Hispania Tarraconensis, Baetica and Lusitania: Vespasian extended Latin status to all the Spanish municipalities. The Senecas, Lucan, Quintilian, Martial and other prominent Latin writers of that age, as well as the emperors Trajan and Hadrian, were of Spanish birth.

These things show how forward-looking was Paul's plan to travel beyond Rome to Spain (Rom. 15:24, 28), a project in which he clearly expects the co-operation of the Roman Christians. Even if his first object was the Hellenized towns, 'it marks the beginning of an entirely new enterprise; behind it lies Gaul and perhaps Germany and Britain. He is about to pass over from the Greek into the distinctly Roman half of the civilized world' (J. Weiss, *History of Primitive Christianity*, 1, 1937, p. 359).

Whether *Paul achieved his ambition remains uncertain. The silence of the Pastorals may indicate a change of plan. Clement of Rome, *c.* AD 95, says that Paul reached 'the boundary of the West' (*1 Clem.* 5)—most naturally interpreted, not of Rome, but of the Pillars of Hercules. The 2nd-century *Acts of Peter* and the Muratorian Fragment are more explicit, but may reflect assumptions based on Rom. 15. The earliest surviving Spanish traditions are too late to help, and later Roman theory was interested in proving that all W churches were founded by Peter's lieutenants (Innocent, *Ep.* 25. 2, AD 416).

BIBLIOGRAPHY. Strabo, 3; C. H. V. Sutherland,

The Romans in Spain 217 BC–AD *117*, 1939; Th. Zahn, *INT*, 1909, 2, pp. 61ff., 73ff.; P. N. Harrison, *The Problem of the Pastoral Epistles*, 1921, pp. 102ff.; F. F. Bruce, *Paul: Apostle of the Free Spirit*, 1977, pp. 445ff. A.F.W.

SPECK. The word occurs in Mt. 7:3–5, and almost identically in the Lucan parallel (Lk. 6:41–42 *bis*). The Gk. word is *karphos* (AV 'mote'), and is cognate with the verb *karphō*, 'to dry up'. The noun means a small, dry stalk or twig, a light piece of straw, or even of wool such as might fly into the eye. Metaphorically it is used by Jesus to denote a minor fault. S.S.S.

SPINNING AND WEAVING. Two implements were used in spinning (Heb. *ṭāwâ*; Gk. *nēthō*). The distaff (Heb. *kîšôr*, Pr. 31:19; AV 'spindle'), on which were wound the unspun fibres, was held with the left hand, while the spindle (Heb. *pelek̲*, Pr. 31:19; AV 'distaff') was worked by the fingers and thumb of the right hand to twist the short natural fibres into yarn. The spindle had a wooden shank 23 to 30 cm long, with a heavy whorl of stone or clay part way down to give momentum to its rotation. A hook at one end held the yarn which, when spun, was twisted on to the spindle shank. A variety of fibres such as flax and wool (Lv. 13:47), goat hair (Ex. 35:26), and camel hair (Mt. 3:4) were used in spinning, though the blending of different kinds of yarn was forbidden, for ritual purity (Lv. 19:19).

In Israel the task of spinning belonged to women (Ex. 35:25; Pr. 31:19). For weaving (Heb. *'āraḡ*; Gk. *hyphainō*), however, both men (Ex. 35:35) and women (2 Ki. 23:7) were employed, and the existence of a guild of weavers is indicated in 1 Ch. 4:21. Whether the horizontal or the vertical loom was more common in Israel is uncertain, though the weaving of the sleeping Samson's hair (Jdg. 16:13) suggests the former in this instance at least. In Egypt horizontal looms were common and such are still in use among Bedouin and peasants in Palestine. Egyp. weavers seem to have been famed particularly for their white cloth (Is. 19:9).

The weaver's beam (*mānôr*), to which the massive shaft of Goliath's spear is compared (1 Sa. 17:7), was the means of raising and lowering the longitudinal warp threads (*šeṯî*) to allow the shuttle carrying the transverse woof thread (*'ēreb̲*, Lv. 13:48) to pass between them. The woof was then beaten tight by a stick or 'pin' (*yāṯēḏ*, Jdg. 16:14) to produce firm cloth.

The familiar art of weaving supplies some striking similes in the OT; the speed of the weaver's shuttle portrays the swift passing of man's life (Jb. 7:6), and death is likened to the cutting of finished cloth from the thrums (*dallâ*) attached to the loom (Is. 38:12). Spinning and weaving are singled out as examples of unremitting human toil from which the world of nature is free (Lk. 12:27, RSV mg.).

BIBLIOGRAPHY. R. J. Forbes, *Studies in Ancient Technology*, 4, 1956; A. Neuburger, *The Technical Arts and Sciences of the Ancients*, 1930. G.I.E.

SPIRIT, HOLY SPIRIT. OT, Heb. *rûaḥ* 378 times (plus 11 Aramaic in Dn.); NT, Gk. *pneuma* 379 times.

I. Basic range of meaning of *rûaḥ* and *pneuma*

From earliest Heb. thought *rûaḥ* had various meanings, all more or less equally prominent. **1.** *Wind*, an invisible, mysterious, powerful force (Gn. 8:1; Ex. 10:13, 19; Nu. 11:31; 1 Ki. 18:45; Pr. 25:23; Je. 10:13; Ho. 13:15; Jon. 4:8), regularly with the notion of strength or violence present (Ex. 14:21; 1 Ki. 19:11; Pss. 48:7; 55:8; Is. 7:2; Ezk. 27:26; Jon. 1:4). **2.** *Breath* (*i.e.*, air on a small scale), or *spirit* (Gn. 6:17; 7:15, 22; Pss. 31:5; 32:2; Ec. 3:19, 21; Je. 10:14; 51:17; Ezk. 11:5), the same mysterious force seen as the life and vitality of man (and beasts). It can be disturbed or activated in a particular direction (Gn. 41:8; Nu. 5:14, 30; Jdg. 8:3; 1 Ki. 21:5; 1 Ch. 5:26; Jb. 21:4; Pr. 29:11; Je. 51:17; Dn. 2:1, 3), can be impaired or diminished (Jos. 5:1; 1 Ki. 10:5; Ps. 143:7; Is. 19:3) and revive again (Gn. 45:27; Jdg. 15:19; 1 Sa. 30:12). That is, the dynamic force which constitutes a man can be low (it disappears at death), or there can be a sudden surge of vital power. **3.** *Divine power*, where *rûaḥ* is used to describe occasions when men seemed to be carried out of themselves—not just a surge of vitality, but a supernatural force taking possession. So particularly with the early charismatic leaders (Jdg. 3:10; 6:34; 11:29; 13:25; 14:6, 19; 15:14f.; 1 Sa. 11:6), and the early prophets—it was the same divine *rûaḥ* which induced ecstasy and prophetic speech (Nu. 24:2; 1 Sa. 10:6, 10; 19:20, 23f.).

These should not be treated as a set of distinct meanings; rather we are confronted with a spectrum of meaning where the different senses merge into each other. Note, *e.g.*, the overlap between **1** and **2** in Ps. 78:39, between **1** and **3** in 1 Ki. 18:12; 2 Ki. 2:16; Ezk. 3:12, 14, between **2** and **3** in Nu. 5:14, 30; 1 Sa. 16:14–16; Ho. 4:12, and between **1, 2** and **3** in Ezk. 37:9. Initially at least these are all seen simply as manifestations of *rûaḥ*, and the meanings of *rûaḥ* are not kept strictly separate. In particular, therefore, we may not presuppose an initial distinction in Heb. thought between divine *rûaḥ* and anthropological *rûaḥ*; on the contrary, man's *rûaḥ* can be identified with God's *rûaḥ* (Gn. 6:3; Jb. 27:3; 32:8; 33:4; 34:14f.; Ps. 104:29f.).

It also becomes immediately evident that the concept *rûaḥ* is an existential term. At its heart is the *experience* of a mysterious, awesome power—the mighty invisible force of the wind, the mystery of vitality, the otherly power that transforms—all *rûaḥ*, all manifestations of divine energy.

In later usage the meanings human spirit, angelic or demonic spirit, and divine Spirit predominate and are more distinct. Thus in the NT *pneuma* is used nearly 40 times to denote that dimension of the human personality whereby relationship with God is possible (Mk. 2:8; Acts 7:59; Rom. 1:9; 8:16; 1 Cor. 5:3–5; 1 Thes. 5:23; Jas. 2:26). Slightly more frequent is the sense of unclean, evil, demonic spirit, a power which man experiences as an affliction, an injurious limitation to full relationship with God and with his fellows (chiefly in the Synoptic Gospels and Acts: Mt. 8:16; Mk. 1:23, 26f.; 9:25; Lk. 4:36; 11:24, 26; Acts 19:12f., 15f.; 1 Tim. 4:1; Rev. 16:13f.). Occasionally there is reference to heavenly (good) spirits (Acts 23:8f.; Heb. 1:7, 14), or to spirits of the dead (Lk. 24:37, 39; Heb. 12:23; 1 Pet. 3:19; *cf.* 1 Cor. 5:5). But by far the most frequent reference in the NT is to the Spirit of God, the Holy Spirit (more than 250 times). At the same time the earlier, wider range of meaning is still reflected in the ambiguity of Jn. 3:8; 20:22; Acts 8:39; 2 Thes. 2:8; Rev. 11:11; 13:15; and in particular there are several passages where it is not possible to decide with finality whether it is human spirit or divine Spirit that is meant (Mk. 14:38; Lk. 1:17, 80; 1 Cor. 14:14, 32; 2 Cor. 4:13; Eph. 1:17; 2 Tim. 1:7; Jas. 4:5; Rev. 22:6).

II. Characteristics of pre-Christian usage

In the earliest understanding of *rûaḥ* there was little or no distinction between natural and supernatural. The wind could be described poetically as the blast of Yahweh's nostrils (Ex. 15:8, 10; 2 Sa. 22:16 = Ps. 18:15; Is. 40:7). And man's God-breathed *rûaḥ* was from the first more or less synonymous with his *nep̄eš* (soul) (especially Gn. 2:7). *rûaḥ* was precisely the same divine, mysterious, vital power which is to be seen most clearly in the wind or in the ecstatic behaviour of prophet or charismatic leader.

Initially also the *rûaḥ* of God was conceived more in terms of power than in moral terms, not yet as the (Holy) Spirit of God (*cf.* again Jdg. 14:6, 19; 15:14f.). A *rûaḥ* from God could be for evil as well as for good (Jdg. 9:23; 1 Sa. 16:14–16; 1 Ki. 22:19–23). At this early stage of understanding, God's *rûaḥ* was thought of simply as a supernatural power (under God's authority) exerting force in some direction.

The earliest leadership in the emergence of Israel as a nation rested its claim to authority on particular manifestations of *rûaḥ*, of ecstatic power—so with the judges (references above, 3), Samuel who had the reputation of a seer and was evidently the leader of a group of ecstatic prophets (1 Sa. 9:9, 18f.; 19:20, 24), and Saul (1 Sa. 11:6; *cf.* 10:11f.; 19:24). Note the part apparently played by music in stimulating the ecstasy of inspiration (1 Sa. 10:5f.; 2 Ki. 3:15).

Various developments are evident in subsequent periods. We can recognize a tendency to open up a distinction between the natural and supernatural, between God and man. Just as the vivid anthropomorphisms of the earlier talk of God are abandoned, so *rûaḥ* becomes more clearly that which characterizes the supernatural and distinguishes the divine from the merely human (particularly Is. 31:3; so Jn. 4:24). So too a distinction between *rûaḥ* and *nep̄eš* begins to emerge: the *rûaḥ* in man retains its immediate connection with God, denoting the 'higher' or Godward dimension of man's existence (*e.g.* Ezr. 1:1, 5; Ps. 51:12; Ezk. 11:19), while *nep̄eš* tends more and more to stand for the 'lower' aspects of man's consciousness, the personal but merely human life in man, the seat of his appetites, emotions and passions (so regularly). Thus the way is prepared for the sharper Pauline distinction between the psychical and the spiritual (1 Cor. 15:44–46).

Also evident is a tendency for the focus of authority to shift from the manifestation of *rûaḥ* in ecstasy to a more institutionalized concept. Possession of the Spirit of God is now conceived as permanent, and capable of being passed on (Nu. 11:17; Dt. 34:9; 2 Ki. 2:9, 15). So presumably the anointing of the king was more and more thought of in terms of an anointing with Spirit (1 Sa. 16:13; and the implication of Ps. 89:20f.; Is. 11:2; 61:1). And prophecy tended to become more and more attached to the cult (the implication of Is. 28:7; Je. 6:13; 23:11; it is likely that some of the psalms began as prophetic utterances in the cult; Hab. and Zc. were quite probably cult prophets). This development marks the beginning of the tension within the Judaeo-Christian tradition between charisma and cult (see especially 1 Ki. 22:5–28; Am. 7:10–17).

The most striking feature of the pre-exilic period is the strange reluctance (as it would appear) of the classical prophets to attribute their inspiration to the Spirit. Neither the 8th-century prophets (Am., Mi., Ho., Is.) nor those of the 7th century (Je., Zp., Na., Hab.) refer to the Spirit to authenticate their message—with the possible exception of Mi. 3:8 (often regarded as a later interpolation for that reason). In describing their inspiration they preferred to speak of the word of God (especially Am. 3:8; Je. 20:9) and the hand of God (Is. 8:11; Je. 15:17). Why this was so we cannot tell: perhaps *rûaḥ* had become too much identified with the ecstatic both in Israel and in other near-Eastern religions (*cf.* Ho. 9:7); perhaps they were reacting against cult professionalism and abuse (Is. 28:7; Je. 5:13; 6:13; 14:13ff.; *etc.*; Mi. 2:11); or perhaps already emerging was the conviction that the work of God's *rûaḥ* would be primarily eschatological (Is. 4:4).

In the exilic and post-exilic period the work of the Spirit came to renewed prominence. The role of divine *rûaḥ* as inspirer of prophecy was reasserted (Pr. 1:23; *cf.* Is. 59:21—Spirit *and* word together; Ezk. 2:2; 3:1–4, 22–24; *etc.*—Spirit, word *and* hand). The inspiration of the earlier prophets too was freely attributed to the Spirit (Ne. 9:20, 30; Zc. 7:12; *cf.* Is. 63:11ff.). The sense that God is present through his Spirit, expressed for example in Ps. 51:11, appears also in Ps. 143:10; Hg. 2:5; Zc. 4:6. And 2 Ch. 20:14; 24:20 may reflect a desire to bridge the gap between charisma and cult.

The tradition which attributed the artistic skills and craftsmanship of Bezalel and others to the activity of the Spirit (Ex. 28:3; 31:3; 35:31), forged a link between the Spirit and more aesthetic and ethical qualities. It is perhaps with this in view, or simply out of the consideration that the Spirit is the Spirit of the holy and good God, that some authors specifically designate the Spirit as God's 'holy Spirit' (only three times in the Old Testament—Ps. 51:13; Is. 63:10f.) or as God's 'good Spirit' (Ne. 9:20; Ps. 143:10).

Another emphasis which appears only infrequently and at different periods is the association of the Spirit with the work of creation (Gn. 1:2; Jb. 26:13; Pss. 33:6; 104:30). In Ps. 139:7 *rûaḥ* denotes the cosmic presence of God.

Probably most important of all from a Christian perspective is the growing tendency in prophetic circles to understand the *rûaḥ* of God in eschatological terms, as the power of the End, the hallmark of the new age. The Spirit would effect a new creation (Is. 32:15; 44:3f.). The agents of eschatological salvation would be anointed with God's Spirit (Is. 42:1; 61:1; and later particularly *Psalms of Solomon* 17:42). Men would be created anew by the Spirit to enjoy a relationship with God much more vital and immediate (Ezk. 36:26f.; 37; *cf.* Je. 31:31–34), and the Spirit would be freely dispensed to all Israel (Ezk. 39:29; Joel 2:28f.; Zc. 12:10; *cf.* Nu. 11:29).

In the period between the Testaments the role attributed to the Spirit is greatly diminished. In Hellenistic Wisdom literature the Spirit is not given any prominence. In speaking about the divine/human relationship Wisdom is wholly dominant, so that 'spirit' is simply one way of defining Wisdom (Wisdom 1:6f.; 7:22–25; 9:17), with even prophecy ascribed to Wisdom rather than to the Spirit (Wisdom 7:27; Ecclus. 24:33). In Philo's attempt to merge Jewish theology and Gk. philosophy the Spirit is still the Spirit of prophecy, but his concept of prophecy is the more typically Gk. one of inspiration through ecstasy (*e.g.*, *Quis Rerum Divinarum Heres Sit* 265). Elsewhere in his speculation about creation the Spirit still has a place, but the dominant category of thought is the Stoic Logos (the divine reason immanent in the world and in men).

In the apocalyptic writings references to the human spirit outweigh those to the Spirit of God by nearly 3:1, and references to angelic and demonic spirits outweigh the latter by 6:1. In only a handful of passages is the Spirit spoken of as the agency of inspiration, but this is a role which is thought of as belonging to the past (*e.g.*, *1 Enoch* 91:1; *4 Ezra* 14:22; *Martyrdom of Isaiah* 5:14).

In rabbinic Judaism the Spirit is specifically (almost exclusively) the Spirit of prophecy. But here, even more emphatically, that role belongs to the past. With the rabbis the belief becomes very strong that Haggai, Zechariah and Malachi were the last of the prophets and that thereafter the Spirit had been withdrawn (*e.g.*, *Tosefta Sotah* 13:2; earlier expressions in Ps. 74:9; Zc. 13:2–6; 1 Macc. 4:46; 9:27; *2 Baruch* 85:1–3). Most striking is the way in which the Spirit to all intents and purposes is subordinated to the Torah (law). The Spirit inspired the Torah—a view of course also carried over into early Christianity (Mk. 12:36; Acts 1:16; 28:25; Heb. 3:7; 9:8; 10:15; 2 Pet. 1:21; *cf.* 2 Tim. 3:16). But for the rabbis this means that the law is now in effect the only voice of the Spirit, that the Spirit does not speak apart from the law. 'Where there are no prophets there is obviously no Holy Spirit' (*TDNT* 6, p. 382). Likewise in the rabbinic hope for the age to come Torah fills a far more prominent role than Spirit. This diminished role for the Spirit is reflected too in the Targums where other words denoting divine activity become more prominent (Memra, Shekinah); and in the Babylonian Talmud 'Shekinah' (glory) has more or less completely supplanted talk of the Spirit.

Only in the Dead Sea Scrolls does 'Spirit' come back into prominence in speaking of present experience (especially 1QS 3. 13–4. 26), reflecting a conviction of living in the last days not dissimilar to the eschatological consciousness of the first Christians.

III. The Spirit in the teaching of John the Baptist and ministry of Jesus

(1) *In early Judaism*, at the time of Jesus, God was tending to be thought of as more and more distant from man, the transcendent holy God, high and lifted up, dwelling in unapproachable glory. Hence the hestitation even to speak the divine name and the increasing talk of intermediary figures, the name, angels, the glory, wisdom, *etc.*, these all being ways of speaking about God's activity in the world without compromising his transcendence. In early days 'the Spirit' had been one of the chief ways of speaking about the presence of God (note, *e.g.*, the implication of 1 Sa. 16:13f. and 18:12, and of Is. 63:11f., that the Spirit of the Lord is the presence of the Lord). But now that consciousness of divine presence was lacking too (with the exception of Qumran). The Spirit, understood principally as the Spirit of prophecy, had been active in the past (inspiring prophet and Torah) and would be poured out in the new age. But in the present, talk of the Spirit had become wholly subordinate to Wisdom and Logos and Torah, and in particular with the rabbis, Torah was becoming more and more the exclusive focus of religious life and authority.

In this context John the Baptist created considerable excitement. Not that he himself claimed to have the Spirit, but he was widely recognized to be a prophet (Mt. 11:9f.; Mk. 11:32) and so to be inspired by the Spirit of prophecy (*cf.* Lk. 1:15, 17). More striking was his message, for he proclaimed that the outpouring of the Spirit was imminent—the one who was coming would baptize in Spirit and fire (Mt. 3:11; Lk. 3:16; Mk. 1:8 and Jn. 1:33 omit the 'and fire'). This vigorous metaphor was probably drawn partly from the 'liquid' metaphors for the Spirit familiar in the OT (Is. 32:15; Ezk. 39:29; Joel 2:28; Zc. 12:10), and partly from his own characteristic rite of water baptism—his drenching with or immersion in water was a picture of an overwhelming experience of fiery Spirit. It would be an experience of judgment (note the emphasis of John's message in Mt. 3:7–12 and particularly on fire in 3:10–12), but not necessarily wholly destructive, the fire could purge as well as destroy (Mal. 3:2f.; 4:1). The Baptist here was probably thinking in terms of 'the Messianic woes', the period of suffering and tribulation which would introduce the age to come—'the birth pangs of the Messiah' (Dn. 7:19–22; 12:1; Zc. 14:12–15; *1 Enoch* 62:4; 100:1–3; *Sibylline Oracles* 3. 632–651). The idea of entry into the new age by immersion in a stream of fiery *rûaḥ* which would destroy the impenitent and purify the penitent was not a strange or surprising one for John to formulate in view of the parallels in Is. 4:4; 30:27f.; Dn. 7:10; 1QS 4. 21; 1QH 3. 29ff.; *4 Ezra* 13:10f.

(2) *Jesus* created an even bigger stir, for he claimed that the new age, the kingdom of God, was not merely imminent but was already effective through his ministry (Mt. 12:41f.; 13:16f.; Lk. 17:20f.). The presupposition of this was clearly that the eschatological Spirit, the power of the End, was already working through him in unique measure, as evidenced by his exorcisms and successful deliverance of Satan's victims (Mt. 12:24–32; Mk. 3:22–29), and by his proclamation of good news to the poor (Mt. 5:3–6 and 11:5, echoing Is. 61:1f.). The Evangelists of course were in no doubt that Jesus' whole ministry had been in the power of the Spirit from the beginning (Mt. 12:18; Lk. 4:14, 18; Jn. 3:34; also Acts 10:38). For Matthew and Luke this special working of the Spirit in and through Jesus dates from his conception (Mt. 1:18; Lk. 1:35), with his birth in Luke announced by an outburst of prophetic activity heralding the beginning of the end of the old age (Lk. 1:41, 67; 2:25–27, 36–38). But all four Evangelists agree that at Jordan Jesus experienced a special empowering for his ministry, an anointing which was also evidently bound up with his assurance of sonship (Mt. 3:16f.; Mk. 1:10f.; Lk. 3:22; Jn. 1:33f.), hence in the subsequent temptations he is enabled to maintain his assurance and to define what sonship involves, sustained by the same power (Mt. 4:1, 3f., 6f.; Mk. 1:12f.; Lk. 4:1, 3f., 9–12, 14).

Jesus' emphasis in his message was significantly

different from that of the Baptist, not just in his proclamation of the kingdom as present, but in the character he ascribed to the present kingdom. He saw his ministry in terms more of blessing than of judgment. In particular, his reply to the Baptist's question in Mt. 11:4f. seems deliberately to highlight the promise of blessing in the passages he there echoes (Is. 29:18–20; 35:3–5; 61:1f.) and to ignore the warning of judgment which they also contained (*cf.* Lk. 4:18–20). On the other hand, when he looked towards the end of his earthly ministry he did evidently speak of his death in terms probably drawn from the Baptist's preaching (Lk. 12:49–50, baptism and fire), probably seeing his own death as a suffering of the Messianic woes predicted by John, as a draining of the cup of God's wrath (Mk. 10:38f.; 14:23f., 36). He also held out the promise of the Spirit to sustain his disciples when they experienced tribulation and trial in their turn (Mk. 13:11; more fully in Jn. 14:15–17, 26; 15:26f.; 16:7–15). Otherwise, however, 'the Holy Spirit' in Lk. 11:13 is almost certainly an alternative to the less explicit 'good things' (Mt. 7:11); and the repetition of the Baptist's promise in Acts 1:5 and 11:16 is probably intended by Luke as a word of the risen Jesus (*cf.* Lk. 24:49; perhaps also Mt. 28:19).

IV. The Spirit in Acts, Paul and John

The main NT writers agree on their understanding of the Spirit of God, albeit with differing emphases.

a. The gift of the Spirit marks the beginning of the Christian life

In Acts the outpouring of the Spirit at Pentecost is the time when the disciples first experienced 'the last days' for themselves (the free dispensing of the eschatological Spirit being the hallmark of the new age), the time when their 'fully Christian' faith began (Acts 11:17). So in Acts 2:38f. the promise of the gospel to the first enquirers centres on the Spirit, and in other evangelistic situations it is the reception of the Spirit which is evidently seen as the crucial factor manifesting the respondents' acceptance by God (8:14–17; 9:17; 10:44f.; 11:15–17; 18:25; 19:2, 6).

Similarly in Paul the gift of the Spirit is the beginning of Christian experience (Gal. 3:2f.), another way of describing the new relation of justification (1 Cor. 6:11; Gal. 3:14; so Tit. 3:7). Alternatively expressed, one cannot belong to Christ unless one has the Spirit of Christ (Rom. 8:9), one cannot be united with Christ except through the Spirit (1 Cor. 6:17), one cannot share Christ's sonship without sharing his Spirit (Rom. 8:14–17; Gal. 4:6f.), one cannot be a member of the body of Christ except by being baptized in the Spirit (1 Cor. 12:13).

Likewise in John the Spirit from above is the power effecting new birth (Jn. 3:3–8; 1 Jn. 3:9), for the Spirit is the life-giver (Jn. 6:63), like a river of living water flowing from the Christ bringing life to him who comes and believes (7:37–39; so 4:10, 14). In 20:22 the language deliberately echoes Gn. 2:7; the Spirit is the breath of the life of the new creation. And in 1 Jn. 3:24 and 4:13 the presence of the Spirit is one of the 'tests of life'.

It is important to realize that for the first Christians the Spirit was thought of in terms of divine power clearly manifest by its effects on the life of the recipient; the impact of the Spirit did not leave individual or onlooker in much doubt that a significant change had taken place in him by divine agency. Paul refers his readers back to their initial experience of the Spirit again and again. For some it had been an overwhelming experience of God's love (Rom. 5:5); for others of joy (1 Thes. 1:6); for others of illumination (2 Cor. 3:14–17), or of liberation (Rom. 8:2; 2 Cor. 3:17), or of moral transformation (1 Cor. 6:9–11), or of various spiritual gifts (1 Cor. 1:4–7; Gal. 3:5). In Acts the most regularly mentioned manifestation of the Spirit is inspired speech, speaking in tongues, prophecy and praise, and bold utterance of the word of God (Acts 2:4; 4:8, 31; 10:46; 13:9–11; 19:6). This is why possession of the Spirit as such can be singled out as the defining characteristic of the Christian (Rom. 8:9; 1 Jn. 3:24; 4:13), and why the question of Acts 19:2 could expect a straightforward answer (*cf.* Gal. 3:2). The Spirit as such might be invisible, but his presence was readily detectable (Jn. 3:8).

The gift of the Spirit was thus not simply a corollary or deduction drawn from baptism or laying on of hands but a vivid event for the first Christians. It is most probably to the impact of this experience that Paul refers directly in passages like 1 Cor. 6:11; 12:13; 2 Cor. 1:22; Eph. 1:13; also Tit. 3:5f., though many refer them to baptism. And although Rom. 6:3 and Gal. 3:27 ('baptized into Christ') are usually understood as references to the baptismal act, they could as readily be taken as an abbreviation of the fuller allusion to the experience of the Spirit, 'baptized in Spirit into Christ' (1 Cor. 12:13). Certainly according to Acts the first Christians adapted their embryonic ritual in accordance with the Spirit rather than vice versa (Acts 8:12–17; 10:44–48; 11:15–18; 18:25–19:6). And though Jn. 3:5 probably links baptism ('water') and the gift of the Spirit closely together in the birth from above, the two are not to be identified (*cf.* 1:33) and birth by the Spirit is clearly the primary thought (3:6–8).

Acts, Paul and John know of many experiences of the Spirit, but they know of no distinctively second or third experience of the Spirit. So far as Luke is concerned Pentecost was not a second experience of the Spirit for the disciples, but their baptism in Spirit into the new age (Acts 1:5 and above, **III**), the birth of the church and its mission. Attempts to harmonize Jn. 20:22 with Acts 2 at a straightforwardly historical level may be misguided, since John's purpose may be more theological than historical at this point, that is, to emphasize the *theological* unity of Jesus' death, resurrection and ascension with the gift of the Spirit and mission (Pentecost, Jn. 20:21–23; *cf.* 19:30, literally, 'he bowed his head and handed over the spirit/Spirit'). Similarly in Acts 8, since Luke does not conceive of the coming of the Spirit in a silent or invisible manner, the gift of the Spirit in 8:17 is for him the initial reception of the Spirit (8:16, 'they had only been baptized in the name of the Lord Jesus'). Luke seems to suggest that their earlier faith fell short of commitment to Christ or trust in God (8:12—'they believed Philip'—as a description of conversion would be without parallel in Acts).

b. The Spirit as the power of the new life

According to Paul the gift of the Spirit is also a beginning that looks to final fulfilment (Gal. 3:3; Phil. 1:6), the beginning and first instalment of a life-long process of transformation into the image of Christ which only achieves its end in the resurrection of the body (2 Cor. 1:22; 3:18; 4:16–5:5; Eph. 1:13f.; 2 Thes. 2:13; also 1 Pet. 1:2). The Spirit is the 'first fruits' of the harvest of resurrection, whereby God begins to exercise his claim over the whole man (Rom. 8:11, 23; 1 Cor. 3:16; 6:19; 15:45–48; Gal. 5:16–23).

Life for the believer is therefore qualitatively different from what it was prior to faith. His daily living becomes his means of responding to the Spirit's claim, enabled by the Spirit's power (Rom. 8:4–6, 14; Gal. 5:16, 18, 25; 6:8). This was the decisive difference between Christianity and rabbinic Judaism for Paul. The Jew lived by law, the deposit of the Spirit's revelatory work in past generations, an attitude which led inevitably to inflexibility and casuistry, since revelation from the past is not always immediately appropriate to the needs of the present. But the Spirit brought an immediacy of personal relationship with God, which fulfilled the ancient hope of Jeremiah (31:31–34) and which made worship and obedience something much more free, vital and spontaneous (Rom. 2:28f.; 7:6; 8:2–4; 12:2; 2 Cor. 3:3, 6–8, 14–18; Eph. 2:18; Phil. 3:3).

At the same time, because the Spirit is only a *beginning* of final salvation in this life, there can be no final fulfilment of his work in the believer so long as this life lasts. The man of the Spirit is no longer dependent on this world and its standards for his meaning and satisfaction, but he is still a man of human appetites and frailty and part of human society. Consequently to have the Spirit is to experience tension and conflict between the old life and the new, between flesh and Spirit (Rom. 7:14–25; 8:10, 12f.; Gal. 5:16f.; *cf.* Heb. 10:29). To those who saw the characteristic life of the Spirit in terms of visions, revelations and the like, Paul replied that grace comes to its full expression only in and through weakness (2 Cor. 12:1–10; *cf.* Rom. 8:26f.).

Luke and John say little of other aspects of the ongoing life of the Spirit (*cf.* Acts 9:31; 13:52), but focus attention particularly on the life of the Spirit as directed towards mission (Acts 7:51; 8:29, 39; 10:17–19; 11:12; 13:2, 4; 15:28; 16:6f.; 19:21; Jn. 16:8–11; 20:21-23). The Spirit is that power which bears witness to Christ (Jn. 15:26; Acts 1:8; 5:32; 1 Jn. 5:6–8; also Heb. 2:4; 1 Pet. 1:12; Rev. 19:10).

c. The Spirit of community and of Christ

A distinguishing feature of the Spirit of the new age is that he is experienced by all and works through all, not just the one or two (*e.g.*, Acts 2:17f.; Rom. 8:9; 1 Cor. 12:7, 11; Heb. 6:4; 1 Jn. 2:20). In Paul's teaching it is only this common participation (*koinōnia*) in the one Spirit that makes a group of diverse individuals one body (1 Cor. 12:13; 2 Cor. 13:14; Eph. 4:3f.; Phil. 2:1). And it is only as each lets the Spirit come to expression in word and deed as a member of the body that the body grows towards the maturity of Christ (1 Cor. 12:12–26; Eph. 4:3–16). This is why Paul both encourages a full range and free expression of the Spirit's gifts (Rom. 12:3–8; 1 Cor. 12:4–11, 27–31; Eph. 5:18f.; 1 Thes. 5:19f.; *cf.* Eph. 4:30) and insists that the community test every word and deed which claims the authority of the Spirit by the measure of Christ and the love he embodied (1 Cor. 2:12–16; 13; 14:29; 1 Thes. 5:19–22; *cf.* 1 Jn. 4:1–3).

The same twin emphasis on a worship which is determined by immediate dependence on the Spirit (rather than in terms of sacred place or sanctuary) and in accordance with the truth of Christ is present in Jn. 21:24 (*cf.* Rev. 19:10). Similarly John emphasizes that the believer may expect an immediacy of teaching by the Spirit, the Counsellor (Jn. 14:26; 16:12f.; 1 Jn. 2:27); but also that the new revelation will be in continuity with the old, a reproclaiming, reinterpretation of the truth of Christ (Jn. 14:26; 16:13–15; 1 Jn. 2:24).

It is this tie-in with Christ which finally distinguishes the Christian understanding of the Spirit from the earlier, less well-defined conception. The Spirit is now definitively the Spirit of Christ (Acts 16:7; Rom. 8:9; Gal. 4:6; Phil. 1:19; also 1 Pet. 1:11; *cf.* Jn. 7:38; 19:30; 20:22; Acts 2:33; Heb. 9:14; Rev. 3:1; 5:6), the other Counsellor who has taken over Jesus' role on earth (Jn. 14:16; *cf.* 1 Jn. 2:1). This means that Jesus is now present to the believer only in and through the Spirit (Jn. 14:16–28; 16:7; Rom. 8:9f.; 1 Cor. 6:17; 15:45; Eph. 3:16f.; *cf.* Rom. 1:4; 1 Tim. 3:16; 1 Pet. 3:18; Rev. 2–3), and that the mark of the Spirit is both the recognition of Jesus' present status (1 Cor. 12:3; 1 Jn. 5:6–12) and the reproduction of the character of his sonship and resurrection life in the believer (Rom. 8:11, 14–16, 23; 1 Cor. 15:45–49; 2 Cor. 3:18; Gal. 4:6f.; 1 Jn. 3:2).

The roots of subsequent Trinitarian theology are perhaps evident in Paul's recognition that the believer experiences through the Spirit a twofold relation, to God as Father (Rom. 8:15f.; Gal. 4:6) and to Jesus as Lord (1 Cor. 12:3).

(*COUNSELLOR, *ANGELS, *BAPTISM, *BODY OF CHRIST, *CONVERSION, *DEMONS, *ESCHATOLOGY, *EXORCISM, *GUIDANCE, *INSPIRATION, *LIFE, *POWER, *PROPHECY, *SPIRITUAL GIFTS, *TRINITY, *WIND.)

BIBLIOGRAPHY. G. M. Burge, *The Anointed Community*, 1987; Church of England Doctrine Commission, *We Believe in the Holy Spirit*, 1991; Y. Congar, *I Believe in the Holy Spirit*, 3 vols., 1983; J. D. G. Dunn, *Baptism in the Holy Spirit*, 1970; *idem*, *Jesus and the Spirit*, 1975; *idem*, 'Spirit, Holy Spirit', *NIDNTT* 3, pp. 689–709; *idem*, 'Rediscovering the Spirit', *ExpT* 84, 1972–3, pp. 7–12, 40–44; 94, 1982–3, pp. 9–18; B. Gaybba, *The Spirit of Love*, 1987; M. Green, *I Believe in the Holy Spirit*, 1975; M. E. Isaacs, *The Concept of Spirit*, 1976; G. F. Hawthorne, *The Presence and the Power*, 1991; A. Heron, *The Holy Spirit*, 1983; F. W. Horn *ABD* 3, pp. 260–280; G. T. Montague, *The Holy Spirit: Growth of a Biblical Tradition*, 1976; C. F. D. Moule, *The Holy Spirit*, 1978; T. S. Smail, *Reflected Glory: The Spirit in Christ and Christians*, 1975; E. Schweizer, *The Holy Spirit*, 1980; J. V. Taylor, *The Go-Between God*, 1972. *On (human) spirit see:* H. W. Robinson, *The Christian Doctrine of Man*, 1926; W. D. Stacey, *The Pauline View of Man*, 1956.

J.D.G.D.

SPIRITS IN PRISON. The single explicit reference is 1 Pet. 3:19, with a possible hint at 4:6. The patristic exegesis of 3:19f. regarded the 'disobedient' of Noah's day as typical of sinners who before the incarnation had no chance of hearing the gospel and repenting. The interval between the death and resurrection of Jesus came later to be understood, especially in the Eastern church, as the occasion when Christ, by his *descent into their 'prison', offered these spirits life. Another suggestion for the meaning of this phrase (Reicke,

Dalton) links it with the proclamation of Christ's victory after his passion (with or without the offer of life) to the *angels* who fell (*cf.* 2 Pet. 2:4f.; Jude 6; note also the possible influence of *1 Enoch*). This is supported by the unqualified use of *pneumata* ('spirits'), which is used elsewhere in the Bible only of supernatural beings, never of departed humans.

BIBLIOGRAPHY. Bo Reicke, *The Disobedient Spirits and Christian Baptism*, 1946; E. G. Selwyn, *The First Epistle of St Peter*, 1946, pp. 314–362; W. J. Dalton, *Christ's Proclamation to the Spirits*, 1965.

S.S.S.

SPIRITUAL GIFTS.

I. Name and nature

The term 'spiritual gifts' represents the common rendering in Eng. of the Gk. neuter plural noun *charismata*, formed from *charizesthai* (to show favour, give freely), which is related to the noun *charis* (grace); they are the concrete expression of *charis*, grace coming to visible effect in word or deed. The singular form is used of God's gift of salvation through Christ (Rom. 5:15f.; 6:23) and of any special grace or mercy (Rom. 1:11; 1 Cor. 1:7; 7:7; 2 Cor. 1:11). The plural form is used chiefly in a technical sense to denote the extraordinary gifts of the Holy Spirit bestowed on Christians for special service, and in a few instances the singular form is similarly employed in a distributive or semi-collective sense (1 Tim. 4:14; 2 Tim. 1:6; 1 Pet. 4:10).

A general diffusion of the gifts of the Holy Spirit, marking the new dispensation, was foretold by the prophet Joel (2:28), and confirmed by the promises of Christ to his disciples (Mk. 13:11; Lk. 12:11f.; Jn. 14:12; Acts 1:8; *cf.* Mt. 10:1, 8 and parallels; Mk. 16:17f.). On the day of Pentecost these prophecies and promises were fulfilled (Acts 2:1–21, 33). Later, numerous spiritual gifts are frequently mentioned by Luke (Acts 3:6ff.; 5:12–16; 8:13, 18; 9:33–41; 10:45f., *etc.*), by Peter (1 Pet. 4:10), and by Paul (Rom. 12:6–8; 1 Cor. 12–14), who also describes them as 'spiritual things' (Gk. *pneumatika*, 1 Cor. 12:1; 14:1), and 'spirits', that is, different manifestations of the Spirit (Gk. *pneumata*, 1 Cor. 14:12). The gifts are distributed by the Holy Spirit according to his sovereign will (1 Cor. 12:11) and an individual believer may receive one or more of them (1 Cor. 12:8f.; 14:5, 13).

II. Purpose and duration

The purpose of these charismatic gifts is primarily the edification of the whole church (1 Cor. 12:4–7; 14:12), and, secondarily, the conviction and conversion of unbelievers (1 Cor. 14:21–25; *cf.* Rom. 15:18f.). A disputed question is whether they should be regarded as permanently bestowed on the church or only as a temporary endowment.

The once popular view that the *charismata* were given for the founding of the church and ceased during the 4th century when it became strong enough to continue without their assistance is contrary to historical evidence (B. B. Warfield, *Counterfeit Miracles*, 1972, pp. 6–21). Warfield himself held the view that the *charismata* were given for the authentication of the apostles as messengers of God, one of the signs of an apostle being the possession of those gifts and the power to confer them on other believers. The gifts gradually ceased with the death of those on whom the apostles had conferred them (*op. cit.*, pp. 3, 21ff.). W. H. Griffiths Thomas saw the *charismata* as a testimony to Israel of the Messiahship of Jesus, becoming inoperative after the end of Acts when Israel had refused the gospel (*The Holy Spirit of God*, 1972, pp. 48f.; *cf.* O. P. Robertson, *WTJ* 38, 1975, pp. 43–53). Those holding these views naturally tend to deny the authenticity of subsequent allegedly charismatic manifestations.

On the other hand, strong evidence for the permanence of *charismata* in the church is found in 1 Cor. 13:8–12, where Paul envisages them as continuing to be manifest until the *parousia*. In that case their intermittent appearance in later history may have been affected by the fluctuating faith and spirituality of the church and by the sovereign purpose of the Spirit himself who distributes the gifts 'as he wills' (1 Cor. 12:11).

III. Individual gifts

The lists of *charismata* in the NT (Rom. 12:6–8; 1 Cor. 12:4–11, 28–30; *cf.* Eph. 4:7–12) are clearly incomplete. Various classifications of the gifts have been attempted, but they fall most simply into two main categories—those which qualify their possessors for the ministry of the word and those which equip them for practical service (*cf.* 1 Pet. 4:10f.).

a. Gifts of utterance

(i) **Apostle* (Gk. *apostolos*, lit. 'one sent forth', envoy, missionary, 1 Cor. 12:28f.; *cf.* Eph. 4:11). The title of 'apostle' was originally given to the Twelve (Mt. 10:2; Lk. 6:13; Acts 1:25f.), but was later claimed by Paul (Rom. 1:1; 1 Cor. 9:1f., *etc.*), and applied in a less restricted sense to Barnabas (Acts 14:4, 14), Andronicus and Junias (or Junia) (Rom. 16:7), and possibly to Apollos (1 Cor. 4:6, 9), Silvanus and Timothy (1 Thes. 1:1; 2:6), and James the Lord's brother (1 Cor. 15:7; Gal. 1:19). The special function of an apostle was, as its meaning suggests, to proclaim the gospel to the unbelieving world (Gal. 2:7–9).

(ii) **Prophecy* (Gk. *prophēteia*, Rom. 12:6; 1 Cor. 12:10, 28f.; *cf.* Eph. 4:11). The chief function of the NT prophet was to convey divine revelations of temporary significance which proclaimed to the church what it had to know and do in special circumstances. His message was one of edification, exhortation (Gk. *paraklēsis*) and consolation (1 Cor. 14:3; *cf.* Rom. 12:8), and included occasional authoritative declarations of God's will in particular cases (Acts 13:1f.), and rare predictions of future events (Acts 11:28; 21:10f.). His ministry was primarily directed to the church (1 Cor. 14:4, 22). Some prophets were itinerant (Acts 11:27f.; 21:10), but there were probably several attached to every church (Acts 13:1), as at Corinth, and a few of them are named (Acts 11:28; 13:1; 15:32; 21:9f.).

The ability to 'distinguish between spirits' (Gk. *diakriseis pneumatōn*, 1 Cor. 12:10; *cf.* 14:29) was complementary to that of prophecy, and enabled the hearers to judge claims to prophetic inspiration (1 Cor. 14:29) by interpreting or evaluating prophetic utterances (1 Cor. 2:12–16), thus recognizing successfully those of divine origin (1 Thes. 5:20f.; 1 Jn. 4.1–6), and distinguishing the genuine prophet from the false.

(iii) *Teaching* (Gk. *didaskalia*, Rom. 12:7; 1 Cor. 12:28f.; *cf.* Eph. 4:11). In contrast to the prophet, the teacher did not utter fresh revelations, but expounded and applied established Christian doctrine, and his ministry was probably confined to the local church (Acts 13:1; *cf.* Eph. 4:11). The 'utterance of knowledge' (Gk. *logos gnōseōs*, 1 Cor. 12:8), an inspired utterance containing or embodying knowledge, is related to teaching; but the 'utterance of wisdom' (Gk. *logos sophias*, 1 Cor. 12:8), expressing spiritual insight, may be related rather to the apostles and evangelists (*cf.* 1 Cor. 1:17–2:5, esp. 1:24–30), or to the prophets.

(iv) *Kinds of tongues* (Gk. *genē glōssōn*, 1 Cor. 12:10, 28ff.) and the *interpretation of* * *tongues* (Gk. *hermēneia glōssōn*, 1 Cor. 12:10, 30).

b. Gifts for practical service

(i) *Gifts of power.* **1.** Faith (Gk. *pistis*, 1 Cor. 12:9) is not saving faith, but a higher measure of faith by which special, wonderful deeds are accomplished (Mt. 18:19f.; 1 Cor. 13:2; Heb. 11:33–40). **2.** Gifts of healings (Gk. plural *charismata iamatōn*, 1 Cor. 12:9, 28, 30) are given to perform miracles of restoration to health (Acts 3:6; 5:15f.; 8:7; 19:12, *etc.*). **3.** Working of miracles (Gk. *energēmata dynameōn*, 1 Cor. 12:10, 28f.), lit. 'of powers'. This gift conferred the ability to perform other miracles of varied kinds (Mt. 11:20–23; Acts 9:36f.; 13:11; 20:9–12; Gal. 3:5; Heb. 6:5).

(ii) *Gifts of sympathy.* **1.** Helpers (Gk. *antilēmpseis*, lit. 'acts of helping', 1 Cor. 12:28) denotes the aid given to the weak by the strong (see LXX of Pss. 22:19; 89:19; the verb occurs in Acts 20:35), and refers to special gifts to care for the sick and needy. It probably includes **2.** the liberal almsgiver (Gk. *ho metadidous*, Rom. 12:8) and **3.** the one who performs works of mercy (Gk. *ho eleōn*, Rom. 12:8). **4.** The service (Gk. *diakonia*, Rom. 12:7; *cf.* Acts 6:1) of the deacon is doubtless in view (Phil. 1:1; 1 Tim. 3:1–13).

(iii) *Gifts of administration.* **1.** Administrators (Gk. *kybernēseis*, lit. 'acts of guidance, giving directions') enjoyed the gifts and authority to govern and direct the local church. **2.** The 'leader' (Rom. 12:8, NEB, Gk. *ho prohistamenos*) apparently shares the same gift (the Gk. word recurs in 1 Thes. 5:12; 1 Tim. 5:17), unless the term is to be translated (with RSV, Rom. 12:8), 'he who gives aid', in which case a gift of sympathy is indicated.

Some gifts, such as those of apostleship, prophecy and teaching, were exercised in regular ministry; other gifts like tongues and healing were manifested occasionally. In some instances the gifts appear to involve a release or enhancement of natural ability, for example, the gifts of teaching, helping or leadership; others are clearly a special endowment: faith, gifts of healing and the power to work miracles.

BIBLIOGRAPHY. H. Conzelmann, *TDNT* 9, pp. 402–406; D. Bridges and D. Phypers, *Spiritual Gifts and the Church*, 1973; J. D. G. Dunn, *Jesus and the Spirit*, 1975; R. B. Gaffin, *Perspectives on Pentecost*, 1979; R. Stronstad, *The Charismatic Theology of St Luke*, 1984; M. M. B. Turner, *Vox Evangelica* 15, 1985, pp. 7–61; D. A. Carson, *Showing the Spirit*, 1987; J. Ruthven, *On the Cessation of the Charismata*, 1992. W.G.P.

SPITTING. From early times the Oriental gesture of spitting upon or in the face of a person conveyed deep enmity (Nu. 12:14). Christ submitted to this indignity as the suffering Servant (Is. 50:6; Mt. 26:67).

The Essenes punished spitting in their assembly with a 30-day penance (Jos., *BJ* 2. 147, and the Qumran *Manual of Discipline*, 7. 13).

'Saliva' (Gk. *ptysma*) was used by Christ to cure the blind (Mk. 8:23; Jn. 9:6) and a deaf mute (Mk. 7:33). It was probably placed in the mouth to facilitate speech in the latter case. Its use with clay in Jn. 9:6 was said by Irenaeus to be creative. The healing technique was common to both Jews and Greeks. Suetonius says Vespasian cured a blind man by spittle. The rabbis condemned its use when accompanied with incantations. The usage persisted with the word *ephphatha* in baptismal rites in Rome and Milan. See A. E. J. Rawlinson, *The Gospel according to St Mark*[5], 1942, p. 102. D.H.T.

SPOKESMAN. The *rhētōr* was a professional teacher of rhetoric, or, as Tertullus (Acts 24:1, AV 'orator') a speech-writer who might accept a barrister's brief himself. The extreme refinement of the rhetorical art, which formed the hallmark of higher education, and the difficulties of a hearing before a foreign court, made his services indispensable to the Jews. They were rewarded with a fine speech, notable for its ingratiating exordium. Paul, a master of the art himself, was able to reply in his own person. Elsewhere (1 Cor. 2:4) he disdained professional skill.

BIBLIOGRAPHY. G. A. Kennedy, *The Art of Rhetoric in the Roman World*, 1972. E.A.J.

STACHYS. A friend of Paul (Rom. 16:9) with an uncommon Gk. name (but see instances in Arndt). Lightfoot (*Philippians*, p. 174) finds one Stachys a *medicus* attached to the Imperial household near this time. (* AMPLIAS.) A.F.W.

STARS

I. General use of the term

Stars (Heb. *kôḵāḇîm*; Gk. (LXX, NT *asteres*) are nowhere in the Bible the subject of scientific curiosity. The term is used generally of any luminous non-terrestrial body, other than sun and moon. The great number of the stars is symbolic of God's prodigality (Ex. 32:13; Dt. 1:10; 10:22; 28:62; 1 Ch. 27:23; Ne. 9:23; Heb. 11:12). God promises Abram that his seed shall be numerous as the stars (Gn. 15:5; 22:17; 26:4). Pre-Christian astronomers (*e.g.* Hipparchus, 150 BC) mapped about 3,000 stars; not until the beginning of telescopic astronomy by Galileo in 1610 was it appreciated how many stars there were. This is, however, implied by the Bible references given above.

They are seen poetically as a majestic manifestation of God's 'otherness' in relation to men. He alone makes, controls, numbers them. Man's arrogant pride sometimes endeavours to usurp this authority (Gn. 1:16; Pss. 8:3; 136:9; 147:4; Am. 5:8; Jb. 9:7; Je. 31:35; Is. 14:13; Ob. 4; Na. 3:16; *cf.* Gn. 37:9). A constant temptation was to worship stellar deities; but the stars are insignificant compared with Yahweh himself (Dt. 4:19; Je. 7:18; Am. 5:26; Acts 7:43). He is at the zenith of the heavens (Jb. 22:12).

God's final acts of redemption and judgment are foreshadowed by astronomical signs. The prophets and our Lord foretell such signs; and in Revelation they are prominent (Is. 13:10; Ezk. 32:7; Dn. 8:10;

Joel 2:10; 3:15; Mt. 24:29; Mk. 13:25; Lk. 21:25; Rev. 6:13; 8:10–12; 9:1).

The word 'star' is also used metaphorically without astronomical reference, usually to imply dignity, either innate or usurped (Jb. 38:7; Dn. 12:3; Rev. 1:16, 20; 2:1; 3:1; 12:1; 22:16).

II. Named constellations

A few constellations are mentioned in the Bible by name.

a. The Bear (AV 'Arcturus') (Jb. 9:9; 38:32). The prominent circumpolar constellation Ursa Major. Hence, 'with its children'—the seven main stars of the group. NEB renders 'Aldebaran'.

b. Mazzaroth (Jb. 38:32). Meaning obscure. Possibly the (twelve) zodiacal signs (so NEB), or the S ones only. (Aram. *Mazzaloth*, 'girdling stars', *i.e.* the Zodiacal circle.)

c. Orion (Jb. 9:9; 38:31; Am. 5:8). 'The Hunter'—an outstanding S constellation, containing the first magnitude stars Betelguese (top left, red) and Rigel (bottom right, blue). The range of colour and brightness of these and adjacent stars is an interesting illustration of 1 Cor. 15:41.

d. Pleiades (Jb. 9:9; 38:31; Am. 5:8). A compact cluster of seven faint stars in Taurus, constituting a connected system enveloped in nebulous material about 300 light-years from the sun. The expressions 'binding the chains' and 'loosing the cords' may refer to the supposed heralding of spring and autumn respectively by the Pleiades and Orion. An attractive but probably unacceptable alternative is that the 'binding' of the Pleiades by their mutual attraction, or (poetically) by the nebulosity surrounding them, is contrasted with the 'loosing' of Orion, the stars of which are physically unconnected, and associated for us only by our line of sight.

e. Chambers of the south (Jb. 9:9). Obscure; possibly the constellations which appear over the horizon as one travels S along the trade route to Arabia. NEB renders 'the circle of the southern stars'.

Particularly interesting is the NEB rendering of Jb. 9:12–15, with its twofold mention of the Dog-star and its description of dawn, 'when the light of the Dog-star is dimmed and the stars of the Navigator's Line go out one by one'—a rendering which makes sense of an otherwise unintelligible passage.

III. The star of Bethlehem

The star heralding the birth of Jesus is mentioned in Mt. 2 only, though seemingly foretold in Nu. 24:17 and Is. 60:3. It has historically been explained in three ways: as a major comet; as a planetary conjunction or sequence of conjunctions; or as a supernova.

A planetary conjunction occurs when two or more major planets appear to stand very close to each other, as Jupiter and Saturn did three times in 7 BC. The location of such an event in the sky would also be seen as significant in an age when astrology and astronomy were largely undifferentiated.

A supernova occurs when a star explodes with great violence and becomes extremely brilliant (perhaps a hundred million times as bright as the sun) for a short time before sinking back, usually into insignificance. Although no such stars have been observed within our own galaxy since 1604, they would be very spectacular indeed, and could easily dominate the night sky.

In recent years, many astronomers and scientific historians have taken the story of the star of Bethlehem very seriously indeed, and have put much effort into trying to identify it in relation to the astonishingly detailed and accurate Chinese astronomical records for that period. Their conclusions do, of course, vary (see bibliography), but a very attractive treatment by Humphreys suggests that planetary conjunctions were seen by the Magi as a sign that an important event was about to happen. A tailed comet observed by the Chinese for over 70 days in 5 BC could have been the actual 'star' that led them to Bethlehem.

IV. Astronomy

There is no real 'astronomy' in the Bible and the scientific approach of, for example, the Babylonians, who by the 4th century BC could predict many astronomical events, is not found there. But a view of the universe is assumed which is not inconsistent with modern scientific cosmology. It is, of course, easy to find references to a primitive and unacceptable world-view comparable, for example, with the Babylonian creation myths. But to judge the Bible only by these is as uncritical as to judge our modern knowledge of the universe by our use of such terms as 'sunrise' and 'the canopy of heaven'. (*CREATION.)

Our own star system, or galaxy, is estimated to contain at least 100 billion stars: light takes 100,000 years to cross it. Our sun is an average star about two-thirds of the way out from the centre. But billions of other similar galaxies may be observed, up to about ten billion light years away from us. (Estimates as of 1994; a billion is a thousand million.) The contrast between this cosmos and the three-decker universe of Semitic mythology is striking. The Bible is often closer to the former than the latter in spirit. For the universe of the biblical writers is rational, and of awe-inspiring immensity. Ps. 104, for example, speaks of a world which is completely rational, and depends entirely on God's laws; this is typical of the outlook of the biblical writers. In the promise to Abram, God couples the number of stars with the number of grains of sand. Only *c.* 3000 stars are visible to the naked eye, so on the face of it this is a feeble comparison. But the total number of stars in the galaxy *is* comparable with the number of grains of sand in all the world! The Bible is full of such implications of vastness quite beyond the knowledge of its day.

We assert, then, that the Bible consistently assumes a universe which is fully rational, and vast in size, in contrast to the typical contemporary world-view, in which the universe was not rational, and no larger than could actually be proved by the unaided senses. The books of I. Velikovsky (*Worlds in Collision*, 1950, *etc.*), though highly controversial, are written from a Jewish standpoint and are full of interest to the OT student who is also interested in astronomy.

BIBLIOGRAPHY. G. R. Driver and L. W. Clarke, 'Stars', *HDB*², 1963, pp. 936ff.; R. A. Rosenberg, 'The "Star of the Messiah" reconsidered', *Bib* 53, 1972, pp. 105ff.; W. Foerster, *TDNT*, 1, pp. 503–505; D. A. Hagner, *NIDNTT*, 3, pp. 734–736; D. Hughes, *The Star of Bethlehem Mystery*, 1979; C. J. Humphreys, 'The Star of Bethlehem', *TynB* 43.1, 1992.

M.T.F.

STEPHANAS. A Corinthian, whose family, one of the few baptized by Paul himself (1 Cor. 1:16), was known for its exertions in voluntary Christian service; Paul, perhaps thinking of the Corinthian factions, bespeaks recognition of such leadership (1 Cor. 16:15ff.). The phrase 'the first converts of Achaia' (*cf.* Rom. 16:5) has been taken to indicate an Athenian origin (Acts 17:34), but it may rather indicate the first Christian *family* in the province, and thus the earnest of the church there (*cf.* Ramsay, *BRD*, pp. 385ff.). The link sometimes made with the apostolic ordination of their 'first-fruits' in *1 Clement* 42 is purely verbal.

Stephanas, with *Fortunatus and *Achaicus, delighted Paul with a visit at Ephesus (1 Cor. 16:17): no doubt they carried the Corinthians' letter and returned with 1 Cor. No connection with the 'household of *Chloe' is likely.

The name is a pet-form (from *Stephanēphoros*?). Two late MSS of Acts 16:27 identify him with the Philippian jailor. A.F.W.

STEPHEN (Gk. *stephanos*, 'crown'). Stephen was one of the seven men chosen by the disciples soon after the resurrection to look after the distribution of assistance to the widows of the church, so that the apostles themselves should be free for their spiritual tasks (Acts 6:1–6). All seven had Gk. names, which suggests that they were Hellenistic Jews (one of them indeed, Nicolas of Antioch, was a proselyte). Stephen is recorded as standing out from the others in faith, grace, spiritual power, and wisdom (6:5, 8, 10). He had time to do more than the special work assigned to him, for he was among those foremost in working miracles and preaching the gospel.

He soon fell foul of the Hellenistic synagogue, which brought him before the Sanhedrin on charges of blasphemy (6:9–14). Stephen, with angelic face, replied to the charges with a survey of the history of Israel and an attack upon the Jews for continuing in the tradition of their fathers and killing the Messiah (6:15–7:53). This brought upon him the fury of the council, and when he claimed to see Jesus standing at the right hand of God (probably as his advocate or witness in his defence) he was seized and stoned to death (7:54–60). He met his end courageously, as did his Master, on accusations by false witnesses of seeking to overthrow the Temple and law (*cf.* Mt. 26:59–61). He prayed as Jesus had done (Lk. 23:34) for his persecutors to be forgiven and committed his soul into Christ's keeping (*cf.* Lk. 23:46). Whether it was a legal execution or not, it seems that Pilate, who normally lived in Caesarea, turned a blind eye to it all.

There were striking consequences from Stephen's death. The persecution which followed (Acts 8:1) led to a more widespread preaching of the gospel (8:4; 11:19). Stephen's death was also undoubtedly a factor in bringing Saul of Tarsus to Christ (7:58; 8:1, 3; 22:20). But above all, Stephen's speech was the beginning of a theological revolution in the early church, as the principles of the universal mission were clearly stated for the first time. Luke records it at great length, and this surely indicates the importance he attached to it.

Stephen's theme in reviewing the history of Israel was that God's presence cannot be localized, and that the people have always rebelled against the will of God. He showed first of all that Abraham lived a pilgrim life, not inheriting the land promised to him (7:2–8). Then he demonstrated how Joseph likewise left Canaan, sold by his brothers through jealousy (vv. 9–16). A long section deals with Moses, against whom Stephen was alleged to have spoken (vv. 17–43). Moses also was shown to have been rejected by his brethren when he came to deliver them. Yet God vindicated him by sending him back to Egypt to bring his people out. Again they turned aside to idolatry in the wilderness and refused to obey Moses. This idolatry continued until the Babylonian Exile owing to their desire to have visible gods.

The next section (vv. 44–50) deals with the tabernacle and the Temple. The tabernacle was mobile and went with God's people on their pilgrimage. The Temple was static and too easily gave rise to a localized view of God. But the Most High does not dwell in manufactured houses (*cf.* Mk. 14:58). The Jewish religion had become static and failed to move on towards the new Temple, the body of Christ.

The references to the tabernacle and the whole idea of the real but invisible Christian cultus is developed in the Epistle to the Hebrews, which has been seen to have close affinities with this speech. It is certain that Paul, too, worked out the principles stated by Christ and developed here by Stephen. When these principles were understood by the church there ensued a break with the old Temple worship (Acts 2:46). The Christians saw in practice that they were not just a sect of the old Israel. They were the new people of God, with the true temple, altar and sacrifice, living the truly pilgrim life, and rejected, as the prophets and as Jesus had been, by the Jews.

BIBLIOGRAPHY. R. J. McKelvey, *The New Temple*, 1969; F. F. Bruce, *New Testament History*, 1969, pp. 206ff.; M. Hengel, 'Between Jesus and Paul. The "Hellenists", the "Seven" and Stephen', in *Between Jesus and Paul*, 1983; *BAICS* 6, f.c. R.E.N.

STEPS (Heb. *maʿalôṯ*, from *maʿalâ*, 'a going up', 'ascent', *cf.* Lat. *gradus*; Gk. *bathmos*, 'a step' (so LXX), 'ascent'). That the shadow should go back ten steps was the sign by which the Lord confirmed to Hezekiah his recovery from mortal illness (2 Ki. 20:8–11; *cf.* Is. 38:8). Josephus (*Ant.* 10. 29) suggested that the stairs of the king's palace may have constituted a type of sun-dial, but for a detailed discussion of the whole incident and possible interpretations, see C. F. Keil, *The Books of the Kings*, 1854, pp. 463–465 and S. Iwry, 'The Qumrân Isaiah and the End of the Dial of Ahaz', *BASOR* 147, 1957.

The word is found also in the titles of Pss. 120–134, which in AV are called Songs of Degrees (RSV 'ascents') and said to have been sung by processions of pilgrims while ascending Mt Zion during the great Temple festivals (*PSALMS).

The term occurs once in the NT (1 Tim. 3:13), where the Gk. word denotes 'good standing'. According to Arndt, a technical term of the mysteries may be involved here, implying a 'step' in the soul's journey heavenward. J.D.D.

STEWARD. In the OT a steward is a man who is 'over a house' (Gn. 43:19; 44:4; Is. 22:15, *etc.*). In the NT there are two words translated steward:

epitropos (Mt. 20:8; Gal. 4:2), *i.e.* one to whose care or honour one has been entrusted, a curator, a guardian; and *oikonomos* (Lk. 16:2–3; 1 Cor. 4:1–2; Tit. 1:7; 1 Pet. 4:10), *i.e.* a manager, a superintendent—from *oikos* ('house') and *nemō* ('to dispense' or 'to manage'). The word is used to describe the function of delegated responsibility, as in the parables of the labourers, and the unjust steward.

More profoundly, it is used of the Christian's responsibility, delegated to him under 'Christ's kingly government of his own house'. All things are Christ's, and Christians are his executors or stewards. Christians are admitted to the responsibilities of Christ's overruling of his world; so that stewardship (*oikonomia*) can be referred to similarly as a dispensation (1 Cor. 9:17; Eph. 3:2; Col.1:25). C.H.D.

STOCKS (Heb. *mahpeḵeṯ*, 'pillory'; *saḏ*, 'fetters'; *ṣînōq*, 'a collar'). Referred to in later OT passages only, this instrument of punishment comprised two large pieces of wood into which were inserted the feet, and sometimes also the hands and neck, of the prisoner. The prophets Jeremiah (Je. 20:2–3; *cf.* 29:26) and Hanani (2 Ch. 16:10) were subjected to it, and Job uses the idea figuratively in mourning his affliction (Jb. 13:27; 33:11).

In the NT Gk. *xylon*, 'wood', is used in describing the Philippian incident when Paul and Silas were put in the stocks (Acts 16:24). (*PRISON.) J.D.D.

STOICS. The Stoic school of philosophy derived its name from the Stoa Poikile, the portico in Athens where Zeno of Citium (335–263 BC) first taught its characteristic doctrines. His teaching was systematized and extended by Chrysippus (*c.* 280–207 BC), the 'second founder' of Stoicism. By the time when Paul encountered Stoics at Athens (Acts 17:18) their general attitude had been modified by elements taken from Platonism; of this more syncretist Stoicism Posidonius was a leading exponent.

Grappling with that same uncertainty of life which led the Epicureans to seek happiness in serene detachment, the Stoics sought salvation in aligning the will with the inherent Reason of the universe, *Logos. Man is happy when he does not want things to be any other than they are; let him, then, seek clear knowledge of the cycle of nature and cultivate a willing acceptance of it. Though a man must play his part willy-nilly in the outworking of universal Reason, for his own peace of mind it is essential that he do so consciously and willingly; he must seek out the things which befit his place in the natural order (*ta kathēkonta*) and pursue them not with desire, which might be disappointed, but with disinterested virtue. His fellow men he must serve not from love, which would make him suffer if service failed to help them, but from a pure recognition that the life of service is the 'natural' life for man. The universal Reason is God; traditional mythologies were given a symbolic interpretation in this sense.

All this seems very formal and austere, but individual Stoics, including the Roman emperor Marcus Aurelius, set a high standard of personal conduct. The form could, moreover, in part be adapted to receive a Christian content; much of Paul's language in the apologetic discourse on Mars' Hill (*AREOPAGUS) is drawn from that of Stoicism.

BIBLIOGRAPHY. H. von Arnim, *Stoicorum Veterum Fragmenta*, 1903–5; J. M. Rist, *Stoic Philosophy*, 1969; F. H. Sandbach, *The Stoics*, 1975. M.H.C.

STOMACH, BELLY. Principally, Heb. *beṭen* or *mēʿîm*; Gk. *koilia.* Indistinguishable from *bowels or *womb in OT and NT, these words being translated by 'stomach' or 'belly' generally when referring to eating, or wounding (Jdg. 3:21; Ezk. 3:3; Jon. 1:17; Lk. 15:16 [RSVmg.]; often translated 'body' in RSV [*e.g.* Nu. 5:21]).

Once in the NT the word *stomachos* is used (1 Tim. 5:23) of the stomach. In early Gk. usage it referred to an opening, or the *mouth (*stoma*), later the opening of the stomach, so having a more precise physiological reference than in the OT. B.O.B.

STOMACHER. The somewhat misleading AV translation of Heb. *peṯîḡîl*, a word of uncertain meaning which occurs only in Is. 3:24 as an antithesis for 'a girding of sackcloth'. RSV 'a rich robe' seems to fit this requirement. J.D.D.

STONE. The chief biblical words are Heb. *'eḇen* and Gk. *lithos* and *akrogōniaios* ('cornerstone').

The common word 'stone' is used in the Bible with a variety of reference. Small stones made a convenient weapon (1 Sa. 17:40), were a means of attack and even execution (Nu. 35:17; *cf.* Jn. 8:59; Acts 7:58f.), formed a handy measure of weight (Lv. 19:36, where *'eḇen* is so translated), and were used, when sharpened, as knives (Ex. 4:25). Larger stones were used to cover wells (Gn. 29:2), to close the mouth of caves (Jos. 10:18) and of tombs (Mt. 27:60), to serve as a landmark (2 Sa. 20:8), as a memorial (Jos. 4:20ff.), and as a pillar or altar which had specifically religious associations (Gn. 28:18; Dt. 27:5). Stones were also, of course, a primary building material.

Figurative as well as literal uses of the term 'stone' occur in the Bible. Notably, the 'stone' image is used in the NT to describe the person of Jesus. In the Synoptic Gospels, for example, the parable of the vineyard (Mk. 12:1–11 and parallels) is followed by the Lord's citation of Ps. 118:22, which is obviously applied to himself ('The very stone which the builders rejected has become the head of the corner'). This provides us with an important clue to the self-understanding of Jesus. The meaning of 'head stone' (LXX, *eis kephalēn gōnias*) in this psalm is 'top stone' or 'coping stone', that is, the carefully chosen and perfectly made stone which completes a building (*cf.* Zc. 4:7). Probably the immediate reference here was to Israel herself, rejected by men but chosen by God. The real significance of the passage in its NT setting is made abundantly clear from Peter's quotation of Ps. 118:22, with reference to Jesus, during his speech before the Jewish court in Jerusalem (Acts 4:11). God has vindicated him whom the Jews cast out, and exalted him to the headship of the new Israel. In the *Epistle of Barnabas* (6:4) these words are quoted directly from the LXX (Ps. 118), and also applied to Christ.

The only OT occurrences of the phrase 'corner stone' are Jb. 38:6 (LXX *lithos gōniaios*) and Is. 28:16 (LXX *akrogōniaios*); and these are both figurative (*cf.* Ps. 144:12). But unlike 'head of the corner', the stone referred to here would seem to be part of the foundation of a building, and to bear its weight. This is evidently the meaning of *akrogōniaios* in 1 Pet. 2:6, where the writer quotes Is. 28:16 itself. Christ is now the corner-stone of the church, the location of which is the heavenly Zion (*cf.* Eph. 2:20, where the same Gk. word is used, and 1 Cor. 3:11). In v. 7 of the same passage, however, the writer goes on to quote the psalmic reference we have noted (118:22, echoed in v. 4), and he thus gives us the complementary truth that Christ is also the *head* of the church, exalted by God the Father to that position of vindication. In this exaltation, moreover, believers will share. The writer's use of *lithos* in v. 8 with reference to stumbling suggests a confusion of images; although it is possible, as J. Y. Campbell points out (*TWBR*, p. 53), that a stone at the corner of the foundation of a building might also form a stumbling-stone (*cf.* also Rom. 9:32f.). Christ is described in the same passage (v. 4) as a 'living stone' (*lithon zōnta*), alive and giving life to those who as believers are incorporated into him, and built up as *lithoi zōntes* into the spiritual building of his church for purposes of worship (v. 5) and witness (v. 9).

BIBLIOGRAPHY. J. R. Harris, *Testimonies*, 1, 1916, pp. 26–32; S. H. Hooke, 'The Corner-Stone of Scripture', *The Siege Perilous*, 1956, pp. 235–249; F. F. Bruce, 'The Corner Stone', *ExpT* 84, 1972–3, pp. 231–235; J. Jeremias in *TDNT* 4, pp. 268–280; W. Mundle *et al.*, *NIDNTT* 3, pp. 381–394.

S.S.S.

STONING (Heb. *sāqal*, 'to stone', 'to be stoned'; Heb. *rāḡam*, 'to collect or cast stones'; Gk. *katalithazō*, 'to stone (thoroughly)'; Gk. *lithazō*, 'to stone'; Gk. *lithoboleō*, 'to cast stones'). Stoning was the usual Heb. form of execution (Ex. 19:13; Lv. 20:27; Lk. 20:6; Acts 7:58, *etc.*). The prosecution witnesses (the law required at least two such) had to cast the first stone (Dt. 13:9f.; *cf.* Jn. 8:7), and afterwards if the victim still lived the spectators carried out the sentence, and the body was suspended until sunset (Dt. 21:23).

For an excellent summary of offences for which stoning was prescribed, and further details of the execution, see W. Corswant, *A Dictionary of Life in Bible Times*, E.T. 1960, p. 261.

J.D.D.

STORE-CITIES. Towns (Heb. *'ᵃrê-miskᵉnôṯ*) where provisions, often revenue paid in kind (grain, oil, wine, *etc.*), and weapons were laid up in magazines or storehouses by the central government, for maintaining frontier and defence forces, and as reserve supplies, *etc.* The Hebrews had to labour on Pharaoh's store-cities Pithom and Ra'amses on the eve of the Exodus (Ex. 1:11). The Delta-residence Ra'amses (Egyp. *Pi-Ramessē*) was frequently boasted of in Egyp. texts as being in a region of plenty, with stores and treasuries abundantly filled (*ANET*, 1955, pp. 470–471; *JEA* 5, 1918, pp. 186f., 192, 194f.). Solomon had store-cities and depots in Israel and Hamath (1 Ki. 9:19; 2 Ch. 8:4–6). When summoned against Baasha of Israel by Asa of Judah, Ben-hadad I of Aram-Damascus smote stores in ('of') cities of Naphtali (2 Ch. 16:4). Jehoshaphat built store-cities in Judah (2 Ch. 17:12), and Hezekiah was proud of his well-filled storage-magazines for revenue in grain, wine and oil (2 Ch. 32:28). And likewise some of his contemporaries: Asitawanda king of Cilicia (*c.* 725 BC) 'filled the storehouses (or, depots) of (the city) Pa'ar' (*ANET*, p. 499; *cf.* Dupont-Sommer, *Oriens* 1, 1948, pp. 196–197). Remains, possibly those of government storehouses, have been excavated in Palestine. For remains at Beth-shemesh and Lachish, *cf.* Wright, *Biblical Archaeology*, 1957, p. 130. For Hazor and Samaria, *cf.* K. M. Kenyon, *Archaeology in the Holy Land*, 1960, pp. 271–272, 279, and Y. Yadin, *Hazor*, BM Exhibition Guide, 1958, p. 17 and fig. 30.

K.A.K.

STORM. The more violent activities of nature are usually associated with rain- and hail-storms. Generally the incidence of violent rain-storms and cloud-bursts occurs at the commencement of the rainy season, or at the beginning of each renewed spell of rain during the cooler months. At Haifa, for example, on 9 December 1921, 28 cm fell in 24 hours. Thunder-storms are most frequent in Nov. and Dec. and occur most commonly in the Jordan Valley. Hail not infrequently accompanies thunder between Dec. and March. Scripture vividly describes its disastrous effects upon the growing crops (Ps. 78:47; Is. 28:2; Ezk. 13:13–14; Hg. 2:17). The wind-storms that sweep down upon the Sea of Galilee are vividly recorded in the events of Mk. 4:37ff., and perhaps in the parable of the badly founded house sited in some dried-up water-bed, when 'the rain fell, and the floods came, and the winds blew and beat against that house' (Mt. 7:27).

God spoke in the thunderstorm (Ex. 9:28; 19:16, 19; 1 Sa. 7:10; 12:18; Jb. 37:1–5; Pss. 18:13; 29:3–9; 104:7), as he judged in the earthquake (Je. 4:24–26; Na. 1:5). The Hebrews in conceiving how 'thy glory passed through the four gates of fire and earthquake and wind and ice' (2 Esdras 3:19) had to learn, however, that Yahweh was more revelatory to them in the Exodus than in storm and earthquake. This certainly was the experience of Elijah, who had the consciousness of 'the still small voice' as more expressive of the divine presence and power than earthquake, wind and fire (1 Ki. 19:11–13). (*EARTHQUAKE, *EUROCLYDON, *RAIN, *THUNDER, *WHIRLWIND, *WIND.)

J.M.H.

STRANGLED (THINGS). Gk. *pnikta* (Acts 15:20, 29; 21:25) refers to animals killed without shedding their blood, to eat which was repugnant to Jews (*cf.* Lv. 17:13; Dt. 12:16, 23). For general principles involved, see *IDOLS, MEATS OFFERED TO.

J.D.D.

STRIPES. The rendering of several Heb. and Gk. words, only one of which (Gk. *plēgē*) occurs more than twice. The Deuteronomic law limited to forty the number of blows which a judge could prescribe (Dt. 25:2–3). The punishment was generally carried out by a three-thonged scourge, and the executioner himself was punished if the stipulated number were exceeded. Thus, what Paul describes in his 'foolish boasting' (2 Cor. 11:24) was in fact the maximum penalty, for the forty strokes were in practice reduced by one on the principle of 'setting a hedge around the law'.

Stripes can be a symbol of salutary correction (Ps. 89:32; *cf.* Pr. 13:24) and a reminder of the Lord's sacrifice (Is. 53:5; 1 Pet. 2:24). (*SCOURGING.) J.D.D.

STUMBLING-BLOCK. In the OT the Heb. root *kāšal*, 'to stagger', 'to stumble', forms the basis of *mikšôl, makšēlâ*, 'that against which anyone stumbles' (Lv. 19:14). It is used figuratively of idols (Is. 57:14; Ezk. 7:19, 14:3–4; Zp. 1:3).

In the NT two Gk. words are used. *proskomma* (*tou lithou*), 'stone of stumbling' (Rom. 9:32–33; 14:13; 1 Cor. 8:9; 1 Pet. 2:8), is used of any form of barrier. *skandalon* (Rom. 11:9; 1 Cor. 1:23; Rev. 2:14), originally the trigger stick of a trap, is used in LXX to translate Heb. *mikšôl*, but also *môqēš*, 'a snare', 'a trap' (*cf.* Pss. 69:22; 140:5). *Cf.* also Mt. 16:23, 'you are a hindrance (*skandalon*; AV 'offence') to me'. See W. Barclay, *New Testament Wordbook*, 1955 (*s.v. skandalon, skandalizein*). J.B.TT.

SUBURB. In AV and RV most commonly the equivalent of Heb. *migrāš*, more accurately rendered 'pasture lands' in RVmg. and 'common land' in RSV in Lv. 25:34. It is used specially, but not exclusively, with regard to the uncultivated land, suitable for the pasturing of cattle, surrounding the levitical cities; its alienation from levitical ownership was forbidden (Lv. 25:34, *etc.*).

In 2 Ki. 23:11, AV, the word 'suburbs' is the rendering of Heb. *parwārîm* (RV and RSV 'precincts'), a word of doubtful origin and meaning, but possibly derived, like 'Parbar' in 1 Ch. 26:18, from Old Persian *frabada*, 'forecourt'. F.F.B.

SUCCOTH. 1. First site on the journey of the Israelites during the Exodus, possibly equivalent to the Old Egyp. *ṯkw* (Pithom), which was in the E part of Wadi Tumilat (Ex. 12:37; 13:20; Nu. 33:5–6). This was the normal way in or out of Egypt for displaced persons. We find it mentioned in the Story of Sinuhe, in Papyrus Anastasi V and VI. (*ENCAMPMENT BY THE SEA, *PITHOM.)

2. City of the tribe of Gad (Jos. 13:27) in the Jordan Valley not far from a water passage (Jdg. 8:5, 16) and from Zarethan (1 Ki. 7:46). It is perhaps the modern Tell Akhsâs or Tell Dêr Allah.

The name Succoth is explained in Gn. 33:17, where it is connected with 'booths', since Jacob established himself there. C.D.W.

SUCCOTH-BENOTH. The name of an object made by Babylonians exiled in Samaria *c.* 722 BC and named among the pagan deities worshipped there (2 Ki. 17:30). The *MT sukkôṯ-bᶜnôṯ* implies an interpretation as 'booths of daughters' (*cf.* Gk. *sokchōthbenithei*). This has been explained either as places of prostitution or as shrines in which were carried images of female deities, *e.g.* Banitu (an epithet of the Babylonian goddess Ishtar).

The parallelism with Nergal of Cutha seems to require the name of a deity here also. Following Rawlinson, Zēr-bānīt (Zarpanitum) the consort of Marduk (*MERODACH) has been proposed, but this is very doubtful. D.J.W.

SUFFERING. In the Bible suffering is regarded as an intrusion into this created world. Creation was made good (Gn. 1:31). When sin entered, suffering also entered in the form of conflict, pain, corruption, drudgery and death (Gn. 3:15–19). In the new heaven and earth suffering has been finally abolished (Rev. 21:4; Is. 65:17ff.). The work of Christ is to deliver man from suffering, corruption and death (Rom. 8:21; 1 Cor. 15:26), as well as from sin (Mt. 1:21). Though Satan is regarded as having power to make men suffer (2 Cor. 12:7; Jb. 1:12; 2:6), they suffer only in the hand of God, and it is God who controls and sends suffering (Am. 3:6; Is. 45:7; Mt. 26:39; Acts 2:23).

The burden of suffering was always keenly felt by God's people (Gn. 47:9; 2 Sa. 14:14). Its presence often became a problem, since it was regarded as sent by God (Ps. 39:9), and thus had to be related to the fact of God's love and righteousness (Ps. 73). Therefore, in the midst of suffering, man was forced to decide how far he could live by faith, and resist the demand for a rational explanation. The problem was not so acute at times when the sense of solidarity within the community was strong, and the individual, as a responsible member of his tribe or family in all circumstances, was able to accept the judgment and suffering that fell on his people as his own responsibility (Jos. 7). But the problem became more urgent as the responsible relation of each individual to God was emphasized (Je. 31:29; Ezk. 18:2–4).

True faith, wrestling with the problem and burden of suffering, does not require an immediate and complete justification of God. It can wait in the darkness (Hab. 2:2–4).

It finds in the reality of God's presence and goodness a more decisive factor in the present situation than even the bitterness of pain (Ps. 73:21–23), and is willing to set against the distorted shape of things present the perfect new order of things in the kingdom of God, of which it has already received a foretaste (Ps. 73:24–26; Rom. 8:18; 2 Cor. 4:16–18). But the man of faith is not insensitive to the baffling nature of the problem. The book of Job shows him experiencing in an extreme degree the bitterness and perplexity of unexplained suffering, refusing to acquiesce in rational theories that make God's ways subject to simple human calculation, temporarily losing his balance, but able ultimately to recover, and finally, through an overwhelming vision of God himself, reaching a certainty in which he can triumph over all his difficulties even though he is not yet, and knows he never will be, able to provide a rational explanation for all circumstances in this life.

Though it is thus asserted that such solutions are inadequate when applied generally, yet sometimes definite understandable reasons are given for instances of suffering (*cf.* Ps. 37), and several lines of thought on the problem appear and converge. Suffering can be the harvest of sin (Ho. 8:7; Lk. 13:1–5; Gal. 6:8), both for the individual (Ps. 1) and for the community and nation (Am. 1–2). It can be regarded at times as a punishment administered by God, or a chastisement designed to correct the ways of his people (Pr. 3:12; Jdg. 2:22–3:6), or a means whereby men are tested or purified (Ps. 66:10; Jas. 1:3, 12; 1 Pet. 1:7; Rom. 5:3) or brought closer to God in a new relationship of dependence and fellowship (Ps. 119:67; Rom. 8:35–37). Thus suffering can be for good (Rom.

8:28f.), or it can have the opposite effect (Mt. 13:21).

In bearing their witness to the sufferings of the coming Messiah (1 Pet. 1:10–12) the OT writers are taught how God can give a new meaning to suffering. Their own experience of serving God in his redemptive purposes in Israel taught them that the love of God must involve itself in sharing the affliction and shame of, and in bearing reproach from, those he was seeking to redeem (Ho. 1–3; Je. 9:1–2; 20:7–10; Is. 63:9). Therefore his true Servant, who will perfectly fulfil his redeeming will, will be a *suffering Servant.* Such suffering will not simply arise as a result of faithfulness to God in pursuing his vocation, but will indeed constitute the very vocation he must fulfil (Is. 53). A new vicarious meaning and purpose is now seen in such unique suffering in which One can suffer in the place of, and as the inclusive representative of, all.

Suffering can have a new meaning for those who are members of the body of Christ. They can share in the sufferings of Christ (2 Cor. 1:5ff.; Mk. 10:39; Rom. 8:17), and regard themselves as pledged to a career or vocation of suffering (Phil. 1:29; 1 Pet. 4:1–2), since the members of the body must be conformed to the Head in this respect (Phil. 3:10; Rom. 8:29) as well as in respect of his glory. Whatever form the suffering of a Christian takes it can be regarded as a cross which may be taken up in following Christ in the way of his cross (Mt. 16:24; Rom. 8:28–29). Such suffering is indeed the inevitable way that leads to resurrection and glory (Rom. 8:18; Heb. 12:1–2; Mt. 5:10; 2 Cor. 4:17f.). It is by tribulation that men enter the kingdom of God (Acts 14:22; Jn. 16:21). The coming of the new age is preceded by birth pangs on earth, in which the church has its decisive share (Mt. 24:21–22; Rev. 12:1–2, 13–17; *cf.*, *e.g.*, Dn. 12:1; Mi. 4:9–10; 5:2–4). Since the sufferings of Christ are sufficient in themselves to set all men free (Is. 53:4–6; Heb. 10:14), it is entirely by grace, and not in any way by necessity, that the sufferings in which his people participate with him can be spoken of as filling up what is lacking in his affliction (Col. 1:24), and as giving fellowship in his vicarious and redemptive suffering.

BIBLIOGRAPHY. H. E. Hopkins, *The Mystery of Suffering*, 1959; J. Scharbert and J. Schmidt, in *EBT*, 3, 1970, pp. 890–897; J. Bowker, *The Problem of Suffering in the World Religions*, 1970; B. Gärtner, *NIDNTT* 3, pp. 719–726; W. C. Kaiser, *A Biblical Approach to Personal Suffering*, 1982; D. A. Carson, *How Long O Lord?*, 1990, E. S. Gerstenberger and W. Schrage, *Suffering*, 1982; J. C. Beker, *Suffering and Hope*, 1987; T. E. Fretheim, *The Suffering of God*, 1984. R.S.W.

SUKKIIM (Egyp. *ṯktn, ṯk*). Libyan auxiliaries in the Egyp. army when *Shishak invaded Palestine (2 Ch. 12:3). They were employed as scouts from 13th to 12th centuries BC. See references in R. A. Caminos, *Late Egyptian Miscellanies*, 1954, pp. 176–177, 180. K.A.K.

SUMER is the land of the **SUMERIANS**, Sumerian its language. Sumer derives from the Akkadian term for the land, *šumeru*. Sumerians called their land, KI-EN-GI(R) and their language EME-GI_7(R). Downstream from the later city of Baghdad, Sumer's chief cities (*e.g.* Eridu, Kish, Lagash, Nippur, Ur and Uruk) lay near the Euphrates River. Sumerian civilization flourished in the 3rd millennium BC. Archaic texts of Uruk from as early as 3100 BC attest to the presence of the Sumerian language. Because the names of cities in this region seem unrelated to the Sumerian language, many have argued that Sumerians emigrated from outside the country. However, no one has identified Sumerian language and culture elsewhere. The Sumerian name for Babylonians and other peoples as 'black headed', and Sumerian references to the Indus Valley may suggest Indian origin. The waters of the Persian Gulf moved N throughout the millennia, reaching their present level about 4000 BC (Roux 1982). Earlier Sumerian habitation in this region may have disappeared under Gulf waters.

The Sumerian language and its literature became the most enduring legacy of this civilization. Sumerian is not a Semitic language. It has no relationship to any known language. There is some discussion as to whether the Sumerians designed the cuneiform script that they used or imported it. Scholars have reconstructed much of the earlier history of Sumer, *c.* 3000–2500 BC, from later myths and legends. Contemporary seals, uncovered in the excavations of the Royal Tombs of Ur (*c.* 2600–2500 BC), feature early leaders such as Meskalamdug. The historicity of the most famous figure, Gilgamesh, is not certain. If he did live, he may exemplify the manner in which early figures took on semi-divine status as the mythological literature developed. This common tendency has no parallel in the biblical literature with its monotheism and consequent exclusion of other deities.

Detailed histories of Sumer focus on the kings of a succession of dominant city states through the 3rd millennium BC, relying on compositions that often date from later periods. The political history of Sumer divides between the earlier period of the 3rd millennium BC and the later period in the final century of that millennium. The earlier period ended in the 23rd century with the conquest by the Semitic king, Sargon of Akkad. The city of Ur dominated the second period and caused a revival of Sumerian culture. The kings, Ur-Nammu and Shulgi, dominated this third dynasty of Ur. The city fell *c.* 2000 BC. The Old Babylonian period that flourished in the following centuries preserved Sumerian as a language of scribes and special literary compositions. This began a practice, continued well into the 1st millennium BC, of writing literary and religious texts of special significance in Sumerian. Sumerian became the religious language of the Assyro-Babylonian worlds and beyond.

Some have identified Shinar, first mentioned in Gn. 10:10, with Sumer. However, Zadok (1984) has related Shinar to a name for Babylonia and its foreign rulers used by the Hittites and others in the Late Bronze Age (1550–1200 BC), *i.e.* Shanḫar. There are two reasons why Sumer and Sumerians do not appear in the Bible. First, the Sumerians flourished earlier than most of the events of the Bible. Second, they lived in a region at the geographic periphery of the Bible. The exception to this is the departure of Abram from Ur of the Chaldees, a site often associated with the Ur of Sumer. If Abram lived in the 2nd millennium BC then Abram's association would date from the period subsequent to Ur's conquest by non-Sumerians. Sumer had an impact on the Bible in two important ways: the development of literary forms and the world of Gn. 1–11.

Walton (1989) and Hallo (1992) compare

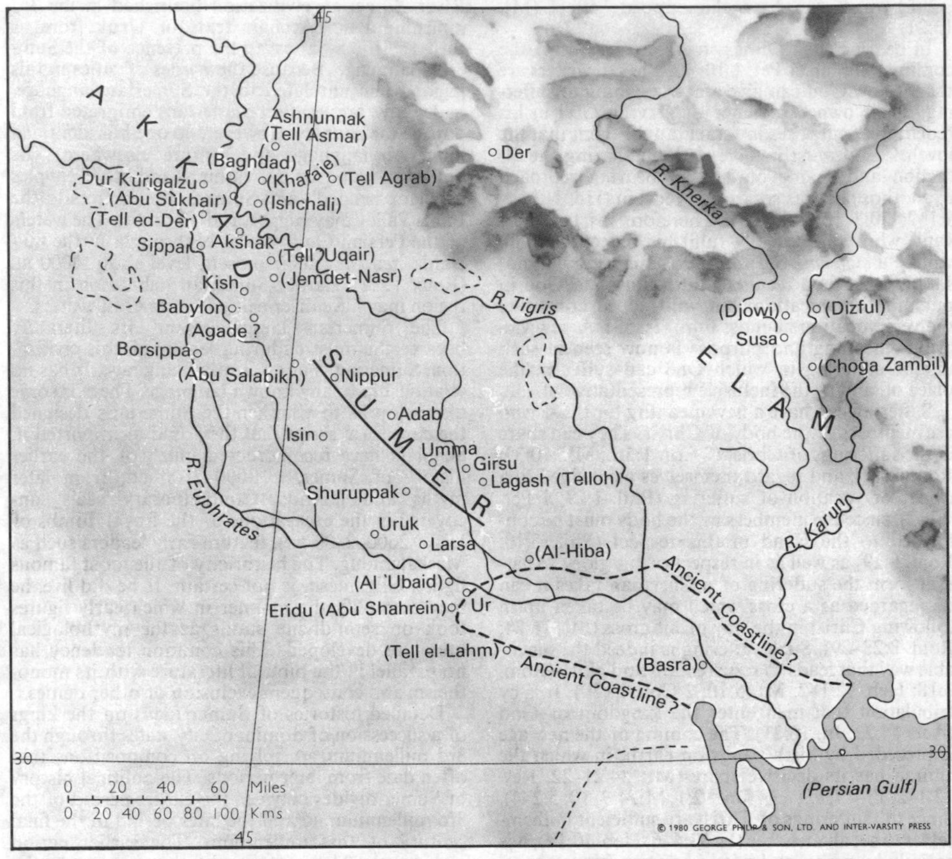

Sumer, the S part of Babylonia.

Sumerian literature with that of the Bible. Most types have parallels in other Near Eastern literature. There was no direct borrowing between the Bible and Sumerian. However, an identification of the types of literature serves as an important tool in the interpretation of the biblical texts. In the pre-Sargon era Hallo identifies incantations, hymns, epics, and wisdom literature. Of these, incantations have no parallel in the Bible. Incantations ascribe a magical power to the words recited to manipulate the spirit world. The Bible rejects contacts with the spirit world (Lv. 19:31; 20:6, 27; Dt. 18:10–12; 1 Sam. 28). It emphasizes the power of God's Word that the believer should hear and obey (Dt. 6–8; Is. 55).

Hymns praise deities and temples. This form occurs in the Psalms where many hymns praise the God of Israel (Pss. 33; 93; 96–99) and express love for the Temple of Jerusalem (Pss. 46; 76; 87). Epics and mythologies recite the achievements of divine and human heroes (*cf.* the Judges of the Bible). There are no deities involved other than the God of Israel but hymns to God's anointed as king appear in the Psalms (2, 110). Elegies to fallen kings also contain similarities to the Sumerian descriptions of the achievements of the kings (2 Sa. 1:19–27). Congregational laments over the destruction of a city occur in Sumerian. The best known one is the lamentation over the destruction of Ur. Sumerian treaties and legal collections have the sort of Ancient Near Eastern literary forms followed in the covenant and law codes found in the Pentateuch and Joshua.

Sumerian wisdom literature begins in the early period and continues into the 2nd millennium BC. Most frequent are the collections of proverbs. They are similar to the Proverbs of the Bible. 'A petition to a man's personal god' laments the loss of health and wealth until the deity restores them. This form continues in the Akkadian theme of the righteous sufferer and appears in the book of Job.

The most important influences from Sumer occur in Gn. 1–11. Scholars have compared the accounts of creation and the flood, as well as the genealogies (Hess and Tsumura, 1994). A Sumerian version of the Atra-Ḫasis epic demonstrates that it formed part of that language's literary corpus. Similar in general structure to the creation and flood stories of Genesis, it diverges on many points of detail and in its overall purpose. The Bible describes the purpose of flood as moral; the cuneiform myths as the reduction of the population of humans because they trouble the gods.

The genealogies of Gn. 4, 5 and 11 contain similarities and differences when compared with the Sumerian king list. The king list names only rulers. The Bible lists members of a family. While the Sumerian king list (and others) establishes the legitimacy of one dynasty over other rivals, the biblical genealogies demonstrate God's gracious preservation of his chosen line through which blessing to all nations of the world would come (Gn. 12:1–3). The Sumerian king list also contains names of the apkallu, wisdom figures associated with antediluvian kings. Insofar as these resemble specific cultural achievements, they appear similar to the figures in Cain's line of Gn. 4 whose names and epithets connect them with similar accomplishments. Some have also found here parallels to the Enoch who ascends to heaven (Gn. 5:24) and to the mysterious 'giants' of Gn. 6:1–4. Lambert (1988) suggests that the long lives of the pre-Flood figures and other matters have similarities with cuneiform king lists and wisdom figures associated with them. This material entered Israelite tradition before the 1st millennium, probably during the international period of the Amarna Age (14th century BC).

BIBLIOGRAPHY. J. S. Cooper, 'Sumer, Sumerians', *ABD* 6, 1992, pp. 231–234; W. W. Hallo, 'Sumerian Literature', *ABD* 6, 1992, pp. 234–237; R. S. Hess and D. Tsumura (eds.), *'I Studied Inscriptions From Before the Flood'. Ancient Near Eastern Linguistiac and Literary Approaches to Genesis 1–11.* Sources for Biblical and Theological Study 4. Eisenbrauns, 1994; T. Jacobsen, *The Treasures of Darkness. A History of Mesopotamian Religion*, 1976; S. N. Kramer, *The Sumerians. Their History, Culture, and Character*, 1963; W. G. Lambert in *Congress Volume. Jerusalem 1986*, 1988, pp. 124–143; *VT Supp.* 40, Leiden; G. Roux, *L'historie* 45, 1982, pp. 46–59; J. H. Walton, *Ancient Israelite Literature in Its Cultural Context*, 1989; R. Zadok, *Zeitschrift für Assyriologie* 74, 1984, pp. 240–244; For texts in translation: *ANET*, pp. 37–59 *et passim*; T. Jacobsen, *The Harps that Once . . . Sumerian Poetry in Translation*, 1987. R.S.H.

SUN (Heb. *šemeš*; Gk. *hēlios*). In addition to many references which merely indicate the time of day, the Bible mentions natural effects of the sun, such as causing the fruits of the earth to grow (Dt. 33:14; 2 Sa. 23:4), withering growth that is insufficiently rooted (Mt. 13:6), producing physical injury (Ps. 121:6; Is. 49:10; Jon. 4:8; Rev. 7:16; 16:8, *etc.*), and inspiring the desire for life (Ec. 11:7). Such poetical allusions as 'a tabernacle for the sun' (Ps. 19:4) and the 'habitation' of the sun (Hab. 3:11) may have been suggested by the Heb. term for the setting sun, *bô'*, meaning literally 'to go in'. A parallel idea finds expression on certain Bab. seals, which represent the sun issuing from a gate. Sun-worship, which was expressly forbidden (Dt. 4:19; 17:3), assumed various forms in Judah (2 Ki. 23:11; Ezk. 8:16–17). Several passages indicate God's control of the sun (Jos. 10:12–14; 2 Ki. 20:8–11; Is. 38:7–8). Ahaz's sundial (2 Ki. 20:11; Is. 38:8) probably had the form of a stairway (*STEPS).

In the book of Psalms the sun is thrice mentioned as an emblem of constancy (Pss. 72:5, 17; 89:36) and God himself is said to be a sun (Ps. 84:11), implying that he is the source of spiritual light and gladness. The face of Jesus at the time of the transfiguration is compared to the shining sun (Mt. 17:2) and it appeared to John in Patmos 'like the sun shining in full strength' (Rev. 1:16). On the other hand the glory of God and of Christ is declared to be greater and more enduring than sunlight (Is. 24:23; 60:19; Acts 26:13; Rev. 21:23; 22:5). Malachi foretells that in the day of the Lord 'the sun of righteousness' shall rise with healing in its rays for them that fear God. In its context this implies that not only will the wicked be punished, but the justice of God will be vindicated and the desire for righteousness of person and environment fully met (Mal. 4:2). The Fathers understood the expression as referring to Christ, and the objection that *šemeš* is feminine cannot be pressed in view of its use in Ps. 84:11 (see above). Part of the imagery associated with 'the day of the Lord' in Scripture is an eclipse of the sun (Is. 13:10; Joel 2:10; 3:15; Am. 8:9; Mt. 24:29; Rev. 6:12), while a third of the sun ceases to function after the fourth trumpet sounds (Rev. 8:12). W.J.C.

SUPERSCRIPTION (Lat. *superscriptio*, 'a writing on or above', = Gk. *epigraphē*, which it translates). The word is used on two occasions in the NT.

1. In Mt. 22:20 (Mk. 12:16; Lk. 20:24) it is used with the word *eikōn* to refer to the head of the

מלך היהודים

REX IVDAEORVM

ΟΒΑϹΙΛΕΥϹΤΩΝΙΟΥΔΑΙΩΝ

The superscription 'The King of the Jews', put on the cross, was written in Hebrew, Latin and Greek (Jn. 19:19–20). Here reproduced in letters of styles current in the 1st cent. AD.

emperor and accompanying inscription on the obverse of a silver *denarius* (*MONEY). The *denarius* then in circulation bore the *eikōn* of the head of Tiberius and the *epigraphē* TI. CAESAR DIVI AUG. F. AUGUSTUS ('Tiberius Caesar Augustus, son of the divine Augustus').

2. In Mk. 15:26 (Lk. 23:38) the superscription is the placard, consisting of a board smeared with white gypsum and bearing in black letters the name of a condemned criminal and the offence for which he was being executed. Hence Mt. 27:37 calls it an *aitia* (accusation): Jn. 19:19–20 uses the official Roman word *titulus*, calling it a *titlos*. This was usually hung about the criminal's neck on the way to execution, and subsequently affixed to the cross over his head. The superscription written by Pilate for Jesus in Hebrew, Greek and Latin was 'This is Jesus of Nazareth, the King of the Jews'. D.H.W.

SUPH. In Dt. 1:1 this may be a place-name (so in RV, RSV, 'over against Suph') whose location is quite uncertain (*cf. GTT*, §431, p. 255, n. 223). In rendering 'over against the Red Sea', AV understands Suph as standing for *yam-sûp̄*, referring to the Gulf of Aqabah, which is also possible (*RED SEA). In Nu. 21:14, Suph(ah), 'storm'(?), is perhaps an area in which Waheb is located, in the brief quotation from the *Book of the Wars of the Lord*. Its relation to Suph in Dt. 1:1 is uncertain. Musil suggested it might be Khirbet Sufah, some 6 km SSE of Madaba (*GTT*, §441, pp. 261–262, n. 229 end). On Suph and Suphah, *cf.* also E. G. Kraeling, *JNES* 7, 1948, p. 201. K.A.K.

SURETY. A surety is a person who undertakes responsibility for a debt, or the fulfilment of an engagement by another. The word is also used to describe a pledge deposited as a security against loss or damage. It means also 'certainty'. In the latter sense we find the word used in the AV of Gn. 15:13; 18:13; 26:9; Acts 12:11 (RSV translates variously: 'indeed', 'I am sure', *etc.*).

Scripture counsels extreme caution in standing surety (Pr. 11:15; 17:18; 22:26–27). The phrase 'to strike hands' (AV) is equivalent to being surety (Pr. 6:1–2; 17:18).

Judah undertook to be a personal surety for Benjamin's safety (Gn. 43:9; 44:32). The giving of hostages (2 Ki. 18:23; Is. 36:8) is a similar idea. The word is used of our Lord (Heb. 7:22; *cf.* Ps. 119:122). M.R.G.

SUSA (AV Shushan), the ruins of which lie near the river Karun (*ULAI), SW Persia, was occupied almost continuously from prehistoric times until it was abandoned by the Seleucids. Here was the capital of *Elam, whose royal inscriptions of the 2nd millennium have been recovered. It maintained its importance under the Kassites and its independence until sacked in 645 BC by Ashurbanipal, who sent men of Susa (Susanchites) to exile in Samaria (Ezr. 4:9). Under the Achaemenids Susa flourished as one of the three royal cities (Dn. 8:2; Ne. 1:1). Darius I built his palace here, the ruins of which, restored by Artaxerxes I (Longimanus) and II (Mnemon), remain, with the Apadana, one of the outstanding Persian architectural features of the 5th century BC. This palace figures prominently in the book of *Esther (1:2, 5; 2:3; 3:15, *etc.*). (*AHASUERUS.) The site was first excavated by Loftus in 1851, and subsequently extensive operations have been undertaken there by the French.

BIBLIOGRAPHY. R. Ghirshman, *Iran*, 1963; E. M. Yamauchi, *Near East Archaeological Society Bulletin* 8, 1976, pp. 5–14. D.J.W.

SYCHAR. The Samaritan town whence the woman came to fetch water from Jacob's well, where she met Jesus who taught her the nature of spiritual worship (Jn. 4). Sychar is commonly identified with Askar, a village 1 km N of Jacob's well, on the E slope of Mt Ebal. A.R.M.

SYENE (AV Sinim, Sinites). **1.** Heb. *sînîm*. A distant land from which the people will return (Is. 49:12), named with the N and W, so either in the far S or E (so LXX 'land of the Persians'). Scholars have looked for a connection with classical Sinae (China), but it is unlikely that Jews had settled in so distant a place by this period. Therefore Sin (Pelusium, Ezk. 30:15) or Sin in Sinai (Ex. 16:1) has been proposed. Most likely is identification with Syene of Ezk. 29:10; 30:6, on the far S border of Egypt. This is Egyp. *swn* 'market', Coptic *Suan*, modern *'Aswān*. A Jewish community living there in the 5th century BC has left us many Aram. papyri in which the place name is written *swn*, hence RV, RSV *Seveneh in Ezk. 29 and 30, better taken as 'to Seven'. 'From Migdol (AV, RV 'tower') to Syene' means from one end of Egypt to the other. Syene, on the first cataract of the Nile, was a fortress and base for expeditions into Nubia (Cush), a terminus for river traffic and a source of red granite for monumental buildings (syenite). The Qumran MS of Isaiah (1Q Is[a]) suggests that 'Syenites' should replace *sînîm* (Is. 49:12); LXX has *Syene* for *Sin* in Ezk. 30:16.

2. Sinites (Heb. *sînî*) were a Canaanite people (Gn. 10:17; 1 Ch. 1:15), probably to be identified with a region, near Arqā, on the Lebanon coast, named in texts from *Mari and possibly *Ebla. The name survives in Nahr as-Sinn and is Ugaritic *syn*, Akkad. *siyanu*.

BIBLIOGRAPHY. E. G. Kraeling, *BA* 15, 1952, pp. 50–68; *The Brooklyn Museum Aramaic Papyri*, 1953, p. 21. D.J.W.

SYMBOL. This word is not found in the Bible, but the use of symbols is common to all religions. The Gk. word *symbolon* had several uses, *e.g.* as a sign, pledge, token, and its importance derived from the fact that it was a representative object which guaranteed the reality of that which it symbolized. The *Concise Oxford Dictionary* defines a symbol as a 'thing regarded by general consent as naturally typifying or representing or recalling something (esp. an idea or quality) by possession of analogous qualities or by association in fact or thought'. This clear distinction between object and symbol is inevitable in analytical philosophy, but is not found in primitive thought. Malinowski emphasized that symbolism is founded, not in a relationship between an object and a sign, but in the influence that a sign or action has upon a receptive organism (*A Scientific Theory of Culture*, 1944). It is important to remember this when examining symbolism in the Bible.

I. In the Old Testament

a. Personal symbols

In early Israelite thought the clan or the family was the fundamental unit, not the individual. The life (*nep̄eš*) of the individuals made up the life of the group; the life of the group was extended through all the individuals. This psychological conception has been termed corporate personality (Wheeler Robinson) or group consciousness (Radcliffe Brown), and helps to explain how one person could symbolize a group of people (2 Sa. 18:3) or the presence of God (Ex. 7:1).

There is an expression, *'îš hā'ᵉlōhîm*, used more than 70 times and translated 'man of God', which could be translated 'divine man'. 27 times it refers to Elisha, and in the remaining instances to prophets such as Elijah and Samuel, or Moses and David. Elisha is credited with divine powers, such as restoring life (2 Ki. 4:35) and mind reading (2 Ki. 5:26). He stands in the place of God, does the works of God, and is the symbol of God's presence. Similarly, Moses was as God to Aaron (Ex. 4:15) and to pharaoh (Ex. 7:1), in word and deed (Ex. 14:16; 17:9). All the prophets spoke the word of God, and when the Israelites heard them they heard God himself; consequently, the person of the prophet was immune from harm. There is little evidence to show that the Israelite monarchy was regarded as divine, but it is possible that Solomon set himself up as a symbol of God.

b. Objective symbols

External objects were also used to symbolize the presence of God, in representative or conventional manner. The rainbow was accepted as the assurance that God's wrath had passed and that he would remember his covenant (Gn. 9:13). Moses made a bronze serpent, symbolizing the wisdom and healing power of God (Nu. 21:9); golden calves were made to symbolize the great power of God (Ex. 32 and 1 Ki. 12). More frequently objects were made without representing particular characteristics of God, one important example being the altar. The Heb. word *mizbēaḥ*, from the root *zbḥ* ('slaughter'), suggests the place where the animal was prepared for sacrifice. One should note, however, that in the earliest accounts the Patriarchs erected altars after an appearance by God, to mark the site and claim it for him for ever. In Israelite worship the altar symbolized the meeting-place of God with man, while the ark symbolized the presence of God because it contained the tablets of the Decalogue, and where the Word of the Lord was, there was the Lord himself.

When the Temple was built it symbolized the universal power of God. The Temple itself was a symbol of the earth, the brazen laver a symbol of the sea and the golden candlestick a symbol of the sun. It was necessary that a priest should be properly vested when he entered the tabernacle or Temple, and the vestments were clearly symbolic. They were made of linen (Ex. 28:39), which was regarded as having protective qualities (Lv. 6:8–12). Two reasons are possible. As the sacrifices were animal, the flax as vegetable conferred an immunity which would not have been found in woollen or leather garments. But it is more likely that, as in many folk stories, flax was regarded as the symbol of immortality or indestructibility. Jewish scholars have suggested symbolic meanings for the colours of the vestments, and for each separate item. The ephod and breastpiece symbolized the 12 tribes and judgment, and as the priest put them on they gave him power of judgment in the name of the Lord. His robe was decorated with pomegranates and bells—symbols of fertility and warnings to evil spirits. On his head was a mitre engraved with the words 'Holy to the Lord' (Ex. 28:36), which made the priest himself the extension of the presence of God—the divine symbol.

c. Acted symbols

These symbols were actions that were illustrative or purposive beyond their immediate context. They demonstrated or introduced new circumstances. They must be distinguished from magic, which was designed to compel a particular action from God. When an Israelite slave preferred to surrender himself to permanent slavery rather than accept his freedom, the owner pierced the slave's ear and fastened him to the doorpost to signify that the slave was from then on part of the household (Ex. 21:6). Other symbolic actions of a domestic nature were the surrender of a shoe to symbolize the surrender of all personal rights of inheritance (Ru. 4:7) and the cutting of hair to symbolize the offering of the mourner's life to a dead relative (Is. 22:12).

Among religious symbolic actions, *circumcision has always been a significant rite; originally connected with marriage, it was performed to avert the evil intentions of spirits that watch over the bridal chamber, but in Israel it was pushed back into childhood and then into infancy, and represents the dedication of the reproductive powers to divine guidance, and the incorporation of the child into the community.

The ceremony of the scapegoat by which the sins of the people were transferred to a goat on the Day of Atonement was a ritual of a type well known in many countries; it has been described as a clear instance of the principle of vicarious solidarity, here between priest, people and goat (C. Lattey, *VT* 1, 1951, p. 272).

Other instances of transference by symbolic action are the red heifer (Nu. 19), which transferred uncleanness, and anointing, which transferred spiritual power (*e.g.* 1 Sa. 16:13).

Special attention should be paid to the importance of the symbolic actions of the prophets. These men not only proclaimed their message but performed actions to demonstrate what God would do, and thereby helped to bring about the result. They did not perform these actions to influence the will of God, but to prepare the way for that which he had decreed. Thus, Isaiah went about naked as a sign that God would bring poverty and exile upon Israel (Is. 20:2). Jeremiah buried a new girdle in damp earth and later dug it up, spoilt, to show how Israel, once so close to God, had now been rejected and would be despoiled (Je. 13). Ezekiel drew a city on a tile and set model siege-engines round it to demonstrate the destruction of Jerusalem which God had already decided (Ezk. 4:1–3). Other examples are in 1 Sa. 15:27; Je. 19:11; 28:11.

II. In the New Testament

Here the situation is quite different. There are no symbolic persons; Jesus Christ was not a symbol of God, for he *was* God, as he claimed in the words, 'I and my Father are one' (Jn. 10:30). Neither could one describe the disciples as symbols, because they were servants under discipline, not representatives.

But Jesus performed symbolic actions and approved them for the church. His healing miracles were not merely deeds of sympathy, but symbols or signs demonstrating the approach of the kingdom of God. Similarly, when he took the bread and the wine and gave them to the disciples, saying, 'Do this in remembrance of me', he was not simply exhorting them to good fellowship, but giving them a rite by which they could symbolize his presence eternally with his church. So the church has accepted the symbolism of the sacraments. In the bread and the wine the worshipper receives by faith the true body and blood of the Lord. In the waters of baptism sin is symbolically washed away and the person made a member of Christ's flock. In these actions the church symbolizes its faith; the *sacraments are not only illustrations but the appointed channels of divine grace.

In addition to the sacramental symbols, the church has used the symbol of the cross. This is a true symbol in that it is a pictorial representation of a historical fact, a visual summary of certain essential features of the Christian faith, and at the same time a means of grace to the worshipper. In the history of Christian art there have crystallized accepted pictorial symbols of the 12 apostles, *e.g.* the keys for St Peter and the symbols of the four Evangelists. At one time the fish was a popular symbol of the Christian faith as the letters of the Gk. word for fish, *ichthys*, formed the initials of words meaning 'Jesus Christ, son of God, Saviour'. The Christian church has never forbidden the use of symbols, because they are rooted in the nature and experience of man, but it has not encouraged them, lest in stressing the symbol the Christian should lose the Lord Jesus Christ himself.

BIBLIOGRAPHY. F. W. Dillistone, *Christianity and Symbolism*, 1955; G. Cope, *Symbolism in the Bible and the Church*, 1958; Å. Viberg, *Symbols of Law*, 1992. A.A.J.

SYNAGOGUE. In the OT 'synagogue' occurs only in Ps. 74:8, AV (RSV 'meeting places'), where it is a translation of Heb. *mô'ēḏ*. It is not definite that the reference has its present connotation. The Gk. term *synagōgē* is used frequently in the LXX for the assembly of Israel, and occurs 56 times in the NT. The basic sense is a place of meeting, and thus it came to denote a Jewish place of worship. The Heb. equivalent of the Gk. noun is *k^e^nēseṯ*, a gathering of any persons or things for any purpose. In the Scriptures it is a gathering of individuals of a locality for worship or common action (Lk. 12:11; 21:12). It came to refer to the building in which such meetings were held.

I. Its significance

The importance of the synagogue for Judaism cannot be overestimated. More than any other institution it gave character to the Jewish faith. Here Judaism learnt its interpretation of the law. Ezk. 11:16, 'I have been a sanctuary to them for a while', was interpreted by Jewish authorities to mean that in world-wide dispersion Israel would have the synagogue as a sanctuary in miniature to replace the loss of the Temple. Unlike the Temple, it was located in all parts of the land, and put the people in touch with their religious leaders. A. Menes states: 'On the Sabbaths and holy days the loss of the Temple and the absence of the solemn sacrificial celebrations were keenly felt by the exiles . . . the synagogue . . . served as a substitute for the Temple. In the synagogue there was no altar, and prayer and the reading of the Torah took the place of the sacrifice. In addition the prayer house performed an important social function . . . it was a gathering point and a meeting place where the people could congregate whenever it was necessary to take counsel over important community affairs. The synagogue became the cradle of an entirely new type of social and religious life and established the foundation for a religious community of universal scope. For the first time Jewish monotheism emancipated itself in religious practice from its bonds to a specific and designated site. God was now brought to the people wherever they dwelt' ('The History of the Jews in Ancient Times', *The Jewish People*, 1, pp. 78–152). Today the synagogue is still one of the dominant institutions of Judaism, and the centre of the religious life of the Jewish community. The book of Acts indicates the significant role the synagogue played in the propagation of the new Messianic faith.

II. Its origin

Neither OT nor NT furnishes any definite information about the origin of the synagogue, nor do the Apocryphal books mention any burning of synagogues during the persecutions of Antiochus Epiphanes in the 2nd century BC. Many see the Exile, when worship in the Temple at Jerusalem was an impossibility, as the time when the synagogue arose.

The oldest references to synagogues are in Gk. inscriptions from Egypt of the 3rd century BC. At Delos in the Aegean there was a synagogue in the 1st century BC, termed a *proseuche*, a 'place of prayer'. The Gk. inscription of Theodotos, a 'ruler of the synagogue' (*archisynagogos*), found in Jerusalem and archaeological discoveries in Palestine (see **III**) prove the existence of synagogues there in the first century.

III. General description

In the 1st century AD synagogues existed wherever Jews lived. *Cf.* Acts 13:5 (Salamis in Cyprus); 13:14 (Antioch in Pisidia); 14:1 (Iconium); 17:10 (Beroea). Large cities, such as Jerusalem and Alexandria, had numerous synagogues. One legend has it that there were 394 synagogues in Jerusalem when Titus destroyed the city in AD 70; another legend sets the number at 480.

The Gospels speak of the synagogues of Nazareth (Mt. 13:54; Lk. 4:16) and Capernaum (Mk. 1:21; Jn. 6:59) as places where our Lord ministered. The apostle Paul found them wherever he went in Palestine, Asia Minor and Greece. According to the Talmud (*Shabbath* 11a), it was required that synagogues be built on high ground or above surrounding houses. Archaeological evidence does not confirm such a practice for Palestine. Examples excavated at Gamala, E of Galilee, and at Herodium and Masada reveal a common plan, a hall with columns at the edges of the floor and benches in tiers along each wall. There might be a cupboard to house the scrolls of the Law and the Prophets. For the readings, they would be carried to a reading desk or platform (*bemâ' Megillah* 3.1) in the centre of the hall. In later synagogues the *bema* often lay against one wall, facing towards Jerusalem. Seats near the reading desk were the more honourable (Mt. 23:6; Jas. 2:2–3), and there was a special place, 'the seat of Moses' (Mt. 23:2). Maimonides said, 'They put a platform in the middle of the house, so that he who reads from the Law, or he who speaks words of exhortation to the people, may stand upon it, and all may hear him.' There is no evidence for men and women sitting separately in the early synagogues.

IV. Its purpose and practice

The synagogue was, literally, a meeting-place, the term used in Theodotus' inscription when he records his building of 'a synagogue for reciting the Law and studying the commandments'. It was especially a place for prayer (*proseuche*), like the Temple (see Mt. 21:13, *etc.*; Acts 16:13). Subject to the law of the land, the synagogue had its own government (Jos., *Ant.* 19. 291). The congregation was governed by elders who were empowered to exercise discipline and punish members. Punishment was by scourging and excommunication. The chief officer was the ruler of the synagogue (*cf.* Mk. 5:22; Acts 13:15; 18:8). He supervised the service to see that it was carried on in accord with tradition. The attendant (Lk. 4:20) brought the scrolls of Scripture for reading, replaced them in the ark, punished offending members by scourging and instructed children to read. The dispenser of alms received the alms from the synagogue and distributed them. Finally, a competent interpreter was required to paraphrase the Law and the Prophets into the vernacular Aramaic.

Those qualified were permitted to conduct the services (Christ, Lk. 4:16; Mt. 4:23; Paul, Acts 13:15). The Sabbath was the appointed day for public worship (Acts 15:21). The Mishnah (*Megillah* 4. 3) indicates that the service consisted of five parts. First, the *Shema'* was read. This prayer covers Dt. 6:4–9; 11:13–21; Nu. 15:37–41. Then synagogical prayers were recited, the most ancient and best known being the eighteen petitions and benedictions.

The first of the 'Eighteen Benedictions' reads: 'Blessed art Thou, the Lord our God, and the God of our fathers, the God of Abraham, the God of Isaac, and the God of Jacob: the great, the mighty and the terrible God, the most high God Who showest mercy and kindness, Who createst all things, Who rememberest the pious deeds of the patriarchs, and wilt in love bring a redeemer to their children's children for Thy Name's sake; O King, Helper, Saviour and Shield! Blessed art Thou, O Lord, the Shield of Abraham.'

Another prayer is worded: 'And to Jerusalem, Thy city, Thou wilt return in mercy and wilt dwell in her midst, as Thou hast said. And do Thou build her soon in our days an eternal building, and the throne of David Thou wilt speedily establish in the midst of her.'

The restoration of Israel to the land of their fathers, the return of the Shekinah glory to the Temple and rebuilt city of Jerusalem, and the re-establishment of the Davidic dynasty are recurring themes in the prayers.

These were followed by the reading of the Law. The Pentateuch, which is now read in the synagogues in annual cycles, was originally covered in 3 years. After the reading from the first portion of the OT Canon a selection from the Prophets was read. In the time of Christ this portion was not yet fixed, but the reader was permitted to make his own choice (Lk. 4:16ff.). The reading of Scripture was central. The portion of the Prophets was expounded, and an exhortation drawn from it. The benediction concluded the service. Later additions were the translation and exposition of the Scripture portions read. To conduct public worship in the synagogue ten adult males were required.

'Synagogue of the Libertines' (AV) (*libertinoi*, from Lat. *libertini*, *'freedmen', RSV) was the name given to worshippers in a synagogue in Jerusalem who disputed with Stephen (Acts 6:9). They were Jews who had been captured in Pompey's campaign, then were freed later by their masters. Thus the privileges of Roman citizenship were accorded them.

Reference is made in Rev. 2:9 and 3:9 to the 'synagogue of Satan'. Since the citations are general in character, it is impossible with certainty to identify those who are meant by John. A heretical party within the infant church would seem to be indicated.

BIBLIOGRAPHY. Articles in *JewE*, *HDB*, *HJP*, *EJ*; G. F. Moore, *Judaism*, 1, 1927, pp. 281–307; I. Abrahams, *Studies in Pharisaism and the Gospels*, 1, 1917; L. I. Levine, *Ancient Synagogues Revealed*, 1981; C. W. Dugmore, *The Influence of the Synagogue upon the Divine Office*, 1944; A. E. Guilding, *The Fourth Gospel and Jewish Worship*, 1960; L. Coenen, *NIDNTT* 1, pp. 291–307; *NEAEHL*, pp. 1421–1424, with references.

C.L.F.

SYNZYGUS. Gk. *synzygos* (*syzygos*), 'yokefellow' (Phil. 4:3), is treated as a personal name by *WH* mg. and others, as though Paul meant 'Yokefellow by name and yokefellow by nature'. The word, however, is certainly to be taken as a common noun, the person addressed being (not Lydia, supposed by S. Baring-Gould and others to have been Paul's wife, but) possibly Luke, who seems to have stayed in Philippi for the 7 years separating the first 'we' section of Acts (ending 16:17) from the second (beginning 20:5). (This identification presupposes that the letter, or at least this part of it, was sent from Ephesus.) F.F.B.

SYRACUSE. A city with a large harbour on the E coast of Sicily. Founded in 734 BC by Corinthian colonists, it had by the end of the 5th century BC become the most important city, politically and commercially, in Sicily, especially under the tyrants Gelon and Dionysius I. With its allies it was strong enough to defeat the great Athenian expedition to Sicily in 415–413 BC. The Romans captured it in 212 BC, in spite of a defence strengthened by the inventions of the great mathematician Archimedes, and made it the seat of government of the province of Sicily, which became one of the sources of grain for Rome. Syracuse continued to flourish down to the 3rd century AD.

On the last stage of his journey to Rome Paul's ship stayed there for 3 days (Acts 28:12), presumably waiting for a suitable wind. K.L.McK.

SYRIA, SYRIANS. 1. In the Eng. OT this merely denotes *Aramaeans.

2. The geographical entity Syria is bounded by the Taurus Mountains in the N, the W bend of the Euphrates river and the Arabian desert-edge from there to the Dead Sea in the E, the Mediterranean

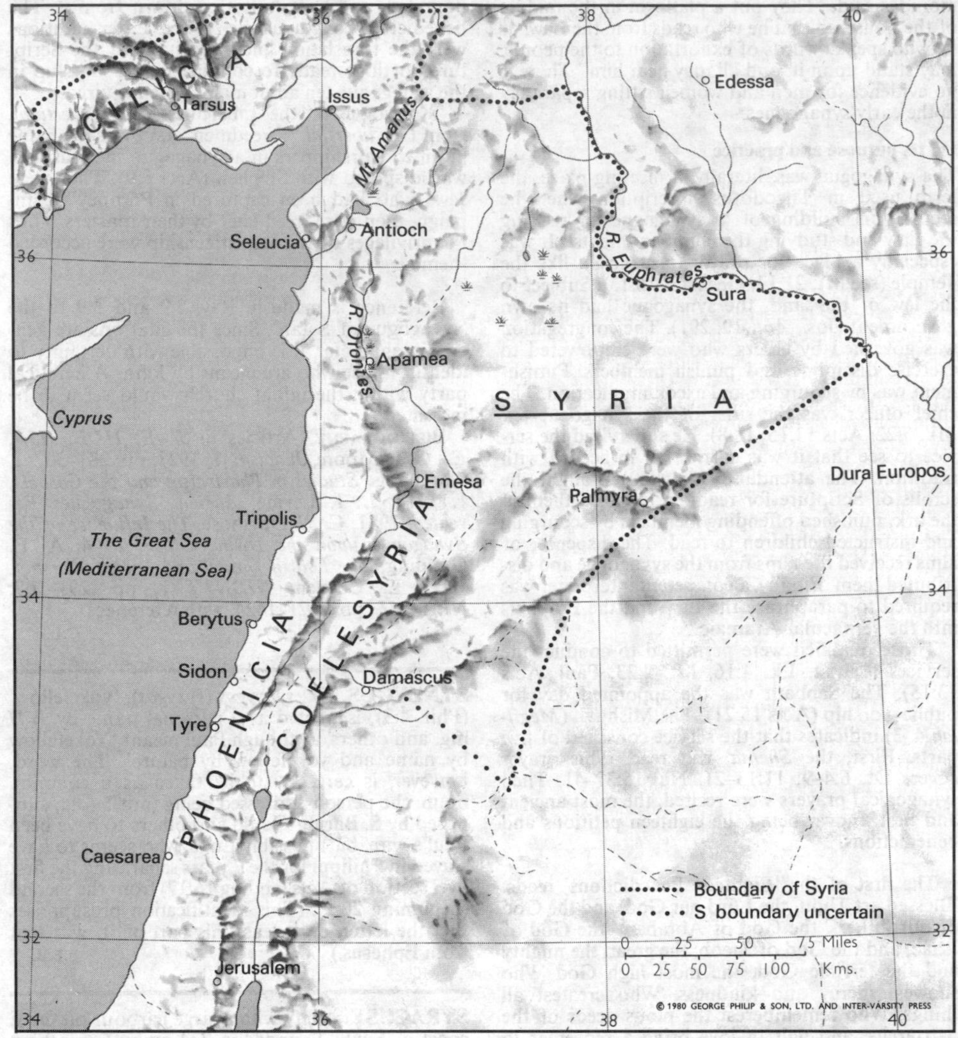

Syria in NT times.

Sea on the W, and the Sinai isthmus at the extreme S (R. Dussaud, *Topographie Historique de la Syrie Antique et Médiévale*, 1927, pp. 1–2, *etc.*; see this work generally).

3. 'Syria' is a Gk. term; Nöldeke derived it from *Assyrios*, 'Assyria(n)', and this suggestion is open to the least objection. *Cf.* F. Rosenthal, *Die Aramaistische Forschung*, 1939, p. 3, n. 1.

4. Historically, ancient Syria existed as a political *unit* only during the period of the Hellenistic Seleucid monarchy, founded by Seleucus I (312–281 BC), who ruled over a realm that stretched from E Asia Minor and N Syria across Babylonia into Persia to the border of India; in 198 BC all 'Syria' belonged to this kingdom when Antiochus III finally gained Palestine from Ptolemy V of Egypt. But from 129 BC, with the death of Antiochus VII, everything E of the Euphrates was lost, and the Seleucids held Syria only. After this, internal dynastic strife disrupted the shrinking state until Pompey annexed the region for Rome in 64 BC. Syria as defined in **2** above constituted the Rom. province of Syria, with which Cilicia was closely associated (Judaea being separate from AD 70). *ANTIOCH (Syrian), *ANTIOCHUS, *UGARIT, *ALALAH, *etc.*, and also *CAH*. K.A.K.

SYROPHOENICIAN. An inhabitant of Phoenicia, which in NT times was part of the Rom. province of Cilicia and Syria. It was a Syrophoenician woman (*syrophoinikissa*), a Greek from the region of Tyre and Sidon, who pleaded with Jesus to heal her daughter (Mk. 7:26; *cf.* Mt. 15:21–28). The parallel verse in Mt. 15:22 calls the woman a Canaanite, using the ancient name by which these people were known. The name Syrophoenician combines the area of Phoenicia which included Tyre and Sidon, and the larger Rom. province of Syria. Phoenicians who lived in Carthage were called Libyphoenicians. J.A.T.

T

TAANACH. Modern Tell Ta'annek on the S edge of the valley of Jezreel, guarding a pass across Mt Carmel following the Wadi Abdullah.

Thothmes III mentions Taanach in the account of his conquest of W Palestine (*c.* 1450 BC; *ANET*, pp. 234ff.), as does *Shishak. Amarna letter 248 complains of a raid by men of Taanach on Megiddo, which was loyal to Egypt. The Israelites defeated the king of this city, but the tribe to which it was allotted, Manasseh, was unable to take possession of it (Jos. 12:21; 17:11; Jdg. 1:27). It was one of the levitical cities (Jos. 21:25) and was also occupied by Issachar (1 Ch. 7:29). Taanach and Megiddo are closely associated in Solomon's administrative division of Israel (1 Ki. 4:12) and in the Song of Deborah, where 'Taanach, by the waters of Megiddo' (Jdg. 5:19) is the site of the Canaanite defeat. Excavations in 1901–4, 1963, 1966 and 1968 revealed an Early Bronze Age city, a Middle Bronze II occupation with typical glacis fortification, destroyed violently, and a prosperous town of Late Bronze I (14 Akkad. cuneiform tablets were found). At the end of the Late Bronze Age there was another destruction, perhaps the work of Deborah's men. In the debris a clay tablet inscribed in a Canaanite cuneiform alphabet was found. The Early Iron Age city, containing a supposed cultic building with stone stelae, numerous pig bones and an elaborate pottery incense-stand, appears to have been destroyed by Shishak. Thereafter the city declined.

BIBLIOGRAPHY. E. Sellin, *Tell Ta'annek*, 1904; P. W. Lapp, *BA* 30, 1967, pp. 1–27; *BASOR* 173, 1964, pp. 4–44; 185, 1967, pp. 2–39; 195, 1969, pp. 2–49; D. R. Hillers, *BASOR* 173, 1964, pp. 45–50; A. Glock, *BASOR* 204, 1971, pp. 17–30; *NEAEHL*, pp. 1428–1433.

A.R.M.

TABERNACLE. 1. The tabernacle of the congregation (AV), more properly 'tent of meeting', as in RV, RSV: a small, provisional meeting-place of God and his people in use before the large tabernacle was built (Ex. 33:7–11). This tent of meeting was pitched outside the camp. Moses would enter it and the Cloud, marking the divine Presence, would descend and stand outside it at the door. In this the function of the tent resembled that of the cleft of the rock in which Moses was placed (Ex. 34:22–23), and that of the cave in which Elijah stood (1 Ki. 19:9–18), to be addressed by God while the glory of God passed by outside. The tabernacle, by contrast, was erected in the midst of the camp, and the Cloud of glory rested not outside but inside it, so that at first Moses had to stay outside (Ex. 40:34–35).

2. The tabernacle commonly so-called was the portable sanctuary in which God dwelt among the Israelites in the desert. After their entry into Canaan, it was stationed successively at Shiloh (Jos. 18:1), at Nob (1 Sa. 21) and at Gibeon (1 Ch. 16:39). Eventually Solomon brought it up to the Temple (1 Ki. 8:4). It is called simply *miškān* = 'dwelling' (EVV 'tabernacle'), as in Ex. 25:9; or *miškān* YHWH = 'dwelling of Yahweh' as in Lv. 17:4; or *miškān ha'ēḏûṯ* = 'dwelling of the *covenant terms' (AV, RSV 'of the testimony'), because it housed the covenant tablets, as in Ex. 38:21; or *'ōhel mô'ēḏ* = tent (AV 'tabernacle') of meeting', *i.e.* the appointed meeting-place between God and his people, as in Ex. 28:43; or *miškān 'ōhel mô'ēḏ* = 'dwelling of the tent of meeting', as in Ex. 39:32; or *miqdāš* = 'sanctuary' as in Ex. 25:8; or *qôḏeš* = ' 'holy place' (AV, RSV 'sanctuary'), as in Ex. 38:24. It is also called *beṯ* [6] *YHWH* = 'house of Yahweh', as in Ex. 34:26.

The materials used in its construction are listed at Ex. 25:3–7. The metal translated 'bronze' (AV 'brass') was more probably copper. The colour 'blue' was probably a violet-blue and the colour 'purple' a reddish-purple. The material translated 'goatskins' (RSV; AV 'badgers' skins') was probably dugong (or 'porpoise', NEB) skin.

I. Tabernacle, tent, coverings and frames

In its stricter technical meaning the term 'tabernacle' refers to a set of ten linen curtains, which when draped round a structure of wooden frames formed God's dwelling-place. The curtains were of linen with figures of cherubim woven into the violet-blue, reddish-purple and scarlet tapestry-work. Each measuring 28 cubits by 4, they were sewn together along their length into two sets of five, which when assembled were held together by fifty golden clasps (AV 'taches') passing through loops on the edge of each set (Ex. 26:1–6). The tabernacle was covered by eleven goats'-hair curtains, called in strict terminology 'the tent' (Ex. 26:7–15). They each measured 30 cubits by 4, were sewn together into two sets, one of five, the other of six, which when assembled were held together, like the tabernacle, by loops and clasps, only their clasps were of copper.

Over the tent went a covering of tanned (literally, 'reddened') rams' skins, and over that again (*cf.* NEB 'an outer covering'; AV, RV 'above') a covering of dugong skin (Ex. 26.14).

These curtains were spread over the top, back and two sides of a framework (Ex. 26:15–30) assembled from forty-eight units, each 10 cubits high and 1½ wide, called *q'rāšîm.* The most likely interpretation of these *q'rāšîm* is that given by A. R. S. Kennedy (*HDB*, 4, pp. 659–662); they were not solid boards (as AV, RV), nor planks (as NEB), but open frames, each consisting of two long uprights (*yāḏôṯ*: not 'tenons' as in most versions) joined by cross-rails somewhat like a ladder. Such frames would have three advantages over solid planks:

they would be much lighter, less liable to whip, and instead of hiding the beautiful tabernacle curtains would allow them to be seen from the inside all round the walls. The feet of the two uprights in each frame stood in sockets made of silver obtained from the census tax (Ex. 30:11–16; 38:25–27). Twenty frames in their sockets, stationed side by side, formed each side of the tabernacle; six formed the rear. In each corner at the rear was an extra frame. The purpose of these extra frames, to give rigidity to the whole structure, is clear; but the details of the specification are not.

Perhaps the best explanation is that given by U. Cassuto: each corner frame was coupled (not 'separate' as RSV) at the bottom and the top so as to form a twin with the end frame in the side, and then clamped to its twin by means of a metal ring (translating v. 24 'into the one ring' and not 'at the first ring', as RSV). To keep the frames in alignment five bars ran along the sides and rear through gold rings attached to the cross-rails of each frame. The middle bar ran the whole length, the other four only part of the way. The frames and bars were made of acacia wood overlaid with gold.

When the frames were assembled the distance from the top of the frames at the front along the roof and down to the bottom of the frames at the rear was $20 \times 1\frac{1}{2} + 10 = 40$ cubits. The assembled tabernacle curtains measured 28 cubits by $10 \times 4 = 40$ cubits. They were spread over the frames so that the 40 cubits ran from the top front of the frames to the rear bottom. The assembled tent curtains measured 30 cubits by $11 \times 4 = 44$ cubits. When they were spread over the tabernacle curtains, the extra 2 cubits (30 as against 28) gave an overhang of 1 cubit on each side (Ex. 26:13). The extra 4 cubits in the other direction (44 as against 40) were disposed as follows: at the rear the tent extended 2 cubits beyond the tabernacle curtains (v. 12), and at the front the other 2 cubits were doubled back and, presumably, tucked under the tabernacle curtains all the way along the top and sides, so protecting what otherwise would have been an exposed edge of tabernacle curtain (v. 9). The word used for arranging the curtains over the frames is not the normal word for pitching a tent, *naṭâ*, but *pāraś*, which means 'to spread' (it is used of wrapping cloths round the furniture). The roof was flat. To prevent the curtains from sagging at the roof and so causing the frames to collapse inwards, there were probably (the text does not say so, but it omits many details which one would need to know to make a tabernacle) wooden struts running across the top of the framework from side to side (see, for comparison, the portable pavilion of Hetep-heres). J. Fergusson (*Smith's Dictionary of the Bible*, 3, pp. 1452–1454) and many others have argued unconvincingly that the curtains must have been spread over a ridge-pole. Some of their arguments presuppose that the sides and rear of the tabernacle were formed of solid planks; since they were formed not of planks but of open fragments, their arguments are invalid, and would lead to the impossible result of exposing the holy place and the most holy to view from the outside. Other arguments are invalidated by their failure to observe that the term 'tabernacle' in Ex. 26:1–13 refers not to the building in general but to the ten linen curtains.

II. The interior

The interior of the dwelling was divided into two compartments by a veil hung under (not 'from' as RSV) the clasps that joined the tabernacle curtains (Ex. 26:31–34). Hence we know that the first compartment was 20 cubits long, the second 10. The height of the frames, 10 cubits, gives us the second dimension, and in all probability the breadth of both compartments was 10 cubits likewise: for while the six frames at the back give a total breadth of 9 cubits, allowance must be made for the thickness of the side frames and corner frames. The first compartment is called 'the holy place', the second 'the holy of holies', *i.e.* the most holy place, or simply 'the holy place' (Lv. 16:2–3; Heb. 9:12; 10:19, RV. RSV 'sanctuary' in these latter two verses is misleading: entry into the holy of holies is intended). Again, the first compartment is sometimes called 'the first tabernacle' and the second 'the second tabernacle' (Heb. 9:6–7, AV, RV; RSV 'the outer tent' and 'the second' respectively). The dividing veil (*pārōḵeṯ*: a term used of no other hanging), made of the same material, colours and design as the tabernacle curtains, was hung by gold hooks on four acacia-wood pillars overlaid with gold and standing in silver sockets. The pillars had no capitals. At the door (= doorway) was a linen screen of violet-blue, reddish-purple and scarlet (but without cherubim). It hung by gold hooks on five acacia-wood pillars overlaid with gold standing in copper sockets. These pillars did have capitals and were overlaid with gold, as were their fillets (Ex. 26:36; 37:38). To distinguish the *pārōḵeṯ* from this screen, the *pārōḵeṯ* is sometimes called the second veil.

III. The furniture

In the most holy place stood the *ark of the covenant (Ex. 25:10–22). A slab (AV, RSV 'mercy seat') of pure gold with a cherub at each end rested on top. The name of this slab, *kappōreṯ*, means not 'lid' but 'propitiatory', *i.e.* place where the blood of propitiation was sprinkled. This is how the LXX (*hilastērion*) understood it, as does the NT (Heb. 9:5; RSV 'mercy seat'). The poles for carrying the ark ran through rings attached to the feet (not 'corners', as in AV) of the ark (Ex. 25:12). There is no implied discrepancy between Ex. 25:15 and Nu. 4:8. The latter verse indicates that to facilitate the covering of the ark for transport the poles were temporarily removed and immediately replaced: the former verse directs that at all other times the poles were to be left in their rings even when the ark was not travelling.

In the holy place in front of the veil was the incense-altar (Ex. 30:1–10). Made of acacia wood and overlaid with pure gold—hence its other name, 'the golden altar'–it was a cubit square and 2 cubits high, with horns projecting at the four corners and an ornamental gold moulding round the top. (For a pagan, stone incense-altar with horns, see *ALTAR.) For transport, two poles were shot through gold rings attached just under the moulding. The altar stood directly opposite the ark (note the emphasis of 30:6), and so was regarded as 'belonging to' the most holy place (*cf.* 1 Ki. 6:22 and Heb. 9:4, where 'golden altar of incense' and not 'censer' seems to be the right translation). With the position of the altar compare the position of the two incense-altars in the temple at Arad (*BA* 31, 1968, pp. 22ff.).

On the N side (Ex. 26:35) stood a table for the Bread of the Presence (AV 'shewbread'; *SHOWBREAD) (Ex. 25:23–29). One such table and a lampstand (see below) from Herod's Temple are represented on Titus' Arch at Rome. Some doubt is cast, however, on the accuracy of these sculptures, since on the lampstand's base various non-Jewish figures appear. The detail of v. 25 is uncertain. Some translators envisage an 8-cm wide horizontal border, some an 8-cm high vertical rim, or frame, running round the top of the table, others, in agreement with apparent vestiges on Titus' Arch, envisage 8-cm broad cross-struts between the legs of the table.

The vessels connected with the table were: plates, presumably for the bread; dishes (*kappōṯ*: for incense, so RSV; *cf.* *kap̄*, in Nu. 7:14 = AV 'spoon'); and flagons and bowls for drink-offerings (not as AV 'to cover withal').

On the S side (Ex. 26:35) stood the *lampstand, *m*ᵉ*nōrâh* (AV 'candlestick') (Ex. 25:31–40), in the form of a stylized tree. In strict technical parlance the base and central shaft form the lampstand proper; the six branches are then described as 'going out of the lampstand' (v. 33). In v. 31 the RSV's literal translation, 'its cups, its capitals, and its flowers', *i.e.* three items, is to be preferred to interpretative renderings such as that of NEB 'its cups, both calyxes and petals', *i.e.* one item made up of two parts. The capitals were round protuberances of some kind, in the arms and shaft of the lampstand (not, as 'capital' might suggest, on the ends of them). It is probable, but not completely certain, that the six branches rose to the same height as the central shaft. The seven lamps were presumably placed one on the end of each of the six branches and one on the central shaft. There were provided *snuffers and *trays.

IV. Court

The tabernacle stood in the W half of a courtyard, 100 × 50 cubits, the long sides running N and S (Ex. 27:9–19). The tabernacle door faced E.

The courtyard was bounded by a linen screen (EVV 'hangings') 5 cubits high hung on pillars. There was an opening for a gate, 20 cubits wide, set centrally in the E end. The gate screen was linen, embroidered in violet-blue, reddish-purple and scarlet.

The pillars were apparently made of acacia wood (they are not mentioned in the list of copper articles, Ex. 38:29–31), and stood in copper sockets. They were stabilized by guy-ropes and pegs, and had capitals overlaid with silver, and silver bands, called fillets, round the neck.

Three main methods are advocated for spacing the pillars:

(1) On the basic assumption that there was one pillar per 5 cubits of hanging, and that no pillar was counted twice, sixty pillars in all are placed to make twenty spaces along the two long sides and ten spaces along the two ends. The gate screen then hangs on four of its own pillars and one of the others.

It is questionable whether this satisfies the direction for the 20 cubits of gate-screen '. . . *their pillars four* . . .'.

(2) The *Baraitha on the Erection of the Tabernacle*, 5, has it that the pillars stood in the middle of each imaginary space of 5 cubits and that there were no pillars in the corners. (For an attempted solution of the difficulties this would create at the corners and the gate, see M. Levine, *The Tabernacle*, 1969, pp. 76, 81.).

(3) Since the text nowhere says that the pillars were 5 cubits apart, maybe at the corners the two end pillars stood together. Or perhaps the corner pillars were counted twice (the text does not explicitly state that the total was sixty). The gate could then be recessed (or advanced). But this system gives very awkward measurements for the spaces between the pillars.

In the E half of the court stood an altar. It was called the copper altar from its covering material and the altar of burnt-offering from the chief *sacrifice offered on it (Ex. 27:1–8). It was a hollow framework of acacia wood, 5 cubits square and 3 high, with projecting horns at the top corners. The whole was overlaid with copper. Halfway up the altar, on the outside, was a horizontal ledge (AV 'compass') running all round. (For a stone altar of comparable dimensions with horns, see Y. Aharoni, *BA* 37, 1974, pp. 2–6; *ALTAR.) Running vertically all round from the ground up to the ledge (not 'extending halfway down the altar' as RSV) was a grating of copper network, on the four corners of which were the rings for the carrying-poles. The grating was not a hearth, and the altar was topless and hollow. Some suppose that in use it was filled with earth and stones, others that it acted like an incinerator, draught being supplied through the grating. Its service vessels were *pots for ashes, *shovels, *basins, *forks (AV *'fleshhooks') and *firepans.

Between the altar and the door of the tabernacle stood the laver (Ex. 30:17–21; 38:8; 40:29–32). It was a copper basin standing on a copper base. Nothing is told us of its size, shape and ornamentation (nor of its means of transport, though the absence of this detail from the *MT* of Nu. 4 may be accidental: LXX gives the expected information). It held water for the priests' ablutions.

In camp the tabernacle court was surrounded first by the tents of the priests and Levites, and outside them by those of the twelve tribes (Nu. 2; 3:1–30).

V. Problems arising

Revision of source-critical theories, particularly those relating to the so-called Priestly texts, together with archaeological discoveries have considerably modified the earlier arguments of the liberal school against the historicity of the tabernacle. See *e.g.* G. Henton-Davies, *IDB*, 3, pp. 503–506; Y. Aharoni, *Orient and Occident* (ed. H. A. Hoffner, Jr), 1973, p. 6; C. L. Meyers, *IDBS*, p. 586. Allegations that the instructions for the building of the tabernacle are in parts impracticable, and thus evidently the work of an idealist, would be valid only if the records were intended to be fully detailed blueprints. They are not that, of course, but records 'for our learning'. Hence many practical details of no aesthetic, symbolic or spiritual value are omitted. At the same time portable pavilions, employing practically the same constructional techniques as the tabernacle, are known to have been in actual use in Egypt long before the time of Moses; see K. A. Kitchen, *Eretz Israel* 24, 1993, pp. 119–129. From the fact that the instructions for the making of the incense-altar stand in Ex. 30, and not as expected in Ex. 25, it used to be argued that its description is a late addition to Exodus and that the incense-altar was not introduced into Israel's worship until a comparatively late date. But since incense-altars have been discovered at Arad and at various Canaanite sites dating from the 10th century BC, it is highly improbable that Israel lacked one in the early period. Similarly, on the basis of the wide divergence of the LXX from the *MT* in Ex. 36–40, it used to be argued that the last chapters of Exodus in Heb. had not yet reached their final form when the LXX was translated, and that the LXX followed in part a Heb. tradition which knew of no incense-altar. But the argument is not valid: see D. W. Gooding, *The Account of the Tabernacle*, 1959.

VI. Significance

Theologically the tabernacle as a dwelling-place of God on earth is of immense importance, as being the first in the series: tabernacle, Temple, the incarnation, the body of the individual believer, the church. It follows from the fact that the tabernacle was built to God's design as 'a copy and shadow of heavenly things' (Heb. 8:5) that its symbols conveyed spiritual meaning to the Israelites of the time. What that meaning was is often stated explicitly, as with the ark and mercy seat (Ex. 25:16, 22; Lv. 16:15–16), the veil and the two-compartment structure (Lv. 16:2; Heb. 9:8), the incense-altar (Ps. 141:2; *cf.* Lk. 1:10–13; Rev. 5:8; 8:3–4), the laver (Ex. 30:20–21), the copper altar (Lv. 1:3–9; 17:11); and where it is not stated explicitly, as with the table and the lampstand, it is self-evident from their declared function. How far these symbols were also types of spiritual realities later to be revealed to us is disputed. Understandably, the extravagant interpretations that from the early centuries have been placed upon the subject have brought it into disrepute. But the NT declares that the law had 'a shadow of the good things to come', which good things actually came with Christ (Heb. 10:1; 9:11). So Christ is said to have entered through the veil (Heb. 6:19–20), and to be set forth as a propitiatory, or mercy seat (Rom. 3:25, *hilastērion*; *cf.* LXX Ex. 25:17–22; Lv. 16:15–16. RSV 'expiation' is scarcely exact); while the writer to the Hebrews indicates that he could have expounded in this fashion all the tabernacle vessels and not simply the one feature which was relevant to his immediate argument (Heb. 9:5).

BIBLIOGRAPHY. M. Haran, *HUCA* 36, 1965, pp. 191–226; U. Cassuto, *A Commentary on the Book of Exodus*, 1967, pp. 319ff.; R. K. Harrison, *IOT*, 1970, pp. 403–410; R. P. Gordon, in G. C. D. Howley (ed.), *An Old Testament Commentary*, 1979; N. M. Sarna, *Exploring Exodus*, 1986.

D.W.G.

TABERNACLES, FEAST OF. Heb. *ḥag̱ hassukkôṯ*, 'festival of booths' (Lv. 23:34; Dt. 16:13), or *ḥag̱ hā'āsîp̱*, 'festival of ingathering' (Ex. 23:16; 34:22). This was one of the three great pilgrimage-festivals of the Jewish year; it was kept for 7 days from the 15th to the 22nd day of the 7th month. It came at the end of the year when the labours of the field were gathered in, and was one of the three annual festivals at which every male was required to appear (Ex. 23:14–17; 34:23; Dt. 16:16). It was a time of rejoicing (Dt. 16:14). The designation 'feast of booths (tabernacles)' comes from the requirement for everyone born an Israelite to live in booths made of boughs of trees and branches of palm trees for the 7 days of the feast (Lv. 23:42). Sacrifices were offered on the 7 days, beginning with thirteen bullocks and other animals on the 1st day and diminishing by one bullock each day until on the 7th seven bullocks were offered. On the 8th day there was a solemn assembly when one bullock, one ram and seven lambs were offered (Nu. 29:36). This is the last day, 'that great day of the feast', probably alluded to in Jn. 7:37. As a feast, divinely instituted, it was never forgotten. It was observed in the time of Solomon (2 Ch. 8:13), Hezekiah (2 Ch. 31:3; *cf.* Dt. 16:16), and after the Exile (Ezr. 3:4; Zc. 14:16, 18–19). The ceremony of water-pouring, associated with this festival in post-exilic times and reflected in Jesus' proclamation in Jn. 7:37f., is not prescribed in the Pentateuch. Its recognition of rain as a gift from God, necessary to produce fruitful harvests, is implied in Zc. 14:17 (*cf.* 1 Sa. 7:6).

This feast had a historical reference to the Exodus from Egypt and reminded the Jews of their wandering and dwelling in booths in the wilderness (Lv. 23:43). However, this is not evidence of the conversion of the agricultural festival to a historical one. Rather it points to the truth that Israel's life rested upon redemption which in its ultimate meaning is the forgiveness of sin.

This fact separates this feast from the harvest festivals of the neighbouring nations whose roots lay in the mythological activity of the gods.

BIBLIOGRAPHY. N. Hillyer, *TynB* 21, 1970, pp. 39–51.

D.F.

TABLE. 1. A table as an article of furniture (Heb. *šulḥān*; Gk. *trapeza*). The table in the steppe, or wilderness (Pss. 23:5; 78:19), was a prepared area or skin laid out on the ground (Heb. *šlḥ*). Elsewhere the word is used, as its modern counterpart, for the table made of wood or metal which was a common item of furniture (2 Ki. 4:10). To eat 'at the king's table' was a signal honour (2 Sa. 9:7; *cf.* Lk. 22:21), while to eat at 'one's own table', as well as having its literal meaning, denoted living at one's own expense (1 Ki. 18:19; Ne. 5.17). 'The table of the Lord' (Mal. 1:7, 12; Ezk. 41:22; 44:16; 1 Cor. 10:21; *ALTAR) implies that at which he is the host. Ps. 69:22 is of uncertain meaning.

2. For AV 'table' standing for writing-tablet (RSV 'tablet', Lat. *tabula*) see *WRITING. The AV also has 'table' for Heb. *lûaḥ*, for a plank used in the construction of the altar (Ex. 27:8), a ship (Ezk. 27:5), a door (Ct. 8:9), and the metal plates at the base of Solomon's lavers (1 Ki. 7:36). All these were also potential surfaces for inscriptions.

D.J.W.

TABOR. If Jos. 19:22; Jdg. 8:18; and 1 Ch. 6:77 refer to the same place, Tabor was on the Zebulun–Issachar border: and it was presumably on or near Mt Tabor. The 'oak', or 'terebinth' (NEB), of 1 Sa. 10:3 must have been at a different Tabor, in Benjaminite territory.

D.F.P.

TABOR, MOUNT. A notable mountain rising from the Plain of Jezreel to 588 m above sea-level. Its slopes are steep, and the views from the summit magnificent; hence it was considered worthy of comparison with Mt Hermon, in spite of the latter's much greater bulk and height (*cf.* Ps. 89:12). It was the scene of Barak's mustering (Jdg. 4:6) and of an idolatrous shrine in Hosea's day (*cf.* Ho. 5:1). In later times there was a town on the summit, which was taken and then fortified by Antiochus III in 218 BC. In 53 BC it was the scene of a battle between the Romans and Alexander the son of Aristobulus. Josephus, in his role as Jewish general,

OFFERINGS	MONTH OF TISRI DAY 15	DAY 16	DAY 17	DAY 18	DAY 19	DAY 20	DAY 21	DAY 22	TOTALS
BULLOCKS	13	12	11	10	9	8	7	1	71
Related cereal offerings▽ (in ephahs)	3.9	3.6	3.3	3.0	2.7	2.4	2.1	0.3	21.3
RAMS	2	2	2	2	2	2	2	1	15
Related cereal offerings○ (in ephahs)	0.4	0.4	0.4	0.4	0.4	0.4	0.4	0.2	3
MALE LAMBS*	14	14	14	14	14	14	14	7	105
Related cereal offerings☆ (in ephahs)	1.4	1.4	1.4	1.4	1.4	1.4	1.4	0.7	10.5
MALE GOATS	1	1	1	1	1	1	1	1	8

* Yearlings without blemish
▽ $\frac{3}{10}$ of an ephah for each bullock
○ $\frac{2}{10}$ of an ephah for each ram
☆ $\frac{1}{10}$ of an ephah for each lamb

Chart showing the daily offerings during the Feast of Tabernacles (*Nu.* 29:12–35).

gave the town on the summit a defensive rampart in AD 66; remains of this wall can still be seen. The mountain also figured in the events of Crusader times.

Since the 4th century AD, and perhaps earlier, tradition has held that Mt Tabor was the scene of the transfiguration. This is not very likely; more probable is the view that Mt Tabor is intended in Dt. 33:19. The Arabs called the mountain Jabal al-Tur; the Israelis have given it its old Heb. name, *Har Tāḇôr.* D.F.P.

TADMOR. This place-name occurs twice in AV (1 Ki. 9:18; 2 Ch. 8:4), and is usually identified with mod. Tudmur, 'Palmyra', 200 km NE of Damascus; mentioned as *Tadmar* in Assyr. texts *c.* 1110 BC. Tadmor in AV in 1 Ki. 9:18 is based on *qᵉrē'* and the ancient versions. The *kᵉṯîḇ* is *tāmār.* The ancient versions have 'Palmyra' (Gk. for 'palm tree' = Heb. *tāmār*). The problem is whether the Tamar of 1 Ki. 9:18 (RV, RSV) is identical with the Tadmor of 2 Ch. 8:4. The following solutions are proposed: **1.** Later in the time of the Chronicler, when the government of Solomon was idealized, the unimportant Tamar of the Judaean desert was changed to the then well-known, illustrious Tadmor in the Syrian desert. **2.** *Qᵉrē'* and the ancient versions are to be followed in identifying the place in 1 Ki. 9:18 with Tadmor, the later Palmyra in the Syrian desert. **3.** Tamar of 1 Ki. 9:18 and Tadmor of 2 Ch. 8:4 are different places. Tamar, the modern *Kurnub*, called *Thamara* in the *Onomasticon* of Eusebius, was situated on the route between Elath and Hebron. This city was fortified to protect the trade with S Arabia and the seaport Elath. Tadmor was the famous trading-centre NE of Damascus and could have been brought under Solomon's rule with the operations against the Syrian Hamath and Zobah.

The third solution is acceptable, because Tamar in 1 Ki. 9:18 is expressly called 'in the land' and thus in Israelite territory (*cf.* also Ezk. 47:19; 48:28).

BIBLIOGRAPHY. J. Starcky, *Palmyra*, 1952.

F.C.F.

TAHPANHES. An important Egyptian settlement in the E Delta, named with Migdol, Noph (Memphis), *etc.* (Je. 2:16; 44:1; 46:14; Ezk. 30:18 as Tehaphnehes), to which certain Jews fled *c.* 586 BC, taking thither the prophet Jeremiah (Je. 43). The same consonantal spelling *Tḥpnḥs* recurs in a Phoen. papyrus letter of the 6th century BC found in Egypt (*cf.* A. Dupont-Sommer, *PEQ* 81, 1949, pp. 52–57). The LXX form Taphnas, Taphnais, probably equates Tahpanhes with the Pelusian Daphnai of Herodotus (2. 30, 107) where the 26th Dynasty pharaoh Psammetichus I (664–610 BC) established a garrison of Gk. mercenaries. On grounds of geographical location, the equivalence of Arabic Defneh with Daphnai, and the excavation at Defneh of Gk. pottery and other objects, Tahpanhes-Daphnai is located at modern Tell Defneh ('Defenneh'), about 43 km SSW of Port Said. The Egyptian for Tahpanhes is not inscriptionally attested, but may be *T'-ḥ(wt)-p'-nḥsy*, 'mansion of the Nubian', names compounded with *nḥsy*, 'Nubian', being known elsewhere in Egypt (so Spiegelberg).

'Pharaoh's house in Tahpanhes' and the 'brickwork' (RV) at its entry in which Jeremiah hid stones to presage Nebuchadrezzar's visitation there (Je. 43:9) may just possibly be the fortress of Psammetichus I, with traces of a brick platform on its NW side, excavated by Petrie (*Nebesheh* (*Am*) *and Defenneh* (*Tahpanhes*) bound with *Tanis II*, 1888).

K.A.K.

TAHPENES. An Egyp. queen whose sister the pharaoh married off to Hadad of Edom (I Ki. 11:19-20; *PHARAOH, II. 6). B. Grdseloff (*Revue de l'Histoire Juive en Égypte*, No. 1, 1947, pp. 88–90) took Heb. *tḥpns* as a transcription of the Egyp. title *t(')-ḥ(mt)-p(')-ns(w)*, 'Royal Wife'. W. F. Albright (*BASOR* 140, 1955, p. 32) postu-lated an Egyp. name *T(')-ḥ(nt) -p(')-*(or *pr-*) *-ns(w)*, for which partial parallels exist.

K.A.K.

TAHTIM-HODSHI. In 2 Sa. 24:6 a place in the N of David's realm, near the frontier with the kingdom of Hamath, mentioned in his census record. On the basis of LXX, *MT 'ereṣ taḥtîm ḥoḏšî* (AV 'the land of Tahtim-hodshi') has been very plausibly emended to *qāḏēš 'ereṣ ha-ḥittîm* (RSV 'Kadesh in the land of the Hittites'). (*KADESH; *HITTITES.)

F.F.B.

TALE. The AV rendering of four Heb. words, each of which is thus translated once only. Three of them mean 'number': *mispār* (1 Ch. 9:28); *maṯkōneṯ*, 'measure', 'proper quantity' (Ex. 5:8); and *tōḵen*, 'a weight', 'measure' (Ex. 5:18).

In the fourth occurrence the Heb. word is *heḡeh*, which could mean 'meditation' or 'utterance' and is found in the phrase 'as a tale that is told' (Ps. 90:9), a rendering much disputed. LXX and Vulg. read 'as a spider's web'. The literal translation is 'like a sigh', and this is retained by RSV.

J.D.D.

TALEBEARING, SLANDER. These words translate, in the OT, expressions implying secrecy (Pr. 18:8, 'whisperer'), evil report (Nu. 14:36), the giving out (Ps. 50:20) or carrying (Pr. 11:13) of slander, or the (wrong) use of tongue (Ps. 101:5) or feet (2 Sa. 19:27). In the NT the words translate accusation (1 Tim. 3:11, *diabolos*), speaking against (2 Cor. 12:20; 1 Pet. 2:1, *katalalia*) or defaming (Rom. 3:8, *blasphēmeō*). All talebearing, whether false (*cf.* Mt. 5:11) or not (*cf.* Dn. 3:8), malicious (Ps. 31:13; Ezk. 22:9) or foolish (Pr. 10:18; *cf.* 18:8 = 26:22; Mt. 12:36), especially between neighbours (Je. 9:4) or brothers (Jas. 4:11), is condemned (Lv. 19:16) and punished (Ps. 101:5) by God, and causes quarrelling (Pr. 26:20). Slander springs from the heart (Mk. 7:22) of the natural man (Rom. 1:30), excludes from God's presence (Ps. 15:3), and must be banished from the Christian community (2 Cor. 12:20; Eph. 4:31; Col. 3:8; 1 Pet. 2:1; *cf.* [of women] 1 Tim. 3:11; Tit. 2:3), which itself suffers slander (Mt. 5:11; *cf.* Rom. 3:8).

P.E.

TALITHA CUMI. 'Little girl, . . . arise.' Mk. 5:41 records these words spoken by Jesus in a Galilean Aramaic dialect to the daughter of Jairus, the Jewish leader. The word used for girl comes from a root meaning 'lamb' and is an affectionate term, like the Eng. 'lambkin'. MSS N, B, C read *koum* for *koumi.* This is due to the fact that the final vowel is not pronounced in some dialects.

R.A.H.G.

TALMAI. 1. A descendant of 'Anaq, a 'giant' (*ANAK), resident in Hebron at the time of the Conquest (Nu. 13:22) but driven out by Caleb (Jos. 15:14). He is described as a Canaanite in Jdg. 1:10, which records his death.

2. The son of Ammihud and ruler of Geshur. David married his daughter Maacah, who bore Absalom (2 Sa. 3:3; 13:37; 1 Ch. 3:2). After the assassination of Amnon Absalom fled for refuge with Talmai in *Geshur (2 Sa. 13:37). The (Hurrian?) name Talmai occurs in texts from *Alalaḫ and *Ugarit of the 14th century BC and as a later Nabataean name.

D.J.W.

TALMUD AND MIDRASH.

I. Talmud

The Talmud is composed of the *Mishnah*, the oral law which was in existence by the end of the 2nd century AD, and was collected by Rabbi Judah the Prince; and the *Gemara*, the comments of the Rabbis from AD 200 to 500 on the Mishnah. The Talmud contains *Halakhah*, legal enactments and precepts with the elaborate discussions whereby decisions were reached; and *Haggadah*, non-legal interpretations. The Talmud is the source from which Jewish law is derived. It is binding for faith and life on orthodox Jews. Liberal Jews do not consider it authoritative, though interesting and venerable. It is important for our knowledge of how the Jews interpreted the OT. It also throws light on portions of the NT.

The position is taken that the law of Moses had to be adapted to changing conditions in Israel. The claim is made that the 'Great Synagogue' (120 men) had such authority, but there is no proof to support the assertion. Rabbi Akiba (*c.* AD 110–35) or an earlier scholar made a comprehensive collection of traditional laws. Rabbi Judah the Prince utilized this material along with other portions in his edition of the Mishnah. The earliest collection of Mishnah may be assigned to the time of the noted schools of Hillel and Shammai, who flourished at the time of the second Temple.

The Mishnah is divided on three principles: (1) subject-matter; (2) biblical order; and (3) artificial devices, such as numbers. The Mishnah is found in six orders or main divisions (called *s^eḏārîm*), which contain the material of sixty treatises. The main categories are subdivided into tractates, chapters and paragraphs. The first order (*Seeds*) treats of agricultural laws and religious duties relating to cultivation of the land, including commandments concerning the tribute of agricultural products to be given to the priest, the Levite, and the poor. The second division (*Feasts*) sets forth the various festivals of the religious calendar, including the observance of the sabbath, with the ceremonies and sacrifices to be brought on those days. The third order (*Women*) deals with the laws of marriage, divorce, the levirate marriage, adultery and regulations for the Nazirite.

The fourth division of the Mishnah (*Fines*) handles civil legislation, commercial transactions of different kinds, legal procedures and a collection of the ethical maxims of the Rabbis. *Sacred Things*, the fifth order of the Mishnah, presents legislation concerning sacrifices, the first-born, clean and unclean animals, together with a description of Herod's Temple. The sixth part of the Mishnah (*Purifications*) lays down the laws touching levitical cleanness and uncleanness, clean and unclean persons and objects, and purifications. In all these portions it was the aim of Rabbi Judah to differentiate between current and obsolete law, and between civil and religious practices.

The Mishnah is marked by brevity, clarity and comprehensiveness, and was employed as a textbook in rabbinical academies. After the editing of the Mishnah, it soon became the official standard of the Academies of Palestine (Tiberias, Caesarea, Sepphoris and Lydda) and Babylonia (Sura, Pumbedita and Nehardea), resulting in the Palestinian Talmud and the Babylonian Talmud respectively. Discussion in these seats of learning became the nucleus for the study of the law, which became known as the Talmud.

The greater part of the discussions in the Talmud is in dialogue form. The dialogue introduces questions and seeks after causes and origins. There are numerous lengthy digressions into the Haggadah. This is actually a literary device to relieve the complexity and monotony of legal discussions. The extant Talmud is a commentary on only two-thirds of the Mishnah. It contains rejected as well as accepted decisions of the law. The observation of A. Darmesteter is amply justified: 'The Talmud, exclusive of the vast Rabbinic literature attached to it, represents the uninterrupted work of Judaism from Ezra to the sixth century of the common era, the resultant of all the living forces and of the whole religious activity of a nation. If we consider that it is the faithful mirror of the manners, the institutions, the knowledge of the Jews, in a word of the whole of their civilization in Judaea and Babylonia during the prolific centuries preceding and following the advent of Christianity, we shall understand the importance of a work, unique of its kind, in which a whole people has deposited its feelings, its beliefs, its soul' (*The Talmud*, p. 7).

II. Midrash

The term *midrash* derives from the Heb. root *dāraš*, 'to search out, investigate', that is, to discover a thought not seen on the surface. It has reference, then, to a didactic or homiletic exposition. It occurs twice in the OT, in 2 Ch. 13:22, where the 'story' (AV, RSV) or 'commentary' (RV) of the prophet Iddo is spoken of, and in 2 Ch. 24:27, where the 'story' (RV; RSV 'Commentary') of the book of the Kings is referred to. 'They were probably didactic developments of the historical narratives we possess, making use of these narratives to emphasize some religious truth; but nothing is known of them beyond their titles' (*HDB*, 1, p. 459).

Our term has received its widest usage in extra-biblical context. Midrash is sometimes used in contrast to Mishnah, in which case it denotes that branch of rabbinic learning which has especially to do with the rules of traditional law. It is impossible at this stage of our knowledge to state which is the older method of study, Midrash or Mishnah. (See G. F. Moore, *Judaism*, 1, pp. 150ff.) Suffice it to say, after the return of the Jews from Babylon with the activity of Ezra and his school on behalf of the law, exposition and commentary for the congregation became a necessity.

The oral form of these commentaries was later crystallized into writing. Since the greater portion of the important works is no longer extant in the original composition, the date of compilation is almost impossible to ascertain. Midrashic activity came to an end soon after the completion of the Babylonian Talmud. In time the Midrash was displaced by the disciplines of history, grammar and theology.

Midrashim are divided into expositional and homiletical. The former comment on the text of Scripture according to their present order, or join to them tales, parables and the like (H. L. Strack, *Introduction to Talmud and Midrash*, pp. 201–205). The latter deal with individual texts, mostly from the beginnings of Scriptural lections. Midrashim exist on the Pentateuch, the Five Rolls, Lamentations, the Psalms, Proverbs and other books.

Bibliography. *HDB* (*s.v.* 'Commentary'); B. Cohen, 'Talmudic and Rabbinical Literature', *The Jewish People*, 3, pp. 54–79; G. F. Moore, *Judaism*, 3 vols., 1927–30; H. L. Strack, *Introduction to*

Talmud and Midrash, 1931; *JewE* (*s.v.* 'Midrash'); *EJ* (*s.vv.* 'Midrash', 'Mishnah', 'Talmud'). C.L.F.

TAMAR (Heb. *tāmār*, 'palm'). **1.** The wife, first of Er the eldest son of Judah, then of *Onan (Gn. 38:6ff.). After Onan's death his father Judah, not recognizing Tamar, became by her the father of twins, Perez and Zerah. The story of Tamar reveals something of the marriage customs in early Israel. (*MARRIAGE, IV.)

2. Daughter of David, violated by Amnon her half-brother, and avenged by Absalom (2 Sa. 13:1ff.; 1 Ch. 3:9). **3.** A daughter of Absalom (2 Sa. 14:27). **4.** A city in SE Judah (Ezk. 47:19; 48:28), near the Dead Sea. For discussion of location, see *TADMOR. J.D.D.

TAMMUZ. The deity whose cult was characterized by ritual offerings and lamentations. In a vision Ezekiel saw women sitting in the N gate of the *Temple in Jerusalem weeping for 'the Tammuz' (8:14). The Tammuz cult is little known and it is by no means certain that mourning for this god was made in the 4th month of the Babylonian *calendar which was named after him.

Tammuz was a predeluvian Sumerian shepherd and ruler who married the goddess *Ishtar. When he died she followed him into the underworld to try for his release and all fertility ceased on the earth. It was once thought that the death and resurrection of Tammuz was reflected in the disappearance of the vegetation in June and its revival in the following spring.

However, it now seems to be more likely from textual evidence that he did not rise (*JSS* 7, 1962, p. 153), or if he did it was for no more than for half the year when his place below was taken by the goddess Geshtinanna (*BASOR* 183, 1966, p. 31), or he was but a ghost coming with others for the funerary offerings prepared for him (*JSS* 11, 1966, pp. 10–15). Babylonian sources provide hymns and lamentations for the god but little about his worship. Tammuz seems to have had devotees at Air and Arad (*BASOR* 208, 1970, pp. 9–13) and later in *Phoenicia and Syria where a similar legend is told of Adonis (identified in *Egypt with Osiris) and Aphrodite whose temple at Byblos (Gebal) was a centre of the cult in Hellenistic times.

BIBLIOGRAPHY. T. Jacobsen in W. L. Moran (ed.), *Towards the Image of Tammuz*, 1970, pp. 73–103; B. Alster, *Dumuzi's Dream*, 1972, pp. 9–15; *ANET*, 1969, pp. 637–642. D.J.W.

TAPPUAH ('quince'?). **1.** A village in the *Shephelah, E of Azekah (Jos. 15:34, 53, Beth-tappuah), sometimes identified with Beit Netif, *c.* 18 km W of Bethlehem. The place-name may derive from a Calebite from Hebron (1 Ch. 2:43). **2.** A town in Ephraim territory (Jos. 16:8) on the S border of Manasseh (Jos. 17:7–8), possibly mod. Sheikh Abu Zarad, *c.* 12 km S of Shechem. Its Canaanite king was defeated by Joshua (Jos. 12:17; *Test. Judah* 3:2; 5:6). If 2 Ki. 15:16 refers to this same place (so RSV, after LXX; *cf.* AV Tiphsah), it was later attacked by Menahem of Israel. D.J.W.

TARGUMS. The Heb. word *targum* (plural *targumîm*) denotes an Aram. translation or paraphrase of some part of the OT. Targums are extant for every book except Ezra, Nehemiah and Daniel.

I. Historical survey

Targums gradually came into being as the *synagogue evolved. After the Babylonian Exile, Aramaic came to predominate over Hebrew as the language of the Jews; in consequence it became customary for the reading of the Heb. scriptures to be followed by an oral rendering into Aramaic for the benefit of the worshippers. Perhaps *cf.* Ne. 8:8. No doubt such renderings were free and spontaneous at first, but they became more and more fixed and 'traditional' as time passed. The next stage was to commit such material to writing; the earliest extant targumic material is from the 2nd century BC, from Qumran.

In the 1st millennium AD Judaism had two chief centres, Babylonia and Palestine. It would seem that most if not all the traditional targumic material originated in Palestine; some of it was transmitted to Babylonia, where in due course Targum Onkelos for the Pentateuch and Targum Jonathan on the Prophets (see below) were given official status. (N.B. References to 'the Targum' without further definition are normally to Onkelos or Jonathan.) Onkelos is claimed by TB (*Megillah* 3. 1) to have been a 1st-century AD proselyte, while Jonathan ben Uzziel lived in the 1st century BC; but considerable doubt surrounds the appropriateness of both names (*cf.* M. McNamara, *Targum and Testament*, p. 174). Neither Targum is likely to be so early; but both were in final, standard form by the 5th century.

Meanwhile an independent targumic tradition developed inside Palestine, and some of it attained a semi-official status there. It is convenient to call this tradition 'the Palestinian Targum', in spite of its varied and rather disparate character. The dating of the various individual targums has been and remains much disputed; it is even more difficult to decide the date of origin of specific features within any targum.

II. General characteristics

At one extreme, Targum Onkelos is for the most part an accurate, word-for-word rendering of the Hebrew. In view of their synagogue purpose, however, it is not surprising that targums were used as a medium of interpretation and instruction. Even the more literal of them display interpretative traits: *e.g.* place-names are brought up to date, difficulties are smoothed over and obscurities clarified. In the more paraphrastic targums (*e.g.* Pseudo-Jonathan), the text is expanded to a marked degree. Not only can the whole sense of a verse or passage be altered, but a great deal of additional material ('midrash') may be incorporated. Thus a targum may be scarcely recognizable as a translation of the Heb. original (see, *e.g.*, the translation of Is. 53 in J. F. Stenning, *The Targum of Isaiah*, 1949).

III. List of Targums

The targums follow the divisions of the Heb. Bible (*CANON OF THE OT, III).

a. The Law

(i) Targum Onkelos (or Onqelos): the official version of Babylonian Jews, among whom it was authoritative no later than the 4th century.

(ii) The Palestinian Targum is extant in three recensions. The only complete version is Neofiti I, probably of the 3rd century AD, although its first editor has claimed a pre-Christian date. Incomplete are the Jerusalem Targums I and II (often known as 'Pseudo-Jonathan', due to a mediaeval error, and 'Fragment Targum' respectively). The former is very complex, at times identical with Onkelos, elsewhere extremely paraphrastic. Fragments of the Palestinian Targum on the Pentateuch are also extant among the Cairo Genizah scrolls.

b. The Prophets

(i) Targum Jonathan ben Uzziel: the official Babylonian version, authoritative from the 4th century AD.

(ii) The Palestinian Targum has not survived, apart from fragments and occasional citations.

c. The Writings

Separate targums are extant on Job–Psalms, Proverbs, the Five Scrolls and Chronicles. These, which were never official, were later in origin than those on the Law and Prophets. From Qumran there are fragments of a much earlier and totally different targum on Job (4Qtg Job; 11Qtg Job).

IV. Value

a. Language

Targumic material offers some of the major evidence for the vernacular speech of ancient Palestine. It is therefore of special importance for the study of the *ipsissima verba* of Jesus and of the Aramaic substratum of the NT as a whole. Major problems remain, however, in view of uncertainties about the date of the various targums, and the problem of the existence of various dialects within Palestine.

b. Text

The targums offer an important witness to the text of the OT, comparable in value with the LXX, Peshitta and Vulgate (*TEXTS AND VERSIONS, I). The evidence is much more reliable in literal than in paraphrastic targumic material, for obvious reasons. Occasionally NT quotations from the OT are closer to the targums than to other Versions or to the *MT*.

c. New Testament background

The targums bear witness to Jewish modes of expression, exegetical methods and current interpretations in the early Christian centuries. Many of them are reflected, whether directly or in a more diffuse way, in the NT. The targums therefore often throw light on the NT, although their evidence is not to be used in isolation from all other rabbinic sources.

BIBLIOGRAPHY. *Major texts:* A. Sperber, *The Bible in Aramaic*, 1957–73; A. Díez Macho, *Neophyti* 1, 1968– ; M. McNamara (ed.), *The Aramaic Bible*, 1987– ; E. Schürer, *HJP*, pp. 99–114; M. McNamara, *The New Testament and the Palestinian Targum to the Pentateuch*, 1966; *idem*, *Targum and Testament*, 1968; J. Bowker, *The Targums and Rabbinic Literature*, 1969; R. Le Déaut, *The Message of the New Testament and the Aramaic Bible*, 1982; B. H. Young, *ISBE* 4, pp. 727–733. See also B. Grossfeld, *A Bibliography of Targumic Literature*, 1972; *Newsletter for Targumic Studies*, 1974– .

D.F.P.

TARSHISH. 1. A grandson of Benjamin, son of Bilhan (1 Ch. 7:10). **2.** One of the seven notable princes of Ahasuerus, ruler of Persia (Est. 1:14).

3. The son of Javan, grandson of Noah (Gn. 10:4; 1 Ch. 1:7). The name Tarshish (*taršîš*), which occurs 4 times in AV as Tharshish (1 Ki. 10:22 (twice); 22:48; 1 Ch. 7:10), refers both to the descendants and to the land.

Several of the references in the OT are concerned with ships and suggest that Tarshish bordered on the sea. Thus Jonah embarked on a ship sailing to Tarshish (Jon. 1:3; 4:2) from Joppa in order to flee to a distant land (Is. 66:19). The land was rich in such metals as silver (Je. 10:9), iron, tin, lead (Ezk. 27:12), which were exported to places like Joppa and Tyre (Ezk. 27). A land in the W Mediterranean where there are good deposits of mineral seems a likely identification, and many have thought of Tartessus in Spain. According to Herodotus (4. 152), Tartessus lay 'beyond the Pillars of Hercules', and Plinius and Strabo placed it in the Guadalquivir Valley. Certainly the mineral wealth of Spain attracted the Phoenicians, who founded colonies there. Interesting evidence comes from Sardinia, where monumental inscriptions erected by the Phoenicians in the 9th century BC bear the name Tarshish. W. F. Albright has suggested that the very word Tarshish suggests the idea of mining or smelting, and that in a sense any mineral-bearing land may be called Tarshish, although it would seem most likely that Spain is the land intended. An old Semitic root found in Akkad. *rašāšu* means 'to melt', 'to be smelted'. A derived noun *taršīšu* may be used to define a smelting-plant or refinery (Arab. *ršš*, 'to trickle', *etc.*, of liquid). Hence any place where mining and smelting were carried on could be called Tarshish.

There is another possibility as to the site of Tarshish. According to 1 Ki. 10:22 Solomon had a fleet of ships of Tarshish that brought gold, silver, ivory, monkeys and peacocks to Ezion-geber on the Red Sea, and 1 Ki. 22:48 mentions that Jehoshaphat's ships of Tarshish sailed from Ezion-geber for Ophir. Further, 2 Ch. 20:36 says that these ships were made in Ezion-geber for sailing to Tarshish. These latter references appear to rule out any Mediterranean destination but point to a place along the Red Sea or in Africa. The expression *'ᵒnî taršîš*, navy of Tarshish or Tarshish fleet, may refer more generally to ships which carried smelted metal either to distant lands from Ezion-geber or to Phoenicia from the W Mediterranean. For the view that Tarshish vessels were deep seagoing vessels named after the port of Tarsus, or Gk. *tarsos*, 'oar' see *SHIPS AND BOATS.

These ships symbolized wealth and power. A vivid picture of the day of divine judgment was to portray the destruction of these large ships in that day (Ps. 48:7; Is. 2:16; 23:1, 14). The fact that Is. 2:16 compares the ships of Tarshish with 'the pleasant place' (RSV 'beautiful craft') suggests that whatever the original identification of Tarshish may have been, it became in literature and in the popular imagination a distant paradise from which all kinds of luxuries might be brought to such areas as Phoenicia and Israel.

BIBLIOGRAPHY. W. F. Albright, 'New Light on the Early History of Phoenician Colonization', *BASOR* 83, 1941, pp. 14ff.; W. S. Lasor, *ISBE* 4, p. 734.

J.A.T.

TARSUS. A city on the Cilician plain, watered by the Cydnus, and some 16 km inland after the fashion of most cities on the Asia Minor coast. To judge from the extent of its remains, Tarsus must have housed a population of no less than half a million in Roman times. The lower Cydnus was navigable, and a port had been skilfully engineered. A major highway led N to the Cilician Gates, the famous pass through the Taurus range some 50 km distant.

Nothing is known of the foundation of Tarsus. It was probably a native Cilician town, penetrated at a very early date by Gk. colonists. The name of Mopsus is traditionally associated with Gk. settlement in Cilicia, and may indicate, as Ramsay believed (*The Cities of St. Paul*, 1907, pp. 116f.), early Ionian settlement. Gn. 10:4, 'The sons of Javan, Elishah, Tarshish . . .' may support this theory. Josephus' identification of Tarshish with Tarsus in this passage does not preclude a different interpretation in other contexts. The antiquity of Gn. 10 is a graver objection, but the words may be evidence of Ionian intrusion of very remote date.

Tarsus appears sporadically in history. It is mentioned in the Black Obelisk of Shalmaneser as one of the cities overrun by the Assyrians in the middle of the 9th century BC. Median and Persian rule followed, with that typically loose organization which permitted the rule of a Cilician subject-king. Xenophon, passing through in 401 BC, found Tarsus the royal seat of one Syennesis, ruling in such capacity. This petty king may have been deposed for his association with Cyrus' revolt which brought Xenophon and the Ten Thousand to Cilicia, for Alexander, in 334 BC, found the area in the hands of a Persian satrap. The coinage of the period suggests a mingling of Greek and Oriental influence, and gives no indication of autonomy. Ramsay professes to trace a decline of Greek influence under the Persian rule.

Nor did the Seleucid kings, who ruled after Alexander, promote the influence of the Greeks in Tarsus. Their general policy, here as elsewhere, was to discourage the Greek urge to city autonomy and its attendant liberalism. It is possible that the shock of the Roman defeat of Antiochus the Great and the peace of 189 BC reversed the process. The settlement limited the Syrian domain to the Taurus, and Cilicia became a frontier region. The fact seems to have prompted Syria to some reorganization, and the granting of a form of autonomy to Tarsus. The Tarsus of Paul, with its synthesis of East and West, Greek and Oriental, dates from this time.

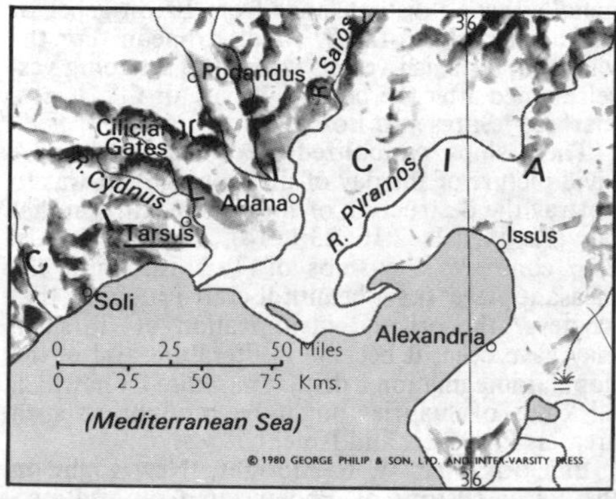

Tarsus, a city of Cilicia.

A story in 2 Macc. 4:30–36 reveals the rapid growth of independence, and the reorganization of the city which a Tarsian protest won from Antiochus Epiphanes in 171 BC. The formation of a 'tribe' of Jewish citizens after the Alexandrian fashion may date from this time. (Antiochus' anti-semitism was against metropolitan recalcitrance.) Tarsian history in the rest of the 2nd century BC is obscure. The 1st century BC is better known. Roman penetration of Cilicia began in 104 BC, but Roman and Greek influence were both overwhelmed in Asia by the Oriental reaction under Mithridates (83 BC). Pompey's settlement in 65–64 BC reconstituted Cilicia as a 'sphere of duty', which is the basic meaning of 'province', rather than a geographical entity, and the governors, Cicero among them (51 BC), had a roving commission to pacify the pirate coast and hinterlands and to protect Roman interests.

In spite of Roman experimentation with the land at large, Tarsus flourished, played some part in the civil wars, was visited by Antony, and favoured by Augustus as the home town of Athenodorus, his teacher at Apollonia and life-long friend. The Roman citizenship of some Tarsian Jews dates probably from Pompey's settlement.

E.M.B.

TARTAK. The name of an idol or deity (Heb. *tartāq*) worshipped by the men of *Avva who were settled in Samaria after its capture by the Assyrians in 722 BC (2 Ki. 17:31). The identification must remain open until the location of Avva itself is sure. TB (*Sanhedrin* 63b) ascribes the form of an ass to Tartak, but this is probably conjecture, as is the suggestion that the deity Atargatis is intended.

D.J.W.

TARTAN. The title of a high Assyrian officer. Two are mentioned in the OT. The first was sent by Sargon II to besiege and capture Ashdod in 711 BC (Is. 20:1, AV). The second came from Sennacherib with other officials (*RABSARIS, *RABSHAKEH) and a military force to demand the surrender of Jerusalem in 701 BC (2 Ki. 18:17). In neither case is the personal name of the officer given. The Assyr. *turtanu* is listed in the Assyrian Eponym texts as the highest official after the king. He was also titular head of the province of which Harran was the capital.

D.J.W.

TATTENAI (Heb. *tatt'nai*; AV 'Tatnai'; *cf.* Gk. *Sisinnes*, 1 Esdras 6:3; 7:1, RSV). The Persian governor, successor of Rehum, of the Samaria district during the reign of Darius Hystaspes and Zerubbabel (Ezr. 5:3, 6; 6:6, 13). He investigated and reported in a sympathetic manner on complaints made from Jerusalem against Jews in his district. He is called 'Tattanni, of the District across the River' (as Ezr. 5:6) in a cuneiform inscription from Babylon, dated 5 June 502 BC (*JNES* 3, 1944, p. 46), and appears to be under the satrap of Babylon Ushtani at this time.

D.J.W.

TAVERNS, THREE (Lat. *Tres Tabernae*). This was a station about 50 km from Rome on the Via Appia, which led SE from the city. It is mentioned by Cicero in his correspondence with Atticus (2. 10). When the apostle Paul and his company were on their way from Puteoli to Rome, Christians came out of the city and met him here (Acts 28:15). B.F.C.A.

TAX COLLECTOR. The Gk. word *telōnēs* (AV 'publican') means a collector of tax or custom on behalf of the Romans, employed by a tax farmer or contractor. As early as 212 BC there existed in Rome a class of men (*ordo publicanorum*, Livy, 25. 3. 8–19) who undertook state contracts of various kinds. They were closely associated with, and supported by, the equestrian order; and at a later date were active in a number of provinces (Cicero, *In Verrem*, 2. 3. 11, §§ 27–28), where their work included the collection of tithes and various indirect taxes. The system was very open to abuse, and the *publicani* seem to have been prone to extortion and malpractice from the very beginning, so that while the grossest excesses were restrained by the government, and cases sometimes brought to justice, a generally bad reputation has come down to us. Cicero considered such occupations as that of customs officer vulgar on account of the hatred they incurred (*de Officiis*, 1. 42, § 150) and Livy records the opinion, expressed in 167 BC, that where there is a *publicanus* allies have not liberty (45. 18. 3–4). The central contractors were often foreign to the provinces whose taxes they farmed, though there was nothing to prevent their being natives, and they might employ native sub-contractors. (The expression *architelōnēs* in Lk. 19:2 seems to imply that Zacchaeus was the contractor for the whole of the taxes of Jericho and had collectors under him—*SB*, 2, p. 249.) But the collectors were usually from the native population, for they needed to know local people and their ways to avoid being deceived. Their generally extortionate practices (*cf.* what amounts to an admission in the words of Zacchaeus, Lk. 19:8, and the conditions implied by the counsel of John the Baptist, Lk. 3:13) made them an especially despised and hated class, so that our Lord could refer to them as typical of a selfish attitude (Mt. 5:46). For the strict Jew, however, this quite natural attitude of hatred was aggravated and altered in character by the religious consideration that the *telōnēs* was regarded as ceremonially unclean, on account of his continual contact with Gentiles, and his need to work on the sabbath. This uncleanness, and the rabbis' teaching that their pupils should not eat with such persons, account for the attitude evidenced by the expressions *tax collectors and sinners* (Mt. 9:10f.; 11:19; Mk. 2:15f.; Lk. 5:30; 7:34; 15:1) and *tax collectors and harlots* (Mt. 21:31), and for the questions of Mt. 9:10f.; 11;19; Mk. 2:15f.; Lk. 5:29f. (*cf. SB*, 1, pp. 498f.), and indicates the intention of the command of Mt. 18:17. This also lends point to both the negative and positive aspects of the denunciation of the chief priests and elders in Mt. 21:31b, to the statement of Mt. 11:19; Lk. 7:34, and to the story of the Pharisee and the tax collector, Lk. 18:10ff.

BIBLIOGRAPHY. E. Schürer, *HJP*, 1, 1973, pp. 372ff.; *SB*, 1, pp. 377f., 498f., 770f.; 2, p. 249; N. Hillyer, *NIDNTT* 3, pp. 755–759; P. Garnsey and R. Saller, *The Roman Empire: Economy, Society and Culture*, 1987. J.H.H.

TAXES. Regular payments extracted from a state and its provinces by its own rulers are taxes, distinct from wealth received from conquered states which is *tribute.

In Israel's infancy the only taxes required were to maintain the tabernacle and its ministers, a practice renewed after the Exile (Dt. 18:1–5; 14:22–27, *etc.*; Ne. 10:32–39; *TITHES). With the Monarchy came heavier demands as listed by Samuel (1 Sa. 8:15, 17), comparable with the habits of all ancient kings. Occasionally there were exceptional levies to pay tribute to foreign conquerors (2 Ki. 15:19–20; 23:35).

In NT times Roman provinces paid regular taxes to Caesar in Roman coin, as Mt. 22:17; Mk. 12:14 are aware, whereas Herodian rulers collected dues in their realms (Mt. 17:24–27). In these passages Mt. and Mk. used Gk. *kēnsos*, borrowed from Lat. *censum*, 'poll-tax', while Lk. has the more general *phoros*, 'tribute, tax' (Lk. 20:22). (*CENSUS; *TAX COLLECTOR.)

BIBLIOGRAPHY. A. N. Sherwin-White, *Roman Society and Roman Law in the New Testament*, 1963, pp. 125–127; M. J. Harris, C. Brown, N. Hillyer, in *NIDNTT* 3, pp. 751–759. A.R.M.

TEKOA. 1. A town in Judah, about 10 km S of Bethlehem, the home of Amos (Am. 1:1). When Joab 'perceived that the king's heart went out to Absalom' he sent to Tekoa for a wise woman who might reconcile David and Absalom (2 Sa. 14:1f.). Rehoboam fortified the town (2 Ch. 11:6). Later, when Jehoshaphat was faced by Ammonites and Moabites, he consulted with the people in 'the wilderness of Tekoa' (2 Ch. 20:20). Jeremiah called for the blowing of a trumpet in Tekoa in the face of the advancing enemy (Je. 6:1). After the Exile the town was re-inhabited (Ne. 3:5, 27). In Maccabean and Roman times the place was known, and the name lingers today as Khirbet Taqû'a, a ruined village of some 5 acres, which has seen little excavation. Tombs of the Iron Age have been found nearby.

2. A descendant of Hezron, the grandson of Judah, belonging to the general Calebite stock (1 Ch. 2:24; 4:5).

BIBLIOGRAPHY. D. Baly, *Geography of the Bible*², 1974, pp. 89, 182; J. J. Davis, *Bulletin of the Near East Archaeological Society* 4, 1974, pp. 27–49; C. E. DeVries, *ISBE* 4, p. 746. J.A.T.

TELAIM. The place where Saul gathered his army before his attack on the Amalekites (1 Sa. 15:4). The incident described in 1 Sa. 15, in which Saul disobeyed God's word given by the prophet Samuel, provoked the severe rebuke of 1 Sa. 15:22–23, 'to obey is better than sacrifice'. Telaim (Heb. *ṭᵉlā'îm*) is identified by some with Telem (Jos. 15:24), in the Negeb. Some MSS allow of an occurrence of the word in 1 Sa. 27:8, and read 'they of Telaim' for 'of old'. J.A.T.

TELASSAR. A place inhabited by the 'children (sons) of Eden' and cited by Sennacherib's messengers to Hezekiah as an example of a town destroyed in previous Assyr. attacks (as also * GOZAN, * HARAN, * REZEPH). The name *tᵉla'śśār* (2 Ki. 19:12) or *tᵉlaśśār* (Is. 37:12) represents Tell Assur ('mound of Assur'). The *bᵉnê 'eḏen* probably lived in the area between the Euphrates and Baliḫ rivers, called in Assyr. Bît-Adini (Beth-Eden), but no Til-Assur has been found in this region, although the area does suit the context. A Til-Aššur named in the annals of Tiglath-pileser III and Esarhaddon appears to lie near the Assyr. border with Elam. The common form of the place-name means that it may not yet be identified. There is no need to emend to Tell Bassar (Basher), SE of Raqqa on the Euphrates (as L. Grollenberg, *Atlas of the Bible*, 1956, p. 164). D.J.W.

TEMA. The name (Heb. *tēmā'*) of the son and descendants of Ishmael (Gn. 25:15; 1 Ch. 1:30) and of the district they inhabited (Jb. 6:19). It is mentioned, with Dedan and Buz, as a remote place (Je. 25:23) and as an oasis in the desert on a main trade route through Arabia (Is. 21:14). Aramaic stelae of the 5th century BC were found in the ruins of Taima' about 400 km NNW of Medina in NW Arabia. The city (Bab. *Tema'*) is also named in documents recording its occupation by Nabonidus during his exile (*AS* 8, 1958, p. 80; *ANET*³, p. 562). D.J.W.

TEMAN. The grandson of Esau (Gn. 36:11; 1 Ch. 1:36), who may have given his name to the district, town or tribe of that name in N Edom (Je. 49:20; Ezk. 25:13; Am. 1:12). The inhabitants were renowned for wisdom (Je. 49:7; Ob. 8f.). Eliphaz the Temanite was one of Job's comforters (Jb. 2:11, *etc.*). A chief (*'allûp̄*) of Teman (*têmān*) is named among the chiefs of Edom (Gn. 36:15, 42; 1 Ch. 1:53), and Husham was one of the early rulers (Gn. 36:34). The prophets include Teman among Edomite towns to be destroyed (Je. 49:20; Ezk. 25:13; Am. 1:12; Ob. 9). Habakkuk in his great vision saw God the Holy One coming from Teman (Hab. 3:3).

N. Glueck (*The Other Side of Jordan*, 1940, pp. 25–26) identified it with Tawilân, since excavated to show a large Edomite town of the 8th to 6th centuries BC (*RB* 76, 1969, pp. 386ff.). R. de Vaux argued that it denoted S Edom (*RB* 77, 1969, pp. 379–385). J.A.T.

TEMPLE.

I. Historical background

Some of the earliest structures built by man were temples or shrines where he could worship his god in his 'house' (see K. M. Kenyon, *Archaeology in the Holy Land*⁴ pp. 24, 33, for the Mesolithic and Neolithic shrines at Jericho). The Tower of * Babel is the first structure mentioned in the Bible which implies the existence of a temple (Gn. 11:4). Although this seems to have been intended as a place where man might meet God, it symbolized the self-confidence of man attempting to climb up to heaven, and for such pride it was doomed.

In Mesopotamia, which Abraham left, each city had a temple dedicated to its patron deity. The god was looked upon as the owner of the land, and if it was not blessed by him it would be unproductive, resulting in poor revenues for his temple. The local king or ruler acted as steward for the god.

There was no purpose in the semi-nomadic Patriarchs building one particular shrine for their God. He revealed himself as and where he pleased. Such occasions were sometimes the scene of a sacrificial * altar. They might be commemorated by a * pillar (Gn. 28:22).

After Israel had grown into nationhood a central shrine became a necessity, as a gathering-point for all the people, a symbol of their unity in the worship of their God. This need was supplied by the * tabernacle during the trek through the wilderness and by recognized shrines during the period of the judges (*e.g.* Shechem, Jos. 8:30ff.; 24:1ff.; Shiloh, 1 Sa. 1:3).

The nations of Canaan had their own temples, simply called 'Dagon's house' or the house of whoever the patron deity was (Heb. *bêṯ dāḡôn*, 1 Sa. 5:5; *bêṯ 'aštārôṯ*, 1 Sa. 31:10; *cf. bêṯ yhwh*, Ex. 23:19). A variety have been uncovered at Beth-shan, Hazor and other sites.

The lack of a shrine of Yahweh appeared invidious when David had consolidated his power and built a permanent palace for himself. The king said, 'I dwell in a house of cedar, but the ark of God dwells in a tent' (2 Sa. 7:2). It was not given to him to build the Temple because he was stained with the blood of his enemies, but he collected materials, gathered treasure and bought the site (1 Ch. 22:8, 3; 2 Sa. 24:18–25). Solomon began the actual construction in his 4th year, and the Temple was completed 7 years later (1 Ki. 6:37–38).

II. Solomon's Temple

a. The site

That it stood within the area now called 'Haram esh-Sherif' at the E side of the 'Old City' of * Jerusalem is undisputed. The precise location within the vast enclosure is less certain. The highest part of the rock (now covered by the building known as 'The Dome of the Rock') may have been the site of the innermost sanctuary or of the altar of burnt-offering outside (2 Ch. 3:1). This rock was presumably part of the threshing-floor of * Araunah, bought by David for a sum given as 50 silver shekels (2 Sa. 24:24) or 600 gold shekels (1 Ch. 21:25).

Nothing of Solomon's structure remains above ground, nor were any definite traces found in the diggings sponsored by the Palestine Exploration Fund. Indeed, it is likely that the work of levelling the rock and building up the great retaining walls for the courtyard of Herod's Temple obliterated earlier constructions.

b. Description

The passages 1 Ki. 6–7 and 2 Ch. 3–4 must be the bases of any reconstruction of Solomon's Temple. These accounts, while detailed, do not cover every feature, are not entirely understood and contain some apparent discrepancies (*e.g.* 1 Ki. 6:2 and 16f.). They may be supplemented by incidental references and by the description of Ezekiel's Temple, an elaborated version of Solomon's building (Ezk. 40–43). The Temple proper was an oblong, orientated E and W. It is reasonable to assume that, like Ezekiel's Temple, it stood on a platform (*cf.* Ezk. 41:8). No dimensions are given for the surrounding area. Again following Ezekiel's plan, it seems that there were two courtyards, inner and outer; a suggestion supported by 1 Ki. 6:36; 7:12; 2 Ki. 23:12; 2 Ch. 4:9.

The bronze altar for burnt-offerings stood in the inner court (1 Ki. 8:22, 64; 9:25). It was 20 cubits square and 10 cubits high (2 Ch. 4:1). Between this and the porch was the bronze laver holding water for ritual washings (AV 'molten' or 'brazen sea', 1 Ki. 7:23–26). This great basin, 10 cubits in diameter, rested upon four groups of four bronze oxen orientated to the four compass-points. These were removed by Ahaz (2 Ki. 16:17).

At the dedication of the Temple, Solomon stood on a bronze 'scaffold' (2 Ch. 6:12f., Heb. *kîyyôr*, the word used for 'laver' elsewhere, Ex. 30:18, *etc.*; here it may denote an inverted basin), which has parallels in Syr. and Egyp. sculptures and possibly in Akkadian (see W. F. Albright, *Archaeology and the Religion of Israel*[3], 1953, pp. 152–154).

A flight of steps would have led up from the inner court to the *porch (Heb. *'ûlām*). The entrance was flanked by two pillars, *Jachin and Boaz, with elaborately ornamented capitals. Their purpose remains indeterminate; they were not part of the structure. Gates probably closed the passage (*cf.* Ezk. 40:48).

The porch was 10 cubits long and 20 cubits wide (on the length of the cubit, see *WEIGHTS AND MEASURES). Its height is given as 120 cubits (2 Ch. 3:4), but this is surely erroneous, as the remainder of the building was only 30 cubits high. W of the porch was the large chamber in which the ordinary rituals were performed. This 'holy place' (AV 'temple'; Heb. *hêkāl*, a word derived through Canaanite from Sumerian *é. gal*, 'great house') was 40 cubits long, 20 in breadth, and 30 high. It was shut off from the porch by double doors of cypress wood, each composed of two leaves. The doorposts were 'a fourth' (Heb. *mᵉzûzôṯ mē'ēṯ rᵉḇi'îṯ*, 1 Ki. 6:33; RSV 'in the form of a square' follows LXX); possibly the doorway was one-quarter of the width of the dividing wall (see A. R. Millard, *Eretz Israel* 20, 1989, pp. 135–139).

Latticed windows near the ceiling lighted the holy place (1 Ki. 6:4). Here stood the golden incense-*altar, the table for *showbread, and five pairs of *lampstands, together with the instruments of *sacrifice. The double doors of cypress leading to the inner sanctuary (Heb. *dᵉḇîr*, 'innermost place'; AV 'oracle' is an unlikely rendering) were rarely opened, probably only for the high priest at the atonement ceremony. The doorposts and lintel are said to have been a fifth (Heb. *hā'ayil mᵉzûzôṯ ḥᵃmiššîṯ*, 1 Ki. 6:31). As with the *hêkāl*, this may be explained as one-fifth of the dividing wall, 4 cubits.

The inner sanctuary was a perfect cube of 20 cubits. Although it might be expected that the floor was raised above the *hêkāl*, there is no hint of this. Within stood two wooden figures side by side, 10 cubits high. Two of their wings met in the centre above the *ark of the covenant, and the other wing of each touched the N and S walls respectively (1 Ki. 6:23–28; *CHERUBIM). In this most holy place the presence of God was shown by a cloud (1 Ki. 8:10f.).

Each room was panelled with cedar wood and the floor planked with cypress (or pine, Heb. *bᵉrôš*; *TREES). The walls and doors were carved with flowers, palm trees and cherubim, and overlaid with gold in the way approved for ancient temples, as inscriptions testify. No stonework was visible.

The outer walls of the inner sanctuary and the holy place were built with two offsets of 1 cubit to support the joists of three storeys of small chambers all around. Thus the ground-floor chambers were 5 cubits wide, those above 6, and the uppermost 7. A door in the S side gave access to a spiral staircase serving the upper floors. These rooms doubtless housed various stores and vestments, and offerings of goods and money, and maybe provided accommodation for the priests in course (see K. A. Kitchen, *Eretz Israel* 20, 1989, pp. 107–112).

Much has been made of the proximity of the royal palace to the Temple and the inference drawn that it was the 'Chapel Royal'. While admitting such a relationship (emphasized by the passage connecting the two buildings, 2 Ki. 16:18), it should be remembered that it was appropriate for the viceroy of Yahweh to reside near to the house of God; entry was not restricted to the king.

Solomon hired a Tyrian to take charge of the work and used Phoenician craftsmen (1 Ki. 5:10, 18; 7:13–14). It is not surprising to find parallels to the design of the Temple and its decoration in surviving examples of Phoenician or Canaanite handiwork. The ground plan is very similar to that of a small shrine of the 9th century BC excavated at Tell Tainat on the Orontes. This shows the three rooms, an altar in the innermost and two columns in the porch, but supporting the roof (for full report see R. C. Haines, *Excavations in the Plain of Antioch*, 2, 1971). At Hazor a Late Bronze Age shrine is also tripartite and was constructed with timbers between the stone-courses (Y. Yadin, *Hazor*, 1972, pp. 89–91; *cf.* 1 Ki. 5:18; 6:36). Numerous carved ivory panels (from the walls or furnishings of palaces) found throughout the ancient East are Phoenician work, often with Egyp. themes. Among the common subjects are flowers, palms and winged sphinxes, undoubtedly comparable with the carvings in the Temple. As with the Temple's panelling, these carvings were overlaid with gold and set with coloured stones.

c. Later history

Ancient temples generally served as state treasuries, emptied to pay tribute or filled and decorated with booty according to the power of the land. If, for some reason, a ruler paid little attention to the temple it would lose its revenue and rapidly fall into disrepair (*cf.* 2 Ki. 12:4–15). Solomon's Temple was no exception. The treasures which he had gathered in the Temple were raided in the reign of his son, Rehoboam, by Shishak of Egypt (1 Ki. 14:26). Later kings, including even Hezekiah, who had adorned the Temple (2 Ki. 18:15f.), used the treasure to purchase allies (Asa, 1 Ki. 15:18) or to pay tribute and buy off an invader (Ahaz, 2 Ki. 16:8). The idolatrous kings added the appurtenances of a Canaanite shrine, including the symbols of pagan deities (2 Ki. 21:4; 23:1–12), while Ahaz introduced an altar of foreign type, displacing the laver, at the time of his submission to Tiglath-pileser III (2 Ki. 16:10–17). By the time of Josiah (*c.* 640 BC), 3 centuries after its construction, the Temple was in need of considerable repair, which had to be financed by the contributions of the worshippers (2 Ki. 22:4). In 587 BC it was looted by Nebuchadrezzar and sacked (2 Ki. 25:9, 13–17). Even after the destruction men came to sacrifice there (Je. 41:5).

III. Ezekiel's Temple

The exiles were heartened in their grief (Ps. 137) by the vision of a new Temple granted to Ezekiel

(Ezk. 40–43, *c.* 571 BC). More details are given of this than of Solomon's structure, although it was never built. The actual shrine was different in little other than its size (porch 20 cubits wide, 12 long; holy place 20 cubits wide and 40 long; inner sanctuary 20 cubits each way). The walls were again panelled and carved with palms and cherubim. The building was set on a platform mounted by ten steps which were flanked by two bronze pillars. Three tiers of rooms enfolded the inner sanctuary and the holy place. The vision gives a description of the surrounding area, something lacking from the account of the first Temple. An area of 500 cubits square was enclosed by a wall pierced by a single gateway on each of the N, E and S sides. Three more gates, opposite the former, led to an inner courtyard, where the altar of sacrifice stood before the shrine. All these gates were well fortified to prevent the entry of any but Israelites. There were various buildings in the courtyards for storage and for the use of the priests.

IV. The Second Temple

This stood for almost 500 years, longer than either the first or Herod's Temple. Yet it is only vaguely known from incidental references. The exiles who returned (*c.* 537 BC) took with them the vessels looted by Nebuchadrezzar, and the authorization of Cyrus for the rebuilding of the Temple. Apparently the site was cleared of rubble, an altar built and the laying of the foundations commenced (Ezr. 1; 3:2–3, 8–10). A stretch of walling on the E side of the present enclosure, abutting the Herodian stonework, may be a part of these foundations. When eventually finished it was 60 cubits long and 60 cubits high, but even the foundations showed that it would be inferior to Solomon's Temple (Ezr. 3:12). Around the shrine were store-places and priests' rooms. From some of these Nehemiah expelled the Ammonite Tobiah (Ne. 13:4–9). 1 Macc. 1:21; 4:49–51 give information about the furnishings. The ark had disappeared at the time of the Exile and was never recovered or replaced. Instead of Solomon's ten lampstands, one seven-branched candelabrum stood in the holy place with the table for showbread and the incense altar. These were taken by Antiochus IV Epiphanes (*c.* 175–163 BC), who set up the 'desolating sacrilege' (a pagan altar or statue) on 15 December 167 BC (1 Macc. 1:54). The triumphant *Maccabees cleansed the Temple from this pollution and replaced the furniture late in 164 BC (1 Macc. 4:36–59). They also turned the enclosure into a fortress so strong that it resisted the siege of Pompey for 3 months (63 BC).

V. Herod's Temple

The building of Herod's Temple, commenced early in 19 BC, was an attempt to reconcile the Jews to their Idumaean king rather than to glorify God. Great care was taken to respect the sacred area during the work, even to the training of 1,000 priests as masons to build the shrine. Although the main structure was finished within 10 years (*c.* 9 BC), work continued until AD 64.

As a basis for the Temple buildings and to provide a gathering-place, an area about 450 m from N to S and about 300 m from E to W was made level. In places the rock surface was cut away, but a large part was built up with rubble and the whole enclosed by a wall of massive stone blocks (normally about 1m high and up to 5 m long; *cf.* Mk. 13:1). At the SE corner, overlooking the Kidron ravine, the inner courtyard was about 45 m above the rock. Perhaps the parapet above this corner was the pinnacle of the Temple (Mt. 4:5). Stretches of this wall still stand. One gateway pierced the N wall (Tadi Gate), but was apparently never used, and one led through the wall on the E (under the present Golden Gate). Traces of the two Herodian gates on the S side are still visible beneath the Mosque of el-Aqsa. Ramps led upwards from these to the level of the court. Four gates faced the city on the W. They were approached by viaducts across the Tyropoeon valley (*JERUSALEM). At the NW corner the fortress of Antonia dominated the enclosure. This was the residence of the procurators when in Jerusalem, and its garrison was always at hand to subdue any unrest in the Temple (*cf.* Lk. 13:1; Acts 21:31–35). The high priest's robes were stored therein as a token of subjection.

A portico surrounded the outer court. Josephus describes the South or Royal Porch as having four rows of columns (*Ant.* 15. 410–416). The porticoes of the other sides each had two rows. Solomon's Porch stretched along the E side (Jn. 10:23; Acts 3:11; 5:12). In these colonnades the scribes held their schools and debates (*cf.* Lk. 2:46; 19:47; Mk. 11:27) and the merchants and money-changers had their stalls (Jn. 2:14–16; Lk. 19:45–46). The inner area was raised slightly above the court of the Gentiles and surrounded by a balustrade. Notices in Gk. and Lat. warned that no responsibility could be taken for the probable death of any Gentile who ventured within. Two of these inscriptions have been found. Four gates gave access on the N and S sides and one on the E. This last had doors of Corinthian bronze-work and may be the Beautiful Gate of Acts 3:2.

The first court inside (Women's Court) contained the chests for gifts towards the expenses of the services (Mk. 12:41–44). Men were allowed into the Court of Israel, raised above the Court of the Women, and at the time of the Feast of Tabernacles could enter the innermost (Priests') Court to circumambulate the *altar. This was built of unhewn stone, 22 cubits away from the porch (*cf.* Mt. 23:35). The plan of the shrine copied Solomon's. The porch was 100 cubits wide and 100 cubits high. A doorway 20 cubits wide and 40 high gave entry, and one half that size led into the holy place. This was 40 cubits long and 20 cubits wide. A curtain divided the holy place from the inner sanctuary (the veil, Mt. 27:51; Mk. 15:38; *cf.* 2 Ch. 3:14). The inner sanctuary was 20 cubits square and, like the holy place, 40 cubits high. An empty room above the holy place and the inner sanctuary rose to the height of the porch, 100 cubits, thus making a level roof. Three storeys of chambers surrounded the N, S and W sides to a height of 40 cubits. Golden spikes were fixed on the roof to prevent birds from perching there.

Masonry uncovered since 1967 reveals the magnificence of the structure in beautifully cut cream stone with elaborately carved vaults. The building was barely finished (AD 64) before Roman soldiers destroyed it (AD 70). The golden candelabrum, the table of showbread and other objects were carried in triumph to Rome, as depicted on the Arch of Titus.

For organization of the Temple, see *Priests and Levites.

BIBLIOGRAPHY. The best summary is A. Parrot,

The Temple of Jerusalem, 1957, with a comprehensive bibliography. For a detailed survey, see L. H. Vincent, *Jérusalem de l'Ancien Testament*, 1–2, 1954; M. Ben-Dov, *In the Shadow of the Temple*, 1985. T. A. Busink, *Der Tempel von Jerusalem*, 1970; L. H. Vincent, 'Le temple hérodien d'après la Mišnah', *RB* 61, 1954, pp. 1–35; C. J. Davey, 'Temples of the Levant and the Buildings of Solomon', *TynB* 31, 1980, pp. 107–146. For reconstructions of Solomon's Temple, see G. E. Wright, *BA* 18, 1955, pp. 41–44. A.R.M.

VI. 'Temple' in the New Testament

Two Gk. words, *hieron* and *naos*, are translated 'temple'. The former refers to the complex of buildings which comprised the Temple of Jerusalem, the latter refers more specifically to the sanctuary. The term preferred by the NT writers to describe the church as the temple of God is *naos*, but not too much should be made of the distinction between *naos* and *hieron*. In Mt. 17.5 *naos* is almost certainly to be understood in the sense of *hieron*, otherwise we have the formidable difficulty of explaining how Judas penetrated the area which was closed to all except priests. The statement in Jn. 2:20, that 46 years were spent in building the *naos*, must have more than the sanctuary in mind. The use of *naos* as a synonym for *hieron* is also present in Herodotus (2. 170) and Jos. (*BJ* 5, 207–211).

With the literal use of 'temple' in the NT, *cf.* 'house' (*oikos*) and 'place' (*topos*). For a description of the Temple of Jerusalem in the time of Jesus, see V, above. The metaphorical use of 'temple' should be compared with the metaphorical use of 'house', 'building' (*oikodome*), 'tent' (*skene*), 'habitation' (*katoiketerion*; NRSV 'dwelling place').

a. 'Temple' in the Gospels

The gospels reflect two opposing attitudes on the part of Jesus to the Temple of Jerusalem. On the one hand, Jesus respected the temple; on the other hand, he attached relatively little importance to it. Thus, he called it the 'house of God' (Mt. 12:4; *cf.* Jn. 2:16) and said that everything was sanctified by God who dwelt in it (Mt. 23:17ff.). Concern for the abuses of the temple made him cleanse it (Mk. 11:11f. and parallels) and thought of the impending doom of Jerusalem caused him to weep (Lk. 19:41ff. *cf.* Mt. 23:37f.; parallels). In contrast are those passages in which Jesus relegated the temple to a subordinate position. It had become a cover for the nation's spiritual barrenness (Mk. 11:12–26 and parallels). Soon it would perish, for a terrible desecration would render it unfit to exist (Mk. 13:1f., 14ff.). Climatically, the death of Jesus caused the veil of the temple to be rent in two (Mk. 14:38 and parallels). See also Mk. 14:57f., 15:29f. and parallels. These differing attitudes are not, however, without explanation.

At the beginning of his ministry Jesus addressed himself to the Jews and summoned all Israel to repentance. (Mk. 1:14ff.). In spite of mounting opposition, we find him appealing to Jerusalem (Mk. 11:1ff. and parallels). The Temple was cleansed with a view to reforming the existing order (11:15ff. and parallels). But the implications of this action (Mal. 3:1ff.; *cf. Psalms of Solomon* 17:32ff.; Mk. 11:27ff.) engendered still greater hostility on the part of the religious leaders, and Judaism, persistently unreformable, was in the end judged as unworthy of the divine presence (Mk. 12:1–12). So Jesus, who began by venerating the Temple, finally announced that his rejection and death would issue in its destruction. The accusation produced at the trial which asserted that Jesus had taught, 'I will destroy this temple that is made with hands, and in three days I will build another not made with hands' (Mk. 14:58; *cf.* 15:29) would therefore be a fitting peroration to the appeal of our Lord. Mark attributes the saying, however, to false witnesses, and what constituted the falsity of the witness is a matter of conjecture among scholars. It is probably wisest to understand the charge as an unscrupulous combination of the prediction of Jesus that the Temple of Jerusalem would be destroyed (Mk. 13:2 and parallels) and the logion that the Son of man would be destroyed and rise again on the third day (Mk. 8:31; 9:31; 10:34 and parallels). That is to say, the falsity lay in misrepresentation of what Jesus actually had taught. One reason why Mark did not trouble to correct the misrepresentation may be due to the fact that the accusation was true in a deeper sense than the witnesses had in mind. The death of Jesus did in fact result in the supersession of the Temple of Jerusalem, and his resurrection put another in its place. The new temple was the eschatological congregation of Jesus Messiah (Mt. 18:20; *cf.* Jn. 14:23). Luke and John, therefore, made no reference to the false witness because when they wrote their Gospels the accusation was no longer seen to be groundless.

b. 'Temple' in the Acts of the Apostles

Some time elapsed, however, before the full ramifications of the work of Christ became apparent, and in the Acts we find the apostles continuing to worship at the Temple of Jerusalem (Acts 2:46; 3:1ff.; 5:12, 20f., 42; *cf.* Lk. 24:52). It appears that the Hellenistic-Jewish party represented by Stephen was the first to discover that belief in Jesus as Messiah meant the abrogation of the order symbolized by the Jerusalem Temple (Acts 6:11ff.). Accordingly, Stephen's defence became an attack on the Temple, or, more correctly, on the attitude of mind to which the Temple gave rise (Acts 7). But whether it is justifiable to find in Stephen's denunciation of the Temple a hint of the new temple made without hands, as some commentators do, is not at all certain. The 'tabernacle of David' of Am. 9:11 is used in Acts 15:13–18, but it is doubtful if this is hinting that the church is God's new temple, even though the same OT text is spiritualized at CDC 7.16, *cf.* 4Q Florilegium 1:11–12. But the use of Am. 9:11 in the eschatology of the Covenanters of Qumran to support their novel conception of a spiritual temple (CDC 3. 9) permits us to see here an adumbration of the doctrine of the church as God's new temple which is so common a feature of the Epistles.

c. 'Temple' in the Epistles

The doctrine of the church as the realization of the eschatological temple of OT and intertestamental writings is most prominent in the epistles of Paul. See 1 Cor. 3:16–17; 6:19; 2 Cor. 6:16–7:1; Eph. 2:19–22. The appeal to prophecy is particularly strong in the case of 2 Cor. 6:16ff., where we have an OT couplet (Lv. 26:12; Ezk. 37:27) which was already in use in Jewish eschatology on the Messianic temple (*Jubilees* 1:17). Also characteristic of the temple image in 1 and 2 Cor. is its hortatory and admonitory application. Since Christians are the realization of the long-cherished hope of the glorious temple, they ought to live holy lives (2 Cor. 7:1; *cf.* 1 Cor. 6:18ff.). Unity is likewise enjoined upon them. Since God is one, there is only one habitation in which he can dwell. Schism is tantamount to profanation of the temple, and merits the same terrible penalty of death (1 Cor. 3:5–17). In Eph. the figure of the temple is employed in the interests of doctrinal instruction. Uppermost in the mind of the writer is the interracial character of the church. The language of the context of 2:19–22 makes it plain that the apostle borrowed liberally from the OT hope of the ingathering of Israel and the nations to the eschatological temple at Jerusalem. For example, the words 'far' and 'near' of vv. 13 and 17 (*cf.* Is. 57:19; Dn. 9:7) were rabbinic technical terms for the Gentiles and the Jews (*Numbers Rabbah* 8:4). Similarly, the 'peace' mentioned in vv. 14 and 17 is an allusion to the eschatological peace which was to prevail when Israel and the nations were united in the one cult at Zion (Is. 2:2ff.; Mi. 4:1ff.; *Enoch* 90:29ff.). Paul undoubtedly regarded the fruits of his Gentile mission as the fulfilment of Jewish faith at its widest and most generous expression. He spiritualized the ancient hope of a reunited mankind, and represented Jews and Gentiles as the two walls of one building, joined by and resting upon Christ, the foremost cornerstone (Eph. 2:19–22). The statement that the building 'grows' (*auxein*) into a 'temple' introduces a different figure, *viz.* that of the body, and reveals a certain fusion of images. 'Temple' and 'body' are largely coterminous ideas of the church. Note the juxtaposition of the two conceptions in Eph. 4:12, 16.

Parallels for Paul's use of the metaphor in 1 and 2 Cor. are sometimes sought in the writings of Philo and the Stoics, where the individual is called a 'temple'. The practice is scarcely justifiable, however. 1 Cor. 6:19–20 does indeed have the individual in mind, but only as a member of the community which corporately comprises the temple of God. Philo and the Graeco-Roman humanists spiritualized the word 'temple' for the sake of anthropology, whereas the NT was occupied with ecclesiology and eschatology and had only a very secondary interest in anthropology. If comparisons are desired one may look for them with greater justification in the writings of the Jews of Qumran (1QS. 5. 6; 8. 4–10; 9. 5–6).

With 'temple' in the Pauline corpus *cf.* 'house' in 1 Pet. 2:4–10, where it is manifest that the numerous allusions in the NT to the priestly and sacrificial character of Christian life stem from the conception of the church as God's sanctuary. See also 'house' in Heb. 3:1–6.

d. 'Temple' in Hebrews and Revelation

The idea of a heavenly temple, which was common among the Semites and which helped to sustain Jewish hope when the exigencies of the intertestamental period made it appear that the Temple of Jerusalem would never become the metropolis of the world, was adopted by the early Christians. Allusions to it are present in Jn. 1:51; 14:2f.; Gal. 4:21ff.; and possibly in Phil. 3:20. The 'building from God . . . eternal in the heavens' in the notoriously difficult passage 2 Cor. 5:1–5 may also bear some connection with the idea. The conception is, of course, most developed in Heb. and Rev.

According to the writer to the Hebrews the sanctuary in heaven is the pattern (*typos*), *i.e.* the original (*cf.* Ex. 25:8f.), and the one on earth used by Jewry is a 'copy and shadow' (Heb. 8:5). The heavenly sanctuary is therefore the true sanctuary (Heb. 9:24). It belongs to the people of the new covenant (Heb. 6:19–20). Moreover, the fact that Christ our High Priest is in this sanctuary means that we, although still on earth, already participate in its worship (10:19ff.; 12:22ff.). What is this temple? The writer supplies a clue when he says that the heavenly sanctuary was cleansed (9:23), *i.e.* made fit for use (*cf.* Nu. 7:1). The assembly of the first-born (Heb. 12:23), that is to say, the church triumphant, is the heavenly temple (*TABERNACLE).

The heavenly temple in Rev. is part of the grand scheme of spiritualization undertaken by the author, and note should also be taken of the heavenly Mt Zion (14:1; 21:10) and the new Jerusalem (3:12; 21:2ff.). In point of fact, the prophet of Patmos was shown two temples, one in heaven and the other on earth. The latter is in mind in 11:1ff. The harassed church on earth is depicted under the guise of the Temple of Jerusalem, or, more accurately, the sanctuary of the Temple of Jerusalem, for the forecourt, that is, the lukewarm who are on the fringe of the church, is excluded from the measurement. The imagery owes something to Zc. 2:5, and appears to have the same meaning as the sealing of the 144,000 in 7:1–8. Those measured, alias the numbered, are the elect whom God protects.

Similar spiritualizing is evident in the author's vision of the temple in heaven. On the top of Mt Zion he sees not a magnificent edifice, but the company of the redeemed (14:1; *cf.* 13:6). That John intends his readers to regard the martyr-host as taking the place of a temple is hinted at in 3:12: 'He who conquers, I will make him a pillar in the temple of my God.' The heavenly temple thus 'grows', like its earthly counterpart (see above on Eph. 2:21f.), as each of the faithful seals his testimony with martyrdom. The building will eventually be completed when the decreed number of the elect is made up (6:11). It is from this temple of living beings that God sends out his judgment upon impenitent nations (11:19; 14:15ff.; 15:5–16:1), just as he once directed the destinies of the nations from the Temple of Jerusalem (Is. 66:6; Mi. 1:2; Hab. 2:10).

The new Jerusalem has no temple (21:22). In a document like Rev. which follows the traditional images and motifs so closely, the idea of a Jerusalem without a Temple is surely novel. John's statement that he 'saw no temple in the city' has been taken to mean that the whole city is a temple; note that the shape of the city is cubical (21:16), like the holy of holies in Solomon's Temple (1 Ki. 6:20). But that is not what John says. He states plainly that God and the Lamb is the Temple. What he very likely means is that in the place of the temple is God and his Son. Such indeed would appear to be the grand dénouement for which the writer prepares his readers. First he dramatically announces that the temple in heaven is opened and its contents laid bare for human eyes to see (11:19). Later he drops the hint that the divine dwelling may be none other than God himself (21:3; note the play on the words *skēnē* and *skēnōsei*). Finally, he states quite simply that the temple is the Lord God Almighty and the Lamb. One after another the barriers separating worshippers from God are removed until nothing remains to hide God from his people. 'His servants . . . shall see his face' (22:3f.; *cf.* Is. 25:6ff.).

This is the glorious privilege of all who enter the new Jerusalem.

The use made of the ancient motif of the ingathering and reunion of Israel and the nations at the eschatological temple by the author of Rev. is thus different from, although complementary to, that of Paul. Paul, as we noted above, applied it to the terrestrial church; John projects it into the heavenly realm and into the world to come. The difference is another illustration of the flexibility of the Temple image.

BIBLIOGRAPHY. P. Bonnard, *Jésus Christ* édi *fiant son Église*, 1948; Y. M. J. Congar, *The Mystery of the Temple*, 1961; A. Cody, *Heavenly Sanctuary and Liturgy in the Epistle to the Hebrews*, 1960; J. Comblin, 'La Liturgie de la Nouvella Jérusalem (Apoc. 21.1–22.5)', *Ephremerides Theologicae Lovanienses 29*, 1953, pp. 5–40; C. J. Davey, *TynB* 31, 1980, pp. 107–146; M. Fraeyman, 'La spiritualisation de l'idée du Temple dans épîtres paulininennes', *ETL* 23, 1947, pp. 378–412; B. Gärtner, *The Temple and the Community in Qumran and the New Testament*, 1965,; J. Jeremias, 'Eckstein-Schlusstein', *ZNW* 36, 1937, pp. 154–157; D. Juel, *Messiah and Temple*, 1977: G. Kittel, *TDNT*, *s.v. hieron, naos, oikodome, oikos, skene: C. R. Koester, The Dwelling of God*: 1989; I. H. Marshall, 'Church and Temple in the New Testament', *TB* 40:2, 1989, pp. 203–222; R. J. McKelvey, *The New Temple*, 1969, C. F. D. Moule, 'Sanctuary and Sacrifice in the New Testament', *JTS* (n.s.) 1, 1950, pp. 29–41; E. P. Sanders, *Jesus and Judaism*, 1985; M. Simon, 'Le discours de Jésus sur la ruine de Temple', *RB* 56, 1949, pp. 70–75; R. Schnackenburg, 'Die Kirche als Bau: Epheser 2:19–22 unter ökumenischem Aspekt'; *Paul and Paulinism*, M. D. Hooker and S. G. Wilson (eds.) 1982, pp. 258–270; W. R. Telford, *The Barren Temple and the Withered Tree*, 1980; P. Vielhauer, *Oikodome*, 1989; H. Wenschkewitz, 'Die Spiritualisierung der Kultusbegriffe Tempel, Priester und Opfer im Neuen Testament', *Angelos* 4, 1932, pp. 77–230. R.J.McK.

TEMPTATION. The biblical idea of temptation is not primarily of seduction, as in modern usage, but of making trial of a person, or putting him to the test; which may be done for the benevolent purpose of proving or improving his quality, as well as with the malicious aim of showing up his weaknesses or trapping him into wrong action. 'Tempt' in AV means 'test' in this unrestricted sense, in accordance with older English usage. It is only since the 17th century that the word's connotation has been limited to testing with evil intent.

The Heb. noun is *massâ* (EVV 'temptation'); the Heb. verbs are *māsâ* (EVV usually 'tempt') and *bāḥan* (EVV usually 'prove' or 'try': a metaphor from metal refining). The LXX and NT use as equivalents the noun *peirasmos* and the verbs *(ek)peirazō* and *dokimazō*, the latter corresponding in meaning to *bāḥan*.

The idea of testing a person appears in various connections throughout the Bible.

1. Men test their fellow human beings, as one tests armour (1 Ki. 10:1; *cf.* 1 Sa. 17:39; *māsâ* both times), to explore and measure their capacities. The Gospels tell of Jewish opponents, with resentful scepticism, 'testing' Christ ('trying him out', we might say) to see if they could make him prove, or try to prove, his Messiahship to them on their terms (Mk. 8:11); to see if his doctrine was defective or unorthodox (Lk. 10:25); and to see if they could trap him into self-incriminating assertions (Mk. 12:15).

2. Men should test themselves before the Lord's Supper (1 Cor. 11:28: *dokimazō*), and at other times too (2 Cor. 13:5: *peirazō*), lest they become presumptuous and deluded about their spiritual state. The Christian needs to test his 'work' (*i.e.* what he is making of his life), lest he go astray and forfeit his reward (Gal. 6:4). Sober self-knowledge, arising from disciplined self-scrutiny, is a basic element in biblical piety.

3. Men test God by behaviour which constitutes in effect a defiant challenge to him to prove the truth of his words and the goodness and justice of his ways (Ex. 17:2; Nu. 14:22; Pss. 78:18, 41, 56; 95:9; 106:14; Mal. 3:15; Acts 5:9; 15:10). The place-name Massah was a permanent memorial of one such temptation (Ex. 17:7; Dt. 6:16). Thus to goad God betrays extreme irreverence, and God himself forbids it (Dt. 6:16; *cf.* Mt. 4:7; 1 Cor. 10:9ff.). In all distresses God's people should wait on him in quiet patience, confident that in due time he will meet their need according to his promise (*cf.* Pss. 27:7–14; 37:7; 40; 130:5ff.; La. 3:25ff.; Phil. 4:19).

4. God tests his people by putting them in situations which reveal the quality of their faith and devotion, so that all can see what is in their hearts (Gn. 22:1; Ex. 16:4; 20:20; Dt. 8:2, 16; 13:3; Jdg. 2:22; 2 Ch. 32:31). By thus making trial of them, he purifies them, as metal is purified in the refiner's crucible (Ps. 66:10; Is. 48:10; Zc. 13:9; 1 Pet. 1:6f.; *cf.* Ps. 119:67, 71); he strengthens their patience and matures their Christian character (Jas. 1:2ff., 12; *cf.* 1 Pet. 5:10); and he leads them into an enlarged assurance of his love for them (*cf.* Gn. 22:15ff.; Rom. 5:3ff.). Through faithfulness in times of trial men become *dokimoi*, 'approved', in God's sight (Jas. 1:12; 1 Cor. 11:19).

5. Satan tests God's people by manipulating circumstances, within the limits that God allows him (*cf.* Jb. 1:12; 2:6; 1 Cor. 10:13), in an attempt to make them desert God's will. The NT knows him as 'the tempter' (*ho peirazōn*, Mt. 4:3; 1 Thes. 3:5), the implacable foe of both God and men (1 Pet. 5:8; Rev. 12). Christians must constantly be watchful (Mk. 14:38; Gal. 6:1; 2 Cor. 2:11) and active (Eph. 6:10ff.; Jas. 4:7; 1 Pet. 5:9) against the devil, for he is always at work trying to make them fall; whether by crushing them under the weight of hardship or pain (Jb. 1:11–2:7; 1 Pet. 5:9; Rev. 2:10; *cf.* 3:10; Heb. 2:18), or by urging them to a wrong fulfilment of natural desires (Mt. 4:3f.; 1 Cor. 7:5), or by making them complacent, careless and self-assertive (Gal. 6:1; Eph. 4:27), or by misrepresenting God to them and engendering false ideas of his truth and his will (Gn. 3:1–5; *cf.* 2 Cor. 11:3; Mt. 4:5ff.; 2 Cor. 11:14; Eph. 6:11). Mt. 4:5f. shows that Satan can even quote (and misapply) Scripture for this purpose. But God promises that a way of deliverance will always be open when he allows Satan to tempt Christians (1 Cor. 10:13; 2 Pet. 2:9; *cf.* 2 Cor. 12:7–10).

The NT philosophy of temptation is reached by combining these last two lines of thought. 'Trials' (Lk. 22:28; Acts 20:19; Jas. 1:2; 1 Pet. 1:6; 2 Pet. 2:9) are the work of both God and the devil. They are testing situations in which the servant of God faces new possibilities of both good and evil, and is exposed to various inducements to prefer the latter. From this standpoint, temptations are Satan's work; but Satan is God's tool as well as his foe (*cf.*

Jb. 1:11f.; 2:5f.), and it is ultimately God himself who leads his servants into temptation (Mt. 4:1; 6:13), permitting Satan to try to seduce them for beneficent purposes of his own. However, though temptations do not overtake men apart from God's will, the actual prompting to do wrong is not of God, nor does it express his command (Jas. 1:12f.). The desire which impels to sin is not God's, but one's own, and it is fatal to yield to it (Jas. 1:14ff.). Christ taught his disciples to ask God not to expose them to temptation (Mt. 6:13), and to watch and pray, lest they should 'enter into' temptation (*i.e.* yield to its pressure) when at any time God saw fit to try them by it (Mt. 26:41).

Temptation is not sin, for Christ was tempted as we are, yet remained sinless (Heb. 4:15; *cf.* Mt. 4:1ff.; Lk. 22:28). Temptation becomes sin only when and as the suggestion of evil is accepted and yielded to.

BIBLIOGRAPHY. *BAGD*; H. Seeseman in *TDNT* 6, pp. 23–26; M. Dods in *DCG*; R. C. Trench, *Synonyms of the New Testament*[10], pp. 267ff.; W. Schneider, C. Brown, H. Haarbeck, *NIDNTT* 3, pp. 798–811. J.I.P.

TEN COMMANDMENTS. The 'ten words' (Heb. *d^ebārîm*; *cf.* Ex. 34:28; Dt. 4:13; 10:4) were originally uttered by the divine voice from Sinai in the hearing of all Israel (Ex. 19:16–20:17). Afterwards, they were twice written by the finger of God on both sides of two tables of stone (Ex. 31:18; 32:15–16; 34:1, 28; *cf.* Dt. 10:4). Moses shattered the first pair, symbolizing Israel's breaking of the covenant by the sin of the golden calf (Ex. 32:19). The second pair were deposited in the ark (Ex. 25:16; 40:20). Later, Moses republished the Ten Commandments in slightly modified form (Dt. 5:6–21).

The common designation of the contents of the two tables as 'the Decalogue', though it has biblical precedent, has tended to restrict unduly the general conception of their nature. To classify this revelation as law is not adequate; it belongs to the broader category of covenant. The terminology 'covenant' (Heb. *b^erîṯ*; Dt. 4:13) and 'the words of the covenant' (Ex. 34:28; *cf.* Dt. 29:1, 9) is applied to it. It is also identified as the 'testimony' (Heb. *'ēḏûṯ*; Ex. 25:16, 21; 40:20; *cf.* 2 Ki. 17:15), which describes the covenant order of life as one solemnly imposed and sworn to so that *'ēḏûṯ* becomes practically synonymous with *b^erîṯ*. The two tables are called 'the tables of the covenant' (Dt. 9:9, 11, 15) or 'testimony' (Ex. 31:18; 32:15; 34:29).

The historical occasion of the original giving of this revelation was the establishment of the theocratic covenant. The principles of Ex. 20:2–17 as elaborated and applied in casuistic form in the book of the covenant (Ex. 20:22–23:33) served as a legal instrument in the ratification of that covenant (Ex. 24:1–8). The later, Deuteronomic, version is part of a document of covenant renewal.

When, therefore, the Scripture designates the revelation of the two tables as 'the ten words', it clearly does so as *pars pro toto.* At the same time, this terminology and the preponderance of law content which it reflects indicates that the type of covenant involved is essentially the establishment of a kingdom order under the lordship of the covenant suzerain.

The covenantal character of the Decalogue is illuminated and corroborated by ancient international treaties of the type used to formalize the relationship of a suzerain and vassal (*COVENANT). Suzerainty treaties began with a preamble identifying the covenant lord, the speaker (*cf.* Ex. 20:2a), and a historical prologue recounting especially the benefits previously bestowed on the vassal through the favour and might of the lord (*cf.* Ex. 20:2b). The obligations imposed on the vassal, the longest section, followed. The foremost stipulation was the requirement of loyalty to the covenant lord or negatively the proscription of all alien alliances (*cf.* Ex. 20:3–17, the first and great principle of which is whole-hearted love of Yahweh, who is a jealous God). Another section enunciated the curses and blessings which the gods of the covenant oath would visit on the vassals in accordance with their transgressions or fidelity. These sanctions were sometimes interspersed among the stipulations (*cf.* Ex. 20:5b, 6, 7b, 12b). Among other parallels are the 'I–thou' style, the practice of placing a copy of the treaty in the sanctuaries of the two parties, and the administrative policy of renewing the covenant with the successive generations of the vassal kingdom. In covenant renewal documents, modification of the stipulations to meet new conditions was customary. That explains the various differences between the Ex. 20 and Dt. 5 forms of the Decalogue. For example, Dt. 5:21 adds 'his field' because of the relevance of land ownership to Israel's now imminent inheritance of Canaan.

In brief, the two tables contained the essence of the Sinaitic Covenant. Yahweh, Creator of heaven, earth, sea and all that is in them, is presented as covenant Suzerain. The theocratic covenant relationship is traced to Yahweh's redemptive election and deliverance, and its continuance to the thousandth generation is attributed to his faithful mercies. The covenant way of life is sovereignly dictated in ten commandments, the standard of Israel's consecration to her Lord.

The very fact that the law is embedded in divine covenant disclosure points to the religious principle of personal devotion to God as the heart of true fulfilment of the law. But there is no incompatibility between the divine demand communicated in concrete imperatives and the call of God to personal commitment to him in love. Yahweh describes the beneficiaries of his covenant mercy as 'those who love me and keep my commandments' (Ex. 20:6; *cf.* Jn. 14:15). The biblical ethic is rooted in biblical religion, and biblical religion is not shapeless mysticism but a structured order.

The revelation of the law in the context of redemptive covenant action indicates that conformity to the law must be a gracious accomplishment of Yahweh, saving from bondage. In this context even the preponderantly negative form of the Decalogue serves to magnify the grace of God, who presents this protest against man's sin not as a final condemnation but as a summons to the godliness which is the goal of restored covenantal communion. The negative form thus becomes a divine promise to the redeemed servants of perfect ultimate triumph over the demonic power that would enslave them in the hell of endless alienation from God. An ethic rooted in such religion possesses the dynamic of faith, hope and love.

The laws of the Decalogue are formulated in terms appropriate to the covenantal order for which it was the treaty-constitution. For example, the specific form of the sabbath law reflects the OT eschatological perspective and the promise appended to the fifth word (and elsewhere related to the entire law, *cf.* Dt. 5:33–6:3) employs the imagery of the contemporary, typical manifestation of God's kingdom. This does not mean the Ten Commandments are not normative for covenant life today; but in determining their precise application we must always reckon with our eschatological location.

As for the division into ten words, the Decalogue's parallelism with the suzerainty treaty structure shows the error of regarding the preamble and historical prologue as a commandment. Also, the variant forms of the prohibition of covetousness in Ex. 20:17 and Dt. 5:21 contradict the division of it into two commandments, and that obviates the associated error of combining into one what most Protestants, following the oldest tradition, have regarded as the first and second commandments. The customary division of the Decalogue into 'two tables' stems from failure to recognize the two tables as duplicate treaty texts.

Speculative higher criticism, though postulating an early (even Mosaic) Decalogue, regards the canonical form as the result of later expansive revisions. Such a reconstruction is incompatible with the form-critical identification of the treaty-nature of the Decalogue, for treaties were not subject to revisionary tampering. Moreover, the treaty form called for by the covenantal context of Sinai would be lost in the shrunken hypothetical original. The theory that Ex. 34:11–26 is a primitive cultic 'decalogue' rests on a mistaken identification of this passage with the 'ten words' mentioned in Ex. 34:28. The actual relation of Ex. 34:5–27 to the second two Decalogue texts (Ex. 34:1–4, 28) is akin to that of Ex. 20:22–23:33 to the original tables.

BIBLIOGRAPHY. R. E. Davies, *Making Sense of the Commandments*, 1990; B.-Z. Segal (ed.), *The Ten Commandments in History and Tradition*, 1990.

M.G.K.

TENT. A collapsible structure of cloth or skins supported on poles, and often held firm by cords stretched from the poles to pegs or stakes fixed in the ground all round. Compare Is. 54:2, which mentions the curtains, cords, stakes or tent-pegs (but not the poles); the tent-cloth was often dark in colour (Ct. 1:5). Tents were among the earliest habitations made by man himself (Gn. 4:20; 9:21). They were the normal dwelling of both nomadic and semi-nomadic people. The Heb. Patriarchs lived in tents (Gn. 18:1, 6, 9–10, *etc.*); and the womenfolk sometimes had their own tents (Sarah, Gn. 24:67; Jacob, Leah, the maids, Rachel, Gn. 31:33), doubtless adjoining those of their husbands. On their journeyings from Egypt to Canaan, Israel lived in tents (Ex. 16:16; 33:8, 10; Nu. 16:26; 19:14), taking up more permanent dwellings when occupying Canaan. In the days of Jeremiah, the Rechabite sect held to the nomadic ideal of dwelling in tents and scorned the ways of sedentary life (Je. 35:7), but even the romantic ideal of independent tent-nomadism was not to be treasured above devotion to God (Ps. 84:10). Death is compared to packing up the tent in Jb. 4:21; *cf.* 2 Cor. 5:1.

Among other peoples, Scripture mentions the tents of the Midianites (Jdg. 6:5; 7:13), of Kedar (Ct. 1:5), and Cushan (Hab. 3:7, also Midian), all dwellers in the desert fringes of Transjordania and NW Arabia. Tents had specific uses in settled nations. Besides the peaceful shepherd tenting in his pastures (Ct. 1:8; Is. 38:12), kings and armies camped in tents in the field, *cf.* 1 Sa. 17:54 (David); 2 Ki. 7:7–8 (Aramaeans). Finally, 'tent' in ordinary speech came to be used of any kind of dwelling (not only literally; *cf.* 1 Ki. 8:66; 2 Ki. 13:5, both rendered 'homes' in RSV), perhaps because the tent was largely used in the summer by many town and village dwellers. The external data on tents illustrate that in Scripture. In the patriarchal period the Egyptian Sinuhe in Canaan had a tent and encampment and plundered that of his adversary (*ANET*, p. 20b, line 145). In the period following Israel's Exodus and initial settlement, Rameses III (*c.* 1192–1161 BC) records that he 'devastated Se'ir (*i.e.* Edom) among the nomadic tribes, and pillaged their tents (*'hr*, from Heb. *'ōhel*) of people and goods' (*ANET*, 262a). *Cf.* Midian, Cushan or Kedar. For pictures of Assyr. military tents (round, supported on poles and sticks), see *ANEP*, figs. 170–171, 374 (royal war-tent). Tents of patriarchal age, *cf.* D. J. Wiseman, in G. A. Tuttle (ed.), *Biblical and Near Eastern Studies* (Essays in Honor of W. S. LaSor), 1978. (*TABERNACLE.)

K.A.K.

TERAH. 1. The father of Abram, Nahor and Haran (Gn. 11:27; AV 'Thara', Lk. 3:34). Heb. *teraḥ* is usually taken as connected with the moon-god and compared with Turaḫi, a place near Harran. Terah emigrated from Ur of the Chaldees and settled in Harran, where he died long after Abram's departure (Acts 7:4 is an oral slip). In Jos. 24:2 he is described as an idolater.

2. An unidentified Israelite encampment in the wilderness between Tahath and Mithkah (Nu. 33:27–28; AV 'Tarah').

J.W.C.

TERAPHIM. These objects are mentioned in every OT period: the Patriarchs (Gn. 31:19); the judges (Jdg. 17:5–18:30); early and late Monarchy (1 Sa. 15:23; 19:13–16; 2 Ki. 23:24; Ho. 3:4; Ezk. 21:21; and post-exile (Zc. 10:2). When mentioned in Israelite contexts they are almost always condemned, directly (1 Sa. 15:23; 2 Ki. 23:24) or indirectly (Jdg. 17:6; Zc. 10:2). In their use, they are mostly associated with *divination: note the pairing of ephod and teraphim in the idolatrous religion of Micah (Jdg. 17:5, *etc.*); the association with divination by arrows and hepatoscopy (Ezk. 21:21), and with spiritist practices (2 Ki. 23:24). Nowhere are we told how they were consulted, nor even what their appearance was. While Gn. 31:34 suggests that they were small objects, 1 Sa. 19:13–16 suggests a life-size figure, or at least a life-size bust. However, it is possible that Michal placed the teraphim 'beside' rather than 'in' the bed, and that they were considered to have some prophylactic or curative propensity. W. F. Albright (*Archaeology and the Religion of Israel*, 1942, p. 114) reasonably urges that all available evidence is against the former view in that 'no "idols" of comparable size have ever been found in Palestine excavations'. He further suggests (*op. cit.*, p. 207) that, from a Canaanite *trp*, 'to wear out', the 'teraphim' in question here might not be any sort of figure but 'old rags', presumably used to simulate the recumbent figure of David.

These last two references (also Jdg. 17:5ff.) associate *tᵉrāpîm* with the home, and Laban, at least, considered them as household gods (Gn. 31:30). The suggestion that Rachel's theft of her father's gods (Gn. 31:19, 30–35) signified an inheritance claim on the basis of Nuzi custom can no longer be sustained, however. Possession of household gods at Nuzi probably indicated family headship, but such a privilege was given, not seized (see M. Greenberg, *JBL* 81, 1962, pp. 239–248; see further, M. J. Selman, *TynB* 27, 1976, pp. 123–124). Rachel's purpose can only be surmised, but examples from Mesopotamia suggest that she may have desired protection on the dangerous journey to Palestine.

Heb. *tᵉrāp̄îm* is a plural form, for which the corresponding singular is unknown. Possible derivations have been proposed from *rāp̄ā'*, 'to heal', or post-biblical *tōrep̄*, 'obscenity' (W. F. Albright, *From the Stone Age to Christianity*, 1957, p. 311), but the most likely association is with Hittite *tarpiš*, a type of spirit, sometimes evil, sometimes protective (H. A. Hoffner, *POTT*, pp. 215ff.; *JNES* 27, 1968, pp. 61–68). Other suggestions have connected *tᵉrāp̄îm* with ancestor worship, perhaps in the form of an ancestor's mask (A. Phillips, *Ancient Israel's Criminal Law*, 1970, p. 61) or mummified human heads (H. L. Ellison, *Ezekiel: The Man and his Message*, 1956).

BIBLIOGRAPHY. H. A. Hoffner, *BS* 124, 1967, pp. 230–238; *idem*, *JNES* 27, 1968, pp. 61–68; K. van der Toorn, *CBQ* 52, 1990, pp. 203–222.

J.A.M.
M.J.S.

TERTIUS. The amanuensis who wrote Romans at Paul's dictation (Rom. 16:22); on the process, see B. M. Metzger, 'Stenography and Church History', in *TCERK*, 2, pp. 1060f., and references there. He appends his own greetings, perhaps at the point where he resumes his pen after Paul has written some personal greetings in autograph (*cf.* Gal. 6:11; Col. 4:18; 2 Thes. 3:17). This may suggest that he had Roman connections himself. The name is Latin and appears in a 1st-century inscription in the Roman cemetery of St Priscilla (cited in *MM*).

A.F.W.

TERTULLUS. A fairly common Rom. name, in origin a diminutive of Tertius. Nothing is known of the orator Tertullus who accused Paul before Felix except what can be deduced from Acts 24:1ff.

From his use of the first person in vv. 3–4 and 6–7 (although found only in the Western Text, v. 7 is undoubtedly genuine) it seems probable that Tertullus was a Jew. The words 'this nation' (v. 2) and 'the Jews' (v. 5) are not inconsistent with this deduction. It was not uncommon for Jews at this period to have Gentile names, and it was possible for a good Jew to be also a Roman citizen, with a Roman name, like Paul.

The fulsome flattery of Felix in Tertullus' opening sentences is in accordance with the rhetorical fashion of the period, but the rest of the speech is unimpressive. Even in his précis Luke makes it clear that Tertullus was trying to cover up a weak case with rhetorical padding.

In addition to the real charge that Paul had attempted to 'profane the temple', Tertullus tries to represent him as one of the sedition-mongers and Messianist politicians who were so often a problem to the Rom. rulers of Palestine.

K.L.McK.

TETRARCH. This title (Gk. *tetraarchēs*, contracted *tetrarchēs*) was used in classical Gk. to denote the ruler of a fourth part of a region, and especially applied to the rulers of the four regions of Thessaly. The Romans gave it to any ruler of part of an Oriental province. When Herod the Great, who ruled Palestine as a client-king under the Romans, died in 4 BC, his sons disputed their father's will. Appeal on their part to Augustus Caesar led to the division of the territory among three sons: Archelaus being appointed *ethnarch of Judaea, Samaria and Idumaea; Antipas tetrarch of Galilee and Peraea; and Philip tetrarch of Batanea, Trachonitis, Ituraea, Gaulanitis and Auranitis, areas NE of the Sea of Galilee. In the NT the noun is used solely in reference to Herod Antipas (Mt. 14:1; Lk. 3:19; 9:7; Acts 13:1), though in Lk. 3:1 the cognate verb is applied to *Antipas, *Philip and *Lysanias, tetrarch of Abilene.

BIBLIOGRAPHY. S. Perowne, *The Later Herods*, 1958; H. W. Hoehner, *Herod Antipas*, 1972.

D.H.W.

TEXTS AND VERSIONS. Texts and versions provide the raw materials for the discipline known as textual criticism. The ultimate aim is to provide a text in the form intended by its author. Generally speaking, the greater the age of a document, the greater is its authority. There may be cases, however, where this does not hold; for instance, of two MSS, the older may have been copied from a recent and poor exemplar, while the other goes back to a very much earlier and better one. The history of a document must be taken into consideration before a verdict can be given on readings.

Documents are exposed to the ravages of time and the frailty of human nature, and the latter gives rise to most of our problems. The errors of scribes, however, seem to run in well-defined channels. Among common errors are:
1. *haplography* (failure to repeat a letter or word); 2. *dittography* (repeating what occurs only once); 3. *false recollection* (of a similar passage or of another MS); 4. *homoeoteleuton* (omission of a passage between identical words); 5. *line omission* (sometimes through homoeoteleuton); 6. *confusion of letters of similar form*; 7. *insertion into body of text of marginal notes.* The comparative study of texts can help towards the elimination of corruptions. Here numerical preponderance is not decisive: several representatives of the same archetype count as only one witness. The form of textual transmission is best depicted as a genealogical tree, and the facts of the genealogical relations can be applied to the assessment of evidence for any given reading.

1. OLD TESTAMENT: HEBREW

The documentary evidence for the OT text consists of Heb. MSS from 3rd century BC to 12th century AD, and ancient versions in Aramaic, Greek, Syriac and Latin.

From earliest times the Jews had at their disposal the means of producing written records. The Semitic alphabet was in existence long before the time of Moses (*WRITING). Moses would have been familiar with Egyp. writing and literary methods. He may, too, have been acquainted with cuneiform, for the el-*Amarna and other letters show that Akkadian was widely used during the

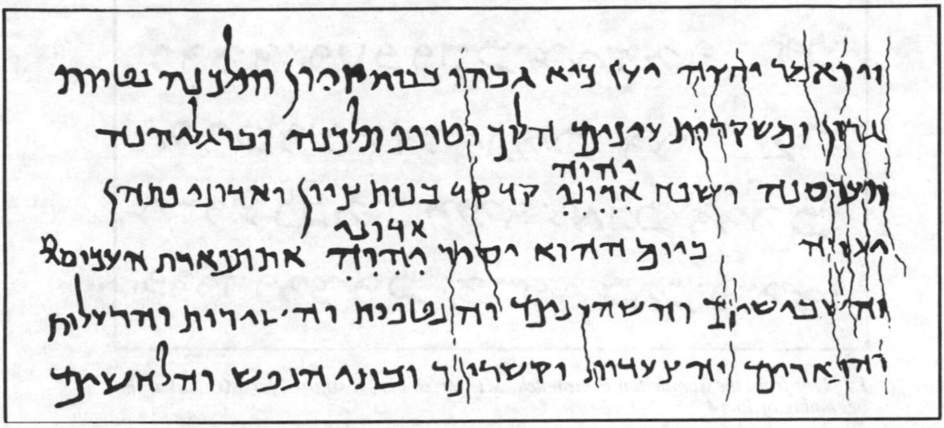

Is. 3:16–20 in the Dead Sea Scroll (1Q Is^a*) showing alterations to the divine Name (from* 'aḏōnāy *to* Yahweh *in line 3 and from* Yahweh *to* 'aḏōnāy *in line 4).*

15th to 13th centuries BC as a diplomatic language. If the Bible did not expressly state that Moses was literate (Nu. 33:2 and *passim*), we should be compelled to infer it from collateral evidence. There is, therefore, no need to postulate a period of oral tradition. Analogies drawn from peoples of disparate culture, even if contemporary, are irrelevant. The fact is, that the peoples of the same cultural background as the Hebrews were literate from the 4th millennium BC onwards, and from the 3rd millennium men were being trained not merely as scribes but as expert copyists. It is unlikely that under Moses the Hebrews were less advanced than their contemporaries or that they were less scrupulous in the transmission of their texts than the Egyptians and Babylonians (*cf.* W. J. Martin, *Dead Sea Scroll of Isaiah*, 1954, pp. 18f.).

Before describing the sources at our disposal for the restoration of the text of the OT, it is important to recall the attitude of the Jews to their Scriptures. It can best be summed up in the statement by Josephus: 'We have given practical proof of our reverence for our own Scriptures. For, although such long ages have now passed, no one has ventured either to add, or to remove, or to alter a syllable; and it is an instinct with every Jew, from the day of his birth, to regard them as the decrees of God, to abide by them, and, if need be, cheerfully to die for them. Time and again ere now the sight has been witnessed of prisoners enduring tortures and death in every form in the theatres, rather than utter a single word against the laws and the allied documents' (*Against Apion* 1. 42f.).

That Josephus is merely expressing the attitude of the biblical writers themselves is clear from such passages as Dt. 4:2 ('You shall not add to the word which I command you, nor take from it, that you may keep the commandments of the Lord your God which I command you') or Je. 26:2 ('. . . all the words which I command you to speak to them; do not hold back a word'). There is no reason to suppose that the Jews ever abandoned these principles. Many of the divergences in texts may be due to the practice of employing the same scribes to copy both biblical texts and Targums. As the latter are frequently paraphrastic in their treatment of the text, this laxity could subconsciously easily affect the copyists.

I. The transmission of the text

Measures for the preservation of the text were already in use in the pre-Christian era, for in the Dead Sea Scroll of Isaiah (*e.g.* plate XXIX, lines 3 and 10) dots are put over doubtful words, just as the Massoretes did later. In NT times the scribes were too well established to be a recent innovation. It was doubtless due to their activity that terms such as *'jot' and 'tittle' owed their currency. The Talmud states that these scribes were called *sōp̄*^{e}*rîm* because they counted the letters in the Torah (*Qiddushin* 30a). Since their intensive preoccupation with the text of Scripture qualified them as exegetes and educationalists, the transmission of the text ceased to be regarded as their prime responsibility.

II. The Massoretes

The writing of the consonants only was sufficient as long as Heb. remained a spoken language.

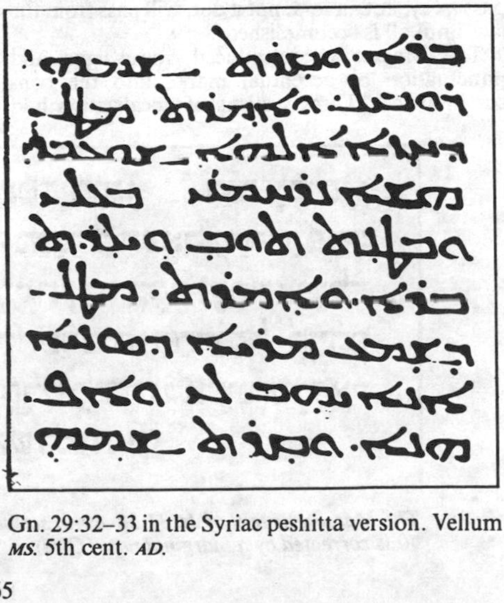

Gn. 29:32–33 in the Syriac peshitta version. Vellum *MS.* 5th cent. *AD.*

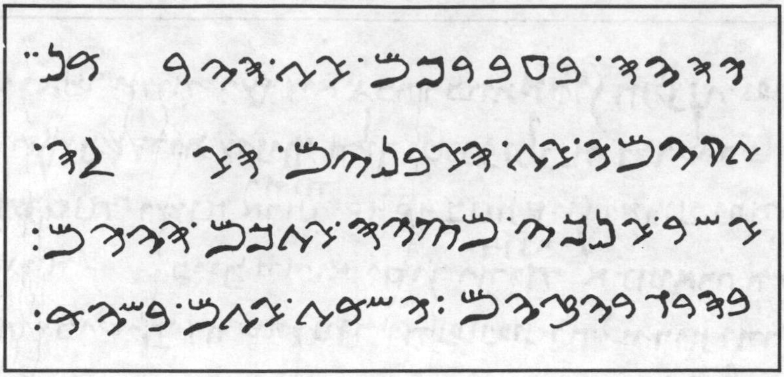

Dt. 27:4 from the Samaritan Pentateuch. Mt Gerizim is substituted for Mt Ebal at the beginning of line 4.

Where a word might be ambiguous 'vowel-letters' could be used to make the reading clear. These 'vowel-indicators' were in origin residual: they arose through 'waw' (*w*) and 'yod' (*y*) amalgamating with a preceding vowel and losing their consonantal identity, but they continued to be written, and in time came to be treated as representing long vowels. Their use was then extended to other words, where etymologically they were intrusive. Their insertion or omission was largely discretionary. Consequent variants have no significance. It was not until about the 7th century of our era that the Massoretes introduced a complete system of vowel-signs.

The Massoretes (lit. 'transmitters') succeeded the old scribes (*sōp̄ᵉ rîm*) as the custodians of the sacred text. They were active from about AD 500 to 1000. The textual apparatus introduced by them is probably the most complete of its kind ever to be used. Long before their time, of course, others had given much thought to the preservation of the purity of the text. Rabbi Akiba, who died about AD 135, was credited with the saying, 'The (accurate) transmission is a fence for the Torah.' He stressed the importance of preserving even the smallest letter. In this he was by no means the first, as the statement in Mt. 5:18 shows: 'Till heaven and earth pass away, not an iota, not a dot, will pass from the law, until all is accomplished.'

The Massoretes introduced vowel-signs and punctuation or accentual marks into the consonantal text. Three systems of vocalization had been developed: two supralinear (Babylonian and Palestinian) and one infralinear, except for one sign. This system, called the Tiberian, supplanted the other two, and is the one now used in Heb. texts.

As it was the resolute purpose of the Massoretes to hand on the text as they had received it, they left the consonantal text unchanged. Where they felt that corrections or improvements should be made, they placed these in the margin. Here the word preferred and which they intended to be read (called the *Qᵉrē'*, 'that which is to be read') was placed in the margin, but its vowels were placed under the consonants of the word in the inviolable text (called the *Kᵉṯîḇ*, 'the written'). It is possible that a form given in the margin (*Qᵉrē'*) was sometimes a variant reading. The view held in some quarters that the scribes or Massoretes boggled at giving variant readings, and in fact deliberately suppressed them, is contrary to what we know of the actual practice of the copyists.

The Massoretes retained, for instance, certain marks of the earlier scribes relating to doubtful words and listed certain of their conjectures (*sᵉḇîrîn*). They used every imaginable safeguard, no matter how cumbersome or laborious, to ensure the accurate transmission of the text. The number of letters in a book was counted and its middle letter was given. Similarly with the words, and again the middle word of the book was noted. They collected any peculiarities in spelling or in the forms or positions of letters. They recorded the

ישראל על־כל־אשר עשו נאם־יהוה׃ הנה ימים °
נאם־יהוה ונבנתה העיר ליהוה ממגדל חננאל שער הפנה׃
ויצא עוד קוה המדה נגדו על גבעת גרב ונסב געתה׃ וכל־ מ
העמק הפגרים והדשן וכל־השרמות עד־נחל קדרון
עד־פנת שער הסוסים מזרחה קדש ליהוה לא־ינתש ולא־
יהרס עוד לעולם׃ ° v. 40. השדמות ק׳

The Massoretic text of Je. 31:38–40. A scribal error (haššārēmoṯ *for* haššāḏēmot) *in verse 40 is corrected by a marginal note (Qᵉrē).*

ΛΙΘΩΝΚΑΙΠΑΝ
ΑϹ
ΤΕϹΑΡΗΜΩΘ
ΕΩϹΝΑΧΑΛΚΕ
ΔΡΩΝΕΩϹΓΩΝΙ

The LXX *of Je. 38:40 (in* MT *Je. 31:40) from the Codex Sinaiticus. The translators have copied into Greek letters* (sar möth) *a Hebrew word which they did not understand because of a scribal error in the Hebrew* MS.

number of times a particular word or phrase occurred. Among the many lists they drew up is one containing the words that occur only twice in OT. Their lists finally included all orthographic peculiarities of the text.

The textual notes supplied by the Massoretes are called the *Massorah.* The shorter notes placed in the margin of the codices are referred to as the *Massorah Parva.* They were later enlarged and arranged into lists and placed at the top or bottom of the page. In this form they were called *Massorah Magna.* This fuller form may give, for instance, the references to the passages where a certain form occurs, whereas the shorter would give only the number of the occurrences. The notes provide the results of their analysis or textual peculiarities. They give variant readings from recognized codices, such as the Mugah and Hilleli (both now lost).

Among the names of Massoretes known to us is that of Aaron ben Asher, who was active in the first half of the 10th century AD. Five generations of his family seem to have worked on the Heb. text, and under Aaron the work reached a definitive stage. The best codex of this school is thought to be the one formerly in Aleppo, now in Israel. Another noted family of Massoretes was that of ben Naphtali, one of whom was apparently contemporary with Aaron ben Asher. The differences between them in their treatment of the text was largely confined to matters of vocalization. The 'Reuchlin' codex in Karlsruhe is a representative of the ben Naphtali approach.

The text edited by Jacob ben Chayyim for the second rabbinic Bible published by Daniel Bomberg in Venice in 1524–5 came to be accepted practically as a standard text. The text was eclectic in character, and scholars have been aware for some 250 years that it could be improved. It is significant, however, that M. D. Cassuto, a scholar who probably had a finer sense for Heb. than any other in this field, and who had an unrivalled knowledge at first hand of the Aleppo Ben Asher codex, evidently saw no reason for preferring this to the Ben Chayyim text, which he retained for his fine edition of the Hebrew Bible (Jerusalem, 1953). The non-expert might easily be misled by the somewhat hyperbolic language used of the extent of the differences to be found in the various MSS. They relate mostly to matters of vocalization, a not altogether indispensable aid in Semitic languages. Linguistically considered they are largely irrelevant minutiae, at the most of diachronistic interest. Belief in the golden age of the phoneme dies hard; it ranks with the naïveté that believes 'honour' is a better spelling than 'honor'. Vocalization in a Semitic language belongs primarily to orthography and grammer, and to exegesis, and only to a limited extent to textual criticism. There never was an original *vocalized* text to restore. It is clear that the Massoretic text is a single type which became recognized as authoritative after the Fall of Jerusalem in AD 70. All Hebrew Bible fragments found with relics of the Second revolt (AD 132–135) in caves near the Dead Sea belong to it, in contrast to the situation at Qumran before AD 70 (see **III**, below).

III. The Dead Sea Scrolls

The discovery of biblical MSS, in caves to the W of the Dead Sea, has revolutionized the approach to the OT text by going some 800 years behind the Massoretic apparatus. It has also been a salutary reminder that the purpose of the discipline is the restoration of a consonantal text. The original find included one complete MS of Isaiah and another containing about one-third of the book. The later discoveries brought to light fragments of every book of the Bible, with the exception of Esther, as well as Bible commentaries and works of a religious nature.

The Dead Sea biblical MSS give us for the first time examples of Heb. texts from pre-Christian times, about 1,000 years earlier than our oldest MSS; thus they take us behind the alleged suppression of all divergent texts in AD 100. According to the Talmud, an attempt was made to provide a standard text with the help of three Scrolls formerly belonging to the Temple, by taking in cases of disagreement the reading that had the support of two (TJ, *Ta'anith* 4. 2; *Soferim* 6. 4; *Sifre* 356). The finds have helped to relegate questions of vocalization to their proper sphere, that of orthography and grammar, and have deprived of much of its pertinency the work done in the field of Massoretic studies by providing us with MSS much older than any hitherto at our disposal.

The Isaiah MSS provide us with a great variety of scribal errors, but all of them familiar to textual criticism. We find examples of haplography, dittography, harmonization (*i.e.* alteration to something more familiar), confusion of letters, homoeoteleuton, line omission and introduction into the text of marginal notes.

The great significance of these MSS is that they constitute an independent witness to the reliability of the transmission of our accepted text. There is no reason whatever to believe that the Qumran community would collaborate with the leaders in Jerusalem in adhering to any particular recension. They carry us back to an earlier point on the line of transmission, to the common ancestor of the great Temple scrolls and the unsophisticated scrolls from Qumran. Beside MSS close to the *MT*, fragments of others display Heb. texts that differ. Until all the material is published, it is hard to evaluate them; by their nature these have attracted most attention (see *DEAD SEA SCROLLS for details). That any are generally superior to *MT* or represent an older text is questionable; each passage has to be considered separately in the light of known scribal customs.

IV. The Cairo Genizah

The MSS discovered from 1890 onwards in the Genizah of the Old Synagogue in Cairo are of considerable importance for the vocalized text. (A Genizah was the depository for scrolls no longer considered fit for use.) The lack of uniformity in vocalization and the virtual absence of variations from the consonantal text show that the vocalization was secondary. Among the fragments of biblical MSS from this Genizah are some with supralinear vowel-signs. In the collection were also quantities of fragments of Targum and of rabbinic literature. Some of the MSS may be older than the 9th century.

V. The Hebrew Pentateuch of the Samaritans

The Heb. Pentateuch preserved by the *Samaritans is unquestionably derived from a very ancient text. The Samaritans, probably the descendants of the mixed population of Samaria, the result of a partial deportation of Jews by Sargon in 721 BC, followed by the plantation of foreigners (*cf.* 2 Ki. 17:24; 24:15–16), were refused a share in the rebuilding of the Temple by the Jews returning under Ezra and Nehemiah. The breach which followed (probably in the time of Nehemiah, *c.* 445 BC) led to the establishment of a separate Samaritan cultic centre at Mt *Gerizim, near Shechem. Contacts between the two communities virtually ceased during the 2nd century BC, and it is to this period that the distinctive Samaritan text form is assigned. It is probably a revision of a form current much earlier. All copies are written in a derivative of the 'Phoenician' alphabet akin to that on Jewish coins of the 2nd century BC, not the Aramaic 'square' script used for Hebrew after the Exile.

The oldest MS is in all probability the one traditionally accredited to Abishua, the great-grandson of Aaron (1 Ch. 6:3f.). The MS itself, written on thin vellum, is not uniformly old; the oldest part seems to be that from the end of Nu. onwards. Expert opinion would assign this scroll to the 13th century AD, or not much earlier than its alleged discovery by the high priest Phinehas in 1355.

The first copy of the Samaritan Pentateuch reached Europe in 1616 through Pietro della Valle, and in 1628 an account of it was published by J. Morinus, who claimed it to be far superior to the Massoretic text. This seems to be the case with every new discovery of documents, prompted either by a preference for the LXX or an innate hostility to the traditional Jewish text. There was in this instance another motive at work: the desire on the part of certain scholars to weaken the position of the Reformers in their stand for the authority of the Bible. Gesenius, probably Germany's greatest Hebrew scholar, brought this barren controversy to an end and demonstrated the superiority of the Massoretic text (1815). We are witnessing in our day an attempt to reinstate the Samaritan Pentateuch. Some of its protagonists betray by their faith in the trustworthiness of the Samaritan transmission an ingenuousness never surpassed by the most extreme conservatives. It is true that in some 1,600 places the Samaritan agrees with the LXX, but the disagreements are equally numerous. It is not easy to account for the agreements; one possibility is that when corrections had to be made in the Samaritan Hebrew Pentateuch an Aram. *targum was used (the Samaritan dialect and Aram. are practically identical, and the Samaritan version, that is, the translation of the Pentateuch into Samaritan, in places agrees verbatim with the Targum of Onkelos). There are numerous traces of the influence of the targums in the LXX.

For many of the variants a simple explanation can be given: the attempt to show that God had chosen Gerizim. After the Ten Commandments in Ex. 20 and in Dt. 5, the Samaritan inserts the passage Dt. 27:2–7 with 'Mount Ebal' replaced by 'Mount Gerizim', and Dt. 11:30 changes 'over against Gilgal' into 'over against Shechem'.

Many of the variants are due to a misunderstanding of grammatical forms or syntactical constructions. Others consist of gratuitous additions from parallel passages. Some stem from dialect influence. Many arise from their effort to remove all anthropomorphic expressions.

There is no evidence that the Samaritans ever had a body of trained scribes, and the absence of any proper collations of MSS, as attested by the numerous variations, is not compatible with any serious textual knowledge. Neither do the deliberate changes or superfluous additions distinguish them as conscientious custodians of the sacred text. Therefore, its variants must be treated with extreme caution. See the important survey by B. K. Waltke, in J. B. Payne (ed.), *New Perspectives on the Old Testament*, 1970, pp. 212–239.

BIBLIOGRAPHY. C. D. Ginsburg, *Hebrew Bible*, 1926– ; R. Kittel, *Biblia Hebraica*, 1952; C. D. Ginsburg, *Introduction to the Massoretico-Critical Edition of the Hebrew Bible*, 1897; F. Buhl, *Kanon und Text*, 1891; F. Delitzsch, *Die Lese- und Schreibfehler im Alten Testament*, 1920; O. Eissfeldt, *The Old Testament: An Introduction*, 1965; P. E. Kahle, *The Cairo Geniza*[2], 1959; F. G. Kenyon, *Our Bible and the Ancient Manuscripts*, 1939 (new edn., 1958); B. J. Roberts, *The Old Testament Text and Versions*, 1951; E. Würthwein, *The Text of the Old Testament*, 1979; M. Burrows, *Dead Sea Scrolls of St. Mark's Monastery*, 1950; W. J. Martin, *Dead Sea Scrolls of Isaiah*, 1954; F. M. Cross, *The Ancient Library of Qumran and Modern Biblical Studies*, 1958; P. E. Kahle, *Der hebräische Bibeltext seit Franz Delitzsch*, 1958; F. M. Cross, S. Talmon, *Qumran and the History of the Biblical Text*, 1975.

W.J.M.
A.R.M.

2. THE SEPTUAGINT

The oldest and most important Gk. translations of OT books are to be found in the so-called Septuagint (commonly denoted by 'LXX').

I. Its varied contents and uncertain limits

The LXX is a collection of very varied works: it contains at least one translation into Gk. of each of the OT canonical books, and sometimes, as with Dn. and Ezr.–Ne., more than one. The translations were later radically revised, some more than once, and the LXX MSS now present varying mixtures of revised and unrevised translations. Some of the canonical books, such as Est. and Dn., are enlarged by the insertion of apocryphal material, though again not all MSS contain the same amount of insertion. Then, of course, the LXX nowadays contains many apocryphal books, though these do not coincide in number (it tends to have more), nor always in name, with the books of the English *Apocrypha. Moreover the early LXX codices do not themselves agree on the number of apocryphal books they include, and in consequence neither do the modern editions. Some of the latter even include Christian canticles and hymns. The apocryphal books likewise differ among themselves in that some are translations from an original Heb. (or Aram.), while some were originally composed in Gk. The date of all this varied material is equally varied: the translation of the Pentateuch was made in Alexandria in the first half of the 3rd century BC; the translation of Ec. is probably the work of Aquila, and if so, was done in Palestine in the 2nd century AD. Some scholars think that the Pss. may have first been translated in Palestine and then taken to Alexandria. Some believe that parts of Sa.–Ki. were originally translated in Ephesus, and some apocryphal books composed in Antioch. Originally this varied material would have stood as single books, or as groups of small books, on separate scrolls; nor was it even possible to collect it together in one volume until advancing technology (and wealth) made available to the Christians of the 2nd century AD onwards the large-codex format. The so-called LXX, then, is far from homogeneous: different accounts must be given of its different parts.

II. Origins

a. Pentateuch

The earliest source of information on the origin of the LXX Pentateuch is the Alexandrian Jewish philosopher, Aristobulus (*c.* 170 BC), the surviving fragments of whose writings have in recent years been proved authentic. Aristobulus asserts that a translation of the Law was made in the reign of Ptolemy II Philadelphus (285–247 BC), and we have no reason to doubt it. He adds that Demetrius of Phalerum made the arrangements for it. Since upon accession Philadelphus banished Demetrius, there is a discrepancy here, unless Aristobulus means that Demetrius had made some preliminary arrangements before being banished.

The next source is Aristeas, author of the so-called *Letter to Philocrates*. He purports to be a Greek who was present in Ptolemy's court when Demetrius suggested that the Jewish Law should be translated, and who was subsequently sent to request from the high priest at Jerusalem an accurate copy of the Law and 72 Jewish experts to translate it (whence in part has come the name Septuagint, which later generations applied to the whole Gk. OT). Aristeas, however, was not a Greek, but a Jew, and wrote not in the time of Philadelphus, but at some point between *c.* 170 and 100 BC. Despite the extravagantly unhistorical details of his story, his basic claim that the Law was translated in the reign of Ptolemy II agrees with that of Aristobulus, and is generally accepted.

Josephus relates Aristeas' story and so is not an independent witness. Philo (*Vit. Mos.* 2. 5ff.) may perhaps be independent of Aristeas; he likewise attributes the translation to Ptolemy II's reign, but adds miraculous details to the story.

Of the Christian fathers some soberly follow Aristeas' story, others follow Philo, and add yet more miraculous elements. Justin Martyr (*c.* AD 100–165) is the first to extend Aristeas' account to cover the whole OT; Augustine (AD 354–430) observes that it was customary in his day to call the translation 'the Septuagint'.

In the rabbinic literature the tradition persists that the translation of the Law was made in the time of a Ptolemy; but there is disagreement over the number of the translators: TB *Megillah* 9a gives it as 72, but *Massekhet Soferim* 1. 7–10 as five (though some scholars regard this as a scribal error).

Both Aristobulus and Aristeas assert that there had been earlier translations before the time of Ptolemy II. But Aristobulus' assertion is made in order to explain how, according to Aristobulus, Plato was able to incorporate material from Moses into his philosophy; while Aristeas asserts that, although there was an earlier translation, divine

ETRESPONDENSDIXITILLISIHS
UIDETEHASMAGNASSTRUCTURAS
AMENDICOUOBIS
QUIANONRELINQUETURHICLAPIS
SUPERLAPIDEMQUINONDESTRUATUR
ETPOSTTERTIUMDIEM
ALIUTRESUSCITETURSINEMANIBUS

The Latin text of Mk. 13:2 with the addition 'and after three days another shall be raised up without hands'. From the Codex Bezae (D).

intervention had prevented any Gentile from ever citing it. This conflicting testimony is of little worth. Scholars nowadays leave open the question whether there may in fact have been earlier translations; but unlike Paul Kahle, whose theories were widely accepted in the 50s and 60s, they find no evidence of such translations either within the LXX MS tradition or without.

b. The other canonical books

From remarks made by Ben Sira's grandson in the Prologue to his translation of his grandfather's book, translations of 'the Law, the prophets and the rest of the books', *i.e.* of the whole of the OT, seem to have been in existence by the end of the 2nd century BC, though, as noted above, the translation of Ec. that now stands in the LXX comes from the 2nd century AD, and the revised and considerably enlarged edition of the Gk. Est. which we now have was introduced into Egypt, as we learn from the colophon, in the year 78–77 BC.

c. The non-canonical books

Dates of translation (or composition) vary widely from the 2nd century BC to the 1st century AD.

III. Revisions

The original translations (designated OGr. = Old Greek), were many of them subsequently subjected in whole or part to a series of revisions. The most important of these revisions were:

1. *The so-called kaige recension.* Made probably in Palestine, but perhaps in Alexandria, around the turn of the two eras, it aimed at making the Gk. represent the Heb. extremely literalistically. Its original extent is unknown, but it survives in parts of a number of books.

2. *Origen's recension.* Completed about 245 AD, Origen's edition was arranged in six parallel columns (hence the name Hexapla) containing: (1) the Heb. text; (2) the Heb. text transliterated into Gk. letters; (3) Aquila's translation; (4) Symmachus' translation; (5) the LXX as revised by Origen himself; (6) Theodotion's translation, or some other such as Quinta. Sometimes, as in the Minor Prophets, Theodotion's translation was placed in a 7th column. The chief purpose of the edition, which covered the whole OT, was to show where the LXX had material that was not in the Heb., and where the LXX lacked material present in the Heb.

3. *Hesychius' recension.* Little is known about this recension; some scholars even dispute its existence, while those who argue for it cannot identify it in many parts of the OT. Its author, a bishop in Egypt, died AD 311.

4. *The Lucianic recension.* Made by Lucian the martyr towards the end of the 3rd century AD, this recension has long been famous because in some books, notably Sa., it presents readings that appear to be based on a Heb. text of better quality than the *MT.* Nowadays however it is thought that these better readings were not supplied by Lucian, who in fact contributed little of importance, but were already present in the MSS on which he based his recension. The better readings may in fact be the OGr., and the variants in the other MSS the result of revisions. Unfortunately the Lucianic tradition, while prominent in some books, seems entirely absent or unidentifiable in others.

The results of these major, and many other minor, revisions are spread in varying mixtures throughout the surviving MSS, and in consequence care is needed in using popular editions of the LXX to check whether the printed text in any one place represents the OGr., translated in the 3rd–2nd century BC, or some later revision, emanating from Egypt, Palestine, or Asia Minor in the course of the next 3 centuries.

IV. Character of the LXX translations

Here two questions arise: (1) how accurately does the Gk. convey the meaning of its original Heb., and (2) how idiomatic is the Gk.? On both counts the translations and revisions vary enormously. Nowhere is the Gk. of the translated books straightforward *koinē* Gk. At its best it abounds with Hebraisms; at its worst it is little more than Heb. in disguise. The literalistic translations follow the Heb. so closely that the result would have been largely unintelligible to a Greek who knew no Heb. The more idiomatic translations may, like that of the Pentateuch, convey the meaning of the Heb. fairly accurately, or may like Pr. be free paraphrase, including material and ideas that never stood in the Heb. at all. However, even translators who normally follow their Heb. closely, on occasions deliberately depart from the Heb. Sometimes reverence dictates the change: *e.g.* in Ex. 24:10 'they saw the God of Israel' has been altered to 'they saw the place where the God of Israel stood'. Sometimes the translator, or some subsequent reviser—it is not always possible to tell which—substitutes for straight translation a midrashic interpretation which patently goes beyond, or even contradicts, the plain meaning of the Heb., and not seldom such midrashic interpretations can be paralleled in later rabbinic literature. The strange interpretation of the dimensions of width and height of the E end of the tabernacle court given in the Gk. of Ex. 27:14–16, for instance, is also to be found in TB *'Erubin* 2b and *Zebaḥim* 59b, where it arises not from some non-*MT*-type Heb. text, but from rabbinic exegesis. Similarly in the historical books the characters of David, Solomon and Ahab are in the LXX 're-interpreted' to their advantage according to principles of exegesis which were later formally enunciated in talmudic schools. The mere fact that the Pentateuch was translated in Egypt is enough to account for some of its departures from the Heb. text. Egyp. influence is marked in Is., and in Lv. the technical terms for the various Temple sacrifices are inexactly and inconsistently rendered: perhaps in Alexandria, where such sacrifices could not be offered, accuracy and consistency were of no great importance. In addition to making deliberate alterations, the translators, when faced with Heb. words of which they did not know the meaning, were obliged to conjecture. The conjectures of course were not necessarily always correct.

V. Status of the translations

This is a topic on which widely differing views have been, and still are, held. Philo, for instance, claims that the translators of the Law 'became as it were possessed, and under inspiration wrote, not each several scribe something different, but the same word for word, as though dictated to by an invisible prompter . . . the Gk. words used corresponded literally with the Chaldaean' (*Vit. Mos.* 2. 37–38). This exaggerated claim contrasts vividly with the realism of the earlier, Palestinian Jew, the grandson of Ben Sira. Recently arrived in Alexandria, and having experienced the difficulties involved in translating his grandfather's work into

Gk., he remarks in the Prologue to his translation: 'For what was originally expressed in Heb. does not have exactly the same sense when translated into another language. Not only this work, but even the Law itself, the prophecies, and the rest of the books differ not a little as originally expressed.'

Aristeas, for his part, is aware that the Heb. MSS circulating in Alexandria are not of the best quality (30), and he is doubtless aware also of criticisms that the Gk. translation is not everywhere accurate. He therefore invents a story designed to invest the Gk. translation of the Law, now already 100, perhaps 150 or more, years old, with supreme cultural authority, that of the reigning Ptolemy, with supreme religious authority, that of the high priest at Jerusalem, and with supreme academic authority, that of Demetrius of Phalerum (who he wrongly supposes was the head of the famous library at Alexandria). In saying moreover that the translation was done by 72 translators, six drawn from each of the twelve tribes, and that upon completion it was solemnly read before the assembled Jewish community along with their priests and elders, who received it with great acclaim and pronounced curses on any who should subsequently alter it, Aristeas, as H. M. Orlinsky has pointed out, is doubtless claiming canonicity for the translation. It is therefore the more remarkable that, unlike Philo, he does not claim that the translators produced their work by divine inspiration, but rather that they used the normal scholarly procedures, 'making all details harmonize by comparing their work each with the other' (302). Aristeas' story would hardly have convinced his near contemporary, Ben Sira's grandson; but his keenness to assert the authority of the translation of the Law suggests that it was currently the official translation used in the synagogues of Alexandria. For the translations of the other canonical books Aristeas makes no claim, even though by his time most, if not all, of them had been, or were in the process of being, translated. Of the exact origin and immediate purpose of these translations we know practically nothing. Were they scholarly products made in the course of study by historians and theologians? Or were they made primarily to serve as translations in the synagogues? Some may have had this latter purpose in mind, but others, like the translation of Pr., surely not. 1 Ki., even at the OGr. level, often reads more like a midrash than a Gk. targum. Its peculiar timetable of events, and its re-ordering of the book's contents to agree with that timetable, may well have originated in the discussions conducted in schools such as that led by the Alexandrian Jewish chronographer, Demetrius (early 2nd century BC).

It is almost unnecessary to say that the non-canonical books would never have been regarded as inspired even by Alexandrian Jews. 2 Macc., for instance, a confessedly uninspired book, composed directly in Gk., was aimed by Palestinian Jews at persuading their Alexandrian brethren to observe certain festivals, recently introduced in Palestine in connection with the Maccabean victories, in spite of the fact that they had no biblical authority. 1 Macc., likewise, was translated into Gk. to impress Gk.-speaking Jews with the devotion of the Hasmoneans to the Temple and the Law. But it freely admits that in certain matters they had been unable to decide what to do, since Scripture gave no guidance and they had no inspired prophet among them to direct them.

As early as the 2nd century BC Palestinian Jews became interested in the Gk. translations of the OT. Eupolemus, the friend of the Maccabees, seems in his history to be dependent on the Gk. translation of Ch. In the following 2 centuries it would seem that Palestine as well as Alexandria spent a good deal of effort on revising the Gk. translations to make them conform more closely to the Heb., which incidentally shows where the Jews as a whole considered the ultimate authority lay. When later the Christians began using the translations in their controversies with the Jews, the latter, already dissatisfied with the translations, eventually abandoned them and produced fresh versions of their own (see below). In the Talmud two attitudes to the LXX are to be found, one favourable and one hostile. They probably reflect the earlier and the later views of Judaism respectively.

The NT writers frequently cite LXX-translations, particularly in formal quotations. But they do not quote them exclusively: when it suits them they cite other versions. In their day, in addition to the so-called LXX translation of Dn., there was available another, more exact, translation (later commonly, but wrongly, attributed to Theodotion). They cited the latter rather than the former. In later centuries, however, some church Fathers who could not read Heb. for themselves came to regard the LXX translations as equally inspired as the Heb. originals, and, in case of disagreement, to be preferred. In support of this claim (and to Jerome's great annoyance), they embroidered Aristeas' and Philo's stories with additional marvels and miracles, and extended them to cover not only the Law but the other canonical and non-canonical books as well. Jerome eventually discarded the Old Lat. versions of the LXX and made new Lat. translations of the canonical books direct from the Heb. It is these translations that stand today in the Vulgate.

VI. Other translations

a. Aquila. Produced in AD 128, Aquila's version was extremely literalistic: it was designed to express in Gk. the minutiae of the Heb. language which were important to the rabbinic exegesis of the time. Only fragments (though some are extensive) survive.

b. Theodotion. Traditionally associated with Ephesus, Theodotion, whoever he was, seems to have produced sometime towards the end of the 2nd century AD a version which was in reality merely a revision of an older version or revision, commonly called nowadays Ur-Theodotion. Opinions, however, differ on who this Ur-Theodotion may have been and on the extent of his work. Some think he belonged to Asia Minor and there translated a great deal of the OT which the Alexandrian Jews had not completed, but which they eventually took over from him. Others believe that he was a Palestinian and none other than Jonathan ben Uzziel, author of the kaige recension.

c. Symmachus. Produced towards the end of the 2nd century AD, or the beginning of the 3rd, Symmachus' version stands at the opposite extreme from Aquila's, being both idiomatic and elegant.

Of the origin and nature of other versions, known as Quinta, Sexta and Septima, little is known: indeed it is uncertain whether they were independent versions or merely revisions.

VII. History of the text

The LXX translations were themselves translated by the early Christian missionaries into Latin, Syriac, Coptic, Armenian, Ethiopic, Gothic, Georgian and Arabic. Moreover they were copiously cited by the Gk.-speaking church Fathers, and the Lat. version(s) by the Lat.-speaking Fathers. These translations and citations, together with the hundreds of LXX MSS, ranging in date from the 3rd century BC to the advent of printing, form the evidence from which we must try to reconstruct the history of the text. Ideally the prime aim should be to recover the text of the original translations as they left the pen of the translator(s), by removing all changes brought about either by error or by revision. In many books the aim is attainable, within reasonable limits. In some books, however, the text-history is exceedingly problematic, and it is doubtful if it will ever be possible to identify the original with any certainty, though the more limited and necessary task of showing what the text looked like at various major stages in its history may still be possible.

VIII. Importance

The LXX translations are valuable for four major reasons among others: (1) they are a witness to the influence of Hellenism on Judaism both in the Diaspora and in Palestine; (2) they form a linguistic bridgehead between the theological vocabulary of the OT and that of the NT; (3) they were the translations in which the church Fathers read their OT in the centuries when they were building their formal theologies; (4) they are an important part of the evidence for the reconstruction of the history of the text of the Heb. OT. The translators undoubtedly sometimes had before them a Heb. text superior to the *MT*; and the NT itself sometimes (*e.g.* in Heb. 11:21) follows the LXX rather than the *MT*. Moreover the Dead Sea Scrolls have shown us that the LXX's disagreements with the *MT* are more often based on non-*MT*-type Heb. MSS than some scholars had previously thought. On the other hand the fact that some ancient Heb. MS agrees with the LXX against the *MT*, does not necessarily mean that MS automatically represents the original better than the *MT* does. The matter still has to be decided by the ordinary canons of textual criticism. Moreover, where the LXX disagrees with the *MT* and no non-*MT* Heb. MS survives, the use of the LXX to reconstruct the original Heb. is fraught with difficulties. Obviously in books where the LXX translation is paraphrastic, it is almost impossible to be sure in any one place what stood in its Heb. But even in books where the translators have followed their Heb. closely, certainty in knowing what Heb. they had before them in any one place is for various reasons often more difficult to attain than might at first be thought. And even where the *MT* makes no sense and the LXX offers what seems to make very good sense, that does not necessarily mean that the LXX translators found their good sense in the Heb. MS before them: like modern scholars, faced with a Heb. text difficult to construe, and having to put something in their translation, they may have resorted to conjecture. And finally when one attempts to retrovert a Gk. word or phrase into Heb., it not seldom happens that more than one retroversion is possible. That does not mean that we should not call on the LXX's evidence; but we need to use it with great caution. Major problem areas are the OGr. text of Jb. (one-sixth shorter than the *MT*), of Je. (one-eighth shorter than the *MT* and with a different order of contents, finding some support in the Qumran Heb. MS 4Q Jer^{b}), of the last six chapters of Ex., and of parts of Sa.–Ki. Much more research needs to be done before we can properly understand and interpret the LXX evidence: and until it is done, it is ill-advised to fill new translations with disputable conjectures based on the LXX.

BIBLIOGRAPHY. S. Jellicoe, *The Septuagint and Modern Study*, 1968, repr. 1993; S. P. Brock *et al.*, *A Classified Bibliography of the Septuagint*, 1973; J. W. Wevers, *Text History of the Greek Genesis*, 1974, *Exodus*, 1992, *Leviticus*, 1986, *Numbers*, 1982, *Deuteronomy*, 1978; D. W. Gooding, *Current Problems and Methods in the Textual Criticism of the Old Testament*, 1978; D. Barthelemy *et al.*, *The Story of David and Goliath*, 1986; E. Tov, *The Text-Critical Use of the Septuagint in Biblical Research*, 1981; *Textual Criticism of the Hebrew Bible*, 1992; Bulletins of *IOSCS* 1–, 1968–.

D.W.G.

3. THE SYRIAC VERSION

After the LXX, the oldest and most important translation of the Heb. Scriptures is the Syriac Version. This translation, used by the Syriac church, was described since the 9th century as the Peshitta (Syr. *pšiṭṭâ*) or 'simple' translation.

I. Origins

No direct information of the authorship or date of the version has been discovered, and as early as Theodore of Mopsuestia (died 428) details concerning its provenance were unknown.

Internal evidence, however, indicates its probable origin. Linguistic affinities have been noted between the Palestinian Aram. Targum and the Syriac translation of the Pentateuch, whereas Syriac (the name usually given to Christian Aram.) is an E Aram. language, and an explanation of this phenomenon offered by P. Kahle throws some light on the possible origin of the version.

These linguistic traces of W Aram., in a version otherwise in E Aram. dialect, reveal some acquaintance with a Palestinian Targum to the Pentateuch. Similarly, A. Baumstark has shown the direct agreement of the Peshitta text of Gn. 29:17 with a Genizah text and the Palestinian Targum as against Targum Onkelos and Pseudo-Jonathan ('Neue orientalische Probleme biblischer Textgeschichte', *ZDMG* 14, 1935, pp. 89–118). These facts suggest that the Peshitta Pentateuch originated in an E Aram. district which had some relationship with Jerusalem.

The ruling house of Adiabene was converted to Judaism about AD 40. Judaism spread among the people of Adiabene, and they needed the Heb. Scriptures in a language they could understand, *i.e.* Syriac, so it is probable that parts of the Syriac OT, and at first the Pentateuch, were introduced into the kingdom in the middle of the 1st century. The Palestinian Targum composed in the W Aram. dialect of Judaea was in current use at that time in Palestine, and we must suppose that this was transposed into the Aram. dialect spoken in Adiabene.

This, however, is not a complete solution, as Baumstark has shown that the original text of the Syriac version goes back even farther than the Palestinian Targum. The Palestinian Targum contains haggadic explanations which in general are not found in the Syriac Bible. On the other hand, the oldest preserved fragment of this Targum containing part of Ex. 21 and 22 does not possess any haggadic explanation, while the Syriac version of Ex. 22:4–5 follows the usual Jewish interpretation. Hence it is supposed that this fragment represents an older type of the Targum than that which might have been sent to Adiabene.

MSS of the Peshitta Pentateuch indicate the early existence of two recensions, one a more literal translation of the Heb. and the other a rendering, as has been described above, closely related to the Palestinian Targum. Many scholars think that the literal translation is the earlier as Syriac church Fathers show more familiarity with a text which followed the Heb. more closely than did the text in common use in the 6th century, *e.g.* W. E. Barnes, *JTS* 15, 1914, p. 38. However, against this view is the fact that Aphraates and Ephrem did not always quote the 'literal' translation.

It would seem that the literal translation made by Jewish scholars for the Jewish community was taken over by the Syriac church improved in style, and this text was accepted as standard about the 5th century AD. This Syriac church had taken root in the district of Arbela, the capital of Adiabene, before the end of the 1st century, and in the course of the 2nd century Edessa, E of the Upper Euphrates, was the centre of Mesopotamian Christianity.

When at the beginning of the 4th century the Christian faith was declared the official religion of the Roman empire, codices of the LXX were produced, and B. J. Roberts writes (*The Old Testament Text and Versions*, 1951, p. 222), 'It is reasonable to suppose that a similar development was taken with the Peshitta version. Thus it is held that an attempt was made to revise the Syriac version in order to bring it more into harmony with the LXX. It took place shortly after the NT Peshitta was revised, but it is obvious that the recension was not carried out in the same way for all the sacred books. Thus the Psalter and the Prophetic books, because of their relatively greater importance for the NT, were more carefully collated with the Gk. version. Job and Proverbs, on the other hand, were scarcely touched and the same may be said to be true, but to a lesser degree, of Genesis.'

An alternative view concerning origin is advanced by R. H. Pfeiffer (*IOT*, 1941, p. 120), quoting F. Buhl (*Kanon und Text des Alten Testaments*, 1890, p. 187) that 'the Peshitta owed its origin to Christian efforts: in part older individual Jewish translations were utilized, in part the remainder was commissioned to Jewish Christians for translation'. Such a view is possible, as the Syriac Christians included a large Jewish element and came possibly from an originally Jewish congregation.

Concerning the influence of the LXX on the Peshitta, the conclusion of W. E. Barnes may also be quoted (*JTS* 2, 1901, p. 197): 'The influence of the Septuagint is for the most part *sporadic*, affecting the translation of a word here and of a word there. The Syriac translators must indeed have known that their knowledge of Hebrew was far in advance of the knowledge possessed by the Septuagint, and yet the stress of Greek fashion had its way now and again. The Syriac transcribers on the contrary were ignorant of Hebrew and ready to introduce readings found in a Greek version or recommended by a Greek Father. So the Peshitta in its later text has more of the Septuagint than in its earlier form. It is only in the Psalter (so it seems to me at the present stage of my work) that any general Greek influence bringing in a new characteristic is to be found. That characteristic is a dread of anthropomorphisms from which the Syriac translators of the Pentateuch were free.'

II. Language and translation

An examination of the character of the Syriac translation in the various books of the OT shows there is no uniformity of rendering between the various books, and this implies a variety of authors. Of the Peshitta of Samuel S. R. Driver has written (*Notes on the Hebrew Text and the Topography of the Books of Samuel*[2], 1913, p. lxxi): 'The Hebrew text presupposed by the Peshitta deviates less from the Massoretic text than that which underlies the LXX, though it does not approach it so closely as that on which the Targums are based. It is worth observing that passages not infrequently occur, in which Peshitta agrees with the text of *Lucian*, where both deviate from the Massoretic text. In the translation of the books of Samuel the Jewish element alluded to above is not so strongly marked as in that of the Pentateuch; but it is nevertheless present, and may be traced in certain characteristic expressions, which would hardly be met with beyond the reach of Jewish influence. . . .'

For the character of the translation in other books we may quote B. J. Roberts (*The Old Testament Text and Versions*, 1951, pp. 221f.): 'The book of Psalms, for example, is a free translation showing considerable influence of the Septuagint; Proverbs and Ezekiel closely resemble the Targumim. Isaiah and the Minor Prophets, for the most part, are again fairly freely translated. The book of Job, although a servile translation, is in parts unintelligible, due partly to textual corruption and partly to the influence of other translations. The Song of Songs is a literal translation, Ruth a paraphrase. Chronicles more than any other book is paraphrastic, containing Midrashic elements and exhibiting many of the characters of a Targum. This book did not originally belong to the Syriac Canon, and it is conjectured that the Syriac version was composed by Jews in Edessa in the third century AD. Christian tendencies, perhaps emanating from an early Christian re-editing, are to be observed in the translation of many passages, prominent among them being Gn. 47:31; Is. 9:5; 53:8; 57:15; Je. 31:31; Ho. 13:14; Zc. 12:10. Many Psalms evidently derive their superscriptions from Christian origins, although in places they also embody some Jewish traditions. How far, however, these may be due to later redactoral activity cannot be determined.'

III. Later history of the Peshitta text

A schism in the Syriac church at the end of the 1st quarter of the 5th century resulted in Nestorius and his followers withdrawing E. Nestorius was expelled from the bishopric of Constantinople in 431 and he took with him the Peshitta Bible. Following the destruction of their school at Edessa in 489, the Nestorians fled to Persia and established a new school at Nisibis. The two branches of the church kept their own Bible texts, and from the time of Bar-Hebraeus in the 13th century others have been distinctive Eastern and Western. The Eastern, Nestorian, texts have undergone fewer revisions based on Heb. and Gk. versions on account of the more isolated location of this church.

IV. Other translations

Other Syriac translations were made at an early date, but there remains no complete MS evidence. Fragments exist of a Christian Palestinian Syriac (Jerusalem) translation, a version of the OT and NT dating from the 4th to the 6th centuries. This was made from the LXX and intended for the religious worship of the Melchite (Palestinian-Syriac) church. It is written in Syriac characters, and the language is Palestinian Aram.

Philoxenus of Mabbug commissioned the translation of the whole Bible from Gk. (*c.* AD 508); of this only a few fragments remain, giving portions of the NT and Psalter. Baumstark states that the extant remains are confined to fragments which are based on a Lucianic recension of the text of Is. These belong to the early 6th century AD.

Another Syriac version of the OT was made by Paul, Bishop of Tella in Mesopotamia, in 617 and 618. This follows the text of the Gk. and also keeps the Hexaplaric signs in marginal notes. Readings are given from Aquila, Symmachus and Theodotion. As this is really a Syriac version of the LXX column of Origen's Hexapla, it is known as the Syro-Hexaplaric text, and it is a valuable witness to the Hexaplar text of the LXX.

V. The manuscripts and editions of the Peshitta

The oldest *dated* biblical MS yet known, British Museum MS Add. 11425, dated AD 464, contains the Pentateuch except the book of Lv. (MS 'D'). Other extant MSS of Is. and Pss. date to the 6th century. The important W Syriac Codex Ambrosianus in Milan of the 6th or 7th century has been published photolithographically by A. M. Ceriani (*Translatio Syra Pescitto Veteris Testamenti*, 1867). This consists of the whole of the OT and is close to the *MT*.

The writings of the Syriac church Fathers, *e.g.* Ephrem Syrus (died AD 373) and Aphraat (letters dated 337–345), contain quotations from the OT, giving textual readings of an early date. The commentaries of Philoxenus, Bishop of Mabbug 485–519, give Jacobite readings. The most valuable authority for the text is the *'Auṣar Raze* of Bar-Hebraeus, composed in 1278.

The *editio princeps* of the Peshitta was prepared by a Maronite, Gabriel Sionita, for inclusion in the Paris Polyglot of 1645. He used as his main source the MS *Codex Syriaque* b in the Bibliothèque Nationale in Paris. This is an erratic 17th-century MS.

The Peshitta text in Brian Walton's Polyglot of 1657 is that of the Paris Polyglot; S. Lee's *Vetus Testamentum Syriace*, 1823, is essentially a reprint of the texts of the Paris and Walton Polyglots, although Lee had access to Codex B (the Buchanan Bible, 12th century) and three MSS, p, u and e, W Syriac MSS of the 17th century.

The Urmia edition was published in 1852, and in many places follows the readings of Nestorian MSS. In 1887–91 the Dominican monks at Mosul published both OT and NT, also depending upon an E Syriac tradition.

A critical edition of the Syriac version is in preparation by the Peshitta Commission of the International Organization for the Study of the OT.

BIBLIOGRAPHY. P. B. Dirksen and M. J. Mulder (eds.), *The Peshitta*, 1988; S. P. Brock, *The Bible in the Syrian Tradition*, 1989.

4. ARAMAIC

I. Aramaic text of the Old Testament

See * LANGUAGE OF THE OT, II.

II. Aramaic in the New Testament

From the time of the Exile Aram. spread as the vernacular language in Palestine, and was the commonly spoken language in the country in NT times, probably more so than Gk., introduced at the time of the conquests of Alexander the Great.

The Gospels record Christ's words in Aram. on three occasions: Mk. 5:41—* Talitha cumi; Mk. 7:34—*ephphatha*, representing a dialect form of *'iṯpattaḥ*; and his cry upon the cross, Mk. 15:34 — * *Eloi, Eloi, lama sabachthani?* (*cf.* Mt. 27:46). When Jesus prayed in the Garden of Gethsemane he addressed God the Father as * *'Abbā'*, Aram. for 'father'.

In Rom. 8:15 and Gal. 4:6 Paul also uses this intimate form '*Abba*, Father', as an intimation that God has sent the Spirit of his Son into the hearts of believers in Christ when they pray, '*Abba*, Father'. Another Aramaism current in early churches, * *Maranatha* (*maranā ṯā'*), 'Our Lord, come!' is recorded by Paul in 1 Cor. 16:22. Other Aram. words found in the NT are * *Akeldama* ('field of blood', Acts 1:19), and several place-names and personal names.

Acts 26:14 mentions that Paul heard the risen Christ speaking to him 'in the Hebrew tongue', for which we should undoubtedly understand Aram. (see F. F. Bruce, *The Book of the Acts*, 1954, p. 491, n. 18), as also in Acts 22:2. See also * LANGUAGE OF THE NT.

5. OTHER VERSIONS

Of the other translations of the OT the Coptic is based on the LXX. It was probably made in the 3rd century AD. There are two versions: one in Bohairic, the dialect of Lower Egypt; the other and older in Sahidic, the dialect of Thebes.

The Ethiopic translation, apparently made from the LXX, is too late to be of any real value.

The best-known Arabic translation is that of Saadia ha-Gaon (892–942). It would be surprising if this was the first translation into such an important language as Arabic. A midrashic reference to an Arabic translation of the Torah may have been prompted by an existing one. Arabic translations known to us are all too late to provide material for the textual criticism of the OT.

BIBLIOGRAPHY. F. F. Bruce, *The Books and the Parchments*[3], 1963, pp. 54ff., 191ff. and bibliography pp. 268f.; P. Kahle, *The Cairo Geniza*, 1947, pp. 129ff., 179–197; R. H. Pfeiffer, *IOT*, 1941, pp. 120f.; B. J. Roberts, *The Old Testament Text and Versions*, 1951, pp. 214–228 and bibliography pp. 309f.; T. H. Robinson, in *Ancient and English Versions of the Bible* (ed. H. Wheeler Robinson), 1940; E. R. Rowlands, *VT* 9, 1959, pp. 178ff.; H. H. Rowley (ed.), *OTMS*, pp. 257f.; E. Würthwein, *The Text of the Old Testament*, 1957, pp. 59ff. and bibliography p. 172; M. Black, *An Aramaic Approach to the Gospels and Acts*[3], 1967; G. H. Dalman, *The Words of Jesus*, 1902; *Jesus–Jeshua*, 1929; C. C. Torrey, *Documents of the Primitive Church*, 1941; G. M. Lamsa (tr.), *The Holy Bible from Ancient Eastern Manuscripts*, 1957; P. K. McCarter Jr., *Textual Criticism*, 1986.

R.A.H.G.

6. THE NEW TESTAMENT

The NT has been handed down amidst many hazards encountered by all the literature of antiquity. The mistakes of the scribe and the corrections of the redactor have left their mark upon all the sources from which we derive our knowledge of its text (or wording). Before we may ascertain the original text, we have to apply to the prolific mass of material a series of disciplines, *viz.* (1) *Codicology*—the study of ancient documents and their interrelation, closely linked with palaeography, the science of ancient writing. In some cases stemmata (family trees) may be established: the stages of transmission ascertained (with or without stemmatic precision), and, in ideal conditions, an archetypal text. (2) *Rational criticism*—the method of informed choice between the variants of the documents or their archetypes where these differ uncompromisingly and cannot be explained in terms of simple error. (3) *Conjectural emendation* may be invoked where insoluble difficulties remain. In the text of the NT, there is much still to be done in the study of single documents and their interrelationship, although there has been much work of this kind: recent decades have laid greater stress on rational criticism as a way towards the original text. The sources of information are many and very few scholars seek recourse to conjectural emendation.

The Gk. sources are very numerous. The standard list of Gk. NT MSS begun by C. R. Gregory (*Die griechischen Hss. des NTs*, 1908, reprinted 1973), is superseded by K. Aland, *Kurzgefasste Liste der griechischen Hss. des N.T.*, 1963; *Materialien z. nt. Handschriftkunde*, 1, 1969, pp. 1–53; *Bericht der Stiftung z. Foerderung der nt. Textforschung*, 1972–4; *idem*, 1975–6. In this there now appear 88 papyri, 274 uncial MSS, 2,795 minuscule MSS, and 2,209 lectionary MSS. Here indeed is *embarras de richesse.* Moreover, besides sources in the original Gk., recourse may be had to the ancient translations (usually termed 'versions') in the languages of Christian antiquity and to the citations made by Christian writers from the Scriptures. Both these prove to be sources of the most important evidence for the establishment of the text and its history.

I. Manuscripts

Our primary source is in Gk. MSS, which are found in a number of different materials. The first of these is *papyrus*; this is a durable writing material made from reeds. It was used throughout the ancient world, but has been preserved mainly in the sands of Egypt. Among the most significant of the 88 listed papyri of the NT (indicated in the list of Gregory–von Dobschütz–Aland by a 'p' in Gothic style, followed by a numeral) are the following.

(i) *Of the Gospels.* P^{45} (Chester Beatty papyrus of the Gospels, Dublin), *c.* AD 250, contains large parts of Lk. and Mk., somewhat less of Mt. and Jn.; P^{52} (John Rylands University Library, Manchester), *c.* AD 100–150, is our earliest fragment of the NT; P^{66} (Bodmer papyrus II, Geneva), *c.* AD 200, contains the Gospel of Jn., with some gaps in chs. 14–21; P^{75} (Bodmer papyrus XIV–XV), 2nd century, contains Lk. 3–14; Jn. 1–15.

(ii) *Of the Acts of the Apostles.* P^{38} (Michigan pap. 1571, Ann Arbor), dated by some in the 3rd century, by some in the 4th, contains Acts 18:27–19:6; 19:12–16; P^{45} (Chester Beatty, as above) contains parts of Acts 5:30–17:17; P^{48} (Florence) from the 3rd century, a single leaf containing Acts 23:11–29.

(iii) *Of the Pauline Epistles.* P^{46} (Chester Beatty papyrus of the Epistles, Dublin), *c.* AD 250, contains considerable parts of Rom., Heb., 1 and 2 Cor., Gal., Eph., Phil., Col., 1 Thes., in this order.

(iv) *Of the Catholic Epistles.* P^{72} (Bodmer papyrus VII–VIII), 3rd or 4th century, contains Jude, 1 Pet., 2 Pet. (mingled with apocryphal and hagiographical writings, and Pss. 33, 34).

(v) *Of the Revelation.* P^{47} (Chester Beatty papyrus of Rev., Dublin) contains Rev. 9:10–17:2.

All these papyri make significant contributions to our knowledge of the text. It should be particularly noted, however, that it is the age of these MSS, not their material or place of origin, which accords such significance to them. A late papyrus need not of necessity have any great importance.

The second material of which Gk. MSS were made is *parchment*. This was the skin of sheep and goats dried and polished with pumice; it made a durable writing material resistant to all climates. It was used from antiquity till the late Middle Ages, when paper began to replace it. The form of the manuscript book was originally the scroll, but few Christian writings survive in this form. The Christian book was usually the codex, *i.e.* the form of binding and pagination familiar to us. (*WRITING, IV.) Many parchment codices survive (the papyri are also in this form) and some are works of great beauty. Some were even 'de luxe' editions coloured with purple and written in gold or silver ink. At certain periods, however, parchment became scarce and the writing on old MSS would be erased and the parchment re-used. Such re-used MSS ARE CALLED *palimpsests*: it is often the erased writing which is of importance to modern scholarship, in which case the use of chemical reagents, photography and other modern technical methods is frequently required before it can be deciphered.

The parchment MSS of the NT (together with the relatively few paper MSS of the 15th and 16th centuries) are divided by a threefold classification. The first main demarcation is that between MSS containing continuous texts and those arranged according to the lections for daily services and church festivals. The latter are termed lectionaries or *evangelistaria*; they are indicated in the Gregory–von Dobschütz–Aland list by the letter 'l' followed by a numeral ('l' alone indicates a gospel lectionary; 'l^a' indicates a lectionary of the Epistles; 'l + ^{a}', a lectionary containing both Gospels and Epistles). This group of MSS was formerly little studied in any systematic way: the series *Studies in the Lectionary Text of the Greek New Testament* (1933–1966), and R. E. Cocroft (*Studies and Documents* 32, 1968) have redressed much of the balance. The former group is further divided into two sub-groups distinguished by the style of writing employed in their execution and roughly consecutive in point of time. The relatively older group is that of the *Uncials, i.e.* MSS written in capital letters: the relatively younger group is that of the *Minuscules* or *Cursives, i.e.* MSS written in the stylized form of the lower case perfected by scribes of the 10th century and thereabouts, and perhaps popularized from the Stoudios monastery.

As in the case of the papyri it should be noted that an uncial MS is not *ipso facto* a better representative of the NT text than a minuscule. Some older uncials rightly occupy a chief place in critical apparatus; some younger are comparatively worthless. Similarly, minuscules, though later in date, may prove to be faithful copies of early MSS; such then have as great importance as uncials.

Uncials are indicated in the Gregory–von Dobschütz–Aland list by capital letters of the Lat. and Gk. alphabets or by a numeral preceded by a zero. Important among the uncials are the following: (1) Codex Sinaiticus ℵ or 01), a 4th-century MS of OT and NT; in addition to its intrinsically important text it contains a series of corrections made in the 6th century and probably to be connected with the critical work of Pamphilus of Caesarea. (2) Codex Vaticanus (B or 03), a MS of similar content, but lacking the latter part of the NT from Heb. 9:14 to the end of Rev. Both these MSS are probably of Egyp. origin. (3) Codex Alexandrinus (A or 02), a 5th-century MS containing OT and NT, probably of Constantinopolitan origin. (4) Codex Ephraemi Rescriptus (C or 04), a 5th-century palimpsest MS of OT and NT re-used in the 13th century for the works of Ephraem the Syrian in Gk. translation. (5) Codex Bezae (Cantabrigiensis) (D or 05), 4th or 5th century and of uncertain provenance—suggestions range from Gaul to Jerusalem; it presents a Gk. text on the left page, a Lat. on the right, and contains an incomplete text of the Gospels and Acts with a few verses of 1 Jn. (6) Codex Washingtonianus (the Freer Codex) (W or 032), probably a 4th-century MS, containing the Gospels of which the text-type varies considerably from place to place. (7) Codex Koridethianus (Θ or 038), which it is impossible to date, since it was apparently written by a scribe unaccustomed to Gk., probably a Georgian; the MS copied by him was apparently a late uncial of the 10th century. (8) Codex Laudianus (E^a or 08), a 6th- or 7th-century Graeco-Lat. MS of the Acts. (9, 10, 11) Codices Claromontanus, Boernerianus, Augiensis (D^{paul} or 06; G^{paul} or 012; F^{paul} or 010), a group of Graeco-Lat. MSS, the former of the 6th, the two latter of the 9th century, containing the Pauline Epistles. (12) Codex Euthalianus (H^{paul} or 015), 6th-century MS much fragmented and scattered, containing the Pauline Epistles connected, according to a colophon (*i.e.* appended note), with a MS in the library of Pamphilus of Caesarea.

These MSS give the varying text-types existing in the 4th century; it is around these that debate has centred in the last 100 years and on these MSS that critical texts have been based. As an exploratory investigation this is justifiable, but, as more recent discoveries have shown, the complexity of the data is greater than this procedure would imply.

The researches of Lake, Ferrar, Bousset, Rendel Harris, von Soden, Valentine-Richards and many others have made it abundantly plain that a fair proportion of minuscules of all dates contain in larger or smaller measure important ancient texts or traces of such texts: to give then even an approximate indication of all important minuscules is virtually impossible. The following remarks give some idea of the significance of this material. Two MSS numbered 33 and 579 in Gregory's list are very closely allied to the text of B; 579 has even been described as presenting a text older than B itself. The text of Θ, otherwise unknown in the uncials save in part of W, is also found in 565, 700 and some others; as such a text was known to Origen, these are of great significance. Closely allied texts are found in the minuscule families known as family 1 and family 13 and in MSS 21, 22 and 28. In the Acts some of the peculiarities of D and E are attested by various minuscules, pre-eminent among which are 383, 614 and 2147. In the Pauline Epistles the minuscule evidence has not been so thoroughly sifted yet, save in the unsatisfactory work of von Soden. However, 1739 has attracted much study, and with its congeners 6, 424, 1908, and the late uncials erroneously placed together as M^{paul}, proves to attest a text of equal antiquity and comparable significance to that of P^{46} and B. In Rev., 2344 is an ally of A and C, the best witnesses to the original text of that book.

II. Versions

By the mid-3rd century parts at least of the NT had been translated from the Gk. original into three of the languages of the ancient world: Lat., Syriac and Coptic. From that time on, these versions were revised and expanded: and in their turn became the basis of other translations. Especially in the E, Bible translation became an integral part of the missionary work of both Gk.-speaking and Syriac-speaking Christians. As churches developed and theology flourished, versions would be revised to the standard of the Gk. text then prevalent. So, both by reason of their ultimate antiquity and by their contacts with the Gk. at various historical points, the versions preserve much significant material for textual criticism.

From this outline it will be plain that each version has a history. There is need, then, for internal textual criticism of any version before it can be used in the determination of the Gk. text; and in scarcely any case may we speak of 'such and such a version' but need to speak of such MSS or such a form or stage of the version in question. This, already observed for the Lat. and Syriac versions, should become the general rule.

In tracing the internal history of a version we have the advantage of the phenomenon of 'rendering' to aid us, which is not to be found in dealing with the Gk. text. In the Gk., text-types can be differentiated by variant readings alone: in any version even the same reading may be found differently rendered in particular MSS. Where this is so, different stages in the evolution of the version may be traced.

Difficulties are to be met, however, in the use of any version for the criticism of the Gk. text. These arise because no language can reproduce any other with complete exactness. This is so even in the case of cognates of Gk. such as Lat. or Armenian; it is more strikingly true of languages of other linguistic type such as Coptic or Georgian. Particles essential to the one are found to have no equivalent or no necessary equivalent in the other; verbs have no equivalent conjugation; nuances and idioms are lost. Sometimes a pedantic translator will maltreat his own language in order to give a literal rendering of the Gk.; in such a case we may have an almost verbatim report of the Gk. model. But in the earliest versions pedantry has no place and we encounter the difficulties of racy idiom and sometimes paraphrase. Nevertheless, the evidence of the versions needs to be mastered in the quest for the original text.

Some have claimed that an important factor in the history of many versions is the *Diatessaron*, a harmony of the four Gospels and some apocryphal source made *c.* AD 180 by Tatian, an Assyr. Christian converted in Rome and a disciple of Justin Martyr (*CANON OF THE NT). Unfortunately for research, no unequivocal evidence of it has been available, until recently, in Syriac, its probable original language. The most important witnesses to it are a commentary upon it by Ephrem the Syrian preserved in Armenian (a considerable portion of the Syriac original of this commentary came to light in 1957); a translation into Arabic extant in several MSS, but apparently much influenced before its translation by the text of the Syriac Peshitta; the Lat. Codex Fuldensis, similarly influenced by the Lat. Vulgate; and a fragment in Gk. found at Dura-Europos. Its widespread vogue and influence may be shown by the existence of harmonies in Old High German, Middle High German, mediaeval Dutch, Middle English, the Tuscan and Venetian dialects of mediaeval Italian, Persian and Turkish. It is quite clear that a *Diatessaron* lies beneath the oldest stratum of the Syriac, Armenian and Georgian versions, but the view that it influenced the Lat. has many flaws. These matters are still an area for research and debate.

The three basic versions made directly from Gk. are the Lat., Syriac and Coptic. Of none of these is the earliest stage certainly known. Tertullian usually translated directly from the Gk., with wide variety of rendering, in which his acquaintance with an early form of the Old Lat. translation shows itself. Our MS evidence for the pre-Vulgate stage of the Lat. consists of about 30 fragmentary MSS. These show a somewhat bewildering richness of variants well meriting the *bon mot* of Jerome, '*tot sunt paene* (*exemplaria*) *quot codices*'. Scholars usually distinguish two or three main types of text (*viz.* 'African', 'European' and sometimes 'Italian') in the various parts of the NT before Jerome; the Vetus Latina Institute of Beuron is presenting in its edition a more precise analysis with alphabetical sigla for text-types and sub-text-types.

But in the Gospels at least there is more interconnection between types than is usually thought: and even in the 'African' Lat. of MSS k and e there may be discerned more than one stage of translation and revision. Jerome undertook a revision of the Lat. Bible (normally known as the Vulgate) at the request of the Pope Damasus about AD 382. It is uncertain how far his revision actually extended. The latter books of the NT are probably very little revised. In the course of time this revision itself became corrupt and a number of attempts at purification figure in its history, most notably those of Cassiodorus, Alcuin and Theodulph.

The Syriac church, after using an apocryphal Gospel, was first introduced to the canonical Gospels in the form of the *Diatessaron*: this remained long in vogue, but was gradually supplanted by the separated Gospels in the form known to us in the Curetonian and Sinaitic MSS and in citations. This retained much of Tatian's language in a four-Gospel form. We have no MSS of a parallel version of the Acts and Epistles, but the citations made by Ephrem indicate its existence. Towards the end of the 4th century a revision was made of an Old Syriac base to a Gk. standard akin to Codex B of the Gk.; this was the Peshitta, which in course of time became the 'Authorized Version' of all the Syriac churches. Its author is unknown: more than one hand has been at work. The version comprises in the NT the canonical books apart from 2 Pet., 2 and 3 Jn., Jude and Rev. Later scholarly revisions—by Polycarp, at the command of Mar Xenaia (Philoxenus) of Mabbug (AD 508) and by Thomas of Harkel (AD 616) made good the omission. Few MSS of either remain, and the existence of a separate Harklean version (as distinct from the addition of scholarly marginal apparatus to the Philoxenian) is still a matter of debate. The version in the quite distinct Palestinian Syriac dialect is generally thought to be unconnected with this stream of translation, but otherwise its origins are at present obscure. Much of the NT is extant in lectionary form.

Biblical remains are found in several dialects of Coptic: the entire NT in Bohairic, the dialect of Lower Egypt and the Delta; almost the whole in Sahidic, the dialect of Upper Egypt; considerable fragments in Fayyumic and Achmimic; and the Gospel of John in sub-Achmimic. To trace in detail the history of the versions in these dialects and in the various parts of the NT is still an unaccomplished task: neither the dates of the versions nor the interrelations between them, if any, have yet been elucidated from the abundant materials to hand. The Sahidic is usually dated in the 3rd or 4th century, while for the Bohairic dates as diverse as the 3rd century and the 7th have been proposed. In the main these versions agree with the Gk. text-types found in Egypt: the Diatessaric element discerned in the Lat. and Syriac texts is scarcely present here, and it may be concluded that, whatever the internal relations of the versions in the different dialects, the Coptic as a whole stands in a direct relation to the Gk. text.

The majority of other versions are dependent on these. From the Latin come mediaeval versions in a number of W European languages: while these mainly reflect the Vulgate, traces of Old Lat. readings are to be found. Thus, Provençal and Bohemian versions preserve an important text of the Acts. The Syriac versions served as base for a number of others, the most important being the Armenian (from which the Georgian was in its turn translated), and the Ethiopic. These have complex internal history, their ultimate form conformed to the Gk., but their earlier stages less so. Persian and Sogdian versions derive from the Syriac, while the many Arabic versions and the fragmentarily preserved Nubian have both Syriac and Coptic ancestry. The Gothic and the Slavonic are direct translations from the Gk. in the 4th and 10th centuries respectively.

III. Patristic citations

For dating different text-types and for establishing their geographical location, we rely on the data provided by scriptural citations in early Christian writings. Much significant work has been done in this field, the most important results being in respect of Origen, Chrysostom and Photius among Gk. writers, of Cyprian, Lucifer of Cagliari and Novatian among the Latins, and of Ephrem and Aphraat among the Syrians. About the effects of the work of Marcion and Tatian on the NT text and concerning the text attested by Irenaeus—all matters of great importance—we are still in some uncertainty.

The whole field is much complicated by the vagaries of human memory and customs of citation. We also find instances where the writer on changing his domicile changed his MSS or on the contrary took a particular text-type with him. For these reasons few would accept a reading attested in citation alone; yet F. Blass and M.-E. Boismard have dared to do this in works on the text of the Gospel of Jn.

IV. Analysis

In many cases of classical literature it is found that the material available for the establishment of the text may be analysed into one *stemma* or line of descent, leading down from the archetype which may be adequately reconstructed even where a careful transcript is not to be discovered among the MSS, as is often the case. The NT material is not patient of such analysis in spite of the efforts of a number of scholars to apply a genealogical method to it. Westcott and Hort used the criterion of conflate readings as the primary stage in such an analysis. In this way they established the inferiority of the text of the mass of the late MSS, a conclusion corroborated by their second criterion, the evidence of patristic citation. They were then faced, however, with two main types of text, *viz.* that attested by B ℵ and that attested by D lat. Between these texts of equal antiquity they were unable to decide by these two objective criteria, and so fell back on a third, inevitably somewhat subjective, namely, that of intrinsic probability. By this means they were enabled to follow the B ℵ text in most cases and to reject the D lat text.

H. von Soden's analysis of the same material arrived at a system of three recensions, all dating in his view from the 4th century: by a simple arithmetical procedure he thought himself able to arrive at a pre-recensional text, always allowing for the factor of harmonization which he considered all-pervasive (and due in the Gospels to the corrupting influence of the *Diatessaron*).

Neither theory has met with unqualified approval subsequently. Von Soden's methodology is open to criticism because of the sometimes artificial rigidity of his triple pattern, and his uncritical use of the Arabic *Diatessaron*. He is, in Lake's phrase, 'so often instructive, so rarely correct'. Hort's theory has a whole history of subsequent debate. Slavishly followed at first, it was then put in doubt by the growing knowledge of the Lat. and Syriac versions, and of minuscule families with early patristic links, both of which helped to create a picture of an early complex of 'mixed texts' rather than a simple clearcut twofold division of text-types. But more recently, anticipated by rational–critical approbation of the codex B and its allies by Lagrange and Ropes, new discoveries and fresh examination have resulted in a growing consensus that the P^{75}-B text in Lk. and Jn., the P^{46}-B text in the Pauline Epistles, is in most of its features an intrinsically good text. Presence of possible corruption within it is not, however, denied. Hort's fault was to suggest, whether intentionally or not, that the third criterion of intrinsic probability had the 'objectivity' of the genealogical method exemplified in the first and second. In fact, he was using rational criticism, and in many of his conclusions, although probably not in all, his judgment appears to have been sound. We need the analysis of text-types and their history and the definition of recensions if these existed: but the concluding stage of any search for the original text can only be pursued by rational criticism, *i.e.* the practice of scientific judgment by intrinsic probability. A number of objective criteria may be established for this purpose.

V. Criteria

In this matter stylistic and linguistic standards play a large part. In every part of the NT enough remains without serious variation to enable studies of the characteristic style and usage of individual writers to be made. In cases of textual doubt we may use such knowledge of the accustomed style of the book in question. Furthermore, we shall in the Gospels prefer variants where the influence of parallel Synoptic passages is absent; or those in which a strongly Aram. cast in the Gk. reveals the underlying original tradition. Throughout, we shall avoid constructions of Attic or Atticizing Gk., preferring those of the Hellenistic vernacular. In other places, factors from a wider sphere may be discerned. Palaeography can elucidate variants which derive from primitive errors in the MS tradition. The history or economics of the 1st century AD can sometimes show us the choice between variants by providing information on technical terms, value of currency, *etc.* Church history and the history of doctrine may reveal where variants show accommodation to later doctrinal trends.

It will be plain from the fact that such criteria can be applied that in spite of the profusion of material the text of the NT is fairly well and accurately preserved, well enough at least for us to make stylistic judgments about, *e.g.*, Paul or John, or to judge in what case doctrine has transformed the text. The text is in no instance so insecure as to necessitate the alteration of the basic gospel. But those who love the Word of God will desire the greatest accuracy in the minutest details, knowing the nuances of meaning made possible by word-order, tense, change of particle, *etc.*

VI. History of the text

In brief outline we may thus sketch the history of the NT text. Many of the factors earliest at work are those described in the history of the growth of the * Canon of the NT. The circulation of separate Gospels, but of the Pauline letters as a corpus; the chequered history of the Acts and Rev.; the overshadowing of the Catholic Epistles by the rest: all these are reflected in the textual data for the several books. During the period of the establishment of the Canon a number of factors were at work. There was a tendency as early as we can trace to attempt emendation of the Gk. according to prevailing fashions or even scribal whim; in the case of the Gospels a close verbal identity was sought, often at the expense of Mk. In some cases, 'floating tradition' was added; or items were taken away from the written word. Such heretical teachers as Marcion and Tatian left the mark of tendentious correction upon their editions of the text, and doubtless their opponents were not blameless in this. In the Acts, alterations were made perhaps for purely literary or popularizing motives. Nevertheless, good texts were to be found, whether preserved by miracle or by philology, although no text known is without some corruption. In the 2nd and 3rd centuries, we find a mixture of good and bad, in differing proportions, in all our evidence.

It has seemed to a number of scholars that at some time in the late 3rd or early 4th century attempts at recensional activity took place. But there is little direct evidence of this, and recent discovery and discussion have put a completely new look on the question. We now know from the close affinity of P^{75} and B that the text-type of the latter, known in the Alexandrian Fathers, was not a creation of the shadowy Hesychius (named, with Lucian, by Jerome in his letter to Damasus, as author of a recension), but existed in the 2nd century. Since, however, as we know from the papyri, other types were known in Egypt, scholarly work may have rescued that one which commended itself on traditional philological grounds. The Byzantine text has been associated with the name of Lucian, and this has been supported by the similarity of many of its features to those of the Lucianic recension of the LXX. That recension, however, may antedate Lucian, at least in some of its elements, and likewise in the NT we have some evidence of Byzantine readings in papyri earlier than his date. The so-called Caesarean text, which Streeter and Lake were confident to have found in the citations of Origen and Eusebius, and in codex Θ and various minuscules, has disintegrated upon closer examination. While there may be a recensional form in some of the witnesses adduced, there was a pre-recensional stage, known, for instance, in P[45]. In other words, Christian scholars, where their activity may be discerned, were not creating new texts so much as choosing from a variety which already existed. In the Epistles their scope for choice was apparently less since only three forms (Alexandrian, Byzantine and 'Western') are found, but in Rev. there is a distinct fourfold pattern, yet one unrelated to the textual divisions of the Gospels. The data which earlier generations termed 'Western text' exemplify the way in which ancient readings could co-exist in specific traditions with material evidently secondary. It is the principles of choice utilized by the Christian scholars of the 3rd and 4th centuries which demand our scrutiny, and the general sobriety of Alexandrian judgment shows itself more and more. Yet no critic today would follow a single text-type alone, even if he were to give pride of place to one in particular.

In the Middle Ages the Alexandrian text seems to have suffered eclipse. Various forms of Caesarean and Byzantine wrestled for supremacy till about the 10th century. After this, the Byzantine text may be said to have been supreme in the sense that many MSS of nearly identical type were produced and have been preserved. But variants from even the earliest times are recrudescent in late MSS, and important MSS of other recensions and even of pre-recensional type come from very late dates, while some late MSS in fact change their allegiance in a bewildering fashion from text-type to text-type.

VII. Conclusion

Thus the task of NT textual criticism is vast and unfinished. Certainly, advances have been made since the material began to be collected and examined in the 17th century. Both Hort and von Soden present texts better than the printed texts of the Renaissance, and provide a sound basis upon which satisfactory exegesis may proceed. It is evident that many of the principles behind the Alexandrian text were sound. But it must be constantly borne in mind that even the best philological work of antiquity demands critical scrutiny if we seek the original text. The textual critic will be as the scribe discipled in the kingdom of heaven, bringing forth from his treasures things new and old. The busy textual projects of the post-war years should bring us nearer to the apostolic *ipsissima verba* than previous generations were favoured to come; yet we cannot but build on other men's foundations.

BIBLIOGRAPHY. P. Maas, *Textkritik*[2], 1950 (E.T. 1958); G. Pasquali, *Storia della Tradizione e Critica del Testo*[2], 1952; A. Dain, *Les Manuscrits*[2], 1964; C. Tischendorf, *Novum Testamentum Graece*, 8a Editio Maior, 1869–72; B. F. Westcott and F. J. A. Hort, *The New Testament in the Original Greek*, 1881; K. Lake, *The Text of the New Testament*[6], 1928; M.-J. Lagrange, *Critique Textuelle*, 2: *La Critique Rationelle*[2], 1935; G. D. Kilpatrick, *The Principles and Practice of New Testament Textual Criticism*, 1990; Jean Duplacy, *Études de critique textuelle du Nouveau Testament*, 1987; G. Zuntz, *The Text of the Epistles*, 1953; A. J. F. Klijn, *A Survey of the Researches into the Western Text of the Gospels and Acts*, 1, 1949; 2, 1969; J. Schmid, *Studien zur Geschichte des griechischen Apokalypse-Textes*, 1955; S. Éphrem, *Commentaire de l'évangile concordante, Texte syriaque édite et traduite par D. Louis Leloir*, 1963; *Fonds Additionels*, 1990; J. N. Birdsall, 'The New Testament Text', *Cambridge History of the Bible*, 1, 1970, pp. 308–377. *New Testament Textual Criticism: 1881 to the Present*, 1992; K. Aland, *Die alten Übersetzungen des neuen Testaments, die Kirchenväterzitate u. Lektionare*, 1972; B. and K. Aland, *The Text of the New Testament*. E.T. 1989; D. C. Parker, *Codex Bezae*, 1992.

Edition with select apparatus: *Novum Testamentum Graece* . . .Nestle–Aland[26], 1979. J.N.B.

THADDAEUS. This name occurs only in the list of the 12 apostles (Mt. 10:3; Mk. 3:18). The equivalent in Lk. 6:16 is 'Judas the son of James' (*cf.* also Acts 1:13). AV in Mt. 10:3 reads 'Lebbaeus, whose surname was Thaddaeus'. Most textual critics now read simply 'Thaddaeus' and treat 'Lebbaeus' as an intrusion from the Western Text, though some have suggested 'Lebbaeus' to be correct and 'Thaddaeus' to have been introduced from Mk. 3:18. 'Thaddaeus' is probably derived from Aram. *taḏ*, meaning the female breast, and suggests warmth of character and almost feminine devotedness. 'Lebbaeus' comes from Heb. *lēḇ*, 'heart', and it may therefore be an explanation of the other name. Attempts have been made to derive 'Thaddaeus' from 'Judah' and 'Lebbaeus' from 'Levi'.

There seems little doubt that Thaddaeus is to be identified with 'Judas of James' (see F. F. Bruce, *The Acts of the Apostles*[3], 1990, p. 105). The name 'Judas' would not be popular with the deed of Judas Iscariot in mind, and this may be why it is not used in Mt. and Mk. The post-canonical literature does not help us to obtain a clear picture, but Jerome says that Thaddaeus was also called 'Lebbaeus' and 'Judas of James', and that he was sent on a mission to Abgar, king of Edessa. Eusebius, on the other hand, reckoned him to be one of the Seventy. The mention of the Gospel of Thaddaeus in some MSS of the *Decretum Gelasii* is thought to be due to a scribal error. R.E.N.

THEATRE. Gk. theatres were usually cut in some naturally concave hillside such as might be afforded by the acropolis of the town concerned. There was thus no limit to size, provided the acoustic properties were adequate, and some theatres seated many thousands of persons. The seats rose precipitously in a single tier around the *orchēstra*, or dancing space. Behind this the theatre was enclosed by a raised stage, the *skēnē*. Together with the gymnasium, the theatre was the centre of cultural affairs, and might be used as a place for official assemblies, as at Ephesus (Acts 19:29). This particular theatre stood facing down the main thoroughfare of the city towards the docks, and as in most Gk. states remains the most substantial relic of the past. E.A.J.

THEBES (Heb. *No*, as AV). Once Egypt's most magnificent capital. Heb. *No* corresponds to the Egyp. *nlw*(*t*), 'the City' *par excellence*, and No-Amon to the Egyp. phrase *nlw*(*t*)-*'Imn*, 'the City of (the god) Amūn'. In Gk. it is called both Thebes, the usual term in modern writings, and Diospolis magna. Some 530 km upstream from Cairo as the crow flies, its site on the two banks of the Nile is marked on the E side by the two vast temple-precincts of the god Amūn (*AMON), now known by the Arab. names Karnak and Luxor, and on the W side by a row of royal funerary temples from modern Qurneh to Medinet Habu, behind which extends a vast necropolis of rock-cut tombs.

Thebes first rose to national importance in the Middle Kingdom (early 2nd millennium BC), as the home town of the powerful pharaohs of the 12th Dynasty (*EGYPT, History); however, the land was then administered not from Thebes in the far S, but from the better-placed Itjet-Tawy just S of ancient *Memphis and modern Cairo. During the Second Intermediate Period Thebes became the centre of Egyp. opposition to the foreign Hyksos kings, and from Thebes came the famous 18th Dynasty kings, who finally expelled them and established the Egyp. empire (New Kingdom). During the imperial 18–20th Dynasties, *c.* 1550–1070 BC, the treasures of Asia and Africa poured into the coffers of Amūn of Thebes, now state god of the empire. All this wealth plus the continuing gifts of Late Period pharaohs such as *Shishak fell as spoil to the conquering Assyrians under Ashurbanipal in 663 BC amid fire and slaughter. In predicting mighty Nineveh's fall, no more lurid comparison could Nahum (3:8–10) draw upon than the fate of Thebes. The force of this comparison rules out attempts occasionally made to identify Nahum's No-Amon with a Lower Egyp. city of the same name. The Nile, Nahum's 'rivers', was truly Thebes' defence. The Late Period pharaohs made full use of its E Delta branches and irrigation and drainage canals as Egypt's first line of defence, with sea-coast forts at the Nile mouths and across the road from Palestine —perhaps alluded to in the phrase 'wall(s) from the sea' (coast inwards?). To this protection was added Thebes' great distance upstream, which invaders had to traverse to reach her. In the early 6th century BC Jeremiah (46:25) and Ezekiel (30:14–16) both spoke against Thebes. See C. F. Nims, *Thebes*, 1965. K.A.K.

THEBEZ (Heb. *tēḇēṣ*, 'brightness'). A fortified city in Mt. Ephraim, in the course of capturing which *Abimelech was mortally wounded by a millstone hurled down on him by a woman (Jdg. 9:50ff.; 2 Sa. 11:21). Thebez is the modern Tūbās, about 16 km N of Nablus, and NE of Shechem on the road to Beth-shan. J.D.D.

THEOPHILUS (Gk. *theophilos*, 'dear to God', 'friend of God'), the man to whom both parts of Luke's history were dedicated (Lk. 1:3; Acts 1:1). Some have thought that the name indicates generally 'the Christian reader', others that it conceals a well-known figure, such as Titus Flavius Clemens, the emperor Vespasian's nephew (so B. H. Streeter, *The Four Gospels*, 1924, pp. 534ff.). But it is most probably a real name. The title 'most excellent' given to him in Lk. 1:3 may denote a member of the equestrian order (possibly in some official position) or may be a courtesy title (*cf.* Acts 23:26; 24:3; 26:25). Theophilus had acquired some information about Christianity, but Luke decided to supply him with a more orderly and reliable account. He may have been a representative of that class of Rom. society which Luke wished to influence in favour of the gospel, but scarcely the advocate briefed for Paul's defence before Nero (so J. I. Still, *St Paul on Trial*, 1923, pp. 84ff.). F.F.B.

THESSALONIANS, EPISTLES TO THE.

I. Outline of contents

1 Thessalonians

a. Greeting (1:1).

b. Thanksgiving for the Thessalonian Christians' faith and steadfastness (1:2–10).

c. Paul's explanation of his recent conduct (2:1–16).

d. Narrative of events since he left Thessalonica (2:17–3:10).

e. His prayer for an early reunion with them (3:11–13).

f. Encouragement to holy living and brotherly love (4:1–12).

g. Concerning the parousia (4:13–5:11).

h. Some exhortations (5:12–22).

i. Prayer, final greeting and benediction (5:23–28).

2 Thessalonians

a. Greeting (1:1–2).

b. Thanksgiving and encouragement (1:3–12).

c. Events which must precede the day of the Lord (2:1–12).

d. Further thanksgiving and encouragement (2:13–3:5).

e. The need for discipline (3:6–15).

f. Prayer, final greeting and benediction (3:16–18).

II. Authorship

Both the Epistles to the Thessalonians are superscribed with the names of Paul, Silvanus (= Silas) and Timothy; but in both Paul is the real author, although he associates with himself his two companions who had recently shared his missionary work in Thessalonica. In 1 Thes. Paul speaks by name in the first person singular (2:18) and refers to Timothy in the third person (3:2, 6); in 2 Thes. he appends his personal signature (3:17) and is therefore to be identified with the 'I' of 2:5. His use of 'we' and 'us' when he is referring to himself alone is as evident in these Epistles as in others, especially so in 1 Thes. 3:1: 'we were willing to be left behind at Athens alone' (*cf.* Acts 17:15f.).

There has been little difficulty about the Pauline authorship of 1 Thes.; F. C. Baur's ascription of it to a disciple of Paul's who wrote after AD 70 to revive interest in the parousia is but a curiosity in the history of criticism.

Greater difficulty has been felt with 2 Thes. Its style is said to be formal as compared with that of the first Epistle; this judgment, based on such expressions as 'we are bound' and 'as is fitting' in 1:3, is not of great moment; it certainly needs no such explanation as that offered by M. Dibelius—that this Epistle was written to be read in church—for the same is true of the first Epistle (*cf.* 1 Thes. 5:27). More serious is the argument that the eschatology of 2 Thes. contradicts that of 1 Thes. The first Epistle stresses the unexpectedness with which the day of the Lord will arrive, 'like a thief in the night' (1 Thes. 5:2), whereas the second Epistle stresses that certain events will intervene before its arrival (2 Thes. 2:1ff.), and does so in a passage whose apocalyptic character is unparalleled in the Pauline literature.

A. Harnack accounted for the difference with the suggestion that 1 Thes. was written to the Gentile section of the church of Thessalonica, and 2 Thes. to the Jewish section. This is not only rendered improbable by the direction of 1 Thes. 5:27 that that Epistle be read to 'all the brethren' but is incredible in the light of Paul's fundamental insistence on the oneness of Gentile and Jewish believers in Christ. Equally unconvincing is F. C. Burkitt's supplement to Harnack's theory—that both Epistles were drafted by Silvanus and approved by Paul, who added 1 Thes. 2:18 ('I Paul') and 2 Thes. 3:17 in his own hand.

Alternative suggestions to the Pauline authorship of both letters raise greater difficulties than the Pauline authorship does. If 2 Thes. is pseudonymous, it was an unbelievable refinement of subtlety on the writer's part to warn the readers against letters forged in Paul's name (2:2); the salutation in 2 Thes. 3:17 is intelligible only as Paul's safeguard against the danger of such forged letters. The difficulties raised by the Pauline authorship can best be accounted for by considering the occasion and relation of the two letters. Both letters were included in the earliest ascertainable edition of the Pauline corpus.

III. Occasion

a. The First Epistle

Paul and his companions had to leave *Thessalonica hastily in the early summer of AD 50, after making a number of converts and planting a church in the city (Acts 17:1–10). The circumstances of their departure meant that their converts would inevitably be exposed to persecution, for which they were imperfectly prepared, because Paul had not had time to give them all the basic teaching which he thought they required. At the earliest opportunity he sent Timothy back to see how the Thessalonian Christians were faring. When Timothy returned to him in Corinth (Acts 18:5) he brought good news of their steadfastness and zeal in propagating the gospel, but reported that they had certain problems, some ethical (with special reference to sexual relations) and some eschatological (in particular, they were concerned lest at the parousia those of their number who had died should be at a disadvantage as compared with those who were still alive). Paul wrote to them immediately, expressing his joy at Timothy's good news, protesting that his recent abrupt departure from them was through no choice of his own (as his detractors urged), stressing the importance of chastity and diligence in daily work, and assuring them that believers who died before the parousia would suffer no disadvantage but would be raised to rejoin their living brethren and 'meet the Lord in the air' at his coming.

b. The Second Epistle

Before long, however, further news reached Paul which indicated that there were still some misapprehensions to be removed. He suspected that some of these misapprehensions might be due to misrepresentations of his teaching to the Thessalonian church. Some members of the church had inferred that the parousia was so imminent that there was no point in going on working. Paul explains that certain events must take place before the parousia; in particular, there will be a worldwide rebellion against God, led by one who will incarnate the forces of lawlessness and anarchy, which at present are being held in check by a power which he need not name in writing, since his readers know what he means. (The allusiveness of his reference to this power makes it likely that he had in mind the Roman empire, whose maintenance of law and order gave him cause for gratitude several times in the course of his apostolic service.) As for those who were disinclined to work, he speaks to them even more sharply than in the former Epistle; to live at the expense of others is unworthy of able-bodied Christians, who had seen an example of the worthier course in the conduct of Paul himself and his colleagues. Spongers and slackers must be treated by their fellow-Christians in a way that will bring them to their senses.

An attempt has sometimes been made to relieve the difficulties felt in relating the two Epistles to each other by supposing that 2 Thes. was written first (*cf.* J. Weiss, *Earliest Christianity*, 1, 1959, pp. 289ff.; T. W. Manson, *Studies in the Gospels and Epistles*, 1962, pp. 268ff.; R. G. Gregson, 'A Solution to the Problems of the Thessalonian Epistles', *EQ* 38, 1966, pp. 76ff.). But 2 Thes. does presuppose some previous correspondence from Paul (2:15), while the language of 1 Thes. 2:17–3:10 certainly implies that 1 Thes. was Paul's first letter to the Thessalonian Christians after his enforced departure.

IV. Teaching

With the possible exception of *Gal., the two Thessalonian letters are Paul's earliest surviving writings. They give us an illuminating, and in some ways a surprising, impression of certain phases of Christian faith and life 20 years after the death and resurrection of Christ. The main lines have already been laid down; the Thessalonian Christians (formerly pagan idolaters for the most part) were converted through hearing and accepting the apostolic preaching (1 Thes. 1:9f.); Jesus, in whom they had put their trust, is the Son of God who can be freely and spontaneously spoken of in terms which assume rather than assert his equality with the Father (*cf.* 1 Thes. 1:1; 3:11; 2 Thes. 1:1; 2:16); the gospel which has brought them salvation carries with it healthy practical implications for everyday life. The living and true God is holy, and he desires his people to be holy too; this holiness extends to such matters as relations with the other sex (1 Thes. 4:3) and the honest earning of their daily bread (1 Thes. 4:11f.; 2 Thes. 3:10–12). The apostles themselves had set an example in these and other matters (1 Thes. 2:5ff.; 2 Thes. 3:7ff.).

Both Epistles reflect the intense eschatological awareness of those years, and the unhealthy excesses to which it tended to give rise. Paul does not discourage this awareness (indeed, eschatology had evidently been prominent in his preaching at Thessalonica), but he teaches the Thessalonians not to confuse the suddenness of the parousia with its immediacy, and he impresses on them the ethical corollaries of Christian eschatology. He himself did not know then whether he would still be alive at the parousia; he hoped he would be, but he had received no assurance on the point. His prime concern was to discharge his appointed work so faithfully that the day would not find him unprepared and ashamed. So to his converts he presents the parousia as a comfort and hope for the bereaved and distressed, a warning to the careless and unruly, and for all a stimulus to holy living. The parousia will effect the ultimate conquest of evil; it will provide the universal manifestation of that triumph which is already guaranteed by the saving work of Christ.

BIBLIOGRAPHY. Commentaries on the Gk. text by J. E. Frame, *ICC*, 1913; B. Rigaux, *Études Bibliques*, 1956; F. F. Bruce, *WBC*, 1982; on the Eng. text by C. F. Hogg and W. E. Vine, 1914; E. J. Bicknell, *WC*, 1932; W. Neil, *MNT*, 1950; *idem*, *TBC*, 1957; J. W. Bailey, *IB*, 11, 1955; W. Hendriksen, 1955; L. Morris, *NIC*, 1991; *TNTC*², 1984; A. L. Moore, *NCB*, 1969; D. E. H. Whiteley, *NCIB*, 1969; E. Best, *BNTC*, 1972; I. H. Marshall, *NCIB*, 1983; also J. B. Lightfoot, *Biblical Essays*, 1893, pp. 235ff.; *Notes on the Epistles of St Paul*, 1895, pp. 1ff.; K. Lake, *Earlier Epistles of St Paul*, 1911, pp. 61ff.; T. W. Manson, *Studies in the Gospels and Epistles*, 1962, pp. 259ff; B. C. Johanson, *To all the Brethren*, 1987. F.F.B.

THESSALONICA. Founded after the triumph of Macedonia to grace her new position in world affairs, the city rapidly outstripped its older neighbours and became the principal metropolis of Macedonia. Situated at the junction of the main land route from Italy to the E with the main route from the Aegean to the Danube, her position under the Romans was assured, and she has remained a major city to this day. Thessalonica was the first place where Paul's preaching achieved a numerous and socially prominent following (Acts 17:4). His opponents, lacking their hitherto customary influence in high places, resorted to mob agitation to force the government's hand. The authorities, neatly trapped by the imputation of disloyalty towards the imperial power, took the minimum action to move Paul on without hardship to him. In spite of his success, Paul made a point of not placing himself in debt to his followers (Phil. 4:16f.; 1 Thes. 2:9). Not that they were themselves without generosity (1 Thes. 4:10); Paul was apparently afraid that the flourishing condition of the church would encourage parasites unless he himself set the strictest example of self-support (2 Thes. 3:8–12). The two Epistles to the *Thessalonians, written soon after his departure, reflect also his anxiety to conserve his gains from rival teachers (2 Thes. 2:2) and from disillusionment in the face of further agitation (1 Thes. 3:3). He need not have feared. Thessalonica remained a triumphant crown to his efforts (1 Thes. 1:8).

BIBLIOGRAPHY. E. Oberhummer, *RE*, *s.v.* 'Thessalonika'. E.A.J.

THEUDAS. 1. In Acts 5:36 an impostor (possibly a Messianic pretender) who some time before AD 6 gathered a band of 400 men, but he was killed and his followers dispersed. His activity was probably one of the innumerable disorders which broke out in Judaea after Herod's death in 4 BC. Origen (*Contra Celsum*, 1. 57) says he arose 'before the birth of Jesus', but that may simply be an inference from this passage, where Gamaliel speaks of his rising as having preceded that of *Judas.

2. In Josephus (*Ant.* 20. 97–99) a magician who led many followers to the Jordan, promising that the river would be divided at his command, so that they could cross it dry-shod. They were attacked by cavalry sent against them by the procurator Fadus (*c.* AD 44–46), and Theudas' head was brought to Jerusalem. F.F.B.

THIGH. Heb. *yārēḵ*, also translated 'side' in RSV, of altar or tabernacle (Nu. 3:29; 2 Ki. 16:14). The variant form *yarᵉḵâ* is almost always used of objects or places generally, mostly in the dual, *i.e.* derived from the thought of the two thighs. The other word translated 'thigh' in RSV (Ex. 29:22, 27) refers to the *leg. The Gk. *mēros* is used once (Rev. 19:16), where it probably refers to the locality of the inscription on the garment. (See *NBCR*, p. 1304.)

The Heb. word is found in similar usage to *motlomacri;nayim* or *ḥᵃlāṣayim* and Gk. *osphys*, 'loins', in respect of the parts of the body usually clothed (Ex. 28:42; *cf.* Is. 32:11), and especially of the position where a sword is worn (Ps. 45:3); also of the locality of the genital organs, and so by figure of speech to one's offspring (Gn. 46:26; *cf.* Gn. 35:11; Acts 2:30; *moṯnayim* is not used in this sense). The custom of making an oath by placing the hand under another's thigh (Gn. 24:2f.; 47:29ff.) signifies the association of the peculiar power of these parts, perhaps with the idea of invoking the support of the person's descendants to enforce the oath. For association in a particular form of oath, see Nu. 5:21ff.

Smiting upon the thigh is a sign of anguish (Je. 31:19). For a discussion of the custom of not eating the sinew of the thigh joint (Gn. 32:32), see *SINEW. B.O.B.

THOMAS. One of the twelve apostles. In the lists of the Twelve which are arranged in three groups of four each, Thomas occurs in the second group (Mt. 10:2–4; Mk. 3:16–19; Lk. 6:14–16; Acts 1:13). He is linked with Matthew in Mt. 10:3 and with Philip in Acts 1:13. The name comes from Aram. *tᵉ'ômā'*, meaning 'twin'; John three times uses the Gk. version of it, 'Didymus' (11:16; 20:24; 21:2). The question whose twin he was cannot be answered with certainty. Various traditions (Syriac and Egyp.) suggest that his personal name was Judas.

It is only in the Fourth Gospel that there are any personal references to Thomas. He was prepared to go with Jesus to the tomb of Lazarus and to possible death at the hands of the Jews (Jn. 11:16). He confessed himself unable to understand where Jesus was going when he warned the Twelve of his impending departure (Jn. 14:5). The chief incident for which he has always been remembered, and for which he has been called 'Doubting Thomas', is his disbelief in the resurrection. He missed the appearance of Christ to the other apostles (Jn. 20:24) and said that he needed visual and tactual proof of the resurrection (20:25). A week later Christ ap-

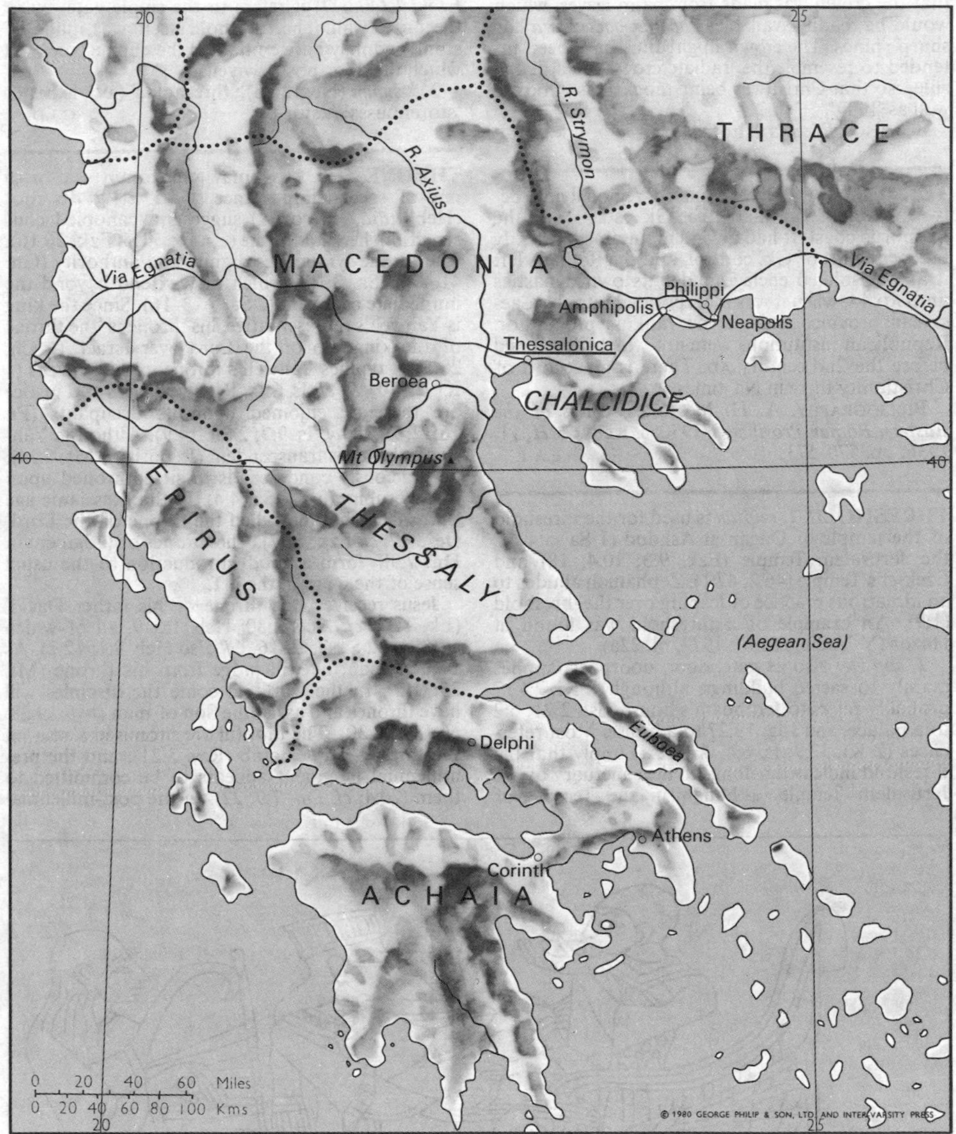

Thessalonica, a major city of Macedonia.

peared again to the Eleven and he offered Thomas the opportunity to test the reality of his body.

Thomas' confession of faith, 'My Lord and my God' (20:28), marks the climax of the Fourth Gospel; blessing is promised to those who can come to faith without the aid of sight. R.E.N.

THORNS, CROWN OF. This was made by the Roman soldiers and placed on the head of Christ when he was mocked before the crucifixion (Mt. 27:29; Mk. 15:17; Jn. 19:2).

It was, with the sceptre of reed and the purple robe, symbolic of the fact that he had been said to be King of the Jews. The superscription on the cross likewise proclaimed this in mockery. Yet Christians have seen the life of Jesus as a royal road from the manger of Bethlehem to the cross of Calvary, and the very incidents in which he least seemed to be a king have won their allegiance more than anything else. For John especially the moment of Christ's humiliation is the moment of his glory (12:31–33; *cf.* Heb. 2:9).

It is uncertain exactly what plant is signified by *akantha.* There are a number of plants with sharp spines which grow in Palestine. Christians have seen the thorns as symbolic of the effects of sin (Gn. 3:18; Nu. 33:55; Pr. 22:5; Mt. 7:16; 13:7; Heb. 6:8).

H. St J. Hart (*JTS* n.s. 3, 1952, pp. 66ff.) suggests

that the crown was made from palm leaves, which would be readily available. *Phoenix dactylifera* has sharp spines. The crown might thus have been intended to resemble the 'radiate crown' of a divine ruler, so that Christ was being mocked as 'God' as well as 'king'.

See also *PLANTS (Thorns). R.E.N.

THRACE. A tribally organized region lying between Macedonia and the Gk. states of the Bosporus coast. It had always maintained a sturdy independence of Gk. control, and the Romans left it as an isolated enclave under its own dynasties until AD 44, when it was incorporated into the Caesarean province under a low-ranking procurator. Republican institutions were not widely developed before the 2nd century AD. There is no record of Christianity there in NT times.

BIBLIOGRAPHY. A. H. M. Jones, *Cities of the Eastern Roman Provinces*², 1970; J. Keil, *CAH*, 11, 1936, pp. 570–573. E.A.J.

THRESHOLD. 1. *mip̄tān* is used for the threshold of the temple of Dagan at Ashdod (1 Sa. 5:4–5), the Jerusalem Temple (Ezk. 9:3; 10:4, 18) and Ezekiel's Temple (46:2; 47:1). Zephaniah alludes to an idolatrous practice of leaping over the threshold (1:9). An example of a threshold was found at Hazor (Y. Yadin, *Hazor*, 1972, pl. 22a).

2. *sap̄* (AV also as gate, door, doorpost) applies mainly to sacred buildings, although 1 Ki. 14:17 probably refers to Jeroboam's house, Est. 2:21; 6:2 to a palace, and Jdg. 19:27 to a house. Most references (2 Ki. 12:9; Is. 6:4; Am. 9:1) imply that the threshold indicated belongs to the sanctuary of the Jerusalem Temple, although in the Temple of Ezekiel (40:6–7) it refers to the single gateway in the outer wall. The threshold itself was made of stone and may have contained the cupped socks in which the door-posts swivelled.

3. *'ᵃsup̄îm* (Ne. 12:25), 'thresholds' (AV), is better 'storehouses' (RSV). C.J.D.

THRONE. Heb. *kissē'* may refer to any seat or to one of special importance (1 Ki. 2:19). Its root (Heb. *kāsâ*, 'to cover') suggests a canopied construction, hence a throne (*e.g.* Ex. 11:5; Ezk. 26:16). The throne symbolizes dignity and authority (Gn. 41:40; 2 Sa. 3:10), which may extend beyond the immediate occupant (2 Sa. 7:13–16). Since the king is Yahweh's representative, his throne is 'the throne of the kingdom of the Lord over Israel' (1 Ch. 28:5); it typifies Yahweh's throne in the heavens (1 Ki. 22:10, 19; *cf.* Is. 6:1). Righteousness and justice are therefore enjoined upon its occupants (Pr. 16:12; 20:28; *cf.* Is. 9:7; 2 Sa. 14:9). Although Yahweh's throne is transcendent (Is. 66:1; *cf.* Mt. 5:34), he graciously condescends to sit enthroned upon the cherubim (*e.g.* 1 Sa. 4:4). In the Messianic age 'Jerusalem shall be called the throne of the Lord' (Je. 3:17; *cf.* Ezk. 43:7). The thrones of judgment in Dn. 7:9ff. form a good introduction to the usual sense of the word in the NT.

Jesus receives 'the throne of his father David' (Lk. 1:32; *cf.* Acts 2:30; Heb. 1:5–9, all of which allude to 2 Sa. 7:12–16. *Cf.* also Heb. 8:1; 12:2). As Son of man, he will judge from his throne (Mt. 25:31ff.). In the world to come the disciples will have thrones and assist the Son of man (Mt. 19:28; *cf.* Lk. 22:30). The faithful are promised a seat on the throne of the Lamb (Rev. 3:21), and the premillennial judgment appears to be committed to them (20:4; *cf.* Dn. 7:9, 22). In the post-millennial

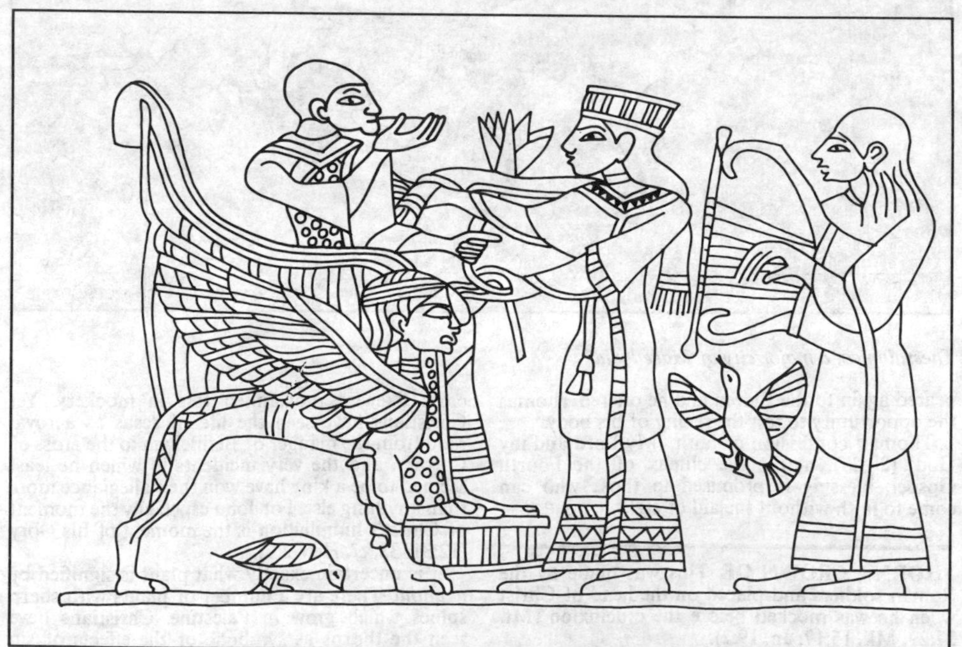

A prince receives tribute, seated on a throne supported by a winged cherubim (cf. 1 Sa. 4:4). Ivory from Megiddo. Height 4 cm. 8th cent. BC

judgment, however, there is only the great white throne (20:11). The disparity is more apparent than real, for Dn. 7 forms the background of each vision. Similarly, the vision of the august throne of God and the Lamb in Rev. 22:3 compares with Mt. 19:28 and Lk. 22:30, because John, in adding 'and they shall *reign* . . .' (22:5), undoubtedly has in mind the thrones of the faithful. *Cf.* 'throne of grace' (Heb. 4:16). R.J.MCK.

THUMB. Heb. *bōhen*, in the OT equally and always together, of the thumb and big toe, differentiated by the designation, 'of the hand' or 'of the foot'. The root is related to an Arabic word meaning 'to cover' or 'shut', hence of that member which closes or covers the hand.

The practice of placing blood from the sacrificial beast upon the right thumb, great toe and also *ear of the priests probably indicated the dedication of the prominent organs of hearing, doing and walking, symbolizing the securing of the whole man (Ex. 29:20; Lv. 8:23, *etc.*). Similarly, the practice of cutting off the thumbs and great toes of a defeated enemy probably symbolized his being rendered powerless (Jdg. 1:6f.), and also ceremonially incompetent to discharge any sacral duties. B.O.B.

THUNDER. Most frequent during the winter season, thunder is vividly described in Jb. 37 and Ps. 29. The few rainstorms of summer are usually associated with thunder (*e.g.* 1 Sa. 12:17); the coincidence of this event with Samuel's message helped to deepen the warning to Israel when they desired a king. A desert thunderstorm seems the most plausible explanation for the narrative of 2 Ki. 3:4–27, when 'the country was filled with water', presumably as a result of a desert thunderstorm on the plateau E of the Zered valley. In another military campaign a thunderstorm decided the result of the battle between Israel and the Philistines (1 Sa. 7:10).

Thunder is frequently associated with the voice of God and is spoken of as a voice in Pss. 77:18; 104:7. The creative voice of God which bade the waters go to their appointed place (Gn. 1:9) is identified with thunder (Ps. 104:7). It was associated with the giving of the law at Sinai (Ex. 19:16; 20:18), and the voice out of heaven which answered Christ (Jn. 12:28f.) was identified by those present as a thunder-peal. Voices like thunder are referred to in the Apocalypse (Rev. 6:1; 14:2; 19:6), where they are even given articulate meaning (Rev. 10:3f.).

(*Plagues of Egypt.) J.M.H.

THYATIRA. A city in the Roman province of Asia, in the W of what is now Asiatic Turkey. It occupied an important position in a low-lying 'corridor' connecting the Hermus and Caicus valleys. It was a frontier garrison, first on the W frontier of the territory of Seleucus I of Syria, and later, after changing hands, on the E frontier of the kingdom of Pergamum. With that kingdom, it passed under Roman rule in 133 BC. But it remained an important point in the Roman road-system, for it lay on the road from Pergamum to Laodicea, and thence to the E provinces. It was also an important centre of manufacture; dyeing, garment-making, pottery

Thyatira, one of the 'seven churches of Asia' (Rev. 1–3).

and brass-working are among the trades known to have existed there. A large town (Akhisar) still stands on the same site.

The Thyatiran woman Lydia, the 'seller of purple' whom Paul met at Philippi (Acts 16:14), was probably the overseas agent of a Thyatiran manufacturer; she may have been arranging the sale of dyed woollen goods which were known simply by the name of the dye. This 'purple' was obtained from the madder root, and was still produced in the district, under the name 'Turkey red', into the present century.

The Thyatiran church was the fourth (Rev. 1:11) of the 'seven churches of Asia'. Some of the symbols in the letter to the church (Rev. 2:18–29) seem to allude to the circumstances of the city. The description of the Christ (v. 18) is appropriate for a city renowned for its brass-working (*chalkolibanos*, translated 'fine brass', may be a technical term for some local type of brassware). The terms of the promise (vv. 26–27) may reflect the long military history of the city. 'Jezebel' (the name is probably symbolic) was evidently a woman who was accepted within the fellowship of the church (v. 20). Her teaching probably advocated a measure of compromise with some activity which was implicitly pagan. This is likely to have been membership of the social clubs or 'guilds' into which the trades were organized. These bodies fulfilled many admirable functions, and pursuance of a trade was almost impossible without belonging to the guild; yet their meetings were inextricably bound up with acts of pagan worship and immorality. (See C. J. Hemer, *The Letters to the Seven Churches of Asia in their Local Setting*, 1986; E. M. Yamauchi, *New Testament Cities in Western Asia Minor*, 1980.)

M.J.S.R.
C.J.H.

TIBERIAS. A city on the W shore of the Sea of *Galilee which subsequently gave its name to the lake. It was founded by Herod Antipas about AD 20 and named after the emperor Tiberius. The principal factors influencing Herod's choice of site seem to have been: (1) a defensive position represented by a rocky projection above the lake; (2) proximity to some already-famous warm springs which lay just to the S. Otherwise, the site offered little, and the beautiful buildings of the city (which became Herod's capital) rose on ground that included a former graveyard, and so rendered the city unclean in Jewish eyes.

Tiberias is mentioned only once in the Gospels (Jn. 6:23; 'sea of Tiberias' appears in Jn. 6:1; 21:1), and there is no record of Christ ever visiting it. It was a thoroughly Gentile city, and he seems to have avoided it in favour of the numerous Jewish towns of the lake shore. By a curious reversal, however, after the destruction of Jerusalem it became the chief seat of Jewish learning, and both the Mishnah and the Palestinian Talmud were compiled there, in the 3rd and 5th centuries respectively.

Of the towns which surrounded the Sea of Galilee in NT times, Tiberias is the only one which remains of any size at the present day.

BIBLIOGRAPHY. *NEAEHL*, pp. 1464–1473.

J.H.P.

TIBERIUS. The stepson of Augustus Caesar, reluctantly adopted as his heir when all other hope of a direct succession was lost. On Augustus' death in AD 14, Tiberius at 56 years of age had a lifetime's experience of government behind him. It was nevertheless a momentous decision when the Senate transferred Augustus' powers bodily to him, thus recognizing that the *de facto* ascendancy of Augustus was now an indispensable instrument of the Roman state. For 23 years Tiberius loyally and unimaginatively continued Augustus' policies. His dourness gradually lost him the confidence of the nation, and he withdrew to a disgruntled retirement on Capri until his death. In his absence treason trials and the intervention of the praetorian guard set dangerous new precedents in Roman politics. He is referred to in Lk. 3:1 and indirectly wherever 'Caesar' is mentioned in the Gospels.

BIBLIOGRAPHY. R. Seager, *Tiberius*, 1972; B. M. Levick, *Tiberius the Politician*, 1976.

E.A.J.

TIBHATH. A town in the Aramaean kingdom of Zobah (*ṣôḇâ*). After David defeated a composite force of Aramaeans, including men from Zobah and Damascus, he pressed on to the towns of Tibhath (*ṭiḇḥaṯ*) and Chun, from which he took booty (1 Ch. 18:8).

J.A.T.

TIDAL. One of four kings who subdued five kings of the cities of the plain (Sodom, Gomorrah, *etc.*), quelling their revolt 13 years later, in Abraham's time (Gn. 14:1–9). Heb. *tiḏ'āl* derives from the old Anatolian name *Tudḫali(y)a*, based on that of a sacred mountain (E. Laroche, *Les noms des Hittites*, 1966, pp. 191, 276, 283), attested also in the alphabetic texts at Ugarit as *tdgl*, *ttgl* (C. Virolleaud, *Palais royal d'Ugarit*, 2, 1957, pp. 64–66 (No. 39:21), 92 (No. 69:4)).

'Tidal king of *gōyîm*' (nations, groups) cannot be identified at present. The Hittite kings Tudkhalia II–IV (15th–13th centuries BC) are chronologically too late, likewise the Ugaritic occurrences. The name does go back, however, to the first half of the 2nd millennium BC. A possible Tudkhalia I (17th century BC?), father of Pusarruma, occurs in Hittite royal offering-lists ('C'; H. Otten, *Mitteilungen d. Deutsch. Orient-Gesellschaft* 83, 1951, pp. 62ff.; K. A. Kitchen, *Suppiluliuma and the Amarna Pharaohs*, 1962, p. 53, and Otten, *Die hethitischen historischen Quellen und die altorientalische Chronologie*, 1968, p. 26). In the story of the siege of Urshu, a little later, occurs back-reference to an official(?) named Tudkhalia (H. G. Güterbock, *ZA* 44, 1938, pp. 122/3:17; p. 135). Still earlier (*c.* 19th/18th centuries BC), Tudkhalia occurs at least twice as a private personal name in Old-Assyrian tablets from Cappadocia (Laroche, *op. cit.*, p. 191:1389:1; P. Garelli, *Les Assyriens en Cappadoce*, 1963, p. 160).

In the early 2nd millennium BC, alliances of kings are commonly attested in Mesopotamia; likewise in Anatolia then, the existence of paramount chiefs and their vassal-rulers—several such are solidly attested (A. Goetze, *Kleinasien*, 1957, p. 75; Garelli, *op. cit.*, pp. 61ff., 206, n. 4), but by no means exhaust the total of all that once existed. Therefore, it is a reasonable hypothesis that Tidal of Gn. 14 was some such Anatolian chief who (like Anum-hirbi) penetrated S into the Levant. *Cf.* also Kitchen, *Ancient Orient and Old Testament*, 1966, pp. 44–46, with references.

K.A.K.

TIGLATH-PILESER, TILGATH-PILNESER. This king of Assyria is known by more than one name. *tiḡlaṯ-pil'eser* (2 Ki. 15:29; 16:7–10) is close to Assyr. *Tukulti-apil-Ešarra* ('My trust is in the son of Ešarra') and the Aram. *tgltpl'sr* (Zinjirli Stele; Ashur ostracon. The variant *tilgaṯ-piln'eser* (1 Ch. 5:6; 2 Ch. 28:20; LXX *Algathphellasar*) may be an inner-Hebrew form (*JSS* 21, 1976, p. 7). The king's other name, Pul, is given in both the OT (2 Ki. 15:19; 1 Ch. 5:26) and the Babylonian Chronicle (*Pulu*).

Tiglath-pileser III (745–727 BC) was a son of Adad-nirari III (*AfO* 3, 1926, p. 1, n. 2). The history of his reign is imperfectly known owing to the fragmentary nature of the extant inscriptions, mainly found at Nimrud (*CALAH), but the primary events are listed in the Assyrian Eponym canon.

The first campaign was directed against the Aramaeans in Babylonia, where Pul 'took the hands of Bel' and regained control until the rebellion of Ukīn-zēr in 731 and the siege of Sapia, following which the Chaldean chief Marduk-apla-iddina (*MERODACH-BALADAN) submitted to the Assyrians. Other campaigns were directed against the Medes and Urartians (Armenia).

In 743 BC Tiglath-pileser marched to subdue the N Syrian city states which were under Urartian domination. During the 3-year siege of Arpad he received tribute from Carchemish, Hamath, *Tyre, Byblos, Rezin of Damascus and other rulers. Among those listed, *Menahem (*Menuhimme*) of Samaria, who was to die soon afterwards, raised his contribution by collecting 1 mina (50 shekels) from each of the 60,000 men of military age 'so that his hands (*i.e.* Tiglath-pileser's) would be with him to confirm the kingdom in his hands' (2 Ki. 15:19–20; *cf. Iraq* 18, 1956, p. 117).

While Tiglath-pileser himself was fighting Sarduri of Urarṭu, a revolt was instigated by 'Azriyau of Yaudi' (Annals). It would seem that when the Urartians imposed control on Carchemish, Bît-Adini (Beth-eden) and Cilicia, the weakened Aramaean states in S Syria came under the leadership of Azariah of Judah, who at this time was stronger than Israel. Azariah-Uzziah (the names *'zr* and *'zz* are variants; G. Brin, *Leshonenu* 24, 1960, pp. 8–14), however, died soon afterwards (2 Ki. 15:7), and 'Judaeans' are named among captives settled in Ullubu (near Bitlis). N Syria was organized into an Assyrian province (Unqi) under local governors.

When opposition to Assyria continued, Tiglath-pileser marched again to the W in 734. The Phoenician seaports were plundered and heavy tribute imposed on Ashkelon and on Gaza, whose ruler Hanun fled to Egypt. Statues of the Assyrian king were set up in their temples.

The army which had marched through the W border of Israel (Bit-Humri; the earlier reading of the names Galilee and Naphtali in these Annals is now disproved) turned back at the 'River of Egypt' (*naḫal-muṣur*). Rezin of Damascus, Ammon, Edom, Moab and (Jeho)ahaz of Judah (*Iauḫazi* [mat]*Iaudaia*) paid tribute to the king of Assyria. (2 Ch. 28:19–21).

Ahaz, however, received no immediate help from Assyria against the combined attacks of Rezin and Pekah of Israel, who, with Edomites and Philistines, raided Judah (2 Ch. 28:17–18). Jerusalem itself was besieged (2 Ki. 16:5–6) and relieved only by the Assyrian march on Damascus late in 733 BC. When Damascus fell in 732 BC, Metenna of Tyre also capitulated and Israel, including Ijon, Abel of Beth-Maachah, Janoah, Kadesh, Hazor, Gilead, Galilee and all Naphtali, was despoiled and captives were taken (v. 9). A destruction level at *Hazor is attributed to this period. Tiglath-pileser claims to have replaced Pekah (*Paqaḫa*) on the throne of Israel by Hoshea (*Ausi'*) and may well have plotted the murder of the former as described in 2 Ki. 15:30.

Ahaz paid for Assyrian help by becoming a vassal, which probably required certain religious concessions and practices to be observed (*cf.* 2 Ki. 16:7–16). Tiglath-pileser extended his control to include Samsi, queen of Aribi (Arabia), Sabaeans and Idiba'il (Adbeel of Gn. 25:13). With captive labour Tiglath-pileser III built himself a palace at Calah, from which have been recovered reliefs depicting the king himself and his campaigns. Although Tiglath-pileser I (1115–1077 BC) invaded Phoenicia, there is no reference to him in the OT.

BIBLIOGRAPHY. D. J. Wiseman in *Iraq* 13, 1951, pp. 21–24; *ibid.*, 18, 1956, pp. 117–129; H. W. F. Saggs in *Iraq* 19, 1957, pp. 114–154; *ZDPV*, 1974, pp. 38–49; R. D. Barnett and M. Falkner, *Sculptures of Tiglath-pileser III*, 1962; H. Tadmor, *Inscriptions of Tiglath-pileser III*, 1978. D.J.W.

TIGRIS. The Gk. name for one of the four rivers marking the location of Eden (*Hiddekel*; Gn. 2:14; Akkad. *Diglat*; Arab. *Dijlah*). It rises in the Armenian Mountains and runs SE for 1,900 km via Diarbekr through the Mesopotamian plain to join the river *Euphrates 64 km N of the Persian Gulf, into which it flows. It is a wide river as it meanders through Babylonia (Dn. 10:4) and is fed by tributaries from the Persian hills, the Greater and Lesser Zab, Adhem and Diyala rivers. When the snows melt, the river floods in Mar.–May and Oct.–Nov. Nineveh, Calah and Assur are among the ancient cities which lay on its banks. D.J.W.

TILE, TILING. Ezekiel was commanded to scratch a representation of Jerusalem on a sun-dried brick (4:1; Heb. *lᵉḇēnâ*, AV 'tile'). Plans engraved on clay tablets have been found (*e.g. ANEP*, no. 260). When Moses and the elders were given a vision of the God of Israel (Ex. 24:10) there was beneath him 'as it were a pavement of sapphire stone'. This may well be a comparison with the contemporary dais built for Rameses II at Qantir which was covered with blue glazed tiles; *cf.* 'Sapphire' under *JEWELS AND PRECIOUS STONES and W. C. Hayes, *Glazed Tiles from a Palace of Rameses II at Kantir*, 1937. Roof tiles were not used in ancient Palestine, so far as is known, so in Lk. 5:19 Gk. *keramos* should be translated more generally 'roofing'. (*HOUSE.) A.R.M.

TIME. Biblical words for time are not in themselves a sound basis for reflection on biblical concepts of time. These must be gathered from the contexts in which the words are used.

I. Times and seasons

The Hebrews had their ways of measuring the passing of time (*CALENDAR) but the most frequent contexts for the words translated 'times' and 'seasons' suggest a concern for appointed times, the right time, the opportunity for some event or action. The commonest word is *'ēṯ* (*cf.* Ec. 3:1ff. for a characteristic use); *zᵉmān* has the same meaning. *môʿēḏ* comes from a root meaning 'appoint' and is used of natural periods such as the new moon (*e.g.* Ps. 104:19) and of appointed festivals (*e.g.* Nu. 9:2). In particular, all these words are used to refer to the times appointed by God, the opportunities given by him (*e.g.* Dt. 11:14; Ps. 145:15; Is. 49:8; Je. 18:23). In NT the Gk. *kairos* often occurs in similar contexts, though it does not in itself mean 'decisive moment' (*cf.* Lk. 19:44; Acts 17:26; Tit. 1:3; 1 Pet. 1:11).

The Bible thus stresses not the abstract continuity of time but rather the God-given content of certain moments of history. This view of time may be called 'linear', in contrast with the cyclical view of time common in the ancient world; God's purpose moves to a consummation; things do not just go on or return to the point whence they began. But calling the biblical view of time 'linear' must not be allowed to suggest that time and history flow on in an inevitable succession of events; rather the Bible stresses 'times', the points at which God himself advances his purposes in the world (*DAY OF THE LORD).

God is sovereign in appointing these times, and so not even the Son during his earthly ministry knew the day and hour of the consummation (Mk. 13:32; Acts 1:7). God's sovereignty extends also to the times of an individual life (Ps. 31:15).

In the Aramaic of the book of Daniel the word *'iddān* refers to chronological periods of time (*e.g.* 2:9; 3:15), often apparently a year (*e.g.* 4:16; 7:25, though not all interpreters agree that years are meant). God's sovereignty is still stressed (2:21).

The word *chronos* sometimes refers in the NT, as in secular Gk., simply to the passing of time (*e.g.* Lk. 20:9; Acts 14:28). The context may give it the sense of 'delay', 'time of tarrying or waiting' (*e.g.* Acts 18:20, 23); this is probably the meaning of Rev. 10:6 rather than that 'time shall have an end'.

II. Eternity

Heb. has the words *'aḏ* and *'ôlām* for lengthy or remote time such as that which brings an end to man's life (*cf.* 1 Sa. 1:22, 28) or the age of the hills (Gn. 49:26). Above all, these words are applied to God, whose being is unlimited by any bound of time (Ps. 90:2). This absence of temporal limit also belongs to all God's attributes and to his grace towards his people (*cf.* Je. 31:3; 32:40; Ho. 2:19). To express more intensely the conviction that God is not limited to any fixed span Heb. uses a poetic intensive plural (*e.g.* Ps. 145:13; Dn. 9:24) or a double form (*e.g.* Ps. 132:14).

The NT usage of *aiōn* is similar; it can be used of a lifetime (1 Cor. 8:13, Phillips) or of a remote time in the past (Lk. 1:70) or future (Mk. 11:14). It is intensively used in phrases such as *eis tous aiōnas tōn aiōnōn* (*e.g.* Gal. 1:5); that such uses are intensive rather than true plurals envisaging a series of world periods, 'ages of ages', is suggested by Heb. 1:8, where the genitive is in the singular. God is also described as active *pro tōn aiōnōn*, 'before the ages' (1 Cor. 2:7).

These uses in both OT and NT correspond to the Eng. use of 'eternal, eternity' to point to that which always has existed and will exist; the language used in the Bible does not itself determine the philosophical questions concerning time and eternity, which are discussed briefly below.

The adjective *aiōnios* corresponds to the use of *aiōn* with reference to God, and therefore adds to its temporal sense of 'everlasting' a qualitative overtone of 'divine/immortal'. This tendency is helped by the fact that in late Heb. *'ôlām* is used in the spatial sense of 'the world'; *cf.* the AV translation of *aiōn* in, *e.g.*, Mk. 10:30; Eph. 1:21.

III. The two ages

The NT picks out one of the times appointed by God as decisive. The first note of Jesus' preaching was 'The time is fulfilled' (Mk. 1:15). The life and work of Jesus mark the crisis of God's purposes (Eph. 1:10). This is the great opportunity (2 Cor. 6:2) which Christians must fully seize (Eph. 5:16; Col. 4:5). Within the period of Jesus' earthly ministry there is a further narrowing of attention to the time of his death and resurrection (*cf.* Mt. 26:18; Jn. 7:6).

It is the fact that this decisive time is in the past which makes the difference between the Jewish and Christian hopes for the future: the Jew looks for the decisive intervention of God in the future; the Christian can have an even keener expectation of the consummation of all things because he knows that the decisive moment is past 'once for all'. The last times are with us already (Acts 2:17; Heb. 1:2; 1 Jn. 2:18; 1 Pet. 1:20).

The NT makes a striking modification of the contemporary Jewish division of time into the present age and the age to come. There is still a point of transition in the future between 'this time' and 'the world to come' (Mk. 10:30; Eph. 1:21; Tit. 2:12–13), but there is an anticipation of the consummation, because in Jesus God's purpose has been decisively fulfilled. The gift of the Spirit is the mark of this anticipation, this tasting of the powers of the world to come (Eph. 1:14; Heb. 6:4–6; *cf.* Rom. 8:18–23; Gal. 1:4). Hence John consistently stresses that we now have eternal life, *zōē aiōnios* (*e.g.* Jn. 3:36). It is not simply that *aiōnios* has qualitative overtones; rather John is urging the fact that Christians now have the life into which they will fully enter by resurrection (Jn. 11:23–25). This 'overlapping' of the two ages is possibly what Paul has in mind in 1 Cor. 10:11.

IV. Time and eternity

Many Christian philosophers have maintained that the intensive time language of the Bible points to aspects of the Being of God which in philosophy can best be expressed in terms of an eternity in some way qualitatively different from time.

Others have held that any talk of God's Being as timeless is unscriptural; that our language is necessarily time-referring and we cannot talk about timeless being without the risk of so abstracting it from the world that it cannot be thought to influence the world's life directly at all. Thus if the Christian view of God as active in history is to be preserved, we must adhere to biblical language rather than use any Platonist terminology which contrasts the world of time 'here' with a world of eternity 'there'. Nevertheless, the NT goes beyond a simple antithesis of this world and the next, 'now' and 'then', by its doctrine of anticipation.

Whatever the outcome of the philosophical debate, Scripture roundly asserts that God is not limited by time as we are, that he is 'the king of ages' (1 Tim. 1:17; *cf.* 2 Pet. 3:8).

BIBLIOGRAPHY. J. Barr, *Biblical Words for Time*, 1962; O. Cullmann, *Christ and Time*, 1951; H. Sasse, *TDNT* 1, pp. 197–209; H. W. Wolff, *Anthropology of the OT*, 1973, ch. 10; J. Guhrt, H.-C. Hahn, *NIDNTT* 3, pp. 826–850. M.H.C.

TIMNA. 1. A concubine of Eliphaz the son of Esau, mother of Amalek (Gn. 36:12). **2.** A daughter of Seir and sister of Lotan (Gn. 36:22). **3.** A chief of Edom (1 Ch. 1:51; wrongly called 'Timnah' in Gn. 36:40, AV). J.D.D.

TIMNAH (Heb. *timnâh*). **1.** A town on the N boundary of Judah, formerly counted as Danite (Jos. 15:10; 19:43). It changed hands more than once between Israelites and Philistines (Jdg. 14:1; 2 Ch. 28:18). Samson's first wife lived there. This may be the place Tamnā, later mentioned in the annals of Sennacherib, *c.* 701 BC (ii. 83). Tell Batashi, 9 km S of Gezer, is probably the site, though Khirbet Tibneh (4 km SE) has the name; see B. Mazar, *IEJ* 10, 1960, pp. 65–73; *NEAEHL*, pp. 152–157.

2. S of Hebron (Gn. 38:12; Jos. 15:57); copper was mined here (B. Rothenberg, *Timna*, 1972). J.P.U.L

TIMNATH-HERES, TIMNATH-SERAH (Heb. *timnaṯ-ḥeres*, *timnaṯ-seraḥ*). The personal inheritance of Joshua, where he was buried (Jos. 19:50; 24:30; Jdg. 2:9). The Samaritans claimed Kafr Haris, 16 km SW of Shechem, as the site; but H. W. Hertzberg (*PJB* 22, 1926, pp. 89ff.) proposed Khirbet Tibneh, a Late Bronze and Early Iron site 27 km from Shechem and from Jerusalem. It lies on the S side of a deep ravine (*cf.* Jos. 24:30); the traditional tomb of Joshua, mentioned by Eusebius, is in the side of the valley towards the E.

ḥeres is a rare word for 'sun' (Jdg. 1:35; 8:13; Job. 9:7; Is. 19:18, where AV 'destruction' reads *ḥerem*). If it had idolatrous implications, the variant *seraḥ* ('extra') was perhaps intended to avoid them (G. F.

Moore, *Judges*, *ICC*, 1895, on 2:9); but this leaves unexplained the retention of *ḥeres* in 2:9 and of *šemeš* in other place-names. See C. F. Burney, *Judges*, 1918, p. 32. J.P.U.L.

TIMOTHY. The son of a mixed marriage; his mother, who evidently instructed him in the Scriptures, was a Jewess and his father a Greek (Acts 16:1; 2 Tim. 1:5). He was a native of Lystra (Acts 16:1) and was highly esteemed by his Christian brethren both there and in Iconium (Acts 16:2). When he became a Christian is not specifically stated, but it is a reasonable inference that he was a convert of Paul's first missionary journey, which included Lystra in its itinerary, and that on that occasion he witnessed Paul's sufferings (2 Tim. 3:11). It is not certain when Timothy's mother Eunice became a Christian, perhaps before Timothy, but certainly before Paul's second missionary journey.

The apostle was strongly attracted to the young man and although he had only recently replaced Barnabas by Silas as his travelling companion he added Timothy to his party, perhaps as a substitute for John Mark whom he had refused to take (Acts 15:36f.). This choice appears to have had other endorsement, for Paul later refers to prophetic utterances which confirmed Timothy's being set apart for this work (*cf.* 1 Tim. 1:18; 4:14). He had received at this time a special endowment for his mission, communicated through the laying on of the hands of the elders and of Paul (1 Tim. 4:14; 2 Tim. 1:6). To allay any needless opposition from local Jews, Timothy was circumcised before setting out on his journeys.

He was first entrusted with a special commission to Thessalonica to encourage the persecuted Christians. He is associated with Paul and Silvanus in the greetings of both Epistles directed to that church, and was present with Paul during his preaching work at Corinth (2 Cor. 1:19). He is next heard of during the apostle's Ephesian ministry, when he was sent with Erastus on another important mission to Macedonia, whence he was to proceed to Corinth (1 Cor. 4:17). The young man was evidently of a timid disposition, for Paul urges the Corinthians to set him at ease and not to despise him (1 Cor. 16:10–11; *cf.* 4:17ff.). From the situation which resulted in Corinth (see 2 Cor.) Timothy's mission was not successful, and it is significant that, although his name was associated with Paul's in the greeting to this Epistle, it is Titus and not Timothy who has become the apostolic delegate. He accompanied Paul on his next visit to Corinth, for he was with him as a fellow-worker when the Epistle to the Romans was written (Rom. 16:21).

Timothy also went with Paul on the journey to Jerusalem with the collection (Acts 20:4–5) and is next heard of when Paul, then a prisoner, wrote Colossians, Philemon and Philippians. In the latter Epistle he is warmly commended and Paul intends soon to send him to them in order to ascertain their welfare. When the apostle was released from his imprisonment and engaged in further activity in the E, as the Pastoral Epistles indicate, it would seem that Paul left Timothy at Ephesus (1 Tim. 1:3) and commissioned him to deal with false teachers and supervise public worship and the appointment of church officials. Although Paul evidently hoped to rejoin Timothy, the fear that he might be delayed occasioned the writing of the first letter to him, and this was followed by another when Paul was not only re-arrested but on trial for his life. Timothy was urged to hasten to him, but whether he arrived in time cannot be ascertained. Later Timothy himself became a prisoner as Heb. 13:23 shows, but no details are given, and of his subsequent history nothing definite is known.

He was affectionate (2 Tim. 1:4) but very fearful (2 Tim. 1:7ff.), needing not a few personal admonitions from his father in the faith; he is warned not to give way to youthful lusts (2 Tim. 2:22) and not to be ashamed of the gospel (2 Tim. 1:8). Yet no other of Paul's companions is so warmly commended for his loyalty (1 Cor. 16:10; Phil. 2:19ff.; 2 Tim. 3:10ff.). It is fitting that the apostle's concluding letter should be addressed so affectionately to this almost reluctant successor, whose weaknesses are as apparent as his virtues. D.G.

TIMOTHY AND TITUS, EPISTLES TO. The two Epistles to Timothy and one to Titus, commonly grouped together as the *Pastoral Epistles, belong to the period at the close of Paul's life and provide valuable information about the great missionary apostle's thoughts as he prepared to pass on his tasks to others. They are addressed to two of his closest associates, and for that reason introduce a different kind of Pauline correspondence from the earlier church Epistles.

I. Outline of contents

1 Timothy

a. Paul and Timothy (1:1–20)

The need for Timothy to refute false teaching at Ephesus (1:3–11); Paul's experience of God's mercy (1:12–17); a special commission for Timothy (1:18–20).

b. Worship and order in the church (2:1–4:16)

Public prayer (2:1–8); the position of women (2:9–15); the qualifications of bishops and deacons (3:1–13); the church: its character and its adversaries (3:14–4:5); the church: Timothy's personal responsibilities (4:6–16).

c. Discipline within the church (5:1–25)

A discussion of the treatment suitable for various groups, especially widows and elders.

d. Miscellaneous injunctions (6:1–19)

About servants and masters (6:1–2); about false teachers (6:3 5); about wealth (6:6–10); about the aims of a man of God (6:11–16); more about wealth (6:17–19).

e. Concluding admonitions to Timothy (6:20–21)

2 Timothy

a. Paul's special regard for Timothy (1:1–14)

Greeting and thanksgiving (1:1–5); exhortations and encouragements to Timothy (1:6–14).

b. Paul and his associates (1:15–18)

The disloyal Asiatics and the helpful Onesiphorus (1:15–18).

c. Special directions to Timothy (2:1–26)

Encouragements and exhortations (2:1–13); advice on the treatment of false teachers (2:14–26).

d. Predictions about the last days (3:1–9)

The times of moral deterioration to come.

e. More advice to Timothy (3:10–17)

A reminder of Paul's early experiences of persecution (3:10–12); an exhortation to Timothy to continue as he had begun (3:13–17).

f. Paul's farewell message (4:1–22)

A final charge to Timothy (4:1–5); a confession of faith (4:6–8); some personal requests and warnings (4:9–15); Paul's first defence and his future hope (4:16–18); greetings and benediction (4:19–22).

Titus

a. Paul's greeting to Titus (1:1–4)

The apostle's consciousness of his high calling.

b. The kind of men Titus must appoint as elders (*or bishops*) (1:5–9)

c. The Cretan false teachers (1:10–16)

Their character and the need to rebuke them.

d. Christian behaviour (2:1–10)

Advice about the older and younger people and about slaves.

e. Christian teaching (2:11–3:7)

What the grace of God has done for Christians (2:11–15); what Christians ought to do in society (3:1–2); how Christianity contrasts with paganism (3:3–7).

f. Closing admonitions to Titus (3:8–15)

About good works (3:8); about false teachers (3:9–10); about Paul's companions and his future plans (3:11–15).

II. The historical situation

It is difficult to reconstruct this period of Paul's life, because there is no independent court of appeal such as the Acts supplies in the case of the earlier Epistles. But certain data may be ascertained from the Epistles themselves. At the time of writing 1 Tim. and Tit., Paul is not in prison, but when 2 Tim. was written he is not only a prisoner (1:8; 2:9), but appears to be on trial for his life, with the probability that an adverse verdict is imminent which will result in his execution (4:6–8). From 1 Tim. 1:3 it is clear that Paul had recently been in the vicinity of Ephesus, where he had left Timothy to fulfil a specific mission, mainly of administration. The Epistle to Titus provides additional historical data, for from 1:5 it may be inferred that Paul had paid a recent visit to Crete, on which occasion he must have had opportunity to ascertain the condition of the churches and to give specific instructions to Titus for rectifying any deficiencies. At the conclusion of the letter (3:12) the apostle urges Titus to join him at Nicopolis for the winter, and it is fairly safe to assume that this was the city situated in Epirus, in which case it is the sole reference to Paul visiting that district. Titus is also instructed to help Zenas and Apollos on their journey (3:13), but the precise point of this allusion is obscure.

2 Tim. is much more specific in historical information. In 1:16 Paul refers to Onesiphorus as having sought him out while in Rome, which suggests that the writer is still in Rome as a prisoner. In 4:16 he mentions an earlier trial which is generally regarded as the preliminary examination preparing for the official trial before the Roman authorities. Paul makes an interesting request in 4:13 for a cloak which he had left behind at the house of Carpus at Troas, which would seem to imply that he had recently visited there. In the same passage Paul mentions that he recently left Trophimus sick at Miletus (4:20), while Erastus, an associate of his, had stayed behind at Corinth.

It is impossible to fit all these historical data as they stand into the Acts history, and there is therefore no alternative if their authenticity is to be maintained (see later discussion) but to assume that Paul was released from the imprisonment mentioned at the close of Acts, that he had a period of further activity in the E, and that he was rearrested, tried and finally executed in Rome by the imperial authorities. The data available from the Pastorals are insufficient to facilitate a reconstruction of Paul's itinerary, but further activity in Greece, Crete and Asia is at least certain. Some scholars, on the basis of Rom. 15:24, 28, have also fitted into this period a visit to Spain, and if this assumption is correct this W visit must have preceded Paul's return to the E churches. But if Col., Phm. and Phil. are assigned to the Roman imprisonment (see separate articles) it seems clear that Paul's face was turned towards the E and not the W at the time of his release. (*CHRONOLOGY OF THE NEW TESTAMENT.)

III. Purpose

Assuming therefore that all three of these Epistles were written within a comparatively short interval of time, it must next be noted that they have a common purpose. They are all designed to supply Paul's associates with exhortations and encouragements for both present and future responsibilities. There is a good deal of instruction about ecclesiastical administration, but it would be wrong to assume that such instruction wholly accounts for the underlying purpose of each. Of the three Epistles the motive for writing 2 Tim. is clearer than that of the others. The apostle is delivering his final charge to his timid successor, and in the course of it reminds Timothy of his early history (1:5–7) and exhorts him to act worthily of his high calling. Many times throughout the Epistle solemn exhortations are directed to him (1:6, 8, 13f.; 2:1, 22; 3:14; 4:1f.), which suggest that Paul was not too certain of his courage in face of the heavy responsibilities now falling upon him. The apostle yearns to see him again and twice urges him to come as soon as possible (4:9, 21), although the tone of the concluding part of the letter suggests that Paul is not convinced that circumstances will permit a reunion (*cf.* 4:6). There are warnings about ungodly men who cause trouble to the church both in the present and in the last days (3:1f.), and Timothy is urged to avoid these. He is to entrust to worthy men the task of passing on the traditions already received (2:2).

The purpose behind the other two Epistles is less plain, for in both instances Paul has only recently left the recipients, and the need for such detailed instructions is not immediately apparent. It would seem probable that much of the subject-matter had already been communicated orally, for in both Epistles detailed qualifications are given for the main office-bearers of the church, and it is inconceivable that until this time neither Timothy nor Titus had received any such instruction. In all probability the Epistles were intended to strengthen the hands of Paul's representatives in their respective tasks. Timothy appears to have had some difficulty in commanding respect (*cf.* 1 Tim. 4:12f.), while Titus had a particularly unenviable constituency in Crete according to Tit. 1:10ff. Both men are to have sober concern for sound doctrine and right conduct and to teach it to others (1 Tim. 4:11; 6:2; Tit. 2:1, 15; 3:8).

It is not to be expected that in these letters the apostle would present to his closest friends anything in the nature of a theological treatise. There was no need to dwell on the great Christian doctrines, oral expositions of which both Timothy and Titus must often have heard from their master's lips. But they did need to be reminded of the futility of wasting time with certain groups of false teachers whose teachings were dominated by irrelevances and wordy combats which led nowhere (see 1 Tim. 1:4; 4:1f.; 6:3f., 20). There does not appear to be any close connection between these heresies in the Ephesian and Cretan churches and that combated by Paul in his letter to Colossae, but they may have been different forms of the tendency which later developed into 2nd-century Gnosticism.

IV. Authenticity

Modern criticism has so much challenged the Pauline authorship of these Epistles that the attestation of the early church is of prime importance in a fair examination of the whole question. There are few NT writings which have stronger attestation, for these Epistles were widely used from the time of Polycarp, and there are possible traces in the earlier works of Clement of Rome and Ignatius. The omission of the Epistles from Marcion's Canon (*c.* AD 140) has been thought by some to be evidence that they were not known in his time, but, in view of his propensity to cut out what did not appeal to him or disagreed with his doctrine, this line of evidence can hardly be taken seriously. The only other possible evidence for the omission of the Epistles is the Chester Beatty papyri, but since these are incomplete it is again precarious to base any positive hypothesis upon their evidence, especially in view of the fact that the Epistles were known and used in the E at an earlier period than the papyri represent.

Objections to authenticity must therefore be regarded as modern innovations contrary to the strong evidence from the early church. These objections began seriously with Schleiermacher's attack on the genuineness of 1 Tim. (1807) and have been developed by many other scholars, among whom the most notable have been F. C. Baur, H. J. Holtzmann, P. N. Harrison and M. Dibelius. They have been based on four main problems. At different periods of criticism different difficulties have been given prominence, but it is probably the cumulative effect which has persuaded some modern scholars that these Epistles cannot be by Paul.

a. The historical problem

The historical situation cannot belong to the period of the Acts history and the consequent need for postulating Paul's release has caused some scholars to suggest alternative theories. Either all the personal references are the invention of the author, or else some of them are genuine notes which have been incorporated into the author's own productions. There has never been anything approaching unanimity among the advocates of the latter alternative as to the identification of the 'notes', which in itself raises suspicions against the theory. Moreover, the notion of a fiction-writer producing personal notes of such verisimilitude is improbable, and neither theory is necessary if the perfectly reasonable supposition that Paul was released from his first Roman imprisonment is maintained.

b. The ecclesiastical problem

It has been claimed that the ecclesiastical situation reflects a 2nd-century state of affairs, but this line of criticism has been widely influenced by the assumption that: (i) 2nd-century Gnosticism is combated in the Epistles, and (ii) the church organization was too developed for the primitive period. The force of the first assumption is reduced to nothing by the increasing modern recognition that Gnosticism had much earlier roots than was at one time imagined and that the form of heresy combated in these Epistles is far removed from developed Gnosticism. The second assumption is equally insecure in view of the fact that the church organization is certainly more primitive than in the time of Ignatius and betrays no anachronism with the period of the apostle.

c. The doctrinal problem

The absence of the great Pauline doctrinal discussions as found in the earlier letters and the presence of stereotyped expressions such as 'the faith' and 'sound doctrine', which suggest a stage of development when Christian doctrine had reached fixity as tradition, have given rise to further doubts about Pauline authorship. But the recognition of the mainly personal character of these communications and of the knowledge that both Timothy and Titus already had of Paul's main teaching is sufficient to account for the first objection, while the second may be annulled by the valid assumption that Paul as a far-sighted missionary pioneer, however creative and dynamic his earlier pronouncements may have been in his church Epistles, could not have been unmindful of the need to conserve true doctrine, and the aptness of the terms used for this purpose must be admitted.

d. The linguistic problem

These Epistles contain an unusually large number of words used nowhere else in the NT and a number not found anywhere else in Paul's writings, and these indications are claimed to demonstrate their un-Pauline character, especially when supported by the absence of many pronouns, prepositions, and particles used by the apostle. But word-counts of this kind can be effective only if sufficient data exist to serve as a fair basis of comparison, and this cannot be maintained in the case of the Pauline Epistles, where the total vocabulary does not exceed 2,500 different words. There appears to be no valid reason why the differences of vocabulary and style could not have taken place in the writings of one man. Some, who in all other respects regard the Epistles as genuine but find some difficulties in the linguistic problem, resort to the hypothesis that Paul used a different amanuensis.

In conclusion, it may be stated that these objections, even when cumulatively considered, do not provide adequate reason for discarding the acknowledged and unchallenged conviction of the Christian church until the 19th century that these three Epistles are genuine writings of the apostle Paul.

V. Value

Throughout the history of the church these Epistles have been used to instruct the ministers of Christ in their duties and demeanour, and have been invaluable in providing a pattern of practical behaviour. Yet their usefulness and appeal have not been restricted to this, for they contain many gems of spiritual encouragement and theological insight which have greatly enriched the devotional life of the church. Such passages as 1 Tim. 3:16 and Tit. 2:12ff.; 3:4ff., among many others, draw the reader's attention to some of the great truths of the gospel, while the last chapter of 2 Tim. preserves the moving swan-song of the great apostle.

BIBLIOGRAPHY. C. K. Barrett, *The Pastoral Epistles*, 1963; J. N. D. Kelly, *The Pastoral Epistles, BNTC*, 1963; M. Dibelius and H. Conzelmann, *Die Pastoralbriefe*, *Hermeneia*, 1955; D. Guthrie, *The Pastoral Epistles, TNTC*[2], 1990; *idem*, *New Testament Introduction*[3], 1970; A. T. Hanson, *Studies in the Pastoral Epistles*, 1968; P. N. Harrison, *The Problem of the Pastoral Epistles*, 1921; W. Hendriksen, *Commentary on I & II Timothy and Titus, NTC*, 1957; J. Jeremias, *Die Briefe an Timotheus und Titus, NTD*, 1953; E. K. Simpson, *The Pastoral Epistles*, 1954; G. D. Fee, *1 and 2 Timothy, Titus, NIBC*, 1984; M. Prior, *Paul the Letter-Writer and the Second Letter to Timothy*, 1989.

D.G.

TIPHSAH (Heb. *tip̄saḥ*, 'a ford', 'a passage'). Probably Thapsacus, an important crossing on the W bank of the Middle Euphrates. At the NE boundary of Solomon's territory (1 Ki. 4:24), it was placed strategically on a great E–W trade route.

J.D.D.

TIRAS (Heb. *tîrās*). A son of Japheth, and brother of Gomer, Madai, Javan and Muški (Gn. 10:2; 1 Ch. 1:5), all probably N peoples (*NATIONS, TABLE OF). The name is commonly identified with the Tursha (*Trš.w*) mentioned among the N invaders in the 13th century BC by Merenptah (*EGYPT). These are in turn often equated with the *Tyrrēnoi* (dialectal form of *Tyrrhēnoi*) of Gk. literature, connected by many with the Etruscans, though this identification is still questioned.

BIBLIOGRAPHY. A. H. Gardiner, *Ancient Egyptian Onomastica*, Text, 1, 1947, p. 196*; M. Pallottino, *The Etruscans*, 1955, pp. 55–56; see also *AS* 9, 1959, pp. 197ff.; N. K. Sanders, *The Sea Peoples*, 1978.

T.C.M.

TIRHAKAH. The pharaoh Taharqa of Egypt's 25th ('Ethiopian') Dynasty; he reigned 26 years, *c.* 690–664 BC. 2 Ki. 19:9 (= Is. 37:9) appears to indicate that Tirhakah led those Egyp. forces which *Sennacherib had to defeat at *Eltekeh in 701 BC while attacking Hezekiah of Judah. If so, Tirhakah was then only the army-commander, as he was not king until 11 years later. The epithet 'king of Ethiopia' is that of the source used in Is. and 2 Ki., and would date from 690 BC or after. An alternative view, namely that Sennacherib again invaded Palestine early in Tirhakah's actual reign (*c.* 688 BC?), requires two major assumptions: a second Palestinian campaign by Sennacherib, otherwise unknown, and a conflation of the two campaigns into one by the OT narrators; references in W. F. Albright, *BASOR* 130, 1953, pp. 8–9. The theory of M. F. L. Macadam (*Temples of Kawa*, 1, 1949, pp. 18–20) that Tirhakah was born *c.* 709 BC, and so could not command troops in 701 BC, is unnecessary and open to other objections; see J. Leclant and J. Yoyotte, *Bulletin de l'Institut Français d'Archéologie Orientale* 51, 1952, pp. 17–27; K. A. Kitchen, *The Third Intermediate Period in Egypt*[2], 1986; pp. 383–386, 552–558, 584–586.

K.A.K.

TIRSHATHA. A title used of the governor of Judaea under the Persian empire (AV, Ezr. 2:63; Ne. 7:65, 70; 8:9; 10:1). It is probably a Persian form (*cf.* Avestan *taršta*, 'reverend') roughly equivalent to the Eng. 'His Excellency'. The title puzzled the Gk. translators, who either omit it or render it as a proper name, 'Athersastha', 'Attharates' or 'Atharias'.

J.S.W.

TIRZAH. 1. The youngest daughter of Zelophehad (Nu. 26:33; 27:1; Jos. 17:3).

2. A Canaanite town noted for its beauty (Ct. 6:4) which lay in the N part of Mt Ephraim at the head of the Wadi Far'ah along which passed the road from Transjordan to the central hill country where Shechem, Samaria, Dothan and other towns lay. It was captured by Joshua (Jdg. 12:24) and was assigned to Manasseh (Jos. 17:2–3). Jeroboam I lived at Tirzah (1 Ki. 14:17) and the town became the capital of the N kingdom in the time of Baasha (1 Ki. 15:21, 23; 16:6), Elah and Zimri (1 Ki. 16:8–9, 15). Zimri burnt the palace over his own head when trapped there by Omri (1 Ki. 16:17–18). After 6 years Omri transferred the capital to Samaria which was more central and easier to defend. In *c.* 752 BC Menahem, a resident of Tirzah, was able to overthrow Shallum and usurp the throne (2 Ki. 15:14, 16).

De Vaux identified the large mound of Tell el-Far'ah, about 11 km NE of Nablus, as the site of Tirzah and over the course of several years excavation revealed the archaeological story of the site. There was continuous settlement here from Chalcolithic times, before 3000 BC, down to Assyrian times. The last period of the city's life (Level I) represents the years of Assyrian domination culminating in the destruction of the city at the end of the 7th century, possibly by Nebuchadrezzar. The Israelite occupation during the days of the N kingdom is represented by levels I to III. The 9th-century level showed a standard type of house over a wide area with one larger administrative building near the gate (Level III). By the 8th century there were several large houses, a great administrative building and a considerable number of very poor houses, confirming the picture drawn by the 8th-century prophets (Am. 5:11; Is. 9:8–10). This latter phase of the city ended with the Assyrian invasion of 723–721 BC (Level II).

BIBLIOGRAPHY. R. de Vaux and A. M. Steve, several articles in *RB* from 1947 (vol. 54) to 1962 (vol. 69), especially vol. 62, 1955, pp. 587–589; 'Tirzah' in *AOTS*, pp. 371–383; 'The Excavation at Tell el-

Far'ah and the site of ancient Tirzah', *PEQ*, 1956, pp. 125–140; A. F. Rainey, *ISBE* 4, pp. 860–861; R. de Vaux, *NEAEHL* 2, pp. 433–440. J.A.T.

TISHBITE, THE (Heb. *hattišbî*). An epithet of Elijah (1 Ki. 17:1; 21:17, 28; 2 Ki. 1:3, 8; 9:36). Generally seen as denoting one from a town Tishbeh in Gilead. N. Glueck read 1 Ki. 17:1 as 'Jabeshite, from Jabesh-Gilead'. A town Tishbeh in Gilead is not otherwise known (Tobit 1:2 places one in Naphthali), but tradition locates it at al-Istib, 12 km N of the Jabbok. The word has been read as *hattōšᵉḇî*, 'the sojourner', related to the following word 'settlers' (RSVmg.).

BIBLIOGRAPHY. N. Glueck, *AASOR* 25–28, 1951, pt. 1, pp. 218, 225–227; F. M. Abel, *Géographie de la Palestine*, 2, 1937, p. 486. D.W.B.

TITHES. The custom of tithing did not originate with the Mosaic law (Gn. 14:17–20), nor was it peculiar to the Hebrews. It was practised among other ancient peoples. There are three main questions to consider.

1. What were the Hebrews required to tithe? The Torah legislated that 'the seed of the land' (crops), 'the fruit of the trees' and 'herds and flocks' (Lv. 27:30–32) were to be tithed. The manner of tithing livestock was as follows: the owner counted the animals as they passed out to pasture, and every tenth one was given to God. In this way there was no possibility of selecting inferior animals for the tithing of the flocks and herds (Lv. 27:32f.). If a Hebrew preferred to dedicate the tenth of his cereal and fruit yields in the form of their monetary value he was free to do so, but a fifth of that sum had to be added to it. He was not allowed to redeem the tenth of his flocks and herds in this way (Lv. 27:31, 33).

2. To whom were the tithes paid? They were to be given to the Levites (Nu. 18:21ff.). But in Heb. 7:5 it is said to be the sons of Levi 'who receive the priestly office' who are to be the recipients of the tithes. This departure from the Law may have been due to the Levites' unwillingness to fulfil their duties in Jerusalem after the return under Ezra (Ezr. 8:15ff.). The Levites, because of the nature of their status and functions in the community, had no means of income, livelihood or inheritance to ensure their support; therefore, and in return 'for their service which they serve, the service in the tent of meeting', they were to receive 'the tithe of the people of Israel' (Nu. 18:21, 24). This passage in Nu. 18 mentions only the tithing of cereal and fruit crops (v. 27). The Levites, however, were not allowed to keep the whole of the tenth. They were directed to present an offering which was to be taken out of the tenth, which represented 'a tithe of the tithe' (Nu. 18:26). This 'tithe of the tithe' was to be 'from all the best of them' (v. 29) and was to be given to the priests (v. 28; Ne. 10:39).

3. Where were the Hebrews to offer their tithes? They were to bring them to 'the place which the Lord your God will choose out of all your tribes, to put his name there' (Dt. 12:5f., 17f.); *i.e.* Jerusalem. And the offering of the tithes was to take the form of a ritual meal, in which the Levite was to share (Dt. 12:7, 12). If Jerusalem was a long way off from a man's village the transporting of the tithe of his crops might create a problem, but he could always take his tithe in the form of money (Dt. 14:22–27). Every third year the tithe was to be offered in each man's own locality (Dt. 14:28f.), although on these occasions he was still obligated to go up to Jerusalem to worship after the offering of his tithes in his home community (Dt. 26:12ff.).

To these comparatively simple laws in the Pentateuch governing tithing there were added a host of minutiae which turned a beautiful religious principle into a grievous burden. These complex additions are recorded in the Mishnaic and Talmudic literature. This unfortunate tendency in Israel undoubtedly contributed to the conviction that acceptance with God could be merited through such ritual observances as tithing (Lk. 11:42), without submitting to the moral law of justice, mercy and faith (Mt. 23:23f.).

The tithes paid by Abraham, the ancestor of Israel and, therefore, of the Aaronic priesthood, to Melchizedek (Gn. 14:20), and his receiving the blessing of this priest-king (Gn. 14:19), signify in Heb. 7:1ff. that Melchizedek's priesthood was infinitely superior to the Aaronic or levitical priesthood. Why Abraham paid tithes to Melchizedek is not explained in Gn. 14:18–20.

The NT reference to the tithing of 'mint and dill and cummin' (Mt. 23:23; Lk. 11:42) illustrates a Talmudic extension of the Mosaic law, ensuring that 'everything that is eaten . . . and that grows out of the earth' must be tithed. J.G.S.S.T.

TITUS. Although not mentioned in Acts, Titus was one of Paul's companions in whom he placed a considerable amount of trust. He is first heard of at the time of the Gentile controversy when he accompanied Paul and Barnabas to Jerusalem (Gal. 2:1). He provided a test case, since he was a Gentile, but he was apparently not compelled to be circumcised (Gal. 2:3). Titus probably accompanied Paul on his subsequent journeys, but no definite information of his work is available until the time of the Corinthian crisis. He had evidently been acting as Paul's representative at Corinth during the year preceding the writing of 2 Cor. (*cf.* 8:16) with a special commission to organize the collection scheme there. The task was unfinished, for Titus is later urged by Paul to return to Corinth to see its completion (2 Cor. 8:6).

A more delicate task was the smoothing over of the tense situation which had arisen between Paul and the Corinthians, a task which clearly demanded a man of great tact and force of character. He appears to have been a stronger personality than Timothy (*cf.* 1 Cor. 16:10; 2 Cor. 7:15) and possessed ability as an administrator. A comparison of 2 Cor. 2 and 7 suggests that he carried a letter from Paul to the Corinthians which has since been lost (the 'severe letter') and in which the apostle took them to task with much anguish of heart for their high-handed attitude. Titus eventually rejoined Paul in Macedonia (2 Cor 7:6) with good news, and as a result 2 Cor. was written and was willingly carried by Titus (2 Cor. 8:16f.), who seems to have possessed a particular affection and serious concern for the Corinthians. He is described by the apostle as his 'partner and fellow worker' (8:23), who would not think of taking advantage of those entrusted to his care (12:18).

From the Epistle addressed to him it may be surmised that Titus accompanied Paul to Crete subsequent to the latter's release from the Roman imprisonment and was left there to consolidate the work (Tit. 1:5f.). The letter urges the use of authority in establishing a worthy ministry, in overcoming opposition, and in the teaching of sound doctrine. He was summoned to rejoin Paul at Nicopolis when relieved by either Artemas or Tychicus (Tit. 3:12), and may possibly have been further commissioned at Nicopolis for an evangelistic mission to Dalmatia on which he was engaged at the time when Paul wrote 2 Tim. (2 Tim. 4:10). Later tradition, however, assumed his return to Crete and described him as bishop there until his old age (Eusebius, *EH* 3. 4. 6). For the possibility that he was Luke's brother (which might explain the absence of his name from Acts), see W. M. Ramsay, *SPT*, p. 390. D.G.

TOB. The name of an Aramaean city and principality lying N of Gilead, mentioned in connection with Jephthah and David (Jdg. 11:3; 2 Sa. 10:6); the district named in 1 Macc. 5:13 is probably identical. The likely location of the city is al-Taiyiba (preserving the ancient name), some 20 km ENE of Ramoth-gilead. For its history, *cf.* B. Mazar, *BA* 25, 1962, pp. 98–120. D.F.P.

TOBIAH. 1. One of *Nehemiah's principal opponents, Tobiah is described by him as 'the servant (or 'slave', NEB), the Ammonite' (Ne. 2:10). 'Servant' may well be an honourable title for a high-ranking Persian official; 'Ammonite' could refer to his ancestry, though he seems at least half Jewish, since his name means 'Yahweh is good', his son is called Jehohanan ('Yahweh is merciful'; Ne. 6:18), and he has many important friends among the Jews (6:18f.; 13:4f.). Some have seen him as Persian governor of the sub-province of Ammon, or even governor of Jerusalem before Nehemiah's arrival (*cf.* Ne. 5:15), but his close association with Sanballat, governor of Samaria (4:7; 6:1) suggests rather that he was Sanballat's deputy. It is uncertain whether this Tobiah had any connection with the famous family of the Tobiads, who in the 3rd century BC ruled a large area of Ammon from their fortress at 'Araq el-Amir, 20 km NW of Heshbon, and were one of the most influential pro-Greek families in Jerusalem (Josephus, *Ant.* 12. 160–236). The inscription at 'Araq el-Amir mentioning a Tobiah is now thought to be no earlier than the 2nd century BC.

2. The name of a clan unable to prove its authentic Israelite ancestry at the time of the 6th-century return from exile (Ezr. 2:60; Ne. 7:62; 1 Esdras 5:37). The *Tobijah of Zc. 6:10, 14, a leading nobleman in Jerusalem, *c.* 520 BC, may perhaps belong to the Tobiah family.

BIBLIOGRAPHY. B. Mazar, *IEJ* 7, 1957, pp. 137–145, 229–238; C. C. McCown, *BA* 20, 1957, pp. 63–76; P. W. Lapp, *BASOR* 171, 1963, pp. 8–39. D.J.A.C.

TOGARMAH. The third son of Gomer, grandson of Japheth and brother of Ashkenaz and Riphath (Gn. 10.3; 1 Ch. 1:6). (Beth-) Togarmah, with Tubal, *Javan and *Meshech, supplied horses and mules to Tyre (Ezk. 27:14) and soldiers to *Gog (Ezk. 38:6). During the 2nd millennium BC Old Assyrian and Hittite texts locate Tegarama near Carchemish and Harran on a main trade-route. It was called Til-garimmu in the Annals of Sargon and Sennacherib, and was the capital of Kammanu on the border of Tabal (*TUBAL), until destroyed in 695 BC. Perhaps to be identified with classical Gauraena, modern Gürün, 120 km W of Malatya. D.J.W.

TOLA (Heb. *tôlā'*). **1.** A family name in a clan of Issachar (Gn. 46:13; Nu. 26:23; 1 Ch. 7:1–2). **2.** Tola ben Puah, of Shamir, an unknown village in Mt Ephraim, who was a national judge for 23 years after Abimelech's reign (Jdg. 10:1). Puah was also a family name in Issachar. J.P.U.L.

Reconstruction of the façade of a shrine built by the Tobiad family at Araq el-Emir, Jordan. c. 175 BC.

TONGUE. Heb. *lāšôn*, Gk. *glōssa*, both of the tongue of man and, by extension, of man's language. The Heb. is also used of the tongue of animals and reptiles (Jb. 20:16), with the still common misapprehension that the poison of a snake lies in its tongue. It is also used of tongue-shaped objects or phenomena, *e.g.* a wedge of gold (Jos. 7:21) or a bay of the sea (Jos. 15:2).

It was apparently believed in biblical times that dumbness was due to some paralysis or binding of the tongue or its cleaving to the palate (Ps. 137:6; Mk. 7:35; Lk. 1:64) (see *BODY for a statement on the apparent belief among the Hebrews that the organs functioned semi-independently).

The tongue is used in parallel with or interchangeably for *lip and *mouth, as the instruments of speech or related concepts, and is spoken of as good or evil (Ps. 120:2; Pr. 6:17; 10:20), taught (Is. 50:4), singing (Ps. 51:14) and speaking (Ps. 71:24). As the mouth can be said to contain something, so wickedness can be hidden under the tongue (Jb. 20:12).

The metaphor of a sharp tongue was used in OT times. The tongue was spoken of as being whetted like a sword (Ps. 64:3; *cf.* Ps. 140:3; Heb. 4:12; Rev. 1:16) and the simile of a bow and arrow is also used (Je. 9:3, 8). The tremendous influence of words for good or ill is expressed by attributing power to the tongue (Pr. 18:21; Jas. 3:5–6).

Famine and thirst are described as causing the tongue to cleave to the palate (La. 4:4), and it rots through disease (Zc. 14:12).

The tongue is used in Ps. 55:9 figuratively to refer to the confusion of language as at Babel (Gn. 11:1ff., where the word for language is 'lip', *śāpâ*; *cf.* Is. 19:18). The alienation of man from man due to the gulf created by language difference, cutting, as it does, across the whole area of instinctive feelings, common interests and co-operation, is attributed in the Gn. passage to the sinful pride of man, bringing upon them this form of visitation by God.

The word 'tongue' is thus used to describe the different nations, or tribes, which generally have distinctive languages (Is. 66:18; Rev. 5:9).

(*TONGUES, GIFT OF.) B.O.B.

TONGUES, GIFT OF. Speaking in tongues, or glossolalia (a 19th-century formation from Gk. *glōssa*, tongue, and *lalia*, speech), is a spiritual gift mentioned in Mk. 16:17, RSVmg.; Acts 10:44–46; 19:6, and described in Acts 2:1–13; 1 Cor. 12–14. The same phenomenon may lie behind such passages as 1 Thes. 5:19; Rom. 12:11.

When the assembled disciples were filled with the Holy Spirit on the day of Pentecost they began 'to speak in other tongues (*lalein heterais glōssais*), as the Spirit gave them utterance' (Acts 2:4), so that many Jews of the Dispersion were astonished to hear the praises of God in their own native languages (*glōssa*, v. 11; *dialektos*, vv. 6, 8). Although it is generally agreed that Luke intended the phrase 'to speak in other tongues' to mean that the disciples spoke in foreign languages, this explanation has not been universally accepted. From the days of the early Fathers some have seen in v. 8 evidence for a miracle of hearing performed on the audience. Gregory Nazianzen (*Orat.* 41. 10, *In Pentecosten*) rejected this view on the ground that it transfers the miracle from the disciples to the unconverted multitude. It also overlooks the fact that speaking in tongues began before there was any audience (v. 4; *cf.* v. 6) and some bystanders thought what they heard was drunken babbling (v. 13).

In the opinion of most modern scholars the glossolalia of Acts 2:1–13 was similar to that described in 1 Cor. 12–14, and consisted of unintelligible ecstatic utterances. They advance various theories to explain why Luke wrote instead about foreign languages. Some think he may have misinterpreted his sources and inserted 'other' (Acts 2:4) on his own initiative; others suggest that he may have interpolated the reference to foreign languages as a more favourable explanation when glossolalia fell into disrepute. Yet others regard his narrative as a dogmatic creation combining reports of ecstatic glossolalia with legends of the giving of the law at Sinai in the 70 languages of mankind (Midrash *Tanḥuma* 26c), the conception of Pentecost as a reversal of the curse of Babel (Gn. 11:1–9) and his own universalism. However, it is unlikely that Luke, a careful historian (Lk. 1:1–4) and close companion of Paul (who spoke in tongues, 1 Cor. 14:18), misunderstood the nature of glossolalia. If the disciples did not actually speak in foreign languages at Pentecost, then the most satisfactory explanation is that Luke records from his sources the convictions of those present who believed they had recognized words of praise to God in other languages. The straightforwardness of the narrative and the scorn of the mockers (v. 13) count against the mediating view that the disciples' speech was delivered from its peculiarities (v. 7; *cf.* Mk. 14:70) and made intelligible to their hearers, most of whom would probably know Greek or Aramaic.

Speaking 'in new tongues' (*glōssais kainais*) is mentioned in Mk. 16:17 (not an original part of the Gospel) as a sign following faith in Christ. It accompanied the outpouring of the Holy Spirit upon the first Gentile converts (Acts 10:44–46; 11:15), and was doubtless one of the manifestations among the earliest Samaritan believers (Acts 8:18). The isolated group of disciples at Ephesus, who may have been early believers in Christ unaware of Pentecost (N.B. Stonehouse, *WTJ* 13, 1950–1, pp. 11ff.) also spoke in tongues when the Holy Spirit came on them (Acts 19:6). In each case spontaneous glossolalia was perceptible evidence of the repetition, in association with the ministry of an apostle (*cf.* 2 Cor. 12:12), of the initial bestowal of the Spirit at Pentecost, and apparently served to endorse the inclusion of new classes of believers into the cautious Jewish-Christian church (*cf.* Acts 10:47; 11:17–18). If tongues serve as a sign of covenantal judgment for Israel (Is. 28:10ff.; *cf.* Dt. 28:49; 1 Cor. 14:21ff.), and the tongues of Pentecost represent the taking of the kingdom from Israel and giving it to men of all nations (see O. P. Robertson, *WTJ* 38, 1975, pp. 43–53), the pattern of glossolalic occurrences in Acts emphasizes this transition.

Corinthian glossolalia differed in some respects from that described in Acts. In Jerusalem, Caesarea and Ephesus, whole companies on whom the Spirit fell immediately broke into tongues, whereas at Corinth not all possessed the coveted gift (1 Cor. 12:10, 30). Glossolalia in Acts appears to have been an irresistible and possibly temporary initial experience, whereas Paul's instructions to the Corinthians imply a continuing gift under the control of the speaker (1 Cor. 14:27–28). At Pentecost 'tongues' were understood by the hearers, but at Corinth the additional gift of interpretation was necessary to make them intelligible (1 Cor. 14:5, 13, 27). Only at Pentecost is speaking in foreign languages explicitly mentioned. On the other hand, glossolalia is everywhere represented as consisting of meaningful utterances inspired by the Holy Spirit and employed primarily for worship (Acts 2:11; 10:46; 1 Cor. 14:2, 14–17, 28).

The 'various kinds of tongues' (1 Cor. 12:10) may include unlearned languages, non-languages, or other forms of utterance (*cf.* S. D. Currie, *Int* 19, 1965, pp. 274–294). At Corinth they were apparently not foreign languages, which Paul denotes by a different word (*phōnē*, 14:10–11), because a special gift, not linguistic proficiency, was necessary to understand them; nor were they for him meaningless ecstatic sounds, though the mind was inactive (v. 14) and the utterances, without interpretation, unintelligible even to the speaker (v. 13), because words (v. 19) and contents (vv. 14–17) were recognized, and interpreted tongues were equivalent to prophecy (v. 5). A definite linguistic form is suggested by the Gk. words for 'to interpret', which elsewhere in the NT, except Lk. 24:27, always mean 'to translate' (*cf.* J. G. Davies, *JTS* n.s. 3, 1952, pp. 228ff.; R. H. Gundry, *JTS* n.s. 17, 1966, pp. 299–307), and Paul probably regarded them as special heavenly languages not having ordinary human characteristics, inspired by the Holy Spirit for worship, for a sign to unbelievers (O. P. Robertson, *op. cit.*; J. P. M. Sweet, *NTS* 13, 1966–7, pp. 240–257), and, when interpreted, for the edification of believers. The Corinthians so overrated and abused glossolalia that Paul strictly limited its exercise in public (1 Cor. 14:27–28), and emphasized the superior value of prophecy for the whole church (1 Cor. 14:1, 5). Whilst it is uncertain how far later manifestations of glossolalia resemble the NT phenomenon, recent studies evaluate them as cadences of vocalization, not languages.

BIBLIOGRAPHY. J. Behm, *TDNT* 1, pp. 722–727; W. E. Mills, *Glossolalia: A Bibliography*, 1985; *idem*, *A Theological/Exegetical Approach to Glossolalia*, 1985; *idem* (ed.), *Speaking in Tongues: A Guide to Research on Glossolalia*, 1986; W. J. Samarin, *Tongues of Men and Angels*, 1972; A. C. Thiselton, 'The "Interpretation" of Tongues?' *JTS* n.s. 30, 1979; C. G. Williams, *Tongues of the Spirit: A Study of Pentecostal Glossolalia and Related Phenomena*, 1981. W.G.P.

TOPHEL. Mentioned only in Dt. 1:1 as the locality where Moses addressed the Israelites. The identification with el-Tafileh, 25 km SE of the Dead Sea, is philologically unlikely (N. Glueck, *AASOR* 18–19, 1939, pp. 42–43). Tophel may well have been a stopping-place in the Israelites' wilderness itinerary. D.J.W.

TOPHETH (AV **TOPHET**). This was a 'high place' in the valley of *Hinnom just outside Jerusalem, where child sacrifices were offered by fire to a deity *Molech. Josiah defiled this idolatrous shrine (2 Ki. 23:10), and Jeremiah prophesied that the place would be used as a cemetery (Je. 7:32f.). The root of the noun seems to be the *tpt* of Aram. and Arab. denoting 'fireplace'. The vowels are artificial, taken from the Heb. noun *bōšeṯ*, 'shame'. D.F.P.

TORCH. The word is usually a translation of Heb. *lappîḏ* in OT and of Gk. *lampas* in NT. *lappîḏ* signifies the traditional torch consisting of a long pole with rags soaked in oil wrapped round the top of it. The word is translated as 'lightnings' in Ex. 20:18. *lampas* is normally translated 'torch' in Jn. 18:3 and Rev. 4:5; 8:10. In Acts 20:8, where the scene is a domestic one, translations generally render it as 'lamp' or 'light' (RSV). The other occurrences are all in Mt. 25:1–8, the parable of the wise and foolish maidens. While most translations favour the rendering 'lamp', it would probably be more appropriate to see a reference to the torches which were used in wedding processions. R.E.N.

TOWN CLERK. The *grammateus* (Acts 19:35) was frequently the secretary of a board of magistrates, responsible for the accurate recording of official decisions. At Ephesus he was clearly the president of the assembly. His punctilious regard for legal niceties, and anxiety about Roman intervention, mark him as a member of the Romanized aristocracy, among whom Paul found support (v. 31). His speech has been much admired as a little masterpiece of political *savoir faire*. E.A.J.

TRACHONITIS. The only biblical reference is Lk. 3:1, where, linked with *Ituraea, it is called the tetrarchy of Philip (the brother of Herod, tetrarch of Galilee). Trachonitis must have been the district around Trachon (Josephus uses both names); Trachon corresponds with the modern al-Laja', a pear-shaped area of petrified volcanic rock some 900 square km in area, to the E of Galilee and S of Damascus. It is on the whole extremely unproductive, but here and there are patches of fertile ground, with a spring or two. The cracked and broken nature of its terrain made it ideal for outlaws and brigands. Among others Varro (governor of Syria under Augustus), Herod the Great and Herod Agrippa I endeavoured to civilize the area, with varying success. Later on a Roman road was built through it. Targum Jonathan identifies the OT *Argob with Trachonitis. D.F.P.

TRADE AND COMMERCE.

I. In the Old Testament

*Palestine has always been the only natural bridge between Europe and Asia on the N and Africa on the S. This accounts for the fact that, although she was a poor country, she was constantly enriched by the trade and commerce that went through her land. Ezk. 27:12–25 presents a cross-section of the world commerce that passed through her territory.

Palestine's major contributions to commerce in OT times were agricultural products and metals. Phoenicia just to the N was a manufacturing area forced to import food. Israel supplied her with grain, oil and wine. Egypt to the S had a surplus of grain, but was short of olive oil and wine. As the desert peoples to the E became more influential after David's day they too absorbed Palestine's agricultural products.

Iron, which had been earlier introduced by the Philistines, appeared in such quantity after David's wide conquests in Syria that it could also be passed on to iron-hungry Egypt. Solomon traded down the Red Sea to the backward peoples of Arabia and Africa. These lands in return sent precious incense, spices and gold to the Mediterranean *via* Palestine as well as Egypt. This Arabian commerce in Palestine was at its peak in Nabataean times. During the intertestamental period the asphalt traffic from the Dead Sea was so important that this body of water was called the Asphalt Sea, and it entered into international politics. Perfumes and spices were always items of exchange, some varieties moving out of the country and others moving in. Both were more important in ancient times than today. Spices, for example, were a common method of varying a rather monotonous menu.

Palestine's flocks produced a surplus of wool, which was probably exported both in bulk and as manufactured goods. Moab was a major wool producer. The excavations at Tell beit Mirsim have shown that this was a manufacturing city devoted exclusively to weaving and dyeing of cloth. Flax was also used for clothing. If it was exported, then it was sent to Phoenicia, since Egypt was a heavy producer of linen. The wide distribution of expensive garments is shown by the finding of a Babylonian garment at the time of Joshua's conquest of Jericho, although that city was of minor importance. The value of good raiment is seen in the fact that it was commonly included in the list of booty taken in war.

*Egypt was the outstanding manufacturing nation along the Mediterranean in early days, but Phoenicia began to cut into her trade by imitating and modifying Egyp. craftsmanship. With Phoenicia's expanding manufacturing and shipping trade, Israel had a constantly increasing market for her agricultural products. Palestine itself entered the manufacturing field about the time of the written prophets. Indeed, much of their social criticism deals with the inevitable economic crises which come when any agricultural people shifts into full-scale manufacturing. An early date to Pentateuchal laws is demonstrated by the absence of any manufacturing code. Palestine used modern assembly-line techniques and standardization of forms and sizes. Their mass-production material was of good quality, although they were often using poorer materials and cheaper labour. Their manufactured goods, however, seemed to have been primarily for local consumption. Trade guilds came in at this time, and trade marks were used by the pottery manufacturers. (*ARTS AND CRAFTS.) In OT times agricultural taxes were largely paid in kind, and the government had its own potteries making official government standardized containers with the government seal stamped on the handles.

Coined *money came into Palestine towards the close of OT times. Previously gold and silver in ingots, bars and rings were weighed out. Jewels offered a more convenient and fairly safe method of investing and transporting larger sums than would be convenient in bullion. After Alexander the Great, coined money was common. During the intertestamental period, Jewish bankers came into prominence, and the synagogues of Asia Minor in NT times are in part due to Jewish influence in banking and commerce. During this same period Alexandria, which had become probably the greatest manufacturing city of the world, attracted a heavy Jewish population.

Only in the days of Solomon and Jehoshaphat did sea commerce play an important part in Palestinian trade, and both ventures were short-lived. Sea commerce was predominantly in the hands of foreigners, first Philistines and other sea peoples, then later Phoenicians and Greeks.

For land travel the ass was the beast of burden until about David's day, when the camel, previously used primarily for war, also became available for the caravan trade. Part of Palestine's commercial wealth came from these caravans, which purchased necessary supplies from farmers and craftsmen as they moved through the country. At the local market-place the population absorbed foreign news, and the efficacy of this news medium can be seen in the sermons of Amos, with their broad picture of world affairs. Ishmaelites and Midianites handled much of the early commerce on the desert fringe. Later the Ammonites took over from them and became the dominant camel-owning people before the Nabataeans, who brought desert commerce to its financial peak.

Ben-hadad and the Omri dynasty had business depots in each other's capital city, and this was probably common practice between adjacent nations. Israel and Phoenicia were normally on far better terms with each other than Israel and Syria. A good source of income for the government was the tax on commerce entering the country. This source of wealth, of course, was at its peak in the days of David and Solomon. But there was a second peak of prosperity under Jeroboam II in Israel and Uzziah in Judah.

The major trade routes of Palestine ran N and S. The most important came out of Egypt, crossed the Philistine plain, continued along the E edge of the plain of Sharon, crossed the Carmel ridge at Megiddo, and then went on to Dan either *via* Hazor of Galilee or *via* Beth-shan and the upland road just N of the Yarmuq river. The high ridge road *via* Beersheba, Hebron, Jerusalem, Shechem and Beth-shan handled more local traffic than through commerce. E of the Jordan valley was the King's Highway coming out of the Gulf of Aqabah and touching the key cities of Kir, Dibon, Medeba, *etc.*, along the centre of the populated areas. A second road followed a parallel track to the E of the King's Highway and just inside the desert fringe. Today a modern road follows the former and the railway the latter. These routes picked up the Arabian trade at such points as Petra, Amman and Edrei.

E and W roads were less profitable, except the most S one, where Arabian commerce came *via* Nabataean Petra to Gaza. Commerce also came out of the caravan city of Amman, down the Jabbok valley, up to Shechem and over to the Mediterranean. More commerce, however, probably came through the Hauran down to Beth-shan and up the plain of Esdraelon to the Mediterranean. The great grain fields of the Hauran sold their wheat down this route. A shorter road cut across Galilee from the Sea of Galilee to Accho. The major seaports used in OT times were Joppa, Dor and Accho. Ashkelon was the Philistine seaport, and Gaza was the Mediterranean outlet for the Nabataean trade.

BIBLIOGRAPHY. D. Baly, *The Geography of the Bible*[2], 1974; data from ancient Near East: *cf.* W. F. Leemans, H. Hirsch, in D. O. Edzard (ed.), *Reallexikon der Assyriologie*, 4, 1973, pp. 76–97; from Egypt: W. Helck, in Helck and Otto (eds.), *Lexikon der Ägyptologie*, 2, 1976, cols. 943–948.

J.L.K.

II. In the New Testament

Trade and commerce have no large place in the NT. The coast of Palestine is harbourless and swept with surf, and no natural port formed a cross-road for trade. The sea in Heb. metaphor is a barrier, not a pathway, and such an attitude was natural in a land which fronted the unbroken border of the waters. The ruins of artificial harbours are common enough, and suggest rather the futility than the success of man's attempts to tame the E end of the Mediterranean (see G. A. Smith, *The Historical Geography of the Holy Land*[25], 1931, pp. 127–144).

Caravan routes, on the other hand, naturally converged on Palestine, and the NT is aware of the activities of the trader. Such parables as those of the talents and the merchant who found 'a pearl of great price' were obviously meant to be understood by the audience to which they were addressed. But this was the petty trade of a small, poor and under-privileged land.

Major activities in trade and commerce, all through NT times, were in the hands of the Romans and Italians. State interference with the processes of trade, which became a sombre feature of late imperial times, was already visible in the 1st century. The legal machinery by which a 'mark in hand or head' could prevent the non-conformist from buying and selling (Rev. 13:16–17) was early apparent. The foreign trade of the empire was extensive and varied. There is also evidence that it was unbalanced, for the hoards of Rom. coins found commonly in India are clear indication of a perilous leakage of bullion, and one cause of the creeping paralysis of inflation.

Lat. and Gk. words in early Irish, German, Iranian, Indian and even Mongolian tongues are evidence of the wide influence of Rom. trade. Archaeology, especially on the S Indian coast, has a similar word to say. An excavation at Pondicherry has established the fact of a large Rom. trade with India in the 1st century. Rom. merchants, indeed, were ubiquitous. There was a Rom. market, the remains of which may still be seen, outside the sacred precincts at Delphi. Trade was no doubt brisk in amulets and souvenirs, and may have been typical of petty Italian enterprise abroad wherever crowds were gathered. Similar activity in the Temple of Jerusalem had been cannily kept in the hands of the Sadducean chief priests.

From the 2nd century before Christ a Rom. city stood on Delos, the Aegean centre of the slave-trade, and when Mithridates in 88 BC massacred the Italian residents of Asia Minor and the Aegean islands, 25,000 fell in Delos alone out of a total of 100,000 victims. They must have been mostly traders and the agents of commerce. The capital itself, whose population in the 1st century was something like one million, was a vast market, and a grim, satiric chapter in the Apocalypse (Rev. 18), constructed after the fashion of an OT 'taunt-song', and in imitation of Ezk. 27, speaks of the wealth and volume of Rome's luxury trade, and the economic disruption sure to follow the loss of a market so rich. Ostia, Rome's port, is full of warehouses.

Rom. trade extended far beyond the boundaries of the empire. The 'far country' of Mt. 25:14 is quite literal. Merchants from Italy carried their foods into unsubdued Germany, along the 'amber route' to the Baltic, to India and perhaps China. All this activity sprang from Rome's dominance, the peace which she policed, and above all from the absence of political frontiers over significant areas of the world. Petronius' Trimalchio, the *nouveau riche* of the *Satiricon*, could make fortunes and lose them, and make them again. Of Augustus the merchants said that 'through him they sailed the seas in safety, through him they could make their wealth, through him they were happy'.

The account of the last journey of Paul to Rome, so ably told by Luke, first in a ship of Adramyttium of Asia Minor, and then in an Alexandrian freighter, probably under charter to the Rom. government for the transport of Egyp. corn, gives a vivid picture of the hazards of trade and navigation.

Apart from the list of Rev. 18, which may have been deliberately selected in accordance with the polemic and satirical purpose of the passage, the commodities of export trade are not widely known. No cargo lists survive. Oysters came from Britain to Rome in barrels of sea-water. Cornish tin, no doubt, came down the same sea-route. N Gaul seems to have had the rudiments of an exporting textile industry, and Gaul certainly exported cheap Samian pottery. Underwater archaeology on wrecked ships has revealed that large cargoes of wine were carried. A monogram device of a double S in a trident seems to indicate that one such freighter, wrecked near Marseilles, was the property of one Severus Sestius, who occupied 'the House of the Trident' on Delos.

On the subject of mass production for such trade there is little information, and none on the business organization necessarily involved. Certain localities, however, became famous for special products, and the resultant commerce would have been in the control of specialist traders who would create and operate their own markets. A striking example is Lydia, 'a seller of purple goods', from the city of Thyatira in Asia Minor (Acts 16:14), whom Paul's party met at Philippi in Macedonia. Corinthian bronze, in ornaments and mirrors (1 Cor. 13:12), and the *cilicium* or goats'-hair cloth, which was either the product or the raw-material of Paul's tent-making (Acts 18:3), were probably distributed by similar private enterprise. The imagery of John's letter to Laodicea (Rev. 3:14–18) is partly derived from the trade and commerce of the town. Ramsay has established the existence of a Laodicean trade in valuable black woollen garments. Laodicea and Colossae produced black fleeces, the evidence of which is still genetically apparent, it is said, in the sheep of the area today. There was also a Laodicean eye-salve, based probably on the kaolin of the thermal area at Hierapolis, 10 km away. Hence the taunt about 'white garments' and 'eye-salve' (see W. M. Ramsay, *The Letters to the Seven Churches of Asia*, chs. 29–30).

*Thyatira, of the earlier letter, was also a centre of trade and commerce, though probably without Laodicea's export emphasis. Lydia has already been mentioned, and archaeological evidence speaks of wool- and linen-workers, dyers, leather-workers, tanners, potters, slave-traders and bronze-smiths. The dyers, and Lydia was probably one of them, dealt in a purple dye made from the madder root, which undercut the expensive sea-dye from the murex shell.

It is curious to note that, in writing to Thyatira, John uses the figure of Jezebel, sign and symbol of Israel's compromising trade partnership with

Phoenicia, to describe a local 'Nicolaitan'. 'Jezebel' of Thyatira had no doubt taught some form of compromise with the surrounding pagan world. In a town of brisk trade activity some such adjustment would appear more urgently necessary because of the power of the trade guilds.

These organizations were a source of major difficulty to Christians, who sought, in their daily converse with the pagan world around, to keep a clear conscience. The trade guilds or *collegia* appear in Acts 19 as a force of organized opposition to Christianity. An important trade commodity of Ephesus, now that the harbour was silting, and commerce was passing to Smyrna, was the manufacture of silver souvenirs and cult objects of Artemis, for sale to the pilgrims who visited the famous shrine. Ephesus saw the guilds concerned exercise sufficient pressure to end Paul's ministry. A famous letter of Pliny (*Ep.* 10. 96), which vividly describes the suppression of a vigorous church in Bithynia in AD 112, is also a clear indication of such influence. The guild of the butchers, alarmed at the falling sales of sacrificial meat, successfully stirred up official action against the church. It was difficult for Christians, whose trade depended upon a measure of goodwill, to carry on their daily activities if they obviously abstained from fellowship with their colleagues. On the other hand, since all the callings of trade and commerce were under the patronage of pagan deities, fellowship, and indeed membership of a trade *collegium*, involved the compromising act of libation or sacrifice at the guild dinner. Records exist of a considerable number of such organizations, and the strictures of Jude, Peter and John against the 'Nicolaitans', the 'followers of Balaam' and 'Jezebel', suggest that the simple functions of trade and commerce may have proved a source of deep division in the early church.

BIBLIOGRAPHY. R. Duncan-Jones, *The Economy of the Roman Empire: Quantitative Studies*, 1982; P. Garnsey and R. Saller, *The Roman Empire: Economy, Society and Culture*, 1987. E.M.B.

TRADITION (Gk. *paradosis*). That which is handed down, particularly teaching handed down from a teacher to his disciples. The concept is often present without the word being mentioned. The main references in the Gospels occur in Mt. 15 and Mk. 7, and concern Jewish tradition.

I. Jewish tradition

The word tradition does not occur in the OT, but between the Testaments much teaching in explanation of the OT was added by the rabbis. Tradition was handed down from teacher to pupil, and by Jesus' day had assumed a place alongside Scripture. This equation of human commentary with divine revelation was condemned by the Lord. By such tradition the Word of God was 'transgressed', 'made of none effect', laid aside, and rejected (Mt. 15:3, 6; Mk. 7:8–9, 13). The doctrines taught by tradition were 'the commandments of men' (Mt. 15:9; Mk. 7:6–7).

II. Christian tradition

Jesus placed his own teaching alongside the Word of God as an authoritative commentary, which he handed down to his disciples. Thus in the Sermon on the Mount Jesus quoted from the Law, but put beside it his own words, 'but I say to you' (Mt. 5:22, 28, 32, 34, 39, 44; *cf.* 6:25). His justification for so doing is found in his Person. As the Spirit-anointed Messiah, the Word made flesh, he alone could make a valid and authoritative commentary on the Spirit-inspired Word of God. Likewise the Epistles emphasize the Person of Christ in contrast to tradition. In Col. 2:8 Paul warns against falling prey to 'philosophy and empty deceit . . . according to human tradition . . . and not according to Christ'. So in Gal. 1:14, 16 Paul abandoned the elders' tradition when God revealed his Son in him; Christ not only created the true tradition but constitutes it.

Christian tradition in the NT has three elements: (*a*) the facts of Christ (1 Cor. 11:23; 15:3; Lk. 1:2, where 'delivered' translates *paredosan*); (*b*) the theological interpretation of those facts; see, *e.g.*, the whole argument of 1 Cor. 15; (*c*) the manner of life which flows from them (1 Cor. 11:2; 2 Thes. 2:15; 3:6–7). In Jude 3 the 'faith . . . once for all delivered' covers all three elements (*cf.* Rom. 6:17).

Christ was made known by the apostolic testimony to him; the apostles therefore claimed that their tradition was to be received as authoritative (1 Cor. 11:2; 2 Thes. 2:15; 3:6). See also Eph. 4:20–21, where the readers had not heard Christ in the flesh but had heard the apostolic testimony to him. Christ told the apostles to bear witness of him because they had been with him from the beginning; he also promised the gift of the Spirit who would lead them into all truth (Jn. 15:26–27; 16:13). This combination of eyewitness testimony and Spirit-guided witness produced a 'tradition' that was a true and valid complement to the OT. So 1 Tim. 5:18 and 2 Pet. 3:16 place apostolic tradition alongside Scripture and describe it as such.

One influential form-critical school of theology questions the historical validity of NT tradition saying that in this tradition Christians were concerned with proclaiming the Christ of faith rather than passing on facts of history. This concern in turn led to their account being coloured by their belief, and therefore the biblical scholar's task is seen as identifying that which originally belonged to Christ and that which was added by early believers. B. Gerhardsson challenges the validity of this form-critical presupposition. He points out that the very thorough methods of transmission of tradition in the rabbinic schools later can be traced back to NT times. Methods such as learning by heart, memorizing the actual words of the teacher, condensing the material into short texts and the use of notebooks were common in the days of Christ. The apostles and the early church were also seriously concerned with a conscious handing down of a valid tradition of Christ and not just with an unconscious transmission of a diluted tradition through preaching. When the uniqueness of Jesus in the eyes of the early church is also taken into account, the likelihood of additions to the story becomes even more suspect.

Gerhardsson's work provoked strong reaction, which questioned the reading back of later rabbinic methods into the early church period and pointed to the distinctiveness of Christian teaching over against contemporary Jewish teaching. Although Gerhardsson may have overstated his case, he has shown that the environment in which the Gospels were written was deeply concerned for the correct handing on of tradition and not as interested in supplementing fact with imagined improvement, as some scholars believe. The exhortations of Paul regarding the 'tradition' gain added significance in this context. The apostolic office was limited to eyewitnesses, and, as only eyewitnesses could bear a faithful witness to Christ as he lived and died and rose again, true tradition must also be apostolic. This was recognized by the church in later years when the Canon of the NT was eventually produced on the basis of the apostolic nature of the books concerned. Apostolic tradition was at one time oral, but for us it is crystallized in the apostolic writings containing the Spirit-guided witness to the Christ of God. Other teaching, while it may be instructive and useful and worthy of serious consideration, cannot claim to be placed alongside OT and NT as authoritative without manifesting the same defects as condemned Jewish tradition in the eyes of our Lord.

BIBLIOGRAPHY. O. Cullmann, 'The Tradition', in *The Early Church*, 1956, pp. 59ff.; B. Gerhardsson, *Memory and Manuscript*, 1961, especially pp. 122–170; *idem*, *Tradition and Transmission in Early Christianity*, 1964; R. P. C. Hanson, *Tradition in the Early Church*, 1962; Y. M. J. Congar, *Tradition and Traditions*, 1966; F. F. Bruce, *Tradition Old and New*, 1970.

D.J.V.L.

TRANCE. The Gk. word *ekstasis* (lit. 'standing outside' or 'being put outside', *i.e.* of one's normal state of mind) is rendered 'trance' in Acts 10:10; 11:5; 22:17, where it forms the condition of a vision. The trance state has never been fully explained, but it involves an overriding of normal consciousness and perception. In the only two occurrences of the strange Heb. word *sanwērîm*, translated 'blindness' in Gn. 19:11 and 2 Ki. 6:18, it is clear that a trancelike state of hypnotic suggestibility is indicated. J.S.W.

TRANSFIGURATION. The transfiguration is recorded in Mt. 17:1–8; Mk. 9:2–8; Lk. 9:28–36. Its absence from John is usually accounted for on the ground that the whole of Christ's life was a manifestation of the divine glory (Jn. 1:14; 2:11, *etc.*). There is also a reference to it in 2 Pet. 1:16–18.

In the Synoptic Gospels the event takes place about a week after Peter's confession of the Messiahship of Jesus. He took his three closest disciples, Peter, James and John, up to a mountain (probably Hermon, which rises to a height of 2,814 m above sea-level). There he was transformed (rather than changed in appearance) and his garments shone with heavenly brightness. Moses and Elijah then appeared and talked to him, and Peter suggested making three tents for them. A voice then came from a cloud declaring Christ's Sonship and his authority, after which the vision ended. The narrative suggests that the whole event was objective, though many modern scholars have sought to describe it in terms of a subjective experience of Jesus or of Peter.

The transfiguration marks an important stage in the revelation of Jesus as the Christ and the Son of God. It is an experience similar to his baptism (Mt. 3:13–17; Mk. 1:9–11; Lk. 3:21f.). Here his glory is revealed not just through his deeds, but in a more personal way. The glory denotes the royal presence, for the kingdom of God is in the midst of his people.

There are many features about the account which derive significance from the OT. Moses and Elijah represent the Law and the Prophets witnessing to the Messiah and being fulfilled and superseded by him. Each of them had had a vision of the glory of God on a mountain, Moses on Sinai (Ex. 24:15) and Elijah on Horeb (1 Ki. 19:8). Each of them left no known grave (Dt. 34:6; 2 Ki. 2:11). The law of Moses and the coming of Elijah are mentioned together in the last verses of the OT (Mal. 4:4–6). The two men at the empty tomb (Lk. 24:4; Jn. 20:12) and at the ascension (Acts 1:10) and the 'two witnesses' (Rev. 11:3) are sometimes also identified with Moses and Elijah. The heavenly voice, 'This is my beloved Son; listen to him' (Mk. 9:7), marks Jesus out not only as the Messiah but also as the Prophet of Dt. 18:15ff.

The cloud symbolizes the covering of the divine presence (Ex. 24:15–18; Ps. 97:2). There is a cloud to receive Christ out of his disciples' sight at the ascension (Acts 1:9). The return of Christ will be with clouds (Rev. 1:7).

In Luke we are told that the subject of their conversation was the *exodos* which he was to accomplish at Jerusalem. This seems to mean not simply his death but the great facts of his death and resurrection as the means of redemption of his people typified by the OT Exodus from Egypt.

The transfiguration is therefore a focal point in the revelation of the kingdom of God, for it looks back to the OT and shows how Christ fulfils it, and it looks on to the great events of the cross, resurrection, ascension and parousia. Peter was wrong in trying to make the experience permanent. What was needed was the presence of Jesus alone and attention to his voice.

BIBLIOGRAPHY. L. D. Hurst & N. T. Wright, *The Glory of Christ in the New Testament*, 1987; B. E. Reid, *The Transfiguration*, 1993. R.E.N.

TRAVAIL. 17th-century English made no distinction between the words 'travel' and 'travail', the two spellings being employed indiscriminately for the two ideas in the earlier editions of the AV. Later editions have, on the whole, conformed to the changing usage, as does RSV. The Eng. word translates a number of Heb. and Gk. words, all of which are normally connected with childbirth. The word is sometimes employed metaphorically, notably in Rom. 8:22 and Gal. 4:19, and in simile as in Ps. 48:6 and Mi. 4:9–10.

BIBLIOGRAPHY. G. Bertram, *TDNT* 9, pp. 667–674; R. K. Harrison, *NIDNTT* 3, pp. 857f.

G.W.G.

TRAVEL IN BIBLICAL TIMES. Travel in the world of biblical times was governed by the available land and water routes. Early in the history of the ancient Near East, especially in Mesopotamia and Egypt, rivers and coastal waters provided the best means for trade or travel. Bridle tracks developed to link villages and villages grew up at crossroads in a continuing double process. As trade developed international sea and land routes came into being. The Mediterranean world was greatly privileged for sea travel because of its climate, coastal pattern and access to other areas (*cf.* 1 Ki. 9:26ff.; Paul's journeys). Palestine was a vital land-bridge between Eurasia and Africa for both sea and land travellers, and so played an important role in communication and *trade. With the establishment of the Roman peace and road system, travel in the biblical world was greatly facilitated, playing an important part in the spread of the gospel.

I. Old Testament times

Land travel in the early OT period was relatively restricted, caravans and military forces being the main groups on the move. Although individuals tended to remain in their home areas so as not to lose their status as citizens, there is evidence of group migrations during the Middle Bronze age. The relatively widespread trade empire of *Ebla in the latter 3rd millennium, from the Mediterranean to the Persian Gulf, indicates reasonable communications and the possibility of travel in the Near East well before the patriarchal age.

A number of Heb. words are used for roads or paths. Of these *dereḵ*, that which is trodden underfoot, and *m*ᵉ*sillâh*, the levelling and filling of a track, suggest best the nature of ancient roads. Although the evidence is not final, it does appear that properly constructed roads were unknown before the Roman road system. Prior to this roads were paths followed regularly by men and animals. Some tracks were better maintained, such as to provincial centres or the cities of refuge (Dt. 19:3), but this meant essentially the clearing of stones and limited levelling (*cf.* Is. 40:3; 62:10). Tiglath-pileser I (1115–1077 BC) of *Assyria used engineers to lay bridges and level tracks for carts and siege-engines. An Egyp. writer, a century earlier, described Palestinian roads as 'filled with boulders and pebbles, . . . overgrown with reeds, thorns and brambles' (*ANET*, p. 478a). Such references indicate unpaved roads but tracks which could be maintained. Even the royal roads of the Persians, including the 2,600 km major link between Sardis and Susa, were probably formed but not paved except perhaps in immediate city areas. Paved streets seem to have been limited to some towns (*e.g.* Nineveh, Babylon). Travellers, caravans, official messengers and armies would use these tracks, travellers normally going with caravans for safety (*cf.* Jdg. 5:6).

Usually travellers would walk, although the ass was used for both riding and as a pack animal from early times. Chariots and horses were used for military purposes. The ox wagon carried heavy loads and probably people (Gn. 46:5). In later times the camel was also utilized. Throughout river and coastal traffic remained very important modes of travel. Little is known of resting-places, but it seems that the traveller prior to Roman times needed to provide and fend for himself (Jos. 9:3–14). People would travel mainly to trade, sometimes to attend religious festivals, and on occasions when migrating due to war, famine or similar reasons.

Roads may be classified as international or internal routes. Often local roads linked international highways, as the E–W roads of Palestine sometimes ran between the 'way of the sea' (Is. 9:1; the so-called Via Maris) and the 'King's Highway' (Nu. 20:17). The former ran from Egypt along the coast of Palestine then inland to Megiddo where it divided, although the main route continued N to Damascus and on to Mesopotamia. The *'King's Highway' also ran N–S between Bozrah in Edom to Damascus, linking both Arabia and Egypt with the N. Lesser N–S roads in Palestine followed the Jordan Valley and the central mountain ridge. Numerous latitudinal roads linked these highways, including the road from Jerusalem to Jericho (see *LOB*). Sea travel was not normally a feature of Israelite life, although ships traversed the coast of Palestine and sailed from Ezion-geber on the Gulf of Aqabah. Jonah's flight illustrates that some individuals did travel on cargo ships in OT times (*SHIPS AND BOATS; *TRADE AND COMMERCE).

International land routes linked important cities of Egypt, Mesopotamia, Syria and Asia Minor. The two highways through Palestine linked Arabia and Egypt with Damascus. From thence one road ran to Babylon via Tadmor (2 Ch. 8:4) and Mari; another went N to Carchemish, W to Haran and Ashur, then S to Babylon and the Persian Gulf. Finally a road N from Carchemish linked up with the Hittite city of Kanish in Asia Minor.

II. New Testament times

By NT times the Roman peace and authority had made travel relatively safe and constant. The simple acceptance in the Gospels and Acts of both short and long journeys as normal demonstrates this. Although some classical writers give the impression that travel, especially by sea, was to be avoided, those who really knew the world of their day, like Pliny and Philo, confirm the NT picture. Extensive plans for travel by land and sea were made and executed, and assurances given of return visits despite the distances involved (*e.g.* Rom. 15:24–25; Acts 15:36; 18:18–21). Such journeys were within the Roman empire: travel in foreign lands, although not unknown, was exceptional.

Within Palestine the Gospels indicate regular movement of people, including annual visits to Jerusalem for the Passover (Lk. 1:39; 2:3–5, 41ff.; Jesus' ministry). These journeys were usually made on foot and lasted a number of days, *e.g.* 5 from Nazareth to Jerusalem. As the Roman road system was not extended to Palestine until late in the 1st century AD, such internal travel would have been on the older road system (*IEJ* 1, 1950, pp. 54ff.). Journeys were also made to or from Palestine (Mt. 2:1, 13–15). Most significant are the extensive travels of *Paul. He utilized to the full the free access to travel within the Roman world. The government's support for shipping, the extermination by Augustus of pirates at sea and much brigandage on land, and the extensive road system leading to Rome, all helped the early Christian traveller. In fact, Christianity first spread directly along the great roads which led to Rome. The great E road illustrates this, with the diversion to Macedonia through divine guidance as a corollary (Acts 16:6 10); the route ran from Caesarea via Syrian Antioch, Tarsus, Derbe, Iconium, Pisidian Antioch, Laodicea, Ephesus, by sea to Corinth, and then to Brundisium or Puteoli, and by land along the Appian Way to Rome.

Begun in 312 BC the Appian Way was the first great Roman highway built. These roads, well planned and constructed, running as much as possible on a straight course, provided ready travel unequalled until the coming of the railway many centuries later. Major roads were paved over a width of 6–8 m; minor roads surfaced with sand or gravel were cambered to ditches 6 m or 3 m apart. Because of their strategic importance it was the army that often built these roads, although Augustus appointed permanent road boards in 22 BC. Josephus records that Vespasian had road-surveyors with his army during the 1st Jewish Revolt (*BJ* 3. 118). Milestones set at 1,000 paces (1,480 m) recorded the distance from the road-head or nearest city. These are valuable sources of information today. Maps of roads, and certainly lists of resting-places and distances both by land and sea were available for travellers to plan their journeys. Such itineraries, more or less complete, have been found belonging to post-NT times, but they must have existed earlier as Strabo (64 BC–AD 19) and other geographers obviously drew information from them.

Apart from the army the road system was used for the imperial post and by other travellers. The royal courier service not only handled communications but also provided transport for officials. Ordinary travellers had to make their own arrangements; so did private persons wishing to send correspondence to others, as in Paul's case. Resting-places with fresh horses were provided at cities or every 25 Roman miles, with probably two intermediary stops in between. Again only couriers and officials were catered for. The ordinary traveller could stay at inns run by private owners. Some provided food and lodging; some lodgings only. Those in the E provinces seem to have been superior in quality, but the over-all picture of inns and innkeepers suggests a generally poor standard. Many were little removed from brothels. Hence the stress in early Christian literature on providing *hospitality. Normal distances travelled would be 16 Roman miles a day by foot, and about 25 by horse or carriage. On some occasions couriers or officials covered 100 miles a day, but on the other hand letters to Cicero from Syria took respectively 50 and 100 days for delivery. Winter months hampered or stopped travel, especially in mountainous regions or plateaux, just as most shipping ceased between mid-November and mid-March at least, preferring to sail between 26 May and 14 September (Acts 27:9ff.). Prevailing winds also determined the courses followed by the ships. Paul used trading ships, whose movements were regulated by considerations of freight, and seems to have avoided ships apparently especially provided for Jews of the Dispersion to go to Jerusalem for the Passover (Acts 20:1ff.). His final journey to Rome was by two grain ships (*SHIPS AND BOATS).

Travel on land would have been similar to that in OT times. Most would go by foot. Officials with permits could use the facilities of the courier system, both horses and carriages. Various light carriages were used (*cf.* Acts 8:29—a travelling chariot?) and some ordinary travellers rode on the heavier ox-wagons, both open and covered. There was even a drive-yourself carriage, the *essedum*! The horse, with a cloth but no saddle, was used by messengers, troops (with Paul, Acts 23:23f., 32) and some travellers; the ass continued its burden-bearing task as it does today. Both personal and group travel were common in NT times. People moving around the empire included government officials, traders, workers seeking employment, especially in large cities, students going to centres of study and the infirm seeking healing sanctuaries. In particular people in large numbers would attend games and great religious festivals. These included not only the Jewish feasts but major events in Greece and Italy. Not least among the travellers were the early Christians using the facilities provided by Rome as they spread the Gospel and corresponded with one another.

BIBLIOGRAPHY. *LOB*; M. Avi-Yonah, 'The Development of the Roman Road System in Palestine', *IEJ* 1, 1950–1; C. Singer *et al.* (ed.), *A History of Technology*, 1, 1967; 2, 1972; D. Baly, *The Geography of the Bible*, 1967; L. Casson, *Travel in the Ancient World*, 1974. G.G.G.

TRAYS. Heb. *maḥtôṯ* (AV 'snuff dishes') were vessels made of gold, used for removing the trimmings from the lamps in the tabernacle and Temple (Ex. 25:38; 37:23; Nu. 4:9). To be distinguished from the copper firepans and censers, likewise called *maḥtôṯ* (Ex. 27:3; Nu. 16:6). D.W.G.

TREASURE, TREASURY. 'Treasure' usually refers to valuables, such as silver or gold. 'Treasures of darkness' (Is. 45:3) are hoarded riches; 'treasures of wickedness' (Mi. 6:10; *cf.* Pr. 10:2) are ill-gotten gains. In Mt. 2:11 'treasures' are boxes containing valuables.

'Treasury' and 'treasure house' frequently signify a place where treasure is stored, generally attached to a sanctuary (Jos. 6:19, 24; 1 Ki. 7:51; Dn. 1:2) or belonging to a king (2 Ki. 12:18; Est. 3:9). In Ezr. 2:69; Ne. 7:70f., 'treasury' is a fund for rebuilding the Temple. In Mk. 12:41; Lk. 21:1 it refers to the thirteen trumpet-shaped offertory boxes placed in the Court of the Women in the Temple; it is apparently used of the vicinity of these boxes in Jn. 8:20.

'Treasure' also has the wider meaning of a store. In 2 Ki. 20:13 'treasure house' is a storage place in the palace (*cf.* v. 15). In Mt. 13:52 it is a storeroom.

The Bible uses 'treasure' and 'treasury' metaphorically too. Yahweh keeps sin in the treasuries of his memory (Dt. 32:34). Wisdom is to be treasured in the mind, *i.e.* valued and taken to heart (Pr. 2:1; 7:1). Awe of Yahweh is Zion's treasure (Is. 33:6). The sky is Yahweh's 'good treasury' containing rain (Dt. 28:12); in poetry, snow, hail (Jb. 38:22) and the wind (Ps. 135:7; Je. 10:13; 51:16) also have 'storehouses' or treasuries. In Zc. 11:13 *MT hayyôṣēr*, 'potter' (RSVmg.), has been emended to *hā'ôṣār*, 'treasury' with Pesh., but it is possible that *MT* can mean 'foundry worker' (*cf.* LXX, NEBmg. 'foundry').

In the Synoptic Gospels Jesus often uses 'treasure' figuratively. Since God rewards whole-hearted service in the hereafter, it is termed laying up treasure in heaven, which is contrasted with money-making in Mt. 6:19f.; Mk. 10:21 and parallels; Lk. 12:33 (*cf.* Mt. 19:21; Lk. 18:22). As the storehouse of either good or evil the heart controls conduct (Mt. 12:35; Lk. 6.45). A man's heart is where his treasure is (Mt. 6:21; Lk. 12:34), *i.e.* his interests are determined by what he values most.

Paul's phrase 'treasure in earthen vessels' (2 Cor. 4:7) contrasts the glory of the divine gospel with the weakness of its human ministers. Wisdom and knowledge are treasures to be found only in Christ (Col. 2:3).

'Peculiar treasure' was the AV and RV rendering of *s^e^gullâ* in Ex. 19:5; Ps. 135:4; Ec. 2:8. The RV also translated it thus in Mal. 3:17 (AV 'jewels'). The Heb. word occurs with 'people' in Dt. 7:6; 14:2; 26:18. It means 'personal property', and the RSV generally renders one's 'own possession' or the like. Apart from 1 Ch. 29:3; Ec. 2:8, where it is used literally of kings' possessions (RSV 'treasure'), *s^e^gullâ* is applied to Israel as Yahweh's very own people. Tit. 2:14; 1 Pet. 2:9 and possibly Eph. 1:14 use the LXX equivalents of the new Israel.

BIBLIOGRAPHY. *BAGD*. L.C.A.

TREES. Comments in the article on *PLANTS concerning the uncertainty of identifications apply equally to the trees.

Trees and timber are frequently mentioned in the Bible. The Holy Land itself can never have been thickly afforested, though woodlands are known to have occurred in areas now devoid of trees. Deciduous oaks covered parts of the Plain of Sharon, while evergreen oaks occurred on much of the hill country, including Carmel where remnants still exist. Aleppo pines also grew on suitable soils in the hills. Bashan and Lebanon were important sources of timber and the cedar of Lebanon is famous. Timber was required for buildings (although rough branches would suffice for humbler dwellings), ships, wooden musical instruments, farm implements, household items and even idols.

Acacia (Heb. *šiṭṭim*, AV shittah, shittim). Several species of acacia (*Acacia albida*, *A. tortilis*, *A. iraqensis*) occur in the desert wadis of Sinai and the hot Jordan valley, where the place Shittim was named after them (Jos. 2:1). The hard timber was used by the Israelites for the ark and parts of the *tabernacle or tent of meeting (Ex. 25). These spreading, thorny trees were some of the few available in Sinai and likely to produce pieces of wood of sufficient size.

Algum (Heb. *'algûmmîm*, 2 Ch. 2:8; 9:10–11). Apparently a tree native to Lebanon, and possibly the coniferous tree called the Cilician fir (*Abies cilicia*). The eastern savin or Grecian juniper (*Juniperus excelsa*) and the evergreen cypress (*Cupressus sempervirens*) have also been suggested. A doubtful suggestion is that the algum is identical with the almug tree of Ophir and that it was re-exported to Judah from Lebanon and thought by the Chronicler to be native there. The reference to 'algum trees' in 2 Ch. 9:10–11 appears to be an example of metathesis, or it may be simply an alternative form.

Almond. The almond (*Prunus dulcis* or *Amygdalus communis*) blooms in the Holy Land as early as Jan. Its Heb. name, *šāqēḏ*, 'waker', suggests the first of the fruit trees to awake after the winter. Blossoms are pink-flushed white, demonstrating an analogy with the hoary-headed patriarch (Ec. 12:5). The almond's beauty was often copied in ornamental work (Ex. 25:33–34). As well as being oil-producing, the kernel was a favourite food in Palestine, and an acceptable gift when sent by Jacob to Egypt (Gn. 43:11). It is probably denoted in Gn. 30:37, where AV renders 'hazel', and is mentioned in Je. 1:11–12, where a play on the words (*šāqēḏ* and *šōqēḏ*) illustrates God's prompt fulfilment of his promises. See A. Goor and M. Nurock, *Fruits of the Holy Land*, 1968, pp. 241–254.

Almug (Heb. *'almûggîm*, 1 Ki. 10:11–12). Imported into Judah with gold from Ophir. The location of Ophir remains a matter of conjecture, and the identity of the tree is uncertain. The traditional identification is with red sandal-wood (*Pterocarpus santalinus*), a large leguminous tree native to India and Ceylon. Others argue, however, that *'algûmmîn* and *'almûggîm* should both be identified with a Lebanese tree.

Apple (Heb. *tappûaḥ*). Referred to chiefly in Canticles, this fruit's identity has long been discussed in view of the (untenable) objection that Palestine is too hot and dry to allow satisfactory cultivation of the true apple (*Malus pumila* or *Pyrus malus*). The Heb. and Arab. words, however, favour this reading; the tree affords good shade, the fruit is sweet (Ct. 2:3) and the perfume is much appreciated (Ct. 7:8). The cultivated apple may have originated in the Caucasus area and it certainly grows well in cultivation in parts of the Holy Land. Though most of these attributes apply also to the apricot (*Armeniaca vulgaris* or *Prunus armeniaca*), about which the image in Pr. 25:11 concerning 'apples of gold' would be more apposite, it is questionable whether the apricot was established in Palestine at this time. This objection is even more serious in the case of the Chinese citron (*Citrus medicus*), a third suggestion. A W Asiatic fruit, the quince (*Cydonia oblonga*), has been proposed also, but its taste is somewhat bitter, and the Mishnah renders it by a different Heb. word. See Goor and Nurock, *op. cit.*

Cedar (Heb. *'erez*; Gk. *kedros*). *Cedrus libani*, the cedar of Lebanon, a large spreading coniferous tree formerly abundant in Mt Lebanon where it is now reduced to scattered remnants and is protected. The wood was highly esteemed for its durability and was used, for example, for building David's house (2 Sa. 5:11, *etc.*), Solomon's Temple (1 Ki. 5:6–10, *etc.*) and the new Temple built after the Babylonian Exile (Ezr. 3:7). Extra-biblical texts speak of Nebuchadrezzar's exploitation of the Lebanese forests (*cf.* Hab. 2:17). Solomon had chariots, or more probably sedans (Heb. *'appiryôn*), made of cedar (Ct. 3:9). Cedars may attain a height of 40 m and OT writers used them as a figure of stature in man (Ezk. 31:3; Am. 2:9), grandeur (Ps. 92:12) and majesty (2 Ki. 14:9). The meaning of Heb. *'ezrāḥ* in Ps. 37:35 is obscure (AV 'bay tree', RSV 'cedar of Lebanon'), but elsewhere in OT means 'native', and a plant indigenous to Palestine is indicated here.

The cedar-wood burnt by a priest during levitical cleansing (Lv. 14:4–6, 49–52; Nu. 19:6) would not have been the cedar of Lebanon but a small tree of the Sinai desert, the Phoenician juniper, *Juniperus phoenicea*, which is fragrant when burnt. See **Pine**, below.

Cypress. A tree (*Cupressus sempervirens*) with a dense habit 13–20 m high, with numerous branchlets having scale leaves and providing excellent timber. Often planted in Mediterranean cemeteries as the columnar variety (var. *pyramidalis*). RSV renders as 'cypress' the Heb. *b^e^rôš* (Is. 41:19; 55:13; AV 'fir'), yet the variant *b^e^rôṯîm* (Ct. 1:17) is taken to be 'pine'. Evidence favours cypress as being Heb. *t^e^'aššûr* (Is. 41:19; 60:13; AV 'box tree'). The reference in Ho. 14:8 to an 'evergreen cypress' (RSV) or 'green fir tree' (AV) continues with a mention of its fruit, which is presumably edible. This is probably the stone pine (*Pinus pinea*), which has a spreading crown and edible seeds in the cone.

Ebony (Heb. *hoḇnîm*, Ezk. 27:15; Egyp. *hbny*). The reddish black heart-wood of *Dalbergia melanoxylon*, a leguminous tree of the drier parts of tropical Africa. It was used extensively in ancient Egypt for fine furniture, valuable vessels, veneers, sceptres and idols. Only later was this Egyp. word transferred to the jet black timbers of the genus *Diospyros* obtained from tropical Africa, and now especially to *D. ebenum* of Ceylon. See A. Lucas and J. R. Harris, *Ancient Egyptian Materials*[4],

1962, pp. 434–435; F. N. Hepper, 'On the transference of plant names', *PEQ* 109, 1977, pp. 129f.

Fir. The RSV renders Heb. *b^e^rôš, b^e^rôṯîm* as 'cypress' and 'fir', which popularly applies to coniferous trees in general. Heb. scholars accept these names as applying to the tall Grecian juniper, *Juniperus excelsa*, of which the timber was imported from Lebanon for the construction of Solomon's house and Temple (1 Ki. 5:8, 10), from Senir (Hermon) for ship boards (Ezk. 27:5) and also for musical instruments (2 Sa. 6:5).

Holm (Heb. *tirzâ*, Is. 44:14). A wood used for making a heathen idol. If the 'holm tree' of RSV indicates the timber of the evergreen holm oak (*Quercus ilex*) of the central Mediterranean area, it would have had to be imported. But an indigenous tree, such as one of the native oaks, is evidently intended by the context. AV renders the Heb. word as 'cypress' (*Cupressus sempervirens*), other versions as 'plane-tree' (*Platanus orientalis*); both are native in Palestine. The Heb. word *tirzâ* is similar to the Ugaritic *tisr* for cypress.

Oak (Heb. *'allôn, ēlôn*). In Palestine there are three species of oak (*Quercus*). The kermes oak (*Q. coccifera*, also known as *Q. calliprinos*) is evergreen and inhabits the hills where it is often seen as a shrub, although the Palestinian variety may form a rounded tree with a stout trunk when protected. One of the deciduous oaks (*Q. infectoria*) is unlikely to be referred to in the Bible owing to its limited occurrence at high altitudes. The other one, the Vallonea or Tabor oak (*Q. aegilops*, also known as *Q. ithaburensis*), occurs in lowland Palestine, but extensive felling has eliminated the woodlands that used to cover the Sharon Plain. Oaks are sturdy, hardwood trees which live to a great age, and the fruit, or acorn, is set in a cup. There is some confusion with the terebinth which has a similar stature and Heb. name, although botanically it is distinct.

An oak was a favourite tree under which to sit (1 Ki. 13:14), or to bury the dead (Gn. 35:8; 1 Ch. 10:12). Solitary trees were landmarks (1 Sa. 10:3, AV 'plain'). Its timber is seldom mentioned: it is hard and was used for oars (Ezk. 27:6). Bashan was renowned for its oaks (Is. 2:13; Ezk. 27:6; Zc. 11:2), and to this day there are many finely grown trees of *Q. aegilops* in that region. The scarlet or crimson dye, used in Heb. rites (Ex. 25:4; 26:1; Heb. 9:19, *etc.*), was obtained from a scale-insect that covered branchlets of the kermes oak. Absalom was caught by his hair in an oak (2 Sa. 18:9–10).

Heb. *'^a^šērâ* is translated in AV (following LXX *alsos*) as an idolatrous 'grove' or a 'high place' (Ex. 34:13; Dt. 16:21; 2 Ki. 17:16, *etc.*) since it was thought to refer to a clump of oaks. But recent scholarship holds that the reference is not to trees but to an image or cult-pole of the Canaanite goddess Asherah, consort of El, hence the RSV use of 'Asherah' and 'Asherim'. However, trees were often involved, too: 'You shall not plant any tree as an asherah' (Dt. 16:21); 'They sacrifice . . . under oak, poplar, and terebinth, because their shade is good' (Ho. 4:13). To this day 'sacred' groves of oaks and terebinths may be seen in various parts of Palestine.

Palm (Heb. *tāmār*, Gk. *phoenix*). The date palm, *Phoenix dactylifera*, a tall, slender, unbranched tree with a tuft of feather-like leaves 3–4 m long at its crown. The male and female flower clusters among the leaves are borne on separate trees. It flourishes in groves in the hot Jordan valley and appears, from the numerous references, to have been commonly planted as an isolated tree (Jdg. 4:5) in biblical times, although the fruit from highland trees was of poor quality. The palm often gave its name to the place where it grew, *e.g.* Tamar (Ezk. 47:18–19; 48:28); Hazazon-tamar (Gn. 14:7, *etc.*). Jericho was called 'the city of palm trees' (2 Ch. 28:15). The palm typified grace, elegance and uprightness (Ps. 92:12; Je. 10:5), and Tamar was used as a woman's name (2 Sa. 13:1; 14:27). It was also a symbol of victory and rejoicing, and the use of palm leaves ('branches') during Jesus' entry into Jerusalem (Jn. 12:13) was significant (*cf.* Rev. 7:9). The form of the palm was used in architectural ornamentation (1 Ki. 6:29, 32; Ezk. 40:31). See Goor and Nurock, *op. cit.*, pp. 121–151.

Pine. There is reason to believe that Heb. *'ōren* of Is. 44:14 applies to the Aleppo pine (*Pinus halepensis*), and not the cedar (RSV) or ash (AV). This pine occurs on the Palestinian hills where the soil is suitable. It is a tall slender tree with pairs of needle leaves and soft, workable timber.

Plane (Heb. *'armôn*, Gn. 30:37; Ezk. 31:8). A large deciduous tree, the plane (*Platanus orientalis*) grows in rocky stream beds in N Palestine. It has digitate leaves and round hanging flower-heads. In AV the Heb. is rendered 'chesnut' (chestnut), which is not native to that region.

Pomegranate (Heb. *rimmôn*). A small tree or bush (*Punica granatum*) growing wild in some E countries, but much prized and cultivated from earliest times, several places in Palestine bearing its name, *e.g.* Rimmon (Jos. 15:32), Gath-rimmon (Jos. 19:45), En-rimmon (Ne. 11:29). It has numerous spreading branches, dark green deciduous leaves, occasional thorns, large persistent calyx and bright red flowers. When fully ripe the apple-shaped fruit is a mixture of yellow, brown and maroon in colour, and contains multitudinous seeds covered with thin skin and surrounded by watery pink pulp. There are two varieties, sweet and acid. A refreshing drink is made from the juice, a syrup (grenadine) from the seeds and an astringent medicine from the blossoms. Ornamental pomegranates decorated the high priest's robe (Ex. 28:33), the capitals of Solomon's Temple pillars (1 Ki. 7:20) and the silver shekel of Jerusalem in circulation 143–135 BC. See Goor and Nurock, *op. cit.*, pp. 70–88.

Poplar (Heb. *liḇneh; b^e^ḵā'îm*, 2 Sa. 5:23–24; 1 Ch. 14:14–15; RSV 'balsam tree', AV 'mulberry'). Rods of poplar, almond and plane were peeled in Jacob's deception of Laban (Gn. 30:37). The poplar tree (*Populus euphratica*) is tall with rustling leaves (2 Sa. 5:23–24; 1 Ch. 14:14–15) and, like willow (see below), grows beside the Jordan and streams where its branches root easily (Ho. 14:5). It is therefore unlikely to be found on the top of mountains as one of the shady trees under which sacrifices and offerings were made (Ho. 4:13) and this may refer to the storax (*Styrax officinalis*) which has leaves white on the lower surface. The 'ben-tree' of Gn. 49:22 (NEBmg.) is thought to have been the Euphratean poplar.

Sycamine (Gk. *sykaminos*, Lk. 17:6). The black mulberry or sycamine (*Morus nigra*), a small, sturdy tree with blood-red, edible fruits, is cultivated in Palestine. Some consider this may refer to the sycomore fig, but there is no reason to doubt that the black mulberry had been introduced by NT times.

Sycomore (Heb. *šiqmâ*, Gk. *sykomōraia*). The

sycomore-fig (sycamore, RSV), *Ficus sycomorus*, a sturdy tree 10–13 m high, with a short trunk, widely spreading branches and evergreen leaves. It was, and still is, planted in Egypt and the lowlands of Palestine (1 Ki. 10:27; 2 Ch. 1:15; 9:27). Its timber was important in Egypt, where trees were scarce, for the construction of coffins and other wooden objects. The fruits are edible and were sufficiently important for King David to appoint an overseer to look after the olive-trees and sycomore-trees (1 Ch. 27:28) and for the psalmist to regard the destruction of the sycomores by frost as a calamity for the Egyptians comparable with the destruction of their vines (Ps. 78:47). In Am. 7:14 the AV translation, 'a gatherer of sycomore fruit', is incorrect, since the Heb. means a dresser or tender of the fruit. This is the operation of cutting the top of each fig to ensure its ripening as clean, insect-free fruit. Zacchaeus climbed a sycomore to see Jesus pass (Lk. 19:4); sycomore trees are still to be seen as street trees in some Palestinian towns. This should not be confused with the European sycamore (*Acer pseudoplatanus*) or the N American plane (*Platanus*) also known as sycamore.

Tamarisk (Heb. *'ēšel*, Gn. 21:33; 1 Sa. 22:6; 31:13; AV 'grove', 'tree'). A soft-wooded tree of desert wadis with numerous slender branchlets, scale-like leaves and small tassels of pink or white flowers. Several similar species grow in Palestine (*Tamarix aphylla*, *T. nilotica*, *T. pentandra*, *T. tetragyna*) especially around Beersheba where Abraham planted one. (*MANNA.)

Terebinth, turpentine tree (Heb. *'ēlâ*, Is. 6:13, AV 'teil tree'; Ho. 4:13, 'elm'). The Palestine terebinth (*Pistacia terebinthus* var. *palestina*, or *P. palestina*) is a small tree occurring very frequently in the hills. The much larger Atlantic terebinth (*P. atlantica*) of hotter drier places resembles an oak and having a similar name may be confused with it in OT. The terebinth was one of the trees under which sacrifice and offerings were made 'because their shade is good' (Ho. 4:13).

Thyine Wood (Gk. *thyinos*, Rev. 18:12, RSV 'scented wood'). Timber from the sanderac-tree (*Tetraclinis articulata*), a small coniferous tree native to NW Africa. The wood is dark, hard and fragrant, and was valued by the Greeks and Romans for cabinet-making. Another name for it is citron wood (botanically unrelated to *Citrus*), and some versions use that name here; others identify it with the almug tree.

Willow (Heb. *'ᵃrāḇîm*, *ṣap̄ṣāp̄â*). Willows (*Salix acmophylla* and other species) are commonly found beside perennial streams in the Middle East, and in the biblical references are usually linked with their habitat (Jb. 40:22; Is. 25:7; 44:4; Ezk. 17:5). They are shrubs or small trees forming thickets. The 'willows of the brook' (Lv. 23:40) and the 'willows' of Babylon (Ps. 137:2) are now usually regarded as being poplar (*Populus euphratica*). Indeed M. Zohary (*Flora Palaestina*, 1, 1966, p. 29) states that in post-biblical literature the Heb. names for willow and poplar were exchanged.

The 'green withs' or new ropes used by Delilah to bind Samson (Jdg. 16:11) may have been willow bark or the fibrous twigs of the desert shrub *Thymelaea hirsuta*. F.N.H.

TRIAL OF JESUS. The arrest of our Lord in the garden is followed, in the Synoptic tradition, by his removal to a meeting of the Jewish leaders (Mk.14:53). Jn. 18:12–13 preserves an independent account of a preliminary examination before Annas, the father-in-law of the high priest Caiaphas. There follows an interrogation concerning his disciples and his teaching, which is inconclusive because Jesus refuses to answer direct questions put by the high priest (Jn. 18:19). He is abused (Jn. 18:22) and sent as a prisoner to Caiaphas (Jn. 18:24).

The reference to 'the high priest' in Jn. 18:19 has raised a difficulty. If the Lord is questioned by Caiaphas in 18:19, why does Annas remit him to the same person in 18:24? It is tempting to see in this preliminary investigation the first of the two Jewish 'trials' which are described in Mk. 'The high priest' in Jn. 18:19 will then be Caiaphas, but the enquiry will be of an informal character. Its chronological placing will be the evening of the arrest. Jn. 18:24, which records the official appearance before Caiaphas and the full Sanhedrin, will be dated the following morning (*cf.* Jn. 18:28) and be parallel with the consultation of Mk. 15:1.

John, however, makes no mention of the issues which are so prominent in the Synoptic report of the first 'trial': the question of Jesus' Messiahship and the accusation of blasphemy.

Mk. 14:53–65 describes an appearance of the prisoner before an assembly of 'all the chief priests and the elders and the scribes' (Mk. 14:53), under the presidency of the high priest. The gravamen of the charge is the witnesses' statement that Jesus had prophesied the destruction of the Jerusalem sanctuary (*cf.* Mk. 13:2; Acts 6:13–14) and the establishment of a new temple. The claim to be the builder of a new temple seems to be the equivalent to the claim to Messiahship, according to contemporary Jewish expectation. But it was the new temple of his body, the church (Jn. 2:19; 1 Cor. 3:16; Eph. 2:21), that he had in view. (See R. J. McKelvey, *The New Temple*, 1969.)

The incriminating challenge of the high priest, 'Are you the Christ, the Son of the Blessed?' drew from him the reply, 'I am,' according to Mk. 14:62. Further, his use of the title 'the Son of man' and his quotation of Ps. 110:1 and Dn. 7:13 are an unmistakable claim to his unique status and destiny, which Caiaphas was quick to grasp and interpret as overt blasphemy. 'It was not blasphemy to claim to be the Messiah, but to speak with assurance of sharing the throne of God and of the fulfilment of Daniel's vision in himself and his community was blasphemy indeed' (Vincent Taylor).

The symbolic action of the high priest's tearing of his clothes, as laid down in the Mishnah, is the prelude to the verdict, 'guilty of death' (Mk. 14:64), and the horseplay of the officers (14:65).

A second meeting of the Sanhedrin the following morning was necessary if, with Vincent Taylor, we take Mk. 14:64 to record a condemnation of Jesus as deserving of death but not the judicial verdict which was required to be passed by 'the whole council' (15:1). The prisoner is then led away to the Roman governor Pilate for the sentence of death to be pronounced. Whether the Jewish council had the power to pronounce and carry out the death sentence on religious grounds (as Juster and Lietzmann believe) or not (so Jn. 18:31: see Barrett's full note) is a complicated question. There is evidence for the view that the Jewish leaders had the power to carry out death sentences at this time. For example, in the Mishnah the tractate *Sanhedrin* gives a variety of regulations for the different types of execution. The warning inscription on Herod's Temple, promising death to any foreigner who is caught inside the barrier and fence around the sanctuary, does not read like an idle threat. Stephen is put to death following a session of the Jewish Sanhedrin. These pieces of evidence seem hardly to harmonize with the admission of Jn. 18:31: 'It is not lawful for us to put any man to death'. E. C. Hoskyns in his commentary (pp. 616f.) sees in the use of the verb 'put to death' (*apokteinai*) a veiled and subtle reference to death by crucifixion as distinct from the customary method of capital punishment for blasphemy, *viz.* stoning. The Jewish admission, then, that they cannot carry out a judicial sentence by crucifixion is recorded by the Evangelist who means his readers to see in it (v. 32) the way in which it fulfilled unconsciously yet providentially God's age-old plan adumbrated in such verses as Dt. 21:23; Ex. 12:46; Nu. 9:12; *cf.* Jn. 19:36. See G. D. Kilpatrick's brochure, *The Trial of Jesus*, 1953; T. A. Burkill in *VC* 10, 1956, and 12, 1958.

Before Pilate the allegation turns on Jesus' claim to kingship (Mk. 15:2; Lk. 23:2) which the Jews would wish Pilate to construe in a political sense. Thus the main charge preferred is one of *majestas* or treason against the Roman imperial authority. See Jn. 19:12. Pilate, however, from the first, is suspicious of these charges and sees through the accusers' motives (Mk. 15:4, 10). He tries to extricate himself in three separate ways from the task of sentencing Jesus to death. He tries to pass the responsibility to Herod (Lk. 23:7ff.); then to offer to punish Jesus by flogging and release him (Lk. 23:16, 22); finally to release Jesus as an act of clemency at the feast (Mk. 15:6; Jn. 18:39). All these expedients fail. Herod sends him back; the fickle and disappointed crowd will not be content with any punishment less than the death sentence (Lk. 23:18, 23); and Barabbas, a condemned murderer, is preferred to Jesus the Christ. And, in spite of the repeatedly confessed innocence of the prisoner (Lk. 23:14–15, 22), he is sentenced to the death of the cross by the judgment of the procurator (Mk. 15:15), and as the Lord himself had foreseen (Jn. 12:33; 18:32).

Bibliography. A. N. Sherwin-White, *Roman Society and Roman Law in the New Testament*, 1963; J. Blinzler, *The Trial of Jesus*, 1959; E. Bammel (ed.), *The Trial of Jesus*, 1970; D. R. Catchpole, *The Trial of Jesus*, 1971; G. S. Sloyan, *Jesus on Trial*, 1973 (bibliography); P. W. Walasky, *JBL* 94, 1975, pp. 81–93; B. Corley, *DJG*, pp. 841–854. R.P.M.

TRIBES OF ISRAEL. When the Israelites entered Canaan they entered as twelve tribes, and portions of the land were assigned to each of the twelve (*cf.* Jos. 13:1ff.). These twelve tribes were descended from the twelve sons of Jacob who had gathered themselves about their father and heard his prophecies uttered concerning them and their future (Gn. 49).

Modern scholarship has proposed a number of possible revisions of the biblical picture. First, it was held (by M. Noth and others) that Israel infiltrated gradually from disparate origins into Palestine, where it formed into a tribal alliance centred on the worship of Yahweh at a central sanctuary, that worship having been imported by a group which had experienced an 'exodus' from Egypt. Second, it has been argued by others (notably N. Gottwald, G. Mendenhall) that 'Israel' arose from the indigenous Canaanite population as a result of a kind of 'peasants' revolt' against the despotic city-states of Canaan, with the egalitarianism of Yahwism as a motivating and binding force for social revolution. Variations on these themes include the view that Israel was formed originally from refugees from political victimization outside Canaan, who settled in the inhospitable hill-country of Judah and Samaria (N. P. Lemche). In all these cases the tribal picture is secondary to historical actuality.

According to the Pentateuchal narrative, however (Nu. 32:33–42; 34:1–35:8), Moses himself made a division between tribes to inhabit the E and those to inhabit the W side of the Jordan river. On the E side portions were allotted to the tribes of Reuben and of Gad, together with the half-tribe of Manasseh. This last was to occupy the territory S of the Sea of Galilee, including the villages of Jair together with Ashtaroth and Edrei. Gad was to occupy the land immediately S of that of Manasseh extending to the N end of the Dead Sea, and S of this section was the territory of Reuben, which reached as far S as Aroer and the Arnon.

On the W side of the Jordan in Canaan proper the remainder of the tribes were to settle. Their inheritance was to be determined by lot, save that to the tribe of Levi no inheritance was to be given. Eventually the tribes became divided into N and S, represented respectively by Ephraim and Judah. The N kingdom came to be designated by the term Israel.

In the S territory was allotted to Simeon, who appears to have occupied land in the Negeb. Above him was the allotment of Judah, including the Judaean hill country and extending as far N as to include Bethlehem and almost to the city of Jerusalem itself. Immediately above the territory of Judah and extending E to the Jordan was the territory of Benjamin. This section reached to the N only a few kilometres and only as far W as the edge of the hill country. To its W was the small section given to the tribe of Dan.

Above the two tribes of Dan and Benjamin was the territory which had been allotted to Ephraim which reached as far N as the river Kanah and Shechem. Then came the large section assigned to the half-tribe of Manasseh, comprising everything between the Mediterranean and the Jordan river and extending N to Megiddo. Above Manasseh was Issachar and Zebulun, and on the sea-coast, reaching N from Carmel, the territory of Asher.

As time went on the tribe of Judah gained more and more in significance, for it really embraced Benjamin, and Jerusalem became the capital. In the N the tribal distinctions seemed to become less important than at first, and the N kingdom as such became the enemy of Judah. Tribal distinctions became of less and less significance, and practically disappeared after the Exile.

Bibliography. J. J. Bimson, 'The Origins of Israel in Canaan: an examination of recent theories', *Them.* 15, 1989, pp. 4–15; J. Bright, *A History of Israel*[3], 1981, pp. 105–182; G. W. Ramsey, *Quest for the Historical Israel*, 1982. J.G.McC.

TRIBULATION. The Heb. word most commonly translated as tribulation in the Eng. Bible is *ṣārā* and its cognates. The root meaning is 'narrow' (*cf.*

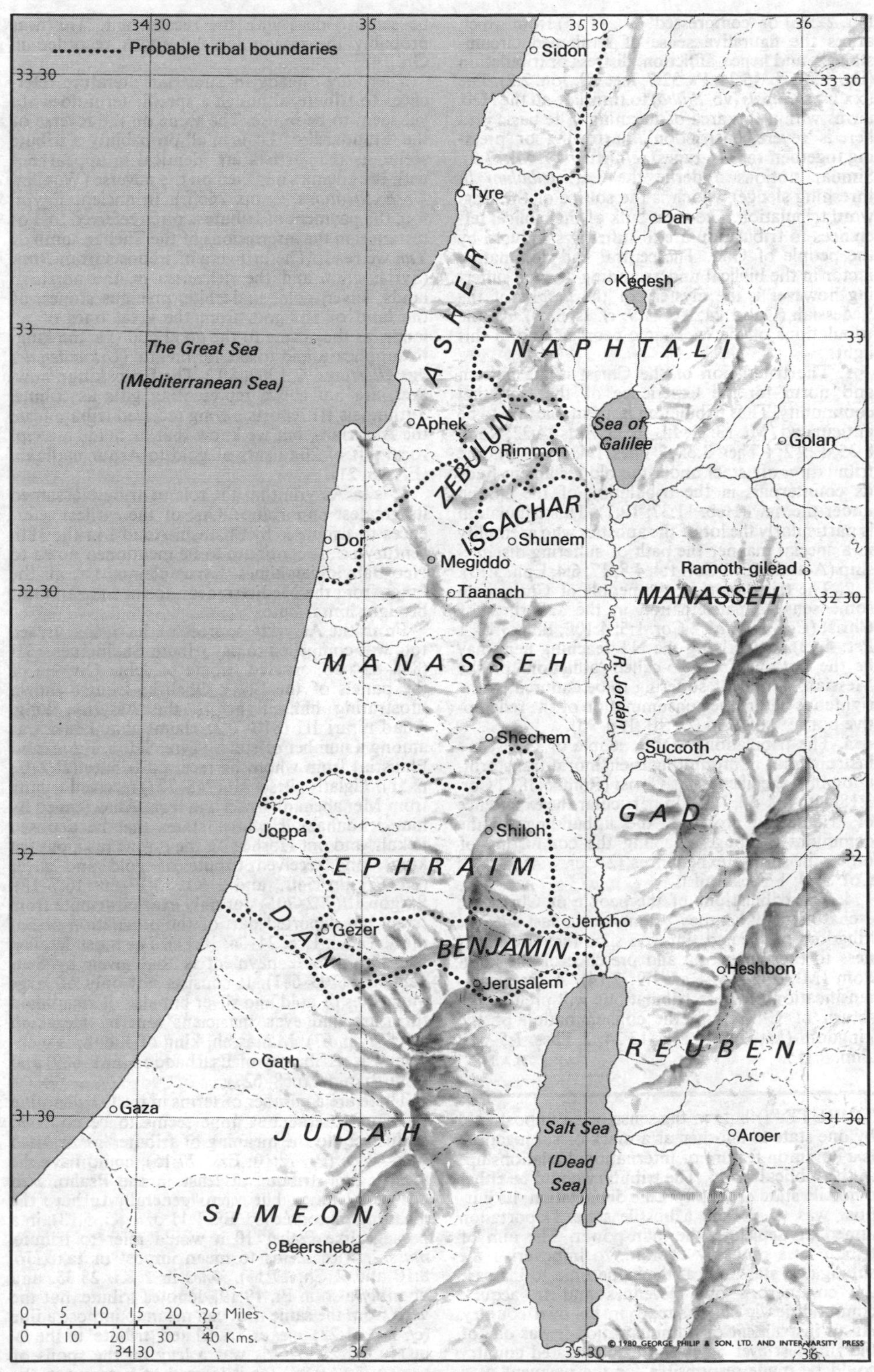

The tribes of Israel.

Nu. 22:26) or 'compressed' (Jb. 41:15) from which arises the figurative sense of straitened circumstances, and hence, affliction, distress or tribulation (Dt. 4:30; Jb. 15:24; Ps. 32:7; Is. 63:9; Jon. 2:2). The LXX uses *thlipsis* (vb. *thlibō*) to translate all the Heb. terms within this area of meaning. The basic idea here is 'severe constriction', 'narrowing' or 'pressing together' (as of grapes) (*cf.* Mt. 7:14; Mk. 3:9). Similar notions underlie the Lat. *tribulum* (a threshing sledge), which is the source of the Eng. word tribulation. The great bulk of the biblical references to tribulation are to sufferings endured by the people of God. The central and dominating factor in the biblical understanding of such suffering however is the mystery of the *thlipsis* of the *Messiah (Col. 1:24; Rev. 1:9; *cf.* Is. 63:9). All the tribulations of the Messianic people stand in this light.

1. The tribulation of the Christ is the pattern and norm for the experience of the Christian community. Thus tribulation is inevitable and to be anticipated (Mt. 13:21; Jn. 16:33; Acts 14:22; Rom. 8:35; 12:12; 1 Thes. 3:3f.; 2 Thes. 1:4; Rev. 1:9). The tribulation of Israel under the old testament finds its counterpart in the tribulation of the church under the new (Heb. 11:37; 12:1). This tribulation is particularly the lot of the apostles who exemplify in a special manner the path of suffering discipleship (Acts 20:23; 2 Cor. 1:4; 4:8, 17; 6:4; Eph. 3:13).

2. The tribulation of the people of Christ is in some sense a participation in the sufferings of Christ (Col. 1:24; *cf.* 2 Cor. 1:5; 4:10f.; Phil. 3:10; 1 Pet. 4:13). Underlying the NT teaching here may be the notion of the so-called 'afflictions of the Messiah', a tally of suffering to be endured by the righteous before the consummation of the redemptive purpose of God (*cf.* SB, 1, p. 95).

3. The tribulations of the people of Christ are instrumental in promoting their moral transformation into the likeness of Christ (Rom. 5:3f.; 2 Cor. 3:18 with 4:8–12, 16f.). In particular the experience of tribulation promotes the upbuilding of the community through enabling the comforting of others in similar experiences (2 Cor. 1:4f.; 4:10f.; Col. 1:24; 1 Thes. 1:6f.).

4. The tribulations of the people of Christ are eschatological; *i.e.* they belong to the last age, the kingdom of the end time. As such they are a witness to the inbreaking and presence of the kingdom (Mt. 24:9–14; Rev. 1:9; 7:14). A certain intensification of these tribulations will prelude the return of Christ and the consummation of the kingdom (Mt. 24:21; Mk. 13:24; 2 Thes. 1:5–6; 2 Tim. 3:1f.). B.A.M.

TRIBUTE. Tribute in the sense of an impost paid by one state to another, as a mark of subjugation, is a common feature of international relationships in the biblical world. The tributary could be either a hostile state or an ally. Like deportation, its purpose was to weaken a hostile state. Deportation aimed at depleting the man-power. The aim of tribute was probably twofold: to impoverish the subjugated state and at the same time to increase the conqueror's own revenues and to acquire commodities in short supply in his own country. As an instrument of administration it was one of the simplest ever devised: the subjugated country could be made responsible for the payment of a yearly tribute. Its non-arrival would be taken as a sign of rebellion, and an expedition would then be sent to deal with the recalcitrant. This was probably the reason for the attack recorded in Gn. 14.

There are already in Sumerian literature references to tribute, although a specific term does not yet seem to be in use. The scene on the reverse of the 'Standard' of Ur is in all probability a tribute scene, as the carriers are identical in appearance with the enemies depicted on the obverse (Woolley, *Ur Excavations*, 2, pp. 266ff.). In ancient Egypt, too, the payment of tribute is often referred to. For instance, in the inscriptions of the Theban tomb of *Tnn* we read: 'The bringing of imposts from *Rtnw* (Syria, *etc.*), and the deliveries of the northern lands: silver, gold, malachite, precious stones, of the land of the god, from the great ones of all lands, as they came to the good god (*i.e.* the king) to supplicate, and to ask for breath' (*Urkunden des äg. Altertums*, 4, 1007, 8ff.). The Egyp. kings, however, are not above representing gifts as tribute. Tuthmosis III reports having received tribute from the Assyrians, but we know that he made a reciprocal gift of 20 talents of gold to Ashur-nadinahi (EA 16, 21).

It is in Assyria that the role of tribute assumed its greatest importance. One of the earliest references to tribute is by Shamshi-Adad I in the 18th century BC. It continues to be mentioned down to Neo-Babylonian times. Cyrus claims that all the kings from the Mediterranean to the Persian Gulf brought him tribute.

From the Assyrian sources we learn that Israel, too, was compelled to pay tribute. Shalmaneser III (858–824 BC) exacted tribute of Jehu. On one of the panels of the Black Obelisk, Jehu is shown prostrating himself before the Assyrian king. Adad-nirari III (810–782) claims that Israel was among a number of states (Tyre, Sidon, Edom and Philistia) from whom he received tribute (*DOTT*, p. 51). Tiglath-pileser III (745–727) received tribute from Menahem of Israel and from Ahaz (called by him Jehoahaz). He later states that he deposed Pekah, and put Hoshea on the throne (as a puppet king), and received tribute of gold and silver (*DOTT*, pp. 54ff., and 2 Ki. 15:17–30; 16:7–18). Sargon II (722–705) not only exacted tribute from Israel but deported part of the population of Samaria (2 Ki. 17:6, 24–34; 18:11). The most detailed list of a tribute payment is that given by Sennacherib (705–681). It consists not only of large quantities of gold and silver but also of rich inlaid furniture and even musicians sent by Hezekiah (*DOTT*, p. 67). Manasseh, king of Judah, is mentioned as a tributary of Esarhaddon (681–669) and Ashurbanipal (668–627).

There are a number of terms in the OT denoting taxes in general, but none seems to be confined exclusively to the meaning of tribute. *'eškār*, used only twice (Ps. 72:10; Ezk. 27:15), could have the meaning of tribute, at least in the Psalm. *mas* occurs 22 times, but seems generally to have the meaning of corvée (*cf.* Ex. 1:11 or 1 Ki. 5:13); in a passage like Esther 10 it would refer to tribute. *maśśā'* twice seems to mean impost or tax (Ho. 8:10 and 2 Ch. 17:11). *'ōneš* in 2 Ki. 23:33, and possibly also in Pr. 19:19, denotes tribute, but the verb from the same root can mean to impose a fine (*cf.* Ex. 21:22). *meḵes*, translated 'tribute' in the AV in Nu. 31:28, 37–41, was a levy on the spoils of war. *bᵉlô* (Aram.), as it is used of a group in the community, cannot refer to 'tribute' in the strict sense (Ezr. 4:13, 20; 7:24). *middâ*, used in both Heb.

and Aram. contexts (Ezr. 4:13, 20; 6:8; 7:24; Ne. 5:4), may refer to tribute.

In several passages the Heb. *minḥâ* may refer to tribute, as RSV at 2 Sa. 8:2, 6, brought by conquered Moabites and Syrians to David, or 2 Ki. 17:4, sent by Egypt to Assyria, but it is clearly a gift in 2 Ki. 20:12, for *Merodach-baladan was no vassal of Hezekiah.

That tribute is not given greater prominence in the OT may be due to the fact that Israel, being a small nation, had few opportunities of imposing tribute. The gifts that Hiram, king of Tyre, brought to Solomon were the gifts of an ally and a friend, and it was probably taken for granted that Solomon would reciprocate (1 Ki. 5:10 and *passim*; 9:11).

(*Tax; *Temple; *Money; *Treasure.)

Bibliography. W. J. Martin, *Tribut und Tributleistungen bei den Assyrern*, 1936; J. N. Postgate, *Neo-Assyrian Royal Grants and Decrees*, 1969, pp. 9–16; J. Nougayrol, *PRU*, 3, pp. 31–32. W.J.M.
A.R.M.

TRINITY. The term 'Trinity' is not itself found in the Bible. It was first used by Tertullian at the close of the 2nd century, but received wide currency and formal elucidation only in the 4th and 5th centuries. Three affirmations are central to the historic doctrine of the Trinity: **1.** there is but *one* God; **2.** the Father, the Son and the Spirit is each fully and eternally God; **3.** the Father, the Son, and the Spirit is each a distinct person. Nowhere does the Bible explicitly teach this combination of assertions. It may, nevertheless, be claimed that the doctrine of the Trinity is a profoundly appropriate *interpretation* of the biblical witness to God in the light of the ministry, death and resurrection-exaltation of Jesus – the 'Christ event'.

I. The biblical basis for Trinitarian confession

The OT witness is fundamentally to the *oneness* of God. In their daily prayer, Jews repeated the *Shema* of Dt. 6:4, 'The Lord our God, the Lord is one'. In this they confessed the God of Israel to be the transcendent creator, without peer or rival. Without the titanic disclosure of the Christ event, no one would have taken the OT to affirm anything but the *exclusive*, *i.e.* unipersonal monotheism that is the hallmark of Judaism and Islam. It was NT writers, exploring the implications of the revelation of God in the Son, who first provided the basis for interpreting this monotheism *inclusively*, *i.e.* as involving more persons than one. Initially this took Christocentric shape in various forms of the affirmation that Jesus was one with the Father. Recognition of the divine personhood of the Spirit was then seen to follow especially from Jesus' exaltation Lordship of the Spirit. Once this step had been taken, it was natural for the later Church, which affirmed the unity of the Testaments in one Bible, to seek the Trinity in the OT too.

a. In the Old Testament

The robust monotheism of the OT concedes only a few hints of plurality within the One God. Principal amongst these are: **1.** the enigmatic plurals in God's own speech in Gn. 1:26; 3:22; 11:7; Is. 6:8; **2.** occasions where two separate figures appear to be addressed as 'God' or 'the Lord' (Pss. 45:6–7; 110:1); **3.** the 'divine' angelic trio who come to Abraham in Gn. 18:1–22; **4.** the 'word' of God active in creation (Gn. 1:3; Ps. 33:6) and redemption (Is. 55.11); **5.** the creative 'wisdom' figure of Pr. 8:22–31; **6.** the Spirit of God, regularly portrayed as bringing God's revelation, wisdom and empowering to his people. It is unlikely that any of these was understood by the OT authors or their contemporary readers to denote eternal personal distinctions within Israel's one God. They would take **4** as poetic reference to God's powerful command, and **5** as literary personification for God's own wisdom. **2** and **3** would naturally be taken as instances of the common phenomenon of divine agency (an exalted creature indwelt by and representing God). The Spirit, **6**, was considered the extension of God's own 'life', 'vitality' and 'person' (after the analogy of the human spirit: *cf.* 1 Cor. 2:10–11!). The deliberative plurals (**1**) would be perceived as plurals of divine council. Only developments reflected in the NT make it appropriate to read a deeper (Trinitarian) sense into these passages.

b. In the life and teaching of Jesus

The gospels clearly present Jesus as the supreme agent of God's messianic redemption and revelation. As the 'Son of God' (a Messianic title, rather than an ascription of divinity, in the Synoptic Gospels, though filial uniqueness of some kind is indicated in Mt. 11:27; Mk. 12:6; 13:32; Lk. 1:35), and as the Isaianic liberator empowered by the Spirit (*cf.* Lk. 4:18–21), Jesus brings God's eschatological reign into the present. He does this through miracles of deliverance and healing (Mt. 12:15–21, 28; Lk. 7:18–23; Acts 10:38, etc.), through the extension of divine forgiveness and sonship to the marginalized (*cf.* Mk. 2:3–12; Lk. 7:36–50; 14:15–24; 15:1–32, etc.), and through transformative teaching which fulfils and surpasses the law of Moses in authority (Mt. 5:17–20; 12:5–6; Mk. 2:23–28; 7:14–23, etc.). In the fourth gospel, Jesus claims to be: the true Bethel (1:51 – *i.e.* the place where heaven comes down to earth); the true temple (2:19–21); the source of the water of life and salvation (4:10, 14; 7:37–39); the true bread from heaven (6:25–59); the light of the world (8:12), and the life of the world to come (11:25). He pre-exists Abraham (8:58), he descends from the Father (3:13, 31–36), and he is so much one with the Father that to see and hear him is to see and hear the Father revealed (10:30, 38; 14:6–11; *cf.* 1:18). According to all four gospels, Jesus also anticipated ascension to the Father, and (in the Synoptics) that he would sit at his right hand (Mk. 14:62 par.).

These claims are entirely consistent with Trinitarian (or, at least, binitarian) thinking. But, taken on their own, they stop somewhat short of an outright claim to eternal, divine Sonship. The claims above are thus overpressed when taken (with the resurrection) as hard 'proofs' of Jesus' divinity. It needs to be remembered that the disciples too worked miracles, were given the authority to forgive sins (*cf.* Jn. 20:23), and were called to share in the sort of unity with the Father and the Son, that the Son himself had evinced (so Jn. 17:21–22). Even Jesus' claim to pre-exist Abraham does not itself 'prove' eternal divinity, for the angels and other heavenly creatures were considered to pre-exist the world. Similarly, at least some rabbis considered David might be given the seat at God's right hand, in accordance with Ps. 110:1. In short, the claims above could all be accounted for (*e.g.*)

on the understanding that Jesus thought of himself as a pre-existent Messiah – *i.e.* an exalted divine agent of great glory, endowed with extraordinary powers and prerogatives, but a creature, nevertheless, in whom God dwelt uniquely – rather than God the Son.

But in one line of affirmation, Jesus makes a claim that goes beyond anything that could be considered possible of any creature, however exalted. In Jn. 15:26, 16:6 and Lk. 24:49, Jesus promises he will send/commission the Spirit to the disciples from heaven, and in Jn. 14:16–23 he teaches that the Spirit will mediate to them the presence of the Father and the Son (*i.e.* it is through the promised Spirit that Jesus and the Father are to make their self-revealing dwelling with the disciples). As the phrase 'Spirit of God' was understood as referring to God himself in action (speaking, revealing, empowering, etc.), Jesus' implicit claim to be Lord of the Spirit goes beyond the bounds of creaturely possibility. The same claim also pushes pneumatology in a Trinitarian direction. The Spirit can no longer be thought of as a way of speaking of the Father himself, without making Jesus' commissioning of the Spirit tantamount to his being Lord in some respect over the Father! It is not surprising that in the very context in which the Spirit is revealed as the One who will come as the Spirit of Jesus (*i.e.* in the Paraclete discourses of Jn. 14–16), the Spirit also emerges as a divine person, distinguishable from both the Father and the Son. Thus, (**1**) he comes from the Father and the Son as a full personal replacement for Jesus ('another Paraclete of the same kind': 14:16), (**2**) he is so united with them that he mediates their presence and activity (as Jesus had the Father's), and (**3**) he glorifies the Son in his teaching, just as the Son had glorified the Father (Jn. 16:14; *cf.* 17:4). A similar perspective is perhaps encapsulated in the great commission of Mt. 28:19, where disciples are instructed to baptize in the *one* name of the Father and of the Son and of the Spirit.

c. The New Testament church and its writings

Peter's Pentecost speech chimes well with the teaching in the Johannine Farewell Discourses. The apostle affirms, 'This Jesus . . . being . . . exalted at the right hand of God, and having received from the Father the promise of the Holy Spirit, he has poured out this which you see and hear' (Acts 2:32–33). Jesus is hereby declared to fulfil the promise of Joel 2:28–32 that *God* would pour out his Spirit (*cf.* 2:17). Accordingly, in 2:36, 38, Peter concludes that Jesus has become one with 'the Lord' of Joel 2:32 (*cf.* Acts 2:21) on whose name people should call for salvation.

While Trinitarian theology could have taken off from such proclamation, it is perhaps not surprising that the early church devoted more time to elucidating its Christology than its pneumatology. This was the appropriate response to the Christ-event, which was a scandal to unbelievers, but was perceived as the definitive revelation of God's saving love by Christians. In seeking to demonstrate the proclamation about Jesus as the fulfilment of Israel's faith and hopes, much attention naturally focused on Jesus as the resurrected Messiah, exalted to the throne at God's right hand (*e.g.* Acts 2:25–36), and as the Danielic 'Son of Man' who would come again in glory at the Parousia to exercise God's judgment. But some of these attempts to integrate the unity of the new faith with that of the OT pushed more towards a divine Christology. As early as 1 Cor. 8:6, the Father and Jesus are identified as the one God and one Lord of Dt. 6:4 (Israel's prototypical monotheistic confession has thus become a binitarian confession!), and both are portrayed as the wisdom that brought creation into being and sustains it (*cf.* also Col. 1:15–20; Heb. 1:2–3; Jn. 1:1–18). Similarly, the assertion of Phil. 2:6, that Jesus was 'in the form of God' but 'did not count equality with God as something to be exploited' provides another early hymnic confession of Jesus' pre-existent divinity. That this is the intent of the language is confirmed in 2:9–10, where the exalted Jesus is revealed as the Lord of Is. 45:21–24 – as fiercely monotheistic a passage as can be found anywhere in the OT! Despite their conservative tendency to keep the title *ho theos* ('God') for the Father, on seven or eight occasions NT writers specifically apply the title 'God' to Jesus (Heb. 1:8 – citing Ps. 45:6–7; Jn. 1:1, 18 – some MSS; 20:28; 1 Jn. 5:20; Rom. 9:5; Tit. 2:13 and 2 Pet. 1:1). Beyond these lie many less direct affirmations of divinity. Amongst them we may make special mention of two striking phenomena. **1.** The opening salutations of Paul's letters (Rom. 1:7; 1 Cor. 1:3, *etc.*) invoke divine grace from both God and the Lord Jesus (no Jew thought of any human or heavenly creature as the source of divine grace!). **2.** Even more significantly, Jesus is offered the community's prayer and worship (*cf.* Mt. 28:17; Jn. 20:28; Acts 7:59; 1 Cor. 16:22b (*Maranatha*!); Rev. 5:11–14; 22:1–5, 17, 20, *etc.*, not to mention the hymnic confessions mentioned earlier). It was widely considered unthinkable and blasphemous to worship any but God alone within the Judaism from which Christianity sprang, yet worship here is directed to Jesus.

Scholars have not found it easy to explain how Christians came to this startling conviction that the crucified and resurrected Messiah was somehow one God with the Father, and that it was appropriate to offer him worship. But the readiest explanation is the church's continuing experience of the risen Lord as presented to them through the Spirit. By the Spirit they had visions of him (*cf.* Acts 7:55–56; 9:10–16; 18:9–10; 22:17–21; 2 Cor. 12:1–7, *etc.*), including the telling visions in Revelation which saw the Lamb on God's throne, receiving the worship of the heavenly congregation (Rev. 5, *etc.*). Also they themselves received words and guidance from the risen Lord (*cf.* Acts 16:17; 2 Cor. 12:8–9, *etc.*). More important, they experienced the Spirit of God as bearing the *character* of Jesus and impressing this on their own lives (*cf.* Rom. 8:9–10, 15; Gal. 4:6). If the Spirit of God had become the 'Spirit of Jesus Christ' too (*cf.* Acts 16:7; Gal. 4:6; Rom. 8:9–10; Phil. 1:19), the means of the presence of Jesus' grace and gifts (*cf.* Acts 2:33; 1 Cor. 12:4–6), then this could hardly mean anything less than that he shared in the divinity of the Father and the Spirit. Indeed the presence of this Spirit-of-God-and-of-Jesus would probably have been understood to evoke the response of confession, prayer and worship in question (*cf.* 1 Cor. 12:3; 14:14–16; Rom. 8:26–27).

All this takes us back from incipient binitarianism to incipient Trinitarianism. Once Jesus is seen to give his character to the Spirit, and to exercise Lordship through the Spirit, the church can no longer be content with the Jewish understanding of the Spirit as the invisible inner life of a unipersonal Father, extending into the world in action and self-revelation (lest the person now acknowledged as the Son be made Lord of the Father). For the Spirit to mediate the Father and the Son, implies his own divine personhood. Accordingly, Paul can even posit sufficient personal 'space' between God the Father and the Spirit to say that God 'knows the mind of the Spirit' who intercedes through the saints (Rom. 8:27): *i.e.* the Father knows the Spirit in the same way as he knows the Son, in intimate unity yet with a real distinction between them. It is not surprising that Paul links Father, Son and Spirit in a triadic, indeed triune pattern as for example in Gal. 4:4–6, 1 Cor. 12:4–6, Rom. 1:1–4, Eph. 4:4–6 (*cf.* 2 Pet. 1:2), and in what are probably Paul's most often repeated words, the closing 'grace' of 2 Cor. 13:13.

While no NT writer fully articulates a 'doctrine of the trinity', the implicitly Trinitarian thought-forms of the teaching of Paul and John (especially) provide much of the basis for that later formulation.

II. The doctrinal development of the doctrine of the Trinity

Whilst the 'incipient Trinitarianism' of the NT remained implicit and as yet undefined, it was clearly demarcated by both the biblical belief in God's oneness (monotheism) and the threefold naming of God as Father, Son and Spirit (Trinitarianism). Positively, this combination of unity and plurality controlled all subsequent discussions of the identity of God. Theologians such as Origen, Irenaeus and Tertullian essentially continued the biblical way of thinking and speaking with little change beyond highlighting the Son's identity as cosmic *logos* (word). The formal doctrine of the Trinity was the result of several inadequate attempts to analyse who and what the Christian God really is. The first major attempt was that of Sabellius. He proposed that whilst God is Father, Son and Spirit, he is not eternally and intrinsically so but only in relation to creation and salvation. In addition, God is only ever *one* of the three at any given time. This was rejected on the grounds that it undermined both the biblical witness and the eternal identity of God.

If Sabellius raised the problem of God's plurality, Arius raised the problem of monotheism. In order to defend God's radical oneness, he argued that the Son was created. This was rejected, however, on the grounds that it undermined the eternal identity of God as Father: if there was a time when the Son was not, then God's real identity cannot be that of Father. Ultimately, on Arius's view, we do not know God's real identity.

To deal with these problems the Church Fathers met in 325 at the Council of Nicaea to set out an orthodox biblical definition concerning the divine identity. Here it was established that the Son is *homoousios* (of the same substance) with the Father. God, it was affirmed, is definitely Father and Son. Then in 381, at the Council of Constantinople, the divinity of the Spirit was affirmed with equal explicitness, due mainly to the efforts of the Cappadocian Fathers, Basil the Great, Gregory of Nazianzus and Gregory of Nyssa. At this point in the history of Christian faith, believers were given words in which to affirm their belief in God as one, because the Father, the Son and the Spirit have the same nature, as partakers of the single reality of divine being; they are fully but only distinct in the sense that each is a different *hypostasis* (person-in-relation) within that unitary nature. Thus, when talking about God's unity Christians have used *essence* (=being, or traditionally substance) and *nature* language. When referring to that which makes God three, however, we refer to the relations or personal identities of Father, Son and Spirit.

This distinction between the One and the Three is reflected in the subsequent development of the doctrine of the Trinity. In the Gk. E, the emphasis has always been on the personal relations of Father, Son and Spirit, the Father being understood as the personal or relational 'origin' of the Son and Spirit. The personal identity of the Son and the Spirit is determined by their relation to the Father alone: the Son is 'begotten' of the Father; the Spirit 'proceeds' from the Father. Consequently, when W bishops in 1014 officially asserted that the Spirit proceeds from the Father and the Son (*Filioque*), deep divisions arose between the E and W churches. Easterners have always rejected this view on the grounds that it confuses the personal identities of Father and Son in relation to the Spirit. However, due to the fact that the Latin W, following Augustine and ratified by Aquinas, has habitually begun its thinking with the One not the Three, the usual starting point for W Trinitarianism is the divine substance. If the E temptation was to a kind of monarchianism (through placing the Father as superior to Son and Spirit) that of the W was to various kinds of modalism (through over-emphasizing the oneness).

Each tradition has unpacked itself culturally. Some commentators see in the W interpretation the seeds of present-day individualism. Stress on the oneness of God, it is argued, leads to its individual and human counterpart, while the relational and communitarian dimension of the E understanding has led to a more communal and inter-related culture. The truth seems to be that only in holding together both the W and the E perspectives do we arrive at a robust and balanced understanding of divine being and, as a consequence, of what it means to be made in God's image as individual and as church.

*COMMUNITY, *CHURCH, *FATHER, *GOD; *IMAGE, *JESUS CHRIST, TITLES OF; *KINGDOM OF GOD; *SPIRIT, HOLY SPIRIT; *WORD; *WISDOM.

BIBLIOGRAPHY. W. Grudem, *Systematic Theology*, 1994, ch. 14; R. P. C. Hanson, *The Search for the Christian Doctrine of God*, 1988; M. J. Harris, *Jesus as God*, 1992; A. I. Heron (ed.), *The Forgotten Trinity* (3 vols.), 1991; L. W. Hurtado, *One God, One Lord*, 1988; C. B. Kaiser, *The Doctrine of God*, 1982; C. M. LaCugna, *God For Us: The Trinity and Christian Life*, 1991; M. Turner, 'The Spirit of Christ and "Divine" Christology' in J. B. Green and M. Turner (eds.), *Jesus of Nazareth: Lord and Christ*, 1994, pp. 413–436; A. W. Wainwright, *The Trinity in the New Testament*, 1962.

M.T.
G.M.

TROAS. The principal seaport of NW Asia Minor, established some 20 km SSW of the site of Troy (Ilium) by the successors of Alexander the Great, and named Alexandria after him. 'Troas' was originally a distinguishing epithet, but it became the usual designation of the city after Augustus made it a Roman colony. The place grew rapidly around its artificial harbour-basins, which provided neces-

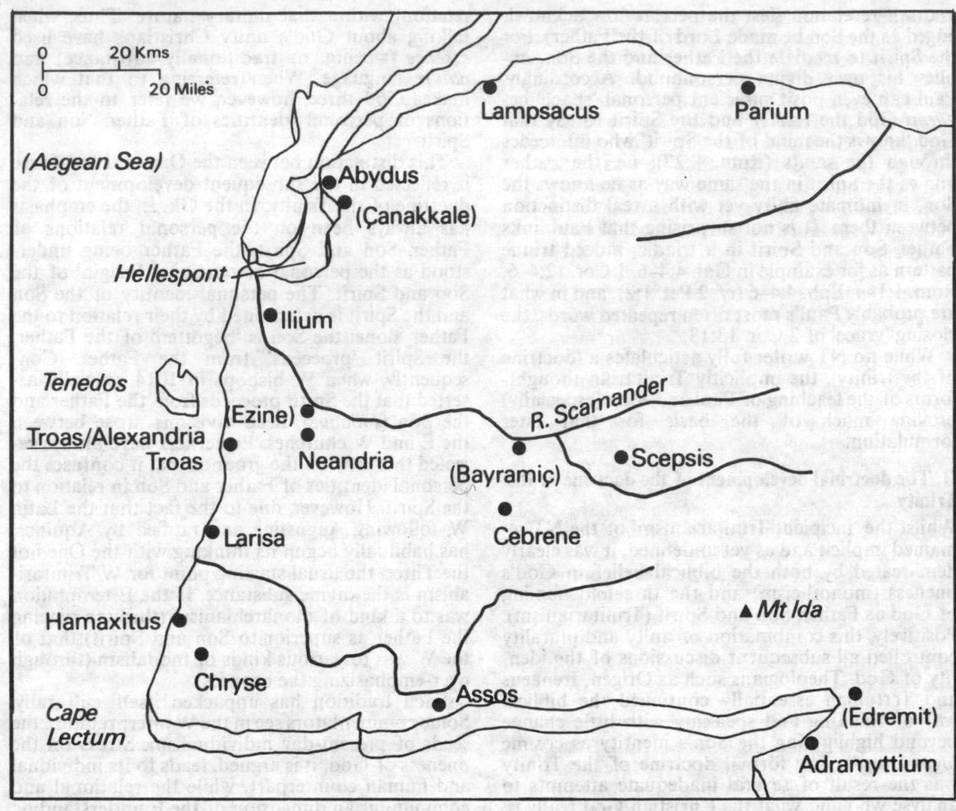

Troas, the principal seaport of NW Asia Minor at the time of Alexander the Great.

sary shelter from the prevailing northerlies at a focal meeting-point of sea-routes, close to the mouth of the Hellespont (Dardanelles). Troas was the port for the crossing to *Neapolis in Macedonia for the land-route to Rome. Though rarely mentioned in secular literature, it had a strategic function in the Roman system of communication, and its importance emerges clearly from unobtrusive references both in Acts and the Epistles. It was the scene of the vision of the 'man of Macedonia' (Acts 16:16–11) and the raising of Eutychus (Acts 20:5–12). The former incident was the occasion of the coming of the gospel from Asia to Europe, though this aspect is not stressed in Acts. Perhaps this also marks the meeting of Paul with luke, for the 'we-passages' begin at Acts 16:10. Later Paul found an 'open door' at Troas (2 Cor. 2:12), and again stayed there as long as possible when in haste to reach Jerusalem (Acts 20:6, 13). Paul's urgent request in 2 Tim. 4:13 may reflect a hurried departure from Troas under arrest. Ignatius, too, after sending three of his epistles from Troas, had to sail in haste for Neapolis as a prisoner bound for Rome (*Ep. to Polycarp* 8), when the weather permitted.

The site of Troas at Daylan is now deserted, but there are remains of the harbour, baths, stadium and other buildings, and several kilometres of the walls may be traced.

BIBLIOGRAPHY. C. J. Hemer, 'Alexandria Troas', *TynB* 26, 1975, pp. 79–112. C.J.H.

TROGYLLIUM (or Trogyllia). A promontory of the W coast of Asia Minor between Ephesus and Miletus, and reaching to within 2 km of Samos. Paul's delay there (Acts 20:15) was no doubt due to the difficulty of navigating a strait in darkness. The Alexandrian text omits reference to this delay at Trogyllium, but is almost certainly at fault here.

K.L.McK.

TROPHIMUS. An Ephesian Christian who evidently accompanied Paul to Europe after the Ephesian riot, later re-crossing and awaiting Paul at Troas for the journey to Jerusalem—doubtless as one of the delegates of the Asian churches with the collection (Acts 20:1–5; *cf.* 1 Cor. 16:1–4). In Jerusalem, however, Jewish pilgrims from Asia recognized him in Paul's company, and afterwards, finding Paul in the Temple with four others, jumped to the false conclusion that he had introduced Trophimus there (Acts 21:27ff.). Trespass beyond the Court of the Gentiles would for Trophimus be to risk the death penalty. The incident issued in a riot, and Paul's arrest.

2 Tim. 4:20 states that Paul left Trophimus sick at Miletus. This was near Trophimus' own city; but if Timothy was himself in the Ephesus area it may seem strange that he needed this information. The circumstances and intention of the verse are, how-

ever, uncertain: it may be connected with greetings, like the immediate context, or perhaps Paul's mind has reverted to the diminution of his band of helpers (*cf.* vv. 10–12). P. N. Harrison (*Problem of the Pastoral Epistles*, 1921, pp. 118ff.) argues that Paul was *en route* for Troas (*cf.* 2 Cor. 2:12) when he left Trophimus; G. S. Duncan (*St. Paul's Ephesian Ministry*, 1929, pp. 191ff.) that he was returning from Corinth to Asia (*cf.* 2 Cor. 1:8). Preferable to these intricate hypotheses is the view that Paul was heading W, destined for his second Roman imprisonment. A.F.W.

TRUMPETS, FEAST OF. 'Day of blowing the trumpets' (Heb. *yôm tᵉrûʻâ*, Nu. 29:1) or 'memorial of blowing of trumpets' (Lv. 23:24). The 7th month in the Jewish * calendar, *tišri* (Sept./Oct.), was the beginning of the civil year. The first day of the month was to be 'a day of solemn rest', in which 'no laborious work' was to be done. The LXX of Nu. 29:1 renders the phrase *yôm tᵉrûʻâ* by *hēmera sēmasias*, 'a day of signalling', but the Mishnah and traditional Jewish practice have understood by this the use of the *šôpār*, usually, though not always, made of ram's horn. Tradition is not clear as to what precisely was meant by the trumpet-blowing, which was accompanied by reading of relevant passages of Scripture (H. G. Friedmann, *JQR* 1, 1888, pp. 62ff.).

BIBLIOGRAPHY. N. H. Snaith, *The Jewish New Year Festival*, 1947. T.H.J.

TRUTH. Truth, like its relation * knowledge, is used in the OT in two senses: (1) the intellectual, of facts which may be ascertained to be true or false (Dt. 17:4; 1 Ki. 10:6); (2) far more commonly, the existential and moral, of truth as the attribute of a person. Joseph's brothers are detained in prison 'that your words may be tested, whether there is truth in you' (Gn. 42:16), *i.e.* whether they are dependable, consistent, of reliable character. It is significant that of the Heb. words translated 'truth' (*'ᵉmeṯ*, *'ᵉmûnâ*), the latter is sometimes rendered by the EVV as 'faithfulness' (Dt. 32:4; Ho. 2:20) (*AMEN). The OT thinks much more of the basis of truth in a reliable person than of the mere facts of the case. This reliability is basically an attribute of God (Ps. 31:5; Je. 10:10), whose truth 'reaches to the clouds' (Ps. 108:4). The God of the Bible is thus very far removed from the capricious pagan deities. He is true, *i.e.* consistent, both in his loving care for his children (Gn. 32:9f.) and in his implacable hostility against sin (Ps. 54:5).

It is no far cry from truth as an attribute of God himself to one of his activity. So he judges truly (Ps. 96:13), and sends truth forth (Ps. 57:3, AV). His word is true in the sense that it is permanently valid. 'As Thou art truth, so is Thy word truth, for it is written "Thy word, O God, stands fast in heaven" (Ps. 119:89)' (Exodus Rabbah on 29:1). Truth is demanded of man as his response to God in obedience to the law (Ps. 119:151) and in his inmost nature (Ps. 51:6), and is the bedrock of all human relationships (Ex. 20:16; Dt. 5:20).

In Gk. literature, the words for truth (*alētheia, alēthēs, alēthinos*) do not have the same personal and moral connotation. Rather, truth is intellectual. It is 'the full or real state of affairs . . . As in judicial language the *alētheia* is the actual state of affairs to be maintained against different statements, so historians use it to denote real events as distinct from myths, and philosophers to indicate real being in the absolute sense' (R. Bultmann, *TDNT* 1, p. 238).

In the NT these Gk. words occur commonly, and bring with them both their OT and their classical and Hellenistic Gk. meanings, so that it is often an extremely delicate matter to decide which nuance predominates. It is possible, however, to distinguish three broad senses in which the words are used, even though these may overlap.

1. Dependability, truthfulness, uprightness of character (the Heb. sense predominating). This applies to God (Rom. 3:7; 15:8) and to men (2 Cor. 7:14; Eph. 5:9) alike. The use of the actual word 'truth' in this sense is not common, but the thought of a God who can be trusted to keep his word is implicit throughout the NT.

2. Truth in the absolute sense of that which is real and complete as opposed to what is false and wanting (Mk. 5:33; Eph. 4:25). The Christian faith in particular is the truth (Gal. 2:5; Eph. 1:13). Jesus claimed that he was truth personified (Jn. 14:6; *cf.* Eph. 4:21). He mediates the truth (Jn. 1:17) and the Holy Spirit leads men into it (Jn. 16:13; *cf.* 14:17; 1 Jn. 4:6), so that Jesus' disciples know it (Jn. 8:32; 2 Jn. 1), do it (Jn. 3:21), abide in it (Jn. 8:44), and their new birth as God's children rests upon it (Jas. 1:18). This truth is more than a credal formula, it is God's active word which must be obeyed (Rom. 2:8; Gal. 5:7).

3. The adjective *alēthinos* especially sometimes carries the 'Platonic' sense of something real as opposed to mere appearance or copy. The Christ is thus a minister of the true tabernacle (Heb. 8:2) in contrast with the shadows of the levitical ritual (Heb. 8:4f.). In clear allusion to the words of institution of the Lord's Supper, Jesus declares that he is the true bread (Jn. 6:32, 35) and the true vine (Jn. 15:1), *i.e.* that he is the eternal reality symbolized by the bread and wine. Similarly, the true worshippers (Jn. 4:23) are not so much sincere as real. Their worship is a real approach to God who is spirit, in contrast to the ritual which restricts God to Jerusalem or Mt Gerizim (Jn. 4:21), and which can at best symbolize and at worst distort him.

BIBLIOGRAPHY. R. Bultmann, *TDNT* 1, pp. 232–251; C. H. Dodd, *The Interpretation of the Fourth Gospel*, 1953, pp. 139f., 170–178; D. J. Theron, '*Aletheia* in the Pauline Corpus', *EQ* 26, 1954, pp. 3–18; A. C. Thiselton, *NIDNTT* 3, pp. 874–902. F.H.P.

TRYPHAENA AND TRYPHOSA. Two women, probably—from the manner of mentioning them and the similarity of their names—sisters, and possibly twin sisters, greeted in Rom. 16:12. Like other women addressed there (Mary, v. 6; Persis, v. 12), they were noted for 'work'—the recurrence of this term may indicate some regular form of service (*cf.* W. Sanday and A. C. Headlam, *Romans*, *ICC*, 1902, p. xxxv). The names ('Delicate' and 'Dainty') were widely used, including in Rome, where Lightfoot (*Philippians*, pp. 175f.) pointed to several examples in 'Caesar's household' in Paul's time. Another contemporary Tryphaena was the daughter of Polemon I of Pontus, mother of three kings, who appears in the *Acts of Paul and Thecla*. A.F.W.

TUBAL-CAIN. The son of Lamech by Zillah (Gn. 4:22) and half-brother of *Jabal and *Jubal. In the words of AV he was 'an instructer of every artificer in brass and iron', but this could be as well translated 'a hammerer of every cutting tool of copper or iron', and could mean either that he was a metal-smith, the most commonly held view, or that he discovered the possibilities of cold forging native copper and meteoric iron, a practice attested archaeologically from the pre-historic times.

T.C.M.

TYCHICUS. An Asian—the 'Western' Text says an Ephesian—who accompanied Paul to Jerusalem, doubtless as a delegate of his church, with the collection (Acts 20:4; *cf.* 1 Cor. 16:1–4). He was the apostle's personal representative—probably (taking 'sent' as an epistolary aorist) the bearer of the letters—to the Colossians (Col. 4:7–9) and Ephesians (Eph. 6:21–22), and, should *Ephesians be a circular letter, to other Asian churches as well. Paul seems to have considered him a possible relief for Titus in Crete (Tit. 3:12), and to have sent him to Ephesus (bearing 2 Tim.?) just when Timothy was needed elsewhere (2 Tim. 4:12). These commissions reflect that trustworthiness which Paul commends (Eph. 6:21; Col. 4:7). His designation as a 'minister' in these contexts probably relates to service to the church, possibly to service to Paul, most improbably to the status of *deacon. Some who have questioned the authenticity of Eph. have connected Tychicus with its origin (*cf.* W. L. Knox, *St. Paul and the Church of the Gentiles*, 1939, p. 203; C. L. Mitton, *Epistle to the Ephesians*, 1950, p. 268).

A.F.W.

TYPOLOGY (Gk. *typos*, 'seal-impression'). A way of setting forth the biblical history of salvation so that some of its earlier phases are seen as anticipations of later phases, or some later phase as the recapitulation or fulfilment of an earlier one.

I. In the Old Testament

There are two archetypal epochs in the OT which are repeatedly presented in this way: the creation and the Exodus from Egypt. The Exodus is viewed as a new creation, or at least as a repetition of the original creative activity. He who in the beginning constrained the unruly sea within bounds, saying, 'Thus far shall you come, and no farther' (Gn. 1:9f.; Jb. 38:8–11), manifested the same power when he restrained the waters of the sea of reeds at the Exodus (Ex. 14:21–29). This parallelism is specially emphasized when the Creator's overthrow of the primeval symbols of chaos, *Rahab and the dragon (Jb. 26:12f.), is taken up and applied to his victory at the Exodus (Pss. 74:12–14; 89:8–10). Rahab becomes a 'type' of Egypt (*cf.* Is. 30:7) and the dragon (Leviathan) of Pharaoh (*cf.* Ezk. 29:3).

The restoration of Israel from the Babylonian captivity is portrayed as both a new creation and a new exodus. The verbs which are used of the Creator's workmanship in Gn. 1 and 2 (Heb. *bārā'*, *yāṣar*, *'āśâ*) are used of his activity in the restoration of the exiles (*cf.* Is. 43:7, where all three verbs appear together). The dragon-typology of creation, which had already been taken over as a picture of Yahweh's victory at the Exodus, now became a means of describing this new victory. When the arm of Yahweh is called upon to 'awake . . . as in days of old', when it 'cut Rahab in pieces' and 'didst pierce the dragon' (Is. 51:9), God is being urged to repeat in this new situation the mighty acts of creation and Exodus. If at the Exodus he saved his people by making 'a way in the sea, a path in the mighty waters' (Is. 43:16), so he will be with the returning exiles when they pass through the waters (Is. 43:2), making 'a way in the wilderness and rivers in the desert' (Is. 43:19). As the Exodus generation was led by a pillar of cloud by day and fire by night, which moved behind them when danger threatened from the back, so the exiles receive the promise: 'The Lord will go before you, and the God of Israel will be your rear guard' (Is. 52:12). Of the later generation as of the earlier it would be true that 'they thirsted not when he led them through the deserts; he made water flow for them from the rock' (Is. 48:21).

In the language of typology, the earlier series of events constituted a 'type' of the later; the later series was an 'antitype' of the earlier. Or it may be said that the successive epochs of salvation-history disclose a recurring pattern of divine activity, which the NT writers believed to have found its definitive expression in their own day.

II. In the New Testament

The typological relation between the two Testaments was summed up in Augustine's epigram: 'In the OT the NT lies hidden; in the NT the OT stands revealed.' In the NT the Christian salvation is presented as the climax of the mighty works of God, as the 'antitype' of his 'typical' mighty works in the OT. The Christian salvation is treated as a new creation, a new exodus, a new restoration from exile.

a. New creation. 'It is the God who said, "Let light shine out of darkness," who has shone in our hearts to give the light of the knowledge of the glory of God in the face of Christ' (2 Cor. 4:6). The Fourth Gospel perhaps provides the clearest instance of creation typology, with its exordium 'In the beginning . . .' echoing the opening words of Gn.: the divine Word which called the old creation into being has now become flesh to inaugurate a new creation. Those who are 'in Christ', according to Paul, constitute a 'new creation' (2 Cor. 5:17; Gal. 6:15). Paul and the seer of Patmos join in seeing the curse of the primordial fall reversed by the redemptive work of Christ (Rom. 8:19–21; Rev. 22:1–5). The gospel establishes 'new heavens and a new earth in which righteousness dwells' (2 Pet. 3:13; *cf.* Rev. 21:1).

b. New exodus. The exodus typology is particularly pervasive in the NT. Matthew seems to view the infancy of Jesus as a recapitulation of the early experiences of Israel, which went down to Egypt and came up again (Mt. 2:15). John, by the chronology of his Gospel and otherwise, implies that Christ is the antitypical Passover lamb (*cf.* Jn. 19:14, 36). Peter's language points in the same direction (1 Pet. 1:19), while Paul makes the thought explicit: since 'Christ, our paschal lamb, has been sacrificed', the ensuing festival should be celebrated by his people 'with the unleavened bread of sincerity and truth' (1 Cor. 5:7f.). As the Israelites passed through the Sea of Reeds, so Christians have been baptized into Christ; as the Israelites received bread from heaven and water from the rock, so Christians have their distinctive 'supernatural food and drink' (1 Cor. 10:1–4). As, despite all those blessings, the Exodus generation died in the wilderness because of unbelief and disobedience and so failed to enter the promised land, Christians for their part are exhorted to take warning lest they fall (1 Cor. 10:5–12; *cf.* Heb. 3:7–4:13; Jude 5). For these things befell the Israelites 'as a warning (*typikōs*), but they were written down for our instruction, upon whom the end of the ages has come' (1 Cor. 10:11). This typology has an intensely ethical and paraenetic emphasis.

c. New restoration. The very word 'gospel' (*euangelion*) and its cognates are probably derived by the NT writers from their occurrences in Is. 40–66 to denote the 'good tidings' of return from Exile and rebuilding of Zion (Is. 40:9; *cf.* 52:7; 61:1). No stretch of OT prophecy has provided such a fertile 'plot' of gospel *testimonia*, from the 'voice' of Is. 40:3 through the ministry of the Servant in Is. 42–53 to the new heavens and new earth of Is. 65:17; 66:22.

d. Typical persons. In Rom. 5:14 Adam is called 'a type (*typos*) of the one who was to come' (*i.e.* of Christ, the last Adam). Adam, as head of the old creation, is an obvious counterpart to Christ, head of the new creation. All humanity is viewed as being either 'in Adam', in whom 'all die', or 'in Christ', in whom all are to 'be made alive' (1 Cor. 15:22).

No other OT character is expressly called a *typos* of Christ in the NT. But other OT characters typify him in some degree, by comparison or contrast—Moses, as prophet (Acts 3:22f.; 7:37), Aaron, as priest (Heb. 5:4f.), David, as king (Acts 13:22). The writer to the Hebrews, taking his cue from Ps. 110:4, sees in Melchizedek a specially apt counterpart of Christ in his priestly office (Heb. 5:6, 10; 6:20ff.). He also hints that the details of the apparatus and services of the wilderness tabernacle might yield typical significance although, from what he says in Heb. 9:6–10, this significance would involve the difference rather than the resemblance between that order and the new order introduced by Christ. It is only in the light of the antitype that the relevance of the type can be appreciated.

III. Post-biblical developments

The post-apostolic age witnessed the beginning of a more unfettered Christian typology. From the first half of the 2nd century the *Epistle of Barnabas* or Justin's *Dialogue with Trypho* illustrate the length to which the typological interpretation of OT episodes could be carried in the absence of exegetical controls. The result was that the OT acquired its chief value in Christian eyes as a book of anticipatory pictures of the person and work of Christ—pictures presented in words and even more in visible art. Perhaps the most impressive example in art is Chartres Cathedral, where the sculptures and windows on the N side depict a wealth of OT analogies to the NT story depicted by their counterparts on the S side. Thus Isaac carrying the wood is a counterpart to Christ carrying his cross, the sale of Joseph for 20 pieces of silver is a counterpart to Christ's being sold for 30 pieces, and so forth. The whole OT is thus made to tell the Christian story in advance, but not on principles which the biblical writers themselves would have recognized.

What was spontaneous in the early Middle Ages tends to become studied and artificial when attempts are made to revive it at the present day. 'If the appeal to Scripture is to be maintained in its proper sense, and Christian doctrine is to be set on a less unstable foundation than the private judgment of ingenious riddle-solvers, some attempt is urgently needed to establish a workable criterion for the legitimate use of the typological method, and so to smooth the path of biblical theology' (G. W. H. Lampe, *Theology* 56, 1953, p. 208).

BIBLIOGRAPHY. G. W. H. Lampe and K. J. Woollcombe, *Essays on Typology*, 1957; S. H. Hooke, *Alpha and Omega*, 1961; D. Daube, *The Exodus Pattern in the Bible*, 1963; A. T. Hanson, *Jesus Christ in the Old Testament*, 1965; G. von Rad, *Old Testament Theology*, 2, 1965, pp. 319–409; F. F. Bruce, *This is That*, 1968; *idem*, *The Time is Fulfilled*, 1978; J. W. Drane, *EQ* 50, 1978, pp. 195–210; R. M. Davidson, *Typology in Scripture*, 1981; L. Goppelt, *Typos. The Typological Interpretation of the Old Testament in the New*, 1982; J. Barton, *Oracles of God*, 1986; G. W. Buchanan, *Typology and the Gospel*, 1987. F.F.B.

TYRANNUS. There is no known reference to Tyrannus apart from Acts 19:9, in which Paul at Ephesus is said to have reasoned daily in the *scholē* of Tyrannus. The word *scholē* (AV 'school', RSV 'hall') means a group or place where lectures are given and discussed. It is not known whether Tyrannus was the founder of the lecture-hall or its owner at the time of Paul's stay. The word translated 'one' in AV, which would support the latter view, is not in the best MSS. D.R.H.

TYRE, TYRUS. The principal seaport on the Phoenician coast, about 40 km S of Sidon and 45 N of Akko, Tyre (mod. Ṣûr; Heb. *ṣôr*; Assyr. *Ṣur(r)u*; Egyp. *Ḏaru*; Gk. *Tyros*) comprised two harbours. One lay on an island, the other 'Old' port on the mainland may be the Uššu of Assyrian inscriptions. The city, which was watered by the river Litani, dominated the surrounding plain, in the N of which lay Sarepta (*ZAREPHATH).

I. History

According to Herodotus (2. 44), Tyre was founded *c.* 2700 BC, and is mentioned in Execration Texts from *Egypt (*c.* 1850 BC) and in a Canaanite poem (Keret, *ANET*, pp. 142f.) from Ras Shamra (*UGARIT). It took an early and active part in the sea-trade in trade and luxuries with Egypt which led to the Egyptian campaigns to control the Phoenician coast. During the Amarna period the local ruler of Tyre, Abimilki, remained loyal, writing to Amenophis III of the defection of surrounding towns and requesting aid against the Amorite Aziru and king of Sidon. When the Philistines plundered Sidon (*c.* 1200 BC) many of its inhabitants fled to Tyre, which now became the 'daughter of Sidon' (Is. 23:12), the principal Phoenician port. By the late 2nd millennium BC it was counted as a strongly defended city on the border of the land allocated to Asher (Jos. 19:29), and this reputation continued (2 Sa. 24:7; RSV 'fortress').

With the decline of Egypt Tyre was independent, its rulers dominating most of the Phoenician coastal cities, including the Lebanon hinterland. Hiram I was a friend of David and supplied materials for building the royal palace at Jerusalem (2 Sa. 5:11; 1 Ki. 5:1; 1 Ch. 14:1), a policy he continued during the reign of Solomon, when he sent wood and stone for the construction of the Temple

(1 Ki. 5:1–12; 2 Ch. 2:3–16) in return for food supplies and territorial advantages (1 Ki. 9:10–14). Tyrians, including a bronze-caster also named Hiram, assisted in Solomon's projects (1 Ki. 7:13–14). During his reign Hiram I linked the mainland port with the island by an artificial causeway and built a temple dedicated to the deities Melqart and Astarte. As part of his policy of colonial expansion and trade he assisted Solomon's development of the Red Sea port of Ezion-geber for S voyages (1 Ki. 9:27), his ships reaching distant places (1 Ki. 9:28; *OPHIR). From this time, often called 'the golden age of Tyre', the people became the merchant princes of the E Mediterranean (Is. 23:8), and were henceforth noted for their seafaring prowess (Ezk. 26:17; 27:32). The primary trade was in their own manufactured *glass and the special scarlet-purple dyes, called 'Tyrian', made from the local *murex* (*ARTS AND CRAFTS; *PHOENICIA).

The Canon of Ptolemy is still a primary source for the king list, though, despite correlations with Assyrian and Hebrew history, there remains a divergence of about 10 years in the chronology of the earlier rulers. Thus Hiram I is dated *c.* 979–945 BC (*cf.* Albright, Katzenstein, *c.* 969–936 BC). His successor Baal-eser I (= Balbazeros) was followed by Abd-Ashtart, who was murdered by his brothers, the eldest of whom, Methus-Astartus, usurped the throne. Phelles, who succeeded Astarymus *c.* 897 BC, was overthrown by the high priest Ethbaal (Ithobal), whose daughter Jezebel was married to Ahab of Israel to confirm the alliance made between their countries (1 Ki. 16:31). Ethbaal was also a contemporary of Ben-hadad I. His success against Phelles may have been connected with the invasion of Ashurnasirpal II of Assyria, who took a heavy tribute from Tyre.

The port suffered another blow in 841 BC, when, in his 18th regnal year, Shalmaneser III of Assyria received tribute from Ba'alimanzar at the same time as Jehu paid him homage at the Nahr-el-Kelb (*Sumer* 7, 1951, 3–21). Baalezer II was followed by Mattan I (*c.* 829–821) and by Pygmalion (Pu'm-yaton), in whose 7th year (825 BC; others 815 BC) Carthage was founded from Tyre.

Assyrian pressure on Phoenicia continued, and Tyre paid tribute to Adad-nirari III of Assyria in 803 BC and its king Hiram II sent gifts to Tiglath-pileser III, who claims that his *Rabshakeh took 150 talents of gold from Mattan II, the next king of Tyre (*c.* 730 BC; *ANET*, p. 282). By peaceful submission the city retained a large measure of autonomy. According to Josephus (*Ant.* 9. 283), Shalmaneser V of Assyria (whose own records are wanting) laid siege to Tyre in 724, and the city fell with Samaria into the hands of Sargon II in 722 BC. Local Assyrian officials supervised the return of taxes in kind to Nineveh, but considerable unrest was fomented from Egypt, to whom the Tyrians turned for help. This led to denunciation of Tyre by the Heb. prophets who followed Isaiah and by Joel (3:5–6) for their selling them as slaves to the Greeks. Tyre came under the domination of Sidon, and when Sennacherib approached its ruler Luli (Elulaeus) fled and died in exile. This saved the city from assault, for the Assyrians installed their nominee Tuba'alu (Ethbaal III) in 701 BC.

Esarhaddon, who was keeping the route open to attack Egypt, executed Abdi-milkitti of Sidon (*c.* 677 BC) and set Ba'ali (I) on the throne, binding him by treaty to Assyria. However, Tyre, instigated by Tirhakah of Egypt, rebelled and Esarhaddon besieged the port, which did not, however, fall since Ba'ali submitted. His influence and independence must have been great in Phoenicia, since he retained the throne throughout his life. When he rebelled again in 664 BC the city fell to Ashurbanipal, who made Azi-Baal king, taking his sisters and many officials as hostages to Nineveh.

With the decline of Assyria at the end of the reign of Ashurbanipal (*c.* 636–627 BC), Tyre regained her autonomy and much of her former seatrade. Nevertheless, Jeremiah prophesied Tyre's subjection to the Babylonians (25:22; 27:1–11), as did Ezekiel later (26:1–28:19; 29:18–20) and Zechariah (9:2ff.). Nebuchadrezzar II besieged Tyre for 13 years, *c.* 587–574 BC (Jos., *Ant.* 10. 228; *JBL* 51, 1932, pp. 94ff.), but no contemporary record of this remains (*cf.* Ezk. 29:18–20). The city (under Ba'ali II) eventually recognized Babylonian suzerainty, and a number of Babylonian contracts confirm this and give the names of the local Babylonian officials. For a decade the city was ruled by 'judges' (*špṭ*).

In 332 BC Alexander the Great laid siege to the island port for 7 months and captured it only by building a mole to the island fortress. Despite heavy losses, the port soon recovered under Seleucid patronage. Herod I rebuilt the main temple, which would have been standing when our Lord visited the district bordering Tyre and Sidon (Mt. 15:21–28; Mk. 7:24–31). People of Tyre heard him speak (Mk. 3:8; Lk. 6:17), and he cited Tyre as a heathen city which would bear less responsibility than those Galilean towns which constantly witnessed his ministry (Mt. 11:21–22; Lk. 10:13–14). Christians were active in Tyre in the 1st century (Acts 21:3–6), and there the scholar Origen was buried (AD 254).

II. Archaeology

The main extant ruins date from the fall of the Crusader city in AD 1291, but excavations from 1921 (*Syria* 6, 1922), and from 1937 in the harbour, have traced some of the earlier foundations. The many coins minted in Tyre from the 5th century BC onwards, found at sites throughout the ancient Near East and Mediterranean, attest its greatness.

The 'ladder of Tyre' (Jos., *BJ* 2. 188), which marked the division between Phoenicia and Palestine proper (1 Macc. 11:59), is identified with the rocky promontory at Ras en-Naqara or Ras el-'Abyad.

BIBLIOGRAPHY. N. Jidejian, *Tyre through the Ages*, 1969; H. J. Katzenstein, *The History of Tyre*, 1973.

D.J.W.

U

UGARIT is modern Ras Shamra, located 1 km from the Mediterranean Sea and 10 km N of Syrian Latakia. C. F. A. Schaeffer began excavations in 1928, first at Ugarit's port by the bay of Minet el-Beida, then at Ras Shamra until 1969. M. Yon has directed the work since 1978. Although occupied as early as the 7th millennium BC, the site flourished in the 2nd millennium. In the Late Bronze Age (1550–1200 BC) the city-state controlled a region of 2,000 square kms, including a large agricultural plain and an excellent port (Yon). It enjoyed a moderate Mediterranean climate. Historical archives begin with King Niqmaddu II (1360–1330 BC) followed by the Hittite domination of the region through the intermediary Carchemish at the end of the 14th century. The Hittite-Egyptian treaty (*c.* 1270 BC) allowed the kingdom to develop with an increasing centralization of power. The king controlled a large palace that formed the centre of a fortified acropolis within the city. This and the towering temple of Baal were the two most impressive landmarks. Ugarit disappeared shortly after 1200 BC for reasons unknown but perhaps related as much to climatic change and internal problems as to any invasion from the sea (Dupont).

Excavators of Ugarit have unearthed thousands of inscriptions from the Late Bronze Age. Texts preserving Egyptian, Cypro-Minoan, Hurrian and Hittite languages occur, but most of the clay tablets preserve writing in Akkadian and Ugaritic languages. Ugaritic script represents one of the earliest alphabets, composed of twenty-nine letters written in cuneiform. The Ugaritic language is one of the earliest West Semitic languages attested by a sizeable corpus and variety of inscriptions. Rivalled only by the Dead Sea Scrolls, the texts from Ugarit represent the most important collection of written evidence yet discovered for better interpreting the OT. Study of the Ugaritic language has demonstrated a flexibility in the use of prepositions and other syntactical features, and has expanded the West Semitic vocabulary of known words and their usage. When applied to biblical Heb., this has provided for new interpretations of difficult texts and rendered unnecessary many textual emendations of previous generations.

Although the citizens of Ugarit distinguished themselves from 'Canaanites', they shared a common culture. Religious, epistolary, lexical, administrative, legal and contractual texts have been discovered at Ugarit (Pardee and Bordreuil). Scholars have made many comparisons between aspects of the Ugaritic mythologies and the OT. Canaanite deities are attested such as Asherah, Anat, Ashtart (Ugaritic Athtart), Baal and El as well as divine personifications of the sea, (Yam) and death (Mot). Leviathan also occurs. El appears as the senior deity who grants the requests of gods and humans. Baal acts to defeat Yam and to build a palace. Mot kills him but Baal reappears and brings fruitfulness. Kings such as Keret and Danel (*cf.* Ezk. 28:3) request sons to inherit their thrones. Other myths emphasize marriage (Nikkal) and procreation, sometimes in a crude fashion (Birth of Shahar and Shalim) that recalls the condemnation by the biblical prophets of the sexual excesses of Canaanite religion. Other texts include lists of deities and offerings they receive. Mesopotamian traditions brought inscribed liver models and other omen texts, the flood story of Atrahasis, the 'Babylonian Job' and other 'wisdom' compositions.

The texts from Ugarit have affected almost every area of OT studies (Brooke, Curtis and Healey). We may consider examples from law, history, poetry and prophecy (Craigie, 1983, pp. 67–90). Although no legal collections have yet appeared at Ugarit, ritual instructions parallel biblical law. Sacrificial texts use similar terms to describe 'whole burnt' (*kll*), 'communion' (*šlmn*) and 'gift' (*mnḥh*) offerings as in Lv. 2, 3 and 6. Other OT terms such as 'priest' (*khn*), 'sacrifice' (*zbḥ*), 'cultic functionary' (*qdš*) and 'tent of meeting' (*'hlm'd*) occur at Ugarit (Smith, 1990, pp. 2–3). A ritual text (*KTU* 1.40) describes how to deal with sins such as anger and impatience by animal sacrifice (Pardee). *'Il ib* 'god of the father' also occurs at Ugarit, and invites comparison with the patriarchal God of the fathers (Ex. 3:16) as a deity associated with one's ancestors.*'El brt* occurs in a Hurrian religious text. Some have compared this to El-Berith, *i.e.* El of the Covenant, as at Shechem (Jdg. 9:46). However, the Hurrian context renders this translation unlikely and illustrates the dangers of making comparisons without careful linguistic controls.

Although Ugarit flourished before Israel settled in Canaan, its administrative records demonstrate a continuity between city-states of the Late Bronze Age Levant and the Jerusalem administration as it developed under David and Solomon (Heltzer). In both cases the 'servants of the king' formed the administrative core of the kingdom, as royal dependents, with specific skills for tasks at the palace and in the governing apparatus. Similarities exist between the description of Baal's construction of his palace or temple, and the rituals surrounding it, and David's transport of the Ark into Jerusalem (2 Sa. 6; Seouw). Letter writers of Ugarit sometimes addressed requests to the queen mother instead of going directly to the king, reflecting her influential role (*cf.* 1 Ki. 2:13–25; 15:11–13; 22:52; 2 Ki. 11). Many personal names correspond to biblical names, though they designate different people. Administrative records mention inhabitants of Palestinian sites such as Ashdod. Girgashites (Dt. 7:1; Jos. 3:10) are attested at Ugarit (*grgš*). The role of Ugaritic Rephaim as dead warriors and ancestors may relate to the biblical group of the same name (Dt. 3:10).

An understanding of the Canaanite background is useful for the study of biblical *poetry (Craigie). Ps. 29 contains many similar ideas and even phrases used of Baal in Ugaritic poetry. However, the biblical psalmist wishes to affirm that Yahweh, not Baal, is Lord of nature. Like God in Ps. 104:3, Baal is a rider on the clouds. Fire and flame assist Baal as well as God (v.4). The voice of Baal is also thunder (v.7) and the cedars of Lebanon form Baal's palace (*cf.* v.16). The psalmist transforms the Canaanite motifs by confessing that the God of Israel is creator of the whole world, not merely a temple in Jerusalem. As the Heb. psalms do with 'selah', 'sheminith', *etc.*, Hurrian poetical compositions contain musical annotations. Poems throughout the Bible describe God as a warrior coming from a distant mountain to do battle on behalf of Israel with the power of the storm (Ex. 15; Dt. 33; Jdg. 5; Ps. 68; Heb. 3). This motif occurs in the Baal cycle from Ugarit (*KTU* 1.4, 29–35; 1.101.1–4; Smith 1990: 49). However, the Bible transforms these images. Thus Ex. 15, the Song of the Sea, celebrates Israel's deliverance from Egypt. Although its confession of God's reign resembles the confession of Baal's reign at Ugarit, the distinction between Baal's victory over the sea god, Yam, differs from God's victory over Egypt. The God of Israel acts in history to redeem; the deities of Ugarit and Canaan act within the cycles of nature. In addition, many similarities exist in the form and structure of Ugaritic and Heb. poetry (Watson).

The taunt of the Babylonian king, Helel, 'the shining one' of Is. 14:12–14, who tries and fails to take God's place, resembles that of Athtar, also called 'the shining one', who tries and fails to occupy Baal's throne in his absence (Craigie). Athtar's feet are too short! Am. 1:1 notes that the prophet was a shepherd. The term used (*nōqēd*) is rare in the Bible. Its occurrences in the administrative texts from Ugarit suggest that it describes owners and managers of large herds, engaged in marketing wool and other produce. This sophisticated background helps to explain the international character of Amos' prophecies and rhetoric. Texts from Ugarit also attest to the marzeah, a religious banquet, associated with the drinking of wine. Je. 16:5–9 and perhaps Am. 6:4–7 describe the practice and condemn it (King). However, it continued into the Christian era.

BIBLIOGRAPHY. Texts: J. Nougayrol and C. Virolleaud, *PRU*, 2–6, 1955–1970; C. H. Gordon, *UT*, Analecta Orientalia 38, 1965; *UG* 5, 1968; *UG* 7, 1978; J. C. L. Gibson, *CML*, 1977; J. C. De Moor and K. Spronk, *A Cuneiform Anthology of Religious Texts from Ugarit*, 1987; P. Bordreuil, *Une bibliotheque au sud de la ville*, 1991; M. Dietrich, O. Loretz and J. Sanmartin, *KTU* 2, 1994. Translations: French – *PRU*; *UG*; Bordreuil texts volumes; A. Caquot, M. Sznycer and A. Herdner, *LAPO* 7, 1974; A. Caquot, J.-M. Tarragon and J.-L. Cunchillos, *LAPO* 14, 1989. English – *ANET*, pp. 129–155 *et passim*; *CML*; J. C. De Moor, *An Anthology of Religious Texts from Ugarit*, 1987; M. S. Smith, *The Ugaritic Baal Cycle* 1, 1994. Other series: *ALASP*; *Newsletter for Ugaritic Studies*; *RSP* 1–3; *Ras Shamra-Ougarit*; *Syria*; *UF*; *UBL*. Sources cited: G. J. Brooke, A. H. W. Curtis and J. F. Healey, *UBL* 11, 1994; P. C. Craigie, *Ugarit and the Old Testament*, 1983; F. R. Dupont, *The Late History of Ugarit*, 1987; M. Heltzer, *Society and Economy in the Eastern Mediterranean*, M. Heltzer and E. Lipinski (eds.), 1988, pp. 7–18; P. J. King, *Amos, Hosea, Micah*, 1988; D. Pardee and P. Bordreuil, *ABD* 6, 1992, pp. 706–721; C. L. Seouw, *Myth, Drama and the Politics of David's Dance*, 1989; M. S. Smith, *The Early History of God*, 1990; W. G. E. Watson, *JSOT*, supp. 26, 1984; M. Yon, *ABD* 6, 1992, pp. 695–706; G. D. Young (ed.), *Ugarit in Retrospect*, 1981.

R.S.H.

ULAI. The canal or river flowing E of Susa in Elam (SW Persia) where Daniel heard a man's voice (Dn. 8:16). The river (Heb. *'ûlāi*; Assyr. *Ulai*; classical *Eulaeus*) has changed its course in modern times, and the present Upper Kherkhah and Lower Karun (Pasitigris) rivers may then have been a single stream flowing into the delta at the N of the Persian Gulf. The river is illustrated in the Assyrian reliefs showing Ashurbanipal's attack on Susa in 646 BC (R. D. Barnett, *Assyrian Palace Reliefs*, 1960, plates 118–127).

D.J.W.

UNBELIEF. Expressed by two Gk. words in the NT, *apistia* and *apeitheia*. According to *MM*, the word *apeitheia*, together with *apeitheō* and *apeithēs*, 'connotes invariably disobedience, rebellion, contumacy'. So Paul says that the Gentiles have obtained mercy through the rebellion of the Jews (Rom. 11:30). See also Rom. 11:32; Heb. 4:6, 11. This disobedience springs from *apistia*, 'a want of faith and trust'. *apistia* is a state of mind, and *apeitheia* an expression of it. Unbelief towards himself was the prime sin of which Christ said that the Spirit would convict the world (Jn. 16:9). Unbelief in all its forms is a direct affront to the divine veracity (*cf.* 1 Jn. 5:10), which is why it is so heinous a sin. The children of Israel did not enter into God's rest for two reasons. They lacked faith (*apistia*, Heb. 3:19), and they disobeyed (*apeitheia*, Heb. 4:6). 'Unbelief finds its practical issue in disobedience' (Westcott on Heb. 3:12).

BIBLIOGRAPHY. O. Becker, O. Michel, in *NIDNTT* 1, pp. 587–606.

D.O.S.

UNCTION. In its three NT occurrences, *i.e.* 1 Jn. 2:20, 27 (twice), AV renders Gk. *chrisma*, 'unction', and RSV has 'anointed', *'anointing'. Christians who, by virtue of their 'unction' (vv. 20, 27), are all able to discern schism (v. 19) and heresy (denial of the incarnation, v. 22) are exhorted to adhere to the apostolic message (v. 24), which led them to confess the Father and the Son. Grammatically, 'unction' must be either (*a*) 'that which is smeared on' (so B. F. Westcott, *The Epistles of John*, 1892); or (*b*) 'the act of anointing' (so A. E. Brooke, *ICC*, 1912); but in either case the word refers to the gift of the Holy Spirit, of which baptism is the outward sign, and whose sensible reception, leading to awareness of dangers to the church, is the consequence of true incarnational faith. This exegesis is compatible with, though not necessarily proving, the belief that the anointing of the Spirit leads to spoken prophecy within the church.

BIBLIOGRAPHY. D. Müller, *NIDNTT* 1, pp. 121–124; I. H. Marshall, *The Epistles of John*, *NIC*, 1978, pp. 153–156; D. H. Engelhard, *ISBE* 1, 129.

M.R.W.F.

UNKNOWN GOD (Gk. *agnōstos theos*). In Acts 17:23 Paul refers to an Athenian altar-dedication 'To the unknown God' which forms the text of his *Areopagus address. Pausanias (*Description of Greece*, 1. 1. 4) says that in Athens there are 'altars of gods called unknown' and Philostratus (*Life of Apollonius of Tyana*, 6. 3. 5) similarly speaks of 'altars of unknown divinities' as set up there. They are frequently associated with a story told by Diogenes Laertius (*Lives of Philosophers*, 1. 110) about the setting up of 'anonymous altars' in and around Athens on one occasion to avert a pestilence. Similar dedications are attested elsewhere, if the name of a local deity was uncertain or the wording of an original dedication had become lost.

BIBLIOGRAPHY. E. Norden, *Agnostos Theos*, 1912; K. Lake, 'The Unknown God', in *BC*, 5, pp. 240–246; B. Gärtner, *The Areopagus Speech and Natural Revelation*, 1955, pp. 242ff.; E. Haenchen, *The Acts of the Apostles*, 1971, pp. 516ff. F.F.B.

UPHAZ. An unidentified location from which came fine gold (Je. 10:9; Dn. 10:5). It may, however, be a technical term for 'refined gold' itself (so 1 Ki. 10:18, *mûp̄āz*; *cf. mippāz*, Is. 13:12) similar to the definition 'pure gold' (*zāhāḇ ṭāhôr*; 2 Ch. 9:17). Others, with some support from VSS, read *'ûp̄îr* (*OPHIR; *cf.* Je. 10:9) for *'ûp̄āz* owing to the similarity of Heb. *z* and *r*. D.J.W.

UR OF THE CHALDEES. The city which Terah and Abram left to go to Harran (Gn. 11:28, 31; 15:7; Ne. 9:7). Considered by Stephen to be in Mesopotamia (Acts 7:2, 4). An old identification of Heb. *'ûr* with Urfa (Edessa), 32 km NW of Harran, is unlikely on philological grounds, and *Ura'* is the name of several places known in Asia Minor. Moreover, such an identification would require Abraham to retrace his steps E before setting out W towards Canaan. This identification requires that the 'Chaldea' which identifies the location must be equated with *Ḫ*aldai (part of ancient Armenia). The *Chaldeans were a Semitic people known in Babylonia from at least the end of the 2nd millennium BC, but there are no references to their presence in N Mesopotamia. LXX wrote 'the land (*chōra*) of the Chaldees', perhaps being unfamiliar with the site. However, Eupolemus (*c.* 150 BC) refers to Ur as a city in Babylonia called Camarina ('the moon') or Ouria. The Talmudic interpretation of Ur as Erech is unlikely since the latter is distinguished in Gn. 10:10.

The most generally accepted identification is with the ancient site of Ur (*Uri*), modern Tell el-Muqayyar, 14 km W of Nasiriyeh on the river Euphrates in S Iraq. Excavations at this site in 1922–34 by the joint British Museum and University Museum, Philadelphia, expedition under Sir C. L. Woolley traced the history of the site from the 'Al 'Ubaid period (5th millennium BC) until it was abandoned about 300 BC. Many spectacular discoveries were made, especially in the royal cemeteries of the early Dynastic 3 period (*c.* 2500 BC). Beneath these a layer of silt was at first equated with the flood of the Epic of Gilgamesh and Genesis (see now *Iraq* 26, 1964, pp. 65ff.). The ruins of the temple tower (*ziggurat*) built by Ur-Nammu, the founder of the prosperous 3rd Dynasty (*c.* 2150–2050 BC) still dominate the site (*BABEL). The history and economy of the city is well known from thousands of inscribed tablets and the many buildings found at the site. The principal deity was Nannar (Semitic Sin or Su'en), who was also worshipped at Harran. The city was later ruled by the Neo-Babylonian (Chaldean) kings of Babylonia.

BIBLIOGRAPHY. P. R. Moorey and C. L. Woolley, *Ur of the Chaldees*, 1982; *Ur Excavations Texts* 1–7, 1928–74; *Excavations at Ur* 1–10, 1934–74; *CAH* 1/2, 1971, pp. 417–468, 595–617.

URBANUS. Latin servile (*cf.* A. Deissmann, *Bible Studies*², 1909, pp. 271ff.) recurrent in inscriptions of the imperial household (*e.g. CIL*, 6. 4237)—perhaps the Urbanus greeted in Rom. 16:9 (AV, Urbane) belonged to it (*cf.* Phil. 4:22; Lightfoot, *Philippians*, p. 174). 'Our fellow-worker' need not imply service with Paul personally. Paul, exact with pronouns, uses '*my* fellow-worker' for companions (*cf.* Rom. 16:3, 21). (*AMPLIAS.) A.F.W.

URIAH (Heb. *'ûriyyâ*, *'ûrriyyāhû*, 'Yahweh is my light'). **1.** A Hittite whose name may be Hurrian *Ariya* conformed to Heb. Uriah, one of several non-Israelites among David's mighty warriors (2 Sa. 23:39; 1 Ch. 11:41). While Uriah was away with the army besieging *Rabbah, David committed adultery with his wife *Bathsheba in Jerusalem (2 Sa. 11:1–4; *cf.* 1 Ki. 15:5). In order to legalize this relationship, David had Uriah placed in a vulnerable position in battle so that he was killed (2 Sa. 11:6–21). He is mentioned in the genealogy of Jesus as the husband of Bathsheba, mother of Solomon (Mt. 1:6).

2. A priest and one of two 'reliable witnesses' to the prophecy concerning Maher-shalal-hash-baz (Is. 8:2). He aided *Ahaz in introducing a foreign-inspired altar and in making other unorthodox changes in the cult (2 Ki. 16:10–16).

3. A prophet from Kiriath-jearim, whose message supported his contemporary, Jeremiah. Flight to Egypt to escape Jehoiakim's wrath, which his prophecies had incited, did not protect him since he was extradited to Judah and executed there (Je. 26:20–24).

4. Father of Meremoth, a priest during the time of Ezra (Ezr. 8:33; *cf.* N. 8:4). D.W.B.

URIEL (Heb. *'ûrî'ēl*, 'God is my light'). **1.** Chief of the Kohathites in the reign of David. He assisted in the bringing up of the ark from the house of Obed-edom (1 Ch. 15:5, 11). He is perhaps the same as in 1 Ch. 6:24. **2.** The maternal grandfather of Abijah (2 Ch. 13:2). M.A.M.

URIM AND THUMMIM. In association with the office of high priest, God made a provision for giving guidance to his people (Dt. 33:8, 10) but particularly to the leaders of his people (Nu. 27:21, *cf.* below). Almost everything, however, about this provision remains unexplained. The words Urim and Thummim have received no satisfactory etymology and the technique whereby guidance was made plain has not been recorded. A further mystery is the apparent disappearance of the Urim and Thummim from national life between the early monarchy (*e.g.* 1 Sa. 23:6) and some revival of the usage envisaged in Ezr. 2:63; Ne. 7:65.

Three passages are of particular interest. Abiathar came to David (1 Sa. 23:6) with the 'ephod'. It is reasonable to assume that this was the high-priestly ephod, not the ordinary ephod of priestly wear (1 Sa. 22:18), for otherwise why should it be mentioned? In the light of the remainder of the story we must assume that 'ephod' here acts as a comprehensive term for that whole unit of high-priestly garb: ephod-breastpiece-Urim (*cf.* Ex. 28:28–30; see 1 Sa. 14:18, where 'ark' [LXX reads 'ephod'] seems similarly to summarize the oracular equipment of the priest). David (1 Sa. 23:9–12) asks direct questions and elicits affirmative answers. In point of fact no examples of negative answers are anywhere recorded. The second passage is 1 Sa. 14 and it presents similarities: *cf.* 14:3, 41 with 23:6, 9; note the identical title in 14:41; 23:10 (a customary formula?). According to *MT* Saul requests: 'Give perfect things' (*tāmîm*, related, presumably, to Thummim). RSV accepts the reconstruction of the text here, helped by LXX, and reads 'If this guilt is in me or in Jonathan . . . give Urim . . . if this guilt is in thy people . . . give Thummim.' The third passage shows that the Urim and Thummim could not be compelled to give an answer: 1 Sa. 28:6; *cf.* 14:36–37.

It is extremely difficult if not impossible to offer a coherent suggestion on the basis of this evidence. H. H. Rowley conjectures that Urim (related to *'ārar*, to curse) gives the negative answer and Thummim (related to *tāmam*, to be perfect) gives the affirmative. On the assumption that the Urim and Thummim were two flat objects each with a 'yes' side and each with a 'no' side, then on being taken or tossed out of the pouch (*cf.* Pr. 16:33) a 'yes' (two Thummim) and 'no' (two Urim) and a 'no reply' (one Urim and one Thummim) were all possible. This is intriguing and plausible but, of course, must rest in part on the reconstruction of 1 Sa. 14:41 and ignore the lack of evidence for negative replies.

BIBLIOGRAPHY. H. H. Rowley, *The Faith of Israel*, 1956, pp. 28ff.; *VT* 12, 1962, pp. 164ff.; Josephus, *Ant.* 3. 214–218; S. R. Driver, *Notes on the Hebrew Text of the Books of Samuel*, 1913, p. 117; J. Mauchline, *I and II Samuel*, 1971.

J.A.M.

UZ. 1. Son of Aram and grandson of Shem (Gn. 10:23). In 1 Ch. 1:17 Uz (Heb. *'ûṣ*, perhaps related to Arab. *'Awḍ*, the name of a deity) is named among the sons, *i.e.* descendants, of Shem. **2.** Son of Nahor and Milcah and brother of Buz (Gn. 22:21, where AV reads Huz). **3.** Son of Dishan and grandson of Seir, the Horite (Gn. 36:28).

4. The land of Uz was Job's homeland (Jb. 1:1; *cf.* Je. 25:20 and La. 4:21), the location of which is uncertain. Of the numerous suggestions (*e.g.* near Palmyra, near Antioch, or in N Mesopotamia) the two most likely are Hauran, S of Damascus, and the area between Edom and N Arabia. The former is supported by Josephus (*Ant.* 1. 145) and both Christian and Muslim traditions. On this view (favoured by F. I. Andersen, *Job*, 1976) Uz is the land settled by the son of Aram.

Many modern scholars (*e.g.* E. Dhorme, *Job*, E.T. 1967) incline towards the more S location. Job's friends seem to have come from the vicinity of Edom, *e.g.* Eliphaz the Temanite (Jb. 2:11). Uz appears to have been accessible both to Sabaean bedouin from Arabia and Chaldean marauders from Mesopotamia (Jb. 1:15, 17). The postscript to the LXX locates Uz 'in the regions of Idumaea and Arabia', but partly on the basis of a spurious identification of Job with Jobab (Gn. 36:33). Uz in Je. 25:20 is coupled with Philistia, Edom, Moab and Ammon, while La. 4:21 indicates that the Edomites were occupying the land of Uz. However, the LXX omits Uz in both of these passages, and the identity of this land of Uz with Job's is not certain. The fact that Job is numbered with the people of the E (1:3; *cf.* Jdg. 6:3, 33; Is. 11:14; Ezk. 25:4, 10) seems to substantiate a location E of the great rift (Arabah) in the area where Edom and W Arabia meet.

D.A.H.

UZAL. 1. Heb. *'ûzāl* in Gn. 10:27 and 1 Ch. 1:21 signifies an Arabian descendant of Joktan, perhaps connected with 'Azal, given by Arab historians as the ancient name of San'a in Yemen.

2. Ezk. 27:19, AV translates 'Dan also and Javan going to and fro occupied in thy fairs' from Heb. *w^eḏān w^eyāwān m^e'ûzzāl b^e'izbônayiḵ nāṯānû*, which RVmg. renders 'Vedan and Javan traded from Uzal for thy wares', while RSV reads 'and wine from Uzal they exchanged for your wares' (following LXX). Uzal may be identified with Izalla in NE Syria, whence Nebuchadrezzar obtained wine (S. Langdon, *Neubabylonische Konigsinschriften*, no. 9, I, l. 22; *cf.* l. 23 'wine from *Ḫilbunim*' with Helbon of Ezk. 27:18). The alteration of *w^eyāwān* to *w^eyayin*, 'and wine', is very slight. Although *w^eḏān* may be omitted as a scribal error due to the proximity of Dedan (v. 20), it might be a cognate of Akkad. *dannu* (and Ugaritic *dn*), 'a large jar or vat used for storing wine or beer'. This would lead to a translation, 'and vat(s) of wine from Uzal they exchanged for your wares'; *cf.* NEB.

See A. R. Millard, *JSS* 7, 1962, pp. 201–203.

A.R.M.

UZZA (Heb. *'uzzā'*). **1.** A descendant of Ehud, a Benjaminite (1 Ch. 8:7). **2.** A son of Merari (1 Ch. 6:29). **3.** The head of a family of Nethinim who returned from the Exile (Ezr. 2:49). **4.** A son of Abinadab, probably a Levite (*cf.* 1 Sa. 7:1), who drove the new cart carrying the ark when it was removed from Kiriath-jearim (2 Sa. 6:3). When the oxen stumbled he 'put out his hand to the ark of God and took hold of it', for which irreverent handling of the ark he was struck dead by God (2 Sa. 6:6–7). **5.** The otherwise unknown owner of a garden in which Manasseh and Amon were buried (2 Ki. 21:18, 26).

M.A.M.

UZZI. A priest in the line of descent from Eleazar (1 Ch. 6:5; Ezr. 7:4), probably contemporary with *Eli. For others of the same name in Benjaminite families, see 1 Ch. 7:7; 9:8; in Issachar, 1 Ch. 7:2–3; and Levites (Ne. 11:22; 12:19, 42).

D.J.W.

UZZIAH (Heb. *'uzziyyâ*, *'uzziyāhû*, 'Yahweh is my strength'. An alternative form is Azariah, *'^azaryâ*, *'^azaryāhû*, 'Yahweh has helped', the difference in spelling is one letter in Heb. The two words, 'strength' and 'help', became almost synonymous, and they were apparently interchangeable.

1. Son of *Amaziah who was made tenth king of Judah by the people upon the assassination of

A limestone plaque, found in Jerusalem, inscribed in Aramaic, 'Hither were brought the bones of Uzziah, king of Judah. Not to be opened'. Probably to be dated in the 1st cent. AD *at a time of reburial of the bones. Height 35 cm.*

his father (*c.* 767 BC; 2 Ki. 14:18–21; 2 Ch. 25:27–26:1). He was probably co-regent from *c.* 791 BC when his father was imprisoned (*cf.* 2 Ki. 14:13; 2 Ch. 25:23). Although this is not explicit in the text, it is required by the *chronology in the light of his 52-year reign (2 Ki. 15:2; 2 Ch. 26:3).

Uzziah extended Judah's borders, regaining control of the Red Sea port of Elath and rebuilding it (2 Ki. 14:22), as well as successfully campaigning against the Philistines, Arabs and Ammonites (2 Ch. 26:6–8). For his internal security he strengthened the fortifications of Jerusalem, perhaps introducing new defensive techniques (vv. 9–15; Y. Yadin, *The Art of Warfare in Biblical Lands*, 1963, p. 326), and maintaining a standing army. A king Azriyau who is mentioned by *Tiglath-pileser III as leader of a revolt against Assyria has been identified with Azariah-Uzziah (*DOTT*, pp. 54–56; *ANET*, p. 282; H. Tadmor, *Scripta Hierosolymitana* 8, 1961, pp. 232–271), but a more recent examination of the sources throws considerable doubt on this (N. Na'aman, *BASOR* 214, 1974).

For a cultic misdemeanour, Uzziah was struck with leprosy, and his son Jotham became co-regent (2 Ch. 26:16–21). Josephus (*Ant.* 9. 225) retains a tradition that the earthquake occurred at that moment which was long remembered (Am. 1:1; Zc. 14:5).

A stone slab found in Jerusalem bears an Aramaic notice of the 1st century AD recording the reburial of the king's remains: 'Hither were brought the bones of Uzziah, king of Judah—do not open!'

2. A Kohathite Levite (1 Ch. 6:24 = Azariah, v. 36). **3.** A Judaean who lived in Jerusalem after the exile (Ne. 11:4). D.W.B.
A.R.M.

UZZIEL (Heb. *'uzzî'ēl*, 'God is my strength'). **1.** A Levite, son of Kohath and father of *Mishael, *Elzaphan and Sithri (Ex. 6:22). **2.** The founder of a levitical family subdivision (Nu. 3:19, 30), twice called Uzzielites (Nu. 3:27; 1 Ch. 26:23) whose members helped David bring the ark to Zion and were subsequently assigned responsibility in the Temple (1 Ch. 23:12, 20; 24:24). D.W.B.

V

VAGABOND. In RSV only at Pr. 6:11, where the sluggard is warned that poverty will come upon him like a vagabond (AV 'as one that travelleth'). 'Highwayman' is apt (C. H. Toy, *Proverbs*, *ICC*, 1899). Vagabond occurs in AV for (1) Heb. *nûḏ*, 'to wander', to describe Cain's lot after God's sentence, Gn. 4:12, 14; *cf.* *NOD; (2) *nûa'*, 'to wander about' (like beggars), Ps. 109:10; (3) Gk. *perierchomai*, 'to go around', to refer to Jewish exorcists, Acts 19:13 (RV, NEB 'strolling'; RSV 'itinerant'; *cf.* Lat. *vagari*, 'to wander'). N.H.

VALE, VALLEY. In Palestine, where rain falls only at a certain time of year, the landscape is cut by many narrow valleys and stream-beds (wadis), wet only in the rainy season (Heb. *naḥal*; Arab. *wadī*). Often water may be found below ground in such wadis during the dry months (*cf.* Gn. 26:17, 19). Perennial rivers flow through wider valleys and plains (Heb. *'ēmeq*, *biq'â*) or cut narrow gorges through the rock. Heb. *šᵉp̄ēlâ* denotes low ground, especially the coastal plain (*SHEPHELAH); *gay'* is simply a valley. For geographical details, see under proper names: *HINNOM; *JEHOSHAPHAT; *SALT (VALLEY OF); *etc.* A.R.M.

VANITY, VAIN. The three main Heb. words translated in EVV 'vanity' are distributed broadly as follows: *hebel*, Pss., Ec., Je.; *šāw'*, Jb., Ezk.; *tōhû*, Is. *heḇel*, lit. 'a vapour', 'a breath' (*cf.* Pss. 78:33; 94:11; Is. 57:13, *etc.*), indicates the fruitlessness of human endeavours. Such is man's natural life (Jb. 7:3; Ps. 39:5). Figuratively *heḇel* conveys the idea of unsubstantial, worthless, thus 'the vanity of idols' (*cf.* Je. 10:15; 51:18, AV). The worship of such is consequently unprofitable (Dt. 32:21; 1 Sa. 15:23; Pss. 4:2; 24:4, *etc.*). Unprofitable, too, are those who turn to such vain things (1 Sa. 12:21; 2 Ki. 17:15; Is. 41:29; 44:9). Idolatry is the worship of a 'no-god', by which God is provoked (Dt. 32:21; 1 Ki. 16:13, 26, *etc.*), in contrast with the true worship of God (*cf.* Is. 30:7; 40). Because idols and their worship raise vain hopes, worthless likewise must be the proclamation of false prophets (Je. 23:16; Ezk. 13:1–23; Zc. 10:2). A 'vain offering' (Is. 1:13) is ritual without righteousness. Wealth got by vanity dwindles (Pr. 13:11; LXX, Vulg., 'in haste'; *cf.* 21:6). *heḇel* has reference to man's human life: 'man at his best estate' (Heb. 'standing firm') is 'a few handbreadths' (Pss. 39:5; *cf.* v. 11; 62:9; 78:33, *etc.*). This *heḇel* of all human existence is fully treated in the book of Ecclesiastes.

With *šāw'* the idea of 'foul', 'unseemly', 'evil' is introduced. Jb. 31:5 illustrates this with reference to behaviour; Pss. 12:2; 41:6; Ezk. 13:8 to speech; Ezk. 13:6, 9 (*cf.* v. 23); 21:29; 22:28 to sight. The word *'āwen* meaning 'breath' is also translated 'vanity' (*e.g.* Jb. 15:35; Ps. 10:7; Pr. 22:8; Is. 41:29; 58:9; Zc. 10:2). It inclines, however, more to the idea of iniquity, and is thus translated by such terms as 'deceit', 'iniquity', 'calamity', 'delusion', 'wickedness', 'nonsense', in the RSV. *tōhû*, lit. 'a waste' (*cf.* Gn. 1:1; Dt. 32:10, *etc.*), then figuratively 'emptiness', 'uselessness'; so God the Lord regards the nations (Is. 40:17, *cf.* v. 23). Ps. 4:2; Hab. 2:13 have the word *rîq*, translated 'vanity' in EVV, lit. 'emptiness' (*cf.* Je. 51:34), in the figurative sense a useless thing.

In the NT the word vanity occurs three times only in the AV, but not at all in the RSV, where the purely biblical and ecclesiastical *mataiotēs* is used (LXX for *heḇel* and *šāw'*). (1) In Eph. 4:17 (RSV 'futility') it refers to behaviour and there 'includes moral as well as intellectual worthlessness or fatuity. It is of all that is comprehended under the word *nous*, the understanding of the heart, that this vanity is predicated. Everything included in the following verses respecting the blindness and depravity of the heart is therefore comprehended in the word vanity' (C. Hodge, *The Epistle to the Ephesians*, 1856, *ad loc.*). (2) In Pet. 2:18 (RSV 'folly') the reference is to speech with the idea of 'devoid of truth', 'inappropriate'. (3) In Rom. 8:20 (RSV 'futility') the thought is 'frailty', 'want of vigour' (*cf.* use of verb in Rom. 1:21 'to make empty', 'foolish'). 'The idea is that of looking for what one does not find—hence of futility, frustration, disappointment. Sin brought this doom on creation; it made a pessimistic view of the universe inevitable. *hypetagē*: the precise time denoted is that of the Fall, when God pronounced the ground cursed for man's sake' (J. Denney in *EGT*).

Heathen deities are vanities, vain things (Acts 14:15; *cf.* Je. 2:5; 10:3, *etc.*). Cognate with the word 'vanity' is 'vain', literally 'devoid of force or purpose'. Our Lord pronounced Gentile worship and Pharisaic piety so (Mt. 6:7; 15:9; Mk. 7:7); so too Paul estimated pagan philosophy (Rom. 1:21; Eph. 5:6, *etc.*). It is possible through faithlessness in Christian service to become so (*cf.* 1 Cor. 9:15; 2 Cor. 6:1; 9:3; Phil. 2:16; 1 Thes. 3:5). Where Christ's resurrection is denied, preaching is 'false' (1 Cor. 15:14) and faith without force (1 Cor. 15:17). Allegiance to the law robs faith of its worth (Rom. 4:14), and Christ's death of its effect (Gal. 2:21). Yet faith without works is as vain as works without faith (Jas. 2:20).

BIBLIOGRAPHY. E. Tiedtke *et al. NIDNTT* 1, pp. 546–553. H.D.McD.

VASHNI. According to AV, following the *MT* of 1 Ch. 6:28, Vashni was the elder son of Samuel. RV and RSV following the Syriac, and Lagarde's recension of the LXX and the parallel text 1 Sa. 8:2 supply Joel as the name of Samuel's elder son; the

Hebrew letters of 'Vashni' are then repointed with 'the' inserted to give the meaning 'and the second' Ahijah. R.A.H.G.

VEGETABLES (Heb. *zērō'îm,* 'seeds', AV 'pulse', Dn. 1:12; *zēr^{e}'ōnîm*, seeds, RVmg. 'herbs', Dn. 1:16). A general term for something that is sown, but usually denoting edible seeds which can be cooked, such as lentils, beans, *etc.* In the biblical context the word is used of the plain vegetable food sought by Daniel and his friends, instead of the rich diet of the king's table.

The Heb. word *pôl* (2 Sa. 17:28) denotes the beans brought for David and his men. Ezk. 4:9 refers to them as a substitute for grain meal in famine bread. Ezekiel's bread probably did not break the levitical law against mixing diverse kinds (see *ICC*, *ad loc.*) The Mishnah uses the same word with the national adjective for Egyptian beans, as do the Greek writers with *kyamos.* The precise species is open to question since the modern Arabic word has wide scope, but there were several plants of the pea family available in biblical times, such as broad bean (*Vicia faba*), chick pea (*Cicer arietinum*) and lentil (*Lens culinaris*).

Vegetables were grown in gardens (Dt. 11:10, 1 Ki. 21:2), and other crops such as leeks, onions and melons were cultivated. Many wild plants were gathered for use as vegetables and *herbs. See also *AGRICULTURE.

Cucumber (Heb. *qiššu'îm*). One of the articles of food which made the discontented Israelites, wandering in the wilderness of Paran, hanker after the pleasures of Egypt (Nu. 11:5). This is most likely to have been the snake cucumber, *Cucumis melo*, which was well known in ancient Egypt, rather than the present-day cucumber, *Cucumis sativus*, which is a native of India and reached the Mediterranean area much later.

The 'lodge' referred to in Is. 1:8 as being in 'a cucumber field' (Heb. *miqšâ*) was a crude wooden hut on four poles or other rough booth. It sheltered the watchman who protected the plants, but after the season was over it was abandoned and allowed to disintegrate, presenting a picture of utter desolation.

Garlic (Heb. *šûmîm*). A kind of onion well known in ancient Egypt and craved after by the wandering Israelites (Nu. 11:5). Garlic (*Allium sativum*) differs from other onions in having scales ('cloves') instead of the usual tunicated bulb; it never sets seeds and is unknown in the wild state.

Leeks (Heb. *ḥāṣîr*, 'herb'). Only in Nu. 11:5; the Heb. word is elsewhere translated 'grass' or 'herb'. The leek of ancient Egypt, judging by samples from the tombs, was the salad leek (*Allium kurrat*) with grass-like leaves narrower than those of the familiar common larger leek (*A. porrum*). Both are evidently cultivated varieties of the wild *A. ampeloprasum.*

Lentils (Heb. *'^{a}ḏāšîm*). A small pea-like plant (*Lens culinaris*, formerly called *L. esculenta* or *Ervum lens*) of the pea family, lentils are easily grown and are still a favourite food throughout the Near East. The parched seeds are regarded as the best food to carry on a long journey or in an emergency (*cf.* Ezk. 4:9). Lentils formed the 'pottage' associated with Esau (Gn. 25:29–34), and were among the foods offered to David at Mahanaim (2 Sa. 17:28). A field of lentils is mentioned in 2 Sa. 23:11–12 as the scene of an Israelite warrior's doughty deeds against the Philistines. See D. Zohary, 'The wild progenitor and the place of origin of the cultivated lentil', *Economic Botany* 26, 1972, pp. 326–332.

Melons (Heb. *'^{a}ḇaṭṭiḥîm*). Mentioned in Nu. 11:5. The reference is to the water-melon (*Citrullus vulgaris*), a member of the marrow family *Cucurbitaceae*, with white or red flesh of the fruit, cultivated from the earliest times in Egypt and the Orient, and seeds of which have been frequently found in Egyp. tombs.

Onions (Heb. (*b^{e}ṣālîm*). The onion (*Allium cepa*) is mentioned only once in the Bible (Nu. 11:5). It has always been a common and much appreciated food, and regarded, moreover, as possessing medicinal qualities. Cultivated by the Egyptians from the earliest times, the onion is represented on some of their tomb-paintings. F.N.H.

VESSELS. Before the invention of pottery (during the 6th millennium BC) vessels were containers made from skins, rushes, wood and stone. These, made of perishable materials, have seldom survived. The dry sands of Egypt have preserved some leather and basketry (see S. Cole, *The Neolithic Revolution*, BM (Natural History), 1959, Plate XI). The peculiar geological conditions at Jericho have resulted in the preservation of a quantity of wooden dishes and trays in tombs of the mid-2nd millennium BC (K. M. Kenyon, *Jericho* 2, 1965). Such wooden vessels, together with leather containers, baskets and sacks, all widely used by the modern Palestinian peasants, were probably as important as pottery in daily life (*cf.* Lv. 11:32). Bottles for carrying both water and wine were simply skins sewn up tightly (Heb. *'ōḇ*, Jb. 32:19; *ḥēmeṯ*, Gn. 21:14; *n^{e}'ōḏ*, Jos. 9:4; *nēḇel*, 1 Sa. 1:24; Gk. *askos*, Mt. 9:17). Soft stones, limestone, alabaster, basalt and even obsidian were cut and ground into shape as bowls, jars, dishes, *etc.* After the introduction of metal tools (*ARCHAEOLOGY) elaborately carved stone vessels were produced, and these often formed part of the equipment of a temple (*e.g.* at Hazor, see Y. Yadin, *Hazor*, 1958, plates 21, 23). Large jars of stone or earthenware were used for storing liquids. The porous earthenware of which the vessels were made absorbed a little of the liquid, thus hindering evaporation and keeping the contents cool (Heb. *kaḏ*, 'pitcher', Gn. 24:14; *cf.* 1 Ki. 17:12ff., AV 'barrel'; Gk. *lithinai hydriai*, 'stone water-jars', Jn. 2:6). The rich could afford vessels of metal, glass and ivory (Jb. 28:17; Rev. 18:12). Metal vessels are rarely found in Palestine, but bronze bowls of Phoenician workmanship found at Nimrud (H. Frankfort, *Art and Architecture of the Ancient Orient*, 1954, plates 141–143) show the type in use during the Monarchy. Gold and silver vessels were a convenient method of storing wealth before the introduction of coined money, and formed the bulk of temple and royal treasures and payments of tribute (see *DOTT*, p. 48, c). Some metal shapes were imitated in pottery. *Glass and *ivory were mainly used for small cosmetic flasks and toilet instruments (see *BA* 20, 1957; *IEJ* 6, 1956).

Definition of the various Heb. terms describing vessels is not usually possible. Many containers, although differently named, could serve the same purpose (1 Sa. 2:14). For the types and proposed identifications of earthenware vessels, see *POTTER. The following terms seem to describe metal vessels only, mostly used in the tabernacle and the Temple: **1.** Heb. *'ᵃḡarṭāl* (Ezr. 1:9), a large bowl; **2.** *gullâ* (Zc. 4:2; *cf.* 1 Ki. 7:41), a round bowl for holding the oil in a lamp, in Ec. 12:6 perhaps a hanging lamp; **3.** *kap̄* (Nu. 7:14), a shallow open dish for holding incense; **4.** *kᵉp̄ôr* (1 Ch. 28:17), a small bowl; **5.** *mᵉnaqqiyyâ* (Ex. 25:29), the golden bowl from which libations were poured; **6.** *merqāḥâ* (Jb. 41:31), an apothecary's compounding jar, possibly pottery; **7.** *mizraq* (Ex. 27:3), a large basin used at the altar of burnt-offering, probably to catch the blood, and also a large banqueting bowl (Am. 6:6); **8.** *ṣinṣeneṯ* (Ex. 16:33), the golden jar in which the specimen of manna was kept (*cf.* Heb. 9:4); **9.** *qᵉ'ārâ* (Ex. 25:29; Nu. 7:13), a plate; **10.** *qaśwâ* (Ex. 25:29), the golden pitcher containing wine for libations. For Heb. *dûḏ*, *sîr* and *qallaḥaṯ* translated 'caldron', see *POTTER; in Jb. 41:20 Heb. *'aḡmôn* is not 'caldron' but possibly 'rushes' (*cf.* Is. 58:5 where *'aḡmôn* is 'rush').

The Gk. *chalkion* (Mk. 7:4) is simply any bronze vessel. Heb. *kᵉlî*, Aram. *mā'n*, Gk. *skeuos* are general words for implements, equipment (1 Sa. 8:12; Acts 9:15) and hence, in many contexts, vessels both actual (1 Sa. 9:7; Jn. 19:29) and metaphorical (1 Pet. 3:7).

BIBLIOGRAPHY. J. L. Kelso, *The Ceramic Vocabulary of the Old Testament*, *BASOR* Supplementary Studies 5–6, 1948. A.R.M.

VESTURE. An archaic word denoting *dress used once in RSV for the obscure *sûṯ*, which appears only in Gn. 49:11 (AV 'clothes', JB 'coat', NEB 'robes'). In AV 'vesture' translates: Heb. *beḡeḏ*, 'cloak', 'garment', 'covering' (Gn. 41:42); Heb. *kᵉsûṯ*, 'a covering' (Dt. 22:12, *FRINGES); Heb. *lᵉḇûš*, 'clothing', 'dress', 'attire' (Pss. 22:18; 102:26); Gk. *himation*, 'an outer garment' (Rev. 19:13, 16), possibly a large square piece of cloth which could be used as a shawl or as a cloak (so rendered in Mt. 5:40; 'raiment' in Lk. 9:29); Gk. *himatismos*, 'dress', 'apparel' (Mt. 27:35; Jn. 19:24); Gk. *peribolaion*, 'what is thrown round one' (Heb. 1:12).

In 2 Ki. 10:22 there is a reference to the one who was over the 'vestry' (*meltāḥâ*; *cf.* 'keeper of the wardrobe', 2 Ki. 22:14), who cared for the 'vestments' (*malbûš*) or sacred dresses used by priests in the temple of Baal. J.D.D.

VIAL. 1. Heb. *paḵ*, 'a flask'. A vial of oil was used in anointing Saul (1 Sa. 10:1) and Jehu (2 Ki. 9:1, 3, AV *'box', RSV 'flask'). **2.** Gk. *phialē*, a broad shallow 'bowl' (RSV) used for incense and drink offering. The word is translated by AV as 'vial' eight times in Revelation (Rev. 5:8, *etc.*). (*POTTER.) J.D.D.

VICTORY. The primary biblical assertion is that victory belongs to God (Jon. 2:9; 1 Cor. 15:54–57; Rev. 7:10). This is succinctly expressed in the phrase 'the battle is the Lord's' (1 Sa. 17:47), *i.e.* victory belongs exclusively to the Lord: it is his to bestow at will.

There are three special features of the Lord's victory which enable us to glimpse its inner character. In the first place, sometimes the Lord's victory is the defeat of his people (*e.g.* Jdg. 2:14; Is. 42:24–25; Je. 25:8–9). The Lord's victory is the exercise of holy sovereignty in the course of history. 'Victory' is another way of saying that the government of the world rests in the hands of a holy God, who orders all things according to inflexible principles of morality, so that sometimes his holiness must be asserted against his people, and becomes 'his strange deed' (Is. 28:21).

Secondly, this holy government of the world will issue in the great victory of the eschatological *'Day of the Lord'. The power of victory is annexed to the holy rule of the only God. Therefore the issue of that conflict is not in doubt. Just as, at creation, there was no possibility of opposing the Creator's will, so, at the new creation, he will speak and it shall be done (Ezk. 38–39; Rev. 19).

Thirdly, the people of God enter upon victory by the obedience of faith: *i.e.* they experience victory in God's victory (Ex. 14:13–14; Dt. 28:1–14; Ps. 20; Eph. 6:16; 1 Jn. 5:4–5). As the Lord Jesus said, only the Son can set men free (Jn. 8:36); those who abide in his word know the truth, and the truth sets them free (Jn. 8:31–32).

The OT associates *'peace', *'righteousness' and *'salvation' with victory. The peace of the victor (*e.g.* 1 Ki. 22:28; Is. 41:3, Heb. text) is not simply cessation of hostilities—even the defeated have that! It is the enjoyment of total well-being which victory brings. Salvation is, positively, the personal enlargement, and negatively, the deliverance, which victory effects (1 Sa. 14:45; Jdg. 6:14). Righteousness is the personal quality which guarantees victory (Is. 59:16–17). All these cluster in a unique way round the cross of the Lord Jesus Christ, the supreme victory of God: peace (Eph. 2:14ff.), salvation (Tit. 3:4–7) and righteousness (Rom. 1:17; 3:21–27).

BIBLIOGRAPHY. J.-J. von Allmen, *Vocabulary of the Bible*, 1958, *s.v.* 'Victory'; N. T. Wright, *Jesus and the Victory of God*, 1994. J.A.M.

VILLAGE. The biblical village was usually, as today, a small group of dwellings, distinct from a *city (Lv. 25:29, 31, *etc.*) in being unwalled and without defences (Ezk. 38:11). Many OT and NT 'cities' (so RSV, NIV, AV) could well be translated 'village' in the British sense. However, the distinction between town and village is not always maintained, *e.g.* Bethlehem is called a town (Gk. *polis*) in Lk. 2:4 and a village (*kōmē*) in Jn. 7:42. A village might be enlarged into a town or city (1 Sa. 23:7).

Villages were often grouped as 'daughters' (lit. Heb.; Nu. 21:25, *etc.*) around the city on which as agricultural communities they depended politically and economically (Jos. 15:13–63). The inhabitants would retreat within the nearest city defences in time of war. The common Semitic word for village (Heb. *kāp̄ār*; Akkad. *kapru*) may not necessarily relate to this 'protection' so much as denote a hamlet or village set in open country (hence *prz* of Jdg. 5:7, 11 (see AV); *cf.* Est. 9:19), farmsteads or suburban settlement around a city. Nomadic camps were also designated 'villages' (Gn. 25:16; Is. 42:11), and names like *Havvoth-jair may reflect this. A village might have its own local government of elders (Ru. 4:2), and sometimes a shrine or sacred place. D.J.W.

VINE, VINEYARD. The common grape-vine, *Vitis vinifera* L., is a slender plant which trails on the ground or climbs supports by means of tendrils. It is mentioned throughout Scripture, frequently in a symbolic sense. First named in connection with Ararat (Gn. 9:20), perhaps its original habitat, it was also cultivated in ancient Egypt. Paintings found on the walls of Egyp. tombs depicted the various stages of wine-making, while inscriptions and sculptures attested to the importance of the vine.

Viticulture was practised in Canaan prior to the Hebrew invasion, as is indicated by the provisions set out by Melchizedek (Gn. 14:18), the report of the spies (Nu. 13:20, 24) and the references of Moses to the Promised Land (Dt. 6:11). That Judah was already renowned for its viticulture may be inferred from the blessing of Jacob (Gn. 49:11). The valley of Eshcol ('grape-cluster') then as now was a particularly productive locality, as was the valley of Sorek in the Philistine plain (Jdg. 14:5; 15:5; 16:4). The En-gedi vineyards were also notable (Ct. 1:14), as were those of Sibmah (Je. 48:32), for whose ruin Jeremiah lamented. Ezekiel recorded that the wine of Helbon was exported to Tyre (Ezk. 27:18), while Hosea referred to the scent of the wine of Lebanon (Ho. 14:7). The ideal of the invading nomadic Israelite was realized when sedentary occupation made it possible for every man to sit 'under his vine and under his fig tree' (1 Ki. 4:25).

The preparation of a vineyard (Is. 5:1ff.; Mk. 12:1) usually involved terracing the hillsides and clearing the stones. These were used for the retaining walls, which were thicker than necessary if the stones were abundant, with still more piled in heaps (*cf.* Ho. 12:11). A living hedge of boxthorn (*Lycium*) —in modern times the American *Opuntia* cactus was substituted and then *Acacia farnesiana*—was planted, or a low wall built and topped with dead spiny burnet (*Poterium spinosum*) to deter animals and thieves. A watch-tower or stone hut served as a cool shelter during the summer when the labourers lived in the vineyards. The enclosed area of ground was dug over carefully, and when the soil was friable young vines were planted. Normally they were arranged in rows about 2·5 m apart, and when the fruit-bearing branches developed they were raised above the ground on supports (Ezk. 17:6). The vines were pruned each spring (Lv. 25:3; Jn. 15:2) by means of pruning-hooks (Joel 3:10). The vine-dressers, who pruned and cultivated the vines, appear to have belonged to the poorer classes (Is. 61:5). A covered wooden structure, the watchtower, was erected on an elevation overlooking the vineyard (Mk. 12:1), where the householder and his family kept a watch throughout the vintage period (Jb. 27:18; Is. 1:8).

When the grapes had reached maturity they were gathered in baskets and taken to the wine-presses (Ho. 9:2), which were hewn out of the solid rock. The grapes were trodden out by helpers (Am. 9:13), who shouted and sang together (Is. 16:10; Je. 25:30). The fermenting wine was stored in strong new goatskin bags (Mt. 9:17) or in large pottery containers. Tax-collectors claimed their share of the produce (*cf.* Is. 3:14), and accumulated debts were often discharged in terms of wine (2 Ch. 2:10). Exemption from military service was granted to men engaged in the vintage. No other plants were to be sown in a vineyard (Dt. 22:9), and the vines were allowed to lie fallow every 7th year (Ex. 23:11; Lv. 25:3). When the harvest had been gathered in, the poor were permitted to enter the vineyard to glean any remaining bunches (Lv. 19:10; Dt. 24:21). When a vineyard had become completely unproductive it was abandoned (*cf.* Is. 16:8) and the dry vines used for fuel and making charcoal (Ezk. 15:4; Jn. 15:6).

Apart from their use in the form of wine, grapes constituted an important item in the diet of the Hebrews, supplying iron and other essential minerals. A certain proportion of the harvest was preserved in the form of raisin cakes. Raisins (Heb. *ṣimmûqîm*, 'dried fruits') have from earliest times been a staple food in biblical lands (*cf.* Nu. 6:3). The grapes were laid out, often on house-tops, to dry in the hot sun (Pliny, *NH* 16). A welcome food for the hungry, being full of energizing sugars (1 Sa. 30:12; 1 Ch. 12:40), raisins were an easily carried and acceptable gift (1 Sa. 25:18; 2 Sa. 16:1).

Used symbolically, the vine was the emblem of prosperity and peace among the ancient Hebrews. More particularly it symbolized the chosen people. They were the vine which God had taken out of Egypt (Ps. 80:8–14; Is. 5:1–5) and planted in a particularly choice land. They had been given all the attention necessary for the production of outstanding fruit, but instead yielded only wild grapes. For this they were to be abandoned to the depredations of their enemies.

No fewer than five parables of Jesus related to vines and their culture. These were the fig in the vineyard (Lk. 13:6–9); labourers in the vineyard (Mt. 20:1–16); new wine in old wineskins (Mt. 9:17); the two sons (Mt. 21:28–32); and the wicked husbandmen (Mt. 21:33–41; Mk. 12:1–11; Lk. 20:9–18). Particularly significant was Christ's description of himself as the true vine (Jn. 15:1ff.), with whom all true believers are in organic relationship. At the Last Supper the fruit of the vine symbolized Christ's atoning blood, becoming the sacramental wine of the Christian Communion service. In Christian art the fruitful vine has often symbolized the union of Christ with his followers.

BIBLIOGRAPHY. H. N. and A. L. Moldenke, *Plants of the Bible*, 1952, pp. 28ff., 239f.; A. Goor and N. Nurock, *Fruits of the Holy Land*, 1968, pp. 18–45; D. Zohary and M. Hopf, *Domestication of Plants in the Old World*, 1988, pp. 136–142; F. N. Hepper, *IEBP*, pp. 96–102.

R.K.H.
F.N.H.

VINEGAR (Heb. *ḥōmeṣ*, Gk. *oxos*). A sour liquid resulting from acetous fermentation in wine or other strong drink. The acid nature of vinegar is indicated in Pr. 10:26; 25:20, while a reference in Ps. 69:21 not merely attests to its nauseous flavour but implies that it was used in punishment.

The vinegar of Ru. 2:14 is typical of the fermented acid drinks enjoyed by labourers in wine-growing countries. The *posca* of the Romans was very similar in nature, and formed part of the soldiers' rations. It was this which was offered to the crucified Christ as refreshment (Mk. 15:36; Jn. 19:29–30), and was different from the myrrh-flavoured anodyne which he had refused earlier (Mt. 27:34; Mk. 15:23). Wine or vinegar was prohibited to Nazirites (Nu. 6:3), hence the gravity of the offence in Am. 2:12. R.K.H.

VIRGIN. Heb. *bᵉṯûlâ* comes from a root meaning 'to separate' and is the common word for a woman who has never had sexual intercourse (Gk. *parthenos*). Metaphorically it is used of nations and place-names, *e.g.* the virgin of Israel (Je. 18:13;

31:4, 21; Am. 5:2); the virgin daughter of Zion (Is. 37:22); Judah (La. 1:15); Sidon (Is. 23:12); Babylon (Is. 47:1); Egypt (Je. 46:11). *'almâ* derives from a root meaning 'to be sexually mature', and refers to a woman of marriageable age who has not yet borne children, though she may be married. It occurs seven times and is translated 'young woman' (Gn. 24:43; Is. 7:14), 'maiden' (Ct. 1:3; 6:8; Pr. 30:19; Ps. 68:25) and 'girl' (Ex. 2:8). The Gk. equivalent is usually *neanis*, 'a young woman', but in Gn. 24:43 (of Rebekah) and in Is. 7:14 *parthenos* is used. As a result, the Isaiah passage has been regarded since early Christian times as a prophecy of the *virgin birth of Christ (Mt. 1:23).

The primary meaning of Isaiah's sign to Ahaz is probably that in less than 9 months (reading RSVmg., 'with child and shall bear') the tide would turn in such a way that a child would be given the name of Immanuel, 'God is with us'. The Messianic interpretation is based on the coincidence of the name Immanuel, which expressed so well the early Christians' belief in the deity of the Christ, and the LXX rendering 'the virgin (*hē parthenos*) shall be with child and shall bear a son', which is a legitimate translation of the Heb. words but which imports into the sign to Ahaz the implication that the mother of Immanuel was a specific woman who was at the time of writing still a virgin (*i.e.* in at least 9 months' time a son would be called Immanuel). The door is thus left open for Matthew and the early church to see a remarkable verbal correspondence with what happened at the birth of Jesus Christ. For a fuller study of this passage, and a different viewpoint, see *IMMANUEL.

BIBLIOGRAPHY. R. E. Brown, *The Birth of the Messiah*, 1977; G. Delling, *TDNT* 5, pp. 826–837; O. Becker, C. Brown, *NIDNTT* 3, pp. 1071–1073; H. A. Hoffner, *TDOT* 1, pp. 287–291. On the various explanations of Paul's teaching on virgins in 1 Cor. 7:25–38, see L. Morris, *'I Corinthians*[2], *TNTC*, 1985; F. F. Bruce, *1 & 2 I Corinthians, NCB*, 1971. (*MARRIAGE.)

J.B.Tr.

VIRGIN BIRTH. By 'virgin birth' Protestants generally mean 'virginal conception'. Roman Catholicism and Orthodoxy believe also in a literal virgin birth, whereby the baby passed out of Mary's body in such a way as to leave her virginity anatomically unimpaired (virginity *in partu*, 'in giving birth', as well as *ante partum*, 'before ...'). This belief is found first in writings of Syrian origin from the mid-2nd century, such as the *Protevangelium of James.* It quickly became a standard part of the doctrine of Mary's 'perpetual virginity', *i.e.* including also virginity *post partum*, 'after giving birth' to Jesus (so that *'the brethren of the Lord' could not have been Mary's children). The Reformers were virtually unanimous in holding to Mary's perpetual virginity. This article will follow common practice in using 'virgin birth' to denote virginal conception.

The two accounts of the birth of Jesus in Matthew and Luke are clearly independent of one another, and both record that he was born through the direct action of the Holy Spirit, without a human father (Mt. 1:18–25; Lk. 1:34). So the only two gospels that record the circumstances of Jesus' birth present him as born from a virgin – although greater stress falls on conception by the Spirit than on Mary's virginity.

Yet the historicity of the virgin birth is doubted or denied by many scholars, who often regard the birth-narratives in Matthew and Luke not as historical record but as some form of imaginative literature, expressing the significance of Jesus' birth in symbolic, poetic, mythical or midrashic terms. The absence of explicit reference to the virgin birth elsewhere in the NT, especially Mark and Paul, is held to confirm that it was not part of the earliest traditions about Jesus.

However there may well be supporting evidence in the rest of the NT. Although a person may not say directly what he believes, he shows his belief by a turn of phrase. Thus Mark has no birth narrative, since he starts where the preachers in Acts start, namely, with the baptism by John. Yet in 6:3 he alone of the Synoptists quotes objectors as saying, 'Is not this the carpenter, the son of Mary?' By contrast Mt. 13:55 has 'the carpenter's son', and Lk. 4:22 'Joseph's son'. Identifying a son by his mother was highly unusual, and perhaps disparaging, in a Jewish context.

John also begins Christ's earthly ministry with the Baptist. Later he indicates that there were rumours about the illegitimacy of Jesus when in 8:41 the Jews declared, '*We* (emphatic pronoun and emphatic position) were not born of fornication'. Less evidential, although accepted by some Christian writers from Tertullian onwards, is the reading in the Verona Latin codex on Jn. 1:13, which has the singular, 'who was born not of blood, nor of the will of the flesh, but of God'. (This reading is not attested in any Gk. MS.)

Paul, the companion of Luke, uses language that implies acceptance of the virgin birth. When he speaks of the coming, or birth, of Jesus Christ, he uses the general verb, *ginomai*, not *gennao*, which tends to associate the husband (*e.g.* Rom. 1:3; Phil. 2:7). This is particularly marked in Gal. 4:4, where 'God sent forth his Son, coming (*genomenon*) from a woman'. By contrast, in 4:23 Ishmael 'was born', *gegennētai* (from *gennao*).

There is no evidence that a virgin birth was part of Jewish Messianic expectations. Is. 7:14 is not specific enough to have given rise to such a belief; its use by Matthew presupposes the prior existence of such a conviction about Jesus' birth. Nor do pagan stories of gods in human form impregnating women provide a credible source for the gospels' account. Matthew and Luke do not present Mary as impregnated by the Holy Spirit – as though Jesus had a human mother and a divine father – but as conceiving miraculously without male intervention at all.

Theologically it has been argued that the reason given for the title 'the Son of God' in Lk. 1:35 cannot be reconciled with the idea of the eternal Son of God of the epistles. This argument assumes that Mary and Joseph would have been given a full theological statement. The two records give the contents of what they were told, namely, that Mary was to be the mother of the promised Messiah, the Son of God and 'God with us'. The fact that Matthew and Luke do not here reflect later theology is a further argument for the authenticity of their records.

Theologically it is also commonly alleged that someone born of only one parent could not truly be said to share our real humanity. This objection misses the significance of a proper concentration on conception. From that point onwards, there are no grounds for seeing Jesus' birth as other than wholly normal. (The objection also sounds increasingly weak in the light of modern medical techniques to facilitate child-bearing.)

A general prejudice against the miraculous in general and the incarnation in particular, often animates denial of the virgin birth. Yet it is wonderfully congruent with the much more fundamental truth of the incarnation itself. To hold to the latter as Christian faith has traditionally believed in it, while rejecting the former, is rather like straining out a gnat while swallowing a camel. Although theologians have given different interpretations of Jesus' birth from a virgin, it at least attests that the entry of God's Son fully into human life was a gift of divine initiative, a new beginning independent of normal male action. The start of the new creation is God's *fiat*, grounded in his grace alone.

BIBLIOGRAPHY. J. Orr, *The Virgin Birth of Christ*, 1907; J. G. Machen, *The Virgin Birth of Christ*, 1930; D. Edwards, *The Virgin Birth in History and Faith*, 1943; T. Boslooper, *The Virgin Birth*, 1962; R. E. Brown, *The Birth of the Messiah*, 1977; D. F. Wright (ed.), *Chosen by God. Mary in Evangelical Perspective*, 1989; B. Witherington III, in *DJG* 70–74 (with biblio.); T. F. Torrance, 'The Doctrine of the Virgin Birth', *SBET* 12, 1994, pp. 8–25.

D.F.W.
J.S.W.

VIRTUE. The word used in the OT is Heb. *ḥayil*, 'ability', 'efficiency', often involving moral worth, as in Ru. 3:11; Pr. 12:4; 31:10 (*'ēšeṯ ḥayil*, 'a woman of worth', 'a virtuous woman'); *cf.* Pr. 31:29 (*'āśâ ḥayil*, 'to do worthily').

In the NT AV renders two words as 'virtue'. **1.** Gk. *aretē*, meaning any excellence of a person or thing (1 Pet. 2:9, RSV 'wonderful deeds', AV 'praises'; 2 Pet. 1:3, 5). In Homer the word is used especially of manly qualities (*cf.* Phil. 4:8). In the LXX it is the equivalent of Heb. *hôḏ*, 'splendour', 'majesty' (of God, Hab. 3:3), and *tᵉhillâ*, 'praise' (Is. 42:12; 43:21, quoted in 1 Pet. 2:9). **2.** *dynamis*, 'power', 'influence' Mk. 5:30; Lk. 6:19; 8:46), is used of the healing influence proceeding from our Lord. The word is commonly translated 'power' (*e.g.* 2 Cor. 12:9; Heb. 11:11). D.O.S.

VISION. The border-line between vision and dream or trance is difficult, if not impossible, to determine. This is reflected in the biblical vocabulary of 'vision'.

Heb. *ḥāzôn* comes from a root used to describe the beholding of a vision by the seer while in an ecstatic state (Is. 1:1; Ezk. 12:27); while the word *mar'â*, from the ordinary root 'to see', means vision as a means of revelation (Nu. 12:6; 1 Sa. 3:15). The NT uses two words in this connection: *horama* (Acts 9:10, 12; 10:3, 17, 19) and *optasia* (Lk. 1:22; Acts 26:19; 2 Cor. 12:1). They signify 'appearance' or 'vision'.

The emphasis here seems to be upon the ecstatic nature of the experience, and the revelatory character of the knowledge, which came to the biblical prophets and seers. The experience points to a special awareness of God shared by saintly men (*e.g.* Je. 1:11; Dn. 2:19; Acts 9:10; 16:9), and to God's readiness to reveal himself to men (Ps. 89:19; Acts 10:3).

The circumstances in which the revelatory visions came to the seers of the Bible are varied. They came in men's waking hours (Dn. 10:7; Acts 9:7); by day (Acts 10:3) or by night (Gn. 46:2). But the visions had close connections with the dream-state (Nu. 12:6; Jb. 4:13).

In the OT the recipients of revelatory visions were the prophets, 'writing' (Is. 1:1; Ob. 1; Na. 1:1) and 'non-writing' (2 Sa. 7:17; 1 Ki. 22:17–19; 2 Ch. 9:29). But the outstanding examples were Ezekiel and Daniel.

In the NT Luke manifests the greatest interest in visions. He reports, *e.g.*, the visions of Zechariah (Lk. 1:22), Ananias (Acts 9:10), Cornelius (10:3), Peter (10:10ff.) and Paul (18:9); although Paul treated visions with much reserve (2 Cor. 12:1ff.). The supreme set of visions in the NT is that in the book of the *Revelation.

Biblical visions concerned both immediate situations (Gn. 15:1f.; Acts 12:7) and the 'far-off divine event' of the kingdom of God, as the writings of Isaiah, Daniel and John testify. In this connection the passages in 1 Sa. 3:1; Pr. 29:18 are especially relevant.

BIBLIOGRAPHY. J. M. Lower, *ZPEB*, 5, p. 889; R. Schnackenburg, *EBT*, 3, pp. 947–952; K. Dahn, *NIDNTT* 3, pp. 511–518; D. E. Aune, *ISBE* 4, pp. 993–994. J.G.S.S.T.

VOW. The idea of 'vow' in Semitic thought may well have been derived from the name of a deity. If so, it illustrates the fact that in biblical usage a vow is always used with reference to God and offers a new interpretation for such passages as Je. 32:35: they must then be construed as the sacrificing of children, not 'to Molech' (*mōleḵ*), but 'as a *mōleḵ*', *i.e.* a votive or 'vowed' offering. On Jdg. 11:30f., see *JEPHTHAH. A vow may be either to perform (Gn. 28:20ff.) or abstain from (Ps. 132:2ff.) an act in return for God's favour (Nu. 21:1–3) or as an expression of zeal or devotion towards God (Ps. 22:25). It is no sin to vow or not to vow, but, if made—presumably uttered (Dt. 23:23)—a vow is as sacredly binding as an *oath (Dt. 23:21–23). Therefore, a vow should not be made hastily (Pr. 20:25); for the person vowing, *e.g.* to offer a sacrifice, then enters into 'the sphere of the offering' and is released only when the sacrifice is made (Pedersen). To have this fulfilment is the state of the happy man (Jb. 22:27), and the character of Israel's future blessedness (Na. 1:15). On the other hand, to substitute a blemished animal for the one vowed reveals a sin and brings God's curse (Mal. 1:14).

What is already the Lord's (*e.g.* firstlings, tithes (Lv. 27:26)), or an abomination to the Lord (Dt. 23:18), cannot be vowed or consecrated; but since a first-born child might be redeemed (Lv. 27; Nu. 3:44ff.), it is proper for Hannah to give Samuel to the Lord as a *Nazirite (1 Sa. 1:11). A vow has no virtue in itself (Ps. 51:16ff.), and may be only the pious pretence of a treacherous (2 Sa. 15:7ff.) or immoral (Pr. 7:14) person. Thus, in the NT the religionist's vow of Corban is condemned by Christ (Mk. 7:11). Paul's (probably not Aquila's) vow (*euchē*) no doubt was a temporary Nazirite vow—a sincere and proper expression of the ancient Hebrew faith (Acts 18:18, *cf.* 21:23).

BIBLIOGRAPHY. A. R. Johnson, *Sacral Kingship in Ancient Israel*, 1955, p. 40 n.; J. Pedersen, *Israel, Its Life and Culture*, 4, 1959, pp. 265f., 324–330; R. de Vaux, *Ancient Israel*, 1961, pp. 465ff. E.E.E.

WAFER. Heb. *rāqîq*, 'thin cake', refers to home-made *bread, named from its thinness (Ex. 29:2; Nu. 6:15, *etc.*; *cf.* Arab. *warak*, 'foliage', 'paper'). Heb. *ṣappîḥit*, 'a cake', appears once only (Ex. 16:31). J.D.D.

WAGES. Basically the payment made for services rendered. The frequency of the term in the Bible is somewhat obscured in that the Heb. and Gk. terms are sometimes translated 'reward' or 'hire'.

In OT society the hired labourer was not common. The family worked the farm. The family group included slaves and relatives whose wages would be in kind, *e.g.* those of Jacob as he worked for Laban. But a Levite received money as well as his keep for his service as family priest (Jdg. 17:10). And when Saul consulted Samuel, the seer, he first planned to pay the fee in kind, but finally resolved on a monetary fee (1 Sa. 9:7–8).

In primitive communities the employer had great power in fixing wages, and Jacob could complain that Laban had changed his wages ten times (Gn. 31:41). But the OT legislated to protect the wage-earner. Unscrupulous employers must not take advantage of his economic weakness. He must be given a fair wage, and paid promptly each day (Dt. 24:14–15).

Men working for wages meet us in the NT, both in actuality (Mk. 1:20) and in parable (Mt. 20:1–2; Lk. 15:17, 19; Jn. 10:13, *etc.*). The principle is laid down in the maxim, 'the worker earns his pay' (Lk. 10:7, NEB). Paul makes use of this to lay bare the essential truth at the heart of the gospel. 'To one who works,' he says, 'his wages (Gk. *misthos*) are not reckoned as a gift but as his due' (Rom. 4:4). Then he goes on to point out that men are saved, not by working for a heavenly wage but by trusting 'him who justifies the ungodly' (Rom. 4:5). By contrast the lost receive an exact if grim wage, for 'the wages of sin is death' (Rom. 6:23; *cf.* 2 Pet. 2:13, 15).

There is a sense in which the preachers of the gospel receive wages from those to whom they preach (*misthos* is used in this connection in Lk. 10:7; 2 Cor. 11:8; 1 Tim. 5:18). Our Lord himself enjoined the principle that 'those who proclaim the gospel should get their living by the gospel' (1 Cor. 9:14; *cf.* D. L. Dungan, *The Sayings of Jesus in the Churches of Paul*, 1971, pp. 3–80). This must not be misinterpreted, however, for in both OT and NT those who teach for the sake of money are castigated (Mi. 3:11; Tit. 1:7; 1 Pet. 5:2).

There are many passages which speak of God as giving wages or reward for righteousness (*e.g.* Lk. 6:23, 35; 1 Cor. 3:14; 2 Jn. 8). The metaphor is striking, but Scripture makes it clear that we are not to think of any rewards that God may give as merited in any strict sense. They are the acts of grace of a beneficent God who delights to give his people all things richly to enjoy. The knowledge of these gratuitous rewards is given to us in order to strengthen our perseverance in the way of righteousness. D.B.K.

WALK. Of the very many occasions when this verb is used in Scripture, the vast majority have the strictly literal sense of moving along or making one's way. It was the normal activity of men, but where the ability to walk had been lost it was capable of being restored by Christ. This outward healing corresponded to an inward renewal which Jesus claimed to be able to effect (Mk. 2:9). Jesus is further represented in the Gospels as walking and enabling others to walk under conditions not normally given to men (Mk. 6:48). Here again, as Matthew's Gospel makes clear, the physical act has a spiritual significance (Mt. 14:31). Walking can be understood as representative of the whole range of human activity to which an impotent man is restored (Acts 3:6).

The term is used in an anthropomorphic sense of God who walks in the garden in the cool of the evening (Gn. 3:8), and metaphorically it is applied to the heart (Jb. 31:7), to the moon (Jb. 31:26), to the tongue of the wicked (Ps. 73:9) and to the pestilence (Ps. 91:6). More frequently it stands for the whole manner of a man's life and conduct, and to the attitude which God takes up towards him, so that God can say: 'If you . . . walk contrary to me, then I also will walk contrary to you' (Lv. 26:23–24).

On occasion the term can be used in a more limited sense, referring to specific laws and observances enjoined upon men (Acts 21:21; *cf.* Heb. *h^{a}lāḵâ*, 'rule', lit. 'walk'), while in John's Gospel it sometimes assumes the connotation of unwearied activity (Jn. 11:9), and sometimes of public appearance (Jn. 7:1). Metaphorically it denotes a studied observance of the new rule of life, and it is this sense which dominates the usage of all the forms in the Epistles, where there is a frequent contrasting of the walk which was characteristic of believers in their unregenerate days, and that to which they are called through faith in Christ. Baptism is to mark decisively the dividing-point between these two (Rom. 6:4), which is as clear as the distinction between the life of Christ before and after his resurrection. This renewal of life can equally well be expressed as walking in the spirit in contrast to walking according to the flesh. The word *stoicheō*, which appears once in Acts and four times in the Pauline Epistles, is used of the setting of plants in rows, and of soldiers walking in file, but the choice of verb appears to have no special significance.

BIBLIOGRAPHY. G. Ebel, *NIDNTT* 3, pp. 933–947. F.S.F.

WALLS. To build his earliest houses, man used any available stone or lumps of unbaked mud, roughly shaped, *e.g.* Jarmo in E Iraq (*Antiquity* 24, 1950, pp. 185–195), Jericho (*PEQ* 88, 1956, plates X–XI). In Palestine stone foundations were often surmounted by brick walls. The enormous city walls of the mid-2nd millennium BC consisted of a strong stone footing to contain a sloping rampart which was smoothed over with plaster, with thick brick walls, sometimes containing chambers inside them, rising above (for those at Jericho, see *ANEP*, no. 715; *PEQ* 84, 1952, plate XVI. 1; see also P. J. Parr, *ZDPV* 84, 1968, pp. 18–45).

Wooden baulks were frequently incorporated into brickwork; in Egypt at least, this served to prevent warping as the mud-brick structure dried out, and to bind the whole (Petrie, *Egyptian Architecture*, p. 9). In Asia Minor, the Aegean and N Syria such beams were commonly inserted on stone foundations under or in mud-brick or stone walls (R. Naumann, *Architektur Kleinasiens*, 1955, pp. 83–86, 88–104, and figs. 63–66, 72–89)—so in houses of 14th–13th centuries BC at Canaanite Ugarit (Schaeffer, *Ugaritica*, 1, 1939, plate 19, with pp. 92–96 and fig. 90). This widespread and venerable use of brick upon wood over stone is apparently referred to in 1 Ki. 6:36; 7:12, as used by Solomon in buildings at Jerusalem. This technique was actually found at the Israelite Megiddo of Solomon or Ahab's day (Guy, *New Light from Armageddon*, Oriental Institute Communication No. 9, 1931, pp. 34–35; *cf.* building illustrated in Heaton, *Everyday Life in Old Testament Times*, 1956, fig. 106 opposite p. 207. See also H. C. Thomson, *PEQ* 92, 1960, pp. 57–63).

(*ARTS AND CRAFTS; *BRICK; *FORTIFICATION AND SIEGECRAFT; *HOUSE.) A.R.M.
K.A.K.

WAR. Heb. *milḥāmâ*, 313 times in the OT from *lāḥam*, 'to fight'; *cf.* Arab. *laḥama*, 'fit close together', denoting the army in battle array (*BDB*). NT Gk. *polemos*, used 18 times.

I. Strategic importance of Palestine

The position of Palestine in relation to Mesopotamia and Egypt was truly axial. And the existence of the great Arabian desert between these two ancient centres of civilization further ensured that contact was almost always via Palestine. This contact was frequently of an inimical sort, so that Palestine could not avoid being the theatre of war—and a prize of war—for considerable periods during the last two millennia BC. Added to this was the fact that the people of Israel secured a kingdom for themselves only by embarking on a war of conquest and that, once established, they had to engage in defensive wars to fend off the Philistines who were challenging their claim to the title-deeds of Canaan. Neither were David's territorial gains made without military engagements beyond the borders of Israel. The imperial era was short-lived, however, and the divided kingdoms of Israel and Judah are soon to be seen defending themselves against their immediate neighbours, and finally against the unrelenting might of Assyria and Babylonia. It is no wonder, then, that war so stalks the pages of the OT.

II. War and religion

In the Near East generally war was a sacred undertaking in which the honour of the national god was very much at stake. The OT writers' conception of Israel's wars bears a superficial resemblance to this. The difference was that the God of Israel was transcendent and did not rise and fall with the fortunes of his people. For all that, he is 'the God of the armies of Israel' (1 Sa. 17:45) and far more involved in the struggles of his people than Marduk or Asshur were ever thought to be (*cf.* 2 Ch. 20:22). God himself is described as a 'man of war' (Ex. 15:3; Is. 42:13) and one of his titles is 'Lord of hosts'. This latter may refer to heavenly hosts (1 Ki. 22:19) or to Israelite armies (1 Sa. 17:45). It was God who led the armies of Israel into battle (Jdg. 4:14) so that the earliest account of Israelite triumphs was called 'the Book of the *Wars of the Lord' (Nu. 21:14). Indeed, at every stage in preparations for battle Israel's dependence upon God was acknowledged. First, enquiry was made as to whether this was the propitious moment for attack (2 Sa. 5:23–24); then sacrifice had to be offered. So vital did the latter preliminary seem that Saul in desperation arrogated priestly privilege to himself, lest battle be joined before the favour of the Lord had been sought (1 Sa. 13:8–12).

The battle cry had a religious significance (Jdg. 7:18, 20) and, further, acclaimed the presence of God as symbolized in the *ark of the covenant (1 Sa. 4:5–6; *cf.* the manner in which the arrival of the ark in Jerusalem was greeted, 2 Sa. 6:15). Because of the divine presence the Israelites could join battle in confidence of victory (Jdg. 3:28; 1 Ch. 5:22), even if the forces of nature had to be invoked to secure the victory (Jos. 10:11–14).

After battle it often happened that the Israelites observed a *'ban' (*ḥērem*), which meant that a whole city or country, people and possessions, would be set apart for God. No Israelite was permitted to appropriate for personal needs anything or anyone belonging to a place which had been put under a ban; failure in this matter met with the direst consequences (Jos. 7; 1 Sa. 15). Sometimes the ban might not be so comprehensive as in the case of Jericho (Jos. 6:18–24), but always the right of God to the fruit of victory was being asserted. The ban was God's way of dealing with 'the iniquity of the Amorites' (Gn. 15:16) and is central to the OT concept of 'the holy war'. Moreover, if pagan tendencies were discovered among the Israelites themselves, the offending community was likewise to be put under a ban (Dt. 13:12–18). And if the whole nation incurred God's displeasure, as they often did, then the agents of retribution could be the very pagans whom God had previously repudiated (Is. 10:5–6; Hab. 1:5–11). The ultimate is reached at the end of the monarchical period, when God announces his intention of himself fighting against Judah and on the side of the Babylonians (Je. 21:5–7). For a considerable time, however, the prophetic community had enjoyed the assurance of a better hope—nothing less than the eradication of war from the earth and the inauguration of a new era of peace by a Davidic 'Prince of Peace' (Is. 9:6; *cf.* Is. 2:4; Mi. 4:3).

III. Method of warfare

In the days before Israel had a standing army the national militia was summoned for action by means of the trumpet (Jdg. 3:27) or by messenger (1 Sa. 11:7). When on the offensive the Israelites set much store by military intelligence (Jos. 2; 2 Ki. 6:8–12); since there was no such thing as a declaration of war, the advantage for the assailant was all the greater. Usually expeditions were undertaken in spring when the roads were suitable (2 Sa. 11:1). Tactics naturally depended on the terrain and on the numbers involved, but in general the Israelite commanders were able, in defensive engagements at least, to exploit their superior knowledge of local geography. When it was a case of a head-on confrontation, as between Josiah and Pharaoh Neco at Megiddo, the Israelites do not seem to have fared so well. As well as the trumpet, signalling could be done by means of fires—to which practice one of the *Lachish ostraca bears testimony. The conventional methods of warfare are all represented in the OT; foray (1 Sa. 14), siege (1 Ki. 20:1) and ambush (Jos. 8) figure alongside the set piece. (*ARMOUR; *ARMY.)

IV. War in the New Testament

Extending Christ's kingdom by military means is clearly not part of the ideal of the NT. 'My kingship is not of this world; if my kingship were of this world, my servants would fight' (Jn. 18:36) was the principle enunciated by our Lord when he stood before Pilate. And his words to Peter as recorded in Mt. 26:52 cast a certain shadow on the use of force whatever the circumstances may be. But the Christian is a citizen of two worlds and has duties to both; tension between the conflicting demands is inevitable, especially since the secular powers have been ordained by God and do not 'bear the sword in vain' (Rom. 13:4). Paul availed himself not only of Roman citizenship but also of the protection of Roman troops, as when his life was threatened in Jerusalem (Acts 21). Piety was not regarded as incompatible with the pursuit of a military career, moreover, and those soldiers who inquired of John the Baptist as to their higher duty were not encouraged to desert (see Acts 10:1–2; Lk. 3:14). We are to assume, on the other hand, that the cause which bound together Matthew the tax collector and Simon the Zealot in the original Twelve required *both* to abandon their erstwhile occupations. In the early church a military career for the Christian was generally frowned upon; Tertullian is representative in his view that the two callings were incompatible, though he made allowances for those already committed to military service before conversion.

The Christian's warfare is pre-eminently a spiritual warfare and he has been equipped with all the armour necessary if he is to obtain victory (Eph. 6:10–20). It follows that he should be under military discipline, and to this end the NT abounds in injunctions couched in military terms (*cf.* 1 Tim. 1:18; 1 Pet. 5:9) and in military metaphors generally (*cf.* 2 Tim. 2:3–4; 1 Pet. 2:11). The critical battle was won at Calvary (Col. 2:15) so that the emphasis in a passage like Eph. 6:10–20 is not so much on the gaining of new ground, but on the holding of what has already been won. Victory ultimate and complete will come when Christ is revealed from heaven at the end of the age (2 Thes. 1:7–10). The final clash between Christ and the minions of darkness is depicted in chs. 16, 19 and 20 of Revelation. A decisive battle is fought at a place called *Armageddon (or Har-Magedon) according to Rev. 16:16. The most likely explanation of the name is that which links it with the hill (Heb. *har*) of Megiddo(n). Megiddo was the scene of many great battles in history (*cf.* 2 Ch. 35:22) and its appearance in an apocalyptic context is most fitting. For the enemies of Christ this encounter will mean destruction (Rev. 19:17–21). But thus will Ps. 110 and a host of OT passages find their fulfilment as the era of Messianic rule begins. The harbingers of that blessed age will indeed be 'wars and rumours of wars' (Mt. 24:6), but when Messiah reigns 'of the increase of his government and of peace there will be no end' (Is. 9:7).

V. The Qumran War Scroll

Among the first *Dead Sea Scrolls to be discovered was one which has become known as 'The War of the Sons of Light against the Sons of Darkness'. It is undoubtedly a product of the community which was once installed at Qumran and it issues directions to the community in anticipation of a protracted war between the forces of good—represented by the sectaries—and the forces of evil. The war will be fought in accordance with all the laws of warfare which Moses laid down, and although victory is predetermined by God there will be serious setbacks. Prominent among the 'sons of darkness' are the 'Kittim', and these are almost certainly to be identified as the Romans. It would seem that this scroll was one of the more exotic products of the age of Rom. domination of Palestine, an age when apocalyptic was at a premium and Messianic expectation at fever pitch.

BIBLIOGRAPHY. G. von Rad, *Der heilige Krieg im alten Israel*, 1951; Y. Yadin, *The Scroll of the War of the Sons of Light against the Sons of Darkness*, 1962; *idem*, *The Art of Warfare in Biblical Lands*, 1963; R. de Vaux, *Ancient Israel*[2], 1965, pp. 247–267; C. Brown, J. Watts, 'War', *NIDNTT* 3, pp. 958–967; M. Langley, 'Jesus and Revolution', *NIDNTT* 3, pp. 967–981. R.P.G.

WARS OF THE LORD, BOOK OF THE. A document mentioned and quoted in Nu. 21:14f. The quotation ends with the word 'Moab' (v. 15), but possibly fragments of poetry in vv. 17–18 and 27–30 come from the same source. The work was evidently a collection of popular songs commemorating the early battles of the Israelites. The name indicates that the Israelites viewed Yahweh virtually as their commander-in-chief, and credited him with their victories. Another similar work was probably the Book of Jashar of 2 Sa. 1:18; it is evident that this document was compiled after the time of David, and probably the Book of the Wars of the Lord appeared at the same period. A few scholars, following the LXX, would emend the text of Nu. 21:14 to excise the reference to any such document. D.F.P.

WASHBASIN (Heb. *sîr raḥaṣ*). Probably a wide, shallow bowl in which the feet were washed. The word is applied in triumphant scorn to Moab's inferiority (Pss. 60:8; 108:9; AV 'washpot'). A.R.M.

WATCH. 1. The 'guard' (RSV) of soldiers (Gk. *koustōdia*) mentioned in Mt. 27:65 as being deputed to watch over our Lord's tomb.

2. A measure of time into which the 12 hours of the night were divided. In Israelite times the division was threefold (Jdg. 7:19). In NT times the Rom. division into four watches seems to have been used (*cf.* Mk. 6:48).

BIBLIOGRAPHY. H.-G. Schütz, C. Brown, in *NIDNTT* 2, pp. 132–137. J.D.D.

WATCHMAN, WATCH-TOWERS. Watchman is in Heb. *ṣōp̄eh* and *šōmēr*, in Gk. *phylax* and *tērōn*; watch-tower is in Heb. *miṣpâ*, *miḡdāl* and *baḥan*. Watch-towers were used for two different purposes in biblical times: (1) Towers were built from the earliest times (*cf.* Gn. 35:21) in the pastures to protect cattle and sheep against wild animals and thieves (*cf.* 2 Ch. 26:10; Mi. 4:8). It is possible that towers were erected in vineyards and cornfields for protection against thieves (*cf.* Is. 27:3). (2) Towers of a more complex structure were built in the defence works of larger cities. The oldest Israelite tower of this kind as yet known was excavated by W. F. Albright at Tell el-Ful, the citadel of Saul. It is a corner tower which forms part of a casemate wall.

Important is the discovery by Albright at Tell beit Mirsim in S Palestine of a gate tower with a rectangular court. This court gives access to six paved rooms probably for guests (*ARCHITECTURE). Excavations at Tell en-Nasbeh show that towers were constructed in the city's defence wall at distances of about 30 m apart and extending about 2 m to the outside. Square towers were built in early Israelite times, but later round ones were favoured. Herod erected in *Jerusalem three massive towers, called Hippicus, Phasael and Mariamne. The ground structure of the so-called 'tower of David' is possibly that of Phasael (8 m × 40 m). The *miḡdāl* and *millô'* (Jdg. 9:6, 20; 2 Sa. 5:9; 1 Ki. 9:15) were citadels or a kind of acropolis in a walled city. This citadel was used as a final place of refuge after the city was conquered. A good example of a *miḡdāl* was excavated at Beth-shean (*cf.* C. Watzinger, *Denkmäler*, 2, 1935, plates 19–21).

In the watch-towers were watchmen on the alert for hostile action against the city. They were also there to give word to the king of any person approaching the city wall (*e.g.* 2 Sa. 18:24–27; 2 Ki. 9:17–20). In time of hostility the dangers of the night were especially feared and the watchmen eagerly looked forward to the break of day (Is. 21:11). (*FORTIFICATION AND SIEGECRAFT.)

F.C.F.

WATER (Heb. *mayim*, Gk. *hydōr*). In a part of the world where water is in short supply, it naturally features significantly in the lives of the people of the Bible. Nothing is more serious to them than absence of water (1 Ki. 17:1ff.; Je. 14:3; Joel 1:20; Hg. 1:11), and conversely rainfall is a sign of God's favour and goodness. An equally serious menace to life is water that has been polluted or rendered undrinkable. This was one of the plagues of Egypt (Ex. 7:17ff.). The Israelites found the water at Marah bitter (Ex. 15:23), and the well at Jericho was unpleasant in Elisha's day (2 Ki. 2:19–22).

It was common practice in time of warfare for an invading army to cut off the water-supply of beleaguered cities, as did Jehoshaphat with the wells of Moab (2 Ki. 3:19, 25), and Holofernes at Bethulia (Judith 7:7ff.). Hezekiah averted this danger by the construction of the tunnel which exists to this day in Jerusalem, running from the Virgin's fountain (Gihon), outside the city walls of his day, to the Pool of *Siloam (2 Ch. 32:30). Under conditions when water had to be rationed (La. 5:4; Ezk. 4:11, 16), the phrase 'water of affliction' could fittingly be used (Is. 30:20), but the context usually suggests punishment (1 Ki. 22:27; 2 Ch. 18:26).

Frequently water is symbolical of God's blessing and of spiritual refreshment, as in Ps. 23:2; Is. 32:2;

The 'pool of Siloam' and the mouth of Hezekiah's tunnel.

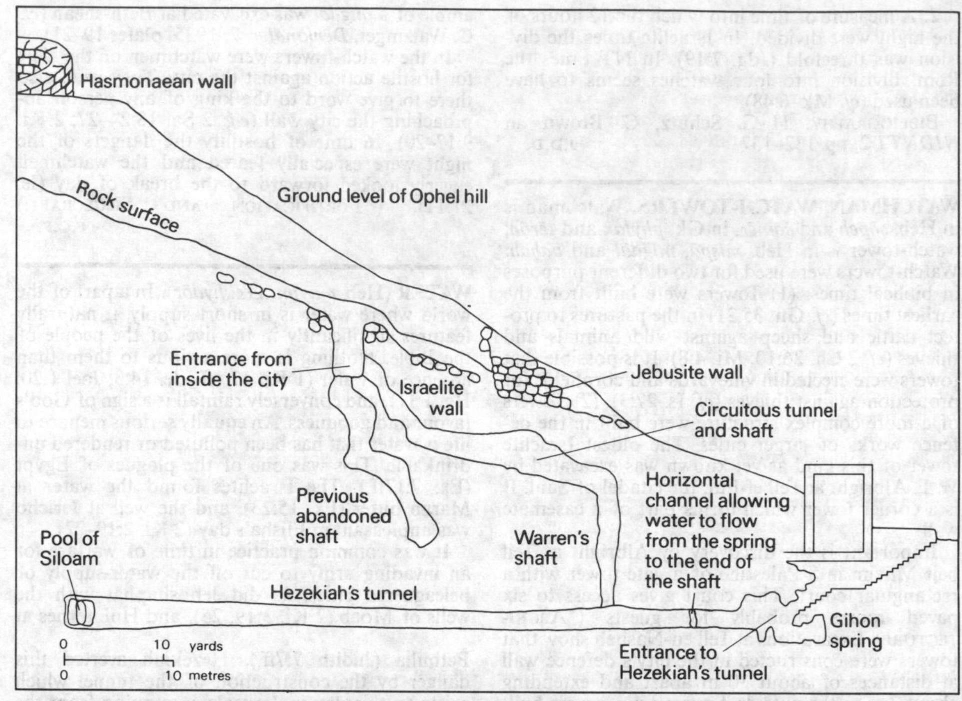

Cross-section of the water-system of ancient Jerusalem, including Hezekiah's tunnel.

35:6–7; 41:18, *etc.*, and the longing for it indicates spiritual need (Pss. 42:1; 63:1; Am. 8:11). In Ezekiel's vision of God's house (47:1–11) the waters that poured out from under the threshold represented the unrestricted flow of Yahweh's blessings upon his people (*cf.* Zc. 14:8). Jeremiah describes Yahweh as 'the fountain of living waters' (2:13; 17:13), a phrase that is echoed in Jn. 7:38 of the Holy Spirit. In the NT water is connected with eternal life as the supreme blessing that God gives (Jn. 4:14; Rev. 7:17; 21:6; 22:1, 17), but in Eph. 5:26; Heb. 10:22, the predominant idea is that of baptismal cleansing for forgiveness of sins.

The idea of cleansing comes next to that of refreshment. In the ceremonial system washing was a prominent feature. Priests were washed at their consecration (Ex. 29:4); Levites too were sprinkled with water (Nu. 8:7). Special ablutions were demanded of the chief priest on the Day of Atonement (Lv. 16:4, 24, 26), of the priest in the 'water of separation' ritual (Nu. 19:1–10), and of all men for the removal of ceremonial defilement (Lv. 11:40; 15:5ff.; 17:15; 22:6; Dt. 23:11). The laver before the *tabernacle was a constant reminder of the need for cleansing in the approach to God (Ex. 30:18–21). A developed form of this ritual ablution was practised by the Qumran sect and by a variety of Jewish baptist sects which flourished before and after the turn of the Christian era. These provide the background to John's baptism of repentance and to the Christian *baptism of cleansing, initiation and incorporation into Christ.

A third aspect is that of danger and death. The story of the Flood, the drowning of the Egyptians in the Red Sea, and the general fear of the sea and deep waters expressed by the psalmist (18:16; 32:6; 46:3; 69:1ff., *etc.*) indicate that water could in Yahweh's hands be an instrument of judgment, although at the same time there was the thought of salvation through danger for the faithful people of God (*cf.* Is. 43:2; 59:19). It is hard to say to what extent these ideas were moulded by the Canaanite myths of the contest of Baal with the tyrannical waters of the sea, recounted in the Ras Shamra texts. Scandinavian scholars and Hooke's 'Myth and Ritual' school saw in these OT references, especially in the Psalms, a clue to the existence in Israel of an annual kingly festival at which the victory of Yahweh, personified by the king, was reenacted. That Heb. thought and poetry echoed the language of Near Eastern mythology is clear (*cf.* the references to Rahab, Leviathan, the dragon, *etc.*), but to hold that the Canaanite rituals themselves or the doctrinal beliefs underlying them were taken over by the religion of Israel goes beyond the evidence. See A. R. Johnson, 'The Psalms', *OTMS*, 1951.

Bibliography. J. Bonnin, *L'Eau dans l'Antiquité*, 1984; W. H. Propp, *Water in the Wilderness*, 1987. O. Böcher, R. K. Harrison, in *NIDNTT* 3, pp. 982–993.

J.B.Tr.

WAY. 1. OT usage. Apart from the obvious literal uses, there are a number of closely linked metaphorical ones. They derive from the fact that one on a public path becomes known and his goal and purposes are revealed by the road he takes. Most important is the sense of God's purposes and will, *e.g.* Ex. 33:13; Jb. 21:14, 31; Ps. 67:2; Pr. 8:22; Ezk. 18:25. There follows the idea of God's commandments, *cf.* especially Ps. 119. 'Way' is used generally of man's conduct, good or bad, and even of that of animals, *e.g.* Ps. 1:1, 6; Pr. 30:19–20. These usages are common in the Qumran literature.

2. NT usage. There are two developments of OT usage that call for comment. In Mt. 7:13–14 (*cf.* Lk. 13:24) we have the two ways in which man can walk contrasted. The earliest evidence for this thought is found at Qumran (1QS 3. 13–4. 26); it is common in rabbinic literature and was developed in the *Didache*, the *Epistle of Barnabas* and later patristic writings. From Acts 9:2; 19:9, 23; 22:4; 24:14, 22 we learn that 'the Way' was the oldest designation of the Christian church for itself. This is partly an extension of a use already found in the OT; *cf.* Is. 40:3 with 40:10–11, where God's people are seen being led along God's way. It can also be explained from Mt. 7:14 as the Way to salvation. Probably Jn. 14:6 was most influential of all, for here Christ claims to be the summing up of all 'the Way' means in relationship to God.

BIBLIOGRAPHY. E. Repo, *Der 'Weg' als Selbstbezeichnung des Urchristentums*, 1964; G. Ebel, *NIDNTT* 3, pp. 933–947. H.L.E.

WAYMARK. A conspicuous mark, monument or sign, usually made of a heap of stones, to mark a track (Je. 31:21, plural; AV 'high heaps'). The meaning is clear from the context and parallelism: Heb. *ṣiyyûn*, *cf.* Arab. *ṣuwwah*, 'guide-stone'; Syr. *ṣwāyâ*, 'stone-heap'. The same Heb. word is used of a monument or pile of stones used to mark the burial-place of the dead (Ezk. 39:15, 'sign'; 2 Ki. 23:17, AV 'title'). The standing stone over Rachel's grave may have been such a marker (Gn. 35:20; *PILLAR). D.J.W.

WEALTH. The view of the OT and of the NT is that wealth is a blessing from God. Abraham is a typical example of a wealthy God-fearing man (Gn. 13:2). The psalmists celebrate material blessings. The godly man flourishes 'like a tree planted by streams of water' (Ps. 1:3). 'Wealth and riches' are in the house of the man that 'fears the Lord' (Ps. 112:1, 3). God is beneficent, and material wealth is a consequence of his bounty: 'God . . . richly furnishes us with everything to enjoy' (1 Tim. 6:17).

The possession of wealth, however, brings with it the duty of generous liberality towards those in need (1 Tim. 6:18; 2 Cor. 8 and 9). (*ALMS.) Such is Christ's own example, 'Though he was rich, yet for your sake he became poor, so that by his poverty you might become rich' (2 Cor. 8:9). Faithfulness in the use of riches brings spiritual reward (Lk. 16:11); for true wealth and true riches are the spiritual blessings which God gives, rather than his material blessings (Lk. 12:33; 16:11).

The Bible recognizes that the possession of material wealth brings with it great dangers. For example, there is the danger of failing to acknowledge that God is the source of the blessing (Dt. 8:17–18; Ho. 2:8). There is the related danger of trusting in riches (Ps. 52:7). This danger of trusting in riches is so great that our Lord said that it was extremely difficult for a rich man to enter the kingdom of heaven, explaining the hard saying by the paraphrase 'those who have riches'. The disciples rightly concluded that all men have this besetting sin; to which our Lord replied that God alone can change the heart (Mk. 10:23, 27). Another spiritual danger associated with riches is materialism, that is, making riches the centre of one's interest. This was the case of the wealthy farmer in Lk. 12:21, who was not rich towards God; and of the church of Laodicea (Rev. 3:17). This temptation that wealth brings is described in the parable of the sower (Mt. 13:22), where the deceitfulness of riches chokes the word, so that it becomes unfruitful in the life. (*MAMMON.)

Covetousness, or the desire to be rich, is an evil against which the Scriptures frequently warn. The love of money is described as the root of all kinds of evil (1 Tim. 6:9–10). Consequently a spirit of contentment with such things as God has given is a virtue inculcated in both Testaments (Ps. 62:10; 1 Tim. 6:8; Heb. 13:5).

Because of the dangers of riches into which the possessor so frequently falls, rich men are, as a class, denounced in several passages of the Scriptures, *e.g.* Lk. 6:24f. and Jas. 5. Blessings are, however, pronounced on the poor (Lk. 6:20ff.); for poverty should quicken faith in God, which riches so frequently in practice deadens.

BIBLIOGRAPHY. D. B. Knox, *Not by Bread Alone*, 1990. D.B.K.

WEIGHTS AND MEASURES.

1. IN THE OLD TESTAMENT

Metrology, an exact science, requires legal sanction to enforce the authority granted to any particular system. In the ancient Near East standards varied between districts and cities, and there is no evidence that Israel had or used an integrated system. David (2 Sa. 14:26) and Ezekiel (45:10) pronounced certain basic standards of weight and measurements. Rabbinic tradition that standard measures were deposited in the Temple is unverified (*cf.* 1 Ch. 23:29). The law, however, prescribed that the Hebrew keep a just weight, measure and balance (Lv. 19:35–36; Ezk. 45:10). The prophets spoke against those merchants who, by increasing or decreasing their weights (Dt. 25:13), or using deceitful weights (Mi. 6:11) or false balances (Pr. 11:1; 20:23), defrauded their fellows. Since ancient balances had a margin of error of up to 6% (*PEQ* 74, 1942, p. 86), and few Heb. weights yet found of the same inscribed denomination have proved to be of exactly identical weight, the importance of this exhortation can be seen. These, and other variants, mean that ancient weights and measures can be given only their approximate equivalent in modern terms.

I. Weights

Ancient weights were stones (Heb. *'eḇen*) carved in shapes, usually with a flat base, which made them easy to handle or recognize (*e.g.* turtles, ducks, lions). They were often inscribed with their weight and the standard followed. Weights were carried in a pouch or wallet (Dt. 25:13; Mi. 6:11; Pr. 16:11) in order that the purchaser could check with the 'weights current among the merchants' at a given place (Gn. 23:16).

a. Talent (Heb. *kikkār*, 'a round'; Akkad. *biltu*, 'a burden'; Gk. *talanton*, 'a weight'). This was the largest unit, probably named after the characteristic shape in which large metal lumps were moulded, as in the lead cover of the ephah (Zc. 5:7). It was used to weigh gold (2 Sa. 12:30, *etc.*), silver (1 Ki. 20:39), iron (1 Ch. 29:7) and bronze (Ex.

OLD TESTAMENT MEASURES

Length

		Metric*
1 finger		1.85 cm
4 fingers	= 1 palm	7.40 cm
3 palms	= 1 span	22.25 cm
2 spans	= 1 cubit	44.5 cm
(1 royal cubit (Ezk.))		= 51.81 cm
6 cubits	= 1 reed	= 2.67 m
(1 reed (Ezk.))		= 3.10 m

Capacity – dry and liquid

		Metric*
1 log†		0.3 litres
4 logs	= 1 cab	1.2 litres
	1 omer ('iśśārôn)	2.4 litres
2½ cabs	= 1 hin†	3.6 litres
2 hins	= 1 seah	7.3 litres
3 seahs	= 1 ephah (bath)†	22 litres
5 ephahs	= 1 half-homer (leṯeḵ)	110 litres
2 half-homers	= 1 homer (kor ††)	220 litres

† liquid measure only
†† dry and liquid measure

Weights

		Metric*
1 gerah		0.5 gm
10 gerahs	= 1 beka	5.0 gm
1.33 bekas	= 1 pim	7.0 gm
1.5 pims	= 1 shekel	10 gm
50 shekels	= 1 mina	500 gm
60 minas	= 1 talent	30 kg

*Metric equivalent approx. only

Two examples of measurements in proportion:

Right: OT weights
Below: OT length

1 finger
1 palm
1 span
1 cubit
1 reed

NEW TESTAMENT MEASURES

Length

		Metric*
1 cubit		44.5 cm (Roman)
		52.5 cm (Palestinian)
4 cubits	= 1 fathom	2.10 metres
		1.8 metres (Greek)
100 fathoms	= 1 stade	185 metres
8 stades	= 1 mile	1478.5 metres

Capacity – dry

		Metric*
1 choinix		1 litre
48 choinikes	= 1 medimnos	52.5 litres
10 medimnoi	= 1 koros	525 litres

Capacity – liquid

		Metric*
1 sextarius		500 cc
16 sextarii	= 1 modius	8.75 litres
4.5 modii	= 1 batos or 1 metrētēs	39.5 litres
6 modii	= 1 medimnos	52.5 litres

*Metric equivalent approx. only

1 talent
1 mina
1 shekel

Old and New Testament measures with modern equivalents.

38:29). 666 talents of gold were included in Solomon's annual revenue (1 Ki. 10:14).

The 30 talents of gold paid by Hezekiah as tribute (2 Ki. 18:14) corresponds with the amount Sennacherib claims to have received (Annals), implying a similar talent in use in Judah and Assyria at this time. This might be the 'light' talent of about 30 kg, as inscribed Babylonian duck-weights of this value range 29·76–30·27 kg. A weight found at Tell Beit Mirsim (4,565 gm) has been interpreted as this talent of 30·43 kg or, more likely, of 28·53 kg (*i.e.* 8 minas of 570·6 gm = 8 × 50 shekels of 11·41 gm; see below).

Other Babylonian weights show that a 'heavy' or double standard talent was also in use, weighed examples ranging from 58·68 to 59·82 kg, *i.e.* about 60 kg.

b. Mina (AV 'maneh'; Heb. *māneh*; Akkad. *manû*) was a weight used to measure gold (1 Ki. 10:17), silver (Ezr. 2:69; Ne. 7:71–72) and other commodities. The talent was subdivided into 60 minas of 50 shekels or 50 minas of 60 shekels. There is some evidence that in Palestine, as at Ras Shamra, the 50-shekel mina was in use in pre-exilic times. The payment by 603,550 men of a poll-tax of ½ shekel (see *f. beka*) produced 100 talents, 1,775 shekels, *i.e.* 3,000 shekels to the talent (as at Ras Shamra), but could be interpreted by either standard. However, multiples of 50 shekels (*e.g.* 400—Gn. 23:15; 500—Ex. 30:24; 5,000—1 Sa. 17:5; 16,750—Nu. 31:52) seem to be conclusive evidence for the use of a 50-shekel mina.

Ezekiel's metrological reforms included the redefinition of the mina to 60 shekels (45:12, *MT*, 20 + 25 + 15). Thus the new Heb. mina at 20 (gerahs) 60 (shekels) kept the value of the mina unchanged in relation to the Babylonian, which comprised 24 (*girū*) 50 (*šiqlu*) = 1,200 gerahs.

c. The *shekel* (Heb. *šeqel*; Akkad. *šiqlu*; Aram., Ugar. *ṯql*) was common to all Semitic metrologies and was the basic weight (*šāqal*, 'to weigh'). Its value varied considerably at different times and areas:

(i) The royal shekel, set by 'the king's weight' (2 Sa. 14:26), was a standard known also in Babylonia. This was probably the 'heavy shekel' of Ras Shamra (*kbd*). Analysis of weights discovered at Gibeon, Gezer, Megiddo and Tell en-Nasbeh show a 'heavy' shekel of 12·5–12·88 gm, *i.e.* about 13 gm (0·457 oz).

(ii) The common shekel was often used to weigh metal objects (1 Sa. 17:5; Goliath's armour of 5,000 shekels = 56·7 kg or 125 lb), foodstuffs (2 Ki. 7:1; Ezk. 4:10), and commonly gold and silver, thus implying its use as a means of payment. Silver shekel coins (*sigloi*) first appeared in the reign of Darius I (* MONEY).

Some fifty inscribed weights of a shekel or multiples upwards show a variation 11·08–12·25; average 11·38 gm. This compares well with calculations based on the inscribed weights of smaller denominations (see below), which confirm a possible devaluation in post-exilic times to about 11·7–11·4 gm (0·401 oz) for the shekel.

Inscriptions on the weights use the symbols I : II : III : ᒣ : Λ : IΛ : IIΛ : T : TΛ : – : Λ : = : ≡ : × . Interpreted by Y. Yadin (*Scripta Hierosolymitana* 8, 1961, pp. 1–62) as 1, 2, 3, 4, 5, 6, 7, 8, 9, 10, 20, 30, royal (*lmlk*). Others (Scott, Aharoni) however equate these markings as the equivalent of the shekel in terms of Egyp. weights, 8 shekels = 1 *deben* = 10 *qedets* (1 *deben* = about 91 gm). Thus Egyp. hieratic numerals were engraved on the weights to show their value; I and II for 1 and 2 shekels, 4 and 8 shekel weights bearing the numbers 5 and 10 (ᒣ and Λ), then values in *qedets*.

(iii) The temple shekel or 'shekel of the sanctuary' (Ex. 30:13; Lv. 5:15, *etc.*) was related to a *bega* or ½ shekel (RSV 'beka', AV 'bekah', Ex. 38:26) and 20 gerahs (Ezk. 45:12), though later with revaluation it equalled ⅓ shekel (Ne. 10:32). This shekel is believed to be the *nṣp* (see *d.* below), of which examples have been discovered weighing 9·28–10·5 gm, *i.e.* about 10 gm (0·353 oz) depreciating to about 9·8 gm (0·349 oz).

d. nṣp or 'part' was ⅚ shekel. Thirteen examples give it a weight of about 10 gm (see *c.* above).

e. pim (Heb. *pîm* or *payim*) is mentioned only in 1 Sa. 13:21 (AV 'Yet they had a file [with mouths]') which should be translated 'and the charge was a *pim* for the ploughshares . . .' (so RSV). This weight was ⅔ of a unit (*cf.* Akkad. [šini]pu), probably of the common shekel, since twelve inscribed *pim* weights (from Lachish, Jerusalem, Gezer, Tell en-Nasbeh, *etc.*) average 7·8 gm.

f. beka (Heb. *beqa'*, 'fraction, division', AV 'bekah') was used for weighing gold (Gn. 24:22) and for paying the poll-tax said to be the equivalent of 'half a shekel, after the shekel of the sanctuary' (Ex. 38:26). Since seven inscribed weights inscribed *bq'* or abbreviated as *b* have been found (at Lachish, Jerusalem, Gezer and Beth-zur), this enables a check to be made of the value of the shekel. These *bq'* have an average weight of 6·02 gm.

g. ḥmš, '⅕' was inscribed on a turtle-shaped weight from Samaria weighing 2·499 gm. This compares with another inscribed '¼ *nṣp*, ¼ *šql*', implying a subdivision of the Ezekiel shekel.

h. gerah (Heb. *gērâ*; Assyr. *girû*). This was defined as ½ shekel (Ex. 30:13; Ezk. 45:12).

i. Other weights. The *peres* (Aram. pl. *parsin*) of Dn. 5:25, 28 was a subdivision of the shekel in use at Babylon (*cf.* Old Bab. *paras*), and like the *parisu* (Alalaḫ) possibly equal to ½ shekel since a term for any weight (here 'fraction') had a precise value. Thus the writing on the wall superficially implied a statement of weight 'Mina, mina, shekel, half-shekel'. The *qᵉśîṭâ* (*qesitah*, RSVmg., Gn. 33:19; Jos. 24:32; Jb. 42:11) appears to be a unit of as yet unknown weight. A stone weight of Darius II is inscribed 120 *krš* = 20 mina.

The table on p. 1246 indicates the relation of these weights to each other and gives approximate modern equivalents, which should be used with caution owing to the varying standards in use in antiquity.

II. Linear measures

Linear measures were based on the 'natural' units which could be easily applied.

a. The *reed* (*qāneh*), though often denoting a measuring instrument rather than a measure (*ARTS AND CRAFTS), was of 6 cubits length and exact enough to be reckoned as a unit of length (Ezk. 40:5; *cf.* 'rod', Rev. 21:15).

b. The *cubit* (Heb. *'ammâ*; Akkad. *ammātu*; Lat. *cubitus*) was the distance from elbow to finger tip. This 'natural' cubit (AV 'cubit of a man', RSV 'common cubit', Dt. 3:11) was used to indicate the general size of a person (4 cubits the height of a man; *cf.* 1 Sa. 17:4; 1 Ch. 11:23) or object (Est. 5:14; Zc. 5:2). It described depth (Gn. 7:20) or distance (Jn. 21:8).

A more precisely defined cubit was used for exact measurement. This *standard Hebrew cubit* was 17·5 inches (44·45 cm), slightly shorter than the common Egyp. cubit of 17·6 inches (44·7 cm). This generally accepted figure compares closely with the length given for the Siloam tunnel as '1,200 cubits', equivalent to a measured 1,749 feet (533·1 m), giving a cubit of 17·49 inches or 44·42 cm. Excavated buildings at Megiddo, Lachish, Gezer and *Hazor reveal a plan based on multiples of this measure. Also Solomon's bronze laver of 1,000 *bath* capacity (*i.e.* 22,000 litres; 1 Ki. 7:23–26; 2 Ch. 4:2, 5), when calculated for the capacity of a sphere, gives a cubit of 17·51 inches or 44·48 cm (R. B. Y. Scott, *JBL* 77, 1958, pp. 210–212).

The *long* or 'royal' *cubit* was a handbreadth ('palm') longer than the standard cubit of 6 palms (Ezk. 40:5), *i.e.* 20·4 inches or 51·81 cm. With this compare the Babylonian cubit of 50·3 cm (of 30 fingers length marked on a statue of Gudea) which was '3 fingers' shorter than the Egyp. cubit of 52·45 cm (Herodotus, *Hist*. 1. 178).

c. The *gōmeḏ* (AV, RSV 'cubit') occurs only in Jdg. 3:16, where it measures a weapon, probably a dagger rather than a sword, and has thus been interpreted as a subdivision (perhaps ⅔) of the cubit, or as the short cubit of 5 palms mentioned in the Mishnah.

d. The *span* (*zereṯ*), or outstretched hand from the thumb to the little finger (Vulg. wrongly *palmus*), was a half-cubit (1 Sa. 17:4; Ex. 28:16; Ezk. 43:13), though 'half a cubit' could be expressed literally (Ex. 25:10).

e. The *palm* (*ṭep̄aḥ*; *ṭōp̄aḥ*) or 'handbreadth' was the width of the hand at the base of the 4 fingers (hence Vulg. *quattuor digitis*), *i.e.* 7·37 cm. Thus was measured the thickness of the bronze laver (1 Ki. 7:26 = 2 Ch. 4:5), the edge of the tabernacle table (Ex. 25:25; 37:12), and of that in Ezekiel's Temple (40:5; 43:13). A man's life is but (a few) handbreadths in length (Ps. 39:5).

f. The *finger* or digit (*'eṣba'*) was a ¼ handbreadth (Je. 52:21), and the smallest subdivision of the cubit in common use in Palestine, as in Egypt and Mesopotamia. It is generally taken to be 1·85 cm.

g. Distance, as opposed to the measurement of objects, was in pre-exilic times reckoned by equation with a known average. It is reckoned as a 'bowshot' (Gn. 21:16), the length of a ploughed furrow (1 Sa. 14:14), 'a day's journey' (Nu. 11:31; 1 Ki. 19:4), or 'a journey of three days' (Gn. 30:36; Ex. 3:18; Jon. 3:3). It is not proved that the latter is to be taken merely as general indication of 'a long distance' (*cf.* 'a seven days' journey', Gn. 31:23), for exact standards were used by the Babylonians; *e.g. bēru*, 'double-hour' march of 10·692 km (*AfO* 16, 1953, p. 20, n. 138).

The step (*peśa'*) in 1 Sa. 20:3 was used metaphorically rather than in the exact manner of the contemporary Assyrian 'foot' (= 32·92 cm). Similarly the 'stretch of the ground' (*kiḇraṯ hā'āreṣ*, RSV 'some distance', Gn. 35:16; 48:7; 2 Ki. 5:19) was only a vague indication of distance.

In Maccabean times Hellenistic measures were introduced. Thus Beth-zur was about 5 *schoinoi* from Jerusalem (2 Macc. 11:5, RSV 'leagues'), *i.e.* 30·5 km at the Ptolemaic value of a *schoinos* of 6·1 km. The Alexandrian *stadion* of 184·9 m was employed. Jerusalem to Scythopolis was 600 *stades* (2 Macc. 12:29, RSVmg.), which corresponds well with the known distance of 110 km between these two cities.

III. Measures of area

Superficial areas were not specifically expressed but described by giving the necessary dimensions. Thus the square was of four sides of equal dimension (*mᵉrubbā'aṯ*, AV 'foursquare', 1 Ki. 7:31; Ezk. 40:47; 45:2), the circumference of a circle (1 Ki. 7:23) and the diameter the distance 'from brim to brim' (2 Ch. 4:2).

The area of land was calculated empirically. Thus vineyards (Is. 5:10) or a field (1 Sa. 14:14) could be measured by the *ṣemeḏ* ('acre'), *i.e.* the area a pair of yoked animals could plough in a day (*cf.* Arab. *faddan*). In Babylonia this was defined as 6,480 square cubits = ⅖ acre (1,618 sq m). This in later times was the Lat. *jugum*, *jugerum* of 28,800 square Rom. feet = ⅝ acre (2,529 sq m). Another method was to estimate the area by the amount of seed (*zᵉra'*) required to sow it (Lv. 27:16; 1 Ki. 18:32). In the Hellenistic period this was 3⅗ seahs to a *jugerum* of land, *i.e.* 0·173 acre (700 sq m) per seah or 5·19 acres (2·1 hectares) per homer of 30 seahs (*JBL* 64, 1945, p. 372), which seems to have improved to 0·193 and 5·79 acres respectively by the 2nd century AD.

The specific measurement of the pastures round the levitical cities (Nu. 35:4–5) presents difficulties. It may have been an area 2,000 cubits square (v. 5), the centres of the sides of which were also reckoned as at a radius of 1,000 cubits from the city walls (v. 4).

IV. Dry measures of capacity

The terms used derive originally from the receptacles which contained an agreed amount and thus served as a measure.

a. Homer (Heb. *ḥōmer*; Akkad. *imēr*), 'a donkey load', was commonly used throughout Asia S of Anatolia and W of Euphrates in the 2nd millennium and thereafter as a measure for cereals. The *homer* is older than the *kor* (*RA* 67, 1973, p. 78); *cf.* Lv. 27:16; Ezk. 45:13. The collection of 10 homers of quails (Nu. 11:32) implied gluttony, whereas the return of only an ephah of wheat from a homer of seed was a picture of failure (Is. 5:10), there being 10 ephahs to the homer, which equalled about 220 litres (48·4 gallons).

b. Kor (RSV 'cor') (Heb. *kōr*; Sum. *gur*; Akkad. *kurru*) was a large dry measure equal to the homer (Ezk. 45:14) used of fine flour (*sōleṯ*), meal (*qemaḥ*, 1 Ki. 4:22), wheat and barley (2 Ch. 2:10; 27:5). It also appears as a liquid measure for oil (Ezk. 45:14), though 2 Ch. 2:10 and Gk. reads *bath* (*cf.* the parallel passage, 1 Ki. 5:11).

c. Half-homer (Heb. *leṯeḵ*) occurs only in Ho. 3:2 as a measure for barley. As it is mentioned after the homer, Aq., Sym. and Vulg. interpret as ½ *kōr* or ½ homer, but there is no confirmatory evidence for this. The *leṯeḵ* may be a Phoenician measure.

d. Ephah (Heb. *'ēp̄â*; Egyp. *ipt*) is the name of a vessel large enough to hold a person (Zc. 5:6–10), and thence of an exact measure (Lv. 19:36). Used only of cereals, and with subdivision of ⅙ (Ezk. 45:13; 46:14) or ⅒ (Lv. 5:11), it was in common use from an early period (Jdg. 6:19). The ephah must never be diminished (Am. 8:5) but always be of equal (just) measure (Dt. 25:14; Pr. 20:10). The ephah was equal to the liquid measure *bath*, both being ⅒ of a homer (Ezk. 45:11).

e. Seah (Heb. *sᵉ'â*; Akkad. *sûtu*) was also a measure for flour and cereals (Gn. 18:6; 1 Ki. 18:32).

f. Omer (Heb. *'ōmer*, *cf.* Arab. *'umar*, 'a small

bowl') occurs only in the account of the collection of manna (Ex. 16), being used both of the measure itself (vv. 18, 32–33) and of the amount measured (vv. 16, 22). The *'ōmer* was equal to ⅒ ephah (v. 36).

g. A *'tenth* deal' (AV; Heb. *'iśśārôn*) was a measure used for flour (Ex. 29:40; Nu. 15:4) equal to ⅒ ephah (Nu. 28:5), and therefore equal to the omer.

h. Cab (Heb. *qaḇ*), a measure of capacity which occurs only in 1 Ki. 6:25, where among the inflated prices at the siege of Samaria ¼ *qaḇ* of carob pods was sold for 5 (shekels) of silver. The cab = 4 log = ⅓ seah = ⅙ hin = about 2 pints.

i. The 'measure' (Heb. *šālîš*) of Ps. 80:5; Is. 40:12 is literally '⅓', but no unit is expressed, so that the measure of capacity is unknown.

It will be noted that these dry measures combine the Babylonian sexagesimal reckonings (1 *kur* = 30 *sutu* = 180 *qa*) with the decimal system (also employed by the Assyrians). See the table on p. 1246.

V. Liquid measures of capacity

a. Bath (Heb. *baṯ*; Gk. *batos*, Lk. 16:6 only) was the equivalent in liquid of the ephah (Ezk. 45:11, 14). It was used to measure water (1 Ki. 7:26), wine (Is. 5:10) and oil (2 Ch. 2:10; so also 1 Ki. 5:11). It was an exact and standard measure (Ezk. 45:10, about 22 litres).

b. Hin (Heb. *hîn*; Egyp. *hnw*, 'a pot') was used of the vessel employed as a measure (Lv. 19:36) and of the measure of water (Ezk. 4:11), oil (Ex. 29:40) or wine (Lv. 23:13). According to Josephus (*Ant.* 3. 197; 4. 234), the *hin* was equal to ⅙ *bath.*

c. Log (Heb. *lōḡ*) is used only in Lv. 14:10 as a measure of oil in the ceremony for the purification of the leper. According to the Talmud, this was equal to 1/12 *hin.*

The values of these liquid measures depend upon that of the *bath.* This is uncertain, since the only inscribed vessels marked *bt* (Tell beit Mirsim) and *bt lmlk* (Lachish) are fragmentary and cannot be reconstructed with certainty; thus the value of the *bath* has been variously calculated between 20·92 and 46·6 litres. On the assumptions that the *bath* measure was half the size of the 'royal *bath*' and that these inscriptions denoted the full capacity of the vessels, the proposal of 22 litres in biblical times (Albright) and 21·5 litres in Hellenistic times is usually adopted as a basis for calculation, since it receives some support from the comparison with the capacity of Solomon's laver, which held 1,000 *baths* = 22,000 litres. For weights in the Talmud, see *EJ*, 16, 1971, pp. 388–392.

BIBLIOGRAPHY. A. H. Gardiner, *Egyptian Grammar*³, 1957, pp. 197–200 (for Egyp. metrology); R. de Vaux, *Ancient Israel*, 1961, pp. 195–209; R. B. Y. Scott, *BA* 22, 1951, pp. 22–40; *PEQ* 97, 1965, pp. 128–139; Y. Aharoni, *BASOR* 184, 1966, pp. 13–19; M. A. Powell, *ABD* 6, pp. 847–909. D.J.W.

2. IN THE NEW TESTAMENT

I. Weights

Only two weights are mentioned in the NT. The *litra* of Jn. 12:3; 19:39 (*cf.* Lat. *libra*: 'pound'—from this weight we have our abbreviation *lb* for pound) was a Rom. measure of weight equivalent to 327·45 gm. In Rev. 16:21 the adjective *talantiaios*, 'weighing a talent'; RSV 'hundredweight', is used to describe hailstones: Arndt maintains that this talent equalled 125 librae, and so would be about 41 kg in weight, but *HDB* calculates it as weighing about 20·5 kg.

II. Linear measures

a. The *cubit.* As in OT times, measurements were related to the parts of the body, and the basic unit was still the *pēchys* ('forearm') or cubit. Under the Rom. empire there were two different measurements for a cubit: the Rom. cubit of 6 handbreadths of 74 mm = 44·4 cm, and the Philetarian cubit of 52·5 cm. Julian of Ascalon relates that the latter system of measurement was customary in Palestine and Egypt (Jeremias, p. 11n.), and this is probably the length indicated in Jn. 21:8; Rev. 21:17. In Mt. 6:27; Lk. 12:25 the term is also used.

b. The *orgyia* ('fathom', Acts 27:28) was the length of the outstretched arms, and so was approximately 1·8 m. This was a Gk. unit of measure, derived from the verb *oregō*, 'I stretch'. Herodotus (2. 149) says that it equalled 6 Gk. feet or 4 Gk. cubits.

c. The *stadion* ('furlong' AV, Lk. 24:13; Jn. 6:19; 11:18; Rev. 14:20; 21:16) was 100 *orgyiai* and equalled about 185 m. As the race-course at Olympia was supposed to be exactly a stade long, the word was used for an arena, as in 1 Cor. 9:24—hence the English 'stadium'.

d. The *milion* ('mile', Mt. 5:41) was a Gk. transliteration of the Rom. measurement *mille passuum*, 'a thousand paces'. This was 1,478·5 m, or 8 stades, and was calculated on the basis of 5 Rom. feet (each of 29·57 cm) to the pace (1·48 m).

e. The sabbath day's journey mentioned in Acts 1:12 was not a proper measurement, but rather the product of rabbinical exegesis of Ex. 16:29 and Nu. 35:5 (*cf.* Lumby in *CGT*, *ad loc.*). It was fixed at 2,000 cubits (Talmud *'Erubin* 51a) and was called *t^{e}ḥûm ha-šabbāṯ*—the limit of the sabbath.

III. Measures of area

None is used in the NT, but the basic unit under the Rom. empire was the *jugerum*, or acre, calculated on the amount of land a yoke of oxen could plough in a day. This was estimated at one *actus*, or furrow (36·6 m), by two (73·2 m); so the *jugerum* was the equivalent of 2 square *actus*, or 0·27 hectares, about ⅔ acre.

IV. Dry measures of capacity

a. The *choinix* ('quart', Rev. 6:6), is variously estimated at 1½–2 pints, and the best calculation would be just over 1 litre. It was a Gk. measure, and Herodotus (7. 187) narrates that it was the daily ration of grain per man in Xerxes' invasion army.

b. The *saton* (Aram. *sā'ṯâ*, Heb. *s^{e}'â*) was the *s^{e}'â* of OT times: Josephus (*Ant.* 9. 85) rates this as equivalent to 1½ *modii* (see below). It is the measure mentioned in Mt. 13:33; Lk. 13:21, where leaven is added to 3 *sata* of wheat-flour: each would be about 12·3 litres.

c. The *koros* of Lk. 16:7 (a 'measure of wheat') was Heb. *kōr*. Josephus (*Ant.* 15. 314) equates it to 10 Attic *medimnoi*, and, as the *medimnos* contained 48 *choinikes*, this would rate the *koros* at 525 litres. Since Ezk. 45:11 rates the *baton* as the tenth of a *koros*, it is generally regarded that Josephus here mistook the *medimnos* for the *metrētēs*, and that the *koros* contained 10 *metrētai*, about 395 litres. It was used for both dry and liquid measure.

d. The *modios* ('bushel') of Mt. 5:15; Mk. 4:21; Lk. 11:33 was Lat. *modius*, and all three references use the word to denote the vessel used to measure this amount. It was a grain measure containing 16 *sextarii*: 6 *modii* equalled the Gk. *medimnos* (Cornelius Nepos, *Attica* 2). Thus the *modius* contained 8 *choinikes* and was about 8·75 litres.

V. Liquid measures of capacity

a. The *xestēs* of Mk. 7:4 (RSV 'pot') is again a reference to the vessel used for measuring this capacity, and is taken by most scholars (but see Moulton and Howard, *Grammar of New Testament Greek*, 2, 1929, p. 155) to be a corruption of the Lat. *sextarius*. This was a liquid and dry measure of ⅙ *modius*, about 500 cc.

b. The *batos* ('measure' of oil in Lk. 16:6) is a Gk. form of Heb. *baṯ* (see above). According to Josephus (*Ant.* 8. 57), it contains 72 *sextarii* or 4½ *modii*—about 39·5 litres.

c. The *metrētēs* mentioned in Jn. 2:6 (AV 'firkin') was a Gk. liquid measure approximately equivalent to the *baṯ*, and so containing about 39·5 litres. Thus the stone water-pots used in the wedding-feast at Cana held between 80 and 120 litres each.

BIBLIOGRAPHY. R. G. Bratcher, 'Weights, Money, Measures and Time', *BTh* 10.4, 1959; R. Gower, *The New Manners and Customs of Bible Times*, 1987. D.H.W.

WELL. 1. An artificial shaft sunk to reach underground water, percolating or collected (Heb. *bᵉ'ēr*; Arab. *bir*; Gk. *phrear*), whereas a spring (Heb. and Arab. *'ayin*; Gk. *pēgē*) is the work of nature. AV confusion of terminology is due to the same confusion in 17th-century English, reflected also in Milton. Heb. and Gk. are unambiguous.

2. An artificial shaft sunk to reach a natural underground spring—a fusion of concepts in which the terms could be interchanged correctly. There is a reasonable presumption that the well from which Rebekah drew (Gn. 24) was of this type—likewise Jacob's well at Shechem, where Jesus met the woman of Samaria (Jn. 4). This would explain satisfactorily the puzzling alternation of words in these two chapters.

3. A *cistern or pit, large or small, public or private, for collecting rain-water: Heb. *bôr*; Gk. *lakkos*. The well at Bethlehem (1 Ch. 11:17–18) was probably an example.

4. A shaft, dry or with miry clay, used as a dungeon, for which the same Heb. word is used (Gn. 37:24; Ps. 40:2; Je. 38:6, *etc.*). The praise of the well of living water in folk-song is reflected in Nu. 21:17–18.

In the arid parts of the E *water may become as precious as gold. Wells were, and still remain, the subjects of fierce disputes and even strife (*cf.* Gn. 21:25, *etc.*). They became hereditary, and were exploited by human monopolies at an earlier date than land. R.A.S.

WHEEL. The earliest attested wheels (Heb. *galgal*, *'ôpān*) are clay models of chariot wheels and fragments of a potter's wheel (*cf.* Je. 18:3, Heb. *'oḇnayim*) of the 4th millennium BC (see C. L. Woolley, *Ur Excavations*, 4, 1956, p. 28, plate 24). Early wheels were made from wooden planks pegged together, with leather tyres (see *ANEP*, nos. 163, 169, 303), but with the displacement of the ass by the horse *c.* 1500 BC lighter spoked wheels came into use (see *ANEP*, nos. 167–168, 183–184). The bronze stands made for Solomon's Temple were miniature chariot wheels, with axles, rims, spokes and hubs (1 Ki. 7:33). Daniel saw the Ancient of Days seated on a throne with wheels of fire (7:9), and Ezekiel gives a description of the wheels in his visions of the chariot of God (1; 10). The rumble of chariot wheels betokened the approach of an enemy (Je. 47:3; Na. 3:2), but all those hostile to God's people will be blown away like whirling dust (Ps. 83:13; Is. 17:13). In later Heb. *galgal* is used *pars pro toto* for wagon (Ezk. 23:24; 26:10). Wheels were also used as part of the machinery for drawing water (Ec. 12:6). On the wheel of birth (Jas. 3:6, AV 'course of nature'), see D. J. Mo., *James*, *TNTC*, 1985, pp. 125f. A.R.M.

WHIRLWIND. The Eng. translation of Heb. *sûpâ* applies loosely to any violent storm and is not restricted to a rotary movement of air (Jb. 37:9; Pr. 1:27; 10:25; Is. 5:28; 17:13; 21:1; 66:15; Je. 4:13; Am. 1:14; Na. 1:3). In AV it is translated 'storm' in other passages (Jb. 21:18; Ps. 83:15; Is. 29:6). *sᵉ'ārâ* is used synonymously, translated 'whirlwind' when it stands alone (*e.g.* 2 Ki. 2:1; Jb. 38:1; 40:6; Is. 40:24; 41:16) but sometimes 'storm' (Ps. 107:29). RV uses the expression only once in its technical sense (Je. 23:19).

The whirlwind is used aptly as a figure for the sudden attack of the invader (Is. 5:28; Je. 4:13; Dn. 11:40; Am. 1:14f.). It also symbolizes divine judgment because of its sudden motion (Ps. 18:10; Na. 1:3) and divine wrath (Ps. 58:9; Pr. 10:25; Is. 17:13; 28:17; 66:15; Ho. 8:7). It is similarly used of the Messianic wrath, described in Mt. 7:24–27. (*WIND.) J.M.H.

WICKED. In the OT, Heb. *rāšā'*, 'wicked, ungodly', and *ra'*, 'evil', are most common; Gk. *ponēros*, 'bad, malignant', as contrasted with *chrēstos*, is the usual NT word, although *athesmos*, *anomos* and *kakos* are also used. While the term is often used in the general sense of 'wrong' (Ps. 18:21), it refers more specifically to evil, not in its moral or judicial sense, but in its active form, *i.e.* mischief (Nu. 16:26). As such, it denotes perversity of mind (Pr. 15:26; Rom. 1:29) by which the natural man surrenders himself to evil impulses (Ps. 10:1–11). Wickedness has its seat in the heart (Je. 17:9; Mk. 7:21–23), and is inspired by Satan (Mt. 13:19; 1 Jn. 3:12). It is progressive (Gn. 6:5) and contagious (1 Sa. 24:13) in its manifestation. The wicked man is utterly perverse, finding unholy delight in the infliction of injury (Pr. 21:10). Jesus often characterized the *sin of his contemporaries as wickedness (Mt. 16:4), while Peter declares that wicked men crucified the Saviour (Acts 2:23).

The Psalms frequently contrast the righteous and the wicked, raising the question of the prosperity of the wicked, and offering suggestions which provide a partial answer (Pss. 37:35–36; 9:15, *et passim*). But this question, which is part of the general problem of evil, is insoluble in the light of the OT revelation. Throughout the Scriptures there is a strong insistence on the certainty of punishment for all who are wicked (Ps. 9:17; Je. 16:4; Mt. 13:49). It is significant to note that *ponēros* is never applied to believers; in 1 Cor. 5:13 the reference is to a nominal member of the Christian community. It is by wicked works that unbelievers are alienated from God (Col. 1:21), but those who are progressing in faith have overcome 'the wicked one' (1 Jn. 2:13), for the shield of faith is a sure defence against his attack (Eph. 6:16). A.F.

WIDOW.

I. In the Old Testament

Heb. legislation has always been solicitous for widows and, together with the fatherless and strangers, made special provision for them (*e.g.* Ex. 22:21f.; Dt. 14:29; 16:11, 14; 24:17; *cf.* Je. 7:6). Even in pre-Mosaic times there was recognition of the predicament of the childless widow and arrangements made for her (Gn. 38; *MARRIAGE, IV), and these were formally enjoined under Moses (Dt. 25:5ff.; *KIN).

Since the bearing of children was accounted a great honour, and one still more enhanced later when the nation looked for Messiah (Is. 11:1), widowhood in such as were not past the age of childbearing, as well as *barrenness, was reckoned a shame and a reproach (Is. 4:1; 54:4). The widows of kings, however, continued in their widowhood, and were the property, though not always the wives, of the new king. To ask any of them in marriage was tantamount to a claim to the kingdom (1 Ki. 2:13ff.).

As widows are often overlooked by men, God has a peculiar concern for them (Pss. 68:5; 146:9; Pr. 15:25), and kindness to them was commended as one of the marks of true religion (Jb. 29:13; Is. 1:17). The oppression and injury of widows, on the other hand, would incur dire punishment (Ps. 94:6; Mal. 3:5). Jerusalem and Babylon are likened in their desolation to widows (La. 1:1; Is. 47:8), and the effect of violent death compared to that of wives becoming widows (La. 5:3; Ezk. 22:25). (*ORPHAN.)

II. In the New Testament

The Christian church inherited from Judaism the duty of providing for the widow. The Jewish-Christian author of James states categorically that to give assistance to widows in their distress is a mark of the kind of religion with which God can find no fault (1:27). Even if widows were left comparatively well-off, they needed to be protected from the unscrupulous. One of the things that Jesus condemned in some Pharisees was that they 'devoured widows' houses' (Mk. 12:40); and he was probably drawing an illustration from contemporary life when he told the story of the widow who by her persistence in demanding justice was wearing out the judge! (Lk. 18:1–5). More often widows were left in penury. One of the earliest good works that engaged the attention of the church at Jerusalem was an organized daily distribution of alms to widows in need; and seven men were appointed to see that the Gk.-speaking widows were not overlooked in favour of those who spoke Aramaic (Acts 6:1–4). Acts also gives a striking illustration of charity shown by one individual when, after the death of Tabitha, it records that 'all the widows' at Joppa assembled to testify before Peter to the kindness she had shown to them (9:39).

Paul told the Corinthians that he thought it good that widows should not marry again, but he was far from making this a rule. Remarriage, however, should be within the Christian fellowship (see 1 Cor. 7:8–9, 39). On the other hand, in writing to Timothy, he expresses his desire that *young* widows should marry again; and urges that widows 'in the full sense', *i.e.* those who have no relatives to support them, and who are regular in their religious duties, should be given a special status and be a charge upon the church. A roll should be kept of these, and only those should be placed upon it who were over 60 years of age and who had given evidence of their good works, by caring for children, by hospitality or by rendering service to those of God's people who were in distress (1 Tim. 5:9–10).

In Rev. 18:7 'widow' is used metaphorically of a city bereaved of its inhabitants and stricken by plague and famine.

BIBLIOGRAPHY. S. Solle, *NIDNTT* 3, pp. 1073–1075. J.D.D. R.V.G.T.

WILDERNESS. In Scripture the words rendered 'wilderness' or 'desert' include not only the barren deserts of sand dunes or rock that colour the popular imagination of a desert, but also steppe-lands and pasture lands suitable for grazing livestock.

The commonest Heb. word is *miḏbār*, a word already well-attested in Canaanite epics from Ugarit (14th century BC, going back to earlier origin) as *mdbr* (Gordon, *Ugaritic Manual*, 3, 1955, p. 254, No. 458). This word can indicate grassy pastures (Ps. 65:12; Joel 2:22), supporting sheep (*cf.* Ex. 3:1), sometimes burnt up by the summer droughts (Je. 23:10; Joel 1:19–20), as well as denoting desolate wastes of rock and sand (Dt. 32:10; Jb. 38:26). The same applies to Gk. *erēmos* in the NT; note that the 'desert' (AV; RSV 'lonely place') of Mt. 14:15 does not lack 'much grass' (Jn. 6:10).

The Heb. *y^e šîmôn*, sometimes rendered as a proper name 'Jeshimon', is used of relatively bare wildernesses in Judaea in 1 Sa. 23:19, 24; 26:1, 3. The wilderness viewed from Pisgah (Nu. 21:20; 23:28; *cf.* Dt. 34:1ff.) would doubtless include the marly waste-lands on either side of the Jordan's channel before it entered the Dead Sea, the slopes of Pisgah and its range into the Jordan valley, and perhaps the edges of the Judaean wilderness opposite, behind Jericho and N and S of Qumran. For general references, *cf.* Dt. 32:10; Ps. 107:4; Is. 43:19. Besides its use as a proper name for the long rift valley from the Dead Sea to the Gulf of Aqabah, the term *ʿ^a rāḇâ* can be used as a common noun for steppe or scrubland where wild creatures must seek out their food (Jb. 24:5; Je. 17:6) or else of barren desert (Jb. 39:6 in parallel with saltflats). The words *ṣiyyâ*, 'dry lands' (Jb. 30:3; Ps. 78:17) and *tōhû*, 'empty waste' (Jb. 6:18;12:24; Ps. 107:40) likewise refer to barren, uninhabitable deserts. K.A.K.

WILDERNESS OF WANDERING.

I. Limits

After leaving Egypt by crossing the Sea of Reeds (Ex. 14:10–15:27), and until they finally by-passed Edom and Moab to reach the Jordan (Nu. 20ff.), Israel spent long years in the intervening territory, comprising (1) the peninsula of Sinai flanked by the Gulfs of Suez and Aqabah and separated from the Mediterranean on the N by the dusty 'way of the land of the Philistines' that linked Egypt to Palestine, (2) the long Arabah rift-valley extending

S from the Dead Sea to the Gulf of Aqabah, and (3) the wilderness of Zin S of Beersheba.

II. Physical features

The road from Egypt by 'the way of the land of the Philistines' to Raphia (Rafa) and Gaza, runs roughly parallel with the Mediterranean coast, passing through and along the N fringes of a barren sandy desert—the wilderness of *Shur—which lies between the line of the modern Suez Canal and the Wadi el-'Arish (River of *Egypt), and then through cultivable land which becomes more evident between El-'Arish and Gaza (*Negeb; *cf.* A. H. Gardiner, *JEA* 6, 1920, pp. 114–115; C. S. Jarvis, *Yesterday and Today in Sinai*, 1931, p. 107); 30–60 km S of the coast road runs the 'way of the wilderness of Shur', from Egypt to the region of Kadesh and NE to Beersheba. S of this road there gradually rise the hills and wadis of the limestone plateau of Et-Tih which, from a 'base-line' N of a line drawn between the heads of the Suez and Aqabah Gulfs, occupies a great semi-circle projecting into the peninsula of Sinai. Across the plateau to Aqabah ran an ancient trade-route. S of the plateau is a triangular-shaped area of granite, gneiss and other hard, crystalline rocks forming mountain ranges, which include the traditional Mt Sinai, several peaks rising to 2,000 m. This region is separated at its NW and NE corners from the limestone plateau by sandstone hills containing deposits of copper ores and turquoise. In the E the limestone plateau of Et-Tih gives way to the jumbled rocks and wadis of the S Negeb, bounded by the Rift Valley of the Arabah between the Dead Sea and the Gulf of Aqabah.

There are wells and springs at intervals of a day's journey all down the W coast from the Suez region to Merkhah; the water-table is usually close to the gravelly ground-surface. The wadis usually have some kind of scanty vegetation; where more permanent streams exist, notably in the broad Wadi Feiran (the finest oasis in Sinai), the vegetation flourishes accordingly. There is a 'rainy season' (up to 20 days) during winter, with mists, fogs and dews.

In the past, there has been much and persistent wholesale destruction of tamarisk and acacia groves for firewood and charcoal, there being a steady export of the latter to Egypt in the 19th century (Stanley, *Sinai and Palestine*, 1905 edn., p. 25). Thus, in ancient times the Sinai peninsula may have had more vegetation in its wadis and consequently better rains; but there has apparently been no fundamental climatic change since antiquity.

III. The route of the journeyings

The precise route taken by Israel from the Sea of Reeds (between Qantara and Suez; *Red Sea) to the edges of Moab is still conjectural, as almost none of the names of Israelite stopping-places has survived in the late, fluid and descriptive Arabic nomenclature of the peninsula of Sinai. Various stopping-places were named by the Israelites in relation to events that occurred on their travels, *e.g.* Kibroth-hattaavah, 'graves of craving' (Nu. 11:34), and they left no sedentary population behind to perpetuate such names. Furthermore, the traditions attaching to the present Mt Sinai (Gebel Musa and environs) have not been traced back beyond the early Christian centuries; this does not of itself prove those traditions wrong, but permits of no certainty. The traditional route ascribed to the Israelites is certainly a possible one. From the wilderness of *Shur they are usually considered to have passed S along the W coast-strip of the Sinai peninsula, Marah and Elim often being placed at 'Ain Hawarah and Wadi Gharandel respectively. That the camp after Elim (Ex. 16:1) is 'by the *yam sûp̄*' (Heb. of Nu. 33:10), *i.e.* the Sea of Reeds, or here by extension the Gulf of Suez (*cf.* *Red Sea), indicates clearly that Israel had kept to the W side of the Sinai peninsula and not gone N (the way of the Philistines). The Gulf of Aqabah is too far away to be the *yam sûp̄* in this passage. Somewhat later, Israel encamped at Dophkah. This name is sometimes considered to mean 'smeltery' (G. E. Wright, *Biblical Archaeology*, 1957, p. 64; Wright and Filson, *Westminster Historical Atlas of the Bible*, 1957 edn., p. 39) and so to be located at the Egyp. mining centre of Serabit el-Khadim. For copper and especially turquoise mining in that area, see Lucas, *Ancient Egyptian Materials and Industries*, 1962, pp. 202–205, 404–405; J. Cerný, A. H. Gardiner and T. E. Peet, *Inscriptions of Sinai*, 2, 1955, pp. 5–8.

As Egyp. expeditions visited this region only during January to March (rarely later), and did not live permanently at the mines (*cf.* Petrie, *Researches in Sinai*, 1906, p. 169), the Israelites would not meet them there, as they left Egypt in the month Abib (Ex. 13:4), *i.e.* about March (*cf.* *Plagues of Egypt), and left Elim a month later (Ex. 16:1), *i.e.* about April. However, Dophkah could be any copper-mining spot in the metalliferous sandstone belt across S-central Sinai (which favours a S route for Israel in any case). Rephidim is sometimes identified with Wadi Feiran, sometimes with Wadi Refayid, and Mt Sinai with the summits of Gebel Musa (or, less likely, Mt Serbal near Feiran). See the works of Robinson, Lepsius, Stanley and Palmer (Bibliography below). Beyond Mt Sinai, Dhahab on the E coast might be Di-zahab (Dt. 1:1; so Y. Aharoni, *Antiquity and Survival*, 2. 2/3, 1957, pp. 289–290, fig. 7); if so, Hud-erah on a different road is less likely to be the Hazeroth of Nu. 11:35; 33:17–18. The next fixed points are Kadesh-barnea (*Kadesh) on the borders of the wilderness(es) of Zin and Paran (Nu. 12:16; 13:26) at 'Ain Qudeirat or 'Ain Qudeis and the surrounding region, including 'Ain Qudeirat, and Ezion-geber at the head of the Gulf of Aqabah (Nu. 33:35f.).

For the phenomenon of the earth swallowing up Korah, Dathan and Abiram (Nu. 16), a most interesting explanation was offered by G. Hort, *Australian Biblical Review* 7, 1959, pp. 2–26, especially 19–26. She would locate this incident in the Arabah Rift Valley between the Dead Sea and the Gulf of Aqabah. Here are to be found mudflats known as *kewirs.* A hard crust of clayey mud overlying layers of hard salt and half-dry mud, about 30 cm thick, eventually forms over the deep mass of liquid mud and ooze. When this crust is hard it may be walked on with impunity, but increased humidity (especially rainstorms) will break up the crust and turn the whole into gluey mud. Dathan, Abiram and Korah's adherents withdrew from the main camp probably to one of these deceptively level, hard mudflats. From his long years of experience in Sinai and Midian (Ex. 2–4), Moses had probably learnt of this phenomenon, but not so the Israelites. When a storm approached he saw the danger and called the Israelites away from the tents of the rebels. The crust broke up and the rebels, their families and their possessions were all swallowed up in the mud. Then the storm broke, and the 250 men with censers were struck by lightning—smitten down by the fire of the Lord.

Miss Hort thought that this incident occurred at Kadesh-barnea, and therefore that Kadesh should be located in the Arabah. But there are possible reasons for locating *Kadesh in the region of 'Ain Qudeis and 'Ain Qudeirat, and in fact Nu. 16 does *not* state that the revolt(s) of Korah, Dathan and Abiram occurred at Kadesh. It should be noted that it is the whole, unitary account of the twin rebellions in Nu. 16 and their awesome end that alone makes sense and fits the physical phenomena in question; the supposed sources obtained by conventional documentary literary analyses severally yield fragmentary pictures that correspond to no known realities.

The long list of names in Nu. 33:19–35 fall into the 38 years of wandering, and cannot be located at present. The precise route past Edom (Nu. 20:22ff.; 21; 33:38–44) is also obscure. Some of the incidents in these long journeys reflect the natural phenomena of the area. The repeated phenomenon of water coming from the smitten rock (Ex. 17:1–7; Nu. 20:2–13) reflects the water-holding properties of Sinai limestone: an army NCO once produced quite a good flow of water when he accidentally hit such a rock face with a spade! See Jarvis, *Yesterday and Today in Sinai*, 1931, pp. 174–175. The digging of wells as recorded in Nu. 21:16–18 (*cf.* Gn. 26:19) reflects the known occurrence of sub-surface water in various regions of Sinai, the Negeb and S Transjordan (see references above, and N. Glueck, *Rivers in the Desert*, 1959, p. 22). The references to the catching of quail (Ex. 16:13; Nu. 11:31–35) have been interpreted by some as requiring a N route for the Exodus along the Mediterranean (*e.g.* Jarvis, *op. cit.*, pp. 169–170; *cf.* J. Bright, *A History of Israel*, 1960, p. 114, after J. Gray, *VT* 4, 1954, pp. 148–154; G. E. Wright, *Biblical Archaeology*, 1957, p. 65). But that route was explicitly forbidden to Israel (Ex. 13:17f.), and in any case the quails land on the Mediterranean coast of Sinai (from Europe) only in the *autumn* and at dawn, whereas Israel found them in the *spring* in the evening, in or following Abib, *i.e.* March (Ex. 16:13), and a year and a month later (Nu. 10:11; 11:31). These two points exclude the Mediterranean coast from Israel's route on these two occasions, and directly favour the S route by the Gulfs of Suez and Aqabah *via* 'Mt Sinai'. The quails return to Europe in the spring—the season when Israel twice had them—across the upper ends of the Gulfs of Suez and Aqabah, and in the evening (Lucas, *The Route of the Exodus*, 1938, pp. 58–63 and refs., and p. 81, overstressing Aqabah at the expense of Suez).

A minority view would make Israel cross the Sinai peninsula more directly to the head of the Gulf of Aqabah and locate Mt Sinai in Midian. Among the best advocates of such a view is Lucas (*The Route of the Exodus*, 1938) who does not invoke non-existent active volcanoes as some have done. However, this view is no freer of topographical difficulties than any other, and fails entirely to account for the origin of the traditions of the Christian period that attached themselves to the peninsula now called Sinai and not to Midian or NW Arabia.

For a good comparative table of the data on the route and stopping-places on Israel's wanderings in Exodus–Numbers, Nu. 33 and Deuteronomy, see J. D. Davis and H. S. Gehman, *WDB*, pp. 638–639; literary background, *cf.* G. I. Davies, *TynB* 25, 1974, pp. 46–81; Bronze Age sites in Sinai, *cf.* T. L. Thompson, *The Settlement of Sinai and the Negev in the Bronze Age*, 1975.

IV. The numbers of the Israelites

When Israel left Egypt there went '600,000 men on foot' besides their families and the mixed multitude, while from a census of the men from the tribes other than Levi held at Sinai comes the total of 603,550 men over 20 who could bear arms (Nu. 2:32). These figures are commonly held to imply a total number of Israelites—men, women and children—of somewhat more than two million. That the slender resources of Sinai were of themselves insufficient to support such a multitude is indicated by the Bible itself (as well as suggested by exploration) in that Israel's chief sustenance came from God-given *manna (Ex. 16; *cf.* vv. 3–4, 35). Israel never went wholly without (Dt. 2:7), although the water-supply sometimes nearly failed them (*e.g.* at Rephidim, Ex. 17:1; Kadesh, Nu. 20:2). In any case, they would soon learn to subsist on very little water per head indeed, as illustrated by Robinson's guide in Sinai, who was able to go without water for a fortnight by living on camel's milk, while sheep and goats as well as camels can sometimes go without water for 3–4 months if they have had fresh pasture (E. Robinson, *Biblical Researches*, 1, 1841 ed., p. 221).

Furthermore, it is wholly misleading to imagine the Israelites marching in long 'columns of four' up and down Sinai, or trying to encamp all together *en masse* in some little wadi at each stop. They would be spread out in their tribal and family groups, occupying a variety of neighbouring wadis for all their scattered encampments; after they left Sinai with the ark and tabernacle (as baggage when on the move), the sites where these were successively lodged would be the focus of the various tribal camps, as in Nu. 2. In various parts of Sinai the water-table is near the ground-surface; the scattered Israelite encampments would thus often get the little they needed by digging small pits over an area. *Cf.* Robinson, *Biblical Researches*, 1, 1841, pp. 100 (general observations), 129; Lepsius, *Letters, etc.*, 1853, p. 306; Currelly in Petrie, *Researches in Sinai*, 1906, p. 249; Lucas, *The Route of the Exodus*, 1938, p. 68.

There have been many attempts down the years to interpret the census-lists in Nu. 1 and 26 and related figures in Ex. 12:37; 38:24–29, besides the levitical reckoning (Nu. 4:21–49) and other figures (*e.g.* Nu. 16:49), in order to gain from the Heb. text a more modest total for the number of the people of Israel involved in the Exodus from Egypt through Sinai to Palestine. For recent attempts, see R. E. D. Clark, *JTVI* 87, 1955, pp. 82–92 (taking *'lp* as 'officer' instead of '1,000' in many cases); G. E. Mendenhall, *JBL* 77, 1958, pp. 52–66 (taking *'lp* as a tribal sub-unit instead of '1,000'), who refers to earlier treatments; and J. W. Wenham, *TynB* 18, 1967, pp. 19–53, esp. 27ff., 35ff. While none of these attempts accounts for all the figures involved, they indicate several possible clues to a better understanding of various apparently high figures in the OT. The fact is that these records must rest on some basis of ancient reality; the apparently high figures are beyond absolute disproof, while no alternative interpretation has yet adequately accounted for all the data involved. (*NUMBER.)

V. Later significance

Theologically, the wilderness period became the dual symbol of God's leading and providing and of man's rebellious nature typified by the Israelites (*cf.*, *e.g.*, Dt. 8:15–16; 9:7; Am. 2:10; 5:25 (*cf.* Acts 7:40–44); Ho. 13:5–6; Je. 2:6; Ezk. 20:10–26, 36; Pss. 78:14–41; 95:8–11 (*cf.* Heb. 3:7–19); 136:16; Ne. 9:18–22; Acts 13:18; 1 Cor. 10:3–5).

BIBLIOGRAPHY. E. Robinson, *Biblical Researches in Palestine, Mount Sinai and Arabia Petraea*, 1, 1841 edn., pp. 98–100, 129, 131, 179; C. R. Lepsius, *Letters from Egypt, Ethiopia and the Peninsula of Sinai*, 1853, pp. 306–307; A. P. Stanley, *Sinai and Palestine*, 1905 ed., pp. 16–19, 22, 24–27; E. H. Palmer, *The Desert of the Exodus*, 1, 1871, pp. 22–26; W. M. F. Petrie and C. T. Currelly, *Researches in Sinai*, 1906, pp. 12, 30, 247–250, 254–256 (Feiran), 269; C. L. Woolley and T. E. Lawrence, *Palestine Exploration Fund Annual*, 3, 1915, p. 33; C. S. Jarvis, *Yesterday and Today in Sinai*, 1931, p. 99; A. E. Lucas, *The Route of the Exodus*, 1938, pp. 19, 44–45, 68; W. F. Albright, *BASOR* 109, 1948, p. 11 (El-'Arish rains; scrub vegetation in N). For Sinai scenery, see G. E. Wright, *Biblical Archaeology*, 1957, pp. 62–64, figs. 33–35; or L. H. Grollenberg, *Shorter Atlas of the Bible*, 1959, pp. 76–77; Petrie, *Researches in Sinai*, 1906, *passim*; B. Rothenberg, *God's Wilderness*, 1961, *passim*. K.A.K.

WIND (Heb. *rûaḥ*). **1.** The Hebrews conceived of climate as influenced by the four winds from the four corners of the earth (Je. 49:36; Dn. 7:2; Rev. 7:1). The wind may be a source of blessing or a curse, according to its source. Its vast power suggests the wind is the breath of God (Is. 40:7), controlled by him (Ps. 107:25; Pr. 30:4; Mk. 4:41), created by him (Am. 4:13) and creative for his purposes (Gn. 1:2; Ezk. 37:9).

2. As compound names for winds are impossible in Hebrew, the four cardinal points are used freely to describe other directions (Ezk. 37:9; Dn. 8:8; Zc. 2:6; Mt. 24:31; Rev. 7:1).

a. The N wind (*rûaḥ ṣāp̄ôn*) is associated with cold conditions, the NE wind dispersing the rain (Jb. 37:9, 22; Pr. 25:23).

b. The S wind (*rûaḥ dārôm*) is variable in its effects, whether tempestuous (Is. 21:1; Zc. 9:14) or gentle (Acts 27:13). The sirocco, usually associated with the S wind, is particularly hot and desiccating, a katabatic wind which descends from the highlands of Sinai and Arabia (Jb. 37:16–17; Je. 4:11; Ho. 12:1; Lk. 12:55). But the katabatic effects can be caused wherever there is a sudden change of gradient, so that its effects are also described as E winds (Is. 27:8; Ezk. 17:10; Ho. 13:15; Jon. 4:8). It destroys the grass, and all vegetation wilts (Ps. 103:16; Is. 40:6–8; Jas. 1:11).

c. The E wind (*rûaḥ qāḏîm*) is similarly described as a dry wind from the wilderness (Jb. 1:19; Je. 4:11; 13:24), strong and gusty (Ex. 14:21; Jb. 27:21; 38:24; Je. 18:17) and with scorching heat (Am. 4:9; Ho. 13:15), affecting the vegetation (Gn. 41:6, 23, 27; Ezk. 17:10; 19:12).

d. The W wind (*rûaḥ yām*) is in Arabic described as 'the father of rain' (1 Ki. 18:44–45; Lk. 12:54). Distinction, however, should be made between the diurnal sea breezes which are a marked feature of the coast in summer, bringing down the high temperatures, and the westerlies which blow strongly in winter, exposing all anchorages to NW gales. The wind is symbolic of nothingness (Is. 41:29) and of the transitoriness of man (Ps. 78:39), and is used also in connection with the Spirit of God (Jn. 3:8; Acts 2:2; *SPIRIT, HOLY).

e. Euraquilo (RV, rightly, for AV 'Euroclydon'), a hybrid formation from Gk. *euros*, 'east wind', and Lat. *aquilo*, 'north wind', and probably a nautical term, is the name given to the typhonic storm described at Paul's shipwreck (Acts 27:14). J. Smith has made a strong case for the wind being the 'north-easter' (so RSV, NEB), and that the shipwreck was, in fact, off the coast of *Malta. Recently, A. Acworth argued that the shipwreck was situated off Mljet in the Adriatic and that the wind was a south-easter. This has been conclusively challenged by C. J. Hemer, who reaffirms the location off Malta. Maltese sailors use the term 'gregale' to refer to violent winds, accompanied by sea-storms in the winter season, associated with depressions over Libya or the Gulf of Gabes. A small Rom. ship, caught in such a storm, having crossed Sicily, would welcome the sighting of the Maltese islands. For there stretched another 320 km or more of open sea between them and safety on the Tunisian coast.

BIBLIOGRAPHY. J. Smith, *Voyage and Shipwreck of St. Paul*[4], 1880, pp. 287–291; see also A. Acworth, 'Where was St. Paul shipwrecked? A re-examination of the evidence', *JTS* n.s. 24, 1973, pp. 190–192; C. J. Hemer, 'Euraquilo and Melita', *JTS* n.s. 26, 1975, pp. 100–111. J.M.H.

WINE AND STRONG DRINK.

I. In the Old Testament

Among a considerable number of synonyms used in the OT the most common are *yayin* (usually translated 'wine') and *šēḵār* (usually translated 'strong drink'). These terms are frequently used together, and they are employed irrespective of whether the writer is commending wine and strong drink as desirable or warning against its dangers. A third word, *tîrôš*, sometimes translated 'new' or 'sweet wine', has often been regarded as unfermented and therefore unintoxicating wine, but an example such as Ho. 4:11, together with the usage of the Talmud, makes clear that it is capable of being used in a bad sense equally with the others. Furthermore, while there are examples of the grapes being pressed into a cup and presumably used at once (Gn. 40:11), it is significant that the term 'wine' is never applied to the resultant juice.

The term 'new wine' does not indicate wine which has not fermented, for in fact the process of fermentation sets in very rapidly, and unfermented wine could not be available many months after the harvest (Acts 2:13). It represents rather wine made from the first drippings of the juice before the winepress was trodden. As such it would be particularly potent and would come immediately to mind as a probable explanation of what seemed to be a drunken state. Modern custom in Palestine, among a people who are traditionally conservative as far as religious feasts are concerned, also suggests that the wine used was fermented. It may be said, therefore, that the Bible in employing various synonyms makes no consistent distinction between them.

Naturally in a land and climate particularly suited to the cultivation of the vine, we find that wine was often associated with grain, and together they stand for a full and adequate supply of food and of the good gifts of life. They can be promised therefore as the tokens of the blessing of God (Gn. 27:28), and they are acceptable to him when offered back upon the altar (Ex. 29:40). As a discipline, however, they are on occasion to be dispensed with, as when a man engages in priestly service (Lv. 10:9), or in the case of a *Nazirite during the course of his vow (Nu. 6:3). The abstinence of the *Rechabites falls within a different category, for it was in an attempt to preserve the nomadic life that they dwelt in tents, and their refusal of wine was not on account of the dangers of its abuse, but because they were associated with the planting of vineyards, the sowing of seed and the building of houses (Je. 35:7). Evidence is by no means lacking, however, that even to those who accepted the agricultural way of life the dangers of strong drink were apparent. The warnings of the book of Proverbs are clear, and in the time of Isaiah even the priests fell into the snare.

These two aspects of wine, its use and its abuse, its benefits and its curse, its acceptance in God's sight and its abhorrence, are interwoven into the fabric of the OT so that it may gladden the heart of man (Ps. 104:15) or cause his mind to err (Is. 28:7), it can be associated with merriment (Ec. 10:19) or with anger (Is. 5:11), it can be used to uncover the shame of Noah (Gn. 9:21) or in the hands of Melchizedek to honour Abraham (Gn. 14:18).

In metaphorical usage the same characteristics are to be observed. Wine may represent that which God himself has prepared (Pr. 9:5), and which he offers to as many as will receive it from his hand (Is. 55:1); yet, on the other hand, it may equally well represent the intoxicating influence of Babylonian supremacy which brings ruin (Je. 51:7).

II. In the New Testament

In the NT the common word is Gk. *oinos* (*cf.* Heb. *yayin*). Once we find *sikera*, 'strong drink' (Lk. 1:15), a loan-word from Semitic (*cf.* Heb. *šēḵār*), and once *gleukos*, 'new wine' (Acts 2:13). This last word means literally 'sweet wine'; the vintage of the current year had not yet come, but there were means of keeping wine sweet all year round.

The references in the NT are very much fewer in number, but once more the good and the bad aspects are equally apparent, and many of the points which we noticed in the OT have their counterpart in the NT. John the Baptist is to abstain from wine in view of his special commission (Lk. 1:15), but this does not imply that of itself wine is evil, for Jesus is not only present at the wedding in Cana of Galilee, but when the wine fails he replenishes the supply in extraordinarily ample measure, and later his readiness to eat and drink with publicans and sinners draws forth the accusation that he is gluttonous and a wine-bibber. The refusal of Jesus to drink the wine offered to him in accordance with Jewish custom at his crucifixion (Mk. 15:23) was not based upon an objection to wine as such, but was due to a determination to die with an unclouded mind. Later he accepted the wine (vinegar) which was the ordinary drink of labourers in the field and of the lower class of soldiers.

On more than one occasion Jesus used wine to illustrate his teaching. Mk. 2:22 points to the current practice of putting new wine into new skins and emphasizes the impracticality of doing otherwise. Commentators differ regarding the interpretation of this parable. For, while the new wine clearly points to the lively and powerful working of Christ's new teaching, the skins which are broken may equally well refer to certain conventional forms or to the whole Judaistic system or to the human heart, all of which need to be recast in accordance with the challenge of the new age which has arrived. Unfortunately the Pharisees were unwilling to face the changes which would have been involved, and obstinately clung to the system upon which their livelihood depended (Lk. 5:39).

Metaphorically in the NT the word 'wine' is again used in both a good and a bad sense. The latter is found several times in Revelation, where the inhabitants of the earth are depicted as having been made drunk by the fornication of Babylon (Rev. 17:2) while she herself is drunk with their blood (Rev. 17:6). On the other hand, Paul exhorts his readers to be filled with the Spirit (Eph. 5:18) in contrast with their being intoxicated with wine. There are, of course, certain similarities between the two conditions, a consideration which may well have led Paul to express himself in this way. Certainly on the Day of Pentecost there were many who took the evidences of the Spirit to be nothing else than the result of strong drink. This same interpretation had been placed long before upon the movement of the lips of Hannah as she prayed in the presence of Eli, a supposed fault which Eli was quicker to rebuke in her than in his own sons (1 Sa. 1:14).

Timothy is exhorted by Paul to take a little wine because of its medicinal properties (1 Tim. 5:23; *cf.* its application in a different form in the story of the good Samaritan), but in the Pastoral Epistles there is a recognition of the grave dangers of excess, and those who bear office or in any way give leadership within the Christian community, both men and women, are specifically warned against this fault, which would unfit them for their task (1 Tim. 3:8; Tit. 2:3). This abuse is particularly unfitting within the church, for if it is true that drunkenness is in general a sign of heedlessness in spiritual matters, and a disregard of the imminent return of Christ (Rom. 13:13), how much more is it to be deplored at the Lord's table, where it reveals not only a spirit of complete indifference towards God but a spirit of utter thoughtlessness in regard to those who stand together within the Christian fellowship (1 Cor. 11:21).

To sum up, then, it may be said that while wine is not condemned as being without usefulness, it brings in the hands of sinful men such dangers of becoming uncontrolled that even those who count themselves to be strong would be wise to abstain, if not for their own sake, yet for the sake of weaker brethren (Rom. 14:21). If it is argued that there are many other things which may be abused besides wine, the point may be immediately conceded, but wine has so often proved itself to be peculiarly fraught with danger that Paul names it specifically at the same time as he lays down the general principle. That this principle has application within the setting of modern life is beyond dispute among those who take their Christian responsibility seriously.

BIBLIOGRAPHY. C. Seltman, *Wine in the Ancient World*, 1957; J. P. Free, *Archaeology and Bible History*, 1950, Appendix II, pp. 351ff.; 'Wine' in *TWBR*; 'Food' in *HDB*, 2, p. 32; C. Brown, *NIDNTT* 3, pp. 918–923. F.S.F.

WISDOM.

I. In the Old Testament

Like all Heb. intellectual virtues, wisdom (generally *ḥokmâ*, though other words are used; *e.g.*: *bînâ*, 'understanding', Jb. 39:26; Pr. 23:4; *tᵉbûnâ*, 'insight', Ps. 136:5; *śekel* or *śēkel*, 'prudence', Pr. 12:8; 23:9) is intensely practical, not theoretical. Basically, wisdom is the art of being successful, of forming the correct plan to gain the desired results. Its seat is the heart, the centre of moral and intellectual decision (*cf.* 1 Ki. 3:9, 12).

Those who possess technical skill are called wise: Bezalel, chief artisan of the tabernacle (Ex. 31:3; RSV 'ability'); artificers of idols (Is. 40:20; Je. 10:9); professional mourners (Je. 9:17); navigators or shipwrights (Ezk. 27:8–9). Practical wisdom may take on a sinister aspect, as in Jonadab's crafty advice (2 Sa. 13:3).

Kings and leaders were in special need of wisdom. On them hung the responsibility for correct decisions in political and social affairs. Joshua (Dt. 34:9), David (2 Sa. 14:20), Solomon (1 Ki. 3:9, 12; 4:29ff.) were granted wisdom to enable them to deal with their official duties. The Messianic King predicted by Isaiah (11:2) was to be equipped with wisdom to judge impartially. 'Wonderful Counsellor' (9:6) avers that his advice would be amazingly successful. See N. W. Porteous, 'Royal Wisdom', in *Wisdom in Israel and in the Ancient Near East*.

A special class of wise men (or women, *cf.* 2 Sa. 14:2) seems to have developed during the Monarchy. By Jeremiah's time they had taken their place beside prophets and priests as a major religious and social influence. Their task was to formulate workable plans, to prescribe advice for successful living (Je. 18:18). For the view that 'wise men' described not a professional class but persons of uncommon intelligence whose wisdom was sought after by their fellow citizens, see R. N. Whybray, *The Intellectual Tradition in the Old Testament* (1974). The wise man or counsellor stood in a parental relationship to those whose well-being hinged on his advice: Joseph was a 'father' to the pharaoh (Gn. 45:8); Deborah, a 'mother' in Israel (Jdg. 5:7). See P. A. H. de Boer, 'The Counsellor' in *Wisdom in Israel and in the Ancient Near East*.

Wisdom in the fullest sense belongs to God alone (Jb. 12:13ff.; Is. 31:2; Dn. 2:20–23). His wisdom is not only completeness of knowledge pervading every realm of life (Jb. 10:4; 26:6; Pr. 5:21; 15:3) but also 'consists in his irresistible fulfilment of what he has in his mind' (J. Pedersen, *Israel: Its Life and Culture*, 1–2, p. 198). The universe (Pr. 3:19f.; 8:22–31; Je. 10:12) and man (Jb. 10:8ff.; Ps. 104:24; Pr. 14:31; 22:2) are products of his creative wisdom. Natural (Is. 28:23–29) and historical (Is. 31:2) processes are governed by his wisdom, which includes an infallible discrimination between good and evil and is the basis for the just rewards and punishments which are the lot of the righteous and the wicked (Pss. 1; 37; 73; Pr. 10:3; 11:4; 12:2, *etc.*). Such wisdom is inscrutable (Jb. 28:12–21): God in his grace must reveal it if man is going to grasp it at all (Jb. 28:23, 28). Even wisdom derived from natural abilities or distilled from experience is a gracious gift, because God's creative activity makes such wisdom possible.

Biblical wisdom is both religious and practical. Stemming from the fear of the Lord (Jb. 28:28; Ps. 111:10; Pr. 1:7; 9:10), it branches out to touch all of life, as the extended commentary on wisdom in Proverbs indicates. Wisdom takes insights gleaned from the knowledge of God's ways and applies them in the daily walk. This combination of insight and obedience (and all insight must issue in obedience) relates wisdom to the prophetic emphasis on the knowledge (*i.e.* the cordial love and obedience) of God (*e.g.* Ho. 2:20; 4:1, 6; 6:6; Je. 4:22; 9:3, 6; and especially Pr. 9:10).

Pagan wisdom, though it, too, may be religious, has no anchor in the covenant-God and, therefore, is doomed to failure, as the prophets frequently point out (Is. 19:11ff.; Ezk. 28:2ff.; Ob. 8). When secularism, materialism and disdain of the covenant-ideals squeezed the fear of God out of Israel's wisdom, it became practical atheism, as vapid as its pagan counterpart, and drew Isaiah's fire: 'Woe to those who are wise in their own eyes' (5:21; *cf.* 29:14; Je. 18:18).

A special problem is the personification of wisdom in Pr. 8:22ff. Jb. 28 anticipates this personification by depicting wisdom as a mystery inscrutable to men but apparent to God. In Pr. 1:20–33 wisdom is likened to a woman crying in the streets for men to turn from their foolish ways and to find instruction and security in her (*cf.* also Pr. 3:15–20). The personification continues in Pr. 8 and reaches its climax in vv. 22ff., where wisdom claims to be the first creation of God and, perhaps, an assistant in the work of creation (8:30; *cf.* 3:19; the difficult *'āmôn*, 'as one brought up' in AV, should be translated 'master workman', as in RV, RSV; see W. F. Albright in *Wisdom in Israel and in the Ancient Near East*, p. 8). The purpose of wisdom's recitation of her credentials is to attract men to pay her rightful heed, as 8:32–36 indicates. Therefore, caution must be exercised in reading into this passage a view of hypostatization, *i.e.* that wisdom is depicted as having an independent existence. The Hebrews' characteristic resistance to speculation and abstraction frequently led their poets to deal with inanimate objects or ideals as though they had personality. See H. W. Robinson, *Inspiration and Revelation in the Old Testament*, 1946, p. 260; H. Ringgren, *Word and Wisdom*, 1947. For the influence of the personification of wisdom on the Logos idea of the Fourth Gospel, see * LOGOS.

II. In the New Testament

By and large NT wisdom (*sophia*) has the same intensely practical nature as in the OT. Seldom neutral (although *cf.* 'the wisdom of the Egyptians', Acts 7:22), it is either God-given or God-opposing. If divorced from God's revelation it is impoverished and unproductive at best (1 Cor. 1:17; 2:4; 2 Cor. 1:12) and foolish or even devilish at worst (1 Cor. 1:19ff.; Jas. 3:15ff.). Worldly wisdom is based on intuition and experience without revelation, and thus has severe limitations. The failure to recognize these limitations brings biblical condemnation on all (especially the Greeks) who haughtily attempt to cope with spiritual issues by human wisdom.

The truly wise are those to whom God has graciously imparted wisdom: Solomon (Mt. 12:42; Lk. 11:31), Stephen (Acts 6:10), Paul (2 Pet. 3:15), Joseph (Acts 7:10). One of Christ's legacies to his disciples was the wisdom to say the right thing in times of persecution and examination (Lk. 21:15). A similar wisdom is necessary for understanding the apocalyptic oracles and enigmas (Rev. 13:18;

17:9). Wisdom is essential not only for leaders of the church (Acts 6:3) but for all believers that they may perceive God's purposes in redemption (Eph. 1:8–9) and may walk worthily of God (Col. 1:9; Jas. 1:5; 3:13–17) and discreetly before unbelievers (Col. 4:5). As Paul has taught his hearers in all wisdom (Col. 1:28), so they who are mature enough to understand this spiritual wisdom (1 Cor. 2:6–7) are to instruct others in it (Col. 3:16).

God's wisdom is clearly demonstrated in his provision of redemption (Rom. 11:33), which is manifested in the church (Eph. 3:10). It is supremely revealed 'not in some esoteric doctrine . . . addressed to . . . initiates of some secret cult, but in action, God's supreme action in Christ on the Cross' (N. W. Porteous, *op. cit.*, p. 258). This wisdom, previously veiled to human minds, brooks no philosophical or practical rivals. The best attempts of men to untangle the problems of human existence are shown to be foolishness in the light of the cross.

The incarnate Christ grew in wisdom (Lk. 2:40, 52) as a boy and astonished his audiences by his wisdom as a man (Mt. 13:54; Mk. 6:2). His claims included wisdom (Mt. 12:42) and a unique knowledge of God (Mt. 11:25ff.). Twice he personifies wisdom in a manner reminiscent of Proverbs: Mt. 11:19 (= Lk. 7:35) and Lk. 11:49 (Mt. 23:34ff.). In both passages Christ may be alluding to himself as 'Wisdom', although this is not certain, especially in the latter instance. (See Arndt for suggested interpretations.) Paul's wisdom Christology (1 Cor. 1:24, 30) was probably influenced both by Christ's claims and by the apostolic consciousness (grounded in Christ's teachings in Matthew) that Christ was the *new Torah*, the complete revelation of God's will, replacing the old law. Since the commandments and wisdom are linked in Dt. 4:6, and especially in Jewish thought (*e.g.* Ecclus. 24:23; *Apocalypse of Baruch* 3:37ff.), it is not unexpected that Paul would view Jesus, the *new Torah*, as the wisdom of God. That Paul saw in Christ the fulfilment of Pr. 8:22ff. seems apparent from Col. 1:15ff., which strongly reflects the OT description of wisdom.

Paul's wisdom Christology is a dynamic concept, as is shown by the emphasis on Christ's activity in creation in Col. 1:15ff. and in redemption in 1 Cor. 1:24, 30. The latter verses affirm that in the crucifixion God made Jesus our wisdom, a wisdom further defined as embracing righteousness, sanctification and redemption. As the slain yet exalted Lord of the church, he is lauded for wisdom (Rev. 5:12). 'Receive' in this verse implies acknowledgment of attributes which are already Christ's; for in him 'are hid all the treasures of wisdom' (Col. 2:3).

BIBLIOGRAPHY. W. D. Davies, *Paul and Rabbinic Judaism*, 1948, pp. 147–176; R. E. Murphy, *The Tree of Life*, 1990; M. Noth and D. W. Thomas (eds.), *Wisdom in Israel and in the Ancient Near East*, 1955; L. G. Perdue, *Wisdom and Creation*, 1994; G. von Rad, *Wisdom in Israel*, 1972; E. J. Schnabel, *Law and Wisdom from Ben Sira to Paul*, 1985; B Witherington III, *Jesus the Sage*, 1994.

D.A.H.

WISDOM LITERATURE. A family of literary *genres* common in the ancient Near East in which instructions for successful living are given or the perplexities of human existence are contemplated. There are two broad types: proverbial (*PROVERB) wisdom—short, pithy sayings which state rules for personal happiness and welfare (*e.g.* Proverbs), and speculative wisdom—monologues (*e.g.* Ecclesiastes) or dialogues (*e.g.* Job) which attempt to delve into such problems as the meaning of existence and the relationship between God and man. This speculative wisdom is practical and empirical, not theoretical. Problems of human existence are discussed in terms of concrete examples: 'There was a man . . . whose name was Job.'

The roots of wisdom literature are probably to be found in short, crisp popular sayings which express rules for success or common observations concerning life. OT examples are found in 1 Ki. 20:11; Je. 23:28; 31:29, *inter al.* The transition from oral to literary wisdom took place in Egypt *c.* 2500 BC (*e.g. Instruction of the Vizier Ptah-Hotep*) and in Sumer shortly after. Throughout the Near East, a class of scribes or wise men arose whose highly honoured task was to create or collect and polish sagacious sayings (Ec. 12:9), usually under the patronage of court or temple. The sources of these sayings may have been clan wisdom, instruction in schools or sayings circulated among the nobility. Two of Israel's kings are credited with important contributions in this area: Solomon (1 Ki. 4:29–34) and Hezekiah (Pr. 25:1). By the 7th century BC the wise man (*ḥāḵām*) had assumed sufficient prominence in Judah to be classed with prophet or priest (Je. 8:8–9; 18:18), although there is some question as to whether he was yet viewed as a professional or merely as an unusually wise citizen. As the phenomenon of prophecy faded in the Persian and Greek periods, the wise men gained in stature, as the important apocryphal works, Ecclesiasticus and Wisdom of Solomon, and the Mishnaic tractate *Pirqe Aboth* (Sayings of the Fathers), show.

The wise men employed several literary devices as aids to memory. The most frequent device was the use of poetic parallelism of either a synthetic (*e.g.* Pr. 18:10) or antithetic (*e.g.* Pr. 10:1) type. Comparisons are common (*e.g.* Pr. 17:1), as are numerical sequences (*e.g.* Pr. 30:15ff.). Alliteration and acrostic patterns (*e.g.* Ps. 37; Pr. 31:10–31) are employed occasionally. Riddles (Jdg. 14:12ff.; *cf.* 1 Ki. 10:1), fables (*e.g.* Jdg. 9:7–15; Ezk. 17:3ff.; 19:1ff.), parables, which are extensions of the comparisons mentioned above (*e.g.* 2 Sa. 12:1–4; Is. 28:4), and allegories (*e.g.* Is. 5:1–7) are part of the wise man's repertoire. This sampling testifies to the impact made by wisdom literature on historical and prophetic writings. H. Gunkel has categorized certain psalms as wisdom poetry: Pss. 127; 133 (simple proverbial type); Pss. 1; 37; 49; 73; 112; 128. S. Mowinckel has called these psalms examples of 'learned psalmography'. Whether stories that teach responsible conduct as a key to success like those of Joseph (Gn. 37;39–50), the succession narrative (2 Sa. 9–20; 1 Ki. 1f.), Esther and Daniel bear wisdom's stamp is still under debate. *Cf.* R. N. Whybray, *The Intellectual Tradition in the Old Testament*, 1974; *contra* J. L. Crenshaw, 'Method in Determining Wisdom Influence upon "Historical" Literature', *JBL* 88, 1969, pp. 129–142). Wisdom's contribution is most readily discernible when its peculiar vocabulary, techniques and didactic content are all present in a text. Such influence is detectable in the NT, both in the teaching methods of Christ, who as the Master Sage employs parables and proverbs, and also in the Epistle of James (*e.g.* 1:5ff.; 3:13ff.).

Though an international phenomenon, as the

OT freely recognizes (Edom in 1 Ki. 4:31; Ob. 8; Je. 49:7; and Egypt in Gn. 41:8; 1 Ki. 4:30; Is. 19:11–15 were particularly renowned), wisdom literature has not escaped Israel's peculiar stamp. Israel's sages confessed that true wisdom stemmed from God (*cf.* Jb. 28). The impact of Israel's prophets upon her sages cannot be ignored. H. Wheeler Robinson (*Inspiration and Revelation in the Old Testament*, 1946, p. 241) goes so far as to define the wisdom movement as '*the discipline whereby was taught the application of prophetic truth to the individual life in the light of experience*'.

At the same time prophets like Amos, Isaiah and Jeremiah occasionally used the forms, techniques and teachings of wisdom literature to enrich and reinforce their oracles, as S. Terrien ('Amos and Wisdom', in *Israel's Prophetic Heritage*, ed. B. W. Anderson and W. Harrelson, 1962, pp. 108–115), H. W. Wolff (*Amos, the Prophet: the Man and His Background*, E.T. 1973) and J. W. Whedbee (*Isaiah and Wisdom*, 1970) have shown.

BIBLIOGRAPHY. J. L. Crenshaw (ed.), *Studies in Ancient Israelite Wisdom*, 1976; J. G. Gammie & L. G. Perdue (eds.), *The Sage in Israel and the Ancient Near East*, 1990; R. Murphy, *The Tree of Life: An Exploration of Biblical Wisdom Literature*, 1990; L. G. Perdue, *Wisdom and Creation: The Theology of Wisdom Literature*, 1994; G. von Rad, *Wisdom in Israel*, 1972. D.A.H.

WITNESS. In EVV 'to witness', 'to bear witness', a 'witness', 'to testify', 'testimony' (with a few minor additional renderings) represent a somewhat arbitrary and not always consistent rendering of the following Heb. and Gk. words. In the OT: *'ānâ* (lit. 'to answer'), *'ûḏ* (verb), *'ēḏ*, *'ēḏâ*, *'ēḏûṯ*, *tᵉ'ûḏâ*; in the NT: *martyreō* (verb) and compounds, *martys*, *martyria*, *martyrion*. Though 'to witness' is used with a wide range of connotations, the forensic often being virtually forgotten, it never occurs in the frequent modern Eng. usage as a synonym of 'to see'.

'ēḏ and its rare synonym *'ēḏâ* always refer to the person or thing bearing witness, examples of the latter being Gn. 31:48, 52; Jos. 22:27–28, 34; 24:27; Is. 19:20. The NT equivalent, *martys*, is used only of persons, there being no example of a thing as bearer of witness.

Heb., disliking abstracts, rarely speaks of witness in the sense of evidence given. In the three cases it does (Ru. 4:7; Is. 8:16, 20) it uses *tᵉ'ûḏâ*. Gk. uses the conception frequently, but distinguishes between *martyria*, the act of testifying or the testimony, and *martyrion*, that which may serve as evidence or proof or the fact established by evidence.

'ēḏûṯ, always rendered 'testimony' except in the AV of Nu. 17:7–8; 18:2; 2 Ch. 24:6, where it is 'witness', has lost its forensic meaning completely and is a technical religious term (*COVENANT), rendered by *KB* 'monitory sign, reminder, exhortation'. The outstanding example of *'ēḏûṯ* is the tables of the Ten Commandments (Ex. 16:34; 25:16, 21, *etc.*). Hence the ark which contained them became 'the ark of the testimony' (Ex. 25:22, *etc.*), the tent which sheltered them, 'the tent of the testimony' (Nu. 17:7), and the veil dividing off the Holy of holies, 'the veil of the testimony' (Lv. 24:3). The term is then enlarged to cover the law as a whole, *e.g.* Pss. 78:5; 119:2 and frequently. The meaning in 2 Ki. 11:12 is doubtful (see *ICC*, *ad loc.*).

AV translation 'martyr' in Acts 22:20; Rev. 2:13; 17:6 (in the last of these also RV, RSV) is hardly justified, though *martys* quickly developed this meaning; *cf.* Arndt, p. 495b.

BIBLIOGRAPHY. L. Coenen, A. A. Trites, *NIDNTT* 3, pp. 1038–1051; A. A. Trites, *The New Testament Concept of Witness*, 1977; *BA1CS* 6, f.c. H.L.E.

WOE. The rendering of the Gk. interjection *ouai*, meaning 'Alas for'. When Jesus says 'Woe unto you', he is not so much pronouncing a final judgment as deploring the miserable condition in God's sight of those he is addressing. Their wretchedness lies not least in the fact that they are living in a fool's paradise, unaware of the misery that awaits them. The state of the materially-minded blinded by wealth to their spiritual needs, of the self-satisfied, of the impenitent and unsympathetic, and of those who are universally popular is declared by Jesus to be wretched (Lk. 6:24–26). Similarly, the woeful condition of the Pharisees and scribes (Lk. 'lawyers') lies, Jesus tells them, in the hypocritical zeal, the lack of proportion, the love of display and the self-complacency which disfigure their religion (Mt. 23:13–33; Lk. 11:42–52). When Jesus addresses the words 'Woe to you' to the unrepentant cities Chorazin and Bethsaida, he follows them with a prophecy of the doom that awaits them (Mt. 11:21) as they are in a woeful state for having refused the gospel. Paul says he would be in a woeful state if he failed to preach it (1 Cor. 9:16). The seer in the Revelation uses the word *ouai* as an interjection in his dirge over fallen Babylon (Rev. 18:10–16), and as a noun to describe three 'woes', a comprehensive term covering various plagues and disasters which will herald the final judgment (Rev. 9:12; 11:14).

BIBLIOGRAPHY. N. Hillyer, *NIDNTT* 3, pp. 1051–1054. R.V.G.T.

WOMAN (Heb. *'iššâ*, Gk. *gynē*). The common humanity and equal value of woman and man, created 'in the image of God', is a theme of Gn. 1:27. Complementarity and the incompleteness of each without the other is a theme of Gn. 2:20, where woman is created to be man's helper or partner. (*EVE). Gn. 3:16 speaks of the pain of dependence and domination between women and men in a sinful world.

Monogamy was the OT ideal, but widespread polygamy was regulated rather than condemned in the Law. Parenthood was highly prized. Women in biblical narratives mainly operate within a household, naming the children and being responsible for their early education. Mothers were to be honoured (Ex. 20:12), feared (Lv. 19:3) and obeyed (Dt. 21:18ff.). Men took responsibility for and protected women family members but, if there were no male heirs, a woman could independently inherit land (Nu. 27:1–8).

Women and men met together for worship (Ezr. 10:1). Individual women made sacrifices and took Nazirite vows of dedication to Yahweh (Nu. 6:2). They sometimes exercised spiritual leadership as prophets, such as Miriam and Huldah, or intellectual leadership as 'wise' counsellors (2 Sam 14:1; 20:16). Deborah, the judge, was the nation's leader at a crucial time.

Partnership of men and women of faith plays a

key role in Luke's account of Jesus' birth. The amazed parents, Elizabeth and Zechariah, Simeon, and the Prophet Anna witnessed the dawning of God's salvation. *Mary, supported by Joseph, trusted God's Word despite the shame and ridicule involved, pondering what she did not yet fully understand (Lk. 2:19). God took flesh and became a man; a woman had the privilege of bringing him to birth. He obeyed her in childhood, separated from her to undertake his ministry (Mk. 3:31–35), and cared for her even on the cross.

Later rabbinical writings tended to undervalue women's spiritual contribution but Jesus showed them love and respect. He forgave them, healed them, taught them. They served him with provisions, hospitality and deeds of love. Women visiting his tomb became the first eyewitnesses of his resurrection.

Jesus included them in his teaching illustrations. He used a woman searching for a lost coin as a parable for God's search for his lost ones. He demanded the same standards from both sexes and offered the same way of salvation.

After the resurrection, women disciples are together with the men, praying, electing a new apostle (Acts 1:12–26) and receiving the power and gifts of the Holy Spirit at Pentecost (Acts 2:17–18).

Acts and the epistles mention many women playing a full part in the church. Dorcas, the carer, is raised by Peter. Lydia, the businesswoman, is Paul's first convert in Europe. Priscilla, with Aquila, taught the gifted Apollos. Philip's four daughters prophesied. Paul mentions many women workers, including Phoebe the deacon and Junia (now widely admitted to be a female name) who, with Andronicus, was prominent among the apostles (Rom. 16:1, 7).

Unlike circumcision, the sign of baptism was for women as well as men. Paul stressed the church as a community without prejudice based on race, class or gender; 'all are one in Christ Jesus' (Gal. 3:28). Christians, however, have to live in a fallen world with existing power structures and conventions. He urged Christian wives, slaves and citizens to submit to authority within such structures. There is ongoing debate about how his metaphor of man and woman as head and body should be applied to relationships within the church today, but agreement that it emphasizes a united, faithful, loving partnership in *marriage.

BIBLIOGRAPHY. B. Witherington, *Women in the Ministry of Jesus*, 1984; *idem. Women in the Earlier Churches*, 1988; M. Evans, *Women in the Bible*, 1983; Shirley Lees (ed.), *The Role of Women*, 1984; R. T. France, *Women in the Church's Ministry: A Test-case for Biblical Hermeneutics*, 1995.

V.M.S.
M.B.

WOMB. Heb. *beṭen*, *mēʿîm* and *reḥem* or *raḥam*; Gk *gastēr*, *koilia* or *mētra*, the former two in both cases being used also of the belly generally, indicating the Heb. vagueness about the internal physiology (*STOMACH, *BOWELS). The reference is generally to the place or time of life's beginning (Jb. 1:21; Is. 49:1), and so figuratively of the origin of anything (Jb. 38:29). The formation of the babe in the womb is a wonderful mystery to the biblical writers, who, understandably enough, attribute it to the direct action and care of God (Jb. 31:15; Ec. 11:5). The presence of the living babe in the womb some time before birth is mentioned in the NT (Lk. 1:41). *Barrenness is attributed to the closing up of the womb, sometimes specifically stated to be done by God (1 Sa. 1:5). This is a great cause of sorrow and shame to the woman concerned (v. 6). The *first-born, referred to as that which opens the womb, is regarded as holy (Ex. 13:2; Lk. 2:23).

B.O.B.

WOOL. The high value set upon wool as the basic fabric for clothing (Jb. 31:20; Pr. 31:13; Ezk. 34:3) is reflected in its inclusion among the first fruits to be offered by the priests (Dt. 18:4) and as an important item in Mesha's tribute (2 Ki. 3:4). Damascus wool was prized at Tyre market (Ezk. 27:18); the LXX compares its quality to that of Miletus which was famous in the ancient world (Pliny 8. 73). The reason for the Mosaic prohibition against wearing cloth made of a mixture of wool and linen (Dt. 22:11) is not clear. Josephus (*Ant.* 4. 208) claims that garments of wool and linen mixture were reserved for priests, but gives no evidence. Static electricity in such a mixture would be uncomfortable to the wearer (*NBCR*, p. 223). The brilliant whiteness of wool after thorough washing is used to illustrate purity (Is. 1:18) and beautiful teeth (Ct. 4:2) and is likened to snowflakes (Ps. 147:16).

N.H.

WORD. In the OT 'the word (*dāḇār*) of God' is used 394 times of a divine communication which comes from God to men in the form of commandment, prophecy, warning or encouragement. The usual formula is 'the word of Yahweh came (lit. was) to . . .' but sometimes the word is 'seen' as a vision (Is. 2:1; Je. 2:31; 38:21). Yahweh's word is an extension of the divine personality, invested with divine authority, and is to be heeded by angels and men (Ps. 103:20; Dt. 12:32); it stands for ever (Is. 40:8), and once uttered it cannot return unfulfilled (Is. 55:11). It is used as a synonym for the law (*tôrâ*) of God in Ps. 119, where alone its reference is to a written rather than a spoken message.

In the NT it translates two terms, **logos* and *rhēma*, the former being supremely used of the message of the Christian gospel (Mk. 2:2; Acts 6:2; Gal. 6:6), though the latter also bears the same meaning (Rom. 10:8; Eph. 6:17; Heb. 6:5, *etc.*). Our Lord spoke of the word of God (in the parable of the sower, Lk. 8:11; see also Mk. 7:13; Lk. 11:28), but in the Synoptic Gospels he always used the plural of his own message ('my words', Mt. 24:35 and parallels; Mk. 8:38; Lk. 24:44). In the Fourth Gospel, however, the singular is often found. To the early church the word was a message revealed from God in Christ, which was to be preached, ministered and obeyed. It was the word of life (Phil. 2:16), of truth (Eph. 1:13), of salvation (Acts 13:26), of reconciliation (2 Cor. 5:19), of the cross (1 Cor. 1:18).

BIBLIOGRAPHY. H. Haarbeck *et al.*, in *NIDNTT* 3, pp. 1078–1146; A. Debrunner *et al.*, in *TDNT* 4, pp. 69–143.

J.B.Tr.

WORK. The main words here are the Heb. *maʿᵃśeh* (181 times), 'an act', 'a doing' (*cf.* Gn. 5:29; Ex. 5:4, *etc.*, and especially in the Psalms of God's act, see Pss. 8:3, 6; 19:1, *etc.*); *mᵉlā'ḵâ* (117 times; *cf.* Gn. 2:2–3; Ex. 20:9, *etc.*); *pōʿal* (30 times), 'a deed' (*cf.* Dt. 32:4, *etc.*). Gk. *ergon* (142 times) is found frequently in Jn., Heb., Jas. and Rev. Less frequent is the abstract *energeia*, literally 'energy' (EVV 'working'). This is a specific Pauline word (Eph. 1:19; 3:7; 4:16; Phil. 3:21; Col. 1:29; 2 Thes. 2:9). Note should be taken also of the Heb. *yᵉgîʿâ*, 'labour', 'weariness', and *ʿāmāl*, 'labour', 'misery'; *cf.* Gk. *kopiaō*, 'to labour', 'to be wearied out' (*cf.* Mt. 11:28; Jn. 4:38, *etc.*), and *ergatēs*, 'a worker' (Mt. 9:37–38; 20:1–2, 8; Lk. 10:2, 7; Jas. 5:4).

In classical Gk. the verb *kopiaō* has reference to the weariness which labour produces (*cf. LSJ*, *ad loc.*), but in the NT it signifies the toil itself (*cf.* Mt. 6:28; 11:28; Lk. 5:5; 12:27; Jn. 4:38). The word *ergatēs* has reference to the business or the trade by which men gain their subsistence (Acts 19:25), and it is also used to denote the profit which results from their activity (Acts 16:16, 19) as well as the toil which the pursuit of their gain involves. *ergasia* occurs in an ethical sense in Eph. 4:19 and means literally 'to make a trade of'; *cf.* 'worker' (*ergatēs*) in Lk. 13:27; 2 Cor. 11:13; Phil. 3:2, and in a good sense Mt. 10:10; 2 Tim. 2:15. Luke's usage of the Latinism *dos ergasian*, 'make an effort' (AV 'give diligence') (Lk. 12:58), to emphasize Christ's warning concerning reconciliation with an adversary is thought by some to be derived from his medical studies, where the term had reference to the making of some mixture, the mixture itself, and the work of digestion, and of the lungs, *etc.* (*cf.* W. K. Hobart, *The Medical Language of St Luke*, 1882, p. 243). The phrase, however, occurs in the LXX (*cf.* Wisdom 13:19) with which Luke was familiar.

I. The general sense

It is clear from the interchangeable use of certain words to indicate God's activity and man's that work is itself a God-ordained thing. Work was from the beginning God's purpose for men, and is set forth in Ps. 104:19–24 and Is. 28:23–29 as a provision of the divine wisdom. Creation itself 'works' (*cf.* Pr. 6:6–11). The fact of work as forming an integral part of the pattern of the divine purpose for man is implied in the fourth commandment. But the entrance of sin changed work from a joy to a toil (*cf.* Gn. 3:16–19). Work has thus become a burden instead of a blessing, and, although not bad in itself, it has lost its true value. It has become an occasion for sin; idolatry results when it becomes an end in itself (*cf.* Ec. 2:4–11, 20–23; Lk. 12:16–22). By some it has become the means of exploitation and oppression (*cf.* Ex. 1:11–14; 2:23; Jas. 5:4). But in redemption, work is again transformed into a means of blessing. From the beginning Christianity has condemned idleness even when this has been indulged in in the name of religion (*cf.* 1 Thes. 4:11; also Eph. 4:28; 1 Tim. 5:13). Our Lord, working as a carpenter (Mk. 6:3), has sanctified common toil, and Paul set an example in honest labour (Acts 18:3). He virtually established a law of social economics in his announcement in 2 Thes. 3:10: 'this we commanded you, that if any would not work, neither should he eat'. On the other side the principle proclaimed by our Lord remains the basis of society, 'the labourer deserves his wages' (Lk. 10:7).

In the experience of grace human tasks are given a new value and become more worth while. They are performed for the sake of the Name. And in their fulfilment in this context they are thrice blessed. The one who works is himself blessed in his reception of divine grace to carry through his labours for the glory of God; those who receive the results of such tasks done in a new spirit and with a new quality are benefited also; and in all God is himself glorified. Such work is done 'in' and 'for' the Lord (*cf.* Rom. 14:7–8; Eph. 6:5–9; Col. 3:23–24). In this way man becomes a steward of God's riches (1 Cor. 4:1–2; *cf.* Mt. 25:14–30) and a servant of his neighbour (Mt. 25:40; Gal. 5:13; 1 Pet. 4:10). The genuineness of man's faith is proved in the end by the quality of his works (*cf.* Mt. 16:27, *praxis*). Yet in the end the acceptance of the labourer will be an act of divine grace (*cf.* 1 Cor. 3:8–15; note especially v. 10).

II. The spiritual and ethical reference

The word 'work' is used with reference to God's act of creation and providence. In the Psalms this note is given special emphasis. God's work or works are great and manifold (*cf.* Pss. 92:5; 104:24; 111:2, *etc.*). They give him everlasting praise (*cf.* Ps. 145:4, 9–10), declare his righteousness (145:17) and bring him joy (104:31). It is the same in the NT (*cf.* Heb. 4:10; Jn. 1:3; Acts 13:41; Rev. 15:3). The term is used also for the work of salvation committed by the Father to the Son. This is specifically a Johannine idea.

The Son has come to do the Father's work (*cf.* Jn. 4:34; 5:36; 9:4; 10:25, 37, *etc.*), which work he has finished (Jn. 15:24; 17:4). This means that nothing can be added to the work he has done, since it is once and for all. *Salvation is therefore not a matter of works or merit but of *grace. But the redeemed man will work and serve and labour and thus commend himself in the Lord. He will be fruitful in every good work (Col. 1:10; *cf.* Gal. 6:4; 2 Thes. 2:17; 2 Tim. 2:21; *etc.*). Those who undertake special work for God are to be esteemed for their work's sake (*cf.* 1 Thes. 5:13; also Phil. 2:29). Yet no work for God can be done apart from the inworking of his grace (*cf.* Eph. 2:10; 3:20; Phil. 2:13; Col. 1:29, *etc.*). Such is the 'work of faith, and labour of love' (1 Thes. 1:3; *cf.* 2 Thes. 1:11).

BIBLIOGRAPHY. A. Richardson, *The Biblical Doctrine of Work*, 1952; J. Murray, *Principles of Conduct*, 1957, pp. 82–106; R. Clark, *Work in Crisis*, 1982; H.-C. Hahn, F. Thiele, in *NIDNTT* 3, pp. 1147–1159. H.D.McD.

WORKS. The three main uses of this term, although distinct, are essentially related: the works of God, the works of Jesus Christ and the works of man in relation to faith.

1. In the OT the works of God are presented as evidence of God's supreme power, authority, wisdom and benevolence. The OT defines the Deity not by abstract terms such as omnipotence, but by his activity. Moses adduced the works of God as evidence of his unique distinction from other gods (Dt. 3:24). In the Psalms the works of God are frequently proclaimed as providing confidence in his power and authority and his sole right to receive worship. These works are his creative activity (Ps. 104:24) and his sovereign acts in relation to his redeemed people (Ps. 77:11–20) and to the nations (Ps. 46:8–10).

2. It was by his works that Jesus revealed that he was both Messiah and Son of God, exemplified by his answer to John the Baptist (Mt. 11:2–5). John's Gospel records the significant activity of Jesus with set purpose to reveal his Messiahship and deity so as to induce faith in his Person (Jn. 20:30–

31). Frequently Jesus pointed to his works as evidence that he was sent by the Father (Jn. 5:36; 10:37–38). Being the very works of God (Jn. 9:3–4), his works are sufficient ground for faith in him as being uniquely related to the Father (Jn. 10:38; 14:10–11). It was through equating his work with that of God that he was accused of blasphemy in identifying himself with God (Jn. 5:17–23). His death completed that work (Jn. 17:4; 19:30).

3. The believer also demonstrates by his good works the divine activity within him (Mt. 5:16; Jn. 6:28; 14:12). Conversely, the man who has no faith demonstrates by his evil works his separation from God (Jn. 3:19; Col. 1:21; Eph. 5:11; 2 Pet. 2:8, *etc.*). Good works are therefore the evidence of living faith, as James emphasizes in opposition to those who claim to be saved by faith alone without works (Jas. 2:14–26). James is in harmony with Paul, who also repeatedly declared the necessity for works, *i.e.* for behaviour appropriate to the new life in Christ following our entry into it by faith alone (Eph. 2:8–10; 1 Cor. 6:9–11; Gal. 5:16–26, *etc.*). The works rejected by Paul are those which men claim as earning God's favour and securing their discharge from the guilt of sin (Rom. 4:1–5; Eph. 2:8–9; Tit. 3:5). Since salvation is given by God in grace, no degree of works can merit it. The good works of the heathen are therefore unavailing as a means of salvation, since the man himself relies on the flesh and not on the grace of God (Rom. 8:7–8). J.C.C.

WORLD. The Gk. word *kosmos* means by derivation 'the *ordered* world'. It is used in the NT, but not in LXX, sometimes for what we should call the 'universe', the created world, described in the OT as 'all things' or 'heaven and earth' (Acts 17:24). The 'world' in this sense was made by the Word (Jn. 1:10); and it was this 'world' of which Jesus was speaking when he said it would not profit a man anything if he gained the whole of it and lost his soul in the process (Mt. 16:26).

But, because mankind is the most important part of the universe, the word *kosmos* is more often used in the limited sense of human beings, being a synonym for *hē oikoumenē gē*, 'the inhabited earth', also translated in the NT by 'world'. It is into this 'world' that men are born, and in it they live till they die (Jn. 16:21). It was all the kingdoms of this world that the devil offered to give to Christ if he would worship him (Mt. 4:8–9). It was this world, the world of men and women of flesh and blood, that God loved (Jn. 3:16), and into which Jesus came when he was born of a human mother (Jn. 11:27).

It is, however, an axiom of the Bible that this world of human beings, the climax of the divine creation, the world that God made especially to reflect his glory, is now in rebellion against him. Through the transgression of one man, sin has entered into it (Rom. 5:18) with universal consequences. It has become, as a result, a *disordered* world in the grip of the evil one (1 Jn. 5:19). And so, very frequently in the NT, and particularly in the Johannine writings, the word *kosmos* has a sinister significance. It is not the world as God intended it to be, but '*this* world' set over against God, following its own wisdom and living by the light of its own reason (1 Cor. 1:21), not recognizing the Source of all true life and illumination (Jn. 1:10). The two dominant characteristics of '*this* world' are *pride*, born of man's failure to accept his creaturely estate and his dependence on the Creator, which leads him to act as though he were the lord and giver of life; and *covetousness*, which causes him to desire and possess all that is attractive to his physical senses (1 Jn. 2:16). And, as man tends in effect to worship what he covets, such covetousness is idolatry (Col. 3:5). Accordingly, worldliness is the enthronement of something other than God as the supreme object of man's interests and affections. Pleasures and occupations, not necessarily wrong in themselves, become so when an all-absorbing attention is paid to them.

'*This* world' is pervaded by a spirit of its own, which has to be exorcized by the Spirit of God, if it is not to remain in control over human reason and understanding (1 Cor. 2:12). Man is in bondage to the elements which comprise the world (Col. 2:20) until he is emancipated from them by Christ. He cannot overcome it till he is himself 'born of God' (1 Jn. 5:4). Legalism, asceticism and ritualism are this world's feeble and enfeebling substitutes for true religion (Gal. 4:9–10); and only a true knowledge of God as revealed by Christ can prevent men from relying upon them. It was because the Jews relied upon them that they did not recognize either the Christ in the days of his flesh (Jn. 1:11) or his followers (1 Jn. 3:1). Similarly, false prophets who advocate such things, or antichrists who are antinomian in their teaching, will always be listened to by those who belong to this world (1 Jn. 4:5).

Christ, whom the Father sent to be the Saviour of this world (1 Jn. 4:14), and whose very presence in it was a judgment upon it (Jn. 9:39), freed men from its sinister forces by himself engaging in mortal combat with its 'prince', the perpetual instigator of the evil within it. The crisis of this world came when Jesus left the upper room and went forth to meet this prince (Jn. 14:30–31). By voluntarily submitting to death, Jesus brought about the defeat of him who held men in the grip of death, but who had no claims upon himself (Jn. 12:31–32; 14:30). On the cross, judgment was passed on the ruler (AV 'prince') of this world (Jn. 16:11); and faith in Christ as the Son of God, who offered the sacrifice which alone can cleanse men from the guilt and power of sin (a cleansing symbolized by the flow of water and blood from his stricken side, Jn. 19:34), enables the believer to overcome the world (1 Jn. 5:4–6), and to endure the tribulations which the world inevitably brings upon him (Jn. 16:33). The love of a Christian for God, the Father of Jesus Christ his Redeemer, who is the propitiation for the sins of the whole world (1 Jn. 2:2), acts with the expulsive power of a new affection; it makes it abhorrent to him to set his affections any longer upon 'this world', which, because it is severed from the true source of life, is transitory and contains within itself the seeds of its own decay (1 Jn. 2:15–17). A man who has come to experience the *higher* love for God, and for Christ and his brethren, must abandon the lower love for all that is contaminated by the spirit of the world: friendship of the world is of necessity enmity with God (Jas. 4:2).

Jesus, in his last prayer in the upper room, did not pray for the world, but for those whom his Father had given him out of the world. By this 'gift', these men whom Jesus described as 'his own' ceased to have the characteristics of the world; and Jesus prayed that they might be kept safe from its evil influences (Jn. 17:9), for he knew that after his own departure they would have to bear the brunt of the world's hatred which had hitherto been directed almost entirely against himself. As the risen and ascended Christ he still limits his intercessions to those who draw near to God through him (Heb. 7:25); and he continues to manifest himself not to the world but to his own that are in the world (Jn. 14:22).

But it is very certain that Christ's disciples cannot and must not attempt to retreat from this world. It is into this world, *all* the world (Mk. 16:15), that he sends them. They are to be its light (Mt. 5:14); and the 'field' in which the church is to do its work of witnessing to the truth as it is in Jesus is no less comprehensive than the world itself (Mt. 13:38). For the world is still God's world, even though at present it lies under the evil one. In the end, 'earth's true loveliness will be restored'; and, with all evil destroyed and the sons of God manifested, the whole creation will be 'set free from its bondage to decay and obtain the glorious liberty of the children of God' (Rom. 8:21). Then God will be 'everything to every one' (1 Cor. 15:28); or, 'present in a total manner in the universe' (J. Héring in *Vocabulary of the Bible*, 1958). The seer of Rev. envisages the day when great voices in heaven will proclaim: 'The kingdom of the world has become the kingdom of our Lord and of his Christ, and he shall reign for ever and ever' (Rev. 11:15). R.V.G.T.

WORSHIP. 'Worship' (Old English 'weorthscipe' = 'worth-ship') originally referred to the action of human beings in expressing homage to God because he is worthy of it. It covers such activities as adoration, thanksgiving, prayers of all kinds, the offering of sacrifice and the making of vows. Nowadays, however, 'worship' is used for any kind of interaction between God and his people, expressed in (but not confined to) cultic or formal activity by a religious group or individuals. It therefore includes not only the human approach to God but also the communications of God with his people, and the whole communal activity that takes place when the people gather together religiously. Such activity is the formal expression of spiritual attitudes which should characterize God's people at all times (Rom. 12:1). Insofar as serving other people is a divine command, the fulfilment of it is a part of worship.

The term 'worship' is misunderstood if it gives the impression that the major element is what *human beings* do or offer to God. Biblical religion is primarily concerned with what *God* does for his people (Mk. 10:45). This is particularly evident in the NT, where words expressing the human activity of worshipping God are surprisingly rare in descriptions of church meetings (Heb. 13:15f.; 1 Pet. 2:5). Worship is human response to a gracious God, and it needs to be placed in this context if it is to be properly understood.

In the OT there is an extensive vocabulary of words expressing this response to God (especially *histaḥ^{a}wâ*; Gk. *proskynein*, 'to bow in reverence'). The activities carried on at the Temple (or the earlier tabernacle) were largely human offerings to God, although it should not be forgotten that the priests were also intended to instruct people. The danger that ritual might not be the outward expression of a spiritual attitude was frequently criticized (Ps. 40:6–8; Am. 5:21–24).

By NT times local synagogues were replacing the temple as the regular meeting places of the Jews, the majority of whom were too far distant from the Temple to visit it other than on special occasions. Activity here centred on the reading of Scripture, accompanied by a 'sermon' based on the text, and placed in the context of prayers and praises to God.

Christians met in house-groups, in meetings that were primarily for themselves but were not closed to outsiders. These meetings reflected the temple in that the living community of believers was now the place where God was present and revealed to his people (1 Cor. 14:25). The influence of the synagogue was important. The Scriptures and Christian documents (such as Paul's letters) were read and expounded (1 Thes. 5:27). Instruction and prophecy were given by persons gifted by the Spirit, and prayer was offered. Thus God's communication with his people and their human response took place in an informal, largely unstructured gathering. Paul lays emphasis on the need for all that happens in the church meeting to 'build up' the congregation in Christian character. The contrast, however, is not between worshipping God and edifying the congregation, but between activities (like prophecy) which are intelligible and helpful and others (like speaking in tongues) which are not (1 Cor. 14:26). From an early date Christians met weekly on the Lord's Day (Acts 20:7; 1 Cor. 16:2). An Easter celebration (1 Cor. 5:7f.) is also likely. At Corinth certainly a weekly church gathering was usual and included a meal with sacramental significance as the proclamation of the death of Jesus (1 Cor. 11: 17–34).

BIBLIOGRAPHY. R. Banks, *Paul's Idea of Community*, 1980; P. Bradshaw, *The Search for the Origins of Christian Worship*, 1992; J. G. Davies (ed.), *A New Dictionary of Liturgy and Worship*, 1986; R. P. Martin, *Worship in the Early Church*², 1974; *idem, The Worship of God*, 1982; C. F. D. Moule, *The Birth of the New Testament*³, 1981; D. Peterson, *Engaging with God*, 1992. I.H.M.

WRATH. The permanent attitude of the holy and just God when confronted by sin and evil is designated his 'wrath'. It is inadequate to regard this term merely as a description of 'the inevitable process of cause and effect in a moral universe' or as another way of speaking of the results of sin. It is rather a personal quality, without which God would cease to be fully righteous and his love would degenerate into sentimentality. His wrath, however, even though like his love it has to be described in human language, is not wayward, fitful or spasmodic, as human anger always is. It is as permanent and as consistent an element in his nature as is his love. This is well brought out in the treatise of Lactantius, *De ira Dei*.

The injustice and impiety of men, for which they have no excuse, *must* be followed by manifestations of the divine wrath in the lives both of individuals and of nations (see Rom. 1:18–32); and the OT contains numerous illustrations of this, such as the destruction of Sodom and Gomorrah and the downfall of Nineveh (see Dt. 29:23; Na. 1:2–6). But until the final 'day of wrath', which is anticipated throughout the Bible and portrayed very vividly in Rev., God's wrath is always tempered with mercy, particularly in his dealings with his chosen people (see, *e.g.*, Ho. 11:8ff.). For a sinner, however, to 'trade' upon this mercy is to store up wrath for himself 'on the day of wrath when God's righteous judgment will be revealed' (Rom. 2:5). Paul was convinced that one of the main reasons why Israel failed to arrest the process of moral decline lay in their wrong reaction to the forbearance of God, who so often refrained from punishing them to the extent they deserved. They were presuming upon 'the riches of his kindness and forbearance and patience', and failed to see that it was intended to lead them to repentance (Rom. 2:4).

In their unredeemed state men's rebellion against God is, in fact, so persistent that they are inevitably the objects of his wrath (Eph. 2:3), and 'vessels of wrath made for destruction' (Rom. 9:22). Nor does the Mosaic law rescue them from this position, for, as the apostle states in Rom. 4:15, 'the law brings wrath'. Because it requires perfect obedience to its commands, the penalties exacted for disobedience render the offender more subject to the divine wrath. It is, to be sure, only by the merciful provision for sinners made in the gospel that they can cease to be the objects of this wrath and become the recipients of this grace. The love of God for sinners expressed in the life and death of Jesus is the dominant theme of the NT, and this love is shown not least because Jesus experienced on man's behalf and in his stead the misery, the afflictions, the punishment and the death which are the lot of sinners subject to God's wrath.

Consequently, Jesus can be described as 'the deliverer from the wrath to come' (see 1 Thes. 1:10); and Paul can write: 'Since, therefore, we are now justified by his blood, much more shall we be saved by him from the wrath of God' (Rom. 5:9). On the other hand, the wrath of God remains upon all who, seeking to thwart God's redemptive purpose, are disobedient to God's Son, through whom alone such justification is rendered possible.

BIBLIOGRAPHY. R. V. G. Tasker, *The Biblical Doctrine of the Wrath of God*, 1951; G. H. C. Macgregor, 'The Concept of the Wrath of God in the New Testament', *NTS* 7, 1960–1, pp. 101ff.; H.-C. Hahn, *NIDNTT* 1, pp. 105–113. R.V.G.T.

WRITING. Throughout the ancient Near East, from at least *c.* 3100 BC onwards, writing was a hallmark of civilization and progress. In the 2nd millennium BC there were several experiments which led to the development of the alphabet, with a consequent general increase in literacy. Although the number of documents from the pre-exilic period found in Palestine is small when compared with the many thousands from Egypt, Mesopotamia and Syria, they show it is reasonable to assume that proximity to other cultural centres stimulated the art of writing there through all periods. The commonest words for writing (Heb. *kāṯaḇ*; Aram. *kᵉṯaḇ*; Gk. *graphō*) occur more than 450 times in OT and NT.

I. Biblical references

Moses is said to have written (Ex. 17:14) the Decalogue (Ex. 24:12; 34:27), the words of Yahweh (Ex. 24:4), the Law (Torah, Jos. 8:31), and spoken about a written copy of it (Dt. 27). He also wrote all the statutes (Dt. 30:10) and judgments (Ex. 34:27; *cf.* 2 Ki. 17:37), as well as legal enactments (Dt. 24:1; Mk. 10:4), details of the journeys made by the Israelites (Nu. 33:2), and the words of the victory song (Dt. 31:19, 22). In these he was helped by officials (probably literate *šoṭᵉrîm*, Nu. 11:16, 'officers'; *cf.* Akkad. *šaṭāru*, 'to write') who, by reason of their ability to record decisions, were closely connected with the judiciary (Dt. 16:18; 1 Ch. 23:4; Jos. 8:33). During the Exodus wanderings priests also wrote down curses (Nu. 5:23) and names of objects (17:3). Joshua wrote a copy of the Ten Commandments (Jos. 8:32) and of the renewed covenant (24:26).

Samuel wrote down the charter of the newly created kingship of Saul (1 Sa. 10:25). David wrote letters to his commander Joab (2 Sa. 11:14) and details of the Temple administration, as did his son Solomon (2 Ch. 35:4), who corresponded with Hiram of Tyre in writing (2 Ch. 2:11). The king of Syria wrote a letter to the king of Israel about Naaman (2 Ki. 5:5). As in all periods, court *scribes were frequently employed to write lists of persons (1 Ch. 4:41; 24:6; see also Nu. 11:26; Is. 10:19; Je. 22:30; Ne. 12:22).

Isaiah the prophet wrote (2 Ch. 26:22; Is. 8:1) and dictated to a scribe (30:8). In his time Hezekiah both wrote letters (*'iggereṯ*) to Ephraim and Manasseh (2 Ch. 30:1; *cf.* Is. 38:9 entitled 'the writing [*miḵtāḇ*] of Hezekiah') and received them from the Assyr. king Sennacherib (Is. 37:14; 39:1; 2 Ch. 32:17). Jeremiah dictated to his amanuensis Baruch (Je. 30:2; 36:27; 45:1), as probably did Hosea (8:12) and Malachi (3:16), for the written word was an important part of prophecy (2 Ch. 21:12), its value being emphasized also by Job (19:23).

Daniel and the Babylonian savants could read, and therefore presumably could themselves write, Aramaic (Dn. 5:24f.). There was an active correspondence within the empire as in earlier periods (*RUNNERS, *ASSYRIA, *BABYLONIA). Nehemiah wrote down the covenant (Ne. 9:38), while his opponents in Samaria wrote to the Persian king (Ezr. 4:6–7), as did other district-governors (Ezr. 5:7; 6:2). Ezra himself was a scribe who wrote decrees or state documents in the local dialects (8:34), in the style of court officials, including Mordecai, on behalf of the king (Est. 9:28f.), who affixed his *seal (Dn. 6:25).

Jesus Christ and his apostles made constant reference to the written Scriptures (*e.g.* 'it is written'—*gegraptai*—occurs 106 times). Our Lord himself was literate (Jn. 7:14–15), reading (Lk. 4:16–19) and writing publicly on at least one occasion (Jn. 8:6). Zechariah the priest wrote on a wax-covered writing-board (Lk. 1:63), and the Roman governor Pilate had a trilingual inscription written to be placed on the cross (Jn. 19:19, 22).

John (21:24), Luke (1:3; Acts 1:1), and Paul himself (Gal. 6:11; Phm. 19; Rom. 15:15), though often using an amanuensis such as Tertius (Rom. 16:22), wrote the historical records and letters which have come down to us. Through to Rev. there is constant reference to writing in its use for letters, legal evidence and record (Rev. 1:11; 21:5). Since writing, by its nature, is a means of communication, declaration and testimony, it is used to illustrate the impression, written in (*engraphō*, 2 Cor. 3:2f.) or upon (*epigraphō*, Heb. 8:10; 10:16) the mind and heart (*cf.* Je. 31:33; Pr. 3:3) by the Holy Spirit.

II. Materials

Almost any smooth surface was used for writing.

Proto – Sinaitic c. 1500 BC	Canaanite c. 1400 – 1100 BC	Represents	S. Arabian c. 300 BC	Phoenician c. 1000 BC	Early Hebrew Siloam c. 700 BC	Early Hebrew Lachish c. 586 BC
		ox				
		house				
		throw-stick				
		fish				
		man with raised arms				
		prop				
		weapon?				
		fence?				
		palm of hand				
		staff				
		water				
		snake				
		fish				
		eye				
		mouth				
		plant?				
		monkey?				
		head				
		bow?				
		cross-mark				

Chart showing the development of the alphabet in various scripts in use in ancient Palestine.

Aramaic, Elephantine c. 450 BC	Hebrew 1st cent. AD	Hebrew name	Phonetic value	Early Greek 8th cent. BC	Classical Greek: Athens 5th cent. BC	Greek name	Roman
𐡀	א	'alep̄	'	Α	Α	alpha	A
𐡁	ב	bêṯ	b	Β	Β	bēta	B
𐡂	ג	gîmel	g	Γ, (	Γ	gamma	G
𐡃	ד	dāleṯ	d	Δ	Δ	delta	D
𐡄	ה	hē	h	Ε	Ε	epsilon	E
𐡅	ו	waw	w	Ϝ	Υ	(digamma) upsilon	FY
𐡆	ז	zayin	z	Ι	Ζ	zēta	Z
𐡇	ח	ḥêṯ	ḥ	⊟	Η	ēta	H
𐡈	ט	ṭêṯ	ṭ	⊕	Θ	thēta	
𐡉	י	yôḏ	y	ς, Ι	Ι	iota	I
𐡊	כ	kap̄	k	Κ	Κ	kappa	K
𐡋	ל	lāmeḏ	l	Λ, Γ	Λ	lambda	L
𐡌	מ	mēm	m	Μ	Μ	mu	M
𐡍	נ	nûn	n	Ν	Ν	nu	N
𐡎	ס	sāmeḵ	s	Ξ	Ξ	xi	
𐡏	ע	'ayin	'	Ο	Ο	omicron	O
𐡐	פ	pê	p	Γ	Π	pi	P
𐡑	צ	ṣāḏê	ṣ	Μ		(san)	
𐡒	ק	qôp̄	q	Ϙ		(koppa)	Q
𐡓	ר	rêš	r	P, R	Ρ	rhō	R
𐡔	ש	šîn	š	Σ, Σ	Σ	sigma	S
𐡕	ת	taw	t	Τ	Τ	tau	T

a. Stone

Inscriptions were carved on stone or rock surfaces (Jb. 19:24), monumental texts being cut on a prepared stele, obelisk or cliff-face (*e.g.* Heb. tomb inscription, *SHEBNA, *IBA*, fig. 53, *cf.* 43, 48). The softer or more rugged surfaces could be covered with a plaster coating, before inscription, as in Egypt, and on the altar stones (Jos. 8:32; Dt. 27:2f.). Stone tablets were normally used for royal, commemorative or religious texts or public copies of legal edicts (*HAMMURAPI). Stone tablets, no larger than 45 × 30 cm (they fitted inside the Ark), were used for the Ten Commandments (Ex. 32:16). These tablets (*luḥôt ᵃḇānîm*) were like the stone flakes used as writing material in Egypt (*PAPYRI & OSTRACA **I***b*). The 'writing of God' (*miktaḇ ᵉlōhîm*) is taken to be a clear, well-formed script. There is no reason to suppose these were clay tablets with cuneiform writing. See A. R. Millard, 'Recreating the Tablets of the Law', *Bible Review* 10, 1994, pp. 48–53.

b. Writing-boards

The tablets used by Isaiah (30:8) and Habakkuk (2:2) may have been writing-boards made of wood or ivory with a recess to hold a wax surface (Akkad. *lē'u*). Such writing-boards, usually hinged to form a diptych or polyptych, could be used for writing in any script. The individual leaf was called a 'door', a term also used for a column of writing (Je. 36:23, AV 'leaves'). The earliest known comes from a Late Bronze Age shipwreck off the coast of S Turkey, but the writing had disappeared (R. Payton, *AS* 41, 1991, pp. 99–110). At Nimrud in Assyria, a set of twelve ivory wax-covered leaves contained a composition of 6,000 lines, copied *c.* 705 BC (D. J. Wiseman, 'Assyrian Writing Boards', *Iraq* 17, 1955, pp. 3–13). Assyrian and other sculptures show scribes with such boards (*IBA*, fig. 60; *ANEP*, p. 460) and they were common in Gk. and Roman times (Lk. 1:63; *pinakidion*, a small writing-tablet, AV 'table').

c. Clay tablets (see also **IV**. a).

The 'brick' (*lᵉḇēnâ*) used by Ezekiel (4:1) was probably of clay similar to the tablets used for plans and surveys in Babylonia, though the word could be used to describe any flat tile. The great 'tablet' on which Isaiah had to write with the 'pen of a man' (as opposed to that of a skilled scribe?) was a sheet or 'blank surface' of an unspecified material (Is. 8:1, *gillāyôn*).

d. Papyrus

Papyrus is not directly mentioned in the OT as a writing-material (Egyp. *ni[t]r[w]*; Akkad. *ni'aru*). It was, however, obtainable from Phoenicia, Lake Huleh and the Jordan (*PAPYRI) from the 11th century BC onwards, and its use is attested by the marks on the backs of seal impressions originally attached to this perishable substance (*e.g.* the reverse of the seal of *GEDALIAH). One example of ancient Heb. writing on papyrus was found in a cave near the Dead Sea (see Gibson, 1, pp. 31ff.). Papyrus (from which the Eng. word 'paper' is derived) was also known to the Assyrians and Babylonians in the 7th century (R. P. Dougherty, 'Writing on Parchment and Papyrus among the Babylonians and the Assyrians', *JAOS* 48, 1928, pp. 109–135). Used extensively in Egypt in all periods, papyri were found among the *Dead Sea Scrolls of the 2nd century BC–2nd century AD period. Isaiah's 'paper reed' (19:7 [AV], *'ārôṯ*), though possibly an indirect reference to papyri, is better interpreted as 'bare place'. The 'paper' used by John (2 Jn. 12) was probably papyrus (Gk. *chartēs*).

e. Leather and parchment

Leather was sometimes used in Egypt for working records because the ink could be washed off and the surface re-used (K. A. Kitchen, *TynB* 27, 1976, p. 141). During at least the Persian period skins were prepared for writing in Babylonia where papyrus did not grow. Skins of goats and sheep would have been available to the Israelites, and their use for copies of the biblical texts by the NT period (*DEAD SEA SCROLLS) may reflect earlier practice.

f. Ostraca

Potsherds or ostraca were another common writing material, since their low cost and availability made them especially useful for the writing of short memoranda with pen or brush and ink. Such potsherds have been recovered in considerable quantity from Palestine, being all but indestructible unless the ink was rubbed. About 240 have been found from the period of the Monarchy. See A. Lemaire, *Inscriptions Hebräiques*, 1, *Les Ostraca*, 1977 (*PAPYRI AND OSTRACA).

Pottery sometimes had characters inscribed on it before or after firing. They usually give the owner's name or the content or capacity of the vessel (*PEKAH; *SEAL, **I**. *f*).

III. Writing implements

1. Metal chisels and gravers were readily available for inscribing stone, metal, ivory or clay (*ARTS AND CRAFTS; *SEAL). The 'stylus' (*ḥereṭ*) or 'pen' (*'ēṭ*) used by Jeremiah (17:1) with its 'iron' point has been interpreted either as used for writing with a soft 'nib' or as a hard (emery?) point for use on iron, lead or other hard surface (Is. 8:1, Vulg. *stylus*; see also Jb. 19:24). None of the many pointed instruments so far excavated can be identified beyond question as used for writing a linear script. The 'pen of the scribes' (Je. 8:8) used for writing with ink on ostraca, papyrus or other smooth surfaces was a reed, split or cut to act as a brush. In ancient Egypt such pens were cut from rushes (*Juncus maritimus*) 15–40 cm long, the end being cut to a flat chisel shape so that the thick or thin strokes might be made with the broad or narrow edges. In Graeco-Roman times reeds (*Phragmites communis*) were cut to a point and split like a quill-pen (A. Lucas, *Ancient Egyptian Materials and Industries*, 1948, p. 417). This type of pen was the *kalamos* used in NT times (3 Jn. 13). The stylus used for writing the cuneiform script was a square-ended reed. For a discussion of the shape, method of use and illustrations of scribes with pens, chisels and styli, see G. R. Driver, *Semitic Writing*³, 1976, pp. 17ff.

2. Ink was usually a black carbon (charcoal) mixed with gum or oil for use on parchment or with a metallic substance for papyrus. It was kept as a dried cake on which the scribe would dip his moistened pen. The ink of the Lachish ostraca was a mixture of carbon and iron (as oak-galls or copperas). The Romans also used the juice of cuttle-fish (Persius, *Satires* 3. 13), which, like most inks, could easily be erased by washing (Nu. 5:23) or by scratching with the 'penknife' (Je. 36:23, Heb. *ta'ar sōp̄ēr*, 'scribe's knife') normally used for trimming

or cutting pens or scrolls. It has been suggested that Heb. *d'yô*, 'ink' (Je. 36:18), should be emended to *r'yô* (= Egyp. *ryt*, 'ink'; T. Lambdin, *JAOS* 73, 1953, p. 154), but this is not certain. The ink used by Paul (2 Cor. 3:3) and John (2 Jn. 12) is simply designated 'black' (*melan*).

The 'inkhorn' (Ezk. 9:2–3, 11; Heb. *qeset*) may be the palette (Egyp. *gsti*), the narrow rectangular wooden board with a long groove to hold the rush pens and circular hollows for the cakes of black and red ink. For illustrations of these palettes, *etc.*, see W. C. Hayes, *The Sceptre of Egypt*, 1, 1953, pp. 292–296; J. B. Pritchard, *The Ancient Near East*, 1958, figs. 52, 55; *IBA*, p. 32, fig. 27. Similar palettes were in use in Syria, being carried by the scribe 'by his side' (Ezk. 9:2–3, 11), as shown on the Aram. stele of Bar-Rekub (*ANEP*, p. 460).

IV. Forms of documents

a. Tablets

The clay documents on which cuneiform script was inscribed vary in size (about 6 mm square to 45 × 30 cm) according to the amount of space required for the text. The inscription from left to right ran in lines (sometimes ruled) down the obverse (flat) side along the lower edge, then on down the reverse (convex) side, the upper and left edges. Where more than one tablet was needed to complete a work each text in the series was linked by a catchline and colophon (see **VI**, below) to indicate its correct place.

Contracts were often enclosed in a clay envelope on which the text was repeated and the *seals of the witnesses impressed. Larger historical or commemorative inscriptions were written on clay prisms or barrel-shaped cylinders which were often placed as foundation deposits. Wooden tablets or writing-boards varied both in size and in the number of leaves as required.

b. The roll

The usual form of the 'book' in Bible times was a roll or scroll (*m'gillâ*) of papyrus, leather or parchment in which the text was written 'within' (recto) and, when necessary, continued 'without' on the back (verso) as described by Ezekiel (2:10). This was sometimes called the 'roll of a book' (*m'gillat sēper*; Ps. 40:8; Ezk. 2:9); the LXX (B) of Je. 36:2, 4 (*chartion biblion*) implies the use of papyrus. The term for scroll (*cf.* Bab. *magallatu*) is not necessarily a late one in Heb. (*BDB*) and it is likely that the Jewish tradition requiring copies of the law to be made on a leather roll (*Soferim* 1. 1–3) reflects earlier practice.

The Heb. *sēper*, usually translated 'book' in AV, could refer to a roll or scroll (so AV Is. 34:4, correctly). It denotes any parchment or papyrus document (R. P. Dougherty, *op. cit.*, p. 114) and means a 'writing, document, missive, or book' (*cf.* Akkad. *šipru*). It is synonymous with the term for 'letter' (*'iggeret*, Est. 9:25), being also used for a letter or order from the king (2 Sa. 11:14; 2 Ki. 5:10; 10:1; Is. 37:14) or published decree (Est. 1:22).

sēper, as a general term for writing, is used of the communication from a prophet (Je. 25:13; 29:1; Dn. 12:4); a legal certificate of divorce (Dt. 24:1; Je. 3:8; Is. 50:1); a contract for the purchase of real estate (Je. 32:11); or an indictment (Jb. 31:35). It also denotes a general register (Ne. 7:5; Gn. 5:1), a covenant (Ex. 24:7) or law book (Dt. 28:61; Jos. 8:31), a book of poems (Nu. 21:14; Jos. 10:13) as well as collections of historical data (1 Ki. 11:41; 14:19; 1 Ch. 27:24; 2 Ch. 16:11; 25:26). Once 'the books' (plural *s'pārîm*) refers to the canonical scriptures of the time (Dn. 9:2). It refers to the divine records (Pss. 69:28; 139:16; Mal. 3:16; Ex. 32:32; Dn. 12:1) and once to book-learning in general (Is. 29:11; *cf.* Dn. 1:4). The word and its cognates were current with similar meanings in the texts of *Ugarit, and *sēper*, 'scribe', appears as a loan word in Egypt during the 13th century BC.

The scroll, as the writing-boards and clay tablets, was inscribed in as many columns (*d'lātōt*), and therefore of any length, as required (Je. 36:23).

In NT times the 'book' (*biblion*) was a roll as used for the law (Mk. 12:26; Lk. 4:17–20). It formed a scroll (Rev. 6:14) made up of sections of *papyrus, the inner bark of which (*byblos*) was used. Like the Heb. *sēper*, the Gk. *biblion* could be used of any (or unspecified) form of written document, including registration lists (Phil. 4:3; Rev. 13:8). 'The books' (plural *ta biblia*; Jn. 21:25; 2 Tim. 4:13, hence our 'Bible') came to be a term for the collected Scriptures. Where a small scroll was in mind *biblaridion* was used (Rev. 10:2, 8–10).

c. The codex

About the 2nd century AD the roll began to be replaced by the codex, a collection of sheets of writing-material folded and fastened together at one edge and often protected by covers. This was an important step in the development of the modern 'book', and was based on the physical form of the writing-tablet. At first these papyrus or parchment notebooks were little used for pagan literature, but were used in Palestine (Mishnah, *Kelim* 24. 7), and especially in Egypt, for biblical writings where the adaptation of 'the codex form to receive all texts both OT and NT used in Christian communities . . . was complete, as far as our present evidence goes, before the end of the 2nd century, if not earlier'. See C. H. Roberts, T. C. Skeat, *The Birth of the Codex*, 1983. Outside Christian circles the codex form was generally accepted by the 4th century AD. It has even been suggested, but not proved, that this form was developed by the early Christian church because of the ease of transport and reference. Certainly the *membranai* requested by Paul (2 Tim. 4:13) could have been a papyrus notebook of his own addresses or other writings or, more likely, an early Christian writing, perhaps the second Gospel or the Book of Testimonies, an anthology of OT passages used to support the Christian claim. These writings were a contrast to 'books' (*ta biblia*), in general probably rolls (of the LXX?). For the significance of the early codices in the history of the *Canon of Scripture, see C. H. Roberts in P. R. Ackroyd (ed.), *Cambridge History of the Bible*, 1, 1970, p. 57.

V. Scripts

a. Hieroglyphs

(i) *Egyptian.* The native script of pharaonic Egypt appears in three forms: hieroglyphic (Gk. *hieros*, 'sacred', and *glyphē*, 'carving'), hieratic (Gk. *hieratikos*, 'priestly'), and demotic (Gk. *demotikos*, 'popular').

1. The *hieroglyphic* system. The Egyp. hieroglyphs are pictorial signs, originally pictures to express the things they represent; many of them were soon used to express sounds—specifically the con-

sonants of the Egyp. word for the thing represented by the picture-hieroglyph. Such a sign could then be used to stand for the same consonants in spelling out other words. Some of these phonetic signs came to stand for just one such consonant, becoming thus the world's first alphabetic signs. However, the Egyptians never isolated these as a separate alphabet as did their W Semitic neighbours. After most Egyp. words as spelt out by phonetic or sound signs, there comes a picture-sign or 'determinative' which signifies the general class into which the word falls. However, in very many cases it would be more accurate to say that the phonetic signs were actually added in front of the picture-sign (so-called 'determinative') as complements to determine the precise reading or sound of the latter, and thus its correct meaning, rather than that the picture-sign acted as classifier to the phonetically written word (*cf.* H. W. Fairman, *Annales du Service des Antiquités de l'Égypte* 43, 1943, pp. 297–298; *cf.* P. Lacau, *Sur le Système hiéroglyphique*, 1954, p. 108). Where a phonetic sign could have more than one sound-value, supplementary alphabetic signs could be added to show which reading was intended, though these were sometimes added even where no ambiguity existed.

2. *Hieratic and demotic.* The other two Egyp. scripts, hieratic and demotic, are adaptations of the hieroglyphic script which retained its splendid pictorial shapes throughout Egyp. history. The hieratic script is a cursive form of hieroglyphic script, written with pen and ink on papyrus, reduced to formal symbols no longer pictorial, for ease of rapid writing. Hieratic is to hieroglyphs what our long-hand script is to printed characters. The hieroglyphs first appear in Egypt just before the foundation of the pharaonic monarchy (1st Dynasty) *c.* 3000 BC, and hieratic came into use soon after. The third form of Egyp. script, demotic, is simply an even more rapid and abbreviated form of hieratic handwriting that first appears about the 7th century BC, and like the other two scripts lasted until the 5th century AD.

3. *Decipherment.* The ancient scripts of Egypt finally passed out of use in the 4th (hieroglyphic) and the 5th (demotic) centuries AD, and remained a closed book for 13 centuries until the discovery of the Rosetta Stone in 1799 during Napoleon's Egyptian expedition made possible the decipherment of Egypt's ancient scripts and language. The Rosetta Stone is a bilingual decree of Ptolemy V, 196 BC, in Gk. and Egyp., the latter in both hieroglyphic and demotic scripts. This and the Bankes obelisk eventually enabled the Frenchman, J. F. Champollion, to achieve the basic decipherment of the Egyp. hieroglyphs in 1822, showing that they were largely phonetic in use and that the Egyp. language was in fact simply the parent of Coptic, the language of the native Egyp. church.

4. *Scope.* From the very beginning, the Egyp. hieroglyphs were used for all purposes: historical records, religious texts and the mundane purposes of administration. They were accordingly drawn on papyrus or ostraca, carved on stone monuments, and engraved in wood or metal wherever inscriptions were required. However, from early in the 3rd millennium, the more rapid cursive script—hieratic —became customary for writing on papyrus, and so for all the records of daily life and administration, while hieroglyphs continued in use for all formal texts, stone inscriptions and monumental purposes. Eventually, from the 7th century BC, demotic largely replaced hieratic as the script of business and administration, and hieratic from the 10th century BC onwards became largely the script of religious papyri.

BIBLIOGRAPHY. On the Egyp. scripts, see A. H. Gardiner, *Egyptian Grammar*, 1957, pp. 5–8. On the hieroglyphs themselves as pictures, see N. M. Davies, *Picture Writing in Ancient Egypt*, 1958, illustrated in colour. On the origin and early development of the hieroglyphic system, see S. Schott, *Hieroglyphen: Untersuchungen zum Ursprung der Schrift*, 1950, and P. Lacau, *op. cit.* For the Rosetta Stone, see BM brochure *The Rosetta Stone*, and, for its discoverer, W. R. Dawson, *JEA* 43, 1957, p. 117, with *ibid.*, 44, 1958, p. 123. On the decipherment of the hieroglyphs, see F. Ll. Griffith, *JEA* 37, 1951, pp. 38–46, or A. H. Gardiner, *op. cit.*, pp. 9–11; *Egypt of the Pharaohs*, 1961, pp. 11–14, 19–26.

(ii) *Hittite.* The system of hieroglyphs used by the Hittites in Anatolia and Syria, mainly in the latter half of the 2nd millennium BC, was deciphered in 1946 (see *AS* 3, 1953, pp. 53–95) and this script is now being studied in detail and used for comparison with the Hittite dialects written in the cuneiform script. It is a series of simple syllables (*ba, da, etc.*) with word-signs for common nouns (earth, king); see E. Laroche, *Les Hiéroglyphes Hittites*, 1, 1960.

b. Cuneiform scripts

(i) ***Akkadian.*** In Babylonia pictographs were used for writing on clay and stone from *c.* 3100 BC onwards. It was, however, soon found difficult to draw curved lines on clay, and the pictograph was gradually replaced by its representation made by a series of wedge-shaped incisions. A further change for convenience from writing down columns from right to left resulted in the classical script being written horizontally in columns, the lines running from left to right. In a major development, word-signs (ideograms) were used to represent words with the same sounds but differing meanings (*e.g.* meat, meet) or syllables in other words (*e.g.* meat, metre). Certain signs were also used as determinatives placed before or after words of a distinct class (*e.g.* deities, personal and place-names, animals, wooden objects, *etc.*). By 2800 BC the cuneiform script had fully developed, though the forms of signs were modified at different periods (for a table illustrating this development see *IBA*, fig. 22).

From the 3rd millennium BC, the cuneiform, using at least 500 different signs, was widely in use outside Mesopotamia (where it was employed for the Sumerian, Bab. and Assyr. languages). It was adapted for writing other languages, notably W Semitic dialects, Hurrian, the various Hittite tongues. During the 15th–13th centuries BC in Palestine the chief cities used it for diplomacy and administration. Thirty-three cuneiform tablets have been found at Palestinian sites, including *Taanach (13), *Aphek (8), *Shechem (2), *Megiddo (2). The fragment of the Epic of Gilgamesh from Megiddo (*Atiqot* 2, 1959, pp. 121–128) and lexical texts from Aphek show scribes were trained in traditional Babylonian style, using standard texts.

(ii) *Ugaritic.* At Ras Shamra scribes employed cuneiform Akkadian for international correspondence and some economic texts in the 15th–13th centuries BC. Parallel with this, however, a unique system of writing was developed. It combined the simplicity of the existing Canaanite (Phoenician) alphabet with the Mesopotamian system of writing with a stylus on clay, thus transcribing the consonantal alphabet by means of cuneiform writing. Since it was employed for both Semitic and non-Semitic (Hurrian) languages, 29 signs were developed (by the addition of a few wedges in a simple pattern bearing little or no relation to Akkadian) to represent the consonants and three *'ālep̄* signs with variant vowels ('a 'i 'u). A number of scribal practice tablets give the order of the alphabet which prefigured the Hebrew order (C. Virolleaud, *Palais royal d'Ugarit*, 2, 1957).

This script was used for both religious, literary (mythological) and administrative texts and for a few letters. Although easier to learn than Akkadian, there is as yet little evidence of it being widely used; but a few examples of a variant form have been found as far afield as Beth-shemesh, Tabor and Taanach in Palestine, and places in S Syria. The invention appears to have come too late to oust the already established and simplified Phoenician linear script. For a general survey, see C. H. Gordon, *Ugaritic Textbook*, 1967.

(iii) *Old Persian.* By the late 7th century BC the Aramaic alphabetic script had largely displaced the cuneiform script, except in a few traditional centres and types of temple documents for which, as at Babylon until AD 75, the Bab. cuneiform script continued to be used.

Under the Achaemenid Persians a special system, derived from the cuneiform of Babylonia, was employed alongside the Aramaic script for their Indo-Iranian (Aryan) language. This simplified cuneiform is mainly known from historical texts of the reigns of Darius I and Xerxes. An inscription of the former written on a rock at Behistun in Old Persian, Bab. and Elamite provided the key to the decipherment of the cuneiform scripts, the Old Persian version being deciphered soon after Rawlinson's copy of 1845 had been published. This cuneiform script comprises 3 vowel signs, 33 consonantal signs with inherent vowel plus 8 ideograms and 2 word dividers. A variant form of cuneiform script was used for the Elamite (SW Persia) language in its earliest forms, and later for more than 2,000 economic texts from Persepolis *c.* 492–460 BC (G. G. Cameron, *Persepolis Treasury Tablets*, 1948; R. T. Hallock, *Persepolis Fortification Tablets*, 1969).

c. Linear scripts

(i) Wide use of Egyp. hieroglyphs and Bab. cuneiform in Syro-Palestine from the 3rd millennium BC on (*e.g.* *EBLA) stimulated the production of simpler writing systems for local languages. At Byblos (*GEBAL) a system of about 100 syllabic signs flourished during the 2nd millennium BC, but they are as yet not fully understood. At the same time Linear A and Linear B scripts arose in Crete with a related script in Cyprus of which examples have been found at Ugarit (Cypro-Minoan). Isolated discoveries attest the existence of other scripts at this period, notably three clay tablets from Tell Deir 'Alla in the Jordan valley, and a stele from Balu'ah in Moab.

(ii) *Alphabetic*. Early in the 2nd millenium BC, it would seem that a scribe living in Syro-Palestine, perhaps at Byblos, realized that his language could be represented by many fewer signs than any of the current more cumbrous syllabaries employed; each consonant could be shown by one symbol. The symbols adapted were pictures on the Egyp. model. The hieroglyphic script included pictures which stood for the initial sounds of their names only, *e.g. r'* 'mouth' for *r*. The value of the alphabetic principle lay in reducing the number of symbols until there was only one for each consonantal sound in the language. Vowels were not separately represented until the Greeks took over the alphabet. It is probable that the symbols were treated initially as consonants plus appropriate vowel (*e.g. ba, du, gi*). With this outstanding invention mankind gained a simple means of recording which eventually broke the monopoly of the *scribes and placed literacy within the reach of everyone (see VI, below).

Examples of this ancestor of all alphabets have been found in Palestine and can be dated shortly before 1500 BC. These exhibit a few signs only, probably personal names, scratched on pottery and metal. The full range of signs—about thirty—appears in the only early group of texts written in a form of this alphabet recovered so far, the 'Proto-Sinaitic' inscriptions. These are short prayers and dedications scratched on the surfaces by Canaanites employed in the Egyp. turquoise mines at Serbit el-Khadim in SW Sinai during the 16th century BC. During the next 500 years the signs were simplified, losing their pictorial form. Examples from sites in Canaan show widespread use and growing standardization (*e.g.* potsherds from Lachish, Hazor, arrowheads from near Bethlehem and the Lebanon) see B. Sass, *The Genesis of the Alphabet and its Development in the Second Millennium* BC, 1988.

The order of the letters is attested by the cuneiform alphabet of Ugarit (13th century BC), an early imitator, by an ostracon from 'Izbet Ṣarṭah, near Aphek (*c.* 1100 BC; M. Kochari, *Tel Aviv* 4, 1977, pp. 1–13). Heb. acrostics also display it (Na. 1:2–14; Pss. 9, 10, 25, 34, 37, 111, 112, 119, 145; La. 1–4; Pr. 31:10–31; Ecclus. 5:13, 29). The Greeks borrowed the letters in the same order. The reason for the arrangement is uncertain. Mnemonic needs and similarities in names or the nature of sounds expressed have been suggested (Driver, *op. cit.*, pp. 180–185, 271–273).

(iii) *Phoenician–early Hebrew.* In the main from 1000 BC onwards we can trace the history of the letters clearly, although there are few specimens written between 1000 and 800 BC. The direction of the writing was standardized, from right to left, as in Egypt. Most documents were made of papyrus and so have perished in the damp soil. Those that survive, on stone, pottery and metal, prove the ready acceptance of the script for all purposes. It was evidently well established before the end of the 2nd millennium BC, a ready tool for the Israelites to employ in recording and teaching the laws of God and the history of his works on their behalf (see A. R. Millard, *EQ* 50, 1978, pp. 67 ff.).

1. The major *monumental* inscriptions for the study of Heb. epigraphy are: (*a*) The agricultural calendar from *Gezer, variously attributed to an archaic or unskilled hand and dated to the 10th century BC (*DOTT*, pp. 201–203). (*b*) The stele of Mesha', king of Moab (*MOABITE STONE). This 34-line inscription is important historically and as an example of the development of the monumental Heb. script in use in a remote place *c.* 850 BC. The well-cut letters already show a tendency to become cursive. This is further seen in (*c*) the *Siloam Inscription (*IBA*, fig. 56), dating from the reign of Hezekiah, *c.* 710 BC, and (*d*) the Tomb

inscription of the Royal Steward from Siloam of about the same date (*SHEBNA; *IBA*, fig. 53). For the lapidary form of the script, see *seals. By this time Phoenician and Aram. letters had taken their own distinctive forms.

2. The *cursive* hand which the OT writers would have originally employed is seen in the inscribed arrow-heads and other smaller writings of *c.* 1000 BC. The earliest body of texts is 75 ostraca from Samaria, some assigned to the reign of Jeroboam II (*c.* 760 BC; A. Lemaire, *op. cit.* (**II.***f*), pp. 23–81; *DOTT*, pp. 204–208). These show a clear, flowing script written by scribes long practised in the art. The unvocalized words are divided by small dots. Inscribed sherds from many sites show the development of the script down to the time of the *Lachish Letters and most of the ostraca from *Arad at the end of Judah's history (*DOTT*, pp. 212–215; *ANET*, pp. 568–569; A. Lemaire, *op. cit.*).

(iv) *Aramaic.* Aramaeans adopted the Canaanite alphabet as they settled in Syria and gradually gave it distinctive features. The earliest texts (*c.* 850–800 BC) are the Tell Fekheriye Statue inscription (A. Abou Assaf, P. Bordreuil, A. R. Millard, *La Statue de Tell Fekherye et son inscription bilingue assyro-araméenne*, 1982, the partly illegible Melqart Stele of Bar-hadad (*BEN-HADAD; *DOTT*, pp. 239–241, but note the second line cannot be read 'son of Tabrimmon'), the *Dan Stele and two pieces of ivory bearing the name of *Hazael. Soon after 800 BC Zakkur, king of *Hamath, erected a stele with 46 lines of inscription, and about 750 BC a treaty between the unknown Bar-ga'ayah and Mati'-el of *Arpad was recorded on three stelae. An increasingly cursive style is attested by the Bar-rakkab Stele (*ANEP*, p. 460). As Aramaic spread, the alphabet quickly took root in Assyria and Babylonia, to the disadvantage of the cuneiform script. Papyrus documents have perished, but a list of names on a sherd from Nimrud (*CALAH) in Assyria of the early 7th century BC (J. B. Segal, *Iraq* 19, 1957, pp. 139–145), notes scratched on clay tablets, and a long letter written on a potsherd and sent from Erech to Ashur about 650 BC, show its use. Papyrus documents found in Egypt show the script developing from *c.* 600 BC (letter from Philistia to Egypt) until the end of the Persian period, notably in the 5th-century documents from Elephantine (*DOTT*, pp. 256–269) and other places (G. R. Driver, *Aramaic Documents of the Fifth Century BC*, 1954).

(v) *Early Jewish scripts.* The discoveries of MSS from the Wadi Qumran (*DEAD SEA SCROLLS), Judaean caves (especially the dated texts from Murabba'at) and inscribed ossuaries from the Jerusalem area have produced a wealth of material for the study of the formal and cursive Palaeo-Hebrew and early Jewish scripts from the 3rd century BC to the 2nd century AD. The fall of the Persian empire and the displacement of the common Aramaic of the imperial court led to many local variations.

1. The Archaic or proto-Jewish script of Judah, *c.* 250–150 BC, as reflected in the Qumran MSS, shows a formal hand derived from the Persian Aramaic which, by the late 3rd century, is a cross between the formal and cursive scripts and close to the common Aramaic scripts of Palmyra and Nabataea which also emerged at this time. While these national scripts cannot yet be more precisely dated, formal, semi-formal and true cursive hands can sometimes be distinguished. This script is also to be seen on coins of the period.

2. The Hasmonaean period (*c.* 150–30 BC) saw the development of the formal, squarer and more angular hand seen in its first stages in the Nash Papyrus, now dated *c.* 150 BC.

3. The Herodian period (30 BC–AD 70) was a time of swift development, and texts can thus be closely dated.

4. The post-Herodian period (after AD 70) is now well known from dated commercial and legal documents. The cursive script is not a literary but highly involved hand. The development of all these Jewish hands is illustrated and discussed in detail by F. M. Cross (*The Bible and the Ancient Near East*, ed. G. E. Wright, 1961, pp. 133–202). Study of early Heb. writing, the scribes' habits and letter forms, is of especial value in considering how errors may, or may not, have crept into the OT text.

(vi) *Greek.* The Gk. alphabet was by tradition attributed to a Phoenician trader Cadmus (Herodotus, *Hist.* 5. 58–59) and, by comparison between the early Gk. alphabets at Athens, Crete, Thera, Corinth and Naxos and dated Phoenician texts (see above), this view is justified. It would seem probable from the form of the letters that the Greeks had by the middle of the 9th century BC adapted the script to the needs of their Indo-European language. They used the Phoenician symbols for sounds which they did not possess (' h *ḥ* ' u [w] y), for the vowel sounds they required (a e ē o y i respectively), and thus created the first true alphabet in which consonants and vowels were represented by distinct signs.

The abundance of monumental and manuscript evidence makes the study of Gk. epigraphy and palaeography an important and exact science for the background of the biblical Gk. texts. From W Greece the alphabet reached the Etruscans, and thus through the Roman script entered Europe.

(vii) *Other scripts.* As well as the development of the Phoenician script for use in the Gk., and thence Roman and subsequently European scripts, the early Canaanite script was developed for writing S Semitic dialects. Examples have been found in S Palestine and S Babylonia from *c.* 600 BC, and from S Arabian sites from slightly later.

VI. Literacy and literary methods

Evidence for the degree of literacy, which varied according to time and place, is small. Gideon was able to lay hands on a young man of Succoth in Jordan who wrote down a list of the city elders (Jdg. 8:14; Heb., RSV, AVmg., RVmg. 'write', AV, RV, unjustifiably 'describe'). Such ability among the young to write (Is. 10:19) was enhanced by the advent of the alphabet and by the establishment of *schools for scribes attached to temples and shrines. Every Israelite householder had to write the words of the Law (Dt. 6:9; 11:20). Writing, though not so well attested in the West as in Babylonia, was certainly widespread in Syria and Palestine by the 2nd millennium, when at least five scripts were in use, *viz.* Egyp. hieroglyphs, Byblian syllabary, Canaanite alphabet, Akkad. cuneiform and the Ugaritic alphabetic cuneiform (see above).

Writing was generally undertaken by trained *scribes. who could be drawn from any class of the population (*contra* E. Nielsen, *Oral Tradition*, 1954, pp. 25, 28), though most higher officials in administration were literate. The mass of cuneiform tablets, ostraca and papyri so far found shows the prominent place of the written word throughout the ancient Near East. A percentage is difficult to estimate owing to the incompleteness of the records, but the six scribes to a population of about 2,000 at Alalaḫ in Syria in *c.* 1800–1500 BC is probably indicative of the literacy in important towns (D. J. Wiseman, *The Alalakh Tablets*, p. 13). Recent studies show that scribes may have learnt their Akkadian at main 'university' centres such as Aleppo in Syria or Babylon itself.

Documents were stored in baskets, boxes or jars (Je. 32:14) and laid up in the local temple (1 Sa. 10:25; Ex. 16:34; *cf.* 2 Ki. 22:8) or special archive stores (Ezr. 6:1). Specific reference books were held by scribes (as, *e.g.*, at Nippur, *c.* 1950 BC). Tiglath-pileser I (*c.* 1100 BC) at Assur and Ashurbanipal (*c.* 650 BC) at Nineveh collected copies of texts or had them written for their libraries. When copying texts a scribe would often quote the source, giving the condition of the document from which he copied, and stating whether the text had been checked with the original document, or only copied down from oral tradition, which was considered a less reliable method (J. Læssøee, 'Literacy and Oral Tradition in Ancient Mesopotamia', *Studia Orientalia Ioanni Pedersen*, 1953, pp. 205–218). Oral tradition was conceived as existing alongside the written word but not taking the place of primary authority. The colophon (both Akkadian and Egyp.) would also give the title or catchline which designated the work; but authorship was often, though not invariably, anonymous. It is likely that the Heb. writers used similar methods.

BIBLIOGRAPHY. See references given in text above; also, for a full description, G. R. Driver, *Semitic Writing*[3], 1976; I. J. Gelb, *A Study of Writing*[2], 1963; J. Naveh, *Early History of the Alphabet*[2], 1987; J. Cerny, *Paper and Books in Ancient Egypt*, 1952; J. C. L. Gibson, *Syrian Semitic Inscriptions*, 1, *Hebrew*, 1971; 2, *Aramaic*, 1975; 3, *Phoenician*, 1982. For books in the ancient world, see *Cambridge History of the Bible*, 1, 1970, pp. 30–66.

D.J.W.
K.A.K.
A.R.M.

YARN. In the Bible the yarns mentioned are goats' hair, camels' hair, cotton (Heb. *karpas*; Est. 1:6; *cf. EBi,* 1, p. 915), linen and silk (Ezk. 16:10; Rev. 18:12). Cotton, from the lint around the seeds produced by the shrub *Gossypium herbaceum*, originated in ancient India, but spread E only in the Gk. period. The 'linen yarn' in the AV of 1 Ki. 10:28 and 2 Ch. 1:16 is due to a misunderstanding of the Heb. text. The correct translation, referring to a country called Kue (*i.e.* * CILICIA), is to be found in the RSV. F.N.H

YOKE. The rendering of several Heb. and Gk. words, used either literally for the wooden frame joining two animals (usually oxen), or netaphoretically as describing one individual's subjection to another. The words are *môṭ* (Na. 1:13) and and *Môṭâ* (Is. 58:6; Je. 27:2, *etc.*), 'a bar'; *'ôl* (Gn. 27:40; La. 1:14, *etc.*), 'a yoke'; *ṣemeḏ* 1 sa. 11:7; Jb. 1:3, *etc.*), 'yoke of oxen'; *zeugos* (Lk. 14;19), 'a pair'; *zygos* (Mt. 11:29; 1 Tim. 6:1, *etc.*), ' a yoke', 'a balance' (*AGRICULTURE).

In 2 Cor. 6:14 Paul uses *heterozygeō*, ' to be yoked with one of another kind'. For the 'yokefellow' of Phil. 4:3 see *SYNZYGUS. J.D.D.

Z

ZAANAN. A place mentioned in Mi. 1:11, the inhabitants of which remained in their city when invading forces passed through the land. It may be identical with Zenan in the Shephelah of Judah listed in Jos. 15:37. J.D.D.

ZAANANNIM, ZAANAIM (Heb. *ṣaʿᵃnannîm*). On the S border of Naphtali, near Kedesh (Jos. 19:33); Heber the Kenite camped there (Jdg. 4:11; AV, *Kᵉṯîḇ* 'Zaanaim'); perhaps Elon ('Oak')-in-Zaanannim, *cf.* G. F. (G. F. Moore, *ICC*, 1903, on Jdg. 4:11).

Khan et-Tuggar, 4 km NE of Tabor, preserves the name in its Arabic equivalent ('traveller'). Khan Leggun near Tell abu Qedeis, 4 km N of Taanach, has been suggested as a more likely refuge for Sisera (Jdg. 4:17), but would have been the wrong side of the flooded Kishon; *cf.* R. Boling, *Judges*, 1975, pp. 96f.; J. Soggin, *Judges*, 1987, pp. 66, 75. J.P.U.L.

ZABAD. 1. An Ephraimite (1 Ch. 7:21). **2.** A man of Judah, of the lineage of Hezron (1 Ch. 2:36f.). **3.** One of David's mighty men (1 Ch. 11:41), probably to be equated with **2**; note the name Ahlai in the parentage of both. **4.** A conspirator against Joash (2 Ch. 24:26). The correct form of the name is *Jozachar. *Cf.* 2 Ki. 12:21. **5, 6, 7.** Three laymen who put away their foreign wives, as directed by Ezra (Ezr. 10:27, 33, 43). D.F.P.

ZABBAI. Possibly a shortened form of Heb. *zāḇaḏyâ*, 'The Lord bestowed upon' (W. Rudolph). This name is found in Ezr. 10:28 and Ne. 3:20. Zabbai was forced by Ezra, according to Ezr. 10:28, to put away his foreign wife. Zabbai in Ne. 3:20 is problematic. He was the father of Baruch who helped with the rebuilding of the walls of Jerusalem. Either he is the same person as in Ezra, or a different person with the same name, or Zabbai must be replaced by Zakkai (*cf.* Ezr. 2:9 and various MSS, Vulg. and Syr.). F.C.F.

ZABDI. 1. The grandfather of Achan who took some of the devoted spoil at Jericho (Jos. 7:1, 17–18). He is also called Zimri (1 Ch. 2:6). **2.** A Benjaminite (1 Ch. 8:19). **3.** An officer of David's vineyards (1 Ch. 27:27). **4.** A Levite (Ne. 11:17), also called Zichri (1 Ch. 9:15). R.A.H.G.

ZACCHAEUS, from Heb. and Aram. *Zakkai*, a reduced form of Zechariah. A chief tax-collector at Jericho who became a disciple of Christ (Lk. 19:1–10). He was probably the general tax-farmer of Jericho and undoubtedly had abused his position on occasions to enrich himself. Being a small man, he climbed a tree to see Jesus, who then asked to stay at his house. Zacchaeus welcomed him and showed practical repentance in giving half his goods to the poor and fourfold compensation to any whom he had defrauded. Christ said that this showed him to be a true son of Abraham and declared that salvation had come, not only to him, but to his house. The self-righteous in the crowd were critical of Jesus' action, but he declared his mission to be the seeking and saving of the lost.

BIBLIOGRAPHY. P. Kariamadam, *The Zacchaeus Story*, 1985. R.E.N.

ZADOK (Heb. *ṣāḏôq*, 'righteous'?). **1.** Son of Ahitub, who was, according to 1 Ch. 6:1ff., 50ff., a descendant of Eleazar, third son of Aaron. He was priest at David's court along with Abiathar (2 Sa. 8:17) and had charge of the ark (2 Sa. 15:24f.); he took part in the anointing of Solomon as David's successor when Abiathar supported Adonijah (1 Ki. 1:7ff.). He and his descendants discharged the chief-priestly duties in Solomon's Temple until its destruction in 587 BC. Ezekiel restricts the priestly privileges in his new commonwealth to the Zadokite family on the ground that they alone were innocent of apostasy under the Monarchy (Ezk. 44:15ff.). In the second Temple the Zadokites retained the high priesthood continuously until 171 BC, when it was transferred to Menelaus by Antiochus IV; even after that a Zadokite priesthood presided over the Jewish temple at Leontopolis in Egypt until Vespasian closed it soon after AD 70. The Qumran community remained loyal to the Zadokite priesthood and looked forward to its restoration.

2. A descendant of Zadok, grandfather of Hilkiah (1 Ch. 6:12; 9:11; Ne. 11:11). **3.** Father-in-law of King Uzziah and grandfather of Jotham (2 Ki. 15:33; 2 Ch. 27:1). **4, 5.** Two builders of the wall under Nehemiah (Ne. 3:4, 29); one or the other of these may be the same as Zadok, a signatory to the covenant (Ne. 10:21), and 'Zadok the scribe' (Ne. 13:13).

BIBLIOGRAPHY. H. H. Rowley, 'Zadok and Nehushtan', *JBL* 58, 1939, pp. 113ff., *idem*, 'Melchizedek and Zadok' in *Festschrift für A. Bertholet* (ed. W. Baumgartner), 1950, pp. 461ff.; R. de Vaux, *Ancient Israel*, 1961, pp. 372–405; J. R. Bartlett, 'Zadok and his successors at Jerusalem', *JTS* n.s. 19, 1968, pp. 1–18. F.F.B.

ZAIR. 2 Ki. 8:21 records that King Joram passed over to Zair to crush a revolt of the Edomites, hence its probable location was on the border of Edom. Some MSS of the LXX read here Z(e)ior, and

Zair may possibly be identical with *Zior, listed in Jos. 15:54, in the Judaean hill-country.

R.A.H.G.

ZALMON. 1. A personal name. One of David's mighty men, said to be an Ahohite (2 Sa. 23:28). He is called Ilai in 1 Ch. 11:29.

2. The name of a mountain in the vicinity of the tower of Shechem (Jdg. 9:48). Its identification is far from certain; both Gerizim and Ebal have been suggested.

3. Another mountain, mentioned in Ps. 68:14 (spelt Salmon in AV). Some have equated it with the foregoing, but this mountain would appear to have been to the E of the Jordan and is usually identified with Jebel Ḥaurân.

D.F.P.

ZAMZUMMIM (*zamzummim*, meaning uncertain; possibly 'whisperers', 'murmurers', from a root known in Arabic). The name given by the *Ammonites to the people (known also as *Rephaim) whom they themselves displaced from their territory in central Transjordan (Dt. 2:20–23). It is at present difficult to associate them with any particular archaeological remains but, assuming that the Ammonites settled in the 13th century BC, one might consider these people as the Middle Bronze/Late Bronze Age occupants of the region, whose presence is attested by a few recent discoveries (*cf. IDBS*, p. 20). Whether the *Zuzim in Gn. 14:5 are the same people remains uncertain.

J.G.G.N.
G.I.D.

ZANOAH (Heb. *zānôaḥ*). **1.** A town in the Shephelah (Jos. 15:34; Ne. 3:13; 11:30); Khirbet Zanu', 3 km S of Beth-shemesh, W of modern Zanoah. **2.** A town in the hills near Juttah (Jos. 15:56; 1 Ch. 4:18); may be Khirbet Beit Amra, overlooking the Wadi el-Halil (W Hevron), part of which is called Wadi Abu Zenah (Grollenberg, Abel); or Khirbet Zanuta, SW of Eshtemoa (Rudolph, *Chronikbucher*, 1955, *ad loc.*; Israeli Survey); or Khirbet Yaqin, 6 km SE of Hebron (Noth, *Josua, ad loc.*, citing LXX to read 'Zanoah of Kain'; but the readings are doubtful).

J.P.U.L.

ZAPHENATH-PANEAH. An Egyp. name bestowed by the pharaoh upon Joseph at his investiture (Gn. 41:45). The search for its Egyp. original has produced many widely divergent suggestions. Steindorff's *Ḏ(d)-p'-nṯ(r)-fiw.f-'nḫ* is phonetically good, but is circumstantially inappropriate in meaning and of too late a date. Most other suggestions are either phonetically unacceptable or else lack any real Egyp. parallels. However, the Heb. consonantal form *ṣ-p-n-t p-'-n-ḥ* may, with one slight change (for euphony in Heb.) to *ṣ-t-n-p p-'-n--ḥ*, stand for (*yôsēp̄*) *ḏd-n.f 'Ip-'nḫ* '(Joseph), who is called *'Ip̄'ankh'; ḏd-n.f* would be the well-known construction introducing a second name, the name itself being 'Ip'ankh, a common name in the Middle Kingdom and Hyksos periods, *i.e.* in the patriarchal and Joseph's age.

K.A.K.

ZAPHON. A town referred to in Jos. 13:27 and Jdg. 12:1, lying in Gadite territory in the Jordan valley. TJ identifies it with the Amathus of Josephus, which is to be located at Tell 'Ammatah; but this is improbable. Other proposed locations for Zaphon are Tell al-Sa'idiya and Tell al-Qos.

D.F.P.

ZAREPHATH ('smelting place'). Akkad. *ṣariptu*; *cf. ṣarāpu*, 'to refine (metals), to fire (bricks)'. A small Phoenician town (mod. Sarafand), originally belonging to *Sidon, it appears in late 13th century Papyrus Anastasi 1 (*ANET*[3], p. 477). It was captured by Sennacherib in 701 BC (Zarebtu, *ANET*[3], p. 287) and by Esarhaddon, *c.* 680–669 BC, who gave it to Ba'ali, king of Tyre (J. B. Pritchard, 'Sarepta in History and Tradition', in J. Reumann (ed.), *Understanding the Sacred Text*, 1971, pp. 101–114).

Situated about 13 km S of Sidon on the Lebanese coast on the road to *Tyre, it is mentioned in 1 Ki. 17:9ff. as the place to which *Elijah went during the drought in Ahab's reign and where he restored life to the son of the widow with whom he lodged. Lk. 4:26 refers to this incident, the town there being called by the Gk. and Lat. name, Sarepta.

Obadiah prophesied that in the Day of the Lord those of the children of Israel who were deported by Sargon after the fall of Samaria should possess Phoenicia as far as Zarephath.

For excavations begun in 1969, see *AJA* 74, 1970, p. 202; 76, 1972, p. 216; *Archaeology* 24, 1971, pp. 61–63; J. Pritchard, *Sarepta*, 1975.

R.A.H.G.

ZARETHAN. This town is spelt variously Zaretan, Zartanah and Zarthan in AV; and the name appears as Zeredah (AV Zeredathah) in 2 Ch. 4:17. Zarethan is mentioned in connection with Bethshean, Adam and Succoth, and lay in the Jordan valley, near a ford over the river. Its exact site has been debated, but it almost certainly lay W of the Jordan. One suggested location, Qarn Sartaba, perhaps recalls the name Zarethan; but most authorities prefer Tell al-Sa'idiya. (Excavated 1964–7; 1985 onwards, see *NEAEHL*, pp. 1295–1300.) Tell Umm Ḥamâd is another possibility.

D.F.P.

ZEAL. In modern Eng. usage, fervour in advancing a cause or in rendering service. But the corresponding Heb. and Gk. words in the Bible can have a bad sense. Thus *qānā'* (verb), *qin'â* (noun), are often rendered *'envy', 'envious' (as in Gn. 26:14; Ps. 37:1), or *'jealous', 'jealousy' (Gn. 37:11; Jb. 5:2), and once 'passion' (Pr. 14:30), as well as 'zeal' in a positive sense (2 Sa. 21:2).

The phrase 'the zeal of the Lord (of hosts)' occurs several times (2 Ki. 19:31; Is. 9:7; 37:32; *cf.* Is. 26:11; 63:15) and means his jealous concern for his own people and their welfare: their relationship to him is as a wife to a husband, hence NEB's 'jealous anger' in Is. 59:17 (Heb. *qin'â*; RSV 'fury').

Similarly, in NT the Gk. terms *zēloō* (verb) and *zēlos* (noun) can have a bad or a good sense, according to context. Thus RSV gives 'jealous' (Acts 7:9), 'jealousy' (Acts 5:17) and 'covet' (Jas. 4:2), but translates in a good sense as 'earnestly desire' (1 Cor. 12:31), 'make much of' (Gal. 4:17) or 'zeal' (2 Cor. 7:7). But 'jealous' can have a positive meaning. In 2 Cor. 11:2 Paul is 'jealous' (*zēloō*) over his converts 'with a divine jealousy' (*zēlos*), not meaning the human jealousy of selfish possessiveness or a concern for his own reputation, but the jealousy which a lover feels for his beloved; and a 'divine' jealousy because it is as felt by God himself for his own people, who stand as in the marriage relationship to him (*cf.* Ex. 20:5; 34:14; Dt. 5:9, *etc.*).

zēlōtēs, *'zealot', is applied to the apostle Simon (Lk. 6:15; Acts 1:13), called in Mt. 10:4 and Mk. 3:18 Simon the Cananean, where *ho kananaios* may translate Aram. *qan'ān*, 'zealot'. *zēlōtēs* also occurs in 1 Cor. 14:12, where Paul's readers who are zealots (RSV 'eager') for manifestations of the Spirit are bidden to strive (*zēteō*) to excel in building up the church, *i.e.* to realize that the purpose of spiritual gifts is communal and not for selfish ends. Elsewhere *zēlōtēs* is translated by RSV as 'zealous' (Acts 21:20; 22:3; Gal. 1:14; Tit. 2:14; 1 Pet. 3:13).

The verb *spoudazō* is translated 'zealous' (2 Pet. 1:10, 15; 3:14), but also 'eager' (Gal. 2:10; Eph. 4:3; 1 Thes. 2:17), 'do your best' (2 Tim. 2:15; 4:9, 21; Tit. 3:12), 'strive' (Heb. 4:11). The adjective *spoudaios* occurs in 2 Cor. 8:17, 22 ('earnest'), and the adverb *spoudaiōs* in Lk. 7:4 ('earnestly'), Phil. 2:28; 2 Tim. 1:17 ('eagerly'), Tit. 3:13 ('do your best'). RSV renders *spoudē* as 'zeal' (Rom. 12:8, 11; 2 Cor. 7:12), 'haste' (Mk. 6:25; Lk. 1:39), 'eagerness' (2 Cor. 8:7–8, 16; Heb. 6:11), 'effort' (2 Pet. 1:5).

BIBLIOGRAPHY. H.-C. Hahn, *NIDNTT* 3, pp. 1166–1168; A. Stumpf, *TDNT* 2, pp. 877–888; G. Harder, *TDNT* 7, pp. 559–568. N.H.

ZEALOT (Gk. *zēlōtēs*). One of the twelve apostles is called Simon the Zealot (Lk. 6:15; Acts 1:13), either because of his zealous temperament or because of some association with the party of the Zealots (*CANANAEAN). Paul speaks of himself as having been a religious zealot (Acts 22:3; Gal. 1:14), and the many members of the church of Jerusalem are described as all 'zealots for the law' (Acts 21:20).

The party of the Zealots, described by Josephus as the 'fourth philosophy' among the Jews (*BJ* 2. 117; *Ant.* 18. 23), was founded by *Judas the Galilean, who led a revolt against Rome in AD 6 (*CENSUS). They opposed the payment of tribute by Israel to a pagan emperor on the ground that this was treason to God, Israel's true King.

These men were called Zealots because they followed the example of Mattathias and his sons and followers, who manifested zeal for the law of God when Antiochus IV tried to suppress the Jewish religion (1 Macc. 2:24–27), and the example of Phinehas, who showed comparable zeal in a time of apostasy in the wilderness (Nu. 25:11; Ps. 106:30f.). When the revolt of AD 6 was crushed they kept its spirit alive for 60 years. Members of Judas's family were Zealot leaders; two of his sons were crucified by the procurator Alexander *c.* AD 46 (Jos., *Ant.* 20. 102), and a third, Menahem, attempted to seize the leadership of the anti-Roman revolt in AD 66 (Jos., *BJ* 2. 433). Zealots were active throughout the war of AD 66–73; the last Zealot stronghold, Masada, fell in May AD 74, but even then the Zealot spirit was not completely quenched. (*ASSASSINS.)

BIBLIOGRAPHY. W. R. Farmer, *Maccabees, Zealots and Josephus*, 1956; Y. Yadin, *Masada: Herod's Fortress and the Zealots' Last Stand*, 1966; D. M. Rhoads, *Israel in Revolution 6–74 C.E.: A Political History based on the Writings of Josephus*, 1976; R. A. Horsley and J. S. Hanson, *Bandits, Prophets and Messiahs*, 1985; M. Hengel, *The Zealots*, 1989. F.F.B.

ZEBAH (Heb. *zeḇaḥ*, 'slaughter', 'sacrifice'). One of two kings of Midian who raided Palestine in the days of Gideon the judge. Some of Gideon's people had been slain in a Midianite raid (Jdg. 8:18f.). Gideon carefully selected 300 and pursued the raiders. The people of Succoth and Penuel refused to help him and were later punished. At Karkor (v. 10) Gideon captured the two chiefs Zebah and Zalmunna and slew them. Following this exploit, Gideon was invited to be king over Israel, but refused (Jdg. 8:22–23). In Ps. 83:1–12 this incident finds a place among the list of victories God gave his people. J.A.T.

ZEBEDEE (Gk. *Zebedaios* from Heb. *ziḇdiyāhû*, 'the gift of Yahweh'). The father of the apostles James and John (Mk. 1:19) and husband of Salome (Mt. 27:56; Mk. 15:40). A Galilean fisherman, probably of some means (*cf.* Mk. 1:20); he evidently lived at or near Bethsaida. J.D.D.

ZEBOIIM (NEB **ZEBOYIM**). One of the cities of the plain (Gn. 14:2) eventually destroyed with *Sodom and Gomorrah (Dt. 29:23). Its location seems to have been in the vicinity of *Admah. D.F.P.

ZEBOIM. 1. A valley near Michmash in Benjaminite territory (1 Sa. 13:18), modern Wadi Abu Daba'. The Heb. phrase means 'ravine of hyenas' (*gê ṣ'ḇō'îm*). **2.** A Benjaminite town of post-exilic times, near Lydda (Ne. 11:34). D.F.P.

ZEBUL (Heb. *z'ḇûl*, 'exalted', *i.e.* prince, or height). Ruler of Shechem under the self-styled 'king' Abimelech, whom he rescued from Gaal's revolt (Jdg. 9:26–41). In Ugaritic, *zbl* (I), 'prince', is used of Baal, lord of the earth, while *zbl* (II) is 'sick (man)'; *cf.* (*e.g.*) C. H. Gordon, *Ugaritic Textbook*, 3, 1965, p. 393, Nos. 815–816. K.A.K.

ZEBULUN. The tenth son of Jacob and the sixth son of Leah (Gn. 30:19f.). The original form of the name may have been Zebulon or Zebul, the name of Abimelech's lieutenant (Jdg. 9:26–41). In the account of his birth a double derivation is suggested: *zāḇal* to 'honour' and *zāḇaḏ* to 'endow' or 'bestow'. Similar forms are found in Egyp., Akkad. and Canaanite sources. Before the descent into Egypt Zebulun had three sons, Sered, Elon and Jahleel (Gn. 46:14), founders of their respective tribal clans.

Zebulun was able to possess more of its allotted territory than most of the tribes, possibly because it comprised largely virgin country, with no great cities (Jos. 19:10–16). Kitron (perhaps the Kattath of Jos. 19:15) and Nahalol are mentioned as incompletely conquered (Jdg. 1:30). Generally speaking, Zebulun occupied a broad wedge in S Galilee between Asher and Naphtali with Manasseh to the SW and Issachar to the SE. The S boundary was probably the river Kishon in the

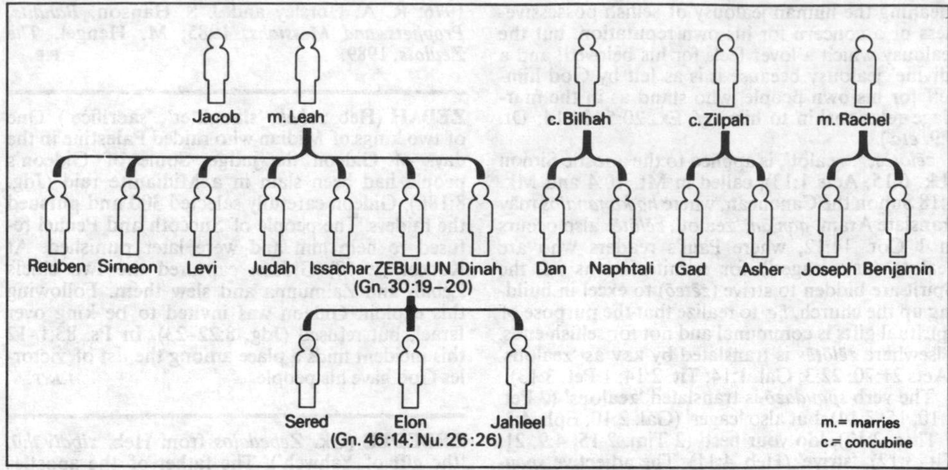

The genealogy of Zebulun.

Valley of Esdraelon, which gave Zebulun, like Issachar, control over the trade routes. The Blessing of Jacob (Gn. 49:13) promises Zebulun access to the sea, although it is not clear whether Galilee or the Mediterranean is meant. In either case this was never realized, but the reference may be to the strategic commercial position shared with Issachar (*cf.* Dt. 33:18f.). These tribes also shared the same holy mountain (Dt. 33:19), probably Tabor (*cf.* Jdg. 4:6), on the fringe of Zebulun's territory. Although one of the smaller tribal areas, it was fertile, being exposed to the rain-bearing W winds. With 57,400 and 60,500 warriors respectively in the two census lists (Nu. 1:31; 26:27), it was the fourth largest tribe.

In the great covenant-renewal ceremony at Shechem, Zebulun was assigned an inferior place with Reuben and the 'handmaiden' tribes (Dt. 27:13). But in the Judges period it distinguished itself in the conflicts against the Canaanites and Midianites (Jdg. 4:6, 10; 5:14, 18; 6:35). One of the minor judges, Elon, came from Zebulun (Jdg. 12:11). When David became king over a united Israel, considerable initial military and economic support was supplied (1 Ch. 12:33, 40). The prophet Jonah was a Zebulunite from Gath-hepher (2 Ki. 14:25; *cf.* Jos. 19:18). Zebulun suffered severely in the Assyr. invasion under Tiglath-pileser (2 Ki. 15:29; *cf.* Is. 9:1), many of its inhabitants were deported and its territory was assimilated into the Assyr. empire. However, its tribal identity survived, and its inhabitants are included among the participants in Hezekiah's Passover (2 Ch. 30:10–22). In the NT, apart from the quotation in Mt. 4:13–16, Zebulun is mentioned only in Rev. 7:8, but Nazareth, where Jesus spent his early years, was within its traditional borders.

BIBLIOGRAPHY. *LOB*, pp. 200, 212, 233, 237.

A.E.C.

ZECHARIAH, ZACHARIAH, ZACHARIAS. Some 28 men bear this name in the Bible, most of them mentioned only once or twice, including the last king of Jehu's line (2 Ki. 14:29; 15:8, 11). The best known is the prophet, who is mentioned with Haggai in Ezr. 5:1; 6:14, and whose prophecies are found in the book that bears his name. As these two prophets were enthusiasts for the rebuilding of the Temple in 520 BC, one must account for their silence during the period 536–520 BC, when the Temple building was neglected. Either their parents had brought them as infants in the return in 537 BC or they did not return until about 520 BC; in this case also they must have been infants in 537 BC, or their enthusiasm would have brought them back then. This means that Zechariah was a young man when he began to prophesy, and indeed it may be he, and not the man with the measuring line, who is referred to as 'this young man' in Zc. 2:4. It is likely that the second part of his book belongs to his old age (* ZECHARIAH, BOOK OF).

In the NT Zechariah is the father of John the Baptist (Lk. 1:5, *etc.*). There is also a mention of 'Zechariah son of Barachiah, whom you murdered between the sanctuary and the altar' (Mt. 23:35; *cf.* Lk. 11:51). Since the prophet Zechariah was the son of Berechiah (Zc. 1:1), it is possible that he was martyred, although there is no independent record of this. Others suppose that the reference is to the martyrdom of Zechariah the son of Jehoiada in 2 Ch. 24:20–22, and that the error of the father's name is due either to the Evangelist, or, since it does not occur in the best MSS of Lk., to a copyist's addition. Since Chronicles is the last book in the Heb. Bible, the naming of Abel and Zechariah in this verse would be the equivalent of our phrase 'from Genesis to Revelation'. There is also a Zechariah the son of Jeberechiah, who is called as a witness in Is. 8:2, but there is no reason to suppose that he is the one referred to by Christ.

J.S.W.

ZECHARIAH, BOOK OF.

I. Outline of contents

a. Prophecies dated between 520 and 518 BC, during the rebuilding of the Temple, 1:1–8:23

(i) Introduction. Zechariah in the line of the true prophets (1:1–6).

(ii) First vision. Angelic riders are told that God will restore Jerusalem (1:7–17).

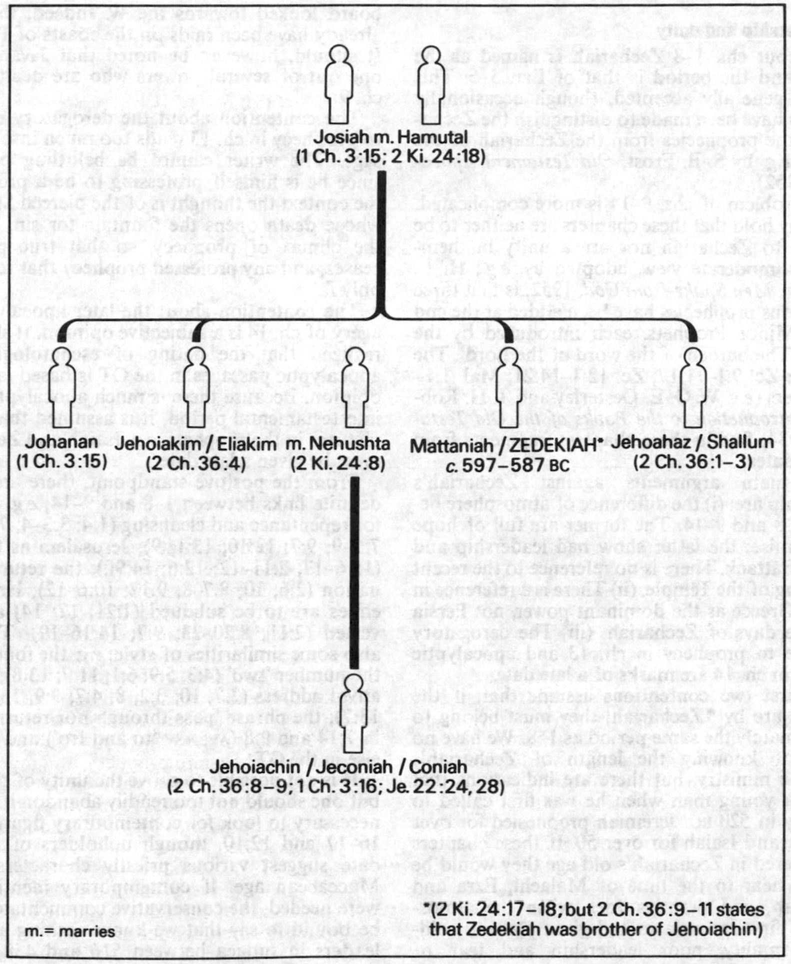

An interpretation of King Zedekiah's family tree.

(iii) Second vision. Four destroying horns are destroyed by four smiths (1:18–21).

(iv) Third vision. The new Jerusalem cannot be contained by walls, but will be the home of Jews and Gentiles (2:1–13).

(v) Fourth vision. Joshua the high priest, accused by Satan, is vindicated by God, given access to his presence and made a type of the Branch-Messiah (3:1–10).

(vi) Fifth vision. A seven-branched candlestick, or lamp, fed by two branches (probably Joshua and Zerubbabel), from two olive trees. A special word of encouragement to Zerubbabel (4:1–14).

(vii) Sixth vision. An immense flying scroll carries God's words of condemnation of sin (5:1–4).

(viii) Seventh vision. A woman in an ephah measure, symbolizing sin, is removed to the unclean land of Babylon, the place of exile (5:5–11).

(ix) Eighth vision. Four chariots go out through the earth as God's executives (6:1–8).

(x) Joshua is crowned as a symbol of the Branch-Messiah who builds the Temple, and who rules as Priest-King (6:9–15).

(xi) A question about observing fasts that had been instituted to commemorate the fall of Jerusalem in 587 BC. Fasts will become feasts, and all nations will share the blessing (7:1–8:23).

b. Undated prophecies, which could be from a later period in Zechariah's ministry, 9:1–14:21

(i) The judgment of Israel's enemies is seen in the light of the coming of the Prince of Peace (9:1–17).

(ii) Evil shepherds give place to God's Leader, who gathers in his people (10:1–12).

(iii) The Good Shepherd confounds the evil shepherds, but is rejected by the flock, who consequently suffer under yet another evil shepherd (11:1–17).

(iv) Jerusalem in distress looks to the One whom her people have pierced, and repents with true sorrow (12:1–14).

(v) Jewish prophecy ceases when the Good Shepherd is smitten and opens the fountain that cleanses from sin (13:1–9).

(vi) The distress of Jerusalem is followed by the blessings and judgments of God's kingdom (14:1–21).

II. Authorship and unity

Throughout chs. 1–8 Zechariah is named as the author, and the period is that of Ezr. 5–6. This claim is generally accepted, though occasionally attempts have been made to distinguish the Zechariah of the prophecies from the Zechariah of the visions (*e.g.* by S. B. Frost, *Old Testament Apocalyptic*, 1952).

The problem of chs. 9–14 is more complicated, and many hold that these chapters are neither to be ascribed to Zechariah nor are a unity in themselves. A moderate view, adopted by, *e.g.*, H. L. Ellison in *Men Spake from God*, 1952, is that three anonymous prophecies have been added at the end of the Minor Prophets, each introduced by the phrase, 'The burden of the word of the Lord'. The three are Zc. 9:1–11:17; Zc. 12:1–14:21; Mal. 1:1–4:6. Others (*e.g.* W. O. E. Oesterley and T. H. Robinson, *Introduction to the Books of the Old Testament*, 1934) find in these chapters fragments from various dates.

The main arguments against Zechariah's authorship are: (i) the difference of atmosphere between 1–8 and 9–14. The former are full of hope and promise; the latter show bad leadership and threat of attack. There is no reference to the recent rebuilding of the Temple. (ii) There is a reference in 9:13 to Greece as the dominant power, not Persia as in the days of Zechariah. (iii) The derogatory reference to prophecy in ch. 13 and apocalyptic pictures in ch. 14 are marks of a late date.

The first two contentions assume that, if the chapters are by *Zechariah, they must belong to approximately the same period as 1–8. We have no means of knowing the length of Zechariah's prophetic ministry, but there are indications that he was a young man when he was first called to prophesy in 520 BC. Jeremiah prophesied for over 40 years, and Isaiah for over 50. If these chapters were uttered in Zechariah's old age they would be drawing near to the time of Malachi, Ezra and Nehemiah, and perhaps Joel, when the atmosphere of first enthusiasm had given place to coldness, formality, poor leadership and fear of attack.

The reference to Greece is not, then, a serious objection, even if one does not give any weight to belief in divine prediction, which is certainly present in the King and the Shepherd references in these chapters. Greece, or Javan, is named by Ezk. 27:13, 19, and also by Is. 66:19, as one of the places to which missionaries will go to declare God's glory. It is worth noting for the sake of the argument that many commentators would make 'Trito-Isaiah' (Is. 56–66) a contemporary of the actual Zechariah who wrote 1–8. It is probable that Zechariah had seen the vision of the chariots going 'toward the west country' (6:6), and in 8:7 he foresees captives returning from the W. Later Joel 3:6 refers to Jews who had been sold by the Phoenicians as slaves to the Greeks.

From about 520 BC onwards the Greeks in Asia Minor were a continual source of trouble to Darius, and in 500 BC a great Ionian revolt occurred. In 499 BC the Athenians burnt the Persian stronghold of Sardis, and in 490 BC and 480 BC the Persians, in a full-scale invasion of Greece, were defeated at Marathon and Salamis. From a purely human point of view, Zechariah could have looked to Greece as a power that would harass the countries in the Persian empire whose seaboard looked towards the W. Indeed, there may already have been raids on the coasts of Palestine. It should, however, be noted that Javan is only one out of several powers who are dealt with in ch. 9.

The contention about the derogatory reference to prophecy in ch. 13 reads too much into the passage. The writer cannot be belittling prophecy, since he is himself professing to be a prophet. In the context the thought is of the pierced Shepherd, whose death opens the fountain for sin, as being the climax of prophecy, so that true prophecy ceases, and any professed prophecy that remains is only false.

The contention about the later apocalyptic imagery of ch. 14 is a subjective opinion. It should be realized that the dating of eschatological and apocalyptic passages in the OT is based largely on opinion. Because there is much apocalyptic in the intertestamental period, it is assumed that similar pictures in the prophets, *e.g.* Isaiah and Zechariah, must be given a late date.

From the positive standpoint, there are certain definite links between 1–8 and 9–14; *e.g.* the need for repentance and cleansing (1:4; 3:3–4, 9; 5:1–11; 7:5–9; 9:7; 12:10; 13:1, 9); Jerusalem as the head (1:16–17; 2:11–12; 12:6; 14:9f.); the return of the nation (2:6, 10; 8:7–8; 9:12; 10:6–12); Israel's enemies are to be subdued (1:21; 12; 14) and converted (2:11; 8:20–23; 9:7; 14:16–19). There are also some similarities of style: *e.g.* the fondness for the number 'two' (4:3; 5:9; 6:1; 11:7; 13:8); the vocatival address (2:7, 10; 3:2, 8; 4:7; 9:9, 13; 11:1–2; 13:7); the phrase 'pass through nor return' occurs in 7:14 and 9:8 (AV; RSV 'to and fro') and nowhere else in the OT.

It is not possible to prove the unity of the book, but one should not too readily abandon it. It is not necessary to look for contemporary figures in 9:8, 16–17 and 12:10, though upholders of the later date suggest various priestly characters of the Maccabean age. If contemporary identifications were needed, the conservative commentator would be bound to say that we know nothing about the leaders in Judaea between 516 and 458 BC, and personal intrigues and assassinations were as likely then as in Maccabean times.

BIBLIOGRAPHY. H. G. Mitchell, *ICC*, 1912; C. H. H. Wright, *Zechariah and his Prophecies*, 1878; M. F. Unger, *Zechariah*, 1963; J. G. Baldwin, *Haggai, Zechariah, Malachi*, *TOTC*, 1972; L. G. Rignell, *Die Nachtgesichte des Sacharja*, 1950; P. Lamarche, *Zacharie IX–XIV*, 1961; B. Otzen, *Studien über Deuterosacharja*, 1964; F. F. Bruce, *BJRL* 43, 1960–1, pp. 336ff.; R. K. Harrison, *IOT*, 1968; C. L. Meyers, *Zechariah 9–14*, 1993. J.S.W.

ZEDAD. One of the sites on the N border of the promised land (Nu. 34:8), mentioned also in Ezekiel's vision of the limits of restored Israel (Ezk. 47:15). There are two main candidates for identification with it, corresponding to the two views that are taken about the line of the N border described in these texts as a whole. The dominant view (*e.g.* Aharoni) sees the name as preserved at Ṣadad, *c.* 110 km ENE of Byblos; this accords well with the preferred location for the 'entrance of *Hamath', the adjacent point on the boundary. A minority of scholars advocate a more S position, at Kh. Ṣerādā, a few miles N of Dan, reading the name as Zerad, with LXX and the Samaritan text.

BIBLIOGRAPHY. G. B. Gray, *Numbers*, 1903, p. 459; G. A. Cooke, *Ezekiel*, *ICC*, 1936, p. 527; Y. Aharoni, *LOB*, pp. 65–67. R.A.H.G.
G.I.D.

ZEDEKIAH (Heb. *ṣiḏqiyyāhû—ṣiḏqiyyâ*, only in 1 Ki. 22:11; Je. 27:12; 28:1; 29:3—'Yahweh is (my) righteousness'). **1.** One of 400 court prophets under *Ahab who lied by prophesying his victory over Syria (1 Ki. 22:1–12; 2 Ch. 18:1–11). When Micaiah revealed the truth, Zedekiah symbolically called him a liar by striking his cheek (1 Ki. 22:13–28; 2 Ch. 18:12–27).

2. A false prophet among the exiles in Babylon whose death at the hand of Nebuchadrezzar is foretold by Jeremiah (Je. 29:21–23).

3. A prince of Judah who heard the scroll of Jeremiah read during the reign of Jehoiachin (Je. 36:11–13).

4. The twenty-first, and last, king of Judah (*c.* 597–587 BC). The third son of Josiah (1 Ch. 3:15), he was placed on the throne by Nebuchadrezzar in the place of *Jehoiachin, his nephew. His name was also changed from *Mattaniah, showing his vassalage to Babylon (2 Ki. 24:17). Enthroned at the age of 21, he reigned for 11 years (v. 18; 2 Ch. 36:11).

Since the leading citizens had been deported with Jehoiachin (2 Ki. 24:14–16), Zedekiah was left with the undesirables, whose advice, which he was not able to refuse, finally led to Yahweh's punishment (Je. 24:8–9; 29:16–19; Ezk. 11:14–21). Rebellion in Babylonia in *c.* 594 BC (A. K. Grayson, *Assyrian and Babylonian Chronicles*, 1975, p. 102, Ezk. 11:21–24) gave the W vassals an opportunity to conspire to throw off their subjugation, sending to Judah, where there was evidence of an anti-Babylonian faction (Je. 28:1–10), for support (27:3). Jeremiah saw the Babylonian overlordship as divinely ordained (Je. 27; *cf.* 28:12–14). Zedekiah went to Babylon in 593 BC, possibly to allay suspicion concerning his involvement in the plot (Je. 51:59).

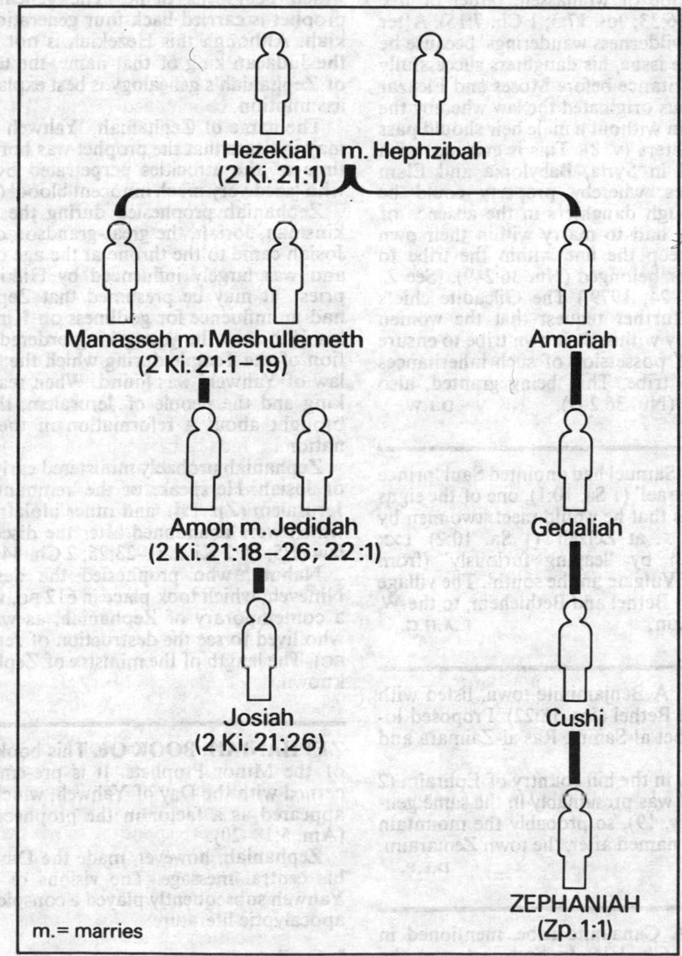

The genealogy of Zephaniah, based on the assumption that 'Hezekiah' (Zp. 1:1) was King Hezekiah of Judah.

Zedekiah finally did revolt (2 Ki. 24:20), breaking a covenant with Babylon (Ezk. 17:12–13). This was possibly related to the arrival of the pharaoh Hophra (Apries; Je. 44:30), whose aid, as indicated by Lachish Letter 3, might have been sought by Judah (*DOTT*, p. 214). In 588 BC, Nebuchadrezzar and his army invaded Judah and laid siege to Jerusalem. The siege was lifted for a period to meet the approaching Egyptians (Je. 37:5) but, as Jeremiah predicted (vv. 6–10; 34:21–22), the siege was resumed. When the famine inside the city had reached its peak, the wall was breached in July, 586 BC, and the city fell (2 Ki. 25:3–4; Je. 52:6–7). The Temple was plundered and burnt and people exiled (2 Ki. 25:17–20). Zedekiah fled towards the Jordan, where he was captured and taken to Nebuchadrezzar's military headquarters at Riblah. There his sons were executed before him. He was then blinded and led off to Babylon (2 Ki. 25:4–7; Je. 52:7–11). D.W.B.

ZELOPHEHAD. The son of Hepher, grandson of Gilead of the tribe of Manasseh, father of five daughters (Nu. 26:33; Jos. 17:3; 1 Ch. 7:15). After his death in the wilderness wanderings, because he was without male issue, his daughters successfully claimed the inheritance before Moses and Eleazar (Nu. 27:1, 7). Thus originated the law whereby the property of a man without a male heir should pass first to his daughters (v. 8). This is evidence of a custom, attested in Syria, Babylonia and Elam from early times, whereby property could be transmitted through daughters in the absence of male heirs. They had to marry within their own family and so keep the line within the tribe to which their father belonged (Nu. 36:2–9). (See Z. Ben-Barak, *JSS* 24, 1979.) The Gileadite chiefs later made the further request that the women should marry only within their own tribe to ensure the continuity of possession of such inheritances within the same tribe. This, being granted, also became Heb. law (Nu. 36:2–9). D.J.W.

ZELZAH. After Samuel had anointed Saul 'prince over his people Israel' (1 Sa. 10:1), one of the signs given to Saul was that he would meet 'two men by Rachel's tomb . . . at Zelzah' (1 Sa. 10:2). LXX translates Zelzah by 'leaping furiously' (from *ṣōlᵉḥîm*), and the Vulgate 'in the south'. The village Beit Jala between Bethel and Bethlehem, to the W, may be the location. R.A.H.G.

ZEMARAIM. 1. A Benjaminite town, listed with Beth-arabah and Bethel (Jos. 18:22). Proposed locations are Khirbet al-Samra, Ras al-Zaimara and Ras al-Tâḥûna.

2. A mountain in the hill country of Ephraim (2 Ch. 13:4). Bethel was presumably in the same general locality (*cf.* v. 19), so probably the mountain was near to, and named after, the town Zemaraim. D.F.P.

ZEMARITES. A Canaanite tribe, mentioned in Gn. 10:18 and 1 Ch. 1:16. In both instances the name is listed between Arvadites and Hamathites. The tribe's home was the Ṣumur of the Tell el-Amarna letters, the Ṣimirra of Assyr. texts. Its modern name is Sumra, and it lies on the Mediterranean coast N of Tripoli (Tarablus). D.F.P.

ZENAS. Gk. pet-name from Zenodorus (*cf.* Lightfoot on Col. 4:15); a lawyer (*nomikos*), accompanying Apollos to an unknown destination: Titus was to provide them with supplies and a good send-off (Tit. 3:13). They doubtless brought Titus Paul's letter (*cf.* Zahn, *INT*, 2, p. 49). Despite the association with Apollos, *nomikos* here probably does not refer to expertise in the Torah. Zenas' proficiency was probably in Roman law: *nomikos* is used of eminent jurists like Mucius Scaevola (Plutarch, *Sulla* 36) or of humble notaries (*cf.* examples in *MM*).

An *Acts of Titus* (5th century) claims his authority, and menologies include him in the Seventy. A.F.W.

ZEPHANIAH. The only biographical reference to Zephaniah appears in the first verse of the book which bears his name. The genealogy of the prophet is carried back four generations to Hezekiah. Although this Hezekiah is not identified as the Judaean king of that name, the unusual form of Zephaniah's genealogy is best explained on that assumption.

The name of Zephaniah, 'Yahweh has hidden', may indicate that the prophet was born during the time of the atrocities perpetrated by Manasseh, who 'shed very much innocent blood' (2 Ki. 21:16).

Zephaniah prophesied during the reign of his kinsman, Josiah, the great-grandson of Hezekiah. Josiah came to the throne at the age of 8 (640 BC) and was largely influenced by Hilkiah the high priest. It may be presumed that Zephaniah also had an influence for godliness on King Josiah. In his 18th year the young king ordered the renovation of the Temple during which the 'book of the law of Yahweh' was found. When read before the king and the people of Jerusalem, this Scripture brought about a reformation in the life of the nation.

Zephaniah probably ministered early in the reign of Josiah. He speaks of the 'remnant of Baal' in Jerusalem (Zp. 1:4), and other idolatrous customs which were abandoned after the discovery of the law (1:5; *cf.* 2 Ki. 22:1–23:25; 2 Ch. 34:1–7).

Nahum, who prophesied the destruction of Nineveh, which took place in 612 BC, was probably a contemporary of Zephaniah, as was Jeremiah, who lived to see the destruction of Jerusalem (587 BC). The length of the ministry of Zephaniah is not known. C.F.P.

ZEPHANIAH, BOOK OF. This book is the ninth of the Minor Prophets. It is pre-eminently concerned with the Day of Yahweh, which had earlier appeared as a factor in the prophecies of Amos (Am. 5:18–20).

Zephaniah, however, made the Day of Yahweh his central message. The visions of the Day of Yahweh subsequently played a conspicuous part in apocalyptic literature.

I. Outline of contents

a. Warning of the impending Day of Yahweh, 1:1–2:3

(i) Superscription (1:1).
(ii) The destruction of all things (1:2–3).
(iii) Judgment on Judah and Jerusalem (1:4–13).
(iv) Judgment described (1:14–18).
(v) Judgment may be avoided (2:1–3).

b. Judgment on foreign nations, 2:4–15
(i) Philistia (2:4–7).
(ii) Moab and Ammon (2:8–11).
(iii) Egypt (2:12).
(iv) Assyria (2:13–15).

c. Judgment on Jerusalem and subsequent blessing, 3:1–20
(i) The sins of Jerusalem judged (3:1–8).
(ii) The remnant of Judah blessed (3:9–20).

II. Historical background

The religious state of the kingdom of Judah deteriorated markedly following the death of Hezekiah. Manasseh, his son, rebuilt the altars to Baal which Hezekiah had destroyed (2 Ch. 33:1–11). Religion was debased to the level of crass externalism. The revival of idolatrous worship, common in the days of Ahaz (2 Ki. 16:3–4), was from the prophetic viewpoint a rejection of Israel's covenant with Yahweh.

Scythian invaders attacked Assyria in 632 BC. Josiah was able to carry out his reforms without fear of Assyr. interference. The Scythians moved into W Asia and reached the Egyp. border where they were bought off by pharaoh Psammetichus I. They do not appear to have attacked Israel, although the ferocity of their assault provided a background against which Zephaniah pictured the wrath of Yahweh.

III. Message of the book

Zephaniah's prophecies begin with a message of gloom. The prophet denounced the idolatry which he saw in Jerusalem, where there had been no spiritual revival since the days of Hezekiah. Zephaniah declared that God's judgment was imminent both on Judah's idolatrous neighbours (2:4–15) and on Judah and Jerusalem (1:4–18; 3:1–7).

The prophet, however, is not a pessimist. Beyond the impending doom he sees a better day. God must bring his people through the afflicting fires in order to prepare them to be a means of blessing to all mankind.

Some of the abuses denounced by Zephaniah were removed in Josiah's reformation (621 BC).

BIBLIOGRAPHY. J. H. Eaton, *Obadiah, Nahum, Habakkuk, Zephaniah, TBC*, 1961; J. D. W. Watts, *Joel, Obadiah, Jonah, Nahum, Habakkuk and Zephaniah*, *CBC*, 1975; D. W. Baker, *Nahum, Habakkuk and Zephaniah*, 1988; P. R. House, *Zephaniah, A Prophetic Drama*, 1988; A. Berlin, *Zephaniah*, 1994. C.F.P.

ZEPHATHAH (Heb. *ṣ^ep̄aṯâh*). 'The valley of Zephathah at (*l^e*) Mareshah', 2 Ch. 14:10 (v. 9 *MT*). The LXX apparently read *baggai miṣṣāp̄ôn* ('in the valley to the north') for *b^eḡê' ṣ^ep̄aṯâh*. Complex re-entrants in gently-sloping country lie N and S of *Mareshah. J.P.U.L.

ZER. A fortified city in the territory of Naphtali (Jos. 19:35). It is not necessary to adopt the LXX reading *Tyros, i.e.* Tyre, which presupposes a Heb. reading *ṣōr* instead of *MT ṣēr.* J.D.D.

ZERAH. From Heb. *zāraḥ*, 'to rise, shine/come forth', especially of the sun.

1. Son of Reuel son of Esau and Basemath (Gn. 36:4, 10, 13, 17; 1 Ch. 1:35, 37), who might be same as: **2.** Father of Jobab, second of the early kings of Edom (Gn. 36:33; 1 Ch. 1:44).

3. Son of Judah by Tamar, and twin of Perez (Gn. 38:29–30; 1 Ch. 2:4); progenitor of the Judaean clan of Zerahites (Nu. 26:20), among whom was Achan who sinned at Jericho (Jos. 7:1, 17–18, 24; 22:20; 1 Ch. 2:6), besides others (1 Ch. 9:6; Ne. 11:24).

4. Son of Simeon and progenitor of a Simeonite clan of Zerahites (Nu. 26:13; 1 Ch. 4:24); the Zohar of Gn. 46:10; Ex. 6:15. **5.** Descendant of Levi through Gershom (1 Ch. 6:21, 41).

6. An Ethiopian who invaded Judah with large Ethiopian and Libyan forces (2 Ch. 14:9–15; 16:8) and was routed in battle at Mareshah by Asa in his 14th year, *c.* 897 BC (*cf.* 2 Ch. 15, especially v. 10, and E. R. Thiele, *The Mysterious Numbers of the Hebrew Kings*², 1965, pp. 58–60, on 2 Ch. 15:19; 16:1). Whether Zerah's starting-point was Egypt or Arabia is disputed. The only point favouring Arabia is the Semitic form of the name Zerah. His retreat by Gerar might hint, and the presence of Libyans in his forces strongly indicates, that Zerah had come from Egypt. Note that Zerah is *not* called king; hence he cannot be the Libyan pharaoh Osorkon I (*c.* 924–889 BC) in whose reign the battle occurred. The clear difference between Heb. *ḥ* and Egyp. *k* probably excludes identification of the names Zerah, *zrḥ*, and Osorkon, *(w)srk(n)*; no convincing Egyp. or Ethiopian original for Zerah's name is yet forthcoming. Zerah would therefore probably be an Ethiopian army-commander leading the Egyp. forces on behalf of Osorkon I, who was seeking to follow up the success of his father Shishak; Zerah's ignominious defeat is unlikely to appear in the scanty Egyp. records of the period. K.A.K.

ZERED, a mountain-torrent (Heb. *naḥal*) or wadi crossed by the Israelites on their journey round the frontiers of Edom and Moab (Nu. 21:12; Dt. 2:13f.). In Nu. it is mentioned as a camping-ground, which accords with the order to 'rise up' in Dt. 2:13. Its identification is disputed; probably it is mod. Wadi el-Hesâ, which runs into the Dead Sea from the SE. The comments which follow in Dt. 2:14ff. show that its crossing was regarded as an important stage in the journey. G.T.M.

ZERUBBABEL. The exact meaning of the name is uncertain; perhaps it is from Akkad. *zeru-Babili*, 'seed of Babylon'. He was the son of Shealtiel, or Salathiel, and thus grandson of King Jehoiachin (Ezr. 3:2; Hg. 1:1; Mt. 1:12). In 1 Ch. 3:19 the Heb., though not LXX, makes him the son of Pedaiah, Shealtiel's brother. If this is not a copyist's error, there may have been a levirate marriage. It is most unlikely that Zerubbabel is to be identified with *Sheshbazzar, since the account given in the letter sent to Darius (Ezr. 5:6–17) is hardly intelligible unless Sheshbazzar was dead at the time of the interview which it records, whereas Zerubbabel is actively building the Temple. Sheshbazzar may have been Zerubbabel's uncle, Shenazzar (1 Ch. 3:18), but, whoever he was, he was more of a figurehead, while Zerubbabel and Joshua were the active leaders. Zerubbabel returned with the main party under Sheshbazzar in 537 BC, and laid the foundations of the Temple (Ezr. 3). Ezra records that the work was hindered until 520 BC, when a fresh beginning was made, with Zerubbabel and Joshua again in the lead (Ezr. 5–6; Hg. 1–2). In Hg. 1:1; 2:2 Zerubbabel is called 'governor'.

The visions of Zechariah encourage both Joshua and Zerubbabel in their work, and Zc. 4:6–10 promises that the mountain of opposition (probably that of Ezr. 5) will be removed, and Zerubbabel will complete the work. It is often held that the crowning of Joshua in Zc. 6:9–15 was really the crowning of Zerubbabel, but there is no MS evidence for this, and in 3:8 it appears to be Joshua who is the type of the Messianic Branch, as here. Since E. Sellin in 1898 it has been increasingly assumed, on the basis of the crowning and the promise of protection in Hg. 2:20–23, that Haggai and Zechariah induced the Jews to crown Zerubbabel as king, though this act of rebellion was speedily crushed by Persia. There is no shred of evidence for or against this theory.

BIBLIOGRAPHY. A. C. Welch, *Post-Exilic Judaism*, 1935; J. S. Wright, *The Building of the Second Temple*, 1958; P. R. Ackroyd, *Exile and Restoration*, 1968; S. Japhet, *ZAW* 94, 1982, pp. 66–98; 95, 1983, pp. 218–229.

J.S.W.

ZERUIAH (Heb. *ṣᵉrûyâ, ṣᵉruyâ*; possibly from Arab. root, either (1) 'run blood, bleed', or (2) the name of an odoriferous tree, or its gum). The mother of Abishai, Joab and Asahel, David's officers (1 Sa. 26:6; 2 Sa. 2:18; 8:16, *etc.*). Her husband is never mentioned, for which there are several explanations. He may have died young, or she may have been the more significant character. It may reflect the ancient custom of tracing kinship through the female line, or she may have married a foreigner, remaining in her own clan, her children being reckoned as belonging to that clan. She was also David's sister (1 Ch. 2:16), though 2 Sa. 17:25 may imply that she was strictly a step-sister, Jesse's wife being earlier married to Nahash; however, the text of this verse is uncertain. J.G.G.N.

ZEUS. The Gk. deities, *Zeus* and *Hermēs (Acts 14:12), rendered in AV by their Roman equivalents, Jupiter and Mercurius, presumably in turn represent unknown local gods, whom the Lycaonian-speaking people of Lystra recognized in Barnabas and Paul. Why a miraculous healing should have prompted this particular identification is not clear. Hermes, the divine wayfarer and messenger of Zeus, suggested himself for Paul 'because he was the chief speaker'. The fact that there was a local cult of Zeus (v. 13) may have clinched the identity of Barnabas. The two gods were associated as wanderers on earth in the tale of Philemon and Baucis (Ovid, *Metamorphoses* 8. 618–724), who secured their favour by being the only ones to give them hospitality. This possibly explains the anxiety of the Lycaonians not to miss their opportunity.

Paul and Barnabas were naturally greatly distressed and managed only with difficulty to divert the people from their plan to offer sacrifice to them. But Paul also improved the occasion with remarkable dexterity: rising to his role of Hermes, he takes up the familiar picture of Zeus as the god of the sky who displays himself in the phenomena of the weather, and with delicacy and restraint reinterprets it to display the principles of the gospel.

BIBLIOGRAPHY. A. B. Cook, *Zeus*, 1914–40; W. K. C. Guthrie, *The Greeks and their Gods*, 1950.

E.A.J.

ZIBA (Heb. *ṣîḇā'*, *ṣiḇā'*, 'a post'). A servant of Saul (2 Sa. 9:2) who introduced Mephibosheth to David when he desired to honour Jonathan's memory. When Mephibosheth was given a place at court, Ziba was appointed steward of Saul's estates bestowed on Mephibosheth (2 Sa. 9). When David was driven out by Absalom's rebellion Ziba brought him food and also falsely accused Mephibosheth of deserting the king. David accepted his story, did not ascertain the other side, and gave the property to Ziba (2 Sa. 16:1–4). On David's return, Ziba hastened to meet him (2 Sa. 19:7), but later his treachery was revealed. David, in a difficult position, divided the property between them, and Mephibosheth was seemingly content (2 Sa. 19:24–30). J.G.G.N.

ZIKLAG. Ziklag appears in Jos. 15:31 as being near the Edomite boundary, in the S of Judah. It was apportioned to the Simeonites, but later fell into Philistine hands. David, when a Philistine vassal, ruled it and was later able to retain and incorporate it in his own realm. It remained in the hands of Judah in both pre-exilic and post-exilic times. At least four locations have been proposed, of which Tell al-Shari'a (Tel Sera', see *NEAEHL*, pp. 1329–1335), *c.* 25 km SE of Gaza, seems the most probable. D.F.P.

ZILPAH. The handmaid of Jacob's first wife Leah, given to Leah by her father Laban (Gn. 29:24). Leah later gave her to Jacob as a concubine, and she bore him Gad and Asher. J.D.D.

ZIMRAN (Heb. *zimrān*, meaning uncertain). Possibly derives from *zimrâ*, 'song, fame', thus 'the celebrated one', *i.e.* in song or fame. Alternatively, it may derive from *zemer*, 'mountain-sheep or goat'. A son of Abraham by the concubine Keturah (Gn. 25:2; 1 Ch. 1:32). J.D.D.

ZIMRI (Heb. *zimrî*). **1.** A Simeonite prince (Nu. 25:6–15) who was put to death by Phinehas, the grandson of Aaron, for his audacious wickedness in bringing a Midianitess into the camp in contempt of the general spirit of penitence among the Israelites for the apostasy of *Baal-peor.

2. King of Israel *c.* 876 BC (1 Ki. 16:9–20). He reigned in Tirzah for only a week following his assassination of Elah in fulfilment of the prophecy against the dynasty of Baasha (1 Ki. 16:1–4). He lacked popular support, the majority following Omri, who immediately laid siege to Tirzah. When the city fell, Zimri burnt down the palace over his own head. J.C.J.W.

ZIN (Heb. *ṣin*). A name loosely applied to the Wilderness of Zin traversed by the Israelites in the Exodus, close to the borders of Canaan (Nu. 13:21). It refers to the extensive area between the camping-place of the Israelites at the oasis of Kadesh-barnea in NE Sinai, to the Ascent of Aqrabbim or Scorpion Pass constituting the limit between Edom and Judah (Jos. 15:1–4; *cf.* Nu. 34:1–5). The wilderness of Paran lay to the S of it, though Kadesh appears to have been included in both territories, and the two wildernesses occur within the broader term *'Negeb'.

BIBLIOGRAPHY. C. L. Woolley and T. E. Lawrence, *The Wilderness of Zin*, 1936. J.M.H.

ZIOR. A city listed in Jos. 15:54 in the Judaean hill-country NE of Hebron and allocated to the tribe of Judah; modern Si'ir (*ZAIR). J.D.D.

ZIPH. 1. A town in S Judah, near the Edomite boundary (Jos. 15:24), perhaps to be located at al-Zaifa. **2.** A town in the hill-country of Judah (Jos. 15:55), associated with David and with Rehoboam, who fortified it. It is identified with Tell Zif, 7 km SE of Hebron. Named on royal jar-handle stamps found at *Lachish and other sites, which probably points to its importance as a major Judaean administrative centre in the reign of Hezekiah. The adjoining area was known as the Wilderness of Ziph. **3.** A man of Judah (1 Ch. 4:16). D.F.P.

ZIPPOR (Heb. *ṣippôr*, *ṣippōr*, 'little bird', perhaps 'sparrow'). Father of Balak, the Moabite king who suborned Balaam to curse Israel (Nu. 22:2, 4, 10, 16; 23:18; Jos. 24:9; Jdg. 11:25). Some think the name implies totemistic associations. J.G.G.N.

ZIPPORAH. Daughter of Jethro priest of Midian and wife of *Moses. She apparently opposed the circumcision of their second son Gershom, but felt compelled to perform the duty herself when Moses' life was endangered because of its omission (Ex. 4:24–26). M.A.M.

ZIZ. The name of an ascent used by the Moabites and Ammonites in a campaign against Jehoshaphat of Judah (2 Ch. 20:16). Their army lay previously at Engedi, on the W shore of the Dead Sea; and they reached the wilderness of Tekoa. These details make the Wadi Hasasa, just N of Engedi, a virtually certain identification.

D.F.P.

ZOAN. Ancient city, Egyp. *ḏ'n(t)* to which Heb. *Ṣō'an* exactly corresponds. The Gk. Tanis and modern site of the San el-Hagar near the S shore of Lake Menzaleh in NE Delta. The curious note in Nu. 13:22 that Hebron was built 7 years before Zoan in Egypt may indicate a refounding of Zoan in the Middle Kingdom (c. 2000–1800 BC); or more probably by the Hyksos kings in the 16th century BC, whose N capital Avaris Zoan may possibly be. For the era of Tabnis, see *Chronology of the Old Testament. **III.** *b.* Ps. 78:12, 43 places the Exodus miracles in 'the field of Zoan', precisely the Egyp. *sḫt ḏ'(nt)*, 'field of Dja'(ne)', a term apparently applied to the region near Zoan; the possible identity of Zoan and *Ra'amses is now unlikely. From 1100 BC until about 660 BC, Zoan was the effective capital of Egypt in the 21st to 23rd Dynasties, and the N base of the Ethiopian 25th Dynasty. Hence the prominence of Zoan as the seat of pharaoh's counsellors and princes (Is. 19:11, 13; 30:4) and among Egypt's great cities in Ezekiel's (30:14) word of judgment. On Zoan/Tanis, see A. H. Gardiner, *Ancient Egyptian Onomastica*, 2, 1947, pp. 199*–201*, and P. Montet, *Les Énigmes de Tanis*, 1952; H. Kees, *Tanis*, 1964. K.A.K.

ZOBAH. An Aramaean kingdom which flourished during the early Heb. Monarchy, and which took the field against Saul and David. One of its kings was Hadadezer (2 Sa. 8:3). It lay between Hamath, to its N, and Damascus to its S, and at its height its influence reached these cities. It is unnecessary to postulate two Zobahs, one of them S of Damascus, merely because it is listed with Beth-rehob and Maacah in 2 Sa. 10:6 (both S of Damascus).

BIBLIOGRAPHY. B. Mazar, *BAR* 2, 1977, pp. 127–151; W. Pitard, *Ancient Damascus*, 1987, pp. 88–97.

D.F.P.

ZOPHAR. The third of the friends of *Job was Zophar the Naamathite (Jb. 2:11). We have no knowledge where his home was, except that it was presumably E of Jordan. He is distinguished by the brutality of his commonsense position. He speaks in chs. 11, 20, and possibly in 27:13–23. H.L.E.

ZOPHIM. This place-name comes from Heb. *ṣōpîm*, 'watchers'. The location of 'the field of the watchers' (Nu. 23:14, AV) is difficult to determine. It must have been on a high part of the Pisgah Mts, from which Balaam could see the encampment of the Israelites at Shittim. Some propose to take the Heb. *śāḏeh* here in the meaning of the Akkad. *šâdû*, 'mountain' ('the mountain of the watchers'). The word 'watcher' is sometimes used in the sense of prophet (*cf.* Is. 52:8; 56:10) and is thus especially applicable to Balaam (*cf.* Ramathaim-zophim; Ramah, 1 Sa. 1:1). F.C.F.

ZORAH. A town in the lowlands of Judah (Jos. 15:33), closely connected with the Samson stories. Its site is Ṣar'a, on the N side of the Wadi al-Ṣarar, the biblical valley of Sorek. The Tell el-Amarna letters refer to it as Zarkha. It was fortified by Rehoboam (2 Ch. 11:10) and reoccupied after the Babylonian Exile (Ne. 11:29). The references to Hebron and Beersheba in these two passages, however, may suggest that there was another similarly named city a considerable distance S of Samson's territory. D.F.P.

ZUZIM (Heb. *zûzîm*; Gk. *ethnē ischyra*, 'strong peoples'). A people, conquered by Chedorlaomer, whose territory lay E of Jordan (Gn. 14:5). Their principal city, Ham, is probably to be identified with the modern village of the same name NE of the Gilboa Mts in N Jordan. Tristram (*Moab*, pp. 182ff.) and others, however, have sought to identify them with the Moabite village of Ziza, between

Bozra and Lejūn. Because the Zuzim are mentioned in parallel with the Rephaim and Emim, it may be that it is descriptive of the inhabitants (so LXX) rather than a tribal name. For this reason some equate them with *Zamzummim who are identified with, or described as, Rephaim (Dt. 2:20), whose territory was later overrun by Ammonites.

D.J.W.

Index

Maps and diagrams
There is no separate index of maps and diagrams, but references are distinguished by the use of different styles of type, divided by semi-colons.

References in bold roman type indicate an article or principal reference within an article under that title.

References in ordinary type indicate significant appearance(s) of the word in the body of the Dictionary.

References in bold italic type indicate diagrams, charts or line drawings.

References in medium italic type indicate maps and serve as a gazeteer.

An abbreviated key appears at the head of each page.

Asterisks
Asterisks mean 'see' or 'see also', referring the reader to other index entries.

Principal refererences: bold type; text refs: roman; ***illustrations and chart refs: bold italic***; *maps: medium italic*

Principal refererences: bold type; text refs: roman; ***illustrations and chart refs: bold italic***; *maps: medium italic*

Principal refererences: bold type; text refs: roman; ***illustrations and chart refs: bold italic***; *maps: medium italic*

Principal refererences: bold type; text refs: roman; ***illustrations and chart refs: bold italic***; *maps: medium italic*

Principal refereerences: bold type; text refs: roman; ***illustrations and chart refs: bold italic***; *maps: medium italic*

Principal refererences: bold type; text refs: roman; ***illustrations and chart refs: bold italic***; *maps: medium italic*

Principal refererences: bold type; text refs: roman; ***illustrations and chart refs: bold italic***; *maps: medium italic*

Principal refererences: bold type; text refs: roman; ***illustrations and chart refs: bold italic***; *maps: medium italic*

Principal refererences: bold type; text refs: roman; ***illustrations and chart refs: bold italic***; *maps: medium italic*

Principal refererences: bold type; text refs: roman; ***illustrations and chart refs: bold italic***; *maps: medium italic*

Principal refererences: bold type; text refs: roman; ***illustrations and chart refs: bold italic***; *maps: medium italic*

Principal refererences: bold type; text refs: roman; ***illustrations and chart refs: bold italic***; *maps: medium italic*

Principal refererences: bold type; text refs: roman; ***illustrations and chart refs: bold italic***; *maps: medium italic*

Principal refererences: bold type; text refs: roman; ***illustrations and chart refs: bold italic***; *maps: medium italic*

Principal refereremces: bold type; text refs: roman; ***illustrations and chart refs: bold italic***; *maps: medium italic*

Principal refererences: bold type; text refs: roman; ***illustrations and chart refs: bold italic***; *maps: medium italic*

Principal refererences: bold type; text refs: roman; ***illustrations and chart refs: bold italic***; *maps: medium italic*

Principal refererences: bold type; text refs: roman; ***illustrations and chart refs: bold italic***; *maps: medium italic*

Principal refererences: bold type; text refs: roman; ***illustrations and chart refs: bold italic***; *maps: medium italic*

Principal refererences: bold type; text refs: roman; ***illustrations and chart refs: bold italic***; *maps: medium italic*

Principal refererences: bold type; text refs: roman; ***illustrations and chart refs: bold italic***; *maps: medium italic*

List of animals, birds, reptiles and insects referred to under 'ANIMALS'

Acknowledgments

Relief maps
Cartography by George Philip and Son Limited, 12–14 Long Acre, London WC2E 9LP, England.

Diagrams and town plans
Designed by Thumb Design Partnership Limited, 20–21 D'Arblay Street, London W1V 3FN, England.

Acknowledgment of the sources of illustrations
The publishers have made every effort to trace the copyright holders of illustrations in this book. Should any have been inadvertently missed, copyright holders are asked to contact the publishers.
The publishers are glad to acknowledge their indebtedness to a variety of sources as indicated below.
In acknowledging the source, 'After' indicates that the material remains essentially as it appears in the source acknowledged but has been redrawn. 'Based on' means that the substance of the source material has been retained but reinterpreted.
For abbreviations see pp. (x)–(xiv).

ANTIOCH, p. 51
After *ACA*, p. 222.

ARCHITECTURE, p. 77
After C. L. Woolley, *History of Mankind* (Allen and Unwin, 1963), vol. 1, part 2.

ATHENS, p. 101
Based on *ACA*, pp. 148f.

BABEL, p. 109 (Temple-tower)
After D. J. Wiseman, *IBA*, fig. 18.

BABYLON, p. 111 (Sites of ziggurats)
Based on A. Parrot, *Ziggurats et tour de Babel* (© Albin Michel), fig. 27, p. 53.

BRICK-KILN, p. 148
Based on information from B. Meissner, *Babylonien und Assyrien* (Carl Winters, Heidelberg, 1920), vol. 1, p. 234, figs. 55 and 56.

CISTERN, p. 205
After *BASOR* 185, 1967, p. 24.

CROSS, p. 246
Based on N. Haas, 'Skeletal Remains from Giv'at ha-Mivtar', *IEJ* 20, 1970, pl. 24.

DAGON, p. 252
Plan after *EAEHL*, vol. 1, p. 216. Reconstruction after A. Rowe, *Four Canaanite Temples of Bethshan* (University of Pennsylvania, 1940), fig. 5.

DEUTERONOMY, p. 273
Based on information supplied by Kenneth Kitchen.

ESSENES, p. 340
Based on J. Murphy and O. O'Connor, 'The Essenes in Palestine', *Biblical Archaeologist*, September 1977, p. 122.

FEASTS, p. 366
Based on information from *Encyclopaedia Judaica*, 1971, vol. 6.

FLOOD, p. 372
Based on information from M. E. L. Mallowan, *Iraq XXVI* (British School of Archaeology in Iraq, 1964), p. 82, pl. 20.

FOOD, pp. 376f.
Based on information from R. J. Forbes, *Studies in Ancient Technology* (E. J. Brill, Leiden, 1955), p. 54.

GEZER, p. 408 (Gate, plan)
After *EAEHL*, vol. 2, p. 437.

GEZER, p. 408 (Gate, reconstruction)
After material supplied by C. J. Davey.

GIBEON, p. 411 (Jar handle)
After J. B. Pritchard, *Hebrew Inscriptions and Stamps from Gibeon*, fig. 1, no. 1.

HOUSE (Ur), p. 488
After material supplied by C. J. Davey.

HOUSE (villa), p. 489
Based on W. F. Albright, *Archaeology of Palestine* (Penguin, 1947), fig. 17.

JERUSALEM (David, Solomon and Herod), pp. 558ff.
Based on Walter de Gruyter (ed.), *Atlas of Jerusalem*, Maps 3:1, 3:2 and 3:6 (Jewish History Publications, 1973).

JOT AND TITTLE, p. 615
Supplied by A. R. Millard.

MENE, p. 750
Supplied by A. R. Millard.

MINING, p. 767
After material supplied by C. J. Davey.

MOABITE STONE, p. 778
Courtesy of Maurice Chuzeville/Louvre Museum.

MUSIC, pp. 790f.
Based on J. Rimmer, *Ancient Musical Instruments of Western Asia* (British Museum, 1969), pp.50f.

NERO, p. 815
After M. Grant, *Nero* (Weidenfeld and Nicolson, 1970), p. 265.

OHOLIBAMAH, p. 843
After B. Rothenberg, *Timna* (Thames and Hudson, 1972), p. 152.

PERSIA, p. 904 (Rulers)
Based on E. Porada, *The art of Ancient Iran* (Holle Verlag, Baden-Baden, 1965), p. 256.

SACRIFICE AND OFFERING, pp. 1036, 1040
Based on A. R. S. Kennedy, *Leviticus and Numbers, CB*, 1910, p. 349.

SHECHEM, p. 1089 (Plan)
Based on G. E. Wright, *Shechem* (Gerald Duckworth, 1964), fig. 41.

SHECHEM, p. 1089 (Reconstruction)
After material provided by C. J. Davey.

SHISHAK, p. 1097
From *Hazor* by Yigael Yadin (Weidenfeld and Nicolson, 1975).

SOLOMON, p. 1118
Based on *IDB*, vol. 2, p. 657.

SUPERSCRIPTION, p. 1139
Supplied by A. R. Millard.

THRONE, p. 1184
Oriental Institute, University of Chicago.

WATER, p. 1232 (cross-section)
Based on W. G. Dever and S. M. Paul, *Biblical Archaeology* (Keter Publishing House, Jerusalem, 1973), p. 132, fig. b.

WRITING, pp. 1252–53
After information provided by A. R. Millard.